Music
Guide to

Jazz

2nd
Edition

Edited by
Michael Erlewine
Vladimir Bogdanov
Chris Woodstra
Scott Yanow

MF Miller
Freeman
Books
San Francisco

Published by Miller Freeman Books, 600 Harrison Street, San Francisco, CA 94107
Publishers of *Guitar Player, Bass Player,* and *Keyboard* magazines
A member of the United Newspapers Group

un Miller Freeman

Distributed to the book trade in the U.S. and Canada by
    Publishers Group West, P.O. Box 8843, Emeryville, CA 94662
Distributed to the music trade in the U.S. and Canada by
    Hal Leonard Publishing, P.O. Box 13819, Milwaukee, WI 53213

ISBN 0-87930-407-3

Cover Photo: Sonny Stitt, New York City, 1953; photo copyright © Herman Leonard
Production Editor: Dorothy Cox
Production: Carolyn Keating, Ellyn Hament, Stephen Wolford, Karen Hager, Wendy Davis and Adolfo Cabral

Printed in the United States of America
96 97 98 99   5 4 3 2 1

CONTENTS

FOREWORD

The second edition of the *All Music Guide to Jazz* is the most complete consumer guide to jazz recordings ever made available. It includes biographies of 1,440 jazz artists and groups with more than 13,200 of their finest recordings rated and/or reviewed.

Thanks to the efforts of guest editor Scott Yanow and the unflagging work of AMG staff Chris Woodstra, Vladimir Bogdanov, and Stephen Thomas Erlewine, this revised edition of the *All Music Guide to Jazz* contains a number of enhancements including more (and longer) reviews and artist biographies plus additional music maps and essays.

AMG jazz editor Scott Yanow is a frequent contributor to *DOWN BEAT*, *Cadence*, *Jazz Times*, and a contributor to the *New Grove Dictionary of Jazz* and *Leonard Feather's Encyclopedia of Jazz*.

Aside from this volume, the All Music Guide series includes our main guide (*All Music Guide*), and the *All Music Guide to Rock*. Additional volumes in preparation include the *All Music Guide to the Blues*, *All Music Guide to Country Music*, and the *All Music Guide to World Music*.

The complete AMG guide is also available on CD-ROM from Corel Corporation. Also, be sure to visit our home page on the World-Wide Web at:

http://AllMusic.com

The *All Music Guide* is an ongoing database project, the largest collection of substantive album reviews ever assembled, and we welcome your feedback. Perhaps we have left out some of your favorite albums, and/or included ones that you don't consider essential. Let us know about it. We welcome criticism, suggestions, and additions. Perhaps you are an expert on the complete output of a particular artist or group and would like to participate in future editions of this book and/or our larger computer database. We would be glad to hear from you.

Michael Erlewine
Executive Editor
All Music Guides

ALL MUSIC GUIDE DATABASE

The *All Music Guide* is more than this book. It is an ongoing database project, the largest collection of substantive album ratings and reviews ever assembled. In fact, the 14,000+ albums listed in this book represent a rather small subset (albeit an important one) of a very much larger collection of over 300,000 albums and reviews. The All Music Guide is also available in the following formats:

Books:
All Music Guide (Miller Freeman Books, 3rd Edition Fall 1996)
All Music Guide to Rock (Miller Freeman Books, 1995)
All Music Guide to the Blues (Miller Freeman Books, available Summer 1996)
All Music Guide to World Music (Miller Freeman Books, available 1997)
All Music Guide to Country Music (Miller Freeman Books, available 1997)
VideoHound & *All-Movie Guide Stargazer* (Visible Ink, 1995)

Electronic Formats:
All Music Guide CD-ROM (Corel, available Summer 1996)
All-Movie Guide CD-ROM (Corel)
MusicRoms (music and data) for Blues, Jazz, R&B, Latin, etc.
(Selectware/Compton's)
All Music Guide (hard disk version) (Great Bear Technology)
World Beat CD-ROM (Medio)

In Store Kiosks:
Musicland's Soundsite
Phonolog's the Source
Sam Goody's

Online:
Internet AMG sites:
ALLMUSIC.COM
ALLMOVIE.COM
THENEWAGE.COM

Other Internet Sites:
Compact Disc Connection (BBS 408-730-9015)
CDNow! (CDNOW.COM)
Entertainment Connection (ECONNECTION, BBS 914-426-2285)
Music Boulevard (www.MusicBlvd.com)
CDUniverse (www.CDUNIVERSE.COM)

Billboard Online
Dimple Records
Reason Ware
Apple's E-World: Hollywood Online
The Microsoft Network: New Age Forum: New Age Music

We welcome your feedback. Perhaps we have left out some of your favorite albums, and/or included ones that you don't consider essential. Let us know about it. We welcome criticism, suggestions, additions, and/or deletions. The All Music Guide is a continuing project. Perhaps you are an expert on the complete output of a particular artist or group and would like to participate in future editions of the book and/or our larger computer database. We would be glad to hear from you. Call or write:

ALL MUSIC GUIDE
315 Marion Avenue
Big Rapids, MI 49307

616-796-3437
FAX 616-796-3060
A division of Matrix Software

All Music Guide to Jazz, 2nd Edition

Editors
Michael Erlewine
Vladimir Bogdanov
Chris Woodstra
Stephen Thomas Erlewine
Scott Yanow

AMG Production Staff
Jonathan Ball
Sherry Batchelder
Nancy Beilfuss
Sandra Brennan
John Bush
Julie Clark
Mark Donkers
Brandy Ellison
Mary Anne Henry
Steve Huey
Debbie Kirby
Luda Lobenko
Sara Sytsma

Matrix Staff
Kyle Alexander
Irene Baldwin
Richard Batchelder
Susan Brownlee
Stephanie Clement
Walt Crocket

Teresa Swift-Eckert,
Iotis Erlewine
Margaret Erlewine
Phillip Erlewine
Stephen Erlewine
Kevin Fowler
Jeff Jawer,
Rock Jensen,
Mary King
Madeline Koperski
Jennifer Page
Forest Ray
Robert Walker

Contributors
Steve Aldrich
Bob Blumenthal
Myles Boisen
Kenneth M. Cassidy
Bill Dahl
Hank Davis
Michael P. Dawson
Bruce Eder
Michael Erlewine
Stephen Thomas Erlewine
John Floyd
Mark C. Gridley
Scot Hacker
Terri Hinte

Michael Katz
Cub Koda
Linda Kohanov
Paul Kohler
Stuart Kremsky
Richard Lieberson
Les Line
Brian Mansfield
David Nelson McCarthy
Alex Merck
Dan Morgenstern
Michael G. Nastos
Buz Overbeck
Barry Lee Pearson
Harvey Pekar
Bob Porter
Bruce Raeburn
Bruce Boyd Raeburn
John Storm Roberts
William Ruhlmann
Bob Rusch
Max Salazar
Ned Sublette
David Szatmary
Blue Gene Tyranny
Richie Unterberger
Charles S. Wolfe
Ron Wynn
Scott Yanow

ABOUT THE EDITORS

Michael Erlewine

All Music Guide editor Michael Erlewine helped form the Prime Movers Blues Band in Ann Arbor, Michigan in 1965. He was the lead singer and played amplified harmonica in this pace-setting band (the first of its kind). The original band included a number of now well-known musicians including Iggy Pop (drums), "Blue" Gene Tyranny (piano; now a well-known avant-garde classical composer); Jack Dawson (bass; became bass player for Siefal-Schwall Blues Band); and Michael's brother Dan Erlewine (lead guitar; now monthly columnist for *Guitar Player* magazine). Michael has extensively interviewed blues performers, both in video and audio, and, along with his band, helped to shape the first few Ann Arbor Blues festivals. Today Michael is a systems programmer and director of Matrix Software. Aside from the company's work in music and film data, Matrix is the largest center for astrological programming and research in North America. Michael has been a practicing astrologer for more than 30 years and has an international reputation in that field.

Michael is also very active in Tibetan Buddhism and serves as the director of the Heart Center Karma Thegsum Choling, one of the main centers in North America for the translation, transcription, and publication of psychological texts and teachings of the Karma Kagyu Lineage of Tibetan Buddhism. Michael has been married for 23 years, and he and his wife Margaret live in Big Rapids, Michigan. They have four children.

Vladimir Bogdanov

Russian mathematician and programmer Vladimir Bogdanov has been involved in the design and development of *All Music Guide* databases since 1991. Having experience in many different fields such as nuclear physics, psychology, social studies and ancient chronology he now applies his knowledge to the construction of unique music reference tools utilizing the latest computer technologies. His personal interest lies in applying artificial intelligence and other mathematical methods to areas with complex semantic structures, like music, film, literature. Vladimir's ultimate goal is to provide people with the means to find what they need, even if they don't know what they are looking for.

Chris Woodstra

Chris Woodstra has had a lifelong obsession with music and is an avid record collector. He has worked many years in music retail, he was a DJ, hosting programs in every genre of music, and has been a contributing editor for several local arts and entertainment magazines. Working as an editor for the *All Music Guide* database has given him the opportunity to combine his technical skills, a B.S. in Physics and Mathematics, and his love of music for the first time in his life. Being a perfectionist by nature, Chris makes sure that that any information that goes into the database has been carefully researched and verified.

Stephen Thomas Erlewine

Stephen Thomas Erlewine studied English at the University of Michigan and was the arts editor of the school's newspaper, *The Michigan Daily*. In addition to editing the *All Music Guide*, Erlewine is a freelance writer and musician.

Scott Yanow

Scott Yanow has been writing about jazz since 1975. He was the jazz editor of *Record Review* during its entire existence (1976-84), has been a freelancer since 1983 and has written for *Down Beat, Jazz Times* and *Jazz Forum*. He is currently a regular contributor to ten magazines including *Jazziz, Cadence, Coda*, the *L.A. Jazz Scene*, the *Mississippi Rag* and the *Jazz Report*. In addition he has written over 100 liner notes, was a contributor to the *New Grove Dictionary of Jazz* and assisted on the fourth edition of Leonard Feather and Ira Gitler's *Encyclopedia of Jazz*. It is his goal to collect every good jazz record ever made, and to have time to listen to them.

HOW TO USE THIS BOOK

ARTIST NAME   (Alternate name in parentheses).

VITAL STATISTICS   Date and place of birth and death, if known.

INSTRUMENT(S) / STYLE OF JAZZ   Major instruments for each performer, and other performace-related credits (bandleader, composer, arranger) are listed here, followed by one or more styles of jazz associated with each performer. A description of these styles is provided in a section at the beginning of the book.

BIOGRAPHY   A quick view of the artist's life and musical career. For major performers, proportionately longer biographies are provided.

MAJOR ALBUMS   These are the 14,000+ albums selected by our editors and contributors. An album listed here (even one without a bullet or comment) is considered an important recording. It's worth a listen. Undistinguished albums are not included here.

KEY TO SYMBOLS   ○ ☆ ★

○ LANDMARK RECORDINGS   Albums marked with an open circle are singled out as landmark or career turning points for the particular artist. These are classic albums—prime stuff. A land-mark recording is either a pivotal recording that marked a change in their career or a high point in their recording output.

☆ ESSENTIAL COLLECTIONS   Albums marked with a star should be part of any good collection of the genre. Often, these are also a good first purchase (filled star). By hearing these albums, you can get a good overview of the entire genre. These are must-hear and must-have recordings. You can't go wrong with them.

★ FIRST PURCHASE   Albums marked with a filled star should be your first purchase. This is where to begin to find out if you like this particular artist. These albums are representative of the best this artist has to offer. If you don't like these picks, chances are this artist is not for you. In the case of an artist (like Miles Davis) who has a number of distinct periods, you will find an essential pick marked for each period. It might be best to start with an earlier album (the albums are listed chronologically when possible) and work up to the later ones.

Booker Ervin (Booker (Telleferro, II) Ervin)

b. 1930, Denison, TX, **d.** Jul. 31, 1970
Tenor saxophone / Hard bop, blues & jazz

Flamboyance, excitement, and bluesy fervor were the trademarks of tenor saxophonist Booker Ervin. He was an aggressive, animated soloist whose repertoire of honks, swaggers, smears, and slurs were matched by his thorough harmonic knowledge and his complete command of the sax. He had one of the hardest tones and biggest sounds among '50s and '60s stylists, something that was even more impressive when he played the blues. Ervin's father was a trombonist who had worked with Buddy Tate. Ervin first played the trombone, then taught himself sax while in the air force. He studied music in Boston for two years, then made his earliest recordings with Ernie Fields's R&B band. This association was Ervin's professional debut as well. During the late '50s and early '60s, he was in Charles Mingus's Jazz Workshop, providing energized, powerful solos. Ervin also played in a group with Horace Parlan, George Tucker, and Al Harewood, and with Randy Weston. He recorded with Weston, and began cutting acclaimed albums as a leader in the '60s. Ervin recorded for Bethlehem, Savoy, and Candid. His crowning achievement was nine albums he did for Prestige in the mid and late '60s. These included such memorable dates as his "books." There were also sessions for Blue Note, Fontana, Pacific Jazz, and a partial album for Enja. Ervin spent most of 1964, 1965, and part of 1966 in Europe, and returned in 1968. Ervin died in 1970. Only a handful of Ervin sessions are currently in print, though others, like *Settin' the Pace*, are being reissued steadily. —*Ron Wynn*

○ **Soulful Saxes** / **i.** Jun. 1960 / Affinity

★ **Book Cooks, The** / Jun. 1960 / Affinity
Robust, earthy Ervin throughout. This tremendous combo date was originally on Bethlehem. —*Ron Wynn*

Down in the Dumps / Nov. 26, 1960-Jan. 5, 1961 / Savoy
An explosive set from Ervin's prime period, reissued on disc with additional material from the following year (1961), with trombonist Dr. Billy Howell. —*Ron Wynn*

○ **Cookin'** / Nov. 26, 1960 / Savoy Jazz

That's It / Jan. 6, 1961 / Candid

☆ **Back From the Gig** / Feb. 15, 1963+May 24, 1968 / Blue Note
Tenor saxophonist Booker Ervin's *Back from the Gig* is a perplexing volume. It is perplexing because it took Blue Note nearly seven years after Ervin's untimely death to release these valuable and infectious recordings. Apparently, both sessions, one recorded under the tutelage of pianist Horace Parlan (whom Michael Cuscuna thoughtfully documents in his liner notes), were scheduled for release years ago but never materialized. The Parlan sextet (1963) was a tough, no-nonsense blues unit. Ervin, trumpeter Johnny Coles, and guitarist Grant Green are the lead voices and are sly, raw, and often dirty. Ervin, in particular, plays with an inciting bounce and masterful range, lean and to the core. His own 1968 recordings, in cahoots with saxophonist Wayne Shorter and pianist Kenny Barron, are more expansive, evincing a knack for melding his blues romanticism to modal foundations and professing some plain big-band-inspired truths. —*Mikal Gilmore*, Down Beat

HOW TO USE THIS BOOK

ALBUM TITLE   The name of the album is listed in bold as it appears on the original when possible. Very long titles have been abbreviated, or repeated in full as part of the comment, where needed.

DATE   The recording date is given as completely as possible. We have made every attempt to verify album dates. However, if you have more accurate information, please write us; we are continually updating and refining our listings.

RECORD LABEL   Record labels indicate the current (or most recent) release of this recording.

REVIEWERS   The name of each review's author (and the magazine where the review originally appeared, if applicable) are given at the end of the review.

○ **Soulful Saxes** / Jun. 1960 / Affinity
★ **Book Cooks, The** / Jun. 1960 / Affinity
Robust, earthy Ervin throughout. This tremendous combo date was originally on Bethlehem. —*Ron Wynn*

Down in the Dumps / Nov. 26, 1960-Jan. 5, 1961 / Savoy
An explosive set from Ervin's prime period, reissued on disc with additional material from the following year (1961), with trombonist Dr. Billy Howell. —*Ron Wynn*
○ **Cookin'** / Nov. 26, 1960 / Savoy Jazz
That's It / Jan. 6, 1961 / Candid
☆ **Back From the Gig** / Feb. 15, 1963+May 24, 1968 / Blue Note
Tenor saxophonist Booker Ervin's *Back From the Gig* is a perplexing volume. It is perplexing because it took Blue Note nearly seven years after Ervin's untimely death to release these valuable and infectious recordings. Apparently, both sessions, one recorded under the tutelage of pianist Horace Parlan (whom Michael Cuscuna thoughtfully documents in his liner notes), were scheduled for release years ago but never materialized. The Parlan sextet (1963) was a tough, no-nonsense blues unit. Ervin, trumpeter Johnny Coles, and guitarist Grant Green are the lead voices and are sly, raw, and often dirty. Ervin, in particular, plays with an inciting bounce and masterful range, lean and to the core. His own 1968 recordings, in cahoots with saxophonist Wayne Shorter and pianist Kenny Barron, are more expansive, envincing a knack for melding his blues romanticism to modal foundations and professing some plain big-band-inspired truths. —*Mikal Gilmore*, Down Beat

ABBREVIATIONS

The following abbreviations are used in some reviews following the musicians' names to indicate instruments played on a particular recording or session.

as	alto saxophone	org	organ
b	bass	p	piano
bcl	bass clarinet	per	percussion
bj	banjo	pkt-t	pocket-trumpet
bs	baritone saxophone	sno	sopranino saxophone
cnt	cornet	ss	soprano saxophone
cl	clarinet	syn	synthesizer
clo	cello	tpt	trumpet
d	drums	tb	trombone
euph	euphonium	tba	tuba
f	flute	ts	tenor saxophone
flhn	flugelhorn	vib	vibraphone
frhn	french horn	vn	violin
g	guitar	vtb	valve trombone
k	keyboards		

INTRODUCTION

The word *jazz* has been used, misused and abused throughout the decades. Because it covers such a wide span of music, from dixieland to solo explorations, it has eluded an easy definition, until now!

Jazz is music that emphasizes improvisation and always has the feeling of the blues. All of the other potential qualities (including swing, a steady rhythm, high musicianship, individuality and even the ability to play in tune) are optional if often desired. What makes music jazz is the fact that a particular piece is not played the same way every time, and that individual and collective expression are considered much more significant than trying to duplicate a recorded performance in concert; the exact opposite of most pop music! Ragtime is entirely written out while New Age and forms of Indian music have improvisation but lack any blues feeling, so each of those styles fall outside of jazz.

Because there have been many different approaches to playing jazz since its birth over 100 years ago, it is desirable to categorize the music to an extent as a way of describing to other listeners what a performance sounds like. The *All Music Guide* uses around 15 different style names to give readers an idea what to expect when approaching an individual's recordings. However it should be understood that this categorization is a necessary simplification. Not every musician listed as playing "bop" sounds alike; nor are necessarily every one of their recordings in the same restricted style. The best jazz players continue to evolve and develop throughout their careers and are expected to take chances and stretch themselves. In addition, since around 1975 it has become more and more difficult to answer the question "What do you call it?" about someone's music. The jazz world has become greatly affected by developments in pop and World Music, and the willingness of many creative musicians to open their playing to nonjazz styles has resulted in fusions of idioms that are born quicker than one can come up with an accurate name.

In general (other than for those musicians who have chosen to perform in a historic style), today's players are classified in this book as playing "Post Bop" (creative acoustic-oriented improvising), "Modern Mainstream" (essentially hard bop tied to the Art Blakey tradition), "Avant-Garde" (more advanced improvising than "Post Bop"), "Fusion" (a combination of jazz and rock), "Free Funk" (avant-garde jazz and funk rhythms), "Crossover" (a combination of jazz, R&B and pop music) or "Instrumental Pop" (pop music with a jazz feel). Obviously many musicians do not stay in any one of these styles all of the time and the descriptions are only intended as general guides. Jazz musicians should always be encouraged to be themselves and be as creative as their imaginations allow, categories and conservative critics be damned!

Another common question is "What is a jazz singer?" The definition that seems to work best is: "A jazz singer is a vocalist who brings his or her own personal interpretation to a song and improvises using notes, sounds, words and/or phrasing." Jazz singers do not ever have to scat (Billie Holiday is a good example) but they have to be creative in at least a subtle way. Because Frank Sinatra and Tony Bennett do not improvise much, their work falls outside of jazz, as do some other singers who might appear in a jazz setting but essentially just sing the melody.

The quantity of jazz recordings exploded in the 1980s and has steadily accelerated throughout the 1990s. It is the goal of the *All Music Guide To Jazz* to have a review of every recording that has appeared on CD or LP in our online database, which is available through the various computer services. However, for this book it is impossible to include everything. What we have done is stick exclusively to CDs or LPs (most of which are still in print or reasonably available) that, taken as a whole, represent each artists' most significant recordings. We have used an open-minded approach in the reviews, never condemning music because it is too advanced or unpredictable but only if it did not live up to its potential.

Our thanks go to all of those writers who have contributed directly or indirectly to this book and to Bob Rusch of Cadence for granting me permission to adapt my reviews for the *All Music Guide*. I would also like to personally thank Michael Erlewine for his confidence and trust in allowing me to put together this important project and to my wife Kathy for her patience!

--Scott Yanow

JAZZ STYLES

Although modern-day publicists sometimes divide jazz into "traditional" (meaning that the music utilizes a 4/4 walking bass) and "contemporary" (having the bass play funky danceable lines), that division is fairly meaningless; is Kenny G. more contemporary than Cecil Taylor? "Traditional" and contemporary are relative and instantly dated terms that are of little use in describing jazz for the best music is both traditional and contemporary!

Because jazz in its 100 years has consistently inspired musicians

Ragtime

Although not really jazz (ragtime does not have improvisation or the feeling of the blues), this early style (which was at its prime during 1899-1915) was a strong influence on the earlier forms of jazz. Best-known as a piano music, ragtime (which is totally written-out) was also performed by orchestras. Its syncopations and structure (blending together aspects of classical music and marches) hinted strongly at jazz and many of its melodies (most notably "Maple Leaf Rag") would be played in later years by jazz musicians in a dixieland context.

New Orleans Jazz

The earliest style of jazz, the music played in New Orleans from about the time that Buddy Bolden formed his first band in 1895 until Storyville was closed in 1917 unfortunately went totally unrecorded. However with the success of the Original Dixieland Jazz Band in 1917 and the many performances documented in the 1920's, it became possible to hear what this music sounded like in later years. Ensemble-oriented with fairly strict roles for each instrument, New Orleans jazz generally features a trumpet or cornet providing a melodic lead, harmonies from the trombone, countermelodies by the clarinet and a steady rhythm stated by the rhythm section (which usually consists of piano, banjo or guitar, tuba or bass and drums). This music is a direct descendant of marching brass bands and, although overlapping with dixieland, tends to de-emphasize solos in favor of ensembles featuring everyone playing and improvising together. Due to its fairly basic harmonies and the pure joy of the ensembles, it is consistently the happiest and most accessible style of jazz.

Classic Jazz

Not all jazz from the 1920's can be described as "New Orleans Jazz" or "Dixieland." The 1920's were a rich decade musically with jazz-influenced dance bands and a gradual emphasis on solo (as opposed to collective) improvisations. Whether it be the stride pianists, the increasingly adventurous horn soloists or the arranged music that predates swing, much of the jazz from this decade can be given the umbrella title of "Classic Jazz." Some of the modern-day revivalists (many who can be heard on the Stomp Off label) who look beyond the dixieland repertoire into the music of Fletcher Henderson, Clarence Williams and Bix Beiderbecke (to name three examples) can be said to be playing in this open-ended style

Dixieland

Because the dixieland revival (one could say fad) of the 1950's was eventually overrun by amateurs, corny trappings (such as straw hats and suspenders) and cliches, many musicians playing in that idiom grew to dislike the term and wanted it to be changed to "traditional" or "classic." But rather than blame the term or the style,

to develop their own individual approaches to self-expression, there are almost as many different styles as there are innovators. The 17 categories listed in this section and throughout the book are a necessary simplification making it possible to give readers a hint as to what particular musicians sound like. It should be assumed that the most original players do not fit neatly into any one style and that the boundaries between these different terms are not absolute or uncrossable.

it seems more justifiable to separate the professionals from the poor imitators. Dixieland, a style that overlaps with New Orleans jazz and classic jazz, has also been called "Chicago jazz" because it developed to an extent in Chicago in the 1920's. Most typically the framework involves collective improvisation during the first chorus (or, when there are several themes, for several choruses), individual solos with some riffing by the other horns, and a closing ensemble or two with a four bar tag by the drummer being answered by the full group. Although nearly any song can be turned into dixieland, there is a consistent repertoire of forty or so songs that have proven to be consistently reliable. Despite its decline in popularity since the 1950's, dixieland (along with the related classic jazz and New Orleans jazz idioms) continues to flourish as an underground music.

Swing

While New Orleans jazz has improvised ensembles, when jazz started becoming popular in the 1920's and demand was growing for larger dance bands, it became necessary for ensembles to be written down, particularly when a group included more than three or four horns. Although swing largely began when Louis Armstrong joined Fletcher Henderson's Orchestra in 1924 and Don Redman began writing arrangements for the band that echoed the cornetist's relaxed phrases, the swing era officially started in 1935 when Benny Goodman's Orchestra caught on. Swing was a major force in American popular music until the big band era largely ended in 1946. Swing differs from New Orleans jazz and dixieland in that the ensembles (even for small groups) are simpler and generally filled with repetitious riffs while in contrast the solos are more sophisticated. Individual improvisations still paid close attention to the melody but due to the advance in musicianship, the solo flights were more adventurous. The swing-oriented musicians who continued performing in the style after the end of the big band era (along with later generations who adopted this approach) can also be said to be playing "Mainstream."

Bebop

Also known as bop, bebop was a radical new music that developed gradually in the early 1940's and seemed to explode in 1945. The main difference between bop and swing is that the soloists engaged in chordal (rather than melodic) improvisation, often discarding the melody altogether after the first chorus and using the chords as the basis for the solo. Ensembles tended to be unisons, most jazz groups were under seven pieces and the soloist was free to get as adventurous as possible as long as the overall improvisation fit into the chord structure. Since the musicians were getting away from using the melodies as the basis for their solos (leading some listeners to ask "Where's the melody?"), the players were generally virtuosos and some of the tempos were very fast, bop divorced itself during the early years of bop from popular music and a dancing audience, uplifting jazz to an art music but cutting deeply into its potential commercial success. Ironically the once-radical bebop style has become the foundation for all of the innovations that followed and now can be almost thought of as establishment music!

Cool Jazz (or West Coast Jazz)

In the late 1940's and 1950's cool jazz evolved directly from bop. Essentially it was a mixture of bop with certain aspects of swing that had been overlooked or temporarily discarded. Dissonances were smoothed out, tones were softened, arrangements became important again and the rhythm section's accents were less jarring. Because some of the key pacesetters of the style (many of whom were studio musicians) were centered in Los Angeles, it was nicknamed "West Coast Jazz." Some of the recordings were experimental in nature (hinting at classical music) while some overarranged sessions were bland but in general this was a viable and popular style. By the late 1950's hard bop from the East Coast had succeeded cool jazz although many of the style's top players had long and productive careers.

Mainstream

The term "Mainstream" was coined by critic Stanley Dance to describe the type of music that trumpeter Buck Clayton and his contemporaries (veterans of the swing era) were playing in the 1950's. Rather than modernize their styles and play bop or join dixieland bands (which some did on a part-time basis in order to survive), the former big band stars (which included such players as Coleman Hawkins, Lester Young, Harry "Sweets" Edison and Roy Eldridge among many others) jammed standards and riff tunes in smaller groups. Mainstream, which was fairly well documented in the 1950's, was completely overshadowed by other styles in the 60's and its original players gradually passed away. However with the rise of tenor- saxophonist Scott Hamilton and trumpeter Warren Vache in the 1970's and the beginning of the Concord label (which emphasized the music), mainstream has made a comeback that, with its hints of both bop and dixieland, survives up to this day.

Third Stream

Third-stream (a term invented by composer Gunther Schuller in 1957) essentially means a mixture of jazz and classical music. Most attempts at fusing the two very different idioms have been at best mixed successes with string sections weighing down jazz soloists. Paul Whiteman in the 1920's, tried to (in his own words) "make a lady out of jazz" and alternated between symphonic string sections and classic jazz solos. Strings were used in some swing bands in the 1940's (most inventively by Artie Shaw and Stan Kenton's dissonant works of 1950-51) but in all cases the added musicians were merely reading their parts and backing the improvisers. Starting with Charlie Parker in 1949 jazz players recorded now and then while joined by strings but it was not until the mid-to-late 1950's that more serious experiments began to take place. Schuller, John Lewis, i.i. Johnson and Bill Russo were some of the more significant composers attempting to bridge the gap between jazz and classical musics. Most musical forecasters in the mid-1950's would have predicted that jazz's next phase would involve a fusion of sorts with classical music but the rise of the avant-garde (which has a spontaneity and an extrovertism that most pseudo-classical works lack) ended the Third Stream movement before it came close to catching on beyond academic circles.

Latin Jazz

Of all the post-swing styles, Latin Jazz has been the most consistently popular and it is easy to see why. The emphasis on percussion and Cuban rhythms make the style quite danceable and accessible. Essentially it is a mixture of bop-oriented jazz with Latin percussion. Among the pioneers in mixing together the two styles in the 1940's were the big bands of Dizzy Gillespie and Machito and the music (which has never gone out of style) has remained a viable force through the 1990's, played most notably by the bands of Tito Puente and Poncho Sanchez. The style has not changed much during the past 40 years but it still communicates to today's listeners.

Hard Bop

Although some history books claim that hard bop arose as a reaction to the softer sounds featured in cool jazz, it was actually an extension of bop that largely ignored West Coast jazz. The main differences between hard bop and bop are that the melodies tend to be simpler and often more "soulful," the rhythm section is usually looser with the bassist not as tightly confined to playing four-beats-to-the-bar as in bop, a gospel influence is felt in some of the music and quite often the saxophonists and pianists sound as if they were quite familiar with early rhythm and blues. Since the prime time period of hard bop (1955-70) was a decade later than bop, these differences were a logical evolution and one can think of hard bop as bop of the 50's and 60's. By the second half of the 1960's, the influence of the avant-garde was being felt and some of the more adventurous performances of the hard bop stylists (such as Jackie McLean and Lee Morgan) fell somewhere between the two styles. With the rise of fusion and the sale of Blue Note (hard bop's top label) in the late 1960's, the style fell upon hard times although it was revived to a certain extent in the 1980's. Much of the music performed by the so-called Young Lions during the latter decade (due to other influences altering their style) can be said to play Modern Mainstream although some groups (such as the Harper Brothers and T.S. Monk's Sextet) have kept the 1960's idiom alive.

Bossa-Nova

For a period in the early 1960's, it seemed as if everyone was playing bossa-nova. To simplify it a bit, the bossa-nova rhythm softly hits 16 beats every two bars (double time) with the accent on one, four, seven, eleven and fourteen (spaced out as 3-3-4-3-3). In ways it is the Brazilian version of cool jazz with soft tones (such as Stan Getz's tenor, Astrud Gilberto's quiet voice and the acoustic guitar in general) being in the forefront. Antonio Carlos Jobim's compositions perfectly fit the popular rhythm and, even though the music went through a short fad period, it has survived. Not many jazz musicians play bossa-nova on a fulltime basis but many will play an occasional tune or two in the very likable style.

Free Jazz

Dixieland and swing stylists improvise melodically and bop, cool and hard bop players follow chord structures in their solos. Free Jazz was a radical departure from past styles for typically after playing a quick theme, the soloist does not have to follow any progression or structure and can go in any unpredictable direction. When Ornette Coleman largely introduced Free Jazz to New York audiences (although Cecil Taylor had preceded him with less publicity), many of the bop musicians and fans debated about whether what was being played would even qualify as music; the radicals had become conservatives in less than 15 years! Free Jazz, which overlaps with the avant-garde (the latter can utilize arrangements and sometimes fairly tight frameworks), remains a controversial and mostly underground style, influencing the modern mainstream while often being ignored. Having dispensed with many of the rules as far as pitch, rhythm and development are concerned (although it need not be atonal or lack a steady pulse to be Free Jazz), the success of a Free Jazz performance can be measured by the musicianship and imagination of the performers, how colorful the music is and whether it seems logical or merely random.

Avant-Garde

Avant-garde Jazz differs from Free Jazz in that it has more structure in the ensembles (more of a "game plan") although the individual improvisations are generally just as free of conventional rules. Obviously there is a lot of overlap between Free Jazz and Avant-Garde; most players in one idiom often play in the other "style" too. In the best Avant-Garde performances it is difficult to tell when compositions end and improvisations begin; the goal is to have the solos be an outgrowth of the arrangement. As with Free Jazz, the Avant-Garde came of age in the 1960's and has continued almost unnoticed as a menacing force in the jazz underground, scorned by the mainstream that it influences.

Fusion

The word "fusion" has been so liberally used during the past quarter-century as to become almost meaningless. Fusion's original definition was best: a mixture of jazz improvisation with the power and rhythms of rock. Up until around 1967 the worlds of jazz and rock were nearly completely separate. But as rock became more creative and its musicianship improved, and as some in the jazz world became bored with hard bop and did not want to play strictly avant-garde music, the two different idioms began to trade ideas and occasionally combine forces. By the early 1970's fusion had its own separate identity as a creative jazz style (although sneered upon by many purists). Unfortunately as it became a moneymaker and as rock declined artistically from the mid-1970's on, much of what was labelled fusion was actually a combination of jazz with easy-listening pop music and lightweight r&b; crossover. The promise of fusion to an extent went unfulfilled although it continues to exist today in groups such as Tribal Tech and Chick Corea's Elektric Band.

Post Bop or Modern Mainstream

It has become increasingly difficult to categorize modern jazz. A large segment of the music does not fit into any historical style, is not as rock-oriented as fusion or as free as the avantgarde. Starting with the rise of Wynton Marsalis in 1979, a whole generation of younger players chose to play an updated variety of hard bop that was also influenced by the mid-1960's Miles Davis Quintet and aspects of free jazz. Since this music (which often features complex chordal improvisation) has become the norm for jazz in the 1990's, the terms "Modern Mainstream" or "Post Bop" are used for every-

thing from Wallace Roney to John Scofield and symbolize the eclectic scene as jazz enters its second century.

Crossover

With the gradual decline of rock (from an artistic standpoint) starting in the early 1970's, fusion (a mixture of jazz improvisations with rock rhythms) began to become more predictable since there was less input and inspiration from the rock world. At the same time, now that it was proven that electric jazz could sell records, producers and some musicians searched for other combinations of styles in order to have big sellers. They were quite successful in making their brand of jazz more accessible to the average consumer. Many different combinations have been tried during the past two decades and promoters and publicists enjoy using the phrase "Contemporary Jazz" to describe these "fusions" of jazz with elements of pop music, r&b and World music. However the word "Crossover" (which describes the intent of the performances as well as the usual results) is more accurate. Crossover and Fusion have been quite valuable in increasing the jazz audience (many of whom end up exploring other styles). In some cases the music is quite worthwhile while in other instances the jazz content is a relatively small part of the ingredients. When the style is actually pop music with only an insignificant amount of improvisation (meaning that it is largely outside of jazz), the term "Instrumental Pop" applies best of all

–Scott Yanow

TERMS

Arco

The bow of a violin. While anyone who uses the bow playing the bass or cello is said to be playing arco, the actual term is *coll' arco* or "with the bow."

Arpeggio

A term for the sounding of the notes of a chord in succession, rather than simultaneously. It also refers to a chord sounded in the same manner.

Arrangement

An adaptation of a work for an instrumentation or scoring for which it was not originally intended that preserves as much as possible of the piece's original character. The term does not quite have a fixed meaning in jazz terminology. Sometimes a new arrangement may change instrument orders or it may use a melody in one song taken from another. Sometimes rhythmic patterns are changed within songs, and there's a question whether this constitutes a new arrangement or fresh composition. Many well-known jazz pieces are frequently rearranged to the point that they're not necessarily new songs but are quite different from their original version.

Articulation

This refers either to the shaping of a musical phrase or the formation of vowels and consonants in singing. It is another important element in the analysis and evaluation of talent and performance in jazz.

Beat

A beat is the basic pulse of measured music.

Blue notes

The flattened third and flattened seventh note of the scale in any particular key. (The flattened fifth is also heard as a blue note when used as a melodic replacement or variation of the normal fifth, but not when it is a harmonic coloring in dense chordal textures.) These notes are often bent or slurred and underlined or embellished through techniques ranging from growls to slurs. They occur in other musical styles as well as jazz, and their sound and expression are far more important than simply their existence in a strict scalar sense.

Cadence

The concluding part of a phrase, movement, or work that affirms the tonality, modality, or musical language of that phrase, movement, or work through resolving dissonance or in some other fashion.

Cadenza

A virtuoso passage, normally designed for a solo instrument or lead vocal (voice). It is intended to be improvised or have an improvisatory character, can be short or extended, and may have structural importance.

Charts

In jazz and sometimes pop parlance, another word for musical scores, particularly arrangements for a band or ensemble. Now the word more often refers to the weekly surveys tabulated by music magazines, usually *Billboard*, but other publications like *Radio and Records, Cash Box, Gavin Report*, and even *Rolling Stone* have their own "charts" as well.

Chord

The sounding of two or more notes simultaneously defines a chord. The term "changes" refers to harmonic chord progressions, or chord "changes."

Chorus

This has multiple meanings in the jazz lexicon. Normally, a chorus means going through the entire number one time, whether that means as few as 12 bars, as many as 32, or any other number. It dates back to the days when popular songs contained a verse that could be tossed or omitted, followed by "the chorus." It's often used in critical parlance to refer to an extended solo chorus; for example, on Paul Gonsalves's celebrated performance at the 1956 Newport Jazz Festival.

Circular breathing

A technique used principally by players of wind instruments, but also by some brass players. The player breathes in through the nose while the cheeks push air out through the instrument. This enables the musician to produce an unbroken column of air, and hold a note indefinitely, since there's no need to pause and breathe. The creative value is directly proportional to the musician utilizing the technique.

Composition

One of jazz's more misunderstood and widely used terms. It does not have the strict meaning employed in classical or even other popular styles. Its pure meaning is simply any piece that has been written, but jazz "compositions" can range from extensively noted and prepared works to rearranged melodies or revised riffs and licks. There's also extensive debate over whether improvisation constitutes composition. The use of classical standards of composition in evaluating jazz authors, a tricky (at best) proposition, has added difficulty. Basically, when composition is used in jazz circles, it refers strictly to the piece in question. The more intricate matter of what exactly defines or determines jazz composition remains unresolved.

Counterpoint

The interweaving of different melodic lines. It is present in many styles, notably free jazz and New Orleans traditional, but it is rhythmic counterpoint, rather than melodic counterpoint, that is most critical in jazz.

Dissonance

A sound which, in the primary harmonic system, is unstable and must be resolved to a consonant, or stable, sound. When used skillfully, this can be a most creative element in jazz circles; when misused it can be frightening.

Double time

A technique in which the apparent tempo of a performance is increased by doubling the number of notes played.

Downbeat

The first beat of a performance, or the first beat of each bar (often referred to as "one").

Embouchure

This has a dual meaning in jazz. It's both the position of the mouth and lips in playing reed and brass instruments, and also the mouthpiece of a reed instrument.

Ensemble

A general term referring to the entire jazz group, big band, combo, or orchestra. When critics talk about "ensemble" interaction, they're usually talking about the interplay among group members during the performance of a piece. Often unison sections are called "ensemble" portions of a piece.

Harmony

The combination of two or more tones, which produces a chord. These tones may be actual notes sounded simultaneously or they may be implied (chords derived from the context of a melodic line). The term generally connotes the presence of a tonality, and chords are said to contain harmonic and nonharmonic tones, depending on whether the tones are part of the current tonality.

Improvisation

This is the lifeblood of jazz, and it is also sometimes called "spontaneous creation." This is playing without premeditation. It's also among the more misunderstood premises within jazz. Jazz is not the only music to use improvisation, nor should composition be considered the enemy of improvisation. The act may involve departing from the established melody, distorting it, or coloring it. It can also involve inserting quotes from other compositions into the improvisation being crafted. Some composers, notably Duke Ellington, wrote with improvisations in mind for particular players.

Jam session

A group improvisation session and an outgrowth of the term "jam." This has long been a musician's term for an occasion when informal extended playing occurred apart from regular jobs. Jams were often held late nights or in the early morning hours following gigs. During the '30s and '40s, jam sessions were regular occurrences, but in the late '40s the Musicians' Union started to discourage members from participating in jam sessions, even in situations with invited audiences. But the term stuck and now is used to identify almost any setting where musicians gather. Norman Granz's Jazz at the Philharmonic concerts and recordings are perhaps the prime example of "jam sessions," despite the fact they soon became quite predictable and were hardly spontaneous affairs.

Key

The tonal center of a composition as defined by the relationship between the other notes of a scale to a certain note known as the tonic or key note.

Lick

A phrase of a player that's been copied, learned, and/or repeatedly used by another player. It's become an established jazz practice for musicians to copy the phrases of artists they admire. One thing that separates innovators from journeymen is the ability to develop one's own licks. Another is the ability to create new phrases rather than simply recycle favorite licks.

Measure

The space between two bar lines.

Medley

A performance linking a number of songs or other musical works. The songs are usually, but not always, related.

Melisma

A group of notes sung to the same syllable. This is a marvelous technique when done by masters, and is interesting even in the hands of journeymen, though it can be excruciating when performed by hacks.

Melody

A succession of musical tones, usually with a definite rhythm and having a characteristic musical shape.

Meter

The arrangement of the rhythmic units of a composition in a manner that produces a regular pattern of beats that are then grouped into measures. The number of beats in a measure is indicated by the time signature.

Modal

A style of jazz improvisation on a series of scales instead of a sequence of chords. This style, which became popular in the late '50s and early '60s, wasn't that much removed from bop, but tried to avoid the amount of harmonic movement and direction of bop sequences. The emphasis on the part of the soloist was toward melodic creativity rather than simply relying on chord-derived material.

Mode

In its simplest definition, mode is a designation for types of scales or melodies, indicating the range, the pitch center, and the whole- and half-step relationships between the notes. Many non-Western cultures, particularly Asian ones, apply the concept quite differently. George Russell developed an entire system (The Lydian Concept of Tonal Organization) from the seven seven-note scales used in ancient Greece, which, along with certain five- and six-note scales, constitute the basis of all European music.

Multiphonics

A term describing multiple simultaneous tones produced on a wind instrument from a single fingering. Although the technique is most commonly used in contemporary classical music, such jazz artists as John Coltrane and Albert Mangelsdorff are among its most skillful proponents.

Note

A single sound of a specific pitch and duration.

Original

Another all-purpose term with a somewhat confusing meaning. An original refers to a song performed and written by the same person, as opposed to an "original" playing style, of which there have been precious few. Actually, there aren't that many "original" compositions either, at least in the strictest sense of the term.

Ostinato

A musical figure repeated, usually at the same pitch, throughout a composition.

Overblowing

The practice of blowing into a wind instrument with more than usual force and changing the pitch, producing an overtone rather than the customary tone.

Overdubbing

At one time this was considered something radical, but it is now a commonplace studio practice in every category of popular music. Overdubbing came about through the introduction of sound into films, where it became necessary to find ways of blending dialog, sound effects, and music and replacing one actor's voice with another. Sidney Bechet's 1941 recording of five instruments (which to this day is widely celebrated in some circles and just as widely debunked in others) was an overdubbing milestone. Les Paul invented the multitrack tape machine, and gradually the practice gained popularity and, finally, total acceptance. Now almost no pop albums are done without overdubbing, and more and more jazz works use it as well. Many reissues are even including pieces with new parts overdubbed. Overdubbing has led to additional practices. These include "tracking," where the ensemble arrangement gets recorded first and then the improvised solos are taped and inserted. There is also "layering," whereby each instrument gets recorded in turn, or the rhythm section arrangement first and then other parts, and then everything gets spliced together later. Numerous country "duets" are actually each participant singing a part with the performances linked later in studio.

Phrasing

The grouping and articulation of a sequence of notes to form a logical unit or phrase. A musician's phrasing is an integral factor in evaluating his or her skills.

Pizzicato

An indication for string players to pluck rather than bow the strings, though in jazz most bassists play with the fingers far more often than with the bow.

Rhythm

The distinctive grouping of sounds and silence in time based on, among other things, the duration of tone, strong and weak stresses, and other factors like harmony and melodic contour.

Rhythm section

A term for players in a band whose primary function is to maintain the rhythm. Initially, rhythm was kept mainly by guitar and bass, or piano and drums. Later, during the '20s, both large bands and small combos used four rhythm players with banjo and brass rather than guitar or string bass. During the '30s, the rhythm role reverted again to predominantly piano and drums. Today, in the basic jazz combo, rhythm section instruments are usually bass and drums, with piano (and in some bands guitar) alternating as part of the rhythm section and also as a lead/solo instrument. Many bands now employ additional percussionists on African and/or Latin instruments for extra rhythmic support.

Riff

A repeated phrase of pronounced rhythmic character, often not strikingly melodic. Riffs occur often in solo work, particularly from players who customarily think along such lines.

Scales

Sequences of notes in ascending or descending order of pitch, customarily beginning and ending on the fundamental note of a tonality or mode and considered to have a scope of one or more octaves.

Sideman

Due to nonsexist language requirements, this term has fallen out of favor in some parts of the jazz universe. It refers to anyone not the group leader on a particular session or date.

Solo

This has at least two meanings in jazz terminology. One refers to any performance that is unaccompanied. Coleman Hawkins's "Picasso" was the first solo saxophone example. It is most frequently the case with pianists, though a number of saxophonists have also recorded some celebrated albums, and some string and brass musicians as well. It also refers to any passage in a performance where one person is engaged in prominent melodic improvisation or on a specific chord sequence. Usually, some or all of the other group members are backing or supporting the "soloist."

Staccato

A type of articulation in which each note so marked is separated from the following note and may receive a greater or lesser accent, depending on the notation and the context.

Standard

A designation usually applied to popular songs from the pre-rock era whose appeal has outlived the original publication and, in many instances, the lifetimes of the composers. These are often songs from musicals, plays, or films, but are also Tin Pan Alley works and even some numbers that were novelty tunes. Some songs, such as "My Favorite Things" or "Green Dolphin Street," are so identified with jazz that their origins have been forgotten. There are also now jazz "standards," that is, works by jazz composers that have become part of the language, like "Perdido," "Tune Up," or "Ornithology."

Syncopation

In European music, syncopation is a simple and steady pulse that is disturbed by an anticipated or delayed accent. In jazz terms, syncopation has a slightly different meaning, as most jazz is naturally polyrhythmic and thus not syncopated in that sense.

Tempo

The rate of speed of a musical passage, indicated by a suggestive word or phrase or by a precise indication. In jazz and popular music a fast tempo is called uptempo, a slow one down tempo, though few contemporary critics use down tempo in their copy, preferring to talk about ballads or slow songs. Out of tempo usually refers to a group or a soloist with a poor sense of rhythm.

Timbre

The color or tonal quality of a sound, determined by its overtones.

Time signature

An indication of the meter of a piece that's placed at the beginning of a composition and at the beginning of any measure where a change in the prevailing meter occurs. The signature is usually a fraction whose numerator is the number of beats per measure and whose denominator is the unit of beat.

Tone

One of the terms with multiple meanings that can greatly confuse the nonjazz listener and someone trying to understand the jazz lexicon. In jazz parlance, tone refers to the qualities that make up a performer's sound. The term also means a musical sound or pitch, but when critics refer to someone's tone, they're describing or evaluating that individual's sound.

Upbeat

The second beat of a piece. In jazz, the upbeat is usually deemed the stronger in the piece. The term also has widespread nonmusical usage as denoting a positive development or personality.

Virtuoso

An often overused word in jazz circles (criminally misused in pop ones), as it is sometimes applied to merely talented people rather than genuine virtuosos. The strictest meaning is a performer with highly developed technical skill. The difference (or similarity) between a virtuoso and a genius makes for interesting discussion.

—*Ron Wynn*

A

Ahmed Abdul-Malik (Sam Gill)

b. Jan. 30, 1927, New York, NY, **d.** Oct. 2, 1993, Long Branch, NJ
Bass, Oud / Hard Bop, World Music
An early pioneer in fusing African, African-American and Middle Eastern musical concepts, Ahmed Abdul-Malik divided his time between playing strong, supportive bass and soloing on oud. He was among the earliest to use the oud in a jazz context, playing it on some '50s sessions. Abdul-Malik studied African and Middle Eastern music, plus violin and bass. He played with Art Blakey in the late '40s, Randy Weston and Thelonious Monk in the '50s, Herbie Mann and Earl Hines in the '60s and Ken McIntyre in the '70s. Abdul-Malik became a Muslim in the '50s, and played oud on a South American tour sponsored by the State Department in the early '60s and at the first jazz festival held in Tangiers, Morocco in 1972. He also recorded on oud with Johnny Griffin in the '50s, John Coltrane in the '60s and Hamiet Bluiett in the '70s. Abdul-Malik began teaching at New York University in 1970, and later also became an instructor in the department of African Studies at Brooklyn College. He was given BMI's "Pioneer in Jazz Award" in 1984. Abdul-Malik's *Jazz Sahara* session was reissued on CD in 1993. It's currently his only recording date available, though he recorded others for New Jazz in the '60s. *—Ron Wynn and Michael G. Nastos*

● **Jazz Sahara** / Oct. 1958 / Riverside ✦✦✦✦
This CD reissue is an early example of fusing jazz with world music. Abdul-Malik switches between bass and oud, interacts closely with the droning violin of Naim Karacand, Jack Ghanaim's kanoon (a 72-string instrument) and Mike Hamway's darabeka (a percussive drum), and mixes in Al Harewood's drums and (on three of the four selections) the tenor of Johnny Griffin. The music is a qualified success, essentially Middle Eastern folk music with Griffin added in. This set is interesting and in its own way innovative but not essential. *—Scott Yanow*

East Meets West / Mar. 16, 1959+Mar. 31, 1959 / RCA ✦✦✦✦

The Music of Ahmed Abdul-Malik / May 23, 1961 / New Jazz ✦✦✦

Sounds of Africa / Aug. 22, 1962 / New Jazz ✦✦

Eastern Moods of Ahmed Abdul Malik / Jun. 11, 1963 / New Jazz ✦✦✦

Spellbound / Mar. 12, 1964 / Status ✦✦✦✦

Ahmed Abdullah

b. May 10, 1947, New York, NY
Trumpet / Avant-Garde
An exciting but still little-known trumpeter, Ahmed Abdullah began playing music when he was 13. He started to get notice during the 1970s, performing in New York's loft scene. Since then he has played with Chico Freeman, Charles Brackeen and Marion Brown, led his own Solomonic Quintet and recorded for Silkheart and Cadence Jazz. This powerful avant-garde trumpeter deserves much greater recognition. *—Scott Yanow*

● **Live at Ali's Alley** / Apr. 24, 1978 / Cadence ✦✦✦✦
Trumpeter Ahmed Abdullah featured French horn and cello in his instrumental configuration, while also working alongside tenor saxophonist Chico Freeman on this 1978 date. It's symbolic of the decade's "loft" jazz, a free-wheeling date with uneven, but often compelling solos as well as periods of rambling, unproductive and ragged ensemble work. Freeman's blistering tenor sax is uni-

formly inspired, while Abdullah's solos are also aggressive and energetic. Vincent Chancey's French horn and Muneer Abdul Fataah's cello contributions provide interesting contrast, while bassist Jerome Hunter and drummer Rashied Sinan are competent and effective, though not memorable. *—AMG*

Life's Force / 1978–1979 / About Time ✦✦✦
A progressive trumpeter with sextet in an all-original program, it includes Jay Hoggard on vibes and Vincent Chancey (French horn). *—Michael G. Nastos*

Liquid Magic / Feb. 16, 1987 / Silkheart ✦✦✦
Trumpeter Abdullah's debut for Silkheart resulted in him sometimes being eclipsed on his session. That wasn't due so much to Abdullah lacking verve or skill, as to the brilliance exhibited by tenor saxophonist Charles Brackeen and bassist Malachi Favors, whose acrobatics threaten to stretch and pull some songs beyond their harmonic fabric. *—Ron Wynn*

And the Solomonic Quintet / Dec. 3, 1987+Dec. 4, 1987 / Silkheart ✦✦✦
Trumpeter Ahmed Abdullah sprays around dissonant solos and spearheads an often frenzied set on his second release for Silkheart. The lineup is exceptional, notably the powerful tenor saxophonist David S. Ware, dynamic bassist Fred Hopkins, and underrated drummer Charles Moffett. *—Ron Wynn*

John Abercrombie

b. Dec. 16, 1944, Port Chester, NY
Guitar / Post-Bop
Perhaps the most skilled of the contemporary jazz guitarists who've embraced and utilized rock techniques and electronic devices in an improvising framework, John Abercrombie has made many superb recordings since the early '70s. He's used phase shifters, volume pedals and guitar synthesizers on a regular basis, as well as the electric mandolin. Abercrombie is cited (or blamed) in many circles for helping create the "ECM sound," a patchwork of acoustic and electric sounds made by eclectic musicians who combine jazz, European and Asian/Indian sources, elements and influences. But Abercrombie can also swing, play in the distorted, jagged rock style, execute bebop changes, improvise in 12-bar blues patterns or engage in free dialogues. He began playing guitar at 14, taking lessons from a local teacher. He attended Berklee in the mid-'60s, while also playing in rock bands. Abercrombie studied guitar with Jack Petersen, and in 1967 and 1968 toured with Johnny "Hammond" Smith. He moved to New York in 1969, working briefly with the group Dreams, then playing with Chico Hamilton, in whose band he made his first visit to Europe. Abercrombie later played with Jeremy Steig, Gil Evans and Gato Barbieri, while recording with Dave Liebman and playing in Billy Cobham's Spectrum. He recorded with them and attracted extensive critical attention. Abercrombie began recording with Jack DeJohnette and also as a leader in the mid-'70s, working mainly for ECM. Since that time, he's done duo albums with Ralph Towner, played in various DeJohnette bands and headed various groups. Abercrombie's recorded with Jan Hammer, Dave Holland, Mike Brecker, Richie Beirach, George Mraz, Peter Donald, Marc Johnson, Adam Nussbaum, Peter Erskine, Vince Mendoza and Jon Christensen, among others. He has many titles currently available on CD. Recently John Abercrombie had a reunion of his early 1970s trio Timeless with Dave Holland and Jack DeJohnette. *—Ron Wynn and David Nelson McCarthy*

Friends / 1971 / Oblivion ✦✦

● **Timeless** / Jun. 21, 1974–Jun. 22, 1974 / ECM ✦✦✦✦
Guitarist John Abercrombie debuted on ECM in 1974 working in a format that would become familiar: a trio setting. Jan Hammer on synthesizer, organ and piano, and drummer Jack DeJohnette accompanied him on a date that included crisp, taut riffs and solos from Abercrombie, sparse and tasty fills and licks by DeJohnette and a bonus in long stretches of first-rate organ work by Hammer, minus the rock gimmicks that eventually plagued his keyboard work. —*AMG*

Gateway / Mar. 1975 / ECM ✦✦✦
The first of two fine trio albums that matched guitarist John Abercrombie, bassist Dave Holland and drummer Jack DeJohnette. This album managed the trick of being both reflective and dynamic, thanks to Abercrombie's intelligent, finely crafted solos and DeJohnette's first-rate, sympathetic rhythms. Though Holland didn't play with his usual vigor, he remained enough of a force to successfully interact with Abercrombie and DeJohnette. —*AMG*

Pilgrim & The Stars / 1976 / ECM ✦✦✦

Untitled / 1976 / ECM ✦✦✦

Sargasso Sea / May 1976 / ECM ✦✦
A nice session, though not as spectacular as anticipated, matching guitarists John Abercrombie and Ralph Towner, who also plays piano. Towner's 12-string solos are stronger than his classical ones, which are frequently beautiful but don't make much of an impression contrasted to Abercrombie's more energetic improvisations. The title track's the best cut on the sessions; the others are more decorative than intriguing. —*AMG*

Cloud Dance / 1976 / ECM ✦✦✦

Gateway 2 / Jul. 1977 / ECM ✦✦✦
This second meeting between Abercrombie, bassist Dave Holland and drummer Jack DeJohnette in 1977 features more electric guitar fireworks and less exacting, thoughtful jazz solos. Holland's bass playing is more intense, while DeJohnette once more is rhythmically diverse, supportive and in control. Those who prefer hearing the rock-tinged side of Abercrombie's musical personality get their wish on the majority of *Gateway 2*. —*AMG*

Characters / Nov. 1977 / ECM ✦✦

Pictures / 1977 / ECM ✦✦

Arcade / Dec. 1978 / ECM ✦✦✦

Straight Flight / Mar. 19, 1979–Mar. 20, 1979 / Jam ✦✦✦✦

Abercrombie Quartet / Nov. 1979 / ECM ✦✦✦

M / Nov. 1980 / ECM ✦✦✦

Five Years Later / Mar. 1981 / ECM ✦✦✦
This album was recorded with Ralph Towner (g). Abercrombie is more electric in this duet setting. Three pieces were co-written by the duo. Two vastly different sounds mesh nicely. —*Michael G. Nastos*

Solar / May 1982 / Palo Alto ✦✦✦

Drum Strum / Oct. 1982 / 1750 Arch ✦✦

Night / Apr. 1984 / ECM ✦✦✦
This spirited original features Jan Hammer on keyboards. It's a favorable group setting for guitarist Abercrombie and timeless trio. Michael Brecker on tenor sax. —*Michael G. Nastos*

Current Events / Sep. 1985 / ECM ✦✦✦
Excellent trio date featuring Abercrombie playing with bassist Marc Johnson and drummer Peter Erskine. The three take chances, converge, collide, alternate time in the spotlight, and make emphatic, unpredictable music while never staying locked into one groove or style. —*Ron Wynn*

Witchcraft / Jun. 24, 1986–Jun. 25, 1986 / Justin Time ✦✦✦

Getting There / Apr. 1987 / ECM ✦✦✦

John Abercrombie, Marc Johnson, & Peter Erskine / Apr. 21, 1988 / ECM ✦✦✦
An excellent trio outing with Abercrombie, inventive bassist Marc Johnson, and careening drummer Peter Erskine. The trio sometimes unite for piercing interpretations as on "Stella by Starlight," and other times collide and interact on furious rhythm dialogues and extended improvisations. —*Ron Wynn*

Animato / Oct. 1989 / ECM ✦✦

While We're Young / Jun. 1992 / ECM ✦✦✦

November / Nov. 1992 / ECM ✦✦✦

Speak of the Devil / Jul. 1993 / ECM ✦✦

Gateway: Homecoming / Dec. 1994 / ECM ✦✦✦✦
The trio heard on this CD (guitarist John Abercrombie, bassist Dave Holland and drummer Jack DeJohnette) recorded *Gateway* and *Gateway 2* for ECM back in 1975 and 1977. Although each of the musicians has grown musically since that time and has piled up plenty of accomplishments, the style of music that they perform when they come together as Gateway has remained largely unchanged. One could call it "creative fusion" or "post bop"; whatever the name, the music's success depends on a great deal of intuitive interplay between the talented players. John Abercrombie's often-distorted tone and use of color show hints of Bill Frisell (who must have learned from the example of the older guitarist). Dave Holland's bass is never predictable or subservient to Abercrombie and, even if the other musicians were allowed to coast, Jack DeJohnette's constantly rumbling drumming would keep the performances from ever getting too comfortable. Although the original music (which concludes with a quiet piece for DeJohnette's piano) is not for all jazz fans (Abercrombie's rockish sound may scare some off), the high improvisational level makes this a set deserving of close listens. —*Scott Yanow*

Muhal Richard Abrams

b. Sep. 19, 1930, Chicago, IL
Piano, Composer, Leader / Avant-Garde
Although somewhat underrated through the years due to his behind-the-scenes work, Muhal Richard Abrams was one of the most important figures to emerge from the Association for the Advancement of Creative Musicians (AACM), an organization whose successes would have been much fewer without his participation. Influential as an avant-garde pianist who bridged the gap between hard bop, free jazz and (to a certain extent) contemporary classical music, Abrams' additional significance as a composer, arranger and bandleader has long put him near the top of the avant-garde field. Although he went to music college when he was 17, Muhal Richard Abrams was essentially self-taught, learning his craft on the job and through his own explorations. Influenced early on by pianist Bud Powell, Abrams performed in a wide variety of jobs during the 1950s, gained some early attention for his playing on the MJT+3's album *Branching Out*, and through the years gigged and/or recorded with such musicians as Max Roach, Sonny Stitt, Dexter Gordon, Eddie Harris, Ruth Brown and Woody Shaw. In 1961 Abrams formed a short-lived orchestra (the Experimental Band) and then on May 8, 1965, he became a founder of the AACM, a still-active Chicago-based organization that emphasizes self-reliance by performing original compositions, organizing one's own concerts and educating the community (including younger musicians) about the new music. The innovators who emerged from the AACM (including the Art Ensemble of Chicago, Anthony Braxton and Henry Threadgill) invigorated the avant-garde, taking the music out of the potential dead-end of consistently intense improvisations into an appreciation of the value of space and silence and a logical mix of compositions with individual expression. As the AACM's first president, Abrams established the organization as a vital force on the Chicago jazz scene. Fortunately he did not neglect his own playing, and through the years, most notably on Delmark (starting with the groundbreaking *Levels and Degrees of Light* in 1967) and continuing on India Navigation, Arista/Freedom and Black Saint, Abrams (who moved to New York in 1977) has recorded in a wide variety of settings, from solo piano to leader of his own innovative big band. He has stuck consistently to his principles (which became the philosophy of the AACM) and forged his own singular path in jazz. —*Scott Yanow*

Levels and Degrees of Light / Jun. 7, 1967+Dec. 21, 1967 / Delmark ✦✦✦✦
This was one of Muhal Richard Abrams' early gems, a 1967 session that included him playing both piano and synthesizer and heading a quartet with Anthony Braxton on clarinet, Thurman Barker on drums and Gordon Emmanuel on vibes. Abrams' superbly interspersed free, hard bop, and blues elements, along with Braxton's solos and the intriguing frontline and contrasts

provided by vibes and drums rather than bass, resulted in some unusual and striking compositions. This has been reissued on CD. —AMG

Young at Heart, Wise in Time / Jul. 2, 1969+Aug. 20, 1969 / Delmark ✦✦✦
Muhal Richard Abrams, as the founder of the AACM in Chicago, has been one of the unsung leaders of the avant-garde ever since the mid-'60s. A versatile pianist, Abrams is heard in two different settings on this, his second session as a leader. "Young at Heart" finds him stretching out on a solo piano performance that hints at earlier styles while exploring the potential sounds and silence of free jazz. "Wise in Time" has Abrams functioning as part of an explorative quintet with trumpeter Leo Smith and altoist Henry Threadgill, both of whom were unknown youngsters at the time. Fascinating music, it is recommended strictly for the open-eared listener who does not demand that all jazz swing conventionally. —Scott Yanow

Things to Come from Those Now Gone / Oct. 10, 1972 / Delmark ✦✦✦✦
A masterpiece and one of the finest works in the contemporary (post-'50s free) jazz vernacular. Muhal Richard Abrams' compositions and piano solos illuminate multiple traditions, from stride and ragtime to the percussive style of the '50s and '60s. —Ron Wynn

Afrisong / Sep. 9, 1975 / India Navigation ✦✦✦
Muhal Richard Abrams seamlessly blends elements of stride, bebop, blues, and free music on this collection of solo piano pieces recorded in 1975 for the Japanese label Trio/Whynot. It was also available briefly on India Navigation. Top numbers include "Hymn to the East," "Blues for M" and the title track. Abrams displays his instrumental facility and underrated keyboard skills, which often take a back seat to his arranging, compositions and bandleading. —AMG

Sightsong / Oct. 13, 1975–Oct. 14, 1975 / Black Saint ✦✦✦
Duets 1976 / Aug. 1, 1976–Aug. 2, 1976 / Black Saint ✦✦
This was not Muhal Richard Abrams session, but Anthony Braxton's, and was issued on Arista under his name. The duo teamed for intriguing, sometimes intense and other times more introspective performances on material ranging from Braxton's numerical compositions to their unusual version of "Maple Leaf Rag." Braxton plays alto and soprano saxophones, plus contrabass clarinet and sax and standard clarinet, while Abrams concentrates on piano and adds everything from bop riffs to stride accents, rag-time and blues lines. —AMG

1–OQA+19 / Nov. 1977–Dec. 1977 / Black Saint ✦✦✦
Muhal Richard Abrams hasn't presided over many small combos with a more imposing lineup than on this 1977 session. Anthony Braxton and Henry Threadgill plays numerous instruments from alto, tenor and soprano saxes to flutes and clarinets, even adding background vocals. Fiery percussionist Steve McCall and bassist Leonard Jones, who also adds some vocals, complete the lineup. The unit makes demanding, harmonically dense and rhythmically unpredictable material, with Braxton's scurrying solos ably matched by Threadgill's bluesier lines and Abrams' leadership and inventive blend of jazz, blues, and other sources holding things together. —AMG

Lifea Blinec / Feb. 1978 / Novus ✦✦✦
Muhal Richard Abrams heads one of his finest small combos on this intense quintet session from 1978. Joseph Jarman provides riveting bass saxophone and bassoon contributions in addition to playing alto clarinet, flute, soprano sax, percussion and vocals. His multiple contributions are matched by Douglas Ewart on an equal array of reed instruments, including bass and soprano clarinet, bassoon, alto and tenor sax and percussion. Abrams divides his time between keyboards, conducting and percussion, while Amina Claudine Myers adds vibrant, bluesy riffs and statements. Thurman Barker takes care of drum duties and doubles on percussion. —AMG

Spiral Live at Montreux 1978 / Jul. 22, 1978 / Novus ✦✦✦✦
Muhal Richard Abrams performs unaccompanied throughout this concert appearance from the 1978 Montreux Jazz Festival. The relatively brief "String Song" features some odd sound explorations as Abrams plays the strings from inside the piano along with gongs. "D Song" and "Voice Song" find Abrams sticking to the piano and offering a slightly mellower alternative to Cecil Taylor in exploring new music. Abrams' occasional use of devices from

earlier styles (including a bit of dissonant stride and basslines à la Lennie Tristano) make this music a bit more accessible than one might expect at times, but in general this set is for listeners who enjoy hearing new approaches to musical freedom. —Scott Yanow

Spihumonesty / Jul. 1979 / Black Saint ✦✦✦
Mama and Daddy / Jun. 16, 1980+Jun. 19, 1980 / Black Saint ✦✦✦
This was a first-rate big band/large group session from 1980, with Muhal Richard Abrams' compositions being played by a masterful ensemble which included French horn and tuba in its instrumental mix. There are wonderful solos, dashing arrangements and fiery rhythm support from Thurman Barker on drums, marimba and percussion, with Andrew Cyrille adding additional percussive assistance. The group also features Baikida Carroll on trumpet and fluegelhorn, Wallace McMillan on various reeds, violinist Leroy Jenkins, bassist Brian Smith, Abrams on keyboards, trombonist George Lewis, Bob Stewart on tuba and Vincent Chancey on French horn. They present adventurous, disciplined, frequently exciting music. —AMG

Duet / May 11, 1981–May 12, 1981 / Black Saint ✦✦✦
Muhal Richard Abrams recorded several memorable and successful duet sessions during the 1970s and '80s. Few covered more territory or were as invigorating as this album with Amina Claudine Myers, a capable player on either organ or piano. Myers discarded the organ for this date, as both she and Abrams use Yamaha C3D pianos. While Myers displays her gospel and blues influences, Abrams' muscular riffs and solos result in exciting dialogues and marvelous complementary, contrasting and dueling passages. This is an intense, yet also swinging, enjoyable session, one in which Abrams displays the mastery of multiple genres that's distinguished his music, and Myers her distinctive mix of secular and spiritual elements. —Ron Wynn

Blues Forever / Jul. 20, 1981–Jul. 27, 1981 / Black Saint ✦✦✦✦
A tremendously large orchestra session, with Abrams heading a crew that includes the cream of '70s and '80s improvisers, plus some '60s survivors. Although every arrangement doesn't click, the band successfully romps and stomps through enough cuts to show that the big band sound doesn't just mean "ghost" groups recreating dusty numbers from the '30s and '40s. —Ron Wynn

● **Rejoicing with the Light** / Jan. 8, 1983–Jan. 25, 1983 / Black Saint ✦✦✦✦✦
Muhal Richard Abrams blends vintage and progressive sensibilities on this outstanding 1984 session. It is a large band outing, and Abrams assembled many of the finest active improvisers. His orchestra does not include just saxophones and trumpets but also French horns, bass clarinets, cello, guitar, vibes and timpani. This assures Abrams a varied, rich sound with multiple options. He leads the orchestra through pieces that are sometimes introspective and other times jubilant and swinging, but never simple or predictable. This session is a challenging, instructive and entertaining lesson in modern big-band writing, arranging and performing. —Ron Wynn

View from Within / Sep. 22, 1984+Sep. 27, 1984 / Black Saint ✦✦✦
Abrams' work for mid-sized groups varies markedly from his solo, trio, or large orchestra material. Compositions are even more unpredictable; there's more emphasis on mood and less on rhythm, and solos are crisper and shorter. This '84 date included some intriguing instrumental configurations at times (vibes/flute/percussion, piano/clarinet/bass clarinet) and ranked among his best '80s dates. —Ron Wynn

Roots of Blue / Jan. 7, 1986 / RPR ✦✦✦✦
Colours in Thirty-Third / Dec. 19, 1986 / Black Saint ✦✦
Muhal Richard Abrams constantly varies the lineups on the seven numbers that constitute this 1986 session, alternating between trio, quartet, quintet and sextet pieces. The title track and "Introspection" feature the entire group, and were the most striking works, though the trio tunes offered the most musically challenging material. John Purcell on soprano and tenor sax and bass clarinet provided several stirring solos, while violinist John Blake was a solid contributor on several selections and the rhythm tandem of bassist Fred Hopkins and drummer Andrew Cyrille were also consistent and engaging, particularly Cyrille. Abrams as usual was an inspiring force as an instrumentalist and conceptualist. —AMG

The Hearinga Suite / Jan. 17, 1989–Jan. 18, 1989 / Black Saint
✦✦✦✦✦
Pianist Muhal Richard Abrams leads an 18-piece orchestra on his seven originals that make up the *Hearinga Suite*. Much of the music is quite adventurous, although "Oldfotalk" is fairly conventional. Although the personnel includes such fine players as trumpeters Jack Walrath and Cecil Bridgewater and saxophonists John Purcell and Marty Ehrlich, the emphasis is on group interplay and the colorful arrangements. Throughout this very interesting set, Abrams shows how a big band can logically be utilized in freer forms of jazz. —*Scott Yanow*

Blu Blu Blu / Nov. 9, 1990–Nov. 10, 1990 / Black Saint ✦✦✦
His finest pure big band date. Abrams leads a surging, eclectic aggregation through numbers that are mostly uptempo and aggressive. Whistler Joel Brandon gets honors as the most distinctive stylist, but the entire crew is showcased favorably in this '90 session. Things are further enhanced by some of Abrams' most intense pieces, especially "One For The Whistler" and "Stretch Time." —*Ron Wynn*

Family Talk / Feb. 26, 1993–Mar. 1, 1993 / Black Saint ✦✦✦
Muhal Richard Abrams' compositions are never structured in a usual manner. This is a quintet outing that pairs trumpeter Jack Walraith and multi-reed player Patience Higgins in the front line, with Abrams on piano and synthesizer, Warren Smith on vibes, marimba, gongs and timpani and bassist Brad Jones. Over the album, Abrams varies the moods, instrumentation, voicings and solo order, with lengthy numbers that have both carefully crafted sections and places that allow the musicians to soar. His music does not have catchy hooks; it is rewarding and captivating but requires some effort and attention, the kind of thing that separates great fare from merely good material. —*Ron Wynn*

One Line, Two Views / Jun. 23, 1995–Jun. 24, 1995 / New World
✦✦✦

George Adams

b. Apr. 29, 1940, Covington, GA, **d.** Nov. 14, 1992, New York, NY
Tenor Saxophone, Flute / Avant-Garde, Post-Bop
A passionate tenor and flute player who did not hesitate to break up chordal improvising with an unexpected scream or roar, George Adams was an original voice who (like his friend Don Pullen) crossed over several stylistic boundaries. He started on piano but by the time he was in high school he was playing tenor in funk bands. In 1961 he toured with Sam Cooke and in 1963 Adams moved to Ohio where he played with organ groups the next few years. In 1968 he relocated to New York where he played with Roy Haynes, Gil Evans and Art Blakey, among others. However, it was his association with Charles Mingus (1973–76) that gave him his initial fame. After playing a bit with McCoy Tyner, Adams co-led a stimulating quartet with Don Pullen that made many records. Late in life Adams (who enjoyed taking an occasional raspy blues vocal) teamed up with James "Blood" Ulmer in the group Phalanx and occasionally played with Mingus Dynasty. —*Scott Yanow*

Suite for Swingers / Jul. 28, 1976 / Horo ✦✦✦
These extended compositions, with Don Pullen, feature one of the great jazz quartets of the last two decades. All of their albums are worthwhile. —*Michael G. Nastos*

Sound Suggestions / May 1979 / ECM ✦✦✦✦

Don't Lose Control / Nov. 2, 1979–Nov. 3, 1979 / Soul Note ✦✦✦
Tenor saxophonist George Adams and pianist Don Pullen first joined forces in Charles Mingus' band of the 1970s and, upon the great bassist's death, they formed their own dynamic quartet, resulting in many recordings (mostly for European labels). *Don't Lose Control*, although their fourth record together, was the first to gain much recognition. On the five originals (all written by either Adams or Pullen), the two principals are in fine form with bassist Cameron Brown and drummer Dannie Richmond contributing stimulating support. Adams' raspy vocal on the title track is fun. This set is not quite as essential as some of the Adams-Pullen Quartet's later releases, but worth picking up. —*Scott Yanow*

Paradise Space Shuttle / Dec. 21, 1979 / Timeless ✦✦✦

Hand to Hand / Feb. 13, 1980–Feb. 14, 1980 / Soul Note ✦✦✦

Earth Beams / Aug. 3, 1981–Aug. 5, 1981 / Timeless ✦✦✦
The usual spinning, chaotic, yet coherent George Adams tenor

solos, contrasted by Don Pullen's ever-striding, attacking piano solos, were the attraction on this 1981 session. Bassist Cameron Brown, now comfortable in the quartet setting, and drummer Dannie Richmond filled their roles admirably as the Adams/Pullen foursome continued a great string of top-flight '80s releases. —*Ron Wynn*

Melodic Excursions / Jun. 6, 1982+Jun. 9, 1982 / Timeless ✦✦✦

Gentleman's Agreement / Jan. 11, 1983–Jan. 12, 1983 / Soul Note
✦✦✦

Live at the Village Vanguard, Vol. 1 / Aug. 19, 1983 / Soul Note
✦✦✦✦
The first of two powerhouse live sessions from 1983 that caught the George Adams/Don Pullen quartet in smashing form at the famed Village Vanguard. Adams, always a dynamo, seemed even more explosive and ambitious on his loping tenor solos, while Pullen rivaled him in energy and scope, and the Cameron Brown/Dannie Richmond bass and drum tandem stretched out the rhythms without ever losing control. —*Ron Wynn*

Live at the Village Vanguard, Vol. 2 / Aug. 19, 1983 / Soul Note
✦✦✦✦
This second '83 Village Vanguard set was just as frenzied and experimental as its predecessor. While Adams and Pullen moved ever further to the outside, Cameron Brown and Dannie Richmond held the inside, challenging the soloists, then bringing things back to a mutually satisfying conclusion. —*Ron Wynn*

Nightingale / Aug. 19, 1988–Aug. 20, 1988 / Blue Note ✦✦
A controversial effort when initially issued in 1988. After carving out a niche as a bombastic, furious improviser, George Adams turned almost timid, doing pre-rock pop ballads and standards on *Nightingale*. The tenor solos aren't anywhere as riveting or searing, while his once raspy, catchy vocals are here more diffuse and uneven. Still, it had its charms, and Hugh Lawson's tidy piano solos underneath cleaned up a lot of problems caused by Adams' leads. —*Ron Wynn*

● **America** / May 24, 1989–Jul. 18, 1989 / Blue Note ✦✦✦✦✦
Saxophonist George Adams was nearing the end of his creative road on 1989's *America*, so it was appropriate for him to go back to his roots and play some blues. He alternates between terse, rippling solos and impassioned, almost serene ones, something that puzzled many critics when this was released. Pianist Hugh Lawson, bassist Cecil McBee, and drummer Marc Johnson took their cues from Adams, mostly playing it straight in their roles and when in the spotlight keeping things simple and restrained, except when Adams himself turned up the intensity. —*Ron Wynn*

Old Feeling / Mar. 11, 1991–Mar. 12, 1991 / Blue Note ✦✦✦✦
Old Feeling ranks as one of George Adams' most exciting and happily eccentric sessions. Unlike some other avant-gardists who seem to lose their personality and purpose when they play standard material, Adams turns even overplayed songs into his own inventive devices; three standards get the "Adams treatment" on this CD. —*Scott Yanow*

Pepper Adams (Pepper Park Adams III)

b. Oct. 8, 1930, Highland Park, MI, **d.** Sep. 10, 1986, New York, NY
Baritone Sax / Hard Bop
Pepper Adams was one of the all-time great baritonists, ranking at the top with Harry Carney, Serge Chaloff and Gerry Mulligan. But Mulligan overshadowed Adams throughout virtually his entire career, which is a little strange because Pepper had a much different sound (heavier and more intense) than the light-toned and playful Mulligan.

Adams grew up in Rochester, NY, and when he was 16 he moved to Detroit, where he became an important part of the very fertile local jazz scene. Other than a period in the military (1951–53), Adams was a major fixture in Detroit, playing with such up-and-coming musicians as Donald Byrd, Kenny Burrell, Tommy Flanagan, Barry Harris and Elvin Jones. Adams had opportunities to tour with Stan Kenton, Maynard Ferguson and Chet Baker, and he moved to New York in 1958. In addition to recording both as a leader and a sideman, Adams played with Benny Goodman (1958–59) and Charles Mingus (off and on between 1959–63) and co-led a quintet with Donald Byrd (1958–62). He was a longtime member of the Thad Jones–Mel Lewis band (1965–78) and a major stylist up until his death. —*Scott Yanow*

Jazzmen: Detroit / Apr. 28, 1956 / Savoy ✦✦✦

Introducing Curtis Fuller / 1956–1957 / Transition ✦✦✦

Pepper Adams Quintet / Jul. 12, 1957 / VSOP ✦✦✦
Pepper Adams ranked among modern jazz's finest baritone saxophonists. His mastery of the middle and lower registers and his technical acumen enabled him to play the cumbersome baritone with a speed, facility, and style usually restricted to smaller horns. This '57 quintet date featured him in a more relaxed context with West Coast jazz types like trumpeter Stu Williamson and pianist Carl Perkins. Bassist Leroy Vinnegar added his famous "walking" lines and drummer Mel Lewis provided a steady, smooth, rhythmic pace, while Adams contributed two originals and did three standards in his usual impeccable fashion. —*Ron Wynn*

Critics Choice / Aug. 23, 1957 / World Pacific ✦✦✦

Pure Pepper / Nov. 19, 1957 / Savoy ✦✦
A reissued Savoy set from '57 with Pepper Adams establishing the robust hard bop sound that made him one of the era's greatest baritone sax stylists. He's backed by a group that includes the then-named Bernard McKinney (subsequently Kiane Zawadi) on euphonium, Hank Jones on piano, George Duvivier on bass, and Elvin Jones laying down the patented bursts and rhythms that became immortalized in the '60s when he provided them for John Coltrane. —*Ron Wynn*

Adams, Pepper Quintet / Mar. 25, 1958 / Mode ✦✦✦

● **10 to 4 at the 5-Spot** / Apr. 5, 1958 / Original Jazz Classics ✦✦✦✦✦
The best example of the bebop baritone saxophonist from Detroit includes a young Donald Byrd (tpt) and pianist Bobby Timmons. —*David Szatmary*

Stardust / 1960 / Bethlehem ✦✦✦

Out of This World / 1961 / Fresh Sound ✦✦✦

Plays Compositions of Charles Mingus / Sep. 9, 1963 / Fresh Sound ✦✦✦

Encounter! / Dec. 11, 1968–Dec. 12, 1968 / Prestige ✦✦✦✦

Ephemera / Sep. 10, 1973 / Spotlite ✦✦✦

Julian / Aug. 13, 1975 / Inner City ✦✦✦✦

Reflectory / Jun. 14, 1978 / Muse ✦✦✦✦

The Master / Mar. 11, 1980 / Muse ✦✦✦
A brilliant example of bebop on the baritone sax, it also featured Tommy Flanagan (p), George Marz (b), and Leroy Williams (d). —*David Szatmary*

Urban Dreams / Sep. 30, 1981 / Palo Alto ✦✦

● **Conjuration: Fat Tuesday's Session** / Aug. 19, 1983–Aug. 20, 1983 / Reservoir ✦✦✦✦✦
The great baritonist Pepper Adams is teamed up with the adventurous trumpeter Kenny Wheeler and veteran pianist Hank Jones for this live quintet date. Wheeler, although often associated with the avant-garde, has never had any difficulty playing changes and his strong style clearly inspired Adams. Together they perform three of the baritonist's originals, Thad Jones' "Tis," Wheeler's "Old Ballad" and the standard "Alone Together." —*Scott Yanow*

Generations / Jan. 25, 1985 / Muse ✦✦

Adams Effect / Jun. 25, 1985–Jun. 26, 1986 / Uptown ✦✦✦

Cannonball Adderley (Julian Edwin Adderley)

b. Sep. 15, 1928, Tampa, FL, d. Aug. 8, 1975, Gary, IN
Alto Saxophone, Leader / *Hard Bop, Soul Jazz*
One of the great alto saxophonists, Cannonball Adderley had an exuberant and happy sound (as opposed to many of the more serious stylists of his generation) that communicated immediately to listeners. His intelligent presentation of his music (often explaining what he and his musicians were going to play) helped make him one of the most popular of all jazzmen.

Adderley already had an established career as a high-school band director in Florida when during a 1955 visit to New York he was persuaded to sit in with Oscar Pettiford's group at the Cafe Bohemia. His playing created such a sensation that he was soon signed to Savoy and persuaded to play jazz full-time in New York. With his younger brother, cornetist Nat, Cannonball formed a quintet that struggled until its breakup in 1957. Adderley then joined Miles Davis, forming part of his super sextet with John Coltrane and participating on such classic recordings as *Milestones* and *Kind of Blue*. Adderley's second attempt to form a

quintet with his brother was much more successful, for with pianist Bobby Timmons he had a hit recording o Here." From then on, Cannonball always was able to work ally with his band.

During its Riverside years (1959–63), the Adderley Quintet p marily played soulful renditions of hard bop, and Cannonba really excelled in the straight-ahead settings. During 1962–63 Yusef Lateef made the group a sextet and pianist Joe Zawinul was an important new member. With the collapse of Riverside, Adderley signed with Capitol, and his recordings gradually became more commercial. Charles Lloyd was in Lateef's place for a year (with less success) and then with his departure the group went back to being a quintet. Zawinul's 1966 composition "Mercy, Mercy, Mercy" was a huge hit for the group, Adderley started doubling on soprano and the Quintet's later recordings emphasized long melody statements, funky rhythms and electronics. However, during his last year, Cannonball Adderley was revisiting the past a bit and on *Phenix* he recorded new versions of many of his earlier numbers. But before he could evolve his music any further, Cannonball Adderley died suddenly from a stroke. —*Scott Yanow*

The Adderleys: Cannonball & Nat / Jun. 26, 1955-Jul. 26, 1955 / Savoy ✦✦
This CD features altoist Cannonball Adderley and his brother Nat at the beginning of their recording careers, starting just seven days after Cannonball caused a sensation when he sat in with Oscar Pettiford's group at the Cafe Bohemia. Actually, a close look at the recording details shows that the first six selections are alternate takes taken from their first sessions and that the remainder of this set features Nat without Cannonball, mostly in a quintet with Jerome Richardson (who doubles on flute and tenor). Collectors who already have the original Cannonball recordings will find these alternates of great interest. In general the music is high-powered bop by two fine musicians in the early stages of developing their own styles. —*Scott Yanow*

Discoveries / Jun. 28, 1955 / Savoy ✦✦
This enjoyable LP gives listeners alternate takes from the two Cannonball Adderley sessions that are heard in their original form on the two-fer *Spontaneous Combustion*. The music (even in these rejected versions) is quite enjoyable, swinging with youthful enthusiasm. In addition to altoist Cannonball and his brother cornetist Nat, other soloists include trumpeter Donald Byrd, Jerome Richardson on tenor and flute and pianists Horace Silver and Hank Jones. —*Scott Yanow*

Spontaneous Combustion / Jun. 28, 1955-Jul. 14, 1955 / Savoy ✦✦✦
This valuable two-LP set features altoist Cannonball Adderley's first recordings, cut just days after the unknown had greatly impressed musicians when he sat in with Oscar Pettiford's group at the Cafe Bohemia. He is quite impressive throughout, holding his own in an all-star octet led by drummer Kenny Clarke with trumpeter Donald Byrd, brother Nat on cornet, Jerome Richardson on reeds and pianist Horace Silver. The second half of this two-fer is the first of many quintet dates he led with Nat. This near-classic music is highlighted by "Bohemia After Talk," Nat's feature on "We'll Be Together Again," "A Little Taste" and the title cut. —*Scott Yanow*

Presenting Cannonball Adderley / Jul. 14, 1955 / Savoy ✦✦
These are Cannonball's first recordings. Featuring Donald Byrd (tpt), Horace Silver (p), Paul Chambers (b), Kenny Clarke (d), Nat Adderley (cnt), and Jerome Richardson (ts, fl). —*Michael Erlewine*

Cannonball / Jul. 21, 1955-Aug. 5, 1955 / EmArcy ✦✦

Compact Jazz: Cannonball Adderley / Jul. 1955-Jan. 1962 / EmArcy ✦✦
A decent anthology of Cannonball Adderley's mid- and late-period material, weighted toward both recognizable, popular soul-jazz material and shorter, less involved songs with plenty of hard-charging solos by Cannonball, Nat, and the crew. Like most compilations, it provides a good introduction to his work, and works best for those with limited knowledge. —*Ron Wynn*

With Strings/Jump For Joy / Oct. 27, 1955-Aug. 21, 1958 / Mercury ✦✦✦

In the Land of Hi-Fi / Jun. 8, 1956+Jun. 18, 1956 / EmArcy ✦✦✦

Sophisticated Swing / Feb. 6, 1957+Feb. 8, 1957 / EmArcy ✦✦

Cannonball En Route / Feb. 7, 1957-Feb. 8, 1957 / Mercury ✦✦
Cannonball Adderley's Mercury albums find the youthful altoist

to keep his quintet with brother Nat togeth-
~~~werful bop-oriented music they consistently
~~~d would break up in a year, only to regroup with
~~~n 1959. This set is highlighted by romps on "A
~~~'I'll Remember April" and "The Way You Look
~~~ith fine solos contributed by the two Adderleys and
~~~unior Mance. —*Scott Yanow*

Cannonball's Sharpshooters / Mar. 4, 1958–Mar. 6, 1958 /
EmArcy ✦✦✦
Excellent bebop from the great altoist Cannonball Adderley and
his original quintet (which co-starred cornetist Nat Adderley and
pianist Junior Mance). Strange that this group was on the verge of
breaking up, for their renditions of such standards as "Our
Delight," "Straight No Chaser," "If I Love Again" and "I'll
Remember April" are often quite exciting. Fortunately this CD
preserves the group, for most of its other recordings have been
out of print for years. —*Scott Yanow*

★ **Somethin' Else** / Mar. 9, 1958 / Blue Note ✦✦✦✦✦
Shortly after Adderley broke up his original quintet and joined
Miles Davis' sextet, he recorded this LP with Davis in the rare role
of a sideman. Actually Davis dominates several of the selections
(including "Autumn Leaves," "Love for Sale" and "One for Daddy-
o") but both hornmen (backed by pianist Hank Jones, bassist Sam
Jones and drummer Art Blakey) sound quite inspired by each
other's presence. —*Scott Yanow*

Portrait of Cannonball / Jul. 1, 1958 / Original Jazz Classics ✦✦✦
Adderley's first album for Riverside, recorded while he was working as a sideman in Miles Davis' classic sextet. With Blue Mitchell
(tpt), Bill Evans (p), Sam Jones (b), and Philly Joe Jones (d). —
Michael Erlewine

Cannonball & Eight Giants / Jul. 1, 1958–Oct. 28, 1958 /
Milestone ✦✦✦
This two-LP set contains two complete Riverside albums by the
great altoist Cannonball Adderley during the period when he was
a sideman with the Miles Davis Sextet. Both sets are quite enjoyable, for Adderley is featured with trumpeter Blue Mitchell and
pianist Bill Evans (highlighted by "Nardis," "A Little Taste" and
two takes of "Minority") and in jubilant form with vibraphonist
Milt Jackson and pianist Wynton Kelly on another date; their versions of "Things Are Getting Better" and "The Sidewalks of New
York" are very enjoyable. —*Scott Yanow*

Alabama Concerto / Jul. 28, 1958–Aug. 2, 1958 / Original Jazz
Classics ✦✦✦

Alabama/Africa / Jul. 28, 1958–Jul. 1962 / Milestone ✦✦✦
This two-LP set contains a pair of very unusual Cannonball Adderley
albums. The earlier set features a quartet comprised of the altoist,
trumpeter Art Farmer, guitarist Barry Galbraith and bassist Milt
Hinton performing John Benson Brooks' nine-part four-movement
"Alabama Concerto," a major work filled with folk melodies. The
remainder of this two-fer (music originally on the LP *African Waltz*)
features Adderley accompanied by a big band for a set of concise
and funky charts recorded with hopes of getting a hit single. Despite
its commercial objectives, the songs (many of which are jazz standards) and arrangements hold one's interest. —*Scott Yanow*

Jump for Joy / Aug. 20, 1958–Aug. 21, 1958 / EmArcy ✦✦

☆ **Things Are Getting Better** / Oct. 20, 1958 / Original Jazz Classics
✦✦✦✦✦
First pairing of Milt Jackson with Cannonball for an all-star
blowin' session. This one works. With Wynton Kelly (p), Milt
Jackson (vib), Percy Heath (b), and Art Blakey (d). Recorded while
Adderley was a sideman with the classic Miles Davis Sextet. —
Michael Erlewine

● **Cannonball and Coltrane** / Feb. 3, 1959 / EmArcy ✦✦✦✦✦
This LP (whose contents have been reissued many times) features
the Miles Davis Sextet of 1959 without the leader. Altoist
Cannonball Adderley and tenor saxophonist John Coltrane really
push each other on these six selections with this version of
"Limehouse Blues" really burning. Coltrane's very serious sound
is a striking contrast to the jubilant Adderley alto; the latter is
showcased on "Stars Fell on Alabama." With pianist Wynton Kelly,
bassist Paul Chambers and drummer Jimmy Cobb playing up to
their usual level, this gem is highly recommended. —*Scott Yanow*

**Cannonball Adderley Collection, Vol. 6: Cannonball Takes
Charge** / Apr. 23, 1959–May 12, 1959 / Landmark ✦✦✦
Adderley was on the verge of leaving Miles Davis' Sextet when he

recorded the seven titles and two alternates that comprise this LP,
the sixth in a seven-volume series of Riverside dates reissued by
producer Orrin Keepnews. Accompanied by pianist Wynton Kelly
and alternating bassists and drummers, Adderley is in fine form
on these standards with the emphasis leaning a bit toward ballads
and blues. Highlights include "Serenata," "Poor Butterfly" and two
versions of "I Remember You." —*Scott Yanow*

● **Cannonball Adderley Quintet in San Francisco** / Oct. 18,
1959+Oct. 20, 1959 / Original Jazz Classics ✦✦✦✦✦
This live date with Bobby Timmons (p), Nat Adderley (cnt), Sam
Jones (b), and Louis Hayes (d) contains the classic and soulful
"This Here." —*Hank Davis*

Coast to Coast / Oct. 18, 1959–Jan. 14, 1962 / Milestone ✦✦✦✦
This two-LP set combines together two of Cannonball Adderley's
finest recordings. The earlier session, recorded live at The Jazz
Workshop in San Francisco, made his new quintet (which also fea-
tured cornetist Nat Adderley, pianist Bobby Timmons, bassist Sam
Jones and drummer Louis Hayes) into a very popular attraction.
In addition to a previously unissued version of "Straight No
Chaser," a classic rendition of "High Fly" and two originals by the
altoist, this is the set that featured the debut recording of Bobby
Timmons' hit "This Here," which by itself defined the term "soul-
jazz" or "funk." The second half of this two-fer is not exactly lightweight material either, a live album by Adderley's 1962 sextet
with the great tenor Yusef Lateef and pianist Joe Zawinul. Their
version of "Dizzy's Business" is quite memorable. These two sessions (which are also available on CD) contain plenty of essential
music. —*Scott Yanow*

Cannonball Adderley Collection, Vol. 1: Them Dirty Blues /
Feb. 1, 1960 / Landmark ✦✦✦
The first of seven LPs that reissue recordings from his period with
Riverside contains several notable selections. The first side (which
has pianist Bobby Timmons well-featured with bassist Sam Jones,
drummer Louis Hayes, cornetist Nat Adderley and the
leader/altoist) includes the original versions of Timmons' "Dat
Dere" (his follow-up to "This Here" which is heard here in two
takes), Sam Jones' "Del Sasser" and Nat's "Work Songlo; the latter
was previously unissued. On the flip side (with Barry Harris in
Timmons' place), the quintet performs the initial "official" version
of "Work Song," a heated "Jeannine," "Easy Living" and "Them
Dirty Blues." Lots of classic music comes from this influential
soul-jazz band. —*Scott Yanow*

Cannonball Adderley Collection, Vol. 4: The Poll Winners /
May 21, 1960–Jun. 5, 1960 / Landmark ✦✦✦
The "Poll-Winners" at the time of this recording were Adderley,
guitarist Wes Montgomery and bassist Ray Brown; together with
Victor Feldman doubling on piano and vibes and drummer Louis
Hayes they cut this excellent quintet date. This was the only meet-
ing on records by Adderley and Montgomery and, although not
quite a classic encounter, the music (highlighted by "The Chant,"
"Never Will I Marry" and two takes of "Au Privave") swings hard
and is quite enjoyable. —*Scott Yanow*

**Cannonball Adderley Collection, Vol. 5: The Quintet at The
Lighthouse** / Oct. 16, 1960 / Landmark ✦✦✦
This is a fine all-around set from the Cannonball Adderley Quintet
of 1960 with the altoist/leader, cornetist Nat Adderley, pianist
Victor Feldman, bassist Sam Jones and drummer Louis Hayes.
The fifth of seven LPs reissued by Orrin Keepnews and taken
from Adderley's Riverside years finds his band in top form on the
original version of "Sack O' Woe," a previously unissued "Our
Delight," Jimmy Heath's "Big 'P'" and "Blue Daniel" among others. It's a strong introduction to the music of this classic hard bop
group. —*Scott Yanow*

What Is This Thing Called Soul? / Nov. 1960 / Pablo ✦✦✦
Cannonball Adderley's 1960 Quintet (with cornetist Nat Adderley
and pianist Victor Feldman) was in top form during their tour of
Europe. Norman Granz did not release the music heard on this LP
until almost 25 years after the fact, but the strong solos and
enthusiastic ensembles had not dated or faded with time. These
versions of "The Chant," "What Is This Thing Called Love?" and
"Big 'P'" make for interesting comparisons with the better-known
renditions. Adderley fans will want this set. —*Scott Yanow*

What I Mean / Jan. 27, 1961–May 11, 1961 / Milestone ✦✦✦✦
This two-LP set combines two fine sessions from 1961. The great
altoist is heard with his quintet in 1961 (featuring cornetist Nat
Adderley, Victor Feldman on vibes and piano and guest pianist

Wynton Kelly) and in a quartet date with pianist Bill Evans. The former has some nice music but it is the latter session (which is highlighted by "Waltz for Debby," "Who Cares," "Nancy (With the Laughing Face)" and two versions of "Know What I Mean?" that is the main reason to acquire this excellent two-fer. —*Scott Yanow*

African Waltz / Feb. 8, 1961–May 9, 1961 / Original Jazz Classics ✦✦

The Quintet Plus / May 11, 1961 / Riverside ✦✦✦
This out-of-print LP, whose contents have been reissued several times since, features the 1961 Cannonball Adderley Quintet (which includes cornetist Nat Adderley and pianist Victor Feldman) plus their guest Wynton Kelly on piano during four of the six tracks; Feldman switched to vibes for those songs. The music is quite enjoyable, high-quality funky jazz that could also be called hard bop. "Well You Needn't" and "Star Eyes" are highpoints. —*Scott Yanow*

Nancy Wilson/Cannonball Adderley / Jun. 27, 1961–Aug. 24, 1961 / Capitol ✦✦✦✦
Adderley's abilities as a talent scout have long been overlooked. He helped discover Nancy Wilson early in her career and by 1961 she was already on her way to becoming a popular middle-of-the-road singer. This CD (which adds a previously unissued "Little Unhappy Boy" to the original LP), instead of alternating instrumental performances by his quintet with Wilson's vocals, as on the LP, sounds like two separate sets due to the placement of the seven vocals at the beginning of the program. Nancy Wilson, who was never really a jazz singer, sounds more influenced by jazz in these numbers (particularly on "Never Will I Marry," "The Masquerade Is Over" and "A Sleepin' Bee") than she would later on. The instrumentals include fine versions of "I Can't Get Started" and "Unit 7." —*Scott Yanow*

In New York / Jan. 12, 1962–Jan. 14, 1962 / Original Jazz Classics ✦✦✦
Live date at The Village Vanguard in NYC. W/ Nat Adderley (cnt), Yusef Lateef (ts, fl), Joe Zawinul (p), Sam Jones (b), and Louis Hayes (d). —*Michael Erlewine*

The Adderley Brothers in New Orleans / May 1962 / Milestone ✦✦
This unusual LP features Cannonball and Nat Adderley (along with bassist Sam Jones) playing with three of the top modern New Orleans musicians of the 1960s: tenor saxophonist Nat Perrilliat, drummer/composer James Black and pianist Ellis Marsalis (who was unknown at the time outside of his hometown). Together they perform a fresh repertoire full of originals by New Orleans players (including two songs from clarinetist Alvin Battiste) and Nat's "In the Bag." This excellent music served as a change of pace in the career of Cannonball Adderley. —*Scott Yanow*

Cannonball Adderley Collection, Vol. 7: Cannonball in Europe / Aug. 5, 1962 / Landmark ✦✦✦✦
Adderley led what was arguably his finest group during 1962–63, a sextet with brother Nat on cornet, Yusef Lateef on flute, oboe and tenor, pianist Joe Zawinul, bassist Sam Jones and drummer Louis Hayes. This excellent LP (whose contents were never previously available in the U.S.) is highlighted by Jimmy Heath's "Gemini," "Work Song," a lengthy "Trouble in Mind" and the exciting "Dizzy's Business." Lateef fit into this band perfectly, giving the unit a fresh and distinctive voice. All of his recordings with Adderley are easily recommended. —*Scott Yanow*

The Sextet / Sep. 21, 1962–Jul. 19, 1963 / Milestone ✦✦✦
This excellent LP features the Cannonball Adderley Sextet (with cornetist Nat Adderley and Yusef Lateef on tenor and flute) of 1962–63. Because most of this material had been recorded just a couple years earlier, these versions of such songs as "This Here," "Bohemia After Dark" and "New Delhi" were unissued until the 1980s. The music remains quite exciting and fresh for, although somewhat overshadowed at the time, this was one of the great jazz groups of the 1960s. —*Scott Yanow*

Cannonball Adderley Collection, Vol. 3: Jazz Workshop Revisited / Sep. 22, 1962–Sep. 23, 1962 / Landmark ✦✦✦
Three years after having a surprise hit ("This Here") recorded live at The Jazz Workshop in San Francisco, Cannonball Adderley and his sextet (featuring cornetist Nat Adderley and Yusef Lateef on tenor, flute and oboe) returned to the club and recorded this particularly rewarding LP, reissued by Orrin Keepnews on his Landmark label. The material was challenging but hard-swinging, including "Primitivo," "Jessica's Days," "Mellow Buno" and Nat

Adderley's new composition "The Jive Samba." A previously unknown version of the classic "Unit 7" was substituted for the Sam Jones ballad "Lillie" with this issue. Every recording by this particular unit is well worth acquiring. —*Scott Yanow*

Cannonball Adderley Collection, Vol. 2: Bossa Nova / Dec. 7, 1962–Dec. 11, 1962 / Landmark ✦✦
Recorded when the bossa nova craze was generating steam, this was one of the better albums of the genre. Cannonball Adderley wisely cut his lone bossa nova record with South American musicians, a group called The Bossa Rio Sextet that included pianist Sergio Mendes and future Weather Report member Dom Um Romao on drums. Adderley's sound on alto was well-attuned to this music (as was his happy musical personality), as can be heard on "Once I Loved" and two versions of "Corcovado." —*Scott Yanow*

Japanese Concerts / Jul. 9, 1963–Jul. 15, 1963 / Milestone ✦✦✦✦✦
Cannonball Adderley's finest group (his sextet with cornetist Nat Adderley, Yusef Lateef on tenor, flute and oboe, pianist Joe Zawinul, bassist Sam Jones and drummer Louis Hayes) is heard at the peak of their powers on this two-LP set. The first half was previously released as *Nippon Soul* while the second LP was only issued for the first time in 1975. After a period of stable personnel (all but Zawinul and Lateef had been in the band since 1959), these musicians were very familiar with each other's playing and they had grown together. The enthusiastic Japanese crowds inspired the all-star band to some of their most rewarding playing, which can be heard on such standouts as "Nippon Soul," "Come Sunday," "Work Song," "Dizzy's Business" and "Jive Samba" among others. It's a definitive portrait of a classic group. —*Scott Yanow*

Cannonball Adderley—Live! / Aug. 1, 1964–Aug. 2, 1964 / Capitol ✦✦
When Riverside Records went into bankruptcy, Adderley signed with Capitol, a label whose interest in jazz tended to be shortlived. As a result, Cannonball's recordings would become more commercial as the 1960s developed but this early Capitol effort is quite good. Charles Lloyd had just joined Adderley's Sextet and his tenor and flute were major assets; he contributed two of the four songs ("Sweet Georgia Bright" and "The Song My Lady Sings") to this fine session which also includes Nat Adderley's "Little Boy with the Sad Eyes" and yet another version of "Work Song." —*Scott Yanow*

Live with the New Exciting Voice of Ernie Andrews / Oct. 4, 1964 / Capitol ✦✦
This LP teams the Cannonball Adderley Quintet with singer Ernie Andrews, a combination that should have resulted in more explosive music. This brief set (under 28 minutes) has its moments (particularly "I'm Always Drunk In San Francisco") but the performances are too concise and not much room is given the musicians. It's a slight disappointment. —*Scott Yanow*

Fiddler on the Roof / Oct. 19, 1964–Oct. 21, 1964 / Capitol ✦✦✦
It is a bit strange that none of the eight songs performed on this LP found their way into Adderley's permanent repertoire, for the altoist was quite inspired throughout this surprising set. With strong assists from cornetist Nat Adderley, Charles Lloyd on tenor and flute, pianist Joe Zawinul, bassist Sam Jones and drummer Louis Hayes, Cannonball plays near his peak; this is certainly the finest album by this particular sextet. —*Scott Yanow*

Domination / Apr. 26, 1965 / Capitol ✦✦
Cannonball and Nat Adderley are joined by an unidentified orchestra arranged by Oliver Nelson for this decent outing. None of the eight performances are all that memorable (and pale next to Cannonball's earlier recordings with Gil Evans) but the music is enjoyable enough. This LP has been out of print for years. —*Scott Yanow*

Great Love Themes / Apr. 6, 1966–Apr. 7, 1966 / Capitol ✦

Cannonball Live in Japan / Aug. 26, 1966 / Capitol ✦
Performing some of their finest songs ("Work Song," "Mercy, Mercy, Mercy," "This Here," "Money in the Pocket," "The Sticks" and "Jive Samba"), the Cannonball Adderley Quintet is strangely uninspired during this Japanese concert, just going through the motions. Perhaps they were already tired of this material or maybe it was jet lag. In any case, this CD is a disappointment. —*Scott Yanow*

Mercy, Mercy, Mercy / Oct. 20, 1966 / Capitol ✦✦✦✦
This set (reissued on CD) is one of Cannonball Adderley's finest

albums of his last decade. "Mercy, Mercy, Mercy," a soulful Joe Zawinul melody that is repeated several times without any real improvisation, became a surprise hit but the other selections on this live date ("Fun," "Games," "Sticks," "Hippodelphia" and "Sack O'Woe") all have plenty of fiery solos from the quintet (which is comprised of the leader on alto, cornetist Nat Adderley, pianist Joe Zawinul, bassist Victor Gaskin, and drummer Roy McCurdy). Cannonball sounds quite inspired (his expressive powers had expanded due to the unacknowledged influence of the avant-garde) and Nat shows just how exciting a player he was back in his prime. "Sack O'Woe" is particularly memorable. This CD, which is far superior to most of Cannonball's later Capitol recordings, is highly recommended. —*Scott Yanow*

Why Am I Treated So Bad? / 1967 / Capitol ♦♦
The follow-up album to Cannonball Adderley's major hit *Mercy, Mercy, Mercy* is surprisingly forgettable. The group originals are run-of-the-mill and the solos by the altoist/leader, cornetist Nat Adderley and keyboardist Joe Zawinul, although decent enough, are hardly inspiring. This LP has been out of print for quite some time. —*Scott Yanow*

Radio Nights / 1967–1968 / Night ♦♦♦
This CD contains private recordings of Cannonball Adderley's groups during 1967–68 playing at the Half Note in New York City. The music is quite worthy with altoist Cannonball Adderley featured in a quartet setting on "Stars Fell on Alabama," performing three songs with his quintet (including "Fiddler on the Roof") and playing three other pieces (highlighted by "Work Song" and "Unit Seven") with the sextet he had that featured Charles Lloyd on tenor. This music is generally superior to Adderley's commercial Capitol recordings of the period. —*Scott Yanow*

In Person / Sep. 23, 1968–Oct. 7, 1968 / Capitol ♦♦
This interesting LP has surprise guest appearances by Lou Rawls ("I'd Rather Drink Muddy Water") and Nancy Wilson ("Save Your Love for Me"), the debut of Joe Zawinul's "Rumpelstiltskin," a feature for Cannonball Adderley's alto on "Somewhere" and a bit of his soprano on "The Scavenger." Keyboardist Zawinul and cornetist Nat Adderley are also heard from. It's a loose but fun live session. —*Scott Yanow*

Cannonball Adderley and His Quintet / Mar. 27, 1969 / RTE ♦♦
This concert recording, released for the first time in the U.S. in 1994, features Cannonball Adderley's 1969 quintet that also included cornetist Nat Adderley, keyboardist Joe Zawinul, bassist Victor Gaskin and drummer Roy McCurdy. Cannonball, whose music had gradually moved beyond bop as it became influenced by rock, funk and the avant-garde, is actually booed a bit on this set by the French audience, who expected him to be playing the same songs as a decade earlier. Actually the altoist is in excellent form and the music (which includes "Black Orpheus" and "Work Song" along with newer material by Zawinul) is generally superior to his Capitol studio recordings of the era. Despite the mixed reaction (which makes Cannonball's usually enthusiastic talks to the audience a bit downbeat), this is an excellent example of late-period Adderley. —*Scott Yanow*

Country Preacher / Oct. 1969 / Capitol ♦♦
This live benefit for Jesse Jackson's Operation Breadbasket in 1969 has been reissued as a CD. There are some decent moments (particularly "Walk Tall" and the original version of "Hummin'," but there are also quite a few weak spots, including cornetist Nat Adderley's vocal on "Oh Babe," the unmemorable four-part Afro-Spanish "Omelet" and the title cut (which is in a similar vein to the then-recent hit "Mercy, Mercy, Mercy"). Cannonball Adderley, although fine in his brief alto and soprano spots, at this point in his career was delegating far too much solo space to his rhythm section, making this a lesser effort. —*Scott Yanow*

The Price You Got to Pay to Be Free / Sep. 14, 1970–Sep. 19, 1970 / Capitol ♦♦

Black Messiah / 1970 / Capitol ♦♦
This is an odd double LP in that the music, which sounded so contemporary in 1972, now comes across as a bit dated. The Cannonball Adderley Quintet (which at the time featured George Duke on keyboards) is joined by percussionist Airto and on some tracks tenor saxophonist Ernie Watts, guitarist/vocalist Mike Deasy, clarinetist Alvin Batiste and percussionist Buck Clark. The rhythm section is excessively funky at times and the many stylists clash a bit (Batiste in particular is out of place). The strongest performances are "The Black Messiah," "Dr. Honouris Cousa" and

"The Chocolate Nuisance," but there is a lot of fat on this rather loose two-fer. —*Scott Yanow*

Inside Straight / Jun. 4, 1973 / Fantasy ♦♦
After seven years with Capitol, Cannonball Adderley switched labels to Fantasy, where he reunited with producer Orrin Keepnews and the quality of his music immediately improved. With Hal Galper as the band's keyboardist (he contributed three of the seven group originals to this LP), this version of the Quintet (actually Sextet with the addition of percussionist King Errison) was more jazz-oriented than previously while remaining modern and funky. —*Scott Yanow*

Pyramid / 1974 / Fantasy ♦♦♦
Cannonball Adderley is in generally good form on this 1974 recording. His Quintet at the time featured cornetist Nat Adderley, keyboardist Hal Galper, bassist Walter Booker and drummer Roy McCurdy. Guests on some selections include guitarist Phil Upchurch, keyboardist George Duke and (on "Bess, Oh Where's My Bess") veteran pianist Jimmy Jones. The emphasis is on recent group originals including the three part "Suite Cannon," two Galper compositions and Cannonball's "Pyramid." Nothing too earthshattering occurs but this is an improvement over many of Adderley's Capitol recordings. —*Scott Yanow*

Phenix / Feb. 1975–Apr. 1975 / Fantasy ♦♦♦♦
Adderley's next-to-last recording (cut just four months before he died of a stroke at age 46) was ironically a retrospective of his career. While his then-current group (with cornetist Nat Adderley, keyboardist Mike Wolff, bassist Walter Booker and drummer Roy McCurdy) is featured on half of this two-LP set (highlighted by "Stars Fell on Alabama," "74 Miles Away" and a medley of "Walk Tall" and "Mercy, Mercy, Mercy"), on the remainder of this two-fer The Adderleys welcome back several alumni (keyboardist George Duke, bassist Sam Jones and drummer Louis Hayes) for new versions of "High Fly," "Work Song," "Sack O'Woe," "Jive Samba," "This Here" and "The Sidewalks of New York." A recommended set with plenty of excellent music, it serves as a fine overview of Cannonball Adderley's career. —*Scott Yanow*

Lovers / Jun. 24, 1975–Oct. 31, 1975 / Fantasy ♦♦
Cannonball Adderley's death on Aug. 18, 1975 was a major surprise to the jazz world because, although he had long been overweight, he was only 46 when he died from a stroke. This particular LP was already more than half completed with Adderley taking his last solos on three of the selections. The group he had utilized was quite unusual, with Cannonball and cornetist Nat Adderley joined by Alvin Batiste (on electric clarinet, flute and tenor), keyboardist George Duke, bassist Alphonso Johnson, drummer Jack DeJohnette and percussionist Airto. Batiste and Nat have individual features, but unfortunately none of the music is all that memorable; Hermeto Pascoal's "Nascente" comes the closest. After Cannonball's death "Lovers" (which had been planned for the album) was recorded as a memorial with Flora Purim on the vocal, Nat Adderley, Batiste, Duke and Nat Adderley Jr. on keyboards, bassists Johnson and Ron Carter, DeJohnette and Airto. The intentions were honorable but the music is pretty forgettable. —*Scott Yanow*

Nat Adderley

b. Nov. 25, 1931, Tampa, FL
Cornet / Hard Bop, Soul Jazz
Nat Adderley's cornet (which in its early days was strongly influenced by Miles Davis) was always a complementary voice to his brother Cannonball in their popular quintet. His career ran parallel to his older brother for quite some time. Nat took up trumpet in 1946, switched to cornet in 1950 and spent time in the military, playing in an Army band during 1951–53. After a period with Lionel Hampton (1954–55), Nat made his recording debut in 1955, joined Cannonball's unsuccessful quintet of 1956–57 and then spent periods with the groups of J.J. Johnson and Woody Herman before hooking up with Cannonball again in Oct. 1959. This time the group became a major success and Nat remained in the quintet until Cannonball's death in 1975, contributing such originals as "Work Song," "Jive Samba" and "The Old Country" along with many exciting hard bop solos. Nat Adderley, who was at the peak of his powers in the early to mid-'60s and who became adept at playing solos that dipped into the subtone register of his horn, has led his own quintets since Cannonball's death; his most notable sidemen were altoists Sonny Fortune (in the early '80s) and Vincent Herring. Although his own playing has declined some-

what (Adderley's chops no longer have the endurance of his earlier days), Nat has continued recording worthwhile sessions. Many of his recordings through the years (for such labels as Savoy, EmArcy, Riverside, Jazzland, Atlantic, Milestone, A&M, Capitol, Prestige, SteepleChase, Galaxy, Theresa, In & Out and Landmark) are currently available. —*Scott Yanow*

That's Nat Adderley / Jul. 26, 1955 / Savoy ✦✦✦
Early material from Nat Adderley. His pithy, pungent trumpet and cornet work is effective in a hard bop context, although his own work outside his brother's group has never seemed quite as effective. His backing group included Kenny Clarke in a non-Modern Jazz Quartet role, plus pianist Hank Jones, bassist Wendell Marshall, and Jerome Richardson on tenor sax and flute, playing with more punch than on either his Quincy Jones or Oliver Nelson large group dates. —*Ron Wynn*

Introducing Nat Adderley / Sep. 6, 1955 / EmArcy ✦✦✦

To the Ivy League from Nat / Jul. 12, 1956 / EmArcy ✦✦✦

Branching Out / Sep. 1958 / Original Jazz Classics ✦✦✦✦
This 1958 date had some of his hottest playing as a leader. Adderley concentrates on cornet, and there haven't been many on that instrument to take it into more abrupt and challenging harmonic contexts. Johnny Griffin's bluesy, taut tenor keeps things moving, while using pianist Gene Harris, bassist Andy Simpkins and drummer Bill Dowdy (better known as The Three Sounds) for a rhythm section was inspiring. —*Ron Wynn*

Much Brass / Mar. 23, 1959+Mar. 27, 1959 / Original Jazz Classics ✦✦✦

● **Work Songs** / Jan. 25, 1960–Sep. 15, 1960 / Original Jazz Classics ✦✦✦✦✦
Guitarist Wes Montgomery was aboard for *Work Song*, a Nat Adderley date with Bobby Timmons (piano), Louis Hayes (drums), Sam Jones and Ketter Betts or Percy Heath (cello, bass). This was, of course, Nat Adderley's date and Montgomery's role was not so much that of guitarist extraordinaire, but as one of the plucked strings which give this date its particular ambience...A thoughtful and varied set with a multi-dimensional personality, this has been previously issued as part of a two-fer. —*Bob Rusch, Cadence*

That's Right!: Nat Adderley & The Big Sax Section / Aug. 9, 1960+Sep. 15, 1960 / Original Jazz Classics ✦✦✦✦
Nat Adderley has seldom played with more fire, verve and distinction than he did on *That's Right!* It placed him in the company of an expanded sax section that included his brother Cannonball on alto, Yusef Lateef on tenor, flute and oboe, Jimmy Heath and Charlie Rouse on tenor, and baritone saxophonist Tate Houston. Solos crackled, the backing was tasty and stimulating, and the eight songs ranged from brisk standards to delightful originals. This CD reissue, despite lacking any new or alternate material, is most welcome due to the full, striking sound that the big reed section provided. —*Ron Wynn*

Naturally! / Jun. 20, 1961+Jul. 1, 1961 / Jazzland ✦✦✦

In the Bag / May 9, 1962 / Original Jazz Classics ✦✦
It's an interesting album with New Orleans musicians Nat Perilliat (reeds), Ellis Marsalis (piano). —*Michael G. Nastos*

Natural Soul / Sep. 23, 1963 / Milestone ✦✦✦

Autobiography / Dec. 21, 1964–Jan. 7, 1965 / Atlantic ✦✦✦✦

Sayin' Somethin' / Feb. 16, 1966 / Atlantic ✦✦✦

Live at Memory Lane / Oct. 30, 1966 / Atlantic ✦✦✦

The Scavenger / Jan. 18, 1968–Jan. 19, 1968 / Milestone ✦✦

You Baby / Mar. 26, 1968–Apr. 4, 1968 / A&M ✦✦

Calling Out Loud / Nov. 19, 1968+Nov. 21, 1968 / A&M ✦✦

Love, Sex and the Zodiac / 1970 / Fantasy ✦

Soul of the Bible / Oct. 14, 1972 / Capitol ✦✦

Double Exposure / 1974 / Prestige ✦✦

Don't Look Back / Aug. 9, 1976 / Inner City ✦✦✦

Hummin' / Oct. 1976 / Little David ✦✦✦

A Little New York Midtown Music / Sep. 18, 1978–Sep. 19, 1978 / Galaxy ✦✦✦
Cornetist Nat Adderley is heard with an all-star quintet also featuring tenor saxophonist Johnny Griffin and keyboardist Victor Feldman on this enjoyable set. Except for "Come Rain or Come Shine," all of the melodies are group originals (including four by Nat). The music is essentially modern hard bop and is as well-

played as one would expect from such strong personnel. —*Scott Yanow*

On the Move / Oct. 1982 / Theresa ✦✦
Nat Adderley teamed with alto saxophonist Sonny Fortune on two albums for Theresa in the mid-'80s, including this six-cut outing. Fortune, capable of playing with as much invention, energy, and drive as any contemporary alto player, is uniformly aggressive and intense. He dominated the proceedings, followed closely by the outstanding rhythm section duo of underrated bassist Walter Booker and drummer Jimmy Cobb. But neither Adderley nor pianist Larry Willis, who supplied half the date's songs, were in top form. Willis played some nice melodies but did not offer much during his solos, while Adderley was plagued by sloppy articulation. However, the work of Fortune, who has not recorded nearly often enough, salvages things somewhat. —*Ron Wynn*

Blue Autumn / Oct. 1982 / Evidence ✦✦
This '83 live set at the Keystone Korner was certainly an uneven, sometimes curious event. The opening number is a solo alto workout for Sonny Fortune, who seems to amble through midway before he becomes recharged at the end. The last track, "The Tallahassee Kid," fades out early and Adderley provides a run-down of band personnel until the disc ends. There are some fine cuts with punchy, snappy melodies, taut solos, and nice rhythm section interaction between Willis, drummer Jimmy Cobb and bassist Walter Booker. But overall, this proves a good but not essential Nat Adderley date. —*Ron Wynn*

We Remember Cannon / Nov. 18, 1989 / In + Out/Rounder ✦✦✦

Autumn Leaves / May 12, 1990–May 13, 1990 / Evidence ✦✦✦

Talkin' About You / Nov. 8, 1990–Nov. 9, 1990 / Landmark ✦✦
A '90 date that found Nat Adderley sometimes struggling to maintain his tone, but holding things together anyhow. The star proved to be young lion Vincent Herring, whose interaction with Adderley was sometimes reminiscent of how the brothers used to mesh. Former Adderley combo bassist Walter Booker and drummer Jimmy Cobb were peerless in their support, while pianist Rob Bargad was effective, but not outstanding. —*Ron Wynn*

The Old Country / Dec. 5, 1990–Dec. 6, 1990 / Enja ✦✦✦
Adderley has evidently found a soul mate in alto saxophonist Vince Herring, with whom he works once more on this 1990 date. Herring's voice has grown more impressive with each release, and he now offers more than just dazzling lines and phrases; he's constructing and completing confident statements. Pianist Rob Bargad, another regular, is on board, with bassist James Genus and drummer Billy Drummond. —*Ron Wynn*

Workin' / Mar. 26, 1992 / Timeless ✦✦

Good Company / Jun. 20, 1994–Jun. 21, 1994 / Jazz Challenge ✦✦

Larry Adler

b. Feb. 10, 1914, Baltimore, MD
Harmonica / Swing, Pop
Larry Adler, who can play jazz but has spent most of his career in other fields, did more than anyone else to make the harmonica accepted as a legitimate instrument, playing everything from classical music to pop. A virtuoso musician, Adler's most interesting jazz-related recordings were with Django Reinhardt and Stephane Grappelli in 1938, John Kirby's Sextet in 1944 and on later sessions with pianist Ellis Larkins. Among his many movie appearances were *Many Happy Returns* with Duke Ellington and *Blues in the Night* with John Kirby. Adler has remained active into the mid-'90s. —*Scott Yanow*

● **Live at the Ballroom** / 1986 / Newport Classics ✦✦✦✦✦

Air

Group / Avant-Garde, Free Jazz
Comprised originally of Henry Threadgill on reeds, bassist Fred Hopkins and drummer Steve McCall. Air emphasized equality of roles by the instruments (without any clear-cut leader) and a smooth mixture of advanced arrangements and free improvisations. In 1971 Threadgill was asked to arrange some of Scott Joplin's songs for a production at Columbia College in Chicago. He teamed up with Hopkins and McCall as the trio Reflection. A few years later, in 1975, the musicians came together again as Air, touring Europe, Japan and America and recording 11 records for such labels as Nessa, India Navigation, Black Saint, Novus and

Antilles. By far their most popular release was 1979's *Air Lore*, which found the group performing abstract versions of tunes by Joplin and Jelly Roll Morton. In 1982 when McCall returned to Chicago and was replaced by Pheeroan AkLaff, the group changed its name to New Air. A year before their breakup in 1986, Andrew Cyrille took over the drum slot. Since then all of the musicians (other than McCall who passed away in 1989) have had very productive careers. —*Scott Yanow*

Air Song / Sep. 10, 1975 / India Navigation ✦✦✦
Air Song was the first recording by Air, a trio comprised of altoist Henry Threadgill (who also plays tenor, baritone and flute on this date), bassist Fred Hopkins, and drummer Steve McCall. The idea behind this unit was always to have all three members on an equal footing and, although Threadgill consistently comes across as the lead voice, their advanced interplay and consistently strong solos make these four lengthy performances make this a rather successful outing. —*Scott Yanow*

Live Air / Jul. 1, 1976+Oct. 28, 1977 / Black Saint ✦✦✦

Air Raid / Jul. 15, 1976 / India Navigation ✦✦✦✦

Air Time / Nov. 17, 1977–Nov. 18, 1977 / Nessa ✦✦✦
The trio Air aimed to have close interplay between three musical equals. This Nessa release (their first recording for an American label) has plenty of explorative solos and is highlighted by Threadgill's three extended compositions; check out his hubka-phone feature on "G.V.E." —*Scott Yanow*

Open Air Suit / Feb. 21, 1978–Feb. 22, 1978 / Novus ✦✦✦
Although in actuality a suite, this LP is called *Open Air Suit* with the five compositions supposedly approximating a five-piece suit. The music played by this talented trio is complex yet ultimately logical. The talented musicians seem to communicate instantly with each other and they consistently develop their music in the same direction on this stimulating set. —*Scott Yanow*

Live at Montreux 1978 / Jul. 22, 1978 / Novus ✦✦✦

● **Air Lore** / May 11, 1979–May 12, 1979 / RCA/Bluebird ✦✦✦✦✦
This was the most unusual and accessible recording ever made by Air. Instead of performing their complex originals as usual, this group (in addition to Threadgill's brief "Paille Street") stretches out on two songs apiece by Jelly Roll Morton and Scott Joplin. Most memorable is their investigation of Joplin's "The Ragtime Dance." Threadgill's solos in particular really fit the mood of these classic pieces. —*Scott Yanow*

Air Mail / Dec. 28, 1980 / Black Saint ✦✦✦✦
The Chicago trio Air is at a high point on this 1980 date, thanks in part to remarkable percussive foundations provided by the late Steve McCall and his interaction with bassist Fred Hopkins, plus the amazing solos and versatility of nominal leader Henry Threadgill. Besides alto and tenor sax, flute, and bass flute, Threadgill plays his own unique instrument called the hubka-phone and makes it just as memorable a weapon as the other horns. —*Ron Wynn*

80 Degrees Below '82 / Jan. 23, 1982–Jan. 24, 1982 / Antilles ✦✦✦
This was Air's ninth LP and the final one featuring drummer Steve McCall. The avant-garde trio stretches out on three of the saxophonist's originals and Jelly Roll Morton's "Chicago Breakdown." This blues-oriented set is more accessible than many of Air's previous recordings without watering down the explorative nature of this always-interesting group. —*Scott Yanow*

New Air: Live at the Montreux Int'l Jazz Festival / Jul. 1983 / Black Saint ✦✦
New drummer Pheeroan Ak Laff brought a fresh approach and crackling edge to the trio Air on this 1983 live date, done at the Montreux Festival. Hopkins didn't mesh as smoothly with Ak Laff on this date, although they found a comfortable meeting place by mid-album. Henry Threadgill, as always, was a compelling soloist, especially on alto sax. —*Ron Wynn*

Air Show No. 1 / Jun. 2, 1986–Jun. 3, 1986 / Black Saint ✦✦✦
The second and final Air recording after drummer/percussionist Pheeroan AkLaff took Steve McCall's place is a bit unusual, for vocalist Cassandra Wilson is heard on three of the six selections. She does an expert job of fitting into this complex music, giving a strong blues feeling to some of altoist Henry Threadgill's originals; bassist Fred Hopkins is also in top form on these unpredictable and dynamic performances. —*Scott Yanow*

Toshiko Akiyoshi

b. Dec. 12, 1929, Dairen, China
Piano, Arranger, Composer, Leader / Bop, Hard Bop
As an arranger, Toshiko Akiyoshi (influenced originally by Gil Evans and Thad Jones) has been particularly notable for incorporating elements of traditional Japanese music into her otherwise boppish charts. A strong (and underrated) pianist in the Bud Powell tradition, Akiyoshi was born in China but moved to Japan in 1946. She played locally (Sadao Watanabe was among her sidemen) and, after being noticed and encouraged by Oscar Peterson, studied at Berklee during 1956–59. Married for a time to altoist Charlie Mariano, she co-led the Toshiko-Mariano quartet in the early '60s. After working with Charles Mingus for a period in 1962 (including Town Hall Concert), Toshiko returned to Japan for three years. Back in New York by 1965, she did a radio series and formed a quartet with her second husband Lew Tabackin in 1970. After moving to Los Angeles in 1972, Toshiko Akiyoshi put together her very impressive big band, which featured such fine soloists as Bobby Shew, Gary Foster and Tabackin. They recorded several notable albums before Akiyoshi decided in 1981 to move back to New York. Since their relocation, Akiyoshi and Tabackin have both been quite active, although her reformed big band has actually received less publicity than it did in L.A. She ranks as one of the top jazz arrangers of the past 25 years. —*Scott Yanow*

Toshiko's Piano / Nov. 13, 1953–Nov. 14, 1953 / Norgran ✦✦✦

The Toshiko Trio / 1954 / Storyville ✦✦✦

United Nations / Jun. 13, 1958 / Metrojazz ✦✦✦

Toshiko & Modern Jazz / Jul. 16, 1964 / Denon ✦✦

At Top of the Gate / Jul. 30, 1968 / Denon ✦✦✦

Kogun / Apr. 3, 1974+Apr. 4, 1974 / RCA ✦✦

Long Yellow Road / Apr. 4, 1974–Mar. 4, 1975 / RCA ✦✦✦✦
Toshiko Akiyoshi's second big-band album (closely following *Kogun*) is a hard-swinging and consistently exciting set that has strong solos from the likes of trumpeter Don Rader, fluegelhornist Bobby Shew, altoist Gary Foster, and Toshiko's husband Lew Tabackin on tenor in addition to the pianist/leader. Akiyoshi draws on her culture successfully on "Children in the Temple Ground" and shows throughout this memorable set (which deserves to be reissued on CD) that she had by this early point already developed into one of the most distinctive big-band arrangers around. —*Scott Yanow*

Tales of a Courtesan / Dec. 1, 1975–Dec. 3, 1975 / RCA ✦✦✦✦✦
Virtually every Toshiko Akiyoshi big-band recording is well worth acquiring for not only does Akiyoshi have a highly appealing and original arranging style, but her orchestra always boasts top soloists. In addition to Lew Tabackin on tenor and flute, *Tales of a Courtesan* features worthy improvisations by altoists Gary Foster and Dick Spencer, trombonist Britt Woodman, trumpeter Bobby Shew and pianist Akiyoshi. "Road Time Shuffle" and "Strive for Jive" are particularly memorable. —*Scott Yanow*

Road Time / Jan. 30, 1976–Feb. 8, 1976 / RCA ✦✦✦✦
This two-LP set, which, like most of the Toshiko Akiyoshi Orchestra's recordings, is currently out of print gives one a definitive look at her 1970s orchestra. Akiyoshi's arrangements are colorful and swinging; the best charts on this two-fer are "Tuning Up," the nearly 23-minute "Henpecked Old Man," "Kogun" (which pays tribute to her Japanese heritage), and "Road Time Shuffle." This edition of the orchestra includes such major players as trumpeter Steve Huffstetter and Bobby Shew, trombonist Jimmy Knepper, altoists Dick Spencer, and Gary Foster and Lew Tabackin on tenor and flute. It's highly recommended, if it can be found. —*Scott Yanow*

Insights / Jun. 22, 1976–Jun. 24, 1976 / Novus ✦✦✦

Dedications / Jul. 19, 1976–Jul. 21, 1976 / Inner City ✦✦
One of her few trio recordings. —*Michael Erlewine*

The Tribute to Billy Strayhorn / Apr. 3, 1978–Apr. 4, 1978 / Jam ✦✦✦

Finesse / May 8, 1978 / Concord Jazz ✦✦
The material on *Finesse* was mostly ballads interspersed with a few things done at medium tempo; although this had been pianist/bandleader/composer Toshiko Akiyoshi's domain in the past, this time she brought to it a dirge-like sound that bred impatience in the listener. In her writing for big band, alongside the drama created by her unusual horn voicings, there was an emo-

tionalism, at turns humorous or reflective, introduced by her sense of rhythmic juxtaposition. It was this later feature that was lacking in all but three of the selections on "Finesse." Akiyoshi was not the only culprit, as bassist Monty Budwig, who shared much of the solo space, plodded through most of his solos as if his bass strings were coated with molasses. The three tunes that broke out of this somber pattern were "Mr. Jelly Lord," an original from The Akiyoshi-Tabackin band book, "Warning," and an arrangement of a Grieg piece, "Solvejg's Song." The Jelly Roll Morton tune was played as a ballad, but this time instead of a facile explication of the melody, Akiyoshi explored the emotional beauty of the notes, pausing in reflection before continuing. "Warning" and "Solvejg's Song" were both taken at a medium tempo. —*Bob Rusch, Cadence*

Notorious Tourist from the East / Dec. 5, 1978–Dec. 6, 1978 / Inner City ◆◆◆
Fine set showcasing the tasty Akiyoshi piano in a non-big band setting. Akiyoshi is a good ballad interpreter, excellent composer, and accomplished soloist, qualities that have been obscured by her conducting and arranging skills. This album put those talents in the forefront. —*Ron Wynn*

Farewell to Mingus / Jan. 10, 1980–Jan. 11, 1980 / Jam ◆◆◆◆

Tanuki's Night Out / Mar. 24, 1981–Mar. 25, 1981 / Jam ◆◆◆◆

European Memoirs / Sep. 21, 1982–Sep. 22, 1982 / Ascent ◆◆◆◆

Wishing Peace / Jul. 21, 1986–Jul. 22, 1986 / Ken Music ◆◆◆

Interlude / Feb. 1987 / Concord Jazz ◆◆◆
A nice trio outing from 1987, with Akiyoshi displaying more accomplished pianistic skills than she was generally given credit for while heading The Akiyoshi/Tabackin big band. She emerges as the dominant instrumentalist among the three, with bassist Dennis Irwin and drummer Eddie Marshall content to let her set the pace and work off her leads, rather than seeking to influence the sound themselves. —*Ron Wynn*

Remembering Bud: Cleopatra's Dream / Jul. 31, 1990–Aug. 1, 1990 / Evidence ◆◆◆
Bandleader and pianist Toshiko Akiyoshi is a far better player than she claims, and she demonstrates her abilities on these 10 tracks recorded in 1990. Akiyoshi displays an accomplished rhythmic style, nice harmonic sense and good command of the keyboard. While her touch and volume are not as emphatic as some other pianists, Akiyoshi's melodic sense and her floating lines are strong enough to express what is necessary within each song. For those unaccustomed to hearing Akiyoshi outside the big band arena, this will be a pleasant departure. —*Ron Wynn*

● **Carnegie Hall Concert** / Sep. 20, 1991 / Columbia ◆◆◆◆

Desert Lady-Fantasy / Dec. 1, 1993–Dec. 3, 1993 / Columbia ◆◆◆

Toshiko Akiyoshi At Maybeck / Jul. 10, 1994 / Concord Jazz ◆◆◆

Joe Albany (Joseph Albani)
b. Jan. 24, 1924, Atlantic City, NJ, d. Jan. 11, 1988, New York, NY
Piano / Bop
Looking at pianist Joe Albany's life in hindsight, it is miraculous that he lived to almost reach 64. Serious problems with drugs and alcohol resulted in a series of harrowing incidents, and his domestic life would never be described as tranquil (his second wife committed suicide while his third almost died from a drug overdose). Albany's life was so erratic that he only recorded once during 1947–71. However, Joe Albany's real importance is as one of the early bop pianists. After playing accordion as a child, he switched to piano in high school and in 1942 joined Leo Watson's group. He had short-term associations with Benny Carter, Georgie Auld, Boyd Raeburn and most significantly Charlie Parker. Albany's live recordings with Parker and some brilliant studio sides with Lester Young in 1946 (the latter later reissued on Blue Note) were the highpoints of his career. Decades of struggle followed (which he frankly described in the excellent 1980 documentary *Joe Albany ...A Jazz Life*) with Riverside's *The Right Combination* (a rehearsal session with tenor saxophonist Warne Marsh) being the only documentation from the lost years. Other than a short stint with Charles Mingus in the mid-'60s, it was not until 1972 that Albany started to have a comeback. He recorded a set with violinist Joe Venuti and was a leader on albums for Revelation, Horo, Inner City, SeaBreeze and Interplay. The 1982 Elektra/Musician

set *Portrait of an Artist* were the final (and one of his finest) recordings from this troubled but talented pianist. —*Scott Yanow*

● **Right Combination** / 1957 / Original Jazz Classics ◆◆◆◆
The only early documentation of the swinging bebop pianist features Warne Marsh (ts). —*David Szatmary*

At Home Alone / Aug. 31, 1971 / Revelation ◆◆

Proto Bopper / Feb. 14, 1972–Oct. 10, 1972 / Revelation ◆◆◆

Birdtown Birds / Apr. 25, 1973–Apr. 30, 1973 / SteepleChase ◆◆◆

Albany Touch / Jul. 5, 1977 / Sea Breeze ◆◆◆◆
One of the early boppers, Albany issued several solo piano records in the '70s. This one was among his finest, with glittering versions of standards and bop anthems like "Night In Tunisia." —*Ron Wynn*

Bird Lives / Jan. 4, 1979 / Storyville ◆◆◆

Portrait of an Artist / 1982 / Elektra ◆◆◆◆
A good example of Albany's hard-driving and infectious style. —*David Szatmary*

Gerald Albright
b. 1957
Tenor Saxophone / Instrumental Pop, Crossover
Gerald Albright has occasionally shown the ability to play jazz (most notably on his Atlantic set *Live at Birdland West*) but has chosen to make his career as an R&B saxophonist. Originally he studied piano before switching to tenor, and in college he began doubling on electric bass. Through the years Albright has performed in a variety of R&Bish settings (with Patrice Rushen, Anita Baker, Quincy Jones, the Temptations, etc.), content to play simplistic music and disappointingly little jazz. —*Scott Yanow*

Just Between Us / 1988 / Atlantic ◆◆

Bermuda Nights / 1988 / Atlantic ◆◆

Dream Come True / Nov. 6, 1990 / Atlantic ◆◆◆
Albright, among the most popular instrumental pop/fusion saxophonists around, plays both high-octane, uptempo tunes and slick covers of Urban Contemporary hits. It's well produced, with a minimum of improvisational content, but should attract those who like light jazz. —*Ron Wynn*

● **Live at Birdland West** / 1991 / Atlantic ◆◆◆◆◆
Virtually all of saxophonist Gerald Albright's previous recordings were in the pop/R&B field, making this mostly straight-ahead session a major surprise. Albright, alternating between alto and tenor, plays quite well throughout this set, which is highlighted by versions of "Impressions," "Georgia on My Mind" and "Limehouse Blues." Tenorman Kirk Whalum helps out on three tracks and Eddie Harris makes a guest appearance on "Bubblehead McDaddy." This is easily Gerald Albright's most rewarding session to date. —*Scott Yanow*

Smooth / Feb. 22, 1994 / Atlantic ◆◆
The title to *Smooth* is appropriate—the album is a collection of slick fusion, drawing more from urban R&B than jazz. However, smooth can be good, as Gerald Albright proves throughout the album. The saxophonist is a proficient, graceful player and he can create a romantic atmosphere rather effortlessly. Jazz purists may disdain it, but *Smooth* would please any of the saxist's fans. —*Stephen Thomas Erlewine*

Giving Myself to You / 1995 / Atlantic Jazz ◆◆

Howard Alden
b. Oct. 17, 1958, Newport Beach, CA
Guitar / Swing
Howard Alden is to the guitar what Scott Hamilton, Warren Vache, Dan Barrett, and Ken Peplowski are to the tenor, trumpet, trombone and clarinet. Part of a youthful swing movement that gained momentum in the 1980s, Alden plays the earlier prebop styles quite effectively but also has the ability to perform the music of Thelonious Monk and Bill Evans as well as being equally talented on electric guitar, acoustic guitar, and his rarely played banjo. Alden began playing guitar at age ten and he counts his early influences as guitarists Barney Kessel, Charlie Christian and George Van Eps in addition to Louis Armstrong, Benny Goodma,n and Count Basie. He began gigging professionally in Los Angeles as a teenager and became good friends with trombonist Dan Barrett. In 1979 Alden played with vibraphonist Red Norvo and in

1982 he followed Barrett to New York, where he quickly became established as a major guitarist. He performed and recorded with the who's who of mainstream jazz (including Joe Bushkin, Ruby Braff, Joe Williams, Woody Herman, Benny Carter, Flip Phillips, Bud Freeman, Clark Terry and Dizzy Gillespie) and by the mid-'80s was one of the most popular artists on the Concord label. A very consistent and inventive musician, Alden has been in great demand for recording sessions, jazz parties and festivals for the past 15 years. His many recordings (which include a quintet co-led with Barrett, sessions on the seven-string guitar with his idol George Van Eps and duets with Peplowski) are all enjoyable and perfect examples of modern swing. — *Scott Yanow*

No Amps Allowed / 1985 / Chiaroscuro ✦✦

● **Swing Street** / Sep. 1986 / Concord Jazz ✦✦✦✦✦

Plays the Music of Harry Reser / Dec. 7, 1988+Dec. 21, 1988 / Stomp Off ✦✦✦✦

The Howard Alden Trio Plus Special Guests / Jan. 1989 / Concord Jazz ✦✦✦✦
The emphasis of this excellent session is on lesser-known swing standards. Guitarist Howard Alden (in a trio with bassist Lynn Seaton and drummer Mel Lewis) welcomes either Ken Peplowski (doubling on tenor and clarinet) or cornetist Warren Vache on eight of the 11 selections. It is particularly rewarding to hear such songs as "You Showed Me the Way," Duke Ellington's "Purple Gazelle," Charlie Parker's "Back Home Blues" and Django Reinhardt's "Tears" getting revived. — *Scott Yanow*

The ABQ Salutes Buck Clayton / Jun. 1989 / Concord Jazz ✦✦✦✦✦

Snowy Morning Blues / Apr. 1990 / Concord Jazz ✦✦

Thirteen Strings / Feb. 1991 / Concord Jazz ✦✦✦

Misterioso / Apr. 1991 / Concord Jazz ✦✦✦

Good Likeness / Aug. 1992 / Concord Jazz ✦✦✦

Your Story: The Music Of Bill Evans / May 19, 1994–May 20, 1994 / Concord Jazz ✦✦✦

Live At Centre Concord / Aug. 15, 1994 / Concord Jazz ✦✦✦✦

Concord Jazz Guitar Collective / May 23, 1995–May 24, 1995 / Concord Jazz ✦✦✦

Monty Alexander (Montgomery Bernard)

b. Jun. 6, 1944, Kingston, Jamaica
Piano / Bop, Hard Bop
Monty Alexander long ago combined the influence of Oscar Peterson with the soul of Gene Harris and Nat King Cole to form his own appealing and personable style. Long a bit underrated (due to the shadow of Peterson), Alexander has recorded more than a score of excellent albums. He began piano lessons when he was six and played professionally in Jamaica clubs while still a teenager; his band, Monty and the Cyclones, was quite popular locally during 1958–60. He first played in the U.S. when he appeared in Las Vegas with Art Mooney's Orchestra. Soon he was accompanying a variety of top singers, formed a friendship with vibraphonist Milt Jackson and began gigging with bassist Ray Brown. With the recording of a pair of Pacific Jazz albums in 1965, an RCA date in 1967 and a Verve session in 1969, Alexander began to gain a strong reputation. His series of exciting albums for MPS during 1971–77 found him in prime form, and later recordings (most notably on Pablo and Concord) found him building on his original style. Alexander has occasionally paid tribute to his Jamaican heritage, but most of the time performs with his trio and swings hard in his own voice. — *Scott Yanow*

Spunky / 1965 / Pacific Jazz ✦✦✦

Monty Alexander / 1965 / Pacific Jazz ✦✦✦

Live! Montreux Alexander / Jun. 10, 1976 / Verve ✦✦✦
Pianist Monty Alexander did some of his finest recordings for the MPS label. This live trio set with bassist John Clayton and drummer Jeff Hamilton (reissued on CD) features Alexander playing his usual repertoire of the period with blues, standards ("Satin Doll," "Work Song" and "Battle Hymn of the Republic") and a version of "Feelings" that uplifts the song a bit (although not enough). His soulful approach to the generally familiar melodies makes them sound fresh and swinging. — *Scott Yanow*

Soul Fusion / Jun. 1, 1977–Jun. 2, 1977 / Pablo ✦✦✦✦

Cobilimbo / Sep. 8, 1977–Sep. 9, 1977 / MPS ✦✦✦

Jamento: The Monty Alexander 7 / Jun. 15, 1978–Jun. 16, 1978 / Pablo ✦✦✦

Monty Alexander in Tokyo / Jan. 22, 1979 / Pablo ✦✦✦

Facets / Aug. 1979 / Concord Jazz ✦✦✦✦

Ivory & Steel / Mar. 1980 / Concord Jazz ✦✦✦

Trio / Aug. 1980 / Concord Jazz ✦✦✦

Overseas Special / Mar. 1982 / Concord Jazz ✦✦✦✦

● **Triple Treat 1** / Mar. 1982 / Concord Jazz ✦✦✦✦✦
One can excuse pianist Monty Alexander if his playing on this Concord set recalls Oscar Peterson, for his sidemen in the trio are O.P.-alumni guitarist Herb Ellis and bassist Ray Brown. The combination lives up to its potential with the group romping on such songs as "The Flintstones," Blue Mitchell's "Fungi Mama" and an uptempo "Small Fry." — *Scott Yanow*

Reunion in Europe / Mar. 27, 1983 / Concord Jazz ✦✦✦

Duke Ellington Songbook / Mar. 29, 1983 / Verve ✦✦✦✦

The River / Oct. 1985 / Concord Jazz ✦✦✦
On this Concord CD, pianist Monty Alexander performs religious hymns plus a few of his originals that also fit comfortably in that tradition. Accompanied by bassist John Clayton and drummer Ed Thigpen, Alexander's sensitive, but generally swinging, interpretations of these timeless melodies communicate very well. — *Scott Yanow*

Threesome / Nov. 30, 1985–Dec. 2, 1985 / Soul Note ✦✦✦

Full Steam Ahead / 1985 / Concord Jazz ✦✦✦

Triple Treat 3 / Jun. 1987 / Concord Jazz ✦✦✦✦
Recorded at the sessions that resulted in *Triple Treat II*, this Concord release follows the same format with the trio of pianist Monty Alexander, guitarist Herb Ellis and bassist Ray Brown being joined by violinist John Frigo for about half of the selections. The music consists of boppish interpretations of standards ranging from "I Told You I Love You, Now Get Out," and "High Heel Sneakers" to "Corcovado." Fans of these veteran players will be very satisfied with the results. — *Scott Yanow*

Triple Treat 2 / Jun. 1987 / Concord Jazz ✦✦✦✦
Five years after the original *Triple Treat*, pianist Monty Alexander has a reunion with guitarist Herb Ellis and bassist Ray Brown in a program that is in the tradition of both Oscar Peterson and Nat King Cole. A special bonus is violinist John Frigo, who sits in on four of the eight songs. Highpoints include Ray Brown's "Lined with a Groove," "Straighten up and Fly Right," "Seven Come Eleven" and "Lester Leaps In." — *Scott Yanow*

Jamboree: Monty Alexander's Ivory and Steel / Feb. 1988–Mar. 1988 / Concord Jazz ✦✦✦
Alexander featured his band "Ivory and Steel" for a session that blended driving jazz feel and breezy Caribbean flavor in an effective, catchy fashion. As usual, Alexander's piano solos were upbeat, brisk, and captivating. — *Ron Wynn*

Caribbean Circle / Jun. 3, 1992–Jun. 4, 1992 / Chesky ✦✦✦✦
First-rate example of connecting diverse styles and traditions. Alexander, a solid soloist well versed in Caribbean music, integrates rhythms from the islands into his solos, yet retains the jazz edge and drive. A great supporting cast as well which includes Slide Hampton and Jon Faddis. — *Ron Wynn*

Maybeck Recital Hall Series, Vol. 40 / Sep. 26, 1994 / Concord Jazz ✦✦✦✦

Lorez Alexandria

b. Aug. 14, 1929, Chicago, IL
Vocals / Standards
A solid singer who is superior at interpreting lyrics, gives a soulful feeling to each song and improvises with subtlety, Lorez Alexandria has been a popular attraction for several decades. She sang gospel music with her family at churches starting in the mid-'40s and worked in Chicago nightclubs in the 1950s. With the release of several albums for King during 1957–59, Alexandria became popular beyond her hometown and by the early '60s was living and working in Los Angeles. Despite a long period off records (only a few private recordings during the 1965–76 period), Alexandria has survived through the many changes in musical styles and in the 1990s can be heard in excellent form. In addi-

tion to King her earlier recording sessions were for Argo and Impulse! while her later albums have been for Discovery and Muse. —*Scott Yanow*

● **Alexandria the Great/More of the Great** / 1964 / MCA ✦✦✦✦
Recorded in 1964-65, this two-fer features fine jazz vocal stylings and combines two Impulse! albums. —*Hank Davis*

How Will I Remember You? / Jan. 16, 1978+Jan. 23, 1978 / Discovery ✦✦✦
Late '70s material with Alexandria essentially sounding the same as she did in the late '50s and early '60s, except that her voice has a weary, wavering quality. She still does pre-rock pop and is backed by another good group of session professionals. —*Ron Wynn*

A Woman Knows / Dec. 19, 1978 / Discovery ✦✦✦
Another late '70s album with Alexandria doing more upbeat, varied material, supported by a sextet with Charles Owens and Brian Atkinson. Things range from pleasant to tepid, with most performances falling somewhere in between. —*Ron Wynn*

Sings the Songs of Johnny Mercer, Vol. 1 / Dec. 5, 1980 / Discovery ✦✦✦
This excellent recent work features jazz vocals and classy material with solid four-piece backing. —*Hank Davis*

Sings the Songs of Johnny Mercer, Vol. 2: Harlem Butterfly / Mar. 27, 1984 / Discovery ✦✦✦

Sings the Songs of Johnny Mercer, Vol. 3: Tangerine / Dec. 13, 1984 / Trend ✦✦✦
With the Mike Wofford Quartet, this excellent recent work features jazz vocals. It's classy material with a solid four-piece backing. —*Hank Davis*

Dear to My Heart / Mar. 24, 1987-Apr. 14, 1987 / Trend ✦✦✦

May I Come In? / Aug. 16, 1990-Aug. 17, 1990 / Muse ✦✦✦

I'll Never Stop Loving You / 1992 / Muse ✦✦✦✦
This is one of singer Lorez Alexandria's finest recordings of her later years. Alexandria has an expressive style and improvises through her phrasing and placing of words. Backed by a particularly attentive quintet featuring Herman Riley (on tenor and flute) and pianist Gildo Mahones, Alexandria is in particularly fine form on nine superior standards that are highlighted by "Love Walked In," "No Moon at All" and a ten-minute version of "For All We Know." —*Scott Yanow*

Rashied Ali (Robert Patterson)

b. Jul. 1, 1935, Philadelphia, PA
Drums / Free Jazz, Avant-Garde
Rashied Ali made history in the mid-'60s when he was recruited by John Coltrane to serve as second drummer in his expanded band. Ali didn't remain in that role very long as Elvin Jones quickly departed, leaving him the lone percussionist. Ali was praised for his ability to play what Trane labeled "multi-directional" rhythms, giving the soloist maximum freedom. This could be heard at its fullest on the duet album *Innerstellar Space*, issued posthumously, where Ali's rhythms spiraled around Coltrane's furious wails and screams, neither conflicting with nor necessarily guiding Coltrane's playing, but meshing and complementing it while establishing a counter direction. Ali studied at the Granoff School in Philadelphia, and played drums with both R&B bands and jazz groups before joining Sonny Rollins in 1963 for a tour of Japan. He then moved to New York, where he played with Pharoah Sanders, Bill Dixon, Paul Bley, Sun Ra, Albert Ayler and Sunny Murray before starting his tenure with Coltrane in 1965. He continued working with Alice Coltrane after John's death in 1967, then began heading his own groups. Ali began efforts in the '70s to improve the lot of jazz musicians, especially their ability to control their music and its proceeds and find venues to work. He helped organize the New York Musicians Festival in 1972, and formed Survival Records in 1973, issuing his own recordings. He also opened a club, Ali's Alley, which he operated as a place for noncommercial and "loft" jazz acts until 1979. Ali participated in a "Dialogue of the Drums" concert with Milford Graves and Andrew Cyrille in the mid-'70s. But he's had a low profile in the '80s and '90s. In the 1990s Rashied Ali has played with the group Phalanx and occasionally emerged with David Murray. —*Ron Wynn*

Rashied Ali Quintet / 1973 / Survival ✦✦✦

Carl Allen

Drums / Hard Bop
Carl Allen, a fine drummer who has worked with Freddie

Music Map

Accordion

Early Uses of Accordion in Jazz
Buster Moten (1929-31 with Bennie Moten orchestra)
Jack Cornell (1929-30, Irving Mill's Hotsy-Totsy Gang)
Cornell Smelser (recorded "Accordion Joe" with Duke Ellington 1930)
Charles Melrose (1930-31, Cellar Boys)

Accordion Popular in Europe
Nisse Lind (1935-36, Sweden)
Kamil Behounek (1936-46, Czechoslovakia)
Buddy Bertinat (1940-48, Switzerland)

Pianists Occasionally Doubling on Accordion
George Shearing
Pete Jolly

Bop and Beyond
Joe Mooney
Mat Mathews (1953-54, group with Herbie Mann)
Art Van Damme
Leon Sash (1957, recorded at Newport Jazz Festival)
Tommy Gumina (1960-63, group with Buddy DeFranco)
Gordie Fleming (1977, recorded with Buddy DeFranco)
Frank Morocco
(1980s-'90s, featured with Most Brothers)
Guy Klucevsek (1993, recorded with Bill Frisell)

Hubbard, Jackie McLean, George Coleman, Art Farmer and Benny Green, fit right in with the band The Message: A Tribute to Art Blakey in the late '80s. He has since led his own sessions for Timeless and Atlantic and been working on producing albums by other top Young Lions. —*Scott Yanow*

Piccadilly Square / Dec. 6, 1989-Dec. 7, 1989 / Timeless ✦✦✦

Pursuer / Sep. 26, 1993-Sep. 27, 1993 / Atlantic ✦✦✦✦
Drummer Carl Allen welcomed some of The Young Lions to his Atlantic CD, including altoist Vincent Herring, Teodross Avery on tenor and trumpeter Marcus Printup. The music, essentially modern mainstream jazz circa 1967, is comprised mostly of Allen's originals. Printup sounds like a mixture of Freddie Hubbard and Wynton Marsalis. Herring is content to emulate Cannonball Adderley and Avery looks toward early John Coltrane; in other words the soloists are generally pretty derivative. Despite that fault, the performances (which have colorful guest appearances from tenor saxophonist George Coleman and trombonist Steve Turre) are generally enjoyable and hard-swinging. —*Scott Yanow*

● **Testimonial** / Dec. 6, 1994-Dec. 7, 1994 / Atlantic ✦✦✦✦

Geri Allen

b. Jun. 12, 1957, Pontiac, MI
Piano / Post-Bop
A shining light among '80s pianists, Geri Allen has achieved a synthesis of bebop, free, hard bop and funk/R&B influences, melding them into an individualistic, exciting style. Her touch, phrasing, melodic and rhythmic abilities are superb, and she's been both a busy session player with numerous credits and recording dates and a featured artist on the Soul Note, DIW, JMT/Polygram and Blue Note labels. Allen cites the unpre-

dictability of Thelonious Monk and Herbie Nichols, and virtuosity of Eric Dolphy as sources that have had strong impact on her style. She's noted for her ability to solo in a quiet, yet intense fashion, and this skill has been illuminated on some remarkable trio dates with Charlie Haden and Paul Motian. Allen once backed The Supremes during her early days in Detroit. After studying music at Howard University and the University of Pittsburgh with Nathan Davis, she studied privately with Roscoe Mitchell. Allen moved to New York in the early '80s, working with James Newton and Lester Bowie before recording her debut for Minor. She's also played with Marcus Belgrave, Kenny Garrett, Robert Hurst, Jeff Watts, Oliver Lake, Andrew Cyrille and Robin Eubanks. Allen has worked closely with both Coleman's M-Base and the Black Rock Coalition, an organization of musicians, artists and cultural activitists working to improve conditions and opportunities for African-Americans in every area of American music. She's also played with Betty Carter. Recently she has played in several settings with Wallace Roney and in 1994 she toured with Ornette Coleman's acoustic quartet. —*Ron Wynn*

The Printmakers / Feb. 8, 1984–Feb. 9, 1984 / Minor Music ✦✦✦
The pianist's first album is a beauty, with Anthony Cox (b) and Andrew Cyrille (d). —*Michael G. Nastos*

Open on All Sides in the Middle / Dec. 1986 / Minor Music ✦✦
One of the lesser items in Geri Allen's discography, this erratic set features such soloists as David McMurray on soprano and flute, trombonist Robin Eubanks, altoist Steve Coleman and on one song, fluegelhornist Marcus Belgrave. Unfortunately, vocalist Shahita Nurallah is also well-showcased and the material is comparatively lightweight for a Geri Allen recording, often only bordering on jazz. She can do (and has done) much better than this so-so affair. —*Scott Yanow*

Twylight / 1989 / Verve ✦✦✦✦
Twylight, which looks from its cover as if it could be a reggae session, is actually a strong example of Geri Allen's originality. —*Scott Yanow*

In the Year of The Dragon / Mar. 1989 / Verve ✦✦✦✦
Throughout *In the Year of the Dragon,* whether the music is classic bop or very free, this trio is creative, colorful and right on the mark. The musical communication between the three musicians seems telepathic; each of them obviously possesses large ears. —*Scott Yanow*

Segments / Apr. 6, 1989–Apr. 8, 1989 / DIW ✦✦✦

The Nurturer / Jan. 5, 1990–Jan. 6, 1990 / Capitol ✦✦✦✦

● **Maroons** / 1992 / Blue Note ✦✦✦✦✦
Allen has developed into one of the major voices of the modern jazz piano. On *Maroons* she brings out the best in trumpeter Wallace Roney, welcomes her mentor, trumpeter Marcus Belgrave on a few tracks and performs 15 fresh compositions, 13 of them her originals. The music is unpredictable and explorative but still tied enough to the tradition to make the results quite coherent. This is a strong example of Allen's playing and compositional talents. —*Scott Yanow*

Twenty One / 1994 / Blue Note ✦✦✦✦
Pianist Geri Allen has thus far been a very consistent performer and all of her recordings are easily recommended. This particular set finds her in a trio with bassist Ron Carter and drummer Tony Williams performing six of her originals along with six jazz standards. Allen's style is fairly original (with hints of Herbie Nichols) and her chance-taking but logical solos are generally quite stimulating. —*Scott Yanow*

Harry Allen

b. Oct. 12, 1966, Washington, D.C.
Tenor Saxophone / Swing
A swing revivalist in the tradition of Scott Hamilton and Ken Peplowski, Harry Allen started playing tenor and clarinet while in high school. Since graduating from Rutgers he has worked with Bucky Pizzarelli, John Colliani, Keith Ingham and as a leader, showing great potential for the future. —*Scott Yanow*

Blue Skies / May 13, 1994 / John Marks ✦✦✦✦
The young tenor Harry Allen, assisted by pianist John Bunch, bassist Dennis Irwin and drummer Duffy Jackson, is in excellent form on a variety of swing standards. Allen seems poised at this point to follow in the footsteps of Scott Hamilton, for he also has a warm tone, a melodic approach to improvising and swings at any tempo. —*Scott Yanow*

Henry Allen (Henry "Red" Allen)

b. Jan. 7, 1908, New Orleans, LA, d. Apr. 17, 1967, New York, NY
Trumpet / New Orleans Jazz, Dixieland, Swing
One of the last great New Orleans trumpeters to emerge during the post-Louis Armstrong era, Henry "Red" Allen has long been overshadowed by Satch and his successors but actually had a fresh new approach of his own to offer. Allen sounded modern no matter what the setting and the rhythmic freedom he achieved made his solos consistently unpredictable and exciting. The son of Henry Allen, Sr. (a famous New Orleans brass band leader), he learned trumpet early on and played in his father's parade band along with other local groups. After working on the riverboats with Fate Marable and with Fats Pichon, Allen joined King Oliver in Chicago. He recorded in New York with Oliver and Clarence Williams, and then Red Allen joined Luis Russell's superb orchestra and began his own solo recording career. Signed by Victor as an alternative to Okeh's Louis Armstrong, Allen's solos were original and brilliant from the start (particularly "It Should Be You"); throughout the 1930s his trumpet and gruff vocals would be heard on dozens of recordings and, even when the material was indifferent, Allen was usually able to uplift the music. After notable stints with Luis Russell (1929–32), Fletcher Henderson (1933–34) and the Mills Blue Rhythm Band (1934–37), Allen became part of Louis Armstrong's backup band for three years, secure but somewhat anonymous work. However, starting in 1940 Red Allen led a series of impressive combos that were Dixieland-based but also open to certain aspects of rhythm & blues. Trombonist J.C. Higginbotham (a lifelong friend) and altoist Dan Stovall were on many of his recordings. From 1954–65 Allen's frequently riotous group played regularly at New York's Metropole (Coleman Hawkins was occasionally among his sidemen), visited Europe several times (including in 1959 with Kid Ory's band) and was one of the most memorable participants in the CBS TV special *The Sound of Jazz.* Red Allen remained very active up until his death and was proclaimed in the 1960s by Don Ellis as "the most creative and avant-garde trumpeter in New York." The European Classics label documents his recordings of the 1930s and many (but not all) of his later performances are also available on CD. —*Scott Yanow*

The Henry Allen Collection, Vol. 2 (1929–1930) / Jul. 16, 1929–Dec. 17, 1930 / JSP ✦✦✦
This English import is a perfect complement to the Classics series, for the CD consists of all of the alternate takes from Red Allen's 1929–30 sessions (including two very different versions of "It Should Be You") and his meetings with singers Victoria and Addie Spivey. In addition, Luis Russell's rare recordings from Oct. 24 and Dec. 17, 1930 (which feature Allen's trumpet) wrap up this gap-filling CD.—*Scott Yanow*

● **Henry "Red" Allen 1929–1933** / Jul. 16, 1929–Nov. 9, 1933 / Classics ✦✦✦✦✦
The first of a five-volume CD series released by the European Classics label that reissues all of the recordings led by trumpeter Red Allen during 1929–41 is one of the best. The great trumpeter is first heard fronting the Luis Russell Orchestra for such classics as "It Should Be You" and "Biff'ly Blues," he then interacts with blues singer Victoria Spivey, and on the selections from 1933 (two of which were previously unreleased) he co-leads a group with tenor saxophonist Coleman Hawkins. Not all of the performances are gems but there are many memorable selections including "How Do They Do It That Way," "Pleasin' Paul," "Sugar Hill Function," and "Patrol Wagon Blues." Other soloists include trombonists J.C. Higginbottham and Dicky Wells, clarinetist Albert Nicholas and altoist Charlie Holmes. —*Scott Yanow*

Henry "Red" Allen / Jul. 16, 1929–Mar. 21, 1957 / RCA ✦✦✦
This entry from the RCA Vintage LP series is comprised of 15 recordings that span 28 years and features trumpeter Red Allen; the first ten songs are from 1929–30. Highlights include "It Should Be You," Fletcher Henderson's "Hocus Pocus," Allen's heated "The Crawl" and a classic version of "I Cover the Waterfront." —*Scott Yanow*

Henry "Red" Allen / Jul. 16, 1929–Jul. 19, 1959 / Time-Life ✦✦✦
This attractive three-LP set gives one a good overview of the early recordings of trumpeter Red Allen, with the first two records covering just a six-year period (1929–35); unfortunately only four selections are from after 1940. Completists will want to pick up the Classics CDs instead, but this reissue does have a large and

informative booklet (with notes by Richard Sudhalter) and serves as a fine introduction to the great trumpeter. —*Scott Yanow*

The Henry Allen Collection, Vol. 1 (1929–1930) / Jul. 16, 1929–Dec. 17, 1930 / JSP ✦✦✦✦

A Recorded Documentary 1933–1941 / Aug. 18, 1933–Jul. 22, 1941 / Meritt ✦✦✦
This hard-to-find double LP from the collectors label Meritt has a great deal of valuable material. Allen and a variety of All-Stars are heard on previously unissued alternate takes by Fletcher Henderson's Orchestra in 1933 (including a version of "King Porter Stomp") bands led by trombonist Benny Morton, clarinetist Buster Bailey and blues singer Victoria Spivey in 1937, and a few numbers with singers Ruby Smith and Ida Cox. In addition, the complete Red Allen sessions of April 17 and July 22, 1941 (including all alternate takes and breakdowns) wrap up the two-fer with many fine solos from trombonist J.C. Higginbotham, clarinetist Edmond Hall and pianist Ken Kersey. Vintage jazz collectors and Red Allen fans are advised to search for this memorable set of heated swing music. —*Scott Yanow*

Henry "Red" Allen 1933–1935 / Nov. 9, 1933–Jul. 19, 1935 / Classics ✦✦✦✦
The second of five CDs put out by the European Classics label that document trumpeter Red Allen's 1929–41 recordings has three titles from a session co-led with tenor saxophonist Coleman Hawkins, eight songs from 1934 and a dozen from the following year. Allen takes vocals on most of the tracks and, even if not all of the songs are gems, there are many highlights including "Pardon My Southern Accent," "Rug Cutter Swing," "Believe It, Beloved," "Rosetta" and "Truckin." The strong supporting cast includes trombonists Dickie Wells and J.C. Higginbotham, clarinetists Buster Bailey and Cecil Scott and, on one date, tenorman Chu Berry. All five of the Red Allen Classics CDs are recommended. —*Scott Yanow*

Henry "Red" Allen 1935–1936 / Nov. 8, 1935–Aug. 31, 1936 / Classics ✦✦✦✦
The third of five Classics CDs that cover Red Allen's recordings of the 1930s has the contents of six complete sessions from a 10-month period. Allen (who has vocals on all but one of the 24 selections) is assisted by such classic players as trombonist J.C. Higginbotham, Cecil Scott (on tenor and clarinet), altoist Tab Smith and several strong rhythm sections. Among the more memorable swing performances are "On Treasure Island," "Take Me Back to My Boots and Saddle," "Lost," "Algiers Stomp" and "I'll Sing You a Thousand Love Songs." The fairly obscure recordings (cut during an era when the big bands really ruled) have long been underrated. —*Scott Yanow*

Henry "Red" Allen 1936–1937 / Oct. 12, 1936–Apr. 29, 1937 / Classics ✦✦✦
The fourth in the Classics label's five-CD series of Red Allen recordings reissues 20 obscure performances from a seven-month period. Although Red Allen was mostly playing with big bands during the 1930s, these small-group sides gave him a chance to be showcased quite a bit more than usual. Allen takes vocals on each of the tunes and, although many of the songs are long forgotten, his trumpet solos and the improvisations of altoist Tab Smith, clarinetist Buster Bailey and Ted McRae on tenor keep one's interest. This is actually the weakest of the five CDs but all are worth picking up. —*Scott Yanow*

Henry "Red" Allen 1937–1941 / Jun. 19, 1937–Jul. 22, 1941 / Classics ✦✦✦✦✦
The final of the five Classics CDs that document the early recordings of trumpeter Henry "Red" Allen covers music from three very different bands. First Allen is heard singing and playing trumpet on eight pop tunes he uplifts with a recording group in 1937 that features altoist Tab Smith. Allen also plays four Dixieland standards with a hot septet in 1940 that includes trombonist Benny Morton, clarinetist Edmond Hall and pianist Lil Armstrong. The final eight numbers (four of which were previously unreleased) showcase his regular band from 1941 (with trombonist J.C. Higginbotham and clarinetist Edmond Hall) really romping through some hard-swinging performances, including "K.K. Boogie" and a two-part version of "Sometimes I'm Happy." All five of these Classics CDs are easily recommended; this is one of the better ones. —*Scott Yanow*

Henry "Red" Allen / Mar. 9, 1939–Apr. 17, 1941 / Everybody's ✦✦
Although trumpeter Red Allen gets first billing, he is actually the

leader on only four of the 15 selections included on this [LP]. However, Allen is a strong force in the recordings of James P. Johnson (two sessions from 1939 that also feature singer Anna Robinson, trombonist J.C. Higginbotham and the tenor of Gene Sedric) and in the backup group (along with Higginbotham and clarinetist Edmond Hall) that accompanies blues singer Ida Cox. The final numbers ("K.K. Boogie," the two-part "Sometimes I'm Happy" and "Ol' Man River") find Allen in top form with his regular band of 1941. The music throughout this collector's LP is excellent but most of it is currently available elsewhere. —*Scott Yanow*

Red Allen & The Blues Singers, Vol. 1 / Nov. 17, 1939–Sep. 23, 1940 / Jazz Archives ✦✦
The now-defunct Jazz Archives label came out with two LPs in 1980 that featured trumpeter Red Allen as a sideman in the late '30s, accompanying blues and vaudevillian singers. The first set has four numbers apiece with Frankie "Half Pint" Jaxon and Blue Lu Barker, six on which Allen backs Lee Brown and two with Johnny Temple. Clarinetists Buster Bailey, Rupert Cole and Fess Williams also help out in spots. Unfortunately the same extensive liner notes are used on both LPs, so the one on the first volume refers to Rosetta Howard and Helen Proctor, neither of whom appear. Collectors of 1930s blues and novelty singers in particular will enjoy this hard-to-find LP. —*Scott Yanow*

The Very Great / Apr. 17, 1941–Jul. 16, 1946 / Rarities ✦✦✦✦
The valuable music on this now-rare European LP is well-deserving to be reissued on CD. Trumpeter Red Allen is heard on four numbers with his 1941 sextet (which also features trombonist J.C. Higginbotham, clarinetist Edmond Hall and pianist Ken Kersey) and on 12 heated jams with his band of 1944–46, an ensemble that found Higginbotham and the underrated altoist Don Stovall holding their own with Allen. The latter group combined the excitement and drive of R&B with the spontaneity and hot solos of Dixieland. "The Crawl" is a classic and several of the other performances are close behind. It's well worth the search. —*Scott Yanow*

Nice / 1946–Feb. 1963 / Phoenix ✦✦✦
This long out-of-print LP has seven titles (two previously unreleased) from Red Allen's exciting 1946 band (with trombonist J.C. Higginbotham and altoist Don Stovall), the two selections ("Wild Man Blues" and "Rosetta") performed by Allen with an all-star group on *The Sound of Jazz* television broadcast and four Dixieland standards played in 1963 with a sextet including trombonist Cutty Cutshall, clarinetist Tony Parenti and pianist Ralph Sutton. Red Allen collectors (and listeners who enjoy the spirit of classic jazz) will enjoy this fine LP. —*Scott Yanow*

Jazz from Bill Green's Rustic Lodge, 1949–1951 / 1949–1951 / Jass ✦✦✦

★ **World on a String** / Mar. 21, 1957–Apr. 10, 1957 / Bluebird ✦✦✦✦✦
This CD is a true classic. Trumpeter Red Allen is heard at the peak of his creative powers with a remarkable octet also featuring trombonist J.C. Higginbotham, clarinetist Buster Bailey and the great tenor Coleman Hawkins. "I Cover the Waterfront" has a wonderfully abstract statement from Allen, "Love Is Just Around the Corner" is joyous Dixieland, "Let Me Miss You, Baby" is a particularly strong blues (featuring Allen's vocal) and the simple blues line that serves as a melody on "Algiers Bounce" is quite catchy. The other seven selections from the classic veterans are also quite enjoyable. Although the music has its basis in Dixieland and swing, the solos of Allen and Hawkins in particular look ahead toward the future. There is nothing dated about these essential performances; highly recommended. —*Scott Yanow*

Red Allen, Jack Teagarden & Kid Ory at Newport / Jul. 4, 1957 / Verve ✦✦
At the 1957 Newport Jazz Festival Louis Armstrong, when confronted with a variety of his alumni from his past, preferred to instead play his standard show with his regular group. The veterans had their own separate set and that is what is heard on this LP. Trumpeter Red Allen, trombonist J.C. Higginbotham and clarinetist Buster Bailey play spirited versions of "Struttin' with Some Barbeque" and "St. James Infirmary"; trombonist Jack Teagarden joins up for "China Boy" and an overly loose "Basin Street Blues"; trombonist Kid Ory struts and sings on "Muskrat Ramble" and Ory, Teagaren and Higginbotham perform a somewhat incoherent "High Society." A happy if somewhat streaky affair, this historic

...as its strong moments but at 27 minutes it is all over soon.—*Scott Yanow*

...ed Allen Quartet "Live" / Sep. 15, 1961+Sep. 22, 1961 / ...nfare ✦✦✦
...n this LP trumpeter Red Allen is heard during two performances at Chicago's London House in 1961. Assisted by pianist Sammy Price (who is featured on James P. Johnson's "Snowy Morning Blues"), bassist Frank Skeet and drummer Jerry Potter, Allen is in excellent form. Although he sticks to Dixieland-oriented standards, his trumpet playing is surprisingly modern with many hints of advanced harmonies and surprising placements of notes. This LP is becoming difficult to find and has yet to surface on CD. —*Scott Yanow*

Rare Red Allen Trio Performances / Mar. 1962–Mar. 22, 1963 / Flutegroove ✦✦✦
Trumpeter Red Allen is heard with his quartets of 1962–63 (which include either Sammy Price or Lannie Scott on piano, bassist Frank Skeet and drummer Jerry Potter) playing an odd variety of material ranging from "That's a Plenty" and a remake of "Biff'ly Blues" to "I've Grown Accustomed to Her Face" and "Hava Nagila!" Throughout, Allen's New Orleans-based but unclassifiable solos are much more modern than expected in spots while still being accessible enough to the audience at Chicago's London House. —*Scott Yanow*

Henry Red Allen Memorial Album / Jun. 5, 1962 / Prestige ✦✦✦
This very enjoyable if brief (under 29 minutes) LP gives one a definitive look at Red Allen in his later years. Allen (who is accompanied by pianist Lannie Scott, bassist Franklin Skeete and drummer Jerry Potter) plays melodic yet advanced trumpet solos on six standards, "There's a House in Harlem" and his "Biff'ly Blues." His solos are unpredictable and he has expressive vocals on "I Ain't Got Nobody" and "Cherry." This LP (the material has not yet been reissued on CD) is worth searching for.—*Scott Yanow*

Feeling Good / Jun. 29, 1965–Aug. 18, 1965 / Columbia ✦✦✦

Marshall Allen

b. May 25, 1924, Louisville, KY
Alto Saxophone / Avant-Garde
Marshall Allen's name will always be closely linked with that of Sun Ra. Although he was 32 when he started playing regularly with Ra (and had performed previously with pianist Art Simmons in Paris during 1949–50 and toured Europe with James Moody), the altoist was a virtual unknown at the time. However from 1956 up until Sun Ra's death in 1993 (with only brief periods off, such as to record with Paul Bley in the mid-'60s), Allen was an integral part of Ra's sound. On alto, flute, piccolo and oboe Marshall Allen's intense flights could be quite violent and out of tune (sounding like Johnny Hodges from a different dimension) but there was no doubting his sincerity, passion or the directness of his musical message. —*Scott Yanow*

Mose Allison

b. Nov. 11, 1927, Tippo, MS
Vocals, Piano / Hard Bop, Folk Jazz
The multi-talented Mose Allison has long been in his own category. A folkey singer reminiscent of the country blues tradition and a lyricist whose unusual messages are usually quite true and unexpected, Allison is also a bop-based pianist whose playing has evolved greatly through the years. Many of his solos give one the impression of taking a trip in a pickup truck, with colorful stops along the way!
Mose Allison started playing piano when he was five, took up the trumpet in high school (he would later record a couple of songs on it) and, after serving in the military and getting out of college, moved to New York in 1956. He played with Stan Getz, Gerry Mulligan, Al Cohn and Zoot Sims before leading his own trios. His early Prestige recordings mostly featured Allison as a pianist but once he switched to Atlantic, his vocalizing began to be emphasized (although he has achieved an excellent balance through the years). Allison, who has written such pieces as "Parchman Farm" and "Your Mind Is on Vacation," has worked steadily into the mid-'90s and continued to be a unique artist, retaining his popularity after 35 years of steady output. —*Scott Yanow*

Back Country Suite / Mar. 7, 1957 / Original Jazz Classics ✦✦✦
A wonderful date mixing his country blue warblings, dynamic

piano playing, and cabaret-from-the-backwoods styles. —*Ron Wynn*

● **Allison Wonderland: Anthology** / Mar. 7, 1957–Dec. 7, 1989 / Rhino/Atlantic ✦✦✦✦✦

Local Color / Nov. 8, 1957 / Original Jazz Classics ✦✦✦

● **Greatest Hits** / Nov. 8, 1957–Feb. 13, 1959 / Original Jazz Classics ✦✦✦✦✦
Basic, no-frills anthology of 13 of his better late-'50s Prestige sides, all of which feature his vocals. It has most of his most famous songs, particularly to listeners from a rock background, including his versions of "The Seventh Son," "Eyesight to the Blind" (covered by The Who on *Tommy*, though Sonny Boy Williamson did it before Allison), "Parchman Farm" (done by John Mayall), and "Young Man's Blues" (also covered by The Who). Were it not for the significant omission of "I'm Not Talking" (retooled by The Yardbirds), this would qualify as the basic collection for most listeners, although more thorough retrospectives are available (particularly Rhino's *Anthology*). *Greatest Hits* does include liner notes by Pete Townshend, originally penned for a 1972 collection. —*Richie Unterberger*

Ol' Devil Mose / 1958 / Prestige ✦✦✦
This was actually a two-album set combining songs from the Allison releases *Rambling With Mose* and *Autumn Song*. They are trio dates, and feature prime Allison vocals, excellent solos, and great interaction between the pianist, bassist Addison Farmer, and drummer Ronnie Free. —*Ron Wynn*

Creek Bank / Jan. 24, 1958+Aug. 15, 1958 / Prestige ✦✦✦✦
When Mose Allison recorded his six early albums for Prestige, he was best-known as a bop-based pianist who occasionally sang. This single CD (which reissues in full *Young Man Mose* and *Creek Bank*) has 15 instrumentals including a rare appearance by Allison on trumpet ("Stroll"), but it is his five typically ironic vocals that are most memorable, particularly Allison's classic "The Seventh Son" and "If You Live." His piano playing, even with the Bud Powell influence, was beginning to become original and he successfully performs both revived swing songs and moody originals. —*Scott Yanow*

Mose Allison Trilogy: High Jinks! / Dec. 21, 1959–May 23, 1961 / Columbia/Legacy ✦✦✦✦

I Don't Worry About a Thing / Mar. 15, 1962 / Rhino/Atlantic ✦✦✦✦✦
Mose Allison was already 34 and had recorded nine records as a leader before cutting his debut for Atlantic (which has been reissued on CD by Rhino), but this was his breakthrough date. One of jazz's greatest lyricists, at the time, Allison was making the transition from being a pianist who occasionally sang to becoming a vocalist who also played his own unusual brand of piano. In addition to the original versions of "Your Mind Is on Vacation," "I Don't Worry about a Thing (Because I Know Nothing Will Turn out Right)" and "It Didn't Turn out That Way," he sings bluish versions of two standards ("Meet Me at No Special Place" and "The Song Is Ended") and plays five instrumentals with his trio. There are only 33 1/2 minutes of music on this straight reissue of the original LP, but the set is one of Mose Allison's most significant recordings. —*Scott Yanow*

Your Mind Is on Vacation / Apr. 5, 1976–Apr. 9, 1976 / Atlantic ✦✦✦

Middle Class White Boy / Feb. 2, 1982 / Elektra ✦✦✦
This Elektra LP finds the unique Mose Allison well-featured in a sextet also including Joe Farrell on tenor and flute and guitarist Phil Upchurch. Allison's unusual mixture of bop, country-blues and his own eccentric personality have long given him a distinctive sound on piano, but it is his ironic vocals and superb lyric-writing abilities that make him a major figure. In addition to such originals as "How Does It Feel? (To Be Good Looking)," "I Don't Want Much" and "I'm Nobody Today," Allison brings new life to such standards as "When My Dreamboat Comes Home," "I'm Just a Lucky So-and-So" and "The Tennessee Waltz." —*Scott Yanow*

Lesson in Living / Jul. 21, 1982 / Elektra ✦✦✦
Lou Donaldson (as) brings a welcome blues and soul-jazz flavor to an already impressive cast and musical menu. —*Ron Wynn*

Ever Since the World Ended / May 11, 1987–Jun. 2, 1987 / Blue Note ✦✦✦
A wonderful update of his sound, with dauntless work by Mose with Arthur Blythe (as), and Kenny Burrell (g). —*Ron Wynn*

My Backyard / Dec. 5, 1989–Dec. 7, 1989 / Blue Note ✦✦

Earth Wants You / Sep. 8, 1993–Sep. 9, 1993 / Blue Note ✦✦✦✦
Mose Allison, one of the top lyricists of the '90s, shows throughout this entertaining CD that his powers as a pianist and singer are also very much intact. The album introduces a few new classics in "Certified Senior Citizen," "This Ain't Me" and "Who's in, Who's Out." His voice is still in prime form and his piano playing remains quite unique. It is true that the guests on the set (guitarist John Scofield, altoist Joe Lovano, Bob Malach on tenor and trumpeter Randy Brecker) are not all that necessary but Allison's performance makes this an excellent showcase for his music. —*Scott Yanow*

Parchman Farm / Original Jazz Classics ✦✦✦

Karrin Allyson

b. Great Bend, KS
Vocals / Standards
One of the more impressive jazz singers to emerge in the 1990s, Karrin Allyson is a great scat singer but also highly expressive on ballads. She grew up in Omaha, NB, and the San Francisco Bay Area and graduated from the University of Nebraska in 1987. After performing regularly at a Minneapolis club, Allyson moved to Kansas City, which has been her home base ever since. Thus far she has had three fine recordings on Concord. —*Scott Yanow*

I Didn't Know About You / 1992 / Concord Jazz ✦✦✦

● **Sweet Home Cookin'** / Jun. 9, 1993–Jun. 10, 1993 / Concord ✦✦✦✦✦
Karrin Allyson has a small and sometimes hoarse voice but she does so much with it that her bop session is easily recommended. Her all-star sextet (comprised of trumpeter Randy Sandke, the late tenor Bob Cooper, guitarist Danny Embrey, pianist Alan Broadbent, bassist Putter Smith and drummer Sherman Ferguson) has plenty of short solos on colorful charts by Alan Broadbent. Allyson sounds perfectly at ease, whether scatting on "No Moon at All," finding fresh melodic variations on "I Cover the Waterfront" or singing her original blues "Sweet Home Cookin' Man." She always swings. —*Scott Yanow*

Azure-Te / Nov. 14, 1994–Nov. 16, 1994 / Concord Jazz ✦✦✦✦

Laurindo Almeida

b. Sept. 2, 1917, Sao Paulo, Brazil, d. Jul. 6, 1995, Los Angeles, CA
Guitar / Brazilian Jazz
Laurindo Almeida helped introduce the Brazilian guitar to jazz, and in his 1953 recordings with Bud Shank was essentially playing bossa nova seven years before Stan Getz! After spending time as a staff guitarist in Los Angeles and was a member of Stan Kenton's Orchestra (1947–48). A studio guitarist in L.A. from 1950 on, Almeida also continued playing jazz along with classical music. A decade after the Shank sessions, Almeida recorded some best-selling bossa nova dates for Capitol. He co-founded the L.A. Four in the mid-'70s (which reunited him with Bud Shank), collaborated on recordings with Charlie Byrd and made several worthwhile sessions for Concord. —*Scott Yanow*

Brazilliance, Vol. 1 / Apr. 15, 1954–Apr. 2, 1954 / World Pacific ✦✦✦✦✦
With Bud Shank (as, fl) on both albums, and Gary Peacock (b) and Chuck Flores (d) on the second album. It is almost possible to hear the birth of bossa nova in these albums. —*Michael Erlewine*

Brazilliance, Vol. 2 / Mar. 1958 / World Pacific ✦✦✦
With Bud Shank (as, fl) Gary Peacock (b) and Chuck Flores (d). —*Michael Erlewine*

Concierto De Aranjuez / Mar. 27, 1978–Mar. 28, 1978 / Inner City ✦✦✦
This solo album includes songs from *Black Orpheus* and a Gershwin medley. —*Michael Erlewine*

Chamber Jazz / Sep. 1978 / Concord Jazz ✦✦✦
There are classical and Third Stream influences throughout this 1978 set. It is very introspective, sometimes almost detached, with Almedia, bassist Bob Magnusson, and drummer Jeff Hamilton playing such songs as "Unaccustomed Bach" and "Chopin a la breve." —*Ron Wynn*

First Concerto for Guitar & Orchestra / Nov. 1979 / Concord Jazz ✦✦✦
Guitarist Laurindo Almeida spins delicate melodies and frequently beautiful riffs and solos, backed by The Los Angeles Orchestra de Camera under the direction of Elmer Ramsey. The program on this 1979 set includes both classical and Afro-Latin compositions. —*Ron Wynn*

Brazilian Soul / Dec. 1980 / Concord Jazz ✦✦✦
Here's two acoustic guitars, played by one of Brazil's greatest guitarists and the man who probably introduced the bossa nova to the U.S., backed by (marvelous) bass and percussion. There's also pre-bossa Brazilian standards like "Carioca", Jobim's "Stone Flower," even "Don't Cry for Me Argentina." It's elegant, gentle, urbane, both light and deep. —*John Storm Roberts*

Latin Odyssey / Dec. 1982 / Concord Jazz ✦✦✦

● **Artistry in Rhythm** / Apr. 1983 / Concord Jazz ✦✦✦✦
With Bob Magnusson (bass) and Milt Holland (percussion). This is lovely easy-listening music, in the best sense of the term. —*Michael Erlewine*

Tango: Laurindo Almeida and Charlie Byrd / Aug. 1985 / Concord Jazz ✦✦✦
This unusual CD finds guitarists Laurindo Almeida and Charlie Byrd (who have both mastered bop and Brazilian music) performing 11 tangoes with the assistance of bassist Joe Byrd and drummer Chuck Redd. Although the two acoustic guitarists have their short solos, the emphasis in this delightful set is on their ensemblework, respectful interpretations of the melodies and those infectious tango rhythms. —*Scott Yanow*

Music of the Brazilian Masters / 1989 / Concord Jazz ✦✦✦

Outra Vez / Oct. 5, 1991 / Concord Jazz ✦✦✦

Barry Altschul

b. Jan. 6, 1943, New York, NY
Drums / Avant-Garde
Both a superb drummer in free and hard bop circles and an instructor, Barry Altschul provides any rhythmic style needed for a session. He's an excellent timekeeper, can drive a date, solo with verve or participate in collective improvisations. A self-taught drummer, Altschul later studied with Charlie Persip in the '60s. He worked with Paul Bley from the mid-'60s until 1970, and then periodically until 1980. Altschul was also in the Jazz Composers Guild and Jazz Composers Orchestra in the '60s. After spending a few months in Europe, he studied with Sam Ulano. Altschul was part of the great free band Circle with Chick Corea, Anthony Braxton and Dave Holland in the late '60s and early '70s. When they disbanded, Altschul, Holland, Braxton and Sam Rivers recorded the seminal *Conference of the Birds*, and he and Holland played in Braxton's quartet. Altschul was also part of the innovative Sam Rivers band of the late '70s. He recorded as a leader for Muse in the late '70s and Sackville and Soul Note in the '80s and '90s, while teaching drums since the late '70s.—*Ron Wynn*

Virtuosi / Jun. 28, 1967 / IAI ✦✦✦
Whether drummer Barry Altschul, pianist Paul Bley and bassist Gary Peacock are *virtuosi* is actually fairly irrelevant to the success of this record. What matters is the interplay between these three masterful players on the two lengthy improvisations, "Butterflies" and "Gary." Unfortunately, the music only totals around 33 minutes (this CD is a straight reissue of the original LP) but, even if the quantity is low, the quality is quite high. The subtle improvising (which finds the three musicians operating as equals) rewards repeated listenings. —*Scott Yanow*

● **You Can't Name Your Own Tune** / Feb. 8, 1977–Feb. 9, 1977 / Muse ✦✦✦✦✦
Although Barry Altschul is showcased on a solo performance on "Hey Toots!" and there is a trio piece with pianist Muhal Richard Abrams and bassist Dave Holland, the highlights of this excellent LP are the other selections, which feature interplay between Sam Rivers (on tenor, flute and soprano) and trombonist George Lewis. Lewis in particular has rarely been heard in this type of relatively straightforward (if still adventurous) setting and really excels. —*Scott Yanow*

Another Time, Another Place / Mar. 13, 1978–Mar. 14, 1978 / Muse ✦✦✦✦

For Stu / Feb. 18, 1979 / Soul Note ✦✦✦

Brahma / Jan. 23, 1980 / Sackville ✦✦

Irina / Feb. 12, 1983 / Soul Note ✦✦✦

That's Nice / Nov. 25, 1985–Nov. 26, 1985 / Soul Note ✦✦✦

Franco Ambrosetti

b. Dec. 10, 1941, Lugano, Switzerland
Trumpet, Fluegelhorn / Hard Bop
Franco Ambrosetti has had dual careers as a very successful busi-

nessman and as a fine trumpeter and fluegelhornist inspired by Freddie Hubbard and Miles Davis. His father Flavio Ambrosetti was an excellent saxophonist. Franco had piano lessons for eight years but is self-taught on trumpet, which he did not take up until he was 17. In 1972 he was one of the founders of the George Gruntz Concert Jazz Band and through the years he has recorded quite a few worthy hard-boppish albums for Enja in addition to leading his own groups. —*Scott Yanow*

Close Encounter / Mar. 21, 1978 / Enja 3017 ✦✦✦

Heartbop / Feb. 10, 1981–Feb. 11, 1981 / Enja ✦✦✦
Nice lineup that didn't always get maximum results on this 1981 date featuring Swiss trumpeter Franco Ambrosetti. He plays with flair, but fails to ignite things on several songs. He gets good assistance from a group that includes Phil Woods on alto sax and clarinet and pianist Hal Galper. They still make some impressive music; it's just not the glittering date you'd expect. —*Ron Wynn*

Gin & Pentatonic / Dec. 1, 1983–Dec. 2, 1983 / Enja ✦✦✦✦
A reissue of an LP better known as *Wings*, several bonus tracks are included on this excellent session featuring Michael Brecker (ts), and Kenny Kirkland (p). —*AMG*

Tentets / Mar. 13, 1985–Mar. 14, 1985 / Enja ✦✦✦✦

Movies / Nov. 24, 1986–Nov. 25, 1986 / Enja ✦✦✦✦
A superb album, even though the subject matter could restrict less dynamic players. But trumpeter Ambrosetti rose to the occasion this time, and his spirited playing set the tone for a fine band that included keyboardist Geri Allen and guitarist John Scofield. Although songs like "Yellow Submarine" are shopworn, the band injects some life into them. —*Ron Wynn*

Movies Too / Mar. 22, 1988–Mar. 23, 1988 / Enja ✦✦✦✦
Brilliant playing from Swiss-born trumpet/fluegelhorn player Franco Ambrosetti, with Geri Allen (p) and all-star cast. Included is "Superman," "Angel Eyes" and "Peter Gunn." —*Michael G. Nastos*

★ **Music for Symphony & Jazz Band** / 1990 / Enja ✦✦✦✦✦
Involved, often sprawling work that seeks to link symphonic and improvisational traditions, and also work in guest stars and a national Radio Orchestra. Things do hold together, and alto saxophonist Greg Osby adds some torrid licks when he gets space. —*Ron Wynn*

Live at the Blue Note / Jul. 13, 1992 / Enja ✦✦✦

Albert Ammons

b. Sep. 23, 1907, Chicago, IL, **d.** Dec. 2, 1949, Chicago, IL
Piano / Boogie-Woogie, Swing
Albert Ammons was one of the big three of late-'30s boogie-woogie along with Pete Johnson and Meade Lux Lewis. Arguably the most powerful of the three, Ammons was also flexible enough to play swing music. Ammons played in Chicago clubs from the 1920s on, although he also worked as a cab driver for a time. Starting in 1934 he led his own band in Chicago and he made his first records in 1936. In 1938 Ammons appeared at Carnegie Hall with Pete Johnson and Meade Lux Lewis, an event that really helped launch the boogie-woogie craze. Ammons recorded with the other pianists in duets and trios, fit right in with the Port of Harlem Jazzmen on their Blue Note session, appeared regularly at Cafe Society, recorded as a sideman with Sippie Wallace in the 1940s and even cut a session with his son, the great tenorman Gene Ammons. Albert Ammons worked steadily throughout the 1940s, playing at President Harry Truman's inauguration in 1949; he died later that year. Many of his recordings are currently available on CD. —*Scott Yanow*

Master of Boogie / Dec. 23, 1938–Feb. 13, 1939 / Milan ✦✦
● **The First Day** / Jan. 6, 1939 / Blue Note ✦✦✦✦
☆ **Complete Blue Note Albert Ammons and Meade Lux Lewis** / Jan. 6, 1939–Aug. 22, 1944 / Mosaic ✦✦✦✦✦
This is everything you thought you knew about the Albert Ammons–Meade Lux Lewis Blue Note recordings plus eight previously unissued sides. This was a three record set, on which producers Mike Cuscuna and Charlie Lourie had a limited run of 5,000 copies…Ammons played his music, poised with excitement, but paced by a rich blues as swampy as it was concrete, while Lux Lewis, with frumpy deliberateness, pounds out poetry on the piano. —*Bob Rusch*

King of Boogie Woogie (1939–1949) / Jan. 6, 1939–1949 / Blues Classics ✦✦✦
Classic early '30s and '40s boogie-woogie from a giant in the

genre. Albert Ammons began emulating the style of Pinetop Smith, then gradually developed his own voice to the point where he was a master player. These cuts include both solos and duets between Ammons and Meade Lux Lewis, and are seminal recordings. —*Ron Wynn*

Gene Ammons

b. Apr. 14, 1925, Chicago, IL, **d.** Aug. 6, 1974, Chicago, IL
Tenor Saxophone / Bop, Hard Bop, Soul Jazz
Gene Ammons, who had a huge and immediately recognizable tone on tenor, was a very flexible player who could play bebop with the best (always battling his friend Sonny Stitt to a tie) yet was an influence on the R&B world. Some of his ballad renditions became hits and, despite two unfortunate interruptions in his career, Ammons remained a popular attraction for 25 years.

Son of the great boogie-woogie pianist Albert Ammons, Gene Ammons (who was nicknamed "Jug") left Chicago at age 18 to work with King Kolax's band. He originally came to fame as a key soloist with Billy Eckstine's orchestra during 1944–47, trading off with Dexter Gordon on the famous Eckstine record *Blowing the Blues Away*. Other than a notable stint with Woody Herman's Third Herd in 1949 and an attempt at co-leading a two tenor group in the early '50s with Sonny Stitt, Ammons worked as a single throughout his career, recording frequently (most notably for Prestige) in settings ranging from quartets and organ combos to all-star jam sessions. Drug problems kept him in prison during much of 1958–60 and, due to a particularly stiff sentence, 1962–69. When Ammons returned to the scene in 1969 he opened up his style a bit, including some of the emotional cries of the avant-garde while utilizing funky rhythm sections, but he was still able to battle Sonny Stitt on his own terms. Ironically the last song that he ever recorded (just a short time before he was diagnosed with terminal cancer) was "Goodbye." —*Scott Yanow*

Jug Sessions / Jun. 17, 1947–Oct. 4, 1949 / EmArcy ✦✦✦✦
This double LP is perfectly done. The great tenor Gene Ammons is heard on his earliest sessions as a leader and each of the six four-song sessions are reissued here complete, in chronological order and with extensive liner notes by Dan Morgenstern. In addition his one session with his father (the legendary boogie-woogie pianist Albert Ammons) is also included; how many listeners have noticed that Albert's original "Hiroshima" has the same chord changes as the standard "Nagasaki"? Throughout these performances Gene Ammons shows that his tone and style were already largely fully formed. Highlights include the original version of "Red Top" (which is heard both with and without the later overdubbed vocal), several heated jams and some warm ballads. This two-fer is highly recommended although it will be hard to find. —*Scott Yanow*

Red Top / Oct. 4, 1947–Jun. 1953 / Savoy ✦✦✦
Tenor saxophonist Gene Ammons is well-featured on this LP, playing as a sideman with baritonist Leo Parker's sextet on four numbers from 1947 and heading two sessions of his own from 1952–53. The latter performances (which also include trumpeter Johnny Coles and pianist John Houston in the octet) are highlighted by a remake of Ammons' hit "Red Top," warm ballad versions of "Street of Dreams," "Travellin' Light" and "Stairway to the Stars" and an extended tenor battle with Mack Easton on "Big Slam." —*Scott Yanow*

Early Visions / Oct. 12, 1948–May 1951 / Chess ✦✦✦
This two-LP set (some of the material has since been reissued on the CD *Young Jug*) is quite definitive of Gene Ammons' early years. All 24 of his Chess recordings are here including a couple of tenor battles with Tom Archia, the happy "Swingin' for Xmas" some warm ballad renditions (including "My Foolish Heart" and "You Go to My Head") and boppish stomps that also hint strongly at rhythm and blues. His flexibility and distinctive tone are very much in evidence throughout this well-conceived reissue. —*Scott Yanow*

Young Jug / Oct. 12, 1948–Mar. 24, 1952 / Chess ✦✦
This is a CD that will most likely frustrate Gene Ammons collectors a bit. During 1948–51 the great tenor recorded 24 titles for Chess and its related labels and all were reissued on the double LP *Early Visions*. This CD has 16 of the songs plus a very rare four-song session from 1952 for Decca that had not been reissued previously; completists are therefore stuck acquiring both sets. But discographical details aside, the music on the Chess CD is excellent, with Ammons sounding quite lyrical on the ballads

(which showcase his huge tone), quoting a dozen Christmas songs on "Swingin' for Xmas" and romping happily with his combos on the jump material. This CD is recommended to those listeners not already owning the two-fer. —*Scott Yanow*

Blues Up and Down, Vol. 1 / Mar. 5, 1950–Jun. 28, 1950 / Prestige ✦✦✦
This LP documents the Gene Ammons-Sonny Stitt combo of 1950, a two-tenor group that had a minor hit in "Blues Up and Down." The set has all of the music from the March 5 session (including three versions of "Blues Up and Down" and two of "You Can Depend on Me") plus four selections that showcase Ammons (during which Stitt switched to baritone) and a couple of ballad features for him in a quartet setting from June 28. Most but not all of this swinging music has since been reissued on CD. —*Scott Yanow*

All Star Sessions / Mar. 5, 1950–Jun. 16, 1955 / Original Jazz Classics ✦✦✦✦
This enjoyable and frequently exciting CD contains a variety of performances mostly featuring the tenors of Gene Ammons and Sonny Stitt. The two combative saxophonists battle it out on "Blues Up and Down" (heard in three takes), the superior "New Blues Up and Down" and two versions of "You Can Depend on Me." In addition Ammons has a few ballad features and there are a pair of extended jams from 1955 matching him in a sextet with trumpeter Art Farmer, altoist Lou Donaldson, pianist Freddie Redd, bassist Addison Farmer and drummer Kenny Clarke. The music is perhaps not essential but has enough exciting moments to fully satisfy bebop collectors. —*Scott Yanow*

Woofin' and Tweetin': Gene Ammons All Star Session / Mar. 5, 1950–Jun. 16, 1955 / Prestige ✦✦✦

The Gene Ammons Story: The 78 Era / Mar. 5, 1950–Nov. 4, 1955 / Prestige ✦✦✦✦
This CD contains 26 of the 30 selections included on the two-LP set of the same name (and catalog number). Although mostly cut during an era when Ammons co-led a two-tenor group with Sonny Stitt, the focus is almost entirely on Ammons. All but the final five titles are from the 1950–51 period and these concise performances were originally on 78s. Even at this early stage Ammons' tone was quite distinctive and he was able to combine the innovations of bop with the simplicity of R&B in his forceful and direct solos; also, few could play ballads with the passion he possessed. This CD is recommended to listeners who do not already own the two-fer. —*Scott Yanow*

Juganthology / Jun. 15, 1955–Apr. 12, 1957 / Prestige ✦✦✦
This double LP contains eight of the tenor saxophonist's finest jam session performances of the 1950s. All of the music has since been reissued on CD but this two-fer acts as an excellent introduction to these strong recordings. Best is "Happy Blues," but all of the selections (which feature such fine players as trumpeters Art Farmer, Donald Byrd and Idrees Sulieman, altoists Lou Donaldson and Jackie McLean, guitarist Kenny Burrell and pianists Freddie Redd, Duke Jordan and Mal Waldron) are easy to enjoy. True Gene Ammons collectors will want the complete sessions, though. —*Scott Yanow*

● **The Happy Blues** / Apr. 23, 1956 / Original Jazz Classics ✦✦✦✦✦
This is one of the great studio jam sessions. Tenor saxophonist Gene Ammons is teamed up with trumpeter Art Farmer, altoist Jackie McLean, pianst Duke Jordan, bassist Addison Farmer, drummer Art Taylor and the congas of Candido for four lengthy selections. Best is "The Happy Blues" which has memorable solos and spontaneous but perfectly fitting riffing by the horns behind each other's playing. The other numbers ("The Great Lie," "Can't We Be Friends" and "Madhouse") are also quite enjoyable, making this a highly recommended set. —*Scott Yanow*

Jammin' with Gene / Jul. 13, 1956 / Original Jazz Classics ✦✦✦✦
Tenor saxophonist Ammons led a series of excellent all-star jam sessions for the Prestige label during the mid-'50s that took advantage of the extra time available on LPs (as opposed to the three-minute 78) This CD is a straight reissue of the original LP and features versions of "Jammin' with Gene" (a blues), "We'll Be Together Again" (which evolves from being an Ammons ballad feature into a group jam and then back again) and "Not Really the Blues" that clocks in between ten and over 16 minutes. With such sidemen as trumpeters Art Farmer and Donald Byrd, altoist Jackie McLean, pianist Mal Waldron, bassist Doug Watkins and drummer Art Taylor, this is an excellent (and rather spontaneous) straight ahead session. —*Scott Yanow*

Funky / Jan. 11, 1957 / Original Jazz Classics ✦✦✦
A blues-oriented bop album that is not "funky" in the soul-jazz sense of that word. An exception is the title cut, a bluesy tune with Kenny Burrell on guitar. With Jackie McLean (as), Art Farmer (tpt), and Mal Waldron (p). Recorded in NYC. —*Michael Erlewine*

Jammin' in Hi Fi with Gene Ammons / Apr. 12, 1957 / Original Jazz Classics ✦✦✦✦
Tenorman Gene Ammons headed a series of notable studio jam sessions in the 1950s and this is one of the better ones. With such young players as trumpeter Idrees Sulieman, altoist Jackie McLean, pianist Mal Waldron, guitarist Kenny Burrell, bassist Paul Chambers and drummer Art Taylor, Ammons and his friends jam through four numbers, all of which clock in between 11:59 and 13:01. The results are an accessible and often exciting brand of bebop. —*Scott Yanow*

Groove Blues / Jan. 3, 1958 / Original Jazz Classics ✦✦✦
On Jan. 3, 1958, Gene Ammons led one of his last all-star jam sessions for Prestige. The most notable aspect to this date (which resulted in two albums of material) is that it featured among its soloists John Coltrane on alto. This CD, a straight reissue of one of the original LPs, includes baritonist Pepper Adams, the tenor of Paul Quinichette, Coltrane on two of the four selections and Jerome Richardson's flute during three of the songs in addition to a fine rhythm section (pianist Mal Waldron, bassist George Joyner and drummer Art Taylor). This set consists of three of Waldron's originals in addition to the standard ballad "It Might as Well Be Spring" and it (along with the CD *The Big Sound*) fully documents the productive day. —*Scott Yanow*

Big Sound / Jan. 3, 1958 / Original Jazz Classics ✦✦✦
Along with its fellow CD *Groove Blues*, this reissue fully documents all of the music recorded by tenor saxophonist Gene Ammons on the busy day of Jan. 3, 1958. Although there were many guest soloists, only one of the four songs on this half of the set (Mal Waldron's "The Real McCoy") has appearances by John Coltrane (on alto) and the tenor of Paul Quinichette. However, baritonist Pepper Adams is aboard for two of the performances and flutist Jerome Richardson (along with pianist Mal Waldron, bassist George Joyner and drummer Art Taylor) are on all four. Ammons is easily the main star (he really excelled in this setting) and he is in generally fine form on the two standards ("That's All" and "Cheek to Cheek"), his own "Blue Hymn and the Waldron original. —*Scott Yanow*

Blue Gene / May 3, 1958 / Original Jazz Classics ✦✦✦
The final of his series of jam sessions for Prestige features an excellent septet (the leader on tenor, trumpeter Idrees Sulieman, baritonist Pepper Adams, pianist Mal Waldron, bassist Doug Watkins, drummer Art Taylor and Ray Barretto on congas) stretching out on three original blues and the ballad "Hip Tip"; all four pieces were written by Waldron. Few surprises occur but everyone plays up to their usual high level. This enjoyable straight ahead CD is a reissue of the original LP. —*Scott Yanow*

Boss Tenor / Jun. 16, 1960 / Original Jazz Classics ✦✦✦✦
There are many Gene Ammons recordings currently available on CD in Fantasy's Original Jazz Classics since the versatile tenorman was a longtime Prestige recording artist. Unlike his earlier jam sessions, this particular outing finds Ammons as the only horn, fronting a talented rhythm section (pianist Tommy Flanagan, bassist Doug Watkins, drummer Art Taylor and Ray Barretto on congas). Jug explores standards (including a near-classic version of "Canadian Sunset"), blues and ballads in his usual warm, soulful and swinging fashion. This is a fine outing by one of the true "bosses" of the tenor. —*Scott Yanow*

The Gene Ammons Story: Organ Combos / Jun. 17, 1960+Nov. 28, 1961 / Prestige ✦✦✦
Gene Ammons recorded frequently for Prestige during the 1950s and early '60s and virtually all of the tenor's dates were quite rewarding. This two-LP set reissues *Twistin' the Jug* plus part of *Angel Eyes* and *Velvet Soul*. Ammons, a bop based but very versatile soloist, sounds quite comfortable playing a variety of standards and lesser-known material in groups featuring Jack McDuff or Johnny "Hammond" Smith on organ and either trumpeter Joe Newman or Frank Wess on tenor and flute. This version of "Angel Eyes" became a surprise hit. —*Scott Yanow*

The Gene Ammons Story: Gentle Jug / Jan. 26, 1961+Apr. 14, 1962 / Prestige ✦✦✦
This single CD reissues the two-LP set of the same name.

Included are two sessions originally cut for Prestige's subsidiary Moodsville (*Nice an' Cool* and *The Soulful Mood of Gene Ammons*) which are purposely relaxed and strictly at ballad tempos. Fortunately Ammons (who had a distinctive and huge tone) was long a master at interpreting ballads and, although these performances do not quite reach the heights of his greatest recordings, the lyrical music is quite easy to enjoy. Ammons (who is accompanied by either Richard Wyands or Patti Bown on piano, Doug Watkins or George Duvivier on bass and J.C. Heard or Ed Shaughnessy on drums) is tasteful and creative (in a subtle way) throughout these successful dates. — *Scott Yanow*

Jug / Jan. 27, 1961 / Original Jazz Classics ♦♦
Tenor saxophonist Gene Ammons recorded many albums during 1961–62, a busy period that was brought to an abrupt halt by his arrest for narcotics abuse. *Jug* finds the great tenor in excellent form, interpreting six standards and two of his originals with the assistance of pianist Richard Wyands, bassist Doug Watkins, drummer J.C. Heard and the congas of Ray Barretto; Sleepy Anderson replaces Wyands on two songs, one of which he takes on organ. Few surprises occur but fans will not be disappointed by his soulful and lyrical playing. — *Scott Yanow*

Soul Summit / Jun. 13, 1961–Apr. 13, 1962 / Prestige ♦♦♦
This single CD reissues all of the music from two LPs titled *Soul Summit* and *Soul Summit, Vol. 2*. The latter session is one of the lesser known of the many collaborations of tenors Gene Ammons and Sonny Stitt, who are joined by organist Jack McDuff and drummer Charlie Persip. Their six performances are primarily riff tunes with "When You Wish upon a Star" taken at a medium pace and "Out in the Cold Again" the lone ballad. The second half of this CD features Ammons on two songs ("Love I've Found You" and a swinging "Too Marvelous for Words") with a big band arranged by Oliver Nelson, jamming "Ballad for Baby" with a quintet, sitting out on "Scram" (which stars McDuff and the tenor of Harold Vick) and backing singer Etta Jones on three numbers, of which "Cool, Cool Daddy" is the most memorable. Overall, this is an interesting and consistently swinging set that adds to the large quantity of recordings that the great Ammons did during the early '60s. — *Scott Yanow*

We'll Be Together Again / Aug. 26, 1961 / Original Jazz Classics ♦♦♦♦
The title of this exciting meeting between the tenors of Gene Ammons and Sonny Stitt was rather poignant because this recording was released in the late '60s when Ammons was serving a long jail sentence for possession of heroin and it appeared that he and Stitt might never meet up again. Backed by pianist John Houston, bassist Buster Williams and drummer George Brown, Ammons and Stitt (who had co-led a regular group a decade before) proved once again to be a perfect team, jamming on a variety of standards, blues and ballads in addition to revisiting "New Blues Up and Down." The two tenors always brought out the best in each other and happily they would get back together in the early '70s. This is high-quality bebop. — *Scott Yanow*

Live! in Chicago / Aug. 29, 1961 / Original Jazz Classics ♦♦♦
The tenor saxophonist is heard in a surprisingly sparse setting for this live set, in a trio with organist Eddie Buster and drummer Gerald Donovan, two Chicago-based musicians. Ammons performs standards, blues and ballads, sounding at his best on an emotional "Please Send Me Someone to Love" and a hard-charging "Sweet Georgia Brown." This is one of many Gene Ammons recordings from the 1961–62 period; virtually all are worth getting. The CD reissue adds two previously unreleased selections to the original program. — *Scott Yanow*

● **Prime Cuts** / Aug. 1961+Feb. 1962 / Verve ♦♦♦♦♦
Gene Ammons and Sonny Stitt always made for a perfect team and it is a real pity that the music on this double LP has not yet surfaced on CD. The two tenors (with Stitt doubling on alto) are heard at their most combative during these consistently exciting performances; one session is with a piano trio led by John Houston while the other features organist Donald Patterson. Highpoints include "John Brown's Body," "Bye, Bye Blackbird," "Blues Up and Down" and "There Is No Greater Love." — *Scott Yanow*

Up Tight / Oct. 17, 1961–Oct. 18, 1961 / Prestige ♦♦♦♦
Gene Ammons recorded many albums for Prestige, but this CD is a good start for listeners unfamiliar with his playing. A reissue of two LPs (*Up Tight* and *Boss Soul*) recorded during the same two-

day period, these performances find Ammons backed by a pair of four-piece rhythm sections (with either Walter Bishop or Patti Bown on piano and Ray Barretto's congas a major asset) and taking the lion's share of the solo space. Ammons sounds particularly warm and emotional throughout this CD, particularly on such numbers as "The Breeze and I," "I'm Afraid the Masquerade Is Over," a cooking "Lester Leaps In" and "Song of the Islands." His sound and style effectively bridged the gap between bop and soul jazz. — *Scott Yanow*

Brother Jack Meets the Boss / Jan. 23, 1962 / Prestige ♦♦♦
On *Brother Jack Meets the Boss*, one of the fathers of Chicago tenor, Gene Ammons, teamed with Jack McDuff in a quintet setting (Harold Vick, tenor sax; Eddie Diehl, guitar; Joe Dukes, drums) for the usual blues-based romp. Here McDuff was in particularly good form and Jug maneuvered with as much subtlety and changes as the genre and drummer allowed. — *Bob Rusch, Cadence*

Blue Groove / Apr. 27, 1962 / Prestige ♦♦
Ammons recorded many worthy albums for Prestige during the 1950s and early '60s. This particular LP, released for the first time in 1982, is an average, although enjoyable enough, outing. Ammons, along with Sleepy Anderson (doubling on piano and organ) and an otherwise unknown rhythm section, plays a variety of ballads and blues-oriented tunes with swing and creativity. Nothing that unusual occurs but fans should enjoy this set. — *Scott Yanow*

Preachin' / May 3, 1962 / Original Jazz Classics ♦♦♦♦
This is a most unusual session. The great tenor performs 11 religious hymns with accompaniment by organist Clarence "Sleepy" Anderson (along with bassist Sylvester Hickman and drummer Dorral Anderson) that is straight from the church. Ammons mostly sticks very closely to the themes but gives such melodies as "Abide with Me," "You'll Never Walk Alone," "What a Friend" and "Holy Holy" passion, soul and honest feelings. This little-known album (now available on CD) is a rather touching and emotional outing and quite unique. — *Scott Yanow*

Jug and Dodo / May 1962 / Prestige ♦♦♦
This CD (which completely reissues a double LP with the same title) is a bit unusual, for it teams together the great tenor Gene Ammons with the very talented (but now obscure) bop pianist Dodo Marmarosa, whose mental problems kept him from pursuing his career. Actually Ammons is only half of this set (which also includes bassist Sam Jones and drummer Marshall Thompson), but Marmarosa is in top form; it's strange that the music was not released for the first time until the mid-'70s. This historical curiosity contains plenty of hard-swinging performances (including two versions apiece of "Yardbird Suite" and "Falling in Love with Love") and is worth picking up. — *Scott Yanow*

Nothing' But Soul / May 1962 / Up Front ♦♦
This budget LP (which has also been reissued by some other semi-legitimate labels) contains four similar and lengthy blues that match tenor saxophonist Gene Ammons and trumpeter Howard McGhee with an obscure and pianoless rhythm section. The music is surprisingly forgettable and there are many more valuable Ammons recordings around although completists might want to get this one anyway. — *Scott Yanow*

Bad! Bossa Nova / Sep. 9, 1962 / Original Jazz Classics ♦♦♦
This was Ammons' final recording before "being made an example of" and getting a lengthy jail sentence for possession of heroin; his next record would be cut over seven years later. Surprisingly the music is upbeat with Ammons joined by two guitars (Bucky Pizzarelli and Kenny Burrell), a fine rhythm section (pianist Hank Jones, bassist Norman Edge and drummer Oliver Jackson) and the bongos of Al Hayes for a set of Latin-flavored jazz that was masquerading as bossa nova. The music is offbeat if not all that memorable, a decent effort but not essential. — *Scott Yanow*

The Boss Is Back / Nov. 10, 1969–Nov. 11, 1969 / Prestige ♦♦♦♦
The executives at Prestige must have been ecstatic when they heard Gene Ammons first play after his release from a very severe seven-year jail sentence. The great tenor proved to still be in his prime; his huge sound was unchanged and he was hungry to make new music. This CD, which completely reissues the first two LPs Ammons cut after his return (*The Boss is Back!* and *Brother Jug!*) rewards repeated listenings. The first date (in an

acoustic quintet with pianist Junior Mance) hints at his earlier bop-based music, while the numbers from the following day (with organist Sonny Phillips) find Ammons playing over a couple of boogaloo vamps very much of the period. Actually it is his ballad statements (particularly "Here's That Rainy Day," "Feeling Good" and even "Didn't We") that really make this CD memorable, although on "He's a Real Gone Guy" Ammons shows that he had not forgotten how to jam the blues either. —*Scott Yanow*

Night Lights / Feb. 2, 1970 / Prestige ♦♦
One of Ammons' first recording sessions after he returned to the scene following a rather severe jail sentence was this tribute to Nat King Cole. As it turned out, the quartet date with pianist Wynton Kelly, bassist George Duvivier and drummer Rudy Collins was quickly forgotten as Ammons recorded some more commercial material and this set was not released for the first time until 1985. Ammons is in excellent form on such ballads as "Nature Boy," "Lush Life," "Sweet Lorraine" and "The Christmas Song," making one wish that the contents of this LP were available on CD. —*Scott Yanow*

The Chase / Jul. 26, 1970 / Prestige ♦♦
Tenors Gene Ammons and Dexter Gordon had a famous tradeoff on Billy Eckstine's 1944 recording of "Blowin' the Blues Away." This reunion (recorded live in Chicago) has its moments but does not reach the heights one would hope for. While Jug and Gordon do trade off on "The Chase," their only other meeting ("Lonesome Lover Blues") has an aimless vocal by Vi Redd and rambles on much too long. Otherwise Gordon is fine on "Polka Dots and Moonbeams" while Ammons takes "The Happy Blues" as his feature. Overall this is a good set that, with some planning, might have been a great one; it is not yet available on CD. —*Scott Yanow*

My Way / Jun. 21, 1971–Jul. 26, 1971 / Prestige ♦♦
Few of Gene Ammons' recordings from his final period (1969–74) have been reissued on CD and it is doubtful that many people are waiting anxiously for this one. The great tenor is heard mostly tackling commercial material such as "What's Going On," "A House Is Not a Home" and "My Way" on this R&B-ish effort. While Ammons sounds fine (his tone was never to be denied), the dated arrangements and unimaginative playing by the rhythm section (what is Roland Hanna doing on electric piano?) largely sink this effort. —*Scott Yanow*

Chicago Concert / Nov. 21, 1971 / Prestige ♦♦♦
This meeting between Gene Ammons and James Moody is not as memorable as one might hope. Backed by pianist Jodie Christian, bassist Cleveland Eaton and drummer Marshall Thompson, the two tenors square off on "Just in Time," "Have You Met Miss Jones?," "C-Jam Blues" and Ammons' "Jim-Jam-Jug" but, although there are a few sparks, they do not blend together that well and the results are surprisingly workmanlike. Ammons is actually best on his two features "Work Song" and "I'll Close My Eyes." This set has not yet been reissued on CD. —*Scott Yanow*

Big Bad Jug / Oct. 28, 1972–Nov. 1, 1972 / Prestige ♦♦
After he made his comeback, Gene Ammons recorded a series of somewhat commercial albums for Prestige on which he was backed by electric R&B rhythm sections. This particular set finds the veteran tenor joined by electric piano, organ, guitar (either Maynard Parker or Joe Beck), Ron Carter (mostly on electric bass) and drums (Billy Cobham, Idris Muhammad or Mickey Roker). The repertoire, which includes a couple of funky originals, Dave Grusin's "Fuzz" and "Papa Was a Rolling Stone," is not too inspiring on this LP (as of yet not reissued on CD) but Ammons makes the best of it. —*Scott Yanow*

Got My Own / Oct. 28, 1972–Nov. 1, 1972 / Prestige ♦♦♦
Recorded at the same sessions that resulted in the more commercial *Big Bad Jug*, this LP (whose contents have not yet been reissued on CD) is the better of the two thanks to the inclusion of four Billie Holiday-associated songs. Ammons (even with the electric rhythm section) is in prime form on "Lady Sings the Blues," "God Bless the Child," "Strange Fruit" and "Fine and Mellow." The other three pieces (which include the theme from *Ben* and a Neal Diamond tune) are not as inspiring, but Ammons' huge sound makes the music worthwhile. —*Scott Yanow*

Gene Ammons and Friends at Montreux / Jul. 7, 1973 / Prestige ♦♦♦♦
This is a Prestige LP well-deserving of being reissued on CD. Ammons, whose studio recordings of the period were somewhat

commercial, is heard in excellent form playing a blues and three standards with the backing of a fine rhythm section: Hampton Hawes (who unfortunately sticks to electric piano), electric bassist Bob Cranshaw, drummer Kenny Clarke and Kenneth Nash on congas. Best of all is a 17-minute blues on which Ammons welcomes fellow tenor Dexter Gordon, cornetist Nat Adderley and altoist Cannonball Adderley; the four horns all get to trade off with each other. This is one of the better late-period Gene Ammons records. —*Scott Yanow*

Brasswind / Oct. 30, 1973 / Prestige ♦♦
Veteran tenor saxophonist Ammons is accompanied by a funky 12-piece band arranged by David Axelrod on this commercial but interesting release, one of his last recordings. The repertoire consists of a couple of Ammons originals, two by Axelrod, Wes Montgomery's "Cariba," Antonio Carlos Jobim's "Once I Loved" and the Monk standard "'Round Midnight." Ammons plays well and even if the arrangements are somewhat dated (George Duke's keyboards do not help), this set has its strong moments. —*Scott Yanow*

Together Again for the Last Time / Nov. 20, 1973–Dec. 10, 1973 / Prestige ♦♦♦
Gene Ammons and Sonny Stitt had a longtime musical partnership and friendship. The two tenors first teamed up on a regular basis in 1950 and they recorded together on an irregular basis over the next two decades. Their similar styles and combative approach made their musical encounters quite exciting and this Prestige LP, their last joint recording, has some strong tradeoffs. Actually the two saxophonists only appear together on three of the six selections (all Ammons originals) while Gene takes "The More I See You" and "I'll Close My Eyes" as his ballad features and Stitt is the only horn on "For All We Know." With pianist Junior Mance leading the rhythm section, this is a fine date (which has yet to be reissued on CD) that is recommended to fans of the two tenors. —*Scott Yanow*

Goodbye / Mar. 18, 1974–Mar. 20, 1974 / Prestige ♦♦♦♦
It is ironic that on his final recording date, the last song he performed was the standard "Goodbye." That emotional rendition is the highpoint of this LP (which has not been reissued on CD yet), a septet date with cornetist Nat Adderley, altoist Gary Bartz, pianist Kenny Drew, bassist Sam Jones, drummer Louis Hayes and Ray Barretto on congas. In contrast to the somewhat commercial studio albums he had recorded during the past couple of years, this set was much more freewheeling for Ammons, and the distinctive tenor was clearly happy to perform the material (which included "It Don't Mean a Thing," "Alone Again (Naturally)" and "Jeannine") without any tight arrangements, in the spirit of his Prestige jam sessions of the 1950s. It's a fine ending to a colorful career. —*Scott Yanow*

David Amram
b. Nov. 17, 1930, Philadelphia, PA
French Horn / Bop, World Fusion, Classical
A knowledgeable, eclectic bandleader and versatile composer, David Amram is an outstanding French horn player and has written classical and jazz works and film scores. Amram attended Oberlin College Conservatory in the late '40s, then worked as a horn player in Paris while serving in the European Army. He recorded with Lionel Hampton and as a leader during 1955 in Paris. Amram moved to New York the next year, and performed with Charles Mingus and Oscar Pettiford's band. Amram and Julius Watkins dueled on French horns on the piece "Two French Fries," recorded while he was playing with Pettiford. He co-led a band with George Barrow that recorded in 1957, and played regularly at the Five Spot in the mid-'60s. Amram wrote music for the New York Shakespeare Festival, composed orchestral pieces, was The New York Philharmonic's composer-in-residence in 1966 and 1967, and conducted concerts and workshops for children on international folk music and jazz. His fluency with world rhythms enabled Amram to record the magnificent *Havana/New York* album in the late '70s, a great union of jazz and Afro-Latin music featuring him working with members of Irakere, Candido, Thad Jones and Pepper Adams. Amram's Triple Concerto for Woodwind, Brass, and Jazz Quintets and Orchestra was recorded in the '70s by various orchestras. —*Ron Wynn and Michael G. Nastos*

Triple Concerto / 1977 / Flying Fish ♦♦♦
This album finds Amram playing his own compositions with the

assistance of his jazz quintet, featuring Pepper Adams, and with the Rochester Philharmonic. —*AMG*

● **Havana New York** / Jun. 1977–Jul. 1977 / Flying Fish ✦✦✦✦
A landmark 1977 recording with Amram, Thad Jones, Pepper Adams, and Irakere. —*Ron Wynn*

No More Walls / 1978 / Flying Fish ✦✦✦
Variety of different settings. Large ensemble orchestra. With Lynn Sheffield (v). This '70s reissue is eclectic and tuneful. —*Michael G. Nastos*

At Home/Around the World / 1980 / Flying Fish ✦✦

Autobiography / May 8, 1990 / Flying Fish ✦✦✦

Arild Anderson

b. Oct. 27, 1945, Lillestrom, Norway
Bass / Post-Bop
Arild Andersen is best known in the United States for his duet album with Sheila Jordan, which preceded the singer's collaborations with Harvie Swartz. Andersen studied with George Russell and during 1967–73 played regularly with both Jan Garbarek and Karin Krog. While in the U.S. during 1973–74, Andersen worked with Sam Rivers and Paul Bley. In addition to leading his own groups, Andersen has played with Kenny Wheeler and Paul Motian (1979), Bill Frisell (1981) and a group he co-led in the mid-'80s, Masqualero. He has recorded frequently for the ECM label through the years. —*Scott Yanow*

If You Look Far Enough / Sept. 1988–Feb. 1992 ECM ✦✦✦✦

Cat Anderson (William Alonzo Anderson)

b. Sep. 12, 1916, Greenville, SC, d. Apr. 29, 1981, Norwalk, CA
Trumpet / Swing
Cat Anderson was arguably the greatest high note trumpeter of all time. His solo on "Satin Doll" from Duke Ellington's *70th Birthday Concert* is a perfectly coherent chorus consisting of notes that are so high that it is doubtful if another trumpeter from all of jazz history could hit more than one or two! He first learned trumpet while at the Jenkins Orphanage in Charleston and toured with the Carolina Cotton Pickers, a group in which he made his recording debut. During 1935–44 Anderson played with many groups, including those of Claude Hopkins, Lucky Millinder, Erskine Hawkins and Lionel Hampton. Hampton loved his high-note mastery, although Hawkins reportedly fired Cat out of jealousy. In 1944 Cat Anderson was hired by Duke Ellington and it ended up being the perfect setting for him. Duke enjoyed writing impossible parts for Cat to play and Anderson received publicity and a steady income. He was more than just a high-note player, being a master with mutes and having a fine tone in lower registers, but no one could really challenge him in the stratosphere (although Maynard Ferguson, Jon Faddis and Arturo Sandoval have come close!). Anderson was with Ellington during 1944–47, 1950–59 and off and on during 1961–71. Occasionally he would go out on his own to lead his own bands but he always came back. After Ellington's death, Cat Anderson settled on the West Coast where he often played with local big bands including an exciting one led by Bill Berry. —*Scott Yanow*

Cat on a Hot Tin Horn / Aug. 23, 1958 / EmArcy ✦✦✦

Cat Anderson & The Ellington All Stars in Paris / Oct. 30, 1958–Mar. 20, 1964 / Disques Swing ✦✦✦
Nice, relaxed, swinging set delivered by longtime Ellington trumpeter Cat Anderson. As with many projects done by Ellingtonians outside the orchestra, it shared many things with standard Duke projects. These include song selection, mood, feel, pacing, and production. —*Ron Wynn*

Cat Speaks / Jun. 4, 1977 / Classic Jazz ✦✦✦

● **Plays W.C. Handy** / May 5, 1978 / Black & Blue ✦✦✦✦

Ernestine Anderson

b. Nov. 11, 1928, Houston, TX
Vocals / Standards
A fine vocalist equally gifted at singing upbeat, spirited blues, big band/swing numbers and jazzy pop standards, Anderson began her career in the early '40s, singing with the bands of Russell Jacquet, Eddie Heywood, Shifty Henry and Johnny Otis. Her version of "K.C. Loving" in 1947 with Henry was a mild hit. These orchestras modified swing arrangements, added shouting vocalists and divided their musical menus between their vocals, jump

blues and fast-paced instrumentals. This formula was eventually labeled Rhythm & Blues or R&B. But Anderson moved away from that style in the '50s, and became a prominent jazz stylist. She worked with Lionel Hampton in 1952 and 1953, and also sang in New York City clubs. While in Hampton's band she met saxophonist Gigi Gryce. Anderson recorded with Quincy Jones in 1953, and Gryce in 1955, then toured Sweden in 1956 with Rolf Ericson's band, which included Duke Jordan and Cecil Payne. While there she recorded *Hot Cargo* with Harry Arnold's orchestra, which was well received when it was issued in America on Mercury. Her 1958 album *Ernestine Anderson* with Pete Rugolo was also praised, and Anderson won the New Star award from *Downbeat*'s critics in 1959. She did more recording for Mercury, but encountered difficult times in the early '60s, moving to England in 1965. Anderson recorded "He Says He Loves Me" for the soundtrack of Sidney Poitier's film *The Lost Man* in 1969. The song attracted some attention. Ray Brown heard her singing at Turnwater Conservatory in 1975 during a weekend festival in Canada, became her manager, and helped her get a contract with Concord Records. The 1976 album *Hello Like Before* generated great response throughout the jazz community. Anderson was suddenly an in-demand singer. There were recordings with Hank Jones, Ray Brown and Monty Alexander, and by the mid-'80s Anderson was cutting sessions with her own quartet. Her 1981 album *Never Make Your Move Too Soon* received a Grammy nomination, and she continued making strong sessions with Benny Carter in 1984 and the Capp-Pierce big band in 1987. She's more visible today than ever, and has become an established star. Her roots weren't fully in bebop, but she's firmly in the jazz camp, though she does include pop and blues material on her albums. —*Ron Wynn*

Ernestine Anderson / 1958 / PolyGram ✦✦✦
This CD brings back singer Ernestine Anderson's first full-length U.S. recording session. The program only clocks in at 31 1/2 minutes and some of the performances are remarkably brief (including a 59-second version of "There Will Never Be Another You"). Backed by an orchestra arranged by Pete Rugolo, Anderson (who at the time was influenced by Dinah Washington) is in good voice and swings without getting very far from the melodies. The highlights are "Stardust," "Social Call," "A Sleepin' Bee" and a particularly touching "My Ship." Although this brief program should have been combined with another Mercury release for this reissue, the music should please Ernestine Anderson's fans. —*Scott Yanow*

Live from Concord to London / Aug. 1, 1976–Oct. 11, 1977 / Concord Jazz ✦✦✦

Hello Like Before / Oct. 8, 1976–Oct. 10, 1976 / Concord Jazz ✦✦✦✦
A wonderful session marking Anderson's return to the scene in 1976. Classy, brassy, and delightful swing and vocals. —*Ron Wynn*

Sunshine / Aug. 1979 / Concord Jazz ✦✦✦
More toward the contemporary, flashy side, but a nice basic jazz set. —*Ron Wynn*

● **Never Make Your Move Too Soon** / Aug. 1980 / Concord Jazz ✦✦✦✦✦

Big City / Feb. 1983 / Concord Jazz ✦✦✦
With sublime Hank Jones (p) and fine vocals. Solid, swinging arrangements. —*Ron Wynn*

When the Sun Goes Down / Aug. 1984 / Concord Jazz ✦✦✦✦

Be Mine Tonight / Dec. 1986 / Concord Jazz ✦✦✦
Backed by a fine rhythm section (pianist Marshall Otwell deserves a date of his own) and assisted by Benny Carter's alto on several selections, Anderson sounds as if she is really enjoying this session. Best are a rare vocal version of "In a Mellotone" and a Dinah Washington-inspired treatment of "Christopher Columbus," the two most jazz-oriented tracks on this well-rounded album. —*Scott Yanow*

Boogie Down / Sep. 1989 / Concord Jazz ✦✦✦

Now & Then / Sep. 24, 1992–Feb. 12, 1993 / Qwest ✦✦✦

Ivie Anderson

b. Jul. 10, 1905, Gilroy, CA, d. Dec. 28, 1949, Los Angeles, CA
Vocal / Swing
Ivie Anderson was a classy yet swinging singer, the best that Duke Ellington ever had. Early on she worked at the Cotton Club in

shows and sang with Anson Weeks, Curtis Mosby, Paul Howard's Quality Serenaders and Earl Hines (1930). Then from February 1931 until 1942, Ivie Anderson was an integral part of the Duke Ellington Orchestra, introducing "It Don't Mean a Thing" and singing such numbers as "Stormy Weather," "I'm Checkin' Out Goombye" and a variety of pop tunes. When she left Ellington it was because of asthma. She opened up a restaurant in Los Angeles and recorded eight songs in 1946 but her illness eventually struck her down. — *Scott Yanow*

Ray Anderson

b. Oct. 16, 1952, Chicago, IL
Trombone / Avant-Garde
A boisterous trombonist who has greatly expanded the range of the trombone and is masterful at multiphonics, Ray Anderson's playing is often hilarious. His main fault is a tendency to repeat the same joke over and over again, namely "look how high I can play!" Anderson began playing the trombone when he was eight and early on had a wide variety of experience ranging from classical lessons to Dixieland, playing blues and funk and going to some concerts by the AACM. After spending some time in California, he moved to New York in 1972 and freelanced. In 1977 Anderson joined Anthony Braxton's Quartet (replacing George Lewis) and started working with Barry Altschul's group. From this point forward he started ranking high in polls and becoming influential himself. In addition to leading his own groups since the late '70s (including the funk-oriented Slickaphonics), Anderson has worked with George Gruntz's Concert Jazz Band. In recent times he has begun taking an occasional good-humored vocal during which he shows the ability to sing two notes at the same time (a minor third apart). — *Scott Yanow*

Harrisburg Half Life / Jun. 1980 / Moers ✦✦

Right Down Your Alley / Feb. 3, 1984 / Soul Note ✦✦✦
A typically fine, frequently electrifying set from trombonist Ray Anderson, among the best players of his generation. This is a tricky set, a trio work for trombone/bass/drums. Anderson, Mark Helias, and Gerry Hemingway are more than up to the test of keeping things moving and interesting without any sax or piano for contrast and counterpoint. — *Ron Wynn*

Old Bottles, New Wine / Jul. 14, 1985–Jul. 15, 1985 / Enja ✦✦✦✦✦
Trombonist Ray Anderson, best-known for his avant-garde recordings, surprised many with these explorations of standards. His high-note outbursts are often hilarious, yet on this program he really digs into the material. "Love Me or Leave Me," "La Rosita" and "In a Mellotone" are among the highpoints and Anderson takes an interesting vocal on "Wine." The all-star rhythm section (pianist Kenny Barron, bassist Cecil McBee and drummer Dannie Richmond) is also a strong asset to this memorable date. — *Scott Yanow*

It Just So Happens / Jan. 31, 1987–Feb. 1, 1987 / Enja ✦✦✦

Blues Bred in the Bone / Mar. 27, 1989–Mar. 28, 1989 / Gramavision ✦✦
Unlike on his previous *Old Bottles, New Wine* recording, trombonist Ray Anderson's high-note technique gets the better of him on this set. He often comes across as a one-line Las Vegas comedian who constantly exclaims, "Look how high I can play!" Whether it be a rather absurd version of "Mona Lisa" or a potentially sensitive ballad such as "A Flower Is a Lonesome Thing," the results are consistently silly if colorful. Even with a supporting cast that includes guitarist John Scofield and pianist Anthony Davis, this has to be considered one of Anderson's lesser efforts. — *Scott Yanow*

What Because / Dec. 16, 1989–Dec. 18, 1989 / Gramavision ✦✦✦✦
Surging, arresting session led by a fine trombonist who is certainly among the best in his generation. Anderson can play standards or originals with verve, go outside or inside, display gimmicks, and execute rapid-fire chord changes. — *Ron Wynn*

Wishbone / Dec. 1990 / Gramavision ✦✦✦

Every One of Us / 1992 / Gramavision ✦✦✦
A '92 session that equals the past high level of Ray Anderson releases. There are tingling trombone solos and excellent support from bassist Charlie Haden and the late Ed Blackwell on drums; besides, Anderson's originals are never predictable. — *Ron Wynn*

● **Big Band Record** / 1994 / Gramavision ✦✦✦✦✦
Ray Anderson has nine of his originals performed by the 17-piece George Gruntz Concert Jazz Band on this Gramavision CD and the results are quite spirited and very satisfying. The often riotous trombonist is fortunate to have his complex but always lively music interpreted by quite an all-star group and Gruntz's arrangements give each musician at least one opportunity to solo. When one considers that the orchestra contains such individualists as trumpeters Lew Soloff, Ryan Kisor, John D'Earth and Herb Robertson, altoist Tim Berne, Marty Ehrlich on several reeds, Ellery Eskelin on tenor and violinist Mark Feldman, it is little surprise that this was one of the top jazz albums released in 1994. — *Scott Yanow*

Don't Mow Your Lawn / Mar. 23, 1994–Mar. 25, 1994 / Enja ✦✦✦✦
Trombonist Ray Anderson is typically uninhibited throughout this joke-filled set. His high-note screams are well-matched by trumpeter Lew Soloff and some of the vocals (most notably on the title cut) are memorable. There is some strong playing by the two horns (who are joined by the funky rhythm section of guitarist Jerome Harris, bassist Gregory Jones, drummer Tommy Campbell and percussionist Frank Colon) but, with titles like "Damaged but Good," "Alligatory Pecadillo" and "What'cha Gonna Do with That?," the humor and philosophizing are often dominant. — *Scott Yanow*

Azurety / Apr. 21, 1994–Apr. 22, 1994 / Hat Art ✦✦✦

Ernie Andrews

b. Dec. 27, 1927, Philadelphia, PA
Vocals / Blues, Swing, Bop
Ernie Andrews has managed to be both popular and underrated throughout his lengthy career. After his family moved to Los Angeles he sang in a church choir and while still attending high school had a few hits for the G&G label. Billy Eckstine and Al Hibbler were early influences and, after reaching maturity, Andrews was somewhat in the shadow of Joe Williams (who has a similar style). He recorded for Aladdin, Columbia and London in the late '40s, spent six years singing with the Harry James Orchestra and cut a couple of big band dates for GNP/Crescendo during 1958–59. Despite his unchanging style, Andrews was mostly in obscurity during the 1960s and '70s, just making a couple of albums for Dot during 1965–66. A 1980 Discovery date found him in excellent form and in the '80s he was rediscovered. Andrews recorded with the Pierce/Capp Juggernaut, Gene Harris' Superband, Jay McShann and with the Harper Brothers in addition to making a few sets in the 1990s for Muse. He is also prominent in the documentary *Blues for Central Avenue*. — *Scott Yanow*

Travelin' Light / Mar. 1959 / GNP ✦✦✦
Prototype big band and jazz-based vocals by Ernie Andrews cut in the late '50s for GNP. Andrews, a fine blues, ballad, and standards stylist, with good sound and excellent phrasing, was backed on these dates by apolished orchestra that sometimes included Benny Carter on alto sax. The sessions have been reissued on CD. — *Ron Wynn*

From the Heart / Nov. 15, 1980 / Discovery ✦✦✦✦

● **No Regrets** / Aug. 2, 1992 / Muse ✦✦✦✦

The Great City / Feb. 16, 1995 / Muse ✦✦✦

Lori Andrews

b. Jan. 23, 1958, Philadelphia, PA
Harp / Bop, Crossover
The harp is rarely thought of as a jazz instrument, but in the 1990s Lori Andrews and Deborah Henson-Conant have proved that their instrument is not restricted to producing pretty backgrounds. Lori Andrews graduated from Temple University in 1979, played regularly in Atlantic City during 1980–85, moved to Los Angeles in 1985 and from 1992 on has had a regular gig at the Warehouse in Marina Del Rey in addition to working in the studio and touring with John Tesh. She had brief on-camera appearances in such films as *Bird*, *The Mambo Kings* and *In the Line of Fire*. More importantly from the jazz standpoint, she founded her own label JazHarp Records and has documented her music since 1993, showing that the harp (at least when played by her) is a viable jazz instrument. — *Scott Yanow*

Suspended / 1993 / JazHarp ✦✦✦
Jazz harpist Lori Andrews' first recording as a leader finds the tal-

ented musician showing that the electric harp can be adapted to play jazz. Her music on this CD (which features groups ranging from a sextet to the unaccompanied title track) is often quite funky but also explorative, and it features plenty of variety. The local players who are heard as sidemen do a fine job of complementing the colorful harpist. —*Scott Yanow*

● **Bossame Mucho** / 1994 / JazHarp ✦✦✦✦✦
Jazz harpists are a real rarity but, even if they were plentiful, Lori Andrews would rank near the top of her field. On this set of unaccompanied solos, Andrews performs selections from the likes of Kenny Dorham ("Blue Bossa"), Sting, Grover Washington, Jr., Jobim, Clare Fischer ("Morning") and Michael Franks, among others. No matter the source, she turns all of the music into swinging and sometimes funky jazz. Her playing is very self-sufficient, with often two independent lines and rhythm being heard, yet there was no overdubbing on this date. Listeners who think of the harp as only capable of producing pretty background music are in for a surprise, particularly when hearing the harder-swinging performances! —*Scott Yanow*

Swinging Strings / 1995 / JazHarp ✦✦✦✦
This is a very impressive outing. Lori Andrews plays solo harp throughout this disc and, without using overdubbing, she sounds very much like a full orchestra. Her creative treatments of such standards as "Popsicle Toes," "Take Five" and a delightful "Is You Is or Is You Ain't My Baby" are highpoints, but her original material is also quite enjoyable. Andrews de-emphasizes the prettiness of her instrument and digs in with some soulful statements. —*Scott Yanow*

Lil Armstrong

b. Feb. 3, 1898, Memphis, TN, **d.** Aug. 27, 1971, Chicago, IL
Piano, Vocal / New Orleans Jazz, Swing
Lil Harden Armstrong will always be best-known for her influence in shaping Louis Armstrong's career (persuading him to leave King Oliver's band and accept Fletcher Henderson's offer in New York) and for her work with Louis' Hot Five and Seven, but she actually had an interesting career after she parted with Armstrong. Early on she worked in Chicago demonstrating new songs at a music store. She worked with Sugar Johnny's Creole Orchestra and then Freddie Keppard's Original Creole Orchestra before becoming a member of King Oliver's Creole Jazz Band. Lil's rhythmic piano helped keep the ensembles solid and she made her recording debut with Oliver in 1923. She met Louis Armstrong while in the band and their marriage lasted from 1924–38, although they separated in 1931. Lil played piano and occasionally sang on Louis' famous Hot Five and Seven recordings and she composed "Struttin' with Some Barbeque." During the latter half of the 1930s she was house pianist at Decca, recording 26 titles as a leader (mostly as a vocalist) during 1936–40, including her "Just For a Thrill." Although she rarely recorded during the remainder of her career (12 titles during 1945–47, six songs in 1953–54, two selections in 1959 and an album in 1961), Lil remained active during her last 30 years in Chicago. She recorded a talking record in 1959 on which she reminisced about her days with Louis Armstrong, and ironically she died of a heart attack while playing "St. Louis Blues" at an Armstrong tribute concert less than two months after Louis himself had passed away. —*Scott Yanow*

● **1936–1940** / Oct. 27, 1936–Mar. 18, 1940 / Classics ✦✦✦✦✦
Chicago: The Living Legends / Sep. 7, 1961 / Original Jazz Classics ✦✦✦

Louis Armstrong

b. Aug. 4, 1901, New Orleans, LA, **d.** Jul. 6, 1971, New York, NY
Trumpet, Vocal, Leader / New Orleans Jazz, Swing, Dixieland
Louis Armstrong was the most important and influential musician in jazz history. Although he is often thought of by the general public as a lovable, clowning personality, a gravel-voiced singer who played simple but dramatic trumpet in a New Orleans-styled Dixieland setting, Armstrong was much, much more.
One of the first soloists on record (although he was preceded by Sidney Bechet), Louis, more than anyone else, was responsible for jazz changing from an ensemble-oriented folk music into an art form that emphasized inventive solo improvisations. His relaxed phrasing was a major change from the staccato style of the early '20s (helping set the stage for the swing era), and Armstrong demonstrated that it was possible to have both impressive technique and a strong feeling for the blues. One of jazz's first true virtuosos, his influence over his contemporaries

was so powerful that nearly every trumpeter to record between 1927 and 1940 sounded to an extent like one of his followers!
Louis Armstrong's unique singing voice was imitated by a countless number of listeners through the years. He popularized scat singing (using nonsense syllables rhythmically rather than words), and his phrasing (carried over from his horn playing) affected virtually every singer to emerge after 1930, including Bing Crosby, Billie Holiday and Frank Sinatra. In addition, Louis Armstrong's accessible humor and sunny stage personality were major assets in popularizing jazz with larger audiences. Many youngsters were inspired to take up the trumpet after hearing or seeing him and millions more were introduced to jazz through Armstrong; in later years Louis Armstrong's worldwide tours resulted in him being widely known as "America's goodwill ambassador."
Few would have predicted greatness for Louis Armstrong based on his humble beginnings. Born in New Orleans on Aug. 4, 1901 (until his birth certificate was discovered in the late '80s, Armstrong's birth date was believed to have been July 4, 1900), Louis grew up in the poorest part of the city, sometimes singing in a vocal quartet on the street for pennies. On New Year's Eve of 1912 he got his hands on a pistol, shot it in the air in celebration and was quickly arrested and sent to live in a Waif's home that functioned as a type of juvenile hall. This would be the turning point of his life, for it was at the Waif's home that he learned to play the cornet. Released after two years, Armstrong began playing with jazz groups and brass bands in New Orleans, developing quickly. When King Oliver, who had befriended Louis, left New Orleans in 1918 he recommended the young player as his replacement in a popular band led by trombonist Kid Ory. Four years later, Oliver sent for his protege to join his Creole Jazz Band in Chicago as second cornetist.
During 1922–24 King Oliver led the top classic jazz orchestra of the era, an octet which, although emphasizing group improvisation, also left room for short solos. While Oliver was a fine cornetist (more an inspiration than a direct influence on Louis' playing), it soon became obvious that Armstrong was surpassing him. Fortunately this very significant band recorded 41 tracks in 1923 for four labels, for by the following year pianist Lil Harden (who became Louis' second of four wives) talked him into leaving Oliver and joining Fletcher Henderson's big band in New York.
Although considered the top jazz orchestra of the time, Henderson's band had not yet learned how to swing, really improvise or play the blues; at the time New York musicians were generally behind those from Chicago. However Armstrong's playing soon inspired the musicians and it was at this point that his impact was first really felt. Armstrong also began to record as an accompanist to blues singers (including Bessie Smith and Ma Rainey), teamed up with Sidney Bechet in Clarence Williams' Blue Five and in 1925 (after he left Henderson and moved back to Chicago) he began his remarkable series of Hot Five and Hot Seven recordings.
With clarinetist Johnny Dodds, trombonist Kid Ory, pianist Lil Armstrong and banjoist Johnny St. Cyr, Armstrong recorded one classic after another during 1925–27, music that can be thought of as both the height of New Orleans jazz and the death of it due to the increasing emphasis on Armstrong's virtuosity. "Cornet Chop Suey" amazed fellow trumpeters (Louis switched from cornet to the similar-sounding trumpet in 1927), "Heebies Jeebies" was a hit that greatly popularized scat singing and both "Potato Head Blues" and "Struttin' with Some Barbecue" had perfectly constructed and thrilling solos. In 1928 Armstrong led a completely different group in the studio, the Savoy Ballroom Five, that used the trombone and clarinet more as color than as competing voices and put the emphasis on the interplay between the trumpeter and the remarkable pianist Earl Hines. "West End Blues," with its remarkable opening trumpet cadenza, was considered by many (including Louis himself) to be his greatest recording, while "Weather Bird" is a duet between Armstrong and Hines that found the two taking many chances with time; Louis' classic versions of "St. James Infirmary" and "Basin Street Blues" (which helped to introduce the two future standards) are almost afterthoughts next to these other remarkable records.
The odd part is that, with the exception of one appearance, the Hot Five and Hot Seven never played in public. Louis Armstrong was later featured in Chicago with big bands led by Erskine Tate and Carrol Dickerson and began developing his talents as a showman. Starting in 1929 he began recording almost exclusive-

ly as the head of a variety of big bands, emphasizing superior pop standards of the era (such as "I Can't Give You Anything but Love"). During the next decade he became a household name, making two acclaimed visits to Europe during 1932–34, appearing in small but memorable roles in movies and leading a swing-oriented big band that mostly functioned as a backdrop for his vocals and trumpet solos. Although the most advanced playing of his career took place with Earl Hines in 1928 and his Decca recordings of 1935–44 often involved novelties and commercial material, Armstrong provided some musical magic to nearly all of the records and his singing voice was at its peak in the early '40s.

However, by the mid-'40s Louis Armstrong was considered out of style. His orchestra had declined and his own solos and clowning sounded at odds with his younger more bop-oriented sidemen. But after appearing with a variety of veteran players in the interesting if flawed Hollywood film New Orleans and having success playing with a small group at an acclaimed Town Hall concert in 1947, Armstrong broke up his big band and formed the All-Stars. His sextet (which originally included trombonist Jack Teagarden and clarinetist Barney Bigard and soon had Earl Hines) was an immediate success, playing Dixieland and swing standards along with some comedy numbers, and Armstrong began a schedule of nearly non-stop travelling that lasted until his death.

After a few years the routines became fairly predictable and critics tired of them, while some in the Civil Rights community thought of Armstrong as an Uncle Tom. However they all missed the point. While Armstrong was quick to make fun of himself and his nickname of "Satchmo" (short for "Satchelmouth") could be considered objectionable, Armstrong always stood up for his race (most notably during the struggle to integrate schools in the South) and spread more goodwill than anyone; his brilliant trumpet playing set an example that busted stereotypes. Audiences the world over loved the joy of Louis Armstrong's music, his inspiring trumpet and vocals; his main concern was always to please the people who paid to see him. And although Armstrong's music did not evolve much after the 1940s, neither did the playing of Johnny Hodges and Thelonious Monk!

In the 1950s Hines left the All-Stars and Teagarden and Bigard were replaced by Trummy Young and Edmond Hall, but the basic sound of the group did not change. Armstrong, who also occasionally recorded with larger orchestras and with Ella Fitzgerald, found his celebrity status continuing to grow. He had major hits in "Blueberry Hill," "Mack the Knife" and "Hello Dolly" and when he died on July 6, 1971, there was no jazz musician who could approach him in popularity. With all of the reissues and continued acclaim (including a postage stamp), there is little chance that Louis Armstrong will ever be forgotten! —Scott Yanow

Louis Armstrong and King Oliver / Apr. 6, 1923–Dec. 22, 1924 / Milestone ✦✦✦✦✦
King Oliver's Creole Jazz Band was the most important jazz group to record in 1923 and did wonders to popularize the new music beyond Chicago. With Louis Armstrong on second cornet, clarinetist Johnny Dodds and trombonist Honore Dutrey, cornetist King Oliver was able to feature jazz that was state of the art for 1923, emphasizing melodic group improvisations during that presolo age. This Milestone CD is a duplicate of the original two-LP set except that the two King Oliver-Jelly Roll Morton duets have been moved to a Morton reissue. The 18 performances by Oliver's band (with "Chimes Blues," "Dippermouth Blues," "Snake Rag" and "Mabel's Dream" among the classics) are joined by the 1924 recordings by The Red Onion Jazz Babies, a small group with Armstrong, soprano great Sidney Bechet and singer Alberta Hunter. —Scott Yanow

Portrait of the Artist As a Young Man / Apr. 6, 1923–Oct. 1934 / Columbia ✦✦✦
This very attractive four-CD box set has definitive liner notes from Dan Morgenstern and draws its 81 selections from Louis Armstrong's prime period. Why then does it not receive the highest rating? Armstrong's Immortal Hot Five and Hot Seven record ings, along with his early big-band sides, had already been reissued complete and in chronological order on seven Columbia CDs and his less interesting performances as an accompanist to various blues singers (some of which are on this set) have also been reissued in similar fashion. Therefore this box is of no real interest to veteran collectors and, although a good introduction to beginners just starting to explore Satch's classic music, they too will eventually be moved to duplicate many of these recordings

by getting the more complete series. As for the music, this set has literally dozens of influential classics and 19 performances that actually predate the Hot Fives but, since everything is available elsewhere, this box is recommended only for the informative booklet. —Scott Yanow

Highlights From His Decca Years / Oct. 10, 1924–Feb. 4, 1958 / Decca ✦✦
Music aside (and there are many fine moments here), this two CD sampler is a real mess. Rather than reissue complete sessions or at least repackage the music in chronological order, the 36 selections are divided into four overlapping sections ("In the Beginning," "The Decca Sessions, Part 1," "The Collaborations," "The Decca Sessions, Part 2") and range from sideman stints in the 1920s with clarinetist Johnny Dodds and Fletcher Henderson ("Shanghai Shuffle") to streaky big-band performances from the swing era, five vocal duets and commercial performances (including "Your Cheatin' Heart") from the 1950s. It is a real mish-mash (with some classics like "I Double Dare You" being overlooked) and Armstrong's important Decca recordings deserve much better. Get the CD releases from the European Classics label instead. —Scott Yanow

Louis Armstrong And The Blues Singers / Oct. 16, 1924–Jul. 16, 1930 / Affinity ✦✦✦✦
During 1924–26 (and to a lesser extent 1927–30), Louis Armstrong appeared as a sideman on a series of sessions by a variety of blues-oriented singers. All of these recordings are included on this attractive six-CD set issued by the English Affinity label (which also includes a lengthy booklet),.Armstrong's cornet (and, by 1928, trumpet) is heard backing and occasionally taking solos on record dates led by singers Ma Rainey, Virginia Liston, Eva Taylor, Alberta Hunter, Margaret Johnson, Sippie Wallace, Maggie Jones, Clara Smith, Bessie Smith, Trixie Smith, Billy Jones, Grant and Wilson, Perry Bradford, Chippie Hill, Blanche Calloway, Hociel Thomas, Baby Mack, Nolan Welsh, Butterbeans and Susie, Lillie Delk Christian, Seger Ellis, Victoria Spivey and even the country pioneer Jimmie Rodgers ("Blue Yodel No. 9"). The Bessie Smith recordings are the most powerful but there are other memorable selections, including those with the remarkably nasal Lillie Delk Christian (Armstrong even joins in and scats during "Too Busy"), Eva Taylor (during "Mandy Make up Your Mind" soprano-great Sidney Bechet switches to the remarkable sarrusophone), Eva Taylor (Armstrong's solo on "Cake Walking Babies from Homete" was one of his first great ones), Chippie Hill (the original version of "Trouble in Mind") and Ma Rainey (the earliest recording of "See See Rider"). These recordings on a whole are not as essential as his own classic sessions from the 1920s, so this perfectly packaged set is recommended mostly to the more fanatical early jazz and blues collectors rather than the more general listeners who are advised to get Armstrong's Hot Five recordings first. —Scott Yanow

☆ **Hot Fives, Vol. 1** / Nov. 12, 1925–Jun. 23, 1926 / Columbia ✦✦✦✦
With these first 16 recordings by Louis Armstrong's Hot Five, the trumpeter revolutionized jazz, changing it from an ensemble-oriented folk music into an art form dominated by virtuoso soloists. Among the historic gems on this CD (which also features classic solos by the great clarinetist Johnny Dodds and trombone stylist Kid Ory) are "Come Back, Sweet Papa," Louis' highly influential scat chorus on "Heebies Jeebies" and his dazzling solo on "Cornet Chop Suey," which made many of his contemporaries reevaluate how they played.. —Scott Yanow

☆ **Hot Fives and Sevens, Vol. 2** /Jun. 28, 1926– May 13, 1927 / Columbia ✦✦✦✦✦
Eight apiece from Louis Armstrong's Hot Five and Seven with some stunning trumpet on "Willie the Weeper" and "Potato Head Blues" and Johnny Dodds very distinctive clarinet at its best during "Weary Blues." Classic and very influential New Orleans jazz. —Scott Yanow

★ **Hot Fives and Sevens, Vol. 3** / May 1927–1928 / Columbia ✦✦✦✦✦
The last (and some of the best) of the Hot Sevens and Fives with Armstrong in brilliant form and followed closely by clarinetist Johnny Dodds and guest guitarist Lonnie Johnson. Armstrong is stunning on "Struttin' With Some Barbeque," "Hotter Than That" and (with his new pianist Earl Hines) "A Monday Date." —Scott Yanow

Armstrong Collection, Vol. 4: Louis Armstrong and ...nes / 1928 / Columbia ✦✦✦✦✦

...mstrong was at its most advanced at the time of these ...ss recordings with pianist Earl Hines. Hines constantly challenged Satch to stretch himself. Their duet "Weather Bird" is futuristic for 1928, their version of "Basin Street Blues" was that standard's earliest recording, and the stunning "West End Blues" was Armstrong's personal favorite recording ever. —*Scott Yanow*

Louis Armstrong Collection, Vol. 5: Louis in New York / Mar. 5, 1929–Nov. 26, 1929 / Columbia/Legacy ✦✦✦✦

By 1929, Louis Armstrong had switched from New Orleans jazz to fronting a variety of larger orchestras, widening his repertoire to include pop tunes but always leaving room for closing trumpet solos. This set includes all known versions (including a few new alternates) of his recordings of this era, including appearances by backing singers Seger Ellis and Victoria Spivey. Highpoints include "Mahogany Hall Stomp" and "Ain't Misbehavin'." —*Scott Yanow*

Louis Armstrong Collection, Vol. 6: St. Louis Blues / Dec. 10, 1929–Oct. 9, 1930 / Columbia/Legacy ✦✦✦✦

Using different big bands purely as a backdrop by 1930, Louis Armstrong was free to stretch out with flashy virtuosic trumpet solos and often scat-filled vocal choruses. "St. Louis Blues," "Body and Soul" and "Tiger Rag" are classics but his rendition of "I'm a Ding Dong Daddy" (which has a solo that gradually builds to a tremendous finish) is a true gem. —*Scott Yanow*

From the Big Band to the All Stars (1946–56) / Aug. 12, 1932–Jan. 8, 1956 / RCA ✦✦✦✦

With the exception of the alternate take of "Hobo, You Can't Ride This Train" from 1932 and a couple of numbers with a big band in 1956, this two-CD set (a straight reissue of the RCA Jazz Tribune two-LP release of the same name) concentrates on the 1946–47 period. Most of the music has been reissued several times by RCA (including in their Bluebird series), but it is still quite valuable and enjoyable. The great trumpeter/vocalist Louis Armstrong is heard on a couple of numbers with the Esquire All-Americans, on his final dozen recordings with his swing big band, with trombonist Kid Ory for a few songs (highlighted by the earliest version of "Do You Know What It Means to Miss New Orleans"), with "The Leader's Band" (a group taken from the film *A Song Is Born*) and with trombonist Jack Teagarden in a couple of all-star bands; their version of "Jack-Armstrong Blues" is a real classic while "Please Stop Playing Those Blues" and "A Song Was Born" are close behind. Very enjoyable music, highly recommended in one form or another. —*Scott Yanow*

Laughin' Louis (1932–1933) / 1932 / Bluebird ✦✦✦

Here is his orchestra before The Joe Glaser connection. Included are great versions of "Mahogany Hall Stomp," "Basin Street Blues," plus some medleys of Armstrong favorites. —*Bruce Boyd Raeburn*

1932–1933 / 1932–Apr. 26, 1933 / Classics ✦✦✦

The European Classics label may or may not be a "legitimate" record label but it currently has the best reissue series for those listeners wanting the complete output of vintage jazz artists. These 24 selections, as with the less-complete Laughin' Louis set, find Armstrong mostly overcoming an inferior big band to play some pacesetting trumpet. —*Scott Yanow*

1934–1936 / Nov. 7, 1934–Feb. 4, 1936 / Classics ✦✦✦✦

This valuable CD includes Armstrong's often riotous Paris session from 1934 ("St. Louis Blues" and "Tiger Rag" almost get out of control!) and then Satch's first 17 Decca recordings, smooth renditions of pop tunes that he turns into classic jazz. It duplicates and exceeds Decca's *Rhythm Saved the World.* —*Scott Yanow*

Rhythm Saved the World / Oct. 3, 1935–Feb. 4, 1936 / GRP ✦✦✦

This is the first domestic volume on CD of Armstrong's swing-era recordings for Decca in chronological order. Joined by the musical, but by then somewhat anonymous, Luis Russell Orchestra, Armstrong's melodic variations turn these pop tunes into fine jazz, even "La Cucaracha." —*Scott Yanow*

The Best of the Decca Years, Vol. 2 / Nov. 21, 1935–Jan. 28, 1957 / Decca ✦

This hodge-podge set has some fine examples of Armstrong's playing from both the '30s and the '50s, but it is somewhat pointless compared to the more complete collections available elsewhere, particularly when it lists "Struttin' with Some Barbeque" (a Lil Armstrong composition) as Louis'. —*Scott Yanow*

1936–1937 / Feb. 4, 1936–Apr. 7, 1937 / Classics ✦✦✦✦

Continuing the complete chronological reissue of Louis Armstrong's output for Decca during the swing era, this set finds Satch at his most exhibitionistic (hitting dozens of high notes on "Swing That Music"), fronting Jimmy Dorsey's orchestra, doing a "Pennies from Heaven" medley with Bing Crosby, joining in for two collaborations with The Mills Brothers and, on four selections, even making charming (if weird) music with a group of Hawaiians! Not essential but quite enjoyable. —*Scott Yanow*

Jazz Heritage: Satchmo's Collectors Items / Feb. 4, 1936–Jun. 29, 1937 / MCA ✦✦✦

This LP contains some of his lesser big-band items from 1936 as well as five successful performances that match Armstrong with the Mills Brothers. Like most of the *Jazz Heritages*, this has been since eclipsed by other, more recent reissue programs. —*Scott Yanow*

New Discoveries / Apr. 16, 1937–Dec. 17, 1961 / Pumpkin ✦✦✦

This unusual LP should greatly interest collectors. Included is a variety of previously unreleased material spanning a 24-year period in the great trumpeter's career. Armstrong is featured on broadcast versions of "Dinah" and "Twelfth Street Rag" with his big band, singing "Flat Foot Floogie" with The Mills Brothers, backing Frank Sinatra on "Blue Skies," rehearsing a couple of songs in 1947 with the all-star cast of the film *A Song Was Born*, performing five numbers at his famous Town Hall concert (including four on which he is backed only by a rhythm section) and playing two songs in a small group with Duke Ellington recorded a few months after their famous joint recording. Most of this music has still not surfaced on CD. —*Scott Yanow*

1937–1938 / Jun. 29, 1937–May 13, 1938 / Classics ✦✦✦✦

22 of Armstrong's big-band recordings and a couple selections with The Mills Brothers are taken in chronological order. A few ("I Double Dare You," "On the Sunny Side of the Street" and his first version of "The Saints") are classics but mostly it is a matter of Armstrong joyfully uplifting mundane material, often higher up than it deserves! —*Scott Yanow*

1938–1939 / May 18, 1938–Apr. 5, 1939 / Classics ✦✦

A mixed bag of Armstrong, these 23 selections, if taken complete and in chronological order, include routine swing, three enjoyable numbers with The Mills Brothers, a few spirituals, an odd two-part sermon and some remakes of Armstrong's earlier classics. His career was drifting a bit but there is enough enjoyable music to make this a worthwhile acquisition. —*Scott Yanow*

Live in 1943: On the Sunny Side of The Street / Jun. 13, 1938–Aug. 4, 1946 / Jass ✦✦

Other than the soundtrack version of "Jeepers Creepers" and two other items, all of this CD is taken from broadcasts of Armstrong's little-known and unrecorded orchestra of 1943. Much of the music is fairly routine swing, but the Armstrong trumpet (which always sounds so enthusiastic) and features for The Mills brothers ("Paper Doll") and clarinetist Barney Bigard make this rarity of some interest. —*Scott Yanow*

1939–1940 / Apr. 5, 1939–May 1, 1940 / Classics ✦✦

Armstrong's Decca years by the late '30s found him treading water. He plays well on these orchestra recordings (four songs find him having a good time with The Mills Brothers), but the remakes are generally more interesting than the newer novelty material from the swing era. —*Scott Yanow*

1940–42 / May 1, 1940–Apr. 17, 1942 / Classics ✦✦✦✦

While MCA continues to release incomplete samplers of his Decca recordings, the European Classics series has reissued the great trumpeter's performances the best possible way: complete and in chronological order. This final CD has 18 mostly rare big-band selections from 1940–42 (highlighted by "I Cover the Waterfront," a remake of "When It's Sleepy Time Down South," "Coquette" and "I Never Knew") along with the four songs recorded by Armstrong during a reunion session with the great soprano saxophonist Sidney Bechet (including a heated "Down in Honky Tonk Town"). Ignore the better publicized MCA Louis Armstrong reissues and get this series instead. —*Scott Yanow*

Pops: 1940's Small Band Sides / Sep. 6, 1946–Oct. 16, 1947 / RCA/Bluebird ✦✦✦✦

Recorded at the time Armstrong was in the film *New Orleans*, when he broke up his orchestra and formed his very popular "All-Stars," these 20 tracks feature Satch in prime form, whether play-

Music Map

Arrangers

Pioneers
Jelly Roll Morton
Don Redman
(with Fletcher Henderson and his own groups)
Bill Challis (with Jean Goldkette and Paul Whiteman)

Most Significant Arranger
Duke Ellington

Other Important Arrangers of the 1930s and '40s
Fletcher Henderson
Benny Carter
Gene Gifford (with the Casa Loma Orchestra)
Sy Oliver (with Jimmy Lunceford and Tommy Dorsey)
Edgar Sampson (with Chick Webb)
Mary Lou Williams (with Andy Kirk)
Horace Henderson • Jimmy Mundy • Glenn Miller
Bill Finegan (with Glenn Miller)
Eddie Sauter (with Red Norvo and Benny Goodman)
Billy May (with Charlie Barnet)

Bop Innovator
Tadd Dameron

Other Top Bop Arrangers
Ralph Burns (with Woody Herman)
George Handy (with Boyd Raeburn)
Gil Fuller (with Dizzy Gillespie)
Gerry Mulligan • Shorty Rogers

The Great Stan Kenton Arrangers
Pete Rugolo　　　　　Bill Russo
Bill Holman　　　　　Marty Paich
Johnny Richards

1950s
Gil Evans • Neal Hefti (with Count Basie)
Ernie Wilkins • Frank Foster • Jimmy Heath
Benny Golson • Slide Hampton • Melba Liston
Quincy Jones

Third Stream
John Lewis • Gunther Schuller • J.J. Johnson

1960s
Oliver Nelson
Hank Levy (with Stan Kenton and Don Ellis)
Thad Jones
Bob Brookmeyer

Avant-Garde
Bob Graettinger　　　　George Russell
Sun Ra　　　　　　　　Muhal Richard Abrams
Julius Hemphill　　　　Carla Bley
Maria Schneider　　　　George Gruntz
Willem Brueker

Crossover
Don Sebesky • Bob James • Eumir Deodato

Modern Mainstream
Gerald Wilson　　　　Francy Boland
Rob McConnell　　　　Bob Florence
John Clayton　　　　　Toshiko Akiyoshi
Wynton Marsalis

ing relaxed standards, New Orleans gems or duetting with trombonist/vocalist Jack Teagarden. Highpoints include a reunion with his old boss trombonist Kid Ory, five selections from his classic 1947 Town Hall concert (including definitive versions of "Ain't Misbehavin," "Rockin' Chair" and "Back O'Town Blues"), sharing the spotlight with Jack T. on "A Song Was Born" and "Please Stop Playing Those Blues, Boy," and taking one of his greatest ever solos on "Jack-Armstrong Blues." An outstanding set. —*Scott Yanow*

The Complete Town Hall Concert, Vols. 3 & 4 / May 17, 1947 / RCA ✦✦✦
One of the key turning points of Louis Armstrong's career occurred at the Town Hall concert fully documented on this two-CD set, a reissue of the earlier two-LP release. Armstrong, who had been leading a big band for 18 years, was showcased with some musical friends who were all very complementary players (including trombonist Jack Teagarden, clarinetist Peanuts Hucko and cornetist Bobby Hackett), and the results were so exciting that Armstrong soon broke up his orchestra to form a similar all-star

sextet. The recording quality of some of the numbers from this concert is erratic, but the magic of the music definitely comes through. Highlights include a few tunes on which Louis is backed by just a rhythm section (including "Cornet Chop Suey" and an emotional "Dear Old Southland"), definitive versions of "Ain't Misbehavin" and "Back O'Town Blues" and a memorable feature for Jack Teagarden on "St. James Infirmary." Recommended for all Louis Armstrong fans who wish to hear the real birth of his All-Stars. —*Scott Yanow*

And His All-Stars / Jun. 10, 1947–1949 / Laserlight ✦✦
Laserlight CDs are very low-priced and have a budget-series look about them, but quite often the music is very enjoyable (despite the lack of worthwhile liner notes and details). This concert recording finds Louis Armstrong's All-Stars (featuring trombonist Jack Teagarden, clarinetist Barney Bigard and pianist Earl Hines) on solid and occasionally exciting live performances. This set concludes with the out-of-place studio version of "Jack-Armstrong Blues," a classic from 1947 that is available elsewhere. —*Scott Yanow*

Satchmo at Symphony Hall, Vol. 1 / Nov. 30, 1947 / Decca ✦✦✦✦✦

The first and best version of Louis Armstrong's All-Stars is heard in inspired form throughout this program of standards, played live before an enthusiastic crowd. Trombonist Jack Teagarden and clarinetist Barney Bigard clearly enjoy playing what was then fresh material, and Armstrong (whether leading the ensembles on "Royal Garden Blues," singing a touching "Black and Blue" or jiving with Velma Middleton on a very funny "That's My Desire") is consistently delightful. —*Scott Yanow*

The Complete Decca Studio Louis Armstrong All Stars / Apr. 26, 1950–Oct. 8, 1958 / Mosaic ✦✦✦✦

This attractive limited-edition six-CD set features all of the studio small-group sides done by Armstrong in the 1950s for Decca. The first disc in particular is quite rewarding for it contains a full program by his 1950 sextet with trombonist Jack Teagarden, clarinetist Barney Bigard and pianist Earl Hines. While the second disc has a variety of odds and ends (including the first version of "A Kiss to Build a Dream On" and two vocal duets with Gary Crosby), most of the final four CDs are from an ambitious project (originally titled "A Musical Autobiography") in which the great trumpeter/vocalist revisited many of the songs that he had recorded in the 1920s and '30s; some of the newer versions are actually better than the earlier ones. The one fault is that Mosaic's decision to reissue the latter in strict chronological order mixes up the original program with some of the '30s selections preceding the ones from the decade before; also Armstrong's verbal introductions (which are often charming) have been deleted. But musically this excellent box set serves as proof that Louis Armstrong was still a very vital trumpeter in the 1950s. —*Scott Yanow*

The California Concerts / Jan. 30, 1951–Jan. 21, 1955 / GRP ✦✦✦✦

Armstrong's All-Stars, giving one a very good idea of the type of performance the great trumpeter/vocalist put on every night. Some dated comedy aside, Satch is in exciting form, assisted by trombonists Jack Teagarden and Trummy Young, clarinetist Barney Bigard and, for the earlier concert, pianist Earl Hines. Actually, it is the later session (which takes up most of the last three CDs) that is quite spirited and lively, with Armstrong enthusiastically leading his All-Stars through timeworn but fresh Dixieland standards. —*Scott Yanow*

Louis Armstrong Plays W.C. Handy / Jul. 12, 1954–Jul. 14, 1954 / Columbia ✦✦

This is considered, along with his Fats Waller tribute, Louis Armstrong's most rewarding recording of the '50s, but Columbia, when they reissued it in 1986, thought they were doing collectors a favor by substituting alternate takes on six of the songs for the originals. If they had merely augmented the set with the extra material it would have increased its value, but instead the original (and superior) versions of many of these songs are out of print. The result is an interesting but flawed tribute with Armstrong's monumental version of "St. Louis Blues" replaced by an imposter. —*Scott Yanow*

Satch Plays Fats: The Music of Fats Waller / Apr. 26, 1955–May 3, 1955 / Columbia ✦✦

The same criticisms levelled at the CD version of Armstrong's W.C. Handy set apply to this version of his tribute to Fats Waller. Six of the nine songs heard here are actually alternate takes inferior to the original releases. The music is still decent but only a shadow of the real version. —*Scott Yanow*

The Sullivan Years: Louis Armstrong / Jul. 15, 1956–Sep. 11, 1966 / TVT ✦✦

Louis Armstrong was always a welcome guest on *The Ed Sullivan Show*, where his happy renditions of Dixieland tunes and pop songs were a consistent crowd pleaser. This CD has 18 selections from nine of his appearances, performing everything from "Hello, Dolly" and "Mack the Knife" to "Muskrat Ramble" and "Basin Street." Although one cannot see these performances (at least not until they are released on videotape), one can certainly feel the joy and love. —*Scott Yanow*

Porgy and Bess / Aug. 18, 1957 / Verve ✦✦✦✦

Louis Armstrong and Ella Fitzgerald, great mutual admirers, team up for 16 songs from the famous George Gershwin opera. Although this would not be considered either's finest moment on record, it may very well be the most satisfying jazz version of *Porgy & Bess*. Russ Garcia's arrangements for the large orchestra work very well with the two singers. —*Scott Yanow*

Happy Birthday, Louis! Armstrong & His All-Stars / Jul. 1, 1960 / Omega ✦✦✦

Armstrong and the 1960 version of his All-Stars (which included trombonist Trummy Young, clarinetist Barney Bigard, pianist Billy Kyle, bassist Mort Herbert, drummer Danny Barcelona and singer Velma Middleton) are heard putting on their usual show at that year's Newport Jazz Festival. The repertoire (which includes "Indiana," a slapdash "Tiger Rag," two songs from the film *High Society*, individual features for the musicians and "Mack the Knife") offers no real surprises but Armstrong's enthusiasm and beautiful tone on the trumpet make this joyful CD (whose contents were released for the first time in 1994) worth having. —*Scott Yanow*

What A Wonderful World / Nov. 1960 / Milan ✦✦

With this CD only containing 35 minutes of music and a so-so and rather predictable performance from Louis Armstrong's All-Stars in 1960, only completists will want to go out of their way to pick this one up. Armstrong, trombonist Trummy Young and clarinetist Barney Bigard are in reasonable form, but the lack of surprises and shaky recording quality are definite minuses. This very brief set is augmented by a version of "What a Wonderful World" that is probably from around 1969. —*Scott Yanow*

Louis Armstrong and Dke Ellington / Apr. 3, 1961–Apr. 4, 1961 / Roulette ✦✦✦✦✦

Armstrong/Ellington: Together for the First Time/The Great Reunion / Apr. 3, 1961–Apr. 4, 1961 / Mobile Fidelity ✦✦✦✦

Formerly available as a two-LP set and also released on CD by Roulette, these 17 selections are the entire results of the only meeting in the studios by Louis Armstrong and Duke Ellington. Although it might have been preferable to have Armstrong perform with Duke Ellington's orchestra, Ellington's performance as pianist with Satch's All-Stars is quite satisfying. The all-Ellington program gave Armstrong a rest from his usual repertoire and permitted him an opportunity to work his magic on fresh material. Lots of surprises, some sensitive vocalizing, and fine supporting work from trombonist Trummy Young and clarinetist Barney Bigard make this a gem. —*Scott Yanow*

Blueberry Hill / 1961 / Milan ✦✦

An obscure concert performance, probably from around 1961–63 (no date is given) The erratic recording quality and somewhat typical repertoire keep this from being highly recommended but it has its strong moments, most notably a beautiful version of "That's My Home" and a relaxed run-through of "Jazz Me Blues." —*Scott Yanow*

Armstrong And His All Stars / Apr. 24, 1962 / RTE ✦✦✦

Louis Armstrong and his All-Stars are heard during a typical concert performance in 1962. There are no real surprises in the repertoire or the solos but the enthusiasm shown by Armstrong, trombonist Trummy Young and clarinetist Joe Darensbourg (somehow Armstrong makes this music sound quite fresh and timely) and the excellent recording quality result in a happy Dixieland set that should be of interest to Satch's many fans. —*Scott Yanow*

Hello, Dolly! / Dec. 3, 1963–Apr. 18, 1964 / Kapp ✦✦✦✦

Not only does this wonderful LP have the original hit version of "Hello, Dolly" but a great rendition of "A Kiss to Build a Dream On" and Louis Armstrong's last extended trumpet solo during a hot version of "Jeepers Creepers." No matter how many times one hears "Hello, Dolly" it is still a joy. —*Scott Yanow*

The Essential Louis Armstrong / Jun. 4, 1965 / Verve ✦✦✦✦

Maybe it is not "essential," but this two-CD set is a definitive look at the Louis Armstrong All-Stars in their later years, when Tyree Glenn was on trombone and the group was riding high from the success of "Hello, Dolly." Armstrong's trumpet solos were briefer and stuck closer to the melody (age was taking its toll), yet were still full of beauty and feeling. —*Scott Yanow*

Here's Louis Armstrong / 1968 / Vocalion ✦✦✦

Disney Songs the Satchmo Way / Mar. 1968 / Disney ✦✦

Only Louis Armstrong could turn songs like "Heigh Ho," "Bibbidi-Bobbidi-Boo" and "The Bare Necessities" into worthwhile jazz. The matchup of Armstrong with Walt Disney tunes is quite logical and an unexpected success. This CD can appeal to tolerant jazz fans and children alike. —*Scott Yanow*

Louis Armstrong and His Friends / May 26, 1970–May 29, 1970 / Flying Dutchman ✦✦✦

Louis Armstrong, trombonist Jack Teagarden and clarinetist

Barney Bigard team up with a West Coast rhythm section (pianist Charlie Lavere, bassist Morty Corb and drummer Nick Fatool) for a typical live set from 1951. Actually the enthusiasm of the audience and the utilization of a different-than-usual rhythm section makes most of these songs (which include "Royal Garden Blues," "Rockin' Chair," "Blueberry Hill" and several features for Teagarden) vary a bit from the more familiar versions. Satch's many fans will want this spirited CD. —*Scott Yanow*

Lynne Arriale

b. Milwaukee, WI
Piano / Post-Bop
Lynne Arriale gained her initial fame when she won the 1993 International Great American Jazz Piano competition and was immediately signed to DMP. A fine advanced bop pianist, Arriale graduated from the Wisconsin Conservatory of Music and toured Japan in 1991 with "100 Golden Fingers," which matched her along with nine veteran pianists, an honor that preceded her contest victory by two years. Lynne Arriale has strong potential for the future. —*Scott Yanow*

The Eyes Have It / Nov. 16, 1993 / DMP ✦✦✦✦
Winner of the 1993 International Great American Jazz Piano Competition, Lynne Arriale makes her recording debut on this CD. Her style at this early point falls easily into the modern mainstream (with the usual influences of Bill Evans, McCoy Tyner, Chick Corea and Herbie Hancock). Arriale does take some chances, opening her release with a moody version of "My Funny Valentine," taking "Yesterdays" at a rapid pace and having the tempo purposely speed up during the early part of "Witchcraft." With attentive support from bassist Jay Anderson and drummer Steve Davis, Lynne Arriele (who contributes four diverse originals) shows a great deal of potential and this CD is a strong start to her career. —*Scott Yanow*

Art Ensemble of Chicago

Group / Avant-Garde, Free Jazz
The Art Ensemble of Chicago has long been one of the most significant avant-garde jazz groups and the most famous band to come out of the AACM. At a time when most musicians involved with the free jazz movement were playing at a consistently intense level, the Art Ensemble showed how to use space and dynamics creatively and how to mix together free form passages with arranged sections. Not averse to hinting at earlier styles while playing originals, the Art Ensemble also helped introduce the concept of "little instruments" (such as bicycle horns, gongs, sirens and unusual percussive devices) to jazz. The group began as saxophonist Roscoe Mitchell's band. After trumpeter Lester Bowie, saxophonist Joseph Jarman and bassist Malachi Favors joined, it became a co-op. Its original drummer was Phillip Wilson but, when he departed to tour with the Butterfield Blues Band, the Art Ensemble continued for a time as a drumless quartet. During the early part of a two-year period spent in Paris (1969–71) Don Moye permanently took over the drum slot. The Art Ensemble was in its prime during the 1970s but by the '80s individual projects began to result in fewer performances. The group has continued on a part-time basis into the mid-'90s and has remained influential. —*Scott Yanow*

Art Ensemble: 1967/68 / May 18, 1967–Mar. 11, 1968 / Nessa ✦✦✦
This limited-edition five-CD set available directly from Nessa not only reissues the important free jazz albums *Old/Quartet*, *Numbers 1 & 2* and *Congliptious* but contains quite a bit of music taken from rehearsals by the members of the group that would by 1969 become known as the Art Ensemble of Chicago. With such advanced improvisers as trumpeter Lester Bowie, Roscoe Mitchell and Joseph Jarman on reeds, bassist Malachi Favors, drummer Phillip Wilson and appearances from bassist Charles Clark, drummers Robert Crowder and Thurman Barker, the music is usually very emotional and sometimes quite scary. There are meandering sections and individual performances that do not work all that well, but in general the music is quite colorful, adventurous and innovative; in many ways the beginning of the modern avant-garde. Open-eared listeners are advised to search for this important historical set. —*Scott Yanow*

Jackson in Your House / Jun. 23, 1969–Aug. 1969 / Affinity ✦✦✦
Vitality was the key to the success of the Art Ensemble of Chicago's *A Jackson in Your House*, which reissued the material from the BYG LP of the same name. This was recorded with just the quartet of Lester Bowie, Roscoe Mitchell, Joseph Jarman and

Malachi Favors (Philip Wilson [drums] had left and Don Moye had yet to link up). —*Bob Rusch, Cadence*

Eda Wobu / Oct. 5, 1969 / JMY ✦✦✦✦✦
● **Live** / 1972 / Delmark ✦✦✦✦
The Art Ensemble of Chicago fuse theatrical fireworks, improvisational elan and rhythmic flexibility in their concerts, and they successfully displayed all these elements and more on this date, which was previously available on vinyl. The Mandel Hall concert included lengthy, sprawling sax and brass dialogues, verbal thrusts, and multiple African, Afro-Latin and funk beats and textures. They were all performed in a non-stop fashion with the volume and pace building, exploding, easing, and rebuilding, and the music is presented in various movements. It can be joyful, furious, comical, cohesive and chaotic, and sounds even more thrilling in digital. —*Ron Wynn*

Fanfare for the Warriors / Sep. 6, 1973 / Atlantic ✦✦✦✦
The Art Ensemble of Chicago's first (and arguably most significant) period concluded with this high-quality studio session. The quintet (trumpeter Lester Bowie, Roscoe Mitchell and Joseph Jarman on reeds, bassist Malachi Favors and drummer Don Moye), with guest pioanist Muhal Richard Abrams, provides concise but adventurous performances. Highpoints include Mitchell's "Nonnaah," Bowie's humorous "Barnyard Scuffle Shuffle" and "Tnoona," but all of the selections have their own musical personality. It's a fine showcase for this important avant-garde unit. —*Scott Yanow*

Nice Guys / May 1978 / ECM ✦✦✦✦
The Art Ensemble of Chicago's first studio album in six years finds the dynamic quintet incorporating elements of other musics into their own style, including earlier forms of jazz. "Dreaming of the Master" is an expert tribute to the Miles Davis Sextet of 1958, "Ja" hints strongly at reggae and "Nice Guys" is spacey in a humorous way. This fairly accessible set serves as a fine introduction to this important band's legacy. —*Scott Yanow*

Full Force / Jan. 1980 / ECM ✦✦
Not quite up to the level of their previous *Nice Guys*, *Full Force* is nevertheless a decent effort from The Art Ensemble of Chicago. Although there is one composition apiece from each of the bandmembers except drummer Don Moye, trumpeter Lester Bowie emerges as the most memorable soloist and his "Charlie M" (a tribute to Charles Mingus) is the most interesting performance. It's not essential but is worth picking up. —*Scott Yanow*

Urban Bushmen / May 1980 / ECM ✦✦✦
The Third Decade / Jun. 1984 / ECM ✦✦
Art Ensemble of Soweto / Dec. 1989–Jan. 1990 / DIW ✦✦
America South Africa / Dec. 19, 1989–Jan. 1990 / DIW ✦✦
Welcome return to American recording scene for the premier Chicago outside band. This mixes African rhythms, township melodies, and The Ensemble's usual array of blistering solos, vocal effects, percussive colors, and furious collective improvisations. —*Ron Wynn*

Dreaming of the Masters Suite / Jan. 12, 1990–Mar. 24, 1990 / DIW ✦✦✦
Thelonious Sphere Monk: Dreaming of the Masters, Vol. 2 / Jan. 16, 1990–Mar. 11, 1990 / DIW ✦✦

Dorothy Ashby

b. Aug. 6, 1932, Detroit, MI, **d.** Apr. 13, 1986, Santa Monica, CA
Harp / Cool, Hard Bop
There have been very few jazz harpists in history and Dorothy Ashby was one of the greats. Somehow she was able to play credible bebop on her instrument. As a pianist she studied at Wayne University and in 1952 she switched to harp. Within two years Ashby was gigging in jazz and in 1956 she made her first recording as a leader. Between 1956–70 she led ten albums for such labels as Savoy, Prestige, New Jazz, Argo, Jazzland, Atlantic and Cadet, guested on many records and was firmly established as a top studio and session player. She moved to the West Coast in the 1970's and was active up until her death. —*Scott Yanow*

● **In a Minor Groove** / Mar. 21, 1958–Sep. 19, 1958 / Prestige ✦✦✦✦✦

Harold Ashby

b. Mar. 27, 1925, Kansas City, MO
Tenor Saxophone / Swing
An excellent Ben Webster-inspired tenor saxophonist, Harold

Ashby fit right in during his period with Duke Ellington. He had played in Kansas City (starting in 1946) and from the early '50s in Chicago. While most of his previous work was in R&B and blues bands, he was always a fine swing-based improviser. In 1957 Ashby moved to New York, met Ben Webster and through the older tenor was introduced to Duke Ellington. During the next decade he was on the periphery of Duke's world, playing with Mercer Ellington's short-lived band, recording with Ellington stars and appearing in Duke's *My People* show. Ashby was more than ready when he joined Ellington in 1968, and he was a major asset to the band up until the leader's death. Since then he has free-lanced with Benny Goodman and Sy Oliver (among others), led a few record dates of his own and appeared often in Europe. *—Scott Yanow*

Presenting Harold Ashby / Aug. 7, 1978 / Progressive ✦✦✦
A longtime Ellingtonian steps away from the orchestra and shows his swing roots. Ashby played with wit, drive, and style, keeping things going even when they threatened to bog down due to average material or arrangements. A pleasant surprise and nice vehicle for someone known more as part of an organization than on his own. *—Ron Wynn*

The Viking / Aug. 4, 1988 / Gemini ✦✦✦✦
Tenor saxophonist Harold Ashby has had relatively few opportunities to record as a leader, making this date for the Norwegian Gemini label a notable effort. Ashby, who is heavily influenced by Ben Webster, gets to stretch out while accompanied by the Norman Simmons Trio (with Simmons on piano, bassist Paul West and drummer Gerryck King). The repertoire includes four mostly basic Ashby originals plus a quartet of swing standards; "I Got It Bad" and "Whispering" are highlights. A strong effort by the very underrated veteran tenor. *—Scott Yanow*

What Am I Here For? / Nov. 30, 1990 / Cross Cross Jazz Crisis ✦✦✦

● **I'm Old Fashioned** / Jul. 25, 1991 / Stash ✦✦✦✦

Svend Asmussen
b. Feb. 28, 1916, Copenhagen, Denmark
Violin / Swing
It seems strange that Svend Asmussen is not better known in the United States, for he has been a top swing violinist since the mid-'30s. He started playing violin when he was seven and in 1933 made his professional debut. Always based in Scandinavia (hence his obscurity in the U.S.), Asmussen made his first records as a leader in 1935 and has been consistently popular in his homeland ever since. He played with the Mills Brothers and Fats Waller in the 1930s when they passed through Denmark, but when Benny Goodman tried to get him in the mid-'50s for his small group, strict immigration laws made it impossible for him to get to the U.S. Asmussen recorded with John Lewis (1962), Duke Ellington (as part of a 1963 violin summit), Toots Thielemans, Lionel Hampton (1978), and on a few occasions with Stephane Grappelli in addition to many dates with his own groups. *—Scott Yanow*

● **Musical Miracle Vol. 1, 1935–1940** / Nov. 6, 1935–Dec. 4, 1940 / Phontastic ✦✦✦✦✦

Prize Winners / Feb. 12, 1978+Feb. 17, 1978 / Matrix ✦✦✦

June Night / Aug. 18, 1983–Aug. 19, 1983 / Doctor Jazz ✦✦✦

Fred Astaire (Franz Austerlitz)
b. May 10, 1899, Omaha, NB, d. Jun. 22, 1987, Los Angeles, CA
Vocals, Dancer / Swing, Standards
While he's rated as a magnificent all-round talent, many people would deem singing the least of Fred Astaire's skills, ranking it well behind dancing and acting. Yet Irving Berlin once said he'd rather hear Fred Astaire sing his compositions than any other vocalist. He was an excellent interpreter of classic American tunes, and could interact with great musicians without being overwhelmed or threatened. Astaire began his professional career as a five year old, and was starring in vaudeville with his sister Adele until 1916; they equalled that success on the Broadway stage until 1932, when she gave up show business for marriage. George Gershwin penned "Lady Be Good" for them in 1924, and they did his "Funny Face" in 1927, and the Arthur Schwartz/Howard Dietz number "The Band Wagon" in 1931. A role in Cole Porter's "The Gay Divorce" in 1932 led to a screen test in which the book on Astaire supposedly was "can't act, slightly bald, can dance a little." No matter, he teamed with Ginger Rogers and became the epito-

me for most Americans (particularly those unaware of or unwilling to consider Bill Robinson) of grace and flair as a dancer. But throughout his extraordinary film, stage and television career, Astaire made superb recordings. He did transcendent versions of "Lady Be Good," "Fascinating Rhythm," "Dancing In The Dark," "Night and Day" and many, many others. Whether doing songs in theatrical productions or interpreting them in the studio, Astaire brought to every number a quiet charm, casual elegance and exquisite timing, as well as distinctive enunciation and understated sense of swing. He made outstanding records in the '30s for Brunswick, and Decca in the '40s. The 1953 four-disc set *The Fred Astaire Story* was a collection of songs long been associated with him, and featured him backed by array of session and jazz greats. He also made *Swings and Sings Irving Berlin* during that same period and recorded with Oscar Peterson, Ray Brown and Charlie Shavers. While his vocal triumphs will never get as much ink as his film and dance exploits, Astaire deserves mention as an important singer in the pre-swing era, with links to, if not a complete foothold in, jazz. *—Ron Wynn and Bruce Eder*

Starring Fred Astaire / Jun. 19, 1935–Sept. 1940 / Columbia ✦✦✦✦✦
This 36-track album traces Fred Astaire's recordings from June 1935 to September 1940, including his #1 hits with "Cheek To Cheek," "I'm Putting All My Eggs In One Basket," "The Way You Look Tonight," "A Fine Romance," "They Can't Take That Away From Me," "Nice Work If You Can Get It," and "Change Partners." In addition to his movie stardom, Astaire was a major recording success in the second half of the '30s, introducing songs that would become standards by some of the great songwriters of the era—Irving Berlin, Jerome Kern and Dorothy Fields, and the Gershwins, especially. These recordings, which are studio efforts, not identical to the same songs in the movies, show Astaire to be as effortless a singer as he is a dancer (and you get to hear the tapping of those famous feet now and then, too). *—William Ruhlmann*

● **The Astaire Story** / Dec. 1952 / Verve ✦✦✦✦✦

Eden Atwood
b. 1970, Memphis, TN
Vocals / Standards
A fine interpreter of lyrics, Eden Atwood has started out with three Concord recordings. Raised in Montana, Atwood studied drama and musical theater at college but became interested in jazz and at 19 she began singing locally. Although she worked as a model and an actress, Atwood has focused her attentions on singing; she made her debut in New York in 1992 and sings in a style somewhere between jazz and cabaret. *—Scott Yanow*

No One Ever Tells You / 1992 / Concord ✦✦✦✦

● **Cat on a Hot Tin Roof** / Oct. 1993 / Concord ✦✦✦
Eden Atwood is a young singer whose appeal sometimes compensates on her second Concord release for a few shortcomings. She has a clear and attractive voice and is at her best on ballads, but occasionally (as on "Not While I'm Around") borders on being a cabaret singer. In contrast, on the uptempo material her scatting and improvising skills are not fully mature or all that adventurous. To her credit she gives her sidemen (particularly Ken Peploski on clarinet and tenor) plenty of solo space on the more cooking material. Atwood does write intelligent lyrics (best are "Silent Movie" and "Cat on a Hot Tin Roof"), is quite expressive on the ballads and shows versatility, but at this point she does not stand apart from the crowd of young jazz vocalists. Her future progress should be worth watching though. *—Scott Yanow*

There Again / Dec. 7, 1994–Jan. 9, 1995 / Concord Jazz ✦✦
Eden Atwood has a lovely voice but this CD (which is dominated by ballads) features little improvising and much of the material has been overdone through the years. Her versions of "It Never Entered My Mind" (a song she is too young to sing) and "The Nearness of You" are far from definitive. Atwood interprets "Sonny Boy" with such seriousness that one wonders if she ever heard Al Jolson's version, and by speeding up "You're My Thrill" she drains that song of all its sensuality. Her rhythm section (pianist Dave Berkman, bassist Michael Moore and drummer Ron Vincent) is supportive without making an impression, while the guest appearances of pianist Marian McPartland and tenorman Chris Potter are not enough to uplift this set. Eden Atwood, 26 at the time of this recording (her third Concord CD) is fine as a middle-of-the-road pop singer, but she will have to work on her

improvising abilities before she can be taken all that seriously by the jazz world. — *Scott Yanow*

Georgie Auld (John Altwerger)

b. May 19, 1919, Toronto, Ontario, Canada, **d.** Jan. 8, 1990, Palm Springs, CA
Tenor Saxophone, Leader / Swing, Bop
Georgie Auld had a long and varied career, changing his tenor sound gradually with the times and adapting to many different musical situations. He moved from Canada to the U.S. in the late '20s and, although originally an altoist, he switched to tenor after hearing Coleman Hawkins. While with Bunny Berigan during 1937–38, Auld sounded like a dead ringer for Charlie Garnet. After spending a year with Artie Shaw in 1939 (including leading the band briefly after Shaw ran away to Mexico), Auld sounded much closer to Lester Young when he joined Benny Goodman. With BG, Auld was a major asset, jamming with a version of Goodman's Sextet that also included Cootie Williams and Charlie Christian. He was back with Shaw in 1942 and then led his own big band (1943–46), an excellent transitional unit between swing and bop that at various times included such young modernists as Dizzy Gillespie, Erroll Garner and Freddie Webster; Sarah Vaughan also guested on a couple of his recordings. After the band's breakup, Auld led some smaller groups that tended to be bop-oriented. He was with Count Basie's octet in 1950 and then freelanced for the remainder of his career, maintaining a lower profile but travelling frequently overseas and not losing his enthusiasm for jazz. Some may remember that in 1977 he played Tommy Dorsey in a scene from the otherwise forgettable Liza Minelli movie *New York, New York.* — *Scott Yanow*

Good Enough to Keep / Sep. 5, 1959 / Xanudu ✦✦✦✦

Teodross Avery

b. Jul. 2, 1973, Fairfield, CA
Tenor Saxophone / Hard Bop
A promising young tenor saxophonist, Teodross Avery made his recording debut as a leader on GRP when he was a few days short of turning 21. He studied classical guitar when he was ten, switched to alto at 13 and a few years later took up the tenor. Avery then studied with Joe Henderson, attended Berklee and soon was leading his own group. In 1993 he appeared on a Carl Allen record and then utilized his quartet on his GRP date. — *Scott Yanow*

In Other Words / Jun. 27, 1994–Jun. 29, 1994 / GRP ✦✦✦
Teodross Avery, a few days shy of turning 21 at the time of his GRP release, sounds quite mature on his debut as a leader. His tenor tone is attractive, his style is very influenced by Joe Henderson and John Coltrane, and he is surprisingly relaxed on the ballads. Avery contributed nine of the 11 selections (all but "What's New" and Wayne Shorter's "Edda"). Three of the songs find trumpeter Roy Hargrove making the group a quintet. The music is very much in the hard bop vein and nothing too innovative or unexpected occurs, but this is an impressive initial effort from Teodross Avery, who will hopefully have a long and productive career. — *Scott Yanow*

● **My Generation** / Oct. 10, 1995–Oct. 12, 1995 / GRP ✦✦✦✦

Roy Ayers

b. Sep. 10, 1940, Los Angeles, CA
Vibes / Instrumental Pop, Soul Jazz
A very talented vibist, Ayers was among the top jazz players of the '60s. He had speed, technique, and the good fortune to appear on some high-profile albums with Herbie Mann. He turned more and more to R&B and funk in the '70s. His group Ubiquity began with prototype jazz-based R&B, then moved more into straight R&B/funk through the '70s. By the late '70s and early '80s, Ayers was essentially an R&B bandleader, with eight albums making the *Billboard* charts in 1976-1979.

During the '80s and '90s Roy Ayers has divided his time between bandleading, performing, writing and producing. He issued *Love Fantasy* in 1980, then toured Africa the next year, performing with Nigerian Afrobeat king Fela Anikulapo-Kuti. Kuti appeared on Ayers' 1981 LP *Africa, Center of The World.* Ayers departed Polydor after 1982's *Feeling Good,* which contained the single "Turn Me Loose," formed the company Uno Melodic Records and worked with Bobby Humphrey, Eighties Ladies, and Sylvia Striplin. He co-wrote "Turned on to You" with

Edwin Birdsong for Eighties Ladies and produced "Give Me Your Love" for Striplin, as well as recording and issuing his own *Lots of Love* LP for Uno Melodic. Ayers signed with Columbia in 1984 and landed one Top-20 R&B single in 1986, "Hot," while cutting a number of LPs. He began recording with Ichiban in 1989. Ayers has also returned to jazz: He recorded a live LP at Ronnie Scott's in 1991 and did a guest stint on the hip-hop/jazz release *Jazzamatazz* in 1993. The session was produced by Gang Starr's Guru, and Ayers has also made club appearances with Guru and Donald Byrd in New York. His LPs with Ubiquity are being reissued. — *Ron Wynn*

● **Virgo Vibes** / Jan. 18, 1967–Mar. 6, 1967 / Atlantic ✦✦✦
Daddy's Back / Mar. 11, 1969–Mar. 12, 1969 / Atco ✦✦
Pop-soul & funk touches, but fine vibes solos. — *Ron Wynn*
Evolution: The Polydor Anthology / 1970 / Polydor/A&M ✦✦✦
Containing several first-rate cuts of funky soul jazz, *Evolution* captures many of the highlights from Roy Ayers' stint with Polydor Records during the '70s. — *Stephen Thomas Erlewine*

Albert Ayler

b. Jul. 13, 1936, Cleveland, OH, **d.** Nov. 5, 1970, New York, NY
Tenor Saxophone, Alto Saxophone / Free Jazz
One of the giants of free jazz, Albert Ayler was also one of the most controversial. His huge tone and wide vibrato were difficult to ignore and his 1966 group sounded like a runaway New Orleans brass band from 1910. It could be said of Ayler's music that he was so far advanced that he came in at jazz's beginning!

Unlike John Coltrane or Eric Dolphy, Albert Ayler was not a virtuoso who had come up through the bebop ranks. His first musical jobs were in R&B bands, including one led by Little Walter, although oddly enough he was nicknamed "Little Bird" in his early days because of a similarity in sound on alto to Charlie Parker! During his period in the Army (1958–61) he played in a service band and switched to tenor. Unable to find work in the U.S. after his discharge due to his uncompromising style, Ayler spent time in Sweden and Denmark during 1962–63, making his first recordings (which reveal a tone with roots in Sonny Rollins) and working a bit with Cecil Taylor. Ayler's prime period was during 1964–67. In 1964 he toured Europe with a quartet that included Don Cherry and that was generally quite free and emotional. The following year he had a new band with his brother Donald Ayler on trumpet and Charles Tyler, and the emphasis in his music began to change. Folk melodies (which had been utilized a bit with Cherry) had a more dominant role, as did collective improvisation and yet, despite the use of spaced-out marches, Irish jigs and brass-band fanfares, tonally Ayler remained quite free. His ESP recordings from this era and his first couple of Impulses find Ayler at his peak and were influential; John Coltrane's post-1964 playing was definitely affected by Ayler's innovations. However during his last couple of years Albert Ayler's career seemed to become a bit aimless and his final Impulse! sessions, although experimental (with the use of vocals, rock guitar and R&Bish tunes), were at best mixed successes. A 1970 live concert that was documented features him back in top form, but in November 1970 Ayler was found drowned in New York's East River under mysterious circumstances. — *Scott Yanow*

Albert Ayler: The First Recordings, Vol. 1 / Oct. 25, 1962 / GNP Crescendo ✦✦
The problem with the trio recordings heard on this LP is that bassist Torbjorn Hultcrantz and drummer Sune Spangberg sound as if they are completely ignoring what tenor saxophonist Albert Ayler is playing. While Ayler improvises quite freely on a lengthy "I'll Remember April" and versions of "Rollins' Tune," "Tune Up" and his original "Free," Ayler's sidemen just play conventionally, never reacting to the tenor's flights or any of his ideas. It is a pity, for the lack of interplay weighs down what could have been an innovative outing. The second half of this interesting but flawed session has been released on CD by the Japanese DIW label. — *Scott Yanow*

The Albert Ayler: The First Recordings, Vol. 2 / Oct. 25, 1962 / DIW ✦✦
This should have been a memorable and possibly innovative session since this CD reissue features the avant-garde tenor saxophonist Albert Ayler interpreting four standards ("Softly As in a Morning Sunrise," "I Didn't Know What Time It Was," "Moanin'" and "Good Bait"). Unfortunately, the Swedish sidemen (bassist Torbjorn Hultcrantz and drummer Sune Spangberg) completely ignore what Ayler is playing and just act as if they were backing

a conventional bop musician. The lack of communication between the musicians defeats this effort, although Ayler collectors will find the results quite interesting. —Scott Yanow

My Name Is Albert Ayler / Jan. 14, 1963 / Fantasy ◆◆◆
Albert Ayler's second recording has its moments of interest. The avant-garde tenorman is backed by a bop-based Swedish rhythm section (comprised of pianist Niels Bronsted, 16-year-old bassist Niels Pedersen and drummer Ronnie Gardiner) that swings behind his intense flights on four standards ("Bye Bye Blackbird," "Billie's Bounce," "Summertime" and "On Green Dolphin Street") and his tribute to Cecil Taylor "C.T." that is in reality a free improvisation. The musicianship of the backup group generally makes up for the lack of interaction with Ayler, while the tenor innovator gives hints of his original influence, Sonny Rollins. This hard-to-find LP (originally put out by Fantasy in their Debut series) will hopefully be reissued on CD someday in the OJC program. —Scott Yanow

Witches and Devils / Feb. 24, 1964 / Freedom ◆◆◆◆
This album was recorded the same day as a lyrical spiritual album, and on this session, tenor saxophonist Albert Ayler really lets his emotions loose. Teamed with primitive trumpeter Norman Howard, Henry Grimes and/or Earle Henderson on bass and drummer Sunny Murray, Ayler plays quite freely on his four originals, "Witches and Devils" (a dirge), "Spirits," the melodic "Holy Holy" and "Saints." The often-intense music (which has been reissued on CD) is not for everyone, and this is one of Ayler's more forbidding releases, but open-eared listeners will find these radical explorations quite colorful. —Scott Yanow

Goin' Home / Feb. 24, 1964 / Black Lion ◆◆◆
1964 was a busy year on records for avant-garde tenor Albert Ayler, and it began with this unusual set. Imagine hearing Ayler play "When the Saints Go Marching In"; did Wild Bill Davison ever record "Ghosts?" Assisted by pianist Call Cobbs, bassist Henry Grimes and drummer Sonny Murray, Ayler plays seven unlikely folk melodies including an overly emotional "Ol' Man River," "Swing Low, Sweet Chariot" and "Nobody Knows the Trouble I've Seen." The highpoint is a jubilant "Down by the Riverside" on which Ayler sounds surprisingly close to Rahsaan Roland Kirk both in tone and ideas. This CD reissue adds the two versions of "Riverside" plus a pair of other alternate takes to the original program and is certainly more accessible than most of Ayler's recordings. —Scott Yanow

Prophecy / Jun. 14, 1964 / ESP ◆◆◆
The first of Albert Ayler's ESP recordings (but one of the last to be released) is this live session with bassist Gary Peacock and drummer Sunny Murray. The tenor is heard on the earliest versions of his most famous theme "Ghosts" (two renditions are included) along with such melodies as "Spirits," "Wizard" and "Prophecy." Ayler alternated the simple march-like themes with wild and very free improvisations which owe little if anything to the bop tradition or even his contemporaries in the avant-garde. Ayler always had his own individual message and his ESP sessions find him in consistently explorative form. —Scott Yanow

Spiritual Unity / Jul. 10, 1964 / ESP ◆◆◆◆
Tenor saxophonist Albert Ayler seemed to burst on the scene in 1964, playing heated free-form solos that put an emphasis on emotion over melodic development. Ironically, many of his themes (particularly "Ghosts," which is heard twice on this brief set) were quite catchy, reminiscent of pre-1910 folk music, but his improvisations need an open mind for one to fully appreciate them. On this ESP date (reissued on CD but under a half-hour long), Ayler also performs "The Wizard" and "Spirits" with bassist Gary Peacock and drummer Sunny Murray. The intense music has not lost any of its fire through the decades. —Scott Yanow

New York Eye and Ear Control / Jul. 17, 1964 / ESP ◆◆◆
This is a very interesting set: music that was freely improvised and used as the soundtrack for the 34-minute short film New York Eye and Ear Control. Tenor saxophonist Albert Ayler leads the all-star sextet (which also includes trumpeter Don Cherry, altoist John Tchicai, trombonist Roswell Rudd, bassist Gary Peacock and drummer Sunny Murray) on two lengthy jams. The music is fiery but with enough colorful moments to hold one's interest throughout. —Scott Yanow

Vibrations / Sep. 14, 1964 / Freedom ◆◆◆◆
1964 was a busy year for Albert Ayler, who recorded at least seven albums' worth of material. This particular session, a quartet date

with trumpeter Don Cherry, bassist Gary Peacock and drummer Sunny Murray, was probably his most significant of the period. Switching between tenor and alto, Ayler is often ferocious on the six performances, jumping from simple melodies (of which "Ghosts" is the most memorable) to intense sound explorations overflowing with emotion; he even makes Cherry seem conservative. It helps greatly to have open ears to appreciate this music, although Ayler's jams would become a bit more accessible the following year. Recommended. —Scott Yanow

The Hilversum Session / Nov. 9, 1964 / Osmosis ◆◆
The first part of Albert Ayler's career found the tenor saxophonist playing rather violent solos and searching for the right sidemen to interact with. This set (recorded in the Netherlands) features Ayler with a fairly ideal group: a quartet with cornetist Don Cherry, bassist Gary Peacock and drummer Sunny Murray. Together they perform five of Ayler's themes (including "Ghosts") along with Cherry's "Infant Hapiness." It's not for the faint of heart. —Scott Yanow

Bells / May 1, 1965 / ESP ◆◆◆
Albert Ayler teamed up with his brother, trumpeter Donald Ayler, on this record for the first time, with the exception of one slightly earlier track issued on an Impulse! sampler. The concert performance with both Aylers, Charles Tyler on alto, bassist Lewis Worrell and drummer Sunny Murray is their entire 20-minute set from a Town Hall concert, and originally came out as a one-sided LP (with the flipside being blank). What is here is quite interesting, with some ferocious ensembles, military-like themes (most of the music is taken up by "Holy Ghost") and a couple of tenor solos from Albert. This music should have been combined with some other dates so the release would not be so ridiculously brief, but it's worth getting (if found at a budget price) anyway. —Scott Yanow

● **Spirits Rejoice** / Sep. 1965 / ESP ◆◆◆◆
Tenor saxophonist Albert Ayler's 1965 group (with trumpeter Donald Ayler, altoist Charles Tyler, both Henry Grimes and Gary Peacock on basses, drummer Sunny Murray and an appearance by Call Cobbs on harpsichord) is a fairly strong and sometimes riotous effort. As is often true of the ESP releases, the playing time is brief (32 minutes), but the quality of the free-form improvisations is high and the music is somewhat groundbreaking while always being stimulating. —Scott Yanow

At Slug's Saloon, Vol. 1 / May 1, 1966 / ESP ◆◆◆◆
One of two CDs that originated from the Albert Ayler Quintet's May Day 1966 appearance at Slug's in New York, this is the better of the pair, although Ayler fans will want both. The leader's tenor is both melodic and ferocious in spots and his group (with trumpeter Donald Ayler, violinist Michel Sampson, bassist Lewis Worrell and drummer Ronald Shannon Jackson was one of his finest. The adventurous performances of lengthy versions of "Truth Is Marching In," "Our Prayer" and "Bells" often sound a bit like a runaway turn-of-the-century marching band and, although the droning violin sometimes gets in the way, the spirit of this rambunctious and often-wild set is memorable. —Scott Yanow

At Slug's Saloon, Vol. 2 / May 1, 1966 / ESP ◆◆◆
The second of two CDs from the Albert Ayler Quintet's engagement at Slug's on May 1, 1966, has long versions of "Ghosts" (over 23 minutes) and "Initiation" performed by the tenor/leader, trumpeter Donald Ayler, violinist Michel Sampson, bassist Lewis Worrell and drummer Ronald Shannon Jackson. The music is both futuristic (with extroverted emotions expressed in free improvisations) and ancient (New Orleans marching band rhythms, group riffing and folkish melodies). Although Vol. 1 gets the edge, most avant-garde collectors will want both releases. —Scott Yanow

Live at Lorrach: Paris, 1966 / Nov. 7, 1966+Nov. 13, 1966 / Hat Art ◆◆◆◆◆
Originally released as a double LP (with the second half being a 45), this single CD finds tenor saxophonist Albert Ayler in top form in 1966. At the time, his music could be considered to have been so advanced that it came in at the beginning of jazz. The folk melodies and some of the ensembles sound very much like an out-of-control New Orleans brass band circa 1900, yet the individual improvisations are as explorative as any heard in free jazz. Ayler heads a quintet with his brother Donald on trumpet, violinist Michel Sampson (whose sawing often sets a drone effect), bassist William Folwell and drummer Beaver Harris. Together

they perform two versions of "Ghosts" and such group originals as "Bells," "Jesus," "Our Prayer," "Spirits," "Holy Ghost" and "Holy Family." Due to the accessible nature of some of the melodies, this is the perfect place for open-eared listeners unfamiliar with Albert Ayler's unique music to start. —*Scott Yanow*

In Greenwich Village / Dec. 18, 1966+Feb. 26, 1967 / Impulse! ✦✦✦

During 1967–69 avant-garde innovator Albert Ayler recorded a series of albums for Impulse! that started on a high level and gradually declined in quality. This LP, Ayler's first Impulse! set, was probably his best for that label. There are two selections apiece from a pair of live appearances, with Ayler having a rare outing on alto on the emotional "For John Coltrane" and the more violent "Change Has Come" while backed by cellist Joel Friedman, both Alan Silva and Bill Folwell on basses and drummer Beaver Harris. The other set (with trumpeter Donald Ayler, violinist Michel Sampson, Folwell and Henry Grimes on basses and Harris) has a strong contrast between the simple childlike melodies and the intense solos. However this LP (which was augmented later on by the two-LP set *The Village Concerts*) will be difficult to find. —*Scott Yanow*

Albert Ayler: The Village Concerts, Vol. 7 / 1967 / ABC/Impulse! ✦✦✦✦

On this two-LP set, the avant-garde innovator Albert Ayler is heard in top form. The tenor saxophonist, teamed with his brother trumpeter Donald Ayler, violinist Michel Sampson, two bassists, drummer Beaver Harris and sometimes cellist Joel Freedman, really stretches out on these often-melodic and occasionally violent improvisations. Ayler stretched free jazz to the breaking point, yet his use of simple melodies during this phase of his career, in conjunction with Donald Ayler's primitive trumpet, often recalled the sound of a very early New Orleans brass band. Sampson's violin does not really fit in and sounds a bit jarring, but otherwise this is one of Ayler's strongest recordings. —*Scott Yanow*

Love Cry / Aug. 31, 1967 / Impulse! ✦✦✦✦

The strongest of his Impulse! recordings (all of which are from the last part of his career), this set avoids the weak attempts at commercialism that plagued most of Ayler's other Impulse!s. The CD reissue, in addition to the eight original tracks (all but one under four minutes long and "Universal Indians" now restored to its unedited full length) also adds three additional tracks. Ayler's three vocals are a bit difficult to sit through, but his tenor and alto solos (along with those of trumpeter Donald Ayler) are worthwhile even if the use of Call Cobbs on harpsichord comes across as merely eccentric. —*Scott Yanow*

New Grass / Sep. 5, 1968+Sep. 6, 1968 / Impulse! ✦✦

This LP (which has not yet been reissued on CD) attempts to combine the avant-garde tenor of Albert Ayler with R&B and the results are quite a mess. Ayler himself sings a bit, over half of the selections feature an unidentified vocal group called The Soul Singers, and the use of a horn section on several tracks sounds very dated. There are a few moments of interest (particularly "New Ghosts," a remake of "Ghosts"), but in general, this attempt at commercialism flops. —*Scott Yanow*

The Last Album / Aug. 26, 1969 / Impulse! ✦✦

Despite the title, this was not Albert Ayler's final album. *Music Is the Healing Force* was recorded at the same sessions (although it came out first) and a concert from a year later was released on two albums. In any case this date is a bit infamous due to the R&Bish material and a few throwaway tracks. Albert Ayler, an important avant-garde tenor innovator, plays bagpipes (!) on a weird duet with the rock guitarist Henry Vestine, takes an odd vocal on "Desert Blood," backs Mary Maria's singing on "Again Comes the Rising of the Sun" and does what he can on a few passionate but weak instrumentals; Ayler sounds as if he has definitely lost his way. This album is of more interest for its novelty value and historical importance than it is musically. —*Scott Yanow*

Music Is the Healing Force of the Universe / Aug. 26, 1969–Aug. 29, 1969 / Impulse! ✦✦

At a peak of experimentation, Ayler used bagpipes, blues instrumentals, and vocals to expand his challenging sound and keep his music at the center of controversy. —*Myles Boisen*

Fondation Maeght Nights, Vol. 1 / Jul. 25, 1970–Jul. 27, 1970 / Jazz View ✦✦✦✦

A little over three months before he was found drowned, Ayler was caught performing in concert at the height of his powers. Unlike his Impulse! releases which often featured him trying to incorporate commercial elements into his music, the release from the European label Jazz View (the first of two CDs) allows Ayler to stretch out and "preach" in his emotional and unique style with just sparse backing (pianist Call Cobbs, bassist Steve Tintweiss and drummer Allen Blairman). This and the second volume would be Albert Ayler's final recordings and are quite memorable. —*Scott Yanow*

Fondation Maeght Nights, Vol. 2 / Jul. 27, 1970 / Jazz View ✦✦✦

While the avant-gardist's later Impulse! albums were erratic and half-hearted attempts at commercialism, his final recordings (two CDs recorded live in concert) feature him in peak form. Ayler, one of the most controversial of the free jazz players of the 1960s, has rarely sounded more viable or creative than on these special recordings. *Volume 2*, as with the first set, finds him stretching out on four of his free yet melodic originals. Both sets are recommended. —*Scott Yanow*

B

B Sharp Jazz Quartet

Group / Post-Bop

The B Sharp Quartet made a strong impression with their first two recordings for the MAMA Foundation label. Consisting of drummer Herb Graham, Jr., Randall Willis on reeds, pianist Eliot Douglass (later replaced by Rodney Lee) and bassist Reggie Carson, the L.A.-based group plays advanced hard bop that looks toward the avant-garde but always swings. One of the finest new jazz groups of the 1990s. —*Scott Yanow*

● **B Sharp Jazz Quartet** / 1994 / MAMA Foundation ✦✦✦✦

Mirage / Jun. 3, 1995–Jun. 4, 1995 / MAMA Foundation ✦✦✦

The second recording by The B Sharp Jazz Quartet, one of the more creative regularly working jazz units based in Los Angeles, is as interesting for its departures as for the bulk of its performances. Three of the nine selections are a bit unusual. On "The Velvet Touch" guest singer Carmen Bradford vocalizes wordlessly and matches wits quite favorably with the tenor of Randall Willis. Joe Henderson's "Inner Urge" is given a light funk rhythm along with some atmospheric organ from Rodney Lee and, although it does not live up to its potential, it hints at possible innovations. Also the closing "C.R.S." has an African-flavored group vocal by the band along with Carmen Bradford. Otherwise the music is more conventional. Best are the driving "Beside Jo'Self," "Mirage" and Freddie Hubbard's "Intrepid Fox." In contrast "Spirit Of J.C." is a disappointment, lacking the passion one would expect from a song with its title. In general this is an excellent session even though some of the music sounds as if The B Sharp Quartet (which also includes drummer Herb Graham, Jr. and bassist Reggie Carson) is treading water a bit. —*Scott Yanow*

Harry Babasin

b. Apr. 19, 1921, Dallas, TX

Bass, Cello / Bop, Cool

Harry Babasin's main significance to jazz is that he was its first soloing cellist, predating Oscar Pettiford by a couple of years. After playing bass with territory bands in the Midwest, he spent 1945 with the orchestras of Gene Krupa, Boyd Raeburn and Charlie Garnet. Moving to the West Coast, Babasin worked again with Raeburn and with Benny Goodman (1946–47). In 1947 he first recorded on cello, taking jazz solos in a bop setting. In 1948 he was with Woody Herman and then became a busy studio musician in Los Angeles. Occasionally through the years Babasin would appear in a jazz setting, as when he formed his own label Nocturne and recorded his group in 1954. In 1956 he recorded on cello with his Jazzpickers and he was briefly with Harry James in 1959. —*Scott Yanow*

● **Harry Babasin and the Jazz Pickers** / Jul. 1957 / VSOP ✦✦✦✦

Harry Babasin was (along with Oscar Pettiford) probably the first bassist to play jazz cello. This LP reissue of a set originally for the MOD (Music of the Day) label features Babasin's Jazz Pickers (a quartet with guitarist Dempsey Wright, bassist Ben Tucker and drummer Bill Douglas) plus guest vibraphonist Terry Gibbs. The music (five Babasin originals and three veteran standards) swings hard but lightly with Babasin's cello solos being the date's most unusual feature. —*Scott Yanow*

Benny Bailey (Ernest Harold Bailey)

b. Aug. 13, 1925, Cleveland, OH

Trumpet / Bop, Hard Bop

A tremendous hard bop soloist and exciting trumpeter, Benny Bailey has resided in Europe since the '60s. His extensive range, dynamic sound and tone and often striking high note solos have been heard on many albums with European orchestras, all-star groups and combos. Bailey learned piano and flute as well as trumpet, studying at the Cleveland Conservatory of Music, and privately with George Russell. He worked in the early '40s with Bull Moose Jackson and Scatman Crothers, then toured with Jay McShann and played with Teddy Edwards. Bailey joined Dizzy Gillespie's big band in the late '40s, touring Europe with them. He was one of the principal soloists in Lionel Hampton's orchestra from 1948 to the mid-'50s, before he settled in Europe. Bailey played with Harry Arnold's band and recorded with Stan Getz in Sweden during the late '50s. He joined Quincy Jones' orchestra in 1959. Bailey returned to America briefly in 1960, then moved to Germany. He recorded with Eric Dolphy in 1961, and contributed many splendid solos to the huge hit album *Swiss Movement* with Eddie Harris and Les McCann in 1969. Bailey was a soloist with The Kenny Clarke-Francy Boland big band from the early '60s until 1973. He played with George Gruntz in the '70s, as well as various radio bands, before joining The Paris Reunion Band in 1986. They've frequently toured both America and Europe. Bailey has recorded for Candid, Enja, Ego and Jazzcraft among others. Some of his session mates have included Mal Waldron, Kenny Clarke, Sal Nistico, Charlie Rouse, Billy Hart, Richard Wyands, Sam Jones, Albert Dailey, Buster Williams and Keith Copeland. —*Ron Wynn and Michael Erlewine*

● **Big Brass** / Nov. 25, 1960 / Candid ✦✦✦✦✦

Trumpeter Benny Bailey has had an on-and-off recording career and due to his longtime residency in Europe has been underrated through the years. This CD reissue of his Candid date is one of the highpoints of his career. Bailey is joined by an all-star septet including altoist Phil Woods, Julius Watkins on French horn and pianist Tommy Flanagan and the high-quality arrangements (some by Quincy Jones) give a lot of variety to this highly recommended set. —*Scott Yanow*

Grand Slam / Oct. 14, 1978 / Jazzcraft ✦✦✦✦

Trumpeter Benny Bailey teamed with veteran tenor saxophonist Charlie Rouse on this hard-blowing quintet date. The fresh material (two songs by Fritz Pauer who arranged the date, a pair from Bailey and one by Pepper Adams) inspires the soloists to play near their peak. With a fine rhythm section (pianist Richard Wyands, bassist Sam Jones and drummer Billy Hart) pushing the horns, this set is even better than expected. —*Scott Yanow*

While My Lady Sleeps / Apr. 1990 / Gemini ✦✦✦

Buster Bailey (William C. Bailey)

b. Jul. 19, 1902, Memphis, TN, d. Apr. 12, 1967, New York, NY

Clarinet, Saxophone / Big Band, Swing

Buster Bailey was a brilliant clarinetist who, although known for his smooth and quiet playing with John Kirby's Sextet, occasionally really cut loose with some wild solos (including on a recording called "Man with a Horn Goes Berserk!"). Expertly trained by the classical teacher Franz Schoepp (who also taught Benny Goodman), Bailey worked with W.C. Handy's band in 1917. He moved to Chicago in 1919 and was soon working with Erskine Tate and King Oliver's Creole Jazz Band. He gained some fame in 1924 when he joined Fletcher Henderson's Orchestra in New York. Bailey was with Henderson off and on during 1924–34 and 1936–37, also playing with Noble Sissle and the Mills Blue

Rhythm Band (1934–35). Next up was the cool-toned swing of John Kirby's Sextet (1937–46), a role he fit perfectly. With the end of the Kirby band, Bailey was mostly employed in Dixieland settings with Wilbur DeParis (1947–49), Big Chief Russell Moore (1952–53), Henry "Red" Allen (1950–51 and 1954–60), Wild Bill Davison (1961–63) and the Saints and Sinners (1963–65), finishing up with the Louis Armstrong All-Stars (1965–67). One of the most technically skilled of the clarinetists to emerge during the 1920s, Buster Bailey never modernized his style or became a leader, but he contributed his talents and occasional wit to a countless number of rewarding and important recordings. —*Scott Yanow*

All About Memphis / Feb. 13, 1958 / Felsted ✦✦✦✦
Buster Bailey was one of the top clarinetists to emerge during the 1920s but he led relatively few sessions throughout his long career. This LP features Bailey with a quartet (along with pianist Red Richards, bassist Gene Ramey and drummer Jimmie Crawford) and, with the horns of trumpeter Herman Autrey, trombonist Vic Dickenson and altoist Hilton Jefferson added, a septet. In addition to W.C. Handy tunes, the other five songs are Bailey originals that mix together swing and the flavor of New Orleans jazz. It's a fine outing for the classic clarinetist. —*Scott Yanow*

Derek Bailey

b. Jan. 29, 1932, Sheffield, England
Guitar / Free Jazz
British musician Derek Bailey is one of the world's foremost guitarists, as well as a distinct and unusual player. His arsenal of effects, splintering riffs, flailing lines and at times seemingly atonal music comes close to being the guitar equivalent of Cecil Taylor, minus the percussive elements. Rhythmic and harmonic patterns can be identified (occasionally) with some effort, but Bailey's a spontaneous improviser whose solos explode and evolve in a powerful, highly unpredictable fashion. Both his unaccompanied works and collaborations with Anthony Braxton and fellow European improvisers like Evan Parker are not designed for most tastes. Calling them non-commercial doesn't even address their uniqueness; outside of musicians and critics, it's hard to fathom many listeners who'd even want to sit through much of Bailey's music despite the fact he's an exceptional talent. But his work is quite different from anything one could hear elsewhere; it's sometimes abstract, other times lyrical, alternately acoustic and electric. Bailey's arsenal includes a 19-string guitar, ukelele and crackle-box. Bailey worked in the '50s and early '60s in theaters, dance halls and other settings all over Sheffield. He moved to London from Sheffield in 1966, and began playing free music with John Stevens, Parker, Paul Rutherford and others. He joined The Spontaneous Music Ensemble for a while before working for five years in Tony Oxley's sextet, where he began to attract international attention. Bailey formed a trio with Rutherford and Barry Guy in 1970, and started the Incus label with Oxley and Parker. He's been featured on over 50 albums since the late '60s, and Incus has also issued numerous recordings featuring Parker and many other European free musicians. Bailey led the group Company during the '70s, which played in Europe, Africa, North and South America and in Japan. He's done more solo dates in the '80s, while continuing to play in duos and small groups. He published a book on improvisation in 1980 in England that's been translated into several languages. Besides Braxton and his fellow English musicians, Bailey's played with Steve Lacy, Dave Holland, George Lewis and John Zorn, among others. His CDs can be located via mail order. —*Ron Wynn*

Improvisations for Cello and Guitar / Jan. 1971 / ECM ✦✦✦
Solo Guitar / Feb. 1971 / Incus ✦✦✦✦
Royal, Vol. 1 / Jul. 2, 1974 / Incus ✦✦✦
London Concert / Feb. 14, 1975 / Incus ✦✦✦
Diverso N. 2 / Sep. 16, 1975–Sep. 18, 1975 / Cramps ✦✦✦
Throughout his career, Derek Bailey has primarily been involved with atonal sound explorations on his guitar. This solo session (available as an Italian LP) features Bailey on 14 sketches getting a wide variety of noises and sounds out of his instrument. All but the most open-eared listeners will probably think of these performances as random noise, but there is a method to Derek Bailey's apparent madness. —*Scott Yanow*

Time / Apr. 23, 1979–Apr. 24, 1979 / Incus ✦✦✦
Dart Drug / Aug. 1981 / Incus ✦✦
● **Yankees** / 1982 / Celluloid ✦✦✦✦
Cyro / Oct. 1982 / Incus ✦✦
Han / Mar. 15, 1986–Mar. 22, 1986 / Incus ✦✦✦✦
Moments Précieux / Oct. 4, 1986 / Victo ✦✦
Wireforks / 1995 / Shanachie ✦✦✦✦

Mildred Bailey

b. Feb. 27, 1907, Tekoa, WA, **d.** Dec. 12, 1951, Pougakeepsie, WA
Vocals / Swing, Standards
Although her high-pitched childlike voice (which contrasted with her plump body) takes a bit of getting used to for some, Mildred Bailey was one of the finest jazz singers to emerge during the 1930s. She learned from her predecessors Ethel Waters, Bessie Smith and Connie Boswell, and had her own lightly swinging style. After singing locally, Bailey sent a demonstration record to Paul Whiteman in 1929; he immediately added her to his band. During her four years with Whiteman, Bailey mostly sang ballads and became identified with "Rockin' Chair" and "Georgia on My Mind." In 1933 she married Red Norvo and they eventually were known as "Mr. and Mrs. Swing." Mildred Bailey was famous and well-paid throughout the 1930s, appearing regularly on radio, recording some superb small-group jazz dates and featuring with Red Norvo's Orchestra during 1936–39. Unfortunately her insecurities about her appearance made her an erratic personality. Bailey's marriage ended in divorce in 1943, although she worked with Norvo on and off in the '40s. After 1945 her health faded and the singer died in 1951 when she was 44. Many of Mildred Bailey's records are currently available and she would probably be shocked to know that she is on a postage stamp! —*Scott Yanow*

Volume One / Oct. 5, 1929–Mar. 2, 1932 / TOM ✦✦✦
The first of two Mildred Bailey CDs from the TOM label contains 21 of the vocalist's first 23 recordings; the two bypassed selections are included on the second volume. The superior swing singer is mostly heard on ballads (some of which are a bit dated) with orchestras led by Eddie Lang ("What Kind O' Man Is You?"), Frankie Trumbauer ("I Like to Do Things for You"), Jimmie Noone, Glen Gray and Paul Whiteman in addition to her initial sessions as a leader; this release is accurately subtitled "Sweet Beginnings" and the jazz content is generally not all that high. Although there are fairly long liner notes (the same ones are used on both volumes), the personnel for these early recordings are not included. Despite that inexcusable omission, fans of Mildred Bailey should be delighted to have these interesting sides reissued; highlights include "Concentratin' on You," "Home," "All of Me" and her original version of "Georgia on My Mind." —*Scott Yanow*

● **Her Greatest Performances (1929–1946)** / Oct. 5, 1929–Oct. 1946 / Columbia ✦✦✦✦✦
This three-LP box set (which deserves to be reissued on CD) lives up to its name. Bailey was one of the top singers of the 1930s and this package, which features highlights from her career (mostly dating from 1933–39), shows why. She holds her own with a variety of all-star groups including such classic players as trumpeters Bunny Berigan, Buck Clayton, Charlie Shavers and Roy Eldridge (the latter is great on "I'm Nobody's Baby"), trombonist Tommy Dorsey, clarinetist Benny Goodman, altoist Johnny Hodges, tenors Coleman Hawkins and Chu Berry, pianists Teddy Wilson and Mary Lou Williams, and her husband, xylophonist Red Norvo. There are lots of gems on this definitive set. —*Scott Yanow*

The Rockin' Chair Lady / Sep. 15, 1931–Apr. 25, 1950 / Decca ✦✦✦✦
The superior swing singer is heard on 20 studio performances throughout this diverse CD that spans virtually her entire recording career. The best selections are the first four, a complete session from 1935 that has Bailey joined by an all-star quartet comprised of trumpeter Bunny Berigan, altoist Johnny Hodges, pianist Teddy Wilson and bassist Grachan Moncur. In addition she sings four ballads from 1931 with The Casa Loma Orchestra, accompanied on ten songs by The Delta Rhythm Boys, a quartet led by pianist Herman Chittison and by Harry Sosnick's octet in 1941–42. This interesting CD concludes with Mildred Bailey's final studio session, two numbers ("Cry, Cry, Cry" and "Blue Prelude") from 1950. Some of the material was formerly rare, making this an essential CD for swing collectors. —*Scott Yanow*

Volume 2 / Dec. 1, 1931–Feb. 2, 1934 / TOM ✦✦✦
The second of two CDs from the TOM ("The Old Masters") label
finishes the documentation of singer Mildred Bailey's earliest
recordings. Bailey is featured with Paul Whiteman, the Dorsey
Brothers Big Band, the Casa Loma Orchestra ("Heat Wave"), an
all-star group with Benny Goodman (and tenor-great Coleman
Hawkins) and on a few of her own sessions. Although the
emphasis is on ballads, the program generally holds on to one's
interest (despite a few songs with racist lyrics, notably
"Snowball") and the Goodman session (which is rounded off with
an instrumental version of "Georgia Jubilee") is a near-classic.
Other highlights include "I'll Never Be the Same," "Love Me
Tonight," a touching "There's a Cabin in the Pines" and Bailey's
earliest version of her future theme song "Rockin' Chair." —*Scott
Yanow*

Legendary V-Disc Series / 1940–1951 / Vintage Jazz Classics
✦✦✦✦
Mildred Bailey fans will find this to be a very interesting CD for
the talented swing singer is heard on some previously unavailable
V-Disc sessions from the war years (including a few false starts)
along with some radio appearances. There is a complete radio
show with her guests The Delta Rhythm Boys, four duets with
pianist Teddy Wilson, three selections with vibraphonist Red
Norvo's quintet, a few songs with either Paul Baron's studio
orchestra or the Ellis Larkins Trio, one number ("There'll Be a
Jubilee") with Benny Goodman's big band and two selections
("Lover, Come Back to Me" and "It's So Peaceful in the Country")
from a 1951 radio aircheck that ended up being her last recordings. Any listener who wonders why Mildred Bailey was awarded
her own postage stamp should be required to get this CD. —*Scott
Yanow*

Mildred Bailey Radio Show / Nov. 24, 1944–Jan. 1945 /
Sunbeam ✦✦✦
These radio performances, taken from three different shows, find
singer Mildred Bailey in particularly stirring form. While she
sticks mostly to ballads, there are also instrumentals featuring
trombonist Trummy Young, the Teddy Wilson Sextet and the Paul
Baron Orchestra; in addition Woody Herman drops by to sing a
blues. This hard-to-find LP is easily recommended to those who
can find it. —*Scott Yanow*

All Of Me / Dec. 1945 / Monmouth-Evergreen ✦✦✦
This difficult-to-find LP features Bailey singing 16 songs recorded
during 1945–47, when she was still in her prime. Some feature her
former husband, vibraphonist Red Norvo, while the selections on
Side Two include some of her most mature ballad statements.
Highpoints include "I've Got the World on a String," "I'm Glad
There Is You," "Me and the Blues" and the title cut. —*Scott Yanow*

Majestic Mildred Bailey / Mar. 5, 1946–Nov. 1947 / Savoy ✦✦✦
During 1946–47 Mildred Bailey recorded four sessions for the
Majestic record label; these late sides were among her finest
recordings. This Savoy LP reissues most of the music from these,
including bassist Neil Swainson and drummer Jerry Fuller). This
Montreal recording features four of Ballantyne's originals along
with the standard "You and the Night and the Music" and is a
strong example of modern straight-ahead jazz. It's well worth
picking up. —*Scott Yanow*

Chet Baker (Chesney Henry Baker)

b. Dec. 23, 1929, Yale, OK, **d.** May 13, 1988, Amsterdam,
Netherlands
Trumpet, Vocals / Cool
What a strange life Chet Baker had! A popular cool-toned trumpeter and a fragile singer whose charisma made up for his limited voice, with his good looks Baker probably could have been a
movie star. Instead he became a drug addict in the mid-'50s and
had an extremely erratic lifestyle with horrific episodes alternating with some wonderful musical moments.
Chet Baker certainly started out on top. After getting out of the
Army, he gigged with Charlie Parker on the West Coast in 1952
and then joined the Gerry Mulligan Quartet, a pianoless unit that
soon became among the most popular in jazz. After Mulligan was
jailed for his own drug problems, Baker (who had helped make
"My Funny Valentine" into a hit) formed a quartet with pianist
Russ Freeman. He began to win polls on both trumpet and vocals,
toured Europe in 1955 and seemed on his way to a lucrative
career. But by 1960 Baker was in an Italian jail and, although he
made a few worthy recordings in the '60s, by the end of the

decade his teeth had been knocked out after a botched drug deal
and he was out of music.
Against all odds Chet Baker made a gradual comeback in the
1970s. Although Baker recorded far too much during his final 15
years and his nomadic lifestyle (never kicking drugs and essentially wandering all over Europe) was unstable and his occasional vocals (always an acquired taste) were generally poor, his trumpet playing improved as the decade progressed. In fact despite
everything, Chet Baker was still in his musical prime when he fell
out of a second-story window (pushed or slipped?) to his death in
1988. He remains one of the great cult figures of jazz. —*Scott
Yanow*

Live at the Trade Winds / Mar. 24, 1952–Aug. 4, 1952 / Fresh
Sound ✦✦✦

Pacific Jazz Years / Oct. 15, 1952–Dec. 9, 1957 / Pacific Jazz ✦✦✦
This attractive four-CD box set gives one a good overview of
trumpeter Chet Baker's 1952–57 recordings, a period when he
became unexpectedly popular. Baker is heard on four numbers
with Gerry Mulligan, with his own quartet (which featured pianist
Russ Freeman), in quintets with either altoist Art Pepper or tenor
saxophonist Phil Urso and with larger groups that also include
altoist Herb Geller, valve trombonist Bob Brookmeyer, and altoist
Bud Shank among others. Perfect as an introduction for those just
beginning to appreciate Chet Baker, this set will also interest veteran collectors for, in addition to its attractive booklet, it contains
four previously unissued selections with Stan Getz (including a
17-minute version of "All the Things You Are") and four selections
from what was thought to be a long-lost session in which the
trumpeter is backed on some Bob Zieff arrangements by French
horn, bass clarinet, bassoon, cello and bass. —*Scott Yanow*

★ **Complete Pacific Jazz Studio Recordings of the Chet Baker
Quartet with Ross Freeman**/ Jul. 24, 1953–Nov. 6, 1956 /
Mosaic ✦✦✦✦✦
This essential four-LP box set features trumpeter Chet Baker lead-
ing his own group during the 1953–56 period (shortly after the
breakup of the Gerry Mulligan Quartet) with pianist Russ
Freeman, either Bob Whitlock, Carson Smith, Joe Mondragon,
Jimmy Bond or Leroy Vinnegar on bass and Bobby White, Larry
Bunker, Shelly Manne, Bob Neel, Peter Littman or Lawrence
Marable on drums. Baker is heard at his coolest (mostly before he
became influenced by Miles Davis); some of the later selections
also feature his first recorded vocals. Because the Mosaic box sets
are limited editions, they should be acquired as soon as possible.
—*Scott Yanow*

Witch Doctor / Sep. 13, 1953 / Contemporary ✦✦
This album features Baker sitting in at the legendary Lighthouse
with some of the top exponents of West Coast jazz. In addition to
Baker, the lineup is quite impressive: trumpeter Rolf Ericson, Bud
Shank on alto and baritone, Jimmy Guiffre and Bob Cooper alternating on tenors, either Russ Freeman or Claude Williamson on
piano, bassist Howard Rumsey and Max Roach or Shelly Manne
on drums. The recording quality of these live performances is so-
so but the music ("I'll Remember April", "Winter Wonderland" and
three originals) is full of spirit and excitement. —*Scott Yanow*

Grey December / Dec. 22, 1953–Feb. 28, 1955 / Pacific Jazz ✦✦✦✦
This excellent CD reissues two Chet Baker sessions. The trumpeter is heard in a septet from 1953 with tenor saxophonist Jack
Montrose (who contributed the arrangements), altoist Herb Geller,
baritonist Bob Gordon and p.ianist Russ Freeman, and backed by
strings on four vocal numbers from 1955. The latter cuts are passable but the former session (which is augmented by five alternate
takes, two being issued for the first time) is frequently superb,
West Coast jazz at its best. —*Scott Yanow*

Chet Baker with Strings / Dec. 30, 1953–Feb. 20, 1954 /
Columbia ✦✦✦
Trumpeter Chet Baker (who fortunately does not sing on this CD)
is heard backed by a string section on these generally enjoyable
selections from his early period. In addition to the strings, Zoot
Sims (and on some tracks altoist Bud Shank) sits in with Baker's
quartet, resulting in an enjoyable easy-listening set. —*Scott
Yanow*

The Best of Chet Baker Sings: Let's Get Lost / 1953–1956 /
Capitol/Pacific Jazz ✦✦✦
To much of the pop (as opposed to the jazz) audience, Chet Baker
was known not as an able cool jazz trumpeter, but as a romantic
balladeer. The two classifications were not mutually exclusive;

Baker's vocal numbers would also feature his trumpet playing, as well as fine instrumental support from West Coast cool jazzers. For those who prefer the vocal side of the Baker canon, this is an excellent compilation of his best vintage material in that mode. The 20 tracks draw from sessions covering the era when he was generally conceded to be at his vocal peak (1953-56), and are dominated by standards from the likes of Rodgers-Hart, Carmichael, Gershwin, and Kern. Baker's singing was white and naive in the best senses, with a quavering, uncertain earnestness that embodied a certain (safe) strain of mid-'50s bohemianism. That's the Chet we hear on this collection, which contains some of his most famous interpretations, including "My Funny Valentine," "Time After Time," "There Will Never Be Another You," and "Let's Get Lost." —*Richie Unterberger*

Boston / Mar. 16, 1954–Oct. 19, 1954 / Uptown ♦♦♦
Released for the first time in the early '90s, this CD consists of three radio broadcasts by the Chet Baker Quartet from the Storyville Club in Boston. In each case the trumpeter/leader is joined by pianist Russ Freeman, bassist Carson Smith and drummer Bob Neel. Baker, who takes a vocal on "Time After Time," is in excellent form performing his standard repertoire of the period. It's easily recommended to all Chet Baker fans. —*Scott Yanow*

● **Complete Pacific Jazz Live Recordings** / May 9, 1954–Oct. 1954 / Mosaic ♦♦♦♦♦
Chet Baker and his popular Quartet (pianist Russ Freeman, bassist Carson Smith and drummer Bob Neel) recorded live for Pacific Jazz on three different occasions in 1954. While their appearance at Ann Arbor was released, last than half of the music recorded in Los Angeles and none of the five selections cut in Santa Cruz, CA, were issued until this limited-edition four-LP box set was put out by Mosaic. Throughout this instrumental set Baker and Freeman are in their early peak form, showing that their variations of bop was not as cool as the stereotype of West Coast jazz might lead one to expect. Get this gem while you can. —*Scott Yanow*

Chet Baker Big Band / Sep. 9, 1954–Oct. 26, 1954 / Pacific Jazz ♦♦♦
Despite the title, only four of the 16 titles that comprise this CD are actually performed by a big band. Trumpeter Chet Baker is featured with an 11-piece group for those selections, plays in a nonet for six others and with a sextet for the remainder. The arrangements of Jimmy Heath, Jack Montrose, Johnny Mandel, Bill Holman, Christian Chevallier, Pierre Michelot and Phil Urso really bring out the best in Baker, making this a highly enjoyable and varied set. —*Scott Yanow*

Chet in Paris, Vol. 1 / Oct. 11, 1955–Oct. 25, 1955 / EmArcy ♦♦♦♦
The first of four CDs documenting Baker's first visit to Europe has nine selections on which the trumpeter is heard in a quartet with the ill-fated pianist Dick Twardzik and four other numbers with a fine French sextet. Baker shows that his "cool" style actually had plenty of fire. All of the sets in this valuable series contain rewarding music. —*Scott Yanow*

Chet in Paris, Vol. 2: Everything Happens to Me / Oct. 24, 1955–Nov. 28, 1955 / EmArcy ♦♦♦♦
The second in a four-CD series that documents his first trip to Europe has the studio sides from two separate sessions in which the trumpeter was teamed with French rhythm sections. The music (all but one are standards) finds Baker in top early form, making this cool-toned bop music well worth hearing. —*Scott Yanow*

Chet in Paris, Vol. 4: Alternate Takes / Oct. 25, 1955–Feb. 10, 1956 / EmArcy ♦♦♦
The final CD in this four-volume series features alternate versions of the many selections recorded by Chet Baker while in Europe for his first visit. Taken from four different sessions, he is heard with a quartet, a sextet and two different quintets (including one with the fine tenor saxophonist Bobby Jaspar). Each of these sets are essential for true Chet Baker fans. —*Scott Yanow*

Chet in Paris, Vol. 3: Cheryl / Dec. 26, 1955–Mar. 15, 1956 / EmArcy ♦♦♦♦
The third of four CDs in this valuable series continues the documentation of Baker's first trip to Europe with three interesting sessions. Baker is teamed with tenor saxophonist Bobby Jaspar and pianist Rene Urtreger for four selections, interacts with the tenor of Jean-Louis Chautemps and pianist Francy Boland on the next

four songs and is finally heard with a fine French octet. Throughout this entire series, the trumpeter is in fine form. —*Scott Yanow*

Chet Baker & Crew / 1956 / Pacific Jazz ♦♦♦
This CD brings back one of his lesser-known bands, the quintet with tenor saxophonist Phil Urso and pianist Bobby Timmons. Urso's cool tenor blended in perfectly with Baker's relaxed trumpet while Timmons' funky piano (which in three years would make him famous with Art Blakey and Cannonball Adderley) inspired the soloists. The fresh repertoire heard on this consistently enjoyable set contains many songs begging to be revived. —*Scott Yanow*

At the Forum Theater / Jul. 24, 1956–Jul. 26, 1956 / Fresh Sound ♦♦♦

The Route / Jul. 26, 1956 / Pacific Jazz ♦♦♦
One of two CDs that team Baker and altoist Art Pepper, this one also features tenor saxophonist and pianist Pete Jolly; all four players get their own showcases. The often-heated results make it obvious that there was no strict borderline between artists associated with West Coast jazz and hard bop ,for some of these performances burn. It's strange that both Baker and Pepper could play such consistent music while conducting chaotic lifestyles. —*Scott Yanow*

Playboys / Oct. 31, 1956 / Pacific Jazz ♦♦♦
This is the second CD (following *The Route*) to team trumpeter Chet Baker and altoist Art Pepper, two masterful players who had similar (and rather strange) life stories, with so many ups and downs as to be almost unbelievable. None of the chaos of their lives appears in the fine music they created. This sextet session (which has five Jimmy Heath compositions in addition to two originals from Pepper) also contains spots for excellent solos by tenor saxophonist Phil Urso and pianist Carl Perkins. —*Scott Yanow*

Reunion with Chet Baker / Dec. 3, 1957–Dec. 17, 1957 / EMI-Manhattan ♦♦♦♦
The Gerry Mulligan Quartet of 1952-53 was one of the best-loved jazz groups of the decade, and it made stars out of both the leader and trumpeter Chet Baker. Mulligan and Baker had very few reunions after 1953, but this particular CD from 1957 is an exception. Although not quite possessing the magic of the earlier group, the music is quite enjoyable and the interplay between the two horns is still special. With expert backup by bassist Henry Grimes and drummer Dave Bailey, these 13 selections (plus two new alternate takes) should please fans of both Mulligan and Baker. —*Scott Yanow*

Embraceable You / Dec. 9, 1957 / Pacific Jazz ♦♦
This is a ballad CD that puts the emphasis on Chet Baker's vulnerable vocals. Only one selection ("Trav'lin' Light") was previously released when this set came out in 1995, all of the songs (with the exception of the two versions of "Little Girl Blue") clock in around the three-minute mark and just six of the 13 tunes (five of which are instrumentals) have any of Baker's trumpet. Backed by guitarist David Wheat and bassist Ross Savakus, Baker largely sticks to the melodies (both instrumentally and vocally) with the main improvisations taking place in his phrasing rather than his notes. Although he was rarely in better voice than during this period, those listeners who think of Chet Baker as chiefly a trumpeter are advised to look elsewhere. —*Scott Yanow*

Chet Baker Sings It Could Happen to You / Aug. 1958 / Original Jazz Classics ♦♦
Baker's singing has always been an acquired taste. Completely untrained, his high voice sometimes sounded similar to Chris Connor's low tones, and his interpretations of innocent lyrics almost seem absurd when one considers his lifestyle. Still, it has its charm and remains popular among a select audience. This vocal-dominated session finds Baker (who is backed by trios led by pianist Kenny Drew) interpreting ten songs plus two that were only discovered in 1987. —*Scott Yanow*

Chet Baker in New York / Sep. 1958 / Original Jazz Classics ♦♦♦
West Coast cool (trumpeter Chet Baker) meets East Coast hard bop (tenor saxophonist Johnny Griffin, pianist Al Haig, bassist Paul Chambers and drummer Philly Joe Jones) on this fine straight-ahead reissue. Not too surprisingly the musicians have little difficulty finding common ground, with Baker clearly enjoying playing with the top-notch rhythm section; half of the six selec-

tions are actually quartet features. Not quite essential, this music can easily be enjoyed by fans of the era. — *Scott Yanow*

Chet Baker Introduces Johnny Pace / Sep. 1958 / Riverside ✦✦
One of the more obscure Chet Baker dates, this LP (which has since been reissued on CD in the OJC series) finds the trumpeter and a quintet that includes Herbie Mann on tenor and flute and pianist Bill Evans backing a young singer on his debut session. Johnny Pace, although he sounds fine on these superior standards, seems to have since disappeared and this is probably his only recording in a jazz setting. It's worth picking up. — *Scott Yanow*

Chet (The Lyrical Trumpet of Chet Baker) / Dec. 30, 1958–Jan. 19, 1959 / Original Jazz Classics ✦✦✦
The shifting personnel on this excellent CD finds Baker joined by such players as baritonist Pepper Adams, flutist Herbie Mann, pianist Bill Evans and guitarist Kenny Burrell. This reissue of an LP adds one selection ("Early Morning Mood") formerly only available on a sampler. Fine straight-ahead music comes from the tail-end of the West Coast jazz era. — *Scott Yanow*

Chet Baker Plays the Best of Lerner and Loewe / Jul. 21, 1959–Jul. 22, 1959 / Original Jazz Classics ✦✦✦
Chet Baker is featured on eight Lerner and Loewe tunes (including four from *My Fair Lady*) along with a frontline that includes flutist Herbie Mann, Zoot Sims on alto and tenor, and baritonist Pepper Adams. Although not up to the historical level of his slightly earlier Pacific Jazz dates, this Riverside date is a fine example of the modern mainstream jazz scene of 1959. — *Scott Yanow*

Chet Baker with Fifty Italian Strings / Oct. 1959 / Original Jazz Classics ✦✦
In 1959 while in Italy, Baker was showcased playing trumpet and (on five of the ten songs) singing a set of ballads while backed by a large string section. Fans will want this set but, due to the mundane string arrangements and the lack of variety, more general collectors should acquire his earlier jazz-oriented dates first. — *Scott Yanow*

● **The Italian Sessions** / Jan. 5, 1962 / RCA/Bluebird ✦✦✦✦
Throughout the 1950s Chet Baker gained fame as a quiet low-register trumpeter with a cool tone and a relaxed style. This CD therefore should be a major surprise to listeners who believe he was incapable of playing heated material or of utilizing the upper register of his horn. Assisted by a fine European sextet (including Bobby Jaspar on tenor and flute and guitarist Rene Thomas), Baker is heard in peak form throughout this memorable and frequently exciting bop date. — *Scott Yanow*

Baker's Holiday: Plays & Sings Billie Holiday / May 1965 / EmArcy ✦✦✦
This CD finds him effectively paying tribute to Billie Holiday with mellow trumpet solos and occasional vocals. Baker is backed by a full sax section and a four-piece rhythm section that includes pianist Hank Jones; Jimmy Mundy contributed the colorful arrangements. His performance of ten songs associated with Lady Day (most of which he had not recorded previously) is often exquisite. — *Scott Yanow*

Live at Pueblo, Colorado, 1966 / 1966 / Baker ✦✦
This CD features the trumpeter with his good friend tenor saxophonist Phil Urso and pianist Dave MacKay in a quintet performing live in his hometown. The playing is excellent but the recording quality is a bit disappointing, making this potentially valuable set (a straight-ahead session performed at a time when Baker's studio recordings were very commercial) of greatest interest to Chet Baker completists. — *Scott Yanow*

Albert's House / 1969 / Par ✦
In 1968 Baker had his teeth knocked out by a group of thugs. In 1969 he recorded this remarkably bad set of music. Of the dozen songs, 11 are forgettable melodies by Steve Allen. Baker, who sounds as if he is struggling to get any air at all out of his horn, rarely ventures out of the lower register or away from the themes. He sounds in sad shape, so why does this music repeatedly get reissued? — *Scott Yanow*

Blood, Chet & Tears / 1970 / Verve ✦

In Concert / 1974 / India Navigation ✦✦✦
The matchup of the cool-toned trumpeter Chet Baker with the advanced but equally mellow-toned altoist Lee Konitz (in a pianoless quartet with bassist Michael Moore and drummer Beaver Harris) was a very logical combination. This CD reissues the orig-

inal five-song LP program while adding three more selections from the same concert, all of them jazz standards. Baker and Konitz very much inspired each other on this frequently superb and exciting set. — *Scott Yanow*

She Was Too Good to Me / Jul. 19, 1974–Nov.. 1974/ Columbia ✦✦✦
Baker began his comeback after five years of musical inactivity with this excellent CTI date. Highlights include "Autumn Leaves," "Tangerine" and "With a Song in My Heart." Altoist Paul Desmond is a major asset on two songs and the occasional strings give variety to this fine session. — *Scott Yanow*

The Best Thing for You / Feb. 16, 1977–May 13, 1977 / A&M ✦✦✦
This CD features previously unissued material from the same sessions that resulted in *You Can't Go Home Again* and, if anything, the music is a touch better. While an alternate take of Don Sebesky's "El Morro" uses a larger group, the other five performances find Baker accompanied just by a rhythm section (pianist Kenny Barron, bassist Ron Carter, drummer Tony Williams and, on one song, guitarist Gene Bertoncini). As a special bonus, altoist Paul Desmond makes memorable appearances on three songs during what would be his final recording session. Throughout, Chet Baker shows that his playing during his much documented final period would be equal if not superior to his more acclaimed recordings of the 1950s. — *Scott Yanow*

Once upon a Summertime / Feb. 20, 1977 / Galaxy ✦✦✦
Artists House, a classy if short-lived label, released this attractive Chet Baker LP, a quintet date with tenor saxophonist Gregory Herbert, pianist Harold Danko, bassist Ron Carter and drummer Mel Lewis. The challenging material ("The Song Is You" is the only one of the five songs that is a standard) inspires the musicians to play creative solos. It is particularly interesting to hear Baker interpret the Wayne Shorter tune "ESP." This set has been reissued on CD in the OJC series. — *Scott Yanow*

Live at Nick's / Nov. 30, 1978 / Criss Cross ✦✦✦

Broken Wing / Dec. 28, 1978 / Inner City ✦✦
A 1978 Paris recording with Baker heading a group that includes Phil Markowitz and Jeff Brillinger. Baker at this point isn't doing anything spectacular, but often plays bright, warm solos. Far from his worst, but not essential with the wealth of Baker flooding the market. — *Ron Wynn*

Ballads for Two / Jan. 8, 1979–Jan. 9, 1979 / Sandra ✦✦✦

The Touch of Your Lips / Jun. 21, 1979 / SteepleChase ✦✦✦
This was the perfect setting during his later years. The trumpeter (who also sings on two of the six songs) sounds very relaxed and comfortable while accompanied by the duo of guitarist Doug Raney and bassist Niels Pedersen, taking some consistently lyrical solos on the six standards. — *Scott Yanow*

No Problem / Oct. 2, 1979 / SteepleChase ✦✦✦
Pianist Duke Jordan's presence adds some punch and spark to this quartet session, which is further helped along by bassist Niels Henning-Orsted Pedersen and selections that are suited for Baker's increasingly mellow and wavering playing. — *Ron Wynn*

Day Break / Oct. 4, 1979 / SteepleChase ✦✦✦
This follow-up to *The Touch of Your Lips* also has the trumpeter/vocalist joined by guitarist Doug Raney and bassist Niels Pedersen but differs in that the repertoire (Jimmy Heath's "For Minor's Only," Hoagy Carmichael's "Daybreak," Richard Beirach's "Broken Wing" and Miles Davis' "Down") avoids standards in favor of lesser-known pieces. Baker is in fine form, stretching out on these 6-to 11-minute performances. — *Scott Yanow*

Someday My Prince Will Come / Oct. 4, 1979 / SteepleChase ✦✦✦

Chet Baker with Wolfgang Lackerschmid / Nov. 1979 / Inakustik ✦✦✦
This was a record not so much of rhythm as of tonal coloring, pitch and reverberation. This was also an avant-garde Chet Baker, without gimmicks, just meeting an interest to expand and further develop: to invent, expand, create. This was also very beautiful creativity; art for art's sake. Wolfgang Lackerschmid played vibes in a manner owing itself more to Red Norvo and Gary Burton than Milt Jackson, and proved himself to be a creator and artist in his ebb and flow with the trumpeter. Bravos for both artists. — *Bob Rusch, Cadence*

And The Boto Brasilian Quartet / Jul. 21, 1980–Jul. 23, 1980 / Dreyfus ✦✦
Chet Baker is in lyrical form throughout this Dreyfus CD, per-

forming six of keyboardist Rique Pentoja's compositions plus two other obscure pieces. None of the laidback performances are all that memorable and Baker's vocal on "Forgetful" is forgettable. It is unusual to hear Baker joined by both an electric keyboardist and an accordion player, although Richard Galliano (who is on the latter instrument) is only heard from occasionally. The results are quite musical and not without their moments of charm, but fall very much into the easy-listening vein and are overly sleepy. — *Scott Yanow*

Live at Fat Tuesday's / Apr. 28, 1981 / Fresh Sound ✦✦✦

Peace / Feb. 2, 1982 / Enja ✦✦
This one is a bit unusual since the trumpeter is accompanied by David Friedman (on vibes and marimba), bassist Buster Williams and drummer Joe Chambers. The music (which includes two takes of "3+15") is somewhat challenging ("The Song Is You" is the only standard) and it inspires Baker to come up with some lyrical statements. There are many Chet Baker recordings from his final decade and his true fans will want to pick up this one. — *Scott Yanow*

Out of Nowhere / Dec. 24, 1982 / Milestone ✦✦
Baker made a rare appearance in his home state of Oklahoma for this live gig with a group of local players. The trumpeter (who sings "There Will Never Be Another You") is in good form on these jazz standards and the other musicians (which include Frank Adams on alto and flute and guitarist Frank Brown) are inspired by his presence. This posthumously issued set should satisfy Chet Baker's many fans. — *Scott Yanow*

Mr. B / May 25, 1983 / Timeless ✦✦✦
Baker recorded many albums (mostly in Europe) during his final decade and it is surprising how consistent his trumpet playing generally was (as opposed to his singing) despite a very hectic and disorganized life. This Timeless set finds him accompanied by pianist Michel Graillier and bassist Ricardo del Fra for a variety of modern material including "Beatrice" (although the liners state that it is Baker's original, this was actually composed by Sam Rivers), Horace Silver's "Strollin'" and Dave Brubeck's "In Your Own Sweet Way." — *Scott Yanow*

The Improviser / Aug. 15, 1983–Aug. 30, 1983 / Cadence ✦✦✦
Baker recorded this Cadence LP in Norway, backed by a pair of fine Norweigan trios that in both cases include pianist Per Husby. In addition to Sam Rivers' "Beatrice" (a song that the trumpeter recorded numerous times) and the standard "Polka Dots and Moonbeams," this fine set includes interpretations of two Hal Galper songs ("Margarine" and "Night Bird") and Tadd Dameron's lesser-known "Gnid." Although a little loose in spots, this is an excellent date by the colorful trumpeter. — *Scott Yanow*

Live in Sweden / Sep. 29, 1983 / Dragon ✦✦✦

At Capolinea / Oct. 1983 / Red ✦✦
For this Italian session, the trumpeter was joined by a flute-soprano-piano-bass-drums quintet of Italians. Although four of the six straight-ahead songs are group originals, Baker somehow sounds comfortable playing the new music, an impressive feat when one considers that he barely read music. It's not essential but enjoyable. — *Scott Yanow*

Blues for a Reason / Sep. 30, 1984 / Criss Cross ✦✦✦

Diane: Chet Baker and Paul Bley / Feb. 27, 1985 / SteepleChase ✦✦✦
On first glance this duet session between Chet Baker and pianist Paul Bley should not have worked. Bley is primarily interested in freer improvising while Baker loved playing melodies, but for this encounter the pianist compromised and laid down a fairly solid foundation for the veteran trumpeter. The results contain some chance-taking moments but sounds more comfortable than one might have expected. — *Scott Yanow*

Chet's Choice / Jun. 6, 1985–Jun. 25, 1985 / Criss Cross ✦✦✦✦
One of the best settings for trumpeter Chet Baker was when he was accompanied by a guitar bass duo. On this excellent Criss Cross CD, Baker is joined by guitarist Philip Catherine and bassist Jean-Louis Rassinfosse on a variety of high-quality standards that include such songs as "If I Should Lose You," Horace Silver's "Doodlin'," "Conception" and "Love for Sale." A special treat is hearing the talented but forgotten Bob Zieff's "Sad Walk." This is one of Baker's better albums from his later period. — *Scott Yanow*

Strollin' / Jun. 1985 / Enja ✦✦✦
Baker always sounded at his best when performing in a trio with

guitar and bass. Guitarist Philip Catherine and bassist Jean Louis Rassinfosse (both of whom had recorded with the trumpeter previously) are major assets to the subtle but swinging session. Each of the performances (Bob Zieff's "Sad Walk," Horace Silver's "Strollin'," "Love for Sale," "But Not for Me" and a 15-minute version of Richard Beirach's "Leaving") are extended versions, but there are no rambling or wandering moments during this set of lyrical jazz. — *Scott Yanow*

Symphonically / Jul. 6, 1985 / Soul Note ✦✦✦

When Sunny Gets Blue / Feb. 23, 1986 / SteepleChase ✦✦✦

The Legacy, Vol. 1 / Nov. 14, 1987 / Enja ✦✦✦
On first glance, this CD might be mistaken for the pair of Enja releases titled *The Last Great Concert*, which took place April 28, 1988. A few of the songs are the same and in both cases Baker was accompanied by the German NDR Big Band, but this particular set is taken from a previously unreleased concert from five months earlier and should delight his followers. Although Baker's singing voice had greatly declined through the years, his trumpet playing experienced a renaissance starting in the late '70s and he is in fine form throughout this purely instrumental set, a rare opportunity for the trumpeter to be showcased with a big band. Altoist Herb Geller and pianist Walter Norris (two of Baker's old friends) have occasional solos but the focus is almost entirely on Baker's horn and he proves up to the task, particularly on songs such as "In Your Own Sweet Way," "All of You" and "Look for the Silver Lining." — *Scott Yanow*

In Memory of / Mar. 13, 1988 / Optimism ✦✦

My Favourite Songs, Vols. 1 and 2: The Last Great Concert / Apr. 28, 1988 / Enja ✦✦✦✦
Despite a rough and-up-down life, Baker remained an excellent trumpeter to the end of his career. This concert, performed two weeks before his mysterious fall out of an Amsterdam hotel window (and his last known recording), is a near-perfect summation of his career. The emphasis is on his trumpet playing and Baker, whether backed by a symphony orchestra, a big band or playing in a small group with altoist Herb Geller, is in inspired form. This double-CD set is also available as two separate CDs and, in one form or another, is highly recommended. — *Scott Yanow*

Ginger Baker

b. London, England
Drums / Rock, Post-Bop
Although he made his fame and fortune playing rock with Cream, Ginger Baker rates inclusion in this book due to his brilliant Atlantic release *Going Back Home*, which finds him performing quite effectively in a trio with Bill Frisell and Charlie Haden. As with apparently many of the best late-'60s rock musicians, Baker had an early period when he played jazz; his experiences ranged from Dixieland and modern styles to Alexis Korner's Blues Incorporated. One could argue that Cream, with its long improvised solos and Eric Clapton's blues playing, was closely related to jazz. In the late '80s Baker investigated world music, and then in 1994 came *Going Back Home*. One hopes that he will continue exploring jazz in the future! — *Scott Yanow*

● **Going Back Home** / 1994 / Atlantic ✦✦✦✦

Shorty Baker (Harold J. Baker)

b. May 26, 1914, St. Louis, MO, **d.** Nov. 8, 1966, New York, NY
Trumpet / Swing
Harold "Shorty" Baker had a mellow sound and a lyrical style that was the modern successor to Arthur Whetsol in the Duke Ellington Orchestra. Originally a drummer, Baker switched to trumpet as a teenager. A fine section player and a warm soloist, Baker played with Fate Marable on riverboats, Erskine Tate, Don Redman (1936–38), Teddy Wilson's Orchestra (1939–1940) and Andy Kirk (1940–42). He married Mary Lou Williams (Kirk's pianist at the time). Baker was with Duke Ellington's Orchestra off and on during 1942–62 (particularly 1943–51 and 1957–59), during which he was well-featured despite being in a trumpet section that at times also included Ray Nance, Clark Terry, Taft Jordan, Willie Cook and Cat Anderson among others. He was with Johnny Hodges' group in the early '50s and after the Ellington years primarily led a quartet. Baker also recorded in later years with Bud Freeman and Doc Cheatham. — *Scott Yanow*

Shorty & Doc / Jan. 17, 1961 / Original Jazz Classics ✦✦✦
This CD reissue brings back a rare Swingville session that match-

es together the trumpets of Harold "Shorty" Baker and Doc Cheatham. At the time Baker, a veteran of Duke Ellington's Orchestra, was much better-known and his soft tone and lyrical style often takes honors on this blowing date with pianist Walter Bishop, Jr., bassist Wendell Marshall and drummer J.C. Heard. For Doc Cheatham, then 55 and (unknown to everyone) only at the halfway mark of his career, this was just his second opportunity to lead a record date, 11 years after an obscure session in France. The results of this meeting are generally quite friendly rather than combative with Cheatham's Dixielandish phrasing sounding slightly old-fashioned next to Baker. They perform appealing swing-oriented material and sound fine in their many tradeoffs. —*Scott Yanow*

Burt Bales

b. Apr. 20, 1916, Stevensville, MO, **d.** Oct. 26, 1989, San Francisco, CA
Piano / Ragtime, Stride
Although well established as a pianist, Burt Bales was also quite effective on mellophone and baritone horn. He loved ragtime and early jazz styles, but added his own flavor and distinctiveness with his "rocking" style. Bales started with dance bands in the '30s, but then responded to the '40s "traditional" New Orleans jazz revival in the Bay Area. He played and recorded with Bunk Johnson during his heralded 1944 appearance in San Francisco, and led his own bands during the mid-'40s. Bales also worked with Lu Watters, Turk Murphy, Bob Scobey and Marty Marsala in the '40s and '50s. He recorded with Murphy, Scobey, and Marsala as a leader from the late '40s until the mid-'50s. Bales recorded as a soloist for Good Time Jazz in 1949 and 1955, and played at San Francisco clubs from 1954–1966, and from 1975 into the '80s. —*Ron Wynn and Bruce Boyd Raeburn*

After Hours Piano / Oct. 22, 1949 / Good Time Jazz ✦✦✦
● **They Tore My Playhouse Down** / Oct. 22, 1949–Feb. 11, 1952 / Good Time Jazz ✦✦✦✦
Burt Bale's testament to Jelly Roll Morton has numbers such as "Wild Man Blues," "New Orleans Joys," and "Midnight Mama," backed with Paul Lingle's mixed bag of W.C. Handy and Morton's blues and stomps, including "Memphis Blues" and "Black Bottom Stomp" (1953). —*Bruce Raeburn*

New Orleans Ragtime / 1974 / Euphonic ✦✦✦
Burt Bales, a superior trad jazz pianist best known for his associations with Turk Murphy and Bob Scobey, did not record enough during his career. This Euphonic LP helped fill the gap a bit. The set of solos leans heavily on Jelly Roll Morton with some Scott Joplin and early jazz classics also included. Lovers of pre-bop piano will enjoy this hard-to-find album. —*Scott Yanow*

Kenny Ball

b. May 22, 1930, Ilford, Essex, England
Trumpet, Leader / Dixieland
Kenny Ball will always be associated with his huge 1961 hit "Midnight in Moscow," cut in the days when it was possible for a Dixieland song to make it in the charts. He started playing trumpet at 15 and gained experience playing in the bands of Charlie Galbraith, Eric Delaney and Sid Phillips. In 1958 he formed his own group and quickly became a leader in Britain's Trad Jazz movement. "I Love You Samantha" was his first hit and after "Midnight in Moscow" and "So Do I," Ball was set. He has remained active into the mid-'90s (touring the Soviet Union in 1985) and remains a household name in England. —*Scott Yanow*

Midnight in Moscow / Apr. 1961–Sep. 1961 / Kapp ✦✦✦✦
Kenny Ball's surprise hit of "Midnight in Moscow" in 1961 helped accelerate the trad jazz movement in England. Already a popular trumpeter, Ball's hit briefly made him an internationally known figure. This LP mostly has infectious versions of Dixieland standards featuring Ball, trombonist Johnny Bennett and clarinetist Dave Jones. —*Scott Yanow*

It's Trad / 1962 / Kapp ✦✦✦
Kenny Ball's follow-up album to *Midnight in Moscow* did not result in any new pop hits, but the results do contain a great deal of joyous Dixieland. Trumpeter Ball (who is also a fine singer) formed an excellent frontline with trombonist John Bennett and clarinetist Dave Jones, as can be heard on a diverse set highlighted by "Cornet Chop Suey," "Potato Head Blues," "I Shall Not Be Moved," "The Green Leaves of Summer" and a tune called "My Old Man Said Follow the Van!" —*Scott Yanow*

● **In Concert In The U.S.A., Vol. 1** / May 9, 1965 / Jazzology ✦✦✦✦
In 1965 English trad trumpeter Kenny Ball was still riding high from the unexpected success of his 1961 hit "Midnight in Moscow." This LP (the first of two) features a rather definitive concert showcasing all of the members of Ball's band on some of their favorite songs. Highly recommended to fans of Dixieland, this set features Kenny Ball at his best. —*Scott Yanow*

In Concert In The U.S.A., Vol. 2 / May 9, 1965 / Jazzology ✦✦✦✦
The second of two LPs taken from a 1965 concert holds its own with the first half, highlighted by versions of "Midnight in Moscow," "I Shall Not Be Moved" and "Tiger Rag." The popular Kenny Ball has long been a talented trumpeter and an enjoyable singer and his sidemen have always been quite musical. —*Scott Yanow*

Gabe Baltazar

b. Nov. 1, 1929, Hilo, HI
Alto Saxophone / Bop, Hard Bop
Gabe Baltazar was one of the last great graduates from the Stan Kenton Orchestra but, because he lives in Hawaii, he is greatly underrated. Baltazar moved to the mainland from Hawaii in the mid-'50s, recording with Paul Togawa in 1957 and spending a brief unrecorded period in 1960 with the Lighthouse All-Stars. He gained recognition for his years with Kenton (1960–65) during which he recorded quite a few rewarding solos. Baltazar worked with Terry Gibbs (1965) and recorded with Gil Fuller and Oliver Nelson before returning to Hawaii in 1969. In recent times he has visited California fairly often and recorded as a leader for the Fresh Sound and V.S.O.P. labels, showing the jazz world just how strong a soloist he is. —*Scott Yanow*

Stan Kenton Presents Gabe Baltazar / Jan. 9, 1979–Jan. 1979 / Creative World ✦✦✦
Gabe Baltazar was one of the last significant soloists to graduate from the Stan Kenton Orchestra. Because he has spent much of his career living in Hawaii and has recorded relatively little, he has been underrated for the past 30 years. This out-of-print LP, his debut as a leader, features Baltazar's alto in front of a big band with strings, playing a program mostly arranged by Don Menza. It is a good but not quite definitive showcase for Gabe Baltazar, one of the few he has had on record as a leader to date. —*Scott Yanow*

● **Back in Action** / Oct. 18, 1992–Oct. 1992 / VSOP ✦✦✦✦
Gabe Baltazar has long been one of the most underrated alto saxophonists in jazz. Because he long ago chose to live in Hawaii, his talents (which were earlier heard with the Stan Kenton Orchestra) have been overlooked but this V.S.O.P. CD signalled a higher profile on the mainland when it was released. Backed by pianist Tom Rainier, bassist Richard Simon and drummer Steve Houghton, Baltazar is in brilliant form, interpreting standards and blues in his bop-oriented style. His reshapings of "Is It True What They Say About Dixie?" and "The Birth of the Blues" are among the highpoints. —*Scott Yanow*

Birdology / Oct. 24, 1992–Oct. 25, 1992 / Fresh Sound ✦✦✦✦

Billy Bang

b. Sep. 20, 1947, Mobile, AL
Violin / Avant-Garde
One of the most stimulating, bluish and accessible violinists in the avant-garde, Billy Bang had a false start on his instrument as a youth and then became serious in 1968. Along the way he studied with Leroy Jenkins and by 1972 he was gigging. In 1977 Bang helped form the co-op group The String Trio of New York with guitarist James Emery and bassist John Lindberg, leaving in 1986. Bang, who has played with Ronald Shannon Jackson's Decoding Society and Material, has recorded frequently as a leader (including an intriguing Stuff Smith tribute set with Sun Ra in a quartet). —*Scott Yanow*

Changing Seasons / June 28, 1980 / Bellows ✦✦✦
This is a difficult record to find, out of print but worth looking for. The opening track, "Summer Night (With Crickets)," lays down an irresistibly funky groove—not in the fusion sense of the word, but in the acoustic sense. bassist William Parker and drummer Toshi Tsuchitori bring an almost Asian rhythmic influence to the setting, though this is strictly jazz. At 13 minutes, there is plenty of elbow room for everyone to stretch out in, and they do take advantage of that fact. The proceedings have an organic, woody

feel to them, as if they are playing deep within a forest. After the first track, things grow somewhat denser, and more complex. The closing "Winter Rains" brings everythng back down to earth. This particular group did not stay together long, which is a shame. There is the feeling that they are just beginning to become family. —*Scot Hacker*

Rainbow Gladiator / Jun. 10, 1981–Jun. 1981 / Soul Note ✦✦✦✦
Ever since his emergence in the late '70s, Billy Bang has been one of the top violinists in the jazz avant-garde (along with his predecessor Leroy Jenkins), a musician not shy to play either melodies or sound explorations. This set, his first as a leader, finds Bang holding his own with a strong cast of players including Charles Tyler on alto and baritone and pianist Michele Rosewoman. All six compositions are Bang's, making this a good introduction to his music for those who have an open mind toward adventurous jazz. —*Scott Yanow*

Invitation / Apr. 13, 1982–Apr. 14, 1982 / Soul Note ✦✦✦

Outline, No. 12 / Jul. 1982 / Celluloid ✦✦✦
Fine, animated, but tough-to-find album featuring violinist Billy Bang, arguably the most striking to emerge on the jazz scene since Leroy Jenkins. The songs on this set weren't gentle, demure or bluesy; they were explosive, searching, and combative and, as such, were ideal for Bang's sawing effects and sweeping solos. —*Ron Wynn*

The Fire from Within / Sep. 19, 1984–Sep. 29, 1984 / Soul Note ✦✦✦
Billy Bang, one of the top violinists of the avant-garde, combines a classical technique with a rough rural sound. On this release he performs seven of his diverse originals with a sextet that also features trumpeter Ahmed Abdullah, guitarist Oscar Sanders, Thurman Barker on marimbas, bassist William Parker and drummer John Betsch. The music is abstract but often melodic and more accessible than one might expect. —*Scott Yanow*

● **Live at Carlos 1** / Nov. 23, 1986 / Soul Note ✦✦✦✦
Violinist Billy Bang uses the same instrumentation on this set as on his previous *The Fire from Within,* although his sextet had two new members: trumpeter Roy Campbell and drummer Zen Matsuura. A more rhythmic album, this melodic avant-garde set rewards repeated listenings and has an impressive amount of variety. —*Scott Yanow*

Valve, No. 10 / Mar. 8, 1988–Mar. 9, 1988 / Soul Note ✦✦✦
This very intriguing set finds the adventurous jazz violinist Billy Bang leading a quartet that includes tenor saxophonist Frank Lowe, bassist Sirone and drummer Dennis Charles. The music is often quite melodic (particularly Lowe's relaxed solos) yet is utterly unpredictable. Bang combines a strong technique with a primitive sound and it may take listeners a little while to get used to his tone. —*Scott Yanow*

Tribute to Stuff Smith / Sep. 1992 / Soul Note ✦✦✦
The connections to the past are worth pointing out here: Sun Ra and violinist Stuff Smith once played together, back in 1953 or 1954. Bassist John Ore has also been a staple in Ra's bands, and Andrew Cyrille is no stranger to any of this crew. That said, those who like their violin "inside" will want to start their Bang collections with this recording: it is the least avant-garde of his oeuvre. For Sun Ra lovers, this recording will be important for being probably the very last thing he did before passing on to the interplanetary spaceways. The entire date is relaxed and highly structured. Like Smith, Bang plays here well within established boundaries, but still manages to place his notes somewhere just out of reach, in a place that's difficult to put a finger on, and all the more rewarding because of this enigma. —*Scot Hacker*

Paul Barbarin (Adolphe Paul Barbarin)

b. May 5, 1899, New Orleans, LA, **d.** Feb. 17, 1969, New Orleans, LA

Drums / New Orleans Jazz

A member of one of New Orleans' most renowned musical dynasties, Paul Barbarin developed his drumming style on the streets of the Crescent City playing with bands like Buddy Petit's Young Olympians while still a teenager. In 1917 he left home to find work in the stockyards of Chicago but soon found more conducive employment playing with transplanted homeboys like King Oliver and Jimmie Noone, as well as a number of Chicago outfits. Over the course of his career he maintained a strong association with New Orleans artists, working with Oliver's Dixie Syncopators

in the mid-'20s before joining Luis Russell's Orchestra in 1928, a move which afforded opportunities to play with Jelly Roll Morton and Louis Armstrong in the '30s. By 1939 Barbarin was back in New Orleans, but he returned to Chicago in 1942–1943 to join Henry "Red" Allen's Sextet and in the following year Sidney Bechet. After World War II he stayed in his hometown, performing with a variety of small combos and brass bands, including The Onward Brass Band (formed in 1960 and named after the original Onward, which his father Isidore had led at the turn of the century). In the last decade of his life he became affiliated with many of the musicians who worked at Preservation Hall, such as Sweet Emma Barrett, with whom he recorded. During this period he also made several recordings under his own leadership, for Atlantic, Nobility, and Southland. His death in 1969 occurred while he was leading The Onward for a street parade, ending his career as he first began it.

As a drummer, Paul Barbarin excelled in the simple, straightforward approach which is associated with New Orleans, reflecting the parade beats which pervade the city's festival traditions. His forte was the press roll, and he required no more than a basic kit of snare, bass drum, tom tom, and wood block to get his message across. Cymbals were used primarily to accent the upbeat on "out choruses," and he almost never engaged in extended drum solos. His approach, like that of Warren "Baby" Dodds, was to play for the band, to provide just enough swing and lift to hold the band together and inspire the front-line soloists. For players like Barbarin, less was always more. In addition to his contributions as a "rhythm man," he was also known for several of his musical compositions, particularly "Bourbon Street Parade" and "The Second Line," which have become standards among New Orleans jazz bands, both on the street and in the dance halls. —*Bruce Boyd Raeburn*

Paul Barbarin and Percy Humphrey / 1951 / Storyville ✦✦✦
The first of ten volumes put out by the Storyville label (all of which consist of live performances of New Orleans jazz bands from the early to mid-'50s), this CD has excellent performances from drummer Paul Barbarin's group (which features trumpeter Ernie Cagnolatti, clarinetist Albert Burbank and trombonist Eddie Pierson) and a decent outing from what was billed as "Percy Humphrey's Jam Session" (with solo space divided between the trumpeter-leader, clarinetist Raymond Burke, trombonist Joe Avery and pianist Sweet Emma Barrett). New Orleans jazz fans will want to acquire the entire series, which has more than its share of spirited and fun music. —*Scott Yanow*

New Orleans Jamboree / Dec. 1954 / Jazztone ✦✦✦✦
This hard-to-find LP showcases drummer Paul Barbarin's excellent New Orleans jazz group of the 1950s, a band featuring trumpeter John Brunious, trombonist Bobby Thomas, clarinetist Willie Humphrey and Danny Barker on banjo. They romp on such tunes as "Gettysburg March," "Tiger Rag," "L'il Liza Jane" and "The Second Line," not to mention "The Saints." This set is long overdue to be reissued. —*Scott Yanow*

● **And His New Orleans Jazz** / Jan. 7, 1955 / Atlantic ✦✦✦✦✦
Drummer Paul Barbarin (a fine composer whose "Bourbon Street Parade" is included on this set) always had New Orleans bands that played in tune, knew how to solo and could jam coherent and often exciting ensembles. This Atlantic release features his 1955 septet (with trumpeter John Brunious, clarinetist Willie Humphreys, trombonist Bob Thomas, pianist Lester Santiago, Danny Barker on banjo and guest bassist Milt Hinton) playing a variety of traditional and ancient themes. These performances, ranging from three to nine minutes, find the band really stretching out and creating memorable and easily enjoyable music. —*Scott Yanow*

Paul Barbarin and Punch Miller / Jul. 5, 1962 / Atlantic ✦✦✦
Recorded with Punch Miller, this album offers a mixed bag featuring Paul Barbarin's Band/Punch Miller's Bunch & George Lewis (cl). It's worth acquiring for the Barbarin composition "The Second Line" alone, but offers much more. —*Bruce Raeburn*

Chris Barber

b. Apr. 17, 1930, Welwyn Garden City, Hertfordshire, England
Trombone / Dixieland

One of the leaders of England's early-'60s trad jazz movement, Chris Barber (a solid trombonist) has been leading his own bands since 1948. In 1954 trumpeter Pat Halcox joined Barber and with the later additions of clarinetist Monty Sunshine, banjoist/singer

Lonnie Donegan and blues singer Ottilie Patterson, Barber had an all-star crew. Sunshine's hit version of "Petite Fleur" made both Barber and the clarinetist into big names. Although his group was based in Dixieland, Barber has long been open-minded toward ragtime, swing, mainstream, blues, R&B and rock. He has collaborated with many artists including Louis Jordan, Russell Procope, Wild Bill Davis and Dr. John and has toured the U.S. several times since 1959. — *Scott Yanow*

Petite Fleur / Apr. 12, 1953–Sep. 12, 1957 / Hallmark ✦✦✦
This long out-of-print LP gives one a good overview of trombonist Chris Barber's recordings of the mid-'50s. His English trad band had an unexpected hit with their version of Sidney Bechet's "Petite Fleur," a feature for clarinetist Monty Sunshine. That recording is included on this LP along with hot versions of a variety of well-known (such as "The Saints" and "Sweet Georgia Brown") and obscure (including "Olga" and "Thriller Rag") tunes from the 1920s. Pat Halcox's trumpet solos and Ottilie Patterson's vocals are major assets. — *Scott Yanow*

In Budapest / Jul. 7, 1962 / Storyville ✦✦✦✦
The 1962 Chris Barber English trad band (featuring trumpeter Pat Halcox, Ian Wheeler on clarinet and alto, and singer Ottilie Patterson) shows a lot of versatility on this CD, playing everything from Duke Ellington's "Mood Indigo" and Ruth Brown's "Mama, He Treats Your Daughter Mean" to the ancient "Whistling Rufus" and a spirited "Ice Cream." It's a happy set of Dixieland and blues. — *Scott Yanow*

Live in East Berlin / Nov. 26, 1968 / Black Lion ✦✦✦✦
This CD features the 1968 Chris Barber band playing music that ranges from English trad to early Duke Ellington and even some gospel numbers. The trombonist/leader, his longtime trumpeter Pat Halcox and John Crocker (on clarinet and alto) form a potent frontline for spirited renditions of such numbers as "Royal Garden Blues," "Saratoga Swing," "Wild Cat Blues" and Johnny Hodges' "Sweet as Bear Meat." — *Scott Yanow*

Take Me Back to New Orleans / Apr. 4, 1980–Apr. 9, 1980 / Black Lion ✦✦
Although Chris Barber gets first billing on this CD, singer/pianist Dr. John dominates much of the music, which attempts to depict several scenes in New Orleans including a funeral, a concert on Canal Street and visits to Bourbon Street and Basin Street. In general the music is merely routine and the jazz content is not as strong as one might hope. Chris Barber has recorded many better albums. — *Scott Yanow*

● **Copulatin Jazz** / 1993 / Great Southern ✦✦✦✦✦
The repertoire performed by Chris Barber's band on this CD may be full of warhorses but the hot Dixieland performances are full of such enthusiasm and high musicianship that this set is highly recommended. With trumpeter Pat Halcox and the reeds of John Crocker and Ian Wheeler joining trombonist Barber on the frontline, this band infuses such songs as "Down by the Riverside," "Swanee River," "My Old Kentucky Home" and even "The Saints" with new life. Dixieland fans should consider this CD to be essential for their collections. — *Scott Yanow*

Patricia Barber

b. Chicago, IL
Vocals, Piano / Post-Bop, Cabaret
Patricia Barber is a difficult performer to easily categorize. A singer with an unusual voice and a talented jazz pianist, Barber has sought to expand the repertoire that singers have today by not only taking obscurities from the pop world but writing her own material. A fixture at Chicago's Gold Star Sardine Bar since 1984 (switching in more recent years to the Green Mill), Barber is the daughter of a saxophonist who played with Glenn Miller (Floyd Barber). She studied classical piano, played saxophone in her high-school band and mostly stuck to classical while at the University of Iowa before switching permanently to jazz. She worked locally in Iowa, moved back to Chicago and formed a regular trio. Beginning in 1989 Barber started appearing regularly at the North Sea Jazz Festival. Thus far she has three recordings: 1989's *Split* (on her own Floyd Records), 1992's *A Distortion of Love* (on Antilles) and 1994's *Cafe Blue* for Premonition. — *Scott Yanow*

A Distortion of Love / Nov. 25, 1991–Nov. 29, 1991 / Antilles ✦✦✦
Interesting, if uneven, contemporary jazz vocal recording featur-

ing Barber backed by musicians such as Wolfgang Muthspiel, Marc Johnson, and Adam Nussbaum. This isn't a typical standards/blues/ballads date, although Barber does do "Summertime" and "You Stepped Out Of A Dream." But she also does suites, rock, and fusion, while the band behind her adds an array of sounds, textures and accompaniment. — *Ron Wynn*

● **Cafe Blue** / 1994 / Premonition ✦✦✦✦
Patricia Barber, who is both a fine keyboardist and an atmospheric singer, contributes roughly half of the material to her Premonition debut. Her dark voice and the generally esoteric program takes awhile to get used to (listeners will have to be patient) but after two or three listens this thought-provoking and rather moody set becomes more accessible. The music ranges stylewise from sophisticated pop sensitivities to the avant-garde and even touches of minimalism while not fitting securely into any category. Barber gives a new slant to "The Thrill Is Gone," "Ode to Billy Joe" and even "A Taste of Honey" and her vocals are all quite haunting and contemporary. An added plus to this unusual music is the adventurous guitarist John McLean. — *Scott Yanow*

Gato Barbieri (Leandro J. Barbieri)

b. Nov. 28, 1934, Rosario, Argentina
Tenor Saxophone / Avant-Garde, Latin Jazz, Pop
Gato Barbieri has enjoyed success in several contexts from the late '60s through the '90s. He's played free, jazz-rock, traditional South American, film and light pop material, and scored crossover hits in the '70s and '80s. His early work was heavily influenced by late '60s John Coltrane and Pharoah Sanders sessions; his tenor sax solos echoed their voice-like effects, with screams, overblowing and false fingering, honks and bleats, plus their accompaniments, which were based on long stretches of simple, repeating two-chord sequences in minor keys to support soaring, sustained-tone solo lines. He used a wide vibrato and would sometimes hum and blow at the same time, producing a high-pitched, wailing tone. Later Barbieri began playing in a more mellow, sentimental fashion on ballads while retaining the energy style on uptempo dates. He still sometimes utilizes the rising, upper register approach, but has exchanged his once fiery method for a more restrained approach on pop and fusion dates. A native of Argentina, Barbieri's family included several musicians, and he studied clarinet as a child. He moved to Buenos Aires in 1947, where he learned alto sax and made an early impact in Lalo Schifrin's band in 1953. Barbieri switched to tenor and formed his own quartet. He moved to Rome in the early '60s, and joined Don Cherry's group in Paris during 1963. He appeared on such fierce dates as *Complete Communion* on Blue Note in 1966 and recorded with Steve Lacy and Abdullah Ibrahim (then Dollar Brand). Barbieri combined free jazz and traditional South American rhythms. His late '60s album *The Third World* for Flying Dutchman won him his first widespread recognition, though earlier ESP dates introduced the formula. Barbieri's early '70s Flying Dutchman LPs included contributions from Stanley Clarke, John Abercrombie, Nana Vasconcelos and one live date pairing him with Oliver Nelson and Eddie "Cleanhead" Vinson. But the album that made Barbieri a genuine star was his Grammy-winning soundtrack for the film *Last Tango In Paris* in 1972. He changed directions in 1973, forming a band of South American musicians and recording several traditional Latin albums. *Chapter One: Latin America* inaugurated the series, and Barbieri's band was a popular college attraction in the early '70s. Barbieri appeared at various festivals through the '70s, among them Newport, Montreux and Bologna. During the '80s he had another smash with the LP *Caliente*. Barbieri essentially played pop and fusion while recording for A&M in the '80s. But in 1989 he returned to the traditional South American vein with *Gato . . . Para Los Amigos* for Bob Thiele's Signature label. He's continued working in the '90s, but hasn't enjoyed similiar exposure or popularity through '93. — *Ron Wynn*

In Search of Mystery / Mar. 15, 1967 / ESP ✦✦✦
Gato Barbieri's ESP album finds the Argentine tenor playing some ferocious solos on four of his originals. Joined by cellist Calo Scott, bassist Sirone and drummer Bobby Kapp, Barbieri is virtually the whole show, so this set is mainly interesting for listeners who enjoy the intense tone he had in his early days. — *Scott Yanow*

Obsession / May 1967–Jun. 1967 / Affinity ✦✦✦
Backed by bassist Jean-Francois Jenny Clark and drummer Aldo Romano on this LP, tenor saxophonist Gato Barbieri plays with

great intensity and fire during these lengthy performances (two versions of "Obsession" and "Michelle"; the latter has no relation to the Beatles tune). Barbieri's playing would become, if not more mellow,, much more melodic a few years later, but at this early stage he was in his avant-garde stage, playing with ferocious energy. —*Scott Yanow*

Confluence / Mar. 16, 1968 / Arista/Freedom ✦✦✦✦
In 1968 tenor saxophonist Gato Barbieri and pianist Abdullah Ibrahim (then known as Dollar Brand) recorded a surprisingly successful set of duets. Although their collaboration was unexpected (Barbieri at the time was mostly known for his intense solos and Brand for his melodic qualities), they seemed to bring out the best in each other, performing two originals apiece and finding a great deal of common ground. —*Scott Yanow*

El Pampero / Jun. 18, 1971 / RCA ✦✦✦
After making his initial reputation as a passionate avant-gardist in Europe, Gato Barbieri rediscovered his Third World roots in the early 1970s. *El Pampero* finds him at a transitional point in his career. Performing with a percussion-filled sextet live at the 1971 Montreux Jazz Festival, Barbieri's playing is as intense as previously but there is more of an emphasis on melody, particularly on his version of "Brasil." —*Scott Yanow*

Under Fire / 1971 / Flying Dutchman ✦✦✦

Last Tango in Paris / Nov. 20, 1972–Nov. 25, 1972 / United Artists ✦✦✦✦
An incredibly popular soundtrack, dreamy and lush. Still sounds great 20 years later. Grammy-winning, sensual soundtrack to the controversial film. —*Ron Wynn*

Chapter 1: Latin America / Apr. 18, 1973–Oct. 17, 1973 / MCA/Impulse! ✦✦✦✦
The four "Chapters" in this series found Gato Barbieri rediscovering his South American roots and displaying his intense tone in melodic settings where his energy would be better focused than it had been on his earlier avant-garde albums. Joined by a large group of Argentinian musicians, Barberi is in top form throughout this heated set, particularly on "Encunetros" and "India." Each of the "Chapters" is recommended, although *Chapter Three* is the only one currently available on CD. —*Scott Yanow*

Chapter 2: Two Hasta Siempre / Apr. 18, 1973–Oct. 17, 1973 / Impulse! ✦✦✦✦
As with *Chapter One*, this follow-up album features Gato Barbieri's fiery tenor playing strong melodies while joined by top Latin American musicians with an emphasis on percussionists. Barbieri was at his peak in the mid-'70s and this "Chapter" (along with the three others) is easily recommended as examples of him at his best. —*Scott Yanow*

The Third World Revisited / 1974 / Bluebird ✦✦✦
Tenor saxophonist Gato Barbieri is in particularly fine form on this release, stretching out on four selections which include "Yesterdays," "Carinoso" and a song simply titled "A John Coltrane Blues." Backed by a six-piece rhythm section that includes Jorge Dalto's keyboards and guitarist Paul Metzke, Barbieri is often exuberant on this spirited and emotional set. —*Scott Yanow*

● **Chapter 3: Viva Emiliano Zapata** / Jun. 25, 1974 / Impulse! ✦✦✦✦✦
On the third of four "Chapters," the intense tenor saxophonist Gato Barbieri is accompanied by a big band playing Chico O'Farrill arrangements. The charts really showcase Barbieri at his peak, performing four of his melodic originals, "Milonga Triste" and "What a Difference a Day Makes." This CD (a straight reissue of the original LP) is highly recommended. —*Scott Yanow*

Yesterday / 1974 / Flying Dutchman ✦✦✦

Chapter 4: Alive in New York / Feb. 20, 1975–Feb. 23, 1975 / ABC/Impulse! ✦✦✦✦
As with the first three "Chapters" in this series, this LP (which has not yet been reissued on CD) is easily recommended. Gato Barbieri was frequently heard at his best in the mid-'70s, featuring his very emotional tenor in melodic and highly rhythmic settings. This live set matches Barbieri with multi-instrumentalist Howard Johnson (who on this date plays the unusual triple of fluegelhorn, tuba and bass clarinet) and a strong rhythm section for four extended workouts. —*Scott Yanow*

Caliente / 1976 / A&M ✦✦✦

Ruby, Ruby / Feb. 1978 / A&M ✦✦✦
An overproduced, but at times hypnotic, release from Barbieri. He achieved success with *Caliente*, an album filled with lush, sentimental material, so he copied that formula for *Ruby, Ruby*. It didn't yield any big hit, but did get consistent airplay on Adult Contemporary stations. —*Ron Wynn*

Tropico / May 1978 / A&M ✦✦

Euphoria / Mar. 1979 / A&M ✦✦

Para Los Amigos!! / Jun. 1981 / Doctor Jazz ✦✦✦

Apasionado / Oct. 1982 / Doctor Jazz ✦✦✦
After his successes of the mid-'70s, Barbieri, on the heels of his hit "Last Tango in Paris," went the commercial route for awhile. This Doctor Jazz LP was one of his better recordings of the '80s, a spirited workout with a large Latin rhythm section during which he interprets six lesser-known tunes (four written by Gato) plus a remake of "Last Tango." —*Scott Yanow*

Eddie Barefield

b. Dec. 12, 1909, Scandia, IA, **d.** Jan. 3, 1991, New York, NY
Clarinet, Tenor Saxophone / Swing
A fine journeyman saxophonist and arranger, Eddie Barefield never gained much fame but he had a productive 60-year career. Barefield came to musical maturity in the 1930s, playing with Bernie Young (1930) in Chicago and then with Bennie Moten (1932), Zack Whyte (1933), the McKinney's Cotton Pickers (1933), Cab Calloway (1933–36), Les Hite (1937), Fletcher Henderson (1938) and Don Redman (1938). Barefield recorded with several orchestras, most notably Moten, Calloway and Henderson.

He supplied arrangements during the swing era to several top big bands (including Calloway, Glenn Miller, Benny Goodman and Jimmy Dorsey), was a staff musician for ABC in the 1940s and also was briefly with Benny Carter (1941), Ella Fitzgerald (1942) and Duke Ellington (1947). After playing with Fletcher Henderson's final band in 1950, Barefield mostly worked in the studios during the '50s and on Broadway in addition to returning now and then to Cab Calloway. He also played with Sammy Price (1958), Wilbur DeParis and the Saints and Sinners before joining the circus band of Ringling Brothers (1971–82). Barefield freelanced in many situations during his last two decades and recorded a fine 1977 album as a leader for Famous Door. —*Scott Yanow*

The Indestructible Eddie Barefield / 1977 / Famous Door ✦✦✦✦
A respected journeyman throughout his long career, Eddie Barefield led relatively few small-group sessions. For this rare outing, he teamed together the contrasting trumpets of Jon Faddis and Warren Vache in a septet with pianist John Bunch and guitarist Bucky Pizzarelli and performed six of his swinging originals. It's an unusual album well worth searching for. —*Scott Yanow*

Blue Lou Barker

b. Nov. 13, 1913, New Orleans, LA
Vocals / Swing / Blues
Blue Lu Barker was a reluctant singer with a limited range who had a huge hit with "Don't You Make Me High" in 1938. She married Danny Barker in 1930 (a marriage that lasted until his death in 1994) and made a series of popular recordings for Decca in the late '30s (all of which are currently available on a Classics CD). Because she disliked singing in public (although she felt more comfortable in the recording studio), Barker only performed on a rare basis after the 1940s. —*Scott Yanow*

1938–1939 / Aug. 11, 1938–Dec. 13, 1939 / Classics ✦✦✦
This is one of the lesser entries put out by the European Classics label. Blue Lou Barker was a so-so singer who had the novelty hit "Don't You Make Me High"; all 21 of her prewar recordings are included on this CD. The more memorable moments are provided by the sidemen, which include trumpeters Red Allen and Charlie Shavers, clarinetist Buster Bailey, tenor saxophonist Chu Berry and her husband, guitarist Danny Barker. —*Scott Yanow*

Danny Barker

b. Jan. 13, 1909, New Orleans, LA, **d.** Mar. 14, 1994, New Orleans, LA
Banjo, Guitar, Vocals / New Orleans Jazz, Swing
A humorous personality as important for his storytelling and teaching as for his playing, Danny Barker had a long and colorful career. He played with the Boozan Kings early on in New Orleans and toured Mississippi with Little Brother Montgomery. In 1930 he moved to New York, switching from banjo to guitar and work-

ing with Dave Nelson, Sidney Bechet, Fess Williams, Albert Nicholas, James P. Johnson, Lucky Millinder (1937-38), Benny Carter (1938) and Cab Calloway (1939-46). He wrote "Don't You Feel My Leg" for his wife Blue Lu Barker (with whom he recorded frequently) and also had a hit with "Save the Bones for Henry Jones" (recorded by Nat King Cole). By 1947 Barker was fully involved in the Dixieland revival (he never cared for bebop), appearing on the *This Is Jazz* radio series, recording with Bunk Johnson and returning to the banjo. He performed at Ryan's throughout the 1950s (often with Conrad Janis or Wilbur DeParis) and then returned to New Orleans in 1965 where he worked as the assistant curator of the New Orleans Jazz Museum (1965-75), led the Onward Brass Band, encouraged younger players and wrote about his experiences. Danny Barker, who appeared at the 1993 Monterey Jazz Festival with Milt Hinton, penned his memoirs (*A Life in Jazz*) in 1986 and was active in keeping New Orleans jazz alive up until to the end. His definitive recording is a solo set for Orleans; Barker can also be heard late in life on records by Wynton Marsalis and the Dirty Dozen Brass Band. — *Scott Yanow*

● **Save the Bones** / 1988 / Orleans ◆◆◆◆◆
Veteran guitarist Danny Barker made a countless number of sessions through a five-decade period as a sideman but only two full-length dates as a leader. This CD is quite definitive, for Barker is heard singing and playing guitar unaccompanied on a variety of ancient standards and obscurities. Barker's version of "St. James Infirmary" (which contains many of his own lyrics and asides) is classic. — *Scott Yanow*

Emile Barnes

b. Feb. 18, 1892, New Orleans, LA, **d.** Mar. 2, 1970, New Orleans, LA

Clarinet / New Orleans Jazz

A respected New Orleans clarinetist, Emile Barnes made relatively few recordings during his career but can be heard on sessions for Folkways in 1951 and 1952 (which were issued in the 1970s on LPs) and for Jazzology during 1961 and 1963. He was the brother of Polo Barnes and learned from the early clarinetists including Lorenzo Tio, Jr. and Alphonse Picou. Barnes worked with Buddy Petit and Chris Kelly (the latter throughout the 1920s). He spent much of the 1930s and '40s outside of music but by the late '40s was gigging with Kid Howard and he remained fairly active in the 1950s and '60s. — *Scott Yanow*

● **Early Recordings, Vol. 1** / Jul. 11, 1951 / Folkways ◆◆◆◆
During a period of time when there were not that many recordings being made in New Orleans, the legendary (and at that point unrecorded) clarinetist Emile Barnes was documented playing with a fine pickup group that also included trumpeter Lawrence Toca and trombonist Harrison Brazlee. On this LP, the first of two volumes, Barnes is in good form on ten standards (including two versions of "St. Louis Blues"), playing a style of New Orleans jazz rarely heard anymore. There are some rough moments from the other players but the spontaneity and joy of this music should win most New Orleans jazz fans over. — *Scott Yanow*

Early Recordings, Vol. 2 / Jul. 11, 1951–Sep. 8, 1952 / Folkways ◆◆◆
The second of two LPs documenting the earliest recordings of the legendary New Orleans clarinetist Emile Barnes contains six alternate takes from his 1951 sextet session with trumpeter Lawrence Toca and trombonist Harrison Brazlee heard in *Volume 1*, plus six selections from the following year that feature a quintet with Barnes and trumpeter Charlie Love. Even with some erratic moments from the band, these two sets are recommended to New Orleans jazz fans; Barnes in particular is in good form. — *Scott Yanow*

George Barnes

b. Jul. 17, 1921, South Chicago Heights, IL, **d.** Sep. 5, 1977, Concord, CA

Guitar / Swing

A pivotal guitarist, George Barnes actually recorded on electric before Charlie Christian, accompanying blues vocalists. He was a rarity among '30s players in that he developed his own single-string style and had a joyful, melodic approach that was influenced by saxophonists. Barnes designed his guitar to get the individualistic sound he desired. His great inflections and nuances broke fresh ground for the guitar, and influenced many in the '40s

generation who heard him on radio. Barnes made the instrument as important a lead weapon as saxophones or trumpets. His first dates were with blues singers Big Bill Broonzy, Blind John Davis and Washboard Sam. Barnes toured the Midwest with his quartet in the mid-'30s, then was an NBC staff musician in the late '30s and early '40s, and played with Bud Freeman. He joined ABC after an Army stint in the mid-'40s and early '50s. Barnes later signed an extended contract with Decca as a guitarist, composer and arranger in New York. He formed a duo with Carl Kress in the early '60s that toured nationally. They recorded with United Artists, but the duo ended when Kress died in 1965. Barnes teamed with Bucky Pizzarelli in the late '60s and early '70s, then worked with Ruby Braff in a quartet until 1975; he also played with Joe Venuti and teamed a final time with Freeman. — *Ron Wynn and Richard Lieberson*

The Uncollected: George Barnes and His Octet 1946 / 1946 / Hindsight ◆◆◆
George Barnes, a pioneering electric guitarist, was a very valuable studio musician during the 1940s and '50s. This Hindsight LP of previously unissued transcriptions made for radio has an unusual instrumentation. In addition to Barnes and a standard four-piece rhythm section (with drummer Frank Rullo doubling on vibes), there are four woodwind players utilizing clarinets, bass clarinets, an English horn, an oboe, flutes and a piccolo. Barnes is pretty much the only soloist on these 15 selections but his colorful and unpredictable arrangements give the other studio musicians plenty to do. The unusual set is quite enjoyable and somewhat unique. — *Scott Yanow*

Two Guitars / 1962 / Stash ◆◆◆
In the early '60s, the two great guitarists Carl Kress and George Barnes teamed up for a Town Hall concert and some rare recordings. This Stash LP finds Barnes playing single-note lines over Kress' sophisticated chordings. Their collaborations on this easily recommended set find the duo interpreting a variety of superior veteran standards along with Kress' "Golden Retriever Puppy Dog Blues" and an original by Barnes. — *Scott Yanow*

● **Two Guitars & A Horn** / 1962 / Stash ◆◆◆◆◆
On the follow-up to *Two Guitars*, the great guitarists George Barnes (who emphasizes single-note lines) and Carl Kress (whose chord voicings were unique) once again team up, this time for seven additional standards. The second side of this LP has the duo becoming a trio with the addition of tenor saxophonist Bud Freeman who contributes the colorfully titled originals "The Eel's Nephew" and "Disenchanted Trout." Timeless small-group swing music, it is well worth acquiring. Both of these sets should be reissued on CD. — *Scott Yanow*

Guitars Anyone / 1964 / Audiophile ◆◆◆
During 1962-65, George Barnes and Carl Kress often teamed up to play guitar duets although they made relatively few recordings. This Audiophile LP was their last meeting on records and it finds the pair in happy form on a dozen standards and their collaboration "Don't Be Nervous." Highlights of this enjoyable set include "Blue Moon," "Undecided" and "Tea for Two." — *Scott Yanow*

Swing Guitar / Aug. 3, 1972 / Famous Door ◆◆◆
This hard-to-find LP from the now-dormant Famous Door catalog features the great swing guitarist George Barnes in a pair of all-star quartets with either Dick Hyman or Hank Jones on piano, bassist Milt Hinton and drummer Jo Jones. A few traditional themes are mixed in with the swing standards and Barnes is in top form throughout. — *Scott Yanow*

Plays So Good / Apr. 17, 1977 / Concord Jazz ◆◆◆
Guitarist George Barnes' final recording is rather brief (32 minutes) but this LP (which contains fine versions of nine standards) has its enjoyable moments. Accompanied by rhythm guitarist Duncan James, bassist Dean Reilly and drummer Benny Barth, George Barnes shows that he never did decline. His hornlike lines are always a joy to hear. — *Scott Yanow*

Charlie Barnet

b. Oct. 26, 1913, New York, NY, **d.** Sep. 4, 1991

Tenor Saxophone, Leader / Swing

Charlie Barnet was unusual in several ways. One of the few jazzmen to be born a millionaire, Barnet was a bit of a playboy throughout his life, ending up with a countless number of ex-wives and anecdotes. He was one of the few White big band leaders of the swing era to openly embrace the music of Duke Ellington (he also greatly admired Count Basie), Barnet was a pioneer in leading integrated bands (as early as 1935) and, although chiefly a tenor saxophonist (where he developed an original sound out of the style of Coleman Hawkins), Barnet was an effective emulator of Johnny Hodges on alto in addition to being virtually the only soprano player (other than Sidney Bechet) in the 1930s and '40s.

And yet Charlie Barnet was only significant in jazz for about a decade (1939–49). Although his family wanted him to be a lawyer, he was a professional musician by the time he was 16 and ironically in his career made more money than he would have in business! Barnet arrived in New York in 1932 and started leading bands on records the following year but his career was quite erratic until 1939. Many of Barnet's early records are worthy but some are quite commercial as he attempted to find a niche. Best is a sideman appearance on a 1934 Red Norvo date that also includes Artie Shaw and Teddy Wilson.

In 1939, with the hit recording of his theme "Cherokee" and a very successful run at the Famous Door in New York, Charlie Barnet soon became a household name. In addition to the fine trumpeter Bobby Burnet (who soloed on many of Barnet's Bluebird records), such sidemen as guitarist Bus Etri, drummer Cliff Leeman, singers Lena Horne, Francis Wayne and Kay Starr, pianist Dodo Marmarosa, clarinetist Buddy DeFranco, guitarist Barney Kessel and even trumpeter Roy Eldridge spent time with Barnet's bands. Although at the height of his popularity during 1939–42 (when his orchestra could often play a close imitation of Ellington's), Barnet's recordings for Decca during 1942–46 were also of great interest with "Skyliner" being a best-seller.

By 1947 Barnet was starting to look toward bop. Clark Terry was his star trumpeter that year and in 1949 his screaming trumpet section included Maynard Ferguson, Doc Severinsen, Rolf Ericson and Ray Wetzel. Barnet however soon lost interest and near the end of 1949 he broke up his band. Semi-retired throughout the remainder of his life, Charlie Barnet occasionally led swing-oriented big bands during short tours and appearances, making his last recording in 1966. — *Scott Yanow*

Complete Charlie Barnet, Vol. 1 (1939–1942) / Jan. 21, 1935–Jan. 20, 1939 / Bluebird ♦♦♦
Charlie Barnet's entire output for Bluebird has been reissued on six two-LP sets. The first two-fer is actually the weakest for it finds Barnet during five sessions in 1936–37 searching for a sound of his own. There are a few hot swing numbers ("Growlin'," "Nagasaki," Benny Carter's arrangement of "Devil's Holiday" and a fine feature for the modernaires on "Make Believe Ballroom") but there is also an excess of sweet sides, erratic vocals (including eight by Barnet himself) and dull arrangements. It is not until the final two numbers on this set (both from early 1939) that the familiar Barnet sound emerges. Historically significant, Barnet collectors may want to acquire this initial volume last. — *Scott Yanow*

Complete Charlie Barnet, Vol. 2 / 1939 / Bluebird ♦♦♦♦
In 1939 Charlie Barnet, after several years of struggling and cutting a variety of erratic recordings, found his sound. His orchestra, featuring trumpeter Bobby Burnet and the leader's tenor, quickly became one of the better swing bands of the era. This second of six two-fers that reissue all of Barnet's Bluebird recordings has among its many highlights "Knockin' at the Famous Door," "The Gal from Joe's," "Jump Session," "Scotch and Soda," "Miss Annabelle Lee," "I Never Knew" and the band's big hit, "Cherokee." — *Scott Yanow*

Complete Charlie Barnet, Vol. 6 (1941–1942) / Jan. 20, 1939–Jan. 20, 1942 / Bluebird ♦♦♦
The sixth and final two-LP set in this very valuable Bluebird series has all of Charlie Barnet's recordings from Jan. 23, 1941 through Jan. 20, 1942, plus early alternate takes of two numbers from 1939. Barnet had one of the finest White swing bands and this set contains a few real gems, including three Duke Ellington numbers ("Merry Go Round," "Birmingham Breakdown" and "Harlem Speaks"). Not as essential as *Volumes 2–5*, this final set is still well worth picking up, especially by Charlie Barnet completists. — *Scott Yanow*

Complete Charlie Barnet, Vol. 3 / Jul. 17, 1939–Feb. 7, 1940 / Bluebird ♦♦♦♦
The third of six two-fers that reissue all of Charlie Barnet's Bluebird recordings finds the Duke Ellington-influenced orchestra

progressing into 1940. Bobby Burnet contributes many fine trumpet solos, Barnet is generally memorable on tenor, and even on the slower numbers the band always swings. With such hot performances as "The Last Jump," "The Duke's Idea," "The Count's Idea," "The Right Idea" and "Clap Hands Here Comes Charlie," the Charlie Barnet band shows that it could hold its own with its top contemporaries. And, with the inclusion of the hilarious "The Wrong Idea" (a satire of sweet bands with a remarkable vocal from Billy May), this set is essential for swing fans. — *Scott Yanow*

Complete Charlie Barnet, Vol. 4 (1940) / Feb. 27, 1940–Jun. 19, 1940 / Bluebird ♦♦♦♦
The fourth of six two-LP sets in this perfectly done reissue series contains all of the Charlie Barnet big-band's recordings from a busy four-month period. Highpoints include "Leapin' at the Lincoln," "Afternoon of a Moax," "Flying Home," "No Name Jive" and "Rockin' in Rhythm." The brief electric guitar solos of Bus Etri are quite interesting and, even if there are an excess of vocals, those of Mary Ann McCall are generally worth hearing. — *Scott Yanow*

Complete Charlie Barnet, Vol. 5 (1940–1941) / Jul. 15, 1940–Jan. 23, 1941 / Bluebird ♦♦♦♦
The fifth of six two-LP sets that reissue all of Charlie Barnet's Bluebird recordings from 1935–42 finds his "Cherokee" big band at its prime on such memorable numbers as "Pompton Turnpike," "Ring Dem Bells," "Southern Fried," "Redskin Rumba," "Charleston Alley" and "Little John Ordinary." With Bobby Burnet taking some fine trumpet solos, Bernie Privin impressive as lead trumpeter, the forgotten electric guitarist Bus Etri getting some spots and Barnet adding his distinctive voices on tenor, alto and soprano, this was one of the top swing bands of the era. All six volumes of this superb series are worth searching for, particularly *Vols. 2, 3* and *5*. — *Scott Yanow*

Best Of Charlie Barnet / Apr. 30, 1942–May 20, 1946 / ♦♦♦
This long out-of-print double LP (which lacks any liner notes) is not really "the best" of Charlie Barnet's recordings but some of his better ones for Decca. "Skyliner," "Drop Me Off in Harlem," and "The Great Lie" are among the highpoints. Most of this fine swing music has since been reissued on CD. — *Scott Yanow*

● **Drop Me off in Harlem** / Apr. 30, 1942–Jun. 16, 1946 / Decca ♦♦♦♦
Charlie Barnet reached his greatest popularity during his years with Bluebird (1939–42) but the orchestra he led during his period with Decca (1942–46) was even more powerful. This CD contains 20 of their best recordings and, even if "Skyliner" was their only commercial hit, such top soloists as trumpeters Peanuts Holland, Al Killian and Roy Eldridge, clarinetist Buddy DeFranco, pianists Dodo Marmarosa and Al Haig, guitarist Barney Kessel and singer Kay Starr (not to mention Barnet himself) make strong appearances on this well-conceived and hard-swinging set. — *Scott Yanow*

Charlie Barnet In Disco Order, Vol. 21 / Sep. 2, 1947–Mar. 1949 / Ajaz ♦♦♦
The collector's label reissued on LP in chronological order most of Charlie Barnet's studio recordings. The first 20 volumes cover the more familiar years but *Vol. 21* finds the big band making a quick transition from swing to bop. In addition to some remakes from 1947 that often feature the young Clark Terry, the orchestra is heard on their lone 1948 recording ("The Redskin Rhumba") and then playing some heated bop in 1949 including Gil Fuller's "Cuba," "Charlie's Other Aunt" and "Overtime." Since most of these relatively obscure recordings are rare (as are those in *Vol. 22*) and unlikely to be reissued on CD soon, this LP is essential for Charlie Barnet collectors. — *Scott Yanow*

Charlie Barnet In Disco Order, Vol. 22 / Mar. 17, 1949 / Ajaz ♦♦♦
The 22nd LP in the collector's label Joyce's Charlie Barnet series contains a great deal of valuable (and mostly rare) recordings. All but the final selection (a fine version of "Spain") dates from March–August 1949, a period when Charlie Barnet led a very spirited bop big band. The trumpet section featured Rolf Ericson, John Howell, Ray Wetzel, Doc Severinsen and Maynard Ferguson, and could really scream. This set has extended versions of "Portrait of Edward Kennedy Ellington" and "Rhapsody in Blue"; an arrangement of "All the Things You Are" (featuring Maynard Ferguson) that was so radical that the Jerome Kern estate succeeded in having the record withdrawn; modern charts by Manny

Albam, Pete Rugolo and Tiny Kahn ("Over the Rainbow"); and a showcase for the vocals of Dave Lambert and Buddy Stewart on "Bebop Spoken Here." This is an essential but hard-to-find release. When will Capitol get around to reissuing this valuable music on CD? —*Scott Yanow*

1949 / Jun. 22, 1949–Oct. 1949 / Alamac ✦✦✦
This budget LP features Charlie Barnet's 1949 bop big band, a short-lived unit that featured a screaming trumpet section (with Maynard Ferguson, Doc Severinson and Ray Wetzel), modern arrangements and hot solos from the likes of altoist Vinnie Dean, tenor saxophonist Dick Hafer, pianist Claude Williamson, bassist Eddie Safranski and Barnet himself on tenor, alto and soprano. These broadcasts increase the slim discography of this forgotten but talented band. —*Scott Yanow*

More / Sep. 3, 1958–Sep. 29, 1958 / Evidence ✦✦
This CD reissue brings back an Everest session that was one of Charlie Barnet's odder recordings. For this big-band set the distinctive swing tenor sticks exclusively to alto and soprano where his personality is much less unique. Actually, except for some moments from trumpeter Charlie Shavers, not much is memorable during these dozen performances which are mostly updates of swing hits. Bill Holman contributed the arrangements but his charts are much less interesting than usual and, although Phil Woods is in the sax section, the altoist does not have a single solo. Also, the sound quality on a few of the pieces (particularly "Evergreens") is a bit distorted. —*Scott Yanow*

Charlie Barnet Big Band: 1967 / Nov. 21, 1966 / Mobile Fidelity ✦✦✦
This LP was not only Charlie Barnet's final recording before he retired but is also the last album that veteran altoist Willie Smith ever made. With arrangements for the orchestra from Billy Byers and Bill Holman, solos by Barnet (on alto and soprano), Smith, pianist Jack Wilson and trumpeter Conte Candoli, and a fine Ruth Price vocal on "Something to Live For," this set wraps up Charlie Barnet's 32-year recording career quite nicely. —*Scott Yanow*

Joey Baron

b. June 26, 1955, Richmond, VA
Drums / Avant-Garde
Joey Baron is chiefly associated with the avant-garde but he is versatile enough to fit into a wide variety of jazz-oriented settings. He has had a longtime association with Bill Frisell, co-led a group with Tim Berne and Hank Roberts, led an unusual trio (Barondown) with trombonist Steve Swell and tenorman Ellery Eskelin, and recorded with John Zorn but was also quite comfortable supporting Jim Hall and Toots Thielemans. —*Scott Yanow*

● **Raised Pleasure Dot** / 1993 / New World ✦✦✦✦
Drummer Joey Baron has played with such unorthodox types as John Zorn, Wayne Horowitz and Tim Berne, so it's not surprising that his own sessions are equally diverse and ambitious. This date presents an unusual instrumental lineup and a free-wheeling, constantly changing musical menu. Baron heads a trio with trumpet and trombone; the absence of bass, keyboards, or guitar results in intriguing voicings, and the pieces are solely dependent on the interaction of his drumming with Ellery Eskelin's saxophone and Steve Sewell's trombone contributions. Elements of free jazz, contemporary funk, Afro-Latin, and even modern classical are incorporated into the mix, and it's an outstanding example of Joey Baron's scope and range as a composer, bandleader and player. —*Ron Wynn*

Tongue in Groove / Jun. 22, 1993 / PolyGram ✦✦✦
Joey Baron does the near-impossible on this CD, making music in a trio comprised of his drums, trombonist Steve Swell and tenor saxophonist Ellery Eskelin; no piano, guitar or bass! Some of the originals find the unusual group resembling a high school band a bit while other pieces are quite explorative and interesting. The fact that the spirited group sounds complete much of the time is particularly notable. —*Scott Yanow*

Dan Barrett

b. Dec. 14, 1955, Pasadena, CA
Trombone / Swing, Dixieland
A major player in the small-group swing movement of the 1980s and '90s, Dan Barrett's trombone is equally at home in Dixieland and swing settings. He started on trombone in high school and played in California with the South Frisco Jazz Band and the

Golden Eagle Jazz Band, two fine trad groups. At the urging of Howard Alden, Barrett moved to New York in 1983 where he worked with the Widespread Depression Orchestra, played at Eddie Condon's club and in 1985 was with Benny Goodman's Orchestra. Barrett came to fame through his series of recordings (both as a leader and as a sideman) with Concord; among his many projects were co-leading a quintet with Howard Alden that was reminiscent of John Kirby's band of the 1940s despite having very different instrumentation. Dan Barrett, who also played with Buck Clayton's Big Band, switched to the Arbors label in the 1990s where his became musical director and has recorded frequently. —*Scott Yanow*

● **Strictly Instrumental** / Jun. 1987 / Concord Jazz ✦✦✦✦
Trombonist Dan Barrett utilizes some of the top younger players of pre-bop in this delightful octet session. In addition to Barrett, the lineup includes cornetist Warren Vache, Ken Peplowski on clarinet and tenor, altoist Chuck Wilson, the late great pianist Dick Wellstood, guitarist Howard Alden, bassist Jack Lesberg and drummer Jackie Williams. Together they play a variety of high-quality standards including relative obscurities such as "No Regrets," Hoagy Carmichael's "Moon Country" and "There's Honey on the Moon Tonight." The concise solos and Barrett's clever arrangements make this a particularly memorable release. —*Scott Yanow*

Jubilesta / Dec. 3, 1991–Feb. 17, 1992 / Arbors ✦✦✦✦
Dan Barrett, probably the top young trombonist to be currently playing classic jazz, is very well featured on this quartet set with pianist Ray Sherman (himself in superior form), bassist David Stone and drummer Jake Hanna. Barrett revives such songs as "Why Can't You Behave?," "Then I'll Be Happy," "Wherever There's Love," "Wait 'Til You See 'Ma Cherie,'" and "Little Jazz," making one wonder why such attractive pieces are not performed more often. —*Scott Yanow*

Sweet Emma Barrett

b. Mar. 25, 1897, New Orleans, **d.** Jan. 28, 1983, New Orleans, LA
Piano, Vocals / New Orleans Jazz
A stalwart performer with powerhouse vocal technique and a bluesy, driving pianist as well, Barrett's career began in the early '20s, and she became known as the "bell gal" for her habit of wearing red garters with bells that jingled while she sang and played. Barrett was part of The Original Tuxedo Orchestra in the '20s and '30s. Barrett also sang and played with Sidney Desvigne, John Robichaux and A. J. Piron. She appeared at Happy Landing in the '50s, and became a Preservation Hall regular after 1961. Barrett toured with their traveling band overseas, and also did dates outside New Orleans. She overcame a 1967 stroke that caused paralysis on her left side, and kept performing playing only with her right hand until her death. —*Ron Wynn*

● **Sweet Emma—New Orleans: The Living Legends** / Jan. 25, 1961 / Original Jazz Classics ✦✦✦✦✦
This CD reissue of the future members of The Preservation Hall Jazz Band is at such a high level it makes one wonder why this group had so many erratic recordings. Pianist Emma Barrett (who also takes four vocals) is in fine form and trombonist Jim Robinson was always a major asset to any New Orleans jazz band but it is the performances of trumpeter Percy Humphrey (who never sounded better on record) and his brother, clarinetist Willie, that really makes this music special. Together the septet plays such songs as "Bill Bailey," "Just a Little While to Stay Here" and "The Saints" with drive, enthusiasm and surprising musicianship. It's essential music for all New Orleans jazz fans. —*Scott Yanow*

Sweet Emma Barrett and Her New Orleans Music / Sep. 1963 / Southland ✦✦✦
This is both classic blues, done in the requisite sassy, double-entendre fashion, and traditional jazz that also touches on gospel, brass band, and other pop styles. Although not the finest pure singer, Sweet Emma could belt out numbers and make suggestive remarks with abandon. —*Ron Wynn*

Sweet Emma and Her Preservation Hall Jazz Band / Oct. 18, 1964 / Southland ✦✦✦
This LP features The Preservation Hall Jazz Band in its early days when pianist/vocalist Sweet Emma Barrett was the leader. Clarinetist Willie Humphrey and trumpeter Percy Humphrey, although not up to the level they attained on the Riverside CD, are in better than usual form and trombonist Jim Robinson is his usual consistent self. This band clearly enjoys themselves, jam-

ming mostly on warhorses, making this a happy set of New Orleans jazz. —*Scott Yanow*

Ray Barretto

b. Apr. 29, 1929, Brooklyn, NY
Percussion / Latin Jazz

A legend among Latin jazz musicians and fans, Ray Barretto helped popularize the conga in jazz, salsa and other Latin styles, as well as R&B and rock. He's arguably the most recorded Latin musician of all time, with numerous recordings either as a leader or session player from the '50s through the '90s. While not quite a polyrhythmic dynamo like Mongo Santamaria or rhythmic innovator like Chano Pozo, Barretto has displayed remarkable flexibility, foresight and tremendous accompaniment skills, while also being a superb soloist and first-class talent scout. He began on conga while in the Army stationed in Germany. Upon his return to America, Barretto began working with New York jazz musicians. His first major job was with Eddie Bonnemere's Latin Jazz Combo. After working with Jose Curbelo, Barretto joined Tito Puente, replacing Mongo Santamaria. While staying in Puente's band four years, he also did R&B and jazz session work, playing on singles and working with Red Garland, Gene Ammons, and Lou Donaldson in the late '50s. Barretto made his recording debut as a leader in the early '60s on a Riverside session. *Pachanga With Barretto* featured arrangements by Hector Rivera. Barretto later took many of the same musicians and established his own band. He recorded with Kenny Burrell, Freddie Hubbard and Cal Tjader during the '60s, while cutting albums for Riverside and on Tico for the Latin market. Barretto scored a crossover hit with the single "El Watusi." He helped modernize the charanga style by incorporating brass into his band. Barretto's Tico LPs blended traditional Latin sounds, jazz improvisation and even pop and rock covers such as his version of "If I Had A Hammer." He subsequently recorded for United Artists before joining Fania in 1967. Barretto eventually became music director of the all-star lineup known as The Fania All Stars. Barretto won many honors during the '70s. He was voted top conga player by *Latin New York* magazine in 1975, 1976 and 1980, and Musician of the Year in 1977 and 1980. Barretto remained in the spotlight during the '80s. His CTI LP *La Cuna* with Tito Puente, Charlie Palmieri and Joe Farrell among others was hailed as a Latin jazz masterpiece and was also a good seller (despite the fact it had been withheld nearly two years). He continued introducing fresh faces, among them vocalists Willie Torres, Cali Aleman and Ray Babu. Barretto was music director of the *Bravisimo* television show and got some high profile rock exposure when he appeared in the anti-apartheid video and on the album *Sun City.* He hasn't slowed down in the '90s, with recent albums issued by Messidor and Concord Picante, as well as others on Latin labels. His contributions to Latin jazz, jazz and popular music are immeasurable. Barretto currently has a few titles available on American jazz labels on CD; many more can be obtained through Latin specialty stores. —*Ron Wynn*

Carnaval / 1962 / Fantasy ✦✦✦
These tough, energetic Afro-Latin and Latin jazz sessions were originally cut in 1962, when Barretto organized his first band as a leader and made albums in different styles. One was a charanga date, the other a surging jam session. They were subsequently reissued in a two-record vinyl package, and now are available as a single disc set. —*Ron Wynn*

Hard Hands / 1968 / Charly ✦✦✦
A '68 album with Barretto in the midst of his most productive period. He had made inroads into pop and jazz markets and was a dominant figure on the Latin jazz and salsa circuit. The album not only provided the great conga player and percussionist with a nickname, it yielded hit single "Abidjan" and also brought personnel changes. Joseph Roman replaced Rene Lopez on trumpet (he'd been drafted), and Tony Fuentes joined the group on bongos. —*Ron Wynn*

Eye of the Beholder / 1977 / Atlantic ✦✦
Percussionist Ray Barretto has been a valuable sideman for a couple of decades. This Atlantic LP, however, finds Barretto's brand of Latin-jazz somewhat overshadowed by funk rhythms and commercial elements with a lot of faceless solos. There are some worthwhile moments, but in general this set is a bit of a disappointment. —*Scott Yanow*

Music Map

Banjo

Pioneering Ragtime Banjoists
Vess Ossman
Fred Van Eps

1920s
Johnny St. Cyr • Bud Scott • Charlie Dixon
Mike Pingitore (with Paul Whiteman)
Freddy Guy (with Duke Ellington)
Ikey Robinson
Eddie Lang
(his switch to guitar helped seal the banjo's fate)

Early Virtuoso
Harry Reser

New Orleans Revival
Lawrence Marrero (with George Lewis)
Emanuel Sayles
Clancy Hayes
Danny Barker

Fusion Banjo
Bela Fleck

Aqui Se Puede / 1987 / Fania ✦✦✦
Barretto has a long history of producing a series of faintly disappointing albums followed by a blockbuster. This one doesn't really bust any blocks, but it works the classic trumpet/trombone expanded conjunto sound to fresher effect than he has contrived for a while, helped by a very gutty trombonist in Jimmy Bosch. — *John Storm Roberts, Original Music*

● **Handprints** / Mar. 1991 / Concord Picante ✦✦✦✦
Percussionist Ray Barretto, best-known as a sideman, had a rare chance to lead a session in 1991 and his Concord Picante debut is quite impressive. With saxophonist Steve Slagle, trumpeter Tim Ouimette and trombonist Barry Olson leading the frontline of this septet, Barretto mostly sticks to group originals for an infectious Latin jazz session. —*Scott Yanow*

Live in New York / 1992 / Messidor ✦✦✦
Recent release by Messidor of the still-dynamic Ray Barretto heading a group for a live New York concert. He ranks alongside Mongo Santamaria for consistency, staying power, and impact in both Latin and jazz circles, and his conga playing and presence drive a band like almost no other. —*Ron Wynn*

Ancestral Messages / Dec. 1992–Jan. 1993 / Concord Picante ✦✦✦
Although overshadowed during this era by Tito Puente and Poncho Sanchez, veteran percussionist Ray Barretto led one of the top Latin-jazz groups around a two-horn septet. This fine release includes a few standards (including "Freedom Jazz Dance" and "Killer Joe") along with a variety of excellent group originals, all of them both stimulating and danceable. —*Scott Yanow*

Taboo / 1994 / Concord Picante ✦✦✦✦
Ray Barretto's group New World Spirit quickly became one of the top Latin jazz bands of the mid-'90s. Trumpeter Ray Vega, saxo-

phonist Adam Kolker and pianist Hector Martignon create some worthy solos, Barretto takes some strong improvisations on congas and the band's repertoire finds the middle ground between salsa and jazz. —*Scott Yanow*

Bill Barron

b. Mar. 27, 1927, Philadelphia, PA, **d.** Sep. 21, 1989, Middletown, CT
Soprano Saxophone, Tenor Saxophone / Hard Bop, Post-Bop
The brother of pianist Kenny Barron, tenor saxophonist Bill Barron had a sturdy tone and resourceful style. He was adaptable enough to record in bop and hard bop contexts, yet also work with Cecil Taylor and co-lead a band with Ted Curson. Barron played with Jimmy Heath and Red Garland in Philadelpia before moving to New York in 1958. Barron directed the Muse Jazz Workshop at the Children's Museum in Brooklyn and taught at City College in the '60s and '70s, then served as chairman of Wesleyan University's Music Department in the mid-'80s. He recorded for Savoy, Audiophile and Muse among others. —*Ron Wynn*

Nebulae / Feb. 21, 1961 / Savoy ✦✦✦
Good, frequently fiery quartet date with trumpeter Ted Curson always threatening to break out of the harmonic framework, and Barron managing to interact with him, then solo in totally different fashion. Bassist Jimmy Garrison also played with a lot less abandon than he would later in the Coltrane quartet. —*Ron Wynn*

Hot Line / Mar. 31, 1962 / Savoy ✦✦✦✦
Tremendous two-tenor hard bop and blues set from the early '60s, matching Bill Barron and Booke Ervin. The ringer on the date is drummer Andrew Cyrille, light-years away from the music that would make him a rhythm institution years later. This was reissued on CD in 1986. —*Ron Wynn*

Jazz Caper / Aug. 1978 / Muse ✦✦✦

● **Variations in Blue** / Aug. 23, 1983–Aug. 2, 1983 / Muse ✦✦✦✦
Fine release by Bill Barron: a 1983 quintet set with him playing in a familiar, warm manner, able to either shift into a more animated pace or move into an interpretative, somber ballad style with ease. Steady, consistent contributions from trumpeter Jimmy Owens, pianist Kenny Barron, bassist Ray Drummond, and drummer Ben Riley. —*Ron Wynn*

The Next Plateau / Mar. 1987 / Muse ✦✦✦✦

Kenny Barron

b. June 9, 1943, Philadelphia, PA
Piano / Hard Bop, Post-Bop
In recent years Kenny Barron has been recognized as one of the giants of modern mainstream piano. The younger brother of the late saxophonist Bill Barron (who was 16 years older), he started on piano when he was 12 and played with Mel Melvin's R&B band in 1957. Barron moved to New York in 1961 where he worked briefly with James Moody, Lee Morgan, Roy Haynes and Lou Donaldson. Most significant were his four years (1962–66) playing and recording with Dizzy Gillespie. Barron followed that important association with periods in the groups of Freddie Hubbard (1966–70), Yusef Lateef (1970–75) and Ron Carter's two-bass quartet (1976–80). Barron was a co-leader of the group Sphere in the 1980s and since then has generally been the leader of his own trios. The pianist was on Stan Getz's final session (a series of brilliant duets) and has recorded many dates as a leader. In the 1990s Barron received long overdue recognition for his talents. —*Scott Yanow*

Sunset at Dawn / Apr. 2, 1973 / Muse ✦✦✦

Peruvian Blue / Mar. 14, 1974 / Muse ✦✦✦
A more experimental, diverse album than Barron has made in quite some time. This '74 date saw him playing in varied settings and alternating the size and personnel according to the song. There were solos, duos, tunes with bass and drums, one with multiple percussion. Barron's playing has grown since then, but his albums, while beautifully played, aren't anywhere as unusual. —*Ron Wynn*

Golden Lotus / Apr. 4, 1980 / Muse ✦✦✦
Solid 1980 session with the always vibrant, challenging pianist Kenny Barron and the underrated saxophonist John Stubblefield in fiery form. Steve Nelson began generating interest on vibes with his playing on this session. It has been reissued on CD. —*Ron Wynn*

At the Piano / Feb. 13, 1981 / Xanadu ✦✦✦✦

Green Chimneys / Jul. 9, 1983 / Criss Cross ✦✦✦✦
Fine trio date, as Barron, bassist Buster Williams, and drummer Ben Riley prove you can inject life into warhorses and constantly played standards. They recorded this for the Criss Cross label in Holland. —*Ron Wynn*

1 + 1 + 1 / Apr. 23, 1984–Apr. 24, 1984 / Blackhawk ✦✦✦
This out-of-print LP finds the talented if underrated pianist Kenny Barron in excellent form during duets with either Ron Carter or Michael Moore on bass. The one exception is a creative solo version of "'Round Midnight." Barron has never recorded a bad record and this set is above average with seven standards and Carter's "United Blues" all receiving favorable and subtly swinging treatment. —*Scott Yanow*

Autumn in New York / Dec. 14, 1984 / Uptown ✦✦✦✦

Scratch / Mar. 11, 1985 / Enja ✦✦✦✦
Kenny Barron, one of those talented pianists who always seems to be underrated, breaks away from playing standards and conventional bebop on this frequently exciting trio date. Matched up with bassist Dave Holland and drummer Daniel Humair, Barron explores five of his originals and Carmen Lundy's "Quiet Times." The fresh material and close interplay between the musicians make this set one of Barron's best trio recordings to date. —*Scott Yanow*

What If? / Feb. 17, 1986 / Enja ✦✦✦✦

Two As One / Jul. 1986 / Red ✦✦✦

Live at Fat Tuesdays / Jan. 15, 1988–Jan. 16, 1988 / Enja ✦✦✦
Barron stretches out and plays both flashy and easy, hot and cool, on this '88 set cut at Fat Tuesday's in New York. Bassist Cecil McBee and drummer Victor Lewis drive the rhythms a bit harder than The Riley/Drummond team, while Eddie Henderson and John Stubblefield on trumpet and tenor sax add some welcome intensity and contrasting solo voices. —*Ron Wynn*

Rhythm-A-Ning / Sep. 3, 1989 / Candid ✦✦✦✦

● **Live at Maybeck Recital Hall, Vol. 10** / Jan. 3, 1990 / Concord Jazz ✦✦✦✦✦

The Only One / Jun. 6, 1990 / Reservoir ✦✦✦
Standards galore, each played with care, artistry, and brilliance by the Kenny Barron trio. If there must be continued recording of "Love For Sale" and "Surrey With The Fringe On Top," then these are the people to do it. —*Ron Wynn*

Invitation / Dec. 20, 1990 / Criss Cross ✦✦✦

Lemuria-Seascape / Jan. 17, 1991 / Candid ✦✦✦
The Barron/Drummond/Riley trio step forward into the '90s and churn out another impressive collection, this one containing mostly either Barron or group originals rather than tons of standards. Exacting, carefully constructed, and consistently brilliant playing all around. —*Ron Wynn*

Quickstep / Feb. 18, 1991 / Enja ✦✦✦

Moment / Aug. 22, 1991 / Reservoir ✦✦✦

Mitchell's Talking / Dec. 1991 / Capri ✦✦✦

Sambao / May 19, 1992 / Verve ✦✦✦

Other Places / Feb. 1, 1993–Feb. 2, 1993 / Verve ✦✦✦

Wanton Spirit / Feb. 22, 1994–Feb. 23, 1994 / Verve ✦✦✦✦

Gary Bartz

b. Sep. 26, 1940, Baltimore, MD
Alto Saxophone, Soprano Saxophone / Post-Bop
When Gary Bartz burst upon the scene in the late '60s and particularly when he led his Ntu Troop in the early '70s, he showed the potential of becoming one of the important leaders of jazz. Although he spent an aimless period in commercialism and never quite fulfilled the initial potential, by the late '80s Bartz had returned to jazz in prime form. He had started on alto at age 11 and, after studying at Juilliard and the Peabody Conservatory, Bartz worked with the Max Roach-Abbey Lincoln group in 1964. He followed that up by stints with Art Blakey's Jazz Messengers (1965–66), McCoy Tyner and Blue Mitchell. Bartz made a strong impression with Miles Davis' 1970–71 fusion group, emerging as perhaps the strongest soloist on the recording *Live/Evil*. The altoist, who had recorded as a leader for Milestone and Prestige fairly regularly since 1967, did some of his finest work at the 1973 Montreux Jazz Festival (released on Prestige as *I've Known Rivers*

and Other Bodies). From that point on his recordings became funkier and more commercial; 1978's *Love Affair* on Capitol (which featured a discofied versionsof "Giant Steps") was an obvious lowpoint. However by 1987 Bartz started recording stronger albums for Mapleshade, SteepleChase and Candid. Now, instead of being a potential giant, Gary Bartz is an underrated (and often totally overlooked) jazz great. —*Scott Yanow*

Libra / May 31, 1967+Jun. 1, 1967 / Milestone ✦✦✦
Featured are excellent compositions and playing in mainstream mode. It includes Kenny Barron on piano and Jimmy Owens on trumpet. This is the more lyrical side of Bartz. —*Michael G. Nastos*

Another Earth / Jun. 19, 1968–Jun. 25, 1968 / Milestone ✦✦✦✦
The album that brought alto saxophonist Gary Bartz close to stardom in the late '60s. It's got lengthy songs, intense, sometimes dramatic solos, and a guest spot from Pharoah Sanders. When he turned in a less challenging direction in the early '70s, many were puzzled and disappointed. —*Ron Wynn*

Home / Mar. 30, 1969 / Milestone ✦✦✦

Harlem Bush Music: Taifa / Nov. 19, 1970+Nov. 23, 1970 / Milestone ✦✦✦

Juju Street Songs / Oct. 1, 1972 / Prestige ✦✦✦

Follow the Medicine Man / Oct. 1972 / Prestige ✦✦✦

I've Known Rivers and Other Bodies / Jul. 7, 1973 / Prestige ✦✦✦✦
At the time of this Montreux Festival concert (which has been released almost complete), altoist Gary Bartz was one of the most promising players in jazz. Already a veteran of the Miles Davis and McCoy Tyner bands, Bartz's future appeared limitless. Although he has not quite lived up to his potential and maintained a rather low profile since the 1970s, Bartz is still playing well over 20 years after this impressive effort. His 1974 quartet (which consisted of pianist Hubert Eaves, bassist Stafford James and drummer Howard King) is in top form on this lengthy two-LP set of original music, creating a new modern mainstream of fresh material that never really caught on. —*Scott Yanow*

Singerella: A Ghetto Fairy Tale / Nov. 1973+Feb. 1974 / Prestige ✦✦

Music Is My Sanctuary / 1975 / Capitol ✦✦

Jujuman / Oct. 1976 / Catalyst ✦✦✦

Bartz / 1980 / Arista ✦✦

Monsoon / Apr. 1988 / SteepleChase ✦✦✦

Reflections of Monk / Nov. 1988 / SteepleChase ✦✦✦✦

● **West 42nd Street** / Mar. 31, 1990 / Candid ✦✦✦✦
Another fine recent release by Gary Bartz, who seems determined not to let his reputation slip in the '90s. From burning hard bop to convincing blues with a touch of funk, this is someone with something to say, rather than another instrumentalist confused and plugging into the latest trends. —*Ron Wynn*

There Goes the Neighborhood / Nov. 11, 1990–Nov. 12, 1990 / Candid ✦✦✦✦
Although he dismissed notions about a comeback, this '90 album was the triumphant, exuberant vehicle Gary Bartz hadn't made in quite a while. His rippling solos and dominant presence were welcome for fans who wondered if he had squandered the potential he'd shown in the '60s. —*Ron Wynn*

Shadows / Jun. 11, 1991–Jun. 12, 1991 / Timeless ✦✦✦

Episode One Children Of Harlem / Jan. 20, 1994 / Jazz Challenge ✦✦
Although the theme of this CD is ostensibly supposed to be nostalgia for Harlem, the music (which includes the "Amos N'Andy Theme") actually has little to do with the subject. However Bartz (who is heard on alto and soprano) is in fine form playing with a top-notch quartet that also includes pianist Larry Willis, bassist Buster Williams and drummer Ben Riley. The hard-bop oriented music includes a few standards (including "Tico Tico" and "Crazy She Calls me") and three originals by either Bartz or Willis. It's not essential but enjoyable. —*Scott Yanow*

Red & Orange Poems / Sep. 24, 1994–Sep. 25, 1994 / Atlantic Jazz ✦✦✦✦
Alto-veteran Gary Bartz may not have made it as big as originally predicted but, as shown on this 1994 studio date, he developed a sound of his own and was always capable of coming out with exciting yet thoughtful music. Joined by such associates as trumpeter Eddie Henderson, John Clark on French horn, pianist Mulgrew Miller, bassist Dave Holland, drummer Greg Bandy and percussionist Steve Kroon, Bartz is in excellent form on a variety of standards (including "By Myself" and "But Not for Me") and originals. —*Scott Yanow*

Paul Bascomb

b. Feb. 12, 1912, Birmingham, AL, **d.** Dec. 2, 1986, Chicago, IL
Tenor Saxophone / Swing, Early R&B
It is easy to divide Paul Bascomb's career in two for he was a top soloist with Erskine Hawkins' swing orchestra and later on recorded a popular series of early rhythm 7 blues records. The brother of trumpeter Dud Bascomb (another star of the Hawkins band), the tenorman was one of the founding members of the 'Bama State Collegians (which eventually became the Erskine Hawkins Big Band) in the early '30s and, except for a period in 1938-39 when he replaced the late Herschel Evans with Count Basie's Orchestra, he was with Hawkins until 1944. Bascomb co-led groups with Dud (1944-47) and in the early '50s recorded extensively for the United label; the accessible performances have been partially reissued by Delmark. Paul Bascomb was active (if maintaining a low-profile) into the mid-'80s. —*Scott Yanow*

● **Bad Bascomb!** / Mar. 3, 1952 / Delmark ✦✦✦✦
Tenor saxophonist Paul Bascomb was a prototype first-generation R&B instrumentalist. His huge tone and swing-influenced sound were featured on several singles issued by Leonard Allen on his United label in the early '50s. Some of the songs were reissued on vinyl in the 1970s and have recently been released on CD. The disc includes ten unissued tracks, with Bascomb's robust licks featured alongside three other saxophonists, plus trumpeter Eddie Lewis, bassist James McCrary and drummer George DeHart. Bascomb adds a good-natured vocal on "Pink Cadillac," with alto saxophonist Frank Porter doubling as a singer on several other numbers. —*Ron Wynn*

Count Basie (William Basie)

b. Aug. 21, 1904, Red Bank, NJ, **d.** Apr. 26, 1984, Hollywood, CA
Piano, Leader / Swing
Throughout his career the name of Count Basie was synonymous with swing. Basie, whose influence remains huge over a decade after his death, not only led two of the finest jazz orchestras ever but he redefined the role of the piano in the rhythm section. Originally a stride pianist in the vein of his idol Fats Waller, Basie had such a strong rhythm section in the mid-'30s that he pared down his style drastically, eliminating the oom-pah timekeeping function of his left hand. With bassist Walter Page, rhythm guitarist Freddie Green and drummer Jo Jones filling in the spaces, Count stuck to simple phrases that were strategically placed to add momentum to the ensembles, and he unwittingly acted as a transitional figure toward the bop of Bud Powell.

But Count Basie was really an institution by himself. Born as William Basie, he played for silent movies (under the tutelage of Waller), learned from the great stride pianists of New York and played the vaudeville circuit. Stranded in Kansas City in 1927 he soon joined Walter Page's Blue Devils (the best small group in the city) and eventually when Bennie Moten (himself a pianist) made Basie a better offer, he became the main pianist with Moten's Kansas City Orchestra, recording with Moten during 1929-32. The final session of Moten's band sound very much like a predecessor of Count Basie's Orchestra.

After Moten's premature death in 1935, Basie formed his own group (known originally as The Barons Of Rhythm) and was based in Kansas City's Reno Club. The nine-piece band had a regular radio program and in 1936 producer John Hammond happened to hear them on his car radio. He was so impressed that he quickly travelled to Kansas City in hopes of signing up Basie to Columbia. However his articles (which raved about the great unknown band) alerted Decca and scouts from the rival label beat Hammond to it (although Basie would switch to Columbia in 1939).

After a period of struggle in which the orchestra (which was immediately expanded) had some rough moments, by late 1937 the Count Basie band had caught on. With such important soloists as the cool-toned tenor Lester Young (whose sound was an alternative to Coleman Hawkins), trumpeters Buck Clayton and Harry "Sweets" Edison, trombonist Dickie Wells, vocalist Jimmy Rushing (and for a period Billie Holiday) and the classic rhythm section, Basie's orchestra could hold its own against any other swing band. Its theme "One O'Clock Jump" soon became widely recorded (almost serving as an anthem for the era) and "Jumpin' at the Woodside" became a standard.

In the 1940s the band's arrangements (many of which were originally thought up by sidemen while on the bandstand) became more formalized. While Lester Young's departure in late 1940 left a hole, such other fine soloists as tenors Don Byas, Illinois Jacquet, Lucky Thompson and Paul Gonsalves, altoist Tab Smith, trumpeters Joe Newman and Clark Terry, and trombonist Vic Dickenson kept the band's music swinging. Bad money management and the change in the public's musical taste led Basie to reluctantly break up his orchestra at the end of 1949 and use a small group (ranging from a sextet to an nonet) for the next two years; it often featured Terry, Wardell Gray on tenor and clarinetist Buddy DeFranco.

In 1952, during a period when very few jazz orchestras were being formed, Count Basie put together what became known as his "New Testament" (as opposed to the earlier "Old Testament") band. Against all odds, Basie's orchestra caught on, especially after recording "April in Paris" and after singer Joe Williams signed on the following year. Although it featured more than its share of top soloists including trumpeters Joe Newman and Thad Jones, and tenors Frank Wess (who helped introduce the flute to jazz) and Frank Foster, it was the arrangements (particularly those of Neal Hefti, Ernie Wilkins, Wess, Foster, Thad Jones and later on Sammy Nistico) and the sound of the swinging ensembles (along with the distinctive rhythm section) that were emphasized.

Although there was a lot of turnover in the 1960s, the Basie sound never changed and the orchestra did not decline or stop travelling. A series of indifferent commercial records in the mid-to-late '60s (which often found famous singers using the Basie band as a prop) were far inferior to the band's live performances, but when Basie renewed his ties with producer Norman Granz in the 1970s and signed with Pablo Records, his recordings (which by then often featured Jimmy Forrest on tenor and trombonist Al Grey) were greatly improved. Count Basie's health gradually failed in the 1980s and his death was greatly mourned. However his orchestra (under the direction first of Thad Jones then Frank Foster and most recently Grover Mitchell) became the only viable ghost band in jazz history. —*Scott Yanow*

Basie's Basement / Oct. 23, 1929–Dec. 13, 1932 / Bluebird ✦✦✦✦
The genesis of the Count Basie band can be heard in these recordings by Bennie Moten's Kansas City Orchestra. With Basie on piano, trumpeter Hot Lips Page, tenor saxophonist Ben Webster and such future Basieites as trombonist/guitarist Eddie Durham, baritonist Jack Washington, bassist Walter Page and the great singer Jimmy Rushing, there are times when Moten's orchestra almost sounds like Basie's. Eight selections from the 1929–30 period are followed by eight numbers recorded at Moten's last and greatest sesssion (from Dec. 13, 1932). Such tunes as "Moten's Swing," "Lafayette" and "Blue Room" are prime examples of early swing. —*Scott Yanow*

Essential Count Basie, Vol. 1 / Oct. 9, 1936–Jun. 24, 1939 / Columbia ✦✦✦
Rather than release all of Count Basie's studio recordings (as Decca recently has or as French Columbia did in two large LP sets over a decade ago), CBS has put together three samplers that contain some (but not all) of the essential Basie recordings from the 1939–41 period. This first volume has Lester Young's great solo on 1936's "Lady Be Good," the classics "Rock-A-Bye Basie" and "Taxi War Dance," and fine examples of the Basie orchestra throughout 1939. —*Scott Yanow*

Super Chief / Oct. 9, 1936–Jul. 24, 1942 / Columbia ✦✦✦
This very interesting two-LP set has quite a variety of material from the 1936–42 period, including a few airchecks, small-group sessions led by Mildred Bailey, Harry James, Glenn Harriman and Teddy Wilson (all feature Basie sidemen), and some studio sessions by both Basie's orchestra and small groups from his big band. Along with the rarities is the very first post-Bennie Moten session, a quintet date (under the pseudonym of Jones-Smith Incorporated) from 1936 that served as the recording debut of Lester Young; "Lady Be Good" was one of his greatest solos. This two-LP set is highly recommended, if you can find it. —*Scott Yanow*

At the Chatterbox: 1937 / Jan. 10, 1937–Feb. 12, 1937 / Jazz Archives ✦✦✦
This historic LP features broadcasts by Count Basie's orchestra in Pittsburgh during its first visit to the East Coast. The music is primarily head arrangements and charts borrowed from other bands. Two of the soloists (trumpeter Carl "Tatti" Smith and violinist/guitarist Claude Williams) would eventually be replaced. It is fascinating to hear what this orchestra sounded like at this early stage. Tenor saxophonist Lester Young and trumpeter Buck Clayton (along with Basie) quickly emerge as the most impressive soloists. —*Scott Yanow*

☆ **The Complete Decca Recordings (1937–1939)** / 1937–Feb. 4, 1939 / GRP ✦✦✦✦✦
This magnificent three-disc set has the first 63 recordings by Count Basie's Orchestra, all of his Deccas. The consistency is remarkable (with not more than two or three turkeys) and the music is the epitome of swing. With such soloists as Lester Young and Herschel Evans on tenors, trumpeters Buck Clayton and Harry "Sweets" Edison, the great blues singer Jimmy Rushing and that brilliant rhythm section of Basie, guitarist Freddie Green, bassist Walter Page and drummer Jo Jones, the music is timeless. It's all here: "One O'Clock Jump," "Sent for You Yesterday," "Blue and Sentimental," "Jumpin' at the Woodside," "Jive at Five" and many others. This is the first Count Basie collection to acquire and should be in every jazz collection. —*Scott Yanow*

Rock-A-Bye Basie, Vol. 2 / Aug. 9, 1938–Mar. 7, 1940 / Vintage Jazz Classics ✦✦✦
These broadcasts (all but one selection from 1938–39) capture Count Basie's orchestra live from the Famous Door. This CD contains 24 performances, a few of which are incomplete or poorly recorded. However the enthusiastic solos of Lester Young, fellow tenors Herschel Evans and Buddy Tate, trumpeters Buck Clayton and Harry "Sweets" Edison and Basie himself are fresh and creative, and the ensembles are consistently swinging. These are the best pre-World War II live recordings of the Count Basie Orchestra and well worth acquiring. —*Scott Yanow*

Count Basie, Vol. 1 (1939) / Jan. 1939–Apr. 1939 / Classics ✦✦✦✦
Count Basie, Vol. 2 (1939) / May 1939–Nov. 1939 / Classics ✦✦✦✦

Essential Count Basie, Vol. 2 / Aug. 4, 1939–May 31, 1940 / Columbia ✦✦✦
A fine sampler of the 1939–40 Count Basie orchestra, it features such classic performances as "Dickie's Dream," "Lester Leaps In" and "Tickle Toe." Lester Young and fellow tenor Buddy Tate, trumpeters Buck Clayton and Harry Edison, and trombonist Dickie Wells all have their chances to star; they can't help swinging with that light but solid Basie rhythm section. Count's Columbia recordings deserve to be reissued in full (with all of the alternate takes), but until CBS gets around to it, this is a good introduction to that period. —*Scott Yanow*

Count Basie, Vol. 3 (1939–1940) / Nov. 1939–Oct. 1940 / Classics ✦✦✦✦

Blues by Basie / 1939–1950 / Columbia ✦✦✦
Because Basie streamlined his piano style down to the bare basics, it is often forgotten how strong a pianist he could be when he was inspired. This intriguing LP features live performances taken from a variety of settings and time periods (dating from 1941–67), all of which put the focus on Basie's piano. Not too surprisingly, most of the numbers are blues but he is in consistently fine form, and there is enough variety to keep one's interest throughout this excellent set. —*Scott Yanow*

Essential Count Basie, Vol. 3 / Aug. 8, 1940–Apr. 10, 1941 / Columbia ✦✦✦
This is the third and thus far final volume in a sampler series picking out some of the highpoints of Count Basie's 1939–42 period on Columbia. Lester Young's departure in December 1940 robbed the orchestra of their top soloist but the band still outswung all of its competitors and the personnel was consistently outstanding. Coleman Hawkins' guest appearance on "9:20 Special" and "Feedin' the Bean" round out this enjoyable set, but when is Columbia going to reissue all of their Count Basie recordings instead of always recycling the same ones? —*Scott Yanow*

Count Basie (1940–1941) / Nov. 1940–Apr. 1941 / Classics ✦✦✦✦

Count Basie V Discs, Vol. 2: 1943–1945 / Jun. 1943–May 14, 1945 / Jazz Society ✦✦✦
This second volume of V Discs almost reaches the great heights

of the first LP. Covering a slightly wider span of time, the Basie band is heard during one of its peak periods, the otherwise poorly documented war years. The music is consistently exciting and tops much of what Basie would record during the following five years. —*Scott Yanow*

Count Basie (1944) / Jan. 10, 1944 / Circle ✦✦
This is the first of two LPs of transcriptions recorded by Count Basie's orchestra during a time when the musicians union was on strike and no commercial recordings were being made. These 11 performances are particularly valuable because they document Lester Young's all-too-brief return to the Basie band and also feature fine moments by trumpeter Harry Edison and the tenor of Buddy Tate. A few too many Earle Warren vocals and the skimpy playing time are the only drawbacks. —*Scott Yanow*

1944–1945 / Jan. 10, 1944–May 25, 1944 / Circle ✦✦✦
The second LP of transcriptions from a period when the musicians union strike resulted in no commercial recordings being made, this set (which is actually superior to the first volume) features Lester Young back with Count Basie in 1944. Trumpeter Harry Edison, trombonist Dickie Wells, Buddy Tate on tenor and Basie all have their strong moments and it is nice to hear the orchestra playing such fresh material, some of which they never got around to recording commercially. —*Scott Yanow*

Count Basie V Discs, Vol. 1: 1944–1945 / May 27, 1944–Jan. 11, 1945 / Jazz Society ✦✦✦✦
Among the very best recordings cut by Count Basie's orchestra in the '40s are the V Discs they recorded exclusively for distribution to servicemen. The first of two volumes, the 11 performances on this LP are quite inspired with Harry Edison, Dickie Wells, Lester Young (during the half when he is present), Buddy Tate and Lucky Thompson taking heated solos. This version of "Taps Miller" is a real classic; there are no weak cuts on this excellent set. —*Scott Yanow*

Beaver Junction (1944—1946) / May 27, 1944–Nov. 12, 1947 / Vintage Jazz Classics ✦✦✦✦
A worthy CD full of Basie rarities, it includes unissued and alternate versions of V Discs and two radio broadcasts; the one from 1944 features drummer Buddy Rich filling in for the recently drafted Jo Jones. Rich had so much fun being part of the swing machine that when Basie handed him a blank check for his services, he tore it up! The music throughout this CD will be equally fun for the listener. —*Scott Yanow*

Count Basie: the Orchestra and The Octet / Jan. 9, 1946–Apr. 10, 1951 / CBS ✦✦✦✦
This French CBS two-LP set has 13 recordings by the 1946 edition of Count Basie's orchestra (including several features for the exciting tenor of Illinois Jacquet), 12 performances by Basie's octet in 1950 (which starred trumpeter Clark Terry, clarinetist Buddy DeFranco and tenor great Wardell Gray among others) and Basie's first session with his new big band in 1951 (Wardell Gray's showcase "Little Pony" is considered a classic). The music throughout this two-fer is consistently memorable and the octet performances are so swinging that it makes one regret that he could not keep it going along with his new orchestra. —*Scott Yanow*

Brand New Wagon: Count Basie 1947 / Jan. 3, 1947–Dec. 12, 1947 / Bluebird ✦✦✦✦
While French RCA put out a three-LP set documenting 48 of Count Basie's recordings for that label during 1947–50, its American counterpart instead just reissued 21 of those sides (all from 1947) on this highly enjoyable CD. Best are the octet and nonet recordings of May 20–21, but none of these tracks are weak. Trumpeter Harry "Sweets" Edison, the tenors of Paul Gonsalves and Buddy Tate and the long underrated baritonist Jack Washington star, along with vocalist Jimmy Rushing and the rhythm section. Even during what is sometimes written off as a declining period, the Basie orchestra was near the top in quality, if not popularity. —*Scott Yanow*

Count Basie—Vols. 1–3 / Jan. 3, 1947–Feb. 2, 1950 / RCA ✦✦✦✦
This three-LP box set from French RCA skips around a bit and fails to give complete personnel information but it is a gem. 95% of Count Basie's studio recordings for RCA during the 1947–50 period are included and, even during the weaker and more commercial numbers, the band always swings. There are quite a few obscure gems (Basie's orchestra was not getting much publicity during this era) including features for baritonist Jack Washington and the tenor of Paul Gonsalves, a nonet date from 1947 and

Basie's octet session of February 2, 1950, cut shortly after economics forced him to disband his classic orchestra. This box is becoming increasingly difficult to locate but it far exceeds anything put out thus far by its American counterpart. —*Scott Yanow*

Paradise Squat / Jul. 22, 1952–Dec. 12, 1952 / Verve ✦✦✦
In 1952 Count Basie put together his second big band after two years of work with six- to eight-piece units. This double LP documents his recordings of that year and it is very interesting to hear the beginnings of his second great orchestra. The soloists are mostly different than he would feature during the remainder of the '50s with the most impressive voices being the two contrasting tenors of Eddie "Lockjaw" Davis and Paul Quinichette. With new charts by Neal Hefti and Ernie Wilkins, it seems apparent that the band was on its way even if Al Hibbler was at this point Basie's vocalist; his version of "Goin' to Chicago" sounds a bit odd. This two-fer also has a pair of combo performances that are Count Basie's first matchup with pianist Oscar Peterson. —*Scott Yanow*

Sixteen Men Swinging / Dec. 12, 1953–Jun. 1954 / Verve ✦✦✦
The second Count Basie Orchestra stabilized its sound and its personnel on the two solid sessions from 1953–54 featured on this two-LP set. With Joe Newman and Thad Jones in the trumpet section and the two tenors of Frank Foster and Frank Wess, the band had more than its share of talented soloists, but it was the clean ensemble sound, the lightly but firmly swinging rhythm section and the inventive and uncluttered arrangements of Ernie Wilkins and Neal Hefti that made this band a surprise success in 1954. This two-fer (which includes "Blues Backstage" and "Down for the Count") has 25 examples of '50s Basie swing. —*Scott Yanow*

Swinging the Fifties / Jun. 26, 1954–Jun. 11, 1955 / IAJRC ✦✦
Two unrelated radio airchecks occupy one side apiece of this collector's LP. The Count Basie Orchestra is heard live at Birdland on a strong set highlighted by versions of "April in Paris" and "Everyday I Have the Blues" that predate the classic studio recordings (for the latter song by just six days). The flip side has the otherwise unrecorded Horace Henderson Orchestra of 1954, a very musical but not particularly distinctive aggregation that did not catch on. It is interesting to hear Henderson (Fletcher's younger brother) performing a modern chart like the Stan Kenton-associated "Artistry Jumps." —*Scott Yanow*

Class of '54 / Sep. 2, 1954–Sep. 7, 1954 / Black Lion ✦✦✦
This fine CD consists of two radio airchecks from 1954, featuring Count Basie with a nonet and his full orchestra. The smaller group also has trumpeter Joe Newman, trombonist Henry Coker and the tenors of Frank Wess and Frank Foster well-featured while the big-band tracks (which mostly sport Neal Hefti arrangements) finds the orchestra on the brink of great success. —*Scott Yanow*

Count Basie, Lester Young & The Stars of Birdland / Feb. 1955 / Jass ✦✦✦✦
This live CD documents a tour by top performers who appeared regularly at Birdland. Count Basie's orchestra backs Basie alumnus Lester Young on three tracks, welcomes Stan Getz to sit in for four numbers (including an exciting version of "Little Pony"), accompanies Sarah Vaughan during eight songs and performs seven tunes by itself, four of which feature Joe Williams (who had just recently joined the band). This historic set will be prized by collectors. —*Scott Yanow*

★ **Count Basie Swings, Joe Williams Sings** / Jul. 17, 1955–Jul. 26, 1955 / Verve ✦✦✦✦✦
Joe Williams' debut on records with the Basie orchestra was so successful in every way that the band's future was secure for the next few decades. Included on this essential set are the classic versions of "Every Day I Have the Blues," "The Comeback," "Alright Okay, You Win," "In the Evening" and "Teach Me Tonight," hits that Williams and Basie would have to perform nightly for the remainder of the '50s. Highly recommended. —*Scott Yanow*

☆ **April in Paris** / Jul. 26, 1955–Jan. 5, 1956 / Verve ✦✦✦✦✦
A true classic, this studio album includes Count Basie's hit versions of "April in Paris," "Shiny Stockings" and "Corner Pocket"; these three tunes have remained in the Basie band's repertoire ever since. Actually all ten selections are very enjoyable, and this exciting and of course swinging record is definitive of '50s Count Basie. —*Scott Yanow*

The Greatest! Count Basie Plays . . . Joe Williams Sings Standards / Apr. 28, 1956 / Verve ✦✦✦
Joe Williams never wanted to be typecast as just a blues singer, so

on his second full album with Count Basie he concentrated on standards. The swinging treatments given to songs such as "Thou Swell," "My Baby Just Cares for Me" and even "Singin' in the Rain" works quite well even if the band is mostly confined to a supporting role. —*Scott Yanow*

Count Basie in London / Sep. 7, 1956 / Verve ✦✦✦
The origin of this session's title is a bit of a mystery since this album was actually recorded live in Sweden. The Count Basie Orchestra plays its usual repertoire (including "Jumpin' at the Woodside," "Shiny Stockings" and "Corner Pocket") with enthusiasm, concise solos and typical Basie swing. Joe Williams takes a few vocals and this CD is rounded by three previously unreleased performances. —*Scott Yanow*

• **Count Basie at Newport** / Sep. 7, 1957 / Verve ✦✦✦✦✦
At the 1957 Newport Jazz Festival the music was consistently inspired and often historic. Count Basie welcomed back tenor-great Lester Young and singer Jimmy Rushing for part of a very memorable set highlighted by "Boogie Woogie" and "Evenin'"; Young plays beautifully throughout and Rushing is in prime form. An exciting full-length version of "One O'Clock Jump" features Young, Illinois Jacquet and trumpeter Roy Eldridge, the Basie band stretches out on "Swingin' at Newport"; and five previously unreleased selections (put out for the first time on this CD) include four Joe Williams vocals. It's a great set of music. —*Scott Yanow*

Atomic Mr. Basie / Oct. 21, 1957–Oct. 22, 1957 / Roulette ✦✦✦✦✦
Known as the "Atomic" album due to the cover picture of an A-Bomb exploding, this is one of the great Count Basie records, ranking with *April in Paris*. The 1957 edition of the Basie orchestra romps through "The Kid from Red Bank" (a superlative feature for its leader), "Whirly Bird" and "Lil' Darlin'" among others; everything works on this essential album. —*Scott Yanow*

The Complete Roulette Studio Count Basie / Oct. 21, 1957–Jul. 26, 1962 / Mosaic ✦✦✦✦✦
Some of Count Basie's finest recordings were cut for the Roulette label during 1957–62 and all of his studio performances are included on this massive Mosaic ten-CD boxed set. Among the classic former LPs that are reissued here are *The Atomic Mr. Basie*, *Basie Plays Hefti*, *Chairman of the Board*, *Everyday I Have the Blues* and *Kansas City Suite*. With such soloists as trumpeters Thad Jones and Joe Newman, the tenors of Frank Foster and Eddie Lockjaw Davis and Frank Wess on alto and flute, vocals by Joe Williams and the timeless arrangements of Neal Hefti, Thad Jones, Frank Foster, Ernie Wilkins and Frank Wess among others, this essential (but unfortunately limited-edition) set features the second Count Basie Orchestra at its very best.

Corner Pocket / 1958 / Laserlight ✦✦✦
This is the first of two Laserlight CDs documenting Count Basie's orchestra, sometime in the late '50s, playing before a live audience. Even with the presence of "Corner Pocket," "Cutell," and "Li'l Darling," the repertoire is pretty fresh, with baritonist Charlie Fowlkes having a rare feature on "Spring Is Here," altoist Marshall Royal getting a few spots and Snooky Young leading the powerful rhythm section. Add trombonist Al Grey and tenor saxophonist Billy Mitchell to the other strong soloists of the period and one has a very enjoyable and swinging set of Basie music. The playing time is a bit brief but Laserlight is a very moderately priced label and the music on this CD is superior. —*Scott Yanow*

One O'clock Jump / 1958 / Laserlight ✦✦
The second of Laserlight's live Count Basie CDs from sometime in the late '50s, this one has fewer high points with remakes of various Basie standards (such as "Jumpin' at the Woodside," "Little Pony," and "One O'Clock Jump") offering solid but unremarkable music, pleasing swing but with no real surprises. —*Scott Yanow*

Basie Plays Hefti / Apr. 3, 1958–Apr. 14, 1958 / Roulette ✦✦✦✦
The Count Basie Orchestra is in top form for this set of Neal Hefti arrangements. Hefti had been one of the main architects of the new Basie sound of the '50s and on this memorable date he utilizes the flute of Frank Wess prominently. "Cute" (heard here in its initial recording) became a standard. —*Scott Yanow*

Basie / May 1958 / Roulette ✦✦✦✦

Sing Along with Basie / May 26, 1958–Sep. 3, 1958 / Roulette ✦✦✦✦
The extraordinary jazz vocal group Lambert, Hendricks and Ross had debuted in 1957 with *Sing a Song of Basie* during which they

recreated his orchestra with their overdubbed voices. That album was so successful that the following year they were able to actually team up with the Basie band. Frank Foster put down on paper the original head arrangements of the '30s and '40s for the orchestra, leaving space for the vocalists to recreate the original solos. The result is a colorful and swinging set. Best is a version of "Goin' to Chicago Blues" that has Joe Williams taking his original vocal while L.H. & Ross sing around him. —*Scott Yanow*

One More Time / Dec. 18, 1958–Jan. 24, 1959 / Roulette ✦✦✦
For this studio album from late 1958 and early 1959, the Count Basie Orchestra performs ten Quincy Jones compositions; he also contributed all of the arrangements. "I Needs to Be Beed With," "For Lena and Lennie" and "The Midnight Sun Never Sets" all caught on and Jones' charts helped expand the Basie sound without altering it. An excellent CD. —*Scott Yanow*

Basie: Eckstine / May 22, 1959–May 23, 1959 / Roulette ✦✦✦✦

The Complete Roulette Live Recordings of Count Basie and His Orchestra (1958–1962) / May 31, 1959–Aug. 1, 1962 / Mosaic ✦✦✦✦
This consistently exciting eight-CD set features the Count Basie Orchestra at three different locations and time periods: at a convention in Florida in 1959, at Birdland on two nights in 1961 and in Stockholm during a four-day period. Of the 133 selections, only 28 were released before, making these hard-swinging performances (which would be essential for Basie fans on the basis of the music alone) of even greater interest. During this era Basie had such top soloists as Frank Wess on alto and flute, the tenors of Frank Foster and Billy Mitchell, trumpeters Thad Jones and Joe Newman and trombonists Al Grey and Quentin Jackson. In addition, drummer Louis Bellson is featured throughout the Stockholm engagement and such guests as trumpeter Harry "Sweets" Edison and singers Joe Williams, Sarah Vaughan and Jon Hendricks are heard from. But it is the swinging Basie rhythm section and the enthusiasm of the ensembles that make this a truly classic and somewhat historic set. —*Scott Yanow*

Everyday I Have the Blues / Sep. 24, 1959 / Roulette ✦✦✦✦
One of Joe Williams' most rewarding recordings with Count Basie came on this set of blues-oriented material. Williams does a fine remake of "Everyday I Have the Blues" and a classic version of "Going to Chicago," but all ten selections are quite enjoyable. —*Scott Yanow*

Paris Jazz Concert / Mar. 29, 1960+May 5, 1962 / RTE ✦✦✦
This two-CD set documents a pair of hour-long performances by the Count Basie big band that are quite complementary despite being recorded two years apart. No real surprises occur (the Basie Orchestra was nothing if not predictably swinging) but neither are there any low points. Most of the material was recorded elsewhere at least once during this productive period and the repertoire alternates Basie standards with dance music and blues. Singers O.C. Smith ("All Right, OK, You Win") and Irene Reid ("The Blues") only have one vocal apiece and fail to make much of an impression. With such soloists (who are unfortunately unidentified in the liner notes) as Thad Jones, Joe Newman, Al Grey, Quentin Jackson, Frank Wess, Frank Foster and Basie himself (among others), this is a well-recorded and enjoyable set that Basie fanatics and completists will want. —*Scott Yanow*

Kansas City Suite: The Music of Benny Carter / Sep. 1960 / Roulette ✦✦✦
These two 1960 sessions gave Benny Carter a unique chance to write a full program for Count Basie's orchestra. Arranged as a type of suite, the ten originals pay tribute to the various Kansas City clubs that were active in the '30s when Basie was a resident. The band swings throughout as usual, with concise solos adding color to this memorable modern session. —*Scott Yanow*

The Count Basie Story / 1961 / Roulette ✦✦
These sessions found Count Basie's orchestra remaking the repertoire of his first band's arrangements from 1936–45. Although this 1960 two-LP box set is well-done, one misses the great soloists of the earlier orchestra like Lester Young, Buck Clayton and Dickie Wells, so this hi-fi revival is a bit pointless. —*Scott Yanow*

First Time! the Count Meets The Duke / Jul. 6, 1961 / Columbia ✦✦✦✦
This session was an impossible dream come true, the teaming of the entire Count Basie and Duke Ellington orchestras, including the principals on joint pianos. Whether it be "Take the 'A' Train," "Jumpin' at the Woodside," or "Until I Met You," everything works

on this album and somehow the ensembles avoid sounding overcrowded. This version of "Segue in C" is the outstanding performance of a unique and highly enjoyable set. —*Scott Yanow*

Count Basie and the Kansas City 7 / Mar. 21, 1962 / MCA ✦✦✦✦
One of Count Basie's few small-group sessions of the '60s was his best. With trumpeter Thad Jones and tenors Frank Foster and Eric Dixon filling in the septet, Basie is in superlative form on a variety of blues, standards and two originals apiece from Thad Jones and Frank Wess. Small-group swing at its best. —*Scott Yanow*

Live in Sweden / Aug. 1962 / Roulette ✦✦✦
First-rate 1991 reissue of Basie in Sweden with a good group including Frank Wess and Frank Foster. The CD version has two bonus cuts. —*Ron Wynn*

Frankly Basie: Count Basie Plays the Hits of Frank Sinatra / Apr. 8, 1963–Jan. 14, 1965 / Verve ✦✦
Originally titled *More Hits of the 50's and 60's*, this salute to Frank Sinatra by Count Basie's Orchestra is mostly closer to dance music than jazz. Billy Byers' arrangements are pleasing enough but in general the music is rather easy-listening with few exciting moments and most solos being quite brief. The original 12-song program is augmented by a "new" alternate take of "Hey, Jealous Lover" and two selections ("My Kind of Town" and "Come Rain or Come Shine") taken from the LP *Basie Picks the Winners*. Considering the personnel and the material, the results are disappointingly sleepy; only "All of Me" is at all memorable. —*Scott Yanow*

Showtime / Aug. 18, 1966–Jan. 16, 1967 / MCA ✦
Big bands found it very rough going in the '60s. Although he always led a superb band, Count Basie's recordings during this decade were quite streaky, with the orchestra often misused behind a variety of dubious vocalists. *Showtime* is an instrumental set but mostly pretty horrendous with the big band playing commercial arrangements written for 20 unsuitable showtunes. Just imagine Basie's crew roaring through "Strangers in the Night", it's even worse than one would expect. —*Scott Yanow*

Live in Antibes (1968) / Jul. 1968 / Esoldun ✦✦✦
The late-'60s Count Basie Band, featuring the frenetic, surging tenor sax of Eddie "Lockjaw" Davis, was spotlighted on this 17-cut CD reissue, part of a series issued by the French Esoldun label and available as an import. The band stuck to its predictable pattern of alternating mid-tempo and fast-paced numbers, blues and vocal change-of-pace items, plus slower treatments, all done in a relaxed, highly professional fashion. The menu included "Going to Chicago Blues," "In a Mellow Tone," "Lil' Darlin," "Stormy Monday Blues" and "Cherokee," as well as the expected closer "Jumping At the Woodside." The arrangements, ensemble interaction and general performances were good, if not exceptional, and Basie's customary sparse piano licks were timely and right in the groove. —*Ron Wynn*

Jazz Fest Masters: Count Basie / Jun. 1969 / Scotti Bros. ✦✦✦
If one judged them by their studio albums of the 1963–70 period, it would seem that Count Basie's orchestra was in its decline, but this recently released live CD proves otherwise. Recorded at the 1969 New Orleans Jazz Festival, the Basie band swings such tunes as "Whirlybird," "Corner Pocket," "Cherokee" (an Eddie "Lockjaw" Davis feature) and "April in Paris" with enthusiasm and power. A fine session. —*Scott Yanow*

Afrique / Dec. 22, 1970–Dec. 23, 1970 / Doctor Jazz ✦✦✦✦
Possibly the most unusual album by Count Basie, it's certainly the most modern. For this session Oliver Nelson arranged eight recent songs including avant-gardist Albert Ayler's "Love Flower" and Pharoah Sanders' "Japan," giving the Basie band a more "contemporary" setting (utilizing electric bass on half the songs) while not altering its basic sound. Nelson's "Kilimanjaro" and "Hobo Flats" are highlights of this very successful but never repeated "experiment." —*Scott Yanow*

Loose Walk / Apr. 24, 1972 / Pablo ✦✦✦
Ironically, the earliest recording by Count Basie for Norman Granz's Pablo label was one of the most recent to be released. This jam session features trumpeter Roy Eldridge, trombonist Al Grey and tenor saxophonist Eddie "Lockjaw" Davis on a set of jammable standards. The results are quite fun. —*Scott Yanow*

Basie Jam, Vol. 1 / Dec. 10, 1973 / Pablo ✦✦
The official start of Count Basie's decade-long association with Norman Granz's Pablo label was a bit disappointing, an all-star cast (with trumpeter Harry "Sweets" Edison, trombonist J.J.

Johnson and tenors Eddie Davis and Zoot Sims) playing one blues after another. Reasonably pleasing but uninspired; there would be many better Basie dates coming up. —*Scott Yanow*

The Bosses / Dec. 11, 1973 / Original Jam Classics ✦✦✦✦
Count Basie and an all-star band (including trumpeter Harry Edison, trombonist J.J. Johnson and the tenors of Eddie Davis and Zoot Sims) back up veteran Kansas City blues singer Big Joe Turner on one of his better later albums. The many fine solos inspire Turner, who is in top form on such tunes as "Night Time Is the Right Time," "Wee Baby Blues" and "Roll 'Em Pete." —*Scott Yanow*

For the First Time / May 22, 1974 / Pablo ✦✦✦
Throughout his career, Count Basie was modest about his own abilities as a pianist, and his success at streamlining his style to the bare essentials often made listeners underrate his playing talents. This 1974 session was a rarity, an opportunity for Basie to be featured in a trio setting (with bassist Ray Brown and drummer Louie Bellson), during which he provides enough variety to hold one's interest and enough technique to lead many to reassess his piano skills. —*Scott Yanow*

Satch and Josh / Dec. 2, 1974 / Pablo ✦✦✦
Producer Norman Granz occasionally got carried away with the quantity of his recording projects. In 1974 he recorded a full album teaming fellow pianists Count Basie and Oscar Peterson in a rhythm quintet; little did anyone realize that this then-unique matchup would eventually result in five albums. This first one, which finds Basie doubling on organ, is among the best. Peterson's virtuosic style somehow worked very well with Basie's sparse playing and these ten numbers really swing. —*Scott Yanow*

Basie and Friends / Dec. 2, 1974–Nov. 1, 1981 / Pablo ✦✦
This is a hodgepodge collection focusing on Basie's piano-playing from four different sessions. Five selections find him in trios while the other three numbers are meetings with Oscar Peterson during which they both double on organ. All of these performances are unavailable elsewhere and are enjoyable if not too unique. —*Scott Yanow*

The Last Decade / 1974–1980 / Artistry ✦✦✦
The well-recorded live performances on this two-LP set date from three different periods: Count Basie's pre-Pablo 1974 band with tenor-great Eddie "Lockjaw" Davis, the star-studded 1977 orchestra (featuring Jimmy Forrest's tenor, trombonist Al Grey and drummer Butch Miles) and the very solid 1980 group. Throughout, the various Basic orchestras are consistently exciting and swinging. —*Scott Yanow*

● **Basie and Zoot** / Apr. 9, 1975 / Original Jazz Classics ✦✦✦✦✦
Pianist/bandleader Count Basie and tenor saxophonist Zoot Sims were beautiful and this was a fine pairing–Sims being at an age when he had caught up to the Count and the Count was hip enough to pass the baton and keep right up with him. There were no musical cliches here; the music sustained itself. John Heard's bass was a pleasure, sensitively walking itself throughout the album. Drummer Louis Bellson was near perfect, keeping the music Kansas City light and rolling, only pushing and prodding Sims and Basie with a delicate tension on "I Surrender Dear." The mark of Norman Granz's productions for Pablo was a give and response relationship between producer, artist, and listener, and the level remained incredibly high on the album; inventive, timeless and classic. —*Bob Rusch, Cadence*

Fun Time: Count Basie Big Band at Montreux '75 / Jul. 19, 1975 / Pablo ✦✦✦
This big-band performance from the 1975 Montreux Jazz Festival introduces what could be called Count Basie's third great orchestra (although in style it was a continuation of the second one he formed in 1952). With trombonist Al Grey, Jimmy Forrest on tenor and the fiery drummer Butch Miles giving this early Pablo version of the band its own personality, the Basie orchestra is in top form for a strong set. Of special note are two fine vocals by Bill Caffey, who would quickly drift into obscurity. —*Scott Yanow*

Basie Jam at Montreux '75 / Jul. 19, 1975 / Pablo ✦✦✦✦
On one of the earliest and best of the Count Basie jams for Pablo, Basie sounds very happy pushing the combative trumpeter Roy Eldridge, tenor saxophonist Johnny Griffin and vibraphonist Milt Jackson on two blues and a lengthy version of "Lester Leaps In." Plenty of sparks fly. —*Scott Yanow*

The Basie Big Band / Aug. 16, 1975–Aug. 27, 1975 / Pablo ✦✦
The Count Basie Orchestra's initial studio album for Pablo mostly features pleasant but lightweight arrangements by Sammy Nestico. The music is quite recognizable as Basie's but the results are somewhat forgettable and predictable. —*Scott Yanow*

For the Second Time / Aug. 28, 1975 / Original Jazz Classics ✦✦✦
On Count Basie's second trio album for Pablo, he is reunited with bassist Ray Brown and drummer Louie Bellson. In addition to the expected blues, the main joy of this set is hearing Basie stretch out on such numbers as "If I Could Be with You," "On the Sunny Side of the Street" and "The One I Love," tunes he did not play much with his orchestra in this later period. —*Scott Yanow*

I Told You So / Jan. 12, 1976–Jan. 14, 1976 / Original Jazz Classics ✦✦✦✦
This is one of Count Basie's best big-band studio recordings for Norman Granz during his Pablo years. The arrangements by Bill Holman are both challenging and swinging, containing enough surprises to make this session a real standout. —*Scott Yanow*

Basie Jam, Vol. 2 / May 6, 1976 / Original Jazz Classics ✦✦✦✦
For this enjoyable jam session, Count Basie heads up a very impressive cast of players, including altoist Benny Carter, Eddie "Lockjaw" Davis on tenor, trumpeter Clark Terry, trombonist Al Grey and guitarist Joe Pass. The four lengthy performances give each of the principals plenty of solo space and the results are predictably exciting. It's a big improvement over the first *Basie Jam*. —*Scott Yanow*

Basie Jam, Vol. 3 / May 6, 1976 / Original Jazz Classics ✦✦✦
From the same recording session that resulted in *Basie Jam—Vol. 2*, these four performances of standards also feature Count Basie, guitarist Joe Pass, trumpeter Clark Terry, altoist Benny Carter, trombonist Al Grey and tenorman Eddie Lockjaw Davis, all in fine form. Norman Granz always preferred Basie in a small group and the success of these jams helped bolster his argument. —*Scott Yanow*

Prime Time / Jan. 18, 1977–Jan. 20, 1977 / Pablo ✦✦✦✦
One of arranger Sammy Nestico's most enjoyable sessions for Count Basie, these eight selections (six composed by Nestico, including the title cut and "Ya Gotta Try") are performed by an inspired Basie orchestra. Tenor saxophonist Jimmy Forrest and trombonist Al Grey star among the soloists. —*Scott Yanow*

Kansas City 5 / Jan. 26, 1977 / Pablo ✦✦✦
This studio session from 1977 features Count Basie in a quintet with vibraphonist Milt Jackson and guitarist Joe Pass. The predictably excellent group performs spirited versions of some of Basie's "hits" (including "Jive at Five" and "One O'Clock Jump"), some blues and a few standards. It is always interesting to hear Basie in a hornless setting like this one where he gets opportunities to stretch out on the piano. —*Scott Yanow*

The Gifted Ones / Feb. 3, 1977 / Pablo ✦✦
Norman Granz got this one backwards. Instead of featuring Dizzy Gillespie with the Count Basie Orchestra, he put Gillespie and Basie together in a quartet which the trumpeter naturally dominates. The music is generally quite rewarding, including an unusual version of "St. James Infirmary," but never reaches the great heights one might have expected. —*Scott Yanow*

Basie Jam: Montreux '77 / Jul. 14, 1977 / Original Jazz Classics ✦✦✦
From Norman Granz's marathon series of performances recorded at the 1977 Montreux Jazz Festival, this set finds Count Basie fronting a jam session featuring trumpeter Roy Eldridge, altoist Benny Carter, Zoot Sims on tenor and the trombones of Vic Dickenson and Al Grey. Despite the possibility of being overcrowded, a bit of planning by Basie made this into a very coherent set with a blues, a long ballad medley and the closing "Jumpin' at the Woodside." Lots of nice moments. —*Scott Yanow*

Basie Big Band: Montreux '77 / Jul. 15, 1977 / Original Jazz Classics ✦✦✦
The Count Basie Orchestra is heard performing a fine set, recorded at the 1977 Montreux Jazz Festival. There are no surprises in the repertoire (which includes tunes by Sammy Nestico, Neal Hefti and some Basie standards) but the band seems inspired by the surroundings and tenor saxophonist Jimmy Forrest is in particularly solid form. —*Scott Yanow*

Satch and Josh.....Again / Sep. 20, 1977 / Pablo ✦✦✦
Recorded three years after their first full album together, this second encounter between Count Basie and Oscar Peterson on twin pianos (this time with a quartet) is as strong as the original, alternating standards with blues. Both Peterson and Basie have one number apiece on electric piano, making this album historic as well as quite musical. —*Scott Yanow*

Milt Jackson & Count Basie & The Big Band, Vol. 1 / Jan. 18, 1978 / Pablo ✦✦

Milt Jackson & Count Basie & The Big Band, Vol. 2 / Jan. 18, 1978 / Pablo ✦✦

Yessir, That's My Baby / Feb. 21, 1978 / Pablo ✦✦✦
From the same week that resulted in *Night Rider* and *Timekeepers*, this is the fifth album that documents the matchup of Count Basie and Oscar Peterson. The two pianists (backed by bassist John Heard and drummer Louis Bellson) play five standards and three blues with predictable swing, finding much more in common with each other than one might have originally suspected. —*Scott Yanow*

Night Rider / Feb. 21, 1978–Feb. 22, 1978 / Original Jazz Classics ✦✦✦
When they first met up for a full album in 1974, the two-piano team of Count Basie and Oscar Peterson must have seemed like an unlikely matchup. After all, Peterson is known for filling up his rapid solos with virtuosic passages while Basie is the master of the "less-is-more" approach, making every note count. But because Peterson has such high respect for Basie, he showed great self-restraint and left more room for Basie's percussive solos. *Night Rider*, like their two previous joint albums, emphasizes the similarities rather than the differences in these two masters' styles. —*Scott Yanow*

The Timekeepers / Feb. 21, 1978–Feb. 22, 1978 / Original Jazz Classics ✦✦✦
From the same sessions that resulted in *Night Rider* and *Yessir*, this quartet date also features the two pianos of Oscar Peterson and Count Basie collaborating and interacting on swing standards and blues. Any of their five albums together are worth acquiring. —*Scott Yanow*

Live in Japan (1978) / May 21, 1978 / Pablo ✦✦✦✦
By 1978 the Count Basie Orchestra no longer had trombonist Al Grey and tenor saxophonist Jimmy Forrest as their stars, but this superb ensemble band was also no longer dependent on famous names. In fact, one does not miss their presence on this superior live performance which features such Basie standbys as "Freckle Face," "All of Me," "Shiny Stockings" and "Jumpin' at the Woodside." Although the soloists were no longer household names, they all fare well, particularly Eric Dixon on tenor and flute. —*Scott Yanow*

On the Road / Jul. 12, 1979 / Original Jazz Classics ✦✦✦
This release gives one a definitive look at the Count Basie Orchestra during its final years. Trumpeter Pete Minger, trombonist Booty Wood and Eric Dixon on tenor and flute are the main soloists, but it is the classic Basie ensemble sound (which never seems to get dated or lose its charm and power) that carries the day. Whether it is "Wind Machine," "Splanky" or "In a Mellow Tone," this is a highly enjoyable set. —*Scott Yanow*

Get Together / Sep. 4, 1979 / Pablo ✦✦✦
This typically enjoyable Basie all-star jam is particularly noteworthy because it includes the great (but underrated) tenor of Budd Johnson along with Eddie "Lockjaw" Davis and trumpeters Clark Terry and Harry "Sweets" Edison. The music is quite delightful, topped by a fine ballad medley. —*Scott Yanow*

Kansas City Shout / Apr. 6, 1980–Apr. 7, 1980 / Pablo ✦✦✦
This session from 1980 helps to recreate the atmosphere of '30s Kansas City. Featured are the great blues singer Joe Turner and the strong singer and altoist Eddie "Cleanhead" Vinson, along with the Count Basie Orchestra. "Just a Dream," "Everyday I Have the Blues," "Cherry Red" and "Stormy Monday" receive very spirited renditions, as do some newer blues. Since all of the principals are no longer with us, Norman Granz deserves special thanks for organizing this special session. —*Scott Yanow*

Kansas City 7 / Apr. 10, 1980 / Original Jazz Classics ✦✦✦✦
Norman Granz recorded Count Basie in many different settings during his decade with Granz's Pablo label. This jam session set was a little unusual in that, along with the tenor of Eddie "Lockjaw" Davis, guitarist Joe Pass and trombonist J.J. Johnson, trumpeter Freddie Hubbard is in the cast along with Basie; pity

he never recorded with the Count Basie Orchestra! This happy session is a strong consolation prize, with plenty of fine solos taking over familiar chord changes. —*Scott Yanow*

Warm Breeze / Sep. 1, 1981–Sep. 2, 1981 / Pablo ✦✦✦
This big-band album finds Count Basie (at age 77) and his orchestra performing seven charts by longtime friend Sammy Nestico, including six originals and "Satin Doll." Trumpeter Harry "Sweets" Edison sits in on "How Sweet It Is" and trumpeter Willie Cook as a couple of strong spots, but it is the classic Basie ensemble sound that is this enjoyable studio session's strongest asset. —*Scott Yanow*

Kansas City 6 / Nov. 1, 1981 / Original Jazz Classics ✦✦✦
This is one of many small-group jam sessions organized by Norman Granz to feature pianist Count Basie. This time around the proceedings (utilizing a sextet) have plenty of solo space for trumpeter Willie Cook, altoist Eddie "Cleanhead" Vinson (who also takes a vocal) and guitarist Joe Pass. As usual, when Basie had his way, the emphasis is on the blues and the music always swings. —*Scott Yanow*

Farmers Market Barbecue / May 4, 1982 / Original Jazz Classics ✦✦✦
This was an excellent outing by the Count Basie Orchestra during its later years. Actually, half of this album features a medium-sized group from Basie's big band, but his orchestra usually had the feel of a small group anyway. Soloists at this late stage include Eric Dixon and Kenny Hing on tenors, trombonist Booty Wood, altoist Danny Turner and four different trumpeters. The rhythm section is of course instantly recognizable and the music is very much in the Basie tradition. —*Scott Yanow*

Me and You / Feb. 22, 1983–Feb. 28, 1983 / Pablo ✦✦✦
Five big-band selections (including a remake of the half-century-old "Moten Swing") and four songs featuring an octet from the orchestra comprise this excellent outing by Count Basie recorded only a little more than a year before his death. However, the spirit of this music (helped out by some Ernie Wilkins arrangements) make Count Basie seem ageless. —*Scott Yanow*

88 Basie Street / May 11, 1983–May 12, 1983 / Original Jazz Classics ✦✦✦✦
One of Basie's final albums, the very appealing title cut seems to sum up his career, a lightly swinging groove with a strong melody. Two small-group performances with guest Joe Pass on guitar and the tenor of Kenny Hing add variety to a particularly strong set. —*Scott Yanow*

Mostly Blues...and Some Others / Jun. 22, 1983 / Pablo ✦✦✦
Count Basie's final small-group studio session (one of a countless number for Norman Granz during Basie's last decade), this outing features trumpeter Snooky Young (who was last with the orchestra in the early '60s), tenor great Eddie "Lockjaw" Davis and the dependable guitarist Joe Pass (along with rhythm guitarist Freddie Green). The repertoire lives up to the album's title: blues and swing standards all played with joy and spirit. —*Scott Yanow*

Fancy Pants / Dec. 1983 / Pablo ✦✦✦
Count Basie's last-known album (recorded four months before his death), this big-band record gives no hints of the end nearing; in fact the music is quite upbeat and typically spirited. The Count Basie Orchestra never declined and its leader (who remained in his musical, if not physical prime) went out swinging. —*Scott Yanow*

Long Live the Chief / Jun. 24, 1986–Jun. 25, 1986 / Denon ✦✦✦
After Count Basie's death, his orchestra went through an expected period of turmoil, almost declaring bankruptcy and having a new short-term leader (the late trumpeter Thad Jones). By 1986 its fortunes had improved and under the leadership of tenor saxophonist Frank Foster it has become the only "ghost" orchestra to still play viable music after the death of its leader. *Long Live the Chief* was recorded only weeks after Foster assumed command, but already his arrangements and leadership were giving fresh life to this great jazz institution. In addition to remakes of "April in Paris," "Lil' Darlin'," "Corner Pocket" and "Shiny Stockings," there was already some new material in the band's books and this enjoyable CD shows just how strong the orchestra was even during this period of transition. —*Scott Yanow*

The Legend: The Legacy / May 16, 1989–May 17, 1989 / Denon ✦✦✦
Three years after Frank Foster had become leader of the Count Basie Orchestra, the group continued to place very well in jazz polls; few big bands were in its class. This fine CD finds Foster extending the tradition of Count Basie with new arrangements and features for both veterans (including trumpeter Sonny Cohn, altoist Danny Turner, and the tenors of Kenny Hing and Eric Dixon) and the newer members (such as trumpeter Byron Stripling and pianist Ace Carter). With Carmen Bradford proving to be the band's best vocalist since Joe Williams, Frank Foster had succeeded in not only reviving the Count Basie Orchestra but restoring it to its prime. The lengthy "Count Basie Remembrance Suite," "Booze Brothers" and a new version of Neal Hefti's "Whirly Bird" are among this enjoyable CD's highlights. —*Scott Yanow*

Live at El Morocco / Feb. 20, 1992–Feb. 21, 1992 / Telarc ✦✦✦
Even without its original leader, the Count Basie Orchestra is today one of the finest jazz big bands in existence. Frank Foster has kept the instantly recognizable sound while welcoming younger soloists and infusing the band's repertoire with new charts. This strong live program is typical of the Basie band in the '90s, performing older tunes (such as "Corner Pocket" and "Shiny Stockings") that alternate with newer and no less swinging originals, all of which leaves room for the orchestra's many promising soloists. —*Scott Yanow*

Basie's Bag / Nov. 1992 / Telarc ✦✦✦✦
Count Basie may have died in 1984 but his orchestra continues to roll on without any loss of quality. The 1992 edition is filled with strong soloists and swinging arrangements. Leader Frank Foster wrote most of the charts for this CD (including the fine four-part "Count Basie Remembrance Suite") and allocated solo space to 12 of the 14 horn players. There are good individual features for Kenny Hing on tenor, trombonist Clarence Banks, electric guitarist Charlton Johnson and Foster himself ("Here's That Rainy Day") but it is the strong ensembles that make this a rewarding set. —*Scott Yanow*

Basin Street Six

Group / Dixieland
The New Orleans-based Basin Street Six was most notable for featuring clarinetist Pete Fountain and trumpeter/vocalist George Girard at the beginning of their careers. A Dixieland sextet that also included trombonist Joe Rotis and pianist Roy Zimmerman among the soloists, the Basin Street Six worked steadily for a time in New Orleans and recorded for 504, Circle and Mercury; the Circle recordings have been reissued on CD by GHB. —*Scott Yanow*

● **Dixieland from New Orleans** / Aug. 28, 1950+Nov. 30, 1950 / Circle ✦✦✦✦

Strictly Dixie / Mar. 1952 / Mercury ✦✦✦

Django Bates

b. Oct. 2, 1960, Beckenham, England
Tenor Horn, Keyboards / Avant-Garde
A talented chance-taking improviser with a wicked sense of humor, Django Bates had extensive musical training. In 1979 he started the group Human Chain and was in the quartet Bordering during 1981–84. In 1983 he joined Dudu Pukwana's band and became a founding member of the unusual English big band Loose Tubes. Bates played and recorded with Bill Bruford's Earthworks from the mid-'80s until 1994, when he decided that he preferred to lead his own bands. In addition to heading the big band Human Precipice, working with George Russell and George Gruntz and fulfilling commissions, Django Bates has recorded as a leader for JMT and as a sideman for ECM. —*Scott Yanow*

Music for the Third Policeman / Jan. 31, 1990–Feb. 2, 1990 / Ah Um ✦✦✦

● **Autumn Fires (And Green Shoots)** / Feb. 15, 1994–Feb. 16, 1994 / JMT ✦✦✦
English pianist Django Bates has a crazy sense of humor, the ability to use dissonance and noise as a logical part of his music and a fresh approach to group playing. On this CD, a solo piano outing, he is more subtle than on his group albums and the music takes a little while to cut loose. Bates plays with great reverence on "Solitude," tears conventionally into "Giant Steps" and does a close imitation of Keith Jarrett on "Hollyhock." However, Bates' unusual take on the world eventually comes to the surface on the overcrowded "Rat King" and a wonderfully titled piece called "The Loneliness of Being Right." He often displays a classical technique

that is bent a bit to his purposes and, although his previous JMT group recording ("Summer Fruits") is recommended first, this solo set rewards repeated listenings. —*Scott Yanow*

Alvin Batiste

b. 1937, New Orleans, LA
Clarinet / Avant-Garde
Although sometimes called a "New Orleans clarinetist" (his Columbia album even billed him as a "Legendary Pioneer of Jazz"), in reality Alvin Batiste is an avant-garde player who does not fit easily into any classification. Under recorded throughout his career, Alvin Batiste was a childhood friend of Ed Blackwell and he spent time in Los Angeles in 1956 playing with Ornette Coleman. However Batiste chose the life of an educator in Louisiana. He did make some little-known records with the AFO ("all for one") quintet in New Orleans, popped up on a couple of Cannonball Adderley dates and toured with Ray Charles in 1958 but was an obscure legend until he made three albums with Clarinet Summit in the 1980s (a quartet also including John Carter, David Murray and Jimmy Hamilton. Batiste recorded as a leader for India Navigation and made the 1993 Columbia album *Late*. He remains a very explorative (and under-recognized) player. —*Scott Yanow*

● **Musique D'afrique Nouvell Orleans** / 1984 / India Navigation ✦✦✦✦

Bayou Magic / 1988 / India Navigation ✦✦✦

Late / 1993 / Columbia ✦✦✦✦
Alvin Batiste has spent much of his career as an educator, so he tends to get overlooked when one thinks of the top jazz clarinetists. He has a conventional and pleasing tone that he utilizes to improvise in an unusual and harmonically advanced style. Most of this CD teams the avant-gardist with a bop-based trio led by Kenny Barron, and the clarinetist is constantly bending the material. The well-paced set (only a dumb modal version of "The Saints" is a disappointment) has among its highpoints a slow atmospheric New Orleans blues ("Late"), a relative of Coltrane's "Giant Steps" ("Imp and Perry"), a Ray Charles lick ("Ray's Segue") and the lengthy vamp-filled "Kinshasa." It's a strong introduction to the rarely recorded clarinetist. —*Scott Yanow*

Billy Bauer

b. Nov. 14, 1915, New York, NY
Guitar / Cool
Billy Bauer will always be best-known for his late-'40s association with Lennie Tristano, playing cool-toned lines that perfectly fit in with the pianist, Lee Konitz and Warne Marsh. He originally started out on banjo, switching to guitar in the early '30s. Bauer worked with Jerry Wald's Orchestra, Woody Herman's First Herd (1944–46), Chubby Jackson (1947) and then (on several occasions) Benny Goodman. With Tristano during his most significant years (1946–49), Bauer participated in the first recorded free improvisations and the classic early Konitz-Marsh dates. He won *Downbeat* and *Metronome* polls during 1949–53. Bauer spent most of the 1950s as a busy studio musician, although he did find time to record with the popular J.J. Johnson-Kai Winding Quintet (1954), Bobby Hackett (1957), Cootie Williams (1957) and Lee Konitz (1955 and 1957). In 1961 he opened his own jazz club in Long Island, NY, and then worked in lounges. In 1970 Bauer opened up his own guitar school. He cut back drastically on his freelancing after a serious ear infection hit in 1975 but has remained active as a teacher. —*Scott Yanow*

Anthology / 1959–Dec. 1969 / Interplay ✦✦✦
Guitarist Billy Bauer, best-known for his early associations with Lennie Tristano and Woody Herman, only recorded three albums as a leader. While his first dates were in 1953 and 1956, this Interplay LP collects together private solo performances from 1959, 1960 and 1969 and a trio gig in 1969 (with bassist John Sherin and drummer Charles Kay) that were taped but originally not planned for release. Fortunately they were saved and in 1987 (when it finally came out) this album showed that Bauer's creative abilities had not diminished with time even though he lacked the drive to have a fulltime performing career. Most of the music is introspective but there are some swinging moments (most notably on the trio's rendition of "I'll Remember April"). Guitarists

and bop historians will be most interested in this quiet set. —*Scott Yanow*

Mario Bauza

b. Apr. 28, 1911, Havana, Cuba, **d.** Jul. 11, 1993, New York, NY
Leader, Arranger / Afro-Cuban Jazz
A talented section player who rarely soloed, Mario Bauza's main importance to music was behind the scenes as one of the main instigators of Afro-Cuban jazz, the potent mixture of Latin rhythms with jazz improvisation. A multi-instrumentalist, Bauza played clarinet and oboe with the Havana Philharmonic before moving to New York in 1930. During a stint with Noble Sissle in 1932 he switched to trumpet. As musical director with Chick Webb (1933–38), Bauza helped convince the drummer of the potential greatness of Ella Fitzgerald. He was with Don Redman during 1938–39 and then Cab Calloway (1939–41). Bauza was largely responsible for Calloway hiring Dizzy Gillespie and in 1947 he would introduce Dizzy to Chano Pozo. Bauza became the longtime musical director of his brother-in-law Machito's orchestra (1941–76), encouraging Machito to add jazz solos to his music. In the 1980s and early '90s as the head of his own Afro-Cuban Orchestra, Mario Bauza (who had long since given up playing trumpet) recorded three excellent albums of his arrangements and finally received some recognition for his important contributions to music. —*Scott Yanow*

● **The Tanga Suite** / Jul. 29, 1992 / Messidor ✦✦✦✦
Mario Bauza's place as one of the key founders of Latin-jazz was overlooked for decades until he formed the exciting orchestra found on this Messidor CD. His 23-piece big band, along with a variety of singers, performs a full set of Bauza's originals including the five movements of his Afro-Cuban jazz suite "Tanga." Victor Paz's lead trumpet drives the ensembles and Paquito D'Rivera has a strong appearance sitting in on alto. —*Scott Yanow*

944 Columbus / May 27, 1993–May 28, 1993 / Messidor ✦✦✦
During his final two years, Mario Bauza and his newly formed Afro-Cuban Jazz Orchestra recorded three albums, of which *944 Columbus* (made just two months before his death) was the last. Three of the ten selections on the CD are dominated by vocals but jazz is a very strong element throughout these sessions, with a variety of fine solos, particularly from trumpeter Michael Mossman. The percussion section blends in well with the horns in this 19-piece orchestra and the final statement from the Father of Afro-Cuban jazz is a memorable one. —*Scott Yanow*

Jeff Beal

b. San Francisco, CA
Piano, Trumpet / Post-Bop
A superior trumpeter, Jeff Beal is thus far most notable for his advanced writing abilities. While studying at the Eastman School of Music, Beal won 11 *Downbeat* student awards. He also received three Exxon/Meet the Composer grants during 1986–87. Beal moved to New York after graduating, recorded his debut *Liberation* for Antilles and then moved to the West Coast to work on film scores. He has since recorded a second date for Antilles (*Perpetual Motion*) and three sets for Triloka. Beal's writing has been featured on albums by Spyro Gyra, Dave Samuels and John Patitucci, but he has not neglected his unpredictable trumpet playing, gigging often in the Los Angeles area. —*Scott Yanow*

Liberation / Apr. 1988 / Antilles ✦✦✦
A contemporary trumpeter steadily building his reputation, Beal began to attract attention with this 1988 release. It's neither fully fusion nor traditional, blends electric and acoustic instrumentation, and shows Beal's musical vision rather than a repertory effort. —*Ron Wynn*

Perpetual Motion / Nov. 2, 1988–Nov. 4, 1988 / Antilles ✦✦

Objects in the Mirror / Feb. 1990–Jun. 25, 1991 / Triloka ✦✦✦

● **Three Graces** / Jan. 1993 / Triloka ✦✦✦✦
Trumpeter Jeff Beal's compositions do not contain catchy melodies but instead set mysterious and often melancholy moods with interesting frameworks, using occasional funklines creatively. Much of the music builds logically to unexpected heights with surprising turns. Beal's fine trumpet playing is generally quite original (even if he hints strongly at Miles Davis' sound when he is muted) and his sextet (with Steve Tavaglione's tenor, pianist

John Beasley and bassist John Patitucci) is flexible enough to interpret his complex compositions. —*Scott Yanow*

Contemplations / Aug. 1993–Dec. 1993 / Triloka ✦✦✦

Sidney Bechet

b. May 14, 1897, New Orleans, LA, **d.** May 14, 1959, Paris, France

Clarinet, Soprano Saxophone / New Orleans Jazz, Dixieland

Sidney Bechet was the first important jazz soloist on records in history (beating Louis Armstrong by a few months). A brilliant soprano saxophonist and clarinetist with a wide vibrato that listeners either loved or hated, Bechet's style did not evolve much through the years but he never lost his enthusiasm or creativity. A master at both individual and collective improvisation within the genre of New Orleans jazz, Bechet was such a dominant player that trumpeters found it very difficult to play with him. Bechet wanted to play lead and it was up to the other horns to stay out of his way!

Sidney Bechet studied clarinet in New Orleans with Lorenzo Tio, Big Eye Louis Nelson and George Baquet and he developed so quickly that as a child he was playing with some of the top bands in the city. He even taught clarinet and one of his students (Jimmie Noone) was actually two years older than him! In 1917 he travelled to Chicago and in 1919 he joined Will Marion Cook's Orchestra, touring Europe with Cook and receiving a remarkably perceptive review from Ernst Ansermet. While overseas he found a soprano sax in a store and from then on it was his main instrument. Back in the U.S. Bechet made his recording debut in 1923 with Clarence Williams and during the next two years he appeared on records backing blues singers, interacting with Louis Armstrong and playing some stunning solos. He was with Duke Ellington's early orchestra for a period and at one point hired a young Johnny Hodges for his own band. However from 1925–29 Bechet was overseas, travelling as far as Russia but getting in trouble (and spending jail time) in France before being deported.

Most of the 1930s were comparatively lean times for Bechet. He worked with Noble Sissle on and off and had a brilliant session with his New Orleans Feetwarmers in 1932 (featuring trumpeter Tommy Ladnier). But he also ran a tailor's shop which was more notable for its jam sessions than for any money it might make. However in 1938 he had a hit recording of "Summertime," Hugues Panassie featured Bechet on some records and soon he was signed to Bluebird, where he recorded quite a few classics during the next three years. Bechet worked regularly in New York, appeared on some of Eddie Condon's Town Hall concerts and in 1945 he tried unsuccessfully to have a band with the veteran trumpeter Bunk Johnson (whose constant drinking killed the project). Jobs began to dry up about this time and Bechet opened up what he hoped would be a music school. He only had one main pupil, but Bob Wilber became his protégé.

Sidney Bechet's fortunes changed drastically in 1949. He was invited to the Salle Pleyel Jazz Festival in Paris, caused a sensation, and decided to move permanently overseas. Within a couple years he was a major celebrity and a national hero in France even though the general public in the U.S. never did know who he was! Bechet's last decade was filled with exciting concerts, many recordings and infrequent visits back to the U.S. before his death from cancer. His colorful (if sometimes fanciful) memoirs *Treat It Gentle* and John Chilton's magnificent Bechet biography *The Wizard of Jazz* (which traces his life nearly week-by-week) are both highly recommended. Many of Sidney Bechet's recordings are currently available on CD. —*Scott Yanow*

The Chronological Sidney Bechet, 1923–1936 / Oct. 1923–Mar. 1936 / Classics ✦✦✦✦

The first in a series of Classics CDs focusing on the recordings of Sidney Bechet, this disc features the clarinetist/soprano saxophonist on two early titles with blues singer Rosetta Crawford, his torrid 1932 session with The New Orleans Feetwarmers (which also features trumpeter Tommy Ladnier and is highlighted by "Shag" and "Maple Leaf Rag") and sides from Noble Sissle's somewhat commercial orchestra. Fortunately Sissle was wise enough to give Bechet plenty of solo space on some of his selections, most notably "Polka Dot Rag." Even with a few indifferent vocals, this CD is recommended to those not already owning this music. —*Scott Yanow*

The Complete, Vol. 1/2 / Sep. 15, 1932–Jan. 8, 1941 / RCA ✦✦✦✦

Of all the overlapping Bechet reissue series, this series of two-LP sets released by French RCA is easily the best, with all of the

Victor sides by the great soprano saxophonist and clarinetist (including the valuable alternate takes) being issued complete and in chronological order. The first two-fer is highlighted by the blazing session by The New Orleans Feetwarmers from 1932, four selections from the "Really the Blues" date with trumpeter Tommy Ladnier and clarinetist Mezz Mezzrow, and such Bechet classics as "Indian Summer," "Old Man Blues" and "Nobody Knows The Way I Feel 'Dis Mornin.'" —*Scott Yanow*

● **Master Takes: Victor Sessions (1932–1943)** / Sept. 15, 1932–Dec. 8, 1943 / Bluebird ✦✦✦✦✦

A three-disc set containing the bulk of Bechet's recordings made in the U.S., it covers 17 different combinations of musicians (including the renowned one-man-band session in which Bechet accompanied himself in 1941). This is the epitome of passion by one of New Orleans' greatest clarinet/soprano masters. —*Bruce Raeburn*

The Chronological Sidney Bechet, 1937–1938 / Apr. 1937–Nov. 1938 / Classics ✦✦✦

The second in a series of CD reissues featuring Sidney Bechet has quite a bit of variety. The unique soprano saxophonist is heard with Noble Sissle's showband, dominating a small group sponsored by Sissle, backing blues singer Trixie Smith and the team of Grant & Wilson, and leading his own session with a sextet that includes baritonist Ernie Caceres, and on "Hold Tight," a vocal by "The Two Fish Mongers." Enjoyable if not quite essential music. —*Scott Yanow*

The Complete, Vol. 5/6 / Nov. 21, 1938–Dec. 8, 1943 / RCA ✦✦✦✦

The third and final two-fer in this definitive series concludes the reissuance of every Sidney Bechet recording on Victor (including the alternate takes) with sessions from 1941 (highlighted by a classic rendition of "What Is This Thing Called Love?") and a quintet set from two years later with trombonist Vic Dickenson. Filling out this two-LP set are what was known as the "Panassie sessions," the recordings organized by French critic Hugues Panassie during a visit to New York in 1938–39. Mezz Mezzrow is heard at length on performances with trumpeters Tommy Ladnier and Sidney DeParis, but it is the six progressive swing tracks from trumpeter Frankie Newton's septet (with pianist James P. Johnson) that are most memorable, particularly a brilliant version of "Rosetta." —*Scott Yanow*

1938–1940 / Nov. 28, 1938–Feb. 5, 1940 / Classics ✦✦✦

This entry in Classics' chronological reissue of the master takes of Bechet's early recordings finds the soprano-great playing with trumpeter Tommy Ladnier and Mezz Mezzrow on the famous "Really the Blues" session, performing a hit version of "Summertime," overshadowing the other members of the all-star Port of Harlem Seven and recording "Indian Summer" and a hot version of "One O'Clock Jump" in a 1940 session for Victor. However, half of this CD is taken up by an odd and surprisingly restrained marathon date with pianist Willie The Lion Smith in which they perform Haitian folk songs. —*Scott Yanow*

★ **Complete Blue Note Recordings** / June 8, 1939–Aug. 25, 1953 / Mosaic ✦✦✦✦✦

Mosaic, a mail-order company, has compiled a series of remarkable box sets that feature the complete recordings of various immortal musicians at the peak of their careers. This limited-edition six-LP set (get it while you can) has all of Sidney Bechet's recordings for Blue Note including three songs with The Port of Harlem Seven (climaxed by his hit version of "Summertime"), two blues with guitarist Josh White, and Bechet's sessions from 1940, 1944, 1945, 1946, 1949, 1950, 1951 and 1953 in which he shares the frontline with such trumpeters as Sidney DeParis, Max Kaminsky, Bunk Johnson, Wild Bill Davison and Jonah Jones. The music ranges from hot swing to exuberant Dixieland, and Bechet somehow always sounds inspired. —*Scott Yanow*

1940 / Mar. 7, 1940–Jun. 4, 1940 / Classics ✦✦✦✦

Classics' chronological reissue of Bechet's recordings (at least the regular takes) continues with a pair of songs made with blues singer Josh White, eight very enjoyable performances cut with a quartet consisting of cornetist Muggsy Spanier, guitarist Carmen Mastren and bassist Wellman Braud, and a pair of Bechet's Victor sessions. This is one of the strongest entries in this valuable series. —*Scott Yanow*

Double Dixie / Mar. 28, 1940–1957 / Drive Archive ✦✦✦

This CD contains music from two different sessions. The first half of this reissue has seven of the eight selections recorded by the Bechet Big Four in 1940 (a group comprised of the leader on soprano and clarinet, cornetist Muggsy Spanier, guitarist Carmen Mastren and bassist Wellman Braud) and it is highlighted by several classics such as "China Boy" (which has some stunning Bechet), "That's a Plenty" and "Sweet Lorraine." The remainder of the set has seven of the dozen numbers recorded by Spanier in 1957 with his Dixieland band (which also includes clarinetist Joe Barufaldi and trombonist Bill Johnson). The latter sides are quite predictable as the sextet does its best to uplift such warhorses as "The Saints," "Muskrat Ramble" and "St. James Infirmary." Dixieland fans should enjoy this set. —*Scott Yanow*

1940–1941 / Sep. 6, 1940–Oct. 14, 1941 / Classics ✦✦✦✦
Classics' Sidney Bechet series continues with this CD, a generous set full of the soprano's prime Victor recordings, including appearances by cornetist Rex Stewart and pianist Earl Hines, Bechet's guest shot with The Chamber Music Society of Lower Basin Street, and his innovative "one-man-band" recordings of "The Sheik of Araby" and "Blues of Bechet." —*Scott Yanow*

The Complete, Vol. 3/4 / Jan. 8, 1941–Oct. 24, 1941 / RCA ✦✦✦✦
The second of three two-LP sets released by French RCA continues the complete chronological repackaging (including alternate takes) of all of Bechet's Victor recordings. During the ten-month period covered in this valuable set, he recorded such classics as "Egyptian Fantasy," "Swing Parade," "The Mooche" and even the odd "Laughin' in Rhythm." Bechet, a remarkable soprano saxophonist who made traditional jazz sound modern, also is heard on six instruments during his innovative overdubbed "one-man-band" performances of a blues and "The Sheik of Araby." This series is highly recommended but is becoming increasingly difficult to find. —*Scott Yanow*

Masters of Jazz, Vol. 4 / Aug. 29, 1945–Dec. 20, 1947 / Storyville ✦✦✦
The dozen performances on this CD are all taken from Sidney Bechet's famous sessions for Mezz Mezzrow's King Jazz label; in fact the CD (along with four other Storyville releases titled *The King Jazz Story Vols. 1–4*) is part of the complete reissuance of that label's output. Since this is by far the briefest of the five CDs (at around 41 minutes), this one can be acquired last. However the music (hot quintet/sextets featuring Bechet, Mezzrow and sometimes trumpeter Hot Lips Page) is often quite exciting with the emphasis on blues and heated ensembles. —*Scott Yanow*

La Legende De Sidney Bechet / Oct. 14, 1949–Jul. 4, 1958 / Vogue ✦✦✦
This CD features a cross-section of soprano-great Bechet's '50s European recordings. A national hero in France during this time, although relatively unknown to the general public in the U.S., Bechet really dominates this set. The music ranges from his 1949 hit "Les Oignons," an early version of "Petite Fleur" and a passionate "Summertime" to romping jams on "Royal Garden Blues" and "When the Saints Go Marchin' In." A fine introduction to late-period Bechet, one of the true giants of jazz history. —*Scott Yanow*

Live In New York, 1950–51 / Apr. 1, 1950–Oct. 19, 1951 / Storyville ✦✦✦
Neglected in his homeland, the great sopran saxophonist Sidney Bechet first moved to France (where he quickly became known as a national hero) in 1949 but made a couple of trips back to the United States during the next few years. His Storyville CD features Bechet in the U.S. during two occasions, leading a quartet/quintet with only a trombone joining him in the frontline; at least he was not compelled to battle for the lead with a trumpeter. There are eight selections with trombonist Vic Dickenson, pianist Ken Kersey, bassist Herb Ward and drummer Cliff Leeman that include individual features for Dickenson and Kersey along with spirited renditions of "Muskrat Ramble," "High Society" and "Royal Garden Blues"; in addition Bechet caresses the melody of "Laura" and romps through "Just One of Those Things." However it is the other 11 numbers (which were only previously released on LP by Pumpkin) that are most notable, for these are probably the finest recordings of the underrated trombonist Big Chief Russell Moore. With pianist Red Richards and drummer Art Trappier functioning quite well as the entire rhythm section (without a bassist), the trombonist stays out of Bechet's way and adds some robust and humorous solos of his own. During memorable versions of "I Found a New Baby," "Bugle Call Rag," "Panama"

and even "Casey Jones," Bechet never runs out of infectious riffs and is in consistently exciting form. —*Scott Yanow*

Salle Pleyel: 31 January 52 / Jan. 31, 1952 / Vogue ✦✦
Bechet is heard on this CD in concert with Claude Luter's orchestra before a semihysterical audience. The crowd shows one just how popular Bechet was in France during the '50s; if only America treated its jazzmen as well. The music is generally rewarding if without many surprises, a variety of standards and Dixieland tunes with Bechet's soprano rightfully dominating the proceedings. —*Scott Yanow*

Sidney Bechet in Paris, Vol. 1 / May 18, 1953+1964 / Vogue ✦✦
This Vogue CD is a bit unusual for, rather than featuring the masterful soprano saxophonist Sidney Bechet in his usual Dixieland settings, it contains his original music for two ballets as performed by a pair of symphony orchestras. "La Nuit Est Une Sorciere" from 1953, after some narration in French, has the orchestra playing dramatic themes with a few token appearances by Bechet himself. "La Colline Du Delta," a lively tribute to Louisiana, was recorded posthumously in 1964 with Claude Luter (a close Sidney Bechet disciple) in Bechet's place; Luter gets to stretch out a bit. Overall this is an interesting, but not essential, set. —*Scott Yanow*

Jazz at Storyville / Oct. 1953 / Black Lion ✦✦✦
Taken from Sidney Bechet's last major tour of the United States, this live session teams his passionate soprano with the subtle wit of trombonist Vic Dickenson and a fine rhythm section (including George Wein on piano). This set may just contain familiar standards, but the general enthusiasm and the interplay between Bechet and Dickenson makes the music well worth hearing and easy to enjoy. —*Scott Yanow*

Olympia Concert, October 19, 1955 / Oct. 19, 1955 / Vogue ✦✦✦
Bechet is heard on this CD at a 1955 concert held before an adoring crowd in Paris where he was continually honored as a national hero. Backed by a pair of alternating French trad bands, Bechet plays some fresher material than usual, bringing back such classics as "Wild Man Blues," "Wild Cat Rag" and "Viper Mad." —*Scott Yanow*

When a Soprano Meets a Piano / 1957 / Inner City ✦✦✦
One of Sidney Bechet's final recordings was this relatively modern quartet session, which also features pianist Martial Solal. This LP finds Bechet playing melodically and with invention on superior swing (rather than Dixieland) standards, meeting the modern 25-year-old pianist halfway. Bechet's sound was still beautiful, even at this late stage. —*Scott Yanow*

Paris Jazz Concert / May 27, 1957–Aug. 3, 1958 / RTE ✦✦✦
This Sidney Bechet CD is comprised of previously unreleased material taken from three Paris concerts that was fortunately broadcast over the radio and properly preserved through the years. The classic master of the soprano sax is heard in reasonably inspired form quite late in his career. The first two sets feature Bechet being accompanied by French groups that, although not overly distinctive, offer contrasting solos that do not get in the way; both Guy Lognon and Roland Hug are fine on trumpet. The other band has much bigger names including trumpeter Buck Clayton, trombonist Vic Dickenson and pianist George Wein but, even with Clayton being showcased on "All of Me," there is no doubt that Sidney Bechet is the leader. It's easily recommended to Dixieland fans. —*Scott Yanow*

Parisian Encounter / Jul. 4, 1958 / Vogue ✦✦✦
One of the most competitive of all jazzmen, Bechet was well-teamed with the Louis Armstrong-influenced trumpet of Teddy Buckner on this spirited set from late in Bechet's life. Buckner is reasonably respectful but gets in plenty of hot licks during this Dixielandish session; a concert shortly afterward by the two would be very combative. This fine CD shows that Sidney Bechet never did decline or lose any of his formidable power. —*Scott Yanow*

And Friends / PolyGram ✦✦
A sampler which is part of the Walkman jazz series. It features Bechet during latter stages in France, playing with his comrades. Some songs are delightful, especially "The Onions" with Claude Luter. —*Ron Wynn*

Bix Beiderbecke

b. May 10, 1903, Davenport, IA, **d.** Aug. 6, 1931, New York, NY
Cornet / Classic Jazz
Bix Beiderbecke was one of the greatest jazz musicians of the

1920s. His colorful life, quick rise and fall and eventual status as a martyr made him a legend even before he died, and he has long stood as proof that not all the innovators in jazz history were black. Possessor of a beautiful distinctive tone and a strikingly original improvising style, Bix's only competitor among cornetists in the '20s was Louis Armstrong and (due to their different sounds and styles) one really could not compare them.

Beiderbecke was a bit of a child prodigy, picking out tunes on the piano when he was three. While he had conventional training on the piano, he taught himself the cornet. Influenced by the original Dixieland Jazz Band, Beiderbecke craved the freedom of jazz but his straight-laced parents felt he was being frivolous. He was sent to Lake Forest Military Academy in 1921 but by coincidence it was located fairly close to Chicago, the center of jazz at the time. Bix was eventually expelled as he missed so many classes! After a brief period at home he became a full-time musician. In 1923 Beiderbecke became the star cornetist of the Wolverines and a year later this spirited group made some classic recordings.

In late 1924 Bix left the Wolverines to join Jean Goldkette's Orchestra, but his inability to read music resulted in him losing the job. In 1925 he spent time in Chicago and worked on his reading abilities. The following year he spent time with Frankie Trumbauer's Orchestra in St. Louis. Although already an alcoholic, 1927 would be Beiderbecke's greatest year. He worked with Jean Goldkette's Orchestra (most of their records are unfortunately quite commercial), recorded his piano masterpiece "In a Mist" (one of his four Debussy-inspired originals), cut many classic sides with a small group headed by Trumbauer (including his greatest solos: "Singin' the Blues,' "I'm Comin' Virginia" and "Way Down Yonder in New Orleans") and then signed up with Paul Whiteman's huge and prosperous orchestra. Although revisionist historians would later claim that Whiteman's wide mixture of repertoire (much of it outside of jazz) drove Bix to drink, he actually enjoyed the prestige of being with the most popular band of the decade. Beiderbecke's favorite personal solo was his written-out part on George Gershwin's "Concerto in F."

With Whiteman, Bix's solos tended to be short moments of magic, sometimes in odd settings; his brilliant chorus on "Sweet Sue" is a perfect example. He was productive throughout 1928 but by the following year his drinking really began to catch up with him. Beiderbecke had a breakdown, made a comeback and then in September 1929 was reluctantly sent back to Davenport to recover. Unfortunately Bix made a few sad records in 1930 before his death at age 28. The bad liquor of the Prohibition era did him in.

For the full story, *Bix: Man & Legend* is a remarkably detailed book. Beiderbecke's recordings (even the obscure ones) are continually in print, for his followers believe that every note he played was special. This writer agrees. —*Scott Yanow*

And the Chicago Cornets / Feb. 18, 1924–Jan. 26, 1925 / Milestone ++++
Not only does this superior double-LP set contain all of cornetist Bix Beiderbecke's recordings with The Wolverines in 1924 (much of which is classic), but it features him with The Sioux City Six and his Rhythm Jugglers (highlighted by the original version of "Davenport Blues"), the two titles cut by The Wolverines after Beiderbecke departed (with Jimmy McPartland in his spot) and seven performances by The Bucktown Five in 1924 (the recording debut of cornetist Muggsy Spanier). Collectors of '20s jazz should be familiar with most of this music, especially The Wolverines sides. Bix Beiderbecke, although only 21 years old at the time, already demonstrated the lyricism, inventiveness and beautiful tone that one associates with him. —*Scott Yanow*

Singin' The Blues / Jun. 2, 1924–Sep. 15, 1930 / Drive Archive +++
Cornetist Bix Beiderbecke's recordings have been reissued in more complete fashion elsewhere, but this single budget CD contains 14 of his greatest performances. Highlights include "Singin' the Blues," "I'm Comin' Virginia," "Riverboat Shuffle" and early versions (with The Wolverines in 1924) of "Royal Garden Blues" and "Tiger Rag." This set does a good job of introducing newer listeners to the classic music. —*Scott Yanow*

The Indispensable / Nov. 24, 1924–Sep. 15, 1930 / RCA ++++
This double-CD from French RCA in their Jazz Tribune series (a reissue of an earlier double-LP) gives one a good overview of cornetist Bix Beiderbecke's Victor recordings. More serious collectors will want to acquire this music as part of a more complete series (since all of his solos are significant) while beginning collectors

are advised to pick up his Columbia reissue CDs (which feature Beiderbecke in smaller groups) first. The 36 performances on this two-fer mostly focus on his sideman appearances with the large dance orchestras of Jean Goldkette and Paul Whiteman during 1926–28, although there is one 1924 track ("I Didn't Know") with Goldkette and a few later sessions from 1930. Highlights include "Clementine," "San," "There Ain't No Sweet Man," "From Monday On" and "You Took Advantage of Me." —*Scott Yanow*

★ **Bix Beiderbecke, Vol. 1: Singin' the Blues** / Feb. 4, 1927–Sep. 30, 1927 / Columbia +++++

At the Jazz Band Ball, Vol. 2 / Oct. 1927–Apr. 3, 1928 / Columbia +++++

Bix Lives / 1927–1930 / RCA ++++
This album includes Jean Goldkette and Whiteman material. It's a nice compliment to the Columbia Records compilations (*Vols. 1 & 2*). —*Richard Lieberson*

Richie Beirach
b. May 23, 1947, New York, NY
Piano / Post-Bop
Although somewhat underrated, Richie Beirach is a consistently inventive pianist whose ability to play both free and with lyricism makes him an original. After studying classical piano, Beirach switched to jazz. He studied at Berklee and the Manhattan School of Music and took lessons with Stan Getz, Dave Holland and Jack DeJohnette. Beirach played electric piano while with Dave Liebman's Lookout Farm in 1974 but has mostly stuck to acoustic piano ever since. He has teamed up with Liebman on many occasions (including the early-'80s group Quest) and has recorded frequently during the past 20 years. Among his many jobs as a sideman were important stints with Getz, Lee Konitz, John Abercrombie and Chet Baker, and Beirach has played music ranging from hard bop to totally free. His classical training can sometimes be heard in his more advanced improvisations, along with the sensitivity of a Bill Evans. —*Scott Yanow*

Eon / Nov. 1974 / ECM +++

Leaving / Aug. 17, 1976–Aug. 18, 1976 / Storyville +++

Hubris / Jun. 1977 / ECM +++

Elm / May 1979 / ECM ++++

Rendevous / Jan. 24, 1981–Jan. 25, 1981 / IPI +++

Breathing of Statues / Sep. 1982 / Magenta +++

Antarctica / Sep. 12, 1985–Sep. 14, 1985 / Evidence ++++
Ambitious, erratic but interesting concept album by pianist Beirach originally made for the Pathfinder label. It's a solo piano suite with all original pieces. He hits sometimes and misses at other times, but it's certainly good to hear something besides standards and hard bop, even when it's more mood than substance. —*Ron Wynn*

Emerald City / Feb. 23, 1987–Feb. 25, 1987 / Evidence +++
Depending on how you choose to define "jazz," this duet session linking pianist Richie Beirach with John Abercrombie (playing guitar synthesizer) may or may not fit your criteria. There are certainly passages with a rock sensibility, and Abercrombie's use of a guitar synthesizer may distress those who instinctively distrust electronics in any improvising context. But if you rank jazz pedigree on skills, individuality, and the willingness to take chances, then this date qualifies on all counts. Beirach and Abercrombie don't fall into quickly identifiable patterns. If you aren't appalled by Abercrombie's embrace of technology and want to hear material that doesn't fit any rigid definition, here's something right up your alley. —*Ron Wynn*

Common Heart / Sep. 28, 1987–Sep. 29, 1987 / Owl +++
Alternately stunning and uneven solo piano work from 1987, with Beirach covering originals, spinning out melodies, pacing the set, and trying something different from conventional theme/solo/theme arrangements. This has been reissued on CD. —*Ron Wynn*

Some Other Time / Apr. 17, 1989–Apr. 18, 1989 / Triloka +++

● **Convergence** / Nov. 10, 1990–Nov. 11, 1990 / Triloka ++++
Great communications on this one, duets with pianist Richard Beirach and tenor saxophonist George Coleman. —*Michael G. Nastos*

Live at Maybeck Recital Hall, Vol. 19 / Jan. 5, 1992 / Concord Jazz ✦✦✦

Bob Belden

b. Oct. 31, 1956, Charleston, SC
Arranger, Composer, Tenor Saxophone / Post-Bop
One of the most adventurous arrangers of the 1990s, Bob Belden has taken the music of Puccini, Prince and (with the most success) Sting and turned it into jazz. After graduating from the University of North Texas in 1978 he was with Woody Herman's Orchestra for 18 months, worked with Donald Byrd off and on during 1981–85, played with the Mel Lewis Orchestra and produced a couple of Red Rodney records. In 1983 Belden settled in New York as a writer for studio sessions. Influenced by Gil Evans, Belden debuted on Sunnyside with *Treasure Island* before working on transforming nonjazz material into jazz. Belden has also been assisting with Columbia Records' Miles Davis reissue program. — *Scott Yanow*

Treasure Island / Aug. 12, 1989–Aug. 13, 1989 / Sunnyside ✦✦✦
This compositional jazz in the tradition of George Russell and Gil Evans is a very good effort. — *Michael G. Nastos*

● **Straight to My Heart: Music of Sting** / Dec. 1, 1989–May 9, 1991 / Blue Note ✦✦✦✦✦
Arranger Bob Belden skillfully takes the music of pop-star Sting and arranges it for a jazz ensemble with stunning results. Featured are Rick Margitza (ts), Joey Calderazzo (p), and Dennis Chambers (d). — *Paul Kohler*

When the Doves Cry: The Music of Prince / May 5, 1993–Sep. 27, 1993 / Metro Blue ✦✦

Marcus Belgrave

b. 1936, Chester, PA
Trumpet / Post-Bop
Because he has spent most of his career in Detroit and has not recorded enough, Marcus Belgrave has often been overlooked. A flexible and talented trumpeter able to play both hard bop and free, Belgrave was tutored by Clifford Brown a bit when he was 17. He toured with Ray Charles during 1954–1959 and had opportunitites to play with the groups of Charles Mingus and Max Roach. In 1963 Belgrave moved to Detroit where he has been continually active as an educator and a studio player. He has recorded with (among others) McCoy Tyner, David Newman, Art Hodes (duets), David Murray, Geri Allen (one of his former students), swing tenor Franz Jackson and Sammy Price, mostly since the 1980s. Belgrave has also been featured with the Lincoln Center Jazz Orchestra. Among his other former students are Bob Hurst, Kenny Garrett and James Carter, so at least indirectly Marcus Belgrave is making a strong impact on jazz. — *Scott Yanow*

Gemini I i / 1975 / Tribe ✦✦✦
The nonet with the master trumpeter is sometimes funky, spacy, or swinging, but always potent. On this LP with Roy Brooks, Wendell Harrison, Harold McKinney, and Phil Ranelin, the band sounds twice its size due to the expansive compositional stance of the leader. — *Michael G. Nastos*

Louie Bellson
(Luigi Paulino Alfredo Francesco Antonion Balassoni)

b. Jul. 26, 1924, Rock Falls, IL
Drums, Leader / Swing, Bop
One of the great drummers of all time (and one of the few whose name can be said in the same sentence with Buddy Rich), Louie Bellson has the rare ability to continually hold one's interest throughout a 15-minute solo. He became famous in the 1950s for using two bass drums simultaneously, but Bellson was never a gimmicky or overly bombastic player. In addition to being able to drive a big band to exciting effect, Bellson can play very quietly with a trio and sound quite satisfied.
Winner of a Gene Krupa talent contest while a teenager, Bellson was with the big bands of Benny Goodman (1943 and 1946), Tommy Dorsey (1947–49) and Harry James (1950–51) before replacing Sonny Greer with the Duke Ellington Orchestra. A talented writer, Bellson contributed "Skin Deep" and "The Hawk Talks" to Duke's permanent repertoire. He married Pearl Bailey in 1952 and the following year left Ellington to be her musical director. Bellson toured with Jazz at the Philharmonic

(1954–55), recorded many dates in the 1950s for Verve and was with the Dorsey Brothers (1955–56), Count Basie (1962), Duke Ellington (1965–66) and Harry James (1966). He has been continually active up to the present day, leading big bands (different ones on the East and West Coasts), putting together combos for record dates, giving clinics for younger drummers and writing new music. Bellson has recorded extensively for Roulette (early '60s), Concord, Pablo and most recently Music Masters. — *Scott Yanow*

150 M.P.H. / May 25, 1974 / Concord Jazz ✦✦✦

The Louis Bellson Explosion / May 21, 1975–May 22, 1975 / Pablo ✦✦✦
A fine mid-'70s date that was both a showcase for Bellson's drumming and also a nice straight-ahead date with great contributions from Blue Mitchell, Snookey Young, Dick Mitchell and others. It's been reissued on CD. — *Ron Wynn*

Louie Bellson's 7 / Jul. 25, 1976 / Concord Jazz ✦✦✦

Ecue Ritmos Cubanos / Jan. 21, 1977–Jan. 21, 1977 / Original Jazz Classics✦✦
Drummer Louis Bellson is co-leader on this CD reissue of a Pablo set with percussionist Walfredo De Los Reyes, but it is very much Reyes' set. Actually, there are eight percussionists on this date and, even with the presence of keyboards, two bassists (including the legendary Cachao) and up to three horns (Cat Anderson and Alejandro Vivar on trumpets and Lew Tabackin contributing some flute and tenor), the five selections are essentially percussion displays. This would have been a fun date to see live with all of the colorful sounds being made but, as a pure listening experience, the lack of variety and the emphasis on fairly simple (if dense) rhythmic vamps makes this a surprisingly forgettable affair. — *Scott Yanow*

Prime Time / Nov. 4, 1977 / Concord Jazz ✦✦✦✦

Sunshine Rock / Dec. 21, 1977–Dec. 23, 1977 / Pablo ✦✦✦

Intensive Care / Mar. 17, 1978–Mar. 18, 1978 / Voss ✦✦

Raincheck / May 3, 1978 / Concord Jazz ✦✦✦

Note Smoking / Aug. 14, 1978–Aug. 15, 1978 / Voss/Allegiance ✦✦✦

Louis Bellson Jam / Sep. 28, 1978–Sep. 29, 1978 / Original Jazz Classics ✦✦✦

Matterhorn: Louie Bellson Drum Explosion / Dec. 11, 1978–Dec. 13, 1978 / Pablo ✦✦

● **Side Track** / Jun. 1979 / Concord Jazz ✦✦✦✦

Dynamite / Aug. 1979 / Concord Jazz ✦✦✦

Live At Ronnie Scott's / Oct. 25, 1979–Oct. 26, 1979 / DRG ✦✦✦

London Scene / Oct. 13, 1980 / Concord Jazz ✦✦✦

The London Gig / Nov. 1, 1982 / Pablo ✦✦✦

Cool Cool Blue / Nov. 9, 1982 / Original Jazz Classics ✦✦✦

Don't Stop Now! / 1984 / Bosco ✦✦✦

Classics in Jazz / Oct. 14, 1986–Oct. 15, 1986 / Music Masters ✦✦✦✦

Live at Joe Segal's Jazz Showcase / Oct. 1987 / Concord Jazz ✦✦✦

Hot / Dec. 7, 1987–Dec. 9, 1987 / Music Masters ✦✦✦

East Side Suite / Dec. 7, 1987–Dec. 9, 1987 / Music Masters ✦✦✦

Jazz Giants / Apr. 30, 1989 / Music Masters ✦✦✦

Peaceful Thunder / Sep. 24, 1991–Sep. 25, 1991 / Music Masters ✦✦✦
Good combo date from a veteran drummer with substantial swing and big band credentials. Bellson's recent records adhere to established musical values, yet seem to have a freshness that escapes some of the recent traditional dates. Marvin Stamm and Derek Smith are examples of critically unheralded players who seldom fail to elevate a session. — *Ron Wynn*

Black Brown & Beige / Oct. 20, 1992–Oct. 22, 1992 / Music Masters ✦✦✦
Rather than try to recreate Duke Ellington's famous "Black, Brown & Beige," Louie Bellson's big band does a reinterpretation of the 50-minute work on this CD that takes a lot of liberties with the composition. A little more space is allocated to solos, Johnny Hodges' famous "Come Sunday" melody statement is given to Clark Terry, Joe Williams sings "The Blues" and such players as

Music Map

Bass (acoustic)

Pioneers

Bill Johnson (first to develop plucked string style)
Ed Garland
Steve Brown
John Lindsay
Wellman Braud (with Duke Ellington 1927-35)
Pops Foster

Swing Era

Israel Crosby (1935 solo on "Blues of Israel")
Walter Page (with Count Basie)
John Kirby
Bob Haggart
Gene Ramey
Milt Hinton

Three Great Innovators

Jimmy Blanton (with Duke Ellington 1939-41)
Oscar Pettiford
Charles Mingus

1940s

Slam Stewart	Tommy Potter
Curly Russell	Red Callender

Bop to Modern Mainstream

Ray Brown	Percy Heath
George Duvivier	Major Holley
Wendell Marshall	Ed Safranski
Red Mitchell	Monty Budwig
Leroy Vinnegar	Eugene Wright
Paul Chambers	Doug Watkins
Sam Jones	Wilbur Ware
Richard Davis	Ron Carter
Buster Williams	Miroslav Vitous
George Mraz	Harvie Swartz
Dave Friesen	Brian Torff
Glen Moore	John Clayton
Christian McBride	Reginald Veal
Robert Hurst	Charnett Moffett
John Patitucci	Charles Fambrough
Niels Henning-Orsted Pedersen	

Bill Evans' Bassists

Scott LaFaro
Chuck Israels
Eddie Gomez
Marc Johnson

Avant-Garde

Buell Neidlinger (with Cecil Taylor 1955-61)
Charlie Haden
Gary Peacock
Reggie Workman
Art Davis
Jimmy Garrison
Henry Grimes
David Izenzon (with Ornette Coleman 1961-68)
Malachi Favors
(a founder of the Art Ensemble Of Chicago)
Dave Holland
Sirone
Johnny Dyani
Barre Phillips
Cecil McBee
Fred Hopkins
Mark Helias
Anthony Cox
John Lindberg
William Parker
Barry Guy

trumpeter Barrie Lee Hall, Art Baron on plunger trombone, pianist Harold Danko and baritonist Joe Temperley are heard from. This version does give some new life to the classic suite. In addition, Bellson's band plays five of the drummer's originals including the boppish "Hawk Talks" and "Skin Deep." The shorter orchestral pieces fit into the general mood of the respectful but fairly creative tribute. —*Scott Yanow*

● **Live From New York** / Jan. 20, 1994 / Telarc ✦✦✦✦
At 71 Louie Bellson on this CD displays more energy than most drummers half his age. Bellson not only takes solos on more than half the selections (including a lengthy workout on "Santos") but

he composed all seven originals; the only surprise is that Bellson decided to let some of his musical friends (including Matt Catingub, Tommy Newsom and Bob Florence) arrange the charts instead of writing them himself. With concise solos from such sidemen as trumpeters Marvin Stamm and Glenn Drewes, tenorman Ted Nash, altoists Joe Roccisano and Steve Wilson and trombonist Keith O'Quinn, Bellson's music is given perfectly suitable interpretations. But just in case, the equally ageless fluegelhornist Clark Terry (at 75) stars on two songs including the exquisite ballad "Blow Your Horn." With Louie Bellson constantly driving the ensembles, this is a big-band disc well worth acquiring. —*Scott Yanow*

Sathima Bea Benjamin

b. Oct. 17, 1936, Cape Town, South Africa
Vocals / Post-Bop
An enchanting, evocative vocalist, Satima Bea Benjamin has made several recordings as a leader since establishing herself in Abdullah Ibrahim's (her husband) band during the '70s. Benjamin's performed and recorded show tunes and standards, traditional South African and African music, and improvised on her originals and other jazz pieces. The two met in South Africa at the end of the '50s. After leaving their homeland, they met Duke Ellington in Switzerland in the early '60s. He invited them to Paris for a recording session. Though only Ibrahim's date was issued of the two, Benjamin eventually sang with Ellington's orchestra at Newport in 1965. She recorded an Ellington tribute album in 1979, and has since done sessions for Blackhawk and Enja. Ricky Ford, Buster Williams, Billy Higgins, and Kenny Barron are some other musicians who've played and worked with Benjamin. *—Ron Wynn*

Sathima Sings Ellington / Apr. 1979 / Ekapa ✦✦✦✦

Windsong / Jun. 17, 1985 / Black Hawk ✦✦✦

● **Love Light** / Sep. 5, 1987 / Enja ✦✦✦✦
A fine set. Carlos Ward almost steals the show on alto sax. *—Ron Wynn*

Southern Touch / Dec. 14, 1989 / Enja ✦✦✦
Evocative, expressive ballads and love songs done by wonderful vocalist Satima Bea Benjamin, wife of Abdullah Ibrahim. She sings without a trace of self-indulgence and has the right touch to make even the most sentimental lyric seem convincing and genuine. *—Ron Wynn*

Tony Bennett

b. Aug. 3, 1926, New York, NY
Vocals / Middle-of-the-Road Pop
Tony Bennett has enjoyed a resurgence of popularity in the late '80s and early '90s that matches his success in the '50s and '60s. He's been the model of consistency, singing with warmth, choosing ideal material and making excellent albums with their foundation in jazz regardless of lyric content. Bennett's admiration for jazz musicians has often been expressed, and he's said to have modeled his phrasing on Art Tatum's piano technique and delivery on Mildred Bailey's vocal style. He sang while waiting tables as a teenager, then performed with military bands during World War II, and later had vocal studies at the American Theatre Wing school. Comedian Bop Hope noticed him working with Pearl Bailey, and made some career suggestions; from them he changed his name from Joe Bari to Tony Bennett. Bennett's initial success came via several Columbia singles in the '50s. These included "Because of You," a chart topper in 1951, "I Won't Cry Anymore" and a remake of Hank Williams Sr.'s "Cold, Cold Heart" which also made it to the number one spot. Bennett had an impressive run of chart entries, with 24 songs making the Top 40 from 1950 to 1964, and hits for almost 16 consecutive years. "Stranger in Paradise," "Just in Time," "Rags to Riches," and "There'll Be No Teardrops Tonight" were other big '50s hits, and in the early '60s came the signature tune "I Left My Heart in San Francisco," which also won a Grammy, plus "I Wanna Be Around," "The Good Life" and "Who Can I Turn To." Bennett made the transition in the '60s and '70s to an album artist, with 25 LPs making the charts between 1962 and 1972. Robert Farnon provided arrangements for four major ones. Bennett didn't merely churn out hits; he recorded with Count Basie, Duke Ellington and Woody Herman. In the '70s, he played with Bill Evans and Jimmy and Marian McPartland. Later came sessions of Rogers and Hart songs with Ruby Braff that yielded two volumes of material. Bennett took a sabbatical from the recording studios in the '70s and '80s, concentrating on touring, performing and painting. Columbia filled the void with reissues until his '86 release *The Art of Excellence*. It primarily featured Bennett with Ralph Sharon's trio, but also included an intriguing duet with Ray Charles. A two-volume 1987 anthology *Tony Bennett/Jazz* featured an unissued track from 1964 with Bennett and Stan Getz. George Benson, Dizzy Gillespie and Dexter Gordon were guests on the 1987 new album *Bennett and Berlin*. His profile hasn't decreased in the '90s, thanks to the hit album *Perfectly Frank* devoted to songs popularized by Frank Sinatra and another album with numbers sung by Fred Astaire. Not only does he continue performing all over the world,

Bennett's making new inroads; he appeared on *MTV Unplugged* in 1993. *—Ron Wynn and William Ruhlmann*

Tony's Greatest Hits / 1951 / Columbia ✦✦✦✦✦
Tony Bennett's first hits collection chronicles his initial seven years as a recording artist, during which he frequently was found in the singles charts. Among this album's 12 selections are nine chart songs: "Because Of You" (#1 for 10 weeks, 1951), "Cold, Cold Heart" (#1 for six weeks, 1951), "Rags To Riches" (#1 for eight weeks, 1953), "Stranger In Paradise" (#2, 1954), "There'll Be No Teardrops Tonight" (#7, 1954), "Just In Time" (#46, 1956), "In The Middle Of An Island" (#9, 1957), "Ca, C'est L'amour" (#22, 1957), and "Young And Warm And Wonderful" (#23, 1958). Also featured is Bennett's non-charting debut single, "Boulevard Of Broken Dreams," a tango complete with castanets that first gained him notice. In retrospect, early Bennett is not Bennett at his best— the song selection and arrangements are often so idiosyncratic and gimmicky they border on being novelty material, and Bennett often oversings in a mock-operatic style. But his intonation is always clear, his confidence always apparent. And there remains a historical interest—this is Tony Bennett as pop idol, and he carries it off. *—William Ruhlmann*

☆ **Jazz** / 1954 / Columbia ✦✦✦✦✦
What a wonderful idea. This is a compilation album ranging across Tony Bennett's early career, from 1954 to 1967, highlighting some of his more adventurous sessions with jazz musicians, including Count Basie, Herbie Hancock, Herbie Mann, Art Blakey, Stan Getz, and others, and featuring jazz standards like "Green Dolphin Street," along with a healthy dose of Duke Ellington compositions. Bennett not only holds his own, he sounds delighted on every track. The ironic thing, of course, is that Columbia frowned on these kinds of side excursions from his pop career in the '50s. Now, all is forgiven, and this proves an unusually imaginative repackaging that illuminates an important part of Bennett's talent and further contributes to his '80s renaissance. (The album contains a previously unreleased 1964 performance of "Danny Boy" featuring Stan Getz. Originally released as a two-LP set, *Jazz* was compressed to a 68-minute CD by excising two tracks.) *—William Ruhlmann*

More Tony's Greatest Hits / 1958 / Columbia ✦✦
It had been only two years since Tony Bennett's first hits collection when Columbia released this, his second. In that time, he hadn't scored many hits. In fact, he'd had only three chart entries: "Firefly" (#20, 1958), "Smile" (#73, 1959), and "Climb Ev'ry Mountain" (#74, 1960). So, the album's title was a misnomer, but it signalled that here was a collection of Bennett performances of either contemporary songs or older songs in contemporary arrangements, intended for the hit parade even if they didn't get there. There is a light, optimistic tone to much of the material— "Smile," "Put On A Happy Face," "You'll Never Get Away From Me"—and although much is also slight, Bennett brings his trademark warmth to the settings. *—William Ruhlmann*

Strike Up The Band / Jan. 3, 1959–Jan. 5, 1959 / Roulette ✦✦✦
Tony Bennett recorded two albums with Count Basie and His Orchestra under a contractual agreement giving one of the records to Bennett's label, Columbia, and the other to Basie's, Roulette. The Columbia album, *In Person!*, was released once, while the Roulette album, initially issued under the title *Strike Up The Band*, has been re-released by various labels under various titles endlessly. This is one of those reissues, and while one may deplore the duplicitous marketing scheme, the pairing between Bennett and Basie remains impressive. The band races through tunes like "With Plenty Of Money And You," and Bennett matches them, drawing strength from the bravura arrangements, while band and singer achieve a knowing tenderness on "Growing Pains." This is an album well worth owning; just make sure you don't buy it twice. *—William Ruhlmann*

To My Wonderful One / 1960 / Columbia ✦✦✦
Working with arranger/conductor Frank DeVol, Tony Bennett here recorded a string-filled ballad session featuring standards like "September Song" and "Autumn Leaves." In so doing, he demonstrated how far he had come in controlling his instrument in his ten years of recording. There was none of the oratorical style of his early hits. The restraint was especially noticeable on a song like "Till," which could have allowed for some of the old bel canto belting. Instead, Bennett's interpretations now had a detail and a nuance that marked him as a master interpreter. *—William Ruhlmann*

☆ **I Left My Heart In San Francisco** / 1962 / Columbia ✦✦✦✦✦
Along with his producer, Ernest Altschuler, and his arranger/pianist Ralph Sharon, Tony Bennett had been searching for a repertoire and a musical approach beyond his long-gone pop work with Mitch Miller of the early 1950s and his artistically pleasing but commercially dicey jazz work of the mid-to-late '50s. It seemed to be a combination of Broadway songs and other contemporary material, carefully selected and arranged to show off Bennett's now-burnished vocals, which, as he approached the end of his thirties, were starting to be located in a more comfortable range closer to a baritone than a tenor. With this album, they found the key, not only by happening across a signature song in the title track, but also in the approach to songs like "Once Upon A Time," a gem from the flop musical *All American*, and Cy Coleman and Carolyn Leigh's "The Best Is Yet To Come," which Bennett helped make a standard. (Frank Sinatra didn't do it until two years later.) From here on until the world changed again toward the late '60s, Bennett would not have to feel that he had to compromise his art for popularity, making uptempo singles in an attempt to meet the marketplace while longing to do ballads and swing material instead. *I Left My Heart In San Francisco*, a gold-selling Top 10 hit that stayed in the charts almost three years, demonstrated that he could have it all. (Tony Bennett won two 1962 Grammy Awards for the title song: Record of the Year and Best Solo Vocal Performance, Male.) — *William Ruhlmann*

Mr. Broadway / 1962 / Columbia ✦✦
In the search for new, non-rock material in the late 1950s and early 1960s, Tony Bennett had turned increasingly to Broadway shows. His second greatest hits collection, for example, found him singing songs from *The Sound Of Music*, *Gypsy*, *Bye Bye Birdie*, and *Flower Drum Song*. On this compilation, subtitled "Tony's Greatest Broadway Hits," Columbia Records culled those tracks, plus others taken from shows like *Bells Are Ringing* and *Kismet* that had been chart singles for Bennett. It's a fair idea, but doesn't make for an essential Bennett release. — *William Ruhlmann*

● **At Carnegie Hall** / 1962 / Columbia ✦✦✦✦✦
Recorded on June 9, 1962, one week before the release of the *I Left My Heart In San Francisco* album that would catapult Tony Bennett's career into the stratosphere, this concert album effectively sums up his accomplishments so far. Some of the hits— "Stranger In Paradise," "Rags To Riches," "Because Of You"—are still on the set list (although drastically rearranged), but clearly he has found his true repertoire in reinventions of older material like "All The Things You Are" (the version here is exquisite) and good choices of new songs—he champions the team of Cy Coleman and Carolyn Leigh, and introduces "San Francisco," which some in the audience already know. (Released as a single in advance of the *San Francisco* album, it was in the charts already.) And on the album's original four LP sides, Bennett managed to find time for such experiments as an uptempo "Ol' Man River" featuring percussionist Candido, a throwback to his innovative *Beat Of My Heart* album. As a consistent demonstration of Bennett's strengths, the album earns its designation as a "pick." More than his greatest hits collections of the '50s and early '60s, it gives a broad sense of Bennett's work, and it does so in the format with which he's most comfortable—live in concert. — *William Ruhlmann*

I Wanna Be Around / 1963 / Columbia ✦✦✦✦✦
As the studio album followup to Tony Bennett's breakthrough record, *I Left My Heart In San Francisco*, *I Wanna Be Around* had a lot to live up to, but since *San Francisco* was a culmination of Bennett's development, not a fluke, *I Wanna Be Around* turned out to be almost on a par with its predecessor. "The Good Life" and "I Wanna Be Around" became Top 20 hits, showing that Bennett had somehow found a line into good new pop material, and there were also some excellent arrangements, courtesy of Marty Manning, including a percussion-and-flute reading of "Let's Face The Music And Dance" that echoed the *Beat Of My Heart* album and a nod to the South American trend with Antonio Carlos Jobim's "Quiet Nights (Corcovado)." A worthy successor. — *William Ruhlmann*

This Is All I Ask / 1963 / Columbia ✦✦✦
Tony Bennett got a #70 hit out of the title track, a warm ballad written by Gordon Jenkins, and elsewhere he turned to old standbys like Cy Coleman and Carolyn Leigh, pulling another song from their show *Little Me*, in this case "On The Other Side Of The Tracks" ("I've Got Your Number" had appeared on *I Wanna Be*

Music Map

Bass (electric)

Pioneer
Monk Montgomery
(electric bass with Lionel Hampton in 1953)

Innovator
Jaco Pastorius

Other Important Electric Bassists
Stanley Clarke
Steve Swallow
Eberhard Weber
John Patitucci
Tyrone Brown (with Max Roach since 1984)
Jamaaladeen Tacuma
Albert MacDowell
Alphonso Johnson
Mark Egan
Victor Bailey
Brian Bromberg
Marcus Miller
Gerald Veasley
Bill Laswell
Bob Cranshaw (with Sonny Rollins)

Around), and included a drum track, "Tricks," with Chico Hamilton. If you hadn't heard Bennett's previous two albums, *I Left My Heart In San Francisco* and *I Wanna Be Around, This Is All I Ask* would sound like a varied, satisfying collection, but if you had, you recognized the formula and realized it had been done slightly better before. — *William Ruhlmann*

Tony & Gene—Fascinatin' Rhythm / 1963 / Columbia ✦✦
This is a 1963 radio show by drummer Gene Krupa and His Orchestra, with vocals on some tracks by Tony Bennett. Bennett trades remarks with disc jockey Martin Block and then sounds overjoyed to be fronting a big band, especially on the frantic title track. It's an energetic session with modest fidelity, a minor addition to the Bennett catalog. — *William Ruhlmann*

The Many Moods of Tony / 1964 / Columbia ✦✦
Tony Bennett's Columbia Records contract in the 1960s called for three albums a year, and the result was occasional releases like this one, whose title gives away the truth: it's a hodgepodge of previously released singles ("Spring In Manhattan," "Don't Wait Too Long," "The Little Boy") and sessions held at various times with various arrangers and musicians, all stitched together to meet the release schedule. What rescues it is a remarkable new ballad, "When Joanna Loved Me," that immediately went onto the Bennett concert short list. He even named his daughter after it. Other highlights are a delicate arrangement of "A Taste Of Honey" and one of Bennett's patented drum duets with Chico Hamilton on "Caravan." But on the whole, this album does not meet the standard Bennett had set with recent releases. — *William Ruhlmann*

Who Can I Turn To / 1964 / Columbia ✦✦✦
Tony Bennett returned to the Top 40 in late 1964 with his version of the Leslie Bricusse-Anthony Newley anthem "Who Can I Turn To (When Nobody Needs Me)," from Newley's Broadway show *The Roar Of The Greasepaint, The Smell Of The Crowd*. That song, like the rest of this album, was arranged and conducted by George Siravo, who made detailed ballad arrangements, using individual

instruments and groups to echo and counterpoint the Bennett vocals. Still searching for new material, and finding it in works by Cy Coleman and Carolyn Leigh, as well as Mel Tormé (whose "Got The Gate On The Golden Gate" recalled Bennett's musical connection to San Francisco), Bennett didn't discover anything to match the title track, and he re-recorded "Autumn Leaves" in a more uptempo framework. But the match of singer and arranger made for a consistent and effective album. — *William Ruhlmann*

If I Ruled the World: Songs for the Jet Set / 1965 / Columbia ✦✦✦

Employing Sinatra arranger Don Costa, Tony Bennett put together a concept album similar to Sinatra's *Come Fly With Me.* Travel was the loose theme that united Antonio Carlos Jobim's "Song Of The Jet" (set in Rio de Janeiro, a photograph of which graces the album cover), "Fly Me To The Moon," and the title song, a Leslie Bricusse-Cyril Ornadel tune from the show *Pickwick* that was Bennett's latest hit single. There were also two songs from the Richard Rodgers-Stephen Sondheim musical *Do I Hear A Waltz?*, which was set in Venice. Other sections might not justify the flight theme—Duke Ellington's "Love Scene" was given a "destination" of Harlem on the back cover, and that neighborhood is on no known flight plan—but with such high-quality material, it was hard to complain. — *William Ruhlmann*

★ Tony's Greatest Hits, Vol. 3 / 1965 / Columbia ✦✦✦✦✦

Tony Bennett's third hits collection isn't only the best of his best-ofs, it's a classic "classic pop" album. Bennett's career hit its second and highest artistic peak in the first half of the 1960s, starting with "I Left My Heart In San Francisco" and continuing through a series of magnificent ballad hits—"I Wanna Be Around," "The Good Life," "This Is All I Ask," "When Joanna Loved Me," "Who Can I Turn To," "If I Ruled The World"—all of which are here, along with such equally impressive album tracks as "Once Upon A Time" and "The Best Is Yet To Come." As a result, this album became Bennett's second gold seller, and it remains the definitive statement of a major pop singer at his zenith. A complete understanding of his work requires a listen to his 1991 box set, *Forty Years: The Artistry Of Tony Bennett.* But this 12-song set, covering the years 1962-1965, remains the brightest jewel in his crown. — *William Ruhlmann*

Tony Bennett's Greatest Hits, Vol. 4 / 1965 / Columbia ✦✦

The fourth and final volume of Columbia's series of Tony Bennett hits (although the label would issue many compilations after be left in 1972), covering the years 1965-1969, traces the gradual decline in his popularity over the period. None of the hits got higher than #84 in the Hot 100, although seven got into the Easy Listening charts. These are mid-level standards—"The Shadow Of Your Smile," "Fly Me To The Moon"; respectable efforts, but not on a par with the best pop songwriting or the best of Bennett. — *William Ruhlmann*

A Time for Love / 1966 / Columbia ✦✦

A couple of movie themes, a few standards, and some new songs, this mixed selection, which featured four different arranger/conductors, had some nice moments here and there—a good duet with cornetist Bobby Hackett on "The Very Thought Of You," a late-night trio version of "In The Wee Small Hours Of The Morning"—but was not one of Tony Bennett's more outstanding efforts. Also notable was that it marked a commercial marginalization for Bennett that all non-rock recording artsts were experiencing. Thus began the pressures Columbia would apply to Bennett to contemporize his image and his music. — *William Ruhlmann*

Movie Song Album / 1966 / Columbia ✦✦✦

By the mid-1960s, retreating from the rock & roll onslaught, that old-time staple of the pre-rock days, the big romantic ballad, had been relegated to Hollywood, where it turned up in the opening and closing credits of movies. Like other classic pop singers, Tony Bennett had sought it out there, and with this album, coincident with his first (and last) acting role in *The Oscar,* he devoted himself exclusively to movie themes, everything from "The Trolley Song" (*Meet Me In St. Louis*) to "Days Of Wine And Roses." Some of the tunes were not first-rate, but in "The Shadow Of Your Smile" and "The Second Time Around" (previously recorded by Frank Sinatra), Bennett found material worthy of him, and even when he was faced with minor material, he sang movingly. — *William Ruhlmann*

For Once In My Life / 1967 / Columbia ✦✦

Those of you who think of "For Once In My Life" as a Stevie

Wonder song, reconsider. True, Wonder took it to #2 in 1968, but Tony Bennett's ballad version was a pop chart entry (his last) and an Easy Listening Top 10 more than a year earlier. On the accompanying album Bennett made his by-now usual selections of standards ("They Can't Take That Away From Me"), Broadway and Hollywood material, and choices from the catalogs of songwriter favorites such as Leslie Bricusse and Cy Coleman. He was a faithful friend and a dependable talent, but, while maintaining his usual standard, this album didn't feature any standout performances to lift it to higher grade. — *William Ruhlmann*

I've Gotta Be Me / 1969 / Columbia ✦✦

Bennett, whose sales had nosedived in recent years, was coming under pressure from his record label to take a more contemporary approach. This album demonstrated that he was willing to bend, but not break. The title song, a hit earlier in the year for Sammy Davis, Jr., "What The World Needs Now Is Love" (in a ludicrous swing arrangement), and "Alfie" were current pop material, which Bennett covered gamely, but it was songs like the Gershwins' "They All Laughed" that he obviously felt more comfortable with. Bennett's real failure to deal with contemporary pop was most apparent on his version of Andre and Dory Previn's "Theme From *Valley Of The Dolls*," on which he just sang his way through the hesitant, fragmented, uncertain lyric as though it was a dramatic ballad on the scale of "Who Can I Turn To." — *William Ruhlmann*

Tony Sings The Great Hits Of Today! / 1970 / Columbia ✦

Disaster strikes. Accompanied by a sleeve note from company president Clive Davis, who forced this record down his throat, Tony Bennett is presented on the album cover in a garish illustration, wearing bellbottoms and a psychedelic tie. On the record, he sings "MacArthur Park" (well, some of it, anyway), "Eleanor Rigby" (most of which he recites instead of singing), "Something," and other "great hits of today." You'd think he might make peace at least with numbers like "The Look Of Love," but the only song he shows any real enthusiasm for is "Is That All There Is?," and even that is too cynical for his style. — *William Ruhlmann*

Tony Bennett's Something / 1970 / Columbia ✦✦

Columbia Records took Tony Bennett's recording of the Beatles' "Something," which had appeared on the previous year's *Tony Sings The Great Hits Of Today!* and been a #23 Easy Listening hit the previous spring, and put it at the top of his 1970 album, which otherwise was a collection arranged and conducted by Peter Matz (who handled the early Barbra Streisand albums) and produced by Teo Macero (who handled jazz artists like Miles Davis). While Bennett still wasn't comfortable with songs like "The Long And Winding Road" and "Everybody's Talkin'," he did manage to place favorites like Antonio Carlos Jobim's "Wave") and Cy Coleman on the songlist, and Matz's tasteful arrangements assured that this record wouldn't be the debacle *Great Hits* had been. Not that Bennett was out of the woods yet. — *William Ruhlmann*

The Best of Tony Bennett / 1972 / Capitol ✦✦

This is not the best of Tony Bennett by any stretch of the imagination, but it is an interesting record from the collector's point of view, because it contains a set of recordings that are not otherwise available. In 1972, after 22 years with Columbia Records, Bennett left for MGM/Verve, where he stayed for only a year or so. This album presents some of the recordings he made then, recordings that were out of print on LP for a long time. It's not great stuff, unless your idea of great Tony Bennett includes hearing him sing George Harrison's "Give Me Love (Give Me Peace On Earth)," and no one looking for a Bennett hits collection should touch it. But fans curious about this small, previously hard-to-find area of Bennett's catalog will want to seek it out. — *William Ruhlmann*

Rodgers & Hart Songbook / Sep. 1973 / DRG ✦✦✦

In sessions recorded in September 1973, Tony Bennett cut a series of songs by Richard Rodgers and Lorenz Hart, backed by the Ruby Braff-George Barnes Quartet. Originally, they resulted into two albums on Bennett's Improv Records, each containing ten selections. The 20-track DRG disc brings the entire collection together. Bennett is a sterling interpreter, and the backup is sympathetic. — *William Ruhlmann*

The Tony Bennett Bill Evans Album / 1975 / ✦✦✦

Tony Bennett has always had an affinity for good pianists, and many of his best performances have been with trios or solo piano, so when he got the chance to make the kind of records he wanted to in the mid-1970s, a pairing with jazz pianist Bill Evans was a natural. This is a true duet, with Evans getting considerable solo time. A low-key effort, but an effective one. — *William Ruhlmann*

Tony Bennett Sings ... "Life Is Beautiful" / 1975 / ✦✦✦
After 22 years with Columbia Records and a brief sojourn on MGM, Tony Bennett launched his own record label with this release. The title track was co-written by Fred Astaire, and the album also features such Bennett favorites as Duke Ellington, Cole Porter, Richard Rodgers and Lorenz Hart, and Irving Berlin, plus a Bennett reading of Herman Hupfield's "As Time Goes By." The result was a record that had nothing to do with pop music trends in 1975, which was exactly the way that Bennett wanted it. Decades later, it sounds fresher than many of his late '60s/early '70s attempts to be contemporary. — *William Ruhlmann*

Together Again / 1976 / DRG ✦✦✦
The second Tony Bennett-Bill Evans duet album was recorded a year after the first and took an essentially similar approach, mixing Bennett's warm, relaxed vocals with the reflective, melodic, and spare piano work of Evans. If anything, Evans dominates this encounter more than he did the first, but it's still a good showcase for Bennett, too. (Originally released on Bennett's own Improv Records label, *Together Again* was reissued on CD by DRG.) — *William Ruhlmann*

Tony Bennett/ the McPartlands and Friends Make Magic / May 13, 1977–May 14, 1977 / DRG ✦✦✦
"Sit down, make yourselves comfortable," Tony Bennett says near the beginning of this album, as he introduces an entertaining live club performance, taped in May 1977. Note, however, that the co-billing in the title indicates that different songs are given over to Marian and Jimmy McPartland and their jazz band, or to Bennett and his trio. The McPartland material is fine, but unremarkable; Bennett shines as usual, but there isn't enough of him. — *William Ruhlmann*

The Special Magic of Tony Bennett / 1979 / DRG ✦✦
On the last of his independent albums before he gave up recording for seven years, Tony Bennett puts together a 12-song medley of Cole Porter songs (it's okay, but why not just devote the whole album to complete versions?) and adds songs drawn from his *Life Is Beautiful* album, plus a couple of new numbers. — *William Ruhlmann*

Chicago / 1984 / DCC ✦✦✦

Astoria: Portrait of the Artist / 1986 / Columbia ✦✦✦✦✦
Like *The Art Of Excellence*, the album that marked Tony Bennett's return to recording in 1986, *Astoria: A Portrait Of The Artist* was a non-thematic collection of new and old songs on which Bennett was backed both by his regular trio, led by pianist Ralph Sharon, and the U.K. Orchestra. Bennett's new songwriting discovery was Charles DeForest, three of whose songs—"When Do The Bells Ring For Me," "Where Do You Go From Love," and "I've Come Home Again"—were included, along with songs by the Gershwins and Jerome Kern, standards like "Body And Soul," and even a re-recording of Bennett's initial Columbia recording, "The Boulevard Of Broken Dreams." That recording had come in 1950, and the point of *Astoria* (which featured a cover photo of the young Bennett in the old neighborhood, with Bennett today standing in the same spot on the back) was to celebrate that 40-year anniversary while looking into both the past and the future, a task it accomplished admirably. — *William Ruhlmann*

Bennett/Berlin / 1987 / Columbia ✦✦✦
With his warmth and upbeat attitude, Tony Bennett makes an excellent interpreter of Irving Berlin, whose songs share exactly those qualities. This was Bennett's second newly recorded album in his return to recording and to Columbia Records, and it's a classy collection, with Bennett breathing life into songs like "Isn't This A Lovely Day" and "Cheek To Cheek." He stuck to the backing of his regular piano-bass-drums trio, led by Ralph Sharon, with extra colors provided by guests Dexter Gordon, Dizzy Gillespie, and George Benson. The result is an understated, informal session that brings out the best in the already impressive material. The only real criticism of the album is that it's so short—just over 30 minutes—which, in the emerging CD era, seems pretty skimpy. — *William Ruhlmann*

Perfectly Frank / 1992 / Columbia ✦✦✦✦✦
Think no one can touch The Chairman on his own turf? Think again. Bennett's tribute is such an obvious move. It's odd that it's taken this long to materialize. Sinatra has made no secret of his admiration of Bennett, who puts his spin on this collection of

Francis Albert classics. In the process, we wind up with Bennett's best in years. — *Steve Aldrich*

Art of Excellence / Mar. 4, 1992 / Columbia ✦✦✦✦✦
This album marked Tony Bennett's return to recording after half a dozen years, his return to Columbia Records after 14 years, and the beginning of the third stage in his career. Back with the Ralph Sharon Trio and backed by The U.K. Orchestra, Bennett demonstrates that he had spent his time off from recording gathering a bunch of good songs and refining his singing. The older material, such as "A Rainy Day" and "I Got Lost In Her Arms," is better than the new discoveries, like "How Do You Keep The Music Playing?" and "Everybody Has The Blues," but the new ones aren't bad, and with this album Bennett joins and helps to lead the swelling trend toward classic pop. It became his best-selling album in 15 years. — *William Ruhlmann*

MTV Unplugged / 1994 / Columbia ✦✦✦
Of course, Tony Bennett never was "plugged," so the concept here is redundant, but what the hell. It's been a while since a Tony Bennett live album, and he's always terrific in concert. Certainly, he is here, singing 22 pop standards, including many of his hits and many other songs he's made his own. Elvis Costello and k.d. lang drop by, but they're feeding off Bennett's energy and star power, not the other way around. The album may be part of a successful marketing plan, but forget that and revel in the singing of a masterful song interpreter still, after 40 years, at the top of his game. — *William Ruhlmann*

Here's To The Ladies / 1994 / Columbia ✦✦✦
For years, it was rumored that Frank Sinatra was going to record an album called *Here's to the Ladies*, but the Chairman of the Board never got around to actually making the record. However, Tony Bennett did and his record covers a wider range of artists and styles than Sinatra's scheduled record. Naturally, Bennett turns in a thoroughly entertaining, professional performance. It's a solid contribution to his impressively assured and diverse comeback. — *Stephen Thomas Erlewine*

☆ **Forty Years: The Artistry of Tony Bennett** / Columbia/Legacy ✦✦✦✦✦

Han Bennink

b. Apr. 17, 1942, Zaandam, Netherlands
Drums / Free Jazz, Avant-Garde
One of Europe's top drummers and percussionists, Han Bennink employs multiple rhythms, colors and accents in a similiar manner to American free-oriented drummers. He's known for using any and everything as part of his arsenal, including playing on the floor or walls, and on wood blocks, chimes, cowbells and assorted percussion instruments from around the world. But while Bennink's associated primarily with free players, he's also backed Ben Webster, Dexter Gordon, Don Byas, Johnny Griffin, Sonny Rollins and Lee Konitz during various tours. Bennink's father was in a radio orchestra and backed singers and dancers in the Netherlands. He began on clarinet, and still occasionally plays it during performances, as well as sometimes performing on banjo, viola and various saxophones. Bennink played with Eric Dolphy during his final European visit in 1964 and is featured on the *Last Date* album. He's worked with Derek Bailey, Evan Parker and Peter Brotzmann, recording with all these musicians and others such as Misha Mengelberg, John Tchicai, Dudu Pukwana and Willem Breuker in the '60s, '70s, and '80s. He's also done solo percussion albums, and recorded as a leader for FMP, Incus and ICP among others. None of Bennink's sessions as a leader are available on CD via American labels, but can be obtained by mail order. He can be heard on various Soul Note dates with Steve Lacy, Roswell Rudd, Mengelberg and others. — *Ron Wynn*

Solo / Oct. 13, 1978 / FMP ✦✦✦

David Benoit

b. 1953, Bakersfield, CA
Piano / Crossover
One of the more popular performers in the idiom somewhat inaccurately called "contemporary jazz," David Benoit has mostly performed light melodic background music, what critic Alex Henderson has dubbed "New Age with a beat." Benoit has done a few fine jazz projects (including a tribute to Bill Evans and a collaboration with Emily Remler) but most of his output for GRP has been aimed clearly at the charts. He studied composition and

piano at El Camino College and in 1975 played on the soundtrack of the film *Nashville*. After recording with Alphonse Mouzon and accompanying singer Gloria Lynne, he was signed to the AVI label when he was 24, recording sets that paved the way toward his later output. Benoit has been been a solo artist for GRP since 1986. —*Scott Yanow*

Freedom at Midnight / 1987 / GRP ✦✦✦
This popular fusion keyboardist added a string section and a large supporting cast on this session. Part of the assembled group included fellow label superstars Eric Mariental and Dave Valentin. This was elaborately produced and mastered, heavily arranged, and extremely successful on the light jazz and adult contemporary circuit. —*Ron Wynn*

Every Step of the Way / 1987 / GRP ✦✦✦

Best of David Benoit 1987–1995 / 1987 / GRP ✦✦

Urban Daydreams / 1988 / GRP ✦✦

● **Waiting for Spring** / Feb. 5, 1989–May 25, 1989 / GRP ✦✦✦✦

Inner Motion / Apr. 1990–May 1990 / GRP ✦✦

Shadows / 1991 / GRP ✦✦

Letter to Evan / 1992 / GRP ✦✦✦

Shaken Not Stirred / 1994 / GRP ✦✦
The popular pianist's release is supposed to be a series of tributes to aspects of the 1960s but the music is essentially crossover jazz-pop of the 1990s. As usual Benoit plays reasonably well but few of the melodies are all that memorable and there is little to distinguish this set from his last few. Benoit is heard in a variety of settings, from the solo "Jacqueline" and a few quartets (including two songs with Eric Mariental on alto and tenor) to a string orchestra, but jazz listeners will find little of interest here. —*Scott Yanow*

George Benoit

b. Mar. 22, 1943, Pittsburgh, PA
Guitar, Vocals / Hard Bop, Crossover, Pop
George Benson has emulated two of his strongest influences in career path and direction: Wes Montgomery and Nat "King" Cole. As with Montgomery and Cole, Benson is a supremely talented individual whose highly marketable skills have often required him to compromise his musical talents. Benson's guitar playing has a swinging flexibility and bluesy, soulful grit. His solos are deftly played and nicely executed, performed in a manner that makes him the equal of any contemporary stylist. He can accompany a vocalist or band, work with, off or against the beat, play tasteful ballads or torrid solos, do wailing soul jazz or slow, steamy blues. His singing has the sentimental, lush touches of Cole, but recalls the gospel-tinged delivery of Donny Hathaway. Benson rode to fame in the '70s on the strength of songs just a cut above easy listening; he became an urban contemporary celebrity with a blend of mellow vocals and light instrumental filler, and has sought to keep record labels and urban radio outlets happy with hit fodder while retaining his integrity doing occasional jazz projects. Benson sang in clubs as a youngster, and formed a rock band at 17. He played with Jack McDuff's quartet twice in the '60s, appearing at the Antibes-Juan-les-Pins Jazz Festival in 1964 and playing on a Swedish television broadcast with Jean Luc-Ponty. He briefly had his own trio in Pittsburgh before reteaming with McDuff. Benson later led and recorded with groups that included Ronnie Cuber and Jimmy Smith. He recorded with Billy Cobham, Miles Davis (who sought in vain to get Benson to join his group), Herbie Hancock, Freddie Hubbard, Ron Carter and Lee Morgan in the '60s. When Creed Taylor, formerly Wes Montgomery's producer, sought a replacement for his departed star he signed Benson to A&M, cutting with him the same string-laden, lightweight pop and rock filler that made Montgomery a star. When Taylor began a new label, CTI, Benson was one of his first signees. Benson continued making pleasant, at times interesting records through the early and mid-'70s until he switched to Warner Bros. His cover of a Leon Russell tune "This Masquerade" took Benson to the next level, crossover success. The single was a Top 10 pop hit and the subsequent *Breezin'* album eventually topped the pop charts and won Grammy awards. Not only did both Columbia and A&M promptly reissue his earlier albums, Benson began a run of hit records that continued into the early '80s. He had seven Top 40 singles between 1976 and 1983, and four more Top 10 albums. But even Benson expressed displeasure at the content of these

albums after awhile, and in the '80s began to try and expand without losing his urban contemporary base. He did make a command appearance at the White House in 1979, showing everyone he hadn't lost his jazz chops. Benson recorded with fellow guitarist Earl Klugh in the late '80s, and in '90 did a nice album with the Count Basie orchestra. Almost every album Benson's done over the '60s, '70s, '80s and '90s has been reissued on CD, while Columbia has reissued anthologies collecting his soul jazz and blues cuts, and Prestige has reissued an anthology of his work with McDuff. —*Ron Wynn*

The New Boss Guitar / May 1, 1964 / Original Jazz Classics ✦✦✦✦
A definitive early album, it features Brother Jack McDuff (organ). —*Michael G. Nastos*

Benson Burner / 1965–1966 / Columbia ✦✦✦
Hot, soulful mid-'60s organ combo material from a period when George Benson was playing with bluesy abandon and reflecting the considerable influence of Grant Green. Anyone hearing these songs shouldn't be surprised at his eventual crossover success, but these weren't as overproduced and orchestrated as his A&M or Warner Bros. recordings. —*Ron Wynn*

The Cookbook / Aug. 1, 1966–Oct. 19, 1966 / Columbia ✦✦✦
Simmering interplay, fueled by guitarist Benson and baritone saxophonist Ronnie Cuber make this early-'60s effort one to savor. Six Benson originals and four standards are included. It was produced by John Hammond. Lonnie Smith (organ), Bennie Green (tb). —*Michael G. Nastos*

The Other Side of Abbey Road / Oct. 22, 1969–Nov. 5, 1969 / A&M ✦✦
The albums that George Benson made for A&M in the late '60s were trial runs for the huge hits he enjoyed in the '70s. This session follows almost the same formula as later releases like *Breezin'*: light, yet immaculately played pop instrumentals, orchestrations, and the inclusion of vocals for counterpoint and contrast. —*Ron Wynn*

Beyond the Blue Horizon / Feb. 2, 1971–Feb. 3, 1971 / Columbia ✦✦✦✦
Essentially a glorified guitar-organ date, this was topnotch in its field. Clarence Palmer's organ was economical and workmanlike, George Benson's guitar was an honest effort and dug in with ideas, though I still think the best George Benson is found in side men roles. —*Bob Rusch, Cadence*

● **White Rabbit** / Nov. 23, 1971–Nov. 30, 1971 / Columbia ✦✦✦✦
This is the best collaboration between Benson and guitarist Earl Klugh (g). —*Ron Wynn*

Body Talk / Jul. 17, 1973–Jul. 18, 1973 / Columbia ✦✦✦
Decent Benson CTI dates, although not as fluid or expressive as either *White Rabbit* or *Beyond The Blue Horizon*. This was an attempt at both recreating the soul jazz he played in the '60s and also retaining a pop audience. —*Ron Wynn*

Bad Benson / May 1974 / Columbia ✦✦✦✦

In Concert at Carnegie Hall / Jan. 11, 1975 / Columbia ✦✦✦

Good King Bad / Jul. 1975–Dec. 1975 / Columbia ✦✦✦
This is a good place to hear Benson playing at his jazz best, rather than his commercial best. —*Michael Erlewine*

Breezin' / Jan. 6, 1976–Jan. 9, 1976 / Warner Brothers ✦✦✦
This was the definitive Benson album commercially; a counterpart to Wes Montgomery's pop works of the 60s. —*Ron Wynn*

Benson & Farrell / Mar. 1976–Sep. 1976 / Columbia ✦✦✦
Within the confines of the material, Benson and Farrell found ways to do more than spew out rote solos and execute the arrangements. Although this is far from their best work, they managed to retain enough integrity to make it worth hearing for the non-fusion audience. —*Ron Wynn*

In Flight / Aug. 1976+Nov. 1976 / Warner Brothers ✦✦

Weekend in L A / Feb. 1, 1977 / Warner Brothers ✦✦
A double-album release and extremely popular, particularly the remake of "On Broadway." It's dominated by vocals, but the few times Benson gets to solo, he displays enough artistry and flair to make it memorable. This has been reissued on CD. —*Ron Wynn*

In Your Eyes / 1978 / Warner Brothers ✦✦
Another in the lengthy run of George Benson hit singles and albums, although this one didn't have either the integrity of *Breezin'* or the chart success of "Give Me The Night" or *20/20*. It

did moderately well, but is not among his best commercial dates. —*Ron Wynn*

Livin' Inside Your Love / 1978 / Warner Brothers ♦♦

20/20 / 1978 / Warner Brothers ♦♦
Guitarist/vocalist George Benson was at his crossover peak with this two-record set, doing more singing than playing and soloing only when necessary. Even operating within these restrictions, however, Benson still demonstrated both a pleasant, occasionally moving voice and a crafty, soulful guitar style. This made up for the heavy-handed production. —*Ron Wynn*

Give Me the Night / 1980 / Warner Brothers ♦♦
The last in his Warner Bros. string of hit crossover albums done in the late '70s and early '80s. The title track was another big smash, and like its predecessors, the album emphasized the vocals, offering just enough guitar moments to remind listeners of Benson's background. —*Ron Wynn*

While the City Sleeps / 1986 / Warner Brothers ♦♦
Decent, more jazz-oriented '86 album Benson made with Warner Bros. under the provisions of a new pact that would give him more creative freedom. Although still not as expansive and loose as he wanted it, Benson got more room to play and present his guitar in contexts other than accompanying wordless vocals. —*Ron Wynn*

Collaboration / 1987 / Warner Brothers ♦♦♦

Tenderly / 1989 / Warner Brothers ♦♦♦♦

Big Boss Band / 1990 / Warner Brothers ♦♦♦♦

Bob Berg

b. Apr. 7, 1951, New York, NY
Soprano Saxophone, Tenor Saxophone / Hard Bop, Post-Bop
A fine tenor and soprano saxophonist most influenced by Wayne Shorter, Bob Berg studied at the High School of Performing Arts and Juilliard. Although he was originally attracted to free jazz, by 1969 (when he joined Jack McDuff), Berg was more intrigued by bop. He had stints with Horace Silver (1974–76) and Cedar Walton (1976–81), spent a couple years (1981–83) in Europe and then was with Miles Davis' electric group during 1984–86. Associated on an occasional basis with Chick Corea, Berg has mostly appeared in hard bop settings, recording as a leader early on for Xanadu and more recently for Denon, Red and Stretch. —*Scott Yanow*

New Birth / May 12, 1978 / Xanadu ♦♦♦
Tenor saxophonist Bob Berg's debut as a leader is mostly in the bop vein although he does his best to break down the boundaries a bit. With trumpeter Tom Harrell sharing the frontline and Cedar Walton (on both acoustic and electric piano) heading the fine rhythm section, Berg performs four group originals, the classic ballad "You're My Thrill" and a reworking of "This Masquerade." It's an impressive debut for the young tenor. —*Scott Yanow*

Steppin': Live in Europe / Dec. 8, 1982 / Red ♦♦♦

Short Stories / Mar. 1987 / Denon ♦♦♦

Back Roads / 1990 / Denon ♦♦♦
A departure from his usual path, Berg explores different musical idioms such as country, jazz, and fusion. —*Paul Kohler*

In the Shadows / 1990 / Denon ♦♦
On his third Denon release Berg ventures into a few jazz standards while maintaining a strong hold on his fusion roots. Jim Beard is featured on keyboards. —*Paul Kohler*

Cycles / Mar. 3, 1992 / Denon ♦♦♦
The follow-up recording to Berg's first Denon release, *Short Stories, Cycles* carries on the legacy with even more convincing results. Featured are Mike Stern (g) and Dennis Chambers (d). —*Paul Kohler*

Virtual Reality / Aug. 1992 / Denon ♦♦
This CD is a disappointment. Many of the selections use unimaginative funk rhythms and Berg (on tenor and soprano) comes across as an anonymous blending of Ernie Watts and Michael Brecker. In addition, this has to be about the dumbest version of "Can't Help Lovin' That Man" that has ever been recorded. There are some good solos from Berg here and there but not enough to justify the purchase of this set. —*Scott Yanow*

● **Enter the Spirit** / 1993 / Stretch ♦♦♦♦
Although Bob Berg has still not developed a strikingly original tone, his talents on tenor and soprano are so consistent as to be taken for granted. With either Chick Corea, David Kikoski or Jim

Beard on keyboards, Berg is in fine form on this quartet session, which is highlighted by two of Corea's tunes, "Sometime Ago" and Sonny Rollins' "No Moe," the latter a duet with drummer Dennis Chambers. —*Scott Yanow*

Riddles / Apr. 29, 1994–May 10, 1994 / ♦♦♦
Bob Berg, whose tenor playing often hints at Michael Brecker, is heard leading a medium-sized group (ranging from five to seven pieces) that often includes Gil Goldstein's accordion and Jim Beard's keyboards on this CD. The music is a bit poppish in spots but the solos are of a generally high caliber with Berg sounding most original on soprano. —*Scott Yanow*

Karl Berger

b. Mar. 30, 1935, Heidelberg, Germany
Piano, Vibes / Avant-Garde
Though he began as a bebop player, German vibist Karl Berger was among the more challenging soloists on his instrument during the '60s and '70s. He became a top free player, expanding the vibes' role and making them a more percussive instrument through solos that stressed colors and tones more than fast lines or pretty phrases. He also was an early advocate for more jazz/international music interaction, and during the mid-'80s took a leave from his teaching post to tour and perform at percussion festivals in India, play with African drummer Olatunji and record with shakuhachi player Hozan Yahamoto. Berger studied classical piano at ten then later served as house pianist at the Club 54 in Heidelberg. He learned bebop from visiting American musicians stationed there like Don Ellis, Leo Wright, Cedar Walton and Lex Humphries. Berger switched to vibes on the advice of French vibist Michel Hausser, with whom he'd played in Germany and Paris. He studied both musicology and philosophy in Heidelberg and Berlin, earning a doctorate in 1963. Berger then joined Don Cherry's free jazz quintet in Paris in 1965. He worked with him 18 months, then worked a month with Steve Lacy before rejoining Cherry. When they recorded in America, Berger remained in the country playing in schools for the organization Young Audiences, Inc. with Horacee Arnold's group from 1967 to 1971. He also periodically toured with his own bands, playing and recording with Marion Brown and Roswell Rudd. Berger and Ornette Coleman co-founded the Creative Music Studio in Woodstock, New York in 1972. He served as director and helped craft programs that helped the students determine their own interests rather than establishing a set curriculum. The studio held many workshops and concerts in the '70s and '80s, with Berger attracting such musicians as Anthony Braxton, Lee Konitz, Jack DeJohnette, and Sam Rivers to assist or play at concerts. He led a 28-piece orchestra that appeared at the 1982 Kool Jazz Festival as part of the "Jazz and World Music" segment. He made an international tour in 1985 and 1986, and served as guest conductor and composer for The Westdeutscher Rundfunk in Cologne, Germany. Berger continued to record periodically for Black Saint/Soul Note and Enja in the '70s and '80s, and is featured on a trio date with Dave Holland and Edward Blackwell issued by Enja in 1993. It's one of only three Berger titles cited as available on CD. —*Ron Wynn*

Karl Berger Quartet / Dec. 8, 1966 / ESP ♦♦♦

All Kinds Of Time / Apr. 26, 1976 / Sackville ♦♦♦
Ambitious, free-tinged date with solid Berger vibes. —*Ron Wynn*

Transit / Aug. 25, 1988–Aug. 26, 1988 / Black Saint ♦♦♦♦

Around / May 9, 1990–May 10, 1990 / Black Saint ♦♦♦

● **Crystal Fire** / Apr. 4, 1991–Apr. 5, 1991 / Enja ♦♦♦♦

Bunny Berigan (Rowland Bernart Berrigan)

b. Nov. 2, 1908, Hilbert, WI, **d.** Jun. 2, 1942, New York, NY
Trumpet, Vocals / Swing
Bunny Berigan during 1935–39 was arguably the top trumpeter in jazz (with his main competition being Louis Armstrong and Roy Eldridge). Blessed with a beautiful tone and a wide range (Berigan's low notes could be as memorable as his upper register shouts), Bunny brought excitement to every session he appeared on. He was not afraid to take chances during his solos and could be a bit reckless, but Berigan's successes and occasional failures were always colorful to hear, at least until he drank it all away.

Bunny Berigan played in local bands and then college groups in the Midwest. He tried out for Hal Kemp's Orchestra unsuccessfully in 1928 (rejected because of his thin tone!) but showed tremendous improvement by 1930 when he was hired. After a few recordings and a trip to Europe, Bunny joined Fred Rich's CBS studio band in 1931 where (except for a few months with Paul Whiteman) he would remain up to 1935. Berigan soon gained a strong reputation as a hot jazz soloist and he appeared on quite a few records with studio bands, the Boswell Sisters and the Dorsey Brothers. In 1935 he spent a few months with Benny Goodman's Orchestra, but that was enough to launch the swing era. Berigan had classic solos on Goodman's first two hit records ("King Porter Stomp" and "Sometimes I'm Happy") and was with BG as he went on his historic tour out West, climaxing in the near-riot at the Palomar Ballroom in Los Angeles.

Berigan soon returned to the more lucrative studio scene, making his only film appearance in 1936 with Fred Rich. In 1937 he joined Tommy Dorsey's band and was once again largely responsible for two hits: "Marie" and "Song of India." Bunny's solos on these tunes became so famous that in future years Dorsey had them written out and orchestrated for the full trumpet section! After leaving Dorsey, Bunny Berigan finally put together his own orchestra. He scored early on with his biggest hit "I Can't Get Started." With Georgie Auld on tenor and Buddy Rich on drums, Berigan had a potentially strong band. Unfortunately he was already an alcoholic and a reluctant businessman. By 1939 there had been many lost opportunities and the following year Bunny (who was bankrupt) was forced to break up his band. He rejoined Tommy Dorsey for a few months but never stopped drinking and was not happy being a sideman again. Soon Berigan formed a new orchestra, but his health began declining and on June 2, 1942, he died when he was just 33. What would this brilliant swing trumpeter have done in the bop era?

Bunny Berigan's life is definitively profiled in Robert Dupuis' book *Elusive Legend of Jazz.* — *Scott Yanow*

● **The Pied Piper** / Jul. 1, 1935–Aug. 3, 1940 / Bluebird ✦✦✦✦✦
This is the best single-CD compilation of Bunny Berigan recordings issued to date. Although all of the trumpeter's big-band sides for Bluebird have come out on three double-LPs, this set gives more general collectors a better overview of his talents. One of the top trumpeters to be active during the 1935–39 period (only Louis Armstrong and the up-and-coming Roy Eldridge were on his level), Berigan was largely responsible for the success of important hit records for Benny Goodman ("King Porter Stomp" and "Sometimes I'm Happy") and Tommy Dorsey ("Marie" and "Song of India") in addition to having a best-seller of his own ("I Can't Get Started"). Unfortunately Berigan's alcoholism eventually did him in, but this CD has all of the hits plus appearances with Gene Gifford's Orchestra (a majestic solo on "Nothin' but the Blues"), Frankie Trumbauer, Fats Waller in a jam session and with The Metronome All-Stars in addition to more titles as a leader, with BG and with Dorsey (including a radio broadcast version of "I've Found a New Baby" from 1940). This is a well-conceived reissue of important and often-exciting swing by one of the greats. —*Scott Yanow*

Sing! Sing! Sing!, Vol. 1: 1936–1938 / Jul. 20, 1936–Jun. 27, 1938 / Jass ✦✦✦
The first of CDs reissuing all of Bunny Berigan's radio transcriptions, this set features him with a studio orchestra on 20 selections in 1936 and with his 1938 big band for the last five numbers. In addition to Berigan (who is generally in superb form), the early tracks feature some vocals by Peggy Lawson and spots for tenor saxophonist Artie Drelinger and a clarinetist who might be Artie Shaw. The later performances give one brief glimpses of tenor saxophonist Georgie Auld and trombonist Ray Coniff. —*Scott Yanow*

Down By The Old Mill Stream / Oct. 22, 1936–1939 / Jazz Archives ✦✦✦✦
This set of radio appearances by Bunny Berigan finds the great swing trumpeter at his best. On "Down by the Old Mill Stream" he shows off his entire (and very impressive) range and the other selections (mostly from 1938) find him romping with his big band. The music on this collector's LP has not been reissued elsewhere and is well worth searching for. Hopefully it will appear on CD eventually. —*Scott Yanow*

The Complete Bunny Berigan, Vol. 1 / Apr. 1, 1937–Oct. 7, 1937 / Bluebird ✦✦✦✦
This two-LP set is the first of three reissues that contained all of the Victor studio recordings of the Bunny Berigan Orchestra. This initial two-fer covers a six-month period when there seemed to be

a great deal of potential for this big band. Berigan's hit "I Can't Get Started" is on this set, as are such near-classics as "The Prisoner's Song," "Mahogany Hall Stomp," "A Study in Brown" and "Mama I Wanna Make Rhythm." Since this is a "complete" series, there are also some turkey songs mixed in, but in general the music is swinging and very enjoyable. —*Scott Yanow*

The Complete Bunny Berigan, Vol. 2 / Oct. 7, 1937–Jun. 8, 1938 / Bluebird ✦✦
At the tail-end of RCA's two-fer LP reissue series, they managed to sneak in all of Bunny Berigan's Victor recordings on three volumes. *Vol. 2* is by far the weakest (although the packaging here is beyond criticism) for, during the eight months covered by this set, Berigan's band was being given some of the worst possible material to record: tunes such as "An Old Straw Hat," "Never Felt Better, Never Had Less," "'Round the Old Deserted Farm," "I Dance Alone" and "Rinka Tinka Man." Truth be told, there are only around five or six worthwhile songs on this set of 28, but completists will want to acquire this two-fer anyway, for it will fill many gaps. —*Scott Yanow*

Complete Bunny Berigan, Vol. 3 / Jun. 8, 1938–Nov. 28, 1939 / Bluebird ✦✦✦✦
The third and final volume of two-fers that reissue all of the Bunny Berigan big-band's Victor recordings is a large improvement over *Vol. 2.* Covering a chaotic 17-month period in Berigan's life (the orchestra had several disasters before collapsing completely), strangely enough, their output in 1938 seemed to improve as they went along. At one point, Berigan had strong soloists in trombonist Ray Coniff and tenor saxophonist Georgie Auld, and a young Buddy Rich (who is heard here prior to joining Artie Shaw's Orchestra) really propelled the ensembles. "Livery Stable Blues," "High Society," "Sobbin' Blues," "I Cried for You," "Night Song" and a six-song Bix Beiderbecke tribute set are among the highpoints of this excellent reissue. —*Scott Yanow*

Devil's Holiday, Vol. 2: 1938 / Jun. 27, 1938–Aug. 9, 1938 / Jass ✦✦✦
The second of three Jass CDs that reissue all of Berigan's radio transcriptions, this set has 15 numbers from June 27 (a consistently strong session) and 12 from August 8–9, 1938. Even with a few dull vocal numbers, the emphasis here is on hard-driving swing with his mighty trumpet, trombonist Ray Coniff, clarinetist Joe Dixon and tenor saxophonist Georgie Auld—all in fine form. It's recommended as a fine example of his exciting chance-taking style. —*Scott Yanow*

Tim Berne

b. 1954, Syracuse, NY
Alto Saxophone / Avant-Garde
One of the top avant-garde saxophonists of the 1980s and '90s, Tim Berne was even able to keep his non-compromising music intact during a short association with Columbia Records. After moving to New York in 1974 and studying with Julius Hemphill, Berne recorded a few records for his own Empire label. He later recorded for Soul Note, Columbia and JMT. Although he participated in John Zorn's Ornette Coleman tribute (*Spy vs. Spy*), Berne has mostly played as a leader, carving out his own unique path in improvised music. —*Scott Yanow*

The Five Year Plan / Apr. 25, 1979 / Empire ✦✦✦

7x / Jan. 8, 1980 / Empire ✦✦✦✦
Ever since his debut, altoist Tim Berne has pursued his own musical vision, forming an original style that is very much in the avant-garde yet not derivative of any of his predecessors. On this, his second session as a leader, Berne teams up with some of the West Coast's top musicians (including Vinnie Golia on a variety of reeds, guitarist Nels Cline and bassist Robert Miranda) to perform some very creative music that deserves more than one close listen. —*Scott Yanow*

Songs and Rituals in Real Time / Jul. 1, 1981 / Empire ✦✦✦

Ancestors / Feb. 1983 / Soul Note ✦✦✦
Tim Berne's playing on *Ancestors* is fluid, warm and conveys a relaxed levity. For this live recording Berne enlarges his regular quartet (Mack Goldsburg, tenor sax, soprano sax; Ed Schuller, bass; Paul Motian, percussion) to include Herb Robertson (trumpet) and Ray Anderson, perhaps the finest trombonist of the past five years. As usual, the tunes are all Berne originals and display the sectional and harmonic structures that so much of his music seems to exhibit. —*Bob Rusch, Cadence*

Mutant Variations / Mar. 5, 1983–Mar. 6, 1983 / Soul Note ✦✦✦✦
Definitely not part of the new traditional scene, alto saxophonist
Tim Berne keeps moving forward. This '84 quartet set of all originals is reminiscent at times of mid-'50s Ornette Coleman, notably
due to Herb Robertson's pocket trumpet solos and the dynamics
generated by Berne and Robertson's interaction with bassist Ed
Schuller and percussionist Paul Motian. —*Ron Wynn*

Theoretically / Aug. 1983–1984 / Empire ✦✦✦✦

Fulton Street Maul / Aug. 10, 1986–Aug. 14, 1986 / Columbia
✦✦✦✦
How did avant-gardist Tim Berne get signed to Columbia? During
his relatively brief alliance with that media giant, the passionate
altoist was somehow able to continue recording his uncompromising music with apparently no real interference. On this set, he
teams up with the amazing guitarist Bill Frisell, cellist Hank
Roberts and percussionist Alex Cline for five explorative pieces that
one can safely bet did not receive much airplay. —*Scott Yanow*

Sanctified Dreams / Oct. 13, 1987–Oct. 15, 1987 / Columbia ✦✦✦
Alto saxophonist Tim Berne ranks among the more progressive
players around, someone who keeps looking ahead rather than
behind. This 1988 set was no different; it contains odd passages,
moments of indecision, and segments where Berne and associates
blazed away. —*Ron Wynn*

Fractured Fairy Tales / Jun. 1989 / JMT ✦✦
Dynamic and uneven, but ambitious. With Herb Robertson, Mark
Feldman, Hank Roberts, Mark Dresser, and Joey Baron. —*Ron Wynn*

Pace Yourself: Tim Berne's Caos Totale / Nov. 1990 / JMT ✦✦
● **Diminutive Mysteries** / Sep. 1992 / JMT ✦✦✦✦
This is certainly the most unusual David Sanborn recording to
date. Avant-gardist Tim Berne (heard here on alto and baritone)
and the popular R&B star Sanborn (mostly leaving his trademark
alto behind to play soprano) share a great respect for altoist Julius
Hemphill and the St. Louis free jazz movement. Along with guitarist Marc Ducret, cellist Hank Roberts and drummer Joey Baron,
they perform seven often-emotional Hemphill pieces plus Berne's
"The Maze." Sanborn is to be congratulated for successfully stretching himself although this is very much Berne's date. —*Scott Yanow*

Nice View / Aug. 1993 / JMT✦✦✦

Lowlife / Sep. 22, 1994–Sep. 25, 1994 / JMT ✦✦✦

Poisoned Minds / Sep. 22, 1994–Sep. 25, 1994 / JMT ✦✦✦

Warren Bernhardt

b. Nov. 1938, Wausau, WI
Piano, Keyboards / Fusion, Post-Bop
A fine soloist who is influenced by Bill Evans but has his own
musical identity, Warren Bernhardt has appeared in many different settings through the years. He studied classical piano, played
in Chicago while attending college and was with Paul Winter's
sextet during 1961–64. After moving to New York, Bernhardt was
with Gerry Mulligan, Clark Terry, George Benson and Jeremy
Steig in addition to doubling as a studio musician on many pop
dates. He was with Jack DeJohnette's Directions (1976) and Steps
Ahead (1984–85) and has frequently led his own trios. Bernhardt
has recorded several fine dates for DMP. —*Scott Yanow*

Blue Montreux / Jul. 21, 1978–Jul. 22, 1978 / Arista ✦✦✦

Blue Montreux 2 / Jul. 21, 1978–Jul. 22, 1978 / Arista ✦✦✦

Trio '83 / Jan. 17, 1983–Jan. 19, 1983 / DMP ✦✦✦✦

Hands On / Oct. 17, 1986–Oct. 18, 1986 / DMP ✦✦

Heat of the Moment / Mar. 1, 1989–Mar. 5, 1989 / DMP ✦✦✦
● **Ain't Life Grand** / Apr. 19, 1990–Apr. 20, 1990 / DMP ✦✦✦✦

Reflections / Dec. 1, 1991–Dec. 3, 1991 / DMP ✦✦✦
A '91 quintet set alternating between good renditions of shopworn jazz standards and some extended blowing on original
numbers. Bernhardt plays in a steady, sometimes vibrant manner
while heading a group with tenor saxophonist and clarinetist Bob
Mintzer, guitarist Chuck Loeb, bassist Jay Anderson, and drummer Jeff Hirshfield. It was cut live at the Carriage House in
Stamford, CT. —*Ron Wynn*

Bill Berry

b. Sep. 14, 1930, Benton Harbor, MI
Trumpet, Leader / Swing
Bill Berry has been leading big bands in the Los Angeles area

since the early '70s, still inspired by his years with Duke Ellington.
After being discharged from the Air Force in 1955 he studied at
the Cincinnati College of Music and Berklee. Berry worked in the
big bands of Woody Herman and Maynard Ferguson before joining Ellington (1961–64). After leaving Duke he was with the Thad
Jones-Mel Lewis Orchestra (1966–68), led his own New York Big
Band and did studio work. After he moved to Los Angeles in 1971,
Berry formed the L.A. Big Band, which he has continued leading
on a part-time basis up to the present time. He has also toured
with Louie Bellson and been involved in the jazz education program run by the Monterey Jazz Festival. Bill Berry is an excellent
veteran mainstream trumpet player who has recorded several sets
(with both small groups and his big band) for Concord. —*Scott
Yanow*

● **Hello Rev** / Nov. 1977 / Concord Jazz ✦✦✦✦✦

The Ellington All-Stars / Jan. 11–12, 1978 / Drive Archive ✦✦✦
This CD reissues an award-winning (for sound quality) Real Time
direct-to-disc album, adding alternate takes of "Mood Indigo" and
"I Got It Bad" to the original program. Cornetist Bill Berry gathered together a variety of veterans (altoist Marshall Royal, trombonist Britt Woodman, pianist Nat Pierce, bassist Ray Brown and
drummer Frankie Capp) along with the young tenor Scott
Hamilton to perform eight numbers associated with Duke
Ellington. Each of the horns get some solo space with Royal's feature on "I Got It Bad" and the full group's jamming on "Perdido"
and "Cotton Tail" being highpoints. —*Scott Yanow*

Shortcake / May 3, 1978 / Concord Jazz ✦✦✦✦

Chu Berry (Leon Brown Berry)

b. Sep. 13, 1910, Wheeling, WV, d. Oct. 30, 1941, Conneaut, OH
Tenor Saxophone / Swing
Chu Berry was considered one of the top tenor saxophonists of
the 1930s, just below Coleman Hawkins (his main influence),
Lester Young and Ben Webster. Particularly strong on uptempo
numbers (although his ballad statements could be overly sentimental), Berry might have become an influential force if he had
not died prematurely. After playing alto in college, he switched to
tenor in 1929 when he joined Sammy Stewart's band. In 1930 he
moved to New York, playing with Benny Carter's band and
Charlie Johnson's Orchestra. He was prominently featured in
Spike Hughes 1933 recording sessions, was a star with the bands
of Teddy Hill (1933–35) and Fletcher Henderson (1936) (to whom
he contributed his song "Christopher Columbus") and then found
a permanent home with Cab Calloway in 1937. Berry was used on
many sessions including with his friend Roy Eldridge, Lionel
Hampton (a classic version of "Sweethearts on Parade"), Teddy
Wilson and Calloway (his version of "Ghost of a Chance" became
well-known); in addition he led a couple of his own fine dates.
Chu Berry died from the effects of a car crash when he was just
33. —*Scott Yanow*

Chu Berry Story / 1937–1938 / Zeta ✦✦✦
● **A Giant of Tenor Sax** / Nov. 10, 1938–Aug. 28, 1941 /
Commodore ✦✦✦✦

Eddie Bert

b. May 16, 1922, Yonkers, NY
Trombone / Bop
A good trombone soloist known for his flexibility and firm, strong
tone, Eddie Bert has recorded successfully in big bands and sextets playing swing or bebop. He studied with Benny Morton as a
teen, then joined Sam Donahue's band at 18. Bert made his
recording debut with Red Norvo's orchestra in 1942, and also
played with Charlie Barnet, Woody Herman, Herbie Fields, Stan
Kenton and Benny Goodman in the '40s. Though he spent part of
that decade in the Army, Bert recorded with Fields, Kenton and
Goodman in the late '40s and with Kenton, Herman, Ray
McKinley and Les Elgart in the early and mid-'50s. He joined a
three-trombone unit led by Bill Harris in 1952, and also headed
groups on Monday nights at Birdland in 1955. Bert played with
Charles Mingus' Jazz Workshop in 1955 and 1956, while also
recording as a leader. He eventually got his degree in music education from the Manhattan School of Music in 1957, and worked
again with Goodman in the late '50s and Mingus in 1962, as well
as Gil Melle. Bert worked with Thelonious Monk in 1963 and
1964. He'd started playing in Broadway theaters with Elliot
Lawrence in 1954, and continued until 1968. That year he joined

Dick Cavett's television show orchestra, and remained with them until 1972. He also toured Europe with the Thad Jones—Mel Lewis orchestra. Bert continued recording in the late '70s and early '80s, making albums with Sal Salvador's sextet and with Lionel Hampton in 1978, and with Teo Macero in 1983. He recently had one of his early Savoy albums, *Eddie Bert With The Hank Jones Trio* reissued on CD, and also *Live At Birdland* with J.R. Monterose. —*Ron Wynn and Michael G. Nastos*

Kaleidoscope / May 11, 1953–Nov. 3, 1954 / Savoy ✦✦✦
Straight-ahead date juggling bop and cool styles from the mid-'50s recently reissued on CD under another title. It was issued on Discovery in 1953, reissued by Savoy/Denon as *Kaleidoscope*. The session was unusual, mainly because Bert was the trombonist, and a lineup of trombone/piano/guitar/bass/drums certainly is an uncommon musical blend. —*Ron Wynn*

● **Encore** / Sep. 1, 1955 / Savoy ✦✦✦
Trombonist Eddie Bert has had a long and honorable musical career, but relatively few opportunities to record as a leader. He is heard in two different settings on this CD reissue; with a piano-less quartet that includes guitarist Joe Puma and with a quintet that includes pianist Hank Jones and the complementary tenor of J.R. Monterose. The repertoire is comprised entirely of originals by either Bert or Puma, but the style is very much of the era: cool-toned and lightly swinging bop. Despite the extreme brevity of this CD (under 35 minutes), the music is worth exploring. —*Scott Yanow*

Let's Dig Bert / Nov. 1955 / Transworld ✦✦✦
Brilliant bebop session by the neglected trombonist includes the equally neglected saxophonist Dave Schildkraut. —*David Szatmary*

Gene Bertoncini

b. Apr. 6, 1937, New York, NY
Guitar / Cool
One of the more elegant, tasteful and sensitive guitarists, Gene Bertoncini has perfected the art of playing soft, sentimental music and presenting it in a light, fluid fashion, yet retaining a degree of feeling and spontaneity. He began on guitar at nine, and was a professional at 16, playing on a children's television show. Bertoncini took architecture at Notre Dame rather than music, though he later returned to full-time playing. He played with a group led by Buddy Rich that also included Mike Mainieri and Sam Most. Bertoncini worked with Clark Terry, Paul Winter,and Nancy Wilson and in the television orchestras of Merv Griffin and Skitch Henderson in the '60s. He also backed Tony Bennett and worked with The Metropolitan Opera House orchestra. During the '70s, Bertoncini played with Wayne Shorter and Charles McPherson, then formed a duo with Mike Moore. They've played and recorded together over parts of two decades, with Bertoncini selecting the material and writing arrangments. Their performances blend classical, light (not "lite") jazz, Latin and popular material. Bertoncini and Moore were joined by Michael Urbaniak in a trio date in 1981, and he's also led workshops and taught at the Eastman School. Bertoncini has recorded for Stash, Chiaroscuro and Omisound. He and Moore have several releases available on CD. —*Ron Wynn*

O Grande Amor / 1986 / Stash ✦✦✦

Strollin' / 1987 / Stash ✦✦✦

Art of the Duo / 1987–1987 / Stash ✦✦✦

● **Two in Time** / Mar. 10, 1989+Mar. 20, 1989 / Chiaroscuro ✦✦✦✦

Ed Bickert

b. Nov. 29, 1932, Hochfeld, Manitoba, Canada
Guitar / Cool
Ed Bickert, a cool-toned guitarist with a boppish style, has been a fixture in Toronto since the 1950s. While he played steadily in the studios from 1956 on and had associations with Moe Koffman and (more importantly) Rob McConnell, it was not until he performed and recorded with Paul Desmond during 1974–75 that Ed Bickert received much recognition in the U.S. He has since been featured on records with Rob McConnell's Boss Brass and small groups, Oscar Peterson (1980), Rosemary Clooney, Benny Carter and on his own Concord and Sackville dates. —*Scott Yanow*

At the Garden Party / Jan. 1978 / Sackville ✦✦✦

Mutual Street / Mar. 1982–May 1984 / Innovation ✦✦✦

● **At Toronto's Bourbon Street** / Jan. 1983 / Concord Jazz ✦✦✦✦
At Toronto's Bourbon Street is the guitarist's definitive live date. —*Michael G. Nastos*

Bye Bye Baby / Aug. 1983 / Concord Jazz ✦✦✦
Nice set with a discernible swing influence, although pianist Dave McKenna sometimes seems ready to break into a stride or rag-time progression. The quartet never hurried or rushed their playing, and bassist Steve Wallace and drummer Jake Hanna were sometimes barely audible. This is smooth, sophisticated, and wonderfully played, although the energy level sometimes seems quite low. —*Ron Wynn*

I Wished on the Moon / Jun. 1985 / Concord Jazz ✦✦✦

Third Floor Richard / Jan. 1989 / Concord Jazz ✦✦✦✦

This Is New / Dec. 1989 / Concord Jazz ✦✦✦

Barney Bigard (Albany Leon Bigard)

b. Mar. 3, 1906, New Orleans, LA, d. Jun. 27, 1980, Culver City, CA
Clarinet / Swing, New Orleans Jazz
Barney Bigard was one of the most distinctive clarinetists in jazz and a longtime asset to Duke Ellington's Orchestra. Although he took clarinet lessons with Lorenzo Tio, Bigard's initial reputation was made as a tenor saxophonist; in fact, based on a few of his recordings (particularly those with Luis Russell), Bigard was number two behind Coleman Hawkins in the mid-'20s. After working with several groups in New Orleans, Bigard moved to Chicago in 1924, where he played with King Oliver during 1925-27. He would also record with Jelly Roll Morton, Johnny Dodds and future boss Louis Armstrong in the 1920s but, after short stints with Charles Elgar and Luis Russell, Bigard found his true home with Duke Ellington's Orchestra, with whom he almost exclusively played clarinet. Between 1927-42 he was well featured on a countless number of recordings with Ellington, who understood Bigard's musical strengths and wrote to showcase him at his best. From "Mood Indigo" (which he co-composed) to "Harlem Air Shaft," Bigard was an important fixture of the Ellington Orchestra.

When he quit the band in 1942 (due to tiring of the road) Bigard played with Freddie Slack's big band, Kid Ory's New Orleans group and appeared in the 1946 film *New Orleans*. Bigard then joined the Louis Armstrong All-Stars, constantly travelling the world during 1947-55 and 1960-61; he spent 1958-59 with Cozy Cole's band. Bigard became largely semi-retired after 1962 but still played now and then, recording with Art Hodes, Earl Hines and as a leader. However Barney Bigard, whose swing style was sometimes out-of-place with Armstrong, really sounded at his best during his Duke Ellington years. —*Scott Yanow*

Paris: December 14–15, 1960 / Dec. 14, 1960–Dec. 15, 1960 / Vogue ✦✦✦✦

● **Bucket's Got a Hole in It** / Jan. 29, 1968–Jan. 30, 1968 / Delmark ✦✦✦✦
This is one of clarinetist Barney Bigard's best recordings of his later period. On four of the eight selections he is well-featured on swing standards with a quartet that also includes the great pianist Art Hodes. The other four tracks are more in the Dixieland vein with trumpeter Nappy Trottier and the veteran trombonist George Brunis making the band a sextet. Throughout, Bigard (whose tone was instantly recognizable) is the main star and in splendid form. —*Scott Yanow*

Clarinet Gumbo / Jun. 25, 1973–Jul. 18, 1973 / RCA ✦✦✦

Barney Bigard & The Pelican Trio / 1976 / Crescent ✦✦✦

Acker Bilk (Bernard Stanley Bilk)

b. Jan. 29, 1929, Pensford, Somerset, England
Clarinet / Trad Jazz, Pop
Best known for his left field hit "Stranger On The Shore" in the early '60s, Acker Bilk was among the leaders in England's trad jazz boom during the '60s. An entertaining, if not particularly original, clarinetist in the early New Orleans style, Bilk worked as a semi-professional musician in England before joining Ken Colyer's band as a clarinetist in the mid-'50s. He scored his first hit in England with the song "Summer Set" in 1958. Bilk and The Paramount Jazz Band were celebrities during the early '60s, performing in their uniform of bowler hats and striped coats. After

landing British successes with the songs "Buona Sera" and "That's My Home," Bilk struck gold with "Stranger On The Shore," recorded with The Young String Chorale. It broke a British record for staying on the charts, remaining there 55 weeks. Bilk kept recording and performing through the '60s, '70s and '80s, even returning to the hit parade with the '76 song "Aria." A fine Dixieland clarinetist, Bilk has several sessions available on American labels including GNP/Crescendo, Stomp Off, Pickwick and K-Tel. — *Ron Wynn*

Stranger on the Shore / 1962 / Philips ◆◆◆
● **Acker Bilk in Holland** / Feb. 8, 1983 / Timeless ◆◆◆◆
Blaze Away / Jan. 19, 1987 / Timeless ◆◆◆

Walter Bishop, Jr.

b. Apr. 10, 1927, New York, NY
Piano / Bop, Hard Bop
A fine bop and hard bop pianist and the son of songwriter Walter Bishop, Walter Bishop, Jr. has been an effective bandleader, composer and educator. He played with Art Blakey in the late '40s, played with Charlie Parker, Miles Davis and Oscar Pettiford in the '50s, and with Curtis Fuller in 1960 before forming his own trio with Jimmy Garrison and G.T. Hogan. Bishop toured with Terry Gibbs in the mid-'60s and studied with Hall Overton at Juilliard. He combined studies and recording after moving to the West Coast in 1969, cutting dates with Supersax and Blue Mitchell. Bishop became an instructor before he moved back to New York in the '70s. He wrote a book on jazz theory in 1976, was in Clark Terry's big band in the late '70s, and toured Switzerland while leading various bands. He taught at the University of Hartford in the early '80s, and had a solo Carnegie Hall concert in 1983. Bishop's recorded for DIW, Prestige, Black Lion, Seabreeze, Muse, Red and Black Jazz among others. — *Ron Wynn*

Speak Low / Mar. 14, 1961 / Muse ◆◆◆
Bish Bash / Aug. 1964+May 1968 / Xanadu ◆◆◆◆
Valley Land / Dec. 30, 1974 / Muse ◆◆◆
Bishop demonstrates his proficiency with rapid-fire bop tunes and standards, playing superbly throughout this trio date, backed by bassist Sam Jones and drummer Billy Hart. — *Ron Wynn*
Soliloquy / Oct. 21, 1976 / Sea Breeze ◆◆◆
Soul Village / Jun. 1977 / Muse ◆◆◆
Interesting, often intriguing work that plays off a village concept on the title track, but is otherwise a pretty standard, although expertly performed, batch of standards and bop originals. Bishop utilizes the classic Messenger three-horn lineup, except that he substitutes a second saxophonist for a trombonist and uses Randy Brecker as trumpeter. — *Ron Wynn*
Hot House / Mar. 14, 1978 / Muse ◆◆◆
Excellent bebop session by this pianist, assisted by Junior Cook (ts) and Bill Hardman (tpt). — *David Szatmary*
Cubicle / Jun. 21, 1978 / Muse ◆◆◆◆
The fine bop pianist heads a large group of distinguished stars, among them Curtis Fuller, Pepper Adams, Randy Brecker, and Billy Hart, plus vocalist Carmen Lundy on this 1978 session. It's a different atmosphere for Bishop, usually featured in small combos or trios. The songs are nicely played, and there are several sparkling solos. — *Ron Wynn*
Just in Time / Sep. 10, 1988 / Interplay ◆◆◆
● **What's New** / Oct. 25, 1990 / DIW ◆◆◆◆◆
Pianist Walter Bishop, Jr. displayed his bop proficiency on this 1991 release, one of his finest. His solos are electric, nicely constructed, and often brilliantly executed. He seldom got much recognition except from musicians, but Bishop was certainly among the finest bop and mainstream pianists of his era. — *Ron Wynn*
Midnight Blue / Dec. 1991 / Red ◆◆◆

Big Bill Bissonnette

b. Bridgeport, CT
Trombone / New Orleans Jazz
A strong advocate of New Orleans jazz as played by the veteran Black musicians, Big Bill Bissonnette in the 1960s ran his own group (the Easy Riders Jazz Band), formed his own label (Jazz Crusade) and organized Northern tours for such veteran players as Kid Thomas Valentine, George Lewis and Jim Robinson. After

a period off the scene, with the successful publication of his 1992 memoirs *The Jazz Crusade* (which has many stories about the New Orleans musicians), Bissonnette reactivated his label and began to play again. Although a somewhat primitive trombonist, Bissonete (whose idol is Jim Robinson) is a boisterous player with plenty of spirit. — *Scott Yanow*

Rhythm Is Our Business / Sep. 1985–Nov. 1986 / Jazz Crusade ◆◆◆
● **Big Bill's British Band** / Oct. 9, 1993 / Jazz Crusade ◆◆◆◆
Trombonist Big Bill Bissonnette has stated that his goal is "to lead the mouldiest jazz band in the world" and, from the evidence of this often-riotous set, he may well have succeeded. A partisan of New Orleans jazz as performed by Kid Thomas Valentine and Captain John Handy in the 1960s, Bissonnette's trombone is heard as a part of a spirited octet/nonet jamming such unusual swing tunes as "Smile Darn You Smile," "On Moonlight Bay" and "On a Coconut Island." The slightly out-of-tune ensembles make up in color and spontaneity for the rough moments. Trumpeter Ken Pye has a clipped, almost staccato style that recalls Valentine while Bissonnette harks back to his idol Jim Robinson, but this band's unusual personality is actually formed by its saxophonists. Norman Field (who doubles on clarinet) also plays a lot of alto as does guest John R.T. Davies, while Sarah Bissonnette's tenor emerges as the most impressive solo voice. Although this ensemble-oriented band does not boast any virtuosos, its extroverted emotions and boisterous spirit should make it of strong interest to fans of New Orleans jazz. — *Scott Yanow*

Cindy Blackman

b. Nov. 18, 1959, Yellow Springs, OH
Drums / Hard Bop
An accomplished, yet not flamboyant or showy drummer, Cindy Blackman has become a well respected percussionist in a short time. Both her mother and grandmother were classical musicians, and her uncle a vibist. Blackman began playing drums as a child, and studied classical percussion at the University of Hartford and Berklee. Alan Dawson and Lennie Nelson were two of her instructors. Blackman moved to New York in the early '80s, and played with Freddie Hubbard and Sam Rivers. She became Jackie McLean's regular drummer in 1987, and began recording as a leader that year for Muse. Blackman was a big attraction at jam sessions organized at the Blue Note by Ted Curson, and played with Don Pullen's trio in 1990 at several festivals. She has a few sessions available on CD. — *Ron Wynn*

Arcane / Aug. 1987–Dec. 1987 / Muse ◆◆◆
Trio + Two / Aug. 1990 / Free Lance ◆◆◆
Code Red / Oct. 1990 / Muse ◆◆◆
● **Telepathy** / 1992 / Muse ◆◆◆◆
Drummer Cindy Blackman's third Muse album shows a maturity, confidence and assertiveness that her two previous sessions lacked. She is the unquestioned leader, sparkling in her playing and punctuating the songs with the vigor you'd expect from a veteran percussionist. This is an ensemble sound, with Blackman's drums prominent but no less important than any other element on the 11 numbers; among them are sharp readings of "Tune Up" and "Well You Needn't," plus her own "Persuasion," "Spank," "Missing You" and the title cut. While hard bop, as well as some funk tinges, are present, Cindy Blackman shows signs of being much more than another neobop follower on this date. — *Ron Wynn*

Ed Blackwell

b. Oct. 10, 1929, New Orleans, LA, d. Oct. 8, 1992, Hartford, CT
Group, Drums / Avant-Garde, Free Jazz
Ed Blackwell was one of the greatest melodic drummers in modern jazz history. His ringing rhythms frequently sounded like vocals transferred to drums, and his conception linked traditional New Orleans jazz, marching band beats, Afro-Latin and Caribbean elements, R&B and blues voicings with free, multiple accents and textures. His ability to provide a quick, incisive history of New Orleans styles turned his solos into exciting, free-wheeling events. Blackwell patterned his early playing after that of the great traditional drummer Paul Barbarin, and during his teens worked in several R&B bands. During the late '40s he played in Plas Johnson and Raymond Johnson's groups. Blackwell moved to Los Angeles in 1951, where he first met and played with Ornette

Coleman. They worked together again a couple of years later in Texas, before Blackwell returned to New Orleans in 1956. He toured with Ray Charles in 1957, then moved to New York in 1960, and shortly afterward replaced Billy Higgins in Coleman's band. During the '60s, Blackwell emerged as a seminal percussionist, playing on such Coleman sessions as *Science Fiction* and *Free Jazz*. He also recorded with Don Cherry and John Coltrane, Cherry in duets, Eric Dolphy and Booker Little at the Five Spot, Randy Weston, Dewey Redman and Archie Shepp. He toured Africa with Weston in the mid-'60s, and lived in Morocco in 1968. Blackwell was an artist-in-residence at Wesleyan in the mid-'70s, and the next year toured and recorded with former Coleman band members Cherry, Redman and Charlie Haden in the group Old And New Dreams. During the '80s, Blackwell again played with Cherry, was in Anthony Braxton's band, and also in groups led by Redman and David Murray. He toured England and Scotland in the late '80s working in Cherry's group Nu. He also did recordings as a leader and sideman for the Black Saint/Soul Note label. Blackwell suffered severe kidney problems through the '80s, and began undergoing dialysis treatment. He finally died of kidney failure. —*Ron Wynn*

● **Boogie Live . . . 1958** / 1958 / Record ✦✦✦✦
When Ed Blackwell returned to New Orleans after a brief early stint with Ornette Coleman in Los Angeles, he joined The American Jazz Quintet, which on this CD also includes clarinetist Alvin Batiste, Nat Perrillat on tenor, pianist Ellis Marsalis and bassist Otis Deverney. This live concert, performed at a high school in 1958, was previously unissued until 1994 and features these strong players in top early form. Alvin Batiste shows that, although he would be buried in the jazz education field (and would therefore be greatly underrated), he was an excellent hard bop clarinetist early in his career. Nat Perilliat is a bit of a revelation because he had already absorbed John Coltrane's sheets of sound style at this early period and was developing his own sound. Ellis Marsalis and Otis Deverney are fine while Ed Blackwell (who has several colorful solos) shows that he was already a giant. The group's six originals are generally based on earlier standards, most obviously Batiste's "Fourth Month" (which uses the chords of "I Remember April"). An excellent set. —*Scott Yanow*

What It Be Like? / Aug. 8, 1992 / Enja ✦✦✦

What It Is / Aug. 8, 1992 / Enja ✦✦✦

Eubie Blake (James Hubert Blake)

b. Feb. 7, 1883, Baltimore, MD, d. Feb. 12, 1983, New York, NY
Piano, Composer / Ragtime
Eubie Blake had a rather unique career. Although his main importance was as a songwriter for Broadway shows in the 1920s, late in life he became known as the last living link to ragtime. Blake always had a colorful life. He wrote his first rag "The Charleston Rag" in 1899, spent years playing with medicine shows and in sporting houses and by 1915 was teaming up with singer Noble Sissle in vaudeville. Sissle and Blake wrote for the 1921 hit show *Shuffle Along* (the first all-Black musical) and it was followed by *Revue Negre, Plantation Review, Rhapsody in Black* and *Bamville Review*. The team of Sissle and Blake, in addition to making recordings, were filmed for some early experimental sound shorts. Among Blake's hit songs of the 1920's were "I'm Just Crazy About Harry," "You're Lucky to Me" and "Memories of You."

Although he made some recordings in 1931, Eubie Blake generally had a lower profile for the next three decades. He worked with Sissle now and then and earned a degree from New York University but was largely forgotten until 1969. That year he recorded a double-LP for Columbia (*The Eighty-Six Years of Eubie Blake*) that amazed listeners who had never heard of him. During his remaining 14 years, Eubie Blake was a very popular performer, playing and singing ragtime-era pieces, charming audiences, making new records, appearing on Broadway in the 1978 show *Eubie* (he was 95 at the time) and running his own label Eubie Blake Music. He continued performing until he was 98 and Eubie Blake made it to his 100th birthday with five days to spare. —*Scott Yanow*

● **The 86 Years of Eubie Blake** / Mar. 12, 1969 / Columbia ✦✦✦✦✦

Live Concert / May 22, 1973 / Eubie Blake Music ✦✦✦
Pianist/singer/composer Eubie Blake (who was 90 years old at the time) is in pretty good shape on this LP, telling stories and play-

ing piano continuously for 37 minutes before an enthusiastic audience. Some of his stories (and playing) might be a bit fanciful, but it is all quite enjoyable. In addition to performing some of his own tunes (including "Tricky Fingers" and "Memories of You"), Blake sounds fine on a James P. Johnson Medley. —*Scott Yanow*

Eubie Blake Introducing Jim Hession / 1974 / Eubie Blake Music ✦✦✦

John Blake

b. Jul. 3, 1947, Philadelphia, PA
Violin / Post-Bop, Crossover
A dashing, eclectic violinist, John Blake has been a crowd favorite in groups as diverse as Isaac Hayes' Movement and McCoy Tyner's combo. Blake played with Hayes and Alice Coltrane in the '70s, then worked with Tyner in the '80s. He's been a more captivating player as a sideman, contributing broken lines, strumming and dynamic solos to dates by Hayes, Coltrane and Tyner. Blake's rare solo albums have been less interesting; he recorded a pair of unimpressive sessions for Gramavision in the mid-'80s that failed to adequately showcase Blake's violin and instead were heavily produced instrumental pop vehicles. Blake's date for Sunnyside in the early '90s is a more traditional, satisfying effort. He's working with Joey Calderazzo, Charles Fambrough, and Joe Ford among others. Blake also studied traditional Indian music. Only his Sunnyside session is available on CD. —*Ron Wynn*

Maiden Dance / Dec. 1983 / Gramavision ✦✦
Decent set alternating experimental, jazz-based songs and more R&B or pop outings. Violinist Blake can provide slashing, dynamic solos or gripping melodies, but also will sometimes rely on gimmicks rather than substance. —*Ron Wynn*

Twinkling of an Eye / Jan. 1985 / Gramavision ✦✦✦

● **Rhythm and Blues** / Jun. 1986 / Gramavision ✦✦✦✦

Adventures of the Heart / Feb. 1987 / Gramavision ✦✦

Quest / Mar. 31, 1992–Apr. 1, 1992 / Sunnyside ✦✦✦

Ran Blake

b. Apr. 20, 1935, Springfield, MA
Piano / Avant-Garde
A champion of "Third Stream" music (mixing together aspects of jazz and classical music), Ran Blake has long had a very individual and unusual piano style. His solos are generally very dramatic, making inventive use of explosive outbursts and silence. When performing standards he often keeps the melody intact but drops the chord structure, creating fresh new music. Blake graduated from Bard College, attended the Lenox School of Jazz during several summers and starting in 1957 had an association with singer Jeanne Lee; they toured Europe in 1963 and performed some fairly free piano-vocal duets. Blake, who recorded for ESP in 1965, became very involved in jazz education at the New England Conservatory of Music, where he has worked since 1967. He has recorded on an infrequent basis throughout his career including solo dates on several labels and collaborations with Ricky Ford, Anthony Braxton, Houston Person and Jeanne Lee. —*Scott Yanow*

The Newest Sound Around / Nov. 15, 1961–Dec. 7, 1961 / Bluebird ✦✦✦

Blue Potato / Apr. 9, 1969–Apr. 10, 1969 / Milestone ✦✦✦✦
Ran Blake has always had such an unusual piano style that it is not surprising that he is far from a household name. A very emotional improviser (whose unexpected explosions of sound sometimes punctuate otherwise introspective performances), Blake is a true original. This Milestone LP, only his third recording in eight years, shows Ran Blake really finding unusual things to say on a variety of standards (highlighted by "God Bless the Child," "Chicago," "Stars Fell on Alabama" and even "Never on Sunday") in addition to some originals. On this solo piano date, Blake makes political (if nonverbal) statements on many of these pieces, improvising off of the titles rather than the chord changes. —*Scott Yanow*

Breakthru / Dec. 2, 1975+Dec. 5, 1975 / IAI ✦✦✦✦
Excellent, haunting melodies and compositions, delivered in a piano style that's completely distinctive and personal. Ran Blake is one of the few Third Stream pianists who never deserted or

abandoned the concept or the style, but his playing is never rhythmically vapid or harmonically predictable. He's also great at building and varying moods in his pieces. —*Ron Wynn*

Third Stream Recompositions / Jun. 23, 1977 / Owl ✦✦✦

Portfolio of Doktor Mabuse / Oct. 1977 / Owl ✦✦✦

Rapport / Apr. 30, 1978–May 3, 1978 / Novus ✦✦

Film Noir / Jan. 23, 1980+Jan. 27, 1980 / Novus ✦✦✦✦✦
Intriguing third-stream arrangements, all-star lineup. Blake's most hypnotic concept statement. Solo piano. —*Ron Wynn*

Improvisations / May 25, 1981–May 26, 1981 / Soul Note ✦✦✦

● **Duke Dreams** / May 27, 1981–Jun. 2, 1981 / Soul Note ✦✦✦✦✦
Ran Blake's tribute to Billy Strayhorn and Duke Ellington, *Duke Dreams,* was recorded May 27 and June 2, 1981. Now, a tribute to these men might appear to be an "in-the-tradition" gambit, but Blake's realization of his own tribute (the title cut), Dave Brubeck's "The Duke," and the other material was a glance backward actually looking toward the present/future. Some of the very familiar tunes were given a most creative reworking. None of the original intent/feeling was destroyed…but instead developed and distilled through this unique artist whose quirky voicings, rhythms and lines make everything he does unmistakeably Blake. —*Bob Rusch, Cadence*

Suffield Gothic / Sep. 28, 1983–Sep. 29, 1983 / Soul Note ✦✦✦
His best concept album, with introspective, teeming melodies and alternately limp and joyful rhythms. Ran Blake's piano solos don't bowl anyone over with their speed or intensity, nor are they filled with clever counterpoint or multiple rhythms or constant reworkings of pop tunes. They're dialogues which shift and evolve according to Blake's vision of the moment; this requires listeners to simply respond, rather than to anticipate. —*Ron Wynn*

Painted Rhythms: The Compleat Ran Blake, Vol. 1 / Dec. 1985 / GM ✦✦✦✦
First in a projected series dedicated to the work of pianist/composer Ran Blake, a genuine iconoclast. His songs can be moving, muddled, dense, or aggressive, but they're never dull. His playing is the same way; always changing, seldom flashy, and usually rewarding for listeners with open ears. —*Ron Wynn*

Painted Rhythms: The Compleat Ran Blake, Vol. 2 / Dec. 1985 / GM ✦✦✦
The first volume of *Painted Rhythms,* from the same sessions as its partner, was an excellent introduction to pianist Ran Blake's style, for it included his reharmonizations of a variety of jazz standards and obscurities. The second volume ranges from Blake's often-scary originals ("Shoah!"/Babbit/Storm Warning") to 1,000-year-old melodies written by Spanish Jews and a fourth re-interpretation of "Maple Leaf Rag" (the first three were on the first volume). Throughout, Blake was quite concise (only "Shoah!" exceeded four minutes and seven other sketches were under two), very expressive and, as usual, totally individual. —*Scott Yanow*

Short Life of Barbara Monk / Aug. 26, 1986 / Soul Note ✦✦✦
Interesting concept work, with Blake's love of Third Stream (jazz and modern classical concepts merging) and film noir uniting in a series of related, yet divergent compositions. Blake's lines, phrasing, rhythms, and voicings defy easy analysis or fixed patterns. They're as diffuse and diverse as his interests, making every Blake album both a challenge and a delight. —*Ron Wynn*

You Stepped Out of a Cloud / Aug. 11, 1989 / Owl ✦✦✦✦
This is pianist Blake and vocalist Jeanne Lee's first record since the early-'60s. —*Michael G. Nastos*

Masters From Different Worlds / Dec. 26, 1989–Dec. 30, 1989 / Mapleshade ✦✦✦

That Certain Feeling / Jul. 3, 1990–Jul. 4, 1990 / Hat Art ✦✦✦
More rhythmic and beat-oriented than the usual Blake release, as he displays his love of gospel and spiritual rhythms, as well as the familiar Third Stream and film noir sounds. Blake has been among jazz's least acclaimed players for years, and that probably won't change, but this should refute the notion that his work is too obsessed with cerebral concerns rather than emotions. —*Ron Wynn*

Epistrophy / 1991 / Soul Note ✦✦✦✦
Ran Blake's re-interpretations of 12 Thelonious Monk songs and four standards that Monk enjoyed playing are quite different than everyone else's. He states the basic melody but, rather than improvising off the chord changes, Blake's flights on these solo piano performances stay close to the mood of the melodies, alternating silence with unexpected emotional flurries. —*Scott Yanow*

Round About / Dec. 19, 1992+Sep. 29, 1993 / Music & Arts ✦✦✦

Art Blakey

b. Oct. 11, 1919, Pittsburgh, PA, **d.** Oct. 16, 1990, New York, NY
Drums, Leader / Hard Bop
Art Blakey was hard bop's guru, the percussive anchor of countless brilliant bands, and its ultimate talent scout. Blakey's technique was famous, with his frequent, high volume snare and bass drum accents. Though he sometimes dismissed the idea of an African/jazz rhythm connection, Blakey incorporated some African devices after visiting in the '40s. These included the habit of rapping on the side of the drum and using his elbow on the tom-tom to alter the pitch. He was also known for the dramatic closing of the hi-hat on every second and fourth beat. Blakey played with such force and fury he eventually lost much of his hearing, and at the end was often playing strictly on instinct. But he maintained The Jazz Messengers as the idiom's foremost repertory band from its beginnings in the late '40s and mid-'50s into the '90s. The roster of greats whose careers Blakey nurtured include Donald Byrd, Hank Mobley, Jackie McLean, Johnny Griffin, Bobby Timmons, Benny Golson, Lee Morgan, Wayne Shorter, Curtis Fuller, Cedar Walton, Freddie Hubbard, Billy Harper, Joanne Brackeen, Valery Ponomarev, Bill Pierce, Bobby Watson, Wynton Marsalis, Branford Marsalis, James Williams, Terence Blanchard, Donald Harrison, Wallace Roney, Javon Jackson and Brian Lynch among others; even Keith Jarrett and Chuck Mangione! Blakey had a few piano lessons in his childhood, and was playing full-time by the seventh grade, heading a band. He switched to drums, essentially teaching himself through listening to such players as Chick Webb and Sid Catlett. He joined Mary Lou Williams in 1942, then played with the Fletcher Henderson Orchestra in 1943 and 1944, touring the south. He briefly led a big band in Boston, then joined Billy Eckstine's new band. During his years with Eckstine, Blakey met many bebop pioneers, including Miles Davis, Fats Navarro and Dexter Gordon. Blakey organized a rehearsal band he called the 17 Messengers upon leaving Eckstine. He later recorded with an octet called The Jazz Messengers. Blakey traveled to Africa in the late '40s, living there more than a year and learning about African music and Islam (he eventually converted to Islam and took the name Buhaina). He performed and did radio broadcasts in the '50s with Charlie Parker, Clifford Brown and Miles Davis, as well as Horace Silver. Blakey was in the Buddy DeFranco quartet from 1951 to 1953. He and Silver formed a co-operative group with Hank Mobley and Kenny Dorham in 1955, using the familiar name Jazz Messengers. When Silver departed in 1956, Blakey became the band's leader, and held that position the remainder of its existence. They became the prototype hard bop ensemble, playing aggressive, exciting bebop material with a vivid blues foundation. Blakey took pride in holding onto musicians just long enough to develop them, seeing them move on and fresh ones arrive. The coveted position of Messengers' music director belonged to a host of superb players, from Wayne Shorter to Bobby Watson. At the same time, Blakey never confined his duties to the Messengers. He found time to record with Monk, the Modern Jazz Quartet, John Coltrane, various African, jazz and Latin drummers on a summit session, do a film soundtrack with Benny Golson, tour with the Giants of Jazz (Gillespie, Monk, Sonny Stitt, and Al McKibbon), often appear as a soloist at the Newport Jazz Festival, and keep abreast of changes and fresh faces. The Messengers recorded from the '50s until the '90s primarily on Blue Note, but also on Impulse!, Timeless, Concord, and Bethlehem, plus some foreign labels. Though it seemed he would live forever, Blakey finally passed in 1992. His spirit and presence are celebrated in the music of the '80s and '90s hard bop revivalists. Mosaic issued a tremendous boxed set featuring the complete 1960 recordings of his group in 1995. Blue Note issued a three disc greatest hits collection, and there are also many single disc reissues from the different Messengers periods. —*Ron Wynn*

New Sounds / Dec. 22, 1947–1948 / Blue Note ✦✦✦
This historically significant CD collects together two sessions led by tenor saxophonist James Moody in 1948 (when he was a member of Dizzy Gillespie's big band) along with drummer Art Blakey's first recording date as a leader. Moody's music features boppish arrangements by Gil Fuller and solos by trumpeter Dave

Burns, altoist Ernie Henry and baritonist Cecil Payne while the Blakey set (originally released under the title of *Art Blakey's Messengers*) features an octet that includes trumpeter Kenny Dorham, altoist Sahib Shihab and pianist Walter Bishop. Classic and formerly rare music. —*Scott Yanow*

A Night at Birdland, Vol. 1 / Feb. 21, 1954 / Blue Note ✦✦✦✦
Just prior to forming the first edition of The Jazz Messengers, drummer Art Blakey led a superb quintet at Birdland for a brief gig in 1954. The band featured the great trumpeter Clifford Brown, altoist Lou Donaldson, pianist Horace Silver and bassist Curly Russell in addition to the leader/drummer. All of the music has since been reissued as part of a Clifford Brown box set for Mosaic, but this is the original LP. The first volume is highlighted by "A Night in Tunisia," "Quicksilver" and "Once in a While" and finds all of the participants in inspired form. Classic bop. —*Scott Yanow*

A Night at Birdland, Vol. 2 / Feb. 21, 1954 / Blue Note ✦✦✦✦
The second volume taken from Art Blakey's pre-Jazz Messengers gig at Birdland features the immortal trumpeter Clifford Brown, altoist Lou Donaldson, pianist Horace Silver, bassist Curly Russell and the leader/drummer romping through the blues "Wee-Dot," two Charlie Parker tunes, an alternate version of "Quicksilver" and a Donaldson ballad feature on "If I Had You." All of the musicians are inspired, none more than Blakey, who would soon form The Jazz Messengers as a permanent outlet for his hard-swinging drums. —*Scott Yanow*

At the Cafe Bohemia, Vol. 1 / Nov. 11, 1955 / Blue Note ✦✦✦
This first of two LP volumes features the original version of The Jazz Messengers, the quintet co-led by drummer Art Blakey and pianist Horace Silver that also featured trumpeter Kenny Dorham, Hank Mobley on tenor and bassist Doug Watkins. Caught live, the band stretches out on such numbers as "Soft Winds," "Minor's Holiday," "Alone Together" and Dorham's "Prince Albert." Highly enjoyable and still timeless music. —*Scott Yanow*

The Jazz Messengers at the Cafe Bohemia, Vol. 2 / Nov. 23, 1955 / Blue Note ✦✦✦
The second of two LP volumes showcasing the 1955 Jazz Messengers features Art Blakey, Horace Silver, Kenny Dorham, Hank Mobley and Doug Watkins digging into such strong material as Mobley's "Sportin' Crowd," "Avila and Tequila" and three standards. This band has influenced jazz up to the present day and was in fine form for this live appearance. —*Scott Yanow*

Art Blakey with the Original Jazz Messengers / Apr. 5, 1956–May 4, 1956 / Columbia ✦✦✦
The original version of The Jazz Messengers only lasted around a year, cutting four albums before the departure of pianist and chief composer Horace Silver. This LP (which also features trumpeter Donald Byrd, Hank Mobley's tenor and bassist Doug Watkins) is highlighted by the earliest recordings of two of Silver's songs, "Nica's Dream" and "Ecaroh," and plenty of typically hard swinging from the band. —*Scott Yanow*

Originally / May 4, 1956+Jun. 25, 1956 / Columbia ✦✦
This LP contains valuable performances by the early Jazz Messengers that sat unissued until decades later. Four selections feature the band when drummer Art Blakey and pianist Horace Silver were co-leaders; trumpeter Donald Byrd, Hank Mobley on tenor and bassist Doug Watkins were also in that quintet. Two numbers from June 1956 find Blakey as sole leader of The Messengers for the first time, heading an otherwise unrecorded unit with Byrd and multi-instrumentalist Ira Sullivan. This LP concludes with a humorous Gershwin medley from later in the year with altoist Jackie McLean and trumpeter Bill Hardman in prominent roles. Although not an essential set, Art Blakey fans will find this album to be a valuable gapfiller in the history of The Jazz Messengers. —*Scott Yanow*

The Jazz Messenger / May 4, 1956–Dec. 13, 1956 / Columbia ✦✦
This CD is a sampler of Art Blakey's 1956 recordings and will be frustrating for Jazz Messengers' collectors. None of the eight selections were previously unissued and they are taken from three separate sessions, none of which are offered here complete. Four selections feature the Art Blakey-Horace Silver quintet during their final recording dates (including "Ecaroh" and "Carol's Interlude"), one has multi-instrumentalist Ira Sullivan joining trumpeter Donald Byrd in the frontline and the remaining selections feature altoist Jackie McLean and trumpeter Bill Hardman. A good sampler for beginners, but Blakey fans should try to acquire the complete sessions instead. —*Scott Yanow*

Hard Bop / Dec. 12, 1956+Dec. 13, 1956 / Columbia ✦✦✦
This LP features The Jazz Messengers shortly after pianist Horace Silver departed to form his own band. With altoist Jackie McLean and trumpeter Bill Hardman as the key soloists (pianist Sam Dockery and bassist Spanky DeBrest completed the quintet), this group was already a potentially great outfit although its most glorious days were still to come. Three group originals (including McLean's "Little Melonae") and two standards are performed during this fine set. —*Scott Yanow*

Once upon a Groove / Jan. 14, 1957+Feb. 11, 1957 / Blue Note ✦✦✦
Following the original all-star version of The Jazz Messengers and preceding the Lee Morgan-Benny Golson band of late 1958, the group that drummer Art Blakey led in 1957 has tended to be overlooked. Featuring altoist Jackie McLean and trumpeter Bill Hardman, this particular outfit soon set the standard for the many versions of The Jazz Messengers that would follow, featuring originals by Blakey's young sidemen, hard-swinging ensembles and increasingly distinctive solos. This hard-to-find LP is worth a search. —*Scott Yanow*

Mirage / Mar. 8, 1957–Mar. 9, 1957 / Savoy ✦✦✦
The 1957 edition of The Jazz Messengers heard throughout this enjoyable LP features altoist Jackie McLean, trumpeter Bill Hardman, pianist Sam Dockery, bassist Spanky DeBrest and leader/drummer Art Blakey. Already at this early stage, the band was the epitome of hard bop and just beginning to become an influential force. Although none of these six selections (three by tuba player Ray Draper) would become standards, the music is consistently excellent and typically hard swinging. —*Scott Yanow*

Jazz Messengers Play Lerner and Loewe / Mar. 13, 1957 / VIK ✦✦✦
One of the rarest of all Art Blakey records, this LP finds The Jazz Messengers (featuring new member Johnny Griffin on tenor and trumpeter Bill Hardman) performing jazz versions of six show tunes by Lerner and Loewe including three ("Almost Like Being in Love," "I Could Have Danced All Night" and "On the Street Where You Live") that would soon become standards. Despite some of the musicians' unfamiliarity with the songs, this date is quite successful and should be reissued on CD someday. —*Scott Yanow*

Art Blakey/John Handy: Messages / May 13, 1957 / Roulette ✦✦✦
This double LP combines together two totally unrelated sessions that happened to be recorded on the same day for Roulette. Art Blakey's Jazz Messengers (with tenor great Johnny Griffin, trumpeter Bill Hardman and guest Sabu Martinez on congas) stretches out on four numbers which include "Woodyn' You" and Charlie Shavers' "Dawn on the Harvest" while altoist John Handy (heard in his first session as a leader), who would join Charles Mingus the following year, mostly sounds pretty individual on his six selections with a quartet. Enjoyable if not essential music, hard bop from the late '50s. —*Scott Yanow*

Art Blakey's Jazz Messengers with Thelonious Monk / May 14, 1957+May 15, 1957 / Atlantic ✦✦✦✦
This was an ideal matchup, one that should have been repeated in future years. Art Blakey was always one of the perfect drummers for Thelonious Monk's music, matching the innovative pianist's percussive excitement while leaving him plenty of space. Blakey's tenorman Johnny Griffin also proved to have a perfect understanding of Monk's music, joining Monk's quartet the following year. With trumpeter Bill Hardman and bassist Spanky DeBrest completing the quintet, five of Monk's finest compositions plus Griffin's "Purple Shades" are explored on this LP. When will this timeless music be reissued on CD? —*Scott Yanow*

Hard Drive / Oct. 9, 1957–Oct. 11, 1957 / Bethlehem ✦✦✦
The final recording by the second version of Art Blakey's Jazz Messengers features trumpeter Bill Hardman, tenor saxophonist Johnny Griffin, either Junior Mance or Sam Dockery on piano and bassist Spanky DeBrest along with leader/drummer Blakey performing four group originals, two Jimmy Heath compositions and the obscure "Late Spring." Although this was not the most famous edition of The Messengers, it set a standard that its successors would uphold to, training its members to be bandleaders in their own right. The music on this LP is typical hard bop of the period, well played and full of enthusiasm and fire. —*Scott Yanow*

Art Blakey Big Band / Dec. 1957 / Bethlehem ✦✦✦
Throughout his long career as a bandleader, drummer Art Blakey

very rarely played with big bands. This Bethlehem date was a one-shot affair, an opportunity for his powerful drumming to be heard propelling a 15-piece orchestra through a set of mostly new material. With such soloists as John Coltrane (who is also featured on two quintet numbers), trombonist Jimmy Cleveland and trumpeters Donald Byrd and Ray Copeland, this was a potentially mighty band; its arrangers included Melba Liston and Al Cohn. This LP is worth searching for. —*Scott Yanow*

★ **Moanin': Art Blakey and the Jazz Messengers** / Oct. 30, 1958 / Blue Note ✦✦✦✦✦
The third version of Art Blakey's Jazz Messengers debuted with this stunning LP which has since been reisssued (along with an alternate version of "Moanin'") on CD. Tenor saxophonist Benny Golson helped give the quintet its own personality with his compositions and arrangements (contributing "Blues March," "Along Came Betty," "Are You Real" and "The Drum Thunder Suite" to this set), 20-year old trumpeter Lee Morgan quickly emerged as a powerful soloist and the funky pianist Bobby Timmons' "Moanin'" became The Messengers' first real hit. This classic album, a major influence on hard bop, is highly recommended. —*Scott Yanow*

1958: Paris Olympia / Nov. 22, 1958+Dec. 17, 1958 / Fontana ✦✦✦✦
The 1958 version of The Jazz Messengers was widely recorded during their stay in Paris, but this CD does not duplicate any of the other recordings previously released. This band (with trumpeter Lee Morgan, Benny Golson on tenor and pianist Bobby Timmons) was particularly strong, and it is quite enjoyable to hear them stretch out on such songs as "I Remember Clifford," "Moanin'," "Blues March" and "Whisper Not." Hard bop at its best, all of it propelled by the powerful drumming of Art Blakey. —*Scott Yanow*

Paris 1958 / Dec. 18, 1958–Dec. 19, 1958 / Bluebird ✦✦✦✦
Originally part of an 11-song three-LP set, this six-song CD (not counting the 28-second "Theme") features the Lee Morgan-Benny Golson-Bobby Timmons version of The Jazz Messengers stretching out on their "hits" (including "Blues March," "Moanin'" and "Whisper Not"), giving one alternate versions of their studio recordings. This was one of the finest bands of the period, and this CD serves as a perfect introduction to the exciting music of The Jazz Messengers. —*Scott Yanow*

Des Femmes Disparaissent / Dec. 18, 1958–Dec. 19, 1958 / Fontana ✦✦✦
This three-LP box set from French RCA (part of which was reissued on the CD *Paris 1958*) features the 1958 Jazz Messengers live in Paris stretching out on 11 songs. Trumpeter Lee Morgan, tenor saxophonist Benny Golson and pianist Bobby Timmons formed a potent team, backed up by bassist Jymie Merritt and the powerful drumming of leader Art Blakey. This hard-to-find set gives one a definitive look at the influential band. —*Scott Yanow*

At The Jazz Corner of the World / Apr. 15, 1959 / Blue Note ✦✦✦✦
Drum legend Art Blakey was heading a streamlined edition of The Messengers when they came to Birdland on April 15, 1959. It was a two-horn, piano, bass, and drum configuration, with trumpeter Lee Morgan, tenor saxophonist Hank Mobley, bassist Jymie Merritt and pianist Bobby Timmons in the lineup alongside Blakey. This two-CD set combines the original two volumes issued as *At The Jazz Corner Of The World*, and it was galvanizing hard bop at its best. No recent Blue Note series has been more on target than the Doubletime line; this one is no exception. —*Ron Wynn*

Africaine: Art Blakey and His Jazz Messengers / Nov. 10, 1959 / Blue Note ✦✦✦
Not released until over 20 years after it was recorded, this LP features tenor saxophonist Wayne Shorter in his first recording with The Jazz Messengers. The quintet at the time also featured the great trumpeter Lee Morgan, pianist Walter Davis Jr, bassist Jymie Merritt and the drummer/leader Art Blakey. The highpoint is easily Shorter's memorable composition "Lester Left Town" (written after Lester Young's passing). Overall, this forgotten session contains plenty of excellent hard bop. —*Scott Yanow*

Live in Stockholm (1959) / Nov. 23, 1959 / Dragon ✦✦✦

Paris Jam Session / Dec. 18, 1959 / EmArcy ✦✦✦
This very interesting CD features Art Blakey's Jazz Messengers (with trumpeter Lee Morgan and their new tenor saxophonist

Wayne Shorter) on fine versions of Morgan's "The Midget" and "A Night in Tunisia" but is highlighted by the guest appearances of altoist Barney Wilen and particularly pianist Bud Powell on two Powell classics ("Dance of the Infidels" and "Bouncing with Bud"). Exciting music, most highly recommended to veteran Art Blakey collectors. —*Scott Yanow*

Les Liaisons / Jul. 8, 1959–Jul. 9, 1959 / Fontana ✦✦
An interesting set of music originally recorded as the soundtrack for the French film *Les Liaisons Dangereuses*, the majority of these tracks feature Art Blakey's Jazz Messengers of mid-1959 with trumpeter Lee Morgan, tenorman Barney Wilen, pianist Bobby Timmons and bassist Jymie Merritt joining the explosive drummer/leader. In general, the music manages to stand on its own with the ensemble getting to stretch out a bit on the rare material. —*Scott Yanow*

The Big Beat / Mar. 6, 1960 / Blue Note ✦✦✦✦✦
In 1960, Art Blakey led one of the greatest versions of his Jazz Messengers. The particular edition heard on this CD features three distinctive soloists (trumpeter Lee Morgan, tenor saxophonist Wayne Shorter and pianist Bobby Timmons). Highlights of *The Big Beat* include Timmons' "Dat Dere" and Shorter's "Lester Left Town" in addition to a colorful arrangement of "It's Only a Paper Moon," heard in two versions. A gem. —*Scott Yanow*

★ **The Complete Blue Note Recordings of Art Blakey's 1960 Messengers** / Mar. 6, 1960–May 27, 1961 / Mosaic ✦✦✦✦
This six-CD limited-edition box set from Mosaic is quite remarkable. It includes all of the music from The Jazz Messenger albums *The Big Beat*, *A Night in Tunisia*, the two volumes of *Meet You at the Jazz Corner of the World*, *The Freedom Rider*, *Like Someone in Love*, *The Witch Doctor*, *Roots and Herbs* and *Pisces* (the latter was originally only issued only in Japan) along with two previously unissued alternate takes. More importantly, the music is consistently brilliant, featuring one of the great editions of Art Blakey's band, the group with trumpeter Lee Morgan, tenor saxophonist Wayne Shorter, pianist Bobby Timmons and bassist Jymie Merritt. But one will have to act fast to get this essential music before it goes out of print and starts showing up on auction lists! —*Scott Yanow*

Like Someone in Love / Aug. 7, 1960 / Blue Note ✦✦✦
Taken from the same sessions that resulted in *A Night in Tunisia*, this fine CD features the 1960 version of The Jazz Messengers starring trumpeter Lee Morgan, tenor saxophonist Wayne Shorter and pianist Bobby Timmons. The title cut is the most impressive performance, but this excellent program of high-quality hard bop also allows listeners to hear three more obscure Wayne Shorter compositions and Lee Morgan's forgotten "Johnny's Blue." —*Scott Yanow*

Night in Tunisia / Aug. 14, 1960 / Blue Note ✦✦✦✦
The lengthy title track on this CD easily overshadows the rest of the program for it is one of the most exciting versions ever recorded of Dizzy Gillespie's "A Night in Tunisia." Trumpeter Lee Morgan (then only in his early 20s), tenor saxophonist Wayne Shorter, pianist Bobby Timmons and bassist Jymie Merritt formed one of the strongest of the many versions of Art Blakey's Jazz Messengers and are actually in fine form during the remainder of the satisfying (if anticlimatic) set. The CD augments the LP by adding a version of "When Your Lover Has Gone" and an alternate take of "Sincerely Diana" to the original program. —*Scott Yanow*

Meet You at the Jazz Corner of the World, Vol. 1 / Sep. 14, 1960 / Blue Note ✦✦✦
Art Blakey's 1960 Jazz Messengers recorded so many excellent records that the "good" rating given this LP is relative. With trumpeter Lee Morgan, tenor saxophonist Wayne Shorter and pianist Bobby Timmons all receiving plenty of solo space, the band is in fine form on Hank Mobley's "The Opener," Lee Morgan's "What Know" and two standards. Little unexpected occurs, but fans of hard-swinging jazz will want to pick up both volumes in this series. —*Scott Yanow*

Meet You at the Jazz Corner of the World, Vol. 2 / Sep. 14, 1960 / Blue Note ✦✦✦
The much-recorded 1960 Jazz Messengers are in fine form for both of the LP volumes in this series of "Live at Birdland" recordings. Trumpeter Lee Morgan, tenor saxophonist Wayne Shorter and pianist Bobby Timmons all take excellent solos on Wayne Shorter's "The Summit," a standard ("The Things I Love") and two Hank Mobley songs. Not essential hard bop music but quite enjoyable in its own right. —*Scott Yanow*

Live in Stockholm (1960) / Dec. 6, 1960 / Dragon ✦✦✦
Recorded from a radio broadcast in Sweden, this LP finds The Jazz Messengers near their peak. This edition of the band (with trumpeter Lee Morgan, Wayne Shorter on tenor and pianist Bobby Timmons) was the most celebrated and most frequently recorded of all the versions of The Jazz Messengers. This album (which includes strong versions of "Blues March," "Lester Left Town," "Along Came Betty," "A Night in Tunisia" and Wayne Shorter's lesser-known "The Summit") is easily recommended as a strong example of their legacy. —*Scott Yanow*

Pisces / Feb. 12, 1961 / Blue Note ✦✦✦

Roots & Herbs / Feb. 18, 1961 / Blue Note ✦✦✦

The Witch Doctor / Mar. 14, 1961 / Blue Note ✦✦✦
The 1960-61 Jazz Messengers featured three distinctive soloists (trumpeter Lee Morgan, Wayne Shorter on tenor and pianist Bobby Timmons), perfectly suitable accompaniment by bassist Jymie Merritt and typically powerful drumming from its leader, Art Blakey. *Witch Doctor* has two compositions apiece from Morgan and Shorter in addition to Timmons' "A Little Busy" and Clifford Jordan's "Lost and Found." None of these songs became standards, but the fine solos and strong group sound make this LP worth picking up. —*Scott Yanow*

Paris Jazz Concert / May 13, 1961 / RTE ✦✦✦

The Freedom Rider / May 27, 1961 / Blue Note ✦✦✦✦
The final recording by this edition of The Jazz Messengers (featuring trumpeter Lee Morgan, tenor saxophonist Wayne Shorter, pianist Bobby Timmons, bassist Jymie Merritt and drummer/leader Art Blakey) finds the group consolidating their year-and-a-half of experience into yet another exciting document. Blakey's unaccompanied drum feature on "The Freedom Rider" is full of drama while the rest of the program (two compositions apiece by Morgan and Shorter) makes this last chapter for this particular band quite memorable. —*Scott Yanow*

Jazz Messengers / Jun. 13, 1961-Jun. 14, 1961 / MCA ✦✦
Trumpeter Lee Morgan's final recording in his initial stint with Art Blakey's Jazz Messengers (and trombonist Curtis Fuller's first) is a curiously lackluster affair. Perhaps Morgan and pianist Bobby Timmons already knew that they would be departing soon. In any case, this set (which includes five standards and Fuller's "A La Mode") is only an average outing for this talented group; nice music but nothing that special. —*Scott Yanow*

Mosaic / Oct. 2, 1961 / Blue Note ✦✦✦
The first studio recording by Art Blakey's all-star Messengers of 1961-64 features five group originals (including "Mosaic," "Arabia" and "Crisis") and exciting solos from the great frontline (trumpeter Freddie Hubbard, trombonist Curtis Fuller and tenor saxophonist Wayne Shorter). All of the recordings by this classic hard bop group are well worth acquiring. —*Scott Yanow*

Buhaina's Delight / Nov. 28, 1961+Dec. 18, 1961 / Blue Note ✦✦✦
There have been several classic editions of Art Blakey's Jazz Messengers including the sextet heard on this CD, which adds four alternate takes to the original LP's program. With trumpeter Freddie Hubbard, tenor saxophonist Wayne Shorter, trombonist Curtis Fuller and pianist Cedar Walton (all of whom would be major names in jazz for the next 30 years) taking consistently excellent solos, it is not surprising that this CD (which is highlighted by "Moon River," "Bu's Delight" and "Backstage Sally"), as with all of the other recordings by this group, is easily recommended to lovers of hard bop. —*Scott Yanow*

Three Blind Mice, Vol. 1 / Mar. 9, 1962-Mar. 18, 1962 / Blue Note ✦✦✦✦
The first of two volumes in this brief CD series greatly expands upon the original LP, adding Wayne Shorter's "Children of the Night" and an alternate version of Freddie Hubbard's "Up Jumped Spring" to an already strong set of memorable material. Other highlights by this all-star sextet (featuring trumpeter Hubbard, Shorter's tenor and trombonist Curtis Fuller) include Fuller's reworking of "Three Blind Mice," "Blue Moon" and "When Lights Are Low." —*Scott Yanow*

Three Blind Mice, Vol. 2 / Mar. 9, 1962-Mar. 18, 1962 / Blue Note ✦✦✦✦
The second of two CDs that greatly expand the original *Three Blind Mice* LP captures the all-star Jazz Messengers sextet of 1961-62 at two separate concerts. The five extended perfor-

mances, which consist of four group originals (including "Mosaic" and "Ping Pong") and "It's Only a Paper Moon," include many strong solos from trumpeter Freddie Hubbard, trombonist Curtis Fuller, tenor saxophonist Wayne Shorter and pianist Cedar Walton, all future bandleaders. Both of the CD volumes are highly recommended. —*Scott Yanow*

Caravan / Oct. 23, 1962-Oct. 24, 1962 / Original Jazz Classics ✦✦✦

Ugetsu / Jun. 16, 1963 / Original Jazz Classics ✦✦✦
Blakey's best sextet, with Wayne Shorter (sax), Freddie Hubbard (tpt), and Curtis Fuller (tb). Cedar Walton is prominent as music director, arranger, and composer. Live at Birdland, NYC. Famous tunes "One by One," "On the Ginza," and title track rank this among his best work. —*Michael G. Nastos*

A Jazz Message / Jul. 16, 1963 / MCA ✦✦
Drummer Art Blakey took time off from his busy schedule as leader of The Jazz Messengers to participate in this quartet session with saxophonist Sonny Stitt, pianist McCoy Tyner and bassist Art Davis. Although this session was under Blakey's leadership, Stitt (on both tenor and alto) emerges as the main soloist, playing his trademark bebop lines with creativity and typical enthusiasm. —*Scott Yanow*

Blues Bag / 1964 / Affinity ✦✦✦
This LP is a real curiosity in the history of Art Blakey's Jazz Messengers, for it found his band utilizing two trumpets (Lee Morgan and Freddie Hill) and welcoming Buddy DeFranco as the only reed player, with the clarinetist sticking exclusively to bass clarinet! Even the repertoire, which includes John Coltrane's "Cousin Mary," Ornette Coleman's "Blues Connotation" and Leonard Feather's "Twelve Tone Blues," is unusual. DeFranco is the main soloist throughout this unique (if consistently swinging) set. —*Scott Yanow*

Free for All / Feb. 10, 1964 / Blue Note ✦✦✦
During most of 1961-64 Art Blakey's Jazz Messengers (except for bassist Reggie Workman replacing Spanky DeBrest) managed to keep the same personnel, a remarkable feat when one considers the strong talent (which included trumpeter Freddie Hubbard, trombonist Curtis Fuller, Wayne Shorter on tenor and pianist Cedar Walton). *Free for All* was this particular group's last recording before Freddie Hubbard went out on his own, and it includes lengthy versions of two Shorter tunes, Hubbard's "The Core" and the standard "Pensativa." Fine music. —*Scott Yanow*

Kyoto / Feb. 20, 1964 / Original Jazz Classics ✦✦✦
Reissued on Fantasy's OJC series, this LP (also available as a CD) finds Art Blakey's Jazz Messengers paying tribute to Japan (where they had toured to great acclaim) on two selections, featuring Art Blakey's cousin as a vocalist on "Wellington's Blues" (a real rarity in The Jazz Messengers' discography) and debuting Curtis Fuller's "The High Priest." With trumpeter Freddie Hubbard, tenorman Wayne Shorter and trombonist Fuller in fine form, this is one of literally dozens of recommended Jazz Messengers recordings. —*Scott Yanow*

Indestructible / Apr. 24, 1964+May 15, 1964 / Blue Note ✦✦✦
In 1964, trumpeter Lee Morgan rejoined The Jazz Messengers, replacing his original replacement, Freddie Hubbard. The hard-swinging style of this influential unit remained unchanged with drummer/leader Art Blakey still insisting on distinctive solos and constant new material. Typically, the music on this fine LP consists of five then-recent compositions by bandmembers, one apiece from Morgan, pianist Cedar Walton ("When Love Is New") and tenor saxophonist Wayne Shorter and two from trombonist Curtis Fuller. Enjoyable music. —*Scott Yanow*

Soul Finger / May 12, 1965-May 13, 1965 / Limelight ✦✦
After six years of very consistent personnel (with only a few gradual changes), Art Blakey's Jazz Messengers in 1965 were in a state of transition. This particular LP found both Lee Morgan and Freddie Hubbard making farewell appearances on trumpet, pianist John Hicks and bassist Victor Sproles joining up as short-term members and veteran Lucky Thompson being well featured on both tenor and soprano sax. The music is more relaxed than usual but still contains some of that distinctive Jazz Messengers fire. This rare set is worth searching for. —*Scott Yanow*

Buttercorn Lady / Jan. 1, 1966-Jan. 9, 1966 / Limelight ✦✦✦
Few jazz followers would think of trumpeter Chuck Mangione and pianist Keith Jarrett as former members of Art Blakey's Jazz Messengers, but in 1966, they both worked in the drummer's clas-

sic hard bop unit and the stint gave them needed exposure and helped the pair to develop their own individual voices. With tenor saxophonist Frank Mitchell and bassist Reggie Workman completing the quintet, this particular version of The Jazz Messengers only had the opportunity to record this one excellent live LP (which is currently out of print) but proved to be a worthy successor to their more acclaimed predecessors. A brilliant and unique set. — *Scott Yanow*

Hold On, I'm Coming / May 27, 1966 / Limelight ♦♦
One of the few out-and-out commercial recordings made by drummer Art Blakey during his long career, this attempt at jazzing up some pop tunes features so-so arrangements by Tom McIntosh and Melba Liston on such songs as "Hold on, I'm Coming," "Secret Agent Man," "Mame" and "Monday, Monday"! A real curiosity (finding Blakey using organist Malcom Bass as a particularly unlikely sideman), it would not be an understatement to say that this is not one of the more essential Art Blakey recordings. — *Scott Yanow*

Art Blakey and the Jazz Messengers / Aug. 1968 / Everest ♦♦♦
After a decade of steady recording, Art Blakey's Jazz Messengers found their hard bop music somewhat out-of-fashion by the late '60s; in fact, they only recorded two sessions (both live) between 1967–71. This particular one (a budget LP from Everest) is most unusual for the solos of tenor saxophonist Billy Harper are much more advanced than those of Blakey's usual sidemen. With trumpeter Bill Hardman, trombonist Julian Priester, pianist Ronnie Mathews and bassist Larry Evans completing the group, much of the music on these four selections is actually closer to free jazz than to hard bop, making this one of Blakey's most adventurous sets. — *Scott Yanow*

Art Blakey and the Jazz Messengers / Feb. 19, 1970 / Catalyst ♦♦♦
One of only two albums recorded by Art Blakey's Jazz Messengers during 1967–71, this LP is quite unusual, for not only does it feature veteran trumpeter Bill Hardman, but the avant-garde tenor of Carlos Garnett and pianist Joanne Brackeen (the first female member of The Jazz Messengers). Mostly performing durable standards such as "Moanin'," "Whisper Not" and "A Night in Tunisia," the quintet casts new light on these tunes, making them sound fresh and flexible. This unusual set is recommended to longtime followers of Art Blakey; it deserves to be reissued on CD. — *Scott Yanow*

Art Blakey and the Jazz Messengers, Vol. 1 / May 23, 1972–Mar. 1973 / Prestige ♦♦♦

Backgammon / Mar. 15, 1976–Mar. 16, 1976 / Roulette ♦♦♦

Gypsy Folk Tales: Art Blakey and the Jazz Messengers / Feb. 14, 1977–Mar. 1, 1977 / Roulette ♦♦♦
The 1977 version of The Jazz Messengers introduced two new voices to jazz (altoist Bobby Watson and the Russian trumpeter Valeri Ponomarev) in addition to featuring tenor saxophonist Dave Schnitter, veteran pianist Walter Davis and bassist Dennis Irwin. This Roulette LP includes six fairly recent originals in addition to a pair of numbers co-written by drummer Art Blakey with saxophonist Bob Mintzer. Davis' "Gypsy Folk Tales" and "Jodi" are the best-known songs and the hard-bop oriented solos are consistently fresh. — *Scott Yanow*

In My Prime, Vol. 1 / Dec. 29, 1977 / Timeless ♦♦♦♦
Leader of The Jazz Messengers at the time of this recording for over 22 years, drummer Art Blakey was still discovering new talent. In addition to altoist Bobby Watson, trumpeter Valeri Ponomarev and David Schnitter on tenor, this particular session introduced the great pianist James Williams to The Messenger fold. Despite the changes in musical fashions, Art Blakey and his hard-bop ensemble were still turning out new material and solos in the late '70s that sound fresh and alive today. — *Scott Yanow*

In This Korner / May 8, 1978 / Concord Jazz ♦♦♦♦
Although one of the lesser-known editions of The Jazz Messengers, the sextet featured on this Concord LP (trumpeter Valeri Ponomarev, altoist Bobby Watson, tenor saxophonist David Schnitter, pianist James Williams and bassist Dennis Irwin in addition to the leader/drummer) could hold its own with its more acclaimed predecessors and successors. Blakey always encouraged his sidemen to write new music, so on this set Williams, Watson and Ponomarev contributed fresh material for the hard-bop ensemble. Blakey fans should enjoy this underrated set. — *Scott Yanow*

Reflections in Blue / Dec. 4, 1978 / Timeless ♦♦♦
The 1978 Jazz Messengers was one of Art Blakey's strongest groups in years, although it would soon be overshadowed by its successor (which introduced a young Wynton Marsalis). With trumpeter Valerie Ponomarev, altoist Bobby Watson and a tenor saxophonist forming a potent frontline and new material from each of the principals (plus pianist James Williams) in addition to a lengthy ballad medley, this is a fine all-around set, last available on LP. — *Scott Yanow*

And the Jazz Messengers Big Band / Jul. 13, 1980–Jul. 17, 1980 / Timeless ♦♦♦
Art Blakey, leader of the highly influential hard-bop group The Jazz Messengers (which was usually a quintet or a sextet), made a rare tour with an 11-piece little big band in mid-1980. Included among the personnel were such unknown youngsters as trumpeter Wynton Marsalis (then age 18), Branford Marsalis on baritone and alto, trombonist Robin Eubanks and guitarist Kevin Eubanks. The remarkable group also included the regular members of The Jazz Messengers (trumpeter Valeri Ponomarev, altoist Bobby Watson, tenor saxophonist Billy Pierce and pianist James Williams) and even a second drummer, John Ramsey. The music (three Bobby Watson compositions, the standard "Stairway to the Stars" and Williams' blues "Minor Thesis") is consistently excellent and all of the musicians get their chance to solo. A historically significant and rather enjoyable release. — *Scott Yanow*

Live at Bubba's / Oct. 11, 1980 / Who's Who In Jazz ♦♦♦
The teenage trumpeter Wynton Marsalis (then most heavily influenced by Freddie Hubbard) made his recording debut as a member of Art Blakey's Jazz Messengers on this fine LP and, as his feature on "My Funny Valentine" shows, he was more than ready for the spotlight. This version of The Messengers was particularly strong, with such future bandleaders as altoist Bobby Watson, tenor saxophonist Billy Pierce, pianist James Williams and bassist Charles Fambrough (along with the leader/drummer) rompin' on such pieces as "Moanin'," "Soulful Mr. Timmons" and "Free for All." — *Scott Yanow*

In Sweden / Mar. 9, 1981 / Evidence ♦♦♦
This CD (a straight reissue of an Amigo LP) documents a live appearance by Art Blakey's Jazz Messengers at a period when he was featuring quite an all-star lineup (although its young members were then fairly unknown): trumpeter Wynton Marsalis (showcased on "How Deep Is the Ocean"), altoist Bobby Watson (heard throughout "Skylark"), tenorman Billy Pierce, pianist James Williams and bassist Charles Fambrough. This CD gives one classic hard bop and a chance to hear Wynton Marsalis at the beginning of his productive career. — *Scott Yanow*

Album of the Year / Apr. 12, 1981 / Timeless ♦♦♦♦
The 1981 edition of The Jazz Messengers featured more than its share of young greats (trumpeter Wynton Marsalis, altoist Bobby Watson, tenor saxophonist Billy Pierce, pianist James Williams and bassist Charles Fambrough), reinforcing drummer Art Blakey's recognition as jazz's greatest talent scout. This high-quality set, recorded in Paris, includes new material (highlighted by James Williams' "Soulful Mister Timmons"), Wayne Shorter's "Witch Hunt" and the Charlie Parker blues "Cheryl." — *Scott Yanow*

Straight Ahead / Jun. 1981 / Concord Jazz ♦♦♦♦♦
One of the best recordings by Art Blakey's 1981 Jazz Messengers, this set features Wynton Marsalis (then 19) on "How Deep Is the Ocean" and other illustrious sidemen (including altoist Bobby Watson, tenor saxophonist Bill Pierce and pianist James Williams) playing such group pieces as "Falling in Love with Love," "My Romance" and Watson's "E.T.A." Highly recommended. — *Scott Yanow*

Killer Joe: Art Blakey & George Kawaguchi / Dec. 4, 1981 / Storyville ♦♦♦
This unusual LP finds Art Blakey and the Jazz Messengers adding a second drummer, the fine Japanese player George Kawaguchi, to a set featuring three standards and two Kawaguchi pieces. Recorded at a time when Wynton Marsalis was on leave (touring with Herbie Hancock), this date showcases such players as trumpeter Wallace Roney, altoist Branford Marsalis and veteran trombonist Slide Hampton. Fine music, although a bit of an oddity. — *Scott Yanow*

Keystone 3 / Jan. 1982 / Concord Jazz ♦♦♦♦
Wynton Marsalis' final recording as a member of Art Blakey's Jazz

Messengers finds his brother Branford taking Bobby Watson's place on alto. The remainder of this superb sextet includes tenor saxophonist Bill Pierce, pianist Donald Brown, bassist Charles Fambrough and the veteran drummer/leader. All concerned sound in top form on both new (Wynton's "Waterfalls" and Watson's "Fuller Love") and old ("In Walked Bud" and "In a Sentimental Mood") material alike. Mostly high-powered hard bop in the best tradition of The Jazz Messengers. —*Scott Yanow*

Art Blakey and the All Star Messengers / Apr. 11, 1982 / RCA ✦✦✦

Drummer Art Blakey could have formed quite a few all-star groups drawn exclusively from the alumni of his Jazz Messengers. One of his few one-shot bands of that nature sounds fine on this LP featuring trumpeter Freddie Hubbard, trombonist Curtis Fuller, Benny Golson's tenor, pianist Cedar Walton and bassist Buster Williams. In addition to newer Golson tunes, this unit clearly enjoys themselves playing such classics as "Moanin'," "Blues March," "A Night in Tunisia" and "I Remember Clifford." Few surprises occur, but the music should satisfy Blakey's many fans. —*Scott Yanow*

Oh, by the Way / May 20, 1982 / Timeless ✦✦✦

When the Marsalis brothers left The Jazz Messengers in early 1982, Wynton suggested that Art Blakey take a close listen to trumpeter Terence Blanchard (then 19) and 21-year-old altoist Donald Harrison. The drummer took his advice, and after also adding young pianist Johnny O'Neal, Blakey soon had an exciting new version of The Jazz Messengers. Tenor saxophonist Bill Pierce and bassist Charles Fambrough were still present from the older band for this excellent LP. In the Blakey tradition, this set has five new compositions from bandmembers in addition to Wayne Shorter's "One by One" and the standard "My Funny Valentine"; the music is a fine example of high-quality hard bop. —*Scott Yanow*

New York Scene / May 1984 / Concord Jazz ✦✦✦

Nearly 30 years after forming the first version of The Jazz Messengers, drummer Art Blakey was still jazz's top talent scout. For this Concord LP such new members as tenor saxophonist Jean Toussaint, pianist Mulgrew Miller and bassist Lonnie Plaxico joined the team of trumpeter Terence Blanchard and altoist Donald Harrison (who had hooked up with Blakey two years earlier) to create a fine set of hard bop. Miller has a ballad medley to himself, Blanchard is well featured on "Tenderly" and the rest of the program features the full band on stimulating group originals. —*Scott Yanow*

Blue Night / Mar. 17, 1985 / Timeless ✦✦✦

The last time that drummer Art Blakey was able to keep a consistent personnel in his Jazz Messengers together for a lengthy period of time was the version he had with trumpeter Terence Blanchard and altoist Donald Harrison in the mid-'80s (a band which also included Jean Toussaint on tenor, pianist Mulgrew Miller and bassist Lonnie Plaxico). This excellent Timeless CD has a version of "Body and Soul" along with seven stimulating (if not overly memorable) recent originals by bandmembers. Fine modern hard bop. —*Scott Yanow*

Live at Sweet Basil: Art Blakey and the Jazz Messengers / Mar. 24, 1985 / GNP ✦✦✦✦

This excellent all-around session showcases the 1985 edition of Art Blakey's Jazz Messengers, a band that boasted such fine young soloists as trumpeter Terence Blanchard, altoist Donald Harrison, tenor saxophonist Jean Toussaint and pianist Mulgrew Miller. In addition to Harrison's "Mr. Babe" and Walter Davis' "Jodi," the ensemble successfully updates two Jazz Messenger classics: "Blues March" and "Moanin'." —*Scott Yanow*

Hard Champion: Art Blakey and the Jazz Messengers / Mar. 24, 1985–May 3, 1987 / Evidence ✦✦

Three of the four selections on this CD are taken from the same session as *Live at Sweet Basil*, but despite some fine playing, the music is not all that memorable or unique. Trumpeter Terence Blanchard, altoist Donald Harrison and tenor saxophonist Jean Toussaint did make a potent frontline, so completists may want to pick up this reissue of Paddle Wheel material that was only previously released in Japan. A final throwaway track (the three-minute "Theme of 'Hard Champion'") was actually recorded two years later by a different version of The Jazz Messengers. —*Scott Yanow*

Live at Kimball's / Apr. 1985 / Concord Jazz ✦✦✦

Art Blakey's mid-1980's version of The Jazz Messengers made

many recordings, but since the group (featuring trumpeter Terence Blanchard, altoist Donald Harrison, tenor saxophonist Jean Toussaint, pianist Mulgrew Miller, bassist Lonnie Plaxico and the leader/drummer) was particularly talented, all of its sessions are well worth acquiring by lovers of modern hard bop. This particular LP has ballad features for Blanchard ("Polka Dots and Moonbeams"), Toussaint ("I Love You") and Miller ("Old Folks" and "You and the Night and the Music") along with three flagwavers for the full ensemble. —*Scott Yanow*

New Year's Eve at Sweet Basil: Art Blakey and His Jazz Messengers / Dec. 30, 1985–Dec. 31, 1985 / Evidence ✦✦✦

One of two CDs recorded by The Jazz Messengers during the last two days of 1985 documents one of the final appearances by the Terence Blanchard-Donald Harrison version of this jazz institution. With trombonist Tim Williams (along with tenor saxophonist Jean Toussaint, pianist Mulgrew Miller and bassist Lonnie Plaxico) added on, The Messengers were temporarily a septet, but their blend of hard bop and youthful enthusiasm was unchanged. Three group originals and Billy Eckstine's "I Want to Talk About You" are performed by this fine group. The Evidence CD is a reissue of music formerly issued by the Japanese Paddle Wheel label. —*Scott Yanow*

Dr. Jeckyle / Dec. 30, 1985–Dec. 31, 1985 / Evidence ✦✦✦

The second of two CDs documenting one of the last appearances by The Jazz Messengers before trumpeter Terence Blanchard and altoist Donald Harrison decided to go out on their own finds Blakey's group expanded temporarily to a septet with the addition of trombonist Tim Williams. The ensemble is in particularly strong form on Bobby Watson's "Fuller Love," Jackie McLean's "Dr. Jeckyle," Wayne Shorter's "One by One" and the advanced Ron Carter tune "81." —*Scott Yanow*

Feeling Good / Sep. 8, 1986–Sep. 9, 1986 / Delos ✦✦✦

After nearly a decade of relative stability, the turnover in Art Blakey's Jazz Messengers greatly increased during the veteran drummer's last four years. This was not due to dissatisfaction with his dedication to hard bop and hard-swinging but to Blakey's desire to play with as many of the promising young jazzmen as possible. The CD *Feeling Good*, The Jazz Messengers' only recording from 1986–87, features a septet with trumpeter Wallace Roney, altoist Kenny Garrett and holdovers Jean Toussaint (on tenor), trombonist Tim Williams and pianist Donald Brown. The repertoire includes both new originals and a few Messenger standbys; the music is consistently enjoyable. —*Scott Yanow*

Not Yet: Art Blakey and His Jazz Messengers / Mar. 19, 1988 / Soul Note ✦✦✦

The 1988 edition of The Jazz Messengers, which drummer Art Blakey had been leading for 33 years, showed a great deal of promise. Comprised of trumpeter Philip Harper (soon to form The Harper Brothers), trombonist Robin Eubanks, the tenor of Javon Jackson, pianist Benny Green and bassist Peter Washington, this band (whose average age without counting Blakey was around 25) performs one original apiece by Green and Jackson along with five older songs on this enjoyable release. The music may not have contained too many surprises or been startlingly new, but the results are quite pleasing. —*Scott Yanow*

I Get a Kick out of Bu / Nov. 11, 1988 / Soul Note ✦✦✦

Even after heading The Jazz Messengers for over three decades, drummer Art Blakey kept true to his original vision, using the band as a forum for talented young players to swing hard and grow rapidly. Certainly his crop of players in 1988 (which included trumpeter Philip Harper, trombonist Robin Eubanks, tenor saxophonist Javon Jackson and pianist Benny Green) could compete favorably with many of his earlier bands. This Soul Note release, which includes a nine-minute drum solo by the leader, mostly sticks to inventive reworkings of standards along with a song apiece from Eubanks and Harper. Excellent music. —*Scott Yanow*

Chippin' In: Art Blakey and His Jazz Messengers / Feb. 1, 1990–Feb. 2, 1990 / Timeless ✦✦✦✦

Thirty-five years after first officially forming The Jazz Messengers, drummer Art Blakey entered his final year still at it. Due to the many promising young players around at the time, Blakey expanded The Messengers from its usual quintet or sextet into a septet for this fine recording session. In addition to trumpeter Brian Lynch, pianist Geoff Keezer and bassist Essiet Okon Essiet, this version of The Messengers had two tenors (Javon Jackson and Dale Barlow) and a pair of alternating trombonists (Frank Lacy and Steve Davis). Quite typically, other than Wayne Shorter's obscure "Hammerhead" and two standards, all of the material on this CD was new and composed by Blakey's sidemen. Because Blakey constantly persuaded his musicians to write music, The Jazz Messengers stayed young in spirit, just like its leader. A fine effort. —*Scott Yanow*

One for All / Apr. 10, 1990–Apr. 11, 1990 / A&M ✦✦✦
The final recording by Art Blakey's Jazz Messengers found the 70-year-old drummer (just months before his death) doing what he loved best, leading a group of young players through hard-swinging and generally new music in the hard-bop style. The last edition of The Jazz Messengers (a septet with trumpeter Brian Lynch, trombonist Steve Davis, the tenors of Dale Barlow and Javon Jackson, pianist Geoffrey Keezer and bassist Essiet O. Essiet) was comprised, as usual, of future bandleaders and stylists. Blakey, although pretty well deaf by this time, still pushed the ensembles and the individual players to play above their heads. A satisfying final effort from an irreplaceable drummer and bandleader. —*Scott Yanow*

Terence Blanchard

b. Mar. 13, 1962, New Orleans, LA
Trumpet / Hard Bop, Post-Bop
Although he originally rose to prominence in the shadow of Wynton Marsalis, Terence Blanchard was one of the first Young Lions to develop his own sound, mixing in elements of Freddie Hubbard and Marsalis. He studied piano from the age of five and took up trumpet in 1976. Blanchard was with Lionel Hampton during 1980–82 and then replaced Marsalis with Art Blakey's Jazz Messengers. He found fame while with Blakey during 1982–86 and then co-led a group with Donald Harrison. After taking time off to work on his embouchure (and returning with a greatly increased range), Blanchard became active writing film scores for Spike Lee. He played in the films *Do the Right Thing* and *Mo' Better Blues* and then wrote for *Jungle Fever* and *Malcolm X*, launching a potentially lucrative second career. Fortunately Blanchard has not neglected his own playing and in the 1990s he has recorded several superior sets of advanced hard bop music. —*Scott Yanow*

New York Second Line / Oct. 15, 1983–Oct. 16, 1983 / George Wein Collection ✦✦✦✦
Blanchard-Harrison. The 1984 set that helped cement their status in the emerging crop of 80s young lions. —*Ron Wynn*

Discernment / Dec. 1984 / George Wein Collection ✦✦✦

Nascence / Jan. 28, 1986+Jan. 31, 1986 / Columbia ✦✦✦

Eric Dolphy & Booker Little Remembered Live at Sweet Basil / Oct. 3–4, 1986 / Evidence ✦✦✦

Fire Waltz: Eric Dolphy and Booker Little Remembered / Oct. 3, 1986–Oct. 4, 1986 / Projazz ✦✦✦
Terence Blanchard and Donald Harrison continued their homage to the Eric Dolphy/Booker Little duo with a second set of performances recorded at Sweet Basil. They featured "Fire Waltz" and "Bee Vamp," two more tunes the duo immortalized during their Five Spot performances. Their versions are well intentioned, frequently exciting, and superbly played. But they are not transcendent for the simple reason that Harrison lacks Dolphy's fluency on either alto sax or bass clarinet, and Blanchard does not possess Little's command of the upper register or his embouchure. That is not a knock; they certainly clicked with the rhythm section of pianist Mal Waldron, bassist Richard Davis, and drummer Ed Blackwell, who did play on the originals. Both of these volumes are highly recommended, but if you have not heard the originals, do whatever it takes to get them. —*Ron Wynn*

Crystal Stair / Apr. 1, 1987–Apr. 3, 1987 / Columbia ✦✦✦
The fourth of five albums co-led by trumpeter Terence Blanchard and altoist Donald Harrison, this quintet session (with pianist Cyrus Chestnut, bassist Reginald Veal and drummer Carl Allen) has seven originals by the co-leaders plus "God Bless the Child" and "Softly as in a Morning Sunrise." Although an outgrowth of Art Blakey and hard bop, the stimulating music contains more than its share of surprises and chancetaking, stretching the boundaries of the mainstream a bit. —*Scott Yanow*

Black Pearl / 1988 / Columbia ✦✦✦✦
Blanchard-Harrison. This is the best by trumpeter Blanchard and saxophonist Donald Harrison, especially the title track. —*Michael G. Nastos*

Terence Blanchard / 1991 / Columbia ✦✦✦✦

Simply Stated / 1992 / Columbia ✦✦✦
Nice date from a youthful New Orleans prodigy, one of the first done after he and onetime alto sax partner Donald Harrison parted. Blanchard was battling embouchure problems, but still manages some compelling solos. Antonio Hart makes a fine replacement for Harrison on alto and a good second solo voice. —*Ron Wynn*

Malcolm X [Original Motion Picture Score] / Nov. 20, 1992 / 40 Acres & A Mule ✦✦

● **Malcolm X Jazz Suite** / Dec. 10, 1992–Dec. 14, 1992 / Columbia ✦✦✦✦✦
Trumpeter Terence Blanchard continues to grow and develop with each year. He wrote the score for *Malcolm X* and this set finds him exploring 11 of his themes from the movie with his quintet (which also includes Sam Newsome on tenor, pianist Bruce Bath, bassist Tarus Matten and drummer Troy Davis). Many moods are explored and the fresh material really invigorates the quintet. Newsome's Trane-isms blend well with Blanchard (whose range has become quite impressive) and the performances (which easily stand apart from the film) are quite memorable. It's one of Terence Blanchard's finest recordings. —*Scott Yanow*

Clockers: Original Orchestral Score / 1994 / Sony ✦

Romantic Defiance / Dec. 12, 1994–Dec. 15, 1994 / Columbia ✦

The Billie Holiday Songbook / Columbia ✦✦
Trumpeter Terence Blanchard's tribute to Billie Holiday is a rather melancholy and often downbeat affair. Sounding less original than usual (he displays a strong Wynton Marsalis influence and also hints at times at both Miles Davis and Thad Jones), there is little joy to these renditions of Lady Day material other than the second half of "I Cried for You." The trumpeter's arrangements for the unswinging string section are occasionally oppressive, sometimes border on muzak and tend to weigh down the music. The only bright spot are the five fine vocals by Jeanie Bryson, who wisely does not try to sound like Holiday and comes across quite well. Otherwise this is a disappointing outing. —*Scott Yanow*

Jimmy Blanton

b. Oct. 1918, Chattanooga, TN, d. Jul. 30, 1942, Los Angeles, CA
Bass / Swing
Jazz's first great bassist outside the traditional New Orleans idiom, Jimmy Blanton expanded the instrument's possibilities and rewrote its vocabulary. His full, round tone, unparalled agility, extremely accurate intonation, swinging style and harmonic knowledge made Blanton the model for a generation, especially such players as Oscar Pettiford, Charles Mingus and Ray Brown. He contributed remarkably advanced solos, departing from what had become the norm, the fixed "walking" style, and demonstrating great command and flexibility. Blanton played in Chattanooga, Tennessee, in groups led by his mother, who was a pianist. He attended Tennesse State a short time, then moved to St. Louis. He played in Fate Marable's riverboat bands and The Jeter-Pillars Orchestra, where he was discovered in 1939 by Duke Ellington. Ellington quickly tapped him for his orchestra, and the results were immediate and impressive. He enriched the band's sound and rhythmic drive, and helped inspire Ellington into a period of great compositional productivity. Blanton's bass was a prominent factor in such compositions as "Ko-Ko," "Jack The Bear" and "Concerto For Cootie." Blanton also participated in small group sessions led by Johnny Hodges and duets with Ellington. He was a member of several early sessions at Minton's, the laboratory from whence the sounds that became bop were nurtured. Blanton's health declined in 1941. He suffered from congenital tuberculosis that took his life. He can be heard on a number of Ellington reissues. —*Ron Wynn*

Carla Bley

b. May 11, 1938, Oakland, CA
Piano, Composer, Leader / Post-Bop
A wonderful composer whose madcap personality and humor carries over into her songwriting, Carla Bley has been at the forefront of many music cooperatives and bands since the '60s. While her piano playing has the unpredictability of Thelonious Monk's, her compositions reflect multiple music genres. She includes early jazz references, improvisational and symphonic elements, and snippets of any and everything from bebop to rock. Bley's father,

a church musician, taught her a few fundamentals, but she otherwise trained herself. She moved to New York from Oakland at 17, and divided her time between playing piano and writing songs for such musicians as George Russell, her husband Paul Bley and Jimmy Giuffre. Bley worked with Pharoah Sanders and Charles Moffett in 1964, then became a full-time musician. She and Michael Mantler co-formed The Jazz Composers Guild Orchestra in the mid-'60s; he became her second husband. The Orchestra gave a concert at Town Hall in 1964 and Bley went to Europe with a quintet in 1965, recording and appearing on radio and television. Bley also co-founded the Jazz Composer's Orchestra Association in 1966, a nonprofit organization that commissioned, produced and distributed a wide range of material ignored by the major labels. The JCOA distributed many labels into the '70s before money woes forced them to close shop. They recorded a two-record (now disc) album on their own label that year. Bley's 1967 work "A Genuine Tong Funeral," recorded by Gary Burton's Quartet, brought her widespread public and critical attention, as did several compositions and arrangements for Charlie Haden's Liberation Music Orchestra album on Impulse! in 1969. Her most acclaimed composition was 1971's "Escalator Over The Hill." The album was hailed by both the national and international jazz press, and Bley received many composing grants. She's divided her time in the '70s, '80s and '90s between recording, leading various large bands and composing. She and Mantler began their own company, Watt Records, which is now distributed by ECM. Bley and Mantler have issued many records on Watt, and Bley's worked with Roswell Rudd and others in the '80s. She provided the soundtrack for a 1985 film *Mortelle randonnee.* Bley contributed new compositions to another Haden Liberation Music Orchestra session in 1983, a Monk tribute album in 1984 and a Kurt Weill tribute in 1986. She played organ on a Steve Swallow album in 1986 and did her own session in 1988. She continued recording with a nine and ten-piece band into the '90s, and in 1993 did another album with Swallow.—*Ron Wynn*

Escalator over the Hill / Nov. 1968–Jun. 1971 / ECM ◆◆

Tropic Appetites / Sep. 1973–Feb. 1974 / Watt ◆◆◆

Dinner Music / Jul. 1976–Sep. 1976 / ECM ◆◆◆◆
First excursion on a funky trail, executed immaculately. Near essential. —*Michael G. Nastos*

● **European Tour (1977)** / Sep. 1977 / ECM ◆◆◆◆◆
One of Carla Bley's most rewarding recordings, this set features her tentet playing such numbers as "Wrong Key Donkey," "Drinking Music" and the 19-minute "Spangled Banner Minor and Other Patriotic Songs." Bley's wry humor is often felt and she utilizes such colorful players as trumpeter Michael Mantler, Gary Windo on tenor, trombonist Roswell Rudd and Bob Stewart on tuba in this unusual, somewhat innovative and always fun music. —*Scott Yanow*

Musique Mecanique / Aug. 1978–Nov. 1978 / ECM ◆◆◆◆
Carla Bley's tentet performs some of her most colorful themes on this often-humorous and generally stimulating set. "Jesus Maria and Other Spanish Strains" and the three-part "Musique Mecanique" are particularly memorable. This is the perfect setting for Bley's music, with such musicians as trumpeter Michael Mantler, Gary Windo on tenor and bass clarinet, trombonist Roswell Rudd and Bob Stewart on tuba making their presence felt. —*Scott Yanow*

Social Studies / Sep. 1980–Dec. 1980 / ECM ◆◆◆

I Hate to Sing / Aug. 19, 1981–Aug. 21, 1981 / ECM ◆◆◆

Live! / Aug. 1981 / Watt ◆◆◆

Heavy Heart / Sep. 1983–Oct. 1983 / ECM ◆◆◆

Night-Glo / Jun. 1985–Aug. 1985 / ECM ◆◆◆
As usual, Carla Bley's albums offer provocative arrangements, unorthodox playing, and interesting guest musicians. Randy Brecker and Paul McCandless are among those who provide interesting solos, while ECM's patented lush, overwhelming production adds atmosphere and color. —*Ron Wynn*

Sextet / Dec. 1986–Jan. 1987 / ECM ◆◆

Fleur Carnivore / Nov. 1988 / ECM ◆◆◆

Duets: Carla Bley and Steve Swallow / 1988 / ECM ◆◆◆◆◆

The Very Big Carla Bley Band / Oct. 29, 1990–Oct. 30, 1990 / ECM ◆◆◆

Go Together / 1992 / ECM ◆◆◆◆
After years spent emphasizing her compositions and bandleading

abilities, in the late '80s, Carla Bley finally started featuring her own piano playing to a much greater degree. A melodic but explorative player, Bley (whose use of space sometimes recalls Thelonious Monk) interacts closely with the electric bass of Steve Swallow on this excellent duet session, performing six of her originals and two of Swallow's. —*Scott Yanow*

Big Band Theory / Jul. 2, 1993–Jul. 3, 1993 / Watt ◆◆◆

Songs with Legs / Dec. 1995 / Watt ◆◆◆

Paul Bley

b. Nov. 10, 1932, Montreal, Quebec
Piano / Avant-Garde, Free Jazz
Paul Bley has long offered avant-garde pianists an alternative approach to improvising than that of Cecil Taylor. Bley has been able to use melody and space in inventive ways while performing fairly free improvisations. He started on piano at age eight, studied at Juilliard during 1950–52 and in 1953 played with Charlie Parker on a Canadian television show; the soundtrack serves as his recording debut. After recording for Charles Mingus' Debut label in 1953, he moved to New York. Following a stint with Jackie McLean's quintet, he relocated to Los Angeles. Bley played with Chet Baker and then in 1958 played at the Hillcrest with musicians who would soon form the Ornette Coleman Quartet: Coleman, Don Cherry, Charlie Haden and Billy Higgins. He soon returned to New York, played and recorded with Charles Mingus and Don Ellis, was part of the Jimmy Giuffre Three (which also included Steve Swallow) and was married to the talented up-and-coming pianist/composer Carla Bley. After leading his own trio, Paul Bley spent much of 1963 with Sonny Rollins' group. He participated in the famous October Revolution in Jazz in 1964 and was a founding member of the Jazz Composers Guild. He recorded frequently with his trios, for a few years experimented with electronics with his second wife Annette Peacock, and then in 1974 founded his Improvising Artists label. Virtually all of that short-lived label's output has been reissued on CD by Black Saint/Soul Note. Since the mid-'70s, Paul Bley has recorded a countless number of albums for literally dozens of labels (once cutting two albums in the same day, in two different countries!). A key link between Bill Evans and Keith Jarrett, Bley's adventurous yet thoughtful playing sounds like no one else. —*Scott Yanow*

Improvisations: Introducing Paul Bley / Nov. 30, 1953 / Original Jazz Classics ◆◆◆
This was pianist Paul Bley's debut. Recorded 11/30/53, this has been a most elusive LP over the years. Fantasy added "Santa Claus Is Coming to Town," originally issued only on a sampler, to the original ten-inch program, but it would seem the two unissued tracks from this session with Art Blakey (drums) and Charles Mingus (bass) are lost. What's here is refreshing music. The harmonics and openness (freedom) suggested by the lines remain remarkably in touch with the times over 30 (1985) years later. Paul Bley has a solid recorded history, yet I still think he remains generally overlooked as a strong and continuing original voice in improvising music. One might start right here, at the beginning with this record. —*Bob Rusch, Cadence*

Paul Bley / Feb. 3, 1954 Aug. 27, 1954 / EmArcy ◆◆◆

Solemn Meditation / 1958 / GNP ◆◆◆

Live at the Hillcrest Club (1958) / Oct. 1958 / Inner City ◆◆◆◆
This out-of-print LP is quite valuable, for it features altoist Ornette Coleman live in concert shortly after making his first studio sessions. Musicians from what would be the Coleman Quartet (with trumpeter Don Cherry, bassist Charlie Haden and drummer Billy Higgins) are heard at a live gig in Los Angeles under the leadership of pianist Paul Bley. Bley's piano is mostly pretty sparse and Coleman is the dominant force, particularly on his melodic "The Blessing" and the well-titled "Free." It is particularly interesting to hear Coleman and Cherry improvising freely on Charlie Parker's "Klactoveesedstene" and Roy Eldridge's "I Remember Harlem." The recording quality is decent for the period, and avant-garde collectors will want to search for this pioneering effort. —*Scott Yanow*

The Floater Syndrome / Aug. 17, 1962+Sep. 12, 1963 / Savoy ◆◆◆
1962 and 1963 trio sessions with Steve Swallow (b) and Pete La Roca (d). Paul and Carla Bley and Ornette Coleman wrote the music for this dense and wide-ranging trio. —*Michael G. Nastos*

Footloose / Aug. 17, 1962+Sep. 12, 1963 / Savoy Jazz ✦✦✦
Paul Bley with Gary Peacock / Apr. 13, 1963 / ECM ✦✦✦
Good 60s session with bassist Gary Peacock, Paul Motian on drums. —*Ron Wynn*

Syndrome / Sep. 12, 1963 / Savoy ✦✦✦
The follow-up to *Floater* features more music from Carla Bley. The Savoy albums really introduced her work (through her then-husband) to the world. —*Michael G. Nastos*

Turns / Feb. 9, 1964 / Savoy ✦✦✦
Turning Point / Mar. 9, 1964 / Improvising Artists ✦✦✦
Barrage / Oct. 20, 1964 / ESP ✦✦✦
Copenhagen and Harlem / Nov. 5, 1965+Nov. 4, 1966 / Arista ✦✦✦✦
This out-of-print double LP from Arista's *Freedom* series features Paul Bley with his trios (either Kent Carter or Mark Levenson on bass along with drummer Barry Altschul) at two different sessions recorded in Scandinavia during 1965-66. Cut during a time when Bley's style was becoming progressively freer, the improvisations (on melodies by Bley, Carla Bley and Annette Peacock) are pretty loose and abstract but perfectly coherent. As has been stated elsewhere, Bley's groups were a logical extension of the Bill Evans Trio, venturing into freer areas than Evans ever chose to travel. —*Scott Yanow*

Closer / Dec. 18, 1965 / ESP ✦✦✦
On *Closer,* the setting for pianist Paul Bley was the more familiar trio format (Barry Altschul, percussion; Steve Swallow, bass)... This LP is characteristic of the Paul Bley style, understated, probing and occasionally passionately percussive, but always with a gently searching ambiance. —*Bob Rusch, Cadence*

Virtuosi / Jun. 27, 1967 / Improvising Artists ✦✦✦
Synthesizer Show / Dec. 9, 1970-Mar. 9, 1971 / Milestone ✦✦
● **Open for Love** / Sep. 11, 1972 / ECM ✦✦✦✦✦
This set is one of Paul Bley's finest solo outings which, considering how often he has recorded during the past 30 years, is really saying something. His rendition of "Ida Lupino" is classic and his other interpretations (of originals by Carla Bley and Annette Peacock in addition to his own "Harlem") are close to definitive. Loose yet logical, these piano solos (which make expert use of space) always hold one's interest. —*Scott Yanow*

Scorpio / Oct. 22, 1972-Oct. 24, 1972 / Milestone ✦✦
Paul Bley/Nhop / Jun. 24, 1973+Jul. 1, 1973 / SteepleChase ✦✦✦
Paul Bley / Jun. 16, 1974 / IAI ✦✦✦
Alone Again / Aug. 8, 1974-Aug. 9, 1974 / IAI ✦✦✦
Bley is an engaging, thoughtful and highly individualistic player who doesn't fit any rigid category. At the time, he was returning to acoustic music after having worked almost exclusively on electric keyboards for several years. This seven-song session (recently reissued on CD) was done in two days in Oslo, Norway, in 1974. Bley wrote four numbers, with two others by his ex-wife and frequent collaborator Carla Bley and one by Annette Peacock. No composition was that rhythmically arresting, as Bley stayed mainly in the piano's center, creating nimble melodies, working off them and crafting alternate directions or intriguing counterpoints. It was intellectual, occasionally stiff, but never dull or detached. —*Ron Wynn*

Quiet Song / Nov. 14, 1974 / Improvising Artists ✦✦✦
Japan Suite / Jul. 25, 1975 / IAI ✦✦
Axis/Solo Piano / Jul. 1, 1977-Jul. 3, 1977 / IAI ✦✦✦✦
An excellent solo date by Paul Bley, his improvisations on three brief pieces (including George Gershwin's "Porgy") and a 16-minute version of his own "Axis" are thoughtful and sometimes introspective explorations. Bley has long given the avant-garde an alternative approach to piano from Cecil Taylor's and this is a good example of his artistry. —*Scott Yanow*

Tango Palace / May 21, 1983 / Soul Note ✦✦✦
Sonor / May 22, 1983 / Soul Note ✦✦✦
Questions / Feb. 26, 1985 / SteepleChase ✦✦✦
Hot / Mar. 10, 1985 / Soul Note ✦✦✦
Excellent playing by Bley keeps things moving on this '85 date. The songs vary in quality, but Bley's moving, teeming solos are consistently impressive, and the production and sound are excellent. —*Ron Wynn*

My Standard / Dec. 8, 1985 / SteepleChase ✦✦✦
When one considers that Paul Bley is a constant improviser, the repertoire he chose for this set (ten standards, most of which are from the '40s and '50s) is rather surprising. But even on tunes such as "Santa Claus Is Coming to Town," "Long Ago and Far Away" and "I Can't Get Started," pianist Bley (accompanied by bassist Jesper Lundgaard and drummer Billy Hart) avoids the obvious and comes up with something new to say. —*Scott Yanow*

Notes / Jul. 3, 1987-Jul. 4, 1987 / Soul Note ✦✦✦
Solo / Dec. 1987 / Justin Time ✦✦✦✦
Live At Sweet Basil / Mar. 1, 1988-Mar. 6, 1988 / Soul Note ✦✦✦
Solo Piano / Apr. 1988 / SteepleChase ✦✦✦
The Nearness of You / Nov. 21, 1988 / SteepleChase ✦✦✦
Life of a Trio: Sunday / Dec. 17, 1989 / Owl ✦✦✦
Bebopbebopbebopbebop / Dec. 22, 1989 / SteepleChase ✦✦✦✦
A surprising album from Bley, long considered an outside player with little, if any, affinity for straight bop. He shatters that myth on this set, going through a dozen songs, including such anthems as "Ornithology" and "The Theme," with vigor, harmonic distinction, and rhythmic edge. He's brilliantly backed by bassist Bob Cranshaw, providing some of his best, least detached playing in quite a while, and drummer Keith Copeland, navigating the tricky changes with grace. —*Ron Wynn*

In a Row / May 23, 1990-May 24, 1990 / Hat Art ✦✦✦
Memoirs / Jul. 1990 / Soul Note ✦✦✦✦
If We May / Apr. 1993 / SteepleChase ✦✦✦✦
Paul Bley has long enjoyed engaging in fairly free improvising, making this set of standards (along with the title cut, an original blues) a bit of a surprise. With bassist Jay Anderson and drummer Adam Nussbaum, Bley plays such songs as "Long Ago and Far Away," "All the Things You Are" and "Confirmation" fairly straight at first, almost as if he were normally a bop-based improviser. The music is quite accessible to straight-ahead fans even if Bley gives these warhorses some new twists, and he shows that he can swing with the best of them (not that anyone really doubted it). —*Scott Yanow*

Synth Thesis / Aug. 23, 1993-Aug. 24, 1993 / Postcards ✦✦✦
Time Will Tell / Jan. 1994 / ECM ✦✦✦
This CD contains a series of mostly thoughtful free improvisations featuring three of the giants of the idiom: pianist Paul Bley, Evan Parker (doubling on tenor and soprano) and bassist Barre Phillips. Surprisingly enough, Bley and Parker had never played together before (although Phillips had performed often with both musicians), but they communicate very well, including on the lengthy "Poetic Justice," their initial meeting. Nothing was preplanned for the set, and in general, it is very much a Paul Bley session. The emphasis is on free ballads and mood pieces with Parker sounding somewhat restrained. He actually cuts loose much more on his two duets with Phillips than he does on the trios. Although the results overall are not classic, the music never fails to hold on to one's interest as the three musicians continually think and evolve together. —*Scott Yanow*

Outside In / Jul. 8, 1994 / Justin Time ✦✦✦
This duet set by pianist Paul Bley and guitarist Sonny Greenwich, after two melodic solos by Greenwich and Bley's feature on "Arrival," becomes a loose bop session. "Meandering" is a blues and, in the tradition of Lennie Tristano, the origins of the originals "Willow" and "You Are" are not too difficult to figure out. The music does meander a bit but mostly swings in a floating way. Although there are some freer moments, this is as straight as Paul Bley has played on records in years and Sonny Greenwich also sounds fairly conservative, at least if one does not listen too closely. It's a relaxed and very interesting set. —*Scott Yanow*

Jane Ira Bloom

b. 1955, Newton, MA
Soprano Saxophone / Avant-Garde, Post-Bop
One of the great soprano saxophonists, Jane Ira Bloom studied at Berklee and Yale. She recorded two albums for her own Outline label and then around 1980 moved to New York. Bloom has since that time recorded for JMT, Columbia, Enja and Arabesque. Notable for sometimes using live electronics on stage, Bloom has a distinctive tone and an adventurous style. —*Scott Yanow*

Second Wind / Jun. 1980 / Outline ✦✦✦

Mighty Lights / Nov. 17, 1982–Nov. 18, 1982 / Enja ✦✦✦

As One / Sep. 1984 / JMT ✦✦✦

Modern Drama / Feb. 9, 1987–Feb. 13, 1987 / Columbia ✦✦✦✦
Jane Ira Bloom, one of the finest soprano saxophonists of the past decade, is in fine form on this Columbia LP. In addition to her soprano and a bit of alto, Bloom makes creative use of live electronics. Key among her sidemen on these nine originals is keyboardist Fred Hersch. The music is explorative yet generally melodic and worth searching for. —*Scott Yanow*

Slalom / Jun. 6, 1988–Jun. 9, 1988 / Columbia ✦✦✦✦
Jane Ira Bloom is teamed with pianist Fred Hersch in a quartet that explores a variety of melodic material in unexpected ways. Bloom, one of the top soprano saxophonists around and a creative user of electronics, has a fairly original tone and her improvisations are consistently full of surprises. Check out her transformations of "I Loves You Porgy" and "If I Should Lose You" on this Columbia LP. —*Scott Yanow*

● **Art & Aviation** / Jul. 22, 1992–Jul. 23, 1992 / Arabesque ✦✦✦✦

Hamiet Bluiett

b. 1940, Lovejoy, IL
Baritone Saxophone / Avant-Garde
The finest baritone saxophonist of the '70s and beyond, Hamiett Bluiett has demonstrated a huge, impressive sound, superb technique and mastery of his horn in every register, plus the ability to provide an array of tonal colors and harmonic options in his solos. A first-rate free player who's just as proficient on standards and bebop, Bluiett has played in many excellent groups, led his own bands and been featured on numerous magnificent recordings. He began taking music lessons from his aunt, who was a choral director. Bluiett started on clarinet at nine. He attended Southern University, where he studied flute and baritone. Following a stint in the Navy, Bluiett moved to St. Louis in the mid-'60s. He played with Lester and Joseph Bowie, Charles "Bobo" Shaw, Julius Hemphill and Oliver Lake and worked with the Black Artists Group (BAG), that city's equivalent of Chicago's Association for the Advancement of Creative Musicians (AACM). He moved to New York in 1969, joining Sam Rivers large ensemble. Bluiett worked with various bands before joining Charles Mingus' quintet in 1972, remaining until 1975. A pair of mid-'70s Bluiett concerts were later issued as albums on India Navigation. Bluiett, Hemphill, Lake and David Murray formed a quartet in 1976 for a New Orleans concert. They decided to remain intact as a working unit and named themselves The World Saxophone Quartet. They've continued recording and performing into the '90s, though Arthur Blythe replaced Hemphill. Bluiett has also worked with other bands; he was a co-leader of The Clarinet Family group that featured seven clarinetists. They recorded with Black Saint in the '80s. Bluiett recorded on his own for Black Saint, Soul Note, Chiaroscuro, Enja and Tutu among others in the '70s, '80s and '90s. He played with Lester Bowie, Hemphill, Abdullah Ibrahim, Phillip Wilson, Marcello Melis, Famadou Don Moye, Don Pullen, Fred Hopkins, Billy Hart, Buddy Collette and Ronnie Burrage during the '70s and '80s. —*Ron Wynn*

Endangered Species / Jun. 19, 1976 / India Navigation ✦✦✦✦
Baritonist Hamiet Bluiett's first full album as a leader is quite impressive. His style on baritone, even at this early point, owed little to his predecessors. In a quintet with trumpeter Olu Dara and Jumma Santos on balafon, Bluiett takes a lot of chances during this adventurous performance. The four selections (three are fairly lengthy) are his originals and fit firmly in the avant-garde mainstream of the day. —*Scott Yanow*

S.O.S. / Aug. 15, 1977 / India Navigation ✦✦✦
Explosive live quartet set that includes slashing piano from Don Pullen. —*Ron Wynn*

Resolution / Nov. 21, 1977–Dec. 1, 1977 / Black Saint ✦✦✦

Orchestra Duo and Septet / Nov. 1977–Dec. 1977 / Chiaroscuro ✦✦✦✦
Array of pieces by Bluiett. Excellent duet with Pullen, good sextet numbers, interesting orchestral piece. —*Ron Wynn*

Birthright / Jun. 1978 / India Navigation ✦✦✦✦✦
This concert performance is quite unusual: an unaccompanied recital by the great baritonist Hamiet Bluiett. Although its subtitle is "A Solo Blues Concert," the "blues" refers to the feeling that

Bluiett puts into his music rather than the structure of his originals itself. "In Tribute to Harry Carney" is a highpoint. Bluiett is in top form during this adventurous but fairly melodic performance. —*Scott Yanow*

Dangerously Suite / Apr. 9, 1981 / Soul Note ✦✦✦

Ebu / Feb. 1, 1984–Feb. 15, 1984 / Soul Note ✦✦✦

The Clarinet Family / Nov. 1984 / Black Saint ✦✦✦

Sankofa/Rear Garde / Oct. 2, 1992–Oct. 3, 1992 / Soul Note ✦✦✦

● **Young Warrior, Old Warrior** / Mar. 1, 1995–Mar. 3, 1995 / Mapleshade ✦✦✦✦

Arthur Blythe

b. Jul. 5, 1940, Los Angeles, CA
Alto Saxophone / Post-Bop, Avant-Garde
Alto saxophonist Arthur Blythe is a gifted soloist with a wide vibrato, a pungent style that reflects several artists from Charlie Parker to Cannonball Adderley, and an interest in unusual configurations and harmonic/melodic possibilities that's seen him lead bands with tuba, guitar and cello. Blythe excels at playing traditional bebop, hard bop or free music, and has also worked effectively in funk, blues and R&B situations. His solos are tasteful, swinging and superbly played. But from his days as "Black Arthur" on the West Coast (which made some think he was a reincarnated Malcom X on alto) to his ill-fated Columbia era, when they marketed him as "the greatest saxophonist in the world" Blythe has suffered exaggerated expectations and false impressions. These haven't affected his output as much as they've created a climate that makes it seem as if he's underachieving when he's actually accomplished as much, if not more, than virtually any other player of his generation. Blythe played in school bands as a youngster, then studied with Kirtland Bradford, a one-time member of Jimmie Lunceford's orchestra, as a teen. He worked with Horace Tapscott during the '60s and early '70s in Los Angeles; both were founding members of the Union of God's Musicians and Artists Ascension. Blythe was part of the West Coast exodus to New York in the '70s that also saw David Murray, James Newton and Stanley Crouch move east. He played with Chico Hamilton in the mid-'70s and Gil Evans in the late '70s and early '80s, as well being in the "loft jazz" movement of the '70s. Blythe recorded and played with Lester Bowie and Jack DeJohnette's Special Edition in the late '70s and early '80s. He signed with Columbia in the late '70s, and led two groups in the early '80s. One was known as In The Tradition, and was a bebop and swing-oriented ensemble with Fred Hopkins, Steve McCall and either Stanley Cowell or John Hicks. The other was an unnamed quintet with Abdul Wadud, Bob Stewart, Bobby Battle and sometimes James "Blood" Ulmer and Kelvyn Bell. They did more challenging, nontraditional material as well as some hard bop and even some pop, R&B and funk. Blythe joined The Leaders in the mid-'80s, replaced Julius Hemphill in The World Saxophone Quartet and did more sessions with Stewart, Bell and Battle. He began recording with Crouch in the late '60s and early '70s. His own albums started with sessions in the mid-'70s for India Navigation and Adelphi. The Columbia dates began in the late '70s and continued until the mid-'80s. Blythe also recorded for Blackhawk and has recently done sessions for Enja. —*Ron Wynn*

Metamorphosis / The Grip-Concert / Feb. 26, 1977 / India Navigation ✦✦✦✦

The Grip / Feb. 26, 1977 / India Navigation ✦✦✦✦
The debut album as a leader by altoist Arthur Blythe is quite impressive. Even at this early stage, Blythe's tone is instantly recognizable. His band (playing five of his originals plus "Spirits in the Field") includes trumpeter Ahmed Abdullah, cellist Abdul Wadud, tuba player Bob Stewart, drummer Steve Reid and percussionist Muhamad Abdullah, and together they live up to their potential. —*Scott Yanow*

Metamorphosis / Feb. 26, 1977 / India Navigation ✦✦✦✦
Taken from the same concert as *The Grip*, this album features the distinctive altoist Arthur Blythe fairly early in his career, a year before he signed with Columbia. His sextet (which consists of trumpeter Ahmed Abdullah, cellist Abdul Wadud, tuba player Bob Stewart, drummer Steve Reid and percussionist Muhamad Abdullah) is heard on two selections (including the colorful title cut) while the nearly 18-minute "Duet for Two" is an adventurous collaboration between Blythe and cellist Wadud. —*Scott Yanow*

Bush Baby / Dec. 1977 / Adelphi ✦✦✦

In the Tradition / Oct. 1978 / Columbia ✦✦✦✦
Sometimes the easiest way to get "in" to someone's music is to see how they handle standards. Altoist Arthur Blythe, who—although he has been associated somewhat with the avant-garde—does not fit easily into any category, is heard on this 1978 studio session exploring four veteran songs plus two of his originals. The instrumentation of his quartet is conventional but the musicianship is exceptionally high (pianist Stanley Cowell, bassist Fred Hopkins and drummer Steve McCall), and it is quite interesting to hear how they stretch such songs as "In a Sentimental Mood," "Jitterbug Waltz" and "Caravan," making them sound fresh and original. —*Scott Yanow*

Lenox Avenue Breakdown / Oct. 19,-Nov. 1978 / Columbia ✦✦✦✦
The signing of Arthur Blythe to Columbia in 1978 received a great deal of attention. Fortunately, the adventurous altoist was able to record for that giant label for a few years without being pressured to water down his sound or his music. This set matches Blythe with such talents as flutist James Newton, guitarist James "Blood" Ulmer, bassist Cecil McBee, drummer Jack DeJohnette, tuba player Bob Stewart and percussionist Guillermo Franco; no weak spots in this group. The band performs four of Blythe's diverse originals with creativity and a strong bluesy feeling. —*Scott Yanow*

Illusions / Apr. 1980–May 1980 / Columbia ✦✦✦
It is surprising how artistically productive altoist Arthur Blythe was during his period on Columbia. Despite the hype and Columbia's reputation for pressuring artists to play mass appeal music, Blythe's recordings for that label are inventive and creative. For this, his third Columbia release, Blythe uses two different groups: an "in the tradition" quartet with pianist John Hicks, bassist Fred Hopkins and drummer Steve McCall, and a more eccentric unit with guitarist James Blood Ulmer, cellist Abdul Wadud, tuba player Bob Stewart and drummer Bobby Battle. No matter the setting, the distinctive alto of Blythe is heard in top form on six of his unusual originals. It's recommended and well deserving of reissue on CD. —*Scott Yanow*

Blythe Spirit / 1981 / Columbia ✦✦✦

Elaboration / 1982 / Columbia ✦✦✦

Light Blue: Arthur Blythe Plays Thelonious Monk / Jan. 27, 1983 / Columbia ✦✦✦

Put Sunshine in It / 1984 / Columbia ✦✦

Basic Blythe / 1987 / Columbia ✦✦✦✦
A classic case of questionable judgment turning what could have been a great album into an uneven one. The assembled quartet is a fine one, with pianist John Hicks, bassist Anthony Cox, and drummer Bobby Battle. Blythe played with conviction, force, and fury, but the string section and orchestrations diluted his impact and greatly muddled the process. —*Ron Wynn*

Hipmotism / Mar. 15, 1991–Mar. 17, 1991 / Enja ✦✦✦✦

● **Retroflection** / Jun. 25, 1993–Jun. 26, 1993 / Enja ✦✦✦✦✦
Arthur Blythe, whose alto tone has been quite original ever since the start of his career, is joined by pianist John Hicks, bassist Cecil McBee and drummer Bobby Battle on this superior quartet date from Enja. Blythe really stretches out on this "Live at the Village Vanguard" set, with six of the seven songs being over nine minutes long. "Jana's Delight" (which is based on a five-note pattern), "JB Blues," a remake of Blythe's "Lenox Avenue Breakdown" and one of the best versions ever of Thelonious Monk's "Light Blue" are the highpoints of the explorative program. Arthur Blythe fans are strongly advised to pick up this particularly strong effort. —*Scott Yanow*

Jimmy Blythe

b. Jan.1901, Louisville, KY, **d.** Jun. 21, 1931, Chicago, IL
Piano / Classic Jazz
A wonderful accompanist and leader who often helped elevate sessions by inspiring otherwise routine performers to extend themselves,. Blythe at various times was house pianist for Paramount, Vocalion and Gennett, and his rolling, steady barrelhouse licks were heard in a number of groups. These included Blythe's Owls and Blue Boys, the State Street Ramblers, Chicago Stompers, Midnight Ramblers and Jimmy Bertrand's Washboard Wizards. —*Ron Wynn*

● **Jimmy Blythe** / Apr. 1924–Mar. 20, 1931 / RST ✦✦✦✦✦
From his first recordings to his last, the short musical life of Jimmy Blythe is fully covered on this imported CD from the Austrian RST label. All of his sessions as a leader (with the exception of his duets with Buddy Burton) are on this very definitive CD. The music ranges from piano solos (early examples of boogie-woogie and stride) to blues records with singers Viola Bartlette and Alexander Robinson, combo performances with Blythe's Sinful Five, the Midnight Rounders and Jimmy Bertrand's Washboard Wizards and piano duets with Charlie Clark. There is plenty of variety on this excellent program of early jazz and blues, highly recommended to 1920s collectors. —*Scott Yanow*

Willie Bobo (William Correa)

b. Feb. 28, 1934, New York, NY, **d.** Sep. 15, 1983, Los Angeles, CA
Percussion / Latin Jazz
Willie Bobo was a superb percussionist who made major inroads in jazz, Latin jazz, R&B and pop. Bobo's father was a musician, and he began on bongos at 14, then played congas, timbales and trap drums. Bobo was a band boy for Machito's Afro-Cubans, then studied with Mongo Santamaria in the late '40s. Santamaria taught him percussion and Bobo served as Santamaria's translator. He recorded with Mary Lou Williams in the early '50s, who gave him his nickname. Bobo replaced Manny Oquendo in Tito Puente's band in 1954. He would double on timbales when Puente took vibes solos. Bobo later played in Shearing's group on drums and timbales with Armando Peraza, Cal Tjader and Santamaria. He appeared on radio in the '50s as Willie Boborosa. Bobo worked in the late '50s with Cal Tjader, and also played with a short-lived Puente splinter group Orquesta Manhattan. He and Santamaria co-formed La Saborsa, a charanga (flute & violin) band in the early '60s; their recording of "Afro-Blue" became both a hit and a standard. Bobo also played on Santamaria's *Our Man In Havana* before starting his own band with Victor Panoja on congas. He recorded for Tico and Roulette in the mid-'60s. Bobo participated in Cal Tjader's hit album *Soul Sauce* for Verve in the mid-'60s. He issued his own albums in the mid-'60s, combing soul and funk with Latin beats. The single "Spanish Grease" became an R&B hit. Bobo worked with Miles Davis, Stan Getz, Cannonball Adderley, Sonny Stitt, Herbie Mann, Terry Gibbs and Herbie Hancock on various '60s sessions. He worked on the West Coast in the late '60s, and made weekly appearances on Bill Cosby's television show. Bobo recorded for Sussex, Blue Note and Columbia through the '70s. —*Ron Wynn*

● **Spanish Grease** / Jun. 8, 1965–Sep. 8, 1965 / Verve ✦✦✦✦
One pass through the title cut, and you know that Carlos Santana was listening. The easy R&B-Latin-jazz shuffle on this Bobo original, with its mix of Spanish and English vocals, is an obvious touchstone of cuts like "Evil Ways" on Santana's first two albums. What a shame, then, that the rest of the record is primarily comprised of covers of pop hits of the day like "It's Not Unusual" (a vocal *and* an instrumental version!) and "Our Day Will Come." The timbales player and his band lay down respectable grooves, but "Spanish Grease" is the only original on the album, and by far the most rewarding number. *Spanish Grease* has been combined with the 1966 LP *Uno Dos Tres 1-2-3* on one CD reissue. —*Richie Unterberger*

Uno, Dos, Tres / Jan. 26, 1966–Apr. 26, 1966 / Verve ✦✦✦
As with his previous album *Spanish Grease*, the toughest and most memorable track is the one Bobo original, "Fried Neck Bones And Some Home Fries." Its creeping Latin soul groove was, like "Spanish Grease," an obvious inspiration for Carlos Santana. But on most of the rest of the recording, Bobo coasts through interpretations of period hits like "Michelle," "Goin' Out Of My Head," and Jay & The Americans' (!) "Come A Little Bit Closer," with some jazz and pop standards as well. *Uno Dos Tres* has been combined with the 1965 LP *Spanish Grease* on one CD reissue. —*Richie Unterberger*

Hell of an Act to Follow / 1978 / Columbia ✦✦✦

Phil Bodner

b. Jun. 13, 1919, Waterbury, CT
Clarinet / Swing
Essentially a swing-based clarinetist, Phil Bodner has spent most of his career as a studio musician. Among his more notable jazz gigs have been with Benny Goodman (1955), the Gil Evans Orchestra with Miles Davis (1958), Oliver Nelson (1962), J.J.

Johnson (1965–68) and Bill Evans (1974). He has recorded just a few sets as a leader (most recently for Stash and Jazz Mania), making one regret that he could not have spent a larger portion of his career playing jazz. —*Scott Yanow*

Fine and Dandy / 1980 / Stash ◆◆◆

● **Jammin' At Phil's Place** / Jan. 25, 1990 / JazzMania ◆◆◆◆
Phil Bodner has long been known as a flexible studio musician so this outing for JazzMania (on which Bodner is joined by pianist Derek Smith, bassist Milt Hinton and drummer Bob Rosengarden) was a special event. Sticking to clarinet, Bodner jams his way through 11 familiar standards, sounding quite individual and occasionally heated in the swing idiom. The strong supporting cast and the attractive (if familiar) chord changes of songs such as "Them There Eyes," "After You've Gone" and "Bill Bailey" make this an easily enjoyable set. —*Scott Yanow*

Buddy Bolden

b. Sept. 6, 1877, New Orleans, LA, **d.** Nov. 4, 1931, Jackson, LA
Cornet, Leader / Classic New Orleans Jazz
Although no one knows when jazz music was "invented," a good starting point is when cornetist Buddy Bolden formed his first band in 1895. The first important name in jazz history, Bolden's career has long been buried in legend but Donald Marquis' definitive book *In Search of Buddy Bolden* successfully pieced together a factual and coherent biography. Bolden left school in 1890, learned cornet and originally played dance music. Because he never recorded (a legendary 1898 cylinder has never been found), one can only guess how Bolden sounded but according to reports he was very blues-oriented. He was the most popular musician in New Orleans by 1900 and an influence on later cornetists but by 1906 he was going slowly insane. The following year Bolden was committed to Jackson Mental Institute where he remained completely forgotten for his final 24 years. —*Scott Yanow*

Claude Bolling

b. Apr. 10, 1930, Cannes, France
Piano, Leader / Swing, Pop
Claude Bolling has found his greatest fame in the U.S. for his jazzy classical collaborations with Jean-Pierre Rampal, Maurice Andre, Elena Duran and Yo Yo Ma, while in Europe he is best-known as the leader of various swing big bands. Bolling formed his first group when he was 14 in 1944. In 1948 he recorded with Rex Stewart and accompanied blues singer Chippie Hill at a jazz festival. Bolling also recorded with Roy Eldrige (1951) and Lionel Hampton (1953 and 1956), led big bands since the 1950s and recorded ragtime, tributes to Duke Ellington and his own original music. Although not an innovator, Claude Bolling has been an important fixture in the French jazz scene since the 1950s. —*Scott Yanow*

Original Ragtime / Mar. 16, 1966–Mar. 18, 1966 / Columbia ◆◆◆
With the Help of My Friends / 1975 / Who's Who In Jazz ◆◆◆
● **Suite for Flute and Jazz Piano** / 1975 / CBS Masterworks ◆◆◆
California Suite / 1977 / CBS ◆◆◆
Bolling Plays Ellington, Vol. 1 / 1985 / Columbia ◆◆◆
Bolling Plays Ellington, Vol. 2 / 1985 / Columbia ◆◆◆
Black, Brown & Beige / Jan. 3, 1989–Jan. 4, 1989 / Milan ◆◆◆
Claude Bolling brings back Duke Ellington's classic "Black, Brown and Beige" on this enjoyable CD. Since Ellington's three-part suite did not feature extensive solos by his unique sidemen, Bolling is able to hint at their presence in his adaptation of Ellington's arrangements for the big band. Forgiving a slightly cutesy interpretation of "Sugar Hill Penthouse," this is a fine recreation of a much-neglected work. —*Scott Yanow*

Cross over U.S.A. / Jun. 8, 1993 / Milan ◆
The music on this fluffy release is so sweet that it's surprising the number of calories are not listed. Classical players are added to Bolling's regular rhythm section in different pairs for three numbers apiece (including flutist Jean-Pierre Rampal) but the results are consistently insipid and saccharine with very little improvisation by anyone but the pianist/leader. There is not much here to interest jazz listeners. —*Scott Yanow*

Victory Concert / Jun. 5, 1994–Jun. 7, 1994 / Milan ◆◆
Claude Bolling's big band has been performing at some World War II anniversary tributes and it is this orchestra which performs a dozen 1940s favorites on this CD. The problem is that, other

than Bolling and trumpeter Charles Martinez, none of the soloists are all that impressive and quite a few were expected to play note-for-note recreations of the original recorded solos. This then is essentially predictable dance music laced with nostalgia and falls far short of its potential. —*Scott Yanow*

Joe Bonner

b. 1948, Rocky Mount, NC
Piano / Post-Bop
A fine pianist who was originally heavily influenced by McCoy Tyner, Joe Bonner is an excellent interpreter of modal-based music and advanced hard bop. He studied music at Virginia State College and early on played with Roy Haynes (1970–71), Freddie Hubbard (1971–72), Pharoah Sanders (1972–74) and Billy Harper (late '70s). Bonner, who recorded as a leader for Muse, Theresa and most prominently SteepleChase, has been based in Colorado since the 1980s and remains a talented improviser. —*Scott Yanow*

Angel Eyes / Oct. 1974 / Muse ◆◆◆

● **The Lifesaver** / Nov. 1974 / Muse ◆◆◆◆◆
Although Joe Bonner's *Angel Eyes* was actually recorded a month earlier, *Lifesaver* was his first album to be released. This solo piano date is still one of Bonner's best. The influence of McCoy Tyner is strong but Bonner's six originals give the set an impressive amount of diversity and even at the relatively young age of 26, Joe Bonner had a lot to say. It is surprising that he has not become very well-known. —*Scott Yanow*

Impressions of Copenhagen / 1978 / Evidence ◆◆◆
Pianist Joe (then known as Joseph) Bonner turned in an intriguing variation on the shopworn concept of a jazz artist recording with strings. He conceived a set mixing piano, brass, chimes, woodwinds, and a string quartet, generating an array of enticing backgrounds, frameworks, and delightful sounds around and behind his own lush, sentimental solos. The results were a gentle, enchanting '81 session which Evidence has reissued with an extra track. The full date spotlights Bonner's tremendous piano and chimes, augmented by the bass/drum interplay of Paul Warburton and J. Thomas Tilton (who also produced) and the trumpet and trombone playing of Eddie Shu and Gary Olson. —*Ron Wynn*

Parade / Feb. 8, 1979 / SteepleChase ◆◆◆
Suburban Fantasies / Feb. 18, 1983 / SteepleChase ◆◆◆
Devotion / Feb. 20, 1983 / SteepleChase ◆◆◆
Suite for Chocolate / Nov. 4, 1985 / SteepleChase ◆◆◆
The Lost Melody / Mar. 29, 1987 / SteepleChase ◆◆◆
New Beginnings / 1988 / Theresa ◆◆◆

Bopsicle

Vocal Group / Bop
Bopsicle, which has one release out thus far on the Why Not label, features the witty lyrics of bassist Jack Prather as sung by Stephanie Haynes and Prather. Their debut set also has contributions by trumpeter Ron Stout, guitarist Mark Waggoner and drummer Charlie Landis. —*Scott Yanow*

● **Bopsicle** / 1994 / Why Not ◆◆◆◆◆
Bopsicle features the lyrics and compositions of bassist Jack Prather and the vocals of Stephanie Haynes and Prather along with excellent work from trumpeter Ron Stout (who has many fine solos), guitarist Mark Waggoner and drummer Charlie Landis. The main strengths of this bop-oriented group are Prather's witty and often-incisive lyrics and Haynes' beautiful voice. During an era when there are few songwriters of standards, Jack Prather's talents are very welcome. This recommended set is highlighted by tributes to several jazz greats, "A Little Jazz" (which makes fun of the pop scene) and the new lyrics to Sonny Rollins' "Pent up House." —*Scott Yanow*

Earl Bostic

b. Apr. 25, 1913, Tulsa, OK, **d.** Oct. 28, 1965, Rochester, NY
Alto Saxophone / R&B, Swing
Earl Bostic's roots and foundation were steeped in jazz and swing, but he later became one of the most prolific R&B bandleaders. His searing, sometimes bluesy, sometimes soft and moving, alto sax style influenced many players, including John Coltrane. His many King releases, which featured limited soloing and basic melodic and rhythmic movements, might have fooled novices into thinking Bostic possessed minimal skills; but Art Blakey once said

"Nobody knew more about the saxophone than Bostic, I mean technically, and that includes Bird." Bostic worked in several Midwest bands during the early '30s, then studied at Xavier University. He left school to tour with various groups, among them a band co-led by Charlie Creath and Fate Marable. He moved to New York in the late '30s, where he was a soloist in the bands of Don Redman, Edgar Hayes, and Lionel Hampton. Bostic also led his own combos, whose members included Jimmy Cobb, Al Casey, Blue Mitchell, Stanley Turrentine, Benny Golson and Coltrane. Bostic toured extensively through the '50s, while cutting numerous sessions for King. His recording of "Flamingo" in 1951 was a huge hit, as were the songs "Sleep," "You Go to My Head," "Cherokee" and "Temptation." Bostic recorded for Allegro, Gotham and King from the late '40s to the mid-'60s. He made more than 400 selections for King; the label would use stereo remakes of songs with different personnel, then use the same album numbers. After a heart attack, Bostic became a part-time player. His mid-'60s albums were more soul jazz than R&B. Several of his King LPs are available on CD. *—Ron Wynn and Michael Erlewine*

● **The Best of Earl Bostic** / Deluxe ✦✦✦✦
A nice cross-section of this fiery alto saxist's '50s output, it includes his hits "Sleep" and "Flamingo." *—Bill Dahl*

Showcase of Swinging Dance Hits / King ✦✦✦
Perhaps his best rocking and uptempo instrumental pop and R&B material. This album was aimed at the jukebox market and weighted toward the hottest, most furiously played cuts in the Bostic repertoire. Bostic was as technically accomplished as any alto saxophonist in his era, but he wasn't able to show that while on King. This album was one of the few times that he was able to really show his skills on uptempo material. *—Ron Wynn*

The Boswell Sisters
Vocal Group / Classic Jazz, Swing
The Boswell Sisters were the greatest jazz vocal group prior to Lambert, Hendricks and Ross 30 years later. Consisting of Connee (1907–76), Martha (1908–58) and Helvetia (1909–88), the trio (which often used Martha on piano) featured hard-swinging choruses and group scatting with numerous key and tempo changes. Connee received all of the solos but Martha and Helvetia both had very appealing voices too. The Boswells grew up in New Orleans where they all learned how to play numerous instruments. They recorded "Nights When I'm Lonely" (and Connee cut "I'm Gonna Cry") in 1925 and they soon were appearing regularly on Los Angeles radio. The group really got going in 1930 with four recordings for Okeh. They were soon signed to Brunswick where they recorded regularly during 1931–35. Their records usually featured top jazz soloists (including Bunny Berigan, the Dorsey Brothers and Joe Venuti) and were often quite exciting. During this period the Boswell Sisters appeared in several films (both shorts and full-length movies) and were a popular radio attraction. They recorded four numbers for Decca in 1936 but by that year all three sisters were married. Martha and Helvetia retired and Connee Boswell (who had been recording solo sides on an occasional basis for several years) went out on her own. A highpoint was her recordings with Bob Crosby but otherwise Connee's career (although reasonably satisfying) did not live up to its potential. In the 1950s for a time she had a major role on the television series *Pete Kelly's Blues*. Ella Fitzgerald always stated that Connee Boswell was her main influence. *—Scott Yanow*

Syncopating Harmonists from New Orleans / 1930–1935 / Take Two ✦✦✦
The Boswell Sisters were the premiere jazz vocal group (along with the early Mills Brothers) of the 1930s. This Take Two CD not only has nine enjoyable (but mostly fairly common) studio recordings from the 1932–35 period but nine numbers from a 1930 radio show and two ("I'll Never Say 'Never Again' Again" and "Lullaby of Broadway") that are taken from a 1935 program. Unfortunately the personnel is not given for the studio sides but the rarity of the 1930 show (which exclusively features songs not recorded elsewhere by this very appealing group) will make classic jazz collectors want to get this release anyway. *—Scott Yanow*

★ **Boswell Sisters, Vol. 1** / Mar. 19, 1931–Apr. 9, 1932 / Collector's Classics ✦✦✦✦✦
Most vocal groups that attempt to sing jazz instead end up in the genre of middle-of-the-road pop music. The Boswell Sisters (comprised of Connee, Vet and Martha) were a strong exception,

always swinging and, by changing tempos and keys frequently while including some other surprises, performing creative jazz of the early '30s. This Collector's Classics CD unfortunately skips their first seven recordings but then reissues complete and in chronological order 24 of the Boswells' finest performances. With a supporting cast frequently including trumpeters Bunny Berigan and Manny Klein, trombonist Tommy Dorsey and clarinetist Jimmy Dorsey (all of whom receive a generous amount of solo space), the sisters are heard at their best throughout this consistently exciting set. Highlights include "Roll on Mississippi, Roll On," "Shine on, Harvest Moon," "Heebies Jeebies," "River Stay 'Way from My Door," "Put That Sun Back in the Sky" and "There'll Be Some Changes Made." This is an essential acquisition. *—Scott Yanow*

Okay America!: Alternate Takes and Rarities / May 25, 1931–Jul. 19, 1935 / Vintage Jazz ✦✦✦✦
That's How Rhythm Was Born / Sony ✦✦✦
That's How Rhythm Was Born compiles 20 of The Boswell Sisters' greatest hits of the '30s, including "The Darktown Strutter's Ball" and "Between the Devil and the Deep Blue Sea." All of the tracks feature musical support from The Dorsey Brothers Orchestra. *—Stephen Thomas Erlewine*

Lester Bowie

b. Oct. 11, 1941, Frederick, MD
Trumpet / Avant-Garde
While he's well known as a member of The Art Ensemble of Chicago, Lester Bowie's amassed almost as many credentials as a leader. His remarkable bag of trumpet and fluegelhorn tricks includes half-valve effects, growls, slurs, smears, bent notes and a wide vibrato punctuating one of the most humorous, yet striking solo styles among modern brass players. His eclecticism has led Bowie to issue harsh denunciations of contemporary artists who feels revere only the bebop and hard bop jazz tradition, and he's led such groups as Brass Fantasy and The New York Organ Ensemble through wild versions of Michael Jackson and James Brown compositions. He's also ventured to the furthest reaches during extended free dialogues, blowing frenetic upper register solos. Bowie played in many blues and R&B bands growing up in St. Louis, among them Albert King and Little Milton. He moved to Chicago in 1965 to become music director for R&B/soul singer Fontella Bass, who was his wife at the time. Bowie met Joseph Jarman, Roscoe Mitchell, Malachi Favors and Don Moye through the Association for the Advancement of Creative Musicians (AACM) which was just getting organized. Bowie eventually became its second president (Muhal Richard Abrams was the first). The album *Numbers 1&2* was issued as a Lester Bowie LP on Nessa in 1967, but was actually the first Art Ensemble release, though the group hadn't yet formally begun calling themselves by that name. That occurred in Paris during 1969, where he, Jarman, Mitchell and Favors officially formed The Art Ensemble of Chicago. Moye joined the next year. While the Art Ensemble has been a steady proposition since '69, Bowie's never rested on his laurels. He worked in the early '70s with the 50-piece Baden Baden Free Jazz Orchestra along with Jarman and Roscoe Mitchell. He co-led the group From The Root To The Source, which blended jazz, rock, soul and gospel and included both Bass and Martha Peaston in the '70s. He later founded and still heads both Brass Fantasy and The New York Organ Ensemble. Bowie recorded albums as a leader in the '70s for Muse, Black Saint and IAI. He played in Jack DeJohnette's New Directions band in the late '70s and did guest spots on other albums. During the '80s he recorded for ECM, Muse and Venture, as well as DIW. He's recorded with The New York Organ Ensemble for DIW in the '90s. *—Ron Wynn*

Numbers 1 & 2 / Aug. 11, 1967+Aug. 25, 1967 / Nessa ✦✦✦

Fast Last / Sep. 10, 1974 / Muse ✦✦✦
Mid-'70s album that indicated the array of talent rising to the surface. It's neither outside nor inside, with songs that threaten to explode and others that are more funky than experimental. Besides Bowie, guests include Julius Hemphill in torrid form, Cecil McBee on bass, and Phillip Wilson on drums. It has not yet been issued on CD. *—Ron Wynn*

Rope-A-Dope / Jun. 17, 1975 / Muse ✦✦✦
Sometimes funny, sometimes chaotic, Bowie worked on this session with Art Ensemble mates Malachi Favors (bass) and Don Moye (drums). Compositions were mostly strong, but the playing

was uniformly excellent. This has not been reissued on CD. —*Ron Wynn*

Duet / Jan. 1, 1978 / IAI ✦✦✦

The 5th Power / Apr. 12, 1978+Apr. 17, 1978 / Black Saint ✦✦✦✦
1978 quintet with Arthur Blythe (as) and Amina Myers (p). Creative jazz and a progressive gospel segment. Bowie at his eclectic best. Essential. —*Michael G. Nastos*

● **The Great Pretender** / Jun. 1981 / ECM ✦✦✦✦✦
This is one of trumpeter Lester Bowie's most accessible albums; certainly his brief versions of "It's Howdy Doody Time" and "When the Moon Comes over the Mountain" are not difficult to understand. But actually the bulk of this album is taken up with the 16-minute title cut and a variety of Bowie's colorful originals. The highly expressive trumpeter is mostly heard with a quartet (although "The Great Pretender" also adds two vocalists and baritonist Hamiet Bluiett) and this set offers many fine examples of his original approach to making music, technically avant-garde but also borrowing aspects of earlier styles in unusual combinations. —*Scott Yanow*

All the Magic! / Jun. 1982 / ECM ✦✦✦
Bowie's pop/soul band sometimes smokes and falters at other times, but generally makes entertaining music. Bowie's trumpet crackles and roars when he gets space, and his array of devices and effects are often impressive. Ari Brown on soprano and tenor sax, and Art Matthews on piano are fine, as are bassist Fred Wilson and drummer Phillip Wilson. Vocalists David Peaston and Fontella Bass made more vivid, exciting records on their own cutting soul tracks. Here, they fit into the concept, but don't illuminate or expand it. —*Ron Wynn*

I Only Have Eyes for You / Feb. 1985 / ECM ✦✦✦

Avant Pop / Mar. 1986 / ECM ✦✦

Twilight Dreams / Apr. 1987 / Venture ✦✦✦
Lester Bowie's Brass Fantasy, which is comprised of four trumpets, two trombones, French horn, tuba and drums, has rarely lived up to its potential on records. Bowie has enjoyed having the band take pop tunes ("Personality" and "Night Time Is the Right Time" on this album) and distort (and sometimes satirize) them, but one imagines that this approach works better in concert than on record. There are some strong moments on this hard-to-find LP (such as Bowie's trumpet-drums duet with the late Phillip Wilson on "Duke's Fantasy"), but this is a hit-and-miss affair. —*Scott Yanow*

Serious Fun / Apr. 4, 1989–Apr. 6, 1989 / DIW ✦✦✦

My Way / Jan. 22, 1990–Jan. 30, 1990 / DIW ✦✦

Funky T, Cool T / Jan. 14, 1991–Jan. 16, 1991 / DIW ✦✦✦

The Fire This Time / May 1, 1992 / In + Out ✦✦✦

Charles Brackeen

b. 1940, White's Chapel, OK
Tenor Saxophone / Free Jazz, Avant-Garde
An excellent avant-garde tenor who has always been a bit underrated, Charles Brackeen originally studied violin and piano. Settling on tenor, he worked in both New York and Los Angeles, meeting and marrying pianist Joanne Brackeen. In New York he was associated with "the new thing" and in 1968 recorded an interesting set for Strata-East with three of the members of the Ornette Coleman Quartet (Don Cherry, Charlie Haden and Ed Blackwell). After a long period of obscurity he began playing with Paul Motian (with whom he recorded for ECM) and in 1987 he started making records for Silkheart. An explorative high-energy player, Charles Brackeen's performances are always stimulating. —*Scott Yanow*

Rhythm X / Jan. 1968 / Strata East ✦✦✦✦
Avant saxophonist on early date. Wild, uninhibited. —*Michael G. Nastos*

Bannar / Feb. 13, 1987 / Silkheart ✦✦✦✦

Attainment / Nov. 29, 1987 / Silkheart ✦✦✦

● **Worshippers Come Nigh** / Nov. 29, 1987 / Silkheart ✦✦✦✦
Rousing, declarative session from a grossly underrecorded tenor and soprano saxophonist. Charles Brackeen was persuaded to return to the recording scene in 1986 by the Silkheart label's managing director, and this was one of three great albums he made in '86 and '87. The pithy, crisp cornet solos supplied by Olu Dara are

almost as striking as Brackeen's sax lines, and there aren't better bassists and drummers in this style than Fred Hopkins and Andrew Cyrille. —*Ron Wynn*

Joanne Brackeen

b. Jul. 26, 1938, Ventura, CA
Piano / Post-Bop
A brilliant pianist flexible enough to play free, modal music and standards, Joanne Brackeen has been a major player for 25 years. She taught herself to play jazz piano. During 1958-59 Brackeen worked in Los Angeles with Teddy Edwards, Harold Land, Dexter Gordon and Charles Lloyd. After marrying Charles Brackeen (they later divorced) she took time off to bring up their four children. Brackeen moved to New York in 1965, worked with Woody Shaw and David Liebman and became the first female member of Art Blakey's Jazz Messengers (1969–72). After working regularly with Joe Henderson (1972-75) and Stan Getz (1975-77), Brackeen (an original stylist) has mostly performed as a leader of her own trios, making numerous records for Choice, Timeless, Tappan Zee and Concord. —*Scott Yanow*

Snooze / Mar. 1975 / Choice ✦✦✦
Pianist Joanne Brackeen's debut album (after a barely documented period with Art Blakey's Jazz Messengers) is a very impressive effort. Teamed with bassist Cecil McBee and drummer Billy Hart, Brackeen plays in a complex and already original style, interpreting four of her tunes plus "Nefertiti," Miles Davis' "Circles" and "Old Devil Moon." Her chord voicings are thick and sometimes quite dense, but this music is strangely accessible. —*Scott Yanow*

Tring-A-Ling / Mar. 20, 1977 / Choice ✦✦✦✦
Brilliant pianist/composer with powerful modern modal music (all originals). With Michael Brecker on sax plus two bassists. —*Michael G. Nastos*

Aft / Dec. 30, 1977 / Timeless ✦✦✦✦
This is one of the more obscure Joanne Brackeen recordings. Although the pianist is heard in a trio with guitarist Ryo Kawasaki and bassist Clint Houston, the music sounds nothing like Nat King Cole or Oscar Peterson. Actually Brackeen long ago developed her own distinctive chord voicings and, even when one hears touches of McCoy Tyner or Chick Corea in her solos, in reality she sounds like no one else. Her close interplay with Kawasaki and Houston on the six group originals (four by Brackeen) is consistently impressive and unpredictable. —*Scott Yanow*

Ancient Dynasty / 1980 / Columbia ✦✦✦
Bob James surprised many when he signed the adventurous pianist Joanne Brackeen to his Tappan Zee subsidiary of Columbia. As it turned out, James signed her for the simple reason that he was impressed by her music, and Brackeen's Columbia recordings fortunately ended up not being any "simpler" or more "accessible" than her earlier small-label dates. This now out-of-print album features Brackeen with an all-star quartet featuring her former boss, Joe Henderson, on tenor, bassist Eddie Gomez and drummer Jack DeJohnette. The four complex Brackeen originals are all at least nine minutes long and are quite challenging for both the musicians and the listener alike. —*Scott Yanow*

Special Identity / Dec. 8, 1981+Dec. 9, 1981 / Antilles ✦✦✦

Havin' Fun / Jun. 1985 / Concord Jazz ✦✦✦✦
Good trio session by the underrated pianist Joanne Brackeen. She's complemented by bassist Cecil McBee and drummer Al Foster, and shows rhythmic verve, harmonic strength, and good solo technique throughout the album. This has been reissued on CD. —*Ron Wynn*

● **Fi-Fi Goes to Heaven** / 1986 / Concord Jazz ✦✦✦✦✦
CD version features this energized, capable pianist at her best, with some sharp assistance from Branford Marsalis (ts) and Terence Blanchard (tpt). —*Ron Wynn*

Live at Maybeck Recital Hall / Jun. 1989 / Concord Jazz ✦✦✦✦

Breath of Brazil / Apr. 18, 1991–Apr. 19, 1991 / Concord Jazz ✦✦✦

Where Legends Dwell / Sep. 3, 1991–Sep. 4, 1991 / Ken Music ✦✦✦✦
Extraordinary trio with Eddie Gomez on bass and Jack DeJohnette on drums, this is her best work of the past decade.

Twelve tracks are all originals. Over 70 minutes of incredibly ingenious jazz included. This is easy to dig into. —*Michael G. Nastos*

Take A Chance / Jun. 15, 1993–Jun. 16, 1993 / Concord ♦♦
Joanne Brackeen previously tackled Afro-Latin and Brazilian music with authority on *Breath Of Brazil*. This sequel isn't quite as dynamic or energetic as its predecessor, but it doesn't miss by much. The main difference is that Brackeen is more light than assertive on several numbers, opting to showcase Brazil's romantic/sentimental side as much as its steamy, rhythmic element. But she doesn't spare any energy on "Recade Bossa Nova," "Ducka" or the title track. This isn't a CD for those who only want the classic Brazilian sound; Brackeen is interested in current affairs, although she can and does occasionally return to the glorious bossa nova and samba past. —*Ron Wynn*

Bobby Bradford

b. Jul. 19, 1934, Cleveland, MS
Cornet / Avant-Garde, Post-Bop
One of the best trumpeters to emerge from the avant-garde, Bobby Bradford largely fulfilled the potential of Don Cherry (whose chops declined through the years due to the amount of time allocated to performing on flute and other instruments). Bradford grew up in Dallas, playing trumpet locally with such local players as Cedar Walton and David Newman. In 1953 he moved to Los Angeles where he met and played with Ornette Coleman and Eric Dolphy. Bradford spent time in the military and in school before becoming Don Cherry's replacement with the Ornette Coleman Quartet in 1961–63, a period when the group unfortunately rarely worked. After moving to Los Angeles, Bradford became a school teacher and also began a longtime association with clarinetist John Carter; his mellow trumpet blended in well with Carter's dissonant flights. He recorded with Ornette Coleman in 1971 but otherwise is best-known for his playing and recordings with Carter. Since the clarinetist's death, Bradford has frequently led a quintet (the Mo'tet) featuring Vinny Golia and occasionally Marty Ehrlich. He has also performed since the early '90s with John Stevens' Freebop, the David Murray Octet and Charlie Haden's Liberation Music Orchestra. —*Scott Yanow*

With John Stevens and the Spontaneous Music Ensemble, Vol. 1 / Jul. 9, 1971 / Nessa ♦♦♦
In the first of two LPs, trumpeter Bobby Bradford fits right into drummer John Stevens' Spontaneous Music Ensemble, a quintet with leader-drummer Trevor Watts on alto and soprano, trombonist Bob Norden, bassist Ron Herman and (on two of the four selections) the haunting voice of Julie Tippetts. Tippetts' wordless vocals give an otherworldly quality to her appearances, while the two instrumentals (including a tribute to Louis Armstrong titled "His Majesty Louis") look more toward the free bop of Ornette Coleman. Stimulating and adventurous music. —*Scott Yanow*

Lost in L.A. / Jun. 7, 1983–Jun. 8, 1983 / Soul Note ♦♦♦
● **One Night Stand** / Nov. 11, 1986 / Soul Note ♦♦♦♦♦
A melodic player with a healthy sense of humor who has become more expressive through the years, Bobby Bradford really got a chance to stretch out on this fine session. Although pianist Frank Sullivan is essentially a bop player, he did a good job of keeping up during the more adventurous performances. Bassist Scott Walton (who has learned from the innovations of Charlie Haden) and drummer Billy Bowker were excellent in support. "Ashes" (a calypso version of "I Got Rhythm") and the mysterious "Woman" were the highpoints of this highly recommended disc. —*Scott Yanow*

Comin' On / May 29, 1988 / Hat Art ♦♦
An uneven 1988 date that still contains some glorious moments, mostly when Bradford and his longtime cohort, clarinetist John Carter, play together. Bradford's solos aren't as universally sharp or focused as usual, but he doesn't totally falter. Drummer Andrew Cyrille and bassist Richard Davis dominate in the rhythm section. —*Ron Wynn*

Will Bradley

b. Jul. 12, 1912, Newton, NJ, **d.** Jul. 1989, Flemington, NJ
Trombone / Swing
Will Bradley was a reluctant celebrity. His name became closely associated with boogie-woogie due to the commercial success of

Music Map

<table>
<tr><td align="center">

Bassoon

</td></tr>
<tr><td align="center">

1920s
Frankie Trumbauer
Garvin Bushell

</td></tr>
<tr><td align="center">

Later Bassoonists
Yusef Lateef
Illinois Jacquet
Frank Tiberi

</td></tr>
<tr><td align="center">

Virtually the Only Full-time Jazz Bassoonists
Karen Borca (free jazz)
Janet Grice (crossover)

</td></tr>
</table>

"Beat Me Daddy, Eight to the Bar" but he much preferred to play ballads. A technically skilled trombonist, Bradley was a busy studio musician throughout much of his career. He worked with Red Nichols (1931–32) and Ray Noble (1935–36) but was an unknown (except to his fellow musicians) when he formed a big band in 1939 with Ray McKinley. McKinley's drumming and vocals along with Freddie Slack's piano solos helped the group catch on. But by 1942 Bradley had tired of the project and he returned to the security and anonymity of studio work, only emerging to play Dixieland, ballads or boogie-woogie on an occasional basis. — *Scott Yanow*

● **Best of Big Bands** / Sep. 19, 1939–Jun. 23, 1941 / Columbia ♦♦♦♦

Ruby Braff

b. Mar. 16, 1927, Boston, MA
Cornet / Swing, New Orleans Jazz
One of the great swing/Dixieland cornetists, Ruby Braff went through long periods of his career unable to find work because his music was considered out-of-fashion, but his fortunes improved by the 1970s. A very expressive player who in later years liked to build his solos up to a low note, Braff's playing is instantly recognizable.

Braff mostly worked around Boston in the late '40s. He teamed up with Pee Wee Russell when the clarinetist was making a comeback (they recorded live for Savoy) and after moving to New York in 1953 he fit easily into a variety of Dixieland and mainstream settings. Braff recorded for Vanguard as a leader and with Vic Dickenson, Buck Clayton and Urbie Green. He was one of the stars of Buck Clayton's Columbia jam sessions and in the mid-'50s worked with Benny Goodman. But despite good reviews and occasional recordings, work was hard for Braff to come by at times. In the 1960s he was able to get jobs by being with George Wein's Newport All-Stars and at jazz festivals, but it was not until the cornetist formed a quartet with guitarist George Barnes in 1973 that he became more secure. Since that time Braff has been heard in many small-group settings including duets with Dick Hyman and Ellis Larkins (he had first met up with the latter in the 1950s), quintets with Scott Hamilton and matching wits with Howard Alden. He remains one of the greats of mainstream jazz. —*Scott Yanow*

Hustlin' and Bustlin' / Mar. 1955 / Black Lion ♦♦♦♦
Nice date putting Braff in the company of a large group filled with traditional and mainstream jazz greats like clarinetist Edmond Hall, trombonist Vic Dickenson, and bassist Milt Hinton. The songs are vintage, the solos exuberant, and the ensemble's playing and interaction reflects the musicians' love for this classic sound. —*Ron Wynn*

Adoration of the Melody / Mar. 17, 1955–Mar. 18, 1955 / Bethlehem ✦✦✦✦✦

Two by Two: Ruby and Ellis Play Rodgers and Hart / Oct. 14, 1955 / Vanguard ✦✦✦✦

Braff! / Jun. 26, 1956–Jul. 10, 1956 / Portrait ✦✦✦

This Is My Lucky Day / Aug. 19, 1957–Dec. 26, 1957 / Bluebird ✦✦✦

This Bluebird CD reissue brings back seven of the nine selections that trumpeter Ruby Braff recorded with an impressive octet that also included trombonist Benny Morton, clarinetist Pee Wee Russell, tenor saxophonist Dick Hafer and a rhythm section led by pianist Nat Pierce. The material, superior swing standards highlighted by "It's Been So Long," "I'm Comin' Virginia" and "Did I Remember," features several tributes to the great Bunny Berigan, putting the emphasis on Braff's passionate horn although Russell gets in some of his unique licks. The remainder of this CD reissues half of an earlier LP, the complete session of Aug. 19, 1957. Braff is matched with fellow trumpeter Roy Eldridge for an interesting but slightly inhibited affair; there are few of the expected fireworks between these normally fiery players. Despite the excess of mutual respect, there are quite a few strong moments, particularly on "Give My Regards to Broadway," "This Is My Lucky Day" and "The Song Is Ended." —*Scott Yanow*

With the Newport All Stars / Oct. 28, 1967 / Black Lion ✦✦✦
With Buddy Tate (ts), George Wein (p), Jack Lesberg (b), and Don Lamond (d). Both Tate and Braff are in top form on this one. —*Michael Erlewine*

The Ruby Braff-George Barnes Quartet / Apr. 22, 1974 / Chiaroscuro ✦✦✦✦

Plays Gershwin / Jul. 26, 1974 / Concord Jazz ✦✦✦

Salutes Rodgers & Hart / Oct. 1974 / Concord Jazz ✦✦✦✦
Superb small combo repertory fare, with Braff's terse cornet finding excellent company with guitarist Wayne Wright and George Barnes. Bassist Michael Moore more than makes up for the absence of a drummer. —*Ron Wynn*

To Fred Astaire with Love / 1975 / RCA ✦✦✦

With the Ed Bickert Trio / Jun. 14, 1979 / Sackville ✦✦✦

Very Sinatra / Dec. 12, 1981 / Red Baron ✦✦

America the Beautiful / Apr. 24, 1982 / George Wein Collection ✦✦✦

Mr. Braff to You: The Ruby Braff Quintet / Dec. 15, 1983 / Phontastic ✦✦✦✦
This is a very enjoyable set. The veteran cornetist Ruby Braff is teamed with the hot young swing tenor player Scott Hamilton in a quintet for a set of nine songs associated with Benny Goodman. Braff and Hamilton are both in top form, playing off of each other and sounding mutually inspired. Backed by a supportive drumless rhythm section led by pianist John Bunch, the two classic horn players are subtle and often a bit restrained but bring some fresh insights to these familiar standards. This is a fine release from the Swedish Phontastic label. —*Scott Yanow*

A First / 1985 / Concord Jazz ✦✦✦

● **A Sailboat in the Moonlight** / Feb. 1985 / Concord Jazz ✦✦✦✦✦

Me, Myself & I / Jun. 1988 / Concord Jazz ✦✦✦

Bravura Eloquence / Jun. 1988 / Concord Jazz ✦✦✦
A wonderful set from a great cornetist, with Howard Alden (g) and Jack Lesberg (b). —*Michael Erlewine*

Music from My Fair Lady / 1989 / Concord Jazz ✦✦✦

Music from *South Pacific* / Jun. 12, 1990–Jun. 13, 1990 / Concord Jazz ✦✦✦✦

Cornet Chop Suey / Mar. 27, 1991–Mar. 28, 1991 / Concord Jazz ✦✦✦

Ruby Braff & His New England Songhounds, Vol. 1 / Apr. 29, 1991 / Concord Jazz ✦✦✦✦

Ruby Braff & His New England Songhounds, Vol. 2 / Apr. 30, 1991 / Concord Jazz ✦✦✦✦

Live At The Regattabar / Nov. 22, 1993 / Arbors ✦✦✦

Controlled Nonchalance, Vol. 1 / Nov. 26, 1993–Nov. 27, 1993 / Arbors ✦✦✦✦
Cornetist Ruby Braff has teamed up with tenor saxophonist Scott Hamilton on several occasions and the combination always proves to be exciting. This live sextet session, which also features

the great swing pianist Dave McKenna and guitarist Gray Sargent, finds the classic players bringing new life to eight veteran standards including "Rosetta," "Struttin' with Some Barbecue" and "The Lady Is a Tramp." Braff in particular is full of subtle surprises and sly humor, spontaneously concluding a slower-than-usual version of "Sunday" with a quick tribute to Louis Armstrong. Dixieland and swing fans should go out of their way to get this one. —*Scott Yanow*

Calling Berlin, Vol. 1 / Jun. 28, 1994–Jul. 1, 1994 / Arbors ✦✦✦✦
Cornetist Ruby Braff and pianist Ellis Larkins recorded a classic album of duets in 1955 and had a reunion in 1972. They waited another 22 years before cutting their third set but, despite the passing of time, the magic heard on their earlier recordings is still very much present on their Arbors release. Both Braff and Larkins love melodies and rarely leave the themes behind in their improvisations. They perform 15 Irving Berlin tunes, ranging from the famous ("Alexander's Ragtime Band," "Easter Parade" and "How Deep Is the Ocean") to the more obscure ("My Walking Stick," "You're Laughing at Me" and "Steppin' out with My Baby"). In all cases the interpretations are loving, personal and uplifting. Guitarist Bucky Pizzarelli makes the group a trio on two numbers and his mellow playing fits right in to the intimate setting. Because Braff (who has always had his own sound) has long been a jazz giant and Larkins is rightfully considered an extraordinary accompanist and perfect on melodic ballads, their most recent matchup is quite successful and delightful. —*Scott Yanow*

Wellman Braud

b. Jan. 25, 1891, St. James Parish, LA, d. Oct. 27, 1966, Los Angeles, CA
Bass/Swing
One of the top string bassists of the 1920s, Wellman Braud was the first of the great Duke Ellington bass players, a tradition that would later include Jimmy Blanton, Oscar Pettiford and even Charles Mingus. Braud grew up playing music in New Orleans occasionally switching to guitar or drums. By the time he moved to Chicago in 1917, Braud was strictly a bassist. He was with Charlie Elgar (1920–22) and toured Europe with Will Vodery's Plantation Revue before freelancing to New York. Braud became a key member of Duke Ellington's Orchestra (1927–35) and his well-recorded bass (his only close competitor on his instrument during the period was Pops Foster) really drove the band during their many records. After leaving Ellington, Braud played with the Spirits of Rhythm (1935–37) before forming his own trio. He recorded with Jelly Roll Morton (1939–40) and Sidney Bechet (1940–41) but opened a poolroom in New York in 1940 and thereafter became a part-time player. Among his later musical experiences were reunions with Duke Ellington (1944 and 1961) and stints with Bunk Johnson (1947) and Kid Ory's Creole Jazz Band (1956). —*Scott Yanow*

Anthony Braxton

b. Jun. 4, 1945, Chicago, IL
Alto Saxophone, Clarinet, Contrabass Clarinet, Reeds, Piano / Avant-Garde
Of all the current leaders of the avant-garde, Anthony Braxton's music has possibly the least chance of ever being accepted by the bebop establishment. His complex lines, staccato attack and enormous quantity of compositions have a logic all their own. Some detractors (like Wynton Marsalis) may deny that Braxton's music is even jazz but, because it does contain a large amount of improvisation and the feeling of the blues, it is unquestionably jazz. And for what it is worth, this writer regards him as an obvious genius although the huge quantity of his work can be rather daunting.

Braxton began studying music when he was 17 and after serving in the military he became involved in Chicago's AACM in 1966. He made his recording debut in 1968 and from the start Braxton's approach was unusual; he used diagrams as songtitles and wrote difficult-to-understand liner notes. Although alto has always been his main ax (and his second recording as a leader was an unprecedented double-LP of unaccompanied alto explorations), Braxton eventually mastered virtually every reed instrument from the clarinet and sopranino to the contrabass clarinet and bass sax. He went to France for a period in 1969 and the following year teamed up with Chick Corea, Dave Holland and Barry Altschul in the mostly free form unit Circle. When Corea decided to quit the group so as to play more accessible music,

Braxton kept Holland and Altschul and added trumpeter Kenny Wheeler to his quartet; in 1976 trombonist George Lewis took his place. From this point forward Braxton's chronology is difficult to follow because each of his recordings seemed to use a different combination of musicians and a large amount of his projects were documented. Luckily Braxton had a good relationship with Arista in the 1970s; since that time he has recorded extensively for many European labels (including Hat Art and Black Saint) and recently the American company Music and Arts. Braxton has cut duet albums with Joseph Jarman, Muhal Richard Abrams, Evan Parker, Derek Bailey and Max Roach, utilized a big band (The Creative Music Orchestra), performed standards with a trio headed by Tete Montoliu (with very advanced improvisations from the altoist), come out with a three LP-set of wholly written-out orchestral works, paid tribute (in an abstract way) to the music of Charlie Parker, Thelonious Monk and Warne Marsh, and recorded more unaccompanied alto solos. Since 1984 Braxton has often toured with a quartet comprised of the brilliant pianist Marilyn Crispell, either John Lindberg or Mark Dresser on bass and drummer Gerry Hemingway. In addition, Braxton has been a teacher at Mills College and Wesleyan College.

Anthony Braxton's accomplishments and contributions to jazz will take decades to fully assess. —*Scott Yanow*

Three Compositions of New Jazz / Mar. 27, 1968–Apr. 10, 1968 / Delmark ✦✦✦

For Alto Saxophone / Oct. 1968 / Delmark ✦✦✦✦

The Complete Braxton / Feb. 4, 1971+Feb. 5, 1971 / Arista ✦✦✦
This two-LP set features the innovative multireedist in a variety of settings. Recorded while he was a member of the group Circle, Braxton is heard in two duets with pianist Chick Corea, three fairly exciting quartet tracks with trumpeter Kenny Wheeler, bassist Dave Holland and drummer Barry Altschul, an unaccompanied solo on contrabass clarinet, a piece (which Braxton wrote but does not play on) for five tubas, and a selection in which he overdubbed four sopranino saxes. Lots of very interesting performances come from a master of the avant-garde who has always followed his own musical path. —*Scott Yanow*

In the Tradition, Vol. 1 / May 29, 1974 / SteepleChase ✦✦
The great avant-gardist Anthony Braxton threw the jazz world a curve with this album (and its second volume). Braxton, filling in for an ill Dexter Gordon, was joined by pianist Tete Montoliu, bassist Niels Pedersen and drummer Tootie Heath for a set of five jazz standards. After playing the melodies fairly straight, Braxton tears into Warne Marsh's "Marshmallow," "Just Friends" and "Lush Life" with very complex and abstract improvisations that are generally ignored by the rhythm section, who go about playing in their usual bop-oriented style. An exception is a duet with bassist Pedersen on a very spooky "Goodbye Pork Pie Hat," one of two songs on which Braxton plays contrabass clarinet. His solo on "Ornithology" on that instrument is a bit silly, for the contrabass clarinet is so low that one has difficulty telling some of its notes apart from each other. A historical curiosity, this set is not as essential as Braxton's explorations of his own music. —*Scott Yanow*

In the Tradition, Vol. 2 / May 29, 1974 / SteepleChase ✦✦
Braxton's set of vintage bop and mainstream songs, done with reverence and, for the most part, extreme competence. These seemed to be Braxton's answer to those who claimed he knew little about jazz tradition and even less about how to present it on album. Reaction to both albums was strong; fellow alto saxophonist Bob Mover even cut an album in answer to them. —*Ron Wynn*

New York (Fall 1974) / Sep. 27, 1974 / Arista ✦✦✦✦
Anthony Braxton, who switches here between alto, flute, clarinet, sopranino and contrabass clarinet, is heard interpreting six of his originals in a wide variety of settings. Most accessible are his three performances with a quartet also including trumpeter Kenny Wheeler, bassist Dave Holland and drummer Jerome Cooper. Braxton also adds violinist Leroy Jenkins to the group on one piece and has a duet with Richard Teitelbaum's moog synthesizer. However, the most historic performance is by an unaccompanied saxophone quartet consisting of Braxton, Julius Hemphill, Oliver Lake and Hamiet Bluiett; this band (with David Murray in Braxton's place) would soon emerge as The World Saxophone Quartet. The wide amount of variety on this set makes this album a perfect introduction to Anthony Braxton's potentially forbidding but logical music. —*Scott Yanow*

Five Pieces (1975) / Jul. 1, 1975–Jul. 2, 1975 / Arista ✦✦✦

Creative Orchestra Music (1976) / Feb. 1976 / Arista ✦✦✦
This is one of Braxton's most interesting recordings. Six of his compositions are performed by groups ranging from 15-20 pieces and featuring such soloists as trumpeters Cecil Bridgewater, Leo Smith, Kenny Wheeler and Jon Faddis, baritonist Bruce Johnstone, trombonist George Lewis, reed player Roscoe Mitchell, bassist Dave Holland, pianist Muhal Richard Abrams and Braxton himself. There is a lot of variety on this set. One of the pieces finds Braxton combining free elements with a Sousa-type march while another one looks toward Ellington. There are quite a few memorable moments on this program. —*Scott Yanow*

Elements of Surprise: Braxton/Lewis Duo / Jun. 7, 1976 / Moers ✦✦✦

Duets (1976) / Aug. 1, 1976–Aug. 2, 1976 / Arista ✦✦

Donaueschingen (Duo) 1976 / Oct. 23, 1976 / Hat Art ✦✦✦

★ **Dortmund (Quartet–1976)** / Oct. 31, 1976 / Hat Art ✦✦✦✦✦
This is the perfect Anthony Braxton recording for listeners to start with. The innovative multireedist (heard here on alto, clarinet, soprano, flute and the remarkable contrabass sax) led a particularly strong group during part of 1976, a quartet with trombonist George Lewis, bassist Dave Holland and drummer Barry Altschul. This CD releases for the first time the often-stunning music they performed at their final concert. Braxton's complex and exciting compositions are among his most accessible (one of them is based on a circus march and another is a hard-swinging original dedicated to Lou Donaldson), both Braxton and Lewis take consistently emotional solos, Holland really drives the group, Altschul contributes his colorful percussion and the ensembles are very spirited. Give this recording to a bebopper who claims that what Anthony Braxton plays is not jazz. —*Scott Yanow*

For Four Orchestras / May 18, 1978–May 19, 1978 / Arista ✦✦

Alto Saxophone Improvisations (1979) / Nov. 28, 1978–Jun. 21, 1979 / Arista ✦✦✦

Performance (9–1–1979) / Sep. 1, 1979 / Hat Hut ✦✦✦

With Robert Schumann String Quartet / Nov. 10, 1979 / Sound Aspects ✦✦

Seven Compositions (1978) / Nov. 1979 / Moers ✦✦✦

Composition 96 / Jan. 24, 1981 / Hat Art ✦✦✦

Six Compositions: Quartet / Oct. 21, 1981–Oct. 22, 1981 / Antilles ✦✦✦
More fierce, often shattering compositions from Anthony Braxton on his usual horn arsenal, backed by a wonderful quartet featuring the welcome presence of drummer Ed Blackwell. Even in this setting, Blackwell finds ways to include enticing accents and rhythms, while pianist Anthony Davis ranked alongside Marilyn Crispell as Braxton's best keyboard partners. Bassist Mark Heilas was also a substantial contributor. —*Ron Wynn*

Open Aspects (1982) / Mar. 18, 1982 / Hat Art ✦✦✦

Six Duets (1982) / Jul. 19, 1982 / Cecma ✦✦✦

Four Compositions (1983) / Mar. 9, 1983–Mar. 10, 1983 / Polydor ✦✦✦

Composition 113 / Dec. 6, 1983 / Sound Aspects ✦✦

Seven Standards (1985), Vol. 1 / Jan. 30, 1985–Jan. 31, 1985 / Magenta ✦✦✦
Saxophonist plays straight-ahead with the Hank Jones (p) Trio. Very enjoyable. *Vol. 2* is also excellent. —*Michael G. Nastos*

London (Quartet–1985) / Nov. 13, 1985 / Leo ✦✦✦

Five Compositions (1986) / Jul. 2, 1986–Jul. 3, 1986 / Black Saint ✦✦✦
Anthony Braxton's 1986 quartet, although fairly strong, is not quite on the level of the longtime group he would have with pianist Marilyn Crispell. Pianist David Rosenboom, bassist Mark Dresser and drummer Gerry Hemingway do an expert job of interpreting Braxton's five difficult compositions (all of which are identified by numbers and humorous pictures). The leader (switching between alto, tenor, sopranino, C-melody sax, clarinet and flute) is in top form, as usual, and is the dominant voice throughout this complex music. —*Scott Yanow*

Six Monk's Compositions (1987) / Jun. 30, 1987+Jul. 1, 1987 / Black Saint ✦✦✦✦
This may be Braxton's finest straight jazz release, and among his best in any style. Bassist Mal Waldron and bassist Buell

Neidlinger are fully equipped to handle Monk's tricky passages, chord structures, and movements, while Braxton displays an affinity for Monk's work that his legion of detractors would find astonishing. Drummer Bill Osborne isn't intimidated by Neidlinger or Waldron and drives the session effectively. —*Ron Wynn*

19 (Solo) Compositions (1988) / Apr. 1988 / New Albion ✦✦✦✦

Ensemble (Victoriaville–1988) / Oct. 8, 1988 / Victo ✦✦✦

Eugene (1989) / Jan. 31, 1989 / Black Saint ✦✦

Seven Compositions (Trio) 1989 / Mar. 21, 1989 / Hat Art ✦✦✦

Vancouver Duets (1989) / Jul. 20, 1989 / Music & Arts ✦✦✦✦
Blistering, compelling duets that are intense, effective, and often frightening in style, volume, and energy. Searing, surging alto sax and piano. —*Ron Wynn*

2 Compositions (Ensemble) 1989/1991 / Oct. 23, 1989+Feb. 23, 1991 / Hat Art ✦✦

Tristano Compositions (1989) / Dec. 10, 1989–Dec. 11, 1989 / Hat Art ✦✦✦✦
Braxton tackles works by another keyboard genius—Lennie Tristano, and shows he's just as able to handle his pieces as those of Monk. Bassist Cecil McBee and drummer Andrew Cyrille threaten, but don't overwhelm, baritone saxophonist John Raskin and pianist Dred Scott. The album is dedicated to Warne Marsh, a saxophonist whose influence resounds in much of Braxton's work. —*Ron Wynn*

Eight Duets / Feb. 21, 1991–Feb. 23, 1991 / Music & Arts ✦✦✦

Willisau (Quartet) / Jun. 2, 1991–Jun. 5, 1991 / HatArt ✦✦✦

Composition No. 165 / 1992 / New Albion ✦✦

Wesleyan (12 Alto solos) 1992 / Nov. 14, 1992 / Hat Art ✦✦✦✦

4 (Ensemble) Compositions—1992 / Dec. 5, 1992 / Black Saint ✦✦✦

Duets (1993) / Jan. 4, 1993 / Music & Arts ✦✦✦

Twelve Compositions / Jul. 13, 1993–Jul. 16, 1993 / Music & Arts ✦✦✦✦
Of all of the avant-garde players of the past 30 years, Anthony Braxton has been perhaps the most diligent at documenting his work. The brilliant multireedist has been very fortunate to have a stable quartet for the past nine years with the frequently astounding pianist Marilyn Crispell, bassist Mark Dresser and drummer Gerry Hemingway doing justice to his very complex originals. This double-CD set features Braxton and his group on two continuous and complete live performances. Not only do the musicians tackle a dozen of Braxton's complicated originals, but during part of four of them individual members are assigned the task of playing a different composition than the rest of the group! Obviously this is not music to be taken lightly or merely played in the background. However listeners with the time and interest will find much to enjoy in the very lively explorations from these masterful musicians. —*Scott Yanow*

Charlie Parker Project 1993 / Oct. 21, 1993–Oct. 23, 1993 / Hat Art ✦✦✦
On this double CD the innovative altoist Anthony Braxton (who also plays a bit of his sopranino and the remarkable contrabass clarinet) interprets 13 bebop songs (two taken twice), 11 of which were composed by Charlie Parker. However, do not mistake these performances (which are comprised of both a studio session and a club set) with the type of music often played by The Young Lions. In fact, those listeners who consider themselves bop purists are advised to look elsewhere. Performing with an adventurous sextet that also includes Ari Brown on tenor and soprano, trumpeter Paul Smoker, pianist Misha Mengelberg (the most consistently impressive of the supporting cast), bassist Joe Fonda and either Han Bennink or Pheeroan AkLaff on drums, Braxton uses the melodies and some of the original structures of such tunes as "Hot House," "Night in Tunisia," "Bebop" and "Ko Ko" as the basis for colorful and often-stunning improvisations. He does not feel restricted to the old boundaries of the 1940s and '50s, preferring to pay tribute to the spirit and chancetaking of Charlie Parker rather than to merely recreate the past. The passionate and unpredictable results are quite stimulating and full of surprises, fresh ideas and wit. It's highly recommended to those jazz followers who have very open ears. —*Scott Yanow*

Knitting Factory (Piano/Quartet) 1994, Vol. 1 / 1994 / Leo ✦✦✦

Composition No. 174 / Feb. 6, 1994 / Leo ✦✦

Joshua Breakstone

b. 1955, Elizabeth, NJ
Guitar / Cool
A fine bop-based guitarist, Joshua Breakstone discovered jazz when he was 14. He studied for several years with Sal Salvador yet at the time was gigging regularly with a rock group. He attended Berklee and in 1977 toured Canada with the reed player Glen Hall, making his recording debut on Hall's Sonora release. During and after teaching guitar at the Rhode Island Conservatory of Music (1979–81), Breakstone worked in New York with Warne Marsh, Kenny Remler, Dave Schnitter and Vic Juris. In 1983 he recorded his first album (*Wonderful!*) for Sonora. While that date had Barry Harris on piano, his follow-up featured Kenny Barron. Breakstone has since recorded for Contemporary (including a quartet date featuring Pepper Adams), Capri and Evidence, helping keep the legacy of quiet bop guitar alive. —*Scott Yanow*

Wonderful / May 24, 1983 / Sonora ✦✦✦
This studio date for the guitarist with the Barry Harris Trio features two Breakstone tunes and five standards from Tristano, Dameron, Gershwin, and Django. This was a good portent of things to come. —*Michael G. Nastos*

4/4 =1 / Jun. 1984 / Mobile Fidelity ✦✦✦
With the Kenny Barron (p) Trio, this one features two more from Breakstone, Frank Lacy's great "Theme for Ernie," and four standards. —*Michael G. Nastos*

Echoes / Feb. 19, 1986 / Contemporary ✦✦✦✦

● **Evening Star** / Dec. 11, 1987 / Contemporary ✦✦✦✦

Self-Portrait in Swing / Feb. 1990 / Contemporary ✦✦✦
Relaxed, smooth guitar date with the accent on easy swinging standards and originals. Breakstone is solidly in the Joe Pass/Barney Kessel school, someone who plays with a minimum of intensity but does display total command and confidence. His solos don't so much impress as they tend to comfort, and nothing here will either bore or amaze anyone. —*Ron Wynn*

9 by 3 / Oct. 30, 1990 / Contemporary ✦✦✦
Includes seven trio tracks with Dennis Irwin on bass, Kenny Washington on drums. Includes lots of Monk. —*Michael G. Nastos*

Walk Don't Run / Aug. 1991 / Evidence ✦✦✦
Although it is not noted anywhere except in the liner notes, this '91 session could be subtitled "tribute to the Ventures." Guitarist Joshua Breakstone covers ten tunes originally recorded by the surf guitar legends, but does not rip through them or make any concession to a more rock or pop approach. Instead, he takes them as he does any composition, playing in a gentle, relaxed pace, investigating the melody, slowly interpreting and revising via his solos. Breakstone's sound and approach are reminiscent of Jim Hall's, although his voicings are not as full, and his comping and tone are his own. Breakstone and company give Ventures fans and jazz audiences something to ponder with their explorations of these ten tunes. —*Ron Wynn*

Sittin' On The Thing With Ming / Jan. 29, 1993 / Capri ✦✦✦
Joshua Breakstone's guitar solos are almost entirely single-note runs (without any chording) and are quite hornlike. His outing for Capri puts the emphasis on his originals and finds Breakstone heading a top quartet comprised of pianist Kenny Barron, bassist Ray Drummond and drummer Keith Copeland. The guitarist is heard in typically swinging form on these straight-ahead pieces, playing in a smooth-toned boppish style that has a few surprising twists and turns. —*Scott Yanow*

Lenny Breau

b. Aug. 5, 1941, Auburn, ME, d. Aug. 12, 1984, Los Angeles, CA
Guitar / Post-Bop
An outstanding finger-style jazz guitarist who performed on both acoustic and electric guitars. Breau's right hand drew on classical, flamenco, and country (Travis/Atkins) finger-picking techniques. He was among the first guitarists to digest the impressionistic, post-bop chord voicings of pianist Bill Evans. Breau developed the ability to simultaneously comp chords and improvise single-string melodies, creating the illusion of two guitarists playing together. His facility with artificial harmonics remains the envy of many guitarists. Late in his career, Breau began using a seven-string

guitar that extended the instrument's range in the upper register. Breau's early RCA recordings are eclectic and technically dazzling. His later work is less flashy, but communicates on a deeper level.

Born to Canadian country music singers, Lenny Breau started out playing country in a sophisticated manner. Chet Atkins himself helped Breau get an RCA recording contract in 1968. However Breau's jazz-oriented style and remarkable tehnique caused him to quickly be uncategorizable. Problems with drugs made his career erratic and he is now considered an underground guitar legend. A new label (Guitararchives) was formed in 1995 specifically to release private tapes of his performances. —*Richard Lieberson and Scott Yanow*

The Livingroom Tapes, Vol. 1 / Oct. 1978 / MHS ✦✦✦
These recordings, which were recorded live at different venues, were all made with the intention that someday they might be released. Shortly after Breau's passing, Brad Terry decided to share his recordings with the rest of the world. Of all Breau's work, this recording and its companion, *Volume 2*, contain some of his most exhilarating guitar playing. —*Paul Kohler*

The Livingroom Tapes, Vol. 2 / Oct. 1978 / MHS ✦✦✦✦
The follow-up to *Volume 1* features both Brad Terry on clarinet and Breau on guitar. At least eighty percent of this CD is Breau playing solo guitar. —*Paul Kohler*

● **Live At Bourbon St.** / Jun. 14, 1983 / Guitararchives ✦✦✦✦✦
The late Lenny Breau, an underground hero, is considered such a masterful guitarist by his admirers that it somehow does not seem surprising that the Guitarchives label was started specifically to release his music. This two-CD set (which was put out in 1995) contains a previously unreleased duet concert from 1983 featuring Breau and bassist Dave Young. The music (full of close musical communication) is subtle and quiet yet consistently inventive. It is obvious after a few minutes of listening that Breau had complete control of his guitar and an original voice of his own. Although most of the repertoire is standards (with just two fairly basic originals), there is little predictable about the playing. Highlights include Breau's interpretations of "There Is No Greater Love," "All Blues," McCoy Tyner's "Vision," "Beautiful Love" and a cooking "There Will Never Be Another You" but all 17 performances have their rewarding moments. Overall this two-fer gives one a definitive portrait of the nearly-forgotten legend. —*Scott Yanow*

Michael Brecker

b. Mar. 29, 1949, Philadelphia, PA
Tenor Saxophone / Post-Bop, Crossover
A remarkable technician and a highly influential tenor saxophonist (the biggest influence on other tenors since Wayne Shorter), Michael Brecker took a long time before getting around to recording his first solo album. He has spent much of his career as a top-notch studio player who often appeared backing pop singers, leading some jazz listeners to overlook his very strong improvising skills.

Michael Brecker originally started on clarinet and alto before switching to tenor in high school. Early on he played with rock and R&B-oriented bands. In 1969 he moved to New York and soon joined Dreams, an early fusion group. Brecker was with Horace Silver during 1973-74, gigged with Billy Cobham and then co-led the Brecker Brothers (a commercially successful funk group) with his brother-trumpeter Randy Brecker for most of the 1970s. He was with Steps (later Steps Ahead) in the early '80s, doubled on an EWI (electronic wind instrument) and made a countless number of studio sessions during the 1970s and '80s, popping up practically everywhere (including with James Taylor, Yoko Ono and Paul Simon). With the release of his first album as a leader in 1987 (when he was already 38), Brecker started appearing more often in challenging jazz settings. He recorded additional sets as a leader (in 1988 and 1990), teamed up with McCoy Tyner on one of 1995's most rewarding jazz recordings and toured with a reunited Brecker Brothers band. —*Scott Yanow*

Cityscape / Jan. 4, 1982-Jan. 8, 1982 / Warner Brothers ✦✦✦
● **Michael Brecker** / Dec. 1986-1987 / MCA/Impulse! ✦✦✦✦✦
The highlight of this very good album is "Nothing Personal." With Pat Metheny (g), Charlie Haden (b), and Jack DeJohnette (d). —*Michael G. Nastos*

Don't Try This at Home / 1988 / MCA/Impulse! ✦✦✦✦
Good follow-up to Brecker's 1987 debut for the revived Impulse!

label, although it wasn't quite as energized or as passionate as his debut. He had another excellent supporting cast, but the songs didn't seem as interesting, and the session at times sounds like merely a less intense continuation of its predecessor. —*Ron Wynn*

Now You See It . . . Now You Don't / 1990 / GRP ✦✦✦
For *Now You See It*, Brecker's third recording as a leader, the tenor great used different personnel on most of the selections, but played consistently well. Jim Beard's synthesizers were used for atmosphere, to set up a funky groove or to provide a backdrop for the leader. Some of the music sounded like updated John Coltrane (Joey Calderazzo's McCoy Tyner-influenced piano helped) but other pieces could have almost passed for Weather Report, if Wayne Shorter rather than Joe Zawinul had been the lead voice. Most of the originals (either by Brecker, Jim Beard or producer Don Grolnick) projected moods rather than featured strong melodies, but Michael Brecker's often-raging tenor made the most of every opportunity. —*Scott Yanow*

Randy Brecker

b. Nov. 29, 1945, Philadelphia, PA
Trumpet / Bop, Crossover
Randy Brecker is essentially a fine hard bop trumpet soloist but one versatile enough to fit into nearly any setting including in the pop world, funk bands and electronic fusion. He studied classical trumpet and attended Indiana University. Brecker was with Blood, Sweat & Tears in 1967 and spent 1968-69 playing with Horace Silver's Quintet. He also appeared with the big bands of Clark Terry, Duke Pearson, Frank Foster and the Thad Jones-Mel Lewis Orchestra. After playing with the early fusion group Dreams in 1969, he worked with Larry Coryell's Eleventh House and Billy Cobham in addition to keeping very busy with studiowork. He teamed up with Michael Brecker in the popular funk-oriented Brecker Brothers (1974-79), in the 1980s often collaborated with his wife, pianist/vocalist Eliane Elias, and in the '90s toured with the reunited Brecker Brothers. But Randy Brecker still sounds best when in a freewheeling bebop combo and fortunately he occasionally records in that type of spontaneous setting. —*Scott Yanow*

Score / Jan. 24, 1969-Feb. 3, 1969 / Blue Note ✦✦✦
Good octet date with Brecker exploring both jazz-rock and straight mainstream material. This was his debut as leader outside the Brecker Brothers, and he displayed the wit, fire, and style that characterized his work as a session player. The musicians assembled include guitarist Larry Coryell, playing both nice bop and more interesting rock-tinged solos, and bassist Eddie Gomez. —*Ron Wynn*

Amanda / Feb. 1985-Mar. 1985 / Passport ✦✦
In the Idiom / Oct. 19, 1986-Oct. 25, 1986 / Denon ✦✦✦✦
Just how strong a trumpeter Brecker could be was demonstrated well on "Little Miss P," a freeish cooker which wound down into near orgasmic playing between trumpet, bass and drums...But while suggestive of a by-gone era, the music—or perhaps more accurately, the playing—was fresh. —*Bob Rusch, Cadence*

Toe to Toe / Aug. 1989 / MCA ✦✦
● **Live at Sweet Basil: Randy Brecker Quintet** / Jan. 11, 1992 / GNP ✦✦✦✦

Willem Breuker

b. Nov. 4, 1944, Amsterdam, Netherlands
Clarinet, Reeds / Avant-Garde
A leader in the European avant-garde and free music community, Dutch saxophonist, clarinetist, composer and bandleader Willem Breuker has worked to ensure recording and performance opportunities for many performers. His compositions incorporate several influences: free jazz, contemporary and avant-garde classical and new music, plus film themes, dance and European folk sounds. Breuker also includes a large dose of humor and even absurdist lyrics and sentiments into his works. That same humor carries over into his playing, which blends screams, shrieks and various effects with honking bleats and also moments of almost straight, bebop-inspired soloing. He helped form The Instant Composers Pool, a nonprofit organization that sponsors performances and recordings of music by European free players. Breuker has played and recorded with the Globe Unity Orchestra, Peter Brotzmann, Misha Mengelberg, Hans Bennink, Alexander Schlippenbach, Gunther Hampel and many others. He formed

The Kollektief in the mid-70s, and toured Europe. They visited America and Canada in the '80s. Breuker was awarded the Duth National Jazz Prize in 1970 and the Jazz Prize of the West German Music Critics in 1976. As a leader he has recorded for MPS, Marge and About Time but most notably for his own BVHaast label. — *Ron Wynn*

De Onderste Steen / Dec. 1974–Jan. 1991 / Entr'acte ✦✦✦

The European Scene / Oct. 19, 1975 / MPS ✦✦✦

Live in Berlin / Nov. 5, 1975 / FMP ✦✦✦✦
This was one of reedman Willem Breuker's works for larger groups and while there was an obvious set of structures within these, it was quite open. — *Bob Rusch, Cadence*

On Tour / Mar. 3, 1977 / BVHaast ✦✦✦

Summer Music / Feb. 4, 1978 / Marge ✦✦✦

. . . Superstars / Mar. 26, 1978 Mar. 27, 1978 / FMP ✦✦✦

In Holland / Apr. 21, 1981–May 6, 1981 / BVHaast ✦✦✦

Driebergen-Zeist / Sep. 12, 1983–Sep. 13, 1983 / BVHaast ✦✦✦

● **In New York** / Oct. 31, 1983 / About Time ✦✦✦✦

De Klap / Jan. 3, 1985 / BVHaast ✦✦✦

Metropolis / Nov. 5, 1987–Apr. 1989 / BVHaast ✦✦

Bob's Gallery / Dec. 1987 / BVHaast ✦✦✦✦✦

Plays Gershwin / Dec. 19, 1987 / BVHaast ✦✦✦✦

To Remain / Jan. 1989–Apr. 1989 / BVHaast ✦✦✦

Parade / Oct. 19, 1990 / BVHaast ✦✦✦

Teresa Brewer

b. May 7, 1931, Toledo, OH
Vocals / Pop, Swing
Specializing in bright, chirpy melodies, spunky Teresa Brewer was one of the top pop thrushes of the '50s. Raised in Toledo, Ohio, she was a regular on "The Major Bowes Amateur Hour" as a child. Brewer scored her first huge hit in 1950 at the tender age of 18 with "Music! Music! Music!" and followed it up with an impressive string of smashes that spanned the entire decade. Several of Brewer's mid-50s hits—Fats Domino's "Bo Weevil," Ivory Hunter's "Empty Arms"—were sanitized R&B covers. Brewer has pursued jazzier directions in recent years, still retaining her youthful vocal delivery. Since marrying producer Bob Thiele in 1972 she has recorded with Duke Ellington, Count Basie, Stephane Grappelli, Ruby Braff, the World's Greatest Jazz Band and Earl Hines. — *Bill Dahl and Scott Yanow*

● **Songs of Bessie Smith** / Feb. 1973–Apr. 1973 / Signature ✦✦✦✦

Live at Carnegie Hall & Montreaux, Switzerland / Apr. 5, 1978–Jul. 22, 1983 / Doctor Jazz ✦✦✦

We Love You Fats / Jul. 24, 1978–Jul. 25, 1978 / Doctor Jazz ✦✦✦

A Sophisticated Lady / 1980 / Columbia ✦✦
There are those who love her. I do not, though her albums are well produced and tasteful, and she sings with energy and style. — *Ron Wynn*

On the Road Again / Oct. 20, 1981–Oct. 21, 1981 / Doctor Jazz ✦✦✦

In London / 1982 / Signature ✦✦

Midnight Cafe (A Few More for the Road) / 1982 / Doctor Jazz ✦✦✦

I Dig Big Band Singers / 1983 / Doctor Jazz ✦

American Music Box, Vol. 1 (Songs of Irving Berlin) / Jul. 7, 1983–Jul. 8, 1983 / Doctor Jazz ✦✦

Cotton Connection / Jan. 24, 1985–Jan. 28, 1985 / Doctor Jazz ✦✦

What a Wonderful World / 1989 / Signature ✦✦✦

Memories of Louis / Jan. 15, 1991–Mar. 12, 1991 / Red Baron ✦✦✦

Softly I Swing / Mar. 21, 1991–Mar. 22, 1991 / Red Baron ✦✦

American Music Box, Vol. 2 / Sep. 7, 1993–Sep. 8, 1993 / Red Baron ✦✦
Teresa Brewer albums are generally frustrating affairs. She is usually joined by great musicians (in this case cornetist Ruby Braff, pianist John Bunch, guitarist Bucky Pizzarelli, bassist Jay Leonhart and drummer Grady Tate) and is generous enough to allocate a liberal amount of solo space to her sidemen. But Brewer's wide vibrato and overly cute phrasing ruin most of her recordings;

even after all these years she has not learned how to sing jazz. This CD (which has ten fine Harry Warren songs) is therefore only recommended to Ruby Braff completists. — *Scott Yanow*

Cecil Bridgewater

b. Oct. 10, 1942, Urbana, IL
Trumpet / Hard Bop
An excellent hard bop trumpeter, Cecil Bridgewater has been the longtime trumpeter with the Max Roach quartet. After studying music at the University of Illinois, he teamed up with tenorman Ron Bridgewater in the Bridgewater Brothers Band (1969). He was married to singer Dee Dee Garrett (aka Bridgewater) for part of the 1970s. In 1970 the trumpeter was with Horace Silver and then he worked with the Thad Jones-Mel Lewis Orchestra (1970–76). Bridgewater started playing with Max Roach in the early '70s and has been a key part of his groups ever since. He recorded his long overdue debut as a leader on a Bluemoon disc in 1993. — *Scott Yanow*

● **I Love Your Smile** / Dec. 4, 1992 / Blue Moon ✦✦✦✦
For one of trumpeter Cecil Bridgewater's few sessions as a leader, the longtime Max Roach sideman welcomes Roach to a few of these selections along with altoist Antonio Hart, trombonist Steve Turre, pianist Roland Hanna, singer Vanessa Rubin (on "Never Too Young To Dream") and others. A highpoint of this modern hard bop set is Bridgewater's duet with Hanna on "Sophisticated Lady." — *Scott Yanow*

Dee Dee Bridgewater

b. May 27, 1950, Memphis, TN
Vocals / Standards
One of the best jazz singers of her generation, Dee Dee Bridgewater (who was married to trumpeter Cecil Bridgewater in the early '70s) had to move to France to find herself. She performed in Michigan during the 1960s and toured the Soviet Union in 1969 with the University of Illinois big band. She sang with the Thad Jones-Mel Lewis Orchestra (1972–74) and appeared in the Broadway musical *The Wiz* (1974–76). Due to erratic records and a lack of direction, Dee Dee Bridgewater was largely overlooked in the jazz world by the time she moved to France in the 1980s. She appeared in the show *Lady Day* and at European jazz festivals, and eventually formed her own backup group. By the late '80s Bridgewater's Verve recordings were starting to alert American listeners as to her singing talents. Her 1995 Horace Silver tribute disc (*Love and Peace*) is a gem and resulted in the singer extensively touring the U.S. — *Scott Yanow*

Dee Dee Bridgewater / 1976 / Atlantic ✦✦

Just Family / 1977 / Elektra ✦✦

Live in Paris / Nov. 24, 1986–Nov. 25, 1986 / MCA ✦✦✦✦
Bridgewater shows her roots in both Carmen McRae and Sarah Vaughan but brings a new sense of maturity and fullness to her singing; she can now be, and is, in command. And the surroundings on this live recording are loose enough to allow the entire group to blow. — *Bob Rusch, Cadence*

In Montreux / Jul. 18, 1990 / Verve ✦✦✦✦
Dee Dee Bridgewater's move to France awhile back has resulted in her having a relatively low profile in jazz. This excellent live set should help restore her reputation. Whether it be a three-song Horace Silver medley, the warhorse "All of Me," Jobim's "How Insensitive," "Night in Tunisia" or the rarely performed "Strange Fruit," Bridgewater (who is backed by a French rhythm section) is in top form, singing with swing and sensitivity. — *Scott Yanow*

Keeping Tradition / Dec. 8, 1992–Dec. 10, 1992 / Verve ✦✦✦

● **Love And Peace: A Tribute to Horace Silver** / Dec. 1994 / Verve ✦✦✦✦✦

Nick Brignola

b. Jul. 17, 1936, Troy, NY
Baritone Saxophone, Soprano Saxophone / Hard Bop
A strong baritone soloist in the tradition of Pepper Adams, Nick Brignola has long been overshadowed by Adams and Gerry Mulligan but actually ranks near the top. He occasionally doubles on other instruments (soprano, alto and flute). After studying at Ithaca College and Berklee he played and recorded with Reese Markewich in the late '50s, Herb Pomeroy, Cal Tjader and the Mastersounds. Brignola worked with Woody Herman's Orchestra (1963), Sal Salvador and Ted Curson (1967) but has generally

been a leader of his own small groups. For a time he played fusion in the early '70s but since then has mostly performed hard bop. Among the many labels Nick Brignola has recorded for are Priam (his own company), Beehive, Interplay, SeaBreeze, Discovery and Reservoir. —*Scott Yanow*

Baritone Madness / Dec. 22, 1977 / Bee Hive ✦✦✦
This album lives up to its title. Nick Brignola is matched up with fellow baritone great Pepper Adams in a sextet also including trumpeter Ted Curson, pianist Derek Smith, bassist Dave Holland and drummer Roy Haynes. The personnel differs throughout the program with the full group being heard on "Billie's Bounce" and "Marmaduke," Curson sitting out on "Donna Lee," "Body and Soul" being a feature for Brignola and "Alone Together" showcasing the rhythm section. It is obvious from the song titles that this is very much a bebop jam session date and happily quite a few sparks do fly. —*Scott Yanow*

New York Bound / Oct. 30, 1978 / Interplay ✦✦✦

Burn Brigade / Jun. 19, 1979 / Bee Hive ✦✦✦

"L.A. Bound" / Oct. 17, 1979 / Sea Breeze ✦✦✦✦

Signals . . . In from Somewhere / Jun. 21, 1983 / Discovery ✦✦✦
Nice release, although not as frenetic or exciting as past Brignola dates. He doubles on soprano and baritone, playing with skill and depth. His supporting cast is good, reliable pros in pianist Bill Dobbins, bassist John Lockwood, and drummer John Calarocco, although none equals the leader in raw talent. —*Ron Wynn*

Northern Lights / Jul. 3, 1984 / Discovery ✦✦✦

Raincheck / Sep. 12, 1988+Sep. 13, 1988 / Reservoir ✦✦✦✦
The fine baritonist Nick Brignola (who here also plays a bit of soprano, tenor and clarinet) is well-featured on a wide range of superior standards and obscurities. With the strong assistance of pianist Kenny Barron, bassist George Mraz and drummer Billy Hart, Brignola is heard at his best playing everything from bop and swing to Ralph Towner's ballad "North Star." —*Scott Yanow*

On a Different Level / Sep. 25, 1989 / Reservoir ✦✦✦

What It Takes / Oct. 9, 1990 / Reservoir ✦✦✦✦
Brignola is matched with playing equals, and he comes out burning. He also plays alto sax and clarinet in addition to his customary baritone and soprano. Pianist Kenny Barron and bassist Rufus Reid lift any session, while drummer Dick Berk defers to them, but doesn't lose the reins while doing so. Randy Brecker takes a welcome break from fusion and studio work to show that his trumpet chops can handle hard bop and mainstream fare. —*Ron Wynn*

It's Time / Dec. 2, 1991 / Reservoir ✦✦✦

Live at Sweet Basil-First Set / Aug. 28, 1992 / Reservoir ✦✦✦

● **Like Old Times** / May 19, 1994 / Reservoir ✦✦✦✦
Some jazz recordings take pages to explain and analyze. Such is not the case with Nick Brignola's Reservoir release for the great baritonist (who ranks up with Gerry Mulligan, Hamiet Bluiett and Ronnie Cuber as pacesetters on his instrument in the mid-'90s) happily jams four standards and three straight-ahead originals with an all-star quintet also featuring trumpeter Claudio Roditi and pianist John Hicks. In addition to his many robust baritone solos, Brignola has excellent outings on clarinet ("More than You Know") and soprano. With bassist George Mraz and drummer Dick Berk ably supporting the group and both Roditi and Hicks heard at the peak of their powers, Brignola's album is a strong set of bop-oriented music. —*Scott Yanow*

Bob Brookmeyer

b. Dec. 19, 1929, Kansas City, MO
Arranger, Piano, Valve Trombone / Cool, Post-Bop
Bob Brookmeyer has long been the top valve trombonist in jazz and a very advanced arranger whose writing is influenced by modern classical music. He started out as a pianist in dance bands but was on valve trombone with Stan Getz (1953). He gained fame as a member of the Gerry Mulligan quartet (1954–57), was part of the unusual Jimmy Giuffre Three of 1957–58 (which consisted Giuffre's reeds, Brookmeyer's valve trombone and Jim Hall's guitar) and then rejoined Mulligan as arranger and occasional player with his Concert Jazz Band. Brookmeyer, who was a strong enough pianist to hold his own on a two-piano date with Bill Evans, occasionally switched to piano with Mulligan. He co-led a

part-time quintet with Clark Terry (1961–66), was an original member of the Thad Jones-Mel Lewis orchestra (1965–67) and became a busy studio musician. Brookmeyer was fairly inactive during much of the 1970s but made a comeback in the late '70s with some very advanced arrangements for the Mel Lewis band (of which he became musical director for a time). Brookmeyer has since moved to Europe where he continually writes and occasionally records on his distinctive valve trombone. —*Scott Yanow*

The Dual Role of Bob Brookmeyer / Jun. 30, 1955 / Original Jazz Classics ✦✦✦

Brookmeyer / Sep. 19, 1956–Oct. 15, 1956 / VIK ✦✦✦

Traditionalism Revisited / Jul. 13, 1957–Jul. 16, 1957 / World Pacific ✦✦✦✦

Street Swingers / Dec. 13, 1957+Dec. 16, 1957 / World Pacific ✦✦✦

Kansas City Revisited / Oct. 23, 1958 / United Artists ✦✦✦✦

The Ivory Hunters / Mar. 12, 1959 / United Artists ✦✦✦
This is a rather surprising session since Bob Brookmeyer, normally a valve trombonist, switched to piano and is heard playing in a quartet with pianist Bill Evans, bassist Percy Heath and drummer Connie Kay. The two-piano experiment was supposed to be for just a couple of songs but the interplay between Brookmeyer and Evans was so delightful that they decided to make a full album out of it. Brookmeyer brought out the playful side of Evans on the six standards, making this straight CD reissue of the original LP a happy (and swinging) success. —*Scott Yanow*

Brookmeyer and Guitars / Dec. 13, 1959–Dec. 16, 1957 / Kimberly ✦✦

Jazz Is a Kick / Jun. 1960 / Mercury ✦✦✦

Gloomy Sunday and Other Bright Moments / Nov. 6, 1961–Nov. 8, 1961 / Verve ✦✦✦✦

And Friends / May 25, 1964–May 27, 1964 / Columbia ✦✦✦
This somewhat obscure session was reissued on LP by Columbia in 1980. Valve trombonist Bob Brookmeyer and tenor-great Stan Getz (who had played together regularly a decade ago) had a reunion for this date, performing five standards and three Brookmeyer originals. The young rhythm section (pianist Herbie Hancock, vibraphonist Gary Burton, bassist Ron Carter and drummer Elvin Jones) uplifts what would have been a fairly conventional (although high-quality) bop date. —*Scott Yanow*

The Power of Positive Swinging / Dec. 1964 / Mainstream ✦✦✦

Back Again / May 23, 1978–May 25, 1978 / Sonet ✦✦✦✦

● **Bob Brookmeyer Small Band, Vols. 1 & 2** / Jul. 28, 1978–Jul. 29, 1978 / Gryphon ✦✦✦✦
Live at Sandy's in Beverly, MA, in 1978. With Michael Moore (b), Jack Wilkins (g), Joe LaBarbera (d). Mostly standards, some music of Andy Laverne. Two Brookmeyer originals. All arrangements by Brookmeyer. Fine group effort. but out-of-print two-LP set —*Michael G. Nastos*

Dreams / Aug. 1988 / Dragon ✦✦

Oslo / Jan. 25, 1992 / Concord Jazz ✦✦✦

Roy Brooks

b. Sep. 3, 1938, Detroit, MI
Drums / Hard Bop
Roy Brooks is a flexible drummer able to play anything from bop to the avant-garde. He gained early experience gigging with Yusef Lateef and became known for his period with the Horace Silver Quintet (1959–64). During the next few years he played with a wide variety of top musicians including Pharoah Sanders, Wes Montgomery, Sonny Stitt, Jackie McLean, Dexter Gordon, Abdullah Ibrahim, Randy Weston, Charles Mingus, Milt Jackson and Lateef. In 1970 he became a founding member of Max Roach's M'Boom, an all-percussion group that allows him to play some musical saw. In 1976 Roy Brooks moved to Detroit where he became very involved in teaching jazz. He has continued performing to the present time and recorded a set of stimulating duets on Enja. —*Scott Yanow*

Beat / 1963 / Jazz Workshop ✦✦✦

● **The Free Slave** / Apr. 26, 1970 / Muse ✦✦✦✦
Recorded at Left Bank Jazz Society in Baltimore, Maryland, this

All Star quintet features George Coleman (ts), Woody Shaw (tpt), Hugh Lawson (p), Cecil McBee (b), and Brooks (d/per). There are four originals, all extended, with room to stretch for musicians. Wild club date. —*Michael G. Nastos*

The Smart Set / Apr. 12, 1979 / Baystate ✦✦✦

Duet in Detroit / Aug. 26, 1983–Feb. 25, 1989 / Enja ✦✦✦✦
This CD features drummer Roy Brooks (who also plays musical saw on one piece) on two duets apiece (recorded live over a period of six years) with trumpeter Woody Shaw and pianists Randy Weston, Don Pullen and Geri Allen. The music is full of surprises and generally holds one's interest with the trumpet-drums duets being the most unusual. —*Scott Yanow*

Tina Brooks (Harold Floyd Brooks)

b. Jun. 7, 1932, Fayetteville, NC, **d.** Aug. 13, 1974, New York, NY
Tenor Saxophone / Hard Bop
A fine hard bop tenor player who after a burst of activity largely faded out of jazz in 1962 (due to continual drug problems), Tina Brooks never reached his potential but did record some rewarding music. He made his recording debut in 1951 on four titles with Sonny Thompson's R&B band. After time spent touring with Amos Milburn and Lionel Hampton and freelancing in New York, Brooks began to record for Blue Note in 1958. In addition to four sessions as a leader cut between 1958–61, he appeared on Blue Note dates as a sideman with Jimmy Smith, Kenny Burrell, Freddie Hubbard, Freddie Redd, Jackie McLean and with Howard McGhee on Felsted. But his last session was on June 17, 1961 and, although he continued playing (mostly Latin and R&B jobs in New York), Brooks let his drug habit ruin his life. He died of kidney failure when he was 42. Ironically Tina Brooks is probably better-known now (due to the release of a definitive Mosaic four-LP box set) than he was in his lifetime. —*Scott Yanow*

● **Complete Blue Note Recordings** / Mar. 16, 1958–Mar. 2, 1961 / Mosaic ✦✦✦✦✦
A tenor saxophonist with four different bands, including Lee Morgan, Freddie Hubbard, Blue Mitchell, and Johnny Coles (trumpets). Also Jackie McLean. Trios led by pianists Sonny Clark, Duke Jordan, and Kenny Drew. Fifteen Brooks originals, seven standards. Brooks was an unsung hero. His work deserves your investigation. —*Michael G. Nastos*

Peter Brotzmann

b. Mar. 6, 1941, Remschied, Germany
Tenor Saxophone, Baritone Saxophone, Bass Saxophone / Free Jazz, Avant-Garde
This tenor saxophonist was a longtime champion of Europe's avant-garde, and a self-taught saxophonist famous for animated, swirling solos and lengthy, twisting dialogues. Brotzmann played initially in local Dixieland bands in Germany, then was an early member of The Fluxus movement and began playing free jazz by 1964. A year later, Brotzmann, Peter Kowald and Seven-Ake Johannsson formed a group. Brotzmann toured Europe in 1966 with a quintet that included Mike Mantler and Carla Bley. He also began working with The Globe Unity Orchestra, and continued with them until 1981. Brotzmann was a founder of the cooperative FMP in 1969, an organization that sponsors and issues free jazz releases. He also founded a trio with Han Bennink and Fred Van Hove that became extremely influential through its blend of European theater and folk music and African rhythms. Van Hove left the group in 1976, but continued playing with Bennink until 1979. During the '80s his associations included Harry Miller, Louis Moholo, Willie Kellers, Andrew Cyrille, the Alarm Orchestra, Cecil Taylor and Last Exit. Among the most ferocious of the free jazz players, Peter Brotzmann has also recorded on baritone, bass sax, clarinet, alto, soprano and bass clarinet. —*Ron Wynn*

● **For Adolphe Sax** / Jun. 1967 / FMP ✦✦✦✦✦

Machine Gun / Mar. 28, 1968 / FMP ✦✦✦

Balls / Aug. 17, 1970 / FMP ✦✦✦

Outspan No. 1 / Apr. 14, 1974–Apr. 15, 1974 / FMP ✦✦✦

Outspan No. 2 / May 4, 1974 / FMP ✦✦✦

Solo / May 1976 / FMP ✦✦✦

Three Points and a Mountain / Jan. 26, 1979 / FMP ✦✦✦

The Nearer the Bone, The Sweeter The Meat / Aug. 27, 1979 / FMP ✦✦✦✦

Opened, But Hardly Touched / Nov. 5, 1980–Nov. 6, 1980 / FMP ✦✦✦

Pica Pica / Sep. 18, 1982 / FMP ✦✦✦

14 Love Poems / Aug. 21, 1984–Aug. 23, 1984 / FMP ✦✦✦

Berlin Djungle / Nov. 4, 1984 / FMP ✦✦✦

Low Life / Jan. 3, 1987–Jan. 6, 1987 / Celluloid ✦✦✦

Reserve / Nov. 4, 1988 / FMP ✦✦✦

No Nothing / Dec. 14, 1990–Dec. 15, 1990 / FMP ✦✦✦

Dare Devil / Oct. 9, 1991 / DIW ✦✦✦

Clifford Brown

b. Oct. 30, 1930, Wilmington, DE, **d.** Jun. 26, 1956, PA
Trumpet / Hard Bop
Clifford Brown's death in a car accident at the age of 25 was one of the great tragedies in jazz history. Already ranking with Dizzy Gillespie and Miles Davis as one of the top trumpeters in jazz, Brownie was still improving in 1956. Plus he was a clean liver and was not even driving; the up-and-coming pianist Richie Powell and his wife (who was driving) also perished in the crash.

Clifford Brown accomplished a great deal in the short time he had. He started on trumpet when he was 15 and by 1948 was playing regularly in Philadelphia. Fats Navarro, who was his main influence, encouraged Brown as did Charlie Parker and Dizzy Gillespie. After a year at Maryland State University he was in a serious car accident in June 1950 that put him out of action for a year. In 1952 Brown made his recording debut with Chris Powell's Blue Flames (an R&B group). The following year he spent some time with Tadd Dameron and from August to December was with Lionel Hampton's band, touring Europe and leading some recording sessions. In early 1954 he recorded some brilliant solos at Birdland with Art Blakey's quintet (a band that directly preceded the Jazz Messengers) and by mid-year had formed a quintet with Max Roach. Considered one of the premiere hard bop bands, the group lasted until Brown's death, featuring Harold Land (and later Sonny Rollins) on tenor and recording several superb sets for EmArcy. Just hours before his death, Brownie appeared at a Philadelphia jam session that was miraculously recorded and played some of the finest music of his short life.

Clifford Brown had a fat warm tone, a boppish style quite reminiscent of the equally ill-fated Fats Navarro and a mature improvising approach; he was as inventive on melodic ballads as he was on rapid jams. Amazingly enough, a filmed appearance of him playing two songs in 1955 on a Soupy Sales variety show has recently turned up after being lost for 40 years, the only known footage of the great trumpeter. Fortunately, virtually all of his recordings are currently available including his Prestige dates (in the OJC series), his work for Blue Note and Pacific Jazz (on a four-CD set) and his many EmArcy sessions (reissued on a magnificent ten-disc set). But the one to pick up first is Columbia's *The Beginning and the End* which has Brown's first and last recordings. —*Scott Yanow*

★ **The Beginning and the End** / Mar. 21, 1952+Jun. 25, 1956 / Columbia ✦✦✦✦✦
Side One has his earliest recordings of some Caribbean-influenced R&B material; Side Two is a live recording of his last performance, the night before he died. It includes the famous "Donna Lee" solo and is a touching tribute album. —*David Nelson McCarthy*

Complete Blue Note-Pacific Jazz / Jun. 9, 1953–Aug. 13, 1954 / Pacific Jazz ✦✦✦✦✦
This four-CD set has the exact same music as an earlier Mosaic five-LP box, but is highly recommended to those listeners not already possessing the limited-edition set. Trumpeter Clifford Brown is heard on the most significant recordings from the first half of his tragically brief career. Whether co-leading a date with altoist Lou Donaldson, playing as a sideman with trombonist J.J. Johnson, interacting with an all-star group of West Coast players or jamming with the first (although unofficial) edition of Art Blakey's Jazz Messengers (a two-disc live performance with a quintet that also includes the drummer/leader, Donaldson and pianist Horace Silver), Brownie is the main star. Highlights are many, including versions of "Brownie Speaks," Elmo Hope's "De-Dah," "Cherokee," "Get Happy," "Daahoud" and "Joy Spring." The attractive packaging, with its 40 pages of text and many rare pictures, is an added bonus. —*Scott Yanow*

Clifford Brown Memorial Album, Vol. 1 / Jun. 11, 1953 Sep. 15, 1953 / Original Jazz Classics ✦✦✦

Clifford Brown Big Band in Paris / Sep. 28, 1953–Oct. 11, 1953 / Original Jazz Classics ✦✦✦
Although Lionel Hampton forbid his sidemen from recording during their trip to France in 1953, many of the musicians fortunately ignored his orders; the band broke up soon anyway. Trumpeter Clifford Brown is heard on this LP mostly with a big band actually put together by Gigi Gryce. A few of these tracks are excerpts but the two takes of "Brownskins" and "Keeping up with Jonesy" are fairly long as is a nearly eight-minute "Chez Moi." The music is not essential but Brownie did not live long enough to record anything less than excellent. —*Scott Yanow*

The Clifford Brown Sextet in Paris / Sep. 29, 1953+Oct. 8, 1953 / Original Jazz Classics ✦✦✦✦
Despite the fact that Lionel Hampton forbid the sidemen in his big band to record while visiting Paris in 1953, an awful lot of records resulted. Trumpeter Clifford Brown, who also recorded in a quartet and a big band during this busy period, is easily the star of this sextet set which also includes altoist Gigi Gryce (who contributed some of the originals), guitarist Jimmy Gourley and a French rhythm section led by pianist Henri Renaud. "Minority" and "Salute to the Band Box" are most memorable on this solid early hard-bop date. —*Scott Yanow*

Clifford Brown Quartet in Paris / Oct. 15, 1953 / Original Jazz Classics ✦✦✦✦
This CD is most highly recommended to the true Clifford Brown collector. The great trumpeter only performs six songs but there are also six alternate takes. Backed by a quiet French rhythm section (pianist Henri Renaud, bassist Pierre Michelot and drummer Benny Bennett), Brownie is in excellent form throughout this set, particularly on the two takes of "The Song Is You," and a superb version of "It Might as Well be Spring." —*Scott Yanow*

The Best of Max Roach and Clifford Brown in Concert / Apr. 1954+Aug. 30, 1954 / GNP ✦✦✦

Jazz Immortal / Jul. 11, 1954–Aug. 13, 1954 / Pacific Jazz ✦✦✦

Brown and Roach, Inc. / Aug. 2, 1954–Aug. 6, 1954 / EmArcy ✦✦✦

☆ **Brownie: The Complete EmArcy Recordings of Clifford Brown** / Aug. 2, 1954–Feb. 16, 1956 / EmArcy ✦✦✦✦✦
Comprehensive multi-disc set that contains Clifford Brown's output for the EmArcy label. This is wonderful material, particularly the sessions by the quintet Brown co-led with Max Roach. But he's also heard here with big bands, backing Dinah Washington, and on other occasions outside the quintet. Brown's tone, speed, command, and phrasing were immaculate and amazing; had he lived past his mid-20s, he certainly would have become an icon, and he's still influenced hosts of players anyhow. —*Ron Wynn*

Best Coast Jazz / Aug. 11, 1954 / EmArcy ✦✦✦

Clifford Brown with Strings / Jan. 18, 1955–Jan. 20, 1955 / EmArcy ✦✦

A Study in Brown / Feb. 23, 1955–Feb. 25, 1955 / EmArcy ✦✦✦

Live at the Bee Hive / Nov. 7, 1955 / Columbia ✦✦
On first glance this two-LP set should be a classic. Recorded at a Chicago jam session, trumpeter Clifford Brown, drummer Max Roach and their regular bassist George Morrow meet up for the initial time with the great tenor Sonny Rollins (who was emerging from his first retirement); other participants include Nicky Hill on tenor, pianist Billy Wallace and guitarist Leo Blevins. They are heard stretching out on lengthy versions of five bop standards but unfortunately the recording quality is horrendous. The drums are way overmiked, often making the rest of the rhythm section inaudible. There is some strong playing from the horns (particularly Brownie) but this record is very difficult to listen to, making it only of historical interest. —*Scott Yanow*

At Basin Street / Jan. 4, 1956–Feb. 16, 1956 / EmArcy ✦✦✦✦

Pure Genius / 1956 / Elektra ✦✦✦

Donald Brown

b. 1954, Hernando, MI
Piano / Hard Bop
A fine pianist and an educator, Donald Brown has also been a prolific composer. He grew up in Memphis and actually started out on drums and trumpet. By the time he attended Memphis

State University (1972–75) he was playing jazz piano. After years of local work Brown replaced James Williams with the Jazz Messengers (1981–82) before arthritis forced him to leave. He has since taught at Berklee (1983–85) and the University of Tennessee (starting in 1988), recorded albums as a leader for Sunnyside and Muse, and had his compositions performed and recorded by a wide variety of top modern jazz players. —*Scott Yanow*

Early Bird / Jun. 4, 1987–Jun. 5, 1987 / Sunnyside ✦✦✦✦
Pianist Donald Brown, who has been often overshadowed by his contemporaries, is a talented modern mainstream pianist with a sound of his own. This CD, his debut as a leader, features Brown in a sextet that also stars altoist Donald Harrison (quite explorative), trumpeter Bill Mobley, vibraphonist Steve Nelson and Wynton Marsalis' rhythm section of the time (bassist Bob Hurst and drummer Jeff "Tain" Watts). Together they perform six of Brown's diverse and generally colorful originals plus "Speak Low" and the pianist's solo showcase "If You Could See Me Now." It's an impressive and easily enjoyable outing. —*Scott Yanow*

The Sweetest Sounds / Jun. 1988 / Jazz City ✦✦✦

Sources of Inspiration / Aug. 11, 1989 / Muse ✦✦✦✦
With the exception of "Embraceable You" (one of two songs on this CD that are "bonus" cuts not on the LP version), pianist Donald Brown wrote all of the material. The strong quintet (which also features Eddie Henderson and altoist Gary Bartz) really digs into the diverse originals which are often reminiscent of a Blue Note date circa 1967. —*Scott Yanow*

People Music / Mar. 19, 1990–Mar. 21, 1990 / Muse ✦✦✦
Fine '90 date by a Memphis pianist. He plays nice bluesy chords and gospel-influenced phrases, but is also an effective straight-ahead and hard bop improviser. He's backed by a large group that features an interesting configuration with a trumpet/alto sax/vibes front line, and also uses vocals at times. Vincent Herring plays with fire on alto, while Steve Nelson adds a different dimension on vibes. —*Ron Wynn*

Cause & Effect / Aug. 16, 1991–Aug. 18, 1991 / Muse ✦✦✦

Send One Your Love / Jun. 29, 1992–Jun. 30, 1992 / Muse ✦✦✦✦
Pianist Donald Brown continues to play with authority, bluesy edge and gusto, and his writing remains intriguing, even though only three of the nine numbers on this disc are originals. Instead, he displays his ability to interpret and lead his group through quality versions of classics by Benny Golson ("Whisper Not") and Barry Harris ("Crazeology"), plus a contemporary number from Mulgrew Miller ("The Sequel"). Brown's playing on Stevie Wonder's title track and the standards "The Second Time Around" and "The Sweetest Sounds" caresses the melody, then takes off and presents his impressive variations and statements. —*Ron Wynn*

● **Cartunes** / Sep. 2, 1993 / Muse ✦✦✦✦

Jeri Brown

b. MS
Vocals / Standards, Bop
One of the finest jazz singers, the Montreal-based Jeri Brown came from a musical family (her grandfather played sax and her uncle was a trumpeter). After growing up in St. Louis and graduating college, she toured Europe singing light opera and spirituals before switching to jazz. An excellent scat singer and an expressive interpreter of lyrics, Jeri Brown has recorded several excellent sets for Justin Time. —*Scott Yanow*

Mirage / Feb. 19, 1991 / Justin Time ✦✦✦

● **Unfolding The Peacocks** / Feb. 1992 / Justin Time ✦✦✦✦✦
A talented improviser blessed with a lovely voice and a wide range, Jeri Brown's expressive powers are heard at their best on this set during her lengthy wordless interplay with Michel Dubeau's flute on "The Peacocks" and on the two bop-era standards "If You Could See Me Now" and "Woody 'n You." Backed by pianist Kirk Lightsey, guitarist Peter Leitch, bassist Rufus Reid and drummer Wali Muhammad, Brown does overwhelm "Orange Colored Sky" a bit to humorous effect but otherwise is in superlative form throughout the impressive date. —*Scott Yanow*

Lawrence Brown

b. Aug. 3, 1907, Lawrence, KS, **d.** Sep. 5, 1988, Los Angeles, CA
Trombone / Swing
One of the great swing trombonists, Lawrence Brown tends to be

underrated because he spent so much of his career with Duke Ellington's Orchestra. Actually Brown's initial solos with Ellington upset some of Duke's fans because it was feared that his virtuosity did not fit into a band where primitive effects and mutes were liberally utilized. But over time Brown carved out his own place in the Ellington legacy.

Lawrence Brown learned piano, violin and tuba before deciding to stick to the trombone. He recorded with Paul Howard's Quality Serenaders (1929–30) and Louis Armstrong (with Les Hite's Orchestra in 1930) in Los Angeles before joining Ellington in 1932, staying until 1951 when he left to join Johnny Hodges' new small group. After 1955 Brown became a studio musician in New York but then spent 1960–70 back with Ellington (where he reluctantly had to play some solos with a plunger mute) before retiring. Although he only led two albums of his own (a 1955–56 outing for Clef and 1965's *Inspired Abandon* for Impulse!), Brown was well-featured on many recordings with Ellington through the years; "The Sheik of Araby" (1932) and "Rose of the Rio Grande" (1938) were favorites. —*Scott Yanow*

Inspired Abandon / Mar. 8, 1965 / Impulse! ✦✦✦✦

Les Brown

b. Mar. 14, 1912, Reinerton, PA
Leader / Swing
The leader of a first-class jazz-oriented dance band for nearly 60 years, Les Brown's music was never innovative but was generally quite pleasing. While attending Duke University in 1935 he put together his first big band, the Duke Blue Devils. After the group broke up in 1936, Brown worked as an arranger before forming a permanent orchestra in 1938. Influenced by the swing of Benny Goodman but gradually forging its own sound, the Les Brown Orchestra had major hits in "Sentimental Journey" (featuring Doris Day in 1944) and a catchy arrangement of "I've Got My Love to Keep Me Warm." Several excellent soloists spent time with the band (including Abe Most and Ted Nash). In 1947 Brown started working with Bob Hope and the association, although putting the band in a subsidiary role, made it possible for the orchestra to stay together for so many decades. The Dave Pell Octet, which was quite popular in the mid-'50s, was comprised of some of Brown's sidemen. —*Scott Yanow*

Les Brown And His Great Vocalists / Jul. 1, 1941–Nov. 14, 1950 / Columbia ✦✦✦

● **Best of the Big Bands** / Sep. 17, 1941–Mar. 14, 1961 / Columbia ✦✦✦✦

The Uncollected Les Brown & His Orchestra, Vol. 1 (1944–1946) / 1944–1946 / Hindsight ✦✦✦
Top-rate big-band swing from the man who backed Bob Hope and discovered Doris Day. —*David Szatmary*

The Uncollected Les Brown & His Orchestra, Vol. 2 (1949) / 1949 / Hindsight ✦✦✦

The Uncollected Les Brown & His Orchestra, Vol. 3 (1949) / 1949 / Hindsight ✦✦✦

Lullaby In Rhythm / Dec. 1954–Jan. 1955 / Drive Archive ✦✦✦
Les Brown had one of his finest big bands during the mid-'50s but the previously unissued live performances heard on this CD are more notable for being among the first stereo recordings than for their musical content. The 14 selections (mostly veteran swing standards) are given overly concise interpretations and the danceable arrangements allocate relatively little space for solos. Trumpeter Don Fagerquist's three choruses on "Our Love Is Here to Stay" are a highlight while Jo Ann Greer does a good job on her three straightforward vocals. —*Scott Yanow*

Les Brown All-Stars / Jun. 15, 1955–Jun. 27, 1955 / Capitol ✦✦✦✦

22 Original Big Band Recordings (1957) / 1957 / Vanguard ✦✦✦

Les Brown And His Band Of Renown / 1957 / Hindsight ✦✦
Although Les Brown gets top billing on this set of 1957 radio airchecks, his big band actually functions as a backup orchestra for singers Julie London, Jo Ann Greer, June Christy and (on "Oh Baby") bandmember Stumpy Brown; only "My Baby Just Cares for Me" is an instrumental. Each of the vocalists are in fine form with Greer holding her own with the better-known Christy and London. Since most of these selections are only about two minutes long, the band has little to do other than read its parts, so this CD is recommended mostly to fans of the singers. —*Scott Yanow*

Digital Swing / Nov. 21, 1986–Jan. 27, 1959 / Fantasy ✦✦✦
Anything Goes / 1990 / USA Music Group ✦✦

Marion Brown

b. Sep. 8, 1935, Atlanta, GA
Flute, Alto Saxophone / Free Jazz, Avant-Garde
One of the brightest and most lyrical voices of the 1960s avant-garde, Marion Brown participated in many stimulating recordings during the '60s and '70s while never really becoming an influential force. He played alto in high school and in Army bands and attended Clark College. In 1965 Brown moved to New York and recorded the monumental *Ascension* with John Coltrane and *Fire Music* with Archie Shepp. Soon Brown was leading his own dates for ESP and Impulse!. He worked with Sun Ra, lived in Europe during 1968–70 and in the early '70s in the U.S. played with Leo Smith. Since recording with Gunter Hampel in 1983 and making an unaccompanied solo date in 1985, ill health has limited Marion Brown's musical activities. —*Scott Yanow*

Marion Brown Quartet / Nov. 1965 / ESP ✦✦✦✦
Why Not? / Oct. 23, 1966 / ESP ✦✦✦
Juba-Lee / Nov. 1966 / Fontana ✦✦✦
● **Three for Shepp** / Dec. 1, 1966 / Impulse! ✦✦✦✦✦
Porto Nova / Dec. 13, 1967 / Arista ✦✦✦
Afternoon of a Georgia Faun / Aug. 10, 1970 / ECM ✦✦✦
Vista / Feb. 18, 1975–Feb. 19, 1975 / Impulse! ✦✦
Altoist Marion Brown, one of the potentially great high-energy saxophonists to emerge in the mid-'60s (he was on John Coltrane's famous *Ascension* record), has had somewhat of a directionless career. This out-of-print LP certainly boasts an impressive backup crew (including both Anthony Davis and Stanley Cowell on keyboards along with bassist Reggie Workman and some appearances by drummer Ed Blackwell) but does not seem to know what it wants to be. The solos are relatively short, there is a poppish vocal by Allen Murphy on a Stevie Wonder tune and little that is all that memorable actually occurs. Better to acquire Marion Brown's earlier recordings. —*Scott Yanow*

La Placita / Live in Willisau / Mar. 26, 1977 / Timeless ✦✦✦
Reed 'n Vibes / Jan. 30, 1978 / IAI ✦✦✦✦
Back to Paris / Feb. 14, 1980 / Freelance ✦✦✦
At La Dreher in Paris. Quartet with pianist Hilton Ruiz. Excellent, moving music. —*Michael G. Nastos*
Gemini / Jun. 13, 1983 / Birth ✦✦✦
Recollections: Ballads and Blues for Saxophone / Jan. 23, 1985 / Creative Works ✦✦✦
Native Land / Mar. 9, 1990–Mar. 10, 1990 / ITM ✦✦

Norman Brown

b. Kansas City, MO
Guitar / R&B, Soul Jazz
One of the first artists signed to Motown's jazz division, Norman Brown has issued *Just Between Us*, a fusion and contemporary jazz session. The keyboardist and composer has also done R&B and pop dates, and his album mixes these styles, with guest stints from Kirk Whalum, Gerald Albright, Ronnie Laws, Stevie Wonder and Boyz II Men. —*Ron Wynn*

Just Between Us / 1992 / Mojazz ✦✦✦
● **After the Storm** / 1994 / MoJazz ✦✦✦

Oscar Brown, Jr.

b. Oct. 10, 1926, Chicago, IL
Vocals, Lyricist / Bop, Standards
The multi-talented Oscar Brown, Jr. has written several classic pieces including the lyrics to "Dat Dere," "Work Song," "Watermelon Man" and "The Entertainer" (the latter a bittersweet biography of Scott Joplin) and the compositions "Signifyin' Monkey" and "But I Was Cool." An important social commentator and playwright, Oscar Brown, Jr. acted on a regular network radio soap opera while in high school. After a wide variety of careers (including public relations, real estate, ad copy and running unsuccessfully for political office), he became a professional songwriter, starting with "Brown Baby" (which was recorded by Mahalia Jackson) and collaborating with Max Roach on the "Freedom Now Suite." A dramatic singer, Brown was signed to

Columbia in 1960 where he recorded several classic albums. In 1962 he was the M.C. on the legendary *Jazz Scene USA* television series (some episodes of which have been made available on video). Brown has performed and written many shows through the years and served as artist-in-residence at several colleges. After recording steadily, he was off records altogether during 1975-94 until returning with *Then & Now* for the Weasel Disc label in 1995, a disc full of both fresh remakes and new material. —*Scott Yanow*

Sin & Soul / Jun. 20, 1960-Oct. 23, 1960 / Columbia ✦✦✦✦✦
● **Then & Now** / 1995 / Weasel ✦✦✦✦✦

Ray Brown

b. Oct. 13, 1926, Pittsburgh, PA
Bass / Bop
The huge and comfortable sound of Ray Brown's bass has been a welcome feature on loop-oriented sessions for a half-century. He played locally in his native Pittsburgh in his early days.

Arriving in New York in 1945, on his first day in town Brown met and played with Dizzy Gillespie, Charlie Parker and Bud Powell! He was hired by Gillespie for his small groups and his big band; "One Bass Hit" and "Two Bass Hit" were early features and he can be seen with Dizzy in the 1947 film *Jiving in Bebop*. Although not a soloist on the level of an Oscar Pettiford, Brown's quick reflexes and ability to accompany soloists in a swinging fashion put him near the top of his field. After playing with Jazz at the Philharmonic, he married Ella Fitzgerald (their marriage only lasted during 1948-52) and for a time led his own trio to back the singer. Brown recorded with an early version of the Modern Jazz Quartet (under Milt Jackson's leadership) and then became a permanent member of the Oscar Peterson Trio (1951-66).

With Peterson the bassist travelled the world, guested with other top jazz artists, was featured on JATP tours, became famous and recorded constantly. He began playing cello in the late '50s and used it on a few of his own dates. After leaving Peterson, Brown settled in Los Angeles, worked in the studios, continued recording jazz and worked as a manager of several artists (including the Modern Jazz Quartet and Quincy Jones). He played with the L.A. 4 starting in 1974, did a great deal to revive the careers of Ernestine Anderson and Gene Harris and recorded extensively for Pablo and Concord. The Ray Brown Trio of the 1990s features pianist Benny Green and drummer Greg Hutchison and has recorded for Telarc. —*Scott Yanow*

This One's for Blanton / Dec. 5, 1972 / Original Jazz Classics ✦✦✦✦
One of Duke Ellington's last small-group sessions (which is mistakenly dated on this album as Dec. 5, 1973), this is a set of duets between the pianist and bassist Ray Brown. Performed in tribute to bassist Jimmy Blanton, the duo plays "See See Rider," four of Ellington's standards (including "Pitter Panter Patter" which was originally recorded as an Ellington-Blanton duet) and the four movements of "Fragmented Suite for Piano and Bass." Brown's solid swing and large tone bring out the best in Ellington's playing, making this an easily enjoyable and consistently swinging date. —*Scott Yanow*

Brown's Bag / Dec. 1975 / Concord Jazz ✦✦✦
Good, occasionally exciting combo set with some pithy trumpet solos by Blue Mitchell, good tenor sax from Kamauca, and generally excellent playing by all involved, even fusion ace Dave Grusin on piano. —*Ron Wynn*

Something for Lester / Jun. 22, 1977-Jun. 197 / Original Jazz Classics ✦✦✦
This excellent trio session forms a sort of transition between bassist Ray Brown's work with the Oscar Peterson Trio and his own small group sessions of the '80s and '90s. With pianist Cedar Walton and drummer Elvin Jones, Brown explores seven strong melodies (four standards, two by Walton and the bassist's "Slippery") in typically swinging and bluish fashion. —*Scott Yanow*

As Good As It Gets / Dec. 22, 1977 / Concord Jazz ✦✦✦

Live at the Concord Jazz Festival / Aug. 1979 / Concord Jazz ✦✦✦✦

Tasty / Oct. 1979 / Concord Jazz ✦✦✦

Ray Brown Three / Feb. 1982 / Concord Jazz ✦✦✦
Brown took a fresh approach for this 1982 date, retaining the trio

format but substituting flute for drums and using Monty Alexander instead of regular pianist Gene Harris. The results were intriguing; most provided colors and sounds that haven't been on a Brown date since, while Alexander added some Caribbean flavor and a bit more adventurous sound. —*Ron Wynn*

Bye Bye Blackbird / Apr. 11, 1984 / Paddle Wheel ✦✦

Soular Energy / Aug. 1984 / Concord Jazz ✦✦✦✦

Don't Forget the Blues / May 1985 / Concord Jazz ✦✦✦

The Red Hot Ray Brown Trio / Nov. 12, 1985 / Concord Jazz ✦✦✦

Summer Wind: the Ray Brown Trio Live at The Loa / Jul. 1988 / Concord Jazz ✦✦✦

Summer Wind / Jul. 1988 / Concord Jazz ✦✦✦✦
Brown's trio with Gene Harris (k) and Jeff Hamilton (d). Perhaps Brown's very best. —*Michael G. Nastos*

Bam Bam Bam / Dec. 1988 / Concord Jazz ✦✦✦

Super Bass / 1989 / Capri ✦✦✦

Black Orpheus / 1989 / Evidence ✦✦✦✦
Whether accompanying or leading a band, bassist Ray Brown has long been among jazz's greatest players. These cuts, mostly from 1989 except for two numbers done in 1991, feature Brown backing soulful pianist Gene Harris and steady drummer Jeff Hamilton on a program combining Afro-Latin material with standards from Johnny Mercer, Fats Waller and others, as well as an excellent rendition of Percy Mayfield's blues/R&B standard "Please Send Me Someone to Love." The songs are long enough to display each musician's skills, but not so lengthy that they become repetitious. It's a well-played, delightful example of the kind of high-powered material that's been Ray Brown's stock-in-trade. —*Ron Wynn*

Moore Makes 4 / May 22, 1990 / Concord Jazz ✦✦✦
Prime release in which Brown departed from his usual trio format and added tenor saxophonist Ralph Moore. Although it seemed like a snap decision, Moore put some edge and juice in the session and even relaxed stars Brown and pianist Gene Harris, and drummer Jeff Hamilton seemed to appreciate the lift. —*Ron Wynn*

New Two Bass Hits / Apr. 29, 1991 / Capri ✦✦✦

Three Dimensional / Aug. 4, 1991 / Concord Jazz ✦✦✦
Excellent trio date with Brown's formidable bass interaction with drummer Jeff Hamilton and pianist Gene Harris. Harris plays with his usual bluesy punch and delicate touch, while Hamilton fits like a glove with Brown. This is heady, solidly professional material. —*Ron Wynn*

Bass Face / Apr. 1993 / Telarc ✦✦✦
For this Telarc CD, bassist Ray Brown and pianist Benny Green split the solo chores almost evenly with drummer Jeff Hamilton, giving them stellar and creative support. Green has his best improvisations on "Phineas Can Be" and "Taking a Chance on Love" and the trio plays very close attention to dynamics (often swinging very quietly) and quickly reacting to each other's ideas. Rather than merely jamming the songs (the majority of which are standards), the bop-oriented group gives each melody a colorful framework filled with plenty of subtle surprises. —*Scott Yanow*

● **Don't Get Sassy** / Apr. 21, 1994-Apr. 22, 1994 / Telarc ✦✦✦✦

Some Of My Best Friends Are ... The Piano Players / Nov. 18, 1994+Nov. 21, 1994 / Telarc ✦✦✦
On his Telarc disc Ray Brown teams up with five different piano players but, rather than this being a tribute to the veteran bassist (who has solo space on every selection), the CD ends up being a celebration of the great Oscar Peterson because Benny Green, Dado Moroni and Geoff Keezer have, to various degrees, based their styles on O.P. The individual standout is actually Ahmad Jamal, who had never previously recorded with Brown. Together with Lewis Nash they perform two blues and "Love Walked In," all renditions that make a liberal use of space and pay close attention to dynamics. Benny Green, who plays his "Ray of Light" along with two standards, had performed regularly with Brown in recent years and his selections offer few surprises. Dodo Moroni is fine on "My Romance" and inserts a bit of Erroll Garner on "Giant Steps" while Geoff Keezer (who had also never played with Brown) swings well on "Close Your Eyes." The CD concludes with a reunion between Oscar Peterson (who had recently recovered from a stroke) and Brown on "St. Tropez" and the upbeat "How Come You Do Me like You Do?" The results overall are pleasing

and swinging (serving as a sampler of the pianists' styles) but not all that innovative. — *Scott Yanow*

Dave Brubeck

b. Dec. 6, 1920, Concord, CA
Piano, Leader, Composer / Cool

Dave Brubeck has long served as proof that creative jazz and popular success can go together. Although critics who had championed him when he was unknown seemed to scorn him when the Dave Brubeck Quartet became a surprise success, in reality Brubeck never watered down or altered his music in order to gain a wide audience. Creative booking (being one of the first groups to play regularly on college campuses) and a bit of luck resulted in great popularity and Dave Brubeck today remains as one of the few household names in jazz.

From nearly the start Brubeck enjoyed utilizing polyrhythms and polytonality (playing in two keys at once). He had classical training from his mother but fooled her for a long period by memorizing his lessons and not learning to read music. Dave studied music at the College of the Pacific during 1938–42. Brubeck led a service band in General Patton's Army during World War II, and then in 1946 he started studying at Mills College with the classical composer Darius Milhaud, who encouraged his students to play jazz. Brubeck led a group mostly consisting of fellow classmates and they recorded as the Dave Brubeck Octet; their music (released on Fantasy in 1951) still sounds advanced today with complex time signatures and some polytonality. The octet was too radical to get much work so Brubeck formed a trio with drummer Cal Tjader (who doubled on vibes) and bassist Ron Crotty. The trio's Fantasy recordings of 1949–51 were quite popular in the Bay Area but the group came to an end when Brubeck hurt his back during a serious swimming accident and was put out of action for months.

Upon his return in 1951, Brubeck was persuaded by altoist Paul Desmond to make the group a quartet. Within two years the band had become surprisingly popular. Desmond's cool-toned alto and quick wit fit in well with Brubeck's often heavy chording and experimental playing; both Brubeck and Desmond had original sounds and styles that owed little to their predecessors. Joe Dodge was the band's early drummer but after he tired of the road the virtuosic Joe Morello took his place in 1956 while the revolving bass chair finally settled on Eugene Wright in 1958. By then Brubeck had followed his popular series of Fantasy recordings with some big sellers on Columbia and had appeared on the cover of *Time* (1954). The huge success of Paul Desmond's "Take Five" (1960) was followed by many songs played in "odd" time signatures such as 7/4 and 9/8; the high-quality soloing of the musicians kept these experiments from sounding like gimmicks. Dave and Iola Brubeck (his wife and lyricist) put together an anti-racism show featuring Louis Armstrong (*The Real Ambassadors*) which was recorded, but its only public appearance was at the Monterey Jazz Festival in the early '60s.

The Dave Brubeck Quartet constantly travelled around the world until its breakup in 1967. After some time off during which he wrote religious works, Brubeck came back the following year with a new quartet featuring Gerry Mulligan, although he would have several reunions with Desmond before the altoist's death in 1977. Brubeck joined with his sons Darius (keyboards), Chris (electric bass and bass trombone) and Danny (drums) in Two Generations of Brubeck in the 1970s. In the early '80s tenor saxophonist Jerry Bergonzi was in the Brubeck Quartet and since the mid-'80s clarinetist Bill Smith (who was in the original Octet) has alternated with altoist Bobby Militello.

There is no shortage of Dave Brubeck records currently available, practically everything he has cut for Fantasy, Columbia, Concord and Telarc (his most recent label) are easy to locate. Brubeck, whose compositions "In Your Own Sweet Way," "The Duke" and "Blue Rondo a La Turk" have become standards, has remained very busy (despite some bouts of bad health) into the mid-'90s. — *Scott Yanow*

The Dave Brubeck Octet / 1946–Jul. 1950 / Original Jazz Classics ++++

On infrequent occasions during 1946–50, pianist Dave Brubeck led an octet that was dominated by students of the composer Darius Milhaud. This pioneering West Coast outfit combined bop with modern classical music to form an interesting new blend of styles but, since they only recorded one LP's worth of material (which has remained obscure through the decades), the octet's life and general influence were limited. With such players as trumpeter Dick Collins, altoist Paul Desmond, Bill Smith on clarinet and baritone, tenor saxophonist Dave Van Kreidt and a rhythm section comprised of Brubeck, bassist Ron Crotty and Cal Tjader

on drums, this fascinating group performs highly original music throughout this CD reissue. — *Scott Yanow*

● **Time Signatures: A Career Retrospective** / 1946–May 7, 1991 / Columbia ++++

This four-CD boxed set does a near-perfect job of summing up Dave Brubeck's extensive recorded legacy. Drawing its recordings from not only Columbia but Fantasy, Atlantic and Music Masters, the attractive package also includes an extensive booklet written by Doug Ramsey that can serve as a mini-biography. The focus is naturally on Brubeck's quartet with altoist Paul Desmond but there is also music from before and after their association, even including one otherwise unissued performance, a remarkable polytonal polyrhythmic version of "Tritonis." Although completists will prefer to acquire Dave Brubeck's individual releases, this set is perfect for those just beginning to explore the magic of his music. — *Scott Yanow*

24 Classic Original Recordings / Sep. 1949–Nov. 1950 / Fantasy ++++

During 1949–51 pianist Dave Brubeck led a San Francisco-based trio with bassist Ron Crotty and Cal Tjader doubling on drums and vibes. This double LP has all 24 of this group's recordings, interpretations of standards that are full of surprising moments. Even at this early stage, Brubeck had his own style and sounds nothing at all like Bud Powell, the dominant influence of the era. — *Scott Yanow*

Stardust / Aug. 1951–Jun. 1955 / Fantasy +++

This double LP features the Dave Brubeck Quartet in its early days. Although the dates are unaccountably left off of this two-fer, most of the music is from 1951–52 and features such short-term sidemen as bassists Norm Bates, Fred Dutton (who doubled on bassoon) and Wyatt "Bull" Reuther and drummers Herb Barman and Lloyd Davis in addition to pianist Brubeck and altoist Paul Desmond. Highlights include "Crazy Chris," "Lyons Busy," "Look for the Silver Lining" and "Alice in Wonderland." Two later selections ("Stardust" and a 14-1/2-minute version of "At a Perfume Counter") are from 1954–55 when the personnel stabilized with bassist Bob Bates and drummer Joe Dodge. — *Scott Yanow*

Modern Complex Diaglogues / Dec. 15, 1951–Jan. 24, 1952 / Alto ++

This bootleg LP contains music from several broadcasts from Birdland by the Dave Brubeck Quaartet with altoist Paul Desmond, bassist Wyatt Reuther and drummer Herb Barman. The recording quality is not the greatest but the music is generally quite worthwhile, not only giving listeners different versions of such songs as "At a Perfume Counter," "Crazy Chris" and "Stardust" but a rare example of the Brubeck Quartet playing "Jingle Bells." — *Scott Yanow*

Dave Brubeck and Paul Desmond / Sep. 1952–Mar. 30, 1954 / Fantasy +++

This two-LP set reissues two earlier Fantasy LPs titled *Jazz at the Black Hawk* and *Jazz at Storyville*. Pianist Dave Brubeck and altoist Paul Desmond are the two main constants while bassists Ron Crotty and Wyatt Ruther and drummers Lloyd Davis, Herb Barman and Joe Dodge are heard on some tracks. The many highpoints to this interesting set include Brubeck-Desmond duets on "Over the Rainbow" and "You Go to My Head," an unaccompanied piano solo on "My Heart Stood Still" and quartet versions of "Jeepers Creepers," "Trolley Song" and "Crazy Chris." — *Scott Yanow*

Jazz at Oberlin / Mar. 2, 1953 / Original Jazz Classics ++++

Featuring Paul Desmond in Concert / Mar. 2, 1953–Dec. 14, 1953 / Fantasy +++

The Art Of Dave Brubeck / Mar. 2, 1953–Dec. 14, 1953 / Atlantic ++++

Although taken from the Fantasy catalog, this two-LP set (which reissues *Jazz at Oberlin* and *Jazz at College of Pacific*) actually came out on Atlantic; the music has since been reissued on CD. Pianist Dave Brubeck and altoist Paul Desmond rarely sounded more adventurous together. On "These Foolish Things," Brubeck's percussive solo almost sounds like Cecil Taylor (who would not emerge for another two years) and the interplay between the two principals on "Perdido" is nearly miraculous. This is essential music in one form or another for every jazz collection. — *Scott Yanow*

Brubeck & Desmond at Wilshire-Ebell / Jun. 20, 1953 / Fantasy
◆◆◆
One of the rarest of all early Dave Brubeck recordings, this Fantasy LP features pianist Brubeck, altoist Paul Desmond, bassist Ron Crotty and drummer Lloyd Davis in top form on six standards. Although Brubeck would record most of this material again (including "Let's Fall in Love," "Stardust" and "All the Things You Are"), these versions are often quite a bit different than the more familiar recordings. There was plenty of magical interplay to be heard during that era between Brubeck and Desmond, making this set worth an extensive search. *—Scott Yanow*

Jazz at the College of the Pacific / Dec. 14, 1953 / Original Jazz Classics ◆◆◆
This was one of two live concerts featuring the Dave Brubeck quartet on college campuses in 1953. Pianist Brubeck's quartet was unique and was soon to become the rage with white America ...It was equally hip (and has remained so) for critics to say Brubeck didn't swing and suggest Desmond was wasting his talents...Nonsense. This group did swing, had emotional depth and great humor. *—Bob Rusch, Cadence*

Brubeck & Desmond: Jazz at Storyville (1954) / Dec. 1953-Jul. 22, 1954 / Columbia ◆◆◆
Taken from three separate occasions, this LP features the Dave Brubeck Quartet (with altoist Paul Desmond, drummer Joe Dodge and either Ron Crotty or Bob Bates on bass) romping through five standards and "Back Bay Blues." The beautiful cool tone of Desmond, although criticized by writers who felt that everyone should sound like Charlie Parker, was always a major asset to the Quartet, contrasting with the complex chord voicings of Brubeck; they made a perfect team. This long out-of-print LP is long overdue to be reissued on CD. *—Scott Yanow*

Jazz Collection / Mar. 9, 1954-1970 / Columbia ◆◆◆
This two-CD set gives one a fine overview of the Dave Brubeck Quartet during their years on Columbia. All of the 28 selections are available elsewhere so longtime collectors will want to skip this reissue, but those listeners just beginning to discover Brubeck's special music may want to acquire this set for a start. The main "hits" ("Take Five," "Blue Rondo A La Turk," etc.) are here but, even with guest appearances by Carmen McRae, Louis Armstrong, Charles Mingus and Jimmy Rushing (along with two later selections that have baritonist Gerry Mulligan in altoist Paul Desmond's place), the emphasis is very much on the classic Quartet. *—Scott Yanow*

Jazz Interwoven / Mar. 30, 1954-Jun. 1955 / Fantasy ◆◆◆
● **Jazz Goes to College** / Mar. 1954 / Columbia ◆◆◆◆◆
A true classic, this CD reissues the original LP. Altoist Paul Desmond's lengthy solo on the blues "Balcony Rock" was one of the greatest of his career with one fresh idea leading (through repetition and gradual development) logically into another; pianist Brubeck's improvisation on this piece almost reaches the heights of Desmond's. Bassist Bob Bates and drummer Joe Dodge give a solid and quiet accompaniment to Desmond and the unpredictable pianist/leader with other highlights including "Out of Nowhere," "The Song Is You" and "Don't Worry 'Bout Me." This is the Brubeck Quartet at its best. *—Scott Yanow*

Jazz: Red, Hot and Cool / Oct. 12, 1954-Aug. 8, 1955 / Columbia ◆◆◆
Recorded live at the Basin Street Club in New York, this LP (half of the contents have since been reissued on the CD *Interchanges '54*) is most notable for introducing Dave Brubeck's composition "The Duke." In addition the pianist/leader, altoist Paul Desmond, bassist Bob Bates and drummer Joe Dodge are in fine form on a variety of standards including "Little Girl Blue," "Sometimes I'm Happy" and "Love Walked In." *—Scott Yanow*

Brubeck Time / Oct. 1954-Nov. 1954 / Columbia ◆◆◆
This LP (which has been reissued on CD as part of *Interchanges '54*) introduced Paul Desmond's beautiful ballad "Audrey" and found the early Dave Brubeck Quartet (with pianist Brubeck, altoist Desmond, bassist Bob Bates and drummer Joe Dodge) making a rare studio recording, up to this point all of their most popular records were club performances. With fresh versions of such songs as "Jeepers Creepers," "Pennies from Heaven" and "A Fine Romance," this music is certainly worth acquiring. *—Scott Yanow*

Interchanges '54: Featuring Paul Desmond / Oct. 1954-Nov. 1954 / Columbia ◆◆◆
This excellent CD reissues the LP *Brubeck Time* plus half of *Red*

Hot and Cool. One of the few early studio (as opposed to club) recordings by the early Dave Brubeck Quartet (this version has bassist Bob Bates and drummer Joe Dodge in addition to pianist Brubeck and altoist Paul Desmond), the fine unit performs nine standards plus three new compositions: "Stompin' for Mili," "Audrey" (dedicated to Audrey Hepburn) and Brubeck's classic, "The Duke." *—Scott Yanow*

Brubeck Plays Brubeck / Mar. 1956-Apr. 1956 / Columbia ◆◆◆
Dave Brubeck has had a strikingly original style ever since he appeared on records, avoiding the usual Bud Powell runs and instead expressing his training in classical music and his interest in polyrhythms and polytonality while never forgetting to swing. On his first solo piano record, Brubeck not only plays quite well but introduces such new compositions as "In Your Own Sweet Way" and "One Moment Worth Years" in addition to performing a remake of "The Duke." Long out-of-print, it's still worth searching for. *—Scott Yanow*

Dave Brubeck And Jay & Kai At Newport / Jul. 6, 1956 / Columbia ◆◆◆
This historic LP finds the Dave Brubeck Quartet performing two standards ("Take the 'A' Train" and "I'm in a Dancing Mood") along with the pianist/leader's "In Your Own Sweet Way" and "Two-Part Contention." Altoist Paul Desmond is in fine form as is the supportive drummer Joe Dodge, who would soon leave the Quartet; Joe Morello was his eventual replacement. The second part of this LP is the final performance by the two-trombone J.J. Johnson-Kai Winding Quintet before they broke up after two years of steady work. Overall, this album gives one a good look at two of the most popular jazz groups of 1956. *—Scott Yanow*

Jazz Impressions of the U.S.A. / Nov. 16, 1956-Nov. 26, 1956 / Columbia ◆◆
For this new musical adventure, pianist Dave Brubeck wrote eight diverse songs, of which "Summer Song" would be the best-known. This out-of-print LP was the debut of drummer Joe Morello with Brubeck's Quartet, which at the time also featured altoist Joe Morello and bassist Norman Bates. Excellent music, although it's not quite as essential as their live performances of the era. *—Scott Yanow*

Plays and Plays And ... / Feb. 8, 1957 / Original Jazz Classics ◆◆◆
Dave Brubeck's second solo piano album differs from the first in that only two of the nine songs he performs are his originals. However Brubeck's versions of such standards as "Imagination," "Our Love Is Here to Stay" and "You'd Be So Nice to Come Home To" sound quite fresh and contain more than their share of surprises. Fortunately the formerly rare music is now available on this CD. *—Scott Yanow*

Reunion / Feb. 1957 / Original Jazz Classics ◆◆
Tenor saxophonist Dave Van Kreidt, a former member of Dave Brubeck's octet in the late '40s, had a reunion with the pianist, altoist Paul Desmond and bassist Bob Bates for this unusual session; Brubeck's new drummer Joe Morello made the group a quintet. Van Kreidt supplied all of the compositions (some of which are fairly complex), giving this set a sound very much different than the usual Brubeck Quartet outing. Interesting if not essential classical-influenced music that predates The Third Stream movement. *—Scott Yanow*

Jazz Goes to Junior College / May 1, 1957-May 2, 1957 / Columbia ◆◆◆◆

Dave Digs Disney / Jun. 29, 1957-Aug. 3, 1957 / Columbia/Legacy ◆◆◆
This CD contains the original LP of the same name plus two previously unissued songs ("Very Good Advice" and "So This Is Love"). Inspired by a trip with his family to Disneyland, Dave Brubeck recorded eight songs taken from four Disney movies (*Alice in Wonderland*, *Pinocchio*, *Snow White* and *Cinderella*), including such melodies as "Give a Little Whistle," "Heigh Ho," "When You Wish Upon a Star" and "Someday My Prince Will Come." The funny part is that all of these songs were already in the Brubeck Quartet's repertoire. The results are pleasing although, due to a misprint, the CD booklet only contains half of the original liner notes. *—Scott Yanow*

The Dave Brubeck Quartet in Europe / Mar. 3, 1958 / Columbia ◆◆◆
Although many people associate the Dave Brubeck Quartet's great

popularity with their recording of "Take Five," the band was actually a major attraction several years before cutting that hit record. This LP, recorded in concert in Copenhagen, finds the Quartet (which for the first time featured bassist Eugene Wright and drummer Joe Morello along with altoist Paul Desmond) performing such numbers as "Tangerine," "Like Someone in Love" and "Wonderful Copenhagen." —*Scott Yanow*

Jazz Impressions of Eurasia / Jul. 28, 1958–Aug. 23, 1958 / Columbia ✦✦✦
In 1958 Dave Brubeck's Quartet, one of the most popular jazz groups in the world, played 80 concerts in 14 countries during a three-month period. To salute the marathon road trip, the pianist/leader composed six songs for a new recording (which is now out on this CD). "Nomad" and "Brandenburg Gate" are the best-known originals but all of the other selections are equally enjoyable, featuring fine solos from Brubeck and altoist Paul Desmond. —*Scott Yanow*

Newport (1958) / Jul. 1958 / Columbia ✦✦✦
For their appearance at the 1958 Newport Jazz Festival, The Dave Brubeck Quartet performed a set of tunes associated with Duke Ellington including "Things Ain't What They Used to Be," "Perdido," an excerpt from the "Liberian Suite" and "C Jam Blues." Rounding off this excellent LP (which features pianist Brubeck, altoist Paul Desmond, bassist Eugene Wright and drummer Joe Morello) is Brubeck's original, "The Duke." It is well deserving of being reissued on CD. —*Scott Yanow*

Gone with the Wind / Apr. 22, 1959 / Columbia ✦✦
For this LP, Dave Brubeck and his Quartet (featuring altoist Paul Desmond) interpret eight songs (including two versions of "Camptown Races") associated with the South such as "Swanee River," "Georgia on My Mind" and "Ol' Man River." Although not one of their most significant recordings, the Brubeck Quartet is still in good form for these interesting performances. —*Scott Yanow*

★ **Time Out** / Jun. 25, 1959–Aug. 18, 1959 / Columbia ✦✦✦✦✦
This is one of the most popular jazz recordings of all time. Altoist Paul Desmond's memorable "Take Five" became a huge hit, showing that it is possible for creative jazz to sell. In addition to "Take Five" (which is still a standard), other highpoints of this classic album include "Blue Rondo A La Turk" and "Three to Get Ready." It's essential for all jazz collections. —*Scott Yanow*

The Riddle / Aug. 12, 1959 / Columbia ✦✦
Clarinetist Bill Smith, a member of Dave Brubeck's octet in the late '40s and a future soloist with Brubeck's Quartet starting in the '80s, recorded three albums with the pianist in the interim. *The Riddle* finds him temporarily taking altoist Paul Desmond's place with the Quartet and contributing all eight compositions which utilize folkish melodies that are related to the English song "Heigh, Ho, Anybody Home." Although not too essential, this little-known set gives Dave Brubeck a chance to play some unusual material. —*Scott Yanow*

Southern Scene / Sep. 10, 1959–Oct. 29, 1959 / Columbia ✦✦
For some reason Dave Brubeck was motivated to record a second album of songs associated with the South (as a follow-up to *Gone with the Wind*) and the results form this LP, a trio set without altoist Paul Desmond. The eight standards range from "Oh Susanna" and "Little Rock Getaway" to "Darktown Strutters Ball" and "Darling Nellie Gray"; in addition two originals in the style round out the well-played but somewhat forgettable program. —*Scott Yanow*

Brubeck and Rushing / Jan. 29, 1960–Aug. 4, 1960 / Columbia ✦✦✦
Although associated with the more modern styles of jazz, Brubeck always had a great respect (if not reverence) for the masters of the past. On ten standards Brubeck, altoist Paul Desmond and the Quartet fit in perfectly behind the great swing/blues singer Jimmy Rushing, who sounds rejuvenated by the fresh setting. This LP, a surprising success, is well worth searching for. —*Scott Yanow*

Brubeck Plays Bernstein / Jan. 30, 1960–Feb. 14, 1960 / Columbia ✦✦✦
For this historic LP, the Dave Brubeck Quartet met with The New York Philharmonic under the direction of Leonard Bernstein for a program subtitled "Bernstein Plays Brubeck Plays Bernstein." Together they perform Howard Brubeck's sidelong "Dialogues for Jazz Combo and Orchestra" along with five Bernstein songs (including four from *West Side Story*). This is one of the more suc-

cessful "Jazz Meets the Symphony" ventures and deserves to be reissued on CD. —*Scott Yanow*

Brubeck a La Mode / May 1960 / Original Jazz Classics ✦✦
One of Brubeck's three recordings of the 1959–61 period that featured clarinetist Bill Smith in the place of altoist Paul Desmond with the Quartet, this one finds Smith contributing ten originals that use various modes and unusual scales. The music generally swings and there are some fine solos but none of the individual pieces are all that memorable. —*Scott Yanow*

Tonight Only! / Sep. 9, 1960 / Columbia ✦✦
One of the more obscure Dave Brubeck albums is really a showcase for the young singer Carmen McRae, who performs nine numbers: six composed by the pianist/leader, one song apiece by altoist Paul Desmond and bassist Eugene Wright and the lesser-known standard "Paradiddle Joe." McRae is in fine voice but strangely enough all of the songs (except for "Strange Meadowlark") have been long forgotten. Stronger material would have resulted in a more memorable session. —*Scott Yanow*

Summit Sessions / 1960–1973 / Columbia ✦✦✦
It would not be an understatement to say that these 13 performances, mostly dating from the 1960s, cover quite a bit of ground. Brubeck is heard with such performers as Tony Bennett, Indian percussionist Palghat Raghu, the folk team of Addis & Crofut, in a remarkable piano duet with Thelonious Monk on "C Jam Blues," with son Darius Brubeck on second piano, on "Blues in the Dark" with singer Jimmy Rushing and in separate recordings with Peter, Paul & Mary, Charles Mingus, Carmen McRae, Gerry Mulligan, Leonard Bernstein and the New York Philharmonic and Louis Armstrong! There's quite a lot of contrast on this largely successful LP. —*Scott Yanow*

Time Further Out / May 3, 1961–Jun. 8, 1961 / Columbia ✦✦✦✦
Unlike most sequels, *Time Further Out* is a worthy successor to *Time Out*. Among the numbers introduced on this impressive set are "It's a Raggy Waltz" and "Unsquare Dance" (the latter an ancestor of Don Ellis' "Pussy Wiggle Stomp"). The selections, which range in time signatures from 5/4 to 9/8, are handled with apparent ease (or at least not too much difficulty) by pianist Brubeck, altoist Paul Desmond, bassist Eugene Wright and drummer Joe Morello on this near-classic. —*Scott Yanow*

Countdown/Time in Outer Space / May 3, 1961–Jun. 28, 1961 / Columbia ✦✦✦
One of Dave Brubeck's more adventurous albums, this LP (not yet available on CD) finds his Quartet exploring originals in a variety of potentially difficult time signatures including 11/4 and a polyrhythmic version of the date's one standard "Someday My Prince Will Come." Other highlights include "Countdown," "Castilian Drums" and "Three's a Crowd." It's highly recommended along with Brubeck's other *Time* recordings. —*Scott Yanow*

Brandenburg Gate Revisited / Aug. 21, 1961–Aug. 22, 1961 / Columbia ✦✦✦
Dave Brubeck's Quartet is joined by a symphony orchestra for the nearly 20-minute "Brandenburg Gate" and four shorter pieces on this LP. The solos of the pianist/leader and altoist Paul Desmond add a great deal of spontaneity to what could have been a weighed-down Third Stream effort. —*Scott Yanow*

Near-Myth with Bill Smith / Aug. 1961 / Original Jazz Classics ✦✦✦
The third and final of the Dave Brubeck albums from 1959–61 that feature clarinetist/composer Bill Smith in Paul Desmond's place with the Quartet has some unusual moments, as when Smith utilizes multiphonics or actually has a mute on his horn. As usual Smith provided all of the music which displays his interest in classical music and academia. —*Scott Yanow*

Real Ambassadors / Sep. 1961–Dec. 1961 / Columbia ✦✦✦
In 1961 Dave Brubeck put together a remarkable musical show. Using the talents of Louis Armstrong and his All-Stars, Carmen McRae, the innovative bop vocal group Lambert, Hendricks and Ross and his own rhythm section, Brubeck and his wife, lyricist Iola, wrote a largely upbeat play full of anti-racism songs and tunes that celebrated human understanding. Although it had only one live performance (at the 1962 Monterey Jazz Festival), *The Real Ambassadors* was recorded for posterity and now, with its reissue on CD, the original 15 selections have been augmented by five more. It is important to listen to this music without prior expectations because Paul Desmond is nowhere to be found, Louis Armstrong does not play that much trumpet here and

Music Map

Big Bands

First Important Jazz Big Bands
Fletcher Henderson
Paul Whiteman

1920s
Jean Goldkette	Ben Pollack
King Oliver	McKinney's Cotton Pickers

Beyond Category
Duke Ellington

Early Swing Bands
Earl Hines	Luis Russell
Cab Calloway	Casa Loma Orchestra
Benny Carter	Jimmy Lunceford
Don Redman	

Swing Era
Benny Goodman	Tommy Dorsey
Jimmy Dorsey	Chick Webb
Louis Armstrong	Artie Shaw
Count Basie	Glenn Miller
Charlie Barnet	Andy Kirk
Bob Crosby	Harry James
Erskine Hawkins	Jay McShann
Gene Krupa	Lionel Hampton
Buddy Johnson	

Bop Era Big Bands
Billy Eckstine
Dizzy Gillespie
Woody Herman (First and Second Herds)
Claude Thornhill
Boyd Raeburn
Machito

Uncategorizable
Stan Kenton

1950s
Count Basie • Dizzy Gillespie • Maynard Ferguson

1960s
Gerry Mulligan Concert Jazz Band
Gerald Wilson
Buddy Rich
Don Ellis
Thad Jones-Mel Lewis Orchestra
Kenny Clarke-Francy Boland

Avant-Garde Orchestras
Sun Ra Arkestra
Jazz Composers Orchestra
Charlie Haden's Liberation Music Orchestra
Globe Unity Orchestra
Anthony Braxton's Creative Music Orchestra
Vienna Art Orchestra
George Gruntz Concert Jazz Band
Pierre Dorge's New Jungle Orchestra
David Murray Big Band
Maria Schneider
London Jazz Composers Orchestra

1970s
Toshiko Akyoshi/Lew Tabackin
Gil Evans
Bill Watrous
Louie Bellson
Bill Berry

1980s
Capp-Pierce Juggernaut
Rob McConnell's Boss Brass
Jaco Pastoriu's Word Of Mouth Orchestra
Illinois Jacquet
Irakere
Mel Lewis

1990s
Mingus Big Band
McCoy Tyner
Carla Bley's Rather Large Orchestra
Bob Florence's Limited Edition
Clayton-Hamilton Jazz Orchestra
Bill Holman
Either/Orchestra

Lambert, Hendricks and Ross essentially function as background singers. However Satch and Carmen McRae make for a very potent team and there are many touching and surprising moments. —*Scott Yanow*

Bossa Nova USA / Jan. 3, 1962–Jul. 12, 1962 / Columbia ♦♦♦
With the popularization of bossa nova in the early '60s, practically every recording artist had to have at least one bossa nova

album. This effort by the Dave Brubeck Quartet is better than most due to the high quality of the compositions of which the title cut is best-known. The date's two standards ("This Can't Be Love" and "Trolley Song") also fare well on this happy session. —*Scott Yanow*

My Favorite Things / Jun. 11, 1962–Sep. 22, 1965 / Columbia ♦♦♦
Although recorded in sessions in 1962 and 1965, this set of

Richard Rodgers tunes by the Dave Brubeck Quartet has a strong unity about it due to the consistent performances of the veteran group. With altoist Paul Desmond and the pianist-leader contributing some fine solos (and bassist Eugene Wright and drummer Joe Morello excellent in support), the Rodgers songs are treated with respect and swing. This comparatively gentle version of "My Favorite Things" would never be mistaken for John Coltrane's. —Scott Yanow

Angel Eyes / Jul. 2, 1962–Feb. 15, 1965 / Columbia ✦✦✦
As with Dave Brubeck's Richard Rodgers set (My Favorite Things), his tribute to composer Matt Dennis was recorded partly in 1962 with the remainder three years later. Each of these seven standards (which include "Let's Get Away from It All," "Violets for Your Furs" and "Will You Still Be Mine?") are given superior and swinging treatments with fine solos from Brubeck and altoist Paul Desmond. —Scott Yanow

Brubeck in Amsterdam / Dec. 3, 1962 / Columbia ✦✦✦
One of the Dave Brubeck Quartet's lesser-known albums, this LP features the group performing six instrumental versions of songs from The Real Ambassadors plus "Dizzy Ditty" and a 12-minute rendition of "Brandenburg Gate." Brubeck, altoist Paul Desmond, bassist Eugene Wright and drummer Joe Morello seem inspired during this concert by the fresh material, making this hard-to-find album a bit of a collector's item. —Scott Yanow

At Carnegie Hall / Feb. 22, 1963 / Columbia ✦✦✦✦✦
The Dave Brubeck Quartet's Carnegie Hall concert found the popular band at the height of its powers. This two-LP set is highlighted by definitive versions of "St. Louis Blues," "Bossa Nova U.S.A.," "Pennies from Heaven," "Three to Get Ready," "Eleven-Four," "It's a Raggy Waltz" and especially "Blue Rondo A La Turk." Only an overly rapid "Take Five" (which was apparently the only time that drummer Joe Morello counted off the tempo for the Quartet) misses the mark. This essential music should be reissued in full on CD. —Scott Yanow

Time Changes / Nov. 20, 1963–Jan. 8, 1964 / Columbia ✦✦✦
For this entry in Dave Brubeck's series of Time albums, his Quartet with altoist Paul Desmond performs "Elementals" with an orchestra and plays five briefer originals including four that have unusual time signatures; "World's Fair" is in 13/4 time! It's not an essential purchase but a good example of Dave Brubeck's music. —Scott Yanow

Jazz Impressions of Japan / Jun. 16, 1964–Jun. 17, 1964 / Columbia ✦✦✦
Inspired by a tour of Japan in the Spring of 1964, Brubeck composed eight songs that pay tribute to the Quartet's visit. "Koto Song" is the best-known of these originals but all of the melodies are enjoyable. Even after being together 13 years, the Quartet was able to consistently perform new music with enthusiasm and creativity. —Scott Yanow

Jazz Impressions of New York / Jun. 16, 1964–Aug. 21, 1964 / Columbia ✦✦
This CD, a straight reissue of the original LP, contains 11 songs written for the soundtrack of the long-forgotten television series Mr. Broadway. It pays tribute to New York in a more abstract way than Jazz Impressions of Japan celebrated Japan, for Brubeck had to concern himself with having the music fit in with the show. In general these themes and the melodic improvisations of Brubeck and altoist Paul Desmond hold their own without the show, although none of the songs became standards. —Scott Yanow

The Canadian Concert Of Dave Brubeck / Aug. 22, 1965 / Can-Am ✦✦✦
The Dave Brubeck Quartet (with altoist Paul Desmond, bassist Eugene Wright and drummer Joe Morello) is in excellent form for this typical program from the mid-'60s. In addition to standards such as "St. Louis Blues," "Tangerine" and "These Foolish Things," they perform Brubeck's originals "Cultural Exchange" and "Koto Song" along with a brief version of "Take Five." This LP is worth searching for. —Scott Yanow

Time In / Sep. 20, 1965–Oct. 13, 1965 / Columbia ✦✦✦
The last of the Dave Brubeck Time albums introduced eight new Brubeck originals including "40 Days," "Travellin' Blues" and "He Done Her Wrong" (the latter based on "Frankie and Johnny"). The consistently swinging (if occasionally complex) music is easily enjoyable and adds evidence to the belief that there are no unworthy Dave Brubeck albums. —Scott Yanow

Anything Goes: the Music of Cole Porter / Dec. 8, 1965–Feb. 17, 1966 / Columbia ✦✦✦
The Quartet performs eight of Cole Porter's most famous songs on this enjoyable outing. Few surprises occur but the music often swings hard, pianist Brubeck and altoist Paul Desmond take several excellent solos and bassist Eugene Wright and drummer Joe Morello really push the group. —Scott Yanow

Jackpot / Jun. 14, 1966–Jun. 15, 1966 / Columbia ✦✦
One of the lesser Dave Brubeck albums, this LP features eight songs built around the theme of gambling towns such as "Ace in the Hole," "Chicago" and the title cut. The music is certainly upbeat but the out-of-tune piano and crowd noises (this date was recorded live in Las Vegas) are a bit distracting. It's strictly for Brubeck completists. —Scott Yanow

Bravo! Brubeck! / May 12, 1967–May 14, 1967 / Columbia ✦✦✦✦
One of the better Dave Brubeck LPs from the later period of the Quartet with altoist Paul Desmond, this set is unusual in that it only contains one Brubeck original. On such tunes as "Cielito Lindo," the beautiful "La Paloma," "Besame Mucho" and "Estrellita," the Quartet is augmented by guitarist Chamin Correa and percussionist Rabito Agueros. The results are melodic but swinging treatments of a variety of famous themes. —Scott Yanow

The Last Time We Saw Paris / Nov. 13, 1967 / Columbia ✦✦✦✦
Taken from the final tour of the Quartet before their breakup, this LP is full of timeless performances. All six selections are worth mentioning: "Swanee River," a 12-minute version of "These Foolish Things," "Forty Days," "One Moment Worth Years," "La Paloma Azul" and "Three to Get Ready." Throughout these extended renditions, Brubeck and altoist Paul Desmond rekindle some of the magic from their concerts of the early '50s while also simultaneously showing just how far they had grown as musicians. This LP is long overdue to be reissued on CD. —Scott Yanow

Compadres / May 23, 1968–Mar. 25, 1968 / Columbia ✦✦✦
This fine LP was the debut of Brubeck's new Quartet, a group featuring baritonist Gerry Mulligan, bassist Jack Six and drummer Alan Dawson. Recorded live in Mexico, the album (unlike the previous Bravo! Brubeck which mostly stuck to traditional folk melodies) has three originals apiece from Brubeck and Mulligan, although the most memorable pieces are the two standards "Adios, Mariquita Linda" and "Amapola." This enjoyable set showed that for Brubeck there was life after Paul Desmond. —Scott Yanow

Blues Roots / Oct. 4, 1968 / Columbia ✦✦✦
Although this is a blues-oriented set, there is plenty of variety in tempos and grooves. The 1968 Quartet featured the leader/pianist, baritonist Gerry Mulligan, bassist Jack Six and drummer Alan Dawson. The repertoire on this LP ranges from "Limehouse Blues" (which is not really a blues) to "Things Ain't What They Used to Be" and several originals. —Scott Yanow

Elementals for Jazzcombo, Orchestra and Baritone-Solo / May 26, 1970 / Decca ✦✦✦
The Dave Brubeck Quartet (featuring baritonist Gerry Mulligan) collaborated with The Cincinnati Symphony Orchestra for a version of "Elementals" and four more concise Brubeck originals, including "The Duke." This is one of the more successful "jazz meets the symphony" recordings, with the orchestra being logically integrated into Brubeck's music. —Scott Yanow

Last Set at Newport / Jul. 3, 1971 / Atlantic ✦✦✦✦
The Dave Brubeck-Gerry Mulligan Quartet is heard in a very inspired performance at the Newport Jazz Festival on this LP, just a short time before a riot by the audience closed the festival. These versions of "Take Five" and "Open the Gates" are memorable but it is the extended "Blues for Newport" that is truly classic. Mulligan and Brubeck (backed by bassist Jack Six and drummer Alan Dawson) constantly challenge each other during this exciting performance, making this set well worth searching for. —Scott Yanow

We're All Together Again (for the First Time) / Oct. 26, 1972–Nov. 4, 1972 / Atlantic ✦✦✦✦
During 1968–72, Brubeck's Quartet usually featured baritonist Gerry Mulligan, bassist Jack Six and drummer Alan Dawson. For this very logical record, altoist Paul Desmond (who was with Brubeck from 1951–67) makes the group a quintet and his interplay with Mulligan is consistently delightful. Together they are heard live in Europe on "Truth," Mulligan's "Unfinished Woman,"

"Rotterdam Blues" and a definitive 16-minute rendition of "Take Five." In addition, Desmond is showcased on "Koto Song" and as an encore Brubeck plays a lighthearted if brief "Sweet Georgia Brown." —*Scott Yanow*

All the Things We Are / Jul. 17, 1973 / Atlantic ✦✦✦✦
This album is a bit unusual in the Dave Brubeck discography. The pianist is heard in a quartet with altoist Lee Konitz on "Like Someone in Love" and a brief "Don't Get Around much Anymore," avant-garde giant Anthony Braxton (also on alto) is featured on "In Your Own Sweet Way" and both Konitz and Braxton team up for "All the Things You Are." In addition, the Brubeck Trio (with bassist Jack Six and drummer Alan Dawson) plays an exquisite and frequently exciting 21-minute five-song "Jimmy Van Heusen Medley." A total success, this "experimental" Brubeck set is highly recommended. —*Scott Yanow*

Two Generations of Brubeck / Aug. 3, 1973–Aug. 20, 1973 / Atlantic ✦✦✦
This very interesting set features the pianist with three of his sons (Darius on keyboards, Chris doubling on trombone and bass and Danny on drums), and a wide variety of musicians including tenor saxophonist Jerry Bergonzi, clarinetist Perry Robinson and Peter "Madcat" Ruth on harmonica. To hear such numbers as "Three to Get Ready," "Blue Rondo A La Turk" and "Unsquare Dance" (along with some newer pieces) performed by these younger players casts new light on the durability and flexibility of these classic Brubeck songs. This fine LP (along with its follow-up) is not yet available on CD. —*Scott Yanow*

Brother, the Great Spirit Made Us All / Jun. 27, 1974 / Atlantic ✦✦✦
Pianist Dave Brubeck and three of his sons (keyboardist Darius, drummer Danny and Chris on trombone and bass), with the assistance of such players as Jerry Bergonzi (on tenor and soprano), clarinetist Perry Robinson and Madcat Ruth on harmonica, perform colorful treatments of a wide variety of swinging pieces. Highlights include "It's a Raggy Waltz," "Temptation Boogie" and "Christopher Columbus"; Dave Brubeck takes "The Duke" solo. This fine music was last available on LP. —*Scott Yanow*

Brubeck & Desmond: Duets (1975) / Jun. 10, 1975–Apr. 16, 1975 / A&M ✦✦✦
Pianist Dave Brubeck and altoist Paul Desmond had a reunion for this set of lyrical duets. They had performed "You Go to My Head" onboard a jazz cruise and that duet was so enjoyable that this full LP resulted. In addition to four standards, the duo plays three Brubeck originals (including "Koto Song" and "Summer Song") and the blues "Balcony Song." This near-classic set, like too many of Brubeck's recordings, has not come out yet on CD. —*Scott Yanow*

25th Anniversary Reunion / Mar. 10, 1976–Mar. 12, 1976 / A&M ✦✦✦✦
This classic LP was the last time that pianist Dave Brubeck recorded with the late altoist Paul Desmond. The reunion of the most famous version of Brubeck's Quartet (which also included bassist Eugene Wright and drummer Joe Morello) found all of the players enthusiastic and still in their prime (although Morello's eyesight was failing). "St. Louis Blues," the tender "Don't Worry 'Bout Me," "Three to Get Ready" and yet another version of "Take Five" are among the highpoints of this historic final session. —*Scott Yanow*

Live at Montreux / Jul. 17, 1977 / Tomato ✦✦
For a period in 1977–78 (after the death of altoist Paul Desmond), pianist Dave Brubeck had a quartet with his sons keyboardist Darius, drummer Dan and Chris on bass and trombone. This Montreux concert features five of Dave Brubeck's originals (including "It's a Raggy Waltz" and "In Your Own Sweet Way") along with the standard "It Could Happen to You" and finds father Dave in fine form even if Desmond is clearly missed. —*Scott Yanow*

A Cut Above / Feb. 27, 1978–Feb. 28, 1978 / Direct-Disk ✦✦
This direct-to-disk double LP is "a cut below" the usual Dave Brubeck recordings. Pianist Brubeck is in good form and his rhythm section (with bassist Chris Brubeck and drummer Dan Brubeck) is fine but keyboardist Darius Brubeck's electronic effects get tiring quickly. Also, some of the performances are much too long and these renditions of "Blue Rondo A La Turk" and "Take Five" are not in the same league with most of the other versions. —*Scott Yanow*

Back Home / Aug. 1979 / Concord Jazz ✦✦✦
The first of three Concord LPs by this particular edition of the Quartet (with Jerry Bergonzi on tenor, Chris Brubeck doubling on electric bass and trombone, and drummer Butch Miles, whose successor would soon be Randy Jones), found Brubeck enthusiastically playing three of his originals along with the standards "Yesterdays," "Caravan" and "The Masquerade Is Over." Bergonzi's Coltrane-influenced tenor gave this unit a different sound than the earlier Quartets and meshes surprisingly well with the pianist/leader. —*Scott Yanow*

Tritonis / Mar. 1980 / Concord Jazz ✦✦✦
This underrated but talented version of the Dave Brubeck Quartet (featuring tenor saxophonist Jerry Bergonzi, drummer Randy Jones and Chris Brubeck on electric bass and bass trombone) performs "Brother, Can You Spare a Dime?," a sparkling version of "Like Someone in Love," Howard Brubeck's "Theme for June" and three fairly recent Dave Brubeck compositions. Bergonzi's Coltranish tenor acts as a perfect foil for Brubeck's unpredictable piano, making this LP worth searching for. —*Scott Yanow*

Paper Moon / Sep. 1981 / Concord Jazz ✦✦✦✦
The third of three Concord albums by this version of the Quartet (with Jerry Bergonzi on tenor, Chris Brubeck on bass and bass trombone and drummer Randy Jones) is the most rewarding of the trio although each one is recommended. Brubeck and the Coltrane-influenced tenor Bergonzi take consistently exciting solos on seven standards which are highlighted by "Music, Maestro, Please," "I Hear a Rhapsody" and "It's Only a Paper Moon"; Brubeck's solo version of "St. Louis Blues" is also noteworthy. —*Scott Yanow*

Concord on a Summer Night / Aug. 1982 / Concord Jazz ✦✦✦
In 1982 pianist Dave Brubeck welcomed clarinetist Bill Smith (who he had played with back in his octet days in the late '40s) as a permanent member of his Quartet along with drummer Randy Jones and Chris Brubeck on electric bass and occasional bass trombone. This album features the new Quartet at the Concord Jazz Festival playing what would become their typical mixture of songs: three Brubeck compositions ("Benjamin," "Koto Song" and "Softly, William, Softly"), a standard ("Black and Blue") and yet another remake of "Take Five." These are fine performances. —*Scott Yanow*

Marian McPartland's Piano Jazz with Guest Dave Brubeck / Mar. 1984 / Jazz Alliance ✦✦✦

For Iola / Aug. 1984 / Concord Jazz ✦✦✦
In addition to the standard "I Hear a Rhapsody" and Dave Brubeck's "Summer Song," this enjoyable CD has five of his lesser-known originals including one called "Big Bad Basie." This particular Quartet (with clarinetist Bill Smith, drummer Randy Jones and Chris Brubeck on electric bass and bass trombone) has been together for quite awhile and all of their releases have their memorable moments. —*Scott Yanow*

Reflections / Dec. 1985 / Concord Jazz ✦✦✦
This is one of Dave Brubeck's more obscure recordings but not because of its quality. Somewhat lost in the shuffle, this excellent quartet session with clarinetist Bill Smith, Chris Brubeck on electric bass and bass trombone) and drummer Randy Jones finds the pianist/leader performing eight of his compositions; only "Blues for Newport" caught on a little. The emphasis is on slower tempos and wistful solos (particularly on the Paul Desmond-tribute "We Will All Remember Paul") but the music is stimulating enough to hold one's interest throughout. Dave Brubeck has never allowed himself to become predictable. —*Scott Yanow*

Blue Rondo / Nov. 1986 / Concord Jazz ✦✦✦✦
The 1987 edition of the Brubeck Quartet featured pianist Brubeck, his son Chris on electric bass and bass trombone, clarinetist Bill Smith and drummer Randy Jones. In addition to remakes of "Blue Rondo A La Turk," "Strange Meadowlark" and "Swing Bells," the leader contributed six new originals including "I See, Satie" and a tribute to Dizzy Gillespie and Stan Getz called "Dizzy's Dream." Bill Smith, who uses electronics with taste on his clarinet during a few songs, has long been a major asset to the later Brubeck Quartets. This is one of their better Concord CDs. —*Scott Yanow*

Moscow Nights / Mar. 1987 / Concord Jazz ✦✦✦✦
In 1987 Brubeck, after decades of trying, finally had an opportunity to perform with his Quartet in the Soviet Union. The enthusiastic crowd (many of whom had grown up on Brubeck's music) clearly inspired the musicians, which included clarinetist Bill

Smith, electric bassist Chris Brubeck and drummer Randy Jones. Together they perform exciting versions of a variety of the leader's tunes plus Howard Brubeck's "Theme for June," "St. Louis Blues" and of course "Take Five." —*Scott Yanow*

New Wine / Jul. 3, 1987 / Music Masters ✦✦✦
The Quartet (which for the past five years had included clarinetist Bill Smith, electric bassist Chris Brubeck and drummer Randy Jones in addition to the pianist/leader) teamed up with the Montreal International Jazz Festival Orchestra for this live recording. Featured are six Brubeck compositions (including "Blue Rondo A La Turk" and "Koto Song") along with "Take the 'A' Train," all of which was in the Quartet's repertoire. In general the orchestra (which has some members of The Montreal Symphony) does not weigh down the proceedings and the music, although not all that "new," is enjoyable. —*Scott Yanow*

Quiet As the Moon / Sep. 20, 1988–May 8, 1991 / Music Masters ✦✦✦
Brubeck is heard at three separate recording sessions on this CD playing music that was used in the *Peanuts* cartoon series. The music ranges from such standards as "Bicycle Built for Two" and "When You Wish Upon a Star" and Vince Guaraldi classics (including "Cast Your Fate to the Wind") to Brubeck originals. The varying personnel includes Bobby Militello (sitting in for Bill Smith) on flute, alto and tenor, either Chris Brubeck or Jack Six on bass, Dan Brubeck or Randy Jones on drums and cellist Matthew Brubeck. This well-paced set stands by itself apart from the *Peanuts* series. —*Scott Yanow*

Once When I Was Young / May 6, 1991–May 7, 1991 / Music Masters ✦✦✦
On this nostalgic and often wistful set, Dave Brubeck and his 1991 Quartet (clarinetist Bill Smith, bassist Jack Six and drummer Randy Jones) play eight songs from the pianist's childhood, such numbers as "Shine on Harvest Moon," "Stardust" and "Among My Souvenirs." In addition Brubeck (who is in top form) contributed "Dancin' in Rhythm" and the title cut, which in its second version is performed by a choral group. —*Scott Yanow*

Trio Brubeck / Jun. 8, 1993 / Music Masters ✦✦✦
Pianist Dave Brubeck and two of his sons (Chris Brubeck on electric bass and bass trombone and drummer Dan Brubeck) are in happy form on this rather spontaneous trio set. Highlights include "I Cried for You," "Broadway Bossa Nova," "One Moment Worth Years" and "Over the Rainbow." —*Scott Yanow*

Late Night Brubeck / Oct. 1993 / Telarc ✦✦✦
Dave Brubeck teams up with Bobby Militello (heard here on alto, tenor and flute), bassist Jack Six and drummer Randy Jones for a set that emphasizes ballads and slower tempos. Militello brings back the spirit of Paul Desmond while Brubeck's own playing continues to be full of surprises. On "Theme for June" he breaks out into stride, a Duke Ellington medley seems to develop quite spontaneously and "Mean to Me" really works well. With bassist Jack Six and drummer Randy Jones fine in support, this CD is a strong effort from Dave Brubeck, who has nearly 100 worthwhile recordings currently in print. —*Scott Yanow*

Nightshift / Oct. 5, 1993–Oct. 10, 1993 / Telarc ✦✦✦✦
This is a particularly well-balanced set with pianist Dave Brubeck (then 73) in typically creative form. Although Brubeck (who is accompanied throughout by bassist Jack Six and drummer Randy Jones) is actually the real star of every selection (coming up with continually inventive ideas whether in ensembles, behind soloists or during his own solos), he is joined by three of his favorite horn players on some of the numbers. Bobby Militello shows a great deal of versatility with some blazing alto on "Yesterdays," melodic playing in a Paul Desmond vein on "I Can't Give You Anything but Love," soulful tenor on "Travelin' Blues" and plenty of intensity on "Knives." Clarinetist Bill Smith is well featured on "You Go to My Head" and the boisterous bass trombone of Chris Brubeck makes several welcome appearances. This recommended set has more than its share of variety and surprising moments. —*Scott Yanow*

Just You Just Me / Jan. 4, 1994–Jun. 29, 1994 / Telarc ✦✦✦
It had been nearly 40 years since Dave Brubeck's last solo piano recording when he recorded this relaxed set. Brubeck sounds typically creative yet often wistful on the seven standards, four originals and a "Tribute to Stephen Foster." This is a fine addition to Brubeck's extensive yet consistently satifying discography. —*Scott Yanow*

Young Lions & Old Tigers / Jun. 29, 1994–Jun. 27, 1995 / Telarc ✦✦✦
To celebrate his 75th birthday, Dave Brubeck recorded one number apiece with quite a variety of top jazz stars, both young and old. Some of the performances (which alternate duets with quartets) work better than others (eight are recent Brubeck compositions) but all of the musicians display mutual respect and it is obvious that the guests are all fans of the still-masterful pianist. Trumpeter Roy Hargrove plays beautifully on his lyrical feature but Jon Hendricks, who sings "How High the Moon" as a ballad, takes it at such a slow tempo as to be dreary. Tenor saxophonist Michael Brecker is fine on "Michael Brecker Waltz" although he sounds a bit restrained, the wittily-titled "Here Comes McBride" is a good-humored romp with bassist Christian McBride, Joe Lovano (on tenor) works well with Brubeck, and particularly memorable is the first meeting on record between Brubeck and fellow pianist George Shearing, a chancetaking interpretation of "In Your Own Sweet Way." Joshua Redman performs fine hard bop on one song, "Together," is a well-conceived duet for baritonist Gerry Mulligan and Brubeck, James Moody plays tenor, sings and yodels on the minor blues "Moody," Mulligan returns for the contrapuntal "Gerry-Go-Round," and, although the obscure fluegelhornist Ronnie Buttacavoli sounds very out of place on his boring feature, the set closes with one of the strongest performances, a solo piano showcase for Brubeck on "Deep in a Dream." Overall this is quite a mixed bag but, even with its occasional misses, the CD is a must for Dave Brubeck fans because the pianist is consistently inventive throughout the unusual set. —*Scott Yanow*

Clora Bryant

b. Dennison, TX
Trumpet / Bop
It seems very strange that Clora Bryant has thus far only led one record session, a 1957 date that has been reissued by V.S.O.P. A fine trumpeter who ranges from bop to Dixieland, Bryant has mostly lived in Los Angeles throughout her career. She made some headlines when she played in the Soviet Union during the Gorbachev years and she was a member of the Cheathams for a time but otherwise has been greatly underrated. —*Scott Yanow*

● **Gal with a Horn: Clora Bryant** / Jun. 1957 / VSOP ✦✦✦✦
It seems strange that trumpeter Clora Bryant, who has been active in jazz for over 40 years, has thus far only had one opportunity to lead her own record date. This V.S.O.P. CD (which reissues a Mode LP from 1957) features Bryant heading a quartet (comprised of pianist Roger Fleming, bassist Ben Tucker and drummer Bruz Freeman) that is sometimes augmented by Walter Benton on tenor and trumpeter Normie Faye (who sticks to section work). Bryant, who also sings, does a fine job of interpreting eight standards with the highlights including "Sweet Georgia Brown," "Tea for Two" and "This Can't Be Love." —*Scott Yanow*

Ray Bryant (Raphael Bryant)

b. Dec. 24, 1931, Philadelphia, PA
Piano / Bop, Swing, Soul Jazz
Although he could always play bop, Ray Bryant's playing combines together older elements (including blues, boogie-woogie, gospel and even stride) into a distinctive, soulful and swinging style; no one plays "After Hours" quite like him.

The younger brother of bassist Tommy Bryant and the uncle of Kevin and Robin Eubanks (his sister is their mother), Bryant started his career playing with Tiny Grimes in the late '40s. He became the house pianist at the Blue Note in Philadelphia in 1953 where he backed classic jazz greats (including Charlie Parker, Miles Davis and Lester Young) and made important contacts. He accompanied Carmen McRae (1956–57), recorded with Coleman Hawkins and Roy Eldridge at the 1957 Newport Jazz Festival (taking a brilliant solo on an exciting version of "I Can't Believe That You're in Love with Me") and played with Jo Jones' trio (1958). Bryant settled in New York in 1959, played with Sonny Rollins, Charlie Shavers and Curtis Fuller and soon had his own trio. He had a few funky commercial hits (including "Little Susie" and Cubano Chant"), which kept him working for decades. Bryant has recorded often throughout his career (most notably for Epic, Prestige, Columbia, Sue, Cadet, Atlantic, Pablo and EmArcy) and even his dates on electric piano in the '70s are generally rewarding. However Ray Bryant is heard at his best when playing the blues on unaccompanied acoustic piano. —*Scott Yanow*

Ray Bryant Trio / Apr. 5, 1957 / Original Jazz Classics ✦✦✦
Pianist Ray Bryant solidified his reputation with this outstanding 1957 trio release. It displayed his facility with the blues, speed, gospel influence and interpretative abilities on such songs as John Lewis' "Django" and Clifford Brown's "Daahoud." It also contained Bryant's funky originals "Splittin" and "Blues Changes," and was punctuated by Ike Isaacs' careful bass work and Specs Wright's loose, in the groove drumming. This set has recently been reissued by Fantasy, and the remastering provides a fine sonic framework for Bryant's heady, unpredictable, and often exciting playing. —*Ron Wynn*

Me and the Blues / Apr. 5, 1957+Dec. 19, 1958 / Prestige ✦✦✦✦
Ray Bryant Plays / Oct. 29, 1959–Nov. 6, 1959 / Signature ✦✦✦
Little Susie / Dec. 10, 1959–Jan. 19, 1960 / Columbia ✦✦✦
Con Alma / Nov. 25, 1960–Jan. 26, 1961 / Columbia ✦✦✦
This is a definitive early Ray Bryant album, and includes "Cubano Chant." —*Michael G. Nastos*

MCMLXX / Mar. 4, 1970–Apr. 14, 1970 / Atlantic ✦✦✦
Alone at Montreux / Jul. 6 23, 1972 / Atlantic ✦✦✦✦✦
Ray Bryant has long been a well-rounded and versatile yet distinctive pianist. His style, modern compared to the swing and stride players but traditional when matched against the boppers, is flexible enough to fit into many settings. This solo outing finds Bryant playing swing standards, blues, soulful versions of a couple of current pop tunes and even a bit of boogie. This LP's only fault is that it is out of print. —*Scott Yanow*

Hot Turkey / Oct. 15, 1975 / Classic Jazz ✦✦✦
Here's Ray Bryant / Jan. 10, 1976–Jan. 12, 1976 / Original Jazz Classics ✦✦✦
Pianist Ray Bryant teams up with bassist George Duvivier and drummer Grady Tate for a set of soulful and bluesy interpretations of five standards and three originals. Oddly enough there are no 12-bar blues on this date (a Pablo session reissued on CD in the OJC series) but Bryant infuses such songs as "Girl Talk," "Good Morning Heartache" and "Li'l Darlin" with plenty of blues feeling anyway. A relaxed outing, not essential but enjoyable. —*Scott Yanow*

Solo Flight / Dec. 21, 1976 / Pablo ✦✦✦
Tremendous collection of standards, blues, and ballads from Ray Bryant. He shows his knowledge of early tunes like "Blues in de Big Brass Bed," while ripping through "Moanin'" and nicely reworking "Take The 'A' Train" and "St. Louis Blues." —*Ron Wynn*

● **Montreux '77** / Jul. 13, 1977 / Original Jazz Classics ✦✦✦✦
All Blues / Apr. 10, 1978 / Original Jazz Classics ✦✦✦✦
Bryant has always had a wide repertoire but he sounds most at home when playing the blues. This trio date with bassist Sam Jones and drummer Grady Tate allows him to do just that with "Please Send Me Someone to Love" being the only nonblues on the program. Whether it be "All Blues," "Billie's Bounce" or "Jumpin' with Symphony Sid," Bryant explores an impressive variety of blues styles and grooves, leaving listeners with a happy feeling. —*Scott Yanow*

Potpourri / May 13, 1980–May 14, 1980 / Pablo ✦✦✦
Ray Bryant Trio Today / Feb. 13, 1987–Feb. 14, 1987 / EmArcy ✦✦✦
With Ray Bryant Trio. Loaded with standards and two Bryant classics: "Tonk" and "Slow Freight." Recommended. —*Michael G. Nastos*

Blue Moods / Feb. 15, 1987–Feb. 16, 1987 / EmArcy ✦✦✦✦
Outstanding trio date with Bryant offering teeming phrases, sweeping statements, and some wonderful ballads, backed by bassist Rufus Reid and drummer Freddie Waits. Not only great playing all around, but an excellent recording as well. —*Ron Wynn*

Plays Basie and Ellington / Feb. 15, 1987–Feb. 16, 1987 / EmArcy ✦✦✦
Golden Earrings / Jan. 23, 1988–Jun. 26, 1988 / EmArcy ✦✦✦
The Bryant/Reid/Waits team cranks out another fine session, this one neatly balancing glittering ballads and joyous uptempo numbers. Bryant has gradually earned the respect he's due as a consummate pianist, while Reid's sympathetic bass work and Waits' nicely controlled drumming complete the package with style. —*Ron Wynn*

All Mine…And Yours / Oct. 19, 1989–Oct. 20, 1989 / EmArcy ✦✦✦

Jeanie Bryson

Vocals / Standards
Jeanie Bryson is a subtle and somewhat sensuous singer with a small and appealing voice. Dizzy Gillespie's illegitimate daughter (a fact hidden from the general public during his lifetime), her mother is the songwriter Connie Bryson. She graduated from Livingston College in 1981 and freelanced for a decade, visiting Europe several times. Bryson recorded several fine albums for Telarc starting in 1992 including a Peggy Lee tribute; she also sang on Terence Blanchard's recorded set of Billie Holiday-associated songs. —*Scott Yanow*

● **I Love Being Here with You** / Jan. 1993 / Telarc ✦✦✦✦
Jeanie Bryson, Dizzy Gillespie's daughter, made her recording debut on this CD. Her voice is highly appealing and often sensuous, hinting at Peggy Lee and Susannah McCorkle. A fine middle-of-the-road song stylist (rather than a jazz singer), Bryson does an excellent job on a set dominated by standards. She mostly concentrates on melody statements with subtle improvising and is at her best on ballads. Steve Nelson's vibes fit in well during his appearances and trumpeter Wallace Roney (as usual sounding like Miles Davis) also takes some good solos. This is a promising beginning for Jeanie Bryson. —*Scott Yanow*

Tonight I Need You So / Jan. 25, 1994–Feb. 20, 1994 / Telarc ✦✦✦
Bryson's soft warm voice at times recalls Maxine Sullivan and on "Solamente Tu" she comes very close to the fragility of Astrud Gilberto. There are a few memorable selections on her second Telarc disc, most notably the exuberant "Simple Song" (which has some jubilant playing from altoist Paquito D'Rivera), a sensuous "Honeysuckle Rose" and a fine version of "Skydive." Unfortunately the set also has an excess of forgettable poppish material that weighs down the content somewhat. However Bryson mostly overcomes the material and her likable and easygoing style compensates. This release is not essential but is enjoyable. —*Scott Yanow*

Milt Buckner

b. Jul. 10, 1915, St. Louis, MO, **d.** Jul. 27, 1977, Chicago, IL
Organ, Piano / Swing
Milt Buckner had a dual career. As a pianist he largely invented the "locked hands" style (parallel chords) that was adopted by many other players including George Shearing and Oscar Peterson. And as an organist he was one of the top pre-Jimmy Smith stylists, helping to popularize the instrument.
The younger brother of altoist Ted Buckner (who played with Jimmie Lunceford), Milt Buckner grew up in Detroit and gigged locally in addition to arranging for McKinney's Cotton Pickers in 1934. He came to fame as pianist and arranger with Lionel Hampton (1941-48, 1950-52 and occasionally in later years) where he was a crowd pleaser. During 1948-50 Buckner led his own bands and after 1952 he generally played organ with trios or quartets. In later years he sometimes teamed up with Illinois Jacquet or Jo Jones. Buckner recorded many dates as a leader, particularly for Black & Blue in the 1970s. —*Scott Yanow*

Them There Eyes / Dec. 7, 1967 / Black & Blue ✦✦✦
Crazy Rhythm / Dec. 7, 1967–Sep. 1968 / Black & Blue ✦✦✦
Midnight Slows, Vol. 3 / Aug. 1, 1973 / Black & Blue ✦✦✦
Straight-ahead jazz with Gatemouth Brown (g), Arnett Cobb (sax), and Candy Johnson (sax). —*Michael G. Nastos*

● **Green Onions** / Feb. 21, 1975 / Inner City ✦✦✦✦
With French rhythm section, guitarist Roy Gaines, drummer Panama Francis. Funky and groove-laden. —*Michael G. Nastos*

Midnight Slows, Vol. 6 / Black & Blue ✦✦✦

Ted Buckner

b. Jul. 16, 1909, Sherman, TX, **d.** Sept. 22, 1994 , Los Angeles, CA
Trumpet / Dixieland
A strong Dixieland player, Teddy Buckner spent most of his career emulating his idol Louis Armstrong, not really developing a sound of his own despite having impressive technique. He worked on the West Coast in the 1930's and was with Buck Clayton's orchestra in Shanghai, China (1934). Louis Armstrong's stand-in on the 1936 film *Pennies from Heaven,* Buckner never attempted to advance with the times. He worked with Benny Carter (1945-48), Lionel Hampton (1947-1948) and most notably with

Kid Ory's Creole Jazz Band (1949-54). Starting in 1955 Buckner led his own Dixieland group and he held his own with the fiery Sidney Bechet at a few French concerts in 1958. Buckner worked regularly for a long period with his band at Disneyland (1965–81) and through the years recorded several albums for GNP/Crescendo and its subsidiary Dixieland Jubilee. —*Scott Yanow*

Teddy Buckner / Feb. 6, 1955 / GNP ✦✦✦

Teddy Buckner in Concert at the Dixieland Jubilee / Oct. 15, 1955 / Dixieland Jubilee ✦✦✦

A Salute to Louis Armstrong / 1957-1958 / GNP ✦✦✦

● **On the Sunset Strip** / 1960 / Dixieland Jubilee ✦✦✦✦
Good traditional jazz session from 1960, with Buckner leading a sextet through 12 vintage New Orleans stomps, blues, and standards, and adding a vocal on "Mack The Knife." His trumpet work is spry and energetic, while Caughey Roberts adds some exuberant soprano sax and clarinet solos. —*Ron Wynn*

Midnight in Moscow / 1961 / GNP ✦✦✦

Teddy Buckner and the All Stars /Apr. 1958 / GNP ✦✦✦
Session modeled along the lines of Louis Armstrong small combo dates, with Buckner operating in Armstrong's role as leader and trumpet soloist, and band members including frequent Armstrong collaborators Trummy Young and Billy Kyle. There are some clichéd moments and other numbers where Buckner and company mesh, particularly on "Mahogany Hall Romp." —*Ron Wynn*

Teddy Bunn

b. 1909, Freeport, NY, d. Jul. 20, 1978, Lancaster, CA
Guitar / Swing, Classic Jazz
A fine single-note acoustic guitar soloist, Teddy Bunn was one of the top jazz guitarists of the 1930s. Largely self-taught, Bunn first gained recognition when he recorded with Duke Ellington in 1929 and played with the Washboard Rhythm Kings in the late-'20s/early-'30s period. A few years later he was one of the stars with the Spirits of Rhythm (which played regularly at the Onyx Club). During 1938–40 Bunn recorded with Jimmie Noone, Johnny Dodds, Trixie Smith, J.C. Higginbotham, Sidney Bechet, Lionel Hampton and was on the famous Mezz Mezzrow-Tommy Ladnier sessions; in addition he made four unaccompanied solos for Blue Note. Switching to electric guitar Bunn led his own groups in the 1940s and rejoined the Spirits of Rhythm; in the '50s he played R&B with a variety of groups (including Jack McVea, Edgar Hayes and Louis Jordan). Although fairly obscure after the early '40s, Bunn worked regularly until the late '60s when health problems forced his retirement. —*Scott Yanow*

● **Teddy Bunn (1929–1940)** / Sep. 16, 1929–Mar. 28, 1940 / RST ✦✦✦✦✦
Teddy Bunn was one of the finest acoustic jazz guitarists of the 1930s, although he had relatively few opportunities to be showcased on record. This CD (from the Austrian RST label) features Bunn on a series of hokum vocal duets with Spencer Williams (Clarence Profit or James P. Johnson provide the piano accompaniment), backing singers Buck Franklin, Fat Hayden and Walter Pichon, jamming with clarinetist Mezz Mezzrow and trumpeter Tommy Ladnier (six alternate takes from the famous Panassié sessions) and leading a session of his own. The latter (which is also included on a Mosaic box set) features Bunn on two memorable unaccompanied guitar solos and on three occasions (including an alternate take of "Blues Without Words") backing his own vocals. It is strange that Bunn recorded so rarely after 1940 for he lived until 1978. This is his definitive set. —*Scott Yanow*

Jane Bunnett

b. Toronto, Canada
Flute, Soprano Saxophone / Post-Bop
One of the finest soprano saxophonists in jazz of the 1990s, Jane Bunnett originally studied classical piano but tendonitis cut short that career. After seeing the Charles Mingus group in San Francisco, Bunnett was inspired to play advanced jazz. On soprano she recalls Steve Lacy a bit (who she has studied with) while her flute playing is quite distinctive. Bunnett has always had major players on her records; in addition to her husband, trumpeter Larry Cramer, the late pianist Don Pullen had been a fixture on her records, her 1988 debut for Dark Light also featured Dewey Redman and she has utilized Sheila Jordan and Jeanne Lee.

Bunnett has recorded for Dark Light, Music & Arts (a series of duets with Pullen) and Denon. Her most adventurous work thus far is 1991's *Spirits of Havana*, which matches her playing with many of Cuba's top jazz musicians in Cuba. In recent years Jane Bunnett has been living in Paris. —*Scott Yanow*

In Dew Time / Feb. 1988 / Dark Light ✦✦✦✦

New York Duets / 1989 / Music & Arts ✦✦✦

Live at Sweet Basil / 1990 / Denon ✦✦✦

★ **Spirits of Havana** / Sep. 27, 1991–Oct. 4, 1991 / Denon ✦✦✦✦✦
Bunnett, a Canadian musician, went to Havana in 1991 and recorded there with a wealth of Cuban talent. (Canada has full relations with Cuba so, unlike U.S. musicians, she can do this.) Singer Mercedita Valdes appears, as does her husband, percussionist Guillermo Barretto (who died a few months after this album was recorded). You certainly couldn't hire a better crew of pianists—Gonzalo Rubalcaba, Hilario Duran (of Perspectiva) and 72-year-old Frank Emilio. —*Ned Sublette*

Water Is Wide / Aug. 18, 1993–Aug. 19, 1993 / Evidence ✦✦✦✦
This intriguing set has more than its share of variety. Jane Bunnett pays tribute to Rahsaan Roland Kirk with some speech-like flute on "Serenade to a Cuckoo," recalls Steve Lacy a bit with her soprano on two Thelonious Monk pieces ("Pannonica" and "Brake's Sake") and her originals (along with those of trumpeter Larry Cramer) range from advanced bop to fairly free improvising. Vocalists Sheila Jordan (wonderful on "You Must Believe in Spring") and Jeanne Lee have individual features and are both major parts of the ancient hymn "The Water Is Wide" while the rhythm section (pianist Don Pullen, bassist Kieran Overs and drummer Billy Hart) consistently displays flexibility and creative reactions to the directions of the lead voices. —*Scott Yanow*

Rendez-Vous / Mar. 20, 1995–Mar. 21, 1995 / Justin Time ✦✦✦

Dave Burrell (Herman Davis Burrell)

b. Sep. 10, 1940, Middletown, OH
Piano / Avant-Garde
A heavily percussive, rhythmic pianist, Dave Burrell has adeptly merged African and Caribbean influences into his compositions and playing style. His solos are often aggressive, sparse and animated, though he's also effective on ballads and standards, and is a steady accompanist and bandleader. Burrell's mother was a vocalist, and helped generate an early interest in jazz. He attended the University of Hawaii in the late '50s and early '60s, and graduated from Berklee in the mid-'60s. Burrell worked in Boston with Tony Williams and Sam Rivers, then moved to New York. He played with Grachan Moncur III and Marion Brown, before forming the Untraditional Jazz Improvisational Team with Byard Lancaster. This group included Sirone and Bobby Kapp. In addition, Burrell helped initate The 360 Degree Music Experience with Moncur and Beaver Harris in 1968. He served as a music instructor for Harlem's Community Thing Organization and appeared at the 1969 Pan African Festival in Algiers. Burrell worked and recorded with Pharoah Sanders, Alan Silva, Sunny Murray, Harris and particularly Archie Shepp. Burrell wrote a jazz opera, "Windward Passages, in the late '70s. He continued recording and playing both solo dates and with such musicians as David Murray, Hamiet Bluiett and Cecil McBee. Burrell's recorded for Black Saint, Victor, Denon, Hat Hut, Douglas, Gazell and BYG. He has a few sessions available on CD. —*Ron Wynn*

High One High Two / Feb. 6, 1968–Apr. 9, 1968 / Arista ✦✦✦✦

Plays Ellington and Monk / Apr. 2, 1978–Apr. 3, 1978 / Denon ✦✦✦

● **Windward Passages** / Sep. 13, 1979 / Hat Hut ✦✦✦✦

Daybreak / Mar. 30, 1989 / Gazell ✦✦✦

Jelly Roll Joys / 1991 / Gazell ✦✦

In Concert / Oct. 12, 1991 / Victor ✦✦✦

Brother To Brother / 1993 / Gazell ✦✦✦

Kenny Burrell

b. Jul. 31, 1931, Detroit, MI
Guitar / Bop
Kenny Burrell has been a very consistent guitarist throughout his career. Cool-toned and playing in an unchanging style based in bop, Burrell has always been the epitome of good taste and solid swing. Duke Ellington's favorite guitarist (though he never actu-

ally recorded with him), Burrell started playing guitar when he was 12 and he debuted on records with Dizzy Gillespie in 1951. Part of the fertile Detroit jazz scene of the early '50s, Burrell moved to New York in 1956. Highly in-demand from the start, Burrell has appeared on a countless number of records during the past 40 years as a leader and as a sideman. Among his more notable associations have been dates with Stan Getz, Billie Holiday, Milt Jackson, John Coltrane, Gil Evans, Sonny Rollins, Quincy Jones, Stanley Turrentine and Jimmy Smith. Starting in the early '70s Burrell began leading seminars and teaching, often focusing on Duke Ellington's music. He toured with the Phillip Morris Superband during 1985–86 and has led three-guitar quintets but generally Kenny Burrell plays at the head of a trio/quartet. —*Scott Yanow*

Introducing Kenny Burrell / May 29, 1956 / Blue Note ♦♦♦
Despite its title, this LP was actually guitarist Kenny Burrell's second Blue Note album, although the first to be released. Teamed with pianist Tommy Flanagan, bassist Paul Chambers, drummer Kenny Clarke and the conga of Candido, Burrell displays what was already an immediately recognizable tone. At 24, Burrell had quickly emerged to become one of the top bop guitarists of the era, and he is in particularly excellent form on "This Time the Dream's on Me," "Weaver of Dreams" and "Delilah." A bonus of this set is a percussion duo by Clarke and Candido on "Rhythmorama." Enjoyable music. —*Scott Yanow*

Monday Stroll / Dec. 17, 1956+Jan. 5, 1957 / Savoy ♦♦♦
Although this LP was reissued under guitarist Kenny Burrell's name, it was originally led by Frank Wess, who is heard doubling on flute and tenor. With the assistance of Burrell, rhythm guitarist Freddie Green, bassist Eddie Jones and either Kenny Clarke or Gus Johnson on drums, Wess is in excellent form on a set very reminiscent (not too surprisingly considering the personnel) of the Count Basie band. Wess contributed four of the songs, Burrell brought in "Southern Exposure" and the quintet also plays "Over the Rainbow" and the obscure "Woolafunt's Lament." This out-of-print LP (put out by Arista in 1978) is a fine straight-ahead date, with Wess' flute taking solo honors. —*Scott Yanow*

All Night Long / Dec. 28, 1956 / Original Jazz Classics ♦♦♦♦
Two of guitarist Kenny Burrell's best sessions from the 1950s were this release (reissued on CD in the OJC series) and its companion *All Day Long*. Burrell is teamed with an impressive group of young all-stars, including trumpeter Donald Byrd, tenor saxophonist Hank Mobley, Jerome Richardson on flute and tenor, pianist Mal Waldron, bassist Doug Watkins and drummer Art Taylor. In addition to the lengthy "All Night Long" and three group originals (two by Mobley and one from Waldron), the LP program has been augmented by a medley of "Body and Soul" and "Tune Up" from the same session. Jam sessions such as this one are only as good as the solos; fortunately, all of the musicians sound quite inspired, making this an easily recommended set. —*Scott Yanow*

All Day Long / Dec. 28, 1956+Jan. 4, 1957 / Original Jazz Classics ♦♦♦♦
For this CD reissue, "C.P.W." has been added to the original LP program. Guitarist Kenny Burrell and the young all-stars (trumpeter Donald Byrd, Frank Foster on tenor, pianist Tommy Flanagan, bassist Doug Watkins and drummer Art Taylor) sound fine on the four group compositions, but the 18-minute blues "All Day Long" is easily the most memorable selection. Well worth picking up, as is *All Night Long*, which was recorded a week earlier. —*Scott Yanow*

Kenny Burrell, Vol. 2 / Feb. 1, 1957 / Original Jazz Classics ♦♦♦
Guitarist Kenny Burrell, 25 at the time, is heard during one of his earlier sessions playing in his already recognizable straight-ahead style with a quintet that also features the underrated baritonist Cecil Payne, pianist Tommy Flanagan, bassist Doug Watkins and drummer Elvin Jones. This CD reissue of the original LP is a bit brief in time (just over 36 minutes) but contains plenty of fine swinging on tunes such as "Don't Cry Baby," "Drum Boogie," "All of You" and Bud Powell's "Strictly Confidential." It's easily enjoyable music. —*Scott Yanow*

Two Guitars / Mar. 5, 1957 / Original Jazz Classics ♦♦♦
For this 1957 studio session (which has been reissued on CD in the OJC series), the two distinctive but complementary guitarists Kenny Burrell and Jimmy Raney are teamed together in a septet with trumpeter Donald Byrd, altoist Jackie McLean, pianist Mal Waldron, bassist Doug Watkins and drummer Art Taylor. The full

group gets to stretch out on originals by Watkins, McLean ("Little Melonae"), and three from Waldron, while the two standards ("Close Your Eyes" and "Out of Nowhere") are individual features for Burrell and Raney. This is a well-rounded set that may not contain any real surprises but will be enjoyed by collectors of hard bop. —*Scott Yanow*

The Cats / Apr. 1957 / Original Jazz Classics ♦♦♦

Kenny Burrell & John Coltrane / Mar. 7, 1958 / Prestige ♦♦♦♦
John Coltrane recorded many interesting jam session-type dates in the 1950s. This matchup with guitarist Kenny Burrell (in a quintet with pianist Tommy Flanagan, bassist Paul Chambers and drummer Jimmy Cobb) finds the group stretching out on two Flanagan compositions: Burrell's "Lyresto" and the standard "I Never Knew." In addition, Coltrane and Burrell play a short duet on "Why Was I Born." Overall the music is excellent for the time period with Coltrane displaying some of his "sheets of sound" and Burrell sounding happy with 'Trane's presence. It was formerly available as the first half of a two-LP set, *Kenny Burrell/John Coltrane*. —*Scott Yanow*

Blue Lights, Vol. 1 / May 14, 1958 / Blue Note ♦♦♦♦
On the first of two CD reissues, guitarist Kenny Burrell leads a strong jam session that features the talented but very underrated trumpeter Louis Smith (who sounds a bit like Lee Morgan), the similar but contrasting tenors of Junior Cook and Tina Brooks, pianist Duke Jordan, bassist Sam Jones and drummer Art Blakey. Jordan's tongue-in-cheek "Scotch Blues" and "I Never Knew" (the latter was not on the original LP) are among the highpoints of this easily enjoyable straight-ahead session. —*Scott Yanow*

Blue Lights, Vol. 2 / May 14, 1958 / Blue Note ♦♦♦♦
The second of two CD reissues of a jam session led by guitarist Kenny Burrell features the talented if forgotten trumpeter Louis Smith, both Junior Cook and Tina Brooks on tenors, pianist Bobby Timmons (Duke Jordan was on the first volume), bassist Sam Jones and drummer Art Blakey. The all-star group performs two standards ("Caravan" and the guitarist's feature on "Autumn in New York"), Sam Jones' "Chuckin'" and Burrell's "Rock Salt." This is excellent music that easily fits into the bop mainstream of the period. —*Scott Yanow*

Moonglow / Nov. 7, 1958–Sep. 14, 1962 / Prestige ♦♦
It seems strange that the music on this double-LP was reissued in the early '80s under guitarist Kenny Burrell's name for two of the three sessions were originally headed by tenor saxophonist Coleman Hawkins. Reissued is the complete album *The Hawk Relaxes* plus half of *Bluesy Burrell* and *Soul*. The emphasis is on ballads (particularly during the first two dates, which were cut for the Moodsville label) and, although everyone plays well, it would have been preferable to hear Hawkins and Burrell roaring on some uptempo material too. The supporting cast includes pianists Ronnell Bright, Tommy Flanagan and Ray Bryant. Enjoyable but not essential. —*Scott Yanow*

On View at the Five Spot Cafe / Aug. 25, 1959–Aug. 26, 1959 / Blue Note ♦♦♦
This likable live set from guitarist Kenny Burrell has a strong supporting cast (Tina Brooks on tenor, either Bobby Timmons or Roland Hanna on piano, bassist Ben Tucker and drummer Art Blakey) and the original five-song program has been expanded on this CD to eight tunes. The swinging music, highlighted by "Lady Be Good," "Birks Works," the blues "36-23-36" and Burrell's feature on "Lover Man," is quite mainstream for the period and predictably excellent. —*Scott Yanow*

A Night at the Vanguard / Sep. 16, 1959–Sep. 17, 1959 / Chess ♦♦♦
For this CD reissue (which adds versions of "I Can't See for Lookin'" and "Cheek to Cheek" to the original Chess LP), guitarist Kenny Burrell is heard in a sparse trio setting with bassist Richard Davis and drummer Roy Haynes. The focus is almost exclusively on Burrell, who is tasteful, swinging and melodically creative on such numbers as "Will You Still Be Mine," Erroll Garner's "Trio," "Broadway" and Thelonious Monk's "Well You Needn't." —*Scott Yanow*

Bluesin' Around / Nov. 21, 1961–Apr. 30, 1962 / Columbia ♦♦
Released for the first time on this 1983 LP, the music on the set features guitarist Kenny Burrell in quartet/quintets with either tenor great Illinois Jacquet, trombonist Eddie Bert or altoist Leo Wright and either pianist Hank Jones or organist Jack McDuff. It is odd that Columbia did not issue any of the straight-ahead

music at the time, considering McDuff's popularity, for the results, even with a few dated numbers such as "Mambo Twist," are excellent. After a short while, this LP went out of print and the music has yet to resurface on CD. —*Scott Yanow*

Midnight Blue / Jan. 7, 1963 / Blue Note ✦✦✦✦✦
This album was one of guitarist Kenny Burrell's best-known sessions for the Blue Note label, although it has yet to be reissued on CD. Burrell is matched with tenor saxophonist Stanley Turrentine, bassist Major Holley, drummer Bill English and Ray Barretto on conga for a blues-oriented date highlighted by "Chitlins Con Carne," "Midnight Blue," "Saturday Night Blues" and the lone standard "Gee Baby Ain't I Good to You." —*Scott Yanow*

Soul Call / Apr. 7, 1964 / Original Jazz Classics ✦✦
Guitarist Kenny Burrell alternates blues and ballads on this swinging quintet set with pianist Will Davis, bassist Martin Rivera, drummer Bill English and Ray Barretto on congas. The music is melodic and boppish, although no real surprises occur. By this time, Burrell was a very respectful player, upholding the tradition rather than offering any real innovations. This CD reissue will still be enjoyed by his fans. —*Scott Yanow*

Guitar Forms / Dec. 4, 1964–Apr. 12, 1965 / Verve ✦✦✦✦
This LP is a near-classic, matching guitarist Kenny Burrell (who is heard at his most versatile) with the Gil Evans Orchestra. Actually, three numbers are performed by a quintet (with pianist Roger Kellaway) and Gershwin's "Prelude #2" is taken solo, but the five numbers, which range from bossa novas to classical and ballads, feature Burrell matched by a 13-piece band playing Gil Evans arrangements. Although Burrell is the only soloist throughout the set, there is plenty of variety. This is considered one of Kenny Burrell's finest recordings of the 1960s. —*Scott Yanow*

Sylvia Is! / 1965 / Fantasy ✦✦✦
Sylvia Sims' greatest notoriety has come in the world of cabaret singing. Sims' jazz roots were in evidence, though, on this recently reissued 1965 session, even though her diction, pacing, and tone are still as much pop and show business as anything. Kenny Burrell's steady, immaculate phrasing and guitar riffs offer a welcome grounding in more conventional jazz time and tone, as do the bass and drum interplay of Milt Hinton and Osie Johnson. Sims takes turns with Afro-Latin material on "Brazil" and "Cuando Te Fuiste De Mi," while also handling "Smile" and "God Bless The Child" in a distinctive, if somewhat unorthodox, fashion. —*Ron Wynn*

A Generation Ago Today / Dec. 15, 1966–Mar. 28, 1967 / Verve ✦✦✦
Guitarist Kenny Burrell interprets eight swing standards associated with the Benny Goodman Sextet and Charlie Christian on this Verve album. Burrell is joined by bassist Ron Carter, drummer Grady Tate and either altoist Phil Woods or (on "Wholly Cats") pianist Richard Wyands; vibraphonist Mike Mainieri guests on "As Long as I Live." Unfortunately the playing time of this LP is brief (a touch under 32 minutes) and the now-obscure set has been out of print for quite awhile but the music is excellent. Highlights include "Poor Butterfly," "Stompin' at the Savoy," "Rose Room" and "A Smooth One." —*Scott Yanow*

God Bless the Child / May 1971 / CTI ✦✦
Guitarist Kenny Burrell's one CTI album is a decent but not essential affair, featuring three of his originals plus lengthy versions of the ballads "A Child Is Born" and "God Bless the Child." Trumpeter Freddie Hubbard helps out and flutist Hubert Laws is on one track, while the arrangements for a cello section are provided by Don Sebesky. This generally lyrical LP has been long out of print. —*Scott Yanow*

★ **Ellington Is Forever, Vol. 1 & 2** / Feb. 4, 1975–Feb. 5, 1975 / Fantasy ✦✦✦✦✦
This two-CD set is a splendid and well-conceived tribute to Duke Ellington by guitarist Kenny Burrell. In a variety of settings, he utilizes such special players as trumpeters Thad Jones, Snooky Young and Jon Faddis, tenors Joe Henderson and Jerome Richardson, organist Jimmy Smith and a fine rhythm section headed by pianist Jimmy Jones. Ernie Andrews has two vocals, all of the horn players get their chances to solo and 15 Ellington and Strayhorn songs receive tasteful yet inventive treatments. It's recommended along with the second volume. —*Scott Yanow*

★ **Ellington Is Forever, Vol. 2** / 1977 / Fantasy ✦✦✦✦✦
The second two-CD set to result from guitarist Kenny Burrell's marathon tribute to Duke Ellington is even wider ranging than

the first. In addition to such stars as guitarist Burrell, trumpeters Snooky Young and Thad Jones, tenors Joe Henderson and Jerome Richardson, organist Jimmy Smith, pianist Jimmy Jones, and singer Ernie Andrews, this release has solo space for cornetist Nat Adderley, trombonist Quentin Jackson, altoist Gary Bartz and pianist Roland Hanna. By varying the personnel and instrumentation from track to track, Kenny Burrell pays homage in a memorable fashion to 15 classic songs by Ellington and Strayhorn. It comes recommended, as does the first volume. —*Scott Yanow*

Tin Tin Deo / Mar. 23, 1977 / Concord Jazz ✦✦✦
Another in a string of trio dates cut in the '70s. Burrell works with bassist Reggie Johnson and drummer Carl Burnett. It's a good menu featuring standards, originals, and soul-jazz tunes alternating with mid-tempo and sentimental ballads. There's also one good Afro-Latin song, "La Petite Mambo." —*Ron Wynn*

Handcrafted / Feb. 27, 1978–Mar. 1, 1978 / Muse ✦✦✦
Steady, consistently swinging trio date with Burrell's fine guitar playing as the focus, and bassist Reggie Johnson and drummer Sherman Ferguson effective but subdued in a supporting mode. There's nothing exceptional here, but the breezy pace and bluesy feel are nice. —*Ron Wynn*

When Lights Are Low / Sep. 1978 / Concord Jazz ✦✦✦

Live at the Village Vanguard / Dec. 15, 1978 / Muse ✦✦✦
Trio date at the famed Village Vanguard, with Burrell backed by bassist Larry Gales and drummer Sherman Ferguson. The location and live context combine to make this a more exuberant session than many Burrell cut in the '70s. His playing has more fire, and he takes longer solos and puts more fervor behind them. —*Ron Wynn*

In New York / Dec. 15, 1978 / Muse ✦✦✦

Moon and Sand / Dec. 1979 / Concord Jazz ✦✦

Heritage / May 27, 1980–May 28, 1980 / AudioSource ✦✦
By 1980 it seemed as if guitarist Kenny Burrell was spending at least as much time looking backwards (paying tribute to the past greats) as he was creating new music. This out-of-print LP from the obscure AudioSource label features Burrell performing nine jazz standards ranging from "Night in Tunisia" and "A Child Is Born" to "Struttin' with Some Barbeque" and even "When the Saints Go Marching In." The personnel varies but often includes trumpeter Oscar Brashear, Patrice Rushen or Pete Jolly on piano and occasionally the reeds of Marshall Royal, Jerome Richardson, Don Menza and Matt Catingub. A worthwhile if not particularly innovative set. —*Scott Yanow*

Listen to the Dawn / Dec. 9, 1980–Dec. 10, 1980 / Muse ✦✦✦
Sharp trio set. Burrell is backed by the excellent bass/drums duo of Rufus Reid and Ben Riley, both of whom are Burrell's playing equals. The results are uniformly solid, sometimes more emphatic than others. Burrell is still playing in a relaxed, easy groove, but occasionally increases the energy level. —*Ron Wynn*

Groovin' High / Jul. 14, 1981–Jul. 15, 1981 / Muse ✦✦✦

Ellington a la Carte / Aug. 19, 1983–Aug. 20, 1983 / Muse ✦✦✦
This quiet live set features duets from guitarist Kenny Burrell and bassist Rufus Reid. The emphasis (as is often the case on Burrell's recordings) is on material from the Duke Ellington songbook. In fact, except for "Don't Worry 'Bout Me" and Burrell's "Blues for Duke," all of the music (including a four-song 11 1/2 minute medley) are from Ellington's repertoire. The playing is excellent and the interplay creative in a subtle way, but nothing out of the ordinary or particularly memorable occurs. However Kenny Burrell fans will enjoy this. —*Scott Yanow*

Togethering / Apr. 5, 1984–Apr. 23, 1984 / Blue Note ✦✦
This CD matches together guitarist Kenny Burrell with the popular saxophonist Grover Washington, Jr., in a quintet also including bassist Ron Carter, drummer Jack DeJohnette and percussionist Ralph Macdonald. The settings gives Washington a rare chance to play strictly straight-ahead jazz but unfortunately he mostly sticks to his comparatively lightweight soprano instead of playing his gutsier tenor. The music is therefore merely pleasing rather than really being all that historic. Highpoints include "A Beautiful Friendship" and "What Am I Here For." —*Scott Yanow*

Generation / Oct. 24, 1986–Oct. 25, 1986 / Blue Note ✦✦✦
On this set, Kenny Burrell teams up with a couple of younger players in what he calls his "Jazz Guitar Band." The only trouble is that it is next to impossible to tell Burrell apart from Rodney Jones or Bobby Broom; they all sound nearly alike! With bassist

Dave Jackson and drummer Kenny Washington giving the three guitarists fine support, the result is some fine bop-oriented music (on such songs as "High Fly," "Jumpin' the Blues" and "Fungii Mama"), but little that is very memorable. —*Scott Yanow*

Pieces of Blue and the Blues / Oct. 24, 1986–Oct. 25, 1986 / Blue Note ✦✦✦

Taken from the same "Live at the Village Vanguard" gig that resulted in *Generation*, Kenny Burrell is teamed up with two younger guitarists (Rodney Jones and Bobby Broom), both of whom have styles and sounds very similar to the older player; it is fortunate that the liners tell who is playing what! Bassist Dave Jackson and drummer Kenny Washington are fine in support of the three guitarists on a variety of blues and bop standards including "Raincheck," "Jeannine" and "'Round Midnight." Nothing all that unexpected or surprising occurs but this is a fine straight-ahead set. —*Scott Yanow*

Guiding Spirit / Aug. 4, 1989–Aug. 5, 1989 / Contemporary ✦✦✦✦

This "live at the Village Vanguard" CD has a combination that works: guitarist Kenny Burrell, vibist Jay Hoggard, bassist Marcus McLaurine and drummer Yoron Israel. Burrell and Hoggard blend together quite well, and the superior tunes they picked for this date (including two from Duke Ellington, Mal Waldron's "Soul Eyes," John Coltrane's "Moment's Notice" and Hoggard's title cut) challenge the soloists. This strong straight-ahead outing is one of Kenny Burrell's better sets from the past decade. —*Scott Yanow*

Sunup to Sundown / Jun. 10, 1991–Jun. 12, 1991 / Contemporary ✦✦✦

Guitarist Kenny Burrell has a strong all-around showcase on this release from Contemporary. Assisted by pianist Cedar Walton, bassist Rufus Reid, drummer Lewis Nash and percussionist Ray Mantilla, Burrell swings harder than he usually does when paying tribute to the past, coming up with fresh statements on the varied material. Although there are a few standards in the program (such as "I'm Old Fashioned," "Autumn Leaves" and "Speak Low"), there are also such obscurities as "Out There" (a medium-uptempo blues), "Sunup to Sundown" and "Love Dance." This set serves as an excellent introduction to Kenny Burrell's enjoyable brand of straight-ahead playing. —*Scott Yanow*

Midnight at the Village Vanguard / Aug. 28, 1993 / Evidence ✦✦✦

Lotus Blossom / Jun. 12, 1995–Jun. 15, 1995 / Concord Jazz ✦✦✦

Buddy Burton

b. Feb. 1890, Louisville, KY, **d.** Jul. 6, 1977, Louisville, KY
Piano / Classic Jazz

A talented if generally overlooked pianist, Buddy Burton also played organ, drums and percussion as well as kazoo. After free-lancing both in and out of music, Burton moved from Louisville to Chicago in 1923. He recorded on drums (1923) and kazoo (1925) with Jelly Roll Morton and in 1928 did the bulk of his recordings including as a soloist (both singing and playing piano), in piano duets with Jimmy Blythe, backing blues singers Tillie Johnson and Mae Mathews and playing with the Dixie Four and the Harlem Trio. Other than two numbers in 1929, duets with pianist Bob Hudson in 1932 and accompanying singer Irene Sanders in 1936, little is known of Burton's later life except that he probably remained active (although off records) in Chicago for decades until returning to Louisville in 1965. —*Scott Yanow*

● **W.E. "Buddy" Burton & Ed "Fats" Hudson** / Feb. 1928–Apr. 2, 1936 / RST ✦✦✦✦

Buddy Burton (also known as W.E. Burton), a minor figure in jazz history, was a fine pianist and a spirited vocalist. His recordings as a soloist; dates backing singers Tillie Johnson, Mae Matthews, and Irene Sanders; duets with fellow pianist Jimmy Blythe (their "Dustin' the Keys" is a near-classic) and performances with The Dixie Four, The Harlem Trio and drummer Marcus Norman (the latter under the title "Alabama Jim and George!") are all on this definitive CD. In addition, the only four recordings by the even more obscure pianist Bob Hudson (heard dueting with Burton, backing trombonist Roy Palmer and playing banjo with pianist Jimmy Blythe) round out this generous 25-cut set. The goodtime music may not be essential but 1920s collectors will love this very complete reissue. —*Scott Yanow*

Gary Burton

b. Jan. 23, 1943, Anderson, IN
Vibes / Post-Bop, Early Fusion

One of the two great vibraphonists to emerge in the 1960s (along with Bobby Hutcherson), Gary Burton's remarkable four-mallet technique (best displayed on an unaccompanied version of "No More Blues" from 1971) can make him sound like two or three players at once. He has recorded in a wide variety of settings and always sounds distinctive. Self-taught on vibes, Burton made his recording debut with country guitarist Hank Garland when he was 17, started recording regularly for RCA in 1961 and toured with George Shearing's Quintet in 1963. He gained some fame while with Stan Getz's pianoless quartet during 1964–66 and then put together his own groups. In 1967 with guitarist Larry Coryell, he led one of the early "fusion" bands; Coryell would later be succeeded by Sam Brown, Mick Goodrick, John Scofield, Jerry Hahn and Pat Metheny. Burton recorded duet sets with Chick Corea (they also toured extensively), Ralph Towner, Steve Swallow and Paul Bley and collaborated on an album apiece with Stephane Grappelli and Keith Jarrett. Among his sidemen in the late '70s/'80s were Makoto Ozone, Tiger Okoshi and Tommy Smith. Very active as an educator at Berklee since joining its faculty in 1971, Burton (who teamed up with Eddie Daniels in the early '90s for an interesting Benny Goodman/Lionel Hampton tribute tour and recording) has remained a prominent stylist up until the present time. He recorded during different periods of his career for RCA, Atlantic, ECM and GRP. —*Scott Yanow*

New Vibe Man in Town / Jul. 6, 1961–Jul. 7, 1961 / RCA ✦✦✦✦

3 in Jazz / Feb. 14, 1963 / RCA ✦✦✦✦

This CD, a straight reissue of an RCA LP, has three unrelated but consistently interesting sessions that were recorded in 1963. Three selections with tenor saxophonist Sonny Rollins (the only performances currently available elsewhere) are rather free (and fascinating) versions of standards and also feature cornetist Don Cherry, bassist Henry Grimes and drummer Billy Higgins. Vibraphonist Gary Burton's quartet (with trumpeter Jack Sheldon, bassist Monty Budwig and drummer Vernell Fournier) is fine if not overly memorable on their four numbers but fluegelhornist Clark Terry (with pianist Hank Jones, bassist Milt Hinton, drummer Osie Johnson and Willie Rodriguez on Latin percussion) is in superior form, playing with great exuberance on "When My Dream Boat Comes Home" and "Cielito Lindo." Well worth picking up. —*Scott Yanow*

● **Artist's Choice** / Aug. 15, 1963–Aug. 16, 1967 / Bluebird ✦✦✦✦

This session traces vibist Gary Burton's musical evolution during 1963–1968 with selections taken from eight of Burton's 13 RCA LPs. Burton was among the very first to incorporate elements of rock, pop and freer forms of jazz into his own music without trivializing any of the styles. *Artist's Choice* is a fine retrospective of the early Gary Burton, although one wishes these sessions were available in full rather than piecemeal. —*Scott Yanow*

The Time Machine / Apr. 5, 1966+Apr. 6, 1966 / RCA ✦✦✦

Tennessee Firebird / Sep. 19, 1966–Sep. 21, 1966 / RCA ✦✦✦

While the concept of "jazz-rock" was in its embryonic stages, Burton was experimenting with a style combining jazz improvisation with rock energy and rhythms. This 1967 session added another ingredient to the musical mix: country and bluegrass sensibility. Burton used Nashville session players like bassist/harmonica player Charlie McCoy, the great Chet Atkins, fiddler Buddy Spicher, and pedal steel guitarist Buddy Emmons. The results were impressive and artistically intriguing; the country players provided a loose, loping feel, while Burton's solos were smooth and delicate but forceful enough to hold the distinct styles together. While it is a short disc at less than 38 minutes, it includes one unissued take and is worth the steep import price. —*Ron Wynn*

Duster / Apr. 18, 1967–Apr. 20, 1967 / RCA ✦✦✦✦

Prophetic session with references to everything from country to rock. Suggested new directions for jazz musicians. —*Ron Wynn*

Lofty Fake Anagram / Aug. 15, 1967–Aug. 17, 1967 / RCA ✦✦✦

Gary Burton Quartet Concert / Feb. 23, 1968 / ✦✦✦

Country Roads and Other Places / Sep. 24, 1968–Sep. 27, 1968 / RCA ✦✦✦

Throb / Jun. 2, 1969+Jun. 3, 1969 / Atlantic ✦✦✦

During his years at Atlantic, Burton became a major player on vibes featuring a cooler, less blues-oriented technique that didn't sacrifice passion or individuality, and he also was among the earliest jazz musicians to incorporate other elements into their style without losing their improvisational outlook. Both areas are displayed on this 14-cut anthology presenting two separate Burton albums. The first five cuts were an LP teaming him with pianist Keith Jarrett; it proved a most intriguing match, with Jarrett reining in his excesses, playing with flair, and never failing to click with Burton. The other nine songs were on the LP *Throb*, in which Burton continued the jazz-cum-rock and country experimentation that marked other LPs like *Tennessee Firebird* and *Duster*. —*Ron Wynn*

Good Vibes / Sep. 2, 1969–Sep. 4, 1969 / Atlantic ✦✦✦

Paris Encounter / Nov. 4, 1969 / Atlantic ✦✦✦✦✦

Gary Burton and Keith Jarrett / Jan. 12, 1971 / Atlantic ✦✦✦✦
This combination works. Vibraphonist Gary Burton and pianist Keith Jarrett (along with guitarist Sam Brown, bassist Steve Swallow and drummer Bill Goodwin) play five Jarrett originals plus Steve Swallow's "Como en Vietnam." Elements of pop music, rock, country and the jazz avant-garde are used in this mixture of styles but the results do not sound logical, merely piecemeal. Burton and Jarrett should have a reunion and see how their styles have grown since this early effort. —*Scott Yanow*

★ **Alone at Last** / Jun. 19, 1971–Sep. 7, 1971 / Atlantic ✦✦✦✦✦

Crystal Silence / Nov. 6, 1972 / ECM ✦✦✦✦✦
Debut on ECM with Chick Corea. The first of many successful pairings of the two. —*Ron Wynn*

The New Quartet / Mar. 5, 1973+Mar. 6, 1973 / ECM ✦✦✦✦
Prelude to *Passengers* with Mick Goodrick (g). —*Michael G. Nastos*

Hotel Hello / May 13, 1974+May 14, 1974 / ECM ✦✦✦

Ring / Jul. 23, 1974+Jul. 24, 1974 / ECM ✦✦✦✦
With Eberhard Weber. These nice arrangements are a bit more energetic than standard ECM. —*Ron Wynn*

Matchbook / Jul. 26, 1974+Jul. 27, 1974 / ECM ✦✦✦

Dreams So Real / Dec. 1975 / ECM ✦✦✦✦
All Carla Bley tunes; with Pat Metheny (g). —*Michael G. Nastos*

Passengers / Nov. 1976 / ECM ✦✦✦✦
Gary Burton Quartet. Includes some stirring originals with Pat Metheny (g), Eberhard Weber (b). —*Michael G. Nastos*

Times Square / Jan. 1978 / ECM ✦✦✦✦

Duet / Oct. 23, 1978+Oct. 25, 1978 / ECM ✦✦✦✦

Easy As Pie / Jun. 1980 / ECM ✦✦✦

Picture This / Jan. 1982 / ECM ✦✦✦

Real Life Hits / Nov. 1984 / ECM ✦✦✦✦

Gary Burton and the Berklee All Stars / Jul. 28, 1985 / JVC ✦✦✦✦
Nice live date with Billy Pierce providing some welcome blues fire on tenor and Burton offering several exciting, intricately constructed vibes solos. There are some rock voicings provided by guitarist Jim Kelly, and Larry Monroe on alto sax makes a good dueling partner for Pierce. —*Ron Wynn*

Whiz Kids / Jun. 1986 / ECM ✦✦✦✦

The New Tango / 1988 / Atlantic ✦✦✦
An interesting, uneven, but often lush and beautiful collaboration between tango master Piazzolla and vibist Gary Burton. Each went out of their way to accommodate the other, with the results being more complementary than challenging. Still, it yielded several enticing selections. —*Ron Wynn*

Times Like These / 1988 / GRP ✦✦✦

Reunion [With Pat Metheny] / May 6, 1989–May 10, 1989 / GRP ✦✦✦✦

Right Time, Right Place / Mar. 29, 1990 / GNP ✦✦✦

Cool Nights / 1991 / GRP ✦✦✦

Six Pack / 1992 / GRP ✦✦✦✦

It's Another Day / May 1993 / GRP ✦✦
Although vibraphonist Gary Burton gets top billing, this CD is actually a showcase for vocalist Rebecca Paris. The material is dominated by newer "contemporary" songs and pop tunes; every song except the closing voice-vibes duet is given a routine funk rhythm. Paris' voice is somewhat dull, her delivery is generally

overpowering and her phrasing usually outside of jazz. Burton's atmospheric vibes are just not enough to save this forgettable set. —*Scott Yanow*

Face To Face / Oct. 31, 1994–Nov. 1, 1994 / GRP ✦✦✦✦
This set of duets between vibraphonist Gary Burton and pianist Makoto Ozone is a bit of a surprise, not the quiet and introverted date one might expect but a consistently exciting outing. The duo (who first started working together back in 1982) clearly inspires each other and a lot of sparks fly. The music ranges from three of Ozone's diverse originals and Astor Piazzola's "Laura's Romance" to a pair of Thelonious Monk tunes, a few standards and a romping version of the Benny Goodman-associated "Opus Half"; on the latter Ozone plays some creditable stride piano. More than half of the selections are taken at medium-to-fast tempos and, whether it be "Blue Monk," a memorable version of Jobim's "O Grande Amor" or a heated rendition of Steve Swallow's "Eiderdown," this is a highly enjoyable outing, one of Burton's finest of the past decade. —*Scott Yanow*

Joe Bushkin

b. Nov. 7, 1916, New York, NY
Piano / Swing
One of the last survivors of the Eddie Condon gang (he recorded with Condon back in 1938), Bushkin has long been a fine swing pianist who shifted easily into middle-of-the-road pop/cabaret by the 1950s. He first played professionally with Frank LaMarr in 1932, worked on 52nd Street from 1935 on, recorded with Billie Holiday in 1936 and was with Bunny Berigan's Orchestra during 1937–38. In addition to jam sessions with Condon, Bushkin was with Louis Prima and Muggsy Spanier in 1939 and during 1940–42 was a member of Tommy Dorsey's Orchestra. A period in the military was followed by a stint with Benny Goodman, an acting role on Broadway in *The Rat Race*, tours with Louis Armstrong in 1953 and a long engagement at the Embers. Bushkin led his own groups throughout the 1950s and '60s, retired for a period, came back to tour with Bing Crosby (1976–77) and has been semi-retired ever since. His two best-known compositions are "Oh Look at Me Now" and "A Hot Time in the Town of Berlin." —*Scott Yanow*

The Road To Oslo & Play It Again Joe / Oct. 4, 1977–1985 / DRG ✦✦
Although Joe Bushkin started his career in swing bands and recordings with Eddie Condon, this CD (which reissues his sessions from 1978 and 1985) has little spontaneity and no real surprises. Bushkin's piano here plays closer to cocktail music than to jazz and his vocals, although charming enough, are not worth hearing twice. Bing Crosby sings on two short numbers from what must have been among his final recordings and a few excellent swing players (including cornetist Warren Vache and clarinetist Phil Bodner) pop up on the later date, but no real excitement occurs. Most of these performances are in the "and then I wrote" vein; Joe Bushkin seemed to have either forgotten his jazz roots or not considered them worth revisiting, making this pleasant set a disappointment from the jazz standpoint. —*Scott Yanow*

Billy Butterfield (Charles William Butterfield)

b. Jan. 14, 1917, Middletown, OH, d. Mar. 18, 1988, North Palm Beach, FL
Trumpet / Dixieland, Swing
A versatile pre-bop trumpeter with a beautiful tone, Billy Butterfield could play pretty ballads and heated Dixieland with equal skill. After early experience in the mid-'30s with the bands of Austin Wylie and Andy Anderson, Butterfield became famous while playing with Bob Crosby's Orchestra (1937–40), taking the main solo on the original version of "What's New," and making numerous records with both the big band and the Bobcats. In 1940 he was with Artie Shaw, participating in the famed Gramercy Five sessions and taking a classic solo on Shaw's rendition of "Star Dust"; in addition Butterfield can be seen and heard playing "Concerto for Clarinet" with Shaw in the film *Second Chorus*. After stints with Benny Goodman (1941) and Les Brown, Butterfield spent time in the military and then led a lyrical (but commercially unsuccessful) big band (1945–47). He worked mostly in the studios during the 1950s and '60s, occasionally emerging for Dixieland dates with Eddie Condon, and was a key member of the World's Greatest Jazz Band (1968–72).

In later years he continued popping up in Dixieland settings both for records and concerts. —*Scott Yanow*

● **The Uncollected Billy Butterfield & His Orchestra (1946)** / 1946 / Hindsight ✦✦✦✦✦

Stardusting / 1950 / Capitol ✦✦✦

Session at Riverside / Mar. 21, 1957 / Capitol ✦✦✦

Songs Bix Beiderbecke Played / Mar. 1, 1959–Mar. 2, 1959 / Epic ✦✦✦✦

Jaki Byard (John A. Byard, Jr.)

b. Jun. 15, 1922, Worcester, MA
Piano / Bop, Stride, Free Jazz

Possessor of a very eclectic style, Jaki Byard has long been able to play stride, swing, bop, completely free and funky in addition to being able to imitate closely both Erroll Garner and Dave Brubeck. His playing fit perfectly with Charles Mingus' band in 1964 during their famous European tour with Eric Dolphy, but otherwise he has never been given the recognition he deserved.

As a youth he played piano and trumpet, switched to trombone while in the Army and then (back on piano) gigged with Earl Bostic (1949–50). Byard (also a fine tenor saxophonist) played with the big bands of Herb Pomeroy and Maynard Ferguson (1959–61) and then gigged and recorded with Dolphy, Don Ellis, Booker Ervin, Charlie Mariano and Mingus (1962–65 and 1970); he also recorded as a leader frequently in the 1960s and collaborated with Rahsaan Roland Kirk. Although he has recorded fairly often through the years (including duet albums with Earl Hines and Ran Blake) and headed a big band (the Apollo Stompers), Byard has been mostly active as an educator since the late '60s. —*Scott Yanow*

● **Blues for Smoke** / Dec. 16, 1960 / Candid ✦✦✦✦✦
An early Byard solo set in which he displays an array of influences, ranging from ragtime and stride to bop and free. —*Ron Wynn*

Here's Jaki / Mar. 14, 1961 / Original Jazz Classics ✦✦✦

Hi-Fly / Jan. 30, 1962 / New Jazz ✦✦✦

Out Front! / May 21, 1964–May 28, 1964 / Original Jazz Classics ✦✦✦
Although Jaki Byard is a very eclectic pianist, this is a surprisingly conventional set. On most selections he is joined by bassist Bob Cranshaw and drummer Walter Perkins (in 1964) for fairly straight-ahead renditions of standards and obscurities. A few of the numbers add Booker Ervin on tenor and trumpeter Richard Williams, and of these by far the most original performance is the episodic "European Episode." Rounding off the set is a 1961 performance (with Byard on both alto and piano) playing "When Sunny Gets Blue." It's fine music but one has to lower their expectations a bit. —*Scott Yanow*

Live! / Apr. 15, 1965 / Prestige ✦✦✦
CD reissue of a fine mid-'60s session spiced by Joe Farrell's exuberant tenor solos and the backing of Byard, bassist George Tucker, and drummer Alan Dawson. The live context adds a fresh element, with the quartet getting looser and more inspired on every number. —*Ron Wynn*

Freedom Together / Jan. 11, 1966 / Prestige ✦✦

On the Spot / Feb. 16, 1967 / Prestige ✦✦✦

Sunshine of My Soul / Oct. 31, 1967 / Prestige ✦✦✦

With Strings / Apr. 2, 1968 / Prestige ✦✦✦✦
Top-notch recording for the brilliant pianist with George Benson (g), Ray Nance (tpt), Ron Carter (b), Richard Davis (b), and Alan Dawson (d). —*Michael G. Nastos*

● **The Jaki Byard Experience** / Sep. 17, 1968 / Prestige ✦✦✦✦✦
Pianist Jaki Byard and the wondrous Roland Kirk (here switching between tenor, clarinet and manzello) were two of the few jazz musicians who could play in literally every jazz style, from New Orleans to bop and free form. If only they had recorded a history of jazz album. Fortunately, they did meet up on a few occasions, including this brilliant quartet session with bassist Richard Davis and drummer Alan Dawson. They romp on Bud Powell's "Parisian Thoroughfare," Thelonious Monk's "Evidence," "Shine on Me" and "Teach Me Tonight." Byard duets with Davis on his own "Hazy Eve" but best of all is the pianist's duet with Kirk on "Memories of You." This set was also reissued as half of the Roland Kirk two-LP set *Pre-Rahsaan*. —*Scott Yanow*

Solo Piano / Jul. 31, 1969 / Prestige ✦✦✦

There'll Be Some Changes Made / Dec. 27, 1972 / Muse ✦✦✦✦

Family Man / Apr. 28, 1978–May 1, 1978 / Muse ✦✦✦
With Major Holley on bass. Includes excerpts from "Family Suite." Challenging listening. —*Michael G. Nastos*

To Them—to Us / May 27, 1981 / Soul Note ✦✦✦

Phantasies, Vol. 1 / Sep. 25, 1984–Sep. 26, 1984 / Soul Note ✦✦
This outing by Jaki Byard's big band The Apollo Stompers does not quite live up to its potential. The 17-piece orchestra has few distinctive soloists (other than the pianist/leader) and all of the performances (which include three medleys) are quite brief; also the two vocals by Byard's daughters are just so-so. The real reason to acquire this admittedly spirited set is for the occasional (and always notable) piano solos. —*Scott Yanow*

Phantasies, Vol. 2 / Aug. 23, 1988+Aug. 24, 1988 / Soul Note ✦✦✦
The second CD featuring Jaki Byard's Apollo Stompers (a young big band) is actually superior to the first one. Although most of the soloists (other than guitarist Peter Leitch and trumpeter Graham Haynes) remain obscure, the material is more stimulating than on the debut set. In addition to a few standards, Byard penned tributes to B.B. King and Count Basie along with a two part "Concerto Grosso." His very versatile piano has its share of short solos, hinting at many jazz styles. —*Scott Yanow*

Foolin' Myself / Aug. 25, 1988 / Soul Note ✦✦✦

Live at Maybeck Recital Hall, Vol. 17 / Sep. 8, 1991 / Concord Jazz ✦✦✦✦
A dynamic, topflight piano soloist and bandleader gets a chance to present his complete package in another superb Maybeck set. Byard employs stride, shuffle, and hard bop rhythms, playing with a density and controlled force that makes each selection a treasure. —*Ron Wynn*

Empirical / Jan. 24, 1992 / Muse ✦✦✦

Don Byas

b. Oct. 21, 1912, Muskogee, OK, d. Aug. 24, 1972, Amsterdam, Netherlands
Tenor Saxophone / Bop, Swing

One of the greatest of all tenor players, Don Byas' decision to move permanently to Europe in 1946 has resulted in him being vastly underrated in jazz history books. His knowledge of chords rivalled Coleman Hawkins and, due to their similarity in tones, Byas can be considered an extension of the elder tenor. He played with many top swing bands including those of Lionel Hampton (1935), Buck Clayton (1936), Don Redman, Lucky Millinder, Andy Kirk (1939–40) and most importantly Count Basie (1941–43). An advanced swing stylist, Byas' playing looked toward bop. He jammed at Minton's Playhouse in the early 1940s, appeared on 52nd Street with Dizzy Gillespie and performed a pair of stunning duets with bassist Slam Stewart at a 1944 Town Hall concert. After recording extensively during 1945–46 (often as a leader), Byas went to Europe with Don Redman's band and (with the exception of a 1970 appearance at the Newport Jazz Festival) never came back to the U.S. He lived in France, the Netherlands and Denmark, often appeared at festivals and worked steadily. Whenever American players were touring, they would ask for Byas who had opportunities to perform with Duke Ellington, Bud Powell, Kenny Clarke, Dizzy Gillespie, Jazz at the Philharmonic (including a recorded tenor battle with Hawkins and Stan Getz), Art Blakey and (on a 1968 recording) Ben Webster. Byas also recorded often in the 1950s but was largely forgotten in the U.S. by the time of his death. —*Scott Yanow*

Savoy Jam Party / Jul. 28, 1944–Aug. 21, 1946 / Savoy ✦✦✦✦
Fun session with a variety of bands from the mid-'40s —*Michael G. Nastos*

● **On Blue Star** / Jul. 4, 1950–Apr. 10, 1952 / Verve ✦✦✦✦✦
Don Byas on Blue Star is a collection of 23 sides cut in Paris between January 13, 1947 and March 1952…The material on this CD is gracious and generally mellow and fans of the mainstream tenor of Byas will have good reason to acquire this CD. —*Bob Rusch*

A Tribute to Cannonball / Dec. 15, 1961 / Columbia ✦✦✦
The title of this LP is misleading for, although Cannonball

Adderley produced the session, no "tribute" takes place. Adderley could always recognize talent and he was wise to get the veteran tenor Don Byas (who had not recorded since 1955) back on record. Teamed in Paris with trumpeter Idrees Sulieman, pianist Bud Powell, bassist Pierre Michelot and drummer Kenny Clarke, Byas proved to be in prime form on a variety of jazz standards including "Just One of Those Things," "Cherokee" and "Jeannine." —Scott Yanow

A Night in Tunisia / Jan. 13, 1963–Jan. 14, 1963 / Black Lion ✦✦✦✦
Consistent mid-'60s quartet date with Byas' sweeping, majestic tenor again sparkling in standards, ballads, and blues format. He's supported by mostly journeyman pros, with the exception of gifted bassist Niels Henning Orsted-Pedersen, who anchors the rhythm section. —Ron Wynn

Walkin' / Jan. 13, 1963–Jan. 14, 1963 / Black Lion ✦✦✦✦
More from a series of mid-'60s sessions done at the Montmarte in Copenhagen. Byas was at his most evocative, playing shopworn anthems and ancient ballads with vigor and conviction. He often soars over the competent but limited rhythm section, although bassist Niels Henning Orsted-Pedersen keeps them from being savaged. —Ron Wynn

Charlie Byrd

b. Sep. 16, 1925, Chuckatuck, VA
Guitar / Bop, Brazilian Jazz
Guitarist Charlie Byrd perfected the application of classical guitar techniques to a jazz setting, and helped introduce American audiences to Latin American sounds in the early '60s, particularly samba and bossa nova. His style is delightful, attractive and impressive, reflecting training he received in the '50s from Sophocles Papas and Andres Segovia. Byrd was born into a musical family, and his brother Joe (Gene) studied at the Peabody Conservatory and has worked in his groups since the mid-'60s. Byrd played with Django Reinhardt while in France during World War II. Following his discharge, he worked with Sol Yaged, Joe Marsala and Freddie Slack. Byrd for a while decided to change fields and become a concert guitarist. He spent half the '50s studying with Papas and Segovia. But he began playing regularly around Washington, D.C., and eventually returned to jazz, working and recording with Woody Herman. He began recording as a leader for Savoy in 1957, and did sessions for Riverside, Prestige, Offbeat, Columbia and Milestone in the '60s. Visits to South America on State Department-sponsored tours led to an interest in Latin sounds. Byrd and Stan Getz made the chart-topping album *Jazz Samba* in 1962. It was Byrd's suggestion that they do some compositions by Antonio Carlos Jobim. Byrd did other Latin dates, working with Keter Betts, Cal Tjader and Clark Terry among others. Along with Barney Kessell and Herb Ellis Byrd formed The Great Guitars group in the '70s. They made several Concord albums, and Byrd also recorded with Nat Adderley and cut his own sessions on Fantasy. He wrote an instruction manual in 1973 that's become widely used. Byrd made other trio dates, as well as quartet and sextet sessions for Concord in the '70s and '80s, working with Laurindo Almeida and Bud Shank. He recorded with the Washington Guitar Quintet in 1990 for the Concord Concerto label. —Ron Wynn

Blues for Night People / Aug. 4, 1957 / Savoy ✦✦✦
Midnight Guitar / Aug. 4, 1957 / Savoy ✦✦✦
A late '50s session that shows another side of Byrd's guitar playing. There are lowdown blues songs and funky soul-jazz numbers, as well as his now-familiar sentimental pieces. But this lineup, particularly bassist Keeter Betts, was more interested in exuberant than understated material, and Byrd proved he could fill this bill. —Ron Wynn

Charlie Byrd at the Village Vanguard / Jan. 15, 1961 / Original Jazz Classics ✦✦✦
Bossa Nova Pelos Passaros / Sep. 28, 1962–Oct. 5, 1962 / Original Jazz Classics ✦✦✦
Once More! Bossa Nova / Feb. 21, 1963+Apr. 4, 1963 / Riverside ✦✦
● **Byrd at the Gate** / May 9, 1963+May 10, 1963 / Original Jazz Classics ✦✦✦✦
Byrd at the Gate presented the unique jazz guitar approach of

Charlie Byrd and his trio (Keter Betts, bass; Bill Reichenbach, drums) live at the Gate. The program was also joined by the guesting of Clark Terry (trumpet) and/or Sheldon Powell (tenor sax) on five of the tracks. —Bob Rusch, Cadence

Brazilian Byrd / Dec. 21, 1964–Feb. 8, 1965 / Columbia ✦✦
Travelin' Man / Mar. 16, 1965 / Columbia ✦✦✦
Byrdland / Aug. 25, 1966–Aug. 27, 1966 / Columbia ✦✦✦
Byrd by the Sea / Mar. 1, 1974–Mar. 3, 1974 / Fantasy ✦✦
Mild, smooth trio date with Byrd playing light jazz, occasional Afro-Latin, and even a mock classical number, backed by bassist Joe Byrd and drummer Bertill Knox. This sometimes comes close to, but never becomes, mood music. —Ron Wynn

Great Guitars / Jul. 28, 1974 / Concord Jazz ✦✦✦✦
Charlie Byrd was teamed up with Barney Kessel and Herb Ellis (along with bassist Joe Byrd and drummer John Rae) for this rather exciting concert. While Ellis and Kessel have three unaccompanied duets, the inclusion of Byrd (thought of as a Brazilian specialist rather than a bopper) is the wild card that makes this set a major success. While Byrd is excellent on his features "Charlie's Blues" and "O Barquinho," it is the three stomps featuring all the guitarists ("Undecided," "Topsy" and "Benny's Bugle") that are most memorable. —Scott Yanow

Blue Byrd / Aug. 1978 / Concord Jazz ✦✦
Fluid, frequently striking guitar solos from Byrd that enliven an otherwise routine set. Things are so mellow that they threaten to become tepid, but Byrd's gentle voicings and fine playing elevate the support of bassist Joe Byrd and drummer Wayne Phillips. —Ron Wynn

Sugarloaf Suite / Aug. 1979 / Concord Jazz ✦✦✦
Great Guitars at the Winery / Jul. 1980 / Concord Jazz ✦✦✦✦
Brazilville / May 1981 / Concord Jazz ✦✦✦
A good quartet date with Bud Shank (as). Shank adds spice to Charlie Byrd's cool Afro-Latin setting. —Ron Wynn

Great Guitars at Charlie's Georgetown / Aug. 1982 / Concord Jazz ✦✦✦
Isn't It Romantic / Mar. 1984 / Concord Jazz ✦✦✦
Byrd and Brass / Apr. 1986 / Concord Jazz ✦✦
It's a Wonderful World / Aug. 1988 / Concord Jazz ✦✦✦✦
The Bossa Nova Years / Apr. 16, 1991–Apr. 17, 1991 / Concord Jazz ✦✦✦✦
The Washington Guitar Quartet / Apr. 15, 1992 / Concord Jazz ✦✦✦
Romanticism, Afro-Latin voicings and classical stylings are the three primary components of Charlie Byrd's most recent release. It blends his playing with that of Carlos Barbosa-Lima, Jeffrey Meyerriecks, Myrna Sislen and Larry Snitzler, and the quintet members expertly complement and contrast each other on a program of American popular standards, compositions by Vivaldi, Mozart, Antonio Carlos Jobim and three superb interpretations of the Bix Beiderbecke masterpieces "In A Mist," "Candlelights" and "In The Dark." It's more structured than improvisatory, but the playing is so compelling and exquisite that it should appeal to both guitar lovers and music fans generally. —Ron Wynn

Aquarelle / Aug. 10, 1993 / Concord Concerto ✦✦✦
Moments Like This / Aug. 9, 1994–Aug. 10, 1995 / Concord Jazz ✦✦✦

Donald Byrd
(Donaldson Toussaint L. Ouverture Byrd, II)

b. Dec. 9, 1932, Detroit, MI
Trumpet / R&B, Hard Bop, Crossover
Donald Byrd has been hailed as a visionary and condemned as a traitor. He's played vigorous hard bop, displayed technical skills that put him at the top of his generation and presided over inspirational, superb record sessions. He's also been responsible for hideous, commercially successful, artistically barren releases that by even the most minimal standards didn't qualify as either good jazz or good pop. He's among the most educated musicians around, has worked tirelessly on behalf of music education and African-American culture, yet also been quoted making highly inflammatory, debatable statements. Byrd may be jazz's ultimate loose cannon now that Miles Davis has departed. His '50s solos,

with their ringing, assertive lines and wonderfully full tone, can stand with anyone's. What he played on many of his '70s dates qualifies as immediately forgettable. Byrd began his music studies at Wayne State University in the early '50s, but they were halted by military service. He played in an Air Force band, then attended the Manhattan School of Music where he earned his MA in music education. Byrd served as Prestige's main studio trumpeter in the late '50s, while cutting dates for Transition, Savoy, Columbia, Discovery, Blue Note and Prestige. He co-led a group with Pepper Adams from the late '50s into the early '60s. Byrd remained an active bandleader in the '60s, recording for Bethlehem, then cutting a string of Blue Note dates, mostly combos in vintage hard bop fashion. At times he'd experiment, as with the mid-'60s *Christo Redentor*, a hymn written and arranged by Duke Pearson. The album included the Coleridge Perkinson Choir. Byrd also studied composition in Europe in 1962 and 1963, and later became an active instructor. He taught at Rutgers, Hampton Institute, Howard and North Carolina Central. Byrd began changing direction in the '70s. He worked with a 12-member group on *Electric Byrd*, then turned more and more toward fusion, urban contemporary and instrumental pop. These albums were big sellers; *Black Byrd* was Blue Note's single biggest hit album in 1973. But the barrage of electronics, funk and urban contemporary arrangements, rigid backbeats and background vocalists generated enormous controversy. Byrd denounced his critics as "jazz snobs." He earned a law degree from Howard and received his doctorate in 1982 from Columbia. He served as chairman of black music at Howard and helped turn an unknown student ensemble into a hugely successful pop fusion act called The Blackbyrds. His late '70s and early '80s albums continued in the fusion/urban contemporary/instrumental pop vein. Then in the late '80s Byrd returned to the music he'd once championed. He played on a Sonny Rollins session, and did an album with Mulgrew Miller and Kenny Garrett. During the '90s he's hedged his bets, cutting jazz material for Landmark and recording with hip-hopper Guru on his rap/jazz project. —*Ron Wynn*

First Flight / Aug. 23, 1955 / Delmark ◆◆◆
An instructive session; you can hear Byrd's trumpet conception taking form. Backing groups include Yusef Lateef (sax), Barry Harris (p). Prototype '80s Detroit/Chicago jazz sound. —*Ron Wynn*

Long Green / Sep. 29, 1955 / Savoy ◆◆◆
This was trumpeter Donald Byrd's second session as a leader, following his lesser-known debut for Transition by a little over a month. Just 22 years old at the time, Byrd did not have his own style yet but already was a promising soloist. Heard in a quintet with tenor saxophonist Frank Foster, pianist Hank Jones, bassist Paul Chambers and drummer Kenny Clarke, Byrd jams on three group originals and a trio of standards. Nothing all that unusual occurs, but there are some strong moments on this enjoyable blowing. —*Scott Yanow*

House of Byrd / Aug. 3, 1956+Nov. 2, 1956 / Prestige ◆◆◆
This two-LP set combines together the music from *Two Trumpets* and *The Young Bloods*. The former session has both Donald Byrd and Art Farmer on trumpets in a sextet with altoist Jackie McLean and pianist Barry Harris while the latter is actually stronger, featuring Byrd, altoist Phil Woods and pianist Al Haig in a quintet. These blowing sessions (typical of Prestige's albums of the 1950s) have their enjoyable moments, with Farmer and Woods taking overall solo honors. —*Scott Yanow*

Modern Jazz Perspective / Aug. 30, 1957–Sep. 5, 1957 / Columbia ◆◆◆

Byrd in Paris, Vols. 1 & 2 / Oct. 22, 1958 / Polydor ◆◆◆◆
Two-volume set of early hard bop done in Paris. Presence of Bobby Jaspar (fl, ts), well-regarded but little-known international musician, increases importance. These two dates helped Jaspar establish his reputation. Walter Davis (p), Doug Watkins (b) and Art Taylor (d) make a fine rhythm section. —*Doug Ramsey*

Off to the Races / Dec. 21, 1958 / Blue Note ◆◆◆

Byrd in Hand / May 31, 1959 / Blue Note ◆◆◆

September Afternoon / May 19, 1959 / Discovery ◆◆

Fuego / Oct. 4, 1959 / Blue Note ◆◆◆
A good one for the Detroit trumpeter, with Jackie McLean (as) and Duke Pearson (p). —*Michael G. Nastos*

Byrd in Flight / Jul. 17, 1960 / Blue Note ◆◆◆◆◆
Donald Byrd at the Half Note Cafe, Vol. 1 / Nov. 11, 1960 / Blue Note ◆◆◆◆
Donald Byrd at the Half Note Cafe, Vol. 2 / Nov. 11, 1960 / Blue Note ◆◆◆◆
This album features two bonus cuts; good though rather standard early-'60s hard bop with Pepper Adams (bar sax) and Duke Pearson (p). —*Ron Wynn*

Chant / Apr. 17, 1961 / Blue Note ◆◆◆◆◆
Not released until 1979, this excellent quintet session features the always formidable team of trumpeter Donald Byrd and baritonist Pepper Adams. The accompanying rhythm section includes pianist Herbie Hancock shortly before he joined Miles Davis. The repertoire consists of six likable tunes including an uptempo "I'm an Old Cowhand," "That's All," "Sophisticated Lady," two Byrd originals and Duke Pearson's "Chant." This is superior hard bop from the early '60s. —*Scott Yanow*

The Cat Walk / May 2, 1961 / Blue Note ◆◆◆
Royal Flush / Sep. 21, 1961 / Blue Note ◆◆◆
Free Form / Dec. 11, 1961 / Blue Note ◆◆◆
Groovin' for Nat / Jan. 12, 1962 / Black Lion ◆◆◆
Solid early-60s session with Byrd meshing alongside Duke Pearson and Bob Cranshaw. Johnny Coles makes effective appearances. —*Ron Wynn*

● **A New Perspective** / Jan. 12, 1963 / Blue Note ◆◆◆◆◆
Includes remarkable "Christo Redentor," a Duke Pearson hymn. Excellent merger of gospel, choral, and jazz sensibility and arrangements. —*Ron Wynn*

I'm Tryin' to Get Home / Dec. 17, 1964–Dec. 18, 1964 / Blue Note ◆◆
Brass with Voices. 1986 reissue of uneven album that takes same tack as *A New Perspective* but with less success. —*Ron Wynn*

Mustang! / Jun. 24, 1966 / Blue Note ◆◆◆
Blackjack / Jan. 9, 1967 / Blue Note ◆◆◆
Perhaps his very best of many recordings with Sonny Red (as), Hank Mobley, (ts), and Cedar Walton (p). —*Michael G. Nastos*

Slow Drag / May 12, 1967 / Blue Note ◆◆◆
The Creeper / Oct. 5, 1967 / Blue Note ◆◆◆

Fancy Free / May 9, 1969–Jun. 6, 1969 / Blue Note ◆◆◆
This CD reissue brings back trumpeter Donald Byrd's final jazz recording before going completely commercial with his R&B group The Blackbyrds; he would not return to jazz until the 1980s and by then the many years of not playing his horn would clearly show. *Fancy Free* was Byrd's first to use electric keyboards and on it the trumpeter found a highly satisfying balance between jazz improvisation and funky rhythms, the acoustic and the electric; pity that he did not continue in that direction. The melody of "Fancy Free" is memorable, a few of the songs are danceable without being simplistic and Byrd and tenor saxophonist Frank Foster have lyrical solos on the ballad "I Love the Girl." —*Scott Yanow*

Kofi / 1969 / Blue Note ◆◆◆◆
This previously unreleased material (taken from two sessions in 1969–70) contains some of trumpeter Donald Byrd's final jazz recordings before he shifted completely to R&B-funk. On "Kofi" Lew Tabackin's flute solo easily takes honors while "Fufu" (which is also from the earlier date) has some fine Byrd trumpet in a Miles Davis vein. The other three performances from a year later feature Byrd and Foster in excellent form on moody material which merges together hard bop with early fusion; it is remarkable how much Byrd sounds like Miles Davis of the period on some of these numbers. Unfortunately he would not be pursuing this path in the future, making this transitional CD a historic and somewhat unique venture that is well worth investigating. —*Scott Yanow*

Electric Byrd / May 15, 1970 / Blue Note ◆◆
Pivotal release with Byrd using 12 piece group. Duke Pearson on electric piano. The arrangements and mood are harbingers of Byrd's shift into pop, funk, and R&B. —*Ron Wynn*

Ethiopian Knights / Aug. 25, 1971–Aug. 26, 1971 / Blue Note ◆◆
Interesting jam-session feel. Top jazz players manage to retain credibility in essentially R&B setting. Album cited by many as reflective of label's trend away from its roots in the 70s. Concept was brainchild of George Butler, now Dr. George Butler of Columbia. —*Ron Wynn*

Street Lady / Jun. 13, 1973+Jun. 15, 1973 / BN ✦✦

Black Byrd / 1974 / Blue Note ✦✦✦

Places and Spaces / Aug. 1975–Sep. 1975 / Blue Note ✦

Caricatures / 1976 / Blue Note ✦✦

Thank You . . . For F.U.M.L. (Funking up My Life) / Feb. 19, 1978 / Elektra ✦

Love Byrd: Donald Byrd and 125th St, N.Y.C. / 1981 / Elektra ✦✦✦✦

Harlem Blues / Sep. 1987 / Landmark ✦✦✦

Getting Down to Business / Oct. 10, 1989–Oct. 12, 1989 / Landmark ✦✦✦

Donald Byrd Sextet. Byrd back to mainstream with old and new players. Top solos by Joe Henderson (sax), Kenny Garrett (sax), Donald Brown on piano. Byrd plays with confidence and edge. — *Ron Wynn*

A City Called Heaven / Jan. 17, 1991–Jan. 19, 1991 / Landmark ✦✦✦

Young Byrd / Milestone ✦✦✦

This reissue of material from two early sessions pairs Byrd with two saxophonists: Art Pepper and Gigi Gryce. The set with Pepper is live at the famous Five Spot Cafe, while the session with Gryce was done in the studio. Here is Donald Byrd in the late '50s at his peak. — *AMG*

Donald Byrd with Clare Fischer and Strings / Discovery ✦✦✦

Don Byron

b. New York, NY

Clarinet, Bass Clarinet / Avant-Garde, Post-Bop, Klezmer

The most intriguing new jazz clarinetist to emerge since Eddie Daniels, Don Byron has eclectic musical interests that are reflected in his playing. He studied classical clarinet but switched to jazz at the New England Conservatory of Music. His 1992 album *Tuskegee Experiments* gave him recognition and since that time, in addition to guesting with such players as Bill Frisell, Ralph Peterson and Bobby Previte, Byron has recorded both advanced (and unpredictable) jazz and klezmer. — *Scott Yanow*

● **Tuskegee Experiments** / Nov. 1990–Jul. 1991 / Elektra/Nonesuch ✦✦✦✦

The album that helped break clarinet sensation Don Byron to a wider audience. Byron's twisting, soaring solos and impressive command of numerous styles had already made him a critical favorite, and he got rave reviews for this release. It contained a mix of social commentary and explosive playing and was expertly produced and mastered. — *Ron Wynn*

Plays the Music of Mickey Katz / 1993 / Elektra Nonesuch ✦✦

C

George Cables

b. Nov. 14, 1944, New York, NY
Piano / Post-Bop, Hard Bop
Equally skilled as a leader or as a sideman, George Cables has helped to define modern mainstream jazz piano of the 1980s and '90s. When he was 18 and at Mannes College he formed the Jazz Samaritans with Steve Grossman and Billy Cobham. Cables gained recognition during his stints with Art Blakey's Jazz Messengers, Sonny Rollins (both in 1969), Joe Henderson (1969–71) and Freddie Hubbard (1971–76). He was with Dexter Gordon (1976–78) during the tenor's successful return to the United States and became known as Art Pepper's favorite pianist (1979–82). In addition to his occasional work with Bebop and Beyond (starting in 1984), Cables has appeared in a countless number of situations through the years and has recorded frequently as a leader, most notably for Contemporary (including the 1979 classic *Cables' Vision*), Concord and SteepleChase. —*Scott Yanow*

Circles / Mar. 27, 1979–Mar. 28, 1979 / Contemporary ✦✦✦
● **Cables' Vision** / Dec. 17, 1979 Dec. 19, 1979 / Original Jazz Classics ✦✦✦✦✦
Strong late '70s release with Cables leading a larger-than-usual group boasting a strong lineup. Freddie Hubbard, Bobby Hutcherson, and Ernie Watts all prove to be fiery, dynamic soloists, while Cables shows the phrasing and pianistic magic that made him Art Pepper's favorite, and the Tony Dumas/Peter Erskine bass and drums duo sparkle behind and underneath the frontline. —*Ron Wynn*

Phantom of the City / May 14, 1985–May 15, 1985 / Contemporary ✦✦✦
For this trio set with bassist John Heard and drummer Tony Williams, pianist George Cables is in excellent form on two standards, four of his originals and the little-known "Waltz for Monday." Cables has long been a talented player in what could be called the "modern mainstream": not breaking down any new boundaries but developing his own style in the flexible boundaries of hard bop. This album is an excellent example of his talents. —*Scott Yanow*

By George / Feb. 27, 1987 / Contemporary ✦✦✦
Assisted by bassist John Heard and drummer Ralph Penland on four of the six tracks, pianist George Cables explores six very familiar George Gershwin compositions. The fact that he was able to come up with fresh statements on these warhorses (and still stay melodic) says a great deal about Cables' inventiveness. —*Scott Yanow*

I Mean You / Apr. 1993 / Steeple Chase ✦✦✦✦
At Maybeck / Jan. 9, 1994 / Concord Jazz ✦✦✦

Joey Calderazzo

b. 1966, New Rochelle, NY
Piano / Post-Bop
A potentially significant pianist playing in the modern mainstream, Joey Calderazzo's career has gotten off to a strong start with a series of fine Blue Note albums. He studied classical piano from age eight, discovered jazz a few years later and hit the big time when he joined Michael Brecker's band in 1987. He has since recorded with Brecker, Bob Belden, Jerry Bergonzi, Rick Margitza and Bob Mintzer in addition to his own projects. —*Scott Yanow*

● **In the Door** / 1990 / Blue Note ✦✦✦
A wonderful debut album with a cast of great sidemen, it included Michael Brecker (sax), Branford Marsalis (tpt), and Jerry Bergonzi (ts). Very modern chord changes. —*Paul Kohler*

To Know One / 1991 / Blue Note ✦✦✦
Although not quite as slashing or dynamic as fellow young lion Bennie Green, pianist Joey Calderazzo provides some interesting moments on his second Blue Note release. But the spotlight gets taken by his impressive band, which includes saxophonists Branford Marsalis and Jerry Bergonzi and first-rate bassist and drummer Dave Holland and Jack DeJohnette. —*Ron Wynn*

The Traveler / 1993 / Blue Note ✦✦✦
Joey Calderazzo, at the time of this CD, was an excellent interpreter of the Herbie Hancock acoustic piano style who, although showing touches of originality here and there, had not yet developed his own voice. However this is a fine trio recording featuring Calderazzo with either John Patitucci or Jay Anderson on bass and Peter Erskine or Jeff Hirshfield on drums. Together they perform five standards, three of the pianist's originals and one song apiece by pianist Larry Willis and Patitucci. Calderazzo does show a great deal of maturity in his playing, sounding just as comfortable on uptempo versions of "Yesterdays" and his "Lunacy" as he does on the ballads. He is a superior middle-of-the-road jazz pianist whose most significant work is most likely in the future. —*Scott Yanow*

Secrets / Oct. 1995 / Audio Quest ✦✦✦

California Ramblers

Group / Classic Jazz
The California Ramblers recorded an enormous amount of performances during 1921–31, most of which have never been reissued. With a repertoire ranging from high-quality dance band music to hot jazz, the California Ramblers had superior musicianship and a strong sampling of the top White jazz players of the day including on some dates Red Nichols, Tommy Dorsey, Jimmy Dorsey and Adrian Rollini. The band's name was revived by manager (and occasional vocalist) Ed Kirkeby for a series of recordings during 1935–36 and used as a pseudonym by Charlie Barnet for a 1937 date. —*Scott Yanow*

● **Hallelujah, Vol. 2** / Jan. 19, 1925–Aug. 1, 1927 / Biograph ✦✦✦✦
Miss Annabelle Lee, Vol. 1 / Apr. 2, 1925–Jun. 20, 1927 / Biograph ✦✦✦✦
Edison Laterals 2 / Nov. 5, 1928–Oct. 9, 1929 / Diamond Cut ✦✦✦
This CD contains 20 performances by The California Ramblers during a one-year period of time, rare selections that were originally released by the Edison label. During the era there weren't any big names in the group, like there had been earlier, but such soloists as trumpeter Fred Van Eps, Jr. (who was influenced by Bix Beiderbecke) and Pete Pumiglio (on alto and clarinet) uplifted the hot dance arrangements of this fine group. Trombonist Miff Mole and bass saxophonist Adrian Rollini have guest appearances but basically this was a no-name unit by 1929. Fans of 1920s jazz will want the attractively packaged set. —*Scott Yanow*

Red Callender (George Sylvester Callender)

b. 1916, Haynesville, VA, **d.** Mar. 8, 1992, Saugus, CA
Bass, Tuba / Bop, Cool, Swing
A busy studio musician who appeared on a countless number of

recordings during his productive (and generally lucrative) career, Red Callender is the only player to turn down offers to join both Duke Ellington's Orchestra and the Louis Armstrong All-Stars! After briefly freelancing in New York, Callender settled in Los Angeles in 1936, debuting on record the next year with Louis Armstrong. In the early '40s he was in the Lester and Lee Young band and then formed his own trio. Callender in the 1940s recorded with Nat King Cole, Erroll Garner, Charlie Parker, Wardell Gray and Dexter Gordon among many others and can be seen and heard taking a bebop break on bass in the 1946 film *New Orleans* (which was supposed to depict the city's music scene of 1915!). After a period spent leading a trio in Hawaii, Callender returned to Los Angeles, becoming one of the first Black musicians to work regularly in the commercial studios. On his 1954 Crown LP *Speaks Low*, Callender was one of the earliest modern jazz tuba soloists and he would occasionally double on that instrument in future years. His composition "Primrose Lane" became a Top Ten hit in 1959 when recorded by Billy Wallace. Keeping busy up until his death, some of the highlights of the bassist's later career include recording with Art Tatum (1955–56), playing with Charles Mingus at the 1964 Monterey Jazz Festival, working with James Newton's avant-garde woodwind quintet (on tuba) and performing as a regular member of the Cheatham's Sweet Baby Blues Band. Callender's mid-'80s autobiography *Unfinished Dream* is quite informative and colorful. —*Scott Yanow*

Red Callender Speaks Low / 1954 / Crown ◆◆◆

Swingin' Suite / 1956 / Modern ◆◆◆◆

The Lowest / Apr. 30, 1958+May 1, 1958 / Metrojazz ◆◆◆

● **Night Mist Blues** / 1984 / Hemisphere ◆◆◆◆

Cab Calloway (Cabell Calloway)

b. Dec. 25, 1907, Rochester, NY, d. Nov. 18, 1994, Delaware
Vocals, Leader / Swing

One of the great entertainers, Cab Calloway was a household name by 1932 and never really declined in fame. A talented jazz singer and a superior scatter, Calloway's gyrations and showmanship on stage at the Cotton Club sometimes overshadowed the quality of his always-excellent bands. The younger brother of singer Blanche Calloway (who made some fine records before retiring in the mid-'30s), Cab grew up in Baltimore, attended law school briefly and then quit to try to make it as a singer and a dancer. For a time he headed the Alabamians but the band was not strong enough to make it in New York. The Missourians, an excellent group that had previously recorded heated instrumentals but had fallen upon hard times, worked out much better. Calloway worked in the 1929 revue "Hot Chocolates," started recording in 1930 and in 1931 hit it big with both "Minnie the Moocher" and his regular engagement at the Cotton Club. Calloway was soon (along with Bill Robinson, Ethel Waters, Louis Armstrong and Duke Ellington) the best-known Black entertainer of the era. He appeared in quite a few movies (including 1943's *Stormy Weather*) and "Minnie the Moocher" was followed by such recordings as "Kicking the Gong Around," "Reefer Man," "Minnie the Moocher's Wedding Day," "You Gotta Hi-De-Ho," "The Hi-De-Ho Miracle Man" and even "Mister Paganini, Swing for Minnie." Among Calloway's sidemen through the years (who received among the highest salaries in the business) were Walter "Foots" Thomas, Bennie Payne, Doc Cheatham, Eddie Barefield, Shad Collins, Cozy Cole, Danny Barker, Milt Hinton, Mario Bauza, Chu Berry, Dizzy Gillespie, Jonah Jones, Tyree Glenn, Panama Francis and Ike Quebec. His 1942 recording of "Blues in the Night" was a big hit.

With the end of the big-band era, Calloway had to reluctantly break up his orchestra in 1948 although he continued to perform with his Cab Jivers. Since George Gershwin had originally modelled the character "Sportin' Life" in *Porgy and Bess* after Calloway, it was fitting that Cab got to play him in a 1950s version. Throughout the rest of his career Calloway made special appearances for fans who never tired of hearing him sing "Minnie the Moocher." —*Scott Yanow*

Cab Calloway and the Missourians (1929–1930) / Jun. 3, 1929–Dec. 23, 1930 / JSP ◆◆◆◆

This English import starts off with the dozen selections recorded by The Missourians (plus two alternate takes) during 1929–30. The excellent group is heard playing a variety of instrumentals, many of which are based on "Tiger Rag." The heated soloing by trumpeters R.Q. Dickerson and Lammar Wright, trombonist De Priest Wheeler and the reeds of Andrew Brown and Walter Thomas makes one surprised that this group was commercially unsuccessful. Cab Calloway permanently took over The Missourians in 1930 and his earliest ten recordings form the second half of this CD. The Calloway performances (which directly precede his hit "Minnie the Moocher") are highlighted by "St. Louis Blues," "Nobody's Sweetheart" and a classic rendition of "St. James Infirmary" and make one know from the start why he was considered one of the most popular and exciting performers of the 1930s. —*Scott Yanow*

● **Cab Calloway (1930–1931)** / Jul. 24, 1930–Jun. 17, 1931 / Classics ◆◆◆◆◆

Calloway is long overdue for a reappraisal. Long put down by some writers as a mere entertainer, he was actually a superior jazz-influenced singer whose vocal abilities were often overshadowed by his showmanship. The ideal way to acquire his best recordings is to get the 11 CDs in Classics' *Complete* series. Not only do these reissues include his hits but some jazz instrumentals and enjoyable obscurities that give one a more well-rounded picture of the "Hi-De-Ho Man." This particular Classics CD has his first 24 recordings; from the start his colorful style was already fully formed. It is particularly interesting to hear Calloway performing some material associated with others, especially "Happy Feet" (Paul Whiteman), "The Viper's Drag" and "I'm Crazy 'Bout My Baby" (the latter two with Fats Waller) along with several Duke Ellington hits. Calloway's band in the early days (one of the better Harlem orchestras) had been formerly known as The Missourians and included several fine soloists, particularly trumpeter Lammar Wright and Walter Thomas on tenor and baritone. Highlights include "St. Louis Blues," "Some of These Days," a classic rendition of "St. James Infirmary," "Nobody's Sweetheart" and the original version of "Minnie the Moocher." —*Scott Yanow*

Jazz Heritage: Mr. Hi-De-Ho (1930–1931) / Jul. 24, 1930–Oct. 21, 1931 / MCA ◆◆◆

This LP from MCA's *Jazz Heritage* series of the early '80s gives listeners a sampling of Cab Calloway's early recordings. Sixteen of his best performances from 1930–31 are here including "St. Louis Blues," "Nobody's Sweetheart," a classic version of "St. James Infirmary," "Bugle Call Rag," "Kickin' the Gong Around," "Trickeration" and the original recording of "Minnie the Moocher." Although superceded by the much more complete Classics CD series, this is a fine set of early material. —*Scott Yanow*

Cab Calloway and Company / Mar. 2, 1931–Nov. 29, 1949 / RCA ◆◆◆◆

This is a very appealing double LP from French RCA's *Jazz Tribune* series. The first 22 of the 34 selections (including four rare alternate takes) feature the Cab Calloway Orchestra of 1933–34, a vastly underrated early swing band which, in addition to its colorful leader/singer, features good soloists in trumpeter Lammar Wright, clarinetist Eddie Barefield and tenor saxophonist Walter "Foots" Thomas. Highlights include "Harlem Hospitality," "The Lady with the Fan," "Harlem Camp Meeting," "Kickin' the Gong Around," "Margie" and two remakes of "Minnie the Moocher." In addition this two-fer (which has all of Calloway's recordings for Victor) contains four long-forgotten items from 1949 including a hilarious version of "I Beeped When I Shoulda Bopped" (in which Calloway satirizes not only bebop but his own style), six numbers from his older sister Blanche Calloway in 1931 (highlighted by "I Need Lovin'") and two obscure items from singer Billy Banks in 1932. Until it is reissued on CD, this two-fer (which contains over 100 minutes of high-quality and entertaining music) is well worth searching for. —*Scott Yanow*

Cab Calloway (1931–1932) / Jul. 9, 1931–Jun. 7, 1932 / Classics ◆◆◆◆

The second of 11 Classics CDs that reissue all of Cab Calloway's recordings from 1930–42 has 23 performances that trace the singer's success during an 11-month period. He shows what he learned from his older sister Blanche on some of the songs, but on "You Rascal You," "Aw You Dawg" and "Kickin' the Gong Around," the singer could be mistaken for no one else but himself. There is a bit of surface noise on some of the tracks (sometimes sounding like a light rain) and even a skip on "Without Rhythm" but the wonderful music far outvalues the minor technical faults. Due to the solos of trumpeter Lammar Wright, clarinetist Arville Harris and the tenor of Walter Thomas, the tight ensembles and Calloway's exuberant (in the case of "Basin Street Blues," rather silly) singing, there are many memorable selections on this set. Highlights include "Bugle Call Rag," "Stardust," "Trickeration," "Kickin' the Gong Around," "Corrine Corrina,"

"The Scat Song" and "Dinah." This is very enjoyable and often-classic music that lets one know immediately why Cab Calloway was so popular during the 1930s. — *Scott Yanow*

Cab Calloway (1932) / Jun. 7, 1932–Dec. 7, 1932 / Classics ✦✦✦✦

The third of 11 Cab Calloway CDs put out by Classics (which on a whole reissues the master takes of all of the popular singer's recordings from 1930–42) covers a busy six-month period. His big band (which tended to be greatly overshadowed) was actually quite excellent with good soloists in trumpeter Lammar Wright, clarinetist Eddie Barefield, Walter Thomas on tenor and pianist Bennie Payne, but of course Calloway was the main star. Highlights of this very enjoyable set include "Old Yazoo," "Reefer Man," "Old Man of the Mountain," "You Gotta Ho-De-Ho," "I've Got the World on a String," the bizarre "Dixie Doorway," "Beale Street Mama" and "The Man from Harlem." Many of the titles on this rewarding release had never been reissued before, making the Classics series a collection worth picking up in a hurry before it disappears. — *Scott Yanow*

Cab Calloway (1932–1934) / Dec. 7, 1932–Sep. 4, 1934 / Classics ✦✦✦✦

The Depression may have been at its height during the two years covered by this Classics CD (the fourth in their series of 11 complete Cab Calloway sets), but there was nothing depressed about Calloway's often-jubilant vocals, the playing of his vastly underrated orchestra or the infectious (and sometimes) crazy lyrics. Trumpeter Lammar Wright, clarinetist Eddie Barefield and Walter Thomas on tenor contribute some fine solos but the focus is very much on the leader's vocals and he is in peak form on such songs as "The Lady with the Fan," "Harlem Camp Meeting," "Kickin' the Gong Around," "Long About Midnight" and "Margie" (even if "Chinese Rhythm" is rather absurd). This easily recommended set also has a remake of "Minnie the Moocher" and an all-star recording of "Doin' the New Lowdown" with The Mills Brothers and Don Redman's Orchestra. — *Scott Yanow*

Cab Calloway (1934–1937) / Sep. 4, 1934–Mar. 3, 1937 / Classics ✦✦✦✦

Cab Calloway, who first became popular in 1930, retained his popularity (despite a lot of competition) throughout the swing era. On this excellent CD (the fifth of 11 in the European label Classics' *Complete* Calloway series), highlights include "Keep That Hi-De-Hi in Your Soul," "Nagasaki," "Copper Colored Gal," "Frisco Flo" and a crazy "That Man Is Here Again." With fine soloists in trumpeters Lammar Wright and Shad Collins, trombonist Claude Jones and (by 1936) the great tenor Ben Webster (along with a top-notch rhythm section that includes bassist Milt Hinton), this was a much better swing orchestra than it is generally rated in jazz history books. — *Scott Yanow*

On Film (1934–1950) / 1934–1950 / Flyright ✦✦
Solid collection of performances taken from soundtracks of his many film appearances. High energy makes up for spotty sound on certain tracks. — *Cub Koda*

The Hi-De-Ho Man / Jul. 2, 1935–Dec. 11, 1947 / RCA ✦✦✦
This double LP from 1974 is a bit brief, only including 20 performances by Cab Calloway and his orchestra (around an hour of music). Several periods are covered with titles from 1935 ("Nagasaki"), the 1938–42 period and nine fairly rare selections from 1945–47. Highpoints include "Jumpin' Jive," "Fifteen Minute Intermission," a 1941 version of "St. James Infirmary," "Hi De Ho Man" and a 1942 rendition of "Minnie the Moocher." On the later tracks Calloway tries to adapt his sound to rhythm & blues but, despite his best efforts, his orchestra would not survive the 1940s. The earlier titles have been reissued on CD by the Classics label and hopefully Columbia will get around to compiling a more generous Cab Calloway package in the future. The music on this two-fer is generally not classic but will be found enjoyable by his fans. — *Scott Yanow*

Cab Calloway (1937–1938) / Mar. 3, 1937–Mar. 23, 1938 / Classics ✦✦✦✦
The swing era may have been at its height during the time covered by this CD (the sixth of 11 put out by the Classics label that reissue all of Cab Calloway's 1930–42 recordings) but the colorful vocalist held onto his national name and remained a household name. With such soloists as Ben Webster or Chu Berry on tenor, trumpeters Shad Collins and Lammar Wright and a rhythm section including guitarist Danny Barker and bassist Milt Hinton,

Calloway had a particularly strong (if generally overlooked) orchestra. Among the more memorable selections of the 24 included on this CD are "Swing, Swing, Swing," "She's Tall, She's Tan, She's Terrific," "Bugle Blues" and "Hi-De-Ho Romeo." — *Scott Yanow*

Penguin Swing / Dec. 10, 1937–Mar. 5, 1941 / Jazz Archives ✦✦✦
The music on this Dutch import CD was last available as a collectors' LP put out by Jazz Archives. The 16 studio recordings by Cab Calloway's Orchestra from the 1937–41 period put the focus on the tenor solos of Chu Berry with eight of the numbers being unissued performances, usually alternate takes. In addition to Berry and of course the leader's exuberant vocals, trumpeters Lammar Wright, Dizzy Gillespie and Jonah Jones also have solo space. Highlights include "Penguin Swing," "Bugle Blues," "Calling All Bars," "Bye Bye Blues" and "Jonah Joins the Cab." This CD is worth picking up (due to the rarer tracks) even by collectors who have been wise enough to get the many Cab Calloway CDs put out by the Classics label. — *Scott Yanow*

Cab Calloway (1938–1939) / Mar. 23, 1938–Feb. 20, 1939 / Classics ✦✦✦✦
The seventh of the Classics label's 11 Cab Calloway CDs traces his progress during an 11-month period through 24 recordings. The band's main soloists at the time included trumpeters Shad Collins and Irving Randolph, trombonists Claude Jones and Keg Johnson and especially tenor great Chu Berry (the band gets four instrumentals on this set). Singer June Richmond has a couple of vocals but obviously Cab Calloway is the main reason that the orchestra was working so steadily. With such songs as "Shout Shout, Shout," "Do You Wanna Jump Children?" and "F.D.R. Jones" among the more memorable tracks, this CD (along with the others in the valuable series) is well worth picking up. — *Scott Yanow*

16 Cab Calloway Classics / Feb. 20, 1939–Nov. 3, 1941 / CBS ✦✦✦
Released in 1973 by French CBS, this LP has 16 performances from Calloway's orchestra that de-emphasize the participation of its vocalist/leader and put the spotlight on his star instrumentalists of the 1939–41 period. Trumpeter Dizzy Gillespie (particularly on "Bye Bye Blues" and a futuristic "Pickin' the Cabbage"), tenor-great Chu Berry (including his famous rendition of "Ghost of a Chance"), bassist Milt Hinton, drummer Cozy Cole and trumpeter Jonah Jones (on "Jonah Joins the Cab") are among the classic players featured on this long out-of-print LP. — *Scott Yanow*

Cab Calloway (1939–1940) / Mar. 28, 1939–Mar. 8, 1940 / Classics ✦✦✦✦
Cab Calloway had one of his strongest orchestras during the period covered by this CD, the eighth of 11 put out by the European Classics label that reissue all of his studio recordings from 1930–42. Trumpeter Dizzy Gillespie joined the band by the time of its Aug. 30, 1939 session and he has several short solos on these tracks in addition to being well-featured on the adventurous "Pickin' the Cabbage." In addition, the great tenor Chu Berry gets plenty of solo space, the impressive rhythm section (with guitarist Danny Barker, bassist Milt Hinton and drummer Cozy Cole) really propels the ensembles and Cab Calloway is in typically exuberant voice. Among the highlights are "The Ghost of Smoky Joe," "Crescendo in Drums" (a feature for Cole), "Pluckin' the Bass" (Hinton's showcase) and even "Jiveformation Please." — *Scott Yanow*

Cab Calloway (1940) / Mar. 8, 1940–Aug. 28, 1940 / Classics ✦✦✦✦
With such soloists as trumpeter Dizzy Gillepie, Chu Berry on tenor and trombonist Tyree Glenn, along with a rhythm section that includes bassist Milt Hinton and drummer Cozy Cole, this was a particularly strong edition of the Cab Calloway Orchestra. There are six instrumentals among the 22 selections on this Classics CD (the ninth of 11 Calloway *Complete* sets) including Berry's famous version of "Ghost of a Chance" and a spot for Gillespie on "Bye Bye Blues," but nearly every performance has its interesting solos; most of the ones with short spots for Gillespie have rarely been reissued. Cab Calloway, who as usual is the main star, is in spirited form. The other highlights include "Hi-De-Ho Serenade," "Fifteen Minute Intermission," "Papa's in Bed with His Britches On" and "Are You Hep to the Jive?" It's recommended, as are all of the CDs in this important series. — *Scott Yanow*

Cab Calloway (1940–41) / Aug. 28, 1940–Jul. 24, 1941 / Classics ✦✦✦✦
Cab Calloway is in superior form throughout this CD (the tenth

of 11 Calloway releases from the European Classics label) but it is often the short solos by his sidemen that hold onto one's interest, particularly those of trumpeter Dizzy Gillespie and tenor Chu Berry. By the last ten numbers (including his feature "Jonah Joins the Cab"), trumpeter Jonah Jones had become a member of the powerful band which could rank at the top echelon of swing orchestras. Calloway is also heard near the peak of his powers and the highlights of this fine set include Benny Carter's "Lonesome Nights" (one of six instrumentals among the 22 numbers), "A Chicken Ain't Nothin' but a Bird," "Ebony Silhouette," "Hep Cat's Love Song" and two versions of "St. James Infirmary." —*Scott Yanow*

Cab Calloway (1941–1942) / Jul. 24, 1941–Jul. 27, 1942 / Classics ✦✦✦✦
The final of the European Classics label's 11 *Complete* Cab Calloway CDs (reissuing all of his studio recordings of 1930–42) has the last recordings of trumpeter Dizzy Gillespie and tenor Chu Berry with Cab; other soloists include trumpeter Jonah Jones and trombonist Tyree Glenn. Calloway retained his popularity throughout the World War II years and was still in prime form during these 22 recordings. Highlights include a memorable "Blues in the Night," "A Smo-o-o-ooth One," "Virginia, Georgia and Caroline" and a new version of "Minnie the Moocher." All of the 11 Classics CDs are highly recommended to Cab Calloway and swing fans; they are perfectly done. —*Scott Yanow*

Jazz Off the Air, Vol. 4 / 1943–1946 / Spotlite ✦✦✦
Cab Calloway and his orchestra are heard on selections taken from four radio broadcasts dating from the 1943–46 era, a period when they were not recording that frequently. Although there are a few spots for Cab Calloway's vocals, the emphasis on this collectors' LP from the English Spotlite label is on such fine soloists as tenors Illinois Jacquet and Ike Quebec, trombonist Tyree Glenn and trumpeter Jonah Jones. Although not essential, swing collectors will enjoy this set. —*Scott Yanow*

Michel Camilo

b. Apr. 4, 1952, Santo Domingo, Dominican Republic
Piano / Hard Bop, Latin Jazz
An exciting and high-powered virtuoso pianist, Michel Camilo came from a very musical family (with all nine of his uncles being musicians). Originally playing accordion, he switched to piano when he was 16. After moving to New York in 1979, his song "Why Not?" became a hit for the Manhattan Transfer and caught on as a standard and "Caribe" entered the repertoire of Dizzy Gillespie. Camilo, who worked with Paquito D'Rivera's band for three years (cutting an album with "Why Not?" as the title cut) has recorded for Electric Bird (sessions reissued by Evidence) and Columbia and worked as a leader for the past decade. —*Ron Wynn*

Why Not / Feb. 25, 1985–Feb. 27, 1985 / Evidence ✦✦✦
Pianist Michel Camilo made his recording debut as a leader with this session for the Japanese King label. Camilo was anxious to show everything, and did so on such cuts as "Thinking Of You" and the title track. He ripped through phrases, added powerhouse chords and rippling lines, switched tempos and meters, and moved from a hard bop feel to an Afro-Latin groove in the middle of a piece. His intensity and energy were impressive, but at times he tried too much and stumbled getting back to the melody. It wasn't an unflawed debut, but Camilo showed that he would be a pianist to be reckoned with down the line. —*Ron Wynn*

Suntan / Jun. 29, 1986–Jun. 30, 1986 / Evidence ✦✦✦
Pianist Michel Camilo did some intensive recording for the Japanese Suntan label over a two-day period in 1986. These five selections were in a trio format with Dave Weckl and Joel Rosenblatt alternating on drums and Anthony Jackson on bass throughout. Camilo displayed the Afro-Latin and Latin jazz side of his keyboard personality with slashing, attacking rhythms and phrases. He sacrificed some of his celebrated speed and thought more about ideas, pace, melodies, and harmonic creativity. Camilo's playing emerged as dominant as Jackson was content to work off his leads, and both drummers were equally willing to interact rather than try to influence the music's direction. As a result, Camilo got the chance to demonstrate his full range and did so in a workmanlike, effective manner. —*Ron Wynn*

Michel Camilo / Jan. 30, 1988–Feb. 1, 1988 / Portrait ✦✦✦✦
● **On Fire** / Jun. 20, 1989–Jun. 25, 1989 / Epic ✦✦✦✦✦
Burning Latin-jazz piano trio. Recommended. —*Michael G. Nastos*

On the Other Hand / Apr. 1990 / Epic ✦✦✦✦
Rendezvous / Jan. 18, 1993–Jan. 20, 1993 / Columbia ✦✦✦
One More Once / May 20, 1994–May 26, 1994 / Sony ✦✦✦✦

John Campbell

b. 1952, Bloomington, IL
Piano / Hard Bop
At this point pianist John Campbell, a powerful player who is creative within the tradition, is best-known for his associations with Mel Tormé and the Terry Gibbs-Buddy DeFranco Quintet. He started piano lessons at seven and in 1977 moved to Chicago. His trio/quartet (known originally as Campbell's Group) was soon in demand to accompany touring artists (including Eddie Jefferson/Richie Cole, Eddie Harris and James Moody) and in 1981 he toured Europe with Clark Terry. In 1984 Campbell moved to New York and he subbed for Jim McNeely with Stan Getz's group. In 1986 he joined Mel Tormé and soon afterward hooked up with Terry Gibbs. In 1993 Campbell recorded a solo disc for Concord (*Live at Maybeck Recital Hall, Vol. 29*). —*Scott Yanow*

After Hours / Aug. 23, 1988 / Contemporary ✦✦✦
Entertaining, occasionally outstanding. Pianist with good group makes slightly above-average mainstream date. —*Ron Wynn*

Turning Point / Jun. 18, 1990–Jun. 19, 1990 / Contemporary ✦✦✦
A good second album for pianist Campbell on the Contemporary label, this one had an added bonus of excellent contributions from jazz immortal Clark Terry. His spry solos and presence elevated both the session and the other participants, particularly Campbell, who played with much more edge and energy than on his previous release. He used different rhythm section personnel as well, this time recruiting Jay Anderson and Joel Spencer. —*Ron Wynn*

● **Live at Maybeck Recital Hall, Vol. 29** / May 1993 / Concord Jazz ✦✦✦✦
Pianist John Campbell stretches out during the eight standards he performs during his Maybeck Recital Hall solo set. An exuberant player, Campbell often switches back and forth between two keys during a song (sometimes during every chorus), a device he sometimes overuses. An uptempo version of "Emily" is a particular surprise and his explorations of "Just Friends," "You and the Night and the Music" and "Easy to Love" are particularly memorable. —*Scott Yanow*

Candido

Group, Percussion / Bop, Latin Jazz
Candido was *the* Latin percussionist of the 1950s, the first person that jazz people would call when they wanted a conga or bongo player. Early on he had recorded in his native Cuba with Machito and he worked regularly with the house band at the Tropicana Club in Havana for six years. Dizzy Gillespie heard him and encouraged him to move to New York in 1952. Soon Candido was performing and recording with Gillespie. During 1953–54 he was in the Billy Taylor quartet and in 1954 he performed and recorded with Stan Kenton. Since that time Candido has recorded with the who's who of jazz including Erroll Garner, Gene Ammons, Art Blakey, Sonny Rollins, Wes Montgomery, Elvin Jones and Lionel Hampton among many others. He remains busy in the studios up to the present time. —*Scott Yanow*

● **Candido Featuring Al Cohn** / Apr. 9, 1956–Apr. 10, 1956 / ABC/Paramount ✦✦✦✦
The Volcanic Candido / Feb. 20, 1957–Feb. 25, 1957 / ABC/Paramount ✦✦✦
In Indigo / Apr. 28, 1958–May 1, 1958 / ABC/Paramount ✦✦✦
Latin Fire / Feb. 20, 1959–Mar. 4, 1959 / ABC/Paramount ✦✦✦
Conga Soul / 1961 / Roulette ✦✦✦
Thousand Finger Man / Sep. 4, 1969–Sep. 9, 1969 / Solid State ✦✦
Beautiful / Oct. 20, 1970–Oct. 27, 1970 / Blue Note ✦✦
Drum Fever / 1973 / Polydor ✦✦✦

Conte Candoli

b. Jul. 12, 1927, Mishawaka, IN
Trumpet / Bop
Conte and Pete Candoli are both solid players in the cool bop

vein, each a trumpeter. Pete Candoli (1923) is the elder, and both are good ballad soloists, fine interpreters and technically accomplished trumpeters with reputations for polished playing with a steady, swinging quality. Pete Candoli played with several swing bands in the '40s, among them Sonny Dunham, Will Bradley, Ray McKinley, Tommy Dorsey, Teddy Powell, Woody Herman and Boyd Raeburn. He moved to the West Coast in the '50s, and worked with Les Brown and Stan Kenton. He and his brother worked together in the late '50s and early '60s, then Pete Candoli led his own band. He started a nightclub act with his wife, Edie Adams, in the early '70s with Candoli singing, dancing, playing and directing the band. The Candoli brothers played the 1973 Monterey Jazz Festival and appeared and recorded at the 1981 Aurex Festival in Japan with Lionel Hampton. They continued playing together through the '80s. Besides the band with his brother, Conte Candoli played in the '40s with Woody Herman, Chubby Jackson, Stan Kenton and Charlie Ventura. He worked in the '50s with Charlie Barnet and Kenton again, before moving to Chicago to head his own group. But he came back to California later in 1954, and played with both his brother's band and Howard Rumsey's Lighthouse All Stars through the end of the '50s. Candoli recorded and played with Terry Gibbs from 1959 to 1962, and recorded with Gerry Mulligan and Sonny Criss during the '60s. He played with Woody Herman at the Monterey Festival and with Kenton's Los Angeles Neophonic Orchestra. Candoli also played regularly with Shelly Manne, worked in the studios on film and television projects, and was in *The Tonight Show* band. During the '70s, he recorded with Frank Strazzeri and Teddy Edwards. Candoli was a member of Supersax in the '70s. The brothers have worked together into the '90s, and have recorded for Dot, Mercury, Crown and Somerset, among others, as a joint band. Conte Candoli has recorded solo sessions for Bethlehem, Atlantic and Andex. —*Ron Wynn and Michael Erlewine*

● **Conte Candoli Quartet** / Jun. 1957 / VSOP ✦✦✦✦✦
Reissued by the VSOP label, this session features the excellent bop trumpeter Conte Candoli in a quartet with pianist Vince Guaraldi, bassist Monty Budwig and drummer Stan Levey. In addition to the joy of hearing Candoli so well-showcased, this set is recommended because of the interesting repertoire. In addition to "Flamingo," "Diane" and "No Moon at All," one gets to hear rare selections penned by the likes of Al Cohn, Osie Johnson, Conte's brother Pete Candoli and the leader himself. —*Scott Yanow*

Mucho Calor / Oct. 1957 / VSOP ✦✦✦✦
Conversation / May 25, 1973 / RCA ✦✦✦
Old Acquaintance / Sep. 30, 1985–Oct. 1, 1985 / PA/USA ✦✦✦✦

Valerie Capers

b. New York, NY
Piano / Hard Bop
Although her 1995 Columbia recording *Come on Home* was released in a *Legendary Pioneers of Jazz* series, Valerie Capers is much too obscure and under recorded to be a legend, and not old enough to be a pioneer! She picked out songs on the piano as a child before losing her sight at the age of six. Her blindness did not stop her from learning to read music in Braille and becoming the first blind graduate from the Julliard School of Music. Although a classical player at the time, she was attracted to jazz and was soon working with Mongo Santamaria. In 1965 Capers recorded for Atlantic; 17 years later she would finally cut her second date (a self-produced effort for the tiny K-M-Arts label) and it would be another 13 years before her Columbia set. Capers did work with Ray Brown, Slide Hampton, James Moody, Max Roach and Dizzy Gillespie in the interim but was mostly employed as a high-level educator. Hopefully she will have more opportunities to record in the future. —*Scott Yanow*

Portrait in Soul / 1965 / Atlantic ✦✦✦
Rare septet, all Capers originals. Worth searching for. —*Michael G. Nastos*
Affirmation / Jun. 29, 1982 / K-M-Arts ✦✦✦
All standards, and well-played. A good one to find. —*Michael G. Nastos*
● **Come On Home** / 1994 / Columbia ✦✦✦✦
Valerie Capers has managed to stay somewhat obscure despite a busy schedule and her obvious talents. When Columbia gave her a rare opportunity to record, she made the most of it. Capers sings several of the songs (most winningly Horace Silver's "Come on Home") but especially notable is her strong bop-based piano playing; her trio also includes drummer Terry Clarke and either John Robinson III or Bob Cranshaw on bass. Trumpeter Wynton Marsalis helps out on two numbers ("Odyssey" and "It's All Right with Me") and altoist Paquito D'Rivera is an asset on four (including "A Night in Tunisia") but the main significance of this long overdue CD is that it gives Valerie Capers her chance to shine. —*Scott Yanow*

Frank Capp (Frank Cappuccio)

b. Aug. 20, 1931, Worchester, MA
Drums, Leader / Bop, Swing
Frank Capp, a flexible and consistently swinging drummer, loves to drive a big band. As leader of the Juggernaut (a group he co-led with Nat Pierce starting in 1975 until the pianist's death in 1992), he gets to push and inspire some of Los Angeles' best. Capp found his initial fame playing with Stan Kenton's Orchestra (1951). Two years later he settled in Los Angeles, became a busy studio musician and played with everyone from Ella Fitzgerald, Harry James and Charlie Barnet to Stan Getz, Art Pepper and Dave Pell. He recorded steadily with Andre Previn's Trio (1957–64) and also made records with Benny Goodman (1958), Terry Gibbs and Turk Murphy. Capp worked steadily on television shows and in the film studios in the 1960s and (starting in the 1970s) has recorded extensively in a variety of settings for Concord. The Capp-Pierce Juggernaut (now known simply as the Juggernaut) sometimes sounds identical to the 1970s Count Basie Orchestra and serves as a perfect format for the drummer's colorful playing. —*Scott Yanow*

Juggernaut / Aug. 8, 1976 / Concord Jazz ✦✦✦✦
● **The Live at the Century Plaza** / Jul. 21, 1978 / Concord Jazz ✦✦✦✦✦
Capp/Pierce Orchestra. Great big band from West Coast. With vocal cameo by Joe Williams. —*Michael G. Nastos*
Juggernaut Strikes Again / Oct. 1981–Nov. 1981 / Concord Jazz ✦✦✦✦
Live at the Alley Cat / Jun. 1987 / Concord Jazz ✦✦✦
The Juggernaut Presents Rickey Woodard / 1991 / Concord Jazz ✦✦✦
An impressive session that spotlights top-flight saxophonist Woodard. —*Ron Wynn*
Quality Time / Oct. 19, 1993–Jan. 1994 / Concord Jazz ✦✦✦
In a Hefti Bag / Nov. 3, 1994–Mar. 21, 1995 / Concord Jazz ✦✦✦

Mutt Carey

b. 1891, Hahnville, LA, **d.** Sep. 3, 1948, Elsinore, CA
Trumpet / New Orleans Jazz
Trumpeter Mutt Carey began playing drums, then guitar and alto horn before switching to cornet in 1912. He worked with brass bands in New Orleans between 1913 and 1917, played with Kid Ory in 1914 and toured on the vaudeville circuit in 1917, playing in Chicago. Carey returned to New Orleans in 1918, then went to California the next year to work with Ory. He became the group's leader when Ory departed in 1925. Carey played with Louis Armstrong's group in the mid-'40s, although the sessions he did weren't included in the film *New Orleans*. Carey rejoined Ory in 1944, then left again in 1947. He recorded that year in New York, making some influential recordings and working with various performers before returning to California, where he again led a group. —*Ron Wynn*
Mutt Carey Plays the Blues / Riverside ✦✦✦

Larry Carlton

b. Mar. 2, 1949, Torrance, CA
Guitar / Blues, Crossover
A very popular guitarist since the 1970s, Larry Carlton has carved out his own style in the crossover field, mixing together blues, rock, pop and some jazz improvising. A busy studio musician since the early '70s, Carlton was a major asset to the Crusaders (1971–75), played with Tom Scott's L.A. Express in the mid-'70s and since 1978 has been a solo artist who occasionally shows the desire to play jazz. —*Scott Yanow*

Sleepwalk / 1981 / MCA ◆◆
Friends / 1982 / MCA ◆◆◆
● **Last Night** / Feb. 17, 1986 / MCA ◆◆◆◆
Alone/But Never Alone / 1986 / MCA ◆◆◆
Discovery / 1987 / MCA ◆◆◆
On Solid Ground / 1989 / MCA ◆◆◆
Renegade Gentleman / Mar. 1991–Apr. 1993 / GRP ◆◆

Hoagy Carmichael (Howard Hoagland Carmichael)

b. Nov. 11, 1899, Blooming, IN, **d.** Dec. 27, 1981, Palm Springs, CA
Piano, Vocals, Composer / Standards, Classic Jazz
One of the great composers of the American popular song, Hoagy Carmichael differed from most of the others (with the obvious exception of Duke Ellington) in that he was also a fine performer. Such Carmichael songs as "Stardust," "Georgia on My Mind," "Up the Lazy River," "Rockin' Chair," "The Nearness of You," "Heart and Soul," "In the Cool, Cool, Cool of the Evening," "Skylark" and "New Orleans" have long been standards, each flexible enough to receive definitive treatment numerous times. Carmichael, who was supposed to become a lawyer, loved jazz almost from the start, and particularly the cornet playing of Bix Beiderbecke. His first composition "Riverboat Shuffle" was recorded by Bix and the Wolverines in 1924 and became a Dixieland standard. Hoagy, as a pianist, vocalist and occasional trumpeter, eventually abandoned law to concentrate on jazz, particularly after recording "Washboard Blues" with Paul Whiteman in 1927. He led a few jazz sessions of his own in the late '20s (including one that interpreted "Stardust" as an uptempo stomp!) but became more popular as a skilled songwriter. By 1935 he was working in Hollywood and he became an occasional character actor, appearing in 14 films including *To Have and Have Not* and *The Best Years of Our Lives*, generally playing a philosophical and world weary pianist/vocalist. In the 1940s Carmichael recorded some trio versions of his hits and in 1956 he cut a full set of vocals while backed by a modern jazz group that included Art Pepper. After that he drifted into semi-retirement, dissatisfied with how the music business had changed. His two autobiographies (1946's *The Stardust Road* and 1965's *Sometimes I Wonder*) are worth picking up. —*Scott Yanow*

● **Classic Hoagy Carmichael** / May 9, 1927–Dec. 15, 1987 / Smithsonian ◆◆◆◆◆
The talented Hoagy Carmichael gained fame in his lifetime for his singing, acting and to a lesser extent his skills at the piano, but his most important contributions to music were made as a composer. This handsome three-LP box set (which includes a classy 64-page booklet) has recordings of Carmichael's songs from a 60-year period and a wide variety of performers. Programmed more or less in chronological order, the box includes no less than six versions of "Stardust" along with fairly definitive versions of his bigger hits along with some obscurities. The music is not strictly jazz although one gets Bix, Louis Armstrong, the Boswell Sisters, Mildred Bailey, Benny Goodman, Artie Shaw, Billie Holiday, Ella, Mel Tormé, Art Pepper and even Wynton Marsalis. In addition, there are selections featuring Bob Hope, Kate Smith, Frank Sinatra, Betty Hutton, Bing Crosby, Jane Wyman, Ray Charles (guess which song) and Margaret Whiting along with ten apperances by Carmichael himself. There are many more than its share of classics in this admirable package which is highly recommended to all. —*Scott Yanow*

Stardust & Much More / Nov. 18, 1927–Mar. 1, 1960 / RCA/Bluebird ◆◆◆◆
A wide-ranging collection of recordings of his work by Carmichael and others, covering 1927 to 1960. A good starter on his work. —*Bruce Eder*

Stardust (1927–1932) / 1927–1932 / Historical ◆◆◆
This session presents a dozen early Hoagy Carmichael sides which make a nice complement to other recently (1982) reissued Decca sides. These tracks are earlier (1927–1932) and have greater jazz interest in both solos and arrangements. There is also a good helping of Carmichael vocals mixed in with Cliff Williams and Scrappy Lambert. Also notable is a hot accordian solo (Jack Cornell) on "High & Dry," which also sports a nice trumpet solo (Manny Klein?). Other supporting musicians include Art Schutt, Joe Tarto, Jimmy and Tommy Dorsey, Stan King, Babe Russin. There are two previously unissued tracks, and the overall sound is fair to good. —*Bob Rusch, Cadence*

The Stardust Road / Feb. 25, 1939–Mar. 1, 1951 / MCA ◆◆
Hoagy Carmichael, The Stardust Road is a set of Decca recordings from the '40s chock full of the Carmichael vocal charm and ambiance, but only of peripheral jazz interest. —*Bob Rusch, Cadence*

Hoagy Carmichael Sings / Sep. 10, 1956–Sep. 13, 1956 / Pacific Jazz ◆◆◆

Judy Carmichael

b. 1952, Lynwood, CA
Piano / Stride, Swing
Judy Carmichael is a real rarity, a pianist that came up since 1950 who specializes in the pre-World War II piano style called stride. Carmichael, who was not even born in 1950, started on piano when her grandfather offered $50 to the first grandchild who could play "Maple Leaf Rag." She played music for the first time professionally when she was 19 and was a ragtime pianist at Disneyland when she discovered stride piano. In 1980 she made her recording debut on Progressive, utilizing four veteran players (including Marshall Royal and Freddie Greene). The following year Carmichael moved to New York and has worked steadily ever since. She recorded more sets for Progressive/Statiras and most recently for her own C&D label. Judy Carmichael plays at the same level as the classic masters. —*Scott Yanow*

Two Handed Stride / Apr. 4, 1980+Apr. 29, 1980 / Statiras ◆◆◆
A contemporary player with a traditional style, Judy Carmichael bangs out stride rhythms with both passion and authenticity. Although she adheres to the genre's exacting beats, she also does more than just recreate; she adds her own quirks and phrasing, making this a fine combination of the old and the new. —*Ron Wynn*

Jazz Piano / Jun. 11, 1983 / Statiras ◆◆◆◆
Solo piano from a lady who knows this music well. Interprets music from Earl Hines, Fats Waller, James P. Johnson, and the like. She is one of a kind, and is a very good player. —*Michael G. Nastos*

Old Friends / Jun. 11, 1983+Nov. 11, 1985 / C&D ◆◆◆
Live session with Warren Vache (cnt) and Howard Alden (g) in 1983 and 1985. More Fats, James P. Johnson, and Jelly Roll Morton. 13 tracks. A very good representation of her capabilities. —*Michael G. Nastos*

Pearls / Sep. 11, 1985–Sep. 12, 1985 / Statiras ◆◆◆◆
With quartet including Warren Vache (cnt), Howard Alden (g), Red Callender (b). All oldish standards, played with considerable wit. —*Michael G. Nastos*

Trio / Jan. 6, 1989–Jan. 7, 1989 / C&D ◆◆◆◆
With Michael Hashim (sax), Chris Flory (g). There are 11 cuts without a bass, but based in early piano swing. Fats Waller, James P. Johnson, Ellington, and Basie repertoire featured. —*Michael G. Nastos*

● **Judy** / Sep. 18, 1994–Sep. 19, 1994 / C&D Productions ◆◆◆◆◆
Although she could certainly recreate the recordings of James P. Johnson and Fats Waller if she wanted to, when the talented pianist Judy Carmichael plays stride it is not as a precious museum piece but rather as a natural part of her musical vocabulary. On this excellent release, she is teamed successfully with electric guitarist Chris Flory, whose solos greatly recall Charlie Christian. Carmichael is in particularly wonderful form on the slower pieces (such as "Gee Baby, Ain't I Good to You?" and "Lazy River") but she also includes several stomps for variety, making this an easily recommended CD. —*Scott Yanow*

Harry Carney

b. Apr. 1, 1910, Boston, MA, **d.** Oct. 8, 1974, New York, NY
Baritone Saxophone / Swing
Although he was not the first jazz baritone-saxophonist, Harry Carney achieved his goal of making the instrument "necessary" in a big band. His tone was huge and definitive and his style mixed together Coleman Hawkins and Adrian Rollini; he was also one of the first jazz musicians to master circular breathing (which he generally used to hold an endless long note). Early on he played piano, clarinet and alto before deciding on baritone. Carney joined Duke Ellington's Orchestra when he was 17 in 1927 and remained for over 46 years, passing away in 1974 a few months after Ellington. Although he originally doubled on alto for Duke, added bass clarinet in later years and traditionally took the clar-

inet solo on "Rockin' in Rhythm," he otherwise stuck exclusively to baritone. Other than two obscure record dates as a leader, Harry Carney can only be heard on Duke Ellington-associated recordings but he has many short solos and his presence was always felt in the ensembles. —*Scott Yanow*

● **Moods for Girl and Boy** / Dec. 14, 1954 / Verve ✦✦✦

Ian Carr

b. Apr. 21, 1933, Dumfries, Scotland
Trumpet, Fluegelhorn / Fusion, Post-Bop

Scottish trumpeter and fluegelhorn player Ian Carr has achieved fame as a player, composer and author. A self-taught trumpeter, Carr has made effective contributions to many bands in the '60s, '70s and '80s. He's played with taste and spark in jazz and jazz-rock bands. He's also composed several pieces and written critically acclaimed books. Carr studied English literature in college before serving in the Army during the late '50s. He played in his brother Mike Carr's band The Emcee Five in the early '60s. Carr co-led a group with Don Rendell from 1962 to 1969; he also played with Joe Harriott, Don Byas and John McLaughlin during this period. He founded Nucleus in 1969, a band that became among the most popular and influential jazz-rock groups of all time. They played at the Montreaux and Newport Jazz festivals during the '70s, did several international tours and recorded 13 albums. They also appeared on many radio and television broadcasts. Carr also recorded with Neil Ardley's New Jazz Orchestra, the Spontaneous Music Ensemble and Keith Tippets' Centipede, and worked with Michael Garrick. He helped form The United Jazz and Rock Ensemble, which performed into the '80s. Carr composed a piece for the 1974 celebration of William Shakespeare's birthday at the Globe Theater in London. His writings on music include *Miles Davis: A Critical Biography*, published in the mid-'70s. He became an associate professor of music at the Guildhall School of Music and Drama in London in 1982. Carr also became a member of The Royal Society of Musicians of Great Britian and won the Calabria Award in 1982. He's recorded for Columbia, Argo and Capitol, as well as English companies Vertigo and Gull, but currently has no sessions available on CD in America. —*Ron Wynn*

Belladonna / Jul. 1972 / Core ✦✦✦

● **Old Heartland** / Apr. 1988–May 1988 / MMC ✦✦✦

Teri Lyne Carrington

b. 1962
Drums / Instrumental Pop, Hard Bop

A drummer who got an early start playing in Boston area clubs as a child, Terri Lyne Carrington parlayed the fame and exposure she got as a charter member of Arsenio Hall's first "posse" into a recording contract. But long before that, she had earned the respect of the jazz community through her contributions to both fusion and more conventional sessions. Carrington's sense of time, disciplined playing and keen rhythmic qualities were about the only interesting thing in Wayne Shorter's late '80s band, and many nights helped elevate otherwise routine filler on Hall's program. She made her recording debut as a leader on an all-star session for Verve/Forecast in the late '80s that was a light fusion and instrumental pop workout with a slight jazz tinge. It included guest appearances by everyone from John Scofield to Greg Osby to Carlos Santana, but wasn't the kind of standout date many anticipated. —*Ron Wynn*

Real Life Story / 1989 / Verve/Forecast ✦✦

Baikida Carroll

b. Jan. 15, 1947, Saint Louis, MO
Trumpet, Fluegelhorn / Avant-Garde

One of the better accompanists and section musicians, Baikida Carroll has added textures, colors and bright solos to various free jazz ensembles and groups, among them the Black Artists Group (BAG) in St. Louis. He's been an active composer, having written film soundtracks and scores and displayed a striking, full sound and solo approach. Carroll attended Southern Illinois University and the Armed Forces School of Music before directing the BAG's free jazz band. He went to Europe with other group members in the mid-'70s, and recorded in Paris in 1974. Carroll's recorded with Oliver Lake, Michael Gregory Jackson, Muhal Richard Abrams, Jack DeJohnette and David Murray in the '70s and '80s, as well as

cutting a solo album in the late '70s and heading a combo in the early '80s. A 1994 session on Soul Note features Carroll in fine form with a quintet.—*Ron Wynn*

● **Shadows and Reflections** / Jan. 13, 1982–Jan. 20, 1982 / Soul Note ✦✦✦✦

Trumpeter Baikida Carroll was once again in the company of alto saxophonist Julius Hemphill for a Jan. 1982 recording with pianist Anthony Davis, bassist Dave Holland and drummer Pheeroan Ak Laff for Soul Note called *Shadows & Reflections*. The material here sounded like it could have been a late Blue Note recording; in fact, there were times when the horns brought back flashbacks of the Jackie McLean-Charles Tolliver front line of the '60s. And for all their avant-garde credentials, this group sounded very comfortable and at-home with the squirrelly free bop displayed here. —*Bob Rusch, Cadence*

Benny Carter (Bennett Lester Carter)

b. Aug. 8, 1907, New York, NY
Alto Saxophone, Trumpet, Arranger, Composer, Leader / Swing

To say that Benny Carter has had a remarkable and productive career would be an extreme understatement. As an altoist, arranger, composer, bandleader and occasional trumpeter, Carter has been at the top of his field since at least 1928 and in 1996 Carter is as strong an altoist at the age of 88 as he was in 1936 (when he was merely 28!). His gradually evolving style has not changed much through the decades but neither has it become at all stale or predictable except in its excellence. Although preceded on record by Doc Cheatham and Benny Waters (who are both still active at this writing), Carter has been a major figure in every decade since the 1920s and his consistency and longevity are unprecedented.

Essentially self-taught, Benny Carter started on the trumpet and, after a period on C-melody sax, switched to alto. In 1927 he made his recording debut with Charlie Johnson's Paradise Ten. The following year he had his first big band (working at New York's Arcadia Ballroom) and was contributing arrangements to Fletcher Henderson and even Duke Ellington. Carter was with Henderson during 1930-31, briefly took over McKinney's Cotton Pickers and then went back to leading his own big band (1932-34). Already at this stage he was considered one of the two top altoists in jazz (along with Johnny Hodges), a skilled arranger and composer ("Blues in My Heart" was an early hit and would be followed by "When Lights Are Low") and his trumpet playing was excellent; Carter would also record on tenor, clarinet (an instrument he should have played more) and piano although his rare vocals show that even he was human!

In 1935 Benny Carter moved to Europe where in London he was a staff arranger for the BBC dance orchestra (1936-38); he also recorded in several European countries. Carter's "Waltzing the Blues" was one of the very first jazz waltzes. He returned to the U.S. in 1938, led a classy but commercially unsuccessful big band (1939-41) and then headed a sextet. In 1943 he relocated permanently to Los Angeles, appearing in the film *Stormy Weather* (as a trumpeter with Fats Waller) and getting lucrative work writing for the movie studios. He would lead a big band off and on during the next three years (among his sidemen were J.J. Johnson, Miles Davis and Max Roach) before giving up on that effort. Carter has written for the studios for over 50 years but he continued recording as an altoist (and all-too-rare trumpeter) during the 1940s and '50s, making a few tours with Jazz at the Philharmonic and participating on some of Norman Granz's jam session albums. By the mid-'60s his writing chores led him to hardly playing alto at all but he made a full "comeback" by the mid-'70s and has maintained a very busy playing and writing schedule even in his advanced age. Even after the rise of such stylists as Charlie Parker, Cannonball Adderley, Eric Dolphy, Ornette Coleman and David Sanborn (in addition to their many followers), Benny Carter still ranks near the top of active altoists! —*Scott Yanow*

Benny Carter (1928-1952) / Jan. 24, 1928-Oct. 2, 1952 / RCA ✦✦✦

This French RCA double LP features the great altoist Benny Carter in a variety of settings, including selections with Charlie Johnson's Paradise Ten in 1928 and with pickup bands led by Mezz Mezzrow, Lionel Hampton, Ethel Waters and Una Mae Carlisle, in addition to his own orchestra on four complete sessions from 1940-41 and seven odd commercial sides cut in 1952. Altogether this package contains Carter's complete output for Victor. The later titles nonwithstanding, there are many swing classics scattered throughout this very enjoyable but out-of-print set. —*Scott Yanow*

The Chronological Benny Carter (1929–1933) / Sep. 18, 1929–May 19, 1933 / Classics ✦✦✦✦
The European Classics series has been reissuing on CD the complete output of many top jazz artists of the '20s and '30s. Benny Carter's music at last receives the treatment it deserves in this program. His first volume features the great altoist with a pickup group (the Chocolate Dandies) from 1929–30 that showcases sidemen from Fletcher Henderson's Orchestra, with his own orchestra in 1932–33 (three of the five numbers have rare vocals from Carter) and on 11 sides with Spikes Hughes' all-star band, an orchestra that also features trumpeter Red Allen, trombonist Dicky Wells, Wayman Carver on flute and the tenors of Coleman Hawkins and Chu Berry. This is wonderful and, in many cases, formerly rare music. —*Scott Yanow*

Symphony in Riffs / 1930–1937 / ASV/Living Era ✦✦✦
Early '30s formative sessions, with Carter's charts and alto sax solos spearheading some great combos. The material on this disc was culled from various recording projects and includes varying personnel, among them some great players like Teddy Wilson, Wilbur de Paris, Chu Berry, and Big Sid Catlett, plus Carter. These cuts are both historic and feature great music. —*Ron Wynn*

The Chronological Benny Carter (1933–1936) / May 19, 1933–Apr. 1936 / Classics ✦✦✦✦
The second volume of the complete early Benny Carter from the European Classics label features Carter on alto, trumpet, clarinet and as arranger (in addition to contributing a bit of piano and even a vocal) on three numbers with Spike Hughes' all-star orchestra, as part of the 1933 edition of The Chocolate Dandies (an interracial outfit put together by Mezz Mezzrow) and with his own big band in 1933–34 and in England two years later. Highlights include "Symphony in Riffs," "Blue Lou" and "Everybody Shuffle." —*Scott Yanow*

● **All of Me** / May 7, 1934–Mar. 1959 / Bluebird ✦✦✦✦
A strong sampling of Benny Carter's music is heard in this hodge-podge CD reissue. Twelve of the altoist's 16 Bluebird big-band recordings of 1940–41 (including a previously unissued version of "Ill Wind") precede nine titles gathered from a wide variety of sessions with one song apiece taken from dates led by Mezz Mezzrow, Willie Bryant, Ethel Waters, Artie Shaw and Lucky Thompson and four performances reissued from Carter's soundtrack album of his score for the *M Squad* in 1959. Obviously not a set recommended to completists (the European Classics series is much preferred), the high quality of the music ("All of Me" has a classic Carter arrangement) makes this a worthwhile purchase for more casual collectors. —*Scott Yanow*

The Chronological Benny Carter (1936) / Jun. 1936–Oct. 19, 1936 / Classics ✦✦✦✦
The third volume in Classics' complete chronological reissue of Benny Carter's recordings of the 1930s covers a four-month period during Carter's long period in Europe. Many of these recordings (cut in London, Copenhagen and Stockholm) were formerly quite rare. Carter (on alto, clarinet, tenor, trumpet and even piano and two vocals) is typically flawless, sophisticated and swinging, whether jamming with a quartet behind singer Elizabeth Welch, matching talents with trumpeter Tommy McQuater in a quintet, heading an English orchestra or guesting with an obscure Danish big band. All of the CDs in this very worthy series are highly recommended. —*Scott Yanow*

The Chronological Benny Carter (1937–1939) / Jan. 11, 1937–Jun. 29, 1939 / Classics ✦✦✦✦
The fourth CD in Classics' complete chronological reissue of Benny Carter's early recordings as a leader finds Carter (on alto, trumpet, clarinet, tenor and even one vocal) leading orchestras in London, Laren, the Hague, Paris and (for the final three selections) New York. Highpoints include "Nagasaki," "I'm in the Mood for Swing," "Blues in My Heart," "I'm Coming Virginia" (from a three-song session that also features Django Reinhardt) and "Melancholy Lullaby." In addition, the great tenor Coleman Hawkins plays a prominent role on four of the performances. Carter is in top form throughout these often formerly rare but very vital swing recordings. His fans should quickly acquire all of these invaluable Classics releases. —*Scott Yanow*

Melancholy Benny / May 20, 1939–Jan. 30, 1940 / Tax ✦✦✦
The Benny Carter big band of 1939–41 was not a huge commer-

cial success but musically this outfit could compete with practically anyone else. Carter (doubling on alto and trumpet) contributed the many colorful arrangements and quite a few compositions as can be heard in this reissue LP that contains three complete studio sessions and a radio broadcast from 1939–40. Other soloists include trumpeter Joe Thomas, trombonist Vic Dickenson, pianist Eddie Heywood and, on one session, the great tenor Coleman Hawkins. Recommended to those Benny Carter collectors who do not have this excellent music yet on CD, the broadcast is particularly rare. —*Scott Yanow*

The Chronological Benny Carter (1940–1941) / May 1940–Oct. 16, 1941 / Classics ✦✦✦✦

The Uncollected Benny Carter . . . / 1944 / Hindsight ✦✦✦
Benny Carter's wartime big band only made a handful of studio recordings but seems to have broadcast fairly regularly, particularly from California. This Hindsight LP gives a fine all-around look at Carter's 1944 band although the complete personnel is not known. Clarinetist Barney Bigard guests on "Tea for Two," the young trombone master J.J. Johnson is heard throughout "J.J. Jump" and Carter himself has three features on trumpet in addition to many alto solos. Although not essential, this swinging music is quite enjoyable. —*Scott Yanow*

In Hollywood 1944–46 / 1944–Oct. 1946 / Jazz Society ✦✦✦
Altoist Benny Carter took his big band to the West Coast in 1944 and soon permanently relocated in L.A. This LP from the Swedish Jazz Society label has 14 selections taken from radio broadcasts dating from 1944–46. Although Carter had many talented sidemen during this era (including trumpeters Emmett Berry, Gerald Wilson and Walter Williams, trombonists J.J. Johnson and Al Grey, tenorman Bumps Myers, pianists Gerald Wiggins and Sonny White and drummer Max Roach), the leader is the most impressive soloist throughout, not only on alto but also occasionally on trumpet. These airchecks are not duplicated on other Benny Carter albums currently available and have among their highlights "Jump Call," "Sunday," "Rose Room," "Sleep" and "La Rosita." —*Scott Yanow*

Jazz Off The Air, Vol. 3 / 1944–1948 / Spotlite ✦✦
Benny Carter's mid-'40s big band is relatively forgotten today because it only made a few studio recordings but, on evidence of the broadcasts heard on this LP, it was a rather significant transition orchestra between swing and bop. Consider that these airchecks, in addition to solos by Carter on alto and trumpet, feature concise statements from such young modernists as trombonists J.J. Johnson and Al Grey, trumpeter Miles Davis and the tenors of Dexter Gordon and Lucky Thompson. In addition, there are guest appearances by pianist Mary Lou Williams, clarinetist Barney Bigard and cornetist Rex Stewart. The recording quality is sometimes just so-so, but obviously the importance of this frequently exciting music overrides other factors. —*Scott Yanow*

Deluxe Recordings, Vol. 1 / Jan. 5, 1946–Aug. 1946 / Contact ✦✦✦
During 1946, Benny Carter led his final regular big band before giving up the struggle and deciding to get involved in studio work and performing in much smaller groups, leading big bands only for special projects. This LP, imported from Denmark, contains Carter's dozen orchestral recordings of 1946, 12 sides that were originally on the rare Deluxe label. Most of these performances feature all-star bands rather than Carter's regular group, allowing the great altoist/arranger to use such musicians as trumpeters Shorty Rogers, Joe Newman and Emmett Berry, trombonists Trummy Young and Dickie Wells, clarinetist Tony Scott, and Dexter Gordon, tenormen Flip Phillips and Don Byas; in addition, Maxine Sullivan has a pair of fine vocals. The music, an interesting mixture of swing and bop, is well worth hearing, if quite obscure. —*Scott Yanow*

The Complete Benny Carter on Keynote / Apr. 22, 1946 / Verve ✦✦✦✦
Here's a fine representative sampling of prime Carter '40s cuts. With Arnold Ross Quintet, his own LA group at the time. —*Ron Wynn*

Swing 1946 / Aug. 23, 1946–Sep. 6, 1946 / Prestige ✦✦✦
The swing era was quickly being supplanted by bop in 1946 but many of the top swing stylists were still recording and playing at their creative peak. Frenchman Charles Delauney visited the U.S. and recorded these three unrelated sessions for his Swing label. Altoist Benny Carter leads a sextet with trumpeter Buck Clayton

and tenor saxophonist Ben Webster, Gene Sedric (on tenor and clarinet) jams with some Fats Waller alumni and trumpeter Lincoln Mills, and Jonah Jones is heard with a fine group of Cab Calloway sidemen (including tenorman Ike Quebec). There are many excellent examples of heated swing on this easily enjoyable and rather historic LP, showing that (contrary to what is written in the more simplistic jazz history books) the best swing players had not run out of gas by the mid-'40s. —*Scott Yanow*

Late Forties / Aug. 1946–May 1949 / Official ✦✦
Imported from Denmark, this LP contains a variety of mostly obscure and overlooked Benny Carter recordings from the 1946–49 era. Carter is heard on two performances with a big band, backing a few decent—but not particularly special—singers and jamming with two hot small groups that also feature trumpeter Buck Clayton, Al Grey or Vic Dickenson on trombone and the great tenor Ben Webster. It is for the latter sessions that this LP is of greatest interest, capturing Carter and Webster during a time when they were being overshadowed by the bebop generation. —*Scott Yanow*

Cosmopolite: The Oscar Peterson Verve Sessions / Sep. 18, 1952–Nov. 12, 1954 / Verve ✦✦✦✦
These timeless Benny Carter performances match the great altoist with pianist Oscar Peterson, bassist Ray Brown, either Barney Kessel or Herb Ellis on guitar, Buddy Rich, J.C. Heard or Bobby White on drums and, on four numbers, trombonist Bill Harris. The 17 standards (four of which are also heard in alternate versions) are treated with respect, taste and swing. Carter always sounds flawless and is in excellent form throughout this easily enjoyable set. —*Scott Yanow*

3, 4, 5: the Verve Small Group Sessions / Mar. 1955 / Verve ✦✦✦✦
Has there ever been a more consistent performer in jazz history over a longer period of time than Benny Carter? The classic altoist, who had fully formed his sound by the early '30s (he first recorded in 1927), has not altered his style much in the past 65 (and counting) years. The music on this Verve reissue CD features Carter in three settings: in a trio with pianist Teddy Wilson and drummer Jo Jones (those performances were only previously out in Japan), heading a quartet with pianist Don Abney, bassist George Duvivier and drummer Louis Bellson and showcased on three previously unissued tracks with the Oscar Peterson trio plus drummer Bobby White. Carter knew most of these standards extremely well and he glides effortlessly over the chord changes, infusing the music with swing and subtle creativity. —*Scott Yanow*

Jazz Giant / Jul. 22, 1957–Apr. 21, 1958 / Original Jazz Classics ✦✦✦✦
Benny Carter had already been a major jazz musician for nearly 30 years when he recorded this particularly strong septet session for Contemporary. With notable contributions from tenor saxophonist Ben Webster, trombonist Frank Rosolino and guitarist Barney Kessel, Carter (who plays a bit of trumpet on "How Can You Lose") is in superb form on a set of five standards and two of his originals. This timeless music is beyond the simple categories of "swing" or "bop" and should just be called "classic." —*Scott Yanow*

Swingin' the Twenties / Nov. 2, 1958 / Original Jazz Classics ✦✦
Combining altoist Benny Carter with pianist Earl Hines in a quartet is an idea with plenty of potential, but the results of this 1958 session are relaxed rather than explosive. Carter and Hines explore a dozen tunes (standards as well as forgotten songs like "All Alone" and "Mary Lou") with respect and light swing, but one wishes that there were a bit more competitiveness to replace some of the mutual respect. —*Scott Yanow*

☆**Further Definitions** / Nov. 13, 1961–Nov. 15, 1961 / Impulse! ✦✦✦✦✦
One of the truly classic sessions and a highpoint in Benny Carter's career, this set of eight tunes (all arranged by him) boasts quite a lineup of players: Carter and Phil Woods on altos, Coleman Hawkins and Charlie Rouse on tenors and a strong four-piece rhythm section. These versions of "Honeysuckle Rose" and "Crazy Rhythm" look back to the 1937 recordings of Carter and Hawk with Django Reinhardt and actually hold their own; both renditions are quite exciting. In addition to a wonderful remake of "Body and Soul" (that lets Coleman Hawkins revisit his famous recording), the other ballads ("The Midnight Sun Will Never Set,"

"Blue Star" and "Cherry") and stomps ("Cotton Tail" and "Doozy") are all memorable in their own way. No serious jazz collection is complete without this very enjoyable recording. —*Scott Yanow*

B.B.B. & Co. / Apr. 10, 1962 / Original Jazz Classics ✦✦✦
One of Benny Carter's last jazz recordings before he became totally immersed in writing for the studios, this set matches his alto and trumpet with tenor great Ben Webster, clarinetist Barney Bigard and trumpeter Shorty Sherock on a pair of lengthy blues and Carter's "Lula" and "When Lights Are Low." All of the swing all-stars are in fine form, making one wish that they were not being so neglected by critics and fans alike during this era; Webster soon left the U.S. permanently for Europe. Although not essential, this set is fun. —*Scott Yanow*

Additions to Further Definitions / Mar. 2, 1966–Mar. 4, 1966 / Impulse! ✦✦✦
This LP is a reprise of Benny Carter's brilliant *Further Definitions* session of 1961 and, like most sequels, it is not quite on the same level as the original. Utilizing five saxes (Bud Shank and his own altos, tenors Buddy Collette and Teddy Edwards and baritonist Bill Hood), Carter's arrangements for six of his originals, "Fantastic, That's You" and "If Dreams Come True" are colorful, although the solos are less memorable than on the earlier session; who could replace Coleman Hawkins? But, evaluated by itself, this date (Carter's only small-group album from 1963–75) has enough enjoyable moments to be recommended. —*Scott Yanow*

The King / Feb. 11, 1976 / Pablo ✦✦✦✦
The great Benny Carter was so much in demand as an arranger/composer in the studios that for 15 years, starting in the early '60s, he rarely recorded or performed in jazz settings, instead choosing to concentrate on writing movie scores. The drought ended when Carter, then in his late 60s, started recording for Pablo. As *The King* (his first small-group session since 1966) proves, the masterful altoist had not lost a thing through the years. In a sextet with vibraphonist Milt Jackson, guitarist Joe Pass and pianist Tommy Flanagan, Benny Carter is in masterful form, stretching out on eight of his own compositions and showing that his name always has to be ranked near the top of jazz improvisers, whether one is considering the 1930s or the 1990s. —*Scott Yanow*

Carter, Gillespie, Inc. / Apr. 27, 1976 / Original Jazz Classics ✦✦✦✦
Although they were from different musical generations (Benny Carter was born ten years before Dizzy Gillespie), it is little wonder that the swing altoist and the bop trumpeter could match up so well on this sextet session; they were quite compatible. Surprisingly, the material they chose to perform could have been better (there is only one Carter composition among the six songs) but on "Broadway" and "A Night in Tunisia," the two veteran hornmen (along with pianist Tommy Flanagan and guitarist Joe Pass) sound at their best. —*Scott Yanow*

Wonderland / Nov. 1976 / Pablo ✦✦✦
For this 1976 LP, the veteran altoist Benny Carter (who was then nearing age 70) was teamed with tenor saxophonist Eddie "Lockjaw" Davis, trumpeter Harry "Sweets" Edison and a strong rhythm section headed by Ray Bryant on a vintage Pablo session. Although it often has the feeling of a jam session, the fact that, in addition to two standards, there are five obscure Carter compositions makes one realize that more planning than usual went into this date, and it shows. —*Scott Yanow*

Live and Well in Japan / Apr. 29, 1977 / Original Jazz Classics ✦✦✦✦
Benny Carter headed a talent-filled tentet for this frequently exciting concert. With trumpeters Cat Anderson and Joe Newman, trombonist Britt Woodman, Cecil Payne on baritone and Budd Johnson doubling on tenor and soprano, it is not at all surprising that the results would be memorable, but this date actually exceeds one's expectations. In addition to fine jam versions of "Squatty Roo," "Them There Eyes" and "It Don't Mean a Thing," there is a remarkable Louis Armstrong medley on which Carter (on trumpet) plays "When It's Sleepy Time Down South," Cat Anderson follows with a high note solo on "Confessin'" and then Joe Newman (who rarely recorded vocals) does a near-perfect imitation of Louis Armstrong singing on "When You're Smiling." —*Scott Yanow*

Benny Carter 4: Montreux 1977 / Jul. 13, 1977 / Original Jazz Classics ✦✦✦✦
For this concert at the 1977 Montreux Jazz Festival, Benny Carter

was in his musical prime, a condition he has thus far stayed at for over 65 years. Joined by the Ray Bryant Trio, the altoist romps through seven standards and plays some tasteful trumpet on "Body and Soul," proving once again that he is really is ageless; Carter was nearly 70 years old at the time. —*Scott Yanow*

Summer Serenade / Aug. 17, 1980 / Storyville ✦✦✦
Benny Carter has recorded so many excellent swing sessions throughout his lengthy career that it is very difficult to pick out the best ones; there's too much competition. This quartet date for the Danish Storyville label matches his alto with pianist Kenny Drew, bassist Jesper Lundgard and drummer Ed Thigpen for four of Carter's originals and three standards. As a bonus, Richard Boone sings the good-humored "All That Jazz." —*Scott Yanow*

Skyline Drive / Sep. 15, 1982 / Phontastic ✦✦✦

All Stars, Featuring Nat Adderley & Red Norvo / Jul. 8, 1985–Jul. 9, 1985 / Gazell ✦✦✦
After recording very few jazz sessions during 1963-75, Benny Carter has returned to the scene with a vengeance, but no one is complaining. Virtually all of Carter's recordings are worth acquiring and this Gazell LP, although not essential, is no exception. Vibraphonist Red Norvo (on one of his last recordings before his retirement) is featured on "Here's That Rainy Day," cornetist Nat Adderley gets to perform yet another version of his "Work Song" (taking a rare vocal) and Carter joins the sextet for "Memories of You" and three of his own compositions. This nice session offers few surprises but satisfying music. —*Steve Yanow*

A Gentleman and His Music / Aug. 1985 / Concord Jazz ✦✦✦
For this 1985 session, altoist Benny Carter (then a week short of turning 78 years old) is teamed with the lyrical trumpeter Joe Wilder and the Concord All-Stars, a contingent that also features tenor saxophonist Scott Hamilton, guitarist Ed Bickert and pianist Gene Harris. The results are predictably excellent with the septet swinging with spirit and creativity on four standards, a blues and Carter's original "A Kiss from You." This LP is well worth tracking down. —*Scott Yanow*

My Kind of Trouble / Aug. 20, 1986 / Pablo ✦✦✦
With the exception of one song, Benny Carter had never previously recorded with an organist during his first 60 years on record. This Pablo set teams the classic Carter alto with organist Art Hillery and guitarist Joe Pass in a fine quintet. Actually, other than the instrumentation, there is little unusual about this date. On four Carter compositions and two standards, Benny Carter (who was nearing age 81) is in typical flawless form, swinging effortlessly. —*Scott Yanow*

Meets Oscar Peterson / Nov. 14, 1986 / Original Jazz Classics ✦✦✦✦
Altoist Benny Carter had recorded with pianist Oscar Peterson back in the early '50s for Norman Granz's Verve label. More than 30 years later he teamed up with Peterson again, this time for Granz's Pablo company. There was no sign of decline or disillusionment in either of the co-leaders' playing; in fact, if anything, they had improved with age. Joined by guitarist Joe Pass, bassist Dave Young and drummer Martin Drew, Carter and Peterson are both in a happy mood and in typically swinging form on six standards and a blues. —*Scott Yanow*

Central City Sketches / 1987 / Music Masters ✦✦✦✦✦
One of the many Benny Carter recordings cut after he returned to jazz on a full-time basis in the mid-'70s, this double-LP set is the jewel among the seemingly countless number of copies. Eight of Carter's compositions are performed by the all-star American Jazz Orchestra ("Doozy" gets two versions) along with his old theme song "Sleep" and his recently written six-part "Central City Sketches." Virtually every player in this big band was a potential star soloist; among the more notable musicians are trombonist Jimmy Knepper, tenors Lew Tabackin and Loren Schoenberg and either John Lewis or Dick Katz on piano. But, as is often the case, Benny Carter frequently steals solo honors and his brief trumpet spot on "Central City Blues" is memorable. —*Scott Yanow*

In the Mood for Swing / Nov. 9, 1987–Nov. 12, 1987 / Music Masters ✦✦✦
All 11 of the songs are somewhat obscure and therefore fresh Carter compositions ("Summer Serenade" is perhaps the best-known) and Dizzy Gillespie sits in with the group for three songs. But even with Gillespie, guitarist Howard Alden and pianist Roland Hanna, the solo star throughout is the ageless Benny

Carter, who at the age of 80 still seemed to be improving. —*Scott Yanow*

Cookin' at Carlos 1 / Oct. 5, 1988–Oct. 9, 1988 / Music Masters ✦✦✦
During the late '80s up to the present, Benny Carter (now an octogenarian) has recorded a string of consistently excellent and frequently superb CDs for Music Masters. This particular effort is a rare live recording for Carter with his regular group, which in 1988 consisted of pianist Richard Wyands, bassist Lisle Atkinson and drummer Al Harewood. The repertoire is typical of his club performances: five standards, a blues and just one of Carter's compositions, "Key Largo." A special treat is Carter's trumpet solo on "Time for the Blues"; otherwise his wonderful alto dominates this fine set. —*Scott Yanow*

Over the Rainbow / Oct. 18, 1988–Oct. 19, 1988 / Music Masters ✦✦✦
Benny Carter has recorded so frequently since the mid-'70s that it must be a constant challenge to come up with new settings for his alto. This particular Music Masters CD finds Carter taking his place in a saxophone section with fellow altoist Herb Geller, the tenors of Jimmy Heath and Frank Wess and baritonist Joe Temperley. The program is split evenly between standards and Carter compositions with the altoist also writing all of the colorful arrangements. This swinging and tasteful Benny Carter recording is a credit to his superb series of Music Masters dates. —*Scott Yanow*

My Man Benny, My Man Phil / Nov. 21, 1989–Nov. 22, 1989 / Music Masters ✦✦✦✦
It is extremely difficult to believe that Benny Carter was 82 years old at the time of this recording, for his strong sound (nothing feeble about his playing) and fertile ideas on alto make him sound as if he were a contemporary of Phil Woods, who was born 24 years later. Together Carter and Woods form a mutual-admiration society which can be heard on "My Man Phil." The repertoire on this CD is particularly inspired (highlighted by "Sultry Serenade," "I'm Just Wild About Harry" and two versions of the atmospheric "Just a Mood"). Carter takes two trumpet solos while, on "We Were in Love," Woods contributes some tasteful clarinet. A special and relaxed but occasionally hard-swinging date, this Music Masters CD is quite enjoyable. —*Scott Yanow*

All That Jazz: Live at Princeton / Nov. 11, 1990 / Music Masters ✦✦✦
For this 1990 concert, altoist Benny Carter teams up with the great fluegelhornist Clark Terry on a set of standards. Vocalist Billy Hill joins the quintet for four numbers (including a humorous collaboration with Clark Terry on Carter's "All That Jazz") but it is the octogenarian altoist who often takes honors. —*Scott Yanow*

Harlem Renaissance / Feb. 7, 1992–Feb. 9, 1992 / Music Masters ✦✦✦✦
Benny Carter is a true marvel. At the time of this recording (a double CD), the classic altoist was already age 84, yet showed no signs of slowing down either his playing or his writing schedule. For his specially assembled big band and The Rutgers University Orchestra (which includes a full string section), Carter wrote entirely new arrangements that demonstrate that his talents have not diminished with age. While the first disc mostly sticks to older material, the second disc is comprised of two new suites, "Tales of the Rising Sun" and "Harlem Renaissance." In addition, Carter's alto is often the solo star, although he does not hog the spotlight; it just naturally drifts back to him. —*Scott Yanow*

Legends / Jun. 16, 1992–Jun. 17, 1992 / Music Masters ✦✦✦✦
For once the term "legend" is not being misused. The great altoist Benny Carter (at age 85) is in typically remarkable form with a quartet, on five duets with pianist Hank Jones and on three selections with the truly remarkable trumpeter Doc Cheatham (who was 87 years old at the time). Whether it be happy jams on "Honeysuckle Rose" and "There Is No Greater Love" or original ballads, there is not a weak track on this classic disc. This set would be recommended even if Carter were 55 rather than 85; the music is timeless and often glorious. —*Scott Yanow*

Elegy In Blue / 1994 / Music Masters ✦✦
Benny Carter, 87 at the time of this recording, could pass musically for 57. His alto playing is as flawless as ever but 79-year-old trumpeter Harry "Sweets" Edison very much sounds his age and falters constantly throughout the date. Pianist Cedar Walton (who

sounds for probably the only time in his career like Oscar Peterson), guitarist Mundell Lowe, bassist Ray Brown and drummer Jeff Hamilton make up a strong rhythm section, but Edison and the so-so material cause this session to fall far short of its potential. —*Scott Yanow*

Songbook / Jun. 26, 1995–Aug. 26, 1995 / Music Masters ♦♦♦♦

Betty Carter (Lorraine Carter)
b. May 16, 1930, Flint, MI
Vocals / Avant-Garde, Bop

A long period of struggling and near-complete obscurity preceded Betty Carter's surprising rise to fame; through it all she never compromised her musical vision. Although she has never cared much for avant-garde jazz, her own interpretations of standards and originals are still so radical (with tonal distortions, a very wide range of tempos and many unexpected changes of direction) that there is simply no other term to describe her unique music. Carter studied piano and worked as a singer in Detroit in 1946. During 1948–51 she toured with Lionel Hampton (where she was nicknamed Betty "Bebop" Carter). After that association ended she settled in New York, gradually developed her style and recorded with Gigi Gryce in 1958. Although she recorded a 1961 duet album with Ray Charles that received some attention, it would be quite awhile before she gained much recognition. After doing some records for Roulette, Carter retired for a few years to raise a family. In 1969 she put together a trio and in 1971 organized her own record label Bet-Car. Gradually Betty Carter's innovative singing began to be recognized, and after she signed with Verve in the early '80s, she finally became a household name (and a consistent pollwinner) in the jazz world. Carter's singing is not to everyone's taste but her willingness to take chances is quite admirable and her ability as a talent scout (her pianists have included John Hicks, Mulgrew Miller, Benny Green, Stephen Scott and Cyrus Chestnut) is beyond criticism. —*Scott Yanow*

Social Call / May 13, 1955–Apr. 25, 1956 / Columbia ♦♦♦♦
This LP contains singer Betty Carter's earliest recordings. On one date she is heard performing six standards with a quartet also featuring pianist Ray Bryant ("I Could Write a Book" and "The Way You Look Tonight" are highpoints). The other session, which was only released for the first time in 1980, has five songs on which Carter is joined by a 14-piece band arranged by Gigi Gryce; this version of "Social Call" is a classic. Naturally Carter sounds much more conventional on these performances than she would 30 to 40 years later, but already her voice was immediately recognizable. —*Scott Yanow*

I Can't Help It / Feb. 1958 / GRP ♦♦♦
Late '50s session with Carter honing her skills, backed by both a moderate-sized group and the Richard Wess Orchestra. The group includes Kenny Dorham, Melba Liston, Wynton Kelly, and Benny Golson. Carter was still building a reputation, and was then more in a standard scat/hard bop mode than in the interpretative style she later patented. —*Ron Wynn*

Out There / Feb. 1958 / Peacock ♦♦♦
A dynamic set with Benny Golson, Melba Liston, and Gigi Gryce that's long since been deleted from the catalog. —*Ron Wynn*

Ray Charles and Betty Carter / 1961 / ABC/Paramount ♦♦♦
This session with Betty Carter has been an elusive treasure for many. Here, the program is augmented by three other Ray Charles items from the back catalog. The collaboration with Betty Carter has become a legendary session...Marty Paich's arrangements are memorable. In this setting Ray Charles is the balladeer and moves back toward his Nat King Cole/Charles Brown roots. —*Bob Rusch, Cadence*

Round Midnight / Aug. 10, 1962–Jan. 15, 1963 / Atco ♦♦♦
Betty Carter recorded only two albums during the 1961–68 period. Her chancetaking style and unusual voice were mostly ignored and it would not be until the late '70s that she was finally "discovered." This Atlantic CD finds Carter backed by orchestras arranged by Claus Ogerman and Oliver Nelson. Her style was a lot freer than it had been in her earlier records but was still more accessible than it would be later. Her repertoire, which includes the title cut, "Theme from Dr. Kildare," "Two Cigarettes in the Dark" and her own "Who What Why Where When" was already becoming eclectic. This is an interesting historic release. —*Scott Yanow*

Inside Betty Carter / Jun. 1964 / United Artists ♦♦♦
Marred only by a ludicrous playing time—25:26—*Inside Betty*

Music Map

Cello

Pioneer Jazz Cello Soloist
Harry Babasin (in late 1940s)

Cellists with Chico Hamilton Quintet
Fred Katz (1955-57)
Nat Gershman (1958-61)

Bassists Doubling on Cello

Oscar Pettiford	Doug Watkins
Ron Carter	Sam Jones
Richard Davis	Eberhard Weber
Dave Holland	

Cellists Since 1970

Diedre Murray	David Darling
David Eyges	Hank Roberts
Abdul Wadud	Tristan Honsinger

Carter is a welcome reissue of a 6/64 session for UA. Save for her stretch on Richard Rodgers' "Look No Further," a brisk "My Favorite Things" and a mostly breakneck "Something Big," this is a showcase for Betty Balladeer, not Betty Bebop. This isn't a scat session, but a study in lyric interpretation and dramatic shading. Her almost uninflected (microshaded) long high notes on "Some Other Time" are alone worth a hear. As on her bossa-nova tinged shuffle "Open the Door," she featured a lighter tonality than one may associate with her power-pipes work. The backing trio (Hal [Harold] Mabern, piano; Bob Cranshaw, bass; Roy McCurdy, drums) was totally at her service, their contributions to the point. With so little time—"Look No Further" and "Something Big" were two minutes or less—there's no room for digression. Carter's restraint should make this a favorite among those who like to hear venerable tunes treated with suitable respect. Only "Favorite Things" might be considered a familiar choice. Carter avoids mannered gestures and crowd-pleasing stunts; lovely, but too friggin' short. —*Bob Rusch, Cadence*

Finally, Betty Carter / Dec. 6, 1969 / Roulette ♦♦♦

At the Village Vanguard / May 1, 1970 / Verve ♦♦♦♦
Betty Carter's remarkable early-'70s LPs were initially available only on her own poorly distributed label. This live date captured Carter when her voice was its most pliable, her delivery in full bloom and her range and power at their peak. She could scat with a fury and rhythmic intensity that were almost magical, then turn a slow tune like "The Sun Died" or "Body And Soul" into a showcase by emphasizing key lyrics, subtly changing each stanza, or increasing the pace at an unexpected moment. This deserves full attention, as it represents Betty Carter still evolving and perfecting her matchless technique. —*Ron Wynn*

The Betty Carter Album / 1972 / Verve ♦♦♦

Now It's My Turn / Mar. 9, 1976–Jun. 22, 1976 / Roulette ♦♦♦♦

● **The Audience with Betty Carter** / Dec. 6, 1979–Dec. 8, 1979 / Verve ♦♦♦♦
Definitive two-fer live set with John Hicks Trio. A must-buy. —*Michael G. Nastos*

Whatever Happened to Love / 1982 / Verve ♦♦♦

Look What I Got / 1988 / Verve ♦♦♦♦
This well-rounded set gives listeners a good look at the adventur-

ous music of Betty Carter. For this CD, she is joined by one of two rhythm sections (with either Benny Green or Stephen Scott on piano) and, on four of the nine songs, tenor saxophonist Don Braden. Carter twists and turns some familiar songs (such as "The Man I Love," "Imagination" and "The Good Life") along with a variety of lesser-known material including two songs of her own. Consistently unpredictable (whether scatting or stretching out ballads) Betty Carter's recordings are always quite stimulating. — *Scott Yanow*

Droppin' Things / May 25, 1990–May 26, 1990 / Verve ✦✦✦

It's Not About the Melody / 1992 / Verve ✦✦✦
A song's melody is simply a reference point and a beginning for Carter; she takes words and inverts, probes and extends them, embellishes themes, changes moods and alters rhythms. She's a vocal improviser in a manner few have equaled, and if her voice lacks the clarity and timbre of the all-time greats, she's more than compensated with incredible timing, flexibility and power. Throughout this 11-track effort, Carter's vocals direct and steer the responses of pianist Cyrus Chestnut, bassist Ariel J. Roland and drummer Lewis Nash. It was yet another memorable outing for Betty Carter, an all-time great. — *Ron Wynn*

Feed The Fire / Oct. 30, 1993 / Verve ✦✦✦

James Carter

b. Detroit, MI
Tenor Saxophone, Bass Clarinet, Alto Saxophone, Baritone Saxophone, Soprano Saxophone / Avant-Garde, Swing, Post-Bop
James Carter caused a sensation in the mid-'90s with his DIW and Atlantic recordings. Similar in some ways to Rahsaan Roland Kirk (although he only plays one instrument at a time!), Carter has the ability to play in any jazz style from the slaptongue staccato of early '20s tenors and Dixieland to swing, bop, 1950s R&B, free form and funk while still sounding like himself. A high-powered player skilled on most reeds (with tenor being his main instrument), Carter often switches quickly and unexpectedly between styles and the effect can be exhilarating or numbing. Carter started played sax when he was 11, performed in the Blue Lake Monster Ensemble with Marcus Belgrave and before he graduated high school in 1986 he gigged with Wynton Marsalis. In 1988 Carter played with Lester Bowie in New York and he soon appeared on two Bowie DIW recordings with the New York Organ Ensemble. He has since worked with the Charles Mingus Big Band, the Lincoln Center Jazz Orchestra, Julius Hemphill, recorded with the Tough Young Tenors and led his own highly versatile group. James Carter has unlimited potential and he seems destined to be one of the giants of jazz. — *Scott Yanow*

● **JC On The Set** / Apr. 14, 1993–Apr. 15, 1993 / DIW/Columbia ✦✦✦✦✦
Twenty-five at the time of this CD, James Carter had already absorbed much of the tradition. His debut as a leader includes compositions by the classic tenors Don Byas and John Hardee, Duke Ellington's "Sophisticated Lady" and even a Sun Ra ballad. He also shows that he has the courage to play completely outside whenever it seems logical to him; in fact on the title cut Carter moves from Gene Ammons and Illinois Jacquet to outbursts a la David Murray in the stratosphere. But most importantly, at this early stage James Carter already had his own sound. He switches between the tenor (his main ax) to alto and baritone, shows self-restraint on the ballads and fills his improvisations with continual surprises. Joined by the supportive pianist Craig Taborn, bassist Jaribu Shahid and drummer Tani Tabbal, James Carter puts on quite a tour-de-force throughout this very impressive set. — *Scott Yanow*

● **Jurassic Classics** / 1994 / DIW/Columbia ✦✦✦✦✦
The young but already great saxophonist James Carter explores seven jazz standards with pianist Craig Taborn (himself a young master capable of playing in several styles), bassist Jaribu Shahid and drummer Tani Tabbal. Among the most versatile and knowledgeable of today's saxophonists, Carter draws on many top stylists during these lengthy solos yet always sounds quite individual. His violent depiction of a train whistle on "Take the 'A' Train" perfectly launches that romp and he also really stretches out on "Epistrophy," plays the blues on John Coltrane's "Equinox" and shows quite a bit of fire on "Oleo." A very stimulating session. — *Scott Yanow*

Real Quiet Storm / Oct. 6, 1994–Nov. 20, 1994 / Atlantic ✦✦✦✦
Despite this CD's title and a slight emphasis on ballads, this is not an easy-listening record! James Carter, one of the great new discoveries of the 1990s (and whose versatility, brilliance on a variety of reed instruments and seeming encyclopedic knowledge of jazz styles makes him a possible successor to Rahsaan Roland Kirk) is heard playing tenor, alto, soprano, baritone, bass clarinet and bass flute on the nine selections with the impressive pianist Craig Taborn, either Dave Holland or Jaribu Shahid on bass and Leon Parker or Tani Tabbal on drums. Although some of the ballad statements (such as his statements on baritone on "'Round Midnight" and "Eventide") are fairly straightforward, Carter also has some explosive moments. His rendition (on soprano) of Don Byas' "1944 Stomp" is memorable as is his interpretations of "Born to Be Blue" and two originals. The results are a bit restrained compared to his live performances, but this is an enjoyable and unpredictable outing, music that will not be played on the "Quiet Storm"! — *Scott Yanow*

John Carter

b. Sep. 24, 1929, Fort Worth, TX, **d.** Mar. 31, 1991, Inglewood, CA
Clarinet / Avant-Garde
John Carter was a major clarinet innovator, turning the swing-associated instrument into a device for very advanced explorations. His upper-register screeches could be grating but his solos had a logic all their own and his five-part suite depicting the history of Blacks in America (released on Black Saint and Gramavision) displayed his compositional talents. Carter taught in the Fort Worth public school system during 1949–61 before switching to Los Angeles (1961–82). He played with Ornette Coleman and Charles Moffett as early as the late '40s and in L.A. of the 1960s he became one of the leaders of the local scene's avant-garde, originally doubling on clarinet and alto. In 1964 he formed the New Art Jazz Ensemble with cornetist Bobby Bradford, who would be his longtime musical partner. Carter (who by 1974 was playing clarinet exclusively) played with Bradford on a fairly regular basis during the remainder of his life in settings ranging from duets to a larger orchestra. By the 1980s with his suite, participation in Clarinet Summit and formation of the Wind College with James Newton, Red Callender and Charles Owens, John Carter finally received some long overdue recognition. — *Scott Yanow*

● **West Coast Hot** / Jan. 3, 1969–Apr. 1, 1969 / Novus ✦✦✦✦✦
This very valuable release documents two important but underrated avant-garde units that were based in Los Angeles. Clarinetist John Carter (here also heard on tenor and alto) and trumpeter Bobby Bradford co-led bands for many years in virtual obscurity. With bassist Tom Williamson and drummer Buzz Freeman, they are both abstract and logical on four originals with Carter's passionate sounds contrasting, as usual, with Bradford's lyricism. The second half of this disc features L.A.'s great undiscovered legend, pianist Horace Tapscott. He is heard in superlative form on four tracks (including the 17-minute "The Giant Is Awakened") in a two bass quintet also co-starring the young altoist Arthur Blythe. Tapscott is still quite active in L.A. When will an enterprising label finally record his working band? — *Scott Yanow*

Seeking / Jan. 16, 1969 / Hat Art ✦✦✦

Flight for Four / Apr. 3, 1969 / Flying Dutchman ✦✦✦✦

Self-Determination Music / 1969–1970 / Flying Dutchman ✦✦✦

Secrets / Sep. 11, 1971–Apr. 4, 1972 / Revelation ✦✦✦

Variations on Selected Themes for Jazz Quintet / Aug. 15, 1979 / Moers ✦✦✦

Castles of Ghana / Feb. 1985 / Gramavision ✦✦✦
The second of clarinetist John Carter's five-part depiction of the history of African Americans deals with the capture of many Africans for shipment as slaves to the New World. Carter's octet on this date features such fine players as bass clarinetist Mary Ehrlich, cornetist Bobby Bradford, trombonist Benny Powell and trumpeter Baikida Carroll, and the music is as dramatic as the episodes it portrays. — *Scott Yanow*

Dauwhe / Feb. 25, 1982–Mar. 8, 1982 / Black Saint ✦✦✦✦✦
This recording brought together some of the best of the West (cornetist Bobby Bradford, flutist James Newton, soprano saxophonist, clarinetist and oboe player Charles Owens, bassist Roberto Miranda, drummer Williams Jeffrey, percussionist/water-

phone player Luis Peralta) for a set of five John Carter compositions. The title track was brilliant both in its open construction and in solos executed by the leader, Bradford, and Newton. In fact, this was arguably Newton's most inspired work. —*Bob Rusch, Cadence*

Suite of Early American Folk Pieces for Solo Clarinet / Aug. 16, 1979 / Moers ✦✦✦

Dance of the Love Ghosts / Nov. 1986 / Gramavision ✦✦✦
Experimental, daring concept work with Andrew Cyrille (d) and Fred Hopkins (b). Excellent clarinet solos and arrangements by Carter. —*Ron Wynn*

Fields / Mar. 1988 / Gramavision ✦✦✦

Shadows on a Wall / Apr. 1989 / Gramavision ✦✦
The fifth and final chapter of John Carter's project to musically portray the history of African Americans deals with the past hundred years. Because the music (despite titles such as "Sippi Strut" and "52nd Street Stomp") does not refer to earlier styles and instead stays unremittingly avant-garde, this set is a bit of a disappointment. Some of the playing by the octet (particularly trumpeter Bobby Bradford and trombonist Benny Powell) is quite excellent but the singing of Terry Jenoure becomes jarring within a short time. This music is easier to respect than to love. —*Scott Yanow*

Ron Carter
....
b. May 4, 1937, Ferndale, MI
Bass, Cello, Piccolo Bass / Post-Bop, Hard Bop
The epitome of class and elegance, though not stuffy, Ron Carter has been a world class bassist and cellist since the '60s. He's among the greatest accompanists of all time, but has also done many albums exhibiting his prodigious technique. He's a brilliant rhythmic and melodic player, who uses everything in the bass and cello arsenal; walking lines, thick, full, prominent notes and tones, drones and strumming effects and melody snippets. His bowed solos are almost as impressive as those done with his fingers. Carter has been featured in clothing, instrument and pipe advertisments; he's close to being the bass equivalent of a Duke Ellington in his mix of musical and extra-musical interests. Carter's nearly as accomplished in classical music as jazz, and has performed with symphony orchestras all over the world. He's almost exclusively an acoustic player; he did play electric for a short time in the late '60s and early '70s, but hasn't used it in many, many years. Carter began playing cello at ten. But when his family moved from Ferndale, Michigan, to Detroit, Carter ran into problems with racial stereotypes regarding the cello and switched to bass. He played in The Eastman School's Philharmonic Orchestra, and gained his degree in 1959. He moved to New York and played in Chico Hamilton's quintet with Eric Dolphy, while also enrolling at the Manhattan School of Music. Carter earned his master's degree in 1961. After Hamilton returned to the West Coast in 1960, Carter stayed in New York and played with Dolphy and Don Ellis, cutting his first records with them. He worked with Randy Weston and Thelonious Monk, while playing and recording with Jaki Byard in the early '60s. Carter also toured and recorded with Bobby Timmons' trio, and played with Cannonball Adderley. He joined Art Farmer's group for a short time in 1963, before he was tapped to become a member of Miles Davis' band. Carter remained with Davis until 1968, appearing on every crucial mid-'60s recording and teaming with Herbie Hancock and Tony Williams to craft a new, freer rhythm section sound. The high profile job led to the reputation that's seen Carter become possibly the most recorded bassist in jazz history. He's been heard on an unprecedented number of recordings; some sources claim 500, others have estimated it to be as many as 1,000. The list of people he's played with is simply too great to be accurately and completely cited. Carter's been a member of The New York Jazz Sextet and New York Jazz Quartet, VSOP tour, Milestone Jazzstars and was in one of the groups featured in the film *Round Midnight* in 1986. He's led his own bands at various intervals since 1972, using a second bassist to keep time and establish harmony so he's free to provide solos. Carter even invented his own instrument, a piccolo bass. Carter's also contributed many arrangements and compositions to both his groups and other bands. He's done duo recordings with either Cedar Walton or Jim Hall. Carter's recorded for Embryo/Atlantic, CTI, Milestone, Timeless, EmArcy, Galaxy, Elektra and Concord. —*Ron Wynn*

● **Where?** / Jun. 20, 1961 / Original Jazz Classics ✦✦✦✦
Essential session with Carter on both bass and cello. Awesome

solos by Eric Dolphy (sax)—stunning pieces. With Mal Waldron. —*Ron Wynn*

Uptown Conversation / Oct. 6, 1969 / Atlantic ✦✦✦✦
Arguably his best release. A 1989 reissue of an Embryo album that features some rangy, vibrant Carter solos. —*Ron Wynn*

Blues Farm / Jan. 10, 1973 / Columbia ✦✦✦
One of his best dates as a leader. A good set with Bob James (k), Richard Tee (k), and Hubert Laws (fl)—revealing jazz chops they've seldom shown otherwise. —*Ron Wynn*

All Blues / Oct. 24, 1973 / CTI ✦✦✦✦
One of bassist Ron Carter's better albums as a leader, this CTI LP features a very compact quartet comprised of tenor saxophonist Joe Henderson, pianist Roland Hanna (keyboardist Richard Tee sits in on one number), drummer Billy Cobham and Carter. All of the music (even the ballad "Will You Still Be Mine?") has a blues feeling although several are not really blues. However, the quality of the solos is high, and this date lives up to one's expectations. —*Scott Yanow*

Spanish Blue / Nov. 1974 / Columbia ✦✦✦

Anything Goes / Jun. 1975–Jul. 1975 / Kudu ✦✦

Yellow and Green / May 1976 / Columbia ✦✦✦

Pastels / Oct. 18, 1976+Oct. 19, 1976 / Original Jazz Classics ✦✦✦
Some tremendous playing by Carter, Kenny Barron (p), and Hugh McCracken (g), though the strings get intrusive. —*Ron Wynn*

Piccolo / Mar. 25, 1977–Mar. 26, 1977 / Milestone ✦✦✦
This double LP is mostly recommended to lovers of bass solos. With Ron Carter functioning as the main soloist on piccolo bass, only the solos of pianist Kenny Barron offer a bit of contrast. Bassist Buster Williams and drummer Ben Riley, who complete the quartet, are mostly featured in support. These performances, which are well-played, are almost all quite long, so listeners who prefer more variety in their music are advised to look elsewhere. —*Scott Yanow*

Third Plane / Jul. 13, 1977 / Original Jazz Classics ✦✦✦
This reunion of Miles Davis' mid-'60s rhythm section (bassist Ron Carter, pianist Herbie Hancock and drummer Tony Williams) has its moments but is not particularly memorable. Performing three of Carter's songs, one apiece from Hancock and Williams and the standard "Stella by Starlight," the solos are fine but on the whole, little special occurs; the magic is missing. —*Scott Yanow*

Peg Leg / Nov. 18, 1977–Nov. 22, 1977 / Original Jazz Classics ✦✦
A 1991 reissue of a decent, though over-arranged, 1977 session. —*Ron Wynn*

A Song for You / Jun. 1978 / Milestone ✦✦✦
A change of pace session for Carter. He pairs his formidable bass lines and playing against a backdrop of four cellists, outstanding drummer Jack DeJohnette, and at various times pianists Kenny Barron or Leon Pendarvis, guitarist Jay Berliner, and percussionist Ralph McDonald. Things generally work, although sometimes the low energy level and lack of tension threaten to turn this into easy listening material. —*Ron Wynn*

1 + 3 / Jul. 29, 1978 / Fantasy ✦✦✦
Exactly the kind of impressive, high level playing and interaction you'd expect from this trio. Pianist Herbie Hancock, bassist Ron Carter, and drummer Tony Williams comprised the rhythm section on many '60s Miles Davis classics; nearly three decades later, they're still in sync with each other. While it's Carter's session, there's really no leader or followers, just three wonderful musicians fully attuned to each other. —*Ron Wynn*

Parade / Mar. 1979 / Milestone ✦✦✦✦
Bassist Carter heads a sterling mid-sized band with three trumpeters and saxophonists and two trombones, but no bass or drums. He handles the job of being both the primary and secondary rhythm support, while guests Joe Henderson, Jon Faddis, and Frank Wess, among others, provide some standout solos. The ensemble interaction clicks as well —*Ron Wynn*

New York Slick / Dec. 1979 / Milestone ✦✦✦

Patrao / May 19, 1980–May 20, 1980 / Original Jazz Classics ✦✦✦✦

Parfait / Sep. 29, 1980 / Milestone ✦✦

Heart and Soul / Dec. 1981 / Timeless ✦✦✦

Etudes / Sep. 1982 / Elektra ✦✦✦
Sophisticated, elegant quartet date from '82, with Art Farmer's

serene trumpet and fluegelhorn playing setting the tone, backed by tenor and soprano saxophonist Bill Evans, who's more restrained than usual. Carter's bass and Tony Williams' drums are both understated and definitive in their support and backing rhythms. —*Ron Wynn*

Live at Village West / Nov. 1982 / Concord Jazz ✦✦✦
The CD reissue of these duets by bassist Ron Carter and guitarist Jim Hall adds two new selections (one original apiece) to the LP program (which was comprised of eight standards). Hall's harmonically advanced style always brings out the best in Carter, and their quiet but passionate interplay is full of subtle surprises. — *Scott Yanow*

☆ **Telephone** / Aug. 1984 / Concord Jazz ✦✦✦✦✦
A live performance—a concert. Lots of space, and a slow pace. Music to listen to, perhaps a tad too intellectual. Still...lovely. — *Michael Erlewine*

All Alone / Mar. 29, 1988 / EmArcy ✦✦✦

Panmanhattan / Jul. 23, 1990 / Evidence ✦✦✦

Meets Bach / Dec. 15, 1991–Dec. 16, 1991 / Blue Note ✦✦✦

Friends / Dec. 27, 1992–Dec. 29, 1992 / Blue Note ✦✦✦✦

Jazz, My Romance / Jan. 4, 1994–Jan. 5, 1994 / Blue Note ✦✦
As with virtually all of Ron Carter's recordings as a leader, this CD is primarily a showcase for his bass solos. The unusual combination of musicians (a trio with guitarist Herb Ellis and pianist Kenny Barron) really does not live up to its potential. There are some short spots for Ellis and Barron, but their roles are mostly in support of the bassist. Some of the selections (particularly "Sweet Lorraine" and the bassist's original "For Toddlers Only") do have their memorable moments but none of the songs are taken at faster than a medium tempo. Since bass solos (as with most drum showcases) often lose a lot when transferred to record (as opposed to being seen live), this CD is recommended mostly to Ron Carter completists. — *Scott Yanow*

Wayman Carver

b. Dec. 25, 1905, Portsmouth, VA, d. May 6, 1967, Atlanta, GA
Flute, Alto Sax, Tenor Sax/ Swing
Although not the first jazz flute soloist, (Albert Socaras preceded him by five years), Wayman Carver was virtualll;y the only flutist to be featured on swing records in the 1930s. He picked up early experience playing with J. Neal Montgomery's band. In 1931 he settled in New York where he recorded with Dave Nelson. After a stint with Elmer Snowden (1931-32), he joined Benny Carter and recorded with Spike Hughes in 1933, taking some of his best solos. Carver was with Chick Webb's band during 1934-39 (mostly playing in the sax section) but was well featured on four 1937 titles by Chick Webb and his Little Chicks, a quintet matching his flute with Chauncey Haughton's clarinet. Carver remained with the orchestra as it continued under Ella Fitzgerald's leadership after Webb's death (1939-41) and then eventually settled in Atlanta as a professor of music at Clark College; among his students were George Adams and Marion Brown. —*Scott Yanow*

Dick Cary

b. Jul. 10, 1916, Hartford, CT, d. Apr. 6, 1994, Glendale, CA
Piano, Trumpet, Alto Horn / Dixieland, Swing
Dick Cary, best-known for his stint with Louis Armstrong's All-Stars (1947-48) was most significant as a behind-the-scenes arranger and freelance musician in the trad jazz movement. He made his recording debut with Joe Marsala (1942), worked as a soloist at Nick's (1942-43) and played for short periods with the Casa Loma Orchestra and Brad Gowans. While in the Army (1944-46) he was able to keep on recording, including with Muggsy Spanier and Wild Bill Davison. After playing with Billy Butterfield and Louis Armstrong, Cary was with Jimmy Dorsey's big band (1949-50), wrote arrangements and played alto horn on Eddie Condon's television shows and throughout the 1950s played and wrote for the Condon gang, recording with Condon, Pee Wee Russell, Max Kaminsky, Bud Freeman, Jimmy McPartland, Bobby Hackett and others. In 1959 he settled in Los Angeles, working as a freelance musician up until his death. In later years Cary led his Tuesday Night Band and performed often at Dixieland jazz festivals . —*Scott Yanow*

Dixieland Goes Progressive / Jun. 11, 1957 / Golden Crest ✦✦✦
Hot and Cool / 1958 / Stereo-Craft ✦✦✦✦
Dick Cary and His Dixieland Doodlers / Oct. 20, 1959–Oct. 30, 1959 / Columbia ✦✦✦
The Amazing Dick Cary / Oct. 27, 1975–Oct. 30, 1975 / Riff ✦✦✦
● **California Doings** / Jun. 1981 / Famous Door ✦✦✦✦

Casa Loma Orchestra

Group / Swing
When originally formed by saxophonist Glen Gray, the Casa Loma Orchestra was a cooperative orchestra. They made their recording debut in 1929 and during the next six years would be one of the top swing-oriented big bands in jazz (even though the term "swing" would not come into general usage until 1935). Although their ensembles were later criticized as sounding mechanical (thanks in part to the complexity of Gene Gifford's arrangements), the band did swing and had several fine soloists including clarinetist Clarence Hutchenrider, the high note trumpeter Sonny Dunham (whose display on "Memories of You" is still impressive) and trombonist/singer Pee Wee Hunt; Kenny Sargent offered smooth ballad vocals. After Benny Goodman's success in 1935 resulted in many new big bands being formed, the Casa Loma Orchestra was never again a pacesetter, but it continued into the 1940s with such players as Red Nichols, Bobby Hackett and Herb Ellis. Glen Gray had top billing from the late '30s on and after he stopped touring (around 1950), he started a commercially successful (if very predictable) series of recordings for Capitol that found the Casa Loma Orchestra (by then mostly studio players) constantly revisiting (and often recreating) the hits of the swing era. But its early original recordings of tunes such as "San Sue Strut," "Casa Loma Stomp," "No Name Jive" and "Smoke Rings" are well worth acquiring. —*Scott Yanow*

● **Best of the Big Bands** / Dec. 18, 1931–Dec. 24, 1934 / Columbia ✦✦✦✦
And the Casa Loma Orchestra (1939) / 1939 / Circle ✦✦
The Uncollected Glen Gray & The Casa Loma Orchestra, Vol. 1 (1939-1940) / 1939-1940 / Hindsight ✦✦✦
And the Casa Loma Orchestra (1940) / 1940 / Circle ✦✦
The Uncollected Glen Gray & The Casa Loma Orchestra, Vol. 2 (1943-46) / 1943-1946 / Hindsight ✦✦✦
Casa Loma in Hi-Fi! / Jun. 18, 1956–Jun. 21, 1956 / Capitol ✦✦✦
This studio recreation of the original Casa Loma band (which recorded sparingly) includes both jazz and sweet aspects of Glen Gray. —*David Szatmary*

Al Casey

b. Sep. 15, 1915, Louisville, KY
Guitar / Swing
Although it has been over half a century since Fats Waller's death and Al Casey has been active during most of that time, he is still closely linked with Waller. He started working with the pianist's group in the early '30s and was his main guitarist (with time off) up until Fats' demise in 1943, recording literally hundreds of performances. Sticking to acoustic guitar during that period, Casey was a very valuable rhythm player who also contributed some excellent single-note solos. Casey, who had worked with Teddy Wilson's big band during part of 1939-40 and recorded with Billie Holiday, Frankie Newton and Chu Berry, briefly led a trio of his own and in 1944 worked with Clarence Profit's group. By that time he had switched to electric guitar and, inspired by Charlie Christian, he himself became influential for a time. Casey has spent the decades since freelancing in swing and blues settings. During 1957-61 he played R&B with King Curtis, in the 1980s he was often featured with the Harlem Blues and Jazz Band and in 1994 Al Casey recorded as a leader for Jazzpoint, a set not surprisingly titled *A Tribute to Fats*. —*Scott Yanow*

● **Buck Jumpin'** / Mar. 7, 1960 / Original Jazz Classics ✦✦✦✦
Al Casey, who will always be best-known as Fats Waller's guitarist, makes one of his few appearances as a bandleader on the CD reissue of his Swingville album. Casey, in a quintet with Rudy Powell (who doubles on alto and clarinet) and pianist Herman Foster, sticks to blues and standards with several of the latter taken from Waller's songbook. The music consistently swings and it is a rare pleasure to hear Casey getting the opportunity to stretch out on acoustic guitar. Two previously unreleased numbers

("Gut Soul" and "I'm Gonna Sit Right Down and Write Myself a Letter") augment the original program. —*Scott Yanow*

Al Casey Quartet / Nov. 10, 1960 / Moodsville ✦✦✦

Genius of Jazz Guitar / Jul. 1981 / JSP ✦✦✦
Side One with pianist Gene Rogers Trio, Side Two with Jay McShann or Mike Carr's Trio. Swing, blues, and gospel standards. —*Michael G. Nastos*

Best of Friends / 1981 / JSP ✦✦✦

Al Casey Remembers King Curtis / Jul. 21, 1985 / JSP ✦✦✦

Dick Cathcart

b. Nov. 6, 1924, Michigan City, IN, d. Nov. 8, 1993
Trumpet, Vocals / Big Band, Dixieland, Traditional Bluegrass, Swing
A fine Dixieland trumpeter, Dick Cathcart became best-known for his role of ghosting the playing of Pete Kelly (as played by Jack Webb) in a radio series, film and television show all titled *Pete Kelly's Blues*. Early on Cathcart played trumpet in the U.S. Army Air Force Band. After stints with Alvino Rey, Ray McKinley and Bob Crosby, he worked in the MGM studios (1946–49), and with the bands of Ben Pollack and Ray Noble. In the 1950s he began recording albums with his own group (which was titled Pete Kelly's Big Seven). Cathcart remained active on the Dixieland circuit (including festivals) off and on until his death. —*Scott Yanow*

Bix MCMLIX / Dec. 12, 1958–Dec. 22, 1958 / Warner Brothers ✦✦✦✦

Philip Catherine

b. Oct. 27, 1942, London, England
Guitar / Swing, Post-Bop
Philip Catherine, who was dubbed "Young Django" by Charles Mingus, can play flashy, flamboyant licks, wondrously beautiful lines, expressive melodies or torrid solos. Catherine's equally accomplished at jazz, classical or Afro-Latin material. He was born in London, but is a Belgian. Catherine played for Belgian radio stations in the '60s, and also worked with Lou Bennett. He got his jazz induction with Jean-Luc Ponty's Experience at a time Ponty was heavily into free music. Catherine came to America after leaving Ponty in the early '70s, enrolled at Berklee, and later formed the band Pork Pie with Charlie Mariano and Jasper van't Hof. They recorded in the mid- and late '70s. Catherine teamed with Niels-Henning Orsted Pedersen in the mid-70s, and the duo worked on various projects into the mid-'80s. Catherine made several dates with Larry Coryell in the '70s, and worked with Stephane Grappelli, Charles Mingus, and Pedersen in the '70s and '80s. —*Ron Wynn*

Nairam / Nov. 1976 / Warner Brothers ✦✦✦

Catherine/Escoude/Lockwood Trio / Sep. 1983–Oct. 1983 / Gramavision ✦✦✦✦

Transparence / Nov. 24, 1986–Nov. 25, 1986 / Timeless ✦✦✦

September Sky / Sep. 1, 1988–Sep. 2, 1988 / September ✦✦✦

● **I Remember You** / Oct. 19, 1990 / Criss Cross ✦✦✦✦

Moods, Vol. 1 / May 19, 1992–May 20, 1992 / Criss Cross ✦✦✦✦

Moods, Vol. 2 / May 19, 1992–May 20, 1992 / Criss Cross ✦✦✦✦

Spanish Nights / 1992 / Enja ✦✦✦

Sidney "Big Sid" Catlett

b. Jan. 17, 1910, Evansville, IN, d. Mar. 25, 1951, Chicago, IL
Drums / Swing
Just as arguments continue today over who's the greatest drummer in jazz, there were similiar disputes during the swing era. Buddy Rich and Gene Krupa got more exposure and ink than "Big Sid" Catlett, but both loved and admired him (as he did them). Catlett was among jazz's premier combo drummers, a sensitive accompanist who knew how to push a beat, but never overpowered or hurried it. He could anticipate a soloist's direction and usually adjusted his timbres to suit a soloist's style. He functioned just as expertly in a big band setting, and was an extraordinary extended soloist; he and Max Roach may be jazz's greatest in building and developing lengthy solos without becoming repetitious, excessively relying on flash or running out of ideas in midstream. He made recordings in every conceivable style, traditional New Orleans jazz, swing, '20s Chicago and bop. Catlett played in several Chicago bands during his youth before moving to New York in 1930. He played during the '30s with Benny Carter, McKinney's Cotton Pickers, the Jeter-Pillars Orchestra, Fletcher Henderson and Don Redman, before joining Louis Armstrong's big band from 1938 to 1942, and working periodically with Benny Goodman in 1941. Catlett recorded for Commodore with Chu Berry and his "Little Jazz" Ensemble in 1938, and Coleman Hawkins and the Chocolate Dandies in 1940. He led his own bands for six years. During this period, there was also a 1943 session with Hawkins and Leonard Feather's All-Stars, and sessions with Dizzy Gillespie and Charlie Ventura. Catlett rejoined Armstrong from 1947 to 1949, this time with the smaller edition of the all-stars. While waiting in the wings at a theater in 1951, Big Sid Catlett died suddenly at 41. —*Ron Wynn*

Page Cavanaugh

b. Jan. 26, 1922, Cherokee, KS
Piano, Vocals / Swing
A talented veteran pianist/vocalist, Page Cavanaugh and his trio (with guitarist Al Viola and bassist Lloyd Pratt) was quite popular during the latter half of the 1940s. Cavanaugh started taking piano lessons when he was nine. He picked up early experience playing with the Ernie Williamson band (1938–39). While in the military he first met up with Viola and Pratt. After their discharge, the trio's swinging playing (inspired by the Nat King Cole Trio) plus their whispered vocals made them a hit during the mid-to-late '40s; among their best-sellers were "The Three Bears," "Walkin' My Baby Back Home" and "All of Me." The group appeared in several movies including *A Song Is Born* and *Romance on the High Seas*. Cavanaugh has worked steadily in the Los Angeles area for the past five decades, heading a septet (The Page 7) in the early '60s and performing regularly with his trio (which once again includes Al Viola) since the late '80s. His earlier RCA dates are difficult to find but he has recorded in recent times for Star Line. —*Scott Yanow*

● **The Digital Page: Page One** / Jan. 12, 1989 / Star Line ✦✦✦✦✦
The Digital Page: Page Two / Jan. 12, 1989 / Star Line ✦✦✦✦

Oscar Celestin

b. Jan. 1, 1884, Napoleonville, LA, d. Dec. 15, 1954, New Orleans, LA
Trumpet, Leader / New Orleans Jazz
Oscar Celestin's legendary career can easily be split into two different parts. A pioneer who moved to New Orleans in 1906, Celestin played with the Algiers Brass Band and the Olympia Band before heading the Tuxedo Brass Band and his original Tuxedo Jazz Orchestra (1917–early '30s). Although not a major trumpeter, Celestin's band was excellent and recorded some enjoyable performances in the 1920s. After the Depression hit, Celestin retired from music, but in 1946 he made a comeback with a new version of the Tuxedo Jazz Orchestra. This group, playing Dixieland standards and hymns, became a major tourist attraction in New Orleans, appearing on TV and radio, making some records and even playing a special concert at Dwight Eisenhower's White House in 1953. —*Scott Yanow*

● **Marie Laveau** / 1950–Apr. 24, 1954 / GHB ✦✦✦✦✦
Papa Celestin's New Orleans Band was one of the most popular jazz groups for a short while in the early '50s. The veteran trumpeter (who was in his mid-60s but seemed older) performed spirited versions of New Orleans standards, even getting to play once at the White House in the Eisenhower years (a rare event during that era for a jazz band). This CD from GHB combines together two former LPs. Celestin is heard mostly singing on four numbers from 1954 (his final recordings and highlighted by the atmospheric title cut and an emotional "Down by the Riverside") and jamming with his sextet (a group including the ancient, but still viable, clarinetist Alphonse Picou) on ten Dixieland standards in 1950–51. The liner notes may be a bit irrelevant (not even giving the recording dates), pianist Octave Crosby gets lost now and then and the ensembles sometimes slip out of tune, but the spirit and the joy of the music make this definitive Oscar Celestin CD a must for New Orleans jazz fans. —*Scott Yanow*

Bill Challis

b. Jul. 8, 1904, Wilkes Barre, PA, d. 1995
Arranger / Swing, Classic Jazz
As staff arranger for Jean Goldkette (1926) and Paul Whiteman (1927–30), Bill Challis was largely responsible for the majority of

the two big bands' most jazz-oriented charts including "Sunday," "My Pretty Girl," "Changes," "Dardanella" and most notably "San." Challis also wrote for Frankie Trumbauer's small-group dates with Bix Beiderbecke and assisted Bix in documenting piano pieces (including "In a Mist"). He contributed arrangements to quite a few big bands including Fletcher Henderson, the Dorsey Brothers, the Casa Loma Orchestra, Artie Shaw ("Blues in the Night"), many radio orchestras and pop sessions. Challis was active into the 1960s and in 1986 many of his best arrangements were recorded by Vince Giordano's Nighthawks and Tom Pletcher (*The Goldkette Project*). —*Scott Yanow*

1936 / Feb. 24, 1936 / Circle ✦✦✦
● **The Goldkette Project** / 1988 / Circle ✦✦✦✦✦

Serge Chaloff

b. Nov. 24, 1923, Boston, MA, **d.** Jul. 16, 1957, Boston, MA
Baritone Saxophone / Bop
One of the great baritone-saxophonists and the first major soloist on that instrument to emerge since Harry Carney (he preceded Gerry Mulligan), Serge Chaloff was a drug addict during his prime years, resulting in broken friendships and lost opportunities. After playing with the orchestras of Boyd Raeburn (1944–45), Georgie Auld (1945–46) and Jimmy Dorsey (1946–47), he found fame as one of the "Four Brothers" with Woody Herman's Second Herd (1947–49). After a stint with Count Basie's octet (1950), Chaloff returned to his native Boston where he eventually worked on kicking his dangerous habit. Ironically when he finally got off drugs, Chaloff contracted spinal paralysis and he played his final recording session (a reunion of the Four Brothers in 1957) seated in a wheelchair. Mosaic's 1993 limited-edition four-CD Serge Chaloff box set has all of his sessions as a leader and his exciting solos still put him near the top of his field. —*Scott Yanow*

● **The Complete Serge Chaloff Sessions** / Sep. 21, 1946–Mar. 14, 1956 / Mosaic ✦✦✦✦✦
This is the type of project the Mosaic label does best: releasing the complete output as a leader of a classic jazz musician including obscurities and a couple of fairly well-known sessions. Serge Chaloff, one of the top baritone-saxophonists in jazz history, is featured as the leader of bop-based small groups on sessions originally out on Dial, Savoy, Futurama, Motif, Storyville and Capitol. Such sidemen as trumpeters Red Rodney and Herb Pomeroy, tenorman Al Cohn, altoist Charlie Mariano and Boots Mussuli, vibraphonist Terry Gibbs and pianists Ralph Burns, George Wallington, Dick Twardzik, Russ Freeman, Barbara Carroll and Sonny Clark have solo space but it is the somewhat forgotten Chaloff who rightfully is the main focus. A definitive booklet rounds out this essential package. —*Scott Yanow*

Boston 1950 / 1950 / Uptown ✦✦✦
The Fable of Mable / Jun. 9, 1954+Sep. 3, 1954 / Black Lion ✦✦✦✦
West Coast jazz's finest baritone saxophonist was in prime, keen form on this 1954 session. Chaloff, playing a group that also included Charlie Mariano and Herb Pomeroy, dominated the proceedings without ever seeming to strain or sweat. His rolling lines and smooth sound on the generally bulky-sounding baritone remains one of jazz's more impressive sounds. —*Ron Wynn*

Boston Blow-Up / Apr. 4, 1955+Apr. 5, 1955 / Capitol ✦✦✦✦
Another swinging, boppish session from a musician who was once a mainstay of Woody Herman's band. —*David Szatmary*

Blue Serge / Mar. 4, 1956 / Capitol ✦✦✦✦
An indispensable session from one of the great underrated baritone sax players, it features Sonny Clark (p) and Philly Joe Jones (d). —*David Szatmary*

Joe Chambers

b. Jun. 25, 1942, Stoneacre, VA
Piano, Drums / Avant-Garde, Post-Bop
A steady, reliable player who's worked in hard bop, big band and free groups, Joe Chambers has never attained stardom, but enjoys healthy respect within the jazz community among musicians and critics. He's not flashy or bombastic, but can provide anything from consistent timekeeping to excellent solos, varied rhythms, multiple accents and colors, plus precise interaction within the rhythm section. Chambers worked in the Washington, D.C. area for a few years in the late '50s and early '60s before moving to New York in 1963. He worked with Eric Dolphy, Freddie Hubbard,

Jimmy Giuffre, Lou Donaldson and Andrew Hill, then in the mid-'60s and early '70s performed and recorded with Bobby Hutcherson. Chambers also played with Donald Byrd's quintet, Duke Pearson's big band and Joe Henderson's group, and recorded with Sam Rivers, Chick Corea, Wayne Shorter and Miroslav Vitous. He was among the originals in M'Boom Re', the percussion ensemble founded by Max Roach in 1970. He played in the '70s with Sonny Rollins, Tommy Flanagan and Art Farmer, while recording and performing with Charles Mingus and Joe Zawinul. Chambers was in the Super Jazz Trio with Reggie Workman and Flanagan in the late '70s, recorded with Chet Baker in the early '80s and played with Ray Mantilla's Space Station. Hubbard, Hutcherson and M'Boom Re have performed Chambers' compositions. They've also been featured on his infrequent albums. Chambers co-led a group with Larry Young in the late '70s, and did albums for Muse and a solo date for Denon. He recorded for Candid in 1992 with Philip Harper, Bob Berg, George Cables and Santi Debriano. —*Ron Wynn*

The Almoravid / Oct. 8, 1973–Nov. 1, 1973 / Muse ✦✦✦✦
Double Exposure / Nov. 16, 1977 / Muse ✦✦✦
This is an unusual date. Joe Chambers, best known as a drummer, is heard on piano on four of these six tracks (including a fine effort on an unaccompanied version of "After the Rain"). The other selections are duets with the great organist Larry Young, who would pass away four-and-a-half months later. The music is somewhat adventurous with Chambers as the lead voice on the numbers on which he plays piano; the final two performances are organ-drum duets that put more of an emphasis on Young's unique sound. This interesting session has some surprising music. —*Scott Yanow*

● **Phantom of the City** / Mar. 8, 1991–Mar. 9, 1991 / Candid ✦✦✦✦
Drummer Joe Chambers works with an intriguing lineup on this '91 quintet set. Young lion trumpeter Phillip Harper teams with journeyman Bob Berg, who holds his own with the lyrical, energetic Harper. Chambers never hurries or crowds the soloists, and he interacts easily and fully with pianist George Cables and bassist Santi Debriano. —*Ron Wynn*

Paul Chambers

b. Apr. 22, 1935, Pittsburgh, PA, **d.** Jan. 4, 1969, New York, NY
Bass / Hard Bop
One of the top bassists of 1955–65, Paul Chambers was among the first in jazz to take creative bowed solos (other than Slam Stewart, who hummed along with his bowing). He grew up in Detroit where he was part of the fertile local jazz scene. After touring with Paul Quinichette, Chambers went to New York where he played with the J.J. Johnson-Kai Winding quintet and George Wallington. He spent the bulk of his prime years (1955–63) as a member of the Miles Davis Quintet, participating in virtually all of Davis' classic recordings of the era. When he left, "Mr. P.C." (as John Coltrane called him in one of his originals) worked with the Wynton Kelly Trio (1963–66) and freelanced until his death. Chambers, a consistently inspired accompanist who was an excellent soloist, made many recordings during his brief period including some with Sonny Rollins, Coltrane, Cannonball Adderley, Donald Byrd, Bud Powell and Freddie Hubbard in addition to a few as a leader —*Scott Yanow*

● **High Step** / Apr. 20, 1955+Nov. 1955 / Blue Note ✦✦✦✦
Complete all-star group sessions from the mid-'50s that include John Coltrane contributions. Rare two-record set that was part of mid-'70s Blue Note reissue line. —*Ron Wynn*

Whims of Chambers / Sep. 21, 1956 / Blue Note ✦✦✦
Go / Feb. 2, 1959–Feb. 3, 1959 / Vee-Jay ✦✦✦
Super late '50s date from Vee Jay, with Cannonball Adderley on the case playing furious alto sax, Freddie Hubbard equally inspired on trumpet, and Chambers interacting with longtime section mates Wynton Kelly (piano) and Philly Joe Jones (drummer). There was an '86 CD reissue. —*Ron Wynn*

1st Bassman / May 12, 1960 / Vee-Jay ✦✦✦✦
Exceptional date with Chambers working in the company of fellow greats Wynton Kelly, Curtis Fuller, and Yusef Lateef, plus solid pros Lex Humphries and Tommy Turrentine. Few have ever equalled Chambers for overall playing quality, whether in ensemble sections, accompaniment, or solo work. The '86 CD contains a bonus cut. —*Ron Wynn*

Dennis Charles

b. Dec. 4, 1933, St. Croix, Virgin Islands

Drums / Avant-Garde, Free Jazz

Dennis Charles is best-known as the drummer with Cecil Taylor's earliest groups (1955–61). Although a steady timekeeper, he was flexible enough to fit in well with Taylor during his formative years. He moved to New York in the mid-'40s and played calypso and mambos before switching to jazz. In addition to his work with Taylor, Charles recorded with Steve Lacy (1957), Gil Evans (1959) and Sonny Rollins (1962) and performed with Lacy's 1963–64 group, Archie Shepp (1967) and Billy Bang (1981–82). Out of music for long periods, Dennis Charles has been more active since the 1980s. —Scott Yanow

● Queen Mary / Apr. 26, 1989–Apr. 27, 1989 / Silkheart ◆◆◆◆

Teddy Charles (Theodore Charles Cohen)

b. Apr. 13, 1928, Chicopee Falls, MA

Vibes / Cool

Teddy Charles' conception and approach have changed considerably from his early days of working with big bands led by Benny Goodman, Chubby Jackson, Artie Shaw, and Buddy DeFranco. In the '50s, both in his own groups and playing with others, Charles began to play aggressively and try newer things, especially as a producer. He created groups for recordings with three trumpets and a rhythm section or a tenor and two baritones; his '50s solos on vibes were far-reaching and a precursor to the things being done currently by Jay Hoggard or Steve Nelson. Charles was both a dedicated and advanced improviser and a superior composer He was a regular participant in Charles Mingus' Jazz Composers Workshop in 1954 and 1955, and he wrote such compositions as "Variations on a Theme By Bud" and others featuring unusual arrangements, modality and polytonality. His 1956 tenet LP has been reissued on CD by Atlantic, as has a 1953 duo effort on Prestige with Shorty Rogers. Charles also has a more recent session on Soul Note and an earlier date on Bethlehem with Zoot Sims (now on Fresh Sound) available on CD. —Ron Wynn

Collaboration: West / Aug. 21, 1953+Aug. 31, 1953 / Original Jazz Classics ◆◆◆

Evolution / Aug. 31, 1953–Jan. 6, 1955 / Original Jazz Classics ◆◆◆

Composition is the thing on this session, which features vibist Teddy Charles on two dates: 8/31/53 and 1/6/55. The earlier date is with Jimmy Giuffre, Shelly Manne, Shorty Rogers and Curtis Counce and the music is highly structured along movements of shifting tempos, colors and instrument features. It is a bit overdrawn and never really flies. The later session included J.R. Monterose, Charles Mingus and Gerry Segal (drums) and it, too, is somewhat overloaded by its careful and often confining scoring and sameness in its sax, bass, vibes color blend. This music has always had distinguishing characteristics, but after living with it more than 30 years I've never felt it lived up to its talents. —Bob Rusch, Cadence

Coolin' / Apr. 14, 1957 / Original Jazz Classics ◆◆◆◆

Although this sextet session was officially a co-op, vibraphonist Teddy Charles and pianist Mal Waldron were really the main organizers. The group plays five originals by bandmembers that often have complex melodies but familiar chord changes. Trumpeter Idrees Sulieman excels on the one standard ("Everything Happens to Me"), altoist John Jenkins (making his recording debut) has some worthy solos and both bassist Addison Farmer and drummer Jerry Segal are fine in support. This obscure session (reissued on CD in the OJC series) is an excellent outing. —Scott Yanow

Of the Museum of Modern Art / Nov. 21, 1959 / Fresh Sound ◆◆◆

● Live at the Verona Jazz Festival (1988) / Jun. 25, 1988 / Soul Note ◆◆◆◆

Concert date with Harold Danko trio. Highlight is the Mingus composition "Nostalgia in Times Square." —Michael G. Nastos

Doc Cheatham (Adolphus Anthony Cheatham)

b. Jun. 13, 1905, Nashville, TN

Trumpet, Vocals / Dixieland, Swing

Doc Cheatham is without question the greatest 90-year-old trumpeter of all time; in fact no brass player over the age of 80 has ever played with his power, range, confidence and melodic creativity. Most trumpeters fade while in their 60s due to the physi-

cal difficulty of their instrument, but Cheatham did not truly find himself as a soloist until he was nearly 70!

Doc Cheatham's career reaches back to the early '20s when he played in vaudeville theaters backing such travelling singers as Bessie Smith and Clara Smith. He moved to Chicago, recorded with Ma Rainey (on soprano sax!), played with Albert Wynn, subbed for Louis Armstrong (his main idol) and had his own group in 1926. After stints with Wilbur DeParis and Chick Webb, he toured Europe with Sam Wooding. Due to his wide range and pretty tone, Cheatham worked as a nonsoloing first trumpeter with McKinney's Cotton Pickers and Cab Calloway throughout the 1930s. He spent time with Teddy Wilson's big band and was with the commercially successful Eddie Heywood Sextet (backing Billie Holiday on some recordings). In the 1950s Cheatham alternated between Dixieland (Wilbur DeParis, guest spots with Eddie Condon) and Latin (Perez Prado, Herbie Mann) bands. He was with Benny Goodman during 1966–67 but it was not until the mid-'70s that Cheatham felt truly comfortable as a soloist. Duet sets with pianist Sammy Price launched his new career and since then he has recorded fairly prolifically, including dates for Sackville, New York Jazz, Parkwood, Stash, GHB, Columbia and several European labels. Cheatham is also a charming singer whose half-spoken, half-sung vocals take nothing away from his chance-taking trumpet flights. —Scott Yanow

Hey Doc! / May 2, 1975 / Black & Blue ◆◆◆

Doc and Sammy / Nov. 17, 1976 / Sackville ◆◆◆

Trumpeter Doc Cheatham has had something of a unique career. A lead trumpeter during much of his life, he did not develop as a soloist until he was nearly 70 years old. This set finally made the jazz world aware of his talents. Doc (who was already age 71) is joined by the 68-year-old pianist Sammy Price for a set of swing and Dixieland standards. This music should appeal to all followers of traditional jazz, and it served as the first real beginning to Cheatham's second career. —Scott Yanow

Good for What Ails Ya / May 2, 1977 / Classic Jazz ◆◆◆◆

This Dixielandish session features the ageless trumpeter Doc Cheatham (who was then 71 and still improving) in a sextet with trombonist Gene "Mighty Flea" Conners, altoist Ted Buckner, pianist Sammy Price, bassist Carl Pruitt and drummer J.C. Heard on eight veteran standards. It is great fun to hear these classic players jam on this LP on such tunes as "Rosetta," "What Can I Say Dear After I Say I'm Sorry?" and "Rose Room." —Scott Yanow

Black Beauty / Oct. 31, 1979 / Sackville ◆◆◆

The second duet session by trumpeter Doc Cheatham (then age 74) and 71-year-old pianist Sammy Price features 11 standards written by Black composers and is as successful as their first recording. Highpoints include such songs as "Some of These Days," "After You've Gone," "Someday You'll Be Sorry" and "Louisiana." This joyful music falls between small-group swing and Dixieland. —Scott Yanow

Too Marvelous For Words / Oct. 25, 1982–Oct. 26, 1982 / New York Jazz ◆◆◆

Veteran trumpeter Doc Cheatham is in fine form on this session with The Hot Jazz Orchestra of New York, an octet that also includes trombonist Dan Barrett, Joe Muranyi's reeds, guitarist Howard Alden and a fine rhythm section; there is one vocal apiece by Cynthia Sayer, Lew Micallef and Eddy Davis. The playing time is a bit brief even for an LP (just over a half-hour) and few surprises occur but this set is still quite enjoyable. —Scott Yanow

I've Got a Crush on You / Oct. 25, 1982–Oct. 26, 1982 / New York Jazz ◆◆◆

The playing time on this LP is brief (under 32 minutes) but this is a particularly strong showcase for trumpeter Doc Cheatham (who was then 77). Cheatham is heard on four duets with guitarist Howard Alden, taking the vocals and playing some heated but relaxed trumpet. The other four selections feature him with an octet that also allocates a generous amount of solo space to bassist Milt Hinton. —Scott Yanow

It's a Good Life / Dec. 6, 1982–Dec. 7, 1982 / Parkwood ◆◆◆◆

The 77-year-old trumpeter proves to be very much in his prime during this excellent session. In fact Cheatham, who is backed by a fine rhythm section led by pianist Chuck Folds, dominates this set, taking melodic but passionate trumpet solos and contributing charming vocals. His versions of "Struttin' with Some Barbecue" and "You're Lucky to Me" are particularly memorable. —Scott Yanow

At the Bern Jazz Festival / Apr. 30, 1983–Jan. 5, 1985 / Sackville ✦✦✦
Veteran trumpeter Doc Cheatham and soprano saxophonist Jim Galloway co-lead these three separate live sessions. The sextet (which also includes trombonist Roy Williams) explores a variety of standards including "Cherry," "Love Is Just Around the Corner," "Swing That Music" and a ballad medley. Everyone is in fine form on this small-group swing CD. — *Scott Yanow*

● **The Fabulous** / Nov. 16, 1983–Nov. 17, 1983 / Parkwood ✦✦✦✦✦
The ageless trumpeter Doc Cheatham (who was 78 years old at the time of this studio session) is remarkable. Most trumpeters fade when they hit their 60s, but he continues to gain in strength, hitting reasonably high notes with confidence and power; his melodic invention also continues to develop. This quartet session with the late pianist Dick Wellstood is one of his finest recordings. Cheatham is in particularly top form on "'Deed I Do," "Swing That Music" and "I Double Dare You," but all nine selections (which also feature his charming whispered vocals) are quite enjoyable. — *Scott Yanow*

Highlights In Jazz / Dec. 12, 1985 / Stash ✦✦
This overly loose LP teams together the great veteran trumpeter Doc Cheatham with tenor saxophonist George Kelly and Joey Cavaseno (doubling on clarinet and alto) for six standards. Although Cheatham sounds fine, the performances tend to be overly long and they ramble a bit. This live, swing-oriented music has its moments but is not too essential. — *Scott Yanow*

Tribute To Billie Holiday / May 13, 1987–May 14, 1987 / Kenneth ✦✦✦
Doc Cheatham (a month short of turning age 82) is in excellent form on this set of eight songs associated with Billie Holiday. Fortunately, the octet avoids the obvious tunes like "God Bless the Child" and "Lover Man" and instead plays songs such as "I Cried for You" and "On the Sunny Side of the Street" that are more adaptable as jazz instrumentals (although Cheatham does take a couple of vocals). Joined by a band filled with top Swedish players, he is in excellent form for this heartfelt and successful tribute. — *Scott Yanow*

Tribute To Louis Armstrong / May 6, 1988–May 7, 1988 / Kenneth ✦✦✦
Listening to Doc Cheatham play trumpet on this Louis Armstrong tribute, it is impossible to believe that he was nearly 83 years old. Cheatham's solos are played with confidence and power and they display a still impressive range; there is nothing feeble about his sound. Cheatham performs ten songs associated with Louis Armstrong assisted by a group of Swedish All-Stars and Armstrong's former pianist Dick Cary. He comes up with fresh interpretations on such songs as "Swing That Music," "Our Monday Date," and "Jeepers Creepers" on this easily recommended LP. — *Scott Yanow*

You're a Sweetheart / Mar. 29, 1992+Nov. 15, 1992 / Sackville ✦✦✦
Trumpeter Doc Cheatham (87 at the time) gets top billing and is well-featured on six of this CD's 11 selections but the release from the Canadian label Sackville is more significant for helping to introduce Rosemary Galloway's Swing Sisters. This fine quintet (originally all women but now just three out of five) features the excellent trumpeter Sarah McElcheran and the local legend Jane Fair on tenor and clarinet. The repertoire mostly consists of swing obscurities and Cheatham is delightful during his two vocals (sharing "Baby It's Cold Outside" with the bassist/leader). The performances without Cheatham sound quite a bit more modern, leaning more toward early-'60s hard bop. This well-rounded set has some fine individual moments. — *Scott Yanow*

Echoes Of New Orleans / Apr. 18, 1992 / Big Easy ✦✦✦
The remarkable Doc Cheatham (two months shy of 87 at the time), leads a fine sextet through a variety of Dixieland and swing numbers on this live set. Clarinetist Sammy Rimington has some good solos, trombonist Jerry Zigmont, pianist Jon Marks and drummer John Russell are competent without leaving much of an impression and bassist Arvell Shaw is in top form, taking a couple of spirited vocals. However it is Cheatham who dominates the happy performances, which range from "Clarinet Marmalade" and "Pennies from Heaven" to "Ain't Misbehavin'" and "Struttin' with Some Barbecue." — *Scott Yanow*

The Eighty-Seven Years of Doc Cheatham / Sep. 17, 1992–Sep. 18, 1992 / Columbia ✦✦✦✦✦
There has never been a trumpeter in recorded history over the age

of 80 on Doc Cheatham's level. Age 87 at the time of this CD, he plays with power, creativity and confidence on this quartet set of swing standards. He dominates the music with his trumpet solos and quiet but charming vocals and, even with the participation of a strong rhythm section led by pianist Chuck Folds, Cheatham is the obvious star. This historic set is a real gem on several levels and is highly recommended. — *Scott Yanow*

Jeannie Cheatham

Vocals, Piano, Leader / Swing, Blues
The husband and wife duo of Jimmy & Jeannie Cheatham have been working together since the mid-'50s and married since the late '50s. Her energetic, joyful vocals and his good-natured trombone riffs and accompaniment have been featured on a succession of fine Concord albums in the '80s and '90s. But their professional affiliation began after they met on stage in Buffalo during the '50s. Jeannie Cheatham had performed in clubs, while Jimmy Cheatham had played in Broadway bands and on television, as well as with Bill Dixon, Duke Ellington, Lionel Hampton, Thad Jones and Ornette Coleman. He'd even been Chico Hamilton's music director. Jeannie Cheatham studied piano as a child, later accompanying Dinah Washington, Al Hibbler and Jimmy Weatherspoon among others. They attended the University of Wisconsin in the '70s and taught in the jazz program, then moved to San Diego in the late '70s. While Jimmy Cheatham taught at the University of California, Jeannie was president of the Lower California Jazz Society. The duo worked in clubs and organized weekly jam sessions. Jeannie Cheatham appeared on a public television special with Sippie Wallace and Big Mama Thornton that was shown in 1983. Concord signed the duo in the mid-'80s, and they've been recording ever since, working with both their regular band and such special guests as Charles McPherson, Eddie "Lockjaw" Davis, Eddie "Cleanhead" Vinson and Red Callendar. — *Ron Wynn*

Sweet Baby Blues / Sep. 1984 / Concord Jazz ✦✦✦
Midnight Mama / Nov. 1985 / Concord Jazz ✦✦✦✦
Homeward Bound / Jan. 1987 / Concord Jazz ✦✦✦
Back to the Neighborhood / Nov. 1988 / Concord Jazz ✦✦✦
Luv in the Afternoon / May 1990 / Concord Jazz ✦✦✦
Basket Full of Blues / Nov. 6, 1991–Nov. 8, 1991 / Concord Jazz ✦✦✦✦✦
The sixth album from the husband and wife blues and swing/trad jazz duo. Jeannie Cheatham has the sassy attitude of classic blues types, but her subject material and style are firmly planted in the urban mode. Jimmy Cheatham keeps things under control and assists the band playing bass trombone, although it's saxophonists like Frank Wess and Curtis Peagler who get the most extensive solo space. — *Ron Wynn*

● **Blues & The Boogie Masters** / Jul. 1993 / Concord Jazz ✦✦✦✦✦
The Kansas City swing blues of The Sweet Baby Blues Band is very difficult not to enjoy. Jeannie Cheatham's exuberant vocals (propelled by her forcefully swinging piano) inspire the many soloists on the blues-oriented material, and there is plenty of variety in tempo and feeling to keep this set continually interesting. Among the main soloists are the ageless trumpeter Snooky Young, tenorman Rickey Woodard (making his debut on clarinet on two cuts) and guest altoist Hank Crawford, who sits in on four songs. — *Scott Yanow*

Gud Nuz Bluz / Sep. 27, 1995–Sep. 28, 1995 / Concord Jazz ✦✦✦✦

Don Cherry

b. Nov. 18, 1936, Oklahoma City, OK, d. Oct. 19, 1995, Malaga, Spain
Flute, Trumpet / Free Jazz, Avant-Garde, World Music
Don Cherry was a pivotal free jazz player/composer/theorist and invigorating, experimental world music improviser. He learned several non-Western instruments while studying and incorporating aspects of Asian, traditional Indian and African sounds into his work. His technique wasn't always the most efficient; frequently his rapid-fire solos contained numerous missed or muffed notes. But he was a master at exploring the trumpet and cornet's expressive, voice-like properties; he bent notes, added slurs and smears, and his twisting solos were tightly constructed and executed regardless of flaws. Among other instruments, he played bamboo flutes, berimbau and various percussive devices along with his unusual pocket cornet (he calls it a "pocket trumpet), trumpet, fluegelhorn and bugle. He played piano in an R&B band with Billy Higgins as a teen, then attracted attention in the late

'50s playing with Ornette Coleman, where his "pocket trumpet" and pithy, brittle sound drew almost as much reaction as Coleman's surging solos and concepts. He was featured on Coleman's first seven albums, and accompanied him to New York in 1959. Cherry and Coleman spent the summer of 1959 at the Lenox School of Music, and the Coleman quartet with Charlie Haden and Billy Higgins made a controversial New York debut that autumn. Then Cherry played with Steve Lacy, Sonny Rollins and John Coltrane in the early '60s, recording with Coltrane. He was in The New York Contemporary Five in 1963 and 1964 with Archie Shepp and John Tchicai, and played in Europe with Albert Ayler. Cherry co-led a quintet with Gato Barbieri in the mid-'60s, and did sessions in Europe and America, some of them later released on Blue Note. He did other dates with Pharoah Sanders and in 1969 recorded in Berlin with an octet that included European musicians Albert Mangelsdorff and Arlid Andersen, plus Sonny Sharrock. Cherry recorded duets with Edward Blackwell for the BYG label. He taught at Dartmouth in 1970, then was based in Sweden for four years. Cherry traveled through Europe and the Middle East extensively, playing informally while rigorously studying non-Western music styles. He continued a busy recording schedule for mostly European and Japanese labels in the early '70s. Cherry recorded in 1973 with The Jazz Composers Orchestra of America, then in Sweden before finally doing some dates for a major American company. He cut albums in the mid-'70s for A&M, Atlantic and Chiaroscuoro, playing with Frank Lowe, Charlie Haden, Billy Higgins, Hamiet Bluiett and Abdullah Ibrahim among others. He, Haden, Blackwell and Dewey Redman recorded in the late '70s for ECM as the quartet Old And New Dreams, and Cherry also recorded with Indian musician Latif Khan. He had a highly publicized collaboration with rock guitarist and vocalist Lou Reed. During the '80s Cherry recorded in the trio Codona with percussionists Colin Walcott and Nana Vasconcelos. He also did another duo session with Blackwell. After Codona disbanded, Cherry formed a new group, Nu, that included Vasconcelos and Carlos Ward. He worked with the more traditional jazz group The Leaders in the mid-'80s. Cherry appeared at the Berlin Jazzfest with Jabbo Smith in 1986, and toured England with Nu in 1987. Mosaic in 1993 issued a fine boxed set covering Cherry's Blue Note recordings. —*Ron Wynn*

Complete Communion / Dec. 24, 1965 / Blue Note ✦✦✦
Trumpeter Don Cherry, best known for his association with altoist Ornette Coleman, matched his innovative—but relatively mellow—horn with ferocious tenors on his three Blue Note albums (all of which have since been reissued in a Mosaic box set). This LP, which finds Cherry, bassist Henry Grimes and drummer Ed Blackwell joined by the passionate tenor of the young Gato Barbieri, consists of two four-song suites that were all composed by Cherry. The unexpected twists and turns of the music and Gato's high-register screams will excite some listeners and turn off others. This is chance-taking and intense music. —*Scott Yanow*

The Complete Blue Note Recordings Of Don Cherry / Dec. 24, 1965–Nov. 11, 1966 / Mosaic ✦✦✦✦
This limited-edition two-CD set reissues trumpeter Don Cherry's three Blue Note albums: *Complete Communion*, *Symphony for Improvisers* and *Where Is Brooklyn*. The avant-garde cornetist is teamed with the tenors of Gato Barbieri and Pharoah Sanders on one album apiece and with both of them on the explosive *Symphony*. All of the music (much of which is performed as continuous medleys) is quite fiery and free and displays Cherry's musical direction during his post-Ornette Coleman and pre-world music phase. These sessions are not essential, but they make for stimulating listening. —*Scott Yanow*

Symphony for Improvisers / Sep. 19, 1966 / Blue Note ✦✦✦
Don Cherry's second of three Blue Note albums (all have been included in a Mosaic box set) is quite a heated affair. That fact is not too surprising when one considers that the lyrical cornetist is joined by the tenors of the young Gato Barbieri and Pharoah Sanders in addition to a four-piece rhythm section that includes two bassists. This stirring music (eight of Cherry's originals) is performed continuously and has plenty of heated moments full of classic avant-garde fire. —*Scott Yanow*

Where Is Brooklyn / Nov. 11, 1966 / Blue Note ✦✦✦
Don Cherry's third Blue Note album (each has been reissued in full on a Mosaic box set) features the cornetist in a quartet with bassist Henry Grimes, drummer Ed Blackwell and the fiery tenor

of Pharoah Sanders. Although the instrumentation is not that much different than it had been with the Ornette Coleman Quartet, the presence of Sanders keeps the music quite passionate and stirring. This group plays the lengthy "Unite" and four shorter pieces, all composed by Cherry and full of the passion of the mid-'60s avant-garde fire. —*Scott Yanow*

Eternal Rhythm / Nov. 11, 1968–Nov. 12, 1968 / Saba ✦✦✦
Beginning of expansion beyond jazz. Cherry is sparkling on cornet, and switches to a variety of flutes and other instruments. Albert Mangelsdorff (tb) and Sonny Sharrock (g) join the party. —*Ron Wynn*

Mu, First Part & Second Part / Aug. 22, 1969 / Actuel ✦✦✦
Electrifying duets with Ed Blackwell (d). This music has been released both as one set and as two separate albums. —*Ron Wynn*

Brown Rice / 1975 / A&M ✦✦
This CD (a reissue of Horizon 717) has always been a bit of a disappointment. Don Cherry's trumpet playing is only heard sparingly (he only plays piano on the title cut) and little memorable occurs. "Brown Rice" is closer to R&B than jazz and Cherry's verbal recitation on "Degi-Degi" is not something one needs to hear twice. He also "vocalizes" a bit on "Chenrezig," and, although bassist Charlie Haden is a strong asset and the leader's trumpet is fine on "Malakauns," this release can be safely passed by. —*Scott Yanow*

Hear and Now / Dec. 1976 / Atlantic ✦✦

El Corazon with Ed Blackwell / Feb. 1982 / ECM ✦✦✦
Trumpet and drum duets are not exactly commonplace, making this collaboration between Don Cherry and Ed Blackwell something special. The music is often quite sparse (Cherry also plays a little bit of piano, melodica and organ) and the colorful Blackwell often steals the show (although the trumpeter's unaccompanied "Voice of the Silence" is a highpoint). The use of space is consistently impressive and those listeners with open ears will find this thoughtful date quite interesting. —*Scott Yanow*

● **Art Deco** / Aug. 27, 1988–Aug. 30, 1988 / A&M ✦✦✦✦
Although it is not mentioned anywhere on the outside of this CD, this session is very much a reunion. Trumpeter Don Cherry is reunited with bassist Charlie Haden and drummer Billy Higgins from the early Ornette Coleman Quartet, and, most importantly, tenor saxophonist James Clay. Clay, who after playing with Cherry in Los Angeles in the 1950s and doing a few recordings moved back to Texas, had been in obscurity for decades. Fortunately, his playing is quite strong on what turns out to be a surprisingly bop-oriented session. Comprised of superior standards, a few group originals and three Ornette Coleman tunes (including the classic "The Blessing"), this set is quite accessible and finds all of the musicians in top form. —*Scott Yanow*

Multi Kulti / Dec. 27, 1988–Feb. 23, 1990 / A&M ✦✦
A '90 patchwork quilt combining things from Asian, African, African-American, and European genres, united by Don Cherry's multi-instrumentalism and presence. Alto saxophonist Carlos Ward adds punch and spark, while special guests include Nana Vasconcelos, Karl Berger, and Ed Blackwell. —*Ron Wynn*

Dona Nostra / Mar. 1993 / ECM ✦✦✦

Billy Childs

b. 1957, Los Angeles, CA
Piano, Composer / Post-Bop
One of the most promising of the pianist-composers of the 1990s, Billy Childs is a superb player and an underrated writer. He toured with J.J. Johnson (with whom he made his recording debut), graduated from USC, had an important association with Freddie Hubbard (1978–84) and led Night Flight (a group with Dianne Reeves). Childs recorded four albums as a leader for Windham Hill Jazz (starting in 1988) and one for Stretch, started writing commissioned works in 1992 (including a 1994 concerto for the Monterey Jazz Festival) and has worked with Allan Holdsworth, Eddie Daniels, Bobby Hutcherson and Branford Marsalis among others in addition to leading his own regular quartet. —*Scott Yanow*

Take for Example This . . . / 1988 / Windham Hill Jazz ✦✦✦
This brilliant debut album has exceptional playing and compositions. —*Paul Kohler*

Twilight Is upon Us / 1989 / Windham Hill ✦✦✦✦
This follow-up album was recorded with Bob Sheppard and Jimmy Johnson (d). —*Paul Kohler*

His April Touch / 1991 / Windham Hill ✦✦✦✦
There is intriguing playing and strong melodic songwriting on this, Childs' third solo album. It has a modern jazz style with great production. —*Paul Kohler*

● **Portrait of a Player** / 1993 / Windham Hill ✦✦✦✦✦
Although relatively underpublicized, Billy Childs is gradually becoming one of the giants of jazz, both as a writer and as a pianist. Two of his compositions (including "Flanagan" a tribute for Tommy Flanagan) are included in this set's repertoire but the emphasis on this trio date is very much on Childs' skills as a pianist. With bassist Tony Dumas and drummer Billy Kilson, Childs explores a variety of high-quality material including John Coltrane's "Satellite," Ivan Lins' "The Island," Cedar Walton's "Bolivia" and Bill Evans' "34 Skidoo." Most impressive is the fact that Billy Childs does not sound like anyone else. —*Scott Yanow*

I've Known Rivers / 1994 / Stretch/GRP ✦✦✦

Herman Chittison

b. Oct. 15, 1908, Flemingsburg, KY, d. Mar. 8, 1967, Cleveland, OH
Piano / Stride
A very talented stride pianist whose great technique in his early days sometimes dominated his style (it was more in balance by the later '30s), Herman Chittison started out with Zack Whyte's Chocolate Beau Brummels (1928–31), a superior territory band. He recorded with Clarence Williams and in 1934 travelled to Europe with Willie Lewis' band. Chittison was featured on Louis Armstrong's European tour that year (he can be seen on film playing three numbers with Satch in Scandinavia) and recorded a series of piano solos. When he left Lewis in 1938, Chittison took some of the other sidemen to Egypt, where they played for two years before returning to the U.S. in 1941. After working with Mildred Bailey in 1941, Chittison led his trio in New York for most of the remainder of his life, appearing regularly on a radio series for nine years, recording on an irregular basis for Musicraft, Columbia and a variety of tiny labels, and ending up playing in Akron, Columbus and Cleveland, OH. —*Scott Yanow*

Herman Chittison / Dec. 8, 1944–May 1, 1945 / Musicraft ✦✦✦

● **P.S. With Love** / Jun. 5, 1964–1967 / IAJRC ✦✦✦
Herman Chittison was one of the top jazz pianists to emerge during the 1930s but, since he spent some of his most important years in Europe and generally recorded for obscure labels, he never achieved much recognition. These previously unreleased piano solos from two separate occasions were made available for the first time on this collector's CD with the second half of the set dating from just two months before the pianist passed away. Overall Chittison sounds fine, relatively modern in spots without losing his melodic style. There are some weak show tunes from the era (such as "Getting to Know You," "The Sound of Music" and "People") but in general Chittison overcomes the material and comes up with some inventive solos. —*Scott Yanow*

Charlie Christian

b. Jul. 29, 1916, Dallas, TX, d. Mar. 2, 1942, New York, NY
Guitar / Swing, Bop
It can be said without exaggeration that virtually every jazz guitarist that emerged during 1940–65 sounded like a relative of Charlie Christian! The first important electric guitarist, Christian played his instrument with the fluidity, confidence and swing of a saxophonist. Although technically a swing stylist, his musical vocabulary was studied and emulated by the bop players and when one listens to players ranging from Tiny Grimes, Barney Kessel and Herb Ellis to Wes Montgomery and George Benson, the dominant influence of Christian is obvious.

Charlie Christian's time in the spotlight was terribly brief. He played locally in Oklahoma and began to utilize an amplified guitar in 1937. John Hammond, the masterful talent scout and producer, heard about Christian (possibly from Mary Lou Williams), was impressed by what he saw and arranged for the guitarist to travel to Los Angeles in August 1939 and try out with Benny Goodman. Although the clarinetist was initally put off by Christian's primitive wardrobe, as soon as they started jamming on "Rose Room," Christian's talents were obvious. For the next two years he would be well featured with Benny Goodman's Sextet, there were two solos (including the showcase "Solo Flight") with the full orchestra and the guitarist had the opportunity to jam at Minton's Playhouse with such up-and-coming players as Thelonious Monk, Kenny Clarke and Dizzy Gillespie. All of

the guitarist's recordings (including guest spots and radio broadcasts) are currently available on CD. Tragically he contracted tuberculosis in 1941 and died at the age of 25 on March 2, 1942. It would be 25 years before jazz guitarists finally moved beyond Charlie Christian. —*Scott Yanow*

Charlie Christian With Benny Goodman and The Sextet / Aug. 10, 1939–Jun. 1941 / Jazz Archives ✦✦✦✦
The collector's label Jazz Archives unearthed these radio broadcast performances in the mid-'70s. The pioneering electric guitarist Charlie Christian is featured throughout with Benny Goodman's Sextet and, on "Solo Flight" (here titled "Chonk, Charlie, Chonk") with Benny Goodman's big band. All of these titles (except for one of the versions of "Wholly Cats") have since been reissued on CD by Vintage Jazz Classics. —*Scott Yanow*

Solo Flight (1939–1941) / Aug. 19, 1939–Jun. 1941 / Vintage Jazz Classics ✦✦✦✦✦
Charlie Christian, who died in 1942 at the age of 25, was the first important electric guitarist and his solos would be the basis of jazz guitar for the next 25 years. This CD is filled with live performances (mostly from radio shows) of the Benny Goodman Sextet featuring Christian solos on every track. With such sidemen as vibraphonist Lionel Hampton and later tenor saxophonist Georgie Auld and trumpeter Cootie Williams, this unit was a perfect outlet for both Christian and Benny Goodman. And, in addition to a big band performance of "Solo Flight" (virtually a tour-de-force for the guitarist), there are five selections from a remarkable all-star group comprised of Goodman, Christian, trumpeter Buck Clayton, Lester Young on tenor and Count Basie along with his rhythm section. This CD is highly recommended as an example of some of the very best in small-group swing and as a tribute to Charlie Christian's highly influential style. —*Scott Yanow*

★ **The Genius of the Electric Guitar** / Oct. 2, 1939–Mar. 13, 1941 / Columbia ✦✦✦✦✦
This set contains some of guitarist Charlie Christian's greatest recordings (although he did not live long enough to record any bad ones). Christian is heard with the Benny Goodman Sextet on famous versions of "Seven Come Eleven," "Benny's Bugle" and "Air Mail Special"; is showcased with Goodman's orchestra on "Solo Flight"; and jams with the members of the Sextet (minus their leader) on "Blues in B" and a fascinating ad-lib, "Waitin' for Benny." This important release belongs in every jazz collection and contains a great deal of essential music. —*Scott Yanow*

Solo Flight: The Genius of Charlie Christian / Oct. 2, 1939–Mar. 13, 1941 / Columbia ✦✦✦✦
Prior to the advent of the CD, this two-LP set was the definitive Charlie Christian release and it is still quite impressive. The great electric guitarist is heard on most of his more famous recordings with the Benny Goodman Sextet (including "Seven Come Eleven," "Air Mail Special," "Royal Garden Blues" and "Breakfast Feud"), on his two features with the Goodman Orchestra ("Honeysuckle Rose" and "Air Mail Special"), with The Metronome All-Stars, leading a jam session that also features Jerry Jerome on tenor (the only selections not yet reissued on CD) and at a practice with the other members of BG's Sextet in which they came up with some hot riffs on the ad-lib "Waitin' for Benny." It's a well-conceived two-fer. —*Scott Yanow*

Charlie Christian/Lester Young: Together 1940 / Oct. 28, 1940–Jan. 15, 1941 / Jazz Archives ✦✦✦
This Jazz Archives LP, which was withdrawn shortly after its release, is a real collector's item. It starts out with the five selections Benny Goodman and Count Basie recorded privately at a period of time when the clarinetist was toying with breaking up his big band and forming this septet (which also included the great electric guitarist Charlie Christian, tenor saxophonist Lester Young and trumpeter Buck Clayton). That material has since been reissued on CD but the other 11 performances are taken from rehearsals of the Benny Goodman Sextet and were apparently not supposed to be released. These alternate versions of their recordings feature one of Goodman's strongest units with creative solos from Christian, trumpeter Cootie Williams, tenorman Georgie Auld and either pianist Count Basie or Ken Kersey. —*Scott Yanow*

Live Sessions at Minton's Playhouse / May 8, 1941+May 12, 1941 / Jass ✦✦✦

Jazz Immortal / May 8, 1941+May 12, 1941 / Everest ✦✦✦
The recording quality is streaky on this budget release and the personnel listing and recording date are omitted but this music

(which has been reissued several times) is classic. Cut live at Minton's Playhouse and Monroe's Uptown House, these jam sessions feature the great pioneering electric guitarist Charlie Christian on the longest solos of his that still exist, really stretching out during "Swing to Bop" (really it's "Topsy"), "Up on Teddy's Hill" and "Stompin' at the Savoy"; his improvisation on the latter was one of the finest of his short life. The trumpeter on those selections is the erratic Joe Guy, but Thelonious Monk can be heard taking some swing-oriented solos, his earliest appearance on records. Some of the other jams (two versions of "Stardust" and "Kerouac") feature Dizzy Gillespie, who at age 24 was still searching for his style. This is very significant music from sessions that led to the birth of bebop and it deserves to be reissued in a more coherent fashion. —*Scott Yanow*

Pete Christlieb

b. Feb. 16, 1945, Los Angeles, CA
Tenor Saxophone / Bop
Though identified with the West Coast where he lives, and thus assumed to be a cool, detached player, Pete Christlieb has always been one of the more powerful soloists in any style. His blistering lines, especially on uptempo numbers, are often red hot, while he can also play effective blues and stirring ballads. Christlieb initially studied violin before starting sax at 13. He played with Si Zentner, Chet Baker and Woody Herman in the '60s, then began working with Louis Bellson. They've maintained a musical relationship through the '80s and into the '90s. Christlieb has worked extensively in the studios doing film and television projects since the late '60s, and was a regular member of the *Tonight Show* orchestra. He played in the backing bands of Della Reese and Sarah Vaughan among other vocalists, and has also done sessions with Count Basie, Quincy Jones, Mel Lewis, Shelly Manne, Gene Ammons, Frank Rosolino, and Carl Fontna. Christlieb headed his own quartet in 1980, and began a record label in 1981. Bosco has issued albums by Bellson, Bob Florence and Christlieb. He's recorded for RAHMP, Capri and Warner Bros. A duet album with Warne Marsh in the late '70s was critically praised. —*Ron Wynn and Michael G. Nastos*

Apogee / 1978 / Warner Brothers ✦✦✦✦
Because this set was produced by the leaders of Steely Dan (Walter Becker and Donald Fagen) for Warner Brothers during a period when that label rarely recorded jazz, this LP received more publicity than expected. The two distinctive tenors of Pete Christlieb and Warne Marsh (backed by pianist Lou Levy, bassist Jim Hughart and drummer Nick Ceroli) are in combative form for the enjoyable blowing session. Joe Roccisano contributed charts for four of the six songs but the main points of interest are the strong tenor solos. It's worth searching for and long overdue for reissue. —*Scott Yanow*

● **Conversations With Warne, Vol. 1** / Sep. 15, 1978 / Criss Cross ✦✦✦✦✦

Going My Way / 1982 / Bosco ✦✦✦

The Pete Christlieb Quartet Live-Dinis '83 / 1983 / Bosco ✦✦✦

Mosaic / Feb. 16, 1990 / Capri ✦✦✦
Recorded at Portland Inn. Christlieb and Bob Cooper swing dual tenors. —*Michael G. Nastos*

June Christy

b. Nov. 20, 1925, Springfield, IL, **d.** Jun. 21, 1990, Los Angeles, CA
Vocals / Cool
Although she originally sounded heavily influenced by Anita O'Day, June Christy's cool-toned yet cheerful style grew to be quite individual and popular, being both sensual and nonthreatening. She sang locally in Chicago and then received her big break, replacing O'Day with Stan Kenton's Orchestra in 1945. She had hits with "Tampico," "Shoo-Fly Pie" and "How High the Moon" and her renditions of ballads and novelties helped to keep the Kenton Orchestra going, contrasting with their more experimental and "progressive" works. Christy married tenor saxophonist Bob Cooper, cut her first solo recordings in 1947 and, after Kenton broke up his band in 1948, she had a very successful career. Her series of Capitol records in the 1950s (particularly *Something Cool* and *The Misty Miss Christy*) defined the "cool jazz" singing style and sold quite well. Christy had occasional reunions with Kenton and, even after she drifted into retirement after 1965, she appeared with the bandleader at the 1972 Newport Jazz Festival.

Though she came back for one final record in 1977, June Christy will always be associated with the 1950s. —*Scott Yanow*

Day Dreams / Mar. 3, 1947–May 19, 1955 / Capitol ✦✦✦

● **Something Cool** / Aug. 14, 1953–Jul. 27, 1955 / Capitol ✦✦✦✦✦
Her classic first album, plus ten other '50s sides, serves as the best introduction. —*Richard Lieberson*

Duet / May 1955 / Capitol ✦✦✦✦
This set of duets between singer June Christy and pianist Stan Kenton is often quite emotional. Christy's cool sound and careful diction hint at darker feelings than appear on the surface during these ballads while Kenton provides sparse but effective piano. Emotions and melody are much more significant in this setting than mere chord changes and this haunting music is surprisingly memorable. —*Scott Yanow*

The Misty Miss Christy / Jul. 26, 1955–May 23, 1956 / Capitol ✦✦✦✦
Fine "torch" and jazzy pop late-'50s recording by Christy, backed by good group with Maynard Ferguson, Laurindo Almeida, Bud Shank, Bob Cooper, and Claude Williamson, among others. It was reissued on compact disc in 1992. —*Ron Wynn*

A Lovely Way to Spend a Evening / 1957 / Jasmine ✦✦✦

June Fair and Warmer / Jan. 3, 1957–Jan. 21, 1957 / Capitol ✦✦✦

Interlude / Jan. 21, 1957–Jul. 15, 1957 / Discovery ✦✦✦
Trademark late-'50s recording, full of delicately performed, lush "torch" numbers that displayed both her jazz roots and pop sophistication. —*Ron Wynn*

Gone for the Day / Jun. 18, 1957–Jul. 15, 1957 / Capitol ✦✦✦

June's Got Rhythm / Jun. 1958–Jul. 14, 1958 / Capitol ✦✦✦

June Christy Recalls Those Kenton Days / 1959 / Capitol ✦✦✦

Impromptu / Jun. 1977 / Discovery ✦✦

Clarinet Summit

Group / Avant-Garde
In 1984 for a concert at the Public Theatre in New York, John Carter organized a unique group consisting of David Murray on bass clarinet and the clarinets of Alvin Batiste, Jimmy Hamilton and himself. Hamilton (who was with Duke Ellington's Orchestra for 26 years) and the flexible Batiste played some spontaneous swing, Carter and Murray went outside during their features and all four had opportunities to inspire each other. The results of the concert were released on two India Navigation LPs (and one reissue CD). In 1987 the unique group came together for a reunion and made a studio record for Black Saint. —*Scott Yanow*

● **Clarinet Summit, Vols. 1 & 2** / 1985 / India Navigation ✦✦✦✦
Southern Bells / Mar. 29, 1987 / Black Saint ✦✦✦

Sonny Clark (Conrad Yeatis Clark)

b. Jul. 21, 1931, Herminie, PA, **d.** Jan. 13, 1963, New York, NY
Piano / Bop, Hard Bop
Before drugs drastically shortened his life, Sonny Clark was one of the top Bud Powell-inspired bop pianists. He worked in San Francisco with Vido Musso and Oscar Pettiford in the early '50s, settled in Los Angeles, made his first recordings with Teddy Charles and then worked with Buddy DeFranco's quartet (1953–56); all of his records with DeFranco have been reissued by Mosaic on a deluxe limited-edition box set. During the same period he worked with Sonny Criss, Frank Rosolino and the Lighthouse All-Stars. Moving to New York in 1957, Clark became a fixture on Blue Note, recording several classics as a leader (*Dial S for Sonny, Cool Struttin'* and *Sonny's Crib* to name three from 1957 alone) and appearing as a sideman with Sonny Rollins, Hank Mobley and Curtis Fuller among many others. Sonny Clark's premature death (at age 31) was a major loss to jazz. —*Scott Yanow*

The Sonny Clark Memorial Album / Jan. 15, 1954 / Xanadu ✦✦✦

Oakland, 1955 / Jan. 13, 1955 / Uptown ✦✦✦
This live concert (which was released for the first time on this 1995 CD) features the great pianist Sonny Clark in prime form in a trio with bassist Jerry Good and drummer Al Randall. The recording quality is a bit primitive (lowering the music's value) but since there are not an excess of Sonny Clark records available and the pianist's interpretations of the dozen selections (mostly

jazz standards) is consistently swinging and inventive, this boppish CD is worth picking up anyway. —*Scott Yanow*

Dial "S" for Sonny / Jul. 21, 1957 / Blue Note ✦✦✦✦

● **Sonny's Crib** / Oct. 9, 1957 / Blue Note ✦✦✦✦
Striking sextet performances. Memorable efforts from John Coltrane (ts), Curtis Fuller (tb), and Donald Byrd (tpt). 1987 CD reissue has three fine bonus cuts. —*Ron Wynn*

Sonny Clark Trio / Nov. 13, 1957 / Blue Note ✦✦✦✦
Captivating trio date. With Paul Chambers (b) and Philly Joe Jones (d). —*Ron Wynn*

Cool Struttin' / Jan. 5, 1958 / Blue Note ✦✦✦✦

High Fidelity / Mar. 23, 1960 / Bainbridge ✦✦✦✦

Leapin' and Lopin' / Nov. 13, 1961 / Blue Note ✦✦✦✦✦
Mainstream, mostly uptempo jazz with a slight taste of funk. One of Clark's best albums as a leader. The CD has two extra tracks. —*Michael Erlewine*

Kenny Clarke

b. Jan. 9, 1914, Pittsburgh, PA, d. Jan. 26, 1985, Paris, France
Drums / Bop
Kenny Clarke was a highly influential if subtle drummer who helped to define bebop drumming. He was the first to shift the time-keeping rhythm from the bass drum to the ride cymbal, an innovation that has been copied and utilized by a countless number of drummers since the early '40s.

Clarke played vibes, piano and trombone in addition to drums while in school. After stints with Roy Eldridge (1935) and the Jeter-Pillars band, Clarke joined Edgar Hayes' Big Band (1937–38). He made his recording debut with Hayes (which is available on a Classics CD) and showed that he was one of the most swinging drummers of the era. A European tour with Hayes gave Clarke an opportunity to lead his own session, but doubling on vibes was a definite mistake! Stints with the orchestras of Claude Hopkins (1939) and Teddy Hill (1940–41) followed and then Clarke led the house band at Minton's Playhouse (which also included Thelonious Monk). The legendary after-hours sessions led to the formation of bop and it was during this time that Clarke modernized his style and received the nickname "Klook-Mop" (later shortened to "Klook") due to the irregular "bombs" he would play behind soloists. A flexible drummer, Clarke was still able to uplift the more traditional orchestras of Louis Armstrong and Ella Fitzgerald (1941) and the combos of Benny Carter (1941–42), Red Allen and Coleman Hawkins; he also recorded with Sidney Bechet. However after spending time in the military, Clarke stayed in the bop field, working with Dizzy Gillespie's big band and leading his own modern sessions; he co-wrote "Epistrophy" with Monk and "Salt Peanuts" with Gillespie. Clarke spent the late '40s in Europe, was with Billy Eckstine in the U.S. in 1951 and became an original member of the Modern Jazz Quartet (1951–55). However he felt confined by the music and quit the MJQ freelance, performing on an enormous amount of records during 1955–56.

In 1956 Clarke moved to France, where he did studio work, was hired by touring American all-stars and played with Bud Powell and Oscar Pettiford in a trio called the Three Bosses (1959–60). Clarke was co-leader with Francy Boland of a legendary all-star big band (1961–72), one that had Kenny Clarke playing second drums! Other than a few short visits home, Kenny Clarke worked in France for the remainder of his life and was a major figure on the European jazz scene. —*Scott Yanow*

The Paris Bebop Sessions / Mar. 2, 1948–Oct. 9, 1950 / Prestige ✦✦✦
Good, although somewhat stiff, sessions done in Paris by Clarke with a French bassist and pianist. Tenor saxophonist James Moody certainly isn't stiff, however, and it's his exuberant, bluesy solos, coupled with Clarke's spinning beats, that keep the date from bogging down, especially when pianist Ralph Schecroun takes the spotlight. —*Ron Wynn*

Kenny Clarke All-Stars / Nov. 1, 1954+Feb. 7, 1955 / Savoy ✦✦✦✦
Recorded with Frank Morgan (sax) and Milt Jackson (vib). —*David Szatmary*

Septet / Mar. 30, 1955 / Savoy ✦✦✦

● **Bohemia After Dark** / Jun. 26, 1955–Jul. 26, 1955 / Savoy ✦✦✦✦
The June 26, 1955 session is most notable for being the recorded

debut of the recently discovered altoist Cannonball Adderley and his brother, cornetist Nat (who is also featured on the lone number from July 26, a quartet version of "We'll Be Together Again"). Although drummer Kenny Clarke is the nominal leader and the other sidemen include trumpeter Donald Byrd, Jerome Richardson on tenor and flute, pianist Horace Silver and bassist Paul Chambers, the impressive performance by the young Adderleys makes this a historic session that has often been reissued under Cannonball's name. —*Scott Yanow*

Klook's Clique / Feb. 6, 1956 / Savoy ✦✦✦
An indispensable session by the bop pioneer, with John LaPorta (sax) and Donald Byrd (tpt). —*David Szatmary*

Kenny Clarke Meets the Detroit Jazzmen / Apr. 30, 1956+May 9, 1956 / Savoy ✦✦✦
Sensational mid-'50s date that exemplifies the Detroit hard bop sound. Clarke rides herd on a great band that includes baritone saxophonist Pepper Adams, pianist Tommy Flanagan, guitarist Kenny Burrell, and bassist Paul Chambers. This has been reissued on both domestic and import CDs. —*Ron Wynn*

Kenny Clarke in Paris, Vol. 1 / Sep. 23, 1957–Nov. 12, 1957 / Disques Swing ✦✦✦

Pieces of Time / Sep. 16, 1983–Sep. 17, 1983 / Soul Note ✦✦✦
Standout session late in his career, with fellow drummers Andrew Cyrille, Milford Graves, and Don Moye. —*Ron Wynn*

Stanley Clarke

b. Jun. 30, 1951, Philadelphia, PA
Bass / Post-Bop, R&B, Fusion
A brilliant player on both acoustic and electric basses, Stanley Clarke has spent much of his career outside of jazz although he has the ability to play jazz with the very best. He played accordion as a youth, switching to violin and cello before settling on bass. He worked with R&B and rock bands in high school but after moving to New York he worked with Pharoah Sanders in the early '70s. Other early gigs were with Gil Evans, Mel Lewis, Horace Silver, Stan Getz, Dexter Gordon and Art Blakey; everyone was impressed by his talents. However Clarke really hit the big time when he started teaming up with Chick Corea in Return to Forever. When the group became a rock-oriented fusion quartet, Clarke mostly emphasized electric bass and became an influential force, preceding Jaco Pastorius. But starting with his *School Days* album (1976) and continuing through his funk group with George Duke (the Clarke/Duke Project) up to his current projects writing movie scores, Stanley Clarke has largely moved beyond the jazz world into commercial music; his 1988 *Portrait* album *If This Bass Could Only Talk* and his 1995 collaboration with Jean Luc Ponty and Al DiMeola on the acoustic *The Rite of Strings* are two of his few jazz recordings of the past decade. —*Scott Yanow*

Children of Forever / Dec. 26, 1972+Dec. 27, 1972 / Polydor ✦✦✦
Early, instructive fusion set from super bassist Stanley Clarke, then establishing his identity as a leader. Clarke had made many mainstream jazz dates in the '60s, and was also part of Chick Corea's Return to Forever. His bass playing, as always, was remarkable, and while the songs and production were predictable, there were enough electric moments to indicate that Clarke had a future in the fusion and pop world. —*Ron Wynn*

Stanley Clarke / 1974 / Epic ✦✦✦✦
Definitive early-period funk/fusion. Clarke's finger-pop bass is up front. —*Michael G. Nastos*

Journey to Love / 1975 / Epic ✦✦✦
Prolific bassist Stanley Clarke's second jazz-rock album in the early '70s marked the beginning of what proved to be an extremely profitable collaboration with keyboardist George Duke. The album includes guest appearances from Chick Corea, John McLaughlin, Lenny White, and rocker Jeff Beck. —*Ron Wynn*

School Days / 1976 / Epic ✦✦

Live (1976–1977) / 1976–1977 / Epic ✦✦

I Wanna Play for You / 1977 / Epic ✦✦✦
A late '70s two-album (now two-disc) set that blends studio and live sessions. Those who only knew Clarke from his heavily produced, sometimes silly Urban Contemporary dates should check out the frequently amazing bass work. He was a top acoustic jazz

Music Map

Clarinet

Pioneers on Record
Larry Shields
(1917, with Original Dixieland Jazz Band)
Leon Rappolo (1922, with New Orleans Rhythm Kings)

New Orleans Early Classic Greats
Sidney Bechet • Johnny Dodds • Jimmy Noone

Other Top Clarinetists of the 1920s
Buster Bailey	Jimmy Dorsey
Frankie Teschemacher	Albert Nicholas
Barney Bigard	Omer Simeon

Commercial Vaudeville Players
Wilbur Sweatman	Ted Lewis
Wilton Crawley	Boyd Senter
Fess Williams	

Clarinet Giants of the Swing Era
Benny Goodman • Artie Shaw

Other Top Pre-Bop Clarinetists
Pee Wee Russell	Joe Marsala
Edmond Hall	Peanuts Hucko
Johnny Mince	Woody Herman
Irving Fazola	Dick Johnson
Abe Most	Bob Wilber
Kenny Davern	Ken Peplowski

New Orleans Revival
Alphonse Picou	George Lewis
Bob Helm	Pete Fountain
Dr. Michael White	

Bop
Stan Hasselgard	Tony Scott
Jimmy Hamilton	Putte Wickman
Eiji Kitamura	

Two Virtuoso Clarinet Innovators
Buddy DeFranco • Eddie Daniels

Saxophonists Who Occasionally Played Clarinet
Lester Young	Eddie Miller
Buddy Collette	Rahsaan Roland Kirk
Art Pepper	Phil Woods
Paquito D'Rivera	

Avant-Garde
John LaPorta	Jimmy Giuffre
Bill Smith	Anthony Braxton
Perry Robinson	Alvin Batiste
John Carter	Marty Ehrlich
Michael Moore	Louis Sclavis
Don Byron	

---

player before switching to electric, and those qualities sometimes can be heard even in his plugged-in solos. The live tracks are more ambitious and impressive than the studio cuts. —*Ron Wynn*

Modern Man / 1978 / Nemperor ♦♦

Rocks, Pebbles and Sand / 1980 / Epic ♦♦

The Clarke/Duke Project, Vol. 1 / 1981 / Epic ♦♦

Let Me Know You / 1982 / Columbia ♦♦

The Clarke/Duke Project, Vol. 2 / 1983 / Columbia ♦♦

Time Exposure / 1984 / Epic ♦♦♦

Find Out / 1985 / Epic ♦♦

Hideaway / 1986 / Epic ♦♦

● **If This Bass Could Only Talk** / 1988 / Portrait ♦♦♦♦

3 / 1989 / Epic ♦♦
Both an accomplished acoustic player and a pioneering electric bassist, Stanley Clarke found new success in two other areas during the '80s and '90s. One was scoring films; the other was cutting Urban Contemporary hits with George Duke. This was their third venture, and it continued in the path of its predecessors: short songs, little solo space, double-tracked background vocals, and lots of wah-wah and synthesizer effects. —*Ron Wynn*

Passenger 57 / 1992 / Epic ♦♦

Live At The Greek / 1993 / Epic ♦♦♦
Bassist Stanley Clarke heads a quintet consisting of guitarist Larry Carlton, saxophonist Najee, keyboardist Deron Johnson and drummer Billy Cobham on this rock-oriented live set. There are some worthwhile solos with Najee being in fine form (his flute on "All Blues" and Ernie Watts-influenced tenor are enjoyable) and Larry Carlton's passionate solos keep the music from getting too mundane. Their version of "School Days" is way too long and the music does get a bit bombastic at times but listeners with an open mind toward fusion will want to acquire this all-star CD. —*Scott Yanow*

Rite of Strings / 1995 / Gai Saber ♦♦♦♦

Benn Clatworthy
b. , London, England
Tenor Saxophone / Hard Bop
A fixture in Los Angeles area clubs since 1980, Benn Clatworthy was originally heavily influenced by late '50s John Coltrane but in recent years has softened his tone and sometimes sounds a little like Warne Marsh with touches of Sonny Rollins. He debuted on record in 1990 with his Discovery release *Thanks Horace* (which also features pianist Cecilia Coleman) and in 1995 released *While My Lady Sleeps* on his own label (featuring Cedar Walton as a guest). —*Scott Yanow*

Thanks Horace / Dec. 16, 1989+Mar. 15, 1990 / Discovery ✦✦✦
● **While My Lady Sleeps** / Feb. 11, 1995+Mar. 11, 1995 / BCM ✦✦✦✦
A fixture in Los Angeles jazz clubs throughout the 1980s and '90s, tenor saxophonist Benn Clatworthy has recorded surprisingly little. This CD from his own private label gives one a strong sampling of his talents; the supporting cast includes pianist Cedar Walton (on three of the nine tunes), guitarist Rick Zunigar, either Larry Gales or Darek Oles on bass and drummer Albert "Tootie" Heath. Clatworthy's style is influenced by John Coltrane (circa 1959) but his tone has gradually become softer and more original. Highlights include a duet version of "My Ship" with Walton, "Blue Room," a rare revival of "While My Lady Sleeps" and several of the tenor's originals. —*Scott Yanow*

James Clay

b. Sep. 8, 1935, Dallas, TX, **d.** 1994
Tenor Saxophone / Hard Bop
A fine tenor saxophonist with an appealing tone and a boppish style, James Clay was an early associate of Ornette Coleman's back in Texas of the 1950s. He came up North, made a few records (including a 1956 date with Lawrence Marable and two Riverside albums in 1960 as a leader) and then went back to Texas. Nearly three decades later he appeared on Don Cherry's *Art Deco* album playing in a style unchanged from the past and just as strong. James Clay recorded a pair of excellent straight-ahead albums for Antilles before his recent death. —*Scott Yanow*

The Sound of the Wide Open Spaces / Apr. 26, 1960 / Original Jazz Classics ✦✦✦
With David Newman. Dueling Texas tenors on an album recorded by Cannonball Adderley. Definitive music. —*Michael G. Nastos*

● **A Double Dose of Soul** / Oct. 11, 1960 / Original Jazz Classics ✦✦✦✦
James Clay only led two record sessions before settling in obscurity in Texas where he would not be rediscovered until the late '80s. Cannonball Adderley helped present him on Riverside in 1960, so it seemed fair that Clay utilized several of Adderley's sidemen on this session (cornetist Nat Adderley or vibraphonist Victor Feldman, bassist Sam Jones and drummer Louis Hayes) along with a young Gene Harris on piano. Clay splits his time between his lyrical flute and tough tenor, proving to be an excellent bop-based improviser. This CD reissue adds two alternate takes to the original LP program and is highlighted by Feldman's "New Delhi," "Come Rain or Come Shine" and Nat's blues "Pockets." —*Scott Yanow*

I Let a Song Go out of My Heart / Jan. 20, 1989 / Antilles ✦✦✦
His first album in years. Excellent collection of standards, most in ballad mode. With Cedar Walton Trio. —*Michael G. Nastos*

Cookin' at the Continental / Jun. 18, 1991–Jun. 19, 1991 / Antilles ✦✦✦✦
With Fathead Newman (sax), Roy Hargrove (tpt). Three old standards, six more from Horace Silver, Bobby Timmons, Charlie Parker, and Babs Gonzalez. An up mode. —*Michael G. Nastos*

Buck Clayton (Wilbur Dorsey Clayton)

b. Nov. 12, 1911, Parsons, KS, **d.** Dec. 8, 1991, New York, NY
Trumpet, Arranger / Swing
Buck Clayton was a valued soloist with the Count Basie orchestra during the '30s and '40s, and later was a celebrated studio and jam session player, writer and arranger. His tart, striking tone and melodic dexterity were his trademark, and Clayton provided several charts for Basie's orchestra and many other groups. Clayton began his career in California, where he organized a big band that had a residency in China in 1934. When he returned, Clayton led a group and played with other local bands. During a 1936 visit to Kansas City, he was invited to join Basie's orchestra as a replacement for Hot Lips Page. Clayton was also featured on sessions with Lester Young, Teddy Wilson and Holiday in the late '30s. He remained in the Basie band until 1943, when he left for Army service. After leaving the Army, Clayton did arrangements for Basie, Benny Goodman, and Harry James before forming a sextet in the late '40s. He toured Europe with this group in 1949 and 1950. Clayton continued heading a combo during the '50s, and worked with Joe Bushkin, Tony Parenti and Jimmy Rushing among others. He organized a series of outstanding recordings for Columbia in the mid-'50s under the title Jam Session (compiled and reissued

by Mosaic in 1993). There were sessions with Rushing, Ruby Braff, and Nat Pierce. Clayton led a combo with Coleman Hawkins and J.J. Johnson at the 1956 Newport Jazz Festival, then reunited with Goodman in 1957 at the Waldorf Astoria. There was another European tour, this time with Mezz Mezzrow. He appeared in the 1956 film *The Benny Goodman Story* and played the 1958 Brussels World Fair with Sidney Bechet. Clayton later made another European visit with a Newport Jazz Festival tour. He joined Eddie Condon's band in 1959, a year after appearing in the film *Jazz On A Summer's Day*. Clayton toured Japan and Australia with Condon's group in 1964, and continued to revisit Europe throughout the '60s, often with Humphrey Lyttelton's band, while playing festivals across the country. But lip and health problems virtually ended his playing career in the late '60s. After a period outside of music, Clayton once again became active in music, this time as a nonplaying arranger, touring Africa as part of a State Department series in 1977. He provided arrangements and compositions for a 1974 Lyttleton and Buddy Tate album, and did more jam session albums for Chiaroscuro in 1974 and 1975. He also became an educator, teaching at Hunter College in the early '80s. Clayton led a group of Basie sidemen on a European tour in 1983, then headed his own big band in 1987 that played almost exclusively his compositions and arrangements. That same year Clayton's extensive autobiography *Buck Clayton's Jazz World* with Nancy Miller-Elliot was published. —*Ron Wynn*

Buck Clayton Rarities, Vol. 1 / Mar. 16, 1945–1953 / Swingtime ✦✦✦
This LP lives up to its name. The fine swing trumpeter Buck Clayton is heard with three different groups (14 selections in all) on consistently obscure but enjoyable performances. Clayton is the solo star with an octet headed by pianist Horace Henderson on two songs, fits right in with trombonist Trummy Young's Lucky Seven (a septet with tenorman Ike Quebec and pianist Ken Kersey) and there are eight songs from a date headed by singer/trumpeter Taps Miller in 1953. Buck solos on five of the tunes and his playing offers a good contrast with Miller's Louis Armstrong-inspired trumpet. This European LP is worth searching for by swing collectors. —*Scott Yanow*

The Classic Swing of Buck Clayton / Jun. 26, 1946–Jul. 24, 1946 / Original Jazz Classics ✦✦✦✦
This limited-edition CD features small-group swing originally issued on the H.R.S. label from three different sessions in 1946. On one date, the great trumpeter Buck Clayton heads an octet with both Trummy Young and Dicky Wells on trombones; on another occasion he leads an unusual pianoless quartet that also includes clarinetist Scoville Brown, guitarist Tiny Grimes and bassist Sid Weiss. In addition, Clayton is heard as a sideman with Trummy Young's septet, which also features clarinetist Buster Bailey. Swing was going very much out of style at the time, and these somewhat obscure dates can be considered among the final small-group swing sessions of the classic era. More importantly, all of the principals sound creative and full of spirit. —*Scott Yanow*

Buck Clayton In Paris / Oct. 10, 1949–Oct. 21, 1953 / Vogue ✦✦✦✦
There are lots of rare and swinging performances on this valuable reissue CD from Vogue. The great swing trumpeter Buck Clayton (for whom critic Stanley Dance coined the phrase "mainstream") is heard in a sextet that co-stars tenor saxophonist Don Byas, heading a nonet that also features fellow trumpeter Bill Coleman (who gets almost as much solo space as Buck) and tenor saxophonist Alix Combelle, and guesting with Combelle's 14-piece orchestra in 1953; the latter group performs eight of its leader's originals, all arranged in swinging fashion by Clayton. This disc is easily recommended to straight-ahead jazz fans. —*Scott Yanow*

Dr. Jazz Series, Vol. 3 / Dec. 13, 1951–Jan. 24, 1952 / Storyville ✦✦✦
Storyville has released a series of CDs taken from the legendary *Dr. Jazz* radio series of 1951–52, a program that each week featured some of the top Dixieland bands then currently playing in New York clubs. Trumpeter Buck Clayton was a swing rather than a Dixieland player but during this era he decided to increase his versatility (and potential for getting jobs) by learning the basic Dixieland repertoire. He fares pretty well in a sextet that also has plenty of solo space for trombonist Herb Flemming, clarinetist Buster Bailey and pianist Kenny Kersey. Highlights of these fairly well-recorded jams include "There'll Be Some Changes Made,"

"Struttin' with Some Barbecue," "'Deed I Do" and "Crazy Rhythm." —Scott Yanow

★ **Complete CBS Buck Clayton Jam Sessions** / Dec. 14, 1953–Mar. 5, 1956 / Mosaic ✦✦✦✦✦
Trumpeter Buck Clayton led a series of exciting studio jam sessions during the mid-'50s. All of the performances are on this superlative three-CD box set including a few "new" alternate takes and several that have been restored to their full length. Among the many soloists (most of them swing-oriented stylists) are Clayton, Joe Newman, Joe Thomas, Billy Butterfield and Ruby Braff on trumpets, trombonists Urbie Green, Benny Powell, Henderson Chambers, Trummy Young, Bennie Green, Dicky Harris, J.C. Higginbotham and Tyree Glenn, altoist Lem Davis, tenors Coleman Hawkins, Al Cohn and Buddy Tate, Julian Dash doubling on tenor and alto, baritonist Charlie Fowlkes, several rhythm sections with pianists Sir Charles Thompson, Jimmy Jones, Billy Kyle, Ken Kersey and the forgotten Al Waslohn and a guest appearance by Woody Herman on clarinet. These generally lengthy performances contain plenty of spontaneous riffing behind soloists and lots of special moments; "How Ili the Fi" is quite memorable. —Scott Yanow

The Essential Buck Clayton / Dec. 30, 1953–Mar. 14, 1957 / Vanguard ✦✦✦✦
This excellent CD contains over 80 minutes of music and reissues 14 of the 16 selections included on a two-LP set from 1977. There are three (rather than five) numbers from a date led by pianist Mel Powell that features trumpeter Buck Clayton and clarinetist Edmond Hall, eight songs from the 1957 Buck Clayton septet (with trombonist Vic Dickenson and altoist Earle Warren) and three tunes from a matchup between the trumpets of Buck Clayton and Ruby Braff (along with the tenor of Buddy Tate and trombonist Benny Morton). The consistently swinging music includes some Count Basie-associated tunes plus seven Clayton originals with fine solos from all of the principals. Mainstream may not have been the dominant form of jazz during this period but many of its exponents (including those heard on this CD) were very much in their prime. —Scott Yanow

Copenhagen Concert / Sep. 17, 1959 / Steeple Chase ✦✦✦
This double-CD documents a concert by a group of swing all-stars dominated by Count Basie alumni: trumpeters Buck Clayton and Emmett Berry, altoist Earle Warren, Buddy Tate on tenor, trombonist Dicky Wells, pianist Al Williams, bassist Gene Ramey and drummer Herbie Lovelle. While the group is fine on the first disc playing five instrumentals (including three of Clayton's lesser-known songs), they really come alive on the second CD when they are joined by the great swing/blues singer Jimmy Rushing. Mr. Five by Five not only is in strong voice on three standards and three famous blues but he inspired the other musicians to play some hard-swinging and colorful solos. It is for Rushing's performance that this set is chiefly recommended. —Scott Yanow

Tenderly / Nov. 16, 1959–Nov. 17, 1959 / Inner City ✦✦✦
This out-of-print Inner City LP has tasteful playing by Buck Clayton with a French quintet comprised of Jean-Claude Pelletier on piano and organ, guitarist Jean Bonal, bassist Roland Lobligeois and expatriate drummer Kansas Fields. The emphasis is on ballads and standards (although there are a pair of obscure Sidney Bechet tunes) but Clayton's appealing sound, naturally melodic style and swinging solos make all of the concise performances of interest to mainstream jazz fans. —Scott Yanow

Buck and Buddy / 1960 / Original Jazz Classics ✦✦✦
Count Basie veterans Buck Clayton and tenorman Buddy Tate teamed up during 1960-61 for a pair of Swingville recordings. This CD reissues the first one, a quintet outing with pianist Sir Charles Thompson, bassist Gene Ramey and drummer Mousie Alexander. The repertoire is split between three standards (including "When a Woman Loves a Man") and three Clayton originals. The melodic music consistently swings and practically defines "mainstream" jazz. Worth picking up. —Scott Yanow

Jammin' at Eddie Condon's, Vol. 1 / 1960 / Jazz Up ✦✦✦
The great swing trumpeter Buck Clayton had many Dixieland gigs in the 1950s, including this decent effort from 1960. Teamed up with either Bennie Morton or Cutty Cutshall on trombones, clarinetist Peanuts Hucko, pianist Dave McKenna, bassist Bob Haggart and drummer Buzzy Drootin, Clayton sounds fine on such warhorses as "Lulu's Back in Town," "At the Jazz Band Ball"

Music Map

Bass Clarinet

Early Days
Harry Carney
(doubles with Duke Ellington's Orchestra)

Clarinetists Playing Bass Clarinet
Omer Simeon (1926, reluctantly takes solo on Jelly Roll Morton's "Someday Sweetheart")
Benny Goodman (1931, two songs with Red Norvo)
Buddy DeFranco (1964, "Blues Bag" with Art Blakey)

No real bass clarinet specialists until the 1960s

Bass Clarinet Innovator
Eric Dolphy

Other Bass Clarinetists
Herbie Mann (switched from flute in 1957 and 1959)
Bennie Maupin
Gunter Hampel
David Murray
Howard Johnson
Roscoe Mitchell
John Surman
John Purcell
Marty Ehrlich
Hamiett Bluiett (alto clarinet)
Doug Ewart
Don Byron

and "Wolverine Blues." Although he was capable of playing more advanced music, Clayton gives a generous amount of spirit to these Dixieland tunes and the results should satisfy trad fans. This CD is the first of two volumes. —Scott Yanow

Jammin' at Eddie Condon's, Vol. 2 / 1960 / Jazz Up ✦✦✦
The second of two CD volumes continues the documentation of a Dixieland session featuring trumpeter Buck Clayton (who was normally a swing player), either Benny Morton or Cutty Cutshall on trombones, clarinetist Peanuts Hucko, pianist Dave McKenna, bassist Bob Haggart and drummer Buzzy Drootin. The repertoire (other than a ballad medley) is a bit stale (including "The Saints," "Ballin' the Jack," "Indiana" and "Bye Bye Blackbird") but the music has plenty of spirit and drive. Clayton generally comes up with something fresh to say in his solos and the ensembles have fire. —Scott Yanow

Goin' to Kansas City / Oct. 5, 1960–Oct. 6, 1960 / Original Jazz Classics ✦✦✦
Although trumpeter Buck Clayton gets top billing, this CD reissue actually features Tommy Gwaltney's Kansas City Nine, an unusual group sporting arrangements by Gwaltney and tenor saxophonist Tommy Newsom (who decades later became famous for his work on The Tonight Show). The group has an unusual combination of major names (Clayton, trombonist Dickie Wells, guitarist Charlie Byrd, pianist John Bunch, bassist Whitey Mitchell and drummer Buddy Schutz) along with Gwaltney (who doubles on reeds and vibes), Newsom and Bobby Zottola (playing second trumpet and peck horn). Although the nonet performs a variety of

songs associated with Kansas City Jazz of the swing era, the arrangements are modern and unpredictable. —*Scott Yanow*

Passport to Paradise / May 15, 1961 / Inner City ✦✦
Trumpeter Buck Clayton was in Paris at the time of this tasteful and typically melodic quintet date. Joined by a four-piece rhythm section that features pianist Sir Charles Thompson and guitarist Jean Bonal, Clayton (who generally states the opening melody muted and then closes the piece with an open horn) never really cuts loose but is quite pleasing to hear on these standards. —*Scott Yanow*

Buck & Buddy Blow the Blues / Sep. 15, 1961 / Original Jazz Classics ✦✦✦

With Humphrey Lyttelton And His Band / Nov. 1964 / Harlequin ✦✦✦✦
For this LP (plus one in 1966), trumpeter Buck Clayton sits in with British trumpeter Humphrey Lyttelton's excellent sextet and together they perform high-quality small-group swing. The fresh repertoire (three underplayed standards, two blues and five originals by either Clayton or Lyttelton), the excellent solos (including some from Tony Coe on tenor and baritonist Joe Temperley) and the happy spirit overcomes any minor technical deficiencies. Recommended to all straight-ahead jazz fans. —*Scott Yanow*

Meets Joe Turner / Jun. 2, 1965 / Black Lion ✦✦✦
Despite its title, trumpeter Buck Clayton and blues singer Big Joe Turner actually perform on three separate songs apiece, only coming together on the concluding "Too Late, Too Late." Recorded in Yugoslavia, these performances also utilize a four-piece Yugoslavian quartet, with vibraphonist Bosko Petrovic the only player to receive much fame through the years. Turner sounds fine on a pair of his blues and "I Want a Little Girl," while Buck jams happily on "Honeysuckle Rose," "I Can't Get Started" and "Perdido." Nothing all that surprising occurs, but the music is quite satisfying. —*Scott Yanow*

Baden, Switzerland 1966 / Feb. 6, 1966 / Sackville ✦✦✦✦
For this Swiss concert, the great swing trumpeter Buck Clayton is joined by three Swiss players (Michel Pilet on tenor, pianist Henri Chaix and bassist Isla Eckinger) in addition to the veteran swing drummer Wallace Bishop. Clayton is in particularly inspired form even though he had played the songs in this repertoire (seven swing standards plus a blues) a countless number of times. His range was at its peak during this period and Clayton comes up with consistently creative ideas on such warhorses as "All of Me," "Stompin' at the Savoy," "You Can Depend on Me" and "One O' Clock Jump." Highly recommended to swing collectors. —*Scott Yanow*

Jam Session / Mar. 25, 1974–Mar. 26, 1974 / Chiaroscuro ✦✦✦
Physical troubles ended trumpeter Buck Clayton's career in the late '60s. However, he was also a talented arranger, and by the mid-'70s he was beginning to emerge from his involuntary retirement. Hank O'Neal of Chiaroscuro Records suggested that Clayton organize and write for some jam sessions that would be in the same spirit as his legendary jams of the mid-'50s. There would be three sessions, one in each year from 1974–76. The 1974 edition, reissued on this CD with two extra cuts, features an outstanding crew of individualists: trumpeters Doc Cheatham and Joe Newman, trombonist Urbie Green, altoist Earle Warren, tenors Budd Johnson and Zoot Sims, baritonist Joe Temperley, pianist Earl Hines, bassist Milt Hinton and drummer Gus Johnson. Although the session doesn't quite reach the excitement level of its 1950s equivalent, there are many fine moments to be heard from these great mainstream all-stars. —*Scott Yanow*

Buck Clayton Jam Session, Vol. 2 / Jun. 5, 1975–Jun. 6, 1975 / Chiaroscuro ✦✦✦
The second of three Buck Clayton-led jam sessions held in the mid-'70s once again features Clayton (who had involuntarily retired from playing trumpet due to health problems) strictly as an arranger. The original three-song LP has been augmented on this CD reissue with one number from the same session originally released on a different album and two alternate takes from band rehearsals. The material all uses fairly basic chord changes, with "Sidekick" based on "Somebody Loves Me," "Change for a Buck" a disguised "Honeysuckle Rose," "The Duke We Knew" a tribute to the recently departed Duke Ellington, and "Glassboro Blues" a medium-tempo blues. A particularly interesting variety

of all-stars participated on this date: trumpeters Joe Newman and Money Johnson, trombonists Vic Dickenson and George Masso, altoists Earle Warren and Lee Konitz, tenors Budd Johnson, Buddy Tate and Sal Nistico, pianist Tommy Flanagan, bassist Milt Hinton and drummer Mel Lewis. In general, the music lives up to one's expectations, even if it isn't at the same high level of Clayton's 1950s jam sessions. Recommended. —*Scott Yanow*

A Buck Clayton Jam Session, Vol. 3 / Sep. 13, 1976 / Chiaroscuro ✦✦✦
The third and final Buck Clayton Jam Session of the mid-'70s, although not as classic as his jams of 20 years earlier, is excellent and swinging. This LP (which has not yet been reissued on CD) once again has a very interesting lineup of all-stars: Harry "Sweets" Edison and Marvin "Hannibal" Peterson on trumpets, trombonists Vic Dickenson and Jimmy Knepper, altoists Earle Warren and Lee Konitz, tenors Buddy Tate and Budd Johnson, Bob Wilber on soprano, pianist Hank Jones, bassist Richard Davis and drummer Bobby Rosengarden. Together they swing hard on four of Clayton's originals, getting some opportunities to trade off and riff behind each other. Fine music. —*Scott Yanow*

A Swingin' Dream / Oct. 23, 1988 / Stash ✦✦✦
The premise for this CD is so logical that it is surprising (and disappointing) that only one recording resulted. Trumpeter Buck Clayton was forced to retire due to lip problems in the late '60s, but he had always been a talented arranger. Finally, in the mid-'80s, he put together a big band to play some new charts he had written. This 13-piece unit has such fine players as trumpeters Spanky Davis and Johnny Letman, trombonist Dan Barrett, altoist Chuck Wilson, baritonist Joe Temperley, guitarist Chris Flory and drummer Mel Lewis, among others. "Avenue C" is the only older tune included on this swinging date; Clayton's big band should have recorded many more sessions! —*Scott Yanow*

Clayton-Hamilton Orchestra

Big Band / Bop, Swing
The Clayton-Hamilton Jazz Orchestra is unusual in that it has three leaders: drummer Jeff Hamilton, altoist Jeff Clayton and bassist John Clayton. While Hamilton (who has played regularly with Oscar Peterson, Ray Brown, Monty Alexander, Gene Harris and the L.A. Four) really drives the band and Jeff Clayton (whose sound is inspired by Cannonball Adderley) is one of the orchestra's top soloists, it is John Clayton's colorful and unpredictable arrangements that really give this big band its own personality. In addition Clayton (who was formerly with Count Basie) is a very talented soloist, particularly when bowing. The swinging orchestra, filled with top Los Angeles players (including such soloists as Rickey Woodard, Charlie Owens, Bobby Bryant, Snooky Young, Oscar Brasher, George Bohanon, Thurman Green and Bill Cunliffe) can hold its own with any other big band of the 1990s as shown on its two Capri sets (*Groove Shop* and *Heart and Soul*) and its Lake Street release *Absolutely*. —*Scott Yanow*

● **Groove Shop** / Apr. 18, 1989–Apr. 19, 1989 / Capri ✦✦✦✦✦
The '89 debut by the orchestra co-led by drummer Jeff Hamilton and bassist John Clayton. They stay in the background, anchoring and fueling the big band that includes several seasoned pros, exciting youngster Ricky Woodard on tenor sax and clarinet, and longtime session trumpeter Snooky Young. —*Ron Wynn*

Heart and Soul / Feb. 1991 / Capri ✦✦✦✦
Nineteen-piece big band plays three standards, four compositions by bassist John Clayton. Great solos from younger and older musicians. Jeff Hamilton (co-leader), Ricky Woodward (ts), Shooley Young, Oscar Brasher, George Bohannon on brass, and Bill Cunliffe (p). —*Michael G. Nastos*

Jimmy Cleveland

b. May 3, 1926, Wartrace, TN
Trombone / Bop, Hard Bop
One of the finest trombonists to emerge during the 1950s, Jimmy Cleveland has been overlooked since moving to Los Angeles in the late '60s. He started on trombone when he was 16 and his first important job was with Lionel Hampton (1950–53). After Hampton's European tour of 1953, Cleveland became a busy free-lance musician in New York, making many recording sessions (including with Dizzy Gillespie, Gil Evans, Oliver Nelson, Oscar Pettiford, Lucky Thompson, James Moody and Gerry Mulligan).

He toured Europe with Quincy Jones in 1959–60 and played with Thelonious Monk's 1967 octet but otherwise stayed in New York until going to the West Coast to play with *The Merv Griffin Show*'s band and to continue recording for Quincy Jones. Jimmy Cleveland remains one of the most technically skilled of the bop-based trombonists and still appears on an irregular basis in Los Angeles clubs. *—Scott Yanow*

● **Introducing Jimmy Cleveland and His All Stars** / Aug. 4, 1955–Nov. 19, 1955 / EmArcy ◆◆◆◆

Cleveland Style / Dec. 12, 1957+Dec. 13, 1957 / EmArcy ◆◆◆
This was a December 12 and 13, 1957 date with trumpeter Art Farmer, saxophonist Benny Golson, pianist Wynton Kelly, drummer Charli Persip, bassist Eddie Jones and Jay McAllister or Don Butterfield on tuba. Looking at the horn line and with the inclusion of tuba, it is hardly surprising that this was a mellifluous jazz date. But the blend here, while smooth, was never sedentary, and this was a good example of some of the excellent thinking and swinging jazz that was being produced between New York and Chicago at the time. There were some loose ends here as far as some solo fitting tightly into the whole, but the overall quality and the Ernie Wilkins charts were such that there was more than one angle to grab your interest. And of course, there was Jimmy Cleveland, one of the best bop trombones—and he can still blow. *—Bob Rusch, Cadence*

Rosemary Clooney

b. May 23, 1928, Maysville, KY
Vocals / Standards
Vocalist Rosemary Clooney remains in the news during the '90s. She's been in the midst of a career revival since the '80s, and was among the artists who performed in 1993 at the White House jazz concert. Clooney's rise to fame in the '50s came on the strength of songs that in many instances were without question novelty tunes; she's not a vocal improviser like McRae, Carter or Sarah Vaughan. She is an excellent lyric interpreter, has fine timing, phrases skillfully and intelligently, and performs with the dramatic quality evident among all great singers. Her background and foundation are jazz, even if her technique doesn't always adhere to rigid jazz scrutiny. Clooney entered amateur events with her sister Betty in Cincinnati, and they sang on radio stations. The duo worked in Tony Pastor's band during the late '40s, then Clooney started as a soloist. She joined the Columbia roster in 1950, and made several hits for them, among them "You're Just In Love," "Beautiful Brown Eyes," "Half as Much," "Hey There," "This Ole House," the number one hit "Come On-A My House" co-written by Ross Bagdasarian of Chipmunks fame and "If Teardrops Were Pennies." Clooney had 13 Top 40 hits in the early '50s, among them duets with Guy Mitchell and Marlene Dietrich. She also appeared in such films as *The Stars Are Singing, Here Come The Girls, White Christmas* and *Red Garters* in 1953 and 1954. Clooney recorded with the Benny Goodman sextet, The Hi-Lo's and Duke Ellington in the '50s. She moved to RCA in the '60s, and recorded with Bing Crosby. There were also dates for Coral, Reprise, and Capitol, among them another session with Crosby. The rock revolution and a decision to spend more time with her family resulted in Clooney going into semi-retirement. She returned in the late '70s, singing with renewed power and confidence while making swing-influenced dates and combo sessions for Concord. She's maintained that relationship in the '80s and '90s, doing standards, repertory albums and demonstrating a resiliency and energy that validates her position among the fine jazz-based vocalists in American music. *—Ron Wynn and Bill Dahl*

Uncollected Rosemary Clooney, 1951–1952 / 1951–1952 / Hindsight ◆◆◆

Blue Rose / 1956 / Columbia ◆◆◆◆
A moody 1956 collaboration with Duke Ellington, it's well worth seeking out. *—Charles S. Wolfe*

● **Everything's Coming up Rosie** / Jun. 7, 1977 / Concord Jazz ◆◆◆◆
Rosemary Clooney's first album for the Concord label set the standard for her work of the next 20 years. Long associated with middle-of-the-road pop music, Clooney really excelled in the jazz-oriented settings with The Concord All-Stars. Although she does not really improvise, her very pleasing voice and subtle phrasing should appeal to most jazz followers. On her Concord debut, Clooney is joined by trumpeter Bill Berry, tenor saxophonist Scott Hamilton, pianist Nat Pierce, bassist Monty Budwig and drummer

Jake Hanna. She lets the band run loose on two instrumentals and then really digs into her eight vocals, finding fresh things to say on eight familiar standards. *—Scott Yanow*

Rosie Sings Bing / Jan. 6, 1978 / Concord Jazz ◆◆◆
Rosemary Clooney sings charming, light, and classic material made famous by Bing Crosby. The jazz content varies, but the musical support provided by a nice band, with excellent solos by Scott Hamilton in particular, makes this well worth hearing. *—Ron Wynn*

Here's to My Lady / Sep. 1978 / Concord Jazz ◆◆◆

Rosemary Clooney Sings the Lyrics of Ira Gershwin / Oct. 1979 / Concord Jazz ◆◆◆
This is the first of a series of '80s albums in which, backed by a jazz combo, she pays tribute to the great pop composers. The whole series is worth having. *—Charles S. Wolfe*

With Love / Nov. 1980 / Concord Jazz ◆◆◆

Sings the Music of Cole Porter / Jan. 1982 / Concord Jazz ◆◆◆
Clooney brings to Porter songs the sophistication, touches, lyric shadings, and performances that only vocal veterans who truly understood them can provide. *—Ron Wynn*

My Buddy / Aug. 1983 / Concord Jazz ◆◆◆
Fine '83 collaboration between Rosemary Clooney and the Woody Herman big band, although Herman is nearing the end of his great career. Excellent arrangements, steadfast vocals, and the usual tidy, though careful, Concord production and engineering. *—Ron Wynn*

Sings the Music of Harold Arlen / 1983 / Concord Jazz ◆◆◆◆
Rosemary Clooney's eighth album for Concord once again gives her the opportunity to interpret the music of a composer, this time Harold Arlen. With a superior sextet that features cornetist Warren Vache, tenor saxophonist Scott Hamilton, pianist Dave McKenna and guitarist Ed Bickert, Clooney sounds very happy and lightly swings such songs as "Hurray for Love," "Ding Dong the Witch Is Dead," "My Shining Hour" and "Stormy Weather." *—Scott Yanow*

Sings the Music of Irving Berlin / Jun. 1984 / Concord Jazz ◆◆◆

Sings Ballads / Apr. 1985 / Concord Jazz ◆◆◆

Sings the Music of Jimmy Van Heusen / Aug. 1986 / Concord Jazz ◆◆◆
Another sparkling repertory work from a topflight standards and pre-rock pop vocalist. Clooney does the same delightful job with Jimmy Van Heusen's music that she did with Harold Arlen's, while everything else (production, arrangements, song sequencing, engineering) is equally satisfying. *—Ron Wynn*

Sings Lyrics of Johnny Mercer / Aug. 1987 / Concord Jazz ◆◆◆

Show Tunes / Nov. 1988 / Concord Jazz ◆◆◆

Sings Rodgers, Hart & Hammerstein / Oct. 1989 / Concord Jazz ◆◆◆

For the Duration / Oct. 15, 1990–Oct. 17, 1990 / Concord Jazz ◆◆◆

Marian Mc Partland's Piano Jazz with Guest Rosemary Clooney / Oct. 1991 / Jazz Alliance ◆◆◆◆

Girl Singer / Nov. 1991–Dec. 1991 / Concord Jazz ◆◆◆
Contemporary set revealing that Clooney's voice hasn't lost its luster or effectiveness. This set featured her singing with a big band comprised of West Coast session pros. The date reflects traditional Concord conservatism in terms of selections and production, but is certainly well done. *—Ron Wynn*

Do You Miss New York? / Sep. 14, 1992–Sep. 17, 1992 / Concord Jazz ◆◆◆◆

Still on the Road / Nov. 22, 1993–Nov. 23, 1993 / Concord ◆◆◆
Rosemary Clooney was in the midst of a major career revival, doing credible jazz tunes and mixing pre-rock pop, standards, and even some pop and country. Clooney didn't falter on Willie Nelson's "On The Road Again" or Paul Simon's "Still Crazy After All These Years," but she seemed more at home on more conventional fare like Cole Porter's "Take Me Back To Manhattan" or Irving Berlin's "How Deep Is the Ocean." Clooney's voice remains clear and confident, her timing and pacing solid, and her range good, if diminished a bit. While some of this isn't jazz, most of it does meet the requirements, and none of it is poorly performed. *—Ron Wynn*

Demi-Centennial / Oct. 10, 1994–Oct. 13, 1994 / Concord Jazz ✦✦✦

Dedicated To Nelson / Sep. 27, 1995–Sep. 30, 1995 / Concord Jazz ✦✦✦✦

Arnett Cobb

b. Aug. 10, 1918, Houston, TX, d. Mar. 24, 1989, Houston, TX
Tenor Saxophone / Swing, Early R&B
A stomping Texas tenor player in the tradition of Illinois Jacquet, Arnett Cobb's accessible playing was between swing and early rhythm & blues. After playing in Texas with Chester Boone (1934–36) and Milt Larkin (1936–42), Cobb emerged in the big leagues by succeeding Illinois Jacquet with Lionel Hampton's Orchestra (1942–47). His version of "Flying Home No. 2" became a hit and he was a very popular soloist with Hampton. After leaving the band, Cobb formed his own group but his initial success was interrupted in 1948 when he had to undergo an operation on his spine. After recovering he resumed touring. But a major car accident in 1956 crushed Cobb's legs and he was reduced to using crutches for the rest of his life. However by 1959 he returned to active playing and recording. Cobb spent most of the 1960s leading bands back in Texas but starting in 1973 he toured and recorded more extensively, including a tenor summit with Jimmy Heath and Joe Henderson in Europe as late as 1988. Arnett Cobb made many fine records through the years for such labels as Apollo, Columbia/Okeh, Prestige (many of the latter are available on the OJC series), Black & Blue, Progressive, Muse and Bee Hive. —*Scott Yanow*

● **Blows for 1300** / May 1947–Aug. 1947 / Delmark ✦✦✦✦
This Delmark CD reissues all 15 of Arnett Cobb's recordings for Apollo. The spirited tenor (who straddled the boundaries between swing and early R&B) is in prime early form with his sextet on a variety of basic material, much of it blues-oriented. Milt Larkins takes vocals on three of the tracks and there are short solos by either Booty Wood or Al King on trombone, but otherwise the main focus is on Cobb's tough tenor. This very accessible music is both danceable and full of exciting performances that were formerly rare. —*Scott Yanow*

Blow, Arnett, Blow / Jan. 9, 1959 / Original Jazz Classics ✦✦✦✦
Seldom has there been any album that could more accurately be termed a blowing session than this 1959 date. It matched a pair of frenetic, furious tenor saxophonists in Arnett Cobb and Eddie "Lockjaw" Davis, and also boasted a propulsive organist in Strethen Davis, a resourceful bassist in George Duvivier, and an ideal drummer in Arthur Edgehill. Edgehill kept the rhythms tight and crashing, while Cobb and Davis exchanged blistering solos, honks, grunts and bluesy dialogues. Duvivier's heavy backbeat and lines, along with Davis' stomping riffs, added vital supporting ingredients and helped make this a soul-jazz and jam session classic. The six cuts here are a delight for fans of steamy, joyous jazz with a soul/blues sensibility. —*Ron Wynn*

Smooth Sailing / Feb. 27, 1959 / Original Jazz Classics ✦✦✦
Noteworthy appearance from undervalued Buster Cooper (tb). Textbook soul power; exemplary sax technique from Cobb. —*Ron Wynn*

Party Time / May 14, 1959 / Original Jazz Classics ✦✦✦
Splendid soul, funk inflections, torrid Cobb at times; reflective and melancholy at other moments. Fine lineup, though Ray Barretto and Art Taylor sometimes seem to dash underneath. —*Ron Wynn*

Blue and Sentimental / Oct. 31, 1960–Nov. 1, 1960 / Prestige ✦✦✦
This CD reissue combines together tenor saxophonist Arnett Cobb's two LPs, *Sizzlin'* and *Ballads by Cobb*. The former session has a good mixture of stomps and ballads with highlights including "Black Velvet," "Georgia on My Mind" and "The Way You Look Tonight." The latter date (originally cut for the Moodsville label) is all slow ballads and, despite the warmth in Cobb's tone, a certain sameness pervades the performances. Pianist Red Garland and drummer J.C. Heard are on both sessions with either George Tucker or George Duvivier on bass. Good music but not quite essential. —*Scott Yanow*

Wild Man from Texas / May 6, 1976–May 30, 1976 / Black & Blue ✦✦✦

Arnett Cobb Is Back / Jun. 27, 1978 / Progressive ✦✦✦✦
One of the great tough Texas tenors, Arnett Cobb roars and stomps throughout this excellent LP. Joined by pianist Derek

Smith, bassist George Mraz and drummer Billy Hart, Cobb sounds quite comfortable on the basic material, which is comprised of blues, ballads, standards and "Flying Home." —*Scott Yanow*

Live at Sandy's! / Aug. 25, 1978–Aug. 26, 1978 / Muse ✦✦✦

More Arnett Cobb and the Muse All Stars Live at Sandy's / Aug. 25, 1978–Aug. 26, 1978 / Muse ✦✦✦✦

Funky Butt / Jan. 22, 1980 / Progressive ✦✦✦

Keep on Pushin' / Jun. 27, 1984 / Bee Hive ✦✦✦
Overlooked soul-jazz, blues, and bop date with sparkling piano by Junior Mance and fine drumming from Panama Francis. —*Ron Wynn*

Showtime / Aug. 10, 1987 / Fantasy ✦✦✦
With Dizzy Gillespie & Jewel Brown. Singer Brown isn't everyone's cup of tea. Cobb & Dizzy (tpt) are just what you'd expect. —*Ron Wynn*

Tenor Tribute, Vol. 1 / Apr. 30, 1988 / Soul Note ✦✦✦
This blowing session (comprised of Charlie Parker's "Steeple Chase," Arnett Cobb's "Smooth Sailing," "Lester Leaps In," a four-song ballad medley and "I Got Rhythm") is of greatest interest for featuring the contrasting styles of tenors Arnett Cobb, Joe Henderson and Jimmy Heath; the latter also plays a bit of soprano and flute. This being one of Cobb's final recordings (he died less than a year later), he holds his own against the younger tenors during this German concert, taking "Smooth Sailing" as his feature. One should have little trouble telling the three tenor masters apart. —*Scott Yanow*

Tenor Tribute, Vol. 2 / Apr. 30, 1988 / Soul Note ✦✦✦

Billy Cobham

b. May 16, 1946, Panama
Drums / Fusion, Post-Bop
Considered the definitive fusion drummer in the 1970s, Billy Cobham's fame has subsided a bit since then but he remains a very capable player who is more flexible than one might think. His family moved to New York from Panama when he was three. After spending time performing with a military band in the Army, Cobham spent eight months with Horace Silver (1968). He then became a busy session musician, played with the jazz-rock band Dreams (1969–70), appeared on some very important Miles Davis records (*Bitches Brew, Live-Evil* and *Jack Johnson*) and joined John McLaughlin in the Mahavishnu Orchestra (1971–73) where he became an influential force. Cobham led his own band (Spectrum) from 1973 on, making a strong initial impact, but by the late '70s he was mostly freelancing. Since that time he has led electric bands on an occasional basis, been involved in teaching and remains a busy studio player. —*Scott Yanow*

● **Spectrum** / May 14, 1973–May 16, 1973 / Atlantic ✦✦✦✦

Shabazz / Jul. 4, 1974–Jul. 13, 1974 / Atlantic ✦✦✦

Crosswinds / 1974 / Atlantic ✦✦✦

Total Eclipse / 1974 / Atlantic ✦✦✦

A Funky Thide of Sings / 1975 / Atlantic ✦✦

Alivemutherforya / Nov. 1977–Dec. 1977 / Columbia ✦✦✦

Magic / 1977 / Columbia ✦✦✦

Flight Time / Jun. 1980 / Inak ✦✦✦

Stratus / Mar. 18, 1981 / Inak ✦✦✦

Observations / 1981 / Elektra ✦✦✦

Smokin' / Jul. 1982 / Elektra ✦✦✦
Recorded live at the Montreux Jazz Festival in Switzerland in 1982 this album picks up where *Observations* leaves off. It's a terrific performance by all. —*Paul Kohler*

Warning / 1985 / GRP ✦✦

Power Play / 1986 / GRP ✦✦

Picture This / 1987 / GRP ✦✦✦

Traveler / Nov. 1993 / Evidence ✦✦✦

Al Cohn

b. Nov. 24, 1925, New York, NY, d. Feb. 15, 1988, Stroudsburg, PA
Tenor Saxophone, Arranger / Bop
An excellent tenor saxophonist and a superior arranger/composer, Al Cohn was greatly admired by his fellow musicians. Early gigs included associations with Joe Marsala (1943), Georgie Auld, Boyd Raeburn (1946), Alvino Rey and Buddy Rich (1947). But it was

when he replaced Herbie Steward as one of the "Four Brothers" with Woody Herman's Second Herd (1948–49) that Cohn began to make a strong impression. He was actually overshadowed by Stan Getz and Zoot Sims during this period but, unlike the other two tenors, he also contributed arrangements including "The Goof and I." He was with Artie Shaw's short-lived bop orchestra (1949), and then spent the 1950s quite busy as a recording artist (making his first dates as a leader in 1950), arranger for both jazz and nonjazz settings and a performer. Starting in 1956 and continuing on an irregular basis for decades, Cohn co-led a quintet with Zoot Sims. The two tenors were so complementary that it was often difficult to tell them apart! Al Cohn continued in this fashion in the 1960s (although playing less), in the 1970s he recorded many gems for Xanadu and during his last few years when his tone became darker and more distinctive, Cohn largely gave up writing to concentrate on playing. He made many excellent loop-based records throughout his career for such labels as Prestige, Victor, Xanadu and Concord; his son Joe Cohn is a talented cool-toned guitarist. —*Scott Yanow*

Al Cohn Quartet / Jul. 29, 1950 / Progressive ◆◆◆
Broadway (1954) / Jul. 29, 1954 / Original Jazz Classics ◆◆◆
This long-lost session was originally cut for the Progressive label in 1954 and was not released until Prestige put it out in 1970. Now available on CD, one can hear tenor saxophonist Al Cohn and bassist Red Mitchell in fine form in a quintet with three lesser-known players: altoist Hal Stein, pianist Harvey Leonard and drummer Christy Febbo. The music (Mitchell's "Help Keep Your City Clean Blues," a four-song ballad medley and two versions apiece of "Broadway" and "Suddenly It's Spring") is fine although there are no surprises. The most interesting aspect to this obscure session is how similar the light-toned Cohn and altoist Stein (who tended to emphasize lower notes) sounded to each other. —*Scott Yanow*

Natural Rhythm / Feb. 3, 1955–Dec. 18, 1955 / RCA ◆◆◆◆
Wonderful mid-'50s date with Freddie Green (g) stepping outside Basie's orchestra; Joe Newman accenting things on trumpet. —*Ron Wynn*

From A to Z / Jan. 23, 1956–Jan. 24, 1956 / Bluebird ◆◆◆
Sterling Cohn with Zoot Sims (ts) pairing. Nice reissue. —*Ron Wynn*

Be Loose / Sep. 29, 1956 / Biograph ◆◆◆
Cohn on the Saxophone / Sep. 29, 1956 / Dawn ◆◆
Al and Zoot / Mar. 26, 1957–Mar. 27, 1957 / MCA/Decca ◆◆◆
Red-letter duet date with the Al Cohn Quintet. Al Cohn, Zoot Sims (ts) dates here are memorable, though you can't say the same thing for MCA's mixes and remastering. W/ Mose Allison. —*Ron Wynn*

Body and Soul / Mar. 23, 1973 / Muse ◆◆◆◆
With Zoot Sims. Immortal tenor pair with Jaki Byard (p), plus George Duvivier (b) and Mel Lewis (d). Can't miss. —*Michael G. Nastos*

Motoring Along / Nov. 25, 1974 / Gazell ◆◆◆
Play It Now / Jun. 19, 1975 / Xanadu ◆◆◆
Silver Blue / Oct. 22, 1976 / Xanadu ◆◆◆
True Blue / Oct. 22, 1976 / Xanadu ◆◆◆
Excellent reissue of mid-'70s duo, quintet, and septet sessions. High-quality pairing of Cohn with Dexter Gordon (ts). —*Ron Wynn*

America / Dec. 6, 1976 / Xanadu ◆◆◆◆
Steady tenor, nice piano from Barry Harris. —*Ron Wynn*

Heavy Love / Mar. 15, 1977 / Xanadu ◆◆◆
Exquisite duets with pianist Jimmy Rowles. —*Ron Wynn*

No Problem / Dec. 18, 1979 / Xanadu ◆◆◆◆
Nonpareil / Apr. 1981 / Concord Jazz ◆◆◆
Stately, pleasant, and occasionally arresting, though Cohn has been in better combos. —*Ron Wynn*

Tour De Force / Aug. 11, 1981 / Concord Jazz ◆◆◆◆
A wonderful meeting between Hamilton, Buddy Tate, and Al Cohn. —*Ron Wynn*

Overtones / Apr. 1982 / Concord Jazz ◆◆◆
Tasty Cohn solos with precise, dignified support from Hank Jones (p) and George Duvivier (b). —*Ron Wynn*

● **Standards of Excellence** / Nov. 1983 / Concord Jazz ◆◆◆◆
Accurate title. Confident veterans going through their paces with

a minimum of flash and a maximum of talent. Herb Ellis (g) shines. —*Ron Wynn*

Al Cohn Meets Al Porcino / Mar. 30, 1987 / Red Baron ◆◆◆
This was one of Al Cohn's last recordings, a live session with trumpeter Al Porcino's European big band. Cohn's Lester Young-influenced tone had darkened quite a bit through the years and his tough tone was now closer to Illinois Jacquet than to Young. However he still swung in a boppish style and is the main soloist throughout this excellent outing, playing eight of his arrangements plus older charts from Gerry Mulligan and Bill Holman among others. Surprisingly Al Porcino does not take a single solo, being content to play in the ensembles and listen to his old friend perform in prime form. —*Scott Yanow*

Rifftide / Jun. 6, 1987 / Timeless ◆◆◆

Dolo Coker (Charles Mitchell Coker)

b. Nov. 16, 1927, Hartford, CT, **d.** Apr. 13, 1983, Los Angeles, CA
Piano / Bop
A fine bop pianist who never became all that famous, Dolo Coker's most high-profile period was when he recorded regularly for Xanadu in the late '70s. Back in the 1950s he had worked and recorded with Sonny Stitt (1955–57), Gene Ammons, Lou Donaldson, Art Pepper (appearing on his Contemporary recording *Intensity*), Philly Joe Jones and Dexter Gordon (1960–61). He settled in Los Angeles in 1961, leading his own trio. In the 1970s Coker worked with Stitt again in addition to Herb Ellis, Blue Mitchell, Red Rodney, Lee Konitz, Sonny Criss and Supersax and many artists associated with the Xanadu label. —*Scott Yanow*

● **Dolo!** / Dec. 26, 1976 / Xanadu ◆◆◆◆
Although by 1976 pianist Dolo Coker had already had a lengthy career, this quintet session was his first opportunity to record as a leader. Four of the six songs are his (three of those were written in 1959) and they are performed in swinging fashion (along with Harold Land's "Smack Up") by Coker, trumpeter Blue Mitchell, Land on tenor, bassist Leroy Vinnegar and drummer Frank Butler. The remaining track, "Never Let Me Go," gives the trio a chance to be featured. The music is as hard-swinging as one would expect from this personnel; happily, Dolo Coker would lead three more Xanadu albums within the next two years. —*Scott Yanow*

California Hard / Dec. 27, 1976 / Xanadu ◆◆◆
Third Down / Nov. 18, 1977 / Xanadu ◆◆◆
All Alone / Jun. 1982 / Xanadu ◆◆◆

Cozy Cole

b. Oct. 17, 1906, East Orange, NJ, **d.** Jan. 29, 1981, Columbus, OH
Drums / Swing
A popular performer throughout much of his career, Cozy Cole was one of the top drummers to emerge during the 1930s. He recorded with Jelly Roll Morton in 1930 (including a song titled "Load of Cole") and played with the big bands of Blanche Calloway (1931–33), Benny Carter (1933–34) and Willie Bryant (1935–36). His stint with Stuff Smith at the Onyx Club (1936–38) gave him some recognition. Cole was well-featured with Cab Calloway's Orchestra (1938–42), playing in a strong rhythm section with Bennie Payne, Danny Barker and Milt Hinton; his showcases included "Crescendo in Drums" and "Paradiddle." Cole popped up in many different types of jazz and studio settings throughout the 1940s and headed several record sessions with swing all-stars. He was with Louis Armstrong's All-Stars (1949–53), opened a drum school with Gene Krupa and in 1957 toured Europe with Jack Teagarden and Earl Hines. A 1958 recording of "Topsy" became a surprise hit, allowing Cole to lead his own band throughout much of the 1960s; he also played with Jonah Jones' quintet later in the decade. —*Scott Yanow*

Topsy Turvy / 1957 / Love ◆◆◆
Cozy's Caravan / Earl's Backroom / Feb. 7, 1958 / Felsted ◆◆◆
● **Lionel Hampton Presents Louis Armstrong Alumni** / Oct. 5, 1977 / Who's Who In Jazz ◆◆◆

Holly Cole

b. 1963, Halifax, Nova Scotia, Canada
Vocals / Cabaret, Standards
Holly Cole's music is difficult to classify. She takes familiar standards and casts them in a new ironic light that is sometimes sinister and occasionally humorous. She also performs sets of diverse

music that have more variety than one would think could possibly be successful; somehow it works. Both of her parents are classical musicians and she studied classical piano for a time. But after discovering Sarah Vaughan when she was 15, she switched to jazz. Cole sang with a big band in Toronto and in 1985 she formed a permanent trio with pianist Aaron Davis and bassist David Piltch. Their first album *Girl Talk* (released only in Canada) was a success and led to three records (thus far) for Manhattan: *Blame It on My Youth, Don't Smoke in Bed* and a nonjazz set of Tom Waits' music. —*Scott Yanow*

Blame It on My Youth / Jun. 1991–Jul. 1991 / Manhattan ◆◆◆

● **Don't Smoke in Bed** / Feb. 1993–Mar. 1993 / Manhattan ◆◆◆◆
Holly Cole explores a number of styles on her second album, *Don't Smoke in Bed*, without overreaching her grasp. Adding pop, blues, country, and a French ballad to her standard, low-key jazz, Cole demonstrates that not only does she have impeccable taste, but she has the talent to make all of the material sound convincing. —*Stephen Thomas Erlewine*

Temptation / 1995 / Metro Blue ◆◆
Holly Cole is one of the most intriguing jazz singers on the scene today, able to turn a standard inside out, pouring on an equal dosage of sensuality and sly wit while often laughing at herself. This CD finds her interpreting 16 Tom Waits compositions but, rather than try to uplift or distort the material, she lets the lyrics mostly speak for themselves and unfortunately few of the surprisingly mundane words would qualify as poetry. Even with the heat that she gives some of the songs (most notably "Take Me Home" and "Temptation"), this set is mostly a bore from the jazz standpoint with relatively little improvisation taking place. —*Scott Yanow*

Nat King Cole (Nathaniel Adams Cole)

b. Mar. 17, 1919, Montgomery, AL, d. Feb. 15, 1965, Santa Monica, CA

Piano, Vocals / Swing, Pop
Nat King Cole had two overlapping careers. He was one of the truly great swing pianists, inspired by Earl Hines and a big influence on Oscar Peterson. And he was a superb pop ballad singer whose great commercial success in that field unfortunately resulted in him greatly de-emphasizing his piano after 1949. Perhaps if his talents had been led to two different people . . . !

Nat Cole grew up in Chicago and by the time he was 12 he was playing organ and singing in church; his three brothers (Eddie, Fred and Isaac) would become jazz musicians. After making his recording debut with Eddie Cole's Solid Swingers in 1936, he left Chicago to lead the band for the revival of the revue *Shuffle Along,* and settled in Los Angeles when the show ended. Cole struggled a bit, put together a trio with guitarist Oscar Moore and bassist Wesley Prince and eventually settled in for a long residency in Hollywood. In the early days (documented on radio transcriptions), most of the group's repertoire was comprised of instrumentals, although the Trio often sang jivey novelty vocals together. However by the time the Trio had its first opportunity to record for Decca in December 1940, Nat King Cole had gained more confidence in his own singing. "Sweet Lorraine" resulted from that session and the Trio soon became quite popular. In future years Art Tatum, Oscar Peterson and Ahmad Jamal would all form piano/guitar/bass combos inspired by Cole's group.

Nat Cole recorded a great deal of exciting jazz during the 1940s including dates featuring Lester Young and Illinois Jacquet, the first Jazz at the Philharmonic concert (1944) and a countless number of selections for Capitol with his trio; all of the latter are included on a gigantic Mosaic limited-edition box set. Although his singing began to become quite popular by the mid-'40s (and particularly after "The Christmas Song" and "Nature Boy"), Cole mostly performed with his Trio during this era; Johnny Miller took over on bass and in 1947 Irving Ashby became the guitarist. Nat Cole was open to the influence of bop and in 1949 started utilizing Jack Constanzo on bongo and conga for some songs. However his career changed permanently in early 1950 with the recording of "Mona Lisa" which became a number one hit. Suddenly Nat King Cole became famous to the nonjazz public as a singer, and many new fans never realized that he also played piano! During the 1950s and '60s he mostly recorded pop ballads although there were a few exceptions (including 1956's *After Midnight* album) and he never lost his ability to play stimulating jazz. Cole had a regular television show during 1956–57 (some of

which has been released on video) but due to the racism of the period he could never find a sponsor. However the popularity of his records and public appearances remained at a remarkable level and the world mourned Nat King Cole's death from lung cancer in early 1965 at age 47. —*Scott Yanow*

From the Very Beginning / Jul. 28, 1936–Oct. 23, 1941 / MCA ◆◆◆◆
This double LP only contains 20 selections (an hour of music) but it perfectly sums up his early period. Cole's first recording date (as a sideman in his brother Eddie Cole's Solid Swingers) is included along with his four sessions for Decca with his trio which at the time featured guitarist Oscar Moore and bassist Wesley Prince. Although there are plenty of early radio transcriptions currently available, this set has all of his most significant studio recordings up until late 1942. Highlights include his first hit "Sweet Lorraine," "Honeysuckle Rose" and "Hit That Jive Jack." —*Scott Yanow*

☆ **Complete Early Transcriptions** / Oct. 1938–Feb. 1941 / Vintage Jazz Classics ◆◆◆◆◆
This four-CD set contains 112 performances by the Trio from 1938–41, radio transcriptions made especially to be played on the air. The early trio is instantly recognizable and, although there is a greater reliance on group vocals and guest singers (including Bonnie Lake, Juanelda Carter, Pauline and Her Perils and the Dreamers) rather than on Cole's solo vocals, the music is not all that different from what The King Cole Trio would be playing a few years later when they became much better known. —*Scott Yanow*

Nat King Cole & the King Cole Trio 1938–39 / Jan. 14, 1939–Jul. 23, 1940 / Savoy ◆◆◆◆
This LP, which does not duplicate the Vintage Jazz Classics set called *The Complete Early Transcriptions,* contains the Nat King Cole Trio's earliest studio recordings, four selections apiece from Jan. 14 and Dec. 1939 that were originally released on the tiny Ammor and Davis & Schwegler labels. In addition, there are 12 radio transcriptions, four of which have vocals by Maxine Johnson. Fans of the Trio will enjoy these swinging obscurities. —*Scott Yanow*

● **Hit That Jive Jack: The Earliest Recordings** / Dec. 1940–Oct. 1941 / Decca ◆◆◆◆◆

The Trio Recordings / 1940–1956 / Laserlight ◆◆◆◆◆
This five-CD set, despite the lack of definitive liner notes, is highly recommended. The bulk of this package (most of four discs) features the Trio on radio transcriptions during 1944–45 and these renditions are easily the equal of their more famous studio recordings. The fifth disc is a hodgepodge that reaches back to 1940 for six numbers and forward to 1956 for a few songs performed on The Dorsey Brothers TV Show and on Nat Cole's own program. Although the music could actually have fit on three discs (averaging around 40 minutes apiece), this set is usually available at a budget price and contains many exciting performances. —*Scott Yanow*

Trio Recordings, Vol. 5 / 1940–1956 / Laserlight ◆◆◆◆
The fifth of five CDs in this series by the budget label Laserlight differs from the first four in that it spans 16 years in pianist/singer Nat King Cole's career. He is heard with his original trio (which included guitarist Oscar Moore and bassist Wesley Prince) on six selections from 1940–41 and with his 1949 quartet (which had Jack Constanzo on congas) for "I Used to Love You." In addition, there are four numbers with Cole's wartime trio and four others from the mid-'50s taken from either The Dorsey Brothers TV show or Cole's own program. Throughout, the emphasis is on his brilliant swing piano rather than his vocals (although there are a generous amount of the latter), making this a series of great interest to jazz collectors. —*Scott Yanow*

WWII Transcriptions / 1941–1944 / Music & Arts ◆◆◆◆
With the exception of a couple of Anita Boyer vocals from 1941, this CD (which contains 30 broadcast transcriptions by Nat King Cole's Trio) dates from 1944. Two numbers apiece feature vocals from a young Anita O'Day and Ida James, but otherwise, Cole and his Trio only sing four other songs. The emphasis is on instrumentals (including two interesting medleys) and the leader's talents as a great swing pianist. Most of this material does not duplicate the Laserlight CDs, making this a recommended set for Nat King Cole's jazz fans. —*Scott Yanow*

☆ **Nat King Cole Meets The Master Saxes** / Jul. 15, 1942–1943 / Spotlite ✦✦✦✦✦
This very interesting LP finds Cole during 1942–43 recording outside of his trio. All of these selections originally came out on obscure 78s from tiny labels, but the personnel is anything but unknown. His piano is heard in a trio with the great tenor Lester Young and bassist Red Callender, with a quintet featuring tenorman Illinois Jacquet and trumpeter Shad Collins, and in a combo with 20-year-old Dexter Gordon on tenor and trumpeter Harry "Sweets" Edison. The late-period swing music is consistently wonderful, historical and formerly quite rare. *—Scott Yanow*

☆ **Complete Capitol Trio Recordings** / Oct. 11, 1942–Mar. 2, 1961 / Mosaic ✦✦✦✦✦
This 18-CD box set lives up to its title, containing not only all of the Nat King Cole Trio's recordings for Capitol during 1943–49 but a remarkable amount of previously unavailable radio transcriptions owned by Capitol. Also, all of Cole's post-1949 recordings that at least have the presence of the trio are here, including the entire *After Midnight* sessions of 1956 and various odds and ends that feature Cole's piano—349 selections in all with a countless number of formerly unissued tracks. Since this is a limited-edition set that will sell out, get this remarkable box as soon as possible. *—Scott Yanow*

Straighten Up and Fly Right / Dec. 1942–Jan. 28, 1948 / Pro Arte ✦✦✦
This CD consists of some of the Nat King Cole Trio's radio appearances, including guest shots on shows hosted by Bing Crosby, Perry Como and Frank Sinatra; Ol' Blue Eyes sits in with the trio on "I've Found a New Baby" and "Exactly like You." Considering that 12 of these 25 songs were never recorded commercially by the Trio, this set is quite valuable for fans of swing and Nat Cole's piano. The colorful music is easily recommended. *—Scott Yanow*

★ **Nat King Cole** / Nov. 30, 1943–Jun. 3, 1964 / Capitol ✦✦✦✦✦
For an overview of Nat King Cole's years as a remarkably popular singer, this four-CD box would be difficult to top. Containing 100 songs spanning a 20-year period, this box has virtually all of Cole's hits, some of his best jazz sides and more than its share of variety including a humorous previously unreleased version of "Mr. Cole Won't Rock & Roll." Recommended to beginners and veteran collectors alike, its attractive booklet is also a major asset. *—Scott Yanow*

The Capitol Collector's Series / Nov. 30, 1943–Jun. 3, 1964 / Capitol ✦✦✦✦
This 20-song single CD gives one an excellent introduction to the very popular singing of Nat King Cole. Concentrating on his hits, it contains virtually all of the biggest, including "Route 66," "The Christmas Song," "Nature Boy," "Mona Lisa" and even "Those Lazy-Hazy-Crazy Days of Summer." It has since been succeeded by the more ambitious four-CD box set *Nat King Cole*, but is recommended to those with a tight budget. *—Scott Yanow*

Trio Recordings, Vol. 1 / 1944–1945 / Laserlight ✦✦✦✦
The first of five CDs featuring Nat King Cole (all are available as part of a five-CD box set), this release from the budget label Laserlight contains 15 concise performances from the Trio on radio transcriptions from 1944–45. Each of the tracks is enjoyable with "What Can I Say After I Say I'm Sorry," "How High the Moon" and "Sweet Lorraine" being most memorable. *—Scott Yanow*

Trio Recordings, Vol. 2 / 1944–1945 / Laserlight ✦✦✦✦
The second of five CDs in this series (which are also all available as a five-CD box set) features the Trio on 17 selections from radio transcriptions dating from 1945. The jazz-oriented program is highlighted by "Is You Is or Is You Ain't My Baby," "On the Sunny Side of the Street," "Rosetta" and "Solid Potato Salad." Each of these sets offer many strong examples of Nat Cole's swing piano. *—Scott Yanow*

Trio Recordings, Vol. 3 / 1944–1945 / Laserlight ✦✦✦✦
The third of five CDs in this series of radio transcriptions features pianist/singer Nat King Cole, guitarist Oscar Moore and bassist Johnny Miller on 17 selections, many of which they never recorded commercially; certainly The King Cole Trio was not known for cutting such numbers as "You Must Be Blind," "If Yesterday Could Only Be Tomorrow," "Wild Goose Chase" or "Bring Another Drink." This very enjoyable swing music is also available (along with the other volumes) in a five-CD set. *—Scott Yanow*

Trio Recordings, Vol. 4 / 1944–1945 / Laserlight ✦✦✦✦
The fourth of five CDs in this series features Nat King Cole's

wartime Trio (with guitarist Oscar Moore and bassist Johnny Miller) on 14 radio transcriptions. Highlights include "After You've Gone," "A Pile of Cole" and "If You Can't Smile and Say Yes (Please Don't Cry and Say No)." A special bonus are five selections on which a young Anita O'Day sits in as guest vocalist. All five of these volumes (or better yet the comprehensive box set) from this budget label are recommended to fans of Nat King Cole's jazz years. *—Scott Yanow*

★ **Jazz Encounters** / Mar. 30, 1945–Jan. 5, 1950 / Blue Note ✦✦✦✦✦
This CD has many of Cole's most interesting Capitol dates away from his trio. The great jazz pianist is heard with the 1947 Metronome All-Stars, jamming with the all-star Capitol International Jazzmen, backing the straight vocals of Jo Stafford and collaborating with Nellie Lutcher, Woody Herman (on a remarkable version of "Mule Train") and Johnny Mercer (highlighted by the joyful "Save the Bones for Henry Jones"). This colorful set is highly recommended. *—Scott Yanow*

Anatomy of a Jam Session / Jun. 9, 1945 / Black Lion ✦✦✦✦
Cole is heard on this quintet session purely as a pianist, co-starring with trumpeter Charlie Shavers and tenor saxophonist Herbie Haymer; bassist John Simmons and drummer Buddy Rich play mainly in support. The quintet only actually performs five songs but seven alternate takes fill in the program and it is very interesting hearing the musicians gradually form the shape of their solos. *—Scott Yanow*

The King Cole Trios Live: 1947–1948 / Mar. 1, 1947–Mar. 13, 1948 / Vintage Jazz Classics ✦✦✦✦
This excellent CD contains five of the Trio's radio shows for NBC during 1947–48. There are some guests (singer Clark Dennis, the Dinning Sisters, Pearl Bailey, Woody Herman and Duke Ellington) for a song apiece, but the focus is on the Trio with occasional vocals from Cole. This historical music is enjoyable although the performances (many around the two-minute mark) are sometimes frustratingly brief. It's still worth acquiring. *—Scott Yanow*

Lush Life / Mar. 29, 1949–Jan. 11, 1952 / Capitol ✦✦✦✦✦
This is a very interesting transitional collection featuring Nat King Cole when he was gradually emphasizing his vocals over his jazz piano playing and phasing out his Trio. All 25 of the selections on this generous set feature the arrangements of Pete Rugolo; highlights include "Lush Life," "Time Out for Tears," "That's My Girl," "Red Sails in the Sunset," "It's Crazy" and "You Stepped out of a Dream." There is enough jazz content and popular appeal on this CD to satisfy both of Cole's audiences. *—Scott Yanow*

Big Band Cole / Aug. 16, 1950–Sep. 6, 1961 / Blue Note ✦✦✦✦✦
Cole's collaborations with the Count Basie and Stan Kenton Orchestras (all of which are included on this CD) found him mostly sticking to singing but enjoying the jazz-oriented backgrounds. He first met up with Kenton in 1950, recording the memorable "Orange Colored Sky" and starring on piano during the instrumental "Jam-Bo." They had a reunion in 1960–61, cutting a remake of "Orange Colored Sky" and two more poppish songs. The matchup with Basie showcased Cole purely as a singer in 1958; Gerald Wiggins took Basie's place at the keyboards. One of Cole's better vocal sessions, he is in top form on a variety of standards (particularly on "The Late Late Show" and "Welcome to the Club"); pity he did not sit in with the band on piano. This CD is recommended for its rare examples of Nat King Cole as a big-band singer. *—Scott Yanow*

The Billy May Sessions / Sep. 4, 1951–Nov. 22, 1961 / Capitol ✦✦✦✦
Nat King Cole recorded with arranger/bandleader Billy May on several occasions and all of their collaborations are on this excellent double CD. Dating from 1951, 1953, 1954, 1957 and 1961, some of the more memorable numbers include "Walkin' My Baby Back Home," "Angel Eyes," "Papa Loves Mambo," "Send for Me," "Who's Sorry Now," "The Party's Over" and "When My Sugar Walks Down the Street." Cole also takes organ solos on three of the selections from 1961 (the only time he ever recorded on that instrument), though he plays no piano on this set. It's recommended for his superior middle-of-the-road singing. *—Scott Yanow*

Piano Stylings / Jun. 7, 1955–Aug. 27, 1955 / Capitol ✦✦✦✦
One of Cole's most obscure albums, these 16 selections from 1955 feature his piano backed by an orchestra arranged by Nelson Riddle; no vocals. Different in style than the earlier recordings by the Trio, these performances put the focus purely on his lyrical

and swinging playing and his improvisations are often quite inspired. This CD deserves to be much better known. — *Scott Yanow*

Complete After Midnight Sessions / Aug. 15, 1956–Sep. 2, 1956 / Capitol ✦✦✦✦
After several years of hearing criticism from the jazz press about his decision to break up his Trio and become a pop singer, Nat King Cole was persuaded to record this jazz set. Joined by a strong rhythm section (including guitarist John Collins), Cole welcomed four guests for several selections apiece: altoist Willie Smith, trumpeter Harry "Sweets" Edison, violinist Stuff Smith and valve trombonist Juan Tizol. The performances on this CD (which include five selections released for the first time) are quite enjoyable, highlighted by "Just You, Just Me," "Sweet Lorraine," "It's Only a Paper Moon" and "Route 66." Cole did hedge his bet a bit by not recording any instrumentals or having any performances feature his trio without a guest. Despite that, this is a great set, and the last time that Nat King Cole would perform an album's worth of jazz material. — *Scott Yanow*

St. Louis Blues / Jan. 29, 1958–Jan. 31, 1958 / Capitol ✦✦✦
The filmed version of W.C. Handy's life, *St. Louis Blues*, is a fictional abomination full of every bad cliché that Hollywood could come up with. Its one saving grace was the dignified performance given by Nat King Cole in the lead role (even if Handy was never a singing pianist). This LP, in addition to featuring Nelson Riddle's "Overture" from the film, finds Cole singing ten of Handy's finest compositions (including "Beale Street Blues," "Careless Love" and the title song) while backed by an orchestra playing Riddle's arrangements. — *Scott Yanow*

Nat King Cole Story / Mar. 22, 1961–Jul. 30, 1961 / Capitol ✦✦✦✦
This double CD finds him revisiting his earlier hits with new versions. The 36 selections mostly focus on his pop successes of the 1950s, although there are a few wistful looks back at his trio days. Not as essential as the original renditions of these popular recordings, these remakes nevertheless find Cole in peak form and form a highly enjoyable retrospective of his vocal career. — *Scott Yanow*

Sings, George Shearing Plays / Dec. 19, 1961–Dec. 22, 1961 / Capitol ✦✦✦✦
Although it would have been interesting to hear Nat Cole play piano behind George Shearing's vocals, this session was a big success. Cole is in prime form on such songs as "September Song," "Pick Yourself Up," and "Serenata." Shearing's accompaniment is tasteful and lightly swinging, and the string arrangements help to accentuate the romantic moods. This CD adds three "new" selections from the same sessions to the original program. — *Scott Yanow*

Richie Cole

b. Feb. 29, 1948, Trenton, NJ
Alto Saxophone / Bop
Back in the mid-'70s when bebop was being greatly overshadowed by fusion, Richie Cole showed that not only was bop not old-fashioned but it could be quite fun. His "Alto Madness" was essentially the idea that any tune, no matter how unlikely its source, could be turned into exuberant bop. Through the years he has successfully recorded such songs as "The *I Love Lucy* Theme," "Holiday for Strings," "Horray for Hollywood," "The White Cliffs of Dover," "Come Fly with Me," "The *Star Trek* Theme," and even "La Bamba!" Influenced by Phil Woods and Charlie Parker, Richie Cole heard jazz from an early age because his father owned a jazz club in New Jersey. He started on alto when he was ten, attended Berklee for two years and joined Buddy Rich's big band in 1969. After a stint with Lionel Hampton Cole formed his own group, doing a great deal to popularize bebop in the 1970s. Some of his finest recordings were his early ones for Muse during a period when he often teamed up with singer Eddie Jefferson. His humor sometimes left critics cold but Cole was one of the top bop-oriented players of the 1980s and his Heads Up releases of the '90s (after a few years off the scene) are excellent. — *Scott Yanow*

Battle of Saxes, Vol. 1 / Mar. 26, 1976–Mar. 27, 1976 / Muse ✦✦✦
Entertaining, stimulating match of alto sax styles of Cole and Eric Kloss. — *Ron Wynn*

New York Afternoon: Alto Madness / Oct. 13, 1976 / Muse ✦✦✦✦
This Muse album features the group that altoist Richie Cole and the late singer Eddie Jefferson co-led in the mid-'70s. They had a

mutually beneficial relationship with Cole learning from the older vocalist and Jefferson gaining extra exposure from associating with the popular young saxophonist. Their happy set (which has two Jefferson vocals) is highlighted by "Waltz for a Rainy Be-Bop Evening," "New York Afternoon," "Stormy Weather" and "Alto Madness." — *Scott Yanow*

Alto Madness / Dec. 1977 / Muse ✦✦✦✦✦
A red-hot album from the late '70s, still one of alto saxophonist Cole's best. Everything, from the surging piano licks provided by Harold Mabern, to Cole's own bustling solos and some sensational vocals from special guest Eddie Jefferson, make this a great tribute to bop's glories. — *Ron Wynn*

Keeper of the Flame / Sep. 6, 1978 / Muse ✦✦✦✦
Cole contributes his usual sparkling, energized alto sax. Pianist Harold Mabern takes second soloist honors, while guitarist Vic Juris, drummer Eddie Gladden, and percussionist Ray Mantilla handle the rhythm section responsibilities. — *Ron Wynn*

● **Hollywood Madness** / Apr. 25, 1979 / Muse ✦✦✦✦✦
Unusual instrumental configuration and lineup for this '79 session. Cole headed a band with two bassists, a drummer, pianist, percussionist, and vocalists Eddie Jefferson and the Manhattan Transfer. This was part concept vehicle, part blowing session, but other than Cole on alto sax, no one else was very decisive. Jefferson and The Manhattan Transfer provide bluesy, flashy singing. — *Ron Wynn*

Side by Side / Jul. 25, 1980+Jul. 26, 1980 / Muse ✦✦✦
This set features a very logical matchup. Richie Cole's main influence has long been Phil Woods, so these concert performances pitting the two altoists together have plenty of fire and extroverted improvisations. With pianist John Hicks, bassist Walter Booker and drummer Jimmy Cobb backing the soloists, Woods and Cole really push each other on "Scrapple from the Apple," "Donna Lee" and "Side by Side." Tenor-great Eddie "Lockjaw" Davis sits in on "Save Your Love for Me," the younger altoist has "Polka Dots and Moonbeams" to himself and Cole and Woods have fun on a brief free-form "Naughayde Reality." It's a generally high-powered and enjoyable set. — *Scott Yanow*

Some Things Speak for Themselves / Feb. 1, 1981 / Muse ✦✦✦

Cool "C" / Feb. 5, 1981–Feb. 8, 1981 / Muse ✦✦✦

Return to Alto Acres / Feb. 16, 1982 / Palo Alto ✦✦✦

Alto Annie's Theme / Jul. 31, 1982 / Palo Alto ✦✦✦✦
Bop altoist Richie Cole features his regular quartet of the early '80s on this hard-to-find album. With pianist Dick Hindman, bassist Brian Bromberg and drummer Victor Jones, Cole (who also plays some tenor and baritone on the extroverted set) is heard at his best on a near-classic rendition of "Jeannine," "Boplicity," "Tangerine" and "Easy to Love." — *Scott Yanow*

Yakety Madness / Aug. 25, 1982–Nov. 15, 1982 / Palo Alto ✦✦✦

Pure Imagination / Nov. 1986 / Concord Jazz ✦✦✦
Fine standards, uptempo cuts. — *Ron Wynn*

Popbop / Jun. 4, 1987–Jun. 6, 1987 / Milestone ✦✦✦

Bossa Nova International / Jul. 16, 1987 / Milestone ✦✦
With Hank Crawford Quintet. Cole and Hank Crawford (sax) make an effective team. — *Ron Wynn*

Signature / Jul. 1988 / Milestone ✦✦✦

Profile / Apr. 5, 1993–Apr. 7, 1993 / Heads Up ✦✦✦
Profile was Cole's first recording in four years and it found the altoist's sound and style virtually unchanged from the earlier days. Joined by a superior rhythm section that includes pianist Dick Hindman and guitarist Henry Johnson, Cole is in top form on diverse material ranging from his original "Presidential Sax" and the lyrical "Street of Dreams" to three Carroll Coates originals and the pop tune "Volare." It's a particularly happy bop session. — *Scott Yanow*

The Music Of Dizzy Gillespie / Dec. 9, 1994 / Heads Up ✦✦✦✦
Altoist Richie Cole makes a full-fledged comeback on this fairly inspired release. He performs nine Dizzy Gillespie compositions (plus "You Go to My Head" which was actually co-written by Haven Gillespie) while joined by groups ranging from a two-guitar trio to a 13-piece band, all arranged in colorful fashion by Bob Belden. In addition to Cole, fellow altoist Paquito D'Rivera battles it out on "Kush" and plays some excellent clarinet on "Salt Peanuts" while trumpeter Jack Walrath has a few spots. Other highlights include "Be-Bop," "Birk's Works," "A Night in Tunisia" and "Manteca." — *Scott Yanow*

Bill Coleman

b. Aug. 4, 1904, Paris, KY, **d.** Aug. 24, 1981, Toulouse, France
Trumpet / Dixieland, Swing
A mellow-toned swing trumpeter with a distinctive sound and a lyrical style, Bill Coleman was a consistent if never particularly famous musician. In 1927 he went to New York with Cecil and Lloyd Scott's band with whom he made his recording debut. He worked with Luis Russell (1929–32) and Charlie Johnson and then in 1933 travelled to France with Lucky Millinder. Coleman recorded with Fats Waller (1934) and played with Teddy Hill's Orchestra (1934–35) but then moved to France for the first time in 1935. While overseas he recorded frequently as a leader (really coming into his own), with Willie Lewis' Orchestra and on dates with Django Reinhardt. He ventured as far as Bombay and spent 1938–40 in Egypt with Herman Chittison. Returning to New York, Coleman played with Benny Carter, Teddy Wilson, Andy Kirk, Mary Lou Williams and John Kirby during 1940–45 and recorded with Lester Young and Coleman Hawkins (both in 1943). However he preferred life in Europe and, after a period with groups led by Sy Oliver and Billy Kyle, in 1948 Coleman moved permanently back to France, staying active and recording fairly regularly up until his death in 1981. *—Scott Yanow*

● **Bill Coleman** / Jan. 31, 1936–Sep. 28, 1938 / Disques Swing ✦✦✦✦✦

From Boogie to Funk / Jan. 21, 1960–Jan. 22, 1960 / Brunswick ✦✦✦

Bill Coleman Meets Guy Lafitte / Jul. 4, 1973 / Black Lion ✦✦✦

Blowing for the Cats / Nov. 15, 1973–Nov. 16, 1973 / DRG ✦✦✦

Really I Do / May 15, 1980 / Black & Blue ✦✦✦✦
This was one of trumpeter Bill Coleman's final recordings (he passed away in Aug. 1981) but there is no hint of his decline on these joyful swing performances. Coleman is teamed up with tenor saxophonist Guy Lafitte (they had recorded together many times previously), pianist Red Richards, bassist Bill Pemberton and drummer Panama Francis for run throughs of familiar standards (such as a heated "Crazy Rhythm," "You've Changed" and "I've Got My Love to Keep Me Warm"), the lesser-known Dickie Wells line "Hello Babe" and two of Coleman's basic originals. The result is a happy set of swinging music featuring Bill Coleman in surprisingly good form. *—Scott Yanow*

Cecilia Coleman

b. 1957, Long Beach, CA
Piano, Leader / Post-Bop
Leader of a stimulating quintet and a talented pianist/composer whose music is becoming more original with each year, Cecilia Coleman performs regularly in Los Angeles clubs. She began on piano when she was six. After graduating from college in 1986, she played in the L.A. area with Charlie Shoemaker, Phil Upchurch and Shelley Moore among others and was a member of the Benn Clatworthy Quartet (with whom she recorded for Discovery) during 1987–91. She made her debut as a leader for the L.A.P. label and then, after forming her quintet (which also includes trumpeter Steve Huffsteter, Andy Suzuki on reeds, bassist Dean Taba and drummer Kendall Kay), recorded two CDs for Resurgent that not only feature her piano playing but her inventive writing. *—Scott Yanow*

● **Young And Foolish** / Dec. 1993 / Resurgent ✦✦✦✦
This CD not only features Cecilia Coleman's increasingly distinctive piano improvisations and seven of her diverse and complex originals but it is the recording debut of her excellent quintet. The soft-toned trumpeter Steve Huffsteter and the harder-edged tenor saxophonist Andy Suzuki offer contrasting solo styles while bassist Dean Taba and drummer Kendall Kay do not just accompany the lead voices but push them to come up with forceful statements. Although she is generous in allocating solo space, the main star throughout is Coleman. Her tricky yet melodic originals cover a variety of moods and force Huffsteter and Suzuki to play at their most creative level. Whether it be the somber "Somalia," the vintage Blue Note sound of "The Real Thing" or an uptempo version of Bud Powell's "Celia," virtually every track on this impressive release by the talented Cecilia Coleman is memorable. *—Scott Yanow*

Earl Coleman

b. Aug. 12, 1925, Port Huron, MI, **d.** 1995
Vocals / Standards
A fine ballad singer with a deep baritone voice influenced by Billy Eckstine, Earl Coleman made his place in history by recording

"This Is Always" and "Dark Shadows" in 1947 while being accompanied by Charlie Parker. He had sung previously with Jay McShann (1943) and Earl Hines (1944). Despite the success of "This Is Always" (which was a minor hit), Coleman never really caught on and was fairly obscure throughout much of his career. He did record now and then with the likes of Fats Navarro (1948), Art Farmer, Sonny Rollins (both in 1956), and on his own dates including two sets for Xanadu (1977 and 1979) and one for Stash (1984). *—Scott Yanow*

● **Earl Coleman Returns** / Mar. 2, 1956–Jun. 8, 1956 / Original Jazz Classics ✦✦✦✦
Earl Coleman was a singer along the lines of Billy Eckstine and Johnny Hartman. And although he's been working professionally for many, many years (since around 1925), he has never been as familiar to the public as Eckstine or Hartman. Part of the reason may be that he has always chosen to record in a solid jazz context with outstanding instrumentalists. While other mellow baritones have had wider commercial exposure, Coleman on occasion can get overly saccharine, but not so on *Earl Coleman Returns*, a Coleman offering worth reissuing for both vocal and instrumental reasons. *—Bob Rusch, Cadence*

A Song for You / Sep. 9, 1977 / Xanadu ✦✦✦

Stardust / Sep. 1984 / Stash ✦✦✦

George Coleman

b. Mar. 8, 1935, Memphis, TN
Tenor Saxophone / Hard Bop
George Coleman's highest visibility occurred when he was a member of the Miles Davis Quintet (1963–64), playing alongside Miles, Herbie Hancock, Ron Carter and Tony Williams. His decision to leave the group after several notable recordings cut short his potential fame (his eventual replacement was Wayne Shorter) but Coleman has created a great deal of rewarding music since. Part of the rich Memphis jazz scene of the early '50s, he started playing in blues bands in The South (including with B.B. King in 1952 and 1955–56). He moved to Chicago in 1957 (where he played with the MJT+3) and to New York the following year. Coleman was with the Max Roach Quintet (1958–59), Slide Hampton's Octet (1959–61) and Wild Bill Davis (1962) before joining Davis. Following that association he was with Lionel Hampton, Elvin Jones and Charles McPherson. Since the mid-'70s George Coleman has mostly led his own groups and has recorded both as a leader (for Timeless, Theresa and Verve) and as a sideman quite frequently; one of his more notable appearances from earlier years was on Herbie Hancock's 1964 classic *Maiden Voyage*. *—Scott Yanow*

Meditation / Feb. 20, 1977 / Timeless ✦✦✦

Big George / Nov. 2, 1977–Nov. 3, 1977 / Charly ✦✦✦

Amsterdam After Dark / Jan. 2, 1977 / Timeless ✦✦✦✦
Legendary tenor saxophonist blows up a storm with the Hilton Ruiz Trio. This has been reissued on CD. Best cut is "New Arrival." *—Michael G. Nastos*

Playing Changes / Apr. 1979 / Ronnie Scott's Jazz House ✦✦✦

Manhattan / 1985 / Theresa ✦✦✦

● **At Yoshi's** / Aug. 1987 / Evidence ✦✦✦✦
George Coleman's animated, anguished tenor sax solos are the hook on this seven-track live set done at Yoshi's in Tokyo during 1989. Coleman offered some lush, sensitive playing, but much of the time ripped through chord changes, expanding through the upper register. Drummer Alvin Queen and bassist Ray Drummond wisely gave Coleman extensive space, spreading and splitting the beat while he roared above. Pianist Harold Mabern added contrasting elements with bluesy, passionate solos or sensitive, subtle understatements that followed and reaffirmed Coleman's emphatic lines. *—Ron Wynn*

My Horns of Plenty / Mar. 4, 1991–Mar. 5, 1991 / Verve ✦✦✦✦
A recent date by Coleman, stepping into the '90s in style. He displays his versatility by playing alto and soprano along with his usual tenor, and scoring on each one. The rhythm trio this time includes his favorite pianist, Harold Mabern, plus bassist Ray Drummond and drummer Billy Higgins. *—Ron Wynn*

Ornette Coleman

b. Mar. 9, 1930, Fort Worth, TX
Trumpet, Violin, Alto Saxophone, Composer, Leader / Free Jazz, Free Funk
One of the most important (and controversial) innovators of the

jazz avant-garde, Ornette Coleman gained both loyal followers and lifelong detractors when he seemed to burst on the scene in 1959 fully formed. Although he and Don Cherry in his original quartet played opening and closing melodies together, their solos dispensed altogether with chordal improvisation and harmony, instead playing quite freely off of the mood of the theme. Coleman's tone (which purposely wavered in pitch) rattled some listeners and his solos were emotional and followed their own logic. In time his approach would be quite influential and the Quartet's early records still sound advanced over 35 years later.

Unfortunately Ornette Coleman's early development was not documented. Originally inspired by Charlie Parker, he started playing alto at 14 and tenor two years later. His early experiences were in R&B bands in Texas including those of Red Connors and Pee Wee Crayton but his attempts to play in an original style were consistently met with hostility both by audiences and fellow musicians. Coleman moved to Los Angeles in the early '50s where he worked as an elevator operator while studying music books. He met kindred spirits along the way in Don Cherry, Charlie Haden, Ed Blackwell, Bobby Bradford, Charles Moffett and Billy Higgins but it was not until 1958 (after many unsuccessful attempts to sit in with top L.A. musicians) that Coleman had a nucleus of musicians who could play his music. He appeared as part of Paul Bley's Quintet for a short time at the Hillcrest Club (which is documented on live records) and recorded two very interesting albums for Contemporary. With the assistance of John Lewis, Coleman and Cherry attended the Lenox School of Jazz in 1959 and had an extended stay at the Five Spot in New York. This engagement alerted the jazz world toward the radical new music and each night the audience was filled with curious musicians who alternately labelled Coleman a genius or a fraud.

During 1959–61 Ornette Coleman recorded a series of classic and somewhat startling quartet albums for Atlantic (all of which have been reissued on a six-CD set by Rhino). With Don Cherry, Charlie Haden, Scott LaFaro or Jimmy Garrison on bass and Billy Higgins or Ed Blackwell on drums, Coleman created music that would greatly affect most of the other advanced improvisers of the 1960s including John Coltrane, Eric Dolphy and the free jazz players of the mid-'60s. One set, a nearly 40-minute jam called *Free Jazz* (which other than a few brief themes was basically a pulse-driven group free improvisation) had Coleman, Cherry, Haden, LaFaro, Higgins, Blackwell, Dolphy and Freddie Hubbard forming a double quartet.

In 1962 Ornette Coleman, feeling that he was worth much more money than the clubs and his label were paying him, surprised the jazz world by retiring for a period. He took up trumpet and violin (playing the latter as if it were a drum!) and in 1965 he recorded a few brilliant sets on all his instruments with a particularly strong trio featuring bassist David Izenzon and drummer Charles Moffett. Later in the decade Coleman had a quartet with the very complementary tenor Dewey Redman, Haden and either Blackwell or his young son Denardo Coleman on drums. In addition Coleman wrote some atonal and wholly composed classical works for chamber groups and had a few reunions with Don Cherry.

In the early '70s Ornette Coleman entered the second half of his career. He formed a "double quartet" comprised of two guitars, two electric bassists, two drummers and his own alto. The group, called "Prime Time," featured dense, noisy and often-witty ensembles in which all of the musicians are supposed to have an equal role but the leader's alto always ended up standing out. He now calls his music "Harmolodics" (symbolizing the equal importance of harmony, melody and rhythm) although "free funk" (combining together loose funk rhythms and free improvising) probably fits better; among his sidemen in Prime Time have been drummer Ronald Shannon Jackson and bassist Jamaaladeen Tacuma in addition to his son Denardo.

Prime Time was a major (if somewhat unacknowledged) influence on the M-Base music of Steve Coleman and Greg Osby. Pat Metheny (a lifelong Ornette admirer) collaborated with Coleman on the intense *Song X*, Jerry Garcia played third guitar on one recording and Ornette had irregular reunions with his original quartet members in the 1980s.

Ornette Coleman, who currently records for Verve, has remained true to his highly original vision throughout his career and, although not technically a virtuoso and still considered controversial, is an obvious giant of jazz. —*Scott Yanow*

The Music of Ornette Coleman: Something Else!!! / Feb. 10, 1958–Mar. 24, 1958 / Original Jazz Classics ◆◆◆
This important CD reissue brings back altoist Ornette Coleman's first recording. His radical free jazz style was already nearly fully developed, even though his quartet had not been formed yet. Coleman is joined by two future quartet members (trumpeter Don Cherry and drummer Billy Higgins), plus pianist Walter Norris (who is out of place) and bassist Don Payne (much more closely tied to the chord structure than Charlie Haden would be). Highlights of this significant recording include two of Coleman's best compositions, "The Blessing" and "When Will The Blues Leave?" —*Scott Yanow*

Coleman Classics, Vol. 1 / Oct. 1958 / Improvising Artists ◆◆◆◆
These fascinating live performances from the Hillcrest Club in Los Angeles feature the original Ornette Coleman Quartet (with Coleman on alto, trumpeter Don Cherry, bassist Charlie Haden and drummer Billy Higgins) all as sidemen with pianist Paul Bley's Quintet. Recorded between Coleman's first and second Contemporary albums, these numbers (extended versions of "When Will the Blues Leave" and "Ramblin" along with briefer renditions of "Crossroads" and "How Deep Is the Ocean") show that Coleman already had his very original style pretty much together at this early stage. Paul Bley was wise enough to mostly stay out of the way and he clearly benefited from this encounter with some of the pioneers of free jazz. —*Scott Yanow*

Tomorrow Is the Question! / Jan. 16, 1959–Mar. 10, 1959 / Original Jazz Classics ◆◆◆
Ornette Coleman's second of two studio albums for Contemporary, which has been reissued on CD in the OJC series, finds him dropping the piano and interacting closely with trumpeter Don Cherry. The rhythm section (Percy Heath or Red Mitchell on bass and drummer Shelly Manne) is still not loose enough for the music (nine Coleman originals, of which "Turnaround" and "Tears Inside" are the best-known), but the freedom heard in the playing of the two horns is quite notable, particularly for 1959. A very interesting session. —*Scott Yanow*

The Shape of Jazz to Come / May 22, 1959 / Atlantic ◆◆◆◆◆
Altoist Ornette Coleman's first Atlantic recording was his first with his somewhat revolutionary quartet, which included cornetist Don Cherry, bassist Charlie Haden and drummer Billy Higgins. Because the solos did not follow any set chord pattern, this music became known as "free jazz." This CD reissue, which has also been included in Rhino's six-CD Ornette Coleman box set, is highlighted by the original version of Coleman's most famous composition, "Lonely Woman," plus "Peace" and "Congeniality." This music would greatly influence jazz of the mid-'60s and still sounds quite advanced. —*Scott Yanow*

Twins / May 22, 1959 / Atlantic ◆◆◆
The five performances on this LP were not released until 1981. Of greatest interest is a shorter version of the nearly 40-minute "Free Jazz," which at 17 minutes was simply titled "First Take." In addition, the innovative altoist is heard on four quartet numbers with cornetist Don Cherry, either Charlie Haden or Scott LaFaro on bass and Ed Blackwell or Billy Higgins on drums; "First Take" has all of these musicians plus bass clarinetist Eric Dolphy and trumpeter Freddie Hubbard. All of this valuable music, which also includes "Little Symphony" and "Monk and the Nun," has been reissued in Rhino's *Complete Ornette on Atlantic* CD box set. —*Scott Yanow*

The Art of Improvisers / May 22, 1959–Mar. 27, 1961 / Atlantic ◆◆◆
The seven selections on this valuable LP are performances by various versions of the Ornette Coleman Quartet that were not released until this 1988 album came out; all of the contents were reissued in Rhino's large Coleman CD box set. The very original altoist is in excellent form and joined by cornetist Don Cherry, either Charlie Haden, Scott LaFaro or Jimmy Garrison on bass and Billy Higgins or Ed Blackwell on drums. The lyrical ballad "Just for You" is one of the highlights, and some of the song titles ("The Legend of Bebop" and "The Fifth of Beethoven") allude both to Coleman's often overlooked wit and his roots. The music is quite advanced, unpredictable and stimulating. —*Scott Yanow*

☆ **Beauty Is A Rare Thing: Complete Atlantic Recordings** / May 22, 1959–Mar. 27, 1961 / Rhino/Atlantic ◆◆◆◆◆
This six-CD box set (which includes a very informative and, colorful 70-page booklet) has all of altoist Ornette Coleman's record-

ings for the Atlantic label. These performances, considered quite revolutionary at the time since Coleman did not use any chord changes, still sound futuristic today. Not only is all the music included from the albums *The Shape of Jazz to Come, This Is Our Music, Free Jazz, Ornette* and *Ornette on Tenor* along with the two later sets of unissued material (*The Art of the Improvisers* and *Twins*) but a record not previously out in Japan (*To Whom Who Keeps a Record*), two songs that feature Coleman on a Gunther Schuller album and six cuts never out before. Although more general listeners may be content with one or two of Ornette Coleman's albums, serious collectors will want to get this very valuable set while it is still around for it contains some of the most important jazz recordings of the early '60s. — *Scott Yanow*

Change of the Century / Oct. 8, 1959–Oct. 9, 1959 / Atlantic ✦✦✦✦
Altoist Ornette Coleman originally recorded six albums for Atlantic (not counting later releases of temporarily discarded tracks), and this particular one was his second. With Don Cherry (on pocket trumpet), bassist Charlie Haden and drummer Billy Higgins, Coleman introduces such interesting and unpredictable "free" pieces as the rhythmic "Una Muy Bonita," "Ramblin'" and "Bird Food." This is important (and still advanced) music that deserves to be heard either in this set or as part of the comprehensive Rhino six-CD box of Coleman's Atlantic recordings. — *Scott Yanow*

This Is Our Music / Jul. 19, 1960–Aug. 2, 1960 / Atlantic ✦✦✦✦
The third of altoist Ornette Coleman's six Atlantic albums (not counting later compilations of unreleased material) is most notable for his lyrical and childlike interpretation of the only non-original recorded during this era, "Embraceable You," and for the memorable "Blues Connotation." The other five numbers are lesser-known, but "Beauty Is a Rare Thing" and "Humpty Dumpty" also stick in one's mind. Ornette, trumpeter Don Cherry, bassist Charlie Haden and drummer Ed Blackwell, the latter making his recording debut with the group, formed a classic unit in which each musician was somehow able to quickly figure out in what direction the others were heading. Their brand of "free jazz" or "avant-garde jazz" caused quite a stir during this era and indirectly influenced many groups later in the 1960s. — *Scott Yanow*

Free Jazz (A Collective Improvisation) / Dec. 21, 1960 / Atlantic ✦✦✦✦✦
This was one of the most controversial jazz recordings of the period, although when compared to John Coltrane's *Ascension* of five years later, *Free Jazz* sounds quite melodic and even slightly conservative. Altoist Ornette Coleman gathered together a "double quartet" comprised of bass clarinetist Eric Dolphy, Don Cherry and Freddie Hubbard on trumpets, Scott LaFaro and Charlie Haden on basses and both Billy Higgins and Ed Blackwell on drums. Although there is an opening melody, a steady pulse and loose but organized parts between the solos, otherwise this music (which is continuous for around 36 1/2 minutes) is completely free. While one player improvises, the other musicians are free to "comment" behind the solo. The ten-minute stretch when Ornette Coleman is the lead voice and the other three horns come up with free "riffs" is the high point of this very interesting recording (which has also been reissued in Rhino's six-CD Coleman box set). — *Scott Yanow*

Ornette! / Jan. 31, 1961 / Atlantic ✦✦✦
This Atlantic session by the Ornette Coleman Quartet is most notable for featuring the ill-fated Scott LaFaro on bass. With the leader's alto, trumpeter Don Cherry and drummer Ed Blackwell all contributing their unpredictable ideas and surprisingly close musical communication, the group is in near-peak form on Coleman's four originals, which are given abbreviated names (such as "W.R.U. and "R.P.D.D."). It would take "free jazz" another four years before it became a dominant force, but it would be recordings such as this one that would influence jazz of the mid-'60s. — *Scott Yanow*

Ornette on Tenor / Mar. 22, 1961+Mar. 27, 1961 / Atlantic ✦✦✦✦
Altoist Ornette Coleman's final album in a series of classic and highly influential Atlantic recordings (which have been reissued in Rhino's *Complete Ornette* six-CD box set) is most unusual because Coleman sticks exclusively to tenor. His gutbucket sound makes his music even more passionate and inaccessible than usual, although listeners who study this record closely will be able to grasp its logic. The "free jazz" improvising by Coleman, trumpeter Don Cherry, bassist Jimmy Garrison (shortly before he

joined the John Coltrane Quartet) and drummer Ed Blackwell is quite original and impressive; the often-startling "Cross Breeding" is a high point. — *Scott Yanow*

Town Hall Concert 1962 / Dec. 21, 1962 / ESP ✦✦✦
Ornette Coleman's decision to temporarily retire from music (this ESP disc was his only recording from a four-year period) was unfortunate. His alto playing was getting stronger and, on evidence of this CD, he had plenty of original ideas that should have been documented. For this Town Hall concert, Coleman debuts with his new trio (a unit that would return in 1965) featuring the remarkable bassist David Izenson and drummer Charles Moffett. Together they perform "Doughnut," "Sadness" and an extensive 23 1/2 minute version of "The Ark." In addition a string quartet performs Coleman's "Dedication to Poets and Writers." Although Ornette's strong writing (which leaves no room for improvising) is pretty well outside of jazz, his playing on the other tracks holds one's interest throughout. — *Scott Yanow*

The Great London Concert / Aug. 29, 1965 / Arista Freedom ✦✦✦✦
Ornette Coleman emerged from three years of retirement in 1965 to bring back the trio he had utilized briefly in 1962, a group also featuring the very impressive bassist David Izenson and drummer Charles Moffett. Coleman's alto playing had become a lot stronger by this time and although his improvising on violin (which he played like a drum) and trumpet were at a much lower level, they were utilized fairly sparingly. This double-LP has the sidelong "Forms and Sounds for Wind Quintet," a wholly written out atonal work for flute, oboe, clarinet, bassoon and French horn that is rather boring. However the trio's performances of the other seven selections is quite stimulating and Coleman (who only plays violin and trumpet on "Falling Stars") is consistently brilliant and explorative. Worth searching for by listeners with open ears. — *Scott Yanow*

● **At the "Golden Circle" in Stockholm, Vol. 1** / Dec. 3, 1965–Dec. 4, 1965 / Blue Note ✦✦✦✦
Ornette Coleman was at the peak of his powers by 1965. His alto playing had become quite a bit stronger than in his early days, and Coleman's trio with bassist David Izenson and drummer Charles Moffett was as exciting as his earlier quartet. On this CD reissue of a Blue Note LP, he stretches out on four of his originals ("Faces and Places," "European Echoes," "Dee Dee" and "Dawn") and plays consistently innovative and surprising solos that probably confused the majority of his audience while delighting others. This set is recommended, as is the second volume. — *Scott Yanow*

At the "Golden Circle" in Stockholm, Vol. 2 / Dec. 3, 1965–Dec. 4, 1965 / Blue Note ✦✦✦✦
The second of two volumes (reissued on CD) documenting a series of concerts in Stockholm, Sweden, by the 1965 Ornette Coleman Trio is almost the equal of the first. Coleman plays his primitive violin and trumpet on "Snowflakes and Sunshine" but sticks to alto (at its prime during this period) during his other three originals ("Morning Song," "The Riddle" and "Antiques"). The interplay between brilliant bassist David Izenson and drummer Charles Moffett is also quite impressive on this recommended set of free jazz. — *Scott Yanow*

Who's Crazy / 1966 / Affinity ✦✦✦
This two-LP set contains the soundtrack Ornette Coleman and his trio contributed for the obscure Belgian film of the same name. Coleman (switching between alto, trumpet and violin), bassist Dave Izenzon and drummer Charles Moffett did not merely provide filler music but full-blown improvisations that stand very much on their own. Fans of Coleman's very explorative music are advised to search for this valuable two-fer. — *Scott Yanow*

Empty Foxhole / Sep. 9, 1966 / Blue Note ✦✦✦
The music on this LP is better than expected. Ornette Coleman uses his son Denardo (who was ten at the time!) on drums along with bassist Charlie Haden and plays either trumpet or violin (instead of his customary alto) on half of the six selections. Although the results are not essential, there are plenty of exciting moments to be heard in this adventurous music and Denardo surprisingly mostly holds his own. — *Scott Yanow*

Forms and Sounds / Mar. 17, 1967+Mar. 31, 1967 / Bluebird ✦✦
Legendary as the performer/composer who freed jazz from the harmony and songforms of Tin Pan Alley ballads, these pieces show more of Coleman's path since his densely chromatic orches-

tral piece "Skies of America" (some movements are entitled "Holiday for Heroes", "Place in Space", "Foreigner in a Free Land", "Sunday in America"). This CD includes "Forms and Sounds"—played by The Philadelphia Woodwind Quartet; densities of melodies alternately freely floating or played to an automaton pulse with commentary-like to bluesy to celebratory trumpet interludes played by Coleman; calls to reconsider life; "Saints and Soldiers"—repression by the religious and political contrasted with saintly discernment; and "Space Flight"—flashes of unidentified fluttering things which suddenly disappear. Performed by The Chamber Symphony of Philadelphia String Quartet. —*Blue Gene Tyranny*

Live in Milano, 1968 / Feb. 5, 1968 / Jazz Up ✦✦✦

Love Call / Apr. 29, 1968+May 7, 1968 / Blue Note ✦✦✦✦
Ornette Coleman's 1968 Quartet featured the explorative tenor of Dewey Redman (who blended in very well with Coleman's alto), bassist Jimmy Garrison and drummer Elvin Jones. For this CD reissue, which was recorded at the same sessions that resulted in *New York Is Now*, the original four songs were augmented by two "new" alternate takes and "Just for You," which was previously available only in Japan. The interplay between Coleman and Redman on these free jazz jams and the similarity of their approaches, even though they had different sounds, make this unit a particularly strong group. This CD is about as accessible as Ornette Coleman ever became. —*Scott Yanow*

New York Is Now / Apr. 29, 1968+May 7, 1968 / Blue Note ✦✦✦✦
Altoist Ornette Coleman had a particularly strong group at the time of his 1968 Blue Note recordings, which resulted in the music heard on this CD and its companion, *Love Call*. Dewey Redman was the equivalent of Coleman on tenor, while bassist Jimmy Garrison and drummer Elvin Jones were alumni of John Coltrane's Quartet. For the CD reissue, a "new" alternate take of "Broad Way Blues" was added to the original program and, although none of the melodies caught on, the complementary playing by Coleman and Redman in particular is quite impressive, making this free jazz set highly recommended. —*Scott Yanow*

Ornette at 12 / Jun. 16, 1968 / Impulse! ✦✦✦

Crisis / Mar. 22, 1969 / Impulse! ✦✦

Friends and Neighbors / Feb. 14, 1970 / Flying Dutchman ✦✦
This out-of-print LP contains one of Ornette Coleman's lesser-known sessions. In addition to his own alto (and occasional trumpet and violin), Coleman is joined by Dewey Redman on tenor, bassist Charlie Haden, drummer Ed Blackwell, and (on one of the two versions of "Friends and Neighbors") a variety of friends who sing along as best they can. Actually, the most notable tracks are the two extended pieces "Long Time No See" and "Tomorrow." The music is typically adventurous, melodic in its own way, yet still pretty futuristic, even if (compared with other releases) the set as a whole is not all that essential. —*Scott Yanow*

Science Fiction / Sep. 9, 1971–Sep. 13, 1971 / Columbia ✦✦✦
This LP has quite a bit of variety and finds altoist Ornette Coleman joined by most of his alumni. Three pieces feature a reunion of his original quartet with trumpeter Don Cherry, bassist Charlie Haden and drummer Billy Higgins; three others match Coleman with trumpeter Bobby Bradford, Dewey Redman on tenor, Haden and drummer Ed Blackwell; and the remaining three pieces utilize either Indian vocalist Asha Puthli or poet David Henderson. The generally dissonant and still radical music will take several listens to absorb, but it is worth the effort. —*Scott Yanow*

Skies of America / May 1972 / Columbia ✦✦

Broken Shadows / Sep. 1972 / Columbia ✦✦✦
This LP contains eight selections taken from Ornette Coleman's three-year period with Columbia that were previously unreleased. Cut prior to Coleman's formation of Prime Time, these performances serve as an unintentional retrospective of his career up to that point. Not that any of the original compositions (all by Coleman) had ever been recorded before, but such alumni as trumpeters Don Cherry and Bobby Bradford, tenor saxophonist Dewey Redman, bassist Charlie Haden, and drummers Ed Blackwell and Billy Higgins appear on most of the selections in one combination or another (and all of them are on two septet selections). In addition, a pair of numbers ("Good Girl Blues" and "Is It Forever") have Coleman, Redman, Haden and Blackwell joined by guitarist Jim Hall, pianist Cedar Walton, a singer and a

woodwind section; these look back a bit at Ornette's guest appearances on a John Lewis/Gunther Schuller album. —*Scott Yanow*

Dancing in Your Head / Jan. 1973+Dec. 1976 / A&M ✦✦
This CD reissue of an A&M album finds altoist Ornette Coleman interacting with musicians from Joujouka, Morocco, on the 4 1/2 minute "Midnight Sunrise" in 1973 and introducing his innovative group Prime Time in 1976 on the nearly 27-minute "Theme from a Symphony." While the playing time would be brief for an LP (and doesn't even fill up half of the CD's capacity), this disc's main fault is that the melody for "Theme from a Symphony" is very repetitive and ultimately annoying. Coleman stretches himself and his group (with Bern Nix and Charlie Ellerbee on guitars, bassist Rudy MacDaniel and drummer Roland Shannon Jackson) shows potential, but much of the music is simply unlistenable. There are many more significant and enjoyable Ornette Coleman sets currently available. —*Scott Yanow*

Body Meta / Dec. 19, 1976 / Artists House ✦✦✦
The short-lived but classy Artists House label debuted with this early Prime Time album by Ornette Coleman. At that point Coleman was utilizing guitarists Bern Nix and Charlie Ellerbee, bassist Jamaaladeen Tacuma and drummer Roland Shannon Jackson. The music (five Coleman originals) features dense ensembles with free funk rhythms. Although the musicians were supposed to be given an equal status, Ornette Coleman's alto always stands out above the complex and overlapping rhythms. This LP will be a hard one to find but will be worth the search for Coleman completists. —*Scott Yanow*

Soapsuds, Soapsuds / Jan. 30, 1977 / Artists House ✦✦✦
This unusual album found Coleman taking time off from his electric free funk group, Prime Time, to record acoustic duets with his longtime associate, bassist Charlie Haden. Coleman switches to tenor and trumpet for the challenging music, which includes three of his originals, Haden's "Human Being" and oddly enough, the theme from the TV show *Mary Hartman, Mary Hartman*. Haden, who had proved to be the perfect bassist for the original Ornette Coleman Quartet (who else could have filled his shoes in 1959?), is the equal of Coleman on this long out-of-print LP, inspiring the saxophonist to play near his peak. —*Scott Yanow*

Of Human Feelings / Apr. 25, 1979 / Antilles ✦✦✦
When one thinks of Ornette Coleman's innovative Prime Time Band, it is of crowded ensembles played by the altoist/leader, two guitars, two electric bassists and two drummers. Actually, Jamaaladeen Tacuma, who plays enough for two musicians, is the only bassist on this date, but guitarists Charlie Ellerbee and Bern Nix, along with drummers Denardo Coleman and Calvin Weston, keep the ensembles quite exciting. None of the eight Coleman originals (which includes a tune titled "What Is the Name of That Song?") would catch on, but in this context they serve as a fine platform for Coleman's distinctive horn and often witty and free (but oddly melodic) style. Hopefully, Antilles will eventually reissue this set on CD. —*Scott Yanow*

Opening the Caravan of Dreams / 1985 / Caravan Of Dreams ✦✦✦✦
Ornette Coleman's innovative Prime Time band is heard at the peak of its powers on this LP from the small Caravan of Dreams label. The altoist/leader is the main voice throughout the otherwise very democratic ensembles, which feature guitarists Bern Nix and Charles Ellerbee, bassists Jamaaladeen Tacuma and Albert MacDowell, and drummers Denardo Coleman and Sabir Kamal. The six originals, which include such titles as "To Know What to Know," "Harmolodic Bebop" and "Sex Spy," feature dense ensembles, equal doses of dissonance and wit, and more than their share of high energy. This was the leading "free funk" band of the 1980s, and this LP, which is worth a search by open-eared listeners, gives one a definitive look into the group's unusual music. —*Scott Yanow*

Prime Design Time Design / 1985 / Caravan Of Dreams ✦✦

In All Languages / Feb. 1987 / Caravan Of Dreams ✦✦✦✦
This is an unusual and very stimulating double album from the tiny Caravan of Dreams label. On the first LP, Ornette Coleman, on alto and tenor, has a reunion with his original quartet, which is comprised of trumpeter Don Cherry, bassist Charlie Haden and drummer Billy Higgins. The second album features Coleman's then-current edition of his "double quartet" Prime Time with guitarists Charlie Ellerbe and Bern Nix, electric bassists Jamaaladeen Tacuma and Al MacDowell, and drummers Denardo Coleman

and Calvin Weston. Five of the ten songs the quartet plays are also heard in versions by Prime Time, and the latter electric group almost makes the acoustic unit sound conservative in comparison. While the quartet displays subtle use of space and interplay between the musicians, Prime Time comes across as overcrowded and loud, but no less stimulating. Highly recommended to fans of Ornette Coleman. —*Scott Yanow*

Virgin Beauty / 1988 / Portrait ◆◆◆
This CD is often quite exciting, if a bit messy. Ornette Coleman (on alto, trumpet and violin) is heard with his "double quartet" Prime Time, which at the time was comprised of guitarists Bern Nix and Charlie Ellerbee, electric bassists Al MacDowell and Chris Walker, and drummers Denardo Coleman (who also plays some keyboards) and Calvin Weston. As if the ensembles are not dense and overcrowded enough, Jerry Garcia sits in on third guitar on three of the 11 Coleman originals. The music is frequently exciting, but will take several listens to absorb. —*Scott Yanow*

Tone Dialing / 1995 / Harmolodic/Verve ◆◆◆◆

Steve Coleman

b. Sep. 20, 1956, Chicago, IL
Alto Saxophone / Free Funk, Post-Bop
The leader of what he termed "M-Base" (short for macro-basic array of structured extemporization), Steve Coleman has a strikingly original alto style (very different from bebop) and his groups through the years have utilized funk rhythms and some nonjazz elements in an unpredictable and creative fashion. Coleman started on alto when he was 15 and played R&B in his early days. After moving to New York in 1978, Coleman played with the Thad Jones-Mel Lewis Orchestra, Cecil Taylor and Sam Rivers. After the mid-'80s he has usually been heard either with his group Five Elements or with such M-Base players as Greg Osby, Gary Thomas, Graham Haynes, Robin Eubanks, Geri Allen and Cassandra Wilson. Coleman has recorded sessions as a leader for JMT and Novus and been a sideman with David Murray, Dave Holland and Branford Marsalis. He is one of the most potentially significant saxophonists of the 1990s. —*Scott Yanow*

Motherland Pulse / Mar. 1985 / JMT ◆◆◆
This shows the jazz side of Coleman. With Geri Allen (p), Lonnie Plaxico (b) and Graham Haynes (tpt). —*Michael Erlewine*

On the Edge of Tomorrow / Jan. 1986+Feb. 1986 / JMT ◆◆◆◆
Modern soul music. This is real contemporary funk, most of it danceable. With Geri Allen (synth) and Cassandra Wilson (v). —*Michael Erlewine*

World Expansion / Nov. 1986 / JMT ◆◆◆
With Geri Allen (k) and Robin Eubanks (tbn). Not his jazziest release, but a lot of good clean funk. —*Michael Erlewine*

Strata Institute Cipher Syntax / 1986 / JMT ◆◆◆◆

Sine Die / Dec. 1987-Jan. 1988 / Pangaea ◆◆◆

Rhythm People (The Resurrection of Creative Black Civilization) / 1990 / Novus ◆◆◆◆
Steve Coleman & The Five Elements. *Rhythm People (The Resurrection of Creative Black Civilization)*. Funky, creative improvisations along the lines of Ornette Coleman's harmedelic music. With Dave Holland (b) and Robin Eubanks (tbn). —*Michael Erlewine*

● **Black Science** / 1991 / Novus ◆◆◆◆

Rhythm in Mind (The Carnegie Project) / Apr. 29, 1991 / Novus ◆◆◆
Erratic but frequently compelling release from Steve Coleman, whose M-base theories have been among the late '80s and early '90s' more controversial subjects. The album has bits and pieces of everything from free jazz to funk and pop, and Coleman's playing has enough straight jazz content to hold the interest of purists. —*Ron Wynn*

Drop Kick / 1992 / Novus ◆◆

The Tao of Mad Phat / May 6, 1993-May 23, 1993 / Novus ◆◆◆

Def Trance Beat (Modalities of Rhythm) / Jun. 14, 1994-Jun. 17, 1994 / Novus ◆◆◆

Johnny Coles

b. Jul. 3, 1926, Trenton, NJ
Trumpet / Hard Bop
A fine trumpeter with a distinctive cry, Johnny Coles has long had

the ability to say a lot with a few notes. He played with a few top R&B bands including Eddie "Cleanhead" Vinson (1948-51), Bull Moose Jackson (1952) and Earl Bostic (1955-56), was with James Moody's group (1956-58) and appeared on several Gil Evans records between 1958-64. Probably his most significant association was with the 1964 Charles Mingus Sextet that toured Europe. Also in the group were Eric Dolphy, Clifford Jordan, Jaki Byard and Dannie Richmond! Coles can be seen holding his own against those giants on a European television show (available on a Shanachie video) but he had to leave the tour halfway through due to a sudden illness. He also played with Herbie Hancock's Sextet (1968-69), Ray Charles (1969-71), Duke Ellington (1971-74), Art Blakey's Jazz Messengers (briefly in 1976), Dameronia, Mingus Dynasty and the Count Basie band when it was under Thad Jones' leadership (1985-86), but fame has managed to elude him. Coles led sessions through the years for Epic, Blue Note, Mainstream and most recently for Criss Cross. —*Scott Yanow*

● **Little Johnny** / Jul. 18, 1963-Aug. 9, 1963 / Blue Note ◆◆◆◆◆
The best of this hard-bop trumpeter was recorded with Leo Wright (as) and Joe Henderson (sax). —*David Szatmary*

New Morning / Dec. 19, 1982 / Criss Cross ◆◆◆
Excellent recent work by infrequently recorded trumpeter. —*David Szatmary*

Buddy Collette (William Marcell Collette)

b. Aug. 6, 1921, Los Angeles, CA
Clarinet, Flute, Tenor Saxophone / Cool
An important force in the Los Angeles jazz community, Buddy Collette was an early pioneer at playing jazz on the flute. Collette started on piano as a child and then gradually learned all of the woodwinds. He played with Les Hite in 1942, led a dance band while in the Navy during World War II and then freelanced in the L.A. area with such bands as the Stars of Swing (1946), Edgar Hayes, Louis Jordan, Benny Carter and Gerald Wilson (1949-50). An early teacher of Charles Mingus, Collette became the first Black musician to get a permanent spot in a West Coast studio band (1951-55). He gained his greatest recognition as an important member of the Chico Hamilton Quintet (1955-56) and he recorded several albums as a leader in the mid-to-late '50s for Contemporary. Otherwise he mostly stuck to the L.A. area, freelancing, working in the studios, playing in clubs, teaching and inspiring younger musicians. Although a fine tenor player and a good clarinetist, Collette's most distinctive voice is on flute; he recorded an album with one of his former students, the great James Newton (1989). In addition Collette participated in a reunion of the Chico Hamilton Quintet and recorded a two-disc "talking record" for the Issues label in 1994 in which he discussed some of what he had seen and experienced through the years. —*Scott Yanow*

Tanganyika / 1954 / VSOP ◆◆◆
This set, presented by disc jockey Sleepy Stein but actually led by multireedist Buddy Collette, slightly predates the Chico Hamilton Quintet and hints strongly at that chamber jazz group. Comprised of Collette, drummer Chico Hamilton, trumpeter John Anderson, pianist Gerald Wiggins, guitarist Jimmy Hall and bassist Curtis Counce—if one substitutes cellist Fred Katz for Anderson and Wiggins and changes the bassist, the result is the Chico Hamilton Quintet of 1955! The music is mostly group originals (five by Collette) and is an excellent example of cool jazz. Happily, VSOP has reissued this worthy recording from the obscure DIG label on CD. —*Scott Yanow*

● **Man of Many Parts** / Feb. 13, 1956-Apr. 17, 1956 / Contemporary ◆◆◆◆◆
Compiled from three 1956 recording sessions—his first as a leader. —*Michael Erlewine*

Nice Day with Buddy Collette / Nov. 6, 1956-Feb. 18, 1957 / Original Jazz Classics ◆◆◆◆
A Nice Day is a nice recording for multireedist Buddy Collette who plays alto, clarinet, flute and tenor during the three sessions heard on the CD reissue. Five of the ten selections are Collette's originals and, although the title cut and "Fall Winds" (which was renamed "Desert Sands") are both better-known for the versions he recorded with the Chico Hamilton Quintet than for these renditions, the original runthroughs are also excellent. Collette is the main voice throughout this set of lightly swinging music, although he gets support from the fine rhythm sections (which

include either Don Friedman, Dick Shreve or Calvin Jackson on piano). Overall this set serves as a good all-around showcase for Buddy Collette's playing and writing talents. —*Scott Yanow*

Jazz Loves Paris / Jan. 24, 1958 / Original Jazz Classics ✦✦✦
Buddy Collette (switching between alto, tenor, flute and clarinet) performs ten songs associated with Paris on this 1958 session originally cut for Specialty. The CD reissue adds four alternate takes to what is still a brief program. Collette utilizes the tuba of Red Callender in some of the ensembles quite colorfully and there is solo space for trombonist Frank Rosolino, guitarist Howard Roberts and bassist Red Mitchell; Bill Douglass or Bill Richmond contribute tasteful support on drums. Such melodies as "I Love Paris," "La Vie En Rose," "C'est Si Bon" and the "Song from 'Moulin Rouge'" are given concise but swinging treatment on this likable date. —*Scott Yanow*

Buddy Collette's Swinging Shepherds / Mar. 5, 1958+Mar. 7, 1958 / EmArcy ✦✦✦

The Buddy Collette Quintet / 1962 / Studio West ✦✦✦
The fourth of four CDs released by Studio West, a subsidiary of VSOP Records, that is taken from previously unissued transcriptions made for the radio show "The Navy Swings" features the Buddy Collette Quintet, which in 1962 was comprised of the leader on flute, clarinet, tenor and alto, guitarist Al Viola, pianist Jack Wilson, bassist Jimmy Bond and drummer Bill Goodwin. As good as Collette (who contributed four melodic originals) plays on these very concise performances (all clocking in around three minutes or less), it is the six often-touching vocals of Irene Kral that particularly make this a recommended disc. Kral's versions of "The Meaning of the Blues," "Nobody Else but Me" and especially "Spring Can Really Hang You Up the Most" are quite definitive and memorable. —*Scott Yanow*

A Jazz Audio Biography / 1993-1994 / Issues ✦✦✦✦
This is an unusual double CD; a talking record. Throughout the 132 minutes, veteran reed player Buddy Collette, who has been part of the Los Angeles jazz scene since the mid-'40s, tells a bit about what he has seen and experienced through the years. Collette actually talks very little about himself, preferring to reminisce about his associates, including Charles Mingus (highlighted by the complete story behind Mingus' infamous Town Hall Concert and a touching interlude about the last time Collette visited the bassist), Charlie Parker (including Bird's explanation of the origin of his nickname), Paul Robeson, Josephine Baker, Eric Dolphy, the Central Avenue scene of the '40s and the long struggle to integrate the Los Angeles Musicians' Union and the studios in the 1950s. The only music heard are brief interludes by Collette on his horns between the spoken sections. The often-fascinating storytelling could have been twice as long. —*Scott Yanow*

Cal Collins

b. May 5, 1933, Medora, IN
Guitar / Bop, Swing
During his period on the Concord label, Cal Collins made a strong impression, although his decision to return to Cincinnati has given him a much lower profile during the past decade. After serving in the Army, he settled in Cincinnati in the 1950s, working in the studios and appearing in clubs locally. Collins was with Benny Goodman for three years in the early '70s at the same time as Scott Hamilton and Warren Vache. The guitarist signed with Concord and recorded often as a leader (six albums during 1978-81) and with Hamilton and Vache. Since returning to Cincinnati, Collins has recorded for Mopro and in 1990 was heard on a quartet date for Concord but has been somewhat forgotten considering his talent. —*Scott Yanow*

Milestones / Aug. 28, 1974 / PA/USA ✦✦✦
The debut album by guitarist Cal Collins, which introduced his brand of fluid, smooth swing-oriented playing. He worked with guitarist Kenny Poole and drummer Terry Moore on an album that had only five songs, but gave the threesome plenty of solo space. The title cut proved to be the album's high point. —*Ron Wynn*

Cincinnati to L.A. / Jan. 5, 1978 / Concord Jazz ✦✦✦✦
Good swing-tinged trio session, the second featuring guitarist Cal Collins as a leader, playing with pianist Monte Budwig and drummer Jake Hanna. The selections were mostly familiar standards, like "Willow Weep For Me" and "Easy Living." All were executed with a modicum of energy and showed the trio's harmonic expertise. —*Ron Wynn*

In San Francisco / Jul. 25, 1978 / Concord Jazz ✦✦✦
The third Collins album and second with pianist Monte Budwig and drummer Jeff Hamilton. There's little deviation from the style used in the previous release; they cover mostly standards, usually doing them in mid-tempo, with Collins' flowing, easy guitar setting the tone and Budwig and Hamilton filling in the spaces underneath or alongside. —*Ron Wynn*

Blues on My Mind / Apr. 1979 / Concord Jazz ✦✦✦✦
Restrained, nicely played swing-tinged late '70s quartet date led by guitarist Cal Collins. He's a fluid, tasteful stylist, not given to excess and leaning more toward light, sentimental solos than energetic or blues-oriented phrasing. He's backed by pianist Larry Vuckovich, bassist Bob Maize, and drummer Jeff Hamilton, who all approach the music the same way. —*Ron Wynn*

By Myself / Dec. 1979 / Concord Jazz ✦✦✦✦

Interplay / Aug. 1980 / Concord Jazz ✦✦✦

Cross Country / Apr. 1981 / Concord Jazz ✦✦✦
Flawless, although sometimes too detached, solo guitar from Collins. The album is designed to present various regional styles as interpreted by Collins. He covers Southwestern swing, West Coast blues, rockabilly (light), train songs, and East Coast mainstream, doing them all in a smooth, sometimes enticing manner. —*Ron Wynn*

● **Crack'd Rib** / Nov. 1983-Mar. 1984 / Mo Pro ✦✦✦✦✦
Finest hour for unsung guitarist with Steve Schmidt Trio. Thoroughly swinging date. —*Michael G. Nastos*

Ohio Style / Nov. 1990 / Concord Jazz ✦✦✦

Joyce Collins Quartet

Group, Piano, Vocals / Bop, Hard Bop
A fine pianist/vocalist based in the Los Angeles area who has also been a popular jazz educator, Joyce Collins was with the Frankie Carle band (1954) and with Oscar Pettiford (1955) before settling in Los Angeles. She worked regularly with Bob Cooper at the Lighthouse in the late '50s and recorded a trio album for Riverside in 1960. Collins toured Europe and Mexico with her trio, gigged with Benny Carter, recorded with Gene Estes Big Band (1969) and toured with Paul Horn in 1969 but has mostly worked locally including in the studios. She played and recorded with Bill Henderson and led record sessions for Discovery (1981) and Audiophile (1990). —*Scott Yanow*

Moment to Moment / Jan. 16, 1981 / Discovery ✦✦✦✦

● **Sweet Madness** / Apr. 9, 1990-Apr. 27, 1990 / Audiophile ✦✦✦✦✦

Lee Collins

b. Oct. 27, 1901, New Orleans, LA, **d.** Jul. 3, 1960, Chicago, IL
Trumpet / New Orleans Jazz
A talented early New Orleans trumpeter, Collins started out his career playing as a teenager in various brass bands including the Young Eagles, the Columbia Band and the Young Tuxedo Band. In 1924 Collins went to Chicago where he was Louis Armstrong's replacement with King Oliver; he also recorded with Jelly Roll Morton. He returned to New Orleans and cut four brilliant sides with the Jones-Collins Astoria Hot Eight in 1929, played briefly in 1930 with Luis Russell in New York and then went back to Chicago. Throughout the 1930s and '40s Collins often accompanied blues singers and was a regular fixture in Chicago clubs. After touring Europe with Mezz Mezzrow in 1951 and 1954, he became ill and had to retire. His autobiography (*Oh Didn't He Ramble*) is filled with priceless stories about the early days of New Orleans jazz. —*Scott Yanow*

Alice Coltrane

b. Aug. 27, 1937, Detroit, MI
Organ, Piano, Harp / Avant-Garde, Free Jazz
Alice Coltrane was a good hard bop pianist with Terry Gibbs, who subsequently altered her style, and became a McCoy Tyner follower when she joined John Coltrane's band in the late '60s. She replaced Tyner in 1966, a move of epic proportions. She added colors and textures to the expansive, constantly shifting wave of sound generated by Coltrane, Pharoah Sanders and Rashied Ali. Alice Coltrane's harp playing, with its rippling, ethereal impact and her swirling organ solos heard on later albums were often more striking than her piano solos. She studied classical music and jazz as a child, playing in church groups. Coltrane worked in

the bands of Kenny Burrell, Johnny Griffin, Lucky Thompson and Yusef Lateef. During the early '60s, while working and recording with Terry Gibbs, she met John Coltrane. They married in 1965, and a year later she was in the group. After his death, Alice Coltrane led various bands, playing with Sanders, Archie Shepp, Joe Henderson, Frank Lowe and Carlos Ward, as well as Cecil McBee, Jimmy Garrison, Ben Riley and Roy Haynes. Her early '70s albums blended strings, Asian and Eastern melodies, rhythms, instrumentation and influences, plus free jazz elements. Alice Coltrane moved to California in the early '70s. She formed the Vedantic Center in 1975, a retreat for the study of Eastern/Asian religions. Since the 1978 album *Transfiguration* Coltrane's seldom performed, although she did play with a quartet including her sons in a 1987 tribute to John Coltrane at the Cathedral of St. John the Divine in New York. Alice Coltrane has only a couple of selections available on CD, but can also be heard on many late period John Coltrane reissues. *—Ron Wynn*

Monastic Trio / Jan. 29, 1968 / Impulse! ✦✦✦

● **Ptah the El Daoud** / Jan. 26, 1970 / Impulse! ✦✦✦✦✦
After John Coltrane's death in 1967, his widow Alice Coltrane recorded a few albums and then dropped out of the jazz scene to raise a family and become much more involved in her religious life. This album was arguably her finest post-1967 recording. Playing piano and harp in a quintet with the tenors of Pharoah Sanders and Joe Henderson, bassist Ron Carter and drummer Ben Riley, Coltrane stretches out on four of her compositions, sounding both soulful and spiritual. She had grown as a pianist during the past three years and it is a pity that she did not continue after this session on a full-time basis. *—Scott Yanow*

Journey in Satchidananda / Jul. 4, 1970+Nov. 8, 1970 / MCA ✦✦✦
Harp and strings with jazz and Indian influences. Extraordinarily beautiful. *—Michael G. Nastos*

Transfiguration / Apr. 16, 1978 / Warner Brothers ✦✦✦

John Coltrane
b. Sep. 23, 1926, Hamlet, NC, d. Jul. 17, 1967, New York, NY
Soprano Saxophone, Tenor Saxophone, Leader, Composer / Hard Bop, Avant-Garde, Free Jazz
The most influential jazz musician of the past 35 years (only Miles Davis comes close), one of the greatest saxophonists of all time and a remarkable innovator, John Coltrane certainly made his impact on jazz!

Unlike most musicians, Coltrane's style changed gradually but steadily over time. His career can be divided into at least five periods: Early days (1947-54), searching stylist (1955-56), sheets of sound (1957-59), the classic quartet (1960-64) and avant-garde (1965-67). Originally an altoist, he played in a Navy band during his period in the military, recording four privately issued songs in 1946. He settled in Philadelphia and then toured with King Kolax (1946-47), switched to tenor when he played with Eddie "Cleanhead" Vinson (1947-48), joined the Dizzy Gillespie big band (1948-49) and was with Dizzy's sextet (1950-51). Radio broadcasts from the latter association find Coltrane sounding heavily influenced by Dexter Gordon and hinting slightly at his future sound. He followed that gig with periods spent with the groups of Gay Crosse (1952), Earl Bostic (1952), Johnny Hodges (1953-54) and in Philadelphia for a few weeks with Jimmy Smith (1955).

The John Coltrane story really starts with his joining the Miles Davis Quintet in 1955. At first some observers wondered what Miles saw in the 28-year-old tenor who had an unusual sound and whose ideas sometimes stretched beyond his technique. However Davis was a masterful talent scout who could always hear potential greatness. Coltrane improved month by month and by 1956 was competing with Sonny Rollins as the top young tenor; he even battled him to a draw on their recording of "Tenor Madness." Coltrane (along with Red Garland, Paul Chambers and Philly Joe Jones) formed an important part of the classic Miles Davis Quintet, recording with Miles for Prestige and Columbia during 1955-56. In addition 'Trane was starting to be featured on many of Prestige's jam-session-oriented albums.

1957 was the key year in John Coltrane's career. Fired by Miles Davis due to his heroin addiction, Coltrane permanently kicked the habit. He spent several months playing with Thelonious Monk's Quartet, a mutually beneficial association that gave Monk long-overdue acclaim and greatly accelerated the tenor's growth.

His playing became even more adventurous than it had been, he recorded *Blue Train* (his first great album as a leader) and, when he rejoined Miles Davis in early 1958, Coltrane was unquestionably the most important tenor in jazz. During his next two years with Davis, 'Trane (whose style had been accurately dubbed "sheets of sound" by critic Ira Gitler) really took the chordal improvisation of bop to the breaking point, playing groups of notes with extreme speed and really tearing into the music. In addition to being one of the stars of Davis' recordings (including *Milestones* and *Kind of Blue*), Coltrane signed a contract with Atlantic and began to record classics of his own; "Giant Steps" (with its very complex chord structure) and "Naima" were among the many highlights.

By 1960 John Coltrane was long overdue to be a leader and Miles Davis reluctantly let him go. 'Trane's direction was changing from utilizing as many chords as possible (it would be difficult to get any more extreme in that direction) to playing passionately over one or two-chord vamps. He hired pianist McCoy Tyner, drummer Elvin Jones and went through several bassists (Steve Davis, Art Davis, Reggie Workman) before settling on Jimmy Garrison in late 1961. The first artist signed to the new Impulse! label, Coltrane was given complete freedom to record what he wanted. He had recently begun doubling on soprano, bringing an entirely new sound and approach to an instrument previously associated with the Dixieland of Sidney Bechet (although Steve Lacy had already started specializing on it) and Coltrane's 1960 Atlantic recording of "My Favorite Things" became a sort of theme song that he revisited on a nightly basis.

John Coltrane continued to evolve during 1961-64. He added Eric Dolphy as part of his group for a period and recorded extensively at the Village Vanguard in late 1961; the lengthy explorations were branded by conservative critics as "anti-jazz." Partly to counter their stereotyping (and short memories), 'Trane recorded with Duke Ellington in a quartet, a ballad program and a collaboration with singer Johnny Hartman; his playing throughout was quite beautiful. But live in concert his solos (which could be 45 minutes in length) were always intense and continually searching. He utilized such songs as "Impressions" (which used the same two-chord framework as Miles Davis' "So What" and "Afro Blue" for long workouts and took stunning cadenzas on the ballad "I Want to Talk About You." In addition to the Impulse! recordings, European radio broadcasts have since been released that show Coltrane's progress and consistency. And in December 1964 he displayed his vast interest in Eastern religion by recording the very popular *A Love Supreme*.

In 1965 it all began to change. Influenced and inspired by the intense and atonal flights of Albert Ayler, Archie Shepp and Pharoah Sanders, Coltrane's music dropped most of the melodies and essentially became passionate sound explorations. *Ascension* from mid-year featured six additional horns (plus a second bassist) added to the quartet for almost totally free improvisations. Fast themes (such as "One Down, One Up" and "Sun Ship") were quickly disposed of on the way to waves of sound. Coltrane began to use Pharoah Sanders in his group to raise the intensity level even more and when he hired Rashied Ali as second drummer, it eventually caused McCoy Tyner (who said he could no longer hear himself) and Elvin Jones to depart.

In 1966 Coltrane had a quintet consisting of his wife Alice on piano, Sanders, Ali and the lone holdover Jimmy Garrison. After a triumphant visit to Japan, Coltrane's health began to fail. Although the cause of his death on July 17, 1967 was listed as liver cancer, in reality it was probably overwork. Coltrane used to practice ten to twelve hours a day and when he had a job (which featured marathon solos), he would often spend his breaks practicing in his dressing room! It was only through such singlemindedness that he could reach such a phenomenal technical level, but the net result was his premature death.

Virtually every recording that John Coltrane made throughout his career is currently available on CD, quite a few books about him have been written and a video (*The Coltrane Legacy*) gives today's jazz followers an opportunity to see him performing in a pair of half-hour television shows. Since Coltrane's passing no other giant has dominated jazz on the same level. In fact many other saxophonists have built their entire careers on exploring music from just one of John Coltrane's periods! *—Scott Yanow*

The Last Giant: Anthology / 1946-1967/ Rhino ✦✦
This deluxe two-CD set is a major disappointment. It contains a few revelations (a brief 1946 recording of "Hot House" featuring

a 20-year-old Coltrane, an aircheck with Dizzy Gillespie and a rare side by Gay Crosse's Good Humor Six in 1952) but mostly repackages familiar material and includes nothing from Coltrane's very important years with Impulse. Why weren't all four of the 1946 sides included and why are only the first 90 seconds heard from Coltrane's final performance before it fades out? The accompanying booklet is quite attractive but this set (which will greatly frustrate completists) only gives an incomplete picture of the great saxophonist. —*Scott Yanow*

Coltrane 1951 / Jan. 13, 1951 / Oberon ✦✦✦✦
It is unusual to give such a high rating to what is essentially a bootleg LP of radio broadcasts, but much of the music on this set is extraordinary. John Coltrane is heard as a featured solost with Dizzy Gillespie's Sextet (which also includes vibraphonist Milt Jackson, pianist Jimmy Foreman, bassist Percy Heath and drummer Art Blakey) four years before he joined Miles Davis. Gillespie has several brilliant trumpet solos ("Good Bait" is quite memorable) and this LP allows one to hear the early influence that Dexter Gordon had on the young Coltrane. It's difficult to find but is well worth searching for. —*Scott Yanow*

First Broadcasts, Vol. 2 / Jan. 13, 1951 / Oberon ✦✦✦✦
The second LP of Dizzy Gillespie broadcasts from early 1951 once again liberally features John Coltrane at the age of 24, four years before he first started recording with Miles Davis. Although Gillespie is clearly the star (he is often in brilliant form), it is fascinating to hear Coltrane this early in his development, sounding like a mixture of Dexter Gordon and Lester Young. This bootlegish set will be hard to find and deserves to be reissued with its counterpart on CD. —*Scot Yanow*

High Step / Apr. 20, 1955 / Blue Note ✦✦✦
Bassist Paul Chambers gets co-billing on this two-LP set, but the main reason to acquire these three sessions is to hear Coltrane during a period when he was just beginning to develop his unique sound. Trane is well featured on six selections in a quartet with Chambers, pianist Kenny Drew and drummer Philly Joe Jones, heard during four numbers with a sextet that includes trumpeter Donald Byrd and on three cuts (two of which were previously unknown until the release of this two-fer) from April 1955 in a group with trombonist Curtis Fuller and baritonist Pepper Adams. Overall the music is not essential but is consistently excellent, fine examples of early hard bop from some of its top young players. —*Scott Yanow*

☆ **John Coltrane: The Prestige Recordings** / May 7, 1956–1958 / Prestige ✦✦✦✦✦
During 1956–58 Coltrane participated in 27 recording sessions for the Prestige label (not counting his three dates with the Miles Davis Quintet), both as a leader and as a sideman. Although these recordings are not as significant on a whole as Coltrane's later Impulse! albums, there are many gems among the jam sessions and all of the music (except The Davis sessions) has been released in its entirety on this somewhat remarkable 16-CD set. Coltrane and a constantly changing all-star cast perform such classics as "Tenor Madness" (his one-time meeting on records with Sonny Rollins), "On a Misty Night," "While My Lady Sleeps," "Like Someone in Love," "Black Pearls" and "Stardust" among many others. This expensive box may not be for all jazz collections, but any true fan of John Coltrane will have to acquire it. —*Scott Yanow*

Tenor Conclave / Sep. 7, 1956 / Original Jazz Classics ✦✦✦
On a Misty Night / Sep. 7, 1956–Oct. 26, 1956 / Prestige ✦✦✦✦
This two-LP set combines together two very different sessions. John Coltrane is just one of four tenor saxophonists (along with Hank Mobley, Zoot Sims and Al Cohn) heard on the four lengthy jam session selections that comprise the first date, while the other one showcases Trane in a quartet with pianist/composer Tadd Dameron (who wrote all six of the songs they perform), bassist John Simmons and drummer Philly Joe Jones. The latter date, with such highpoints as "On a Misty Night," "Mating Call" and "Soultrane," was one of Coltrane's very best early records. —*Scott Yanow*

Interplay for 2 Trumpets and 2 Tenors / Mar. 22, 1957 / Original Jazz Classics ✦✦✦
Dakar / Mar. 22, 1957–Apr. 20, 1957 / Prestige ✦✦✦
On this two-LP set, a pair of his lesser-known Prestige sessions are combined. The great tenor, whose sound was developing month by month during 1957, is heard in an unusual sextet with the bari-

tones of Cecil Payne and Pepper Adams and also in an octet with fellow-tenor Bobby Jaspar and the trumpets of Idrees Sulieman and Webster Young. What these sessions have in common is the emphasis on new compositions, including five from pianist Mal Waldron (highlighted by the original version of "Soul Eyes"), three by Teddy Charles and two from Pepper Adams in addition to Jimmy Heath's "C.T.A." —*Scott Yanow*

John Coltrane with Kenny Burrell / 1957 / Prestige ✦✦✦
Tenor saxophonist John Coltrane and guitarist Kenny Burrell are the alleged co-leaders of the two sessions included on this two-LP set but actually the second date (originally titled *The Cats*) was really under pianist Tommy Flanagan's direction; in fact Flanagan contributed four of the five compositions. Throughout, though, Coltrane is really the most significant soloist, whether on a brief duet with Burrell ("Why Was I Born"), in a quintet or (with the addition of trumpeter Idrees Sulieman) a sextet. —*Scott Yanow*

Wheelin' / Apr. 19, 1957–Sep. 20, 1957 / Prestige ✦✦✦
This two-fer from the excellent Prestige series of two-LP sets features Coltrane at a pair of jam-session-type settings in 1957. He is heard along with fellow tenor Paul Quinichette and Frank Wess on flute and tenor on two long versions apiece of "Wheelin'" and "Dealin'" in addition to a fine rendition of "Things Ain't What They Used to Be" and a 15-minute version of "Robbins' Nest." In addition, there are two numbers from a sextet session with trumpeter Bill Hardman and altoist Jackie McLean. Overall the music is not all that essential (since there are so many other Coltrane recordings available) but is quite enjoyable on its own terms and worth picking up. —*Scott Yanow*

Bahia / May 17, 1957–Dec. 26, 1958 / Prestige ✦✦✦
This two–LP set matches together the very different-sounding tenors of John Coltrane and Paul Quinichette in a jam-session type setting from 1957 (although three of the five songs were actually composed by pianist Mal Waldron) in addition to Coltrane's final Prestige date, which also has appearances by the trumpeters Freddie Hubbard (on "Then I'll Be Tired of You") and an uncredited Wilbur Harden ("Something I Dreamed Last Night"). This is nice if not overly memorable music. —*Scott Yanow*

First Trane / May 31, 1957 / Prestige ✦✦✦✦
More Lasting Than Bronze / May 31, 1957 / Prestige ✦✦✦✦✦
Of the ten double LPs of John Coltrane's recordings reissued by Prestige, this is the one to get. All but one selection dates from 1957 and nearly every number is a gem including three performances ("Like Someone in Love," "I Love You" and "Trane's Slo Blues") on which the great tenor is backed by just bass and drums, a lengthy version of "Lush Life" with trumpeter Donald Byrd, three tunes with a trio led by pianist Red Garland and four other songs (including the very memorable "While My Lady Sleeps") with a sextet. Coltrane is in inspired form on virtually every track. This music has since been reissued on CD in the massive box *The Prestige Recordings*, but for those with a tight budget and the good luck to find this two-fer, the set is highly recommended, for it contains the cream. —*Scott Yanow*

Lush Life / Aug. 16, 1957 / Original Jazz Classics ✦✦✦✦
Fine session in which Coltrane stripped away his usual surrounding sound and recorded in a trio format. He's backed only by bassist Earl May and drummer Art Taylor, working in a pianoless format championed by Sonny Rollins. The extra space seems to benefit him, as his solos on these cuts are emphatic and exuberant. —*Ron Wynn*

Rain or Shine / Aug. 16, 1957 / Prestige ✦✦✦
This particular two-fer (mostly from 1958) contains two alternate takes of "Trane's Slo Blues," two numbers with trumpeter Donald Byrd that emphasize Coltrane's "sheets of sound" approach and five selections that feature Coltrane's tenor with pianist Red Garland in a quartet. Excellent music from Trane's hard bop years will fill some gaps among Coltrane collectors. —*Scott Yanow*

The Last Trane / Aug. 16, 1957–Mar. 26, 1958 / Original Jazz Classics ✦✦✦
Traneing In / Aug. 23, 1957 / Original Jazz Classics ✦✦✦
John Coltrane / Aug. 23, 1957+Feb. 7, 1958 / Prestige ✦✦✦
This two-LP set reissues the full contents of the earlier albums *Traneing In* and *Soultrane*. In both cases tenor saxophonist John Coltrane was joined by pianist Red Garland, bassist Paul Chambers and drummer Art Taylor. Highpoints include "Traneing In," "You Leave Me Breathless," Coltrane's first version of "I Want

to Talk About You" and a lengthy "Good Bait." It's excellent advanced hard bop music, although 'Trane's most significant work was still in the future. —*Scott Yanow*

★ **Blue Train** / Sep. 15, 1957 / Blue Note ✦✦✦✦✦
A landmark album—stunning. This is Coltrane's only Blue Note recording as a leader, and he never made a better album in this particular hard-bop style. A must-hear for all jazz fans, Blue Train includes Coltrane's most impressive early composition, "Moment's Notice." With outstanding performances from sidemen Lee Morgan (tpt), Curtis Fuller (tb), and Kenny Drew (p). —*Michael Erlewine*

The John Coltrane/Ray Draper Quintet / Dec. 20, 1957 / Prestige ✦✦✦
When one thinks of modern jazz instruments, the tuba does not come immediately to mind, but Ray Draper performs well on this quintet session with John Coltrane and a standard rhythm section. Draper's three compositions (along with three jazz standards) comprise this interesting if not essential hard bop session; Coltrane is in fine form throughout. —*Scott Yanow*

Wheelin' and Dealin' / 1957 / Original Jazz Classics ✦✦✦

Black Pearls / Jan. 10, 1958–May 23, 1958 / Prestige ✦✦✦✦
Four of the six performances on this two-LP set are over ten minutes long, giving tenor saxophonist John Coltrane (heard at the peak of his "sheets of sound" period), trumpeter Donald Byrd, pianist Red Garland, bassist Paul Chambers and drummer Art Taylor plenty of space in which to stretch out. 'Trane takes some miraculous solos (by 1958 he was the leading tenor saxophonist in jazz and already long on his way to becoming a giant), sounding ten years ahead of his sidemen. The young trumpeter Freddie Hubbard makes an appearance on "Do I Love You Because You're Beautiful?" and this two-fer also finds Coltrane for the first time playing a McCoy Tyner composition ("The Believer"), two years before Tyner joined his Quartet. —*Scott Yanow*

The Believer / Jan. 10, 1958–Dec. 26, 1958 / Prestige ✦✦✦

Soultrane / Feb. 7, 1958 / Prestige ✦✦✦✦
Coltrane works with the Red Garland trio, a busy unit during this period. He tackles these standards with a quiet confidence, sometimes extending his solos, other times merely expanding the original melody. Garland was an excellent soloist on standards and ballads, while Paul Chambers on bass and drummer Art Taylor provided their own sterling counterpoint. —*Ron Wynn*

Countdown / Mar. 13, 1958 / Savoy ✦✦
This two-LP set is strictly for collectors for, in addition to six competent but not overly original compositions by the obscure fluegelhornist Wilbur Harden, there are three lengthy alternate takes. The previously unreleased title cut (which is heard in two versions) has no relation to John Coltrane's "Countdown" from his *Giant Steps* album. The music, featuring John Coltrane on tenor, Harden and a fine rhythm section (pianist Tommy Flanagan, bassist Doug Watkins and drummer Louis Hayes), is reasonably enjoyable but not all that memorable; just another hard-bop jam session from the 1950s. —*Scott Yanow*

Settin' the Pace / Mar. 26, 1958 / Original Jazz Classics ✦✦✦

Dial Africa / May 13, 1958–Jun. 24, 1958 / Savoy ✦✦✦
For this sextet date with fluegelhornist Wilbur Harden and trombonist Curtis Fuller (which is taken from the same sessions as *Gold Coast*), Coltrane performs four Harden originals (including two versions of "B.J.") and the standard "Once in a While." The music is excellent but much more conservative than most of 'Trane's recordings from this era. This LP is worth picking up but is not essential. —*Scott Yanow*

Gold Coast / May 13, 1958–Jun. 24, 1958 / Savoy ✦✦✦
John Coltrane's Savoy recordings with fluegelhornist Wilbur Harden are enjoyable but not particularly innovative. This LP contains "Tanganyika Strut," "Gold Coast" and alternate takes of "Dial Africa" and "B.J." Despite all of the emphasis on Africa in the song titles, the music is essentially American bebop featuring Coltrane, Harden and trombonist Curtis Fuller. Harden and Fuller contributed two originals apiece. This album is a companion of *Dial Africa*. —*Scott Yanow*

Standard Coltrane / Jul. 11, 1958 / Original Jazz Classics ✦✦✦

The Stardust Session / Jul. 11, 1958+Dec. 26, 1958 / Prestige ✦✦✦✦
This double LP completes John Coltrane's long series of appearances on Prestige sessions from the 1950s. Originally these eight

standards (which include the title cut, "Invitation," "My Ideal" and "I'll Get By") were scattered on three separate LPs even though they all took place on the same day. With strong support from the rhythm section (pianist Red Garland, bassist Paul Chambers and drummer Jimmy Cobb) and good solos from fluegelhornist Wilbur Harden, Coltrane is heard near the end of his "sheets of sound" period, perfecting his distinctive sound and taking colorful and aggressive solos. —*Scott Yanow*

Coltrane Time / Oct. 13, 1958 / Blue Note ✦✦✦
This is a most unusual CD due to the inclusion of Cecil Taylor on piano. Although Taylor and John Coltrane got along well, trumpeter Kenny Dorham (who is also on this quintet date) hated the avant-garde pianist's playing and was clearly bothered by Taylor's dissonant comping behind his solos. With bassist Chuck Israels and drummer Louis Hayes doing their best to ignore the discord, the group manages to perform two blues and two standards with Dorham playing strictly bop, Taylor coming up with fairly free abstractions and Coltrane sounding somewhere in between. The results are unintentionally fascinating. —*Scott Yanow*

Like Sonny / Nov. 1958 / Roulette ✦✦✦
This Roulette CD combines two unrelated sessions. Coltrane is heard in a quintet with the tuba player Ray Draper (their second album together) playing five standards (including "Doxy" and "Oleo") and Draper's "Essii's Dance." The 1960 performances are more significant for they are the earliest recorded collaborations by Coltrane and pianist McCoy Tyner. Together with bassist Steve Davis and drummer Billy Higgins they perform "One and Four," "Like Sonny" and two takes of "Exotica," music that barely predates 'Trane's classic quartet and succeeds on its own terms. —*Scott Yanow*

The Coltrane Legacy / Jan. 15, 1959–May 25, 1961 / Atlantic ✦✦✦
When this LP was released in 1970, it debuted some valuable Coltrane recordings covering a two-year period. Three of the selections are alternates taken from his Atlantic album with vibraphonist Milt Jackson, "Original Untitled Ballad" (later titled "To Her Ladyship") is from the session that resulted in Coltrane's *Ole* album with Eric Dolphy and Freddie Hubbard, and the remaining two numbers ("262" and "Exotica") find 'Trane meeting up with both pianist McCoy Tyner and drummer Elvin Jones (along with bassist Steve Davis) on records for the first time. Historically significant music, it's generally quite enjoyable. —*Scott Yanow*

★ **Heavyweight Champion: The Complete Atlantic Recordings** / Jan. 15, 1959–May 25, 1961 / Rhino/Atlantic ✦✦✦✦✦
The Heavyweight Champion is a box set that lives up to its title. Collecting all of John Coltrane's Atlantic recordings, including a fair number of unreleased takes as well as an entire disc of alternate tracks and studio chatter, the seven-disc box set documents a pivotal moment in Coltrane's career, as he was moving from hard-bop and sweet standards to a more daring, experimental style of playing influenced by the avant-garde. Much of the music is hard-bop (*Giant Steps*) or lushly melodic (*My Favorite Things*), but the latter discs show the saxophonist coming to terms with the more experimental movements in jazz, as he performs with musicians like Ornette Coleman. The scope of this music is, quite simply, breathtaking—not only was Coltrane developing at a rapid speed, the resulting music encompasses nearly every element that made him a brilliant musician and it is beautiful. —*Stephen Thomas Erlewine*

Cannonball and Coltrane / Feb. 3, 1959 / Mercury ✦✦✦✦✦

★ **Giant Steps** / Apr. 1, 1959 / Atlantic ✦✦✦✦✦
This is one of John Coltrane's classic sets; in fact this CD reissue (which adds alternate takes to five of the seven original recordings) almost doubles one's pleasure. In "Giant Steps" Coltrane built a tongue-twister of chord changes (stretching bop to its logical breaking point) which he would soon abandon in favor of long drones on simpler patterns. Not only does this CD give one the two earliest versions of "Giant Steps" but also "Naima," "Cousin Mary," "Spiral," "Syeeda's Song Flute," the underrated but remarkable "Countdown" and "Mr. P.C." Recorded while Coltrane was still with Miles Davis' group, this CD (which mostly features pianist Tommy Flanagan, bassist Paul Chambers and drummer Art Taylor) made it obvious that Coltrane had something very important of his own to say and that he would need his own band in the future to fully express himself. —*Scott Yanow*

Alternate Takes / Apr. 1, 1959 / Atlantic ✦✦✦✦
This LP, released in the mid-'70s, gave listeners their first oppor-

tunity to hear alternate versions of eight John Coltrane recordings from 1959–60. The original versions of five of these songs (including "Giant Steps," "Naima" and "Countdown") were from the *Giant Steps* sessions, "Body and Soul" was from *Coltrane's Sound* and the other two selections were from *Coltrane Jazz.* It is always interesting to hear "new" versions of classic recordings. All of this music has since been reissued on CD (as is true of most Coltrane LPs). —*Scott Yanow*

Coltrane Jazz / Nov. 24, 1959–Dec. 2, 1959 / Atlantic ◆◆◆
This CD contains the original LP program plus alternate takes of "Like Sonny" and "I'll Wait and Pray." With the exception of "Village Blues" (which features Coltrane's 1960 Quartet) and the earlier alternate of "Like Sonny," this set features Coltrane in 1959 with the Miles Davis rhythm section of the time: pianist Wynton Kelly, bassist Paul Chambers and drummer Jimmy Cobb. "My Shining Hour" and "Harmonique" are among the highlights of this excellent release. —*Scott Yanow*

Avant Garde / Jun. 20, 1960–Jul. 8, 1960 / Atlantic ◆◆◆
This CD is a straight reissue of the original LP. Despite the title, it is actually a fairly relaxed and somewhat conservative session for these players. Tenor saxophonist John Coltrane (who on "The Blessing" makes his debut on soprano) works well with the sidemen of the Ornette Coleman Quartet (trumpeter Don Cherry, bassist Charlie Haden or Percy Heath and drummer Ed Blackwell) on three Coleman compositions (this version of "The Blessing" is a classic), Don Cherry's "Cherryco" and Thelonious Monk's "Bemsha Swing." It's an enjoyable set of early freebop. —*Scott Yanow*

Coltrane Plays the Blues / Oct. 24, 1960 / Atlantic ◆◆◆◆
Recorded during the same week as his original version of "My Favorite Things," this LP by John Coltrane features six blues-oriented originals (five by 'Trane) including "Blues to Bechet" and "Mr. Syms." The music is more melodic than usual, with Coltrane playing soprano on two of the six tracks; "Blues to You" is the best showcase for his intense tenor. —*Scott Yanow*

Coltrane's Sound / Oct. 24, 1960 / Atlantic ◆◆◆◆
Although one may not think of *Coltrane's Sound* as being one of John Coltrane's most famous recordings, when one looks at its contents it quickly becomes obvious that this set ranks near the top. This CD reissue contains such classic material as "Central Park West," "Equinox," a reharmonized (and influential) version of "Body and Soul," the underrated "Satellite," "Liberia" and an intense rendition of "The Night Has a Thousand Eyes." Also included on this reissue is an alternate version of "Body and Soul" and the lesser-known "262." Co-starring pianist McCoy Tyner, bassist Steve Davis and drummer Elvin Jones, this set is highly recommended. —*Scott Yanow*

★ **My Favorite Things** / Oct. 24, 1960–Oct. 26, 1960 / Atlantic ◆◆◆◆◆
This LP was very influential when it came out and remains a classic. The first full album by the classic John Coltrane Quartet (with pianist McCoy Tyner, drummer Elvin Jones and their bassist of the time, Steve Davis) consists of a fiery "Summertime," the lyrical "But Not for Me," a nice ballad for 'Trane's soprano on "Everytime We Say Goodbye" and most importantly, the lengthy "My Favorite Things." On the latter Coltrane, who had used a seemingly endless number of chords on the prior year's "Giant Steps," reduces the chords to a minimum and plays passionately over a repetitious vamp, creating startlingly new music. This set has since been reissued on CD and in one form or another is essential. —*Scott Yanow*

Complete Africa/Brass Sessions / May 23, 1961+Jun. 4, 1961 / Impulse! ◆◆◆◆
John Coltrane's first recordings for Impulse! are different than any of his later ones for they feature the saxophonist accompanied by large brass-heavy 14-17 piece groups. This two-CD set has all of the music which was originally released on *Africa/Brass,* the later *Africa/Brass Sessions-Volume Two* and *Trane's Modes.* In general the arrangements are essentially an expansion of the style and sound of the John Coltrane Quartet with much of the improvising ("Blues Minor" excepted) taking place over two-chord vamps. Eric Dolphy wrote all but a pair of the charts (there are one apiece from McCoy Tyner and Calvin Massey) and he based his orchestrations on the piano voicings of Tyner. The only soloists are Coltrane (on both tenor and soprano) and his regular quartet members; it is disappointing that Dolphy, Freddie Hubbard and

Booker Little are not really heard from. While Massey's "The Damned Don't Cry" falters and sounds under rehearsed, the three renditions of "Africa" are quite colorful. But since over half of the performance time is taken up by "Africa," this two-CD set is not for everyone! —*Scott Yanow*

From the Original Master Tapes / May 23, 1961–1962 / MCA ◆◆◆
This early CD sampler of John Coltrane's Impulse! years gives the personnel listing but leaves off the recording dates. All of the music ("Soul Eyes," "Song of the Underground Railroad," "Dear Lord," "Vilia," "India," "Spiritual" and "Big Nick") has been reissued again on CD, making this set of greatest interest to those listeners just beginning to explore the music of the great saxophonist; the emphasis here is the more melodic and conservative performances, although several classics are included. "Vilia" (which was originally released on an LP sampler) was formerly the rarest selection. —*Scott Yanow*

Ole Coltrane / May 25, 1961 / Atlantic ◆◆◆◆
One of John Coltrane's most interesting sessions for Atlantic was also his last before exclusively switching to Impulse. This CD, which contains the original three selections from the LP ("Ole," "Dahomey Dance" and "Aisha") in addition to one item from the same date that was not released until decades later ("To Her Ladyship"), features the great saxophonist leading an all-star group (Eric Dolphy on alto and flute, trumpeter Freddie Hubbard, pianist McCoy Tyner, bassists Reggie Workman and Art Davis and drummer Elvin Jones) on a variety of very interesting material. "Ole" is quite haunting and "Dahomey Dance" became a minor standard. The solos are more concise than is usual on a Coltrane session and this set is quite accessible even to listeners who prefer his earlier "sheets of sound" recordings. —*Scott Yanow*

Other Village Vanguard Tapes / Nov. 1, 1961–Nov. 5, 1961 / Impulse! ◆◆◆
This double LP augments the original *Live at the Village Vanguard* album with six more performances taken from John Coltrane's famous Nov. 1961 engagement. In addition to Coltrane on soprano and tenor, pianist McCoy Tyner and drummer Elvin Jones, the participants include both bassist Reggie Workman and his eventual replacement, Jimmy Garrison, and (for atmosphere) veteran Garvin Bushell on oboe and contrabassoon on two numbers and Ahmed Abdul-Malik added on oud for one. The music is comprised of "India," "Greensleeves," "Chasin' the Trane," two versions of "Spiritual" and a lengthy "Untitled Original." Throughout this two-fer the music is passionate, often intense and innovative with Coltrane reducing the number of chords down to a minimum in favor of drones and vamps. —*Scott Yanow*

Live at the Village Vanguard / Nov. 2, 1961–Nov. 3, 1961 / Impulse! ◆◆◆◆
It is surprising, considering how much additional material from John Coltrane's week at the Village Vanguard in Nov. 1961 has surfaced, that this CD reissue only includes the original LP program. However the music is consistently excellent with the moody "Spiritual" (which features Coltrane's soprano and Eric Dolphy's bass clarinet) living up to its title, 'Trane jamming happily on a beboppish "Softly as in a Morning Sunrise" and roaring on a marathon tenor solo during "Chasin' the Trane." This classic music hopefully will be released someday along with all of the other surviving performances in a larger set. —*Scott Yanow*

Newport '63 / Nov. 2, 1961–Jul. 7, 1963 / Impulse! ◆◆◆◆
Three of the four lengthy performances on this CD are taken from one of the John Coltrane Quartet's greatest performances: the 1963 Newport Jazz Festival. With pianist McCoy Tyner, bassist Jimmy Garrison and drummer Roy Haynes (filling in for an absent Elvin Jones), Coltrane performs what is arguably his greatest version of "My Favorite Things" along with memorable renditions of "Impressions" and "I Want to Talk About You." Two of those selections originally appeared on the LP *Selflessness* while "Impression" was included in a later collection. This set is rounded out by "Chasin' Another Trane," the only recording from 'Trane's famous Nov. 1961 engagement at the Village Vanguard that had Roy Haynes sitting in for Elvin Jones; altoist Eric Dolphy is also heard from on that heated selection. —*Scott Yanow*

Impressions / Nov. 5, 1961 / Impulse! ◆◆◆◆
This LP is a hodgepodge of memorable John Coltrane performances from the 1961–63 period. "India" and "Impressions" are

taken from 'Trane's famous Nov. 1961 engagement at the Village Vanguard; bass clarinetist Eric Dolphy is heard on the former while the latter features a marathon solo from Coltrane on tenor. Also included on this set are 1962's "Up 'Gainst the Wall" and the classic of the album, 1963's "After the Rain." — *Scott Yanow*

The Complete Paris Concerts / Nov. 18, 1961 / Magnetic ✦✦✦✦
John Coltrane collectors will want this double CD. Coltrane's 1961 Quintet (with Eric Dolphy on alto, bass clarinet and flute, pianist McCoy Tyner, bassist Reggie Workman and drummer Elvin Jones) is heard during two different concerts recorded the same night. This set gives us "Impressions" and two versions apiece of "I Want to Talk About You," "Blue Train" and "My Favorite Things"; none of the music was previously issued. The recording quality is good and the solos are quite passionate. — *Scott Yanow*

Live Trane / Nov. 22, 1961–Jul. 28, 1965 / BYG ✦✦✦✦
This Japanese three-LP box set from the German company BYG captures Coltrane at four separate European concerts from a four-year period. At a Stockholm concert from Nov. 22, 1961, Coltrane and his Quintet (with Eric Dolphy on alto, flute and bass clarinet, pianist McCoy Tyner, bassist Reggie Workman and drummer Elvin Jones) perform a 20-minute "My Favorite Things" and much more concise versions of "Naima," "Blue Train" and "Impressions." The classic Quartet (with Tyner, bassist Jimmy Garrison and Jones) interprets "I Want to Talk About You," "Traneing In," "Spiritual" and "Mr. P.C." at a Stockholm concert from Oct. 22, 1963, and the same group at concerts in Antibes and Paris on July 27 and 28, 1965 really tears into "Blue Valse," "Afro Blue," "Naima" and two versions of "Impressions." This hard-to-find set, even if the liner notes are in Japanese, is highly recommended to true John Coltrane fans, for these live recordings are often quite intense and dazzling, particularly the later performances. — *Scott Yanow*

Ballads / Dec. 21, 1961 / GRP/Impulse! ✦✦✦
Stung by criticism from conservative jazz critics, Coltrane decided to show his detractors that he had not forgotten how to embrace a melody; the problem is that on this brief set (reissued on CD by GRP in an attractive fold-out package) he never really gets away from the themes. While Trane (who sticks to tenor) plays quite pretty, pianist McCoy Tyner actually has the more interesting solos. Coltrane shows the tunes an excess of respect, making this outing with his classic quartet enjoyable as background music but lacking much passion. — *Scott Yanow*

The Gentle Side of John Coltrane / 1961–1964 / GRP ✦✦✦

Coltrane / Apr. 11, 1962–Jun. 29, 1962 / Impulse! ✦✦✦✦
John Coltrane and his classic Quartet (pianist McCoy Tyner, bassist Jimmy Garrison and drummer Elvin Jones) are in fine form for this 1962 studio LP. Highpoints include a passionate "Out of This World" (what did Johnny Mercer think of this version?) and a classic version of Mal Waldron's "Soul Eyes." The remainder of the program includes "The Inch Worm" and the two Coltrane compositions "Tunji" and "Miles' Mode." Not as intense as many of 'Trane's other albums, this is still a recommended and easily enjoyable set. — *Scott Yanow*

The Paris Concert / Nov. 17, 1962 / Original Jazz Classics ✦✦✦
This excellent CD by the classic John Coltrane Quartet (with pianist McCoy Tyner, bassist Jimmy Garrison and drummer Elvin Jones) is highlighted by a 26-minute version of "Mr. P.C." Also included on the album are "The Inch Worm" and the ballad "Every Time We Say Goodbye." Although the sound and passion of the group on this date will not surprise veteran listeners, it is always interesting to hear new variations of songs already definitively recorded in the studios. It's recommended to all true Coltrane fanatics. — *Scott Yanow*

The Complete 1962 Stockholm Concert, Vol. 1 / Nov. 19, 1962 / Magnetic ✦✦✦

The Complete 1962 Stockholm Concert, Vol. 2 / Nov. 19, 1962 / Magnetic ✦✦✦

Ev'rytime We Say Goodbye / Nov. 28, 1962 / Natasha ✦✦✦
Taken from a concert in Graz, Austria, this well-recorded outing by the classic John Coltrane Quartet features fresh versions of "The Inch Worm," "Everytime We Say Goodbye" and "Impressions." Although only containing 38 minutes of music, this CD has more than its share of passion and the Quartet really digs into the familiar material. — *Scott Yanow*

The Complete Graz Concert, Vol. 1 / Nov. 28, 1962 / Magnetic ✦✦✦

The Complete Graz Concert, Vol. 2 / Nov. 28, 1962 / Magnetic ✦✦✦

Bye Bye Blackbird / 1962 / Original Jazz Classics ✦✦✦
A straight reissue of the Pablo LP, this CD only contains 36 minutes of music but the quality is quite high. John Coltrane and his Quartet (pianist McCoy Tyner, bassist Jimmy Garrison and drummer Elvin Jones) perform extended versions of "Bye Bye Blackbird" and "Traneing In" that gradually build up to great intensity. Well-recorded, this European concert (of uncertain origin) is worth hearing, particularly by Coltrane collectors who already have his more essential recordings, although it does not quite live up to the label that producer Norman Granz gave it: "His Greatest Concert Performance!" — *Scott Yanow*

John Coltrane Quartet Live At The Half Note / Feb. 23, 1963–May 7, 1965 / Audiofidelity ✦✦✦
Despite the inaccurate information given on this three-LP box set (which states that all of the music was recorded at the Half Note in 1963; none of it actually was), these rare performances are quite fascinating. "I Want to Talk About You" and "One Up, One Down" actually originated from Birdland on Feb. 23, 1963, and, although the other six performances are from the Half Note, they date from March 19 ("Impressions" and "Chim Chim Cheree"), April 12 ("Untitled Original") and May 7 ("Brazilia," "Song of Praise" and "My Favorite Things") of 1965. Coltrane is in particularly fiery form on the later tracks and with four of the eight selections being over 19 minutes long, there is plenty of room for him to stretch out. It's recommended despite the erratic packaging but sure to be hard to find. — *Scott Yanow*

☆ **John Coltrane and Johnny Hartman** / Mar. 7, 1963 / GRP/Impulse! ✦✦✦✦✦
John Coltrane's matchup with singer Johnny Hartman, although quite unexpected, works extremely well. Hartman, who had not recorded since 1956, was in prime form on the six ballads and his versions of "Lush Life" and "My One and Only Love" have never been topped. Coltrane's playing throughout the session is beautiful, sympathetic and still explorative; he sticks exclusively to tenor on the date. At only a half-hour one wishes there were twice as much music but what is here is classic, essential for all jazz collections. — *Scott Yanow*

Dear Old Stockholm / Apr. 29, 1963 / Impulse! ✦✦✦
This CD contains five excellent performances by the John Coltrane Quartet from two occasions when drummer Roy Haynes filled in for Elvin Jones. A definitive "Dear Old Stockholm" and Coltrane's mournful ballad "After the Rain" are from Apr. 29, 1963, while the beautiful "Dear Lord" and two long and raging performances ("One Down, One Up" and "After the Crescent") date from May 26, 1965. Although Haynes had a different approach on the drums than Jones, he fit in perfectly with the group, stimulating Coltrane to play brilliantly throughout these two sessions. — *Scott Yanow*

Selflessness / Jul. 7, 1963 / Impulse! ✦✦✦
In the current CD reissue program run by GRP, this particular LP has been taken apart with its contents put on either *Newport '63* ("I Want to Know About You" and what is arguably the best version of "My Favorite Things") or *The Major Works of John Coltrane* (the atmospheric "Selflessness" from Oct. 1965). The realignment is logical but if one sees this LP at a reasonable price, it is still well worth acquiring, particularly for the passionate "My Favorite Things." — *Scott Yanow*

★ **Live at Birdland** / Oct. 8, 1963+Nov. 18, 1963 / Impulse! ✦✦✦✦✦
Arguably John Coltrane's finest all-around album, this LP (which has since been reissued on CD) has brilliant versions of "AfroBlue" and "I Want to Talk About You"; the second half of the latter features Coltrane on unaccompanied tenor tearing into the piece but never losing sight of the fact that it is a beautiful ballad. The remainder of this album ("Alabama," "The Promise" and "Your Lady") is almost at the same high level. It is highly recommended, either on LP or CD. — *Scott Yanow*

The European Tour / Oct. 22, 1963 / Pablo ✦✦✦✦
Norman Granz produced a couple of the John Coltrane Quartet's European tours, releasing some of their live performances years later. Although this LP states that these performances of "The Promise," "I Want to Talk About You," "Naima" and "Mr. P.C." are from Nov. 1962, they are actually taken from their Stockholm con-

cert of Oct. 22, 1963. Coltrane fans will find these new variations to be of great interest (even if they are not the definitive versions of any of these songs) since the solos vary greatly from the original recordings. —*Scott Yanow*

Afro Blue Impressions / Oct. 22, 1963–Oct. 26, 1963 / Pablo ◆◆◆◆
Taken from several European concerts (producer Norman Granz is vague about the exact dates but those listed are educated guesses), this double CD finds John Coltrane and his classic Quartet playing their standard repertoire of the period. The nine songs include "Chasin' the Trane," "My Favorite Things," "Afro Blue," "I Want to Talk About You," "Impressions" and "Naima." No new revelations occur but this is a strong all-around set of 'Trane near his peak. —*Scott Yanow*

Crescent / Apr. 27, 1964+Jun. 1, 1964 / Impulse! ◆◆◆
One of only two studio albums cut by the John Coltrane Quartet during 1964, *Crescent* is most notable for including five Coltrane compositions including the title cut, "Lonnie's Lament" and the swinging "Bessie's Blues." The music is excellent although not as fiery as the Quartet's live performances of the period. —*Scott Yanow*

★ **A Love Supreme** / Dec. 9, 1964 / Impulse! ◆◆◆◆◆
John Coltrane recorded more exciting albums than this one (which has been reissued on CD by GRP) but the highly influential *A Love Supreme* is the project that meant the most to him, his gift to God. In addition to the famous chanting of the title, Coltrane performs a couple of particularly memorable themes (it is surprising that "Resolution" did not become a standard) and the soloing is on a consistently high level. This recording (which also features pianist McCoy Tyner, bassist Jimmy Garrison and drummer Elvin Jones) closed the book on what could be considered 'Trane's most significant period, for he would begin to more fully explore atonality with the coming of 1965. —*Scott Yanow*

John Coltrane Quartet Plays ... / Feb. 18, 1965–May 17, 1965 / Impulse! ◆◆◆◆
1965 was one of the turning points in the career of John Coltrane. The great saxophonist, whose playing was always very explorative and searching, crossed the line into atonality during that year, playing very free improvisations (after stating quick throwaway themes) that were full of passion and fury. This particular studio album (the CD is a straight reissue of the original LP) has two standards (a stirring "Chim Chim Cheree" and "Nature Boy") along with two recent Coltrane originals ("Brazilia" and "Song of Praise"). Art Davis plays the second bass on "Nature Boy" but otherwise this set (a perfect introduction for listeners to Coltrane's last period) features the classic Quartet comprised of the leader, pianist McCoy Tyner, bassist Jimmy Garrison and drummer Elvin Jones. —*Scott Yanow*

Feelin' Good / Feb. 18, 1965–Sep. 22, 1965 / Impulse! ◆◆◆
This interesting double LP contains a variety of previously unissued performances by the classic John Coltrane Quartet in 1965, their most controversial (and final) year. Two of these selections ("Living Space" and "Joy") were originally issued posthumously by Alice Coltrane with strings and percussion overdubbed but here they are heard as they were originally played. In addition to those tracks, "Feelin' Good," an alternate version of "Nature Boy" and "My Favorite Things" (the latter recorded at the 1965 Newport Jazz Festival), this two-fer includes three unknown Coltrane compositions, only one of which ("Dusk-Dawn") actually has a title. It is most highly recommended to Coltrane collectors. —*Scott Yanow*

Transition / May 26, 1965–Jun. 10, 1965 / Impulse! ◆◆◆◆
The title of this CD (a straight reissue of the LP) fits perfectly, for Coltrane was certainly at an important transitional point in his career at the time. Although he was still utilizing the same Quartet that he had had for over three years (pianist McCoy Tyner, bassist Jimmy Garrison and drummer Elvin Jones) and his music had always been explorative, now he was taking his solos one step beyond into passionate atonality, usually over simple but explosive vamps. Other than the tender ballad "Welcome," most of this set is uncompromisingly intense; in fact the closing 9-minute "Vigil" is a fiery tenor-drums duet. The 21-minute "Suite," even with sections titled "Prayer And Meditation: Day" and "Affirmation," is not overly peaceful. It must have seemed clear, even at this early point, that McCoy Tyner and perhaps Elvin Jones would not be with the band much longer. —*Scott Yanow*

Kulu Se Mama / Jun. 16, 1965–Oct. 14, 1965 / Impulse! ◆◆
Ascension / Jun. 28, 1965 / Impulse! ◆◆◆◆
Coltrane's first album considered tonally "free." —*Michael Erlewine*

The Major Works of John Coltrane / Jun. 1965–Oct. 1965 / GRP ◆◆◆◆◆
New Thing at Newport / Jul. 2, 1965 / GRP ◆◆◆
Sun Ship / Aug. 26, 1965 / Impulse! ◆◆◆
Other than *First Meditations*, which was not released at the time, *Sun Ship* (reissued on CD by Impulse) was the final studio album by John Coltrane's classic quartet (with pianist McCoy Tyner, bassist Jimmy Garrison and drummer Elvin Jones) before Pharoah Sanders joined the band on second tenor. At this point in time, Coltrane was using very short repetitive themes as jumping off points for explosive improvisations, often centered around one chord and a very specific spiritual mood. Tyner sounds a bit conservative in comparison, but Jones keeps up with 'Trane's fire (especially on "Amen"). Even in the most intense sections (and much of this music is atonal), there is a logic and thoughtfulness about Coltrane's playing. —*Scott Yanow*

First Meditations / Sep. 2, 1965–1970 / GRP ◆◆◆
Recorded before *Meditations*, but released in 1970, reissued in 1978 and 1992. CD version has original version of "Joy." "Compassion" is a standout Coltrane anthem. —*Michael G. Nastos*

Live in Seattle / Sep. 30, 1965 / Impulse! ◆◆◆◆
This double CD features John Coltrane at a concert in Sept. 1965 with his expanded sextet (which included pianist McCoy Tyner, bassist Jimmy Garrison, drummer Elvin Jones, Pharoah Sanders on tenor and Donald Garrett doubling on bass clarinet and bass). Coltrane experts know that 1965 was the year that his music became quite atonal and, with the addition of Sanders, often very violent. This music, therefore, is not for fans of Coltrane's earlier sheets of sound period or for those who prefer jazz as melodic background music. The program from the original double LP (the nearly free "Cosmos," an intense workout on "Out of This World," a bass feature and the truly wild "Evolution") is augmented by previously unissued versions of "Body and Soul" and a 34-minute "Afro Blue" that is incomplete because the tape ran out. Throughout much of this set Coltrane plays some miraculous solos, Sanders consistently turns on the heat, Garrett makes the passionate ensembles a bit overcrowded, Tyner is barely audible, Garrison drones in the background and Jones struggles to make sense of it all. This is innovative and difficult music that makes today's young lions (not to mention the pop saxophonists) sound very old-fashioned in comparison. —*Scott Yanow*

Om / Oct. 1, 1965 / MCA ◆◆◆
Perhaps Coltrane's only major release of questionable quality, this was reportedly recorded on his first (and only) LSD trip. Featuring screechy playing and moaning vocals, this is for true believers and historical interest only. —*David Nelson McCarthy*

Meditations / Nov. 23, 1965 / MCA ◆◆◆◆◆
A perfect companion to *A Love Supreme*. As powerful and pure in spiritual content and intent. Long, extended, embellished passages in hymn-like prayer session. With Pharoah Sanders (ts), Elvin Jones (d), Rashied Ali (d), McCoy Tyner (p), Jimmy Garrison (b). —*Michael G. Nastos*

Live at the Village Vanguard Again! / May 28, 1966 / Impulse! ◆◆◆
Live in Japan / Jul. 11, 1966 / GRP/Impulse! ◆◆◆
A multi-disc set containing recordings Coltrane made in Japan late in his career. By this time, he and Pharoah Sanders were regularly engaging in shattering dialogues on alto sax as well as tenor. Alice Coltrane had replaced McCoy Tyner, and Rashied Ali was the drummer instead of Elvin Jones. This was animated, unrelenting, and experimental music, and these discs are not for the casual or new Coltrane listener. —*Ron Wynn*

Stellar Regions / Feb. 15, 1967 / Impulse! ◆◆◆◆
This is a major set, "new" music from John Coltrane that was recorded February 15, 196, (five months before his death), but not released for the first time until 1995. One of several "lost" sessions that were stored by Alice Coltrane for decades, only one selection ("Offering" which was on *Expression*) among the eight numbers and three alternates was ever out before. The music, although well worth releasing, offers no real hints as to what Coltrane might have been playing had he lived into the 1970s. The perfor-

Music Map

Composers

<table>
<tr><td valign="top">

Ragtime Composers
Scott Joplin
Joseph Lamb
James Scott
Tom Turpin

</td><td valign="top">

Major Contributors to Jazz's Modern Repertoire
Billy Strayhorn	Charlie Parker
Dizzy Gillespie	Thelonious Monk
Tadd Dameron	Gil Evans
Lennie Tristano	Gerry Mulligan
Shorty Rogers	Sonny Rollins
Horace Silver	Benny Golson
Kenny Dorham	Randy Weston
John Lewis	Thad Jones
Bobby Timmons	Johnny Mandel
Wayne Shorter	Tony Williams
Wynton Marsalis	Terence Blanchard
Pat Metheny	Antonio Carlos Jobim

</td></tr>
</table>

Pioneers
W.C. Handy
Jelly Roll Morton
James P. Johnson
Elmer Schoebel
Clarence Williams
Spencer Williams
Don Redman

Avant-Garde
Charles Mingus	Herbie Nichols
George Russell	Ornette Coleman
Carla Bley	Muhal Richard Abrams
Anthony Braxton	Julius Hemphill
Henry Threadgill	Maria Schneider
Bob Moses	

Classic Songwriters of the 1920s and 30s
Duke Ellington	Irving Berlin
George Gershwin	Jerome Kern
Harold Arlen	Cole Porter
Hoagy Carmichael	Richard Rodgers
Fats Waller	Edgar Sampson
Benny Carter	

Fusion
Joe Zawinul	Jaco Pastorius
Chick Corea	Herbie Hancock

mances by the quartet (with pianist Alice Coltrane, bassist Jimmy Garrison and drummer Rashied Ali) are briefer (2:48–8:54) than Coltrane's recordings of the previous year but that might have been due to the fact that this music was played in the studio (as opposed to the marathon live blowouts with Pharoah Sanders) or to Coltrane's worsening health. Actually 'Trane (who sticks here exclusively to tenor) is as powerful as usual, showing no compromise in his intense flights and indulging in sound explorations that are as free (but with purpose) as any he had ever done. Coltrane's true fans will want to go out of their way to acquire this intriguing CD. —*Scott Yanow*

Expression / Feb. 15, 1967–Mar. 1967 / Impulse! ✦✦✦✦
This music came from John Coltrane's final recording sessions, although no one at that time knew it. It was emblematic of his work in that era—unpredictable, experimental, restless, sometimes remarkable, sometimes more noteworthy for what was being attempted than presented. GRP's recently reissued CD includes a great bonus cut, the nearly 12-minute "Number One" with surging, raw Coltrane tenor contrasted by Pharoah Sanders' piccolo and flute. But while the new material was valuable, the compelling cut here remains "To Be," the 16-minute-plus Coltrane/Sanders dialogue on flutes and piccolo. It was the only time on record that Coltrane played flute (at least for any lengthy period), and his singing lines, blend of raspy and lyrical phrases and overall approach were as identifiable on that instrument as any of his saxes. —*Ron Wynn*

Interstellar Space / Feb. 22, 1967 / GRP ✦✦✦✦
Posthumously released, free-wheeling date by Coltrane with drummer Rashied Ali in a series of slashing, complementary and explosive duets. Coltrane was now playing more rhythms than anything else, having leaped beyond notions of chord changes, structure, and melody. Ali sometimes supported him, sometimes challenged him, and held things together as best he could. —*Ron Wynn*

Ravi Coltrane

b. Aug. 6, 1965, Huntington, NY
Soprano Saxophone / Post-Bop
The son of John and Alice Coltranc, Ravi was not even two years old when his father died. He was in his early 20s when he seriously started playing jazz and, although his father's music was a slight influence, Ravi Coltrane actually sounds closer to Branford Marsalis and Joe Henderson. He picked up valuable experience playing with Elvin Jones' band during 1991–93 and has since performed as a sideman with many top musicians including Geri Allen, Kenny Barron and Cindy Blackman. —*Scott Yanow*

Ken Colyer

b. Apr. 18, 1928, Great Yarmouth, Norfolk, England, d. Mar. 11, 1988, France
Cornet, Leader / New Orleans Jazz
Cornetist, trumpeter and guitarist Ken Colyer was among England's premier bandleaders and players. He was a self-taught player who in 1949 was a founding member of The Crane River Jazz Band. It made several recordings before disbanding in 1953. He worked with The Christie Brothers' Stompoers in 1951, and visited New Orleans while in the merchant Navy, playing with George Lewis and recording with Emiles Barnes and Albert Glenny in 1953. Colyer returned to England that same year, and led The Jazzmen, a band that included Chris Barber and Sunshine. Colyer began heading his own groups in 1954, while Barber took over The Jazzmen's reins. One Colyer skiffle band included Acker Bilk and Diz Disley. His most influential band in the mid-'50s with Ian Wheeler, Mac Duncan and Ray Foxley became the leading British revival group of the '50s. Its style was heavily influenced by the George Lewis and Bunk Johnson bands. Colyer continued heading groups through the '60s and '70s, despite suffering health problems. He played regularly at his club

Studio 51 in London and played on the film soundtrack *West 11*, which was partly set there. He also had a brief label in the '60s, KC Records. Colyer played with his group The All Star Jazzmen in the early '80s, and toured with Max Collie's "New Orleans Mardi Gras" show in 1986 and 1987. —*Ron Wynn*

● **Painting the Clouds with Sunshine** / Oct. 6, 1979 / Black Lion ✦✦✦

Colyer In Stockholm / Jun. 28, 1986 / Jazz Crusade ✦✦✦
This was Ken Colyer's final recording. By 1986 he no longer had his own regular group and his health was gradually declining (he would pass away less than two years later) but, when he was invited to play a jazz festival in Stockholm, the English trad trumpeter got along well musically and personally with the members of The Classic Jazz Band. A few months later he returned to Stockholm and privately taped one of their joint concerts. The balance of the instruments is a bit off with the horns generally low in the mix, but the music is quite listenable. Ken Colyer's sparse lead (mostly short notes) leaves a lot of space in the ensembles and, although clarinetist Goran Erikson and trombonist Jens Lindgren are fine, the most impressive voice is actually drummer Cacka Ekhe, whose colorful percussive sounds recall Baby Dodds. The pianoless sextet performs a variety of old standards and even if the music is not flawless and is occasionally rather aimless, New Orleans jazz fans should appreciate this historically significant music. —*Scott Yanow*

Eddie Condon (Albert Edwin Condon)

b. Nov. 16, 1905, Goodland, IN, **d.** Aug. 4, 1973, New York, NY
Leader, Guitar / Dixieland
A major propagandist for freewheeling Chicago jazz, an underrated rhythm guitarist and a talented wisecracker, Eddie Condon's main importance to jazz was not so much through his own playing as in his ability to gather together large groups of all-stars and produce exciting, spontaneous and very coherent music.

Condon started out playing banjo with Hollis Peavey's Jazz Bandits when he was 17, he worked with members of the famed Austin High School Gang in the 1920s and in 1927 he co-led (with Red McKenzie) the McKenzie-Condon Chicagoans on a record date that helped define Chicago jazz (and featured Jimmy McPartland, Jimmy Teschemacher, Joe Sullivan and Gene Krupa). After organizing some other record sessions, Condon switched to guitar, moved to New York in 1929, worked with Red Nichols' Five Pennies and Red McKenzie's Blue Blowers, and recorded in several settings including with Louis Armstrong (1929) and the Rhythm Makers (1932). During 1936-37 he co-led a band with Joe Marsala.

Although Condon had to an extent laid low since the beginning of the Depression, in 1938, with the opportunity to lead some sessions for the new Commodore label, he became a major name. Playing nightly at Nick's (1937-44), Condon utilized top musicians in racially mixed groups. He started a long series of exciting recordings (which really continued on several labels up until his death) and his Town Hall concerts of 1944-45 (which were broadcast weekly on the radio) were consistently brilliant and gave him an opportunity to show his verbal acid wit; the GHB label has been at last reissuing them complete and in chronological order. Condon opened his own club in 1945, recorded for Columbia in the 1950s (all of those records have been made available by Mosaic on a limited-edition box set) and wrote three colorful books, including his 1948 memoirs *We Called It Music*. A partial list of the classic musicians who performed and recorded often with Condon include trumpeters/cornetists Wild Bill Davison, Max Kaminsky, Billy Butterfield, Bobby Hackett, Rex Stewart and Hot Lips Page, trombonists Jack Teagarden, Lou McGarity, Cutty Cutshall, George Brunies and Vic Dickenson, clarinetists Pee Wee Russell, Edmond Hall, Joe Marsala, Peanuts Hucko and Bob Wilbur, Bud Freeman on tenor, baritonist Ernie Caceres, pianists Gene Schroeder, Joe Sullivan, Jess Stacy and Ralph Sutton, drummers George Wettling, Dave Tough, and Gene Krupa, a string of bassists and singer Lee Wiley. Many Eddie Condon records are currently available and no jazz collection is complete without at least a healthy sampling. —*Scott Yanow*

Eddie Condon's World Of Jazz / Sep. 28, 1927-Jun. 24, 1954 / Columbia ✦✦✦
This double LP is not strictly an Eddie Condon record (although the rhythm guitarist and bandleader is on a few of the recordings) but a collection of performances that he enjoyed by some of his

friends. The 27 recordings feature a who's who of classic jazz, programmed in alphabetical order from Red Allen to Lee Wiley. Although most of the recordings have since been reissued in more complete fashion on CD, this two-fer is a good introduction to the freewheeling musical personalities that inhabited Condon's world. —*Scott Yanow*

The Commodore Years / Jan. 17, 1938-Nov. 30, 1938 / Atlantic ✦✦✦✦✦
The contents of this two-LP set have fortunately been reissued in various forms on CD, for the music is quite classic. The first album contains three sessions that define the Eddie Condon "Nicksieland" sound and set the standard for Dixieland. Such distinctive players as cornetist Bobby Hackett, trombonists Jack Teagarden and George Brunies, clarinetist Pee Wee Russell, tenorman Bud Freeman and pianists Jess Stacy and Joe Bushkin are in consistently inspired form. Among the many highpoints of this album are Russell's solo on "Love Is Just Around the Corner," Hackett's lyrical lead on "Embraceable You" (a later favorite of Miles Davis), Teagarden's melody statement on "Diane," and versions of "California Here I Come" and "Sunday" that are filled with joyous ensembles and the enthusiastic drumming of Lionel Hampton. The second set, a marvelous trio outing by Bud Freeman, Jess Stacy and drummer George Wettling, is no less exciting. It's essential music in one form or another. —*Scott Yanow*

Dixieland All Stars / Aug. 11, 1939-Mar. 27, 1946 / GRP/Decca ✦✦✦✦
Some but not all of Eddie Condon's studio recordings for Decca are included on this single CD. Since five of the 20 selections are actually previously unissued alternate takes and several songs are bypassed altogether, this release will probably drive some collectors mad, but the music is consistently enjoyable. The rhythm guitarist heads an impressive outfit (with trumpeter Max Kaminsky, valve trombonist Brad Gowans, clarinetist Pee Wee Russell, Bud Freeman on tenor and pianist Joe Sullivan) on four titles from 1939 along with a variety of groups from 1944-46 that feature other top stylists including trumpeters Billy Butterfield, Bobby Hackett, Yank Lawson, Max Kaminsky and Wild Bill Davison, trombonists Jack Teagarden and Lou McGarity, baritonist Ernie Caceres, clarinetist Edmond Hall, Tony Parenti and Joe Dixon; the latter bands perform a variety of standards including eight George Gershwin songs. Dixieland and small-group swing fans will enjoy this set, which serves as a strong example of Eddie Condon's music, at least until a more complete reissue of the valuable recordings takes place. —*Scott Yanow*

Jam Sessions (1944) / Mar. 30, 1944+Dec. 14, 1944 / Jazzology ✦✦✦
A pair of sessions cut as radio transcriptions during 1944 are released in full on this two-LP set. Unfortunately the programming does not always make sense with alternate takes and false starts often separated from the "real" versions, but in general the performances are quite enjoyable, as one would expect from the two all-star groups. The players perform up-to-par and the lineup tells the story: trumpeters Max Kaminsky, Billy Butterfield and Bobby Hackett, trombonists Jack Teagarden and Wilbur DeParis, clarinetist Pee Wee Russell, baritonist Ernie Caceres, pianists Joe Bushkin and Gene Schroeder, bassists Bob Casey and Bob Haggart, drummer George Wettling and vocalists Red McKenzie, Lee Wiley and Teagarden. —*Scott Yanow*

Live at Town Hall (1944) / May 11, 1944 / Jass ✦✦✦✦✦
This consistently exciting CD predates all of the Eddie Condon Town Hall concerts released by Jazzology by a couple of months. Rhythm guitarist Condon, as usual, put together a spontaneous but logical show featuring quite a few top Dixieland all-stars. Trumpeter/vocalist Hot Lips Page takes honors with his "Uncle Sam Blues," but there are also two well-received features apiece for pianists Cliff Jackson and Joe Bushkin and plenty of solo space for trumpeters Billy Butterfield and Max Kaminsky, cornetist Bobby Hackett (whose chops are just a little off), trombonist Miff Mole and clarinetists Edmond Hall and Pee Wee Russell; bassists Bob Casey and Pops Foster and drummers Kansas Fields and George Wettling also make notable contributions. With Condon as the wisecracking M.C. and such highlights as "Muskrat Ramble," "Ja Da" and the lengthy "Impromptu Ensemble," this CD is highly recommended to Eddie Condon and Dixieland fans. —*Scott Yanow*

Town Hall Concerts, Vol. 1 / May 20, 1944–Jun. 10, 1944 / Jazzology ✦✦✦✦✦
Eddie Condon's *Town Hall Concerts* were historic in several ways. These weekly half-hour radio shows were very uncommercial (in fact they could not attract a sponsor), featured interracial bands and gave Condon an opportunity to put together well-paced programs. He would gather together a core band of Condonites who would have ensemble jams and individual features, and there were always a couple of numbers set aside for guest artists who would also join in on the show's concluding jam (titled "Impromptu Ensemble") with the regulars. Plus Condon, despite making a few too many jokes at the expense of Pee Wee Russell, proved to be a perfect host. After decades of only being available as incomplete excerpts, these programs have finally been issued complete and in chronological order on a series of two-CD sets by George Buck of Jazzology. The first volume, which has four complete shows, features such classic players as trumpeters Billy Butterfield, Bobby Hackett, Max Kaminsky, Hot Lips Page and Rex Stewart, clarinetists Pee Wee Russell and Edmond Hall, trombonists Bill Harris, Miff Mole and Benny Morton, the greatly underrated baritonist Ernie Caceres, and pianists James P. Johnson and Gene Schroeder. Although the recording quality of the very first show is subpar (the only one in the series that is less than flawless technically), all of the volumes in this wonderful series (which find the participants at the peak of their powers) are highly recommended. —*Scott Yanow*

Definitive, Vol. 1 / Jun. 8, 1944+Oct. 24, 1944 / Stash ✦✦✦✦
1944 was a busy year for Eddie Condon with the start of his legendary Town Hall concerts and the growing popularity of Chicago jazz. Among his projects at that time were recording selections for radio transcriptions, music made specifically to be played over the air (as opposed to being sold to the general public). Two sessions (complete with alternate takes and breakdowns) are released on this CD and it finds the all-stars in spirited form. As many as 11 musicians play together at a time and Condon drew his talent from this lineup: cornetist Bobby Hackett and Muggsy Spanier, trumpeters Billy Butterfield, Max Kaminsky, and Hot Lips Page, trombonists Benny Morton and Lou McGarity, clarinetists Pee Wee Russell and Edmond Hall, Ernie Caceres on baritone or clarinet, pianists Gene Schroeder and Jess Stacy, bassist Bob Haggart, drummers George Wettling and Joe Grauso and vocals from Lee Wiley, Liza Morrow and Hot Lips Page. This hot music is easily recommended to Dixieland and small-group swing fans. —*Scott Yanow*

Town Hall Concerts, Vol. 2 / Jun. 17, 1944–Jul. 8, 1944 / Jazzology ✦✦✦✦✦
This two-CD set has four complete radio shows featuring Eddie Condon's all-star groups during their legendary series of Town Hall concerts. Despite having large ensembles of classic players, Condon was able to feature virtually everyone on every show, still leaving room for ensemble pieces and interplay between the unique musicians. In addition, the verbal commentary of Condon and announcer Fred Robbins is informative and witty (even if they picked on Pee Wee Russell a bit too much). Among the musicians heard on the well-recorded set (which like the other volumes in this extensive series is highly recommended to fans of Chicago jazz) include trumpeters Bobby Hackett, Hot Lips Page, Max Kaminsky, Jonah Jones and Billy Butterfield, trombonists Bill Harris and Benny Morton, clarinetists Pee Wee Russell, Joe Marsala and Edmond Hall, baritonist Ernie Caceres and pianists James P. Johnson, Willie "The Lion" Smith and Gene Schroeder. —*Scott Yanow*

Town Hall Concerts, Vol. 3 / Jul. 15, 1944–Aug. 5, 1944 / Jazzology ✦✦✦✦✦
The third volume in this very valuable series of two-CD sets contains four half-hour weekly radio shows featuring Eddie Condon's all-star ensembles at Town Hall concerts. Condon (who supplies verbal commentary along with announcer Fred Robbins) programmed each show quite skillfully, featuring the large groups of all-stars in logical fashion. This set (which is highly recommended along with the other volumes in the series to followers of traditional jazz) features quite a roster: trumpeters Bobby Hackett, Jonah Jones, Max Kaminsky and Sterling Bose, trombonist Benny Morton, baritonist Ernie Caceres (who is really in peak form throughout the Condon programs), clarinetists Edmond Hall and Pee Wee Russell, guitarists Carl Kress and Tony Mottola, pianist Harry "The Hipster" Gibson (taking a couple of rare solos), Willie

"The Lion" Smith, Jess Stacy and Gene Schroeder, bassist Bob Haggart, drummers Gene Krupa, Joe Grauso and George Wettling and singer Lee Wiley. —*Scott Yanow*

Town Hall Concerts, Vol. 4 / Aug. 12, 1944–Sep. 2, 1944 / Jazzology ✦✦✦✦✦
Although they were never able to get a paying sponsor, the *Eddie Condon Town Hall Concerts* (a weekly half-hour radio show) was quite popular at the time and became legendary. For *Volume 4* of this colorful series of well-recorded two-CD sets (which is highly recommended to all followers of Chicago jazz), there are four complete programs featuring a remarkable ensemble of top musicians (virtually all of whom are showcased individually and collectively in logical fashion): trumpeters Billy Butterfield, Bobby Hackett, Jonah Jones, Max Kaminsky and Muggsy Spanier, trombonists Bill Harris, Miff Mole and Benny Morton, baritonist Ernie Caceres, clarinetists Edmond Hall, Joe Marsala and Pee Wee Russell and pianists James P. Johnson, Willie "The Lion" Smith, and Gene Schroeder in addition to guest drummer Gene Krupa and singer Lee Wiley. —*Scott Yanow*

Town Hall Concerts, Vol. 5 / Sep. 9, 1944–Sep. 30, 1944 / Jazzology ✦✦✦✦✦
This two-CD set, as is true of the other very valuable releases in the Eddie Condon Town Hall series (which had never before been reissued complete and in chronological order), features four well-recorded radio shows that logically showcase the individual members of Condon's remarkable all-star groups. These Dixielandish (but never corny or overly predictable) performances are generally exciting and the verbal commentary of Eddie Condon adds to the flavor and wit of the music. And check out this lineup of musicians: trumpeters Billy Butterfield, Bobby Hackett, Max Kaminsky and Muggsy Spanier, trombonist Miff Mole, baritonist Ernie Caceres, clarinetists Edmond Hall and Pee Wee Russell, pianists James P. Johnson, Jess Stacy and Gene Schroeder, bassists Bob Haggart, Sid Weiss and Jack Lesberg, drummers Cozy Cole, Joe Grauso and Gene Krupa and singers Red McKenzie and Lee Wiley. The spontaneous yet well-planned performances find the classic players in peak form and the results are quite memorable. —*Scott Yanow*

The Town Hall Concerts, Vol. 6 / Oct. 7, 1944–Oct. 28, 1944 / Jazzology ✦✦✦✦✦
Volume 6 of this very valuable series of two-CD sets has four complete (and well-recorded) half-hour radio shows taken from a legendary program billed as *Eddie Condon's Town Hall Concerts* (even though by late 1944 the performances were actually being held at the Ritz Theatre). Every week Condon gathered together a large ensemble of his favorite players and featured them individually and collectively in exciting fashion, finishing each Dixieland-oriented show with an "Impromptu Ensemble." All of the volumes in this series (which contain shows that had never been coherently reissued before) have more than their share of memorable moments. This particular two-fer features such classic players as trumpeters Billy Butterfield, Max Kaminsky and Muggsy Spanier, trombonists Lou McGarity, Bennie Morton, and Miff Mole, baritonist Ernie Caceres, clarinetists Edmond Hall and Pee Wee Russell, pianists Jess Stacy and Gene Schroeder and singers Lee Wiley and Red McKenzie. Condon somehow manages to feature each of the highly individual musicians and still save some space for his witty and acerbic comments. This is timeless music from an era that can never quite be duplicated. —*Scott Yanow*

The Town Hall Concerts, Vol. 7 / Nov. 4, 1944–Dec. 2, 1944 / Jazzology ✦✦✦✦✦
The *Eddie Condon Town Hall Concerts* were a series of half-hour radio programs during 1944–45 that gave the guitarist-bandleader an opportunity to present many classic jazz greats in spontaneous settings. The seventh volume of this very significant Jazzology reissue series of double CDs differs from the previous ones in that, due to scheduling conflicts, a couple of the shows were shorter than usual so there are five (rather than four) included on the set. Condon features quite an impressive lineup: trumpeters Billy Butterfield, Bobby Hackett, Max Kaminsky, Wingy Manone, Hot Lips Page and Muggsy Spanier, trombonists Lou McGarity and Jack Teagarden, clarinetists Jimmy Dorsey and Pee Wee Russell, baritonist Ernie Caceres, pianists Dick Cary, Cliff Jackson, Gene Schroeder, Jess Stacy and Norma Teagarden, bassists Bob Casey and Jack Lesberg, drummers Johnny Blowers and George Wettling and singers Red McKenzie and Lee Wiley. The Teagarden show is particularly inspired but all of the volumes

in this series are highly recommended to fans of the era, for the well-recorded performances allowed the many stars not only to be featured individually but to interact with each other in "Impromptu Ensembles." — *Scott Yanow*

A Night At Eddie Condon's / Dec. 12, 1944–Aug. 6, 1947 / Decca ✦✦✦

This hard-to-find LP has a dozen performances by Eddie Condon's all-star Chicago jazz bands of 1944–47. Five of the songs feature vocals by the great trombonist Jack Teagarden (including "The Sheik of Araby" and "Aunt Hagar's Blues"), pianist James P. Johnson is showcased on "Just You, Just Me" and the music (much of which has not been reissued on CD) also stars trumpeters Bobby Hackett, Billy Butterfield, Max Kaminsky and Wild Bill Davison, valve trombonist Brad Gowans, clarinetists Pee Wee Russell, Joe Dixon, Peanuts Hucko and Tony Parenti, tenorman Bud Freeman and baritonist Ernie Caceres. The spirited playing is consistently delightful and hard-swinging but unfortunately many of these recordings have not yet appeared on CD. — *Scott Yanow*

The Best Of Eddie Condon / Dec. 12, 1944–Sep. 26, 1950 / MCA ✦✦✦

This budget two-LP set (which inexcusably has no liner notes or even a personnel listing) contains about one hour of music, 20 three-minute selections from Eddie Condon's period with the Decca label. Although the music is not necessarily the best, there are many fine solos and plenty of freewheeling ensembles. The all-star groups include such classic players as trumpeters Bobby Hackett, Billy Butterfield, Max Kaminsky, Wild Bill Davison and Johnny Windhurst, trombonists Jack Teagarden, Cutty Cutshall (who takes a rare vocal on "Everybody Loves My Baby"") and Brad Gowans, clarinetists Pee Wee Russell, Peanuts Hucko, Joe Dixon, Edmond Hall and Tony Parenti, Bud Freeman on tenor, baritonist Ernie Caceres, pianists Gene Schroeder, Ralph Sutton and James P. Johnson, bassists Bob Haggart and Jack Lesberg and drummers George Wettling, Buzzy Drootin and Dave Tough; Bing Crosby even drops by to sing "After You've Gone." — *Scott Yanow*

The Town Hall Concerts, Vol. 8 / Dec. 16, 1944–Jan. 6, 1945 / Jazzology ✦✦✦✦✦

The eighth double CD in this essential series has four more half-hour shows that were billed as *The Eddie Condon Town Hall Concerts*. Condon, who was always more important as an instigator than as a guitarist, was a perfect host for the program, not only offering witty and sometimes sarcastic commentary but designing the shows so all of the all-stars were properly featured, both individually and collectively. The eighth volume has the usual incredible roster: trumpeters Billy Butterfield, Bobby Hackett, Max Kaminsky and Wingy Manone, trombonists Tommy Dorsey, Benny Morton and Jack Teagarden, Sidney Bechet on soprano, baritonist Ernie Caceres, clarinetist Pee Wee Russell, pianists Dick Cary, Gene Schroeder and Jess Stacy, bassists Bob Casey, Jack Lesberg and Sid Weiss, drummers Johnny Blowers and George Wettling and vocalist Lee Wiley. As usual there are dozens of highlights from these spontaneous yet logical jam sessions, easily recommended to Dixieland and Chicago jazz fans. — *Scott Yanow*

The Town Hall Concerts, Vol. 9 / Jan. 13, 1945–Feb. 3, 1945 / Jazzology ✦✦✦✦✦

Eddie Condon certainly had good taste in musicians. On his legendary *Town Hall Concert* series (a regular weekly half-hour radio program reissued by Jazzology on double CDs), he showcased some of the very best New Orleans and Chicago-style players, musicians who in some cases were quite happy to get away from their regular gigs within the confines of a big band and had a rare chance to stretch out. *Volume 9* has four half-hour shows and the usual remarkable lineup of players: trumpeters Billy Butterfield, Wild Bill Davison (the latter making his debut on the show), Max Kaminsky and Muggsy Spanier, trombonists Tommy Dorsey and Lou McGarity, Sidney Bechet on soprano, baritonist Ernie Caceres, clarinetists Pee Wee Russell, Edmond Hall, Joe Marsala and Woody Herman, pianists Earl Hines, Dick Cary, Gene Schroeder and Jess Stacy, bassist Sid Weiss, drummer George Wettling and singers Red McKenzie and Lee Wiley. The music lives up to its potential. — *Scott Yanow*

The Dr. Jazz Series, Vol. 5 / Dec. 24, 1951–Mar. 31, 1952 / Storyville ✦✦✦

The *Doctor Jazz* radio series (which was on from Dec. 1950 to June 1952) presented for a half-hour each week some of the finest Dixieland then being performed regularly in New York City. This particular CD features Eddie Condon's freewheeling band, with

consistently heated solos taken by cornetist Wild Bill Davison, trombonist Cutty Cutshall, clarinetist Edmond Hall and either Gene Schroeder or Ralph Sutton on piano. Together they romp through a variety of veteran standards and a ballad medley. The excellent programming on this Storyville disc (which actually draws its material from eight different broadcasts) makes the results sound like a complete show. Chicago jazz and Eddie Condon fans are advised not only to acquire this CD but to investigate the entire series from this Danish import label. — *Scott Yanow*

Dr. Jazz Series, Vol. 1 / Jan. 21, 1952–Jun. 2, 1952 / Storyville ✦✦✦

★ **The Complete CBS Eddie Condon All Stars** / Nov. 24, 1953–Sep. 4, 1962 / Mosaic ✦✦✦✦✦

Chicago jazz and Dixieland fans should go out of their way to pick up this limited-edition five-CD boxed set. The first four discs date from 1953–57 and feature freewheeling performances (originally out on seven LPs) with such classic soloists as cornetists Wild Bill Davison and Bobby Hackett, trumpeter Billy Butterfield, trombonists Cutty Cutshall, Lou McGarity and Vic Dickenson, clarinetists Edmond Hall, Peanuts Hucko, Bob Wilber and Pee Wee Russell and tenorman Bud Freeman among others. Eddie Condon's comments during his band's waterlogged performance at the 1957 Newport Jazz Festival alone are worth the price. The final disc of material (all from 1962) is somewhat commercial but still has its moments of interest. — *Scott Yanow*

Condon Concert / 1956–1957 / Jazzology ✦✦✦

This somewhat obscure LP from the collector's Jazzology label features the 1956 version of Eddie Condon's band, a septet starring the great cornetist Wild Bill Davison, trombonist Cutty Cutshall and clarinetist Bob Wilber. Nothing all that surprising occurs other than a four-song ballad medley, but these freewheeling performances (best are "At the Jazz Band Ball," "High Society" and Wild Bill's feature on "I Can't Give You Anything but Love") will be easily enjoyed by Dixieland fans. — *Scott Yanow*

Dixieland Jam / Aug. 19, 1957–Sep. 25, 1957 / Columbia ✦✦✦

Tiger Rag and All That Jazz / 1958 / World Pacific ✦✦✦

One of the lesser-known Eddie Condon groups is the one he led in 1958 that featured cornetist Rex Stewart. Of their three albums, this rare World Pacific LP is the most rewarding, featuring the group on eight mostly heated stomps including seven tunes recorded decades earlier by the original Dixieland Jazz Band. With the exception of some animal imitations on "Livery Stable Blues," there is no attempt to recreate the past and the songs are used as a good excuse for some colorful jamming. In addition to Stewart, trombonist Cutty Cutshall, Bud Freeman on tenor, clarinetist Herb Hall, pianist Gene Schroeder, bassist Leonard Gaskin, drummer George Wettling and the guitarist/leader are heard from but the fiery cornetist generally takes solo honors. — *Scott Yanow*

That Toddlin' Town / Feb. 26, 1959–Feb. 27, 1959 / Warner Brothers ✦✦✦✦

To celebrate the 20th anniversary of the first jazz album (meaning a specially released series of 78s that came out in 1939), a variety of Chicago jazz veterans under the leadership of rhythm guitarist Eddie Condon (all of whom gigged regularly with Condon anyway) jammed through ten Dixieland standards. Trumpeter Max Kaminsky, trombonist Cutty Cutshall, tenor saxophonist Bud Freeman and clarinetist Pee Wee Russell formed a particularly potent frontline and their LP (which has yet to be reissued on CD) has such highlights as spirited versions of "Chicago," "I've Found a New Baby," "Love Is Just Around the Corner," "Oh Baby" and "Nobody's Sweetheart Now." — *Scott Yanow*

In Japan / Mar. 1964–Apr. 1964 / Chiaroscuro ✦✦✦✦

Relaxed and often brilliant soloing from Condonites Buck Clayton, Vic Dickenson, and Pee Wee Russell, with three vocals by Jimmy Rushing. "Stompin' at the Savoy," "Three Little Words," "Rose Room," and more are included. — *Bruce Raeburn*

Jazz As It Should Be Played / Dec. 1, 1968 / Jazzology ✦✦✦

This little-known LP would be worth picking up if only for the occasionally hilarious wisecracking of Eddie Condon, trumpeter Wild Bill Davison and trombonist George Brunies. However there is also a fair sampling of fine Chicago Dixieland from these unique veterans along with clarinetist Tommy Gwaltney, pianist Don Ewell, bassist Bill Goodall and drummer Frank Marshall. Particularly enjoyable are "At the Jazz Band Ball," Brunies' vocal on "Sister Kate," "That's a Plenty" and "I've Found a New Baby." —*Scott Yanow*

And His Strolling Reunion Commodores / Dec. 7, 1969 / Fat Cat Jazz ✦✦
By 1969 veteran bandleader and rhythm guitarist Eddie Condon was only performing on a sporadic basis. This LP features his band of the era (cornetist Wild Bill Davison, trombonist George Brunies, clarinetist Tommy Gwaltney, pianist John Eaton, bassist Bill Goodall and drummer Cliff Leeman) playing a variety of Dixieland standards and a four-song ballad medley. The spontaneous concert performances are a bit loose at times (particularly by the later cuts) and there is a lot of joking around, but Condon collectors will want this spirited release. —*Scott Yanow*

Eddie Condon Jam Session / 1970 / Jazzology ✦✦✦
For one of Eddie Condon's final recordings (and what was possibly his last studio session), he largely let cornetist Wild Bill Davison run the show. Two of the five songs ("Time After Time" and "Crazy Rhythm") have arrangements for the septet (which includes Davison, trombonist Ed Hubble, clarinetist Johnny Mince and pianist Dill Jones) while the other three pieces ("How Come You Do Me like You Do," "Them There Eyes" and "Eddie's Blues") are looser and more freewheeling. This LP contains easily enjoyable and somewhat historic music. —*Scott Yanow*

The Spirit Of Condon / Dec. 5, 1971+May 6, 1973 / Jazzology ✦✦✦
This posthumously released LP has five selections from one of bandleader Eddie Condon's final concerts, an appearance at the 1971 Manassas Jazz Festival. "Washboard Blues" features pianist Art Hodes and the other four standards use a couple of overlapping groups with such fine players as cornetist Wild Bill Davison, trumpeter Wallace Davenport, trombonist Herb Gardner, clarinetist Joe Muranyi and Deane Kincaide on tenor and baritone. In addition there is a short parody (titled "Condon") by trombonist George Brunies (who sings and plays piano) which was taped for the ailing rhythm guitarist in 1973 but did not reach him before he passed away. Overall this out-of-print LP is not essential but it does have its strong moments and will be savored by Eddie Condon's many fans. —*Scott Yanow*

Jazz at the New School / Apr. 1972 / Chiaroscuro ✦✦✦✦

Harry Connick, Jr.

b. Sep. 11, 1967, New Orleans, LA
Piano, Vocals / Swing, Middle-Of-The-Road Pop
For a short time Harry Connick, Jr. was praised for helping to popularize standards among younger fans, and then he caught on so big with the media that his faults became obvious; he has not been taken seriously since in the jazz world. Connick studied music at the New Orleans Center for Creative Arts with Ellis Marsalis and played piano in New Orleans before being signed by Columbia. Emerging as an instrumental pianist with somewhat faulty time but a sincere approach toward playing swing and New Orleans standards, Connick evolved quickly into a singer who based his limited voice closely on the style of Frank Sinatra. He was excellent on the soundtrack of the film *When Harry Met Sally*, but then headed a bland big band, essentially hogging the great majority of the solo space himself. He has since recorded in the pop field and had nonmusical roles in films, making one doubt his dedication to jazz. Connick's earliest Columbia records are his best. —*Scott Yanow*

11 / Nov. 4, 1978+Nov. 11, 1978 / Columbia ✦✦

Harry Connick Jr / 1987 / Columbia ✦✦✦
A versatile, nervy pianist whose gift for rhythmic variation and countermelody is well displayed on this debut album, especially when he tackles such standards as "Love Is Here to Stay" and "Sunny Side of the Street." —*William Ruhlmann*

20 / 1989 / Columbia ✦✦✦✦
Even more confident and exuberant than his debut, Connick's second album (the title refers to his age) finds him pulling out the stops on Irving Berlin's "Blue Skies" and trying out his limited but earnest vocal style on a few tunes, notably "Do You Know What It Means to Miss New Orleans?" —*William Ruhlmann*

● **When Harry Met Sally . . .** / Jun. 1989 / CBS ✦✦✦✦✦

Lofty's Roach Souffle / Apr. 4, 1990–Apr. 22, 1990 / Columbia ✦✦✦
Still in a pronounced jazz phase, this shows his debt to James

Booker and New Orleans barrelhouse blues influences. —*Ron Wynn*

Blue Light, Red Light / Jun. 27, 1991–Jul. 14, 1991 / Columbia ✦✦
Connick in a slick, large-orchestra format. —*Ron Wynn*

25 / Oct. 2, 1992–Oct. 9, 1992 / Columbia ✦✦✦

She / 1994 / Sony ✦✦

Chris Connor

b. Nov. 8, 1927, Kansas City, MO
Vocals / Cool
Chris Connor was among the most popular '50s vocalists, famous for altering rhythms on ballads, using little vibrato except on special occasions, and a husky, lush sound. Connor studied clarinet for eight years as a child, then began singing in her late teens. She was the vocalist with a large band at the University of Missouri led by Bob Brookmeyer modeled after the Kenton band. After working with a group in Kansas City, Connor moved to New York in 1949. She sang with Claude Thornhill, Herbie Fields and Thornhill again in the early '50s, performing with Thornhill's vocal group the Snowflakes. She sang with Jerry Wald and then during 1952-53 was with Stan Kenton, recording her most famous performance "All About Ronnie." Connor went solo in 1953 and was with Bethlehem for two years. She moved to Atlantic, and enjoyed success, having two chart singles in the late '50s. They were the songs "Trust In Me" and the title cut from the album *I Miss You So.* Connor switched to ABC-Paramount in 1965, and was highly praised for her 1966 appearance at the Austin Jazz Festival. Following a period of semiretirement, Connor made a comeback in the mid-'70s, cutting albums with Kenton and Maynard Ferguson. She continued recording in the '80s for Progressive, Stash and Contemporary. Her most recent session was a '92 date for Enja. A fair amount of Connor material is available on CD. —*Ron Wynn*

Lullabies at Birdland / Dec. 17, 1953–Aug. 21, 1954 / Evidence ✦✦✦✦

This Is Chris / Apr. 1955 / Bethlehem ✦✦✦

● **Sings the George Gershwin Almanac of Song** / Jun 5, 1956–Jan. 23, 1961 / Atlantic ✦✦✦✦✦
Connor demonstrated her real jazz roots and base on this collection of Gershwin masterpieces. —*Ron Wynn*

A Jazz Date with Chris Connor / Nov. 16, 1956–Mar. 23, 1958 / Atlantic ✦✦✦✦

A Portrait of Chris / Dec. 5, 1960–Jan. 23, 1961 / Atlantic ✦✦✦✦

Sweet and Swinging / Jan. 27, 1978+Feb. 28, 1978 / Progressive ✦✦✦

Lover Come Back to Me / Oct. 1981 / Evidence ✦✦✦

Love Being Here with You / Sep. 12, 1983+Sep. 19, 1983 / Stash ✦✦✦

Classic / Aug. 5, 1987–Aug. 6, 1986 / Contemporary ✦✦✦
Good though mannered set from longtime "torch" favorite. Fine lineup, including Paquito D'Rivera (as). —*Ron Wynn*

New Again / Aug. 17, 1987–Aug. 19, 1987 / Contemporary ✦✦✦✦

As Time Goes By / Mar. 30, 1991–Apr. 2, 1991 / Enja ✦✦✦

Bill Connors

b. Sep. 24, 1949, Los Angeles, CA
Guitar / Fusion, Post-Bop
Bill Connors' great moment of fame occurred when he was with Chick Corea's Return to Forever during 1973-74, recording the influential *Hymn of the Seventh Galaxy*. His decision to leave RTF to concentrate more on acoustic guitar may have been satisfying artistically but it cut short any chance he had at commercial success. Previously he had played electric guitar with Mike Nock and Steve Swallow in San Francisco but his post-1974 work has been primarily acoustic, particularly in the 1970s when he recorded a series of atmospheric albums for ECM (including with Jan Garbarek). In the mid-'80s for Pathfinder Connors' music became more rock-oriented, but those releases did not make much of an impact, despite his talent. —*Scott Yanow*

Theme to the Guardian / Nov. 1974 / ECM ✦✦✦✦
This is an album of terrific solo acoustic guitar from a former member of Return to Forever. —*Paul Kohler*

Of Mist and Melting / Dec. 1977 / ECM ✦✦✦
An atmospheric jazz album, it includes Jack DeJohnette (d), Gary Peacock (b), and Jan Garbarek (ts). —*Paul Kohler*

● **Swimming with a Hole in My Body** / Aug. 1979 / ECM ✦✦✦✦✦
Brilliant solo acoustic guitar with some overdubs. Required listening. —*Paul Kohler*

Step It! / Jun. 12, 1984–Oct. 15, 1984 / Evidence ✦✦
This session accented the funk/R&B and rock elements of Connors' arsenal; the eight selections were dominated both by drummer Dave Weckl's prominent backbeats and Connors' riffs and dashing licks, as well as catchy hooks, progressions, and patterns from bassist Tom Kennedy. Such songs as "A Pedal," "Brody," and the title cut weren't melodically sophisticated, but had a bass-heavy structure and quick, animated solos. Although the date is a bit old, its qualities prove a perfect fit on several new adult contemporary and lite-jazz outlets. —*Ron Wynn*

Double-Up / 1986 / Evidence ✦✦✦
Guitarist Bill Connors has forged a successful career by mixing light, pop-oriented fusion cuts with more ambitious works that showcase his considerable solo abilities and compositional skills. This was a trio date with Connors (who doubled as producer) playing in an introspective vein, showing his funk and rock side, and then playing with more imagination and style. The playing time was quite short (35 minutes-plus), but there was enough of Connors' guitar work presented to satisfy his fans and fusion/pop/light jazz followers. —*Ron Wynn*

Assembler / Jun. 1987 / Evidence ✦✦✦
His third electric release is in an Alan Holdsworth style. All his electric albums are highly recommended. —*Paul Kohler*

Junior Cook (Herman Cook)

b. Jul. 22, 1934, Pensacola, FL, **d.** Feb. 4, 1992, New York, NY
Tenor Saxophone / Hard Bop
An expert hard bop tenor who tended to be overshadowed by more innovative contemporaries, Junior Cook was always a solid improviser. After playing with Dizzy Gillespie in 1958, Cook gained some fame for his longtime membership in the Horace Silver Quintet (1958–64); when he and Blue Mitchell left the popular band, Cook played in Mitchell's quintet (1964–69). Later associations included Freddie Hubbard, Elvin Jones, George Coleman, Louis Hayes (1975–76), Bill Hardman (1979–81) and the McCoy Tyner big band. In addition to many appearances as a sideman, Junior Cook recorded as a leader for Jazzland (1961), Catalyst (1977), Muse and Steeple Chase. —*Scott Yanow*

Junior's Cookin' / Apr. 10, 1961–Dec. 4, 1961 / Jazzland ✦✦✦

Pressure Cooker / Nov. 1, 1977–Nov. 2, 1977 / Affinity ✦✦✦

Good Cookin' / Jun. 7, 1979 / Muse ✦✦✦✦
This all-star hard-bop cast includes Bill Hardman (tpt) and Slide Hampton (tb). —*David Szatmary*

● **Somethin's Cookin'** / Jun. 12, 1981 / Muse ✦✦✦✦✦
Junior Cook, who was best known for playing tenor with the Horace Silver Quintet during the period that Blue Mitchell was the group's trumpeter, recorded relatively few sessions as a leader during his career. The muscular but smooth saxophonist is heard at his best on this Muse quartet release which really showcases his playing (with fine support from pianist Cedar Walton, bassist Buster Williams and drummer Billy Higgins). The original program (which includes originals by Walton and Larry Willis) is augmented by four alternate takes for the CD reissue. —*Scott Yanow*

The Place to Be / Nov. 23, 1988 / Steeple Chase ✦✦✦

On a Misty Night / Jun. 1989 / Steeple Chase ✦✦✦✦

Bob Cooper

b. Dec. 6, 1925, Pittsburgh, PA, **d.** Aug. 5, 1993 , Hollywood, CA
Tenor Saxophone / Cool, Hard Bop
One of the great West Coast tenors, Bob Cooper made even the most complex solos sound swinging and accessible. Coop joined Stan Kenton's big band in 1945 and he was a fixture with several of the editions (including the Innovations Orchestra) through 1951; in 1947 he married Kenton's singer, June Christy. After leaving Kenton, Cooper settled in Los Angeles where he was a busy studio musician for the next four decades. He was a regular member of the Lighthouse All-Stars from 1952–62, sometimes playing oboe and English horn (being the first strong jazz soloist on both of those instruments). The cool-toned tenor (whose sound fit into the "Four Brothers" style) was on many records in the 1950s (including those of Shorty Rogers, Pete Rugolo and June Christy) and continued working steadily in Los Angeles-area clubs up

until his death. He appears on records with the big bands of Frank Capp/Nat Pierce, Bob Florence and the 1980s version of the Lighthouse All-Stars and participated in the 1991 Stan Kenton 50th-anniversary celebration. As a leader Coop recorded for Capitol in the 1950s, Contemporary, Trend, Discovery and Fresh Sound. —*Scott Yanow*

Bob Cooper Sextet / Nov. 7, 1954–Jul. 30, 1954 / Capitol ✦✦✦

● **Coop! the Music of Bob Cooper** / Aug. 26, 1958–Aug. 27, 1958 / Original Jazz Classics ✦✦✦✦✦
Excellent aggregation with delightful work from Cooper and friends. —*Ron Wynn*

Tenor Sax Jazz Impressions / May 6, 1979–Nov. 17, 1986 / Trend ✦✦✦

In a Mellotone / Oct. 27, 1985 / Contemporary ✦✦✦✦
Enchanting mid-'80s collaboration. Snooky Young (tpt) sounds energized. —*Ron Wynn*

For All We Know / Aug. 15, 1990–Aug. 16, 1990 / Fresh Sound ✦✦✦✦

Chick Corea (Armando Anthony Corea)

b. Jun. 12, 1941, Chelsea, MA
Piano, Keyboards, Leader, Composer / Fusion, Post-Bop, Free Jazz
Chick Corea has been one of the most significant jazzmen of the past 30 years. Not content at any time to rest on his laurels, Corea has been involved in quite a few important musical projects and his musical curiosity has never dimmed. A masterful pianist who along with Herbie Hancock and Keith Jarrett was one of the top stylists to emerge after Bill Evans and McCoy Tyner, Corea is also one of the few electric keyboardists to be quite individual and recognizable on synthesizers. In addition he has composed several jazz standards including "Spain," "La Fiesta" and "Windows."

Corea began playing piano when he was four and early on Horace Silver and Bud Powell were influences. He picked up important experience playing with the bands of Mongo Santamaria and Willie Bobo (1962–63), Blue Mitchell (1964–66), Herbie Mann and Stan Getz. He made his recording debut as a leader with 1966's *Tones for Joan's Bones* and his 1968 trio set (with Miroslav Vitous and Roy Haynes) *Now He Sings, Now He Sobs* is considered a classic. After a short stint with Sarah Vaughan, Corea joined Miles Davis as Herbie Hancock's gradual replacement, staying with Miles during a very important transitional period (1968–70). He was persuaded by the trumpeter to start playing electric piano and was on such significant albums as *Filles de Kilimanjaro, In a Silent Way, Bitches Brew* and *Miles Davis at the Fillmore*. When he left Davis, Corea at first chose to play avant-garde acoustic jazz in Circle, a quartet with Anthony Braxton, Dave Holland and Barry Altschul. But at the end of 1971 he changed directions again.

Leaving Circle, Corea played briefly with Stan Getz and then formed Return to Forever which started out as a melodic Brazilian group with Stanley Clarke, Joe Farrell, Airto and Flora Purim. Within a year Corea (with Clarke, Bill Connors and Lenny White) had changed Return to Forever into a pacesetting and high-powered fusion band; Al DiMeola took Connors' place in 1974. While the music was rock-oriented, it still retained the improvisations of jazz and Corea remained quite recognizable, even under the barrage of electronics. When RTF broke up in the late '70s, Corea retained the name for some big-band dates with Clarke. During the next few years he generally emphasized his acoustic playing and appeared in a wide variety of contexts including separate duet tours with Gary Burton and Herbie Hancock, a quartet with Michael Brecker, trios with Miroslav Vitous and Roy Haynes, tributes to Thelonious Monk and even some classical music.

In 1985 Chick Corea formed a new fusion group, the Elektric Band, which eventually featured bassist John Patitucci, guitarist Frank Gambale, saxophonist Eric Marienthal and drummer Dave Weckl. To balance out his music, a few years later he formed his Akoustic Trio with Patitucci and Weckl. When Patitucci went out on his own in the early '90s the personnel changed but Corea has continued leading stimulating groups (including a recent quartet with Patitucci and Bob Berg) up until the present time. He remains an important force in modern jazz and every phase of his development has been well-documented on records. —*Scott Yanow*

☆ **Inner Space** / 1966 / Atlantic ✦✦✦✦✦
This double LP reissues Chick Corea's first album as a leader,

Tones for Joan's Bones, adding two previously unissued tracks from the same session plus a pair of performances from a Hubert Laws date of the period that feature Corea's piano and writing. With such players as Joe Farrell on tenor and flute, trumpeter Woody Shaw, bassist Steve Swallow and drummer Joe Chambers on this Corea date, the pianist performs five of his originals plus "This Is New" while The Laws cuts include Corea's "Windows." Throughout, this advanced hard bop music, which keeps an open attitude toward the avant-garde innovations of the period, is consistently stimulating. Even at this early stage, Chick Corea's playing is quite recognizable. —*Scott Yanow*

Bliss! / May 25, 1967 / Muse ✦✦✦
This 1967 quartet session is quite notable in several respects. Although the Muse reissue makes Chick Corea the leader (and the then-unknown pianist is in fine form), it was actually drummer Pete LaRoca's date, and he contributes seven now-forgotten but quite intriguing originals. But of greatest interest is the playing of tenor saxophonist John Gilmore, heard during one of his few excursions away from Sun Ra. Fine advanced hard bop. —*Scott Yanow*

☆ **Now He Sings, Now He Sobs** / Mar. 14, 1968–Mar. 27, 1968 / Blue Note ✦✦✦✦✦
The original LP (using the same title) only had five selections, but this CD contains 13, with the added eight (from the same sessions) having first been released on the double-LP *Circling In*. Age 26 at the time, and on the brink of gaining major recognition in the jazz world, pianist Chick Corea is featured with a very strong trio that also includes bassist Miroslav Vitous and drummer Roy Haynes. The music includes 11 of Corea's originals including "Matrix," "Windows" and "Samba Yantra," Thelonious Monk's "Pannonica" and the standard "My One and Only Love" and is essentially advanced hard bop with an open-minded attitude toward free jazz. Listen to how part of "Steps–What Was" has hints of Corea's future composition "Spain." —*Scott Yanow*

Is / Jun. 30, 1969 / Solid State ✦✦
Listeners most familiar with Chick Corea through his work with Return to Forever and the Elektric Band will be very surprised if they stumble across this LP. The music on the sextet date (which includes trumpeter Woody Shaw and Hubert Laws on flute) is often quite free and explorative, exploring a variety of moods (some of them rather violent). Rambling and uneven (particularly during the 29-minute "Is"), this set is not essential but has its interesting moments. —*Scott Yanow*

Sundance / 1969 / Groove Merchant ✦✦
Recorded during the same period as *Is*, *Sundance* has four very advanced (if forgettable) Chick Corea compositions interpreted by a septet that includes trumpeter Woody Shaw, Hubert Laws on flute and Bennie Maupin on reeds. Actually, this is a lesser Corea item with plenty of rambling moments (although it is generally not as free as *Is*) and is recommended mostly to completists of the pianist who are interested in his early development. —*Scott Yanow*

Song of Singing / Apr. 7, 1970–Apr. 8, 1970 / Blue Note ✦✦✦
This LP features the rhythm section of Circle (pianist Chick Corea, bassist Dave Holland and drummer Barry Altschul) playing rather advanced improvisations on group originals (highlighted by Holland's "Toy Room") and "Nefertiti." Influenced by the early Art Ensemble of Chicago, this music is rather free and avant-garde but rewards close listenings. —*Scott Yanow*

Early Circle / Apr. 8, 1970–Oct. 18, 1970 / Blue Note ✦✦✦✦
Chick Corea's most esoteric music of his career was performed when he was a member of Circle, an avant-garde quartet that during 1970–71 featured pianist Corea, the reeds of Anthony Braxton, bassist Dave Holland and drummer Barry Altschul. This CD contains some of their briefer performances including bass/piano and clarinet/piano duets, two versions of "Chimes," "Percussion Piece," a free ballad and Braxton's "73 Degrees–A Kelvin." These free explorations are worth listening to closely, but one has to put away any preconceptions that they have about Corea. The title of this CD is a bit silly though, for Circle broke up only a few months after these recordings! —*Scott Yanow*

A.R.C. / Jan. 1971 / ECM ✦✦✦✦
This LP features pianist Chick Corea, bassist Dave Holland and drummer Barry Altschul during the brief period that, along with Anthony Braxton, they were members of the fine avant-garde quartet Circle. The music heard on this set is not quite as free as

Circle's but often very explorative. Four of the six songs are Corea originals which, in addition to Holland's "Vedana" and Wayne Shorter's "Nefertiti," form a very viable set of adventurous jazz, recorded just a few months before Corea changed direction. —*Scott Yanow*

Circle/Paris-Concert / Feb. 21, 1971 / ECM ✦✦✦✦✦
Of all of the recordings from the short-lived avant-garde quartet Circle, this double-LP is the most rewarding. Cut live in Paris, this set features pianist Chick Corea, the reeds of Anthony Braxton, bassist Dave Holland and drummer Barry Altschul playing a wide variety of fairly free explorations. Highlights include their reinterpretation of the standard "There Is No Greater Love," the playful "Toy Room–Q & A," Braxton's "73 Degrees Kelvin" and "Nefertiti." The music is often quite abstract but generally colorful and innovative; Chick Corea would soon break up the band for other musical adventures, but this set remains one of the highpoints of his productive career. —*Scott Yanow*

Piano Improvisations, Vol. 1 / Apr. 21, 1971–Apr. 22, 1971 / ECM ✦✦✦
After spending a year with the avant-garde quartet Circle, Chick Corea's desire to communicate to a wider audience led to him deciding to break up the unit. His first post-Circle recordings were two LPs of piano solos. *Vol. 1* features six of his originals including the eight sketches of "Where Are You Now?," and the debut of the future standard "Sometime Ago." These performances are sometimes a bit precious, but they succeed in being accessible and serve as a transition between Circle and Return to Forever. —*Scott Yanow*

Piano Improvisations, Vol. 2 / Apr. 21, 1971–Apr. 22, 1971 / ECM ✦✦✦
This is the second of two LPs recorded by Chick Corea shortly after he broke up the avant-garde quartet Circle, saying that he wanted to communicate to a larger audience. As with the first set, these brief sketches are melodic and a bit precious but contain some strong moments. In addition to seven Corea originals, he interprets Thelonious Monk's "Trinkle Tinkle" and Wayne Shorter's "Masquellero." Not essential but worth acquiring. —*Scott Yanow*

Return to Forever / Feb. 2, 1972–Feb. 3, 1972 / ECM ✦✦✦✦
Chick Corea's original version of Return to Forever (featuring Joe Farrell on flute and soprano, bassist Stanley Clarke, Airto on drums and percussion and singer Flora Purim along with the pianist/leader) only was in existence long enough to record two albums. This self-titled set is highlighted by a sidelong medley of "Sometime Ago" and "La Fiesta" and demonstrates that it is possible to create music that is both strong jazz and popular. —*Scott Yanow*

● **Light As a Feather** / Sep. 1972 / Polydor ✦✦✦✦✦
Of the three versions of Return to Forever, the initial version is of the greatest interest from the jazz standpoint. With Joe Farrell on reeds, bassist Stanley Clarke, Airto on drums and percussion and Flora Purim contributing vocals, this contingent was one of the finest groups of the 1972–73 period even if they only actually cut two records. This particular set includes the original version of Chick Corea's greatest composition ("Spain") along with versions of "500 Miles High" and "Captain Marvel." This music crosses many boundaries and still sounds fresh two decades later. —*Scott Yanow*

Crystal Silence / Nov. 6, 1972 / ECM ✦✦✦✦
Chick Corea and Gary Burton teamed up for a series of piano/vibraphone duets on November 6, 1972, playing originals by Corea and Steve Swallow along with Mike Gibbs' "Feeling and Things." The most memorable performances on this introspective but fairly joyful set are "Señor Mouse" and "What Game Shall We Play Today." —*Scott Yanow*

Hymn of the Seventh Galaxy / Aug. 1973 / Polydor ✦✦✦✦
The second (and most popular) version of Return to Forever débuted with this strong fusion effort. This was guitarist Bill Connors' only recording with the group, and he is particularly fiery on "Captain Señor Mouse" and "Hymn of the Seventh Galaxy." With Chick Corea on keyboards, Stanley Clarke on electric bass and drummer Lenny White, this was one of the top fusion bands, mixing together the power and sound of rock with the sophisticated improvisations of jazz. Fans of late-'60s rock were able to enter the world of jazz through albums such as this near-classic. —*Scott Yanow*

Where Have I Known You Before / Jul. 1974–Aug. 1974 / Polydor ✦✦✦✦

The Leprechaun / 1975 / Polydor ✦✦
Chick Corea took a break from his fusion group, Return to Forever, to record this slightly more jazz-oriented effort. Such players as saxophonist Joe Farrell, trombonist Bill Watrous and bassist Eddie Gomez are on the date (as is vocalist Gayle Moran) but few of the tracks are all that memorable. A somewhat forgettable effort. —*Scott Yanow*

Romantic Warrior / Feb. 1976 / Columbia ✦✦✦
Return to Forever still had plenty of power left by the time of this later recording. Keyboardist Chick Corea, guitarist Al DiMeola, electric bassist Stanley Clarke and drummer Lenny White brought rock to a high creative level while leaving many jazz listeners behind with efforts such as this high-energy fusion set. —*Scott Yanow*

● **My Spanish Heart** / Oct. 1976 / Polydor ✦✦✦✦✦
Chick Corea has long been one of the most distinctive of all electric keyboardists, being able to transfer his mastery of the acoustic piano successfully to synthesizers. This double-LP, a classic of its genre, is full of delightful new melodies (particularly the last section of "El Bozo") and masterful keyboard playing along with a few guest appearances by a string quartet, a small brass section, singer Gayle Moran, bassist Stanley Clarke and drummer Steve Gadd. —*Scott Yanow*

Music Magic / Jan. 1977–Feb. 1977 / Columbia ✦✦
The third and final edition of Return to Forever gave Chick Corea an excuse to write for a four-piece brass section and to tour with bassist Stanley Clarke, his old friend saxophonist Joe Farrell, drummer Gerry Brown and his future wife, vocalist Gayle Moran. Unfortunately, the compositions are not too memorable on this set and the lyrics are a bit lightweight. Better to acquire this group's live recording if possible. —*Scott Yanow*

R.T.F. Live / May 20, 1977–May 21, 1977 / Columbia ✦✦✦✦
The final Return to Forever album, by Chick Corea's third group to use that name, is a massive four-LP box set that documents a complete concert. This band, in addition to the keyboards of Chick Corea, featured electric bassist Stanley Clarke and singer Gayle Moran plus the reeds of Joe Farrell, drummer Gerry Brown and a five-piece brass section. The music is generally pretty jazz-oriented with extended versions of such songs as "The Musician," "So Long Mickey Mouse," "Musicmagic" and "Spanish Fantasy" along with a piano/bass duet encore version of "On Green Dolphin Street." Worth searching for. —*Scott Yanow*

Live at Midem / Jan. 22, 1978–Feb. 1978 / Who's Who ✦✦✦
With the breakup of the final Return to Forever, Chick Corea began a long period of freelancing, resulting in some unlikely collaborations. For much of this concert performance, the pianist teams up with veteran vibraphonist Lionel Hampton for some swinging music. Corea is heard without Hamp on "Fiesta" and on singer Gayle Moran's feature on "Come Rain or Come Shine" and joins in the ageless vibist for "Moments Notice" and the spirited blues "I Ain't Mad at You." Not essential music, but this LP is fun. —*Scott Yanow*

Homecoming: Corea and Hancock / Feb. 1978 / Polydor ✦✦✦

Chick Corea and Gary Burton in Concert / Oct. 23, 1978+Oct. 25, 1978 / ECM ✦✦✦
During Chick Corea's freelance period after Return to Forever broke up and before he formed his Elektric Band, the pianist collaborated with many of his favorite musicians. This two-LP set contains eight duets with vibraphonist Gary Burton (highlighted by "Señor Mouse," "Bud Powell" and a remake of "Crystal Silence") along with one solo performance apiece by the two masterful musicians. The music is often introspective, but there are some exciting moments. —*Scott Yanow*

Delphi I: Solo Piano Improvisations / Oct. 26, 1978+Oct. 27, 1978 / Polydor ✦✦
This set of acoustic piano improvisations by Chick Corea (the eight-part Delphi series, "Children's Song #20" and the seven-part "Stride Time") is surprisingly dull. In the liner notes, Corea states that whatever the message is that he is trying to get across with this music is not complete without the next two volumes. To date they have never been released! This disappointing LP can be safely passed by. —*Scott Yanow*

Tap Step / Dec. 1978–Jan. 1980 / Warner Brothers ✦✦✦
This interesting collection finds Chick Corea playing seven then-new originals with a variety of musicians including flutist Hubert Laws, tenor saxophonist Joe Farrell, trumpeter Al Vizzutti, bassist Stanley Clarke and, on "Flamenco," tenor saxophonist Joe Henderson. The music is pleasing and spirited if not all that memorable; an average release from a hugely talented jazzman. —*Scott Yanow*

The Mad Hatter / 1978 / Polydor ✦✦✦
This post-Return to Forever Chick Corea LP is a bit of a mixed bag. Corea is heard on his many keyboards during an atmospheric "The Woods," interacts with a string section on "Tweedle Dee," features a larger band plus singer Gayle Moran on a few other songs and even welcomes fellow keyboardist Herbie Hancock for the "Mad Hatter Rhapsody." The most interesting selection, a quartet rendition of "Humpty Dumpty" with tenorman Joe Farrell set the stage for his next project, *Friends*. Overall, this is an interesting and generally enjoyable release. —*Scott Yanow*

Friends / 1978 / Polydor ✦✦✦✦
Although this set contains eight lesser-known Chick Corea compositions, it is in reality a fine blowing date. Corea, on both acoustic and electric pianos, is joined by his old friend Joe Farrell on reeds, bassist Eddie Gomez and drummer Steve Gadd for some fine straight-ahead jazz. —*Scott Yanow*

Secret Agent / 1978 / Polydor ✦✦✦
This orchestral project finds Chick Corea using colleagues from the final version of Return to Forever and singer Gayle Moran along with occasional strings and some newer associates such as trumpeter Al Vizzutti, electric bassist Bunny Brunel and drummer Tom Brechtlein. A bit of a mixed bag, most of the music is quite satisfying, particularly the exciting "Central Park." —*Scott Yanow*

Duet–In Concert, Zurich / Oct. 28, 1979 / ECM ✦✦✦

Live In Montreux / 1981 / Stretch ✦✦✦

Three Quartets / Jan. 1981–Feb. 1981 / Stretch ✦✦✦✦✦
This encounter between Chick Corea (sticking to acoustic piano), tenor saxophonist Michael Brecker, bassist Eddie Gomez and drummer Steve Gadd lives up to its expectations. The original program featured three lengthy "Quartet" pieces including sections dedicated to Duke Ellington and John Coltrane. The CD reissue adds four briefer pieces that were previously unissued, including an unaccompanied Brecker workout on "Confirmation" that would be perfect for "blindfold" tests. This blowing date is highly recommended for all true jazz fans. —*Scott Yanow*

Trio Music / Nov. 1981 / ECM ✦✦✦✦
Pianist Chick Corea had a reunion with bassist Miroslav Vitous and drummer Roy Haynes for this double LP, 13 years after they had recorded *Now He Sings, Now He Sobs*. The first half of this two-fer consists of duet and trio-free improvisations and is sometimes a touch lightweight even with moments of interest; playing free was not as natural to Corea by this time as it had been in the 1960s. However, the second album, seven Thelonious Monk compositions, comes across quite well as Corea does justice to the spirit of Monk without losing his own strong musical personality. —*Scott Yanow*

Touchstone / 1982 / Stretch ✦✦
Chick Corea was involved in a wide variety of projects during the early 1980s, some acoustic, others electric, and everything from solos and duets to orchestral projects. Touchstone really displays quite a bit of diversity with features for flamenco guitarist Paco DeLucia, a one-song ("Compadres") reunion of Return to Forever (with guitarist Al DiMeola, bassist Stanley Clarke and drummer Lenny White), a spot for alto-great Lee Konitz ("Duende") and a conventional sextet outing on "Dance of Chance." A bit uneven but with its interesting moments, *Touchstone* is worth checking out. —*Scott Yanow*

Again and Again / Mar. 23, 1982 / Elektra ✦✦✦
Chick Corea's regularly working band of 1982, a quintet with Steve Kujala on flute, soprano and tenor, took time off from a tour of South Africa to record six of the keyboardist's originals. The music, although sometimes electric, is generally modern mainstream with some adventurous moments. None of the newer songs (such as "Diddle Diddle" and "Twang") caught on and they were all more or less forgotten when this band broke up. However the music is still enjoyable, capturing Corea at a transitional point in his career. —*Scott Yanow*

The Meeting / Jun. 27, 1982 / Philips ✦✦✦
Chick Corea spent the years between the breakup of Return to Forever and the formation of his Elektric Band indulging in many

one-time collaborations with musicians he admired. This LP finds Corea teaming up with fellow pianist Friedrich Gulda for lengthy improvisations that mix together jazz (including "Someday My Prince Will Come") and classical themes. There are some surprising moments during these long performances, with Corea and Gulda inspiring each other to come up with creative ideas. —*Scott Yanow*

Lyric Suite for Sextet / Sep. 1982 / ECM ✦✦✦
For this meeting between pianist Chick Corea and vibraphonist Gary Burton, their duets are augmented by a string quartet. The seven sections of the "Lyrics Suite for Sextet" (which includes a "Sketch" for Thelonious Monk) contain more variety than one might expect and this set rewards repeated listenings. —*Scott Yanow*

Children's Songs / Jul. 1983 / ECM ✦✦
This solo LP finds pianist Chick Corea playing his 20 *Children's Songs*, brief (under three minute) sketches that quickly set a mood and then end; none are fully developed or memorable by themselves. It's one of Corea's less significant efforts. —*Scott Yanow*

Voyage / Jul. 1984 / ECM ✦✦
For this somewhat obscure Chick Corea LP, the pianist teams up with flutist Steve Kujala for a set of duets. Together they perform three of Corea's lesser-known originals along with two melodic free improvisations. It's pleasant music but not particularly memorable compared to Corea's group projects. —*Scott Yanow*

Septet / Jul. 1984–Oct. 1984 / ECM ✦✦

Trio Music: Live in Europe / Sep. 1984 / ECM ✦✦✦
Pianist Chick Corea had a reunion with bassist Miroslav Vitous and drummer Roy Haynes for this well-rounded set of trio performances. In addition to three standards (including "I Hear a Rhapsody" and "Night and Day"), the group performs a touch of classical music and four originals. —*Scott Yanow*

The Elektric Band / 1986 / GRP ✦✦✦✦
Nine years after the breakup of the final version of Return to Forever, Chick Corea ended a long period of freelance projects by forming his Elektric Band. This set, the group's initial release, finds Corea meeting up for the first time with the great bassist John Patitucci and drummer Dave Weckl; half of the selections also have either Carlos Rios or Scott Henderson on guitar. Due to the high musicianship, the personalities of the players and Corea's colorful compositions, The Elektric Band quickly became one of the top fusion groups of the late '80s.—*Scott Yanow*

Light Years / 1987 / GRP ✦✦✦✦✦
The second recording by Chick Corea's Elektric Band was the first to feature altoist Eric Marienthal and guitarist Frank Gambale in addition to bassist John Patitucci, drummer Dave Weckl and the leader/keyboardist. Unlike most other fusion groups, these musicians displayed original musical personalities and Corea's compositions tended to be memorable. This is one of The Elektric Band's better releases. —*Scott Yanow*

Eye of the Beholder / 1988 / GRP ✦✦✦✦✦
During an era when the word "fusion" was applied to any mixture of jazz with pop or funk, Chick Corea's Elektric Band reinforced the word's original meaning: a combination of jazz improvisations with the power, rhythms and sound of rock. *Eye of the Beholder*, which found guitarist Frank Gambale, saxophonist Eric Marienthal and bassist John Patitucci displaying increasingly original solo voices, is one of this group's finest recordings and ranks with the best fusion of the latter half of the 1980s. —*Scott Yanow*

Akoustic Band / 1989 / GRP ✦✦✦✦
As a contrast to his Elektric Band, Chick Corea formed The Akoustic Band with bassist John Patitucci and drummer Dave Weckl. This trio gave him a chance to stretch out acoustically in a straight-ahead setting on a variety of standards and originals. Their debut release is highlighted by "Bessie's Blues," "My One and Only Love," "Someday My Prince Will come" and Corea's "Spain." —*Scott Yanow*

Inside Out / 1990 / GRP ✦✦✦✦
Chick Corea's Elektric Band was always a well-integrated unit, featuring passionate solos from the rockish guitarist Frank Gambale and the R&Bish saxophonist Eric Marienthal in addition to major statements from the distinctive leader, who utilized a battery of keyboards yet remained quite recognizable. With John Patitucci (arguably jazz's top electric bassist) and drummer Dave Weckl pushing the ensemble, this pacesetting fusion unit is heard at its peak on these Corea originals. —*Scott Yanow*

Alive / 1991 / GRP ✦✦✦
The second effort by Chick Corea's Akoustic Band (a trio with

bassist John Patitucci and drummer Dave Weckl) is an easily enjoyable set of straight-ahead jazz with such standards explored as "On Green Dolphin Street," "Sophisticated Lady" and Thelonious Monk's "Hackensack" along with two Corea originals. —*Scott Yanow*

Expressions / 1993 / GRP ✦✦✦✦
Although Chick Corea has recorded quite a few releases throughout his career, solo albums are rare, particularly ones in which he explores standards. This acoustic set (which he dedicated to Art Tatum) finds Corea performing such songs as "Lush Life," "My Ship," Bud Powell's "Oblivion" and even the veteran warhorse "I Want to Be Happy" with individuality, respect and creativity. —*Scott Yanow*

Paint the World / 1993 / GRP ✦✦✦✦
Chick Corea's Elektric Band II found bassist John Patitucci, drummer Dave Weckl and guitarist Frank Gambale going out on their own and being replaced by Jimmy Earl, Gary Novak and Mike Miller. Saxophonist Eric Marienthal was the only sideman from the first Elektric Band to stick with Corea. Although the new members are not as distinctive as their predecessors, the high-quality material played on this release (which includes Jimmy Heath's "CTA," "Blue Miles" and a variety of Corea originals) is very jazz-oriented and occasionally there are straight-ahead sections. This set is recommended even to listeners who have not yet acquired a taste for fusion. —*Scott Yanow*

Time Warp / 1995 / GRP ✦✦✦
Chick Corea features an acoustic quartet on this CD, performing a full set of original material. Although the music is tied to a lengthy, complicated and philosophical fictional piece outlined in great length in the liner notes (which are not really worth bothering with), the performances by the group (which is comprised of Corea on piano, Bob Berg on tenor and soprano, bassist John Patitucci and drummer Gary Novak) are excellent. Berg continues to grow and show individuality beyond the Michael Brecker influence (especially on soprano), the interplay between Corea and Patitucci is as impressive as ever and Novak is alert to the constantly changing musical events. Although none of these songs are destined to become standards, the almost-continuous music holds on to one's attention. —*Scott Yanow*

Larry Coryell

b. Apr. 2, 1943, Galveston, TX
Guitar / Fusion, Post-Bop
Larry Coryell has been a splendid guitar stylist in jazz-rock, bebop, Latin and classical contexts. His only negative attributes have been inconsistency in material selection and supporting musicians for his bands and recording projects. Coryell has marvelous skills; he can play entrancing melodies, lighting fast phrases, spectacular solos or soothing statements. He's equally masterful on electric or acoustic, and has creatively used wah-wah pedals, attachments, distortion, dissonance and feedback. He's played 12-string, hollow-bodied, double neck and guitar synthesizers, as well as conventional acoustic. Coryell has few discernible musical weaknesses besides occasional inconsistency, and his ratio of topflight recorded output to junk has been quite high. Coryell worked in a band with Mike Mandel as a teenager. He moved to New York from Texas in the mid-'60s, where he initially worked with Chico Hamilton and the early jazz-rock band Free Spirits. He played with Gary Burton in 1967 and 1968, doing an intriguing blend of jazz-rock and jazz/country/western swing. Coryell and Mandel formed Foreplay in 1969, and with Steve Marcus continued the group until 1973. Coryell also played in Herbie Mann's band on such crossover hits as *Memphis Underground* and *Memphis Two-Step* during this period. He formed another jazz-rock band with Mandel and Marcus, Eleventh House, in 1973. The group also included Randy Brecker and Alphonse Mouzon, but it degenerated from a promising beginning into an overly loud unit playing second-rate arena rock by its end. Coryell periodically worked with Miroslav Vitous and John McLaughlin; he and McLauglin later recorded some superb duets. Coryell has worked with many duos and small combos, recording and playing with John Scofield, Michael Urbaniak, Steve Khan, Emily Remler, Brian Keane and Philip Catherine. He's also recorded with Charles Mingus, Stephane Grappelli and Sonny Rollins. Coryell began cutting his own albums for Vanguard in the late '60s. He continued in the '70s, '80s and '90s, recording for Vanguard, Flying Dutchman, Arista, Elektra, Atlantic, Mood, Keystone, Flying Fish,

Concord and Shanachie among others. Coryell's worked with a host of great musicians besides guitarists; these include Jimmy Garrison, Ron Carter, Roy Haynes, Joachim Kuhn, Ray Mantilla, Eddie Gomex, Albert Dailey and vocalists Urszula Dudziak. Recent Coryell projects have included a Brazilian session for CTI and some acoustic guitar workouts for Shanachie. He has an ample supply of sessions available on CD, though unfortunately none of his best jazz-rock dates from either his time with Gary Burton or on Flying Dutchman are currently available. —*Ron Wynn*

Basics (1968–1969) / 1968–1969 / Vanguard ✦✦
This album of leftovers from Vanguard sessions is better than it appears but far from essential. The personnel listing is confusing (and inexcusably leaves off the name of tenor saxophonist Jim Pepper). The music, which ranges from basic blues to early fusion and only clocks in at around 31 minutes, also features organist Mike Mandel and several rhythm sections. Fans of guitarist Larry Coryell (a fusion pioneer) may find some moments of interest here. —*Scott Yanow*

The Essential Larry Coryell / 1968–1975 / Vanguard ✦✦✦✦✦
His best work of the '60s and early '70s. —*Michael G. Nastos*

Spaces / Jul. 1970 / Vanguard ✦✦✦

Introducing Larry Coryell & The 11th House / 1972 / Vanguard ✦✦✦
One of three releases spotlighting Coryell's early '70s electric jazz-rock band Eleventh House. The group was erratic, their material often undistinguished, and the volume excessive. Yet they also produced some fine material, most of it done in expansive jam format. Besides Coryell on electric guitar, other players were keyboardist Mike Mandel, trumpeter Randy Brecker, bassist Danny Trifan, and drummer Al Mouzon. —*Ron Wynn*

Offering / Jan. 17, 1972–Jan. 20, 1972 / Vanguard ✦✦✦

At Montreux (1974) / Jul. 4, 1974 / Vanguard ✦✦✦

Twin House / 1976 / Atlantic ✦✦✦

Standing Ovation / Mar. 8, 1978+Mar. 11, 1978 / Mood ✦✦
A mixed bag with classical, traditional Indian songs, originals, and even modified funk played by Coryell and L. Subramaniam on violin and tampura. Coryell also plays a little piano and proves an effective partner, although sometimes the stylistic leaping around can be jarring. —*Ron Wynn*

Tributaries / Aug. 17, 1978–Sep. 1979 / Novus ✦✦✦✦

Bolero / Apr. 18, 1981–Nov. 1983 / Evidence ✦✦✦✦
Guitarist Larry Coryell is a superb player whether on acoustic or electric, doing straight-ahead jazz, classical, Afro-Latin, or even fusion and jazz-rock. He was masterful on this '81 date, displaying on acoustic ornate, expressive flashes, rapid-fire progressions, and darting phrases. He also provided evocative, passionate, sensitive playing on ballads and slower pieces. Coryell was supported by second guitarist Brian Keane, but it is clear from the opening notes of "Improvisation on 'Bolero'" that this is Coryell's date. His riveting leads and accompaniment almost render Keane's contribution superfluous, and that's not a knock on Keane but simply a recognition of Coryell's marvelous abilities. —*Ron Wynn*

A Quiet Day in Spring / Nov. 11, 1983 / Steeple Chase ✦✦✦

● **Together** / Aug. 1985 / Concord Jazz ✦✦✦✦✦
Coryell works easily and decisively with the late Emily Remler. —*Ron Wynn*

Toku Do / Sep. 8, 1987 / Muse ✦✦✦

American Odyssey / May 10, 1989–Nov. 9, 1989 / DRG ✦✦✦

Shining Hour / Oct. 20, 1989 / Muse ✦✦✦
Coryell shows he can work in traditional jazz bands. Marvelous musical assistants available, among them Kenny Banon on piano. —*Ron Wynn*

Coryell Plays Ravel & Gershwin / 1990 / Soundscreen ✦✦✦

Dragon Gate / 1990 / Shanachie ✦✦✦
Nice set with impressionistic, soaring solos by Coryell. —*Ron Wynn*

Twelve Frets to One Octave / 1991 / Shanachie ✦✦✦
A guitar showcase for Coryell, who has always been among the more accomplished players on either electric or acoustic. He goes through old blues, jazz standards, and everything in between. There's absolutely nothing else to support him, enabling Coryell to display his complete technical arsenal. —*Ron Wynn*

Live from Bahia / 1992 / CTI ✦✦✦
Nice Afro-Latin set with Coryell on acoustic guitar, recorded in Bahia. The assembled cast includes drummer Billy Cobham, alto saxophonist Donald Harrison, and several Brazilian musicians, notably vocalist Dori Caymmi. —*Ron Wynn*

Fallen Angel / 1993 / CTI ✦✦

Eddie Costa

b. Aug. 14, 1930, Atlas, PA, d. Jul. 28, 1962, New York, NY
Piano, Vibes / Bop
Eddie Costa was an aggressively rhythmic pianist, known for using the lower half of the keyboard for his rippling lines. He was a highly effective bebop soloist, a fine vibist and first-rate reader always in demand for studio work. Costa taught himself vibes; he had classical piano training. He worked with Joe Venuti as an 18-year-old, then played in Japan and Korea while in the Army. Costa recorded in the mid-'50s with Sal Salvador, and later worked with Tal Farlow, Kai Winding and Don Elliott. A double "New Star" *Downbeat* winner in 1957 on vibes and piano, Costa played in the late '50s with Woody Herman and led a trio with Paul Motian and Henry Grimes. He was just beginning to explore new harmonic areas when he was killed in a 1962 car crash. Costa had recorded for Jubilee, Mode and Coral. Costa recorded in the mid-'50s with Sal Salvador and worked with Kai Winding, Don Elliott and, most notably, Tal Farlow's Trio (1956-58). —*Ron Wynn*

● **Eddie Costa Quintet** / Jul. 13, 1957 / VSOP ✦✦✦✦✦
(Originally released as Mode 118). Eddie Costa's outing on Mode features him both on piano and vibes, in the company of Phil Woods and Art Farmer.—*AMG*

Tom Coster

b. 1941, Detroit, MI
Piano, Keyboards / Fusion, Crossover
A fine keyboardist, Tom Coster originally studied accordion for ten years. He performed music while in the Air Force and in 1969 he was in a jazz/rock group called the Loading Zone on electric piano. After a stint with Gabor Szabo in 1971, Coster spent 1972-78 with Santana. He played at the 1978 Montreux Jazz Festival with Billy Cobham, spent a couple of years outside of music and since then has primarily led his own fusion-oriented bands other than an association with Vital Information. He has since recorded as a leader for Fantasy, Headfirst and JVC and his son Tom Coster, Jr. is also an excellent keyboardist. —*Scott Yanow*

Did Jah Miss Me?!? / 1989 / Headfirst ✦✦✦
An album by ex-Santana keyboardist, it features Frank Gambale and D. Chambers. —*Paul Kohler*

From Me to You / 1990 / Headfirst ✦✦

Gotcha!! / 1992 / JVC ✦✦✦

● **Let's Set the Record Straight** / Sep. 14, 1993 / JVC ✦✦✦✦
Keyboardist Tom Coster looks to the 1970s for inspiration on this set, particularly toward Chick Corea's Return to Forever and Miles Davis. The music mixes together funk and jazz with liberal doses of R&B and Latin, and the passionate rhythms add to the power of the improvisations. Coster, Bob Berg on tenor and guitarist Frank Gambale take strong solos that give the CD plenty of stimulating moments. Acoustic purists are advised to look elsewhere but fusion fans will enjoy this fine set. —*Scott Yanow*

Forbidden Zone / 1994 / JVC ✦✦✦

Curtis Counce

b. Jan. 23, 1926, Kansas City, MO, d. Jul. 31, 1963, Los Angeles, CA
Bass / Hard Bop
A first-rate accompanist and session bassist, Curtis Counce played on numerous recording dates in the '50s. He was a solid, swinging player with a great tone, one of the finest "walking" bassists. Counce studied violin, bass and tuba as a teen, then played in the early '40s with Nat Towles' orchestra. He settled in Los Angeles and worked with Edgar Hayes from 1945 to 1948, followed by stints with Billy Eckstine, Bud Powell, Buddy DeFranco, Wardell Gray and Hampton Hawes. Counce later played in a group co-led by Benny Carter and Ben Webster, while recording with Lester Young. He studied composition and arranging with Spud Murphy. During the '50s, there were recording sessions with Teddy Charles, Shorty Rogers, Buddy Collette, Claude Williamson, Herb Geller, Bob Cooper, Clifford Brown, and Milt Bernhart. Counce

later played with DeFranco again, then toured Europe with Stan Kenton's orchestra. He formed a quintet in the mid-'50s that at various times included Jack Sheldon, Harold Land, Carl Perkins and Frank Butler. Some of Counce's recordings were *Landslide*, *Carl's Blues* and *Councilation* (also known as *You Get More Bounce*). He was also a bass teacher and did some film work. Most of Counce's albums have been reissued on CD. —*Ron Wynn*

● **Landslide** / Oct. 8, 1956+Oct. 15, 1956 / Original Jazz Classics ✦✦✦✦✦

Sonority / Oct. 15, 1956–Jan. 6, 1958 / Contemporary ✦✦✦
A relaxed, yet vibrant date, with Harold Land (ts) and Carl Perkins (p) as standouts. —*Ron Wynn*

You Get More Bounce with Curtis Counce / Apr. 15, 1957–Sep. 3, 1957 / Contemporary ✦✦✦✦

Carl's Blues / Aug. 29, 1957–Jan. 6, 1968 / Contemporary ✦✦✦✦
The Curtis Counce (bass) group was a working group when they recorded *Carl's Blues*. This album, with its cool-hot late night ambiance was a sleeper when it was first released and remains so years later. —*Bob Rusch, Cadence*

Exploring the Future / Apr. 1958 / Boplicity ✦✦✦

Stanley Cowell

b. May 5, 1941, Toledo, OH
Piano / Post-Bop, Hard Bop
An excellent modern mainstream pianist who is adaptable to many acoustic jazz settings, Stanley Cowell has long been under-rated except among knowing musicians. He studied the piano from the time he was four and Art Tatum made an early impact. After attending Oberlin College Conservatory and the University of Michigan, Cowell (who had played with Rahsaan Roland Kirk while at Oberlin) moved to New York in 1966. He played regularly with Marion Brown (1966–67), Max Roach (1967–70) and the Bobby Hutcherson-Harold Land Quintet (1968–71). In the early '70s Cowell worked in Music Inc. with Charles Tolliver and they co-founded the label Strata-East. He played regularly with the Heath Brothers during 1974–83 and since 1981 has been a busy jazz educator. Cowell has recorded as a leader for Arista-Freedom (1969), ECM (1972), Strata East, Galaxy, Unisson, DIW, Concord and Steeple Chase. —*Scott Yanow*

Blues for the Viet Cong / Jun. 5, 1969–Jun. 6, 1969 / Freedom ✦✦✦✦
Stanley Cowell's debut as a leader features his piano (and on two selections rare outings on electric keyboards) with a trio also including bassist Steve Novosel and drummer Jimmy Hopps. Cowell's style at the time was often modal and always quite powerful. After hearing seven of his often-somber pieces, Cowell's stride version of "You Took Advantage of Me" (inspired by Art Tatum) is a welcome change of pace. —*Scott Yanow*

Brilliant Circles / Sep. 25, 1969 / Arista ✦✦✦✦

Illusion Suite / Nov. 29, 1972 / ECM ✦✦✦

Waiting for the Moment / Jul. 6, 1977+Jul. 8, 1977 / Galaxy ✦✦✦

Talkin' 'bout Love / 1978 / Galaxy ✦✦

Equipoise / Nov. 28, 1978+Nov. 30, 1978 / Galaxy ✦✦✦

We Three / Dec. 5, 1987 / DIW ✦✦✦

Back to the Beautiful / Jul. 1989 / Concord Jazz ✦✦✦✦
A good session, with Steve Coleman (reeds) in an unusual mainstream role. —*Ron Wynn*

Sienna / Jul. 1989 / Steeple Chase ✦✦✦✦

● **Live at Maybeck Recital Hall, Vol. 5** / Jun. 1990 / Concord Jazz ✦✦✦✦✦
Cowell displays impressive technique and holds his own in the solo setting. —*Ron Wynn*

Close to You Alone / Aug. 2, 1990 / DIW ✦✦✦
Excellent trio date cut in Japan for the DIW label in '90. Cowell, sometimes more reflective than expressive, had no trouble cutting loose on these numbers. Most are originals, but they conclude the date with a brilliant version of "Stella By Starlight." Cowell is backed by bassist Cecil McBee and drummer Ronnie Burrage. —*Ron Wynn*

Ida Cox

b. Feb. 25, 1896, Toccoa, GA, **d.** Nov. 10, 1967, Knoxville, TN
Vocals / Blues
One of the finest classic blues singers of the 1920s, Ida Cox was

Music Map

Cornet

The cornet was the main brass instrument in jazz until it was succeeded by the trumpet in the mid-1920s.

New Orleans Pioneers
Buddy Bolden
(his 1895 band is considered the first jazz group)
Freddie Keppard
Manuel Perez

Important Cornetists of the 1920s
Nick LaRocca (with the Original Dixieland Jazz Band)
Paul Mares (with the New Orleans Rhythm Kings)
King Oliver
Oscar Celestin
Lee Collins
Punch Miller
Tommy Ladnier
George Mitchell (with Jelly Roll Morton)
Red Nichols

The Two Most Significant Cornetists
Louis Armstrong (switched to trumpet during 1926-27)
Bix Beiderbecke

Other Important Pre-Bop Players
Bunk Johnson
Ray Nance
Jimmy McPartland
Muggsy Spanier
Warren Vache

Rex Stewart
Bobby Hackett
Wild Bill Davidson
Ruby Braff

Bop
Nat Adderley
Thad Jones

Avant-Garde
Don Cherry
Bobby Bradford
Butch Morris
Olu Dara
Joe McPhee

singing in theaters by the time she was 14. She recorded regularly during 1923–29 (her "Wild Woman Don't Have the Blues" and "Death Letter Blues" are her best-known songs). Although she was off record during much of the 1930s, Cox was able to continue working and in 1939 she sang at Cafe Society, appeared at John Hammond's "Spirituals to Swing" concert and made some new records. Ida Cox toured with shows until a 1944 stroke pushed her into retirement; she came back for an impressive final recording in 1961. —*Scott Yanow*

● **Wild Women Don't Have the Blues** / Apr. 11, 1961–Apr. 12, 1961 / Rosetta ✦✦✦✦✦

Lol Coxhill (Lowen Coxhill)
b. Sep. 19, 1932, Portsmouth, England
Soprano Saxophone / Avant-Garde
Famous for his unaccompanied, unorthodox concerts and albums, Lol Coxhill has an immediately identifiable soprano and sopranino style. He's perhaps Steve Lacy's prime rival in getting odd sounds out of the soprano with his wrenching, twisting, quirky solos. While Coxhill's an accomplished saxophonist and can play conventional bebop, it's his winding, flailing soprano and sopranino lines that make him stand out. He actually started playing more conservatively; Coxhill backed visiting American soul and blues vocalists in the '60s, playing behind Rufus Thomas, Lowell Fulson and Champon Jack Dupree. He worked with Steve Miller's group Delivery in 1969 and 1970, and played with them at the Berlin Music Festival. But his debut album *Ear of the Beholder* established a new direction for Coxhill. Since then, he's worked with both bebop and free musicians, among them Chris McGregor, Trevor Watts, Bobby Wellins and Company. Coxhill's also played with such groups as The Recedents, Standard Conversions and The Melody Four.. —*Ron Wynn*

Ear of the Beholder / Jul. 12, 1970–Jul. 18, 1970 / Ampex ✦✦✦✦
The Story So Far . . . Oh Really [1 Side] / 1974 / Caroline ✦✦✦
Fleas in the Custard / 1975 / Caroline ✦✦✦
Digwell Duets / May 11, 1978–Jul. 1978 / Random Radar ✦✦✦
Lid / Jul. 1978 / Ictus ✦✦✦
Slow Music / Apr. 19, 1980–May, 1980/ Pipe ✦✦✦
Johnny Rondo Duo Plus Mike Cooper / May 3, 1980 / FMP ✦✦✦
● **Instant Replay** / Nov. 3, 1981–Sep. 4, 1982 / Nato ✦✦✦✦
Dunois Solos / Nov. 6, 1981 / Nato ✦✦✦
10:02 / Mar. 25, 1985–Mar. 26, 1985 / Nato ✦✦✦

Hank Crawford (Bennie Ross Crawford, Jr.)
b. Dec. 21, 1934, Memphis, TN
Piano, Alto Saxophone / R&B, Soul Jazz, Hard Bop
Hank Crawford's greatest contribution to music has been his soulful sound, one that is immediately identifiable and flexible enough to fit into several types of settings. Early on he played with B.B. King, Bobby Bland and Ike Turner in Memphis before moving to Nashville to study at Tennessee State College. He gained fame with Ray Charles (1958–63), at first playing baritone before switching to alto and becoming the music director. During 1959–69 Crawford recorded a popular series of soul jazz albums for Atlantic that made his reputation. His 1970s sets for Kudu were more commercial and streakier but in 1982 Crawford started recording regularly for Milestone, often matched up with organist Jimmy McGriff or pianist Dr. John. An influence on David Sanborn, Crawford's very appealing sound can still be heard in prime form in the mid-'90s. —*Scott Yanow*

Heart And Soul / Jul. 5, 1958–Aug. 27, 1992 / Rhino/Atlantic ✦✦✦
This two-disc set blends the bland and the bold, but Crawford's shimmering alto even injects life into shopworn numbers like "Imagination." The set includes superb Crawford solos in other settings, particularly his outstanding contribution to B.B. King's "There Must Be A Better World Somewhere" and some dazzling playing backed by Marty Paich's orchestra. The first disc contains several collaborations with fellow blues/soul-jazz stalwart David "Fathead" Newman, including a brisk Ray Charles octet workout "Sherry" from 1958. Despite a tendency to get syrupy, this anthology showcases both sides of Hank Crawford—the sentimentalist and the exuberant wailer. —*Ron Wynn*

More Soul / Oct. 7, 1960 / Atlantic ✦✦✦
Soul of the Ballad / Feb. 16, 1963+Feb. 20, 1963 / Atlantic ✦✦
Lots of blues, mellow numbers, and funky cuts. —*Ron Wynn*
True Blues / 1963–1964 / Atlantic ✦✦✦
First album to establish his reputation as a leader outside the Ray Charles orchestra. —*Ron Wynn*

After Hours / Oct. 19, 1965–Jan. 19, 1966 / Atlantic ✦✦✦✦
Soul-jazz and blues with ensembles of varying size from trio up to octet. Detroiters Ali Jackson and Wendell Harrison appear, as well as stalwarts Howard Johnson, Wilbert Hogan, and Joe Dukes (drums), and John Hunt and Fielder Floyd (trumpet). Four standards including the title track. Originals by Bennie Golson, Ben Tucker, Stanley Turrentine, and the leader. —*Michael G. Nastos*

It's a Funky Thing to Do / Dec. 10, 1970 / Cotillion ✦✦✦
We Got a Good Thing Going / Sep. 19, 1972–Oct., 1972 / Columbia ✦✦✦✦
Wildflower / Jun. 1973 / Columbia ✦✦
Tico Rico / Nov. 1976 / Kudu ✦✦✦
Centerpiece / Oct. 1978–Nov. 1978 / Buddah ✦✦✦
Midnight Ramble / Nov. 4, 1982–Nov. 5, 1982 / Milestone ✦✦✦
Fine blues, bop, and ballads menu. —*Ron Wynn*
Indigo Blue / Aug. 22, 1983–Aug. 23, 1983 / Milestone ✦✦✦✦
With Dr. John (p, organ), David "Fathead" Newman (ts). Good session with soul-jazz leanings. —*Ron Wynn*
Down on the Deuce / Jun. 18, 1984–Jun. 19, 1984 / Milestone ✦✦✦
Roadhouse Symphony / Aug. 5, 1985–Aug. 12, 1985 / Milestone ✦✦✦
Soul Survivors / Jan. 29, 1986+Jan. 30, 1986 / Milestone ✦✦✦✦
With Jimmy McGriff (organ), George Benson (g), Mel Lewis (d). Soul-jazz the way they did it in the '60s (almost). —*Ron Wynn*
Mr. Chips / Nov. 1986 / Milestone ✦✦✦
Steppin' Up / Jun. 15, 1987+Jun. 16, 1987 / Milestone ✦✦✦✦
With Jimmy McGriff (organ), Jimmy Ponder (g). Solid, exuberant soul-jazz. —*Ron Wynn*
Night Beat / Sep. 1988–Mar. 1990 / Milestone ✦✦✦
● **On the Blue Side** / Apr. 4, 1989+Aug. 9, 1989 / Milestone ✦✦✦✦✦
With Jimmy McGriff. Funky, mellow, and gritty. —*Ron Wynn*
Groove Master / Jan. 1990–Mar. 1990 / Milestone ✦✦✦
Portrait / Mar. 19, 1991–Mar. 20, 1991 / Milestone ✦✦✦
South Central / Aug. 11, 1992+Aug. 27, 1992 / Milestone ✦✦✦

Ray Crawford
b. Feb. 7, 1924, Pittsburgh, PA
Guitar / Hard Bop, Soul Jazz
Ray Crawford played tenor and clarinet with Fletcher Henderson during 1941–43 but tuberculosis forced him to give them up. He switched to guitar and was an important part of Ahmad Jamal's early groups (1949–55); his ability to make his guitar sound like bongos by hitting it was soon adopted by Herb Ellis. Crawford also recorded with Gil Evans (1959–60), played off and on with Jimmy Smith from 1958 into the 1980s and in the '60s settled in Los Angeles. He led fairly obscure records for Candid (1961, but not released until the '80s), Dobre (1977) and United National (1978). —*Scott Yanow*
● **Smooth Groove** / Feb. 10, 1961 / Candid ✦✦✦✦

Marilyn Crispell
b. Mar. 30, 1947, Philadelphia, PA
Piano / Avant-Garde
One of the finest pianists of the avant-garde, Marilyn Crispell has been greatly inspired by Cecil Taylor and can be nearly as powerful but also is not shy to use space or occasionally play a spiritual standard. She studied piano at the Peabody Music School in Baltimore from age seven and later went to the New England Conservatory. Crispell was outside of music during 1969–75 but then became very interested in advanced jazz. She met Anthony Braxton, toured Europe with his Creative Music Orchestra in 1978 and has been in his regular quartet since the early '80s. Marilyn Crispell has also led her own groups (both live and on records) since then, recording several notable sets for Leo, Cadence and Music & Arts. She is near the top of her field. —*Scott Yanow*
● **Spirit Music** / May 15, 1981+Jan. 13, 1982 / Cadence ✦✦✦✦✦
Marilyn Crispell is one of the most significant piano voices of the avant-garde. A powerful player influenced by Cecil Taylor but who has her own way of using space, Crispell has been closely associated with Anthony Braxton's group during the past decade. This Cadence release, however, finds her leading her own trio, an unusual group which also includes violinist Billy Bang and drum-

mer John Betsch. On one of the four lengthy improvisations heard on this set, guitarist Wes Brown makes the band a quartet. These stirring performances serve as a fine introduction to the passionate music of Marilyn Crispell. —*Scott Yanow*

Live in Berlin / Nov. 4, 1982 / Black Saint ✦✦✦

Rhythms Hung in Undrawn Sky / May 7, 1983 / Leo ✦✦✦

A Concert in Berlin / Jul. 2, 1983 / FMP ✦✦✦✦

And Your Ivory Voice Sings / Mar. 7, 1985–Mar. 9, 1985 / Leo ✦✦✦

Live in San Francisco / Jun. 30, 1986–Oct. 20, 1989 / Music & Arts ✦✦✦✦

Gaia / Mar. 15, 1987 / Leo ✦✦✦

Labyrinths / Oct. 2, 1987 / Les Disques ✦✦✦

The Kitchen Concerts / Feb. 2, 1989–Feb. 4, 1989 / Leo ✦✦✦

Live in Zurich / Apr. 12, 1989 / Leo ✦✦✦✦
Crispell keeps cranking out furious, aggressive free dates for the European market. They're devoid of any devices now in vogue on the jazz circuit: no standards, no electronics, no hard bop, Adult Contemporary, strings, or fusion. If you enjoy hearing spirited dialogues between Crispell, bassist Reggie Workman, and drummer Paul Motian, this one's for you. —*Ron Wynn*

Overlapping Hands: Eight Segments / Jun. 28, 1990–Jun. 30, 1990 / FMP ✦✦✦

Circles / 1990 / Victo ✦✦✦✦

Marilyn Crispell Trio / 1992 / Music & Arts ✦✦✦✦

Crispell & Hemingway Duo / 1992 / Knitting Factory ✦✦✦✦

Stellar Pulsations / Feb. 2, 1992–Jul. 13, 1992 / Leo ✦✦✦

Inference / Jun. 25, 1992 / Music & Arts ✦✦✦✦

Hyperion / Jun. 25, 1992 / Music & Arts ✦✦✦

Band On The Wall / May 26, 1994 / Matchless ✦✦✦✦
Pianist Marilyn Crispell and drummer Eddie Prevost match together very well on this avant-garde duet concert which was recorded live in Manchester, England. Although 13 songs are listed (all but Denny Zeitlin's "Quiet Now" are originals by one or both musicians), this is actually a continuous performance. Crispell, a very talented pianist who can play with tremendous power and freedom, is also not afraid to occasionally wring out sincere emotions on straightforward melodies. Her performance covers several different moods and, although often very free form and percussive, she leaves space and can be quite lyrical. Prevost follows her musical directions closely and has four solo interludes of his own. The results are a stimulating set of adventurous music that is sometimes surprisingly accessible. —*Scott Yanow*

Sonny Criss (William Criss)

b. Oct. 23, 1927, Memphis, TN, **d.** Nov. 19, 1977, Los Angeles, CA
Alto Saxophone / Hard Bop
A talented bop altoist, Sonny Criss was influenced by Charlie Parker but had his own heavier sound. He spent most of his life in the Los Angeles area starting in 1942. In 1946 he worked in Howard McGhee's band with Charlie Parker and Teddy Edwards and can be heard on several jam sessions on Savoy in 1947. Criss spent periods playing with Johnny Otis, Gerald Wilson, and Billy Eckstine (1950–51) and was with Stan Kenton in 1955. He also worked with Howard Rumsey's Lighthouse All-Stars and Buddy Rich's quartet (1958) in addition to leading his own groups, recording three albums for Imperial in 1956. Criss lived in Europe during 1962–65, recorded some excellent sets for Prestige during 1966–69 and in the 1970s headed sessions for Fresh Sound, Xanadu, Muse and a couple of commercial efforts for Impulse. After European tours in 1973 and 1974, Sonny Criss' career seemed on an upswing. But due to the pain of cancer, he chose to commit suicide in 1977. —*Scott Yanow*

Memorial Album / Oct. 17, 1947–Jun. 15, 1965 / Xanadu ✦✦✦
Good teamup with Hampton Hawes (p). —*Ron Wynn*

Intermission Riff / Oct. 12, 1951 / Pablo ✦✦✦

Sonny Criss and Kenny Dorham, Vol. 1: The Bopmasters / Apr. 4, 1956–1959 / ABC/Impulse! ✦✦✦✦
Released as the first volume in Impulse's short-lived reissue program titled *The Dedication Series*, this two-LP set combines together a pair of unrelated sessions. Trumpeter Kenny Dorham leads his Jazz Prophets, a quintet in 1956 that also stars tenor saxophonist J.R. Monterose and pianist Dick Katz. They ably perform four of Dorham's originals plus the ballad "Don't Explain." The

Sonny Criss session from 1959 has trombonist Ole Hansen and pianist Wynton Kelly among the other soloists but Criss' alto dominates the set. The music by both groups is high-quality hard bop and these rare sides are worth getting. Pity that this valuable series quickly went out of print. —*Scott Yanow*

This Is Criss! / Oct. 21, 1966 / Original Jazz Classics ✦✦✦✦
Early-period recording from this unsung hero. Highly recommended. —*Michael G. Nastos*

Portrait of Sonny Criss / Mar. 12, 1967 / Original Jazz Classics ✦✦✦✦
Valuable reissue of a stalwart date. Criss is in piercing form; high-caliber rhythm section work. —*Ron Wynn*

Sonny's Dream / May 8, 1968 / Original Jazz Classics ✦✦✦✦
For Sonny Criss this was an unusual date. The altoist is backed for the set by a nonet arranged by the great Los Angeles-legend Horace Tapscott. The arrangements are challenging but complementary to Criss' style and he is in top form on the six Tapscott originals. The CD reissue includes two additional alternate takes and is highly recommended for both Criss' playing and Tapscott's writing. —*Scott Yanow*

I'll Catch the Sun / Jan. 20, 1969 / Original Jazz Classics ✦✦✦✦
Altoist Sonny Criss made some of his finest recordings for Prestige during the mid-to-late '60s; *I'll Catch the Sun* was the seventh and final. Since this CD reissue is only 35 minutes long, it is overly brief, but the straight-ahead music (featuring Criss with pianist Hampton Hawes, bassist Monty Budwig and drummer Shelly Manne) is often excellent as the altoist performs two blues, two standards (including a passionate "Cry Me a River") and two forgotten pop tunes from the era. —*Scott Yanow*

★ **Crisscraft** / Feb. 24, 1975 / Muse ✦✦✦✦✦
This is one of the very best Sonny Criss albums. The distinctive altoist, who is here joined by guitarist Ray Crawford, pianist Dolo Coker, bassist Larry Gales and drummer Jimmy Smith, is in prime form on a lengthy "The Isle of Celia," Benny Carter's "Blues in My Heart," the boppish blues "Crisscraft" and two shorter pieces. Criss, who had not recorded as a leader in six years, was really ready for this session, making this his definitive set to get. —*Scott Yanow*

Saturday Morning / Mar. 1, 1975 / Xanadu ✦✦✦✦✦

Out of Nowhere / Oct. 20, 1975 / Muse ✦✦✦✦
Tremendous date that reactivated the memory of Criss among longtime jazz fans who had overlooked him. —*Ron Wynn*

Warm & Sonny / 1975 / Impulse! ✦✦

The Joy of Sax / 1976 / ABC/Impulse! ✦✦

Bing Crosby (Harry Lillis Crosby)

b. May 2, 1904, Tacoma, WA, **d.** Oct. 14, 1977, Madrid, Spain
Vocals / Swing, Standards
A beloved icon whose contributions to American music are so great that they are difficult to describe, Bing Crosby had a major influence on jazz singers. Prior to his rise in the late '20s, most male vocalists (outside of the blues world) were hired as much for their ability to project volume as for anything else. With the exception of Cliff Edwards, few White singers were worth listening to. Bing Crosby's friendly baritone voice and easy sense of swing saved the world from being overrun by Rudy Vallee imitators and boy tenors!

Crosby's main connection to jazz was in his early days. He played drums and sang with jazz groups as a boy. In 1926 he became part of the Rhythm Boys with Al Rinker and the greatly underrated Harry Barris. The colorful trio (one of the few jazz vocal groups) performed regularly with Paul Whiteman's Orchestra during 1926–30 (appearing in the 1930 film *The King of Jazz*) and during this time Crosby was also featured solo on a few recordings, inspired by his friends Bix Beiderbecke and Joe Venuti. Bing, who proved to be a fine scat singer, hit it big singing ballads with Gus Arnheim in the early '30s but always retained a love for jazz, particularly Dixieland. He recorded "St. Louis Blues" with Duke Ellington, teamed up with Louis Armstrong in the films *Pennies from Heaven* (1936) and *High Society* (1956), sang in a Dixieland setting throughout *The Birth of the Blues* (1940) and introduced dozens of songs that became jazz standards. Although he moved beyond jazz by the mid-'30s, Crosby occasionally recorded with top jazz players including Jimmy Dorsey's Orchestra, his brother Bob Crosby's Bobcats, Eddie Condon,

Woody Herman, Louis Jordan, Eddie Heywood's Sextet and Bob Scobey. —*Scott Yanow*

Bing Crosby / Dec. 22, 1926–Feb. 11, 1932 / Timeless ✦✦✦✦

★ **Bing! His Legendary Years, 1931 to 1957** / Nov. 23, 1931–Dec. 27, 1957 / MCA ✦✦✦✦✦
This four-CD set does a superb job of summing up Bing Crosby's years with Decca. After nine titles from 1931 (which were acquired by Decca later on), the program concentrates on the 1934–57 period and, in addition to the expected hits, all aspects of his career are covered. Despite a few Dixieland-flavored selections, Crosby had largely abandoned jazz by the late '30s but his phrasing (which was influenced by Louis Armstrong) and appealing voice should be of interest to jazz listeners. In later years his ballads grew in stature while the uptempo performances tended to be less memorable novelties. Although it should be augmented by collections that focus on his recordings of the 1920s and early '30s, this is the definitive Bing Crosby set. —*Scott Yanow*

And Some Jazz Friends / Aug. 8, 1934–May 27, 1942 / GRP ✦✦✦✦

Bob Crosby (George Robert Crosby)

b. Aug. 25, 1913, Spokane, WA, d. Mar. 9, 1993, La Jolla, CA
Vocals, Leader / Dixieland, Swing
Bob Crosby, Bing's younger brother, often found himself in the odd position of being the least important member of his orchestra! An OK singer, Crosby was much more important as the leader of a memorable swing band that found its own style by looking backwards at the 1920s. To Crosby's credit, he seemed aware of his predicament and not uncomfortable with allocating most of the solo space to his talented sidemen, featuring them with his big band and his Bobcats, the latter a hot Dixieland band taken out of his orchestra. After stints with Anson Weeks in 1932 and The Dorsey Brothers' orchestra during 1934–35, Crosby was voted the frontman of a new big band that was formed out of the remains of Ben Pollack's orchestra. 1935–42 was Crosby's heyday, with his band featuring such classic soloists as Yank Lawson, Billy Butterfield, Eddie Miller, Matty Matlock, Irving Fazola, Joe Sullivan, Bob Zurke, Jess Stacy and Muggsy Spanier. During an era when swing was the thing and New Orleans jazz was considered by many to be ancient history, Crosby's crew led the way to the eventual New Orleans revival. Such classic recordings as "South Rampart Street Parade" and "What's New" (both composed by bassist Bob Haggart) along with the many Dixieland stomps kept the band quite popular. The orchestra broke up in late 1942, Crosby served in the Marines during 1944–45 and then spent the rest of his life in a variety of activities, often bringing back versions of The Bobcats for special concerts and recordings, taking an occasional vocal but mostly letting his sidemen play. Some of Crosby's many Decca recordings are currently available. —*Scott Yanow*

★ **South Rampart Street Parade** / Apr. 13, 1936–Feb. 17, 1942 / GRP ✦✦✦✦✦

1937–1938 / Feb. 8, 1937–Oct. 19, 1938 / DRG ✦✦✦

Bob Crosby & His Orchestra (1938) / 1938 / Circle ✦✦

I Remember You / Sep. 1941–Jul. 1942 / Vintage Jazz Classics ✦✦✦

The Uncollected Bob Crosby & His Orchestra (1941–1942) / 1941–1942 / Hindsight ✦✦✦

Bob Crosby & His Orchestra (1952–1953) / 1952–1953 / Hindsight ✦✦✦

Israel Crosby

b. Jan. 19, 1919, Chicago, IL, d. Aug. 11, 1962, Chicago, IL
Bass / Swing, Cool
One of the finest bassists to emerge during the 1930s, Israel Crosby was young and flexible enough to still sound quite modern in the early '60s. He started on trumpet when he was five and then played trombone and tuba before settling on bass. In 1935 when he was 16, Crosby took one of the first full-length bass solos on record ("Blues for Israel") during a pickup date led by Gene Krupa. He played with Albert Ammons (1935–36), Fletcher Henderson (1936–38), the Three Sharps and a Flat, Horace Henderson (1940), Teddy Wilson (1940–42) and then in the studios. He was with Ahmad Jamal during most of 1954–62, propelling some of the pianist's finest trios. He toured with Benny

Goodman during part of 1955–56 and in 1962 joined the George Shearing Quintet but died of a heart attack two months after recording with Shearing. —*Scott Yanow*

Crusaders

Group / Soul Jazz, Hard Bop, Crossover
Back in 1954 Houston pianist Joe Sample teamed up with high-school friends tenor saxophonist Wilton Felder and drummer Stix Hooper to form the Swingsters. Within a short time they were joined by trombonist Wayne Henderson, flutist Hubert Laws and bassist Henry Wilson and the group became the Modern Jazz Sextet. With the move of Sample, Felder, Hooper and Henderson to Los Angeles in 1960, the band (a quintet with the bass spot constantly changing) took on the name of the Jazz Crusaders. The following year they made their first recordings for Pacific Jazz and throughout the 1960s the group was a popular attraction, mixing together R&B and Memphis soul elements with hard bop; its trombone/tenor frontline became a trademark. By 1971 when all of the musicians were also busy with their own projects, it was decided to call the group simply the Crusaders so it would not be restricted to only playing jazz. After a few excellent albums during the early part of the decade (with guitarist Larry Carlton a strong asset), the group began to decline in quality. In 1975 the band's sound radically changed when Henderson departed to become a full-time producer. 1979's "Street Life" was a hit but also a last hurrah. With Hooper's decision to leave in 1983, the group no longer sounded like the Crusaders and gradually disbanded. In the mid-'90s Henderson and Felder had a reunion as the Crusaders but in reality only Joe Sample has had a strong solo career. —*Scott Yanow*

Looking Ahead / 1961 / Pacific Jazz ✦✦✦✦

At the Lighthouse / Aug. 5, 1962+Aug. 6, 1962 / Pacific Jazz ✦✦✦

Uh Huh / May 15, 1967 / Pacific Jazz ✦✦✦

★ **I** / 1970 / Chisa ✦✦✦✦✦
Their finest modern soul-jazz date. Wilton Felder burns on tenor, and the arrangements meld funk beats and jazz licks to maximum success. —*Ron Wynn*

Second Crusade / 1972 / Chisa ✦✦✦✦

Those Southern Knights / 1975 / MCA ✦✦

Scratch / 1975 / MCA ✦✦✦
One of their best. This is a prime example of The Crusaders doing the soul-jazz they invented and perfected. —*Ron Wynn*

Chain Reaction / 1975 / MCA ✦✦✦

Free As the Wind / Dec. 1976 / MCA ✦✦

Images / 1978 / MCA ✦✦

Street Life / 1979 / MCA ✦✦✦

Rhapsody & Blues / Mar. 1980 / MCA ✦✦

Standing Tall / 1980 / MCA ✦✦

Rhapsody And Blues / Standing Tall / 1980 / MCA ✦✦

Live in Japan / Jan. 1981 / GRP ✦✦✦
This CD consists of a complete concert recorded shortly before drummer Stix Hooper left The Crusaders. Far superior to most of The Crusader's later studio recordings, the funky date (which is an excellent summation of the group's previous five years) was one of the band's last worthwhile recordings. The passionate solos of tenorman Wilton Felder and keyboardist Joe Sample take chances within the genre and make this a particularly spirited date. —*Scott Yanow*

Royal Jam / Sep. 1981 / MCA ✦✦

The Good and the Bad Times / 1986 / MCA ✦✦

Life in the Modern World / 1988 / MCA ✦

Healing the Wounds / 1991 / GRP ✦✦

Ronnie Cuber

b. Dec. 25, 1941, New York, NY
Baritone Saxophone / Hard Bop
A powerful baritonist in the tradition of Pepper Adams, Ronnie Cuber has been making excellent records for over 20 years. He was in Marshall Brown's Newport Youth Band at the 1959 Newport Jazz Festival and was featured with the groups of Slide Hampton (1962), Maynard Ferguson (1963–65) and George Benson (1966–67). After stints with Lionel Hampton (1968), Woody Herman's Orchestra (1969) and as a freelancer, he record-

ed a series of fine albums (both as a leader and as a sideman) for Xanadu and performed with Lee Konitz's nonet (1977–79). In the mid-'80s Cuber recorded for Projazz (in both straight-ahead and R&Bish settings), in the early '90s he headed dates for Fresh Sound and Steepl Chase and performed regularly with the Mingus Big Band. —*Scott Yanow*

● **Cuber Libre** / Aug. 20, 1976 / Xanadu ✦✦✦✦✦
This quartet session was a perfect setting for baritonist Ronnie Cuber, who was 34 years old at the time. Joined by the impeccable pianist Barry Harris, bassist Sam Jones and drummer Albert "Tootie" Heath, Cuber gets to swing hard on such standards as "Star Eyes," "Rifftide" and "Tin Tin Deo." Throughout this bop-oriented date, Cuber shows why he has been considered one of the top masters of the baritone during the past 20 years. —*Scott Yanow*

The Eleventh Day of Aquarius / Jan. 31, 1978 / Xanadu ✦✦✦✦
A quintet with Tom Harrell (tpt) and the Mickey Tucker Trio playing Latin and jazz. —*Michael G. Nastos*

Passion Fruit / Feb. 29, 1985 / King ✦✦✦
George Benson (g) makes a guest appearance on this well-engineered recording. —*Ron Wynn*

Two Brothers / Nov. 21, 1985–Dec. 9, 1985 / Intersound ✦✦✦
Some hard bop, some blues, and a few things in between on this '85 set. Cuber's lumbering baritone is backed by a group proficient at either mainstream or more funky material, fueled by drummer Steve Gadd. "Green Dolphin Street" is a high point. —*Ron Wynn*

Live at the Blue Note / Nov. 3, 1986 / Intersound ✦✦✦✦
Good, sometimes fiery session, featuring baritone and soprano saxophonist Cuber heading a group with Randy Brecker, organist Lonnie Smith, and drummer Ronnie Burrage. There's plenty of blues, soul-jazz, and hard bop.—*Ron Wynn*

The Scene Is Clean / Dec. 1993 / Milestone ✦✦✦

Jim Cullum

b. Sep. 20, 1941, San Antonio, TX
Cornet / Dixieland, Classic Jazz
A powerful cornetist inspired by Louis Armstrong, Jim Cullum has led an exciting jazz band in San Antonio since his father's death in the 1970s. A clarinetist, Jim Sr. led the Happy Jazz Band with Jim Jr. on cornet, recording for their own Audiophile and Happy Jazz labels. The younger Cullum, who has recorded a *Porgy and Bess* jazz set for Sony and tributes to Louis Armstrong and Hoagy Carmichael, has made quite a few rewarding albums for Stomp Off and Audiophile in recent years plus a Christmas record for World Jazz. Among his best sidemen has been the talented clarinetist Allan Vache (brother of Warren). —*Scott Yanow*

Porgy & Bess / Dec. 19, 1985–Jan. 1987 / Columbia ✦✦✦✦

● **Hooray for Hoagy!** / Jan. 1990 / Audiophile ✦✦✦✦✦
Cornetist Jim Cullum leads one of the finest classic jazz/Dixieland bands of the 1990s. For this Audiophile CD his septet (which also includes trombonist Mike Pittsley, clarinetist Allan Vache and pianist John Sheridan) plays 14 Hoagy Carmichael songs including such rarely performed numbers as "Kinda Lonesome," "I Walk with Music" and "Snowball" and a few of the "hits" (including "Star Dust" and "Skylark"). A special highpoint is the multi-tempoed treatment given "Washboard Blues" during its nearly 9 1/2 minutes. Easily recommended both for the melodic ensembles (many of which are arranged) and the strong solo work. —*Scott Yanow*

Shootin' The Agate / Aug. 9, 1992–Aug. 10, 1992 / Stomp Off ✦✦✦✦

Bill Cunliffe

Piano / Post-Bop, Hard Bop
One of the more promising pianists currently based in the L.A. area, Bill Cunliffe has been careful to have each of his recordings have its own personality. He won the 1989 Thelonious Monk piano award, for a time led the fusion band Porcupine, works with Natalie Cole and in the studios, and is a regular member of both the Clayton-Hamilton Jazz Orchestra and the Clayton Brothers Quartet. Cunliffe's recordings for Discovery have included *A Paul Simon Songbook* (on which he turned a dozen of Simon's pop tunes into jazz), *A Rare Connection* (a post bop set filled with new originals) and *Bill in Brazil* (a bossa nova and Latin-jazz program). —*Scott Yanow*

● **Rare Connection** / Jun. 19, 1993 / Discovery ✦✦✦✦✦
Los Angeles-based keyboardist Bill Cunliffe is in excellent form on his Discovery CD, performing two standards, Wayne Shorter's "Miyako" and seven of his originals. Cunliffe utilizes some of L.A.'s top players (Bob Sheppard on tenor and bass clarinet, trumpeter Clay Jenkins, trombonist Bruce Paulson, bassist Dave Carpenter, drummer Peter Erskine and percussionist Kurt Rasmussen) for a set of modern mainstream, jazz that is straight ahead but not without some surprising twists and turns. "Jamaican Lounge Lizards" which Cunliffe describes as going "from having a Jamaican reggae feel to a barroom brawl" is a highlight of this enjoyable disc. —*Scott Yanow*

A Paul Simon Songbook / Jul. 1993–Aug. 1993 / Discovery ✦✦✦

Bill in Brazil / Jul. 25, 1994–Nov. 18, 1994 / Discovery ✦✦✦
Pianist Bill Cunliffe performs Brailizan-flavored music throughout this CD, part of which was actually recorded in Brazil. Cunliffe's regular trio with bassist Dave Carpenter and drummer Joe LaBarbera is also heard from along with a variety of guests. Although the accessible program puts an accent on the strong melodies, Cunliffe (occasionally sounding a little like Herbie Hancock and Chick Corea) digs in and comes up with some consistently rewarding improvisations. —*Scott Yanow*

Bob Curnow

Arranger, Leader / Post-Bop
Bob Curnow toured with Stan Kenton's Orchestra for a time in the mid-'60s, worked as general manager and producer for Kenton's Creative World label in the 1970s and has extensive experience as a jazz educator. In 1994 Curnow wrote arrangements of a dozen pieces by Pat Metheny and/or Lyle Mays for his 20-piece big band and the successful (and unusual) results were released on a MAMA Foundation CD. —*Scott Yanow*

● **Music Of Pat Metheny & Lyle Mays** / 1994 / MAMAa Foundation ✦✦✦✦✦
Arranger Bob Curnow transcribed a dozen compositions by Pat Metheny and/or Lyle Mays (originally recorded by the Pat Metheny Group) and adapted them for his Stan Kenton-influenced big band. The instrumentation differs drastically from Metheny's quartet and some of the pieces were originally very electric but somehow these new renditions make the songs sound as if they were originally designed for this orchestra. The 20-piece big band is full of some of the cream of L.A.'s jazz scene and includes such soloists as trombonists Andy Martin and Rick Culver, saxophonists Bob Sheppard, Rob Lockart and Danny House, pianist Bill Cunliffe and a mighty trumpet section. This is an unusual concept that somehow works perfectly and with surprising logic. —*Scott Yanow*

Ted Curson

b. Jun. 3, 1935, Philadelphia, PA
Trumpet / Avant-Garde, Post-Bop, Hard Bop
An excellent and flexible trumpeter, Ted Curson will always be best-known for his work with Charles Mingus' 1960 quartet (which also included Eric Dolphy and Dannie Richmond). He studied at Granoff Musical Conservatory, moved to New York in 1986 and played in New York with Mal Waldron, Red Garland and Philly Joe Jones and recorded with Cecil Taylor (1961). After the 1959-60 Mingus association (which resulted in some classic recordings), Curson co-led a quintet with Bill Barron (1960-65), played with Max Roach and led his own groups. He spent time from the late '60s on in Europe (particularly Denmark) but has had a lower profile than one would expect since his return to the U.S. in 1976. Ted Curson has led sessions for Old Town (1961), Prestige, Fontana, Atlantic, Arista, Inner City, Interplay, Chiaroscuro and several European labels but has been barely on records at all since 1980. —*Scott Yanow*

Live at La Tete De L'art / Sep. 15, 1962 / CanAm ✦✦✦

● **Fire Down Below** / Dec. 10, 1962 / Original Jazz Classics ✦✦✦✦✦

Flip Top / Aug. 1, 1964 / Freedom ✦✦✦
This is a Paris date from one of the jazz's best trumpeters, with tenor saxophonist Bill Barron. Some of his better originals. —*Michael G. Nastos*

Tears for Dolphy / Aug. 1, 1964 / Freedom ✦✦✦✦
Trumpeter Ted Curson, a distinctive player who is still best-known for his association with Charles Mingus in 1960, is heard here in a pianoless quartet with tenor saxophonist Bill Barron, bassist

Herb Bushler and drummer Dick Berk. Recorded shortly after Eric Dolphy's premature death, this date is highlighted by Curson's tribute to Eric, but the other eight pieces (all originals by either Curson or Barron) are also worthy, ranging from early free bop to conventional swinging with occasional hints of the trumpeter's avant-garde past. *—Scott Yanow*

Ted Curson and Co. / Jul. 1, 1976 / India Navigation ✦✦✦

Jubilant Power / Oct. 16, 1976+Oct. 17, 1976 / Inner City ✦✦✦✦
Slashing, dynamite exchanges, and an intense approach make this the Curson to grab. *—Ron Wynn*

King Curtis (Curtis Ousley)
b. Feb. 7, 1934, Fort Worth, TX, **d.** Aug. 14, 1971, New York, NY
Tenor Saxophone / R&B
King Curtis spent most of his life playing R&B and doing studio work, but on an occasional basis he would perform jazz, as if to show possible detractors that he really could play. After touring with Lionel Hampton (1951) he settled in New York and was soon doing session work with the Coasters as an anonymous but memorable soloist whose identity was unknown to all but fellow musicians. From then on he became a major studio player, appearing on a countless number of pop and rock & roll dates. He became Aretha Franklin's musical director shortly before his tragic death from a stabbing. Curtis' two excellent sets with Nat Adderley in 1960 and his appearance at the 1971 Montreux Jazz Festival in support of Champion Jack Dupree (Curtis' last recording) are the highpoints of his career from a jazz standpoint. *—Scott Yanow*

● **The New Scene of King Curtis** / Apr. 21, 1960 / Original Jazz Classics ✦✦✦✦
Tenor and soprano saxophonist King Curtis made several R&B and pop recordings during his career, and also was a prolific session artist. What's not quite as well known was that he also made some jazz and blues recordings in the early '60s, among them this 1960 date that matched him with Wynton Kelly, Oliver Jackson, and Paul Chambers doing mostly hard bop, plus some blues backing Little Brother Montgomery. It was reissued on CD in 1985. *—Ron Wynn*

Andrew Cyrille
b. Nov. 10, 1959, New York, NY
Drums / Avant-Garde, Free Jazz
Drummer Andrew Cyrille is an outstanding percussionist and among the more far-sighted players of his generation. His ability to interact with pianist Cecil Taylor seemed almost instinctive on many records; he could provide multiple rhythms and accents, compliment Taylor's direction, change the music's pace or support the powerful solos of Taylor, saxophonist Jimmy Lyons and any others involved in the dialogue. He was seldom cast in the customary pattern of pushing the beat with Taylor; Cyrille has also excelled as a session player and bandleader. He began playing drums at 11, and studied at

Juilliard. During the early '50s he worked with Illinois Jacquet doing swing and bebop and played African and funk/rock/R&B with Olatunji. Cyrille recorded with Coleman Hawkins and Walt Dickerson on Prestige sessions, and Bill Barron on Savoy. He also played with Rahsaan Roland Kirk and Cedar Walton before working over a decade with Taylor, including one stint at Antioch College as an artist-in-residence. Cyrille was featured on numerous Taylor records for Blue Note, Arista/Freedom, Leo, Shandar and many other labels. He also recorded with Lyons, The Jazz Composers Orchestra, Grachan Moncur III and Marion Brown. Cyrille, Milford Graves and Rashied Ali played and recorded together in the '70s, and Cyrille also did a duo date with Graves. During the '70s and '80s, he began making more dates as a leader, working with a sextet, leading Maono with Ted Daniel and doing various sessions for Black Saint, FMP and Ictus. These included a solo percussion set, a trio with Lyons and vocalist Jeannie Lee, and another duet date with German multi-instrumentalist Peter Brotzmann. He was featured on a tremendous session for DIW/Sony with Oliver Lake and Hannibal in 1992. A decent amount of Cyrille titles, many of them duets, are available on CD, plus some of his output with Taylor. In recent times the always-adaptable drummer has worked with Reggie Workman, Marilyn Crispell, Billy Bang and Anthony Braxton. *—Ron Wynn*

Dialogue of the Drums / 1974 / Institute Percussive ✦✦✦

● **Metamusicians' Stomp** / Sep. 1978 / Black Saint ✦✦✦✦✦

Nuba / 1979 / Black Saint ✦✦✦
Drummer Andrew Cyrille and alto saxophonist Jimmy Lyons developed an impressive chemistry during their years with Cecil Taylor. Cyrille's array of percussion instruments and mastery of multiple styles, from hard bop to Afro-Latin, enabled him to play rippling rhythms or light, tinkling lines, attack or lay back. Lyons' alto solos were alternately driving and soft, sometimes searing in their intensity, sometimes more laidback and introspective. Those seeking a standard trio or straight jazz date are advised to look elsewhere; there was nothing conventional or predictable about this one. *—Ron Wynn*

Special People / Oct. 21, 1980+Oct. 22, 1980 / Soul Note ✦✦✦

Andrew Cyrille Meets Peter Brotzmann in Berlin / Mar. 19, 1982–Mar. 21, 1982 / FMP ✦✦✦✦

The Navigator / Sep. 21, 1982+Sep. 22, 1982 / Soul Note ✦✦✦
Cyrille displayed his facility at sympathetically and smartly guiding other players throughout this date, interacting with bassist Nick Di Geronimo to design a framework that allowed trumpeter Ted Daniel maximum space and room for his piercing solos, and spurred pianist Sonelius Smith. When necessary, Cyrille soloed with a rigorous discipline and percussive vitality, but was more concerned with overall group dynamics and sound. Daniel was particularly impressive on longer cuts, where his lines, phrases and solos were crisp, expertly articulated and surging. The sound was bright and full, and this is an example of thoughtful, nicely played group improvisation. *—Ron Wynn*

D

Albert Dailey

b. Jun. 16, 1938, Baltimore, MD, **d.** Jun. 26, 1984, Denver, CO
Piano / Post-Bop, Hard Bop
A sorely-neglected and underrated pianist during his lifetime, Albert Dailey's skill and verve as a soloist was greatly appreciated and eulogized following his death. An often hypnotic stylist, his shimmering harmonies and phrases were particularly admired by Stan Getz, with whom he worked in the mid-'70s. Daily began piano studies at an early age, then played in the Baltimore Royal Theater's house band in the early and mid-'50s. He attended Morgan State and Peabody Conservatory in the late '50s. Dailey toured with vocalist Damita Jo from 1960 to 1963, then led a trio at the Bohemia Caverns in Washington, D.C. before moving to New York in 1964. Dailey played with Dexter Gordon, Roy Haynes, Sarah Vaughan and Charles Mingus, while recording with Freddie Hubbard. He performed and recorded with Woody Herman at the 1967 Monterey Jazz Festival, and was in Art Blakey's Jazz Messengers during the late '60s and again in the mid-'70s. Dailey played periodically with Sonny Rollins, toured and recorded with Stan Getz, and also cut sessions with Elvin Jones and Archie Shepp in the '70s. He performed at Carnegie Hall and in the Mobil Summerpier Concerts series in the '80s, while also playing in The Upper Manhattan Jazz Society with Charlie Rouse, Benny Bailey and Buster Williams. He recorded for Columbia, SteepleChase, Muse and Elektra, with his '72 debut *The Day After The Dawn* getting widespread critical praises but not enough sales to keep Columbia from dropping him after that one date. He has only one session currently available on CD. —*Ron Wynn*

That Old Feeling / Jul. 13, 1978 / SteepleChase ✦✦✦

Textures / Jun. 4, 1981 / Muse ✦✦✦
This 1981 session has Dailey working with a pianoless trio keyed by saxophonist Arthur Rhames, plus bassist Rufus Reid and drummer Eddie Gladden. Dailey was a particular favorite of Stan Getz and was especially strong doing uptempo material. —*Ron Wynn*

● **Poetry** / 1983 / Elektra ✦✦✦✦✦

Meredith D'Ambrosio

b. 1941, Boston, MA
Piano, Vocals / Cool
A soft, polished, yet also striking vocalist and pianist, Meredith D'Ambrosio has issued several nice, unimposing albums for Sunnyside. She's sung standards, provided her own lyrics for John Coltrane's "Giant Steps" and Dave Brubeck's "Strange Meadowlark," and added sparse piano accompaniment. D'Ambrosio's style and sound isn't as quirky as Blossom Dearie, nor as captivating as Mose Allison, but she's succeeded in making music that's undeniably distinctive and individualistic. She's not a powerful, gripping or dynamic singer or pianist, yet she retains the listener's attention by an inspired combination of the right material and effective presentation. D'Ambrosio has several sessions available on CD. —*Ron Wynn and Michael G. Nastos*

Another Time / Feb. 6, 1981 / Sunnyside ✦✦✦

Little Jazz Bird / Mar. 2, 1982 / Palo Alto ✦✦✦
Fine '82 combo session in which D'Ambrosio shows her ability to handle a variety of songs supplied by composers as diverse as harpist Deborah Henson-Conant and vocalist David Frishberg. Phil Woods heads a capable backing band and supplies his cus-

tomary heated alto sax solos, while Hank Jones lends some flair on piano. —*Ron Wynn*

It's Your Dance / Mar. 27, 1985+Mar. 28, 1985 / Sunnyside ✦✦✦✦
A first-rate trio date, possibly D'Ambrosio's finest in that format. Her singing has punch, variety, and dimension, and her phrasing is creative and expertly constructed. Kevin Eubanks' guitar contributions are concise, thoughtful, and without any gimmicks or wasted riffs. D'Ambrosio and Harold Danko interact smoothly, and his piano backing is delicate and supportive. —*Ron Wynn*

The Cove / Oct. 27, 1987–Oct. 28, 1987 / Sunnyside ✦✦✦✦

South to a Warmer Place / Feb. 1989 / Sunnyside ✦✦✦
Eddie Higgins Trio joined by trumpeter Lou Columbo. Two lyrics by singer. Sweetness and light. —*Michael G. Nastos*

● **Love Is Not a Game** / Dec. 19, 1990–Dec. 20, 1990 / Sunnyside ✦✦✦✦✦
With husband Eddie Higgins Trio. Dreamy, soft-voiced D'Ambrosio makes a definitive emotional statement. Fifteen tracks, nine standards (three adapted or modified by D'Ambrosio). Five written by her. Nice twisting on "I Love You/You I Love," "Oh, Look at Me Now/But Now Look at Me," and "Lament/This Lament." —*Michael G. Nastos*

Sleep Warm / Feb. 23, 1991 / Sunnyside ✦✦✦

Tadd Dameron

b. Feb. 21, 1917, Cleveland, OH, **d.** Mar. 8, 1965, New York, NY
Piano, Arranger, Composer / Bop
The definitive arranger/composer of the bop era, Tadd Dameron wrote such standards as "Good Bait," "Our Delight," "Hot House," "Lady Bird," and "If You Could See Me Now." Not only did he write melody lines but full arrangements and he was an influential force from the mid-'40s on even though he never financially prospered. Dameron started out in the swing era touring with the Zack Whyte and Blanche Calloway bands, wrote for Vido Musso in New York and most importantly contributed arrangements for Harlan Leonard's Kansas City Orchestra, some of which were recorded. Soon Dameron was writing charts for such bands as Jimmie Lunceford, Count Basie, Billy Eckstine and Dizzy Gillespie (1945–47) in addition to Sarah Vaughan. Dameron was always very modest about his own piano playing but he did gig with Babs Gonzales' Three Bips and a Bop in 1947 and led a sextet featuring Fats Navarro (and later Miles Davis) at the Royal Roost during 1948–49. Dameron co-led a group with Davis at the 1949 Paris Jazz Festival, stayed in Europe for a few months (writing for Ted Heath) and then returned to New York. He wrote for Artie Shaw's last orchestra that year, played and arranged R&B for Bull Moose Jackson (1951–52) and in 1953 led a nonet featuring Clifford Brown and Philly Joe Jones. However drug problems started to get in the way of his music. After recording a couple of albums (including 1958's *Mating Call* with John Coltrane) he spent much of 1959–61 in jail. After he was released, Dameron wrote for Sonny Stitt, Blue Mitchell, Milt Jackson, Benny Goodman and his last record, but was less active in the years before his death from cancer. Tadd Dameron's classic Blue Note recordings of 1947–48, his 1949 Capitol sides and Prestige/Riverside sets of 1953, 1956, 1958 and 1962 are all currently in print on CD. —*Scott Yanow*

Anthropology / Aug. 1949–1949 / Spotlite ✦✦✦

Fontainebleau / Mar. 9, 1956 / Original Jazz Classics ✦✦✦✦
Fontainebleau put greater emphasis on arrangements and those who might have hoped for a blowing date with Kenny Dorham, Henry Coker, Sahib Shihab, Joe Alexander, Cecil Payne, John

Simmons and Shadow Wilson would be advised to look else-where…It was mostly for the arranging that one would pick this up, for it did offer some nice examples of the floating, suspended heat that marked this arranger's touch. —*Bob Rusch, Cadence*

Mating Call / Nov. 30, 1956 / Original Jazz Classics ✦✦✦✦
Super quartet session with John Coltrane (ts). —*Ron Wynn*

● **The Magic Touch of Tadd Dameron** / Feb. 27, 1962 / Original Jazz Classics ✦✦✦✦✦

Dameronia

Group / Bop
In the early '80s drummer Philly Joe Jones, with the strong assis-tance of trumpeter Donald Sickler (who transcribed the arrange-ments), revived the music of Tadd Dameron in a nonet called Dameronia. Two Uptown records resulted (with such sidemen as Walter Davis, Jr., Britt Woodman, Frank Wess and Cecil Payne) before Jones' 1985 death. In 1989 Sickler gathered together the alumni (with Kenny Washington on drums) for a special Paris concert that was documented on Soul Note. —*Scott Yanow*

● **To Tadd with Love** / Jun. 28, 1982 / Uptown ✦✦✦✦✦
Drummer Philly Joe Jones during his last years led the group Dameronia, a band dedicated to performing the music of the great composer Tadd Dameron. Their debut disc for Uptown has Donald Sickler's transcriptions of six Dameron originals (includ-ing "Philly J.J.," "Soultrane" and "On a Misty Night"). The nonet is comprised of many fine veteran players: trumpeters Sickler and Johnny Coles, trombonist Britt Woodman, altoist Frank Wess, Charles Davis on tenor, baritonist Cecil Payne, pianist Walter Davis, Jr., bassist Larry Ridley and Jones himself. This loving trib-ute (which perfectly balances the arrangements with concise solo space) is highly recommended. —*Scott Yanow*

Live at The Theatre Boulogne / May 30, 1989 / Soul Note ✦✦✦✦
Dameronia, a group organized by drummer Phily Joe Jones to perform the great bop-era arrangements of Tadd Dameron, came back together four years after Jones' death for a concert in France. Fortunately it was recorded and released on this Soul Note CD for, since that time, tenor saxophonist Clifford Jordan and pianist Walter Davis, Jr., have also passed away. In addition to those two masters, the 1989 version of Dameronia included trumpeters Don Sickler (whose transcriptions made this group possible) and Virgil Jones, trombonist Benny Powell, Frank Wess on alto and flute, baritonist Cecil Payne, bassist Larry Ridley and drummer Kenny Washington. The ensembles are very much in Dameron's classic style but happily all of the musicians also have plenty of solo space. Tadd Dameron's legacy was very well-served by Dameronia and this set is a fine tribute. —*Scott Yanow*

Eddie Daniels

b. Oct. 19, 1941, New York, NY
Clarinet, Tenor Saxophone / Hard Bop, Post-Bop
One of the truly great jazz clarinetists (ranking at the top with Benny Goodman, Artie Shaw and Buddy DeFranco), Daniels makes the impossible look effortless. On his first GRP release *Breakthrough* in 1984, Daniels switched back and forth on a sec-ond's notice between jazz and classical and he has since explored Charlie Parker, Roger Kellaway tunes, crossover and even swing with consistent brilliance. He is also a dazzling (if underrated) tenor player. Daniels appeared at the 1957 Newport Jazz Festival in Marshall Brown's Youth band (playing alto) and after gradu-ating from Juilliard in 1966 he played tenor with the Thad Jones-Mel Lewis Orchestra for six years. Daniels recorded *First Prize* as a leader (1966) and made albums with Freddie Hubbard (1969), Richard Davis, Don Patterson and duets with Bucky Pizzarelli (1973). Although he recorded as a leader for Muse and Columbia during 1977-78, Eddie Daniels did not make it big until he start-ed specializing on clarinet and recording regularly for GRP in 1984. In 1992 he started doubling on tenor again now that his reputation on clarinet was secure. —*Scott Yanow*

First Prize / Sep. 8, 1966+Sep. 12, 1966 / Original Jazz Classics ✦✦✦✦
When one hears this early Eddie Daniels CD (a straight reissue of the original LP), it is surprising to realize that he would remain in relative obscurity for almost another 20 years. As shown on three of the eight selections on which he plays clarinet, Daniels (even at this early stage) ranked near the top while his tenor play-ing on the remaining numbers was already personal and virtu-

osic. With the assistance of The Thad Jones/Mel Lewis rhythm sec-tion of the time (pianist Roland Hanna, bassist Richard Davis and drummer Mel Lewis), Daniels is in top form on three standards, four originals and the pop tune "Spanish Flea." —*Scott Yanow*

Flower for All Seasons / Feb. 1973 / Choice ✦✦✦
With Bucky Pizzarelli. A good tribute to the compositional mettle of Roger Kellaway. —*Ron Wynn*

Brief Encounter / Jul. 11, 1977 / Muse ✦✦✦
Steady mainstream date by Daniels, who became a clarinet star in the '80s. He plays both clarinet and tenor sax and does straight-ahead material, backed by pianist Andy Laverne, bassist Rick Laird, and drummer Billy Mintz. It was issued on vinyl in 1977 and reissued on CD in 1986. —*Ron Wynn*

Morning Thunder / 1978 / Columbia ✦✦✦

★ **Breakthrough** / 1986 / GRP ✦✦✦✦✦

Memos from Paradise / Dec. 16, 1987-Jan. 4, 1988 / GRP ✦✦✦
Excellent, soaring clarinet solos by Eddie Daniels help overcome occasional compositional defects on this late '80s set. Daniels emerged during this decade as the clarinet's reigning soloist, and showed why with plenty of spiraling, exhaustive contributions. The orchestrations sometimes got sappy, and Roger Kellaway's piano playing was more nice than exuberant. But the disc was very popular with the light jazz and Adult Contemporary audi-ence. —*Ron Wynn*

To Bird with Love / 1987 / GRP ✦✦✦✦

Blackwood / 1989 / GRP ✦✦✦
Eddie Daniels is such a monster on the clarinet that all of his GRP recordings are worth acquiring. This one, however, due to the somewhat commercial nature of some of the tunes (and the light-ly funky rhythm sections), is of lesser interest compared to the classics such as *Breakthrough*. Daniels sounds fine but he is far better than much of the material (generally written by either the clarinetist, Rob Mounsey or Dave Grusin). —*Scott Yanow*

Nepenthe / Dec. 6, 1989-Dec. 9, 1989 / GRP ✦✦✦

This Is Now / 1991 / GRP ✦✦✦

Benny Rides Again / Jan. 14, 1992-Jan. 15, 1992 / GRP ✦✦✦

Under the Influence / 1993 / GRP ✦✦✦✦✦
After a decade of exclusively playing clarinet (and establishing himself as one of the greats), Eddie Daniels began doubling on tenor again on this recording. Switching between his two axes, Daniels sounds in top form on some diverse but consistently rewarding originals and a few standards ("I Hear a Rhapsody," "Weaver of Dreams," "I Fall in Love Too Easily" and an exciting version of Bill Evans' "Five"). Joined by pianist Alan Pasqua, bassist Mike Formanek and drummer Peter Erskine, Eddie Daniels really digs into these tunes and both his virtuosity and his inventive improvisations are quite impressive. —*Scott Yanow*

Real Time / May 26, 1994-May 27, 1994 / Chesky ✦✦✦✦

Five Seasons / Aug. 1995 / Shanachie ✦✦✦

Palle Danielsson

b. Oct. 15, 1946, Stockholm, Sweden
Bass / Post-Bop
Palle Danielsson is best-known for his work as a sideman with a variety of top leaders. He studied violin for five years starting when he was eight. Danielsson then switched to bass and was playing professionally when he was 15. After studying at the Stockholm Royal Academy of Music (1962-66) he began to play with some of the top Scandinavian musicians including Jan Garbarek and Bobo Stenson. When American jazzmen passed through his country, they often asked for Danielsson; he worked with Bill Evans, George Russell, Ben Webster and Charlie Shavers. He gained fame for being part of Keith Jarrett's European quartet (1974-79), a group that also included Jan Garbarek. Danielsson has also toured and recorded with Charles Lloyd (early '80s), Michel Petrucciani and Kenny Wheeler. —*Scott Yanow*

James Dapogny

b. Sept. 3, 1940, Berwyn, IL
Piano, Leader / Swing, Classic Jazz
An excellent stride and swing pianist and an important musicol-ogist, James Dapogny's recordings (particularly his recent ones for Discovery) have helped to keep classic jazz alive. An educator who has taught jazz theory and history at the University of

Michigan since 1966, Dapogny has written a complete book of transcriptions of the work of Jelly Roll Morton. As a pianist/bandleader, he has generally been based in Chicago, giving veteran blues singer Sippie Wallace exciting support in her 1982 Atlantic release and recording an excellent series of CDs with his combo for Discovery; the two most recent sets focus on the music of Morton and small-group swing respectively. —*Scott Yanow*

The Piano Music of J. R. Morton / 1976 / Smithsonian ✦✦✦
Pianist James Dapogny, in his recording debut as a leader, does a good job of interpreting a dozen of Jelly Roll Morton's compositions. Dapogny's improvisations are fairly subtle, mostly sticking close to Morton's written-out music and giving listeners a good introduction to the jazz pioneer's style. This deluxe LP also has extensive and definitive liner notes. —*Scott Yanow*

Chicago Jazz Band / Jun. 17, 1982 / Jazzology ✦✦✦✦
Recorded in a St. Louis studio with an octet. Nine cuts ranging from early Dixieland. Dapogny wrote "Dreamer's Blues." The band plays in an up mode. Paul Klinger (cnt), Peter Ferran, and Russell Whitman (reeds), Hal Smith (d) stand out. A fine display of traditional jazz. —*Michael G. Nastos*

How Could We Be Blue? / Feb. 20, 1988–Feb. 21, 1988 / Stomp Off ✦✦✦
Recorded in Ann Arbor, MI. Duets on twin pianos with Dapogny and Butch Thompson. Great idea to team these two. Twelve cuts. "Today's Blues" written by participants. Material by Morton, Waller, Ellington, Sidney Bechet, and others. Thompson plays clarinet on two tracks. —*Michael G. Nastos*

Laughing at Life / 1992 / Discovery ✦✦✦✦
Dapogny is one of the few traditional jazz bandleaders whose music doesn't sound totally dated. Although he adheres to all the genre's conventions, his band plays with spirit and conviction, putting some energy and life into ancient material. —*Ron Wynn*

Original Jelly Roll Blues [Music of Jelly Roll Morton] / Jul. 1993 / Discovery ✦✦✦✦✦

★ **Hot Club Stomp** / Jun. 17, 1994–Jun. 19, 1994 / Discovery ✦✦✦✦✦
This delightful Discovery disc is subtitled "Small Band Swing" and the description fits perfectly. Pianist James Dapogny, whose previous recording was a tribute to Jelly Roll Morton, moved his music up ten years for this outing with his four-horn octet. Many of the ensembles are arranged but there is plenty of room for spontaneity as Dapogny and his sidemen explore 13 mostly obscure songs from the swing era. The frameworks, constantly swinging rhythm and melodic solos (trumpeter JonErik Kellso is a standout) sound very much from the mid-'30s but yet are quite fresh and full of life. —*Scott Yanow*

David Darling

b. Mar. 4, 1941, Elkhart, IN
Cello / New Age, Post-Bop
David Darling has done substantial improvisational sessions, but his work doesn't fall into hard bop or mainstream context. He learned piano and cello as a child and played bass and alto sax in his high school band, as well as being its leader. Darling studied cello and music education at Indiana University, then taught there from 1966 to 1980. He spent eight years with The Paul Winter Consort, touring the country and also recording with them. Darling made his solo debut in 1979, and also displayed his own homemade cello, an eight-string electric he designed. Darling was a founding member of the group Gallery in 1981, and he has recorded and worked with such musicians as Ralph Towner, Glen Moore, John Clark, Spyro Gyra and Terje Rypdal. —*Ron Wynn*

Kenny Davern (John Kenneth Davern)

b. Jan. 7, 1935, Huntington, NY
Clarinet / Dixieland, Swing
One of the finest clarinetists in traditional jazz of the past 20 years (and able to hit notes far above the normal register) Davern has been an excellent player since the 1950s. He started playing professionally when he was 16 and in 1954 made his recording debut with Jack Teagarden. He picked up experience playing with Phil Napoleon's Memphis Five (1955), Pee Wee Erwin, Wild Bill Davison, Red Allen, Buck Clayton and Jo Jones. Davern led a band at Nick's in the early '60s and was with the Dukes of Dixieland during 1962-63. After associations with Eddie Condon, Herman Autrey and Ruby Braff, Davern co-led Soprano Summit during

1974–79 with Bob Wilber. Up until that point Davern had doubled on clarinet and soprano but after the group's breakup he decided to specialize exclusively on clarinet. He formed the Blue Three (with Dick Wellstood and Bobby Rosengarden) in the early '80s, recorded several fine sets for Music Masters in the 1980s and '90s and in recent times has had several matchups with Bob Wilber in a new Soprano Summit retitled Soprano Reunion. —*Scott Yanow*

★ **Soprano Summit** / Mar. 1976 / Concord Jazz ✦✦✦✦✦
Live at the Concord Festival with Bob Wilber and quintet. Two Wilber originals, one by guitarist Marty Grosz. A fine representation of two artists in Dixie-early-swing mode with blues and a touch of Ellington. —*Michael G. Nastos*

The Hot Three / Jul. 1, 1979 / Monmouth ✦✦✦✦✦

El Rado Scuffle / Jun. 7, 1980 / Kenneth ✦✦✦
A tribute to Jimmy Noone. With Swedish sextet. —*Michael G. Nastos*

The Blue Three at Hanratty's / 1981 / Chaz Jazz ✦✦✦✦✦

Stretchin' Out / Dec. 18, 1983 / Jazzology ✦✦✦
A fine swing/traditional date with Dick Wellstood (p) and Chuck Riggs (d). —*Ron Wynn*

Kenny Davern And Dick Wellstood / Jan. 15, 1984 / Challenge ✦✦✦✦
Clarinetist Kenny Davern and pianist Dick Wellstood make for a potent duo on this live session. Two of the top trad jazz musicians to emerge during the 1940s (thereby making them a bit out-of-place in their generation), both Davern and Wellstood developed their own individual voices. Their strong performance of stomps and ballads also has a bit of storytelling as Wellstood talks about how he got started and the challenges of playing stride piano while Davern recalls his reaction when he first heard fellow clarinetist Pee Wee Russell. But more importantly the music is very enjoyable and often surprisingly wistful. This CD release from the Dutch label Challenge is fortunately readily available in the U.S. —*Scott Yanow*

Kenny Davern Big Three / Nov. 25, 1985 / Jazzology ✦✦✦✦✦

Live Hot Jazz / 1986 / Statiras ✦✦✦

I'll See You in My Dreams / Jan. 1988 / Music Masters ✦✦✦✦

One Hour Tonight / Jan. 1988 / Music Masters ✦✦✦✦

My Inspiration / Sep. 12, 1991 / Music Masters ✦✦✦
Traditional jazz and light swing by distinguished clarinetist Kenny Davern, working with a sympathetic rhythm section and symphony orchestra. His wavery, floating solos aren't subsumed or obscured by the strings, while guitarist Howard Alden, drummer Bobby Rosengarden, and bassist Bob Haggart fall in perfectly in the middle. —*Ron Wynn*

East Side, West Side / Jun. 24, 1994 / Arbors ✦✦✦✦
The most unusual aspect to this trad jazz sextet session led by clarinetist Kenny Davern is that it features trombonist Dan Barrett playing cornet on all but one selection. Although Barrett is not as distinctive as on his normal ax, his solos are quite enjoyable and hold their own with Davern, trombonist Joel Helleny and guitarist Buck Pizzarelli; bassist Bob Haggart and drummer Tony DeNicola complete the fine group. The repertoire is mostly comprised of underplayed standards with the highlights including "There'll Be Some Changes Made," "Delta Bound," "Sidewalks of New York," "There's Yes! Yes! in Your Eyes" and "Please Be Kind," It's recommended to swing and classic jazz fans. —*Scott Yanow*

Anthony Davis

b. Feb. 20, 1951, Paterson, NJ
Piano, Composer / Avant-Garde, Post-Bop
Anthony Davis, a major composer of the late 20th century, stretches beyond jazz into modern classical music although he has recorded quite a few rewarding jazz sessions. He studied classical music as a child and in 1975 graduated from Yale. A member of the New Delta Ahkri during 1974-77 (which was led by Leo Smith), Davis moved to New York in 1977, played with Oliver Lake, Anthony Braxton, Chico Freeman, George Lewis and Leroy Jenkins' trio (1977-79) and worked often with James Newton and Abdul Wadud. Davis formed an octet (Episteme) in 1981 which played both improvised and wholly composed music. Anthony Davis composed the opera X (based on the life of Malcolm X) in the early '80s and he taught at Yale in the early '80s. Davis has recorded for India Navigation, Red, Sackville and Gramavision. —*Scott Yanow*

Past Lives / Jun. 7, 1978 / Red ✦✦✦

Of Blues and Dreams / Jul. 30, 1978–Jul. 31, 1978 / Sackville ✦✦✦
On the cutting edge of avant-garde. With violinist Leroy Jenkins and cellist Abdul Wadud. —*Michael G. Nastos*

Song for the Old World / Jul. 1978 / India Navigation ✦✦✦✦
Pianist/composer Anthony Davis has long been one of the most interesting musicians of his generation. His music is difficult to categorize, ranging from explorative jazz to classical with many stops in between. This early album (with a quartet also featuring vibraphonist Jay Hoggard, bassist Mark Helias and drummer Ed Blackwell) finds Davis performing six of his wide-ranging compositions. In addition to a feature for Hoggard and tributes to the bebop generation and Andrew Hill, the most impressive piece is the title cut, which has fragments of melodies from Africa and Asia. This subtle album rewards repeated listenings. —*Scott Yanow*

Hidden Voices / Mar. 1979 / India Navigation ✦✦✦
This quintet album has great teamwork with George Lewis (tb), James Newton (fl). —*Michael G. Nastos*

Under the Double Moon / Sep. 1, 1980–Sep. 2, 1980 / PA/USA ✦✦✦

● **Lady of the Mirrors** / 1980 / India Navigation ✦✦✦✦✦

Episteme / 1981 / Gramavision ✦✦✦

I've Known Rivers / Apr. 1982 / Gramavision ✦✦✦✦
Top-notch improvisers team up. Sparks fly. With James Newton (fl), Abdul Wadud on cello. —*Michael G. Nastos*

Variations in Dreamtime / 1982 / India Navigation ✦✦✦

Hemispheres / Jul. 1983 / Gramavision ✦✦✦

Middle Passage / 1984 / Gramavision ✦✦
A 1984 set mixing Davis' studio and tape piano solos spotlighting originals weaved around the theme of suffering and degradation. The title refers to the many African slaves who died en route from their homeland to America. —*Ron Wynn*

Undine / Jun. 1986 / Gramavision ✦✦✦

Ghost Factory / Apr. 19, 1987–May, 1988 / Gramavision ✦✦✦
The gifted pianist/composer demonstrates his facility with contemporary classical and jazz pieces, playing sometimes in duos, other times trios, and also interacting with The Kansas City Symphony Orchestra. Percussionists Pheeroan Ak Laff or Gerry Hemingway and violinist Shem Guibbory are his partners, while all the compositions are Davis'. —*Ron Wynn*

Trio, Vol. 2 / 1989 / Gramavision ✦✦✦✦✦

Art Davis

b. Dec. 5, 1934, Harrisburg, PA
Bass / Post-Bop, Hard Bop
A top rate player, Art Davis has attained as much acclaim within the jazz community for his work as an educator and teacher in addition to his playing. Davis came to the bass late; he studied piano and tuba first, winning a national competition as a tuba player before starting on bass in 1951. He played with Max Roach in 1958 and 1959, then toured Europe with Dizzy Gillespie in 1959 and 1960. David was extremely busy in the early '60s; He recorded and played with John Coltrane in 1961 and in 1965, and was featured in the bands of Gigi Gryce, Lena Horne, Booker Little, Quincy Jones, Rahsaan Roland Kirk, Oliver Nelson, Freddie Hubbard, Clark Terry and Art Blakey at various times. In addition, Davis was a member of the NBC, CBS and Westinghouse television orchestras between 1962 and 1970. His teaching career began to expand in the '70s. Davis taught at Manhattan Community College from 1971–1973. He earned a BA from Hunter College in 1972, MA degrees from CUNY and New York University in music and psychology in 1976 and a doctorate in psychology in 1981. Davis has since combined being a psychologist with playing music, doing sessions, playing in a duo with Hilton Ruiz in 1985 and 1986, and recording as a leader in 1984. His 1975 book *The Arthur Davis Method for Double Bass* is one of the finest instructional works for the instrument. —*Ron Wynn*

● **Life** / Oct. 5, 1985 / Soul Note ✦✦✦✦
Bassist Art Davis, who occasionally played with John Coltrane in the early '60s, has led relatively few sessions throughout his career. A very talented player with complete control over his instrument, Davis contributed all four selections to this impressive outing which is highlighted by "Duo" (matching his bass with

tenor saxophonist Pharoah Sanders) and the 19-1/2-minute four-part "Add." Davis' all-star quartet also includes pianist John Hicks and drummer Idris Mohammed. —*Scott Yanow*

Charles Davis

b. 1933, Goodman, MI
Baritone Saxophone / Hard Bop
Although he has performed previously on tenor and alto, Charles Davis is best known for his fine baritone playing, both as a soloist and for his dependable work in sax sections. Early on he gigged with Sun Ra (off and on from 1954 into the 1980s), Brother Jack McDuff, Ben Webster, Billie Holiday and Dinah Washington (1957–58). Davis gained some attention when he was with Kenny Dorham's band (1959–62). He also played with Illinois Jacquet, Lionel Hampton, the Jazz Composers' Orchestra (1966–76), Louis Hayes' Sextet (1972–74), Clark Terry's big band and the Thad Jones-Mel Lewis Orchestra. In the 1980s he was with Dameronia (1981–84), Philly Joe Jones, Barry Harris and Abdullah Ibrahim. Charles Davis has led sessions for Strata-East, West 54, Nilva, Red and L&R. —*Scott Yanow*

Dedicated to Tadd / Mar. 1, 1979–Mar. 2, 1979 / West 54 ✦✦✦✦

Super 80 / Jan. 12, 1982 / Nilva ✦✦✦

● **Reflections** / Feb. 19, 1990 / Red ✦✦✦✦✦

Eddie "Lockjaw" Davis

b. Mar. 2, 1922, New York, NY, **d.** Nov. 3, 1986, Culver City, CA
Tenor Saxophone / Bop, Hard Bop, Swing
Possessor of a cutting and immediately identifiable tough tenor tone, Eddie "Lockjaw" Davis could hold his own in a saxophone battle with anyone. Early on he picked up experience playing with the bands of Cootie Williams (1942–44), Lucky Millinder, Andy Kirk (1945–46) and Louis Armstrong. He began heading his own groups from 1946 and Davis' earliest recordings as a leader tended to be explosive R&B affairs with plenty of screaming from his horn; he matched wits successfully with Fats Navarro on one session. Davis was with Count Basie's Orchestra on several occasions (including 1952–53, 1957 and 1964–73) and teamed up with Shirley Scott's trio during 1955–60. During 1960–62 he collaborated in some exciting performances and recordings with Johnny Griffin, a fellow tenor who was just as combative as Davis. After temporarily retiring to become a booking agent (1963–64), Davis rejoined Basie. In his later years Lockjaw often recorded with Harry "Sweets" Edison and he remained a busy soloist up until his death. Through the decades he recorded as a leader for many labels including Savoy, Apollo, Roost, King, Prestige, Prestige/Jazzland/Moodsville, RCA, Storyville, MPS, Black & Blue, Spotlite, SteepleChase, Pablo, Muse and Enja. —*Scott Yanow*

Jaws N' Stitt at Birdland / 1954 / Roulette ✦✦✦

The Eddie Lockjaw Davis Cookbook / Jun. 20, 1958 / Original Jazz Classics ✦✦✦✦

Jaws / Sep. 12, 1958 / Original Jazz Classics ✦✦✦
Tenorman Eddie "Lockjaw" Davis and organist Shirley Scott co-led a popular combo during 1956–60, recording many albums and helping to popularize the idiom. This particular CD reissue of an LP (which at 37 minutes is a bit brief) finds the quartet (with bassist George Duvivier and drummer Arthur Edgehill) interpreting eight swing standards, alternating ballads with romps. It's a fine all-around showcase for the accessible group. —*Scott Yanow*

Smokin' / Sep. 12, 1958+Dec. 5, 1958 / Original Jazz Classics ✦✦✦✦
Tenor saxophonist Eddie "Lockjaw" Davis recorded many albums with organist Shirley Scott during 1956–60, cutting enough material on two dates to fill up four records. The seven selections included on this brief 36-minute CD (a straight reissue of an LP recorded during the same period as Davis' better-known *Cookbook* albums) also include Jerome Richardson (switching between flute, tenor and baritone) on three of the numbers, bassist George Duvivier and drummer Arthur Edgehill. Together the group swings hard on basic originals, blues and an occasional ballad, showing why this type of accessible band was so popular during the era. —*Scott Yanow*

The Eddie Lockjaw Davis Cookbook, Vol. 2 / Sep. 12, 1958–Dec. 15, 1958 / Original Jazz Classics ✦✦✦✦

The Eddie Lockjaw Davis Cookbook, Vol. 3 / Sep. 12, 1958–Dec. 15, 1958 / Prestige ✦✦✦✦
Tenorman Eddie "Lockjaw" Davis made quite a few records with

organist Shirley Scott during the late '50s. The basic originals in their *Cookbook* series tended to have titles that dealt with cooking; in this case "Heat 'N' Serve," "The Goose Hangs High" and "Simmerin" apply as does the standard "My Old Flame." Jerome Richardson's flute, baritone and tenor gives this CD reissue some variety, bassist George Duvivier and drummer Arthur Edgehill are fine in support and Shirley Scott shows that she was one of the top organists to emerge after the rise of Jimmy Smith. But Davis is the main star and his instantly recognizable sound is the most memorable aspect to this swinging session. —*Scott Yanow*

Jaws in Orbit / May 1, 1959 / Original Jazz Classics ✦✦✦
Includes Shirley Scott on the Hammond organ. This is early Scott, not yet all that funky. Traditional swinging, uptempo music. —*Michael Erlewine*

Trane Whistle / Sep. 20, 1960 / Prestige ✦✦✦✦✦

Afro Jaws / May 4, 1961+May 12, 1961 / Original Jazz Classics ✦✦✦✦
1989 reissue of a wild, dashing date with Clark Terry (tpt) and Ernie Royal (tpt). —*Ron Wynn*

Tough Tenor Favorites / Feb. 5, 1962 / Jazzland ✦✦✦

Streetlights / Nov. 15, 1962 / Prestige ✦✦✦✦
This CD combines together the music from two complete LPs that were recorded the same day with the identical personnel. Eddie "Lockjaw" Davis' tough tenor is well featured with his regular group of the time, a combo consisting of the powerful organist Don Patterson (who dominates many of the ensembles), guitarist Paul Weeden (talented but quite obscure), drummer Billy James and guest bassist George Duvivier. The emphasis is on standards and intense blowing (even on the ballads) with the set being a good example of a strong tenor-organ band. —*Scott Yanow*

Lock the Fox / Jun. 20, 1966-Dec. 14, 1966 / RCA ✦✦✦

Tough Tenors Again 'n Again / Apr. 24, 1970 / PA/USA ✦✦✦✦
Includes robust duet/duels with longtime comrade Johnny Griffin (ts). —*Ron Wynn*

Leapin' on Lennox / Jul. 20, 1974 / Black & Blue ✦✦✦

Chewin' the Fat / Oct. 23, 1974 / Spotlite ✦✦✦

Sweet and Lovely / Jul. 26, 1975 / Classic Jazz ✦✦✦
A very inviting blues, ballads, and bop plate. —*Ron Wynn*

Jaws Strikes Again / Jan. 21, 1976 / Black & Blue ✦✦✦

Swingin' 'til the Girls Come Home / Mar. 1976 / SteepleChase ✦✦✦✦✦
This was almost as fine an Eddie "Lockjaw" Davis album as you could want…Jaws followed a pattern of cool to hot as he advanced through a tune, immediately leading to crescendos of gruff, macho, Ben Websterish vibrato on tenor, stopping just short of excessive romanticism. —*Bob Rusch, Cadence*

Straight Ahead / May 3, 1976 / Original Jazz Classics ✦✦✦
Tommy Flanagan is incredible on the piano. —*Ron Wynn*

Montreux '77 / Jul. 15, 1977 / Original Jazz Classics ✦✦✦

Sweets and Jaws / Dec. 1, 1978 / Vogue ✦✦✦

The Heavy Hitter / Jan. 18, 1979 / Muse ✦✦✦✦
Emphatic and mellow mainstream session. —*Ron Wynn*

Jaw's Blues / Feb. 11, 1981 / Enja ✦✦✦✦

★ **All of Me** / Aug. 23, 1983 / SteepleChase ✦✦✦✦✦
Tenorman Eddie "Lockjaw" Davis had already been a potent force in jazz for 35 years when he recorded this set but as it turned out his SteepleChase date (his next-to-last session) was one of the strongest of his career. Accompanied by a trio led by pianist Kenny Drew, Lockjaw really tears into these standards which are highlighted by "I Only Have Eyes for You," two versions of "There Is No Greater Love" (the alternate version was released for the first time on this CD reissue), "Four" and the title cut. Davis was at the peak of his powers during this recording, making his lone SteepleChase outing one of his very best. —*Scott Yanow*

Jesse Davis

b. Nov. 9, 1965, New Orleans, LA
Alto Saxophone / Hard Bop
A fine altoist whose style comes out of the Cannonball Adderley tradition, Jesse Davis made a strong impression with his Concord recordings. He started on alto when he was 11, attended the New Orleans Center for Creative Arts and learned from Ellis Marsalis. Davis studied at Northeastern Illinois University (1983–86),

playcd locally in Chicago, was in the Illinois Jacquet big band (1987–90) and worked wtih Chico Hamilton. After recording with TanaReid in 1990, he was signed to Concord and today is one of the most promising of the young hard bop stylists. —*Scott Yanow*

Horn of Passion / Jan. 24, 1991–Jan. 25, 1991 / Concord Jazz ✦✦✦
Solid debut from saxophonist who once was in a class taught by Ira Gitler. Decent originals and exuberant performances. —*Ron Wynn*

● **As We Speak** / Feb. 13, 1992 / Concord Jazz ✦✦✦✦✦
Good straight-ahead session that comprises the second album by alto saxophonist Jesse Davis, who hasn't gotten as much ink as many other young lion players. The menu features pre-rock and bop anthems, plus hard bop originals, keyed by Davis' aggressive, often soothing solos and fine assistance from trombonist Robin Trowers, pianist Jacky Terrasson, guitarist Peter Bernstein, bassist Dwayne Burno, and drummer Leon Parker. —*Ron Wynn*

Young at Art / Aug. 24, 1993–Aug. 25, 1993 / Concord Jazz ✦✦✦✦
Jesse Davis comes close to capturing the sound and exuberant spirit of Cannonball Adderley on this release while also hinting strongly at Charlie Parker, Phil Woods and Richie Cole. Davis utilizes a strong backup crew that includes guitarist Peter Bernstein and pianist Brad Mehldau to perform a set of superior tunes. The music is not particularly innovative but is a fine example of high-quality bebop played by some promising young players. —*Scott Yanow*

High Standards / Jun. 13, 1994–Jun. 14, 1994 / Concord Jazz ✦✦✦✦

Miles Davis

b. May 25, 1926, Alton, IL, **d.** Sep. 25, 1991, Santa Monica, CA
Trumpet, Leader, Composer / Bop, Cool, Hard Bop, Avant-Garde, Fusion
Miles Davis had quite a career, one with so many innovations that his name is one of the few that can be spoken in the same sentence with Duke Ellington. As a trumpeter, Davis was never a virtuoso on the level of his idol Dizzy Gillespie, but by 1947 he possessed a distinctive cool-toned sound of his own. His ballad renditions (utilizing a Harmon mute) were exquisite yet never predictable, he mastered and then stripped down the bebop vocabulary to its essentials and he generally made every note count; as with Thelonious Monk, less was more in Miles' music.

But Miles Davis was much more than just a trumpeter. As a bandleader he was a brilliant talent scout, able to recognize potential in its formative stage and bring out the best in his sidemen. Among the musicians who greatly benefitted from their association with Davis were Gerry Mulligan (virtually unknown when he played with Miles' Birth of the Cool Nonet), Gil Evans, John Coltrane, Red Garland, Paul Chambers, Philly Joe Jones, Cannonball Adderley, Bill Evans, Jimmy Cobb, Wynton Kelly, George Coleman, Wayne Shorter, Herbie Hancock, Ron Carter, Tony Williams, Chick Corea, Jack DeJohnette, Dave Holland, John McLaughlin, Joe Zawinul, Keith Jarrett, Steve Grossman, Gary Bartz, Dave Liebman, Al Foster, Sonny Fortune, Bill Evans (the saxophonist), Kenny Garrett, Marcus Miller, Mike Stern and John Scofield. This partial list forms a who's who of modern jazz.

In addition to his playing and nurturing of young talent, Miles Davis was quite remarkable in his rare ability to continually evolve. Most jazz musicians (with the exceptions of John Coltrane and Duke Ellington) generally form their style early on and spend the rest of their careers refining their sound. In contrast Miles Davis every five years or so would forge ahead, and due to his restless nature he not only played bop but helped found cool jazz, hard bop, modal music, his own unusual brand of the avant-garde and fusion. Jazz history would be much different if Davis had not existed.

Born in Alton, Illinois, Miles Davis grew up in a middle-class family in East St. Louis. He started on trumpet when he was nine or ten, played in his high-school band and picked up early experience gigging with Eddie Randall's Blue Devils. Miles Davis has said that the greatest musical experience of his life was hearing the Billy Eckstine Orchestra (with Dizzy Gillespie and Charlie Parker) when it passed through St. Louis.

In September 1944 Davis went to New York to study at Juilliard but spent much more time hanging out on 52nd Street and eventually dropped out of school. He played with Coleman Hawkins, made his recording debut in early 1945 (an impressive and nervous session with Rubberlegs Williams) and by late 1945 was playing regularly with Charlie Parker. Davis made an impression with his playing on Bird's recordings of "Now's the Time" and "Billie's Bounce." Although influenced by Dizzy Gillespie, even at this early stage the 19-year-old had something of his own to contribute.

When Charlie Parker went with Gillespie out to California, Miles followed him a few months later by travelling cross-country with Benny Carter's Orchestra. He recorded with Parker in California and when Bird formed a quintet in New York the following year, Davis was a key member. By late 1948 when he went out on his own, Miles Davis had formed a nonet that with arrangements by Gerry Mulligan, Gil Evans and John Lewis, helped usher in "cool jazz." Although the group only had one paying job (two weeks in September 1948 as an intermission band for Count Basie at the Royal Roost), its dozen recordings for Capitol were highly influential in the West Coast jazz movement.

Typically, by the time his nonet dates were renamed "Birth of the Cool," Miles Davis had moved on. He played at the Paris Jazz Festival in 1949 with Tadd Dameron and during 1951-54 was recording music with such sidemen as J.J. Johnson, Jimmy Heath, Horace Silver, Art Blakey and Sonny Rollins that directly led to hard bop. However this was very much an off period for Miles because he was a heroin addict who was only working on an irregular basis. In 1954 he used all of his willpower to permanently kick heroin and his recording that year of "Walkin'," although overlooked at the time, is a classic.

1955 was Miles Davis' breakthrough year. His performance of "'Round Midnight" at the Newport Jazz Festival alerted the critics that he was "back." Davis formed his classic quintet with John Coltrane, Red Garland, Paul Chambers and Philly Joe Jones and during 1955-56 they recorded four well-received albums for Prestige and 'Round Midnight for Columbia. Davis' muted ballads were very popular and he became a celebrity. Even the breakup of the quintet in early 1957 did not slow up the momentum. Miles recorded the first of his full-length collaborations with arranger Gil Evans (Miles Ahead) which would be followed by Porgy and Bess (1958) and Sketches of Spain (1960); on these recordings Davis became one of the first trumpeters to stretch out on fluegelhorn. In 1957 he went to France to record the soundtrack for Lift to the Scaffold and then in 1958 he formed his greatest band, a super sextet with Coltrane, Cannonball Adderley, Bill Evans, Paul Chambers and Philly Joe Jones. Although Evans and Jones were eventually succeeded by Wynton Kelly and Jimmy Cobb, all of the recordings by this remarkable group somehow live up to their potential with Milestones and Kind of Blue being all-time classics that helped to introduce modal (or scalar) improvising to jazz.

If Miles Davis had retired in 1960, he would still be famous in jazz history, but he had many accomplishments still to come. The sextet gradually changed with Adderley departing and Coltrane's spot being taken first by Sonny Stitt, then Hank Mobley. Although 1960-63 is thought of as a sort of resting period for Davis, his trumpet chops were in prime form and he was playing at the peak of his powers. With the departure of the rhythm section in 1963, it was time for Miles to form another group. By 1964 he had a brilliant young rhythm section (Herbie Hancock, Ron Carter and Tony Williams) who were open to the innovations of Ornette Coleman in addition to funky soul-jazz. With George Coleman on tenor, the sidemen really inspired Davis and, although he was sticking to his standard repertoire, the renditions were full of surprises and adventurous playing. By late 1964 Coleman departed and, after Sam Rivers filled in for a European tour, Wayne Shorter was the new tenor. During 1965-68 Miles Davis' second classic quintet bridged the gap between hard bop and free jazz, playing inside/outside music that was quite unique. Although at the time the quintet was overshadowed by the avant-garde players, in the 1980s the music of this group would finally become very influential, particularly on Wynton and Branford Marsalis.

During 1968-69 Miles Davis' music continued to change. He persuaded Hancock to use electric keyboards, Shorter started doubling on soprano, the influence of rock began to be felt and, after the rhythm section changed (to Chick Corea, Dave Holland and Jack DeJohnette), Davis headed one of the earliest fusion bands. Rock and funk rhythms combined with jazz improvisations to form a new hybrid music and Miles' recordings of In a Silent Way and Bitches Brew (both of which used additional instruments) essentially launched the fusion era.

Many of Miles Davis' fans essentially write off his post-1968

music, not realizing that not all of the recordings sound the same and that some were more successful than others. If Miles Davis had sold out so as to gain a larger audience, than why did he record so many 20-minute jams that could not possibly be played on the radio? During 1970-75 the ensembles of his group (which sometimes utilized two or three guitars and a couple of keyboardists) became quite dense, the rhythms were often intense and Davis unfortunately often used electronics that distorted the sound of his horn. Actually the only album from this era that is a complete failure is On the Corner (Davis is largely absent from that fiasco) and Live/Evil, Jack Johnson and 1975's Panagea all have memorable sections.

And then suddenly in 1975 Miles Davis retired. He was in bad health and, as he frankly discusses in his autobiography Miles, very much into recreational drugs. The jazz world speculated about what would happen if and when he returned. In 1981 Davis came back with a new band that was similar to his '70s group except that the ensembles were quite a bit sparser. The rock influence was soon replaced by funk and pop elements and, as he became stronger, Miles Davis' trumpet playing proved to still be in excellent form. He toured constantly during his last decade and his personality seemed to have mellowed a bit. Where once he had been quite forbidding and reluctant to be friendly to nonmusicians, Davis was at times eager to grant interviews and talk about his past. Although he had never looked back musically, in the summer of 1991 he shocked everyone by letting Quincy Jones talk him into performing Gil Evans arrangements from the past at the Montreux Jazz Festival. Even if he had Wallace Roney and Kenny Garrett take some of the solos, Davis was in stronger-than-expected form playing the old classics. And then two months later he passed away at the age of 65.

There are currently over 120 valuable Miles Davis recordings in print including many live sets issued on European labels. Taken as a whole, these form quite a legacy. —Scott Yanow

First Miles / Apr. 24, 1945-Aug. 14, 1947 / Savoy ✦✦
This unusual set includes Davis' first recording session and his initial date as a leader. The former is more historical than musical: four blues featuring singer Rubberlegs Williams, Herbie Fields' tenor and the noticeably nervous 18-year-old trumpeter who is actually only heard in ensembles. The latter recording finds him much more confident in 1947, heading the Charlie Parker Quintet (with Bird switching to tenor) on "Milestones," "Little Willie Leaps," "Half Nelson" and "Sippin' at Bells"; all of the alternate takes (both complete and partial) are included from both sessions. Since the later date has also been reissued on various Charlie Parker collections, this set is more for completists than for general listeners. —Scott Yanow

Bopping the Blues / Oct. 18, 1946 / Black Lion ✦✦✦
When this CD was initially released, it had quite a few jazz collectors scratching their heads wondering why they had never heard of it. Previously unissued, these formerly unknown performances (just four songs with eight alternate takes) feature the vocals of Earl Coleman and Ann Baker in 1946 but the backup group is of great interest, for it includes trumpeter Miles Davis and tenor saxophonist Gene Ammons. It's not essential music but bop collectors will want to pick it up. —Scott Yanow

Pre Birth of the Cool '49 / Sep. 4, 1948 / Jazz Live ✦✦✦✦
This Italian LP featured the first release of these two important broadcasts, although this music has since been reissued on CD. Miles Davis' Birth of the Cool nonet recorded a dozen influential performances during 1949-50 but only actually appeared in public for one gig: a two-week stint in 1948 as the intermission band at the Royal Roost for Count Basie's Orchestra. This set features nine performances taken from radio broadcasts and is near-classic. This version of the nonet features Davis, baritonist Gerry Mulligan, altoist Lee Konitz, pianist John Lewis and drummer Max Roach in addition to French horn, tuba, trombone and bass. Other than getting to hear "new" and extended versions of some of the Nonet's studio sides, this set offers otherwise unrecorded arrangements of "Why Do I Love You?" and "S'il Vous Plait." —Scott Yanow

Quintet with Lee Konitz; Sextet With Jackie McLean / Sep. 25, 1948-May 3, 1952 / Fresh Sound ✦✦✦

★ **Birth of the Cool** / Jan. 21, 1949-Mar. 9, 1950 / Capitol ✦✦✦✦✦
This CD contains all 12 of the recordings by Miles Davis' highly influential Birth of the Cool nonet. Emphasizing arrangements and softer tones more than bebop, this music led the way for West

Coast jazz of the 1950s. With arrangements by Gil Evans, Gerry Mulligan, John Lewis, Johnny Carisi and Davis, and concise solos from Davis, altoist Lee Konitz, baritonist Mulligan and either J.J. Johnson or Kai Winding on trombones, this music still sounds fresh and exciting today. —*Scott Yanow*

☆ **Blue Note and Capitol Recordings** / Jan. 21, 1949–1958 / Capitol ✦✦✦✦✦
This four-CD set is actually just a repackaging of four CDs that are available separately: the classic Birth of the Cool sessions, Cannonball Adderley's 1958 date with Miles Davis as a sideman (*Somethin' Else*), *Volume One* and *Volume Two*. The latter two sets feature three often-overlooked sessions from 1952–54 that actually are among the earliest hard bop recordings, starring Davis, trombonist J.J. Johnson, tenorman Jimmy Heath, altoist Jackie McLean, pianist Horace Silver and drummer Art Blakey among others. All of this music was quite influential and is essential (in one form or another) to all jazz libraries. —*Scott Yanow*

The Paris Festival International / May 8, 1949–May 11, 1949 / Columbia ✦✦✦✦✦
Miles Davis was best-known during the late '40s for offering an alternative approach to trumpeters Dizzy Gillespie and Fats Navarro, emphasizing his middle register, a softer tone and a more thoughtful approach. This concert performance, which was not released until nearly three decades later, shows that Davis was just as capable of playing hard-driving bebop as most of his contemporaries. In a quintet with tenor saxophonist James Moody and pianist-composer Tadd Dameron, Davis confounded the French audience by playing very impressive high notes and displaying an extroverted personality. Never content to merely satisfy the expectations of his fans, he was already moving in surprising directions. This LP also gives one a very rare opportunity to hear Miles Davis verbally introducing songs in a voice not yet scarred. —*Scott Yanow*

Birdland Days / Feb. 18, 1950–Sep. 29, 1951 / Fresh Sound ✦✦✦
This CD from the Spanish Fresh Sound label consists of three broadcasts originating from Birdland during 1950–51 that feature the early Miles Davis with such notable players as trombonist J.J. Johnson, tenors Stan Getz, Sonny Rollins, Eddie "Lockjaw" Davis and Big Nick Nicholas, pianists Tadd Dameron, Kenny Drew and Billy Taylor, bassists Gene Ramey, Tommy Potter and Charlie Mingus and drummer Art Blakey. The repertoire is filled with bop classics and, although the recording quality is sometimes a little erratic, the enthusiastic solos from these young players (most of whom were still in their 20s) makes this set both historic and enjoyable. —*Scott Yanow*

And Horns / Jan. 17, 1951+Feb. 19, 1953 / Original Jazz Classics ✦✦✦
Instructive early-'50s sessions. Miles emerges out of a "cool" bag, Sonny Rollins (ts) is strong, and Al Cohn (ts) and Zoot Sims (ts) participate. —*Ron Wynn*

☆ **Miles Davis: Chronicle—the Complete Prestige Recordings** (1951–1956) / Jan. 17, 1951–Oct. 26, 1956 / Prestige ✦✦✦✦✦
The complete Prestige recordings. This is an unbelievable eight-disc set of 93 performances containing everything on the Prestige label. —*Ron Wynn*

Dig / Oct. 5, 1951 / Original Jazz Classics ✦✦✦
Tenor saxophonist Sonny Rollins was present as a member of the Miles Davis sextet (alto saxophonist Jackie McLean, pianist Walter Bishop, bassist Tommy Potter, drummer Art Blakey) on *Dig*, which was part of a 10/5/51 session, all of which was also on a two-fer. I love this music, but I have to admit it sounds dated. This wasn't Miles Davis' best, but I've always appreciated it for McLean's cutting sax work. —*Bob Rusch, Cadence*

Our Delight / 1952 / Original Jazz Classics ✦✦
In 1952 during his "off period," Miles Davis sat in with tenor saxophonist Jimmy Forrest's quintet at a club in his hometown of St. Louis. Because the recording quality is not the best and Davis recorded many more significant sessions through the years, this CD only gets an "OK" rating, but collectors may want to acquire it anyway. Included are performances of bop standards including Dizzy Gillespie's "A Night in Tunisia." —*Scott Yanow*

Miles Davis, Vol. 1 / May 9, 1952–Mar. 6, 1954 / Blue Note ✦✦✦✦
Miles Davis' recordings of 1951–54 tend to be overlooked because of his erratic lifestyle of the period and because they predated his first classic quintet. Although he rarely recorded during this era, what he did document was often quite classic. The two sessions

included on this CD (which includes three alternate takes) are among the earliest hard bop recordings and would indirectly influence the modern mainstream music of the 1960s. The first session features Davis in a sextet with trombonist J.J. Johnson, altoist Jackie McLean, pianist Gil Coggins, bassist Oscar Pettiford and drummer Kenny Clarke; highlights include "Dear Old Stockholm," "Woody 'n You" and interpretations of "Yesterdays" and "How Deep Is the Ocean." The remaining six numbers showcase Davis in a quartet with pianist Horace Silver, bassist Percy Heath and drummer Art Blakey, really stretching out on such numbers as "Take Off" and "Well You Needn't." However on "It Never Entered My Mind," Davis' muted statement (his only one on this set) looks toward his treatments of ballads later in the decade. —*Scott Yanow*

Miles Davis, Vol. 2 / Apr. 20, 1953 / Blue Note ✦✦✦✦
This CD contains all of the music recorded by a particularly strong sextet in 1953, six selections plus four alternate takes. With trumpeter Miles Davis, trombonist J.J. Johnson, tenor saxophonist Jimmy Heath, pianist Gil Coggins, bassist Percy Heath and drummer Art Blakey all in fine form, "Tempus Fugit" and "C.T.A." receive definitive treatment along with two Johnson compositions. —*Scott Yanow*

Miles Tones / May 16, 1953–May 17, 1958 / Jazz Tones ✦✦✦
Quite a few albums have been released of Miles Davis live performances from the 1950s, many of them in the bootleg category. This particular LP is of strong interest for, in addition to a forgettable 1953 version of "I Got Rhythm" that is dominated by the scatting of Joe Carroll, there are three tracks with Davis' otherwise undocumented quintet of 1957 (featuring the great tenor of Sonny Rollins) and three numbers by the 1958 quintet with John Coltrane, Bill Evans, Paul Chambers and Philly Joe Jones. Not as essential as his studio albums, this LP still has more than its share of strong moments. —*Scott Yanow*

Blue Haze / May 19, 1953–Apr. 3, 1954 / Prestige ✦✦✦
Fine '50s Davis. Presence of seldom-heard David Schildkraut (as) enhances its value. Supporting cast, which includes Charles Mingus (b), John Lewis (p), Horace Silver (p), et al, isn't too shabby either! —*Ron Wynn*

Tallest Trees / May 19, 1953–Oct. 26, 1956 / Prestige ✦✦✦
Miles Davis' valuable recordings for Prestige were at one time made available on a series of attractive two-LP sets; much of this music has since been reissued on CD. This two-fer has plenty of brilliant music including the four master takes from the classic session with vibraphonist Milt Jackson and pianist Thelonious Monk (Monk's solo on "Bags' Groove" is quite memorable), three selections with a variety of different rhythm sections ("Smooch," "Miles Ahead" and "Blue Haze"), an alternate (and inferior) version of "'Round Midnight" with John Coltrane and four great performances ("Airegin," "Oleo," "But Not for Me" and "Doxy") with a quintet featuring tenor saxophonist Sonny Rollins (composer of three of the four songs) and pianist Horace Silver. —*Scott Yanow*

At Last / Sep. 13, 1953 / Contemporary ✦✦
This set has odds and ends recorded at the Lighthouse on a Sunday when Miles Davis was in town. He jams with the regular sextet (which included trumpeter Rolf Ericson, altoist Bud Shank, Bob Cooper on tenor and drummer Max Roach) on two numbers and has "'Round Midnight" as his feature. Max Roach takes "Drum Conversation" unaccompanied and trumpeter Chet Baker plays "At Last" with pianist Russ Freeman. The recording quality is merely okay but the viable and occasionally exciting historical music makes this a set worth picking up. —*Scott Yanow*

Walkin' / Apr. 3, 1954–Apr. 29, 1954 / Original Jazz Classics ✦✦✦✦✦
In 1954 Miles Davis was on the verge of making a comeback. Somewhat obscure during 1951–53 due to his erratic lifestyle and low-profile gigs, Davis at 28 was entering his creative prime. On April 3 of that year he recorded three fine numbers (including his "Solar") in a quintet with the forgotten altoist Dave Schildkraut and pianist Horace Silver, but the real reasons to acquire this set are for the exciting versions of "Walkin'" and "Blue 'N' Boogie" performed by Davis, Silver, trombonist J.J. Johnson and tenor saxophonist Lucky Thompson. —*Scott Yanow*

★ **Bags' Groove** / Dec. 24, 1954 / Original Jazz Classics ✦✦✦✦✦
This CD (which contains almost 58 minutes of music) has the complete session of Dec. 24, 1954, the classic date that matched together trumpeter Miles Davis, vibraphonist Milt Jackson, pianist

Thelonious Monk, bassist Percy Heath and drummer Kenny Clarke. Davis and Monk actually did not get along all that well and the trumpeter did not want Monk playing behind his solos, but a great deal of brilliant music occurred on the day of their encounter. There are two very different versions apiece of "Bags' Groove" (Monk's solo on the first take was one of his best) and "The Man I Love" along with single performances of "Bemsha Swing" and "Swing Spring"; the shortest selection is eight minutes long. Timeless music that defies easy classification, this set belongs in every jazz collection. —*Scott Yanow*

Green Haze / Jun. 7, 1955–Nov. 16, 1955 / Prestige ✦✦✦
This two-LP set combines together sets originally known as *The Musings of Miles* and simply *Miles* but could have been jointly retitled "The Birth of a Quintet." The great trumpeter is featured in top form with pianist Red Garland, bassist Oscar Pettiford and drummer Philly Joe Jones on two of his originals and four standards for the first session, and with Garland, Jones, bassist Paul Chambers and a tentative-sounding tenor saxophonist named John Coltrane on five standards and the initial version of Benny Golson's "Stablemates" a few months later. Since Coltrane is not heard from much here, it is for the excellent rhythm sections and the playing of Miles Davis that this two-fer is highly recommended. —*Scott Yanow*

☆ **Miscellaneous Miles Davis 1955–1957** / Jul. 17, 1955–Dec. 18, 1957 / Jazz Unlimited ✦✦✦✦✦
One of the great legendary moments took place during the 1955 Newport Jazz Festival (the very first) when Miles Davis unexpectedly sat in on a jam session and (with Thelonious Monk playing behind him) constructed a brilliant solo on "'Round Midnight." Davis had been in danger of being forgotten, but that moment, which took place before many of the top jazz critics, was a minor sensation and gave momentum to his career. Now for the first time the performance (which also includes versions of "Hackensack" and "Now's the Time" with a sextet featuring baritonist Gerry Mulligan and Zoot Sims on tenor) has been made available, and it lives up to its legendary status. Also on this essential CD are three numbers on which Miles plays with the Rene Urtreger Trio (the great Lester Young sits in on "Lady Be Good"), two songs with his 1957 quintet with Bobby Jaspar on tenor and three tunes in which Davis is backed by a European orchestra. This Danish import is highly recommended. —*Scott Yanow*

Quintet/Sextet / Aug. 5, 1955 / Original Jazz Classics ✦✦✦
One of the most obscure of his Prestige recordings, this CD only contains a half-hour of music, but the quality is fairly high. Davis is heard outside of his regular group, playing with vibraphonist Milt Jackson, pianist Ray Bryant (who was left out of the personnel listing), bassist Percy Heath, drummer Art Taylor and, on two of the four numbers, altoist Jackie McLean. This set (formerly known as *Miles Davis and Milt Jackson*) is highlighted by "Dr. Jackle" and "Minor March." —*Scott Yanow*

★ **Round About Midnight** / Oct. 27, 1955–Sep. 10, 1956 / Columbia ✦✦✦✦✦
Davis' first Columbia album is a classic. His quintet (with tenor saxophonist John Coltrane, pianist Red Garland, bassist Paul Chambers and drummer Philly Joe Jones) was quickly becoming one of the pacesetters in jazz and each of these six performances are memorable. In addition to the definitive non-Monk rendition of "'Round Midnight," one hears the quintet making such diverse songs as "Ah-Leu-Cha," Cole Porter's "All of You," "Tadd's Delight" and "Dear Old Stockholm" sound as if they were all written for the group. Their version of "Bye Bye Blackbird" is the ultimate in cool sophistication. —*Scott Yanow*

☆ **Miles & Coltrane** / Oct. 27, 1955–Jul. 4, 1958 / Columbia ✦✦✦✦✦
In addition to two selections ("Little Melonae" and "Budo") from his first session for Columbia, this CD contains his complete performance at the 1958 Newport Jazz Festival. When one considers that Davis' sextet at the time included such giants as tenor saxophonist John Coltrane, altoist Cannonball Adderley, pianist Bill Evans, bassist Paul Chambers and drummer Jimmy Cobb, it is not surprising that fireworks resulted. Still, the power and drive of this intense version of "Ah-Leu-Cha" is a revelation and the band really swings and stretches out on "Straight, No Chaser," "Fran Dance," "Two Bass Hit" and "Bye Bye Blackbird." —*Scott Yanow*

Facets / Oct. 27, 1955–Aug. 23, 1962 / Columbia ✦✦✦
This LP is an interesting hodgepodge of Miles Davis recordings.

Davis is heard with his classic 1955–56 quintet playing "Sweet Sue" and "Budo," with large orchestras performing "Jazz Suite for Brass" and "Three Little Feelings" (early third-stream works that put the spotlight totally on Davis' fluegelhorn), on a couple of odd tracks from 1962 with vocalist Bob Dorough ("Devil May Care" and "Blue Xmas") and, most significantly, on four numbers arranged by Michel Legrand for an 11-piece group in 1958 that also feature altoist Phil Woods, John Coltrane and pianist Bill Evans. Worth searching for, this set will fill gaps in many collections. —*Scott Yanow*

Circle in the Round / Oct. 27, 1955–Jan. 27, 1970 / Columbia ✦✦✦
This two-CD set is highly recommended to collectors for it contains many interesting performances, all but one of which were previously unissued at the time of this two-fer's release. Spanning 15 years, this program includes a 1955 version of "Two Bass Hit" from Davis' first classic quintet, an extended version of "Love for Sale" by his 1958 sextet, a reunion between Miles and drummer Philly Joe Jones in 1961, the side-long "Circle in the Round" from Davis' 1967 quintet (with guest guitarist Joe Beck), a few unfinished works from his transitional 1968 band and a lengthy workout by Davis' fusion group in early 1970. There are lots of unusual performances on this worthy collection. —*Scott Yanow*

☆ **Cookin'** / Nov. 16, 1955–Oct. 26, 1956 / Original Jazz Classics ✦✦✦✦✦
Trumpeter Davis (along with tenor saxophonist John Coltrane, pianist Red Garland, bassist Paul Chambers and drummer Philly Joe Jones) are heard on such tunes as "My Funny Valentine" (Davis' earliest version of this standard), "Blues by Five," "Airegin" and a medley of "Tune Up" and "When Lights Are Low." This classic music has great sound. —*Scott Yanow*

☆ **Workin'** / May 11, 1956+Oct. 26, 1956 / Original Jazz Classics ✦✦✦✦✦
Miles Davis' 1956 quintet was one of his classic groups, featuring tenor saxophonist John Coltrane, pianist Red Garland, bassist Paul Chambers and drummer Philly Joe Jones. They recorded four albums for Prestige in two marathon sessions. Among the highlights are "It Never Entered My Mind," "Four," "In Your Own Sweet Way" and two versions of "The Theme." The music is essential in one form or another. —*Scott Yanow*

☆ **Steamin'** / May 11, 1956+Oct. 26, 1956 / Prestige ✦✦✦✦✦
This classic Prestige session (one of four) has been reissued many times. The release from the audiophile label DCC Jazz is a gold compact disc. Davis is heard with his classic quintet of 1956 (which featured tenor saxophonist John Coltrane, pianist Red Garland, bassist Paul Chambers and drummer Philly Joe Jones) performing six numbers, all of which are somewhat memorable. Highpoints are "Surrey with the Fringe on Top," "Diane" and "When I Fall in Love"; Davis' muted tone rarely sounded more beautiful. —*Scott Yanow*

Relaxin' / May 11, 1956+Oct. 26, 1956 / Original Jazz Classics ✦✦✦✦
Workin' & Steamin' / May 11, 1956–Oct. 26, 1956 / Prestige ✦✦✦✦
This two-LP set combines together a pair of classic albums by the Miles Davis Quintet of 1956, the group that also featured John Coltrane on tenor, pianist Red Garland, bassist Paul Chambers and drummer Philly Joe Jones. Even though all but two of these 14 selections were recorded at the same May 11 session, the music has plenty of variety and does not sound rushed. Highpoints include "It Never Entered My Mind," "Four," "In Your Own Sweet Way," "Surrey with the Fringe on Top" "Diane" and "When I Fall in Love." Davis' beautiful muted statements made these two of his most popular albums. This timeless music has since been reissued on CD. —*Scott Yanow*

Miles Davis / May 11, 1956–Oct. 26, 1956 / Prestige ✦✦✦✦
This two-LP set (which launched Prestige's very valuable reissue series of two-fers) features the two albums originally known as *Cookin'* and *Relaxin'.* With John Coltrane on tenor, pianist Red Garland, bassist Paul Chambers and drummer Philly Joe Jones, Davis was in fine form for these run throughs on the Quintet's usual club repertoire. Most of the music is medium-tempo with the highpoints including "My Funny Valentine," "If I Were a Bell," "I Could Write a Book" and "Oleo." —*Scott Yanow*

Miles Davis/Stan Getz: Tune Up / Nov. 12, 1956–Jul. 1961 / Natasha Imports ✦✦✦
Miles Davis and Stan Getz do not actually play together on this

CD but Davis does perform with Lester Young and the Modern Jazz Quartet on two songs recorded in Germany in 1956; a big band "sits in" on one of those numbers. Prez sounds a bit weak but blends well. Davis also plays two short songs with a fine French rhythm section. Stan Getz's three performances are taken from the 1961 Newport Jazz Festival and find him stretching out with his fine trio (pianist Steve Kuhn, bassist Scott LaFaro and drummer Roy Haynes). Overall this historical music, although not essential, is enjoyable. —*Scott Yanow*

★ **Miles Ahead** / May 6, 1957–May 27, 1957 / Columbia ✦✦✦✦✦
Miles Davis' first collaboration with arranger Gil Evans since *The Birth of the Cool* recordings of 1949–50 resulted in this classic album. The advantage that this CD reissue has over the LP is that since the music was recorded as a continuous suite, this way there is no break between the fifth and sixth songs. Davis' trumpet (backed by Evans' 19-piece orchestra) is heard at its best on such selections as "The Duke," "My Ship," "Miles Ahead," "Blues for Pablo" and "I Don't Wanna Be Kissed." Although a bit brief (just 36 minutes) this set is highly recommended. —*Scott Yanow*

Miles Davis Live In 1958 / Sep. 1957–Nov. 1958 / Bandstand ✦✦✦
This LP contains radio and television appearances by two versions of Davis' groups along with a mystery band. Side One is the main reason to acquire this set for it features versions of "Four," "Bye Bye Blackbird" and "No Blues" performed by the Davis Quintet of 1958 with tenor saxophonist John Coltrane, pianist Bill Evans, bassist Paul Chambers and drummer Philly Joe Jones. There are two other songs ("All of You" and "Four") supposedly played by the same group but actually dating from Sept. 1957 and featuring Davis with Bobby Jaspar on tenor, pianist Tommy Flanagan, Chamber and Jones. Concluding this set is a televised jam-session version of "What Is This Thing Called Love" on which the personnel listing is mostly wrong. Davis is not present (the trumpeter might be Nat Adderley or Art Farmer) but one can hear baritonist Gerry Mulligan, trombonist Bennie Green and percussionist Candido. Miles Davis and 'Trane completists will need to acquire this LP anyway. —*Scott Yanow*

Ascenseur Pour L'echafaud / Dec. 4, 1957–Dec. 5, 1957 / Fontana ✦✦✦
In 1957 Miles Davis went to France for a short tour and while there he recorded the soundtrack for the film *Ascenseur Pour L'Echafaud*. This CD contains the original LP of material plus 19 minutes of unreleased alternate versions. Better than many soundtracks, this music (which also features the tenor of Barney Wilen and pianist Rene Urtreger) does not really stand on its own without the film, so it's of mostly historical interest. —*Scott Yanow*

Complete Amsterdam Concert / Dec. 8, 1957 / Celluloid ✦✦✦
This two-LP set is a real rarity, a performance by trumpeter Miles Davis while he was in Europe in late 1957. Joined by drummer Kenny Clarke and three excellent French players (tenor saxophonist Barney Wilen, pianist Rene Urtreger and bassist Pierre Michelot), the same unit with which Davis recorded a French soundtrack during this period, the quintet jams through ten songs from Davis' repertoire. Although all of this music (around 56 minutes' worth) could have been put on one rather than two LPs, this hard-to-find set is recommended for the rare opportunity to hear Miles Davis stretching out with these musicians. —*Scott Yanow*

★ **Milestones** / Apr. 2, 1958–Apr. 3, 1958 / Columbia ✦✦✦✦✦
Kind of Blue might have received most of the acclaim but *Milestones*, the recorded debut of the Miles Davis Sextet, is in the same league. This remarkable super group (featuring Davis' trumpet, tenor saxophonist John Coltrane, altoist Cannonball Adderley, pianist Red Garland, bassist Paul Chambers and drummer Philly Joe Jones) was arguably the greatest one Miles Davis ever led. "Two Bass Hit" features the two saxes trading off with fire and "Billy Boy" showcases the Red Garland trio (showing what they learned from Ahmad Jamal), but "Straight No Chaser" really demonstrates what a powerhouse band this was. —*Scott Yanow*

'58 Sessions / May 26, 1958–Jul. 28, 1958 / Columbia ✦✦✦✦
Miles Davis had quite an all-star group in 1958: Tenor saxophonist John Coltrane, altoist Cannonball Adderley, pianist Bill Evans, bassist Paul Chambers and drummer Jimmy Cobb (who had recently replaced Philly Joe Jones). This frequently exciting CD has three of the four performances originally on an LP titled *Jazz at the Plaza* ("Straight No Chaser," "My Funny Valentine," and

"Oleo"), a lengthy "Love for Sale" that was unreleased until the 1970s and three other songs ("On Green Dolphin Street," "Fran Dance" and "Stella by Starlight") most notable for the lyricism of Davis and Evans. —*Scott Yanow*

At Newport / May 26, 1958–Apr. 15, 1961 / Columbia ✦✦✦✦
This French Columbia LP features the Sextet (with John Coltrane and Cannonball Adderley) at the 1958 Newport Jazz Festival; their rapid version of "Ah Leu Cha" is thunderous and "Straight No Chaser" swings like mad. This set also includes three laidback selections ("On Green Dolphin Street," "Fran Dance" and "Stella by Starlight") from a slightly earlier studio date along with a different version of "On Green Dolphin Street" from 1961. This classic music has since been reissued on CD. —*Scott Yanow*

☆ **Porgy & Bess** / Jul. 22, 1958–Aug. 18, 1958 / Columbia ✦✦✦✦✦
The second of the three great Miles Davis-Gil Evans collaborations features the trumpeter backed by Evans' 18-piece orchestra on 13 selections from George Gershwin's *Porgy and Bess*. This version of "Summertime" (with Evans' countermelody) is definitive and the entire suite should be savored in one sitting. —*Scott Yanow*

Jazz at the Plaza, Vol. 1 / Jul. 28, 1958 / Columbia ✦✦✦
Recorded at a Columbia press party in 1958, this spontaneous LP features the Miles Davis Sextet that had the giant talents of John Coltrane, Cannonball Adderley and Bill Evans. Their performances of "Straight No Chaser" (mistitled here "Jazz at the Plaza"), "My Funny Valentine" (Davis' feature), "If I Were a Bell" and "Oleo" are consistently exciting. Three of these selections (all but "If I Were a Bell") have since been reissued on CD. —*Scott Yanow*

All Stars / Jan. 3, 1959–Feb. 1959 / Jazz Band ✦✦✦
This LP contains two valuable radio broadcasts of the Miles Davis Sextet of early 1959, a unit that also featured John Coltrane, Cannonball Adderley and (if the personnel listing can be believed) pianist Red Garland. There are only five selections on this set ("All of Me" is actually "All of You") but any surviving recording by this classic group (arguably the greatest band Miles Davis ever led) is well worth getting. —*Scott Yanow*

★ **Kind of Blue** / Mar. 2, 1959–Apr. 22, 1959 / Columbia ✦✦✦✦✦
Miles Davis' most famous recording remains his most influential. It is not just that this album helped popularize modal jazz (improvising based on modes or scales rather than running chord changes) or that it introduced two future standards ("So What" and "All Blues") and three other gems ("Freddie Freeloader," "Blue in Green" and "Flamenco Sketches"). Most impressive is how the solos of Miles Davis, John Coltrane and Cannonball Adderley (what a lineup), despite their differing styles, fit the songs perfectly. *Scott Yanow*

☆ **Sketches of Spain** / Nov. 10, 1959–Mar. 11, 1960 / Columbia ✦✦✦✦✦
The third and final of the great Miles Davis-Gil Evans collaborations of 1957–59 was also their most ambitious. This set finds Davis in the forefront improvising on two numbers associated with Spanish music and three Evans compositions in that idiom. Much of the music is quite dramatic and emotional (notably "Saeta") and Davis plays at his best throughout, really stretching the boundaries of jazz. —*Scott Yanow*

Directions / Mar. 11, 1960–Feb. 27, 1970 / Columbia ✦✦✦
This double LP of leftover items not previously issued features Davis over a ten-year period. "Song of Our Country" is from the sessions that led to *Sketches of Spain* and there is a "new" version of "'Round Midnight" from 1961 along with "So Near, So Far" dating from 1963. Otherwise the remainder of this two-fer is from the transitional 1967–70 period when Davis was experimenting with combining jazz and rock. Some of the selections ramble on a bit too long but the music is mostly quite fascinating, featuring such players as Wayne Shorter, Herbie Hancock, Joe Zawinul, Chick Corea and John McLaughlin. It's most highly recommended to collectors with an open ear toward fusion. *Scott Yanow*

Live in Stockholm 1960 / Mar. 22, 1960 / Royal Jazz ✦✦✦✦✦
This remarkable two-CD set features John Coltrane with the Miles Davis Quintet just a short time before 'Trane went out on his own. Davis sounds inspired by his star tenor and although Coltrane was reportedly bored with the repertoire ("On Green Dolphin Street," "All Blues," "Fran-Dance," "Walkin'" and two versions of "So What"), he is at his most explorative throughout this often-stunning music. In addition, the rhythm section (pianist Wynton

Kelly, bassist Paul Chambers and drummer Jimmy Cobb) had been together for two years and is really tight. This highly recommended set also includes a brief interview with Coltrane from this period. —*Scott Yanow*

Copenhagen 1960 / Mar. 24, 1960 / Royal Jazz ◆◆◆
Miles & Coltrane Quintet / Apr. 9, 1960 / Unique ◆◆◆
This LP from a collector's label features the last documented appearance of John Coltrane with the Miles Davis Quintet before he departed to lead his own group. The repertoire ("On Green Dolphin Street," "Walkin'," "Theme," "So What" and "'Round Midnight") offers no surprises but the soloing of Davis, Coltrane and pianist Wynton Kelly is consistantly excellent and sometimes quite exciting. —*Scott Yanow*

Live In Europe / Oct. 6, 1960–Nov. 4, 1967 / Jazz Up ◆◆◆
This very interesting CD has two unusual live performances. Miles Davis' short-lived Quintet with Sonny Stitt as John Coltrane's replacement (and the strong rhythm section of pianist Wynton Kelly, bassist Paul Chambers and drummer Jimmy Cobb) plays "All of You," but the bulk of this disc features his 1967 band (with Wayne Shorter, Herbie Hancock, Ron Carter and Tony Williams) performing a wandering but coherent 45-minute medley that hints at a variety of older tunes from Davis' repertoire. —*Scott Yanow*

Miles Davis & Sonny Stitt / Oct. 13, 1960 / Dragon ◆◆◆
When John Coltrane departed from the Miles Davis Quintet, it left a major gap that would not be fully filled for several years. Veteran Sonny Stitt was with the band for six months in 1960 but the association was totally unrecorded until this two-LP set came out. Stitt (who plays alto on nine of the 12 numbers and tenor on the remainder) sounded much more conventional than Coltrane did at the time, turning these standards into a bebop jam session. Davis and the great trio (pianist Wynton Kelly, bassist Paul Chambers and drummer Jimmy Cobb) along with Stitt are in fine form on the seven lengthy performances, all but one being over 11 minutes. —*Scott Yanow*

Someday My Prince Will Come / 1961 / Columbia ◆◆◆◆
Miles Davis' 1961 Quintet was more relaxed and less adventurous than his earlier groups with John Coltrane. The trumpeter was at the peak of his powers in the early '60s and comfortable with his own playing. This CD, a straight reissue of the earlier LP, features Davis, tenor saxophonist Hank Mobley, pianist Wynton Kelly, bassist Paul Chambers, either Jimmy Cobb or Philly Joe Jones on drums and, as a special bonus, guest appearances by John Coltrane (the last time he would record with Miles) on "Teo" and the title cut. —*Scott Yanow*

Friday Night at the Blackhawk / Apr. 21, 1961 / Columbia ◆◆◆◆
The first of two sets recorded during a weekend in 1961 features the Miles Davis Quintet at a period of time when Hank Mobley was on tenor and the rhythm section was comprised of pianist Wynton Kelly, bassist Paul Chambers and drummer Jimmy Cobb. Davis is in particularly strong form on "Walkin'," "Bye Bye Blackbird" and "No Blues" and Kelly proved to be the perfect pianist for this hard-driving and swinging set. —*Scott Yanow*

Saturday Night at the Blackhawk / Apr. 22, 1961 / Columbia ◆◆◆
The second of two sets documenting the Miles Davis Quintet in 1961 finds tenor saxophonist Hank Mobley being a minor character (although two of his solos are fully restored from the edited original issue) but the trumpeter/leader and pianist Wynton Kelly play many memorable solos on standards such as "Well You Needn't," "So What," "Oleo" and "If I Were a Bell." Both of these sets, although not innovative, are recommended as strong examples of Miles Davis' trumpet playing. —*Scott Yanow*

Live Miles: More Music from the Legendary Carnegie Hall Concert / May 19, 1961 / Columbia ◆◆◆
This additional music from his Carnegie Hall concert of 1961 once again features the great trumpeter with the Gil Evans Orchestra (for a 16-minute version of "Concierto De Aranguez") and with his quintet of the period (with tenor saxophonist Hank Mobley and pianist Wynton Kelly) for three shorter numbers (the modal "Teo," "Walkin'" and "I Thought About You"). It's not essential but Miles Davis fans will enjoy these performances. —*Scott Yanow*

At Carnegie Hall / May 19, 1961 / Columbia ◆◆◆◆
For this concert, the Quintet (with tenor saxophonist Hank Mobley and pianist Wynton Kelly) are featured along with the Gil Evans Orchestra. The small group plays "So What," "Spring Is Here," "No

Blues," "Oleo" and "Someday My Prince Will Come" before the 21-piece big band backs the trumpeter on three numbers originally recorded for the *Miles Ahead* album. Although nothing all that new occurs in these remakes, this retrospective of Davis' previous four years has fresh solos and enthusiastic performances. —*Scott Yanow*

Miles in St Louis / Jun. 24, 1961–Jun., 1963 / VGM ◆◆◆
This collector's LP mostly features the 1963 Miles Davis Quintet (which included tenor saxophonist George Coleman, pianist Herbie Hancock, bassist Ron Carter and drummer Tony Williams) during a live appearance in St. Louis. The previously unissued music is reasonably well-recorded and gives listeners additional versions of such standards as "I Thought About You," "All Blues" and "Seven Steps to Heaven." This LP is rounded out by a rendition of "Like Someone to Love" from 1961 that showcases the young Herbie Hancock with a trio, two years before he first joined Davis' group. —*Scott Yanow*

Transition / 1961–1963 / Magnetic ◆◆◆
This is the type of CD that should greatly interest Miles Davis collectors although those listeners just getting into his music of the 1960s are advised to acquire his Columbia studio discs first. This CD features Davis with two very different quintets in 1961 (a group with tenor saxophonist Hank Mobley, pianist Wynton Kelly, bassist Paul Chambers and drummer Jimmy Cobb) and 1963 (which included George Coleman on tenor, pianist Herbie Hancock, bassist Ron Carter and drummer Tony Williams). The earlier session is more relaxed and less adventurous while the latter (which is highlighted by lengthy versions of "All Blues" and "Seven Steps to Heaven") finds Miles Davis challenged by his younger sidemen. —*Scott Yanow*

Quiet Nights / Jul. 27, 1962–Nov. 6, 1962 / Columbia ◆◆◆
Davis' final official collaboration with arranger Gil Evans was their weakest project. There are only 27 minutes of music on this LP and six of it is taken up by a Quintet performance of "Summer Night." The six remaining pieces are enjoyable enough (highlighted by "Once upon a Summertime" and "Corcovado") but are rather brief, making one wonder why not more material was not recorded. Still, this set is worth getting if found at a budget price. —*Scott Yanow*

Sorcerer / Aug. 23, 1962–May 24, 1967 / Columbia ◆◆◆◆
Six of the seven selections on this CD (a straight reissue of the earlier LP with newer liner notes) showcase Miles Davis' second classic Quintet, the band with such young talents as tenor saxophonist Wayne Shorter, pianist Herbie Hancock, bassist Ron Carter and drummer Tony Williams. Shorter contributed four of the six group originals (including "Masqualero" and "Limbo") while Hancock's "The Sorceror" and Williams' "Pee Wee" rounded out the advanced set of complex music. An oddity, a 1962 Bob Dorough vocal ("Nothing like You") with Davis and Shorter as sideman, is also on this generally rewarding CD. —*Scott Yanow*

Seven Steps to Heaven / Apr. 16, 1963–May 14, 1963 / Columbia ◆◆◆◆◆
In 1963 Miles Davis was at a transitional point in his career, without a regular group and wondering what his future musical direction would be. At the time he recorded the music heard on this CD (a straight reissue of the earlier LP with new liner notes), he was in the process of forming a new band, as can be seen from the personnel: Tenor saxophonist George Coleman, Victor Feldman (who turned down the job) and Herbie Hancock on pianos, bassist Ron Carter, and Frank Butler and Tony Williams on drums. Recorded at two seperate sessions, this set is highlighted by the classic "Seven Steps to Heaven," "Joshua" and slow passionate versions of "Basin Street Blues" and "Baby Won't You Please Come Home." —*Scott Yanow*

Cote Blues / Jul. 26, 1963 / Jazz Music Yesterday ◆◆◆
These five alternate versions of Davis classics ("All Blues," "Stella by Starlight," "Seven Steps to Heaven," "If I Were a Bell" and "So What") find Davis and his new quintet (with tenor saxophonist George Coleman, pianist Herbie Hancock, bassist Ron Carter and drummer Tony Williams) in superior form, stretching out with creative solos, particularly on the 21-1/2-minute "Seven Steps." —*Scott Yanow*

Miles Davis in Europe / Jul. 27, 1963 / Columbia ◆◆◆◆
The official debut of his new Quintet features the brilliant trio of pianist Herbie Hancock, bassist Ron Carter and drummer Tony Williams along with the fine tenor saxophonist George Coleman

and the 47-year-old trumpeter/leader. These lengthy versions of "Autumn Leaves," "Milestones," "Joshua," "All of You" and a 16-minute "Walkin'" on this hour-long LP really show what this powerful band could do, even in their early days. — *Scott Yanow*

☆ **The Complete Concert: 1964 (My Funny Valentine & Four & More** / Feb. 12, 1964 / Columbia ✦✦✦✦✦
This two-CD set, which completely reissues the two lengthy LPs *My Funny Valentine* (a set of lyrical ballads) and *Four & More* (which is filled with very rapid versions of Davis's standard repertoire), features the 1963-64 Quintet at its best. This particular unit consisted of the greatly underrated tenor saxophonist George Coleman and the young rhythm section of pianist Herbie Hancock, bassist Ron Carter and drummer Tony Williams. Since Davis' future studio albums with this group (after Wayne Shorter replaced Coleman) would be sticking exclusively to group originals, this exciting set gives one the opportunity to hear this band really stretching out on older tunes, showing off the influence of the avant-garde along with the players' own individual styles. It's highly recommended transitional music. — *Scott Yanow*

Miles in Tokyo / Jul. 14, 1964 / Columbia ✦✦✦✦
After George Coleman left the Miles Davis Quintet, tenor saxophonist Sam Rivers took his place for a short period including a tour of Japan. Davis did not care for Rivers' avant-garde style (they failed to develop any chemistry) and soon replaced him, but this live LP (originally only issued in Japan) survived to document the brief association. The music (five lengthy versions of standards) is actually of high quality with both Davis and Rivers in fine form and the young rhythm section (pianist Herbie Hancock, bassist Ron Carter and drummer Tony Williams) pushing the trumpeter/leader to open up his style. — *Scott Yanow*

Miles In Berlin / Sep. 25, 1964 / CBS/Sony ✦✦✦
Originally only released in Japan, this LP contains the earliest documentation of tenor saxophonist Wayne Shorter performing as a regular member of the Quintet. Unlike the band's upcoming studio albums, this set features lengthy versions of four standards ("Milestones," "Autumn Leaves," "So What" and "Walkin'") that had been in Davis' repertoire for at least five years, making for an interesting comparison between this group's treatments of the songs and their predecessors. The rhythm section in particular (pianist Herbie Hancock, bassist Ron Carter and drummer Tony Williams) really opens up this music, exploring fresh avenues in their improvisations. — *Scott Yanow*

Paris, France / Oct. 1, 1964 / Moon ✦✦✦
Wayne Shorter was still a new member of the Davis Quintet at the time of this concert recording. Although the group (which also includes pianist Herbie Hancock, bassist Ron Carter and drummer Tony Williams) would soon begin recording exclusively originals in the studios, their live performances would feature standards for several years to come. In addition to an unidentified "Miles Impro," the group performs such standbys as "Stella by Starlight," "Walkin'," "Autumn Leaves" and "So What" on this date. Recording quality is decent if not great but the improvisations by the fiery young group are excellent, extending the boundaries of bop. This valuable music was released for the first time on this European CD. — *Scott Yanow*

Davisiana / Oct. 8, 1964 / Moon ✦✦✦
Recorded in Germany, this early document from his second classic Quintet features Davis, Wayne Shorter, Herbie Hancock, Ron Carter and Tony Williams stretching the trumpeter's standard repertoire, playing four of his veteran songs ("Autumn Leaves," "Joshua," "So What" and "Milestones") as a pair of adventurous two-song medleys. His young sidemen were really pushing Davis and the result was very stimulating and unpredictable music. — *Scott Yanow*

E.S.P. / Jan. 20, 1965–Jan. 22, 1965 / Columbia ✦✦✦✦✦
The first of six studio albums by Miles Davis' second classic Quintet features seven originals by bandmembers including "Eighty-One," "Agitation," "Iris" and "E.S.P." This music was quite original although somewhat overshadowed at the time by John Coltrane and some of the avant-garde players. Influenced by Ornette Coleman, the soloing by Davis, Wayne Shorter and Herbie Hancock was quite advanced by this time and this band's music would later be a major influence on Wynton and Branford Marsalis. — *Scott Yanow*

☆ **Complete Live At The Plugged Nickel** / Dec. 22, 1965–Dec. 23, 1965 / Columbia ✦✦✦✦✦
All of the music that trumpeter Miles Davis and his second clas-

sic quintet (with tenor saxophonist Wayne Shorter, pianist Herbie Hancock, bassist Ron Carter and drummer Tony Williams) played at the Plugged Nickel in Chicago on two nights in 1965 has been released on this eight-CD box. The packaging is a bit confusing because Davis' group actually performed seven full sets, but, since their second one on the 22nd ran over, it has been issued on two CDs but placed inside the same package! In any case, the music during these two nights, primarily explorative versions of standards (as opposed to Miles' all-original studio albums of the period), is continually fascinating. A few titles are repeated, but the interpretations differ greatly from each other. The trumpeter's chops are actually not quite in peak form (although his creativity is) but Wayne Shorter (who often takes solo honors) is consistently brilliant and the rhythm section (propelled by Tony Williams) was one of the best of the period. Although some of this music had been issued earlier on three LPs, most of it had been out previously only in Japan. This was a very significant group (even if it was somewhat overshadowed by John Coltrane's Quartet at the time) and their advanced versions of such Miles Davis standards as "Walkin'," "My Funny Valentine," "I Fall in Love Too Easily," "If I Were a Bell," "Stella by Starlight" and "So What" are among the many highlights. One of the top releases of 1995. — *Scott Yanow*

Highlights from the Plugged Nickel / Dec. 22, 1965–Dec. 23, 1965 / Columbia ✦✦✦
Replacing the previous records *Cookin' At the Plugged Nickel* and *Live At the Plugged Nickel, Highlights from the Plugged Nickel* collects a handful of tracks from the mammoth eight-CD set *The Complete Live At the Plugged Nickel 1965*. Two of the tracks on *Highlights* are songs that were issued in their complete versions on the box, but that isn't what makes the album preferable to *Cookin'* and *Live*. On *Highlights*, the fidelity is stunning and the selection is first-rate—the disc flows like one of the original concerts captured on the box. For listeners that don't want to invest in the box, *Highlights* is a worthwhile purchase. — *Stephen Thomas Erlewine*

★ **Miles Smiles** / 1966 / Columbia ✦✦✦✦✦
Of the six studio albums recorded by Miles Davis' second classic quintet, *Miles Smiles* is their definitive set. This CD reissue of the original LP (which has been given new liner notes) features the trumpeter/leader, tenor saxophonist Wayne Shorter, pianist Herbie Hancock, bassist Ron Carter and drummer Tony Williams in superb form on adventurous versions of "Freedom Jazz Dance," "Gingerbread Boy," Wayne Shorter's "Footprints" and three lesser-known pieces ("Orbits," "Circle" and "Dolores"). The music is challenging but quite rewarding. — *Scott Yanow*

Nefertiti / Jun. 7, 1967–Jul. 19, 1967 / Columbia ✦✦✦✦
The fourth of the six studio albums by the Miles Davis Quintet of the 1960s was their last all-acoustic session. Wayne Shorter, Herbie Hancock and Tony Williams contributed all of the music to this adventurous set including such classics as "Nefertiti," "Riot" and "Pinocchio." This CD reissue of the original LP (which has new liner notes) is brief at under 40 minutes but the music is consistently stimulating and unpredictable. It's funny that this group's playing had little influence on the music of 1967 for by 1987 it was becoming the mainstream of jazz. — *Scott Yanow*

Water Babies / Jun. 1967–Nov. 1968 / Columbia ✦✦✦
This studio LP was first released almost a decade after it was recorded. The first half features the 1967 Quintet (with Wayne Shorter on tenor and soprano, pianist Herbie Hancock, bassist Ron Carter and drummer Tony Williams) performing three otherwise unknown Shorter compositions. The flip side finds Davis in 1968 leading the same group (with possibly Chick Corea and Dave Holland replacing Hancock and Carter) on two early fusion jams that look a bit toward *Bitches Brew*. Although not an essential set, this album fills in some gaps during Davis' transitional period from adventurous acoustic playing to early electric performances. — *Scott Yanow*

No Blues / Nov. 6, 1967 / Jazz Music Yesterday ✦✦✦✦✦
The Miles Davis Quintet only recorded new material during 1965-68 but in their live performances they still played some of the trumpeter's older standards. Until recent times, few of the live sessions by the Quintet made it onto record, but this very valuable CD features the group in late 1967 playing such songs (for nearly the final time) as "'Round Midnight," "No Blues," "I Fall in Love Too Easily," "Walkin'" and "Green Dolphin Street" in addition to the newer songs "Mascalero" and "Riot." It is utterly fascinating to hear the Quintet at that late date stretching out on these

veteran songs and coming up with fresh new ideas one more time. This Italian import is well worth searching for; it fills an important gap in jazz history. —*Scott Yanow*

Miles in the Sky / Jan. 16, 1968–May 17, 1968 / Columbia ✦✦✦✦
The fifth of the six studio albums by the second classic Quintet found Davis continuing to move ahead. For the first time Herbie Hancock is heard a bit on electric piano, guitarist George Benson guests on "Paraphernalia" and the extended performances were just beginning to open themselves to the influences of pop and rock music. This CD reissues the original LP but has new liner notes. This important set of music which can be seen as either early fusion, the beginning of the end of the Miles Davis Quintet, or both. —*Scott Yanow*

Filles De Kilimanjaro / Jun. 19, 1968–Sep. 24, 1968 / Columbia ✦✦✦✦✦
The sixth and final studio album by Miles Davis' second classic Quintet finds the group looking toward early fusion. Herbie Hancock (who doubles on electric piano) and bassist Ron Carter are replaced by Chick Corea and Dave Holland on the two selections from Sept. 24, 1968, although Wayne Shorter and drummer Tony Williams are still key members of Davis' band. The music is less esoteric than his music of a year or two earlier, with funky rhythms and hints at pop and rock music becoming prevalent although not dominant yet. To many of the jazz purists, this was Miles Davis' final jazz album but to those with open ears toward electronics and danceable rhythms, this set was the predecessor of his next great innovation. This CD reissue of the original LP is well worth checking out. —*Scott Yanow*

☆ **In a Silent Way** / Feb. 18, 1969 / Columbia ✦✦✦✦✦
The beginning of fusion (although other groups such as Gary Burton's Quartet with Larry Coryell had hinted strongly at it), this set found Miles Davis for the first time really combining jazz improvising with the rhythms and power of rock. On this LP, Davis jams with an octet (which includes the magical names of tenor saxophonist Wayne Shorter, keyboardists Herbie Hancock, Chick Corea and Joe Zawinul, guitarist John McLaughlin, bassist Dave Holland and drummer Tony Williams; all future bandleaders) on two lengthy side-long medleys. Those jazz purists with their minds closed toward electronics of any kind are advised to check out this fairly accessible date before tackling *Bitches Brew*. The strong solos on this early fusion classic might very well win them over. —*Scott Yanow*

It's About That Time / Jul. 1969 / Jazz Door ✦✦✦✦
This exciting live set (released for the first time on this European CD in the mid-'90s) finds Miles Davis at a particularly intriguing point in his evolution. He had finished recording *In a Silent Way* five months earlier and was just a few weeks before starting *Bitches Brew*. His working quintet (captured during a seven-song continuous set at the Montreux Jazz Festival) at that time was comprised of Wayne Shorter on tenor and soprano, keyboardist Chick Corea, Dave Holland on electric bass and drummer Jack DeJohnette. In addition to performing versions of "Miles Runs the Voodoo Down" and "Sanctuary" that predate *Bitches Brew,* they also play the last versions thus far released of Davis performing two of his standards: "Milestones" and 'Round About Midnight." The recording quality is excellent and Miles Davis was in fine form for this very interesting transitional date which captures the trumpeter just before he permanently turned his music completely into fusion. —*Scott Yanow*

★ **Bitches Brew** / Aug. 19, 1969–Aug. 21, 1969 / Columbia ✦✦✦✦✦
No jazz collection is complete without this double CD. This very influential set was one of the first successful attempts to form a new music (soon termed fusion) by combining jazz solos with rock rhythms. "Miles Runs the Voodoo Down" is the most memorable of the six lengthy selections, featuring a fascinating ensemble with Davis' trumpet, Wayne Shorter's soprano, Bennie Maupin's bass clarinet, guitarist John McLaughlin, the keyboards of Chick Corea and Larry Young (Joe Zawinul is on some of the other selections), Dave Holland and Harvey Brooks on basses, drummers Jack DeJohnette, Charles Alias and Lenny White and percussionist Jim Riley. Not for the close-minded, this music brought many rock listeners into jazz and gave jazz musicians new possibilities to explore. —*Scott Yanow*

Big Fun / Nov. 19, 1969–Jun. 12, 1972 / Columbia ✦✦
This double LP features Davis on four side-long jams taken from different sessions during 1969–72. "Great Expectations" features

most of the players from *Bitches Brew* along with two sitarists and "Ife" has the trumpeter's 1972 band (with saxophonists Carlos Garnett and Sonny Fortune) but the two best tracks ("Lonely Fire" and "Go Ahead John") are from 1970; the latter features the quintet of Davis, Steve Grossman on soprano, guitarist John McLaughlin, bassist Dave Holland and drummer Jack DeJohnette. Very interesting if erratic music, it's not essential but fans of Davis' fusion years will enjoy much of it. —*Scott Yanow*

Live: Evil / Feb. 6, 1970–Dec. 19, 1970 / Columbia ✦✦✦✦
Forget the inexcusably ugly (and somewhat racist) artwork and a few of the weaker tracks. At its best this double LP has some of Davis' finest playing of the 1970s, and the solos by altoist Gary Bartz, guitarist John McLaughlin and keyboardist Keith Jarrett are not that far behind on such lengthy pieces as "What I Say" and "Funky Tonk." This is fusion at its most adventurous (and sometimes most riotous), before the record labels and radio stations turned it into meaningless "smooth jazz." —*Scott Yanow*

A Tribute to Jack Johnson / Apr. 7, 1970 / Columbia ✦✦✦✦✦
Davis' odd soundtrack for a documentary on the boxer Jack Johnson did not really fit the movie (it was far too modern) but stands alone very well as a strong piece of music. On this straight reissue of the original LP, the two lengthy jams (25-minute-plus versions of "Right Off" and "Yesternow") feature fine playing by a sextet comprised of Davis' trumpet, Steve Grossman's soprano sax, keyboardist Herbie Hancock, guitarist John McLaughlin, electric bassist Michael Henderson and drummer Billy Cobham. Even listeners who write off the fusion years will find moments of interest on this set. —*Scott Yanow*

Black Beauty / Apr. 10, 1970 / CBS ✦✦✦

At the Fillmore / Jun. 17, 1970–Jun. 20, 1970 / Columbia ✦✦✦
The four side-long excursions on this double LP are full of self-indulgent moments, particularly when Chick Corea and Keith Jarrett almost literally battle each other on their arsenal of electric keyboards, but there are also hot solos from Miles Davis and occasionally saxophonist Steve Grossman. This occasionally out-of-control set will not win any converts to Davis' fusion years but it does have its enjoyable and humorous moments. —*Scott Yanow*

Hooray For Miles Davis, Vol. 3 / Nov. 26, 1971 / Session ✦✦✦
The sound quality of this bootleg LP is just okay, but the two medleys played by Davis' 1971 quintet (with altoist Gary Bartz, keyboardist Keith Jarrett, electric bassist Mike Henderson and drummer Jack DeJohnette) combines some of his better groove tunes of the era (including "What I Say," "Miles Runs the Voodoo Down" and "Yesternow"). It's a spirited session of creative fusion. —*Scott Yanow*

On the Corner / Jun. 1, 1972–Jun. 6, 1972 / Columbia ✦✦✦
On the Corner is Miles Davis' most controversial album. Jazz purists detest the album, dismissing it out of hand for the very reason that its fans celebrate it—there are no fully-formed songs on the record, just funky rhythmic vamps. Davis assembled a large group of musicians, who aren't credited on the record, and had them play one groove, which demonstrated a heavy debt to Sly Stone. Miles rarely plays trumpet on the record and when he does, it is distorted and processed. Instead, he plays organ, blending into the dense, electric funk. None of the players take extended solos and all of the songs are brief, but improvisation isn't the point of the record. *On the Corner* is about funk and rhythm, not about jazz. With this record, Davis laid the foundation of the genre-blurring hip-hop and acid jazz revolutions in popular music in the '80s and '90s. —*Stephen Thomas Erlewine*

Get Up with It / Sep. 6, 1972–Oct. 7, 1974 / Columbia ✦✦✦
This double LP, featuring a variety of Miles Davis' electric ensembles of 1974, has plenty of variety, ranging from a sidelong dirge for Duke Ellington ("He Loved Him Madly") and a dumb but interesting "Red China Blues," to heated jams on "Honky Tonk," "Calypso Frelimo" and "Mtume." Although Davis plays organ rather than trumpet half the time, the dense ensembles and passionate improvisations are creative rather than predictable. —*Scott Yanow*

In Concert / Sep. 29, 1972 / Columbia ✦
On the heels of the disastrous *On the Corner,* Davis recorded an utterly forgettable live session. This two-LP set has no song titles, no personnel listing and, more importantly, no purpose. The music consists of self-indulgent rhythmic vamps, Davis' appearances are almost unrecognizable (his horn was electrified throughout) and this set can be safely passed by. —*Scott Yanow*

Dark Magus / Mar. 3, 1974 / Sony ✦✦✦

Pangaea / Feb. 1, 1975 / Columbia ✦✦✦✦

Although Davis' health was shaky at the time of this two-CD set (recorded the same day as the weaker *Agharta*), he has a few strong trumpet solos on these two very lengthy pieces ("Zimbabwe" and "Gondwana"); Davis would drift into retirement for six years shortly after this concert. The music is actually quite rewarding (at least it will be for listeners with open ears) with the dense ensembles and heated solos (Sonny Fortune on soprano, alto and flute and the guitars of Pete Cosey and Reggie Lucas) being quite dangerous, as opposed to the safe fusion of the 1990s. *Pangaea* is the finest recording from the least-understood period of Davis' career (1971-75). —*Scott Yanow*

Agharta / Feb. 1, 1975 / Columbia ✦✦✦

Recorded the same day as *Pangaea* but not up to its level, this two-LP set features Davis just prior to his six-year retirement. He actually sounds a bit weak on this set (although he takes a rare straight-ahead solo on "Interlude") but altoist Sonny Fortune has his moments. The dense and rockish ensembles (with the guitars of Pete Cosey and Reggie Lucas) will scare most jazz listeners away. —*Scott Yanow*

The Man with the Horn / 1981 / Columbia ✦✦✦

Miles Davis' first comeback record finds the trumpeter a bit shaky (he would improve album by album during the next few years) and has a few poppish throwaway tracks; it is doubtful if anyone really remembers the title cut or "Shout." But with Bill Evans on soprano and electric bassist Marcus Miller, the other four selections are more rewarding, with Davis forming the nucleus of his new band. —*Scott Yanow*

We Want Miles / Jun. 27, 1981-Oct. 4, 1981 / Columbia ✦✦✦✦

Davis' second recording since ending his six-year retirement was one of his best of the 1980s. Unlike his bands from the 1970s, this particular unit leaves plenty of space and plays much more melodically. Guitarist Mike Stern lets loose some fury but electric bassist Marcus Miller is not reluctant to walk now and then in a straight-ahead fashion, drummer Al Foster and percussionist Mino Cinelu are tasteful and Bill Evans gets in a few good spots on soprano. As for Davis, he was gradually regaining his earlier form. This double LP is highlighted by "Back Seat Betty," a sidelong investigation of "My Man's Gone Now" and two versions of Davis' childlike "Jean Pierre." —*Scott Yanow*

Star People / Sep. 1, 1982-Jan. 5, 1983 / Columbia ✦✦✦✦

On this 1983 release, Miles Davis rediscovers the blues. He really stretches out on "Star People," making dramatic use of silence and placing each note carefully. "Come Get It" is also memorable although "U 'N' I" (which had the potential to catch on) is only heard in a truncated version. In general Davis is in fine form on this set and, although saxophonist Bill Evans is barely heard from (many of his solos were edited out), the contrasting guitars of Mike Stern and John Scofield hold one's interest. —*Scott Yanow*

Decoy / Jun. 30, 1983-Sep. 11, 1983 / Columbia ✦✦

This rather streaky set of music features Davis with keyboardist Robert Irving III (who has since slipped into obscurity) and guitarist John Scofield contributing most of the compositions and the other solos. There are some moments of interest (Branford Marsalis is heard on some cuts on soprano) but it is doubtful if anyone will be reviving "Robot 415," "Freaky Deaky" or "Code M.D." anytime soon. —*Scott Yanow*

You're under Arrest / Jan. 26, 1984-Jan. 1985 / Columbia ✦✦

Miles Davis' final Columbia recording (other than *Aura*, which was released several years later) includes his straightforward ballad interpretations of Cyndi Lauper's "Time After Time" and the Michael Jackson-associated "Human Nature," two songs he would play in most of his concerts for the remainder of his life. Other tunes (including "You're Under Arrest," "One Phone Call" and "Ms. Morrisine") were quickly discarded. In addition to Davis (who had regained his earlier chops) tenor saxophonist Bob Berg, guitarist John Scofield and guest John McLaughlin get in a few decent solos on this competent but not overly memorable effort. —*Scott Yanow*

Aura / Jan. 31, 1985-Feb. 4, 1985 / Columbia ✦✦✦

Miles Davis' final Columbia release was this two-LP set, an unusual effort from his fusion years. Palle Mikkelborg composed a challenging nine-part suite that finds the trumpeter in fairly inspired form, joined by a colorful big band. Guitarist John McLaughlin and bassists Niels Pedersen and Bo Stief have some solos but oth-

erwise the spotlight is entirely on Davis, who mostly rises to the occasion. —*Scott Yanow*

Tutu / Jan. 6, 1986-Mar. 25, 1986 / Warner Brothers ✦✦✦

This controversial but memorable recording is mostly a duet between Miles Davis and the many overdubbed instruments of producer Marcus Miller (although violinist Michel Urbaniak, percussionist Paulinho da Costa and keyboardist George Duke are among the other musicians making brief appearaances). Certainly the results are not all that spontaneous but Davis is in top form and some of the selections (most notably the title cut) are quite memorable. —*Scott Yanow*

Music from Siesta / Jan. 19, 1987-Mar. 1987 / Warner Brothers ✦✦✦

This collaboration between Davis and producer Marcus Miller (who, except for some cameos, plays all of the other instruments) is quite successful and a bit of a surprise since it is essentially a soundtrack to an obscure film. Dedicated to arranger Gil Evans, the music is greatly influenced by his style with Miller creating an electrified but very warm orchestra to accompany Davis' melodic solos. This was the first of several instances in which Miles Davis, in the twilight of his life, returned to his roots. It's worth searching for. —*Scott Yanow*

Amandla / Dec. 1989, 1988 / Warner Brothers ✦✦✦✦

A particularly strong set by late-period Miles Davis, this set is highlighted by a surprisingly straight-ahead performance titled "Mr. Pastorius." In addition to Davis and his new altoist Kenny Garrett, various guests (including Marcus Miller, guitarist Jean Paul Boureiiy, Joey DeFrancesco on keyboards, Rick Margitza on tenor, pianist Joe Sample and bassist Foley) get their chances to play next to the great legend, who is in top form. An excellent effort, it was really his last studio recording with his regular band. —*Scott Yanow*

Dingo / Mar. 1990 / Warner Brothers ✦✦

In 1990 Miles Davis starred in a movie about a veteran trumpeter (talk about typecasting) and had a rare opportunity to play part of the time in a straight-ahead setting. Fellow trumpeter Chuck Findley performs the solos for a younger musician who befriends Davis and Michel Legrand arranged and composed the music. There are some good moments on these selections (Findley actually overshadows Davis in some places) but since this is a soundtrack, the music does not often stand up that well by itself. It's a worthy effort but is sure to become an obscurity. —*Scott Yanow*

Hot Spot / May 5, 1990-May 10, 1990 / Antilles ✦✦✦

This unusual blues-oriented soundtrack extensively features trumpeter Miles Davis and guitarist/vocalist John Lee Hooker (along with Taj Majal and slide guitarist Roy Rogers). More of a historical curiosity than an essential CD, the music has its strong moments and it is particularly interesting to hear Davis in this setting. —*Scott Yanow*

Doo-Bop / Jan. 19, 1991-Feb. 1991 / Warner Brothers ✦

Miles Davis' final studio album was one of the few totally worthless recordings of his career. Davis, in an attempt to remain contemporary, teamed up with rapper Easy Mo Bee for some meaningless rhythm tracks. Most of the raps have to do with how great Miles is but the trumpeter (whose playing here is consistently mediocre) provides little evidence of his creativity or power. Skip it. —*Scott Yanow*

Live at Montreux / Jul. 8, 1991 / Warner Brothers ✦✦✦

This historically significant set found Miles Davis, just months before his death, doing what he always said he wouldn't: revisiting his past. Backed by a large orchestra (mostly George Gruntz's concert band) conducted by Quincy Jones, Davis plays music from his four collaborations with Gil Evans including "Boplicity" (from the *Birth of the Cool* days) and medleys from *Miles Ahead, Porgy and Bess* and *Sketches of Spain*. Unfortunately, Davis chose to be muted most of the time, leaving more difficult (and exciting) sections to Roney and delegated some other solo space to Garrett. The results are quite emotional, but not up to the level that one would hope, a suitable last hurrah for the innovative true classic greats of jazz. —*Scott Yanow*

Nathan Davis

b. Feb. 15, 1937, Kansas City, KS

Tenor Saxophone / Hard Bop

Nathan Davis has split his career between being a fine tenor saxophonist and a jazz educator. He played briefly with Jay McShann in 1955, attended the University of Kansas, spent time in the Army in Berlin (1960-63) and stayed in Paris where he worked with Kenny Clarke (1963-69), Eric Dolphy (1964) and Art Taylor. He also toured Europe with Art Blakey (1965) and Ray Charles. Since 1969 Davis has been a professor of jazz at the University of Pittsburgh and Moorhead State University. His two most important musical associations have been heading the Paris Reunion Band (1985-89) and leading Roots (which he formed in 1991). — *Scott Yanow*

● **The Hip Walk** / Sep. 1, 1965 / Saba ◆◆◆◆

London by Night / Aug. 17, 1987–Aug. 18, 1987 / Hot House ◆◆◆◆

Richard Davis

b. Apr. 15, 1930, Chicago, IL
Bass / Post-Bop, Hard Bop
One of the most technically skilled of all acoustic bassists, Richard Davis has played in symphony orchestras but fortunately has spent much of his career in the jazz world. His early jazz jobs included stints with Ahmad Jamal (1953-54), Don Shirley (1954-55) and Sarah Vaughan (1957-60). In addition to his symphony work in the 1960s (including for Stravinsky), Davis was a major asset on recordings by Eric Dolphy, Booker Ervin, Rahsaan Roland Kirk, Andrew Hill, Ben Webster, Stan Getz, Earl Hines, Hank Jones and Billy Cobham; in addition he was a regular member of the Thad Jones-Mel Lewis Orchestra during 1966-72. In 1977 he became an educator at the University of Wisconsin. Richard Davis' infrequent albums as a leader include dates for MPS, Muse, Flying Dutchman, Galaxy, Hep and Sweet Basil (1990). — *Scott Yanow*

Muses for Richard Davis / Dec. 9, 1969 / Pausa ◆◆◆

With Understanding / Jan. 1971 / Muse ◆◆◆
Chick Corea (k) center stage with fine Davis support. — *Ron Wynn*

Epistrophy / Now's the Time / Sep. 7, 1972 / Muse ◆◆◆◆
Fine set with stirring Clifford Jordan (ts). CD issue. — *Ron Wynn*

Dealin' / Sep. 14, 1972 / Muse ◆◆◆

As One / Oct. 19, 1975+Oct. 25, 1975 / Muse ◆◆◆

Harvest / May 3, 1977 / Muse ◆◆◆

Fancy Free / Jun. 30, 1977+Jul. 1, 1977 / Galaxy ◆◆◆

Cauldron / Jan. 13, 1979 / Corvo ◆◆◆◆

One for Frederick / Jul. 6, 1989-Jul. 7, 1987 / Hep ◆◆◆

● **Live At Sweet Basil** / Aug. 8, 1990+May 21, 1991 / Evidence ◆◆◆◆◆

Walter Davis, Jr.

b. Sep. 2, 1932, Richmond, VA, d. Jun. 2, 1990, New York, NY
Piano / Bop, Hard Bop
In 1959 Walter Davis, Jr. led one of the great Blue Note sessions, a quintet set with Donald Byrd and Jackie McLean called *Davis Cup*. It seems strange that not only did he not have an opportunity for an encore but his next session as a leader was for Denon, in 1977! An excellent bop-based pianist, Walter Davis picked up early experience in the late '40s working with Babs Gonzales' Three Bips and a Bop before playing and recording with Charlie Parker in 1952. Following were associations with Max Roach (1952-53), Dizzy Gillespie's big band (1956), Donald Byrd (1959) and Art Blakey's Jazz Messengers (1959). After a long period outside of music Davis came back to play with Sonny Rollins (1973-74), the Jazz Messengers (1975-77) and then as leader of his own group. He was on the soundtrack of the film *Bird* and recorded extensively as a leader during 1977-79 (for Denon, Bee Hive, Red and Owl) and in 1987-89 (for Jazz Heritage, Jazz City, Mapleshade and SteepleChase). — *Scott Yanow*

★ **Davis Cup** / Aug. 2, 1959 / Blue Note ◆◆◆◆◆
Propulsive hard bop, it features Donald Byrd (tpt) and Jackie McLean (as). — *David Szatmary*

Blues Walk / Nov. 23, 1979 / Red ◆◆◆◆

400 Years Ago, Tomorrow / Dec. 1979 / Owl ◆◆◆

☆ **In Walked Thelonious** / Apr. 19, 1987 / Mapleshade ◆◆◆◆◆
Some spectacular solo playing by Walter Davis, Jr., a severely underrated pianist. He did 15 Monk classics, among them complex works like "Trinkle, Tinkle" and "Panonica," and made them his own. All the songs were complete first takes, and there was no

overdubbing or multi-tracking—just Davis displaying his brilliance on each cut. — *Ron Wynn*

Illumination / Feb. 1988 / Denon ◆◆◆◆

Wild Bill Davis

b. 1918, Glasgow, MO, d. 1995
Organ / Swing
Prior to the rise of Jimmy Smith in 1956, Wild Bill Davis was the pacesetter among organists. He actually played guitar and wrote arrangements for Milt Larkin's legendary band during 1939-42. Davis played piano with Louis Jordan's Tympany Five (1945-49) before switching to organ in 1950 and heading his own influential organ/guitar/drums trios. Davis was originally supposed to record "April in Paris" with Count Basie's Orchestra in 1955 but when he could not make the session, Basie used his arrangement for the full band and had a major hit. In addition to working with his own groups in the 1960s, Davis made several albums with his friend Johnny Hodges, leading to tours during 1969-71 with Duke Ellington. In the '70s he recorded for *Black & Blue* with a variety of swing all-stars and played with Lionel Hampton, appearing at festivals through the early '90s. — *Scott Yanow*

Con Soul and Sax / Jan. 7, 1965 / RCA ◆◆◆◆

★ **In Atlantic City** / Aug. 10, 1966+Aug. 11, 1966 / RCA ◆◆◆◆◆

Doin' His Thing / Nov. 13, 1967-Nov. 15, 1967 / RCA ◆◆◆

Impulsions / May 9, 1972+May 10, 1972 / Black & Blue ◆◆◆

Wild Bill Davison

b. Jan. 5, 1906, Defiance, OH, d. Nov. 14, 1989, Santa Barbara, CA
Cornet / Dixieland
One of the great Dixieland trumpeters, Wild Bill Davison had a colorful and emotional style that ranged from sarcasm to sentimentality with plenty of growls and shakes. His unexpected placement of high notes was a highlight of his solos and his strong personality put him far ahead of the competition. In the 1920s he played with the Ohio Lucky Seven, the Chubb-Steinberg Orchestra (with whom he made his recording debut), the Seattle Harmony Kings and Benny Meroff. After he was involved in a fatal car accident that ended the life of Frankie Teschemacher in 1932 (his auto was blindsided by a taxi), Davison spent the remainder of the 1930s in exile in Milwaukee. By 1941 he was in New York and in 1943 made some brilliant recordings for Commodore (including a classic version of "That's a Plenty") that solidified his reputation. After a period in the Army, Davison became a fixture with Eddie Condon's bands starting in 1945, playing nightly at Condon's. In the 1950s he was quite effective on a pair of albums with string orchestras, but most of his career was spent fronting Dixieland bands either as a leader or with Condon. Wild Bill toured Europe often from the 1960s, recorded constantly, had a colorful life filled with remarkable episodes and was active up until his death. — *Scott Yanow*

That's a Plenty / Nov. 27, 1943+Nov. 30, 1943 / Commodore ◆◆◆◆◆
Lots of Pee Wee Russell (cl) and George Brunis (tb) from old 78s. Nice album to find. — *Michael G. Nastos*

And His Jazz Band, 1943 / Dec. 3, 1944+Oct. 13, 1955 / Jazzology ◆◆◆◆
This CD contains the complete Wild Bill Davison session of December 3, 1944 (which was originally made as radio transcriptions) and part of a date led by the cornetist in 1955. The former set has five songs, plus five alternate takes, from a particularly mighty outfit also including trombonist George Brunis, clarinetist Pee Wee Russell, pianist Gene Schroeder, Eddie Condon on rhythm guitar, bassist Bob Casey and drummer George Wettling. Highlights include "That's a Plenty," the many different versions of "Royal Garden Blues" and "Muskrat Ramble." Only three songs are included from the later session, which matches Davison with trombonist Lou McGarity, clarinetist Tony Parenti, pianist Hank Duncan, bassist Pops Foster and drummer Zutty Singleton, but there are also 12 false starts and 11 alternate takes, eight of which are incomplete. Obviously this CD is mostly for true Dixieland completists and fanatics, but fans of Wild Bill Davison will find his many consistently colorful variations worth hearing. — *Scott Yanow*

★ **Showcase** / Dec. 27, 1947-Oct. 19, 1976 / Jazzology ◆◆◆◆◆
Two unrelated but rewarding sessions by the great Dixieland cornetist Wild Bill Davison are combined on this delightful CD. The first session, a six-song ballad-oriented date that also includes trombonist Jimmy Archey, Garvin Bushell on clarinet and (on

"Yesterdays") bassoon, pianist Ralph Sutton, bassist Sid Weiss and drummer Morey Feld, has some particularly ferocious playing from Davison (who takes his first recorded vocal on "Ghost of a Chance"). The remaining dozen tunes come from a very successful matchup in 1976 between Davison and the Classic Jazz Collegium Orchestra, a talented ten-member Czechoslovakian group. Some of the numbers (most notably a classic rendition of "Sunday") have inventive arrangements that make the band sound like a unit from the 1920s. Wild Bill is quite inspired throughout, making this one of his most rewarding sets of the 1970s. Highly recommended. —*Scott Yanow*

Individualism Of. . . . / Nov. 6, 1951–Nov. 10, 1951 / Savoy ✦✦✦✦
1951 sessions at Eddie Condon's in Boston. Features Cutty Cutshall (tb), Ed Hall (cl), George Wein (p), Buzzy Drootin (d). Sextet and septet recordings with two different groups. Dixie to swing standards by the master cornetist. 23 cuts. —*Michael G. Nastos*

Pretty Wild / Feb. 22, 1956+Feb. 23, 1956 / Columbia ✦✦✦

Live! Miami Beach (1955) / Nov. 27, 1956+Nov. 29, 1956 / Pumpkin ✦✦✦

Plays the Greatest of The Greats / Sep. 4, 1959–Sep. 5, 1959 / Dixieland Jubilee ✦✦

Blowin' Wild / Oct. 1962 / Jazzology ✦✦✦

Surfside Jazz / Aug. 19, 1965 / Jazzology ✦✦✦

Wild Bill at Bull Run / Sep. 1966 / Jazzology ✦✦✦

Live at the Rainbow Room / Jul. 7, 1973 / Chiaroscuro ✦✦✦

Just a Gig / Nov. 1973 / Jazzology ✦✦

"Wild" Bill Davison/Papa Bue's Viking Jazz Band / Feb. 10, 1974 / Storyville ✦✦✦✦

Together Again / May 23, 1977–May 24, 1977 / Storyville ✦✦✦✦

Plays Hoagy Carmichael / Mar. 12, 1981–Mar. 13, 1981 / Real Time ✦✦✦

All-Stars / Oct. 19, 1986 / Timeless ✦✦✦

Alan Dawson

b. July 14, 1929, Marietta, PA, **d.** 1996
Drums / Hard Bop
Both an outstanding drummer and heralded instructor, Alan Dawson has tutored many first-rate players and been showcased on several excellent recordings. His taste, rhythmic sophistication and drive have been highly praised by musicians and critics alike. Dawson studied with Charles Alden in Boston during the early '50s, and worked with Sabby Lewis. He toured with Lionel Hampton in 1953, played with Lewis again from '53–'56, then joined the faculty at Berklee in 1957. He remained there until the mid-'70s. Some of Dawson's pupils during that stint included Tony Williams, Clifford Jarvis, Harvey Mason and Joe LaBarbera. He was also an early mentor to Terry Lyne Carrington, who he spotted working in Boston clubs as a youngster. Dawson did many local gigs as well, backing visiting greats like Rahsaan Roland Kirk and Sonny Stitt during their dates. His steady, crisply paced drumming with Jaki Byard, Booker Ervin, Tal Farlow and Dexter Gordon was highlighted on several outstanding Prestige albums in the '60s and '70s, and he was in Dave Brubeck's quartet from 1968 to 1974. Dawson continued private teaching after leaving Berklee, and has published several instructional manuals. Though he didn't issue any sessions as a leader, Dawson can be prominently heard on many CD reissues by Brubeck, Ervin, Byard, Gordon, and others. —*Ron Wynn*

Blossom Dearie

b. Apr. 28, 1926, East Durham, NY
Piano, Vocals / Bop, Standards
Blossom Dearie has one of the most unusual styles to be heard in jazz and cabaret music. A fine bop-based pianist, Dearie has a little girl's voice that is definitely an acquired taste but charming in its own way. Early on she sang with the Blue Flames (a vocal group featured with the Woody Herman Orchestra), the Blue Reys (part of Alvino Rey's band) and in 1952 she recorded the original version of "Moody's Mood for Love" with King Pleasure. That year she went to Paris, where she performed with Annie Ross and formed her own vocal group, the Blue Stars. In 1956 Dearie returned to the U.S. and led her own trio, having a successful solo career highlighted by her versions of Dave Frishberg's "Peel Me a

Grape" and her original "Hey John." In 1974 she started recording exclusively for her own Daffodil label. —*Scott Yanow*

★ **Blossom Dearie** / Sep. 11, 1956–Apr. 9, 1959 / Verve ✦✦✦✦✦

Summertime / Sep. 12, 1958–Sep. 13, 1958 / Verve ✦✦✦
Vocalist Blossom Dearie's *Summertime* is a low-key collection of chamber-jazz arranged for a small trio. Working with guitarist Mundell Lowe, bassist Ray Brown, and drummer Ed Thigpen, Dearie sings the material with a gentle conviction; she may never sound passionate, but she never sounds like she doesn't care. The result is a pleasant record, that might never be a compelling listen, but it's never a bad one. —*Stephen Thomas Erlewine*

May I Come In? / Feb. 13, 1964–Feb. 15, 1964 / Daffodil ✦✦✦

John D'Earth

b. Mar. 30, 1950, Holliston, MS
Trumpet / Post-Bop, Hard Bop
An excellent straight-ahead trumpeter who is sometimes adventurous, John D'Earth worked with the big bands of Buddy Rich, Thad Jones-Mel Lewis and Lionel Hampton before recording with Bob Moses, Harvie Swartz and Emily Remler. He led his first session in 1989 for Enja. —*Scott Yanow*

One Bright Glance / Apr. 11, 1989 / Enja ✦✦✦✦

Barrett Deems

b. Mar. 1, 1914, Springfield, IL
Drums / Swing
It is ironic that Barrett Deems' highest profile gig, touring with the Louis Armstrong All-Stars, found him very much out of place, reduced to playing clichés in a Dixieland setting. In reality Deems has had a lengthy career with other lesser-known highpoints. He was with Paul Ash's group when he was just 15 and had his own groups during much of the 1930s. Deems was with the Joe Venuti big band (1937–44), Red Norvo (1948), Charlie Barnet (1951) and Muggsy Spanier (1951–54); during that era he was billed almost accurately as "the world's fastest drummer." Deems was with Louis Armstrong during 1954–58, a period when he was criticized by many jazz writers despite giving the music his best effort. After playing with Jack Teagarden (1960–63) he settled in Chicago where he played locally with many top swing stars. Deems toured Eastern Europe with Benny Goodman's sextet in 1976 and visited South America with Wild Bill Davison. Barrett Deems has for the past few years led a fairly modern big band in Chicago and he recorded a strong set with the orchestra for Delmark after he turned 80; his playing now sounds modeled after Buddy Rich. —*Scott Yanow*

Barrett Deems Big Band / Mar. 6, 1994–Mar. 7, 1994 / Delmark ✦✦✦✦
Barrett Deems, 81 at the time of this recording, will always be best-known for his stint with the Louis Armstrong All-Stars in the 1950s. After settling in Chicago the drummer became the leader of a top-notch jazz orchestra, which made its recording debut on this Delmark release. Deems, whose musical role model is Buddy Rich, is in top form throughout the set, which is a bit surprising considering his shaky health at the time. The performances (which are mostly veteran standards) are usually hard-driving and always swing. The many concise solos are unfortunately unidentified; trumpeter Brad Goode is the only one of the sidemen really known outside of Chicago although vibraphonist Duane Thamm is clearly a strong asset to the 18-piece band. Few surprises occur during this conventional date, but the music is very easy to enjoy and makes one aware of some of the many musical talents that reside in Chicago. —*Scott Yanow*

Joey DeFrancesco

b. 1971, Philadelphia, PA
Organ / Bop, Soul Jazz, Hard Bop
The comeback of the organ in jazz during the late '80s was partly due to the rise of Joey DeFrancesco, a brilliant and energetic player whose style is heavily influenced by Jimmy Smith. He started on piano when he was five and within a year had switched to his father's instrument, the organ. In the first Thelonious Monk International Jazz Piano Competition in 1987 he was a finalist at the age of 16. He toured with Miles Davis in late 1988 and has led his own groups ever since. A decent trumpeter, DeFrancesco is the most important new organist to emerge during the past decade. He has recorded for Columbia and Muse. —*Scott Yanow*

All of Me / 1989 / Columbia ✦✦✦✦

● **Where Were You?** / Jun. 1990 / Columbia ✦✦✦✦✦
Nice mix-and-match quartet sessions. The lineup is split between esteemed veterans like Illinois Jacquet (sax) and Milt Hinton (b) and the younger Wallace Roney (tpt) and Kirk Whalum (ts). —*Ron Wynn*

Part III / 1991 / Columbia ✦✦✦
Substantial fluctuation in material quality and performances. DeFrancesco has a good flair for soul jazz and hard bop but gets bogged down at times in pop-tinged pablum. —*Ron Wynn*

Reboppin' / 1992 / Columbia ✦✦✦✦
Joey DeFrancesco's powerhouse riffs, solos, and soulful phrasing have made DeFrancesco the top mainstream stylist. This set includes contributions from his father and brother on one cut and a good backing band, despite the absence of major names or stars. —*Ron Wynn*

Live at the 5 Spot / 1993 / Columbia ✦✦✦
Organist Joey DeFrancesco clearly had a good time during this jam session. His fine quintet (which has strong soloists in altoist Robert Landham, trumpeter Jim Henry and especially guitarist Paul Bollenback) starts things off with a run through of "rhythm changes" during "The Eternal One" and the hornless trio cuts loose on a swinging "I'll Remember April," but otherwise all of the other selections feature guests. Tenors Illinois Jacquet, Grover Washington, Jr., Houston Person and Kirk Whalum all fare well on separate numbers (Jacquet steals the show on "All of Me") and on the closing blues DeFrancesco interacts with fellow organist Captain Jack McDuff. Few surprises occur overall (the tenors should have all played together) but the music is quite pleasing and easily recommended to DeFrancesco's fans. —*Scott Yanow*

All About My Girl / 1994 / Muse ✦✦✦✦

The Street of Dreams / 1995 / Big Mo ✦✦✦

Buddy DeFranco
(Boniface Ferdinand Leonardo DeFranco)

b. Feb. 17, 1923, Camden, NJ
Clarinet / Bop
Buddy DeFranco is one of the great clarinetists of all time and, until the rise of Eddie Daniels, he was indisputably the top clarinetist to emerge since 1940. It was DeFranco's misfortune to be the best on an instrument that after the swing era dropped drastically in popularity and, unlike Benny Goodman and Artie Shaw, he has never been a household name for the general public.

When he was 14 DeFranco won an amateur swing contest sponsored by Tommy Dorsey. After working with the big bands of Gene Krupa (1941-42) and Charlie Barnet (1943-44), he was with TD on and off during 1944-48. DeFranco, other than spending part of 1950 with Count Basie's septet, was mostly a bandleader from then on. Among the few clarinetists to transfer the language of Charlie Parker onto his instrument, DeFranco has won a countless number of polls and appeared with the Metronome All-Stars in the late '40s. He recorded frequently in the 1950s (among his sidmen were Art Blakey, Kenny Drew and Sonny Clark) and participated in some of Norman Granz's Verve jam sessions. During 1960-63 DeFranco led a quartet that also featured the accordion of Tommy Gumina and he recorded an album with Art Blakey's Jazz Messengers on which he played bass clarinet. However, work was difficult to find in the 1960s, leading DeFranco to accept the assignment of leading the Glenn Miller ghost band (1966-74). He has found more artistic success co-leading a quintet with Terry Gibbs off and on since the early '80s and has recorded through the decades for many labels. —*Scott Yanow*

★ **Complete Verve Recordings of Buddy De Franco/Sonny Clark** / Apr. 7, 1954-Aug. 26, 1955 / Mosaic ✦✦✦✦✦

Blues Bag / 1964 / Affinity ✦✦✦
This is a reissue of a hot date with Lee Morgan (tpt), Curtis Fuller (tb), and a slashing Art Blakey (d). —*Ron Wynn*

Free Sail / Jul. 1974 / Choice ✦✦✦
After a lengthy hiatus, clarinet legend Buddy DeFranco returns to the studios with this '74 set. It opens with a four-part suite, then evolved into a pleasant outing with DeFranco and company doing light standards and originals. His playing is colorful and impressionistic, while pianist Victor Feldman emerges as the lone rhythm section member capable of matching DeFranco. —*Ron Wynn*

Waterbed / Jan. 1977-May 1977 / Choice ✦✦

On Tour: UK / Sep. 28, 1983 / Hep ✦✦✦

Mr. Lucky / 1984 / Pablo ✦✦✦

Holiday for Swing / Aug. 22, 1988-Aug. 23, 1988 / Contemporary ✦✦✦✦
An often intriguing team up with Terry Gibbs (vib). —*Ron Wynn*

Chip Off the Old Bop / Jul. 28, 1992-Jul. 29, 1992 / Concord Jazz ✦✦✦

Jack DeJohnette

b. Aug. 9, 1942, Chicago, IL
Drums, Keyboards, Leader / Avant-Garde, Post-Bop
A premier percussionist and drummer, as well as a fine pianist, composer, electric keyboards and melodica soloist, Jack DeJohnette has been a familiar face on the jazz scene since the '60s. He's often considered the finest modern jazz drummer of the '70s after Elvin Jones and Tony Williams, and has worked and/or led jazz-rock, free, pop, rock, reggae, bebop and hard bop groups, distinguishing himself no matter the context. DeJohnette can provide a steady, sustained pulse indefinitely, or break up the beat and redirect it. He's a marvelous percussionist, can be an equally remarkable timekeeper, uses brushes expertly, and can either provide booming volume or soft underpinning. DeJohnette was an eclectic drummer and artist long before the term became a defining virtue. He's led numerous bands and done even more recording sessions. DeJohnette played drums in a high school concert band in Chicago, and took classical piano lessons for ten years. He graduated from the American Conservatory of Music and spent his early days working in all types of bands in Chicago from R&B and soul to free jazz, while maintaining a busy practice schedule on drums and piano. He moved to New York in 1966, and worked with Big John Patton. DeJohnette later played with Jackie McLean, Betty Carter and Abbey Lincoln. His first job that won him major recognition outside jazz circles came in Charles Lloyd's late '60s quartet. They were the first jazz band to visit the Soviet Union and also play several rock halls. Lloyd's band toured Europe six times, the Far East once, and enjoyed crossover attention via Lloyd's "Forest Flower" cut. DeJohnette kept busy in New York, working with John Coltrane, Thelonious Monk, Freddie Hubbard, Bill Evans, his Lloyd bandmate Keith Jarrett, Chick Corea and Stan Getz. DeJohnette also worked with Miles Davis, playing on the *Bitches Brew* album and joining the band full-time in 1970. He remained with them until 1971. DeJohnette's first band was a jazz-rock group called Compost. He was almost ECM's house drummer in the '70s, appearing on sessions with Kenny Wheeler, Jarrett, John Abercrombie, Jan Garbarek and George Adams. He had a separate deal as a bandleader, and recorded with his groups New Directions in the '70s and Jack DeJohnette's Special Edition in the '80s. New Directions' debut album won the Prix du Jazz Contemporain de l'Academie Charles Cros in 1979. DeJohnette continued recording for ECM in the '80s. He's also recorded for Milestone, Columbia, Landmark, MCA/Impulse! and Prestige. He's played with Bennie Maupin, David Murray, Lester Bowie, Arthur Blythe, Slex Foster, Chico Freeman, Ornette Coleman, Pat Metheny and Nana Vasconcelos among others. During the '90s, DeJohnette has been responsible for some original blends of Native American music and jazz. There are currently several DeJohnette titles available on CD, including a recent trio session with Metheny and Herbie Hancock.

During the 1970s DeJohnette appeared as a sideman on many ECM recordings under the leadership of such players as Kenny Wheeler, John Abercrombie and Jan Garbarek. He led two groups of his own: New Directions (which also included Lester Bowie and Abercrombie) and Jack DeJohnette's Special Edition. The latter band was quite successful, featuring such sidemen at various times as David Murray, Arthur Blythe, Chico Freeman, John Purcell, Peter Warren, Rufus Reid and later on Greg Osby, Gary Thomas and Mick Goodrick; DeJohnette not only played drums with Special Edition, but keyboards. In 1985 he recorded a full trio album on piano and did not sound like he was playing his "second" instrument. In the 1990s DeJohnette has teamed up with Abercrombie and Dave Holland in Gateway and with Keith Jarrett and Gary Peacock in their Standards Trio. He remains one of the most consistently interesting drummers on the modern jazz scene. —*Ron Wynn and Scott Yanow*

The De Johnette Complex / Dec. 26, 1968–Dec. 27, 1968 / Original Jazz Classics ✦✦✦
Early session has some appealing cuts. Outstanding personnel; Jack occasionally doubles on melodica. New reissue. —*Ron Wynn*

Have You Heard? / Jul. 4, 1970 / Epic ✦✦✦

Sorcery / Mar. 1974 / Original Jazz Classics ✦✦
A lot of rambling takes place on this interesting but erratic CD reissue. Drummer Jack DeJohnette (doubling on keyboards) performs three songs with a group featuring bass clarinetist Bennie Maupin and the guitars of John Abercrombie and Mick Goodrick, music that shows the influence of fusion (most obviously on "The Rock Thing") and has its strong moments (much of the nearly 14-minute "Sorcery #1"); however, the attempt at humor on "The Right Time" is self-indulgent. The second half of this release, trios by DeJohnette, bassist Dave Holland and Michael Fellerman on metaphone (whatever that is), are less memorable. While one admires DeJohnette's willingness to take chances, this music has not dated well. —*Scott Yanow*

Cosmic Chicken / Apr. 24, 1975+Apr. 26, 1975 / Prestige ✦✦✦
Funk suggestiveness, improvisatory energy. —*Ron Wynn*

Pictures / Feb. 1976 / ECM ✦✦✦

New Rags / May 1977 / ECM ✦✦✦
Drummer Jack DeJohnette's Directions was a rather unusual quartet. With the leader doubling on piano and matching his creativity with guitarist John Abercrombie, Alex Foster (on tenor and soprano) and bassist Mike Richmond, this was obviously a talented all-star group. The compositions on *New Rags* (all by DeJohnette or Foster) are difficult, rather dry and unpredictable, and the ensemble is not shy about using electronics and the subtle influence of rock. It is easy to see why this unit did not catch on, but its music is still fresh. —*Scott Yanow*

New Directions / Jun. 1978 / ECM ✦✦
New Directions (a quartet with Jack DeJohnette on drums and piano, guitarist John Abercrombie, trumpeter Lester Bowie and bassist Eddie Gomez) is a group that never seemed to live up to its potential. On this set of three DeJohnette compositions (including the wittily titled "Where or Wayne") and two group improvisations, the music is a bit dull, making too much use of space and featuring less of Bowie's trumpet and wit than one would hope. There are some strong moments (particularly from Abercrombie and DeJohnette) but this band (to use a cliché) was less than the sum of its parts. —*Scott Yanow*

★ **Special Edition** / Mar. 1979 / ECM ✦✦✦✦✦
Arguably his finest small combo. David Murray and Arthur Blythe light up the sky. —*Ron Wynn*

New Directions in Europe / Jun. 1979 / ECM ✦✦✦
A tremendous group, with Lester Bowie, John Abercrombie, and Eddie Gomez, elevates a menu that gets ragged at times. —*Ron Wynn*

Tin Can Alley / Sep. 1980 / ECM ✦✦✦✦
Special Edition has long been the best vehicle for Jack DeJohnette's drumming, occasional keyboard work and writing. The 1980 version of this quartet featured Chico Freeman on tenor and bass clarinet, John Purcell's work on baritone and alto, and bassist Peter Warren. The wide-ranging music on this fine set ranges from African rhythms and colors reminiscent of Duke Ellington to some boppish moments and a bit of light funk. Although not the most powerful version of *Special Edition*, this set is recommended. —*Scott Yanow*

Inflation Blues / Sep. 1982 / ECM ✦✦✦
The best of two early-'80s sets with Chico Freeman (d). —*Ron Wynn*

Album, Album / Jun. 1984 / ECM ✦✦✦✦✦
Most of Special Edition's recordings are quite rewarding and this set is no exception. Drummer/keyboardist Jack DeJohnette contributed five of the six compositions (all but "Monk's Mood") and they cover a wide range of styles and moods, from "New Orleans Suite" and "Festival" to the ambitious "Third World Anthem" and a revisit to his "Zoot Suite." This was one of the most stimulating jazz groups of the 1980s and this particular lineup (with John Purcell on alto and soprano, tenor saxophonist David Murray, Howard Johnson doubling on tuba and baritone, and bassist Rufus Reid) was one of DeJohnette's strongest. —*Scott Yanow*

The Jack DeJohnette Piano Album / Jan. 14, 1985+Jan. 15, 1985 / Landmark ✦✦✦
DeJohnette on piano, not drums. Very well done. —*Michael G. Nastos*

Zebra / May 8, 1985–May 10, 1985 / MCA ✦✦

Irresistible Force / Jan. 1987 / MCA ✦✦✦

Audio-Visualscapes / Feb. 1, 1988–Feb. 3, 1988 / MCA ✦✦✦

Parallel Realities / 1990 / MCA ✦✦✦
An overlooked session with Pat Metheny (g) in definite jazz phase. Herbie Hancock shows his steadfast piano form. —*Ron Wynn*

Earthwalk / Jun. 1991 / Somethin' Else ✦✦✦

Music for the Fifth World / Feb. 1992 / Manhattan ✦✦
Jack DeJohnette has long been more than "just" a drummer; he is also a fine keyboardist and a very talented composer. This CD finds him exploring music ranging from American Indian melodies to rockish fusion and his tribute "Miles." His group includes powerhouse guitarists Vernon Reid and John Scofield along with a chanting vocal choir. The music is stimulating if not as essential as DeJohnette's earlier work with Special Edition. —*Scott Yanow*

Extra Special Edition / 1994 / Blue Note ✦✦
The inclusion of Bobby McFerrin to drummer Jack DeJohnette's group should have been a definite plus, since the singer can do so much with his voice (from substituting for a string bass to using his falsetto like a horn) but the mostly original program not only lacks more than one or two strong melodies but any real development as well, particularly on the selections that have McFerrin. Performances often start in what could just as well be the middle and end inconclusively, with many of the pieces being little more than funky riffs for the rhythm section. Despite a few strong moments (mostly from pianist Michael Cain), only "Seventh D" and "Summertime" (both instrumentals) are worth hearing a second time. —*Scott Yanow*

Barbara Dennerlein

b. Sept. 25, 1964, Munich, Germany
Organ / Post-Bop, Hard Bop
Barbara Dennerlein differs from most organists by not sounding all that much like Jimmy Smith. She utilizes MIDI with her organ in order to get a different sound and her baselines (which she operates through her foot pedals) really do sound like a bass. Dennerlein began playing organ at 11 and four years later was already gigging in local clubs. She recorded on her own Bebap label and since 1988 has also made albums for Enja that have created a bit of a stir in the U.S., using such sidemen as Ray Anderson and Mitch Watkins. —*Scott Yanow*

Bebab / Jul. 27, 1985 / Bebap ✦✦✦
German organist Barbara Dennerlein made her recording debut on this release from her Bebap label. Even at this early stage she had a pretty original conception on her instrument, escaping almost completely from the dominant Jimmy Smith influence. Dennerlein performs a loop-oriented set (comprised of seven originals and "Au Privave") with her two-horn quintet and, although the brief liner notes are in German, the swinging music definitely communicates. —*Scott Yanow*

★ **Straight Ahead** / Jul. 18, 1988–Jul. 20, 1988 / Enja ✦✦✦✦✦
Organ-fired and guitar-laced modern jazz from this up-and-coming keyboardist. A solid album throughout. —*Michael G. Nastos*

Hot Stuff / Jun. 6, 1990–Jun. 8, 1990 / Enja ✦✦✦✦
Emerging organ star comes out with adventurous session. —*Ron Wynn*

That's Me / Mar. 3, 1992–Mar. 10, 1992 / Blue Moon ✦✦✦✦
Recent release from a compelling organist whose spinning lines, booming bass pedal, and swirling phrases have made her the most intriguing player to emerge since Larry Young. Dennerlein can take things out one moment, then provide soulful, exuberant passages the next. Tenor saxophonist Bob Berg adds some fiery solos in support. —*Ron Wynn*

Take Off! / Mar. 1995 / Verve ✦✦✦✦

Sidney DeParis

b. May 30, 1905, Crawfordsville, IN, **d.** Sep. 13, 1967, New York, NY
Trumpet / Dixieland
A distinctive trumpeter who fit into both New Orleans jazz and swing settings, Sidney DeParis was particularly expert with mutes. He worked with Charlie Johnson's Paradise Ten (1926–31), Don Redman (1932–36 and 1939), Zutty Singleton (1939–41), Benny Carter (1940–41) and Art Hodes (1941) and recorded on

the famed Panassie sessions (1938) and with Jelly Roll Morton (1939) and Sidney Bechet (1940). DeParis recorded some highly enjoyable and freewheeling sessions as a leader in 1944 (for Commodore and Blue Note) and for Blue Note in 1951. He played with his brother Wilbur DeParis' New New Orleans Jazz Band throughout the 1950s before ill health forced his retirement in the 1960s. — *Scott Yanow*

Wilbur DeParis

b. Jan. 11, 1900, Crawfordsville, IN, **d.** Jan. 3, 1973, New York, NY
Trombone, Leader / Dixieland
Wilbur DeParis, an adequate soloist, was an excellent ensemble player and an important bandleader who helped keep New Orleans jazz alive in the 1950s. He started out on alto horn and in 1922 played C-melody sax while working with A.J. Piron before switching permanently to trombone. In 1925 DeParis led a band in Philadelphia and then had stints in the orchestras of Leroy Smith (1928), Dave Nelson, Noble Sissle, Edgar Hayes, Teddy Hill (1936–37), the Mills Blue Rhythm Band and Louis Armstrong (1937–40). Not as well-known as his brother, the talented trumpet soloist Sidney DeParis, Wilbur was with Roy Eldridge's big band and Duke Ellington (1945–47) and recorded with Sidney Bechet during 1949–50. However it was in 1951 when he put together a band to play at Ryan's that included his brother and clarinetist Omer Simeon that he found his niche. Wilbur DeParis' New New Orleans Jazz Band did not just play Dixieland standards but marches, pop tunes and hymns, all turned into swinging and spirited jazz. Throughout the 1950s the group recorded consistently exciting sets for Atlantic (all of which are unfortunately long out of print) and they were the resident band at Ryan's during 1951–62, touring Africa in 1957. DeParis continued leading bands up until his death but his last recordings were in 1961. — *Scott Yanow*

● **Dr. Jazz Series, Vol. 7** / Dec. 12, 1951–Jun. 5, 1952 / Storyville ✦✦✦✦✦
Trombonist Wilbur DeParis and his brother trumpeter Sidney led one of the most exciting Dixieland bands of the 1950s. Unfortunately, virtually every one of their valuable Atlantic recordings are long out of print (all are worth searching for), making this set of broadcasts from the short-lived Dr. Jazz radio series a major release. With the great clarinetist Omer Simeon completing the frontline, the sextet (no bass at this point) adds a lot of heat to such standards as "Bill Bailey," "Milenberg Joys" and "Alexander's Ragtime Band" but also performs such underplayed tunes as "Too Much Mustard," "Russian Rag" and "Blame It on the Blues." A very colorful band heard in excellent form. — *Scott Yanow*

An Evening At Jimmy Ryan's / 1951–1958 / Jazz Crusade ✦✦✦
Trombonist Wilbur DeParis led one of the most exciting Dixieland bands in the 1950s, a unit that he said specialized in "New New Orleans Jazz." This CD from the Jazz Crusade label features music taken from broadcasts dating from 1951–52 along with the soundtrack of a television show from either 1955 or 1958. The recording quality is decent if not state-of-the-art but the excitement of this unit (which also features cornetist Sidney DeParis and clarinetist Omer Simeon) definitely can be felt on such numbers as "Down in Honky Tonk Town," "Original Dixieland One Step," "Under the Double Eagle" and even "The Marine's Hymn." — *Scott Yanow*

Paul Desmond

b. Nov. 25, 1924, New York, NY, **d.** May 30, 1977, New York, NY
Alto Saxophone / Cool
The definitive "cool" alto saxophonist, Paul Desmond (who had a beautiful floating tone that owed little to Charlie Parker) took his time in his solos (rarely double-timing) but his melodic ideas were full of surprising twists and turns. He played his first and his last gigs with Dave Brubeck and spent his prime years (1951–67) with Brubeck's popular quartet. Early on he studied clarinet in school and then during 1948–50 recorded and gigged on alto with the Dave Brubeck octet. During the years with the quartet, Desmond was a key part of the sound, indulging in counterpoint with the pianist-leader, writing "Take Five" (in his will he left the huge royalties of this hit to the Red Cross) and taking witty and logical solos that inspired Brubeck. Away from the group, Desmond occasionally recorded as a leader (usually in pianoless settings) including a couple of encounters with Gerry Mulligan and a series of

records with Jim Hall. After the quartet broke up, Desmond was mostly semi-retired although a concert with the Modern Jazz Quartet (1971) was recorded and he teamed up with guitarist Ed Bickert on a few live albums. The altoist also had reunions with Brubeck during 1972–75 before his death from cancer. His Jim Hall sets have been reissued in a Mosaic box set, most of the Brubeck albums are currently in print and Desmond also recorded as a leader for Fantasy, A&M, Finesse, CTI, Telarc and Artists House. — *Scott Yanow*

Quintet/Quartet / Feb. 14, 1956 / Original Jazz Classics ✦✦✦✦

East of the Sun / Sep. 5, 1959–Sep. 7, 1959 / Discovery ✦✦✦✦
Quartet. First-rate quartet session. Jim Hall (g), Percy Heath (b), and Connie Kay (d) are super. — *Ron Wynn*

★ **Paul Desmond: Jim Hall Recordings** / Sep. 5, 1959–Jun. 1, 1965 / Mosaic ✦✦✦✦✦
Incredible music! A six-disc boxed set of recordings from 1959–1965 featuring Desmond with Jim Hall. Desmond plays flawless sax, and Jim Hall likewise on guitar. In brief, these are classic cuts; the best. Whether a beginning listener or a jazz expert, this is satisfying music. Mosaic does it again. — *Michael Erlewine*

Late Lament / Sep. 14, 1961–Mar. 15, 1962 / Bluebird ✦✦✦

Two of a Mind / Jun. 26, 1962–Aug. 13, 1962 / Bluebird ✦✦✦✦

Take Ten / Jun. 5, 1963–Jun. 25, 1963 / RCA/Bluebird ✦✦✦
Early '60s sessions reissued on a recent Bluebird CD. The title refers not to a song but the number of cuts that Desmond, guitarist Jim Hall, and others recorded. Bassist Percy Heath and drummer Connie Kay also participated. These sessions were partially reissued on CD before; this is the full date. — *Ron Wynn*

Summertime / Oct. 10, 1968–Dec. 20, 1968 / A&M ✦✦✦
Some beautiful playing by Paul Desmond, coupled with several lovely melodies, help overcome some heavily orchestrated and arranged songs on this 1968 set. Desmond's alto sax solos were pungent and enticing on such cuts as the title song, "Emily," and "Autumn Leaves." The assembled band had many West Coast and session pros, most of whom didn't get any individual space. — *Ron Wynn*

From the Hot Afternoon / Jun. 24, 1969–Aug. 14, 1969 / A&M ✦✦

Bridge over Troubled Water / 1969 / A&M ✦✦
Beautiful Desmond with fine Herbie Hancock on electric piano, but occasionally annoying orchestrations. — *Ron Wynn*

In Concert at Town Hall / Dec. 25, 1971 / DRG ✦✦✦✦
This delightful collaboration with MJQ has been reissued several times. — *Ron Wynn*

Skylark / Nov. 27, 1973–Dec. 4, 1973 / Columbia ✦✦✦
Very glossy, with some beautiful moments. — *Ron Wynn*

Pure Desmond / Sep. 24, 1974–Sep. 26, 1974 / Columbia ✦✦✦✦

Like Someone in Love / 1975 / Telarc ✦✦✦

The Paul Desmond Quartet Live / Oct. 25, 1975–Nov. 1, 1975 / A&M ✦✦✦✦
During his post-Brubeck years, altoist Paul Desmond was semiretired, only playing in public on an occasional basis. When he did perform, it was often with the tasteful Canadian guitarist Ed Bickert in a quiet pianoless quartet. This double LP, put out by John Snyder's Horizon subsidiary for A&M, is melodic, subtle and consistently swinging. Desmond and Bickert (along with bassist Don Thompson and drummer Jerry Fuller) clearly enjoyed themselves matching wits and wisdom on the altoist's "Wendy" and the seven superior standards (which include Desmond's "Take Five"). — *Scott Yanow*

Trudy Desmond

Vocals / Cabaret, Standards
A fine jazz-influenced singer, Trudy Desmond has had several careers. She operated a successful interior design business, worked as an actress, produced cabaret and theater shows and ran a club for vocalists. As a singer the Toronto-based singer has recorded for Unisson (her 1988 debut), Jazz Alliance and Koch. — *Scott Yanow*

Tailor Made / Nov. 14, 1991–Nov. 15, 1991 / Jazz Alliance ✦✦✦✦

Vic Dickenson

b. Aug. 6, 1906, Xenia, OH, **d.** Nov. 16, 1984, New York, NY
Trombone / Dixieland, Swing
A distinctive trombonist with a sly wit and the ability to sound as if he were playing underwater (!), Vic Dickenson was an asset to any session in which he appeared. He started out in the 1920s and

Music Map

Drums

Pioneer
James I. Lent
(recorded "The Ragtime Drummer" in 1904!)

Top 1920s Drummers

Tony Sbarbaro	Ben Pollack
Baby Dodds	Vic Berton
Chauncey Morehouse	Zutty Singleton
Paul Barbarin	

Swing Era
Jo Jones (with Count Basie)
Sonny Greer (with Duke Ellington)
Gene Krupa
Chick Webb
Dave Tough
Big Sid Catlett
Cozy Cole
Ray McKinley

Dixieland
George Wettling
Ray Bauduc
Nick Fatool

Unbeatable Virtuoso
Buddy Rich

Founders of Bebop Drums
Kenny Clarke
Max Roach
Art Blakey

1950s
Roy Haynes
Philly Joe Jones
Chico Hamilton
Connie Kay (with Modern Jazz Quartet)
Shelly Manne
Joe Morello (with Dave Brubeck)
Art Taylor
Jimmy Cobb
Ed Thigpen (with Oscar Peterson)
Stan Levey

Avant-Garde
Ed Blackwell (with Ornette Coleman)
Danny Richmond (with Charles Mingus)
Don Moye (with Art Ensemble Of Chicago)
Gerry Hemingway (with Anthony Braxton)

Elvin Jones	Rashied Ali
Milford Graves	Charles Moffett
Dennis Charles	Andrew Cyrille
Sunny Murray	Philip Wilson
J.C. Moses	Clifford Jarvis
Joe Chambers	Beaver Harris
Pheeroan Ak Laff	Bob Moses
Barry Altschul	Steve McCall
Paul Motian	Joey Baron
Han Bennink	Tony Oxley
Paul Lovens	Bobby Previte

Fusion
Billy Cobham
Lenny White (with Return To Forever)
Alphonse Mouzon
Steve Gadd
Peter Erskine (with Weather Report)
Ronald Shannon Jackson (free funk)
Dave Weckl (with Chick Corea's Elektric Band)
Bill Bruford

Big Band Drummers

Louie Bellson	Mel Lewis
Sonny Payne	Rufus Jones
Frank Capp	Jeff Hamilton
Sam Woodyard (with Duke Ellington)	

1980s-1990s

T.S. Monk	Tony Williams
Jack DeJohnette	Billy Higgins
Jake Hanna	Louis Hayes
Roy McCurdy	Grady Tate
Roy Brooks	Mickey Roker
Alan Dawson	Joe LaBarbera
Al Foster	Billy Hart
Danny Gottlieb	Dennis Chambers
Victor Lewis	Jeff Watts
Herlin Riley	Ralph Penland
Adam Nussbaum	Ralph Peterson
Cyndi Blackman	Leon Parker
Terri Lyne Carrington	Marvin "Smitty" Smith
Kenny Washington	Carl Allen
Lewis Nash	Winard Harper

'30s playing in the Midwest. Associations with Blanche Calloway (1933–36), Claude Hopkins (1936–39), Benny Carter (1939), Count Basie (1940), Carter again (1941) and Frankie Newton (1941–43) preceded a high-profile gig with Eddie Heywood's popular sextet (1943–46); Dickenson also played and recorded with Sidney Bechet. From then on he was a freelancing soloist who spent time on the West Coast, Boston and New York, appearing on many recordings (including some notable dates for Vanguard) and on the legendary *Sound of Jazz* telecast (1957). In the 1960s Dickenson co-led the Saints and Sinners, toured with George Wein's Newport All-Stars and worked regularly with Wild Bill Davison and Eddie Condon. During 1968–70 he was in a quintet with Bobby Hackett, in the 1970s he sometimes played with the World's Greatest Jazz Band and Vic Dickenson was active up until his death. —*Scott Yanow*

★ **The Essential Vic Dickenson** / Dec. 29, 1953+Nov. 29, 1954 / Vanguard ✦✦✦✦✦

Plays Bessie Smith: "Trombone Cholly" / Mar. 21, 1976 / Gazell ✦✦✦✦

This set is unusual for, although it is a tribute to Bessie Smith, there are no vocals. Trombonist Vic Dickenson takes the place of Smith's favorite trombonist Charlie Green, and his witty sound and expressive slides are well-showcased in a sextet with trumpeter Joe Newman and tenor saxophonist Frank Wess; Milt Hinton was the natural choice for the bass spot. Bessie Smith, though known as the "Empress of the Blues," actually recorded a lot of other material throughout her career so there is more variety on this enjoyable set (which is not recommended to 1920s purists) than one might expect. —*Scott Yanow*

Vic Dickenson Quintet / Apr. 13, 1976 / Storyville ✦✦✦

Just Friends / Oct. 1981–Mar. 1985 / Sackville ✦✦✦✦

Walt Dickerson

b. 1931, Philadelphia, PA
Vibes / Post-Bop
A solid soloist noted for his complex harmonies, Walt Dickerson provided an alternative voice on the vibraphone in the '60s before he abruptly stopped playing in 1965. Dickerson uses only two sticks, and dips them in a solution to harden them. His lines, voicings, approach and technique were quite different from anything else done on vibes at the time, and he was named "new star" by *Downbeat* in 1962. A Morgan State graduate, Dickerson served in the Army during the early '50s, played in California leading a group that included Andrew Hill and Andrew Cyrille and recorded with Sun Ra in 1965. But he quit from 1965 until 1975. After his return, Dickerson worked mainly in Europe. He and Sun Ra recorded together again, this time on SteepleChase in the late '70s. He also made a duo session with Pierre Dorge, and recorded other albums on SteepleChase and Soul Note, including a duet date with Cyrille. Dickerson currently has a few sessions available on CD. —*Ron Wynn and Michael G. Nastos*

This Is Walt Dickerson! / Mar. 7, 1961 / Original Jazz Classics ✦✦✦✦

This CD reissue of vibraphonist Walt Dickerson's debut as a leader finds Dickerson (in a quartet with pianist Austin Crowe, bassist Bob Lewis and drummer Andrew Cyrille) performing six of his moody and generally advanced originals. One can hear the influence of Ornette Coleman in the soloing, which does not stick exclusively to standard bebop chordal improvisation. The purposely monotonous backup on "Death and Taxes" and such songs as "The Cry" and "Infinite You" show that Dickerson was trying to get beyond the dominant Milt Jackson influence that affected most of the other vibists at the time. It's an interesting outing. — *Scott Yanow*

● **A Sense of Direction** / May 5, 1961 / Original Jazz Classics ✦✦✦✦✦

Vibraphonist Walt Dickerson's second recording as a leader (reissued on CD in the OJC series) utilizes talented if obscure sidemen (pianist Austin Crowe, bassist Edgar Bateman and drummer Eustis Guillemet, Jr.) on a variety of challenging originals and three standards ("What's New," "You Go to My Head" and "If I Should Lose You"). Although Dickerson would not become an influential force himself, he was one of the first vibraphonists of the era to develop his voice away from Milt Jackson's influence, predating Bobby Hutcherson by a few years. —*Scott Yanow*

Relativity / Jan. 16, 1962 / Original Jazz Classics ✦✦✦✦

Vibraphonist Walt Dickerson always had a fairly unique sound, predating Bobby Hutcherson with his ability to straddle the boundaries between hard bop and the emerging avant-garde. On this quartet date with pianist Austin Crowe, bassist Ahmed Abdul-Malik and drummer Andrew Cyrille, Dickerson plays a fairly accessible program (three standards and four diverse originals) that serves as a strong introduction to his talents for the uninitiated. —*Scott Yanow*

To My Queen / Sep. 21, 1962 / New Jazz ✦✦✦

Divine Gemini / Feb. 9, 1977 / SteepleChase ✦✦✦

Tenderness / Feb. 9, 1977 / SteepleChase ✦✦✦

Shades of Love / Nov. 16, 1977 / SteepleChase ✦✦✦

Visions / Jul. 11, 1978 / SteepleChase ✦✦✦

Neville Dickie

b. Jan. 1,1937, Durham, England
Piano / Stride
A brilliant pianist playing in the stride style of James P. Johnson and Fats Waller (but with a musical personality of his own), Neville Dickie has helped keep traditional jazz alive and healthy. He worked in London during 1958–68 playing in a trio, made his recording debut in 1966, cut four albums in the 1970s and '80s for the Stomp Off label and has led the Rhythmakers since 1985, occasionally appearing in the U.S. —*Scott Yanow*

The Piano Has It / Apr. 14, 1993–Sep. 30, 1993 / Stomp Off ✦✦✦✦✦

On this excellent set of solos, duets and trios (with bassist Micky Ashman and drummer John Petters), the English pianist Neville Dickie interprets classic compositions by the likes of James P. Johnson, James Scott, Joseph Lamb, Spencer Williams and Don Ewell among others. Dickie's enthusiastic playing keeps these ancient works from sounding like museum pieces, infusing them with life and relevance. —*Scott Yanow*

Al DiMeola

b. Jul. 22, 1954, Jersey City, NJ
Guitar / Fusion, World Music
Al DiMeola has had a dual career as a blazing fusion electric guitarist and as an acoustic player eager to explore music from other cultures. DiMeola burst upon the scene by replacing Bill Connors with Return to Forever in 1974 before he turned 20. He had been attending Berklee but essentially started out on top, immediately becoming an influential fusion guitarist. Criticized for playing an excess of notes and not showing enough feeling in his playing (faults he has since overcome), DiMeola has matured through the years. After Return to Forever broke up, he went on several tours with John McLaughlin and Paco DeLucia in an acoustic guitar trio (1980–83). Since that time DiMeola has led his own groups, alternating between electric and acoustic guitars and changing musical direction a few times. DiMeola, who toured with the Rite of Strings in 1995 (a trio with Jean Luc Ponty and Stanley Clarke), has recorded sets as a leader since 1976 including dates for Columbia, Manhattan and Tomato. —*Scott Yanow*

Elegant Gypsy / 1976 / Columbia ✦✦✦
The frenetic, slashing stylist shows his sentimental, restrained, and romantic side. —*Ron Wynn*

Land of the Midnight Sun / 1976 / Columbia ✦✦✦✦✦
One of the guitar heroes of fusion, Al DiMeola was just 22 years old at the time of his debut as a leader but already a veteran of Chick Corea's Return to Forever. The complex pieces (which include the three-part "Suite-Golden Dawn," an acoustic duet with Corea on "Short Tales of the Black Forest" and a brief Bach violin sonata) show DiMeola's range even at this early stage. With assistance from such top players as bassists Jaco Pastorius and Stanley Clarke, keyboardist Barry Miles and drummers Lenny White and Steve Gadd, this was a very impressive beginning to DiMeola's solo career. —*Scott Yanow*

Casino / 1977 / Columbia ✦✦✦
Guitarist Al DiMeola was in his electronic fusion phase when this was recorded in the late '70s. He played frenetic, flashy riffs and solos, and was assisted on a variety of keyboards by Barry Miles, electric bassist Anthony Jackson, and drummer Steve Gadd, who added a steady array of rock and funk beats. —*Ron Wynn*

★ **Splendido Hotel** / 1979 / Columbia ✦✦✦✦✦
Talk about ambitious, this two-LP set finds guitarist Al DiMeola performing with his quintet of the time (featuring keyboardist Philippe Saisse), with studio musicians, solo, in a reunion with pianist Chick Corea, singing a love song and welcoming veteran Les Paul for a version of "Spanish Eyes"! Most of the music works quite well and it shows that DiMeola (best-known for his speedy rock-oriented solos) is a surprisingly well-rounded and versatile musician. —*Scott Yanow*

Friday Night in San Francisco / Dec. 5, 1980 / Columbia ✦✦✦✦
With John McLaughlin (g), Paco De Lucia (g). —*Ron Wynn*

Electric Rendezvous / 1981 / Columbia ✦✦✦

Tour De Force: Live / Feb. 4, 1982 / Columbia ✦✦✦

Scenario / 1983 / Columbia ✦✦

Soaring through a Dream / 1985 / EMI ✦✦✦
This reissued 1985 date has plenty of electric bombast, along with ample examples of DiMeola's piercing acoustic style. What it lacks is the energy and creative integrity that underscores DiMeola's World Sinfonia sessions and his classic *Splendido Hotel*. There are some pretty melodies, an entrancing moment or two, and too many interludes where it seems that something is about to happen, but things cool down or degenerate into blandness. The longer compositions drone on without establishing anything substantial, while the short pieces fade in and out, offering bits and pieces of fine playing, but nothing thematically distinguished. When the CD ends, you realize that DiMeola is an excellent technician, but nothing left any lasting impression. —*Ron Wynn*

Cielo E Terra / 1985 / EMI ✦✦✦

Tirami Su / Apr. 1987 / EMI ✦✦✦✦
Guitar work is aggressive and often superb. —*Ron Wynn*

Kiss My Axe / Sep. 24, 1988–May 1991 / Tomato ✦✦✦✦

World Sinfonia / Oct. 1990 / Tomato ✦✦✦✦
This ia an outstanding venture into the international/Latin arena. —*Ron Wynn*

Heart of the Immigrants / 1993 / Mesa ✦✦✦✦✦
Guitarist Al DiMeola has been alternating electric and acoustic projects for the past few years. For this acoustic affair, he teams up with Dino Saluzzi on bandoneon to pay tribute to the tango master Astor Piazzolla. The music (even a duet version of "Someday My Prince Will Come") has the flavor of Argentina and uses a wide variety of instrumentations, including an occasional string section and the voice of Hernan Romero. It's recommended to lovers of world music, the modern tango and those who think of DiMeola's guitar playing as being one-dimensional and purely based on speed. —*Scott Yanow*

Orange & Blue / 1994 / Tomato ✦✦✦

Danny D'Imperio

b. 1945, Sydney, NY
Drums, Leader / Hard Bop
A fine drummer, Danny D'Imperio is best-known for his leadership and recordings with the Metropolitan Bopera House and his own groups. He picked up early experience playing with the Glenn Miller ghost band (1970–72) and two years apiece with the orchestras of Maynard Ferguson and Woody Herman. He subbed for Buddy Rich when Rich was ill in 1983, was the house drummer at Condon's and has freelanced quite a bit, but it is his VSOP recordings (which often feature obscure bop and hard bop songs being revived with enthusiasm) that have given D'Imperio a certain amount of fame. —*Scott Yanow*

Danny D'Imperio Sextet / May 19, 1988+May 20, 1988 / VSOP ✦✦✦✦

● **Blues for Philly Joe** / Sep. 5, 1991+Sep. 6, 1991 / VSOP ✦✦✦✦✦

Joe Diorio

b. Aug. 6, 1936, Waterbury, CT
Guitar / Post-Bop
A brilliant if generally overlooked guitarist with an adventurous spirit and a boppish style of his own, Joe Diorio has for quite a while made his main living as a teacher at the Guitar Institute in Hollywood. In the 1960s he was based in Chicago, playing with the likes of Sonny Stitt, Eddie Harris and Bennie Green. After moving to Miami (1968–77), Diorio often gigged with Ira Sullivan, Stan Getz, Stanley Turrentine and Freddie Hubbard among others; he also recorded as a leader for the Spitball label starting in 1975. His relocation to Los Angeles has not resulted in higher visibility but Diorio has recorded in recent times in several settings for RAM and has gained influence as an educator. —*Scott Yanow*

Double Take / Apr. 1992 / Ram ✦✦✦

We Will Meet Again / May 1992 / Ram ✦✦✦

● **Breeze and I** / Jun. 9, 1993 / RAM ✦✦✦✦
This duet encounter between Joe Diorio and Ira Sullivan defies one's expectations. Diorio is normally thought of as a firebreathing guitarist and Sullivan as a versatile multi-instrumentalist at his best on both tenor and trumpet. However this set is comprised

entirely of lyrical ballads with Sullivan sticking to flutes, soprano and alto. The music is quite atmospheric, haunting and beautiful, far superior to most one-mood new age performances. These introverted yet friendly duets, in addition to being superior background music, reward close scrutiny. —*Scott Yanow*

The Dirty Dozen Brass Band

Group / New Orleans R&B
The Dirty Dozen Brass Band in its prime successfully mixed together R&B with the instrumentation of a New Orleans brass band. Featuring Kirk Joseph on sousaphone playing with the agility of an electric bassist, the group revitalized the brass band tradition, opening up the repertoire and inspiring some younger groups to imitate their boldness. Generally featuring five horns (two trumpets, one trombone and two saxes) along with the sousaphone, a snare drummer and a bass drummer, the DDBB was innovative in its own way, making fine recordings for Rounder, Columbia and the George Wein Collection (the latter released through Concord); guest artists have included Dr. John, Dizzy Gillespie and Danny Barker. Unfortunately in recent years the group has become much more conventional, still using R&B riffs but now with a standard (and less distinctive) rhythm section. —*Scott Yanow*

★ **My Feet Can't Fail Me Now** / 1984 / Concord Jazz ✦✦✦✦✦

Live: Mardi Gras in Montreux / Jul. 1985 / Rounder ✦✦✦
This live concert featured The Dirty Dozen Brass Band in an exuberant setting, performing at the 1985 Montreux Festival. The musical lineup includes comic/novelty works, stomping R&B covers, an inspired jazz-meets-pop medley of "Blue Monk" and "Stormy Monday," and their own tunes, "Who Took The Happiness Out," "It Ain't What You Think" and "Lickity Split." Besides their matchless ensemble interaction, the group has such brilliant musicians as trumpeters Gregory Davis and Efrem Towns, tenor saxophonist Kevin Harris, baritone/soprano saxophonist Roger Lewis and trombonist Charles Joseph, who also take flamboyant, memorable solos. —*Ron Wynn*

Voodoo / Aug. 1987–Sep. 1987 / Columbia ✦✦✦
Guest stars Dizzy Gillespie (tpt), Dr. John (p), and Branford Marsalis (ts) fit right in with the band's masterful ensemble work. —*Bruce Raeburn*

New Orleans Album / Aug. 1989–Dec. 1989 / Columbia ✦✦✦
This time, veteran Orleanians Danny Barker, Eddie Bo, and Dave Bartholomew join in, plus Elvis Costello—the fun quotient runs off the meter with plenty of solos and absolutely infectious rhythms. —*Bruce Raeburn*

Open Up: Whatcha Gonna Do for the Rest of Your Life? / Jan. 1991–Apr. 1991 / Columbia ✦✦✦✦

Jelly / Aug. 1992–Jan. 1993 / Columbia ✦✦✦
The Dirty Dozen Brass Band, an innovative group that combines R&B with New Orleans parade rhythms, pays tribute to the great Jelly Roll Morton on this CD. Actually the DDBB mostly ignores Morton's original recordings (and leaves out some of his themes) in an unusual set that does not find them neglecting their own individuality. A few Danny Barker monologues add to the authenticity of this music, which takes great liberties with Morton's compositions. Trumpeter Gregory Davis (who duets with guest pianist Eddie Bo on "Dead Man Blues") is the most impressive soloist, though it is the sound of the rollicking ensembles (propelled by the sousaphone of Keith Anderson) that gives this set its sense of purpose. Purists, however, should avoid this one. —*Scott Yanow*

Diva

Big Band / Bop
Diva is a 15-piece all-female big band that made its debut on records on the Perfect Sound label. Founded by Stanley Kay and headed by drummer Sherri Maricle, the group includes among its personnel altoist Carol Chaikin, Virginia Mayhew on tenor and trumpeter Ingrid Jensen. —*Scott Yanow*

● **Something Is Coming** / 1994 / Perfect Sound ✦✦✦✦
The all-female jazz orchestra Diva (which has the subtitle of "No Man's Band") makes their recording debut on this CD from Perfect Sound. Headed by drummer Sherri Maricle (whose Buddy Rich-inspired style had been previously featured on Stash), the 15-piece big band has arrangements by Maricle, Michael Abene, John LaBarbera and Tommy Newsome. The charts are generally fairly conventional (with "Caravan," "Ding Dong the Witch Is Dead" and

"Something's Coming" being the most colorful) but the clean ensembles, hard-swinging rhythm section and many talented soloists make Diva stand out from the crowd. Trumpeter Ingrid Jensen and tenor saxophonist Virginia Mayhew are best-known among the players and they have their spots, but the main stars of this disc are the altoists Sue Terry and Carol Chaikin. Chaikin's soulful rendition of "If I Should Lose You" and Terry's intense interpretation of "My Favorite Things" are among the highpoints. Also notable are a driving "You Stepped out of a Dream," "Three Sisters and a Cousin" (which has Terry, Chiakin and Mayhew all soloing on alto) and a tasteful version of "Stardust." It's recommended for big-band fans. —*Scott Yanow*

Bill Dixon

b. Oct. 5, 1925, Nantucket, MA
Trumpet / Free Jazz, Avant-Garde
Bill Dixon is an unusual trumpeter, one who emphasizes low notes and space. A pioneer in the avant-garde, Dixon has spent much of his career as an educator but has recorded on an occasional basis during the past 30 years. He played with Cecil Taylor in 1958, in 1962–63 he led an advanced jazz group with Archie Shepp and he played with the New York Contemporary Five. In 1964 Dixon presented six concerts (called "The October Revolution in Jazz") which helped to introduce free jazz to New York audiences. Dixon recorded with Cecil Taylor (*Conquistador*) and had his own session for RCA. He also organized the short-lived Jazz Composers Guild. Dixon started teaching at Bennington College in 1968 and has recorded on an occasional basis since for Cadence and Soul Note. —*Scott Yanow*

Collection / 1970–1976 / Cadence ✦✦✦
● In Italy, Vol. 1 / Jul. 11, 1980–Jul. 13, 1980 / Soul Note ✦✦✦✦
This set, one of two Dixon albums issued on vinyl in 1980, was a rare release that showed why he is so admired by musicians, and has such a tough time getting recorded. The four songs contain no prominent beats or riffs, catchy hooks, sentimental melodies, or enticing devices. One is nearly 20 minutes long, with multiple movements ("For Cecil Taylor"); another is almost 13 minutes, with stretches of blistering exchanges between Dixon and fellow trumpeters Arthur Brooks and Stephen Haynes. Even the shorter pieces have exacting unison statements and prickly solos. An unfolding, unpredictable musical dialogue. —*Ron Wynn*

In Italy, Vol. 2 / Jul. 11, 1980–Jul. 13, 1980 / Soul Note ✦✦✦✦
A rare date from a distinctive trumpeter whose approach, clarity of tone, and directness set him apart in the '60s. The set includes a fine three-part song dedicated to Cecil Taylor. The band mixes avant-garde types like bassist Alan Silva with mainstream figures like drummer Freddie Waits. It also has an unusual lineup, with two, sometimes three trumpeters and a saxophonist, bassist, and drummer. Dixon occasionally plays piano. —*Ron Wynn*

November 1981 / Nov. 8, 1981 / Soul Note ✦✦✦
Thoughts / May 16, 1985 / Soul Note ✦✦
Sons of Sisyphus / Jun. 1988 / Soul Note ✦✦✦✦

Baby Dodds

b. Dec. 24, 1898, New Orleans, LA., d. Feb. 14, 1959, Chicago, IL
Drums / Classic New Orleans Jazz
Arguably the first important jazz drummer, Baby Dodds was one of the earliest to vary his patterns during a performance; a strong example of his adventurous style can be heard on a trio performance (with Jelly Roll Morton and Baby's brother Johnny) on "Wolverine Blues" in 1927. A major influence on Gene Krupa, Dodds worked in New Orleans with Willie Hightower, Bunk Johnson, Oscar Celestin and others and played with Fate Marable's riverboat band in 1918. He joined King Oliver in San Francisco in 1922 and settled in Chicago the following year. In addition to recording with Oliver's classic Creole Jazz Band, Dodds was an important part of sessions led by Jelly Roll Morton and Louis Armstrong's Hot Seven. He remained in Chicago for decades, performing and recording regularly with his brother Johnny Dodds until the clarinetist's death in 1940. During the traditional jazz revival, Baby played with Jimmie Noone, Sidney Bechet, Bunk Johnson and Art Hodes, appeared on the *This Is Jazz* radio broadcasts of 1947 and visited Europe with Mezz Mezzrow the following year. During 1945–46 he recorded the first unaccompanied drum solos. Despite ill health in the 1950s, Baby Dodds kept playing until two years before his death; his memoirs are well worth reading. —*Scott Yanow*

Johnny Dodds

b. Apr. 12, 1892, New Orleans, LA, d. Aug. 8, 1940, Chicago, IL
Clarinet / Classic New Orleans Jazz
One of the all-time great clarinetists and arguably the most significant of the 1920s, Johnny Dodds (whose younger brother Baby Dodds was among the first important drummers) had a memorable tone in both the lower and upper registers, was a superb blues player and held his own with Louis Armstrong (no mean feat) on his classic Hot Five and Hot Seven recordings. He did not start on clarinet until he was 17 but caught on fast, being mostly self-taught. Dodds was with Kid Ory's band during most of 1912–19, played on riverboats with Fate Marable in 1917, and joined King Oliver in Chicago in 1921. During the next decade he recorded with Oliver's Creole Jazz Band, Jelly Roll Morton, Louis Armstrong and on his own heated sessions, often utilizing trumpeter Natty Dominique. He worked regularly at Kelly's Stables during 1924–30. Although Dodds continued playing in Chicago during the 1930s, part of the time was spent running a cab company. The clarinetist led recording sessions in 1938 and 1940 but died just before the New Orleans revival movement began. —*Scott Yanow*

Jazz Classics: Great Performances (1923–1929) / 1923–1929 / Mobile Fidelity ✦✦✦
Jazz Heritage: Spirit of New Orleans (1926–1927) / May 29, 1926–Oct. 8, 1927 / MCA ✦✦✦✦
Traditional jazz's greatest clarinetist was featured on some late '20s tracks he cut for Decca. These tracks included contributions from many immortal figures, among them Kid Ory, George Mitchell, Jimmy Blythe, and Lil Hardin Armstrong. —*Ron Wynn*

★ 1926 / May 19, 1926–Dec. 1926 / Classics ✦✦✦✦✦
Dodds was one of the very finest New Orleans clarinetists, and the only non-Creole among them. The peak experiences here, and some of the finest small-group recordings ever made, are The New Orleans Wanderers sessions—Armstrong's Hot Five with George Mitchell instead of Armstrong. Also present are Freddie Keppard's only two recordings and a bunch of marginally lesser cuts that Dodds transmutes into gold. —*John Storm Roberts*

Johnny Dodds and Kid Ory / Jul. 13, 1926–Jul. 4, 1928 / Columbia ✦✦✦✦
Blue Clarinet Stomp / Dec. 11, 1926–Feb. 7, 1929 / Bluebird ✦✦✦✦
This is classic jazz (1927–29) at its best—Dodds with Jelly Roll Morton's Trio, with his own orchestra, his Washboard Band, and The Dixieland Jug Blowers. Alternate takes show the improvisational character of Dodd's approach. The CD has four bonus cuts —*Bruce Raeburn*

☆ 1927 / Jan. 19, 1927–Aug. 10, 1927 / Classics ✦✦✦✦
South Side Chicago Jazz / Apr. 13, 1927–Jul. 24, 1929 / MCA ✦✦✦
Johnny Dodds appears in various combinations (1927–29), from his Trio through The Black Bottom Stompers to Jimmy Blythe's Washboard Wizards and the Beale Street Washboard Band. "Wild Man Blues" shows one of many reasons Dodds was one of the most individual and celebrated clarinetists from New Orleans. —*Bruce Raeburn*

Bill Doggett

b. Feb. 16, 1916, Philadelphia, PA
Organ, Piano / R&B, Swing
Although early on he was known as a fine swing-based pianist, Bill Doggett found his greatest fame in the 1950s as an R&Bish organist, particularly after recording his big hit "Honky Tonk" in 1956. He led his own big band in 1938, which accompanied Lucky Millinder for a year. After stints with Jimmy Mundy's short-lived orchestra (1939) and back with Millinder (1940–42), Doggett arranged for the Ink Spots (1942–44) and recorded with Johnny Otis and Illinois Jacquet (1945–47). He replaced Wild Bill Davis with Louis Jordan's Tympany Five (1948–51) and, following Davis' example, took up the organ. After recording with Eddie "Lockjaw" Davis and Ella Fitzgerald, Doggett led his own groups, recording frequently for King throughout the 1950s. He was heard in more jazz-oriented settings in the 1970s on sessions for the Black & Blue label and recorded for After Hours as recently as 1991. —*Scott Yanow*

● Everybody Dance to the Honky Tonk / 1956 / King ✦✦✦✦
This hugely influential jazz-laced R&B quartet plays their classic

two-part instrumentals and several more groovers, with guitarist Billy Butler and saxist Clifford Scott incendiary throughout the album. —*Bill Dahl*

The Doggett Beat for Dancing Feet / 1958 / King ✦✦✦
Doggett's fatback organ cooks in tandem with Butler's licks and Scott's sax. —*Bill Dahl*

Klaus Doldinger

b. May 12, 1936, Berlin, Germany
Soprano Saxophone, Tenor Saxophone, Leader / Fusion, Post-Bop
One of Germany's most popular players and the head of the '70s fusion band Passport, Doldinger studied classical piano and clarinet in Germany, then began playing traditional jazz in 1952. He won several awards at jazz competitions for his alto sax playing in 1955 and 1956. Doldinger played Chicago and New York in 1960 leading The Feetwarmers, a traditional group, and as part of the hard bop band Oskar's Trio. He later formed his own hard bop group, touring Europe, Africa, Asia and Latin America in the mid- and late '60s. Then he changed gears in 1970, forming Passport and doing lighter, less intense, more pop-oriented material, though he also included songs that allowed the group to stretch out. Passport was among the '70s most popular bands; Doldinger also composed the scores to the films *Das Boot* and *The Eternal Store*. He has not been as prolific in the '80s and '90s. —*Ron Wynn*

Constellation / 1983 / WEA ✦✦✦

Balance of Happiness / Mar. 1990 / Atlantic ✦✦✦

● **Doldinger In New York: Street Of Dreams** / 1994 / Blue Moon ✦✦✦✦✦

Eric Dolphy

b. Jun. 20, 1928, Los Angeles, CA, **d.** Jun. 29, 1964, Berlin, Germany
Flute, Bass Clarinet, Alto Saxophone / Avant-Garde, Post-Bop
Eric Dolphy was a true original with his own distinctive styles on alto, flute and bass clarinet. His music fell into the "avant-garde" category yet he did not discard chordal improvisation altogether (although the relationship of his notes to the chords were often pretty abstract). While most of the other "free jazz" players sounded very serious in their playing, Dolphy's solos often came across as ecstatic and exuberant. His improvisations utilized very wide intervals, a variety of nonmusical speechlike sounds and their own logic. Although alto was his main ax, Dolphy was the first flutist to move beyond bop (influencing James Newton) and he largely introduced the bass clarinet to jazz as a solo instrument. He was also one of the first (after Coleman Hawkins) to record unaccompanied horn solos, preceding Anthony Braxton by five years.

Eric Dolphy first recorded while with Roy Porter's Orchestra (1948–50) in Los Angeles, he was in the Army for two years and then played in obscurity in L.A. until he joined Chico Hamilton's Quintet in 1958. In 1959 he settled in New York and was soon a member of Charles Mingus' Quartet. By 1960 Dolphy was recording regularly as a leader for Prestige and gaining attention for his work with Mingus but throughout his short career he had difficulty gaining steady work due to his very advanced style. Dolphy recorded quite a bit during 1960–61, including three albums cut at the Five Spot while with trumpeter Booker Little, *Free Jazz* with Ornette Coleman, sessions with Max Roach and some European dates. Late in 1961 Dolphy was part of the John Coltrane Quintet; their engagement at the Village Vanguard caused conservative critics to try to smear them as playing "anti-jazz" due to the lengthy and very free solos. During 1962–63 Dolphy played Third Stream music with Gunther Schuller and Orchestra U.S.A. and gigged all too rarely with his own group. In 1964 he recorded his classic *Out to Lunch* for Blue Note and travelled to Europe with Charles Mingus' Sextet (which was arguably the bassist's most exciting band as shown on *The Great Concert of Charles Mingus*). After he chose to stay in Europe, Dolphy had a few gigs but then died suddenly from a diabetic coma at the age of 36, a major loss.

Virtually all of Eric Dolphy's recordings are in print, including a nine-CD box set of all of his Prestige sessions. In addition Dolphy can be seen on film with John Coltrane (on *The Coltrane Legacy*) and with Mingus from 1964 on a video released by Shanachie. —*Scott Yanow*

Outward Bound / Apr. 1, 1960 / Original Jazz Classics ✦✦✦✦✦
Expansive, compelling, and excellent Dolphy with strong Freddie Hubbard and even better Jaki Byard. —*Ron Wynn*

☆ **The Complete Prestige Recordings** / Apr. 1, 1960–Jun. 8, 1961 / Prestige ✦✦✦✦✦

Dash One / Apr. 1, 1960–Jul. 16, 1961 / Prestige ✦✦✦
This LP contains four rare items by Eric Dolphy, alternate takes of "G.W.," "245," "Bee Vamp" and "Serene." The first two selections also feature trumpeter Freddie Hubbard while Booker Little provides the brass on the latter two songs. Needless to say, Dolphy (heard here on alto and bass clarinet) takes completely different improvisation than on the originally released recordings, making this a valuable addition to his discography. —*Scott Yanow*

Status / Apr. 1, 1960–Sep. 8, 1961 / Prestige ✦✦✦
This two-LP set reissues music originally on the two LPs *Here and There* and *Eric Dolphy in Europe, Vol. 2*. Taken from three separate occasions, Eric Dolphy is featured at the Five Spot with trumpeter Booker Little on "Status Seeking" and on unaccompanied bass clarinet for "God Bless the Child," stretching out on five songs with a European trio in 1961 (including two lengthy versions of "Don't Blame Me") and a rendition of "Laura" that clocks in at 13:45) and starring on a flute feature with the Jaki Byard trio, "April Fool." A true original, Dolphy is in typically adventurous form throughout this recommended two-fer. —*Scott Yanow*

Here and There / Apr. 1, 1960–Sep. 8, 1961 / Original Jazz Classics ✦✦✦✦

Other Aspects / Jul. 8, 1960–1962 / Blue Note ✦✦✦✦
This CD contains some unusual music by Eric Dolphy that was released for the first time more than two decades after his death. The lengthy "Jim Crow" matches the multi-instrumentalist with a classical singer and a rhythm section for a stirring performance while "Improvisations and Tukras" finds Dolphy on flute backed by two Indian percussionists. These two selections are unlike anything else in Dolphy's discography. In addition, this album has a duet with bassist Ron Carter and two brief unaccompanied flute solos. Consistently fascinating music. —*Scott Yanow*

☆ **Out There** / Aug. 15, 1960 / Original Jazz Classics ✦✦✦✦✦
Dolphy at his evocative best, with wonderful support from Ron Carter and Roy Haynes. —*Ron Wynn*

Caribe / Aug. 19, 1960 / Original Jazz Classics ✦✦✦
The innovative Eric Dolphy plays alto, flute and bass clarinet solos on this CD while backed by The Latin Jazz Quintet. The problem is that the other musicians essentially ignore Dolphy, never reacting to his explosive flights, seemingly content to play their quiet rhythmic bop music as if he were not present! Still, Dolphy's improvisations make this odd date worth picking up. —*Scott Yanow*

Candid Dolphy / Oct. 20, 1960–Apr. 4, 1961 / Candid ✦✦✦✦
The great Eric Dolphy recorded several albums for the Candid label as a sideman, including dates with bassist Charles Mingus, trumpeter Booker Little, singer Abbey Lincoln and the Newport Rebels. This CD features eight alternate takes from these sessions, six of which were previously unissued. "Reincarnation of a Love Bird" and "Stormy Weather" are with Mingus in a group also featuring trumpeter Ted Curson, two numbers have vocals by Abbey Lincoln (Coleman Hawkins is heard from on "African Lady"), Dolphy is matched with trombonist Jimmy Knepper on "Body and Soul," and the veteran trumpeter Roy Eldridge on "Body and Soul," and he proves to be a perfect partner of Booker Little in a sextet. Even the "complete" box sets that have been issued of these sessions do not include all of this music, which in general is up to the level of the originally issued versions. —*Scott Yanow*

Far Cry / Dec. 21, 1960 / Original Jazz Classics ✦✦✦✦✦
This marks Dolphy's departure from standard jazz repertoire playing, with originals and exciting Parker-isms.—*Myles Boisen*

Magic / Dec. 21, 1960+Jun. 21, 1961 / Prestige ✦✦✦
This two-LP set reissues Eric Dolphy's *Far Cry* and *Where*, a Ron Carter date featuring Dolphy. Together they make for an excellent all-around set that showcases the talents of Dolphy on alto, bass clarinet and flute. The former session matches Eric with trumpeter Booker Little, pianist Jaki Byard, bassist Carter and drummer Roy Haynes; highlights include "It's Magic," "Miss Ann" and an unaccompanied alto feature on "Tenderly." Carter's set features the leader doubling on cello and bass and joined by Dolphy, pianist Mal Waldron, bassist George Duvivier and drummer

Charlie Persip for some stirring music well worth listening to closely. —*Scott Yanow*

Quartet 1961 / 1961 / Jazz Anthology ✦✦✦
Taken from Eric Dolphy's much-recorded European tour of 1961, this set matches the remarkable multi-instrumentalist with pianist Lalo Schifrin, bassist Bob Cunningham and drummer Mel Lewis, performing long versions of "On Green Dolphin Street" (over 23 minutes), "Softly As in a Morning Sunrise" and "The Way You Look Tonight." Although the rhythm section is conventional, Dolphy really tears into these standards, making this imported LP worth searching for. —*Scott Yanow*

Live! at the Five Spot, Vol. 1 / Jul. 16, 1961 / Original Jazz Classics ✦✦✦✦
The first of the immortal Dolphy live dates, with incredible interaction between Dolphy and Booker Little (tpt). Awesome alto sax and bass clarinet, with feverish tempos. —*Ron Wynn*

Live! at the Five Spot, Vol. 2 / Jul. 16, 1961 / Original Jazz Classics ✦✦✦✦
Just as vital as its predecessor. Wondrous solos and compositions. 1987 reissues of a landmark concert. —*Ron Wynn*

The Great Concert of Eric Dolphy / Jul. 16, 1961 / Prestige ✦✦✦✦✦
For two weeks, the multi-instrumentalist (alto, flute and bass clarinet) Eric Dolphy appeared at the Five Spot in New York with a quintet comprised of trumpeter Booker Little (who would pass away before the year ended), pianist Mal Waldron, bassist Richard Davis and drummer Ed Blackwell. One night, July 16, 1961, was fully recorded and the results released on three LPs. This three-LP box set contains all of the music, and, despite an out-of-tune piano, the results are consistently brilliant. The seven selections (all over 12 minutes long with "The Prophet" going on for over 21) give the principals plenty of space in which to stretch out, and the long improvisations consistently hold one's interest. All of the material (except the standard "Like Someone in Love") was composed by Dolphy, Little or Waldron. Classic and adventurous music. —*Scott Yanow*

Berlin Concerts / Aug. 30, 1961 / Enja ✦✦✦✦
This two-LP set features the great multi-instrumentalist Eric Dolphy mostly stretching out on standards, coming up with very original statements on such songs as "Hot House," "When Lights Are Low," "Hi Fly," "I'll Remember April" and "God Bless the Child" (the latter taken as an unaccompanied bass clarinet solo), in addition to two brief originals. With trumpeter Benny Bailey helping out on half of the selections along with a strong rhythm section, the two-fer would be a perfect introduction for listeners not familiar with Eric Dolphy's innovative style, but this set is very difficult to find! —*Scott Yanow*

The Complete Uppsala Concert / Sep. 4, 1961 / Jazz Door ✦✦✦
This two-CD set features the remarkable Eric Dolphy (tripling on alto, bass clarinet and flute) during a concert in Sweden. Accompanied by an obscure but talented rhythm section (pianist Rony Johansson, bassist Kurt Lindgren and drummer Rune Carlsson), Dolphy really stretches out on five of the seven numbers, particularly during a 20-1/2 minute version of his blues "245." Other highlights include "Laura" (featuring Dolphy unaccompanied on alto), "Bag's Groove" (his only recording of that piece) and "I'll Remember April." With the exception of "245," all of the songs are bop standards, but Eric Dolphy's improvisations are typically unpredictable and adventurous. The recording quality is decent, making this a good set to get after acquiring Dolphy's better-known sessions. —*Scott Yanow*

Eric Dolphy in Europe, Vol. 1 / Sep. 6, 1961+Sep. 8, 1961 / Original Jazz Classics ✦✦✦

Eric Dolphy in Europe, Vol. 2 / Sep. 6, 1961+Sep. 8, 1961 / Original Jazz Classics ✦✦✦
These live recordings from two dates are spread over three albums. All feature excellent soloing and capable, if reserved, backing from a Danish trio. —*Myles Boisen*

Eric Dolphy in Europe, Vol. 3 / Sep. 6, 1961+Sep. 8, 1961 / Original Jazz Classics ✦✦✦
These live recordings from two dates are spread over three albums. All feature excellent soloing and capable, if reserved, backing from a Danish trio. —*Myles Boisen*

Copenhagen Concert / Sep. 8, 1961 / Prestige ✦✦✦✦
Eric Dolphy's tour of Europe is one of the best documented peri-

ods of his much-too-short career. This two-LP set is highlighted by a flute/bass duet with Chuck Israels on "Hi-Fly," an unaccompanied bass clarinet exploration on "God Bless the Child" and several numbers on which Dolphy is backed on standards by a European trio led by pianist Bent Axen. The only weak spot is the three straight versions of "In the Blues," none of which really succeed. This two-fer, a reissue of *Eric Dolphy in Europe, Vols. 1 & 3*, is a must for Dolphy collectors. —*Scott Yanow*

Stockholm Sessions / Sep. 25, 1961–Nov. 1, 1961 / Enja ✦✦✦
The music on this CD (the original LP program plus a second version of "Sorino") is taken from a radio aircheck and a TV special, both originating from Stockholm. The remarkable Eric Dolphy (switching between alto, bass clarinet and flute) performed two of his originals plus "Don't Blame Me" with a sympathetic quartet on the aircheck while the television show (does this film still exist?) features him in a quintet with trumpeter Idrees Sulieman playing three more originals, Mal Waldron's "Alone" and his unaccompanied bass clarinet feature "God Bless the Child." This innovative music can serve as a strong introduction of Eric Dolphy's talents to bebop fans who have not yet grasped the avant-garde. —*Scott Yanow*

Softly, As in a Morning / Dec. 2, 1961 / Natasha ✦✦
This CD has a very interesting lineup of musicians: Eric Dolphy (sticking to bass clarinet throughout), pianist McCoy Tyner, bassist Reggie Workman and drummer Mel Lewis. Dolphy was actually touring with the John Coltrane Quintet (of which Tyner and Workman were a part) at the time and apparently Elvin Jones had passport problems so Lewis subbed for him. The playing on these four lengthy standards, including a 23 1/2 minute "On Green Dolphin Street," is fine, but unfortunately, the recording quality from this Munich, Germany, concert is pretty bad, making much of this historic music fairly unlistenable. For Dolphy completists only! —*Scott Yanow*

Vintage Dolphy / Mar. 10, 1962–Apr. 18, 1963 / GM ✦✦✦✦
This posthumous collection features the remarkable Eric Dolphy in prime form. On three songs, Dolphy (switching between alto, bass clarinet and flute) performs two originals and Jaki Byard's "Ode to Charlie Parker" with a quartet that includes trumpeter Edward Armour, bassist Richard Davis and J.C. Moses. In addition, Dolphy is heard on three third stream avant-garde classical pieces by Gunther Schuller (taking a rare clarinet solo on "Densities") and jamming on a wild version of "Donna Lee" with an all-star group including such players as trumpeter Don Ellis, trombonist Jimmy Knepper, Benny Golson on tenor and guitarist Jim Hall; the ensembles are rather uproarious. Highly recommended. —*Scott Yanow*

☆**Jitterbug Waltz** / 1963 / Casablanca ✦✦✦✦✦
In 1963, Eric Dolphy recorded two of his most rewarding sessions which were originally released on two LPs: *Conversations* and *Iron Man*. This music has been reissued numerous times through the years, including in total on this two-LP set; it deserves to come out on CD! These dates are among Dolphy's finest, with the challenging material interpreted by a constantly shifting personnel. Three numbers ("Jitterbug Waltz," "Iron Man" and "Mandrake") find the multi-instrumentalist (alto, flute and bass clarinet) playing unconventional music with a quintet that includes two masterful musicians at the beginning of their careers: vibraphonist Bobby Hutcherson and trumpeter Woody Shaw. Two other pieces ("Burning Spear" and "Music Matador") have Dolphy interacting with a variety of top young avant-gardists including Shaw, Hutcherson, Clifford Jordan on soprano, altoist Sonny Simmons and Prince Lasha on flute. In addition, there are three duets with bassist Richard Davis ("Come Sunday," "Alone Together" and "Ode to Charlie Parker") and an unaccompanied alto piece (an intense "Love Me"). Quite a varied set, essential music for any jazz collection. —*Scott Yanow*

★**Out to Lunch** / Feb. 25, 1964 / Blue Note ✦✦✦✦✦
Eric Dolphy's debut as a leader on Blue Note was also his last American recording before his unexpected death four months later. On this brilliant set, Dolphy performs five of his colorful originals with quite an all-star group (even though at the time none of these young players were all that well-known): trumpeter Freddie Hubbard, vibraphonist Bobby Hutcherson, bassist Richard Davis and drummer Tony Williams. Whether playing alto, flute or bass clarinet, Dolphy had a highly original style, and this set remains one of his finest statements. —*Scott Yanow*

☆ **Last Date** / Jun. 2, 1964 / Verve ✦✦✦✦✦
Although one slighty later session has since been discovered, *Last Date* remains a near-classic with the great Eric Dolphy (heard on alto, flute and bass clarinet) backed by a top European rhythm section—pianist Misha Mengelberg, bassist Jacques Schols and drummer Han Bennink—performing exciting versions of "Epistrophy," "You Don't Know What Love Is" and four of his originals. The innovative music points out what a giant loss Dolphy's premature death was; he passed away just 27 days after this memorable performance. —*Scott Yanow*

Naima / Jun. 11, 1964 / West Wind ✦✦✦✦
Recorded nine days after Eric Dolphy's *Last Date* album and at the same sessions that resulted in the other West Wind release *Unrealized Tapes*, this CD finds the great Eric Dolphy (just 18 days before his death) in excellent form. He plays flute on "Ode to Charlie Parker" and stretches out on alto and bass clarinet during lengthy versions of "Naima" and "Springtime." Although joined by a fine French rhythm section, trumpeter Donald Byrd and Nathan Davis on tenor, Dolphy is easily the dominant voice throughout the spirited set, showing listeners that he still had a great deal to say even though his time had run out. This European import is worth searching for. —*Scott Yanow*

Unreleased Tapes / Jun. 11, 1964 / West Wind ✦✦✦✦
For years, *Last Date* was thought of as Eric Dolphy's final recording until *Unrealized Tapes* (from nine days later) was released; Dolphy passed away only 18 days after performing this music. This LP from the European West Wind label features the great Dolphy on alto and bass clarinet with a sextet that includes trumpeter Donald Byrd, tenor saxophonist Nathan Davis and a French rhythm section performing four of his compositions including the otherwise unknown "Springtime." Eric Dolphy collectors will have to get this gem! —*Scott Yanow*

Natty Dominique (Anatie Dominique)

b. Aug. 2, 1898, New Orleans, LA, d. Aug. 30, 1982, Chicago, IL
Trumpet / Classic Jazz
An erratic trumpeter, Natty Dominique was at his best in the 1920s (such as on "Brush Stomp" and "Oriental Man"). He played in an appealing rhythmic style with plenty of force. However there were also times ("Tack 'Em Down") when his enthusiasm got the best of him. He played in brass bands as a teenager in New Orleans, left town in 1913 and freelanced in Chicago and the Midwest. Dominique recorded with Jelly Roll Morton in 1923 and played with Carroll Dickerson and Jimmie Noone, but he is best remembered for his association with Johnny Dodds; they recorded together frequently. After appearing on Dodds' final records in 1940, Dominique's heart condition forced him to retire and he worked as an airport porter, but in the early '50s he started playing again on a part-time basis, often using Baby Dodds. —*Scott Yanow*

Natty Dominique's Creole Dance Band / Sep. 28, 1953 / American Music ✦✦✦
Natty Dominique is best-known for his erratic but sometimes quite rewarding playing with the great clarinetist Johnny Dodds in the 1920s. He made no recordings after 1940 except for the material on this CD; only two of the songs had been issued before 1993. Dominique is typically streaky in a septet that also includes clarinetist Darnell Howard, trombonist Preston Jackson and drummer Baby Dodds, sounding fine on a few of the ensembles where he plays in a style reminiscent of Freddie Keppard. Most interesting are two excerpts from interviews where Natty talks about playing with Dodds and remembers a lesson that he had from Louis Armstrong about the importance of being original. This is a historically significant if not really essential release. —*Scott Yanow*

Arne Domnérus

b. Dec. 20, 1924, Stockholm, Sweden
Clarinet, Alto Saxophone / Bop, Swing
One of Sweden's top jazz musicians, Arne Domnerus led his first group in 1942, made his earliest recordings in 1945 and led his first record sessions in 1949. An altoist who combines together Johnny Hodges and Lee Konitz and an excellent swing clarinetist, Domnerus has led combos for over 45 years and worked steadily with the Swedish Radio Band and its successors. He has made many recordings for Swedish labels including Phontastic. —*Scott Yanow*

Arne Domnerus and His Favourite Groups / Aug. 20, 1949–Mar. 15, 1950 / Dragon ✦✦✦✦
Duets for Duke / Jul. 27, 1978–Jul. 28, 1978 / Sonet ✦✦✦
Ad 1980 / May 14, 1980–May 15, 1980 / Phontastic ✦✦✦✦
● **Sketches of Standards** / Aug. 28, 1990–Aug. 29, 1990 / Proprius ✦✦✦✦✦

Barbara Donald

b. Feb. 9, 1942, Minneapolis, MN
Trumpet / Free Jazz, Avant-Garde
One of the top female trumpeters of all time, Barbara Donald has a powerful and explorative style that has been showcased on records far too little. She is best known for playing with altoist Sonny Simmons (her husband at the time) during 1963–72. She recorded a couple of impressive efforts for Cadence in the early '80s but little has been heard from her since. —*Scott Yanow*

● **Olympia Live** / Mar. 30, 1981 / Cadence ✦✦✦✦✦
Best known for her collaboration with her then-husband, altoist Sonny Simmons, the powerful trumpeter Barbara Donald recorded two excellent albums for Cadence in the early '80s. This particular set, cut live in Olympia, WA, features Donald with Carter Jefferson (who doubles on tenor and soprano) with a septet. Surprisingly, the music is mostly in a hard bop rather than free vein, with such songs as Cedar Walton's "Bolivia," Thelonious Monk's "Well You Needn't" and Donald's "Blues for You" receiving relatively straight-ahead but passionate treatment. It's worth searching for. —*Scott Yanow*

The Past and Tomorrows / Apr. 16, 1982+Apr. 17, 1982 / Cadence ✦✦✦✦
The powerful trumpeter Barbara Donald leads a strong sextet that also features the tenors of Carter Jefferson and Gary Hammon on Monk's "Pannonica" and several group originals. The music is advanced hard bop with plenty of room for stirring improvisations, particularly by the leader. In view of the fact that the talented Barbara Donald has rarely recorded since this album, someone should give her a recording contract. —*Scott Yanow*

Lou Donaldson

b. Nov. 1, 1926, Badin, NC
Alto Saxophone / Bop, Soul Jazz
A truly great bebop player, alto saxophonist Lou Donaldson strayed from the path in the early '70s, making some decent soul jazz and funk records, and a couple of mediocre fusion dates. But he returned in the late '70s to the style that's his best; hard-edged, searing bop, played with as much vigor as any living performer. Like Frank Morgan and Phil Woods, Donaldson at his best exemplifies the Charlie Parker spirit without being a slavish imitator. He can insert clever quotes, make dazzling harmonic maneuvers at fast or slow tempos and play beautiful, compelling blues and ballads. Donaldson began clarinet studies at 15, and later joined the Navy, continuing his education. He played in a Navy band with Willie Smith, Clark Terry, and Ernie Wilkins, having switched to alto sax. In 1952, Donaldson made his recording debut with Milt Jackson and Thelonious Monk. He began leading various combos, playing with Charlie Parker, Sonny Stitt, Blue Mitchell, Horace Silver, Art Blakey, Clifford Brown and Philly Joe Jones before joining Blakey's Jazz Messengers with Brown in 1954. Since leaving the Messengers, Donaldson has been a busy leader and session contributor, recording numerous albums and touring frequently nationally and overseas. He initially recorded for Blue Note from 1952 to 1962, cutting albums with Silver, Brown, Horace Parlan, Baby Face Willette, and Big John Patton among others. He started including soul jazz material on his Blue Note dates, but began to switch more to funk in 1963, when he moved to Argo (later Cadet). Donaldson recorded again with Patton and made a nine-piece session with Oliver Nelson before returning to Blue Note in 1967. There was another nine-piece group date, and Donaldson also recorded with George Benson, Charles Earland and Lonnie Smith. These were mostly soul jazz and funk but they were earthy and enjoyable. Donaldson's solos still reflected his bebop heritage. During the early '70s Blue Note joined other labels in the jazz-rock/fusion/instrumental pop phase (or craze). Donaldson made albums with overdubbed female vocals, strings and heavy electronic backgrounds. He defended albums like *Cosmos* and *Sweet Lou* in magazine and newspaper interviews at the time, but by the late '70s he returned to the music he knew and played best. His '80s sessions for Timeless, Muse and Blue Note reaffirmed those values; tart, sizzling bop

and animated blues and ballads. He has continued recording in the '90s for Milestone. Donaldson's formative Blue Note dates, both as a leader and with The Jazz Messengers, have been periodically reissued, while the bulk of his other material, except the Argo/Cadet records, is still in print. —*Ron Wynn and Bob Porter*

The Lou Donaldson Quartet/Quintet/Sextet / Jun. 20, 1952–Aug. 22, 1954 / Blue Note ✦✦✦✦✦
Both soul-jazz and more mainstream/hard-pop sessions. Elmo Hope (p), Horace Silver (p), Blue Mitchell (tpt), Kenny Dorham (tpt), and cast of all-stars. —*Ron Wynn*

★ **Blues Walk** / Jul. 28, 1958 / Blue Note ✦✦✦✦✦
This early session from Lou Donaldson is pure bebop with the altoist romping on such pieces as "Blues Walk," "Move," "Play Ray" and "Callin' All Cats." The rhythm section (pianist Herman Foster, bassist Peck Morrison, drummer Dave Bailey) is supportive if not particularly distinctive, although the congas of Ray Barretto add some color to the accompaniment. No matter, Lou Donaldson is the main star of this swinging and easily enjoyable set. —*Scott Yanow*

Sunny Side Up / Feb. 5, 1960+Feb. 29, 1960 / Blue Note ✦✦✦

Midnight Sun / Jul. 22, 1960 / Blue Note ✦✦✦

Natural Soul / May 9, 1962 / Blue Note ✦✦✦✦

At His Best / Aug. 30, 1966 / Cadet ✦✦✦

Lush Life / Jan. 20, 1967 / Blue Note ✦✦✦✦✦
Smooth, moody, suggestive, and enlightening. —*Ron Wynn*

Alligator Bogaloo / Apr. 7, 1967 / Blue Note ✦✦✦
Prototype funk, soul-jazz, blues, boogie, and ballads from a stalwart alto master. —*Ron Wynn*

Midnight Creeper / Mar. 15, 1968 / Blue Note ✦✦✦

Say It Loud! / Nov. 8, 1968 / Blue Note ✦✦

Hot Dog / Apr. 25, 1969 / Blue Note ✦
This CD reissues one of altoist Lou Donaldson's weakest recordings. Dating from the declining years of Blue Note, Donaldson plays decent enough (although when he utilizes a baritone sax it greatly dilutes his sound), but the very weak material features R&B rhythms, endless vamping and automatic pilot riffing from organist Charles Earland. The "glee club" vocal on "Who's Making Love" is incredibly bad, laughably so. Guitarist Melvin Sparks and trumpeter Ed Williams do their best during their solos but the material sinks the date. —*Scott Yanow*

Everything I Play Is Funky / Aug. 22, 1969+Jan. 9, 1970 / Blue Note ✦✦
It is always a bit painful to hear creative jazz musicians play well below their potential and it would not be an overstatement to say that altoist Lou Donaldson is capable of much better than the music heard on this CD. His calypso "West Indian Daddy" is okay (if not at all memorable), he jams reasonably well on the driving blues "Minor Bash" and plays honestly (if overly straight) on "Over the Rainbow." But the three other tracks are throwaways, trumpeter Blue Mitchell shows so little personality that the unknown Eddie Williams (who replaces Mitchell on two cuts) proves to be his equal and the rhythm section (with either Lonnie Smith or Charles Earland on organ) does little except chug away. This set is a major disappointment. —*Scott Yanow*

Pretty Things / Jan. 9, 1970–Jun. 12, 1970 / Blue Note ✦✦
Lou Donaldson has recorded many strong sessions throughout his career but this CD reissue brings back one of the less-significant ones. Organist Leon Spencer dominates the ensembles, the material is a bit trivial and the altoist/leader uses a baritone sax on some of the selections which makes him sound much less individual than usual. Trumpeter Blue Mitchell's solos and a fine closing jam on "Love" help upgrade the music a bit, but there are many better Donaldson recordings to acquire first. —*Scott Yanow*

The Scorpion: Live At The Cadillac Club / Nov. 7, 1970 / Blue Note ✦✦
This previously unreleased live set, which has been issued on Blue Note's *Rare Groove Series*, will bore anyone who listens closely. The repertoire is dominated by lengthy funk grooves that are quite danceable but never develop beyond the obvious. Altoist Lou Donaldson was using a baritone horn at the time that gave him a generic and unappealing tone, the obscure trumpeter Fred Ballard does his best to no avail and the enthusiastic rhythm section (guitarist Melvin Sparks, organist Leon Spencer, Jr., and drummer Idris Muhammad) keeps the grooves repetitious. Bob Porter's liner notes (which colorfully give readers the history of

Newark jazz of the past 30 years) are superlative but, even with the inclusion of a fast blues, musically nothing much happens. —*Scott Yanow*

Sweet Poppa Lou / Jan. 7, 1981 / Muse ✦✦✦

Forgotten Man / Jul. 2, 1981 / Timeless ✦✦✦
Altoist Lou Donaldson was never exactly a "forgotten man," but his boppish style had been largely overlooked since his commercial electric funk sessions for Blue Note in the early to mid-'70s. This is a straight-ahead acoustic quartet date with pianist Herman Foster (whose block chord solos on a couple of numbers are quite exciting), bassist Geoff Fuller and drummer Victor Jones. Donaldson romps through some bop standards, Tadd Dameron's lesser-known "This Is Happiness" and his own "Tracy" and takes a humorous vocal on "Whiskey Drinkin' Woman." Although not essential, this album should easily please Lou Donaldson's fans, for it finds him in exuberant form. —*Scott Yanow*

Back Street / 1982 / Muse ✦✦✦

Live in Bologna / Jan. 1984 / Timeless ✦✦✦

Play the Right Thing / Dec. 19, 1990–Dec. 20, 1990 / Milestone ✦✦✦

Birdseed / Apr. 28, 1992–Apr. 29, 1992 / Milestone ✦✦✦✦
Nice music. Nothing exceptional. Bop and ballads, with one blues (Donaldson sings on this one) and a bossa nova. —*Michael Erlewine*

Caracas / Jul. 1993 / Milestone ✦✦✦

Sentimental Journey / Aug. 14, 1994–Aug. 15, 1994 / Columbia ✦✦✦✦
This Lou Donaldson Quintet set (which also features organist Lonnie Smith, guitarist Peter Bernstein, drummer Fukushi Tainaka and the percussion of Ray Mantilla) offers few surprises but no real disappointments either. Altoist Donaldson plays his usual mixture of blues, ballads and standards with a fine organ trio and the results are predictably swinging. The music could have been performed in 1965, but strangely enough the familiar style heard on this CD has not dated and still communicates. The enthusiasm of the musicians (who sound perfectly at home) has kept this popular idiom alive and sounding reasonably fresh. —*Scott Yanow*

Dorothy Donegan

b. .Apr. 6, 1924, Chicago, IL
Piano / Bop, Swing, Stride, Boogie-Woogie
A brilliant virtuoso, Dorothy Donegan constantly switches between boogie-woogie, bop, stride, Art Tatum-style swing and classical music, sometimes in the same chorus! In concerts she often puts together spontaneous medleys of unrelated songs and is never shy about dancing while she plays. She studied at the Chicago Conservatory and Chicago Music College and made her recording debut in 1942. Donegan made a sensational appearance in the film *Sensations* of 1945 but never caught on that big despite her remarkable technique. She recorded a lot less than one would expect (six obscure albums during 1954–63 and nothing during 1964–74) and was not really that well-known in the jazz world until the mid-'80s. A couple of live Chiaroscuro CDs from 1990–91 find her in peak form, but she has to be seen to be fully appreciated. —*Scott Yanow*

● **Dorothy Romps–a Piano Retrospective (1953–1979)** / 1953–1979 / Rosetta ✦✦✦✦✦
This retrospective of the works of one of the most outstanding pianists in jazz history spans 1953–1979, as *Volume 9* in Rosetta Records' *Foremothers* series. From boogie woogie to honky tonk to blues, pop and even classical, this album demonstrates the spectacular technique and broad-ranging abilities of the artist. It includes "Grieg's Boogie," "Louise," "I Want a Little Girl," "Minuet in G," "Lullaby of Birdland." —*Ladyslipper*

Live at the 1990 Floating Jazz Festival / 1990 / Chiaroscuro ✦✦✦✦

The Incredible Dorothy Donegan Trio / 1991 / Chiaroscuro ✦✦✦✦

Dorothy Donegan Trio with Clark Terry / 1993 / Chiaroscuro ✦✦✦✦

Pierre Dorge

b. Feb. 28, 1946, Copenhagen, Denmark
Guitar, Leader / Avant-Garde, Post-Bop
Pierre Dorge has gained some fame for his work with his New

Jungle Orchestra, a band that plays fresh interpretations of some classics (particularly by Duke Ellington and Thelonious Monk) along with its leader's originals. Dorge led his first band in 1960, was a member of John Tchicai's big band (1969–71), in 1978 headed a quartet called Thermaenius and in 1980 put together the New Jungle Orchestra. Dorge has recorded several very interesting sessions (including a duo with Tchicai) for the SteepleChase label. —*Scott Yanow*

New Jungle Orchestra / Mar. 7, 1982–Mar. 8, 1982 / SteepleChase ✦✦✦✦

● **Even the Moon Is Dancing** / Jul. 30, 1985 / SteepleChase ✦✦✦✦✦

Johnny Lives / Apr. 15, 1987 / SteepleChase ✦✦✦✦

Live in Denmark / Sep. 11, 1987 / Olufsen ✦✦✦

Different Places, Different Bananas / Nov. 8, 1988–Nov. 9, 1988 / Olufsen ✦✦✦

Live in Chicago / Jul. 6, 1990 / Olufsen ✦✦✦

Kenny Dorham

b. Aug. 30, 1924, Fairfield, TX, d. Dec. 5, 1972, New York, NY
Trumpet / Hard Bop
Throughout his career Kenny Dorham was almost famous for being underrated, since he was consistently overshadowed by Dizzy Gillespie, Fats Navarro, Miles Davis, Clifford Brown and Lee Morgan. Dorham was never an influential force himself but a talented bop-oriented trumpeter and an excellent composer who played in some very significant bands. In 1945 he was in the orchestras of Dizzy Gillespie and Billy Eckstine, he recorded with the Be Bop Boys in 1946 and spent short periods with Lionel Hampton and Mercer Ellington. During 1948–49 Dorham was the trumpeter in the Charlie Parker Quintet. After some freelancing in New York in 1954 he became a member of the first version of Art Blakey's Jazz Messengers and for a short time led a group called the Jazz Prophets, which recorded on Blue Note. After Clifford Brown's death, Dorham became his replacement in the Max Roach Quintet (1956–58) and then he led several groups of his own. He recorded several fine dates for Riverside (including a vocal album in 1958), New Jazz and Time but it is his Blue Note sessions of 1961–64 that are among his finest. Dorham was an early booster of Joe Henderson (who played with his group in 1963–64). After the mid-'60s Kenny Dorham (who wrote some interesting reviews for *Downbeat*) began to fade and he died in 1972 of kidney disease. Among his many originals is one that became a standard, "Blue Bossa." —*Scott Yanow*

Kenny Dorham Quintet / Dec. 15, 1953 / Original Jazz Classics ✦✦✦✦
Kenny Dorham's debut as a leader found the 29-year-old trumpeter more than ready to take control; unfortunately he spent virtually his entire career in the shadows of other trumpeters (such as Dizzy Gillespie, Miles Davis, Clifford Brown and Lee Morgan). This set was originally released by the Debut label as a six-song LP and then reissued with two alternate takes as a regular album. Now available on CD with two additional blues and another alternate, the fine playing by the quintet (with Jimmy Heath on tenor and baritone, pianist Walter Bishop, bassist Percy Heath and drummer Kenny Clarke) is not watered down by the extra material. A special bonus is the fine arranging of Dorham for the ensemble, a much overlooked talent of a continually underrated musician. —*Scott Yanow*

★ **Afro-Cuban** / Jan. 30, 1955+Mar. 29, 1955 / Blue Note ✦✦✦✦✦
This is a particularly strong set from trumpeter Kenny Dorham, for it has the debut versions of "Lotus Flower," "Minor Holiday" and "La Villa," three of his most rewarding compositions. The first half of the set is Afro-Cuban in nature due to the inclusion of Carlos "Potato" Valdes' conga; also on the four songs (plus a previously unreleased alternate take of "Minor's Holiday") are trombonist J.J. Johnson, Hank Mobley on tenor, baritonist Cecil Payne, pianist Horace Silver, bassist Oscar Pettiford and drummer Art Blakey. The final four numbers (including a "new" song added to the CD reissue, "K.D.'s Cab Ride") are more straight-ahead in nature and drop out Valdes and Johnson while substituting Percy Heath for Pettiford. In both cases, Dorham has an all-star group of young hard boppers eager to play his challenging and memorable originals. —*Scott Yanow*

And the Jazz Prophets / Apr. 4, 1956 / ABC/Paramount ✦✦✦

'Round About Midnight At The Cafe Bohemia / May 31, 1956 / Blue Note ✦✦✦✦
This is a double-CD reissue of two prior single CD reissues, which

expand the original Kenny Dorham LP from 42 minutes to over two hours. Although not necessarily trumpeter Dorham's finest hour, this surprisingly consistent set features the trumpeter and his sextet (with J.R. Monterose on tenor, guitarist Kenny Burrell, pianist Bobby Timmons, bassist Sam Jones and drummer Arthur Edgehill) performing 17 selections; ten (counting alternate takes) are the trumpeter's hard bop originals, although one also gets fine versions of such standards as "Round Midnight," "A Night in Tunisia" and "My Heart Stood Still." Considering how extensive this recording is (virtually the whole evening's performance), it is fortunate that Kenny Dorham's group (which was a short-lived venture called The Jazz Prophets) was in top form that night. —*Scott Yanow*

Jazz Contrasts / May 21, 1957+May 27, 1957 / Original Jazz Classics ✦✦✦✦✦
Some of trumpeter Kenny Dorham's finest recordings were his sessions as a leader for Riverside in the 1950s, and fortunately all of that music has been reissued on CD. This straight reissue of an original LP is a bit brief in time (41 minutes) but contains many memorable selections. Three of the songs ("Falling in Love with Love" a 12-minute version of "I'll Remember April" and the trumpeter's "La Villa") match Dorham in an all-star quintet with the great tenor Sonny Rollins, pianist Hank Jones, bassist Oscar Pettiford and drummer Max Roach. The other three numbers (of which only "My Old Flame" includes Rollins) adds a fine harp player (Betty Glamman) and focuses on Dorham's lyricism. —*Scott Yanow*

2 Horns, 2 Rhythms / Nov. 13, 1957+Dec. 1957 / Original Jazz Classics ✦✦✦✦
Trumpeter Kenny Dorham was one of the most underrated talents of the bop and hard bop eras. Although he did not hit high notes or influence a lot of players, Dorham's appealing sound and consistently creative ideas should have made him a star in the jazz world instead of just a journeyman. On this CD reissue (which adds an alternate take of "'Sposin'" to the original eight-song LP program), Dorham and altoist Ernie Henry (on his final session) are heard in a pianoless quartet (with either Eddie Mathias or Wilbur Ware on bass and drummer G.T. Hogan) playing three of the trumpeter's originals (including "Lotus Blossom") and four standards. Highlights include "I'll Be Seeing You" and a rare revival of "Is It True What They Say About Dixie?" The sparse setting (unusual for a Dorham session) works quite well. —*Scott Yanow*

This Is the Moment / Jul. 1958–Aug. 1958 / Original Jazz Classics ✦✦
The release of this recording must have surprised most jazz listeners at the time, for trumpeter Kenny Dorham sings on all ten selections. He had never hinted at any desire to sing previously (although he had sung a blues regularly with Dizzy Gillespie's Orchestra in the 1940s) and, as it turned out, this was his one and only vocal album; the sales were probably quite a bit less than Chet Baker's records of the period. Dorham had an okay voice, musical if not memorable, but the arrangements for these selections (which utilize his trumpet and Curtis Fuller's trombone, both of which are muted all the time) are inventive and pleasing. The supportive rhythm section is also an asset; pianist Cedar Walton made his recording debut on this album–which is now available on CD–a historical curiosity. —*Scott Yanow*

Blue Spring / Feb. 18, 1959 / Original Jazz Classics ✦✦✦✦
This is one of trumpeter Kenny Dorham's most intriguing sessions. His arrangements of five songs that have "Spring" in their title plus the tune "Poetic" are colorful, making use of altoist Cannonball Adderley, baritonist Cecil Payne, the French horn of Dave Amram and a fine rhythm section. Plus, Dorham's melodic solos (he was never just a bop stylist) are often memorable. —*Scott Yanow*

Quiet Kenny / Nov. 13, 1959 / Original Jazz Classics ✦✦✦
This CD is a reissue of a Kenny Dorham quartet session that was also previously released as *1959*. Not everything on the set is necessarily quiet but the emphasis is on ballads and the beauty of the trumpeter's tone. Accompanied by pianist Tommy Flanagan, bassist Paul Chambers and drummer Art Taylor, Dorham is heard in fine form throughout, particularly on "Lotus Blossom," "My Ideal," "Alone Together," "Old Folks" and a brief rendition of "Mack the Knife." —*Scott Yanow*

Memorial Album / Jan. 10, 1960 / Xanadu ✦✦✦
This somewhat-obscure Kenny Dorham LP features the excellent

hard bop trumpeter in a quintet with baritonist Charles Davis, pianist Tommy Flanagan, bassist Butch Warren and drummer Buddy Enlow. The straight-ahead music includes features for Davis ("When Sunny Gets Blue") and Warren, but Dorham consistently takes honors, particularly on his "Stage West," "I'm an Old Cowhand," "Stella by Starlight" and "Lazy Afternoon." —*Scott Yanow*

Jazz Contemporary / Feb. 11, 1960 / Bainbridge ✦✦✦
Originally on the Time label, this LP features the excellent (but always underrated) trumpeter Kenny Dorham heading a quintet that also includes baritonist Charles Davis, pianist Steve Kuhn, either Jimmy Garrison or Butch Warren on bass and drummer Buddy Enlow. The results are not quite essential but everyone plays up to par, performing three of Dorham's originals plus "In Your Own Sweet Way," "Monk's Mood" and "This Love of Mine." It's fine hard bop, the modern mainstream music of the period. —*Scott Yanow*

Showboat / Dec. 9, 1960 / Bainbridge ✦✦✦✦
This CD reissue of a Kenny Dorham session that was originally on the Time label features the talented trumpeter and an all-star quintet (with Jimmy Heath on tenor, pianist Kenny Drew, bassist Jimmy Garrison and drummer Art Taylor) playing six famous themes from the Jerome Kern play *Showboat*. All of the melodies ("Why Do I Love You?," "Nobody Else but Me," "Can't Help Lovin' Dat Man," "Make Believe," "Ol' Man River" and "Bill") are heard in likable and swinging versions. This is one of Dorham's better sessions from the era and is easily recommended to his fans and collectors of hard bop. —*Scott Yanow*

Whistle Stop / Jan. 15, 1961 / Blue Note ✦✦✦✦
Kenny Dorham was always underrated throughout his career, not only as a trumpeter but as a composer. This CD reissue features seven of his compositions, none of which have been picked up by any of the "Young Lions" of the 1990s despite their high quality and the many fresh melodies. Dorham teams up with tenor saxophonist Hank Mobley (who he had recorded with previously with Art Blakey and Max Roach), pianist Kenny Drew, bassist Paul Chambers and drummer Philly Joe Jones for a set of lively, fresh and consistently swinging music. This is a generally overlooked near-classic set. —*Scott Yanow*

West 42nd Street / Mar. 13, 1961 / Black Lion ✦✦✦
The date included on this CD reissue was originally led by the obscure tenor Rocky Boyd but has come back under trumpeter Kenny Dorham's name with the six songs augmented by four alternate takes. Boyd (whose style mixes together the influences of Hank Mobley and John Coltrane) blends in well with Dorham, the rhythm section (pianist Walter Bishop, Jr., bassist Ron Carter and drummer Pete La Roca) is excellent and the repertoire (group originals plus "Samba De Orpheus" and two slow versions of "Stella by Starlight") generally inspires the players. It's funny how La Roca's original "Why Not" has exactly the same melody and chord structure as Coltrane's "Impressions." This CD is worth picking up by straight-ahead jazz collectors. —*Scott Yanow*

Osmosis / Oct. 4, 1961 / Black Lion ✦✦✦
Originally released under drummer Dave Bailey's name and given the accurate title *Modern Mainstream*, this Black Lion CD reissue has excellent straight-ahead jazz from Bailey, trumpeter Kenny Dorham, trombonist Curtis Fuller, the obscure but talented tenor Frank Haynes, pianist Tommy Flanagan and bassist Ben Tucker. The CD reissue not only has the original seven selections but four previously unreleased alternate takes. Dorham and Haynes are in fine form but it is pianist Flanagan (well-showcased on "Just Friends" and two versions of "Like Someone in Love") who often takes solo honors. —*Scott Yanow*

Matador / Inta Somethin' / Nov. 1961–Apr. 15, 1962 / Blue Note ✦✦✦✦
Two full LPs are combined on this single CD. Both dates feature trumpeter Kenny Dorham and altoist Jackie McLean (two very compatible players although the rhythm sections (pianist Bobby Timmons or Walter Bishop, bassist Teddy Smith or Leroy Vinnegar and drummer J.C. Moses or Art Taylor) differ between the two sessions. McLean was beginning to look forward and be influenced by the avant-garde; the passion he puts into his tone on such tunes as "Smile," "Beautiful Love," "It Could Happen to You" and "Lover Man" is memorable. Dorham was able to keep up with the times during this era and his three compositions (particularly "El Matador" and "Una Mas") add a lot to the music. This

generous CD is worth picking up as an example of veteran players stretching the boundaries of hard bop. —*Scott Yanow*

Una Mas / Apr. 1, 1963 / Blue Note ✦✦✦✦
When one thinks of great talent scouts in jazz, the name of Kenny Dorham is often overlooked. However many top young players benefitted from playing in his groups, and for proof one need look no further than the lineup on this 1963 CD reissue: tenor saxophonist Joe Henderson, bassist Butch Warren and (before either player joined Miles Davis) pianist Herbie Hancock and drummer Tony Williams. Together the quintet performs three of the trumpeter's originals ("Una Mas" is the most famous) along with the standard ballad "If Ever I Would Leave You." Even if the playing time (under 37 minutes) is a bit brief, the explorative yet swinging music lives up to its potential. —*Scott Yanow*

Scandia Skies / Dec. 5, 1963 / SteepleChase ✦✦
This live performance from the Montmartre in Copenhagen is a disappointment considering the lineup. Both Kenny Dorham and Rolf Ericson are on trumpets and joined by a brilliant rhythm section (pianist Tete Montoliu, a teenaged Niels Pedersen on bass and drummer Alex Riel) but, instead of fireworks, the two trumpeters are overly relaxed and play in similar dull styles on the four standards (plus Dorham's title cut); Montoliu is easily the most impressive soloist. It was an off night, making this CD of limited interest. —*Scott Yanow*

Short Story / Dec. 19, 1963 / SteepleChase ✦✦✦
This SteepleChase CD, taken from a live concert from the Montmartre Jazzhus in Copenhagen, features trumpeter Kenny Dorham, fluegelhornist Allan Botschinsky, pianist Tete Montoliu, bassist Niels Pedersen (then only 17) and drummer Alex Riel stretching out on four standards and Dorham's "Short Story." Dorham (featured on "Manha De Carnival") and Botschinsky (who is showcased on "The Touch of Your Lips") display complementary styles but are not shy to occasionally play fiery phrases. However Montoliu (in exciting form) often steals the show during the relaxed set. —*Scott Yanow*

Trompeta Toccata / Sep. 4, 1964 / Blue Note ✦✦✦✦
It seems strange and somewhat tragic that this was trumpeter Kenny Dorham's last full album as a leader, for he was only 40 at the time and still in his prime. Dorham contributed three of the four selections to the session (Joe Henderson's catchy "Mamacita" also receives its debut) and his very underrated abilities as a writer, trumpeter and talent scout are very much in evidence. This modern hard bop quintet set with Henderson on tenor, pianist Tommy Flanagan, bassist Richard Davis and drummer Albert "Tootie" Heath served as a strong (if premature) ending to Dorham's impressive career as a solo artist. —*Scott Yanow*

Dorsey Brothers

Big Band / Swing
Tommy and Jimmy Dorsey first teamed up together on records as the Dorsey Brothers in 1928, but the groups they led through 1933 were strictly studio affairs, featuring classic jazz and hot dance music along with some ballads. In 1934 they decided to put together a regular orchestra and by 1935, with Bob Crosby (and later Bob Eberle) taking the vocals and Glenn Miller providing many of the arrangements, the group was on the brink of success in the early swing era. However a well-publicized argument at a ballroom over the tempo of "I'll Never Say Never Again Again" led to Tommy Dorsey immediately leaving and starting his own separate orchestra.

By 1953 both brothers had had major success with their bands and had long since patched up their differences. Because both orchestras were struggling, it was decided that Jimmy would break up his band and co-lead Tommy's. For nearly four years the Dorsey Brothers Orchestra featured first-class dance music with occasional solos from trumpeter Charlie Shavers and the two brothers; they also had their own television show. With Tommy's sudden death in November 1956 (Jimmy followed seven months later), the partnership came to an end. —*Scott Yanow*

Dorsey Brothers, Vol. 1 / Feb. 14, 1928–Nov. 2, 1928 / TOM ✦✦✦✦
This LP (the first of two volumes) has the first 16 recordings led by The Dorsey Brothers. There are no personnel or date listings but this set is well worth acquiring, for it includes many fine examples of hot dance music, featuring Tommy's trombone, Jimmy's clarinet and alto, and appearances by trumpeters Leo McConville and Phil Napoleon along with a variety of dated singers. Their version of "My Melancholy Baby" is a classic with

TD playing some fine trumpet and bass-saxophonist Adrian Rollini heard in a prominent role. —*Scott Yanow*

Dorsey Brothers, Vol. 2 / Oct. 1928–Nov. 7, 1930 / TOM ✦✦✦
The second of two LP volumes from the collector's label TOM has 16 more examples of Tommy and Jimmy Dorsey in their early days. The music strikes a balance between hot jazz and commercial dance music with the leaders, tenorman Bud Freeman and guitarist Eddie Lang having many fine spots, even if the varying singers also get plenty of space. It's well worth acquiring since most of this material has not been reissued on CD yet. —*Scott Yanow*

● **Best of the Big Bands** / Sep. 14, 1932–Apr. 23, 1934 / Columbia ✦✦✦✦✦
The Dorsey Brothers Orchestra was actually just a series of studio groups until Jimmy and Tommy decided to hit the road in 1934. This strong jazz-oriented CD covering the 1932–34 period actually finds the exciting trumpeter Bunny Berigan consistently stealing solo honors. Highlights include Bill Challis' torrid arrangement of "Someone Stole Gabriel's Horn," "The Blue Room," the novelty tune "Annie's Cousin Fanny" and the original version of what would later become Tommy Dorsey's theme song, "I'm Getting Sentimental over You." —*Scott Yanow*

Mood Hollywood / Sep. 24, 1932–Oct. 17, 1933 / HEP ✦✦✦✦
This excellent LP features 16 performances (including four alternate takes) by The Dorsey Brothers during 1932–33. Bunny Berigan's trumpet solos are the most memorable aspect of these early swing recordings, many of which feature an octet rather than a big band. Highlights include "Someone Stole Gabriel's Horn," two takes of "I'm Getting Sentimental over You" and the brothers' many fine solos. —*Scott Yanow*

Harlem Lullaby / Feb. 1933–Jul. 1933 / Hep ✦✦✦

The Decca Sessions (1934–1935) / Aug. 15, 1934–Feb. 6, 1935 / MCA ✦✦
This budget LP from MCA includes only ten recordings by The Dorsey Brothers Orchestra (less than a half-hour of music) and has a barely readable personnel listing. The only thing that saves this set is the generally strong jazz-oriented music performed by this first-class dance band (heard only a short time before its breakup) including fine versions of "Dippermouth Blues," "Milenberg Joys" and "Honeysuckle Rose." —*Scott Yanow*

Dorsey Brothers' Orchestra 1935 / Jan. 17, 1935 / Circle ✦✦✦
This LP contains music recorded for radio transcriptions by The Dorsey Brothers Orchestra, one of the most interesting new bands heard during this era. The music by this dance band is generally jazz-oriented (although Bob Crosby's three vocals are quite straight), with fine solos from Tommy's trombone and Jimmy's alto and clarinet; the lead trumpet of Charlie Spivak is also heard from. —*Scott Yanow*

Jimmy Dorsey

b. Feb. 29, 1904, Shenandoah, PA, **d.** Jun. 12, 1957, New York, NY
Clarinet, Alto Saxophone / Swing
The older of the two Dorsey Brothers, Jimmy was the superior jazz player. An excellent clarinetist and one of the finest altoists to emerge during the 1920s, JD's jazz playing was overshadowed during the swing era by the commercial hits of his orchestra. Trumpet was actually his first instrument and Jimmy recorded on it a couple of times in the 1920s but by the time he was a teenager he was specializing on reeds. He started out playing with his brother Tommy in Dorsey's Novelty Six, the Scranton Sirens and the California Ramblers and his solos with Red Nichols' Five Pennies made a strong impression. Dorsey recorded with Frankie Trumbauer (including Bix Beiderbecke's "Singin' the Blues"), Jean Goldkette and Paul Whiteman and became a busy studio musician during the Depression. In addition, starting in 1928 he co-led the Dorsey Brothers Orchestra with Tommy. Strictly a studio group at first, the Dorseys put together a full-time big band in 1934, only to break up in late 1935. Jimmy took over the nucleus of the band and, after a period of struggle, the orchestra hit it big in the early '40s with a series of vocal records featuring Bob Eberle and Helen O'Connell. By late in the decade Dorsey was alternating between some boppish big band performances (Maynard Ferguson was among his sidemen) and Dixieland jams with his Dorseyland Band. In 1953 he broke up the band to join Tommy in a new Dorsey Brothers Orchestra that emphasized dance music. After Tommy's sudden death in late 1956, Jimmy

took over the orchestra and had a surprise hit in "So Rare" before passing away from cancer. —*Scott Yanow*

The Best of Jimmy Dorsey / Jul. 7, 1936–Oct. 6, 1943 / MCA ✦✦
This out-of-print two-LP set only has 20 performances and does not list the personnel or recording dates, but it does contain several fine pictures and offers one a good all-around overview of Jimmy Dorsey's commercial recordings. Of the 20 songs, all but four have vocals, mostly by Helen O'Connell and Bob Eberly, with five being vocal duets. Not much is heard from the leader, but it was the singers that made Jimmy Dorsey's Orchestra one of the most popular in the early '40s, so those listeners who enjoyed the hits should pick this one up; it includes "Tangerine," "Brazil," "Green Eyes" and "Besame Mucho." —*Scott Yanow*

★ **Contrasts** / Jul. 7, 1936–Oct. 7, 1943 / GRP ✦✦✦✦
This CD, virtually the only example of Jimmy Dorsey's orchestra currently available on CD, puts the emphasis on his jazz sides rather than the vocal best-sellers. Popular singer Helen O'Connell does make three appearances (including the hit "Tangerine") but most of these selections are instrumentals with Dorsey's alto and clarinet in outstanding form (it was easy to forget how talented an instrumentalist he was during these commercial years). Most of the other fine soloists are lesser names although they include future bandleaders Ray McKinley (on drums) and pianist Freddie Slack. Highlights are "Parade of the Milk Bottle Caps," "I Got Rhythm," "John Silver," "Ducks in Upper Sandusky," Dorsey's theme "Contrasts," and "King Porter Stomp" although there isn't a weak track on this release. Recommended, this is Dorsey's definitive set. —*Scott Yanow*

The Uncollected Jimmy Dorsey & His Orchestra, Vol. 1 (1939–1940) / 1939–1940 / Hindsight ✦✦✦
The first of five Hindsight LPs to document Dorsey's radio transcriptions, this set gives a good all-around picture of his orchestra shortly before it became a major commercial success. There are four vocals apiece by Helen O'Connell and Bob Eberly along with eight fine instrumentals and, although Dorsey (on alto and clarinet) is the only distinctive soloist, the music overall is first-class swing and dance music. —*Scott Yanow*

The Uncollected Jimmy Dorsey & His Orchestra, Vol. 2 (1942–1944) / 1942–1944 / Hindsight ✦✦✦
The second of five LPs released by Hindsight that contain performances cut for radio airplay by the Jimmy Dorsey Orchestra is more jazz-oriented than his usual recordings. Helen O'Connell has a pair of vocals but there are also hot versions of "Just You, Just Me," "I Got Rhythm," "I Would Do Anything for You" and the boppish "Grand Central Getaway" which was composed and arranged by Dizzy Gillespie himself. Such players as pianist Johnny Guarnieri, trumpeter Ray Linn and tenorman Babe Russin are heard from during this fine overview of Dorsey's wartime orchestra. —*Scott Yanow*

The Uncollected Jimmy Dorsey & His Orchestra, Vol. 3 (1949–1951) / 1949+1951 / Hindsight ✦✦✦
The third of five Hindsight LPs featuring Dorsey's orchestra is particularly interesting because it features his big bands of 1949 and 1951, a period of time when he no longer had hits or prospered financially; in fact in 1952 he disbanded and joined brother Tommy's orchestra. Other than one Claire Hogan vocal, these two sessions are comprised of instrumentals, featuring both Dorsey and many members of his talented but no-name crew. —*Scott Yanow*

Muscat Ramble / 1950 / Swing House ✦✦✦✦
During 1949–50, Dorsey enjoyed leading a small group taken out of his big band and playing Dixieland. This English LP finds the hot band (which featured Charlie Teagarden's trumpet and sometimes Cutty Cutshall's trombone) jamming happily on a set of Dixieland standards. Jimmy Dorsey, who mostly sticks to clarinet, clearly enjoyed playing this music; perhaps he should have spent the 1950s in similar small combos instead of permanently joining his brother's orchestra in 1952. —*Scott Yanow*

The Uncollected Jimmy Dorsey & His Orchestra, Vol. 4 (1950) / 1950 / Hindsight ✦✦✦
The fourth of five LPs issued by Hindsight that feature rare airchecks of Jimmy Dorsey's orchestra showcases his band in its declining days. However, despite the three commercial vocals heard on this set, Dorsey's band in 1950 was potentially a strong jazz outfit, featuring Charlie Teagarden and Shorty Sherock on trumpets along with the leader's alto and clarinet. JD's workout

on "Fingerbustin'" and the renditions of "Lover" and "King Porter Stomp" are highpoints of this swinging set. —*Scott Yanow*

The Uncollected Jimmy Dorsey & His Orchestra, Vol. 5: Dorseyland Band (1950) / 1950 / Hindsight ✦✦✦✦

Although he still struggled to keep his orchestra together, Dorsey during 1949-50 often returned to his roots, leading a small contingent out of his big band that he termed "the Original Dorseyland Band." The seven-piece group, featuring Charlie Teagarden's trumpet, trombonist Frank Rehak, Artie Lyons on tenor and Dorsey mostly on clarinet but also on alto is heard on these transcriptions playing a variety of Dixieland tunes in spirited fashion. —*Scott Yanow*

The Fabulous Jimmy Dorsey / Nov. 11, 1956–Jan. 1958 / Fraternity ✦✦

After Tommy Dorsey's death in 1956, Jimmy Dorsey took over his orchestra, although it turned out that he himself was dying from cancer. Ironically JD's final recording date resulted in his first hit in over a decade, "So Rare." Dorsey's alto is actually only heard on four of the 13 selections on this LP; after he passed away trumpeter Lee Castle took over the band and altoist Dick Stabile filled in on the remaining selections. Despite its historic value, this mostly forgettable dance and pop music from 1956-57 conclusively proves that by then the big-band era was long dead. —*Scott Yanow*

Leon Lee Dorsey

b. Mar. 12, 1958, Pittsburgh, PA
Bass / Post-Bop

Leon Lee Dorsey made a strong impression with his 1995 debut disc as a leader, *The Watcher* (on Landmark). A graduate from Oberlin College, the University of Wisconsin and the Manhattan School of Music, he has played as a sideman with a wide variety of top players including Benny Carter, Max Roach, Freddie Hubbard, Horace Silver and Cassandra Wilson. —*Scott Yanow*

● **The Watcher** / Feb. 5, 1994 / Landmark ✦✦✦✦

This is an intriguing debut as a leader for bassist Leon Lee Dorsey. Dorsey, who has played with everyone from Benny Carter and Freddie Hubbard to Oliver Lake and Don Pullen, has really put together two CDs in one. The first six selections are very modern originals which feature his quintet (starring an inspired Vincent Herring on alto and soprano and the hard-toned tenor of Don Braden along with pianist Lafayette Harris, Jr., and drummer Cecil Brooks) in top form. While "Miles," which has plenty of simultaneous fiery improvising by the two saxes, does not really remind one of Miles Davis' music, it is quite memorable as is the haunting ballad "I Am with You Always" which features Herring's soprano as the lead voice. The second half of the program (a blues "Centre Avenue Shuffle," three standards and Ron Carter's "United") are more straight-ahead and give the principals an opportunity to really swing hard within an older format. Dorsey, who only takes a couple of long solos (most notably on "Misty"), is generous in allocating the spotlight but is clearly responsible for this colorful session's success. —*Scott Yanow*

Tommy Dorsey

b. Nov. 19, 1905, Shenandoah, PA, d. Nov. 26, 1956, Greenwich, CT
Trombone / Swing

Tommy Dorsey was the definitive ballad player of the swing era, possessing a beautiful tone and very impressive breath control. A better jazz player than he thought, Dorsey enjoyed playing Dixieland now and then but preferred later in life to stick to ballads. In his early days he played with older brother Jimmy in Dorsey's Novelty Six and the Scranton Sirens before moving to New York and appearing on records with Jean Goldkette, Paul Whiteman and Red Nichols. TD occasionally doubled on trumpet in the 1920s, playing in a style as rough and primitive as his trombone was smooth. He was a busy studio player during the Depression until agreeing to co-lead the Dorsey Brothers Orchestra in 1934. Late in 1935 a blowup on stage led to Tommy leaving and forming his own big band, taking over the Joe Haymes Orchestra. After a short struggle, major hits in 1937 ("Marie" and "Song of India," both highlighted by classic Bunny Berigan trumpet solos) made the Tommy Dorsey Orchestra into a major attraction. TD, who learned from Paul Whiteman how to mix together a diverse repertoire, alternated swing romps, ballads

(often featuring the vocals of his girlfriend Edythe Wright), novelties and Dixieland from his Clambake Seven (which at times included Yank Lawson and Bud Freeman). In the early '40s with the hiring of Sy Oliver as chief arranger, drummer Buddy Rich and a vocal group featuring Frank Sinatra and Jo Stafford, the orchestra evolved and continued to have hits including "I'll Never Smile Again" and "Opus One." In 1942 Dorsey was able to hire the string section of the Artie Shaw Orchestra, greatly expanding his band. By the end of World War II and the collapse of the swing era, TD had to drop the strings and cut back a bit, even breaking up his band for a period after 1946. He appeared in the unfortunate fictional movie *The Fabulous Dorseys* with Jimmy in 1947, reformed his orchestra and did his best to ignore bop (which he detested). Charlie Shavers was the key soloist in Tommy Dorsey's band from the mid-'40s on. In 1953 Jimmy Dorsey agreed to join forces with his brothers. Tommy Dorsey's band was renamed the Dorsey Brothers Orchestra, emphasizing dance music. The nostalgia formula worked well until Tommy's sudden death in November 1956. —*Scott Yanow*

Trumpets and Trombones, Vol. 1 / Aug. 16, 1927–Nov. 18, 1929 / Broadway Intermission ✦✦✦✦✦

This superb LP contains 20 early selections featuring Tommy Dorsey on both trombone and trumpet; he rarely played the latter after 1930. Most of these performances were quite rare (six were issued on this LP for the first time) and they find him featured with Paul Whiteman, Hoagy Carmichael, Seger Ellis, Arthur Schutt and, on most selections, The Dorsey Brothers Orchestra. This hot dance music contains many fine jazz solos from some of the top New York studio players of the late '20s and gives one a valuable look at Tommy Dorsey years before he became "the Sentimental Gentleman of Swing." —*Scott Yanow*

Trumpets and Trombones, Vol. 2 / Apr. 21, 1930–Feb. 1946 / Broadway Intermission ✦✦✦✦

This second LP of Tommy Dorsey rarities features him both in his early studio days with The Dorsey Brothers' Orchestra and with his successful big band. These 14 selections include soundtracks from films, unissued V-Discs, radio broadcasts and early obscure sides from the early '30s. All of the music is quite interesting with "Three Moods" and "Dust" being dance-band classics. Both volumes from this collectors series are highly recommended to all true swing collectors. —*Scott Yanow*

Complete Tommy Dorsey, Vol. 1 (1935) / Sep. 26, 1935–Dec. 21, 1935 / Bluebird ✦✦✦✦

The most complete series of Tommy Dorsey reissues was a two-fer LP program that succeeded in issuing in chronological order all of his recordings from the beginnings of his big band in September 1935 up to March 1939 (eight volumes in all), before corporate indifference brought the program to a halt at its halfway mark. Since Dorsey led a dance band that performed novelties and commercial vocal features in addition to jazz, not all of their recordings were classics. General collectors might be more satisfied with samplers rather than getting everything. *Volume I* in this series has as its highpoints "Weary Blues," Dorsey's theme "I'm Getting Sentimental over You" and the first sides by his Clambake Seven, including "The Music Goes Round and Round." —*Scott Yanow*

Having a Wonderful Time / Dec. 9, 1935–Mar. 2, 1946 / ✦✦✦

A collection of 16 tracks that Tommy Dorsey's Clambake Seven recorded between 1935 and 1947, *Having a Wonderful Time* is a good sampler of the band's work. —*Stephen Thomas Erlewine*

● **Music Goes Round and Round** / Dec. 9, 1935–Feb. 25, 1947 / Bluebird ✦✦✦✦✦

In 1935, Tommy Dorsey first jammed with musicians from his big band in a Dixieland format, calling the little band The Clambake Seven. He recorded frequently with the unit up until 1939 and then on a rare basis up until 1950. This particular CD has 21 of The Clambake's better performances and, although it would have been preferable to reissue all of the group's recordings, this serves as a strong introduction to their music. With such soloists as trumpeters Yank Lawson, Max Kaminsky and Pee Wee Erwin, clarinetists Johnny Mince and Joe Dixon, tenorman Bud Freeman and TD himself, this music was quite joyous and spirited. Edythe Wright ably sings on many of the songs, which are highlighted by the title cut, "At the Codfish Ball," two versions of "The Sheik of Araby" and "When the Midnight Choo-Choo Leaves for Alabama." These are Dixieland recordings that predated the New Orleans revival of 1940. —*Scott Yanow*

Seventeen Number Ones / 1935–1942 / Bluebird ✦✦✦
Good 1990 overview of their biggest-selling popular music standards. —*Ron Wynn*

Complete Tommy Dorsey, Vol. 2 (1936) / Feb. 3, 1936–Oct. 18, 1936 / Bluebird ✦✦✦✦
The second of eight two-fer LPs that trace complete and in chronological order all of Dorsey's recordings from 1935 up to March 1939, this set (like the others) includes gems and duds. During 1936 his band was popular enough to keep going but had not broken through to the bigtime yet. With trumpeter Max Kaminsky, clarinetist Joe Dixon and the great tenor Bud Freeman contributing solos and Edythe Wright and the commercial singer Jack Leonard heard on vocals, the music ranges from pop schlock to some big-band swing (such as "Royal Garden Blues," "That's a Plenty" and "After You've Gone") and two songs by Dorsey's Clambake Seven. —*Scott Yanow*

Complete Tommy Dorsey, Vol. 3 (1936–1937) / Nov. 18, 1936–Mar. 20, 1937 / Bluebird ✦✦✦✦
The third LP two-fer in this *Complete* series (which died after the eighth volume when Bluebird lost interest), this set is the most essential of the bunch because it includes the 18 selections that the great trumpeter Bunny Berigan cut with Dorsey. Not only do these include the major hits "Marie" and "Song of India" (which made Tommy Dorsey into a household name) but memorable solos on "Mr. Ghost Goes to Town," "Melody in F," "Liebestraum" and "Mendelssohn's Spring Song." Not all of the other songs cut directly before and after Berigan's stint were classics, but there are superior versions of "Keepin' out of Mischief Now," "Black Eyes" and "Jammin'." —*Scott Yanow*

Radio Days, Vol. 1 / Nov. 30, 1936–Jan. 4, 1937 / Starline ✦✦✦
Solid swing music comes from Dorsey's orchestra just before he hit it big with "Marie." Although Bunny Berigan is on a few of these songs, the main soloists on this CD are tenorman Bud Freeman, trumpeter Max Kaminsky and clarinetist Joe Dixon along with Dorsey's trombone. Swinging instrumentals and vocals by Edythe Wright and The Three Esquires are heard in an enjoyable program of Dorsey radio appearances. —*Scott Yanow*

Complete Tommy Dorsey, Vol. 4 (1937) / Apr. 15, 1937–Jul. 10, 1937 / Bluebird ✦✦✦✦
The post-Berigan era found Dorsey heading one of the most popular of all big bands, rivaling Benny Goodman's. This fourth of eight LP two-fers has all of his recordings cut during a three-month period, including 15 selections by Dorsey's Clambake Seven (which was now featuring trumpeter Pee Wee Erwin, Bud Freeman's tenor and clarinetist Johnny Mince in addition to singer Edythe Wright) and a variety of big-band titles, most memorably "Satan Takes a Holiday," "Beale Street Blues" and a truly bizarre version of "Am I Dreaming?" —*Scott Yanow*

Complete Tommy Dorsey, Vol. 5 (1937) / Jul. 10, 1937–Oct. 14, 1937 / Bluebird ✦✦✦✦
The fifth in Bluebird's superb series of LP two-fers that trace *The Complete Tommy Dorsey* up until 1939 is highlighted by 11 performances by his Dixielandish Clambake Seven, along with "Night and Day" and "Once in a While" from his big band. As with the others in this admirable series, there are also plenty of novelties and forgettable vocals included, but Dorsey fanatics should go out of their way to get all of these highly appealing sets. —*Scott Yanow*

Complete Tommy Dorsey, Vol. 6 (1937–1938) / Dec. 6, 1937–Mar. 10, 1938 / Bluebird ✦✦✦✦
The sixth out of the eight volumes in *The Complete Tommy Dorsey* series of two-fer LPs has only two Clambake Seven performances and no major hits but, even with the large amount of so-so Jack Leonard vocals, there are also many examples of first-class dance music and swing from the very versatile orchestra. It's worth picking up by those Dorsey fans who are wise enough to search for all eight volumes. —*Scott Yanow*

Complete Tommy Dorsey, Vol. 7 (1938) / Apr. 11, 1938–Sep. 22, 1938 / Bluebird ✦✦✦✦
The seventh in this series of eight LP two-fers contains all of the recordings made by his orchestra during a five-month period in 1938. Seven commercial Jack Leonard vocals are compensated for by seven performances from Dorsey's Clambake Seven, a Dixieland outfit taken out of his big band. With such tunes as "Music, Maestro Please," "Panama," "Chinatown, My Chinatown," "The Sheik of Araby" and the big hit "Boogie Woogie," this set

(along with all the others in this valuable series) is recommended to all true Tommy Dorsey fans. —*Scott Yanow*

Complete Tommy Dorsey, Vol. 8 (1938–1939) / Sep. 29, 1938–Mar. 8, 1939 / Bluebird ✦✦✦✦
The eighth and unfortunately the final volume in this superb LP two-fer series closed the program of Tommy Dorsey recordings partway through the session of March 8, 1939, thanks to the indifference of RCA Records. This very worthy series reissued all of his studio recordings during the four years since he formed his own band, and, although it necessarily included both gems and duds, the former generally outnumbered the latter. *Volume 8* is highlighted by "Tin Roof Blues," "Hawaiian War Chant," the two-part "Milenberg Joys" and The Clambake Seven's "You Must Have Been a Beautiful Baby." All of the volumes in this increasingly hard-to-find series are recommended to serious swing fans. —*Scott Yanow*

★ **Yes, Indeed!** / Jun. 15, 1939–Sep. 20, 1945 / Bluebird ✦✦✦✦✦
This CD includes many of Tommy Dorsey's very best recordings from 1939–42 along with four selections dating from 1944–45. During this period the sound of his orchestra had changed from the earlier days, thanks in large part to Sy Oliver's arrangements and the hard-driving drums of Buddy Rich. With such soloists as trumpeter Ziggy Elman, tenor saxophonist Don Lodice and clarinetist Johnny Mince (in addition to Dorsey's trombone), this orchestra could play jazz with the best of their contemporaries although many of their other recordings (not included here) actually showcased vocals and dance music. Highlights of this recommended disc include "Well, All Right," "Stomp It Off," "Quiet Please," "Swing High," "Swanee River," "Deep River" and "Well, Git It!," while the later tracks include "Opus #1," the Charlie Shavers feature "At the Fat Man's" and a guest appearance by Duke Ellington on "The Minor Goes Muggin'." —*Scott Yanow*

Sentimental Gentleman / Jun. 1, 1940–Aug. 13, 1944 / RCA ✦✦✦
This two-LP set, released probably in the early '60s and housed in a very attractive box, has a variety of radio appearances by Tommy Dorsey's orchestra in the early '40s, some of which are remakes of his hits, although there are a few unusual items. Most interesting are a heated "Hawaiian War Chant" featuring Buddy Rich and Ziggy Elman, Frank Sinatra singing the Jack Leonard hit "Marie," Ziggy Elman reprising "And the Angels Sing", alternate versions of "Well, Git It!" and "Swanee River," and Frank Sinatra's "The Song Is You" from his farewell appearance with the band. This will be a very difficult set to find. —*Scott Yanow*

All-Time Greatest Dorsey/Sinatra Hits, Vol. 1 / 1940–1942 / RCA ✦✦✦✦
When RCA decided to issue its early '40s Tommy Dorsey recordings containing Frank Sinatra vocals on compact disc, it abandoned the chronological sequencing found on the Grammy-winning album series *The Dorsey/Sinatra Sessions* and instead jumped back and forth through the catalog. This first volume of four contains some of the biggest hits, notably "I'll Never Smile Again" and "I'll Be Seeing You," and thus is the best selection for beginners. But be sure to move on to Vol. 2 and Vol. 3 and, especially, Vol. 4, which contains Sinatra's first solo session. —*William Ruhlmann*

All-Time Greatest Dorsey/Sinatra Hits, Vol. 2 / 1940–1942 / RCA ✦✦✦
With Frank Sinatra. Fine companion volume to first Dorsey/Sinatra overview set. —*Ron Wynn*

All-Time Greatest Dorsey/Sinatra Hits, Vol. 3 / 1940–1942 / RCA ✦✦✦

All-Time Greatest Dorsey/Sinatra Hits, Vol. 4 / 1940–1942 / RCA ✦✦✦

Well Git It! / Sep. 30, 1943–Jan. 4, 1946 / Vintage Jazz ✦✦✦
Tommy Dorsey's wartime orchestra is well featured on these radio airchecks. With such stars as drummer Buddy Rich (and on three songs, Gene Krupa), clarinetist Buddy DeFranco and trumpet Charlie Shavers Dorsey kept up his musical standards despite the change in both the public's taste and the continuing evolution of jazz. With the Sentimentalists, Bonnie Lou Williams and Stuart Foster contributing vocals, the mixture of jazz and dance music heard on this CD is typical of Dorsey's mid-'40s music. —*Scott Yanow*

The Post-War Era / Jan. 31, 1946–Jun. 13, 1950 / Bluebird ✦✦✦
The funny part about this CD is that there is relatively little Dorsey on it. His trombone is mostly heard in a cameo role with

the exception of "Trombonology." The real stars of this fine CD are arranger Bill Finegan (who wrote the charts for the majority of these 22 performances) and the fiery trumpeter Charlie Shavers, although drummer Louis Bellson also gets featured on "Drumology." After 1946, Tommy Dorsey's music was definitely behind the times (he always had a strong resistance to bebop) and some of these later tracks sound like tired dance music, but this CD does an excellent job of summing up his better recordings of the 1946-50 period, leaving out the real dog tunes and bad vocalists he sometimes utilized. —*Scott Yanow*

At the Fat Man's / May 29, 1946–Nov. 8, 1948 / Hep ✦✦✦
This English LP features three different versions of The Tommy Dorsey Orchestra heard in radio performances: his mid-'40s unit, the new big band he reorganized in 1947, and the unit he led the following year that never recorded commercially due to the recording strike. With trumpeter Charlie Shavers, tenorman Don Lodice and drummer Louis Bellson among the stars, there are good examples of Dorsey's postwar music, a period of time when the swing he continued to play with enthusiasm was slipping permanently behind the times. —*Scott Yanow*

Tommy Dorsey (1950–52) / 1950–1952 / First Time Records ✦✦✦
In the early '50s, Tommy Dorsey mostly recorded commercial (and long out of print) music for Decca, so these live performances are quite welcome. Emphasizing Dorsey's jazz side, one not only hears Dorsey's trombone but Charlie Shavers' trumpet and Sam Donahue's tenor featured throughout this LP as well. Bill Finegan contributed some of the arrangements to what would be Tommy Dorsey's last big band before rejoining forces with his brother Jimmy Dorsey for a final nostalgia-based orchestra. —*Scott Yanow*

Ray Draper (Raymond Allen Draper)

b. Aug. 3, 1940, New York, NY, d. Nov. 1, 1982, New York, NY
Tuba / Hard Bop
Ray Draper was an excellent tuba soloist, one of the few in the 1950s to utilize the instrument for bop improvisations. After attending the Manhattan School of Music, he played and recorded with Jackie McLean (1956–57), worked with Donald Byrd and recorded with John Coltrane (1958). Draper was with Max Roach's band (1958–59) and worked with Don Cherry in the early '60s. However from that point on drugs played havoc with his life. He did play later in the 1960s with Horace Tapscott, Archie Shepp, Brother Jack McDuff (recording with him in 1971) and Howard Johnson's group Gravity, but had largely dropped out of music by the time he was killed during a robbery. Draper led sessions during 1957-60 for Prestige, New Jazz, Jubilee and Epic. —*Scott Yanow*

● **Ray Draper Quintet Featuring John Coltrane** / Dec. 20, 1957 / New Jazz ✦✦✦✦

A Tuba Jazz / 1958 / Jubilee ✦✦✦

Kenny Drew

b. Aug. 28, 1928, New York, NY, d. Aug. 4, 1993, Copenhagen, Denmark
Piano / Hard Bop
A talented bop-based pianist (whose son has been one of the brightest pianists of the 1990s), Kenny Drew was somewhat underrated due to his decision to move permanently to Copenhagen in 1964. He made his recording debut in 1949 with Howard McGhee and in the 1950s was featured on sessions with the who's who of jazz including Charlie Parker, Coleman Hawkins, Lester Young, Milt Jackson, Buddy DeFranco's quartet, Dinah Washington and Buddy Rich (1958). Drew led sessions for Blue Note, Norgran, Pacific Jazz, Riverside and the obscure Judson label during 1953-60; most of the sessions are currently available on CD. He moved to Paris in 1961 and relocated to Copenhagen in 1964 where he was co-owner of the Matrix label. He formed a duo with Niels-Henning Orsted Pederson and worked regularly at the Montmartre. Drew recorded many dates for SteepleChase in the 1970s and remained active up until his death. —*Scott Yanow*

Talkin' and Walkin' / Dec. 1955 / Blue Note ✦✦✦
Quartet. Prototype hard-bop/mainstream Blue Note, with Drew immense on piano. —*Ron Wynn*

The Kenny Drew Trio / Sep. 20, 1956+Sep. 26, 1956 / Original Jazz Classics ✦✦✦✦
Kenny Drew, with the assistance of bassist Paul Chambers (whose bowed solos are always welcome) and drummer Philly Joe Jones,

explores six standards and two of his originals. Although Drew would have to move to Europe in the early '60s in order to get the recognition he deserved, it is obvious (in hindsight) from this enjoyable date that he was already a major improviser. —*Scott Yanow*

Trio-Quartet-Quintet / Sep. 20, 1956–Oct. 15, 1957 / Original Jazz Classics ✦✦✦
A wonderful collection of the first-rate pianist in varied contexts, with Donald Byrd (tpt), Paul Chambers (b), and Philly Joe Jones (d) on the job. —*Ron Wynn*

★ **Pal Joey** / Oct. 15, 1957 / Original Jazz Classics ✦✦✦✦✦
It seems strange that (with the exception of a 1960 session for Blue Note) this would be pianist Kenny Drew's last session as a leader until 1973. With bassist Wilbur Ware and drummer Philly Joe Jones, Drew interprets eight Rodgers And Hart tunes, five written for the play *Pal Joey* and three of their earlier hits that were included in the film version. Drew contributes swing and subtle bop-based improvising to these superior melodies (which are highlighted by "Bewitched, Bothered and Bewildered," "I Could Write a Book" and "The Lady Is a Tramp") and the results are quite memorable. —*Scott Yanow*

Undercurrent / Dec. 11, 1960 / Blue Note ✦✦✦✦✦

Duo, Vol. 1 / Apr. 2, 1973 / SteepleChase ✦✦✦✦

Everything I Love / Oct. 1973–Dec. 31, 1973 / SteepleChase ✦✦✦

Duo, Vol. 2 / Feb. 11, 1974–Feb. 12, 1974 / SteepleChase ✦✦✦✦

If You Could See Me Now / May 21, 1974–May 22, 1994 / SteepleChase ✦✦✦✦

Morning / Sep. 8, 1975 / SteepleChase ✦✦✦

In Concert / Feb. 3, 1977 / SteepleChase ✦✦✦

Lite Flite / Feb. 6, 1977 / SteepleChase ✦✦✦✦

Ruby My Dear / Aug. 23, 1977 / SteepleChase ✦✦✦

Home Is Where the Soul Is / Oct. 15, 1978 / Xanadu ✦✦✦
Brilliant, tasty, and exciting piano and compositions. —*Ron Wynn*

For Sure / Oct. 16, 1978 / Xanadu ✦✦✦✦✦
Robust and dynamic session from the late '70s. —*Ron Wynn*

It Might As Well Be Spring / Nov. 23, 1981 / Soul Note ✦✦✦

Your Soft Eyes / Nov. 25, 1981–Nov. 26, 1981 / Soul Note ✦✦✦

And Far Away / Feb. 21, 1983 / Soul Note ✦✦✦
He can still drive a group and play with class, elegance and beauty. —*Ron Wynn*

Recollections / May 14, 1989–May 15, 1989 / Timeless ✦✦✦

Kenny Drew, Jr.

b. 1958, New York, NY
Piano / Hard Bop, Post-Bop
Despite sharing his father's name, Kenny Drew, Jr. was raised by his aunt and grandparents and does not consider Kenny Drew, Sr. to be an influence. He was taught classical music by his mother and grandmother and gigged in clubs as a teenager. He made his recording debut with Charnett Moffett and worked with Stanley Jordan and OTB and recorded with Eddie Gomez, Sadao Watanabe, and the Mingus Big Band. In 1990 Drew won the Great American Jazz Piano competition at the Jacksonville Jazz Festival. He first led sessions for the Japanese label Jazz City and has since had record dates for Antilles, Concord (a solo Maybeck Recital Hall concert) and Claves. —*Scott Yanow*

The Flame Within / Nov. 1987 / Jazz City ✦✦✦

Third Phase / Jun. 1989 / Jazz City ✦✦✦

Kenny Drew, Jr. / Jun. 6, 1991–Jun. 7, 1991 / Antilles ✦✦✦✦
Debut album by the gifted son of a jazz legend. Kenny Drew, Jr. demonstrates that genetics do sometimes play a role in jazz. He doesn't yet have the total command or timing of his famous father, but Kenny Drew, Jr. shows he is well on his way to developing those skills. —*Ron Wynn*

A Look Inside / Jun. 22, 1992–Jun. 24, 1992 / PolyGram ✦✦✦✦

★ **Maybeck Recital Hall Series, Vol. 39** / Aug. 7, 1994 / Concord Jazz ✦✦✦✦✦

Paquito D'Rivera

b. Jun. 4, 1948, Havana, Cuba
Clarinet, Alto Saxophone / Bop, Afro-Cuban Jazz
One of Cuba's finest exports, Paquito D'Rivera is a distinctive altoist with an impressive upper register and a skilled clarinetist.

He studied at the Havana Conservatory from 1960 and played professionally starting when he was 14. After playing in an Army band, D'Rivera joined the Orquesta Cubana de Musica Moderna and Irakere (1973-80); the latter was Cuba's top band. After defecting to the U.S. in 1980, D'Rivera moved to New York and worked with Dizzy Gillespie and McCoy Tyner before starting his own band. He has directed Dizzy Gillespie's last group, the United Nation Orchestra, since Dizzy's death. D'Rivera has recorded an impressive string of albums for Columbia, Chesky, Messidor and Candid. —*Scott Yanow*

Blowin' / 1981 / CBS ✦✦✦✦
Altoist Paquito D'Rivera's first American recording after defecting from Cuba is an often-jubilant affair. D'Rivera, who also plays some soprano and flute on this album, is heard in groups ranging from a duet with pianist Jorge Dalto to a septet. The impressive lineup also includes pianist Hilton Ruiz, bassist Eddie Gomez and drummer Ignacio Berroa, among others. The music is high-quality modern bebop with a strong dose of Latin rhythms—a fine example of D'Rivera's talents. —*Scott Yanow*

Mariel / 1982 / Columbia ✦✦✦✦✦
With pianists Hilton Ruiz and Jorge Dalto. Becoming more funky. Also includes "Moment's Notice." Funk and jazz from Cuban fire-spitter. —*Michael G. Nastos*

Live at Keystone Korner / Jul. 17, 1983-Jul. 18, 1983 / Columbia ✦✦✦✦

Why Not / Jun. 19, 1984-Jun. 21, 1984 / Columbia ✦✦✦✦✦
With a backup crew that includes trumpeter Claudio Roditi, pianist Michel Camilo, guest Toots Thielemans on harmonica and guitar and several fiery percussionists, it is not surprising that this is a very successful date. Paquito D'Rivera, heard here on alto and clarinet, has long had a very distinctive bop-oriented style and his technique (which includes a wide range) and creativity is fully displayed on this well-rounded set. Highpoints include "Manteca" and Camilo's "Why Not." —*Scott Yanow*

Explosion / Jul. 1985 / Columbia ✦✦✦

Manhattan Burn / Sep. 30, 1986-Oct. 1, 1986 / Columbia ✦✦✦

Celebration / Sep. 1987-Oct. 1987 / Columbia ✦✦✦✦
1988 release, some high-flying moments. Claudio Roditi (tpt) is great. —*Ron Wynn*

Return to Ipanema / Mar. 1, 1989-Mar. 2, 1989 / Town Crier ✦✦✦✦

Tico! Tico! / Jun. 28, 1989-Aug. 16, 1989 / Chesky ✦✦✦
Paquito D'Rivera's alto and clarinet skills were ably displayed on this session, which featured him working in Afro-Latin, salsa, funk, swing and hard bop. Compositions ranged from intense, jam-flavored numbers with torrid solos, like "Recife's Blue" and the title tune, to introspective ballads, group pieces with rhythmically explosive sections and numbers displaying classical influences. The unifying force was D'Rivera, who also played tenor, but was most prominent on clarinet, doing both swing-oriented and looser, freer solos. While not as strict a jazz vehicle as his Columbia dates, this session presented a more eclectic, versatile Paquito D'Rivera. —*Ron Wynn*

Reunion / Aug. 1990 / Messidor ✦✦✦✦
Excellent session done for German label, distributed domestically by Rounder. D'Rivera at the top of his game. —*Ron Wynn*

★ **Who's Smoking?!** / May 21, 1991-May 22, 1991 / Candid ✦✦✦✦✦
Hot, surging Afro-Latin set by alto saxophonist Paquito D'Rivera, matching him with both celebrated veterans and established session stars. D'Rivera doesn't falter through any of these pieces and gets strong assistance from special guest James Moody and super trumpet solos by Claudio Roditi. The percussive backgrounds supplied by Danilo Perez and Al Foster are varied and constantly shifting and changing. —*Ron Wynn*

Havana Cafe / Aug. 28, 1991-Aug. 29, 1991 / Chesky ✦✦✦✦

40 Years of Cuban Jam Sessions / 1993 / Messidor ✦✦✦✦
Despite its title, this CD does not offer one a sampler of Cuban jams of the past 40 years but it does contain a recent session featuring 25 of the top Cuban expatriates. Organized to a large extent by altoist Paquito D'Rivera (who is only actually on six of the 11 selections), these performances utilize a wide variety of instrumentations. Carlos Gomez has a vocal, there is a laidback feature for Jose Silva's tenor, Juan Pablo Torres takes a couple of impressive trombone solos and, on "Descarga Para Banda Y

Combo," there is a humorous blending of circus music, Dixieland and a boppish blues. With D'Rivera in fine form on alto and clarinet during his appearances, this is a continually interesting and stimulating set. —*Scott Yanow*

A Night in Englewood / Jul. 1993 / Messidor ✦✦✦✦✦

Ray Drummond
b. Nov. 23, 1946, Brookline, MA
Bass / Hard Bop
Early on Ray Drummond played with Michael White and Bobby Hutcherson in San Francisco. After attending Stanford Business School (1974-77) he has had a countless number of jobs as a supportive bassist with everyone from David Murray to Pharoah Sanders to the New York Quartet, Mingus Dynasty and Kenny Barron. Drummond has also led sessions for Nilva, Criss Cross and DMP. —*Scott Yanow*

Susanita / Jul. 17, 1984-Jul. 19, 1984 / Nilva ✦✦✦

● **Camera in a Bag** / Dec. 28, 1989 / Criss Cross ✦✦✦✦✦

The Essence / Oct. 8, 1990-Oct. 9, 1990 / DMP ✦✦✦✦
The third album with premier bassist Ray Drummond stepping out from the rhythm section to serve as leader. But this trio venture seems more cooperative, as pianist Hank Jones, Drummond, and drummer Billy Higgins zipped through the program of standards and originals sounding almost like one player. —*Ron Wynn*

Excursion / 1993 / Arabesque ✦✦✦

Urszula Dudziak
b. Oct. 22, 1943, Straconka, Poland
Vocals / Fusion, Post-Bop
Urszula Dudziak, wife of violinist Michal Urbaniak, made a big impression in the mid-'70s with three innovative albums for Arista and Inner City, but has maintained a low profile ever since. Dudziak had piano lessons and took up singing in her native Poland in the late '50s. She met Urbaniak in 1962, performed in Scandinavia (1965-69) and in 1974 settled in New York. Dudziak employed electronics to accentuate her wide range and explorative style, recording both with and without Urbaniak and working in the 1980s with Archie Shepp, Lester Bowie and Bobby McFerrin. —*Scott Yanow*

Newborn Light / Nov. 13, 1972 / Cameo ✦✦✦

● **Urszula** / 1976 / Arista ✦✦✦✦✦

Future Talk / Feb. 1979 / Inner City ✦✦✦✦
A showcase for the unusual, sometimes thrilling vocal acrobatics of Urzula Dudziak. She could do a song straight, but seldom chose to do so, leaping octaves, scatting, and reworking lyrics. She was joined occasionally by her husband Michael Urbaniak on lyricon. —*Ron Wynn*

Sorrow Is Not Forever...But Love Is / 1983 / Keytone ✦✦✦

George Duke
b. Jan. 12, 1946, San Rafael, CA
Keyboards / Funk, Instrumental Pop
George Duke showed a great deal of promise early in his career as a jazz pianist and keyboardist but has forsaken creative music to be a pop producer. Inspired early on by Les McCann, he worked with a trio in San Francisco during the mid-'60s. In 1969 Duke accompanied Jean-Luc Ponty, recording with the violinist. After eight months with Don Ellis' Orchestra, he joined Frank Zappa for much of 1970. Duke spent 1971-72 with Cannonball Adderley and then returned to Zappa for 1973-75. In 1975 he worked with Sonny Rollins, co-led a group with Billy Cobham and then formed a funk band (the Clarke-Duke Project) with Stanley Clarke. By the late '70s he was completely outside of jazz, playing R&B and producing projects for pop artists. Although he has since expressed interest in returning to active playing, little of George Duke's post-1976 work is relevant to jazz. —*Scott Yanow*

I Love the Blues: She Heard My Cry / 1975 / Polydor ✦✦✦

● **Solo Keyboard Album** (1976) / 1976 / Epic ✦✦✦✦

Brazilian Love Affair / 1979 / Epic ✦✦✦

Secret Rendezvous / 1983 / Epic ✦✦

Muir Woods Suite / Jul. 12, 1996 / Warner Brothers ✦✦✦

Dukes Of Dixieland
Group / Dixieland
Trumpeter Frank Assunto (who was also a fine singer) and his

brother/trombonist Fred Assunto formed the Dukes of Dixieland in 1948 and won a Horace Heidt talent contest. In 1950 they started a long engagement at the Famous Door in New Orleans. An early member of the group was clarinetist Pete Fountain and the Assuntos' father Papa Jac joined the band in 1955 on banjo and second trombone. The group's first recordings were for Band Wagon in 1951 and Fountain appeared on their 1955 Vik date but the Dukes really caught on with a dozen albums cut for Audio Fidelity during 1956–60. During this period the Dukes also recorded twice with Louis Armstrong. The band hit its peak with their Columbia records of 1961–64 (featuring clarinetist Jerry Fuller), particularly an exciting set recorded at Disneyland. Their Decca and Coral dates of 1965–66, although of some interest, are a step down in quality. Both Fred (1966) and Frank (1974) died of cancer. In the late '70s a new Dukes of Dixieland was formed but this group is somewhat corny and inferior in quality, having no real connection to the original band. —Scott Yanow

The Dukes of Dixieland at the Jazz Band Ball / May 3, 1955 / VIK ✦✦✦

You've Got to Hear It to Believe It, Vol. 1 / Mar. 1956 / Audio Fidelity ✦✦✦

You've Got to Hear It to Believe It, Vol. 2 / 1956 / Audio Fidelity ✦✦✦

Dukes of Dixieland: Marching Along / 1956–1957 / Audio Fidelity ✦✦✦

Dukes of Dixieland, Bourbon Street / 1957 / Audio Fidelity ✦✦✦

Circus Time with the Dukes of Dixieland / Sep. 1957 / Audio Fidelity ✦✦✦

Mardi Gras Time / Sep. 1957 / Audio Fidelity ✦✦✦

Minstrel Time / 1957 / Audio Fidelity ✦✦✦

Up the Mississippi with The Dukes of Dixieland / Mar. 1958 / Audio Fidelity ✦✦✦

The Dukes of Dixieland on Campus / 1958 / Audio Fidelity ✦✦✦

Satchmo and the Dukes of Dixieland / 1959 / Happy Hour ✦✦✦✦

During his latter years, many criticized Louis Armstrong for falling into set patterns and putting more emphasis on entertaining than playing. His critics have since re-evaluated much of his final output and found that there was more substance in his solos and vocals than they had assumed. That's the case on this 1959 date with his favorite New Orleans band, The Dukes of Dixieland. While there's certainly nothing new from a song standpoint, Armstrong and the group made hot, frequently dazzling, traditional jazz. The date was digitally remastered for this 1988 CD, and Armstrong's singing and playing sound even more vivid. —Ron Wynn

Dukes of Dixieland at Carnegie Hall / 1959 / Audio Fidelity ✦✦✦

Dukes of Dixieland Piano Ragtime / 1960 / Audio Fidelity ✦✦✦

Breakin' It up on Broadway / Aug. 29, 1961–Sep. 1, 1961 / Columbia ✦✦✦✦

Now Hear This / Jan. 15, 1962 / Columbia ✦✦✦✦✦

Dixieland Hootnanny / Mar. 16, 1962–Jun. 16, 1962 / Columbia ✦✦✦

★ **The Dukes of Dixieland at Disneyland** / Sep. 29, 1962 / Columbia ✦✦✦✦✦

Struttin' at the World's Fair / Feb. 17, 1964+Mar. 23, 1964 / Columbia ✦✦✦

Live at Bourbon Street / Feb. 1965 / Decca ✦✦✦

Come on and Hear / 1965 / Decca ✦✦

Sunrise Sunset / 1966 / Decca ✦✦

Come to the Cabaret / 1966 / Decca ✦✦

Candy Dulfer

b. Sept. 19, 1969, Amsterdam, Netherlands
Alto Saxophone / Pop, Crossover
Thus far it is very difficult to take Candy Dulfer seriously. She seems to spend more time posing with her sax than learning to play it. Heavily influenced by David Sanborn, Dulfer has decent technique and is modest about her own playing but her first two BMG releases (the subtly titled *Saxuality* and *Sax-a-go-go*) were big sellers anyway. At this point there is not much incentive for her to improve, but one can hope. —Scott Yanow

● **Saxuality** / 1991 / Arista ✦✦✦
Sax-A-Go-Go / 1993 / RCA ✦✦

Cornell Dupree

b. Dec. 1942, Fort Worth, TX
Guitar / Blues, Soul Jazz
Long a top R&B session player, Cornell Dupree led excellent jazz-oriented sets for Amazing and Kokopelli in the early '90s, showing that he was also capable of playing swinging jazz. Dupree was with King Curtis in 1962 before appearing on more than 2,500 records in the studios. He toured with Aretha Franklin (1967–76) and a variety of top pop and R&B acts and in the early '70s worked with the group Stuff. Dupree's blues-oriented playing is quite appealing. —Scott Yanow

Can't Get Through / Jun. 1991 / Amazing ✦✦✦✦

Child's Play / May 26, 1993 / Amazing ✦✦✦

● **Bop 'N' Blues** / Nov. 15, 1994–Feb. 13, 1995 / Kokopelli ✦✦✦✦✦
Guitarist Cornell Dupree has long been famous for his blues and R&B solos, so even he was surprised (and a bit apprehensive) when label-head Herbie Mann suggested he record a variety of bop-oriented standards. As it turned out, several of the tunes were blues anyway (such as "Bags' Groove," "Now's the Time" and "Walkin'") and Dupree was free to adapt the other songs to his own style. "Freedom Jazz Dance" became a funky vamp while "My Little Suede Shoes" was drastically slowed down and stretched out. With backing from a versatile rhythm section and occasional contributions from altoist Bobby Watson, trumpeter Terell Stafford and baritonist Ronnie Cuber, Dupree sounds perfectly at home throughout this fine CD, even on "Manteca" and "'Round Midnight." —Scott Yanow

Eddie Durham

b. Aug. 19, 1906, San Marcos, TX, **d.** Mar. 6, 1987, New York, NY
Guitar, Trombone, Arranger / Swing
Eddie Durham, a somewhat forgotten name in jazz history, was the first important jazz soloist to be featured on electric guitar (in 1938 with the Kansas City Five), predating Charlie Christian by a year. He also played trombone throughout most of his career and was quite significant as a swing-era arranger too. He started playing guitar and trombone with six siblings in the Durham Brothers band. Durham toured in some territory bands in the Midwest, was with Walter Page's Blue Devils and then worked with Bennie Moten (1929–33) with whom he made his recording debut. After moving to New York in 1934, Durham worked as an arranger with Willie Bryant and then played with Jimmie Lunceford (1935–37) and Count Basie (1937–38). He also contributed arrangements to Artie Shaw and Glenn Miller, in 1940 led a short-lived big band of his own and during 1941–43 was the musical director for the International Sweethearts of Rhythm. Durham later led an otherwise all-female group and freelanced mostly as an arranger. In 1969 he returned to active playing with Buddy Tate and in later years played with the Countsmen (with whom he recorded) and the Harlem Blues and Jazz Band. Among Durham's most famous arrangements through the years were "Moten Swing" for Bennie Moten, Jimmy Lunceford's "Lunceford Special," several notable charts for Count Basie ("Topsy," "Swinging the Blues" and "Jumpin' at the Woodside") and Glenn Miller's "In the Mood." —Scott Yanow

Dutch Swing College Band

Group / Dixieland
Formed in May 1945 by clarinetist Peter Schilperoort, the Dutch Swing College Band has long been considered one of Europe's top Dixieland and swing bands. In addition to many albums on their own, the group welcomed such guests as Sidney Bechet (1951), Hot Lips Page, Albert Nicholas, Jimmy Witherspoon, Billy Butterfield, Joe Venuti and Teddy Wilson, recording with all but Page and Nicholas. The band has continued to tour despite the death of Schilperoort in 1990, although its peak years were the 1970s. —Scott Yanow

● **Digital Dixie** / Jul. 12, 1981 / Philips ✦✦✦✦✦
Digital Dutch / Jul. 18, 1982 / Philips ✦✦✦✦
Digital Anniversary / Jul. 12, 1985 / Philips ✦✦✦✦

Johnny Dyani

b. Nov. 30, 1945, East London, South Africa, **d.** Jul. 11, 1986, Berlin, Germany
Bass / Avant-Garde, World Music
One of the top South African expatriates, Johnny Dyani had a lyri-

cal style and an authoritative tone on bass. He was with Chris McGregor's Blue Notes during 1962–65, leaving South Africa with them. He settled in London for five years, working with the top local players and recorded in South America with Steve Lacy and Enrico Rava in 1968. Dyani was also with the Spontaneous Music Ensemble (1969). In the early '70s he moved to Denmark where he worked with John Tchicai, Don Cherry, Abdullah Ibrahim, David Murray and Joseph Jarman. Dyani can be heard on many SteepleChase recordings. —*Scott Yanow*

Witchdoctor's Son / Mar. 15, 1978 / SteepleChase ✦✦✦

★ **Song for Biko** / Jul. 18, 1978 / SteepleChase ✦✦✦✦
With Don Cherry (cnt). Very enjoyable progressive music. —*Michael G. Nastos*

African Bass / Nov. 14, 1979 / Red ✦✦✦

Mbizo / Feb. 24, 1981 / SteepleChase ✦✦✦

Grandmother's Teaching / Mar. 1983 / Jam ✦✦✦

Afrika / Oct. 1, 1983 / SteepleChase ✦✦✦✦✦
The South African bassist/pianist/composer with septet. Well-respected as a musician worldwide. A unique amalgam of styles. —*Michael G. Nastos*

Born under the Heat / Nov. 18, 1983 / Dragon ✦✦✦

Angolian Cry / Jul. 23, 1985 / SteepleChase ✦✦✦✦

Ann Dyer

Vocals / Avant-Garde
An impressive chancetaking singer, Ann Dyer was one of the hits of the 1994 Monterey Jazz Festival, stretching out standards and really pouring a lot of emotion into Ornette Coleman's "Lonely Woman." She graduated from Mills College in 1979 with a modern dance degree and had plans to be a dancer but her singing gained better reviews. Dyer recorded her debut for the Mr. Brown label in 1993. —*Scott Yanow*

● **Ann Dyer & The No Good Time Fairies** / Aug. 30, 1993–Sep. 1, 1993 / Mr. Brown ✦✦✦✦✦
One of the most exciting new singers of the mid-'90s, Ann Dyer is a true improviser who is not afraid to really cut loose and show her emotions. Blessed with a wide range and a very appealing voice, Dyer takes all kinds of wild chances throughout her debut. Among the highlights are a spaced-out "I'll Remember April," an intense version of Ornette Coleman's "Lonely Woman," a nutty rendition of Wayne Shorter's "Pinnochio" and a slightly demented yet swinging interpretation of Gigi Gryce's "Social Call." The singer is greatly assisted by the rockish but versatile guitar of Jeff Buenz, bassist John Shifflett, drummer Jason Lewis and Hafez Modirzadeh on tenor and bass clarinet. Ann Dyer has the same adventurous spirit as the most creative jazz musicians, making this a highly recommended disc. —*Scott Yanow*

E

Allen Eager

b. Jan. 27, 1927, New York, NY
Tenor Saxophone / Bop, Cool
At one point in the early '50s, Allen Eager sounded nearly identical to Stan Getz, Zoot Sims, Al Cohn and Brew Moore; in fact all five tenors (from the Lester Young-influenced "Four Brothers" school) recorded together. But of the five, Eager has had the least impressive career, lacking the desire to really work on jazz full-time. He had played during World War II as a teenager with the bands of Bobby Sherwood, Sonny Dunham, Shorty Sherock, Hal McIntyre, Woody Herman (1943–44), Tommy Dorsey and Johnny Bothwell. By 1945 he was appearing regularly on 52nd Street, and during 1946–48 he recorded as a leader. Eager did well with Tadd Dameron's band in 1948 but by the early '50s he seemed to be losing interest in jazz. He recorded with Gerry Mulligan (1951), Terry Gibbs (1952), played with Buddy Rich and led his own band during 1953–55. After living in Paris during 1956–57 and recording with Mulligan in 1957, he largely dropped out of music. Eager did make a comeback album for Uptown in 1982 but has been little-heard of since, apparently much more interested in racing cars! —*Scott Yanow*

● **Tenor Sax** / Mar. 22, 1946–Jul. 15, 1947 / Savoy ✦✦✦✦✦

Renaissance / Mar. 25, 1982 / Uptown ✦✦
This album was notable for the return of the driving, tenor saxophonist. —*David Szatmary*

Jon Eardley

b. Sep. 30, 1928, Altoona, PA
Trumpet / Bop, Cool
Somewhat forgotten in the United States, Jon Eardley has long been active in Europe. He began playing trumpet when he was 11. After working in an Air Force band (1946–49), he played locally (1950–53) and then worked in New York with Phil Woods (1954). Eardley gained some visibility playing on and off with Gerry Mulligan's quartet and sextet (1954–57) and is still best-known for that association today. After working back in Pennsylvania for several years, the cool-toned bopper moved to Belgium in 1963 and in 1969 relocated to Germany to play in a radio orchestra. Eardley can be heard at his best on three Spotlite albums, all from 1977. —*Scott Yanow*

● **From Hollywood to New York** / Dec. 25, 1954+Mar. 14, 1955 / Original Jazz Classics ✦✦✦✦✦
Trumpeter Jon Eardley's first two sessions as a leader (he would only lead two others during the next 20 years) are combined on this reissue CD. A fine boppish player who mostly stuck to the middle register of his horn, Eardley would soon be joining Gerry Mulligan's group. He is heard on four selections heading a quartet with pianist Pete Jolly (who was just starting his career), bassist Red Mitchell and drummer Larry Bunker, and on four other numbers with tenor saxophonist J.R. Monterose, pianist George Syran, bassist Teddy Kotick and drummer Nick Stabulas. The music (five originals and three standards) is essentially cool-toned bop and was quite modern for the period. —*Scott Yanow*

The Jon Eardley Seven / Jul. 1, 1956 / Original Jazz Classics ✦✦✦

Namely Me / Aug. 12, 1977+Aug. 13, 1977 / Spotlite ✦✦✦✦

Stablemates / Sep. 16, 1977 / Spotlite ✦✦✦

Charles Earland

b. May 24, 1941, Philadelphia, PA
Organ / Soul Jazz, Hard Bop
Charles Earland has played organ and other keyboards plus soprano sax. His style has been influenced by Jimmy Smith and Jimmy McGriff, and combines elements of soul jazz with blues, funk and pop. He doesn't have as heavy a sound as Groove Holmes or Jack McDuff, but has done some solid dates for Prestige, Muse and other labels. He became one of the most popular organists in the '70s using walking and rolling bass pedal lines in either soul jazz or jazz-rock and funk contexts. Earland actually began his career as a saxophonist working with McGriff. He began heading his own band in the '60s, and unable to either attract or keep organists in his bands, switched to the instrument in 1963. Earland played organ with Lou Donaldson in the late '60s, then issued his own albums on Choice and Prestige. His *Black Talk* album in 1969 featured his own compositions. The LP's success won Earland a long-term deal with Prestige. He started mixing soprano sax, synthesizer, electric piano and organ in his bands. During the '70s Earland appeared at the Montreux and Newport jazz festivals and played on the soundtrack for the film *The Dynamite Brothers*. His '70s Prestige albums alternated between combos, large groups and some sessions with vocalists. His '73 date *Leaving This Planet* included guest appearances from Freddie Hubbard, Eddie Henderson and Joe Henderson. After a live session recorded in Montreux in 1974, Earland switched labels to Mercury, cutting one studio date, then Muse for four albums. The first three reunited Earland with guitarist Jimmy Ponder, who'd played on his first album as a leader. He then recorded with Columbia on sessions ranging from large bands to dates with The Brecker Brothers and female vocalists. During the '80s and '90s, Earland returned to Muse for quartet/combo dates, including one co-led by George Coleman. —*Ron Wynn and Michael Erlewine*

★ **Black Talk** / Dec. 15, 1969 / Original Jazz Classics ✦✦✦✦✦
This CD reissue of a Prestige date is one of the few successful examples of jazz musicians from the late '60s taking a few rock and pop songs and turning them into creative jazz. Organist Charles Earland and his sextet, which includes trumpeter Virgil Jones, Houston Person on tenor and guitarist Melvin Sparks, perform a variation of "Eleanor Rigby" titled "Black Talk," two originals, a surprisingly effective rendition of "Aquarius" and a classic rendition of "More Today than Yesterday." Fans of organ combos are advised to pick up this interesting set. —*Scott Yanow*

Black Drops / Jun. 1, 1970 / Prestige ✦✦✦
Early soul-jazz, occasional R&B and pop cuts from organist Charles Earland, just cutting his third album as a leader at that time. His organ solos were sometimes churning and impressive, but at other times bogged down in clichés and repetitive phrases. But the potential Earland showed on most cuts has since materialized. —*Ron Wynn*

Living Black / Sep. 17, 1970 / Prestige ✦✦✦
Funky taste of soul done at the Key Club in Newark. With Grover Washington, Jr. —*Ron Wynn*

Leaving This Planet / Dec. 11, 1973–Dec. 13, 1973 / Prestige ✦✦✦✦✦
Great stints by Joe Henderson (sax), Eddie Henderson (tpt) and Freddie Hubbard (tpt). His most ambitious album. —*Ron Wynn*

Smokin' / 1977 / Muse ✦✦✦
Fine mid-'70s sextet set featuring Earland's customary soul-jazz, blues and funk, with uptempo and ballad originals. Tenor saxophonists David Schnitter and George Coleman excel, as does guitarist Jimmy Ponder. —*Ron Wynn*

Pleasant Afternoon / Apr. 19, 1978 / Muse ✦✦✦

Infant Eyes / 1978 / Muse ✦✦✦

Coming to You Live / 1979 / Columbia ✦✦

Front Burner / Jun. 27, 1988–Jun. 28, 1988 / Milestone ✦✦✦

Third Degree Burn / May 15, 1989–May 16, 1989 / Milestone ✦✦✦✦

Sparkling funky tenor from David "Fathead" Newman and solid organ from Earland. —*Ron Wynn*

Whip Appeal / May 23, 1990 / Muse ✦✦✦

Good, although sometimes lightweight, soul-jazz and funk session from 1990. Fine solos by trumpeter Johnny Coles, tenor saxophonist Houston Person and Earland, plus effective Latin backgrounds from Lawrence Killian on conga. —*Ron Wynn*

Unforgettable / Dec. 6, 1991 / Muse ✦✦✦

Ready 'N' Able / Jan. 1, 1995 / Muse ✦✦✦✦

Madeline Eastman

b. , San Francisco, CA
Vocals / Bop, Standards
A fine singer who takes chances during her solos, Madeline Eastman recorded three excellent albums for the Mad-Kat label during 1990–94. She has been a fixture in the San Francisco area since the late '70s. —*Scott Yanow*

Point Of Departure / 1990 / Mad-Kat ✦✦✦✦

★ **Mad About Madeline!** / Jan. 1991 / Mad-Kat ✦✦✦✦✦

Art Attack / Jun. 1994 / Mad-Kat ✦✦✦

Singer Madeline Eastman's third release for the Mad-Kat label shoots out in a lot of directions, some more successful than others. Eastman is at her best on explorative workouts (such as a wordless version of "Nefertiti" in which she is joined by The Turtle Island String Quartet), uptempo pieces where she can scat and swing and on sensuous ballads such as "The Thrill Is Gone." The supporting cast includes a trio with pianist Kenny Barron and drummer Tony Williams on half of the program; Bay Area musicians were enlisted for most of the other tracks. To Madeline Eastman's credit, she consistently stretches herself and is not afraid to take chances. The hits far outnumber the misses on this very interesting release. —*Scott Yanow*

Billy Eckstine

b. Jul. 8, 1914, Pittsburgh, PA, d. Mar. 8, 1993, Pittsburgh, PA
Vocals / Bop, Standards, Pop
An influential ballad singer with a very appealing baritone voice, Billy Eckstine made a very important contribution to jazz early on, leading one of the first bebop big bands and keeping it together (while turning down lucrative offers to work as a single) as long as possible. He worked in Chicago starting in 1937 and was with the Earl Hines Orchestra during 1939–43, having a few hit records including the blues "Jelly, Jelly." Near the end of his stay with Hines, the big band had become bop-oriented with such sidemen as Dizzy Gillespie, Charlie Parker and the young Sarah Vaughan. After leaving Hines, Eckstine hired those three as part of his very modern orchestra and other members of his band during parts of 1944–47 included Gene Ammons, Dexter Gordon, Frank Wess, Miles Davis, Kenny Dorham, Fats Navarro, Sonny Stitt, Leo Parker and Art Blakey; virtually all of the musicians were fairly unknown at the time. Unfortunately they did not make many recordings in 1944 (and by then Charlie Parker was gone) but they did have a minor hit with "Blowin' the Blues Away" and recorded more frequently during 1945–47; the latter performances have been reissued by Savoy. Eckstine, who occasionally took decent solos on valve trombone and trumpet, alternated ballads with bop instrumentals and made a short film in 1945 but by 1947 was forced financially to give up the band. Switching to middle-of-the-road pop ballads, Mr. B. became a very popular attraction (in a later era he would have been a romantic movie star), recording many string-filled arrangements for MGM that were best-sellers. But he never lost his feeling for jazz, and a 1959 collaboration with Count Basie finds Eckstine swinging with the best. —*Scott Yanow*

● **I Want to Talk About You** / Feb. 13, 1940–Mar. 4, 1945 / Xanadu ✦✦✦✦✦

The warm baritone voice of Billy Eckstine made him one of the most popular vocalists of the '40s and '50s. Although not a jazz singer himself, Eckstine always had a strong sympathy for the music, and his championing of a bebop big band during 1944–47 (when he could have made a lucrative living as a single) was quite heroic. This Xanadu LP features Eckstine's earliest recordings, 13 selections taken from his 1940–41 Victor sides with Earl Hines' Orchestra. Ballads naturally dominate but "Jelly, Jelly" (Eckstine's first hit), "The Jitney Man" and "Stormy Monday Blues" are among the more memorable performances. This set is rounded out by three ballads taken from a 1945 broadcast with his own big band. Bop collectors will prefer to get a full set of orchestral sides by Eckstine's pioneering big band, but fans of his warm vocals should pick up this appealing album. —*Scott Yanow*

Mr. B / Apr. 13, 1944–Sep. 5, 1944 / Audio Lab ✦✦✦✦✦

The Legendary Big Band of Billy Eckstine Together! / Feb. 1945–Mar. 1945 / Spotlite ✦✦✦✦

★ **Mister B and the Band** / May 2, 1945–Apr. 21, 1947 / Savoy ✦✦✦✦✦

These landmark recordings (1945–1946) show the roots of bop. The album has incredible personnel and great vocals. —*Ron Wynn*

Billy Eckstine Sings / 1945 / Savoy ✦✦✦

There are those (Sarah Vaughan was one of them) who consider Eckstine the supreme male jazz vocalist, though (like her) he sometimes was obliged to sing awful songs. He came up in an era and with a ballad-based style that is pretty much forgotten now—a hazard quite common in jazz. He also hired various of the up-and-coming beboppers for his own big band, though he wasn't a bop singer himself. These fine sessions from the mid-'40s include only a couple of inherent turkeys, along with fine minor ballads like "Gloomy Sunday" and a few standards. A major plus is tenor saxist Wardell Gray as soloist on some cuts. —*John Storm Roberts*

MGM Years / May 20, 1947–Apr. 26, 1957 / PolyGram ✦✦✦✦

Basie and Eckstine, Inc. / Mar. 22, 1959–Jul. 28, 1959 / Roulette ✦✦✦✦✦

No Cover, No Minimum / Aug. 1960 / Roulette ✦✦✦✦

An outstanding '60 live set, with Eckstine backed by a good combo doing classics like "Lush Life" and "Moonlight In Vermont." The intimate nightclub setting, coupled with Bobby Tucker's simple, yet effective, arrangements, make this perhaps Eckstine's best album outside his prime '40s and early '50s dates. It has been reissued on CD with 12 previously unissued cuts. —*Ron Wynn*

Billy Eckstine Sings with Benny Carter / Nov. 17, 1986–Nov. 18, 1986 / Verve ✦✦✦

Harry Edison

b. Oct. 10, 1915, Columbus, OH
Trumpet / Swing
Harry "Sweets" Edison gets the most mileage out of a single note, like his former boss Count Basie. Edison, who is immediately recognizable within a note or two, has long used repetition and simplicity to his advantage while always swinging. He played in local bands in Columbus and then in 1933 joined the Jeter-Pillars Orchestra. After a couple years in St. Louis, Edison moved to New York where he joined Lucky Millinder and then in June 1938 Count Basie, remaining with that classic orchestra until it broke up in 1950. During that period he was featured on many records, appeared in the 1944 short *Jammin' the Blues* and gained his nickname "Sweets" (due to his tone) from Lester Young. In the 1950s Edison toured with Jazz at the Philharmonic, settled in Los Angeles and was well-featured both as a studio musician (most noticeably on Frank Sinatra records) and on jazz dates. He had several reunions with Count Basie in the 1960s and by the '70s was often teamed with Eddie "Lockjaw" Davis; Edison also recorded an excellent duet album for Pablo with Oscar Peterson. One of the few swing trumpeters to be influenced by Dizzy Gillespie, Sweets has led sessions through the years for Pacific Jazz, Verve, Roulette, Riverside, Vee-Jay, Liberty, Sue, Black & Blue, Pablo, Storyville and Candid among others. Although his playing faded during the 1980s and '90s, Edison can still say more with one note than nearly anyone. —*Scott Yanow*

Jawbreakers / Apr. 18, 1962 / Original Jazz Classics ✦✦✦✦

Solid, inviting duo work, matching Edison with Eddie "Lockjaw" Davis (ts). —*Ron Wynn*

Home with Sweets / Aug. 1964 / Vee-Jay ✦✦

Oscar Peterson and Harry Edison / 1974 / Original Jazz Classics ✦✦✦✦✦

Just Friends / Jul. 26, 1975 / Black & Blue ✦✦✦✦

★ **Edison's Lights** / May 5, 1976 / Original Jazz Classics ✦✦✦✦✦

Opus Funk / Jul. 6, 1976 / Storyville ✦✦✦✦

Simply Sweets / Sep. 22, 1977 / Pablo ✦✦✦

Trumpeter Harry "Sweets" Edison and tenor saxophonist Eddie "Lockjaw" Davis always made a potent pair. They both possessed immediately identifiable sounds, were veterans of Count Basie's Orchestra and never had any difficulty swinging. The repertoire of this Edison album is not too creative with five blues among its eight songs and one of the others, "Feelings," being quite forgettable. However, the playing of the principals (along with pianist Dolo Coker, who also makes a couple of surprising appearances on electric keyboard) holds one's interest throughout. —*Scott Yanow*

'S Wonderful / Oct. 19, 1982 / Pablo ✦✦✦

Well done '82 set pairing veteran swing trumpeter Harry Edison with tenor saxophonist Zoot Sims and a solid rhythm section anchored by drummer Shelly Manne, with bassist Monte Budwig and pianist Mike Wofford. It was recorded live in Tokyo. —*Ron Wynn*

For My Pals / Apr. 18, 1988–Apr. 19, 1988 / Pablo ✦✦

Can't Get out of This Mood / Oct. 1988–Nov. 1988 / Orange Blue ✦✦✦

Swing Summit / Apr. 27, 1990–Apr. 28, 1990 / Candid ✦✦✦

Teddy Edwards

b. Apr. 26, 1924, Jackson, MS
Tenor Saxophone / Bop, Hard Bop
Teddy Edwards was, with Dexter Gordon and Wardell Gray, the top young tenor of the late '40s. Unlike the other two, he chose to remain in Los Angeles and has been underrated through the years but, even in his early 70s, Edwards remains in prime form. Early on he toured with Ernie Fields' Orchestra, moving to L.A. in 1945 to work with Roy Milton as an altoist. Edwards switched to tenor when he joined Howard McGhee's band and was featured in many jam sessions during the era, recording "The Duel" with Dexter Gordon in 1947. A natural-born leader, Edwards did work briefly with Max Roach and Clifford Brown (1954), Benny Carter (1955) and Benny Goodman (1964), and he recorded in the 1960s with Milt Jackson and Jimmy Smith. But it is his own records for Onyx (1947-48), Pacific Jazz, Contemporary (1960-62), Prestige, Xanadu, Muse, SteepleChase, Timeless and Antilles that best show off his playing and writing; "Sunset Eyes" is Edwards' best-known original. —*Scott Yanow*

★ **Teddy's Ready** / Aug. 17, 1960 / Original Jazz Classics ✦✦✦✦✦

Many feel this album is this West Coast group's finest hour. With Joe Castro (p), Leroy Vinnegar (b) and Billy Higgins (d). —*Michael Erlewine*

Back to Avalon / Dec. 7, 1960–Dec. 13, 1960 / Original Jazz Classics ✦✦✦

Although rejected at the time it was recorded, this octet session by tenor saxophonist Teddy Edwards sounded pretty good when it was finally released in 1995. There are some minor slip-ups in some of the ensembles, and Edwards is the only significant soloist (although altoist Jimmy Woods and baritonist Modesto Brisenio were talented players) but the leader is in fine form, and his arrangements manage to be both complicated and swinging. Five of the nine songs (all but "You Don't Know What Love Is," "Sweet Georgia Brown" and two versions of "Avalon") are Edwards', highlighted by "Our Last Goodbye" and "Good Gravy." A worthwhile if not essential release. —*Scott Yanow*

Together Again! / May 15, 1961+May 17, 1961 / Contemporary ✦✦✦✦✦

Dynamite pairing with Howard McGhee (tpt). Incredible piano by Phineas Newborn, Jr. (p) —*Ron Wynn*

Good Gravy! / Aug. 23, 1961–Aug. 25, 1961 / Original Jazz Classics ✦✦✦

Teddy Edwards has long been one of the most underrated of the bop tenors, due in large part to his decision to settle in Los Angeles. Edwards is in typically swinging form on this quartet date with either Phineas Newborn, Jr., or Danny Horton on piano,

bassist Leroy Vinnegar and drummer Milt Turner. The tenor contributed four originals and also performs the obscure "A Little Later" and four standards with warmth and creativity within the hard bop genre. —*Scott Yanow*

Heart and Soul / Apr. 24, 1962 / Original Jazz Classics ✦✦✦

Nothin' But the Truth! / Dec. 13, 1966 / Original Jazz Classics ✦✦✦✦

This CD reissue is quite brief (just 32 minutes) but it does give one a pretty definitive look into the style of tenor saxophonist Teddy Edwards. Accompanied by pianist Walter Davis, Jr. guitarist Phil Orlando, bassist Paul Chambers, drummer Billy Higgins and percussionist Montego Joe, Edwards plays three of his originals plus a trio of standards. His warm tenor (alternately boppish and soulful) is heard at its best during "On the Street Where You Live" and "But Beautiful." —*Scott Yanow*

Feelin's / Mar. 25, 1974 / Muse ✦✦✦✦

This session finds Edwards in good swinging company. All originals (except "Georgia On My Mind"). Forthright and well done. —*Ron Wynn*

Inimitable / Jun. 25, 1976 / Xanadu ✦✦✦✦✦

Out of This World / Dec. 5, 1980 / SteepleChase ✦✦✦✦

Mississippi Lad / Mar. 13, 1991–Mar. 14, 1991 / Antilles ✦✦✦

☆ **Blue Saxophone** / Jun. 8, 1992–Jun. 10, 1992 / Antilles ✦✦✦✦✦

One of the major tenor saxophonists in jazz since his emergence in the mid-'40s, Teddy Edwards has not led enough sessions throughout his career, considering his great talent. In the 1990s, he has been making up for some of the lost time by putting a great deal of planning into his releases. For this ambitious effort he is joined by five brass, five strings, a harp, a four-piece rhythm section and, on two songs, the fine young singer Lisa Nobumoto. As if that were not enough, Edwards wrote ten of the 12 songs, arranged all of them, takes "Prelude" unaccompanied and plays a bit of clarinet on "Serenade in Blue." It's an impressive effort. —*Scott Yanow*

Mark Egan

b. Jan. 14, 1951, Brockton, MA
Bass / Post Bop, Crossover
Mark Egan, who has a floating sound, is best known for his leadership of Elements with drummer Danny Gottlieb. His first instrument was the trumpet, switching to bass at 16. Egan played with Ira Sullivan's group in Miami during 1974-76 and then moved to New York where he toured with the Pointer Sisters and David Sanborn. Egan's big break was when he became a member of the Pat Metheny Group (1977-80), recording and touring extensively. Since leaving Metheny he has worked in many situations, including with Stan Getz, Jim Hall, the Gil Evans Orchestra (1983-85) and John McLaughlin. Elements, which usually also features Bill Evans on reeds and keyboardist Clifford Carter, was formed in 1982 and has existed on a part-time basis ever since, recording for Philo, Antilles, Novus and Blue Moon. —*Scott Yanow*

Mosaic / 1985 / Hip Pocket ✦✦

Touch of Light / Apr. 19, 1988–May 1988 / GRP ✦✦✦

● **Beyond Words** / 1990 / Blue Moon ✦✦✦✦

Marty Ehrlich

b. 1955, St. Louis, MO
Clarinet, Flute, Bass Clarinet, Alto Saxophone, Soprano Saxophone, Tenor Saxophone / Avant-Garde
A versatile player, Marty Ehrlich has led stimulating sessions and been a valuable sideman in several different situations. He first recorded with the Human Arts Ensemble in 1972. Ehrlich studied at the New England Conservatory of Music, and in 1978 he moved to New York. Since then he has worked with many top musicians including Muhal Richard Abrams, Anthony Braxton, Julius Hemphill and Bobby Bradford (where he fills in for the late John Carter). Ehrlich has also duetted with Anthony Cox, led his Dark Woods Ensemble and recorded as a leader for Cecma, Sound Aspects, Muse, New World and most often Enja. —*Scott Yanow*

The Welcome / Mar. 21, 1984 / Sound Aspects ✦✦✦

Pliant Plaint / Apr. 1987 / Enja ✦✦✦✦

The Traveller's Tale / May 30, 1989–Jun. 1, 1989 / Enja ✦✦✦✦

Solid, energized solos by Marty Ehrlich on a variety of saxophones and flute, plus equally animated playing from co-saxophonist Stan Strickland on tenor, soprano and flute. The two-sax frontline, plus tasteful, probing bass/drum help from Lindsey Horner and Robert Previte, not only fills the spaces open due to the absence of a pianist, but periodically shifts the mood, focus and tempo. —*Ron Wynn*

Falling Man / Oct. 3, 1989–Nov. 3, 1989 / Muse ◆◆◆
An intriguing, but sometimes disjointed, duo outing between multi-instrumentalist Marty Erhlich and bassist Anthony Cox. They venture into free, fusion, funk and rock territory, and while all their duets are exceptionally played, the compositions aren't uniformly interesting. The best cut is their emphatic duet "You Don't Know What Love Is," which was a signature song for Eric Dolphy. —*Ron Wynn*

Emergency Peace / Dec. 14, 1990–Dec. 16, 1990 / New World ◆◆◆◆
It's a fascinating blend of improvisation and original structures. —*Myles Boisen*

Side by Side / Jan. 1991 / Enja ◆◆◆◆

★ **Can You Hear A Motion?** / Sep. 22, 1993–Sep. 23, 1993 / Enja ◆◆◆◆◆
This quartet release matches the cool-toned reeds of Marty Ehrlich (heard on clarinet, alto and soprano) and Stan Strickland (doubling on flute and tenor) with bassist Michael Formanek (who operates as an active partner) and the quietly supportive drummer Bobby Previte. Their unpredictable music ranges from free bop a la Ornette Coleman (including a tenor-alto duet rendition of Coleman's "Comme Il Faut") and a pair of John Carter tributes to Jaki Byard's "Ode to Charlie Parker" (which includes transcriptions of part of trumpeter Booker Little's solo from its original recording) and the modern classical harmonies of "Pictures in a Glass House." Throughout the improvisations are a logical outgrowth of the written sections and vice versa. The musicians constantly react to each other, making this stimulating and passionate but quiet music well worth acquiring. —*Scott Yanow*

Just Before the Dawn / Apr. 10, 1995–Apr. 11, 1995 / New World ◆◆◆◆

Either/Orchestra

b. 1985
Big Band / Post Bop, Avant-Garde
The Either/Orchestra was founded in 1985 by tenor saxophonist Russ Gershon. An adventurous medium-sized seven-horn ten-piece group based in Massachusetts, the ensemble often has the sound of a big band but the looseness of a combo and, although occasionally reminiscent of some of Charles Mingus' groups, it has developed its own sound over time. Gershon in 1987 founded Accurate Records and the Either/Orchestra recorded four memorable albums for the label during 1987-90. —*Scott Yanow*

Dial E / Jul. 4, 1986–Jul. 9, 1986 / Accurate Jazz ◆◆◆◆
First album features two Russ Gershon originals and one each by Thelonious Monk, Sonny Rollins and Roland Kirk. It's a fine debut, as they feel their way around new jazz music. —*Michael G. Nastos*

Radium / Aug. 2, 1987–Jan. 31, 1988 / Accurate Jazz ◆◆◆◆
Includes three standards and five originals. Trombonist Curtis Hasselbring and baritone saxophonist Charles Kohlhase stand out as soloists. "Born in a Suitcase" and Roscoe Mitchell's "Odwallah" are the best tracks. —*Michael G. Nastos*

The Half-Life of Desire / Jan. 31, 1988–Apr. 30, 1989 / Accurate Jazz ◆◆◆◆◆
Led by saxophonist/composer Russ Gershon, this shows progressive sensibilities with jazz aesthetics. Recorded at Van Gelder's, this album features great originals and interesting twists on "Temptation," "Circle in the Round/I Got it Bad and That Ain't Good," and King Crimson's "Red." —*Michael G. Nastos*

The Calculus of Pleasure / Apr. 25, 1990–Jun. 27, 1990 / Accurate Jazz ◆◆◆◆

★ **Brunt** / Apr. 22, 1993–May 11, 1993 / Accurate ◆◆◆◆◆
At the time of its formation The Either/Orchestra asked "why should a seven-horn band only limit themselves in ensembles to playing three basic parts (for trumpets, trombones and reeds) when having seven parts would be much more exciting?" Gradual tempo changes within a song, the use of emotional outbursts, humor and group improvising, and the ability to look both backwards and forwards stylistically at the same time are qualities

that make The Either/Orchestra a logical outgrowth of Charles Mingus' innovations. This CD is full of extroverted solos, wild group interplay, hard-swinging and unpredictable performances and quite a bit of variety. Even with the many strong solos, it is the occasionally overcrowded ensembles of the stimulating group that stick in one's mind. —*Scott Yanow*

Roy Eldridge (David Roy Eldridge)

b. Jan. 30, 1911, Pittsburgh, PA, d. Feb. 26, 1989, Valley Stream, NY
Trumpet / Swing
One of the most exciting trumpeters to emerge during the swing era, Roy Eldridge's combative approach, chancetaking style and strong musicianship were an inspiration (and an influence) to the next musical generation, most notably Dizzy Gillespie. Although he sometimes pushed himself farther than he could go, Eldridge never played a dull solo!

Roy Eldridge started out playing trumpet and drums in carnival and circus bands. With the Nighthawk Syncopators he received a bit of attention by playing a note-for-note recreation of Coleman Hawkins' tenor solo on "The Stampede." Inspired by the dynamic playing of Jabbo Smith (Eldridge would not discover Louis Armstrong for a few years), Roy played with some territory bands including Zack Whyte and Speed Webb and in New York (where he arrived in 1931) he worked with Elmer Snowden (who nicknamed him "Little Jazz"), McKinney's Cotton Pickers and most importantly Teddy Hill (1935). Eldridge's recorded solos with Hill, backing Billie Holiday, and with Fletcher Henderson (including his 1936 hit "Christopher Columbus") gained a great deal of attention. In 1937 he appeared with his octet (which included brother Joe on alto) at the Three Deuces Club in Chicago and recorded some outstanding selections as a leader including "Heckler's Hop" and "Wabash Stomp." By 1939 Roy had a larger group playing at the Arcadia Ballroom in New York. With the decline of Bunny Berigan and the increasing predictability of Louis Armstrong, Eldridge was arguably the top trumpeter in jazz during this era.

During 1941-42 Eldridge sparked Gene Krupa's Orchestra, recording classic versions of "Rockin' Chair" and "After You've Gone" and interacting with Anita O'Day on "Let Me Off Uptown." The difficulties of travelling with a White band during a racist period hurt him as did some of the incidents that occurred during his stay with Artie Shaw (1944-45), but the music during both stints was quite memorable. Eldridge had a short-lived big band of his own, toured with Jazz at the Philharmonic and then had a bit of an identity crisis when he realized that his playing was not as modern as the beboppers. A successful stay in France during 1950-51 restored his confidence when he realized that being original was more important than being up-to-date. Eldridge recorded steadily for Norman Granz in the 1950s, was one of the stars of JATP (where he battled Charlie Shavers and Dizzy Gillespie) and by 1956 was often teamed with Coleman Hawkins in a quintet; their 1957 appearance at Newport was quite memorable. The 1960s were tougher as recording opportunities and work became rarer. Eldridge had brief and unhappy stints with Count Basie's Orchestra and Ella Fitzgerald (feeling unnecessary in both contexts) but was leading his own group by the end of the decade. He spent much of the 1970s playing regularly at Ryan's and recording for Pablo and, although his range had shrunk a bit, Eldridge's competitive spirit was still very much intact. Only a serious stroke in 1980 was able to halt his horn. Roy Eldridge recorded throughout his career for virtually every label. —*Scott Yanow*

★ **Little Jazz** / Feb. 26, 1935–Apr. 2, 1940 / Columbia ◆◆◆◆◆
This CD contains the best recordings from the early years of the fiery trumpeter Roy Eldridge. Eldridge, one of the great swing trumpeters and a powerful player into the 1970s, is heard with Teddy Hill's Orchestra, backing singer Putney Dandridge, on four titles with Fletcher Henderson (including the hit "Christopher Columbus"), starring on a four-song session with Teddy Wilson, joining Billie Holiday on "Falling in Love Again," soloing on two numbers with Mildred Bailey (his "I'm Nobody's Baby" solo is years ahead of its time) and, best of all, leading a small group through six songs (plus an alternate) from his own explosive sessions of Jan. 1937. This brilliant music is essential for all serious jazz collections. —*Scott Yanow*

The Early Years / Feb. 26, 1935–May 9, 1949 / Columbia ◆◆◆◆◆
Next to Louis Armstrong and Bunny Berigan, Roy Eldridge was one of the big three of jazz trumpeters who were active in the sec-

ond half of the '30s. His stirring outbursts were consistently exciting and became a major influence on the playing of his contemporaries. This two-LP set has many of the highpoints of Eldridge's early years, particularly on the first album. He is heard in 1935 with Teddy Hill's Orchestra, guesting with Teddy Wilson in 1939 and on three titles with Mildred Bailey the following year (taking a futuristic solo on "I'm Nobody's Baby") but it is the six numbers that he recorded with his own small group in 1937 that are most outstanding, particularly on "Wabash Stomp," "Heckler's Hop," "That Thing" and his first version of "After You've Gone." The second album is more unusual, for it includes alternate takes of ten numbers that Eldridge recorded with Gene Krupa's Orchestra during 1941–42, including "new" versions of such hits as "Green Eyes," "Let Me Off Uptown," "After You've Gone" and "Rockin' Chair." This two-fer concludes with a pair of numbers from 1949 when Eldridge briefly returned to Krupa's band. —*Scott Yanow*

After You've Gone / Feb. 5, 1936–Sep. 24, 1946 / GRP ✦✦✦✦
This excellent CD features the great swing trumpeter Roy Eldridge shortly after the breakup of the Gene Krupa Orchestra. Eldridge is heard leading his own recording groups (mostly big bands) and, although his own orchestra never really caught on, the trumpet solos are always quite exciting. This CD skips over five of Eldridge's Decca sides (it should have been a "complete" set) but does include three previously unissued performances plus a recently discovered jam on "Christopher Columbus" from 1936. —*Scott Yanow*

Live at the Three Deuces / Feb. 1937 / Jazz Archives ✦✦✦
Trumpeter Roy Eldridge's octet, which recorded six songs in Jan. 1937, is heard on this LP stretching out during a couple of radio broadcasts from later that year. Actually, despite the fine playing of altoists Joe Eldridge and Scoops Carey, tenor Dave Young and the four-piece rhythm section, the focus is generally on the exciting trumpeter/leader. The recording quality is erratic but the performances are often quite heated with Eldridge showing what he learned from listening to Louis Armstrong, most notably how to build a solo gradually up to a high note. Highlights include "Little Jazz," "Basin Street Blues," "Heckler's Hop" and "Chinatown, My Chinatown." —*Scott Yanow*

Arcadia Shuffle / Aug. 5, 1939–Sep. 9, 1939 / Jazz Archives ✦✦✦
On this LP the great swing trumpeter Roy Eldridge is heard leading his ten-piece group at New York's Arcadia Ballroom. These radio broadcasts were somewhat primitively recorded but the excitement of Eldridge's playing shines through. Although this particular band did record eight titles later in the year, most of the music on this set (including "Little Jazz," "Mahogany Hall Stomp," "Shine," "Woodchopper's Ball" and "Lady Be Good") was not recorded by the trumpeter during the era. This album is worth searching for by swing collectors. —*Scott Yanow*

At Jerry Newman's / Nov. 19, 1940 / Xanadu ✦✦
This LP is strictly for collectors. The music at this jam session is loose, with multiple versions of some titles, the musicians (which include altoist Willie Smith, Herbie Fields on tenor, guitarist Mike Bryan and various pianists and drummers) never really come together as a unified band and the recording quality is erratic. But then again, trumpeter Roy Eldridge (who was not documented very well during this period) is in consistently intense and creative form, uplifting the performances and making this a worthwhile (and somewhat historic) album that his fans should enjoy despite its faults. —*Scott Yanow*

Roy Eldridge In Paris / Jun. 9, 1950+Jun. 14, 1950 / Vogue ✦✦✦✦
In 1950 trumpeter Roy Eldridge was having a bit of an identity crisis. Once considered one of the pacesetters, the emergence of Dizzy Gillespie and the bop stylists left Eldridge unsure what to do. But that year when he travelled to France with Benny Goodman, the future seemed clearer. The Parisian audiences demanded that Eldridge play himself rather than try to copy the modernists and he took their advice. This CD reissue features the complete output (including seven alternate takes) from two exciting recording sessions. Eldridge heads a quintet with tenor saxophonist Zoot Sims; two songs have vocals from Anita Love and Roy does a good job of singing on the happy "Ain't No Flies on Me." While "Wrap Your Troubles in Dreams" (heard in two versions) is the classic of that session, the later date features Roy with a quartet and he is in top form on "If I Had You" and "Someone to Watch over Me." —*Scott Yanow*

I Remember Harlem / Oct. 28, 1950–Mar. 29, 1951 / Inner City ✦✦✦✦
This out-of-print LP features Roy Eldridge in generally superb

form. Recorded during his visit to Paris with the Benny Goodman Sextet, the well-rounded set finds him a dominant force on seven selections (six of which are his compositions) with a French septet. In addition, Eldridge is heard in an exciting quintet with tenor saxophonist Don Byas (the trumpeter's "Oh Shut Up" is based on the chords of "Please Don't Talk About Me When I'm Gone"), Eldridge and Claude Bolling perform "Wild Man Blues" and "Fireworks" as duets reminiscent of the interplay of Louis Armstrong and Earl Hines, and Eldridge even takes three loose but fun piano solos. This music is highly recommended but will probably be difficult to find. —*Scott Yanow*

Roy's Got Rhythm / Jan. 1951 / EmArcy ✦✦✦
Between his Paris sessions of 1950 and 1951 for Vogue, trumpeter Roy Eldridge traveled to Sweden and recorded nine spirited selections for Metronome, which were reissued on this EmArcy LP. None of Eldridge's sidemen (except for clarinetist Ove Lind, who is just on two songs) gained much of a reputation outside of Sweden, but they fare well during these fairly basic performances which are based in swing but also influenced a little by early rhythm & blues. Highlights include "The Heat's On," the two-part "Saturday Nite Fish Fry," "School Days," "Echoes of Harlem" and a pair of numbers that feature Charles Norman on harpsichord. A bit of a collector's item, this LP will be difficult to find. —*Scott Yanow*

Dale's Wail / Dec. 13, 1952–Sep. 1954 / Clef ✦✦✦✦✦
This two-LP set features the great swing trumpeter at the peak of his powers. Eldridge is virtually the whole show on these four sessions for, although he is backed by the Oscar Peterson Trio plus either J.C. Heard, Jo Jones, Alvin Stoller or Buddy Rich on drums, Peterson (who is on organ for half of the selections) does not have much solo space. Highpoints include "Little Jazz," "Wrap Your Troubles in Dreams," "Rockin' Chair," "Somebody Loves Me," "Sweethearts on Parade," "The Song Is Ended" and the title cut. —*Scott Yanow*

Little Jazz Live in 1957 / 1957 / Jazz Band ✦✦✦
Rare live performances (all from 1957) featuring trumpeter Roy Eldridge in four different settings are heard on this collectors' LP. He excels with a no-name quintet and a quartet, leads an all-star group (taken from a television show) that includes Bud Freeman on tenor, clarinetist Buddy DeFranco, trombonist J.J. Johnson and Art Van Damme on accordion for two numbers and jams a blues with Freeman and an otherwise-unidentified band. The recording quality is decent and, although the results are not essential, this English import album will be greatly enjoyed by Roy Eldridge's fans, for the fiery trumpeter is heard in his prime. —*Scott Yanow*

Just You Just Me, Live in 1959 / 1959 / Stash ✦✦✦✦
In the late '50s trumpeter Roy Eldridge and tenor saxophonist Coleman Hawkins teamed up on a fairly regular basis. Since they always brought out the best in each other (their solos could be quite competitive and fiery), all of their joint recordings are recommended. Two LPs from their gig at Washington, D.C.'s Bayou Club in 1959 were previously released on the Honeysuckle Rose label. Five of those selections plus four previously unissued cuts are included on this Stash CD. Most of the tunes are medium-tempo jams such as "Just You, Just Me," "Rifftide," and "How High the Moon," but there is also an excellent ballad medley. Backed by a local rhythm section, Eldridge and Hawk are both in superior form, making this a highly recommended disc even for those listeners who already have the earlier LPs. —*Scott Yanow*

Comin' Home Baby / Aug. 25, 1965–Mar. 25, 1966 / Pumpkin ✦✦✦
With the exception of a European date in 1962, it had been five years since trumpeter Roy Eldridge led a record session when he performed the music on this LP, and these two sessions were not initially released until 1978. Teamed with the cool-toned but hard-swinging tenor Richie Kamuca and a rhythm section headed by pianist Dick Katz, the trumpeter is in fine form on five standards plus "Comin' Home Baby." Nothing that surprising occurs but there is enough intensity and passion to make this an album recommended to straight-ahead jazz collectors. —*Scott Yanow*

The Nifty Cat Strikes West / Jul. 1966 / Master Jazz ✦✦✦
Trumpeter Roy Eldridge's first studio album as a leader in six years and only one of two from a 15-year period (his swing-based style was out of vogue) matches his fiery and competitive playing with trombonist Grover Mitchell, the tenor of Eric Dixon, pianist Bill Bell, bassist Norman Keenan and drummer Louis Bellson on

five standards and two group originals. At the time Eldridge was a member of Count Basie's Orchestra (an association that only lasted a brief time) and all of the players on this LP (except of course pianist Bell) were also Basie-ites. It is therefore not too surprising that the music swings, the solos are quite melodic and that no real surprises occur. The results are pleasing if conservative. — *Scott Yanow*

Nifty Cat / Nov. 24, 1970 / New World ◆◆◆◆
One of only two Eldridge-led studio sessions from the 1961-74 period, this CD reissue of a set originally recorded for Master Jazz matches the great swing trumpeter with Budd Johnson (who doubles on tenor and soprano), trombonist Benny Morton, pianist Nat Pierce, bassist Tommy Bryant and drummer Oliver Jackson. All six of the jump tunes are by Eldridge with "5400 North" and "Ball of Fire" being best-known. For this album the veteran trumpeter had a very rare opportunity to call his own shots on a recording date and the generally inspired playing makes this CD a fine example of small-group swing from the early '70s. — *Scott Yanow*

Little Jazz & The Jimmy Ryan All-Stars / Apr. 7, 1975 / Pablo ◆◆◆◆
During the 1970s Eldridge had a regular gig at Jimmy Ryan's in New York playing music that fell between swing and Dixieland. For this Pablo LP he sought to play a program with his regular group (Joe Muranyi on clarinet and soprano, trombonist Bobby Pratt, pianist Dick Katz, bassist Major Holley and drummer Eddie Locke) that, although recorded in the studio, would sound like one of the Jimmy Ryan sets. So, in addition to such standards as "Between the Devil and the Deep Blue Sea" and "All of Me," Eldridge also performs (and takes occasional vocals on) some older tunes like "St. James Infirmary," "Beale Street Blues" and "Bourbon Street Parade." The music is quite joyful and spirited with Eldridge in rather happy form. This LP is recommended and well-deserving of being reissued on CD. — *Scott Yanow*

Jazz Maturity....Where It's Coming From / Jun. 3, 1975 / Original Jazz Classics ◆◆
Teaming together Dizzy Gillespie and Roy Eldridge should result in some classic music, but by 1975, Eldridge (although still a fierce competitor) was past his prime and Gillespie was starting to fade. The material performed for this LP is just not all that inspiring— a few overly played standards and blues. Despite some good efforts by Gillespie and Eldridge, pianist Oscar Peterson easily emerges as the most impressive soloist; better to acquire the magnificent collaborations of the 1950s instead. — *Scott Yanow*

Happy Time / Jun. 4, 1975 / Original Jazz Classics ◆◆◆
This is a fun album. Eldridge actually spends as much time singing as playing the ten standards but the solos he takes (although concise) have their explosive moments. With pianists Oscar Peterson, guitarist Joe Pass, bassist Ray Brown and drummer Eddie Locke providing the support, the music always swings in a happy fashion. This CD reissue, although not essential, is worth acquiring. — *Scott Yanow*

What It's All About / Jan. 16, 1976 / Original Jazz Classics ◆◆◆
"What It's All About" is swinging, building up solos to potentially ferocious levels and going for broke. That was always the philosophy that Roy Eldridge followed and, even though it was rather late in his career by the time he recorded this Original Jazz Classics LP, he was still pushing himself. His septet on the album is full of talented veterans including altoist Norris Turney, Budd Johnson on tenor, pianist Norman Simmons and (on half of the set) vibraphonist Milt Jackson. The music (three Eldridge originals and two obscurities) features plenty of lengthy and spirited soloing. — *Scott Yanow*

★ **Montreux 1977** / Jul. 13, 1977 / Original Jazz Classics ◆◆◆◆◆
Eldridge's final recording as a leader is a real gem. Although his chops were no longer in prime form, he was still pushing himself to the limit. With a brilliant rhythm section egging him on (pianist Oscar Peterson, bassist Niels Pedersen and drummer Bobby Durham), Eldridge still went for the high notes (and generally hit them) during this exciting set from the 1977 Montreux Jazz Festival. Although the musicians did not know it at the time, the last two songs ("Perdido" and "Bye Bye Blackbird") were a perfect ending to a brilliant career. This dramatic CD reissue is highly recommended. — *Scott Yanow*

Elements

Group / Crossover, Post Bop
A group featuring Mark Egan and Danny Gottlieb, who've record-

ed several albums on Antilles and Novus, working with such guest players as saxophonist Bill Evans and guitarist Steve Khan. — *Ron Wynn*

Elements / Jan. 1982 / Antilles ◆◆◆◆
Influential fusion group that began when duo Mark Egan and Danny Gottlieb recorded together in early '80s. They were subsequently joined on this '83 effort by saxophonist Bill Evans and Clifford Carter, and things got more intense and expansive with two additional voices. — *Ron Wynn*

Forward Motion / May 6, 1983–May 7, 1983 / Antilles ◆◆◆
Another from fusion ensemble Elements, this one more introspective and heavily produced than some earlier releases. It was reissued on CD in 1991. Mark Egan and Danny Gottlieb were the central performers and group's compositional backbone. — *Ron Wynn*

Blown Away / Jul. 5, 1985–Jul. 7, 1985 / Blue Moon ◆◆◆

● **Illumination** / Aug. 1987 / Novus ◆◆◆◆◆

Liberal Arts / 1989 / Novus ◆◆◆

Spirit River / Feb. 19, 1990 / Novus ◆◆◆◆
Airto (per) and Flora Purim (v) give session distinction. — *Ron Wynn*

Far East, Vol. 1 / Jul. 1992 / Wavetone ◆◆◆

Eliane Elias

b. Mar. 19, 1960, Sao Paulo, Brazil
Piano / Post Bop, Brazilian Jazz
A versatile pianist, Eliane Elias has played straight-ahead jazz, fusion and Brazilian jazz with equal skill. After working in her native Brazil she moved to New York on Eddie Gomez's advice in 1981, became a member of Steps Ahead and married Randy Brecker in 1983. She debuted as a leader in 1986, signed with Blue Note in 1989 and toured with her trio. Elias has also sung on some of her records but her piano playing is really her most significant musical talent; she held her own with Herbie Hancock on her 1995 release *Solos and Duets*. — *Scott Yanow*

Illusions / Oct. 22, 1986–Oct. 24, 1986 / Denon ◆◆◆

Cross Currents / Mar. 16, 1987–Mar. 21, 1987 / Denon ◆◆◆◆
This Brazilian pianist's best album to date, though it only scratches the surface of her immense talents. — *Michael G. Nastos*

Eliane Elias Plays Jobim / Dec. 1989 / Blue Note ◆◆◆◆◆
Good adaptions by Elias of both classic and contemporary Jobim compositions. Her often sultry, soft voice, although not Portuguese, covers the material with conviction and sincerity. She's backed by bassist Eddie Gomez, drummer Jack DeJohnette and percussionist Nana Vasconcelos. — *Ron Wynn*

So Far So Close / 1989 / Blue Note ◆◆◆◆
With backing from The Brecker brothers. — *Ron Wynn*

A Long Story / 1991 / Blue Note ◆◆◆◆

Fantasia / Mar. 1992 / Blue Note ◆◆◆◆◆
Eliane Elias continues exploring Brazilian music on this latest release, doing both classics such as "The Girl From Ipanema" and a Milton Nacimiento medley, plus several Ivan Lins tunes. She uses alternating bassists and drummers, with Eddie Gomez, Marc Johnson, Jack DeJohnette and Peter Erskine dividing time, plus Nana Vasconcelos on percussion, with Lins helping out on vocals. — *Ron Wynn*

Paulistana / Oct. 5, 1993 / Blue Note ◆◆◆
Eliane Elias continues to revisit and update her Brazilian heritage on this Blue Note CD. The music ranges from South American folk songs and such standards as "Brazil" and "Black Orpheus" to newer originals. Elias mostly sticks to acoustic piano and is primarily heard in a trio format with occasional percussion added. She hints strongly at Keith Jarrett and Bill Evans in spots but by this time had largely formed her own personal style out of her earlier influences. A few vocals (including a collaboration with Ivan Lins) weaken some of the tracks, for Elias' singing is on a much lower level than her more individual playing. Still, even with its minor flaws, *Paulistana* is recommended. — *Scott Yanow*

★ **Solos & Duets** / Nov. 18, 1994+Dec. 1994 / Blue Note ◆◆◆◆◆
This release is a change of pace for Eliane Elias. Instead of interpreting Brazilian songs, fusion or modern bop, Elias shows off her classical technique on a set of acoustic solos, plus six duets with Herbie Hancock. She really digs into the standards (sometimes sounding a little like Keith Jarrett) and creates some fairly free

and unexpected ideas while putting the accent on lyricism. Some of the music is introspective and there are wandering sections but the net results are logical and enjoyable. As for the duets, Elias and Hancock mostly stay out of each other's way, which is an accomplishment when one considers that the four-part "Messages" is a series of free improvisations. There are playful spots (particularly on the adventurous ten-minute rendition of "The Way You Look Tonight") and, since Elias knows Hancock's style well (and was clearly thrilled to have him on the date), their collaborations work quite well. A successful outing. — *Scott Yanow*

Kurt Elling

b. Nov. 2, 1967, Chicago, IL
Vocals / Post Bop
During an era when the number of significant male jazz singers under the age of 60 can be counted on one hand, Kurt Elling's arrival is very welcome. Influenced by Mark Murphy, Elling combines poetry with jazz and is a chancetaking improviser who often makes up lyrics as he goes along. He discovered jazz while attending college and, although he had planned to become a professor in the philosophy of religion, he eventually became a professional singer instead. After a period of struggle Elling recorded a demo tape that was accepted by Blue Note, resulting in the impressive 1995 release *Close Your Eyes*. — *Scott Yanow*

★ **Close Your Eyes** / 1995 / Blue Note ◆◆◆◆◆

Duke Ellington (Edward Kennedy Ellington)

b. Apr. 29, 1899, Washington, D.C., **d.** May 24, 1974, New York, NY
Piano, Composer, Arranger, Leader / Beyond Category
Duke Ellington's contributions to jazz and American music were simply enormous. As a bandleader, his orchestra during 1926–74 was always among the top five, whether it be 1929 or 1969. As a composer, Ellington ranked with George Gershwin, Cole Porter, Irving Berlin and their contemporaries. He wrote literally thousands of songs (the exact number is not known) of which hundreds became standards. As an arranger Ellington was particularly innovative, writing for his very individual players rather than for an anonymous horn section and, not being content to play his songs the same way every time, he constantly rearranged them; "Mood Indigo" sounded different in 1933 than it did in 1953 or 1973. As a pianist Duke Ellington was originally an excellent stride player who gained the respect of such giants as James P. Johnson, Fats Waller and his main influence Willie "The Lion" Smith. Unlike virtually all of his contemporaries (other than Mary Lou Williams), Duke was able to modernize his style through the years, keeping the percussive approach of the stride players but leaving more space and using more complex chords; his playing was an influence on Thelonious Monk and (in a more abstract fashion) Cecil Taylor.

Duke Ellington always considered his orchestra to be his main instrument and with it he recorded constantly from 1926 on. In the early days he recorded for many labels, sometimes under pseudonyms, and by the 1950s he often seemed to live in the studios when not performing before audiences, trying out new material and fresh versions of older songs. The result is that there are currently a countless number of Ellington albums available (way over 200) with "new" (previously unissued) ones coming out nearly every month as if he were still alive. What is more remarkable than the quantity is the consistently high quality; there are few if any throwaways in Ellington's entire discography!

There is simply no explanation for Edward Kennedy Ellington's musical genius. Although he started studying piano when he was seven, for a time it seemed that Duke (who picked up his lifelong nickname early) was going to be an artist. However, he so enjoyed hearing the ragtime and barrelhouse piano players of the era that he soon chose music. Ellington started playing music in Washington, D.C., in 1917 and, after wisely taking out the biggest ad in the telephone yellow pages, was soon leading several bands despite the fact that his repertoire was very limited. Ellington, whose first composition "Soda Fountain Rag" was written during this era, worked on building up his technique by slowing down James P. Johnson piano rolls and analyzing the fingering. A brief visit to New York in 1922 (playing with Wilbur Sweatman) was unsuccessful but Ellington returned the following year and was determined to stick it out. He and such hometown friends as

Sonny Greer, Otto Hardwicke and Arthur Whetsol worked for a period under banjoist Elmer Snowden's leadership and then, after an argument over missing money, Ellington became the leader. His early group was called the Washingtonians.

Duke Ellington soon gained a job at the Hollywood Club (later renamed the Kentucky Club) for his band. For a brief time Sidney Bechet starred on soprano but more important to Duke's development was the playing of trumpeter Bubber Miley, a brilliant plunger specialist who largely founded the "jungle sound" that made Ellington's group sound different than anyone else. Duke recorded two titles with his group in November 1924 ("Choo Choo" and "Rainy Nights") that found his band already sounding recognizable despite only having three horns (with altoist Otto Hardwicke and trombonist Charles Irvis). Oddly enough the eight other selections that he recorded during 1925–26 are quite primitive and disappointing; Miley is absent and the band sounds as if it were struggling. However with the debut of Ellington's early theme song "East St. Louis Toodle-oo" along with "Birmingham Breakdown" on the session of November 29, 1926, the Duke Ellington Orchestra was essentially born. The band was up to 11 pieces including the wonderful wa-wa trombonist Tricky Sam Nanton, who made for a perfect team with Miley.

1927 was the breakthrough year for Duke Ellington. In addition to recording more versions of "East St. Louis Toodle-oo," he debuted "Black and Tan Fantasy" and "Creole Love Call"; the latter used Adelaide Hall's voice as an instrument. Baritonist Harry Carney (who would remain with Duke nonstop through 1974!) became a key member of the ensemble. And Ellington's band (through the help of manager Irving Mills) gained a permanent spot at the Cotton Club. Not only would its radio broadcasts soon make Ellington famous throughout the country, but he had the opportunity to write for the floor shows and the experience led to him growing rapidly as a composer/arranger.

Duke Ellington's life would never be a good topic for a Hollywood movie because from 1927 on it was one success after another. In 1928 clarinetist Barney Bigard and altoist Johnny Hodges became longtime members and Arthur Whetsol (whose lyrical trumpet offered a contrast to the speech-like playing of Miley) gained a more prominent role. In early 1929 Bubber Miley, whose alcoholism led to him becoming increasingly unreliable, was reluctantly let go but his replacement Cootie Williams would eventually be a more flexible soloist. Ellington appeared in his first film (*Black and Tan*) that year, and unlike most other Black celebrities of the 1920s and '30s, his performance did not find him acting as a clown or inferior to White people. Ellington always appeared as a classy and charming genius (just as he did in real life) and, despite the "inconvenience" of being Black in a racist society, Duke Ellington was able to survive (and eventually prosper) due to his brilliance without compromising himself.

While most big bands might have three or four notable soloists, Ellington's Orchestra in the 1930s featured eight: trumpeters Cootie Williams and Rex Stewart (the latter joined on cornet in 1935), trombonists Tricky Sam Nanton and Lawrence Brown, clarinetist Barney Bigard, altoist Hodges, baritonist Carney and the leader on piano; in addition Ivie Anderson was their finger singer. After leaving the Cotton Club in 1931 (although he would return on an occasional basis throughout the rest of the decade), the Ellington Orchestra became a road band, touring Europe and Sweden in 1933 and 1939 and becoming a major attraction in every key city in the U.S. Ellington, who had recorded a two-sided six-minute version of "Tiger Rag" in 1929 began to compose longer works including "Creole Rhapsody" (1931) and "Reminiscing in Tempo" (1935), and his three-minute masterpiece "Daybreak Express" found the orchestra doing an uncanny imitation of a train's journey. Although there was a lot more competition from big bands with the rise of the swing era in 1935, Ellington remained a major name. Such compositions as "Mood Indigo," "Rockin' in Rhythm," "It Don't Mean a Thing If It Ain't Got That Swing," "Sophisticated Lady," "Drop Me Off at Harlem," "In a Sentimental Mood," "Caravan" (written by valve trombonist Juan Tizol), "I Let a Song Go Out of My Heart," "Prelude to a Kiss," "Solitude" and "Boy Meets Horn" became standards.

By 1940 Duke Ellington's Orchestra had become, if anything, even stronger. Ben Webster joined as their first major voice on tenor, the innovative bassist Jimmy Blanton became the first important soloist on his instrument in jazz history and Billy Strayhorn, as arranger and composer, became Ellington's musical partner up until his death in 1967. When Cootie Williams departed in late 1940, Ray Nance (a fine trumpeter, violinist and vocalist) easily fit into the spot. Many critics consider Duke's 1940–42 big band to be his greatest. Certainly there was an explosion of activity with such new pieces as "Concerto for Cootie," "Cotton Tail," "Harlem Air Shaft," "All Too Soon," "Warm Valley," "Take the 'A' Train," "Just A-Settin' and A-Rockin'," "I Got It Bad," "Jump for Joy," "Chelsea Bridge," "Perdido," "The 'C' Jam Blues," "Johnny Come Lately" forming only a partial list of the orchestra's accomplishments.

In 1943 Duke Ellington gave his first Carnegie Hall concert (it would be an annual series lasting until 1950) and debuted his 50-minute work "Black, Brown and Beige" which, although it received mixed reviews, can now be heard and evaluated as a major success. The turnover in his orchestra increased during the latter half of the 1940s but the quality remained consistently high and, despite the collapse of the big-band era and the rise of bebop (a music that Ellington accepted and borrowed from), Duke's orchestra never did break up; his royalty payments from his hits helped keep the big band together. Such new players as trumpeters Taft Jordan, Shorty Baker and the remarkable high-note player Cat Anderson (who had several long stints with Duke), Tyree Glenn (on trombone and vibes), Al Sears on tenor and bassist Oscar Pettiford passed through the band and clarinetist Jimmy Hamilton stayed into the late '60s. "Don't Get Around Much Anymore" was a hit and Ellington also wrote such lengthy works as "The Perfume Suite," "The Deep South Suite" and "The Liberia Suite"; the last theme of "Happy Go Lucky Local" was "borrowed" by Jimmy Forrest and retitled "Night Train."

By the early '50s, Duke Ellington was in the only slump of his career but it was more a commercial slip than artistic. Johnny Hodges, Lawrence Brown and Sonny Greer suddenly left to form a small group under Hodges' leadership. In what was called "The Great James Robbery," Duke persuaded three members of Harry James' Orchestra to join him: drummer Louie Bellson, altoist Willie Smith and Juan Tizol (who had left Ellington in the 1940s). But by 1953–54 the orchestra was struggling a bit during an era when few big bands survived. However in 1955 Hodges returned to the fold and at the 1956 Newport Jazz Festival tenor saxophonist Paul Gonsalves took an exciting marathon solo on "Diminuendo and Crescendo in Blue" that caused a sensation. Ellington was big again and the momentum would continue through the remainder of his life.

With such fine soloists as trumpeters Clark Terry, Ray Nance, Cat Anderson and Willie Cook, trombonists Buster Cooper and Britt Woodman and a reed section that was together for over a decade (Hodges, Carney, Hamilton, Gonsalves and Russell Procope on clarinet and alto), Ellington's late-'50s orchestra could hold its own with any of his groups. Although "Satin Doll" in the early '50s was his last pop hit, Duke continued writing major works with Strayhorn. In the 1960s he turned toward religion, writing music for three sacred concerts and also composing "The Far East Suite," a very impressive and modern work. Duke also recorded albums on which he played piano in a trio with Charles Mingus and Max Roach, sat in with both the Louis Armstrong All-Stars and the John Coltrane Quartet and he had a double big-band date with Count Basie and a combo session with Coleman Hawkins. Constantly travelling the world and receiving long overdue honors (although not a Pulitzer Prize), Duke Ellington was finally recognized as a remarkable national treasure.

By the latter half of the '60s, Ellington's associates were starting to die off. Billy Strayhorn's loss in 1967 was major as was Johnny Hodges' passing in 1970. There were important new members in Harold Ashby on tenor, altoist Norris Turney and (in 1973) trumpeter Barry Lee Hall. But in 1974 Duke Ellington was stricken with cancer and spent his 75th birthday in a hospital. His death four weeks later has left a huge hole that will never be filled. — *Scott Yanow*

The Birth of a Band, Vol. 1 / Nov. 1924–Dec. 1926 / EPM ◆◆◆
This CD contains virtually all of Duke Ellington's recordings before he had developed his own musical identity. Starting off with a piano roll from 1924 and including obscure vocals by Alberta Hunter, Florence Bristol, Alberta Jones and Jo Trent, the valuable set also has all of Ellington's earliest instrumentals, cut during the years that his Washingtonians successfully struggled and landed an important association with the Kentucky Club. Highly recommended to collectors but certainly too primitive for most of Ellington's fans. — *Scott Yanow*

Complete, Vol. 1: 1925–1928 / Sep. 1925–Oct. 1928 / CBS ◆◆◆◆
French Columbia, in the mid-to-late '70s, put out a perfectly conceived Duke Ellington series that eventually totalled 15 double LPs. As with the French RCA program, Columbia reissued every Ellington recording they owned, including all of the alternate takes, but unfortunately both of these definitive series are very difficult to acquire and current CD programs are less complete. All of the Columbia two-fers are worth tracking down if possible. *Volume 1* has four early sides from 1925–26 that find Ellington struggling to find his own musical personality. Then suddenly, with "East St. Louis Toodle-oo" from March 22, 1927, he emerges as a major force. The contrasting trumpets of Bubber Miley and Arthur Whetsol, along with trombonist Tricky Sam Nanton and a variety of emerging soloists, star throughout this wonderful set which is mostly from 1928. — *Scott Yanow*

☆ **Early Ellington (1926–1931)** / Nov. 29, 1926–Jan. 20, 1931 / Decca ◆◆◆◆◆
This three-CD set, which has all of Duke Ellington's recordings for the Brunswick and Vocalion labels, dwarfs all of the earlier reissues that Decca and MCA have put out of this important material. Starting with the first session in which the Ellington Orchestra sounds distinctive ("East St. Louis Toodle-oo" and "Birmingham Breakdown" from Nov. 29, 1926) and progressing through the Cotton Club years, this essential release (which contains 56 performances) adds a few "new" alternate takes and rare items ("Soliloquy" and a few titles by the "Six Jolly Jesters") to make this collection truly complete, at least for MCA's holdings (since Ellington also recorded for Columbia and Victor-owned labels during the same period). With such major soloists as trumpeters Bubber Miley (and his replacement Cootie Williams), Freddy Jenkins and Arthur Whetsol, trombonist Tricky Sam Nanton, clarinetist Barney Bigard, altoist Johnny Hodges, baritonist Harry Carney and the pianist/leader, along with the classic arrangements/compositions, this set is essential for all serious jazz collections. — *Scott Yanow*

The Brunswick Recordings, Vol. 1 (1926–1929) / Dec. 29, 1926–Jan. 8, 1929 / MCA ◆◆◆
The first of two CDs featuring highpoints from the Ellington recordings owned by MCA, this set features music from the Bubber Miley era including "Immigration Blues" (from the first session when Duke Ellington's band established its identity) to early versions of "East St. Louis Toodle-oo" and "Black and Tan Fantasy," an alternate take of "Black Beauty" and the exciting two-part version of "Tiger Rag." Trumpeters Bubber Miley and Arthur Whetsol and trombonist Tricky Sam Nanton star throughout. — *Scott Yanow*

☆ **The Works of Duke, Vols. 1–5** / Jan. 10, 1927–Nov. 21, 1930 / RCA ◆◆◆◆◆
In the '70s, French RCA did a perfect job of reissuing Duke Ellington's priceless recordings for its associated labels, releasing everything cut through 1952 (including all of the alternate takes) on 24 LPs also available in five box sets. No other reissue program conducted by RCA (whether on LP or on CD) comes close, although these sets are unfortunately out of print. The five volumes trace Ellington's legacy from 1927–30 and, along with a few period vocals and novelties, is overflowing with classics. Get it if you can. — *Scott Yanow*

Okeh Ellington / Mar. 22, 1927–Nov. 8, 1930 / Columbia ◆◆◆◆◆
Although generally not as celebrated as his Victor recordings of the same period, Duke Ellington's performances for Okeh (late acquired by Columbia) are among the best of the period, featuring distinctive solos by the likes of trumpeter Bubber Miley (and later his replacement Cootie Williams), trombonist Tricky Sam Nanton (who, like Miley, was an expert with wa-wa mutes), clarinetist Barney Bigard and altoist Johnny Hodges, among others. These 50 performances (which bypass Ellington's alternate takes) contain many classics including his original theme "East St. Louis Toodle-oo," "Black and Tan Fantasy," "The Mooche," "Mood Indigo" and his two earliest solo piano sides. This is one of the best sets of early Ellington currently available. — *Scott Yanow*

Flaming Youth / Oct. 26, 1927–Jan. 6, 1929 / RCA ◆◆◆◆
Of all of the single LPs released of early Duke Ellington in the '60s and '70s, *Flaming Youth* was the definitive one, for it seemed to include the most exciting versions of each of Ellington's classics of the era. These versions of "Black and Tan Fantasy," "Jubilee Stomp," "The Mooche" and especially "East St. Louis Toodle-oo" have never been topped and, if only for the contributions of the

unique trumpeter Bubber Miley, this set was a perfect introduction to early Ellington during the LP era. —*Scott Yanow*

Early Ellington (1927–1934) / Oct. 26, 1927–Jan. 10, 1934 / Bluebird ✦✦✦
Thus far RCA, in its Bluebird series, has released three CDs of early Duke Ellington. Although not comparable in quantity to its earlier "complete" series on French RCA LPs, this first disc is well worth acquiring and is a perfect place for collectors to start in exploring Duke Ellington's music of the '20s and early '30s. Highpoints include "Black and Tan Fantasy," "Creole Love Call," "East St. Louis Toodle-oo," the lyrical "Black Beauty," "Mood Indigo" and the remarkable "Daybreak Express," on which Ellington has his unique orchestra colorfully depicting a train ride. Some of his music still sounds futuristic today. —*Scott Yanow*

Duke Ellington (1927–1928) / Oct. 1927–Mar. 1928 / Classics ✦✦✦✦

Jungle Nights in Harlem / Dec. 19, 1927–Jan. 9, 1932 / Bluebird ✦✦✦
This second of three CDs of early Ellington released by Bluebird has the loose theme of his Cotton Club days as an excuse to release a variety of recordings from a five-year period. Highlights include the two-part "A Night at the Cotton Club" (essentially a medley), some of the hotter songs from the Broadway musical *Blackbirds of 1928* ("Bandanna Babies," in addition to an odd vocal, has one of trumpeter Bubber Miley's greatest solos), some mood pieces and two lengthy medleys from 1932. Although the music deserves to be reissued as complete sessions, this sampler is consistently delightful and shows that, when it came to swing, Ellington (along with Fletcher Henderson) predated everyone. —*Scott Yanow*

Jubilee Stomp / Mar. 26, 1928–May 9, 1934 / Bluebird ✦✦✦
The third of three CDs of early Ellington put out by Bluebird, this set has mostly lesser-known recordings including a few pop tunes and mood pieces. Collectors will want to acquire the complete sessions (hopefully RCA will get around to reissuing this timeless music in a more definitive fashion in the future) but this CD has plenty of fine moments, including memorable versions of "Bugle Call Rag" and the hot title tune. —*Scott Yanow*

Duke Ellington (1928) / Mar. 1928–Oct. 1928 / Classics ✦✦✦✦

Duke Ellington (1928–1929) / Oct. 1928–Mar. 1929 / Classics ✦✦✦✦

Complete, Vol. 2: 1928–1930 / Oct. 1928–Nov. 20, 1929 / CBS ✦✦✦✦
The second volume of this regrettably unavailable series of two-fers contains all of CBS's Ellington recordings from October 1928 up to January 29, 1930, a period when trumpeter Cootie Williams replaced Bubber Miley and altoist Johnny Hodges quickly developed into one of the major soloists in jazz. There are lots of valuable rarities on this highly enjoyable two-fer. —*Scott Yanow*

Brunswick Era, Vol. 2 / Jan. 8, 1929–Jan. 20, 1931 / Decca ✦✦✦
The second of two CDs featuring highlights from MCA's collection of early Duke Ellington (but not as complete as their three LPs from back in the '70s), this enjoyable set is filled with performances from the early Depression years, including the jubilant "Wall Street Wail" (recorded only a short while after the crash of 1929), "Mood Indigo," "Rockin' in Rhythm" and his two-part "Creole Rhapsody." During this period, altoist Johnny Hodges emerged as a major soloist and Cootie Williams became more comfortable as the replacement of the great Bubber Miley. —*Scott Yanow*

Duke Ellington (1929) / Mar. 1929–Jul. 1929 / Classics ✦✦✦✦

Duke Ellington (1929–1930) / Aug. 1929–Jan. 1930 / Classics ✦✦✦✦

The Cotton Club Stomp / 1929–1935 / Biograph ✦✦
For the true Ellington fanatic who needs every one of his recordings, this LP contains the soundtracks from three of his earliest film appearances. One gets the soundtrack of 1929's *Black and Tan* (which featured trumpeter Arthur Whetsol in a prominent role), 1933's *A Bundle of Blues* (including Ivie Anderson singing "Stormy Weather") and 1935's *Symphony in Black*; the latter has one blues chorus by Billie Holiday. A well-done package but not essential. —*Scott Yanow*

Complete, Vol. 3: 1930–1932 / Jan. 29, 1930–Feb. 4, 1932 / CBS ✦✦✦✦
The third of 15 volumes that document every Duke Ellington

recording for CBS and its related labels up to 1940, this hard-to-find double LP has many alternate takes and even more gems from 1930–32, including rare remakes of "The Mooche" and "Black and Tan Fantasy" and the original "It Don't Mean a Thing If It Ain't Got That Swing." —*Scott Yanow*

Duke Ellington (1930) / Jan. 1930–Jun. 1930 / Classics ✦✦✦✦

Duke Ellington (1930), Vol. 2 / Jun. 1930–Nov. 1930 / Classics ✦✦✦✦

☆ **Works of Duke, Vols. 6–10** / Nov. 26, 1930–Jul. 22, 1940 / RCA ✦✦✦✦✦
The second of five priceless box sets put out by French RCA in the '70s, these five LPs cover Ellington from 1930–34 and also when he returned to Victor in 1940. Loads of brilliant music; even the weaker items have their great moments. —*Scott Yanow*

Duke Ellington (1930–1931) / Nov. 1930–Jan. 1931 / Classics ✦✦✦✦

Duke Ellington (1931–1932) / Jan. 1931–Feb. 1932 / Classics ✦✦✦✦

Reflections in Ellington / Feb. 3, 1932–Sep. 26, 1940 / Everybodys ✦✦✦
For this LP there are previously unissued broadcast performances from 1940 (most of them quite rewarding) that feature one of Duke Ellington's greatest orchestras, along with two medleys from 1932 that are heard for the first time in stereo. Apparently the latter items were originally recorded using two sets of microphones and, although the notes are unchanged from the more conventional release, one can hear a bit of separation between the two channels. This LP is well worth searching for. —*Scott Yanow*

Complete, Vol. 4: 1932 / Feb. 4, 1932–Dec. 21, 1932 / CBS ✦✦✦✦
From the French CBS series of two-fer LPs that reissued all of Duke Ellington's output (including alternate takes) for their associated labels, this set finds his orchestra still flourishing musically at the height of the Depression. Most of these titles generally miss getting reissued by "best-of" series but are all worth hearing. Best known are the two versions of "St. Louis Blues" with guest Bing Crosby and Ellington's famous recording of "The Sheik of Araby" that is highlighted by a famous chorus by trombonist Lawrence Brown. —*Scott Yanow*

Solos, Duets and Trios / Feb. 9, 1932–Aug. 30, 1967 / Bluebird ✦✦✦✦
This CD puts the focus on Duke Ellington the piano player, featuring the genius in several different settings. He is heard playing two duets with Billy Strayhorn, taking rare piano solos in 1932, 1941 and 1967, meeting up with Earl Hines in 1965 and leading a trio in 1945. However the real reason to acquire this set is the four duets (plus five alternate takes) with Jimmy Blanton, the first important bass soloist in jazz history. From 1940, those recordings find Blanton sounding like the Charles Mingus of 20 years later and Ellington unselfishly but masterfully playing the role of an accompanist. —*Scott Yanow*

Duke Ellington (1932–1933) / May 1932–Jan. 1933 / Classics ✦✦✦✦

Complete, Vol. 5: 1932–1933 / Dec. 21, 1932–May 16, 1933 / CBS ✦✦✦✦
The fifth of 15 double LPs from French CBS that document Ellington's long period in the '30s on Columbia's labels has many fine recordings that often elude reissue. Among the highpoints are collaborations with guest vocalists like The Mills Brothers, Ethel Waters and Adelaide Hall, a couple versions apiece of two medleys from The Blackbirds of 1928 and the original recordings of "Sophisticated Lady" and "Drop Me Off at Harlem." —*Scott Yanow*

Complete, Vol. 6: 1933–1936 / Aug. 15, 1933–Jan. 20, 1936 / CBS ✦✦✦✦
It would be difficult to improve upon this French CBS reissue series; if only it were made available on CD. *Volume Six* covers a session apiece from 1933 and 1934 and then most of 1935. Among the classics are a spirited version of "In the Shade of the Old Apple Tree," "In a Sentimental Mood," "Truckin'" and the four-part "Reminiscing in Tempo." Recommended if it can be found. —*Scott Yanow*

★ **The Duke's Men: Small Groups, Vol. 1** / Dec. 12, 1934–Jan. 19, 1938 / Columbia ✦✦✦✦✦
In the '30s Ellington started recording prolifically with small groups taken from his big band. It gave him an opportunity to

both debut new works and to let his sidemen stretch out and act as leaders once in awhile (under his direction). This two-disc set contains 45 recordings, almost all of them brilliant, including sessions ostensibly under the leadership of cornetist Rex Stewart (including two selections cut before he joined Ellington), clarinetist Barney Bigard, trumpeter Cootie Williams and altoist Johnny Hodges. In addition to early versions of such future standards as "Caravan," "Stompy Jones" and "Echoes of Harlem," there are many hot stomps performed that feature strong solos from these very distinctive stylists. Brilliant music, highly recommended. —*Scott Yanow*

Complete, Vol. 7: 1936–1937 / Feb. 27, 1936–Mar. 5, 1937 / CBS ✦✦✦✦

From the definitive French CBS reissue program of two-LP sets, this volume covers 1936 and a bit of 1937 with small-group sessions led by Rex Stewart and Barney Bigard (the latter includes the original version of "Caravan") and many lesser-known big-band sides including a pair of rare solo piano performances by Ellington and Rex Stewart's feature "Trumpet in Spades." —*Scott Yanow*

Complete, Vol. 8: 1937 / Mar. 5, 1937–May 20, 1937 / CBS ✦✦✦✦

A continuing French CBS definitive reissue series of Duke Ellington's '30s recordings for its labels, this two-LP set sticks to the first half of 1937. Highlighted by small-group sessions from Cootie Williams and his Rug Cutters, Barney Bigard's Jazzopators and the first part of Johnny Hodges initial session as a leader, there are many gems among even the obscurities. —*Scott Yanow*

Complete, Vol. 9: 1937 / May 20, 1937–Sep. 20, 1937 / CBS ✦✦✦✦

Continuing French CBS's comprehensive mid-'70s reissue of all of Duke Ellington's recordings during the '30s for its labels, this very enjoyable two-fer has small-group sessions led by Johnny Hodges, Barney Bigard and Rex Stewart and such titles by the big band as "Diminuendo in Blue," "Crescendo in Blue" and the exciting "Harmony in Harlem." Other bands during this era may have been better known to the general public, but in reality Duke Ellington's orchestra had no close competitors. —*Scott Yanow*

Complete, Vol. 10: 1937–1938 / Oct. 26, 1937–Mar. 28, 1938 / CBS ✦✦✦✦

The majority of this volume from French CBS's complete reissue of Duke Ellington's '30s recordings focuses on the many rewarding small-group sessions led by his sidemen (and actually directed by Ellington). Cootie Williams, Barney Bigard and Johnny Hodges all get their chances to act as leaders while the big band is heard on such selections as "The New Black and Tan Fantasy" and "I Let a Song Go out of My Heart." —*Scott Yanow*

Complete, Vol. 11: 1938 / Mar. 28, 1938–Aug. 4, 1938 / CBS ✦✦✦✦

This 11th of 15 volumes from French CBS continues the complete reissue of all Duke Ellington's recordings during the '30s for Columbia's associated labels. With small-group sessions led by Cootie Williams and Johnny Hodges and many fine big-band sessions, this set proves that Duke Ellington had a brilliant orchestra before the 1939–42 edition made history. Included are two versions of Lawrence Brown's famous solo on "Rose of the Rio Grande." —*Scott Yanow*

Duke's Men, Vol. 2 / Mar. 28, 1938–Mar. 20, 1939 / Columbia/Legacy ✦✦✦✦✦

This second two-disc set, like the first, includes all of the master takes (no alternates) from the small-group sessions led by Duke Ellington's sidemen. During the year covered on this volume, Johnny Hodges, Cootie Williams and Rex Stewart all had opportunities to head sessions and the results included early versions of "Jeep's Blues," "Pyramid," "Prelude to a Kiss," "The Jeep's Jumping" and "Hodge Podge" along with many hot obscurities. There are few duds and many memorable performances during these 43 recordings. —*Scott Yanow*

Complete, Vol. 12: 1938 / Aug. 4, 1938–Dec. 22, 1938 / CBS ✦✦✦✦

This two-LP set from French CBS's superb reissue series of the mid-to-late '70s covers a five-month period with small-group sessions by Johnny Hodges (including "Prelude to a Kiss" and "The Jeep Is Jumpin'") and Cootie Williams, along with such big-band selections as "Battle of Swing" and Rex Stewart's famous "Boy Meets Horn." —*Scott Yanow*

Complete, Vol. 13: 1938–1939 / Dec. 22, 1938–Jun. 2, 1939 / CBS ✦✦✦✦

Taken from the period just prior to bassist Jimmy Blanton joining his orchestra, this two-LP set finds Duke Ellington playing in several formats, including small groups drawn from his orchestra led by altoist Johnny Hodges, trumpeter Cootie Williams and cornetist Rex Stewart, on a pair of rare piano solos (originally unissued) and some big-band classics. Highpoints include "Dooji Wooji," "Pussy Willow," "Finesse" and two versions of "Portrait of the Lion." —*Scott Yanow*

Complete, Vol. 14: 1939 / Jun. 2, 1939–Oct. 14, 1939 / CBS ✦✦✦✦

The next-to-last volume in French CBS's definitive (but now out-of-print) LP series, this two-fer has combo sides led by altoist Johnny Hodges, clarinetist Barney Bigard and trumpeter Cootie Williams, a pair of numbers with a vocal group called The Quintones and bassist Jimmy Blanton's first recordings with Ellington's full orchestra. Whether it be "I'm Checkin' out Go'om Bye," "The Sergeant Was Shy," "Tootin' Through the Roof" or some of the lesser-known tracks, this music is consistently enjoyable and timeless. —*Scott Yanow*

In Boston 1939–1940 / Jul. 26, 1939+Jan. 9, 1940 / Jazz Unlimited ✦✦✦✦

This CD has two formerly rare broadcasts featuring the Duke Ellington Orchestra near the peak of its powers. The earlier session is highlighted by "Jazz Potpourri," "Rose of the Rio Grande" and "Pussy Willow" while the later date (which finds Jimmy Blanton on bass) has fine versions of "Little Posey," "Tootin' Through the Roof" and "Merry-Go-Round" among others. With trumpeters Cootie Williams and Rex Stewart, trombonist Tricky Sam Nanton and Lawrence Brown, clarinetist Barney Bigard, altoist Johnny Hodges, baritonist Harry Carney and Ellington himself among the main soloists, and Ivie Anderson and Herb Jeffries contributing vocals, it would be surprising if this CD were not on the want lists of many Ellington collectors. —*Scott Yanow*

Complete, Vol. 15: 1939–1940 / Oct. 14, 1939–Feb. 15, 1940 / CBS ✦✦✦✦

The final two-LP set in French CBS's definitive reissue of Duke Ellington's recordings for their associated labels, this package finds the orchestra poised for greatness just prior to switching to RCA. Bassist Jimmy Blanton was now in the band, tenor saxophonist Ben Webster was aboard by the second half of this set, and such longtime stars as trumpeter Cootie Williams, cornetist Rex Stewart, trombonists Tricky Sam Nanton and Lawrence Brown, clarinetist Barney Bigard and altoist Johnny Hodges were very much in their prime. Hodges, Bigard and Cootie get to lead some small-group sessions, Ellington is heard solo on "Blues," there are two Ellington-Blanton piano-bass duets (which were unprecedented for the time) and the full orchestra backs singer Ivie Anderson on one of her finest sessions. Overall, this series is a brilliant effort that should be duplicated on CD. —*Scott Yanow*

Blanton-Webster Band / 1939–1942 / Bluebird ✦✦✦

1939–1942. Important material, but there's some question about the sound quality and production of this set. —*Ron Wynn*

In a Mellotone / May 28, 1940–Jun. 26, 1942 / RCA ✦✦✦

This CD is a straight reissue of an RCA album from the early '60s. Comprised of 16 performances by Duke Ellington's Orchestra during what many consider to be his peak period, the program is highlighted by such classics as the original version of "Take the 'A' Train," "Just A-Settin' and A-Rockin'," "I Got It Bad," "Perdido," "Cotton Tail" and "All Too Soon." With such soloists as trumpeter Cootie Williams (who was replaced by Ray Nance) and Rex Stewart, trombonists Tricky Sam Nanton and Lawrence Brown, altoist Johnny Hodges, clarinetist Barney Bigard, Ben Webster on tenor, baritonist Harry Carney and the innovative bassist Jimmy Blanton (in addition to the leader/pianist), this was one of the all-time great orchestras. Ellington's recordings are available in more complete form elsewhere but this is a strong sampling. —*Scott Yanow*

Jimmy Blanton Years / Jun. 1940–Oct. 9, 1941 / Queen ✦✦✦✦

Longtime Ellington collectors should love this LP, for it includes rare radio broadcasts of the Duke Ellington Orchestra during 1940–41 and four selections that find Ellington and bassist Jimmy Blanton making guest appearances with John Scott Trotter's studio orchestra. A perfect LP for those Ellington fanatics who think they have everything. —*Scott Yanow*

☆ **Works of Duke, Vols. 11–15** / Jul. 24, 1940–Jul. 2, 1941 / RCA
✦✦✦✦✦
The third of three brilliant box sets put out by French RCA in the
'70s, this five-LP package covers a year in the life of Duke
Ellington, one of his very best. Complete with all of the alternate
takes, this music has many more than its share of classic performances. Unfortunately, it is long out of print but worth bidding
for on auction lists. —*Scott Yanow*

The Great Ellington Units / Nov. 2, 1940–Sep. 29, 1941 / RCA
✦✦✦
Beginning in the '30s, Duke Ellington started recording with
small groups taken out of his orchestra under the leadership of
his sidemen. These highly enjoyable recordings offered the musicians some variety and the chance to debut some new material.
All but two of the small-group recordings cut for Victor during
1940–41 are included on this very enjoyable CD including such
future Ellington-associated standards as "Day Dream," "Things
Ain't What They Used to Be," "Passion Flower" and "C Jam Blues."
With altoist Johnny Hodges, cornetist Rex Stewart and clarinetist
Barney Bigard acting as leaders (and bassist Jimmy Blanton
inspiring the soloists), the music is consistently brilliant. —*Scott
Yanow*

At Fargo / Nov. 7, 1940 / Book of the Month Club ✦✦✦✦✦

★ **Fargo ND, November 7, 1940** / Nov. 7, 1940 / Vintage Jazz
Classics ✦✦✦✦✦
One winter night in late 1940, Jack Towers (then a young
Ellington fan) received permission to record the orchestra on his
portable disc cutter at a dance in Fargo, ND. Little did he know
that it was a historic night (as trumpeter Ray Nance made his
debut with the band) and that the band would be in inspired
form. Decades later the music came out on LP and now this double CD includes every scrap of music that has survived. The Duke
Ellington Orchestra was at one of its peaks during this period,
overflowing with distinctive and unique soloists and propelled by
the top bassist in jazz (Jimmy Blanton). With the accelerated writing activity of Ellington and his new musical partner Billy
Strayhorn, there was no better orchestra at the time and rarely
since. tenor saxophonist Ben Webster is heard in top form on
"Star Dust," cornetist Rex Stewart, trombonists Tricky Sam
Nanton and Lawrence Brown, clarinetist Barney Bigard and
altoist Johnny Hodges also have some very strong moments and
Ray Nance does his best to fit in; many in the band were hearing
him for the first time. It is indeed very fortunate that Jack Towers
was present for what would have been a forgotten one-night
stand. —*Scott Yanow*

Take the "A" Train: The Legendary Blanton-Webster / Jan. 15,
1941–Dec. 3, 1941 / Vintage Jazz Classics ✦✦✦✦
During 1941, one of Ellington's peak years, not only did he record
frequently in the studios but made this CD's worth of transcriptions for radio. Of the 26 selections on this generous set, eight of
the songs were never recorded commercially and six others are
heard here in their earliest versions, including his theme "Take
the 'A' Train" and "Perdido." The all-star orchestra is propelled by
the great bassist Jimmy Blanton. Highly recommended.

☆ **The Works of Duke, Vols. 16–20** / Jul. 2, 1941–May 15, 1945 /
RCA ✦✦✦✦✦
The fourth of five mammoth box sets documenting Duke
Ellington's Victor recordings (including all alternate takes), this
one has five LPs. Small group sessions by Rex Stewart, Johnny
Hodges and Barney Bigard alternate with full-band classics
(including two versions of "Chelsea Bridge" and the original renditions of "Perdido" and "C Jam Blues") during the first half of this
set. The remainder traces Ellington's activity in the war years
(including his four-part studio version of "Black, Brown and
Beige" up to 1945, when he remade many of his hits from the
previous decade, most successfully a hot vocal version of "It Don't
Mean a Thing." —*Scott Yanow*

★ **The Carnegie Hall Concerts (January 1943)** / Jan. 23, 1943–Jan.
28, 1943 / Prestige ✦✦✦✦✦
This two-CD set captures one of the milestones in Duke
Ellington's long and extremely productive career, highlighted by
his monumental suite "Black, Brown and Beige" in the only full-
length suite ever recorded by his orchestra; soon it was only
performed as excerpts. In addition, Ellington's all-star orchestra
(including such stylists as trumpeters Rex Stewart, Ray Nance and
Shorty Baker, trombonists Tricky Sam Nanton and Lawrence

Brown and a saxophone section boasting Johnny Hodges, Ben
Webster and Harry Carney) excels on the shorter pieces, a mixture
of older and recent compositions. Every serious jazz library
should contain this set. —*Scott Yanow*

Duke Ellington, Vol. 1: 1943 / Nov. 8, 1943 / Circle ✦✦✦
This is the first in a nine-LP series that contains all of the radio
transcriptions that Duke Ellington and his orchestra recorded for
the World Broadcasting Series, including alternates and some
false starts. Due to the latter, there is generally around five to
eight songs per LP, making this nevertheless valuable series of
primary interest to collectors. *Volume One* has previously rare
versions of "Rockin' in Rhythm," "Blue Skies," "Boy Meets Horn,"
"Do Nothing 'Till You Hear from Me" and "Summertime." —*Scott
Yanow*

Duke Ellington, Vol. 2: 1943 / Nov. 8, 1943–Nov. 9, 1943 / Circle
✦✦✦
The second in this nine-LP series of transcriptions documents the
1943 Duke Ellington Orchestra shortly after tenor star Ben
Webster had departed, but the band had so many talented soloists
that he was barely missed. *Volume Two* is one of the strongest in
this collector's program, containing nine selections (in addition to
alternate takes and false starts) that are highlighted by features
for Johny Hodges and Ray Nance. —*Scott Yanow*

Duke Ellington, Vol. 3: 1943 / Nov. 9, 1943 / Circle ✦✦✦
The third of nine volumes in this collector's series featuring Duke
Ellington's transcriptions from 1943 and 1945; the best tracks are
strong versions of "Caravan" and "Ain't Misbehavin'" (featuring
trumpeter Harold "Shorty" Baker). —*Scott Yanow*

Duke Ellington, Vol. 4: 1943 / Dec. 1, 1943 / Circle ✦✦✦
Part of a nine-LP series of Duke Ellington's transcriptions for the
World Broadcasting System, *Volume Four* has particularly enjoyable versions of "It Don't Mean a Thing," "Johnny Come Lately"
and "Creole Love Call" although, due to the many alternates, it is
recommended mostly to true Ellington collectors. —*Scott Yanow*

Duke Ellington, Vol. 5: 1943–1945 / Dec. 1, 1943–Jan. 2, 1945 /
Circle ✦✦✦
The midway point in this collector's series is reached in *Volume
Five*, which splits the program between performances by Duke
Ellington's orchestras of 1943 and 1945. Although there were
some personnel changes, there is a strong consistency to this
series. Eight fine numbers (along with some alternate takes and
false starts) makes this a worthy release. —*Scott Yanow*

At Carnegie Hall / Dec. 11, 1943 / Everest ✦✦✦✦
Prestige has up to this point released the performances from four
of Duke Ellington's Carnegie Hall concerts, but they have not
acquired this one, his second recital of 1943. This budget LP only
has some highlights but they include exuberant versions of standards and two excerpts from "Black, Brown and Beige." Unless it
is released in a more complete form elsewhere, this LP version is
worth searching for. —*Scott Yanow*

The Carnegie Hall Concerts (December 1944) / Dec. 19, 1944 /
Prestige ✦✦✦✦
The Ellington orchestra was undergoing some personnel (and personality) changes during this era, none of it unexciting. This
Carnegie Hall concert (available on two CDs) introduced
Ellington's "Perfume Suite," and includes a half-hour series of
selections from "Black, Brown and Beige," but also in the shorter
pieces shows the impact of tenorman Al Sears and high-note wizard Cat Anderson on the band's sound, making it a more potentially boisterous and extroverted ensemble. Lots of great moments
from this brilliant orchestra occurred during this concert. —*Scott
Yanow*

Duke Ellington, Vol. 6: 1945 / Jan. 2, 1945–Jan. 3, 1945 / Circle
✦✦✦
The sixth volume in this nine-LP series finds Duke Ellington's
orchestra taking their time perfecting six songs to be used for
radio transcriptions. Best is Rex Stewart's adventurous "Frantic
Fantasy," but the many takes make this one recommended mostly for Ellington collectors. —*Scott Yanow*

Duke Ellington, Vol. 7: 1945 / Jan. 3, 1945–Jul. 31, 1945 / Circle
✦✦
This is one of the lesser volumes in the nine-LP series of radio
transcriptions from Duke Ellington. But even with weaker material, too many false starts and a generous dose of Al Hibbler's
vocals, there are moments of interest on "Bluetopia" and several
individual solos. —*Scott Yanow*

☆ **The Works of Duke, Vols. 21–24** / May 16, 1945–Apr. 25, 1953 /
   RCA ✦✦✦✦✦
The final box set (four LPs this time) put out by French RCA (why
doesn't the American counterpart make all of Ellington's recordings available?) finishes off this program with his studio performances from 1945–46 and a live concert dating from 1952. There
is plenty of surprising material (such as "Indiana," "Lover Man"
and three W.C. Handy tunes), two trio performances, the original
version of "The Perfume Suite," Ellington's appearances with several all-star groups and many other highpoints. The concert also
has a fine version of "Harlem." A strong ending to an exciting but
sadly out-of-print series. —*Scott Yanow*

Duke Ellington, Vol. 8: 1945 / Jul. 31, 1945–Aug. 7, 1945 / Circle
   ✦✦✦
In contrast to *Volume Seven* in this nine-LP series of radio transcriptions by Duke Ellington, this set contains more than its share
of interesting selections, including rarely performed arrangements
of "Metronome All Out," "Esquire Swank," "Downbeat Shuffle"
and "Hollywood Hangover." In addition, Ray Nance's vocal on
"Otto, Make That Riff Staccato" is always a delight. —*Scott Yanow*

Duke Ellington, Vol. 9: 1945 / Aug. 7, 1945 / Circle ✦✦✦
The final set in this nine-LP series has six fine performances
(including a lengthy "In the Shade of the Old Apple Tree"), five false
starts and three complete alternate takes. This is a very valuable
collector's series, although more casual listeners are well-advised to
first acquire Ellington's studio recordings of the era. —*Scott Yanow*

The Great Chicago Concerts / Jan. 20, 1946+Nov. 10, 1946 /
   Music Masters ✦✦✦✦
The 1946 Duke Ellington Orchestra is heard in superior form
throughout this highly recommended set. Split between a pair of
separate concerts that took place in Chicago, this two-CD release
of mostly previously unissued material features such top soloists
as trumpeters Taft Jordan, Cat Anderson, Harold "Shorty" Baker
and Ray Nance, trombonist Lawrence Brown, altoist Johnny
Hodges, clarinetist Jimmy Hamilton, Al Sears on tenor, baritonist
Harry Carney and the pianist/leader. Four selections from the
later concert feature the great guitarist Django Reinhardt as a special guest but, although he plays well, there is virtually no interaction with the band. In addition to fresh versions of many of
Ellington's standards and then-current arrangements, this two-fer
has a lengthy excerpt from "Black, Brown & Beige," Ellington's
three-part "Tonal Group" and the rarely heard "Deep South Suite."
—*Scott Yanow*

The Uncollected Duke Ellington & His Orchestra, Vol. 1 (1946)
   / Mar. 28, 1946 / Hindsight ✦✦✦✦
Hindsight has released five excellent LPs of radio transcriptions
by Duke Ellington from 1946–47, one of his most underrated periods. With the trumpet section now starring Taft Jordan and the
phenomenal high-note virtuoso Cat Anderson, Tricky Sam
Nanton and Lawrence Brown still in the trombone section and
veterans Harry Carney and Johnny Hodges joined in the saxophone section by clarinetist Jimmy Hamilton and tenorman Al
Sears (not to mention the presence of bassist Oscar Pettiford),
Ellington's orchestra was far from in decline. There are lots of colorful moments provided throughout this series by all of the above
and *Volume One* gets it off to a solid start. —*Scott Yanow*

The Uncollected Duke Ellington & His Orchestra, Vol. 2 (1946)
   / Mar. 28, 1946–Nov. 16, 1946 / Hindsight ✦✦✦✦
The second of five Hindsight LPs containing Duke Ellington's
radio transcriptions from 1946–47 has lots of strong moments
including "Perdido," the rousing "Suddenly It Jumped," a version
of "One O'Clock Jump" and the only performance of a feature for
bassist Oscar Pettiford, "Tip Toe Topic." —*Scott Yanow*

The Uncollected Duke Ellington & His Orchestra, Vol. 5 (1947)
   / Mar. 28, 1946–Jun. 10, 1947 / Hindsight ✦✦✦✦
The final volume in this very worthy five-LP series of radio transcriptions, this set features the 1947 Duke Ellington Orchestra on
plenty of material not generally associated with Ellington, including "How High the Moon," "Royal Garden Blues" and
"Embraceable You." The whole series casts a new light on this
often neglected period in his career and there are more highlights
than one can list. For two, try these versions of "Jumpin' Punkins"
and "Jump for Joy." —*Scott Yanow*

The Uncollected Duke Ellington & His Orchestra, Vol. 3 (1946)
   / Jul. 16, 1946–Jul. 17, 1946 / Hindsight ✦✦✦✦
The third of five volumes in this worthy LP series of Duke

Ellington radio transcriptions finds Ellington's orchestra in spirited form on a set of standards and obscurities. Al Sears' tenor is
powerful on "The Suburbanite," and "Just You, Just Me" and
"Indiana" are quite enjoyable but it is the great Tricky Sam
Nonton's solo on "The Mooche" (recorded four days before his
death) that takes honors. —*Scott Yanow*

Sir Duke / Oct. 23, 1946–Dec. 25, 1946 / Drive Archive ✦✦✦
Although many critics think of Duke Ellington's 1946 orchestra
as being a bit less significant than his band of five years earlier,
it still ranked with the very best of the period. Eleven of
Ellington's studio recordings of the period (including the two-part
renditions of "Overture to a Jam Session" and "Happy Go Lucky
Local") are included on this budget CD reissue. Highlights include
the exciting "Jam-A-Ditty," a trumpet battle on "Blue Skies"
(which was renamed "Trumpets No End" by its arranger Mary Lou
Williams), Johnny Hodges' lyrical alto on "Sultry Sunset" and
"Magenta Haze," and the theme from the last part of "Happy Go
Lucky Local" which would later be "borrowed" note-for-note by
Jimmy Forrest to create "Night Train." —*Scott Yanow*

The Golden Duke / Oct. 23, 1946–Nov. 1950 / Prestige ✦✦✦✦
This double LP contains some very valuable Duke Ellington studio recordings that have since been reissued as separate sessions.
The 13 titles from late 1946 include the hot "Jam-A-Ditty," a classic trumpet battle on "Blue Skies," Ray Nance's colorful vocal on
"Tulip or Turnip" and the original version of "Happy-Go-Lucky
Local" which Jimmy Forrest would "borrow" a few years later and
rename "Night Train." The second half of this two-fer features
piano duets by Duke Ellington and Billy Strayhorn (the radical-
sounding "Tonk" is very memorable) and four showcases for
Oscar Pettiford's cello. This music is recommended, in one form
or another. —*Scott Yanow*

Duke Ellington's Orchestra / Nov. 25, 1946–Dec. 18, 1946 /
   Laserlight ✦✦
This budget CD reissues 11 of the 13 selections recorded by Duke
Ellington's orchestra in late 1946 (leaving out the classic "Tulip or
Turnip" and "Overture to a Jam Session"), substituting later ver-
sions of "Satin Doll" and the untraceable "Glory" for some odd
reason. The music is strong even if the packaging and irrelevant
liner notes are not. —*Scott Yanow*

The Uncollected Duke Ellington & His Orchestra, Vol. 4 (1947)
   / Jan. 7, 1947–Jun. 9, 1947 / Hindsight ✦✦✦✦
On this fourth volume of the five-LP series of radio transcriptions
from Duke Ellington's underrated orchestra of 1946–47, all of the
sets are enjoyable, often surpassing the level of Ellington's studio
recordings of the period. Now with a six-member trumpet section
and relatively new soloists in Al Sears, Jimmy Hamilton and Taft
Jordan, Ellington continued his reign as one of the top bandleaders with swinging versions of "Happy Go Lucky Local," three W.C.
Handy tunes and "Jam-A-Ditty." —*Scott Yanow*

The Complete Duke Ellington (1947–1952) / Aug. 14,
   1947–Dec. 22, 1952 / CBS French ✦✦✦✦✦
French CBS did a perfect job on this six-LP set of covering a
somewhat forgotten period in the career of Duke Ellington. Big
bands were breaking up, rhythm & blues and pop vocalists were
taking away the audiences (as was television), yet somehow
Ellington kept his orchestra together. This wonderful box set has
its share of forgettable vocals and attempts at pop hits, but also
contains the "Liberian Suite," "Controversial Suite" and many
three-minute classics. The personnel underwent a lot of turnover
during these five years, giving one the opportunity to hear such
new solo stars as Tyree Glenn (on trombone and vibes), high-note
trumpeter Al Killian and tenor saxophonist Jimmy Forrest (and
eventually Paul Gonsalves) along with the usual Ellington greats.
This set also finds Ellington surviving the defection of altoist
Johnny Hodges in 1951, proving that he never had an off period.
—*Scott Yanow*

Liberian Suite / Dec. 24, 1947 / Sony France ✦✦✦

The Carnegie Hall Concerts (December 1947) / Dec. 27, 1947 /
   Prestige ✦✦✦✦✦
One of Duke Ellington's most enjoyable Carnegie Hall concerts,
this two-CD set contains among its highpoints a superior live version of the "Liberian Suite," a Johnny Hodges medley, the beautiful "On a Turquoise Cloud," a roaring version of "Cotton Tail" (featuring Al Sears' tenor), the nearly atonal "Clothed Woman" and a
trumpet battle on "Blue Skies." Well worth acquiring. —*Scott
Yanow*

Carnegie Hall Concerts (November 1948) / Nov. 13, 1948 / Vintage Jazz Classics ✦✦✦✦✦
The sixth and final of Duke Ellington's acclaimed Carnegie Hall concerts, this two-CD set allows one to hear the largely undocumented 1948 orchestra, which was kept off record because of a musicians union strike. With Ben Webster temporarily back in the band and such solo stylists as altoist Johnny Hodges, Al Sears on tenor, clarinetist Jimmy Hamilton and trumpeters Ray Nance and Shorty Baker, the Ellington orchestra performs both newer material (such as "The Tattooed Bride" and several obscurities) and some surprising older compositions including a revival of "Reminiscence in Tempo" and a "hits medley." An oddity is one of the very few Ellington performances of Billy Strayhorn's classic "Lush Life." —*Scott Yanow*

The 1949 Band Salutes Ellington '90 / Feb. 1, 1949–Feb. 20, 1949 / Marlor Productions ✦✦✦
The 1949 Duke Ellington big band made few worthwhile studio recordings, which makes this LP (consisting of material from radio broadcasts) of great interest to Ellington collectors. Recorded at a time when Al Killian was leading the trumpet section and both Ben Webster and Al Sears were on tenor, this nearly one-hour set contains an extended version of "The Tattooed Bride," superior versions of "How High the Moon," "St. Louis Blues" (and even "Singin' in the Rain") and many fine solos from a somewhat forgotten version of Duke Ellington's orchestra. —*Scott Yanow*

Great Times! Piano Duets with Billy Strayhorn / Oct. 3, 1950–Nov. 1950 / Original Jazz Classics ✦✦✦
Overlooked pairing of Duke and his greatest pupil/cohort, Billy Strayhorn. —*Ron Wynn*

Masterpieces by Ellington / Dec. 19, 1950 / Sony France ✦✦✦
For this record, Duke Ellington for the first time took advantage of the extra time that the LP offered (as opposed to the three-minute 78). Ellington and his orchestra perform stretched-out versions of three of his best-known songs ("Mood Indigo," "Sophisticated Lady" and "Solitude") and the more recently composed "The Tattooed Bride." Superior pacing, careful attention to dynamics and variety and the strong material itself make this a recommended set. —*Scott Yanow*

☆ **Uptown** / Dec. 7, 1951–Dec. 8, 1952 / Columbia ✦✦✦✦✦
Although some historians have characterized the early '50s as Duke Ellington's "off period" (due to the defection of alto-star Johnny Hodges), in reality his 1951-52 orchestra could hold its own against his best. This set has many classic moments, including Betty Roche's famous bebop vocal on "Take the 'A' Train," a version of "The Mooche" that contrasts the different clarinet styles of Russell Procope and Jimmy Hamilton, a hot "Perdido" that is highlighted by some great Clark Terry trumpet, Louie Bellson's drum solo on "Skin Deep," a definitive version of "The Harlem Suite" and the two-part "Controversial Suite" which contrasts New Orleans jazz with futuristic music worthy of Stan Kenton. One of the great Duke Ellington sets. —*Scott Yanow*

1952 Seattle Concert / Mar. 28, 1952 / Bluebird ✦✦✦
The early '50s have often been written about as if they were an off-period for Duke Ellington but in reality his concert performances were very much up to par. This fine CD features drummer Louie Bellson on "Skin Deep" and "The Hawk Talks," showcases trombonist Britt Woodman on "Sultry Serenade," altoist Willie Smith on "Sophisticated Lady," trumpeter Clark Terry throughout an impressive version of "Perdido" and the lead of valve trombonist Juan Tizol on his "Caravan." In addition to a brief hits medley and a typically heated "Jam with Sam," one of the best versions ever of "Harlem Suite" highlights this enjoyable if not quite essential release. —*Scott Yanow*

The Pasadena Concert (1953) / Mar. 30, 1953 / GNP ✦✦✦
Gene Norman often recorded jazz bands live when they appeared in Southern California, including a couple of Duke Ellington concerts. This particular one has its fine moments (particularly a good early version of "Diminuendo and Crescendo in Blue" and a feature on "Perdido" for guest Oscar Pettiford on cello) but three Jimmy Grissom vocals and a long medley of Ellington's hits weigh the music down a bit. —*Scott Yanow*

☆ **The Complete Capitol Recordings Of Duke Ellington** / Apr. 6, 1953–May 19, 1955 / Mosaic ✦✦✦✦✦
This five-CD box set from Mosaic documents Duke Ellington's least-known period, his two years on Capitol. Although thought of by some as his off-years due to the absence of Johnny Hodges, the

set serves as evidence that a great deal of viable music was created. During this period the orchestra had 11 distinctive soloists including four very different trumpeters (Clark Terry, Cat Anderson, Willie Cook and Ray Nance). In addition to a well-known trio set that showcases Ellington's underrated piano playing, there are quite a few unissued selections highlighted by four numbers from 1955 that find Ellington playing electric piano. Even vocalist Jimmy Grissom (best on "Balling the Blues") sounds better than usual and one should not miss Ray Nance's humorous singing and playing on "Basin Street Blues." Toss in the original version of "Satin Doll," the unusual *Ellington '55* album (which found the band playing their versions of swing hits associated with other orchestras) and an oddity such as "Twelfth Street Rag Mambo" and one has a highly enjoyable reissue that Duke Ellington fans should pick up immediately. —*Scott Yanow*

Piano Reflections / Apr. 13, 1953–Dec. 3, 1953 / Capitol ✦✦✦✦
At the time of its release this was a true rarity, a full album of Duke Ellington featured with a trio sans his orchestra. Although his talents at the piano sometimes have been overshadowed by his many accomplishments as a composer, arranger and bandleader, Ellington was actually one of the very few stride pianists (along with Mary Lou Williams) to effectively make the transition into more modern styles of jazz without losing his own musical personality; in fact Duke was an early influence on both Thelonious Monk and Cecil Taylor. Throughout this CD (which contains one previously unissued track), Ellington sounds modern (especially rhythmically and in his chord voicings) and shows that he could have made a viable career out of just being a pianist. —*Scott Yanow*

Happy Birthday, Duke! The Birthday Sessions, Vols. 1–5 / Apr. 29, 1953–Apr. 29, 1954 / Laserlight ✦✦✦
Quite by coincidence, Duke Ellington celebrated his birthday in both 1953 and 1954 by performing with his orchestra at McElroy's Ballroom in Portland, OR. Laserlight has released the results (recorded by engineer Wally Heider) on a five-CD box set which is also available as five separate CDs. The 1953-54 period has never been considered the peak years for Ellington; in fact his orchestra's popularity was low and he was struggling to keep his group together. However, as these performance show, he still had one of the most exciting big bands in the world and its commercial difficulties had little to do with the music. There are not many surprises on these dance dates but it is always fun to hear new solos on Ellington's standards played by his illustrious sidemen. Although only containing around three hours of music (pretty brief for five CDs), the budget price of Laserlight's releases makes this an excellent buy. —*Scott Yanow*

Los Angeles Concert (1954) / Apr. 13, 1954 / GNP ✦✦✦
This LP has an excellent performance by the Duke Ellington Orchestra at a time when its commercial fortunes were near the bottom. The struggles however are not reflected in the music, which is full of enthusiasm and creative invention with trumpeter Clark Terry, tenorman Paul Gonsalves and trombonist Britt Woodman (on "Theme for Trambean") standing out among the many stars during a well-paced program. —*Scott Yanow*

Duke (1956–1962), Vol. 3 / Jan. 1, 1956–Mar. 3, 1961 / CBS ✦✦
Unlike the first two volumes of this series of alternate takes and unissued performances that Duke Ellington recorded for Columbia during 1956-62, this is a single (rather than double) LP that finds the orchestra accompanying a wide variety of vocalists including Rosemary Clooney, Ozzie Bailey, Margaret Tynes, Jimmy Grissom, Lil Greenwood, Milt Grayson and even Johnnie Ray. A well-designed series although this album is not too essential. —*Scott Yanow*

Blue Rose / Jan. 23, 1956–Jan. 27, 1956 / Sony ✦✦✦
Years before she became a jazz singer through her association with Concord Records, Rosemary Clooney recorded this surprisingly effective album with Duke Ellington's orchestra, revisiting some of his compositions from the '30s; the Ellington and Strayhorn arrangements leave a liberal amount of space for the many soloists. —*Scott Yanow*

The Bethlehem Years, Vol. 1 / Feb. 7, 1956–Feb. 8, 1956 / Bethlehem ✦✦✦✦
In this two-volume series, Duke Ellington mostly revisited some of his songs from the '30s but, as was his custom, the standards were rearranged and came out sounding nearly brand new. With Johnny Hodges back in the orchestra, the all-star ensemble once

again had no weak points and, other than an overly rapid "Ko-Ko," this set is a gem. —*Scott Yanow*

Duke Ellington Presents . . . / Feb. 1956 / Bethlehem ✦✦✦
This is actually the second volume of recordings made for Bethlehem in early 1956, a companion to J 4212. In this case, in addition to new versions of "Cotton Tail," "Daydream" and "Everything but You," the emphasis is on Ellingtonian treatments of standards such as "Summertime," "My Funny Valentine" and "Deep Purple." The music is quite enjoyable even if this was not one of his most memorable sets. —*Scott Yanow*

The Private Collection, Vol. 1 / Mar. 17, 1956–Dec. 16, 1956 / Atlantic ✦✦✦
The first of ten CDs of previously unreleased material recorded privately by Ellington between engagements, all of which was eventually reissued first on LMR and then Saja/Atlantic. Each of the sets has its interesting moments, offering previously unknown compositions and performances. *Volume One*, recorded in Chicago during March and December 1956, has plenty of spots for Clark Terry, Ray Nance, Johnny Hodges and Paul Gonsalves among the orchestra's many great soloists. —*Scott Yanow*

Ellington at Newport / Jul. 7, 1956 / Columbia ✦✦✦✦✦
After several years of struggle, Duke Ellington made a spectacular commercial comeback, launched by this memorable appearance at the Newport Jazz Festival. Following an inventive but somewhat overlooked "Newport Jazz Festival Suite" and a routine version of Johnny Hodges' feature "Jeep's Blues," the orchestra launched into "Diminuendo and Crescendo in Blue" with great intensity. The passion really grew during a marathon 27-chorus blues solo by tenor saxophonist Paul Gonsalves that inspired some wild dancing and a near-riot in the audience; the crowd's reaction can easily be heard on this recording. Following Gonsalves, the full ensemble built to a tremendous climax with trumpeter Cat Anderson screaming on top. This performance made headlines all around the world and Ellington's "off period" was finally over. It can all be heard on this classic recording. —*Scott Yanow*

Duke (1956–1962), Vol. 1 / Jul. 7, 1956–Jun. 2, 1959 / CBS ✦✦✦✦
The *Duke 56/62* series (two double LPs and one single album) from French CBS includes a wide variety of unreleased material, alternate takes and rare recordings by the Duke Ellington Orchestra during an era when they recorded 24 albums for Columbia. *Volume 1*, a two-LP set, has many valuable performances including a version of "Black and Tan Fantasy" from his famous appearance at Newport in 1956, the four-part "Piano Improvisations," two "new" renditions of "Mood Indigo" and a rare alternate version of Ellington's "Anatomy of a Murder." —*Scott Yanow*

First Annual Connecticut Jazz Festival / Jul. 28, 1956 / IAJRC ✦✦✦
From the collector's label IAJRC, this CD, recorded three weeks after Ellington's sensational performance at the 1956 Newport Jazz Festival, not only features the orchestra (best on the three-part "Festival Suite"), but has selections by a sextet led by the great swing trumpeter Buck Clayton and three numbers played by the classic pianist Willie "the Lion" Smith. Lots of fine music. —*Scott Yanow*

A Drum Is a Woman / Sep. 1956–Dec. 1956 / Columbia ✦✦
Duke Ellington's fanciful tale of Carribee Joe and his drum, which evolved into a woman known as Madam Zajj (and a very abstract telling of the evolution of jazz) became a television special in the late '50s but does not translate all that well to record. Dominated by vocals and narration, the music often plays a backseat to the story, which is worth hearing twice at the most. —*Scott Yanow*

Duke Ellington, Vol. 7 / Jan. 1957–Jun. 6, 1962 / Atlantic ✦✦✦
One of ten CDs of previously unreleased and even unknown studio and concert performances by Duke Ellington's orchestra, these sets allow one to hear him experimenting with his ensemble. Some selections were essentially works-in-progress that would develop within the next few years, others were quickly discarded originals or rearrangements of older tunes. This seventh volume is split between big-band sessions from 1957 and 1962 and a get-together from an octet that included Ellington's former drummer Sonny Greer in the latter year. Ellington fans will want all ten in this valuable series. —*Scott Yanow*

Duke Ellington, Vol. 8 / Jan. 1957–Jul. 11, 1967 / Atlantic ✦✦✦
The eighth of ten CDs in this valuable series of previously

unknown Duke Ellington recordings is mostly taken from the 1965–67 period (with one selection from 1957) and features particularly strong moments from trumpeter Cat Anderson, altoist Johnny Hodges and tenorman Paul Gonsalves on many little-played Ellington compositions (along with versions of "Cottontail" and "Moon Mist"). Drummer Louie Bellson guests on a few selections. All ten volumes in this series are recommended. —*Scott Yanow*

Happy Reunion / Mar. 1957–Jun. 1958 / Doctor Jazz ✦✦✦
This LP consists of two small-group sessions led by Duke Ellington. From 1957 four numbers feature a septet with trumpeter Clark Terry and altoist Johnny Hodges while the remainder of this set is from 1958 and finds tenor saxophonist Paul Gonsalves showcased in a quartet. A particular highlight is hearing Gonsalves play 31 choruses on "Diminuendo and Crescendo in Blue" in this setting. —*Scott Yanow*

Such Sweet Thunder / Apr. 1957–May 1957 / Sony ✦✦✦✦
Duke Ellington's tribute to Shakespeare is witty, full of fresh melodies and gives his famed sidemen many opportunities to solo in unusual settings. Trombonist Britt Woodman stars on "Sonnet to Hank Cinq," trumpeter Cat Anderson gets to go nuts on "Madness in Great Ones" and there are notable features for Johnny Hodges, Paul Gonsalves and Quentin Jackson. —*Scott Yanow*

Ella Fitzgerald/The Duke Ellington Songbook / Jun. 25, 1957–Sep. 57, 1957 / Verve ✦✦✦✦
The first lady of song meets the genius of jazz on this delightful two-LP set. Unlike many other albums in which a singer is backed by a big band, there are many spots for Ellington's sidemen to shine; in fact the four-part "Portrait of Ella Fitzgerald" is purely instrumental until the final movement. It is wonderful to hear her sing such songs as "Drop Me Off in Harlem," "Rockin' in Rhythm" and "Perdido" along with the ballads. Recommended. —*Scott Yanow*

All Star Road Band, Vol. 2 / Jun. 1957 / Doctor Jazz ✦✦✦
This double LP was recorded at a typical dance date, a one-night stand in Carrolltown, PA, by the Duke Ellington Orchestra. Although Ellington's band could be erratic on gigs like this, playing for a partying dancing crowd, the music is consistently enjoyable, occasionally a bit loose and always full of the spontaneity of jazz. With a few exceptions, most of the songs are standards (including "Take the 'A' Train," "Mood Indigo," "Sophisticated Lady" and "I Got It Bad") but they sound fresh and through Ellington's rearrangements, almost new as played by his all-star orchestra. —*Scott Yanow*

Live at the 1957 Stratford Festival / Jul. 1957 / Music & Arts ✦✦✦
Now that Duke Ellington had regained his former commercial success with his performance at the 1956 Newport Jazz Festival, he was free for the remainder of his career to essentially play what he pleased. This live performance from 1957 ranges from old favorites like "I Got It Bad" and "Sophisticated Lady" to the spectacular Britt Woodman trombone feature on "Theme Trambene," the whimsical "Pretty and the Wolf," a fresh rendition of "Harlem Air Shaft" featuring trumpeter Clark Terry and the extended "Harlem Suite." Baritonist Harry Carney, high-note trumpet wizard Cat Anderson and altoist Johnny Hodges all have their great moments on this enjoyable set. —*Scott Yanow*

Indigos / Sep. 9, 1957–Oct. 10, 1957 / Columbia ✦✦
An easy-listening set of ballads (only three of the ten songs were associated with Ellington), this is a relaxing if unexciting program. On this reissue, two "new" performances ("Night and Day" and a trio version of "All the Things You Are") were added to the original LP, but one song ("The Sky Fell Down") was dropped and an alternate version of "Autumn Leaves" was substituted for the original; all 12 performances could have easily fit. Nice subtle music, but not essential. —*Scott Yanow*

The Girl's Suite and the Perfume Suite / Dec. 9, 1957–Aug. 20, 1961 / Columbia ✦✦✦

Black, Brown and Beige / Feb. 5, 1958–Feb. 12, 1958 / Columbia ✦✦
This album, Duke Ellington's revised version of his formerly 50-minute long "Black, Brown and Beige," has always been a bit of a disappointment. Stung by criticism from 15 years before, Ellington divided the suite into six much shorter sections, leaving in "Come Sunday" (which is hurt by Johnny Hodges' absence due

to a brief illness) and "Work Song" and featuring gospel singer Mahalia Jackson during two of the parts. Despite some good moments, this rendition has little of the power of the original arrangement. — *Scott Yanow*

Blues in Orbit / Feb. 5, 1958–Dec. 3, 1959 / Columbia ✦✦✦
This LP mostly features the Duke Ellington Orchestra in late 1959 on a variety of his shorter originals. At the time, the band's instrumentation was a bit unusual, with Ray Nance temporarily the only trumpeter, but the famous saxophone section was very much intact. The emphasis is on blues-oriented tunes and there are many fine spots for Nance, baritonist Harry Carney, altoist Johnny Hodges, clarinetist Jimmy Hamilton and Ellington himself. Excellent music by a timeless orchestra. — *Scott Yanow*

Duke Ellington, Vol. 2 / Mar. 4, 1958 / Atlantic ✦✦✦
The second of ten CDs of previously unissued recordings of Duke Ellington, this set differs from the others by being from a single live session, a dance concert from 1958. The orchestra at the time boasted such stars as trumpeters Shorty Baker, Clark Terry and Ray Nance, trombonists Quentin Jackson and Britt Woodman and a superb saxophone section (although Johnny Hodges is temporarily absent). The music on this CD sticks to standards (some of which were not usually associated with Ellington) and can be thought of as a live version of Ellington Indigos although the inclusion of some uptempo material (including a totally ad-lib "Lady Be Good") adds more variety. A typically excellent example of 1958 Duke Ellington. — *Scott Yanow*

Duke Ellington, Vol. 6 / Mar. 4, 1958–Mar. 5, 1958 / Atlantic ✦✦✦
The sixth of ten CDs in this series of previously unknown private recordings is actually related to *Volume 2*. Some of these performances are from the same concert at Travis Air Force Base while the remainder were recorded the next day at Mather Air Force Base. Although altoist Johnny Hodges and high-note trumpeter Cat Anderson were absent, the music did not suffer in the slightest, for Ellington still had ten other distinctive soloists. Quite informal and sometimes a bit loose, these spirited performances (mostly of standards) gives such players as trumpeters Shorty Baker, Clark Terry and Ray Nance along with the many other stars plenty of opportunities to stretch out. Recordings like this give one a chance to hear how Ellington re-arranged tunes to make them sound fresh year after year (sometimes decade after decade). — *Scott Yanow*

Duke Ellington at the Bal Masque / Mar. 1958 / Columbia ✦✦✦
One of Duke Ellington's more unusual albums of the '50s, this live session finds the orchestra performing such songs as "Got a Date with an Angel," "The Peanut Vendor," "Indian Love Call" and even "Who's Afraid of the Big Bad Wolf." Amazingly enough the music works quite well for Ellington and his all-star orchestra manage to transform what could be a set of tired revival swing into superior dance music and swinging jazz. While certainly not the most essential Ellington record, *At the Bal Masque* is a surprise success. — *Scott Yanow*

Cosmic Scene: Duke Ellington's Spacemen / Apr. 12, 1958 / Columbia ✦✦✦✦
This is the original LP version of a fine session featuring a small group from Duke Ellington's orchestra which, due to the time period, he dubbed his "Spacemen." For this nonet Duke chose three of his most modern soloists (trumpeter Clark Terry, clarinetist Jimmy Hamilton and tenor saxophonist Paul Gonsalves, along with his trombone section and the rhythm section. In general the tunes are standards that give each of the three main horns plenty of space in which to display their distinctive sounds. Part of this has been reissued on *Blues in Orbit* (Columbia). — *Scott Yanow*

Blues Summit / Aug. 14, 1958–Feb. 20, 1959 / Verve ✦✦✦✦
Partly reissued on CD, this very enjoyable double LP includes two related sessions. The main one is both unusual and delightful for it features altoist Johnny Hodges and trumpeter Harry "Sweets" Edison" leading a sextet that found Duke Ellington on piano. The repertoire is inspired, a variety of jam tunes including several by W.C. Handy, and both Sweets and Hodges are heard at their most expressive. The remainder of this two-fer teams Hodges and trombonist Lawrence Brown with tenor-great Ben Webster and the exciting trumpeter Roy Eldridge; this time Billy Strayhorn is on piano and the music is almost as memorable. Highly recommended in one form or another. — *Scott Yanow*

Jazz at the Plaza, Vol. 2 / Sep. 9, 1958 / Columbia ✦✦✦
In 1958 Columbia Records hosted a jazz party that resulted in two

records, one by the Miles Davis Sextet and the other featuring Duke Ellington's orchestra during a prime period. In addition to features for Johnny Hodges, Clark Terry and Paul Gonsalves (along with the "Jazz Festival Suite"), Ellington welcomes Count Basie's former vocalist, Jimmy Rushing, for three numbers and Billie Holiday (in okay form for this late in her life) stops by for two numbers with a small group that includes trumpeter Buck Clayton. Excellent music. — *Scott Yanow*

At the Blue Note in Chicago / Dec. 28, 1958 / Vogue ✦✦✦
A typically excellent club appearance by Duke Ellington's orchestra near the end of 1958, it exists on CD because CBS happened to broadcast this date. Nearly all of the selections were composed by Ellington and his associates. Johnny Hodges stars throughout while trumpeter Clark Terry is tops among the supporting players. Not essential but well worth owning. — *Scott Yanow*

Jazz Party / Feb. 19, 1959–Feb. 25, 1959 / Columbia ✦✦✦
A most unusual Duke Ellington record, two selections feature nine symphonic percussionists on tympani, vibes, marimbas and xylophones. Dizzy Gillespie makes a historic appearance with Ellington's orchestra on "U.M.M.G." (a meeting that should have been repeated often but sadly never was), Jimmy Rushing (Count Basie's former vocalist) sings "Hello Little Girl" and both Johnny Hodges ("All of Me") and Paul Gonsalves ("Ready Go!") have chances to blow. — *Scott Yanow*

Ellington Suites / Feb. 25, 1959–Dec. 5, 1972 / Original Jazz Classics ✦✦
It took until 1976 before these three extended works ("The Queen's Suite," "The Goutelas Suite" and "The Uwis Suite") were released and their obscurity is somewhat deserved. Although there are some good moments from Ellington's orchestras of 1959 and 1971-72, few of the themes (outside of "The Single Petal of a Rose" from "The Queen's Suite") are all that memorable. But even lesser Ellington is of great interest and veteran collectors may want to pick this up. — *Scott Yanow*

Anatomy of a Murder / May 29, 1959–Jun. 2, 1959 / Rykodisc ✦✦✦
Duke Ellington's music was used surprisingly little in movies. *Anatomy of a Murder* was a landmark film and his writing fit in perfectly. Like all good soundtracks, the music's role was to accompany and enhance the story, so to hear the soundtrack on CD does leave one with a somewhat incomplete feeling. However, Ellington's writing was colorful enough to largely stand on its own even in this setting so this set, although not essential, does not disappoint. — *Scott Yanow*

Newport Jazz Festival (1959) / Jul. 4, 1959 / EmArcy ✦✦✦
Duke Ellington's concert at the 1959 Newport Jazz Festival lacked the excitement and adventure of his appearances in 1956 and 1958. Ellington and his orchestra played their usual program of standards and features with the 14-and-a-half-minute "Idiom '59" being introduced (and then quickly forgotten). Fine music but nothing that historic or essential occurred this time around. — *Scott Yanow*

Live at The Blue Note / Aug. 9, 1959 / Roulette ✦✦✦✦
This two-CD set gives one a good example of how Duke Ellington's Orchestra sounded in 1959. Greatly expanded from the original single LP, the release essentially brings back a full night by the Ellington band, three nearly complete sets. The music ranges from old favorites to some newer material and highlights include Billy Strayhorn sitting in on his "Take the 'A' Train," several selections from the recent *Anatomy of a Murder* soundtrack, versions of "Drawing Room Blues" and "Tonk" that have both Ellington and Shearing on piano, an 11-minute rendition of "Mood Indigo" and quite a few features for altoist Johnny Hodges. — *Scott Yanow*

Festival Session / Sep. 8, 1959 / Columbia ✦✦✦
This LP included Ellington's new works for 1959 along with a superior version of "Perdido"(featuring Clark Terry) and a Johnny Hodges workout on "Things Ain't What They Used to Be." None of the newer pieces ("Duael Fuel," "Copout Extension," "Idiom '59" and "Launching Pad") caught on but all are enjoyable and show that Ellington's creativity at age 60 had not slowed down in the slightest. — *Scott Yanow*

Duke (1956–1962), Vol. 2 / Dec. 2, 1959–Jun. 21, 1962 / CBS ✦✦✦✦
The second of three volumes, this two-LP set from French Columbia includes unissued alternate takes and rarities recorded

by Duke Ellington for Columbia during 1959-62. Of primary interest to veteran collectors, there is much to enjoy here, including new renditions of the "Asphalt Jungle Suite," "Tulip or Turnip," "Paris Blues," two versions of "Jingle Bells" and a pair of selections from the one-time meeting on record between the Ellington and Count Basie Orchestras that were not included on the original set. —Scott Yanow

Three Suites / Mar. 3, 1960–Oct. 10, 1960 / Columbia ✦✦✦✦✦
One of Duke Ellington's most delightful adaptations of another composer's material is his reworking of Tchaikovsky's "Nutcracker Suite" into jazz; this version is a classic and well worth treasuring. Ellington's reworking of Grieg's "Peer Gynt Suites" (including "In the Hall of the Mountain King") and his tribute to John Steinbeck ("Suite Thursday") are also among his better extended works, really utilizing the unique tones of his distinctive sidemen. Highly recommended. —Scott Yanow

Piano in the Background / May 1960–Jun. 1960 / Columbia ✦✦✦
One of Ellington's rarer studio sessions and last out on this French CD, the main plot behind this run-through of his standards is that the leader's piano is featured at some point in every song. His sidemen are also heard from and everyone is in fine form. Ellington's solo abilities were always a bit underrated due to his brilliance in other areas, but this set shows just how modern he remained through the years as a player. —Scott Yanow

Unknown Session / Jul. 14, 1960 / Columbia ✦✦✦
Discovered in Columbia's vaults 19 years after it was performed, this recording features a septet from Duke Ellington's orchestra keeping busy in the studios mostly playing standards and blues. With altoist Johnny Hodges, baritonist Harry Carney, trombonist Lawrence Brown and cornetist Ray Nance all having ample solo space, these renditions are quite enjoyable, swing hard and sound fresh. Ellington fans should pick this one up. —Scott Yanow

Hot Summer Dance / Jul. 22, 1960 / Red Baron ✦✦✦
There have been so many releases of live concert performances by Duke Ellington's orchestra that it is easy to become blasé about them. It is true that one does not really need all of these CDs but, on the other hand, virtually all of the releases contain quite a bit of excellent music. When one considers the consistent high quality of Ellington's material and the many distinctive soloists that he employed, the result is that practically everything released of his orchestra is quite worthwhile. Hot Summer Dance features the 1960 Duke Ellington Orchestra performing their usual repertoire from that era including excerpts from "The Nutcracker Suite" and "Such Sweet Thunder," a three-song medley of jungle pieces from the '20s, several Johnny Hodges features and a new version of "Diminuendo and Crescendo in Blue." It may not be essential, but Ellington collectors will enjoy this CD. —Scott Yanow

Paris Blues / Dec. 14, 1960-1961 / United Artists ✦✦
The soundtrack to the flawed but intriguing jazz movie Paris Blues has a few strong melodies (including "Guitar Amour," the title track and a new version of "Mood Indigo") along with an appearance by Louis Armstrong on "Battle Royal," but there is actually less than a half-hour of music on this LP. Even with the prominence of Paul Gonsalves' tenor, this is of lesser interest. —Scott Yanow

Piano in the Foreground / Mar. 1, 1961 / Columbia ✦✦✦
This rare trio session by Duke Ellington (on which he is joined by bassist Aaron Bell and drummer Sam Woodyard) was the first of several in the early '60s that featured his piano in a variety of settings. It is particularly interesting hearing Ellington, along with three standards and a blues, performing some of his rarer compositions such as "Cong-go," "Fontainbleau Forest," "It's Bad to Be Forgotten" and "A Hundred Dreams Ago." One wishes that today's revivalists when playing "the Duke Ellington Songbook" would bring back some of his true obscurities such as the ones on this somewhat forgotten session. —Scott Yanow

The Duke Ellington-Louis Armstrong Years / Apr. 3, 1961–Apr. 4, 1961 / Roulette ✦✦✦✦✦
Although Duke Ellington and Louis Armstrong were jazz music's most famous and acclaimed musicians, their only meeting on record (other than a couple of isolated selections in the '40s) is the music contained on this two-CD set. Rather than have Armstrong sit in with the orchestra, Ellington temporarily became a member of Satch's All-Stars. For this all-Ellington program, Armstrong is inspired by the fresh repertoire and his vocals are often jubilant. With strong assistance from trombonist Trummy Young and clar-

inetist Barney Bigard (a former Ellington bandmember then travelling with Armstrong), Pops and Ellington created a very memorable and quite unique program of classic music. —Scott Yanow

☆ **First Time! Count Meets Duke** / Jul. 6, 1961 / Columbia ✦✦✦✦✦
At first glance this collaboration should not have worked. The Duke Ellington and Count Basie Orchestras had already been competitors for 25 years but the leaders' mutual admiration (Ellington was one of Basie's main idols) and some brilliant planning made this a very successful and surprisingly uncrowded encounter. On most selections Ellington and Basie both play piano (their interaction with each other is wonderful) and the arrangements allowed the stars from both bands to take turns soloing. "Segue in C" is the highpoint but versions of "Until I Met You," "Battle Royal" and "Jumpin' at the Woodside" are not far behind. —Scott Yanow

Duke Ellington / **Johnny Hodges** / Jan. 9, 1962–Aug. 27, 1964 / Storyville ✦✦✦
This LP contains the soundtrack of a half-hour TV special featuring the 1962 Duke Ellington Orchestra along with four selections from a Johnny Hodges-led small group drawn from the band in 1964. Few surprises occur but the soloing is at a high level. —Scott Yanow

Masters of Jazz, Vol. 6 / Jan. 9, 1962–Feb. 25, 1966 / Storyville ✦✦✦
This LP largely duplicates Duke Ellington & His Orchestra/Johnny Hodges & His Orchestra (Storyville), featuring six of the seven selections performed by the Duke Ellington Orchestra for a half-hour television special. However it is the additional material that is of greatest interest, for Duke Ellington is also heard solo in 1966 playing a lengthy medley of his popular numbers and a version of "New World A-Comin'." For that reason this LP is preferred over the other Storyville set. —Scott Yanow

All American / Jan. 1962 / Columbia ✦✦
Throughout this LP, the Duke Ellington Orchestra is largely wasted playing ten selections from the now-forgotten play All American. None of the melodies caught on, but Ellington does the best he can with them, featuring his many all-stars on concise and respectful performances. The music is harmless enough but there are at least 100 other more worthy Ellington releases currently available. —Scott Yanow

Midnight in Paris / Jan. 1962–Jun. 1962 / Columbia ✦✦
One of the odder Duke Ellington collections, only three of the 13 numbers were written by Ellington or Strayhorn (including a remake of "Paris Blues" and "Guitar Amour") and the music (some of it associated with Paris) sticks pretty much to melodic ballads like "I Wish You Love" and "Comme Ci, Comme Ça." Pretty music but far from essential. —Scott Yanow

The Feeling of Jazz / Feb. 13, 1962–Jul. 3, 1962 / Black Lion ✦✦✦
This is a nice all-around set by the 1962 Duke Ellington Orchestra. Whether it be the lightweight but fun "Taffy Twist," "I'm Gonna Go Fishin'" (the theme from Anatomy of a Murder) or the many songs revived from decades earlier (such as "What Am I Here For?," "Black and Tan Fantasy" and "Jump for Joy"), this CD is filled with consistently swinging music. —Scott Yanow

New Mood Indigo / Jul. 3, 1962–Mar. 29, 1966 / Doctor Jazz ✦✦✦
A very interesting collection of Duke Ellington studio material from 1962-66, it was first issued in 1985. The title cut finds Ellington giving a rare double-time treatment to his classic "Mood Indigo," three selections put the focus on the cornet and vocals of Ray Nance, and a special treat are the four selections from the Mercer Ellington Septet, a combo consisting of six of Ellington's sidemen plus a then-unknown 24-year-old pianist named Chick Corea. It gives one a rare chance to hear Corea playing with the likes of Johnny Hodges, Paul Gonsalves and Harry Carney. —Scott Yanow

Duke Ellington, Vol. 3 / Jul. 25, 1962–Sep. 13, 1962 / Atlantic ✦✦✦✦
This is the third of ten volumes of previously unknown Duke Ellington sessions made available in this valuable CD series. One of the strongest in The Private Collection, these rarities from 1962 include early versions of several selections that would later be included in Duke's Sacred Concerts, two otherwise unknown but fun Paul Gonsalves originals titled "Major" and "Minor," Thelonious Monk's composition "Monk's Dream" (here mistitled "Blue Monk") and "September 12th Blues" which welcomed trum-

peter Cootie Williams back into the band after a 22-year absence. Recommended. —*Scott Yanow*

Duke Ellington Meets Coleman Hawkins / Aug. 18, 1962 / Impulse! ✦✦✦✦
After years of discussions, Duke Ellington and the great tenor saxophonist Coleman Hawkins finally met up in a recording studio for the first and only time in 1962. Hawk sounds quite natural sitting in with a septet from Ellington's orchestra (including cornetist Ray Nance, trombonist Lawrence Brown, altoist Johnny Hodges and baritonist Harry Carney) and these versions of "Mood Indigo," "Self Portrait of the Bean" and a joyous "The Jeep Is Jumpin'" are classic. —*Scott Yanow*

Money Jungle / Sep. 17, 1962 / Blue Note ✦✦✦✦✦
In 1962 Duke Ellington was teamed on record with a trio consisting of bassist Charles Mingus and drummer Max Roach. The setting may have seemed "modern" for a pianist from his generation, but one should realize that he was a major influence on both Thelonious Monk and Cecil Taylor. Ellington, one of the few veterans of the '20s to make a smooth transition to the relatively modern era, is in superlative form on this date, even when challenged on "Money Jungle" by the potentially combative Mingus. This LP version includes four selections not on the original release; the later CD also added a couple of "new" alternate takes. Well worth acquiring. —*Scott Yanow*

☆ **Duke Ellington and John Coltrane** / Sep. 26, 1962 / MCA ✦✦✦✦✦
For this classic encounter, Duke Ellington "sat in" with the John Coltrane Quartet for a set dominated by Ellington's songs; some performances have his usual sidemen (bassist Aaron Bell and drummer Sam Woodyard) replacing Jimmy Garrison and Elvin Jones in the group. Although it would have been preferable to hear Coltrane play in the Duke Ellington Orchestra instead of the other way around, the results are quite rewarding. Their version of "In a Sentimental Mood" is a highpoint and such numbers as "Take the Coltrane," "Big Nick" and "My Little Brown Book" are quite memorable. Ellington always recognized talent and Coltrane seemed quite happy to be recording with a fellow genius. —*Scott Yanow*

Will Big Bands Ever Come Back? / Nov. 29, 1962–Jan. 4, 1963 / Reprise ✦✦
In general the '60s were not a good period for big bands and many veteran jazz artists. The labels often pressured musicians to play the more faddish tunes of the day or to come up with gimmicks that would increase their record sales. In Duke Ellington's case, he largely avoided the traps that were set for so many others of his era, with the exception of four albums. This one found him playing 11 tunes from the swing era and, although not that painful (at least there were no note-for-note recreations), the results are also not all that stimulating. It's interesting to hear Ellington play such material as "Smoke Rings," "Artistry in Rhythm" and "Sentimental Journey," once. —*Scott Yanow*

Afro-Bossa / Nov. 29, 1962–Jan. 5, 1963 / Discovery ✦✦✦
Inspired by their world travels, Duke Ellington and Billy Strayhorn composed 11 new compositions (along with performing the standard "Pyramid") that paid tribute to the rhythms and cultures of many countries. "Purple Gazelle" and "Eighth Veil" became part of the Ellington orchestra's regular repertoire, but each of these dozen selections have their memorable moments. It's one of his better sessions of the '60s. —*Scott Yanow*

The Great London Concerts / Jan. 22, 1963+Feb. 20, 1964 / Music Masters ✦✦✦✦
This previously issued material (released on a single CD by Music Masters) features the Duke Ellington Orchestra during a very busy era. The veteran musicians were getting older but their very individual voices were still powerful, and Ellington was far from running out of gas at this point. The five standards taken from the earlier performance date from the brief period when both Cootie Williams and Ray Nance were in the trumpet section while the later pieces are highlighted by "Caravan" (featuring the mighty Williams), an early version of "Isfahan," a rare Ernie Shephard vocal on "Take the 'A' Train," and a fine rendition of "Harlem." —*Scott Yanow*

The Symphonic Ellington / Jan. 31, 1963–Feb. 21, 1963 / Discovery ✦✦✦
In 1963 Duke Ellington realized a longtime goal of his, to record

some of his extended works using both a symphony orchestra and his regular big band. Included on this fine CD are the three movements of "Night Creature," the relatively brief "Non-Violent Integration," "La Scala" and an adaptation of Ellington's "Harlem Air Shaft." With most of his all-star soloists heard from in this program and a complete avoidance of trying to make his music sound so-called "respectable" or self-consciously third-stream, Ellington's arrangements keep the strings from weighing down the proceedings and the music is actually quite successful. —*Scott Yanow*

The Great Paris Concert / Feb. 1, 1963–Feb. 23, 1963 / Atlantic ✦✦✦✦✦
A definitive look at the early-'60s edition of the Duke Ellington Orchestra, this live two-LP set contains many highlights: fresh versions of "Rockin' in Rhythm," "Concerto for Cootie" (featuring Cootie Williams) and "Jam with Sam," extended renditions of "Suite Thursday" and the "Harlem Suite," and a few newer selections. 11 soloists (without counting the pianist/leader) are heard from in memorable settings, including both Cootie Williams and Ray Nance. Highly recommended music, either as a two-fer or on CD. —*Scott Yanow*

Jazz Violin Session / Feb. 22, 1963 / Atlantic ✦✦✦
This is a unique entry in Duke Ellington's massive discography. During half of this LP, Ellington and his rhythm section are joined by violinists Stephane Grappelli and Ray Nance, and Svend Asmussen on viola; the remainder of the set adds three horns for background work. On both ancient standards and a few newer pieces put together specifically for this date, the contrasting but complementary styles of the three string players and the general infectious enthusiasm makes this a memorable encounter. —*Scott Yanow*

Duke Ellington, Vol. 4: Studio Sessions—New York (1963) / Apr. 17, 1963–Jul. 18, 1963 / Atlantic ✦✦✦
The fourth of ten CDs released in this valuable series, these studio sessions from 1963, in addition to rare revivals of "Harmony in Harlem" and "Blue Rose," are filled with previously unknown Ellington compositions, a stockpile of fresh material well worth a full investigation by contemporary musicians. Throughout all but the four full-band tracks, the focus is on cornetist Ray Nance, who is the only brass player present on most of this set. Johnny Hodges, Jimmy Hamilton and Paul Gonsalves also receive a good sampling of solo space on this strong entry in *The Private Collection* program. —*Scott Yanow*

My People / Aug. 20, 1963–Aug. 28, 1963 / Red Baron ✦✦✦
In 1963 Duke Ellington wrote the music for a short-lived show titled *My People*, which was a sort of combination of his early-'40s *Jump for Joy* play along with some of the music from his "Black, Brown and Beige" suite. Using an orchestra comprising Ellingtonians past, present and future along with a few compatible outsiders and featuring a variety of vocalists that include Joya Sherrill, Jimmy Grissom and Lil Greenwood, Ellington created music whose message of racial harmony remains timeless. Due to the high quality of the "Black, Brown and Beige" suite and the shorter originals, this interesting set is more enjoyable than one might expect. —*Scott Yanow*

Harlem / Mar. 9, 1964 / Pablo ✦✦✦
Taken from a concert in Stockholm, Sweden, this well-recorded CD mostly features trumpeters Cootie Williams and Cat Anderson, tenor saxophonist Paul Gonsalves and altoist Johnny Hodges as the main soloists in a set with Duke Ellington's orchestra. "The Opener," "Blow by Blow" and "The Prowling Cat" have rarely been recorded and even the more familiar pieces are given new life, highlighted by a definitive rendition of "Harlem." —*Scott Yanow*

All Star Road Band, Vols. 1 & 2 / May 31, 1964 / Doctor Jazz ✦✦✦✦
This two-LP set finds Duke Ellington's orchestra in surprisingly inspired form playing at a dance in Chicago. With solo highlights provided by trumpeters Cootie Williams and Cat Anderson, trombonists Lawrence Brown and· Buster Cooper and the very stable saxophone section (Johnny Hodges, Russell Procope, Jimmy Hamilton, Paul Gonsalves and Harry Carney), the all-star ensemble brings new life to the potentially tired repertoire, introduces some relatively new arrangements and seems to have a good time playing for an enthusiastic audience. Excellent music. —*Scott Yanow*

Mary Poppins / Sep. 4, 1964–Sep. 9, 1964 / Reprise ✦✦✦
Live at Carnegie Hall (1964), Vol. 1 / 1964 / New Sound Planet ✦✦✦
Duke Ellington's 1964 Carnegie Hall concert did not find him debuting any major works but it gave his famed orchestra an opportunity to run through some lesser-known new material plus a variety of Ducal standards. The first of two CDs documenting their performance has among its highlights a medley of Ellington songs from the 1920s ("Black and Tan Fantasy," "Creole Love Call" and "The Mooche"), a version of "Perdido" featuring trumpeter Rolf Ericson and an excellent version of "Harlem." Not an essential CD but Ellington collectors will enjoy this set. —*Scott Yanow*
Live at Carnegie Hall (1964), Vol. 2 / 1964 / New Sound Planet ✦✦✦
The second of two CDs taken from Duke Ellington's 1964 Carnegie Hall concert finds trumpeter Cootie Williams in emotional form on "Caravan" and "Tutti for Cootie" and altoist Johnny Hodges typically soulful and bluish on "Isfahan," "Things Ain't What They Used to Be" and the obscure "Banquet." The rest of the set is more routine but still worth hearing, as are all of the recordings in Duke Ellington's massive discography. —*Scott Yanow*
Duke Ellington, Vol. 10 / Mar. 4, 1965–May 6, 1971 / Atlantic ✦✦✦✦
The tenth and final volume of this valuable series of previously unknown Duke Ellington recordings, this CD contains excerpts from his monumental "Black, Brown & Beige" suite recorded in 1965 (with this version of "The Blues" dating from 1971), a lengthy version of "Ad Lib on Nippon" (which was taken from Ellington's "The Far East Suite") and a 1966 rendition of "Harlem." Each of these extended works is rich enough to deserve several interpretations and it is always fascinating to hear how Duke altered his arrangements through the decades. —*Scott Yanow*
Concert in the Virgin Islands / Apr. 14, 1965 / Discovery ✦✦✦
Although in his mid-60s, Duke Ellington proves on this program of mostly new music that he never declined or lost his creativity. Four of the pieces comprise "The Virgin Islands Suite," there are new versions of "Things Ain't What They Used to Be" and "Chelsea Bridge," and also a variety of miniature classics. In 1965 The Ellington orchestra had 11 very distinctive soloists; eight are heard from during this memorable set. —*Scott Yanow*
The Duke at Tanglewood / Jul. 28, 1965 / BMG ✦✦
In 1965 Duke Ellington appeared at a concert with Arthur Fiedler's Boston Pops Orchestra and a recording resulted. Ellington's piano is fine throughout this LP but unfortunately the arrangements were written by Richard Hayman and are hilariously overblown and pompous; "Caravan" is an unintentional scream. Those Ellington collectors without a strong sense of humor are obliged to skip this odd greatest-hits performance. —*Scott Yanow*
Duke Ellington (1965–1972) / 1965–Aug. 2, 1972 / Music Masters ✦✦✦
This is the type of CD that Duke Ellington collectors should love, for it contains a variety of unusual and fascinating performances. Highlights include Jimmy Hamilton's stomping tenor on "The Old Circus Train," the colorful "Trombone Buster," early versions of songs later included in "The New Orleans Suite" and three selections featuring organist Wild Bill Davis. —*Scott Yanow*
Duke Ellington (1966) / Jan. 19, 1966–Jan. 2, 1965 / Reprise ✦✦
A follow-up to *Ellington '65*, this out-of-print LP finds him playing a wide variety of mostly unsuitable pop tunes from the mid-'60s, including "Red Roses for a Blue Lady," "People," "Days of Wine and Roses," "Moon River" and even "I Want to Hold Your Hand." A true historical curiosity but often downright weird. —*Scott Yanow*
Orchestral Works / Apr. 10, 1966 / MCA ✦✦
Duke Ellington's collaboration with Erich Kunzel and the Cincinnatti Symphony Orchestra gives one an opportunity to hear Ellington's "The Golden Broom & the Green Apple" and "New World A'Coming" in rare performances along with a symphonic version of "Harlem." Ellington, who is featured throughout on piano, adds verbal "poetic commentary" between sections and the arrangements (which may have been by Luther Henderson) are fine but one misses his illustrious orchestra. Interesting but not essential music. —*Scott Yanow*
The Pianist / Jul. 18, 1966–Jan. 7, 1970 / Original Jazz Classics ✦✦✦
Duke Ellington had so many talents (composer, arranger, band-

leader, personality) that his skills as a pianist could easily be overlooked. Fortunately he did record a fair amount of trio albums through the years so there is plenty of evidence as to his unique style, which was both modern and traditional at the same time. *The Pianist* has trio performances from 1966 and 1970 and finds Ellington shifting smoothly between styles and moods while always remaining himself. —*Scott Yanow*
Soul Call / Jul. 28, 1966 / Verve ✦✦
The centerpiece of this live album is Ellington's "La Plus Belle Africaine," one of his better late-period works. Otherwise an overly fast "Jam with Sam," two short Paul Gonsalves features and a lengthy drum solo comprise the remainder of the program, making this a lesser Ellington item. —*Scott Yanow*
Ella and Duke on the Cote D'azur / Jul. 28, 1966 / Verve ✦✦✦
Ella Fitzgerald and Duke Ellington did not team up in concerts until relatively late in their careers (although she did record her *Ellington Songbook* with him in the '50s). This live double LP actually finds Fitzgerald singing six numbers with The Jimmy Jones Trio and only "Mack the Knife" and a scat-filled "It Don't Mean a Thing" with the orchestra. Ellington has eight numbers for his band, mostly remakes of older tunes (including a guest appearance by former associate Ben Webster on "All Too Soon," a remarkable Buster Cooper trombone feature and a rowdy version of "The Old Circus Train Turn-Around Blues"). This is a spirited set of music that with better planning could have been great. —*Scott Yanow*
The Far East Suite (Special Mix) / Dec. 19, 1966–Dec. 21, 1966 / Bluebird ✦✦✦✦✦
This CD differs from the previous release of "The Far East Suite" by the inclusion of four "new" alternate takes. This particular nine-part suite was arguably Duke Ellington's finest major work of the 1960s. The haunting ballad "Isfahan" (a showcase for altoist Johnny Hodges) is the best-known section, but several of the other pieces (particularly "Bluebird of Delhi," "Mount Harissa" and "Ad Lib on Nippon") are also quite memorable. Clarinetist Jimmy Hamilton and tenor saxophonist Paul Gonsalves co-star with Hodges, but it is the creative writing of Ellington and Billy Strayhorn that makes this CD quite essential. —*Scott Yanow*
Live in Italy, Vol. 1 / Feb. 22, 1967 / Jazz Up ✦✦✦
The first of two volumes, this CD captures Duke Ellington's orchestra during a European tour late in his career, but when he still retained virtually all of his star sidemen. The inclusion of some lesser-known compositions increase the value of this set as do the excellent solos of tenor saxophonist Paul Gonsalves, trombonist Lawrence Brown, Johnny Hodges and, on "Salome" and "Wild Onions," the phenomenal high-note trumpeter Cat Anderson. Typically brilliant music from Duke Ellington. —*Scott Yanow*
Live in Italy, Vol. 2 / Feb. 22, 1967 / Jazz Up ✦✦✦
Intimacy of the Blues / Mar. 15, 1967–Jun. 15, 1970 / Original Jazz Classics ✦✦✦
Lots of rare music was uncovered when these recordings were first released. Duke Ellington did a remarkable number of private recordings with small groups taken from his orchestra and the selections included on this LP are some of the best. A "Combo Suite" from 1967 introduces Billy Strayhorn's "Intimacy of the Blues" along with five forgotten but worthy originals while the music on Side Two (some of which features organist Wild Bill Davis) dates from 1970; "All Too Soon" showcases Ellington's new tenor Harold Ashby. Excellent music. —*Scott Yanow*
Live at the Rainbow Grill / Aug. 1967 / Moon ✦✦✦
This concert date (released for the first time on this 1993 CD) features Duke Ellington with an octet taken from his big band. Trumpeter Cat Anderson (the most surprising choice) jams on a variety of Ellington standards with trombonist Lawrence Brown, altoist Johnny Hodges, tenorman Paul Gonsalves, bassist John Lamb, drummer Steve Little and the pianist/leader. First Ellington summons the other musicians to the stand by playing piano on "Heaven" and "Le Sucrier Velours." After a few other informal numbers, a radio broadcast begins and Duke sticks to familiar (although enthusiastically) played material such as "Take the 'A' Train," "Perdido" and "Things Ain't What They Used to Be." A good if not essential outing. —*Scott Yanow*
★ **His Mother Called Him Bill** / Aug. 28, 1967–Sep. 1, 1967 / RCA ✦✦✦✦✦
Shortly after Billy Strayhorn's early death in 1967, the Duke

Ellington Orchestra recorded a dozen of his compositions during a series of emotional and passionate sessions. The results are consistently inspired, with such selections as "Blood Count" (Strayhorn's final composition), "Rain Check," "Lotus Blossom" and "The Intimacy of the Blues" receiving definitive versions. In addition, this CD reissue also contains an alternate take of "Lotus Blossom" and remakes of three more Strayhorn classics that were previously unissued. This was one of Duke Ellington's finest sessions and, considering his huge recorded legacy, that is saying a lot. —*Scott Yanow*

Francis A. and Edward K. / Dec. 12, 1967 / Reprise ✦✦✦
Frank Sinatra was never a jazz singer but he always had a strong respect for high musicianship and strong individuals. Since Duke Ellington was recording for Frank's label Reprise during this period, it seemed only right that the two would team up eventually. Actually Ellington's orchestra is primarily stuck in the role of accompanying the singer, who is heard at his best on "I Like the Sunrise" and "Poor Butterfly" (although the inclusion of "Sunny" does not work as well). In reality, this record is more significant in Sinatra's discography than it is in Ellington's. —*Scott Yanow*

Yale Concert / Jan. 26, 1968 / Original Jazz Classics ✦✦✦
The great Duke Ellington Orchestra was still intact and in its late prime at the time of this performance from 1968. With the death of Billy Strayhorn the year before, Ellington (perhaps sensing his own mortality) accelerated his writing activities, proving that even as he neared 70, he was still at his peak. Other than a Johnny Hodges medley and the theme ("Take the 'A' Train"), all of the music on this set was fairly new. Included are showcases for Cootie Williams, Harry Carney, Paul Gonsalves and Cat Anderson, an 11-minute "The Little Purple Flower," "Swamp Goo" (which gives Russell Procope a chance to play some New Orleans-style clarinet) and a jazz version of Yale's famous "Boola, Boola." —*Scott Yanow*

Latin American Suite / Oct. 1968 / Original Jazz Classics ✦✦✦
Written after his orchestra's successful debut in South America, Duke Ellington's seven-part suite celebrates the atmosphere and rhythms of the many south-of-the-border countries that he visited. The usual horn stars have their moments but the pianist himself is the main voice throughout this enjoyable set of fresh music. —*Scott Yanow*

Duke Ellington, Vol. 5 / Nov. 6, 1968–Jun. 15, 1970 / Atlantic ✦✦✦✦
One of the most interesting of the ten volumes released in *The Private Collection* series, this CD contains "The Degas Suite" (music for a soundtrack of an art film that was never produced) and a ballet score titled "The River." Ellington is mostly the lead voice but his star sidemen are heard from on these formerly very rare and somewhat unusual performances. Clearly his genius was strong enough to fill three lifetimes full of new music and this CD contains some melodies that might have been more significant if he had lived long enough to find a place for them. —*Scott Yanow*

Duke Ellington, Vol. 9 / Nov. 23, 1968–Dec. 3, 1968 / Atlantic ✦✦✦
The ninth of ten volumes of music from Duke Ellington's *Private Collection* of unknown tapes, this CD captures him in 1968 shortly after clarinetist Jimmy Hamilton left the band and tenor saxophonist Harold Ashby joined up. Even after 30 years of playing some of these standards, Ellington found new ways to rearrange such songs as "Sophisticated Lady," "Mood Indigo" and "Just Squeeze Me." In addition, there are a few new obscurities such as "Knuf" (which finds Jeff Castleman switching to electric bass), "Reva" and the somewhat dated Trish Turner vocal on "Cool and Groovy." Lots of surprises on this fine CD. —*Scott Yanow*

April in Paris / 1969 / West Wind ✦✦
Recorded in the same period of time as Duke Ellington's acclaimed 70th Birthday Concert, this single CD has its moments. Although subtitled "Featuring Wild Bill Davis," the organist is only on a few of the selections including a version of "Satin Doll" that unfortunately has Cat Anderson's miraculous high-note trumpet solo way off mike. However there are good versions of "Rockin' in Rhythm," "Take the 'A' Train" (starring trumpeter Cootie Williams), a hits medley and Paul Gonsalves' tenor feature on "Diminuendo and Crescendo in Blue." This disc is not essential but Ellington collectors will find it to be an interesting addition to their collections. —*Scott Yanow*

The Intimate Ellington / Apr. 25, 1969–Jun. 29, 1971 / Original Jazz Classics ✦✦
This Pablo set has odds and ends taken from nine different recording/rehearsal sessions that find Ellington experimenting a bit with instrumentation and personnel, even taking a vocal on the tongue-in-cheek "Moon Maiden." Performances range from a couple of vigorous trio workouts and spots for Wild Bill Davis' organ to a few big-band performances. Even this late in his life, Duke Ellington had a great deal to say musically and his band continued to rank near the top. —*Scott Yanow*

Up in Duke's Workshop / Apr. 25, 1969–Dec. 1972 / Original Jazz Classics ✦✦

★ **Seventieth Birthday Concert** / Nov. 25, 1969–Nov. 26, 1969 / Blue Note ✦✦✦✦✦

New Orleans Suite / Apr. 27, 1970 / Atlantic ✦✦✦

The Afro-Eurasian Eclipse / Feb. 11, 1971–Feb. 17, 1971 / Fantasy ✦✦✦

Toga Brava Suite / Oct. 22, 1971+Oct. 24, 1971 / Blue Note ✦✦✦
This single CD reissues all of the contents of the original United Artists double LP. By the time of these concerts from England, the Duke Ellington Orchestra had suffered quite a few losses of veteran personnel with Johnny Hodges having passed away and such greats as Cat Anderson, Ray Nance, Lawrence Brown and Jimmy Hamilton having departed. However the band was still a major force and this set has plenty of highpoints. Ellington's four-part "Togo Brava Suite" contains some memorable themes, there are spirited remakes of "C Jam Blues," "Cotton Tail," "In a Mellotone" and "I Got It Bad" (the latter featuring vocalist Nell Brookshire) and among the solo stars are the ancient-sounding trumpeter Cootie Williams, trombonist Booty Wood, Norris Turney on alto and flute (his "Checkered Hat" is a fine tribute to Hodges), the tenors of Paul Gonsalves and Harold Ashby and pianist Ellington himself. —*Scott Yanow*

This One's for Blanton / Dec. 5, 1972 / Original Jazz Classics ✦✦✦
These are sublime duets. Some of Ray Brown's best bass work on record. —*Ron Wynn*

The Duke's Big Four / Jan. 8, 1973 / Pablo ✦✦✦✦

Eastbourne Performance / Dec. 1, 1973 / RCA ✦✦✦

Mercer Ellington
b. Mar. 11, 1919, Washington, D.C., **d.** 1996
Leader / Swing
Mercer Ellington had the impossible task of trying to escape from his father Duke Ellington's shadow and he never really succeeded, perhaps not trying hard enough. He studied music early on and made several attempts to lead his own band (1939, 1946–49 and 1959) that were all ultimately unsuccessful. During the ASCAP strike of the early '40s when Duke was desperate for new material, Mercer wrote several notable songs including "Things Ain't What They Used to Be," "Jumpin' Punkins," "Moon Mist" and "Blue Serge," but nothing he composed since then approached their stature. Among his many other jobs were working as road manager for Cootie Williams' Orchestra, musical director for Della Reese, and as a salesman, a record-company executive and a disc jockey. Finally in 1965 he gave up trying to be independent and became Duke Ellington's road manager and a nonsoloing section trumpeter. After Duke's death in 1974, Mercer took over the band, but within a couple years it had greatly declined. Mercer wrote a biography in 1978, *Duke Ellington in Person,* directed the so-so musical *Sophisticated Ladies* (1981–83), supervised the release of many previously unavailable Ellington recordings and led the inaccurately titled "Duke Ellington Orchestra" on an occasional basis, recording a few dates that often had all-stars as ringers. —*Scott Yanow*

Continuum / Jul. 14, 1974–May 12, 1975 / Fantasy ✦✦✦✦

Take the Holiday Train / Jul. 28, 1980–Jul. 29, 1980 / Special Music ✦✦

Hot and Bothered / Jun. 22, 1984 / Doctor Jazz ✦✦✦

Digital Duke / 1987 / GRP ✦✦✦✦
The Duke Ellington Orchestra pretty much fell apart after its leader's death in 1974, but his son, Mercer, on an occasional basis has put together pickup bands to perform Duke's music. This particular CD uses quite an all-star group, mixing together such Ellington alumni as fluegelhornist Clark Terry, trumpeter Barry

Lee Hall, altoist Norris Turney, trombonist Britt Woodman and on four cuts, drummer Louie Bellson with such other major players as trumpeter Lew Soloff, clarinetist Eddie Daniels, tenorman Branford Marsalis (on two songs), trombonist Al Grey and pianist Roland Hanna. The big band does a fine job of performing a dozen songs associated with Duke, making this one of the best of Mercer Ellington's efforts. —*Scott Yanow*

● **Music Is My Mistress** / 1988 / Music Masters ✦✦✦✦✦

Don Ellis

b. Jul. 25, 1934, Los Angeles, CA, **d.** Dec. 17, 1978, Hollywood, CA

Trumpet, Leader / Post Bop, Avant-Garde

A talented trumpeter with a vivid musical imagination and the willingness to try new things, Don Ellis led some of the most colorful big bands of the 1965–75 period. After graduating from Boston Unversity, Ellis played in the big bands of Ray McKinley, Charlie Barnet and Maynard Ferguson (he was featured with the latter on "Three More Foxes"), recorded with Charles Mingus and played with George Russell's sextet (at the same time as Eric Dolphy). Ellis led four quartet and trio sessions during 1960–62 for Candid, New Jazz and Pacific Jazz, mixing together bop, free jazz and his interest in modern classical music. However it was in 1965 when he put together his first orchestra that he really started to make an impression in jazz. Ellis' big bands were distinguished by their unusual instrumentation (which in its early days had up to three bassists and three drummers including Ellis himself), the leader's desire to investigate unusual time changes (including 7/8, 9/8 and even 15/16), its occasionally wacky humor (highlighted by an excess of false endings) and an openness toward using rock rhythms and (in later years) electronics. Ellis invented the four-valve trumpet and utilized a ring modulator and all types of wild electronic devices by the late '60s. By 1971 his band consisted of an eight-piece brass section (including French horn and tuba), a four-piece woodwind section, a string quartet and a two-drum rhythm section. A later unrecorded edition even added a vocal quartet.

Among Don Ellis' sidemen were Glenn Ferris, Tom Scott, John Rlemmer, Sam Falzone, Frank Strozier, Dave MacKay and the brilliant pianist (straight from Bulgaria) Milcho Leviev. The orchestra's most memorable recordings (none are out on CD yet) were *Autumn, Live at the Fillmore* and *Tears of Joy* (all for Columbia). After suffering a mid-'70s heart attack, Ellis returned to live performing, playing the "superbone" and a later edition of his big band featured Art Pepper. Ellis' last recording was at the 1977 Montreux Jazz Festival, a year before his heart finally gave out. —*Scott Yanow*

How Time Passes / Oct. 4, 1960–Oct. 5, 1960 / Candid ✦✦✦✦

Out of Nowhere / Apr. 21, 1961 / Candid ✦✦✦
Early '60s Don Ellis, recorded in his pre-big band days, with bassist Steve Swallow and pianist Paul Bley. It's more conventional material, with Ellis playing in a dramatic, high register fashion. —*Ron Wynn*

New Ideas / May 11, 1961 / Original Jazz Classics ✦✦✦✦
The original thinking-jazz-lover's music. Quintet with unsung vibist Al Francis and the Jaki Byard Trio. All originals by Ellis, who has a lot to say with combos like this. Variations, nay mutations, of familiar themes crop up, along with staggered and fractured time signatures. Very innovative musician. —*Michael G. Nastos*

Essence / Jul. 15, 1962–Jul. 17, 1962 / Pacific Jazz ✦✦✦

Don Ellis at Monterey / Sep. 17, 1966–Sep. 18, 1966 / Pacific Jazz ✦✦✦✦✦

Live in 3/4 Time / Oct. 1966 / Liberty ✦✦✦✦
Unorthodox playing in varying time and musical contexts, done live at Monterey in the mid-'60s. —*Ron Wynn*

Electric Bath / Sep. 19, 1967–Sep. 20, 1967 / Columbia ✦✦✦✦✦

Shock Treatment / Feb. 14, 1968–Feb. 15, 1968 / Columbia ✦✦✦

★ **Autumn** / Aug. 1968 / Columbia ✦✦✦✦✦

New Don Ellis Band Goes Underground / Jan. 1969 / Columbia ✦✦✦

Don Ellis at Fillmore / 1970 / Columbia ✦✦✦✦✦
The release that helped break him into a mass audience. It is

live, daring, loud, annoying and distinctive all at once. —*Ron Wynn*

Tears of Joy / May 20, 1971–May 23, 1971 / Columbia ✦✦✦✦

Connection / 1972 / Columbia ✦✦

Haiku / 1973 / BASF ✦✦

Soaring / 1974 / BASF ✦✦✦

Live at Montreux / Jul. 24, 1977 / Atlantic ✦✦✦
Six pieces with big band and strings (21 pieces in all). John McLaughlin-influenced "The Sporting Dance" is a highlight. Lots of interplay, excellent solos from saxophonists Ann Patterson and Ted Nash, and Ellis on quarter-tone trumpet and the superbone. —*Michael G. Nastos*

Music from Other Galaxies and Planets / 1977 / Atlantic ✦

Herb Ellis (Mitchel Herbert Ellis)

b. Aug. 4, 1921, Farmersville, TX

Guitar / Bop, Swing

An excellent bop-based guitarist with a slight country twang to his sound, Herb Ellis became famous playing with the Oscar Peterson Trio during 1953–58. Prior to that he had attended North Texas State Unversity and played with the Casa Loma Orchestra, Jimmy Dorsey (1945–47) and the sadly underrecorded trio Soft Winds. While with Peterson, Ellis was on some Jazz at the Philharmonic tours and had a few opportunities to lead his own dates for Verve, including his personal favorite, *Nothing but the Blues* (1957). After leaving Peterson, Ellis toured a bit with Ella Fitzgerald, became a studio musician on the West Coast, made sessions with the Dukes of Dixieland, Stuff Smith and Charlie Byrd and in the 1970s became much more active in the jazz world. He is on the first three Concord releases, (interacting with Joe Pass on the initial two) and toured with the Great Guitars (along with Byrd and Barney Kessel) through much of the 1970s into the '80s. After a long series of Concord albums, Herb Ellis cut a couple of excellent sessions in the 1990s for Justice. —*Scott Yanow*

☆ **Nothing But the Blues** / Oct. 11, 1957–May 1, 1958 / Verve ✦✦✦✦✦
Guitarist Herb Ellis considers this is his favorite personal album and it is easy to see why. With trumpeter Roy Eldridge and tenor saxophonist Stan Getz contributing contrasting but equally rewarding solos and lots of inspired riffing while bassist Ray Brown and drummer Stan Levey join Ellis in the pianoless rhythm section, these performances have plenty of color and drive. Ellis does indeed stick to the blues during the original eight selections, yet there is also a surprising amount of variety. This CD reissue has been augmented by four numbers from 1958 originally recorded for a European soundtrack. Getz, Eldridge and Coleman Hawkins all have their features, but Dizzy Gillespie fares best. —*Scott Yanow*

Together / Jan. 18, 1963 / Epic ✦✦✦✦

Jazz at Concord / Jul. 29, 1973 / Concord Jazz ✦✦✦
A wonderful collaboration with his old friend Joe Pass (g) on a standard, though nicely played, mainstream date. —*Ron Wynn*

Seven Come Eleven / Jul. 30, 1973 / Concord Jazz ✦✦✦✦
With Joe Pass. Concord's second record. Titans clash. Great music. Good on CD. First-rate band doing prototype arrangements. —*Ron Wynn*

Two for the Road / Jan. 30, 1974–Feb. 20, 1974 / Pablo ✦✦✦
With Joe Pass. Exemplary two-guitar date. —*Ron Wynn*

After You've Gone / Aug. 1974 / Concord Jazz ✦✦✦✦

Soft Shoe / 1974 / Concord Jazz ✦✦✦✦
"Sweets" Edison (tpt) brings some fire to this Ellis/Ray Brown (b) set. —*Ron Wynn*

Hot Tracks / 1975 / Concord Jazz ✦✦✦
With Ray Brown Sextet. 1989 reissue of this session with Ray Brown (b) sharing the spotlight. —*Ron Wynn*

Rhythm Willie / 1975 / Concord Jazz ✦✦✦

Pair to Draw / 1976 / Concord Jazz ✦✦✦

Windflower / Oct. 1977 / Concord Jazz ✦✦✦
Typically restrained, quietly swinging set. —*Ron Wynn*

Soft and Mellow / Aug. 1978 / Concord Jazz ✦✦✦
On-the-money title. Ellis shows the difference between restraint and detachment. With Ross Tompkins (p). —*Ron Wynn*

Herb Ellis at Montreux / Jul. 1979 / Concord Jazz ✦✦✦
Herb Mix / Jun. 1981 / Concord Jazz ✦✦✦
Doggin' Around / Mar. 1988 / Concord Jazz ✦✦✦✦
★ **Roll Call** / 1991 / Justice ✦✦✦✦✦
Well-done recent release with Ellis backed by a solid lineup of session and studio pros, among them trumpeter Jay Thomas and violinist Johnny Frigo. They play a mix of blues, traditional jazz stomps and standards, with organist Mel Rhyne adding soulful support alongside drummer Jake Hanna. —*Ron Wynn*

Texas Swings / 1992 / Justice ✦✦✦✦
Texas-born guitarist Herb Ellis teams up with a variety of country musicians on this Justice CD for a set of Western swing-oriented jazz. Essentially an instrumental country date with Ellis as one of the lead voices, the enjoyable set also has Willie Nelson's guitar added on some of the tracks along with steel guitar, two violinists and a standard rhythm section. The twangy sound of the steel guitar may not appeal to everyone but the fairly basic music (mostly swing standards) is played with plenty of spirit. This recording gives Ellis a fresh setting after years in trios and quartets. —*Scott Yanow*

Ziggy Elman (Harry Finkelman)

b. May 26, 1914, Philadelphia, PA, **d.** Jun. 26, 1968, Los Angeles, CA
Trumpet / Swing
In a word-association game, the name Ziggy Elman will always be followed by "And the Angels Sing," his one hit. He started out playing trombone with Alex Bartha's band, making his recording debut in 1932. In 1936 he hit the big time by joining Benny Goodman's Orchestra, but the hiring of Harry James (who had a similar style) within a year greatly cut Elman's solo opportunities and potential for fame. However he had his moments, as on "Bed Mir Bist Du Schon" in 1937, which had a section similar to "And the Angels Sing." Elman, who was part of BG's famous trumpet section with James and Chris Griffin, had opportunities in 1938-39 to record 20 songs as a leader. One of them, "Fralich in Swing," was soon given a Martha Tilton vocal and recorded as "And the Angels Sing."
In what could be considered a mistake, Ziggy Elman left Goodman in 1940, not to lead his own orchestra but to join Tommy Dorsey. He was well-featured during his long stay (1940-47) but by the time he decided to form his own big band (off and on during 1947-52), the swing era was over. He became a studio musician and gradually faded out of the jazz world without becoming a star or fulfilling his potential. —*Scott Yanow*

Bob Enevoldsen

b. Jan. 11, 1920, Billings, MT
Valve Trombone, Tenor Saxophone / Cool
Bob Enevoldsen has long been the perfect utility jazz player. Although best-known as a valve trombonist, Enevoldsen is also a talented tenorman and has filled in on string bass, too. He had mostly been a music teacher when he moved to Los Angeles in 1951 and became a busy studio musician, appearing on West Coast jazz dates headed by Gerry Mulligan, Shorty Rogers, Shelly Manne and Marty Paich among many others. During 1954-55 he was the bassist in Bobby Troup's trio and during 1962-64 he worked on Steve Allen's television series. He remains active up to the present day, generally playing valve trombone in L.A.-based big bands. Enevoldsen recorded as a leader during 1954-55 for Nocturne, Tampa (reissued on V.S.O.P.) and Liberty. —*Scott Yanow*

● **Bob Enevoldsen Quintet** / 1955 / VSOP ✦✦✦✦
This CD reissue brings back an unusual, but consistently swinging, release from the 1950s Tampa label. Bob Enevoldsen, in one of only three albums that he had as a leader, alternates between valve trombone and tenor and is joined by Marty Paich (tripling on piano, organ and accordion), vibraphonist Larry Bunker (who switches to drums on a lengthy "Blues"), bassist Red Mitchell and drummer Don Heath. The music (three basic originals, "Topsy" and "Don't Be That Way") is more conventional than the instrumentation but is a fine outing for all concerned with plenty of swinging solos. —*Scott Yanow*

Bobby Enriquez

b. 1943, Phillipines
Piano / Bop, Afro-Cuban Jazz
Bobby Enriquez has the nickname of "The Madman," and it is a

title he has earned through his very hyper piano playing. A virtuoso who was largely self-taught from the age of four, Enriquez was a professional by the time he was 14. In the 1960s he played in Manila, Hong Kong and Honolulu, becoming Don Ho's musical director for a time. He arrived on the mainland in the early '70s, toured with Richie Cole during 1980-81 and made his debut on record in 1981. Enriquez cut eight albums for GNP/Crescendo during 1981-85, which made his reputation. Due to putting an excess of song quotes in his solos (some of them very silly), Enriquez is not known for his exquisite taste, but his technique and ability to think very fast are quite impressive. He has also recorded for Portrait (1987) and a 1990 date for the Japanese Paddle Wheel label has been issued domestically on Evidence. —*Scott Yanow*

Wild Man / 1981 / GNP ✦✦✦✦
Although not as explosive as the title suggests, some strong piano work by Bobby Enriquez in an early '80s quartet session. The material is divided between originals and standards like "Sweet Georgia Brown" and bop anthems like "Confirmation." Drummer Alex Acuna and Pancho Sanchez on congas provide solid Afro-Latin backgrounds and interact smoothly with star fusion bassist Abe Laboriel. —*Ron Wynn*

Wildman Meets the Madman / 1981 / GNP ✦✦✦
Espana / 1982 / GNP ✦✦✦
Live! in Tokyo, Vol. 2 / Aug. 6, 1982–Aug. 7, 1982 / GNP ✦✦✦
★ **Wild Piano** / Dec. 22, 1987 / Portrait ✦✦✦✦✦
Filipino "Wild man from Mindanao" plays fiercely probing trio jazz. Look for GNP albums, too. —*Michael G. Nastos*

Wildman Returns / Apr. 19, 1990 / Evidence ✦✦✦✦
Despite his nickname and the disc's title, pianist Bobby Enriquez starts things off laid-back and mellow on the opening numbers. He smartly intersperses parts of the James Bond theme with the *Pink Panther* theme and is smooth and beguiling on "Our Love Is Here To Stay." But he kicks it into gear on "Groovin' High," and for the remainder of the date justifies his reputation with some furious phrases, spinning licks, percussive right-hand lines, booming two-handed riffs and plenty of bluesy block chords. —*Ron Wynn*

Rolf Ericson

b. Aug. 29, 1922, Stockholm, Sweden
Trumpet, Fluegelhorn / Bop, Swing
One of Sweden's finest trumpeters, Rolf Ericson has played in the U.S. often enough to gain a strong reputation. He started on trumpet when he was eight and, after hearing Louis Armstrong play in Stockholm in 1933, he switched to jazz. Ericson recorded in Sweden with Alice Babs and others starting in 1945, moved to New York in 1947 and played with Charlie Barnet (1949) and Woody Herman (1950). After returning to Sweden in 1950, he recorded as a leader and with Arne Domnerus and Leonard Feather's Swinging Swedes. He also toured and recorded with Charlie Parker. Back in the U.S. during 1953-56, Ericson played with the big bands of Charlie Spivak, Harry James, the Dorsey Brothers and Les Brown and was with the Lighthouse All-Stars. In 1956 he toured Sweden and played with Ernestine Anderson and Lars Gullin. During 1956-65 in the U.S., Ericson was with Dexter Gordon, Harold Land, Stan Kenton, Woody Herman, Maynard Ferguson (1960-61), Buddy Rich, Benny Goodman, Gerry Mulligan and Charles Mingus among others. There were also occasional tours with Duke Ellington during 1963-71 and plenty of freelance jobs. In 1971 he settled in Germany as a studio musician but Ericson has returned to the U.S. several times since. His warm tone and creative yet melodic style are always an asset. —*Scott Yanow*

● **Stockholm Sweetnin'** / Aug. 21, 1984–Aug. 22, 1984 / Dragon ✦✦✦✦✦

Peter Erskine

b. Jun. 5, 1954, Somers Point, NJ
Drums / Fusion, Post Bop
A very versatile drummer, Peter Erskine has excelled in several types of jazz settings. He was with Stan Kenton's Orchestra (1972-75) and Maynard Ferguson's big band (1976-78) before gaining fame with Weather Report (1978-82) where he made a perfect team with Jaco Pastorius. Since that time he has been a member of Steps Ahead (which he had originally joined when

they were Steps in 1979), John Abercrombie's band, Bass Desires, and groups headed by Kenny Wheeler in addition to leading his own units. Peter Erskine has led sessions for Contemporary (1982), Denon, Ah-Um, Novus and most recently ECM. —*Scott Yanow*

★ **Peter Erskine** / Jun. 22, 1982–Jun. 23, 1982 / Contemporary ✦✦✦✦✦
First release by a first-rate drummer and lots of New York friends. "All's Well that Ends" is a winning track, as is "Leroy St." —*Michael G. Nastos*

Transition / Oct. 16, 1986–Oct. 17, 1986 / Denon ✦✦✦
Big Theatre / 1986–1989 / Ah Um ✦✦✦
Motion Poet / Apr. 25, 1988–May 1, 1988 / Denon ✦✦
An excellent percussionist makes an uneven, but ambitious statement. —*Ron Wynn*

Aurora / Nov. 14, 1988–Nov. 15, 1988 / Denon ✦✦✦✦✦
Sweet Soul / Mar. 4, 1991–Mar. 5, 1991 / Novus ✦✦✦✦
A terrific date, it features John Scofield (g), Joe Lovano (s), Bob Mintzer (s), Kenny Werner (p). Erskine's abilities as a composer are quite evident on this recording. —*Paul Kohler*

You Never Know / Jul. 1992 / ECM ✦✦✦
Time Being / Nov. 1993 / ECM ✦✦✦
Although it is easy to stereotype Peter Erskine as a fusion drummer due to his notable work with Weather Report, in reality he is a very flexible percussionist. On his trio session for ECM, Erskine is mostly content to back his sidemen (pianist John Taylor and bassist Palle Danielsson). This CD is actually most interesting for the playing of Taylor, who contributes three of the originals and plays in a style not that far from Keith Jarrett. In general the music starts out pretty quiet but builds its intensity and holds one's interest. —*Scott Yanow*

Booker Ervin

b. Oct. 30, 1930, Denson, TX, **d.** Jul. 31, 1970, New York, NY
Tenor Saxophone / Avant-Garde, Hard Bop, Post Bop
A very distinctive tenor with a hard passionate tone and an emotional style that was still tied to chordal improvisation, Booker Ervin was a true original. He was originally a trombonist but taught himself tenor while in the Air Force (1950–53). After studying music in Boston for two years, he made his recording debut with Ernie Fields' R&B band (1956). Ervin gained fame while playing with Charles Mingus (off and on during 1956–62), holding his own with the volatile bassist and Eric Dolphy. He also led his own quartet, worked with Randy Weston on a few occasions in the '60s and spent much of 1964–66 in Europe before dying much too young from kidney disease. Ervin, who is on several notable Charles Mingus records, made dates of his own for Bethlehem, Savoy and Candid during 1960–61, along with later sets for Pacific Jazz and Blue Note, but it is his nine Prestige sessions of 1963–66 (including *The Freedom Book*, *The Song Book*, *The Blues Book* and *The Space Book*) that are among the highpoints of his career. —*Scott Yanow*

The Book Cooks / Jun. 1960 / Bethlehem ✦✦✦
Down in the Dumps / Nov. 26, 1960–Jan. 5, 1961 / Savoy ✦✦✦
An explosive set from Ervin's prime period, reissued on disc with additional material from the following year (1961), with trombonist Dr. Billy Howell. —*Ron Wynn*

That's It / Jan. 6, 1961 / Candid ✦✦✦✦
Back from the Gig / Feb. 15, 1963+Jun. 24, 1968 / Blue Note ✦✦✦✦✦
This two-LP set consists of a pair of classic Blue Note sets that were not originally released until 1976. The great tenor Booker Ervin (whose hard passionate sound was always immediately recognizable) is well-showcased with the Horace Parlan Sextet in 1963 (a group also featuring pianist Parlan, trumpeter Johnny Coles and guitarist Grant Green) and with his own all star quintet from 1968 (which also stars trumpeter Woody Shaw and pianist Kenny Barron). The stimulating group originals and advanced solos (which fall somewhere between hard bop and the avant-garde) still sound fresh and frequently exciting. —*Scott Yanow*

Exultation! / Jun. 19, 1963 / Original Jazz Classics ✦✦✦✦
Booker Ervin's debut for Prestige (which has been reissued on CD with two shorter alternate takes added) matches the intense tenor

with altoist Frank Strozier, pianist Horace Parlan, bassist Butch Warren and drummer Walter Perkins for some bop-based music that is actually quite adventurous. Highlights include "Mour" (based on "Four"), "Black and Blue" and Ervin's "Mooche Mooche." Ervin and Strozier made a mutually inspiring team; pity that this was their only recording together. —*Scott Yanow*

Freedom Book / Dec. 3, 1963 / Original Jazz Classics ✦✦✦✦
Freedom and Space Sessions / Dec. 3, 1963+Oct. 2, 1964 / Prestige ✦✦✦✦✦
Tenor saxophonist Booker Ervin was overshadowed during his lifetime by everyone from Eric Dolphy and John Coltrane to Ornette Coleman and Sonny Rollins. Ervin, whose distinctive sound can be identified within two notes, never received much recognition, but he was one of the top tenors of the 1960s, as can be heard on this excellent two-LP set. The two-fer includes the full contents of both *The Freedom Book* and *The Space Book* plus two other selections originally issued on another LP. Joined by the remarkably versatile pianist Jaki Byard, bassist Richard Davis and drummer Alan Dawson, Ervin is top form on seven of his obscure originals plus three standards and Randy Weston's "Cry Me Not." —*Scott Yanow*

The Song Book / Feb. 27, 1964 / Original Jazz Classics ✦✦✦✦✦
Another in a series of exceptional quartet dates led by tenor saxophonist Booker Ervin in the mid-'60s. This time, Tommy Flanagan replaced Jaki Byard on piano, with absolutely no dip in the quartet's execution. Ervin's solos were once more robust and well played, while The Davis/Dawson bass and drum duo did their customary excellent job. This has been issued on vinyl as part of the two-record set *The Blues Book/The Song Book* and on both vinyl and CD as a single session. —*Ron Wynn*

★ **The Blues Book** / Jun. 30, 1964 / Original Jazz Classics ✦✦✦✦✦
For this CD reissue in his series of *Books*, Ervin and his quintet (with trumpeter Carmell Jones, pianist Gildo Mahones, bassist Richard Davis and drummer Alan Dawson) perform four very different blues: the speedy "One for Mort," a lowdown "No Booze Blooze," the modal "True Blue" and the minor-toned "Eerie Dearie." The consistently passionate Ervin makes each of the fairly basic originals sound fresh and the performances are frequently exciting inside/outside music. —*Scott Yanow*

Space Book / Oct. 2, 1964 / Prestige ✦✦✦✦✦
The fourth and final Booker Ervin "book" release, each done in 1964. Ervin does two exceptional ballads here, stunning versions of "I Can't Get Started" and "There Is No Greater Love," plus his usual arresting uptempo and blues numbers. Jaki Byard is back on piano, and again Richard Davis and Alan Dawson are paired on bass and drums. This has been issued on vinyl as part of the two-record set *The Freedom and Space Sessions* and as a single release under the title *Groovin' High*. —*Ron Wynn*

The Trance / Oct. 27, 1965 / Prestige ✦✦✦✦
Settin' the Pace / Oct. 27, 1965 / Prestige ✦✦✦
With Dexter Gordon. This is an earthy, booming workout with Dexter Gordon (ts) aboard. —*Ron Wynn*

Lament for Booker Ervin / Oct. 29, 1965 / Enja ✦✦✦
Heavy! / Sep. 9, 1966 / Prestige ✦✦✦
Some soul, some funk and lots of power. —*Ron Wynn*

Structurally Sound / Dec. 1966 / Pacific Jazz ✦✦✦
In Between / Jan. 12, 1968 / Blue Note ✦✦✦
The in Between / Jan. 12, 1968 / Blue Note ✦✦✦
For the more adventurous. With Bobby Few on piano and Richard Williams on trumpet. Ervin veers between inside and outside jazz. —*Ron Wynn*

Pee Wee Erwin (George Erwin)

b. May 30, 1913, Falls City, NB, **d.** Jun. 20, 1981, Teaneck, NJ
Trumpet / Dixieland, Swing
An excellent trumpeter who spent most of his career on the fringe of fame, Pee Wee Erwin made many fine records during his career. He began playing trumpet when he was four. Stints with territory bands were followed by gigs with Joe Haymes (1931–33) and Isham Jones (1933–34). Erwin then moved to New York and became a busy studio musician, working often on radio including with Benny Goodman during 1934–35. After playing with Ray Noble in 1935 he succeeded Bunny Berigan in both the Benny Goodman (1936) and Tommy Dorsey (1937–39) orchestras. Erwin

put together an unsuccessful big band in 1941–42 and tried again with little luck in 1946. He worked steadily playing Dixieland at Nick's during the 1950s, ran a trumpet school with Chris Griffin in the 1960s (Warren Vache was one of his students) and played steadily until the end of his life. Pee Wee Erwin led sessions on an occasional basis in the 1950s (including a couple for United Artists) and made six albums during 1980–81, including three for Qualtro and one for Jazzology, still sounding quite good that late in his career. —*Scott Yanow*

Oh, Play That Thing! / Oct. 1958 / United Artists ✦✦✦✦

● **Pee Wee in New York** / Jan. 21, 1980 / Qualtro ✦✦✦✦

Pee Wee in Hollywood / May 26, 1980–May 27, 1980 / Qualtro ✦✦✦

Pee Wee Erwin Memorial / May 28, 1981–May 29, 1981 / Jazz Crooner ✦✦✦

Bruce Eskovitz

b. CA
Tenor Saxophone / Hard Bop
After a couple of crossover records, Bruce Eskovitz really stretched out on his Koch Jazz release (*One for Newk*) as he paid tribute to Sonny Rollins. One selection ("Tenor Madness") features him holding his own with the great Ernie Watts. Eskovitz started playing tenor when he was 11 and at age 20 was composing music for the *Merv Griffin* television show. He has mostly worked as a studio musician and a jazz educator but appears regularly in Los Angeles area clubs. —*Scott Yanow*

Bruce Eskovitz / May 6, 1992 / Cexton ✦✦✦

● **One for Newk** / Nov. 18, 1993–Nov. 19, 1993 / Koch ✦✦✦✦✦
This is a record that all lovers of bebop have to get. tenor saxophonist Bruce Eskovitz has a fat tone and a hard-driving style that is most reminiscent of Don Menza and Lew Tabackin, making him a perfect person to record a tribute to Sonny Rollins. If he sounded exactly like Newk this set would not be all that effective since there is no reason to hear an imitation when the original is also quite prominent on records. But by paying homage to Rollins without directly copying him, Eskovitz has put together a very enjoyable set. With the exception of "Poor Butterfly" and "Count Your Blessings," all ten numbers are Rollins compositions. Eskovitz is greatly assisted by pianist Bill Mays, vibraphonist Charlie Shoemake, bassist Ray Drummond and drummer Larance Marable on such numbers as "No Moe," "Airegin," "Valse Hot," "Strode Rode" and "Pent-Up House." As intense as some of the jam session-style performances are, it is the final number that is the most passionate, for "Tenor Madness" is a ten-minute blowout with guest Ernie Watts challenging (but not overwhelming) Eskovitz. Highly recommended. —*Scott Yanow*

Ruth Etting

b. Nov. 23, 1897, David City, NB, **d.** Sept. 24, 1978
Vocals / Pop, Classic Jazz
One of the most popular singers of the late-'20s/early-'30s period, Ruth Etting was not really a jazz singer (unlike her contemporary Annette Hanshaw) but a superior middle-of-the-road pop singer who was often accompanied by top jazz musicians. She recorded over 200 songs between 1926–37, appeared on stage, was in 35 film shorts and three full-length movies and was a fixture on radio before her bad marriage cut short her career. She made a minor comeback in the late '40s and was still singing on an occasional basis in the mid-'50s when a semifictional Hollywood movie on her life (*Love Me or Leave Me*) was released. A superb torch singer with a cry in her voice even when she smiled, Etting recorded the definitive versions of "Ten Cents a Dance" and "Love Me or Leave Me." —*Scott Yanow*

★ **Ten Cents a Dance** / Apr. 14, 1926–Sep. 29, 1930 / Living Era ✦✦✦✦✦
This English import has 20 recordings featuring the early jazz-influenced pop singer Ruth Etting. Although the music is not programmed in chronological order (and there is no personnel listing given), many of Etting's greatest performances are here: the emotional "Ten Cents a Dance," "Button Up Your Overcoat," "Mean to Me," "Sam, the Old Accordion Man," "You're the Cream in My Coffee" and "Love Me or Leave Me." This CD gives one a definitive look into Ruth Etting's talents during her prime period and is

easily recommended as a fine example of superior pop singing of the 1920s. —*Scott Yanow*

Goodnight My Love (1930–1937) / 1930–1937 / Take Two ✦✦✦

Kevin Eubanks

b. Nov. 15, 1957, Philadelphia, PA
Guitar / Post Bop
During the past couple of years Kevin Eubanks has been seen by millions of viewers nightly due to being the leader of Jay Leno's Tonight Show Band, where his main purpose is to assist the comedian/host rather than play creative jazz. Eubanks comes from a musical family that included Ray and Tommy Bryant as uncles and older brother/trombonist Robin Eubanks. After studying at Berklee, he was with the Art Blakey big band (1980–81), had stints with Roy Haynes, Slide Hampton and Sam Rivers and then in 1983 started leading his own groups. After debuting on Elektra, starting in 1985 Eubanks began recording regularly for GRP. Some of the sets were a bit commercial while others were fairly explorative. Switching to Blue Note in the 1990s, Eubanks has been emphasizing acoustic guitar in more recent years. —*Scott Yanow*

Guitarist / May 1982–Aug. 1982 / Elektra ✦✦✦
Acoustic guitar solos and group works, with Ralph Moore (ts), Roy Haynes (d), Charles David (p) and Robin Eubanks (tb). This is a fine debut album. —*Michael G. Nastos*

Sundance / Dec. 1984 / GRP ✦✦✦

Opening Night / 1985 / GRP ✦✦✦

Face to Face / 1986 / GRP ✦✦✦

The Heat of Heat / 1987 / GRP ✦✦

Shadow Prophets / Jan. 15, 1988–Jan. 24, 1988 / GRP ✦✦✦

The Searcher / Nov. 18, 1988–Nov. 23, 1988 / GRP ✦✦✦

Promise of Tomorrow / Nov. 13, 1989–Nov. 19, 1988 / GRP ✦✦✦

● **Turning Point** / Dec. 16, 1991–Jan. 9, 1992 / Blue Note ✦✦✦✦✦
Blue Note session in which Eubanks disproves those who have questioned his jazz and improvising credentials. There are only four cuts, and they're designed for intense solos and exacting ensemble interaction. Besides Eubanks on electric and acoustic guitar, the cast features alto flutist Kent Jordan, bassist Dave Holland and drummer Marvin "Smitty" Smith. —*Ron Wynn*

Spirit Talk / 1993 / Blue Note ✦✦✦✦
Kevin Eubanks plays acoustic guitar on this Blue Note release as much as he does electric. His nine originals set moods and/or grooves more than they state memorable melodies, but they do provide a stimulating framework for solos from Eubanks, his brother trombonist Robin Eubanks and Kent Jordan on alto flute; the quintet is completed by bassist Dave Holland and either Marvin "Smitty" Smith or Mark Mondesir on drums. Some songs are mildly funky, others are melancholy ballads or straight-ahead but, no matter what the rhythm, none of the music is predictable. This CD, which has the feel of a logical suite, is well worth checking out. —*Scott Yanow*

Spiritalk 2 / Jun. 25, 1994–Jun. 28, 1994 / Blue Note ✦✦✦
The most notable aspect to this CD from Kevin Eubanks is the instrumental blend between his acoustic guitar, trombonist Robin Eubanks and the alto flute of Kent Jordan; bassist Dave Holland and either Marvin "Smitty" Smith or Gene Jackson on drums completes the quintet. Eubanks' originals are moody and thoughtful (even in the more heated moments) but do little more than set introspective moods; none of the themes are particularly memorable. The playing is of a consistent high quality on this set but the music is much easier to respect than to love. —*Scott Yanow*

Robin Eubanks

b. Oct. 25, 1955, Philadelphia, PA
Trombone / Post Bop
The older brother of guitarist Kevin Eubanks, Robin Eubanks has made his mark playing in his brother's groups, on his own JMT releases and interacting with many of the top M-Base players, such as Steve Coleman and Greg Osby. Capable of playing anything from bop to free, Eubanks came to New York in 1980, played with Slide Hampton and Sun Ra, toured with Stevie Wonder and then spent time with Art Blakey's Jazz Messengers. A versatile player, Eubanks has freelanced in many contexts including with the McCoy Tyner big band. —*Scott Yanow*

● **Different Perspectives** / Jun. 1988 / JMT ✦✦✦✦✦
Exceptional first album from this trombonist. A great listening album with many components, mostly in a progressive vein. —*Michael G. Nastos*

Dedication / Apr. 1989 / JMT ✦✦✦✦
With Steve Turre. Two trombonists live up to their reputations with much vital music. —*Michael G. Nastos*

Karma / May 1990 / JMT ✦✦✦
A noteworthy experimental session with both pop and improvisational elements. —*Ron Wynn*

Mental Images / Apr. 1994 / JMT ✦✦✦

Jim Europe

b. Feb. 22, 1881, Mobile, AL, **d.** May 10. 1919, Boston, MS
Leader / Dance Music, Ragtime
An early Black music pioneer, Jim Europe did not live long enough to play jazz, but his large orchestra utilized jazz instruments (including a full banjo section) and performed ragtime, marches and dance music of the 1912-19 period. His pre-World War I group often accompanied the legendary dancers Vernon and Irene Castle. During the war he toured Europe with his huge military band and seemed poised to repeat his success in the U.S. in 1919 when he was stabbed to death by an irate musician. Europe recorded as early as 1912. —*Scott Yanow*

Bill Evans

b. Aug. 16, 1929, Plainfield, NJ, **d.** Sep. 15, 1980, New York, NY
Piano, Leader / Post Bop, Cool
Bill Evans was (along with McCoy Tyner) the most influential pianist in jazz during the 1960s and '70s, and since his death in 1980 his influence has exceeded Tyner's. Evans, who was the next step beyond Bud Powell, had a sophisticated way of voicing chords that has been adopted by a countless number of pianists. Very popular even among nonjazz audiences for his sensitive interpretations of ballads, Evans could always swing as hard as anyone when he was inspired.

After attending Southwestern Louisiana University, working with Mundell Lowe and Red Mitchell and serving in the Army, Evans first emerged on the New York scene playing with Tony Scott in 1956 and that year he made his first trio album, *New Jazz Conceptions*. After working with George Russell and recording with Charles Mingus, Evans was part of the 1958 Miles Davis Sextet with John Coltrane and Cannonball Adderley. Other than a few live dates and "So What" from the 1959 classic *Kind of Blue*, Evans did not record all that much during his months with Davis but he made a strong impact and contributed one future standard, "Blue in Green," which ranks with "Waltz for Debby" as his most famous original.

By 1959 Bill Evans was leading his own trio, which soon utilized the great bassist Scott LaFaro and drummer Paul Motian. The interplay between the three musicians (with an almost equal role by each of the players) was highly influential and nearly telepathic. Tragically, shortly after they recorded extensively at the Village Vanguard in June 1961, LaFaro was killed in a car accident. Evans went into isolation for the remainder of the year. In 1962 he re-emerged with Chuck Israels as his new bassist and recorded the first of two classic albums in a duet with guitarist Jim Hall. In future years Evans would continue touring and recording with his trio which included such sideman as bassists Israels (1962-65), Gary Peacock (1963), Eddie Gomez (1966-77) and Marc Johnson (1978-80) and drummers Paul Motian (1959-62), Larry Bunker (1963-5), Philly Joe Jones (1967), Jack DeJohnette (1968), Marty Morell (1969-75), Eliot Zigmund (1975-78) and Joe LaBarbera (1979-80). Drug addiction cut short Bill Evans' life prematurely, but he fortunately had recorded extensively from 1956 on, most notably for Riverside, Verve, Fantasy and Warner Bros. Several videos are also available of this major force in modern jazz whose innovations helped form the styles of Herbie Hancock and Keith Jarrett. —*Scott Yanow*

New Jazz Conceptions / Sep. 27, 1956 / Original Jazz Classics ✦✦✦✦
This was pianist Bill Evans debut as a leader, a 9/18, 9/27/56 recording. He had backing from bassist Teddy Kotick and drummer Paul Motian. The album swings hard but really did not develop the grace and cutting execution that would be found on *Explorations*. —*Bob Rusch*

Conception / Sep. 27, 1956-Apr. 10, 1962 / Milestone ✦✦✦✦
Although all of Bill Evans' Riverside recordings have been reissued in a massive box set, those listeners who have not invested in that may very well be satisfied to pick up a few of his Milestone two-fers. This particular one reissues the influential pianist's very first session as a leader (which was originally on an LP titled *New Jazz Conceptions*), a trio date with bassist Teddy Kotick and drummer Paul Motian that also includes three unaccompanied piano solos (highlighted by the original version of Evans' most famous composition, "Waltz for Debby"). In addition, there is a full album of previously unreleased music: an alternate take of "No Cover, No Minimum," an unaccompanied version of "Some Other Time" from 1958 and four solo pieces that Evans cut in 1962, his first recordings after the tragic death of his bassist Scott LaFaro. —*Scott Yanow*

☆ **The Complete Riverside Recordings (1956-63)** / Sep. 27, 1956-May 31, 1963 / Riverside ✦✦✦✦✦
12 CDs. Fantasy/1985. All the marvelous Evans one could ever want is on this incredible 18-disc boxed set. It is a wonderful, comprehensive collection of superb performances, with some of his most majestic trio and solo dates. —*Ron Wynn*

Everybody Digs Bill Evans / Dec. 15, 1958 / Original Jazz Classics ✦✦✦✦
A worthy session with the great Philly Joe Jones drumming. —*Ron Wynn*

Peace Piece and Other Pieces / Dec. 15, 1958-Aug. 21, 1962 / Milestone ✦✦✦
This valuable two-LP set reissues pianist Bill Evans' 1958 trio set with bassist Sam Jones and drummer Philly Joe Jones originally titled *Everybody Digs Bill Evans* plus a full previously unreleased 1959 session with bassist Paul Chambers and Philly Joe; in addition there is one piece ("Loose Bloose") from a long-lost quintet date with Zoot Sims on alto and Jim Hall on guitar. Although not quite essential, there is a great deal of worthy and timeless music on this two-fer. —*Scott Yanow*

Undercurrent / May 15, 1959 / Blue Note ✦✦✦✦✦
A must-have reissue of brilliant date with Jim Hall (g). —*Ron Wynn*

Portrait in Jazz / Dec. 28, 1959 / Original Jazz Classics ✦✦✦✦✦
Here is an excellent reissue of a solid concert, with some typically stunning Scott LaFaro on bass. —*Ron Wynn*

Spring Leaves / Dec. 28, 1959-Feb. 2, 1961 / Milestone ✦✦✦✦
Bill Evans' greatest trio was the one with bassist Scott LaFaro and drummer Paul Motian during 1959-61. In addition to their justifiably famous Village Vanguard recordings (performed just two weeks before LaFaro's death in a car accident), Evans' trio also recorded the two studio albums (originally titled *Portrait in Jazz* and *Explorations*) that are included on this two-LP set. The interplay between the three musicians (with LaFaro assuming as important a role as Evans) was very influential on rhythm sections from the 1960s up to the present. "Autumn Leaves" (heard in two versions), "When I Fall in Love," "Blue in Green," "Nardis" and "How Deep Is the Ocean" are among the many highlights of this very significant body of work. —*Scott Yanow*

Explorations / Feb. 2, 1961 / Original Jazz Classics ✦✦✦✦
Pianist Bill Evans, like guitarist Wes Montgomery, was a Riverside "discovery." This session was recorded in 1961 by Evans' trio with bassist Scott LaFaro and drummer Paul Motian. The version of "Israel" on this release remains such a continuing unfolding joy that it alone would justify the album's purchase. Through technique, execution and imagination Bill Evans made some very fine *free* jazz artistically free. This was also issued as part of a two-fer. —*Bob Rusch*

★ **Sunday at the Village Vanguard** / Jun. 25, 1961 / Original Jazz Classics ✦✦✦✦✦
This represents one of the best known sessions from the Village Vanguard and most of the material from this 6/25/61 date was on a previous two-fer. Simply put, it sounds like pianist Bill Evans, bassist Scott LaFaro and drummer Paul Motian, and it sounds like Sunday. —*Bob Rusch, Cadence*

★ **Waltz for Debby** / Jun. 25, 1961 / Original Jazz Classics ✦✦✦✦✦
This second issue of the Bill Evans trio (Scott LaFaro, bass; Paul Motian, drums) had a good run on Riverside, was one of the first Milestone two-fers and also as part of the 19-LP Bill Evans box. The material here has, because of its lasting popularity and the influence of Evans, become somewhat its own cliché, which of

course is really an ironic distortion of time and place. For this date, time, place, artists were right, and for two decades this, for many, continues to be a stimulating comfort. —*Bob Rusch*

How My Heart Sings! / May 17, 1962–Jun. 5, 1962 / Original Jazz Classics ✦✦✦✦
Bill Evans Trio. More from the Evans-Chuck Israels-Paul Motian lineup. —*Ron Wynn*

Moonbeams / May 17, 1962–Jun. 5, 1962 / Original Jazz Classics ✦✦✦✦
Bill Evans Trio. Top trio again features Evans, Israels (b) and Motian (d). —*Ron Wynn*

Interplay / Jul. 16, 1962 / Original Jazz Classics ✦✦✦✦
Quintet. A dazzling small-group date with top-flight Freddie Hubbard (tpt). 1987 reissue. —*Ron Wynn*

Empathy / A Simple Matter of Conviction / Aug. 14, 1962+Oct. 11, 1966 / Verve ✦✦✦✦
Empathy was a collaboration between drummer Shelly Manne and pianist Bill Evans and came almost a year after their first pairing. On this date Monty Budwig was the bassist. This was a bit of an uneven set as there were times when the creative lines taken by Manne and Evans did not really interplay and Budwig tended to straddle between the two. On the other hand, there were individually fine moments and one particular cut, "Washington Twist," matched Manne and Evans equally in creative interplay and involvement. —*Bob Rusch*

Loose Blues / Aug. 21, 1962–Aug. 22, 1962 / Milestone ✦✦✦

V.I.P.S. Theme Plus Others / 1963 / MGM ✦✦

The Solo Sessions, Vol. 1 / Jan. 10, 1963 / Milestone ✦✦✦

The Solo Sessions, Vol. 2 / Jan. 10, 1963 / Milestone ✦✦✦
Tremendous solo piano by Bill Evans, featuring mid-'60s material. There are exceptional reworkings of many standards and show tunes, with Evans displaying the technical command and melodic and harmonic invention that made him a legend. This material has also been issued in a two-record set *Solo Sessions, Vols 1 & 2*, as well as a separate vinyl album and CD. —*Ron Wynn*

Conversations with Myself / Feb. 6, 1963 / Verve ✦✦✦✦✦
Stunning multiple-tracked piano solos. Great playing and admirable use of multitrack technology. —*Ron Wynn*

Bill Evans Trio at Shelly's Manne-Hole / May 30, 1963+May 31, 1963 / Original Jazz Classics ✦✦✦
On this 1987 reissue of a super trio date, Chuck Israels is vastly different from Scott LaFaro on bass, yet equally effective. —*Ron Wynn*

Time Remembered / May 30, 1963+May 31, 1963 / Milestone ✦✦✦

Bill Evans Trio '65 / Jan. 1965 / Verve ✦✦

Trio '65 / Feb. 1965 / Verve ✦✦✦

Paris (1965) / Feb. 13, 1965 / Royal Jazz ✦✦✦✦✦

Bill Evans Trio with Symphony Orchestra / Sep. 29, 1965–Dec. 16, 1965 / Verve ✦✦
Mid-'60s sessions matching the Bill Evans trio with a large orchestra arranged and conducted by Claus Ogerman. The strings provide a nice backdrop, but are otherwise inconsequential. Evans and bassist Chuck Israel are outstanding, with Evans' piano treatments of both classical and jazz material exceptional. Drummer Larry Bunker holds things together as the lone percussive element. —*Ron Wynn*

Time to Remember (Live in Europe 1965–1972) / 1965–1972 / Natasha ✦✦✦

Bill Evans at Town Hall / Feb. 21, 1966 / Verve ✦✦✦✦✦

Intermodulation / Apr. 7, 1966–May 10, 1966 / Verve ✦✦✦✦
A beautiful return engagement with Jim Hall (g). —*Ron Wynn*

A Simple Matter of Conviction / Oct. 4, 1966 / Verve ✦✦✦✦
What separated this from the average good Bill Evans date was the inclusion of Shelly Manne on drums, who inventively pushed and took unexpected chances. This was, I believe, Eddie Gomez' (bass) debut release with Evans (piano) and it was quite impressive. There were numerous takes at this session and judging from Chuck Briefer's liners it might be interesting to hear them released. —*Bob Rusch*

Further Conversations with Myself / Aug. 9, 1967 / Verve ✦✦✦

California Here I Come / Aug. 17, 1967–Aug. 18, 1967 / Verve ✦✦✦✦✦
California Here I Come by pianist Bill Evans was not a re-issue but was in fact previously unreleased material from two nights (8/17 & 8/18/67) at the Village Vanguard. This was first-class material, with textbook Evans and drummer Philly Joe Jones pushing the trio (bassist Eddie Gomez) along quite nicely, especially on the uptempos. —*Bob Rusch*

At the Montreux Jazz Festival / Jun. 15, 1968 / Verve ✦✦✦✦
A superb trio date. Eddie Gomez (b) and Jack DeJohnette (d) are brilliant in accompanying roles. —*Ron Wynn*

What's New / Jan. 30, 1969–Mar. 11, 1969 / Verve ✦✦✦

Jazzhouse / Nov. 24, 1969 / Milestone ✦✦✦

You're Gonna Hear from Me / Nov. 24, 1969 / Milestone ✦✦✦

Bill Evans Alone / Dec. 12, 1969 / Verve ✦✦✦

From Left to Right / 1970 / MGM ✦✦

Montreux, Vol. 2 / Jun. 19, 1970 / CTI ✦✦✦

Bill Evans Album / May 11, 1971–May 20, 1971 / Columbia ✦✦✦

Yesterday I Heard the Rain / 1972 / Bandstand ✦✦✦

The Tokyo Concert / Jan. 20, 1973 / Original Jazz Classics ✦✦✦

☆ **The Complete Fantasy Recordings** / Jan. 20, 1973–May 13, 1979 / Fantasy ✦✦✦✦✦
This gorgeous boxed set is a collection of his '70s selections. It covers everything in all contexts and is a must-have for piano fans. —*Ron Wynn*

Eloquence / Nov. 19, 1973–Dec. 18, 1975 / Original Jazz Classics ✦✦✦

Re: Person I Knew / Jan. 11, 1974–Jan. 12, 1974 / Fantasy ✦✦✦✦
This late trio date was recorded live at the Village Vanguard. Eddie Gomez (b) and Marty Morell (d) also appeared. —*AMG*

Since We Met / Jan. 11, 1974–Jan. 12, 1974 / Fantasy ✦✦✦

Intuition / Nov. 7, 1974–Nov. 8, 1974 / Original Jazz Classics ✦✦✦
This is a wonderful pairing of musically attuned comrades Bill Evans and Eddie Gomez (b). —*Ron Wynn*

The Tony Bennett/Bill Evans Album / Jun. 10, 1975–Jun. 13, 1975 / Original Jazz Classics ✦✦✦✦
Exquisite collaboration between a great romantic vocalist and a tremendous melodic interpreter. Bennett and Evans mesh as though they had been working together for years, never having any problems with tempo, pacing, or mood. This has been reissued on CD. —*Ron Wynn*

Montreux, Vol. 3 / Jul. 20, 1975 / Original Jazz Classics ✦✦✦✦
For this duet set from the 1975 Montreux Jazz Festival (a Fantasy date that has been reissued on CD in the OJC series), Bill Evans alternates between acoustic and electric pianos while Eddie Gomez offers alert support and some near-miraculous bass solos. The audience is attentive and appreciative, as they should be, for the communication between the two masterful players (on such songs as "Milano," "Django," "I Love You" and their encore "The Summer Knows") is quite special. —*Scott Yanow*

Alone (Again) / Dec. 16, 1975 / Original Jazz Classics ✦✦✦
Bill Evans was at his best playing solo piano; his touch, harmonic and rhythmic creativity, phrasing and total technique were so accomplished that he needed ideal accompanists to excel in any trio or group situation. But when playing unaccompanied, he was free to explore any and all directions, developing and exploiting them without concern about other musicians following, fitting in or expanding the territory behind or underneath him. There were only five cuts on this 1975 date, and the superb CD remastering illuminates Evans' brilliant solos. It offers a textbook example of how Evans opened, developed and finished a composition; he examined it to the utmost, explored multiple options with a flair, then concluded it in spectacular fashion. —*Ron Wynn*

Quintessence / May 1976 / Original Jazz Classics ✦✦✦
Most of pianist Bill Evans' recordings were in a trio format, making this quintet date a nice change of pace. Evans' all-star group consists of tenor saxophonist Harold Land, guitarist Kenny Burrell, bassist Ray Brown and drummer Philly Joe Jones, and the results are quite tasteful and explorative in a subtle way. This version of Thad Jones' "A Child Is Born" is most memorable. —*Scott Yanow*

Cross-Currents / Feb. 28, 1977–Mar. 2, 1977 / Original Jazz Classics ✦✦✦✦
A change of pace for the Bill Evans trio, with the usual threesome

paired with saxophonists Warne Marsh and Lee Konitz on some numbers. There's one excellent duet by Evans and Konitz on "When I Fall In Love," and one quartet number without Konitz, but otherwise, Evans shows that he could head a quintet, play solos and interact with a combo as effectively as he did his trio. Konitz and Marsh are superb, while bassist Eddie Gomez and drummer Eliot Zigmund work effectively in a different format. — *Ron Wynn*

I Will Say Goodbye / May 11, 1977–May 13, 1977 / Original Jazz Classics ✦✦✦
Nice, occasionally superior late '70s Evans trio date. Although Evans' impressionistic, shimmering style had been absorbed by countless pianists by this time, he still never failed to provide at least one dazzling solo on every album. For this one, he played brilliantly on "Dolphin Dance" and reinterpreted "A House Is Not A Home." Longtime bassist Eddie Gomez and drummer Eliot Zigmund fit in their respective places perfectly. — *Ron Wynn*

You Must Believe in Spring / Aug. 23, 1977–Aug. 25, 1977 / Warner Brothers ✦✦✦
This well-rounded set (released posthumously) features the highly influential pianist Bill Evans in a set of typically sensitive trio performances. With his longtime bassist Eddie Gomez and his drummer of the period, Eliot Zigmund, Evans explores such songs as "We Will Meet Again," Jimmy Rowles' classic "The Peacocks" and the "Theme from *M*A*S*H*." It's a solid example of the great pianist's artistry. — *Scott Yanow*

New Conversations / Jan. 26, 1978–Feb. 16, 1978 / Warner Brothers ✦✦✦

Affinity / Oct. 30, 1978–Nov. 30, 1978 / Warner Brothers ✦✦✦
With Toots Thielemans (harmonica). A good date from his late-'70s period. — *Ron Wynn*

★ **Marian Mc Partland's Piano Jazz with Guest Bill Evans** / Nov. 6, 1978 / Jazz Alliance ✦✦✦✦✦

We Will Meet Again / Aug. 6, 1979–Aug. 9, 1979 / Warner Brothers ✦✦✦
This was pianist Bill Evans' final studio session, a rare outing with a quintet starring trumpeter Tom Harrell and Larry Schneider on tenor and soprano) and his first recording with the members of his final regular trio (bassist Marc Johnson and drummer Joe LaBarbera). Although a straight CD reissue of the original LP, the playing time is over 61 minutes. The group interprets "For All We Know" and seven Evans originals including "Peri's Scope" and "Five." The thoughtful session is full of lyrical melodies and strong solos; even Evans' electric keyboard work on a few tunes is distinctive. — *Scott Yanow*

Paris Concert, Edition One / Nov. 26, 1979 / Elektra ✦✦✦✦✦
The two LPs recorded at this Paris concert are the last examples of Bill Evans' playing that have been released to date although there are other concert performances from 1980 that are expected to come out eventually. With bassist Marc Johnson and drummer Joe LaBarbera, Evans had one of the strongest trios of his career, as can be heard on such pieces as "My Romance," "I Loves You Porgy" and "Beautiful Love." The close communication between the players is reminiscent of Evans' 1961 unit with Scott LaFaro and Paul Motian. — *Scott Yanow*

Paris Concert, Edition Two / Nov. 26, 1979 / Elektra ✦✦✦✦
Bill Evans' death in 1980 ended the career of the most influential (along with McCoy Tyner) acoustic pianist in jazz of the past 20 years. This second of two LPs features Evans, bassist Marc Johnson and drummer Paul Motian closely interacting on four of the pianist's originals, Gary McFarland's "Gary's Theme" and Miles Davis' "Nardis." The music is sensitive and subtly exciting. Until some later live sessions from 1980 are released, this can be considered Bill Evans' final recording and serves as evidence that, rather than declining, he was showing a renewed vitality and enthusiasm in his last year. — *Scott Yanow*

Bill Evans
b. Feb. 9, 1958, Clarendon Hills, IL
Tenor Saxophone, Soprano Saxophone / Post Bop, Crossover
No relation to the other Bill Evans, this saxophonist has an adventurous spirit and strong improvising skills despite his utilization of a rapper on some recent records. Evans started on piano before switching to tenor. He moved to New York in 1978 and was with Miles Davis during most of 1981–84. He also played with John McLaughlin's short-lived reformed Mahavishnu Orchestra in the

mid-'80s, was with Elements from 1982 on and has recorded as a leader for Lipstick including with his 1990s group Petite Blonde. — *Scott Yanow*

Moods Unlimited / Oct. 28, 1982+Oct. 30, 1982 / Evidence ✦✦✦
This was one of the more unconventional jazz trios assembled in recent years, including veteran bebop and hard bop pianist Hank Jones, equally venerable bassist Red Mitchell and relative youngster Bill Evans, best known from Miles Davis' band of the '80s. They came together for a 1982 session that has been reissued by Evidence, and the results are mostly good, despite occasional flubs and meandering by Evans, who did not always sound confident. But it is easy to understand why when listening to the fluid, smooth, routinely brilliant playing of Jones. The absence of a drummer made the instrumental mix and contrast even more vivid; Evans' tenor and soprano stood almost naked at times without covering rhythms. But he mostly met the challenge well, showing some subtlety and depth on soprano. — *Ron Wynn*

Living in the Crest of a Wave / Nov. 1983 / Elektra ✦✦✦
Alternative Man / Jan. 1985–May 1985 / Blue Note ✦✦
● **Petite Blonde** / Oct. 1992 / Lipstick ✦✦✦✦✦
Push / 1993 / Lipstick ✦✦✦
Live in Europe / Nov. 24, 1994 / Lipstick ✦✦
If it were possible to give this live CD a split rating, it would get both "Best" and "Poor." Saxophonist Bill Evans (switching between tenor and soprano) plays creative jazz-funk on five selections with plenty of heated solos and strong support from a rhythm section including guitarist Gary Poulson and keyboardist Charles Blenzig. If the whole recording were of that quality, this set would be close to essential. Unfortunately Evans then "welcomes" rapper KC Flight to four other numbers, and his monotonous talking and shouting are annoying in the extreme, essentially ruining those performances. So this CD is recommended only if it is sold at half price. — *Scott Yanow*

Doc Evans (Paul Wesley Evans)
b. Jun. 20, 1907, Spring Valley, MN, d. Jan. 10, 1977, Minneapolis, MN
Cornet / Dixieland
A fine Dixieland cornetist, Doc Evans freelanced in the Midwest before leading his own bands in Chicago starting in the 1940s. He recorded extensively for Audiophile during 1949–59. Evans settled in Minneapolis later in life, playing music up until near his death; his last recordings were in 1975. — *Scott Yanow*

● **Doc Evans & His Band, Vol. 1** / Apr. 1953–May 1953 / Audiophile ✦✦✦✦
Doc Evans & His Band, Vol. 2 / Apr. 1953–May 1953 / Audiophile ✦✦✦✦

Gil Evans (Ian Ernest Gilmore Green)
b. May 13, 1912, Toronto, Canada, d. Mar. 20, 1988, Cuernavaca, Mexico
Piano, Arranger, Leader, Composer / Cool, Fusion, Post Bop
One of the most significant arrangers in jazz history, Gil Evans' three album-length collaborations with Miles Davis (*Miles Ahead, Porgy and Bess* and *Sketches of Spain*) are all considered classics. Evans had a lengthy and wide-ranging career that sometimes ran parallel to the trumpeter. Like Davis, Gil became involved in utilizing electronics in the 1970s and preferred not to look back and recreate the past. He led his own band in California (1933–38) which eventually became the backup group for Skinnay Ennis; Evans stayed on for a time as arranger. He gained recognition for his somewhat futuristic charts for Claude Thornhill's Orchestra (1941–42 and 1946–48), which took advantage of the ensemble's cool tones, utilized French horns and a tuba as frontline instruments and by 1946 incorporated the influence of bop. He met Miles Davis (who admired his work with Thornhill) during this time and contributed arrangements of "Moon Dreams" and "Boplicity" to Davis' "Birth of the Cool" nonet. After a period in obscurity, Evans wrote for a Helen Merrill session and then collaborated with Davis on *Miles Ahead*. In addition to his work with Miles (which also included a 1961 recorded Carnegie Hall concert and the half-album *Quiet Nights*), Evans recorded several superb and highly original sets as a leader (including *Gil Evans and Ten, New Bottle Old Wine* and *Great Jazz Standards*) during the era. In the 1960s among the albums he worked on for other artists were notable efforts with Kenny Burrell and Astrud Gilberto. After his own sessions for Verve dur-

ing 1963–64, Evans waited until 1969 until recording again as a leader. That year's *Blues in Orbit* was his first successful effort at combining acoustic and electric instruments; it would be followed by dates for Artists House, Atlantic (*Svengali*) and a notable tribute to Jimi Hendrix in 1974. After 1975's *There Comes a Time* (which features among its sidemen David Sanborn), most of Evans' recordings were taken from live performances. Starting in 1970 he began playing with his large ensemble on a weekly basis in New York clubs. Filled with such all-star players as George Adams, Lew Soloff, Marvin "Hannibal" Peterson, Chris Hunter, Howard Johnson, Pete Levin, Hiram Bullock, Hamiet Bluiett and Arthur Blythe among others, Evans' later bands were top-heavy in talent but tended to ramble on too long. Gil Evans, other than sketching out a framework and contributing his keyboard, seemed to let the orchestra largely run itself, inspiring rather than closely directing the music. There were some worthwhile recordings from the 1980s (when the band had a long string of Monday night gigs at Sweet Basil in New York) but in general they do not often live up to their potential. Prior to his death, Gil Evans recorded with his "arranger's piano" on duets with Lee Konitz and Steve Lacy and his body of work on a whole ranks with the top jazz arrangers. —*Scott Yanow*

Arrangers' Touch / Jun. 11, 1953–Oct. 10, 1957 / Prestige ++++
This two-LP set includes the album *Gil Evans Plus Ten* plus two sessions led by arranger Tadd Dameron. Evans' repertoire includes compositions not only by Irving Berlin, Rodgers & Hart and Cole Porter but Leadbelly and Leonard Bernstein. The 11-piece band heard on these 1957 recordings consists of Evans' piano, two trumpets, trombone, bass trombone, French horn, Steve Lacy's soprano, altoist Lee Konitz, bassoon, bass and drums, quite an unusual combination. The music is as colorful as the instrumentation suggests. But actually, the Tadd Dameron sessions are the main reason to search for this two-fer. Four titles (plus an alternate take) feature trumpeter Clifford Brown in a nonet in 1953 and the other four performances have an octet that includes trumpeter Kenny Dorham and such classics as "Fontainebleau" and "The Scene Is Clean." It's highly recommended. —*Scott Yanow*

★ **Gil Evans and Ten** / Sep. 6, 1957–Oct. 10, 1957 / Original Jazz Classics +++++
Although arranger Gil Evans had been active in the major leagues of jazz ever since the mid-'40s and had participated in Miles Davis' famous *Birth of the Cool* recordings, this set was his first opportunity to record as a leader. The CD reissue features a typically unusual 11-piece unit consisting of two trumpets, trombonist Jimmy Cleveland, Bert Varsalona on bass trombone, French horn player Willie Ruff, Steve Lacy on soprano, altoist Lee Konitz, Dave Kurtzer on bassoon, bassist Paul Chambers and either Nick Stabulas or Jo Jones on drums, plus the leader's sparse piano. As good an introduction to his work as any, this program includes diverse works ranging from Leadbelly to Leonard Bernstein, plus Evans' own "Jambangle." The arranger's inventive use of the voices of his rather unique sidemen make this a memorable set. —*Scott Yanow*

New Bottle, Old Wine / Apr. 9, 1958–May 26, 1958 / Blue Note +++++
Early, intriguing Gil Evans orchestra material, one of the sessions that established his reputation as an arranger and bandleader. The band, which included Johnny Coles, Cannonball Adderley, Paul Chambers and Art Blakey, did rousing, fresh versions of vintage songs like "St. Louis Blues" and "King Porter Stomp." This material has also been issued on vinyl album and CD under the title *Pacific Standard Time.* —*Ron Wynn*

Pacific Standard Time / Apr. 9, 1958–Feb. 5, 1959 / Blue Note +++++
This two-LP set (put out in 1975) combines together a pair of arranger Gil Evans' greatest sessions. Both *New Bottle Old Wine* and *Great Jazz Standards* were reissued for a period on CD before also going out of print. The former session features altoist Cannonball Adderley in peak form as the main soloist on such tunes as "St. Louis Blues," "Struttin' with Some Barbeque," "Lester Leaps In," "Manteca" and a classic reworking of Jelly Roll Morton's "King Porter Stomp"; other soloists include trombonist Frank Rehak, trumpeter Johnny Coles and Evans himself on piano. The second date, highlighted by a very memorable rendition of "Straight No Chaser," also has "Davenport Blues," "Joy Spring" and "Django" among the highlights; key soloists include

trumpeter Johnny Coles, Steve Lacy on soprano and tenorman Budd Johnson. Essential music. —*Scott Yanow*

Great Jazz Standards / 1959 / Blue Note +++++

Out of the Cool / Nov. 18, 1960–Dec. 15, 1960 / MCA ++++
Gil Evans recordings (particularly those without Miles Davis) were not a common occurrence in the pre-1970 era, making this set a special treat. Evans' 14-piece band (which includes trumpeter Johnny Coles, trombonist Jimmy Knepper, Budd Johnson on tenor and soprano and guitarist Ray Crawford among others) investigates a wide variety of complex material including the leader's "La Nevada" and "Sunken Treasure," John Benson Brooks' obscure "Where Flamingos Fly," George Russell's "Stratusphunk" and Kurt Weill's "Biobao"; some reissues of this album also add Horace Silver's "Sister Sadie." The orchestrations are both thoughtful and colorful, the main reason to acquire this music. —*Scott Yanow*

In the Hot / Oct. 10, 1961 / MCA/Impulse! ++++

The Individualism of Gil Evans / Sep. 1963–Oct. 29, 1964 / Verve +++
Although Gil Evans had gained a lot of acclaim for his three collaborations with Miles Davis in the 1950s and his own albums, this CD contains (with the exception of two tracks purposely left off), Evans' only dates as a leader during 1961-68. The personnel varies on the six sessions that comprise the CD (which adds five numbers including two previously unreleased to the original LP) with such major soloists featured as tenorman Wayne Shorter, trombonist Jimmy Cleveland, trumpeter Johnny Coles and guitarist Kenny Burrell. Highlights include "Time of the Barracudas," "The Barbara Song," "Las Vegas Tango" and "Spoonful." Highly recommended to Gil Evans fans; it is a pity he did not record more during this era. —*Scott Yanow*

Gil Evans Orch, Kenny Burrell & Phil Woods / Mar. 4, 1964–Jul. 9, 1964 / Verve +++
When this LP was originally released in 1973, its five selections had never been out before. Three have been since reissued on CD in *The Individualism of Gil Evans*, although two ("Blues in Orbit" which is really "Cheryl," and "Isabel," which is really "Ah Moore") were not, because the arranger considered those recordings little more than orchestral sketches that should not have been released. Despite his feelings, the disputed pair (which have solos from trombonist Jimmy Knepper) are not bad, while the other three selections ("Spoonful," "Concorde" and "Barracuda") have colorful arrangements and solos from guitarist Kenny Burrell, altoist Phil Woods and (on "Barracuda") tenor saxophonist Wayne Shorter. The CD is preferred but Evans completists may want to search for this LP too. —*Scott Yanow*

Where Flamingos Fly / 1971 / Artists House +++
This transitional LP (which has been long out of print) features arranger Gil Evans shortly after he decided to put together a permanent big band. Although the music didn't come out until a decade later, it is actually quite worthwhile. Evans is heard at the head of two different (but overlapping) units ranging from ten to fifteen pieces, and he utilizes synthesizers for the first time. The key soloists are tenor saxophonist Billy Harper and Howard Johnson, mostly on baritone, but the emphasis is on Evans' writing, unlike his later live recordings. Most memorable is "Zee Zee," "Hotel Me," "Where Flamingos Fly" and a 17 1/2 minute version of "El Matador." —*Scott Yanow*

Svengali / May 30, 1973+Jun. 30, 1973 / Atlantic +++++
This is one of Gil Evans' finest recordings of the 1970s. He expertly blended together acoustic and electronic instruments, particularly on an exciting rendition of "Blues in Orbit" (which includes among its soloists a young altoist named David Sanborn). All six selections have their memorable moments (even a 1 1/2 minute version of "Eleven"); colorful solos are contributed by guitarist Ted Dunbar, Howard Johnson on tuba and fluegelhorn, the passionate tenor of Billy Harper and bassist Herb Bushler, among others; and Evans' arrangements are quite inventive and innovative. Rarely would he be so successful in balancing written and improvised sections in his later years. This LP is highly recommended but may be difficult to find. —*Scott Yanow*

Gil Evans' Orchestra Plays the Music of Jimi Hendrix / Jun. 11, 1974–Jun. 13, 1974 / Bluebird +++++
This CD reissue (which adds additional material to the original LP program) is much more successful than one might have expected. Jimi Hendrix was scheduled to record with Gil Evans' Orchestra

but died before the session could take place. A few years later, Evans explored ten of Hendrix's compositions with his unique 19-piece unit, an orchestra that included two French horns, the tuba of Howard Johnson, three guitars, two basses, two percussionists and such soloists as altoist David Sanborn, trumpeter Hannibal Marvin Peterson, Billy Harper on tenor and guitarists Ryo Kawasaki and John Abercrombie. Evans' arrangements uplift many of Hendrix's more blues-oriented compositions and create a memorable set that is rock-oriented but retains the improvisation and personality of jazz. Recommended. —*Scott Yanow*

There Comes a Time / Mar. 6, 1975–Jun. 12, 1975 / Bluebird ✦✦✦✦

This CD reissue differs greatly from the original LP of the same name. Not only are there three previously unreleased performances ("Joy Spring," "So Long" and "Buzzard Variation") but "The Meaning of the Blues" has been expanded from six minutes to 20(!), two numbers ("Little Wing" and "Aftermath the Fourth Movement Children of the Fire") have been dropped (the former was reissued on Evans' Jimi Hendrix tribute) and the remaining four tracks were re-edited and remixed under Evans' direction. So in reality, this 1987 CD was really a "new" record when it came out. The remake of "King Porter Stomp" (with altoist David Sanborn in Cannonball Adderley's spot) is a classic, the "new" version of "The Meaning of the Blues" is memorable and overall the music (which also has solos by Billy Harper and George Adams on tenors along with trumpeter Lew Soloff) is quite rewarding–creative big band fusion that expertly mixes together acoustic and electric instruments. This was one of Gil Evans' last truly great sets. —*Scott Yanow*

Priestess / May 13, 1977 / Antilles ✦✦✦

After the success of his studio sessions of the early to mid-'70s, Gil Evans primarily recorded live in concert during the remainder of his career. This is one of the better sets, for, although two of the four selections are over 12 minutes long ("Priestess" exceeds 19 1/2 minutes), the music is generally under control. Evans' eccentric 16-piece group consists of three trumpets, trombone, French horn, two tubas, three saxes and a five-piece rhythm section including Pete Levin on synthesizer. With such soloists as altoists David Sanborn and Arthur Blyte, trumpeter Lew Soloff and George Adams on tenor, the music is quite stimulating and exciting. —*Scott Yanow*

Little Wing / Oct. 1978 / Inner City ✦✦✦

For a 1978 European tour, Gil Evans used a nonet, a much smaller-than-usual band. However, all of the ingredients (good and bad) from his later groups are very much present on the German concert preserved on this LP (which was originally put out by Circle). The three performances ("Dr. Jekyll," "The Meaning of the Blues" and Jimi Hendrix's "Little Wing") are generally much too long, with "Little Wing" only two seconds short of 26 1/2 minutes. While Evans is on electric piano, his contributions are rather minor, as his sidemen take overly long solos which alternate exciting and somewhat aimless sections. Heard from in prominent roles are altoist Gerry Niewood, trumpeter Terumasa Hino, George Adams on tenor, trumpeter Lew Soloff and the synthesizer of Peter Levin. An interesting set but, as is usually true with Gil Evans' later recordings, not too essential. —*Scott Yanow*

Anti-Heroes / Jan. 11, 1980–Jan. 12, 1980 / Verve ✦✦

Heroes / Jan. 11, 1980–Jan. 12, 1980 / Verve ✦✦

Live at the Public Theater in New York, Vol. 1 / Feb. 8, 1980–Feb. 9, 1980 / Blackhawk ✦✦✦

One of arranger Gil Evans' main talents was his ability to fuse diverse, unique performers into a unified ensemble. He accomplishes that on the first of two LPs taken from a pair of 1980 concerts, even if his presence is felt more than heard. Although Evans is on electric piano, he also employed two other synthesizer players (Masabumi Kikuchi and Pete Levin) in his eclectic band, which at the time included such notables as Lew Soloff, Jon Faddis and Hannibal Marvin Peterson on trumpets, altoist Arthur Blythe, trombonist George Lewis, baritone saxophonist Hamiet Bluiett and drummer Billy Cobham, among others. A lengthy "Anita's Dance" and a remake of "Gone, Gone, Gone" are the more memorable selections. —*Scott Yanow*

Live at the Public Theatre in New York, Vol. 2 / Feb. 8, 1980–Feb. 9, 1980 / Blackhawk ✦✦✦

The second of two Gil Evans LPs originally recorded for the Japanese Trio label and put out in the United States on the now-

defunct Black-Hawk company features the veteran arranger leading a 14-piece group at a pair of 1980 concerts. The five selections (which include Jimi Hendrix's "Stone Free," Charles Mingus' "Orange Was the Color of Her Dress" and Evans' "Zee Zee") are given colorful treatment by the unique band, which consists of three keyboardists, a rhythm section propelled by drummer Billy Cobham, three trumpets (Lew Soloff, Jon Faddis and Hannibal Marvin Peterson), two trombones (including George Lewis), John Clark on French horn, baritone saxophonist Hamiet Bluiett and altoist Arthur Blythe. Although the end results do not quite live up to the potential of this unique ensemble, there are plenty of colorful moments. —*Scott Yanow*

British Orchestra / 1983 / Mole ✦✦✦

Although the 13-piece ensemble heard on this CD is comprised mostly of English players, somehow it still sounds like the Gil Evans Orchestra. Evans travelled to England to lead the all-star group in 1983 and altoist Chris Hunter would eventually join Evans' U.S. outfit. Other impressive soloists include John Surman on baritone and soprano and Stan Sulzmann on tenor and soprano while guitarist Ray Russell is showcased on Jimi Hendrix's "Little Wing." The four selections (which also include "Hotel Me," "London" and Thelonious Monk's "Friday the 13th") tend to be a bit overlong, but the spirit and enthusiasm of the players (who sound thrilled to be working with Evans) make this a worthy set. —*Scott Yanow*

Live at Sweet Basil, Vol. 1 / Aug. 20, 1984+Aug. 27, 1984 / Evidence ✦✦

Despite some exciting moments, this CD (which was originally a Gramavision two-LP set) has always been a bit of a disappointment. By 1984, arranger/keyboardist Gil Evans, who exercised such tight control over his earlier groups, had become very much a laissez-faire leader in that he let his sidemen ramble on and on as long as they felt inspired. During an 18 1/2 minute "Parabola" and the over 24 1/2 minute "Blues in 'C,'" it's as if Evans was not even on the bandstand. His sidemen were obviously quite talented, since they include Lew Soloff and Hannibal Marvin Peterson on trumpets, tenorman George Adams, altoist Chris Hunter, Howard Johnson on tuba, baritone and bass clarinet, guitarist Hiram Bullock and Pete Levin on synthesizer, but the lack of direction by Evans on the eclectic repertoire (which also includes two tunes apiece by Charles Mingus and Jimi Hendrix, in addition to Herbie Hancock's "Prince of Darkness") does not live up to its potential. —*Scott Yanow*

Live at Sweet Basil, Vol. 2 / Aug. 27, 1984 / Evidence ✦✦

This volume (available originally on Gramavision as a two-LP set and reissued on CD by Evidence) has the same faults as the first. Although arranger/keyboardist Gil Evans is the leader of the 14-piece band, he has a very minor presence on the set, letting his talented sidemen get self-indulgent and take seemingly endless solos. Because the supporting cast includes such fine players as trumpeter Lew Soloff, George Adams on tenor, altoist Chris Hunter, guitarist Hiram Bullock and Pete Levin on synthesizer, the music is not without interest. However these endless jams (which range from 11 to almost 23 minutes) on such songs as "Jelly Roll," Thelonious Monk's "Friday the 13th," "Gone" and Jimi Hendrix's "Stone Free" must have been more interesting live than on record. This is a lesser effort that should have been a memorable one. —*Scott Yanow*

Farewell—Live at Sweet Basil / Dec. 1, 1986+Dec. 22, 1986 / Evidence ✦✦✦

This CD (plus *In Memoriam*, another Projazz set taken from the same sessions) contains the last recordings of arranger/pianist Gil Evans with his regular orchestra, other than a set backing rock singer Sting. As was typical for Evans' later-period work, he is content to play quietly while letting his ensemble run somewhat wild. The four pieces, which include the umpteenth remake of Jimi Hendrix's "Little Wing," are all overly long but not without interest; sidemen include trumpeter Lew Soloff, trombonist Dave Bargeron, John Clark on French horn, altoist Chris Hunter, Bill Evans on tenor and soprano, baritone saxophonist Hamiet Bluiett, guitarist Hiram Bullock and both Peter Levin and Gil Goldstein on synthesizers, while fluegelhornist Johnny Coles is a welcome guest. Fans of Gil Evans' 1950s work may not much care for his 1980s electronic band, but this set is fairly coherent and has its exciting moments. —*Scott Yanow*

In Memoriam: Bud and Bird / Dec. 1, 1986+Dec. 22, 1986 / Evidence ✦✦✦

Released posthumously, this CD features the 1986 version of Gil

Evans' Monday Night Orchestra. As was usual in his later years, Evans' presence is felt rather than heard and he lets his 15-piece ensemble stretch out; in fact four of the five numbers (all but Gil's "Bud and Bird") are group originals. In general the players in Evans' band were fairly young at the time, although many of the players have had pretty substantial careers since. Among the soloists are altoist Chris Hunter (who sounds pretty close tonewise to David Sanborn), veteran baritonist Hamiet Bluiett, guest trumpeter Johnny Coles, Bill Evans on tenor and soprano, trumpeter Lew Soloff, trombonist Dave Bargeron, John Clark on French horn and Gil Goldstein on synthesizer. Still, there are times during this music when it would have been beneficial for Gil Evans to have played a bigger part; "Groove from the Louvre" certainly did not need to be nearly 22 minutes long! —*Scott Yanow*

Rhythm-A-Ning / Nov. 2, 1987–Nov. 26, 1987 / EmArcy ◆◆◆
This is a very interesting recording. Aging arranger/pianist Gil Evans agreed after much persuasion to come to Paris and play his music at a few concerts with Laurent Cugny's Orchestra. After only one rehearsal, the first event took place, and it gratified Evans to realize that the young French musicians were not only excellent players but big Gil Evans fans. Their interpretations of Thelonious Monk's "Rhythm-A-Ning," "London" and "La Nevada" rank with the best versions of Evans' regular Monday Night Band, and Cugny's "Charlie Mingus' Sound of Love" (an answer to Mingus' "Duke Ellington's Sound of Love") is also excellent. Few of the sidemen, other than tenor saxophonist Andy Sheppard and percussionist Marilyn Mazur, are known in the U.S., but they did an excellent job of bringing Gil Evans' music to life. —*Scott Yanow*

Paris Blues / Nov. 30, 1987–Dec. 1, 1987 / Owl ◆◆
Recorded just three months before arranger/pianist Gil Evans' death, this duet album teams Evans with the great soprano saxophonist Steve Lacy. In truth, Evans' playing here is generally little more than melody statements and comping behind Lacy and, although the soprano is in top form, little of significance occurs. The duo performs lengthy versions of three Charles Mingus tunes, Duke Ellington's "Paris Blues" and Lacy's "Esteem." Evans was never a masterful keyboardist and clearly was not in Lacy's league as a player, so this CD is of greater interest from a historical rather than musical standpoint. —*Scott Yanow*

Tribute to Gil Evans / Jul. 8, 1988–Jul. 24, 1988 / Soul Note ◆◆◆
Four months after arranger/pianist Gil Evans' death, his Monday Night Band fulfilled their engagements playing at Italian jazz festivals. With several alumni and guests added on, the 16-piece ensemble stretches out on two marathon performances ("Orgone" and "London"), makes very concise (under two-minute) statements on "Moonstruck One" and "Eleven," and features the eccentric singer Urszula Dudziak on "Duet." The results are colorful if not all that memorable; among the soloists are trumpeters Lew Soloff and Miles Evans, altoist Chris Hunter, Alex Foster on tenor, guitarist Bireli Legrene (who is quite rockish on "Prelude to Orgone"), violinist Michal Urbaniak and Pete Levin on synthesizer. Gil Evans would have enjoyed this set. —*Scott Yanow*

Take Me to the Sun / Last Chance Music ◆◆◆

Herschel Evans

b. 1909, Denton, TX, **d.** Feb. 9, 1939, New York, NY
Tenor Saxophone / Swing
One of the earliest "tough Texas tenors," Herschel Evans' hard sound was a perfect contrast to that of the cool-toned Lester Young in the Count Basie Orchestra. He started out playing in territory bands including Troy Floyd (1929–31), with whom he made his recording debut and Benny Moten (1933–35). In 1936 Evans had stints with Lionel Hampton and Buck Clayton in Los Angeles and then joined Count Basie just in time to enjoy the band's success and to participate on many recordings; his most famous solo was on a ballad feature "Blue and Sentimental" from 1938. Sadly Herschel Evans died of a heart ailment before his 30th birthday. —*Scott Yanow*

Don Ewell

b. Nov. 14, 1916, Baltimore, MD, **d.** Aug. 9, 1983, Pompano Beach, FL
Piano / Stride
A major if underrated stride pianist, Don Ewell was inspired by Jelly Roll Morton and Earl Hines, but could stride like Fats Waller too. He started leading his own trios in Baltimore in the mid-'30s, played during the New Orleans jazz revival (starting in the mid-'40s) with Bunk Johnson, Muggsy Spanier, Sidney Bechet and Kid Ory (1953) and was with Jack Teagarden during 1957–64. Ewell sometimes played duets with the weakening Willie "the Lion" Smith in the late '60s before moving to New Orleans, where he worked regularly during his last years. He recorded for Good Time Jazz (three 1956–57 dates are currently available on CD), GHB/Audiophile/Jazzology, Delmark, Fat Cat's Jazz and Chiaroscuro; previously unreleased sets were issued posthumously by Stomp Off and Pumpkin. —*Scott Yanow*

F

Jon Faddis

b. Jul. 24, 1953, Oakland, CA
Trumpet / Bop
When Jon Faddis burst on the jazz scene as a teenager, observers were amazed by his technique and his ability to sound like an identical twin of Dizzy Gillespie (whose complex style had never been successfully duplicated before). After a period he was typecast as a Dizzy imitator, but Faddis' remarkable range (hitting higher notes than Gillespie ever could) and the gradual development of his individual sound have helped him to overcome the early fault. In fact Faddis can now also imitate Roy Eldridge and Louis Armstrong quite well, too. Dizzy was always Jon Faddis' idol, from the time he started playing trumpet at age eight. After moving to New York in the early '70s, Faddis played with Lionel Hampton and Charles Mingus (guesting on a recorded concert with the bassist when Roy Eldridge became ill) and then recorded two notable albums for Pablo including a duet session with Oscar Peterson. After playing a bit with Dizzy Gillespie (their best encounters in the mid-'70s were unfortunately not recorded), Faddis seemed to disappear, sticking to studio work and playing first trumpet with the Thad Jones-Mel Lewis Orchestra. After re-emerging in the mid-'80s, Jon Faddis recorded for Concord and Epic and in 1993 became the musical director of the Carnegie Hall Jazz Orchestra. —*Scott Yanow*

Jon & Billy / Mar. 13, 1974 / Evidence ✦✦✦
Jon Faddis and Billy Harper made an interesting, if, at times, mismatched team on this 1974 date recently reissued by Evidence. Faddis was then laboring to find his own voice on trumpet; his mentor, Dizzy Gillespie, remained both his predominant influence and stylistic guiding light. Harper had won critical attention and praise for his work with Lee Morgan, and his robust tenor sax was well displayed throughout this date. The times were probably responsible for Sir Roland Hanna sometimes turning to electric piano; his elegant figures, precise melodies and harmonic interplay are not as expertly articulated on electric as acoustic, which he also plays. But the date's value is in hearing where Harper and Faddis, as well as jazz itself, were in the mid-'70s and then comparing how far they and the music have and have not come since then. —*Ron Wynn*

Youngblood / Jan. 8, 1976–Jan. 9, 1976 / Pablo ✦✦✦✦
Good and Plenty / Aug. 1978–Sep. 1978 / DRZ ✦✦
★ **Legacy** / Aug. 1985 / Concord Jazz ✦✦✦✦
A tremendous mainstream session to which Harold Land (ts) and Kenny Barron (p) make excellent contributions. —*Ron Wynn*

Into the Faddisphere / May 2, 1989-May 8, 1989 / Epic ✦✦✦
Check out "Ciribiribin" for a taste of Faddis and his trumpet acrobatics. Also has pianist Renee Rosnes and drummer Ralph Peterson. —*Michael G. Nastos*

Hornucopia / 1991 / Epic ✦✦✦✦

Don Fagerquist

b. Feb. 6, 1927, Worcester, MA, **d.** Jan. 24, 1974, Los Angeles, CA
Trumpet / Bop, Cool
An excellent trumpeter of the bop and cool eras who largely faded out in the 1960s, Don Fagerquist only had two sessions as a leader, a half-date for Capitol in 1955 and an excellent outing for Mode (reissued on VSOP) in 1957. Fagerquist was a key soloist with Gene Krupa (off and on during 1944–50), Artie Shaw's Orchestra and Gramercy Five (1949–50) and Woody Herman's Third Herd (1951–52). He was with Les Brown in 1953 and a major soloist with Dave Pell's Octet (1953–59). From 1956 on, Fagerquist worked as a staff musician for Paramount films, although he still recorded jazz now and then with Pete Rugolo, Mel Tormé and Art Pepper among others. —*Scott Yanow*

● **Eight by Eight** / Sep. 14, 1957 / VSOP ✦✦✦✦
With the exception of three selections from 1955, this was the only session that trumpeter Don Fagerquist ever led. Performing in a nonet arranged by Marty Paich (who also plays piano), Fagerquist's attractive and mellow tone is well showcased as is his fine boppish style on this CD reissue. The supporting cast, which includes altoist Herb Geller and valve trombonist Bob Enevoldsen, also gets their chances to shine during the eight standards. Easily recommended to bop fans. —*Scott Yanow*

Charles Fambrough

b. Aug. 25, 1950, Philadelphia, PA
Bass / Post-Bop, Hard Bop
Best-known for his stint with Art Blakey's Jazz Messengers, bassist Charles Fambrough has led three very effective all-star dates for CTI that were filled with his stimulating originals. He originally studied classical piano but switched to bass when he was 13. In 1968 Fambrough began playing with local pit bands for musicals and, after some freelancing in 1970, he joined Grover Washington, Jr.'s band, staying with the popular saxophonist up until 1974. Fambrough was with Airto (1975–77), McCoy Tyner (1978–80) and then Art Blakey (1980–82). Since that time he has freelanced in many different situations. Fambrough's sidemen on his CTI recordings have thus far included Wynton and Branford Marsalis, Roy Hargrove, Kenny Kirkland, Jerry Gonzalez, Steve Turre, Donald Harrison, Kenny Garrett, Abdullah Ibrahim and Grover Washington, Jr.! —*Scott Yanow*

The Proper Angle / May 29, 1991–May 31, 1991 / CTI ✦✦✦✦
Excellent bassist Charles Fambrough steps into the spotlight with his debut album as a leader. While his compositions are straightforward hard bop, he's recruited an impressive guest list. The line-up includes both Wynton and Branford Marsalis, Roy Hargrove, Kenny Kirkland, Jeff Watts, Jerry Gonzalez and Steve Berrios. —*Ron Wynn*

The Charmer / 1992 / CTI ✦✦✦✦
● **Blues at Bradley's** / 1993 / CTI ✦✦✦✦
Charles Fambrough, who first gained recognition as a bassist with Art Blakey's Jazz Messengers, has proven with his releases thus far that he is also a talented composer and bandleader. Four of the five diverse pieces on this CD are his, and Fambrough's octet (which includes altoist Donald Harrison, trombonist Steve Turre and Joe Ford on soprano) does a splendid job of interpreting the often-challenging but swinging repertoire. This is high-quality modern mainstream music. —*Scott Yanow*

Tal Farlow

b. Jun. 7, 1921, Greensboro, NC
Guitar / Bop, Cool
Nearly as famous for his reluctance to play as for his outstanding abilities, guitarist Tal Farlow has been semi-retired since 1958 although, whenever he gets around to playing, he sounds in peak form. He did not take up the guitar until he was 21, but within a year was playing professionally and, in 1948, was with Marjorie

Hyams' band. While with the Red Norvo Trio (which originally included Charles Mingus) from 1949–53, Farlow became famous in the jazz world. His huge hands and ability to play rapid yet light lines made him one of the top guitarists of the era. After six months with Artie Shaw's Gramercy Five in 1953, Farlow put together his own group, which for a time included pianist Eddie Costa. Late in 1958 Farlow settled in New England, became a sign painter and just played locally. He only made one record as a leader during 1960–75 but emerged a bit more often during 1976–84, recording for Concord fairly regularly before largely disappearing again. Profiled in the definitive documentary *Talmage Farlow*, the guitarist can be heard on his own records for Blue Note (1954), Verve, Prestige (1969) and Concord. —*Scott Yanow*

The Tal Farlow Album / Apr. 11, 1954–Jul. 5, 1955 / Verve ✦✦✦✦✦
This album featured two groups working with guitarist Tal Farlow; bassist Oscar Pettiford, pianist Barry Galbraith and drummer Joe Morello were on several numbers, and bassist Red Mitchell and pianist Claude Williamson were on the others. Both it and its companion, *Tal*, are highly recommended. —*Bob Rusch, Cadence*

Tal / Jun. 1956 / Verve ✦✦✦✦✦
This was recorded in 1956 with Eddie Costa on piano and vibes and Vinnie Burke on drums. Tal Farlow is a most listenable guitarist, accessible without compromising either technical brilliance of depth or content. —*Bob Rusch, Cadence*

Fuerst Set / Dec. 18, 1956 / Xanadu ✦✦✦✦
Recorded in 1956 at the home of Ed Fuerst, this was almost 50 minutes of relaxed jamming. The group was working together at the time and were obviously comfortable not only in the setting but with themselves. —*Bob Rusch, Cadence*

Second Set / Dec. 18, 1956 / Xanadu ✦✦✦✦
Tal Farlow was one of the finest guitarists to emerge during the 1950s. The exciting trio he performs with during this record (which was recorded in a friend's apartment) also features pianist Eddie Costa and bassist Vinnie Burke. The recording quality is generally quite good and the lengthy performances of the four standards never loses their momentum, except when the tape ran out during "Let's Do It." These boppish performances (with plenty of impressive interplay by the musicians) will certainly please straight-ahead jazz fans. —*Scott Yanow*

Tal Farlow Returns / Sep. 23, 1969 / Original Jazz Classics ✦✦✦✦
A Sign of the Times / Aug. 2, 1976 / Concord Jazz ✦✦✦
On Stage / Aug. 1976 / Concord Jazz ✦✦✦✦
Farlow's reunion w/ Red Norvo (vib), plus Hank Jones (p) and Ray Brown (b). —*Ron Wynn*

Trinity / Sep. 14, 1976+Sep. 21, 1976 / Inner City ✦✦✦
Tal Farlow 1978 / Sep. 15, 1977 / Concord Jazz ✦✦✦
Chromatic Palette / Jan. 1981 / Concord Jazz ✦✦✦✦
Superior interaction with Tommy Flanagan (p). —*Ron Wynn*

● **Cookin' on All Burners** / Aug. 1982 / Concord Jazz ✦✦✦✦✦
Excellent piano from James Williams, plus outstanding guitar by Farlow. —*Ron Wynn*

The Legendary / Sep. 1984 / Concord Jazz ✦✦✦✦

Art Farmer

b. Aug. 21, 1928, Council Bluffs, IA
Trumpet, Fluegelhorn / Cool, Hard Bop
Largely overlooked during his formative years, Art Farmer's consistently inventive playing has been more greatly appreciated as he continues to develop. Along with Clark Terry, Farmer helped to popularize the fluegelhorn among brass players. His lyricism gives his bop-oriented style its own personality. Farmer studied piano, violin and tuba before settling on trumpet. He worked in Los Angeles from 1945 on, performing regularly on Central Avenue and spending time in the bands of Johnny Otis, Jay McShann, Roy Porter, Benny Carter and Gerald Wilson among others; some of the groups also included his twin brother bassist Addison Farmer (1928–63). After playing with Wardell Gray (1951–52) and touring Europe with Lionel Hampton's big band (1953) Farmer moved to New York and worked with Gigi Gryce (1954–56), Horace Silver's Quintet (1956–58) and the Gerry Mulligan Quartet (1958–9). Farmer, who made many recordings in the latter half of the 1950s (including with Quincy Jones and George Russell and on some jam-session dates for Prestige), co-

led the Jazztet with Benny Golson (1959–62) and then had a group with Jim Hall (1962–64). He moved to Vienna in 1968 where he joined the Austrian Radio Orchestra, worked with Kenny Clarke-Francy Boland Big Band and toured with his own units. Since the 1980s Farmer has visited the U.S. more often and has remained greatly in demand up to the present day. Art Farmer has recorded many sessions as a leader through the years including for Prestige, Contemporary, United Artists, Argo, Mercury, Atlantic, Columbia, CTI, Soul Note, Optimism, Concord, Enja and Sweet Basil. —*Scott Yanow*

Early Art / Jan. 20, 1954+Nov. 9, 1954 / Original Jazz Classics ✦✦✦✦✦
When Farmer Met Gryce / May 19, 1954+May 26, 1955 / Original Jazz Classics ✦✦✦✦
The Art Farmer Quintet / Oct. 21, 1955 / Original Jazz Classics ✦✦✦✦
Two Trumpets / Aug. 3, 1956 / Original Jazz Classics ✦✦✦
W/ Donald Byrd. This nice date puts two top trumpets together. —*Ron Wynn*

★ **Farmer's Market** / Nov. 23, 1956 / Original Jazz Classics ✦✦✦✦✦
Quintet. A top release from the 50s, with precise, deftly-played solos, compositions and arrangements. It has a wonderful all-star lineup and is one of the rare occasions where Farmer worked on record with his brother Addison. —*Ron Wynn*

Last Night When We Were Young / Mar. 28, 1957-Apr. 29, 1957 / Paramount ✦✦✦
Portrait of Art Farmer / Apr. 19, 1958+May 1, 1958 / Original Jazz Classics ✦✦✦✦
Exemplary session, with Roy Haynes dynamic on drums. —*Ron Wynn*

★ **Meet the Jazztet** / Feb. 6, 1960-Feb. 10, 1960 / MCA/Chess ✦✦✦✦✦
Although this CD has the same program as the original LP, it gets the highest rating because it is a hard bop classic. Not only does it include superior solos from trumpeter Art Farmer, trombonist Curtis Fuller, tenor saxophonist Benny Golson and pianist McCoy Tyner (who was making his recording debut), along with fine backup from bassist Addison Farmer and drummer Lex Humphries, but it features the writing of Golson. Highlights include the original version of "Killer Joe" along with early renditions of "I Remember Clifford" and "Blues March." This was Fuller and Tyner's only recording with the original Jazztet and all ten selections (which also include "Serenata," "It Ain't Necessarily So," "It's All Right with Me" and "Easy Living") are quite memorable. —*Scott Yanow*

Blues On Down / Sep. 16, 1960-Mar. 15, 1961 / Chess ✦✦✦✦
Here and Now / Feb. 28, 1962-Mar. 2, 1962 / Mercury ✦✦✦✦
Live at the Half Note / Dec. 6, 1963-Dec. 7, 1963 / Atlantic ✦✦✦
The Time and the Place / Feb. 8, 1967 / Columbia ✦✦✦
Art Farmer Quintet Plays the Great Jazz Hits / May 16, 1967-Jun. 7, 1967 / Columbia ✦✦✦
Gentle Eyes / 1972 / Mainstream ✦✦
Beautiful trumpet and fluegelhorn solos throughout this session by Art Farmer overcome occasionally weak, sappy orchestrations and vocal effects from the Swedish Radio group. This has been reissued on CD. —*Ron Wynn*

To Duke with Love / Mar. 5, 1975 / Inner City ✦✦✦
Summer Knows / May 12, 1976-May 13, 1976 / Inner City ✦✦✦
This relaxed session features fluegelhornist Art Farmer in a quartet with pianist Cedar Walton, bassist Sam Jones and drummer Billy Higgins. The material (which includes such tunes as "Alfie," "When I Fall in Love" and "I Should Care") is given lyrical treatment by these masterful players on this ballad-dominated date. —*Scott Yanow*

Art Farmer Quintet at Boomer's / May 14, 1976-May 15, 1976 / Inner City ✦✦✦
Fine small combo jazz by an underrated group. Trumpet and fluegelhorn player Art Farmer heads a unit with soulful tenor saxophonist Clifford Jordan, plus an excellent rhythm section featuring pianist Cedar Walton, bassist Sam Jones and drummer Billy Higgins. They were among the '70s finest groups, especially those doing mainstream material, but didn't get the recognition they deserved from even the jazz community. —*Ron Wynn*

On the Road / Jul. 26, 1976 Jul. 28, 1976 / Original Jazz Classics ✦✦✦✦

Comparing this to Farmer's 1979 C.T.I. work, and the like, is similar to listening to Sidney Bechet in the '30s and early '40s and then later in the '50s, with those French bands. The magic was always somewhere, but it became little more than reflex motion. —*Bob Rusch, Cadence*

Big Blues / Feb. 2, 1978–Feb. 3, 1978 / Columbia ✦✦✦
Subdued, but has some good work with Jim Hall (g). —*Ron Wynn*

Foolish Memories / Aug. 6, 1981–Aug. 7, 1981 / L & R Music ✦✦✦

Work of Art / Sep. 1981 / Concord Jazz ✦✦✦
This is a crisp, no-nonsense session. —*Ron Wynn*

Manhattan / Nov. 29, 1981-Nov. 30, 1981 / Soul Note ✦✦✦✦

Mirage / Sep. 18, 1982-Sep. 19, 1992 / Soul Note ✦✦✦

Warm Valley / Sep. 1982 / Concord Jazz ✦✦✦✦

Jazztet, The: Moment to Moment / May 30, 1983–May 31, 1983 / Soul Note ✦✦✦✦

In Concert / Aug. 15, 1984 / Enja ✦✦✦

You Make Me Smile / Dec. 13, 1984–Dec. 15, 1984 / Soul Note ✦✦✦
Trumpeter Art Farmer and tenor saxophonist Clifford Jordan combined many times in the '70s and do so here on this excellent mid-'80s quintet date, backed by bassist Rufus Reid, pianist Fred Hersch and drummer Akira Tana. Hersch has since moved into more experimental waters, but shows here he can certainly handle standards and mainstream originals. —*Ron Wynn*

Real Time / Feb. 21, 1986-Feb. 22, 1986 / Contemporary ✦✦✦✦

Back to the City / Feb. 21, 1986–Feb. 22, 1986 / Original Jazz Classics ✦✦✦✦
W/ the Golson Jazztet. This fine update of vintage Jazztet format has high-quality help from Curtis Fuller (tb). —*Ron Wynn*

☆ **Something to Live for: the Music of Billy Strayhorn** / Jan. 14, 1987-Jan. 15, 1987 / Contemporary ✦✦✦✦✦
This is a beautiful tribute to Billy Strayhorn. Clifford Jordan (ts) and James Williams (p) are sublime. —*Ron Wynn*

Azure / Jun. 25, 1987–Sep. 10, 1987 / Soul Note ✦✦✦

Blame It on My Youth / Feb. 4, 1988–Feb. 8, 1988 / Contemporary ✦✦✦✦✦
This is one of the better Art Farmer recordings of the 1980s, which is saying a great deal, for the fluegelhornist is among the most consistent of all jazz musicians. The two ballads that open and close this set ("Blame It on My Youth" and "I'll Be Around") give Farmer an opportunity to display his warm and attractive sound (with fine support from pianist James Williams, bassist Rufus Reid and drummer Victor Lewis) while the other two pieces (Benny Carter's "Summer Serenade" and more obscure material) add the great tenor saxophonist (and so-so soprano player) Clifford Jordan to the group. It's an easily enjoyable and very successful outing. —*Scott Yanow*

Ph.D / Apr. 3, 1989-Apr. 4, 1989 / Contemporary ✦✦✦✦
Quintet. The followup to *Blame It on My Youth*, with Clifford Jordan (sax) and James Williams (p). —*Michael G. Nastos*

Central Avenue Reunion / May 26, 1989–May 27, 1989 / Contemporary ✦✦✦✦

Soul Eyes / May 1991 / Enja ✦✦✦

Live At Sweet Basil / Mar. 27, 1992–Mar. 28, 1992 / Evidence ✦✦✦✦

Company I Keep / Jan. 11, 1994–Jan. 12, 1994 / Arabesque ✦✦✦

Joe Farrell (Joseph Carl Firrantello)

b. Dec. 16, 1937, Chicago Heights, IL, **d.** Jan. 10, 1986, Los Angeles, CA
Flute, Soprano Saxophone, Tenor Saxophone / Hard Bop, Crossover
Joe Farrell's CTI albums of 1970–76, which combined together his hard bop style with some pop and fusion elements, made him briefly popular among listeners not familiar with his earlier work. He began playing clarinet when he was 11 and, after graduating from the University of Illinois in 1959, Farrell moved to New York where he worked with the Maynard Ferguson Big Band (1960–61) and Slide Hampton (1962) and recorded with Charles Mingus, Dizzy Reece and a notable series with Jaki Byard (1965). A mem-

ber of both the Thad Jones-Mel Lewis Orchestra (1966–69) and Elvin Jones' combo (1967–70), Farrell's distinctive sound on tenor and general versatility were assets. A member of the original version of Return to Forever (1971–72), Farrell was fairly prosperous during the 1970s when his solo CTI records sold well, but a drug problem gradually caught up with him. After performing with Mingus Dynasty in the late '70s and recording with Louis Hayes in 1983, he moved to Los Angeles where he scuffled during his last couple of years. In addition to CTI, Farrell recorded as a leader for Warner Bros, Xanadu, Contemporary, Realtime, Timeless and (with Airto and Flora Purim) for Reference. —*Scott Yanow*

★ **Joe Farrell Quartet** / Jul. 1, 1970+Jul. 2, 1970 / Columbia ✦✦✦✦✦
Quartet. Early CTI recordings for this West Coast transplant. Farrell's flute and sax are well-represented. This must-buy also includes John McLaughlin (g) and Chick Corea (p). Includes "Follow Your Heart." —*Michael G. Nastos*

Outback / Nov. 1971 / CTI ✦✦✦✦
Multi-instrumentalist Joe Farrell was among a select crew of jazz veterans who enjoyed unprecedented attention when they recorded for CTI in the early '70s. This session was his second at the label and featured Farrell playing tenor and soprano sax, flute, alto flute and piccolo with equal facility. He headed a first-rate band with pianist Chick Corea, guitarist John McLaughlin, bassist Dave Holland and drummer Jack DeJohnette. This has been reissued on CD. —*Ron Wynn*

Moon Germs / Nov. 21, 1972 / Columbia ✦✦✦
Another early CTI recording. Farrell's flute and sax are well-represented. A must-buy, though a bit electric. —*Michael G. Nastos*

Penny Arcade / Nov. 1973 / CTI ✦✦✦

Upon This Rock / Mar. 1974 / CTI ✦✦✦

Canned Funk / Nov. 1974–Dec. 1974 / CTI ✦✦✦

La Cathedral Y El Toro / Apr. 1978 / Warner Brothers ✦

Night Dancing / 1978 / Warner Brothers ✦✦

Skateboard Park / Jan. 29, 1979 / Xanadu ✦✦✦
A solid date with Chick Corea (p). —*Ron Wynn*

Sonic Text / Nov. 27, 1979–Nov. 28, 1979 / Original Jazz Classics ✦✦✦✦
Joe Farrell was such a successful session musician that he didn't do as much recording under his own name as his skills merited. *Sonic Text* was one of his best recordings, a 1979 quintet set with a stalwart lineup and several songs that were long enough to spotlight everyone without resorting to overkill. Farrell wisely avoided the pop trappings that sometimes weighted down his '70s CTI releases and played with vigor on tenor, soprano and flute, assisted by Freddie Hubbard's vibrant trumpet and George Cables nimble, delightful keyboard forays. —*Ron Wynn*

Darn That Dream / Mar. 23, 1982 / Drive Archive ✦✦✦
Tenor saxophonist Joe Farrell recorded two albums' worth of material for RealTime in March 1982. This CD reissue by Drive Archive has most of the best material including three selections featuring altoist Art Pepper in one of his final recordings; Pepper is best on his showcase "Darn That Dream." Farrell (who is joined by pianist George Cables, bassist Tony Dumas and drummer John Dentz) is in consistently fine form throughout the other selections, sounding particularly adventurous on "Mode for Joe" and coming up with some fresh statements on such standards as "Blue & Boogie," "You Stepped out of a Dream" and "Someday My Prince Will Come." —*Scott Yanow*

Vim 'n' Vigor / Nov. 6, 1983 / Timeless ✦✦✦✦

Malachi Favors

b. Aug. 22, 1937, Chicago, IL
Bass/Avant-Garde, Free Jazz
The long-time bassist with the Art Ensemble of Chicago has also played a variety of miscellaneous instruments (including banjo, zither bells gong harmonica melodica and percussion) on their many records. In his early days he played bop in Chicago with Andrew Hill (mid-50's) and other local musicians. Favors was in the AACM from the start, being a member of Muhal Richard Abrams' Experimental Band as early as 1961. He joined Roscoe Mitchell's quartet in 1966 which soon became the Art Ensemble. In addition to his work with that important group, Favors has recorded with Archie Shepp, Sunny Murray, Dewey Redman, Abrams and Lester Bowie. —*Scott Yanow*

Rick Fay

b. Chicago, IL
Clarinet, Tenor Saxophone, Soprano Saxophone / Dixieland
Unrecorded until 1989, Rick Fay has made up for lost time with many fine records for the Arbors label. He had worked for the Disney Music Department for 24 years (in California and later in Florida) and played regularly at Disney World and in freelance jobs with Wild Bill Davison, Pete Dailey, the Firehouse Five Plus Two and others. On the many Arbors releases, Rick Fay has had the opportunity to record frequently as both a leader and a sideman with such players as Jackie Coon, Dan Barrett and Johnny Varro and he has held his own. —*Scott Yanow*

Hello Horn! / Apr. 23, 1990 / Arbors ✦✦✦

● **Rick Fay's Endangered Species** / Mar. 2, 1993–Mar. 3, 1993 / Arbors ✦✦✦✦
This nine-piece unit boasts quite a few strong talents. While leader Rick Fay is fine on tenor and soprano, he is matched by fluegelhornist Jackie Coon, trombonist Dan Barrett, Betty O'Hara (who plays bass trumpet, double-bell euphonium, cornet and fluegelhorn), clarinetist Bobby Grodon and a four-piece rhythm section led by pianist Johnny Varro. With Fay, Coon, O'Hara and banjoist Eddie Erickson all contributing one or two vocals apiece, there is plenty of variety on this program of swing and Dixieland standards. It's enjoyable and generally hard-swinging music. —*Scott Yanow*

Leonard Feather

b. Sep. 13, 1914, London, England, **d.** Sep. 22, 1994, Sherman Oaks, CA
Piano, Composer / Bop, Swing, Blues
Leonard Feather was best-known as easily the most famous jazz critic in the world, writing at least ten jazz books (including the famed *Encyclopedia of Jazz* series) and thousands of liner notes along with articles and reviews for all of the jazz magazines and most of the daily newspapers. Feather, who was very modest about his piano playing, produced many important sessions from the late '30s on, but his inclusion in this book is due to his skills as a lyricist/composer. He was responsible for such songs as "Evil Gal Blues" (a hit for Dinah Washington), "Blowtop Blues," the memorable "Mighty like the Blues," "I Remember Bird," "Signing Off," "Twelve Tone Blues" and "How Blue Can You Get." Feather also led record dates on an irregular basis starting from 1937 (some of which he played on), most notably two 1971 sets for Mainstream with his Night Blooming Jazzmen, a group including Blue Mitchell and Ernie Watts. —*Scott Yanow*

Night Blooming Jazzmen / Aug. 23, 1971–Aug. 24, 1972 / Mainstream ✦✦✦✦✦

Freedom Jazz Dance / Aug. 19, 1971 / Mainstream ✦✦✦✦
Here is an example of this noted jazz critic's songwriting abilities, though it doesn't match the tunes he penned for Dinah Washington and others in the '40s and '50s. —*Ron Wynn*

Wilton Felder

b. Aug. 31, 1940, Houston, TX
Bass, Tenor Saxophone / Soul Jazz, Crossover
Wilton Felder spent over 30 years with the group known as the Jazz Crusaders (and later the Crusaders). In the mid-'50s while in high school in Houston, Felder, Joe Sample and Stix Hooper became the founding members of the group that soon picked up Wayne Henderson as an additional member. Felder moved to Los Angeles with the other musicians in the late '50s and by 1961 they were recording for Pacific Jazz as the Jazz Crusaders. Felder's soulful blues-based tone and hard bop style fit well in the popular band. Around 1968 he started doubling on electric bass and has backed many top players outside of the group on that instrument. However, his own solo albums (for World Pacific in 1969, MCA and Par) have generally found him cast as a third-rate Grover Washington, Jr. and have not caught on. Felder remained with the Crusaders until its end in the late '80s and had a reunion with Wayne Henderson in the '90s in a new version of the group. —*Scott Yanow*

Secrets / 1983 / MCA ✦

Nocturnal Moods / 1991 / Par ✦✦

● **Forever Always** / 1992 / Par ✦✦✦
Throughout this routine R&B-oriented jazz date, Wilton Felder comes across as a second-rate Grover Washington, Jr., playing predictable solos over a variety of unimaginative funky vamps in a

tired style very similar to his previous albums. Felder has a nice sound (particularly on tenor), but he should stick to being a hired sideman, or at least come up with some original ideas. At best, this is a pleasant dance date. —*Scott Yanow*

Victor Feldman

b. Apr. 7, 1934, London, England, **d.** May 12, 1987, Los Angeles, CA
Percussion, Piano, Drums, Vibes / Cool, Post-Bop, Crossover
Victor Feldman was a child prodigy who was a professional from the age of seven and sat in on drums with Glenn Miller's Army Air Force Band in 1944 when he was ten. He was active in his native England through the bebop years (mostly on drums), debuting as a leader in 1948. By 1952 Feldman was getting better-known for his vibes playing and he recorded extensively during the 1950s. After touring with Woody Herman (1956–57), he decided to move to the U.S. in 1957 where he worked at the Lighthouse with Howard Rumsey. Feldman recorded (on vibes and piano) for Mode, Contemporary and Riverside during 1957–61, a period in which he became a busy studio musician. Feldman was with Cannonball Adderley's Quintet (mostly as a pianist) for six months in 1960–61 and recorded with Miles Davis in 1963 (who offered him a job with his new quintet and recorded his original "Seven Steps to Heaven"), but remained in L.A. and the studios. He cut jazz dates for Choice, Concord, Palo Alto and TBA and, in the 1980s until his death, he led a soulful crossover group (The Generation Band) that often featured his son, Trevor Feldman, on drums. —*Scott Yanow*

★ **Suite Sixteen** / Aug. 19, 1955–Sep. 21, 1955 / Original Jazz Classics ✦✦✦✦✦
This interesting set (a CD reissue of the original LP) features Victor Feldman shortly before he left England for the United States. Feldman, mostly heard on vibes but also making strong appearances on piano and drums, heads several groups filled with English All-Stars including such notable musicians as trumpeters Jimmy Deuchar and Dizzy Reece, tenors Ronnie Scott and Tubby Hayes and pianist Tommy Pollard. The music is boppish with some surprises in the consistently swinging arrangements, giving one a definitive look at Victor Feldman near the beginning of his career. —*Scott Yanow*

With Mallets a Fore Thought / Sep. 1957 / VSOP ✦✦✦✦
This CD reissue of a set from the long-defunct Interlude label brings back an outing by vibraphonist Vic Feldman. Feldman is showcased in a quartet with pianist Carl Perkins, bassist Leroy Vinnegar and drummer Stan Levey on half of the selections, while the remaining tracks add trombonist Frank Rosolino and tenor saxophonist Harold Land. An obscurity ("Chart of My Heart"), two standards and four Feldman originals comprise this easily enjoyable and relaxed bop date. —*Scott Yanow*

The Arrival of Victor Feldman / Jan. 21, 1958–Jan. 22, 1958 / Original Jazz Classics ✦✦✦
This date proclaimed the beginning of Victor Feldman's American recording career as a leader. The January 1958 recording had some strong jazz performances on its program, but not a particularly strong personality. Feldman reached back and forth between vibes and piano making clear, rich, unequivocating pronouncements on both instruments. —*Bob Rusch, Cadence*

Merry Olde Soul / Dec. 16, 1960–Jan. 11, 1961 / Original Jazz Classics ✦✦✦

Your Smile / 1973 / Choice ✦✦✦

The Artful Dodger / Jan. 24, 1977–Jan. 26, 1977 / Concord Jazz ✦✦✦

In My Pocket / Dec. 4, 1977 / Coherent ✦✦✦

Soft Shoulder / 1981 / TBA ✦✦✦✦

Secrets of the Andes / Feb. 26, 1982 / Palo Alto ✦✦✦

To Chopin with Love / May 7, 1983–May 8, 1983 / Palo Alto ✦✦✦
Trio. Impressionistic; outstanding playing. —*Ron Wynn*

Call of the Wild / Jan. 19, 1984 / TBA ✦✦

Fiesta / Jun. 8, 1984–Aug. 1984 / TBA ✦✦
Good arrangements. Feldman plays with some vigor, though not as strongly as on his more jazz-oriented releases. —*Ron Wynn*

High Visibility / Feb. 19, 1985–April 1985 / TBA ✦✦

Maynard Ferguson

b. May 4, 1928, Montreal, Canada
Trumpet, Leader / Bop, Hard Bop, Crossover
When he debuted with Stan Kenton's Orchestra in 1950, Maynard

Ferguson could play higher than any other trumpeter up to that point in jazz history, and he was accurate. Somehow he has kept most of that range through the decades and since the 1970s has been one of the most famous musicians in jazz. Never known for his exquisite taste (some of his more commercial efforts are unlistenable), Maynard Ferguson has nevertheless led some important bands and definitely made an impact with his trumpet playing.

After heading his own big band in Montreal, Ferguson came to the United States in 1949 with hopes of joining Kenton's orchestra, but that ensemble had just recently broke up. So instead, MF gained experience playing with the big bands of Boyd Raeburn, Jimmy Dorsey and Charlie Garnet. In 1950 with the formation of Kenton's Innovations Orchestra, Ferguson became a star, playing ridiculous high notes with ease. In 1953 he left Kenton to work in the studios of Los Angeles and three years later led the all-star "Birdland Dreamband." In 1957 he put together a regular big band that lasted until 1965, recorded regularly for Roulette (all of its recordings with that label are on a massive Mosaic box set) and performed some of the finest music of Ferguson's career. Such players as Slide Hampton, Don Ellis, Don Sebesky, Willie Maiden, John Bunch, Joe Zawinul, Joe Farrell, Jaki Byard, Lanny Morgan, Rufus Jones, Bill Berry and Don Menza were among the more notable sidemen.

After economics forced him to give up the impressive band, Ferguson had a few years in which he was only semiactive in music, spending time in India and eventually forming a new band in England. After moving back to the U.S., Ferguson in 1974 drifted quickly into commercialism. Young trumpeters in high school and colleges were amazed by his high notes, but jazz fans were dismayed by the tasteless recordings which resulted in hit versions of such songs as the themes from *Star Wars* and *Rocky* and much worse. After cutting back on his huge orchestra in the early '80s, Ferguson recorded some bop in a 1983 session, led a funk band called "High Voltage" during 1987–88 and then returned to jazz with his "Big Bop Nouveau Band," a medium-sized outfit with which he still tours the world. Although MF's range finally started to shrink a little in the 1990s, he is still an enthusiastic and exciting player —*Scott Yanow*

Stratospheric / Feb. 19, 1954–May 12, 1956 / EmArcy ♦♦♦♦
This two-LP set from 1976 gives listeners a good overview of trumpeter Maynard Ferguson's four Mercury albums of 1954–56. M.F. is heard in several different settings ranging from octets to a big band with arrangements by Bill Holman and Willie Maiden; among the many other soloists are altoists Bud Shank and Herb Geller, baritonist Bob Gordon, trombonists Herbie Harper and Milt Bernhart, and tenors Bob Cooper and Georgie Auld. Although it would be preferable to get all of the performances from the four albums since those remain out-of-print, this two-fer is worth searching for in the meantime. This is excellent bop-based music with highlights including "The Way You Look Tonight," Ferguson's feature on "Over the Rainbow" and a variety of strong Holman originals. —*Scott Yanow*

The Birdland Dream Band / Sep. 7, 1956–Sep. 25, 1956 / Bluebird ♦♦♦♦♦

Maynard Ferguson And His Original Dreamband / Dec. 1956 / Artistry ♦♦♦
Ferguson's first significant orchestra was the "Dreamband" he had in 1956. This live set (put out on an LP in 1984 by the Artistry label) contains originals by Bill Holman, Al Cohn, Marty Paich, Manny Albam, Ernie Wilkins and Johnny Mandel; one would presume that the arrangements are also by the composers. The music generally jumps and is modern for the period. Such soloists as the leader/trumpeter, altoist Herb Geller and tenors Richie Kamuca and Nino Tempo are heard from and the rhythm section is driven by drummer Mel Lewis. Excellent music, it's also well-recorded. —*Scott Yanow*

A Message from Newport/ Newport Suite / May 6, 1958–Mar. 22, 1960 / Roulette ♦♦♦♦♦
Two of trumpeter Maynard Ferguson's best-ever albums are combined on this double LP; all of the music has since been reissued on Mosaic's massive *M.F. on Roulette* CD box set. Slide Hampton, Willie Maiden and Don Sebesky contributed most of the colorful arrangements and there are strong solos from Ferguson (on trumpet, valve trombone and baritone horn), trombonist Hampton, altoist Jimmy Ford, Carmen Leggio, Maiden and Joe Farrell on tenors and pianist Jaki Byard among others. Highlights include "Tag Team," "Frame for the Blues," "Three Little Foxes,"

"Newport," "Got the Spirit," "Ol' Man River" and "Three More Foxes." —*Scott Yanow*

★ **The Complete Roulette Maynard Ferguson** / May 6, 1958–Mar. 1962 / Mosaic ♦♦♦♦♦
Trumpeter Maynard Ferguson led his greatest big band during the years that he was signed to Roulette and all of the music from his 13 Roulette LPs (plus 11 previously unissued selections) are included on this deluxe, limited-edition, ten-CD box set. Although three of the LPs were originally recorded as dance records (and stick close to the melodies), this box as a whole finds Maynard at his peak and with an orchestra that includes such talented soloists as trombonists Slide Hampton and Don Sebesky (both of whom contributed arrangements), altoist Lanny Morgan, the tenors of Carmen Leggio, Willie Maiden, Joe Farrell and Don Menza, pianists Jaki Byard and Joe Zawinul and drummer Rufus Jones in addition to the leader. The music is very jazz-oriented and contains more than its share of classic moments, particularly the sessions that resulted in *A Message from Newport* and *Newport Suite*. It's highly recommended. —*Scott Yanow*

Si! Si! M.F. / 1962 / Roulette ♦♦♦♦
This single-CD reissues the contents of two former LPs by the Maynard Ferguson Orchestra: *Si! Si!* and *Maynard '64*. These 16 performances have been reissued by Mosaic in a ten-CD box set, but those listeners who do not have that set should get this one. In addition to the high-note trumpet master, the boppish performances feature such soloists as altoist Lanny Morgan, the tenors of Willie Maiden and Don Menza and pianist Mike Abene. The arrangements (by Ernie Wilkins, Marty Paich, Don Sebesky, Don Rader, Maiden, Abene and Menza) took advantage of the band's many strengths and the result is a solid set (actually two) of swinging music. —*Scott Yanow*

The New Sound of Maynard Ferguson / 1964 / Cameo ♦♦♦
The sound was not all that new but the label was as Maynard Ferguson and his orchestra, which had just concluded a long association with Roulette, switched briefly to Cameo. The big band was still in prime form, playing both swing standards and originals with power, swing and spirit. In addition to Ferguson's screaming trumpet, altoist Lanny Morgan, Willie Maiden and Frank Vicari on tenors, baritonist Ronnie Cuber and pianist Mike Abene are heard from prominently while Abene, Maiden and Don Sebesky contribute most of the arrangements. This rare LP (which has not yet been reissued on CD) is worth the search. —*Scott Yanow*

Color Him Wild / Sep. 15, 1964–Sep. 16, 1964 / Mainstream ♦♦♦
After eight years the Maynard Ferguson Orchestra was in its last period when it recorded a couple of LPs for Mainstream. The band's sound and winning spirit were still unchanged from its prime days and this excellent album (which features solos from the trumpeter/leader, valve trombonist Rob McConnell, altoist Lanny Morgan, Willie Maiden on tenor, baritonist Ronnie Cuber and pianist Mike Abene) is a fine example of the orchestra's music. Highlights include "Airegin," "Green Dolphin Street" and a remake of "Three More Foxes" (although their version of "People" can be safely skipped). —*Scott Yanow*

Blues Roar / Dec. 1, 1964–Dec. 11, 1964 / Mainstream ♦♦♦
This rather brief (under 36 minutes) CD is a straight reissue of a Mainstream LP by the Maynard Ferguson Orchestra. M.F. and his crew perform a variety of blues-oriented material including "Every Day I Have the Blues," "Night Train," "What'd I Say" and "I've Got a Woman." Willie Maiden, Don Sebesky and Mike Abene were responsible for the arrangements and the main soloists are Ferguson (on trumpet and valve trombone), altoists Lanny Morgan and Charlie Mariano, Frank Vicari on tenor and pianist Mike Abene. A fine set, it's the last recording by this excellent orchestra. —*Scott Yanow*

Six by Six: Maynard Ferguson and Sextet / Sep. 13, 1965–Sep. 14, 1965 / Mainstream ♦♦♦♦
After trumpeter Maynard Ferguson reluctantly broke up his big band in late 1964 after eight years, he formed a more economical sextet with two of his top soloists (Willie Maiden on tenor and baritone and altoist Lanny Morgan) and his rhythm section (pianist Mike Abene, bassist Ron McClure and drummer Tony Inzalaco). Although this group did not last long, their mainstream recording has excellent performances and good solos from the somewhat forgotten band; highlights include Maiden's ballad "April Fool," the cooking "No More Wood" and "Summertime." —*Scott Yanow*

Trumpet Rhapsody / Dec. 1967 / MPS ++
This is one of the less significant Maynard Ferguson albums but the music is still fairly enjoyable. Accompanied by The German Rolf Hans Muller Orchestra in Dec. 1967, the great trumpeter sticks mostly to ballads, showcasing his tone and sometimes his range with restraint and an accent on lyricism. The music is enjoyable enough but not too essential. With the exception of one obscure record, Ferguson would not record again for over two years when he started his commercial comeback with Columbia. —Scott Yanow

MF Horn / Feb. 1970 / Columbia +++
Trumpeter Maynard Ferguson began his successful "comeback" (after several years of low-profile activity) with this well-received Columbia LP. Featuring his English orchestra (and such soloists as altoist Pete King and Danny Moss on tenor), Ferguson had a minor hit in "MacArthur Park," showcases some Indian musicians on "Chala Nata" and shows throughout that his mind was open toward both newer forms of jazz and pop music. It's an interesting if not essential set. —Scott Yanow

MF Horn 2 / Jan. 1972 / Columbia ++
During his period on Columbia, Maynard Ferguson showed a willingness (and sometimes even an eagerness) to record pop material. His trumpet playing is frequently brilliant throughout this LP with his English orchestra, but not too many jazz purists will be thrilled with his renditions of "Theme from *Shaft*," "Spinning Wheel" and "Hey Jude." The music is actually better than it seems, but do not look here for any bop. —Scott Yanow

MF Horn 3 / Apr. 18, 1973 / Columbia ++
Maynard Ferguson's *M.F. Horn* series for Columbia mixed together jazz versions of pop and rock music, hurting the trumpeter's reputation with the jazz collectors but helping him to become practically a household name. This set has some worthwhile pieces (notably "Awright, Awright," "Round Midnight" and "Nice 'N Juicy") and some spirited ensemble playing; the most notable among Ferguson's sidemen in this English big band are pianist Pete Jackson, drummer Randy Jones and baritonist Bruce Johnstone. The music on the LP is not essential, but has its exciting moments. —Scott Yanow

Maynard Ferguson / Apr. 18, 1973–May 1979 / Columbia +++
Most of trumpeter Maynard Ferguson's recordings for Columbia were rather erratic, alternating very commercial pop performances with occasional jazz selections. This sampler LP reissues eight of the latter, allowing jazz listeners to truly get the "best of" Ferguson from the 1970s. Certainly few but Maynard's greatest fans will want to get his album *Hot* just for this version of "Naima" or *New Vintage* for "Airegin." This consistent sampler lets one avoid his more dated material and sticks to the more rewarding jazz. —Scott Yanow

MF Horn 4 & 5 / Jul. 10, 1973 / Columbia ++++
This double LP is easily Maynard Ferguson's best jazz-oriented recording for Columbia. With the exception of a remake of "MacArthur Park" (which isn't bad), the music sticks exclusively to jazz with the highlights including "I'm Gettin' Sentimental over You," "Two for Otis," "Stay Loose with Bruce," "The Fox Hunt" and "Got the Spirit." In addition to Ferguson's powerful trumpet, other musicians making strong impressions include first trumpeter Lin Biviano, altoist Andy MacIntosh, Ferdinand Povel on tenor, baritonist Bruce Johnstone and keyboardist Pete Jackson. This very enjoyable set is long overdue to be reissued on CD. —Scott Yanow

Chameleon / Apr. 1, 1974+Apr. 4, 1974 / Columbia ++
This is a really streaky CD reissue from Maynard Ferguson's generally commercial Columbia period. The trumpeter's version of Herbie Hancock's hit "Chameleon" is enjoyable, and he does a good job on Chick Corea's "La Fiesta," the standard "I Can't Get Started" and "Superbone Meets the Bad Man" (which cofeatures baritonist Bruce Johnstone). However his renditions of such pieces as "The Way We Were," Paul McCartney's "Jet" and "Livin' for the City" are quite forgettable and lightweight, making this reissue an unnecessary frivolity. —Scott Yanow

Carnival / May 15, 1978 / Columbia ++
Maynard Ferguson's version of "Birdland" from this LP was a bit of a hit and he fares fairly well on "Stella by Starlight" and "Over the Rainbow," but overall this typically commercial Columbia album is of lesser interest. MF, at the height of his popularity, was clearly looking for a hit, which is why he recorded the "Theme from *Battlestar Galactica*" and roughly half of the poppish mate-

rial on this rather forgettable effort. The trumpeter/bandleader would record worse albums than this LP, but this one is weak enough. —Scott Yanow

Storm / Jun. 23, 1982–Jun. 24, 1982 / Palo Alto ++
Maynard Ferguson had led many big bands before recording this Palo Alto LP. This was not one of his more significant units (few of the sidemen have been heard from much since) and the music, although more jazz-oriented than his earlier Columbias (including versions of "Take the 'A' Train" and a vocal feature for MF on "As Time Goes By"), is not really that memorable. It's a lesser effort. —Scott Yanow

Hollywood / 1982 / Columbia +

Live from San Francisco / May 27, 1983 / Palo Alto +++
This LP was Maynard Ferguson's strongest jazz album in quite a few years. Utilizing a small big band comprised of 12 pieces, Ferguson is in consistently fiery form during a session recorded live from the Great American Music Hall in San Francisco. "Bebop Buffet" (which has quotes from many bop classics) is a highpoint and these versions of "Lush Life" and "On the Sunny Side of the Street" (along with four group originals) are quite enjoyable; baritonist Denis DiBlasio's arrangements are a major asset. This fine straight-ahead date deserves to be reissued on CD. —Scott Yanow

Body and Soul / Jan. 1986 / Black Hawk ++
Trumpeter Maynard Ferguson cut back on his big band around this time, utilizing an 11-piece group with six horns and an expanded rhythm section; best known among his sidemen is tenor saxophonist Rick Margitza. MF uses electronics on some of the selections and swings a bit on "Body and Soul." In addition to Margitza, the other soloists include guitarist Michael Higgins, altoist Tim Ries and keyboardist Todd Carlon. The music is pleasing but not all that memorable although Ferguson's mastery of his upper register remains quite impressive. —Scott Yanow

High Voltage, Vol. 2 / Jul. 1988–Sep. 1988 / Intima ++
For a period in the mid-to-late '80s, trumpeter Maynard Ferguson broke up his usual big band and had a funky combo, a septet with just two horns and a large rhythm section. For the second of his two *High Voltage* CD's, Ferguson primarily plays group originals (plus a slower-than-usual "Star Eyes") that comes across as fairly routine and predictable. There is nothing particularly memorable about this pleasant but unadventurous set of music. —Scott Yanow

Big Bop Nouveau / 1988–1989 / Intima +++
Maynard Ferguson broke up his funk combo High Voltage around this time and put together a 15-piece straight-ahead group that emphasized swinging and big band-oriented charts. Although there is a throwaway "Maynard Ferguson Hit Medley," such pieces as "Blue Birdland," "Cherokee" and "But Beautiful" better showcase the remarkable trumpeter. The sidemen include Christopher Hollyday on alto. This is an excellent all-round showcase for MF, but the CD from the now-defunct Intima label will be hard to find. —Scott Yanow

Live from London / 1993 / Avenue Jazz ++++
Utilizing a 13-piece band that includes ten horns, Maynard Ferguson performs bebop with his Big Bop Nouveau on this CD. All of the music is fairly basic, using common chord changes and charts that leave plenty of room for solos. Ferguson shows at age 65 that he still has most of his outstanding range and, assisted by a trumpet section full of screamers, the performances are boisterous and sometimes a bit bombastic. Chip McNeill takes a passionate soprano solo on "A Night in Tunisia," Matt Wallace has a couple of rewarding spots on tenor and trumpeter Walter White fares well on "Fox Hunt," but it is the leader who gives this music its main personality. —Scott Yanow

These Cats Can Swing / 1994 / Concord Jazz ++++

Dale Fielder

b. 1956, East Liverpool, Ohio
Tenor Saxophone / Post-Bop
Dale Fielder has emerged in the 1990s as one of the top up-and-coming saxophonists in the Los Angeles area. He started studying music (clarinet and then alto) at the age of nine and played R&B while in high school. Fielder attended the University of Pittsburgh and played regularly around town. In 1980 he moved to New York and gigged with the calypso band of the Mighty Sparrow. While in New York Fielder formed the Clarion label and recorded an LP, *Scene from a Dream*, that featured Geri Allen. In 1988 he relo-

cated to Los Angeles and since then has played regularly in town and up and down the Coast. Dale Fielder has recorded two CDs recently for his Clarion label including a strong tribute to Wayne Shorter. —*Scott Yanow*

Know Thyself / May 5, 1994-Sep. 20, 1994 / Clarion ✦✦✦✦

Dear Sir / March 5, 1995 / Clarion ✦✦✦✦✦

Brandon Fields

b. 1958, Indiana
Alto Saxophone, Soprano Saxophone / Post Bop, Crossover
A talented altoist influenced by David Sanborn, Brandon Fields has the versatility to be able to play both R&B/crossover and hard bop. Fields grew up in Orange County, CA and started playing alto when he was ten. A freelance musician since he was a teenager, Fields moved to Los Angeles in 1982 and has worked steadily ever since. He toured with George Benson in 1985, was a regular member of the Rippingtons, has long been a busy session player and recorded four CDs as a leader for Nova and one recently for Positive music. —*Scott Yanow*

● **The Other Side of the Story** / Feb. 13, 1985–Feb. 14, 1985 / Nova ✦✦✦✦✦

Other Places / 1990 / Nova ✦✦

Everybody's Business / 1991 / Nova ✦✦✦

Firehouse Five Plus Two

Group / Dixieland
The Firehouse Five Plus Two started out as an amateur Dixieland band mostly comprised of cartoon animators from the Disney Studios. Their spontaneous sessions (led by trombonist Ward Kimball) were so successful that they started recording for Good Time Jazz in 1949 and soon became a poular attraction, while never giving up their day jobs! In addition to colorful Dixieland ensembles and solos, the band often let off a siren during their hotter choruses and was not shy to inject their music with a healthy dose of humor. They recorded regularly for Good Time Jazz during 1949–60 with additional albums cut in 1962, 1964 and 1969. In addition to Kimball, the band included trumpeter Johnny Lucas (for the first session), cornetist Danny Alguire, clarinetist Clarke Mallory and, from 1960 on, George Probert on soprano and clarinet. —*Scott Yanow*

★ **The Firehouse Five Plus Two Story** / May 1949–May 20, 1952 / Good Time Jazz ✦✦✦✦✦

Firehouse Five Plus Two Goes South / Jan. 23, 1954–Oct. 10, 1956 / Good Time Jazz ✦✦✦✦

Firehouse Five Plus Two Plays for Lovers / Sep. 23, 1955+Dec. 19, 1955 / Good Time Jazz ✦✦✦✦

Firehouse Five Plus Two Goes to Sea / Feb. 24, 1957–Nov. 18, 1957 / Good Time Jazz ✦✦✦

Firehouse Five Plus Two Crashes a Party / Sep. 29, 1958–Nov. 10, 1959 / Good Time Jazz ✦✦✦

Dixieland Favorites / Sep. 29, 1958–Mar. 14, 1969 / Fantasy ✦✦✦

Firehouse Five Plus Two Around the World / Nov. 18, 1958–Mar. 27, 1960 / Good Time Jazz ✦✦✦

16 Dixieland Favorites / 195 / Good Time Jazz ✦✦✦✦

The Firehouse Five Plus Two at Dixieland / Jul. 27, 1962–Jul. 28, 1962 / Good Time Jazz ✦✦✦✦

The Firehouse Five Plus Two Goes to a Fire / Apr. 1964–Jun. 1964 / Good Time Jazz ✦✦✦✦
The Firehouse Five Plus Two always played a happy brand of Dixieland and this LP, their next-to-last recording, finds their enthusiasm at a high level. The fine septet (which features solos from cornetist Danny Alguire, trombonist Ward Kimball and soprano saxophonist George Probert) performs a dozen songs with titles having something to do with fires such as "Keep the Home Fires Burning," "Hot Lips," "Fireman, Save My Child," "A Hot Time in the Old Town" and "I Don't Want to Set the World on Fire," etc. Fans of the group will not be disappointed with this spirited effort. —*Scott Yanow*

Twenty Years Later / Oct. 6, 1969–Oct. 8, 1969 / Good Time Jazz ✦✦✦

Clare Fischer

b. Oct. 22, 1928, Durand, MI
Piano, Keyboards, Arranger, Composer / Latin Jazz, Hard Bop
Clare Fischer has had a varied career as keyboardist, composer,

---

Music Map

┌───┐
│   │
│   **Fluegelhorn**   │
│   │
├───┤
│   **Early Uses of Fluegelhorn**   │
│ Joe Bishop (1936 with Woody Herman's   │
│   Orchestra)   │
│   Shorty Rogers (early 1950s')   │
│   Miles Davis (1957, on *Miles Ahead*)   │
├───┤
│ *By the mid-1960s nearly all trumpeters │
│   used the fluegelhorn as a double.*   │
├───┤
│ **Most Important Fluegelhorn Specialists** │
│   Clark Terry   Art Farmer   │
│   Freddie Hubbard   Chuck Mangione   │
│   Thad Jones   Kenny Wheeler   │
│   Jackie Coon   │
└───┘

arranger and bandleader. The composer of two standards, "Pensativa" and "Morning," Fischer has long had an interest in Latin rhythms. After graduating from Michigan State University he moved to Los Angeles in 1957, working as accompanist and arranger for the Hi-Lo's. He wrote for a 1960 Dizzy Gillespie album (*A Portrait of Duke Ellington*) and recorded bossa nova as early as 1962; that same year he recorded two trio sets and the following year he led his first big-band date. Fischer, who has alternated between the two formats through the years, has recorded in a wide variety of settings from solo piano to heading a vocal-dominated Latin group Salsa Picante. Based in Los Angeles, Fischer (who is also an effective organist and a strong electric keyboardist) has recorded extensively through the years for such labels as Pacific Jazz/World Pacific, Revelation, Discovery, MPS and Concord. —*Scott Yanow*

Waltz / Oct. 9, 1968 / Discovery ✦✦✦
CD reissue of a 1968 set by Clare Fischer, the pianist and composer who replaced the late Cal Tjader as the most prominent non-Latin working in the Afro-Latin and Latin jazz idiom. This date was more devoted to mainstream and standards than Latin, but shows he was moving in that direction at the time. —*Ron Wynn*

Memento / Jul. 3, 1969 / Discovery ✦✦✦
Clare Fischer has inherited the crown from Cal Tjader as Latin music's leading non-Latin bandleader and figure. These 13 selections, pulled from three Fischer albums done in the late '60s and early and mid-'80s, show Fischer's straight jazz and big band work. It does include the title song and "Preludio," but this is mostly straight-ahead swing, bop and cool fare, with nice reworkings of such anthems as "Giant Steps," "Jeru" and "Old Folks." His band contains many West Coast household names, like Bill Perkins, Gary Foster and Bud Shank, plus bassist John Patitucci on board part-time. —*Ron Wynn*

Salsa Picante / Jan. 30, 1978 / Discovery ✦✦✦✦
Nice set with Fischer and company in a salsa groove. This is among his hardest, most energetic dates, with plenty of strong solos, intense percussive dialogues and extended jamming. —*Ron Wynn*

Machacha / May 16, 1979–May 17, 1979 / Discovery ✦✦✦✦
Salsa picante at its instrumental best. Latin jazz-hots with Rick Zunigar (g), Gary Foster on saxophone and flute and Alex Acuna and Poncho Sanchez on percussion. —*Michael G. Nastos*

● **Starbright** / Nov. 23, 1982 / Discovery ✦✦✦✦✦

Lembrancas / Jun. 1989 / Concord Jazz ✦✦
This '89 date takes Fischer's Latin sound into a lighter, more pop direction. The leader plays only synthesizer and the rhythms; although they adhere to Latin patterns, they aren't as explosive or

varied as on earlier Fischer sessions. Dick Mitchell isn't as aggressive as other Fischer saxophonists, either. The results are certainly pleasant and competent, but not among his best. —*Ron Wynn*

Just Me: Solo Piano Excursions / Mar. 31, 1995–Apr. 7, 1995 / Concord Jazz ✦✦✦✦

Ella Fitzgerald

b. Apr. 25, 1918, Newport News, VA
Vocals / Bop, Swing

"The First Lady of Song," Ella Fitzgerald was arguably the finest female jazz singer of all time (although some may vote for Sarah Vaughan or Billie Holiday). Blessed with a beautiful voice and a wide range, Ella (who at this writing is retired) could outswing anyone, was a brilliant scat singer and had near-perfect elocution; one could always understand the words she sang. The one fault was that, since she always sounded so happy to be singing, Ella did not always dig below the surface of the lyrics she interpreted and she even made a downbeat song such as "Love for Sale" sound joyous. However, when one evaluates her career on a whole, there is simply no one else in her class.

One could never guess from her singing that Ella Fitzgerald's early days were as grim as Billie Holiday's. Growing up in poverty, Ella was literally homeless for the year before she got her big break. In 1934 she appeared at the Apollo Theater in Harlem, winning an amateur contest by singing "Judy" in the style of her idol, Connee Boswell. After a short stint with Tiny Bradshaw, Ella was brought to the attention of Chick Webb by Benny Carter (who was in the audience at the Apollo). Webb, who was not impressed by the 17-year-old's appearance, was reluctantly persuaded to let her sing with his orchestra on a one-nighter. She went over well and soon the drummer recognized her commercial potential. Starting in 1935, Ella began recording with Webb's Orchestra and by 1937 over half of the band's selections featured her voice. "A-Tisket, A-Tasket" became a huge hit in 1938 and "Undecided" soon followed. During this era, Fitzgerald was essentially a pop/swing singer who was best on ballads while her medium-tempo performances were generally juvenile novelties. She already had a beautiful voice but did not improvise or scat much; that would develop later.

On June 16, 1939 Chick Webb died. It was decided that Ella would front the orchestra even though she had little to do with the repertoire or hiring or firing the musicians. She retained her popularity and when she broke up the band in 1941 and went solo, it was not long before her Decca recordings contained more than their share of hits. She was teamed with the Ink Spots, Louis Jordan and the Delta Rhythm Boys for some best-sellers and, in 1946, began working regularly for Norman Granz's Jazz at the Philharmonic. Granz became her manager, although it would be nearly a decade before he could get her on his label. A major change occured in Ella's singing around this period. She toured with Dizzy Gillespie's big band, adopted bop as part of her style and started including exciting scat-filled romps in her set. Her recordings of "Lady Be Good," "How High the Moon" and "Flying Home" during 1945–47 became popular and her stature as a major jazz singer rose as a result. For a time (1948–52) she was married to bassist Ray Brown and used his trio as a backup group. Ella's series of duets with pianist Ellis Larkins in 1950 (a 1954 encore with Larkins was a successful follow-up) found her interpreting George Gershwin songs, predating her upcoming *Songbook* series. After appearing in the film *Pete Kelly's Blues* in 1955, Ella signed with Norman Granz's Verve label and over the next few years she would record extensive "Songbooks" of the music of Cole Porter, the Gershwins, Rodgers and Hart, Duke Ellington, Harold Arlen, Jerome Kern and Johnny Mercer. Although (with the exception of the Ellington sets) those were not her most jazz-oriented projects (Ella stuck mostly to the melody and was generally accompanied by string orchestras), the prestigious projects did a great deal to uplift her stature. At the peak of her powers around 1960, Ella's hilarious live version of "Mack the Knife" (in which she forgot the words and made up her own) from *Ella in Berlin* is a classic and virtually all of her Verve recordings are worth getting.

Ella's Capitol and Reprise recordings of 1967–70 are not on the same level as she attempted to "update" her singing by including pop songs such as "Sunny" and "I Heard It Through the Grapevine," sounding quite silly in the process. But Ella's later years were saved by Norman Granz's decision to form a new label, Pablo. Starting with a Santa Monica Civic concert in 1972 that is climaxed by Ella's incredible version of "C Jam Blues" (in

which she trades off with and "battles" five classic jazzmen), Fitzgerald was showcased in jazz settings throughout the 1970s with the likes of Count Basie, Oscar Peterson and Joe Pass among others. Her voice began to fade during this era and by the 1980s her decline due to age was quite noticeable. Troubles with her eyes and heart knocked her out of action for periods of time although her increasingly rare appearances found Ella still retaining her sense of swing and joyful style. By 1994, Ella was in retirement but she remains a household name and dozens of her recordings are easily available on CD. —*Scott Yanow*

Ella Fitzgerald 1935–1937 / Jun. 12, 1935–Jan. 14, 1937 / Classics ✦✦✦✦

The first of six Ella Fitzgerald CDs in the European label Classics "complete" series has her earliest 25 recordings with two numbers ("My Melancholy Baby" and "All My Life") from a session with Teddy Wilson, three songs (including "Goodnight My Love") cut with Benny Goodman's big band, four tunes from her initial session as a leader and the remainder with Chick Webb's Orchestra, which mainly acted as a backup band for the young singer. Even at the age of 17, Ella Fitzgerald had a beautiful voice and a strong sense of swing (although she would not seriously scat for another decade). "I'll Chase the Blues Away," "When I Get Low I Get High," "Sing Me a Swing Song" and "You'll Have to Swing It" are among the highpoints of this fine set. —*Scott Yanow*

The Early Years, Pt. 1 / Jun. 12, 1935–Oct. 6, 1938 / GRP ✦✦✦✦

This two-CD set contains 43 of the best recordings that Ella Fitzgerald recorded during her apprentice period with Chick Webb's Orchestra. Although only 16 years old at the time of her recording debut, she already had a strong and likable voice. She would not learn to really scat sing until the mid-'40s but, on the strength of "A-Tisket, A-Tasket," by 1938 Fitzgerald was one of the most popular of all the big-band singers. This set, which only contains a few examples of the Webb Orchestra's instrumental powers, is highlighted by "I'll Chase the Blues Away," "Sing Me a Swing Song," "You'll Have to Swing It," "Organ Grinder's Swing," "If Dreams Come True" and "You Can't Be Mine." —*Scott Yanow*

Ella Fitzgerald 1937–1938 / Jan. 14, 1937–May 2, 1938 / Classics ✦✦✦✦

The second of six CDs in the Classics label's complete reissue of Ella Fitzgerald's early recordings features the singer as a teenager with the Chick Webb Orchestra, in addition to leading two sessions that use Webb's sideman and performing a pair of songs ("Big Boy Blue" and "Dedicated to You") with The Mills Brothers. Highlights include "I Want to Be Happy," "If Dreams Come True" and her big hit "A-Tisket, A-Tasket." Although not yet the brilliant jazz singer she would become, Ella Fitzgerald already had a highly appealing voice and the ability to swing any song she was given. —*Scott Yanow*

Ella Fitzgerald 1938–1939 / May 2, 1938–Feb. 17, 1939 / Classics ✦✦✦✦

After her giant hit of "A-Tisket, A-Tasket," the already-popular Ella Fitzgerald became the main attraction with the Chick Webb Orchestra and the majority of their recordings from 1938 feature the singer who was then 20. She is particularly strong on the ballads (such as "You Can't Be Mine") and had a hit in "Undecided" (the lone 1939 selection on this CD) although her work on the novelties is less memorable. All of these Classics releases are worth picking up for a definitive (and very complete) look at early Fitzgerald. —*Scott Yanow*

☆ **75th Birthday Celebration** / May 2, 1938–Aug. 5, 1955 / GRP ✦✦✦✦✦

This attractive, two-CD set, released to celebrate Fitzgerald's 75th birthday, is a perfect greatest-hits collection spanning the first half of her very productive career. All 39 songs are winners, highlighted by "A-Tisket, A-Tasket," "Undecided," "Flying Home," "Lady Be Good," "How High the Moon," "Smooth Sailing," "Airmail Special," "Lullaby of Birdland" and "Hard Hearted Hannah." During the period covered by this package, she developed from a fine big-band pop vocalist into the definitive jazz singer, one who could scat and swing with the best musicians. This set is a perfect introduction to her magic. —*Scott Yanow*

Best of Ella Fitzgerald / May 2, 1938–Aug. 5, 1955 / ✦✦✦

This deluxe, two-LP set, which was released in the late '50s but stayed in print for quite awhile, has 23 of Ella Fitzgerald's most popular Decca recordings. All but three selections date from the 1944–55 period; highlights are many including "Undecided," "Stairway to the Stars," "Flying Home," "Lady Be Good," "How

High the Moon" and "Smooth Sailing." However, all of the music on this attractive set has since been reissued on CD. —*Scott Yanow*

Ella Fitzgerald 1939 / Feb. 17, 1939–Jun. 29, 1939 / Classics ✦✦✦✦
Unlike GRP, which has merely reissued the "best" of early Ella Fitzgerald domestically, the European Classics label has released all of the great singer's early recordings (from the 1935–41 period) on six CDs. This, the fourth volume, has her final recordings with Chick Webb's Orchestra (before the legendary drummer's premature death) and her first after she took control of his big band. Fitzgerald is best on "Tain't What You Do" and the ballads (particularly "Don't Worry About Me," "Little White Lies," "Stairway to the Stars" and "Out of Nowhere") although she is less memorable on such uptempo novelties as "Chew-Chew-Chew Your Bubble Gum" and "I Want the Waiter with the Water." This CD is well worth acquiring along with the other entries in this definitive series. —*Scott Yanow*

The Early Years, Pt. 2 / Feb. 17, 1939–Jul. 31, 1941 / GRP ✦✦✦✦
GRP on this two-CD set reissues 42 of the 69 recordings that Ella Fitzgerald cut during a two-and-one-half-year period. Not as valuable as the European Classics "complete" series, this set does give one a good introduction to the classic singer's music during a time when she led Chick Webb's Orchestra after the drummer's death. Highlights include "Undecided," "Don't Worry About Me," "Stairway to the Stars," "Taking a Chance on Love," "The One I Love" and "Can't Help Lovin' Dat Man"; the medium-tempo novelties are less significant. It is recommended to the more casual collector. —*Scott Yanow*

Ella Fitzgerald 1939–1940 / Aug. 18, 1939–May 9, 1940 / Classics ✦✦✦✦
This fifth in the six-CD series by the European Classics label documents Fitzgerald's recordings during a nine-month period starting shortly after she took over the late Chick Webb's Orchestra. During this era she was much better on the ballads than on the uptempo novelties, many of which (such as "My Wubba Dolly") were not worth saving. Fortunately, this CD has a good sampling of ballads (such as "My Last Goodbye," "Moon Ray," "Sugar Blues" and "Imagination") along with two rare instrumentals by her band. The music is not essential, but fans will enjoy this look at her early days. —*Scott Yanow*

Sing Song Swing / Mar. 4, 1940–Apr. 30, 1949 / Laserlight ✦✦✦
This budget CD is better than it looks. Although there are two numbers taken from a 1940 broadcast, all of the other selections date from a pair of 1949 performances in which Ella Fitzgerald is backed by a good small combo. Her scatting is very bop-oriented on songs such as "Flying Home," a particularly inspired version of "Mister Paganini," the novelty "Old Mother Hubbard" and "Robbin's Nest." Pity that there is only a half-hour of music included on this disc, particularly when there are four other numbers that exist from the 1949 dates. —*Scott Yanow*

Ella Fitzgerald 1940–1941 / May 9, 1940–Jul. 31, 1941 / Classics ✦✦✦✦
The sixth in Classics' six-CD series that completely reissues all of Ella Fitzgerald's early recordings has her final 23 performances as the head of what was formerly the Chick Webb Orchestra. Just 22 during most of this period, she is generally in superb voice and the ballads (highlighted by "Shake Down the Stars," "Taking a Chance on Love," "The One I Love" and "Can't Help Lovin' Dat Man") are frequently exquisite; her expertise at scatting would come a few years later. It's recommended as are all of the entries in this valuable series (which is superior to GRP's Decca program). —*Scott Yanow*

The Best of Ella Fitzgerald, Vol. 2 / Nov. 8, 1940–Apr. 1, 1955 / MCA ✦✦
Unlike the first volume, which was a very attractive package, the second two-fer put out by MCA of Fitzgerald's Decca recordings is very much a budget affair, to the point of lacking any liner notes, recording dates or listing of personnel. The 20 selections (less than an hour of music) include many memorable performances by the great singer (such as "Lullaby of Birdland," the hit "Stone Cold Dead in the Market," "That Old Feeling," "Cow-Cow Boogie" and "Taking a Chance on Love"), but virtually all of the music is available in more coherent form on CD. —*Scott Yanow*

The War Years / Oct. 6, 1941–Dec. 20, 1947 / GRP/Decca ✦✦✦✦
Covering an important six-year period in Ella Fitzgerald's career,

this two-CD set contains some of the highlights of the period as she develops from a top big-band singer into a masterful jazz improviser. Although one wishes that this survey were "complete," the 43 selections do feature Fitzgerald in a wide variety of settings, including with small groups, collaborating with The Ink Spots, the Delta Rhythm Boys, Louis Jordan, Louis Armstrong and fronting various studio groups. Most of her hits from the period are here along with previously unissued alternate takes of "It's Only a Paper Moon," "Flying Home" and two of "How High the Moon," making this a strong introduction to her early years. —*Scott Yanow*

Ella Fitzgerald Set / Sep. 18, 1949–Sep. 17, 1954 / Verve ✦✦✦
This LP released for the first time selections from Ella Fitzgerald sets that were performed while touring with Jazz at the Philharmonic. Pianist Raymond Tunia, bassist Ray Brown and drummer Buddy Rich give effective support during six numbers from 1953–54 (highlighted by "The Man That Got Away" and "Hernando's Hideaway"), pianist Hank Jones along with Brown And Rich accompany the singer in 1949 on such songs as "Robbins Nest," "Black Coffee" and "Basin St. Blues" (during the latter she imitates Louis Armstrong) and, for a grand finale, five horn players back Fitzgerald on "Flying Home" which also features some hot tenor by Flip Phillips. —*Scott Yanow*

The First Lady of Song / Sep. 18, 1949–Jul. 29, 1966 / Verve ✦✦✦✦
This attractive three-CD set gives listeners an overview of Ella Fitzgerald's Verve recordings, although the inclusion of seven previously unissued cuts (in addition to 44 that are mostly available in more complete form elsewhere) will frustrate some completists. However the careful selection of representative performances along with the informative and lengthy text make this highly enjoyable reissue (which captures her in prime form) recommended even to collectors who have most of the singer's albums. —*Scott Yanow*

Pure Ella / Sep. 11, 1950–Mar. 30, 1954 / GRP/Decca ✦✦✦✦
In 1950, six years before her acclaimed *Songbook* series for Verve, Fitzgerald recorded eight George and Ira Gershwin classics in intimate duets with the sensitive and lightly swinging pianist Ellis Larkins. Four years later she recorded a dozen more songs (this time by a variety of composers) with Larkins and all 20 performances are included on this wonderful CD. Although the emphasis is on ballads and fairly straightforward treatment of the high-quality melodies, she does improvise with subtlety and gives great meaning to the lyrics. The exquisite and very memorable set is highlighted by "But Not for Me," "How Long Has This Been Going On?," "People Will Say We're in Love," "Stardust" and "My Heart Belongs to Daddy." It is highly recommended. —*Scott Yanow*

The Concert Years / Nov. 18, 1953–1983 / Pablo ✦✦✦✦
This four-CD set features highlights from ten concert appearances by Ella Fitzgerald. All of the music (which is taken from a Japanese concert in 1953, collaborations with Duke Ellington in 1966 and 1967, a French concert in 1971, her famous Santa Monica Civic performance of 1972, a gig at Ronnie Scott's in 1974, concerts at the Montreux Jazz Festival in 1975, 1977 and 1979 and a Japanese concert from 1983) has been out previously on Pablo. There are some remarkable moments (particularly 1972's "C Jam Blues" on which she trades off in very humorous fashion with Al Grey, Stan Getz, Harry "Sweets" Edison, Eddie "Lockjaw" Davis and Roy Eldridge) even if she was starting to decline a bit by the later concerts. Completists will want to get the original sets (all of which are still available) but, for those wanting a sampler of live Fitzgerald, this attractive set will fit the bill. —*Scott Yanow*

Sings the Cole Porter Songbook / Feb. 7, 1956–Mar. 27, 1956 / Verve ✦✦✦✦

The Silver Collection: The Songbooks / Feb. 7, 1956–Oct. 21, 1964 / Verve ✦✦✦

☆ **The Complete Ella Fitzgerald Song Books** / Feb. 7, 1956–Oct. 21, 1964 / Verve ✦✦✦✦✦
With her signing to Verve in 1956, Ella Fitzgerald (under producer Norman Granz's guidance) began a series of *Songbook* projects in which the singer (backed by orchestras) performed the works of various major composers. Her *Cole Porter Song Book* was so well-received that it was followed by ones featuring the music of Rodgers And Hart, Duke Ellington (half of which featured his band), Irving Berlin, a massive salute to George and Ira Gershwin, Harold Arlen, Jerome Kern and Johnny Mercer. This 16-CD box

set is not for everyone (due to its cost) and is not the most jazz-oriented of Ella Fitzgerald's recordings (she does not scat much and some of the string arrangements weigh the music down a little), but her voice is in peak form and this was a very classy (and extensive) project. The reissue (which uses miniature reproductions of the original LPs along with a definitive book, all placed in a red box) is a gem, perfectly done. —*Scott Yanow*

For the Love of Ella / Feb. 7, 1956–Jul. 20, 1966 / Verve ✦✦✦
This double CD gives listeners some of the highlights from Ella Fitzgerald's period with Verve, 32 performances divided into "Monuments of Swing" and "Ballads & Blues." Putting all of the uptempo works on one CD is an odd idea and the music is not placed in chronological order. There are many gems on this French import, but the more serious collectors will prefer to get her other more complete reissues instead. —*Scott Yanow*

Ella and Louis / Aug. 16, 1956 / Verve ✦✦✦✦
Ella Fitzgerald and Louis Armstrong make for a charming team on this CD. Accompanied by pianist Oscar Peterson, guitarist Herb Ellis, bassist Ray Brown and drummer Buddy Rich, Fitzgerald and Armstrong perform 11 standards with joy and swing. There are touches of Satch's trumpet, but this is primarily a vocal set with the emphasis on tasteful renditions of ballads. Its follow-up, *Ella & Louis Again*, is also worth getting. —*Scott Yanow*

Sings the Rodgers & Hart Songbook / Aug. 21, 1956–Aug. 31, 1956 / Verve ✦✦✦
The second of Ella Fitzgerald's famed *Songbook* series features her singing 34 of the best songs co-written by Richard Rodgers And Lorenz Hart. The arrangements by Buddy Bregman for the string orchestra and big band only border on jazz, but she manages to swing the medium-tempo numbers and give sensitivity to the ballads. With such songs as "You Took Advantage of Me", "The Lady Is a Tramp," "It Never Entered My Mind," "Where or When" "My Funny Valentine" and "Blue Moon," it is not too surprising that these recordings (originally released on a two-LP set) were so popular. This entire program is currently available in the massive box set *The Complete Ella Fitzgerald Song Books*. —*Scott Yanow*

Sings the Duke Ellington Songbook / Sep. 4, 1956–Oct. 17, 1957 / Verve ✦✦✦✦
Volume 1 is with Ellington's orchestra, *Volume 2* is with smaller groups including Ben Webster, Stuff Smith and Oscar Peterson. Outstanding recordings, worthwhile both as documents of a fertile period for her and simply as the great music they are. —*Michael G. Nastos*

Like Someone in Love / 1957 / Verve ✦✦✦
Ella Fitzgerald was unaccompanied by an orchestra arranged by Frank DeVol on this fine studio session; the CD reissue has been augmented by four selections recorded a month later. Most of the songs are veteran standards, Stan Getz's warm tenor helps out on four tunes and, although not an essential release, her voice was so strong and appealing during this era that all of her recordings from the mid-to-late '50s are enjoyable and easily recommended. —*Scott Yanow*

Ella Fitzgerald and Jazz at the Philharmonic, 1957 / Apr. 28, 1957–Apr. 29, 1957 / Tax ✦✦
Although billed as a Jazz at the Philharmonic tour, the music on this CD from the Swedish Tax label is not as spontaneous or as exciting as one would expect from JATP. Actually the instrumentals feature a scaled-down group with trumpeter Roy Eldridge and violinist Stuff Smith joined by the Oscar Peterson Quartet (which includes guitarist Herb Ellis, bassist Ray Brown and drummer Jo Jones); best is Smith's showcase on "Bugle Call Rag." Otherwise this is strictly an Ella Fitzgerald date and, although she is in fine form on nine numbers, nothing too surprising occurs. —*Scott Yanow*

Ella & Louis Again / Aug. 13, 1957+Aug. 23, 1957 / Verve ✦✦✦
As with their first full-length meeting on records, *Ella and Louis*, this CD features Ella Fitzgerald and Louis Armstrong swinging their way through a dozen standards. Armstrong plays a bit of trumpet (best on "Stompin' at the Savoy") but the emphasis is on their vocals (which are accompanied by pianist Oscar Peterson, guitarist Herb Ellis, bassist Ray Brown and drummer Louie Bellson). The results are quite delightful and charming. —*Scott Yanow*

Porgy and Bess / Aug. 18, 1957–Oct. 15, 1957 / Verve ✦✦✦
There have been many recordings of the music from the

Gershwin opera *Porgy and Bess*, but this is one of the more rewarding ones. Louis Armstrong and Ella Fitzgerald sing all of the parts, performing 16 of the play's best melodies. Unfortunately, there is not much Armstrong trumpet to be heard, but the vocals are excellent and occasionally wonderful, making up for the unimaginative Russ Garcia arrangements assigned to the backup orchestra. —*Scott Yanow*

At the Opera House / Sep. 29, 1957+Oct. 7, 1957 / Verve ✦✦✦
Taken from a Jazz at the Philharmonic tour, Ella Fitzgerald is backed by pianist Oscar Peterson, guitarist Herb Ellis, bassist Ray Brown and drummer Jo Jones on two well-rounded sets. Actually the two dates are quite similar with eight of the ten songs being repeated (although the second "Stompin' at the Savoy" and "Lady Be Good" find her backed by a riffing eight-horn all-star group) so this reissue CD is mostly recommended to her greatest fans. However the music is wonderful, there are variations between the different versions and her voice was at its prime. —*Scott Yanow*

Sings the Irving Berlin Songbook / Mar. 13, 1958–Mar. 19, 1958 / Verve ✦✦✦
This was a great period for Ella Fitzgerald; Norman Granz was her producer and she was in great voice and projection…It was seamless great American music and well suited to Fitzgerald ambiance. This set included all the 32 titles, in the same sequence, as the original issues. There is, however, one extra track which did appear on a "Playboy" collection. —*Bob Rusch, Cadence*

Ella in Rome: The Birthday Concert / Apr. 25, 1958 / Verve ✦✦✦✦✦
This concert performance finds Ella Fitzgerald celebrating her 40th birthday. A top singer for 23 years at that point, she was at the peak of her powers. Backed by her regular rhythm section (with pianist Lou Levy, bassist Max Bennett and drummer Gus Johnson), she puts on her usual show of the period, uplifting the ballads and swinging the faster material. Highlights include "St. Louis Blues," "Caravan," "It's All Right with Me" and "I Can't Give You Anything but Love," during which she imitates both Louis Armstrong and Rose Murphy. This set concludes with a jam version of "Stompin' at the Savoy" with the Oscar Peterson Trio and drummer Gus Johnson. —*Scott Yanow*

Ella Swings Lightly / Nov. 22, 1958–Nov. 23, 1958 / Verve ✦✦✦
CD reissue featuring Ella Fitzgerald's flowing vocals and Marty Paich's Dek-tette band backing her. This was among several hit albums that Fitzgerald enjoyed in the '50s, when she was reaching the mass audience cutting pre-rock standards. —*Ron Wynn*

Ella Swings Brightly with Nelson / Jan. 5, 1959–Dec. 27, 1961 / Verve ✦✦✦✦
Nelson Riddle, whose arrangements were an asset on some of Ella Fitzgerald's *Songbook* projects, also made two albums with her during 1961: this one plus *Ella Swings Gently with Nelson*. The singer has rarely sounded better than during this period. For the *Swings Brightly* set (which gets a slight edge over the other one) Fitzgerald sticks mostly to familiar standards and is particularly memorable on "Don't Be That Way," "What Am I Here For," "I'm Gonna Go Fishin'" and "I Won't Dance." Three slightly earlier "bonus" tracks round out this enjoyable big-band effort. —*Scott Yanow*

☆ **The Complete Ella in Berlin** / Feb. 13, 1960 / Verve ✦✦✦✦✦
Ella Fitzgerald was at the peak of her form during her 1960 tour of Europe. Her Berlin concert is most remembered for her hilariously inventive version of "Mack the Knife" during which she forgot the words and substituted ones of her own that somehow fit, amazing herself in the process. In addition to the original LP program, this CD has two previously unissued titles and a pair of others only briefly released on a very rare LP. With fine support from her quartet (pianist Paul Smith, guitarist Jim Hall, bassist Wilfred Middlebrooks and drummer Gus Johnson), Fitzgerald is brilliant throughout the well-rounded set with highlights including "Misty" (a version very different from Sarah Vaughan's), "The Lady Is a Tramp," "Too Darn Hot" and a scat-filled "How High the Moon." This is essential music. —*Scott Yanow*

The Intimate Ella / Apr. 14, 1960–Apr. 19, 1960 / Verve ✦✦✦✦
This is a most unusual Ella Fitzgerald recording, reissued on CD by Verve. Recorded around the time when she performed some of these songs for the film *Let No Man Write My Epitaph*, the masterful singer is heard in duets with pianist Paul Smith interpreting 13 songs (even "I Cried for You," "I Can't Give You Anything but Love" and "Who's Sorry Now") at slow expressive tempoes.

Listeners who feel that Ella Fitzgerald was mostly a scat singer who had trouble giving the proper emotional intensity to lyrics will be surprised by this sensitive and often-haunting set. —*Scott Yanow*

Sings the Harold Arlen Songbook / Aug. 1, 1960–Jan. 16, 1961 / Verve ++++

Of all of her *Songbooks* (which are now available on the remarkable 16-CD set *The Complete Ella Fitzgerald Song Books*), the Harold Arlen and Duke Ellington sets are the most jazz-oriented. With perfectly suitable arrangements by Billy May for the big band and occasional strings, she really digs into the 26 Arlen songs, giving her own sympathetic interpretations to such classics as "Blues in the Night," "Stormy Weather," "My Shining Hour," "That Old Black Magic," "Come Rain or Come Shine" "It's Only a Paper Moon" and even "Ding-Dong! The Witch Is Dead." —*Scott Yanow*

Ella Returns to Berlin / Feb. 11, 1961 / Verve ++++

Ella Fitzgerald's Berlin concert of Feb. 13, 1960, highlighted by her ad-lib version of "Mack the Knife," is considered a classic. The performance on this CD dates from the following year and is almost as rewarding. Accompanied by pianist Lou Levy, guitarist Herb Ellis, bassist Wilfred Middlebrooks and drummer Gus Johnson, she sings 18 songs in a varied and well-paced set. Highlights include "Take the 'A' Train," "Anything Goes," "If You Can't Sing It You'll Have to Swing It," "Round Midnight," a new (but less humorous) version of "Mack the Knife" and an encore, "This Can't Be Love," that has the singer joined by the Oscar Peterson Trio. —*Scott Yanow*

Ella Swings Gently with Nelson / Nov. 13, 1961–Apr. 10, 1962 / Verve +++

In 1961 Ella Fitzgerald recorded two albums with Nelson Riddle's Orchestra. Her voice was in peak form and, even if the backup band was somewhat anonymous, Fitzgerald uplifted the 15 songs on this set; "All of Me" was from a different obscure sampler and "Call Me Darling" was previously unissued. Although the accent is on ballads, several of the songs are taken at medium tempos and she swings throughout. Highlights include "Georgia on My Mind," "The Very Thought of You," "It's a Pity to Say Goodnight," "Darn That Dream," "Body and Soul" and a cooking "All of Me." —*Scott Yanow*

Sings the Jerome Kern Songbook / Jan. 5, 1963–Jan. 7, 1963 / Verve +++

By 1963, Ella Fitzgerald's *Songbook* series had almost run its course and was becoming much less ambitious in scope. Her Jerome Kern set features her interpretations of 14 songs while backed by an orchestra arranged by Nelson Riddle. Treatments of such classics as "A Fine Romance," "All the Things You Are" and "Yesterdays" are pretty straightforward and would have pleased the composer. All of her songbooks are now included in the massive 16-CD box set *The Complete Ella Fitzgerald Song Books*. —*Scott Yanow*

These Are the Blues / Oct. 28, 1963 / Verve +++

Ella Fitzgerald was never thought of as a blues singer but she does a surprisingly effective job on the ten blues included on this CD reissue including Bessie Smith's "Jailhouse Blues," "See See Rider," "Trouble in Mind" and "St. Louis Blues." She somehow sings more or less in the style of the classic blues vocalists of the 1920s and largely pulls it off. Trumpeter Roy Eldridge, who has few solos and is low in the mix, is largely wasted as organist Wild Bill Davis (with assistance from guitarist Herb Ellis, bassist Ray Brown and drummer Gus Johnson) dominates the ensembles. It's an interesting set. —*Scott Yanow*

Sings the Johnny Mercer Songbook / Oct. 19, 1964–Oct. 21, 1964 / Verve +++

Stockholm Concert, 1966 / 1966 / Pablo Live +++

Ella Fitzgerald was teamed up with the Duke Ellington Orchestra for this spirited concert performance. Ellington himself only appears on a furious "Cottontail" (which features Fitzgerald scatting at her best), but there are some good solo spots for tenor saxophonist Paul Gonsalves, altoist Johnny Hodges and trumpeter Cootie Williams, and she is in good voice throughout this CD reissue. —*Scott Yanow*

Thirty by Ella / Jul. 1968-Aug. 1968 / Capitol +++

This LP is a weird concept that mostly works. Fitzgerald participates in six medleys consisting of five of her vocals and an instrumental with each song ranging from one to two minutes apiece.

Most of the pieces are swing standards and obviously not much development takes place, but altoist Benny Carter, trumpeter Harry "Sweets" Edison, tenor saxophonist Georgie Auld and guitarist John Collins all have some solo space. It's a historical curiosity. —*Scott Yanow*

Ella in Nice / Jul. 21, 1971 / Original Jazz Classics +++

Dream Dancing / Jun. 12, 1972+Feb. 13, 1978 / Pablo ++++

Originally released on Atlantic as *Ella Loves Cole* and then reissued on Pablo with two extra cuts from 1978, this set features the great Ella Fitzgerald (still in excellent form) backed by an orchestra arranged by Nelson Riddle performing an extensive set of Cole Porter songs. Fifteen years earlier Fitzgerald had had great success with her *Cole Porter Songbook* and this date, even with a few hokey arrangements, almost reaches the same level. Trumpeter Harry "Sweets" Edison and pianist Tommy Flanagan are among the supporting cast. Highlights include "I Get a Kick out of You," "I've Got You Under My Skin," "All of You," "My Heart Belongs to Daddy" and "Just One of Those Things." —*Scott Yanow*

Newport Jazz Festival: Live at Carnegie Hall / Jul. 5, 1973 / Columbia +++++

Ella Fitzgerald is heard in several different settings on this double LP, which pays tribute to what (at the time) had been 38 years of musical milestones. She is backed by her regular rhythm section (which is led by pianist Tommy Flanagan), on three songs she is joined by a Chick Webb alumni band and three others find her duetting with pianist Ellis Larkins. The third side of this two-fer is purely instrumental with a ballad medley featuring Flanagan, trumpeter Roy Eldridge, tenorman Eddie "Lockjaw" Davis and trombonist Al Grey along with a heated jam session version of "C Jam Blues." Finally she joins the horns for a few ballads and a combative "Lemon Drop." This enjoyable outing holds its own with most of Ella Fitzgerald's later recordings. —*Scott Yanow*

Take Love Easy / 1973 / Pablo +++

With Joe Pass (g). Nice and smooth. —*Ron Wynn*

Ella Fitzgerald Jams / Jan. 8, 1974 / Pablo +++

Although Ella Fitzgerald was a little past her prime at this point, the all-star group (which includes trumpeters Harry "Sweets" Edison and Clark Terry, the tenors of Zoot Sims and Eddie "Lockjaw" Davis, pianist Tommy Flanagan, guitarist Joe Pass, bassist Ray Brown and drummer Louie Bellson) inspire her to sing at her best for this late period. Highpoints include "I'm Just a Lucky So and So," "Rockin' in Rhythm," and "'Round Midnight." —*Scott Yanow*

★ **Ella in London** / Apr. 11, 1974 / Pablo +++++

This is one of Fitzgerald's most enjoyable recordings from her later years. With pianist Tommy Flanagan, guitarist Joe Pass, bassist Keeter Betts and drummer Bobby Durham serving as a backup group (not a bad band), she swings everything from "Sweet Georgia Brown," and "It Don't Mean a Thing" to "Lemon Drop" and even Carole King's "You've Got a Friend." Her ballad interpretations are only topped by her scatting talents. This set serves as a perfect introduction to the mature Ella Fitzgerald. —*Scott Yanow*

Ella and Oscar Peterson / May 19, 1974 / Pablo +++

At the Montreux Festival / 1975 / Original Jazz Classics ++++

This CD from the 1975 Montreux Jazz Festival has a typical late-period set from Ella Fitzgerald. Backed by the Tommy Flanagan Trio (with bassist Keter Betts and drummer Bobby Durham), she is in fine form on such songs as "Teach Me Tonight," "It's All Right with Me," "How High the Moon" and even "The Girl from Ipanema." This is a good example of Fitzgerald singing in the 1970s with some scatting, a few ballads and lots of swinging. —*Scott Yanow*

Fitzgerald and Pass . . . Again / Jan. 29, 1976–Feb. 8, 1976 / Pablo +++

The second of three duet albums by Ella Fitzgerald and guitarist Joe Pass (which has been reissued on CD) finds the duo uplifting 14 superior standards with subtle improvising and gentle swing. Highpoints include the wordless "Rain," "I Ain't Got Nothin' but the Blues," "That Old Feeling," "You Took Advantage of Me" and "The One I Love"; even "Tennessee Waltz" comes out sounding like classic swing. —*Scott Yanow*

Montreux '77 / Jul. 14, 1977 / Original Jazz Classics +++

Ella Fitzgerald, 42 years after her recording debut, showed on this late concert recording that she still had the magic. Backed by pianist Tommy Flanagan, bassist Keter Betts and drummer Bobby Durham, she sounds pretty strong at times, mostly singing veteran ballads but also getting hot on "Billie's Bounce." It's not essential but worth checking out. —*Scott Yanow*

Lady Time / Jun. 19, 1978–Jun. 20, 1978 / Original Jazz Classics ✦✦✦
This CD places Ella Fitzgerald (then 60) in an unusual setting. Joined only by organist Jackie Davis and drummer Louie Bellson, she tackles a wide variety of material that ranges from "I'm Walkin' " and "I Cried for You" to "Mack the Knife" (which did not need to be remade) and "And the Angels Sing." Not one of her more essential releases, *Lady Time* does show that even at this fairly late stage in her career, Ella Fitzgerald could outswing just about anyone. —*Scott Yanow*

A Classy Pair / Feb. 15, 1979 / Pablo ✦✦✦
This studio album matches together Ella Fitzgerald and the Count Basie Orchestra 16 years after they first recorded together. Basie's sidemen are unfortunately restricted in the Benny Carter arrangements to backup work but Basie has a few piano solos and Fitzgerald is in good voice and in typically swinging form. Highlights include "Just a Sittin' and a Rockin'," "Teach Me Tonight" and "Honeysuckle Rose." —*Scott Yanow*

Live: Digital 3 at Montreux / Jul. 12, 1979 / Pablo ✦✦✦
W/ Count Basie and Joe Pass (g). Pass takes the instrumental honors. —*Ron Wynn*

Perfect Match / Jul. 12, 1979 / Pablo ✦✦✦
Although Count Basie gets cobilling with Ella Fitzgerald on this concert recording from the 1979 Montreux Jazz Festival, the veteran pianist is only on the final of the 11 songs. His big band, along with pianist Paul Smith, backs the veteran singer for a set of standards and, although Fitzgerald was beginning to fade, she could still hint strongly at her former greatness. Highlights include "Sweet Georgia Brown," "'Round Midnight" and "Honeysuckle Rose." —*Scott Yanow*

Ella Abraca Jobim / Sep. 17, 1980–Mar. 20, 1981 / Pablo ✦✦✦
The Best Is Yet to Come / Feb. 4, 1982–Feb. 5, 1982 / Pablo ✦✦
Speak Love / Mar. 21, 1982+Mar. 22, 1982 / Pablo ✦✦✦
Nice Work If You Can Get It / May 23, 1983 / Pablo ✦✦✦
Ella Fitzgerald, who in the late '50s recorded the very extensive *George and Ira Gershwin Songbook*, revisits their music on this duet album with pianist Andre Previn. Her voice was past her prime by this point, but she was able to bring out a lot of the beauty in the ten songs, giving the classic melodies and lyrics tasteful and lightly swinging treatment. This is not an essential CD but is a reasonably enjoyable outing. —*Scott Yanow*

Easy Living / 1986 / Pablo ✦✦
For her third duo recording with guitarist Joe Pass, Ella Fitzgerald swings 15 mostly familiar standards that range from "My Ship" and "Don't Be That Way" to "Why Don't You Do Right?" and "Slow Boat to China." At 66, her voice was visibly fading, although her charm and sense of swing were still very much present. But this CD is not one of her more significant recordings other than being one of the final chapters. —*Scott Yanow*

All That Jazz / Mar. 15, 1989-Mar. 22, 1989 / Pablo ✦
Ella Fitzgerald's final recording is a bit sad. At the age of 69, she no longer had much range or power and she could only hint at her former greatness. Her sidemen (which include such veterans as trumpeters Harry "Sweets" Edison and Clark Terry, trombonist Al Grey, pianists Kenny Barron and Mike Wofford, bassist Ray Brown, drummer Bobby Durham and the apparently ageless altoist Benny Carter) do their best, but this noble effort is more important historically than musically. —*Scott Yanow*

Tommy Flanagan

b. Mar. 16, 1930, Detroit, MI
Piano / Bop, Hard Bop
Known for his flawless and tasteful playing, Tommy Flanagan received long overdue recognition for his talents in the 1980s. He played clarinet when he was six and switched to piano five years later. Flanagan was an important part of the fertile Detroit jazz scene (other than 1951-53 when he was in the Army) until he moved to New York in 1956. He was used for many recordings after his arrival during that era, cut sessions as a leader for New Jazz, Prestige, Savoy and Moodsville and worked regularly with Oscar Pettiford, J.J. Johnson (1956-58), Harry "Sweets" Edison

(1959–60) and Coleman Hawkins (1961). Flanagan was Ella Fitzgerald's regular accompanist during 1963-65 and 1968-78, which resulted in him being underrated as a soloist. However, starting in 1975 he began leading a series of superior record sessions and since leaving Ella, Flanagan has been in demand as the head of his own trio, consistently admired for his swinging and creative bop-based style. Among the many labels that he has recorded for since 1975 have been Pablo, Enja, Denon, Galaxy, Progressive, Uptown, Timeless and several European and Japanese companies. —*Scott Yanow*

The Cats, with John Coltrane and Kenny Burrell / Apr. 18, 1957 / Original Jazz Classics ✦✦✦✦
Tenor saxophonist John Coltrane was part of a April 18, 1957 blowing session along with Idrees Sulieman (trumpet), Kenny Burrell (guitar), Doug Watkins (bass), Louis Hayes (drums) and the obvious leader, though uncredited, Tommy Flanagan (piano). This set was also present on a two-fer. —*Bob Rusch, Cadence*

In Stockholm 1957 / Aug. 15, 1957 / Dragon ✦✦✦✦
Jazz . . . Its Magic / Sep. 5, 1957 / Savoy ✦✦✦
A late '50s quintet date, one of the earliest that established pianist Tommy Flanagan as a tremendous soloist and leader. He headed a superior group, with alto saxophonist Sonny Red, bassist George Tucker, trombonist Curtis Fuller and drummer Louis Hayes. It preceded by two years the sessions he cut with Coltrane that became the *Giant Steps* album and was done the same year he and Coltrane had recorded for Prestige. Although he wasn't yet as accomplished on ballads, his harmonic brilliance was already evident. —*Ron Wynn*

Tommy Flanagan Trio / May 18, 1960 / Original Jazz Classics ✦✦✦
Since this set (reissued on CD) was originally recorded for the Prestige subsidiary Moodsville, most of the selections are taken at slow tempoes. With bassist Tommy Potter and drummer Roy Haynes giving the pianist fine support, the trio cooks a bit on Flanagan's "Jes' Fine" but otherwise plays such songs as "You Go to My Head," "Come Sunday" (which is taken as a solo piano feature) and "Born to Be Blue" quietly and with taste. —*Scott Yanow*

The Tokyo Recital / Feb. 15, 1975 / Original Jazz Classics ✦✦✦✦
An album of tunes by Duke Ellington and Billy Strayhorn, it was recorded during a time when Flanagan was accompanist for Ella Fitzgerald, some three years before he went out on his own. —*AMG*

Trinity / Oct. 1975–Nov. 1975 / Inner City ✦✦✦
Only Tommy Flanagan's second album as a leader in 15 years, this little-known date (a trio session with bassist Ron Carter and drummer Roy Haynes) was recorded at a period when the pianist was suffering from the anonymity (if gaining financial security) of backing singer Ella Fitzgerald. All but four of the nine selections are quite obscure, but the music is accessible and consistently swinging. This out-of-print LP is worth picking up if it can be found. —*Scott Yanow*

Montreux 1977 / Jul. 13, 1977 / Original Jazz Classics ✦✦✦✦
This Pablo recording was cut at a time when pianist Tommy Flanagan, due to his long stint with Ella Fitzgerald's backup band, was almost forgotten. The fine trio outing (with bassist Keter Betts and drummer Bobby Durham) has been reissued on CD in the *Original Jazz Classics* series with one track ("Heat Wave") added to the original program. The two ballad medleys are enjoyable but it is on "Barbados," "Woody 'n You" and "Blue Bossa" that Flanagan shows how hard-swinging a pianist he can be. Happily, his solo career really started to take off a few years after this concert appearance. —*Scott Yanow*

Alone Too Long / Dec. 8, 1977 / Denon ✦✦✦✦
Wonderful solo piano. —*Ron Wynn*

More Delights with Hank Jones / Jan. 28, 1978 / Galaxy ✦✦✦✦
This set is a companion piece to the originally released *Our Delights*. Once again, Tommy Flanagan and Hank Jones, two highly compatible pianists, are heard on a set of duos. Six of these performances are actually alternate takes to the songs included on the first album. These "new" performances (plus duo versions of " 'Round Midnight" and "If You Could See Me Now") are as tasteful and as easily enjoyable as the "older" ones. —*Scott Yanow*

Our Delights / Jan. 28, 1978 / Original Jazz Classics ✦✦✦✦
Piano duets have the potential danger of getting overcrowded and a bit incoherent, but neither happens on this rather delightful set.

Hank Jones and Tommy Flanagan, two of the four great jazz pianists (along with Barry Harris and Roland Hanna) to emerge from Detroit in the '40s and '50s, have similar styles and their mutual respect is obvious. Their renditions of seven superior bop standards (including "Robbins Nest," "Confirmation" and Thad Jones' "A Child Is Born") are tasteful, consistently swinging and inventive within the tradition. —*Scott Yanow*

Something Borrowed, Something Blue / Jan. 30, 1978 / Galaxy ◆◆◆

Plays Music of Harold Arlen / Sep. 30, 1978–Oct. 2, 1978 / Inner City ◆◆◆
A great pianist's wonderful tribute to a great songwriter. —*Ron Wynn*

Ballads and Blues / Nov. 15, 1978 / Enja ◆◆◆
Includes fine duets with George Mraz (b). —*Ron Wynn*

Together with Kenny Barron / Dec. 6, 1978 / Denon ◆◆◆
A fine, well-produced album by two piano masters. —*Michael G. Nastos*

Super-Session / Feb. 4, 1980 / Enja ◆◆◆

You're Me / Feb. 24, 1980 / Phontastic ◆◆◆
A dose of blues and funk with bassist Red Mitchell. —*Ron Wynn*

The Magnificent Tommy Flanagan / Jul. 2, 1981+Jul. 3, 1981 / Progressive ◆◆◆◆
The title of this set is not an overstatement. Tommy Flanagan has long been one of the top bop-based jazz pianists and, although he was somewhat neglected during his stints with Ella Fitzgerald's group, he has been a steady poll-winner since finally going out on his own. This trio session with bassist George Mraz and drummer Al Foster (featuring seven standards and Thad Jones' "Blueish Grey") is as tasteful and consistently swinging as one would expect from players of this caliber. —*Scott Yanow*

Giant Steps / Feb. 17, 1982+Feb. 18, 1982 / Enja ◆◆◆◆◆
Pianist Tommy Flanagan's playing seems to be more direct, edited and stronger as he gets older; certainly his reemergence in the mid-'70s as a solo artist produced his strongest work. *Giant Steps*, was a Feb. '82 tribute to John Coltrane with super backing from bassist George Mraz and drummer Al Foster…This set was particularly inventive; it was Coltrane's music, but it drinks of its own spirit. You won't listen for the familiar Trane solos, but you will listen! —*Bob Rusch, Cadence*

● **Thelonica** / Nov. 30, 1982–Dec. 1, 1982 / Enja ◆◆◆◆◆
Recorded just ten months after Thelonious Monk's death, pianist Tommy Flanagan's tribute features eight of Monk's compositions plus Flanagan's own "Thelonica." Assisted by bassist George Mraz and drummer Art Taylor, Flanagan does not sound at all like Monk but he recaptures his spirit and hints strongly now and then at his style on this fine (and often introspective) outing. —*Scott Yanow*

Nights At The Vanguard / Oct. 18, 1986–Oct. 19, 1986 / Uptown ◆◆◆◆
Pianist Tommy Flanagan (in a trio with bassist George Mraz and drummer Al Foster) mostly sticks to lesser-known material (with a few exceptions such as "More than You Know" and "All God's Children") on this enjoyable live date. Flanagan was very much in his prime during the period, revitalizing the bop and hard bop traditions. Highlights include Phil Woods' "Goodbye Mr. Evans," Benny Golson's "Out of the Past," "A Biddy Ditty" and "I'll Keep Loving You." A good example of the fine pianist's talents —*Scott Yanow*

Jazz Poet / Jan. 17, 1989–Jan. 19, 1989 / Timeless ◆◆◆◆◆

☆ **Beyond the Bluebird** / Apr. 29, 1990+Apr. 30, 1990 / Timeless ◆◆◆◆◆
Veteran pianist Tommy Flanagan, in a quartet with guitarist Kenny Burrell, bassist George Mraz and drummer Lewis Nash, performs blues, ballads and some obscurities during one of his most rewarding recordings. Flanagan has never recorded an indifferent album, but this set seems more inspired than most, making it a perfect introduction to this tasteful, swinging and creative (within the bop mainstream) pianist. —*Scott Yanow*

Let's Play the Music of Thad Jones / Apr. 4, 1993 / Enja ◆◆◆◆◆
This relatively little-known trio set by pianist Tommy Flanagan (with bassist Jesper Lundgaard and drummer Lewis Nash) is a minor classic. Flanagan performs 11 of cornetist Thad Jones' compositions, the majority of which had never been played by a piano

trio before. Easily the best-known selection is "A Child Is Born" with "Mean What You Say," "Three in One" and "Quietude" being the closest of the other songs to being standards. But, despite their relative obscurity, this body of work is quite diverse and flexible enough to be covered by other jazz musicians. Congratulations are due Tommy Flanagan for putting together a consistently swinging and tasteful salute to Thad Jones, a very talented composer. —*Scott Yanow*

Lady Be Good . . . For Ella / Jul. 30, 1993–Jul. 31, 1993 / Verve ◆◆◆◆◆

Bela Fleck
b. 1958, New York, NY
Banjo, Leader / Fusion, Post-Bop, Bluegrass
Bela Fleck, as leader of the Flecktones, has certainly carved out his own place in the music world. Virtually the only banjoist playing modern music (which includes fusion, advanced jazz and bluegrass all mixed together), Fleck began playing banjo when he was 15. In 1978 he moved to Boston to play with the Tasty Licks and in 1979 he recorded his first solo album, *Crossing the Tracks*. During the next few years he co-founded the group Spectrum and played with the New Grass Revival, recording frequently. Then, in 1989, Fleck moved away from bluegrass and new acoustic music into jazz with the formation of the Flecktones, which has thus far recorded four sets for Warner Bros. Originally the often-humorous group was a quartet with Howard Levy on harmonica and piano, but Levy's decision to go out on his own made the band a trio with Fleck's powerful banjo interacting with bassist Victor Wooten and the electronic percussion of Roy "Future Man" Wooten. —*Scott Yanow*

Crossing the Tracks / 1979 / Rounder ◆◆◆

Double Time / 1984 / Rounder ◆◆◆

Inroads / 1986 / Rounder ◆◆◆

Bela Fleck & The Flecktones / 1990 / Warner Brothers ◆◆◆◆◆
After disbanding New Grass Revival, Bela Fleck began re-creating the role of the banjo in the same way Charlie Parker redefined the role of the saxophone. But Fleck may be the least-innovative member of this quartet: Howard Levy gets chromatics from his blues harp, Victor Wooten picks banjo rolls on his bass, and Roy "Future Man" plays a Frankenstein-monster drum-machine/guitar synthesizer. For all the flash, there's little pretense: the group's astonishing musicianship keeps an "aw-shucks" accessibility that lets everybody follow the melody while they marvel. —*Brian Mansfield*

★ **Flight of the Cosmic Hippo** / 1991 / Warner Brothers ◆◆◆◆◆
The Flecktones owe more to bebop than bluegrass, and here the group finally names its style "blu-bop." That's why *Cosmic Hippo* topped the jazz, not the country, chart. The Flecktones continue to make it look easy, adding banjo power chords to "Turtle Rock" and reworking Lennon/McCartney's "Michelle." —*Brian Mansfield*

UFO Tofu / 1992 / Warner Brothers ◆◆◆

Three Flew over the Cuckoo's Nest / 1993 / Warner Brothers ◆◆◆

Tales From The Acoustic Planet / 1994 / Warner Brothers ◆◆◆◆

Bob Florence
b. May 20, 1932, Los Angeles, CA
Piano, Arranger, Composer, Leader / Post-Bop
A top arranger influenced by Bill Holman, Bob Florence regularly leads a big band in the Los Angeles area. He worked as a pianist and arranger for Si Zentner's band during 1959-64; his chart on "Up a Lazy River" was a hit in 1960. Florence has worked extensively in the studios and in commercial music (he is the long-time musical director for Julie Andrews) and played with the 1980s version of the Dave Pell Octet, but has also led his own orchestra off and on since 1958. That year he recorded an obscure trio date and a couple of big-band albums. His orchestra backed Big Miller in 1961 and there were recordings in 1965 and 1968, but Florence hit his stride in 1979 with a big-band album. Since then he has recorded fairly regularly for Trend/Discovery, Bosco, USA and most recently the MAMA Foundation. Florence's arrangements are among the most colorful (and challenging) in jazz. —*Scott Yanow*

Here and Now / 1965 / Liberty ✦✦✦

Live at Concerts by the Sea / Jun. 15, 1979–Jun. 18, 1979 / Trend ✦✦✦✦✦

Westlake / Mar. 3, 1981 / Discovery ✦✦✦✦

Soaring / Oct. 1982 / Bosco ✦✦✦✦

Magic Time / Nov. 29, 1983+Nov. 30, 1983 / Trend ✦✦✦✦

Trash Can City / Nov. 24, 1986–Nov. 25, 1986 / Trend ✦✦✦✦

State of the Art / 1988 / USA Music Group ✦✦✦✦✦
Bob Florence Limited Edition. Five standards, four Florence originals. —*Michael G. Nastos*

Treasure Chest / 1990 / USA Music Group ✦✦✦✦

Funupsmanship / 1993 / MAMA Foundation ✦✦✦✦✦
Bob Florence has long been one of the most stimulating arrangers in jazz and this live set from his big band features some of his most interesting charts. With such soloists as trumpeters Steve Huffsteter and Warren Luening, trombonists Alex Iles, Charlie Loper and Rick Culver, altoist Lanny Morgan and the reeds of Kim Richmond, Don Shelton and Bob Efford (along with the pianist/leader), Florence's dense and often-witty ensembles alternate with fine improvisations. Highlights of this consistently exciting set include "Slimehouse" (based on "Limehouse Blues"), "Funupsmanship," "Lester Left Town" and "All Blues." —*Scott Yanow*

★ **With All The Bells And Whistles** / Feb. 20, 1995–Feb. 21, 1995 / MAMA Foundation ✦✦✦✦✦
Arranger/pianist Bob Florence's release for the MAMA Foundation may very well be his finest; it certainly offers a strong sampling of his talents. Four of the ten songs are standards and "Oceanography" is based closely on "How Deep Is the Ocean," but Florence's complex yet logical arrangements make each piece sound like it was written for the band. To name a few examples, "In a Mellow Tone" appears to be in two keys at once at times, "Laura" (normally an emotional ballad) really cooks and "Teach Me Tonight" is so intense as to be purposely humorous in spots. Among the other highlights of this well-conceived release are Don Shelton's clarinet feature on "Shimmer," the competitive interplay between Dick Mitchell and Terry Harrington throughout "Tenors, Anyone?" and the fluency of trombonist Bob McChesney on "In a Mellow Tone." The ensembles are consistently clean, exciting and remarkably relaxed considering how tricky some of the charts must be. This CD offers modern big-band jazz at its best. —*Scott Yanow*

Chris Flory

Guitar / Swing
An excellent swing-based guitarist, Chris Flory first worked professionally in Providence, Rhode Island in 1974. A long-time associate of Scott Hamilton (who he first played with in 1976), Flory has also worked with Benny Goodman (1979–85), Roy Eldridge, Illinois Jacquet, Bob Wilber, Buddy Tate and Ruby Braff among others, and he toured China in 1992 with Judy Carmichael. He has appeared on many Concord records, leading two sessions of his own and playing regularly with Hamilton. —*Scott Yanow*

For All We Know / Jan. 1988 / Concord Jazz ✦✦✦✦

● **City Life** / Mar. 18, 1993–Mar. 19, 1993 / Concord ✦✦✦✦✦
Chris Flory, a talented swing-based guitarist, tackles standards, Latin tunes and a few hot jam-session numbers on his second Concord CD with a solid quartet that also features pianist John Bunch, bassist John Webber and drummer Chuck Riggs. Highlights include an enjoyable "So Danco Samba," the uptempo blues "Drafting," "Besame Mucho," "S'Posin' " and a spirited rendition of "My Shining Hour." This swinging session is consistent with the high-quality music to be found throughout Concord's impressive catalog. —*Scott Yanow*

Carl Fontana

b. Monroe, LA
Trombone / Bop
A brilliant trombonist who has spent much of the past 40 years playing commercial music in Las Vegas, Carl Fontana occasionally emerges to remind listeners just how technically skilled he is. The son of a saxophonist, Fontana started out playing in his father's group during 1941–45, but did not gain prominence until he was with Woody Herman's Orchestra (1952–53). Fontana spent time in the big bands of Lionel Hampton (1954), Hal McIntyre

(1954–55) and most importantly Stan Kenton (1955–56), with whom he was well-featured. After playing in Kai Winding's four-trombone band (1956–57), Fontana moved to Las Vegas but he has emerged on an occasional basis, touring with Woody Herman in 1966, recording with Supersax (1973), co-leading a group with Jake Hanna (1975), playing with the World's Greatest Jazz Band and appearing at jazz parties. In 1995 Carl Fontana recorded a fine album with Bobby Shew. —*Scott Yanow*

● **The Great Fontana** / Sep. 5, 1985–Sep. 6, 1985 / Uptown ✦✦✦✦✦

Ricky Ford

b. Mar. 4, 1954, Boston, MA
Tenor Saxophone / Hard Bop, Post-Bop
An excellent veteran tenor inspired by Dexter Gordon and Sonny Rollins, Ricky Ford was playing creative hard bop several years before Wynton Marsalis and his talent has been often overlooked. After studying at the New England Conservatory, he recorded in 1974 with Gunther Schuller. After touring with the Duke Ellington Orchestra (under Mercer Ellington's leadership during 1974–76), Ford was with Charles Mingus (1976–77), Dannie Richmond's Quintet (1978–81), Lionel Hampton and Mingus Dynasty (1982); he also played in 1985 with Abdullah Ibrahim. Ricky Ford has recorded as a leader for New World, an excellent string of dates for Muse (1978–89) and more recently for Candid. —*Scott Yanow*

Loxodonta Africana / Jun. 1977 / New World ✦✦✦
Tenor saxophonist Ricky Ford's debut album, done in 1977 as he was just attaining a reputation and name outside the New England area. He spent the previous year working with Charles Mingus and helping him transcibe music. The impact was obvious; these are all Ford compositions, and they display pointed Mingus tendencies in the arrangements and structure. —*Ron Wynn*

Manhattan Plaza / Aug. 1, 1978 / Muse ✦✦✦

Flying Colors / Apr. 24, 1980 / Muse ✦✦✦✦
Although often overlooked (his music is beyond bop but not really in the avant-garde and certainly not in the fusion genre), Ricky Ford was one of the top tenors to emerge during the '70s and early '80s. This Muse set finds him matched with a top-notch rhythm section (pianist John Hicks, bassist Walter Booker and drummer Jimmy Cobb) for "Take the Coltrane," Thelonious Monk's "ByeYa," Billy Strayhorn's "Chelsea Bridge" and four of Ford's originals, including the mournful "Portrait of Mingus." It was a fine showcase for the up-and-coming tenor. —*Scott Yanow*

Tenor for the Times / Apr. 6, 1981+Jul. 1, 1981 / Muse ✦✦✦✦✦
Ricky Ford, a fine tenor saxophonist whose main influences have been Sonny Rollins and Dexter Gordon (although he has his own sound), is in excellent form throughout this quartet date. Accompanied and inspired by pianist Albert Dailey, bassist Rufus Reid, drummer Jimmy Cobb and, on one song, trumpeter Jack Walrath, Ford investigates seven of his diverse originals, really digging into the material. It's a good introduction to his talents. —*Scott Yanow*

Interpretations / Feb. 22, 1982 / Muse ✦✦✦✦
Brilliant lineup, aggressive hard-bop/mainstream format. —*Ron Wynn*

Future's Gold / Feb. 9, 1983 / Muse ✦✦✦✦
What makes this outing by tenor saxophonist Ricky Ford a bit different than his previous ones is that in addition to the fine trio (pianist Albert Dailey, bassist Ray Drummond and drummer Jimmy Cobb), Larry Coryell is an important voice on the record, playing electric guitar on the first four songs and acoustic 12-string guitar on the remaining four tunes. Ford, a vastly underrated but talented tenorman, contributes six originals (including "Centenarian Waltz" for the 100-year-old Eubie Blake) and does a fine job of interpreting "Goodbye, Pork Pie Hat" by former boss Charles Mingus and the standard "You Don't Know What Love Is." An excellent record, it is recommended both for the contributions of Ford and the surprisingly versatile Coryell. —*Scott Yanow*

★ **Shorter Ideas** / Aug. 28, 1984 / Muse ✦✦✦✦✦
An inspired idea that works, Ford, who has usually recorded with small groups, here heads an all-star sextet with altoist James Spaulding and trombonist Jimmy Knepper. They perform four Wayne Shorter numbers, a couple of Ford's originals and Duke Ellington's "Happy Reunion." Ford takes the lion's share of the solo space and is clearly up to the task, making these sometimes-com-

plex compositions seem accessible and logical. Ford has long been underrated (too old to be a Young Lion and too young to be an elder statesman) but, based on the evidence of this recording alone, he clearly deserves much greater acclaim. —*Scott Yanow*

Looking Ahead / Feb. 14, 1986–Oct. 9, 1986 / Muse ✦✦✦✦
An outstanding session, with a first-rate supporting cast. —*Ron Wynn*

Saxotic Stomp / Sep. 4, 1987 / Muse ✦✦✦✦

Hard Groovin' / Feb. 24, 1989 / Muse ✦✦✦✦
The consistent tenor saxophonist Ricky Ford, who was often the youngest player on the bandstand when he first emerged in the late '70s, is easily the oldest musician on this energetic modern bop album. Trumpeter Roy Hargrove, pianist Geoff Keezer, bassist Bob Hurst and drummer Jeff "Tain" Watts are among the main Young Lions of the late '80s and '90s, but Ford (heard on both alto and tenor) is easily the most impressive solo voice on this high-quality outing. Ford and his quintet perform five of his originals, a Geoff Keezer song and the standards "Jitterbug Waltz" and "Minority" with driving swing and personable creativity. —*Scott Yanow*

Manhattan Blues / Mar. 4, 1989 / Candid ✦✦✦✦✦

Ebony Rhapsody / Jun. 2, 1990 / Candid ✦✦✦✦
A high-level date with Jaki Byard immense on piano. —*Ron Wynn*

Hot Brass / Apr. 30, 1991 / Candid ✦✦✦✦✦
Nice session matching tenor saxophone standout Ricky Ford with crew of fiery trumpet and trombone players, plus bassist Christian McBride, drummer Carl Allen and percussionist Danilo Perez. Ford was a young lion back in the '70s, when there was no hype. He's now an experienced, skilled veteran and teams superbly with trumpeters Lew Soloff and Claudio Roditi and trombonist Steve Turre. —*Ron Wynn*

American-African Blues / Sep. 1, 1991 / Candid ✦✦✦✦

Tenor Madness Too / Aug. 12, 1992 / Muse ✦✦✦

Robben Ford

b. Dec. 16, 1951, Ukiah, CA
Guitar / Blues, Fusion, Crossover
Robben Ford has had a diverse career. He taught himself guitar when he was 13 and considered his first influence to be Mike Bloomfield. At 18 he moved to San Francisco to form the Charles Ford Band (named after his father who was also a guitarist) and was soon hired to play with Charles Musselwhite for nine months. In 1971 the Charles Ford Blues Band was re-formed and recorded for Arhoolie in early 1972. Ford played with Jimmy Witherspoon (1972–73), the L.A. Express with Tom Scott (1974), George Harrison and Joni Mitchell. In 1977 he was a founding member of the Yellowjackets, which he stayed with until 1983, simultaneously having a solo career and working as a session guitarist. In 1986 Ford toured with Miles Davis and he had two separate periods (1985 and 1987) with Sadao Watanabe, but he seemed to really find himself in 1992 when he returned to his roots, the blues. Robben Ford formed a new group, the Blue Line, and has since recorded a couple of blues-rock dates for Stretch that are among the finest of his career. —*Scott Yanow*

Talk to Your Daughter / 1988 / Warner Brothers ✦✦✦
Efficient, sometimes electrifying playing but detached, uneven material. —*Ron Wynn*

Robben Ford & The Blue Line / 1992 / Stretch ✦✦✦
An effective combination of fusion and mainstream players unite for a session that alternates between light, pleasant instrumentals and more challenging numbers. Ford's guitar solos try to balance things and sometimes get a bit bland, then loosen up whenever the songs are more involved. The lineup includes outstanding drummer Marvin Smith. —*Ron Wynn*

Mystic Mile / 1993 / Stretch ✦✦✦✦

● **Handful of Blues** / 1994 / Blue Thumb ✦✦✦✦
On *Handful of Blues*, Robben Ford strips his sound back to the basics, recording a set of blues with only a bassist and a drummer. The group runs through a handful of standards, including "Don't Let Me Be Misunderstood" and "I Just Want to Make Love to You," and a number of made-to-order originals. Throughout the album, the musicians play well, but Ford's voice is never commanding. However, this is a minor flaw, since his guitar speaks for itself. —*Stephen Thomas Erlewine*

Music Map

Flute

Pioneer
Albert Soccarras
(with Clarence Williams as early as 1927)

Swing Era
Wayman Carver (with Chick Webb and his Little Chicks)

1950s Cool Bop
Frank Wess (with Count Basie)
Sam Most • Bud Shank • Buddy Collette
Paul Horn • Jerome Richardson • James Moody
Moe Koffman (1957 hit "Swinging Shepherd Blues")
Les Spann • Sahib Shihab • Bobby Jaspar

Post Bop
Jim Walker

1960s Innovators
Eric Dolphy • Yusef Lateef • Rahsaan Roland Kirk

Popularizers of Flute
Herbie Mann • Hubert Laws

Avant-Garde
Sam Rivers	Prince Lasha
Byard Lancaster	Dave Liebman
Henry Threadgill	

Crossover
Jeremy Steig • Dave Valentin • Gerry Niewood

Other Important Flutists
Charles Lloyd	James Spaulding
Lew Tabackin	Ira Sullivan
Holly Hoffman	Kent Jordan
Jane Bunnett	

Recent Innovator
James Newton

Bruce Forman

b. 1956, Springfield, MA
Guitar / Bop
An exciting bop-oriented guitarist who is a fixture at the Monterey Jazz Festival, Bruce Forman moved to San Francisco in 1971. He has mostly headed his own groups in the Bay Area, but played and toured with Richie Cole during 1978–82. Forman has led his own dates for Muse, Concord and Kamei. —*Scott Yanow*

Coast to Coast / Oct. 19, 1978 / Choice ✦✦✦

River Journey / Mar. 10, 1981 / Muse ✦✦✦
An upbeat album from the early '80s by guitarist Bruce Forman, playing with a group that includes torrid alto saxophonist Richie Cole. His fluid, bluesy solos on fast, mid-tempo and slow numbers injects some spark into the date and also makes Forman extend himself. —*Ron Wynn*

20/20 / Sep. 1, 1981 / Muse ✦✦✦

In Transit / Jun. 9, 1982 / Muse ✦✦✦✦
Good trio set, with Forman getting enough room to display his complete technique, with huge tone, good use of overtones and fine solo style. He's backed by Ed Kelly and Eddie Marshall, and the three mesh smoothly. —*Ron Wynn*

The Bash / Nov. 2, 1982 / Muse ✦✦✦✦
Good mid-'80s date by guitarist Bruce Forman, with pianist Albert Dailey, bassist Buster Williams and drummer Eddie Gladden. Forman, a mainstream stylist solidly in the Jim Hall/Herb Ellis/Joe Pass school, plays with a precise, delicate mastery. —*Ron Wynn*

Full Circle / May 1984 / Concord Jazz ✦✦✦✦✦
A good mid-'80s date with a tremendous lineup that includes Bobby Hutcherson and George Cables. —*Ron Wynn*

Dynamics with George Cables / Feb. 1985 / Concord Jazz ✦✦✦
W/ George Cables. This is Forman's best all-round album: good material and outstanding playing. —*Ron Wynn*

There Are Times / Aug. 1986 / Concord Jazz ✦✦✦

Pardon Me! / Oct. 1988 / Concord Jazz ✦✦✦✦✦

Still of the Night / 1991 / Kamei ✦✦✦✦

★ **Forman on the Job** / 1992 / Kamel ✦✦✦✦✦
Recent album by guitarist Bruce Forman with his current band. He's moved more toward swing, although he also includes some Caribbean flavor on some cuts with guest Andy Narrell on steel drums. Forman uses alternating personnel and gets great contributions from pianist Mark Levine and saxophonist Joe Henderson, among others. —*Ron Wynn*

Mitchell Forman
b. Jan., 1956, Brooklyn, NY
Keyboards / Fusion, Post-Bop
Mitchel Forman has had a continually surprising career. After graduating from the Manhattan School of Music (1978), he recorded three solo acoustic piano albums for the Japanese New Wave and Soul Note labels and worked with Stan Getz, Gerry Mulligan, Carla Bley and Mel Tormé. However, he made his strongest impression on electric keyboards, playing with the reformed Mahavishnu Orchestra, Wayne Shorter and recording for Magenta (1985) and Novus (1991). Forman surprised many by performing a very effective Bill Evans tribute for Novus (1992) with an acoustic trio, but then went back to playing modern fusion on *Lipstick* (1993). Talented on both acoustic and electric keyboards, Mitchel Forman's future progress should be well worth watching! —*Scott Yanow*

Childhood Dreams / Feb. 6, 1982-Feb. 7, 1982 / Soul Note ✦✦✦

Only a Memory / Aug. 2, 1982-Aug. 3, 1982 / Soul Note ✦✦✦

Train of Thought / 1985 / Magenta ✦✦✦✦

● **Now & Then: a Tribute to Bill Evans** / Dec. 8, 1992-Dec. 10, 1992 / Novus ✦✦✦✦✦
Mitchel Forman, who usually plays electric keyboards in more "contemporary" settings, sticks to acoustic piano during his heartfelt tribute to Bill Evans. Forman performs eight songs associated with the late pianist along with two of his originals. At times the pianist's style comes remarkably close to his idol, and it helps that his trio has two of Evans' most famous sidemen (bassist Eddie Gomez and drummer Jack DeJohnette) helping out. The music is tasteful and swinging and Forman's title cut is strong enough to possibly become a standard itself in the future. —*Scott Yanow*

Handmade / 1993 / Lipstick ✦✦✦

Michael Formanek
b. May 7, 1958, San Francisco, CA
Bass / Avant-Garde, Post-Bop
An excellent bassist who has emerged as a talented bandleader, Michael Formanek has had a versatile career. He started off playing professionally in 1974 with saxophonist Norman Williams in

San Francisco and then, during the next few years, worked with Eddie Henderson, Joe Henderson, Tony Williams and Dave Liebman among others. After moving to New York in 1978, Formanek was a sideman with Tom Harrell, Herbie Mann and Chet Baker. During much of 1980, he performed with the Media Band in West Germany and then, in 1982, he joined the quintet Gallery. Formanek has since led sessions for Enja and Soul Note that feature such stimulating sidemen as Greg Osby, Mark Feldman, Tim Berne, Dave Douglas and Marty Ehrlich. —*Scott Yanow*

★ **Wide Open Spaces** / Jan. 25, 1990-Jan. 26, 1990 / Enja ✦✦✦✦✦

Extended Animation / Nov. 21, 1991-Nov. 23, 1991 / Enja ✦✦✦✦
Bassist Michael Formanek's second album continues the pattern established on his debut. He features mostly originals and keeps things moving with varied rhythms and arrangements that don't emphasize any particular style. He's assisted by guitarist Wayne Krantz, violinist Mark Feldman and drummer Jeff Hirschfield. —*Ron Wynn*

Loose Cannon / Oct. 26, 1992-Oct. 28, 1992 / Soul Note ✦✦✦✦✦

Jimmy Forrest
b. Jan. 24, 1920, St. Louis, MO, d. Aug. 26, 1980, Grand Rapids, MI
Tenor Saxophone / Swing, Early R&B
A fine all-round tenor player, Jimmy Forrest is best-known for recording "Night Train," a song that he "borrowed" from the last part of Duke Ellington's "Happy Go Lucky Local." While in high school in St. Louis, Forrest worked with pianist Eddie Johnson, the legendary Fate Marable and the Jeter-Pillars Orchestra. In 1938 he went on the road with Don Albert and then was with Jay McShann's Orchestra (1940-42). In New York Forrest played with Andy Kirk (1942-48) and Duke Ellington (1949) before returning to St. Louis. After recording "Night Train," Forrest became a popular attraction and recorded a series of jazz-oriented R&B singles. Among his most important later associations were with Harry "Sweets" Edison (1958-63), Count Basie's Orchestra (1972-77) and Al Grey with whom he co-led a quintet until his death. Forrest recorded for United (reissued by Delmark), Prestige/New Jazz (1960-62) and Palo Alto (1978). —*Scott Yanow*

★ **Night Train** / Nov. 27, 1951-Sep. 7, 1953 / Delmark ✦✦✦✦✦
This is tremendous early-'50s material from Forrest's days on the pioneering United label. The title cut was a huge jukebox and R&B hit. —*Ron Wynn*

All the Gin Is Gone / Dec. 10, 1959-Dec. 12, 1959 / Delmark ✦✦✦✦
Straight bop. Grant Green's (g) first recording session (in Chicago)—he was flown in from St. Louis by Forrest. W/ Harold Mabern (p), Elvin Jones (d). —*Michael Erlewine*

Black Forrest / Dec. 10, 1959-Dec. 12, 1959 / Delmark ✦✦✦
Bop. From the same session as *All the Gin Is Gone*. Includes the lovely "But Beautiful," featuring Grant Green (g), with Forrest sitting this tune out. Recorded in Chicago. —*Michael Erlewine*

Forrest Fire / Aug. 9, 1960 / Original Jazz Classics ✦✦✦✦
An exceptional date, with some instructive early Larry Young (organ) solos. —*Ron Wynn*

Out of the Forrest / Apr. 18, 1961 / Original Jazz Classics ✦✦✦✦
With Joe Zawinul (piano), Tommy Potter (bass) and Clarence Johnston (drums) backing Jimmy Forrest on eight tracks. An honest and rewarding big tenor date with a touch of Lester Young… This was excellent smokey soulful tenor playing, which I think has probably been overlooked by many. —*Bob Rusch, Cadence*

Heart of the Forrest / Mar. 1983 / Palo Alto ✦✦✦

Sonny Fortune (Cornelius Fortune)
b. May 19, 1939, Philadelphia, PA
Flute, Tenor Saxophone, Alto Saxophone / Post-Bop
Sonny Fortune has continued to grow with time and in the mid-'90s he is in prime form. Fortune started his career playing in R&B groups in Philadelphia. He moved to New York in 1967 where he worked with Elvin Jones, Mongo Santamaria (1967-70) and McCoy Tyner (1971-73 and occasionally since). After a stint with Buddy Rich, Fortune played quite effectively with Miles Davis (1974-75). His solo albums during the 1970s for Horizon and Atlantic were generally unsuccesful mixtures of advanced jazz with funk and pop elements. However, he has cut excellent

dates for Konnex (1984, 1991 and 1993) including a well-received Monk set, and Fortune has toured in recent times with Nat Adderley and (on tenor, an instrument he should play more often) with Elvin Jones' Jazz Machine. —*Scott Yanow*

Long Before Our Mothers Cried / Sep. 8, 1974+Sep. 15, 1974 / Strata East ✦✦✦
A large-ensemble recording. A fully realized creative album and very listenable as well. With Charles Sullivan (tpt) and Stanley Cowell (p). —*Michael G. Nastos*

Awakening / Aug. 28, 1975–Sep. 9, 1975 / Horizon ✦✦

Waves of Dreams / Mar. 22, 1976+Mar. 23, 1976 / Horizon ✦✦

Serengeti Minstrel / Apr. 6, 1977–Apr. 8, 1977 / Atlantic ✦✦✦
Studio date from this virile Philadelphia saxophonist/flutist, who tackles the Coltrane legacy in fine fashion with Woody Shaw (tpt) and Kenny Barron (p). —*Michael G. Nastos*

Infinity Is / 1978 / Atlantic ✦✦✦

It Ain't What It Was / Dec. 1991 / Konnex ✦✦✦✦

★ **Four In One** / Jan. 25, 1993–Jan. 26, 1993 / Blue Note ✦✦✦✦✦

A Better Understanding / Feb. 19, 1995 / Blue Note ✦✦✦✦✦

Frank Foster

b. Sep. 23, 1928, Cincinnati, OH
Tenor Saxophone / Swing, Hard Bop
A very talented tenor saxophonist and arranger, Frank Foster has been associated with the Count Basie Orchestra off and on since 1953. Early on he played in Detroit with the many talented local players and, after a period in the Army (1951–53), he joined Basie's big band. Well-featured on tenor during his Basie years (1953–64), Foster also contributed plenty of arrangements and such originals as "Down for the Count," "Blues Backstage" and the standard "Shiny Stockings." In the latter half of the 1960s, Foster was a freelance writer. In addition to playing with Elvin Jones (1970–72) and occasionally with the Thad Jones-Mel Lewis Orchestra, he led his Loud Minority big band. In 1983 Foster co-led a quintet with Frank Wess and he toured Europe with Jimmy Smith in 1985. Although influenced by John Coltrane in his playing, Foster was able to modify his style when he took over the Count Basie ghost band in 1986, revitalizing it and staying at the helm until 1995. Outside of his Basie dates, Foster has led sessions for Vogue, Blue Note (1954 and 1968), Savoy, Argo, Prestige, Mainstream, Denon, Catalyst, Bee Hive, SteepleChase, Pablo and Concord. —*Scott Yanow*

Two Franks Please! / Mar. 5, 1956–Oct. 13, 1957 / Savoy ✦✦✦✦
High-quality hard-bop set with trumpeter Donald Byrd. —*Ron Wynn*

Here and Now / Jun. 1976 / Catalyst ✦✦✦

Roots, Branches and Dances / Dec. 7, 1978 / Bee Hive ✦✦✦
Wonderful arrangements, slashing playing. —*Ron Wynn*

The House That Love Built / Sep. 10, 1982 / SteepleChase ✦✦✦✦

Two for the Blues / Oct. 11, 1983+Oct. 12, 1983 / Original Jazz Classics ✦✦✦✦✦

● **Frankly Speaking** / Dec. 1984 / Concord Jazz ✦✦✦✦✦
One of Foster's many sparkling collaborations with his longtime friend, fellow Basie bandmate Frank Wess. Outstanding rhythm section as well. —*Ron Wynn*

Pops Foster

b. May 18, 1892, McCall, LA, **d.** Oct. 30, 1969, San Francisco, CA
Bass / Classic Jazz, New Orleans Jazz
One of the first important bassists (along with Steve Brown, Bill Johnson and Wellman Braud), Pops Foster had the longest career and he kept the tradition of slap bass solos alive into the late '60s. Foster was playing in bands around New Orleans as early as 1906. He played tuba with Fate Marable's group on riverboats (1918–21) and was with Kid Ory's band in California. Foster was in St. Louis in the mid '20s, working with Charlie Creath and Dewey Jackson. After he arrived in New York in 1928, Foster played with King Oliver and then joined the great Luis Russell Orchestra where his thumping bass really propelled the ensembles. Pops stayed with Russell during the long period (1935–40) when the orchestra was really the backup group for Louis Armstrong. After that stint ended, Foster was in demand during the New Orleans revival period, freelancing with many bands including Art Hodes, Mezz Mezzrow, Sidney Bechet (1945) and Bob Wilber. He toured Europe

with Sammy Price during 1955–56, played with Earl Hines in San Francisco (1956–61) and then spent 1963–64 with Elmer Snowden's trio. He also wrote his autobiography, which was published posthumously in 1971. —*Scott Yanow*

Pete Fountain

b. Jul. 3, 1930, New Orleans, LA
Clarinet / Dixieland
One of the most famous of all New Orleans jazz clarinetists, Pete Fountain has the ability to play songs that he has performed a countless number of times (such as "Basin Street Blues") with so much enthusiasm that one would swear he had just discovered them! His style and most of his repertoire have remained unchanged since the late '50s yet he never sounds bored. In 1948 Fountain (who is heavily influenced by Benny Goodman and Irving Fazola) was a member of the Junior Dixieland Band and this was followed by a stint with Phil Zito and an important association with the Basin Street Six (1950–54) with whom the clarinetist made his first recordings. In 1955 Fountain was a member of the Dukes of Dixieland, but his big breakthrough came when he was featured playing a featured Dixieland number or two on each episode of *The Lawrence Welk Show* during 1957–59. After he left, he moved back to New Orleans, opened his own club and has played there regularly since. Fountain's finest recordings were a lengthy string for Coral during 1959–65 (they turned commercial for a period after that) although he has made relatively few CDs considering his continuing popularity. —*Scott Yanow*

The Blues / 1959 / Coral ✦✦✦
Accompanied by an enthusiastic big band featuring some solos from tenor great Eddie Miller, trombonist Moe Schneider, Jackie Coon on mellophone and the trumpets of John Best and Conrad Gozzo, Pete Fountain is in excellent form on a dozen blues-oriented pieces. Since the swinging arrangements are uncluttered and attention was paid to varying tempos and moods, this LP is one of Fountain's better ones from his earlier days. As is true with all of his Coral recordings (which are generally his most inspired and best planned), none of these performances have appeared yet on CD. —*Scott Yanow*

Pete Fountain's New Orleans / Feb. 1959 / Coral ✦✦✦
This LP is an excellent showcase for Pete Fountain in his early days. The clarinetist (who is the only horn in a quartet with pianist Stan Wrightsman, bassist Morty Corb and drummer Jack Sperling) sounds typically enthusiastic on the Dixieland warhorses, turning "The Saints" into a march and coming up with fresh things to say on such songs as "Do You Know What It Means to Miss New Orleans," "Basin Street Blues" and "Tin Roof Blues." —*Scott Yanow*

Pete Fountain Day / Oct. 29, 1959 / Coral ✦✦✦✦
This attractive LP gives one a definitive look at clarinetist Pete Fountain in his early days. With fine backup from vibraphonist Godfrey Hirsch, pianist Merle Koch, bassist Don Bagley and drummer Jack Sperling, Fountain enthusiastically and melodically swings his way through ten veteran standards. The music falls between swing and Dixieland and is consistently joyous; in other words, it's a typically enjoyable Pete Fountain set. —*Scott Yanow*

At The Bateau Lounge / 1960 / Coral ✦✦✦
Pete Fountain's steady series of recordings for Coral were among the most rewarding of his career. This particular set found him playing live at Dan's Bateau Lounge, his home base in New Orleans prior to opening his own club. The repertoire for the quartet (which also includes pianist Merle Koch, bassist Don Bagley and drummer Jack Sperling) consists of a variety of standards along with a few folk songs (including "Londonderry Air" and "Deep River") and a rare Fountain original "Creole Gumbo." This is excellent music from one of Dixieland's most enduring stars. —*Scott Yanow*

Salutes The Great Clarinetists / 1960 / Coral ✦✦✦
Pete Fountain plays a dozen songs associated with seven different clarinetists ranging from Benny Goodman and Woody Herman to Irving Fazola and even Ted Lewis. Backed by a big band directed by Bud Dant on some of the selections, Fountain is in excellent form playing in his own swing/Dixieland style. Unfortunately, this LP, as with all of his enjoyable Coral dates, is long out-of-print but might be found at secondhand record stores. —*Scott Yanow*

Mr. New Orleans Meets Mr. Honky Tonk / 1960 / Coral ✦✦
This is a hilariously bad LP. Pete Fountain's Dixieland group alter-

nates (often chorus by chorus) with pianist Big Tiny Little's very corny honky tonk band, really tearing apart (quite unintentionally) a dozen veteran standards. Add to the general bedlam quite a few sound effects and the results are remarkable: music to offend everyone. Also quite humorous are Leonard Feather's liner notes, which attempt to justify this nonsense. —*Scott Yanow*

Pete Fountain's French Quarter / 1961 / Coral ✦✦✦✦✦

In the early-to-mid '60s, Pete Fountain recorded a series of rewarding albums for Coral, none of which have been reissued yet on CD. This album, a quintet set with vibraphonist Godfrey Hirsch, pianist Stan Wrightsman, bassist Morty Corb and drummer Jack Sperling, celebrated the opening of the clarinetist's New Orleans club, the French Quarter Inn. Fountain always sounds enthusiastic when he plays (as if he were discovering veteran Dixieland and swing standards for the first time) and he is heard in top form on such songs as "Dear Old Southland," "Someday Sweetheart," "Is It True What They Say About Dixie?," "That Da Da Strain" and even "The Birth of the Blues." —*Scott Yanow*

On Tour / 1961 / Coral ✦✦✦

Pete Fountain (backed by pianist Stan Wrightsman, bassist Morty Corb and drummer Jack Sperling) is in his usual enthusiastic and swinging form on a dozen songs, all of which have a location in their title (such as "New Orleans," "San Antonio Rose," "Manhattan," "Indiana" and "Moonlight in Vermont"). The clarinetist is well-showcased and the frameworks have more variety than one might expect, making this out-of-print LP worth searching for. —*Scott Yanow*

The New Orleans Scene / 1961 / Coral ✦✦✦

Trumpeter Al Hirt gets co-billing with Pete Fountain on this album, but unfortunately only joins the clarinetist on four of the eight selections; best is "Panama." While those performances also include trombonist Jack Delaney and drummer Monk Hazel among the personnel, the other four numbers find Fountain utilizing his usual quartet of the time with pianist Stan Wrightsman. Nothing too unexpected happens on these Dixieland warhorses (which are augmented by Leonard Feather's "Mighty like the Blues"), but this LP should satisfy Dixieland fans; Fountain always sounds so enthusiastic. —*Scott Yanow*

Music from Dixie / Mar. 20, 1961–Mar. 22, 1961 / Coral ✦✦✦✦✦

Clarinetist Pete Fountain's group expands from a quartet to a nonet on this easily enjoyable LP with the addition of trumpeter Charlie Teagarden, trombonist Moe Schneider and tenor great Eddie Miller. The music falls between Dixieland and swing as Fountain leads the spirited crew through a dozen songs including his own "Bye Bye Bill Bailey," "High Society," "Struttin' with Some Barbeque," "Milenberg Joys" and "When You're Smiling." Dixieland fans will want to search for this album along with many of Fountain's other Coral LPs. —*Scott Yanow*

New Orleans at Midnight / Mar. 20, 1961–Mar. 25, 1963 / Coral ✦✦✦

The dozen selections on this excellent Pete Fountain LP are taken from several different sessions, although the music had not been released previously. Fountain, who must have been starting to run out of songs to record by 1963 (since he cut so many albums for Coral during the early-to-middle '60s), swings such material as "Creole Love Call," "Brahms' Lullaby," Rod McKuen's "Midnight Pete" and "Battle Hymn of the Republic" along with a variety of swing and Dixieland standards. The music is enjoyable as is true of all of Pete Fountain's performances from this era, his prime period. Unfortunately, none of Fountain's Coral recordings have surfaced on CD yet. —*Scott Yanow*

Plenty of Pete / Nov. 28, 1962 / Coral ✦✦✦

Coral certainly offered Dixieland fans plenty of Pete Fountain in the early '60s for he recorded at least 16 albums for the label during 1959-63. Fortunately, this was the clarinetist's prime period (although he always sounds good), but unfortunately none of the recordings have been reissued on CD yet. For *Plenty of Pete*, Fountain is heard showcased with an orchestra on five of the eight numbers (including an attempt to capitalize on the success of "Stranger on the Shore") and jams with his rhythm section on the remaining pieces plus a lengthy and rather odd medley. The latter somehow combines together "Stardust," "Is It True What They Say About Dixie?," "The Saints" and "Dixie," shifting back and forth between those unrelated songs! As with most of his output for Coral, this Pete Fountain LP is worth picking up if one is lucky enough to run across it. —*Scott Yanow*

South Rampart Street Parade / Mar. 23, 1963 / Coral ✦✦✦

This is an unusual Pete Fountain record for the popular Dixieland/swing clarinetist's regular group (which at the time had trumpeter Jackie Coon and trombonist Moe Schneider) is joined by four drummers (Godfrey Hirsch, Jack Sperling, Nick Fatool and Paul Barbarin) and four trombones for a set of parade music. Actually, many of the songs (such as "South Rampart Street Parade," "Over the Waves" and "Farewell Blues") are also part of the usual Dixieland repertoire, but plenty of space was left for the drummers to be heard. This is a surprisingly successful and fun outing. —*Scott Yanow*

Walking Through New Orleans / 1963–1968 / Coral ✦✦✦

For this LP, one of Pete Fountain's last ones for Coral, the clarinetist is heard in a variety of settings spanning a five-year period (although none of the performances were released on other albums). Fountain leads a marching band on some songs and otherwise is accompanied by his ten-piece combo of the time; in addition, a harmless vocal group also pops up on one song. The music ranges from swing standards to blues and some Dixieland. This record is not an essential acquisition, but does have its strong moments. —*Scott Yanow*

● Standing Room Only / 1965 / Coral ✦✦✦✦✦

This is one of the best Pete Fountain records for the clarinetist (who recorded so often with just a rhythm section or very subservient horns) is challenged by the presence of trumpeter Charlie Teagarden, trombonist Bob Havens and the great tenor Eddie Miller. With drummer Nick Fatool pushing the rhythm section, the band romps through eight standards (highlighted by "Muskrat Ramble," "Struttin' with Some Barbeque" and "You Are My Sunshine") and a memorable four-song "Ramblin' Medley." This LP, as with all of Pete Fountain's valuable output for Coral, has yet to be reissued on CD. —*Scott Yanow*

Pete Fountain's Crescent City / 1973 / MCA ✦✦

Clarinetist Pete Fountain gives a melodic swing/Dixie approach to a wide variety of material on this obscure LP, ranging from "Muskrat Ramble" and "At the Jazz Band Ball" to "Dream" and even "Tie a Yellow Ribbon Round the Old Oak Tree." Although tenor saxophonist Eddie Miller and drummer Jack Sperling are in the accompanying group, they are very much confined to the background during this so-so set of unsurprising music. —*Scott Yanow*

Alive In New Orleans / 1977 / First American ✦✦

Few sparks occur during this melodic LP by clarinetist Pete Fountain. The tunes include some Dixieland ("Jazz Me Blues" and "Indiana"), a few ballads ("When Your Lover Has Gone" and "Georgia") and a revival of a pop hit ("Stranger on the Shore") but, despite a few solos from Eddie Miller on tenor, the emphasis is very much on Fountain's melodic solos. It's pleasant music, though totally lacking in surprises. —*Scott Yanow*

Swingin' Blues / 1990 / Ranwood ✦✦

Clarinetist Pete Fountain interacts with musicians from both the Dixieland and country music world on this okay effort. Most of the selections on the CD are the usual Dixieland standards but there is also "Walking the Floor over You," "Honky Tonk" and "Amazing Grace." This is fairly predictable but reasonably pleasing melodic music from the always-enthusiastic clarinetist. — *Scott Yanow*

Live At The Ryman / 1992 / Sacramento ✦✦✦

Pete Fountain plays warhorses with such enthusiasm and delight that it often sounds as if he is discovering songs such as "Basin Street Blues" and "Way Down Yonder in New Orleans" for the first time. On this typically excellent live performance Fountain, in a quintet that also features vibraphonist Godfrey Hirsch and pianist Merle Koch, really stretches out on lengthy versions of "Avalon" and "Up a Lazy River." Koch has well-played if somewhat slapdash features on "Little Rock Getaway" and "Kansas City Stomp" while Hirsch's vibes are well-displayed on "Stardust" (in the Lionel Hampton tradition). Even if "Stardust" gets a bit lost in a pointless detour into "Dixie," Fountain and company have a fine time throughout this very accessible swing/Dixie session (which would have benefited from some liner notes) that will probably be enjoyed by his fans. —*Scott Yanow*

Cheek to Cheek / May 1993 / Ranwood ✦✦

Clarinetist Pete Fountain designed this CD as a romantic and very danceable ballad album and even such songs as "Rose Room" and "I Can't Believe That You're in Love with Me" are taken at slow tempos. Accompanied by an inflexible rhythm section that probably regarded jazz as a second language and a dull trombone section, Fountain still sounds enthusiastic. His tone is the only reason to acquire this disappointing set. —*Scott Yanow*

A Touch of Class / 1995 / Ranwood ✦
This CD from Pete Fountain is a bit of a disappointment. The clarinetist does little more than show off his attractive tone on 18 brief songs (many associated with France). The unidentified backing (which often includes a string section) leaves no impression whatsoever and Fountain's fairly straight melody readings do little to uplift the tunes. At best this is superior background music. —*Scott Yanow*

Fourplay

Group / Instrumental Pop, Crossover
This all-star group (comprised of keyboardist Bob James, guitarist Lee Ritenour, bassist Nathan East and drummer Harvey Mason) was formed in 1991 after the quartet all came together on part of James' *Grand Piano Canyon* album. They have since recorded three CDs for Warner Bros. that have all been big-sellers, not surprising considering the popularity of James and Ritenour. The group's music borders on jazz with some strong improvisations mixed in with large doses of pop and R&B, about what one would expect from these studio musicians. —*Scott Yanow*

Fourplay / 1991 / Warner Brothers ✦✦
A pleasant fusion effort, it never really lives up to potential possibilities. —*Steve Aldrich*

Between the Sheets / Aug. 17, 1993 / Warner Brothers ✦✦✦
It is not too surprising that Fourplay started out fairly popular for the group, in addition to bassist Nathan East and drummer Harvey Mason, teams together keyboardist Bob James and guitarist Lee Ritenour. Their playing on this Warner Bros. release results in rather predictable background music, easy-listening crossover with touches of jazz heard in the melodic solos along with poppish R&B rhythms. Nathan East's vocals dominate a few selections. Nothing very substantial occurs. —*Scott Yanow*

● **Elixir** / 1995 / Warner Brothers ✦✦✦

Panama Francis (David Albert Francis)

b. Dec. 21, 1918, Miami, FL
Drums, Leader / Early R&B, Swing
Panama Francis has had a long and versatile career, equally at home in swing and R&B sessions. Playing for church revival meetings were among his earliest gigs and he also gigged with George Kelly's group, the Cavaliers, in Florida (1934–38) before moving to New York. The following year he worked with Roy Eldridge (making his recording debut) and this was followed by a long period at the Savoy with the Lucky Millinder big band (1940–46) and an association with Cab Calloway (1947–52). Francis then became a busy studio drummer, performing anonymously on many pop and rock & roll records. In 1979 when he was in danger of being forgotten, Francis formed the Savoy Sultans, a group based on the small unit that used to play opposite Millinder at the Savoy. The Sultans recorded a steady stream of exciting hot swing records for Black & Blue and Stash during 1979–83. Since that time Panama Francis has continued freelancing including recording and touring with the Statesmen of Jazz (1994–95). —*Scott Yanow*

● **All-Stars 1949** / 1949 / Collectables ✦✦✦✦✦
Sizzling swing set propelled by a truly fine drummer. —*Ron Wynn*

Francis & The Savoy Sultans / Jan. 31, 1979 / Classic Jazz ✦✦✦✦
Panama Francis was one of the great swing-era drummers, often playing in the house band at the Savoy. This late '70s album updates the sound he helped perfect through the heyday of swing and big bands, and on into the early days of R&B. It's dynamic, propulsive and well played. —*Ron Wynn*

● **Savoy Sultans** / Jan. 31, 1979-Feb. 11, 1979 / Classic Jazz ✦✦✦✦✦
Although their recordings do not always show it, The Savoy Sultans in the late '30s were considered one of the hottest small swing groups in existence. Decades later, drummer Panama Francis decided to revive the group's concept by putting together a new *Savoy Sultans*, using occasional alumni but mostly utilizing other surviving veteran players. This Classic Jazz LP finds the group at its best, cooking on such numbers as "Song of the Islands," "Frenzy," "Little John Special" and "Clap Hands, Here Comes Charlie." With George Kelly contributing the arrangements

as well as his tenor and such other fine soloists as trumpeters Francis Williams and Irv Stokes, altoists Norris Turney and Howard Johnson and pianist Red Richards, this is a hot band that could outswing the original group. This LP deserves to be reissued on CD. —*Scott Yanow*

Everything Swings / Oct. 3, 1983–Oct. 10, 1983 / Stash ✦✦✦✦

Free Flight

Group / Post-Bop, Classical, Fusion
Founded originally by the masterful classical flutist Jim Walker and the very versatile keyboardist Milcho Leviev (who, after some internal dissension, was replaced in 1984 by Mike Garson), Free Flight on their recordings for Arabesque, Palo Alto and CBS have successfully fused together classical passages, straight-ahead jazz and fusion, sometimes switching between all three idioms in the same chorus! Walker's long and complex unison choruses with Garson are a highlight of the latter-day group; neither virtuoso seems to ever make a mistake. Bassist Jim Lacefield and drummer Peter Erskine were also founding members of the group. Ralph Humphrey took Erskine's spot by 1982 and, with the death of Lacefield, the bass and drum chairs are filled with a variety of flexible players. Free Flight (now a collaboration between Walker and Garson) has continued on a part-time basis into the mid-'90s. —*Scott Yanow*

Free Flight / 1981 / Voss ✦✦✦

★ **The Jazz/Classical Union** / Mar. 1982 / Palo Alto ✦✦✦✦✦

Soaring / 1983 / Palo Alto ✦✦✦✦

Beyond the Clouds / 1984 / Palo Alto ✦✦✦✦

Illumination / 1986 / CBS ✦✦✦

Slice of Life / 1988 / Columbia ✦✦✦
The most recent of this group's releases. Some good players burdened by lackluster arrangements and production. —*Ron Wynn*

Nnenna Freelon

b. Cambridge, MS
Vocals / Standards
When Nnenna Freelon recorded her debut album for Columbia, a string-filled affair titled *Nnenna Freelon*, she was quickly labelled a Sarah Vaughan imitator. However, her second date, (*Heritage*) which featured her backed by just a trio and occasionally a couple of horns, was a major improvement and she displayed a much more adventurous and original style, showing that first impressions are not always correct. Freelon, after graduating from Simmons College, raised three children and had a career in health services in Durham, NC, before really starting her vocal career. She performed well at an Atlanta jam session with Ellis Marsalis and two years later, on the strength of that jam, she was signed to Columbia. In 1996 she switched to the Concord label and, despite her late start, Nnena Freelon seems to have a productive career ahead of her. —*Scott Yanow*

Nnenna Freelon / Jul. 1, 1992 / Columbia ✦✦✦

● **Listen** / 1994 / Columbia ✦✦✦✦

Bud Freeman (Lawrence Freeman)

b. Apr. 13, 1906, Chicago, IL, **d.** Mar. 15, 1991, Chicago, IL
Tenor Saxophone / Dixieland, Swing
When Bud Freeman first matured, his was the only strong alternative approach on the tenor to the harder-toned style of Coleman Hawkins and he was an inspiration for Lester Young. Freeman, one of the top tenors of the 1930s, was also one of the few saxophonists (along with the slightly later Eddie Miller) to be accepted in the Dixieland world and his oddly angular but consistently swinging solos were an asset to a countless number of hot sessions.

Freeman, excited (as were the other members of the Austin High School Gang in Chicago) by the music of the New Orleans Rhythm Kings, took up the C-melody sax in 1923, switching to tenor two years later. It took him time to develop his playing, which was still pretty primitive in 1927 when he made his recording debut with the McKenzie-Condon Chicagoans. Freeman moved to New York later that year and worked with Red Nichols' Five Pennies, Roger Wolfe Kahn, Ben Pollack, Joe Venuti, Gene Kardos and others. He was starred on Eddie Condon's memorable 1933 recording "The Eel." After stints with Joe Haymes and Ray Noble, Freeman was a star with Tommy Dorsey's Orchestra and

Clambake Seven (1936–38) before having a short unhappy stint with Benny Goodman (1938). He led his short-lived but legendary Summe Cum Laude Orchestra (1939–40), which was actually an octet, spent two years in the military and then from 1945 on alternated between being a bandleader and working with Eddie Condon's freewheeling Chicago jazz groups. Freeman travelled the world, made scores of fine recordings and stuck to the same basic style that he had developed by the mid-'30s (untouched by a brief period spent studying with Lennie Tristano). Bud Freeman was with the World's Greatest Jazz Band (1968–71), lived in London in the late '70s and ended up back where he started, in Chicago. He was active into his 80s, and a strong sampling of his recordings are currently available on CD. —*Scott Yanow*

★ **Jammin' at Commodore** / Jan. 17, 1938–Jun. 13, 1939 / Commodore ✦✦✦✦✦

Midnight at Eddie Condon's / Dec. 5, 1945–Dec. 10, 1945 / EmArcy ✦✦✦✦

Bud Freeman / Jul. 1955 / Bethlehem ✦✦✦

☆ **Chicago/Austin High School Jazz in Hi Fi** / Mar. 7, 1957–Jul. 8, 1957 / RCA Victor ✦✦✦✦✦

The All Stars with Shorty Baker / May 13, 1960 / Original Jazz Classics ✦✦✦✦
Tenor sax great Bud Freeman, who is often associated with the Eddie Condon school of Nicksieland, is heard leading an excellent swing quintet for this 1960 studio session. Trumpeter Harold "Shorty" Baker (best known for his periods with Duke Ellington) made too few small-group recordings throughout his life so this is one of his best. With the often-overlooked but virtuosic stride pianist Claude Hopkins heard in the rhythm section along with bassist George Duvivier and drummer J.C. Heard, the group plays superior standards and a couple of originals on this fine swing date. —*Scott Yanow*

● **Something to Remember You By** / Jan. 15, 1962 / Black Lion ✦✦✦✦✦

The Compleat Bud Freeman / Dec. 10, 1969+Dec. 12, 1969 / Monmouth ✦✦✦✦

The Real Bud Freeman 1984 / Dec. 2, 1983–Dec. 3, 1983 / Principally Jazz ✦✦✦
A mid-'80s album, one of the last made by Bud Freeman, a major figure during the '20s and '30s among Chicago jazz musicians. By this time, he had pretty much passed his peak, but still was a charming, witty soloist. The mix was the usual, some standards, some Freeman originals. The CD reissue has three bonus cuts. —*Ron Wynn*

Chico Freeman (Earl Lavon Freeman, Jr.)

b. Jul. 17, 1949, Chicago, IL
Soprano Saxophone, Tenor Saxophone / Post-Bop
An excellent tenor saxophonist and the son of Von Freeman, Chico Freeman has had a busy and diverse career, with many recordings ranging from advanced hard bop to nearly free avant-garde jazz. He originally played trumpet, not taking up the tenor until he was a junior in college. Freeman graduated from Northwestern University in 1972, played with R&B groups and joined the AACM. In 1977 he moved to New York where he worked with Elvin Jones, Sun Ra, Sam Rivers' big band, Jack DeJohnette's Special Edition and Don Pullen in addition to leading his own groups. He recorded a dozen albums as a leader during 1975–82. Starting in 1984, Freeman has played on a part-time basis with the Leaders, he has recorded on a few occasions with his father and, in 1989, he put together an electric band called Brainstorm. Chico Freeman has recorded through the years as a leader for Dharma, India Navigation, Contemporary, Black Saint, Elektra/Musician, Black Hawk, Palo Alto, Jazz House and In & Out. —*Scott Yanow*

Morning Prayer / Sep. 8, 1976 / India Navigation ✦✦✦
A tremendous quintet date. Wonderful solos by Freeman, plus a strong supporting cast w/ Muhal Richard Abrams (p). —*Ron Wynn*

Beyond the Rain / Jun. 21, 1977-Jun. 23, 1977 / Original Jazz Classics ✦✦✦✦
With the Hilton Ruiz Trio, featuring the compositions of M.R. Abrams and Freeman's hard-charging playing. —*Michael G. Nastos*

Kings of Mali / Sep. 1977 / India Navigation ✦✦✦✦

Chico / 1977 / India Navigation ✦✦✦✦
A standard for creative tenor saxophonists to live up to. With Cecil McBee, Muhal Richard Abrams and Steve McCall. —*Michael G. Nastos*

★ **The Outside Within** / 1978 / India Navigation ✦✦✦✦✦
A sterling quartet session. —*Ron Wynn*

No Time Left / Jun. 8, 1979–Jun. 9, 1979 / Black Saint ✦✦✦

Spirit Sensitive / Sep. 1979 / India Navigation ✦✦✦✦
During an era when tenor saxophonist Chico Freeman was recording frequently and being associated with the avant-garde, he decided to emphasize standards on this quintet date. With pianist John Hicks, bassist Cecil McBee and either Billy Hart or Don Moye on drums, Freeman digs into five familiar songs (including "Autumn in New York," "It Never Entered My Mind" and "Don't Get Around Much Anymore") along with McBee's "Close to You Alone." Although he does not cast any new light on these tunes or really make them his, the music is enjoyable and reasonably accessible. —*Scott Yanow*

Peaceful Heart, Gentle Spirit / Mar. 6, 1980–Mar. 7, 1980 / Contemporary ✦✦✦✦✦
Chico Freeman (a tenor saxophonist who, on this date, also plays soprano, flute, alto flute, clarinet and bass clarinet) recorded many sessions in the late '70s and early '80s but this is one of his very best. Utilizing an unusual instrumentation (flutist James Newton, pianist Kenny Kirkland, vibraphonist Jay Hoggard, cello, bass, drums and two percussionists), Freeman infuses his five challenging—but generally logical—compositions with rich tone colors and shades. This music is stimulating and represents one of the highpoints of Freeman's rather streaky career. —*Scott Yanow*

Destiny's Dance / Oct. 29, 1981–Oct. 30, 1981 / Original Jazz Classics ✦✦✦✦
Chico Freeman established himself in the 1970s as one of that decade's finest, most ambitious and exciting saxophone stylists. He continued his impressive playing on this 1981 date, which was recently reissued on CD (no bonus cuts). While it was a short (37 minutes) session, it was distinguished both by superb tenor sax solos and bass clarinet playing from Freeman, and equally distinctive contributions from a great cast. This lineup included trumpeter Wynton Marsalis, then known solely within the jazz world, vibist Bobby Hutcherson, pianist Dennis Moorman and a rhythm section sparked by bassist Cecil McBee and anchored by drummer Ronnie Burrage and percussionist Paulinho Da Costa. —*Ron Wynn*

Tradition in Transition / 1982 / Elektra ✦✦✦✦

The Search / 1982 / India Navigation ✦✦✦

Pied Piper / Apr. 9, 1984 / Blackhawk ✦✦✦
An outstanding mid-'80s date, with Chico Freeman displaying both his strong solo skills and his versatility. He and fellow multi-instrumentalist John Purcell split duties on 12 horns between them. Kenny Kirkland and Mark Thompson admirably divide the piano chores, while bassist Cecil McBee and powerful drummer Elvin Jones nicely handle rhythm section tasks. —*Ron Wynn*

Tales of Ellington / Apr. 9, 1984–Mar. 7, 1987 / Black Hawk ✦✦✦

Tangents / 1984 / Elektra ✦✦✦
A sometimes-intriguing album, featuring saxophonist Chico Freeman interacting with vocal acrobat Bobby McFerrin on some tracks, while otherwise playing standard but inspired hard bop or venturing into free territory. —*Ron Wynn*

You'll Know When You Get There / Aug. 12, 1988–Aug. 31, 1988 / Black Saint ✦✦✦

Freeman and Freeman / 1989 / India Navigation ✦✦✦
Father and son make a wonderful team on this release with Von and Chico Freeman. —*Ron Wynn*

The Mystical Dreamer / May 1989 / In + Out ✦✦

Up and Down / Jul. 26, 1989-Jul. 27, 1989 / Black Saint ✦✦✦

Sweet Explosion / Apr. 1990 / In + Out ✦✦

In The Moment / Oct. 15, 1992–Oct. 16, 1992 / Edgetone ✦✦✦
For these live performances tenor saxophonist Chico Freeman (who sounds better here than he has on record in at least three years) sits in with the San Francisco Bay Area-based group Jazz on the Line. The fiery music is often quite free although coherent and logical. Aaron Repke (on alto, soprano, baritone and flute)

and trumpeter Jason Olaine co-star on this fine small-label release. —*Scott Yanow*

Threshold / Oct. 27, 1992–Oct. 28, 1992 / In + Out ✦✦

Focus / 1994 / Contemporary ✦✦✦

Russ Freeman

b. May 28, 1926
Piano / Cool
Not to be confused with the leader of the Rippingtons, this Russ Freeman is best-known for his work in the West Coast scene of the 1950s, most noticeably with the first Chet Baker Quartet. He moved to Los Angeles in the mid-'40s and worked with Howard McGhee, sat in with Charlie Parker and recorded with Dexter Gordon (1947), Art Pepper, Wardell Gray, the Lighthouse All-Stars, Shorty Rogers and Baker (1954). Freeman was with Shelly Manne's Men for a long period (1955-66) and toured with Benny Goodman in 1959. After the mid-'60s he appeared less often in jazz settings, (other than a 1978 recording with Art Pepper and a 1982 duet set for Atlas with Shelly Manne), mostly working in the studios; by the mid-'80s he was largely retired. Freeman made records as a leader for Pacific Jazz and Jazz West Coast during 1953-59. His song "The Wind" has been recorded by several other artists including Keith Jarrett. —*Scott Yanow*

● **Trio with Richard Twardzik** / Oct. 27, 1953-Aug. 12, 1957 / Pacific Jazz ✦✦✦✦✦

Von Freeman (Earl Lavon Freeman, Sr.)

b. Oct. 3, 1922, Chicago
Tenor Saxophone / Post-Bop
Veteran tenor Von Freeman is essentially a bop-oriented improviser whose unusual tone (admired by some, disliked by others) is an acquired taste. The father of tenor Chico Freeman and the brother of guitarist George Freeman and drummer Bruz Freeman, Von worked early on with Horace Henderson's Orchestra (1940–41), with a Navy band while in the military (1941–45) and with Sun Ra (1948–49). He was in the house band at the Pershing Hotel in Chicago (1946–50) with his brothers Bruz and George, accompanying the many top bop stars who passed through town. Freeman, who did not record as a leader until 1972 and only three times until 1989, became a local legend, playing with many types of groups in Chicago. He had a quartet with his brothers in the 1950s that used Ahmad Jamal and later Andrew Hill as their pianist. Freeman also worked with many AACM musicians (including Muhal Richard Abrams), played with blues bands in the 1960s and from the early '70s on has generally led his own groups. Von Freeman has recorded as a leader for Atlantic (1972), Nessa, Daybreak, Columbia (a set with his son Chico in 1981), Southport and SteepleChase. —*Scott Yanow*

Doin' It Right Now / 1972 / Atlantic ✦✦✦

Have No Fear / Jun. 11, 1975 / Nessa ✦✦✦✦

● **Serenade and Blues** / Jun. 11, 1975 / Nessa ✦✦✦✦✦
It is surprising that Von Freeman's supporters never seem to grasp why the veteran tenor saxophonist has never become all that popular. Freeman has one of the odder tones of any saxophonist and it takes some getting used to. This Nessa release, which finds Freeman joined by pianist John Young, bassist Dave Shipp and drummer Wilbur Campbell, is as accessible as any of his recordings. Von Freeman performs lengthy versions of two ballads, an original blues and his theme song "After Dark." —*Scott Yanow*

Walkin' Tuff / 1989 / Southport ✦✦✦
The veteran Chicago tenor saxophonist, a blues, ballads and standards master as well as an expert hard bop player, works with a relatively inexperienced band on this recent release. He does an admirable job of meshing with them, while also soaring during his solos. —*Ron Wynn*

Don Friedman

b. May 4, 1935, San Francisco, CA
Piano / Post-Bop, Hard Bop
An excellent if underrated pianist, Don Friedman started off playing on the West Coast in 1956 with Dexter Gordon, Shorty Rogers, Buddy Collette, Buddy DeFranco (1956–57), Chet Baker and even the unknown altoist Ornette Coleman. After moving to New York in 1958, Friedman played in many settings including with his own trio, Pepper Adams, Booker Little (recording with him in 1961), the Jimmy Giuffre Three (1964), a quartet with Attila Zoller, Chuck Wayne's trio (1966–67) and, by the end of the decade, Clark Terry's big band. He has continued working in New York as both

Music Map

French Horn

Claude Thornhill started using French horns in his orchestra in 1942.

Played French Horn with Miles Davis "Birth Of The Cool" Nonet
Junior Collins • Sandy Siegelstein • Gunther Schuller

"Charlie Parker of the French Horn"
Julius Watkins

1950s
John Graas • Willie Ruff • David Amram

More Recent Jazz French Horn Players
Tom Varner
Pete Levin (with Gil Evans, 1970s')
Sharon Freeman
Peter Gordon
Vincent Chancey
John Clark

a jazz educator and a pianist with wide musical interests and he was featured on Concord's Maybeck Recital Hall series (1993). Don Friedman, who also recorded for Riverside, Prestige, Progressive, Owl, Empathy and several Japanese labels, is not to be confused with vibraphonist David Friedman! —*Scott Yanow*

● **A Day in the City** / Jun. 12, 1961 / Original Jazz Classics ✦✦✦✦✦
For his debut as a leader, pianist Don Friedman (in a trio with bassist Chuck Israels and drummer Joe Hunt) performed six variations on a theme taken from an old folk song "The Minstrel Boy." Called "Dawn," "Midday," "Rush Hour," "Sunset," "Early Evening" and "Night," these "Six Jazz Variations on a Theme" are often quite abstract and not as picturesque as one would think considering their titles. However Friedman's playing (which shows the strong influence of modern classical music, particularly in its chords) rewards repdated listenings. —*Scott Yanow*

Hot Knepper and Pepper / Jun. 26, 1978 / Progressive ✦✦✦

Don Friedman at Maybeck / Sep. 5, 1993 / Concord ✦✦✦✦

David Friesen

b. May 6, 1942, Tacoma, WA
Bass / Post-Bop, New Age
David Friesen's music ranges from hard bop to mood music that borders on spiritual new age but on a higher emotional level. While stationed in Germany with the Army in 1961, he taught himself the bass. After short stints with John Handy and Marian McPartland, Friesen worked with Joe Henderson for two years. He toured Europe with Billy Harper (1975), made his recording debut as a leader that same year on Muse, started a longtime musical association with guitarist John Stowell (1976) and appeared with Ted Curson at the 1977 Monterey Jazz Festival. After working with Ricky Ford, Duke Jordan and Mal Waldron and touring the USSR with Paul Horn (1983), Friesen settled in the Pacific Northwest. He often plays the Oregon bass (an electrified acoustic bass) these

days and has recorded as a leader for Muse, Inner City, SteepleChase, Palo Alto, ITM (including an intriguing series of duets during 1992–93) and Global Pacific in addition to some smaller labels. —*Scott Yanow*

Color Pool / Oct. 1, 1975 / Muse ✦✦✦

● **Star Dance** / Nov. 8, 1976 / Inner City ✦✦✦✦
Bassist David Friesen's 1976 outing as a leader remains his finest straight jazz date; it also contains some extraordinary playing, particularly the cut "Duet and Dialogue," where he blends both plucked and bowed work in the same song while using both hands. —*Ron Wynn*

Waterfall Rainbow / Jun. 1977–Aug. 1977 / Inner City ✦✦✦✦

Through the Listening Glass / Jul. 7, 1978 / Inner City ✦✦✦

Other Mansions / Nov. 1979 / Inner City ✦✦✦

Paths Beyond Tracing / Feb. 12, 1980 / SteepleChase ✦✦

Storyteller / Apr. 13, 1981 / Muse ✦✦✦

Amber Skies / Jan. 1983+Apr. 1983 / Palo Alto ✦✦✦✦
Bassist Dave Friesen has marvelous technical skills, but doesn't always stick to a jazz context. This '83 date has him doing quasi-classical, light pop and more conventional jazz; the compositions are erratic, but his bass solos and skills are consistently impressive. —*Ron Wynn*

Inner Voices / 1987 / Global Pacific ✦✦
Bassist Friesen moves into a more atmospheric, lighter and expressionist mode with this session for Global Pacific. He's always been an excellent bassist, but stays in the background, mostly supporting others. There's minimal energy, and arrangements and production are the dominant factors. —*Ron Wynn*

Other Times: Other Places / 1989 / Global Pacific ✦✦✦

Departure / 1990 / Global Pacific ✦✦✦
Good combination of Afro-Latin-jazz and chamber music with guests Airto (per) and Flora Purim (v). —*Ron Wynn*

Johnny Frigo

b. Dec. 27, 1916, Chicago, IL
Violin, Bass / Swing
Johnny Frigo has really had two careers. He started out playing violin in grammar school and, after switching to tuba in order to play in his junior high school band, he took up the bass. Frigo started playing professionally as a bassist in 1934 and had some low-profile jobs until joining Jimmy Dorsey in the mid-'40s. In 1947 he formed a trio with guitarist Herb Ellis and pianist Lou Carter called Soft Winds that was popular for a few years; they co-wrote "Detour Ahead" and "I Told Ya I Love Ya, Now Get Out." After the group disbanded in the early '50s, Frigo became a studio bassist in Chicago for decades, playing sessions, jingles and club dates. Although Frigo had an opportunity to record an album on violin in 1957 for Mercury, it was not until 1988 that he returned to his first instrument, guesting on a Herb Ellis Justice CD and leading two excellent and swinging dates of his own for Chesky that put him near the top of his field. —*Scott Yanow*

Live from Studio A in New York City / Nov. 16, 1988 / Chesky ✦✦✦✦

● **Debut of a Legend** / 1994 / Chesky ✦✦✦✦✦

David Frishberg

b. Mar. 23, 1933, St. Paul, MN
Piano, Vocals, Lyricist / Swing, Bop
Arguably the top living lyricist, Dave Frishberg has written more than his share of witty (yet insightful) classics including "I'm Hip," "Peel Me a Grape," "Dear Bix," "The Underdog," "Saratoga Hunch," "Slappin' the Cakes on Me," "Z's," "My Attorney Bernie," "Blizzard of Lies," "Another Song About Paris," "You Are There," "El Cajon," "Can't Take You Nowhere" and "Let's Eat Home." A fine swing pianist and a world-weary sounding vocalist, the multi-talented Dave Frishberg moved to New York in 1957. He worked early on as a pianist with Carmen McRae, Kai Winding, Gene Krupa (1960–63), Wild Bill Davison, Bud Freeman, Ben Webster, the Al Cohn-Zoot Sims Quintet and Bobby Hackett among others and cut an album with Jimmy Rushing. He recorded a commercial record for CTI (1968) that generated a surprise hit in "Van Lingle Mungo." However, it was not until Frishberg moved to the West Coast (1971) and started recording for the Concord label (1977) as a vocalist/pianist that he began to make a big impres-

sion. Dave Frishberg has since cut albums for Omnisound, Fantasy, Bloomdido and a purely instrumental duet set with Dixieland trumpeter Jim Goodwin (1992) for Arbors. Many of his originals have been recorded by other vocalists. —*Scott Yanow*

Oklahoma Toad / 1968 / CTI ✦✦

Solo and Trio / 1975 / Seeds ✦✦✦

★ **Getting Some Fun out of Life** / Jan. 25, 1977–Jan. 26, 1977 / Concord Jazz ✦✦✦✦✦

You're a Lucky Guy / Feb. 20, 1978–Jul. 10, 1978 / Concord Jazz ✦✦✦✦
Al Cohn (ts) elevates the entire set. —*Ron Wynn*

Dave Frishberg Classics / Apr. 29, 1981–Dec. 1982 / Concord Jazz ✦✦✦✦✦
This hits collection reissued almost all of his most well-known tunes. A must-buy. —*Michael G. Nastos*

☆ **Live at Vine Street** / Oct. 1984 / Original Jazz Classics ✦✦✦✦✦
Arguably the greatest living lyricist, Dave Frishberg sings and plays piano on this very enjoyable solo disc. His nine originals include such memorable (and humorous) tunes as "El Cajon" (a Johnny Mandel melody), "The Dear Departed Past" and "Blizzard of Lies." In addition, Frishberg plays a lengthy medley of Johnny Hodges-associated songs. This witty set is easily recommended. —*Scott Yanow*

Can't Take You Nowhere / Sep. 21, 1986 / Fantasy ✦✦✦✦

Let's Eat Home / Aug. 1989 / Concord Jazz ✦✦✦✦

Where You At? / Mar. 4, 1991 / Bloomdido ✦✦✦✦
This is one of the more obscure Dave Frishberg CDs, made for the French label Bloomdido. On some of the selections the pianist/vocalist/lyricist is joined by baritonist Turk Mauro, trombonist Glenn Ferris and bassist Michel Guadry but he is the main star throughout. Frishberg sounds excellent on a pair of solo instrumental medleys of songs associated with Ivie Anderson and Duke Ellington and introduces his memorable lyrics to "Another Song About Paris." In addition Frishberg is in fine vocal form on "Where You At?" (which was given new words), "I'm an Old Cowhand" and "Tulip or Turnip." An excellent outing. —*Scott Yanow*

Double Play / Oct. 3, 1992–Oct. 4, 1992 / Arbors ✦✦✦✦
Dave Frishberg, best-known for his impressive abilities as a lyricist and vocalist, sticks exclusively to instrumentals on this enjoyable disc. Frishberg the pianist is teamed with cornetist Jim Goodwin on a duet set comprised of 17 trad and swing classics that mostly date from the 1920s and '30s. To their credit the duo constantly walk a musical tightrope, taking chances within the idiom and not being afraid to make mistakes; neither musician felt that the music should be edited afterward. The result is colorful classic jazz interpreted by two strong stylists who, while paying tribute to their predecessors, infuse the music with their own personalities. It is easily recommended to trad fans. —*Scott Yanow*

Quality Time / May 28, 1993–May 29, 1993 / Sterling ✦✦✦
This Dave Frishberg CD is a more specialized project than the lyricist/vocalist/pianist's more definitive Concord releases. Five of the songs were written for a musical about baseball history that was never produced and several of these are of much more limited interest than usual. The most memorable selections on this release are the title cut (which is a near-classic about a Yuppie couple halfheartedly struggling to make time for each other), a bittersweet "The Dear Departed Past" and a remake of "Dear Bix." In addition there are two fine piano solos and short spots for trumpeter Rich Cooper and tenor saxophonist Lee Wuthernow. But, although a sincere effort, this CD is primarily for Frishberg completists who already have his Concord sets. —*Scott Yanow*

Tony Fruscella

b. Feb. 4, 1927, Orangeburg, NY, d. Aug. 14, 1969, New York, NY
Trumpet / Cool
Before drugs fouled up his life, Tony Fruscella was a talented cool-toned trumpeter. A pair of Spotlite albums (1948 and 1953) and a session released by Xanadu (1952) show that Fruscella was a fine player who, although sounding similar to times to Chet Baker, had developed his sound by himself. After serving in the military, Fruscella worked with Lester Young, Gerry Mulligan (1954) and Stan Getz (1955). In 1955 he recorded his one studio album as a leader and was captured at a jam session with Phil Woods (the

latter was released on two Honey Dew LPs). Unfortunately, Fruscella soon became musically inactive and it was not long before he was pretty well forgotten. —*Scott Yanow*

Debut / Dec. 10, 1948–1953 / Spotlite ✦✦✦

Fru 'n Brew / 1953 / Spotlite ✦✦✦

● **Tony Fruscella** / Mar. 29, 1955+Apr. 1, 1955 / Atlantic ✦✦✦✦✦

Curtis Fuller

b. Dec. 15, 1934, Detroit, MI
Trombone / Hard Bop

Curtis Fuller belongs in the select circle with J.J. Johnson, Kai Winding and a few others who make the trombone sound fluid and inviting rather than awkward. His ability to make wide octave leaps and play whiplash phrases in a relaxed, casual manner is a testament to his skill. Fuller's solos and phrases are often ambitious and creative, and he's worked in several fine bands and participated in numerous great sessions. Fuller studied music in high school, then began developing his skills in an Army band, where he played with Cannonball Adderley. He worked in Detroit with Kenny Burrell and Yusef Lateef, then moved to New York. Fuller made his recording debut as a leader on Transition in 1955 and recorded in the late '50s for Blue Note, Prestige, United Artists and Savoy. He was a charter member of The Jazztet with Benny Golson and Art Farmer in 1959, then played in Art Blakey's Jazz Messengers from 1961 to 1965. There were additional recording dates for Warwick, Smash/Trip, Epic and Impulse! in the '60s. Fuller toured Europe with Dizzy Gillespie's big band in 1968, then did several sessions in New York. During the '70s, he experimented for a time playing hard bop arrangements in a band featuring electronic instruments, heading a group with guitarist Bill Washer and Stanley Clarke. He concluded that phase with the '73 album *Crankin'.* Fuller toured with the Count Basie band from 1975 to 1977 and did dates for Mainstream, Timeless and Bee Hive. He co-lead the quintet Giant Bones with Winding in 1979 and 1980 and played with Art Blakey, Cedar Walton and Benny Golson in the late '70s and early '80s. During the '80s, Fuller toured Europe regularly with The Timeless All-Stars and performed and recorded with the revamped Jazztet. There are a few Fuller sessions available on CD, mostly early dates. —*Ron Wynn*

New Trombone / May 11, 1957 / Original Jazz Classics ✦✦✦

This 1957 date, which has recently been reissued on CD, matches Fuller with bluesy, fervent alto sax wailer Sonny Red Kyner. They make both a tight ensemble pair and an excellent contrasting frontline, with Kyner's spewing, flailing delivery featured on such cuts as "Blue Lawson" and "Namely You" operating against Fuller's equally intense, but lighter and smoother trombone lines. With Hank Jones operating as the rhythm section's harmonic link on piano, bassist Doug Watkins and drummer Louis Hayes mesh underneath effectively. It's the type of undiluted, straight-ahead bop and blues number that were par for the course then and now. —*Ron Wynn*

Curtis Fuller with Red Garland / May 14, 1957 / Original Jazz Classics ✦✦✦✦

This CD reissue features trombonist Curtis Fuller in a quintet with altoist Sonny Red, pianist Red Garland, bassist Paul Chambers and drummer Louis Hayes performing a pair of originals, two blues and a couple of ballad features. Red is outstanding on "Moonlight Becomes You" (one of his finest recordings) while Fuller does a fine job on "Stormy Weather." Even with the new material, this set has a feel of a jam session; the blend between the trombone and the alto is particularly appealing. Despite the overly critical liner notes (written in 1962), this is an excellent hard-bop oriented date. —*Scott Yanow*

Curtis Fuller, Vol. 3 / Dec. 1, 1957 / Blue Note ✦✦✦

Blues-Ette / May 21, 1959 / Savoy Jazz ✦✦✦✦✦

A powerhouse session with Fuller leading a stalwart group. Benny Golson (ts) and Tommy Flanagan (p) are sublime. —*Ron Wynn*

The Curtis Fuller Jazztette / Aug. 25, 1959 / Savoy Jazz ✦✦✦✦

Imagination / Dec. 17, 1959 / Savoy Jazz ✦✦✦✦

Four on the Outside / Sep. 18, 1978 / Timeless ✦✦✦✦

Fire and Filigree / Dec. 6, 1978 / Bee Hive ✦✦✦✦

● **Blues-Ette, Pt. 2** / Jan. 4, 1993–Jan. 6, 1993 / Savoy ✦✦✦✦✦

The original *Blues-ette* album was a quintet session from 1959 featuring trombonist Curtis Fuller, tenor saxophonist Benny Golson, pianist Tommy Flanagan, bassist Jimmy Garrison and drummer Al Harewood. Thirty-four years later the same musicians (with bassist Ray Drummond filling in for the deceased Garrison) had a reunion for this Savoy CD. Three of the songs from the original session are given new versions and there are also performances of several recent compositions by both Golson and Fuller in addition to four standards. Although Golson's sound on tenor has evolved since the earlier date, the appealing blend between the two horns remain unchanged as do the styles of Fuller and Flanagan, making this an excellent example of swinging hard bop. —*Scott Yanow*

G

Kenny G (Kenneth Gorelick)
b. 1959, Seattle, WA
Soprano Saxophone / Instrumental Pop, Crossover
During the '80s, Kenny G became the biggest-selling saxophonist of all time. While he did have several pop hits, he carved out a niche in adult contemporary and lite radio stations with his light jazz/pop-fusion instrumentals. Kenny G's soprano sax style is smooth and fluid, spinning out airly melodics tunes like the top five hit "Songbird." Such polished confections have made the saxophonist a commercial heavy-hitter.

Born Kenneth Gorelick, Kenny G began playing saxophone professionally with Barry White's Love Unlimited Orchestra in 1976 when he was 17. Shortly afterward, he left the group to study accounting at the University of Washington. However, he didn't give up music—he recorded with the Seattle funk band Cold, Bold & Together and frequently played in supporting bands for major artists. Once he graduated from college, he became part of the Jeff Lorber Fusion, recording an album with the combo. That appearance led to a solo deal with Arista; he released his self-titled debut album in 1982.

Kenny G's first few records find him experimenting with both jazz and R&B, without developing a real feal for either genre. With 1986's *Duotones* he landed on the formula that would make him an international multi-million seller. Propelled by the number four hit single "Songbird," the record sold over three million copies. In addition to establishing his stardom, the album led to work with Aretha Franklin, Whitney Houston and Natalie Cole, among others.

Every subsequent Kenny G album has subsequently sold at least two million copies a piece in the United States, while shifting impressive numbers in other countries, as well; 1992's *Breathless* has sold over eight million copies in the U.S. alone. Although he has been an unqualified commercial success, Kenny G has suffered at the hands of critics, who have called his music both lightweight and worthless. However, Kenny G's music is not jazz, nor does he claim that it is jazz. There are elements of jazz in his music, as well as R&B, funk and pop. In the end, it is smooth, polished pop music and it rarely has pretensions of being anything more than that. —*Stephen Thomas Erlewine*

Kenny G / 1982 / Arista ✦✦
Although he hadn't perfected his stylish amalgam of pop melodies and jazz improvisation, Kenny G's first album is worthwhile to his fans, simply as a document of his formative era. Parts of *Kenny G* may be rough, but it is sporadically enjoyable. —*Stephen Thomas Erlewine*

G Force / 1983 / Arista ✦✦
Gravity / 1985 / Arista ✦✦
● **Duotones** / 1986 / Arista ✦✦✦✦✦
Kenny G's breakthrough effort featured the hit "Songbird," which is the definitive example of the saxophonist's smooth, lyrical playing; the rest of the album is nearly as good, highlighting his melodic jazzy pop. —*Stephen Thomas Erlewine*

Silhouette / 1988 / Arista ✦✦✦✦
Kenny G was at the top his form with *Silhouette*, the follow-up to his breakthrough *Duotones*, turning in a set of smooth, melodic sax that cemented his position as America's favorite pop instrumentalist. —*Stephen Thomas Erlewine*

Kenny G Live / Aug. 26, 1989–Aug. 27, 1989 / Arista ✦✦✦
Breathless / Oct. 20, 1992 / Arista ✦✦✦
One among many huge hit albums featuring the shimmering,

willowy soprano sax solos of Kenny G. He's the best-selling saxophonist of all time and has never claimed to be a jazz musician, which is accurate. These are simple, sometimes enjoyable, pop tunes with forgettable melodies and no harmonic tension or rhythmic excitement. —*Ron Wynn*

Steve Gadd
b. 1945, Rochester, NY
Drums / Funk, Post-Bop, Crossover
A well-respected drummer who has appeared in many types of settings in many genres, Steve Gadd's impressive technique and flexibility have been influential during the past 20 years. He started playing drums at the age of three, sat in with Dizzy Gillespie when he was 11 and, after extensive study and a stint in the Army, Gadd became an important studio drummer beginning in 1972. Among his more significant jazz associations have been with Chick Corea (starting in 1975), Bob James, Al DiMeola, Tom Scott, Grover Washington, Jr., David Sanborn, the group Stuff, the Manhattan Jazz Quintet and his own impressive band (the Gadd Gang), which recorded for Columbia in 1986 and 1988. —*Scott Yanow*

Slim Gaillard
b. Jan. 4, 1916, Detroit, MI, d. Feb. 25, 1991, London, England
Guitar, Vocals, Piano / Swing, Jive
A cult hero, Slim Gaillard was a frequently hilarious personality whose comedy (inventing his own jive language with a liberal use of the words "vout" and "oreenee") generally overshadowed his music. In the mid-'30s he had a solo act during which he played guitar while tap dancing! In 1936 Gaillard began teaming with bassist Slam Stewart as Slim and Slam. Their very first recording became his biggest hit, "Flat Foot Floogie." Slim and Slam were a popular attraction up to 1942 with such other songs as "Tutti Frutti" and "Laughin' in Rhythm." By 1945 Gaillard had a new bassist, Bam Brown (whose frantic vocals matched well with Slim's cool if nonsensical voice), and "Cement Mixer" and "Poppity Pop" caught on. Gaillard, who played electric guitar influenced by Charlie Christian, fairly basic boogie-woogie piano and vibes, led an unusual date with guests Charlie Parker and Dizzy Gillespie (1945) that was highlighted by "Slim's Jam." Throughout the 1940s in Los Angeles, Gaillard had a strong following, using such sidemen as Zutty Singleton and Dodo Marmarosa, but the popularity of jive singers (which included Harry "The Hipster" Gibson and Leo Watson) ran its course and, after 1953, Gaillard only led two other record sessions (in 1958 and 1982). In the 1960s he was largely outside of music, running a motel in San Diego, but by the late '70s Slim Gaillard was back on a part-time basis, still singing "Flat Foot Floogie" and making one wonder why this comic whiz was neglected for nearly three decades. Many of his key recordings can be found on Tax (a box set has the complete Slim and Slam from 1938–42), Hep and Verve. —*Scott Yanow*

Slim and Slam, Vol. 1 / Feb. 17, 1938–Nov. 9, 1938 / Tax ✦✦✦
★ **Slim & Slam** / Feb. 17, 1938–Apr. 4, 1942 / Affinity ✦✦✦✦✦
Starting with his initial recording "Flat Foot Floogie" (whose original name was actually "Flat Fleet Floogee"), guitarist/singer/jokester Slim Gaillard was a cult hero and a masterful (if somewhat limited) entertainer. Teamed with bassist Slam Stewart (who sang along with his bowed solos), Gaillard became quite popular during the latter part of the swing era. This very complete three-CD

set contains all of Slim Gaillard's 82 performances (usually with Slam) including several taken from radio broadcasts and quite a few alternate takes. Among the other sidemen are the underrated tenorman Kenneth Hollon, trumpeter Al Killan, pianist Loumell Morgan, clarinetist Garvin Bushell and Ben Webster on tenor. A definitive and perfectly realized reissue from the English Affinity label. —*Scott Yanow*

Slim and Slam, Vol. 2 / Nov. 9, 1938–Apr. 19, 1940 / Tax ◆◆◆

Slim and Slam, Vol. 3 / Aug. 2, 1940–Jul. 24, 1941 / Tax ◆◆◆

Cement Mixer, Putti, Putti / Dec. 1, 1945–Sep. 1949 / Folklyric ◆◆◆◆

Best Of: Laughin' In Rhythm / Apr. 22, 1946–Jan. 1954 / Verve ◆◆◆◆
This CD has highlights from Slim Gaillard's 1946–47 and 1951–54 recordings for the Verve label. A fine Charlie Christian-inspired guitarist, an adequate pianist and a unique jive singer, Gaillard was always in his own category. Some of the selections on this CD are hilarious and highlights include the four-part "Opera in Vout," "Serenade to a Poodle" (which of course has plenty of barking), "Laughin' in Rhythm," "Chicken Rhythm," "Potato Chips" and the previously unreleased (and modestly titled) "Genius," which features Gaillard overdubbing himself on trumpet, trombone, tenor, vibes, piano, organ, bass, drums, tap dancing and a vocal full of "McVouties!" Although Gaillard's heyday was really the mid-'40s, this CD is quite memorable. —*Scott Yanow*

Dot Sessions / Nov. 1958 / MCA ◆◆◆

Anytime, Anyplace, Anywhere / Oct. 30, 1982 / Hep ◆◆◆

Eric Gale

b. Sep. 20, 1938, New York, NY, d. May 25, 1994
Guitar / R&B, Instrumental Pop, Blues
A guitarist who was used for many R&B-oriented dates and occasionally played jazz, Eric Gale had an appealing sound and was best while performing lazy melodic blues. He was most significant to the jazz world in the early '70s when he recorded often as a sideman for CTI, later on with the group Stuff and on isolated tracks on his own sessions. Gale's fine 1987 EmArcy set *In a Jazz Tradition* shows what he could really do. —*Scott Yanow*

Ginseng Woman / Multiplication / 1976 / Columbia ◆◆
Standard contemporary jazz. A doubleplay of two of Gale's most popular fusion dates. Minimal jazz content or appeal. —*Ron Wynn*

Touch of Silk / 1980 / Columbia ◆◆◆

Blue Horizon / Oct. 1981–Nov. 1981 / Elektra ◆◆
Nice, basically mainstream session from funk and R&B session star Eric Gale. Gale showed his jazz and blues roots on this one, with several tasty, thoughtfully played solos. —*Ron Wynn*

● **In a Jazz Tradition** / Nov. 29, 1987–Nov. 30, 1987 / EmArcy ◆◆◆◆◆

Let's Stay Together / 1989 / Artful Balance ◆◆

Jim Galloway

b. Jul. 28, 1936, Kilwinning, Scotland
Soprano Saxophone, Tenor Saxophone, Clarinet / Swing, Dixieland
An excellent swing soprano player with a lighter tone than Sidney Bechet, Jim Galloway has made many recordings with like-minded veterans. He played locally in Scotland on clarinet and alto before emigrating to Canada in 1965. He soon began specializing on soprano, led the Metro Stompers (1968), put together the Wee Big Band (1978) and hosted the weekly jazz radio program *Toronto Alive!* (1981–87). Galloway, who has appeared at many jazz festivals and jazz parties, has recorded for Sackville, Hep and Music & Arts along with several smaller Canadian labels with such pianists as Dick Wellstood, Art Hodes and most often Jay McShann. —*Scott Yanow*

★ **Thou Swell** / Jun. 15, 1981–Jun. 16, 1981 / Sackville ◆◆◆◆◆

Jim And Jay's Christmas / Nov. 8, 1992–Nov. 9, 1992 / Sackville ◆◆◆

Wee Big Band / Apr. 23, 1993–Apr. 24, 1993 / Sackville ◆◆◆◆

Hal Galper

b. Apr. 18, 1938, Salem, MA
Piano / Post-Bop
An excellent if generally overlooked advanced hard bop pianist,

Hal Galper studied at Berklee (1955–58) and then worked in many groups including with Chet Baker, Stan Getz, the Brecker Brothers, Bobby Hutcherson and with such singers as Joe Williams, Chris Connor and Anita O'Day. He played electric piano (an instrument he has since dropped) with the Cannonball Adderley Quintet during its last years (1973–75) and spent time playing with Lee Konitz and John Scofield. Galper, who has recorded as a leader for Mainstream, SteepleChase, Enja, Concord (including a solo set at Maybeck Recital Hall) and Blackhawk, gained his greatest notoriety for being pianist with Phil Woods' quartet/quintet during 1981–90. —*Scott Yanow*

Now Hear This / Feb. 15, 1977 / Enja ◆◆◆◆

Redux 1978 / Feb. 1978 / Concord Jazz ◆◆◆◆◆
A follow-up recording to the *Speak with a Single Voice* album. An important document of this great band. —*Michael G. Nastos*

★ **Speak with a Single Voice** / Feb. 1978 / Enja ◆◆◆◆◆
First quintet recording, with The Brecker Brothers, at Rosie's in New Orleans. Essential. —*Michael G. Nastos*

Ivory Forest / Oct. 31, 1979–Nov. 1, 1979 / Enja ◆◆◆

Naturally / Jan. 1982 / Blackhawk ◆◆◆

Dreamsville / Mar. 3, 1986 / Enja ◆◆◆

Portrait / Feb. 1989 / Concord Jazz ◆◆

Live at Maybeck Recital Hall, Vol. 6 / Jul. 1990 / Concord Jazz ◆◆◆◆
First-rate, stately solo piano. —*Ron Wynn*

Invitation to a Concert / Nov. 18, 1990 / Concord Jazz ◆◆◆◆◆

Tippin' / Nov. 16, 1992 / Concord Jazz ◆◆◆

Just Us / Sep. 20, 1993 / Enja ◆◆◆

Rebop / 1995 / Enja ◆◆◆

Frank Gambale

b. Dec. 22, 1958, Canberra, Australia
Guitar / Fusion
Frank Gambale is best-known for his fiery work with Chick Corea's Elektric Band. He was a student at the Guitar Institute of Technology while in his early 20s, wrote instructional books and, during 1983–86, was on the school's faculty. He joined Corea in 1986 and has also performed with Steve Smith's Vital Information and as a leader on his own rock-oriented dates for JVC. —*Scott Yanow*

● **The Great Explorers** / 1990 / JVC ◆◆◆◆

Thunder from Down Under / 1990 / JVC ◆◆◆

Note Worker / 1991 / JVC ◆◆◆

Passages / 1994 / JVC ◆◆◆

Thinking Out Loud / May 1995 / JVC ◆◆
On this JVC CD, guitarist Frank Gambale plays in a surprisingly clear tone, avoiding rock (except for the closing "My Little Viper") and at times sounding unexpectedly close to George Benson. Keyboardist Otmaro Ruiz also plays creatively on his three appearances, but unfortunately the weak Gambale compositions (funky but without soul or any worthwhile melodies) and the remarkably dull automatic pilot drumming of Dave Weckl makes this into a fairly routine set. Next time Gambale should apply his fine guitar playing to much better material; he still has a lot of potential. —*Scott Yanow*

Ganelin Trio

Group / Avant-Garde, Free Jazz
Comprised of pianist Vyacheslav Ganelin (b. 1944), saxophonist Vladimir Chekasin (b. 1947) and drummer Vladimir Tarasov (b. 1947), the Ganelin Trio created quite a stir when they were discovered by the West. The group from the Soviet Union played very explorative avant-garde jazz, a rare example of freedom behind the Iron Curtain. They mixed in ethnic free music and earlier jazz styles in their lengthy, colorful and often-humorous improvisations. In addition to their work for the Russian Melodija company, most of their recordings were made for the enterprising Leo label. The group, which had a few opportunities to tour in the West, broke up when Ganelin emigrated to Israel. —*Scott Yanow*

Poco a Poco / Feb. 1978 / Leo ◆◆◆

Strictly for Our Friends / Mar. 1978 / Leo ◆◆◆

Encores / Jun. 15, 1978–Nov. 15, 1981 / Leo ◆◆

★ **Concerto Grosso** / 1978 / Melodiya ◆◆◆◆◆
Ganelin-Tarasov-Checkasin. Russian trio of wildly pure improvisers. A must-buy for the challenging listener. —*Michael G. Nastos*

Non Troppo / Oct. 13, 1980-1982 / Hat Art ✦✦✦
Ancora Da Capo, Vol. 1 / Nov. 15, 1980–Nov. 16, 1980 / Leo ✦✦✦
Ancora Da Capo, Vol. 2 / Nov. 15, 1980–Nov. 16, 1980 / Leo ✦✦✦
Poi Segue / 1981 / Eastwind ✦✦✦✦
Baltic Triangle / Nov. 15, 1981 / Leo ✦✦✦
New Wine . . . / Jun. 26, 1982 / Leo ✦✦✦✦
Con Affetto / Nov. 20, 1983 / Leo ✦✦✦✦
● **Jerusalem February Cantible** / Feb. 1989 / Leo ✦✦✦✦✦
The avant-garde lives overseas, as demonstrated by this free-wheeling, non-stop Russian trio. This is music as unrelenting and animated as anything that came from the '50s and '60s pioneers and simply isn't being made in America much anymore. —*Ron Wynn*
Opuses / Dec. 24, 1989 / Leo ✦✦✦✦

Jan Garbarek
b. Mar. 4, 1947, Mysen, Norway
Tenor Saxophone, Soprano Saxophone / Post-Bop, New Age
The Norwegian saxophonist Jan Garbarek's icy tone and liberal use of space and long tones has long been perfect for the ECM sound and as a result he is on many recordings for that label, both as a leader and as a sideman. He had won a competition for amateur jazz players back in 1962, leading to his first gigs. Garbarek worked steadily in Norway throughout the remainder of the 1960s, usually as a leader but also for four years with George Russell (who was in Scandinavia for a long stretch). Garbarek began recording for ECM in the early '70s and, although he had opportunities to play with Chick Corea and Don Cherry, his association with Keith Jarrett's European quartet in the mid-'70s made him famous, resulting in the classic recordings *My Song* and *Belonging*. In the 1980s Garbarek's groups included bassist Eberhard Weber and, at various times, guitarists Bill Frisell and David Torn. Garbarek, whose sound is virtually unchanged since the 1970s, collaborated with the Hilliard Ensemble in 1993 (a vocal quartet singing Renaissance music) and the result was a surprisingly popular recording. —*Scott Yanow*
The Esoteric Circle / 1969 / Freedom ✦✦✦✦
The '69 album that introduced the stark, careening soprano sax of Norway's Jan Garbarek to American audiences. Composer and theorist George Russell helped get Garbarek entry to American recording studios, and the rest is history. —*Ron Wynn*
Afric Pepperbird / Sep. 22, 1970–Sep. 23, 1970 / ECM ✦✦✦✦
Sart / Apr. 14, 1971–Apr. 15, 1971 / ECM ✦✦✦
Triptykon / Nov. 8, 1972 / ECM ✦✦✦
The third album featuring Norwegian tenor saxophonist Jan Garbarek, issued in 1972. He was a bit less frenetic and more assured, and he began incorporating non-jazz elements into his work, also experimenting with electronics. —*Ron Wynn*
Red Lanta / Nov. 17, 1973–Nov. 20, 1973 / ECM ✦✦✦
● **Witchi-Tai-To** / Nov. 27, 1973–Nov. 28, 1973 / ECM ✦✦✦✦✦
One of the albums that defined the ECM Records sound. —*Michael G. Nastos*
Belonging / Apr. 24, 1974–Apr. 25, 1974 / ECM ✦✦✦✦✦
Luminescence / Apr. 29, 1974–Apr. 30, 1974 / ECM ✦✦✦✦
Dansere / Nov. 1975 / ECM ✦✦✦
Dis / Dec. 1976 / ECM ✦✦
Places / Dec. 1977 / ECM ✦✦✦
Photo with Blue Sky . . . / Dec. 1978 / ECM ✦✦✦✦
Folk Songs / Nov. 1979 / ECM ✦✦✦
Excellent teaming. Haden & Gismonti awaken the perenially detached Garbarek. —*Ron Wynn*
Aftenland / Dec. 1979 / ECM ✦✦
Eventyr / Dec. 1980 / ECM ✦✦✦
Paths, Prints / Dec. 1981 / ECM ✦✦✦
One of the better, more exciting releases—thanks to Bill Frisell (g). —*Ron Wynn*
Wayfarer / Mar. 1983 / ECM ✦✦✦
It's Ok to Listen to the Gray Voices / Dec. 1984 / ECM ✦✦✦
To All Those Born with Wings / Aug. 15, 1986 / ECM ✦✦
Legend of the Seven Dreams / Jul. 1988 / ECM ✦✦
I Took up the Runes / Aug. 1990 / ECM ✦✦✦
Star / Jan. 1991 / ECM ✦✦✦✦
Madar / Aug. 1992 / ECM ✦✦✦
On this CD Jan Garbarek (doubling on tenor and soprano) is

accompanied only by Anouar Brahem on oud and Ustad Shaukat Hussain's tabla. Garbarek shows off his distinctive tones and lyricism on a set of gradually developing group originals, two of which are based on traditional Norwegian melodies. It may take some time for listeners to get into this music and notice the fire beneath the ice, but the close communication between the players is apparent from the start. Jan Garbarek has succeeded in carving out his own unique niche in improvised music and Madar (which also has individual features for Brahem and Shaukat) is a good example of how he can create a great deal out of what seems like very little. —*Scott Yanow*
Twelve Moons / Sep. 1992 / ECM ✦✦
Officium / Sep. 1993 / ECM ✦✦

Laszlo Gardony
b. 1956, Hungary
Piano / Post-Bop
Laszlo Gardony is a superior jazz improviser who infuses his post bop music with references to his Hungarian folk roots. He studied at the Bela Bartok Conservatory in Budapest, graduating in 1979. Gardony recorded five albums on European labels, toured throughout Europe and then in 1983 emigrated to the U.S. to attend Berklee. He performed with the group Forward Motion, recording two albums for Hep. Since graduating from Berklee, Gardony joined their faculty on a part-time basis, played with John Abercrombie and recorded as a leader for Antilles, Sunnyside and Avenue Jazz. —*Scott Yanow*
The Secret / 1986 / Antilles ✦✦✦✦
● **Changing Standards** / Aug. 15, 1990 / Sunnyside ✦✦✦✦✦
Pianist Laszlo Gardony lives up to the title of his CD, performing a variety of standards (including such classics as "Body and Soul," "Take the 'A' Train," "Naima," "Caravan," "Doxy" and two Thelonious Monk tunes) but he re-invents them, altering the harmonies and chord structrues, inserting large doses of passion and putting the emphasis on his own spontaneity. These performances are full of surprises and unusual interpretations. One should expect the unexpected while listening to this stimulating and consistently inventive session. —*Scott Yanow*
Breakout / 1994 / Avenue Jazz ✦✦✦

Red Garland (William M. Garland)
b. May 13, 1923, Dallas, TX, d. Apr. 23, 1984, Dallas, TX
Piano / Hard Bop
Red Garland mixed together the usual influences of his generation (Nat Cole, Bud Powell and Ahmad Jamal) into his own distinctive approach; Garland's block chords themselves became influential on the players of the 1960s. He started out playing clarinet and alto, switching to piano when he was 18. During 1946-55 he worked steadily in New York and Philadelphia, backing such major players as Charlie Parker, Coleman Hawkins, Lester Young and Roy Eldridge, but still remaining fairly obscure. That changed when he became a member of the classic Miles Davis Quintet (1955-58), heading a rhythm section that also included Paul Chambers and Philly Joe Jones. After leaving Miles, Garland had his own popular trio and recorded very frequently for Prestige, Jazzland and Moodsville during 1956-62 (the majority of which are available in the Original Jazz Classics series). The pianist eventually returned to Texas and was in semi-retirement but came back gradually in the 1970s, recording for MPS (1971) and Galaxy (1977-79) before retiring again. —*Scott Yanow*
Garland of Red / Aug. 17, 1956 / Original Jazz Classics ✦✦✦✦✦
Thirty-three at the time of this, his first recording as a leader, pianist Red Garland already had his distinctive style fully formed and had been with the Miles Davis Quintet for a year. With the assistance of bassist Paul Chambers (also in Davis' group) and drummer Art Taylor, Garland is in superior form on six standards, Charlie Parker's "Constellation" (during which he shows that he could sound relaxed at the fastest tempos) and his own "Blue Red." Red Garland recorded frequently during the 1956-62 period and virtually all of his trio recordings are consistently enjoyable, this one being no exception. —*Scott Yanow*
Red Garland's Piano / Dec. 14, 1956+Mar. 22, 1957 / Original Jazz Classics ✦✦✦
Red Garland's third session as a leader finds the distinctive pianist investigating eight standards (including "Please Send Me Someone to Love," "Stompin' at the Savoy," "If I Were a Bell" and

"Almost Like Being in Love") with his distinctive chord voicings, melodic but creative ideas and solid sense of swing. Joined by bassist Paul Chambers and drummer Art Taylor, Garland plays up to his usual consistent level, making this an easily recommended disc for straight-ahead fans. —*Scott Yanow*

Groovy / May 24, 1957 / Original Jazz Classics ✦✦✦✦
As the liner notes properly state, this CD (Red Garland's fourth as a leader for the Prestige label) has "jazz standards, ballad standards, blues ballads and just plain blues." The pianist's trio (with bassist Paul Chambers and drummer Art Taylor) swings such numbers as "C Jam Blues," "Will You Still Be Mine" (the latter from The Ahmad Jamal songbook) and "What Can I Say After I Say I'm Sorry" with spirit and subtle invention. All of Red Garland's Prestige recordings are worth getting. —*Scott Yanow*

All Mornin' Long / Nov. 15, 1957 / Original Jazz Classics ✦✦✦
Loose, with elements of funk and soul-jazz, plus the usual excellence from Donald Byrd (tpt), Coltrane (ts) and Garland. —*Ron Wynn*

Soul Junction / Nov. 15, 1957 / Original Jazz Classics ✦✦✦✦
Quintet. More Donald Byrd (tpt), John Coltrane (ts), Red Garland. Solos from Coltrane and Byrd are better than on *High Pressure*. —*Ron Wynn*

High Pressure / Nov. 15, 1957+Dec. 13, 1957 / Prestige ✦✦✦

Dig It! / Dec. 13, 1957–Feb. 7, 1958 / Original Jazz Classics ✦✦✦
1989 reissue contains more from the mammoth Garland late-'50s output, with Donald Byrd (tpt), John Coltrane (ts), Paul Chambers (b), Art Taylor (d) and the underrated George Joyner (tpt). —*Ron Wynn*

Manteca / Apr. 11, 1958 / Original Jazz Classics ✦✦✦
Red Garland Trio. Afro-Latin flavoring from Ray Barretto (per) spices up an otherwise proficient but musically standard trio date. —*Ron Wynn*

Rediscovered Masters / Jun. 1958 / Original Jazz Classics ✦✦✦
Rediscovered Masters, Vol. 1 includes a previously unissued track "Satin Doll," from this 1959 set with bassist Doug Watkins and drummer Specs Wright. This previously unissued cut is perhaps notable in that it sounds like the group was unclear on how long solos would stretch. At the time of these recordings, Garland was being prolifically recorded by Prestige and at a faster rate than the records could be realistically issued. He was Prestige's favorite Texas pianist. —*Bob Rusch, Cadence*

Rojo / Aug. 22, 1958 / Original Jazz Classics ✦✦✦✦
Pianist Red Garland recorded frequently with trios for Prestige during the second half of the 1950s. For this set (reissued on CD), Garland, bassist George Joyner and drummer Charlie Persip are joined by Ray Barretto on congas and the emphasis is on forceful swinging. Garland takes such ballads as "We Kiss in a Shadow" and "You Better Go Now" at faster-than-expected tempos. "Ralph J. Gleason Blues" and the Latin feel of "Rojo" are among the highlights of this enjoyable disc. —*Scott Yanow*

Red Garland Trio / Nov. 21, 1958 / Original Jazz Classics ✦✦
This session from pianist Red Garland, reissued on LP in Fantasy's *Original Jazz Classics* series but not yet on CD, originally appeared on the Moodsville label. Its slow tempos (only "And the Angels Sing" moves a little) fit well into the theme of that subsidiary's releases, but it resulted in the set being a bit sleepy. Bassist Paul Chambers and drummer Art Taylor help out and Garland play these two blues and four standards well, but the lack of variety makes this reissue one of Red Garland's lesser efforts. —*Scott Yanow*

All Kinds Of Weather / Nov. 27, 1958 / Original Jazz Classics ✦✦✦
Red Garland was always a consistent pianist and all of his mid-to-late-'50s Prestige dates are worth acquiring. This CD reissue has six titles having to do with seasons and the weather (such as "Rain," "Summertime" and "Winter Wonderland"). The gimmick served as a good excuse for Garland, bassist Paul Chambers and drummer Art Taylor to explore six superior songs and their interpretations always swing and uplift the melodies. —*Scott Yanow*

Red in Bluesville / Apr. 17, 1959 / Original Jazz Classics ✦✦✦
Pianist Red Garland and his trio (with bassist Sam Jones and drummer Art Taylor) explore six veteran blues-based compositions ranging from Nellie Lutcher's "He's a Real Gone Guy" and "St. Louis Blues" to "Your Red Wagon" and Count Basie's "M Squad Theme." Throughout, Garland modernizes each of the selections with his distinctive chord voicings and he makes the

songs sound fresh and new. A solid effort comes from this very consistent pianist, who will always be best remembered for his playing with the classic Miles Davis Quintet. —*Scott Yanow*

★ **Red Garland at the Prelude, Vol. 1** / Oct. 1959 / Prestige ✦✦✦✦✦
Originally released as two LPs (*Red Garland at the Prelude* and *Red Garland/Live*), this single CD (which has around 77 minutes of music) features a particularly strong trio set by the pianist, bassist Jimmy Rowser and drummer Specs Wright. Garland mostly sticks to standards and the highlights include "Perdido," "Bye Bye Blackbird" (which is reminiscent of the famous Miles Davis version) and two versions of "One O'Clock Jump." Straight-ahead jazz fans should get this one. —*Scott Yanow*

The Red Garland Trio with Eddie Lockjaw Davis, Vol. 1 / Dec. 11, 1959 / Original Jazz Classics ✦✦✦

Bright and Breezy / Jul. 19, 1961 / Original Jazz Classics ✦✦✦
During 1961–62, following a long series of recording for Prestige, pianist Red Garland recorded four LPs for the Jazzland label. His style was unchanged from a few years earlier, and this trio set with bassist Sam Jones and drummer Charlie Persip (reissued on CD in the OJC series) is very much up to par. Highlights include Garland's interpretations of "I Ain't Got Nobody," "Blues in the Closet" and "Lil' Darlin'." An enjoyable straight-ahead session. —*Scott Yanow*

Solar / Jan. 30, 1962 / Jazzland ✦✦✦
Pianist Red Garland recorded many sessions during 1955–63, and his distinctive chord voicings and relaxed style was always worth hearing. The wild card on this quartet is Les Spann, who had the unusual double of guitar and flute; his flute is a major asset on "Where Are You?" and "The Very Thought of You." Garland (along with bassist Sam Jones and drummer Frank Gant) is in fine form throughout these underplayed standards; highlights include "Sophisticated Swing," "Solar" and "This Can't Be Love." —*Scott Yanow*

When There Are Grey Skies / Oct. 9, 1962 / Original Jazz Classics ✦✦✦✦
This set was pianist Red Garland's 25th session as a leader since 1956, but it would be eight years before his next record. Garland's influential style had been fully formed since the mid-'50s and his chord voicings were immediately recognizable. With the assistance of bassist Wendell Marshall and drummer Charlie Persip, Garland explores and updates seven veteran songs (including a previously unreleased "My Blue Heaven") dating from the '20s era. This fine CD is highlighted by such unlikely material as "Sonny Boy," "St. James Infirmary," "Baby Won't You Please Come Home" and a 12-minute "Nobody Knows the Trouble I've Seen." —*Scott Yanow*

The Quota / May 3, 1971 / MPS ✦✦✦

Red Alert / Dec. 2, 1977 / Original Jazz Classics ✦✦✦✦
A 1991 issue of an excellent album date with superb Garland piano and top contributions by Nat Adderley (cnt), Harold Land (ts) and Ira Sullivan (tpt). —*Ron Wynn*

Crossings / Dec. 1977 / Original Jazz Classics ✦✦✦
Tremendous update. An example of Garland's ability to heave and create in a trio setting, this time with Ron Carter (b) and Philly Joe Jones (d). —*Ron Wynn*

Feelin' Red / May 15, 1978 / Muse ✦✦✦

I Left My Heart . . . / May 1978 / Muse ✦✦✦

Equinox / Aug. 4, 1978–Aug. 5, 1978 / Galaxy ✦✦✦

Strike up the Band / Jul. 11, 1979–Jul. 12, 1979 / Galaxy ✦✦✦✦
Some stunning solos from George Coleman (ts). Garland is still an impressive player in the final stages of his career, though not as much the driving force as in the past. —*Ron Wynn*

Misty Red / Apr. 13, 1982–Apr. 14, 1982 / Timeless ✦✦✦✦

Erroll Garner

b. Jun. 15, 1921, Pittsburg, PA, d. Jan. 2, 1977, Los Angeles, CA
Piano / Swing, Bop
One of the most distinctive of all pianists, Erroll Garner proved that it was possible to be a sophisticated player without knowing how to read music, that a creative jazz musician can be very popular without watering down his music and that it is possible to remain an enthusiastic player without changing one's style once it is formed. A brilliant virtuoso who sounded unlike anyone else, Erroll Garner on medium-tempo pieces often stated the beat with

his left hand like a rhythm guitar while his right played chords slightly behind the beat, creating a memorable effect. His playful free-form introductions (which forced his sidemen to really listen), his ability to play stunning runs without once glancing at the keyboard, his grunting and the pure joy that he displayed while performing were also part of the Erroll Garner magic.

Garner, whose older brother Linton is also a fine pianist, appeared on the radio with the Kan-D-Kids at the age of ten. After working locally in Pittsburgh, he moved to New York in 1944 and worked with Slam Stewart's trio during 1944–45 before going out on his own. By 1946 Garner had his sound together and when he backed Charlie Parker on his famous "Cool Blues" session of 1947, the pianist was already an obvious giant. His unclassifiable style had an orchestral approach straight from the swing era, but was open to the innovations of bop. From the early '50s, Garner's accessible style became very popular and he never seemed to have an off day up until his forced retirement (due to illness) in early 1975. His composition "Misty" became a standard. Erroll Garner, who had the ability to sit at the piano without prior planning and record three albums in one day (all colorful first takes), made many records throughout his career for such companies as Savoy, Mercury, RCA, Dial, Columbia, EmArcy, ABC-Paramount, MGM, Reprise and his own Octave label. —*Scott Yanow*

The Elf / Sep. 25, 1945–Mar. 29, 1949 / Savoy ✦✦✦
This set allows one to hear the very distinctive pianist Erroll Garner in his early days. Four tracks are with bassist John Levy and drummer George de Hart in 1945, but the lion's share is with bassist John Simmons and drummer Alvin Stoller from 1949. The medium-tempo pieces are the most enjoyable with Garner's slightly behind-the-beat right hand echoing his on-the-beat left hand. The ballads can sometimes get a bit overly rhapsodic, but are still enjoyable. It is no wonder that Garner remained popular for decades without needing to adjust or water down his style. — *Scott Yanow*

Body and Soul / Jan. 11, 1951–Jan. 3, 1952 / Columbia ✦✦✦✦

Too Marvelous for Words, Vol. 3 / May 26, 1954 / EmArcy ✦✦✦✦✦

Erroll Garner Collection, Vols. 4 & 5: Solo Time! / Jul. 7, 1954 / EmArcy ✦✦✦✦

Mambo Moves Garner / Jul. 27, 1954 / Mercury ✦✦✦✦✦
For this lengthy session, pianist Erroll Garner added a conga player (Candido) to his trio (which includes bassist Wyatt Ruther and drummer Eugene Heard) for the first time. Throughout the remainder of his career he would occasionally play in the Latin idiom. This CD reissue (which adds two songs from the same session to the original LP program) finds the pianist in typically enthusiastic form and the highlights include "Mambo Garner," "Night and Day," "Cherokee" and "Sweet Sue." —*Scott Yanow*

The Original Misty / Jul. 27, 1954–Mar. 14, 1955 / EmArcy ✦✦✦✦✦

Afternoon of an Elf / Mar. 14, 1955 / Mercury ✦✦✦
Spectacular, frenzied solo piano from Errol Garner, done in 1955. Sometimes he would probe, pick apart, then reconstruct standards. Other times, he would race through a song, varying the tempo, pulse and pace with each solo. This has been reissued on CD. —*Ron Wynn*

Solitaire / Mar. 14, 1955 / Mercury ✦✦✦
On March 14, 1955, Erroll Garner sat down at the piano and played one interesting solo after another, resulting in two albums of music. Seven pieces (all but "That Old Feeling" are taken as ballads) were originally released as *Solitaire*; this CD reissue adds four additional selections that are taken at faster paces. Although not essential, the rhapsodic and occasionally wandering but always intriguing set should greatly interest fans. —*Scott Yanow*

★ **Concert by the Sea** / Sep. 19, 1955 / Columbia ✦✦✦✦✦
Concert by the Sea was arguably the finest record pianist Erroll Garner ever made, and he made many—a few outstanding—many good recordings. But this live recording (Sept. 19, 1955) with his trio (Eddie Calhoun, bass; Denzil Best, drums) presented a typical Garner program; it was a mixture of originals, show biz and pop standards delivered with his unique delivery and enthusiasm. The rhythms and brilliant use of tension and release was perfectly captured. And while for many jazz listeners, Garner's deliberate structures were too orchestrated, there was an equal spontaneity in the propulsion of these orchestrations that swung as well as anything. —*Bob Rusch, Cadence*

Other Voices / 1956 / Columbia ✦✦
Among his more pop (and popular) releases when it was issued in 1956. This reissue isn't of the highest caliber; it's merely a decent one. Find the original if possible. —*Ron Wynn*

Errol Garner Plays Gershwin and Kern / 1958–1965 / Mercury ✦✦✦✦

Dancing on the Ceiling / Jun. 1, 1961–Aug. 19, 1965 / EmArcy ✦✦✦✦✦
The great pianist Erroll Garner is heard on these 11 selections, happily jamming standards with bassist Eddie Calhoun and drummer Kelly Martin. One number is from 1964 and another from a year later, but the remainder was performed in 1961; all of the selections were previously unreleased. The music is marvelous and sometimes miraculous, with Garner's distinctive style heard at its best throughout. —*Scott Yanow*

Easy to Love / 1961–Aug. 19, 1965 / EmArcy ✦✦✦

Plays Gershwin and Kern / Aug. 5, 1964–Feb. 5, 1968 / EmArcy ✦✦✦
Errol Garner Plays Gershwin and Kern is a reissue of material previously issued in Europe on Bulldog, MPS and Polydor… Either way, the material is quite excellent, often adventuresome and some of his best studio sides. Included here from Feb. 5, 1968 and never issued before is a brief "Nice Work If You Can Get It" with Garner singing along to himself—it's a wonderful gem of a private moment. Backup is Eddie Calhoun or Ike Isaacs on bass, Kelly Martin or Jimmy Smith on drums and Jose Mangual, congas. This was the first domestic issue of this material. —*Bob Rusch, Cadence*

That's My Kick & Gemini / 1967–1972 / Telarchive ✦✦✦✦
This CD from Telarchive (a subsidiary of Telarc) reissues the complete content of two later Errol Garner LPs: *That's My Kick* and *Gemini*. The great pianist was still in prime form and, although his sidemen are fine in support (Wally Richardson is on guitar on the first date and the congas of Jose Mangual add a Latin flavor to the music to both sessions), Garner totally dominates the music as usual. He contributed eight of the 19 compositions and his wit is only exceeded by his creativity. —*Scott Yanow*

Magician & Gershwin And Kern / 1974–1976 / Telac ✦✦✦
Two of Errol Garner's last albums, *Magician* and *Gershwin and Kern*, are reissued on this single CD. The pianist, heading trios or quartets, is in typically whimsical and hard-swinging form; he never did decline on record. The former session includes several of his originals plus versions of "Close to You" and "Watch What Happens" that manage to uplift those pop tunes; the latter date has consistently superior material. Garner's very spontaneous playing is as usual both unpredictable and quite accessible, and these unedited performances were all first takes. No one ever really sounded like Erroll Garner and this highly enjoyable set of formerly rare material gives one a good example of his magical music. —*Scott Yanow*

Kenny Garrett

b. Oct. 9, 1960, Detroit, MI
Alto Saxophone / Post-Bop
Kenny Garrett was one of the last significant graduates of Miles Davis' groups and is one of the potential greats in jazz. He started early on playing in Detroit with Marcus Belgrave and toured with the Mercer Ellington Orchestra before moving to New York in 1980. He made his debut recording for Criss Cross (1984) and was part of the group Out of the Blue before joining Davis for the trumpeter's last few years. Garrett recorded an obscure session for Paddlewheel (1988) and the weak *Prisoner of Love* (1989) and the recommended *African Exchange Student* (1990) as a leader for Atlantic. Since Miles Davis' death, Garrett has led his own groups and recorded for Warner Brothers, justifying Davis' faith in him. —*Scott Yanow*

Introducing Kenny Garrett / Dec. 28, 1984 / Criss Cross ✦✦✦

Prisoner of Love / 1989 / Atlantic ✦✦
Miles Davis makes a guest appearance. The compositions are erratic, but Garrett is a stalwart player. —*Ron Wynn*

African Exchange Student / 1990 / Atlantic ✦✦✦✦✦
Adventurous, robust playing from young lion Garrett, but uneven material. Two bonus cuts on CD. —*Ron Wynn*

Black Hope / 1992 / Warner Brothers ✦✦✦✦
Alto saxophonist Kenny Garrett hasn't been as heavily publicized

as his fellow young lions, but he can play with as much authority, conviction and sheer energy as anyone. Only some uneven material keeps his '92 album from being exceptional, and even on the weak songs, Garrett's playing forces you to pay attention. — *Ron Wynn*

★ **Triology** / 1995 / Warner Brothers ✦✦✦✦✦

Threshold / Warner Brothers ✦✦✦

Jimmy Garrison

b. Mar. 3, 1934, Miami, FL, **d.** Apr. 7, 1976, New York, NY
Bass / Avant-Garde, Post-Bop, Free Jazz
Jimmy Garrison was one of the most advanced bassists of the 1960s, a perfect candidate to play with John Coltrane and Ornette Coleman. He grew up in Philadelphia and came to New York with Philly Joe Jones in 1958. He freelanced for a couple of years with the likes of Bill Evans, Benny Golson, Kenny Dorham and Lennie Tristano and then succeeded Charlie Haden in Ornette Coleman's Quartet (1961). However Garrison will always be associated with John Coltrane (1961–67), not only playing with the classic quartet (which included McCoy Tyner and Elvin Jones) but surviving the tumultuous changes and staying with Trane until the end. Garrison's solos (which were thoughtful and slow to build) were not to everyone's taste, but his ability to play coherent and inspiring lines in the raging ensembles behind Coltrane and Pharoah Sanders was quite impressive. After Coltrane's death, Garrison played in groups led by Alice Coltrane, Archie Shepp and Elvin Jones before lung cancer cut short his life. — *Scott Yanow*

Mike Garson

b. Jul. 1945, Brooklyn, NY
Piano, Keyboards / Post-Bop, Crossover
Mike Garson, a true virtuoso, has had a very diverse career. Heard at his best with his own groups or with Free Flight, Garson has also toured with David Bowie and for a television movie on Liberace he performed the music and had his hands used for the playing sequences of the film! He started playing piano when he was seven, studied classical music for ten years, graduated from Brooklyn College, served in the military and then joined a rock group called Brethren that recorded. Garson soon gained experience freelancing with a wide variety of performers including Mel Tormé, Thad Jones and Annette Peacock; he also studied with Lennie Tristano and had an important six-hour lesson with Bill Evans. Garson toured with Bowie during 1972–74, moved to Los Angeles and worked with Freddie Hubbard and Stanley Clarke (1978). He became a busy studio musician (both composing and performing prolifically) and in 1982 joined Free Flight, a group that switches back and forth between classical, straight-ahead jazz and funkier rhythms. Garson has recorded jazz as a leader for Contemporary (1979), Jazzhounds, Chase and Reference. — *Scott Yanow*

Avant Garson / Nov. 20, 1979–Nov. 21, 1979 / Contemporary ✦✦✦
Pianist Mike Garson, who has worked in every setting from big band to solo, moves to the free and outside edge on this release. He sustains his intensity throughout, and while this album doesn't have as much emotional punch as some others in the genre, he shows he can handle cutting edge material, as well as straight-ahead. — *Ron Wynn*

● **Serendipity** / 1986 / Reference ✦✦✦✦
The best total album thus far by pianist Mike Garson has been a set of trio and combo performances recorded in 1986 titled *Serendipity.* That's partly due to the material's caliber, timeless pieces such as "Autumn Leaves," "My One and Only Love," and "My Romance." It's also partly due to the quality of guest performers like bassist Stanley Clarke, drummer Peter Sprague and saxophonist Gary Herbig. But the biggest reason is Garson, who simply illuminates and communicates the greatness of the songs. — *Ron Wynn*

The Mystery Man / Apr. 1990 / Chase Music Group ✦✦✦

The Oxnard Sessions Vol. 1 / Aug. 1, 1990–Aug. 2, 1990 / Reference ✦✦✦✦
Pianist Mike Garson leads an accomplished group through a mixed bag of jazz standards and recent pop hits on *The Oxnard Sessions, Volume One.* His playing, particularly on the lengthy "Without Self" and a good cover of "Sweet and Lovely," has its provocative, challenging moments, along with the requisite shadings and more impressionistic melodies. The 1990 CD includes

four alternate takes, two of which are longer versions of "Nothing To Do Blues" and "Spontaneity." — *Ron Wynn*

The Oxnard Sessions, Vol. 2 / Aug. 18, 1992–Aug. 19, 1992 / Reference ✦✦✦
Mike Garson has invested in star power to punch up *The Oxnard Sessions, Volume Two.* The recently released disc features a smaller group (piano/bass/drums/sax) and gives Garson a lot more solo room this time out. Drummer Ralph Humphrey shows more facility with a backbeat than Billy Mintz, who does appear on one alternate take. Saxophonist Eric Marienthal, a powerhouse type whose spurts and squeals add some excitement to even his most shrill and pop-oriented solos, also gets room to show his talents. The selections are more jazz and standard-oriented than before, and Garson and his mates demonstrate much more integrity than at any time on the previous release. — *Ron Wynn*

A Gershwin Fantasia / Aug. 23, 1992 / Reference ✦✦✦

Screen Themes '93 / 1993 / Discovery ✦✦

Screenthemes '94 / 1994 / Discovery ✦✦

George Garzone

b. Boston, MA
Tenor Sax / Post-Bop
A powerful tenor saxophonist whose adventurous flights with his longtime band, the Fringe, have made him a legend in the Boston area, George Garzone has spent most of his life as a jazz educator. He began on the tenor when he was six, played in a family band and attended music school in Boston. Garzone first formed his trio the Fringe (a group that in the mid-'90s also included founding member Bob Gullotti on drums and bassist John Lockwood) back in 1972. In addition Garzone has guested in many situations, touring Europe with Jamaaladeen Tacuma and gigging with Danilo Perez, Joe Lovano, Jack DeJohnette, Rachel Z and John Patitucci among others. In 1995 he recorded a fine tribute to Stan Getz on NYC called *Alone.* — *Scott Yanow*

Charles Gayle

b. 1939, Buffalo, NY
Tenor Saxophone / Free Jazz
The logical successor to Albert Ayler (circa 1965), Charles Gayle is a high energy player whose improvisations are filled with extreme emotions and speechlike screams. He did not emerge in the avant-garde scene until the mid-'80s, making his recording debut with three albums cut for Silkheart in 1988 that were cut within a five-day period (April 10–14). Gayle, who recorded frequently for the Knitting Factory label starting in 1992 (he has also made CDs for Black Saint and Victor), is a ferocious tenor player who in recent times has also been playing bass clarinet and fairly basic piano in addition to taking some eccentric vocals full of strange right-wing preaching. Charles Gayle is certainly a talent not to be taken lightly! — *Scott Yanow*

Always Born / Apr. 10, 1988–Apr. 11, 1988 / Silkheart ✦✦✦

Spirits Before / Apr. 13, 1988–Apr. 14, 1988 / Silkheart ✦✦✦

Homeless / Apr. 13, 1988–Apr. 14, 1988 / Silkheart ✦✦✦✦

★ **Repent** / 1992 / Knitting Factory ✦✦✦✦✦
There is absolutely no one currently playing tenor (or any other saxophone) coming close to making the kind of music created by Charles Gayle. While it's reminiscent of Albert Ayler's energetic, twisting 1960s free dates, Gayle's saxophone acrobatics and stamina are astonishing. This two-song CD was recorded live and features one number that runs 23 minutes; it's the short tune. "Jesus Christ and Scripture," the second piece, proceeds for over 50 minutes, much of that featuring Gayle's honks, bleats, turnarounds, moans and anguished cries on tenor. After listening closely to this disc, its lack of repetition and gimmickry is commendable. It's certainly not for all (or even most tastes), but those who listen fairly and intently to Charles Gayle will be rewarded. — *Ron Wynn*

More Live / 1993 / Knitting Factory ✦✦✦✦✦
Tenor saxophonist Charles Gayle plays with such fury and intensity that it seems he won't make it through the performances featured on these two discs. They spotlight his quartet during concerts. Hearing Gayle's overtones, screams and blistering solos, backed by equally spirited playing from bassists Vattel Cherry and William Parker and either Michael Wimberly or Marc Edwards on drums, it's easy to forget you're hearing it as they played it, with

little pacing or variance in volume. It's impossible not to remember the 1960s and '70s free and loft jazz schools, but it's also appropriate to emphasize that Gayle doesn't sound like anyone else currently active and deserves significant attention beyond tiny jazz publications and sympathetic, but small, audiences. – *Ron Wynn*

Translation / Jan. 21, 1993–Jan. 22, 1993 / Silkheart ◆◆◆◆

Raining Fire / Jan. 21, 1993–Jan. 22, 1993 / Silkheart ◆◆◆◆

Consecration / Apr. 17, 1993–Apr. 18, 1993 / Black Saint ◆◆◆

Kingdom Come / 1994 / Knitting Factory ◆◆◆

Herb Geller

b. Nov. 2, 1928, Los Angeles, CA
Alto Saxophone, Soprano Saxophone / Bop, Hard Bop
Herb Geller is a survivor of the Los Angeles jazz scene of the 1950s who is playing better than ever in the mid-'90s. Geller played in 1946 with Joe Venuti's Orchestra and in 1949 he traveled to New York to play with Claude Thornhill. In 1951 he moved back to L.A. and married the excellent bop pianist Lorraine Walsh. Geller was a fixture in L.A., playing with Billy May (1952), Maynard Ferguson, Shorty Rogers, Bill Holman and Chet Baker among others, jamming with Clifford Brown and Max Roach (1954) and leading a quartet that included his wife (1954–55). Lorraine Geller's sudden death in 1958 eventually resulted in the altoist deciding to leave the country to escape his grief. He played with Benny Goodman off and on between 1958–61, spent time in Brazil and, in 1962, moved to Berlin. Geller worked in German radio orchestras for 30 years, played in European big bands and continued to grow as a musician although he was pretty much forgotten in the U.S. From the early '90s on, Herb Geller has begun returning to the States on a more regular basis and he recently recorded a tribute to Al Cohn for Hep. Geller also recorded as a leader in the 1950s for EmArcy, Jubilee and Atco and in the 1980s and '90s for Enja, Fresh Sound and VSOP. – *Scott Yanow*

The Herb Geller Sextet / Aug. 6, 1954+Aug. 9, 1954 / EmArcy ◆◆◆

That Geller Feller / Mar. 1957 / Fresh Sound ◆◆◆◆

Fire in the West / Mar. 1957 / Jubilee ◆◆◆◆

Stax of Sax / 1958 / Jubilee ◆◆◆◆

Rhyme and Reason / Jan. 13, 1975 / Discovery ◆◆

Hot House / Nov. 24, 1984 / Circle ◆◆◆

Birdland Stomp / Jan. 24, 1986-Jan. 25, 1986 / Enja ◆◆◆

Jazz Song Book / Dec. 1988 / Enja ◆◆◆
This is much better than you'd expect from the low-key publicity. Geller deserves a wider profile, having been an active player since the '40s. Walter Morris is a prominent figure on the piano. – *Ron Wynn*

Birdland Stomp / May 24, 1990–May 25, 1990 / Fresh Sound ◆◆◆◆
An outstanding quartet date, with Kenny Drew sharp on the piano. – *Ron Wynn*

★ **Herb Geller Quartet** / Aug. 5, 1993–Aug. 6, 1993 / VSOP ◆◆◆◆◆
This quartet outing with pianist Tom Ranier, bassist John Leitham and drummer Louis Bellson is one of altoist Herb Geller's finest recordings. Geller, whose long period in Europe has resulted in him being somewhat forgotten in the U.S., has actually improved through the years and was even stronger in the mid-'90s than he had been in the mid-'50s. For this date he contributes five originals (including a tribute to Lenny Bruce "Stand-Up Comic" during which Geller sings) and performs six mostly lesser-known standards, highlighted by "The Peacocks," which has its composer Jimmy Rowles sitting in on piano. This CD is easily recommended to bop collectors for it finds Herb Geller at the peak of his powers. – *Scott Yanow*

Stan Getz

b. Feb. 2, 1927, Philadelphia, PA, d. Jun. 6, 1991, Malibu, CA
Tenor Saxophone / Cool, Bossa Nova, Post-Bop
One of the all-time great tenor saxophonists, Stan Getz was known as "The Sound" because he had one of the most beautiful tones ever heard. Getz, whose main early influence was Lester Young, grew to be a major influence himself and to his credit he never stopped evolving.

Stan Getz had the opportunity to play in a variety of major swing big bands while a teenager due to the World War II draft. He was with Jack Teagarden (1943) when he was just 16 and this was followed with stints with Stan Kenton (1944–45), Jimmy Dorsey (1945) and Benny Goodman (1945–46); he soloed on a few records with BG. Getz, who had his recording debut as a leader in July 1946 with four titles, became famous during his period with Woody Herman's Second Herd (1947–49), soloing (along with Zoot Sims, Herbie Steward and Serge Chaloff) on the original version of "Four Brothers" and having his sound well-featured on the ballad "Early Autumn." After leaving Herman, Getz was (with the exception of some tours with Jazz at the Philharmonic) a leader for the rest of his life.

During the early '50s, Getz broke away from the Lester Young style to form his own musical identity and he was soon among the most popular of all jazzmen. He discovered Horace Silver in 1950 and used him in his quartet for several months. After touring Sweden in 1951, he formed an exciting quintet that co-featured guitarist Jimmy Raney; their interplay on uptempo tunes and tonal blend on ballads was quite memorable. Getz's playing helped Johnny Smith have a hit in "Moonlight in Vermont," during 1953–54 Bob Brookmeyer made his group a quintet and, despite some drug problems during the decade, Getz was a constant pollwinner. After spending 1958–60 in Europe, the tenorman returned to the U.S. and recorded his personal favorite album, *Focus*, with arranger Eddie Sauter's Orchestra. Then, in Feb. 1962, Getz helped usher in the bossa nova era by recording *Jazz Samba* with Charlie Byrd; their rendition of "Desafinado" was a big hit. During the next year, Getz made bossa nova flavored albums with Charlie Byrd, Laurindo Almeida, but it was *Getz/Gilberto* (a collaboration with Antonio Carlos Jobim and Joao Gilberto) that was his biggest seller, thanks in large part to "The Girl from Ipanema" (featuring the vocals of Astrud and Joao Gilberto).

Stan Getz could have spent the next decade sticking to bossa nova, but instead he de-emphasized the music and chose to play more challenging jazz. His regular group during this era was a pianoless quartet with vibraphonist Gary Burton, recorded with Bill Evans (1964), played throughout the 1965 Eddie Sauter soundtrack for *Mickey One* and made the classic album *Sweet Rain* (1967) with Chick Corea. Although not all of Getz's recordings from the 1966–80 period are essential, he proved that he was not shy to take chances. *Dynasty* with organist Eddie Louiss (1971), *Captain Marvel* with Chick Corea (1972) and *The Peacocks* with Jimmy Rowles (1975) are highpoints. After utilizing pianist Joanne Brackeen in his 1977 quartet, Getz explored some aspects of fusion with his next unit, which featured keyboardist Andy Laverne. Getz even used an echoplex on a couple of songs but, despite some misfires, most of his dates with this unit are worthwhile. However, purists were relieved when he signed with Concord in 1981 and started using a purely acoustic backup trio on most dates. Getz's sidemen in later years included pianists Lou Levy, Mitchell Forman, Jim McNeely and Kenny Barron. His final recording, 1991's *People Time*, (despite some shortness in the tenor's breath) is a brilliant duet set with Barron.

Throughout his career Stan Getz recorded as a leader for Savoy, Spotlite, Prestige, Roost, Verve, MGM, Victor, Columbia, SteepleChase, Concord, Sonet, Black Hawk, A&M and EmArcy among other labels (not to mention sessions with Lionel Hampton, Dizzy Gillespie and Gerry Mulligan), and there are dozens of worthy records by the tenor currently available on CD. – *Scott Yanow*

Opus De Bop / Dec. 12, 1945–May 5, 1949 / Savoy ◆◆◆
Some of tenor saxophonist Stan Getz's earliest recordings are included on this well-conceived LP. Getz displays a harder sound than one might expect on sextet sides with trombonist Kai Winding and trumpeter Shorty Rogers from late 1945 and on four selections with a quartet from mid-1946. The final four selections (from May 1949) are more typical as Getz (along with fellow tenors Al Cohn and Zoot Sims) plays hard-swinging cool bop; the three tenors can barely be told apart. Bop collectors will want this interesting music. – *Scott Yanow*

Brothers / Apr. 8, 1949 / Original Jazz Classics ◆◆◆

Preservation / Jun. 21, 1949–Jul. 28, 1949 / Original Jazz Classics ◆◆◆

Quartets / Jun. 21, 1949–Apr. 14, 1950 / Original Jazz Classics ◆◆◆◆
Some formative material from 1949 and 1950—instructive and often vital. – *Ron Wynn*

Roost Quartets / May 17, 1950–Mar. 1, 1951 / Roulette ✦✦✦✦✦
After leaving Woody Herman's Orchestra, tenor saxophonist Stan Getz became one of the leaders of the "cool school" due to his attractive light tone and his strong jazz abilities. This CD features his 1950–51 quartets. On the first seven selections, Getz is accompanied by pianist Al Haig, bassist Tommy Potter and drummer Roy Haynes; they play such numbers as "On the Alamo," "Yesterdays" and the appealing "Hershey Bar." By late 1950 Getz had a new band, a rhythm section that he had discovered and immediately hired in Connecticut. Although bassist Joe Calloway and drummer Walt Bolden are obscure, pianist Horace Silver later became a major star. On his recording debut (15 performances including three alternate takes), Silver displays a style that was already recognizable and fit in perfectly with Getz. —*Scott Yanow*

★ **The Complete Recordings of the Stan Getz Quintet with Jimmy Raney** / Aug. 15, 1951–Apr. 23, 1953 / Mosaic ✦✦✦✦✦
This limited-edition, three-CD set will be hard to acquire, but it is a gem. Tenor saxophonist Stan Getz and guitarist Jimmy Raney had very complementary cool-toned but hard-swinging styles. Their gig at Storyville in Boston resulted in some classic music that, along with five studio sessions, is included in this box. The supporting cast includes pianists Al Haig, Horace Silver, Duke Jordan and Hall Overton; the music was originally recorded for Roost, Clef, Norgran and Prestige. This essential set is filled with exciting performances from Stan Getz when he was first becoming a highly influential force in jazz. —*Scott Yanow*

Live 1952, Vol. 1 / Apr. 15, 1952–Aug. 9, 1952 / Jazz & Jazz ✦✦✦
This Italian import features tenor saxophonist Stan Getz in rare Birdland appearances from April 15, 1952 (with a quintet including pianist Horace Silver, guitarist Jimmy Raney, bassist Charles Mingus and drummer Connie Kay) and Aug. 9, 1952 (with a quintet, pianist Duke Jordan, Mingus and drummer Phil Brown). Getz is in excellent form on these eight selections, which are highlighted by "Potter's Luck," "Parker 51" (which is really "Cherokee") and "Move." Getz and Raney had a special chemistry and all of their recordings are excellent, but this LP will be difficult to locate. —*Scott Yanow*

Move! Live 1952-1953 / Aug. 7, 1952–Jan. 15, 1953 / Natasha ✦✦✦✦
This CD is highly recommended not so much for its historic value (guitarist Jimmy Raney, Stan Getz's most stimulating partner during this period, is absent), but for the consistently stimulating playing of tenor saxophonist Getz. These radio broadcasts from Birdland are well-recorded, Getz is in top form and his supporting cast (pianist Duke Jordan, bassist Bill Crow, drummer Kenny Clarke and on three songs trumpeter Dick Sherman) is excellent. Stan Getz, whether coming up with surprising variations on "Moonlight in Vermont" or romping during the title cut, comes up with many colorful solos. —*Scott Yanow*

Plays / Dec. 12, 1952–Jan. 14, 1954 / Verve ✦✦✦✦
Tenor saxophonist Stan Getz is in excellent form playing with one of his finest groups, a quintet with guitarist Jimmy Raney and pianist Duke Jordan. Although the music does not quite reach the excitement level of the Getz-Raney Storyville session, this music (particularly the ballads) really shows off the tenor's appealing tone. This CD is rounded out by four titles that Getz cut with a quartet in 1954 that co-starred pianist Jimmy Rowles. —*Scott Yanow*

Stan Getz at the Shrine / Nov. 8, 1954 / Norgran ✦✦✦✦
Tenor Stan Getz and valve-trombonist Bob Brookmeyer made a mutually beneficial team. Although they had not played together all that much in 1954 (Brookmeyer had left Getz's band earlier in the year to join the Gerry Mulligan Quartet), the strong musical communication between the two horns during this CD reissue is obvious. Eight of the ten selections are from a live concert (with pianist John Williams, bassist Bill Anthony and drummer Art Mardigan) while the final two numbers (on what was originally a pair of LPs) were cut in the studio the following day with the same personnel except that Frank Isola was on drums. Highlights of this cool-toned bop music (which, in addition to the solos, has many exciting ensembles) include "Lover Man," "Pernod," "Tasty Pudding" and "It Don't Mean a Thing." —*Scott Yanow*

Hamp and Getz / Aug. 1, 1955 / Verve ✦✦✦✦✦
The cool tenor of Stan Getz and the extroverted vibraphonist Lionel Hampton might have seemed like an unlikely matchup, but once again producer Norman Granz showed his talents at combining complementary talents. Hampton and Getz really battle hard on "Cherokee" and "Jumpin' at the Woodside" and, other than a ballad medley, the other selections on this CD (which include two previously unreleased performances) are also heated. Classic music from two of the best. —*Scott Yanow*

In Stockholm / Dec. 1955 / Verve ✦✦✦
This excellent LP finds Stan Getz, who had just recovered from a serious illness, in fine form playing standards with a Swedish rhythm section that includes the talented pianist Bengt Hallberg. One of the lesser-known Getz dates, the great tenor (who was 30 at the time) clearly inspired the quietly swinging rhythm section. —*Scott Yanow*

☆ **Stan Getz and J.J. Johnson at the Opera House** / Sep. 29, 1957–Oct. 7, 1957 / Verve ✦✦✦✦✦
On two Jazz at the Philharmonic concerts, tenor saxophonist Stan Getz and trombonist J.J. Johnson (backed by the Oscar Peterson Trio plus drummer Connie Kay) performed an identical repertoire during the two sets of music, one recorded in mono and the other in stereo. All of the music from those dates (with the exception of one number left out due to lack of space) is included on this very exciting release: two versions apiece of "Billie's Bounce," "My Funny Valentine," "Crazy Rhythm" and "Blues in the Closet" plus one try at "Yesterdays" and "It Never Entered My Mind." Surprisingly, Oscar Peterson and guitarist Herb Ellis do not solo at all, but Getz and Johnson make a perfect combination and are in peak form. Bebop at its best, it has plenty of uptempo jamming and no shortage of ideas. —*Scott Yanow*

Stan Getz and the Oscar Peterson Trio / Oct. 10, 1957 / Verve ✦✦✦✦
This very enjoyable CD for the first time gathers together all of the music recorded at this timeless session. Tenor saxophonist Stan Getz is joined by pianist Oscar Peterson, guitarist Herb Ellis and bassist Ray Brown for a well-rounded set filled with appealing standards, three Getz originals (two of which are blues) and a fine ballad medley. Everyone is in top form and Getz clearly enjoyed playing with Peterson. —*Scott Yanow*

Live In Europe / 1958 / Jazz Anthology ✦✦✦
Tenor-great Stan Getz spent several years in Europe in the late '50s. This difficult-to-find French import features Getz in a quartet/quintet with pianist Martial Solal, bassist Pierre Michelot, drummer Kenny Clarke and, on two numbers, guitarist Jimmy Gourley. The results are predictably excellent with such songs as "All God's Children Got Rhythm," "Broadway" and "East of the Sun" among the highpoints. —*Scott Yanow*

Stan Getz with Cal Tjader / Feb. 8, 1958 / Original Jazz Classics ✦✦✦
W/ Cal Tjader. 1987 reissue, super Latin-jazz summit. Billy Higgins fits in nicely on drums. —*Ron Wynn*

Jazz Giants '58 / Aug. 1, 1958 / Verve ✦✦✦✦
This LP contains more than its share of brilliant music. Tenorman Stan Getz meets up with baritonist Gerry Mulligan, trumpeter Harry "Sweets" Edison, the Oscar Peterson Trio and drummer Louie Bellson for three standards and a lyrical ballad medley, but it is the well-constructed solos on the blues "Chocolate Sundae" (during which every note seems to fit perfectly) that are most memorable. —*Scott Yanow*

Stockholm Sessions '58 / Aug. 26, 1958–Sep. 16, 1958 / Dragon ✦✦✦✦
This double LP from the Swedish label Dragon is not only very attractive but the music is both rare and quite rewarding. Taken from Stan Getz's stay in Europe, the great tenor is heard with some of Sweden's top jazz musicians of the era including trombonist Ake Persson, expatriate trumpeter Benny Bailey, baritonist Lars Gullin and either Bengt Hallberg or Jan Johansson. The 18 octet/nonet performances include eight alternate takes and find Getz's cool tenor sound fitting in perfectly with the Swedes. —*Scott Yanow*

In Denmark 1958-59 / Dec. 7, 1958–Oct. 25, 1959 / Olufsen ✦✦✦
In late 1958, Stan Getz lived in Denmark and these recordings, cut at live concerts, are the result. The great tenor is heard with three different quartets (three songs feature expatriate Oscar Pettiford on bass) and featured with Ib Glindemann's Orchestra. The music (all jazz standards) is consistently excellent with the cool tenor clearly rejuvenated by his years in Europe. —*Scott Yanow*

Stan Getz at Large+ Vol. 1 / Jan. 14, 1960–Jan. 15, 1960 / Jazz Unlimited ✦✦✦✦
This music on this CD and the second volume was originally only available as a pair of limited-edition LPs overseas. What makes the first volume of these quartet sessions (with pianist Jan Johansson) special is that much of the material (including "Pammie's Tune," "I Like to Recognize the Tune" and the previously unissued "A New Town Is a Blue Town") is fresh and some of it is quite obscure. Even on "Night and Day" and Dave Brubeck's "In Your Own Sweet Way," Getz's playing is enthusiastic and full of surprising twists. —*Scott Yanow*

Stan Getz at Large+ Vol. 2 / Jan. 14, 1960–Jan. 15, 1960 / Jazz Unlimited ✦✦✦✦
The second of two CDs recorded by Stan Getz while in Copenhagen finds the great tenor performing such fresh material as Johnny Mandel's "Just a Child," Harold Land's "Land's End" and "He Was Good to Me" in addition to two previously unreleased selections with a fine quartet featuring pianist Jan Johansson. These very obscure performances are well-recorded and should delight all Stan Getz fans. —*Scott Yanow*

☆**Focus** / Jul. 1961–Oct. 1961 / Verve ✦✦✦✦✦
Stan Getz's personal favorite recording, this challenging session found the great tenor improvising over a big band performing seven songs composed and arranged by Eddie Sauter. Nothing was written out for Getz but he was up to the challenge, creating beautiful and logical statements and interacting closely with the orchestra. Music worth hearing several times. —*Scott Yanow*

Stan Getz and Bob Brookmeyer / Sep. 12, 1961–Sep. 13, 1961 / Verve ✦✦✦✦
Shortly after returning to the U.S. (following three years in Copenhagen), Stan Getz had a musical reunion with Bob Brookmeyer. As usual, the cool-toned tenor blends in very well with the valve trombonist and, backed by a fine rhythm section (pianist Steve Kuhn, bassist John Neves and drummer Roy Haynes), they perform three Brookmeyer pieces (including one titled "Minuet Circa '61"), two standards and Buck Clayton's "Love Jumped Out." This little-known session is often quite memorable. —*Scott Yanow*

Jazz Samba / Feb. 13, 1962 / Verve ✦✦✦✦✦
This classic session, which launched the bossa nova craze in the early '60s, was originally recorded for Verve. The reissue from DCC Compact Classics improves the sound a bit and adds the shortened 45 version of "Desafinado" to the original program. The music, which matches Stan Getz's cool tenor with guitarist Charlie Byrd and his lightly swinging group, helped introduce Antonio Carlos Jobim's music to the United States through the hit recordings of "Desafinado" and "One Note Samba." It's essential music, no matter in what format one acquires it. —*Scott Yanow*

★ **The Bossa Nova Years (Girl from Ipanema)** / Feb. 13, 1962–Oct. 9, 1964 / DCC ✦✦✦✦✦
This five-LP box set (which has been reissued on CD) contains nearly all of Stan Getz's classic bossa nova sessions, five wonderful yet diverse LPs (*Jazz Samba, Big Band Bossa Nova, Jazz Samba Encore, Stan Getz/Laurindo Almedia* and *Getz/Gilberto*). The cool-toned tenor is heard on his groundbreaking collaboration with guitarist Charlie Byrd (which resulted in the best-selling "Desafinado"), is showcased with a big band arranged by Gary McFarland (introducing "No More Blues" and "One Note Samba"), stars in recordings with guitarists Laurindo Almeida and Luiz Bonfa and is heard at the famous meeting with composer/pianist Antonio Carlos Jobim, guitarist Joao Gilberto and singer Astrud Gilberto, which resulted in the major hit "The Girl from Ipanema." This essential set finishes off with three previously unissued performances from a 1964 Carnegie Hall Concert, concluding with a remake of "The Girl from Ipanema." These recordings stand as proof that it is possible for good music to sell. —*Scott Yanow*

Big Band Bossa Nova / Aug. 27, 1962–Aug. 28, 1962 / Verve ✦✦✦
This is an essential part of his bossa nova period. W/ Gary McFarland. —*Ron Wynn*

Jazz Samba Encore / Feb. 8, 1963–Feb. 27, 1963 / Verve ✦✦✦
Wonderful pairing of Stan Getz and Luiz Bonfa (g). —*Ron Wynn*

● **Getz and Gilberto** / Mar. 18, 1963–Mar. 19, 1963 / Mobile Fidelity ✦✦✦✦✦
This straight CD reissue of Verve's famous *Getz/Gilberto* album was released as part of Mobile Fidelity's Ultradisc II series. The music is timeless with the surprise hit "The Girl from Ipanema"

(during which Astrud Gilberto made her debut not only on records but as a singer), "Corcovado," "So Danco Samba" and "Desafinado" among the highpoints. Stan Getz's tenor fit in perfectly with Antonio Carlos Jobim's music (six of the eight songs are Jobim's) and Joao Gilberto's vocals. —*Scott Yanow*

Stan Getz with Guest Artist Laurindo Almeida / Mar. 21, 1963 / Verve ✦✦✦
W/ Laurindo Almeida (g). Music that is lush, beautiful and substantial. —*Ron Wynn*

Stan Getz and Bill Evans / May 5, 1964–May 6, 1964 / Verve ✦✦✦✦
As musically serene and amazing as you'd expect. Getz and Evans are incredible, while Ron Carter (b), Richard Davis (b) and Elvin Jones (d) aren't too bad either. —*Ron Wynn*

Chick Corea / Bill Evans Sessions / May 5, 1964–Mar. 30, 1967 / Verve ✦✦✦✦✦
This double LP, whose contents have since been reissued on two separate CDs, combines together two of tenor saxophonist Stan Getz's finest albums of his post-bossa nova period. Getz and pianist Bill Evans (along with drummer Elvin Jones and either Ron Carter or Richard Davis on bass) perform lyrical versions of five standards (including "But Beautiful" and "My Heart Stood Still") along with Evans' "Funkallero." The second half of this set has Getz in a quartet with pianist Chick Corea, bassist Ron Carter and drummer Grady Tate. The music is quite a bit more modern, particularly Corea's two originals "Litha" and "Windows." In both cases, the cool-toned tenor is in inspired form, making this music highly recommended in one form or another. —*Scott Yanow*

Getz Au Go Go Featuring Astrud Gilberto / Aug. 19, 1964 / Verve ✦✦✦
This enjoyable LP, the last album recorded by Stan Getz in his bossa nova period, is not included in the Verve box sets documenting the era. Half of the music features Astrud Gilberto's soft vocals (including versions of "Corcovado" and "One Note Samba") while the remainder of the set is more straight-ahead, featuring Getz with his quartet, which at the time co-starred the young vibraphonist Gary Burton. —*Scott Yanow*

The Canadian Concert Of Stan Getz / Mar. 1965 / Can-Am ✦✦✦
This LP is a bit valuable because it documents a group that recorded relatively little, Stan Getz's 1965 quartet with vibraphonist Gary Burton, bassist Gene Cherico and drummer Joe Hunt. Although "Morning of the Carnival" looks back a little at his bossa nova recordings, the remainder of this fine set (taken from a radio broadcast of a Vancouver concert) is straight-ahead and features fairly advanced improvising. —*Scott Yanow*

A Song After Sundown / Aug. 2, 1966–Aug. 3, 1966 / Bluebird ✦✦
For this unusual CD, Stan Getz and his all-star 1966 quintet (which was comprised of guitarist Jim Hall, vibraphonist Gary Burton, bassist Steve Swallow and drummer Roy Haynes) are teamed up with The Boston Pops Orchestra under the direction of Arthur Fielder. Getz plays well enough, but the arrangements are predictably lightweight with the emphasis on ballads; few surprises occur during this slight disappointment. —*Scott Yanow*

Sweet Rain / Mar. 21, 1967–Mar. 30, 1967 / Verve ✦✦✦✦✦
From someone who made so many classics, this might be his best romantic work overall. —*Ron Wynn*

Dynasty / Jan. 11, 1971–Mar. 17, 1971 / Polydor ✦✦✦✦
This double CD finds tenor saxophonist Stan Getz in an unusual setting, playing in a quartet with organist Eddy Louise, guitarist Rene Thomas and drummer Bernard Lubat. Together they perform advanced improvisations on five Louise songs, two by Thomas, Albert Mangelsdorff's "Mona" and just one standard, "Invitation." The music is often fascinating and really challenges Getz. —*Scott Yanow*

● **Captain Marvel** / Mar. 3, 1972 / Columbia ✦✦✦✦✦
This LP (which should be reissued on CD as soon as possible!) was one of Stan Getz's most successful recordings of the 1970s. Teamed up with a younger rhythm section (keyboardist Chick Corea, bassist Stanley Clarke, drummer Tony Williams and percussionist Airto), Getz is in consistently brilliant form on "Lush Life" and five Corea compositions. "Times Lie" and "Five-Hundred Miles High" are memorable, but it is this version of "La Fiesta" (a song that perfectly fit Stan Getz's tone) that is truly classic. Highly recommended. —*Scott Yanow*

The Best of Two Worlds / May 21, 1975 / Columbia ✦✦
Stan Getz's reunion with guitarist/vocalist Joao Gilberto does not live up to expectations. Although the veteran tenor saxophonist sounds fine, the material on this LP (generally more modern Brazilian songs than he had recorded previously) is erratic and surprisingly forgettable. Gilberto has plenty of vocals and the large percussion section and guitarist Oscar Castro Neves help out, but this is definitely a lesser effort. —*Scott Yanow*

The Peacocks / Jul. 1975 / Columbia ✦✦✦✦
Although listed under Stan Getz's name, this CD is really a showcase for pianist Jimmie Rowles, an underrated stylist loved by singers and musicians alike. Rowles is heard in exquisite duets with Getz, solo, in a quartet with Getz, bassist Buster Williams and drummer Elvin Jones, and on "The Chess Players" during which the quartet is joined by four vocalists including three from Jon Hendricks' family. Most memorable are the haunting title cut, "Lester Left Town" and several of Rowles' touching vocals. —*Scott Yanow*

The Master / Oct. 1, 1975 / Columbia ✦✦✦
On this LP the great tenor Stan Getz is heard with a quartet comprised of pianist Albert Dailey, bassist Clint Houston and drummer Billy Hart. Together they stretch out on four extended performances (all between nine and 11 minutes long) that are highlighted by "Lover Man" and "Invitation." More straight-ahead than Getz's other Columbia albums of the period, this set finds him really pushing himself. —*Scott Yanow*

Stan Getz Gold / Jan. 27, 1977–Jan. 30, 1977 / Inner City ✦✦✦
A marvelous, wonderfully played two-record set with plenty of extended, furious Stan Getz tenor, as well as several teeming, gripping ballads. This session unfortunately is no longer in print and has not been reissued thus far on CD. —*Ron Wynn*

★ **Live at Montmartre** / Jan. 1977–Feb. 1977 / SteepleChase ✦✦✦✦✦
This double LP has been reissued on two CDs by Steeplechase for it finds tenor saxophonist Stan Getz in superb form. His modern quartet (featuring pianist Joanne Brackeen, bassist Niels Pedersen and drummer Billy Hart) is heard live at Copenhagen's Montmartre, celebrating Getz's 50th birthday with some brilliant playing. The emphasis is mostly on standards, but there have been few versions of such songs as "Lady Sings the Blues," "Lush Life," "Lester Left Town" and "Eiderdown" that could compare with the lyricism and creativity of these renditions. This is essential music featuring a master at his best. —*Scott Yanow*

Another World / Sep. 13, 1977 / Columbia ✦✦✦
Stan Getz's recordings with his late-'70s group have often been criticized because Andy LaVerne backed the veteran tenor with electric keyboards and the originals by LaVerne and bassist Mike Richmond were open to the influence of fusion. On one selection on this out-of-print double LP, Getz uses a digital delay to create an echo effort that must have distressed some of his longtime fans, but actually the music heard throughout this set is generally quite rewarding. The musicianship is high and Stan Getz was open to new challenges. And for closeminded beboppers, there are versions included of "Willow Weep for Me" and "Blue Serge" along with the newer material. —*Scott Yanow*

Children of the World / Dec. 20, 1978–Dec. 21, 1978 / Columbia ✦✦
It is not the electronics of Andy LaVerne that is bothersome on this LP, but the poppish material (which includes the theme from *Evita*) and the excessive amount of keyboardists and guitarists. Stan Getz cannot be blamed for trying something new (he even uses an echoplex sparingly) and his cool-toned tenor is in fine form, but the overall results are rather forgettable. —*Scott Yanow*

Forest Eyes / Nov. 1979 / Jazz Man ✦✦
Stan Getz performs nine songs from the soundtrack of the film *Forest Eyes* with a Dutch orchestra for this fairly obscure LP. The great tenor is in his usual professional form, but none of the themes are all that memorable and his backing is pretty anonymous. It's not one of the essential Stan Getz albums. —*Scott Yanow*

Legacy / Jul. 3, 1980–Jul. 16, 1986 / Rendezvous ✦✦
The music is generally much better than the recording quality on this CD. Stan Getz is heard with several of his quartets in 1980, 1983 and 1986 and, most importantly, at Woody Herman's 50th-anniversary concert at the Hollywood Bowl. The latter finds Getz joined by Herman's Orchestra on three numbers (including "Easy

Living") and dueting with pianist Jimmy Rowles on the beautiful "Peacocks." Due to the shaky technical quality (an echoey "Lush Life" sounds quite ghostly), this CD is primarily for true Stan Getz collectors. —*Scott Yanow*

The Dolphin / May 1981 / Concord Jazz ✦✦✦
Stan Getz's first recording for Concord finds him returning to the strictly acoustic straight-ahead format, performing six standards with a quartet comprised of pianist Lou Levy, bassist Monty Budwig and drummer Victor Lewis. Getz is in particularly fine form on the title cut, "Joy Spring" and "The Night Has a Thousand Eyes." —*Scott Yanow*

Spring Is Here / May 1981 / Concord Jazz ✦✦✦
This CD was recorded at the same sessions that resulted in *The Dolphin*, but were not released until after Stan Getz's death. Actually, the music (which features pianist Lou Levy, bassist Monty Budwig and drummer Victor Lewis in addition to the leader's tenor) is the equal of the original set, with "How About You," "Easy Living," and "Old Devil Moon" showing off Getz's tone and strong improvising skills at its best. —*Scott Yanow*

Billy Highstreet Samba / Nov. 4, 1981 / EmArcy ✦✦✦
During a period when Stan Getz was recording purely straight-ahead jazz for Concord, he joined up with keyboardist Mitchel Forman, guitarist Chuck Loeb, bassist Mark Egan, drummer Victor Lewis and percussionist Bobby Thomas, Jr., for this obscure session in France. First released in the U.S. in 1990, this finds the veteran tenor playing "contemporary" jazz, doing a good job of fitting into five Loeb and two Forman originals plus "Body and Soul." Not essential music but a fine example of Getz's flexibility and creative instincts. —*Scott Yanow*

Pure Getz / Jan. 1982 / Concord Jazz ✦✦✦✦
Stan Getz's 1982 band featured the harmonically advanced pianist Jim McNeely, bassist Marc Johnson and drummer Victor Lewis; Billy Hart fills in for Lewis on three numbers. This date sticks (with one exception) to high-quality jazz standards, which are not performed all that often. Getz is particularly swinging on "Tempus Fugit" and quite lyrical on Billy Strayhorn's "Blood Count." —*Scott Yanow*

Poetry / Jan. 12, 1983 / Elektra ✦✦✦
This out-of-print duet LP is as much pianist Albert Dailey's date as Stan Getz's. Getz lets Dailey, who passed away a little over a year later, dominate the music, and the lyrical pianist comes up with some fresh ideas during the standards set. "Confirmation," "A Child Is Born" and "Spring Can Really Hang You Up the Most" are highpoints as are Dailey's unaccompanied solo performances of "'Round Midnight" and "Lover Man." Pity that this album is so difficult to find. —*Scott Yanow*

The Stockholm Concert / Feb. 18, 1983 / Gazell ✦✦✦
Stan Getz and his 1983 quartet (which included pianist Jim McNeely, bassist George Mraz and drummer Victor Lewis) are in good form during this performance in Stockholm. With the exception of Alec Wilder's "The Baggage Room Blues" and Jobim's "O Grande Amor," the repertoire is typical for this period in Getz's career, but the veteran tenor was able to come up fresh statements for such standards as "How Long Has This Been Going On" "We'll Be Together Again," "I'll Remember April" and Billy Strayhorn's heartbreaking "Blood Count." If anything, Getz's tone became even more luscious through the years yet he never seemed to lose his fire. —*Scott Yanow*

Line for Lyons / Feb. 18, 1983 / Gazell ✦✦✦✦
This LP (whose contents have since been reissued by Storyville on CD) found trumpeter Chet Baker guesting with Stan Getz's 1983 quartet (which also included pianist Jim McNeely, bassist George Mraz and drummer Victor Lewis). Although Getz and Baker ended up not getting along very well personally, their cool-toned musical personalities fit together perfectly as can be heard on a brief duet version of "Line for Lyons." The remainder of the set finds them successfully revisiting six standards from the 1950s, making one wish it had not been 25 years since their last collaboration. —*Scott Yanow*

Voyage / Mar. 9, 1986 / Blackhawk ✦✦✦
Tenor saxophonist Stan Getz found a perfect accompanist in pianist Kenny Barron who would regularly play in his group for his last five years. This out-of-print Black-Hawk LP finds the pair (along with bassist George Mraz and drummer Victor Lewis) performing two standards and four more recent pieces including two ("Dreams" and "Voyage") by Barron. The music is difficult to clas-

sify (modern bop?), but relatively easy to enjoy; Getz never coasts. —*Scott Yanow*

Anniversary! / Jul. 6, 1987 / EmArcy ✦✦✦✦
As he did to celebrate his 50th birthday, Stan Getz performed at the Montmartre Club in Copenhagen at the time of his 60th birthday. This enjoyable set (mostly lengthy versions of standards) finds the veteran tenor still very much in his prime and greatly assisted by pianist Kenny Barron, bassist Rufus Reid and drummer Victor Lewis. Worth picking up. —*Scott Yanow*

Serenity / Jul. 6, 1987 / EmArcy ✦✦✦✦
From the same sessions that resulted in *Anniversary*, Stan Getz celebrated his 60th birthday as he had his 50th, with a gig at the Cafe Montmartre in Copenhagen. Joined by pianist Kenny Barron, bassist Rufus Reid and drummer Victor Lewis, Getz (who only had four years left) plays in peak form, really stretching out on lengthy versions of three standards, Victor Feldman's "Falling in Love" and Kenny Barron's "Voyage." His solo on "I Remember You" is particularly strong. —*Scott Yanow*

Apasionado / 1989–Mar. 2, 1992 / A&M ✦✦
This rather commercial album (the next to last of Stan Getz's long career) is saved only by the great tenor's tone and creativity. The originals by Eddie del Barrio and Herb Albert are quite forgettable, and the backup by a variety of studio musicians is anonymous. But somehow the wonderful playing of Stan Getz makes this a worthwhile session despite it all. —*Scott Yanow*

● **People Time** / Mar. 3, 1991–Mar. 6, 1991 / Verve ✦✦✦✦✦
Stan Getz's final recording, a two-CD live set of duets with pianist Kenny Barron that was cut just three months before Getz's death, finds the great tenor in surprisingly creative form despite an occasional shortness of breath. Getz's tone is as beautiful as ever and he does not spare himself on this often exquisite set. His version of Charlie Haden's "First Song" is a highlight, but none of the 14 performances are less than great. A brilliant farewell recording by a masterful jazzman. —*Scott Yanow*

Best Of the Verve Years, Vol. 1 / Verve ✦✦✦✦
This two-CD sampler is most highly recommended for listeners not familiar with Stan Getz's recordings of the 1950s and '60s. Starting with a version of "Stella by Starlight" that co-stars guitarist Jimmy Raney, this set matches Getz's cool tenor with such artists as trumpeters Dizzy Gillespie and Conte Candoli, trombonist J.J. Johnson, baritonist Gerry Mulligan, pianists Oscar Peterson, Bill Evans and Chick Corea, valve trombonist Bob Brookmeyer and vibraphonist Gary Burton. Also included are his two main bossa nova hits, "Desafinado" and "The Girl from Ipanema," along with a couple of tracks from Getz's highly rated *Focus* album. It's a fine overview of the great tenor's middle years. —*Scott Yanow*

Terry Gibbs (Julius Gubenko)

b. Oct. 13, 1924, New York, NY
Vibes / Bop
One of the most hyper of all jazzmen (even his ballads are taken mostly doubletime), Terry Gibbs is a consistently exciting and competitive vibraphonist. As a xylophonist, he won an amateur contest when he was 12. After spending three years in the military during World War II, Gibbs played on 52nd Street, gigged with Tommy Dorsey (1946 and 1948), Chubby Jackson (touring Scandinavia during 1947–48), Buddy Rich (1948), Woody Herman's Second Herd (1948–49) and Benny Goodman (1950–52). Gibbs settled in Los Angeles in 1957, worked in the studios, led jazz orchestras (his late-'50s version was callled the Terry Gibbs Dream Band), was the musical director of *The Steve Allen Show* during the 1960s and in the 1980s and '90s has often teamed up in a quintet with Buddy DeFranco. Terry Gibbs, who recorded as a leader for Prestige, Savoy, Brunswick, EmArcy, Mercury, Verve, Time, Impulse, Dot, Xanadu, Jazz a La Carte and Contemporary (among others), had such fine sidemen as his sidemen through the years as Terry Pollard, Pete Jolly (on accordion in 1957), Alice McLeod (in 1963 before she became Alice Coltrane) and John Campbell. —*Scott Yanow*

Jazz Band Ball-Second Set / Sep. 1957 / VSOP ✦✦✦
This reissue is unrelated to another VSOP set simply titled *A Jazz Band Ball*. Terry Gibbs on vibes and marimba matches wits and creativity with Victor Feldman and Larry Bunker, both of whom double on vibes and xylophone. Assisted by pianist Lou Levy, bassist Max Bennett and drummer Mel Lewis, the intriguing

frontline essentially plays bop, but with a great deal of color. The interaction between the vibraphonists, who are all featured and occasionally trade off, is the main reason to acquire this very interesting set. —*Scott Yanow*

Launching a New Band / Feb. 17, 1959 / Mercury ✦✦✦

● **Dream Band, Vol. 1** / Mar. 17, 1959–Mar. 19, 1959 / Contemporary ✦✦✦✦✦

Dream Band, Vol. 3: Flying Home / Mar. 17, 1959–Mar. 19, 1959 / Contemporary ✦✦✦✦

Dream Band, Vol. 2: Sundown Sessions / Nov. 1959 / Contemporary ✦✦✦✦
Terry Gibbs Dream Band. *The Sundown Sessions*. A 1987 reissue of big-band dates. Nicely played, with excellent arrangements but a low-energy level. —*Ron Wynn*

Dream Band, Vol. 4: Main Stem / Jan. 20, 1961–Jan. 22, 1961 / Contemporary ✦✦✦✦

That Swing Thing / Apr. 5, 1961–Apr. 8, 1961 / Verve ✦✦

The Dream Band, Vol. 5: Big Cat / Apr. 6, 1962–Apr. 7, 1962 / Contemporary ✦✦✦✦

El Nutto / Apr. 15, 1963 / Limelight ✦✦

Take It from Me / Jan. 16, 1964 / Impulse! ✦✦

The Latin Connection / May 9, 1986+May 10, 1986 / Contemporary ✦✦✦✦
Fine playing by Frank Morgan (sax) and Tito Puente (per). Gibbs handles Afro-Latin rhythms expertly. —*Ron Wynn*

Chicago Fire / Jul. 24, 1987–Jul. 26, 1987 / Contemporary ✦✦✦✦

Holiday for Swing / Aug. 22, 1988–Aug. 23, 1988 / Contemporary ✦✦✦✦✦

● **Air Mail Special** / Apr. 1990 / Contemporary ✦✦✦✦

Memories of You / Apr. 13, 1991–Apr. 15, 1991 / Contemporary ✦✦✦✦✦

Kings of Swing / Apr. 13, 1991–Apr. 15, 1991 / Contemporary ✦✦✦✦✦
Recorded at Kimball's East, Emeryville, CA, with the Terry Gibbs, Buddy DeFranco, Herb Ellis Sextet. A late and very nice album of cuts like "Body and Soul" and "Stompin' at the Savoy" that features these kings of swing as fresh today as ever. The CD is 68 minutes. —*Michael Erlewine*

Banu Gibson

b. Oct. 24, 1947, Dayton, OH
Vocals / Classic Jazz
During an era when most female singers who interpret music from the 1920s come across as dated "red hot mamas," camp or satirical, Banu Gibson practically stands alone. She performs music from the 1920s and '30s creatively but within the boundaries of the idiom, giving fresh life and excitement to forgotten tunes and swinging hard with her New Orleans Hot Jazz Orchestra. Growing up in Hollywood, FL, Gibson was trained as a dancer, although she studied voice as a child with an opera singer. She gained early experience playing in a Miami club opposite Phil Napoleon (1967–68), toured with Your Father's Mustache (1969–72) and appeared in *Class of '27* (1972–78). She moved to New Orleans in 1973, commuting to Los Angeles and working in N.O. doing choreography and directing. Gibson learned how to play rhythm banjo and, on April 1, 1981, put together her six-piece band which improved steadily throughout the 1980s and became a popular attraction at traditional jazz festivals. Although Banu Gibson has recorded for World, Jazzology and Stomp Off, her most rewarding recordings are for her own Swing Out label and those rank with the top classic jazz of the era. —*Scott Yanow*

Jazz Me Blues / 1974+1980 / World Jazz ✦✦✦
On this out-of-print LP, there are seven selections by the excellent classic jazz singer Banu Gibson from 1980 (early in her career) and six by the 1974 version of The World's Greatest Jazz Band. Banu is joined by a pickup group of Los Angeles-based Dixieland musicians including trumpeter Bill Vogel, the great swing pianist Johnny Varro and drummer Gene Estes; best are Gibson's spirited versions of "Jazz Me Blues," "Happy Days and Lonely Nights" and "Radio." The WGJB, which, at the time, was comprised of quite an all-star lineup (trumpeter Yank Lawson, Bob Wilber on clarinet and soprano, Vic Dickenson and Benny Morton on trombones, Bud Freeman on tenor, pianist Ralph Sutton, bassist Bob Haggart and drummer Gus Johnson), mostly sticks to warhorses,

but Freeman's workout on "Crazy Rhythm," Sutton's feature on "The Sheik of Araby" and a pair of Dickenson vocals are somewhat memorable. Dixieland fans will enjoy this album. —*Scott Yanow*

On Tour / Nov. 28, 1982 / Jazzology ✦✦
Singer Banu Gibson does her best during this loose concert appearance (from the 1982 Manassas Jazz Festival) and there a few good moments, but the poorly organized jam session has plenty of car wrecks as various horn players (including nine horns on "Swing That Music") consistently crash into each other. Trumpeter Billy Butterfield and clarinetist Johnny Mince are the most notable players in the supporting cast, but frankly many of the performances on this LP should not have been released. For much better examples of Banu Gibson's singing, get her Swing Out CDs instead. —*Scott Yanow*

Jazz Baby / Sep. 1, 1983–Dec. 16, 1983 / Stomp Off ✦✦✦
The great classic jazz singer Banu Gibson is heard for the first time with her regular group (the New Orleans Hot Jazz Orchestra), on this Stomp Off LP. Although the group would improve (and swing a lot harder) when the tuba player was replaced eventually by a string bassist, this is an excellent outing. Gibson brings a real understanding to the veteran standards and sounds quite spirited and creative within the idiom on such songs as "Down in Honky Tonk Town," "Changes," "Sweet Man" and "Rose of Washington Square." With fine solos contributed by cornetist Charles Fardella, trombonist Steve Yocum and pianist David Boeddinghaus (the group did not have a clarinetist yet), this was a major first step for Banu Gibson, who would soon be at the top of her field. —*Scott Yanow*

★ **Let Yourself Go** / Jan. 1988 / Swing Out ✦✦✦✦✦
Most singers who attempt to interpret tunes from the 1920s come across as either nostalgia acts, campy or corny. Banu Gibson is a major exception for she sings creatively within the idiom, her voice is both powerful and versatile and she swings without "modernizing" or simplifying the style. This CD from her Swing Out label (along with Swing Out 104) is quite definitive for the material is superior (with "Let Yourself Go," "Love Me or Leave Me," an inventive version of "I Got Rhythm" and "Put That Sun Back in the Sky" among the highlights), there is lots of room for solos from her New Orleans Hot Jazz Orchestra (cornetist Charles Fardella, trombonist David Sager, pianist David Boeddinghaus, bassist James Singleton and drummer Hal Smith) and there are plenty of heated and exciting ensembles. This release is highly recommended to fans of classic jazz. —*Scott Yanow*

★ **You Don't Know My Mind** / Jun. 26, 1989–May 2, 1990 / Swing Out ✦✦✦✦
Banu Gibson ranks at the top of her field, one of the very few creative singers in the 1990s interpreting music from the 1920s in the older style without directly copying any of the past greats. There are plenty of exciting solos on this CD from cornetist Charles Fardella, trombonist David Sager, the reeds (clarinet, tenor and alto) of Tom Fischer and pianist David Boeddinghaus while the hot rhythm section often sounds like Fats Waller's group. Gibson always swings hard and she has a particularly strong (yet appealing) voice that is quite versatile. The material is highlighted by "I've Got My Fingers Crossed," "I Cover the Waterfront," "Ol' Pappy" and "Truckin'," but each of the 16 selections are quite rewarding. All classic jazz collectors should be aware of Banu Gibson and this CD (along with Swing Out 103) features her in prime form. —*Scott Yanow*

Livin' In A Great Big Way / May 22, 1990–Jul. 16, 1990 / Swing Out ✦✦✦✦
This is an unusual Banu Gibson CD in that, instead of using her regular New Orleans Hot Jazz Orchestra, the talented singer is accompanied by just one of two pianists, John Sheridan or David Boeddinghaus. Gibson's repertoire on this set includes both classics from the pre-bop era and obscurities, and the highlights (among many) are "They All Laughed," "It's Been So Long," "About a Quarter to Nine," "I've Got a Feelin' You're Foolin'" and "I'll See You in My Dreams." Arguably the top classic jazz singer to be active in the 1990s, Banu Gibson's attractive voice and versatile swinging style are very much in evidence throughout this excellent outing. —*Scott Yanow*

Harry "The Hipster" Gibson

b. 1914, New York, NY, d. May 9, 1991, California
Piano, Vocals / Swing, Jive
Harry "The Hipster" Gibson, a talented if eccentric pianist-vocalist, had his brief moment of fame before fading into obscurity. He

started out playing on 52nd Street as a stride pianist and, in 1944, even performed "In a Mist" at an Eddie Condon Town Hall concert. But it was his crazy compositions (including "Who Put the Benzedrine in Mrs. Murphy's Ovaltine," "Handsome Harry the Hipster" and "Stop That Dancin' Up There") and frantic singing style (predating rock & roll by a decade) that gave him an underground reputation. Gibson's definitive recordings were made for Musicraft in 1944 and 1947 and his unusual showmanship was captured on a few Soundies during the period. However, Gibson's excessive drug use resulted in his quick decline after 1947. He did record a somewhat demented Christmas album in 1974 and some new songs for Progressive in 1986, but largely wasted his great potential. —*Scott Yanow*

★ **Boogie Woogie in Blue** / Aug. 21, 1944–Feb. 13, 1947 / Musicraft ✦✦✦✦✦

Astrud Gilberto

b. 1940, Bahia, Brazil
Vocals / Bossa Nova
Astrud Gilberto is a limited but strangely memorable singer known mostly for her very first recording. At the famous 1963 collaboration between Stan Getz, Antonio Carlos Jobim, and her then-husband, Joao Gilberto, Astrud was spontaneously asked to sing the English lyrics to "The Girl from Ipanema" even though she was a housewife and not a professional singer. Her cool-toned voice fit the song perfectly and, after it became a giant hit, she unwittingly became a celebrity. Gilberto recorded with Stan Getz again in 1964 and made a series of albums for Verve during 1965–69. Although lightning did not strike again, the easy-listening encounters with string orchestras sold well. Astrud Gilberto has continued singing on a part-time basis, and it is doubtful if she has performed anywhere in the past 33 years without having to sing "The Girl from Ipanema!" —*Scott Yanow*

The Astrud Gilberto Album / Jan. 27, 1965+Jan. 28, 1965 / Verve ✦✦✦
Demure Brazilian vocalist Astrud Gilberton became a hit artist in 1963 with the song "The Girl from Ipanema." She recorded it with her husband, Joao Gilberto, plus tenor saxophonist Stan Getz and Antonio Carlos Jobim. The resulting furor eventually got her a solo album, this 1965 work. It's got some charming moments, and she was ideal for the light bossa nova sound. But the jazz content was and still is minimal. —*Ron Wynn*

The Shadow of Your Smile / May 25, 1965–Jun. 3, 1956 / Verve ✦✦✦

● **Look at the Rainbow** / Nov. 22, 1965–Feb. 4, 1966 / Verve ✦✦✦✦✦
For this CD reissue, the music on singer Astrud Gilberto's LP *Look at the Rainbow* is combined with half of the songs from her following album *A Certain Smile*. The former session was one of the bossa nova singer's best (11 perfectly suitable songs on which her soft voice is accompanied by an orchestra arranged by Gil Evans and Al Cohn) while on the latter she interacts successfully with a trio led by organist Walter Wanderley. —*Scott Yanow*

A Certain Smile, a Certain Sadness / Sep. 20, 1966–Sep. 23, 1966 / Verve ✦✦✦

Astrud Gilberto with Stanley Turrentine / 1971 / Columbia ✦✦
W/ Stanley Turrentine. 1988 reissue of 1971 set that had some mildly entertaining moments. —*Ron Wynn*

Joao Gilberto

b. 1932, Bahia, Brazil
Guitar, Vocals / Bossa Nova
Vocals, guitar, composer. One of the greatest Brazilian singers of all time. It would be difficult to overestimate the influence of Joao Gilberto on Brazilian music. "Everything he did and does," Caetano Veloso has remarked, "illuminates the past and the future of the music in Brazil."
Born in Bahia in 1932, Gilberto electrified the country with his 1958 recording of Jobim's "Chega de Saudade." Just a few years later the colossal hit "The Girl from Ipanema," which he recorded with then-wife Astrud and saxophonist Stan Getz, precipitated the worldwide bossa-nova phenomenon.
Gilberto is generally recognized as the architect of bossa nova: he condenses samba polyrhythms into his syncopated, thoroughly original guitar style, while his cool, caressing, utterly free vocals define intimacy and swing. —*Terri Hinte*

The Legendary Joao Gilberto / 1958 / World Pacific ✦✦✦✦
A 1990 compilation of Gilberto's alluring bossa-nova recordings (1958–1961), contains a generous 75 minutes of music. At the time of its original release, it changed the musical landscape of Brazil and beyond. — *Terri Hinte*

The Boss of the Bossa Nova / Oct. 19, 1962 / Atlantic ✦✦✦
● **Amoroso/Brasil** / Nov. 17, 1976–1980 / Warner Brothers ✦✦✦✦✦
Two of the influential Joao Gilberto's LPs (*Amoroso* and *Brasil*) are combined on this single CD. The former session is pretty definitive with Gilberto interpreting four of Antonio Carlos Jobim's compositions (including "Wave" and "Triste") and four other songs (highlighted by "Besame Mucho," "Estate" and an odd 31-bar rendition of " 'S Wonderful"). The strings (arranged by Claus Ogerman) are unnecessary, but Gilberto proves to be in prime form. The later album also has its moments of interest (including a Brazilian version of "All of Me") and finds Gilberto backed by Johnny Mandel arrangements and assisted by singers Caetano Veloso, Gilberto Gil and Maria Bethania. Overall there is not much variety throughout this gently swinging program, but these are a pair of Gilberto's better post-1970 recordings. — *Scott Yanow*

Dizzy Gillespie (John Birks Gillespie)

b. Oct. 21, 1917, Cheraw, SC, **d.** Jan. 7, 1993, Englewood, NJ
Trumpet, Leader, Composer / Bop
Dizzy Gillespie's contributions to jazz were huge. One of the greatest jazz trumpeters of all time (some would say the best), Gillespie was such a complex player that his contemporaries ended up copying Miles Davis and Fats Navarro instead, and it was not until Jon Faddis' emergence in the 1970s that Dizzy's style was successfully recreated. Somehow Gillespie could make any "wrong" note fit, and harmonically he was ahead of everyone in the 1940s, including Charlie Parker. Unlike Bird, Dizzy was an enthusiastic teacher who wrote down his musical innovations and was eager to explain them to the next generation, thereby insuring that bebop would eventually become the foundation of jazz.

Dizzy Gillespie was also one of the key founders of Afro-Cuban (or Latin) jazz, adding Chano Pozo's conga to his orchestra in 1947 and utilizing complex polyrhythms early on. The leader of two of the finest big bands in jazz history, Gillespie differed from many in the bop generation by being a masterful showman who could make his music seem both accessible and fun to the audience. With his puffed-out cheeks, bent trumpet (which occurred by accident in the early '50s when a dancer tripped over his horn) and quick wit, Dizzy was a colorful figure to watch. A natural comedian, Gillespie was also a superb scat singer and occasionally played Latin percussion for the fun of it, but it was his trumpet playing and leadership abilities that made him into a jazz giant.

The youngest of nine children, John Birks Gillespie taught himself trombone and then switched to trumpet when he was 12. He grew up in poverty, won a scholarship to an agricultural school (Laurinburg Institute in North Carolina) and then, in 1935, dropped out of school to look for work as a musician. Inspired and initially greatly influenced by Roy Eldridge, Gillespie (who soon gained the nickname of Dizzy) joined Frankie Fairfax's band in Philadelphia. In 1937 he became a member of Teddy Hill's Orchestra in a spot formerly filled by Eldridge. Dizzy made his recording debut on Hill's rendition of "King Porter Stomp" and during his short period with the band toured Europe. After freelancing for a year, Gillespie joined Cab Calloway's Orchestra (1939–41), recording frequently with the popular bandleader and taking many short solos that trace his development; "Pickin' the Cabbage" finds Dizzy starting to emerge from Eldridge's shadow. However, Calloway did not care for Gillespie's constant chancetaking, calling his solos "Chinese music." After an incident in 1941 when a spitball was mischievously thrown at Calloway (he accused Gillespie but the culprit was actually Jonah Jones), Dizzy was fired.

By then Gillespie had already met Charlie Parker who confirmed the validity of his musical search. During 1941–43, Dizzy passed through many bands including those led by Ella Fitzgerald, Coleman Hawkins, Benny Carter, Charlie Barnet, Fess Williams, Les Hite, Claude Hopkins, Lucky Millinder (with whom he recorded in 1942) and even Duke Ellington (for four weeks). Gillespie also contributed several advanced arrangements to such bands as Benny Carter, Jimmy Dorsey and Woody Herman; the latter advised him to give up his trumpet playing and stick to full-time arranging!

Dizzy ignored the advice, jammed at Minton's Playhouse and Monroe's Uptown House where he tried out his new ideas and in late 1942 joined Earl Hines' big band. Charlie Parker was hired on tenor and the sadly unrecorded orchestra was the first orchestra to explore early bebop. By then Gillespie had his style together and he wrote his most famous composition "A Night in Tunisia." When Hines' singer Billy Eckstine went on his own and formed a new bop big band, Diz and Bird (along with Sarah Vaughan) were among the members. Gillespie stayed long enough to record a few numbers with Eckstine in 1944 (most noticeably "Opus X" and "Blowing the Blues Away"). That year he also participated in a pair of Coleman Hawkins-led sessions that are often thought of as the first full-fledged bebop dates, highlighted by Dizzy's composition "Woody 'n You."

1945 was the breakthrough year. Dizzy Gillespie, who had led earlier bands on 52nd Street, finally teamed up with Charlie Parker on records. Their recordings of such numbers as "Salt Peanuts," "Shaw Nuff," "Groovin' High" and "Hot House" confused swing fans who had never heard the advanced music as it was evolving and Dizzy's rendition of "I Can't Get Started" completely reworked the former Bunny Berigan hit. It would take two years for the often-frantic but ultimately logical new style to start catching on as the mainstream of jazz. Gillespie led an unsuccessful big band in 1945 (a Southern tour finished it) and late in the year he travelled with Parker to the West Coast to play a lengthy gig at Billy Berg's club in L.A. Unfortunately, the audiences were not enthusiastic (other than local musicians) and Dizzy (without Parker) soon returned to New York.

The following year Dizzy Gillespie put together a successful and influential orchestra that survived for nearly four memorable years. "Manteca" became a standard, the exciting "Things to Come" was futuristic and "Cubana Be/Cubana Bop" featured Chano Pozo. With such sidemen as the future original members of the Modern Jazz Quartet (Milt Jackson, John Lewis, Ray Brown and Kenny Clarke), James Moody, J.J. Johnson, Yusef Lateef and even a young John Coltrane, Gillespie's big band was a breeding ground for the new music. Dizzy's beret, goatee and "bop glasses" helped make him a symbol of the music and its most popular figure. During 1948–49 nearly every former swing band was trying to play bop, and for a brief period the major record companies tried very hard to turn the music into a fad.

By 1950 the fad had ended and Gillespie was forced, due to economic pressures, to break up his groundbreaking orchestra. He had occasional (and always exciting) reunions with Charlie Parker (including a fabled Massey Hall concert in 1953) up until Bird's death in 1955, toured with Jazz at the Philharmonic (where he had opportunities to "battle" the combative Roy Eldridge), headed all-star recording sessions (using Stan Getz, Sonny Rollins and Sonny Stitt on some dates) and led combos that, for a time in 1951, also featured Coltrane and Milt Jackson. In 1956 Gillespie was authorized to form a big band and play a tour overseas sponsored by the State Department. It was so successful that more traveling followed including extensive tours to the Near East, Europe and South America, and the band survived up to 1958. Among the young sidemen were Lee Morgan, Joe Gordon, Melba Liston, Al Grey, Billy Mitchell, Benny Golson, Ernie Henry and Wynton Kelly; Quincy Jones (along with Golson and Liston) contributed some of the arrangements. After the orchestra broke up, Gillespie went back to leading small groups, featuring such sidemen in the 1960s as Junior Mance, Leo Wright, Lalo Schifrin, James Moody and Kenny Barron. He retained his popularity, occasionally made specially assembled big bands and was a fixture at jazz festivals. In the early '70s, Gillespie toured with the Giants of Jazz and around that time his trumpet playing began to fade, a gradual decline that would make most of his 1980s work quite erratic. However, Dizzy remained a world traveler, an inspiration and teacher to younger players, and during his last couple of years he was the leader of the United Nation Orchestra (featuring Paquito D'Rivera and Arturo Sandoval). He was active up until early 1992.

Dizzy Gillespie's career was very well-documented from 1945 on, particularly on Musicraft, Dial and RCA in the 1940s, Verve in the 1950s, Philips and Limelight in the 1960s and Pablo in later years. — *Scott Yanow*

★ **Complete RCA Victor Recordings 1947–1979** / May 17, 1937–Jul. 6, 1949 / Bluebird ✦✦✦✦✦
This two-CD set dwarfs all previous reissues of the trumpeter's Victor output. Gillespie's pioneering bebop big band made many

of their greatest recordings for that label and they are all here including the original version of "Manteca," "Two Bass Hit," "Cubana Be/Cubana Bop," "Good Bait," "Hey Pete! Le's Eat Mo' Meat" and "Jumpin' with Symphony Sid"; among the soloists are tenors James Moody and Yusef Lateef, trombonist J.J. Johnson and Chano Pozo on congas. In addition this essential reissue has Gillespie's three earliest recorded solos (with Teddy Hill's Orchestra in 1937), "Hot Mallets" with Lionel Hampton's all-star group in 1939, a combo session (four songs and three alternate takes) with Don Byas and Milt Jackson in 1946 and the two versions of "Overtime" and "Victory Ball" he made with the 1949 Metronome All-Stars; "Overtime" has a tradeoff between Gillespie, Fats Navarro and Miles Davis. No jazz collection is complete without this innovative and exciting music. —Scott Yanow

Development of an American Artist / 1940–1946 / Smithsonian ✦✦✦✦
1940–1946. A thorough compilation of Gillespie's formative '40s dates. Available by mail-order only from the Smithsonian. —Ron Wynn

Dizzy Gillespie with Charlie Christian / May 1941 / Esoteric ✦✦✦

Shaw Nuff / Feb. 9, 1945–Nov. 12, 1946 / Musicraft ✦✦✦✦✦
This CD has Dizzy Gillespie's classic Musicraft sides (all except "A Handfulla Gimme"), some of the most famous recordings of his long career. These influential performances (which set the standard for bebop) include "Blue 'N' Boogie" (with tenor saxophonist Dexter Gordon), seven gems with Charlie Parker (highlighted by "Groovin' High," "Hot House" and "Salt Peanuts"), a few numbers with Sonny Stitt and nine big-band recordings including "Our Delight," "Ray's Idea" and the futuristic "Things to Come." If Dizzy Gillespie's career had ended after these recordings, he would still be famous in the jazz world. —Scott Yanow

Groovin' High / Feb. 29, 1945–Feb. 22, 1953 / Savoy Jazz ✦✦✦
This budget-price Drive Archive CD features trumpeter Dizzy Gillespie during two different periods. He is heard along with Charlie Parker on classic versions of "Groovin' High," "Dizzy Atmosphere" and "All the Things You Are" from 1945. Much rarer are his 1952 Paris recordings with tenor saxophonist Don Byas and pianist Arnold Ross and his 1953 session with strings; during the latter Gillespie virtually ignores the unswinging string arrangements and comes up with melodic variations for the standard melodies. Although not essential, there are some very interesting performances on this boppish CD. —Scott Yanow

Dizziest / Feb. 22, 1946–Jul. 6, 1949 / Bluebird ✦✦✦✦
Dizziest, a two-LP set (the contents of which have mostly been reissued on CD), contains the entire output (except a couple of alternate takes) by Dizzy Gillespie's innovative bebop orchestra of 1947–49. Sounding light years ahead of Glenn Miller and Benny Goodman, this big band upset a lot of people (particularly would-be dancers) before it broke up in 1950. There are many classics on this set, including "Cubana Be/Cubana Bop" (featuring the percussion of Chano Pozo), "Manteca," "Two Bass Hit," "Good Bait," "Hey Pete! Let's Eat Mo' Meat" and "Jumpin' with Symphony Sid." As a bonus, the four titles from Gillespie's small-group session of Feb. 22, 1946 (with vibraphonist Milt Jackson and tenor saxophonist Don Byas, are included; these hot versions of "A Night in Tunisia" and "Anthropology" should not be missed. —Scott Yanow

One Bass Hit / May 15, 1946–Nov. 12, 1946 / Musicraft ✦✦✦✦
A good reissue spotlighting Gillespie's prime orchestra in the mid '40s. —Ron Wynn

It Happened One Night / Sep. 29, 1947 / Natural Organic ✦✦✦✦
On the night of Sept. 29, 1947, there were three sets of music at Carnegie Hall: the Dizzy Gillespie Big Band, Ella Fitzgerald backed by the orchestra and the Dizzy Gillespie-Charlie Parker Quintet. The second and third parts of the show are included on this very interesting LP. Fitzgerald sounds fine on tunes such as "Lady Be Good" and "How High the Moon," scatting while being backed by the big band. However the reason to search for this set is to get the five titles from Diz and Bird. This version of "Confirmation" has some miraculous Parker. —Scott Yanow

Live at Carnegie Hall / Sep. 29, 1947 / Artistry ✦✦✦✦
This LP documents the same concert (but a different set) as It Happened One Night. The Dizzy Gillespie Orchestra performs ten selections including several that they never recorded commercially (such as "Relaxin' at Camarillo," "Salt Peanuts," "Hot House" and "Toccata for Trumpet") plus "new" versions of "Cubana

Be/Cubana Bop" and "Things to Come." The leader/trumpeter, who is the main soloist throughout, is in particularly fiery form on this very enjoyable (and somewhat historical) set. —Scott Yanow

Bebop Enters Sweden / Dec. 20, 1947-1949 / Dragon ✦✦✦✦
A rather fascinating LP, Bebop Enters Sweden features radio broadcasts from Sweden by three American bop groups. Chubby Jackson & His Fifth Dimensional Jazz Group, an all-star sextet of Woody Herman alumni, performs three numbers, and tenor saxophonist James Moody is heard sitting in with trumpeter Gosta Torner's Jam Session Band for three other songs, but the bulk of this set is taken up by Dizzy Gillespie's orchestra. From early 1948, that classic band provides fresh variations on such songs as "Our Delight," "Manteca" and "Ray's Idea." —Scott Yanow

Dizzy Gillespie And Max Roach In Paris / Feb. 28, 1948+May 15, 1949 / Vogue ✦✦✦✦
The bulk of this CD from the French Vogue label features the Dizzy Gillespie Orchestra in particularly strong form at a Paris concert. In addition to the leader/trumpeter, the main soloists are altoist Howard Johnson, Big Nick Nicholas on tenor, pianist John Lewis and Chano Pozo on congas. The highlights of this date (which was formerly made available domestically on LP by Prestige) include "Woody 'n You," "I Can't Get Started," "Good Bait," "Afro-Cuban Drum Suite" (which is really "Cubana Be") and "Things to Come." In addition, there are four selections from a 1949 quintet led by drummer Max Roach that stars trumpeter Kenny Dorham, James Moody on tenor and pianist Al Haig. —Scott Yanow

Dizzy Gillespie and His Big Band / Jul. 26, 1948 / GNP ✦✦✦✦✦
The Dizzy Gillespie Big Band was the most innovative jazz orchestra of 1946–49, proof that bebop was not exclusively a small group music. All of its recordings are well worth acquiring, and this particular CD gives one a well-rounded picture of the orchestra at a concert before an enthusiastic crowd. With prominence given James Moody's tenor, Cecil Payne on baritone and Chano Pozo on congas (he was killed a short time after this performance) in addition to the remarkable leader/trumpeter, the Dizzy Gillespie Orchestra is heard at its absolute prime. Versions of "Good Bait," "One Bass Hit" and "Manteca" are among the highlights of this recommended CD. —Scott Yanow

Good Bait / Dec. 1948–Jul. 1949 / Spotlite ✦✦✦✦
This LP features the Dizzy Gillespie Orchestra on a pair of extensive radio broadcasts from late 1948 and mid-1949. Considering that its studio recordings were declining during this period (as Capitol records tried to cash in on the "bebop fad") and that the big band would break up altogether in early 1950, these performances are quite valuable. But more importantly, with such soloists as altoist Ernie Henry, tenor saxophonist Yusef Lateef and trombonist J.J. Johnson in addition to Dizzy himself, the music is consistently exciting. It's available from the English Spotlite label. —Scott Yanow

Dizzy's Diamonds: The Best of Verve Years / Jun. 6, 1950–Nov. 6, 1964 / Verve ✦✦✦
Many of trumpeter Dizzy Gillespie's recordings for the Verve label in the '50s and early '60s (when he was at the peak of his powers) have inexcusably been out of print for decades. This three-CD set is a sampler of his legacy, with the discs subtitled "Big Band," "Small Groups & Guests" and "In an Afro Cuban, Bossa Nova, Calypso Groove." The programming jumps all over the place and makes little sense, but this set serves as a good excuse to acquire 40 performances by the great Gillespie and the many all-stars who recorded with him. Few but the most fanatical veteran Gillespie fans will have had all of these selections in their collection. This will fill a void until Verve gets around to doing a much more comprehensive Dizzy Gillespie reissue program. —Scott Yanow

Dee Gee Days: Savoy Sessions / Mar. 1, 1951–Jul. 18, 1952 / Savoy ✦✦✦
During 1951–52, Dizzy Gillespie had his own record label, Dee Gee. Having been forced to break up his big band in 1950 due to the impossible financial situation, he was working regularly with a small group, which, for a short while, included a young tenor named John Coltrane; the future giant's first recorded solo ("We Love to Boogie") is one of the highlights of this CD. Gillespie is heard in a wide variety of novelties, bop romps and ballads on this diverse program. There are many vocals from him and Joe

Carroll, a funny parody of Louis Armstrong on "Umbrella Man," and one extended performance on the fiery "The Champ"; all of the other cuts are in the three-minute range. Enjoyable but not essential music. —*Scott Yanow*

Dizzy Gillespie / Mar. 25, 1952–Feb. 22, 1953 / Everest ✦✦✦
This budget LP gives no personnel or date information so one gets what they pay for. Actually, the half-hour of music is generally quite rewarding. Dizzy Gillespie is teamed with expatriate tenor Don Byas on "Blue and Sentimental" and fronts a rhythm section for strong versions of "Sleepy Time Down South" and "Blue Moon." The other seven tracks find Gillespie performing with "his Operatic Strings," but the results are much more exhilarating than one might fear. He does not let the arrangements inhibit him and he plays brilliantly throughout. This music deserves better treatment than was given it by Everest (it should be reissued complete and in chronological order with all of the discographical data) but, if found at a cheap price, get this. —*Scott Yanow*

Dizzy Gillespie in Paris, Vol. 2 / Mar. 27, 1952–Feb. 22, 1953 / Vogue ✦✦✦✦✦
The second of two CD volumes of Dizzy Gillespie performances put out by Vogue has the full contents from three of his Paris studio sessions. The great trumpeter heads a quintet that includes tenor saxophonist Don Byas and pianist Arnold Ross on four songs (plus three alternate takes); highlights include Gillespie's playing on "I Cover the Waterfront" and his vocal on the two versions of "Say Eh." The most rewarding of the sets finds him leading a septet on such numbers as "Cripple Crapple Crutch" (which has his classic blues vocal), "Somebody Loves Me" and two versions of "Wrap Your Troubles in Dreams." The final eight selections feature Dizzy Gillespie's regular band of 1953 (with trombonist Nat Peck in baritonist Bill Graham's place). Vocalist Joe Carroll helps out on a couple of the numbers and Gillespie is in particularly memorable form on "My Man" and " 'S Wonderful." This highly enjoyable music is easily recommended. —*Scott Yanow*

Dizzy Gillespie/Gerry Mulligan / 1952–1961 / Europa ✦✦✦
The previously unissued performances included on this Italian LP were mostly recorded in Europe and add to the legacy of several of their participants. Trumpet-great Dizzy Gillespie jams five tunes with a group of Europeans plus expatriate tenor Don Byas. Altoist Hubert Fol and the rhythm section from the same date perform a fine version of "Everything Happens to Me," and this LP concludes with a Gerry Mulligan-led jam session that teams the baritonist with trumpeter Ruby Braff and tenor saxophonist Bud Freeman for a fine version of "Rose Room." Nice music, nothing too essential. —*Scott Yanow*

Diz and Getz / Dec. 9, 1953 / Verve ✦✦✦✦
Dizzy Gillespie was at the peak of his powers throughout the 1950s, still the pacesetter among trumpeters. This double CD matches Dizzy with Stan Getz, the Oscar Peterson Trio and drummer Max Roach. Getz, although identified with the "cool" school, thrived on competition and is both relaxed and combative on the uptempo explorations of "It Don't Mean a Thing" and "Impromptu." —*Scott Yanow*

★ **Dizzy Gillespie with Roy Eldridge** / Oct. 29, 1954 / Verve ✦✦✦✦✦
To call this music "classic" would be a great understatement. Producer Norman Granz loved to team together combative musicians in jam sessions, both live and in the studios. Since Roy Eldridge was one of the most competitive of trumpeters and Dizzy Gillespie considered him his original idol, they made a perfect matchup. This two-CD includes a ballad medley and a few slower pieces, but to hear Gillespie and Eldridge battling on "I've Found a New Baby" and "Limehouse Blues" is to hear two of the very best trying to cut each other. Highly recommended for all jazz collections. —*Scott Yanow*

One Night in Washington / Mar. 13, 1955 / Elektra ✦✦✦
This excellent LP documents a meeting between trumpeter Dizzy Gillespie and a Washington, D.C.-based orchestra in 1955. Gillespie is the only significant soloist on the four-part "Afro Suite" (which includes "Manteca"), a couple of Buster Harding pieces, "Tin Tin Deo," "Caravan" and a group original. The big band is fine (if not distinctive) in support of the great trumpeter. —*Scott Yanow*

Dizzy Gillespie and His Big Band at Birdland / 1956 / Sandy Hook ✦✦✦
This LP (put out by a collector's label) contains a couple of radio

broadcasts featuring Dizzy Gillespie's acclaimed big band of 1956, the one that toured the world. With altoist Phil Woods, tenor Billy Mitchell and pianist Walter Davis among the supporting cast, trumpeter Gillespie felt that a big band such as this one was a perfect setting for his music. Among the better selections on this set are "Night in Tunisia," the always humorous "Doodlin' " and "Dizzy's Business." —*Scott Yanow*

The Modern Jazz Sextet / Jan. 12, 1956 / Verve ✦✦✦✦
Producer Norman Granz was a near-genius at matching together jazz musicians in such a way that they would stimulate each other to play above their heads. He always loved jam sessions, but it did not take too much insight to realize that putting trumpeter Dizzy Gillespie and altoist Sonny Stitt together with a strong rhythm section would result in some explosive music. The fireworks really fly on this LP during versions of "Tour De Force," "Dizzy Meets Sonny," "Mean to Me" and "Blues for Bird," with time out taken for a ballad medley. Bebop at its best. —*Scott Yanow*

★ **Birks Works: Verve Big Band Sessions** / May 25, 1956–Apr. 8, 1957 / Verve ✦✦✦✦✦

On Tour With Dizzy Gillespie and His Big Band / Aug. 1956 / Artistry ✦✦✦
The Dizzy Gillespie Big Band of 1956 was caught in concert for this excellent LP. The spirited young orchestra plays such standbys as "The Champ," the humorous "Doodlin' " and "Groovin' High" (featuring altoist Phil Woods) along with Gillespie's showcases "Begin the Beguine" and "Stella by Starlight." Unfortunately, this classic ensemble was disbanded in early 1958. —*Scott Yanow*

"Live" 1957 / Jun. 14, 1957 / Jazz Unlimited ✦✦✦
Although not quite up to the exciting level of their Newport Jazz Festival appearance of a month later, this live CD of the Dizzy Gillespie big band gives one a strong set from the legendary orchestra. In addition to the leader/trumpeter, such soloists as Lee Morgan (who takes the opening trumpet solo on "Night in Tunisia"), altoist Ernie Henry, trombonist Al Grey and Benny Golson on tenor make strong impressions. "Jordu," "I Remember Clifford," a blazing "Cool Breeze" and a humorous "Doodlin' " are among the highlights. —*Scott Yanow*

★ **At Newport** / Jul. 6, 1957 / Verve ✦✦✦✦✦
This CD features Dizzy Gillespie's second great big band at the peak of its powers. On the rapid "Dizzy's Blues" and a truly blazing "Cool Breeze," the orchestra really roars; the latter performance features extraordinary solos by Gillespie, trombonist Al Grey and tenor saxophonist Billy Mitchell. In addition to fine renditions of "Manteca" and Benny Golson's then-recent composition "I Remember Clifford," the humorous "Doodlin' " is given a definitive treatment, there is a fresh version of "A Night in Tunisia" and pianist Mary Lou Williams sits in for a lengthy medley of selections from her "Zodiac Suite." This brilliant CD captures one of the highpoints of Dizzy Gillespie's remarkable career and is highly recommended. —*Scott Yanow*

Dizzy Gillespie Duets / Dec. 11, 1957 / Verve ✦✦✦✦✦

Sonny Rollins / Sonny Stitt Sessions / Dec. 11, 1957–Dec. 19, 1957 / Verve ✦✦✦✦
This two-LP set (whose contents have since been reissued on CD) contains a couple of the very best Norman Granz studio sessions. Dizzy Gillespie is matched with the great tenor Sonny Rollins on two selections, Sonny Stitt (sticking to tenor) takes Rollins' place for a couple of other songs and then the two Sonnys team up with Gillespie for four remarkable selections. Diz sings "On the Sunny Side of the Street" with good humor and "After Hours" is given a fine treatment, but it is Rollins' ferocious stoptime solo on "I Know That You Know" and the pure fire that is felt on a rapid "The Eternal Triangle" that makes this set truly memorable. —*Scott Yanow*

Greatest Trumpet of Them All / Dec. 17, 1957 / Verve ✦✦
The title given this LP may very well be true, but this particular session is surprisingly restrained. Dizzy Gillespie is heard in an octet with tenor saxophonist Benny Golson, altoist Gigi Gryce, trombonist Henry Coker and baritonist Pee Wee Moore, but the Golson arrangements seem to inhibit the trumpeter and the repertoire (mostly by Golson and Gryce) fails to inspire Gillespie. For many other jazz musicians this would be a "good" or even "fine" effort, but Dizzy Gillespie has recorded too much classic music for this disappointment to rate very high. —*Scott Yanow*

Sonny Side Up / Dec. 19, 1957 / Verve ✦✦✦✦✦
W/ Sonny Rollins and Sonny Stitt (sax). The dynamic threesome hit some impressive heights, with Stitt at his peak. —*Ron Wynn*

The Ebullient Mr. Gillespie / Feb. 17, 1959–Feb. 20, 1959 / Verve
✦✦✦

Dizzy Gillespie was certainly in good spirits for this long out-of-print session with his sextet, an ensemble also featuring pianist Junior Mance, Les Spann on flute and guitar and the congas of Chino Pozo (a cousin of the late Chano). Gillespie jokes around on "Swing Low, Sweet Cadillac," sings "Umbrella Man" and otherwise emphasizes more mellow material. A pleasing—if not all that essential—date of melodic music from the masterful trumpeter. —*Scott Yanow*

Have Trumpet, Will Excite! / Feb. 17, 1959–Feb. 20, 1959 / Verve
✦✦✦

With his globetrotting big band now in the past, Dizzy Gillespie headed a quintet featuring pianist Junior Mance and Les Spann on flute and guitar for this excellent effort. Gillespie is at his best on such unlikely material as "My Heart Belongs to Daddy," "My Man" and "I Found a Million Dollar Baby." Pity that Verve has allowed so many of its great Dizzy Gillespie recordings (including this one) to be out of print literally for decades. —*Scott Yanow*

Copenhagen Concert / Sep. 17, 1959 / SteepleChase ✦✦✦
This SteepleChase CD for the first time releases music from a Sept. 17, 1959 Copenhagen concert featuring trumpeter Dizzy Gillespie and his Quintet of the period (which includes altoist Leo Wright, pianist Junior Mance, bassist Art Davis and drummer Teddy Stewart). Wright (who doubled on flute) was a perfectly suitable musical partner for Gillespie (staying with the group until 1962) and was always able to take assertive solos without trying to steal the spotlight from the trumpeter. Diz is in good spirits throughout these two sets, singing a good-humored "Ooh-Shoo-Be-Doo-Bee" and scatting furiously on "Lady Be Good." His trumpet chops are in excellent form and his solos are as complex as ever. Highlights include "My Man," "Wheatleigh Hall," "Night in Tunisia" and "Woody 'n You." —*Scott Yanow*

Gillespiana/Carnegie Hall Concert / Nov. 14, 1960–Mar. 4, 1961 / Verve ✦✦✦✦✦
This CD combines two complete and related LPs. When Lalo Schifrin joined Dizzy Gillespie's Quintet in 1960, he was encouraged by Gillespie to write an extended work for him. "Gillespiana" was the result, an impressive five-movement suite that showcased the trumpeter's talents with a large orchestra. The latter half of this CD was recorded at Carnegie Hall the same day that "Gillespiana" was debuted live, but those five pieces are more conventional, highlighted by remakes of "Manteca" and "Night in Tunisia" (the latter as the more involved "Tunisian Fantasy"). Only an overly silly version of "Ool Ya Koo" with Joe Carroll detracts from this otherwise superb release. —*Scott Yanow*

Dizzy Gillespie Quintet In Europe / 1961 / Unique ✦✦
The 1961 Dizzy Gillespie Quintet (with Mel Lewis subbing on drums) is heard at a European concert playing their standard repertoire. This budget LP from Italy (which lacks any liner notes and the exact recording date) has decent versions of "Lady Be Good," "There Is No Greater Love," "The Mooche," "Night in Tunisia" and "Long Long Summer," but there are better examples of this particular group elsewhere. —*Scott Yanow*

☆ **Electrifying Evening** / Feb. 9, 1961 / Verve ✦✦✦✦✦
Why isn't the exciting music on this LP available on CD? Dizzy Gillespie (along with altoist Leo Wright, pianist Lalo Schfrin, bassist Bob Cunningham and drummer Chuck Lampkin) were in peak form for this live performance. Their versions of "Kush," "Salt Peanuts" and "The Mooche" are all excellent, but it is "A Night in Tunisia," with its absolutely stunning trumpet break (which lasts half a chorus), that is most memorable. —*Scott Yanow*

Perceptions / May 22, 1961 / Verve ✦✦✦
This unusual session (last available on LP) consists of a complex six-movement suite by J.J. Johnson featuring Dizzy Gillespie's trumpet over a brass choir (six trumpets, two trombones, two bass trombones, four French horns and two tubas), bass, drums, percussion and two harps. Often reminiscent of classical music, Johnson's writing allows plenty of room for Gillespie to improvise. The result is a rather unique set of music that is well worth searching for. —*Scott Yanow*

Dizzy on the French Riviera / May 1962–Jul. 1962 / Philips
✦✦✦✦

Long out of print, this highly enjoyable LP finds trumpeter Dizzy Gillespie and his quintet joined by guitarist Elek Bacsik and per-

cussionist Pepito Riestria for some joyous explorations of bossa nova rhythms and related material. This extended version of Antonio Carlos Jobim's "No More Blues" is classic, and the quintet's renditions of "Long Long Summer," "Desafinado" and "Here It Is" are also memorable. In addition to the trumpeter, altoist Leo Wright and pianist Lalo Schifrin have plenty of solo space. All of Gillespie's Philips recordings should be reissued on CD. —*Scott Yanow*

New Wave / May 1962–Jul. 1962 / Philips ✦✦✦✦
It is such a pity that Dizzy Gillespie Philips' LPs have yet to be reissued on CD, for the trumpeter (45 at the time of this recording) was at the peak of his powers in the early '60s. On such songs as "In a Shanty in Old Shanty Town," "Careless Love," "One Note Samba" and the "Theme from *Black Orpheus*," Gillespie and his expanded quintet (with guests Bola Sete or Elec Bacsik on guitar and Charlie Ventura taking a memorable bass sax solo on "No More Blues-Part II") show a great deal of spirit and creativity. Leo Wright (on alto and flute) and pianist Lalo Schifrin are also in fine form throughout this gem. —*Scott Yanow*

Composer's Concepts / Sep. 1962–Apr. 23, 1964 / EmArcy ✦✦✦
This interesting double LP contains Lalo Schifrin's six-movement work for Dizzy Gillespie and a large orchestra titled "The New Continent," three compositions by Tom McIntosh for Gillespie's 1963 quintet and 11 themes from Mal Waldron that were played by Gillespie's group for the soundtrack of *The Cool World*. Little all that memorable occurs, but Diz has plenty of fine trumpet solos. —*Scott Yanow*

Something Old, Something New / Apr. 23, 1963 / Philips ✦✦✦✦
This out-of-print LP features the 1963 Dizzy Gillespie Quintet at its best. With strong soloing by tenor saxophonist James Moody and pianist Kenny Barron, trumpeter Gillespie was inspired to play at his best. These rapid versions of "Be-Bop" and "Dizzy Atmosphere" are classic, "Good Bait" receives definitive treatment and the logical medley of "I Can't Get Started" and "Round Midnight" is also quite memorable. The remainder of this essential (but sadly unavailable) set includes three Tom McIntosh compositions and "This Lovely Feeling." —*Scott Yanow*

Dizzy Gillespie and the Double Six of Paris / Jul. 8, 1963 / Verve ✦✦✦
This odd (but successful) matchup finds The Double Six of Paris singing vocalese in French to a dozen bebop classics associated with Dizzy Gillespie. Gillespie with pianist Bud Powell and a rhythm section take solos that uplift this date; two songs feature his quintet (with James Moody on alto). Not for all tastes, this is a unique addition to Dizzy Gillespie's discography. —*Scott Yanow*

Dizzy Gillespie Goes Hollywood / Sep. 11, 1963–Sep. 14, 1963 / Philips ✦✦✦
On first glance, this LP looks like a dud. Dizzy Gillespie and his quintet (with saxophonist James Moody and pianist Kenny Barron) perform 11 themes from then-recent movies including "Caesar and Cleopatra," "Love Theme from *Lolita*" and "Never on Sunday." However, because the trumpeter was near the peak of his powers and his band does play such songs as "Moon River," "Days of Wine and Roses" and "Carioca" with spirit, the results are quite worthwhile, if not essential. —*Scott Yanow*

Jambo Caribe / Nov. 4, 1964–Nov. 6, 1964 / Limelight ✦✦✦
This fun LP features Dizzy Gillespie and his quintet plus the percussion of Kansas Fields playing eight rhythmic pieces influenced by melodies from South America. Such tunes as "Fiesta Mo-jo," "Jambo" and "Trinidad, Goodbye" never became standards, but "And Then She Stopped" was played by Gillespie in future years. Good music if not one of his classics. —*Scott Yanow*

With Gil Fuller and the Monterey Jazz... / Oct. 1965 / Blue Note ✦✦✦
For this studio session, Dizzy Gillespie was reunited with arranger Gil Fuller who that year led a specially assembled big band for the Monterey Jazz Festival. A bit of a disappointment, this CD failed to generate the fireworks one might expect. There are some good moments, most notably on "The Shadow of Your Smile," "Groovin' High" and "Things Are Here" (the answer to "Things to Come"), but the big band is mostly heard from in a purely accompanying role behind the great trumpeter and little interplay occurs. —*Scott Yanow*

Swing Low Sweet Cadillac / May 25, 1967–May 26, 1967 / MCA
✦✦

The weak material sinks this Dizzy Gillespie CD. "Swing Low,

Sweet Cadillac" (which features a lot of joking routines) is amusing the first few times around, but fades in time. Otherwise "Mas Que Nada," "Something in Your Smile" and "Kush" contain little of interest from Gillespie's Quintet, which at the time included saxophonist James Moody and pianist Mike Longo. There are many finer Gillespie sets available elsewhere. —*Scott Yanow*

Live at the Village Vanguard / Oct. 1, 1967 / Blue Note ✦✦✦✦
This double CD reissues material formerly on LPs, restoring several of the selections that were originally issued in edited form. A pair of unusual jam sessions, on the first (and more eccentric of the two) trumpeter Dizzy Gillespie is paired with baritonist Pepper Adams, pianist Chick Corea, bassist Richard Davis, either Mel Lewis or Elvin Jones on drums and violinist Ray Nance (who is in particularly adventurous form). The second date substitutes Garnett Brown for Nance and is a bit more conventional. These lengthy performances (all but one of the seven songs are over 11 minutes) contain some loose and rambling moments, but also plenty of creative playing by this unusual group of all-stars. —*Scott Yanow*

Reunion Big Band / Nov. 7, 1968 / MPS ✦✦✦✦✦
This little-known LP actually contains one of Dizzy Gillespie's greatest performances of the 1960s. Joined by a particularly strong big band (which includes trombonist Curtis Fuller, altoist Chris Woods, James Moody on tenor, both Sahib Shihab and Cecil Payne on baritones and a screaming trumpet section), Dizzy Gillespie performs the most exciting version of "Things to Come" ever recorded plus "One Bass Hit" and the more recent "Con Alma," "Frisco" and "The Things Are Here." Although already 51, the trumpeter is heard at his best on this hard-to-find but essential LP. —*Scott Yanow*

Enduring Magic / 1970–1985 / Blackhawk ✦✦✦
This LP contains performances by trumpeter Dizzy Gillespie with the Dwike Mitchell-Willie Ruff duo taken from five separate concerts spanning the years 1970–85. Gillespie always sounded comfortable with this group, which featured Mitchell on piano and Ruff playing bass and occasional French horn. The music (which includes "Blue & Boogie," "Take the 'A' Train" and "Love for Sale") is enjoyable, intimate and swinging. —*Scott Yanow*

Dizzy Gillespie and the Dwike Mitchell-Willie Ruff Duo / 1971 / Mainstream ✦✦✦
Trumpeter Dizzy Gillespie sounds quite comfortable playing in an intimate setting with pianist Dwike Mitchell and Willie Ruff (who plays bass and occasional French horn). Gillespie explores a couple of recent collaborations with his sidemen plus "ConAlma," "Woody 'n You" and Ruff's "Bella Bella." This is one of Gillespie's stronger sets of the '70s; he was 54 years old at the time. —*Scott Yanow*

Giants / Jan. 31, 1971 / Perception ✦✦✦
On this live session not yet issued on CD, the great trumpeter is teamed in an all-star quintet with cornetist Bobby Hackett and pianist Mary Lou Williams. The music (seven standards) is generally quite melodic and swinging, but the closer, a classic version of "My Man," steals the show. It is interesting to hear the contrast between the two brassmen. Hackett was always a very complementary player, so the combination works well. —*Scott Yanow*

Giants of Jazz / Nov. 12, 1972 / Atlantic ✦✦✦✦✦
This two-LP set (which should be reissued on CD) features a dream band comprised of trumpeter Dizzy Gillespie, Sonny Stitt on alto and tenor, trombonist Kai Winding, pianist Thelonious Monk (in a very rare stint as a sideman), bassist Al McKibbon and drummer Art Blakey. In general, the all-stars perform up to their usual standards on such standards as "Night in Tunisia," "Woody 'n You," "Tour De Force," "Allen's Alley" and "Blue 'N' Boogie." Monk is well-featured on "Blue Monk" and " 'Round Midnight," but Stitt steals honors on "Everything Happens to Me." A historic and superlative set. —*Scott Yanow*

The Giant / Apr. 1973 / Accord ✦✦✦
This CD finds trumpeter Dizzy Gillespie at age 55, just beginning to slip. Gillespie plays well enough on these nine selections with a fine rhythm section comprised of pianist Kenny Drew, bassist Niels Pederson, drummer Kenny Clarke and the congas of Humberto Canto; Johnny Griffin's tenor is a major asset on four numbers. Still, the edge is missing on these explorations of standards and recent originals although he is in particularly fine form on the ballads such as "I Waited for You" and "The Girl of My Dreams." —*Scott Yanow*

Trumpet Kings Meet Joe Turner / Sep. 19, 1974 / Original Jazz Classics ✦✦✦
This is an excellent collaboration by three established, outstanding trumpeters, plus rollicking Joe Turner (v) near the end of a wonderful career. W/ Roy Eldridge (tpt) & Harry Edison (tpt). —*Ron Wynn*

Dizzy Gillespie's Big Four / Sep. 19, 1974 / Original Jazz Classics ✦✦✦✦✦
Arguably Dizzy Gillespie's most rewarding recording of the 1970s, this quartet date (with guitarist Joe Pass, bassist Ray Brown and drummer Mickey Roker) finds the 57-year-old trumpeter near peak form on three of his compositions and four standards. These versions of "Tanga" and "Be Bop" are brilliant. —*Scott Yanow*

Afro-Cuban Jazz Moods / Jun. 4, 1975+Jun. 5, 1975 / Original Jazz Classics ✦✦✦

The Trumpet Kings at Montreux '75 / Jul. 16, 1975 / Pablo ✦✦✦✦
Putting the competitive trumpeters Dizzy Gillespie, Roy Eldridge, Clark Terry and an Oscar Peterson Trio with bassist Niels Pedersen and drummer Louis Bellson together before a live crowd at the Montreux Jazz Festival was a typically inspired idea by producer Norman Granz. The trumpeters bring out the best in each other on "There Is No Greater Love," "On the Alamo" and "Indiana," although Peterson does not let himself get upstaged during this happy jam session. —*Scott Yanow*

The Dizzy Gillespie Big Seven / Jul. 16, 1975 / Original Jazz Classics ✦✦✦
Recorded at the 1975 Montreux Jazz Festival, this set features trumpeter Dizzy Gillespie (then 58 years old and slightly past his prime) heading an all-star outfit (that also includes vibraphonist Milt Jackson, the tenors of Eddie "Lockjaw" Davis and Johnny Griffin, pianist Tommy Flanagan, bassist Niels Pedersen and drummer Mickey Roker) jamming three standards including a 16-minute version of "Lover, Come Back to Me." There are some fine moments (and some rambling ones) on this generally enjoyable jam session. —*Scott Yanow*

Dizzy's Party / Sep. 15, 1976+Sep. 16, 1976 / Original Jazz Classics ✦✦

Free Ride / Feb. 1, 1977+Feb. 2, 1977 / Original Jazz Classics ✦✦
Recent reissue of a late '70s Pablo session, with Gillespie playing some entertaining originals, backed by the Lalo Schifrin orchestra. The compositions and performances are good, but not great. —*Ron Wynn*

Gifted Ones / Feb. 3, 1977 / Original Jazz Classics ✦✦
This Norman Granz session got it backwards. Instead of featuring Dizzy Gillespie with the Count Basie Orchestra, Basie is heard with a Gillespie-led quartet. The emphasis is on blues and fairly standard chord changes and, even with bassist Ray Brown and drummer Mickey Roker completing the group, there are no surprises. What should have been a classic encounter is instead fairly routine. —*Scott Yanow*

Montreux '77 / Jul. 14, 1977 / Original Jazz Classics ✦✦✦
It wasn't until the mid-'70s that a trumpeter emerged who could not only emulate Dizzy Gillespie but display a larger range: Jon Faddis. Unfortunately, Gillespie and his protege barely recorded together and this 1977 encounter at the Montreux Jazz Festival is quite disappointing. The trumpeters (plus vibraphonist Milt Jackson, pianist Monty Alexander, bassist Ray Brown and drummer Jimmie Smith) play well enough on "Girl of My Dreams," "Get Happy," "The Champ" and a ballad medley, but amazingly enough, there are no tradeoffs between Faddis and Gillespie (the younger trumpeter is much too respectful throughout this session) and few fireworks occur in what should have been an explosive encounter. —*Scott Yanow*

Trumpet Summit Meets Oscar Peterson Big Four / Mar. 1980 / Original Jazz Classics ✦✦✦
W/ Freddie Hubbard, Clark Terry, Joe Pass. Not spectacular, but a satisfying and enjoyable romp by these veterans. —*Ron Wynn*

Digital at Montreux, 1980 / Jul. 19, 1980 / Pablo ✦✦
A 1980 date with trumpeter Dizzy Gillespie playing in an unusual trio setting with guitarist Toots Thielemans and drummer Bernard Purdie. Purdie, a consummate funk and R&B percussionist, makes the switch to mainstream material adequately, while Gillespie and Thielemans establish a quick, consistent rapport. —*Ron Wynn*

Musician-Composer-Raconteur / Jul. 17, 1981 / Pablo ✦✦
This double LP is subtitled "Dizzy Gillespie Plays and Raps in His

Greatest Concert," an exaggeration to say the least. In reality, this set (which contains some of his humorous joking with the audience) is a fine all-around example of Gillespie at a typical concert in 1981. At the age of 63, he was no longer the powerful trumpeter he once was, but he still had something to contribute. His sextet (with vibraphonist Milt Jackson, James Moody on tenor and alto and the fine guitarist Ed Cherry) stretches out on long versions of "A Night in Tunisia," "Con Alma" and "Olinga" along with four other pieces. —*Scott Yanow*

To a Finland Station / Sep. 9, 1982 / Original Jazz Classics ✦✦✦✦
This unique set finds Dizzy Gillespie (who was nearly age 65) sharing the frontline with the great Cuban trumpeter Arturo Sandoval. Backed by a fine Finnish rhythm section, Sandoval and the great trumpeter are both in good spirits playing five of Gillespie's originals including "Wheatleigh Hall" and "And Then She Stopped." Considering that it would be another decade before Sandoval was able to defect from Cuba (and finally play the music he wanted), this recording is of great historic value. —*Scott Yanow*

Closer to the Source / Aug. 24, 1984–Sep. 30, 1984 / Atlantic ✦
It was an open secret that by the 1980s, Dizzy Gillespie was well past his playing prime. A very likable and humorous entertainer and still an expert scat singer, his trumpet playing had unfortunately greatly declined, and in 1984, at the time of this misfire, he was soon to turn age 67. This set of commercial material (with guest spots by Stevie Wonder, tenor saxophonist Branford Marsalis and bassist Marcus Miller) is quite forgettable—throwaway funk tunes with the parts of the sidemen sounding as if they were phoned in. This LP fortunately went quickly out of print. —*Scott Yanow*

New Faces / 1984 / GRP ✦✦✦
Gillespie was teamed up with Branford Marsalis for this decent effort. His own trumpet playing had faded quite a bit by this time (he was already age 67), but he sounds happy on five of his compositions (including "Birk's Works"), "Tin Tin Deo" and Mike Longo's "Every Mornin'," trading ideas with such young turks as Marsalis, pianist Kenny Kirkland and bassist Lonnie Plaxico. —*Scott Yanow*

Endlessly / 1987 / MCA ✦

Live at Royal Festival Hall / Jun. 10, 1989 / Enja ✦✦✦✦
Dizzy Gillespie, who was nearing 72 years old at the time of this concert, headed one of his finest big bands during his later years, The United Nation Orchestra. With such stellar sidemen as trumpeters Arturo Sandoval and Claudio Roditi, trombonists Slide Hampton and Steve Turre, altoist Paquito D'Rivera, James Moody on tenor and alto, pianist Danilo Perez and singer Flora Purim, Gillespie was relieved from having to carry this concert by himself and could concentrate on taking short solos and enjoying listening to the band play. Whether it is "Tanga," "And Then She Stopped" or an 18-minute version of "A Night in Tunisia," every selection on this excellent CD works. —*Scott Yanow*

Symphony Sessions (August 25, 1989) / Aug. 26, 1989–Aug. 27, 1989 / Pro Arte ✦✦
Teaming Dizzy Gillespie with a symphony orchestra may have been a good idea in theory but, by the time of the recordings that comprise this CD, he was already nearing the age of 72, and his trumpet playing had declined quite a bit. Since Gillespie is the main soloist throughout this set (in which his quintet with tenor saxophonist Ron Holloway is accompanied by The Rochester Philharmonic Orchestra conducted by John Dankworth), there are many weak moments. Certainly these versions of "Manteca" and "A Night in Tunisia" pale in comparison to the earlier classic recordings, leading one to the conclusion that this matchup should have occurred 20 years earlier. —*Scott Yanow*

Winter in Lisbon / Aug. 1990 / Milan ✦✦
This CD, featuring Dizzy Gillespie playing on the soundtrack of *The Winter in Lisbon* (a film never properly distributed), is only of minor interest. He wrote the nine themes and Slide Hampton put together the arrangements, but, as with most soundtracks, the music sounds incomplete without the picture. Also, Gillespie's playing at this late date in his life was quite erratic. —*Scott Yanow*

Rhythmstick / Mar. 1991 / CTI ✦✦✦

To Bird with Love: Live at the Blue Note / Jan. 23, 1992–Jan. 25, 1992 / Telarc ✦✦✦
Taken from a month that Dizzy Gillespie was featured at the Blue Note in New York, virtually at the end of his playing career, the 74-year-old trumpeter is quite erratic on this set of bop standards.

However, his supporting cast (heard from in different combinations) includes such major players as altoists Jackie McLean, Antonio Hart and Paquito D'Rivera and tenors Benny Golson, Clifford Jordan and David Sanchez, in addition to a strong trio led by pianist Danilo Perez. The sidemen are in generally fine form and Bobby McFerrin literally came out of the audience to scat on "Oo Pa Pa Da." The good spirits and obvious love that these musicians had for Gillespie make up for his technical lapses. —*Scott Yanow*

To Diz with Love: Diamond Jubilee Recordings / Jan. 29, 1992–Feb. 1, 1992 / Telarc ✦✦✦
Dizzy Gillespie's final recording, taken from a month he spent featured at the Blue Note in New York, matches the aging giant with such fellow trumpeters as Jon Faddis, Wynton Marsalis, Claudio Roditi, Wallace Roney, Red Rodney, Charlie Sepulveda and the ancient—but still brilliant—Doc Cheatham (who cuts both Diz and Faddis on "Mood Indigo"). Although Gillespie was no longer up to the competition, the love that these fellow trumpeters had for him (and some fine solos) makes this historic CD worth getting. —*Scott Yanow*

John Gilmore

b. Sept. 28, 1931, Summit, MS, d. Aug. 20, 1995, Philadelphia, PA
Tenor Saxophone / Avant-Garde, Free Jazz
John Gilmore's decision to play almost exclusively within the realm of Sun Ra's Arkestra long frustrated jazz observers who felt that he could have made a bigger impact if he had had a solo career. Gilmore grew up in Chicago and after a stint in the Army (1948–52), he worked with Earl Hines (1952). In 1953 he joined Ra and 40 years later when the bandleader died, Gilmore was still there. His playing in the 1950s was an influence on the developing John Coltrane. Gilmore, who teamed up with Clifford Jordan for a 1957 Blue Note session, did spend 1964–65 with Art Blakey's Jazz Messengers. However other than a few sideman recordings in the 1960s (including with Freddie Hubbard, McCoy Tyner, Andrew Hill and Pete LaRoca), Gilmore stuck with Ra, being well-featured both on hard bop and free-form material. He briefly headed the Arkestra after Ra's death. —*Scott Yanow*

★ **Blowing in from Chicago** / Mar. 3, 1957 / Blue Note ✦✦✦✦✦

Adele Girard

b. 1913, d. Sept. 7, 1993, Denver, CO
Harp / Swing, Dixieland
Possibly the greatest jazz harpist of all time, Adele Girard showed that it was possible to swing hard on that angelic instrument; only the little-known Casper Reardon had preceded her. Girard played with Harry Sosnick's band and then, in 1937, she joined clarinetist Joe Marsala's combo, marrying him the same year. Her swing and Dixieland recordings with Marsala in the 1930s and '40s (although somewhat obscure) are remarkable to hear today. Little was heard of Girard after the mid-'50s, but she emerged in 1992 to record a fine album with Bobby Gordon for Arbors. —*Scott Yanow*

George Girard

b. Oct. 7, 1930, New Orleans, LA, d. Jan. 18, 1957, New Orleans, LA
Trumpet, Vocals / Dixieland
One of the finest New Orleans jazz players to emerge in the 1950s, George Girard's premature death from cancer cut short a very promising career. He became a professional in 1946 after graduating from high school, played with Phil Zito and then became a key member (along with Pete Fountain) of the Basin Street Six (1950–54). After the breakup of that group, Girard led his own bands and freelanced until bad health forced him to retire in 1956. Girard had an exciting trumpet style and was a rhythmic vocalist whose potential was sadly not realized. In addition to his recordings with the Basin Street Six, Girard led sessions that were later issued by Storyville, GHB and Good Time Jazz in addition to cutting two full albums for Vik. —*Scott Yanow*

● **George Girard** / Sep. 19, 1954–Jul. 1956 / Storyville ✦✦✦✦

Egberto Gismonti

b. Carmo, Brazil
Guitar, Piano / World Fusion
A marvelous Brazilian guitarist, Egberto Gismonti has blended

classical, traditional ethnic and jazz influences into a distinctive, very personal and alternately lyrical and aggressive style. A self-taught guitarist, Gismonti began on six-string in the '70s, later switched to an eight-stringed instrument and finally settled on a 10-string with an extended bass range in the early '80s. Gismonti began studying piano at six and continued until he journeyed to Paris to study orchestration and composition many years later. His teachers were Nadia Boulanger and Jean Barraque. Gismonti became interested in the choro, a Brazilian variation on African-American funk, when he returned home in 1966. While learning guitar, Gismonti closely examined the music of Baden Powell and flutist Pixinguinha. He toured America with Airto and Flora Purim in the mid-'70s and also with Nana Vasconcelos. Gismonti spent extensive time studying the music of the Xingu Indians in 1977 and later included their compositions on a pair of albums. In addition to his many recordings for ECM and EMI, Gismonti has recorded with Paul Horn, Charlie Haden, Jan Garbarek and Nana Vasconcelos. — *Ron Wynn and Terri Hinte*

Danca Das Cabecas / Nov. 1976 / ECM ++++
The initial American release features extended pieces for guitarist and percussionist Nana Vasconcelos. A tour de force, with the pieces segueing together beautifully. — *Michael G. Nastos*

Sol Do Meio Dia / Nov. 1977 / ECM ++++

Solo / Nov. 1978 / ECM +++++

Duas Vozes / Jun. 1984 / ECM +++

★ **Danca Dos Escravos** / 1989 / ECM +++++

Infancia / Nov. 1990 / ECM +++++
This is a stunning effort by Egberto and his current (1991) working group: guitarist/synthesist Nando Carneiro, bassist Zeca Assumpao and cellist Jacques Morelen-baum. — *Terri Hinte*

Musica De Sobrevivencia / Apr. 1993 / ECM +++

Jimmy Giuffre

b. Apr. 26, 1921, Dallas, TX
Flute, Baritone Saxophone, Soprano Saxophone, Tenor Saxophone / Cool, Avant-Garde
Jimmy Giuffre has had many accomplishments in a long career that has never been predictable. Giuffre graduated from North Texas State Teachers College (1942), played in an Army band during his period in the service and then had stints with the orchestras of Boyd Raeburn, Jimmy Dorsey and Buddy Rich. His composition "Four Brothers" became a hit for Woody Herman, an orchestra that Giuffre eventually joined in 1949.

Settling on the West Coast, the cool-toned tenor also started playing clarinet and occasional baritone. He was with Howard Rumsey's Lighthouse All-Stars (1951–52) and Shorty Rogers' Giants (1952–56), recording with many top West Coast jazz players. In 1956 he went out on his own, forming the Jimmy Giuffre 3 with guitarist Jim Hall and bassist Ralph Pena (later Jim Atlas). Giuffre had a minor hit with his recording of "The Train and the River," a song that he played during his notable appearance on the 1957 television special *The Sound of Jazz*. In 1958 Giuffre had a most unusual trio with valve trombonist Bob Brookmeyer and guitarist Hall (no piano, bass or drums!), appearing in the movie *Jazz on a Summer's Day*. After a couple years of reverting back to the reeds-guitar-bass format, in 1961 the new Jimmy Giuffre 3 featured pianist Paul Bley and bassist Steve Swallow and was involved in exploring the more introspective side of free jazz. From 1963 on Giuffre maintained a lower profile, working as an educator although Don Friedman and Barre Phillips were in his unrecorded 1964–65 group. He popped up on records now and then in the 1970s with diverse trios (including a session with Bley and Bill Connors) and his 1980s unit often utilized the synthesizer of Pete Levin. Giuffre, who started late in life playing flute and soprano and seems to have made a career out of playing surprising music, reunited with Bley and Swallow in 1992. He has recorded as a leader through the years for Capitol, Atlantic, Columbia, Verve, Hat Art, Choice, Improvising Artists, Soul Note and Owl. — *Scott Yanow*

Four Brothers and Tangents in Jazz / Feb. 19, 1954–Jan. 31, 1955 / Affinity +++

Tenors West / Nov. 9, 1955–Nov. 10, 1955 / GNP +++
Although this set is often issued under Jimmy Giuffre's name, the tenor saxophonist actually only appears on five of the 11 selec-

tions. The first date of what is actually a Marty Paich album features fellow tenor Bob Cooper in an octet with Paich's piano, trumpeter Conte Candoli, baritonist Jack Dulong, valve trombonist Bob Enevoldsen and flutist Harry Klee; both Enevoldsen And Klee play some of the sections on tenor, giving the ensemble a Four Brothers sound. Giuffre replaces Cooper on the later session and does emerge as the most consistently interesting soloist. The real stars are Paich's inventive arrangements. — *Scott Yanow*

The Jimmy Giuffre Clarinet / Mar. 21, 1956–Mar. 22, 1956 / Atlantic +++

The Jimmy Giuffre Three, Vol. 46 / Dec. 3, 1956–Dec. 2, 1957 / Atlantic ++++
Wonderful recording with guitarist Jim Hall that features the classic "The Train and the River." — *Michael G. Nastos*

The Music Man / Jan. 2, 1958–Jan. 6, 1958 / Atlantic ++++

Trav'lin' Light / Jan. 20, 1958–Jan. 21, 1958 / Atlantic ++++

Four Brothers Sound / Jun. 23, 1958–Sep. 1, 1958 / Atlantic ++++

Western Suite / Dec. 3, 1958 / Atlantic ++++

Ad Lib / Jan. 1959 / Verve +++

Seven Pieces / Feb. 25, 1959–Mar. 2, 1959 / Verve +++

The Easy Way / Aug. 6, 1959–Aug. 7, 1959 / Verve ++++
A compelling trio date with Jim Hall (g). — *Ron Wynn*

In Person / Aug. 1960 / Verve +++

● **1961** / Mar. 3, 1961+Aug. 4, 1961 / ECM +++++
Excellent '92 reissue of a pivotal set featuring multi-instrumentalist Jimmy Giuffre with bassist Steve Swallow and pianist Paul Bley. It's actually two separate, compelling albums issued as one CD, *Fusion* and *Thesis*. The three interacted so completely that there was more emphasis on mood, sound and texture than individual voices. — *Ron Wynn*

Emphasis, Stuttgart 1961 / Nov. 7, 1961 / Hat Art ++++

Flight, Bremen 1961 / Nov. 23, 1961 / Hat Art ++++

Free Fall / Jul. 10, 1962–Nov. 1, 1962 / Columbia ++++
Fine trio pieces with Paul Bley (p) and Steve Swallow (b). — *Ron Wynn*

Music for People, Birds, Butterflies and Mosquitos / Dec. 1972 / Choice ++

Quiet Song / Nov. 1974 / Improvising Artists +++
Exceptional trio output with Paul Bley (p) and Bill Connors (g). — *Ron Wynn*

River Chant / Apr. 1975 / Choice ++

Iai Festival / May 19, 1978 / Improvising Artists ++++

Dragonfly / Jan. 14, 1983–Jan. 15, 1983 / Soul Note +++

Quasar / May 3, 1985-May 5, 1985 / Soul Note +++

Liquid Dancers / Apr. 24, 1989 / Soul Note +++

Diary of a Trio: Saturday / Dec. 1989 / Owl ++++

Diary of a Trio: Sunday / Dec. 1989 / Owl ++++

Tyree Glenn

b. Nov. 23, 1912, Corsicana, TX, **d.** May 18, 1974, Englewood, NJ
Trombone, Vibes / Swing
Tyree Glenn, who had the unusual double of trombone and vibes, was an important asset at various times to both Duke Ellington and Louis Armstrong. Glenn started out working in territory bands in Virginia then moved to the West Coast, playing with groups headed by Charlie Echols and Eddie Barefield. After playing with Ethel Waters and Benny Carter, he became a longtime member of the Cab Calloway Orchestra (1939–46). Glenn visited Europe with Don Redman's big band (1946). During his association with Duke Ellington (1947–51), he was an effective wa-wa trombonist in the Tricky Sam Nanton tradition and Ellington's only vibraphonist, being well-featured on the "Liberian Suite." During the 1950s, Glenn worked in the studios, led his quartet at the Embers and freelanced in swing and Dixieland settings. Other than some European dates in 1947, Glenn's only extensive opportunity to record was for Roulette (1957–58 and 1961–62). During 1965–68 he toured with the world with Louis Armstrong's All-Stars. After leaving Armstrong, Tyree Glenn led his own group during his last few years. — *Scott Yanow*

At the Embers / Mar. 28, 1957–Mar. 29, 1957 / Roulette ◆◆◆◆
● Tyree Glenn at the Roundtable / 1958 / Roulette ◆◆◆◆
The Trombone Artistry / 1962 / Roulette ◆◆◆

Globe Unity Orchestra

b. 1966
Big Band / Free Jazz
Formed in 1966 by pianist Alexander von Schlippenbach to perform his composition "Globe Unity" at the Berlin Jazztage, Globe Unity has been a forum for some of the top free jazz players to get together and engage in collective improvisation. They mostly performed in Germany up until 1974, but have since toured Europe, India, the Far East and Canada. Among its members through the years have been Albert Mangelsdorff, Kenny Wheeler, Evan Parker, Manfred Schoof, Paul Rutherford, Steve Lacy, Peter Brotzmann, George Lewis and Han Bennink. The group (which has recorded for FMP and Japo) has been only occasionally active since celebrating its 20th anniversary in 1986. —*Scott Yanow*

★ Live in Wuppertal '73 / Mar. 25, 1973 / FMP ◆◆◆◆◆
Hamburg '74 / Nov. 19, 1974 / FMP ◆◆◆◆
Evidence / Mar. 31, 1975 / FMP ◆◆◆◆
Jahrmarket / Jun. 5, 1976–Nov. 27, 1975 / Potorch ◆◆◆
Improvisations / Sep. 5, 1977+Sep. 9, 1977 / Japo ◆◆◆
Pearls / Nov. 25, 1977+Nov. 27, 1977 / FMP ◆◆◆◆
Compositions / Jan. 1979 / Japo ◆◆◆
Intergalactic Blow / Jun. 4, 1982 / Japo ◆◆◆

Don Goldie

b. Feb. 5, 1930, Newark, NJ, d. Nov. 1995, Florida
Trumpet / Dixieland
A talented soloist with a wide range, Don Goldie was the son of longtime Paul Whiteman trumpeter Harry Goldfield. Goldie performed with many types of groups, including Buddy Rich and the society band of Lester Lanin, before gaining prominence for his playing with Jack Teagarden's Dixieland sextet (1959 until the trombonist's death in 1964). Goldie eventually settled in Miami where, in the early '70s ,he recorded 11 albums for Jazz Forum, many of which were dedicated to the work of one composer. A fixture in Miami clubs and hotels, Don Goldie committed suicide in 1995. —*Scott Yanow*

● Brilliant / 1961 / Argo ◆◆◆◆◆
Trumpet Caliente / Oct. 3, 1962 / Argo ◆◆◆◆

Larry Goldings

b. 1968, Boston
Organ, Piano / Post-Bop
One of the top organists to emerge since Joey DeFrancesco, Larry Goldings began piano lessons when he was nine. Goldings, who graduated from the New School for Social Research in the late '80s, was Jon Hendricks' accompanist during 1987–89, worked with Jim Hall for three years and (inspired by Jimmy Smith) he led a trio that gave him an opportunity to play organ. He worked on the Hammond B-3 with Maceo Parker and, in 1990, recorded his first set for Minor Music. Since then Goldings has toured and recorded with John Scofield and signed with Warner Bros. —*Scott Yanow*

The Intimacy of the Blues / 1991 / Verve ◆◆◆◆
W/ Fathead Newman (sax) and Bill Stewart (b). —*Ron Wynn*
Light Blue / Sep. 1992 / Minor Music ◆◆◆◆
Caminhos Cruzados / Dec. 19, 1993–Dec. 20, 1993 / Novus/RCA ◆◆◆◆◆
Listening to this CD, it is surprising to note that few bossa nova records up to now have featured organs. Larry Goldings' subtle style (a laidback Jimmy Smith) perfectly fits the idiom and some of the selections performed on his set are given straight-ahead sections for variety. The music is mostly easy-listening with an appealing ensemble sound, consistently excellent concise solos from Goldings and guitarist Peter Bernstein and tasteful backup from drummer Bill Stewart and percussionist Guilherme Franco. The three guest appearances by Joshua Redman make one wish

that he were on more tracks for his tenor fits very comfortably into this setting. —*Scott Yanow*
★ Whatever It Takes / 1995 / Warner Bros. ◆◆◆◆◆

Jean Goldkette

b. Mar. 18, 1899, Valenciennes, France, d. Mar. 24, 1962, Santa Barbara, CA
Leader / Classic Jazz
Although he was a fine, classically trained pianist who emigrated to the United States in 1911, Jean Goldkette's importance to jazz is a bandleader in the 1920s. Goldkette actually had over 20 bands under his name by the mid-'20s, but it was his main unit (which recorded for Victor during 1924–29) that is the only one remembered today. In 1924 the band included Tommy and Jimmy Dorsey and Joe Venuti, with the legendary cornetist Bix Beiderbecke heard on just one selection ("I Didn't Know"); his inability to sightread at the time kept his first stint with Goldkette quite short. However in 1926, Bix became the orchestra's top soloist and the jazz lineup was pretty impressive with such musicians as Spiegle Willcox, Bill Rank, Don Murray, Frankie Trumbauer, Joe Venuti, Eddie Lang, Steve Brown and Chauncey Morehouse among the personnel. With Bill Challis working as chief arranger, the orchestra was among the best of the period, even defeating Fletcher Henderson at a Battle of the Bands contest in New York. Unfortunately, Goldkette's Orchestra was not allowed to cut loose much in the studios and were saddled with indifferent vocalists who were not part of the band. Best among their recordings are "My Pretty Girl" and "Clementine"; Steve Brown's swinging bass is a major asset on many of the other numbers, particularly during the final choruses. In 1927 Paul Whiteman hired away most of Goldkette's top jazz players (including Bix and Tram) and the band's later recordings are of lesser interest although Hoagy Carmichael is heard on two vocals. Goldkette, who also helped organize McKinney's Cotton Pickers and the Orange Blossoms (the latter became the Casa Loma Orchestra), dropped out of the jazz business by the early '30s, working as a booking agent and a classical piano soloist. In 1959 Jean Goldkette revived some of the old arrangements (adding some new ones by Sy Oliver) for a Camden "reunion" LP, but few of the sidemen (other than Chauncey Morehouse) were present. —*Scott Yanow*

Gil Goldstein

b. 1950
Accordion, Keyboards / Post-Bop, World Music
Gil Goldstein, an excellent pianist and synthesizer player, actually started on the accordion. In the late '80s he resumed doubling on it for special occasions, such as a recording project for Michel Petrucciani and for his own sessions. Earlier Goldstein had picked up important experience playing with Pat Martino, Jim Hall, Billy Cobham, the Gil Evans Orchestra (starting in 1983) and Wayne Shorter. In 1991 he helped in reconstructing Gil Evans' arrangements for Miles Davis' Montreux Jazz Festival concert, and he has recorded as a leader for Chiaroscuro (1977), Muse, Blue Note, World Pacific and Big World. Generally, Gil Goldstein's music grooves while utilizing the influences of other cultures (particularly Latin America). —*Scott Yanow*

Pure As Rain / Nov. 14, 1977+Nov. 16, 1977 / Chiaroscuro ◆◆◆
Sands of Time / May 14, 1980–May 15, 1980 / Muse ◆◆◆
City of Dreams / Mar. 1989–Jul. 1989 / Blue Note ◆◆◆
Zebra Coast / Jun. 6, 1991–Jun. 9, 1991 / World Pacific ◆◆◆◆

Vinny Golia

b. Bronx, New York
Reeds / Avant-Garde
One of the unsung heroes of avant-garde jazz, Vinny Golia has been recording prolifically in Los Angeles (on his Nine Winds label) and staging concerts (ranging from solo improvisations and trios to his Large Ensemble) since 1977. He started out as a visual artist and even designed a Chick Corea album cover (*The Song of Singing*), not taking up the saxophone until he was already 21. Within a short time, Golia was playing gigs in settings ranging from blues bands to a folk-rock group and Indian music. He started on the soprano and soon added flute, tenor, piccolo, clarinet, bass clarinet, baritone, bass sax and more, currently playing 19 reeds! In 1973 he moved to Los Angeles, played regularly with

John Carter and Bobby Bradford and became a force in the under-ground new music scene. In 1977 Golia founded New Winds and, although the first few records were of his music, the label has since broadened its scope and put out over 70 releases to date that document the L.A. avant-garde jazz scene. Vinny Golia has played in recent times with the saxophone octet Figure 8 (recording for Black Saint), William Parker's big band in New York, Bradford's quartet and his own many diverse groups. —*Scott Yanow*

Spirits in Fellowship / Oct. 1977 / Nine Winds ✦✦✦✦✦
His first album, quartet recordings with John Carter (cl). "Haiku" is Balinese or Tibetan-like, "The Human Beings" for Louis Armstrong and "Duke Ellington & the American Indian" show Golia's passion and compass for freedom. Boldly inventive. —*Michael G. Nastos*

Openhearted / Feb. 7, 1979 / Nine Winds ✦✦✦✦

In the Right Order / Aug. 25, 1979 / Nine Winds ✦✦✦✦✦

Solo / Jul. 16, 1980 / Nine Winds ✦✦✦

Slice of Life / Jun. 6, 1981 / Nine Winds ✦✦✦✦

Compositions for Large Ensemble / Mar. 14, 1982 / Nine Winds ✦✦✦✦

★ **Goin' Ahead** / Mar. 23, 1985–Mar. 24, 1985 / Nine Winds ✦✦✦✦✦

Pilgrimage to Obscurity / Jul. 1991 / Nine Winds ✦✦✦

Commemoration / Oct. 11, 1991+Apr. 11, 1992 / Nine Winds ✦✦✦✦

On Worldwide & Portable / Dec. 1991 / Nine Winds ✦✦✦

Decennium Dans Axlan / Apr. 11, 1992 / Nine Winds ✦✦✦✦

Against the Grain / 1993 / Nine Winds ✦✦✦✦

Benny Golson

b. Jan. 25, 1929, Philadelphia, PA
Tenor Saxophone, Arranger, Composer / Hard Bop
Benny Golson is a talented composer/arranger whose tenor play-ing has continued to evolve with time. After attending Howard University (1947–50), he worked in Philadelphia with Bull Moose Jackson's R&B band (1951) at a time when it included one of his writing influences, Tadd Dameron on piano. Golson played with Dameron for a period in 1953 and this was followed by stints with Lionel Hampton (1953–54), Johnny Hodges and Earl Bostic (1954–56). He came to prominence while with Dizzy Gillespie's globetrotting big band (1956–58), as much for his writing as for his tenor playing (the latter was most influenced by Don Byas and Lucky Thompson). Golson wrote such standards as "I Remember Clifford" (for the late Clifford Brown), "Killer Joe," "Stablemates," "Whisper Not," "Along Came Betty" and "Blues March" during 1956–60. His stay with Art Blakey's Jazz Messengers (1958–59) was significant and during 1959–62 he co-led the Jazztet with Art Farmer. From that point on, Golson gradually drifted away from jazz and concentrated more on working in the studios and with orchestras including a couple of years (1964–66) in Europe. When Benny Golson returned to active playing in 1977, his tone had hardened and sounded much closer to Archie Shepp than to Don Byas. Other than an unfortunate commercial effort for Columbia (1977), Golson has recorded consistently rewarding albums (many for Japanese labels) since that time, including a reunion with Art Farmer and Curtis Fuller in a new Jazztet. Through the years he has recorded as a leader for Contemporary, Riverside, United Artists, New Jazz, Argo, Mercury and Dreyfus among others. —*Scott Yanow*

★ **Benny Golson's New York Scene** / Oct. 14, 1957+Oct. 17, 1957 / Original Jazz Classics ✦✦✦✦✦
This was one of the first albums to establish Golson's reputation as a soloist and composer. —*Ron Wynn*

The Modern Touch / Dec. 19, 1957+Dec. 23, 1957 / Riverside ✦✦✦✦
W/ Kenny Dorham (tpt), J.J. Johnson (tb), Wynton Kelly (p), Paul Chambers (b) and Max Roach (d). —*Michael Erlewine*

The Other Side of Benny Golson / Nov. 12, 1958 / Riverside ✦✦✦✦
Tenor saxophonist Benny Golson's third recording as a leader was significant in two ways. It was his first opportunity to work with trombonist Curtis Fuller (the two would be members of The Jazztet by 1960) and it was one of his first chances to really stretch out on record as a soloist; up to this point Golson was possibly better known as a composer. Three of the six originals on this CD

reissue of a Riverside date are Golson's ("Are You Real" was the closest one to catching on), but the emphasis is on the solos of the leader, Fuller and pianist Barry Harris; bassist Jymie Merritt and drummer Philly Joe Jones are excellent in support. —*Scott Yanow*

Benny Golson and the Philadelphians / Nov. 17, 1958 / United Artists ✦✦✦

Gone with Golson / Jun. 20, 1959 / Original Jazz Classics ✦✦✦✦
Shortly before the formation of The Jazztet, tenor saxophonist Benny Golson and trombonist Curtis Fuller teamed up for this quintet set with pianist Ray Bryant, bassist Tommy Bryant and drummer Al Harewood. Although Golson contributed three of the six songs ("Blues After Dark" is the best-known one), the empha-sis is on his playing; the tenor is quite heated on the uptempo blues "Jam for Bobbie." The CD reissue adds "A Bit of Heaven" (originally on a sampler but part of the same session) to the orig-inal program, a fine example of hard bop of the late '50s. —*Scott Yanow*

Groovin' with Golson / Aug. 28, 1959 / Original Jazz Classics ✦✦✦
A mainstream date with traces of soul-jazz. Golson is solidly in the pocket on tenor. —*Ron Wynn*

Gettin' with It / Dec. 23, 1959 / Original Jazz Classics ✦✦✦

Killer Joe / 1977 / Columbia ✦✦
This album broke Golson's long hiatus in America and reintro-duced him to the domestic jazz audience, but it wasn't quite the hit for him as for Quincy Jones. —*Ron Wynn*

California Message / Oct. 20, 1980–Oct. 22, 1980 / Baystate ✦✦✦
This set (which is also available on the Timeless label) was Benny Golson's first album (other than a dismal commercial affair for Columbia) since 1964; he had spent the interim writing full-time for the studios. For this happy occasion, Golson reunites with trombonist Curtis Fuller in a septet also including trumpeter Oscar Brashear, trombonist Thurman Green and pianist Bill Mays. The music (seven Golson compositions including his older "Hits" "Blues March," "Whisper Not" and "I Remember Clifford") are not as surprising as his new sound, which had discarded his former roots in Don Byas and Lucky Thompson for a gruffness closer to Archie Shepp. Solidly swinging music. —*Scott Yanow*

One More Mem'ry / Aug. 19, 1981–Aug. 20, 1981 / Timeless ✦✦✦

Time Speaks / Dec. 8, 1982–Dec. 9, 1982 / Timeless ✦✦✦✦

This Is for You, John / Dec. 1983 / Timeless ✦✦

Stardust / Jun. 22, 1987–Jun. 23, 1987 / Denon ✦✦✦✦
A high-caliber session, with Golson and Freddie Hubbard (tpt) more than capably splitting the leadership duties. —*Ron Wynn*

● **Live** / Feb. 3, 1989 / Dreyfus ✦✦✦✦✦

Domingo / Nov. 11, 1991–Nov. 13, 1991 / Dreyfus ✦✦✦✦
Tenor saxophonist Benny Golson reunites with his longtime asso-ciate Curtis Fuller for this enjoyable set of hard bop. With assis-tance from pianist Kevin Hays, bassist James Genus, drummer Tony Reedus and (on "Blues March") trumpeter Jean-Loup Longnon, Golson and Fuller both sound very much in their musi-cal prime. The tenor's sound at this point had become quite a bit harder than previously, at times fairly close to Archie Shepp's, but he swung as hard as ever. Fuller in contrast is unchanged from his earlier days. Together they play in top form on six of Golson's compositions plus Fuller's "A La Mode" and Dave Brubeck's "In Your Own Sweet Way." —*Scott Yanow*

Eddie Gomez

b. Oct. 4, 1944, San Juan, Puerto Rico
Bass / Post-Bop
Eddie Gomez is a brilliant bassist whose flexibility and quick reflexes make him an ideal accompanist (although his own albums tend to be a bit erratic jazzwise). He grew up in New York and was with the Newport Festival Youth Band during 1959–61. After studying at Juilliard, Gomez played with Rufus Jones' sextet, Marian McPartland (1964), Paul Bley (1964–65), Giuseppe Logan, Gerry Mulligan and Gary McFarland among others. Gomez came to fame during his long period with the Bill Evans Trio (1966–77). He has since worked in a countless number of settings filling in for Charles Mingus (1978) and with Steps Ahead (1979–84), Benny Wallace, Joanne Brackeen, Jack DeJohnette, Chick Corea and in commercial settings as a studio musician. Eddie Gomez has recorded as a leader for Columbia, ProJazz and Stretch. —*Scott Yanow*

Down Stretch / Jan. 22, 1976–Jan. 23, 1976 / Blackhawk ✦✦✦

Gomez / Jan. 1984–Feb. 1984 / Denon ✦✦✦

Discovery / Nov. 1985 / Columbia ✦✦✦✦
A powerful recording, it features Michael Brecker on sax and E.W.I., an electronic wind instrument. Musically, this album covers jazz and classical and a little avant-garde. —*Paul Kohler*

Trio / Mar. 4, 1986 / Pro Arte ✦✦✦

Power Play / Nov. 1987 / Columbia ✦✦✦

Street Smart / May 1989 / Columbia ✦✦
A session with a balance between radio-oriented fusion and more ambitious traditional material. —*Ron Wynn*

● **Next Future** / 1992 / Stretch ✦✦✦✦✦
Bassist Eddie Gomez is better as a sideman than as a leader on recording dates, but this is one of his stronger efforts in the latter category (even if one has to get used to him taking or sharing virtually all of the melodies). Chick Corea sticks exclusively to an atmospheric synthesizer but otherwise this is a fairly straight-ahead quintet session featuring Gomez with the Coltranish tenor of Rick Margitza, pianist James Williams, drummer Lenny White and a guest appearance from flutist Jeremy Steig. —*Scott Yanow*

Nat Gonella

b. Mar. 7, 1908, London, England
Trumpet, Vocals / Dixieland
Inspired by Louis Armstrong, Nat Gonella in the 1930s could be considered the Wingy Manone or Louis Prima of England. He started off playing in the jazz-oriented dance bands of Billy Cotton, Roy Fox, Ray Noble and Lew Stone during 1929–34 before leading his own band, the Georgians, named thus because his version of "Georgia on My Mind" was popular. Although he visited and played in the U.S. in 1939, Gonella chose to stay in England where he made many records during 1932–42, a few in the mid-'40s and then became less prominent. In 1958 he formed the New Georgia Jazz Band (which recorded frequently during the next three years) and he remained an active and popular figure into the late '70s. Nat Gonella's recordings are worth investigating by swing and Dixieland fans. —*Scott Yanow*

● **Mister Rhythm Man** / Nov. 2, 1934–Mar. 29, 1035 / EMI ✦✦✦✦✦

Paul Gonsalves

b. Jul. 12, 1920, Boston, MA, d. May 14, 1974, London, England
Tenor Saxophone / Bop, Swing
The greatest moment of Paul Gonsalves' musical career occurred at the 1956 Newport Jazz Festival when, to bridge the gap between "Diminuendo in Blue" and "Crescendo in Blue," Duke Ellington urged him to take a long solo, egging him on through 27 exciting choruses that almost caused a riot. That well-publicized episode resulted in Ellington having a major "comeback," and Gonsalves forever earning Duke's gratitude.

Gonsalves had already earned a strong reputation during his stints with Count Basie (1946–49) and the Dizzy Gillespie Orchestra (1949–50). Joining Ellington in 1950, Gonsalves' warm breathy tone and harmonically advanced solos were a constant fixture for 24 years (except for a brief time in 1953 when he was with Tommy Dorsey) and he was well-featured up until his death, just ten days before Ellington passed on. In addition to his countless number of recorded performances with Ellington, Gonsalves led dates of his own on an occasional basis including for Argo, Jazzland, Impulse! (highlighted by a combative meeting with Sonny Stitt), Storyville, Black Lion and Fantasy. —*Scott Yanow*

Gettin' Together! / Dec. 20, 1960 / Original Jazz Classics ✦✦✦✦

★ **Salt and Pepper** / Sep. 5, 1963 / Jasmine ✦✦✦✦✦
A very good collaboration with Sonny Stitt (as). —*Ron Wynn*

Just A-Sittin' and A-Rockin' / Aug. 28, 1970+Sep. 3, 1970 / Black Lion ✦✦✦
This relaxed session gave three of Duke Ellington's finest sidemen rare opportunities to record outside of Ellington's Orchestra: tenor saxophonist Paul Gonsalves, Ray Nance (who had left Ellington a few years earlier) on trumpet, violin and vocal and (for half of this CD) altoist Norris Turney. The emphasis is on slower material, but there are a few romps (such as "Stompy Jones") to give the session a bit of variety. Good swinging performances on mostly familiar material. —*Scott Yanow*

Paul Gonsalves Meets Earl Hines / Dec. 15, 1970+Nov. 29, 1972 / Black Lion ✦✦✦
Most of this CD was recorded at the earlier date. Duke Ellington's

longtime tenor, Paul Gonsalves, was a perfect match for the inventive pianist, Earl Hines, who (along with bassist Al Hall and drummer Jo Jones) is in top form on five standards, three by Ellington. The music swings hard and has its surprising moments. The one track from 1972 is a solo version of "Blue Sands" played by its composer Earl Hines. Although not essential, this CD should please the fans of Hines and Gonsalves, two masterful players who had only previously recorded together once, on a date shared by the pianist and Johnny Hodges. —*Scott Yanow*

Mexican Bandit Meets Pittsburgh Pirate / Aug. 24, 1973 / Original Jazz Classics ✦✦✦
This album teams tenor saxophonist Paul Gonsalves and trumpeter Roy Eldridge quite late in their careers. Gonsalves would pass away within a year and Eldridge would only be able to play for about five more. Actually, Eldridge is in generally good (and typically combative) form on tunes such as his "5400 North" and "C Jam Blues." The ailing Gonsalves is tentative and streaky in spots and just average throughout despite his best efforts. The rhythm section (pianist Cliff Smalls, bassist Sam Jones and drummer Eddie Locke) is perfectly up to the task and has "It's the Talk of the Town" as its feature. It's an interesting historical album although the leader has sounded much better elsewhere. —*Scott Yanow*

Babs Gonzales

b. Oct. 27, 1919, Newark, NJ, d. Jan. 33, 1980, Newark, NJ
Vocals / Bop
A limited but enthusiastic singer, Babs Gonzales did what he could to popularize bop. He had brief stints with Charlie Barnet and Lionel Hampton and then led his own group (Three Bips and a Bop) during 1946–49, recording 24 numbers during 1947–49 including the earliest version of "Oop-Pop-A-Da" and such songs as "Weird Lullaby," "A Lesson in Bopology," "Professor Bop" and "Prelude to a Nightmare"; among his sidemen on these dates were Tadd Dameron, Tony Scott, Roy Haynes, James Moody, J.J. Johnson, Julius Watkins, Sonny Rollins (making his recording debut), Art Pepper, Wynton Kelly and even Don Redman. However, once the bop "fad" ended, Gonzales became more of a cult figure. He worked with James Moody (1951–53), recorded with Jimmy Smith and Johnny Griffin, ran his own label (Expubidence) and wrote two autobiographies that were more colorful than accurate. —*Scott Yanow*

★ **Weird Lullaby** / Feb. 24, 1947–Nov. 23, 1958 / Blue Note ✦✦✦✦✦
Long unavailable sessions from 1947, 1949, 1956 and 1958. Twenty tracks, including three-bips-and-a-bop sessions with Tadd Dameron, the first Sonny Rollins recording. Also with Don Redman, Ray Nance, Herbie Stewart, Jimmy Smith (organ), Art Pepper (sax) and countless others. A prize. —*Michael G. Nastos*

Dennis Gonzalez

b. 1954, Abilene, TX
Trumpet / Avant-Garde, Post-Bop
A talented trumpeter who has recorded a consistently rewarding string of lesser-known dates, Dennis Gonzalez's playing falls between advanced hard bop and free jazz. He moved to Dallas in 1977 and started the Daagnim label for which he recorded frequently with top local players. Starting in 1986 Gonzalez also made several dates for the Silkheart label (utilizing Charles Brackeen on one session) and Konnex. —*Scott Yanow*

Stefan / Apr. 8, 1986 / Silkheart ✦✦✦
Creative trumpeter and percussionist leads ensemble. All originals and a fresh unconventional sound. —*Michael G. Nastos*

Namesake / Feb. 14, 1987 / Silkheart ✦✦✦✦

Catechism / Jul. 14, 1987 / DAAGNIM ✦✦✦✦

Debenge, Debenge / Feb. 11, 1988–Feb. 12, 1988 / Silkheart ✦✦✦

Jerry Gonzalez

b. Jan. 5, 1949, New York, NY
Trumpet, Percussion, Leader / Afro-Cuban Jazz, Post-Bop
A multi-talented musician, Jerry Gonzalez plays trumpet in the tradition of Miles Davis and Dizzy Gillespie while also being one of the top Latin percussionists. He played in salsa bands as a teenager and freelanced in the 1970s and '80s with (among others) Dizzy Gillespie, Tony Williams, Eddie Palmieri, Tito Puente and McCoy Tyner. In 1980 Gonzales formed the Fort Apache Band, a group that has creatively Latinized all types of challeng-

ing jazz compositions including a full set of Thelonious Monk tunes. Gonzalez and his important group have recorded for Enja and Sunnyside. —*Scott Yanow*

A Yo Me Cure / Jul. 1979–Aug. 1979 / American Clave/Pangaea ◆◆◆
An often spectacular, breakout Afro-Latin album by conga player, bandleader, composer and sometime pianist Jerry Gonzalez. He merged Latin jazz, salsa and Afro-Cuban rhythms, producing an album that had both multiple textures and plenty of explosive improvising. —*Ron Wynn*

The River Is Deep / Nov. 5, 1982 / Enja ◆◆◆◆
And The Fort Apache Band. Powerhouse group; strong material. A sparkling session that helped cement Gonzalez's status among the new crop of Latin-jazz stars. —*Ron Wynn*

Rhumba Para Monk / Oct. 27, 1988–Oct. 28, 1988 / Sunnyside ◆◆◆◆◆
And The Fort Apache Band. Great production by Jim Anderson on eight Monk standards. Stripped to quintet with Carter Jefferson, the tenor sax foil. Very intriguing concept, melding Latin rhythms to Monk's off minorisms. —*Michael G. Nastos*

★ **Obatala** / Nov. 6, 1988 / Enja ◆◆◆◆◆
Latinos have always understood jazz much better than jazz musicians understand Latin music. The Fort Apache Band is typical— a largely Latino group including several heavy NY salsa percussionists, with a couple of excellent Anglos on sax and piano. The numbers range from Shorter, Davis and Monk to the lucumi-inflected title cut. —*John Storm Roberts*

Crossroads / 1994 / Milestone ◆◆◆◆

Pensativo / 1995 / Milestone ◆◆◆◆

Benny Goodman

b. May 30, 1909, Chicago, IL, d. Jun. 13, 1986, New York, NY
Clarinet, Leader / Swing
The greatest jazz clarinetist of all time, Benny Goodman deserved his title as "The King of Swing." Although not the actual founder of swing, BG's phenominal success in 1935 launched the swing era and, without watering down his music or displaying an extroverted show-biz personality, he became a major pop star. His eccentricities (being very self-possessed) resulted in some odd incidents and a great deal of misunderstanding through the years, but they were consistent with the fact that Goodman's main interest in life was playing clarinet and that everything else was secondary.

Benny Goodman began on clarinet when he was 11 and he had two years of study with the classically trained Franz Schoepp (whose other students included Jimmy Noone and Buster Bailey). Goodman, who first played in public doing an imitation of Ted Lewis when he was 12, developed fast. By 1923 he was a member of the Musicians Union and playing regularly in Chicago. In August 1925 when he was 16, Goodman joined Ben Pollack's Orchestra and in December 1926 he made his recording debut with Pollack. Technically gifted from the start, Goodman was a major soloist with Pollack (along with Jimmy McPartland, Glenn Miller and later Jack Teagarden) and had his first opportunities to lead his own recording sessions in 1928 including two songs with a trio. After leaving Pollack in 1929, Goodman worked with Red Nichols' Five Pennies and then became a very busy studio musician, recording a countless number of performances (often in anonymous settings) during 1929–33. He even doubled during this era on alto, baritone and (on one session) trumpet. His own dates in 1933–34 featured Teagarden, Billie Holiday (in her recording debut), Mildred Bailey, Coleman Hawkins and the up-and-coming Gene Krupa. In 1934 Goodman put together his first orchestra, started recording for Columbia and appeared as one of three big bands on the *Let's Dance* radio series; the show's trademark melody would permanently become his own opening theme. Using Fletcher Henderson arrangements, Goodman's well-rehearsed ensemble showed that it was possible to play both jazz and dance music simultaneously.

But when the radio show ended in May 1935, Benny Goodman's future as a bandleader was far from secure. With Bunny Berigan on trumpet, the band made popular records for Victor of "King Porter Stomp" and "Sometimes I'm Happy." The clarinetist also teamed up with Teddy Wilson and Gene Krupa for the first recordings of the Benny Goodman Trio and then agreed to go on a cross-country tour with the orchestra. After some minor

successes and major disasters, the group was well-received in Oakland and then on August 21, 1935 they nearly caused a riot at the Palomar Ballroom in Los Angeles as teenagers went crazy over the band; unknown to BG, his national broadcasts on the *Let's Dance* series had been very popular in California. From that point on, he went from success to success, causing sensations in Chicago and New York. Although Berigan did not stay long with the band, his successors (Ziggy Elman, Harry James and Chris Griffin) formed one of the great trumpet sections, Gene Krupa became the pacesetter among drummers, and pianist Jess Stacy and singer Helen Ward (later Martha Tilton) were major assets. Goodman, by using Teddy Wilson and Lionel Hampton regularly in his Quartet, broke boundaries in race relations. He had the most popular band in the world during 1935–38.

The highpoint to Benny Goodman's success was his historic January 16, 1938, Carnegie Hall concert which was miraculously recorded and released for the first time in the early '50s. "Sing, Sing, Sing" made Krupa such a star that that fact (plus a personality conflict with Goodman) resulted in him being the first of BG's stars to depart. Although BG's popularity was soon matched and then exceeded during the swing era by Artie Shaw and Glenn Miller, his orchestra (even with its turnover) remained a major force. By 1940 James, Wilson and Stacy were gone, but Goodman had the pioneering electric guitarist Charlie Christian playing in his new sextet, he had signed with Columbia, the clarinetist was starting to record challenging arrangements by Eddie Sauter and he was using such fine sidemen as Cootie Williams, Georgie Auld and Johnny Guarnieri. As the 1940s advanced, other top players (such as Mel Powell, Lou McGarity, Red Norvo and even a young Stan Getz) and singers (Helen Forrest and Peggy Lee) made contributions and Goodman remained "King of Swing." He even took some time to show the classical music world that he could play their music, too.

By 1945 and the rise of bebop, Benny Goodman's music started to be thought of as old-fashioned. BG's own playing rarely changed from that point forward, but he remained enthusiastic about performing the old repertoire, and no one played it better. He broke up his band in 1946 and then opened his music temporarily to bebop. Goodman had a 1948 septet with fellow clarinetist Stan Hasselgard and Wardell Gray, used Fats Navarro on one recording and his 1949 orchestra had some very advanced arrangements by Chico O'Farrill in its book. But by the following year, Goodman returned permanently to swing. He led small groups and occasional big bands throughout the remainder of his career. While the orchestras tended to be nostalgic affairs (revisiting the Henderson charts), the combos allowed Goodman to stretch out and display his brilliant style. He had some reunions with his Trio and Quartet, participated in the rather fictional 1956 movie *The Benny Goodman Story* (playing the clarinet solos) and toured the USSR in 1962. Among Goodman's sidemen in the 1950s were Terry Gibbs, Buck Clayton, Ruby Braff, Paul Quinichette, Roland Hanna, Jack Sheldon, Bill Harris, Flip Phillips and Andre Previn. During his last three decades, BG often used alumni and even such youngsters as Herbie Hancock and George Benson. Goodman was less active in the 1960s and made no records during 1973–77. He came back in 1978 to play at his 40th-anniversary Carnegie Hall concert before drifting back into retirement again. However, in the early '80s, Goodman began to show a strong interest in performing and he put together his final big band (which was really founded by Loren Schoenberg), playing on a public television show just a short time before his death.

Due to his continuing popularity, Benny Goodman (still a household name) is represented on more records than any jazz leader other than Duke Ellington. Most of his radio broadcasts and lesser-known recordings from the 1930s and '40s were released on Sunbeam LPs, his output for Victor during the swing era has been fully reissued, his Columbia performances have come out in more piecemeal fashion and there are a countless number of later combo sessions that are available; Music Masters, possessor of BG's private tapes, has thus far come out with ten CDs of previously unreleased material. —*Scott Yanow*

A Jazz Holiday / 1928 10 2 / Decca ◆◆◆◆
This two-LP set contains some of Benny Goodman's most interesting pre-swing recordings. The many highlights include two sides by his very first trio (from 1928), the satirical "Shirt Tale Stomp," Goodman's only recorded trumpet solo (on "Jungle Blues") and some rare spots on alto and baritone, four classic sides by the Joe Venuti-Eddie Lang All-Star Orchestra (including

definitive versions of "Beale Street Blues" and "Farewell Blues" with trombonist/singer Jack Teagarden) and sessions led by Adrian Rollini and Red Nichols (the latter has memorable renditions of "Dinah" and "Indiana" along with a famous version of "The Sheik of Araby"). These many all-star New York bands are full of young and energetic players with BG only 19 on the earliest of these hot sides. Highly recommended in one form or another; some of the material has since been reissued on CD. —*Scott Yanow*

Great Soloists: Featuring Benny Goodman / Mar. 1929–Nov. 22, 1933 / Biograph ✦✦✦
This LP has a grab bag of somewhat rare items, featuring clarinetist Benny Goodman as a sideman during the 1929–33 period. Included are dance sides with Ben Selvin's orchestra, a hot version of "Roll on Mississippi" and strong appearances with Mills Musical Clowns (a pickup group put together by Irving Mills) and Steve Washington's orchestra. Interesting pre-swing sides by the future King. —*Scott Yanow*

Benny Goodman and the Giants of Swing / Apr. 18, 1929–Oct. 23, 1934 / Prestige ✦✦✦✦
This excellent LP collects together some of Benny Goodman's best early recordings, all cut at least a few years before he became known as The King of Swing and also co-starring the great trombonist/singer Jack Teagarden. BG is heard during 1929–31 with Red Nichols' Five Pennies (whose eight selections include "Indiana," "Dinah" and Teagarden's famous vocal on "The Sheik of Araby"), the 1930 session by Irving Mills' Hotsy Totsy Gang that included an ailing Bix Beiderbecke, an Adrian Rollini date from 1934 and four gems by the Joe Venuti-Eddie Lang All-Star Orchestra in 1931. Throughout, Goodman (just barely out of his teens) and Teagarden, (along with other talented jazzmen then earning a living as studio musicians, seem overjoyed to be able to play jazz. This is highly enjoyable music that serves as a fine introduction to early pre-swing jazz. —*Scott Yanow*

B.G. & Big Tea in NYC / Apr. 1929–Oct. 1934 / GRP ✦✦✦✦
CD reissue of some early '30s material that doesn't feature clarinetist Benny Goodman in a leadership role. Instead, he's in bands under the direction of Red Nichols, Arthur Rollini and Irving Mills. Yet, he's the star soloist, along with trombonist Jack Teagarden. —*Ron Wynn*

Swinging '34, Vol. 1 / 1934 / Melodean ✦✦✦✦
These two volumes find Benny Goodman and an impressive nine-piece unit (which includes trumpeter Bunny Berigan, trombonist Jack Jenney and drummer Gene Krupa) jamming anonymously under the bandname of "Bill Dodge and His All-Star Orchestra" (even though there was no Bill Dodge). The music, recorded for radio airplay for use between shows, features excellent examples of early swing with plenty of then-recent compositions and, on the first volume, four vocals by Red McKenzie. Collectors will enjoy comparing these performances to the regular studio versions; both are generally enjoyable. —*Scott Yanow*

Swinging '34, Vol. 2 / 1934 / Melodean ✦✦✦✦
This is the second of two LPs documenting music recorded for anonymous radio airplay in early 1934 by Benny Goodman and a particularly strong nonet (including trumpeter Bunny Berigan and trombonist Jack Jenney). The results are swing performed a year before it became wildly popular; these performances hold their own against their more familiar studio versions. —*Scott Yanow*

Complete Benny Goodman, Vol. 1 (1935) / Apr. 4, 1935–Nov. 22, 1935 / RCA ✦✦✦✦✦
This is the first of eight double LPs that contain all of Benny Goodman's output for Victor during his remarkable 1935–39 period. After recording "King Porter Stomp" and "Sometimes I'm Happy" on July 1, 1935, and then thrilling the crowd at the Palomar Ballroom in Los Angeles on August 21, the Goodman Orchestra became the most popular in the world, not losing its dominance until the rise of Glenn Miller in 1939. This two-fer not only includes the two hits but all of trumpeter Bunny Berigan's solos with Goodman, the debut of the BG Trio (with pianist Teddy Wilson and drummer Gene Krupa) and many other swinging sides, even a hot version of "Jingle Bells." —*Scott Yanow*

★ **The Birth of Swing** / Apr. 4, 1935–Nov. 5, 1936 / Bluebird ✦✦✦✦
This three-CD set includes all of the Benny Goodman's big band's recordings from April 1935 through November 1936, a period when the orchestra became the most popular and influential in

the world, making both swing and Benny Goodman into household words. Augmented by some alternate takes, this set shows just how solid and musical a unit Goodman had from the start. Key soloists include trumpeters Bunny Berigan and Ziggy Elman, pianist Jess Stacy and the band's excellent singer Helen Ward, but BG usually emerges as the main star with the tight and swinging ensembles being a close second. In addition to the hits ("King Porter Stomp," "Sometimes I'm Happy," "When Buddha Smiles," "Stompin' at the Savoy," and "Goody-Goody") even the lesser-known numbers and pop tunes have their strong moments. This music is essential to any serious jazz collection. —*Scott Yanow*

Thesaurus, Vol. 1 / Jun. 6, 1935 / Sunbeam ✦✦✦
June 6, 1935, was a very busy day for Benny Goodman and his big band. The group recorded no less than 51 tunes for transcriptions that were leased to NBC radio stations under the pseudonym of The Rhythm Makers Orchestra. Recorded shortly before BG made it big (otherwise they could not have been disguised as a fictional band), these excellent sides are a fine showcase for Goodman and his sidemen, which at the time included trumpeter Pee Wee Erwin, pianist Frank Froeba and drummer Gene Krupa among others. This first of three LP volumes is highlighted by a surprisingly effective swing version of "Yes, We Have No Bananas." —*Scott Yanow*

Thesaurus, Vol. 2 / Jun. 6, 1935 / Sunbeam ✦✦✦
The second of three LPs documenting one very busy day in the life of Benny Goodman's orchestra, these transcriptions cut for radio are well-recorded and consistently swinging even with the presence of a few fluffs (each performance only received one run-through). The musicians received just $1 apiece per tune (51 songs were cut that day) so listeners definitely receive their money's worth. A fascinating look at the Benny Goodman Orchestra just before it became wildly successful. —*Scott Yanow*

Thesaurus, Vol. 3 / Jun. 6, 1935 / Sunbeam ✦✦✦
This is the third and final volume of LPs chronicling the 51 songs recorded by the Benny Goodman orchestra for radio transcriptions in one day. This set includes interesting versions of "King Porter Stomp" and "Sometimes I'm Happy" performed less than a month before the hit studio renditions and captures The King of Swing only a short time before he unexpectedly became a household name. —*Scott Yanow*

● **The Complete Small Combinations, Vols. 1-2** / Jul. 11, 1935–Jul. 30, 1937 / RCA ✦✦✦✦✦
This two-CD set from the French RCA Jazz Tribune series (a straight reissue of a two-LP set) has the first 30 recordings by the Benny Goodman Trio and Quartets, groups featuring the leader-clarinetist, pianist Teddy Wilson, drummer Gene Krupa and sometimes vibraphonist Lionel Hampton. A special bonus of this historic set is the inclusion of five formerly rare alternate takes (including "After You've Gone" and "Body and Soul" from the first trio session). Although used by BG as a brief departure from his big band, his trio and quartet became famous in their own right and their recordings are essential to any serious jazz collection. This two-fer was followed by a second one tracing Goodman's small groups into 1939. —*Scott Yanow*

Original Benny Goodman Trio and Quartet Sessions, Vol. 1: After You've Gone / Jul. 13, 1935–Feb. 3, 1937 / Bluebird ✦✦✦✦
Although Benny Goodman came to fame as leader of a big swinging orchestra, from nearly the beginning he always allocated some time to playing with smaller groups. On July 13, 1935, the Benny Goodman Trio debuted (featuring drummer Gene Krupa and pianist Teddy Wilson) and 13 months later vibraphonist Lionel Hampton made the unit a quartet. The first interracial group to appear regularly in public, this outlet gave BG an opportunity to stretch out and interact with his peers. The CD *After You've Gone* contains the first ten Trio recordings and the initial twelve studio performances by the Quartet. Helen Ward contributes two fine vocals, but the emphasis is on the close interplay between these brilliant players. —*Scott Yanow*

Complete Benny Goodman, Vol. 2 (1935-1936) / Nov. 22, 1935–Jun. 16, 1936 / RCA ✦✦✦✦✦
The second two-LP set in this eight-volume series has all of Benny Goodman's Victor studio sides that were recorded during a seven-month period when the orchestra consolidated and built on its unexpected success. In addition to such popular recordings as "When Buddha Smiles," "Stompin' at the Savoy," and "Goody Goody," there are six selections by the Benny Goodman Trio,

many enjoyable vocals from Helen Ward (the best of BG's many singers) and four hot numbers by a combo under Gene Krupa's leadership that match the clarinetist with trumpeter Roy Eldridge and tenor great Chu Berry. Essential music in one form or another. —*Scott Yanow*

Benny Goodman from the Congress Hotel / Dec. 27, 1935–Feb. 10, 1936 / Sunbeam ✦✦✦✦
This five-LP boxed set houses the same music as the five individual volumes (even including all of the same liner notes) and is overall a gem. Benny Goodman was booked into the Congress Hotel in December 1935 for a one-month stint; the engagement was eventually extended to six months. These well-recorded aircheks are seven separate but continuous broadcasts that contain plenty of strong examples of BG's early band. Unlike his 1937 version, this orchestra only had its leader and pianist Jess Stacy as memorable soloists (although trombonist Joe Harris did a good job in a Jack Teagarden vein), but the ensembles are remarkably tight, Helen Ward's vocals are enjoyable, the band always swung (even on the pop tunes) and happily the recording quality is quite good. Highly recommended to those who can find this rare box. —*Scott Yanow*

Complete Benny Goodman, Vol. 3 (1936) / Aug. 13, 1936–Dec. 9, 1936 / Bluebird ✦✦✦✦
The third of eight two-LP sets reissuing all of Benny Goodman's Victor recordings from the swing era, this two-fer has such "killer dillers" as "Down South Camp Meeting," "St. Louis Blues" and two versions of "Bugle Call Rag," in addition to performances by the Benny Goodman Trio and his new Quartet (with vibraphonist Lionel Hampton), Ella Fitzgerald as a guest vocalist and trumpeter Ziggy Elman's first recordings with the band. In all there are 32 performances on this set that prove that Benny Goodman really did deserve the title, "the King of Swing." —*Scott Yanow*

Complete Benny Goodman, Vol. 8 (1936-1939) / Dec. 2, 1936–May 4, 1939 / Bluebird ✦✦✦✦✦
The final volume of this definitive series of Benny Goodman's Victor studio recordings not only contains his recordings from April and May 1939 but digs up a variety of alternate takes (most of them previously unissued) from the 1936–39 period. It is fascinating to hear "new" versions of such songs as "Stompin' at the Savoy," "Sing, Sing Sing," "Avalon" and "Sugarfoot Stomp," especially when one is familiar with the original released renditions. In addition, this two-fer has the two recordings (and one alternate) cut by The Metronome All-Star Band, which, in 1939, (with such musicians as Bunny Berigan, Jack Teagarden and Tommy Dorsey) allowed Goodman to reunite with some of his associates from the earlier days. A fitting ending to an essential series. —*Scott Yanow*

Airplay / Dec. 15, 1936–Oct. 11, 1938 / Doctor Jazz ✦✦✦
There are so many CDs and LPs in existence of Benny Goodman radio broadcasts that it seems silly or repetitive to release more, but as long as the musical quality stays as high as on this two-LP set, there is no reason to complain. Most unusual is a broadcast in 1937 that took place when Gene Krupa was ill. Benny Goodman and Teddy Wilson perform a duo version of "Body and Soul" and, with the addition of Lionel Hampton, form an unusual clarinet-vibes-piano trio on "Dinah." An excellent set. —*Scott Yanow*

Complete Benny Goodman, Vol. 4 (1936-1937) / Dec. 30, 1936–Oct. 22, 1937 / Bluebird ✦✦✦✦✦
The fourth of eight volumes (all are two-LP sets) documenting Benny Goodman's highly influential Victor studio sides, the 1936-37 period covered by this set found BG's amazing popularity still on the rise (he was now a household name), Harry James joining the orchestra and Martha Tilton settling in as the band's regular vocalist. Among the many memorable recordings are "Sing, Sing, Sing," the BG Quartet's "Avalon" and "Sugarfoot Stomp." —*Scott Yanow*

● **On the Air 1937-1938** / Mar. 25, 1937–Sep. 20, 1938 / Columbia/Legacy ✦✦✦✦✦
In the early '50s, after the unexpectedly large sales of Benny Goodman's 1938 Carnegie Hall concert, Columbia came out with a two-LP set of broadcasts from 1937-39 that also sold well. This recent double-CD set not only includes the music on the original LPs but adds 14 additional tracks only previously put out on collector's labels. *On the Air* really captures the Benny Goodman big band (along with some examples of the Trio and Quartet) at its peak and shows why the original swing orchestras (as opposed to

the weak nostalgia bands that are currently around) were so popular with younger people in the 1930s and '40s. These performances are still exciting. —*Scott Yanow*

Roll 'em, Vol. 1 / Mar. 25, 1937–Nov. 22, 1939 / Columbia ✦✦✦
Columbia has never coherently reissued their valuable 1939-46 Benny Goodman recordings. This LP is a bit confusing for it includes six aircheck performances from 1937-38 that are available elsewhere, along with ten studio recordings from 1939. The liner notes mistakenly say that the guitar solo on "Honeysuckle Rose" is by Arnold Covey; it is actually Charlie Christian. There is some excellent music on this LP but as a sampler it misses the mark. —*Scott Yanow*

Avalon: the Small Bands, Vol. 2 (1937—1939) / Jul. 30, 1937–Apr. 6, 1939 / Bluebird ✦✦✦✦
This second of two CDs reissuing all of Benny Goodman's Trio and Quartet recordings for Victor starts out with eight performances co-starring the magical team of vibraphonist Lionel Hampton, pianist Teddy Wilson and drummer Gene Krupa (including their famous version of "Avalon") and then finishes off with 14 recordings from the post-Krupa era. The latter have either Dave Tough or Buddy Schutz in the drummer's spot, and three cuts (including a classic version of "I Cried for You") add bassist John Kirby. No matter what the personnel, Benny Goodman is in top form on these highly enjoyable classics from his early prime. —*Scott Yanow*

Benny Goodman at the Madhattan Room / Oct. 13, 1937–Jan. 16, 1938 / Sunbeam ✦✦✦✦
Available originally as a dozen individual sets, these late-1937 broadcasts of Benny Goodman's Orchestra, Trio and Quartet from the Madhattan Room of the Pennsylvania Hotel in New York were also put out as this 12-LP box, containing exactly the same program and liner notes as the original sets. There are many highlights with strong solos from Goodman and trumpeter Harry James, exuberant backup by Gene Krupa, features for the Trio and Quartet and plenty of vocals by Martha Tilton. Since this set gives one a valuable look at the Benny Goodman Orchestra as they seem to be counting down to their famous January 1938 Carnegie Hall concert, it sems fitting that the series concludes with two numbers actually from that historic performance that were left out of the Columbia set due to their rough quality. Few bands could withstand the enormous amount of recordings, broadcasts and performances that Benny Goodman's orchestra underwent at the peak of its popularity without losing some of its quality, but the taskmaster clarinetist kept his troops nearly flawless in their ensemble work and they never failed to swing. This is a great set well worth searcing for. —*Scott Yanow*

Complete Benny Goodman, Vol. 5 (1937-1938) / Oct. 29, 1937–Apr. 8, 1938 / Bluebird ✦✦✦✦✦
It was during the period covered by this two-fer that Benny Goodman played his famous Carnegie Hall concert and his orchestra reached its peak. This fifth of eight two-LP sets documenting Benny Goodman's Victor recordings of the '30s has more than its share of memorable performances including "Don't Be That Way," "One O'Clock Jump" and two versions of "Life Goes to a Party" plus the last recordings of the Benny Goodman Quartet before Gene Krupa (after a dispute with BG) left the band to form his own orchestra. Other sessions include an unusual one that found some of Count Basie's sidemen (including tenor-great Lester Young) sitting in, and there is also a quartet date with Dave Tough sitting and performing ably in the departed Krupa's place. As with all of the two-fers in this series, this one is highly recommended and deserves to be reissued in full on CD. —*Scott Yanow*

Treasure Chest Series, Vol. 1 / 1937-1938 / MGM ✦✦✦✦
This three-LP series features radio aircheks by the Benny Goodman big band and small groups during 1937-38. Since the producers were quite choosy in designing these programs, there are virtually no weak seletions with the big band numbers emphasizing middle and utempo swing and the Trio and Quartet selections up to the level one would expect of Benny Goodman, Lionel Hampton, Teddy Wilson and Gene Krupa. The first volume contains "When Buddha Smiles," "Dear Old Southland," "Madhouse" and a few quartet performances. The biggest surprise is Lionel Hampton's ad-lib appearance on vibes during the big band's "I Know That You Know." —*Scott Yanow*

Treasure Chest Series, Vol. 2 / 1937-1938 / MGM ✦✦✦✦
The second of three LPs in this superior series continues the

issuance of rare (and well-chosen) live performances by Benny Goodman's big band and small groups. Virtually every selection is a gem and there are a few surprises. The big band joins the quartet at the end of a rousing "Avalon" while "Space, Man" finds Lionel Hampton and Jess Stacy sharing the same piano. Overall, this series finds BG and his sidemen at their best — *Scott Yanow*

Treasure Chest Series, Vol. 3 / 1937–1939 / MGM ✦✦✦✦
The third and final LP in this wonderful series of radio airchecks once again features Benny Goodman, his big band and small groups at their best; the producers really cherry-picked the large amount of live documentation to come up with some of the most rewarding performances by BG during one of his prime periods. The biggest surprise of *Volume 3* is the addition of Harry James' trumpet to the quartet on "Twilight in Turkey," but even the selections that should be predictable tend to swing hotter than expected. As a bonus, a 1939 live version of "AC-DC Current" adds a rare performance by guitarist Charlie Christian to his slim discography. Overall, this is a great series that deserves to be reissued on CD. — *Scott Yanow*

★ **Benny Goodman Carnegie Hall Jazz Concert** / Jan. 16, 1938 / Columbia ✦✦✦✦✦
One of the greatest concerts ever captured on record is in itself a turning point in the way jazz is judged by outsiders. Never before had a full jazz concert been held at Carnegie Hall; it is hard to believe that tapes of this momentous event were kept in a closet, forgotten until rediscovered by accident in 1950. There are many many highpoints, including exciting versions of "Don't Be That Way" and "One O'Clock Jump," a tribute to the 20 years of jazz that were then on record, a jam-session version of "Honeysuckle Rose," which found sidemen of the orchestras of Duke Ellington and Count Basie interacting with Goodman's stars, exciting performances by the Trio and Quartet and, of course, "Sing, Sing, Sing" with Gene Krupa's creative (if not too subtle) drumming and Jess Stacy's remarkable ad-lib piano solo. Fortunately, this program has been reissued in full on CD and it belongs in every serious music library, capturing Benny Goodman and the swing era in general at its height. — *Scott Yanow*

Wrappin' It Up: the Harry James Years, Part II / Mar. 9, 1938–May 4, 1939 / Bluebird ✦✦✦
A "best-of" CD, this Bluebird release is somewhat unnecessary since all of Benny Goodman's recordings for the label have already been reissued in more complete form. However this set, which is sure to frustrate completists, includes rare takes of "The Blue Room," "I'll Always Be in Love with You" and "Louise" along with a previously unissued version of "Undecided." The Benny Goodman Orchestra is featured on 22 selections from the period right after drummer Gene Krupa left the band. Trumpeter Harry James is the main star, but there are also good solos from tenors Bud Freeman and Jerry Jerome, pianist Jess Stacy and (on "Ti-Pi-Tin") guest Lester Young. Benny Goodman (still just 29 at the time) is in prime form and, since the emphasis is on instrumentals, there are plenty of killer dillers included. Highlights include "Ti-Pi-Tin," "Big John Special," "Wrappin' It Up," "Bumble Bee Stomp," "Smoke House" and "Estrellita," but all of the music is rewarding. However, more serious collectors will want to get these swing recordings as part of a more complete series. — *Scott Yanow*

Complete Benny Goodman, Vol. 6 (1938) / Apr. 8, 1938–Oct. 13, 1938 / Bluebird ✦✦✦✦✦
This sixth of eight two-LP sets documenting Benny Goodman's Victor studio recordings finds BG in his post-Gene Krupa era. The classic trumpet section of Harry James, Ziggy Elman and Chris Griffin was still intact, but after the Carnegie Hall concert there must have been a feeling of these performances being anti-climactic. Still, there are lots of memorable moments on these big-band and quartet tracks with a liberal amount of Martha Tilton vocals, pop tunes (although superior ones) and jazz standards. The rhythm was now much more subtle (with Dave Tough on drums), but the BG sound in 1938 was not that much different than in 1937 and the music is well worth acquiring. — *Scott Yanow*

Best of Newhouse / May 10, 1938–Apr. 18, 1939 / Phontastic ✦✦✦✦
This two-LP set owes its existence to Jerry Newhouse who, in 1938, was a young swing fan who had just bought a professional record-cutting machine so as to record his favorite musicians off radio broadcasts. The Swedish Phontastic label wisely went through Newhouse's acetates in 1981 and were able to put together this generous package of timeless swing. Mostly dating from 1938, these well-recorded performances do not necessarily shed

new light on Benny Goodman's legacy but they offer "new" versions of BG's standards, including a version of "Sing, Sing, Sing" that lets Lionel Hampton stretch out on drums. — *Scott Yanow*

Complete Benny Goodman, Vol. 7 (1938–1939) / Oct. 13, 1938–Apr. 7, 1939 / Bluebird ✦✦✦✦✦
The seventh two-LP set in this eight-volume series continues the documentation of Benny Goodman's influential studio recordings for Victor in the '30s. Highpoints of this fine two-fer include a version of "Ciribiribin" that predates Harry James' famous recording, the unusual "Bach Goes to Town," a memorable "I Cried for You" by Goodman's quintet (with John Kirby on bass), "Sent for You Yesterday" (featuring a Johnny Mercer vocal) and the big Ziggy Elman hit "And the Angels Sing." Recommended. — *Scott Yanow*

Sing, Sing, Sing / Apr. 4, 1935–Apr. 11, 1939 / Bluebird ✦✦✦
A fine all-around single CD, it sums up Benny Goodman's 1935–38 period on Victor. During this time, BG became jazz's and popular music's number one attraction, achieving this impressive feat without watering down his music or emphasizing novelties. All Goodman did was play the music he loved and the audience magically responded and started dancing. This set has most of BG's better-known recordings from the era including "King Porter Stomp," "Goody Goody," "Roll 'Em," "Don't Be That Way," "One O'Clock Jump" and, of course, the memorable "Sing, Sing, Sing"; it serves as a good beginning for those listeners just starting to explore Benny Goodman's music. — *Scott Yanow*

Jumpin' at the Woodside / May 2, 1939–May 9, 1939 / Giants Of Jazz ✦✦✦
This well-recorded Giants of Jazz LP finds the Benny Goodman Orchestra in transition. Lionel Hampton had temporarily taken over on drums (giving the band a rhythmic drive more enthusiastic than had been heard since Gene Krupa's departure a year earlier) and, while Krupa himself guests on a hot version of "Chicago" by the Quartet, a small-group performance from the later of these two broadcasts finds BG trying out guitarist George Rose. Although Rose did not catch on, the stage was being unwittingly set for Charlie Christian's arrival later that year. Since these two radio airchecks are complete, some time is wasted with dated talk and novelties, but there are enough strong musical moments to make this set worth acquiring. — *Scott Yanow*

Alternate Goodman, Vol. 1 / Aug. 10, 1939–Sep. 13, 1939 / Phontastic ✦✦✦
Although Columbia has never fully reissued Benny Goodman's valuable work for the label during 1939–46, the Swedish Phontastic label did release no less than twelve LPs full of alternate takes and unissued performances from the era, issued chronologically. So, thanks to Phontastic, it is possible to acquire alternate versions of songs while the original takes remains completely unavailable! *Volume 1* contains "new" versions of such classics as "Jumpin' at the Woodside," "Stealin' Apples," "Bolero," and "Boy Meets Horn." With trumpeters Ziggy Elman and Jimmy Maxwell, trombonist Vernon Brown and tenorman Jerry Jerome among the soloists, it quickly becomes obvious that Benny Goodman (even though his popularity was gradually being exceeded by Glenn Miller) had a great band in 1939. — *Scott Yanow*

Legendary Benny Goodman / Aug. 10, 1939–Sep. 26, 1951 / Columbia ✦✦✦✦
Released by Columbia Special Products back in 1981, this five-LP box set contains an excellent cross-section of Benny Goodman's recordings for Columbia, dating from 1939–42, 1945–46 and a few tracks from 1950–51. Since CBS has never reissued BG's recordings in full, this sampler (which has become hard to find) is the best set from this era put out to date, tracing the evolution of Benny Goodman through his second great band (including a few tracks by the Sextet with guitarist Charlie Christian) to some of the clarinetist's first post-war recordings and a few performances where, instead of being the pacesetter, he was looked upon as a nostalgia act. Throughout BG plays quite well and, even with only five selections to a side (for a total of around 150 minutes on the five LPs) this box is worth bidding for. — *Scott Yanow*

Benny Goodman on V-Disc / Aug. 11, 1939–Oct. 1948 / Sunbeam ✦✦✦✦
Originally released as three separate LPs, this three-LP set is a straight reissue with the same liner notes as the individual Sunbeam records. A wonderful acquisition for the true collector, *Benny Goodman on V-Disc* contains a wide variety of perfor-

mances that were issued on V-Discs (limited-edition records specially available for servicemen during World War II), and many of the selections were formerly quite rare. Although a few tracks are from 1939–41 and some others date as late as 1948, the bulk of the music is from 1944–46, not one of The King of Swing's better-known periods. Such star soloists as trumpeter Cootie Williams, guitarist Charlie Christian, Gene Krupa, trumpeter Roy Eldridge, vibraphonist Red Norvo and pianist Mel Powell have their spots, but the clarinetist consistently gets solo honors. Historical and quite enjoyable performances. —*Scott Yanow*

Fletcher Henderson Arrangements / Aug. 11, 1939–Feb. 23, 1953 / Columbia ✦✦✦
Fletcher Henderson was always Benny Goodman's favorite arranger and the clarinetist constantly went out of his way to give Henderson's danceable and swinging charts a great deal of credit for his own success. This particular LP does not include Henderson's earlier "hits" for Goodman (which were recorded for Victor), but does contain highlights from BG's Columbia years, starting with "Stealin' Apples" (Fletcher's old theme song), "Honeysuckle Rose" (which includes a fine Charlie Christian guitar solo) and "Henderson Stomp," continuing through 1945's "Just You, Just Me" and three performances with vocalist Helen Ward that were recorded in 1953 specifically for this LP (including "I'll Never Say 'Never Again' Again"). Since Henderson had died in late 1952, this fine LP served as a tribute to his writing skills and is a good excuse to hear a variety of classic Benny Goodman big-band recordings. —*Scott Yanow*

Best of Big Bands / Aug. 16, 1939–Sep. 12, 1945 / Columbia ✦✦✦
This CD, a sampler from Benny Goodman's 1939–45 period with Columbia, unfortunately does not list any recording dates or personnel (inexcusable omissions), but contains worthwhile music from The King of Swing. The 16 performances (not released in chronological order) have arrangements by both Fletcher Henderson and Eddie Sauter, three vocals apiece by Helen Forrest and Peggy Lee and plenty of fine solos from Goodman. Most of the tracks (other than Peggy Lee's hit "Why Don't You Do Right?") are lesser-known, making this somewhat ill-conceived set worth acquiring if found at a budget price! —*Scott Yanow*

Alternate Goodman, Vol. 2 / Sep. 13, 1939–Nov. 29, 1940 / Phontastic ✦✦✦
The second of twelve LPs that chronologically release alternate and rare versions of Benny Goodman's Columbia recordings, this one has quite a bit of variety, including Sextet versions of "Flying Home," "Soft Winds" and "I'm Confessin'," the 1940 Metronome All-Star Band (which is dominated by BG alumni) romping through "King Porter Stomp" and a dozen Goodman orchestra performances. Goodman fanatics will want to acquire this entire series. —*Scott Yanow*

★ **Featuring Charlie Christian** / Oct. 2, 1939–Mar. 13, 1941 / Columbia ✦✦✦✦✦
Charlie Christian was not the first electric guitarist, but he was its first giant. He elevated the guitar from a member of the rhythm section (where it was often inaudible) to the frontline, taking solos that could challenge any saxophonist. His playing was so appealing to his contemporaries that it was not until the emergence of rock in the mid-to-late '60s that more advanced guitarists emerged. By then it was over a quarter-century since Christian's premature death from tuberculosis. He spent his only two high-profile years as a member of the Benny Goodman Sextet and 18 of their best recordings are on this CD. Christian and Goodman are joined by Lionel Hampton on the first dozen performances while the final six boast the explosive combination of trumpeter Cootie Williams and Georgie Auld's tenor. The riffing inspires heated yet melodic solos, resulting in classic music that is impossible to dislike. —*Scott Yanow*

Clarinet á La King, Vol. 2 / Dec. 27, 1939–Oct. 2, 1941 / Columbia ✦✦✦
Much more coherent than the first LP in this series (R 139615), *Volume 2* consists of 16 of Benny Goodman's studio recordings for Columbia that date from late 1939 through 1941. A fine "best-of" (rather than "complete") set, this LP has among its many highlights "Zaggin' with Zig," "Henderson Stomp," the Cootie Williams trumpet feature "Superman," "Solo Flight" (which showcases guitarist Charlie Christian), "The Earl" and the title cut. A fine introduction to Goodman's underrated early-'40s orchestra. —*Scott Yanow*

Featuring Helen Forrest / Mar. 1, 1940–Jun. 4, 1941 / Columbia ✦✦✦
Helen Forrest was considered one of the top band singers of the swing era, earning prestigious stints with the orchestras of Artie Shaw, Benny Goodman and Harry James. Not a jazz singer, her appealing voice and attractive phrasing were considered major assets to any band. This particular CD has 16 of her many recordings with BG during 1939–41; Goodman and his star sidemen (including trumpeter Cootie Williams) provide most of the jazz interest. —*Scott Yanow*

Alternate Goodman, Vol. 3 / Nov. 29, 1940–Jan. 21, 1941 / Phontastic ✦✦✦
The third of 12 LPs put out by the Swedish label Phontastic (like the others) is comprised of alternate takes and rare studio recordings by the Benny Goodman Orchestra. There are two sextet tracks with trumpeter Cootie Williams, Count Basie and guitarist Charlie Christian, a few Helen Forrest vocals and some advanced instrumentals. Most collectors will take an all-or-nothing approach to this important series. —*Scott Yanow*

Solid Gold Instrumental Hits / Dec. 18, 1940–Mar. 17, 1945 / Columbia ✦✦✦
Despite its dumb title (none of these 20 performances were million sellers), this double LP contains many of the highpoints of what was Benny Goodman's most interesting orchestra. The arrangements of Eddie Sauter and Mel Powell in particular challenged BG (while giving him an entire new book of material) and led to many classic moments. Highpoints include "Air Mail Special," "Clarinet á La King," "Clarinade," "Love Walked In" "String of Pearls" and "Jersey Bounce." —*Scott Yanow*

Eddie Sauter Arrangements / Dec. 18, 1940–Mar. 17, 1945 / Columbia ✦✦✦✦✦
Here is an LP crying to be reissued on CD. Eddie Sauter was Benny Goodman's most advanced arranger. His writing for BG in the early '40s was much more unpredictable than Fletcher Henderson's and often full of surprises and unusual colors. A dozen of Sauter's greatest arrangements (including "Moonlight on the Ganges," "La Rosita," "Superman" and a remarkable reworking of "Love Walked In") are heard on this set and they really challenge Benny Goodman to come up with fresh ideas. A classic album. —*Scott Yanow*

All the Cats Join in, Vol. 3 / 1940 / Columbia ✦✦✦
1988 reissue, fine early-40s material. —*Ron Wynn*

Alternate Goodman, Vol. 4 / Jan. 28, 1941–Mar. 27, 1941 / Phontastic ✦✦✦
On the fourth of 12 LPs released by the Swedish Phontastic label that issue, in chronological order, alternate takes and rarities from Benny Goodman's period with Columbia in the '40s, highpoints include "Perfidia," "Scarecrow," "Solo Flight" (starring guitarist Charlie Christian), Cootie Williams' feature "Fiesta in Blue" and a sextet version of "Airmail Special." —*Scott Yanow*

Alternate Goodman, Vol. 5 / Mar. 27, 1941–Sep. 25, 1941 / Phontastic ✦✦✦
On the fifth volume of a 12-LP series of Benny Goodman alternate takes and rarities, the 1941 Orchestra is heard playing "new" versions of such songs as "Don't Be That Way," "Smoke Gets in Your Eyes," "Clarinet á La King" and "The Earl." Also quite interesting (to hear once) is Peggy Lee's debut on the alternate of "Elmer's Tune"; she sounds scared to death. —*Scott Yanow*

Roll 'em Live: 1941 / Jul. 1941–Oct. 1941 / Vintage Jazz Classics ✦✦✦✦

Featuring Peggy Lee / Aug. 15, 1941–Dec. 10, 1941 / Columbia ✦✦✦✦
When Peggy Lee made her first recording with Benny Goodman's orchestra, she was 19 and scared to death. The result, "Elmer's Tune," is one she probably wished were lost, but the other 15 recordings on this CD (all from 1941) find her improving month by month, struggling gamely through the difficult Eddie Sauter and Mel Powell arrangements. Many of these titles were formerly rare and offer an interesting look at the early Peggy Lee. —*Scott Yanow*

Alternate Goodman, Vol. 6 / Sep. 25, 1941–Nov. 27, 1941 / Phontastic ✦✦✦
The sixth of 12 LPs that contain alternate versions of Benny Goodman's recordings from his period on Columbia in the '40s

Music Map

Guitar

The Early Giants
Eddie Lang • Lonnie Johnson

Rhythm Guitarists
Johnny St. Cyr • Eddie Condon
Freddie Green (with Count Basie 1937-87)
Allan Reuss

Chordal Acoustic Guitar Soloists
Carl Kress • Dick McDonough • George Van Eps

The First Great Virtuoso
Django Reinhardt

Other Swing Guitarists
Oscar Aleman • Bernard Addison • Teddy Bunn

Innovative Electric Guitarist
Charlie Christian

Early Electric Guitarists
Eddie Durham (1937 with Kansas City Six)
Floyd Smith (with Andy Kirk)
George Barnes • Oscar Moore • Tiny Grimes
Al Casey • Les Paul

Bop Soloists	
Barney Kessel	Tal Farlow
Herb Ellis	Kenny Burrell
Emily Remler	Bruce Forman

Cool-Toned Soloists	
Billy Bauer	Jimmy Raney
Johnny Smith	Jim Hall
Ed Bickert	Joshua Breakstone
Doug Raney	Peter Leitch

Brazilian Acoustic Jazz	
Laurindo Almeida	Charlie Byrd
Bola Sete	Egberto Gismonti

1960s Greats	
Wes Montgomery	Grant Green
George Benson	Pat Martino
Gabor Szabo	Attila Zoller

Fusion	
Larry Coryell	John McLaughlin
Al DiMeola	Steve Khan
Terje Rypdal	Hiram Bullock
Allan Holdsworth	Kazumi Watanabe
Frank Gambale	Scott Henderson

Avant-Garde	
Sonny Sharrock	Eugene Chadbourne
Derek Bailey	James "Blood" Ulmer

Two Very Different Masters of Solo Guitar
Joe Pass • Stanley Jordan

Modern Swing		
Bucky Pizzarelli	Marty Grosz	Cal Collins
Chris Flory	Frank Vignola	Howard Alden

Other Modern Guitarists	
John Abercrombie	Philip Catherine
Cornell Dupree	Eric Gale
Ted Dunbar	Lenny Breau
Joe Diorio	Ralph Towner
Mike Stern	Kevin Eubanks

Crossover
Earl Klugh • Lee Ritenour • Larry Carlton

Three Guitar Innovators of the 1990s
Pat Metheny • John Scofield • Bill Frisell

has several highlights: two versions of "Clarinet á La King," several Peggy Lee vocals (including "Let's Do It") and two titles ("If I Had You" and "Limehouse Blues") by Goodman's new sextet with trombonist Lou McGarity and pianist Mel Powell. True Benny Goodman collectors are advised to pick up these worthy 12 LPs in a hurry. —*Scott Yanow*

Small Groups: 1941-1945 / Oct. 28, 1941–Feb. 4, 1945 / Columbia ✦✦✦✦

When one thinks of Benny Goodman's small groups, it is gener-

ally his original Trio and Quartet (with Lionel Hampton, Teddy Wilson and Gene Krupa) or his sextet with Charlie Christian that comes immediately to mind. This superior set dates from a slightly later period and features a sextet with trombonist Lou McGarity (the clarinet-trombone blend works very well) and his 1944-45 quintet/sextet with vibraphonist Red Norvo. Vocalists Peggy Lee, Jane Harvey and Peggy Mann give this set some variety. The music (and the clarinet playing) is consistently brilliant. —*Scott Yanow*

Alternate Goodman, Vol. 7 / Nov. 27, 1941–Feb. 5, 1942 / Phontastic ✦✦✦
Part of a 12-LP series put out by the Swedish label Phontastic, this set (as with the others) is comprised of alternate takes and rarities from the Benny Goodman Orchestra during his period with Columbia. As interesting as the big band alternates are (particularly "A String of Pearls"), it is the two numbers from the Benny Goodman Sextet (which feature trombonist Lou McGarity and pianist Mel Powell) and three performances from the 1941 Metronome All-Star Band that are of greatest interest. —*Scott Yanow*

Alternate Goodman, Vol. 8 / Mar. 10, 1942–Jun. 17, 1942 / Phontastic ✦✦✦
The eighth of 12 LPs of Benny Goodman alternate takes and rarities from the '40s has a hilarious breakdown on "Before" by the big band and four titles from his 1942 sextet (which co-stars trombonist Lou McGarity) and quartet including two contrasting versions of "The World Is Waiting for the Sunrise." As with all of the records in this series, collectors should love comparing these versions to the ones originally approved by Goodman. —*Scott Yanow*

Alternate Goodman, Vol. 9 / Jun. 17, 1942–Feb. 25, 1945 / Phontastic ✦✦✦
The ninth of 12 LPs of alternate takes and rare items from Benny Goodman's '40s orchestra and small groups has more than its share of strong items. Highlights include an alternate to "Mission to Moscow" and ten performances from BG's combos, including a "new" version of "Slipped Disc." —*Scott Yanow*

Way Down Yonder (1943–1944) / Dec. 9, 1943–Jan. 1946 / Vintage Jazz Classics ✦✦✦✦
This valuable CD contains performances from 1943–46 originally recorded for World War II servicemen. VJC has fleshed out the original recordings with alternate takes and breakdowns which, due to the high quality of the music, makes this CD even more interesting. Gene Krupa is heard with Goodman's 1943 big band and in a trio with pianist Jess Stacy while the bulk of this set features the BG Quintet with vibraphonist Red Norvo during 1944 including an early version of the classic "Slipped Disc." —*Scott Yanow*

Complete Capitol Small Group Recordings / Jun. 12, 1944–Dec. 14, 1955 / Mosaic ✦✦✦✦✦
This limited-edition, four-CD set fills some gaps in the huge discography of Benny Goodman. The great clarinetist is primarily featured during the 1947–49 period, heading a diverse assortment of small bands. After performing with a quartet on "After You've Gone" in 1944, BG in 1947 utilizes such sidemen as pianists Jess Stacy, Tommy Todd, Jimmy Rowles, Mel Powell and Teddy Wilson (the latter is featured on ten trio performances), Ernie Felice (on accordion), vibraphonist Red Norvo and Goodman's former singer, Peggy Lee, who drops by for previously unissued versions of "Eight, Nine and Ten" and "Keep Me in Mind." Also quite notable are three titles with the "Hollywood Hucksters" that are highlighted by "Happy Blues," which has humorous vocals by Goodman and Stan Kenton. While all of this music falls in the area of swing (with a touch of bop), Goodman's five recordings from 1948–49 are very boppish, featuring tenorman Wardell Gray and either Fats Navarro (on "Stealin' Apples") or Doug Mettome on trumpet. The remainder of this box dates from 1954–55 with Goodman performing trios with Mel Powell, jamming in a sextet with trumpeter Charlie Shavers and having a reunion with vibraphonist Lionel Hampton. All in all, this attractive box has more than its share of highly enjoyable music. —*Scott Yanow*

King of Swing / Jul. 21, 1944–Jan. 14, 1946 / Giants Of Jazz ✦✦✦
The Giants of Jazz label consistently released well-recorded LPs of Benny Goodman radio appearances. This one is no exception, giving one a rare (if brief) glance at BG's unrecorded big band of 1944 with trumpeter Roy Eldridge, along with more extended performances by Goodman's orchestra (which featured trombonist Lou McGarity and a young Stan Getz on tenor) and quintet in January 1946. The vocals of Art Lund and Liz Morrow do not hurt either. Fine swing from the tail-end of the swing era by its King. —*Scott Yanow*

Slipped Disc (1945–46) / Feb. 4, 1945–Oct. 22, 1946 / Columbia ✦✦✦✦
One of Benny Goodman's greatest combos was the sextet that he led in 1945. With Red Norvo on vibes, either Teddy Wilson or Mel

Powell on piano and the humming bass solos of Slam Stewart, this unit had a lot of personality and yet allowed Goodman to operate throughout as the lead voice. This set has 14 performances by this highly enjoyable band, including their hit "Slipped Disc," "Tiger Rag," "Shine," "China Boy" and two versions of "I Got Rhythm." In addition, there are three selections from two of Goodman's sextets from the following year with vibraphonist Johnny White. Great swing music from Benny Goodman, who is heard throughout at his best. —*Scott Yanow*

Alternate Goodman, Vol. 10 / Feb. 25, 1945–Jun. 18, 1945 / Phontastic ✦✦✦
The tenth of 12 LPs of Benny Goodman alternate takes and rarities from his period with Columbia contains a variety of odds and ends including three "new" versions of "Gotta Be This or That," two of "Love Walked In" and one apiece of "Clarinade," "Ain't Misbehavin' " and the sextet's "Rachel's Dream." Little did Benny Goodman know that his work in 1945, although hardswinging, was already in danger of slipping behind the times. Despite that, this music is quite enjoyable and timeless. —*Scott Yanow*

Goodman on the Air / May 1945–Dec. 23, 1945 / Phontastic ✦✦✦
Benny Goodman had one of his great years in 1945 when we was still only 36. Although history looks at him as being a bit old-fashioned musically by this time, especially when compared to Charlie Parker and Dizzy Gillespie, in reality BG was still the world's top clarinetist, leader of an exciting (if underrated) big band and at the peak of his commercial fame. The LP *Goodman on the Air*, released by the Swedish Phontastic label, is comprised of radio airchecks from 1945 featuring both the Goodman Sextet (on five numbers) and big band on selections that might be familiar to the clarinetist's fans (such as "Slipped Disc," "Clarinet á La King" and "King Porter Stomp"), but actually differ greatly from their studio versions. Worth searching for. —*Scott Yanow*

Alternate Goodman, Vol. 11 / Aug. 29, 1945–Jan. 30, 1946 / Phontastic ✦✦✦
The next-to-last of 12 LPs released by the Swedish label Phontastic continues the documentation of alternate takes and rarities recorded by Benny Goodman during the 1939–46 period. Goodman had an excellent big band in 1945 as one can hear on such selections as "Just You, Just Me," "Give Me Simple Life" and "Fascinating Rhythm," but it is his sextet (heard here on five performances) that really stars. Vibrahonist Red Norvo, pianist Mel Powell and bassist Slam Stewart star on such numbers as "Tiger Rag," "Shine," and "China Boy" and really push the clarinetist to some of his best playing. —*Scott Yanow*

Swing Sessions / Oct. 17, 1945–Jan. 11, 1946 / Hindsight ✦✦✦
This CD contains previously unreleased performances by Benny Goodman that were originally recorded for the Armed Forces Radio Service during 1945–46. Four selections feature his short-lived big band of the era and these sport arrangements by Eddie Sauter, Mel Powell and Fletcher Henderson (a reworking of "Somebody Stole My Gal"). In addition to a vocal apiece from Liza Morrow and Art Lund on the orchestra performances, there are solos from trumpeter Bernie Privin and (on two numbers) the young tenor Stan Getz. However, the bulk of this set features Goodman's small group of the era with the clarinetist/leader, vibraphonist Red Norvo and pianist Teddy Wilson getting plenty of solo space. The enjoyable release is not essential, but collectors will want to pick it up. —*Scott Yanow*

Alternate Goodman, Vol. 12 / Jan. 23, 1946–Aug. 7, 1946 / Phontastic ✦✦✦
The twelfth and final of the dozen LPs released by the Swedish label Phontastic completes the issuance of Benny Goodman alternate takes and rarities from his valuable period (1939–46) with Columbia. Although there are some fine big-band performances on this set (particularly a two-part version of "Oh, Baby!") it is the small-group performances (which co-star pianist Mel Powell) that are most exciting and foretell BG's future. Collectors are well-advised to pick up all 12 of these LPs while they can still be found. —*Scott Yanow*

Undercurrent Blues / Jan. 28, 1947–Oct. 15, 1949 / Blue Note ✦✦✦✦✦
During 1947–49 on an irregular basis, clarinetist Benny Goodman's band recorded bebop for Capitol before he permanently switched back to swing in 1950. All of BG's small group recordings from this period have been reissued on a Mosaic set and five are duplicated on this single CD, but there are also four

previously unissued big-band performances along with six others on this recommended reissue. Goodman and his band interpret a pair of Mary Lou Williams originals and other highlights include "Stealin' Apples" (a septet track with trumpeter Fats Navarro), "Bop-Hop," "Dreazag," "Bedlam" and "Blue Lou." Key soloists include trumpeter Doug Mettome, Wardell Gray on tenor and pianist Buddy Greco while Chico O'Farrill provided most of the big-band charts. It is very interesting to hear the great swing clarinetist adapting to the new music. —*Scott Yanow*

Swedish Pastry / May 24, 1948–Jun. 5, 1948 / Dragon ♦♦♦♦♦
In 1948 the young Swedish clarinetist Stan Hasselgard so impressed Benny Goodman that BG invited him to join his new septet, a unit that also included tenor saxophonist Wardell Gray and pianist Teddy Wilson. Because of the recording strike and Hasselgard's death before year's end in a car accident, no commercial recordings were made of the two-clarinet combo, but luckily the short-lived septet was captured live at the Cique in Philadelphia during a two-week period. Although Goodman is the dominant soloist, Hasselgard has some solo space and even gets to interact with BG. This was one of Goodman's few bop-oriented bands and so this LP fills a major gap in jazz history. —*Scott Yanow*

Sextet / Nov. 24, 1950–Oct. 22, 1952 / Columbia ♦♦♦♦
In 1950 Benny Goodman formed a new sextet and, although he used a big band for some recordings, the small group was his main outlet for the next couple of years. This CD features this somewhat forgotten unit, a hot swing combo featuring vibraphonist Terry Gibbs and usually pianist Teddy Wilson. Rather than repeat his older hits, the clarinetist clearly enjoyed playing other standards not generally associated with him. Excellent and easily enjoyable music. —*Scott Yanow*

Album of Swing Classics / Mar. 25, 1955–Mar. 26, 1955 / Book of the Month Club ♦♦♦
In 1955 Benny Goodman led one of his finest groups of the decade, a septet with trumpeter Ruby Braff, Paul Quinichette's tenor, trombonist Urbie Green and pianist Teddy Wilson. This three-LP boxed set from the Book of the Month Club includes a beautiful booklet and much swinging music. Although most of the 19 songs that Goodman performs are identified with him, these small-group renditions are fresh and lively with BG drawing inspiration from his talented sidemen. Recommended. —*Scott Yanow*

Yale Recordings, Vol. 2: Live at Basin Street / Mar. 26, 1955 / Music Masters ♦♦♦♦♦
The second CD to be compiled from the valuable tapes that Benny Goodman willed to Yale features one of his strongest groups from the '50s, a septet with trumpeter Ruby Braff, tenorman Paul Quinichette and pianist Teddy Wilson. Recorded at the same period as a Book-of-the-Month collection but not duplicating any of the performances, Benny Goodman is heard in top form, clearly inspired by his younger colleagues. Many of the songs are fairly typical of his veteran repertoire, but they sound fresh and different in this setting, making this one of the stronger entries in this valuable series. —*Scott Yanow*

Yale Recordings, Vols. 1–5 / Mar. 26, 1955–Jun. 28, 1967 / Music Masters ♦♦♦♦
In his will, Benny Goodman gave to Yale not only all of his band arrangements (over 1,500) but 400 ten-inch master tapes of unreleased studio and concert recordings. Some of the more rewarding sessions have now been issued by Music Masters and this particular box set includes the first five volumes (and a 40-page booklet), six CDs in all (since *Volume 5* had two CDs by itself) which are also available separately. The music dates from 1955–84 (the second half of Benny Goodman's career) and is taken from quite a few sessions, including a full CD of material by his excellent septet of 1955 (featuring trumpeter Ruby Braff and Paul Quinichette on tenor), big-band performances from 1958 with several vocals by Jimmy Rushing and many selections from a 1959 engagement with a nonet featuring trumpeter Jack Sheldon, trombonist Bill Harris and tenorman Flip Phillips. Although no longer a pacesetter, Benny Goodman remained one of the jazz world's most brilliant performers, making this set well worth acquiring. —*Scott Yanow*

The Benny Goodman Story / Aug. 1955 / Victor ♦♦♦
One of the most successful of the music biography movies of the '50s was *The Benny Goodman Story*. The plot was pure fiction,

but the music was often quite exciting, helped out by the fact that Goodman himself did all of the clarinet playing. This two-LP set contains the movie's soundtrack with strong "roles" played by pianist Teddy Wilson, vibraphonist Lionel Hampton, drummer Gene Krupa, trumpeters Harry James and Buck Clayton, Stan Getz on tenor and of course the mighty clarinetist. —*Scott Yanow*

Yale Archives, Vol. 1 / Sep. 8, 1955–Jan. 17, 1986 / Music Masters ♦♦♦
Shortly after Benny Goodman's death in 1986, trustees at Yale University's Music Library were surprised to find out that, in addition to memorabilia and over 1,500 arrangements, Benny Goodman had left them around 400 ten-inch master tapes of concert and studio performances that had never been heard before, along with the right to lease these recordings for commercial release. *Volume 1* of what is now known as BG's Yale Archives is a hodgepodge collection of performances that skip around between 1955 and 1986. Among the dozen selections on this CD are a couple of tunes by BG's 1955 combo with trumpeter Ruby Braff, an example of the group he led briefly in 1959 with trombonist Bill Harris and Flip Phillips' tenor, some okay big-band performances, Goodman's forgotten 1967 septet with trumpeter Joe Newman and tenor saxophonist Zoot Sims and a version of "Blue Room" played by his last band, Goodman's 1986 orchestra. —*Scott Yanow*

B.G. World Wide / Dec. 14, 1956–Nov. 8, 1980 / TCB ♦♦♦♦♦
This four-CD box set from the European TCB label releases for the first time the music from four Benny Goodman concerts. The great clarinetist is heard at two nostalgic big-band appearances, heading a 13-piece unit in Bangkok, Thailand in 1956 (with fine solos heard from trumpeter Mel Davis and Budd Johnson on tenor) and a 15-piece orchestra in Santiago, Chile in 1961, a band that also features trumpeter Buck Clayton. However it is the other two performances that are of greatest interest. Goodman plays at his most advanced with an all-star group (which includes trumpeter Jack Sheldon, trombonist Bill Harris, the tenor of Flip Phillips and vibraphonist Red Norvo) during a particularly exciting set from Basel, Switzerland in 1959 and his solos from Berlin in 1980 in a quintet with four supportive but obscure musicians are surprisingly inspired. In fact, the German concert is arguably Goodman's finest recording of his last decade. This well-conceived set (which has a different small booklet for each of the CDs) is highly recommended to Benny Goodman's many fans. —*Scott Yanow*

Yale Recordings, Vol. 8: Never Before Released Recordings from Benny Goodman's Private Collection / May 16, 1957–Jan. 24, 1961 / Music Masters ♦♦♦♦
The eighth volume of previously unreleased material willed by Benny Goodman to Yale continues the series with some very interesting selections. Martha Tilton gets to redo her hit "Bei Mir Bist Du Schon" in 1958 with a big band, Goodman's clarinet is well-featured with a quintet that includes pianist Andre Previn on three tracks, and BG has his last musical encounter with pianist Mel Powell on a pair of medleys. But most unusual are eight selections cut with a nine-piece unit in 1961 that are dominated by songs associated with Hawaii including "On the Beach at Waikiki," "Blue Hawaii," "Sweet Leilani" and "My Little Grass Shack." Bill Stegmeyer's creative arrangements and an all-star lineup actually make this into a highly enjoyable and very surprising session. —*Scott Yanow*

Yale Recordings, Vol. 4: Big Band Recordings / May 16, 1957–Jun. 17, 1964 / Music Masters ♦♦♦
This fourth volume of material culled from the tapes willed by Benny Goodman to The Yale University Music Library contains a variety of big-band performances taken from no less than five different sessions held over an eight-year period. Such musicians as baritonist Pepper Adams, Bob Wilber (on tenor), Zoot Sims and BG's former vocalist Martha Tilton get their spots. While several Eddie Sauter arrangements are performed, one has to also sit through a weak version that includes a forgettable version of "People." An interesting if somewhat erratic set. —*Scott Yanow*

Yale Recordings, Vol. 3: Big Band in Europe / May 1958 / Music Masters ♦♦♦♦
The third volume in this important series taken from tapes willed by Benny Goodman to the Yale Music Library focuses on the big band he took to Europe in 1958, a tour that culminated in a week at the Brussels World Fair in Belgium. The orchestra was filled with both young names like Zoot Sims and pianist Roland Hanna

and veterans such as trombonist Vernon Brown and trumpeter Taft Jordan. With the great Jimmy Rushing and Ethel Ennis contributing vocals and the ensemble playing a variety of mostly new charts, Benny Goodman had the right to feel inspired. His playing of this "modern swing" is typically brilliant; collectors will want this entire series. —*Scott Yanow*

Benny Rides Again / Sep. 1958–Nov. 1958 / Chess ♦♦
Goodman leads a big band again for the majority of this LP with few surprises. The instrumentals (all standards except for the recent "Stereo Stomp") are fine, but the unidentified personnel (which has such players as Bob Wilbur, Pepper Adams and Russ Freeman) mostly functions as an anonymous ensemble. Better are the four selections by Goodman and a rhythm section that include pianist Andre Previn. Nice music overall, but there are many more essential Benny Goodman sets available elsewhere. —*Scott Yanow*

Happy Session / Nov. 1958 / Columbia ♦♦♦
Recorded after Benny Goodman returned with his 1958 big band from a European tour that included a happy stint at the Brussels World Fair, this LP alternates between orchestra performances (mostly newer compositions include four by a Yugoslavian composer Bobby Gutesha) and Goodman features with his rhythm section (which co-stars Andre Previn's piano). BG dominates this album and is in excellent form. —*Scott Yanow*

Yale Recordings, Vol. 7: Florida Sessions / Aug. 15, 1959–Aug. 17, 1959 / Music Masters ♦♦♦♦
One of the most interesting bands led by Benny Goodman after the end of the swing era was the forgotten septet featured on this CD. It was essentially a sextet co-led by tenor saxophonist Flip Phillips and trombonist Bill Harris that they willingly let BG take over. Phillips and Harris were alumni of Woody Herman's First Herd and their constant riffing and well-constructed solos really push the competitive clarinetist to play at his best and most fiery. Rather than revisit past glories, during this live gig Benny Goodman and his all-stars play infectious arrangements that perfectly set up the solos, creating exciting new music in the swing tradition. Recommended. —*Scott Yanow*

Legendary Concert / Oct. 28, 1959 / Artistry ♦♦♦♦
In 1959 Goodman (then 50) took over a sextet co-led by two alumni of Woody Herman's First Herd (tenor saxophonist Flip Phillips and trombonist Bill Harris) and eventually expanded it into a short-lived ten-piece group. This LP documents a concert from his European tour and finds The King of Swing successfully exploring both new material and old favorites. The vibes of Red Norvo and trumpeter Jack Sheldon are also strong assets; pity that this group did not stay together longer. —*Scott Yanow*

Yale Recordings, Vol. 5 / Nov. 13, 1959–Jun. 14, 1963 / Music Masters ♦♦♦
The fifth volume of material taken from the tapes that Benny Goodman willed to Yale's Music Library is, for no particular reason, a double-CD set. Two separate and somewhat forgotten Goodman combos are featured: a fine ten-piece unit from 1959-60 that includes trumpeter Jack Sheldon, trombonist Bill Harris and Flip Phillips on tenor and an otherwise totally unrecorded sextet from 1963. The latter not only features cornetist Bobby Hackett and the young bassist Steve Swallow but the forgotten Modesto Bresano, who contributes some fine tenor and flute. Benny Goodman is in fine form with both of these unjustly obscure combos. —*Scott Yanow*

Together Again! (1963 Reunion with Lionel Hampton, Teddy Wilson & Gene Krupa / Feb. 13, 1963–Aug. 27, 1963 / Bluebird ♦♦♦♦
In 1963, almost exactly 25 years after Gene Krupa left Benny Goodman's orchestra, the Benny Goodman Quartet recorded together for the first time in a quarter-century. This CD, a straight reissue of the original LP, finds BG, Lionel Hampton, Teddy Wilson and Gene Krupa clearly happy to be back together, not so much revisiting their older "hits" as having a good time playing songs that they missed the first time around. One can feel the absence of a bass (the more primitive recording quality of the '30s helped cover it up originally), but the music is so joyful and swinging that one does not mind. —*Scott Yanow*

Made in Japan / Feb. 25, 1964 / Capitol ♦♦
One could not blame Benny Goodman for getting a bit bored by the mid-'60s. He had achieved astonishing success by 1935 when he just 26 and, with the passing of the big-band era a decade later, he was no longer a pacesetter in jazz. Despite possessing a fully-formed style, BG led many high-quality groups through the years and continued playing creatively within the swing tradition, but the LP *Made in Japan* is merely a lukewarm affair. Backed by a supportive but faceless rhythm section and limiting the length of the performances (only two exceed four minutes, and three are less than half as long), Goodman plays passable but unmemorable versions of swing standards like "Stompin' at the Savoy" and "Dinah." It's worth acquiring at a budget price, but otherwise there are many far superior Benny Goodman CDs currently available. —*Scott Yanow*

Yale Recordings, Vol. 7: Live at the Rainbow Grill / Jun. 3, 1966–Jun. 29, 1967 / Music Masters ♦♦♦
The seventh volume of music taken from the hundreds of tapes that Benny Goodman willed to Yale University covers a period of time when The King of Swing used pickup (although still all-star) groups, combining veterans with younger talents. This CD has nine selections from a septet with trumpeter Joe Newman, Zoot Sims' tenor and guitarist Attila Zoller. There is nothing surprising about the repertoire (BG generally ignored the novelty pop tunes of the '60s) and this particular unit works well. The remaining six numbers find Goodman sharing the frontline with trumpeter Doc Cheatham (whose solo style was not as well developed as it would become after he passed his 70th birthday), allocating two vocals to the forgotten Annette Saunders and trying out a new pianist who was subbing for Hank Jones, Herbie Hancock. Even with this unusual personnel, the result is a strong set of solid swing. —*Scott Yanow*

Let's Dance Again / Oct. 28, 1969–Nov. 28, 1969 / Mega ♦♦
What to do with The King of Swing by the late '60s? Benny Goodman had already recorded nearly every worthwhile song from the golden age of popular music (1920-50) and his unchanging (although never stale) swing style was too familiar for most jazz listeners of later eras to fully appreciate. So, for this LP, recorded in London with a big band and an octet filled with English musicians, Goodman was persuaded to emphasize more recent items. BG performs such songs as "Yesterday," "This Guy's in Love with You," "On a Clear Day" and "I Talk to the Trees," in addition to a few remakes of swing standards. Since he primarily sticks to the melody in these short renditions and sounds predictably silly and out-of-place in spots, this album is not one of the highpoints of Benny Goodman's career. —*Scott Yanow*

Benny Goodman Today / Feb. 20, 1970 / London ♦♦
By 1970 there seemed little new for Benny Goodman to say musically. A major success 35 years earlier and the possessor of a briliant but unchanging clarinet style, BG was performing less during this period and his big-band projects generally emphasized re-creations of the past. This attractive but routine double LP (which does not list the personnel) features Goodman in a big band mostly comprised of Europeans (other than guitarist Bucky Pizzarelli) running through a program not all that different than what he might have presented in 1940; only four of the 20 songs are of newer vintage. A pleasing but not very stimulating set of music. —*Scott Yanow*

On Stage / Mar. 13, 1972 / London Phase 4 ♦♦♦
While Benny Goodman's big-band projects of his later years overly relied on re-creations and revisits to earlier successes, his small-group work gave the clarinetist a much better opportunity to stretch out. This double LP matches the 63-year old King of Swing with tenor great Zoot Sims, vibraphonist Peter Appleyard and a strong rhythm section for an enjoyable set of standards. —*Scott Yanow*

Fortieth Anniversary Concert / Jan. 17, 1978 / London ♦♦♦♦
In 1978 Benny Goodman celebrated the 40th anniversary of his original pioneering Carnegie Hall concert with a new concert at the palace of classical music. From reviews of the actual event, the music and presentation were quite erratic, but this double LP, which only includes the best moments, is on a higher level. In addition to a strong big band, Goodman was joined by vibraphonist Lionel Hampton, pianist Mary Lou Williams, his late-'30s vocalist Martha Tilton and a newer singer, Debi Craig. With trumpeters Warren Vache and Jack Sheldon (why did he sing "Rocky Raccoon"?) and tenor saxophonist Buddy Tate also getting solo space, Benny Goodman was fairly inspired; he even sings "I Love a Piano." With the exception of a medley, "Loch Lomond" and of course "Sing, Sing, Sing" (which has drummer Connie Kay playing Gene Krupa's famous solo), none of the songs from the 1938

concert were reprised. This set has both historical and musical value and no Benny Goodman collection is quite complete without it. —*Scott Yanow*

Live! Benny, Let's Dance / Oct. 7, 1985 / Musical Heritage Society ◆◆◆

This soundtrack from a PBS special is Benny Goodman's last recording. After a period of semi-retirement, Goodman had recently taken over the big band put together by Loren Schoenberg and he had regained his enthusiasm for touring. The big band almost exclusively played early Fletcher Henderson arrangements and boasted such soloists as trumpeters John Eckert and Randy Sandke, trombonist Eddie Bert and Ken Peplowski on tenor. In addition, for the PBS special, such veterans as pianist Dick Hyman and drummer Louis Bellson helped out. Benny Goodman at the age of 77 still swung with the best and his death three months after this recording meant that he went out on top. This CD is a fine tribute to his remarkable talents. —*Scott Yanow*

Mick Goodrick

b. Jun. 9, 1945, Sharon, PA
Guitar / Post-Bop
A technical genius on guitar, Mick Goodrick's music is well worth study. Goodrick began playing guitar at 12 and then later began attending Stan Kenton's summer camps. A mid-'60s Berklee graduate, Goodrick later taught there for four years. He recorded with Woody Herman in 1970 and played in Boston clubs as part of a trio with pianist Alan Broadbent and bassist Rick Laird, while also working in a duo with guitarist Pat Metheny. Goodrick toured and recorded with Gary Burton from 1973 to 1975 and also recorded and played occasionally with Jack DeJohnette and worked with Joe Williams and Astrud Gilberto. Goodrick recorded with Eddie Gomez, John Surman and DeJohnette in the late '70s for ECM and recorded with Charlie Haden in 1982. Goodrick's recorded for CMP in the '90s. His recordings show an individuality that defies easy description and categorization. —*Ron Wynn and Michael G. Nastos*

● **In Passing** / Nov. 1978 / ECM ◆◆◆◆◆
Guitarist Mick Goodrick once worked alongside Pat Metheny in Gary Burton's band, and they have a similar sound, voicings and eclectic approach. Goodrick's '78 debut as a leader was a strong set that had fusion, straight-ahead and even almost free pieces. He also headed a strong band, with English saxophonist John Surman at his terse, animated best, plus bassist Eddie Gomez and drummer Jack DeJohnette in fine form. —*Ron Wynn*

Biorhythms / Oct. 1990 / CMP ◆◆◆◆

Rare Birds / Apr. 12, 1993–Apr. 13, 1993 / Ram ◆◆◆◆

Bob Gordon

b. Jun. 11, 1928, St. Louis, MO, d. Aug. 28, 1955, California
Baritone Saxophone / Cool
Bob Gordon was a fine West Coast bop-oriented baritonist. He played with Shorty Sherock (1946), Alvino Rey's Orchestra (1948–51) and Billy May (1952) before becoming an in-demand session player for jazz dates with the likes of Shelly Manne, Maynard Ferguson, Chet Baker, Clifford Brown (1954), Shorty Rogers, Tal Farlow and Stan Kenton. While on his way to playing at a Pete Rugolo concert in San Diego, Bob Gordon was killed in a car accident. His lone album as a leader has been reissued by VSOP. —*Scott Yanow*

● **Bob Gordon Memorial** / Dec. 1953–May 1954 / Fresh Sound ◆◆◆◆◆

Moods in Jazz / 1954 / VSOP ◆◆◆◆
On one of two albums led by baritonist Bob Gordon before his tragic death in a 1955 car crash, the cool-toned baritonist blends in well with trombonist Herbie Harper in a quintet that also includes a no-name rhythm section (pianist Maury Dell, bassist Don Prell and drummer George Redman). The emphasis is on slower tempos, in fact, two of the songs are titled "Slow Mood" (the Eddie Miller composition) and "Slow." This CD reissue of a Tampa set is worth picking up by fans of relaxed straight-ahead jazz. —*Scott Yanow*

Bobby Gordon

Clarinet / Swing, Dixieland
Bobby Gordon is best-known for his recent Arbors recordings and for his association with Marty Grosz in the Orphan Newsboys. He

recorded three early albums for Dot (1962–63) that sought to capitalize on the popularity of folk music and Acker Bilk's string hits. Gordon, who sometimes hints at Pee Wee Russell (although his tone is a lot smoother), has recorded more worthy sets in recent times for Jump and Arbors, currently lives in the San Diego area and is sometimes coaxed away to play at jazz parties and festivals. —*Scott Yanow*

Dexter Gordon

b. Feb. 27, 1923, Los Angeles, CA, d. Apr. 26, 1990, Philadelphia, PA
Tenor Saxophone / Bop, Hard Bop
Dexter Gordon had such a colorful and eventful life (with three separate comebacks) that his story would make a great Hollywood movie. The top tenor saxophonist to emerge during the bop era and possessor of his own distinctive sound, Gordon sometimes was long-winded and quoted excessively from other songs, but he created a large body of superior work and could battle nearly anyone successfully at a jam session. His first important gig was with Lionel Hampton (1940–43) although, due to Illinois Jacquet also being in the sax section, Gordon did not get any solos. In 1943 he did get to stretch out on a recording session with Nat King Cole. Short stints with Lee Young, the Fletcher Henderson Orchestra and Louis Armstrong's big band preceded his move to New York in December 1944 and becoming part of Billy Eckstine's Orchestra, trading off with Gene Ammons on Eckstine's recording of "Blowin' the Blues Away." Dexter recorded with Dizzy Gillespie ("Blue 'n Boogie") and as a leader for Savoy before returning to Los Angeles in the summer of 1946. He was a major part of the Central Avenue scene, trading off with Wardell Gray and Teddy Edwards in many legendary tenor battles; studio recordings of "The Chase" and "The Duel" helped to document the atmosphere of the period.

After 1952, drug problems resulted in some jail time and periods of inactivity during the 1950s (although Gordon did record two albums in 1955). By 1960 he was recovered and soon he was recording a consistently rewarding series of dates for Blue Note. Just when he was regaining his former popularity, in 1962 Gordon moved to Europe where he would stay until 1976. While on the continent, he was in peak form and Dexter's many SteepleChase recordings rank with the finest work of his career. Gordon did return to the U.S. on an occasional basis, recording in 1965, 1969–70 and 1972, but he was to an extent forgotten in his native land. It was therefore a major surprise that his return in 1976 was treated as a major media event. A great deal of interest was suddenly shown in the living legend with long lines of people waiting at clubs in order to see him. Gordon was signed to Columbia and remained a popular figure until his gradually worsening health made him semiactive by the early '80s. His third comeback occurred when he was picked to star in the motion picture '*Round Midnight* and, even if his playing by then was past its prime, Gordon's acting was quite realistic and touching. He was nominated for an Academy Award, four years before his death after a very full life. Most of Dexter Gordon's recordings for Savoy, Dial, Bethlehem, Dootone, Jazzland, Blue Note, SteepleChase, Black Lion, Prestige, Columbia, Who's Who, Chiaroscuro and Elektra Musician are currently available. —*Scott Yanow*

Long Tall Dexter / Oct. 30, 1945–Dec. 22, 1946 / Savoy ◆◆◆◆◆
In the mid-to-late '40s, there were three great young tenor saxophonists: Dexter Gordon, Wardell Gray and Teddy Edwards. Of the trio, Dexter Gordon had the greatest influence on upcoming players and was the most bop-oriented. This superb two-LP set contains all 17 selections Gordon cut for Savoy during 1945–47 plus eight alternate takes and a jam session performance (with trumpeter Howard McGhee and altoist Sonny Criss) titled "After Hours Bop." Gordon is heard in a quartet, with several quintets (featuring such major players as pianist Bud Powell, drummers Max Roach and Art Blakey, baritonist Leo Parker and trumpeter Fats Navarro) and in a septet with trumpeter Joe Newman and trombonist J.J. Johnson. Throughout, Gordon holds his own with the slightly older players and gets his career off to a brilliant start. —*Scott Yanow*

Master Takes: The Savoy Recordings / Oct. 30, 1945–Dec. 22, 1947 / Savoy ◆◆◆◆
This single album contains 15 of Dexter Gordon's significant Savoy sides from the prime years of the bop era. Gordon was (along with Wardell Gray and Teddy Edwards) the top young

tenor of the period and his fame and influence would soon dwarf his two competitors. These quartet and quintet performances (featuring such top players as pianist Bud Powell, baritonist Leo Parker and trumpeter Fats Navarro) are concise, swinging and advanced for the time. This set is really more for general collectors since all of this music (plus the alternate takes, an additional session and one jam-session number) were included on the two-fer *Long Tall Dexter*. —*Scott Yanow*

★ **The Chase!** / Jun. 5, 1947–Dec. 4, 1947 / Stash ✦✦✦✦✦
During the mid-to-late '40s, Dexter Gordon, one of the top young tenors to emerge during the bop era, had nightly tenor "battles" in Los Angeles clubs with his two top competitors, Wardell Gray and Teddy Edwards. Fortunately, Gordon also had opportunities to meet up with his fellow tenors on record; "The Chase" (featuring Gray and Gordon) is a classic and "The Duel" (which was recorded twice with Edwards) is close behind. Although issued as part of Stash's budget series, the vintage music on this CD (which has all of Dexter Gordon's recordings for Dial in 1947) is often quite memorable. In addition to the battles, Gordon teams up with trombonist Melba Liston in a quintet, leads a couple of his own quartets and "Blues in Teddy's Flat" features Edwards. Since all of the alternate takes are also included, this highly recommended release is quite definitive and recaptures some of the excitement of the period. —*Scott Yanow*

The Hunt / Jul. 6, 1947 / Savoy ✦✦✦
This two-LP set could be called "A Day in the Life of Central Avenue." These four sidelong performances are jams featuring a nonet comprised of tenors Dexter Gordon and Wardell Gray, trumpeter Howard McGhee, altoist Sonny Criss, trombonist Trummy Young, pianist Hampton Hawes (making his recording debut), guitarist Barney Kessel, either Harry Babasin or Red Callender on bass and Connie Kay or Ken Kennedy on drums. The recording quality is only so-so, but the solos and the many tenor tradeoffs are generally quite heated and often exciting. The two-fer preserves the legacy of a brief but colorful era. —*Scott Yanow*

The Bethlehem Years / Sep. 18, 1955 / Bethlehem ✦✦✦✦
Drug problems plagued Dexter Gordon during the 1950s, and this Bethlehem LP was one of only two albums that the great tenor led during 1953–59. Gordon, heard in a quartet with pianist Kenny Drew, bassist Leroy Vinnegar and drummer Lawrence Marable, is actually in excellent form on these six jams, which are highlighted by "Daddy Plays the Horn" (a medium-tempo blues), "Confirmation" and "You Can Depend on Me." —*Scott Yanow*

Dexter Blows Hot and Cool / Nov. 11, 1955–Nov. 12, 1955 / Authentic/Dootone ✦✦✦
Little was heard of tenor saxophonist Dexter Gordon on record during the 1950s; in fact, this somewhat obscure LP (Savoy in one of their reissue programs also released these performances) was one of Gordon's only three appearances on record (two as a leader) during 1953–59. He fronts a quintet with pianist Carl Perkins, bassist Leroy Vinnegar, drummer Chuck Thompson and the forgotten trumpeter Jimmy Robinson and sounds pretty strong on the straight-ahead material. Few surprises occur, but this collector's item from a dark period in Dexter Gordon's life has its share of fine music. —*Scott Yanow*

The Resurgence of Dexter Gordon / Oct. 13, 1960 / Jazzland ✦✦✦
Originally put out on Jazzland, this important LP was a comeback album by the great tenor Dexter Gordon who had (with the exception of a couple of occasions in 1955) been largely off record since 1952. Teamed up with trombonist Richard Boone (listed on the LP on trumpet), trumpeter Martin Banks and pianist Dolo Coker, Gordon is in excellent form on the six selections, all originals by either the leader or Coker. Because of the large amount of Dexter Gordon recordings from his later years, this LP is not essential, but fans should enjoy it. —*Scott Yanow*

Doin' Alright / May 6, 1961 / Blue Note ✦✦✦✦
The title of this Blue Note set perfectly fit at the time, for tenor saxophonist Dexter Gordon was making the first of three successful comebacks. Largely neglected during the 1950s, Gordon's Blue Note recordings (of which this was the first) led to his rediscovery. The tenor is teamed with the young trumpeter Freddie Hubbard, pianist Horace Parlan, bassist George Tucker and drummer Al Harewood for a strong set of music that is highlighted by "You've Changed" (which would become a permanent part of Dexter's repertoire), "Society Red" (a blues later used in the film *Round Midnight*) and "It's You or No One." —*Scott Yanow*

Dexter Calling.... / May 9, 1961 / Blue Note ✦✦✦✦
Tenor saxophonist Dexter Gordon recorded seven Blue Note albums during 1960–64 and all are easily recommended. The power and creativity he showed during those performances led to his first successful comeback and display him in prime form. This particular CD (the reissue adds a version of "Landslide" not released at the time) showcases the distinctive tenor with a quartet that also includes pianist Kenny Drew, bassist Paul Chambers and drummer Philly Joe Jones. Gordon and Drew contributed six originals to the date, but it is the leader's interpretations of the two standards ("End of a Love Affair" and particularly "Smile") that are most memorable. —*Scott Yanow*

Landslide / May 9, 1961–Jun. 25, 1962 / Blue Note ✦✦✦

Go! / Aug. 27, 1962 / Blue Note ✦✦✦✦
Dexter Gordon is in hard-swinging yet lyrical form throughout this particularly strong release. Accompanied by pianist Sonny Clark, bassist Butch Warren and drummer Billy Higgins, Gordon is heard at his best on "I Guess I'll Hang My Tears Out to Dry," "Where Are You" and "Three O'Clock in the Morning"; three rarely performed standards. All of Dexter Gordon's Blue Note recordings (and in reality 90 percent of his releases) are recommended to lovers of bop and straight-ahead jazz. —*Scott Yanow*

A Swingin' Affair / Aug. 29, 1962 / Blue Note ✦✦✦✦
Recorded just two days after his popular album *Go* and using the same personnel (pianist Sonny Clark, bassisf-Butch Warren and drummer Billy Higgins), tenor-great Dexter Gordon stretches out on two of his originals, Warren's "The Backbone" and (best of all) three standards: "You Stepped out of a Dream," "Until the Real Thing Comes Along" and the highpoint "Don't Explain." This CD is well worth getting. —*Scott Yanow*

Cry Me a River / Nov. 28, 1962 / SteepleChase ✦✦✦
This CD contains two separate European sessions taken from radio broadcasts. Tenor saxophonist Dexter Gordon, who had just moved to Europe, is heard on lengthy versions of "I'll Remember April" and "Cry Me a River" from 1962 with a Danish trio comprised of pianist Atli Bjorn, bassist Marcel Rigot and drummer Williams Schiopffe. The two 1964 numbers ("The Thrill Is Gone" and "Suite") are by Bjorn's 1964 trio with bassist Benny Nielsen and drummer Finn Frederiksen; the talented pianist is well-showcased. —*Scott Yanow* .

Our Man in Paris / May 23, 1963 / Blue Note ✦✦✦✦
Tenor saxophonist Dexter Gordon, who had recently moved to Europe, is featured on this set with the all-star rhythm section sometimes called "the Three Bosses": pianist Bud Powell, bassist Pierre Michelot and drummer Kenny Clarke. The repertoire is strictly bop standards and Powell in particular is in excellent form. Gordon sounds fine, too, on such songs as "Scrapple from The Apple," "Stairway to the Stars" and "A Night in Tunisia." —*Scott Yanow*

One Flight Up / Jun. 2, 1964 / Blue Note ✦✦✦✦
Tenor-great Dexter Gordon and trumpeter Donald Byrd make for an excellent team on this 1964 hard bop quintet date with pianist Kenny Drew, bassist Niels Pedersen (then only 18) and drummer Art Taylor. The Blue Note LP only contains three selections: an 18-minute rendition of Byrd's "Tanya," Drew's minor-toned "Coppin' the Haven" and a quartet version of "Darn That Dream" that finds Gordon in lyrical form. —*Scott Yanow*

Cheesecake / Jun. 11, 1964 / SteepleChase ✦✦✦✦
Dexter Gordon's long stint at the Club Montmartre in Copenhagen during the summer of 1964 included weekly radio broadcasts. Happily, these live performances have been preserved and released by SteepleChase on a series of albums. This particular LP features the great tenor with a rhythm section comprised of Europe's best (pianist Tete Montoliu, bassist Niels Pedersen and drummer Alex Riel) performing Dexter's "Cheese Cake," "Manha De Carnival" and "Second Balcony Jump." Gordon takes long solos that never seem to run out of ideas, making this set a valuable addition to his lengthy discography. —*Scott Yanow*

King Neptune / Jun. 24, 1964 / SteepleChase ✦✦✦✦
Dexter Gordon and his European quartet (pianist Tete Montoliu, bassist Niels-Henning Orsted Pedersen and drummer Alex Riel) played a three-month engagement at Copenhagen's Montmartre Club during the summer of 1964. The group had an hour-long radio broadcast every other Thursday night and the results have been released by SteepleChase on six CDs. *Cheesecake* was the first and its follow-up, *King Neptune*, features the quartet and the

great tenor stretching out on "Satin Doll," "Body and Soul," the happy "I Want to Blow Now" (which Gordon briefly sings) and the otherwise unknown title cut, a Gordon original that was never recorded elsewhere. All of the releases in this valuable *Dexter in Radioland* series are recommended. —*Scott Yanow*

I Want More / Jul. 9, 1964 / SteepleChase ✦✦✦✦
SteepleChase has released on six CDs the radio broadcasts of Dexter Gordon and his 1964 Quartet (with pianist Tete Montoliu, bassist Niels-Henning Orsted Pedersen and on this volume drummer Rune Carlsson) from Copenhagen's Montmartre Club. In addition to the title cut, Dexter and company perform "Come Rain or Come Shine," "Where Are You," the fun "I Want to Blow Now" (which Gordon sings) and "Second Balcony Jump." Fans will want all of the releases in this enjoyable and well-recorded series. —*Scott Yanow*

Love for Sale / Jul. 23, 1964 / SteepleChase ✦✦✦✦
Dexter Gordon and his Quartet of 1964 (pianist Tete Montoliu, bassist Niels-Henning Orsted Pedersen and drummer Alex Riel) had a three-month engagement at the Montmartre Club in Copenhagen, broadcasting on the radio every other Thursday. SteepleChase has released these consistently exciting (and well-recorded) performances on six CDs. *Love for Sale* features the impressive group jamming on the title cut, "Cherokee," two Gordon originals (including "Big Fat Butterfly," which has the tenor taking a brief vocal) and an emotional rendition of "I Guess I'll Hang My Tears Out to Dry." It's recommended, as are all of the releases in this valuable *Dexter in Radioland* series. —*Scott Yanow*

It's You or No One / Aug. 6, 1964 / SteepleChase ✦✦✦✦
The fifth of six SteepleChase CDs taken from the 1964 broadcasts of tenor great Dexter Gordon and his quartet (pianist Tete Montoliu, bassist Niels-Henning orsted Pedersen and drummer Alex Riel) from Copenhagen's Montmartre Club once again finds Gordon in top form. He performs extended versions of four standards ("Just Friends," "Three O'Clock in the Morning," "Where Are You?" and "It's You or No One" with creativity and the music is quite enjoyable, recommended to bop fans. —*Scott Yanow*

Billie's Bounce / Aug. 20, 1964 / SteepleChase ✦✦✦✦
Dexter Gordon and his 1964 Quartet (with pianist Tete Montoliu, bassist Niels-Henning Orsted Pedersen and drummer Alex Riel) broadcast from the Montmartre Club in Copenhagen on six occasions and all of the music has been issued on SteepleChase CDs. This particular set finds the group playing a fairly brief "Night in Tunisia" and long versions of "Billie's Bounce" (over 17 minutes), "Satin Doll" and Gordon's "Soul Sister." The well-recorded performances feature the great bop tenor in peak form and are easily recommended as is this entire *Dexter in Radioland* series. *Scott Yanow*

After Hours / 1964–1965 / SteepleChase ✦✦
Tenor saxophonist Dexter Gordon, the fine trumpeter Rolf Ericson and a Danish rhythm section (pianist Lars Sjosten, bassist Sture Norin and drummer Per Hulten) are heard on four rather lengthy performances: "All the Things You Are," "Darn That Dream," an 18-minute "Straight No Chaser" and a previously unissued nearly 17-minute rendition of "I Remember You." Originating from a club appearance in Stockholm probably from 1964-65 (this CD lacks liner notes), the music is well-played if sometimes a bit long-winded. —*Scott Yanow*

After Midnight / 1964–1965 / SteepleChase ✦✦
This CD has two rather long performances by a quintet led by Dexter Gordon that also features trumpeter Rolf Ericson, pianist Lars Sjosten, bassist Sture Norin and drummer Per Hulten: a 20-minute version of "Three O'Clock in the Morning" and a 26-minute rendition of Miles Davis' "No Blues." Although not essential, these live radio broadcasts (from an often-overlooked period in the great tenor's career) are enjoyable and worth hearing by straight-ahead jazz fans. —*Scott Yanow*

Clubhouse / May 27, 1965 / Blue Note ✦✦✦
Although tenor saxophonist Dexter Gordon had moved to Europe in 1962, he made a return visit to the U.S. in 1965 that resulted in both this album and *Gettin' Around*. Gordon teams up with trumpeter Freddie Hubbard, pianist Barry Harris, bassist Bob Cranshaw and drummer Billy Higgins for three of his originals, two obscurities and a standard that ended up being the date's most memorable performance: "I'm a Fool to Want You." The CD reissue is a reproduction of the original LP, which was not issued

until the mid-'70s. It is excellent music if not quite essential. —*Scott Yanow*

Gettin' Around / May 28, 1965 / Blue Note ✦✦✦✦
Dexter Gordon meets up with vibraphonist Bobby Hutcherson, pianist Barry Harris, bassist Bob Cranshaw and drummer Billy Higgins on this excellent hard bop date. Recorded during one of the great tenor's infrequent U.S. visits (he had moved to Europe in 1962), Gordon is in excellent form on six diverse selections that range from "Manha De Carnaval" and "Shiny Stockings" to "Heartaches" and Gordon's original "Le Coiffeur." Although underrated during this era due to his residence in Europe, Dexter Gordon was at the peak of his powers throughout this period; all of his Blue Note releases are easily recommended. —*Scott Yanow*

Body and Soul / Jul. 20, 1967 / Black Lion ✦✦✦✦
Tenor saxophonist Dexter Gordon recorded three CD's worth of material during a two-day period at Copenhagen's legendary Montmartre Club; *Take the 'A' Train* and *Both Sides of Midnight* have also been released by Black Lion on CD. Gordon and his impressive quartet (pianist Kenny Drew, bassist Neils Henning Orsted Pederson and drummer Albert "Tootie" Heath) play versions of "Like Someone in Love," "Come Rain or Come Shine," "There Will Never Be Another You," "Body and Soul" and "Blues Walk" that clock in between nine and 14 minutes. Ironically, Dexter, who was in peak form during his years in Europe, was somewhat forgotten in the U.S. at the time. This set is recommended along with the two other CDs from this well-documented engagement. —*Scott Yanow*

Both Sides of Midnight / Jul. 20, 1967 / Black Lion ✦✦✦✦
Tenor saxophonist Dexter Gordon is accompanied by an all-star rhythm section (pianist Kenny Drew, bassist Niels Pederson and drummer Albert "Tootie" Heath) on this easily enjoyable club recording from Copenhagen's Montmartre. In addition to Ben Tucker's modal "Divilette," Gordon explores four jazz standards, really digging into the material. Bop fans are advised to pick up this excellent CD. —*Scott Yanow*

Take the 'A' Train / Jul. 21, 1967 / Black Lion ✦✦✦✦
During a two-day period (July 20-21, 1967) tenor saxophonist Dexter Gordon and his quartet (pianist Kenny Drew, bassist Niels Pederson and drummer Albert "Tootie" Heath) recorded enough music to fill up three CDs, all of which have been released by the English Black Lion label. Four of the six standards on this hard-swinging set ("But Not for me," "Take the 'A' Train," "Blues Walk" and "Love for Sale") are over ten minutes long, while the other two ("For All We Know" and "I Guess I'll Have to Hang My Tears Out to Dry") are a little more concise). Throughout, Dexter Gordon is in consistently creative form, making this CD well worth getting by his fans. —*Scott Yanow*

Live at the Amsterdam Paradiso / Feb. 5, 1969 / Affinity ✦✦✦✦
The great tenor Dexter Gordon made so many consistently enjoyable straight-ahead recordings during 1960–78 that it is difficult to come up with any sets that are not recommended to fans of bebop. This double LP finds Gordon in excellent form, performing four jazz standards along with two of his originals ("Fried Bananas" and "Junior") with a Dutch trio (pianist Cees Slinger, bassist Jacques Schois and the future avant-garde innovator Han Bennink on drums). Virtually all of Gordon's records from his productive European period find him at his peak and this two-fer is no exception. —*Scott Yanow*

Day in Copenhagen / Mar. 10, 1969 / Polydor ✦✦✦
Unlike many other American expatriates living in Europe, tenor saxophonist Dexter Gordon always managed to play and record with the top musicians while overseas. This excellent sextet session (with trombonist Slide Hampton, trumpeter Dizzy Reece, pianist Kenny Drew, bassist Niels Pedersen and drummer Art Taylor) finds him exploring three Slide Hampton compositions and a trio of standard ballads. The other soloists are fine, but Gordon easily dominates the set, playing his brand of hard-driving bop. *Scott Yanow*

The Tower of Power / Apr. 2, 1969+Apr. 4, 1969 / Original Jazz Classics ✦✦✦
The highpoint of this boppish CD is a bit of a surprise, tenor Dexter Gordon's emotional rendition of "Those Were the Days." Otherwise fellow-tenor James Moody's guest appearance on "Montmartre" is less exciting than one would hope, although the other two quartet performances (with pianist Barry Harris, bassist Buster Williams and drummer Albert "Tootie" Heath) are good.

Recorded during an infrequent visit to the U.S., this recording (along with its companion *More Power*) failed to create much of a stir. —*Scott Yanow*

More Power / Apr. 2, 1969+Apr. 4, 1969 / Original Jazz Classics ◆◆◆

Recorded at the same two sessions that also resulted in *The Tower of Power* (a title that predated the R&B group), this set features tenor-great Dexter Gordon in the middle of one of his infrequent visits to the U.S., during a long period when he lived in Europe. Gordon, joined by James Moody's tenor on two cuts (Moody only solos on Tadd Dameron's "Lady Bird"), is accompanied throughout by pianist Barry Harris, bassist Buster Williams and drummer Albert "Tootie" Heath. The music (three Gordon originals, including the original version of "Fried Bananas," Jobim's "Meditation" and a Tadd Dameron tune), finds Gordon at the peak of his powers, a place he stayed for 15 years even though he tended to be overshadowed by many younger players during this era. —*Scott Yanow*

Dexter Gordon at Montreux (With Junior Mance) / Jun. 18, 1970 / Original Jazz Classics ◆◆◆◆

Dexter Gordon's set at the 1970 Montreux Jazz Festival is typically exciting with long tenor solos, fine backup (from pianist Junior Mance, bassist Martin Rivera and drummer Oliver Jackson) and a well-rounded repertoire: Gordon's "Fried Bananas," "Sophisticated Lady," Thelonious Monk's "Rhythm-A-Ning," an explorative "Body and Soul," "Blue Monk" and "The Panther." This excellent CD serves as a fine all-around introduction to the music of the great tenor saxophonist. —*Scott Yanow*

The Panther / Jul. 7, 1970 / Original Jazz Classics ◆◆◆◆

Although Dexter Gordon contributed three originals to this American session, it is his rendition of the three standards that are most memorable. The great tenor romps on the familiar line "The Blues Walk," digs into "Body and Soul" (giving this warhorse a fresh new interpretation) and makes a classic statement on "The Christmas Song." With the assistance of pianist Tommy Flanagan, bassist Larry Ridley and drummer Alan Dawson, Gordon is in typically spirited form for this happy set. —*Scott Yanow*

Jumpin' Blues / Aug. 27, 1970 / Prestige ◆◆◆

Amazing piano from Wynton Kelly, fine Gordon. —*Ron Wynn*

The Shadow of Your Smile / Apr. 21, 1971 / SteepleChase ◆◆◆

Tenor saxophonist Dexter Gordon uplifts four warhorses (a cooking "Secret Love," "Polkadots and Moonbeams," "The Shadow of Your Smile" and "Summertime") in lengthy and creative renditions. This live set from Stockholm, Sweden finds Gordon joined by an excellent Swedish rhythm section (pianist Lars Sjosten, bassist Sture Nordin and drummer Fredrik Noren) on an excellent LP of fairly explorative bop. —*Scott Yanow*

Ca' Purange / 1972 / Prestige ◆◆◆

The harmonically advanced trumpeter Thad Jones is a perfect contrast to the tenor of Dexter Gordon on this enjoyable Prestige LP. Gordon was somewhat forgotten in the United States at the time (his "comeback" was still four years away), but is in excellent form on the four numbers, particularly during a passionate version of "The First Time Ever I Saw Your Face." —*Scott Yanow*

Generation / Jul. 22, 1972 / Original Jazz Classics ◆◆◆◆

Veteran tenor saxophonist Dexter Gordon welcomed trumpeter Freddie Hubbard to his recording group several times during his career and each collaboration was quite rewarding. For this Prestige studio set the two horns (who are joined by pianist Cedar Walton, bassist Buster Williams and drummer Billy Higgins) work together quite well on "Milestones" (a second version is included as a bonus track), "Scared to Be Alone," Thelonious Monk's "We See" and Gordon's "The Group." This CD should please collectors. —*Scott Yanow*

Blues a la Suisse / Jul. 7, 1973 / Prestige ◆◆

Tenor-great Dexter Gordon sounds fine on these four extended performances ("Gingerbread Boy," "Blues a la Suisse," "Some Other Spring" and "Secret Love") which, (with the exception of the six-minute "Some Other Spring"), clock in between ten and 15 minutes apiece. The rhythm section (Hampton Hawes on electric piano, electric bassist Bob Cranshaw and drummer Kenny Clarke) is not as attuned to Gordon's music as one would hope (the electronics do not really blend in well), making this a somewhat average (but still fairly enjoyable) bop session. —*Scott Yanow*

The Apartment / May 24, 1974–Sep. 8, 1974 / SteepleChase ◆◆◆◆◆

While in Europe, tenor sax-great Dexter Gordon recorded many

sessions with pianist Kenny Drew, bassist Niels Pedersen and drummer Albert "Tootie" Heath. All are worth acquiring and this one is no exception. In addition to three of his originals (including the original), the quartet performs the old bop line "Wee-Dot" and Horace Silver's "Strollin'," while the ballad "Old Folks" is taken as an emotional Gordon-Pedersen duet. —*Scott Yanow*

More Than You Know / Feb. 21, 1975–Mar. 27, 1975 / SteepleChase ◆◆◆◆

Dexter Gordon's SteepleChase recordings of the early- to mid-'70s are among the most rewarding of his career. This particular session (which finds Gordon backed by a string orchestra arranged by Palle Mikkelborg) is one of the lesser items from this fertile period. Dexter is in memorable form on "Naima" and "More than You Know," but the backup orchestra has little interplay with Gordon and the lush charts offer few surprises. This set does not quite live up to its potential, although Dexter Gordon fans will still find moments to enjoy. —*Scott Yanow*

★ **Stable Mable** / Mar. 10, 1975 / Inner City ◆◆◆◆◆

Dexter Gordon is in frequently exuberant form on this quartet session with pianist Horace Parlan, bassist Niels Pedersen and drummer Tony Inzalaco. The material, which includes "Just Friends," "Misty," "Stablemates" and "Red Cross," is familiar, but the veteran tenor sounds quite inspired throughout the joyous outing. —*Scott Yanow*

Swiss Nights, Vol. 1 / Aug. 23, 1975 / Inner City ◆◆◆◆

The first of three volumes taken from the 1975 Zurich Jazz Festival features tenor saxophonist Dexter Gordon (with his reliable sidemen pianist Kenny Drew, bassist Niels Pedersen and drummer Alex Riel) stretching out on "Tenor Madness," "Wave," "You've Changed" and "Days of Wine and Roses." All of the performances are at least ten minutes long and there are some rambling moments, but in general, the music is quite rewarding. This was one of Dexter Gordon's prime periods. —*Scott Yanow*

Swiss Nights, Vol. 2 / Aug. 23, 1975–Aug. 24, 1975 / SteepleChase ◆◆◆◆

The second of three CDs taken from Gordon's appearances at the 1975 Montreux Jazz Festival showcases the veteran tenor in peak form. With strong support from the talented rhythm section (pianist Kenny Drew, bassist Niels-Henning Orsted Pedersen and drummer Alex Riel), Dexter is particularly exciting on a nearly 15-minute version of "There Is No Greater Love," "Wave" and "Thelonious Monk's "Rhythm-A-Ning"; the latter two songs were issued for the initial time on this six-song CD reissue. Dexter Gordon is heard throughout at his best. —*Scott Yanow*

Swiss Nights, Vol. 3 / Aug. 23, 1975–Aug. 24, 1975 / SteepleChase ◆◆◆◆

The third of three CDs taken from tenor saxophonist Dexter Gordon's appearances at the 1975 Zurich Jazz Festival has more variety than his other two. There are previously unissued versions of "Tenor Madness" and "Days of Wine and Roses" (the latter has a guest appearance by trumpeter Joe Newman), tender ballad renditions of "Didn't We" and "Sophisticated Lady," an effective vocal by Gordon on "Jelly Jelly" and a rollicking rendition of "Rhythm-A-Ning." With pianist Kenny Drew, bassist Niels Pedersen and drummer Alex Riel offering strong support, Dexter Gordon is heard in happy and hard-swinging form. —*Scott Yanow*

Something Different / Sep. 13, 1975 / SteepleChase ◆◆◆◆◆

What is different about this set (recorded in a particularly busy year for Dexter Gordon) is that the veteran tenor is joined by a trio (guitarist Philip Catherine, bassist Niels Pedersen and drummer Billy Higgins) that does not include a pianist. Otherwise, the music is at the same high quality level and in the same modern bop genre as one would expect. In addition to one of his originals and Slide Hampton's "Yesterday's Mood," Gordon stretches out on some standards, making a classic statement on the ballad "When Sunny Gets Blue." All of his SteepleChase albums (particularly those from the 1975–76 period) are well worth acquiring. —*Scott Yanow*

★ **Bouncin' with Dex** / Sep. 14, 1975 / SteepleChase ◆◆◆◆◆

Dexter Gordon recorded nine albums for SteepleChase during 1975–76 (seven in 1975 alone) and was at the peak of his powers. This particular release finds Gordon joined by pianist Tete Montoliu, bassist Niels Pedersen and drummer Billy Higgins on two of his originals and three jazz standards. Gordon is in superlative form, jamming with enthusiasm and melodic creativity on these familiar chord changes. —*Scott Yanow*

Strings and Things / May 17, 1976–May 19, 1976 / SteepleChase ✦✦✦✦

Lullaby for a Monster / Jun. 15, 1976 / SteepleChase ✦✦✦✦
Recorded shortly before his triumphant return to the United States after a dozen years overseas, this Dexter Gordon album features him in a surprisingly sparse setting, accompanied only by bassist Niels Pedersen and drummer Alex Riel. Whether it be the humorous melody "Nursery Blues," Pedersen's title cut or the four jazz standards (of which "Good Bait" was first released on this CD reissue), he is up to the challenge and his lengthy solos never lose one's interest. —*Scott Yanow*

Biting the Apple / Nov. 9, 1976 / SteepleChase ✦✦✦✦✦
Many of Dexter Gordon's finest recordings were cut in Europe just prior to his triumphant return to the United States. This album was recorded just weeks before and it is one of the veteran tenor's best. With strong assistance from pianist Barry Harris, bassist Sam Jones and drummer Al Foster, Dexter plays exciting solos on "I'll Remember April," a warm version of "Skylark" and his two originals, "Apple Jump" and "A La Modal." It is highly recommended, as are all of Dexter Gordon's SteepleChase recordings from this period. —*Scott Yanow*

Featuring Joe Newman / Nov. 1976 / Monad ✦✦✦
This live set is better than it appears at first glance. The recording quality is excellent and Dexter Gordon (who had recently returned to the U.S. after quite a few years in Europe) is in inspired form, really tearing into his solos with intensity. Trumpeter Joe Newman, who obviously had not played much with Gordon, has to fight to find a place for himself in the ensembles and is sometimes overextended in his solos, but his colorful tone is immediately recognizable. The rhythm section is fine in support with drummer Wilbur Campbell really pushing the group and pianist Jodie Christian contributing some excellent solos. Not every number is a classic. Newman's feature on "Ode to Billy Joe" is a bit dull and there are some unfortunate fadeouts with the two parts of "Body and Soul" being lengthy fragments from Dexter Gordon solos, "The Shadow of Your Smile" only comprised of Gordon's statement and "Softly" ending during Newman's spot. However, Dexter Gordon's heated improvisations on "Tangerine" and "Walkin'" are both quite memorable. So, although not essential, this CD is easily recommended to fans. —*Scott Yanow*

Homecoming: Live at the Village Vanguard / Dec. 11, 1976–Dec. 12, 1976 / Columbia ✦✦✦✦✦
The acclaim that met Dexter Gordon when he returned to the United States after 14 years in Europe was completely unexpected. Not only did the jazz critics praise the great tenor, but there were literally lines of young fans waiting to see his performances. This double CD, recorded during his historic first American tour, improved on the original double LP with the inclusion of previously unreleased versions of "Fried Bananas" and "Body and Soul." Gordon in a quintet with trumpeter Woody Shaw, pianist Ronnie Mathews, bassist Stafford James and drummer Louis Hayes frequently sounds exuberant on these lengthy performances; all ten songs are at least 11 minutes long. The excitement of the period can definitely be felt in this excellent music. —*Scott Yanow*

Sophisticated Giant / Jun. 21, 1977–Jun. 22, 1977 / Columbia ✦✦✦✦
This excellent Columbia album was recorded less than a year after Dexter Gordon's well-publicized tour of the United States following a dozen years spent living in Europe. With assistance from such other major players as trumpeters Woody Shaw and Benny Bailey, vibraphonist Bobby Gordon sounds in superlative form on Woody Shaw's "The Moontrame," four standards and his own "Fried Bananas." This set deserves to be reissued on CD. —*Scott Yanow*

Who's Who In Jazz / Nov. 11, 1977 / Who's Who ✦✦
This LP is an unusual one for tenor saxophonist Dexter Gordon. Instead of his usual bop-based group, the backing is more swing-oriented (with vibraphonist Lionel Hampton pianist Hank Jones, guitarist Bucky Pizzarelli, bassist George Duvivier, drummer Oliver Jackson and Candido on congas) as is the repertoire. Gordon plays a few songs on his less-distinctive soprano sax and the music, although reasonably pleasing, is not up to Gordon's earlier recordings. This odd set is a historical curiosity. —*Scott Yanow*

Manhattan Symphonie / 1978 / Columbia ✦✦✦✦
This LP is one of Dexter Gordon's last great albums. The veteran tenor (assisted by pianist George Cables, bassist Rufus Reid and drummer Eddie Gladden) is in superior form on such classic numbers as "As Time Goes By," "Moment's Notice" and most memorably "Body and Soul"; during the latter he shows what he learned from John Coltrane (who was originally most influenced by Gordon). Until Columbia gets around to reissuing it on CD, this superior LP is well worth searching for. —*Scott Yanow*

Nights at the Keystone, Vols. 1-3 / May 13, 1978–Mar. 24, 1979 / Blue Note ✦✦✦✦
Nights at the Keystone dates from a couple of years after Dexter Gordon had returned triumphantly to America (1978-79). He took strong solos on several lengthy performances. One can fault the occasional excess of song quotes (especially "Laura," which seemed to pop up in every solo), but Gordon's authoritative sound, freshness of ideas and confident explorations easily compensated. Pianist George Cables was often in dazzling form (check out "Tangerine") and was continually inventive. Bassist Rufus Reid and drummer Eddie Gladden were perfect in support. In addition, the ambience of the late, lamented Keystone Korner, San Francisco's top jazz club and possessor of one of the most knowledgeable jazz audiences anywhere, can be felt. —*Scott Yanow*

Great Encounters / Sep. 23, 1978 / Columbia ✦✦✦✦
The two great tenors, Dexter Gordon and Johnny Griffin, battle it out on in exciting fashion on live versions of "Blues up and Down" and "Cake," bop singer Eddie Jefferson and trumpeter Woody Shaw join Gordon and his quartet (pianist George Cables, bassist Rufus Reid and drummer Eddie Gladden) on "Diggin' In" and "It's Only a Paper Moon" and Dexter takes Thelonious Monk's ballad "Ruby My Dear" as his feature. Everything works quite well on this diverse but consistent LP, one of Dexter Gordon's later efforts. —*Scott Yanow*

Gotham City / Aug. 11, 1980–Aug. 12, 1980 / Columbia ✦✦✦
Tenor saxophonist Dexter Gordon was still in pretty good form at the time of this later recording. The veteran great is joined by an all-star rhythm section (pianist Cedar Walton, bassist Percy Heath and drummer Art Blakey) along with guest appearances from trumpeter Woody Shaw and guitarist George Benson. Although this boppish set is rather brief (just four songs totalling around 37 minutes), the quality of the solos is quite high. —*Scott Yanow*

Jive Fernando / 1981 / Chiaroscuro ✦✦
The recording quality on this LP is not flawless, the liner notes (which do not list the recording date) are somewhat irrelevant and Dexter Gordon's rhythm section (keyboardist George Duke, bassist Ralph Garrett and drummer Oliver Johnson) is not perfectly suited to his music, but the great tenor plays fairly well on the four extended performances. This obscure session (not essential but worthwhile) is highlighted by "Blue Monk" an "The Shadow of Your Smile." —*Scott Yanow*

American Classic / Mar. 8, 1982 / Discovery ✦✦
Tenor saxophonist Dexter Gordon's final album (not counting his work on the film *Round Midnight*) is a decent effort if not all that notable. Gordon is assisted by Grover Washington, Jr. (who makes some guest appearances on soprano), pianist Kirk Lightsey, organist Shirley Scott, bassist David Eubanks and drummer Eddie Gladden, sounding best on "Besame Mucho" and "Skylark." Worth picking up, but not that essential. —*Scott Yanow*

The Other Side of Round Midnight / Jul. 1, 1985–Jul. 12, 1985 / Blue Note ✦✦✦
Outtakes and alternate cuts from the soundtrack of the film that got Dexter Gordon an Oscar nomination. —*Ron Wynn*

Round Midnight / Jul. 1, 1985–Jul. 12, 1985 / Columbia ✦✦✦

Joe Gordon
b. May 15, 1928, Boston, MA, d. Nov. 4, 1963, Santa Monica, CA
Trumpet / Hard Bop
A fine bop-oriented trumpeter, Joe Gordon's tragic death in a fire cut short any chance he had at fame in the jazz world. He became a professional in 1947 and had stints with George Auld, Lionel Hampton, Charlie Parker (on an occasional basis during 1953-55), Art Blakey (1954) and Don Redman. Gordon was with Dizzy Gillespie's 1956 big band, touring the Mideast and getting a solo on "Night in Tunisia." He was in the Horace Silver quintet, moved back to Boston for a period and then relocated to Los Angeles where he worked and recorded with Barney Kessel, Benny Carter, Harold Land, Shelly Manne, Dexter Gordon and Shelly Manne (1958-60). Joe Gordon, who led dates for EmArcy (1955) and

Contemporary (1961), was on one Thelonious Monk recording and spent his last few years as a freelance musician. —*Scott Yanow*

Introducing Joe Gordon / Sep. 3, 1955+Sep. 8, 1955 / Mercury ✦✦✦✦

● **Lookin' Good!** / Jul. 11, 1961–Dec. 18, 1961 / Original Jazz Classics ✦✦✦✦✦

Danny Gottlieb

b. Apr. 18, 1953, New York, NY
Drums / Post-Bop, Crossover
A flexible and talented drummer, Danny Gottlieb studied with Mel Lewis and Joe Morello. After graduating from the University of Miami (1975), he did session work in the Miami Beach area. Gottlieb joined Gary Burton's Quartet (1976) at a period when Pat Metheny was the guitarist. When Metheny soon formed his Group, Gottlieb became a charter member (1977–83). In 1981 he teamed up with Metheny's bassist Mark Egan in a band that by 1983 was called Elements. He has worked in many other settings since then including with John McLaughlin in the short-lived later version of the Mahavishnu Orchestra (1984) and Al DiMeola (1985). Gottlieb continues to play on a part-time basis with Elements. —*Scott Yanow*

Elements / Jan. 1982 / Philo ✦✦✦

Aquamarine / 1987 / Atlantic ✦✦✦✦
The debut album from this former Pat Metheny Group drummer features guitarist John Abercrombie. —*Paul Kohler*

Whirlwind / 1989 / Atlantic ✦✦✦
This great followup album has an incredible list of sidemen, featuring John Abercrombie (g). —*Paul Kohler*

● **Brooklyn Blues** / Dec. 1990 / Big World ✦✦✦✦

Dusko Goykovich

b. Oct. 14, 1931, Jajce, Yugoslavia
Trumpet, Fluegelhorn / Hard Bop
An excellent bop-based soloist who, in recent times, has been recording rewarding sets for Enja, Dusko Goykovich played in Yugoslavia and Germany before visiting the U.S. for the first time with Marshall Brown's International Youth Band (playing at the 1958 Newport Jazz Festival). Goykovich attended Berklee (1961–63) and played with the orchestras of Maynard Ferguson (1963–64) and Woody Herman (1964–66) before deciding to return to Germany, leading a group with Sal Nistico (1966). He was with the Kenny Clarke-Francy Boland Big Band (1968–73) and had a 12-piece band with Slide Hampton (1974–75). Miles Davis is his main influence, but Dusko Goykovich (who has been quite active during the past two decades in Europe) has his own extroverted style. —*Scott Yanow*

● **Soul Connection** / Jun. 28, 1993–Jun. 29, 1993 / Enja ✦✦✦✦✦
Trumpeter Dusko Goykovich, a fixture in Germany for decades, has had few of his recordings available in the United States. This Enja CD is an exception, an excellent quartet/quintet date with pianist Tommy Flanagan, bassist Eddie Gomez and drummer Mickey Roker; tenor saxophonist Jimmy Heath is on five of the nine selections. Goykovich, whose hero was Miles Davis (one of his eight originals on this session is called "Ballad for Miles"), has a mellow tone and a likable swinging style. This relaxed CD is an excellent example of his talents. —*Scott Yanow*

Bebop City / 1995 / Enja ✦✦✦✦

John Graas

b. Oct. 14, 1924, Dubuque, IA, d. Apr. 13, 1962, Van Nuys, CA
French Horn / Cool, Third Stream
Along with Julius Watkins, John Graas was one of the first jazz French horn soloists. After playing some classical music, in 1942 he became a member of the Claude Thornhill Orchestra. A period in the Army (1942–45) and stints with the Cleveland Orchestra and Tex Beneke's big band preceded Graas' first high-profile gig, playing with Stan Kenton's Innovations Orchestra (1950–51). After leaving Kenton, he settled in Los Angeles and worked as a studio musician in addition to being used on West Coast jazz dates by Shorty Rogers and others. Graas, an excellent composer who sought to combine together jazz and classical music (predating the Third Stream movement), recorded fairly regularly as a leader during 1953-58, sessions that (with the exception of one VSOP

release) have not been reissued. He died of a heart attack at the age of 37. —*Scott Yanow*

● **International Premiere in Jazz** / Oct. 1956+Mar. 18, 1958 / VSOP ✦✦✦✦✦
John Graas was a multi-talented French horn player not shy to take chances in both his solos and his writing. On this VSOP CD reissue of two sessions for Andex, Graas performs his 171/2 minute, three-part "Jazz Chaconne No. 1" and four alternate takes with a nonet including altoist Art Pepper, trumpeter Jack Sheldon and flutist Buddy Collette. In addition, Graas' four-movement "Jazz Symphony No. 1" is played by The Rundfunk-Symphony Orchestra with guest soloists taken from The Erwin Lehn band (German musicians who have remained quite obscure). The lack of liner notes is unfortunate for it would have been interesting to hear what John Graas' goals were in writing this music. Overall, the performances hold one's attention, particularly the "Jazz Chaconne," and this CD is recommended to adventurous listeners. —*Scott Yanow*

Teddy Grace

b. Jun. 26, 1905, Arcadia, LA, d. Jan. 4, 1992, La Mirada, CA
Vocals / Swing, Blues
A superior singer whose career was tragically cut short, most of Teddy Grace's recordings have been reissued on a Timeless CD. She became a professional singer in 1931, sang on the radio in the South, worked for Al Katz (1933), Tommy Christian (1934) and Mal Hallett (on and off during 1934–37) and recorded for Decca during 1937–40, using such sidemen as Bobby Hackett, Jack Teagarden, Charlie Shavers, Buster Bailey, Pee Wee Russell and Bud Freeman. Grace became disenchanted with the music business and quit in 1940. She joined the WACs during World War II and after straining herself singing during a busy schedule of bond rallies and shows, she lost her voice. Although Teddy Grace's speaking voice eventually came back in a weakened form, she was unable to sing again and spent the rest of her life outside of music. —*Scott Yanow*

★ **Teddy Grace** / Oct. 25, 1937–Sep. 26, 1940 / Timeless ✦✦✦✦✦
Even veteran swing collectors might be unaware of the enjoyable recordings that the unfortunately obscure but very talented Teddy Grace made during her relatively brief career. This valuable CD has 22 of the 30 selections that she made as a leader (leaving off two sessions) and finds Grace very much at ease, whether interpreting swinging lesser-known material, a series of high-quality blues or period pieces. The supporting cast, which includes such notables as cornetist Bobby Hackett, trumpeters Charlie Shavers and Max Kaminsky, trombonist Jack Teagarden, clarinetist Pee Wee Russell, tenor saxophonist Bud Freeman and pianist Billy Kyle among others, speaks for the high esteem in which she was held during the era. —*Scott Yanow*

Stephane Grappelli (Stephane Grappelly)

b. Jan. 26, 1908, Paris, France
Violin / Swing
One of the all-time great jazz violinists (ranking with Joe Venuti and Stuff Smith as one of the big three of pre-bop), Stephane Grappelli's longevity and consistently enthusiastic playing has done a great deal to establish the violin as a jazz instrument. He was originally self-taught as both a violinist and a pianist, although during 1924–28 he studied at the Paris Conservatoire. Grappelli played in movie theaters and dance bands before meeting guitarist Django Reinhardt in 1933. They hit it off musically from the start even though their lifestyles (Grappelli was sophisticated while Django was a gypsy) were very different. Together as the Quintet of the Hot Club of France (comprised of violin, three acoustic guitars and bass) during 1933–39 they produced a sensational series of recordings and performances. During a London engagement in 1939, World War II broke out. Reinhardt rashly decided to return to France, but Grappelli stayed in England, effectively ending the group. The violinist soon teamed up with the young pianist George Shearing in a new band that worked steadily through the war. In 1946 Grappelli and Reinhardt had the first of several reunions, although they never worked together again on a regular basis (despite many new recordings). Grappelli performed throughout the 1950s and '60s in clubs throughout Europe and, other than recordings with Duke Ellington (*Violin Summit*) and Joe Venuti, he remained somewhat obscure in the U.S. until he began regularly touring the world in

the early '70s. Since then Grappelli has been a constant traveller and a consistent pollwinner, remaining very open-minded without altering his swing style; he has recorded with David Grisman, Earl Hines, Bill Coleman, Larry Coryell, Oscar Peterson, Jean Luc Ponty and McCoy Tyner among many others. Even at the age of 88, Stephane Grappelli remains at the top of his field. His early recordings are all available on Classics CDs and he has recorded quite extensively since the 1970s. —*Scott Yanow*

★ **Stephane Grappelli 1935-1940** / Sep. 30, 1935-Jul. 30, 1940 / Classics ✦✦✦✦✦
This Classics CD has all of the recordings made under violinist Stephane Grappelli's name during the 1935-40 period. The earlier selections (with his Hot Four) match his violin with Django Reinhardt's guitar in what was essentially the Quintet of The Hot Club of France. There are also nine duets with Reinhardt; a couple find Grappelli switching to piano. The set concludes in 1940 with Grappelli (in London) leading an octet on two numbers that also feature the young pianist George Shearing. —*Scott Yanow*

Stephane Grappelli 1941-1943 / Feb. 28, 1941-Dec. 8, 1943 / Classics ✦✦✦✦✦
This Classics CD reissues some very rare recordings made by violinist Stephane Grappelli: all of his performances as a leader during a difficult three-year period. The violinist had decided to stay in England during World War II (when Django Reinhardt returned to France) and soon had a new group featuring the young pianist George Shearing. This CD has seven sessions with quartets and quintets along with one featuring a larger group that includes other strings and a harp. Although there are vocals on eight of the numbers (by Beryl Davis and Dave Fullerton), the swinging performances and the rarity of the recordings easily compensate. —*Scott Yanow*

Unique Piano Session / 1955 / Jazz Anthology ✦✦✦
Piano was Stephane Grappelli's first instrument and, although he has recorded occasionally on it through the years, this was the first of only two albums to feature Grappelli exclusively on piano. A relaxed stride player, Grappelli mostly performs originals and obscure material with a trio on this interesting but hard-to-find LP. —*Scott Yanow*

Violins No End / May 4, 1957 / Pablo ✦✦✦✦
With Stuff Smith (violin) and the Oscar Petersen Trio. No disappointments; a great session. All standards except two improvised blues. —*Michael G. Nastos*

Feeling + Finesse Jazz / Mar. 7, 1962-Mar. 9, 1962 / Atlantic ✦✦✦
Although he was very active in France during the 1950s and '60s, violinist Stephane Grappelli recorded relatively little until 1969. This Atlantic LP from 1962 finds Grappelli in good form in a quintet with guitarist Pierre Cavalli, performing a Django-dominated repertoire that is not all that different from what he would be playing 30 years later. —*Scott Yanow*

Two of a Kind / Jan. 23, 1965-Jan. 24, 1965 / Storyville ✦✦✦
Although it is hard to believe, discographies list this session (co-led with fellow violinist Svend Asmussen) as Stephane Grappelli's only recording as a leader during 1963-68. Accompanied by two guitarists, bassist Niels Henning Orsted Pedersen and a drummer, the two violinists (contemporaries whose similar styles matured in the 1930s) sound excellent on the LP, playing four standards, Toots Thielemans' "Blue Lady" and three of their originals. —*Scott Yanow*

Limehouse Blues / Jun. 23, 1969-Jun. 24, 1969 / Black Lion ✦✦✦✦
In 1969 violinist Stephane Grappelli and guitarist Barney Kessel teamed up for a few albums. This CD, in addition to five hot performances that originally came out on LP, has five previously unreleased performances from the same sessions. Throughout, the two principals (backed by rhythm guitarist Nini Rosso, bassist Michel Gaudry and drummer Jean-Louis Viale) are in top form, consistently inspiring each other. —*Scott Yanow*

Meets Barney Kessel / Jun. 23, 1969 Jun. 24, 1969 / Black Lion ✦✦✦✦✦
This excellent set features a logical combination. Violinist Stephane Grappelli originally came to fame through his recordings with guitarist Django Reinhardt. Barney Kessel, although more influenced by Charlie Christian than by Django, was one of the top jazz guitarists of the 1950s and '60s and his style was quite complementary to Grappelli's. The two teamed up for several albums' worth of material in 1969. This CD reissues the former

LP *I Remember Django*, adding four additional selections and serving as a perfect introduction to the brilliant playing of Stephane Grappelli. —*Scott Yanow*

Venupelli Blues / Oct. 22, 1969 / Charly ✦✦✦✦✦
Stephane Grappelli and Joe Venuti, arguably the two top violinists in jazz history, only made one recording together, this heated 1969 studio sesion. With pianist George Wein and guitarist Barney Kessel helping out as part of the supporting four-piece rhythm section, Grappelli and Venuti often romp during the title cut and the six standards that comprise this memorable session. This violin "battle" ends up as a dead heat, a joyous and historic occasion for all concerned. —*Scott Yanow*

Afternoon in Paris / Mar. 1971 / Verve ✦✦✦
This is a typically flawless swing set by violinist Stephane Grappelli. Joined by pianist Marc Hemmeler, bassist Eberhard Weber and drummer Kenny Clare for a session originally cut for MPS, Grappelli mixes together sophisticated ballads with hotter stomps and uplifts the somewhat modern rhythm section. —*Scott Yanow*

Jalousie: Music of the 30's / Jun. 14, 1972-Mar. 7, 1973 / Angel ✦✦
This was the first of three albums that matched together the two great violinists Stephane Grappelli and Yehudi Menuhin. They performed a set of superior standards (mostly from the 1920s and '30s) but, unfortunately, Menuhin was unable to improvise. The classical violinist does his best, but his written parts weigh down the jazz content of this merely pleasant session. —*Scott Yanow*

Homage to Django / Jun. 19, 1972-Jun. 22, 1972 / Classic Jazz ✦✦✦✦
Violinist Stephane Grappelli has recorded many Django Reinhardt tributes over the past few decades. This double LP, which includes many originals co-written by Reinhardt and Grappelli in addition to a few 1930s standards, is one of his best. With the assistance of either Alan Clare or Marc Hemmeler on keyboards, guitarist Ernie Cranenburgh, bassist Lennie Bush and drummer Chris Karan, Grappelli is in top form on such rarely played numbers as "Tears," "Clopin Clopant," "Are You in the Mood," "Sweet Chorus" and "Fantaisie." This classic music deserves to be reissued on CD. —*Scott Yanow*

Satin Doll / Nov. 12, 1972-Nov. 13, 1972 / Vanguard ✦✦✦
On this double LP, violinist Stephane Grapelli gets away from his usual tribute to the late Django Reinhardt and plays 15 standards including "Mack the Knife," "The Girl from Ipanema," "You Took Advantage of Me" and two versions of "Body and Soul." Accompanied by organist Eddy Louiss, pianist Marc Hemmeler, guitarist Jimmy Gourley, bassist Guy Pedersen and drummer Kenny Clarke, Grappelli is in typically flawless form for these enjoyable swing sessions. —*Scott Yanow*

Talk Of The Town / Mar. 19, 1973 / Black Lion ✦✦
Violinist Stephane Grappelli plays a set of ballads in duet with pianist Alan Clare on this set. Although one wishes there were more variety in tempos and moods (and perhaps a little less taste), the results are pleasant enough and worth picking up for those who love Grappelli's timeless sound. —*Scott Yanow*

Parisian Thoroughfare / Sep. 5, 1973-Sep. 7, 1973 / Black Lion ✦✦✦✦
Originally titled *Stephane Grappelli Meets the Rhythm Section*, this 1973 studio CD matches the great violinist with keyboardist Roland Hanna, bassist George Mraz and drummer Mel Lewis for a varied program that includes standards, two Roland Hanna compositions and a jazz version of a Chopin piece. The CD reissue adds three more titles to the program and is easily recommended to fans of the veteran violinist. —*Scott Yanow*

★ **Live in London** / Nov. 5, 1973 / Black Lion ✦✦✦✦✦
One of the best groups that violinist Stephane Grappelli collaborated with during the second half of his long career has been The Hot Club of London, a unit led by guitarist Diz Disley and usually including a second rhythm guitarist and a bassist. This Black Lion CD reissues the entire contents of a former two-LP set (*I Got Rhythm*) and even has room for a previously unreleased version of "Them There Eyes." Grappelli sounds particularly inspired playing with this group, very comfortable with the drumless setting and free to dominate the proceedings. —*Scott Yanow*

Stephane Grappelli / Bill Coleman / Dec. 1973 / Classic Jazz ✦✦✦✦✦
Bill Coleman, a fine swing trumpeter, settled in France in the

1930s and (other than during World War II) he remained overseas for the remainder of his life. Somewhat underrated in jazz history books, he had a distinctive sound of his own. Coleman's musical reunion with violinist Stephane Grappelli (they had recorded together 35 years earlier) is a happy occasion with spirited versions of nine standards resulting from their long overdue joint recording. Not yet out on CD, this LP is well worth searching for. —*Scott Yanow*

Stephane Grappelli Meets Earl Hines / Jul. 4, 1974 / Black Lion ✦✦

This unusual duet session by violinist Stephane Grappelli and pianist Earl Hines had the potential for a lot of fireworks, but is disappointingly relaxed. The emphasis is on ballads and, although Hines typically takes some chances with time during his solos, the music on the CD is on a whole overly tasteful and safe, well-played but not as memorable as it could have been. —*Scott Yanow*

The Reunion, with George Shearing / Apr. 11, 1976 / PolyGram ✦✦✦✦✦

Back in 1940, pianist George Shearing made his debut as a sideman with violinist Stephane Grappelli's new band. In 1976, over 30 years since they last played with each other, the two masters had a recorded reunion and they sounded if as they had been performing together for decades. With the assistance of bassist Andy Simpkins and drummer Rusty Jones, Grappelli and Shearing create some musical magic on nine standards and Grappelli's "La Chanson De Rue." —*Scott Yanow*

Tea for Two / Oct. 28, 1977–Oct. 30, 1977 / Angel ✦✦

For the third recorded meeting between violinists Stephane Grappelli and Yehudi Menuhin, the rhythm section is joined by some woodwinds on a few of the selections. Grappelli sounds fine, but Menuhin's classical technique did not prepare him to improvise and he weighs down the proceedings a bit, making some of the ballads sound too sweet. This LP is, therefore, a historical curiosity rather than an essential acquisition. —*Scott Yanow*

Live at Carnegie Hall / Apr. 5, 1978 / Doctor Jazz ✦✦✦

Stephane Grappelli teams up once again with the Diz Disley Trio (which in 1978 was comprised of Disley and John Ethridge on guitars along with bassist Brian Torff) and the results are often quite exciting. Grappelli is heard at his best on such songs as "I Can't Give You Anything but Love," "Crazy Rhythm" and even "Chattanooga Choo Choo." Few surprises occur, but this swinging music is easily enjoyable. —*Scott Yanow*

Uptown Dance / Apr. 1978 / Columbia ✦✦✦✦

On this LP, violinist Stephane Grappelli is heard in a different setting than usual, accompanied by a large orchestra arranged by Claus Ogerman. "Uptown Dance" is particularly catchy and most of the other songs, while new to him (other than "Baubles, Bangles and Beads" and "Angel Eyes") come across quite well. The supporting cast (which has pianist Jimmy Rowles and keyboardist Richard Tee alternating) is a major asset to this enjoyable set. —*Scott Yanow*

Young Django / Jan. 19, 1979–Jan. 21, 1979 / Verve ✦✦✦✦✦

This CD finds veteran violinist Stephane Grappelli joined by bassist Niels Pedersen and guitarists Philip Catherine and Larry Coryell for a memorable tribute to Django Reinhardt. Grappelli has recorded many Reinhardt memorial albums through the years, but this one is particularly special, for both Coryell and Catherine go out of their way to display the unexpected influence that Reinhardt has had on their styles. The guitarists contribute a song apiece and also enjoy playing seven compositions co-written by Django and Grappelli. —*Scott Yanow*

Live at Tivoli Gardens, Copenhagen, Denmark / Jul. 6, 1979 / Original Jazz Classics ✦✦✦✦

Stephane Grappelli's live Pablo album matches his violin in trios with guitarist Joe Pass and bassist Niels Pedersen, two masters who could not only keep up with him but often inspired his solos. The repertoire is unsurprising as is the musical excellence, but those are not good reasons to pass this set by. Recorded live in Copenhagen, Denmark, the trio brings fresh life to such old standards as "It's Only a Paper Moon," "Let's Fall in Love" and "I Get a Kick out of You." —*Scott Yanow*

Stephane Grappelli and Hank Jones: a Two-Fer! / Jul. 20, 1979 / Muse ✦✦✦

The title of this Muse release is a bit inaccurate for this is but a single LP (not a two-fer). Actually its name was meant to signify that two giants were teamed up: violinist Stephane Grappelli and

pianist Hank Jones. Assisted by bassist Jimmy Woode and drummer Alan Dawson, the duo are in fine form on seven familiar standards and the violinist's "Mellow Grapes." Few surprises occur, but this swinging date finds everyone displaying spirit and creativity. —*Scott Yanow*

★ **Stephane Grappelli and David Grisman Live** / Sep. 7, 1979–Sep. 20, 1979 / Warner Brothers ✦✦✦✦✦

One of the most exciting of the many Stephane Grappelli recordings, this live session (a straight CD reissue of the original LP) teams the veteran violinist with mandolist David Grisman's band, an ensemble that (in addition to its leader) boasts hot solos from Mike Marshall on violin, guitarist Mark O'Connor (who switches to violin to battle Grappelli on a memorable "Tiger Rag") and bassist Rob Wasserman. The first two songs ("Shine" and "Pent-Up House") are taken at breakneck tempoes and then, after the group tries to cool off on "Misty," they really burn on "Sweet Georgia Brown" and "Tiger Rag." Essential music with more than its share of great solos. —*Scott Yanow*

Happy Reunion / Feb. 17, 1980–Feb. 18, 1980 / Owl ✦✦✦

This CD's title is a bit ironic, for violinist Stephane Grappelli and pianist Martial Solal (who are heard on a set of duets), although two of France's finest jazzmen, had only recorded together once before and that was for a single selection in which they overdubbed their parts. This 1980 studio recording finds Solal reining in his adventurous style a bit so as to offer solid support for Grappelli. They perform six standards, two of Solal's pieces and a free improvisation. —*Scott Yanow*

At the Winery / Sep. 1980 / Concord Jazz ✦✦✦

Violinist Stephane Grappelli plays his usual repertoire (standards ranging from Stevie Wonder's "You Are the Sunshine of My Life" to "Chicago" and the Reinhardt-associated piece "Minor Swing") in a quartet with the guitars of John Etheridge and Martin Taylor and bassist Jack Sewing. The music, although a bit predictable, is easily enjoyable for Grappelli has never lost his enthusiasm for playing swinging jazz. He performs "Let's Fall in Love" and "Love for Sale" as if he had just discovered those songs. —*Scott Yanow*

Vintage 1981 / Jul. 1981 / Concord Jazz ✦✦✦

For this outing, veteran violinist Stephane Grappelli (then 73) jams a variety of standards (several of which he had not recorded previously) with guitarists Martin Taylor and Mike Gari (in addition to bassist Jack Sewing). Grappelli, who switches to electric piano for Taylor's "Jamie" and adds Stevie Wonder's "Isn't She Lovely" to his repertoire, displays an open mind toward new music while retaining his classic swing style. —*Scott Yanow*

Live in San Francisco / Jul. 7, 1982 / Black Hawk ✦✦✦

This out-of-print LP features violinist Stephane Grappelli in a very comfortable setting with guitarists Diz Disley and Martin Taylor and bassist Jack Sewing; three players who he had recorded with many times in the 1970s and '80s. Performing live at San Francisco's Great American Music Hall, the quartet interprets veteran jazz standards plus The Beatles' "Here, There and Everywhere" and Stevie Wonder's "You Are the Sunshine of My Life." Few surprises occur, but the music consistently swings and Grappelli is in excellent form. —*Scott Yanow*

Stephanova / Jun. 1983 / Concord Jazz ✦✦✦✦

For this Concord LP, violinist Stephane Grappelli is joined by guitarist Marc Fosset for a set of sparse but swinging duets. The repertoire, which includes "Tune Up," Grieg's "Norwegian Dance," Grappelli's "Waltz for Queenie" and two Fosset originals, is fresher than usual and Grappelli is up to the challenge. —*Scott Yanow*

Grappelli Plays Jerome Kern / 1987 / GRP ✦✦✦✦

This CD is much more unusual for the GRP label than it is for violinist Stephane Grappelli. Joined by two guitars (Marc Fossett and Martin Taylor), bass, drums and a subtle string orchestra, Grappelli comes up with fresh statements on 11 Jerome Kern songs including such classics as "The Way You Look Tonight," "All the Things You Are," "Pick Yourself Up" and "I Won't Dance." —*Scott Yanow*

Olympia 1988 / Jan. 24, 1988 / Atlantic ✦✦✦

Violinist Stephane Grappelli has recorded so many fine sets during the past two decades that although virtually all of them are enjoyable, most are not essential. This fine concert performance with a quartet (which also includes the guitars of Marc Fosset and Martin Taylor) is typical of Grappelli's ability to infuse familiar melodies that he has performed a countless number of times with enthusiasm, energy and wit. Pianist Martial Solal and violinist Svend Asmussen make guest appearances, but most of the focus is on the great Grappelli, who never seems to have an off day. —*Scott Yanow*

My Other Love / 1990 / Columbia ✦✦✦
This is one of only two full sets from his entire career that features violinist Stephane Grappelli exclusively on his first instrument, the piano. On this solo CD, Grappelli mostly plays slower and romantic renditions of standards (along with three originals) and shows that he could have made a living for himself through the years on his "Other Love." Tasty music that largely succeeds. —*Scott Yanow*

One on One, with McCoy Tyner / Apr. 18, 1990 / Milestone ✦✦✦✦
Violinist Stephane Grappelli, although a veteran of the swing era, has always kept an open mind toward newer styles even while he has retained his own sound and veteran repertoire. This duet set with pianist McCoy Tyner might seem unlikely at first glance, but it works quite well. The duo sticks to standards (including ones that are associated with John Coltrane) and find plenty of common ground. The mutual respect they have for each other is obvious and they both sound a bit inspired. —*Scott Yanow*

In Tokyo / Oct. 4, 1990 / Denon ✦✦✦✦
Although 82 at the time of this concert, violinist Stephane Grappelli plays with the fire and enthusiasm of a musician half his age. The repertoire is generally pretty familiar, but the music (performed in trios with guitarist Marc Fosset and bassist Jean-Philippe Viret), consistently swings and there is nothing predictable or tired about Grappelli's solos. With Marcel Azzola making a few guest spots on accordion, this fine straight-ahead set is easily recommended as an example of the youthful Stephane Grappelli. —*Scott Yanow*

Live 1992 / Mar. 27, 1992–Mar. 28, 1992 / Verve ✦✦✦✦
Fifty-eight years after the first recordings of The Quintet of the Hot Club of France, its violinist Stephane Grappelli still sounds young on this date. Much of the repertoire on this CD stems from the 1930s (including such pieces as "Minor Swing," "Tears" and "Sweet Chorus," all three of which were co-composed by Grappelli and guitarist Django Reinhardt) but Grappelli has retained his enthusiasm and creativity. Performing in a top-notch quartet with two guitars (Philip Catherine and Marc Fosset) and bassist Niels Pedersen, Grappelli is in excellent form and performs a joyous set of melodic swing. —*Scott Yanow*

Milford Graves

b. Aug. 20, 1941, New York, NY
Drums / Free Jazz
Milford Graves has been among the flashiest drummers in the free mode, known for skillful inclusion of Asian and African rhythmic ingredients into his solos. He studied Indian music extensively, including learning the tabla from Wasantha Singh. He has unfortunately not recorded much in recent years, especially on American labels. Graves played congas as a child, then switched to trap drums at 17, before his tabla studies with Singh. During the '60s, Graves worked with Giuseppi Logan and the New York Art Quartet. He recorded on ESP in the mid-'60s with Logan and was an original member of the Jazz Composers' Orchestra Association. Graves also played with Hugh Masekela and Miriam Makeba in the early '60s. His appearance in the Bill Dixon-sponsored concert series, "The October Revolution In Jazz," helped introduce Graves to a wider audience. He did two albums of duets with pianist Don Pullen at Yale in 1966. Graves worked regularly with Albert Ayler in 1967 and 1968, performing at the '67 Newport Festival. He also played with Hugh Glover and worked in a duo with Andrew Cyrille. During the '70s, Graves participated in a series of mid-'70s concerts called "Dialogue of the Drums" with Cyrille and Rashied Ali, including several shows in black neighborhoods. Graves taught at Bennington College alongside Bill Dixon in the '70s and toured Europe and Japan. During the '80s, he played in percussion ensembles with Cyrille, Kenny Clarke and Don Moye. Philly Joe Jones later replaced Clarke. —*Ron Wynn*

● **Milford Graves Percussion Ensemble** / Nov. 11, 1965 / ESP ✦✦✦✦

The Graves Pullen Duo / Apr. 30, 1966 / Pullen Graves Music ✦✦✦

Anita Gravine

b. Carbondale, PA
Vocals / Bop, Standards
Considering how exciting an album Anita Gravine's *I Always*

Knew was in 1985, it is surprising that she has not caught on yet as one of the top jazz singers. In the mid-'60s she sang with the bands of Larry Elgart, Buddy Morrow and Urbie Green. Gravine made her solo debut with *Dream Dancing* on Progressive in the early '80s; *I Always Knew* really displayed her appealing voice, solid sense of swing and versatility. But since then her only jazz recording, *Welcome to My Dream* (recorded in 1986 but not released on Jazz Alliance until 1993), was a disappointment due to weak material (songs from the Bob Hope/Bing Crosby *Road* pictures) and uninspired arrangements that take the songs too seriously. Hopefully, much more will be heard from Anita Gravine in the future. —*Scott Yanow*

Dream Dancing / Sep. 12, 1983–Sep. 13, 1983 / Progressive ✦✦✦✦

★ **I Always Knew** / Oct. 1984 / Stash ✦✦✦✦✦

Welcome to My Dream / Nov. 1986 / Jazz Alliance ✦✦
Anita Gravine is a particularly talented jazz singer, but this set (which was released for the first time in 1994) is a surprising dud. Gravine interprets ten songs from the Bing Crosby/Bob Hope road movies,but Michael Abene's arrangements for the small big band rob the mostly lightweight ditties of their good-natured humor and they cannot stand the glaring light given them as "contemporary art." Only "Moonlight Becomes You" became a standard and to hear songs such as "Road to Morocco" and "Good-Time Charley" given such serious treatment is unintentionally laughable. Anita Gravine deserves to be recorded under much more logical circumstances. —*Scott Yanow*

Wardell Gray

b. Feb. 13, 1921, Oklahoma City, OK, d. May 25, 1955, Las Vegas, NV
Tenor Saxophone / Bop, Swing
Wardell Gray was one of the top tenors to emerge during the bop era (along with Dexter Gordon and Teddy Edwards). His Lester Young-influenced tone made his playing attractive to swing musicians as well as younger modernists. He grew up in Detroit, playing in local bands as a teenager. Gray was with Earl Hines during 1943–45, recording with him (1945). That same year he moved to Los Angeles and he became a major part of the Central Avenue scene, having nightly tenor battles with Dexter Gordon; their recording of "The Chase" was popular. Gray recorded with Charlie Parker in 1947 and yet his style appealed to Benny Goodman with whom he played the following year. Among his own sessions, his solos on "Twisted" (1949) and "Farmer's Market" (1952) were turned into memorable vocalese by Annie Ross a few years later. Back in New York, Gray played and recorded with Tadd Dameron and the Count Basie septet and big band (1950–51); "Little Pony," his showcase with the Basie orchestra, is a classic. Gray was featured on some Norman Granz jam sessions ("Apple Jam" has a particularly heated solo) and recorded with Louie Bellson (1952–53). Ironically, Wardell Gray, who in the late '40s was an inspiration to some younger musicians due to his opposition to drug use, himself became involved in drugs and died mysteriously in Las Vegas on May 25, 1955, when he was just 34. —*Scott Yanow*

One for Prez / Nov. 23, 1946 / Black Lion ✦✦✦✦

Wardell Gray / Stan Hasselgard / Apr. 29, 1947–Sep. 1948 / Spotlite ✦✦✦✦
This historic Spotlite LP has live performances from 1947–48, important years in the history of bop. Wardell Gray is featured in a Los Angeles-based sextet with trumpeter Howard McGhee, altoist Sonny Criss and pianist Dodo Marmarosa for three lengthy versions of bop anthems; the tenor is showcased with the Count Basie Orchestra on six forward-looking selections and he teams up with the doomed clarinetist Stan Hasselgard in a sextet for two jams. The music is reasonably well-recorded considering its date and source, and the solos are frequently quite exciting. Jazz historians in particular are advised to search for this one. —*Scott Yanow*

★ **Wardell Gray Memorial, Vol. 1** / Nov. 11, 1949–1953 / Original Jazz Classics ✦✦✦✦✦
1949–1951. Legendary tenor is in sympathetic quartets and larger combos where he can duel at big. 1949, 1950, 1952, 1953 sessions in Detroit, LA (live at the Hula Hut) and NYC. Lots of bonus tracks on CD. Participants include Dexter Gordon, Art Mardigan, Art Farmer, Hampton Hawes, Al Haig, Frank Morgan and Teddy

Charles. A must-buy for veteran listeners and newcomers alike. — *Michael G. Nastos*

Wardell Gray Memorial, Vol. 2 / Nov. 11, 1949–Dec. 1951 / Original Jazz Classics ✦✦✦✦✦
Both this and the first volume were originally paired together in the '60s as one of the first two-fers initiated by Prestige. It was a terrific bargain then, a great bargain again almost 10 years later, when it was included in another two-fer, and now in single album incarnation the music remained fine. The material here all came from between Nov. 11, 1949 and Dec. 1951 and contained almost all of Gray's (tenor sax) Prestige material and some classics. —*Bob Rusch, Cadence*

Live at the Haig / Sep. 9, 1952 / Fresh Sound ✦✦✦✦
A hot 1952 session with an excellent lineup. Previously issued on Xanadu and Straight Ahead with different titles. —*Ron Wynn*

Bennie Green

b. Apr. 16, 1923, Chicago, IL, **d.** Mar. 23, 1977, San Diego, CA
Trombone, Saxophone / Bop, Swing
Bennie Green was one of the few trombonists of the 1950s who played in a style not influenced by J.J. Johnson (Bill Harris was another). His witty sound and full tone looked backwards to the swing era yet was open to the influence of R&B. After playing locally in Chicago, he was with the Earl Hines Orchestra during 1942–48 (except for two years in the military). Green gained some fame for his work with Charlie Ventura (1948–50) before joining Earl Hines' small group (1951–53). He then led his own group throughout the 1950s and '60s, using such sidemen as Cliff Smalls, Charlie Rouse, Eric Dixon, Paul Chambers, Louis Hayes, Sonny Clark, Gildo Mahones and Jimmy Forrest. Green recorded regularly as a leader for Prestige, Decca, Blue Note, Vee Jay, Time, Bethlehem and Jazzland during 1951–61 although only one further session (a matchup with Sonny Stitt on Cadet in 1964) took place. Bennie Green was with Duke Ellington for a few months in 1968–69 and then moved to Las Vegas where he spent his last years working in hotel bands, although he did emerge to play quite well at the 1972 Newport Jazz Festival in New York jam sessions. —*Scott Yanow*

● **Bennie Green Blows His Horn** / Jun. 10, 1955+Sep. 22, 1955 / Original Jazz Classics ✦✦✦✦
This is fun music. Bennie Green, one of the few trombonists of the 1950s not to sound somewhat like a J.J. Johnson clone, always had a likable and humorous style. He blends in well with tenor saxophonist Charlie Rouse on these standards, blues and jump tunes, two of which have group vocals. With a fine rhythm section (pianist Cliff Smalls, bassist Paul Chambers, drummer Osie Johnson and Candido on congas), Green and his band show that there is no reason that swinging jazz has to be viewed as overly intellectual and esoteric. This CD (a reissue of the original LP) is a fine example of Bennie Green's talents and winning musical personality. —*Scott Yanow*

With Art Farmer / Apr. 13, 1956 / Original Jazz Classics ✦✦✦
Trombonist Bennie Green and trumpeter Art Farmer (with the assistance of pianist Cliff Smalls, bassist Addison Farmer and drummer Philly Joe Jones) challenge each other on these five selections, which include an original apiece by the two horns and Smalls in addition to cheerful renditions of "My Blue Heaven" and "Gone with the Wind." The playing is not flawless on this CD reissue of a rather brief (under 34 minutes) LP, but the soloists take chances and the music is often exciting. It's recommended to straight-ahead jazz fans. —*Scott Yanow*

Walking Down / Jun. 29, 1956 / Original Jazz Classics ✦✦✦✦
The third of Bennie Green's three Prestige albums from 1955–56 features the personable trombonist in a quintet with the young tenor saxophonist Eric Dixon (here showing a strong Paul Gonsalves influence) and an obscure but swinging rhythm section (pianist Lloyd Mayers, bassist Sonny Wellesley and drummer Bill English). The solos are colorful if occasionally stumbling, and the arrangements of the four standards and Green's "East of the Little Big Horn" have their share of surprises; "Walkin' " and "The Things We Did Last Summer" are taken at two different tempos while "It's You or No One," normally a ballad, really cooks. This straight CD reissue of the original LP is worth picking up. —*Scott Yanow*

The Swingin'est / Nov. 12, 1958 / Vee-Jay ✦✦
The emphasis is on the blues and very basic chord changes on this

relaxed jam session. With trombonist Bennie Green leading an octet that also includes the tenors of Gene Ammons and Frank Foster, trumpeter Nat Adderley, Frank Wess on tenor and flute and a rhythm section led by pianist Tommy Flanagan, everyone has plenty of opportunities to solo. Due to the similarity of the material plus three alternate takes that have been added to augment the original program, it is advisable to listen to this CD in small doses. —*Scott Yanow*

Benny Green

b. Apr. 4, 1963, New York, NY
Piano / Hard Bop
Although not yet an innovator himself, Benny Green has managed to combine the styles of Bobby Timmons, Wynton Kelly, Gene Harris and especially Oscar Peterson in his playing; his fast octave runs are often wondrous. He grew up in Berkeley and played as a teenager with Joe Henderson and Woody Shaw. After moving to New York he spent important periods with Betty Carter (1983–87) and Art Blakey's Jazz Messengers (1987–89), becoming quite well-known during the latter association. In addition to working with Freddie Hubbard, Green popped up in many bop-oriented settings for a few years before joining Ray Brown's Trio in 1992. At the same time, he has worked with his own trio which originally included Christian McBride and Carl Allen. When Oscar Peterson in 1992 was asked to name his protege for a concert, Green was his choice. Benny Green has recorded for Criss Cross and Blue Note in addition to his work with Ray Brown on Telarc and his earlier Blakey dates. —*Scott Yanow*

Prelude / Feb. 22, 1988 / Criss Cross ✦✦✦

In This Direction / Dec. 29, 1988–Jan. 2, 1989 / Criss Cross ✦✦✦✦
Good set from ranking young jazz pianist, along with Geoff Keezer. Green, a former Messenger, plays anything from standards to originals with flair, and his solos are always inventive and nicely crafted. —*Ron Wynn*

Lineage / Jan. 30, 1990–Feb. 1, 1990 / Blue Note ✦✦✦✦
Debut work, with this former Jazz Messenger forging his identity as a leader. —*Ron Wynn*

Greens / Mar. 4, 1991–Mar. 5, 1991 / Blue Note ✦✦✦

★ **Testifyin'!: Live at the Village Vanguard** / Nov. 1991 / Blue Note ✦✦✦✦✦
A former member of Betty Carter's band, Green shows on this set that the word on him was correct; he's both an aggressive and sensitive stylist, able to rip through songs and make quick, yet correct chord changes. Yet he can also play a passionate ballad and not rush through it, instead developing and then completing his solos impressively. —*Ron Wynn*

That's Right! / Dec. 21, 1992–Dec. 23, 1992 / Blue Note ✦✦✦✦✦
At the time of this 1992 recording, Benny Green had developed into a masterful pianist who thought fast, swung hard and played with soul, mixing together Oscar Peterson, Gene Harris and Bobby Timmons. The only problem was that his music had become somewhat predictable, sticking closely to the boundaries of hard bop circa 1962. In his trio with bassist Christian McBride and drummer Carl Allen, Green is heard in top form for the period (his version of Bud Powell's "Celia" is particularly memorable) and performs a program that is easily recommended to lovers of bop. Benny Green plays with such enthusiasm and joy that it almost sounds as if he had invented the style. —*Scott Yanow*

Place To Be / Mar.–May, 1994 / Blue Note ✦✦✦✦

Bunky Green

b. Apr. 23, 1935, Milwaukee, WI
Alto Saxophone / Hard Bop, Post-Bop
Bunky Green has long had his own sound, but unfortunately most of his recordings have gone long out of print as he has conducted a career as an educator (including a term as the president of the International Association of Jazz Educators). After playing locally, in 1960 he had a stint with Charles Mingus. That year Green moved to Chicago where he played with Ira Sullivan, Andrew Hill, Louie Bellson, Yusef Lateef and Sonny Stitt among others. Originally strongly influenced by Charlie Parker, Green spent a period reassessing his style and studying, emerging with a much more distinctive sound. He recorded for Exodus (1960) and Argo (1964–66) but his best work was his mid-to-late-'70s recordings for Vanguard and a 1989 session for Delos. A self-

described "inside/outside" player, Bunky Green has had an influence on the styles of Steve Coleman and Greg Osby. —*Scott Yanow*

Transformation / Nov. 1976 / Vanguard ✦✦✦✦

Places We've Never Been / Feb. 21, 1979+Feb. 22, 1979 / Vanguard ✦✦✦✦✦
With Randy Brecker (tpt), Al Dailey Trio. Modal "East & West" shows alto saxophonist at his improvisational best. —*Michael G. Nastos*

In Love Again / Jun. 27, 1987–Jun. 28, 1987 / Mark ✦✦✦✦
Quintet with trumpeter Willie Thomas. Three by saxophonist Green, one by Thomas, one co-written by the pair, one standard ("You Stepped out of a Dream"). —*Michael G. Nastos*

☆ **Healing the Pain** / Dec. 13, 1989–Dec. 14, 1989 / Delos ✦✦✦✦✦
With Billy Childs Trio, sharp drummer Ralph Penland and the great bassist Art Davis. All standards save two are Bucky's originals. A bright alto voice shines through. —*Michael G. Nastos*

Charlie Green

b. 1900, Omaha, NE, d. 1936, New York, NY
Trombone / Classic Jazz, Blues
One of the finest early trombonists and the first strong jazz soloist in the Fletcher Henderson Orchestra (joining slightly before Louis Armstrong), Charlie Green played locally in Omaha (1920–23) before his two stints with Henderson (July 1924–April 1926 and late 1928–spring 1929). A superior blues player who could also swing fairly early, Green starred on several classic Bessie Smith recordings (including one called "Trombone Cholly"), recorded in the 1920s with several other blues singers and also worked with the bands of Benny Carter (1929–31 and 1933), Chick Webb (several times during 1930–34), Don Redman (1932) and at the end with Kaiser Marshall. His premature death was from passing out on his doorstep on a winter night and freezing to death. —*Scott Yanow*

Freddie Green

b. Mar. 31, 1911, Charleston, SC, d. Mar. 1, 1987, Las Vegas, NV
Guitar / Swing
Freddie Green was known throughout his long career as the definitive rhythm guitarist. He rarely soloed (briefly on a few records early on), he stuck to acoustic guitar and was often more felt than heard. Although he had originally played banjo, Green was playing guitar in New York in early 1937 when producer John Hammond heard him and immediately recommended him to Count Basie. A quick audition and Green had the job, forming a classic rhythm section with Basie, Walter Page and Jo Jones. After 13 years with the orchestra, Green was not originally included in Basie's small group in 1950, but one night sat down uninvited on the bandstand and never left! He stayed with the band even after its leader's death, making a recording with Dianne Schuur and the Frank Foster-led orchestra in 1987 shortly before he passed on after nearly 50 years of service. Freddie Green also composed "Corner Pocket" (later renamed "Until I Met You" for the vocal version) and "Down for Double." —*Scott Yanow*

Natural Rhythm / Feb. 3, 1955+Dec. 18, 1955 / Bluebird ✦✦✦✦
Green's *Mr. Rhythm* & Al Cohn's *Natural Seven* albums combined. A wonderful collaboration between Freddie Green (away from the Basie band) and Al Cohn (ts). —*Ron Wynn*

Grant Green

b. Jun. 6, 1931, St. Louis, MO, d. Jan. 31, 1979, New York, NY
Guitar / Hard Bop, Soul Jazz
A severely underrated player during his lifetime, Grant Green had a beautiful sound and excellent guitar skills. He maintained that he listened to horn players rather than other guitarists, and his single-note linearity and style, which avoided chordal playing, was unique. His extensive foundation in R&B combined with a mastery of bebop and simplicity that put expressiveness ahead of technical expertise. Green was a superb blues interpreter, and his later material was predominantly blues and R&B, though he was also a wondrous ballad and standards soloist. He was a particular admirer of Charlie Parker, and his phrasing often reflected it. Green played in the '50s with Jimmy Forrest, Harry Edison and Lou Donaldson. He also collaborated with many organists, among them Brother Jack McDuff, Sam Lazar, Baby Face Willette, Gloria Coleman, Big John Patton and Larry Young. During the early '60s,

both his fluid, tasteful playing in organ/guitar/drum combos and his other dates for Blue Note established Green as a star, though he seldom got the critical respect given other players. Green played with Stanley Turrentine, Dave Bailey, Yusef Lateef, Joe Henderson, Hank Mobley, Herbie Hancock, McCoy Tyner and Elvin Jones. Sadly, drug problems interrupted his career in the '60s and undoubtedly contributed to the illness he suffered in the late '70s. Green was hospitalized in 1978 and died a year later. Despite some rather uneven LPs near the end of his career, the great body of his work represents marvelous soul jazz, bebop and blues. —*Ron Wynn and Michael Erlewine*

Grant's First Stand / Jan. 28, 1961 / Blue Note ✦✦✦

Green Blues / Mar. 15, 1961 / Black Lion ✦✦✦
Originally issued on *Jazztime* under Dave Bailey's name and now reissued in this format. This is early Green, his second session, and the music is straight-ahead mainstream jazz with a bluesy flavor. —*Michael Erlewine*

Green Street / Apr. 1, 1961 / Blue Note ✦✦✦✦
Most of guitarist Grant Green's recordings of the 1960s feature him in larger groups, making this trio outing with bassist Ben Tucker and drummer Dave Bailey (a CD reissue of the original LP plus two added alternate takes) a strong showcase for his playing. Green, whose main competitor on guitar at the time was Wes Montgomery, already had his own singing sound and a highly individual hornlike approach. He stretches out on a full set of attractive originals plus "Round Midnight" and "Alone Together," so this reissue is an excellent introduction to his appealing and hard-swinging style. —*Scott Yanow*

Sunday Mornin' / Jun. 4, 1961 / Blue Note ✦✦✦

Grantstand / Aug. 1, 1961 / Blue Note ✦✦✦✦
A quartet session with Yusef Lateef (ts, fl) and vintage Jack McDuff on the Hammond organ. The 15-minute "Blues in Maude's Flat" is very nice indeed, and "My Funny Valentine" (with Lateef on flute) is just plain lovely. No one does standards like Green. — *Michael Erlewine*

★ **Complete Blue Note with Sonny Clark** / Dec. 23, 1961–Sep. 7, 1962 / Mosaic ✦✦✦✦✦
Guitarist Grant Green and pianist Sonny Clark recorded together on five separate occasions during the 1961–62 period, but virtually none of the music was released domestically until decades later. These performances were clearly lost in the shuffle for the solos are of a consistent high quality and the programs were well-paced and swinging. Now on this Mosaic limited-edition, four-CD boxed set, the long-lost music (much of which had been previously available only in Japan) is saved for posterity. Green and Clark blend together well, tenor saxophonist Ike Quebec joins their quartet for one session and the final two numbers add Latin percussion. All of this music should be easily enjoyed by hard bop fans. Includes Blue Note albums *Gooden's Corner, Nigeria, Oleo, Born to Be Blue* (w/ Ike Quebec), plus unissued tracks. —*Scott Yanow*

The Latin Bit / Apr. 26, 1962 / Blue Note ✦✦✦

Goin' West / Nov. 30, 1962 / Blue Note ✦✦✦

Feelin' the Spirit / Dec. 21, 1962 / Blue Note ✦✦✦✦
An entire album of spirituals—all jazz instrumentals. Green, already a bluesy guitarist, lets himself out in the gospel format. The result is an album that remains true to both the jazz and gospel genres. Unique. —*Michael Erlewine*

Am I Blue? / May 16, 1963 / Blue Note ✦✦✦✦

★ **Idle Moments** / Nov. 4, 1963+Nov. 11, 1963 / Blue Note ✦✦✦✦✦
Excellent album, with Green in good form. Bobby Hutcherson (vib) in the group produces a somewhat different sound than the usual Green album, so make a note of that. Joe Henderson (ts) is hot. —*Michael Erlewine*

☆ **Matador** / May 20, 1964 / Blue Note ✦✦✦✦✦
With Coltrane sidemen McCoy Tyner (p) and Elvin Jones (d)—still with Coltrane at the time. Green tackles the Coltrane hit "My Favorite Things" and pulls it off in his own style. This is a fine album. —*Michael Erlewine*

Solid / Jun. 12, 1964 / Blue Note ✦✦✦✦✦
Not released until 1979, this set contains more challenging material than many of guitarist Grant Green's other Blue Note sessions. In a state-of-the-art sextet with tenor saxophonist Joe Henderson, altoist James Spaulding, pianist McCoy Tyner, bassist Bob Cranshaw and drummer Elvin Jones, Green performs tunes by Duke Pearson, George Russell ("Ezz-thetic"), Sonny Rollins,

Henderson ("The Kicker") and his own "Grant's Tune." Perhaps this music was considered too uncommercial initially or maybe it was simply lost in the shuffle. In any case, this is one of Grant Green's finer recordings. —*Scott Yanow*

His Majesty, King Funk / May 26, 1965 / Verve ♦♦♦

Iron City / 1967 / Muse ♦♦♦
Powerhouse trio recordings, with stomping organ from Big John Patton. —*Ron Wynn*

Carryin' on / Oct. 3, 1969 / Blue Note ♦♦
Grant Green's recording career was just starting to slip at the time of this release although the talented guitarist always played as well as he could under the circumstances. He manages to uplift the dated R&B-ish and pop material a bit, but his backup band (which includes tenor saxophonist Claude Bartee and either Clarence Palmer or Earl Neal Creque on electric piano) seems content to repeat the same grooves endlessly and play it safe, making this CD reissue of rather limited interest. —*Scott Yanow*

Green Is Beautiful / Jan. 30, 1970 / Blue Note ♦♦♦
Of the five songs included on this CD reissue, the first three are one-chord vamps; none of these renditions were destined to be remembered as classics. "Ain't It Funky Now" makes the set worthwhile for it has tenor saxophonist Claude Bartee doing a close imitation of Eddie Harris and trumpeter Blue Mitchell taking an exciting solo. But the unimaginative material in general does not really inspire guitarist Grant Green and keeps this CD from being too essential. —*Scott Yanow*

Alive! / Aug. 15, 1970 / Blue Note ♦♦
Grant Green was one of the most consistent and versatile guitarists of the 1960s, but once 1970 came around his recording career became quite erratic. This CD reissue brings back a rather weak effort with Green's sextet (which at time included Claude Bartee on tenor, vibraphonist William Bivens and either Ronnie Foster or Earl Neal Creque on organ) playing R&B cliches while laying forever on one chord. There are many more rewarding Grant Green sets than this one. —*Scott Yanow*

Live at the Lighthouse / Apr. 21, 1972 / Blue Note ♦♦♦

Urbie Green (Urbam Clifford Green)
b. Aug. 8, 1926, Mobile, AL
Trombone / Swing, Bop
A fine jazz player with a beautiful tone who has spent most of his career in the studios, Urbie Green is highly respected by his fellow trombonists. He started playing when he was 12, was with the big bands of Tommy Reynolds, Bob Strong and Frankie Carle as a teenager and worked with Gene Krupa during 1947–50. Green had a stint with Woody Herman's Third Herd, appeared on some of the famous Buck Clayton Jam Sessions (1953–54) and was with Benny Goodman off and on during 1955–57. He played with Count Basie in 1963 and spent a period in the 1960s fronting the Tommy Dorsey ghost band (1966–67), but has mostly stuck to studio work. Urbie Green recorded frequently as a leader in the 1950s up to 1963 (for Blue Note, Vanguard, Bethlehem, ABC-Paramount and dance-band-oriented records for RCA and Command). He has appeared much less often in jazz settings since then, but did make two albums for CTI in 1976–77. —*Scott Yanow*

Urbie Green Septet / Sep. 27, 1953 / Blue Note ♦♦♦

Let's Face the Music and Dance / Dec. 19, 1957–Dec. 23, 1957 / Fresh Sound ♦♦♦

● **The Fox** / Jul. 1976–Nov. 1976 / CTI ♦♦♦♦

Sonny Greenwich (Herbert Lawrence Greennidge)
b. Jan. 1, 1936, Hamilton, Canada
Guitar / Avant-Garde
One of Canada's top guitarists, the eccentric playing of Sonny Greenwich is always stimulating and usually surprising. He played locally in Toronto, appeared with Charles Lloyd in New York (1965), toured with John Handy (1966–67) and recorded with Hank Mobley (1967). Greenwich came close to joining Miles Davis in 1969, settled in Quebec (he moved to Montreal in 1974) and has since led sessions for Sackville, PM, Justin Time and his own Kleo label. —*Scott Yanow*

● **Live at Sweet Basil** / 1987 / JustIn Time ♦♦♦♦♦
Live club date in New York City. Three originals and one standard with quartet. This man is an unsung hero, revered by guitarists. —*Michael G. Nastos*

Standard Idioms / Nov. 21, 1991+Sep. 15, 1992 / Kleo ♦♦♦♦

Hymn to the Earth / Oct. 1994 / Kleo ♦♦♦
Sonny Greenwich, long considered one of Canada's most consistently creative guitarists, is very relaxed on this recording for his label Kleo. Simple rhythms and vamps are the basis for most of the originals and Greenwich plays quite slow and melodically, letting his notes really ring while constructing improvisations that develop gradually. Backed by a fine rhythm section, Greenwich's melancholy flights are given such titles as "Hymn to the Earth," "Nature Prays" and "Invocation," but the music is not of the one-mood new age variety. Some of the performances could have been briefer and the development a bit quicker but, except for a throwaway vocal by Ernie Nelson on "Serengeti," Greenwich's latest project (which sometimes crosses over into folk and world music) is rewarding. —*Scott Yanow*

Sonny Greer
b. Dec. 13, 1895, Long Branch, NJ, d. Mar. 23, 1982, New York, NY
Drums / Swing
He was never the greatest timekeeper, but Sonny Greer was perfect for Duke Ellington's Orchestra during 1924–51, adding color and class to the rhythm section. He met Ellington in 1919 when he was a member of the Howard Theatre's orchestra in Washington, D.C. Greer visited New York for the first time with Elmer Snowden and was an original member of Duke's Washingtonians, which was a five-piece group at its start. Greer's playing grew with the band and his large array of sounds (using a drum set that included a gong, chimes, timpani and vibes) added to the Ellington band's "jungle sound." He was with the orchestra until 1951 when, after a few arguments with Duke over his drinking and increasing unreliability, Greer left to join Johnny Hodges' new group. He later worked with Red Allen, Tyree Glenn and J.C. Higginbottham, in 1967 led his own band and played with Brooks Kerr's trio in the 1970s. —*Scott Yanow*

Al Grey
b. Jun. 6, 1925, Aldie, VA
Trombone / Bop, Swing
Al Grey's trademark phrases and often-humorous use of the plunger mute have long made him quite distinctive. After getting out of the service, he was with the orchestras of Benny Carter (1945–46), Jimmie Lunceford (1946–47), Lucky Millinder and Lionel Hampton (off and on during 1948–53). Grey was a well-featured soloist with the classic Dizzy Gillespie globetrotting orchestra during 1956–57 (taking an exciting solo at the 1957 Newport Jazz Festival on a blazing version of "Cool Breeze"). He was with Count Basie's Orchestra on three separate occasions (1957–61, 1964–66 and 1971–77), led a band with Billy Mitchell in the early '60s and had a group with Jimmy Forrest after leaving Count in 1977. In recent years Grey has performed and recorded often with Clark Terry, made a CD with the Statesmen of Jazz and, for a time, led a quintet that featured his son Mike Grey on second trombone. Al Grey recorded as a leader for Argo (1959–64), Tangerine, Black & Blue, Stash, Chiaroscuro and Capri and co-led an excellent Pablo date in 1983 with J.J. Johnson. —*Scott Yanow*

Struttin' and Shoutin' / Aug. 30, 1976 / Columbia ♦♦♦
Trombonist Al Grey, a master of the wah-wah mute, had a rare opportunity to record with a major label in 1976. Needless to say, Columbia almost lost the master, and when it was finally released in 1983, one of the principals (tenor saxophonist Jimmy Forrest) had already passed away. Despite its delayed arrival, this happy set (dominated by soulful blues but also including two standards) was worth the wait. Grey and Forrest are heard as part of a nonet and are the principal soloists, although there are brief spots for trumpeter Waymond Reed and pianist Ray Bryant. This out-of-print LP will be hard to find, but is worth picking up. —*Scott Yanow*

★ **Things Are Getting Better All the Time** / 1983 / Original Jazz Classics ♦♦♦♦♦

Al Grey and Jesper Thilo Quintet / Aug. 1986 / Storyville ♦♦♦♦

The New Al Grey Quintet / May 16, 1988–May 17, 1988 / Chiaroscuro ♦♦♦♦

Al Meets Bjarne / Aug. 5, 1988 / Gemini ♦♦♦♦
Veteran trombonist Al Grey teams up with the talented (if

obscure) Norwegian tenor player Bjarne Nerem and the Norman Simmons Trio (with pianist Simmons, bassist Paul West and drummer Gerryck King) on this informal session for the Norwegian Gemini label. Nerem's playing is a bit reminiscent of Coleman Hawkins and he works well with Grey who is clearly the leader. In addition to two Simmons originals and Grey's blues "Al Meets Bjarne," the quintet performs six swing standards (including "Lester Leaps In," "Tangerine" and "Stompin' at the Savoy") and the results are easily enjoyable and typically swinging. — *Scott Yanow*

Fab / Feb. 4, 1990+Feb. 7, 1990 / Capri ✦✦✦✦

Live at the Floating Jazz Festival / Oct. 22, 1990–Oct. 25, 1990 / Chiaroscuro ✦✦✦

Center Piece, Live at the Blue Note / Mar. 23, 1995–Mar. 26, 1995 / Telarc Jazz ✦✦✦

Johnny Griffin

b. Apr. 24, 1928, Chicago, IL
Tenor Saxophone / Bop, Hard Bop

Once accurately billed as "the world's fastest saxophonist," Johnny Griffin (an influence tonewise on Rahsaan Roland Kirk) has been one of the top bop-oriented tenors since the mid-'50s. He gained early experience playing with the bands of Lionel Hampton (1945–47) and Joe Morris (1947–50) and also jammed regularly with Thelonious Monk and Bud Powell. After serving in the Army (1951–53), Griffin spent a few years in Chicago (recording his first full album for Argo) and then moved to New York in 1956. He held his own against fellow tenors John Coltrane and Hank Mobley in a classic Blue Note album, was with Art Blakey's Jazz Messengers in 1957 and proved to be perfect with the Thelonious Monk Quartet in 1958 where he really ripped through the complex chord changes with ease. During 1960–62, Griffin co-led a "tough tenor" group with Eddie "Lockjaw" Davis. He emigrated to Europe in 1963 and became a fixture on the Paris jazz scene both as a bandleader and a major soloist with the Kenny Clarke-Francy Boland Big Band. In 1973 Johnny Griffin moved to the Netherlands, but has remained a constant world traveller, visiting the U.S. often and recording for many labels including Blue Note, Riverside, Atlantic, SteepleChase, Black Lion, Antilles, Verve and some European companies. — *Scott Yanow*

Introducing Johnny Griffin / Apr. 17, 1956 / Blue Note ✦✦✦✦
A seminal date that shows Griffin's speed, technique and power. — *Ron Wynn*

★ **A Blowing Session** / Apr. 6, 1957 / Blue Note ✦✦✦✦✦
More than just a mere "blowing session," these four jams (on a pair of standards and two Johnny Griffin compositions) match together three very different tenor stylists: Griffin, Hank Mobley and John Coltrane. Although the solos and trade-offs are often quite combative, the result is a three-way deadheat, for each of these tenor greats has a different approach and a distinctive sound. Of all of the 1950s jam sessions, this is one of the most successful and exciting. — *Scott Yanow*

★ **The Congregation** / Oct. 13, 1957 / Blue Note ✦✦✦✦✦
The great tenor saxophonist Johnny Griffin is heard in top form on this near-classic quartet set. Assisted by pianist Sonny Clark, bassist Paul Chambers and drummer Kenny Dennis, Griffin is exuberant on "The Congregation" (which is reminiscent of Horace Silver's "The Preacher"), thoughtful on the ballads and swinging throughout. It's recommended for bop collectors. — *Scott Yanow*

Johnny Griffin Sextet / Feb. 25, 1958 / Original Jazz Classics ✦✦✦✦
The great tenor Johnny Griffin made his debut on Riverside with this sextet set which has been reissued on CD in the OJC series. Griffin is teamed with trumpeter Donald Byrd, baritonist Pepper Adams, pianist Kenny Drew, bassist Wilbur Ware and drummer Philly Joe Jones for three obscure tunes, the ballad "What's New" and a cooking version of "Woody 'n You." High quality hard bop from some of the best. — *Scott Yanow*

Way Out! / Feb. 26, 1958–Feb. 27, 1958 / Original Jazz Classics ✦✦✦✦
This formerly obscure quartet set by tenor saxophonist Johnny Griffin (reissued on CD in the OJC series) features the fiery soloist on five little-known originals written by Chicagoans plus a burning version of "Cherokee." Virtually all of Griffin's recordings are worth getting and, with the assistance of pianist Kenny Drew,

bassist Wilbur Ware and drummer Philly Joe Jones, the tenor is in superior form for this spirited date. — *Scott Yanow*

The Little Giant / Aug. 4, 1959–Aug. 5, 1959 / Original Jazz Classics ✦✦✦

The Big Soul Band / May 24, 1960–Jun. 3, 1960 / Original Jazz Classics ✦✦✦
Tenor saxophonist Johnny Griffin is showcased with a ten-piece group on this CD reissue of a Riverside LP, which is augmented by a previously unreleased version of "Wade in the Water." The repertoire is a bit unusual with some spirituals (including "Nobody Knows the Trouble I've Seen" and "Deep River"), a tune apiece by Bobby Timmons ("So Tired") and Junior Mance and three originals from Norman Simmons who arranged all of the selections. Trumpeter Clark Terry and trombonists Matthew Gee and Julian Priester have some short solos, but the emphasis is on the leader who is in typically spirited and passionate form. — *Scott Yanow*

Jazz Party / Sep. 27, 1960 / Riverside ✦✦✦

Griff and Lock / Nov. 4, 1960+Nov. 10, 1960 / Original Jazz Classics ✦✦✦✦
For a couple of years in the early '60s, tenors Johnny Griffin and Eddie "Lockjaw" Davis co-led a popular quintet, jamming bop standards and occasional originals. Although their sounds were very different (one never had trouble telling them apart), their styles were quite complementary and their combative approaches constantly inspired each other to some heated playing. This former Jazzland LP finds the tough tenors at their best. — *Scott Yanow*

Toughest Tenors / Nov. 4, 1960–Feb. 5, 1962 / Milestone ✦✦✦
During the early '60s, Johnny Griffin and Eddie "Lockjaw" Davis matched forces and put together a consistently exciting quintet. The two tenors (both of whom had very distinctive sounds) brought out the best in each other in these frequently combative encounters. This two-LP set has 13 selections taken from five separate albums and gives one a well-rounded portrait of the legendary group. The music ranges from bop standards to a trio of Thelonious Monk tunes. — *Scott Yanow*

White Gardenia / Jul. 13, 1961–Jul. 17, 1961 / Original Jazz Classics ✦✦✦
Tenor saxophonist Johnny Griffin pays tribute to Billie Holiday, who had died exactly two years earlier, on this ballad-oriented set, which has been reissued on CD. Griffin is joined by a brass section (either five or seven pieces), plus a rhythm section and strings (the latter dominated by cellos), for his warm interpretations of nine songs associated with Billie Holiday, plus his original "White Gardenia." The arrangements, provided by Melba Liston and Norman Simmons, are tasteful, and the lyrical music is well-performed, if not overly memorable. Worth checking out. — *Scott Yanow*

Tough Tenor Favorites / Feb. 5, 1962 / Original Jazz Classics ✦✦✦✦
Johnny Griffin and Eddie "Lockjaw" Davis, the two "tough tenors" in question, always made for an exciting team. With pianist Horace Parlan, bassist Buddy Catlett and drummer Ben Riley completing the quintet for this CD reissue of a Jazzland date from 1962, Griff and Lockjaw are in top form and quite competitive on a variety of standards. Highlights include "Blue Lou," "Ow," "I Wished on the Moon" and "From This Moment On." The main winner in these fiery tenor "battles" is the listener! — *Scott Yanow*

The Man I Love / Mar. 30, 1967–Mar. 31, 1967 / Black Lion ✦✦✦✦

You Leave Me Breathless / Mar. 30, 1967–Mar. 31, 1967 / Black Lion ✦✦✦✦

The Jams Are Coming / Dec. 1975–Oct. 1977 / Timeless ✦✦✦

Return of the Griffin / Oct. 17, 1978 / Galaxy ✦✦✦✦
Johnny Griffin recorded this studio album during his first visit to the United States in 15 years. Accompanied by a very supportive trio (pianist Ronnie Mathews, bassist Ray Drummond and drummer Keith Copeland), the great tenor is in frequently exuberant form on such tunes as "Autumn Leaves," his own "A Monk's Dream" and the funky "The Way It Is." Long one of the underrated masters, Johnny Griffin is heard at the peak of his powers on this modern bop session. — *Scott Yanow*

★ **Bush Dance** / Oct. 18, 1978–Oct. 19, 1978 / Galaxy ✦✦✦✦✦
Johnny Griffin has (at least since the mid-'50s) been one of the masters of the tenor sax, although consistently underrated. This

studio session is one of his great achievements, particularly a fascinating (and cleverly constructed) 17-minute version of "A Night in Tunisia." Whether it be his own "The Jams Are Coming" or a lyrical version of the veteran ballad "Since I Fell for You," Griffin (joined here by guitarist George Freeman, bassist Sam Jones, drummer Albert Heath and percussionist Kenneth Nash) is inspired and quite creative throughout this highly recommended gem. —*Scott Yanow*

NYC Underground / Jul. 6, 1979–Jul. 7, 1979 / Galaxy ✦✦✦
To the Ladies / Nov. 27, 1979–Nov. 28, 1979 / Galaxy ✦✦✦
Call It Whachawana / Jul. 25, 1983–Jul. 26, 1983 / Galaxy ✦✦✦✦
The emphasis is on ballads and slower tempos on this often-exquisite outing by tenor saxophonist Johnny Griffin. With strong support from the young rhythm section (pianist Mulgrew Miller, bassist Curtis Lundy and drummer Kenny Washington), Griffin is heard at his best on a definitive version of "Lover Man," recalls his days (25 years earlier) with Thelonious Monk on "I Mean You" and introduces two recent originals. Superlative music by a masterful player. —*Scott Yanow*

The Cat / Oct. 26, 1990-Oct. 29, 1990 / Antilles ✦✦✦✦
3 Dances of Passion / Apr. 29, 1992-Apr. 30, 1992 / Antilles ✦✦✦
Chicago, New York, Paris / 1995 / Verve ✦✦✦✦

Mario Grigorov

b. 1963, Sofia, Bulgaria
Piano / Post-Bop
Three days after arriving in the United States in 1992, Mario Grigorov was trying out some instruments in a piano store when Bob James walked in, was very impressed and soon signed him to Reprise! Before that remarkable event took place, Grigorov had had extensive classical training in Bulgaria, Iran, East Germany and Austria. By the time his family relocated to Australia, Grigorov was becoming much more interested in jazz and rock. He had a successful composing and recording company, doing a great deal of scoring for films and television, but felt dissatisfied from an artistic level. Grigorov moved to the U.S., met James, recorded *Rhymes with Orange* for Reprise and went out on tour. A virtuoso player, Mario Grigorov infuses his complex but generally melodic improvisations with strong indications of both his classical background and his Bulgarian heritage. —*Scott Yanow*

● **Rhymes With Orange** / 1994 / Reprise ✦✦✦✦✦
The classically trained pianist Mario Grigorov (who is joined on some tracks by bassist Brian Bromberg and percussionist Glen Velez) makes his American debut on this impressive effort. A virtuoso with a very strong classical influence but the ability to improvise masterfully, Grigorov reworks "Body and Soul" and performs 11 of his originals. If he sticks to jazz, he has a great future. —*Scott Yanow*

Henry Grimes

b. Nov. 3, 1935, Philadelphia, PA
Bass / Free Jazz, Hard Bop
In 1967 at the height of the free jazz movement, one of its finest bassists Henry Grimes disappeared, dropping out of music permanently. After attending Juilliard in the 1950s, Grimes toured with Arnett Cobb and Willis Jackson and played with the many talented young players in the Philadelphia scene of the mid-'50s. He was with Anita O'Day and Sonny Rollins in 1957 and a member of Gerry Mulligan's Quartet during 1957-58. A measure of his versatility is that, at the 1958 Newport Jazz Festival, Grimes played with Benny Goodman's Orchestra, Lee Konitz, Sonny Rollins and Thelonious Monk. After stints with Lennie Tristano and Rollins, Grimes became part of the free jazz movement, playing with Cecil Taylor (off and on during 1961-66), Perry Robinson, Rollins again, Albert Ayler (1964-66) and Don Cherry, leading one session of his own for ESP (1965). And then in 1967 (for reasons that are still unclear) Henry Grimes, who was still only 31, left jazz. —*Scott Yanow*

Henry Grimes Trio / Dec. 28, 1965 / ESP ✦✦✦✦

Tiny Grimes (Lloyd Grimes)

b. Jul. 7, 1916, Newport News, VA, d. Mar. 4, 1989, New York, NY
Guitar / Bop, Early R&B
Tiny Grimes was one of the earliest jazz electric guitarists to be influenced by Charlie Christian and he developed his own bluish

swinging style. Early on he was a drummer and worked as a pianist in Washington. In 1938 he started playing electric guitar, and two years later he was playing in a popular jive group, the Cats and a Fiddle. During 1943-44 Grimes was part of a classic Art Tatum Trio, which also included Slam Stewart. In September 1944 he led his first record date, using Charlie Parker; highlights include the instrumental "Red Cross" and Grimes' vocal on "Romance Without Finance (Is a Nuisance)." He also recorded for Blue Note in 1946 and then put together an R&B-oriented group, "the Rockin' Highlanders," that featured the tenor of Red Prysock during 1948-52. Although maintaining a fairly low profile, Tiny Grimes was active up until his death, playing in an unchanged swing/bop transitional style and recording as a leader for such labels as Prestige/Swingville, Black & Blue, Muse and Sonet. —*Scott Yanow*

Blues Groove / Feb. 28, 1958 / Original Jazz Classics ✦✦✦
Callin' the Blues / Jul. 18, 1958 / Original Jazz Classics ✦✦✦✦
Long, informal, laid-back jams. Good guitar, as always, in a jazzier vein than his early work. —*Myles Boisen*

● **Tiny in Swingsville** / Aug. 13, 1959 / Original Jazz Classics ✦✦✦✦✦
Guitarist Tiny Grimes was in a bit of obscurity when he had the opportunity to first record for Prestige in 1958. This particular CD (a reissue of the original LP) was the final of his three Prestige albums and it really puts the focus on Grimes' bluish but swinging guitar playing. With the strong assistance of Jerome Richardson (who is in top form on flute, tenor and baritone), pianist Ray Bryant, bassist Wendell Marshall and drummer Art Taylor, Grimes is heard in excellent form on "Annie Laurie," his "Durn Tootin,' " "Ain't Misbehavin' ," "Frankie and Johnnie" and a couple of original blues. —*Scott Yanow*

Profoundly Blue / Mar. 6, 1973 / Muse ✦✦✦
The veteran swing guitarist Tiny Grimes had relatively few chances to record during the '60s and '70s, particularly for American labels. This enjoyable outing for Muse features Grimes in a sextet with tenor saxophonist Houston Person and pianist Harold Mabern; these versions of "Profoundly Blue" and "Tiny's Exercise" are among the highpoints. Grimes also takes an effective vocal on the blues "Backslider," although the use of electric bass and congas makes the music seem a bit dated in spots. —*Scott Yanow*

Some Groovy Fours / May 13, 1974 / Black & Blue ✦✦✦

Don Grolnick

b. Sept. 23, 1947, Brooklyn, NY
Piano / Post-Bop
Don Grolnick has thus far been a subtle and rather underrated pianist, but his flexibility and talents have made him well-known to his fellow musicians. Grolnick played in rock bands while a teenager but was always interested in jazz. He worked in the early fusion group Dreams (1969-71), the Brecker Brothers (starting in 1975) and in the early '80s with Steps Ahead. He has long been a busy session musician often utilized by pop singers. In the 1980s, Grolnick appeared in many settings including with Joe Farrell, George Benson, Peter Erskine, David Sanborn, John Scofield, Mike Stern and the Bob Mintzer big band. Don Grolnick is heard at his best on his Hip Pocket debut *Hearts and Numbers* (1986) and on his two Blue Note albums. —*Scott Yanow*

Hearts and Numbers / 1985 / Hip Pocket ✦✦✦✦
A very attractive contemporary project. "Pointing at the Moon" and "More Pointing" make for sprightly music. —*Michael G. Nastos*

Weaver of Dreams / Feb. 1989 / Blue Note ✦✦✦✦
● **Nighttown** / Sep. 3, 1992 / Blue Note ✦✦✦✦✦
On his third release, Grolnick returns to his straight-ahead jazz roots with a vengance. Featured are Joe Lovano (s), Dave Holland (b), and Randy Brecker (t). Excellent. —*Paul Kohler*

Steve Grossman

b. Jan. 18, 1951, New York, NY
Soprano Saxophone, Tenor Saxophone / Hard Bop
Although he started out playing in fusion-oriented settings, Steve Grossman has developed into an excellent hard bop tenor in the tradition of Sonny Rollins (although he has developed his own sound). Grossman originally started on alto when he was eight, added soprano at 15 and tenor at 16. He started at the top as Wayne Shorter's replacement with Miles Davis, playing in his fusion group from late 1969 up to September 1970. Grossman

was with Lonnie Liston Smith in 1971, spent a valuable period (1971–73) as part of Elvin Jones' group and in the mid-'70s was with Gene Perla's Stone Alliance. Steve Grossman has mostly led his own bands ever since, recording as a leader for P.M., Owl, Red and Dreyfus. —*Scott Yanow*

Some Shapes to Come / Sep. 4, 1974–Sep. 6, 1974 / PM ✦✦✦

Way out East, Vol. 1 / Jul. 23, 1984–Jul. 24, 1984 / Red ✦✦✦✦

Way out East, Vol. 2 / Jul. 24, 1984 / Red ✦✦✦✦

Love Is the Thing / May 1985 / Red ✦✦✦✦

Steve Grossman Quartet, Vol. 1 / Nov. 1985 / DIW ✦✦✦

Steve Grossman Quartet, Vol. 2 / Nov. 1985 / DIW ✦✦✦

Katonah / Feb. 4, 1986 / DIW ✦✦✦

My Second Prime / Dec. 17, 1990 / Red ✦✦✦✦

Do It / Apr. 1991 / Dreyfus Disques ✦✦✦✦✦

★ **In New York** / Sep. 13, 1991–Sep. 14, 1991 / Dreyfus ✦✦✦✦✦

Marty Grosz

b. Feb. 28, 1930, Berlin, Germany
Guitar, Vocals / Classic Jazz
One of jazz music's great comedians (his spontaneous monologues are often hilarious), Marty Grosz is a brilliant acoustic guitarist whose chordal solos bring back the sound of Carl Kress and Dick McDonough of the 1930s while his vocals are very much in the Fats Waller tradition. It took Grosz a long time to get some visibility. He grew up in New York, attended Columbia University and in 1951 led a Dixieland band with Dick Wellstood that recorded. Based in Chicago, Grosz did record with Dave Remington, Art Hodes and Albert Nicholas in the 1950s, led sessions of his own in 1957 and 1959 for Riverside and Audio Fidelity and tried his best to coax Jabbo Smith out of retirement (some of their rehearsals were later released on LP) but was pretty obscure until he joined Soprano Summit (1975–79). After that association ended, Grosz became a busy freelancer on the classic jazz scene, playing with Dick Sudhalter, Joe Muryani and Dick Wellstood in the Classic Jazz Quartet and, in more recent times, heading the Orphan Newsboys, a superb quartet that also includes Peter Ecklund, Bobby Gordon and bassist Greg Cohen. Marty Grosz, a unique personality, has recorded several delightful sets for Jazzology and Stomp Off. —*Scott Yanow*

I Hope Gabriel Likes My Music / Jun. 25, 1981 Jun. 26, 1981 / Aviva ✦✦✦✦

Sings of Love & Other Matters / May 20, 1986–May 22, 1986 / Jazzology ✦✦✦✦

Swing It! / Jun. 1988–Jul. 1988 / Jazzology ✦✦✦✦

Extra! / Aug. 1989–Sep. 1989 / Jazzology ✦✦✦✦✦

Unsaturated Fats / Jan. 30, 1990–Feb. 22, 1990 / Stomp Off ✦✦✦✦✦

★ **And Destiny's Tots** / Mar. 23, 1992–Jun. 11, 1992 / Jazzology ✦✦✦✦✦

GRP All-Star Big Band

Group / Hard Bop
GRP is best-known as a label specializing in slick and accessible jazz, but in 1992 label-heads Dave Grusin and Larry Rosen decided to put together a conventional but star-studded big band comprised of their company's top players. Three recordings over a four-year period (and one full-length video) have thus far featured such musicians as Arturo Sandoval, Randy Brecker, Chuck Findley, Dave Grusin, Ernie Watts, Bob Mintzer, Dave Valentin, John Patitucci and even Tom Scott, Eric Marienthal, Nelson Rangell and Lee Ritenour playing straight-ahead charts of jazz standards from the 1950s and '60s. The recordings actually offer few surprises (other than the fact that Scott and company still remember how to play bop), but are enjoyable outings. —*Scott Yanow*

● **GRP All-Star Big Band** / 1992 / GRP ✦✦✦✦✦
It would not be an understatement to call the aggregation that Larry Rosen gathered to celebrate GRP's tenth anniversary an "all-star band." Everyone in this unique orchestra has recorded previously as a leader and all but George Bohannon (who makes up for the lack of trombonists on the label) and Randy Brecker are closely associated with the label. Only Chick Corea and Michael Brecker (both of whom were already committed else-

where) are missing among the key GRP players. Rather than perform swing-era tunes on **GRP All-Star Big Band**, this orchestra revisits jazz standards from the roots of these players, mostly from the '50s and '60s. The arrangements (by Michael Abene, Tom Scott, Dave Grusin, David Benoit, Russell Ferrante, Bob Mintzer, Vince Mendoza and Chick Corea) do not offer that many surprises, but they leave plenty of room for individual statements; everyone gets to solo somewhere. A particular joy of this date is hearing some of the musicians who mostly record crossover stretching out in this setting. Nelson Rangell fares well on alto during "Blue Train," and piccolo during a speedy "Donna Lee." Ernie Watts and Tom Scott (on alto) have a torrid tradeoff on "Airegin," and the jazz quality does not drop when Dave Grusin, David Benoit or Russell Ferrante take over for Kenny Kirkland on piano. —*Scott Yanow*

GRP All-Star Band Live! / 1993 / GRP ✦✦✦

All Blues / Jan. 8, 1994–Jan. 9, 1994 / GRP ✦✦
When one considers the large number of great players that participated in this project (including trumpeters Arturo Sandoval, Randy Brecker and Chuck Findley, trombonist George Bohanon, the reeds of Eric Marienthal, Nelson Rangell, Tom Scott, Ernie Watts and Bob Mintzer, such keyboardists as Dave Grusin, Chick Corea, Ramsey Lewis and Russell Ferrante, bassist John Patitucci, drummer Dave Weckl and guests B.B. King and tenor-great Michael Brecker), the rather predictable results are a disappointment. With the exception of Chick Corea's recent "Blue Miles," this album could have been titled "Warhorses" due to the very familiar material. The arrangements by Michael Abene, Scott, Grusin, Mintzer and Ferrante contain no real surprises (other than some unexpected moments on "Misterioso"), and none of the solos are long enough to really build. There is a certain novelty in hearing some of the crossover players like Rangell, Scott And Lewis playing hard bop tunes such as "Birks Works," "Senor Blues" and "Cookin' at the Continental," but why waste B.B. King on yet another version of "Stormy Monday Blues?" —*Scott Yanow*

George Gruntz

b. Jun. 24, 1932, Basel, Switzerland
Piano, Arranger, Composer, Leader / Post-Bop
George Gruntz's Concert Jazz Band, an orchestra that sticks to originals by bandmembers (both past and present) and the leader's arrangements, has long been one of the most stimulating of all jazz big bands. Gruntz, a fine pianist, played locally in Switzerland and then debuted in the United States when he appeared with Marshall Brown's International Youth Band at the 1958 Newport Jazz Festival. His trio in Europe accompanied touring American musicians in the 1960s, including Dexter Gordon and Rahsaan Roland Kirk ,and formed part of Phil Woods' adventurous European Rhythm Machine (1968–69). Gruntz recorded in many different settings including with the Swiss All-Stars, a four-flute septet and with Mideast musicians and Jean-Luc Ponty on 1967's *Noon in Tunisia*. In 1972 he formed the Concert Jazz Band, which, through the years, has featured a who's who of top musicians including Benny Bailey, Woody Shaw, Franco Ambrosetti, Dexter Gordon, Herb Geller, Phil Woods, Eddie Daniels, Ray Anderson, Lew Soloff, Chris Hunter, Bob Mintzer and many other Americans and Europeans; they typically have two tours a year and have even performed in China. Gruntz has also recorded with smaller groups, and his more recent records have been released by Enja and TCB. —*Scott Yanow*

Happening Now! / Oct. 16, 1987–Oct. 17, 1987 / Hat Art ✦✦✦

★ **First Prize** / May 7, 1989–May 8, 1989 / Enja ✦✦✦✦✦
George Gruntz Concert Jazz Band. Live in Zurich. Pianist Gruntz with four compositions, originals by saxophonist Larry Schneider, trumpeters Franco Ambrosetti and Kenny Wheeler and trombonist Ray Anderson. Standout is Gruntz's "Gorby-Chief." Eighteen-piece band, horn and brass-heavy, with dynamite rhythm section of Gruntz, Mike Richmond (b), Adam Nussbaum (d). —*Michael G. Nastos*

Serious Fun / Sep. 21, 1989–Sep. 23, 1989 / Enja ✦✦✦✦
George Gruntz is best known as the leader and arranger of his Concert Jazz Band so this trio date is a real rarity. Gruntz's piano playing, although very much in the tradition, features his own individual voice. Joined by bassist Mike Richmond and drummer Adam Nussbaum (fluegelhornist Franco Ambrosetti makes the group a quartet on "Autumn Again"), Gruntz is in excellent form throughout this enjoyable live set. —*Scott Yanow*

Blues 'n Dues Et Cetera / Jan. 4, 1991–Jan. 29, 1991 / Enja ✦✦✦✦✦

Pianist/composer George Gruntz had led his Concert Jazz Band for nearly 20 years at the time of this Enja CD. Although the personnel changes to a large extent every year, Gruntz's principles for his music (all of which he arranges) have remained the same: utilize flexible virtuosi on a repertoire of originals drawn entirely from the band. This particular release combines such major players as altoist Chris Hunter, guitarist John Scofield, trombonist Ray Anderson, trumpeters Wallace Roney, Jon Faddis, Randy Brecker, Michael Mossman, Marvin Stamm, John D'Earth and Franco Ambrosetti and tenors Bob Mintzer, Bob Malach and Jerry Bergonzi on a diverse and well-rounded set of unpredictable music. Anderson's "Rap for Nap" is particularly odd. It's well worth investigating. —*Scott Yanow*

Live In China / Nov. 11, 1992–Nov. 18, 1992 / TCB ✦✦✦✦

In Nov. 1992 the George Gruntz Concert Jazz Band became one of the very first jazz groups to ever tour China. Gruntz's 16-piece orchestra at the time featured such colorful soloists as trumpeters Lew Soloff, Jack Walrath, Tim Hagans and John D'Earth, trombonist Ray Anderson, altoist Chris Hunter and the tenors of Larry Schneider and Bob Malach. For the tour, Gruntz brought along bluesmen Billy Branch (on harmonica) and guitarist Carl Weathersby, and they are heard singing and playing on three of the six full-length selections, making this set a little more accessible than usual. Ray Anderson's riotous "Literary Lizard" (during which he challenges Lew Soloff in the upper register), Weatherby's emotional guitar solo on "Carl" and the general spirit of this flexible orchestra makes one wonder what the Chinese thought of this extroverted and often eccentric music. —*Scott Yanow*

Dave Grusin

b. Jun. 26, 1934, Denver, CO

Piano, Composer / Crossover, Bop

Dave Grusin, the very successful producer and co-founder of GRP Records, primarily thinks of himself as being a film composer. He worked as a pianist and music director for middle-of-the-road pop singer Andy Williams (1959–66), but did record with Benny Goodman (1960), cut a pair of trio records for Epic (1961–62) and made a quintet set in 1964 for Columbia that featured Thad Jones, Frank Foster and his future GRP partner, Larry Rosen, on drums. Grusin became a prolific writer for television and films, but always retained an interest in jazz. He and Rosen first teamed up as producers under the GRP banner in the early '70s, organizing together some dates for Arista. In the mid-'70s they formed their own separate label and had phenomenal success with lightly funky, jazz-oriented music. Grusin's own records tended to be poppish or emphasize his movie scores, but from the mid-'80s on they were stronger from a jazz standpoint including tribute sets to George Gershwin and Duke Ellington. Although GRP was acquired by MCA in the late '80s, it has retained its own identity through the '90s. —*Scott Yanow*

Discovered Again / Jun. 1, 1976–Jun. 3, 1976 / Sheffield Lab ✦✦✦✦

One of a Kind / 1977 / GRP ✦✦✦

Mountain Dance / Dec. 10, 1979–Dec. 17, 1979 / GRP ✦✦

Out of the Shadows / Jan. 1982–Feb. 1982 / GRP ✦✦

Night-Lines / 1983 / GRP ✦✦

Harlequin / 1985 / GRP ✦✦

● **Sticks and Stones** / 1988 / GRP ✦✦✦✦✦

Migration / 1989 / GRP ✦✦✦

The Gershwin Collection / 1991 / GRP ✦✦✦✦

● **Homage to Duke** / 1993 / GRP ✦✦✦✦✦

Although Dave Grusin is best known as a soundtrack composer and for his jazz-pop recordings, he has always had a great admiration for jazz. This CD (released in a fairly deluxe package) gave Grusin an opportunity to pay tribute to Duke Ellington. He performs ten mostly familiar songs associated with Ellington and wisely features fluegelhornist Clark Terry on five of the selections. Other prominent soloists include tenor saxophonist Pete Christlieb, trombonist George Bohanon, tenor saxophonist Tom Scott (returning to his roots), clarinetist Eddie Daniels (on an orchestrated version of "Mood Indigo") and pianist Grusin himself. This is a respectful and well-conceived tribute. —*Scott Yanow*

The Orchestral Album / 1994 / GRP ✦✦

Don Grusin

b. Apr. 22, 1941, Denver, CO

Keyboards / Crossover

The younger brother of producer/composer Dave Grusin, Don Grusin is an excellent keyboardist who has had his own solo career. He originally avoided music (not wanting to be in his brother's shadow), becoming an economics professor and not becoming a full-time musician until 1975. At that time he put together a band to tour Japan with Quincy Jones, freelanced in Los Angeles and headed the group Friendship, which recorded for Elektra in 1978. Grusin recorded a few albums for JVC in the early '80s and, in 1988, with Sticks And Stones (a collaboration with brother Dave), Don Grusin began recording regularly for GRP, playing music that (although influenced by pop) is also somewhat adventurous within the crossover genre. —*Scott Yanow*

10k-La / Nov.–Dec. 1980 / JVC ✦✦✦

Don Grusin / 1983 / JVC ✦✦✦

Raven / 1990 / GRP ✦✦✦

Zephyr / 1991 / GRP ✦✦✦

No Borders / 1992 / GRP ✦✦✦

The usual array of label superstars are on hand for pianist Don Grusin's latest foray into slick fusion and pop-oriented instrumentals. They include Eric Marienthal, Abraham Laboriel, Alex Acuna, Ricardo Silveira and Brazilian vocalist Dori Caymmi. —*Ron Wynn*

● **Native Land** / 1993 / GRP ✦✦✦✦

Banana Fish / 1994 / GRP ✦✦✦

Gigi Gryce (Basheer Quism)

b. Nov. 28, 1927, Pensacola, FL, d. Mar. 17, 1983, Pensacola, FL

Alto Saxophone / Hard Bop

Gigi Gryce was a fine altoist in the 1950s, but it was his writing skills (including composing the standard "Minority") that were considered most notable. After growing up in Hartford, CT, and studying at the Boston Conservatory and in Paris, Gryce worked in New York with Max Roach, Tadd Dameron and Clifford Brown. He toured Europe in 1953 with Lionel Hampton and led several sessions in France. After returning home in 1954 (including recording with Thelonious Monk), Gryce worked with Oscar Pettiford's groups (1955–57) and led the Jazz Lab Quintet (1955–58), a band featuring Donald Byrd. He had a quintet with Richard Williams during 1959–61, but then stopped playing altogether to become a teacher. During his short career Gigi Gryce recorded as a leader for Vogue (many of the releases have been issued domestically on Prestige), Savoy, Metrojazz, New Jazz and Mercury. —*Scott Yanow*

Nica's Tempo / Oct. 15, 1955–Oct. 22, 1955 / Savoy Jazz ✦✦✦

Gigi Gryce was a good player in the post-Charlie Parker mode and offers some tart solos on this session, whose title track has become a frequently recorded jazz staple. —*Ron Wynn*

● **Gigi Gryce & The Jazz Lab Quintet** / Feb. 27, 1957+Mar. 7, 1957 / Original Jazz Classics ✦✦✦✦✦

During 1957, altoist Gigi Gryce and trumpeter Donald Byrd co-led a quintet that sought to extend and come up with new variations to bebop. Unfortunately the group did not survive the year, but Gryce and Byrd did combine for several memorable recordings, including an excellent Prestige LP reissued on this CD. Their quintet (with pianist Wade Legge, bassist Wendell Marshall and drummer Art Taylor) turn "Love for Sale" into a jazz waltz (an innovation for 1957), introduce Gryce's best-known composition "Minority," swing "Zing Went the Strings of My Heart" and perform a tricky but memorable blues line "Straight Ahead." This is exciting and still fresh-sounding bebop. —*Scott Yanow*

Sayin' Somethin'! / Mar. 11, 1960 / Original Jazz Classics ✦✦✦✦

Altoist Gigi Gryce's last regular group before moving to Africa and largely retiring from music was the quintet featured on this CD, two from Prestige/New Jazz sessions and an album for Trip. Gryce's alto matched well with Richard Williams' impressive trumpet and, with fine support from pianist Richard Wyands, bassist Reggie Workman and drummer Mickey Roker, the two horns explore mostly blues-based originals by Gryce, Curtis Fuller and Hank Jones. There is more variety than expected, and the contrast between Gryce's lyricism and the extroverted nature of Williams' solos makes this set fairly memorable. *—Scott Yanow*

The Hap'nin's / May 3, 1960 / Original Jazz Classics ✦✦✦
A solid, tasteful date, with soul-jazz influences. *—Ron Wynn*

The Rat Race Blues / Jun. 7, 1960 / Original Jazz Classics ✦✦✦✦
As always, very crisp, precise and bluesy Gryce. *—Ron Wynn*

Vince Guaraldi

b. Jul. 17, 1928, San Francisco, CA, d. Feb. 6, 1976, Menlo Park, CA
Piano, Composer / Cool, Latin Jazz
Vince Guaraldi occupies an unusual place in jazz history. Although not a major pianist, his playing in the late '50s on ballads influenced the new age pacesetter George Winston two decades later, he was an Italian whose work in Latin-jazz impressed many and he became best-known for writing the scores for the *Peanuts* television cartoons. Guaraldi was with Cal Tjader's first trio in 1951, gigged with the Bill Harris/Chubby Jackson band (1953), Georgie Auld (1953) and Sonny Criss (1955), toured with Woody Herman's Orchestra (1956–57), gained fame playing with Tjader again (1957–59) and returned to Herman for part of 1959. Guaraldi, who recorded two albums for Fantasy during 1956–57, led his own groups from 1960 on and made seven further records for Fantasy during 1962–66 including a recording of his hit original "Cast Your Fate to the Wind" and his 1965 jazz mass. *—Scott Yanow*

Vince Guaraldi Trio / Apr. 1956 / Original Jazz Classics ✦✦✦
Straightforward trio material. *—Ron Wynn*

Jazz Impressions / Apr. 1956–Apr. 1957 / Original Jazz Classics ✦✦✦
A 1987 reissue of one of Guaraldi's more conventional jazz works. *—Ron Wynn*

A Flower Is a Lovesome Thing / Apr. 16, 1957 / Original Jazz Classics ✦✦✦✦
Vince Guaraldi Trio. Spry playing and interesting, unusual arrangements. *—Ron Wynn*

★ **Jazz Impressions of "Black Orpheus"** / Apr. 18, 1962 / Original Jazz Classics ✦✦✦✦✦
Guaraldi blends jazz improvisation with Afro-Latin and bossa-nova stylings. *—Ron Wynn*

Vince Guaraldi In Person / May 1963 / Fantasy ✦✦✦✦

Guaraldi Sete and Friends / 1963 / Fantasy ✦✦✦

A Boy Named Charlie Brown / 1964 / Fantasy ✦✦✦✦

The Latin Side of Vince Guaraldi / 1964 / Fantasy ✦✦
Pianist Vince Guaraldi performs an easy-listening set of Latin-flavored music on this LP. Joined by a string quartet plus an expanded rhythm section that includes guitarist Eddie Duran and two Latin percussionists, Guaraldi is in melodic form throughout this rather brief 31-minute album. The music (which includes "Corcovado," "Work Song" and four of his originals) is pleasing, but very safe and not too substantial. *—Scott Yanow*

Vince Guaraldi at Grace Cathedral / May 21, 1965 / Fantasy ✦✦✦

Live at the El Matador / 1966 / Fantasy ✦✦✦✦
A hotter-than-normal Guaraldi set, with Bola Sete (g) bringing a whole new ethos to the date. *—Ron Wynn*

Oh! Good Grief / 1968 / Warner Brothers ✦✦✦

Johnny Guarnieri

b. Mar. 23, 1917, New York, NY, d. Jan. 7, 1985, Livingston, NJ
Piano / Swing, Stride
One of the most talented pianists of the 1940s, Johnny Guarnieri had the ability to closely imitate Fats Waller, Count Basie and even Art Tatum. Not too surprisingly he was in great demand during his prime years. Guarnieri started classical piano lessons when he was ten and soon switched to jazz. In 1939 he joined Benny Goodman's orchestra, recording frequently with both the big band and BG's sextet. In 1940 Guarnieri became a member of Artie Shaw's orchestra and gained fame playing harpsichord on Shaw's popular Gramercy Five recordings. After further associations with Goodman (1941) and Shaw (1941–42), he was with Tommy Dorsey (1942–43) and then freelanced. Among

Guarnieri's many recordings during this era were important dates with Lester Young ("Sometimes I'm Happy"), Roy Eldridge, Ben Webster, Coleman Hawkins, Rex Stewart, Don Byas and Louis Armstrong ("Jack-Armstrong Blues"). He also recorded frequently as a leader during 1944–47, including one date on which Lester Young was his sideman. Guarnieri joined the staff of NBC in the late '40s, appeared in the Coleman Hawkins/Roy Eldridge television pilot *After Hours* (1961), moved to California in the '60s where he often played solo piano and toured Europe a few times in the 1970s. Guarnieri's later records often found him playfully performing stride in 5/4 time. He recorded as a leader through the years for such labels as Savoy, Majestic, Coral (1956), Golden Crest, Camden, Dot, Black & Blue, Dobre and Taz-Jazz (1976 and 1978). *—Scott Yanow*

Hot Piano / Sep. 20, 1944–Nov. 7, 1944 / Savoy ✦✦✦

Superstride / Jul. 19, 1976+Jul. 26, 1976 / Taz-Jaz ✦✦✦

● **Echoes of Ellington** / 1984 / Star Line ✦✦✦✦✦

Lars Gullin (Gunnar Victor Gullin)

b. May 4, 1928, Visby, Sweden, d. May 17, 1976, Vissefjarda, Sweden
Baritone Saxophone / Cool, Bop
One of the top baritone-saxophonists of all time and a giant of European jazz, Lars Gullin would be better-known today if he had visited the U.S. often and if excessive drug use had not cut short his career. Early on he learned to play bugle, clarinet and piano and was actually a professional altoist until switching to baritone when he was 21. Sounding somewhere between Gerry Mulligan and Serge Chaloff, Gullin played in local big bands in the late '40s and was in Arne Domnerus' sextet (1951–53), but is best-known for his own small-group recordings. He played with such touring Americans as Lee Konitz (a major influence), James Moody, Clifford Brown, Zoot Sims and Chet Baker and recorded frequently during 1951–60 with "Danny's Dream" being his most famous composition. Gullin also recorded a bit during 1964–65, but made only one later session (1973). Despite a lot of accomplishments in the 1950s, he did not live up to his enormous potential. Gullin can be heard at his best on five Dragon CDs released as *The Great Lars Gullin Vols. 1-5*. *—Scott Yanow*

The Great Lars Gullin, Vol. 2 / Mar. 11, 1953–Dec. 1, 1953 / Dragon ✦✦✦✦✦

The Great Lars Gullin, Vol. 5 / May 25, 1954–Jan. 26, 1955 / Dragon ✦✦✦✦

The Great Lars Gullin, Vol. 3 / Sep. 11, 1954–Jun. 13, 1955 / Dragon ✦✦✦✦

★ **The Great Lars Gullin, Vol. 1** / Apr. 25, 1955–May 31, 1956 / Dragon ✦✦✦✦✦

Lars Gullin Swings / Jul. 1958 / East West ✦✦✦

The Great Lars Gullin, Vol. 4 / Jan. 28, 1959–Sep. 2, 1960 / Dragon ✦✦✦✦

Trilok Gurtu

b. Oct. 30, 1951, Bombay, India
Percussion / World Fusion
Trilok Gurtu gained some recognition when he became the late Collin Walcott's replacement with Oregon in 1985. He studied classical tabla in India, but early on mixed his music with jazz. Gurtu worked in Europe (1973–75), moved to New York (1976) and during the next few years played with Charlie Mariano, Don Cherry, Barre Phillips, Karl Berger and Lee Konitz. He had a duo with Nana Vasconcelos, worked with Jan Garbarek, recorded frequently for ECM, toured with John McLaughlin (late '80s-early '90s) and led his own groups in addition to playing with Oregon. Trilok Gurtu's most recent dates as a leader are for CMP. *—Scott Yanow*

Usfret / 1987, 1988 / CMP ✦✦✦
Includes Mother Shobha Gurtu (v), Don Cherry (tpt), Ralph Towner (g, k), L. Shakar (violin), Jonas Helborg (b). *—Michael G. Nastos*

● **Living Magic** / Aug. 1990+Mar. 1991 / CMP ✦✦✦✦✦
With Jan Garbarek (saxes), Nana (per), Daniel Goyone (k). Septet. Indian, Turkish, Scandinavian and Brazilian world-fusion, very well conceived. One of Garbarek's better recent efforts, as collaborator or leader. *—Michael G. Nastos*

Crazy Saints / May 1993–Jun. 1993 / CMP ✦✦✦✦
Bad Habits Die Hard / 1995 / CMP ✦✦✦

Barry Guy
b. Apr. 22, 1947, London, England
Bass, Leader / Avant-Garde, Free Jazz
The leader of an exciting avant-garde big band called the London Jazz Composers Orchestra since 1970, Barry Guy is one of the top free-form string bassists, able to get a wide variety of unusual sounds out of his instrument. Classically trained, Guy has had simultaneous careers in advanced jazz and contemporary classical music. He was in the Spontaneous Music Ensemble with Trevor Watts and John Stevens (1967–70), has played in a variety of adventurous small groups (including Amalgam and Iskra 1903) and has recorded often with Evan Parker, Derek Bailey and the London Jazz Composers Orchestra, most recently for his Maya label. —*Scott Yanow*

Ode for Jazz Orchestra / Apr. 22, 1977 / Incus ✦✦✦
Stringer / Mar. 26, 1980 / FMP ✦✦✦✦
☆ **Harmos** / Apr. 4, 1989–Apr. 5, 1989 / Intakt ✦✦✦✦✦

☆ **Double Trouble** / Apr. 5, 1989–Apr. 6, 1989 / Intakt ✦✦✦✦✦
Arcus / 1990 / Maya ✦✦✦✦
Theoria / Feb. 1991 / Intakt ✦✦✦✦
Fizzles / Sep. 1991 / Maya ✦✦✦
★ **Study-Witch Gong Game II/1O** / Feb. 26, 1994–Feb. 27, 1994 / Maya ✦✦✦✦✦

Bassist Barry Guy teamed up with the 13-piece New Orchestra Workshop (NOW) for this difficult but sometimes wondrous set of avant-garde music. The 16-minute "Study" makes excellent use of an ensemble drone and space in building up and releasing tension, while the 52-minute "Witch Gong Game II/10" is quite menacing and sometimes even scary. The wide range of tone colors during some of the denser moments make it difficult to know what notes one is hearing and sometimes even what instruments are being played. Among the individual players are the brilliant pianist Paul Plimley, the very flexible vocalist Kate Hammett-Vaughan, six horns, guitar, cello, three bassists (counting Guy) and drums, but it is the intense and sometimes ferocious ensembles that are most memorable. This import from the English label Maya will take several listens to digest. —*Scott Yanow*

H

Bobby Hackett
b. Jan. 31, 1915, Providence, RI, d. Jun. 7, 1976, Chatham, MA
Cornet / Dixieland, Swing
Bobby Hackett's mellow tone and melodic style offered a contrast to the brasher Dixieland-oriented trumpeters. Emphasizing his middle-register and lyricism, Hackett was a flexible soloist who actually sounded little like his main inspiration, Louis Armstrong.

When Hackett first came up he was briefly known as "the new Bix" because of the similarity in his appproach to that of Bix Beiderbecke, but very soon he developed his own distinctive sound. Originally a guitarist (which he doubled on until the mid-'40s), Hackett performed in local bands and by 1936 was leading his own group. He moved to New York in 1937, played with Joe Marsala, appeared at Benny Goodman's 1938 Carnegie Hall concert (recreating Beiderbecke's solo on "I'm Coming Virginia"), recorded with Eddie Condon and by 1939 had a short-lived big band. Hackett played briefly with Horace Heidt and, during 1941–42, was with Glenn Miller's Orchestra, taking a famous solo on "String of Pearls." Next up was a stint with the Casa Loma Orchestra and then he became a studio musician while still appearing with jazz groups. Hackett was a major asset at Louis Armstrong's 1947 Town Hall Concert, in the 1950s he was a star on Jackie Gleason's commercial but jazz-flavored mood music albums and he recorded several times with Eddie Condon and Jack Teagarden. During 1956–57 Hackett led an unusual group that sought to modernize Dixieland (using Dick Cary's arrangements and an unusual instrumentation), but that band did not catch on. Hackett recorded some commercial dates during 1959–60 (including one set of Hawaiian songs and another in which he was backed by pipe organ), he worked with Benny Goodman (1962–63), backed Tony Bennett in the mid '60s, co-led a well-recorded quintet with Vic Dickenson (1968–70) and made sessions with Jim Cullum, the World's Greatest Jazz Band and even Dizzy Gillespie and Mary Lou Williams, remaining active up until his death. Among the many labels Bobby Hackett recorded for as a leader were Okeh (reissued by Epic), Commodore, Columbia, Epic, Capitol, Sesac, Verve, Project 3, Chiaroscuro, Flying Dutchman and Honey Dew.—*Scott Yanow*

The Hackett Horn / Feb. 16, 1938–Jan. 25, 1940 / Epic ◆◆◆◆◆
This set of 16 songs has been reissued intact several times. It includes 12 of the first 16 songs cut at dates led by cornetist Bobby Hackett, featuring a pair of hot combos and a larger big band (why are the other four rewarding sides always left out?) along with two Bix-associated songs recorded under the sponsorship of bandleader Horace Heidt and a pair of jams from a set led by critic Leonard Feather. Throughout, Hackett (then barely in his mid-20s) shows why his original reputation as "the new Bix" never quite fit. Even this early in his career his pretty tone was distinctive. Among the other stars of these swing/trad performances are trombonists George Brunies and Brad Gowans, and clarinetists Pee Wee Russell and Joe Marsala. —*Scott Yanow*

Jazz in New York / Apr. 15, 1944–Sep. 23, 1944 / Commodore ◆◆◆◆
This CD has plenty of hot traditional jazz as played by a variety of top Condonites who were in their prime in the mid-'40s. The three seperate bands feature overlapping personnel with cornetist Bobby Hackett's octet including trombonist Lou McGarity and the great baritonist Ernie Caceres, trombonist Miff Mole's Nicksielanders also showcasing Hackett and Caceres, and cornetist Muggsy Spanier's Ragtimers featuring Mole; clarinetist Pee

Wee Russell is also heard with all three groups. But even if the individual bands are pick-up affairs, a few classic performances resulted, most notably Mole's version of "Peg of My Heart," Spanier's "Angry" and "Alice Blue Gown," and Bobby Hackett's "At Sundown" and "Soon." Fun Dixieland from some of the best. —*Scott Yanow*

Live at the Rustic Lodge / 1949 / Jass ◆◆◆
These radio airchecks feature cornetist Bobby Hackett and clarinetist Tony Parenti sitting in with a fine pickup group in New Jersey for two standards and a lengthy blues medley, the local musicians getting three tunes to themselves, Parenti rejoining them for "That's a Plenty" and the great trumpeter Red Allen dominating "Squeeze Me" and "I Wish I Could Shimmy like My Sister Kate." Nothing unique occurs, but the good feelings generated at the sessions can still be savored (along with the frequently hot music) four decades later. —*Scott Yanow*

Dr. Jazz Series, Vol. 2 / Feb. 11, 1952–Apr. 17, 1952 / Storyville ◆◆◆

Coast Concert / Oct. 18, 1955+Oct. 19, 1955 / Capitol ◆◆◆◆◆
In the 1950s, Hackett's pretty tone was often utilized on mood music albums, most notably by Jackie Gleason, but he never lost his ability to play hot jazz. *Coast Concert* finds him leading a particularly strong octet that also featured clarinetist Matty Matlock and both Jack Teagarden and Abe Lincoln on trombones. On nine familiar standards (including tunes such as "I Want a Big Butter and Egg Man," "Basin Street Blues" and "Struttin' with Some Barbecue"), the top-notch players really inspire each other with some heated ensembles and creative solo work. This is one of Hackett's best sessions of the decade. —*Scott Yanow*

Bobby Hackett's Jazz Band: 1957 / Mar. 30, 1957 / Alamac ◆◆◆
The budget-LP label Alamac dug up a fine aircheck from Bobby Hackett's unusual sextet of 1957. With Hackett's cornet, Johnny Gwaltney on clarinet and vibes, Ernie Caceres doubling on baritone and clarinet, Dick Cary playing piano and Eb horn and fine backing from John Dengler's tuba and Nat Ray's drums, the band plays fresh versions of swing standards and a couple of originals from Cary. —*Scott Yanow*

Bobby Hackett at the Embers / Nov. 1957 / Capitol ◆◆◆
Supper-club jazz from the Bobby Hackett Quartet, the music borders between solid swing and easy-listening with the accent on ballads (other than a couple of exceptions) and mellow sounds from the pretty cornet of Hackett. Nice music but not all that stimulating. —*Scott Yanow*

Hawaii Swings / 1959–1960 / Capitol ◆◆
Because he had a very accessible tone on cornet, Hackett was in demand during the 1950s and '60s for mood music albums in addition to jazz dates. This LP was one of his oddest, for he is heard playing a dozen Hawaiian melodies in a band that includes steel guitar, ukulele, guitar and bongos in addition to a standard rhythm section. Fortunately, the majority of the selections are taken uptempo and Hackett has plenty of solo space to romp over the unusual backing, making this a novelty date well worth picking up. It is doubtful that it will be reissued on CD anytime in the next decade. —*Scott Yanow*

Creole Cookin' / Jan. 30, 1967 / Verve ◆◆◆◆◆
This long-out-of-print LP contains one of his finest all-around recordings. The cornetist is featured on 11 Dixieland standards and joined by a 15-piece, all-star band arranged by Bob Wilber; Wilber and tenor great Zoot Sims also receive some solo space on

this essential release, which is well deserving of reissue on CD. — *Scott Yanow*

Melody Is a Must: Live at the Roosevelt Grill / Mar. 1969–Apr. 1969 / Phontastic ◆◆◆
One of Bobby Hackett's favorite groups was the quintet he co-led with trombonist Vic Dickenson during 1969–71. Fortunately, this relatively short-lived unit made more than its share of recordings (all of them live). Hackett and Dickenson both had soft tones and fluent styles that were flexible enough to bring new life and their own brand of sly wit to these veteran songs. This set does not duplicate any of the Chiaroscuro releases. — *Scott Yanow*

Live from Mannasas / Dec. 7, 1969 / Jazzology ◆◆◆
This LP captures a very spirited set starring cornetist Hackett, trombonist Vic Dickenson, clarinetist Tommy Gwaltney and singer Maxine Sullivan cut live at a jazz festival. Cornetist Wild Bill Davison and trombonist George Brunies really make the ensembles overcrowded by sitting in unexpectedly during the final two numbers. The good spirits make up for some loose moments. — *Scott Yanow*

Featuring Vic Dickenson at the Roosevelt Grill / Apr. 1970–May 1970 / Chiaroscuro ◆◆◆
The Bobby Hackett/Vic Dickenson Quintet of 1969–71 was one of Hackett's favorite bands of his career. The cornet/trombone frontline worked together very well, as did a rhythm section led by pianist Dave McKenna. This LP, released long after the group had become history, differs from the previous releases in that all of the songs are Dixieland (rather than swing) favorites but, no matter, the band's sly wit and subtle creativity remained at a high level. — *Scott Yanow*

★ **Live at the Roosevelt Grill with Vic Dickenson** / Apr. 19, 1970–May, 1970 / Chiaroscuro ◆◆◆◆◆
During 1969–71, Bobby Hackett co-led a memorable reedless quintet with trombonist Vic Dickenson that also featured pianist Dave McKenna. This superb swing combo gave fresh interpretations to a wide variety of tunes (mostly from the 1930s) and featured colorful interplay between the two highly distinctive horns. Of the many live recordings that resulted, this Chiaroscuro CD was the first and best. — *Scott Yanow*

What a Wonderful World / 1973 / Columbia ◆◆◆
One of Hackett's last studio albums, the cornetist is heard in fine form with three different units ranging from seven to 15 pieces. Teresa Brewer's three vocals are typically unfortunate but Hackett, trombonist Vic Dickenson and clarinetist Johnny Mince keep the music (dominated by Dixieland standards) swinging. — *Scott Yanow*

Strike Up The Band / Aug. 3, 1974 / Flying Dutchman ◆◆◆◆
Hackett recorded many excellent performances throughout his life; this LP is one of the more rewarding of his later years. He is teamed successfully with tenor saxophonist Zoot Sims and guitarist Bucky Pizzarelli in a frequently exciting sextet. Highpoints include the uptempo "Strike up the Band," a revisit to "Embraceable You" (Hackett had cut a famous solo on that standard 34 years earlier) and a variety of standards and basic originals. A consistently stimulating and enjoyable set, it is well-deserving of being reissued on CD. — *Scott Yanow*

Charlie Haden

b. Aug. 6, 1937, Shenandoah, IL
Bass, Leader / Free Jazz, Hard Bop
What would Ornette Coleman have done in 1959 if Charlie Haden were not around? There were probably not another jazz bassist who fully understood Coleman's radical music that early. Haden's large and distinctive tone, his unhurried approach and his ability to state a pulse without handcuffing the lead voices to a repeated chord structure were unprecedented at the time. He played country music on a regular radio show with his family as a child, arrived in Los Angeles in the mid-'50s and gigged with Art Pepper, Hampton Hawes, and Paul Bley during 1957–59. It was with Bley at the Hillcrest Club that Haden first performed with Ornette Coleman and Don Cherry and he soon became an important member of their quartet. Haden traveled with Coleman to New York in 1959 and was with him through 1961 including making some innovative records for Atlantic. He worked with Denny Zeitlin during 1964–66, had several reunions with Ornette through the years (including some later recordings), was part of

the Jazz Composers' Orchestra Association in the late '60s and in 1969 formed the Liberation Music Orchestra. Always outspoken against injustice and political repression, Haden's avant-garde orchestra was quite political. He also played often with Keith Jarrett (1967–75) including his excellent quintet that featured Dewey Redman, recorded with Alice Coltrane (1968–72), led a pair of diverse duet albums (1975–76) and was with Old and New Dreams in the mid-to-late '70s. A perennial pollwinner, Haden (who teaches at Cal Arts) had a trio during 1982–83 with Jan Garbarek and Egberto Gismonti and, since 1986, has led the comparatively conservative Quartet West (which also includes Ernie Watts, Alan Broadbent and Larance Marable) in addition to occasionally putting together a new version of the Liberation Music Orchestra. Charlie Haden, composer of the standard "First Song," has recorded as a leader for Impulse, Artists House, Horizon, ECM, Verve, Blue Note, Soul Note and Antilles. — *Scott Yanow*

☆ **Liberation Music Orchestra** / Jul. 27, 1970–Jul. 29, 1970 / Impulse! ◆◆◆◆◆
One of the few message/protest jazz vehicles that works on every level. It has brilliant compositions, arrangements, playing, and lineup, plus passionate material. — *Ron Wynn*

As Long As There's Music / Jan. 25, 1976 / Artists House ◆◆◆◆
Although one would not immediately associate bassist Charlie Haden with pianist Hampton Hawes, they had performed together on an occasional basis since first meeting in 1957. This Artists House LP, a set of five duets, was their last opportunity to play together because Hawes would pass away the following year. The music includes a fairly free improvisation on "Hello/ Goodbye," the duo's interpretation of the title cut, a collaboration on "This Is Called Love" and two originals from the pianist. This quiet and often lyrical set contains a great deal of thoughtful and subtle music by two masters. — *Scott Yanow*

Closeness / Jan. 26, 1976–Mar. 21, 1976 / A&M ◆◆◆◆
This one is absolutely essential. One duet apiece with Ornette Coleman (sax), Alice Coltrane (p), Keith Jarrett (p), Paul Motian (d). — *Michael G. Nastos*

Golden Number / Jun. 7, 1976–Dec. 20, 1976 / A&M ◆◆◆◆
Superb album featuring bassist Charlie Haden in various duet situations, each one a gem. The guest list included Ornette Coleman, Hampton Hawes, and Don Cherry. It was issued on John Synder's Artist House, a treasured label that went defunct, and thus far, few of its CD's have been reissued. — *Ron Wynn*

Gitane / Sep. 22, 1978 / Verve ◆◆◆
The American bassist meets Gypsy guitarist Christian Escoude. — *Michael G. Nastos*

Magico / Jun. 1979 / ECM ◆◆◆◆
w/ Gismonti & Garbarek. Outstanding trio work on this reunion of the group that made the superb "Folk Songs" in 1979. — *Ron Wynn*

Folk Songs / Nov. 1979 / ECM ◆◆◆◆

The Ballad of the Fallen / Nov. 1982 / ECM ◆◆◆

☆ **Quartet West** / Dec. 22, 1986–Dec. 23, 1986 / Verve ◆◆◆◆◆

Etudes / Sep. 14, 1987–Sep. 15, 1987 / Soul Note ◆◆◆

Silence / Nov. 11, 1987–Nov. 12, 1987 / Soul Note ◆◆◆

In Angel City / May 30, 1988–Jun. 1, 1988 / Verve ◆◆◆◆
Charlie Haden Quartet West. This is a solid session, w/ the undervalued Lawrence Marable on drums. Ernie Watts (reeds) does his best playing with Haden. — *Ron Wynn*

Montreal Tapes / Jul. 2, 1989 / Verve ◆◆◆

Dialogues / Jan. 28, 1990–Jan. 29, 1990 / Antilles ◆◆◆
Jazz bassist Haden meets Portuguese guitarist. Stangely beautiful. — *Michael G. Nastos*

★ **Dream Keeper** / Apr. 4, 1990–Apr. 5, 1990 / Blue Note ◆◆◆◆◆

First Song / Apr. 26, 1990 / Soul Note ◆◆◆

Haunted Heart / Oct. 27, 1991–Oct. 28, 1991 / Verve ◆◆◆◆
Charlie Haden loves film as much as music, combining both loves on the critically acclaimed *Haunted Heart*. Haden led his tremendous group Quartet West through 12 numbers, several, like Cole Porter's "Every Time We Say Goodbye," Alan Broadbent's "Lady In The Lake," Arthur Schwartz and Howard Dietz's "Haunted Heart," and even the short introduction, with film ties and/or links. Haden

transferred vocals on some numbers from Jeri Southern, Billie Holiday and Jo Stafford into the mix without disrupting or disturbing the group framework. Quartet West has emerged as a premier small combo, and Haden nicely paid tribute to the past without being held hostage to it. *—Ron Wynn*

Always Say Goodbye / Jul. 30, 1993–Aug. 1, 1993 / Verve ✦✦✦✦

Steal Away / Jun. 29, 1994–Jun. 30, 1994 / Verve ✦✦✦
This is an unusual record. Bassist Charlie Haden and pianist Hank Jones perform a variety of spirituals, hymns and folk songs as duets. The traditional music (which includes such tunes as "Nobody Knows the Trouble I've Seen," "Swing Low, Sweet Chariot," "Sometimes I Feel like a Motherless Child" and "We Shall Overcome") are all performed respectfully and with reverence. These melodic yet subtly swinging interpretations hold one's interest throughout and reward repeated listenings. *—Scott Yanow*

Dick Hafer

b. May 29, 1927, Wyomissing, PA
Tenor Saxophone / Cool
A fine veteran tenor saxophonist who has long been overlooked and underfeatured, Dick Hafer made a strong impression with his 1994 Fresh Sound release *Prez Impressions* (a tribute to Lester Young). He started on clarinet when he was seven, switching to tenor in high school. Hafer's first major job was with Charlie Barnet's bebop orchestra of 1949. (Hafer was featured on some recorded solos the same day he joined the band). Next he was with Claude Thornhill (1949–50), was briefly back with Barnet and then joined Woody Herman (1951–55), soloing most notably on "Wild Apple Honey." Hafer freelanced in New York, played with Tex Beneke (1955), Bobby Hackett (1957–58), Elliott Lawrence (1958–60) and Benny Goodman (1962) and recorded with Charles Mingus (1963) and Johnny Hartman. He moved to Los Angeles in 1974 and worked steadily but was fairly obscure until the Fresh Sound session. Since then an earlier album (1991) from the cool-toned tenor has been released on Progressive. *—Scott Yanow*

★ **Prez Impressions** / Feb. 28, 1994–Mar. 1, 1994 / Fresh Sound ✦✦✦✦✦
Veteran tenor saxophonist Dick Hafer's sudden emergence as a brilliant soloist on his Fresh Sound recording is a very welcome event. A reliable musician for the previous 40 years (mostly as a section player in big bands), Hafer heads a quartet (with pianist Ross Tompkins, bassist Dave Carpenter and drummer Jake Hanna) and displays his own wonderful tenor sound, which not only looks toward Lester Young of the 1930s but Prez of the'50s. Hafer is quite creative within Young's style (not merely copying Prez) and swings hard on ten swing standards and a song apiece by Al Cohn and Zoot Sims. It's a wonderful outing of melodic mainstream music by an often overlooked tenor master. *—Scott Yanow*

Tim Hagans

b. Aug. 19, 1954, Dayton, OH
Trumpet / Hard Bop
Tim Hagans, an excellent hard bop-oriented trumpeter, was with the orchestras of Stan Kenton (1974–77) and Woody Herman (1977) before moving to Sweden (1977–81) where he played with Sahib Shihab, Ernie Wilkins' Almost Big Band, the Danish Radio Orchestra (which was then directed by Thad Jones) and Dexter Gordon. After returning to the U.S., he taught at the University of Cincinnati and recorded for the local MoPro label. Hagans taught at Berklee (1984–86) and then, in 1986, he started working with Joe Lovano and Fred Hersch. Since then he has made records with Bob Belden, Lovano, Rick Margitza, John Hart and the Yellowjackets, and has worked with the big bands of Bob Mintzer, Maria Schneider and the Gil Evans Orchestra. Tim Hagans has recorded two Blue Note albums thus far as a leader. *—Scott Yanow*

From the Neck Down / Apr. 19, 1983–Apr. 20, 1983 / MoPro ✦✦✦

No Words / Dec. 3, 1993 / Blue Note ✦✦✦✦
The impressive trumpeter Tim Hagans holds his own with the tenor of Joe Lovano during a sextet session with guitarist John Abercrombie, keyboardist Marc Copland, bassist Scott Lee and

drummer Bill Stewart that features nine of his originals. The music is essentially advanced hard bop (Lovano and Abercrombie both sound somewhat inspired) and Hagans displays both an attractive tone and a fertile imagination. It's a strong set of modern mainstream jazz. *—Scott Yanow*

★ **Audible Architechture** / Dec. 17, 1994–Dec. 18, 1994 / Blue Note ✦✦✦✦✦
Although Tim Hagans is rightly thought of as a veteran hard bop player, his adventurous spirit has led to him playing pretty freely on this CD. The programming is quite admirable with three pianoless trios followed by four quartet numbers (that also include tenor saxophonist Bob Belden) alternating with separate trumpet-bass ("You Don't Know What Love Is") and trumpet-drums ("Drum Row") duets before a brief unaccompanied trumpet solo closes the set. At times (particularly on "Jasmine in Three" and "Audible Architecture," a pair of his seven originals) Hagans almost sounds like Don Cherry with technique! Of the highlights, "I Hear a Rhapsody" sets the stage, the loose funk played by bassist Larry Grenadier and drummer Billy Kilson (two underrated talents) on "Garage Bands" accompanies the improvised interplay of the horns, Bob Belden is quite memorable (particularly on "Shorts") and the trumpet-drums duet comes off quite well. Actually there is not a throwaway track among the ten with Tim Hagans in prime physical and creative form. Highly recommended. *—Scott Yanow*

Bob Haggart

b. Mar. 13, 1914, New York, NY
Bass, Composer / Dixieland, Swing
One of the last survivors of Bob Crosby's Bobcats, Bob Haggart has been a top bassist for 60 years. Originally a guitarist, Haggart taught himself bass while in high school. He gained fame when he joined Bob Crosby in 1935, not only supplying his supportive and swinging bass but contributing arrangements and writing such songs as "What's New," "South Rampart Street Parade," "My Inspiration" and "Big Noise from Winnetka," the latter a colorful duet with drummer Ray Bauduc. After Crosby broke up his band in 1942, Haggart became a studio musician and was on a countless number of sessions (particularly for Decca). In addition to his studio work, the busy bassist teamed up with Yank Lawson for recordings as the Lawson-Haggart Band. Bob Haggart participated in many Bobcat reunions with Bob Crosby, co-led the World's Greatest Jazz Band with Lawson starting in 1968 and has been a steady fixture at many jazz parties and festivals through the years. *—Scott Yanow*

Jerry Hahn

b. Sep. 21, 1940, Alma, NE
Guitar / Post-Bop
A lesser-known but talented guitarist, Jerry Hahn attended Wichita State University and played in Kansas before moving to San Francisco in 1962. He gained some recognition for his work with John Handy's adventurous band (1964–66), which was the hit of the 1965 Monterey Jazz Festival. Hahn led an album in 1967, toured with the Fifth Dimension the following year and was one of many great guitarists to be part of Gary Burton's group (1968–69). He led the Jerry Hahn Brotherhood in the early '70s and then became a teacher at Wichita State University. Hahn maintained a low profile until 1986 when he moved to Portland and began playing full-time again. In 1993 Jerry Hahn relocated to Colorado, recording his first album in 20 years for Enja. *—Scott Yanow*

Ara-Be-In / Apr. 4, 1967–Apr. 4, 1967 / Arhoolie ✦✦✦

Al Haig

b. Jul. 22, 1924, Newark, NJ, d. Nov. 16, 1982, New York, NY
Piano / Bop
One of the finest pianists of the bop era (and one who learned from Bud Powell's innovations quite early), Al Haig was quite busy during two periods of his career but unfortunately was pretty obscure in the years between. After serving in the Coast Guard (playing in bands during 1942–44) and freelancing around Boston, Haig worked steadily with Dizzy Gillespie (1945–46), Charlie Parker (1948–50) and Stan Getz (1949–51) and was on many recordings, mostly as a sideman (including some classic Diz and Bird sessions), but also as a leader for Spotlite, Dawn and Prestige. However, (other than little-known dates in 1954 for

Esoteric, Swing and Period) Haig did not lead any more albums until 1974. He played fairly often during the 1951–73 period but was generally overlooked. That changed during his last decade when he was finally recognized as a bop giant and recorded for Spotlite, Choice, SeaBreeze, Interplay and several Japanese and European labels. —*Scott Yanow*

Al Haig Meets the Master Saxes, Vol. 1 / 1948 / Spotlite ✦✦✦✦

Al Haig Meets the Master Saxes, Vol. 2 / 1948 / Spotlite ✦✦✦✦

Al Haig Meets the Master Saxes, Vol. 3 / 1948–Sep. 3, 1951 / Spotlite ✦✦✦✦

Live in Hollywood / Aug. 4, 1952 / Xanadu ✦✦✦

Al Haig Quartet / Sep. 13, 1954 / Fresh Sound ✦✦✦

Al Haig Today / Jul. 6, 1965 / Fresh Sound ✦✦✦

Invitation / Jan. 7, 1974 / Spotlite ✦✦✦

Special Brew / Nov. 27, 1974 / Spotlite ✦✦✦✦

★ **Strings Attached** / Mar. 27, 1975 / Choice ✦✦✦✦✦
A stalwart early bopper, pianist Al Haig returned to the recording spotlight briefly in the mid-'70s with this set, which could just as easily have been made in the '40s. Haig's fluidity and ability to navigate blistering passages and make the appropriate chord changes enabled him to survive the turbulent bop era; those skills are now second nature, as he shows with crisp, rippling solos throughout the album. —*Ron Wynn*

Piano Interpretation / Jun. 21, 1976 / Sea Breeze ✦✦✦✦
A fine solo piano set from 1976, with Al Haig displaying the total technical package on standards and bop anthems. He plays some rapid-fire; others, he constructs slowly and carefully, then tears them down and rebuilds the theme with nicely executed, intricate solos. —*Ron Wynn*

Piano Time / Jun. 21, 1976 / Sea Breeze ✦✦✦
The second of two solo piano albums Al Haig made in 1976, both done with exacting precision as well as exuberant force. Haig was disproving the critics who said he was finished, and he showed convincingly that there was still plenty of power in his hands and lots of tricks up his sleeve. —*Ron Wynn*

Interplay / Nov. 16, 1976 / Sea Breeze ✦✦✦
Fine duets featuring pianist Al Haig during a busy period in the mid-'70s. He'd overcome personal problems and was cranking out albums left and right for both domestic and foreign labels. These were cut for Interplay, a small West Coast firm, but then were mostly issued in Japan. They are mostly excellent examples of Haig's surging bop style. —*Ron Wynn*

Expressly Ellington / Oct. 14, 1978 / Spotlite ✦✦✦✦

Al Haig Plays (Music of Jerome Kern) / 1978 / Inner City ✦✦✦
A '78 showpiece for a bop legend. Pianist Al Haig was around during the idiom's early days, playing often with Charlie Parker, Miles Davis, and others, but drug problems reared their head. Haig missed several years during the '50s and '60s, but made a stunning return to the playing arena in the '70s. This was one of his most expressive and finely performed albums among the many he made in the mid- and late '70s. —*Ron Wynn*

Bebop Live / May 27, 1982 / Spotlite ✦✦✦

Edmond Hall

b. May 15, 1901, New Orleans, LA, d. Feb. 11, 1967, Boston, MA
Clarinet / New Orleans Jazz, Swing
It took Edmond Hall a long period to develop his own musical individuality but by the early '40s he had a very distinctive and dirty sound on the clarinet that was recognizable within one note. One of four clarinet playing brothers (including Herbie Hall) that were the sons of an early clarinetist Edward Hall, Edmond worked in many bands in New Orleans (including Buddy Petit during 1921–23) before going to New York in 1928 with Alonzo Ross. He was with Claude Hopkins' Orchestra (1929–35), doubling on baritone and only occasionally sounding like his future self on clarinet. Hall played with Lucky Millinder, Zutty Singleton and Joe Sullivan and had his style together by the time he joined Red Allen in 1940. He was with Teddy Wilson's sextet (1941–44) and turned down an opportunity to be Barney Bigard's successor with Duke Ellington's Orchestra in 1942. In 1944 Hall began working with Eddie Condon (including appearances on his *Town Hall Concert* radio series), he led his own group at Cafe Society, spent a few years based in Boston and then during 1950–55 was in the house band at Condon's club. Edmond Hall toured the world as a

member of Louis Armstrong's All-Stars (1955–58), worked in the 1960s now and then with Condon and made his final recording (before his death from a heart attack) at John Hammond's 1967 *Spirituals to Swing* concert. He recorded as a leader for Blue Note (1941–44), Commodore, Savoy, Storyville, United Artists and some smaller labels. —*Scott Yanow*

● **Edmond Hall: 1937–1944** / 1937–1944 / Classics ✦✦✦✦✦

Edmond Hall/Ralph Sutton Quartet, at Club Hangover / Jul. 24, 1954–Jul. 31, 1954 / Storyville ✦✦✦✦

Edmond Hall in Copenhagen / Dec. 2, 1966–Dec. 7, 1966 / Storyville ✦✦✦✦

Jim Hall

b. Dec. 4, 1930, Buffalo, NY
Guitar / Cool, Post-Bop
A harmonically advanced cool-toned and subtle guitarist, Jim Hall has been an inspiration to many current guitarists, including some (such as Bill Frisell) who sound nothing like him. Hall attended the Cleveland Institute of Music and studied classical guitar in Los Angeles with Vincente Gomez. He was an original member of the Chico Hamilton Quintet (1955–56) and during 1956–59 was with the Jimmy Giuffre Three. After touring with Ella Fitzgerald (1960–61) and sometimes forming duos with Lee Konitz, Hall was with Sonny Rollins' dynamic quartet in 1961–62, recording *The Bridge*. He co-led a quartet with Art Farmer (1962–64), recorded on an occasional basis with Paul Desmond during 1959–65 (all of their quartet performances are collected on a Mosaic box set) and then became a New York studio musician. He has mostly been a leader ever since and in addition to his own projects for World Pacific/Pacific Jazz, MPS, Milestone, CTI, Horizon, Artists House, Concord, Music Masters and Telarc, Jim Hall recorded two classic duet albums with Bill Evans. —*Scott Yanow*

Jazz Guitar / Jan. 10, 1957+Jan. 24, 1957 / Pacific Jazz ✦✦✦✦
Features a brilliant Carl Perkins (p). Hall is a marvel on guitar. —*Ron Wynn*

Where Would I Be? / Jul. 1971 / Original Jazz Classics ✦✦✦
Although the rhythm section was more "modern" than he usually used (keyboardist Benny Aranov, bassist Malcolm Cecil and Airto Moreira on drums and percussion), guitarist Jim Hall (who always had a harmonically advanced style anyway) has little difficulty adapting to the fresh setting. Highlights of the well-rounded CD reissue include Hall's "Simple Samba," "Baubles, Bangles And Beads," an unaccompanied "I Should Care" and Milton Nascimento's "Vera Cruz." —*Scott Yanow*

★ **Alone Together** / Aug. 4, 1972 / Original Jazz Classics ✦✦✦✦✦
With Ron Carter. Best bass/guitar duets. A must-buy. —*Michael G. Nastos*

Concierto / Apr. 16, 1975–Apr. 23, 1975 / Columbia ✦✦✦
A beautiful session. The title cut is a masterpiece. Chet Baker (tpt), Paul Desmond (as), Sir Roland Hanna (p), and Hall are majestic. —*Ron Wynn*

Jim Hall Live! / Sep. 10, 1975+Sep. 11, 1975 / Horizon ✦✦✦✦
Guitarist Jim Hall is heard at his best stretching out on five standards in a quiet trio with bassist Don Thompson and drummer Terry Clarke, two of Canada's finest. Despite the generally low volume, this harmonically rich music frequently burns ("Scrapple from the Apple" is a good example) and is intense and explorative; it's one of Hall's most rewarding recordings from this period. —*Scott Yanow*

Jim Hall and Red Mitchell / Jan. 20, 1978–Jan. 21, 1978 / Musical Heritage Society ✦✦✦✦

Concierto De Aranjue / Jan. 18, 1981 / Evidence ✦✦✦
Jim Hall's warm, fluid guitar and full tones are the anchor for this good but often unexciting session pairing him with the David Matthews orchestra. Hall recorded the title track on two other occasions; this third version is nicely orchestrated and produced, and Hall's solo is superbly played but adds little to the interpretation that he had provided before. The orchestra is wisely kept from getting in Hall's way, and his guitar lines are bright, sometimes arresting, and frequently dazzling. What is missing is the inventive spark and extra dimension Hall usually injects into his material. When these tracks were originally cut in 1981, Hall had been away from the studio for three years. —*Ron Wynn*

Circles / Mar. 1981 / Concord Jazz ✦✦✦
Jim Hall's Three / Jan. 1986 / Concord Jazz ✦✦✦
These Rooms / Feb. 1988 / Denon ✦✦✦
All Across the City / May 1989 / Concord Jazz ✦✦✦✦
Jim Hall & Friends, Vol. 1: Live At Town Hall / Jun. 26, 1990 / MusicMasters ✦✦✦✦
Live at Town Hall, Vol. 2 / Jun. 26, 1990 / Music Masters ✦✦✦✦
On this second concert volume, John Scofield (g) makes an excellent guest appearance. —*Ron Wynn*
Subsequently / Jan. 1991 / Music Masters ✦✦✦
Toots Thielemans on guitar and harmonica lends a hand, and things stay loose and breezy, but never detached or predictable. — *Ron Wynn*
● **Something Special** / Mar. 6, 1993–Jun. 8, 1993 / Music Masters ✦✦✦✦✦
Dialogues / Feb. 3, 1995–Feb. 25, 1995 / Telarc ✦✦✦✦✦
Guitarist Jim Hall has long been one of the most open-minded of the important stylists to emerge during the 1950s and his harmonically advanced style remains quite modern while hinting at its foundations in bop. For this Telarc CD, Hall teams up with five major players on two numbers apiece: Guitarists Bill Frisell and Mike Stern, Joe Lovano on tenor, fluegelhornist Tom Harrell and Gil Goldstein on accordion. Bassist Scott Colley and drummer Andy Watson are on the Frisell and Lovano tracks and part of The Harrell And Stern performances. All of the compositions but "Skylark" are Hall's originals and, although they are usually a bit dry, there are some exceptions; "Uncle Ed" and "Frisell Frazzle" are a little nutty. The emphasis throughout is on interplay between the lead voices and advanced improvising. Despite his strong sidemen (Stern And Harrell fare best), Jim Hall ends up as the dominant voice on virtually every selection, making this a set his fans will enjoy. —*Scott Yanow*

Bengt Hallberg

b. Sep. 13, 1932, Göteborg, Sweden
Piano / Cool, Hard Bop
One of Sweden's top jazz pianists, Bengt Hallberg made his first trio recordings when he was 17. In the 1950s he recorded with Lars Gullin, Arne Domnerus and such traveling Americans as Clifford Brown, Stan Getz and Quincy Jones. He worked as a member of the Swedish Radio Big Band (1956–63) and, although in demand as a writer for films and television, Hallberg has continued playing jazz on a part time basis (often with Domnerus and Karin Krog) up to the present time, mostly recording for Swedish labels such as Metronome, Sonet and Phontastic. —*Scott Yanow*
Kiddin' on the Keys / Dec. 20, 1959–Dec. 30, 1959 / Dragon ✦✦✦✦
At Gyllene Cirkeln / Dec. 29, 1962–Dec. 30, 1962 / Dragon ✦✦✦✦
Hallberg's Happiness / Mar. 1977 / Phontastic ✦✦✦
The Hallberg Touch / Aug. 1979 / Phontastic ✦✦✦
● **Bengt Hallberg in New York** / Sep. 23, 1982 / Phontastic ✦✦✦✦✦
Hallberg's Yellow Blues / Mar. 25, 1987–Nov. 20, 1987 / Phontastic ✦✦✦
Hallberg's Surprise / Mar. 1987–May 1987 / Phontastic ✦✦✦✦

Chico Hamilton (Forestorn Hamilton)

b. Sep. 21, 1921, Los Angeles, CA
Drums, Leader / Cool, Hard Bop, Post-Bop, Crossover
Chico Hamilton, a subtle and creative drummer, will probably always be better-known for the series of Quintets that he led during 1955–65 and for his abilities as a talent scout than for his fine drumming. Hamilton first played drums while in high school with the many fine young players (including Dexter Gordon, Illinois Jacquet and Charles Mingus) who were in Los Angeles at the time. He made his recording debut with Slim Gaillard, was house drummer at Billy Berg's, toured with Lionel Hampton and served in the military (1942–46). In 1946 Hamilton worked briefly with Jimmy Mundy, Count Basie and Lester Young (recording with Young). He toured as Lena Horne's drummer (on and off during 1948–55) and gained recognition for his work with the original Gerry Mulligan pianoless quartet (1952–53). In 1955 Hamilton put together his first Quintet, a chamber jazz group with the reeds of Buddy Collette, guitarist Jim Hall, bassist Carson Smith and cel-

list Fred Katz. One of the last important West Coast jazz bands, the Chico Hamilton Quintet was immediately popular and appeared in a memorable sequence in 1958's *Jazz on a Summer's Day* and the Hollywood film *The Sweet Smell of Success*. The personnel changed over the next few years (with Paul Horn and Eric Dolphy heard on reeds, cellist Nate Gersham, guitarists John Pisano and Dennis Budimir and several bassists passing through the group) but it retained its unusual sound. By 1961 Charles Lloyd was on tenor and flute, Gabor Szabo was the new guitarist and soon the cello was dropped in favor of trombone (Garnett Brown and later George Bohanon), giving the group an advanced hard bop style.
In 1966 Chico Hamilton started composing for commercials and the studios, and he broke up his Quintet. However he continued leading various groups, playing music that ranged from the avant-garde to erratic fusion and advanced hard bop. Such up-and-coming musicians as Larry Coryell (1966), Steve Potts (1967), Arthur Blythe, Steve Turre (on bass!) and Eric Person (who played in Hamilton's 1990s group Euphoria) were among the younger players he helped discover. In 1989 Chico Hamilton had a recorded reunion with the original members of his 1955 Quintet (with Pisano in Hall's place), and in recent times he has been making records for Soul Note. —*Scott Yanow*
Spectacular / Aug. 4, 1955–Aug. 5, 1955 / Pacific Jazz ✦✦✦✦
The Original Hamilton Quintet / Nov. 11, 1955 / World Pacific ✦✦✦
Chico Hamilton Quintet in Hi Fi / Jan. 4, 1956–Feb. 13, 1956 / Pacific Jazz ✦✦✦
Chico Hamilton Quintet / Oct. 21, 1956+Oct. 24, 1956 / Pacific Jazz ✦✦✦
The Music of Fred Katz / Nov. 1956 / Pacific Jazz ✦✦✦
The Chico Hamilton Quintet with Strings Attached / Oct. 26, 1958–Oct. 27, 1958 / Warner Brothers ✦✦✦
● **Gongs East** / Dec. 29, 1958–Dec. 30, 1958 / Discovery ✦✦✦✦✦
This Chico Hamilton date, originally released on Warner Bros., has become somewhat of a collector's item because of the presence of Eric Dolphy (alto sax, flute, bass clarinet). I also should mention, I am a great fan of Dolphy's and, to a lesser extent, Chico Hamilton (drums), but found the recording only of historical interest. I feel Chico Hamilton overreached a bit, the date seemed too calculated, almost an inflexible caricature of the controlled mood jazz he worked successfully at in the early '50s. In addition, the use of gong throughout the date was totally unswinging and ungraceful. Dolphy's role here was mainly on flute and it didn't show his great individualism, sounding closer to Buddy Collegge. The occasional use of bass clarinet will satisfy those looking for (earlier) established Dolphy styles. Dennis Budimir, an exciting guitarist of the time, was also pretty much hobbled by the structure, while Nathan Gershman filled the usual Hamilton cello capacity as expected. —*Bob Rusch, Cadence*
Ellington Suite / Jan. 9, 1959+Jan. 12, 1959 / World Pacific ✦✦✦✦
Transfusion / 1962 / Studio West ✦✦✦
The first four CDs released by Studio West, a subsidiary of VSOP, are all taken from concise (around three minutes apiece) performances that were made to be used as part of the radio show "The Navy Swings." This particular release features performances by one of drummer Chico Hamilton's most stimulating groups, a quintet comprised of Charles Lloyd (on tenor, flute and alto), guitarist Gabor Szabo, trombonist George Bohanon, bassist Albert Stinson and the drummer/leader. Because the individual selections are brief, in many cases only one soloist is featured on each cut, but there is plenty of solo space for Lloyd (very much playing in a Coltrane vein), Bohanon and Szabo. The mixture of seven standards with nine Lloyd originals works quite well with plenty of variety in moods and tempos. An excellent showcase for this underrated but timeless unit. —*Scott Yanow*
Drumfusion / Feb. 19, 1962 / Columbia ✦✦✦
Man from Two Worlds / Sep. 18, 1962–Dec. 11, 1963 / GRP ✦✦✦✦✦
Although it tended to get overlooked at the time, one of drummer Chico Hamilton's finest groups was his 1962–63 quartet/quintet. With Charles Lloyd at his most fiery on tenor and flute and the colorful solos of the up-and-coming Hungarian guitarist Gabor Szabo, this band placed a stronger emphasis on melody and softer sounds than the more avant-garde groups of the time but still pushed away at musical boundaries. Trombonist George Bohanon

is also on the final four numbers of this CD reissue, which brings back all of the music from Hamilton's *Man from Two Worlds* LP and four of the six numbers originally on *Passin' Thru.* Highlights include the original version of Lloyd's most famous song, "Forest Flower." —*Scott Yanow*

A Different Journey / Jan. 19, 1963–Jan. 31, 1963 / Reprise ✦✦✦

Chic Chic Chico / Jan. 4, 1965 / Impulse! ✦✦✦✦

El Chico / Aug. 26, 1965–Aug. 27, 1965 / Impulse! ✦✦✦

The Further Adventures of El Chico / May 2, 1966–May 5, 1966 / Impulse! ✦✦✦
Sometimes super and sometimes ragged cuts with Charlie Mariano (as). —*Ron Wynn*

The Dealer / Sep. 9, 1966 / MCA/Impulse! ✦✦✦
This groundbreaking session heralded the coming of jazz-rock in 1966 and introduced Larry Coryell (g) to the jazz world. —*Ron Wynn*

The Gamut / 1967 / Solid State ✦✦

The Head Hunters / 1969 / Solid State ✦✦✦

Peregrinations / Jul. 9, 1975–Jul. 10, 1975 / Blue Note ✦✦✦
Not always high-caliber material, but the group gets a boost from then largely unknown Arthur Blythe. —*Ron Wynn*

Euphoria / Oct. 1988 / Soul Note ✦✦✦✦

Reunion / Jun. 28, 1989+Jun. 29, 1989 / Soul Note ✦✦✦✦✦
In 1989, 34 years after the formation of the somewhat unique Chico Hamilton Quintet, the original members (with one exception) reunited for a tour and this Soul Note recording. In addition to drummer Hamilton, Buddy Collette (heard on flute, clarinet and alto), cellist Fred Katz and bassist Carson Smith, guitarist John Pisano (who was Jim Hall's first replacement) completes the group. This studio session only includes one standard remake of "I Want to Be Happy," and comprises then-recent originals by bandmembers with two selections ("Brushing with B" and "Conversation") being freely improvised duets by Collette and Hamilton. So, rather than merely being an exercise in nostalgia, this excellent set features the Quintet members as they sounded in the late '80s, creating new music for their classic sound. —*Scott Yanow*

Arroyo / Dec. 11, 1990–Dec. 17, 1990 / Soul Note ✦✦✦✦✦
A recent release for this drummer and the quartet Euphoria, including two standards and four of Hamilton's earthy and electric numbers on the eight cuts. This is easily recomended. —*Michael G. Nastos*

Trio! / May 1, 1992–May 17, 1992 / Soul Note ✦✦✦✦

★ **My Panamanian Friend** / Aug. 21, 1992–Aug. 28, 1992 / Soul Note ✦✦✦✦✦
My Panamian Friend is Hamilton's finest outing in several years. Part of the reason may be its purpose, paying tribute to the great Eric Dolphy. Another plus is that eight of the nine songs are Dolphy compositions, among them "Springtime," "South Street Exit," and "Something Sweet, Something Tender." But the prime reason for this disc's success is alto saxophonist/flutist Eric Person. He plays with sensitivity and a tender, yet strong, dynamic approach that proves more intriguing than his performances on his recent session as a leader. Although he's no Dolphy, Eric Person not only pays ample respects, but matures greatly as a player on this session. —*Ron Wynn*

Jeff Hamilton

b. Aug. 4, 1953, Richmond, IL
Drums / Bop
A reliable and versatile drummer who sounds equally at home with a big band or combo, Jeff Hamilton has a strong reputation in the jazz world. He attended Indiana University, in 1974 was with the Tommy Dorsey ghost band, played briefly with Lionel Hampton and then spent two years as a member of Monty Alexander's Trio (1975–77). Hamilton was with Woody Herman's Orchestra (1977–78), became a member of the L.A. Four (with whom he made six records) and started recording regularly as a sideman for Concord. During 1983–87 he performed with Ella Fitzgerald, the Count Basie Orchestra, Rosemary Clooney and Monty Alexander. In the 1990s Hamilton toured the world with Oscar Peterson and the Ray Brown trio, gigged with the Clayton Brothers' Quartet and has been a co-leader (with John and Jeff Clayton) of the Clayton-Hamilton Orchestra. Jeff Hamilton has

also occasionally led his own trio, recording for Lake Street. —*Scott Yanow*

● **Indiana** / Jan. 1982 / Concord Jazz ✦✦✦✦

It's Hamilton Time / 1994 / Lake Street ✦✦✦

Jimmy Hamilton

b. May 25, 1917, Dillon, SC
Clarinet / Bop, Swing
A longtime member of the Duke Ellington Orchestra, Jimmy Hamilton's cool vibrato-less tone and advanced style (which was ultimately influenced by bop) initially bothered some listeners more accustomed to Barney Bigard's warmer New Orleans sound, but Hamilton eventually won them over with his brilliant playing. As opposed to how he sounded on clarinet, Hamilton's occasional tenor playing was gutsy and emotional. Prior to joining Duke, he had worked with Lucky Millinder, Jimmy Mundy and most noticeably Teddy Wilson's sextet (1940–42) and Eddie Heywood; Hamilton also recorded with Billie Holiday. He was with Ellington for 25 years (1943–68) and was well-featured on clarinet on "Air Conditioned Jungle," "Ad Lib on Nippon" and a countless number of other pieces. After leaving Ellington, Hamilton moved to the Virgin Islands where he taught music in public schools. He did return to the U.S. to play with Clarinet Summit in 1981 and 1985 and gigged a bit in New York during 1989–90 but was otherwise little heard from in his later years. Jimmy Hamilton only had a few opportunities to record as a leader, mostly dates for Urania (1954), Everest (1960), Swingville (two in 1961) and a 1985 set for Who's Who. —*Scott Yanow*

Jimmy Hamilton Rediscovered Live at the Buccaneer / Sep. 24, 1985 / Who's Who In Jazz ✦✦✦✦
An '85 quartet date issued on the Lionel Hampton Presents Who's Who label featuring clarinetist Jimmy Hamilton, longtime Ellingtonian and also a member of Clarinet Summit. He plays with a youthful vigor and swing, although these are mostly standards and shopworn numbers. —*Ron Wynn*

Scott Hamilton

b. Sep. 12, 1954, Providence, RI
Tenor Saxophone / Swing
When Scott Hamilton appeared in the mid-'70s fully formed with an appealing swing style on tenor (mixing together Zoot Sims and Ben Webster), he caused a minor sensation, for few other young players during the fusion era were exploring pre-bop jazz at his high level. He began playing when he was 16 and developed quickly, moving to New York in 1976. Hamilton played with Benny Goodman in the late '70s, but he has mostly performed as a leader, sometimes sharing the spotlight with Warren Vache, Ruby Braff, Rosemary Clooney, the Concord Jazz All-Stars or George Wein's Newport Jazz Festival All-Stars. Scott Hamilton, other than a session apiece for Famous Door and Progressive, has recorded a long string of dates for Concord that are notable for their consistency and solid swing. —*Scott Yanow*

Good Wind Who Is Blowing Us No Ill / Mar. 1, 1977 / Concord Jazz ✦✦✦✦
Tenor saxophonist Scott Hamilton's 1977 debut as a leader astounded the jazz world at the time. Unlike the '80s and '90s generation, whose muses are '50s hard boppers, Hamilton took his inspiration from the lusty swing sound of the '30s; Coleman Hawkins particularly, but also Ben Webster and Lester Young. —*Ron Wynn*

Scott Hamilton 2 / Jan. 7, 1978 / Concord Jazz ✦✦✦✦
Good followup to his first album as a leader. Another straight-ahead swing-influenced session, with Hamilton blowing fierce uptempo tunes one minute, then swaggering, soulful ballads the next. He was still heavily under the spell of Coleman Hawkins and Ben Webster at this time, but was slowly finding his own voice. —*Ron Wynn*

Grand Appearance / Jan. 23, 1978+Feb. 8, 1978 / Progressive ✦✦✦✦

With Scott's Band In New York / Jun. 26, 1978 / Concord ✦✦✦
Tenor saxophonist Scott Hamilton is in typically fine form on his third album as a leader for Concord. While Hamilton is equally skillful on ballads and hot stomps, cornetist Warren Vache sometimes takes a few too many chances on the uptempo material although one admires his brave attempts; he fares best on "Darn That Dream." Singer Sue Melikian sounds fine on two short

vocals, but it is the instrumentals by the sextet (which includes guitarist Chris Flory and pianist Norman Simmons) that are most memorable. — *Scott Yanow*

Back to Back / Sep. 1978 / Concord Jazz ++++
Veteran tenor saxophonist Buddy Tate and the relative youngster Scott Hamilton make for a potent combination on this spirited set of small-group swing. They contribute an original apiece, perform a ballad medley, and indulge in a lot of interplay and trade-offs on the standards. Backed by pianist Nat Pierce, bassist Monty Budwig and drummer Chuck Riggs, the tenors are in excellent form throughout this happy session. — *Scott Yanow*

Skyscrapers / Jul. 1979 / Concord Jazz ++++

Tenorshoes / Dec. 1979 / Concord Jazz +++++

● **Scott's Buddy** / Aug. 1980 / Concord Jazz ++++
This was the second recorded encounter between tenors Buddy Tate and Scott Hamilton and, despite their vast age difference (41 years), it is difficult to tell from their playing who is the older musician. Hamilton is one of the few hornmen from his generation to make the grade as a major swing stylist, and his respect for the elder Tate (who returns the feeling) is obvious. With guitarist Cal Collins, pianist Nat Pierce, bassist Bob Maize and drummer Jake Hanna, the two tenors are in spirited form on these standards and riff-filled originals; this combination works well. — *Scott Yanow*

Apples & Oranges / Jan. 1981+Aug. 1981 / Concord Jazz +++

Close Up / Feb. 1982 / Concord Jazz +++

Scott Hamilton Quintet in Concert / Jun. 1983 / Concord Jazz +++

The Second Set / Jun. 1983 / Concord Jazz +++

The Right Time / Jan. 1986 / Concord Jazz ++++

Major League / May 1986 / Concord Jazz +++++
Dave McKenna (p) and Jake Hanna (d) share the spotlight with Hamilton. — *Ron Wynn*

Scott Hamilton Plays Ballads / Mar. 1989 / Concord Jazz +++
Its title accurately describes the music on this CD. The warm tenor of Scott Hamilton (accompanied by pianist John Bunch, guitarist Chris Flory, bassist Phil Flanigan and drummer Chuck Riggs) brings out a great deal of beauty on 11 ballads including his own "Two Eighteen" and a variety of veteran melodies. This romantic disc is easy to enjoy. — *Scott Yanow*

Radio City / Feb. 1990 / Concord Jazz +++++

Groovin' High / Sep. 17, 1991 / Concord Jazz +++++
Tenor saxophonist Scott Hamilton co-led this '92 session with fellow saxophonists Ken Peplowski and Spike Robinson. It's another swing-tinged date, with the threesome mixing in other horns as well and teaming with guitarist Howard Alden, pianist Gerry Wiggins, bassist Dave Stone, and drummer Jake Hanna for both swing and blues anthems and ballads. — *Ron Wynn*

Race Point / Sep. 18, 1991 / Concord Jazz ++++

East of the Sun / Aug. 1993 / Concord Jazz +++
For this Concord CD, tenor saxophonist Scott Hamilton gave the readers of Japan's *Swing Journal* the opportunity to vote on which songs they would like him to record. With the exception of his original "Setagaya Serenade" (a stomping blues that Hamilton took the liberty of performing) and "Autumn Leaves," he had recorded all of these veteran songs previously, but Hamilton's melodic improvisations do not copy the earlier versions. With the assistance of an English rhythm section (pianist Brian Lemon, bassist Dave Green and drummer Allan Ganley), Hamilton is in typically swinging form on this fine set of standards and ballads. — *Scott Yanow*

Organic Duke / May 18, 1994–May 19, 1994 / Concord Jazz +++

Live At The Brecon Jazz Festival / Aug. 13, 1994 / Concord Jazz +++

Jan Hammer

b. Apr. 17, 1948, Prague, Czechoslovakia
Keyboards / Fusion
One of the more inventive keyboardists of the early fusion days, Jan Hammer has not played much jazz since the late '70s. He studied at Prague Conservatory and, in 1967, played at the Warsaw Jazz Jamboree with Stuff Smith. In 1968 after the Russian invasion of Czechoslovakia, Hammer left for the U.S. He attended

Berklee, worked with Sarah Vaughan (1970–71) and moved to New York where he played with Jeremy Steig and Elvin Jones. Hammer gained fame playing with the Mahavishnu Orchestra during its prime period (1971–73) and with Billy Cobham (1973–75). After leading his own groups (Jeff Beck was a sideman in 1976), he had great success with his score for the television series *Miami Vice* and worked with Al DiMeola in 1982 but has not been heard from much since. — *Scott Yanow*

Make Love / Aug. 30, 1968 / MPS ++++

● **Like Children** / 1974 / Atlantic +++++
The keyboardist and violinist Jerry Goodman away from Mahavishu. They play all instruments (overdubbed). "Country and Eastern Music" and "Steppings Tones" were high-water marks for this new breed (at the time). — *Michael G. Nastos*

The Early Years / 1974–1979 / Nemperor +++
1974–1979. A comprehensive compilation of Hammer's best cuts from the '70s. — *Ron Wynn*

Oh Yeah / 1976 / Nemperor ++++
This is an album of fusion at its best. "Magical Dog" and "Red & Orange" are definitive statements. This was the first exposure for violinist Steve Kindler. David Earle Johnson is on congas. — *Michael G. Nastos*

Escape from Television / 1986 / MCA ++
Late '80s vehicle with synthesizer and keyboardist Jan Hammer, featuring a collection of songs he wrote and prepared for the *Miami Vice* television show and other programs. This is not a jazz album, but has some entertaining themes and arrangements. — *Ron Wynn*

Gunter Hampel

b. Aug. 31, 1937, Gottingen, Germany
Vibes, Clarinet, Flute, Piano / Avant-Garde, Free Jazz
Gunter Hampel, a multi-instrumentalist who in addition to vibes, bass clarinet and flute also plays piano and other reeds, has done a fine job of documenting his avant-garde music since 1969 for his own Birth label. He started leading his own band in 1958, has been playing very advanced jazz in Europe since the early '60s and in the early '70s formed his Galaxie Dream Band. Among his sidemen have been his wife, singer Jeanne Lee, Anthony Braxton, Alexander von Schlippenbach, Willem Breuker, Perry Robinson, Enrico Rava and Mark Whitecage. — *Scott Yanow*

Music from Europe / Dec. 21, 1966 / ESP ++++

July 8, 1969 / Jul. 8, 1969 / Birth +++

★ **Jubilation** / Nov. 1983 / Birth +++++

Fresh Heat: Live at Sweet Basil / Feb. 1985 / Birth +++++

Lionel Hampton

b. Apr. 12, 1909, Louisville
Vibes, Leader, Drums, Piano / Swing
Lionel Hampton was the first jazz vibraphonist and has been one of the jazz giants since the mid-'30s. He has achieved the difficult feat of being musically open-minded (even recording "Giant Steps") without changing his basic swing style. Hamp started out as a drummer, playing with the Chicago Defender Newsboys' Band as a youth. His original idol was Jimmy Bertrand, a 1920s drummer who occasionally played xylophone. Hampton played on the West Coast with such groups as Curtis Mosby's Blue Blowers, Reb Spikes and Paul Howard's Quality Serenaders (with whom he made his recording debut in 1929) before joining Les Hite's band, which, for a period, accompanied Louis Armstrong. At a recording session in 1930, a vibraphone happened to be in the studio, and Armstrong asked Hampton (who had practiced on one previously) if he could play a little bit behind him and on "Memories of You" and "Shine", and Hamp became the first jazz improviser to record on vibes.

It would be another six years before he found fame. Lionel Hampton, after leaving Hite, had his own band in Los Angeles' Paradise Cafe until one night in 1936 when Benny Goodman came into the club and discovered him. Soon Hampton recorded with BG, Teddy Wilson and Gene Krupa as the Benny Goodman Quartet, and six weeks later he officially joined Goodman. An exciting soloist whose enthusiasm even caused BG to smile, Hampton became one of the stars of his organization, appearing in films with Goodman, at the famous 1938 Carnegie Hall Concert and nightly on the radio. In 1937 he started recording regularly as a leader for Victor with specially assembled all-star groups that formed a who's who of swing; all of these timeless performances (1937–41) were reissued by Bluebird on a six-LP set although thus far in piecemeal fashion on CD.

Hampton stayed with Goodman until 1940, sometimes substituting on drums and taking vocals. In 1940 Lionel Hampton formed his first big band and, in 1942, had a huge hit with "Flying Home" featuring a classic Illinois Jacquet tenor spot (one of the first R&B solos). During the remainder of the decade, Hampton's extroverted orchestra was a big favorite, leaning toward R&B, showing the influence of bebop after 1944 and sometimes getting pretty exhibitionistic. Among his sidemen, in addition to Jacquet, were Arnett Cobb, Dinah Washington (who Hampton helped discover), Cat Anderson, Marshall Royal, Dexter Gordon, Milt Buckner, Earl Bostic, Snooky Young, Johnny Griffin, Joe Wilder, Benny Bailey, Charles Mingus, Fats Navarro, Al Gray and even Wes Montgomery and Betty Carter. Hampton's popularity allowed him to continue leading big bands off and on into the mid-'90s and the 1953 edition that visited Paris (with Clifford Brown, Art Farmer, Quincy Jones, Jimmy Cleveland, Gigi Gryce, George Wallington and Annie Ross) would be difficult to top, although fights over money and the right of the sideman to record led to its breakup. Hampton appeared and recorded with many all-star groups in the 1950s including reunions with Benny Goodman, meetings with the Oscar Peterson Trio, Stan Getz, Buddy DeFranco, and as part of a trio with Art Tatum and Buddy Rich. He was also featured in *The Benny Goodman Story* (1956).

Since the 1950s, Lionel Hampton has mostly repeated past triumphs, always playing "Hamp's Boogie Woogie" (which features his very rapid two-finger piano playing), "Hey Ba-Ba-Re-Bop" and "Flying Home." However, his enthusiasm still causes excitement and he remains a household name. Hampton has recorded through the years for nearly every label including two of his own (Glad Hamp and Who's Who) and most recently Mojazz. Despite strokes and the ravages of age, Lionel Hampton, as of this writing, is still a vital force. *—Scott Yanow*

Lionel Hampton (1929–1940) / Apr. 1929–Dec. 1940 / BBC ✦✦✦

Lionel Hampton (1937–1938) / Feb. 8, 1937–Jan. 18, 1938 / Classics ✦✦✦✦✦

Lionel Hampton's Jumpin' Jive, Vol. 2 / Feb. 8, 1937–Oct. 12, 1939 / Bluebird ✦✦✦
Lionel Hampton's small-group swing sessions of 1937–41 were consistently brilliant but, unfortunately, the current Bluebird CD reissue program has issued these performances in almost random fashion on three separate CDs, leaving out many strong sides and often dividing up sessions between two overlapping CDs. The second volume has a little of this and a little of that including a hot session featuring altoist Johnny Hodges, a few of tenor saxophonist Chu Berry's best performances (particularly "Sweethearts on Parade") and the alternate take of "When Lights Are Low", but this CD is primarily for beginners; it'll drive Hampton collectors crazy. *—Scott Yanow*

☆ **The Complete Lionel Hampton** / Feb. 8, 1937–Apr. 8, 1941 / Bluebird ✦✦✦✦✦
Although this six-LP box set is now out of print, it is so definitive that it deserves the highest rating. Consisting of all of the sessions led by vibraphonist Lionel Hampton prior to the formation of his popular big band, these hot swing sides feature a who's who of jazz greats from the 1930s including trumpeters Ziggy Elman, Cootie Williams, Jonah Jones, Harry James, Rex Stewart, Red Allen and Dizzy Gillespie, altoists Benny Carter, Johnny Hodges and Earl Bostic, tenors Herschel Evans, Chu Berry, Coleman Hawkins, and Ben Webster, guitarist Charlie Christian and the Nat King Cole Trio among many others. With Hamp on vibes, two-fingered piano and occasional vocals, this set is overflowing with classic performances. It should have been reissued in complete form on CD instead of in the piecemeal fashion that it has thus far partially reappeared. This box has yet to be matched. *—Scott Yanow*

Hot Mallets, Vol. 1 / Apr. 14, 1937–Sep. 11, 1939 / Bluebird ✦✦✦
While the original six-LP box set correctly reissued all of Lionel Hampton's 1937–41 small-group recordings as a leader, the CD reissue program has been rather erratic, dividing up some of these selections in almost random fashion between three CDs, often splitting up sessions between a pair of discs. The first of these three CDs is the strongest, highlighted by "On the Sunny

Side of the Street" (featuring altoist Johnny Hodges), "I'm Confessin'" with trumpeter Jonah Jones, and the four master takes from a date with Coleman Hawkins, Chu Berry, Ben Webster, Benny Carter and a young Dizzy Gillespie. Great music but dumb programming. *—Scott Yanow*

Lionel Hampton (1938–1939) / Jan. 18, 1938–Jun. 13, 1939 / Classics ✦✦✦✦✦

Lionel Hampton (1939–1940) / Jun. 13, 1939–May 10, 1940 / Classics ✦✦✦✦✦

Tempo and Swing / Oct. 30, 1939–Aug. 21, 1940 / Bluebird ✦✦✦
The third and final CD in a rather flawed reissue program of Lionel Hampton's early small-group recordings as a leader contains most (but not all) of the recordings from six of Hamp's sessions, featuring such players as trumpeter Ziggy Elman, Benny Carter, tenors Ben Webster and Coleman Hawkins, clarinetist Edmond Hall and the Nat King Cole Trio. Best is the Carter-Hall-Hawkins date, which is highlighted by two takes of "Dinah," but this music should have been reissued complete and in chronological order as it had been previously on LP. *—Scott Yanow*

Steppin' out (1942–1944) / Mar. 2, 1942–Oct. 16, 1944 / MCA ✦✦✦✦
Released as part of MCA's *Jazz Heritage* series in the early '80s, this LP contains 14 of the 16 selections from Lionel Hampton's 1942–44 sessions including two versions of "Flying Home" (featuring the contrasting tenor sax solos of Illinois Jacquet and Arnett Cobb) and the original recording of "Hamp's Boogie-Woogie." This is classic music played in an exuberant swing style that Hampton has continued to keep alive for the half-century since. *—Scott Yanow*

All-American Award Concert at Carnegie Hall / Apr. 15, 1945 / Decca ✦✦✦
Lionel Hampton's 1945 Carnegie Hall concert (available on this LP) is a fine all-round showcase for the band, which at the time was evolving rapidly from swing to bop and rhythm & blues. Some of the music on this set is a bit hysterical (including a tenor battle by Arnett Cobb and Herbie Fields) and of course "Flying Home." Dizzy Gillespie makes a memorable guest appearance on "Red Cross" and Dinah Washington sings a fine version of her first hit, "Evil Gal Blues." *—Scott Yanow*

● **Midnight Sun** / Jan. 29, 1946–Nov. 10, 1947 / GRP ✦✦✦✦✦
Although firmly identified with Benny Goodman and the swing era, vibraphonist Lionel Hampton led one of the most bop-oriented and forward-looking big bands of the mid-to-late '40s; for proof of that check out "Mingus Fingers" (by Charles Mingus) on this CD. This set reissues some of Hampton's most boppish sides from 1946–47 along with the original version of "Midnight Sun" and is full of extroverted solos and exciting ensembles. Although tenorman Arnett Cobb (heard in the earlier selections) and pianist Milt Buckner are the best-known sidemen, such musicians as the screaming trumpeters Jimmy Nottingham and Leo "the Whistler" Sheppard and tenors Morris Lane, John Sparrow and the young Johnny Griffin provide their own strong moments. Until Decca gets around to reissuing all of Hamp's big band sides in chronological order, this is one of the sets to get. *—Scott Yanow*

The Original Stardust / Aug. 4, 1947 / Decca ✦✦✦✦✦
Lionel Hampton's classic live version of "Star Dust" at this "Just Jazz" concert is rightfully acclaimed, and remains one of the highpoints of his long career. Oddly enough, Hampton does not appear on the other three selections included on this LP (which has since been reissued on CD), but these fine renditions of "One O'Clock Jump," "The Man I Love" and "Lady Be Good" do benefit from excellent solos by trumpeter Charlie Shavers, altoist Willie Smith, Corky Corcoran on tenor and bassist Slam Stewart. Highly recommended. *—Scott Yanow*

Lionel Hampton with the Just Jazz All Stars / Aug. 4, 1947 / GNP ✦✦✦
Taken from the same concert that produced Lionel Hampton's famous "Stardust" solo, this second LP actually has more Hamp (he dominates all six selections) but never reaches the heights of "Stardust." There are some fine moments from trumpeter Charlie Shavers, altoist Willie Smith and bassist Slam Stewart on such familiar material as "Perdido," "Hamp's Boogie Woogie" and "Flying Home," making it a worthwhile release. *—Scott Yanow*

Hot House / 1948 / Alamac ✦✦✦
This budget (and possibly bootleg) LP of Lionel Hampton radio airchecks from 1948 is notable for a few reasons. Charles Mingus

is heard throughout on bass, the great bop trumpeter Fats Navarro gets a fine spot on "Hot House" and a young Wes Montgomery takes a rare solo during "Brant Inn Boogie." Other key voices include trumpeters Benny Bailey, Teddy Buckner and the remarkable high-note specialist Leo "the Whistler" Sheppard, altoist Johnny Board and Johnny Sparrow on tenor in addition to the leader/vibraphonist. Since this particular orchestra did not get a chance to record commercially (due to the 1948 recording strike), this set is invaluable to jazz historians. —*Scott Yanow*

The Blues Ain't News to Me / Apr. 17, 1951–Aug. 3, 1955 / Verve ◆◆◆◆

This two-LP reissue contains highlights of two Lionel Hampton big-band Verve recordings in 1951 and a full set from 1955. One of the most popular of all bandleaders, Hampton is in fine form during these selections, which are not as hysterical as his live performances of the same era. Mixing rhythm & blues with modern swing and showcasing such soloists as trumpeters Benny Bailey and Wallace Davenport, trombonists Jimmy Cleveland and Al Grey and the tenors of Johnny Board and Eddie Chamblee (along with vocals by Hampton, Sonny Parker, Janet Thurlow and Vicki Lee), this is a fine all-round showcase of Hampton's often-overlooked '50s big band. As an added plus, drummer Buddy Rich drops by for "Air Mail Special" and "Flyin' Home." —*Scott Yanow*

Complete Quartet / Sep. 10, 1953–Jul. 31, 1955 / Verve ◆◆◆

This out-of-print, five-LP box set features the great vibraphonist Lionel Hampton on extensive jams of standards with pianist Oscar Peterson, bassist Ray Brown and drummer Buddy Rich; the final two ballads are from a reunion of Hamp with pianist Teddy Wilson and drummer Gene Krupa (in addition to bassist Red Callender). Few surprises occur and no new ground is broken, but the music is consistently joyful and swinging, a happy set for all concerned. —*Scott Yanow*

Lionel Hampton in Paris / Sep. 28, 1953 / Vogue ◆◆◆

This CD reissue features a loose jam session dominated by vibraphonist Lionel Hampton. The nine selections (which include such titles as "Real Crazy," "More Crazy" and "More and More Crazy"), in addition to many long solos from Hamp, has some spirited playing by trumpeter Walter Williams (who rarely had an opportunity to stretch out like this on records), trombonists Jimmy Cleveland and Al Hayse, clarinetist Mezz Mezzrow, tenors Alix Combelle and Clifford Scott and guitarist Billy Mackell with suitable backup by pianist Claude Bolling, electric bassist Monk Montgomery and drummer Curley Hamner. The results are not innovative or essential but generally quite fun. —*Scott Yanow*

European Concert, 1953 / Sep. 1953 / IAJRC ◆◆◆

Lionel Hampton led one of his most potentially great big bands during a European tour in 1953, but he managed (for unknown reasons) to sabotage it. When Hamp forbid sidemen to record on a freelance basis overseas and most of the key ones disobeyed his orders, the friction eventually led to the breakup of the band. Considering that the orchestra included trumpeters Clifford Brown and Art Farmer, trombonist Jimmy Cleveland, altoist Gigi Gryce, tenor Clifford Scott, pianist George Wallington and Annie Ross on vocals, the dissolution of the orchestra before it made any commercial recordings is a major tragedy. This IAJRC LP contains part of a concert that the band performed and gives hints as to what might have been. Hampton really hogs the spotlight (he is the only soloist on "How High the Moon") but "Blue Boy" has spots for Farmer, Gryce, Scott and, most importantly, Clifford Brown. —*Scott Yanow*

★ **Hamp and Getz** / Aug. 1, 1955 / Verve ◆◆◆◆◆

If one were to believe the cliches and stereotypes common in some jazz history books, this matchup should not have worked. By 1955 Lionel Hampton was a veteran swing vibraphonist while Stan Getz was the leader of the "cool school" of young tenors. But what these two masters had in common (in addition to a healthy respect for each other's talents) was the ability to swing as hard as possible. Joined by a fine trio, the duo really rip into "Cherokee" and "Jumpin' at the Woodside" (listen to their blistering tradeoffs) and, even with a fine ballad medley, it is these torrid jams that make this a highly recommended disc. —*Scott Yanow*

Reunion at Newport 1967 / Jun. 30, 1956–Jul. 3, 1967 / RCA/Bluebird ◆◆◆◆

Most of this CD is taken up by a special Newport Jazz Festival concert featuring a big band full of Lionel Hampton's alumni. With trombonist Al Grey, Frank Foster on tenor and a screaming

trumpet section that boasted Snooky Young, Jimmy Nottingham, Joe Newman and Wallace Davenport, the explosive nature of the music is not too surprising; the climax is provided by guest Illinois Jacquet on "Flying Home." The remainder of this disc contains half of a very effective 1956 session cut in Spain in which the medium-sized group includes a castanet player, and two songs match Hampton with the great Spanish pianist Tete Montoliu. —*Scott Yanow*

You Better Know It / Oct. 26, 1964 / Impulse! ◆◆◆◆

Vibist Lionel Hampton's rhythmic abilities haven't been dulled by age, and he displayed his proficiency on this date, which includes the enjoyable bonus track "Moon Over My Annie." There was no wasted energy or unnecessary or exaggerated solos; just bluesy, assertive, muscular arrangements, accompaniment, and ensemble segments. Highlights included "Vibraphone Blues," "Trick or Treat" and "Swingle Jingle," in which Hampton shifted from vibes to piano. —*Ron Wynn*

Lionel Hampton & Friends: Rare Recordings, Vol. 1 / Apr. 15, 1965–Nov. 13, 1977 / Telarc ◆◆◆

During the mid-to-late '70s, Lionel Hampton sought to recapture the magic of his classic '30s all-star recordings with a series of albums featuring his vibes with musicians who he normally did not encounter in his travels. This particular CD draws one or two selections apiece from seven of these albums (originally on the Who's Who label), all but one from 1977. The lone exception, a version of "Stardust" from 1965, has quite a lineup (trumpeters Clark Terry and Thad Jones, trombonist J.J. Johnson, Lucky Thompson on soprano and tenor great Coleman Hawkins) and is quite listenable but does not live up to its potential. The same can be said for most of these performances, which include meetings with pianists Earl Hines and Teddy Wilson, a workout with baritonist Gerry Mulligan, a version of "Cherokee" featuring Steve Marcus' soprano and drummer Buddy Rich, two selections with Dexter Gordon (who has a rare outing on soprano during "Seven Comes Eleven") and a pair of numbers from what would be bassist Charles Mingus' final recording date. Hopefully, these interesting sessions, even though they do not reach the creative heights of Hampton's earlier recordings, will eventually be reissued on CD complete and in chronological order. —*Scott Yanow*

Lionel Hampton and His Jazz Giants / May 15, 1977 / Black & Blue ◆◆◆

By the time of this 1977 small-group recording, Lionel Hampton had been performing with pickup bands for decades, outfits that usually only lasted as long as particular tours. This studio session found him reuniting with such alumni as Milt Buckner (sticking here exclusively to organ), the remarkable high-note trumpeter Cat Anderson, guitarist Billy Mackel and the two tenors of Eddie Chamblee and Paul Moen. Performing standards and two basic originals, this is a happy, extroverted outing that has yet to be reissued on CD. —*Scott Yanow*

Live in Emmen, Holland / May 13, 1978 / Timeless ◆◆◆◆

In addition to new versions of Lionel Hampton's three "greatest hits" ("Flying Home," "Hamp's Boogie-Woogie" and "Airmail Special"), this live nonet session features him grappling successfully with two of John Coltrane's most notable compositions ("Giant Steps" and "Moments Notice") along with songs by Roland Hanna and Joe Henderson. Clearly Hampton, although always closely identified with the swing era, was one of the few members of his musical generation to keep up with later developments in jazz. With strong solos by trumpeter Joe Newman, Paul Moen on tenor, Eddie Chamblee (alternating between alto and tenor) and Wild Bill Davis on organ and piano, this spirited and diverse set is highly recommended. —*Scott Yanow*

Fiftieth Anniversary Concert Live at Carnegie Hall / Jul. 1, 1978 / Sutra ◆◆◆

One has to completely overlook this double-LP's inadequate packaging (which makes it appear to be a bootleg or a budget series) in evaluating the music of this loose but rather notable set. The lineup includes such brilliant players as trumpeters Cat Anderson, Doc Cheatham and Joe Newman, tenors Arnett Cobb and Paul Moen, altoist Charles McPherson, clarinetist Bob Wilbur, baritonist Pepper Adams and pianist Ray Bryant. Although little prior preparation seems to have taken place (many of the all-stars had rarely played with Hamp in the past), the results are quite spirited, generally musical and consistently fun. —*Scott Yanow*

Sentimental Journey / Mar. 13, 1985–Mar. 14, 1985 / Atlantic ◆◆

A rather forgettable LP, this set mostly features the okay vocals of

Sylvia Bennett on a variety of overplayed swing standards. Lionel Hampton's big band is mostly restricted to background work with occasional short individual spots while Hampton himself is the only soloist on five of the nine selections, including the lone instrumental, "Avalon." The lack of liner notes on this Atlantic LP is surprising since its purpose seemed to be to introduce a new singer. This set can be safely passed by. —Scott Yanow

Mostly Blues / Mar. 10, 1988–Apr. 8, 1988 / Music Masters ✦✦✦
Considering that this program features such songs as "Someday My Prince Will Come," "Take the 'A' Train," "Honeysuckle Rose" and "Gone with the Wind," its title is rather inaccurate; in fact only three of the nine songs are actually blues. In any case, vibraphonist Lionel Hampton is in fine form as the dominant soloist in a quintet also including pianist Bobby Scott and guitarist Joe Beck. Even as he entered his 80s, Hampton still displayed youthful vitality and enthusiasm. —Scott Yanow

Cookin' In The Kitchen / Jun. 7, 1988–Jun. 15, 1988 / Glad Hamp ✦✦✦
The veteran vibraphonist Lionel Hampton (then 79) leads his young big band through recent originals; only Joe Henderson's "Inner Urge" and the Gene Ammons/Sonny Stitt line "Blues Up & Down" were more than a few years old at the time and, to his credit, Hampton avoids his usual repertoire. The music is often funky and played with spirit, although the orchestra occasionally sounds like a somewhat anonymous stage band that had not fully developed its own individual personality yet. Jerry Weldon and Doug Miller have a good tenor battle on "Blues Up & Down," altoist Rob Middleton and his brother Andy (on soprano) are in fine form on "Two Brothers" and Hampton has little difficulty finding fresh statements to make on this modern material. —Scott Yanow

Mostly Ballads / Sep. 8, 1989–Nov. 28, 1989 / Music Masters ✦✦
As with the slightly earlier Mostly Blues CD, the title of this set is inaccurate. True, Hampton performs such ballads as "I'll Be Seeing You," "Lover Man" and "But Beautiful," but many of these songs are taken at medium tempos and this program also includes three Teo Macero originals that are definitely not ballads. The use of synthesizer on several numbers is not particularly interesting and, although trumpeter Lew Soloff contributes a few fine solos, the most rewarding numbers are the ones that focus on Hampton's highly expressive vibes; he is in fine form throughout. It's an erratic but worthy release from the vital octogenarian. —Scott Yanow

Live at the Blue Note / Jun. 11, 1991–Jun. 13, 1991 / Telarc ✦✦✦
In 1991, for a gig at the Blue Note in New York, vibraphonist Lionel Hampton headed a nonet full of classic veterans that were termed "the Golden Men of Jazz": trumpeters Clark Terry and Harry "Sweets" Edison, tenors James Moody and Buddy Tate, trombonist Al Grey, pianist Hank Jones, bassist Milt Hinton and drummer Grady Tate. Even with its many loose moments, these great players came up with some notable moments, including James Moody's humorous vocalizing on "Moody's Mood for Love" and particularly fine playing by Terry and Grey; Tate and Edison do show their age a bit but are welcome participants in what must have been a very happy occasion. —Scott Yanow

Just Jazz: Live at the Blue Note / Jun. 11, 1991–Jun. 13, 1991 / Telarc ✦✦
The second of two volumes by "the Golden Men of Jazz" at the Blue Note in New York, this CD is not at the same level as the first, with several almost chaotic spots; listen to how Lionel Hampton tries to hog the spotlight on "Ring Dem Bells." There are some good moments from Clark Terry, James Moody and Al Grey (although Harry Edison and Buddy Tate show their age a bit), but the earlier release, Live at the Blue Note, is a much better buy. —Scott Yanow

For The Love Of Music / 1994–1995 / Mojazz ✦✦
For his debut on the MoJazz label, the ancient vibraphonist Lionel Hampton was featured with several groups, some more suitable than others. Keyboardist Patrice Rushen largely ruins a funky rendition of "Flying Home" and several of the other songs (the insipid "Jazz Me" and Chaka Khan's feature on "Gossamer Wings" are little more than throwaways). Better is Hampton's collaboration with Tito Puente's band on "Don't You Worry 'Bout a Thing" and his original "Mojazz," even if Grover Washington, Jr., sounds as if he is on automatic pilot on "Another Part of Me." Overall this so-so disc can easily be passed by. —Scott Yanow

Slide Hampton (Locksley Wellington Hampton)

b. Apr. 21, 1932, Jeannette, PA
Trombone, Arrranger / Bop, Hard Bop
Slide Hampton has been a fine trombonist and arranger since the mid-'50s, helping to keep the tradition of bop alive in both his playing and his writing. After working with Buddy Johnson (1955–56) and Lionel Hampton, he became an important force in Maynard Ferguson's excellent big band of 1957–59. He led octets in the 1960s with such sidemen as Freddie Hubbard and George Coleman. After traveling with Woody Herman to Europe in 1968, Hampton settled overseas where he stayed very active. Since returning to the U.S. in 1977, he has led his World of Trombones (which features nine trombonists), played in a cop-op quintet called Continuum and been involved in several Dizzy Gillespie tribute projects, recording in the 1990s for Telarc. —Scott Yanow

World of Trombones / Jan. 8, 1979–Jan. 9, 1979 / Black Lion ✦✦✦✦
Ambitious project with nine trombonists merging their skills under the leadership of Slide Hampton. The list includes both established veterans like Curtis Fuller and Steve Turre and emerging newcomers Janice Robinson and Afro-Latin star Papo Vasquez. Hampton's arrangements are excellent, but there's more emphasis on performance style than real solo development. Pianist Albert Dailey and bassist Ray Drummond were also outstanding. —Ron Wynn

● **Roots** / Apr. 17, 1985 / Criss Cross ✦✦✦✦✦
Tremendous '85 quintet session with trombonist Slide Hampton heading a distinguished group and nicely teaming with tenor saxophonist Clifford Jordan in a first-rate hard bop frontline. The rhythm section's quality isn't far behind, especially pianist Cedar Walton and drummer Billy Higgins. —Ron Wynn

Dedicated to Diz / Feb. 6, 1993–Feb. 7, 1993 / Telarc ✦✦✦

Herbie Hancock

b. Apr. 12, 1940, Chicago, IL
Piano, Keyboards, Leader, Composer / Post-Bop, Fusion, Pop
If not for the amazing reign of Miles Davis, pianist Herbie Hancock might qualify as jazz's most well known, popular performer since the '60s. Hancock had 11 albums chart during the '70s and 17 between 1973 and 1984, including three in 1974, figures that puts him well ahead of any other jazz musician in the '70s and beyond. He's also among jazz's finest eclectics, having played everything from bebop to free, jazz-rock, fusion, funk, instrumental pop, dance, hip-hop and world fusion. Hancock's style, greatly influenced by Bill Evans, mixes introspective and energetic elements, and fuses blues and gospel influences with bebop and classical elements. He's both a great accompanist and excellent soloist, whose voicings, phrasing, melodic and interpretative skills and harmonic facility were impressive early in his career, and remain sharp no matter what style or idiom he's working.

Hancock began studying piano at seven and performed the first movement of a Mozart concerto with The Chicago Symphony Orchestra in a young people's concert at 11. He formed his own jazz ensemble while attending Hyde Park High School. He was influenced harmonically by the arrangements Clare Fischer provided for The Hi-Los and Robert Farnon's orchestrations of pop songs. Hancock had begun working in Chicago jazz clubs with Donald Byrd and Coleman Hawkins when he left Grinnell College in 1960. Byrd invited him to join his group and Hancock moved to New York. After he recorded with Byrd's band, Blue Note offered Hancock his own pact. Hancock's debut Takin' Off was issued in 1962 and yielded a hit with "Watermelon Man." He joined Miles Davis in 1963. Hancock's solo style became an integral part of Davis' evolving '60s approach. His interaction with Ron Carter and Tony Williams was at the core of songs that increasingly became more flexible and less fixed, while Hancock also cut important albums as a leader for Blue Note and gained status as a composer. Some major compositions during the '60s included "Maiden Voyage," "Dolphin Dance," "Speak Like A Child" and "I Have A Dream" dedicated to Dr. Martin Luther King, Jr. During the '70s, Hancock led a sextet that merged jazz, rock, African, and Indian musical references and was mostly electric. This band was one of the great jazz-rock groups, though Hancock finally disbanded it because the group had limited market appeal and financial success. The Sextant group sometimes performed in African garb, and Hancock even issued the album Mwandishi with the musicians African names given along with their English ones. He played many electronic instruments, adding the Hohner Clavinet, various synthesizers and Mellotron to his Fender Rhodes. Hancock disbanded The Sextant in 1973 and formed The Headhunters, a funk, rock and instrumental pop band that scored a huge crossover hit with the album *Headhunters*. Hancock's records were now being played by the emerging upper- and middle-class black professionals, who for the most part, had little or no knowledge of his past sound. The single "Chameleon," which reflected the influence of accompanists in Sly Stone's band, was a club and radio smash in edited fashion. Hancock turned more to strict pop music, though he also did an acoustic VSOP tour in the late '70s and a series of duo concerts with Chick Corea. He repeatedly defended his right to make any and all kinds of music, and often labeled criticism of his commercial projects "elitist," an extension of the charge that some black nationalists leveled against the '60s free players.

During the '80s, Hancock alternated between acoustic and electric material. He had another big hit in 1983 with "Rockit," a song that utilized the scratching technique and predated its popularity in hip-hop production with a multi-textured, heavily edited snippet/rhythm framework. The video and single gained Hancock MTV coverage and exposure, and triggered a fresh round of debate over whether he was selling out. Hancock spent the next two years doing mostly conventional jazz dates, even winning an Oscar for his score of the film *Round Midnight*. Hancock collaborated with African musician Foday Musa Suso for a fine duet album that made the charts as well. He toured Europe in 1987 with Buster Williams and Al Foster, and did a series of American and Japanese dates with a quartet that included Mike Brecker, Ron Carter and Tony Williams. Hancock also hosted a variety show on the Showtime cable television network, and did lecture/performances on public television. He's done numerous albums for Blue Note, Columbia, and Warner Bros. The lengthy list of musicians Hancock's played with reads like a jazz who's who; it includes Joe Henderson, Freddie Hubbard, Wynton Marsalis, George Coleman, Johnny Coles, Bobby Hutcherson, George Benson and Paul Desmond, among many others. His versatility and track record ensure Hancock will never have difficulty getting recording opportunities. It would be silly to insist everything he's done was great, but much of it, even his most commercial, trendy dates, has retained a high level of musicianship and attention to stylistic detail. —*Ron Wynn and William Ruhlmann*

● **Takin' Off** / May 28, 1962 / Blue Note ✦✦✦✦✦
A prophetic title for this session with Dexter Gordon (ts) and Freddie Hubbard (tpt). —*Ron Wynn*

My Point of View / Mar. 19, 1963 / Blue Note ✦✦✦✦

Inventions and Dimensions / Aug. 30, 1963 / Blue Note ✦✦✦✦
First-rate early work. Willie Bobo makes a scintillating percussive contribution. —*Ron Wynn*

Empyrean Isles / Jun. 17, 1964 / Blue Note ✦✦✦✦✦
1985 reissue of one of Hancock's seminal releases. Freddie Hubbard (tpt) is daring and aggressive. —*Ron Wynn*

★ **Maiden Voyage** / Mar. 17, 1965 / Blue Note ✦✦✦✦✦

Blow Up / Oct. 1966 / Atlantic ✦✦✦

Speak Like a Child / Mar. 9, 1968 / Blue Note ✦✦✦✦✦
A simply beautiful title cut, plus wondrous arrangements and playing throughout. —*Ron Wynn*

The Prisoner / Apr. 18, 1969–Apr. 23, 1969 / Blue Note ✦✦✦
A poignant tribute to Dr. Martin Luther King, Jr. from pianist Herbie Hancock, whose '69 album featured Hancock's compositions for large orchestra and was sparked by superb playing from the leader and Joe Henderson on tenor sax. —*Ron Wynn*

★ **Mwandishi: The Complete Warner Bros. Recordings** / Oct. 4, 1969–Feb. 17, 1972 / Warner Archives ✦✦✦✦✦
This two-CD set reissues the complete contents of three LPs: *Fat Albert Rotunda*, *Mwandishi* and *Crossings*. The earliest session (extensions of generally memorable funk themes used in a Bill Cosby cartoon) features the keyboardist in a sextet on most selections with tenor saxophonist Joe Henderson, trumpeter Johnny Coles and trombonist Garnett Brown; two songs use a 15-piece group. However the bulk of this set showcases Hancock's regular sextet of the era (which comprised trumpeter Eddie Henderson, Benny Maupin on bass clarinet, alto flute and soprano, trombon-

ist Julian Priester, bassist Buster Williams and drummer Billy Hart); the later session also adds Patrick Gleeson's moog synthesizer. The unique music is both explorative and loosely funky, avant-garde yet influenced by rock and funk. The results are often quite fascinating, but this group (which only recorded one further album for Columbia) was a commercial flop which Hancock would eventually break up, in favor of The Headhunters. —*Scott Yanow*

Sextant / 1972 / Columbia ✦✦✦

☆ **Headhunters** / 1973 / Columbia ✦✦✦✦✦

Thrust / Aug. 26, 1974 / Columbia ✦✦✦

Death Wish / 1974 / Columbia ✦✦✦

Secrets / Jun. 1976 / Columbia ✦✦✦

VSOP / Jun. 29, 1976 / Columbia ✦✦✦✦

VSOP Quintet / Jul. 16, 1977–Jul. 18, 1977 / Columbia ✦✦✦✦✦

Sunlight / 1977 / Columbia ✦✦✦

An Evening With / Feb. 1978 / Columbia ✦✦✦✦
Since Chick Corea and Herbie Hancock had, by 1978, spent several years mostly playing electric keyboards, their acoustic duet tour surprised many listeners who thought that they would always specialize in fusion. This double LP contains many fine performances including lengthy versions of "Maiden Voyage" and "La Fiesta," but it is the striding by Corea and Hancock on "Liza" that is most unique. —*Scott Yanow*

Feets, Don't Fail Me Now / 1978 / Columbia ✦✦

Live under the Sky / Jul. 26, 1979 / Columbia ✦✦✦
Herbie Hancock's all-star VSOP Quintet reunited the Miles Davis group of the mid-'60s (Wayne Shorter on tenor and soprano, pianist Hancock, bassist Ron Carter and Tony Williams), with trumpeter Freddie Hubbard doing his best to fill Davis' shoes. The Japanese outdoors concert (recorded during a rainstorm) heard on this two-LP set finds the talented players in fine form on extended versions of six group originals (only Williams' "Pee Wee" dates from the Miles Davis years); a Hancock-Shorter duet medley on "Stella by Starlight" and "On Green Dolphin Street" is offered as the encore. Few surprises occur, but it is particularly rewarding to hear Wayne Shorter (after years of being in Weather Report) stretching out again. —*Scott Yanow*

Monster / 1980 / Columbia ✦✦

Mr. Hands / 1980 / Columbia ✦✦

Magic Windows / 1981 / Columbia ✦✦

Quartet / Jul. 25, 1981 / Columbia ✦✦✦✦✦
A fine mainstream set that showed detractors Hancock hadn't lost his jazz chops. Wynton Marsalis (tpt) (then reaping a wave of prodigy/discovery headlines) is in the group. —*Ron Wynn*

Lite Me Up / 1982 / Columbia ✦✦

Future Shock / 1983 / Columbia ✦✦

Sound-System / 1984 / Columbia ✦✦

Village Life / 1985 / Columbia ✦✦
An arresting mix of Hancock's jazz concept with African Foday Suso's rhythmic innovations. —*Ron Wynn*

Perfect Machine / Oct. 1988 / Columbia ✦✦

Dis Is Da Drum / 1994 / Mercury ✦✦

Cap'n John Handy

b. Jun. 24, 1900, Pass Christian, MO, d. Jan. 12, 1971, New York, NY
Alto Saxophone / New Orleans Jazz
Capt. John Handy (no relation to the modern altoist John Handy) was unusual in the New Orleans revival movement because he played Dixieland alto influenced by R&B. A veteran who had been playing clarinet on and off in New Orleans since the 1920s (often with his group the Louisiana Shakers), Handy (who switched from clarinet to alto in 1928) was virtually unknown to the outside world until he started recording in the 1960s. During that decade he played regularly with Kid Sheik Cola's group and the Preservation Hall Jazz Band, toured Europe and recorded for several labels including GHB, RCA (two interesting records) and the Jazz Crusade label. His enthusiastic and very musical playing made him one of the top New Orleans musicians of the 1960s; "Hindustan" was a favorite feature. —*Scott Yanow*

The December Band / 1965 / Jazz Crusade ✦✦✦✦

Capt. John Handy with Geoff Bull and Barry Martyn's Band / Apr. 12, 1966 / Beautiful Dumaine ✦✦✦

● Introducing Cap'n John Handy / Nov. 15, 1966–Nov. 18, 1966 / RCA ✦✦✦✦✦

New Orleans and the Blues / Mar. 19, 1968–Mar. 20, 1968 / RCA Victor ✦✦✦

Craig Handy

b. 1963, Oakland, CA
Tenor Saxophone / Post-Bop
One of the potential greats of the 1990s, Craig Handy's playing ranges from bop to advanced post bop. Since attending North Texas State University (1981–84) he has worked with Art Blakey's Jazz Messengers, Wynton Marsalis, Roy Haynes and Abdullah Ibrahim and recorded with Elvin Jones and Betty Carter among others. Handy's two Arabesque releases from 1991 and 1993 are quite impressive. — *Scott Yanow*

Split Second Timing / Jun. 18, 1991–Jun. 19, 1991 / Arabesque ✦✦✦✦

● Introducing Three For All & One / Apr. 12, 1993–Apr. 13, 1993 / Arabesque ✦✦✦✦✦
The trio of Craig Handy (on tenor and soprano), bassist Charles Fambrough and drummer Ralph Peterson lives up to its potential during a wide-ranging set. The improvisations are explorative yet melodic and logical while the interplay between these talented players is consistently impressive. Together they explore tributes to Clifford Jordan and George Adams and, at times, hint at Coltrane, Sonny Rollins and even Grover Washington, Jr., Pianist David Kikoski is heard on four selections, but his presence is actually unnecessary. Handy's unaccompanied solo on "West Bank: Beyond the Berlin Wall" is a highlight of this recommended disc. — *Scott Yanow*

John Handy

b. Feb. 3, 1933, Dallas, TX
Alto Saxophone, Tenor Saxophone / Post-Bop, Crossover
A talented and adventurous altoist whose career has gone through several phases, John Handy started playing alto in 1949. After moving to New York in 1958, he had a fiery period with Charles Mingus (1958–59) that resulted in several passionate recordings that show off his originality; he also recorded several dates as a leader for Roulette. Handy led his own bands during 1959–64 and played with Mingus at the 1964 Monterey Jazz Festival, but it was at the following year's festival that he was a major hit, stretching out with his quintet (which included violinist Michael White and guitarist Jerry Hahn) on two long originals. Soon Handy was signed to Columbia where he recorded his finest albums (three excellent albums) during 1966–68. Since that time he has performed world music with Ali Akbar Khan, recorded the R&B hit "Hard Work" for Impulse! in 1976, gigged and recorded with Mingus Dynasty and, in the late '80s, led a group (called Class) featuring three female violinists who sing. John Handy (no relation to the Dixieland altoist Capt. John Handy) remains a strong soloist who can hit high notes way above his horn's normal register with ease, but he has mostly maintained a low profile, teaching in the San Francisco Bay area. — *Scott Yanow*

In the Vernacular / Nov. 1959 / Roulette ✦✦✦✦

No Coast Jazz / 1960 / Roulette ✦✦✦✦

★ Live at Monterey / Sep. 18, 1965 / Columbia ✦✦✦✦✦

The Second John Handy Album / Jul. 7, 1966–Jul. 26, 1966 / Columbia ✦✦✦✦✦

New View / Mar. 19, 1967–Jun. 28, 1967 / Columbia ✦✦✦✦

Projections / Apr. 15, 1968 / Columbia ✦✦✦✦

Karuna Supreme / Nov. 1, 1975 / MPS ✦✦

Hard Work / Jan. 1976 / Impulse! ✦✦✦

Carnival / 1977 / ABC ✦✦

Excursion in Blue / Aug. 9, 1988–Aug. 10, 1988 / Quartet ✦✦✦

Centerpiece / Apr. 10, 1989–Apr. 13, 1989 / Milestone ✦✦✦✦

Jake Hanna

b. Apr. 4, 1931, Boston, MA
Drums / Swing
A superior drummer equally at ease driving a big band or play-

ing in small mainstream combos, Jake Hanna has been a strong asset to a countless number of sessions. He started out playing locally in Boston and worked with Toshiko Akiyoshi (1957), Maynard Ferguson (1958), as the house drummer at Storyville in Boston, with Marian McPartland (1959–61) and most significantly with the Woody Herman Orchestra (1962–64). As a studio musician, he was a regular member of the Merv Griffin television program's big band (1964–75), moving with the show to Los Angeles (1970) where he is still based. Hanna co-led a group with Carl Fontana that recorded for Concord in 1975, played with Supersax and has since appeared on many mainstream and swing sessions, becoming a fixture at jazz parties and festivals. He has recorded many dates (mostly as a sideman) for Concord. — *Scott Yanow*

● Live at Concord / Jul. 1975 / Concord Jazz ✦✦✦✦✦

Kansas City Express / Apr. 1976 / Concord Jazz ✦✦✦

Jake Takes Manhattan / Dec. 14, 1976–Dec. 15, 1976 / Concord Jazz ✦✦✦
Nice, restrained light swing quintet session led by drummer Jake Hanna, with contributions from bassist Mike Moore and pianist John Bunch. Although he's cited as the leader, Hanna doesn't dominate, and it's more a cooperative venture than a featured drum date. — *Ron Wynn*

Sir Roland Hanna

b. Feb. 10, 1932, Detroit, MI
Piano / Hard Bop, Swing
A talented pianist with a style diverse enough to fit into swing, bop and more adventurous settings, Roland Hanna was one of the last in an impressive line of great pianists who emerged in Detroit after World War II (including Hank Jones, Barry Harris and Tommy Flanagan). After serving in the Army and studying music at Eastman and Juilliard, Hanna made a strong impression playing with Benny Goodman (1958). He worked with Charles Mingus for a period in 1959 and since then has generally led his own trios. Hanna was an integral part of the Thad Jones-Mel Lewis Orchestra (1967–74) and, in 1974, helped found the New York Jazz Quartet (with Frank Wess). He was given knighthood (thus the "Sir") from the President of Liberia in 1970. Sir Roland Hanna has led sessions for many labels including Atco (1959), MPS, Choice, Freedom, Inner City and Music Masters. — *Scott Yanow*

Sir Elf / Apr. 1973–May 1973 / Choice ✦✦✦✦✦
Pianist Roland Hanna's first solo album is one of his finest recordings. Whether it be a tribute to Art Tatum on "You Took Advantage of Me," a nod to Erroll Garner on "There Is No Greater Love," a humorous "Bye Bye Blackbird" or his original "Morning," Hanna is in top form on this well-paced and inventive set. — *Scott Yanow*

★ Perugia / Jul. 2, 1974 / Freedom ✦✦✦✦✦

Time for the Dancers / Feb. 17, 1977 / Progressive ✦✦✦

Glove / Oct. 15, 1977 / Storyville ✦✦✦

Roland Hanna Plays the Music of Alec Wilder / 1978 / Inner City ✦✦✦
Soaring, dramatic interpretations of classic Jerome Kern tunes by pianist Sir Roland Hanna. He plays them with a sophisticated, yet exuberant flair, perfectly executing the basic melodies, then extending and reworking them through often magnificent solos. — *Ron Wynn*

Bird Tracks / Feb. 22, 1978–Mar. 1, 1978 / Progressive ✦✦✦
Tingling versions of songs by and about Charlie Parker. — *Ron Wynn*

Play For Monk / Apr. 10, 1978+Apr. 12, 1978 / Musical Heritage Society ✦✦✦✦

Impressions / Jul. 17, 1978–Jul. 14, 1978 / Black & Blue ✦✦✦✦

Piano Soliloquy / Jun. 25, 1979–Jun. 26, 1979 / L & R Music ✦✦✦

The New York Jazz Quartet in Chicago / Jul. 27, 1981 / Bee Hive ✦✦✦✦
The New York Jazz Quartet gave pianist Roland Hanna, Frank Wess (doubling on tenor and flute), bassist George Mraz and drummer Ben Riley an opportunity to collaborate and, although the group did not innovate, it did record several excellent albums. This Bee Hive album is one of their extroverted affairs with particularly fine playing on Wess' "Four the Hard Way," Thad Jones' "H and T Blues" and the ballad "You Don't Know What Love Is." — *Scott Yanow*

Romanesque / Jan. 13, 1982 / Black Hawk ◆◆◆

Gershwin Carmichael Cats / Jun. 19, 1982–Jul. 1982 / CTI ◆◆◆

Round Midnight / Mar. 1987 / Town Crier ◆◆◆◆

Duke Ellington Piano Solos / Mar. 22, 1991–Mar. 23, 1991 / Music Masters ◆◆◆◆◆

● **Maybeck Recital Hall, Vol. 32** / Aug. 15, 1993 / Concord ◆◆◆◆◆
Elegance and artistry are the two qualities that best define both Sir Roland Hanna's piano style and this superb CD, the 32nd in Concord's continuing Maybeck solo series. Hanna devotes half the eight selections to Gershwin compositions, and his interpretations of "Love Walked In," "The Man I Love," "How Long Has This Been Going On" and others are sublime, marvelously crafted and magnificent in their ideas and execution. Seldom will you hear a solo date less self-indulgent and more satisfying. —*Ron Wynn*

Susie Hansen

Violin/Latin Jazz
One of the few violinists who specialize in playing Latin-jazz, the talented Susie Hansen works frequently with both her jazz and salsa bands in the Los Angeles area. Her father James Hansen was with the Chicago Symphony for 37 years and was her first teacher. Susie studied jazz in Boston with Charlie Banacos, sat in often with Cedar Walton in Chicago and moved to L.A. in 1988. She has led her own bands since 1989, debuting on the Jazz Caliente label in 1993 with *Solo Flight*. —*Scott Yanow*

Annette Hanshaw

b. Oct. 18, 1910, New York, NY, **d.** Mar. 13, 1985, New York, NY
Vocals / Classic Jazz
One of the first great female jazz singers, in the late '20s Annette Hanshaw ranked near the top with Ethel Waters, the Boswell Sisters and the upcoming Mildred Bailey. Unlike her contemporary Ruth Etting, Hanshaw could improvise and swing while also being a strong interpreter of lyrics. She was not quite 16 when she started her recording career and her recordings (1926–34) included such major jazz players as Red Nichols, Miff Mole, Jimmy Lytell, Adrian Rollini, Joe Venuti, Eddie Lang, Vic Berton, Benny Goodman, Manny Klein, Phil Napoleon, Jimmy Dorsey, Tommy Dorsey and Jack Teagarden. Billed as "The Personality Girl," Annette Hanshaw (whose trademark was saying "That's all" at the end of her record) soon got tired of show business and retired in 1934, at the age of 23! She lived outside of music for the rest of her life, but fortunately most of her records were reissued in British LPs in the 1970s and '80s. —*Scott Yanow*

★ **Sweetheart of the Twenties** / Oct. 1926–Sep. 8, 1927 / Halcyon ◆◆◆◆◆
Solid collection of Hanshaw's earliest sides, 1926–1928, with superb jazz backing. Import. —*Cub Koda*

It Was So Beautiful / 1932–1934 / Halcyon ◆◆◆◆◆
Superlative collection of Hanshaw's last recordings, with "Say It Isn't So," "Give Me Liberty or Give Me Love," and "I'm Sure of Everything but You" being particular standouts. Import. —*Cub Koda*

Twenties Sweetheart / Jasmine ◆◆◆

Fareed Haque

b. 1963, Chicago, IL
Guitar / Post-Bop
Fareed Haque is a flexible guitarist whose own records show off his roots in classical music along with his interest in several styles of jazz. Raised in Chicago, Haque traveled extensively as a youth with his parents who were from Pakistan and Chile; the influence of different country's folk musics can be heard in his playing. He studied jazz at North Texas State University and classical music at Northwestern University in Chicago. Haque made two records with Paquito D'Rivera and played with Tito Puente, Toots Thielemans and Von Freeman among others. He made his debut as a leader for Sting's short lived Pangaea label (1988) and has since recorded two sets for Blue Note, toured with Joe Zawinul and performed with Straight Ahead, Joey Calderazzo, Renee Rosnes and Dianne Reeves among others. —*Scott Yanow*

Voices Rising / 1988 / Pangaea ◆◆◆

Sacred Addiction / Jun. 21, 1993–Jun. 26, 1993 / Blue Note ◆◆◆
Fareed Haque is a talented classical guitarist heard on this set delving into some poppish numbers, light funk, a little bit of

Indian-influenced music and a strong version of Chick Corea's "No Mystery." Not every performance works equally well and there are some premature fadeouts. However, Haque's pretty but authoritative sound carries the day and makes this set worthwhile. —*Scott Yanow*

● **Opaque** / Feb. 9, 1995–Feb. 17, 1995 / Blue Note ◆◆◆

John Hardee

b. Dec. 20, 1918, Corsicana, TX, **d.** May 18, 1984, Dallas, TX
Tenor Saxophone / Bop, Swing
John Hardee's time in jazz's major leagues was brief but memorable. The thick-toned tenor (influenced by Coleman Hawkins and Chu Berry) toured with Don Albert (1937–38) and graduated from college in 1941. After a period as band director at a Texas school and a stint in the Army, Hardee played with Tiny Grimes in 1946 and recorded 18 titles as a leader (1946–48) including eight for Blue Note that were reissued in a Mosaic set; other songs have been released by Savoy and Spotlite. Hardee also had recording dates with Russell Procope, Earl Bostic, Billy Kyle, Helen Humes, Billy Taylor and Lucky Millinder. But in the early '50s he returned to Dallas where he worked in the school system, just playing locally and rarely emerging during his last 30 years. —*Scott Yanow*

Wilbur Harden

b. 1925, Birmingham, AL
Trumpet, Fluegelhorn / Hard Bop
Wilbur Harden is a mystery man in jazz history for he appeared on some important recording sessions (most notably with John Coltrane) and then, after 1960, pretty well disappeared. He played R&B with Roy Brown (1950) and Ivory Joe Hunter and then served in the Navy. Harden emerged in 1957 recording with Yusef Lateef, and led four record dates for Savoy in 1958; three were with Coltrane (who became the leader on reissues) and one in a quartet with Tommy Flanagan. In 1960 Wilbur Harden (who was one of the first trumpeters to double regularly on fluegelhorn) recorded one title with Curtis Fuller, but then ill health forced him to retire at the age of 35. —*Scott Yanow*

Mainstream (1958) / Mar. 13, 1958 / Savoy ◆◆◆◆

● **Tanganyika Suite** / May 13, 1958+Jun. 29, 1958 / Savoy ◆◆◆◆◆

Jazz Way Out / Jun. 24, 1958 / Savoy Jazz ◆◆◆◆

The King and I / Sep. 23, 1958–Sep. 30, 1958 / Savoy Jazz ◆◆◆

Bill Hardman

b. Apr. 6, 1933, Cleveland, OH, **d.** Dec.5, 1990, Paris, France
Trumpet, Fluegelhorn / Hard Bop
A reliable hard bop-oriented trumpeter, Bill Hardman never became famous but he helped out on many sessions. While a teenager Hardman gigged with Tadd Dameron, and after graduating high school, he was with Tiny Bradshaw (1953–55). He debuted on record with Jackie McLean (1955), played with Charles Mingus (1956) and gained recognition for his work with Art Blakey's Jazz Messengers (1956–58). Hardman worked with Horace Silver (1958), Lou Donaldson (on and off during 1959–66), rejoined Blakey twice (1966–69 and in the late '70s), was with Mingus again during parts of 1969–72 and led a group with Junior Cook (1979–81). Bill Hardman had an appealing style in the Clifford Brown tradition and recorded as a leader for Savoy (1961) and Muse. —*Scott Yanow*

Saying Something / Oct. 18, 1961 / Savoy ◆◆◆
An album with topflight blowing from Sonny Red (sax). This is perhaps Hardman's best date; among his most memorable. —*Ron Wynn*

Home / Jan. 10, 1978 / Muse ◆◆◆◆
Bill Hardman had long been a talented—if not overly original—bop trumpet soloist. Best known for his four stints with Art Blakey's Jazz Messengers, Hardman is in excellent form on a pair of Brazilian pieces, two originals by pianist Mickey Tucker and Tadd Dameron's lesser-known "I Remember Love." There are also fine solos throughout this date by Tucker, tenor saxophonist Junior Cook and trombonist Slide Hampton. —*Scott Yanow*

Focus / Apr. 17, 1980 / Muse ◆◆◆

● **Politely** / Jul. 7, 1981 / Muse ◆◆◆◆◆
This quintet date (with trumpeter Bill Hardman, tenor saxophonist Junior Cook, pianist Walter Bishop, Jr., bassist Paul Brown and

drummer Leroy Williams) is very much in the bop vein. Despite its title (the name of a Hardman minor blues), much of the session is actually hard-driving. John Coltrane's "Lazy Bird" and Hardman's ballad feature on "Smooch" are highlights of this excellent album. —*Scott Yanow*

Otto Hardwicke

b. May 31, 1904, Washington DC, **d.** Sept. 5, 1970, Washington DC
Alto Sax/Swing, Classic Jazz
Otto Hardwicke had a sweet tone on alto and a fluid style. Hardwicke grew up with Duke Ellington and was originally a bassist until Duke talked him into switching to C-melody sax in 1920. He was an original member of the Washingtonians and was with Ellington until 1928 when he traveled to Paris, working with Noble Sissle. He had his own band by 1930 but two years later rejoined Ellington. Hardwicke, who took a famous solo on the original version of "Sophisticated Lady" (a standard he co-wrote) was an important player (on alto and occasional baritone and bass saxes with Ellington prior to 1928 but during 1932–46 he was rarely heard from except in section work; Johnny Hodges got virtually all of the alto solos. Personal differences in 1946 resulted in him leaving the band and, after recording two songs as a leader the following year, Otto Hardwicke retired from music. —*Scott Yanow*

Roy Hargrove

b. Oct. 16, 1969, Waco, TX
Trumpet / Hard Bop
Roy Hargrove is a hard bop-oriented Young Lion who has a great deal of potential. A fine straight-ahead player who does not sound overly influenced by any of his predecessors, Hargrove's fiery solos resulted in him winning the *Downbeat* Readers' Poll in 1995. He met Wynton Marsalis in 1987 when the trumpeter visited his high school and impressed Marsalis, who let him sit in with his band. With the help of Wynton, Hargrove was soon playing with major players including Bobby Watson, Ricky Ford, Carl Allen and in the group Superblue. Hargrove attended Berklee (1988–89) and in 1990 released his first of four recordings for Novus; he was 20 at the time. He has been touring ever since with his own group, which for several years included Antonio Hart. In addition to Novus, Hargrove has recorded for Verve and as a sideman with quite a few notables including Sonny Rollins, James Clay, Frank Morgan and Jackie McLean plus the group Jazz Futures. —*Scott Yanow*

Diamond in the Rough / Dec. 1989 / Novus ◆◆◆
Young trumpeter sounds good, especially on originals. —*Michael G. Nastos*

Public Eye / Oct. 1990 / Novus ◆◆◆
Hargrove's second album displays great promise, though things sometimes get ragged. —*Ron Wynn*

Tokyo Sessions / Dec. 4, 1991–Dec. 5, 1991 / Novus ◆◆◆◆
Trumpeter Roy Hargrove and alto saxophonist Antonio Hart, two of the finest contemporary hard boppers, made a potent team on this CD featuring sessions recorded in Tokyo during 1991. Hargrove's fierce trumpet solos and Hart's bluesy, equally energetic and accomplished answering alto statements fueled nine excellent reworkings of standards and jazz repertory. The quintet performed such established material as Oscar Pettiford's "Bohemia After Dark," Thelonious Monk's "Straight No Chaser," and Kenny Dorham's "Lotus Blossom," as well as Cole Porter's "Easy To Love," with confidence and in a smooth yet expressive style. It would still be nice to hear Hart and Hargrove doing their own material rather than simply putting their spin on shopworn, though wonderful, anthems. —*Ron Wynn*

The Vibe / 1992 / Novus ◆◆◆◆
The twenty-something trumpeter's release, features him working with fellow young lions, most notably alto saxophonist Antonio Hart. Hargrove's technique, range, and power have improved with each album, and he's steadily reaching the point where his solos and skill will match the amount of publicity he's received. —*Ron Wynn*

Of Kindred Souls / May 1993 / Novus ◆◆◆◆◆
Of all the "Young Lions" to emerge in jazz after the rise of Wynton Marsalis, trumpeter Roy Hargrove is among the most impressive, filling in the major gap left by the early departure of Lee Morgan. On his fifth session as a leader, Hargrove is heard live with his

quintet (which also features pianist Marc Cary and Ron Blake on tenor and soprano) with cameo appearances on a selection apiece by altoist Gary Bartz and trombonist Andre Hayward. Hargrove is in excellent form on a set of group originals, a brief ballad medley and the standard "My Shining Hour." All of the trumpeter's releases thus far are worth picking up. —*Scott Yanow*

● **With the Tenors of Our Time** / Dec. 18, 1993–Jan. 17, 1994 / Verve ◆◆◆◆◆
Trumpeter Roy Hargrove has the opportunity of a lifetime on this recording, sharing separate songs with five great tenors: Johnny Griffin, Joe Henderson, Branford Marsalis, Joshua Redman and Stanley Turrentine. Everyone fares well, including Hargrove's group (Ron Blake on tenor and soprano, pianist Cyrus Chestnut, bassist Rodney Whitaker and drummer Gregory Hutchinson). The young trumpeter (who is vying for Lee Morgan's unoccupied chair) keeps up with the saxophonists on this generally relaxed affair; recommended for hard bop fans. —*Scott Yanow*

Family / Jan. 26, 1995–Jan. 29, 1995 / Verve ◆◆◆◆

Parker's Mood / Apr. 12, 1995–Apr. 14, 1995 / Verve ◆◆◆◆

Rufus Harley

b. May 20, 1936, Raleigh, NC
Bagpipes, Reeds / Soul Jazz, Hard Bop
Jazz's only bagpipe specialist, Rufus Harley proved that jazz can be played on any instrument! He was originally a saxophonist and took up the bagpipes in the early '60s. Harley recorded two albums for Atlantic (*Bagpipe Blues* and *Scotch and Soul*) during 1965–67 and appeared on one selection apiece on albums by Sonny Stitt, Herbie Mann and in 1974 with Sonny Rollins. Otherwise Rufus Harley has not been heard from much during the past 20 years, but he certainly made his own place in jazz history! —*Scott Yanow*

Bagpipe Blues / 1965 / Atlantic ◆◆◆◆

● **Scotch and Soul** / Apr. 6, 1966–Apr. 29, 1966 / Atlantic ◆◆◆◆◆

Tribute to Courage / 1968 / Atlantic ◆◆◆

Everette Harp

b. Aug. 17, 1961, Houston, TX
Alto Saxophone / Crossover
An emotional R&B-oriented saxophonist, Everette Harp graduated from North Texas State University and played locally in Houston during 1981–88, becoming a studio musician. In 1988 he moved to Los Angeles and was soon playing in major R&B bands (including those of Anita Baker, Sheena Easton and Kenny Loggins). In 1991 Harp toured with George Duke and Marcus Miller and recorded his debut for Manhattan. In 1992 he toured with Rachelle Ferrell and two years later his second album (for Blue Note Contemporary) was released. The popular Everette Harp's background is in gospel and R&B, but he sometimes displays the ability to improvise; hopefully, a jazz album will be in the future. —*Scott Yanow*

● **Everette Harp** / 1992 / Blue Note ◆◆◆

Common Ground / 1994 / Blue Note ◆◆
This CD can be dismissed quickly for Everette Harp (principally on alto) seems content to merely ape the sound of David Sanborn but without the sincere emotions or any pretense at creativity or originality. This pop/R&B date is essentially mindless dance music and even Branford Marsalis' one appearance does not help. —*Scott Yanow*

The Harper Brothers

Group / Hard Bop
One of the most hyped jazz groups of the late '80s, the Harper Brothers (co-led by drummer Winard Harper and trumpeter Phillip Harper) symbolized what was right and wrong about the Young Lions movement. The musicianship in this hard bop unit was excellent and the young players respected their elders, but originality was lacking (they were largely revisiting the past) and the Harper Brothers received an excess of publicity at the expense of more innovative players. Still, during its five years, the group produced four enjoyable bop albums for Verve and its sidemen (altoist Justin Robinson, tenors Javon Jackson and Walter Blanding, pianists Stephen Scott and Kevin Hays, and bassists Michael Bowie and Nedra Wheeler among them) all had strong starts to their career. Both Winard and Phillip Harper have grown musically since the band's breakup. —*Scott Yanow*

● **Harper Brothers** / Jun. 21, 1988 / Verve ✦✦✦✦✦
The introductory album for the jazz-playing brothers who became staples among mainstream fans in the late '80s and early '90s. Winard and Phillip Harper's music reflected the influence of Art Blakey and Horace Silver, but was played with a youthful zest and individualistic flair. This late '80s release was reissued in '92 on CD with a bonus cut. —*Ron Wynn*

Remembrance / Sep. 8, 1989–Sep. 9, 1989 / Verve ✦✦✦✦

Artistry / 1991 / Verve ✦✦✦
'91 session by Winard and Phillip Harper, the brothers whose trumpet/sax sound and conception echoed classic late '50s hard bop material. This was their next-to-last album as a duo, and it was aided by contributions from Javon Jackson, Kevin Hays, and Nedra Wheeler. —*Ron Wynn*

You Can Hide Inside the Music / Oct. 15, 1991–Oct. 16, 1991 / Verve ✦✦✦✦

Billy Harper

b. Jan. 17, 1943
Tenor Saxophone / Post-Bop, Hard Bop
An intense tenor saxophonist whose music has stretched the boundaries of hard bop and modal music, Billy Harper graduated from North Texas State College and in 1966 moved to New York. He worked on and off with Gil Evans for the next ten years, was with Art Blakey's Jazz Messengers (1968–70), played with Elvin Jones (1970), Max Roach, the Thad Jones-Mel Lewis Orchestra (recording a notable solo on "Fingers") and Lee Morgan. Harper has recorded as a leader for Strata-East, Black Saint, Denon and Soul Note and has maintained a low profile during the past decade, but he did record a set for Evidence in 1993. —*Scott Yanow*

Capra Black / Oct. 1973 / Strata East ✦✦✦

★ **Black Saint** / Jul. 21, 1975–Jul. 22, 1975 / Black Saint ✦✦✦✦✦
An important document and the first album for the Italian Black Saint label. A potent quartet, with Harper's most familiar themes. This is essential listening in the modal jazz idiom. —*Michael G. Nastos*

Soran-Bushi, Billy Harper / Dec. 15, 1977+Dec. 17, 1977 / Denon ✦✦✦

Billy Harper Quintet in Europe / Jan. 24, 1979–Jan. 25, 1979 / Soul Note ✦✦✦

In Europe / Jan. 24, 1979–Jan. 25, 1979 / Soul Note ✦✦✦

Destiny Is Yours / Dec. 1989 / SteepleChase ✦✦✦✦

Somalia / Oct. 18, 1993–Oct. 23, 1993 / Evidence ✦✦✦✦

Herbie Harper

b. Jul. 2, 1920, Salina, KS
Trombone / Cool
A fine trombonist active in the West Coast jazz scene of the 1950s, Herbie Harper has spent most of his playing time since 1955 as a studio musician, although he occasionally re-emerges in the jazz world. After playing with Charlie Spivak's Orchestra (1944–47), Harper settled in Los Angeles where he gigged with Teddy Edwards and had short-time associations with Benny Goodman, Charlie Barnet and Stan Kenton (1950). In addition to recording in the 1950s with June Christy, Kenton, Maynard Ferguson, Benny Carter and Barnet, Herbie Harper led five albums of his own during 1954–57 for Nocturne, Tampa, Bethlehem and Mode. He has mostly worked in the studios since then but has emerged to play with Bob Florence's big band and in the 1980s he recorded for SeaBreeze and with Bill Perkins for VSOP. —*Scott Yanow*

Herbie Harper / 1954 / Liberty ✦✦✦
A swinging session from this ex-big-band trombonist, it was recorded with Bud Shank (as), Charlie Mariano (sax), and Bob Gordon (bar sax). —*David Szatmary*

● **Five Brothers** / Jun. 15, 1955 / VSOP ✦✦✦✦✦
Trombonist Herbie Harper, who has not been heard of much as a leader since the 1950s, has always been a talented bop-based trombonist with an attractive tone. For this quintet set, he is teamed with multi-instrumentalist Bob Enevoldsen (mostly sticking to tenor), guitarist Don Overberg, bassist Red Mitchell and drummer Frankie Capp. The West Coast-styled ensembles still sound appealing. This is one of the obscure Tampa sessions that have been rescued and reissued by VSOP. —*Scott Yanow*

Herbie Harper Sextet / Jun. 1957 / VSOP ✦✦✦✦
Trombonist Herbie Harper's fifth and final session as a leader in the 1950s is an excellent outing that also features the little-known tenorman Jay Core, guitarist Howard Roberts, pianist Marty Paich, bassist Red Mitchell and either Frank Capp or Mel Lewis on drums. Core and Capp contributed an original apiece and the sextet also plays five superior standards along with a surprising rendition of "Little Orphan Annie." This set for the defunct Mode label (reissued by VSOP) has plenty of high-quality West Coast jazz. —*Scott Yanow*

Revisited / May 6, 1981–May 7, 1981 / Sea Breeze ✦✦✦

Herbie Harper/Bill Perkins Quintet / Sep. 14, 1989+Sep. 15, 1989 / VSOP ✦✦✦✦✦
Herbie Harper and Bill Perkins have assembled a pianoless quintet similar to what Herbie Harper recorded with in the mid '50s. A fine collaboration with everyone in top form.—*AMG*

Philip Harper

b. May 10, 1965, Baltimore, MD
Trumpet / Hard Bop
A good hard bop trumpeter who in recent years has become a more adventurous improviser, Phillip Harper became well-known during 1988–93 as co-leader (with older brother Winard) of the Harper Brothers. He had previously toured with Art Blakey's Jazz Messengers (where his Lee Morgan-influenced style fit in perfectly) and recorded with Cecil Brooks III, Joe Chambers and Errol Parker. Since the Harper Brothers broke up (having produced four albums for Verve), the trumpeter has recorded as a leader for Muse and played with the Mingus Big Band. —*Scott Yanow*

Soulful Sin / Feb. 22, 1993 / Muse ✦✦✦

● **The Thirteenth Moon** / Jan. 21, 1994 / Muse ✦✦✦✦

Winard Harper

b. Jun 4, 1962, Baltimore, MD
Drums / Hard Bop
An excellent drummer whose creativity stretches beyond the hard bop settings in which he is often featured, Winard Harper (along with younger brother Phillip) gained a great deal of publicity during 1988–93 as co-leader of the Harper Brothers. Before that band he had gained important experience working with Betty Carter, and since then Winard Harper has freelanced and continued to grow as a player. —*Scott Yanow*

● **Be Yourself** / 1994 / Epicure ✦✦✦✦✦
The music on Winard Harper's Epicure release (Art Blakeyish romps, boogaloos, ballads and bop) is straight from vintage Blue Note stylewise, although the majority of the songs are actually group originals. But, as with the best revival Dixieland of the 1950s, the musicianship, enthusiasm and creativity of the musicians (within the genre's boundaries) uplift the music beyond the limits of nostalgia. Trumpeter Eddie Henderson is in top form, altoist Antonio Hart is fine in a Cannonball Adderley bag during his three appearances and tenor saxophonist Don Braden takes a major step forward with these performances. In addition, David "Fathead" Newman has two features on tenor, the rhythm section is excellent and the drummer/leader is content to push the other musicians rather than engaging in lengthy solos himself. It's recommended for hard bop fans. —*Scott Yanow*

Tom Harrell

b. Jun. 16, 1946, Urbana, IL
Trumpet, Fluegelhorn / Hard Bop
Tom Harrell has managed to fight courageously (and thus far successfully) against schizophrenia to become one of jazz's top trumpeters of the 1980s and '90s. On stage he is totally focused on his playing and seems to only come alive when he is improvising. Harrell grew up in Northern California and toured with Stan Kenton (1969), Woody Herman (1970–71) and Horace Silver (1973–77). He moved to New York in the mid-'70s and played during this period with Cecil Payne, Bill Evans (1979), Lee Konitz's Nonet (1979–81) and George Russell (1982). Harrell traveled the world with the Phil Woods Quintet (1983–89) and has since then generally led his own bands, recording for Contemporary and Chesky. His style mixes together the power of Clifford Brown with the lyricism of Chet Baker. —*Scott Yanow*

Aurora/Total / Jun. 24, 1976 / Pinnacle ✦✦✦
Harrell's first album features choice material and Bob Berg (ts). —
Michael G. Nastos

Play of Light / Feb. 11, 1982 / Blackhawk ✦✦✦✦

Moon Alley / Dec. 22, 1985 / Criss Cross ✦✦✦✦✦

Open Air / May 26, 1986 / SteepleChase ✦✦✦✦

Visions / Apr. 18, 1987–Apr. 9, 1990 / Contemporary ✦✦✦✦
This latest session has an all-star lineup, with large-group pieces.
—*Ron Wynn*

Stories / Jan. 26, 1988–Jan. 27, 1988 / Contemporary ✦✦✦
Assisted by Bob Berg (ts), John Scofield (g), Niels Lan Doky (p),
Billy Hart (d), and Ray Drummond (b), fluegelhornist and trumpeter Harrell charts his way through a solid hour of modern jazz
progressions. —*Paul Kohler*

★ **Sail Away** / Mar. 22, 1989–Mar. 23, 1989 / Contemporary
✦✦✦✦✦
Spirited originals and his best effort to date. Featuring Dave
Liebman (sop sax) and Joe Levano (ts). —*Michael G. Nastos*

Form / Apr. 8, 1990–Apr. 9, 1990 / Contemporary ✦✦✦✦✦

Passages / Oct. 10, 1991–Oct. 11, 1991 / Chesky ✦✦✦✦

Upswing / Jun. 11, 1993–Jun. 12, 1993 / Chesky ✦✦✦✦✦

Joe Harriott

b. Jul. 15, 1928, Kingston, Jamaica, **d.** Jan. 2, 1973, London,
England
Alto Saxophone / Post-Bop, Avant-Garde
Jamaica's most prominent straight jazz musician until Courtney
Pine's arrival, Joe Harriott was a hard blowing, experimental
alto saxophonist who had the misfortune to begin making his
break with traditional bebop and hard bop at the same time
Ornette Coleman's innovations were appearing in England.
Those who failed to listen closely pinned the ripoff tag on
Harriott, who was actually moving in a different, though relat-
ed, direction. Harriott's concepts were based on an alternative
for ensemble interaction rather than individual exposition,
something that was later recognized by astute critics. Harriott
initially played in Jamaica with Wilton Gaynair and Dizzy
Reece, then came to England in the early '50s. He did sessions
and freelance dates until he began working with Pete Pitterson.
Harriott played with Tony Kinsey's combo and Ronnie Scott's big
band in the mid-'50s, then formed his own quintet in 1958. His
album *Southern Horizons* illustrated his new notions of playing
in its infancy. Harriott worked further on the concept while hospitalized in 1960. He continued on such early '60s LPs as
Abstract and *Indo-Jazz Fusions*. Harriott later explored other
hybrid styles, mixing jazz with poetry and traditional Indian
music. He did a duet with Michael Garrick for Argo *Black
Marigolds* in 1966. Harriott currently has no sessions available
as a leader on CD. —*Ron Wynn*

● **Southern Horizons** / May 5, 1959–Apr. 21, 1960 / Jazzland ✦✦✦✦

Free Forms / Nov. 1960 / Jazzland ✦✦✦✦

Indo-Jazz Suite / Oct. 10, 1965 / Atlantic ✦✦✦✦

Indo Jazz Fusions: The Joe Harriott-John Mayer Do / Sep. 3,
1966–Sep. 4, 1966 / Atlantic ✦✦✦

Allan Harris

b. 1958
Vocals / Standards
One of the top male jazz singers to emerge in the 1990s, Allan
Harris sometimes sounds a bit like Nat King Cole but also puts
his own personality into his spirited rendition of standards. He
first recorded for his own Love Productions label and has more
recently recorded two sets for Mons: *It's a Wonderful World* (a sextet date with Benny Green, Mark Whitfield and Claudio Roditi)
and an ambitious effort on which he is backed by Germany's 54-
piece Metropole Orchestra. —*Scott Yanow*

Setting The Standard / 1994 / Love Productions ✦✦✦✦
The debut of singer Allan Harris finds the Nat King Cole-inspired
vocalist in a variety of settings that sometimes include three
horns and a string section. Not really an improviser, Harris uplifts
11 standards by embracing the strong melodies and giving fresh
meaning to their lyrics. Highlights include a swinging "On the
Street Where You Live," "You Go to My Head" and a surprisingly
jubilant "I Know What I Got." —*Scott Yanow*

Barry Harris

b. Dec. 15, 1929, Detroit, MI
Piano / Bop
One of the major bop pianists of the past 40 years, Barry Harris
has long had the ability to sound very close to Bud Powell yet
he can also do convincing impressions of Thelonious Monk and
has his own style within the bop idiom. He was an important
part of the Detroit jazz scene of the 1950s and has been a jazz
educator since that era. Harris recorded his first set as a leader
while in 1958 and moved to New York in 1960 where he spent
a short period with Cannonball Adderley's Quintet. He also
recorded with Dexter Gordon, Illinois Jacquet, Yusef Lateef and
Hank Mobley and was with Coleman Hawkins off and on
throughout the decade (including Hawk's declining years). In the
1970s Harris was on two of Sonny Stitt's finest records (*Tune Up*
and *Constellation*) and made many recordings in a variety of
settings for Xanadu. Barry Harris has mostly been working with
his trio during the past 20 years and he has recorded as a leader
for Argo (1958), Riverside, Prestige, MPS, Xanadu and Red. —
Scott Yanow

Barry Harris at the Jazz Workshop / May 15, 1960–May 16,
1960 / Original Jazz Classics ✦✦✦✦
Barry Harris has been remarkably consistent over the years. *At
the Jazz Workshop* captured him live in 1960 with Sam Jones
(bass) and Louis Hayes (drums). Adding to the expected pleasures
of Harris was the slick work of Sam Jones' active bass and the
powerful (as in accomplished) drumming of Louis Hayes. —*Bob
Rusch, Cadence*

Preminado / Dec. 21, 1960+Jan. 19, 1961 / Original Jazz Classics
✦✦✦✦

Barry Harris Plays Tadd Dameron / Jun. 4, 1975 / Xanadu
✦✦✦✦✦
A criminally underrated arranger/composer gets showcase treatment from an equally overlooked pianist. —*Ron Wynn*

★ **Live in Tokyo** / Apr. 12, 1976+Apr. 14, 1976 / Xanadu ✦✦✦✦
Barry Harris has been a major force on piano in keeping the pure
styles of Bud Powell and Thelonious Monk alive. This trio outing
with bassist Sam Jones and drummer LeRoy Williams is quite successful and frequently exciting. Harris is heard at his best on such
numbers as "Tea for Two," "Dance of the Infidels" and "Un Poco
Loco." —*Scott Yanow*

Barry Harris Plays Barry Harris / Jan. 17, 1978 / Xanadu ✦✦✦✦

The Bird of Red and Gold / Sep. 18, 1989 / Xanadu ✦✦✦✦✦

Live at Maybeck Recital Hall, Vol. 12 / Mar. 1990 / Concord Jazz
✦✦✦✦
Barry Harris has long been the perfect bebop pianist. This solo
recital finds Harris paying tribute to Bud Powell and Thelonious
Monk as well as Art Tatum, not so much in their compositions
(although he does perform Bud's "I'll Keep Loving You") but in
aspects of their styles that he has enveloped into his own musical
personality. Harris is even able to make bebop sense out of a
medley consisting of "It Never Entered My Mind" and the themes
from *The Flintstones* and *I Love Lucy!* —*Scott Yanow*

Confirmation / Sep. 1, 1991 / Candid ✦✦✦

Beaver Harris (William Godvin Harris)

b. Apr. 20, 1936, Pittsburgh, **d.** Dec. 22, 1991, New York, NY
Drums / Avant-Garde, Post-Bop
A wildly eclectic drummer, Beaver Harris didn't merely know different styles, he was an accomplished player in each one. He could
drive a band in the swing mode, play free, incorporate Caribbean,
African or Afro-Latin rhythms into his group's musical structure,
or play in hard bop and bebop fashion. Harris began on drums at
20. He served in the Army during the '50s, then returned to his
native Pittsburgh in 1957, where he played with Benny Golson,
Slide Hampton and Horace Silver. Harris moved to New York in
1962, and became active in free and hard bop circles. He played
with Sonny Rollins, Marion Brown, Albert Ayler, Roswell Rudd,
Steve Lacy, Gato Barieri, Thelonious Monk, and Archie Shepp in
the '60s and early '70s. Harris co-formed The 360-Degree Music
Experience in 1968 with Dave Burrell and Grachan Moncur III.
This band continued through the '70s and '80s as a repository of
musical genres. Many fine players passed through the group
including Ken McIntyre, Hamiett Bluiett, Ricky Ford and Don
Pullen and its debut record (1975) even featured Doc Cheatham

and Maxine Sullivan; the versatile drummer also played with Cecil Taylor in the 1970s. Beaver Harris recorded with the 360-Degree Music Experience for 360 Records, Black Saint, Owl, Cadence and Soul Note. —*Ron Wynn*

From Ragtime to No Time / Dec. 11, 1974–Feb. 11, 1975 / 360 ✦✦✦✦
This record opened with a New Orleans march-like drum solo and went into a ragged solo with piano on Dave Burrell's "A.M.Rag." After a short, Roy Haynes-like drum transition, vocalist Maxine Sullivan entered doing "Can There Be Peace." The rest of the ensemble joined in on this (2:21) dirge-like recitative, and then it was uptempo pleasure on "It's Hard But We Do," featuring clarinetist Herb Hall. A few seconds of drum transition and Sullivan returned in similiar fashion. Bringing this side to an end was one last 23 second drum transition. Side Two concerned itself more with explorations of sound and rhythm, shifting position to feature Howard Johnson on tuba and also Burrell. This was all part of "Round Trip Parts 1 & 2" (23 minutes), which covered the second side and was music filled with joy. The album in total had a joyful, universal concept about it that I applaud. —*Bob Rusch, Cadence*

★ **In: Sanity** / Mar. 8, 1976–Mar. 9, 1976 / Black Saint ✦✦✦✦✦
Recording with 360-Degree Music Experience. Improvisational music with world music touches from percussionist Harris and pianist Dave Burrell. An essential purchase for the adventurous listener. —*Michael G. Nastos*

Live at Nyon / Jun. 14, 1979 / Cadence ✦✦✦✦
An ambitious, swinging quintet date, with a welcome appearance from Grachan Moncur III (tb). —*Ron Wynn*

Beautiful Africa / Jun. 23, 1979+Jun. 25, 1979 / Soul Note ✦✦✦
Negcaumongus / Dec. 7, 1979 / Cadence ✦✦✦✦
Brilliant septet cuts. Ricky Ford (ts) and Don Pullen (p) are magnificent. —*Ron Wynn*

Beaver Is My Name / Nov. 1983 / Timeless ✦✦✦
Well Kept Secret with Don Pullen / 1984 / Hannibal ✦✦✦✦

Benny Harris

b. Apr. 23, 1919, New York, NY **d.** May 11, 1975, San Francisco, CA
Trumpet, Composer/Bop
A minor figure in the bop era who had potential but unfortunately retired from music in 1952, Benny Harris played with Tiny Bradshaw (1939) and twice with Earl Hines Orchestra (1941 and 1943). He was a fixture on 52nd Street in the early '40s, taking part in many early bop sessions and playing with Benny Carter, John Kirby, Coleman Hawkins, Don Byas and Thelonious Monk. Harris also was part of Boyd Raeburn's band for a period during 1944–45 and recorded with Clyde Hart in December 1944 and with Byas in 1945. The composer of "Ornithology," "Crazeology," "Reets and I" (often performed by Bud Powell) and "Wahoo" (based on "Perdido"), Benny Harris did not play all that much in the mid-to-late '40s. He was with Dizzy Gillespie's big band briefly in 1949 and recorded with Charlie Parker in 1952 but then permanently dropped out of music. —*Scott Yanow*

Bill Harris

b. Oct. 28, 1916, Philadelphia, PA, **d.** Aug. 21, 1973, Hallandale, FL
Trombone / Bop, Swing
Bill Harris was one of the few modern trombonists of the 1945–60 era who was not influenced by J.J. Johnson. A very distinctive player almost from the start with a strong and highly original wit, Harris became a professional musician in 1938 and toured with the big bands of Gene Krupa, Ray McKinley and Bob Chester. After playing with Benny Goodman (1943–44) and Charlie Barnet and guesting on a couple of Eddie Condon's Town Hall Concerts, Harris became famous for his work with Woody Herman's First Herd (1944–46); "Bijou" was a showcase and the trombonist is heard at his best on Herman's many uptempo (and often riotous) performances. One of the few First Herd members to also be in the Four Brothers Second Herd (1948–50), Harris also rejoined Herman a few times during 1956–59. He co-led a band with Charlie Ventura (1947), teamed up with Chubby Jackson (1953) and was a star with Jazz at the Philharmonic during 1950–54. During the second half of the 1950s, Harris often collaborated

with Flip Phillips and their band formed the nucleus of Benny Goodman's group in 1959. He mostly retired to Florida in the 1960s after a spell in Las Vegas, occasionally leading his own groups and playing with Red Norvo. Bill Harris led dates during 1945–57 for Mercury, EmArcy, Dial, Capitol, Verve, Fantasy and Mode, usually featuring alumni from the Woody Herman Orchestra. —*Scott Yanow*

The Bill Harris Memorial Album / Sep. 30, 1957 / Xanadu ✦✦✦✦
● **Bill Harris and Friends** / Sep. 1957 / Original Jazz Classics ✦✦✦✦✦
Trombonist Bill Harris led relatively few recording sessions throughout his career and this is the definitive one. On the quintet set with the great tenor Ben Webster, pianist Jimmy Rowles, bassist Red Mitchell and drummer Stan Levey, Harris' unique tone is showcased throughout "It Might as Well Be Spring," he jams happily with Webster on a variety of standards and verbally jokes around with Ben on a unique version of "Just One More Chance." —*Scott Yanow*

Craig Harris

b. Sep. 10, 1954, Hempstead, NY
Trombone / Avant-Garde
One of the more esoteric trombonists of the avant-garde, Craig Harris has been an original stylist throughout his career. He played in R&B bands early on, graduated from college in 1976 and had stints with Sun Ra (1976–78) and Abdullah Ibrahim (1979–81). During the 1980s and '90s, he has worked with the who's who of the avant-garde including David Murray's octet and big band, Henry Threadgill, Lester Bowie's Brass Fantasy, Olu Dara, Cecil Taylor, Sam Rivers, Muhal Richard Abrams and Charlie Haden's Liberation Orchestra. Craig Harris has also led a few of his own groups (best-known are Tailgater's Tales and the R&Bish Cold Sweat) and has recorded as a leader for several labels including India Navigation, Soul Note and JMT. —*Scott Yanow*

Aboriginal Affairs / 1983 / India Navigation ✦✦✦✦
Craig Harris, who had spent two years playing with Sun Ra's Arkestra, is a very advanced and generally original trombonist. On his debut as a leader, Harris doubles on the Australian didjeridu. His septet on this set is filled with like-minded players including avant-garde veteran Ken McIntyre (switching between alto, flute and bass clarinet) and pianist/vocalist Donald Smith. Harris' six originals feature all the members of the group on a program of challenging material that rewards repeated listenings. —*Scott Yanow*

Black Bone / Jan. 4, 1983–Jan. 13, 1983 / Soul Note ✦✦✦✦
Outstanding session led by trombonist Craig Harris from '83. His robust, vocalized solos were well supported by an all-star quartet including George Adams on tenor sax, Donald Smith on piano, bassist Fred Hopkins, and drummer Charlie Persip. The pieces ranged from respectful covers of standards to rousing, spirited originals. —*Ron Wynn*

Tributes / 1985 / OTC ✦✦✦
Shelter / Nov. 19, 1986–Dec. 1986 / JMT ✦✦✦✦
W/ Tailgaters Tales. This is an aggressive, never-dull session that operates in the stylistic middle ground between jazz, R&B, blues, and rock. —*Ron Wynn*

★ **Blackout in the Square Root of Soul** / Nov. 1987 / JMT ✦✦✦✦✦
A first-rate example of a fresh direction in jazz that blends improvisatory zeal, funk, and R&B references. —*Ron Wynn*

Cold Sweat Plays J.B. / Nov. 1988 / JMT ✦✦✦
Four Play / Aug. 1990 / JMT ✦✦✦
F Stops / Jun. 24, 1993–Jun. 25, 1993 / Soul Note ✦✦✦

Eddie Harris

b. Oct. 20, 1934, Chicago, IL
Tenor Saxophone / Soul Jazz, Hard Bop
Eddie Harris has had a diverse and erratic recording career, leading to many observers greatly underrating his jazz talents. Harris has had his own sound on tenor since at least 1960, his improvisations range from bop to free, he was a pioneer with utilizing the electric sax (and was much more creative on it than most who followed), he introduced the reed trumpet, is a fine pianist (one of his first professional jobs was playing piano with Gene Ammons),

composed the standard "Freedom Jazz Dance" and, although his vocals are definitely an acquired taste, he is a skilled comedian.

After getting out of the military, Eddie Harris' very first recording resulted in a hit version of "Exodus." His high-note tenor playing (which managed to sound comfortable in the range of an alto or even soprano) was well-featured on a series of strong selling Vee Jay releases (1961–63). After two outings for Columbia (1964), he switched to Atlantic for a decade. In 1966 Harris started utilizing an electric sax and he debuted the popular "Listen Here" (although the 1967 recording is better-known). At the 1969 Montreux Jazz Festival, Harris and Les McCann made for a very appealing combination, recording such songs as "Compared to What" and "Cold Duck Time." Harris' later output for Atlantic was streaky, sometimes rock-oriented and occasionally pure comedy. He has since generally recorded strong jazz sets for such labels as Impulse, Enja and SteepleChase and has remained a unique musical personality. — *Scott Yanow*

Exodus to Jazz / Jan. 17, 1961 / Vee-Jay ✦✦✦✦✦

The Artist's Choice: the Eddie Harris Anthology / Jan. 1961–Feb. 20, 1977 / Rhino ✦✦✦
Eddie Harris' tenure at Atlantic in the 1960s and '70s was his most productive, but until recently it was represented only by a pair of single album collections. Now, a fine two-disc anthology containing selections chosen by Harris and his comments fully cover his Atlantic years. The discs include his huge singles "Exodus" and "Love Theme From *The Sandpiper* (Shadow Of Your Smile)," plus soul/jazz numbers like "Get On Down," "Funkaroma" and "1974 Blues," his most famous single composition, "Freedom Jazz Dance," and his remakes of "Giant Steps" and "Love For Sale." Harris has creatively utilized the varitone attachment on his saxophone and the reed trumpet, while constructing and playing his blues, soul and funk solos with zest and a minimum of gimmickry. — *Ron Wynn*

Mighty Like a Rose / Apr. 14, 1961 / Vee-Jay ✦✦✦✦

Jazz for "Breakfast at Tiffany's" / 1961 / Vee-Jay ✦✦✦

The Lost Album Plus the Better Half / 1962–1963 / Vee-Jay ✦✦✦✦
This CD contains an LP's worth of unissued material plus half of an album that was released. With a supporting cast that on different tracks includes Ira Sullivan on trumpet, altoist Bunky Green, organist Mel Rhyne and guitarist Joe Diorio among others, the underrated but very distinctive tenor is in consistently spirited form. Eddie Harris stretches out on the rhythm changes of "Cuttin' Out" and the blues "Shakey Jake," (both of which are over 15 minutes long) and is heard on a variety of much shorter performances. A few of the briefer pieces are throwaways but all of Eddie Harris' Vee Jay recordings are enjoyable and this one is no exception. — *Scott Yanow*

Eddie Harris Goes to the Movies / 1962–1963 / Vee-Jay ✦✦✦

Bossa Nova / 1963 / Vee-Jay ✦✦✦

Cool Sax, Warm Heart / Jan. 15, 1964–Jan. 16, 1964 / Columbia ✦✦✦

Cool Sax from Hollywood to Broadway / Sep. 22, 1964–Sep. 24, 1964 / Columbia ✦✦✦

The In Sound/Mean Greens / Aug. 9, 1965–Jun. 7, 1966 / Rhino/Atlantic ✦✦✦✦✦
This CD from Rhino's valuable Atlantic reissue program combines together two former LPs from thge 1965-67 period. *The In Sound* is among tenor saxophonist Eddie Harris' most significant recordings, highlighted by the original version of his "Freedom Jazz Dance," and including a memorable rendition of "The Shadow of Your Smile," three standards and a blues. Harris is assisted by an all-star rhythm section (pianist Cedar Walton, bassist Ron Carter and drummer Billy Higgins) and, on three selections, trumpeter Roy Codrington. The lesser-known *Mean Greens* set (comprised entirely of originals except for Harris' high-note treatment of "It Was a Very Good Year") utilizes the same personnel on the first four numbers and is just as exciting with the calypso "Yeah Yeah Yeah" being a highpoint. The final three performances are more unusual for Harris switches to electric piano and jams with a Latin rhythm section; included is the original (and somewaht obscure) recording of "Listen Here," which predates his hit version by over a year. Overall this CD is a well-rounded and highly recommended set. — *Scott Yanow*

The Tender Storm / Sep. 19, 1966 / Atlantic ✦✦✦

Excursions / 1966 / Atlantic ✦✦✦✦
A very underrated, two-record live set with some of Harris' best acoustic and electric sax solos. — *Ron Wynn*

Electrifying Eddie Harris / Apr. 20, 1967 / Atlantic ✦✦✦✦✦
The birth and fruition of Harris' use of varitone and electronics on tenor as a legitimate technique. — *Ron Wynn*

Plug Me In / Mar. 14, 1968–Mar. 15, 1968 / Atlantic ✦✦✦

Silver Cycles / Sep. 4, 1968 / Atlantic ✦✦✦

High Voltage / Oct. 28, 1968–Apr. 19, 1969 / Atlantic ✦✦✦

★ **Swiss Movement** / Jun. 1969 / Atlantic ✦✦✦✦✦
With Les McCann. Contains the monster hit "Compared to What." A must-buy. — *Michael G. Nastos*

Free Speech / Dec. 15, 1969 / Atlantic ✦✦✦

Come on Down! / Mar. 3, 1970 / Atlantic ✦✦✦

Live at Newport / 1970 / Atlantic ✦✦✦

Instant Death / Dec. 7, 1971 / Atlantic ✦✦✦

Second Movement / 1971 / Atlantic ✦✦✦

Sings the Blues / Jul. 25, 1972 / Atlantic ✦✦

Eddie Harris in the UK / 1973 / Atlantic ✦✦

Is It In / Dec. 16, 1973 / Atlantic ✦✦

I Need Some Money / Jul. 15, 1974–Dec. 2, 1974 / Atlantic ✦✦

Bad Luck Is All I Have / 1975 / Atlantic ✦

That Is Why You're Overweight / 1975 / Atlantic ✦✦

Tale of Two Cities / 1975 / Night ✦✦✦

Steps Up / Feb. 20, 1981 / SteepleChase ✦✦✦
Some torrid interchanges and dialogs with pianist Tete Montoliu. — *Ron Wynn*

Homecoming / 1985 / Spindletop ✦✦✦
A very nice, underrated teaming of Eddie Harris and Ellis Marsalis (p). It's understated, bluesy, mellow, and sometimes challenging. — *Ron Wynn*

Eddie Who? / Feb. 27, 1986 / Timeless ✦✦✦

Live in Berlin / Mar. 24, 1988 / Timeless ✦✦✦

There Was a Time (Echo of Harlem) / May 9, 1990 / Enja ✦✦✦✦

For You, for Me, for Everyone / Oct. 1992 / SteepleChase ✦✦✦✦
Tenor saxophonist Eddie Harris was scheduled to record a duet set with pianist Jodie Christian, but for unknown reasons Christian never showed up. Harris made it a solo showcase by first recording on piano and then overdubbing his tenor. The spontaneous experiment worked quite well as Harris performed four originals, lesser-known songs by Gershwin and Donald Byrd and four standards. The music is thoughtful and melodic but has its fiery moments, serving as a reminder (to those who may have forgotten) that Eddie Harris can really play. — *Scott Yanow*

Funk Project: Listen Here! / Nov. 7, 1992–Nov. 9, 1992 / Enja ✦✦✦

The Electrifying Eddie Harris/Plug Me In / 1967–1968 / Rhino ✦✦✦✦✦
This CD combines two fine Harris dates from 1967 and 1968. *The Electrifying Eddie Harris* had bluesy, soulful examples of Harris on baritone sax. "Listen Here" ranked second only to "Freedom Jazz Dance" among his most popular compositions, while he stretched out on "Spanish Bull." "Theme In Search Of A Movie," "Sham Time" and "Judie's Theme" were goodtime concessions to pop and jazz-soul audiences, yet still retained some fiber and spark. Once more, Harris found a good compromise between artistic and commercial concerns. — *Ron Wynn*

Gene Harris

b. Sep. 1, 1933, Benton Harbor, MI
Piano / Soul Jazz, Hard Bop
One of the most accessible of all jazz pianists, Gene Harris' soulful style (influenced by Oscar Peterson and containing the bluesiness of a Junior Mance) is immediately likable and predictably excellent. After playing in an Army band (1951–54), he formed a trio with bassist Andy Simpkins and drummer Bill Dowdy which was by 1956 known as the Three Sounds. The group was quite popular and recorded regularly during 1956–70 for Blue Note and

Verve. Although the personnel changed and the music became more R&B-oriented in the early '70s, Harris retained the Three Sounds name for his later Blue Note sets. He retired to Boise, ID, in 1977 and was largely forgotten when Ray Brown persuaded him to return to the spotlight in the early-'80s. Harris worked for a time with the Ray Brown Trio and has led his own quartets ever since, recording regularly for Concord and heading the Phillip Morris Superband on a few tours. —*Scott Yanow*

● **Introducing the Three Sounds** / Sep. 16, 1958–Sep. 18, 1958 / Blue Note ✦✦✦✦✦

Feelin' Good / Jun. 28, 1960 / Blue Note ✦✦✦✦
Prototypical Three Sounds release. Elements of funk, soul-jazz, and blues merge into a workable jazz concept. —*Ron Wynn*

Anita O'Day and the Three Sounds / Oct. 12, 1962–Oct. 15, 1962 / Verve ✦✦✦
Classy vocals with good trio backing. —*Ron Wynn*

Live at Otter Crest / Apr. 24, 1981 / Bosco ✦✦✦
Underrated latter-period Harris on piano with trio. Great extended "Battle Hymn," Basie's repertoire represented in "Shiny Stockings" and "Cute" and reliable Harris' "A Little Blues There." —*Michael G. Nastos*

The Plus One / Nov. 19,–Dec. 1985 / Concord Jazz ✦✦✦
Live at New York City's legendary Blue Note, a great place to hear live music. Ray Bown is a major player on bass and compositionally. Stanley Turrentine (ts) cameos. —*Michael G. Nastos*

Tribute to Count Basie / Mar. 1987–Jun. 1987 / Concord Jazz ✦✦✦
Gene Harris All Star Big Band. An emphatic big-band tribute to the swing master. —*Ron Wynn*

Listen Here! / Mar. 1989 / Concord Jazz ✦✦✦✦
A solid mainstream date with light soul-jazz flavor. —*Ron Wynn*

Live at Town Hall / Sep. 23, 1989 / Concord Jazz ✦✦✦
A fine, traditional big-band outing. The song selection is predictably conservative, but there's enough boldness in the arrangements and playing to even things out and make this an above-average entry in a domain screaming for fresh blood. —*Ron Wynn*

● **At Last** / May 1990 / Concord Jazz ✦✦✦✦✦
A wonderful teamup of Gene Harris with Scott Hamilton. —*Ron Wynn*

World Tour 1990 / Oct. 18, 1990 / Concord Jazz ✦✦✦
This is a fine big-band showcase. —*Ron Wynn*

Black and Blue / Jun. 29, 1991 / Concord Jazz ✦✦✦✦
Although there are few actual blues on this CD, pianist Gene Harris gives all of the songs (whether complex standards, ballads or near-blues) a bluesy feel, adding soul and a church feeling to each of the melodies. With the assistance of guitarist Ron Eschete, bassist Luther Hughes and drummer Harold Jones, Harris is in typically fine form. —*Scott Yanow*

Like a Lover / Jan. 17, 1992 / Concord Jazz ✦✦✦✦

Live at Maybeck Recital Hall, Vol. 23 / Aug. 3, 1992 / Concord Jazz ✦✦✦

● **Brotherhood** / Aug. 4, 1992–Aug. 5, 1992 / Concord Jazz ✦✦✦✦✦

A Little Piece of Heaven / Jul. 30, 1993–Jul. 31, 1993 / Concord Jazz ✦✦✦✦

Funky Gene's / May 25, 1994–May 27, 1994 / Concord Jazz ✦✦✦

Donald Harrison

b. Jun. 23, 1960, New Orleans
Alto Saxophone, Soprano Saxophone / Post-Bop
A talented post bop altoist with a personal angular style, Donald Harrison came to fame with Art Blakey's Jazz Messengers but has not become a major name in jazz yet despite his talent. He studied at the New Orleans Center for the Creative Arts with Ellis Marsalis, went to Berklee (1979–80), worked with Roy Haynes and Jack McDuff and was with Blakey during 1982–84, sharing the frontline with Terence Blanchard. Harrison and Blanchard co-led a group for a few years, recording frequently before they broke up their band. Donald Harrison reunited with the Jazz Messengers for a few brief occasions, led his own groups and recorded as a leader for Candid, making guest appearances on CTI sessions. —*Scott Yanow*

● **Crystal Stair** / Jan. 22, 1987–Jan. 30, 1988 / CBS ✦✦✦✦✦

Black Pearl / 1988 / CBS ✦✦✦✦

For Art's Sake / Nov. 9, 1990–Nov. 10, 1990 / Candid ✦✦✦✦
A tribute album to great drummer Art Blakey from onetime Jazz Messenger alto saxophonist Donald Harrison. This was one of the first sessions after Harrison and longtime partner Terence Blanchard (trumpet) went their separate ways, and Harrison was working with new trumpeter Marlon Jordan and other young lions, such as pianist Cyrus Chestnut, bassist Christian McBride, and drummer Carl Allen. The results would have made Blakey smile. —*Ron Wynn*

Indian Blues / May 22, 1991–May 23, 1991 / Candid ✦✦✦
Alto saxophonist Donald Harrison explores another area of his New Orleans heritage, the music of the Mardi Gras "Indians." His solos are more bluesy and R&B-flavored, while the supporting cast includes Dr. John on piano, along with Cyrus Chestnut, drummer Carl Allen, bassist Phil Bowler, percussionists Bruce Cox And Howard Smiley Ricks, And Harrison's father on vocals. —*Ron Wynn*

Power Of Cool / 1993 / CTI ✦✦

Wendell Harrison

b. 1942, Detroit, MI
Clarinet / Bop
A fine clarinetist and tenor saxophonist, Wendell Harrison has been an important force in Detroit during the past 25 years. He began clarinet when he was seven, started playing tenor in high school and studied with Barry Harris. In 1960 he moved to New York, playing with Jack McDuff, Elvin Jones, Sonny Stitt, Grant Green and Sun Ra in addition to being in Hank Crawford's band for over four years. In 1970 Harrison moved back to Detroit, starting doing session work and became a jazz educator. He has formed several labels (Tribe, Rebirth and WenHa), recording frequently and utilizing such sidemen as Leon Thomas, Marcus Belgrave, Kirk Lightsey, Charles Tolliver and (with his Clarinet Ensemble) James Carter. —*Scott Yanow*

● **Forever Duke** / 1991 / Wen-Ha ✦✦✦✦✦
Clarinetist leads modern ensemble through five Duke tunes and two originals. Guests include Charles Tolliver (tpt) and Harold McKinney (p). There is a brief appearance by a five-piece clarinet ensemble. —*Michael G. Nastos*

Live in Concert / 1992 / Wen-Ha ✦✦✦
This 1992 performance in Detroit's Museum of African-American history includes a big band and Clarinet Ensemble. Unique music, mostly modern, with three standards. —*Michael G. Nastos*

Rush & Hustle / 1994 / WenHa ✦✦✦✦
This is a fairly unusual record. Wendell Harrison leads his Clarinet Ensemble on six of his colorful originals and the standard "My Shining Hour." The group consists of four clarinets (including Harrison who doubles on tenor), one bass clarinet and two contrabass clarinets; the promising James Carter is among the latter. In addition, a standard rhythm section (with an added percussionist) backs the reeds. Harrison's episodic compositions/arrangements (which range from modern bop, modal and light funk to some free moments) hold one's interest throughout with the leader and pianists Harold McKinney and Pamela Wise getting their share of solo space. The one disappointment is that the bass clarinet and contrabass clarinets are primarily heard in the ensembles; it would have been nice to hear the two contrabass clarinets trading off. —*Scott Yanow*

Nancy Harrow

b. New York, NY
Vocals / Standards
Nancy Harrow made a strong impression with her Candid recording *Wild Women Don't Have the Blues* in 1960, but it was a long time before she was a full-time singer. She had studied classical piano extensively from the age of seven before deciding to become a dancer and later a jazz singer. After her Candid recording and an album for Atlantic (1962), Harrow raised a family and spent time outside of music. In 1975 Nancy Harrow came back and has recorded frequently since then for Audiophile, Finesse, Inner City, Tono, Gazell and Soul Note. She is a talented and swinging bop-based singer who wrote all of the material for her 1993 *Lost Lady* release. —*Scott Yanow*

★ **Wild Women Don't Have the Blues** / Nov. 2, 1960–Nov. 3, 1960 / Candid ✦✦✦✦✦

Anything Goes / Nov. 29, 1978+Dec. 18, 1978 / Audiophile ✦✦✦

Street Of Dreams / Apr. 28, 1988–Oct. 17, 1988 / Gazell ✦✦✦

Secrets / Nov. 21, 1990–Jan. 18, 1991 / Soul Note ✦✦✦✦✦

Lost Lady / Jun. 28, 1993–Nov. 29, 1993 / Soul Note ✦✦✦✦

Antonio Hart

b. 1969, Baltimore, MD
Alto Saxophone / Hard Bop, Post-Bop
An excellent altoist who gained recognition for his work with Roy Hargrove, Antonio Hart studied classical saxophone at the Baltimore School for the Arts for four years. He sat in with Art Blakey's Jazz Messengers, toured with Hargrove for a few years, and in the mid-'90s, formed his own group. Hart, who is most influenced by Cannonball Adderley and Gary Bartz, has recorded for Novus with Hargrove and as a leader of four of his own CDs. —*Scott Yanow*

For the First Time / Feb. 1991–Apr. 1991 / Novus ✦✦✦
Introductory vehicle for yet another young lion, twenty-something alto saxophonist Antonio Hart. The set had the almost obligatory hard bop feel, but Hart's shimmering solos weren't just imitative Charlie Parker licks; he displayed sensitivity and style on every selection, and the album demonstrated genuine potential, as well as technical aptitude. —*Ron Wynn*

Don't You Know I Care / 1992 / Novus ✦✦✦✦
Some beautiful ballads and surging uptempo songs done by alto saxophonist Antonio Hart on his '92 followup release to his '91 debut as a leader. Hart has the tone, style, and skill to be a star, and hasn't succumbed to young lion publicity hype. He's aided by a cast that blends new players such as Gregory Hutchinson and Rodney Whitaker with veterans like Gary Bartz. —*Ron Wynn*

● **For Cannonball & Woody** / 1993 / Novus ✦✦✦✦✦
Altoist Antonio Hart's latest recording starts out with an eerie recreation of the Cannonball Adderley version of "Sticks" from 1968 which, like the original, even has a live audience shouting out encouragement and clapping along more or less in time. After that the music gets more original, featuring trumpeter Darren Barrett (who shows an impressive amount of versatility), either Carlos McKinney or Mulgrew Miller on piano and a guest spot from cornetist Nat Adderley on "Sack O' Woe." In addition to he Adderley tributes, there are several Woody Shaw pieces that generally contain new arrangements for an expanded group, based more on the spirit of the original '70s versions than the notes. Antonio Hart is in top form throughout this well-conceived release. —*Scott Yanow*

It's All Good / 1994 / Novus/RCA ✦✦✦✦

Billy Hart

b. Nov. 29, 1940, Washington, DC
Drums / Post-Bop
A flexible drummer who has been a sideman in many different settings, Billy Hart is a creative player most at home playing advanced jazz. He worked early on in Washington, D.C., with Buck Hill and Shirley Horn and was with the Montgomery Brothers (1961), Jimmy Smith (1964–66) and Wes Montgomery (1966–68). Hart was a member of Herbie Hancock's challenging sextet (1969–73) and played regularly wtih McCoy Tyner (1973–74) and Stan Getz (1974–77) in addition to extensive freelancing (including recording with Miles Davis on 1972's *On the Corner*). His own opportunities to lead sessions have been comparatively rare, but Billy Hart has led interesting dates for Horizon, Gramavision and Arabesque. —*Scott Yanow*

Oshumare / 1985 / Gramavision ✦✦✦

Rah / Sep. 1987 / Gramavision ✦✦✦
Excellent original compositions. This is very listenable, time after time. Many great soloists and ensemble players. Highly recommended. —*Michael G. Nastos*

● **Amethyst** / May 27, 1993–May 29, 1993 / Arabesque ✦✦✦✦

Johnny Hartman

b. Jul. 3, 1923, Chicago, IL, d. Sep. 15, 1983, New York, NY
Vocals / Standards, Ballads
A superior ballad singer with a warm baritone voice, Johnny Hartman was rediscovered to an extent posthumously when some of his recordings were used on the soundtrack of the 1995 Clint Eastwood film *Bridges of Madison County,* but jazz fans had never forgotten him for his classic date with John Coltrane. After

military service, Hartman sang with Earl Hines (1947), the Dizzy Gillespie Big Band (1948–49) and Erroll Garner. Although he recorded two Bethlehem albums in 1956, Hartman was generally overlooked during the 1950s. However his three Impulse! albums (1963–64) were well-received, particularly the Coltrane collaboration, which was highlighted by the definitive version of "Lush Life" and a memorable "My One and Only Love." But it would be 1977 before he recorded again and, despite some fine later sessions (including for Bee Hive), Johnny Hartman was underrated throughout his lifetime. —*Scott Yanow*

First, Lasting and Always ... / Dec. 1947 / Savoy ✦✦✦

Songs from the Heart / Oct. 1955 / Bethlehem ✦✦✦

All of Me / Nov. 1956 / Bethlehem ✦✦✦

★ **John Coltrane and Johnny Hartman** / Mar. 7, 1963 / Impulse! ✦✦✦✦✦
Marvelous love songs, superior playing. —*Ron Wynn*

I Just Dropped by to Say Hello / Oct. 9, 1963+Oct. 17, 1963 / Impulse! ✦✦✦✦✦

The Voice That Is / Sep. 22, 1964–Sep. 24, 1964 / Impulse! ✦✦✦

The Unforgettable Johnny Hartman / Sep. 1966 / ABC Paramount ✦✦✦

For Trane / Nov. 29, 1972–Dec. 1, 1972 / Bluenote ✦✦✦
Culled from two separate 1972 albums by Johnny Hartman, *Harman Meets Hino* and *Trane's Favorites, For Trane* is an 11-track collection that was released in 1995. While both of the albums were fine, they were a little uneven, so *For Trane* does do some good by capturing the best tracks from the records. Nevertheless, dedicated fans and jazz purists will want to stick with the original sessions/albums. For casual fans and listeners intrigued by the *Bridges of Madison County* soundtrack—the record that almost certainly inspired this particular record's release—*For Trane* is a nice addition to a record collection. —*Stephen Thomas Erlewine*

Today / 1973 / Perception ✦✦✦✦

I've Been There / 1975 / Perception ✦✦✦

Live at Sometime / Oct. 13, 1977 / Trio ✦✦✦

Once in Every Life / Aug. 11, 1980 / Bee Hive ✦✦✦✦✦
Johnny Hartman was the best, or certainly one of the best mellow jazz singers. Considering all of Hartman's LPs made previous to this Bee Hive recording, he made two great ones: one with John Coltrane and Impulse, and the other for Perception Records called *Today*. This record ranked with his best. It was vocal honey and beyond words. —*Bob Rusch, Cadence*

This One's for Tedi / Aug. 23, 1980 / Audiophile ✦✦✦

Stan Hasselgard

b. Oct. 4, 1922, Sundsvall, Sweden, d. Nov. 23, 1948, Decatur, IL
Clarinet / Bop, Swing
Stan Hasselgard was (along with Buddy DeFranco and Tony Scott) the first clarinetist to fully explore bebop, and the only one to share the bandstand with Benny Goodman. He played swing in Sweden and recorded with local groups before moving to New York in 1947. Hasselgard sat in with both Dixieland and bop players and recorded in December for Capitol, using Red Norvo and Barney Kessel. For part of 1948 he was in the Benny Goodman Septet along with Wardell Gray and Teddy Wilson and, although a recording strike kept the group off records, broadcasts have been released by Dragon that contrast the two clarinetist's styles. Hasselgard had a quintet with Max Roach later in the year and was planning a new band when he died in a car crash at the age of 26. —*Scott Yanow*

☆ **Ake Stan Hasselgard (1945–1948)** / Oct. 11, 1945–Nov. 18, 1948 / Dragon ✦✦✦✦✦

Hampton Hawes

b. Nov. 13, 1928, Los Angeles, CA, d. May 22, 1977, Los Angeles, CA
Piano, Keyboards / Bop, Hard Bop, Crossover
Hampton Hawes was one of the finest jazz pianists of the 1950s, a fixture on the Los Angeles scene who brought his own interpretations to the dominant Bud Powell style. In the mid-to-late '40s he played with Sonny Criss, Dexter Gordon and Wardell Gray among others on Central Avenue. He was with Howard McGhee's band (1950–51), played with Shorty Rogers and the Lighthouse

All-Stars, served in the Army (1952–54) and then led trios in the L.A. area, recording many albums for Contemporary. Arrested for heroin possession in 1958, Hawes spent five years in prison until he was pardoned by President Kennedy. He led trios for the remainder of his life, using electric piano (which disturbed his long-time fans) for a period in the early-to-mid-'70s but returning to acoustic piano before dying from a stroke in 1977. Hampton Hawes' memoirs *Raise Up off Me* (1974) are both frank and memorable and most of his records (for Xanadu, Prestige, Savoy, Contemporary, Black Lion and Freedom) are currently available. —*Scott Yanow*

Memorial Album / Feb. 12, 1952–Dec. 23, 1952 / Xanadu ✦✦✦✦

Piano: East/West / Dec. 1952–Feb. 28, 1955 / Original Jazz Classics ✦✦✦
Hawes and Freddie Redd (p) split an album, revealing their differing, yet mutually appealing, stylistic tendencies. —*Ron Wynn*

The Trio: Vol. 3 / Jun. 28, 1955 / Original Jazz Classics ✦✦✦
An essential set of powerhouse mid-'50s trio works with Hawes, Red Mitchell (b), and Chuck Thompson (d). —*Ron Wynn*

The Trio: Vol. 2 / Dec. 3, 1955–Jan. 25, 1956 / Original Jazz Classics ✦✦✦✦
The second volume of mid-'50s trio sessions featuring pianist Hampton Hawes. He does moving ballads, reinterprets standards with elan, and pens originals that show his blues and gospel influence, while also exhibiting his voicings and fluidity. —*Ron Wynn*

All Night Session!, Vol. 1 / Nov. 12, 1956 / Original Jazz Classics ✦✦✦✦✦

All Night Session!, Vol. 2 / Nov. 12, 1956 / Original Jazz Classics ✦✦✦✦✦
Hampton Hawes Quartet. Some wondrous, invigorating playing from everyone included, especially Hawes and Jim Hall (g). —*Ron Wynn*

All Night Session!, Vol. 3 / Nov. 13, 1956 / Original Jazz Classics ✦✦✦✦✦

★ **Four! Hampton Hawes!!!!** / Jan. 27, 1958 / Original Jazz Classics ✦✦✦✦✦
This is an outstanding date, with excellent Barney Kessel guitar. —*Ron Wynn*

For Real! / Mar. 17, 1958 / Original Jazz Classics ✦✦✦✦

The Sermon / Nov. 24, 1958–Nov. 25, 1958 / Contemporary ✦✦✦✦
A 1988 reissue of a tight, tough trio work. —*Ron Wynn*

The Green Leaves of Summer / Feb. 17, 1964 / Original Jazz Classics ✦✦✦✦✦

Here and Now / May 12, 1965 / Original Jazz Classics ✦✦✦
Trio. Adept and nimble work from Hawes. Chuck Israels roams and booms on bass. —*Ron Wynn*

The Seance / Apr. 30, 1966–May 1, 1966 / Original Jazz Classics ✦✦✦✦✦
There was an uneasy feeling given by pianist Hampton Hawes as he made little rips in his blues out of which tumbled skittering runs. Hawes' playing here proved more than a backdrop for one's thoughts and action; it drew one's attention to its ideas and body. This set was recorded live, over two days, at Mitchell's Studio Club, where the group had been gigging for most of a year. Hawes' trio and music with bassist Red Mitchell and drummer Don Bailey really had everything going for it, including a solid program of standards and excellent originals, superior support, especially from Mitchell and swinging improvisation that was both inventive and accessible. There was an emotional power here which was subtle but unrelenting, and the tracks seemed so arranged that, if played in order, when one got to the end of "My Romance" one felt as though they had been part of the music's movement. —*Bob Rusch, Cadence*

I'm All Smiles / Apr. 30, 1966–May 1, 1966 / Contemporary ✦✦✦
Pianist Hampton Hawes led a trio during the 1960s and '70s that maintained popularity without compromising its sound or musical integrity. His phrasing and voicings could entice or amaze, and he displayed great range, rhythmic vitality and harmonic excellence during the five selections featured on this 1966 live date now reissued on CD. Hawes moved from the Afro-Latin feel of "Manha De Carnaval" to brilliant chordal exposition on "Spring Is Here" and "The Shadow Of Your Smile," before concluding with a flourish on "Searchin'." Hawes was backed by wonderful bassist

Red Mitchell and steady drummer Donald Bailey, who had both been with him for over a decade. They were not just a cohesive unit, but an intuitive team, maintaining a communication with him that was amazing even within a genre that demands it. —*Ron Wynn*

Hamp's Piano / Nov. 8, 1967 / Saba ✦✦✦

Key for Two / Jan. 1968 / Affinity ✦✦✦
A stomping workout with fellow pianist Martial Solal. —*Ron Wynn*

Blues for Bud / Mar. 10, 1968 / Black Lion ✦✦✦✦

The Challenge / May 7, 1968–May 12, 1968 / Storyville ✦✦✦✦✦
Stunning solo piano. —*Ron Wynn*

Plays Movie Musicals / Aug. 1969 / Fresh Sound ✦✦

High in the Sky / 1970 / Fresh Sound ✦✦✦

Trio At Montreux / Jun. 1971 / Fresh Sound ✦✦✦✦
This CD consists of a continuous 57-minute set performed by pianist Hampton Hawes' Trio with bassist Henry Franklin and drummer Mike Carvin. Two songs (Bert Bacharach's "This Guy's in Love with You" and Hawes' "High in the Sky") are fully explored and, despite the extreme length and some wandering sections, the performance holds one's interest throughout. —*Scott Yanow*

A Little Copenhagen Night Music / Sep. 2, 1971 / Arista/Freedom ✦✦✦
An album where Hawes adds electric piano and synthesizer to his arsenal. —*Ron Wynn*

Live at the Montmartre / Sep. 2, 1971 / Arista/Freedom ✦✦✦✦
Hampton Hawes, a bop-oriented pianist in the '50s, continued to develop and evolve throughout his career without losing his musical identity. For this trio set with bassist Henry Franklin and drummer Michael Carvin, Hawes shows the influence of McCoy Tyner a bit and, by performing Burt Bacharach's "This Guy's in Love with You" (along with four other group originals), he shows his openness to including some pop material in his repertoire (although his explorative version owes little to the original hit tune). This excellent live session has plenty of close interplay by the tight trio. —*Scott Yanow*

Universe / May 19–June 1972 / Prestige ✦✦

Blues for Walls / Jan. 16, 1973–Jan. 18, 1973 / Prestige ✦✦
Good, early-'70s set with pianist Hampton Hawes mixing acoustic and electric keyboard numbers and playing with passion, although the material is uneven. He's backed by electric bassist Carol Kaye, and tries to find balance between the bop and West Coast-style numbers he had done in the past and more contemporary material. —*Ron Wynn*

Live at the Jazz Showcase in Chicago / Jun. 10, 1973 / Enja ✦✦✦✦✦
Vol. 1. As fine as any trio set Hawes ever made, with Cecil McBee (b) and Roy Haynes (d). —*Ron Wynn*

Northern Windows / Jul. 17, 1974–Jul. 18, 1974 / Prestige ✦✦✦

Recorded Live at the Great American Music Hall / Jun. 10, 1975 / Concord Jazz ✦✦✦✦
This album, one of pianist Hampton Hawes' last recordings, is a surprise success. First Hawes, in duets with bassist Mario Suraci, really digs into two rather unpromising pop tunes ("Fly Me to the Moon" and "Sunny") in extended versions ("Sunny" is given over 14 minutes) and brings out surprising beauty in those overdone songs. For the second side of this LP, Hawes performs his own suite for solo piano, an impressive three-movement work that he titled "The Status of Maceo" that has enough variety in its 20-plus minutes to keep one's interest throughout. —*Scott Yanow*

Coleman Hawkins

b. Nov. 21, 1904, St. Joseph, MO, **d.** May 19, 1969, New York, NY
Tenor Saxophone / Classic Jazz, Swing, Bop
Coleman Hawkins was the first important tenor saxophonist and he remains one of the greatest of all time. A consistently modern improviser whose knowledge of chords and harmonies was encyclopedic, Hawkins had a 40-year prime (1925–65) during which he could hold his own with any competitor.

Coleman Hawkins started piano lessons when he was five, switched to cello at age seven and two years later began on tenor. At a time when the saxophone was considered a novelty instrument, used in vaudeville and as a poor substitute for the trombone in marching bands, Hawkins sought to develop his own sound. A professional when he was 12, Hawkins was playing in a Kansas City theater pit band in 1921 when Mamie Smith hired him to play with her Jazz Hounds. Hawkins was with the blues singer until June 1923, making many records in a background role and he was occasionally heard on instrumentals. After leaving Smith, he freelanced around New York, played briefly with Wilbur Sweatman and, in August 1923, made his first recordings with Fletcher Henderson. When Henderson formed a permanent orchestra in January 1924, Hawkins was his star tenor.

Although (due largely to lack of competition) Coleman Hawkins was the top tenor in jazz in 1924, his staccato runs and use of slap-tonguing sound quite dated today. However, after Louis Armstrong joined Henderson later in the year, Hawkins learned from the cornetist's relaxed legato style and advanced quickly. By 1925 Hawkins was truly a major soloist and the following year his solo on "Stampede" became influential. Hawk (who doubled in early years on clarinet and bass sax) would be with Fletcher Henderson's Orchestra up to 1934 and during this time he was the obvious pacesetter among tenors; Bud Freeman was about the only tenor who did not sound like a close relative of the hard-toned Hawkins! In addition to his solos with Henderson, Hawkins backed some blues singers, recorded with McKinney's Cotton Pickers, and with Red McKenzie in 1929 he cut his first classic ballad statement on "One Hour."

By 1934 Coleman Hawkins had tired of the struggling Fletcher Henderson Orchestra and he moved to Europe, spending five years (1934-39) overseas. He played at first with Jack Hylton's Orchestra in England and then freelanced throughout the continent. His most famous recording from this period was a 1937 date with Benny Carter, Alix Combille, Andre Ekyan, Django Reinhardt and Stephane Grappelli that resulted in classic renditions of "Crazy Rhythm" and "Honeysuckle Rose." With World War II coming close, Hawkins returned to the U.S. in 1939. Although Lester Young had emerged with a totally new style on tenor, Hawkins showed that he was still a dominant force by winning a few heated jam sessions. His recording of "Body and Soul" that year became his most famous record. In 1940 he led a big band that failed to catch on so Hawkins broke it up and became a fixture on 52nd Street. Some of his finest recordings were cut during the first half of the 1940s including a stunning quartet version of "The Man I Love." Although he was already a 20-year veteran, Hawkins encouraged the younger bop-oriented musicians and did not need to adjust his harmonically-advanced style in order to play with them. He used Thelonious Monk in his 1944 quartet, led the first official bop record session (which included Dizzy Gillespie and Don Byas), had Oscar Pettiford, Miles Davis and Max Roach as sidemen early in their careers, toured in California with a sextet featuring Howard McGhee and, in 1946, utilized J.J. Johnson and Fats Navarro on record dates. Hawkins toured with Jazz at the Philharmonic several times during 1946-50, visited Europe on a few occasions and, in 1948, recorded the first unaccompanied saxophone solo, "Picasso."

By the early '50s the Lester Young-influenced Four Brothers sound had become a much greater influence on young tenors than Hawkins' style and he was considered by some to be out-of-fashion. However, Hawkins kept on working and occasionally recording and, by the mid-'50s, was experiencing a renaissance. The up-and-coming Sonny Rollins considered Hawkins his main influence, Hawk started teaming up regularly with Roy Eldridge in an exciting quintet (their appearance at the 1957 Newport Jazz Festival was notable) and he proved to still be in his prime. Coleman Hawkins appeared in a wide variety of settings, from Red Allen's heated Dixieland band at the Metropole and leading a bop date featuring Idrees Sulieman and J.J. Johnson to guest appearances on records that included Thelonious Monk, John Coltrane and (in the early '60s) Max Roach and Eric Dolphy. During the first half of the 1960s, Coleman Hawkins had an opportunity to record with Duke Ellington, collaborated on one somewhat eccentric session with Sonny Rollins and even did a bossa nova album. By 1965 Hawkins was even showing the influence of John Coltrane in his explorative flights and seemed ageless.

Unfortunately 1965 was Coleman Hawkins' last good year. Whether it was senility or frustration, Hawkins began to lose interest in life. He practically quit eating, increased his drinking, and quickly wasted away. Other than a surprisingly effective appearance with Jazz at the Philharmonic in early 1969, very little of Hawkins' work during his final 3-1/2 years (a period during which he largely stopped recording) is up to the level one would expect from the great master. However, there are dozens of superb Coleman Hawkins recordings currently available and, as Eddie Jefferson said in his vocalese version of "Body and Soul," "He was the king of the saxophone." —*Scott Yanow*

Body & Soul / Apr. 27, 1927-Jul. 18, 1963 / RCA ✦✦✦✦✦
This single LP is a perfect sampler of the career and talents of Coleman Hawkins. The 16 selections find the great tenor saxophonist in many different settings, ranging from The Fletcher Henderson big band and other groups from the '20s, through the swing and bop years, and concluding with a musical encounter with Sonny Rollins in 1963. Long out-of-print, this well-conceived LP is still quite valuable. —*Scott Yanow*

Three Great Swing Saxophones / Nov. 14, 1929-Aug. 23, 1946 / Bluebird ✦✦✦
This CD is a best-of collection that includes performances showcasing the tenors of Coleman Hawkins and Ben Webster and altoist Benny Carter, mostly from the swing era. Hawk is heard with Fletcher Henderson's Orchestra, playing "One Hour" and "Hello Lola" with The Mound City Blue Blowers, on two versions of "Dinah" with Lionel Hampton, soloing a song with McKinney's Cotton Pickers and performing his famous version of "Body and Soul." Webster is featured with Bennie Moten, Willie Bryant, Lionel Hampton, Duke Ellington (including "Cotton Tail") and Rex Stewart while Carter is heard with McKinney's Cotton Pickers, Mezz Mezzrow, Hampton and with his own bands in 1940-41. Very much a sampler (virtually all of the music is available elsewhere), this set serves as a fine introduction to the early work of these classic players. —*Scott Yanow*

Coleman Hawkins (1929-1934) / Nov. 1929-Mar. 1934 / Classics ✦✦✦✦

☆ **In Europe 1934/39** / Nov. 18, 1934-May 26, 1939 / Jazz Up ✦✦✦✦✦
In 1934 Hawkins, after 11 years as the star soloist with Fletcher Henderson's pioneering jazz big band, was looking for other worlds to conquer. To satisfy his curiosity he travelled to Europe and for the next five years was a major celebrity overseas, only returning to the U.S. when World War II was about ready to start. This magnificent three-CD set contains every recording that the great tenor saxophonist made in Europe, 71 in all (including alternate takes). Whether featured in London, Switzerland, Paris or Holland, Hawkins dominates these recordings, which find him in a variety of settings, from duets with pianist Freddie Johnson to medium-sized bands. Benny Carter and Django Reinhardt also make a few notable appearances. This perfectly done set is highly recommended. —*Scott Yanow*

The Hawk in Europe / Nov. 1934-May 1937 / ASV/Living Era ✦✦✦
Vintage material recorded in Europe by tenor sax legend Coleman Hawkins from 1934-1937, with Hawkins playing with Django Reinhardt, Stephane Grappelli, Freddy Johnson, and Michael Warlop, among others, in both "hot" and swing style. —*Ron Wynn*

Coleman Hawkins (1924-1937) / Nov. 1934-1937 / Classics ✦✦✦✦✦

Hawk in Holland / Feb. 4, 1935-Apr. 26, 1937 / GNP ✦✦✦
This enjoyable LP finds Hawkins guesting with The Ramblers, a fine Dutch swing group, in 1935 and 1937. While pianist Freddie Johnson is the only other distinctive soloist (although Annie de Reuver contributes two haunting vocals), The Ramblers do an excellent job of accompanying their American guest on a variety of standards and a couple of Hawk's originals. The closer, "Something Is Gonna Give Me Away," finds the tenorman romping with just the rhythm section and is quite memorable. This material has since been reissued on CD. —*Scott Yanow*

Coleman Hawkins and Benny Carter / Mar. 2, 1935-Aug. 23, 1946 / Disques Swing ✦✦✦
This attractive LP (which contains quite a few photos in its gateway liners) is drawn from four separate recording sessions. Hawkins is heard as the main soloist with Michel Warlop's orchestra in 1935, and he teams up with Benny Carter, two of Europe's best saxophonists (Alix Combelle on tenor and altoist Andre Ekyan), and Django Reinhardt for the famous "Crazy Rhythm" all-star session of 1937. In addition, Benny Carter is heard in Europe in 1938 and with his Chocolate Dandies (featuring trumpeter

Buck Clayton and Ben Webster on tenor) in 1946. Superb music, all of which has since been reissued. —*Scott Yanow*

Dutch Treat / Apr. 1936–Jun. 14, 1938 / Xanadu ✦✦✦
It was during his period in Europe (1934–39) that Hawkins smoothed out some rough edges in his tenor playing and really matured as an improviser. This Xanadu LP features some of his European sessions, including a meeting with the Swiss group The Berries and a series of duets and trios with pianist Freddy Johnson. Hawkins is the dominant soloist throughout and in fine form. —*Scott Yanow*

Coleman Hawkins (1937–1939) / Apr. 1937–Jun. 1939 / Classics ✦✦✦✦

★ **Body and Soul** / Oct. 11, 1939–Jan. 20, 1956 / RCA/Bluebird ✦✦✦✦✦
Much of the material on this two-LP set has been since reissued on CD but, one way or the other, this music (particularly the first 16 tracks) belongs in every serious jazz collection. In 1939 Hawkins returned to the U.S. after five years in Europe and it took him very little time to reassert his prior dominance as king of the tenors. This set starts off with the session that resulted in Hawk's classic version of "Body and Soul," teams him with Benny Carter (on trumpet) for some hot swing (including a memorable rendition of "My Blue Heaven") and then finds Hawkins using younger musicians (including trumpeter Fats Navarro and trombonist J.J. Johnson) on some advanced bop originals highlighted by "Half Step Down Please." The remainder of this set is also good but less historic with Hawkins well-showcased with three larger groups in 1956, culminating in a remake of "Body and Soul." —*Scott Yanow*

Coleman Hawkins (1939–1940) / Oct. 1939–Aug. 1940 / Classics ✦✦✦✦

April in Paris, Featuring Body and Soul / Oct. 1939–Jan. 1956 / Bluebird ✦✦

Commodore Years: The Tenor Sax / May 25, 1940–Aug. 12, 1954 / Atlantic ✦✦✦✦
This attractive, two-LP reissue (whose contents have since been reissued in Mosaic's massive *Complete Commodore Jazz Recordings* box set) consists of four interesting swing sessions. The first two are quite classic. The great tenor saxophonist Coleman Hawkins is heard with a pianoless sextet in 1940 that also stars altoist Benny Carter and trumpeter Roy Eldridge. Their four selections (plus two alternate takes) are all impressive, but it is this brilliant version of "I Can't Believe That You're in Love with Me" (during which Carter takes solo honors) that is most memorable. The other Hawkins date is with a septet from 1943. Trumpeter Cootie Williams and clarinetist Edmond Hall are in fine form, but it is the participation of the remarkable pianist Art Tatum that makes the set particularly historic. The other two sessions, among the final ones for Commodore, showcase Frank Wess (on tenor and flute) with a variety of Count Basie's sidemen (including trombonists Henry Coker, Benny Powell and Urbie Green, trumpeter Joe Wilder and pianist Jimmy Jones) on some lightly swinging modern jazz. —*Scott Yanow*

1940 / Aug. 4, 1940–Aug. 23, 1940 / Alamac ✦✦✦
The Coleman Hawkins big band only lasted around a year, recording but four songs in the studio. Although Hawkins was a major name in jazz, his orchestra never did catch on, partly because it did not have a strong personality of its own. This Alamac LP is valuable, for it contains performances by the big band from the Savoy Ballroom aired over the radio, including fine versions of "The Sheik of Araby" and "I Can't Believe That You're in Love with Me." Hawkins sounds typically hard-swinging but, other than trumpeter Joe Guy, the rest of the anonymous-sounding band is mostly just used in support of the leader. —*Scott Yanow*

☆ **Classic Tenors: Lester Young & Coleman Hawkins** / Dec. 8, 1943–Dec. 23, 1943 / Flying Dutchman ✦✦✦✦✦
Although this LP is long out-of-print, its brilliant contents have since been reissued by Bob Thiele on a couple of his labels. Hawkins is featured on eight of the 12 selections. Half come from a fine session with trumpeter Bill Coleman, but it is the other four that are of greatest interest, for they find the tenor saxophonist in a quartet with pianist Eddie Heywood, bassist Oscar Pettiford and drummer Shelly Manne. Their rendition of "The Man I Love" has what is arguably Heywood's finest solo, preceding a lengthy roaring statement by Hawkins. The other tracks ("Sweet Lorraine," "Get Happy" and "Crazy Rhythm") are almost as special. In addition, this LP finishes off with an excellent session from tenor sax-

ophonist Lester Young, trombonist Dickie Wells and trumpeter Bill Coleman. Wells' high-note trombone solo on "I'm Fer It Too" is a crackup. —*Scott Yanow*

☆ **Coleman Hawkins on Keynote** / 1944 / Verve ✦✦✦✦✦

★ **Rainbow Mist** / Feb. 16, 1944–May 22, 1944 / Delmark ✦✦✦✦✦
Hawkins was always an open-minded musician. A very advanced player even when he first emerged with Fletcher Henderson's orchestra in the '20s, by the '40s he may have been technically middle-aged but remained a young thinker. For his recording session of February 16, 1944, the great tenor invited some of the most promising younger players (including trumpeter Dizzy Gillespie, bassist Oscar Pettiford and drummer Max Roach) and the result was the very first bebop record. During their two sessions, the large ensemble recorded six selections including Gillespie's "Woody 'n You," Hawk's "Disorder at the Border" and a new treatment of "Body and Soul" by the tenorman, which he retitled "Rainbow Mist." Also on this highly recommended CD are four titles matching together the tenors of Hawkins, Ben Webster and Georgie Auld (with trumpeter Charlie Shavers included as a bonus) and a session from Auld's big band, highlighted by Sonny Berman's trumpet solo on "Taps Miller." —*Scott Yanow*

Thanks for the Memory / May 17, 1944–Dec. 1, 1944 / Xanadu ✦✦✦✦
On this fine LP, Hawkins is heard on four separate sessions from 1944, only one of which has since been reissued on CD. The latter is his encounter with fellow tenors Georgie Auld and Ben Webster; that date led to the little-known original recording of "Salt Peanuts." In addition he is heard with the Esquire All-Stars of 1944, on a date actually led by saxophonist Walter "Foots" Thomas" and in a matchup with trumpeter Charlie Shavers and Hawk's greatest disciple, Don Byas. Hot swing that looks forward toward the rapidly emerging bebop. —*Scott Yanow*

● **Hollywood Stampede** / Feb. 23, 1945–Jun. 1947 / Capitol ✦✦✦✦✦
Hawkins led one of his finest bands in 1945, a sextet with the fiery trumpeter Howard McGhee that fell somewhere between small-group swing and bebop. This CD contains all of that group's 12 recordings, including memorable versions of "Rifftide" and "Stuffy"; trombonist Vic Dickenson guests on four tracks. This CD concludes with one of Hawkins' rarest sessions, an Aladdin date from 1947 that finds the veteran tenor leading a septet that includes 20-year-old trumpeter Miles Davis. —*Scott Yanow*

Coleman Hawkins/Lester Young / Feb. 1945–Apr. 1946 / Spotlite ✦✦✦✦
Hawkins and Lester Young crossed paths constantly throughout their careers but only recorded together on an infrequent basis. This LP from the English Spotlite label features the two great tenors teaming up with trumpeter Buck Clayton for three songs at a jam session; everyone is in fine form. The other side of this set finds Young and Hawkins individually showcased on three numbers apiece. Lester has the benefit of the Nat King Cole Trio plus Buddy Rich on two of his songs, while part of Hawkins' miniset is with the great quintet that he led with trumpeter Howard McGhee. Rare broadcasts containing classic music that was fortunately well-recorded. —*Scott Yanow*

Hawk Variation / 1945–1957 / Contact ✦✦✦
This is an utterly fascinating LP of rare Coleman Hawkins. First the veteran tenor saxophonist is heard on the two-part "Hawk Variation," his initial unaccompanied tenor solo (recorded a couple of years before his more famous "Picasso"). Hawkins is also featured backing singer Delores Martin, on two alternate takes from a 1949 Paris session, guest-starring with a Danish band, uplifting four so-so songs recorded with a quartet in 1950, on a radio transcription made with Elliot Lawrence's All-Stars and soloing on two versions of "Walking My Baby Back Home" that were cut with a pickup band that also included cornetist Rex Stewart, trumpeter Cootie Williams and fellow tenor Bud Freeman. Hawkins collectors will have to own this set. —*Scott Yanow*

The Coleman Hawkins Set / Sep. 18, 1949–Oct. 19, 1957 / Verve ✦✦✦
Coleman Hawkins was frequently featured with Norman Granz's *Jazz at the Philharmonic* during 1946–59 and Granz usually made sure that Hawk had a special spot in addition to participating in the jam sessions. This LP finds Hawkins showcased with two different quartets from 1949 and 1950 (both recorded live at Carnegie Hall); three of the six selections were not released until

the '80s. The repertoire is familiar ("Rifftide," "Stuffy" and ballads including "Body and Soul"), but Hawkins' solos are fresh and creative. The second side of this record features the tenor giant matched with trumpeter Roy Eldridge on two jams and a brief ballad medley. The combative Eldridge always brought out the best in Hawkins and this music is quite exciting. — *Scott Yanow*

Coleman Hawkins And Johnny Hodges In Paris / Dec. 21, 1949–Jun. 20, 1950 / Vogue ✦✦✦✦✦
This CD from the French Vogue label features two unrelated groups, six titles from tenor saxophonist Coleman Hawkins that were formerly on a Prestige LP and a lengthy pair of sessions by altoist Johnny Hodges that were last available in the U.S. on Inner City in the 1970s. Hawkins dominates his sextet date (altoist Hubert Fol and drummer Kenny Clarke are most prominent among the sidemen) and is in superior form on two blues, two ballads and two romps. Hodges allocates much more solo space to his fellow players during his 16 numbers, a wise decision considering that the musicians include Don Byas on tenor, trumpeter Harold Baker, trombonist Quentin Jackson and clarinetist Jimmy Hamilton; all four soloists had their own individual voices. The mixture of bop-tinged jump tunes, blues and ballads is a predecessor to the type of music featured by Hodges' own group a few years later when he temporarily left Duke Ellington's Orchestra to go out on his own. There are lots of highlights to be heard on this highly recommended CD. — *Scott Yanow*

Body and Soul Revisited / Oct. 19, 1951–Oct. 13, 1958 / Decca ✦✦✦
Hawkins had been the dominant tenor saxophonist from the mid-'20s up until 1940, but even though he remained a major force, his influence was waning, due to the emergence of Lester Young and then Charlie Parker. By the early '50s he only recorded on an infrequent basis. Fortunately a few years later (partly due to the rise of Sonny Rollins whose original hero was Hawk), his fortunes were on the rise again. This Decca CD contains quite a variety of music. There are ten selections of melodic "mood" music from 1951-53 in which Hawkins mostly sticks to the melody (an exception is an excellent version of "If I Could Be with You"). Then the great tenor is heard in an occasionally exciting session with Cozy Cole's All-Stars; cornetist Rex Stewart steals the show with a couple of colorful solos. The best music on this CD is taken from a 1955 radio broadcast in which Hawkins plays "Foolin' Around" (based on the chords of "Body and Soul") totally unaccompanied and roars on "The Man I Love." This set concludes with three selections (one previously unissued) from a fine session led by clarinetist Tony Scott. — *Scott Yanow*

Disorder at the Border / Sep. 6, 1952–Sep. 13, 1952 / Spotlite ✦✦✦
Although Hawkins' studio recordings from this era were few and generally found him restricted to playing commercial mood music, his concert and club appearances showed him to still be in prime form. This enjoyable LP has the great tenor leading two different quintets at Birdland on broadcasts that were aired just a week apart. The rhythm section features the then-unknown pianist Horace Silver, bassist Curly Russell and either Art Blakey or Connie Kay on drums. More importantly, trumpeters Roy Eldridge and Howard McGhee (heard separately) inspire the competitive Hawkins to play at his best. A short but very thorough interview wraps up this erratically recorded but very interesting release. — *Scott Yanow*

The Hawk Returns / May 27, 1954 / Savoy ✦✦
This CD features Hawkins on a dozen selections (all around three minutes long) performing with an odd group (organ, piano, bass, drums and sometimes a vocal group). Despite the potentially commercial backing, he really digs into the tunes and creates some magic. Pity that this CD only lasts around 36 minutes. — *Scott Yanow*

1954 / Nov. 8, 1954 / Jazz Anthology ✦✦✦
This relaxed session matches the great tenor with a fine sextet that also includes trumpeter Emmett Berry and trombonist Eddie Bert. Hawk and company sound fine on the nine standards, swinging in a mainstream style that might have been out of fashion at the time but still remains timeless and highly enjoyable. — *Scott Yanow*

Masters of Jazz, Vol. 12 / Nov. 8, 1954–Feb. 13, 1968 / Storyville ✦✦✦
A very interesting release, this set has a version of "Honeysuckle

Rose" from a Hawkins session in 1954 that usually gets left out of reissues (it was originally released in a sampler), four numbers from a live date in Europe that matches his tenor with a superb rhythm section (pianist Bud Powell, bassist Oscar Pettiford and drummer Kenny Clarke) and two songs from what probably was Hawkins' final studio session. Despite being very ill, he is in surprisingly strong form on the latter (from February 1968), easily playing with more fire and strength than he had in 1966 on *Sirius*, his last complete album. — *Scott Yanow*

Hawk in Paris / Jul. 9, 1956–Jul. 13, 1956 / VIK ✦✦✦✦
This CD is a major surprise. Hawkins had always wanted to record with a large string section and he received his wish on the majority of these 12 romantic melodies, all of which have some association with Paris. The surprise is that he plays with a great deal of fire (his doubletiming on "My Man" is wondrous), and that Manny Albam's arrangements mostly avoid being muzaky and quite often are creative and witty. What could have been a novelty or an insipid affair is actually one of Coleman Hawkins' more memorable albums. — *Scott Yanow*

Coleman Hawkins, Roy Eldridge, Pete Brown, Jo Jones, All-Stars / Jul. 5, 1957 / Verve ✦✦✦✦
In 1957 Hawkins underwent a critical renaissance. Fellow musicians and writers alike finally realized that his style (whether currently in fashion or not) was timeless and that the veteran tenor could still blow most of his competitors away. He teamed up with trumpeter Roy Eldridge and altoist Pete Brown for what would be a highly successful set at the Newport Jazz Festival. Their first number ("I Can't Believe That You're in Love with Me") was so explosive it made the rest of the performance (a ballad medley and "Sweet Georgia Brown") anticlimatic. Actually, Brown is just okay on "I Can't Believe," but the long solos of Eldridge and Hawkins are among the most exciting of their career, making this LP well worth searching for. — *Scott Yanow*

Coleman Hawkins Encounters Ben Webster / Oct. 16, 1957 / Verve ✦✦✦✦

The Genius of Coleman Hawkins / Oct. 16, 1957 / Verve ✦✦✦✦
Genius may not be the right word, but "brilliance" certainly fits. At the age of 51 in 1957, Hawkins had already been on records for 35 years and had been one of the leading tenors for nearly that long. This CD matches him with the Oscar Peterson Trio (plus drummer Alvin Stoller) for a fine runthrough on standards. Hawk plays quite well, although the excitement level does not reach the heights of his sessions with trumpeter Roy Eldridge. — *Scott Yanow*

Volume One: Warhorses / Dec. 16, 1957 / Jass ✦✦
Considering the outstanding lineup of players (tenor-great Coleman Hawkins, trumpeter Red Allen and trombonist J.C. Higginbotham among them), this should have been a great session. As it turned out (and is accurately stated in the LP's title), the seven tunes are all overdone standards, most of them from the repertoire of Dixieland bands, like "Bill Bailey," "Battle Hymn of the Republic" and "The Saints." In addition to that liability, there is less than 30 minutes of music on this LP. What is here is fine but not really worth searching for. This music has since been combined with the equally brief LP *High Standards* (Jass 11) on one single CD. — *Scott Yanow*

High and Mighty Hawk / Feb. 18, 1958–Feb. 19, 1958 / Affinity ✦✦✦✦
Although Hawkins had been a major tenor stylist for over 35 years by the time of this recording, he had never felt all that comfortable playing blues, preferring to dig his harmonic talents into more complicated material. For one of the first times, on the lengthy "Bird of Prey Blues" that opens this LP, Hawkins showed that at last he had mastered the blues. His honking and roaring improvisation, although more sophisticated than the usual solos by R&B tenors, captured their spirit and extroverted emotions perfectly. It is the highlight of this otherwise excellent (if more conventional) quintet session with trumpeter Buck Clayton and pianist Hank Jones. — *Scott Yanow*

Blues Groove / Feb. 28, 1958 / Swingville ✦✦✦
Strange as it seems, after over 35 years on the scene, Hawkins seemed to discover the blues in 1958. A harmonic wizard who enjoyed improvising over the most complex chord changes, he finally dug into the blues around this period and learned to emphasize extroverted emotions. This LP finds him jamming happily on two standards and four blues (including "Marchin' Along")

with a sextet that also prominently features guitarist Tiny Grimes. —Scott Yanow

Rare Live Performance / Mar. 18, 1958-Oct. 27, 1959 / Jazz Anthology ✦✦✦
This imported LP features Hawkins playing with two different pickup groups during 1958-59. On Side One he jams on three familiar but appealing numbers with a sextet that includes trombonist Jimmy Cleveland and tenorman Benny Golson (although the latter is left out of the personnel listing), while the second side finds Hawk interacting with guitarist Tiny Grimes and a quintet. The music, which might have been taken from television appearances, is predictable but swinging. —Scott Yanow

High Standards / Aug. 7, 1958 / Jass ✦✦
This impressive lineup (tenor saxophonist Coleman Hawkins, trumpeter Red Allen and altoist Earl Warren, who for some reasons sticks here to clarinet) should have guaranteed a highly recommended LP but the very brief playing time (around 27 minutes) and the predictable music makes this set a bit of a disappointment. This has since been reissued on a CD along with the equally scanty Warhorses. —Scott Yanow

Coleman Hawkins and His Friends at a Famous Jazz Party / Oct. 16, 1958-Nov. 6, 1958 / Enigma ✦✦✦
True, this LP looks like a bootleg and it is probably semi-legitimate at best, but the music is quite exciting. Possibly taken from television shows, such musicians as tenor-great Coleman Hawkins, trumpeters Red Allen, Charlie Shavers and Rex Stewart, trombonists J.C. Higginbotham and Dickie Wells and clarinetist Buster Bailey among others star, and for some reason they seem quite inspired, possibly by each other's presence. "Love Is Just Around the Corner" and a "Bugle Call Rag" that teams Shavers and Stewart are among the highpoints. Probably difficult to find and not too pretty to look at (with a dumb sketch of Hawkins on the front and a totally blank back cover), pick this one up if you see it. —Scott Yanow

Soul / Nov. 7, 1958 / Original Jazz Classics ✦✦
This is a decent but not very exciting outing. Then 52, Hawkins uses a typically young rhythm section (including guitarist Kenny Burrell and pianist Ray Bryant) and plays melodically on a variety of originals and standards. This insipid version of "Greensleeves" is difficult to sit through, but the rest of this CD is enjoyable if not overly inspiring. —Scott Yanow

Just You, Just Me / Jan. 1959 / Stash ✦✦✦✦

Hawk Eyes / Apr. 3, 1959 / Original Jazz Classics ✦✦✦✦
Tenor-great Coleman Hawkins tended to be at his best when challenged by another horn player. On this highly enjoyable CD, Hawkins is joined by the superb trumpeter Charlie Shavers and a strong rhythm section that includes guitarist Tiny Grimes and pianist Ray Bryant. With such superior songs as "Through for the Night," "I Never Knew" and "La Rosita," in addition to long jams, plenty of fireworks occur during this frequently exciting session. —Scott Yanow

Immortal Coleman Hawkins / Jul. 3, 1959-Feb. 1, 1963 / Pumpkin ✦✦✦
There are quite a few recordings (mostly, like this one, on LP) of Coleman Hawkins concert appearances during 1957-65, his final prime period. This Pumpkin set finds Hawk matched with his best partner, trumpeter Roy Eldridge, for fiery versions of "Soft Winds" and "Sweet Sue" in 1959. The second half features the veteran tenor saxophonist with a Swedish rhythm section performing two ballads and the jumping "Rifftide." This is a good example of strong late-period Coleman Hawkins. —Scott Yanow

Blowin' up a Breeze / Aug. 9, 1959-Jun. 12, 1963 / Spotlite ✦✦✦
This LP has two excellent concert performances by Hawkins. First he is heard at the 1959 Playboy Jazz Festival with a Chicago-based rhythm section performing four standards including a remake of his old standby "Body and Soul" and a strong version of "Centerpiece." The flip side moves up to 1963 as Hawkins and the Tommy Flanagan trio explore "The Way You Look Tonight" and two ballads. A nice all-around set of strong mainstream jazz comes from one of its pioneers. —Scott Yanow

With Red Garland Trio / Aug. 12, 1959 / Original Jazz Classics ✦✦✦
One of Hawkins' better Prestige sessions (originally on its Swingville subsidiary) finds him fronting a then-modern rhythm section for a variety of basic originals, the ballad "I Want to Be

Loved" and "It's a Blues World." The lengthy "Bean's Blues" is the highpoint of this generally relaxed session. —Scott Yanow

Dali / 1959-May 1962 / Stash ✦✦✦✦
This Stash CD, despite some silly graphics on the liners, has quite a bit of rewarding music. There are three examples of the fireworks that generally occured when tenor saxophonist Coleman Hawkins and trumpeter Roy Eldridge met up (taken from a live session in 1959) while the remainder of this disc finds Hawk playing in Brussels in 1962. The veteran tenor is particularly strong on "Disorder at the Border" and "Rifftide," but the highpoint is a rare unaccompanied solo on "Dali," the fourth and final time that Hawkins recorded an improvisation by himself. It is a pity he never recorded an entire album like that. —Scott Yanow

Centerpiece / 1959-Sep. 1, 1962 / Phoenix ✦✦✦

At Ease with Coleman Hawkins / Jan. 29, 1960 / Original Jazz Classics ✦✦
Recorded originally for the Prestige subsidiary Moodsville, Hawkins (along with the Tommy Flanagan Trio) sticks exclusively to ballads and slower pieces, all played at a low flame. Although it is nice to hear the veteran tenor interpreting "Poor Butterfly" and "I'll Get By," this CD is more successful as pleasant background music than as creative jazz. —Scott Yanow

Bean Stalkin' / Oct. 1960-Nov. 1960 / Pablo ✦✦✦✦
In contrast to Hawkins' sometimes sleepy studio albums from this era, his live performances were generally quite exciting. This set features the great tenor at two European concerts in 1960, performing three fairly heated numbers with a four-piece rhythm section, matching wits with trumpeter Roy Eldridge on "Crazy Rhythm" and leading two all-star jams with Eldridge, fellow tenor Don Byas and altoist Benny Carter. Some of the music is quite fiery, making this a recommended disc. —Scott Yanow

Night Hawk / Dec. 30, 1960 / Original Jazz Classics ✦✦✦✦
Hawkins was one of the main inspirations of his fellow tenor Eddie "Lockjaw" Davis, so it was logical that they would one day meet up in the recording studio. This CD has many fine moments from these two highly competitive jazzmen, particularly the lengthy title cut and a heated tradeoff on "In a Mellow Tone," on which Davis goes higher but Hawkins wins on ideas. —Scott Yanow

Jazz Reunion / 1961 / Candid ✦✦✦
The reunion referred to in the title was between tenor saxophonist Coleman Hawkins and clarinetist Pee Wee Russell, two legendary players who had recorded a couple of classic sides back in 1929. Still in their musical primes, both Hawkins and Russell were looking much more toward modern material to explore during this era and, although they revisit "If I Could Be with You," they also perform some Duke Ellington tunes, two of Russell's recent originals and the bop standard "Tin Tin Deo." The septet (which also includes trombonist Bob Brookmeyer, trumpeter Emmett Berry and pianist Nat Pierce) is in excellent form with Russell consistently taking solo honors. —Scott Yanow

The Hawk Relaxes / Feb. 28, 1961 / Original Jazz Classics ✦✦
While Hawkins' recordings in the early '60s for Swingville tended to swing (not too suprisingly), his Moodsville dates were dominated by overly relaxed treatments of ballads. That is the case with this CD, which finds the great tenor saxophonist sounding alright on melody statements of such tunes as "When Day Is Done," "More than You Know" and "Moonglow" but failing to develop his solos very much beyond the opening themes. The sameness of tempos makes this affair chiefly viable as background music, although of a high quality within that genre. —Scott Yanow

Hawkins! Alive! at the Village Gate / Aug. 13, 1962-Aug. 15, 1962 / Verve ✦✦✦✦
The great Hawkins (who debuted on records 40 years earlier) gets to stretch out on this live outing by his 1962 quartet (which also features pianist Tommy Flanagan). This CD, which as a former LP had lengthy versions of "All the Things You Are," "Joshua Fit the Battle of Jericho," "Mack the Knife" and "Talk of the Town," is augmented by previously unreleased versions of "Bean and the Boys" and "If I Had You," all of which show that Coleman Hawkins in his late 50s was still a powerful force. —Scott Yanow

Alive! / Aug. 15, 1962 / Verve ✦✦✦✦✦
From the mid-'50s until Coleman Hawkins' death in 1969, the tenor saxophonist frequently teamed up with trumpeter Roy Eldridge to form a potent team. However, Hawkins rarely met

altoist Johnny Hodges on the bandstand, making this encounter a special event. Long versions of "Satin Doll," "Perdido" and "The Rabbit in Jazz" give these three classic jazzmen (who are ably assisted by the Tommy Flanagan Trio) chances to stretch out and inspire each other. The remainder of this CD has Eldridge and Hodges absent while Coleman Hawkins (on "new" versions of "Mack the Knife," "It's the Talk of the Town," "Bean and the Boys" and "Caravan") heads the quartet for some excellent playing. Timeless music played by some of the top veteran stylists of the swing era. — *Scott Yanow*

Duke Ellington Meets Coleman Hawkins / Aug. 18, 1962 / Impulse! ✦✦✦✦✦
This CD documents a historic occasion. Although Coleman Hawkins had been an admirer of Duke Ellington's music for at least 35 years at this point and Ellington had suggested they record together at least 20 years prior to their actual meeting in 1962, this was their first (and only) meeting on record. Although it would have been preferable to hear the great tenor performing with the full orchestra, his meeting with Ellington and an all-star group taken out of the big band does feature such greats as Ray Nance (on cornet and violin), trombonist Lawrence Brown, altoist Johnny Hodges and baritonist Harry Carney. Highpoints include an exuberant "The Jeep Is Jumpin'," an interesting remake of "Mood Indigo" and a few new Ellington pieces. This delightful music is recommended in one form or another. — *Scott Yanow*

Desafinado: Bossa Nova and Jazz Samba / Sep. 12, 1962+Sep. 16, 1962 / MCA ✦✦✦✦
This set seems to have the word "fad" written all over it, but surprisingly it is a major success. During the era when everyone was trying to cash in on the popularity of bossa nova, tenor-great Coleman Hawkins recorded eight selections with a group consisting of two guitars, bass and three percussionists. In addition to a classic version of "O Pato" and such typical songs as "Desafinado" and "One Note Samba," Hawkins and company even turn "I'm Looking over a Four Leaf Clover" into a strong bossa. Although this straight CD reissue of a former LP is a bit brief, the music is highly enjoyable. — *Scott Yanow*

Back in Bean's Bag / Dec. 10, 1962 / Columbia ✦✦✦
Hawkins teamed up with the personable trumpeter Clark Terry for this upbeat set of of solid swing. Terry in particular is in exuberant form on "Feedin' the Bean" and a delightful version of "Don't Worry About Me," but Hawkins' playing (particularly on the trumpeter's ballad "Michelle") is also in fine form. The Tommy Flanagan Trio assists the two classic hornmen on this superior LP. — *Scott Yanow*

Hawk Talk / Mar. 21, 1963–Mar. 25, 1963 / Fresh Sound ✦✦

Today and Now / Sep. 9, 1963+Sep. 11, 1963 / Impulse! ✦✦✦
Of Hawkins' three sessions for Impulse! in the early-to-mid-'60s, this is the most intriguing due to the unusual repertoire. Included are such songs as "Go Lil' Liza," Quincy Jones' recent ballad "Quintessence," "Put on Your Old Grey Bonnet," "Swingin' Scotch" and "Don't Sit Under the Apple Tree." Despite (or perhaps due to) the strange choice of tunes, Hawkins is in inspired form, taking consistently creative solos on the fresh material. — *Scott Yanow*

Wrapped Tight / Feb. 22, 1965–Mar. 1, 1965 / Impulse! ✦✦✦✦
Hawkins' last strong recording finds the veteran, 43 years after his recording debut with Mamie Smith's Jazz Hounds, improvising creatively on a wide variety of material on this CD, ranging from "Intermezzo" and "Here's That Rainy Day" to "Red Roses for a Blue Lady" and "Indian Summer." Best is an adventurous version of "Out of Nowhere" that shows that the tenor saxophonist was still coming up with new ideas in 1965. — *Scott Yanow*

Rifftide / Mar. 1965 / Pumpkin ✦✦✦
Hawkins is heard during this concert performance near the end of his career and shortly before the steep decline that resulted in his death. Joined by the Earl Hines Trio on this LP from the collector's label Pumpkin, Hawkins is in surprisingly good form on five standards, displaying the tone that had made him the main influence on all saxophonists 40 years earlier. — *Scott Yanow*

Supreme / Sep. 26, 1966 / Enja ✦✦
The great tenor Coleman Hawkins started to go downhill in late 1965 (eating too little, drinking too much) and his career became progressively sadder until his death on May 19, 1969. This Enja CD (which is comprised of brand new material taken from a Baltimore club date) has five lengthy performances and strong work from the rhythm section (pianist Barry Harris, bassist Gene

Taylor and drummer Roy Brooks), but Hawkins' solos are consistently aimless and occasionally lost. His lines are shorter than in previous years and he seems to be gasping for air to an extent. The ironic part is that the audience is overly enthusiastic, loving every note no matter how desperate Hawkins sounds. Only on the brief closing "Ow" (where the tenor trades off very advanced phrases with Harris) does Coleman Hawkins sound up-to-par. Skip this set and acquire some of his many valuable earlier recordings instead. — *Scott Yanow*

Sirius / Dec. 20, 1966 / Pablo ✦
Hawkins' final studio session is rather sad. Due to an excess of drink and his unwillingness to eat, the great tenor saxophonist went steadily downhill between 1965 and his death four years later. Recorded in late 1966, this quartet set finds Hawk constantly short of breath and unable to play long phrases. He is able to get away with this deficiency on the faster pieces but the ballads are rather painful to hear. Even at this late stage Hawkins still had his majestic tone, but this recording is only of historical interest. — *Scott Yanow*

Erskine Hawkins

b. Jul. 26, 1914, Birmingham, AL, **d.** Nov. 11, 1993, Willingboro, NJ
Trumpet, Leader / Swing, Early R&B
A talented high-note trumpeter and a popular bandleader, Erskine Hawkins was nicknamed "The 20th Century Gabriel." He learned drums and trombone before switching to trumpet when he was 13. While attennding the Alabama State Teachers College, he became the leader of the college band, the 'Bama Street Collegians. They went to New York in 1934, became the Erskine Hawkins Orchestra, started making records in 1936 and by 1938 were quite successful. With Hawkins and Dud Bascomb sharing the trumpet solos, Paul Bascomb or Julian Dash heard on tenors, Haywood Henry on baritone and pianist Avery Parrish, this was a solidly swinging band that delighted dancers and jazz fans alike. Hawkins had three major hits ("Tuxedo Junction," "After Hours" and "Tippin' In") and was able to keep the big band together all the way until 1953; some of their later sessions were more R&B-oriented yet never without jazz interest. Hawkins led a smaller unit during his last few decades (the survivors of the big band had a recorded reunion in 1971) and the trumpeter kept on working into the 1980s. — *Scott Yanow*

★ **The Original Tuxedo Junction** / Sep. 12, 1938–Jan. 10, 1945 / Bluebird ✦✦✦✦✦
These sessions for 14-piece band include pianist Avery Parrish on his immortal "After Hours" and teaming up with the leader for "Swing Out." Features tenor Julian Dash, baritonist and clarinetist Haywood Henry, Buscomb and Hawkins on trumpet. — *Michael G. Nastos*

Erskine Hawkins 1940–1941 / Nov. 6, 1940–Dec. 22, 1941 / Classics ✦✦✦✦

Clancy Hayes (Clarence Leonard Hayes)

b. Nov. 14, 1908, Caney, KS, **d.** Mar. 13, 1972, San Francisco, CA
Banjo, Vocals / Dixieland
Clancy Hayes was one of the finest vocalists of the Dixieland revival movement, much better than the typical musician who feels compelled to sing. He was a steady fixture in San Francisco from 1927 on, appearing regularly on the radio and in clubs. He hooked up with Lu Watters in 1938, performing with Watters' big band for two years and then ten with the Yerba Buena Jazz Band, mostly as a rhythm banjoist and occasionally on drums. He gained his greatest fame while singing with Bob Scobey's group (1950–59). In the 1960s, Hayes worked with the Firehouse Five Plus Two, Turk Murphy, in an early version of what would be the World's Greatest Jazz Band and with his own groups. Clancy Hayes recorded as a leader for Verve (1950), Audio Fidelity (1960), Good Time Jazz (1963), Delmark, ABC-Paramount and Fat Cat Jazz (1969) and helped make songs such as "Oh by Jingo," "Ace in the Hole" and his own "Huggin' and A-Chalkin'" popular in the trad jazz world. — *Scott Yanow*

★ **Swingin' Minstrel** / 1963 / Good Time Jazz ✦✦✦✦✦

Oh by Jingo / Aug. 13, 1964 / Delmark ✦✦✦✦

Clifford Hayes

Violin / Classic Jazz, Blues
A shadowy figure in jazz history, Clifford Hayes was an okay vio-

linist but more significant as a leader of recording sessions. He recorded with Sara Martin (1924) and often teamed up with banjoist Cal Smith in early jug bands including the Old Southern Jug Band, Clifford's Louisville Jug Band, the well-known Dixieland Jug Blowers (1926–7) and Hayes' Louisville Stompers (1927–29). One of the Dixieland Jug Blowers' sessions featured the great clarinetist Johnny Dodds while pianist Earl Hines was a surprise star with the otherwise primitive Louisville Stompers (a jugless group with a frontline of Hayes' violin and Hense Grundy's trombone). Clifford Hayes' last recordings were in 1931 and all of his sessions (plus those of some other jug bands) are available on four RST CDs. —*Scott Yanow*

Clifford Hayes & The Louisville Jug Bands, Vol. 1 / Sep. 16, 1924–Dec. 10, 1926 / RST ✦✦✦✦
The first of four volumes from the Austrian RST label that reissue the complete output from several historic jug bands from Louisville features violinist Clifford Hayes in several contexts. In 1924 he led the first jug band on record, backing blues singer Sara Martin on some exuberant performances that overcame the primitive recording quality. In addition, this CD has Hayes leading The Old Southern Jug Band, Clifford's Louisville Jug Band And The Dixieland Jug Blowers; all of the groups greatly benefit from the exciting playing of Earl McDonald on jug. The CD is rounded out by four selections from Whistler's Jug Band. Historic and generally enjoyable music, it's recommended to 1920s collectors. —*Scott Yanow*

● **Clifford Hayes & The Louisville Jug Bands, Vol. 2** / Dec. 10, 1926–Apr. 30, 1927 / RST ✦✦✦✦✦
The second of four CDs in a very valuable series from the Austrian RST label has 12 selections from The Dixieland Jug Blowers (a very spirited sextet with violinist Clifford Hayes, the colorful jug blowing of Earl McDonald and on six numbers, clarinetist Johnny Dodds as a guest), eight from Earl McDonald's Original Louisville Jug Band and four by Whistler's Jug Band (its leader Buford Threlkeld doubles on guitar and nose whistle). The monologue on the former group's "House Rent Rag" is quite memorable and still humorous. Of the four CDs, this is the most essential one for it finds these historic groups in their prime. —*Scott Yanow*

Clifford Hayes & The Louisville Jug Bands, Vol. 3 / Jun. 6, 1927–Feb. 6, 1929 / RST ✦✦✦✦✦
The third of four CDs from the Austrian RST label has the final ten selections from The Dixieland Jug Blowers along with 14 by Clifford Hayes' Louisville Stompers. Although the former no longer had the powerful jug playing of Earl McDonald, the mysterious H. Clifford was a good substitute and the three-horn septet (which features two guest vocalists) certainly had plenty of spirit. The Louisville Stompers is essentially a stripped-down jugless version of The Jug Blowers, a jazz-oriented quartet comprised of violinist Clifford Hayes, tromonist Hense Grundy, pianist Johnny Gatewood and the impressive guitarist Cal Smith who makes "Blue Guitar Stomp" a classic. The final seven Stompers performances are a bit surprising for the pianist is the great Earl Hines who has a few short solos although mostly in a supporting role. All four of the CDs are easily recommended to collectors of the era or on a whole they contain the complete output of these unusual groups. —*Scott Yanow*

Clifford Hayes & The Louisville Jug Bands, Vol. 4 / Feb. 6, 1929–Jun. 17, 1931 / RST ✦✦✦✦
The fourth and final CD in this brief but important series from the Austrian RST label features jug bands in a variety of roles. There are the three last performances by Clifford Hayes' Lousville Stompers (the two versions of "You're Ticklin' Me" have Earl Hines on piano while "You Gonna Need My Help" features the classic blues singer Sippie Wallace), The Kentucky Jazz Babies (a quartet with violinist Clifford Hayes and trumpeter Jimmy Strange) does a good job on two numbers and Phillips' Louisville Jug Band (an odd quartet with Hooks Tifford on C-melody sax and Charles "Cane" Adams playing what is called "walking cane flute") performs eight songs. In additio,n Whistler and His Jug Band play two primitive numbers while violinist Clifford Hayes backs the minstrel singer Kid Coley and reunites with the great jug player Earl McDonald behind the vocals of country pioneer Jimmie Rodgers, Ben Ferguson and John Harris. An interesting set, to say the least, all four CDs in this series are recommended to fans of the era. —*Scott Yanow*

Louis Hayes

b. May 31, 1937, Detroit, MI
Drums / Hard Bop
A superior hard bop drummer best-known for supporting soloists rather than taking the spotlight himself, Louis Hayes led a band in Detroit as a teenager and was with Yusef Lateef during 1955-56. He had three notable associations: Horace Silver's Quintet (1956–59), the Cannonball Adderley Quintet (1959–65) and the Oscar Peterson Trio (1965–67). Hayes often teamed up with Sam Jones, both with Adderley and Peterson and in freelance settings. He led a variety of groups during the 1970s including quintets co-led by Junior Cook and Woody Shaw. Louis Hayes has appeared on many records through the years with everyone from John Coltrane and Cecil Taylor to McCoy Tyner, Freddie Hubbard and Dexter Gordon and has led sessions for Vee-Jay (1960), Timeless (1976), Muse (1977) and Candid (1989). —*Scott Yanow*

Louis Hayes (Featuring Yusef Lateef & Nat Adderley) / Apr. 26, 1960 / Vee-Jay ✦✦✦✦
The 1960 Cannonball Adderley Quintet (with drummer Louis Hayes, cornetist Nat Adderley, pianist Barry Harris and bassist Sam Jones) performs on this Vee-Jay CD reissue with tenor saxophonist Yusef Lateef in Cannonball's place. Although one misses the fiery altoist, the contrast between Nat's exciting (if sometimes erratic) cornet and Yusef's dignified yet soulful tenor make this an above-average session of swinging bop. The high-quality originals are augmented by five "new" alternate takes. —*Scott Yanow*

Breath of Life / Feb. 2, 1974 / Muse ✦✦✦
Ichi-Ban / May 5, 1976 / Timeless ✦✦✦
★ **The Real Thing** / May 20, 1977–May 21, 1977 / Muse ✦✦✦✦✦
His best band, with Woody Shaw (tpt), Rene McLean (sax), and Slide Hampton (tb). All originals, all excellent. —*Michael G. Nastos*
Variety Is the Spice / Oct. 9, 1978–Oct. 12, 1978 / Gryphon ✦✦✦✦
Light and Lively / Apr. 21, 1989 / SteepleChase ✦✦✦✦✦
Another good one, with Charles Tolliver (tpt) and Bobby Watson (as). —*Michael G. Nastos*
The Crawl / Oct. 14, 1989 / Candid ✦✦✦✦✦
Live at Birdland, with Charles Tolliver (tpt) and Gary Bartz (sax). Very good. —*Michael G. Nastos*
Una Max / Dec. 19, 1989 / SteepleChase ✦✦✦✦

Tubby Hayes (Edward Brian Hayes)

b. Jan. 30, 1935, London, **d.** Jun. 8, 1973, London, England
Flute, Tenor Saxophone, Vibes / Bop, Hard Bop
One of England's top jazz musicians of the 1950s and '60s, Tubby Hayes was a fine hard bop stylist on tenor and occasionally vibes and flute. A professional at 15, Hayes played with Kenny Baker and in the big bands of Ambrose, Vic Lewis and Jack Parnell during 1951-55. He led his own group after that and started doubling on vibes in 1956. Hayes co-led the Jazz Couriers with Ronnie Scott (1957–59) and appeared in the U.S. a few times during 1961-65. He headed his own big band in London, sat in with Duke Ellington's Orchestra in 1964 and was featured at many European festivals. Heart trouble forced him out of action during 1969-71 and caused his premature death. Tubby Hayes led sessions for Tempo (1955-59), London, Jazzland (1959), Fontana, Epic (a 1961 date with Clark Terry and Horace Parlan), Smash (a 1962 album which matched him with James Moody and Roland Kirk), 77, Spotlite and Mole. —*Scott Yanow*

● **New York Sessions** / Oct. 3, 1961–Oct. 4, 1961 / Columbia ✦✦✦✦✦
Tubby's Back in Town / Jun. 23, 1962 / Smash ✦✦✦✦

Roy Haynes

b. Mar. 13, 1926, Roxbury, Mass.
Drums / Bop, Hard Bop
A veteran drummer long overshadowed by others but finally ,in the 1990s, being recognized for his talents and versatility, Roy Haynes has been a major player for 45 years. He worked early on with the Sabby Lewis big band, Frankie Newton, Luis Russell (1945–47) and Lester Young (1947–49). After some engagements with Kai Winding, Haynes was a member of the Charlie Parker quintet (1949–52); he also recorded during this era with Bud Powell, Wardell Gray and Stan Getz. Haynes toured the world

with Sarah Vaughan (1953–58), played with Thelonious Monk in 1958, led his own group and gigged with George Shearing, Lennie Tristano, Eric Dolphy and Getz (1961). He was Elvin Jones' occasional substitute with John Coltrane's classic quartet during 1961–65, toured with Getz (1965–67) and was with Gary Burton (1967–68). In addition to touring with Chick Corea (1981 and 1984) and Pat Metheny (1989–90), Haynes has led his own Hip Ensemble on and off during the past 28 years. When one considers that he has also gigged with Miles Davis, Art Pepper, Horace Tapscott and Dizzy Gillespie, it is fair to say that Roy Haynes has played with about everyone! He led dates for EmArcy and Swing (both in 1954), New Jazz (1958 and 1960), Impulse! (a 1962 quartet album with Roland Kirk), New Jazz, Pacific Jazz, Mainstream, Galaxy and more recently Dreyfus, Evidence and Storyville. In 1994 Roy Haynes was awarded the Danish Jazzpar prize. His son Graham Haynes is an excellent cornetist. *—Scott Yanow*

Out of the Afternoon / May 16, 1962+May 23, 1962 / Original Jazz Classics ✦✦✦✦✦
Definitive creative music with Roland Kirk (reeds) and Tommy Flanagan (p). *—Michael G. Nastos*

Cracklin' / Apr. 10, 1963 / Original Jazz Classics ✦✦✦✦
A fine date, with Booker Ervin center stage on tenor sax. *—Ron Wynn*

Equipoise / 1971 / Mainstream ✦✦✦✦
This explosive session helped cement the reputations of George Adams (ts) and Hannibal Marvin Peterson (tpt). *—Ron Wynn*

Vistalite / Jul. 12, 1977–Jul. 20, 1977 / Galaxy ✦✦✦
Thank You, Thank You / Jul. 16, 1977–Jul. 20, 1977 / Galaxy ✦✦✦
Roy Haynes, who came up shortly after Max Roach and Art Blakey, has been a major drummer since the late '40s but has never gotten quite the recognition he deserves. This somewhat obscure outing features Haynes in a variety of settings including a duet with percussionist Kenneth Nash, a pair of quartets with either George Cables or Stanley Cowell on piano, a quintet on the title cut featuring the tenor of John Klemmer and vibraphonist Bobby Hutcherson, and a selection with a two-keyboard septet. The music ranges from poppish to more straight-ahead with plenty of diverse moods explored. *—Scott Yanow*

True or False / Oct. 30, 1986 / Freelance ✦✦✦
This live session in Paris with Ralph Moore (ts) is proof that Haynes is a premier jazz drummer. *—Michael G. Nastos*

Homecoming / Jun. 27, 1992 / Evidence ✦✦✦✦
When It's Haynes It Roars / Jul. 24, 1992–Jul. 26, 1992 / Dreyfus Disques ✦✦✦✦✦
★ **Te Vou!** / 1994 / Dreyfus ✦✦✦✦✦
Veteran drummer Roy Haynes only has a single short solo on this CD, but one suspects that his presence helped solidify and inspire the illustrious sidemen (altoist Donald Harrison, guitarist Pat Metheny, pianist David Kikoski and bassist Christian McBride). Harrison and Metheny are the lead solo voices on a program that ranges from compositions by Chick Corea, Thelonious Monk (the difficult "Trinkle Twinkle") and Ornette Coleman to three by Metheny. Strong as the other musicians are, Christian McBride often comes close to stealing the show (as can be heard during his solo on Charlie Haden's "Blues M45"). This all-star matchup works quite well. *—Scott Yanow*

My Shining Hour / Mar. 10, 1994–Mar. 13, 1994 / Storyville ✦✦✦✦

Stephanie Haynes
b. California
Vocals / Standards
Blessed with a beautiful voice, Stephanie Haynes has appeared regularly in Los Angeles and Orange County clubs during the past 15 years. A classically-trained flutist through college, she sang in jazz clubs in Albuquerque, New Mexico in the late '60s and then performed pop music with a Top 40 group for seven years. However, Haynes rediscovered jazz, moved to Orange County, worked frequently with pianist Kent Glenn (1980–85) and recorded for Ortho, Trend and Holt. In recent years she has often performed adventurous duets with pianist Dave MacKay (including cutting a CD for Why Not) and sung with Bopsicle. *—Scott Yanow*

Here's That Rainy Day / Jul. 27, 1988–Jul. 28, 1988 / Trend ✦✦✦✦
Dawn At Dana Point / Aug. 9, 1992–Aug. 10, 1992 / Holt ✦✦✦
The melodies and lyrics (most of which were composed by Dave

Holt) are unfamiliar, but the beautiful voice of Stephanie Haynes (one of the top singers in Los Angeles) makes this CD worth getting. The tasteful backup (from tenor saxophonist Jack Montrose, pianist Pete Jolly, bassist Chuck Berghofer and drummer Nick Martinis) is an added plus on the lightly swinging date of newly composed love songs. *—Scott Yanow*

● **Two On A Swing** / 1993 / Why Not ✦✦✦✦✦
Stephanie Haynes not only possesses a beautiful voice but has the ability to always find the right note, which is fortunate for pianist Dave MacKay really pushes her on their duet recording, sometimes only barely hinting at the more conventional chords to the standards. The results are full of chancetaking with the hair-raising accompaniment inspiring Haynes to really stretch herself. The interplay between voice and piano on "Easy to Love" and the witty "Everything but You" are highpoints on this very satisfying and sometimes unpredictable set. *—Scott Yanow*

Kevin Hays
b. 1968, New York, NY
Piano / Post-Bop
A talented pianist, Kevin Hays grew up in Connecticut and started lessons when he was seven. He made his recording debut with Nick Brignola, toured with the Harper Brothers (1989–90) and worked with Joshua Redman, Benny Golson, Donald Harrison, Roy Haynes and Joe Henderson among others. Kevin Hays recorded three albums with Bob Belden and, in 1994, cut his first record as a leader, *Seventh Sense* (Blue Note). *—Scott Yanow*

● **Seventh Sense** / Jan. 12, 1994–Jan. 13, 1994 / Blue Note ✦✦✦✦
Pianist Kevin Hays' style mixes together the influences of Bill Evans and McCoy Tyner and he helps define the modern mainstream on this Blue Note disc. The quintet set also features plenty of solo space from vibraphonist Steve Nelson and the excellent tenorman Seamus Blake. Opening with three Hays originals and also including Hindermith's "Interlude" (which finds the group sounding a little like The Modern Jazz Quartet) and such standards as "My Man's Gone Now" and "East of the Sun," the music pays tribute to the past without becoming predictable or overly derivative. It's a fine release. *—Scott Yanow*

Go Round / Jan. 21, 1995–Jan. 22, 1995 / Blue Note ✦✦✦✦

J.C. Heard (James Charles Heard)
b. Oct. 8, 1917, Dayton, OH, d. Sept. 27, 1988, Royal Oak, MI
Drums / Swing, Bop
J.C. Heard was a very supportive drummer versatile enough to fit comfortably into swing, bop and blues settings. He was in vaudeville shows as a dancer in his youth. Heard's first important job playing drums was with Teddy Wilson's big band in 1939. He later worked with Wilson's sextet and with Coleman Hawkins and Benny Carter. Heard was with Cab Calloway's Orchestra (1942–45), recorded with top bop musicians, led his own band at Cafe Society (1946–45), was a member of Erroll Garner's trio (1948) and toured with Jazz at the Philharmonic. During 1953–57 he spent time in Japan and Australia, he freelanced in New York during 1957–66 (including playing with the Coleman Hawkins-Roy Eldridge Quintet and in 1961 with Teddy Wilson's trio) and then in 1966 J.C. Heard moved to Detroit where he worked as a bandleader and a mentor to younger musicians into the mid-'80s. *—Scott Yanow*

Some of This, Some of That / Dec. 26, 1986 / Hiroko ✦✦✦✦
Master drummer leads 13-piece band. Loads of blues and modern jazz along with some goofy fun and solid musicianship. Fine "Nica's Dream" and "Sweet Love of Mine, Sweet Samantha." Heard vocalizes frequently on this album, which features trumpeter Walt Szymanski. *—Michael G. Nastos*

Heath Brothers
Group / Hard Bop
Jimmy, Percy and Tootie Heath teamed up in 1975 to form the Heath Brothers. Up until then bassist Percy had been busy with the Modern Jazz Quartet but with the group in "retirement" (temporarily as it turned out), all three brothers were free to join forces. Originally a quartet with pianist Stanley Cowell and expanding after the addition of guitarist Tony Purrone and Jimmy's son Mtume on percussion, the band recorded for Strata East (1975), four albums for Columbia and two for Island. Tootie Heath left the group early on and was replaced by Akira Tana,

although he came back for the final 1983 record. Although the Heath Brothers' music was essentially hard bop, there were occasional departures into jazzy R&B on isolated selections. All of their LPs are worth searching for although none have been reissued on CD yet. —*Scott Yanow*

● **Marchin' on** / Oct. 22, 1975 / Strata East ✦✦✦✦✦

Passing Thru / May 19, 1978 / Columbia ✦✦✦✦

Live at the Public Theater / 1979 / Columbia ✦✦✦
Their first date without Albert on drums. Akira Tana (d) joins the fold. —*Ron Wynn*

Brotherly Love / Dec. 29, 1981–Dec. 30, 1981 / Antilles ✦✦✦✦
A welcome reissue of an album that had consistently good compositions and excellent solos from Jimmy Heath. Stanley Cowell (p) and Tony Purrone (g) are first-rate. —*Ron Wynn*

Brothers and Others / May 16, 1983–May 17, 1983 / Antilles ✦✦✦✦✦
A solid blend of typically sharp Heath Brothers material, with guest contributions by Slide Hampton (tb). A 1991 reissue of a session previously available on Columbia. —*Ron Wynn*

Albert "Tootie" Heath

b. May 31, 1935, Philadelphia, PA
Drums / Hard Bop, Post-Bop
The younger brother of Percy and Jimmy Heath, Albert "Tootie" Heath has long been a top hard bop-based drummer with an open mind toward more commercial styles of jazz. After moving to New York (1957) he debuted on record with John Coltrane. Heath was with J.J. Johnson's group (1958–60) and the Jazztet (1960–61), worked with the trios of Cedar Walton and Bobby Timmons in 1961 and recorded many records as a sideman for Riverside during that era. He lived in Europe in 1965–68 (working frequently with Kenny Drew, Dexter Gordon and backing touring Americans) and, after returning to the U.S., he played regularly with Herbie Hancock's sextet (1968–69) and Yusef Lateef (1970–74). After an additional year in Europe, he joined the Heath Brothers band (1975–78) and then settled in Los Angeles where Tootie Heath has continued freelancing up to the present time, recently recording with the Riverside Reunion Band. —*Scott Yanow*

Kawaida / Dec. 11, 1969 / Trip ✦✦✦
An adventurous octet date with Don Cherry (tpt) and Herbie Hancock (p). —*Ron Wynn*

● **Kwanza (The First)** / Jun. 4, 1973 / Muse ✦✦✦✦
Excellent recording from The Heath Brother's drummer, with brothers Percy (b) and Jimmy (sax), Curtis Fuller (tb), Ted Dunbar (g), and Kenny Barron (p). —*Michael G. Nastos*

Jimmy Heath

b. Oct. 25, 1926, Philadelphia, PA
Flute, Tenor Saxophone, Soprano Saxophone, Arranger / Hard Bop
The middle of the three Heath Brothers, Jimmy Heath has a distinctive sound on tenor, is a fluid player on soprano and flute and a very talented arranger/composer whose originals include "C.T.A." and "Gingerbread Boy." He was originally an altoist, playing with Howard McGhee during 1947–48 and the Dizzy Gillespie big band (1949–50). Called "Little Bird" because of the similarity in his playing to Charlie Parker, Heath switched to tenor in the early '50s. Although out of action for a few years due to "personal problems," Heath wrote for Chet Baker and Art Blakey during 1956–57. Back in action in 1959, he worked with Miles Davis briefly that year in addition to Kenny Dorham and Gil Evans, and started a string of impressive recordings for Riverside. In the 1960s Heath frequently teamed up with Milt Jackson and Art Farmer and he also worked as an educator and a freelance arranger. During 1975–82, Jimmy Heath teamed up with Percy and Tootie in the Heath Brothers and since then has remained active as a saxophonist and writer. In addition to his earlier Riverside dates, Jimmy Heath has recorded as a leader for Cobblestone, Muse, Xanadu, Landmark and Verve. —*Scott Yanow*

The Thumper / Sep. 1959 / Original Jazz Classics ✦✦✦✦
Jimmy Heath at age 33 made his recording debut as a leader on this Riverside session, which has been reissued on CD in the OJC series. The hard bop tenor saxophonist is in superior form, contributing five originals (of which "For Minors Only" is best

known), jamming with an all star sextet (including cornetist Nat Adderley, trombonist Curtis Fuller, pianist Wynton Kelly, bassist Paul Chambers and drummer Albert "Tootie" Heath) and taking two standards as ballad features. The excellent session of late '50s straight-ahead jazz is uplifted above the normal level by Heath's writing. —*Scott Yanow*

Nice People / Dec. 1959–1964 / Original Jazz Classics ✦✦✦
A compilation of Riverside albums. Well programmed. —*Michael G. Nastos*

Really Big / Jun. 24, 1960–Jun. 28, 1960 / Original Jazz Classics ✦✦✦✦
This is one of Heath's earliest as a leader and showcases his savvy as both a leader and a player. —*Ron Wynn*

The Quota / Apr. 14, 1961+Apr. 20, 1961 / Original Jazz Classics ✦✦✦✦

Triple Threat / Jan. 4, 1962+Jan. 17, 1962 / Riverside ✦✦✦✦

Swamp Seed / Mar. 11, 1963 / Riverside ✦✦✦
An early version of The Heath Brothers, with Albert (d) and Percy (b) on board. —*Ron Wynn*

★ **On the Trail** / 1964 / Original Jazz Classics ✦✦✦✦✦
Unlike some of his other Riverside recordings, the accent on this Jimmy Heath CD reissue is very much on his tenor playing (rather than his arrangements). Heath is in excellent form with a quintet that also includes pianist Wynton Kelly, guitarist Kenny Burrell, bassist Paul Chambers and drummer Albert "Tootie" Heath. The instantly recognizable hard bop saxophonist performs four standards and three of his own compositions, including the original versions of "Gingerbread Boy" and "Project S." It's a good example of his playing talents. —*Scott Yanow*

The Gap Sealer / Mar. 1, 1972 / Cobblestone ✦✦✦✦
Some of Heath's finest, most aggressive playing. He is a standout on soprano, flute, and tenor. —*Ron Wynn*

Jimmy / Mar. 1, 1972 / Muse ✦✦✦✦
A typically low-key, yet authoritative and impressive session by saxophonist Jimmy Heath from 1972. He's leading a group with pianist Kenny Barron, bassist Bob Cranshaw, his brother Tootie Heath on drums, and his son Mtume on congas. They run through mainstream, hard bop, standards, and blues with crisp professionalism. —*Ron Wynn*

Love and Understanding / Jun. 11, 1973 / Xanadu ✦✦✦
An outstanding group buttressed by trombonist Curtis Fuller and Billy Higgins (d). —*Ron Wynn*

Picture of Health / Sep. 22, 1975 / Xanadu ✦✦✦✦
A fine quartet. Super playing by Barry Harris (p), Heath, and Higgins (d). —*Ron Wynn*

New Picture / Jun. 18, 1985–Jun. 20, 1985 / Landmark ✦✦✦✦
An assured, consistently productive, and appealing mainstream date, with Tommy Flanagan on piano as a bonus. —*Ron Wynn*

Peer Pleasure / Feb. 17, 1987–Feb. 18, 1987 / Landmark ✦✦✦✦
A smooth session with sharp work from Heath. As usual, it has fine compositions. —*Ron Wynn*

Little Man, Big Band / Jan. 30, 1992–Mar. 3, 1992 / Verve ✦✦✦✦

Percy Heath

b. Apr. 30, 1923, Wilmington, NC.
Bass / Bop, Hard Bop
The oldest of the three Heath Brothers, Percy Heath's association with the Modern Jazz Quartet has been the dominant activity of his career. An excellent soloist and a perfect accompanist with an appealing tone, Percy (who grew up in Philadelphia) was originally a violinist. He switched to bass in 1946, was soon famous locally and the following year he moved to New York with brother Jimmy to join Howard McGhee's band. Heath played with the who's who of bop (Charlie Parker, Dizzy Gillespie, Thelonious Monk, Fats Navarro, Miles Davis and J.J. Johnson) in various settings and recordings. In 1951 he joined Milt Jackson's Quartet, which in 1952 became the Modern Jazz Quartet. For the next 23 years, the MJQ toured and recorded constantly. After its temporary breakup, Percy joined Jimmy and Tootie in the Heath Brothers Band (1975–82), going back to the MJQ (where he is still a key member) when they regrouped in the early '80s. Strangely enough Percy Heath has never led a record date of his own. —*Scott Yanow*

Chuck Hedges

b. Chicago, IL
Clarinet / Dixieland, Swing
A very talented if often overlooked veteran clarinetist, Chuck Hedges is an exciting player whose music falls between swing and Dixieland. He played in the early '50s with George Brunis, Danny Alvin and Muggsy Spanier in Chicago. Later in the decade he was with Dave Remington, in the 1960s Hedges toured with trumpeter Dick Ruedebusch and in the 1970s and '80s he often played with Wild Bill Davison. Although he has long lived in Milwaukee, Chuck Hedges plays often in Chicago and is a regular at several traditional jazz festivals. He co-led a Jazzology album with Allan Vache (1982) and has recorded as a leader for Arbors and Delmark (1992–93). —*Scott Yanow*

No Greater Love / Dec. 1992 / Arbors ✦✦✦✦

★ **Swingtet Live at Andy's** / Mar. 22, 1993–May 3, 1993 / Delmark ✦✦✦✦✦
The talented clarinetist Chuck Hedges is joined by some excellent Chicago-based players (vibraphonist Duane Thamm, guitarist Dave Bany, bassist John Bany and drummer Charles Braugham) for a spirited set of superior swing-based tunes. "Softly as in a Morning Sunrise," "It's Allright with Me," "Breakfast Feud" and "I Don't Wanna Be Kissed" are among the highpoints of this consistently swinging and very enjoyable music, a bit of a throwback to the 1950s. Hedges has rarely been given the opportunity to lead a record session, so that fact (on top of the high quality of the music) makes this successful effort something special. —*Scott Yanow*

Neal Hefti

b. Oct. 29, 1922, Hastings, NE
Arranger, Composer, Trumpet / Swing
One of the top jazz arranger/composers of the 1950s, Neal Hefti first wrote charts in the late 1930s for Nat Towles. He contributed arrangements to the Earl Hines big band, played trumpet with Charlie Barnet, Horace Heidt and Charlie Spivak (1942–43) and toured with Woody Herman's First Herd (1944–46), marrying Woody's singer Francis Wayne. It was with Herman that Hefti began to get a strong reputation, arranging an updated "Woodchopper's Ball" and "Blowin' up a Storm," and composing "The Good Earth" and "Wild Root." He also took a notable solo during a Lucky Thompson session on "From Dixieland to Bop." However, Hefti soon relegated his trumpet playing to a secondary status (although he played it on an occasional basis into the 1960s) and concentrated on his writing. He contributed charts to the orchestras of Charlie Ventura (1946), Harry James (1948–49) and most notably Count Basie (1950–62). For Basie he wrote "Little Pony," "Cute," "Li'l Darling," "Whirlybird" and many other swinging songs, often utilizing Frank Wess' flute in inventive fashion. Neal Hefti also led his own bands off and on in the 1950s but in later years concentrated on writing for films while remaining influenced by his experiences in the jazz world. —*Scott Yanow*

Mark Helias

b. Oct. 1, 1950, Brunswick, NJ
Bass / Avant-Garde
An adventurous and flexible bassist, Mark Helias did not start on his instrument until he was 20. Helias studied at Yale and played locally with such modern players as Leo Smith and Anthony Davis. He recorded with many top avant-garde musicians including Anthony Braxton (1977), Dewey Redman and Muhal Richard Abrams and teamed up with Ray Anderson in the band BassDrumBone and the bizarre funk group Slickaphonics (on and off during 1980–83). Helias was also in the band Nu (1985–87), which included Don Cherry, Carlos Ward and Nana Vasconcelos. Starting in 1984 he has led his own series of explorative sessions for Enja. —*Scott Yanow*

Split Image / Aug. 29, 1984 / Enja ✦✦✦✦
With Dewey Redman (ts), Tim Berne (as), Herb Robertson (tpt), and Gerry Hemingway. Six more Helias originals. —*Michael G. Nastos*

● **The Current Set** / Mar. 4, 1987–Mar. 5, 1987 / Enja ✦✦✦✦✦
Septet with Tim Berne (as), Robin Eubanks (tb), Greg Osby (as), Herb Robertson, Victor Lewis, and Nana Vasconcelos (per). Six originals by leader and bassist, all in strong improvisatory flavor,

while keeping rhythm intact. "Greetings from L.C." a fave. —*Michael G. Nastos*

Desert Blue / Apr. 1, 1989–Apr. 2, 1989 / Enja ✦✦✦✦

Gerry Hemingway

b. 1955, New Haven, CT
Drums / Avant-Garde
A long-time member of the Anthony Braxton Quartet, Gerry Hemingway has become a leader in his own right during the past decade. A very alert drummer who reacts immediately to the playing of other musicians, Hemingway studied at Wesleyan College and Yale. In the mid-'70s he played often with such advanced musicians as George Lewis, Anthony Davis, Leo Smith and Mark Helias. In 1978 he formed the Auricle label to document his music. Hemingway was a member of BassDrumBone with Ray Anderson and Mark Helias and since the early '80s has been with Braxton's Quartet, Marilyn Crispell's group and (starting in 1985) his own quintet. —*Scott Yanow*

Kwambe / Jan. 10, 1978+Feb. 20, 1978 / Auricle ✦✦✦

Solo Works / Jun. 28, 1981+Sep. 12, 1978 / Auricle ✦✦✦

Tubworks / Dec. 1983–Aug. 1987 / Sound Aspects ✦✦

Outerbridge Crossing / Sep. 1985 / Sound Aspects ✦✦✦✦

★ **Special Detail** / Oct. 29, 1990–Oct. 30, 1990 / Hat Art ✦✦✦✦✦
Ambitious, far-reaching mid-'80s session by drummer and percussionist Gerry Hemingway that features Don Byron playing a variety of saxophones in the period before he decided to concentrate on clarinet. He uses an unorthodox trombone/cello pairing instead of a pianist, and buttresses each composition with sympathetic, careful rhythms. —*Ron Wynn*

Down To The Wire / Dec. 8, 1991–Dec. 10, 1991 / Hat Art ✦✦✦✦✦

Demon Chaser / Mar. 2, 1993 / Hat Hut ✦✦✦

Julius Hemphill

b. 1940, Fort Worth, TX, **d.** Apr. 2, 1995
Alto Saxophone, Soprano Saxophone, Composer / Avant-Garde, Free Jazz
One of the giants of the jazz avant-garde, Julius Hemphill had a distinctive sound, a bluish yet dissonant style and was also a talented arranger/composer. An influence on many forward-thinking young players including Tim Berne and (more indirectly) David Sanborn, Hemphill took lessons in Ft. Worth on clarinet from John Carter, studied music at North Texas State and played locally in Texas in addition to serving in the military. After moving to St. Louis in 1968, Hemphill became a major force in the city, forming the Black Artists Group, founding his own label Mbari and recording two albums later reissued on Freedom. He moved to New York in the mid-'70s, recorded with Anthony Braxton and Lester Bowie in 1974 and was part of the loft jazz scene. Hemphill was a founding member of the World Saxophone Quartet (1976) and became the main writer for the group. He was also closely involved in multimedia events and his own individual projects. After being forced out of the WSQ in 1990 (the group has declined ever since), Hemphill had his own saxophone sextet before his health failed. He recorded as a leader for several labels including Freedom, Sackville, Elektra/Musician and Black Saint. —*Scott Yanow*

★ **Dogon A.D.** / Feb. 1972 / Freedom ✦✦✦✦✦
This historic album features four unknowns on three lengthy avant-garde explorations that were quite influential not only in St. Louis (where they were recorded) but eventually on such diverse players as altoists Tim Berne and David Sanborn. Julius Hemphill (on alto and flute), trumpeter Baikida Carroll, cellist Abdul Wadud and drummer Philip Wilson are in superb form, both as soloists and in ensembles where they react instantly to each other. This important music is better heard than described. —*Scott Yanow*

Coon Bid'ness / Feb. 19, 1975 / Freedom ✦✦✦✦
This historic LP includes a 20-minute performance with altoist Julius Hemphill, trumpeter Baikida Carroll, baritonist Hamiet Bluiett, cellist Abdul Wadud and drummer Philip Wilson ("The Hard Blues") taken from the same session that resulted in *Dogon A.D.* In addition, there are four briefer tracks that feature Hemphill, Bluiett, Wadud, altoist Arthur Blythe, drummer Barry Altschul and the congas of Daniel Zebulon. The music throughout is quite avant-garde but differs from the high-energy jams of the

1960s due to its emphasis on building improvisations as a logical outgrowth from advanced compositions. It's well worth several listens. —*Scott Yanow*

Blue Boye / Jan. 1977 / Mbari ✦✦✦

Roi Boye and the Gotham Minstrels / Mar. 1, 1977 / Sackville ✦✦✦
Psycho-theater drama in the form of the free African-American creative-jazz movement at its height. —*Michael G. Nastos*

Raw Materials and Residuals / Nov. 1977 / Black Saint ✦✦✦✦

Buster Beee / Mar. 1, 1978 / Sackville ✦✦✦

Flat out Jump Suite / Jun. 4, 1980–Jun. 5, 1980 / Black Saint ✦✦✦✦
Quartet with Abdul Wadud (cello), Olu Dara on trumpet, and Warren Smith on percussion. Unabashed free music, at times funky. —*Michael G. Nastos*

Georgia Blue / Aug. 31, 1984 / Minor Music ✦✦✦✦

Julius Hemphill Big Band / Feb. 1988 / Elektra ✦✦✦
A 16-piece progressive big band with lots of saxophones. Good dose of Bill Frisell and Jack Watkins on guitar. Trumpets Rasul Siddik and David Hines are outstanding. —*Michael G. Nastos*

☆ **Fat Man and the Hard Blues** / Jul. 15, 1991+Jul. 16, 1991 / Black Saint ✦✦✦✦✦
After leaving The World Saxophone Quartet, the innovative altoist/composer Julius Hemphill recorded with an unaccompanied sax sextet. This CD features such great players as Marty Ehrlich, Carl Grubbs, the young James Carter, Andrew White and baritonist Sam Furnace along with the leader on 14 of Hemphill's compositions. These miniatures (all under seven minutes) are most notable for their fresh melodies, logical arrangements and spirited ensembles. —*Scott Yanow*

Live from the New Music Cafe / Sep. 27, 1991 / Music & Arts ✦✦✦✦

Oakland Duets / Nov. 13, 1992–Nov. 14, 1992 / Music & Arts ✦✦✦

Five Chord Stud / Nov. 18, 1993–Nov. 19, 1993 / Black Saint ✦✦✦✦
Although altoist Julius Hemphill gets top billing on this CD, his heart surgery in 1993 forced him to stop playing. However, this saxophone sextet was his regular group; he contributed six of the eight compositions (the other two are free improvisations) and the chancetaking heard throughout this adventurous music definitely makes most of the performances sound like they came from a Julius Hemphill recording even if his alto is missed. The sextet has a very strong lineup (altoists Tim Berne, Marty Ehrlich and Sam Furnace, tenors James Carter and Andrew White and baritonist Fred Ho) and the resulting CD contains more than its share of variety. The music ranges from the soulful "Spiritual Chairs" and a boppish "Band Theme" to introspective ballads and wild passionate interplay. Other than Fred Ho (who is not heard from enough), each of the players has their chance to star. The generally fascinating music rewards repeated listenings but one has to have an open mind before putting it on. —*Scott Yanow*

Bill Henderson

b. Mar. 19, 1930, Chicago, IL
Vocals / Standards
Bill Henderson sings blues, ballads and swing tunes in the tradition of Joe Williams and Ernie Andrews but with his own personality. He started singing professionally in 1952, performed in Chicago with Ramsey Lewis, moved to New York and started recording as a leader in 1958. He had a hit with "Senor Blues" (recorded with Horace Silver), Jimmy Smith's trio backed Henderson on one date, during his period on Vee-Jay (1959–61) his sidemen included Ramsey Lewis, Booker Little, Yusef Lateef and Eddie Harris and in 1963 Henderson was featured on a full album (for MGM) accompanied by the Oscar Peterson Trio. Although he made one further record in 1965 (for Verve) and was with Count Basie during 1965–66, Bill Henderson never really received the fame that his talents deserved. He settled in Los Angeles, worked as an actor and occasionally led a group containing both pianist Dave MacKay and pianist/vocalist Joyce Collins. Henderson (who recorded a couple of albums for Discovery in the 1970s but very little since) still performs regularly in the Los Angeles area and is in prime form in the mid-'90s. —*Scott Yanow*

Music Map

Harmonica

Although it has been a major instrument in the blues from the 1920s on, the harmonica has only had a very small number of practitioners in jazz.

1930s
Larry Adler (only part-time in jazz)

The One Jazz Virtuoso
Toots Thielemans

Rare Instances of the Harmonica in Jazz
Sonny Terry (1958, guesting with Chris Barber's Band)
Buddy Lucas
Malachi Favors (of the Art Ensemble Of Chicago)
Wally Chambers
(1972, "Red China Blues" with Miles Davis)

1990s
Hendrik Meurkens
Howard Levy

★ **Complete Vee-Jay Recordings, Vol. 1** / Oct. 26, 1959–Nov. 21, 1960 / Vee-Jay ✦✦✦✦✦
Bill Henderson was that rare item on the Vee-Jay label, a certified jazz singer. He worked with many luminaries during his tenure, among them the Ramsey Lewis Trio, Booker Little, the MJT + 3, and Jimmy Jones, all of whom are represented on this first of two reissued sets covering Henderson's Vee-Jay output. The menu ranges from such standards as "My Funny Valentine" and "Bye Bye Blackbird" to jazz anthems like "Moanin'" and originals penned by Dinah Washington, Ray Charles, and Jerome Kern. Henderson did them all in a charming fashion with impeccable swing and timing; his style is in a solid jazz mode—almost no scatting, just delivering and interpreting the songs with zest and flair. —*Ron Wynn*

Complete Vee-Jay Recordings, Vol. 2 / Dec. 5, 1960–Apr. 25, 1961 / Vee-Jay ✦✦✦✦✦
It seems odd that Bill Henderson did not make it big, particularly when one considers how few new male jazz singers emerged during the 1960s. This second of two CDs continues the reissuance of all of his 1959–61 recordings for Vee-Jay. Although there are a few lightweight tracks, most of the selections find Henderson swinging lightly or wringing honest emotion out of the ballads. The backup varies greatly from string orchestras and the Count Basie band to a combo with tenor saxophonist Eddie Harris and a quartet headed by pianist Tommy Flanagan. Both volumes are recommended. —*Scott Yanow*

Please Send Me Someone to Love / 1961 / Vee-Jay ✦✦✦

● **Bill Henderson/Oscar Peterson Trio** / Feb. 1963–May 28, 1963 / Verve ✦✦✦✦
Exceptional release from an unsung hero of jazz vocals. Highly recommended. —*Michael G. Nastos*

Live at the Times / Aug. 1975 / Discovery ✦✦✦
Stylized. Some good moments with Joyce Collins (v). —*Ron Wynn*

Something's Gotta Give / 1979 / Discovery ✦✦✦
Nice session, with Joyce Collins (v) present. —*Ron Wynn*

Tribute to Johnny Mercer / May 5, 1981 / Discovery ✦✦✦✦

Eddie Henderson

b. Oct. 26, 1940, New York, NY
Trumpet / Post-Bop, Fusion
Eddie Henderson was one of the few trumpeters who was strongly influenced by Miles Davis' work of his early fusion period. He grew up in San Francisco, studied trumpet at the San Francisco Conservatory of Music but was trained to be a doctor when he permanently chose music. Henderson worked with John Handy, Tyrone Washington and Joe Henderson in addition to his own group. He gained some recognition for his work with the Herbie Hancock Sextet (1970–73) although his own records (which utilized electronics) tended to be commercial. After Hancock broke up his group, Henderson worked with Art Blakey and Mike Nock, recorded with Charles Earland and later in the 1970s led a rock-oriented group. In recent times he has returned to playing acoustic hard bop (touring with Billy Harper in 1991) while also working as a psychiatrist. —*Scott Yanow*

Realization / Feb. 27, 1973–Feb. 28, 1973 / Capricorn ✦✦

Inside Out / Oct. 1973 / Capricorn ✦✦✦

Sunburst / Mar. 1975–Apr. 1975 / Blue Note ✦✦✦

Heritage / 1975 / Blue Note ✦✦✦

Comin' Through / Jan. 1977 / Capitol ✦✦

Mahal / 1978 / Capitol ✦✦

Running to Your Love / 1979 / Capital ✦✦

● **Inspiration** / Jul. 8, 1994–Jul. 9, 1994 / Milestone ✦✦✦✦✦

Fletcher Henderson

b. Dec. 18, 1897, Cuthbert, GA, d. Dec. 29, 1952, New York, NY
Piano, Leader, Arranger / Classic Jazz, Swing
Fletcher Henderson was very important to early jazz as leader of the first great jazz big band, as an arranger and composer in the 1930s and as a masterful talent scout. Between 1923–39 quite an all-star cast of top young black jazz musicians passed through his orchestra, including trumpeters Louis Armstrong, Joe Smith, Tommy Ladnier, Rex Stewart, Bobby Stark, Cootie Williams, Red Allen and Roy Eldridge, trombonists Charlie Green, Benny Morton, Jimmy Harrison, Sandy Williams, J.C. Higginbottham and Dickie Wells, clarinetist Buster Bailey, tenors Coleman Hawkins (1924–34), Ben Webster, Lester Young (whose brief stint was not recorded) and Chu Berry, altoists Benny Carter, Russell Procope and Hilton Jefferson, bassists John Kirby and Israel Crosby, drummers Kaiser Marshall, Walter Johnson and Sid Catlett, guest pianist Fats Waller and such arrangers as Don Redman, Benny Carter, Edgar Sampson and Fletcher's younger brother Horace Henderson. And yet at the height of the swing era, Henderson's band was little-known.

Fletcher Henderson had a degree in chemistry and mathematics, but when he came to New York in 1920 with hopes of becoming a chemist, the only job he could find (due to the racism of the times) was as a song demonstrator with the Pace-Handy music company. Harry Pace soon founded the Black Swan label and Henderson, a versatile but fairly basic pianist, became an important contributor behind the scenes, organizing bands and backing blues vocalists. Although he started recording as a leader in 1921, it was not until January 1924 that he put together his first permanent big band. Using Don Redman's innovative arrangements, he was soon at the top of his field. His early recordings (Henderson made many records during 1923–24) tend to be both futuristic and awkward with strong musicianship but staccato phrasing. However, after Louis Armstrong joined up in late 1924 and Don Redman started contributing more swinging arrangements, the Fletcher Henderson Orchestra had no close competitors artistically until the rise of Duke Ellington in 1927. By then Henderson's band (after a period at the Club Alabam) was playing regularly at the Roseland Ballroom but, due to the bandleader being a very indifferent businessman, the all-star outfit recorded relatively little during its peak (1927–30).

With the departure of Redman in 1927 and the end of interim periods when Benny Carter and Horace Henderson wrote the bulk of the arrangements, Fletcher himself developed into a top arranger by the early '30s. However, the Depression took its toll

on the band and the increased competition from other orchestras (along with some bad business decisions and the loss of Coleman Hawkins) resulted in Henderson breaking up the big band in early 1935. Starting in 1934 he began contributing versions of his better arrangements to Benny Goodman's new orchestra (including "King Porter Stomp," "Sometimes I'm Happy" and "Down South Camp Meeting") and ironically Goodman's recordings were huge hits at a time when Fletcher Henderson's name was not known to the general public. In 1936 he put together a new orchestra and immediately had a hit in "Christopher Columbus," but after three years he had to disband again in 1939. Henderson worked as a staff arranger for Goodman and even played in BG's Sextet for a few months (although his skills on the piano never did develop much). He struggled through the 1940s, leading occasional bands (including one in the mid-'40s that utilized some arrangements by the young Sun Ra). In 1950 Henderson had a fine sextet with Lucky Thompson, but a stroke ended his career and led to his death in 1952. Virtually all of Fletcher Henderson's recordings as a leader (and many are quite exciting) are currently available on the Classics label and in more piecemeal fashion domestically. —*Scott Yanow*

1921–1923 / Jun. 1921–Jun. 11, 1923 / Classics ✦✦✦
This Classics CD reissues the first 23 recordings of Fletcher Henderson and his orchestra. The music is generally pretty primitive, but historically it is quite significant since Henderson's group would develop into the first real jazz big band; also the 1921–22 sides have rarely ever been reissued. Oddly enough, his only three solo piano recordings date from this period. The earliest orchestra recordings are essentially period dance-band performances but, by the end of this CD, Henderson's big band was already beginning to display a bit of its own musical personality although (needless to say) the best years were still in the future. —*Scott Yanow*

★ **A Study In Frustration/Thesaurus Of Classic Jazz** / Aug. 9, 1923–May 28, 1938 / Columbia ✦✦✦✦✦
Formerly a four-LP set, this three-CD box contains some of the finest recordings of the 1920s and '30s. Fletcher Henderson's big band during this period featured many of the top black jazz soloists including trumpeters Louis Armstrong, Joe Smith, Rex Stewart, Tommy Ladnier, Bobby Stark, Cootie Williams, Red Allen and Roy Eldridge, trombonists Charlie Green, Jimmy Harrison and J.C. Higginbotham, tenors Coleman Hawkins, Ben Webster and Chu Berry, clarinetist Buster Bailey, altoist Benny Carter and guest pianist Fats Waller among others. With Don Redman and later Benny Carter and Fletcher himself contributing advanced arrangements, Henderson had the leading big band of 1923–27 and one of the best jazz orchestras of the next few years. This is an essential acquisition for all serious jazz collections. —*Scott Yanow*

Fletcher Henderson (1924–1927) / Jul. 10, 1924–Apr. 24, 1927 / EPM ✦✦✦✦
This French CD contains many of the best recordings from Louis Armstrong's year with Henderson, including such classics as "Copenhagen," "Everybody Loves My Baby," "Mandy Make up Your Mind" and "Sugar Foot Stomp." During this time, Henderson added other fine soloists (including trombonist Charlie Green and clarinetist Buster Bailey) and Don Redman's arrangements began to swing. The final six numbers from this 22-selection CD are from The Henderson orchestra's zenith in 1927 with "Fidgety Feet" and "Variety Stomp" featuring brilliant work from tenor great Coleman Hawkins, trombonist Jimmy Harrison, clarinetist Bailey and trumpeter Tommy Ladnier. A perfect introduction to Fletcher Henderson. —*Scott Yanow*

Fletcher Henderson and Louis Armstrong / Oct. 10, 1924–Oct. 21, 1925 / Timeless ✦✦✦
This rather unusual CD has 24 selections but most of them are shorter excerpts. The focus is on the brilliant solos that Louis Armstrong took while a member of the Fletcher Henderson Orchestra. Since his cornet flights were years ahead of some of the wheezing arrangements and the attempts by the other sidemen, the producers simply cut out the more dated segments and sometimes spliced in several of his solos from different takes of the same song. Where the producers erred was in not including every Armstrong solo with Henderson and, most importantly, programming the CD in complete chronological order so one could more easily trace the month-by-month growth of this innovative

jazzman. Still, this is a historical curiosity and the music is consistently exciting. — *Scott Yanow*

Fletcher Henderson (1924–1925) / Oct. 1924–Feb. 1925 / Classics ✦✦✦✦
This excellent European LP contains 14 performances (including three alternate takes) from Armstrong's period with Fletcher Henderson's orchestra. Most of these selections are fairly rare (such as "My Rose Marie," "Twelfth Street Blues" and "Me Neenyah") and only one performance is duplicated from the CD *Fletcher Henderson (1924–1927)*. Almost all of these cuts have memorable Louis Armstrong solos that easily take honors and are state-of-the-art for 1925. — *Scott Yanow*

Fletcher Henderson (1925–1926) / Nov. 23, 1925–Apr. 14, 1926 / Classics ✦✦✦✦✦
The Classics series has undergone the admirable task of reissuing on CD in chronological order every selection (although no alternate takes) of Fletcher Henderson's orchestra. This set finds the post-Armstrong edition of this pacesetting big band swinging hard on a variety of standards and obscurities. With cornetist Joe Smith, trombonist Charlie Green, clarinetist Buster Bailey and tenor great Coleman Hawkins contributing many fine solos and Don Redman's often-innovative arrangements inspiring the musicians, at this period Fletcher Henderson's orchestra had no close competitors among jazz-oriented big bands. Even the weaker pop tunes (like "I Want to See a Little More of What I Saw in Arkansas") have their strong moments. — *Scott Yanow*

● **Fletcher Henderson (1926–1927)** / Apr. 14, 1926–Jan. 22, 1927 / Classics ✦✦✦✦✦
This CD, in Classics' chronological series, which captures the Fletcher Henderson Orchestra at its peak, is overloaded with classics: "Jackass Blues," "The Stampede" (which has a very influential tenor solo by Coleman Hawkins), "Clarinet Marmalade" "Snag It" and "Tozo" among others. In addition to Coleman Hawkins, Tommy Ladnier emerges as a major trumpeter and Fats Waller drops by for his "Henderson Stomp." Eight years before the official beginning of the swing era, Fletcher Henderson's orchestra was outswinging everyone. — *Scott Yanow*

● **Fletcher Henderson (1927)** / Mar. 11, 1927–Oct. 24, 1927 / Classics ✦✦✦✦✦
Fletcher Henderson's orchestra was at the peak of its powers during this period, as can be heard on such torrid recordings as "Fidgety Feet," "Sensation," "St. Louis Shuffle," and "Hop Off"; even the overly complex Don Redman arrangement "Whiteman Stomp" (which Paul Whiteman's musicians apparently had trouble learning) is no problem for this brilliant orchestra. Classics' chronological reissue of Henderson's valuable recordings on this CD covers the many highpoints of the peak year of 1927; only Duke Ellington's orchestra was on the level of this pace-setting big band. — *Scott Yanow*

The Complete Fletcher Henderson (1927–1936) / Mar. 11, 1927–Aug. 4, 1936 / RCA/Bluebird ✦✦✦✦
"Complete" is in this case a relative term, meaning every recording by Fletcher Henderson's orchestra owned by RCA/Bluebird rather than every record he made during this period. A perfectly done two-LP set, these 34 songs include three from 1927 (featuring trumpeters Tommy Ladnier and Joe Smith at their best), 12 varying sides from 1931-32 (during which tenor saxophonist Coleman Hawkins and trumpeters Rex Stewart and Bobby Stark make even the most commercial material into worthwhile music), a session from 1934 with trumpeter Red Allen and 15 numbers from 1936 that co-star trumpeter Roy Eldridge and Chu Berry on tenor. Throughout, the consistent high quality of the solos and musicianship (even with some off moments) makes one regret that this classic orchestra was not more commercially successful. — *Scott Yanow*

Hocus Pocus: Classic Big Band Jazz / Apr. 27, 1927–Aug. 4, 1936 / Bluebird ✦✦✦
Highpoints include "St. Louis Shuffle, "Variety Stomp," "Sugar Foot Stomp," the swinging title cut, examples of early Roy Eldridge trumpet and "Strangers," which contrasts a horrendous vocal with some inspired Coleman Hawkins tenor. — *Scott Yanow*

Fletcher Henderson (1927–1931) / Nov. 4, 1927–Feb. 5, 1931 / Classics ✦✦✦✦✦
With its high musicianship and many talented soloists (including trumpeters Rex Stewart and Bobby Stark, trombonist Jimmy Harrison, Coleman Hawkins on tenor and altoist Benny Carter),

the Fletcher Henderson Orchestra should have prospered during this period, but unaccountably its leader (never a strong businessman) seemed to be losing interest in the band's fortunes and made several bad decisions. The result is that by 1931 Henderson's orchestra was struggling while Duke Ellington's was becoming a household name. This Classics CD, in covering over three years, demonstrates how few recordings this band made (only four songs apiece in both 1929 and 1930), although the quality largely makes up for the quantity. The original band version of "King Porter Stomp" and an explosive "Oh Baby" are the highpoints of this satisfying collection. — *Scott Yanow*

Fletcher Henderson (1931) / Feb. 5, 1931–Jul. 31, 1931 / Classics ✦✦✦✦
Even with such strong players as trumpeters Bobby Stark and Rex Stewart, trombonist Benny Morton and tenor saxophonist Coleman Hawkins, the fortunes of Fletcher Henderson's orchestra were slipping during 1931. With the departure of Don Redman several years earlier, the group's arrangements were less innovative, and the pressure was on to perform commercial songs for the Depression audience. Even the jazz standards (such as "Tiger Rag" and "After You've Gone") are less interesting than those of their competitors, although this new version of "Sugar Foot Stomp" is a classic and the strong solos by the all-star cast make this CD well worth acquiring. — *Scott Yanow*

The Crown King of Swing / Mar. 1931–Oct. 1931 / Savoy ✦✦✦
In 1931 the Fletcher Henderson Orchestra recorded ten titles for the low-budget Crown label. This LP includes all ten numbers plus two alternate takes, giving Henderson's band a chance to play material generally not associated with their early brand of swing including such tunes as "After You've Gone," "Stardust," "Tiger Rag" and even "Twelfth Street Rag." Although not essential (only the remake of "Sugar Foot Stomp" is classic), it is interesting to hear trumpeters Bobby Stark and Rex Stewart, trombonist J.C. Higginbottham and tenorman Coleman Hawkins soloing on this unlikely material. — *Scott Yanow*

Fletcher Henderson (1931–1932) / Jul. 31, 1931–Mar. 11, 1932 / Classics ✦✦✦
During this period Fletcher Henderson was often stuck recording commercial leftover like "My Sweet Tooth Says I Wanna (But My Wisdom Tooth Says No)", "I Wanna Count Sheep (Till the Cows Come Home)" and "Strangers," but in most cases his all-star orchestra was able to overcome the material. This CD, part of Classics' complete chronological reissue of Henderson's recordings, also finds the orchestra backing Baby Rose Marie on two songs in addition to attempting (with uneven success) to put its stamp on jazz standards made famous by other musicians (such as "12th Street Rag" and "Casa Loma Stomp"). The music is generally quite good if not essential Henderson. — *Scott Yanow*

Fletcher Henderson (1932–1934) / Dec. 9, 1932–Sep. 12, 1934 / Classics ✦✦✦✦
Although the Fletcher Henderson Orchestra was struggling and missing opportunities during this era, its recordings greatly improved from the ones in 1931. Henderson had finally developed into a top arranger (as can be heard on "Honeysuckle Rose" and "Wrappin' It Up"), the band was full of top soloists (trumpeter Bobby Stark had his greatest moments on "The New King Porter Stomp") and even if Coleman Hawkins chose to move to Europe (after starring on "It's the Talk of the Town") the band should have been poised to flourish in the swing era. These recordings (from Classics' complete chronological program) prove that swing did not begin with Benny Goodman in 1935. — *Scott Yanow*

Fletcher Henderson (1934–1937) / Sep. 25, 1934–Mar. 2, 1937 / Classics ✦✦✦✦✦
In early 1935 Fletcher Henderson broke up his classic orchestra but a year later, with the success of so many other big bands, he formed a new ensemble. This Classics CD includes four songs from 1934, Henderson's entire output from 1936 and his first recording of 1937. The main difference between the two units is that the later one boasted the trumpet of Roy Eldridge and tenor solos from Coleman Hawkins' potential successor, Chu Berry. "Christopher Columbus" became a hit as did the band's new theme song ("Stealin' Apples"), but the brief bit of glory would not last. However, Henderson's brand of swing music still sounds fresh today and this CD is easily recommended. — *Scott Yanow*

Fletcher Henderson (1937–1938) / Mar. 2, 1937–May 28, 1938 / Classics ✦✦✦✦
The Classics chronological reissue of Fletcher Henderson's record-

ings continues with this disc, which traces the decline of his last "permanent" orchestra. With the departure of Roy Eldridge, Henderson, for the first time since the early '20s, lacked any major trumpet soloists, although he still featured the fine tenor of Chu Berry and a variety of up-and-coming players. Unfortunately, the band was far overshadowed by other orchestras influenced by Henderson and since the quality of his recordings was declining, the breakup of his group was hardly noticed. The irony is that the founder of the swing era could not survive when his music (as played by Benny Goodman) caught on. —*Scott Yanow*

1938 / Jul. 11, 1938–Jul. 13, 1938 / Jazz Unlimited ✦✦✦
The Fletcher Henderson Orchestra was in decline in 1938 and its breakup would come the following year. However, despite its eventual commercial failure, it was still a first-class swing band at this late point with fine soloists in trumpeter Emmett Berry, trombonist Ed Cuffee, tenor Elmer Williams and clarinetist Eddie Barefield. The two formerly unknown radio broadcasts included on this CD took place a few months after the band's final studio recordings and are generally excellent. Fletcher Henderson was definitely in Benny Goodman's shadow by this time (even if the announcer calls Henderson "the King of Swing") but, as such numbers as "Down South Camp Meeting," "Bugle Blues" and "Panama" show, there was still plenty of life left in this veteran band. —*Scott Yanow*

Fletcher Henderson's Sextet (1950) / Dec. 20, 1950–Dec. 21, 1950 / Alamac ✦✦✦
Recorded only a day or two before a stroke ended his playing career and, soon afterward, his life, this LP contains a broadcast that finds Fletcher Henderson playing mostly standards with a fine sextet. Trumpeter Dick Vance and clarinetist Eddie Barefield were alumni of his orchestra, but it is tenor saxophonist Lucky Thompson who takes honors on this spirited session of small-group swing. —*Scott Yanow*

The Big Reunion / Nov. 29, 1957–Dec. 2, 1957 / Jazztone ✦✦✦✦
In 1957 cornetist Rex Stewart gathered together a large group dominated by Fletcher Henderson alumni and the result is this excellent tribute. Not every selection was from Henderson's book, but the four main jams ("Sugar Foot Stomp," "Honeysuckle Rose," "Wrappin' It Up" and "King Porter Stomp") both revisit past glories and, with the fresh solos of Coleman Hawkins, Ben Webster, Buster Bailey, J.C. Higginbotham, Dickie Wells and Stewart among others, create some new history. —*Scott Yanow*

Horace Henderson

b. Nov. 22, 1904, Cuthbert, GA, **d.** Aug. 29, 1988, Denver, CO
Piano, Arranger / Swing
While Horace Henderson can't justly be compared to his brother (Fletcher) in terms of achievement, he has a substantial legacy as an arranger and bandleader. More than 30 Henderson arrangements were incorporated into his brother's band, among them "Hot and Anxious/Comin' and Goin'," and "Christopher Columbus." He also led a small splinter group in the early '30s that made some fine recordings for Parlaphone. Henderson's arrangement of "Hot and Anxious" revised the traditional riff that would eventually be recorded by the Glenn Miller Orchestra as "In The Mood"; he also used the melody from the Duke Ellington/Barney Bigard song "Voom" as a reference for his composition "Doin' The Voom." He was an above average pianist, and more rhythmically intense and varied than his brother. Henderson performed in New York during the mid-'20s while still a student at Wilberforce University. He subsequently toured with his band, The Wilberforce Collegians. The roster included Rex Stewart and Benny Carter. Besides heading bands in the '20s, '30s and '40s, Henderson also worked in the groups of Don Redman and Vernon Andrae while arranging and playing in his brother's band from 1931 to 1947. Henderson also did arrangements periodically for Benny Goodman, Charlie Barnet, Jimmie Lunceford and Earl Hines among others. He continued heading bands into the '70s. His work can be heard on Fletcher Henderson reissued CDs. —*Ron Wynn*

● **Horace Henderson (1940)** / Feb. 27, 1940–Oct. 23, 1940 / Tax ✦✦✦✦✦

Joe Henderson

b. Apr. 24, 1937, Lima, Ohio
Tenor Saxophone / Hard Bop, Post-Bop
Joe Henderson is proof that jazz can sell without watering down

the music; it just takes creative marketing! Although his sound and style are virtually unchanged from the mid-'60s, Joe Henderson's signing with Verve in 1992 was treated as a major news event by the label (even though he had already recorded many memorable sessions for other companies). His Verve recordings had easy-to-market themes (tributes to Billy Strayhorn, Miles Davis and Antonio Carlos Jobim), and as a result he became a national celebrity and a constant pollwinner while still sounding the same as when he was in obscurity in the 1970s!

The general feeling is that it couldn't happen to a more deserving jazz musician. After studying at Kentucky State College and Wayne University, Joe Henderson played locally in Detroit before spending time in the military (1960–62). He played briefly with Jack McDuff and then gained recognition for his work with Kenny Dorham (1962–63), a veteran bop trumpeter who championed him and helped Henderson get signed to Blue Note. Henderson appeared on many Blue Note sessions both as a leader and as a sideman, spent 1964–66 with Horace Silver's Quintet and during 1969–70 was in Herbie Hancock's band. From the start he had a very distinctive sound and style which, although influenced a bit by both Sonny Rollins and John Coltrane, also contained a lot of brand new phrases and ideas. Henderson has long been able to improvise in both inside and outside settings, from hard bop to free form. In the 1970s he recorded frequently for Milestone and lived in San Francisco but was somewhat taken for granted. The second half of the 1980s found him continuing to freelance and teach while recording for Blue Note, but it was when he hooked up with Verve that he suddenly became famous. Virtually all of his recordings are currently in print on CD including a massive collection of his neglected (but generally rewarding) Milestone dates. —*Scott Yanow*

The Blue Note Years / Apr. 1, 1963–Feb. 15, 1990 / Blue Note ✦✦✦
Unlike many other box sets currently available, this four-CD package is actually a sampler taken from Joe Henderson's many recordings for Blue Note; all but three selections date from 1963–69. Out of the 36 selections, 26 feature the great tenor as a sideman and some are from sessions not reissued in quite awhile. Henderson is instantly recognizable (his distinctive tone has not changed much since 1963) and an asset to each of these performances. Also included in the box is a very attractive, 40-page booklet that is highlighted by his complete Blue Note discography. This set is particularly recommended to listeners only vauge-ly aware of Joe Henderson's powerful music. —*Scott Yanow*

★ **Page One** / Jun. 3, 1963 / Blue Note ✦✦✦✦✦
Tenor saxophonist Joe Henderson's debut as a leader is a particularly strong and historic effort. With major contributions made by trumpeter Kenny Dorham, pianist McCoy Tyner, bassist Butch Warren and drummer Pete La Roca, Henderson (who already had a strikingly original sound and a viable inside/outside style) performs six generally memorable compositions on this CD reissue. Highlights include the original versions of Dorham's "Blue Bossa" and Henderson's "Recorda Me." It's highly recommended. —*Scott Yanow*

Our Thing / Sep. 9, 1963 / Blue Note ✦✦✦✦✦
Joe Henderson's second recording as a leader features a very strong supporting cast: trumpeter Kenny Dorham (one of Henderson's earliest supporters), pianist Andrew Hill, bassist Eddie Khan and drummer Pete La Roca. Together they perform three Dorham and two Henderson originals, advanced music that was open to the influence of the avant-garde while remaining in the hard bop idiom. The uptempo blues "Teeter Totter" contrasts with the four minor-toned pieces and, even if none of these songs became standards, the playing is consistently brilliant and unpredictable. Even at this relatively early stage, Joe Henderson was a potentially great tenorman. —*Scott Yanow*

In 'n Out / Apr. 10, 1964 / Blue Note ✦✦✦✦✦
Joe Henderson's third Blue Note release (which is reissued here on CD along with the addition of a previously unissued version of the title cut) matches the very distinctive tenor with the veteran trumpeter Kenny Dorham and an unbeatable rhythm section: pianist McCoy Tyner, bassist Richard Davis and drummer Elvin Jones. Henderson, who has always had the ability to make a routine bop piece sound complex and the most complicated free improvisation seem logical, and Dorham provided all of the material and the music still sounds fresh over three decades later. —*Scott Yanow*

Inner Urge / Nov. 30, 1964 / Blue Note ✦✦✦✦✦
The fourth of Joe Henderson's early Blue Note recordings is his first in a quartet setting without trumpeter Kenny Dorham. Henderson (who is accompanied by pianist McCoy Tyner, bassist Bob Cranshaw and drummer Elvin Jones) is in explorative form on three of his originals (including "Inner Urge" and the original version of "Isotope"), Duke Pearson's "You Know I Care" and the standard "Night and Day." The music straddles the boundaries between hard bop and the avant-garde and, while Henderson's improvisations are chordal-based, they are also quite unpredictable and prone to emotional outbursts. This colorful music is highly recommended. *— Scott Yanow*

Mode for Joe / Jan. 27, 1966 / Blue Note ✦✦✦✦
Tenor saxophonist Joe Henderson's fifth and final early Blue Note album is his only one with a group larger than a quintet. Henderson welcomes quite an all-star band (trumpeter Lee Morgan, trombonist Curtis Fuller, vibraphonist Bobby Hutcherson, pianist Cedar Walton, bassist Ron Carter and drummer Joe Chambers) and together they perform originals by Henderson (including "A Shade of Jade"), Walton and Morgan ("Free Wheelin'"). The advanced music has plenty of exciting moments and all of the young talents play up to the level one would hope for. *— Scott Yanow*

● **The Kicker** / Aug. 10, 1967 / Original Jazz Classics ✦✦✦✦✦
Joe Henderson's first recording for Milestone was very much a continuation of the adventurous acoustic music he had recorded previously for Blue Note. For those listeners who do not wish to invest in the tenor saxophonist's "complete" eight-CD Milestone box set, this single CD is a good place to start in investigating his "middle period" music. Henderson is featured in a sextet with trumpeter Mike Lawrence, trombonist Grachan Moncur III, pianist Kenny Barron, bassist Ron Carter and drummer Louis Hayes on a well-rounded set highlighted by "Mamacita," "Chelsea Bridge," "If," "Without a Song" and "Nardis." *— Scott Yanow*

☆ **The Milestone Years** / Aug. 10, 1967–Sep. 26, 1976 / Milestone ✦✦✦✦✦
Tenor saxophonist Joe Henderson's most famous recordings are his early Blue Notes and his more recent Verves, but in between he recorded exclusively for Milestone and, although he was in consistently fine form in the diverse settings, Henderson was somewhat neglected during his middle years. This massive eight-CD set contains all of the music from Henderson's dozen Milestone LPs plus a duet with altoist Lee Konitz and his guest appearances with singer Flora Purim and cornetist Nat Adderley. The music ranges from Blue Note-style hard bop and modal explorations to fusion and '70s funk with important contributions made by trumpeters Mike Lawrence, Woody Shaw and Luis Gasca, trombonist Grachan Moncur and keyboardists Kenny Barron, Don Friedman, Joe Zawinul, Herbie Hancock, George Cables, Alice Coltrane, Mark Levine and George Duke among others. Not all of the music is classic (some of the later sets are unabashedly commercial), but none of the 82 selections are dull and the very distinctive Joe Henderson always plays his best. It's highly recommended. *— Scott Yanow*

Tetragon / Sep. 27, 1967–May 16, 1968 / Original Jazz Classics ✦✦✦✦
Joe Henderson's second Milestone recording (which, as with all the others, is currently available on his massive "complete" eight-CD box set) features the great tenor with two separate rhythm sections: Kenny Barron or Don Friedman on piano, bassist Ron Carter and either Louis Hayes or Jack DeJohnette on drums. Highlights of this LP include the title track, "I've Got You Under My Skin" and "Invitation." *— Scott Yanow*

Four / Apr. 21, 1968 / Verve ✦✦✦✦✦
Released for the first time on this CD in 1994, the previously unknown live session from 1968 features the great tenor Joe Henderson (who was then just a few days short of turning 31) playing for the first and possibly only time with the Wynton Kelly Trio. Henderson, pianist Kelly, bassist Paul Chambers and drummer Jimmy Cobb really stretch out on six standards (including a two-song medley), all of which clock in between 11:47 and 16:05 (except for a three-minute "Theme"). Henderson really pushes the rhythm section (which, although they had not played with the tenor previously, had been together for a decade) and he is certainly inspired by their presence. This is a frequently exciting performance by some of the modern bop greats of the era. *— Scott Yanow*

Power to the People / May 23, 1969+May 29, 1969 / Milestone ✦✦✦✦✦
This LP (which has been included in Joe Henderson's eight-CD complete Milestone box set) has quite a few classic moments. At that point in time tenor saxophonist Henderson was a sideman with Herbie Hancock's Sextet so Hancock was happy to perform as a sideman (doubling on piano and electric piano) with the all-star group (which also includes trumpeter Mike Lawrence, bassist Ron Carter and drummer Jack DeJohnette). Highlights are many including the original version of "Black Narcissus," "Isotope," a lyrical rendition of "Lazy Afternoon" and the free-form "Foresight and Afterthought." *— Scott Yanow*

If You're Not Part of the Problem.... / Sep. 24, 1970–Sep. 26, 1970 / Milestone ✦✦✦✦
This live session from the legendary Lighthouse features a particularly strong version of the Joe Henderson Quintet, which at the time included the leader on tenor, trumpeter Woody Shaw, keyboardist George Cables, bassist Ron McClure and drummer Lenny White. There are excellent remakes of "Mode for Joe" and "Blue Bossa" plus two new originals and a fine rendition of "'Round Midnight." As is typical of Henderson's Milestone recordings, this one did not sell all that well, but blame cannot be placed on the musical quality. All of the performances on this LP are included in Joe Henderson's eight-CD Milestone box set. *— Scott Yanow*

In Pursuit of Blackness / Sep. 24, 1970–May 12, 1971 / Milestone ✦✦✦
This Joe Henderson LP features the great tenor with two very different groups. "Invitation" and "Gazelle" are taken from the same live sessions that resulted in his previous album *If You're Not Part of the Solution* and showcase Henderson's quintet with trumpeter Woody Shaw, keyboardist George Cables, bassist Ron McClure and drummer Lenny White. The remaining three tracks are funkier and freer, adding bassist Stanley Clarke to a rhythm section of Cables and White and featuring the rather ad-lib "Mind over Matter." It's an interesting if slightly erratic set. *— Scott Yanow*

Joe Henderson in Japan / Aug. 4, 1971 / Milestone ✦✦✦✦✦
Tenor saxophonist Joe Henderson toured Japan in the summer of 1971 and performed in Tokyo with an all-Japanese rhythm section (keyboardist Hideo Ichikawa, bassist Kunimitsu Inaba and drummer Notohiko Hino). Henderson really stretches out on two of his compositions ("Out 'n' In" and "Junk Blues"), "'Round Midnight" and Kenny Dorham's "Blue Bossa." The trio gives him strong support and Henderson is heard throughout in top form. The frequently superb performances heard on this LP have been reissued in Joe Henderson's eight-CD "complete" Milestone box set. *— Scott Yanow*

Black Is the Color / Mar. 1972–Apr. 1972 / Milestone ✦✦
For a short period tenor saxophonist Joe Henderson made extensive use of overdubbing. This LP finds him not only playing tenor but adding flute, alto flute, soprano and percussion; he also utilizes extra musicians (most notably David Horowitz on synthesizer and percussionist Airto) to augment his core group of keyboardist George Cables, bassist Dave Holland and drummer Jack DeJohnette. Although the music holds one's interest, it is not up to the same creative level of his earlier Milestone releases; a few of these pieces sound like Henderson was hoping for a hit. *— Scott Yanow*

Multiple / Jan. 30, 1973–Apr. 13, 1973 / Original Jazz Classics ✦✦✦
This CD reissue of the original Joe Henderson LP is one of the few on which the great tenor extensively utilized overdubbing. The main group includes Henderson (who later overdubbed himself on soprano, flute, percussion and even voice), keyboardist Larry Willis, bassist Dave Holland, drummer Jack DeJohnette and percussionist Arthur Jenkins; later on, guitarists James Blood Ulmer and John Thomas were added to some of the tracks. The music is at times funky, dense and a bit aimless although it is generally quite stimulating. This is not an essential release, but those listeners who stereotype Joe Henderson as a strictly acoustic stylist will find the set particularly interesting. *— Scott Yanow*

The Elements / Oct. 15, 1973–Oct. 17, 1973 / Milestone ✦✦
This is one of the odder Joe Henderson recordings. The four lengthy selections not only feature the great tenor saxophonist but the piano and harp of Alice Coltrane (during one of her rare appearances as a sideman), violinist Michael White, bassist Charlie Haden, percussionist Kenneth Nash and Baba Duru

Oshun on tablas. The somewhat spiritual nature of the music (Henderson's compositions are titled "Fire," "Air," "Water" and "Earth") and the presence of Alice Coltrane makes these Eastern-flavored performances rather unique if not all that essential: an early example of world music. This LP has been reissued as part of Henderson's eight-CD Milestone box set. —Scott Yanow

Canyon Lady / Oct. 1973 / Milestone ✦✦✦
This LP has trumpeter Luis Gasca featured as a co-star with tenor saxophonist Joe Henderson. Gasca arranged "Tres Palabras" which is played by a 13-piece group (Oscar Brashear takes the trumpet solo) while the other three originals (two by pianist Mark Levine) use either a sextet or a nonet. Henderson is in fine form on these spirited Latinish performances, which have also been included on his eight-CD Milestone box set. —Scott Yanow

Black Narcissus / Oct. 19, 1974–Apr. 1975 / Milestone ✦✦✦
This Milestone LP (which has been included in Joe Henderson's eight-CD Milestone box set) is a bit of a mixed bag. The tenor recorded four numbers with pianist Joachim Kuhn's trio in Paris and later had percussion and Patrick Gleeson's synthesizer over-dubbed. In addition there is the odd "Amoeba" (which finds Henderson doubling on synth himself) along with a superior version of "Good Morning Heartache" featuring Henderson, Kuhn, bassist Dave Friesen and drummer Jack DeJohnette. This album has its moments although there are many much more consistent Joe Henderson albums around. —Scott Yanow

Black Miracle / Feb. 13, 1975–Sep. 25, 1975 / Milestone ✦✦
Tenor saxophonist Joe Henderson's final Milestone recording has a few attempts at trying to create a hit (including utilizing George Duke's keyboards, overdubbing a horn section and synthesizers and playing Stevie Wonder's "My Cherie Amour"), but this LP did not sell anymore than Henderson's less commercial efforts. Actually, the music is generally pretty good, funky at times but still with searching solos from Henderson. "Soulution" and "Gazelle" are highpoints. As with his other Milestone recordings, this one has been reissued on CD as part of Joe Henderson's eight-CD box set *The Milestone Years*. —Scott Yanow

Barcelona / Jun. 2, 1977–Nov. 15, 1977 / Enja ✦✦✦✦
Tremendous, frenzied trio date by tenor saxophonist Joe Henderson, recently released with bassist Wayne Darling and drummer Ed Soph. After many years of obscurity, Henderson has become famous in the last few years. But the whirling lines, huge tone and astonishing solos that he routinely offers on this album have been prized by jazz fans since the early '60s. —Ron Wynn

Relaxin' at Camarillo / Aug. 20, 1979+Dec. 29, 1979 / Original Jazz Classics ✦✦✦
Originally on Contemporary, this CD reissue teams the great tenor Joe Henderson with pianist Chick Corea, either Tony Dumas or Richard Davis on bass and Peter Erskine or Tony Williams on drums. The repertoire includes two songs by Corea, Henderson's "Y Todavia La Quiero," the standard ballad "My One and Only Love" and Charlie Parker's "Relaxin' at Camarillo." This informal session has plenty of fine solos from the two principals and is recommended to fans of advanced hard bop. —Scott Yanow

Mirror, Mirror / Jan. 1980 / Pausa ✦✦✦✦
Tenor saxophonist Joe Henderson has had a remarkably consistent career. Although he has spent periods (such as the 1970s) in relative obscurity and others as almost a jazz superstar, Henderson's style and sound has been relatively unchanged since the 1960s. This lesser-known LP finds Henderson in typically fine form in an acoustic quartet with pianist Chick Corea, bassist Ron Carter and drummer Billy Higgins. Carter and Corea contribute two songs apiece, Henderson gets to perform his "Joe's Bolero" and the tenor sounds majestic on "What's New." —Scott Yanow

★ **The State of the Tenor (Live at The Village Vanguard)** / Nov. 4, 1985 / Blue Note ✦✦✦✦✦
The very distinctive tenor saxophonist is heard at his best on this two-CD set recorded live at the Village Vanguard. Accompanied only by bassist Ron Carter and drummer Al Foster, Henderson at times recalls Sonny Rollins, but none of his searching improvisations are predictable. Of the 14 selections, 12 were originally released on two Blue Note LPs while the renditions of "Stella by Starlight" and "All the Things You Are" were previously unissued. Highlights of this particularly strong set (recorded over a three-day period) include "Beatrice," several Thelonious Monk tunes (particularly "Friday the Thirteenth" and "Ask Me Now"), "Soulville" and "Isotope." —Scott Yanow

Punjab / Nov. 27, 1986 / Arco ✦✦✦
Evening With / Jul. 9, 1987 / Red ✦✦✦✦
Although Joe Henderson's pianoless trio recordings for Blue Note in 1985 received a fair amount of publicity, this similar date for the Italian Red label has been almost completely overlooked. Joined by bassist Charlie Haden and drummer Al Foster, Henderson is in excellent form, giving "Beatrice," "Invitation," Thelonious Monk's "Ask Me Now" and his own "Serenity" lengthy and rewarding explorations. —Scott Yanow

The Standard Joe / Mar. 16, 1991 / Red ✦✦✦✦
For at least his fourth recording in six years heading a pianoless trio, the great tenor Joe Henderson (along with bassist Rufus Reid and drummer Al Foster) is heard on his own "Inner Urge," an original blues, two lengthy versions of "Body and Soul" and three other jazz standards. This Italian import is particularly recommended to listeners not that familiar with Henderson's playing, for he brings new life to these often overplayed compositions. —Scott Yanow

★ **Lush Life** / Sep. 3, 1991–Sep. 8, 1991 / Verve ✦✦✦✦✦
With the release of this CD, the executives at Verve and their marketing staff proved that, yes indeed, jazz can sell. The veteran tenor Joe Henderson has had a distinctive sound and style of his own ever since he first entered the jazz major leagues, yet he has spent long periods in relative obscurity before reaching his current status as a jazz superstar. As for the music on his "comeback" disc, it does deserve all of the hype. Henderson performs ten of Billy Strayhorn's most enduring compositions in a variety of settings ranging from a full quintet with trumpeter Wynton Marsalis and duets with pianist Stephen Scott, bassist Christian McBride and drummer Gregory Hutchinson to an unaccompanied solo exploration of "Lush Life." This memorable outing succeeded both artistically and commercially and is highly recommended. —Scott Yanow

☆ **So Near, So Far (Musings for Miles)** / Oct. 12, 1992–Oct. 14, 1992 / Verve ✦✦✦✦✦
Joe Henderson's follow-up to his hugely successful *Lush Life* disc is another concept album, this time involving ten songs (including many lesser-known ones) associated with Miles Davis. Henderson only actually played with Davis for a few weekends around 1967, but he shows a great deal of understanding for this potentially difficult music. With particularly strong assistance from guitarist John Scofield, bassist Dave Holland and drummer Al Foster, Henderson revives such forgotten songs as "Teo," "Swing Spring" and "Side Car" in addition to coming up with fresh interpretations of "Miles Ahead," "Milestones" and "No Blues." He is to be congratulated for not taking the easy way out and sticking to the simpler material of Davis' earlier years. —Scott Yanow

Double Rainbow / Sep. 19, 1994–Nov. 6, 1994 / Verve ✦✦✦✦✦
The third of tenor saxophonist Joe Henderson's tribute CDs on Verve was originally supposed to be a collaboration with the great bossa nova composer Antonio Carlos Jobim, but Jobim's unexpected death turned this project into a memorial. Henderson performs a dozen of the composer's works with one of two separate groups: a Brazilian quartet starring pianist Eliane Elias and a jazz trio with pianist Herbie Hancock, bassist Christian McBride and drummer Jack DeJohnette. In general, Henderson avoids Jobim's best-known songs in favor of some of his more obscure (but equally rewarding) melodies and in some cases (such as a very straight-ahead "No More Blues") the treatments are surprising. Highlights of this very accessible yet unpredictable CD include "Felicidade," "Triste," "Zingaro" and a duet with guitarist Oscar Castro-Neves on "Once I Loved" although all of the performances are quite enjoyable. Highly recommended. —Scott Yanow

Scott Henderson

b. 1955
Guitar / Fusion
One of the finest fusion (as opposed to crossover) guitarists of the 1980s and '90s, Scott Henderson's explosive playing is often teamed up with electric bassist Gary Willis in their group Tribal Tech. Originally most influenced by rock, Henderson (who grew up in West Palm Beach, FL) played in local funk and rock bands. In 1980 he moved to Los Angeles to attend the Guitar Institute of Technology, studying with Joe Diorio. After graduating, he became a teacher himself at GIT. Henderson played with Jeff Berlin and Jean-Luc Ponty and, in 1985, toured with the original version of Chick Corea's Elektric Band. During 1987-89 he worked on and off with Joe Zawinul's Syndicate, and since then Tribal Tech has been his main band. As a leader, Scott Henderson

has recorded for Passport, Relativity and Bluemoon. —*Scott Yanow*

Spears / Jun. 1985 / Passport ◆◆◆
Recorded with Tribal Tech, this debut release features Henderson's exceptional guitar tones in a small-group setting. It's well worth a listen. —*Paul Kohler*

Dr. Hee / Mar. 19, 1987 / Relativity ◆◆◆◆
Recorded with Tribal Tech, this exceptional album of jazz, rock, and fusion compositions is a must for guitarists. —*Paul Kohler*

Nomad / May 1988 / Relativity ◆◆◆◆

Tribal Tech with Gary Willis / Nov. 19, 1990 / Relativity ◆◆◆◆◆
An interesting, sometimes enchanting, blend of technology, aggressive rhythms, and improvisatory zeal. —*Ron Wynn*

★ **Illicit** / Apr. 1992 / Blue Moon ◆◆◆◆◆

Tribal Tech / 1993 / Blue Moon ◆◆◆

Face First / Apr. 1993–May 1993 / Blue Moon ◆◆◆◆

Dog Party / Feb. 1994 / Blue Moon ◆◆◆

Reality Check / Nov. 1994 / Blue Moon ◆◆◆◆

Wayne Henderson

b. Sept. 24, 1929, Houston, TX
Trombone / Soul Jazz, Hard Bop, R&B
Wayne Henderson's trombone teamed up with Wilton Felder's tenor in the Jazz Crusaders to give the group its own trademark sound. A fine hard bop soloist who later in his career chose to become an R&B producer instead, Henderson first played regularly with Felder, Joe Sample and Stix Hooper in Houston in the mid-'50s. By the time they moved to Los Angeles and started recording in 1961 they were known as the Jazz Crusaders. After many records for Pacific Jazz, the group in 1971 changed their name to the Crusaders. With Henderson's decision to quit the band in 1975, the Crusaders lost a great deal of their originality. In the mid-'90s Henderson and Felder had a nostalgic reunion with an enlarged group for a recording on the PAR label. —*Scott Yanow*

Back to the Groove / 1992 / Par ◆◆◆

Jon Hendricks

b. Sep. 16, 1921, Newark, OH
Vocals, Lyricist / Vocalese, Bop
The genius of vocalese, Jon Hendricks' ability to write coherent lyrics to the most complex recorded improvisations is quite notable, as were his contributions to the classic jazz vocal group Lambert, Hendricks and Ross. Hendricks grew up in Toledo, OH, and sang in local radio. After a period in the military (1942–46), he studied law but eventually switched to jazz. He spent a period of time playing drums before becoming active as a lyricist and vocalist. In 1952 his "I Want You to Be My Baby" was recorded by Louis Jordan. In 1957 Hendricks made his recording debut (cutting "Four Brothers" and "Cloudburst" while backed by the Dave Lambert Singers). Soon he teamed up with fellow singers Dave Lambert and Annie Ross to form their vocal trio, starting off with a recreation (through overdubbing) of some of Count Basie's recordings. Lambert, Hendricks and Ross (after 1962 Yolande Bavan took Ross' place) stayed together up to 1964 and they have yet to be topped as a jazz vocal group, influencing those that would follow (including the Manhattan Transfer). In 1960 Hendricks wrote and directed the show *Evolution of the Blues* for the Monterey Jazz Festival; he would revive it several times during the next 20 years. During 1968–73 he lived and worked in Europe. After returning to San Francisco, Hendricks wrote about jazz for the *San Francisco Chronicle*, taught jazz and formed a group with his wife Judith, children Michelle and Eric and other singers (including, for a time, Bobby McFerrin) called the Hendricks Family that is active on a part-time basis up to the present time. Although he never recorded often enough, Hendricks did cut a classic Denon album featuring McFerrin, George Benson, Al Jarreau and himself recreating all the solos in the original version of "Freddie the Freeloader." He also recorded through the years as a leader for World Pacific, Columbia, Smash, Reprise, Arista and, most recently, Telarc. —*Scott Yanow*

A Good Git-Together / Oct. 1959 / World Pacific ◆◆◆◆

Evolution of the Blues / Sep. 21, 1960 / Columbia Special Products ◆◆◆◆
Jazz vocalist and lyricist Jon Hendricks conceived a musical pre-

sentation on jazz history for the 1960 Monterey Jazz Festival and called it "Evolution of the Blues." Columbia subsequently issued this similarly titled album, which features Hendricks' stylized vocals and other presentations linked to the theme. This presentation was revived and presented again in 1975. —*Ron Wynn*

Fast Livin' Blues / Sep. 6, 1961–Sep. 27, 1961 / Columbia ◆◆◆

In Person at the Trident / 1963 / Smash ◆◆◆◆
Dynamic, forceful singing and scatting. —*Ron Wynn*

Cloudburst / Feb. 1972 / Enja ◆◆◆◆

Tell Me the Truth / 1975 / Arista ◆◆◆
Jon Hendricks had not recorded in over a decade when he finally got the chance with Arista. This somewhat obscure effort is quite worthwhile. Hendricks sings eight songs (including "Flat Foot Floogie," "Naima," "On the Trail" and "Blues for Pablo"); all but "Old Folks" have his own lyrics. He is assisted by a fine backup crew and, on "Flat Foot Floogie," The Pointer Sisters. Hendricks is in spirited form throughout this rare LP. —*Scott Yanow*

Love / Aug. 1981–Feb. 1982 / Muse ◆◆◆

★ **Freddie Freeloader** / 1990 / Denon ◆◆◆◆◆
Tour-de-force recording with Bobby McFerrin (v), George Benson (v), Al Jarreau (v), and Manhattan Transfer (v). —*Michael G. Nastos*

● **Boppin' At The Blue Note** / Dec. 23, 1993–Dec. 26, 1993 / Telarc ◆◆◆◆◆
Jon Hendricks, the genius of vocalese (writing words to fit the recorded solos of jazz greats) has long been one of the top lyricists in music. However, the emphasis during the first seven songs of this live CD is on scatting and heated bop-oriented improvising. Hendricks, assisted by Michelle Hendricks, is joined by quite an all-star horn section: trumpeter Wynton Marsalis, trombonist Al Grey, altoist Red Holloway and tenor Benny Golson in addition to a supportive four-piece rhythm section. After a warmup on "Get Me to the Church on Time," Jon Hendricks sings some humorous lyrics on "Do You Call That a Buddy," swings hard on his original boppish "Good Ol' Lady" and gets a bit lowdown on "Contemporary Blues." The biggest surprise of the date is "Everybody's Boppin'" which features scatting by Jon Hendricks, Michele Hendricks and Wynton Marsalis. Wynton is quite effective and typically virtuosic in a manner similar to Dizzy Gillespie. Michele is excellent on an uptempo "Almost Like Being in Love" and "Since I Fell for You," Jon sings the blues on "Roll 'Em Pete" and, together with Kevin Burke and Judith, Michele and Aria Hendricks, performs vocalese versions of three Count Basie charts long ago recorded by Lambert, Hendricks And Ross: recreations of recreations! This is Jon Hendricks' best all-round recording in several years and was one of the finest jazz vocal albums to be released in 1995. —*Scott Yanow*

Ernie Henry

b. Sept. 3, 1926, Brooklyn, NY, **d.** Dec. 29, 1957, New York, NY
Alto Saxophone / Hard Bop
Ernie Henry accomplished a lot in a short period of time before passing away prematurely. He had his own sound although his style was clearly heavily influenced by Charlie Parker. He worked during the bop era with Tadd Dameron (1947), Fats Navarro, Charlie Ventura, Max Roach and the Dizzy Gillespie Orchestra (1948–49). He was with Illinois Jacquet's band (1950–52), maintained a low profile for a few years and in 1956 recorded with Thelonious Monk (the *Brilliant Corners* album), worked with Charles Mingus and toured with Dizzy Gillespie's big band (1956–57) before his death. Ernie Henry led three albums for Riverside during 1956-57. —*Scott Yanow*

Presenting Ernie Henry / Aug. 23, 1956–Aug. 30, 1956 / Original Jazz Classics ◆◆◆◆
This presents an artist who died right at the beginning of his solo career and whose promise has continued to interest listeners ever since. Part of that interest comes from the company he kept on his few recordings; on this 1956 date it was Kenny Dorham (trumpet) and Kenny Drew (piano) with Art Taylor and Wilbur Ware on drums and bass, respectively… This was imperfect and the interplay and exchange between the leader and the group was less than smooth, at times almost awkward. Yet there was music, solos in particular, here, which was rewarding and plenty of what must be heard as the spontaneous creating of jazz to be enjoyed. —*Bob Rusch, Cadence*

● **Last Chorus** / Sep. 23, 1957 / Original Jazz Classics ✦✦✦✦✦
Last Chorus presents Ernie Henry, who died Dec. 29, 1957 at the age of 30. Henry's alto playing combined the exigency of the hard alto sound with the big, scooping delivery more associated with the tenor sax and players like Sonny Rollins; a more deliberate sound than fleet register runs. This record found him leading his own groups or in the company of Kenny Dorham or Thelonious Monk. —*Bob Rusch, Cadence*

Seven Standards and a Blues / Sep. 30, 1957 / Original Jazz Classics ✦✦✦
This was recorded just before Ernie Henry's death. The record was issued posthumously. The main problem here was that the leader's alto playing seemed to lack any great emotional invest-ment in the music, often seemed out of focus and occasionally seemed to make glaring musical missteps, which had his name been Ornette Coleman would have been in brilliant character but here sounded more like unintentional miscues and techni-cal goofs...Wynton Kelly (piano), Wilbur Ware (bass) and Philly Joe Jones (drums) were the rhythm backup. —*Bob Rusch, Cadence*

Deborah Henson-Conant

b. Stockton, CA
Harp / Post-Bop, Crossover
One of the finest (and one of the very few) jazz harpists in the world, Deborah Henson-Conant combines storytelling and vocals in her entertaining show. She played piano from age ten and start-ed doubling on harp when she was 13. It became her main instru-ment while in college and, although classically trained, she also enjoyed improvising. In 1982 she began seriously playing jazz, and the following year started amplifying her harp. In 1989 Henson-Conant was signed to GRP, and she recorded three well-received recordings. She has since toured the world and recorded for Laika (a European company) and her own White Cat compa-ny. —*Scott Yanow*

● **'Round The Corner** / 1987 / Golden Cage ✦✦✦✦✦
From the jazz standpoint, this is harpist Deborah Henson-Conant's strongest CD to date. Released by her private label, the program features Henson-Conant (who is accompanied by bassist John Lockwood and drummer Bob Gullotti) playing melodic ver-sions of six jazz standards (including "Georgia on My Mind," "Take Five" and "Summertime") plus her own "'Round the Corner." Actually, the highpoint is a delightful "Over the Rainbow," which starts out as an extensive medley of songs from *The Wizard of Oz.* Deborah Henson-Conant is one of the very few harpists who can improvise jazz, and this fine set is superior to her better-known (and slightly later) GRP releases. Worth search-ing for. —*Scott Yanow*

On the Rise / Oct. 1988 / GRP ✦✦✦

Caught in the Act / 1990 / GRP ✦✦✦
One of that rare breed known as jazz harpists, Henson-Conant is an underrated player and gifted composer. She doesn't have her full talents tested because this set alternates between more expan-sive, ambitious jazz-based tunes and lighter, Adult Contemporary and pop instrumental fare. But hearing harp in a lead role is inter-esting, no matter the context. —*Ron Wynn*

Talking Hands / 1991 / GRP ✦✦✦

Budapest / 1992 / Unity ✦✦✦✦
This CD from harpist Deborah Henson-Conant is a mix of funky grooves, folk melodies, world music mood pieces and happy jams. Henson-Conant's harp (and occasional voice) shines through the ensembles. The backup crew includes Mark Johnson's tenor and soprano, the co-leaders of Special EFX (guitarist Chieli Minucci and percussionist George Jinda) and bassist Victor Bailey. This atmospheric music (which was actually recorded in Budapest) is one of Henson-Conant's stronger efforts. —*Scott Yanow*

Just For You / Jun. 1, 1994–Jun. 12, 1994 / Laika ✦✦✦✦
Harpist Deborah Henson-Conant teams up with bassist Wolfgang Diekmann and percussionist Davey Tulloch for live versions of ten of her originals. Henson-Conant, who also contributes vocals and humorous introductions, proves to be quite a showperson in addition to being a superior harpist. The music falls somewhere between advanced bop, crossover and even cabaret. No matter what it is called, this release from the German label Laika is col-orful and entertaining, not merely a replay of Henson-Conant's GRP recordings. —*Scott Yanow*

Woody Herman (Woodrow Charles Herman)

b. May 16, 1913, Milwaukee, WI, **d.** Oct. 29, 1987, Los Angeles, CA
Clarinet, Alto Saxophone, Soprano Saxophone, Leader / Swing, Bop, R&B
A fine swing clarinetist, an altoist whose sound was influenced by Johnny Hodges, a good soprano saxophonist and a spirited blues vocalist, Woody Herman's greatest significance to jazz was as the leader of a long line of big bands. He always encouraged young talent and, more than practically any bandleader from the swing era, kept his repertoire quite modern. Although Herman was always stuck performing a few of his older hits (he played "Four Brothers" and "Early Autumn" nightly for nearly 40 years), he much preferred to play and create new music.

Woody Herman began performing as a child, singing in vaude-ville. He started playing saxophone when he was 11, and four years later he was a professional musician. He picked up early experience playing with the big bands of Tom Gerun, Harry Sosnik and Gus Arnheim and then, in 1934, he joined the Isham Jones orchestra. He recorded often with Jones and when the vet-eran bandleader decided to break up his orchestra in 1936, Herman formed one of his own out of the remaining nucleus. The great majority of the early Herman recordings feature the band-leader as a ballad vocalist, but it was the instrumentals that caught on, leading to his group being known as "The Band That Plays the Blues." Woody Herman's "At the Woodchopper's Ball" became his first hit (1939). Herman's early group was actu-ally a minor outfit with a Dixieland feel to many of the looser pieces and fine vocals contributed by Mary Ann McCall in addi-tion to Herman. They recorded very frequently for Decca and for a period had the female trumpeter/singer Billie Rogers as one of its main attractions.

By 1943 the Woody Herman Orchestra was beginning to take its first steps into becoming the Herd (later renamed the First Herd). Herman had recorded an advanced Dizzy Gillespie arrangement ("Down Under") the year before, and during 1943 Herman's band became influenced by Duke Ellington; in fact, Johnny Hodges and Ben Webster made guest appearances on some recordings. It was a gradual process, but by the end of 1944 Woody Herman had what was essentially a brand new orchestra. It was a wild goodtime band with screaming ensembles (pro-pelled by first trumpeter Pete Candoli), major soloists in trom-bonist Bill Harris and tenorman Flip Phillips and a rhythm sec-tion pushed by bassist/cheerleader Chubby Jackson and drummer Dave Tough. In 1945 (with new trumpeters in Sonny Berman and Conte Candoli), the First Herd was considered the most exciting new big band in jazz. Several of the arrangements of Ralph Burns and Neal Hefti are considered classics, and such Herman favorites entered the book as "Apple Honey," "Caldonia," "Northwest Passage," "Bijou" (Harris' memorable if eccentric feature) and the nutty "Your Father's Mustache." Even Igor Stravinsky was impressed and he wrote "Ebony Concerto" for the orchestra to perform in 1946. Unfortunately, family troubles caused Woody Herman to break up the big band at the height of its success in late 1946; it was the only one of his orchestras to really make much money. Herman recorded a bit in the interim and then by mid-1947 had a new orchestra, the Second Herd, which was also soon known as the Four Brothers band. With the three cool-toned tenors of Stan Getz, Zoot Sims and Herbie Steward (who a year later was replaced by Al Cohn) and baritonist Serge Chaloff form-ing the nucleus, this orchestra had a different sound than its more extroverted predecessor, but it could also generate excitement of its own. Trumpeter/arranger Shorty Rogers and eventually Bill Harris returned from the earlier outfit and with Mary Ann McCall back as a vocalist, the group had a great deal of potential. But despite such popular numbers as Jimmy Giuffre's "Four Brothers," "The Goof and I" and "Early Autumn" (the latter ballad made Getz into a star), the band struggled financially. Before its collapse in 1949 such other musicians as Gene Ammons, Lou Levy, Oscar Pettiford, Terry Gibbs and Shelly Manne made important contri-butions.

Next up for Woody Herman was the Third Herd which was sim-ilar to the Second except that it generally played at danceable tempoes and was a bit more conservative. Herman kept that band together during much of 1950–56, even having his own Mars label for a period; Conte Candoli, Al Cohn, Dave McKenna, Phil Urso, Don Fagerquist, Carl Fontana, Dick Hafer, Bill Perkins, Nat

Pierce, Dick Collins and Richie Kamuca were among the many sidemen. After some short-lived small groups (including a sextet with Nat Adderley and Charlie Byrd), Herman's New Thundering Herd was a hit at the 1959 Monterey Jazz Festival. He was able to lead a big band successfully throughout the 1960s, featuring such soloists as high note trumpeter Bill Chase, trombonist Phil Wilson, the reliable Nat Pierce and the exciting tenor of Sal Nistico. Always open to newer styles, Woody Herman's boppish unit gradually became more rock-oriented as he utilized his young sidemen's arrangements, often of current pop tunes (starting in 1968 with an album titled *Light My Fire*). Not all of his albums from this era worked, but one always admired Herman's open-minded attitude. As one of only four surviving jazz-oriented bandleaders from the swing era (along with Duke Ellington, Count Basie and Stan Kenton) who was still touring the world with a big band, Herman welcomed such new talent in the 1970s as Greg Herbert, Andy Laverne, Joe Beck, Alan Broadbent and Frank Tiberi; he also recorded with Chick Corea, had a reunion with Flip Phillips and celebrated his 40th anniversary as a leader with a notable 1976 Carnegie Hall Concert.

Woody Herman returned to emphasizing straight-ahead jazz by the late '70s. By then he was being hounded by the IRS due to an incompetent manager from the 1960s not paying thousands of dollars of taxes out of the sidemen's salaries. Herman, who might very well have taken it easy, was forced to keep on touring and working constantly into his old age. He managed to put on a cheerful face to the public, celebrating his 50th anniversary as a bandleader in 1986. However his health was starting to fail and he gradually delegated most of his duties to Frank Tiberi before his death in 1987. Tiberi still leads a Woody Herman Orchestra on a part-time basis, but it has never had the opportunity to record. Fortunately, Herman was well-documented throughout all phases of his career and his major contributions are still greatly appreciated. — *Scott Yanow*

★ **Blues on Parade** / Apr. 26, 1937–Jul. 24, 1942 / GRP ✦✦✦✦✦
This single CD gives a definitive look at Woody Herman's first orchestra, the Decca ensemble he led during 1936–42 billed "the Band That Plays the Blues." Although he also recorded many vocal ballads during this era, the emphasis here is on hot swing with such highlights as the original version of "Woodchopper's Ball," "Blue Prelude," "Blue Flame," the humorous "Fan It" and two takes of "Blues on Parade." Also heard are performances by Herman's early small combos (the Woodchoppers and the Four Chips) along with a Dizzy Gillespie composition/arrangement ("Down Under") that hints at Woody Herman's future. — *Scott Yanow*

First Session / Sep. 23, 1937 / Circle ✦✦✦
This LP features Herman's first orchestra close to its birth, although its title is not really accurate, since the band had already cut some studio recordings. These are radio transcriptions that are superior to his first Decca records. The leader takes four ballad vocals while the band gets to show off their talents on some of the more jazz-oriented selections. Herman's orchestra had not yet found its own musical personality and would not began to catch on until 1939. This fine LP gives one a look at the Herman legacy near its start. — *Scott Yanow*

The Uncollected Woody Herman and His Orchestra (1937) / Sep. 23, 1937–Nov. 1937 / Hindsight ✦✦✦
These 16 selections are taken from two sessions made for radio transcriptions in 1937; most of the first ten numbers are also included on a Circle LP although the final six date from two months later. Better than many of Herman's commercial Decca recordings of this period, these 16 jazz-oriented performances are generally quite enjoyable with tenorman Saxie Mansfield, fluegelhornist Joe Bishop and trombonist Neil Reid being the main soloists next to clarinetist Herman (who also takes two vocals). — *Scott Yanow*

Big Band Bounce & Boogie / Apr. 12, 1939–Nov. 8, 1943 / Affinity ✦✦✦✦
Prior to the release of *Blues on Parade*, a CD that duplicates eight of these 16 selections, this LP had been the best all-around set of early Woody Herman available. *The Band That Plays the Blues* did not feature any outstanding virtuosoes but was a versatile and enthusiastic outfit that could swing hard when given a chance. On this LP one hears many of the orchestra's best instrumentals along with a few examples of Herman's crooning style. — *Scott Yanow*

Turning Point / Nov. 18, 1943–Dec. 12, 1944 / Decca ✦✦✦
This LP has a very accurate title for, during 1943–44, Woody Herman was searching for a new sound. His "Band That Plays the Blues" had been decimated by the draft, and Herman was in the mood for a change anyway. These 14 selections from his transition year found him welcoming guests from other bands onto his records (including Ben Webster, Juan Tizol and Johnny Hodges from the Duke Ellington Orchestra along with tenormen Georgie Auld and Budd Johnson), going through a brief Ellington phase and then encouraging the gradual emergence of The First Herd. Only five members of Herman's November 1943 orchestra were still with him by the time of the last recording on this set (Dec. 12, 1944). The journey between bands (and the highly enjoyable music that was created along the way) are well worth hearing. — *Scott Yanow*

Woodchopper's Ball, Vol. 1 / Aug. 2, 1944–Oct. 18, 1944 / Jass ✦✦✦✦
1944 was a pivotal year in Herman's career, the year his orchestra gradually evolved into The First Herd, his most exciting band. This CD features music from two radio shows in August (actually rehearsals for the broadcasts) plus performances from two prestigious engagements at the Hotel Pennsylvania in August and the Hollywood Palladium that October. With Flip Phillips' jump tenor and Bill Harris' expressive trombone already emerging as the band's top soloists and Francis Wayne contributing a few fine vocals, Ralph Burns and Neal Hefti were hurriedly putting together colorful arrangements to challenge the young sidemen. The music on this set, which precedes The Herd's first commercial recordings, could be titled *The Birth of the Herd*. Recommended, particularly to serious Woody Herman fans. — *Scott Yanow*

The Uncollected Woody Herman and His First Herd / 1944 / Hindsight ✦✦✦
Hindsight's second LP of Woody Herman broadcasts (the first volume dated from 1937) is actually taken exclusively from rehearsals for radio shows and finds Herman at an important transition in his career. The old "Band That Plays the Blues" was making way for The First Herd; already tenor saxophonist Flip Phillips and trombonist Bill Harris were in place as the key soloists. Other than "Apple Honey," most of the material heard on this LP was in the earlier band's repertoire, so it makes for very interesting listening for those fans only familiar with The First Herd's studio recordings. — *Scott Yanow*

Northwest Passage, Vol. 2 / Feb. 18, 1945–Aug. 22, 1945 / Jass ✦✦✦
Unlike the first volume in this CD series, *Volume 2* does not find The First Herd in transition but instead in its early prime. Taken from five separate radio broadcasts, these live performances are generally colorful and sometimes quite exciting, although there are more vocals than normal. More for First Herd fanatics and completists than for general collectors. — *Scott Yanow*

☆ **Thundering Herds 1945–1947** / Feb. 19, 1945–Dec. 27, 1947 / Columbia ✦✦✦✦✦
Since the definitive three-LP box set *Thundering Herds* is out-of-print, this single CD is the best place for listeners to go first when starting to explore the music of Woody Herman. There are 14 selections from what was arguably his best band, his First Herd, and two numbers (including the original version of "Four Brothers") by The Second Herd. A few rarities (such as "A Jug of Wine" and "The Blues Are Brewing") are mixed in with such classics as "Apple Honey," "Northwest Passage," "Your Father's Mustache" and a new version of "Woodchopper's Ball," but there is unavoidably a lot missing from this single disc, a set which will have to suffice until a more complete reissue series comes along. — *Scott Yanow*

★ **Thundering Herds** / Feb. 19, 1945–Dec. 27, 1947 / Columbia ✦✦✦✦✦
This now out-of-print three-LP box set is still the best compilation to date of Herman's First and Second Herds. These 40 selections (the cream of his Columbia recordings) include many classics such as "Apple Honey," "Caldonia," "Northwest Passage," "Bijou," "Your Father's Moustache," eight numbers from Woody Herman's Woodchoppers, "Let It Snow," a new rendition of "Woodchopper's Ball," the four-part "Summer Sequence" and the original version of "Four Brothers." Even the lesser items on this set are memorable, making this the number one Herman release to own. Why hasn't it been reissued in total on CD yet? — *Scott Yanow*

Best of the Big Bands / Feb. 26, 1945–Dec. 22, 1947 / Columbia
✦✦

This CD reissue of classic material from the First and (in two cases) The Second Herds is a bit of a mess. Despite having chatty liner notes, there are no listings of Herman's sidemen or the exact recording dates. Also, some so-so material is mixed in with a few of The First Herd's greatest performances and the whole set is made anonymous by the meaningless title *Best of the Big Bands*. Highlights include "Caldonia," "Laura," "Apple Honey" and "Northwest Passage," so if given a budget price this might serve as a good introduction to Herman, but in general it is advisable to wait until this material comes around again. —*Scott Yanow*

Roadband (1948) / Mar. 1948–May 12, 1948 / Hep ✦✦✦✦

Woody Herman's Second Herd was one of his finest orchestras but, unlike The First Herd, it was a money loser and the Musicians Union strike of 1948 kept it off commercial recordings for much of that important year. Fortunately, a few LPs of broadcasts (including this one) show just how strong a unit it was. With solos by the likes of tenors Stan Getz, Zoot Sims and Al Cohn and baritonist Serge Caloff (who together formed the "Four Brothers" that year) plus the vocals of Woody Herman and Mary Ann McCall made this a memorable outfit, who play at their best on this set imported from Scotland. It is a particular joy to hear The Second Herd performing so much material that they otherwise never recorded. —*Scott Yanow*

★ **Keeper of the Flame: Complete Capitol Recordings** / Dec. 29, 1948–Jul. 21, 1949 / Capitol ✦✦✦✦✦

Subtitled *The Complete Capitol Recordings of the Four Brothers Band*, this CD contains 19 selections from Herman's Second Herd, including three songs never before released. Top-heavy with major soloists (including trumpeters Red Rodney and Shorty Rogers, trombonist Bill Harris, tenors Al Cohn, Zoot Sims, Stan Getz and Gene Ammons and vibraphonist Terry Gibbs, not to mention Herman himself) this boppish band may have cost the leader a small fortune, but they created timeless music. Highlights include "Early Autumn" (a ballad performance that made Stan Getz a star), the riotous "Lemon Drop" and Gene Ammons' strong solo on "More Moon." —*Scott Yanow*

Third Herd, Vol. 1 / May 30, 1952–Sep. 11, 1953 / Discovery ✦✦✦

During 1952–53, when Herman's Third Herd had trouble landing a recording contract (big bands were out), he formed his own label, Mars Records. This first of two Discovery LPs contains ten of The Herd's records for Mars and the music is spirited, swinging and a bit safer than the sounds created by the first two Herds. Unfortunately, Discovery has thus far not reissued all of his Mars sides and this LP clocks in at under 29 minutes, but the music is excellent and Woody Herman fans will want it anyway. —*Scott Yanow*

Third Herd, Vol. 2 / May 30, 1952–Mar. 30, 1954 / Discovery ✦✦✦

The second of two LP volumes released by Discovery documents some more of the recordings Herman and his Third Herd made for their own label, Mars Records, during 1952–54. This melodic but swinging orchestra had its share of fine soloists (such as trombonist Carl Fontana and the tenors of Arno Marsh and Bill Perkins) along with fine arrangements from Nat Pierce and Ralph Burns. Unfortunately, this LP only has 31 minutes of music and many of his Mars recordings have been bypassed (they should all be released in chronological order), but more devoted fans will still want it. —*Scott Yanow*

Music for Tired Lovers / Jul. 8, 1954 / Columbia ✦✦✦

In 1954 Woody Herman recorded one of his most unusual sets, a purely vocal album in which he was accompanied by the Erroll Garner Trio. Herman, who originally sang on half of his band's recordings, was always an expressive ballad singer and he does a fine job on such standards as "My Melancholy Baby," "Let's Fall in Love" and "I'm Beginning to See the Light." The humorous photo on this out-of-print LP is an extra bonus. —*Scott Yanow*

The Woody Herman Band / Sep. 1954 / Capitol ✦✦✦✦

When Herman originally formed his Third Herd in 1950 (after the financial collapse of The Second Herd), he put the emphasis on music for the dancing public first and the jazz public second. However, the jazz content was always strong and, by 1954, the band was less shy to swing hard. This hard-to-find LP was one of that orchestra's finest recordings, a strong all-around set highlighted by the flag-waver "Wild Apple Honey," several Ralph Burns arrangements and solos by such fine players as tenors Bill

Perkins and Dick Hafer, Cy Touff's bass trumpet, Jack Nimitz's baritone (featured on "Sleep") and Herman's alto and clarinet. —*Scott Yanow*

Road Band / Oct. 13, 1954–Jun. 7, 1955 / Capitol ✦✦✦

This out-of-print LP finds Herman's Third Herd in its prime. Rather than just revisiting his celebrated past, he and his orchestra primarily perform then-recent material, much of it arranged by Ralph Burns. Highlights include a big-band version of Horace Silver's "Opus De Funk," Burns' "Cool Cat on a Hot Tin Roof," "I Remember Duke" and Bill Holman's reworking of "Where or When." With tenors Richie Kamuca and Dick Hafer, trumpeter Dick Collins and bass trumpeter Cy Touff as the main soloists, The Third Herd had developed into a particularly strong unit by the mid-'50s. —*Scott Yanow*

Herd Rides Again / Jul. 30, 1958–Aug. 1, 1958 / Evidence ✦✦✦

This CD contains a better-than-expected reunion of Herman's First Herd. Actually, many of the key players from that classic band (such as tenorman Flip Phillips and trombonist Bill Harris) were not on this date while some of the musicians who did participate were Hermanites from a later era or (in the case of trombonist Bob Brookmeyer and tenor saxophonist Sam Donahue) had never been a part of his bands before. Because the music was generally only a decade old, the results are quite satisfying, with fresh solos and spirited ensembles giving new life to such numbers as "Northwest Passage," "Caldonia" and "Blowin' up a Storm," among others. Certainly Brookmeyer's playing on "Bijou" will not remind anyone of Bill Harris. —*Scott Yanow*

Woody Herman, Vol. 3 / Jul. 30, 1958–Dec. 26, 1958 / Everest ✦✦

This budget LP combines six selections from a First Herd reunion (all of which are included on the Evidence CD *The Herd Rides Again*) with four numbers that feature a Herman-led studio orchestra with acoustic guitarist Charlie Byrd cast as the main soloist. The liner notes are pretty useless and do not give a personnel listing so this LP is not one of Herman's essential releases, but the music (from 1958) is generally pleasing and swinging. —*Scott Yanow*

Herman's Heat and Puente's Beat / Aug, 1958 / Evidence ✦✦✦✦

Tito Puente and Woody Herman teamed in 1958 for a mutually satisfying meeting in the same way that Charlie Parker, Dizzy Gillespie, and Machito found commond ground in the late '40s. Puente's Latin rhythms and beats meshed with the swing and bebop of Herman's band on half of the disc's cuts, and the results were hot and delightful. With Puente heading the rhythm section and playing timbales, Robert Rodriquez on bass, and assorted percussion from Gilbert Lopez, Raymond Rodriquez, and Ray Barretto, the band stays locked into the Latin groove while the saxophonists and trumpeters weave in, out, and around the beat. There are also more conventional Herman swing numbers such as "Blue Station" and "Woodchopper's Ball," where the standard Herman stomping sound is in effect. —*Ron Wynn*

The Fourth Herd & The New World of Woody Herman / Jul. 31, 1959–Dec. 27, 1962 / Mobile Fidelity ✦✦✦

This CD is quite a bit different than most audiophile releases, for it contains rare rather than famous recordings. 1959's *The Fourth Herd* (which features an all-star group of studio musicians and Woody Herman alumni along with his octet of the time) was only put out briefly by Jazzland while the music on 1962's *The New World of Woody Herman* was never available commercially before; both were originally cut for the SESAC Transcribed Library and were available only to selected radio stations on a subscription basis. The earlier session has solo spots for tenors Zoot Sims, Al Cohn and Don Lanphere, trumpeters Nat Adderley and Red Rodney, vibraphonist Eddie Costa and Herman on clarinet, a bit of alto and two vocals; Cohn and pianist Nat Pierce wrote most of the colorful and diverse arrangements. By the later session (which has charts by Pierce, Gene Roland, Phil Wilson and Bill Chase), Woody Herman once again was leading an exciting big band of his own. Trombonist Phil Wilson, Duke Ellington's tenor Paul Gonsalves (filling in for the temporarily absent Sal Nistico) and Herman are the solo stars and (as with the first date) the music swings hard and contains its share of surprises. —*Scott Yanow*

Live at Monterey / Oct. 3, 1959 / Atlantic ✦✦✦✦

Woody Herman returned to the big-band wars in 1959 with these two very successful appearances at the Monterey Jazz Festival. His new band featured such major players as trumpeter Conte

Candoli, trombonist Urbie Green, acoustic guitarist Charlie Byrd and a sax section comprised of tenors Zoot Sims, Bill Perkins and Richie Kamuca, Don Lanphere on alto and tenor and baritonist Med Flory in addition to Herman himself. The all-star orchestra romps happily through "Four Brothers," "Monterey Apple Tree" and "Skoobeedoobee," and Urbie Green is well-featured on the ballad "Skylark" and "The Magpie." Excellent music that signalled a "comeback" for Woody Herman. — *Scott Yanow*

Woody Herman (1963) / Oct. 15, 1962–Oct. 16, 1962 / Philips ◆◆◆◆
In 1962 Woody Herman signed a contract with Philips and went on to record some of the finest big-band albums of his long career. Unfortunately, all are currently out-of-print (none have yet appeared on CD), but most are well worth searching for. This version of Herman's Thundering Herd featured high-note trumpet work by Bill Chase, trombonist Phil Wilson, pianist Nat Pierce and the exciting tenor of Sal Nistico. Highpoints of this fine LP are "Sister Sadie" and "Camel Walk." — *Scott Yanow*

Encore: Woody Herman (1963) / May 19, 1963–May 21, 1963 / Philips ◆◆◆◆
Herman led one of his finest orchestras during 1962–66, a hard-swinging outfit filled with enthusiastic young players such as high-note trumpeter Bill Chase, trombonist Phil Wilson and the exciting tenor of Sal Nistico. The LP *Encore* has quite a few high-lights, including the uptempo blues "That's Where It Is," a Nat Pierce arrangement of Herbie Hancock's "Watermelon Man" and Charles Mingus' "Better Git It in Your Soul" and a remake of "Caldonia." Excellent music that deserves to be reissued on CD. — *Scott Yanow*

Woody's Big Band Goodies / May 21, 1963–Sep. 9, 1964 / Philips ◆◆◆
Herman's Swingin' Herd of the early-to-mid '60s was one of his finest big bands, an ensemble that could compare well with his historic First And Second Herds. Their series of LPs on Philips (all now out-of-print and well deserving of a complete reissue on CD) are consistently exciting. *Big Band Goodies* consists of some "left-overs" from Encore and three newer selections from 1964. Actually, the older tracks are on the same high level as those issued previously. No band with such soloists as trumpeters Bill Chase and Dusko Goykovich, trombonist Phil Wilson and the exciting tenor Sal Nistico, not to mention arrangements by pianist Nat Pierce and a rhythm section propelled by drummer Jake Hanna should be taken for granted. *Big Band Goodies* finds this orchestra interpreting some older tunes ("Sidewalks of Cuba," "Bijou" and "Apple Honey"), Thelonious Monk's "Blue Monk," and the well-titled "Wailin' in the Woodshed" with equal success. — *Scott Yanow*

Woody Herman (1964) / Nov. 20, 1963–Nov. 23, 1963 / Philips ◆◆◆◆
All of Woody Herman's recordings for Philips (which, regrettably, remain out-of-print and unissued on CD) are excellent. He was leading one of the finest orchestras of his long career, playing both current and older tunes with creativity (helped out greatly by Nat Pierce's arrangements) and featuring such talented soloists as trumpeter Bill Chase, trombonist Phil Wilson and tenor great Sal Nistico. The release ranges from "Deep Purple" and "After You've Gone" to Oscar Peterson's "Halleluah Time" and even "A Taste of Honey"; everything works. — *Scott Yanow*

Swinging Herman Herd, Recorded Live / Sep. 9, 1964 / Philips ◆◆◆
The Swingin' Herd of the early-to-mid-'60s was one of his great orchestras. This live LP, the final one of Herman's consistently exciting Philips releases, has particularly diverse material with many pop tunes of the era represented. Although Joe Carroll's two vocals and "Everybody Loves Somebody Sometime" were not the band's most significant moments, there are other performances on this set (particularly "Bedroom Eyes," "Just Squeeze Me" and "Dr. Wong's Blues") that compensate. — *Scott Yanow*

My Kind of Broadway / Nov. 27, 1964–Mar. 13, 1965 / Columbia ◆◆◆
Herman's Swinging Herd of the '60s was so successful they were signed up by their old label, Columbia. Their first CBS release (which, like the others, has yet to be reissued on CD) features jazz interpretations of a dozen songs that debuted in Broadway shows. There are some fine solos and the arrangements try hard but some of the selections (such as "Who Can I Turn To?," "My

Favorite Things" and "The Sound of Music") sound out of context in this setting. Nice music but not too essential. — *Scott Yanow*

Woody's Winners / Jun. 28, 1965–Jun. 30, 1965 / Columbia ◆◆◆◆◆
Of the many exciting recordings by The Swinging Herd of the '60s, this is the definitive set. With such soloists as trumpeters Bill Chase, Dusko Goykovich and Don Rader and tenors Sal Nistico, Andy McGhee and Gary Klein, this orchestra rarely had any diffi-culty raising the temperature. Recorded live at Basin Street West in late June of 1965, this set finds the enthusiastic band featuring a three-way trumpet battle on "23 Red," reworking "Northwest Passage" (highlighted by Sal Nistico's long tenor solo) and romp-ing on a lengthy version of "Opus De Funk" along in addition to interpreting a few ballads and blues. This is a very memorable LP that deserves to be reissued on CD so it can be in every jazz col-lector's library. — *Scott Yanow*

Jazz Hoot / Jun. 28, 1965–Mar. 23, 1967 / Columbia ◆◆◆
This collector's LP includes unissued and rare items by Herman's Swingin' Herd of the '60s. Several selections (including "Hallelujah Time," "Watermelon Man" and "Greasy Sack Blues") are alternate versions of tunes released on other albums and a couple others ("The Duck" and "Boopsie") originally came out as singles featuring guitarist Charlie Byrd. All in all, a nice set of music that wraps up Herman's '60s recordings for Columbia. — *Scott Yanow*

The Jazz Swinger / Feb. 28, 1966–Jun. 10, 1966 / Columbia ◆
Apparently, the same Columbia executives who tried to get Miles Davis to record an album of forgettable melodies from the film *Dr. Doolittle* and were unsuccessful in persuading Thelonious Monk to record Beatles songs somehow talked Woody Herman into singing songs associated with Al Jolson. Not only did Herman have a much different singing style than Jolson, but many of the dated lyrics were embarrassing even 30 years ago. As for the arrangements for the orchestra, the more modern they were, the cornier they sounded (particularly Bill Holman's modernization of "Swanee" and "Toot, Toot, Tootsie"). What a mess! The only likable part about this misfire is the album drawing of Herman singing while down on one knee like Jolson; fortunately, he was not drawn in blackface. — *Scott Yanow*

Live in Seattle / 1967 / Moon ◆◆◆
The 1967 edition of Woody Herman's Orchestra is captured live in concert on this well-recorded European import. With fine playing from tenor saxophonist Sal Nistico, baritonist Ronnie Cuber, pianist John Hicks and high-note trumpeter Bill Chase, this is an excellent all-round showcase for the band. Some tunes are stronger than others with "Greasy Sack Blues" and "Jumpin' Blue" highpoints although "Make Someone Happy" and the funky "Hush" are more routine. To Herman's credit, "Four Brothers" is the only one of his older songs to be reprised on this interesting set; the leader sounds good on clarinet, alto and soprano. — *Scott Yanow*

Concerto for Herd / Sep. 1967 / Verve ◆◆◆
1967 found the Woody Herman Orchestra in transition. While tenor saxophonist Sal Nistico and trombonist Carl Fontana were the biggest names, trumpeter Luis Gasca and pianist Albert Daily were up and coming players. This LP, recorded live at the tenth-annual Monterey Jazz Festival, features the sidelong "Concert for Herd," an adventurous work by Bill Holman. In addition, there are three shorter pieces that find Herman and his musicians explor-ing a variety of music including a boogaloo and a feature for Herman's soprano sax ("The Horn of the Fish"). This fine all-around set has been long out-of-print. — *Scott Yanow*

Light My Fire / Oct. 1968 / Cadet ◆◆

Somewhere / May 1969 / Moon ◆◆

Heavy Exposure / Sep. 2, 1969–Sep. 17, 1969 / Cadet ◆◆

Woody / Jul. 29, 1970–Jul. 30, 1970 / Cadet ◆◆

Brand New / Mar. 1971 / Fantasy ◆◆◆
Of all of the big bandleaders who emerged during the swing era, Herman had always been the most receptive toward keeping his music modern and attuned to the music younger people were lis-tening to. This unusual LP found him welcoming the great elec-tric blues guitarist Mike Bloomfield to the band for three num-bers. The other selections include new originals, Ivory Joe Hunter's "I Almost Lost My Mind" and "After Hours." Keyboardist Alan Broadbent arranged most of the material, although Nat

Pierce's chart on "After Hours" was most memorable. With Woody Herman taking a couple of vocals and soloing on clarinet, soprano and alto, this early-'70s release was a surprise success. — *Scott Yanow*

The Raven Speaks / Aug. 28, 1972–Aug. 30, 1972 / Original Jazz Classics ✦✦✦✦✦
The best of his Fantasy releases of the '70s, this well-rounded CD is highlighted by a great jam on "Reunion at Newport" and strong soloing from Herman (on soprano and clarinet), pianist Harold Danko, trumpeter Bill Stapleton and the tenors of Gregory Herbert and Frank Tiberi. The Herman orchestra performs a couple of modern ballads ("Alone Again Naturally" and "Summer of '42"), some blues and a few swinging numbers, showing off their versatility with expertise and spirit. — *Scott Yanow*

Giant Steps / Apr. 9, 1973–Apr. 12, 1973 / Original Jazz Classics ✦✦✦✦
Woody Herman always went out of his way during his long career to encourage younger players, often persuading them to write arrangements of recent tunes for his orchestra. On this LP one gets to hear his band interpret such selections as Chick Corea's "La Fiesta," Leon Russell's "A Song for You," "Freedom Jazz Dance," "A Child Is Born" and "Giant Steps"; what other bandleader from the '30s would have performed such modern material? With strong solo work from tenors Gregory Herbert and Frank Tiberi, trumpeter Bill Stapleton and Herman himself, this is an impressive effort. — *Scott Yanow*

Feelin' So Blue / Apr. 11, 1973–Jan. 7, 1975 / Fantasy ✦✦✦
This LP has a variety of recordings Herman cut for Fantasy during 1973–75 that had not found a place on his other releases. There are some good moments (notably "Brotherhood of Man"), but nothing all that memorable occurs. This is an average release from a jazz institution. — *Scott Yanow*

Thundering Herd / Jan. 2, 1974–Jan. 4, 1974 / Original Jazz Classics ✦✦✦
Woody Herman went out of his way to interpret current material and keep his orchestra young, enthusiastic and modern. For this Fantasy date (reissued on CD in the OJC series), Herman's band not only plays two John Coltrane songs, but material from Frank Zappa ("America Drinks and Goes Home"), Stanley Clarke ("Bass Folk Song") and even Carole King ("Corazon"). This is one of Herman's most successful efforts of the period, for the arrangements (by Alan Broadbent, Bill Stapleton and Tony Klatka) are inventive and generally swinging, with such soloists as Frank Tiberi on tenor, fluegelhornist Klatka and electric keyboardist Andy Laverne keeping the music continually interesting. "Blues for Poland," "Lazy Bird" and the Zappa piece are high points. — *Scott Yanow*

Children of Lima / Oct. 22, 1974–Jan. 8, 1975 / Fantasy ✦✦✦

King Cobra / Jan. 7, 1975–Jan. 9, 1975 / Fantasy ✦✦
As the years passed and Woody Herman continued to age, his orchestra's music stayed young and contemporary. Never willing to have a mere nostalgia band, he continued looking ahead for new music without lowering his standards. On this LP from 1975, the big band performs an excellent version of Chick Corea's "Spain," explores material by Tom Scott and Stevie Wonder and sounds fine on "Come Rain or Come Shine." Herman's vocal on "Jazzman" does not come off so well, but occasional misfires are excused when one considers how many chances he took during his productive career. — *Scott Yanow*

40th Anniversary Carnegie Hall Concert / Nov. 20, 1976 / Bluebird ✦✦✦✦
To celebrate his 40th anniversary as a bandleader, Herman had a celebrated concert at Carnegie Hall. For the first half of the program he welcomed back many of his alumni including such veterans as tenors Flip Phillips, Stan Getz, Zoot Sims, Jimmy Giuffre and Al Cohn, the Candoli brothers, trombonist Phil Wilson and singer Mary Ann McCall. Overall, the concert served as a loving tribute to a major jazz figure. The only major flaw was Herman's tendency to call out soloist's names before they finished playing, pretty much ruining this version of "Four Brothers." It was originally available as a two-LP set although the first half has since been reissued on this CD. — *Scott Yanow*

Lionel Hampton Presents Woody Herman / 1977 / Who's Who In Jazz ✦✦✦
This LP contains a rare small-group session from late in his career. Switching between clarinet, soprano and alto, Herman is

the lead voice throughout these five extended jams on standards. Joined by a six-piece rhythm section including vibraphonist Lionel Hampton, pianist Roland Hanna and guitarist Al Caiola, he is in fine form on this fun session. — *Scott Yanow*

Road Father / Jan. 3, 1978+Jan. 4, 1978 / Century ✦✦✦✦

Woody Herman and Flip Phillips / Jan. 5, 1978 / Century ✦✦✦
Over 30 years after The First Herd broke up, Flip Phillips had a reunion with Woody Herman for this LP. The emphasis is on ballads and Phillips plays beautifully throughout, but this set lacks variety (only "There Is No Greater Love" is taken at a medium pace). Still, within its limitations and with the orchestra itself mostly playing a supporting role, Phillips and Herman (the latter particularly on alto) blend very well together on this pretty music. — *Scott Yanow*

Plays Chick, Donald, Walter and Woodrow / Jan. 25, 1978–Jan. 26, 1978 / Century ✦✦✦
In keeping with his policy of featuring his orchestra on modern material, Herman had his band play compositions by Chick Corea (the three movements of "Suite for a Hot Band") and the team of Donald Fagen and Walter Becker (co-leaders of Steely Dan). In reality, the orchestra's solos are more impressive than the compositions with Tom Scott taking a couple of guest spots and the other strong voices including Joe Lovano and Frank Tiberi on tenors, baritonist Bruce Johnstone and Herman himself on soprano and clarinet. It's a worthy, but not particularly memorable, effort. — *Scott Yanow*

Woody and Friends at the Monterey Jazz Festival / Sep. 1979 / Concord Jazz ✦✦✦✦
Recorded live at the 1979 Monterey Jazz Festival, Herman and his Young Thundering Herd welcomed trumpeters Woody Shaw and Dizzy Gillespie and trombonist Slide Hampton to the bandstand for "Woody 'n You" and "Manteca," and featured guest Stan Getz on a typically beautiful rendition of "What Are You Doing the Rest of Your Life?" The other side of this LP finds The Herd sounding in spirited form on four standards with baritonist Gary Smulyan and tenor saxophonist Frank Tiberi (who doubles on bassoon during "Caravan") taking solo honors. — *Scott Yanow*

Presents, Vol. 1: A Concord Jam / Aug. 1980 / Concord Jazz ✦✦✦✦

Live in Chicago / Mar. 6, 1981 / Status ✦✦✦

Woody Herman Presents . . . , Vol. 2: Four Others / Jul. 1981 / Concord Jazz ✦✦✦✦
The second of three sets that find Herman presenting all-star groups, this one is quite a saxophone summit. The tenors of Al Cohn, Sal Nistico, Bill Perkins and Flip Phillips (referred to as "Four Others" because none of them were on the original recording of "Four Brothers" and each played with a different Herd) and a strong rhythm section form an exciting septet. Al Cohn's arrangements perfectly set up the soloists on these attractive jam tunes. Herman only actually appears on one song, joining the group on alto for "Tenderly," but he must have enjoyed seeing his alumni all still playing at their prime. — *Scott Yanow*

The Live at Concord Jazz Festival (1981) / Aug. 15, 1981 / Concord Jazz ✦✦✦
The Woody Herman Orchestra is in fine form during this live performance from the 1981 Concord Jazz Festival. Other than trumpeter Bill Stapleton, none of the sidemen are all that well-known over a decade later, but they played very well as an ensemble and there are some worthwhile solos on the varied material. Al Cohn guests on "Things Ain't What They Used to Be" and a spirited "Lemon Drop" while the great Stan Getz steals solo honors on "The Dolphin." — *Scott Yanow*

World Class / Sep. 1982 / Concord Jazz ✦✦✦
As with most of the Woody Herman Orchestra's recordings for Concord, this set (taken from concerts in Japan) welcomes guests from Herman's past. In this case, tenors Al Cohn, Med Flory, Sal Nistico and Flip Phillips get to star on half of the eight selections including a remake of "Four Brothers" and Phillips' "The Claw." Phillips has an opportunity to reprise his famous *Jazz at the Philharmonic* solo on "Perdido." The regular Herman sidemen do not sound as distinctive in comparison, but they play quite well on these attractive arrangements, four of them by pianist John Oddo. — *Scott Yanow*

Presents, Vol. 3: Great American Evening / Apr. 1983 / Concord Jazz ✦✦✦✦
The third and final LP volume in the *Woody Herman Presents*

series finds him leading an all-star band, playing clarinet and taking rare late-period vocals on "I've Got the World on a String" and "Caldonia." Actually, there are almost too many talents to hear from during this set, including tenor saxophonist Scott Hamilton, trombonist George Masso, trumpeter/vocalist Jack Sheldon (who does a funny bit on "Leopard-Skin Pill-Box Hat)," Japanese clarinetist Eii Kitamura and even whistler Ron McCroby. It all works somehow on this happy set of swinging music. —*Scott Yanow*

Fiftieth Anniversary Tour / Mar. 1986 / Concord Jazz ♦♦♦♦♦
This set, which is the best of the Woody Herman Orchestra's Concord recordings, celebrates his 50th year as a bandleader, quite an accomplishment. No guest stars are needed for this set, which shows just how strong a big band he still had. With tenor saxophonist Frank Tiberi gradually taking over leadership duties (today he leads the ghost Woody Herman Orchestra) and trombonist John Fedchock contributing the arrangements, the band was in fine shape even if the leader was aging. Whether it be "It Don't Mean a Thing," John Coltrane's "Central Park West" (a great arrangement) or Don Grolnick's "Pools," every selection is excellent. —*Scott Yanow*

Woody's Gold Star / Mar. 1987 / Concord Jazz ♦♦♦♦
Herman's final recording, made just weeks before his health began to seriously fail, is actually quite good. With future leader Frank Tiberi contributing some strong tenor solos, John Fedchock writing some colorful arrangements for a varied program (ranging from "Rose Room" and "'Round Midnight" to Chick Corea's "Samba Song"), and three guest percussionists on some of the pieces, this is an enjoyable release. Herman takes short solos on three of the pieces, recorded approximately 50 years after he formed his first successful big band. This serves as a fine closer to a significant career. —*Scott Yanow*

Vincent Herring

b. Nov. 19, 1964, Hopkinsville, NY
Alto Saxophone / Hard Bop
It was only fitting that Vincent Herring gained his first important recognition playing with Nat Adderley for his sound is strongly influenced by his idol, Cannonball Adderley. Born in Kentucky and raised in California, Herring moved to New York in 1983 and played with a variety of major musicians (including Lionel Hampton, David Murray, Horace Silver and Art Blakey) before joining Adderley (1987-93). Vincent Herring, who has recorded for Landmark and Music Masters, has led his own group since the early '90s. —*Scott Yanow*

American Experience / Oct. 12, 1989 / Music Masters ♦♦♦
The emerging alto saxophonist reveals his debt to Cannonball Adderley and Charlie Parker. Good tone, lots of potential. —*Ron Wynn*

Evidence / Jun. 29, 1990-Jul. 2, 1990 / Landmark ♦♦♦♦
A much sharper, clearer statement than his other release. The compositions are better and the music is more dynamic. —*Ron Wynn*

Dawnbird / Oct. 31, 1991-Feb. 7, 1992 / Landmark ♦♦♦♦♦
Alto saxophonist Vince Herring has steadily developed his own tart, bluesy sound, emerging from the shadow of prime influence Cannonball Adderley. There is more spark, ambition and drive in his playing on this release than any previous date; he tries new things on each number and isn't afraid to stretch out. He is working with two bands and is consistently excellent with both units, and his sparkling sound overcomes the difference in quality between groups and makes this by far his best release. —*Ron Wynn*

● **Secret Love** / 1993 / Music Masters ♦♦♦♦♦
Altoist Vincent Herring's release is an impressive effort. Although he still sounds fairly close to Cannonball Adderley at times, Herring is continuing to develop as a fine modern bop stylist. Accompanied by a strong rhythm section (pianist Renee Rosnes, bassist Ira Coleman and drummer Billy Drummond), Rosnes explores Kenny Barronis "And Then Again" and eight standards including Jobim's lesser-known "If You Never," John Lewis' "Skating in Central Park" and Billy Strayhorn's lyrical "Chelsea Bridge." —*Scott Yanow*

Folklore / Nov. 26, 1993-Nov. 28, 1993 / Music Masters ♦♦♦♦

Don't Let It Go / Oct. 11, 1994-Oct. 12, 1994 / Music Masters ♦♦♦♦

Fred Hersch

b. Cincinnati, OH
Piano / Post-Bop
A superior soloist, accompanist and interpreter of ballads, Fred

Hersch started playing piano when he was four. He moved to New York in 1977 and has worked as a sideman with many players including Stan Getz, Joe Henderson, Toots Thielemans, Art Farmer, Jane Ira Bloom, Eddie Daniels and Janis Siegel in addition to leading his own groups. During 1980-86 he taught at the New England Conservatory and has since been on the faculty of the New School. In addition Hersch has recorded extensively as a leader including for Sunnyside, Concord, Angel/EMI, Red and Chesky. —*Scott Yanow*

Horizons / Oct. 1984 / Concord Jazz ♦♦♦♦
Trio. This session has an adventurous quality and sensibility. —*Ron Wynn*

Sarabande / Dec. 4, 1986-Dec. 5, 1986 / Sunnyside ♦♦♦♦

E.T.C. / May 19, 1988 / Red ♦♦♦

The French Collection / 1989 / Angel ♦♦♦

Heartsongs / Dec. 4, 1989-Dec. 5, 1989 / Sunnyside ♦♦♦♦♦

Forward Motion / Jul. 22, 1991-Jul. 23, 1991 / Chesky ♦♦♦
Fred Hersch Group. This is a release that has components of jazz, chamber, and new-age. The playing is better and more consistent than the material. —*Ron Wynn*

Red Square Blue: Jazz Impressions of Classical ... / Sep. 1, 1992-Oct. 1, 1992 / Angel ♦♦♦

Dancing in the Dark / Dec. 1992 / Chesky ♦♦♦♦♦

Live at Maybeck Recital Hall, Vol. 31 / Oct. 1993 / Concord Jazz ♦♦♦
Hersch downplays his own compositions, including only two of his pieces among the 11-song program. Hersch sparkles on Thelonious Monk's "In Walked Bud," nicely conveying its unpredictable flavor and quick-shifting harmonic flair. He's equally effective on Ornette Coleman's "Ramblin," communicating a mood somewhere between frenetic and calculating. He's quite proficient on the shopworn standards "Embraceable You," "Body and Soul," and "You Don't Know What Love Is," but frankly it's more rewarding to hear Fred Hersch tackling his own work or exploring the ambitious fare of Monk or Coleman than putting his stamp on great songs that have been done many times. —*Ron Wynn*

★ **Fred Hersch Trio Plays ...** / Feb. 16, 1994-Feb. 17, 1994 / Chesky ♦♦♦♦♦

Passion Flower / 1995 / Concord Jazz ♦♦♦♦

Point In Time / Mar. 20, 1995-Mar. 24, 1995 / Enja ♦♦♦♦

Eddie Heywood

b. Dec. 4, 1915, Atlanta, GA **d.** Jan. 2, 1989, Miami Beach, FL
Piano / Swing, Pop
The Eddie Heywood Sextet was very popular in the mid-'40s, playing melodic and tightly arranged versions of swing standards. Heywood's father, Eddie Heywood, Sr., was a strong jazz pianist of the 1920s who often accompanied Butterbeans and Susie. He taught piano to his son who played professionally when he was 14. Heywood, Jr. performed with bands led by Wayman Carver (1932), Clarence Love (1934-37) and, after moving to New York, Benny Carter (1939-40). Heywood led his own group from that period on, backing Billie Holiday on a few occasions starting in 1941. In 1943 Eddie Heywood took several classic solos on a Coleman Hawkins quartet date (most notably "The Man I Love") and put together his first sextet, which also included Doc Cheatham and Vic Dickenson. Their 1944 version of "Begin the Beguine" became a hit and three years of strong success followed. During 1947-50 Heywood was stricken with a partial paralysis of his hands and could not play at all. He made a gradual comeback in the 1950s, mostly performing watered-down commercial music in addition to composing the standard "Canadian Sunset." Despite a second attack of paralysis in the late '60s, Eddie Heywood continued performing into the 1980s. —*Scott Yanow*

John Hicks

b. Dec. 21, 1941, Atlanta, GA
Piano / Post-Bop, Hard Bop
A versatile pianist who is able to retain his own personality whether playing hard bop, free or anything in between, John Hicks has recorded many records throughout his career, both as a leader and as a sideman. After studying music at Lincoln University in Missouri, Hicks attended Berklee and started work-

ing as a freelance musician. He moved to New York in 1963 and was a member of Art Blakey's Jazz Messengers (1964–66) and the groups of Betty Carter (1966–68) and Woody Herman (1968–70). He later worked again with Blakey (1973) and Carter (1975–80) in addition to recording with Oliver Lake, Lester Bowie, Charles Tolliver and Chico Freeman (1978–79). From the early '80s on, Hicks has led his own trio and worked regularly with David Murray, Arthur Blythe, Pharoah Sanders and others. As a leader John Hicks has recorded for Strata-East, Theresa, Limetree, DIW, Timeless, Red Baron, Concord, Evidence, Novus, Reservoir, Mapleshade and Landmark among others. —*Scott Yanow*

Some Other Time / Apr. 14, 1981 / Evidence ✦✦✦

In Concert / Aug. 1984 / Evidence ✦✦✦✦
Pianist John Hicks is alternately calm and aggressive, laid back and attacking on this '84 set newly reissued by Evidence with two bonus cuts. He nicely supports and buttresses Elise Wood's flute on "Say It (Over and Over Again)," adding a delicate voice solo. Bobby Hutcherson's outstanding vibes solo on "Paul's Pal" brings an added bonus, while bassist Walter Booker and drummer Idris Muhammad handle their roles with tact and skill, particularly Muhammad, who sometimes adds light textures and touches and at other times contributes sparks and excitement. —*Ron Wynn*

Sketches of Tokyo / Apr. 11, 1985 / DIW ✦✦✦✦

Luminous / Jul. 31, 1985+Sep. 1985 / Evidence ✦✦✦✦
While he is regarded as being among the finest and most intense jazz pianists currently active, John Hicks is also quite versatile. He has a reflective, lyrical bent throughout the 11 songs on this '88 date. Flutist Elise Wood's entrancing, superbly played solos almost demanded that things be less vigorous and more introspective, but the session was not devoid of energy. Hicks offered soothing melodies and warm, lush solos showing that he could be equally outstanding as a complementary/supporting player. The same held true for bassist Walter Booker, alternating drummers Jimmy Cobb and Alvin Queen, and special guest tenor saxophonist Clifford Jordan. —*Ron Wynn*

Two of a Kind / Jun. 14, 1986–Aug. 4, 1987 / Evidence ✦✦✦
Pianist John Hicks and bassist Ray Drummond had not worked together often when they recorded the 11 tracks on this '80 session. Neither was the consensus star that they are in the '90s, but they were already accomplished soloists. Their union yielded some superb, distinctive playing on this collection of mostly standards. Hicks nicely outlined the basic melodies, then began probing their structure, reworking and restating, finding his own directions and expressing fresh thoughts without distorting the songs. Drummond's heavy yet sometimes barely audible bass lines were both supportive and compelling, at times contrasting Hicks and at other times establishing its own direction. They were a true duo, each player conscious of the other but able to make his own way. —*Ron Wynn*

Eastside Blues / Apr. 8, 1988 / DIW ✦✦✦✦
This album is explosive and substantive, with Curtis Lundy and Victor Lewis. —*Ron Wynn*

Naima's Love Song / Apr. 8, 1988–Apr. 9, 1988 / DIW ✦✦✦✦
Hicks moves into overdrive. Wonderful alto sax from Bobby Watson. —*Ron Wynn*

★ **Power Trio** / May 10, 1990 / Novus ✦✦✦✦✦

Is That So? / Jul. 10, 1990 / Timeless ✦✦✦✦

● **Live at Maybeck Recital Hall, Vol. 7** / Aug. 1990 / Concord Jazz ✦✦✦✦✦
Rollicking, thoughtful, unpredictable, and eclectic solo piano. —*Ron Wynn*

Friends Old and New / Jan. 14, 1992 / Novus ✦✦✦✦
'92 session with pianist John Hicks playing in various combo settings with some excellent musical associates. Bassist Ron Carter, tenor saxophone dynamo Joshua Redman, trumpeter Clark Terry, trombonist Al Grey, and drummer/vocalist Grady Tate are among the friends who join Hicks for some powerhouse numbers. —*Ron Wynn*

Crazy for You / Apr. 3, 1992 / Red Baron ✦✦✦
Marvelous piano playing in a trio format by John Hicks, featured on this '92 session with bassist Wilbur Bascomb, Jr. and drummer Kenny Washington. Hicks' solos have feeling, force, and depth, and he's adept at anything from reinterpreting standards to provocative originals, hard bop, swing, blues, spirituals, and even ragtime or stride. —*Ron Wynn*

Lover Man: Tribute to Billie Holiday / 1993 / Red Baron ✦✦✦
Pianist John Hicks only actually saw Billie Holiday perform once but was enthusiastic about recording this Lady Day tribute. His renditions of ballads and blues (with only "What a Little Moonlight Can Do" being faster than a medium-tempo pace) are tasteful, relaxed, melodic and somewhat predictable. The music (which also features bassist Ray Drummond and drummer Victor Lewis) is consistently excellent but rarely rises above the level of superior background music, lacking the emotional intensity that Holiday could give these songs. The music is solid but not inspired. —*Scott Yanow*

Beyond Expectations / Sep. 1, 1993 / Reservoir ✦✦✦✦

Single Petal Of A Rose / 1994 / Mapleshade ✦✦✦✦✦

In the Mix / Nov. 13, 1994 / Landmark ✦✦✦✦

J.C. Higginbotham (Jay C. Higginbotham)

b. May 11, 1906, Social Circle, GA, d. May 26, 1973, New York, NY
Trombone / New Orleans Jazz, Swing
An extroverted trombonist with a sound of his own, J.C. Higginbotham was heard at his best during the late '20s/early '30s when he was one of the stars with Luis Russell's Orchestra. From that point on he went gradually downhill due to being an alcoholic, but he had worthy moments along the way. He started his career playing in territory bands in the Midwest. Higginbotham was with Russell (1928–31) for some classic recordings, including a few sessions backing Louis Armstrong and two songs on which he fronted the orchestra under the title of "J.C. Higginbotham and his Six Hicks." Higginbotham was a featured soloist with the orchestras of Fletcher Henderson, Chick Webb and Benny Carter during the next six years before rejoining Russell's band when it was playing a purely supportive role behind Armstrong (1937–40); he had a few solos on Satch's better records of the period. Having teamed up with Red Allen while with Luis Russell, J.C. happily joined Allen's hot jump band for a long stint (1940–47). Higginbotham spent a few years in obscurity, led his own groups in the mid-'50s and rejoined Allen for a residency at the Metropole that lasted until 1963. He led sessions for Sonet (1962) and Jazzology (1966) but continued his decline until his death. —*Scott Yanow*

Higgy Comes Home / Dec. 1966 / Jazzology ✦✦✦✦

Billy Higgins

b. Oct. 11, 1936, Los Angeles, CA
Drums / Hard Bop, Free Jazz
A very adaptable drummer, Billy Higgins came to fame playing with Ornette Coleman's Quartet but proved to be an expert bop player, too. He started his career playing R&B and rock in the Los Angeles area, then teamed up with Don Cherry and James Clay in an unrecorded group called the Jazz Messiahs. In the mid-'50s Higgins started rehearsing with Ornette Coleman. He was on Ornette's first records (starting in 1958), came to New York and played with Coleman during 1959-60 before Ed Blackwell (who was actually his predecessor) replaced him. Higgins and Blackwell were both on Coleman's monumental *Free Jazz* album and Higgins would participate in occasional reunions with Ornette through the years. He kept busy during the 1960s, '70s and '80s, freelancing with a countless number of major players including recordings with Thelonious Monk, Steve Lacy, Sonny Rollins, Lee Morgan, Donald Byrd, Dexter Gordon, Jackie McLean, Hank Mobley, Mal Waldron, Milt Jackson, Art Pepper, Joe Henderson, Pat Metheny and David Murray's big band. From 1966 on, Higgins also often played with Cedar Walton's trio and later with the Timeless All-Stars. Based in Los Angeles during most of the 1980s and '90s, Billy Higgins became an inspiration to younger musicians (including the members of the B Sharp Quartet and Black/Note), opening the World Stage as a performance venue and recording label. —*Scott Yanow*

Soweto / Jan. 21, 1979 / Red ✦✦✦✦
Higgins hasn't been a bandleader on many sessions; this date was one of those rare times, as he headed a quartet on this release (recently reissued on CD) for the Italian Red label. Higgins played with intelligence, drive and style, keeping things rhythmically tight while principal soloist Bob Berg on tenor saxophone displayed his thick tone and versatility on a program of mainstream and hard bop featuring compositions by Higgins (two of the five),

pianist Cedar Walton (two others) and one by Berg himself. This was a welcome entry by a good group that unfortunately didn't work together longer. —*Ron Wynn*

The Soldier / Dec. 3, 1979 / Timeless ✦✦✦
This recording with Cedar Walton (p) presents post-bop standards, well-played. —*Michael G. Nastos*

Bridgework / Jan. 4, 1980–Apr. 23, 1986 / Contemporary ✦✦✦✦
A rare Higgins album, with conservative arrangements and compositions, plus outstanding technique and percussive foundations. —*Ron Wynn*

Once More / May 25, 1980 / Red ✦✦✦

● **Mr. Billy Higgins** / Apr. 12, 1984–May 29, 1984 / RIZA ✦✦✦✦
One of jazz's greatest session drummers got a rare date as a leader on this set, but it was tough to tell that it was Billy Higgins' album. He was in his usual place, driving and pacing the session on drums while soprano and tenor saxophonist Gary Bias took the spotlight on such songs as "Morning Awakening" and "Humility." —*Ron Wynn*

Eddie Higgins

b. Feb. 21, 1932, Cambridge, MA
Piano / Hard Bop, Post-Bop
A solid bop-based pianist, Eddie Higgins has never become a major name, but he has been well-respected by his fellow musicians for decades. After growing up in New England, he moved to Chicago where he played in all types of situations before settling in to a long stint as the leader of the house trio at the London House (1957–69). Higgins moved back to Massachusetts in 1970 and has freelanced ever since, often accompanying his wife, vocalist Meredith D'Ambrosio, and appearing at jazz parties and festivals. Eddie Higgins has led sessions of his own for Replica (1958), Vee-Jay (1960), Atlantic and more recently Sunnyside; back in 1960 he recorded as a sideman for Vee-Jay with Lee Morgan and Wayne Shorter. —*Scott Yanow*

Eddie Higgins / 1960 / Vee-Jay ✦✦✦✦

Soulero / Aug. 25, 1965 / Atlantic ✦✦✦

By Request / Aug. 5, 1986 / Statiras ✦✦✦✦

Those Quiet Days / Dec. 21, 1990 / Sunnyside ✦✦✦✦
Nice, sometimes delightful date with pianist Eddie Higgins. Rather than the customary keyboard/bass/drums lineup, he substituted guitarist Kevin Eubanks for a drummer and interacts with bassist Rufus Reid. The results are both satisfactory and revealing; the absence of a percussionist frees everyone to alternate between setting the beat and working off it. —*Ron Wynn*

● **Zoot's Hymns** / Feb. 3, 1994–Feb. 4, 1994 / Sunnyside ✦✦✦✦✦
Pianist Eddie Higgins alternates trio outings (also including bassist Phil Flannigan and drummer Danny Burger) with quartet performances that feature the cool-toned tenor of John Doughten on this consistently swinging set. "Zoot's Hymns" is a Higgins original that sets the tone for the CD (of which many but not all of the songs were formerly performed by Zoot Sims); other highlights include "The Red Door," "In Your Own Sweet Way," "Hi Fly" and "'Tis Autumn." —*Scott Yanow*

Andrew Hill

b. Jun. 30, 1937, Chicago, IL
Piano / Avant-Garde, Post-Bop
Andrew Hill has long been a highly original pianist and composer. Never quite free form but too advanced to be accepted by bop fans, Hill's complex music has never really caught on although he is widely respected as an innovative jazz musician. He started on piano when he was 13, studied with the composer Paul Hindemith and throughout the 1950s freelanced in jazz and R&B settings in Chicago. In 1961 Hill moved to New York and became Dinah Washington's accompanist. After a stint with Rahsaan Roland Kirk in 1962, he has mostly worked as a leader. Hill's series of explorative and advanced Blue Note albums (1963–1966) have been reissued in a Mosaic box set; *Point of Departure* (1964) has such sidemen as Kenny Dorham, Eric Dolphy and Joe Henderson and other dates feature John Gilmore, Freddie Hubbard, Sam Rivers and Henderson. Hill also recorded for Blue Note during 1968–70, became an educator and by the mid-'70s was teaching in public schools in California. He has recorded less frequently during the past couple of decades for labels such as SteepleChase, Freedom, East Wind, Soul Note and Blue Note but

remains a very viable performer who has stuck to his own singular musical vision. —*Scott Yanow*

So in Love / 1956 / Warwick ✦✦✦

★ **Black Fire** / Nov. 8, 1963 / Blue Note ✦✦✦✦✦

Smoke Stack / Dec. 13, 1963 / Blue Note ✦✦✦
This is an early example of Hill's percussive, Afro-Caribbean sound. —*Ron Wynn*

Judgment! / Jan. 8, 1964 / Blue Note ✦✦✦✦

★ **Point of Departure** / Mar. 31, 1964 / Blue Note ✦✦✦✦✦
A 1989 reissue of a remarkable session that still has avant-garde quality today. Eric Dolphy (sax) and Joe Henderson (sax) break barriers with their splendid solos. —*Ron Wynn*

Andrew! / Jun. 25, 1964 / Blue Note ✦✦✦✦

Compulsion / Oct. 8, 1965 / Blue Note ✦✦✦✦
Exacting, dynamic compositions, with intense playing. —*Ron Wynn*

Grass Roots / Aug. 5, 1968 / Blue Note ✦✦✦✦

Dance with Death / Oct. 11, 1968 / Blue Note ✦✦✦

Lift Every Voice / May 16, 1969 / Blue Note ✦✦✦
Andrew Hill incorporates vocals into his concept with ease and skill. —*Ron Wynn*

One for One / Aug. 1, 1969–Jan. 23, 1970 / Blue Note ✦✦✦✦
These are previously unreleased sessions from 1969 and 1970. Group efforts, at times with a string quartet. Hefty solos from B. Maupin, P. Patrick, J. Henderson, F. Hubbard, and C. Tolliver. —*Michael G. Nastos*

Invitation / Oct. 17, 1974 / SteepleChase ✦✦✦

Spiral / Dec. 20, 1974–Jan. 20, 1975 / Freedom ✦✦✦✦
This is a wonderful quintet w/ Ted Curson (tpt), Lee Konitz (sax). —*Ron Wynn*

Divine Revelation / Jul. 10, 1975 / SteepleChase ✦✦✦

Live at Montreux / Jul. 1975 / Freedom ✦✦✦✦
Beautiful, authoritative solo playing. —*Ron Wynn*

Nefertiti / Jan. 25, 1976 / Inner City ✦✦✦✦
Powerful, outstanding trio session cut in '76 for the East Wind label. Hill was at one time Dinah Washington's pianist, then moved from that to writing adventurous outside pieces and playing fiery, experimental music. These songs aren't very outside, but they're certainly done in an aggressive, captivating manner. —*Ron Wynn*

From California with Love / Oct. 12, 1978 / Artists House ✦✦✦✦
One of the major jazz pianists to emerge during the 1960s, Andrew Hill has always performed uncategorizable music that has never been a major commercial success despite (or perhaps because of) its obvious artistic value. The creative pianist is heard on two sidelong solo improvisations on this excellent LP, building his solos from fairly simple themes into works of great complexity and individuality. This deluxe LP (which contains an insightful interview and Hill's discography up to that time) is worth the search. —*Scott Yanow*

Faces of Hope / Jun. 13, 1980–Jun. 14, 1980 / Soul Note ✦✦✦✦
Sometimes loping, sometimes soaring solo piano from Andrew Hill, one of several impressive releases he made in the '80s. Hill often used rhythms from his native Haiti in his compositions. This time, however, it's neither the arrangements nor the songs that score, but Hill's emphatic execution of them. —*Ron Wynn*

Strange Serenade / Jun. 13, 1980–Jun. 14, 1980 / Soul Note ✦✦✦

Shades / Jul. 3, 1986–Jul. 4, 1986 / Soul Note ✦✦✦✦
Both Hill and Clifford Jordan (ts) are impressive. —*Ron Wynn*

Verona Rag / Jul. 5, 1986 / Soul Note ✦✦✦✦✦
Although Andrew Hill in this solo recital does wonders with the standards "Darn That Dream" and "Afternoon in Paris" and contributes two other superior originals, it is his breakdown of his striding "Verona Rag" that is most fascinating, transforming the piece from a spiritual-type rag into a very advanced improvisation. Hill, a true individualist, embodies the best in creative jazz. —*Scott Yanow*

Eternal Spirit / Jan. 30, 1989–Jan. 31, 1989 / Blue Note ✦✦✦✦
This newer material showcases Hill's influence on young lion Greg Osby (as) and includes a reunion with Bobby Hutcherson (vib). —*Ron Wynn*

But Not Farewell / Jul. 12, 1990–Sep. 16, 1990 / Blue Note
✦✦✦✦
A latter-day set with the smouldering Greg Osby on alto sax. Hill
updates his sound. —*Ron Wynn*

Buck Hill (Roger Hill)

b. 1928, Washington, DC
Tenor Saxophone / Hard Bop
Buck Hill received some fame in the 1970s for being a mailman
who also plays tenor. He actually began playing professionally in
1943 but always had a day job in Washington, D.C. He recorded
with Charlie Byrd (1958–59) but had to wait until the late '70s
before getting his own dates. He has since led sessions for
SteepleChase and Muse, displaying a large tone and a swinging
style. —*Scott Yanow*

This Is Buck Hill / Mar. 20, 1978 / SteepleChase ✦✦✦✦
● **Scope** / Jul. 8, 1979 / SteepleChase ✦✦✦✦✦
A studio date with the Kenny Barron Trio. Hill is a D.C. postman
by day, a great tenor saxophonist by night. —*Michael G. Nastos*

Easy to Love / Jul. 10, 1981–Jul. 12, 1981 / SteepleChase ✦✦✦✦
Capital Hill / Aug. 7, 1989 / Muse ✦✦✦✦
Lusty soul-jazz and funk ingredients, plus lots of blues. —*Ron
Wynn*

Buck Stops Here / Apr. 13, 1990 / Muse ✦✦✦✦
The Washington, D.C. vet along with the big buttery sound
gives the warhorse "Harlem Nocturne" one of its most inspired
reading. Elsewhere on his third Muse outing he shares the solo
spotlight with the rarely recorded Johnny Coles, who seldom plays
a superfluous note on his warm-voiced fluegelhorn. This is a nicely balanced set of pretty ballads and jaunty originals like Cole's
infectious "Wip Wop." —*Les Line*

I'm Beginning to See the Light / Jun. 12, 1991 / Muse ✦✦✦
☆ **Impulse** / Jul. 24, 1992 / Muse ✦✦✦✦✦
On Buck Hill's fourth release for Muse, the veteran tenor saxophonist is heard in peak form. This particularly well-rounded set
has many highpoints including a hard-charging "Blues in the
Closet," a couple of rare workouts for Hill's mellow-toned clarinet
and a happy rendition of "Sweet Georgia Brown." However, the
highpoint of the quartet date (which also features fine supportive
work from pianist Jon Ozmont, bassist Carroll Dashiell and drummer Warren Schadd) is Hill's caressing of the beautiful McCoy
Tyner melody "You Taught My Heart to Sing," a song that
deserves to become a standard based on this rendition alone. —
Scott Yanow

Earl Hines

b. Dec. 28, 1903, Dusquesne, PA, d. Apr. 22, 1983, Oakland, CA
Piano, Leader, Composer / Classic Jazz, Swing
Once called "the first modern jazz pianist," Earl Hines differed
from the stride pianists of the 1920s by breaking up the stride
rhythms with unusual accents from his left hand. While his right
hand often played octaves so as to ring clearly over ensembles,
Hines had the trickiest left hand in the business, often suspend-
ing time recklessly but without ever losing the beat. One of the
all-time great pianists, Hines was a major influence on Teddy
Wilson, Jess Stacy, Joe Sullivan, Nat King Cole and even, to an
extent, on Art Tatum. He was also an underrated composer
responsible for "Rosetta," "My Monday Date" and "You Can
Depend on Me" among others.
    Earl Hines played trumpet briefly as a youth before switching
to piano. His first major job was accompanying vocalist Lois
Deppe, and he made his first recordings with Deppe and his
orchestra in 1922. The following year Hines moved to Chicago
where he worked with Sammy Stewart and Erskine Tate's
Vendome Theatre Orchestra. He started teaming up with Louis
Armstrong in 1926 and the two masterful musicians consistently
inspired each other. Hines worked briefly in Armstrong's big band
(formerly headed by Carroll Dickerson) and they unsuccessfully
tried to manage their own club. 1928 was one of Hines' most significant years. He recorded his first ten piano solos including versions of "A Monday Date," "Blues in Thirds" and "57 Varieties."
Hines worked much of the year with Jimmy Noone's Apex Club
Orchestra and their recordings are also considered classic. Hines
cut brilliant (and futuristic) sides with Louis Armstrong's Hot Five,
resulting in such timeless gems as "West End Blues," "Fireworks,"
"Basin Street Blues" and their remarkable trumpet-piano duet

"Fireworks." And on his birthday on December 28, Hines debuted
with his big band at Chicago's Grand Terrace.
    A brilliant ensemble player as well as soloist, Earl Hines would
lead big bands for the next 20 years. Among the key players in
his band through the 1930s would be trumpeter/vocalist Walter
Fuller, Ray Nance on trumpet and violin (prior to joining Duke
Ellington), trombonist Trummy Young, tenor saxophonist Budd
Johnson, Omer Simeon and Darnell Howard on reeds and
arranger Jimmy Mundy. In 1940 Billy Eckstine became the band's
popular singer and in 1943 (unfortunately during the musicians'
recording strike), Hines welcomed such modernists as Charlie
Parker (on tenor), trumpeter Dizzy Gillespie and singer Sarah
Vaughan in what was the first bebop orchestra. By the time the
strike ended Eckstine, Parker, Gillespie and Vaughan were gone
but tenor Wardell Gray was still around to star with the group
during 1945–46.
    In 1948 the economic situation forced Hines to break up his
orchestra. He joined the Louis Armstrong All-Stars but three years
of playing second fiddle to his old friend were difficult to take.
After leaving Armstrong in 1951, Hines moved to Los Angeles
and later San Francisco, heading a Dixieland band. Although his
style was much more modern, Hines kept the group working
throughout the 1950s, at times featuring Muggsy Spanier, Jimmy
Archey and Darnell Howard. Hines did record on a few occasions
but was largely forgotten in the jazz world by the early '60s. Then
in 1964 jazz writer Stanley Dance arranged for him to play three
concerts at New York's Little Theater, both solo and in a quartet
with Budd Johnson. The New York critics were amazed by Hines'
continuing creativity and vitality and he had a major comeback
that lasted through the rest of his career. Hines travelled the world
with his quartet, recorded dozens of albums and remained famous
and renowned up until his death at the age of 79. Most of the
many recordings from his career are currently available on CD. —
Scott Yanow

☆ **Earl Hines (1928–1932)** / Dec. 1928–Jun. 1932 / Classics ✦✦✦✦✦
☆ **Earl Hines** / Feb. 13, 1929–1929 / Raretone ✦✦✦✦✦
Nearly impossible to find now, this LP from the collector's label
has all of the music recorded by Earl Hines as a solo pianist (two
versions of "Glad Rag Doll") and as a bandleader in 1929. Hines,
who would lead orchestras for 20 years, had a particularly strong
big band from the start, with George Mitchell and Shirley Clay on
trumpets and the reeds of Cecil Irwin. This LP allows one to hear
15 performances of nine songs (there are quite a few very interesting alternate takes) and much of the music is exciting. Pity that
the Depression would keep the band out of the studios until 1932,
and that this music is not yet available in complete form on CD.
—*Scott Yanow*

Swingin' Down / Jul. 1, 1932–Mar. 27, 1933 / Hep ✦✦✦✦
This LP and Hep 1003 contain the entire recorded output of Earl
Hines' big band of 1932–33 (including all of the alternate takes),
an underrated orchestra. At the time Hines' featured soloists were
trumpeter/singer Walter Fuller, trombonist Trummy Young, and
the reeds of Darnell Howard, Omer Simeon and Cecil Irwin, in
addition to the brilliant pianist/leader. The fine arrangements
(particularly Jimmy Mundy's) show off this band's power. "Blue
Drag," "Rosetta," "Cavernism," "Madhouse" and "Swingin' Down"
are among the best performances. —*Scott Yanow*

Deep Forest / Jul. 14, 1932–Oct. 27, 1933 / Hep ✦✦✦✦
This LP and Hep 1018 have all of the recordings of Earl Hines'
1932–33 orchestra (including the many alternate takes). This often
overlooked big band featured strong and swinging arrangements
(particularly those of Jimmy Mundy) along with fine solos from
trumpeter Walter Fuller, trombonist Trummy Young (who joined
in mid-1933) and the reeds of Omer Simeon, Cecil Irwin and
Darnell Howard. Both of these LPs are well worth searching out,
for they offer fine examples of early swing and the sparkling virtuosity of Hines' piano. —*Scott Yanow*

Earl Hines (1932–1934) / Jul. 1932–Mar. 1934 / Classics ✦✦✦✦
Harlem Lament / Feb. 13, 1933–Mar. 7, 1938 / Portrait ✦✦✦
This excellent LP (which unaccountably leaves out the recording
dates of its 16 selections) features the best recordings by Earl
Hines' Orchestra during 1932–34 (prior to signing with Decca)
and 1937–38. Highlights include the initial version of "Rosetta,"
such Jimmy Mundy charts as "Cavernism" and "Madhouse," a
small-group romp on "Honeysuckle Rose" and early examples of
Ray Nance's trumpet on the later tracks. Throughout, the music

consistently swings hard and the leader's brilliant piano is a constant joy. —*Scott Yanow*

Earl Hines (1934–1937) / Sep. 1934–Feb. 1937 / Classics ◆◆◆◆

Earl Hines & His Orchestra 1936, 1938 & 1940 / 1936–May 1, 1941 / Alamac ◆◆◆

Sometimes releases from low-budget labels include some very rewarding music. This LP from the 1970s by the long defunct Alamac label features Earl Hines' only recordings from 1936 (solo piano workouts on "Avalon" and "I Surrender Dear"), two numbers from a radio broadcast from his 1938 big band, guest appearances in 1941 with Henry Levine's Barefoot Dixieland Philharmonic and six numbers that catch his 1940 orchestra live. The recording quality is streaky, but collectors will want this valuable set. —*Scott Yanow*

● **Earl Hines (1937–1939)** / Feb. 10, 1937–Oct. 6, 1939 / Classics ◆◆◆◆◆

● **Piano Man** / Jul. 12, 1939–Mar. 19, 1942 / Bluebird ◆◆◆◆◆

This sampler of Earl Hines' Bluebird recordings features five brilliant piano solos from the often-breathtaking pianist, "Blues in Thirds" by Sidney Bechet's Trio with Hines and 16 of the better performances from his big band of 1939–42. An excellent purchase for those not familiar with Hines' big-band days, this CD includes such classics as "Piano Man," "Boogie Woogie on St. Louis Blues" and "Jelly, Jelly" along with many hot swinging performances from this very underrated orchestra. —*Scott Yanow*

☆ **Indispensable Earl Hines, Vol. 1 & 2** / Jul. 12, 1939–Dec. 2, 1940 / RCA ◆◆◆◆◆

The best way to acquire the 1939–45 recordings of Earl Hines' exciting big band is to somehow get the two double LPs released by French RCA, for they include all of their performances plus the alternate takes. The first set is highlighted by "Indiana," "Piano Man," "Riff Medley," two takes of "Boogie Woogie on St. Louis Blues," two versions of "Tantalizing a Cuban" and three typically remarkable Hines solo piano performances. Hard-swinging music from one of the swing era's great orchestras. —*Scott Yanow*

Earl Hines (1939–1940) / Oct. 6, 1939–Dec. 2, 1940 / Classics ◆◆◆◆◆

☆ **Indispensable Earl Hines, Vol. 3 & 4** / Oct. 21, 1939–Jan. 12, 1945 / RCA ◆◆◆◆◆

The second of two "complete" two-fers from French RCA in their sadly discontinued *Jazz Tribune* series starts off with two alternate versions of Hines' piano solos and then includes all of his orchestra's recordings from Dec. 1940 through 1942 plus two numbers from 1945 and four more Hines solos. During this period, both Budd Johnson and Franz Jackson starred on tenor and, although many of the musicians were lesser-known players (other than the increasingly popular vocalist Billy Eckstine), the orchestra was one of the top swing big bands around. Highpoints include the piano solos, "Jelly Jelly" (Eckstine's first hit), "Windy City Jive," "The Father Jumps" and "Second Balcony Jump." This highly recommended set was unfortunately become difficult to find. —*Scott Yanow*

And the Duke's Men / May 16, 1944–May 14, 1947 / ◆◆◆

This very interesting Delmark CD has formerly rare selections from three different groups in the mid-'40s. Pianist Earl Hines heads a septet that also features trumpeter Ray Nance, altoist Johnny Hodges, Flip Phillips on tenor and vocalist Betty Roche. Drummer Sonny Greer leads a group of Ellingtonians that include cornetist Rex Stewart, clarinetist Jimmy Hamilton, trombonist Lawrence Brown and baritonist Harry Carney, and highnote trumpet wiz Cat Anderson is at the helm of a competent (if somewhat anonymous) big band. All of this music is essentially swing with bop overtones and the 15 performances (originally on the Apollo label) are quite enjoyable. —*Scott Yanow*

Earl Hines / Nov. 4, 1949–Nov. 6, 1949 / GNP ◆◆◆

Pianist Earl Hines visited Paris with the Louis Armstrong Quintet and recorded performances (last available on this LP) with a quintet that included trumpeter Buck Clayton, clarinetist Barney Bigard, bassist Arvell Shaw and drummer Wallace Bishop; in addition, the 14 selections include three piano solos. The music overall is somewhere between Dixieland and swing, mainstream pre-bop jazz that swings easily if in this case a bit predictably. —*Scott Yanow*

Varieties / Dec. 15, 1952–Aug. 21, 1954 / Xanadu ◆◆◆

This Xanadu LP features two very different Earl Hines sessions

from the mid-to-early '50s, shortly after leaving the Louis Armstrong All-Stars. Hines is heard on an interesting trio set in which he takes four vocals, switches to celeste on "If I Had You" and romps on "Humoresque." The flip side finds him heading an unusual band with three horns (trumpeter Jonah Jones, trombonist Bennie Green and Aaron Sachs on tenor and clarinet) and three vocalists (the forgotten Lonnie Satin, Helen Merrill on her recorded debut and Etta Jones); Hines himself chips in on "Ella's Fella." It's not essential but a very musical and somewhat unique set. —*Scott Yanow*

Earl Hines at Club Hangover, Vol. 5 / Sep. 10, 1955–Sep. 24, 1955 / Storyville ◆◆

During the mid-'50s, the classic jazz pianist Earl Hines, who was considered a very modern player in the '20s and '30s, was reduced to playing in Dixieland bands in San Francisco so as to earn a living. Fortunately, his groups still featured talented sidemen (on this LP he has trumpeter Marty Marsala, trombonist Jimmy Archey and clarinetist Darnell Howard) and plenty of drive even if the repertoire (which in this case included "Darktown Strutters Ball," "Ballin' the Jack" and "St. James Infirmary") was uninspired and predictable. Dixieland fans will enjoy this set more than most Hines collectors. —*Scott Yanow*

Another Monday Date / Nov. 1955–Dec. 1956 / Prestige ◆◆◆◆

Two of pianist Earl Hines' finest recordings sessions of the 1950s are included on this CD. One is a tribute to Fats Waller on which Hines (with guitarist Eddie Duran, bassist Dean Reilly and drummer Earl Watkins) explores songs associated with Waller. The other date is Hines' only solo session of the decade and features him playing his own compositions (including "Everything Depends on You," "You Can Depend on Me," "Piano Man" and "My Monday Date") along with "Am I Too Late?" During the 1950s, Hines was somewhat forgotten in jazz, reduced to playing Dixieland dates, so this two-fer is far superior to his other sessions prior to his "comeback" of 1964. —*Scott Yanow*

Earl Fatha Hines and His All-Stars, Vol. 1 / 1957–1958 / GNP ◆◆

Spirited and generally high-powered Dixieland is the order of the day on this first of two LPs. The early modern pianist Earl Hines is a bit out of place in this setting but does his best to fit in with the dominating cornetist Muggsy Spanier, trombonist Jimmy Archey and the hyper clarinet of Darnell Howard. The repertoire is somewhat predictable as are the solos, but the frontline's enthusiasm carries the day. —*Scott Yanow*

Earl Fatha Hines and His All Stars, Vol. 2 / 1957–1958 / GNP ◆◆

On the second of two LPs featuring the great pianist Earl Hines with a Dixieland band, it seems strange to hear Hines play such warhorses as "High Society," "That's a Plenty" and "Royal Garden Blues," but the power and enthusiasm of the frequently riotous frontline (cornetist Muggsy Spanier, trombonist Jimmy Archey and clarinetist Darnell Howard) causes the music to be quite exciting rather than routine. It's recommended more for Spanier fans than for Hines collectors. —*Scott Yanow*

Earl's Backroom and Cozy's Caravan / Feb. 3, 1958 / Felsted ◆◆◆

This LP of material originally recorded by Stanley Dance in 1958 features quite a few obscure—but talented—players. On half of the program, the Earl Hines Quartet showcases the great pianist (who was in a long period of critical neglect) and the forgotten tenor and baritonist Curtis Lowe. The other session has drummer Cozy Cole leading a group of complete unknowns: trumpeter Lou Jones, Phatz Morris on the unusual double of trombone and harmonica, tenor saxophonist Boe McCain, pianist June Cole, guitarist Dicky Thompson and bassist Pete Compo. They come up with interesting ideas on a blues, "Caravan" and "Margie." —*Scott Yanow*

A Monday Date / Sep. 7, 1961–Sep. 8, 1961 / Original Jazz Classics ◆◆

Earl Hines, one of jazz's greatest pianists, was a modern stylist who broke up the usual stride piano pattern of the 1920s with unexpected accents and an uncanny ability to play successfully with time; he had the trickiest left hand in jazz history. After his orchestra disbanded in 1947 and he spent a few unfulfilling years as a sideman with the Louis Armstrong All Stars, Hines entered a decade of critical neglect and indifference in which his talents were pretty well forgotten; he found himself playing Dixieland in

San Francisco for several years. This particular CD is a decent Dixieland set with trumpeter Eddie Smith, trombonist Jimmy Archey and clarinetist Darnell Howard. Still, Hines' abilities are somewhat wasted on tunes such as "Bill Bailey," "Yes Sir, That's My Baby" and "Clarinet Marmalade." His renaissance was still three years in the future. —*Scott Yanow*

Legendary Little Theater Concert / Mar. 7, 1964 / Muse ◆◆◆◆
The great pianist Earl Hines had been pretty well forgotten by the jazz establishment at the time of this concert, relegated to playing Dixieland in San Francisco. However this appearance by his quartet (with bassist Ahmed Abdul-Malik, drummer Oliver Jackson and, on three cuts, tenor saxophonist Budd Johnson) caught the attention of New York critics and suddenly Hines was rediscovered and a hot item again. The momentum would last throughout the remainder of his life and he would never be taken for granted again. Some of the music from his *Little Theater Concert* was issued at the time by Contact but this two-LP set contains "new" material including five medleys and fresh versions of "Stealin' Apples" and "Rosetta." Hines would record many sets during the next decade that were superior to this one, but this historic gig made them all possible. —*Scott Yanow*

Spontaneous Explorations / Mar. 7, 1964–Jan. 17, 1966 / Contact ◆◆◆◆◆
This two-CD set contains a pair of very exciting sessions by the great pianist Earl Hines. The earlier set, recorded the same day as his historic "comeback" concert at the Little Theater, was Hines' first solo session since 1956 and is full of stunning performances. The later session finds Hines, a veteran of the 1920s, sounding quite comfortable in a trio with two young modernists: bassist Richard Davis and drummer Elvin Jones. The pianist, in fact, sounds quite youthful throughout these classic recordings, taking wild chances and constantly pushing himself. —*Scott Yanow*

Linger Awhile [1964] / Nov. 5, 1964–Nov. 6, 1964 / Bluebird ◆◆◆
After the success of his Little Theater concert earlier in 1964, Earl Hines was suddenly a hot property; he would record frequently during the next decade and practically all of his recordings are worth getting. This CD is a bit unusual, for Hines (usually heard with a trio or solo) leads a quintet also featuring Ray Nance (for four selections) on cornet and violin and Hines' longtime friend Budd Johnson on tenor, soprano and baritone saxophones. The original 12 selections are augmented by six alternate takes and the results are melodic, swinging and quite enjoyable. —*Scott Yanow*

The New Earl Hines Trio / Nov. 9, 1964–Nov. 10, 1964 / Columbia ◆◆
A relaxed and, at times, lazy set by pianist Earl Hines and his 1964 trio with bassist Ahmed Abdul Malik and drummer Oliver Jackson, the overly concise performances (only one of the dozen songs is over four minutes) contain no real surprises. Hines takes a few pleasing (but forgettable) vocals and since he recorded so frequently during the 1964–77 period, there are many better sets to acquire before this okay LP. —*Scott Yanow*

Grand Reunion / Mar. 14, 1965 / Verve ◆◆◆◆
For a session at the Village Vanguard, pianist Earl Hines and his trio were joined part of the time by the great tenor Coleman Hawkins and trumpeter Roy Eldridge. But on this LP, the three giants only actually play together on a fine version of "Take the 'A' Train." Eldridge has "The Man I Love" and "Undecided" as his features (Hines is absent on the latter), Hawkins gets to roar on "Sweet Georgia Brown" and Hines and his trio play a lengthy "Grand Terrace Medley." The music is excellent but not as explosive as one might expect from these competitive players. —*Scott Yanow*

Earl Hines & Roy Eldridge at The Village Vanguard / Mar. 14, 1965 / Xanadu ◆◆◆
Pianist Earl Hines and trumpeter Roy Eldridge only actually play together on "Blue Moon," but both are in fine form. Hines dominates a couple of lengthy medleys and Eldridge really digs into a nearly 11-minute blues in which he is accompanied by just bass and drums; he is also inspired on a briefer "I Can't Get Started." This LP is worth acquiring even if Hines and Eldridge barely meet. —*Scott Yanow*

Reunion in Brussels / Mar. 17, 1965 / Red Baron ◆◆◆
The "reunion" on this CD is between pianist Earl Hines and drummer Wallace Bishop who had played with Hines' big band over 20 years earlier. With bassist Rolland Haynes completing the trio,

Hines is in good form on a variety of standards (including three medleys), performing a typical mid-'60s set of melodic—but occasionally unpredictable—jazz, one of the many enjoyable examples of his talents currently available. —*Scott Yanow*

Blues in Thirds / Apr. 20, 1965 / Black Lion ◆◆◆◆◆
Earl Hines' solo piano sessions were always a joy. Freed from having to keep a steady rhythm to accommodate a bassist and a drummer, Hines was able to take wild chances with time, with his left hand playing broken patterns rather than sticking to a steady stride. This Black Lion CD augments the eight selections originally released on an LP with two alternate takes and "Black Lion Blues." Hines made many exciting recordings during 1964–77; this set is a good place to start in exploring his frequently dazzling playing. —*Scott Yanow*

Hines (1965) / Apr. 20, 1965 / Master Jazz ◆◆◆◆
Recorded the same day as the CD *Blues in Thirds*, this LP finds Earl Hines in excellent and frequently exciting form playing six standards and two originals as unaccompanied piano solos. Hines was one of the giants and most of his recordings are worth acquiring. —*Scott Yanow*

At the Village Vanguard / Jun. 29, 1965–Jun. 30, 1965 / Columbia ◆◆◆
Recorded one year after his "comeback" began, pianist Earl Hines is featured on this live session with his quartet, which at the time featured bassist Gene Ramey, drummer Eddie Locke and on five of the nine selections, the tenor and soprano of Budd Johnson. The tunes are superior and these versions of "Cavernism," "Rosetta" and "Tea for Two" are highpoints. Most of Hines' post-1964 output is quite enjoyable and this LP is no exception. —*Scott Yanow*

Blues So Low / 1966 / Stash ◆◆
Considering that this is an Earl Hines solo set, it is surprising how routine the music is. Hines performs far too many medleys with unrelated songs and odd song quotes for this to be considered one of his great sessions. A Fats Waller medley is eventful and a collage titled "The Blues and Other Folks," for no particular reason, concludes with a ten-minute version of "Sweet Lorraine." In general, this is a rather trivial performance with its few inspired moments not occuring often enough to justify its purchase. —*Scott Yanow*

Once Upon a Time / Jan. 10, 1966–Jan. 11, 1966 / Impulse! ◆◆◆
For reasons that are unclear, this LP reissue of an Impulse! set drops one of the seven songs ("Black and Tan Fantasy") from the program, reducing the playing time down to a mere 29 minutes. But if one finds this LP at a budget price, it is worth picking up, for the great pianist Earl Hines is featured on three selections with many of the members of the Duke Ellington Orchestra (including on the exciting "Once Upon a Time" and "Cotton Tail"), in a quartet featuring Jimmy Hamilton and with a nonet that also includes clarinetist Pee Wee Russell along with some Ellingtonians. Great music, lousy packaging. —*Scott Yanow*

Dinah / Apr. 29, 1966 / RCA ◆◆◆
This excellent CD finds the great pianist Earl Hines performing solo versions of such superior standards as "Dinah," "Rose Room" (heard in two versions), "Blue Skies" and his own "Blues in Thirds." Hines, who loved to break up the rhythms and take wild chances with time, was generally at his best when performing solo and this set is an example of his pianistic mastery. —*Scott Yanow*

Earl Hines at Home / 1969 / Delmark ◆◆◆
This interesting solo LP features the great pianist Earl Hines performing four of his lesser-known compositions ("Love at Night Is out of Sight," "Minor Nothing," "Moon Mare" and "The Cannery Walk") in addition to two standards and a vocal version of "It Happens to Be Me." For most pianists, this set would be one of the highpoints of their career, but Hines recorded so many superb albums during the 1964–77 period that this fine date is only average for him. —*Scott Yanow*

☆ **Quintessential Recording Session** / Mar. 15, 1970 / Halcyon ◆◆◆◆◆
In 1970, Earl Hines was persuaded to do new versions of the eight solo performances that he had recorded at the beginning of his career, 42 years earlier. Some of these songs (most notably "Chimes in Blues," "Chicago High Life" and "Panther Rag") he had rarely played since the 1920s but, after a quick listen to the original recordings, he came up with new and exciting interpretations. This LP contains one of Earl Hines' finest recordings of his come-

back years, although unfortunately, it is not yet available on CD. —*Scott Yanow*

Earl Hines and Maxine Sullivan / Nov. 1970 / Chiaroscuro ✦✦✦

It Don't Mean A Thing If It Ain't Got That Swing! / Dec. 15, 1970–Nov. 29, 1972 / Black Lion ✦✦✦✦
This recommended set teams the great pianist Earl Hines with Duke Ellington's longtime tenor saxophonist, Paul Gonsalves, in a quartet. Since Hines mostly recorded in trios and unaccompanied during his last decade, it is particularly enjoyable to hear him interacting with a horn player. The repertoire includes three Duke Ellington songs, "Over the Rainbow," "Moten Swing" and, from 1972, a piano solo version of "Blue Sands." —*Scott Yanow*

Earl Hines Plays Duke Ellington / Jun. 1, 1971–Dec. 10, 1971 / New World ✦✦✦✦✦
During a four-year period, pianist Earl Hines recorded enough of Duke Ellington's compositions to fill up four LPs. This double CD contains 20 of his better performances including both Ellington's better-known standards and a few obscurities (most notably lengthy versions of "The Shepherd" and "Black Butterfly"). The music is satisfying, although one wishes that New World had reissued all of the music from this extensive project on three CDs. — *Scott Yanow*

Hines Does Hoagy / Jul. 18, 1971 / Audiophile ✦✦✦✦
Earl Hines pays tribute to composer Hoagy Carmichael on this inventive set of solo piano. Highpoints of this fine LP include a ten-minute version of "Stardust," "Skylark" and "Ole Buttermilk Sky." Pity that Hines did not tackle "Riverboat Shuffle," but he chose to mostly stick to Carmichael's classic ballads. One of three albums recorded by the great pianist in a two-day period, this is one of about fifty recommended Hines sets. —*Scott Yanow*

My Tribute to Louis / Jul. 18, 1971 / Audiophile ✦✦✦✦
Twelve days after Louis Armstrong died, his old friend Earl Hines recorded a solo tribute to the great trumpeter/vocalist. This Audiophile LP, one of three that Hines recorded in a two-day period, features eight songs associated with Satch including "Struttin' with Some Barbeque," "A Kiss to Build a Dream On," "Someday You'll Be Sorry" and two versions of Armstrong's theme "When It's Sleepy Time Down South." This set should be of particular interest to Earl Hines collectors for the pianist rarely performed most of these songs, and he gives fresh heartfelt renditions to the standards. —*Scott Yanow*

Comes in Handy / Jul. 19, 1971 / Audiophile ✦✦✦✦
Earl Hines' third tribute LP to be recorded in a two-day period, this set features five of W.C. Handy's best-known compositions ("St. Louis Blues," "Ole Miss," "Memphis Blues," "Loveless Love" and "Beale Street Blues") along with three unrelated songs of which "For the Past Masters" is the most touching. So many of Hines' solo sets are superb that it is difficult to call any single one definitive, but this is a highly enjoyable and rather emotional set. —*Scott Yanow*

Partners in Jazz / Feb. 14, 1972 / MPS ✦✦✦✦
With Jaki Byard (p). Piano duets from masters of two styles and generations. Definitive. —*Michael G. Nastos*

Hines Plays Hines / Jul. 29, 1972 / Swaggie ✦✦✦✦
During 1971–72, Earl Hines recorded entire sets of the compositions of Louis Armstrong, W.C. Handy, Hoagy Carmichael and Duke Ellington; a George Gershwin program was one year in the future. However, one of the most enjoyable of these tributes is this Swaggie LP, featuring Hines' own compositions. The ten songs include a few that became standards (most notably "My Monday Date" and "You Can Depend on Me") and some enjoyable lesser-known tunes (such as "When I Dream of You," "Tosca's Dance" and "I Can't Trust Myself Alone"). Hines (who takes a vocal on "So Can I") is in superior form for this brilliant set. —*Scott Yanow*

Tour De Force Encore / Nov. 22, 1972–Nov. 29, 1972 / Black Lion ✦✦✦✦✦
The second of two CDs taken from a pair of solo piano sessions (and greatly expanding upon the original LP that came out), this set features the great pianist Earl Hines near the peak of his powers, stretching out on a variety of stimulating standards including "Who's Sorry Now," "I Never Knew," "Stompin' at the Savoy" and "Mack the Knife." Every jazz collection should have at least a few examples of Hines' stimulating and exciting piano; this CD and *Tour De Force* are perfect examples of his virtuosic powers. — *Scott Yanow*

★ **Tour De Force** / Nov. 22, 1972–Nov. 29, 1972 / Black Lion ✦✦✦✦✦
Pianist Earl Hines is in top form on this brilliant set of solo piano. This CD (which has three previously unreleased performances along with five of the six numbers from its counterpart LP) and *Tour De Force Encore* greatly expand upon the original set. Whether it be "Mack the Knife," "Indian Summer" or "I Never Knew," Hines is near the peak of his creativity on this CD, taking wild chances with time and coming up with fresh new variations on these veteran standards. —*Scott Yanow*

An Evening with Earl Hines / 1973 / Chiaroscuro ✦✦✦
This double LP is valuable as documentation of Earl Hines and his band on a typical gig in 1973. Marva Josie has a few vocals and Tiny Grimes contributes some guitar solos, but the leader/pianist is easily the main star, romping on such tunes as "Perdido," "Boogie Woogie on the St. Louis Blues" and "Lester Leaps In." Swinging (if not essential) music. —*Scott Yanow*

Earl Hines Quartet / 1973 / Chiaroscuro ✦✦✦
This LP has a fairly loose set by pianist Earl Hines in a quartet with guitarist Tiny Grimes, bassist Hank Young and drummer Bert Dahlander. Their version of "Watermelon Man" is a bit lightweight and some of the ballads have been overdone through the years, but these renditions of "Second Balcony Jump," "Memories of You" and "Showboat Medley" are quite enjoyable. It's not essential but also not a bad acquisition. —*Scott Yanow*

☆ **Quintessential Continued** / 1973 / Chiaroscuro ✦✦✦✦
In 1970 for the *Quintessential* date, Earl Hines was persuaded to revisit his first eight solo recordings, from 1928. For this sequel (last available on LP), he re-recorded some other selections he had originally cut as solos in 1928 ("73 Varieties" which is a remake of "57 Varieties"), 1929 ("Glad Rag Doll") and 1932 ("Down Among the Sheltering Palms" and "Love Me Tonight"). In addition, Hines performs two pieces his '30s big band used to play ("Deep Forest" and "Cavernism") along with the more recent "Another Child." Perhaps it is the joy of rediscovering the older classics, but Earl Hines was in particularly brilliant form for both of the *Quintessential* sessions; hopefully they will be reissued by Chiaroscuro on CD in the near future. —*Scott Yanow*

☆ **Earl Hines at the New School** / Mar. 1973 / Chiaroscuro ✦✦✦✦✦
Even though it is not yet available on CD, this LP is a first pick because it features pianist Earl Hines at the absolute peak of his powers. Nine years after his renaissance began, Hines seemed to still be getting more daring in his playing. This version of "I've Got the World on a String" is somewhat miraculous (the chances he takes are breathtaking) and the Fats Waller medley (which features six songs) is definitive. The inclusion of "When the Saints Go Marching In" might not have been necessary and "Boogie Woogie on the St. Louis Blues" is a bit exhibitionistic but those are minor complaints about a definitive and classic session by a true jazz master. —*Scott Yanow*

Earl Hines Plays George Gershwin / Oct. 16, 1973 / Classic Jazz ✦✦✦✦
This excellent two-LP set features the great pianist Earl Hines interpreting ten of George Gershwin's compositions. Highlights of this solo piano session include extensive explorations of "Embraceable You" and "They Can't Take That Away from Me" (both are over ten minutes) and more concise readings of "They All Laughed" and "Love Walked In." Hines recorded so many rewarding records throughout his productive career that what would be considered "best" for some is merely "good" for him. This set is worth picking up, if it can still be found. —*Scott Yanow*

Piano Solos / Jan. 29, 1974 / Laserlight ✦✦✦✦
The budget label Laserlight has unearthed an excellent set of Earl Hines piano solos recorded ten years after his rediscovery. Hines was one of the true originals, a chancetaking pianist who loved to play with time and always seemed to make it back safely from his breathtaking flights. He stretches out on six standards (including "Once in Awhile," "Wrap Your Troubles in Dreams" and "Don't Take Your Love from Me") and takes a vocal on his composition "So Can I." This excellent music is frequently quite exciting. —*Scott Yanow*

Masters of Jazz, Vol. 2 / Mar. 23, 1974–Mar. 24, 1974 / Storyville ✦✦✦✦
Earl Hines, age 68 at the time of this solo set, is in fine form on these six explorations of standards. He really digs into "Over the Rainbow" and "My Shining Hour" (the latter is nearly 11 minutes long) and is in particularly inventive form on "I've Got the World

on a String" and "The Devil and the Deep Blue Sea." One of the giants of jazz piano, Earl Hines was still in his prime for this session, which was cut 46 years after his first recording as a leader. —*Scott Yanow*

Live at The New School, Vol. 2 / Apr. 15, 1974 / Chiaroscuro ✦✦✦
Not at the same level as his first Chiaroscuro *Live at the New School* LP (which was titled *I've Got the World on a String*), this Earl Hines solo piano LP has two lengthy medleys (one featuring four of his compositions), a fine version of "Japanese Sandman," "Blue Skies" and "Slaughter on 10th Avenue." The music is excellent enough but just not as classic as some of Hines' other solo sets. —*Scott Yanow*

Earl Hines/Budd Johnson / Jul. 16, 1974 / Classic Jazz ✦✦✦
Tenor saxophonist Budd Johnson (who on this LP doubles on soprano) played with the great pianist Earl Hines off and on from the mid-'30s up to the late '70s. This excellent quartet session features the band stretching out on six numbers including three standards, a blues and two Johnson pieces. Solid small-group swing from a pair of classic veterans. —*Scott Yanow*

Live at Buffalo / 1976 / Improv ✦✦✦
During the mid-to-late '70s Earl Hines utilized the quartet heard on this LP: Rudy Rutherford on reeds, bassist Harley White, drummer Eddie Graham and the singer Marva Josie. This is a fairly typical set by the unit with an uptempo opener ("Second Balcony Jump"), some Ellington ("Black and Tan Fantasy"), a Rutherford feature on "The Man I Love," a blues ("Melodica Blues"), a jazz version of the current pop tune "Close to You," Josie's vocal on "A Sunday Kind of Love," the millionth remake of "Boogie Woogie on the St. Louis Blues" and Hines' closing theme "It's a Pity to Say Goodnight." It's not essential but a fine document of Earl Hines' last regular working group. —*Scott Yanow*

Father of Modern Jazz Piano / Sep. 9, 1977–Dec. 30, 1977 / M.F. Productions ✦✦✦✦
This five-LP box set consists of three albums of piano solos by the great Earl Hines and two LPs in which Hines is joined by tenor saxophonist Budd Johnson, bassist Bill Pemberton and drummer Oliver Jackson. Happily, this excellent package is generally available at budget prices and there are many strong performances. In many ways it is definitive, for Hines is heard performing a wide variety of material including solo renditions of "The One I Love," "Can't We Talk It Over," "The Pearls," "Wolverine Blues," "A Monday Date," a lengthy "Blues in Thirds," "You Can Depend on Me" and of course "Boogie Woogie on the St. Louis Blues." The quartet selections are also consistently excellent. —*Scott Yanow*

Lionel Hampton Presents Earl Fatha Hines / Sep. 26, 1977 / Who's Who ✦✦✦
Although they were both active during the same half-century, pianist Earl Hines and vibraphonist Lionel Hampton rarely had the opportunity to play together. This quintet set from 1977 finds the immortal pair joined by bassist Milt Hinton, drummer Grady Tate and Sam Turner on congas, happily jamming on standards like Hampton's "Earl's Pearl" and Hines' "One Night in Trinidad." Few surprises occur but, the music swings hard and is quite enjoyable. —*Scott Yanow*

Earl Hines in New Orleans / Nov. 7, 1977 / Chiaroscuro ✦✦✦
Virtually all of Earl Hines' solo piano sets (and there are quite a few) are well worth getting. This LP from the later part of his career finds Hines in excellent form on five standards, "I'm a Little Brownbird" and his composition "The Cannery Walk." "Memories of You" (at nearly eight minutes) is the longest performance, but the classic pianist makes the most of every moment on this set; each of the standards sound as if they were written for him. —*Scott Yanow*

Honor Thy Fatha / 1978 / Drive Archive ✦✦✦
This CD reissues one of pianist Earl Hines' last recordings, a Direct to Disc album done originally for RealTime and formerly titled *Hits I've Missed*. Hines (with backup from bassist Red Callender and drummer Bill Douglass) performs nine songs, some of which were more familiar than others. Certainly Hines was well acquainted with Fats Waller's "Squeeze Me" and "Ain't Misbehavin,'" Duke Ellington's "Sophisticated Lady" and James P. Johnson's "Old Fashioned Love," but he had never recorded "Misty," Horace Silver's "The Preacher" or "Blue Monk" before. The real wild card track was his rendition of "Birdland," with Red Callender switching to tuba. This interesting CD (well-played but not really essential) adds alternate versions of "Birdland" and "Blue Monk" to the original program. —*Scott Yanow*

Terumasa Hino

b. Oct. 25, 1942, Tokyo, Japan
Trumpet, Fluegelhorn / Hard Bop, Fusion
A fine trumpeter influenced by Freddie Hubbard and Miles Davis, Terumasa Hino has long been one of Japan's best jazz musicians. A professional since 1955, Hino has mostly become known to Americans since the 1970s due to his Enja recordings although some of his albums were made available domestically by Catalyst, Inner City and Blue Note. He moved to the U.S. in 1975 where he worked with Gil Evans, Jackie McLean, Dave Liebman and Elvin Jones. Hino has spent more time in Japan since the early '80s and has recorded in several different styles ranging from straight-ahead to fusion. —*Scott Yanow*

Vibrations / Nov. 7, 1971 / Enja ✦✦✦

Taro's Mood / Jun. 29, 1973 / Enja ✦✦✦

Double Rainbow / Feb. 19, 1981 / Columbia ✦✦

Bluestruck / Sep. 19, 1989+Sep. 21, 1989 / Blue Note ✦✦✦✦✦
Eight-piece band with John Scofield (g), Bob Watson (as), and Bob Hurst as principals. Hino wrote six of the eight tracks. —*Michael G. Nastos*

From the Heart / Jan. 17, 1991–Jan. 18, 1991 / Somethin' Else ✦✦✦✦
Smaller group with Alan Gumbs Trio and guests. "Free Mandela" and "Lava Dance" stand out. Six by Hino, one by Gumbs, one standard. —*Michael G. Nastos*

Triple Helix / Apr. 18, 1993 / Enja ✦✦✦

★ **Unforgettable** / Apr. 21, 1993–Apr. 22, 1993 / Blue Note ✦✦✦✦✦

Spark / 1994 / Blue Note ✦✦✦✦
This is one of trumpeter Terumasa Hino's more interesting releases. Hino often sounds like an exact duplicate of Freddie Hubbard in his prime on the more hard bop-oriented pieces while mixing in a bit of Miles Davis with Hubbard on the funkier numbers. He is joined by a fine Japanese group (in addition to Jay Hoggard on marimbas and vibes and percussionist Don Alias), which includes two percussionists who keep the rhythms torrid; Hoggard (particularly on marimbas) is a major part of the ensembles. Highlights include memorable versions of Horace Silver's "Song for My Father" (which is given funky Latin rhythms) and Silver's neglected "Calcutta Cutie." Other than the tribute, "Art Blakey," most of the other performances utilize rhythmic vamps while "Suavemente" features the trumpeter's expressive long tones over a synthesizer. Every selection holds one's interest, making this one of Terumasa Hino's most rewarding recordings to date. —*Scott Yanow*

Milt Hinton

b. Jun. 23, 1910, Vicksburg, MS
Bass / Swing
Bassist Milt Hinton has probably appeared on more records than any other musician in the world and he remains a vital figure in jazz even at the age of 86. He grew up in Chicago and worked with many legendary figures from the late '20s to the mid-'30s including Freddie Keppard, Jabbo Smith, Tiny Parham (with whom he made his recording debut in 1930), Eddie South, Fate Marable and Zutty Singleton. He was with Cab Calloway's Orchestra and his later small group during 1936–51. Considered the best bassist before the rise of Jimmy Blanton in 1939, Hinton was featured on "Pluckin' the Bass" (1939) and was an ally of Dizzy Gillespie in modernizing Calloway's music.

After leaving Cab, Hinton worked in clubs with Joe Bushkin, had brief stints with Count Basie and Louis Armstrong's All-Stars and in 1954 became a staff musician at CBS, appearing on a countless number of recordings (jazz and otherwise) during the next 15 years; everything from Jackie Gleason mood music and polka bands to commercials and Buck Clayton jam sessions. By the 1970s Hinton was appearing regularly at jazz parties and festivals and his activities have not slowed down during the past two decades; in 1995 he toured with the Statesmen of Jazz. Although a modern soloist, Hinton has also kept the art of slap bass alive. A very skilled photographer, Hinton has released two books of his candid shots of jazz musicians including one (*Bass Line*) which has his fascinating memoirs. Milt Hinton has recorded as a leader for Bethlehem, Victor (both in 1955), Famous Door, Black & Blue and Chiaroscuro and as a sideman for virtually every label! —*Scott Yanow*

★ **Old Man Time** / Oct. 3, 1989–Mar. 2, 1989 / Chiaroscuro ✦✦✦✦✦
Laughing At Life / 1994 / Columbia ✦✦✦✦
Milt Hinton's major label debut as a leader (at age 85!), other than a 1955 date for Victor, finds the great bassist utilizing two separate rhythm sections on a variety of standards. In addition to fine solos from pianists Richard Wyands and Derek Smith, there are guest appearances by trumpeter Jon Faddis (who defies his stereotype by sounding closer here to Roy Eldridge than to Dizzy Gillespie) and veteran Harold Ashby whose warm tenor recalls Ben Webster. Even if Hinton's three vocals are one too many, his singing has its charm. The finale "The Judge and the Jury" adds four other bassists for a very musical tribute to one of the few veterans of the 1920s still to be heard in his prime in the mid-'90s. —*Scott Yanow*

The Trio: 1994 / Jan. 14, 1994 / Chiaroscuro ✦✦✦✦

Al Hirt (Alois Maxwell Hirt)

b. Nov. 7, 1922, New Orleans, LA
Trumpet / Dixieland
A virtuoso on the trumpet, Al Hirt is often "overqualified" for the Dixieland and pop music that he performs. He studied classical trumpet at the Cincinnati Conservatory (1940–43) and was influenced by the playing of Harry James. He freelanced in swing bands (including both Tommy and Jimmy Dorsey and Ray McKinley) before returning to New Orleans in the late '40s and becoming involved in the Dixieland movement. He teamed up with clarinetist Pete Fountain on an occasional basis from 1955 on and became famous by the end of the decade. An outstanding technician with a wide range along with a propensity for playing far too many notes, Hirt had some instrumental pop hits in the 1960s and also recorded swing and country music but mostly stuck to Dixieland in his live performances. He remains a household name today, although one often feels that he could have done so much more with his talent. Hirt's early Audiofidelity recordings (1958–60) and collaborations with Fountain are the most rewarding of his career. —*Scott Yanow*

Al Hirt: Swingin' Dixie / 1958 / Audio Fidelity ✦✦✦✦
Al Hirt: Swingin' Dixie, Vol. 2 / 1958 / Audio Fidelity ✦✦✦✦
Al Hirt: Swingin' Dixie, Vol. 3 / 1958 / Audio Fidelity ✦✦✦✦
He's the King / Dec. 7, 1960–Dec. 16, 1960 / Victor ✦✦✦
Our Man in New Orleans / Jan. 26, 1962–Jan. 27, 1962 / RCA ✦✦✦
Live at Carnegie Hall / Apr. 22, 1965 / RCA ✦✦
● **That's a Plenty** / Mar. 29, 1988–Mar. 31, 1988 / Pro Arte ✦✦✦✦
Jumbo appears with Peanuts Hocko, Bobby Breaux, Dalton Hagler, and others pouncing on New Orleans favorites like "Royal Garden Blues," "Bourbon Street Parade," and "Saints." —*Bruce Raeburn*

Steve Hobbs

b. Raleigh, NC
Vibes / Hard Bop
One of the more talented vibraphonists to come up in the late '80s, Steve Hobbs' style is bop-based but fairly original. He studied at Berklee, the University of Miami and the University of Northern Colorado in Greeley and freelanced in Denver for six years with such players as Tom Harrell, Joe Bonner, Spike Robinson and Stix Hooper. Hobbs eventually moved back to Raleigh where he works as an educator but keeps up an active performance schedule. He has thus far recorded as a leader for Cexton, Timeless and Candid. —*Scott Yanow*

Escape / Nov. 11, 1988–Nov. 12, 1988 / Cexton ✦✦✦
Cultural Diversity / Aug. 5, 1991–Aug. 6, 1991 / Timeless ✦✦✦✦
● **Lower East Side** / Jul. 21, 1993–Jul. 22, 1993 / Candid ✦✦✦✦✦

Art Hodes

b. Nov. 14, 1904, Nikoliev, Russia, **d.** Mar. 4, 1993, Park Forest, IL
Piano / Dixieland, Blues
Throughout his long career, Art Hodes was a fighter for traditional jazz, whether through his distinctive piano playing, his writings (which included many articles and liner notes) or his work on radio and educational television. Renowned for the feeling he put into blues, Hodes was particularly effective on uptempo tunes where his on-the-beat chordings from his left hand could be quite

exciting. Born in Russia, he came to America with his family when he was six months old and grew up in Chicago. Hodes had the opportunity to witness Chicago jazz during its prime years in the 1920s and he learned from other pianists. In 1928 he made his recording debut with Wingy Manone but spent most of the 1930s in obscurity in Chicago until he moved to New York in 1938. He played with Joe Marsala and Mezz Mezzrow before forming his own band in 1941. Hodes recorded for Solo Art, his Jazz Record label, Signature, Decca and Black & White during 1939–42, but he made more of an impression with his heated Dixieland recordings for Blue Note during 1944–45 (all of which have been reissued on a Mosaic box set). During 1943–47 Hodes edited the important magazine *The Jazz Record*, had a radio show and became involved in the moldy fig vs. bebop wars with Leonard Feather and Barry Ulanov; jazz on a whole lost from the latter. In 1950 he returned to Chicago where he remained active locally and made occasional records. Hodes hosted a television series *Jazz Alley* for a time in the 1960s, wrote for *Downbeat* and was a jazz educator. Art Hodes recorded frequently during the 1970s and '80s and was widely recognized as one of the last survivors of Chicago jazz. His later recordings were for such labels as Audiophile, Jazzology, Delmark, Storyville, Euphonic, Parkwood, Candid and Music & Arts. —*Scott Yanow*

★ **Complete Blue Note Art Hodes Sessions** / Mar. 18, 1944–Dec. 16, 1945 / Mosaic ✦✦✦✦✦
The Funky Piano of Art Hodes / Mar. 22, 1944–May 17, 1945 / Blue Note ✦✦✦
Pianist Art Hodes led a consistently enjoyable series of Dixielandish recordings during 1944–45, all of which have since been issued in a Mosaic five-LP boxed set. This LP, which compiled in 1969, has a strong sampling of the hotter tracks with such fine players as trumpeter Max Kaminsky, trombonists Vic Dickenson and Sandy Williams and clarinetists Omer Simeon, Rod Cless and Edmond Hall getting their spots. —*Scott Yanow*

Apex Blues / Dec. 12, 1944 / Jazzology ✦✦✦
The Trios / Mar. 5, 1953–Dec. 10, 1953 / Jazzology ✦✦✦✦
Plain Old Blues / May 1962 / EmArcy ✦✦✦✦
Friar's Inn Revisited / 1968 / Delmark ✦✦✦✦
The bulk of this excellent album of Dixieland standards features pianist Art Hodes in a sextet with trumpeter Nappy Trottier, trombonist George Brunies (who also sings "Angry") and clarinetist Volly De Faut. Since recording opportunities for these musicians and for traditional jazz in particular were pretty rare in 1968, Delmark documented some very valuable music in this relaxed session. The LP is rounded out by two alternate takes left from a quartet date that Hodes did about the same period of time with the swing veteran clarinetist Barney Bigard. —*Scott Yanow*

Hodes' Art / Oct. 22, 1968–Apr. 23, 1972 / Delmark ✦✦✦
Opportunities for pianist Art Hodes to record in the 1960s were quite rare. In fact during 1963–70, other than a record documenting a concert, Hodes' entire output was three albums cut for Delmark in 1968; traditional jazz was definitely out of style. This particular Delmark CD has brief moments from a variety of veteran greats. "When My Sugar Walks down the Street" matches Hodes and his rhythm section with trombonist George Brunis, trumpeter Nappy Trottier and clarinetist Volly De Faut; the clarinetist (a veteran of the early '20s) also plays on "Struttin' with Some Barbeque." In addition to three piano-bass-drums trio numbers, Hodes is heard on six relaxed selections in a trio with clarinetist Raymond Burke (who is in good form) and veteran bassist Pops Foster. This historic music is easily enjoyable. —*Scott Yanow*

Selections from the Gutter / Oct. 5, 1970–Oct. 10, 1970 / Storyville ✦✦✦✦
Wonderful blues, traditional jazz, and stride numbers by jazz pianist and critic Art Hodes, who cut many superb records for small independents during an extensive career. —*Ron Wynn*

Up in Volly's Room / Mar. 15, 1972–Apr. 1972 / Delmark ✦✦✦✦
Someone to Watch over Me / Aug. 26, 1981 / Muse ✦✦✦✦✦
After a long period of critical neglect, pianist Art Hodes' career was on the upswing in the early '80s. Rightfully celebrated for his blues solos, Hodes' uptempo romps (check out "Grandpa's Spells" and "Struttin' with Some Barbecue" on this solo set) could be quite jubilant with his left hand happily pounding out chords on the beat. This well-rounded set is a fine showcase for his playing talents. —*Scott Yanow*

South Side Memories / Nov. 29, 1983 / Sackville ✦✦✦

Blues in the Night / Jun. 16, 1985 / Sackville ✦✦✦

Solos, Vol. 1 / Apr. 20, 1987–Jul. 10, 1989 / Parkwood ✦✦✦✦
Pianist Art Hodes is heard on two different solo albums on this single CD. First he performs eight Christmas songs, infusing the familiar melodies with a strong dose of blues and rhythm (although the emphasis is on relaxed tempos). The later set has eight of Hodes' blues-oriented originals. Hodes was one of the top pianists in classic jazz with a distinctive voice of his own. This set from his later years is a fine example of his talents. —*Scott Yanow*

Live from Toronto's Cafe Des Copains / 1988 / Music & Arts ✦✦✦✦

★ **Pagin' Mr. Jelly** / Nov. 14, 1988 / Candid ✦✦✦✦✦

Final Sessions / Jul. 30, 1990–Aug. 19, 1990 / Music & Arts ✦✦✦✦
Pianist Art Hodes, one of the leading pianists during the revival years of classic jazz, is surprisingly strong during what would be his final recordings. Already in his mid-'80s, Hodes (three years before his death) explores 13 familiar themes ranging from "Alexander's Ragtime Band" and "Royal Garden Blues" to "America the Beautiful." Six songs are duets with Jim Galloway on soprano, Hodes teams up with clarinetist Kenny Davern for "Summertime," there are four trios with both horns and also two unaccompanied piano solos. Hodes was a very consistent performer throughout his lengthy career and his last album (available as a 71-minute CD) is well worth hearing. —*Scott Yanow*

Johnny Hodges

b. Jul. 25, 1907, Cambridge, MA, **d.** May 11, 1970, New York, NY
Alto Saxophone, Soprano Saxophone / Swing
Possessor of the most beautiful tone ever heard in jazz, altoist Johnny Hodges formed his style early on and had little reason to change it through the decades. Although he could stomp with the best swing players and was masterful on the blues, Hodges' luscious playing on ballads has never been topped. He played drums and piano early on before switching to soprano sax when he was 14. Hodges was taught and inspired by Sidney Bechet although he soon used alto as his main ax; he would regretfully drop soprano altogether after 1940. His early experiences included playing with Lloyd Scott, Chick Webb, Luckey Roberts and Willie "The Lion" Smith (1924) and he also had the opportunity to work with Bechet. However, Johnny Hodges' real career began in 1928 when he joined Duke Ellington's Orchestra. He quickly became one of the most important solo stars in the band and a real pacesetter on alto; Benny Carter was his only close competition in the 1930s. Hodges was featured on a countless number of performances with Ellington and also had many chances to lead recording dates with Duke's sidemen. Whether it was "Things Ain't What They Used to Be," "Come Sunday" or "Passion Flower," Hodges was an indispensable member of Ellington's Orchestra in the 1930s and '40s. It was therefore a shock in 1951 when he decided to leave Duke and lead a band of his own. Hodges had a quick hit in "Castle Rock" (which ironically showcased Al Sears' tenor and had no real contribution by the altoist) but his combo ended up struggling and breaking up in 1955. Hodges' return to Duke Ellington was a joyous occasion and he never really left again. In the 1960s Hodges teamed up with organist Wild Bill Davis on some sessions, leading to Davis joining Ellington for a time in 1969. Johnny Hodges, whose unchanging style always managed to sound fresh, was still with Duke Ellington when Hodges suddenly died in 1970. —*Scott Yanow*

Hodge Podge / Mar. 28, 1938–Oct. 14, 1939 / Legacy/Epic ✦✦✦
This is a good set that should have been a great one. Rather than reissue all 43 of altoist Johnny Hodges' small-group dates for Vocalion and Okeh, this CD (which should have been two) only contains 16. The music is often classic small-group swing ("Jeep's Blues," "Hodge Podge" and "Rent Party Blues" are among the highpoints) and there are several superb examples of Hodges playing soprano (showing off the influence of Sidney Bechet), but many valuable performances are missing. The problem is that the set is a straight reissue (although with some new liner notes) of an Epic LP rather than being an improvement. This important material deserves to be repackaged in a more complete fashion. —*Scott Yanow*

● **Passion Flower** / Nov. 2, 1940–Jun. 9, 1946 / Bluebird ✦✦✦✦✦
For 42 years (with a four-year interruption), altoist Johnny Hodges was the top soloist in Duke Ellington's all-star Orchestra. This excellent CD reissue has the eight selections (plus an alternate take) from Hodges' two Bluebird sessions of 1940–41; among the sidemen on such classics as "Day Dream," "Good Queen Bess," "Passion Flower" and "Things Ain't What They Used to Be" are either Cootie Williams or Ray Nance on trumpet, trombonist Lawrence Brown and Ellington himself. In addition, there are 13 selections by the Duke Ellington Orchestra of 1940–46 that feature Hodges including "Don't Get Around Anymore," "In a Mellotone," "Warm Valley," "I Got It Bad" and "Come Sunday." This is classic music that has been intelligently repackaged. —*Scott Yanow*

On Keynote with Rex Stewart / 1946 / PolyGram ✦✦✦
A thorough collection of sides from Keynote, spotlighting Ellingtonians Hodges and Rex Stewart (cnt). —*Ron Wynn*

Ellingtonia! / Sep. 3, 1946–Aug. 27, 1964 / Onyx ✦✦✦
This long out-of-print 1974 Onyx LP has a variety of fine performances featuring altoist Johnny Hodges. The first two titles ("Esquire Swank" and "Midriff") also have the full Duke Ellington Orchestra and spots for high note trumpeter Cat Anderson and trombonist Lawrence Brown. In addition there are four songs apiece from a 1950 Paris session (featuring trumpeter Harold "Shorty" Baker, trombonist Quentin Jackson and Don Byas on tenor) and a previously unissued four-tune date from 1964 with Anderson, Brown and tenor saxophonist Paul Gonsalves. Johnny Hodges' beautiful alto sound and mastery of blues and ballads is very much in evidence on these fine swing sessions. Well worth a search. —*Scott Yanow*

Caravan / Jun. 1947–Jun. 19, 1951 / Prestige ✦✦✦✦
This single CD, which reissues all of the music from a double-LP, has a variety of formerly rare sessions from 1947–51. Although the great altoist Johnny Hodges gets top billing, and he leads three sessions from 1947 (featuring such top Ellington stars as trombonist Lawrence Brown, tenorman Al Sears, baritonist Harry Carney and either Taft Jordan or Harold Baker on trumpet), he is actually absent on the second half of the release. With Billy Strayhorn and/or Duke Ellington as leader and Willie Smith on alto, these enthusiastic swing performances range in personnel from a three-trombone septet to a version of "Caravan" with Ellington on piano and Strayhorn making a rare appearance on organ. Although the music falls just short of classic, Ellington collectors will love these rarities. —*Scott Yanow*

☆ **Complete Johnny Hodges Sessions (1951–1955)** / Jan. 15, 1951–Sep. 8, 1955 / Mosaic ✦✦✦✦✦
As is true of most Mosaic box sets, it would be very difficult to improve upon this reissue. Altoist Johnny Hodges left Duke Ellington's Orchestra in 1950 after 22 years to try to make it on his own as a bandleader. Five years later, he returned to Ellington for the final 15 years of his life after having recorded the music heard on this six-LP set. Hodges' small group, a unit that emphasized blues, ballads and riff-filled romps, was an extension of the Ellington band. Hodges had a big hit with "Castle Rock" (ironically a feature for tenor saxophonist Al Sears), but otherwise had trouble at the end making ends meet. Other notable sidemen on these easily enjoyable performances include trumpeters Emmett Berry and Harold "Shorty" Baker, trombonist Lawrence Brown and tenors Flip Phillips, Ben Webster and John Coltrane on one session (during which he unfortunately does not solo); the final session, from Sept. 8, 1955 (after Hodges had already returned to Ellington), also has trumpeter Clark Terry and pianist Billy Strayhorn. Most of this music had been long out of print at the time this 1989 box was released. A highly recommended gem of swinging jazz. —*Scott Yanow*

Used to Be Duke / Jul. 2, 1954+Aug. 5, 1954 / Verve ✦✦✦✦
Recorded during his five year "vacation" from Duke Ellington's orchestra, this Johnny Hodges set (reissued on CD) features his band sticking mostly to standards. With trumpeter Harold "Shorty" Baker, trombonist Lawrence Brown, baritonist Harry Carney, pianist Call Cobbs or Richie Powell, bassist John Williams, drummer Louis Bellson and either Jimmy Hamilton or John Coltrane (who unfortunately does not solo) on tenor, Hodges had a particularly strong group. High points include "On the Sunny Side of the Street," the title track and a seven-song ballad medley. This session was also included in Mosaic's six-LP Johnny Hodges set. —*Scott Yanow*

At A Dance, In A Studio, On Radio / 1954–1957 / Enigma ✦✦✦✦
Although this is a bootleg album, the music on this LP is histori-

cally significant, particularly a couple of titles from 1954 on which tenor saxophonist John Coltrane (the year before he joined Miles Davis) gets to solo; trumpeter Harold "Shorty" Baker and trombonist Lawrence Brown are also in the supporting cast. Although the bulk of the album is a 1954 dance date (probably taken from a radio broadcast) there are also a few titles from March 1957 by the full Ellington band. This is worth picking up, particularly for the early Coltrane solos. —*Scott Yanow*

The Big Sound / Jun. 26, 1957+Sep. 3, 1957 / Verve ++++
No surprises, but the session was as good as one might hope. Gathered here was the Ellington band with Billy Strayhorn at the piano. While it was not an Ellington record, the band brought its solid qualities in backing and the occasional solo to all the fine Hodges features. This was an integrated unit, not some detached studio band for Hodges to blow over, under, around, and through. It was wonderful Hodges and fine Ellington. —*Bob Rusch, Cadence*

A Smooth One / Apr. 7, 1959+Sep. 8, 1960 / Verve +++
This attractive double-LP from 1979 includes two complete sessions by altoist Johnny Hodges that were previously unissued at the time. Most unusual is that Hodges contributed 15 of the 19 compositions; the others are "Melancholy Baby," "Lotus Blossom" and two by clarinetist Jimmy Hamilton. Despite the unfamiliar material, the music is very much in the Duke Ellington style, with an emphasis on blues, ballads and riff tunes. In addition to Hodges, the other main soloists are trumpeter Harold "Shorty" Baker, tenor Ben Webster (on the first date) and trumpeter/violinist Ray Nance (on the second). None of this enjoyable music has yet been reissued on CD. —*Scott Yanow*

Masters of Jazz, Vol. 9 / Nov. 22, 1960–Mar. 14, 1961 / Storyville ++++
Here is a CD that is highly recommended for swing collectors. Altoist Johnny Hodges and tenor saxophonist Ben Webster team up for a sextet set from 1960, a club appearance that was released for the first time on this set. Their six performances (all are basic Hodges originals) find the pair of veteran swing stylists in prime form. The remainder of the program (three standards plus Hodges' "Good Queen Bess") is played by a septet dominated by Ellington musicians including the leader/altoist, baritonist Harry Carney, trumpeter Ray Nance and trombonist Lawrence Brown. Excellent music that still has not dated. —*Scott Yanow*

At the Berlin Sportpalast / Mar., 1961 / Pablo ++++
This double-CD, a straight reissue of a Pablo double-LP, documents a fun set. Altoist Johnny Hodges and some fellow members of Duke Ellington's Orchestra (Ray Nance on cornet, violin and vocals, trombonist Lawrence Brown, baritonist Harry Carney, bassist Aaron Bell, drummer Sam Woodyard and guest pianist Al Williams) jam through a mostly typical set of standards and Ellington tunes. Everyone gets featured and, even if there are no real surprises, the musicians are consistently heard in top form. Superior small-group swing by some of the best. —*Scott Yanow*

Blue Hodges / Aug. 23, 1961–Aug. 24, 1961 / Verve +++
This out-of-print LP (which has not yet been reissued on CD) is the earliest of several matchups between altoist Johnny Hodges and organist Wild Bill Davis. With the assistance of Les Spann on guitar and flute, bassist Sam Jones and drummer Louis Hayes, Hodges and Davis mostly stick to fresh material, including three then-recent originals by Gary McFarland. Highlights include "Azure Te," "It Shouldn't Happen to a Dream" and "There Is No Greater Love," in addition to some swinging blues. —*Scott Yanow*

Mess of Blues / Sep. 3, 1963–Sep. 4, 1963 / Verve +++
In the 1960s altoist Johnny Hodges took a brief time off from Duke Ellington's orchestra to record eight albums with organist Wild Bill Davis. For this, their third collaboration, the duo welcome guitarist Kenny Burrell, trumpeter Joe Wilder and either Osie Johnson or Ed Shaughnessy on drums. Hodges plays typically beautifully on such numbers as "I Cried for You," "Lost in Meditation" and "Stolen Sweets" and, although no real surprises occur (and the playing time at around a half-hour is quite brief), the performances are up to par. However, the music on this long out-of-print LP has yet to appear on CD. —*Scott Yanow*

• **Everybody Knows** / Feb. 6, 1964+Mar. 8, 1965 / GRP/Impulse! +++++
This excellent single CD has the complete contents of two Impulse! LPs: *Everybody Knows Johnny Hodges* and *Inspired*

Abandon, which was actually a Lawrence Brown album featuring Hodges. The two similar and equally rewarding swing-oriented albums find Hodges joined by a variety of top Ellington stars, including trumpeters Cat Anderson and Ray Nance, either Harold Ashby or Paul Gonsalves on tenors and trombonist Brown, among others. The renditions of "310 Blues," "The Jeep Is Jumpin'," "Stompy Jones" and "Mood Indigo," in particular, sound quite fresh and inventive. Recommended. —*Scott Yanow*

Johnny Hodges/Wild Bill Davis, Vols. 1 & 2 / Jan. 7, 1965–Sep. 11, 1966 / RCA Jazz Tribune ++++
This enjoyable double-CD from the RCA's Jazz Tribune series combines together a pair of sessions from altoist Johnny Hodges and organist Wild Bill Davis. While the earlier set has the pair joined by two guitarists (Mundell Lowe and Dickie Thompson), bassist Milt Hinton and drummer Osie Johnson while the second session has trombonist Lawrence Brown, Bob Brown on tenor and flute, Thompson returning on guitar and trombonist Bobby Durham. Another difference between the two dates is that the later album (which has been reissued on CD in the Bluebird series) was recorded in concert. The music generally sticks to standards (many written by Duke Ellington), ballads and an occasional blues. Hodges and Davis were a surprisingly complementary team (their collaborations were a brief vacation from their usual settings) and they seem to inspire each other. Fine swing-based music. —*Scott Yanow*

Johnny Hodges with Lawrence Welk's Orchestra / Dec. 20, 1965–Dec. 21, 1965 / Dot +++
This was one of the oddest matchups and yet ended up being fairly logical. Altoist Johnny Hodges had one of the most beautiful tones ever heard and Lawrence Welk always loved beautiful music. This Dot LP features Hodges on a dozen standards while accompanied by a string section, brass and a rhythm section. The concise and melodic interpretations are indeed pretty and the arrangements (by a dozen different writers) are generally fine. Plus the album cover (which has a picture of the unlikely duo) is classic. Recommended for the novelty value although this LP may be hard to find. —*Scott Yanow*

In a Mellotone / Sep. 10, 1966–Sep. 11, 1966 / Bluebird ++++
Altoist Johnny Hodges and organist Wild Bill Davis teamed up successfully on quite a few albums in the 1960s. This set, reissued on CD, was their final one and quite possibly their most rewarding. With solo work provided not only by the co-leaders but trombonist Lawrence Brown, obscure tenor Bob Brown, and guitarist Dickie Thompson (drummer Bobby Durham helps out in support), this is a particularly interesting outing. Unlike most of their other collaborations, this outing by Hodges and Davis sticks mostly to better-known material, including a previously unissued version of Duke Ellington's "Squeeze Me But Please Don't Tease Me" and four Hodges originals. Highlights include "It's Only a Paper Moon," "Taffy," "Good Queen Bess" and "In a Mellotone." This release is recommended as a strong (and swinging) example of Johnny Hodges outside of the Duke Ellington Orchestra. —*Scott Yanow*

Triple Play / Jan. 9, 1967–Jan. 10, 1967 / Bluebird ++++
Altoist Johnny Hodges is heard in three different settings on this reissue CD. Such top swing stars as trumpeters Ray Nance, Cat Anderson and Roy Eldridge, trombonists Buster Cooper, Lawrence Brown and Benny Powell, tenors Paul Gonsalves and Jimmy Hamilton, baritonist Harry Carney, pianists Hank Jones and Jimmy Jones (the latter two sometimes together), guitarists Tiny Grimes, Les Spann and Billy Butler, bassists Milt Hinton, Aaron Bell and Joe Benjamin and drummers Gus Johnson, Rufus Jones and Oliver Jackson are heard in nonets with the great altoist. Despite the many changes in personnel, the music is pretty consistent, with basic swinging originals, blues and ballads all heard in equal proportion. As usual, Johnny Hodges ends up as the main star. —*Scott Yanow*

Holly Hofmann

b. Ohio

Flute / Bop

An excellent bop-oriented flutist, Holly Hofmann began on the flute when she was five. She had extensive classical training and in 1984, when she moved to San Diego, Hofmann began playing jazz fulltime. She worked with James Moody, Slide Hampton and Mundell Lowe among others before making her recording debut on Capri (1989). Hofmann has since recorded fine straight-ahead dates for Jazz Alliance (1992) and Azica (1995), led her own groups and played regularly in the San Diego area. —*Scott Yanow*

Further Adventures / Jun. 28, 1989–Jun. 29, 1989 / Capri ✦✦✦✦

Duo Personality / Apr. 1992 / Jazz Alliance ✦✦✦✦

● **Tales of Hofmann** / Jul. 14, 1995–Jul. 20, 1995 / Azica ✦✦✦✦✦

Jay Hoggard

b. Sep. 24, 1954, New York, NY
Vibes / Avant-Garde, Post-Bop

Jay Hoggard has had a wide-ranging career. One of the top vibraphonists to emerge during the 1970s, Hoggard originally started on piano and saxophone before switching to vibes. By the early '70s he was working in New England with such top avant-garde players as Anthony Davis and Leo Smith. Hoggard moved to New York in 1977 where he played with Chico Freeman and Anthony Davis. In 1978 he recorded a solo avant-garde vibes performance but he followed it up with a more commercial date. Hoggard has worked with such greats as Sam Rivers, Cecil Taylor, James Newton and Kenny Burrell in addition to leading his own group; he has recorded hard bop-oriented dates as a leader for Contemporary, India Navigation and several for Muse. —*Scott Yanow*

Solo Vibraphone / Nov. 18, 1978 / India Navigation ✦✦✦✦✦
The finest, most complete record released thus far by vibist Jay Hoggard. This solo date put him alone in the spotlight, and he used the vehicle to display his total skills, from delicate melodies to aggressive harmonies and expressive solos. —*Ron Wynn*

Days Like These / 1979 / GRP ✦✦
Vibes playing is fine, but it's otherwise forgettable. —*Ron Wynn*

Rain Forest / Nov. 1980 / Contemporary ✦✦✦

Mystic Winds, Tropical Breezes / 1982 / India Navigation ✦✦✦✦✦
Strong, free-wheeling date by vibist Jay Hoggard. He was working with a topflight group, which featured pianist Anthony Davis, bassist Cecil McBee, drummers Billy Hart and Don Moye, and Dwight Andrews on various saxophones. The compositions were loosely structured and extended, and solos were fierce. —*Ron Wynn*

Love Survives / 1983 / Gramavision ✦✦✦✦

Riverside Dance / 1985 / India Navigation ✦✦✦✦

Overview / Jun. 22, 1989 / Muse ✦✦✦✦
Very good, with Geri Allen (p). —*Michael G. Nastos*

The Little Tiger / Jun. 10, 1990 / Muse ✦✦✦✦✦
An album with the vibist at his best. The title track is worth the price alone. With Benny Green. —*Michael G. Nastos*

★ **The Fountain** / Jul. 10, 1991 / Muse ✦✦✦✦✦
Vibraphonist Jay Hoggard has had a diverse recording career, playing everything from very free jazz to a couple of commercial efforts. In the 1990s he seemed to discover straight-ahead jazz and this quintet session (with guitarist Kenny Burrell and pianist James Weidman) is mostly very much in that idiom. Hoggard is fine on standards such as "Stompin' at the Savoy" (a tribute to Lionel Hampton) and Monk's "Epistrophy" but it is on his originals (the soulful "Sweet Potato" and a fairly free "The Fountain") that Hoggard sounds most individual. —*Scott Yanow*

In the Spirit / May 4, 1992 / Muse ✦✦✦✦

Love Is The Answer / Jan. 9, 1994–Feb. 27, 1994 / Muse ✦✦✦✦

Billie Holiday (Eleanora Harris)

b. Apr. 7, 1915, Baltimore, MD, d. Jul. 17, 1959, New York, NY
Vocals / Swing

Billie Holiday remains (37 years after her death) the most famous of all jazz singers. "Lady Day" (as she was named by Lester Young) had a small voice and did not scat but her innovative behind-the-beat phrasing made her quite influential. The emotional intensity that she put into the words she sang (particularly in later years) was very memorable and sometimes almost scary; she often really did live the words she sang.

Her original name and birthplace have been wrong for years but are listed correctly above thanks to Donald Clarke's definitive Billie Holiday biography *Wishing on the Moon*. Holiday's early years are shrouded in legend and rumors due to her fanciful ghostwritten autobiography *Lady Sings the Blues*, but it is fair to say that she did not have a stable life. Her father, Clarence

Holiday, (who never did marry her mother) played guitar with Fletcher Henderson and abandoned his family early on while her mother was not a very good role model. Billie essentially grew up alone, feeling unloved and gaining a lifelong inferiority complex that led to her taking great risks with her personal life and becoming self-destructive.

Holiday's life becomes clearer after she was discovered by John Hammond singing in Harlem clubs. He arranged for her to record a couple of titles with Benny Goodman in 1933 and although those were not all that successful, it was the start of her career. Two years later she was teamed with a pickup band led by Teddy Wilson and the combination clicked. During 1935–42 she would make some of the finest recordings of her career, jazz-oriented performances in which she was joined by the who's who of swing. Holiday sought to combine together Louis Armstrong's swing and Bessie Smith's sound; the result was her own fresh approach. In 1937 Lester Young and Buck Clayton began recording with Holiday and the interplay between the three of them was timeless.

Lady Day was with Count Basie's Orchestra during much of 1937 but, because they were signed to different labels, all that exists of the collaboration are three songs from a radio broadcast. She worked with Artie Shaw's Orchestra for a time in 1938 but the same problem existed (only one song was recorded) and she had to deal with racism, not only during a Southern tour but in New York, too. She had better luck as a star attraction at Cafe Society in 1939. Holiday made history that year by recording the horribly picturesque "Strange Fruit," a strong anti-racism statement that became a permanent part of her repertoire. Her records of 1940–42 found her sidemen playing a much more supportive role than in the past, rarely sharing solo space with her.

Although the settings were less jazz-oriented than before (with occasional strings and even a background vocal group on a few numbers) Billie Holiday's voice was actually at its strongest during her period with Decca (1944–49). She had already introduced "Fine and Mellow" (1939) and "God Bless the Child" (1941), but it was while with Decca that she first recorded "Lover Man" (her biggest hit), "Don't Explain," "Good Morning Heartache" and her renditions of "Ain't Nobody's Business If I Do," "Them There Eyes" and "Crazy He Calls Me." Unfortunately, it was just before this period that she became a heroin addict and she spent much of 1947 in jail. Due to the publicity, she became a notorious celebrity and her audience greatly increased. Lady Day did get a chance to make one Hollywood movie (*New Orleans*) in 1946 and, although she was disgusted at the fact that she was stuck playing a maid, she did get to perform with her early idol Louis Armstrong.

Billie Holiday's story from 1950 on is a gradual downhill slide. Although her recordings for Norman Granz (which started in 1952) placed her once again with all-star jazz veterans (including Charlie Shavers, Buddy DeFranco, Harry "Sweets" Edison and Ben Webster), her voice was slipping fast. Her unhappy relationships distracted her, the heroin use and excessive drinking continued and by 1956 she was way past her prime. Holiday had one final burst of glory in late 1957 when she sang "Fine and Mellow" on *The Sound of Jazz* telecast while joined by Lester Young (who stole the show with an emotional chorus), Ben Webster, Coleman Hawkins, Gerry Mulligan and Roy Eldridge, but the end was near. Holiday's 1958 album *Lady in Satin* found the 43-year old singer sounding 73 (barely croaking out the words) and the following year she collapsed; in the sad final chapter of her life she was placed under arrest for heroin possession while on her deathbed!

Fortunately, Billie Holiday's recordings have been better treated than she was during her life and virtually all of her studio sides are currently available on CD. —*Scott Yanow*

★ **The Quintessential Billie Holiday, Vol. 1 (1933–1935)** / Nov. 27, 1933–Dec. 3, 1935 / Columbia ✦✦✦✦✦
After years of reissuing her recordings in piecemeal fashion, Columbia finally got it right with this nine-CD *Quintessential* series. All of Lady Day's 1933–42 studio recordings (although without the alternate takes) receive the treatment they deserve in this program. *Vol. 1* has Holiday's first two tentative performances from 1933 and along with her initial recordings with Teddy Wilson's all-star bands. Highpoints include "I Wished On the Moon," "What a Little Moonlight Can Do," "Miss Brown to You," and "Twenty-Four Hours a Day." —*Scott Yanow*

Billie Holiday: The Legacy Box 1933-1958 / Nov. 27, 1933-Feb. 19, 1958 / Columbia ✦✦✦
The logic behind this sampler is puzzling. Rather than reissue the very best of Billie Holiday's Columbia recordings on a three-CD box set or a package of her rare alternate takes, CBS tries it both ways by including 60 common selections already available in the *Quintessential* series along with 10 rarities that were either unissued or alternates. This otherwise attractive box (which includes a colorful booklet) will drive completists and veteran collectors crazy. The music (mostly from 1933-42 with three weaker performances from 1957-58) is often classic but duplicates more coherent reissues. —*Scott Yanow*

☆ **Billie Holiday: The Voice of Jazz: The Complete Recordings 1933-1940** / Nov. 27, 1933-Oct. 15, 1940 / Affinity ✦✦✦✦✦

Lady Day / Jul. 2, 1935-Jun. 15, 1937 / Columbia ✦✦✦✦
This LP, whose contents have since been reissued on CD, used to be the one definitive set to acquire of early Billie Holiday. The 12 selections are all classics (particularly "What a Little Moonlight Can Do," "If You Were Mine," "Billie's Blues," "I Must Have That Man," "Easy Living," "Me, Myself and I" and "I Cried for You") and find Lady Day joined by such all-stars as pianist Teddy Wilson, trumpeters Roy Eldridge, Bunny Berigan and Buck Clayton, clarinetist Benny Goodman, the tenors of Lester Young and Ben Webster and altoist Johnny Hodges among others. Wonderful music that is essential to acquire in one form or another. —*Scott Yanow*

★ **The Quintessential Billie Holiday, Vol. 2 (1936)** / Jan. 30, 1936-Oct. 21, 1936 / Columbia ✦✦✦✦✦
The second of nine volumes in this essential series (all are highly recommended) continues the complete reissue of Billie Holiday's early recordings (although the alternate takes are bypassed). This set is highlighted by "I Cried for You" (which has a classic alto solo from Johnny Hodges), "Billie's Blues" (from Holiday's first session as a leader), "A Fine Romance" and "Easy to Love." Holiday's backup crew includes such greats as pianist Teddy Wilson, baritonist Harry Carney, trumpeters Jonah Jones and Bunny Berigan and clarinetist Artie Shaw. There's lots of great small-group swing. —*Scott Yanow*

Don't Explain / Sep. 29, 1936-Jul. 25, 1958 / Audio Fidelity ✦✦
This three-LP box set is one of the more bizarre Billie Holiday reissues with virtually all of the discographical information on its back cover completely inaccurate. A hodgepodge collection of live performances along with a few (presumably illegal) studio cuts, the recordings jump all over the place, from broadcasts with Count Basie in 1937 to TV appearances, concert performances in the 1950s and the 1936 studio version of "I Can't Pretend"; the latter has dubbed in phony applause. The recording quality varies from decent to barely listenable. —*Scott Yanow*

★ **The Quintessential Billie Holiday, Vol. 3 (1936-1937)** / Oct. 28, 1936-Feb. 18, 1937 / Columbia ✦✦✦✦✦
The third of nine CDs that document all of Billie Holiday's studio recordings of 1933-42 for Columbia has classic versions of "Pennies from Heaven," "I Can't Give You Anything but Love" (on which she shows the influence of Louis Armstrong) and "My Last Affair," along with Lady Day's first meeting on record with tenor saxophonist Lester Young. Their initial encounter resulted in four songs including "This Year's Kisses" and "I Must Have That Man." All nine volumes in this admirable series (if only the alternate takes had been included!) are highly recommended. —*Scott Yanow*

☆ **The Quintessential Billie Holiday, Vol. 4 (1937)** / Mar. 31, 1937-Jun. 15, 1937 / Columbia ✦✦✦✦✦
The fourth of nine CDs in this essential series of Billie Holiday's studio recordings of 1933-42 features the great tenor Lester Young on eight of the 16 performances. Prez and Lady Day make a perfect match on "I'll Get By" (although altoist Johnny Hodges steals the honors on that song), "Mean to Me," "Easy Living," "Me Myself and I" and "A Sailboat in the Moonlight." Other strong selections without Young include "Moanin' Low," "Let's Call the Whole Thing Off" and "Where Is the Sun." It's highly recommended along with all of the other CDs in this perfectly done Billie Holiday reissue program. —*Scott Yanow*

★ **The Quintessential Billie Holiday, Vol. 5 (1937-1938)** / Jun. 15, 1937-Jan. 27, 1938 / Columbia ✦✦✦✦✦
The fifth of nine CDs in the complete reissue of Billie Holiday's early recordings (sans alternate takes), this great set has 18 selec-

tions, all but four featuring tenor saxophonist Lester Young and trumpeter Buck Clayton. Among the classics are "Getting Some Fun out of Life," "Trav'lin' All Alone," "He's Funny That Way," "My Man," "When You're Smiling" (on which Prez takes a perfect solo), "If Dreams Come True" and "Now They Call It Swing." All nine volumes in this series are highly recommended, but if one can only acquire a single entry, this is the one. —*Scott Yanow*

The Billie Holiday and Her Orchestra (1937-1939) / 1937-1939 / Classics ✦✦✦✦

☆ **Quintessential Billie Holiday, Vol. 6 (1938)** / May 11, 1938-Nov. 9, 1938 / Columbia ✦✦✦✦✦
The sixth of nine CDs in this very worthy series traces Billie Holiday's recording career throughout much of 1938. Although not containing as many true classics as *Vol. 5*, most of these 18 selections are quite enjoyable, particularly "You Go to My Head," "Having Myself a Time," "The Very Thought of You" and "They Say." All of the sets in this reissue program are recommended, featuring Lady Day when she was youthful and still optimistic about life. —*Scott Yanow*

The Quintessential Billie Holiday, Vol. 7 (1938-1939) / Nov. 28, 1938-Jul. 5, 1939 / Columbia ✦✦✦✦
By 1939 when the bulk of these 17 selections were recorded, Billie Holiday was dominating her own recordings, allocating less space for her sidemen to solo. This was not really a bad thing since Lady Day's voice was getting stronger each year. On the seventh of nine CD volumes that reissue all of Holiday's 1933-42 Columbia recordings (other than the alternate takes, which have been bypassed), Holiday sounds at her best on "More than You Know, Sugar" (featuring a superb Benny Carter alto solo), "Long Gone Blues" and "Some Other Spring." It's recommended along with all of the other entries in the *Quintessential* series. —*Scott Yanow*

I'll be Seeing You / Apr. 20, 1939-Apr. 8, 1944 / Commodore ✦✦✦✦✦
This CD includes all of Billie Holiday's Commodore recordings (the master takes but no alternates): four titles from 1939 (including the still haunting "Strange Fruit" and "Fine and Mellow") and the remainder dating from 1944 when Holiday's voice was at its peak. The latter sessions are highlighted by "I'll Get By," "Billie's Blues," "He's Funny That Way" and "I'm Yours." Pianist Eddie Heywood has many sparkling solos on the 1944 selections. This definitive single CD contains music essential for every jazz collection. —*Scott Yanow*

☆ **Quintessential Billie Holiday, Vol. 8 (1939-1940)** / Jul. 5, 1939-Sep. 12, 1940 / Columbia ✦✦✦✦
The eighth of nine volumes that feature all of the master takes from Billie Holiday's Columbia recordings of 1933-42 is one of the better sets, although all nine CDs are recommended. Highpoints include "Them There Eyes," "Swing, Brother, Swing," "The Man I Love," "Ghost of Yesterday," "Body And Soul," "Falling in Love Again," and "I Hear Music." Among the variety of all-stars backing her, tenor saxophonist Lester Young makes his presence known on eight of the 18 numbers. —*Scott Yanow*

Billie Holiday (1939-1940) / 1939-1940 / Classics ✦✦✦✦

Quintessential Billie Holiday, Vol. 9 (1940-1942) / Oct. 15, 1940-Feb. 10, 1942 / Columbia ✦✦✦✦✦
The final volume in this nine-CD series contains all of Billie Holiday's recordings from her final 16 months with the label. Highlights include "St. Louis Blues," "Loveless Love," "Let's Do It," "All of Me" (arguably the greatest version ever of this veteran standard), "Am I Blue," "Gloomy Sunday" and "God Bless the Child." All 153 of Lady Day's Columbia recordings (even the occasional weak item) are well worth hearing and savoring. —*Scott Yanow*

Billie's Blues / Jun. 12, 1942-Jan. 5, 1954 / Blue Note ✦✦✦✦
Most of this excellent CD features one of Billie Holiday's finest concert recordings of the 1950s. Recorded in Europe before an admiring audience, this enjoyable set finds Lady Day performing seven of her standards with her trio and joining in for jam session versions of "Billie's Blues" and "Lover Come Back to Me" with an all-star group starring clarinetist Buddy DeFranco, vibraphonist Red Norvo and guitarist Jimmy Raney. These performances (which find Holiday in stronger voice than on her studio recordings of the period) have also been included in Verve's massive CD box set. This program concludes with Holiday's four rare sides for Aladdin in 1951 (between her Decca and Verve periods), which are highlighted by two blues and "Detour Ahead," and her

1942 studio recording of "Trav'lin' Light" with Paul Whiteman's Orchestra. —*Scott Yanow*

Masters of Jazz, Vol. 3 / Jan. 18, 1944–1949 / Storyville ✦✦✦
This very interesting CD has a variety of mostly rare Billie Holiday live performances from 1944–49. In addition to two selections with the 1944 Esquire All-Stars, Lady Day is heard with Hot Lips Page, accompanied by pianist Teddy Wilson on a 1947 version of "The Man I Love," backed by Percy Faith's string orchestra on "You Better Go Now" and joined by a Red Norvo-led band in 1949 that also includes trumpeter Neal Hefti and the reeds of Herbie Steward. Collectors are advised to search for this set. —*Scott Yanow*

Fine and Mellow / Jan. 18, 1944–Apr. 15, 1959 / Collectables ✦✦✦
This CD contains 20 selections featuring Billie Holiday in a variety of live performances covering a 15-year period. Starting with two songs in 1944 in which she was backed by the Esquire All-Stars and continuing through TV appearances and club dates, one can hear the gradual aging and decline of Lady Day's voice, which definitely took a turn for the worse between 1955–56. And yet oddly enough the last five numbers, which were performed April 15, 1959 (making them Holiday's final recordings), actually find her sounding stronger than she had in a few years, perhaps in a final gasp of energy. Of great historical value, this set has plenty of strong moments to justify its acquisition. —*Scott Yanow*

★ **The Complete Decca Recordings** / Oct. 4, 1944–Mar. 8, 1950 / Decca ✦✦✦✦✦
Billie Holiday is heard at her absolute best on this attractive two-CD set. During her period on Decca, Lady Day was accompanied by strings (for the first time), large studio orchestras and even background vocalists, so jazz solos from her sidemen are few. But her voice was at its strongest during the 1940s (even with her personal problems) and to hear all 50 of her Decca performances (including alternate takes and even some studio chatter) is a real joy. Among the highpoints of this essential set are her original versions of "Lover Man" (Holiday's biggest-selling record), "Don't Explain," "Good Morning Heartache," "'Tain't Nobody's Business if I Do," "Now or Never," "Crazy He Calls Me" and remakes of "Them There Eyes" and "God Bless the Child." —*Scott Yanow*

☆ **The Complete Billie Holiday on Verve 1945–1959** / Feb. 12, 1945–Mar. 1, 1959 / Verve ✦✦✦✦✦
This is a rather incredible collection, ten CDs enclosed in a tight black box that includes every one of the recordings that Verve owns of Billie Holiday. It includes not only the many studio recordings of 1952–57 (which feature Lady Day joined by such jazz all-stars as trumpeters Charlie Shavers and Harry "Sweets" Edison, altoist Benny Carter and the tenors of Flip Phillips, Paul Quinichette and Ben Webster) but prime performances at Jazz at the Philharmonic concerts in 1945–7, an enjoyable European gig from 1954, her "comeback" Carnegie Hall concert of 1956, Holiday's rather sad final studio album from 1959 and even lengthy tapes from two informal rehearsals. It's a perfect purchase for the true Billie Holiday fanatic. —*Scott Yanow*

Billie Holiday at Storyville / Oct. 29, 1951–1953 / Black Lion ✦✦✦
Billie Holiday is in generally good form for this club appearance. On most of the selections she is accompanied by the Carl Drinkard Trio, but six others find her joined by Buster Harding's Trio; the great tenor Stan Getz sits in on three of these numbers, making one wish that he and Lady Day had collaborated more extensively. This set of standards (most of which had been recorded previously by Holiday) are not up to the quality of her Decca output but are enjoyable nevertheless. —*Scott Yanow*

Lady Sings the Blues / 1954–1956 / Verve ✦✦✦
Immaculate 1954 and 1956 recordings with an all-star lineup and smashing Holiday cuts. One of her last great dates. —*Ron Wynn*

Lady in Satin / Feb. 18, 1958–Feb. 20, 1958 / Columbia ✦✦✦✦✦
This is the most controversial of all Billie Holiday records. Lady Day herself said that this session (which finds her accompanied by Ray Ellis' string orchestra) was her personal favorite and many listeners have found her emotional versions of such songs as "I'm a Fool to Want You," "You Don't Know What Love Is," "Glad to Be Unhappy" and particularly "You've Changed" to be quite touching. But Holiday's voice was essentially totally gone by 1958, and although not yet 43, she could have passed for 73. Ellis' muzaky arrangements do not help; most of this record is very difficult to listen to. Late in life, Billie Holiday expressed the pain of life so effectively that her croaking voice had become almost unbearable to hear. —*Scott Yanow*

The Monterey Jazz Festival with Buddy Defranco / Oct. 5, 1958 / Black Hawk ✦
Appearing at the first Monterey Jazz Festival, Billie Holiday tried gamely to succeed, but during this live set she often sounds a bit out of it. Accompanied by the Mal Waldron Trio (and on the final few numbers baritonist Gerry Mulligan, altoist Benny Carter and clarinetist Buddy DeFranco), Lady Day struggles through the half-hour set, performing old favorites but often sounding quite weak. The results, as heard on this LP (recorded nine months before her death), are historic but often rather sad. —*Scott Yanow*

Last Recordings / Mar. 3, 1959–Mar. 11, 1959 / Verve ✦✦
In many ways, a sad event. 1988 reissue of an album with Ray Ellis and his orchestra. It's poignant in a tragic way. —*Ron Wynn*

Dave Holland

b. Oct. 1, 1946, Wolverhampton, England
Bass / Post-Bop, Avant-Garde
One of the top bassists of free bop and the avant-garde, Dave Holland has long been quite flexible. He started on bass in 1963 and studied extensively in England, playing with many of the British players including Humphrey Lyttelton, John Surman, Evan Parker, Tubby Hayes, Ronnie Scott and Kenny Wheeler (which is quite a variety!). After playing with the Spontaneous Music Ensemble, he worked with Miles Davis during 1968–70 as Ron Carter's replacement, recording several albums including most noticeably *Bitches Brew*. He next teamed up with Chick Corea, Anthony Braxton and Barry Altschul in Circle (1970–71) and after Corea's decision to play more accessible music, Holland became a member of Braxton's quartet up until 1976. He also played with Paul Bley (1972–73) and Stan Getz during the period (1973–75). Holland was in Gateway with John Abercrombie and Jack DeJohnette (1975–77), a group that in the mid-'90s had a reunion. The bassist played regularly with Sam Rivers during 1976–80 and in 1982 formed his own group which through the years have included Kenny Wheeler, Steve Coleman and Robin Eubanks among others. He has been active as an educator, worked with the M-Base players, toured with Pat Metheny, Herbie Hancock and DeJohnette in a quartet and has recorded as a leader since 1971 for ECM. —*Scott Yanow*

Music for Two Basses / Feb. 15, 1971 / ECM ✦✦✦

Conference of the Birds / Nov. 30, 1972 / ECM ✦✦✦✦
Dave Holland Quartet. Definitive progressive music, with Sam Rivers (ts), Anthony Braxton (reeds), and Barry Altschul (d). —*Michael G. Nastos*

Emerald Tears / Aug. 1977 / ECM ✦✦✦✦
Holland is a rare virtuoso who makes solo performance a varied and joyous proposition. —*Myles Boisen*

Life Cycle / Nov. 1982 / ECM ✦✦✦
Wholly original cello solos in jazz and folk flavors. —*Myles Boisen*

★ **Jumpin' In** / Oct. 1983 / ECM ✦✦✦✦✦
Bassist Dave Holland leads one of his most stimulating groups on this superlative quintet date. With the young Steve Coleman on alto and flute, trumpet great Kenny Wheeler, trombonist Julian Priester and drummer Steve Ellington in the band, Holland had a particularly creative group of musicians in which to interpret and stretch out his six originals; Coleman also contributed one composition. This set, which has plenty of variety in moods, tone, colors and styles, is one of Holland's better recordings. —*Scott Yanow*

Seeds of Time / Nov. 1984 / ECM ✦✦✦✦

The Razor's Edge / Feb. 1987 / ECM ✦✦✦✦✦

Triplicate / Mar. 1988 / ECM ✦✦✦✦

Extensions / Sep. 1989 / ECM ✦✦✦✦✦
Dave Holland Quartet. With Kevin Eubanks (g). This was the 1990 *Downbeat* Critic's Album of the Year. Very good band/album music. Percussionist Smitty Smith is unreal. Recommended. —*Michael G. Nastos*

Major Holley

b. Jul. 10, 1924, Detroit, MI, d. Oct. 25, 1990, Maplewood, NJ
Bass / Swing, Bop
Major Holley was best-known for using the Slam Stewart trademark of singing along with his bowed bass solos although he

sang in unison while Stewart vocalized an octave above his bass. Otherwise, Major Holley (known as "Mule") was a fine support-ive bassist. He originally played violin and tuba but switched to bass while playing in Navy bands. He played with Dexter Gordon, Charlie Parker and Ella Fitzgerald in the mid-to-late '40s and in 1950 did a series of duet recordings (never reissued) with Oscar Peterson. After a period of working for the BBC in England, he toured with Woody Herman (1958), played with the Al Cohn-Zoot Sims quintet (1959–60) and worked in the studios in addition to appearing on some jazz recordings and having a stint with Duke Ellington (1964). He taught at Berklee (1967–70), freelanced in New York and recorded with everyone from Roy Eldridge and the Lee Konitz Nonet to Quincy Jones; he even met up on two records with Slam Stewart. —*Scott Yanow*

● **Featuring Gerry Wiggins** / Mar. 21, 1974 / Black & Blue ◆◆◆

Red Holloway

b. May 31, 1927, Helena, AK
Alto Saxophone, Tenor Saxophone / Bop, Swing, Soul Jazz
An exuberant player with attractive tones on both tenor and alto, Red Holloway is also a humorous blues singer. Whether it be bop, blues or R&B, Holloway can hold his own with anyone. Holloway played in Chicago with Gene Wright's big band (1943–46), served in the Army and then played with Roosevelt Sykes (1948) and Nat Towles (1949–50) before leading his own quartet (1952–61) during an era when he also recorded with many blues and R&B acts. Holloway came to fame in 1963 while touring with Jack McDuff, making his first dates as a leader for Prestige (1963–65). Although he has cut many records in R&B settings, Red Holloway is a strong bop soloist at heart as he proved in the 1970s when he battled Sonny Stitt to a tie on their recorded collaboration. He has mostly worked as a leader since then but has also guested with Juggernaut and the Cheathams and played with Clark Terry on an occasional basis. —*Scott Yanow*

Cookin' Together / Feb. 2, 1964 / Original Jazz Classics ◆◆◆◆◆
W/ the McDuff Quartet. A 1988 reissue of a textbook soul-jazz date. —*Ron Wynn*

Brother Red / Feb. 6, 1964–Feb. 7, 1964 / Prestige ◆◆◆◆
The 11 selections included on this CD reissue include seven songs from a session headed by tenor saxophonist Red Holloway that used the members of the Jack McDuff Quintet (with the organist, guitarist George Benson, bassist Wilfred Middlebrooks and drum-mer Joe Dukes), three pieces from a McDuff date in which the lead voices are backed by an orchestra arranged by Benny Golson, and a selection from a sampler. The material varies a bit ("Wives and Lovers" and Holloway's soul ballad "No Tears" are forget-table), but the blues and the uptempo pieces (highlighted by "This Can't Be Love") are quite enjoyable and the underrated saxo-phonist is in excellent form. —*Scott Yanow*

Nica's Dream / Jul. 7, 1984 / SteepleChase ◆◆◆◆

The Early Show, Vol. 1: Blues in the Night / May 1986 / Fantasy ◆◆◆

The Late Show, Vol. 2: Live at Maria's Memory Lane Supper Club / May 1986 / Fantasy ◆◆◆

Red Holloway and Company / Jan. 1987 / Concord Jazz ◆◆◆◆
A fine session that juggles blues, swing feeling, and soul-jazz sen-sibility. —*Ron Wynn*

● **Locksmith Blues** / Jun., 1989 / Concord Jazz ◆◆◆◆◆
Raucous jazz and blues from trumpeter Clark Terry and saxo-phonist Red Holloway. —*Michael G. Nastos*

Ron Holloway

b. 1953, Washington, D.C.
Tenor Saxophone / Hard Bop
An excellent tenor saxophonist with an open mind who is best known for his hard bop-oriented performances and recordings, Ron Holloway started playing music in the seventh grade. He worked in R&B and funk bands early on and sat in with such players as Sonny Rollins, Freddie Hubbard and Dizzy Gillespie. After playing with Gil Scott-Heron during 1981–88, Holloway (sounding a bit like Stanley Turrentine) was in Dizzy Gillespie's last band (1989–92). He has recorded two albums as a leader for Milestone. —*Scott Yanow*

Slanted / Aug. 1993–Sep. 1993 / Milestone ◆◆◆◆
● **Struttin'** / 1995 / Milestone ◆◆◆◆◆

Christopher Hollyday

b. Jan. 3, 1970, New Haven, CT
Alto Saxophone / Hard Bop
One of the "young lions" of the late '80s, altoist Christopher Hollyday created a big stir when he appeared on the scene but has maintained a surprisingly low profile during the past couple of years. He started playing alto when he was nine, developed quick-ly and was playing in clubs when he was 14, the year when he recorded his first album on his own Jazzbeat label. Back then he was heavily influenced by Charlie Parker, but a few years later Hollyday almost sounded like a clone of Jackie McLean. In 1988 he took a group into the Village Vanguard and the following year he toured with Maynard Ferguson's big band. During 1989–92, Hollyday recorded four CDs for Novus and was starting to develop his own voice when he was dropped from the label. —*Scott Yanow*

● **Christopher Hollyday** / Jan. 25, 1989–Jan. 26, 1989 / Novus ◆◆◆◆◆
Teen wizard Hollyday . . . Cedar Walton is around to lend some keyboard seasoning while fabled drummer Billy Higgins and bassist David Williams complete the cast in a session blending McLean, Parker, and Gillespie songs with the occasional Gershwin standard. —*Ron Wynn*

On Course / Jan. 16, 1990–Jan. 17, 1990 / Novus ◆◆◆◆

The Natural Moment / Jan. 21, 1991–Jan. 22, 1991 / Novus ◆◆◆◆

And I'll Sing Once More / 1992 / Novus ◆◆◆◆
Release by youthful saxophonist Christopher Hollyday, this time recording with a large group including several contemporaries. These include Kenny Werney, Scott Robinson, Eric Charry, John Mosca, and Ed Neumeister. He's also experimenting with more ambitious compositions and displaying other aspects of his play-ing style. —*Ron Wynn*

Bill Holman (Willis Leonard Holman)

b. May 21, 1927, Olive, CA
Arranger, Leader, Tenor Saxophone / Hard Bop, Post-Bop
One of the great arrangers, Bill Holman's dense but hard-swing-ing charts often have so much of value going on that they reward repeated listenings. After a stint with Charlie Barnet (1950–51), Holman became well-known for his arrangements for Stan Kenton (1952–56), which helped advance the Kenton sound. Although a fine tenor saxophonist, Holman's writing has always overshadowed his playing. He concentrated on studio work in the 1960s but also wrote through the years for Woody Herman, Maynard Ferguson, Gerry Mulligan, Count Basie and Buddy Rich among others. Holman wrote the charts for Natalie Cole's best-selling *Unforgettable* album (1991) and has led his own part-time big band in the Los Angeles area since 1975. Bill Holman record-ed as a leader for Capitol, Coral (reissued on Sackville), Andex and Hi Fi during 1954–60 and more recently his Los Angeles band has been documented by JVC. —*Scott Yanow*

The Fabulous Bill Holman / Apr. 25, 1957+Apr. 29, 1957 / Sackville ◆◆◆

In a Jazz Orbit / Feb. 11, 1958–Feb. 13, 1958 / VSOP ◆◆◆◆
Considering his talents, arranger Bill Holman has led relatively few recording sessions through the years. This formerly rare big-band set from 1958 (originally on the Andex label and reissued on CD by VSOP) features a 15-piece band filled with West Coast all-stars. Among the soloists on these five standards and four orig-inals are trombonists Frank Rosolino, Carl Fontana and Ray Sims, altoists Charles Mariano and Herb Geller, trumpeter Jack Sheldon, Richie Kamuca on tenor, pianist Victor Feldman and Holman him-self on tenor. The leader's arrangements were quite distinctive (although not as complex as they would become) at this fairly early stage and the results are a big band album that still sounds fresh nearly four decades later. —*Scott Yanow*

Jive for Five / May 29, 1958–Jun. 6, 1958 / VSOP ◆◆◆◆
For a brief time, tenor saxophonist Bill Holman and drummer Mel Lewis led a hard-swinging quintet based in Los Angeles. Trumpeter Lee Katzman, pianist Jimmy Rowles and bassist Wilford Middlebrook complete the group, a band that benefits greatly from the arrangements of Holman. Rowles contributed

"502 Blues Theme," Holman brought in two songs, and the unit also performs the obscure "Mah Lindy Lou" and two originals. This LP (originally on the Andex label) serves as proof that not all jazz recordings from Los Angeles in the 1950s are quiet and cool. —*Scott Yanow*

Bill Holman's Great Big Band / Jun. 29, 1960–Jul. 1, 1960 / Creative World ✦✦✦✦

The Bill Holman Band / Nov. 30, 1987–Dec. 1987 / JVC ✦✦✦✦✦
Bill Holman Band. A very good contemporary recording of modern big-band music. It swings nicely. —*Michael G. Nastos*

★ **A View from the Side** / Apr. 24, 1995–Apr. 25, 1995 / JVC ✦✦✦✦✦
Although he never seems to win any popularity polls, Bill Holman is among the most respected and unique arrangers of the past 40 years. This CD features his band of the mid-'90s, an outfit that includes many of the top Los Angeles-based musicians. Holman's writing is often colorfully overcrowded (rewarding repeated listenings) yet logical with the charts progressing and developing from beginning to end rather than repeating the same basic ideas continuously. Whether it be the many complex themes of "No Joy in Mudville," the showcases for tenor saxophonist Pete Christlieb ("But Beautiful") and Bob Efford's bass clarinet ("The Peacocks"), the very advanced "Make My Day" or the rebuilding of "Tennessee Waltz," this JVC release is a consistently memorable set from a masterful arranger who deserves much greater recognition in the jazz world. —*Scott Yanow*

Richard "Groove" Holmes
(Richard Arnold Holmes)

b. May 2, 1931, Camden, NJ, **d.** Jun. 29, 1991, St. Louis, MO
Organ / Hard Bop, Soul Jazz
A great jazz organist, Groove Holmes taught himself organ and developed a strongly swinging style with powerful bass lines and a superb harmonic and melodic edge, something that reflects Holmes' ability to play acoustic bass and the influence of saxophonists on his approach. He worked in local New Jersey clubs for a number of years. Holmes had successful albums with such guests as Les McCann, Ben Webster, Gene Ammons and Clifford Scott (using the alias Joe Splink) in the early '60s. Though Holmes played well, these sessions got more exposure due to their illustrious guests. He did more trio settings in the mid-'60s, and also got better quality recordings. Holmes scored a huge pop hit with his version of "Misty." His late '60s releases yielded neither hits nor memorable efforts, while his early '70s sessions, particularly those with Jimmy McGriff in a pair of organ battles, were good. Holmes turned in several fine efforts from the late '70s on through the late '80s, often working with Houston Person. But Holmes also experimented with various electronic keyboards during the '70s on dates that are short of his best work. —*Ron Wynn and Bob Porter*

Groove / Mar. 1961 / Pacific Jazz ✦✦✦✦
A 1990 reissue of an interesting meeting between Groove Holmes and Ben Webster (ts). Webster shows he's capable of adapting his robust soul into a soul-jazz context. —*Ron Wynn*

Groovin' with Jug / Aug. 15, 1961 / Pacific Jazz ✦✦✦✦✦
Recorded live at The Black Orchid and at the Pacific Jazz Studio earlier that afternoon. Ammons at his peak of popularity, Holmes just about to become well-known—the only date they ever played together. Both players are on. Holmes, also a bassist and famous for his organ bass lines, can be heard to good advantage on "Morris the Minor." —*Michael Erlewine*

Soul Message / Aug. 3, 1965 / Original Jazz Classics ✦✦✦✦✦
Organist Richard "Groove" Holmes hit upon a successful formula on this Prestige session (reissued on CD in the OJC series), mixing together boogaloo rhythms with emotional solos. His double-time version of "Misty" became a big hit, and the other selections, including Horace Silver's "Song for My Father" and a pair of soulful originals, are in a similar vein. The lone ballad of the set ("The Things We Did Last Summer") is a fine change of pace. With the assistance of guitarist Gene Edwards and drummer Jimmie Smith, Groove Holmes shows that it is possible to create music that is both worthwhile and commercially successful. —*Scott Yanow*

Misty / Aug. 3, 1965–Aug. 12, 1966 / Original Jazz Classics ✦✦✦✦
Organist Richard "Groove" Holmes in the mid-'60s had a hit with his medium-tempo rendition of "Misty." This CD reissue has the original short version (which was cut as a 45) plus other medium-tempo ballads performed in similar fashion. Holmes and his trio

(featuring guitarist Gene Edwards and drummer George Randall) play enjoyable if not overly substantial versions of such songs as "The More I See You," "The Shadow of Your Smile," "What Now My Love" and "Strangers in the Night," trying unsuccessfully for another pop hit; the organist's sound is more appealing than some of the tunes. —*Scott Yanow*

★ **Blue Groove** / Mar. 15, 1966–May 29, 1967 / Prestige ✦✦✦✦✦
This CD, which reissues two former LPs by Richard "Groove" Holmes (*Get Up & Get It* and *Soul Mist*), showcases the organist in a quintet featuring the tenor of Teddy Edwards and guitarist Pat Martino, with his trio, and (on two standards) with trumpeter Blue Mitchell and tenor saxophonist Harold Vick. Overall, this 73-minute set has many fine solos, spirited ensembles and two well-rounded programs. —*Scott Yanow*

Shippin' Out / Jun. 1977 / Muse ✦✦✦✦
There is a lot of fine music here—all of it funky, spacious, clear. This album feels good. It has some of that soul-jazz magic. —*Michael Erlewine*

Good Vibrations / Dec. 19, 1977 / Muse ✦✦✦✦✦
An album of uptempo cookers from his middle period. W/ Houston Person (ts). —*Michael Erlewine*

Broadway / Dec. 2, 1980 / Muse ✦✦✦
W/ Houston Person (ts). Tight band. Later, uptempo but slick. It lacks the space that his early small-combo funk albums have. —*Michael Erlewine*

Blues All Day Long / Feb. 24, 1988 / Muse ✦✦✦✦
W/ Houston Person (ts), Jimmy Ponder (g). Respectable, and enjoyable later effort by Holmes. Slightly uptempo, but funky. Very nice album. —*Michael Erlewine*

Bertha Hope

b. Jun. 23, 1910, Vicksburg, MS
Piano / Hard Bop
Although she recorded three piano duets with her husband Elmo Hope in 1961, few knew that Bertha Hope was a talented pianist until her 1992 Minor Music release *Between Two Kings*. She grew up in California, started studying classical piano when she was three, became interested in jazz through the playing of Bud Powell and in the late '50s worked in Los Angeles clubs with a trio. Bertha was married to Elmo Hope from 1960 up until his death in 1967 but put her own career on hold until emerging in the early '90s. —*Scott Yanow*

Between Two Kings / 1992 / Minor Music ✦✦✦✦

Elmo Hope

b. Jun. 27, 1923, New York, NY, **d.** May 19, 1967, New York, NY
Piano / Bop, Hard Bop
Overshadowed throughout his life by his friends Bud Powell and Thelonious Monk, Elmo Hope was a talented pianist and composer whose life was cut short by drugs. His first important gig was with Joe Morris' R&B band (1948–51). He recorded in New York as a leader (starting in 1953) and with Sonny Rollins, Lou Donaldson, Clifford Brown and Jackie McLean, but the loss of his cabaret card (due to his drug use) made it very difficult for him to make a living in New York. After touring with Chet Baker in 1957, Hope relocated to Los Angeles. He performed with Lionel Hampton in 1959, recorded with Harold Land and Curtis Counce, and returned to New York in 1961. A short prison sentence did little to help his drug problem and, although he sounds fine on his trio performances of 1966, he died less than a year later. Elmo Hope's sessions as a leader were cut for Blue Note, Prestige, Pacific Jazz, Hi Fi Jazz, Riverside, Celebrity, Beacon and Audio Fidelity; his last albums were initially released on Inner City. Hope was also a fine composer although none of his songs became standards. —*Scott Yanow*

★ **Trio and Quintet** / Jun. 1953–Oct. 31, 1957 / Blue Note ✦✦✦✦✦
Three early sessions: 1953, 1954, & 1957. —*Michael Erlewine*

Meditations / Jun. 8, 1955 / Original Jazz Classics ✦✦✦✦
Although Elmo Hope was one of the more interesting jazz composers of the 1950s, the emphasis on his trio set with bassist John Ore and drummer Willie Jones is on Hope's piano playing. Influenced greatly by Bud Powell (his contemporary), Hope performs standards (such as "All the Things You Are" and "Falling in Love with Love") along with some originals, most of which are based on the chord changes of earlier songs. Fans of bop piano

and Bud Powell will want this enjoyable CD reissue. —*Scott Yanow*

Hope Meets Foster / Oct. 4, 1955 / Original Jazz Classics ✦✦✦
This decent bop session features tenor saxophonist Frank Foster and pianist Elmo Hope in a quintet with the forgotten trumpeter Freeman Lee (who is on three of the six songs), bassist John Ore and drummer Art Taylor. They perform three of Hope's originals, two by Foster and an uptempo version of "Georgia on My Mind." None of the originals caught on (when was the last time anyone played "Fosterity"?) and nothing that innovative occurs, but the music should please bop fans. —*Scott Yanow*

The All Star Sessions / May 7, 1956–Nov. 14, 1961 / Original Jazz Classics ✦✦✦✦✦
Includes two sessions, in 1956 & 1961. A gathering of greats, supervised and sparked by Hope on piano. The list includes Coltrane (ts), Donald Byrd (tpt), and Jimmy Heath (sax). —*Ron Wynn*

Elmo Hope Trio / Feb. 1959 / Original Jazz Classics ✦✦✦✦

Homecoming / Jun. 22, 1961+Jun. 29, 1961 / Original Jazz Classics ✦✦✦✦
Probing, introspective piano solos from Elmo Hope on this '61 date issued by Riverside. —*Ron Wynn*

Hope Full / Nov. 9, 1961+Nov. 14, 1961 / Original Jazz Classics ✦✦✦✦
During the early years of the bop revolution, few of its younger pianists recorded unaccompanied solos. Even by 1961, solo albums by the bop musicians were considered a bit unusual, but Elmo Hope (an underrated composer and pianist) fares quite well during this Riverside set, which has been reissued on CD. Hope is joined by his wife Bertha on second piano during three of the eight numbers, most notably on a swinging "Blues Left and Right." Of the solo pieces, Elmo Hope is at his best on "When Johnny Comes Marching Home" and a cocktailish, but appealing, version of "Liza." —*Scott Yanow*

Final Sessions, Vol. 1 / Mar. 8, 1966–May 9, 1966 / Original Jazz Classics ✦✦✦
A 1991 reissue of the excellent set that marked the last work of pianist Elmo Hope. —*Ron Wynn*

Final Sessions, Vol. 2 / Mar. 8, 1966–May 9, 1966 / Original Jazz Classics ✦✦✦

Claude Hopkins

b. Aug. 24, 1903, Alexandria, VA, **d.** Feb. 19, 1984, New York, NY
Piano / Swing, Stride
A talented stride pianist, Claude Hopkins never became as famous as he deserved. He was a bandleader early on and toured Europe in the mid-'20s as the musical director for Josephine Baker. Hopkins returned to the U.S. in 1926, led his own groups and in 1930 took over Charlie Skeete's band. Between 1932–35 he recorded steadily with his big band (all of the music has been reissued on three Classics CDs), which featured Jimmy Mundy arrangements and such fine soloists as trumpeter/vocalist Ovie Alston, trombonist Fernando Arbello, a young Edmond Hall on clarinet and baritone and tenorman Bobby Sands along with the popular high-note vocals of Orlando Roberson. The orchestra's recordings are a bit erratic with more than their share of mistakes from the ensembles and a difficulty in integrating Hopkins's powerhouse piano with the full group, but they are generally quite enjoyable. Mundy's eccentric "Mush Mouth" is a classic and Hopkins introduced his best-known original "I Would Do Anything for You." Although they played regularly at Roseland (1931–35) and the Cotton Club (1935–36) and there were further sessions in 1937 and 1940, the Claude Hopkins Big Band never really caught on and ended up breaking up at the height of the swing era. Hopkins did lead a later unrecorded big band (1944–47) but mostly worked with small groups for the remainder of his career. He played with Red Allen's group during the second half of the 1950s, led his own band during 1960–66 and in 1968 was in the Jazz Giants with Wild Bill Davison. Claude Hopkins led an obscure record for 20th Century Fox (1958) and three Swingville albums (1960–63) but his best later work were solo stride dates for Chiaroscuro and Sackville (both in 1972) and a trio session for Black and Blue in 1974; it is surprising that his piano skills were not more extensively documented. —*Scott Yanow*

● **Claude Hopkins 1932–1934** / May 24, 1932–Jan. 1, 1932 / Classics ✦✦✦✦✦

Claude Hopkins 1934–1935 / Jan. 11, 1934–Feb. 1934 / Classics ✦✦✦✦✦

Claude Hopkins 1937–1940 / Feb. 2, 1937–Mar. 4, 1937 / Classics ✦✦✦✦

Yes Indeed / Mar. 25, 1960 / Swingville ✦✦✦

Let's Jam / Feb. 21, 1961 / Swingville ✦✦✦

Swing Time / May 22, 1963 / Swingville ✦✦✦

● **Soliloquy** / May 13, 1972 / Sackville ✦✦✦✦✦

Crazy Fingers / 1972 / Chiaruscoro ✦✦✦✦

Fred Hopkins

b. Oct. 11, 1947, Chicago, IL
Bass / Avant-Garde
Fred Hopkins has gained his greatest recognition as bassist with the co-op trio Air, but he has played through the years with most of the top avant-garde musicians and his abilities are well-known to his fellow players. He recorded with Kalaparusha Maurice McIntyre in 1970, worked with Henry Threadgill and Steve McCall in the trio Reflection (1971–72), freelanced in Chicago, moved to New York in 1975 and reunited with Threadgill and McCall as Air (1975–mid-'80s); after McCall's departure in 1982 the group (with Pheeroan AkLaff on drums) became known as New Air. Hopkins has also worked and recorded with Anthony Braxton, Marion Brown, Oliver Lake, David Murray, Hamiet Bluiett, Craig Harris, Don Pullen and many others but strangely enough he has never led a record session of his own. —*Scott Yanow*

Paul Horn

b. Mar. 17, 1930, New York, NY
Clarinet, Flute, Alto Saxophone / Hard Bop, World Fusion, New Age
When one evaluates Paul Horn's career, it is as if he were two people, pre- and post-1967. In his early days, Horn was an excellent cool-toned altoist and flutist while, in more recent times, he has been a new age flutist whose mood music is often best used as background music for meditation. Horn started on piano when he was four and switched to alto at the age of 12. After a stint with the Sauter-Finegan Orchestra on tenor, Horn was Buddy Collette's replacement with the popular Chico Hamilton Quintet (1956–58), playing alto, flute and clarinet. He became a studio musician in Los Angeles but also found time during 1957–66 to record cool jazz albums for Dot (later reissued on Impulse), World Pacific, Hi Fi Jazz, Columbia and RCA and he participated in a memorable live session with Cal Tjader in 1959. In addition in 1964 Horn recorded one of the first *Jazz Masses*, utilizing an orchestra arranged by Lalo Schifrin. In 1967 Paul Horn studied transcendental meditation in India and became a teacher. The following year he recorded unaccompanied flute solos at the Taj Mahal (where he enjoyed interacting with the echoes) and in the future would record in the Great Pyramid, tour China (1979) and the Soviet Union, record using the sounds of killer whales as "accompaniment" and found his own label Golden Flute. Most of Paul Horn's work of the past 20 years is of little interest from the jazz standpoint. —*Scott Yanow*

● **Something Blue** / Mar. 1960 / Original Jazz Classics ✦✦✦✦
Years before Paul Horn became famous for his pioneering new age and mood music albums, he was an adventurous bop-based improviser trying to create an alternative to the hard bop music of the era. On this CD reissue of a set cut for Hi Fi, Horn plays alto, flute and clarinet on six complex originals (four are by the leader) in a quintet with vibraphonist Emil Richards, pianist Paul Moer, bassist Jimmy Bond and drummer Billy Higgins. All of the music is pretty episodic with tricky frameworks and some unusual time signatures being utilized. The results are generally stimulating if rarely all that relaxed; Richards is actually the most impressive soloist on the interesting if often dry release. —*Scott Yanow*

The Sound of Paul Horn / Mar. 30, 1961 / Columbia ✦✦✦✦

Inside the Taj Mahal 2 / 1968 / Kuckuck ✦✦✦
Horn's most influential album was captured when Horn slipped into the Taj Mahal one night with his flute and a tape recorder. The resulting set of spontaneous solo flute improvisations took

full advantage of the magical resonances of India's famous monument. Each tone Horn plays hangs suspended in space for 28 seconds, and the acoustics are so perfect you can't tell when the original sound stops and the echo takes over. —*Linda Kohanov*

Inside / Apr. 1968 / Rykodisc ✦✦✦

Inside the Great Pyramid / 1976 / Kuckuck ✦✦✦
The flutist continues his travels, arriving in Egypt to record in the Great Pyramid of Giza. The double-CD set features a powerful introspective suite of 40 spontaneously composed "psalms" created by Horn on piccolo, alto, and C flutes. —*Linda Kohanov*

China / 1983 / Kuckuck ✦✦✦
This exquisite collaboration between Horn and Chinese multi-instrumentalist David Mingyue Liang captures the timeless elegance of oriental music. —*Linda Kohanov*

Traveler / 1985 / Kuckuck ✦✦✦
Originally released in 1987, this album is a striking summation of Horn's many talents. Reverberant solo instrumental episodes are complemented by evocative original compositions involving synthesizers, string quartet, even a boys' choir. —*Linda Kohanov*

Shirley Horn

b. May 1, 1934, Washington, DC
Piano, Vocals / Ballads
A superior ballad singer and a talented pianist, Shirley Horn put off potential success until finally becoming a major attraction while in her 50s. She studied piano from the age of four. After attending Howard University, Horn put together her first trio in 1954 and was encouraged in the early '60s by Miles Davis and Quincy Jones. She recorded three albums during 1963-65 for Mercury and ABC-Paramount but chose to stick around Washington, D.C., and raise a family instead of pursuing her career. In the early '80s she began recording for SteepleChase, but Shirley Horn really had her breakthrough in 1987 when she started making records for Verve, an association that continues to the present day. —*Scott Yanow*

Live at the Village Vanguard / Aug. 1961 / CAM-AM ✦✦✦

Loads of Love/Shirley Horn with Horns / 1963 / Mercury ✦✦✦

Travelin' Light / 1965 / ABC/Paramount ✦✦✦
Vocalist/pianist Shirley Horn was doing the same highly stylized singing and classy, exquisite piano solos in the 1960s that have earned her lavish critical praises in the '80s and '90s. Her newfound notoriety is no doubt responsible for this good, if somewhat low-key, collection of standards from 1965 resurfacing on CD. Horn handles everything from Beatles covers to delicate love tunes, uptempo swingers, and bittersweet ballads with elegance and keen timing, while her piano work adds the right mix of understatement and rhythmic drive. The only sour note is the disc time; it's impossible to justify charging current CD prices for a disc that clocks in at just over 30 minutes. There's no excuse for this, unless MCA is willing to charge consumers the same price they would have paid for a 1965 LP. —*Ron Wynn*

Violets for Your Furs / Jul. 10, 1981-Jul. 12, 1981 / SteepleChase ✦✦✦✦

Garden of the Blues / Nov. 16, 1984 / SteepleChase ✦✦✦✦

I Thought About You / May 12, 1987+May 13, 1987 / Verve ✦✦✦✦✦
This live set (recorded at Hollywood's Vine St. Bar and Grill) was Shirley Horn's "comeback" album after many years in which she purposely maintained a low profile as she raised her daughter. Typical of Horn's music ever since, she sings intimate ballads with her trio (which includes bassist Charles Ables and drummer Steve Williams) and plays very effective piano behind her vocals, taking "Isn't It Romantic" as an instrumental. —*Scott Yanow*

Softly / Oct. 1987 / Audiophile ✦✦✦✦

★ **Close Enough for Love** / Nov. 1988 / Verve ✦✦✦✦✦
Shirley Horn's second Verve recording consolidated the success that she had had with her previous release, *I Thought About You*, and resulted in her gaining a large audience for her ballad vocals and solid jazz piano playing. Performing with her usual trio (which includes bassist Charles Ables and drummer Steve Williams) and guest tenor Buck Hill on five of the 13 tracks, Horn is heard in definitive form throughout these studio sessions. Highlights include "Beautiful Friendship," "Baby, Baby All the Time," "This Can't Be Love," "I Wanna Be Loved," "But Beautiful," "Get out of Town" and "It Could Happen to You." —*Scott Yanow*

You Won't Forget Me / Jun. 12, 1990-Aug. 1990 / Verve ✦✦✦✦
Miles Davis (tpt) and Wynton (tpt) and Branford Marsalis (ts) are part of the guest cast. Great piano and delightful vocals. —*Ron Wynn*

Here's to Life / 1991 / Verve ✦✦✦
Release by Washington, D.C.-based pianist and vocalist Shirley Horn, who was a local legend for many years but couldn't get any recognition, even within jazz circles. This album includes a guest appearance by Wynton Marsalis, plus her regular accompanists Charles Ables and Steve Williams, and she's also backed by a string orchestra. —*Ron Wynn*

I Love You Paris / Mar. 7, 1992 / Verve ✦✦✦

Light out of Darkness (A Tribute to Ray Charles) / Apr. 30, 1993-May 3, 1993 / Verve ✦✦✦✦

Main Ingredient / May 15, 1995-May 18, 1995 / PolyGram ✦✦✦✦✦

Lena Horne

b. Jun. 30, 1917, Brooklyn, NY
Vocals / Swing, Middle-Of-The-Road Pop
An ageless beauty and a very appealing personality, Lena Horne was never really a jazz singer as much as a superior pop vocalist since she does not improvise. Horne started performing when she was six, sang and danced at the Cotton Club as early as 1934, was with Noble Sissle's Orchestra (1935-36), recorded with Teddy Wilson in the late '30s and sang with Charlie Barnet's big band during 1940-41. She also recorded with Artie Shaw (1941) and made major impressions in the films *Boogie Woogie Dream* (actually a jazz short), *Cabin in the Sky* and especially *Stormy Weather*. Married to arranger/pianist Lennie Hayton, Horne has been a popular attraction since the 1940s but her connection with jazz (even when she sings veteran swing standards) is peripheral. A Bluebird compilation of some of her best early recordings is recommended. —*Scott Yanow*

● **Stormy Weather: The Legendary Lena (1941-1958)** / Jan. 7, 1941-Jun. 9, 1941 / Bluebird ✦✦✦✦✦
A wonderful anthology covering her '40s and '50s show tunes, blues, and ballads. —*Ron Wynn*

Lena & Gabor / Oct. 11, 1969 / Gryphon ✦✦✦
Collaboration between Horne and guitarist Gabor Szabo, who proved to be one of her most sympathetic accompanists. They made expert duo recordings, with Szabo's delicate, sometimes emphatic playing smoothly accompanying Horne's distinctive vocals. The '69 session has been reissued on CD. —*Ron Wynn*

Live on Broadway (Lena Horne: The Lady & Her Music) / 1981 / Qwest ✦✦✦✦
A triumphant cast album from 1981 that effectively captured Lena Horne's acclaimed one-woman Broadway show on a two-record set. The album served both as a vinyl autobiography and also as a centerpiece to document her rise to symbolic importance for black performers. —*Ron Wynn*

An Evening With Lena Horne / Sep. 19, 1994 / Blue Note ✦✦✦✦✦
It is difficult not to love Lena Horne. Recorded when she was 77, this live CD finds the ageless singer sounding as if she were 57 at the most (and the photo of her on the cover makes her look 47!). Horne talks the lyrics a little more than in the past but she cuts loose in spots with power, performs superior standards, takes part of a Duke Ellington/Billy Strayhorn medley as a duet with bassist Ben Brown and does not hesitate to hold long notes. On six of the songs 11 horns from the Count Basie Orchestra riff and play harmonies behind her; otherwise Horne is joined by her usual quartet with pianist Mike Renzi and guitarist Rodney Jones. The well-rounded set is Lena Horne's most rewarding recording in years. —*Scott Yanow*

Wayne Horvitz

b. 1955, New York, NY
Keyboards / Avant-Garde
Active as a performer since 1976, Wayne Horvitz has long been a key part of New York's downtown new music scene. In addition to leading his own band the President, he has worked with John Zorn (on both *Naked City* and a tribute to Sonny Clark), Butch Morris, Billy Bang, Fred Frith, Robert Previte and others, recording his unpredictable music for Elektra/Nonesuch, Black Saint and Sound Aspects. —*Scott Yanow*

Some Order, Long Understood / Feb. 1982 / Black Saint ✦✦✦
This New Generation / 1985 / Elektra ✦✦✦✦
Mid-'80s release that established Horovitz among the prime composers and players on the contemporary improvising scene. He's not among either the traditionalists or the fusion/light jazz crowd, but is part of the New York "downtown" school that utilizes everything from hard bop to rock to contemporary classical. Guitarist Bill Frisell was also an important contributor to the date. —*Ron Wynn*

Todos Santos / May 1989 / Sound Aspects ✦✦✦
Explosive, animated session from the late '80s with Horvitz, Butch Morris, and Robert Previte engaging in spirited dialogues that were sometimes nearly chaotic, but always impressive. Horovitz shared space with the duo of Bill Frisell and Doug Wieselman and played compositions done by his wife Robin Holcomb. —*Ron Wynn*

● **Bring Your Camera** / Dec. 11, 1991 / Elektra ✦✦✦✦
A downtown NYC supergroup led by keyboardist Wayne Horvitz hybridizes jazz, rock, improv, and dashes of blues guitar from Elliot Sharp. —*Myles Boisen*

George Howard

b. Philadelphia, PA
Soprano Saxophone / Instrumental Pop, R&B
George Howard would deny that his music is jazz but since his recordings always placed on *Billboard*'s nonsensical "contemporary jazz" charts and he occasionally appears at jazz festivals, he deserves a brief mention. Heavily influenced by Grover Washington, Jr.'s (with whom he toured in 1979) sound but not his improvising style, Howard's recordings are essentially R&B/funk with an emphasis on backbeats, lightweight vocals and melody statements with very little spontaneity. From the jazz standpoint ,his dates for Palo Alto/TBA, GRP and MCA have very little to offer. —*Scott Yanow*

Asphalt Gardens / Jun. 21, 1982+Aug. 31, 1982 / Palo Alto ✦✦
Steppin' Out / 1984 / GRP ✦✦
Dancing in the Sun / 1985 / GRP ✦✦
A Nice Place to Be / 1986 / MCA ✦✦
Personal / Aug. 14, 1990 / MCA ✦✦✦
Love Will Follow / Dec. 30, 1991 / GRP ✦✦✦✦
● **Do I Ever Cross Your Mind?** / 1992 / GRP ✦✦✦✦
Unlike most of the soprano blowers out there in the pop-jazz market, Howard avoids the "Fuzak" plague, and keeps a stronghold on his R&B roots. At the same time, Howard's latest stays away from the vocal-dominated tracks, which pop up all the more frequently in this genre. A solid, masterful set of funk/fusion. —*Steve Aldrich*

Love and Understanding / Jan. 13, 1992 / GRP ✦✦✦
When Summer Comes / 1993 / GRP ✦✦
Home Far Away / 1994 / GRP ✦✦
George Howard has never claimed to be a jazz artist and his recordings are of minor interest to followers of improvised music. There are a few times on this recording when the soprano saxophonist (who has made a career out of copying Grover Washington, Jr.) sounds like a solo might cut loose, but the electronic rhythms keep that impulse in check. This set is only passable as background music and will immediately disappoint anyone who gives it a close listen. —*Scott Yanow*

Attitude Adjustment / 1995 / GRP ✦✦

Freddie Hubbard (Frederick Dewayne Hubbard)

b. Apr. 7, 1938, Indianapolis, IN
Trumpet, Fluegelhorn / Hard Bop, Post-Bop
One of the great jazz trumpeters of all time, Freddie Hubbard formed his sound out of the Clifford Brown/Lee Morgan tradition and by the early '70s was immediately distinctive and the pacesetter in jazz. However a string of blatantly commercial albums later in the decade damaged his reputation and, just when Hubbard in the early '90s (with the deaths of Dizzy Gillespie and Miles Davis) seemed perfectly suited for the role of veteran master, his chops started causing him serious troubles.

Born and raised in Indianapolis, Hubbard played early on with Wes and Monk Montgomery. He moved to New York in 1958, roomed with Eric Dolphy (with whom he recorded in 1960) and

Music Map

Harp

Pioneer
Caspar Reardon (recorded with Jack Teagarden in 1934)

Hard-Swinging Harpist
Adele Girard
(many sessions with husband clarinetist Joe Marsala)

1950s - Bop and Studio Work
Dorothy Ashby
Corky Hale

Avant-Garde
Alice Coltrane

1980s
Deborah Henson-Conant

1990s
Lori Andrews

was in the groups of Philly Joe Jones (1958–59), Sonny Rollins, Slide Hampton and J.J. Johnson before touring Europe with Quincy Jones (1960–61). He recorded with John Coltrane, participated in Ornette Coleman's *Free Jazz* (1960), was on Oliver Nelson's classic *Blues and the Abstract Truth* album (highlighted by "Stolen Moments") and started recording as a leader for Blue Note that same year. Hubbard gained fame playing with Art Blakey's Jazz Messengers (1961–64) next to Wayne Shorter and Curtis Fuller. He recorded *Ascension* with Coltrane (1965), *One Step Beyond* (1964) with Eric Dolphy and *Maiden Voyage* with Herbie Hancock and, after a period with Max Roach (1965–66), he led his own quintet, which at the time usually featured altoist James Spaulding. A blazing trumpeter with a beautiful tone on fluegelhorn, Hubbard fared well in freer settings but was always essentially a hard bop stylist.

In 1970 Freddie Hubbard recorded two of his finest albums (*Red Clay* and *Straight Life*) for CTI. The follow-up, *First Light* (1971), was actually his most popular date, featuring Don Sebesky arrangements. But after the glory of the CTI years (during which producer Creed Taylor did an expert job of balancing the artistic with the accessible), Hubbard made the mistake of signing with Columbia and recording one dud after another; *Windjammer* (1976) and *Splash* (a slightly later effort for Fantasy) are lowpoints. However in 1977 he toured with Herbie Hancock's acoustic VSOP Quintet and in the 1980s on recordings for Pablo, Blue Note and Atlantic he showed that he could reach his former heights (even if much of the jazz world had given up on him). But by the late '80s Hubbard's "personal problems" and increasing unreliability (not showing up for gigs) started to really hurt him and a few years later his once-mighty technique started to seriously falter. Whether Freddie Hubbard will ever make a serious comeback is open to question, but his fans can certainly enjoy his many recordings for Blue Note, Impulse, Atlantic, CTI, Pablo and his first Music Masters sets. —*Scott Yanow*

Open Sesame / Jun. 19, 1960 / Blue Note ✦✦✦✦
Freddie Hubbard's first recording as a leader, *Open Sesame* fea-

tures the 22-year old trumpeter in a quintet with tenor saxophonist Tina Brooks, the up-and-coming pianist McCoy Tyner, bassist Sam Jones and drummer Clifford Jarvis. The CD reissue adds two alternate takes to the original six-song program and shows that even at this early stage Hubbard had the potential to be one of the greats. On the ballad "But Beautiful" he shows maturity and other highlights include "Open Sesame," a driving "All or Nothing at All" and "One Mint Julep." It's an impressive start to what would be a very interesting career. — *Scott Yanow*

Goin' Up / Nov. 6, 1960 / Blue Note ++++
For his second recording as a leader, trumpeter Freddie Hubbard (22 at the time) performs two compositions apiece by Kenny Dorham and Hank Mobley, the obscure "I Wished I Knew" and his own "Blues for Brenda." Hubbard (featured in a quintet with tenor saxophonist Mobley, pianist McCoy Tyner, bassist Paul Chambers and drummer Philly Joe Jones) takes quite a few outstanding solos, playing lyrically on the ballads and building his own sound out of the Clifford Brown/Lee Morgan tradition. It's an excellent set of advanced hard bop. — *Scott Yanow*

Hub Cap / Apr. 9, 1961 / Blue Note +++

Here to Stay / Apr. 9, 1961–Dec. 27, 1962 / Blue Note ++++
This two-LP set, which was released in 1979 as part of United Artists' Blue Note reissue series, brought back trumpeter Freddie Hubbard's early album *Hub Cap*, a sextet session with tenor saxophonist Jimmy Heath, trombonist Julian Priester and pianist Cedar Walton. Although that session (comprised of four Hubbard compositions, one of Walton's songs and Randy Weston's "Cry Me Not") is excellent, it is the full album of previously unreleased material from an all-star quintet that is of greatest interest. Hubbard teams up with fellow Jazz Messengers Wayne Shorter (on tenor), Walton, bassist Reggie Workman and (in Blakey's spot) drummer Philly Joe Jones for some advanced hard bop. Highpoints include the fiery "Philly Mignon" and a strong version of "Body and Soul." — *Scott Yanow*

Minor Mishap / Aug. 2, 1961 / Black Lion ++++
This is one of Freddie Hubbard's more obscure sessions of the 1960s. Actually, it was originally led by the forgotten trombonist Willie Wilson (who died in 1963) but has been reissued by Black Lion on CD under Hubbard's name. The 23-year-old trumpeter is teamed with Wilson, baritonist Pepper Adams and the Duke Pearson Trio (with bassist Thomas Howard and drummer Lex Humphries) for originals by Wilson, Pearson, Adams, Donald Byrd and Tommy Flanagan in addition to two standards that feature the trombonist; the reissue adds five alternate takes to the original seven-song program. Hubbard and Adams both have plenty of solos on this excellent hard bop date, one that is worth picking up by straight-ahead jazz fans. — *Scott Yanow*

★ **Ready for Freddie** / Aug. 21, 1961 / Blue Note +++++
Trumpeter Freddie Hubbard really came into his own during this Blue Note session. He is matched with quite an all-star group (tenor saxophonist Wayne Shorter, pianist McCoy Tyner, bassist Art Davis and drummer Elvin Jones in addition to Bernard McKinney on euphonium), introduces two of his finest compositions ("Birdlike" and "Crisis") and is quite lyrical on his ballad feature "Weaver of Dreams." Hubbard's sidemen all play up to par and this memorable session is highly recommended; it's one of the trumpeter's most rewarding Blue Note albums. — *Scott Yanow*

The Artistry of Freddie Hubbard / Jul. 2, 1962 / Impulse! ++++
Trumpeter Freddie Hubbard leads a particularly talented sextet (with trombonist Curtis Fuller, a rare outing away from Sun Ra for tenor saxophonist John Gilmore, pianist Tommy Flanagan, bassist Art Davis and drummer Louis Hayes) on three of his originals and strong versions of "Summertime" and "Caravan." This advanced hard bop music deserves to be reissued on CD. — *Scott Yanow*

Hub-Tones / Oct. 10, 1962 / Blue Note +++++
Trumpeter Freddie Hubbard teams up on record with James Spaulding (who doubles on alto and flute) for the first time on this excellent set. With the assistance of pianist Herbie Hancock, bassist Reggie Workman and drummer Clifford Jarvis, the quintet performs four of the trumpeter's originals (including "Lament for Booker" and the title cut) plus an advanced version of the standard "You're My Everything." John Coltrane's modal music was starting to influence Hubbard's conception and his own playing was pushing ahead the modern mainstream without really entering the avant-garde. — *Scott Yanow*

Body and Soul / Mar. 8, 1963–May 2, 1963 / Impulse! ++++
The second of trumpeter Freddie Hubbard's two Impulse! albums features the 25-year old in three separate settings. He is heard along with tenor saxophonist backed by with strings ("Skylark," "I Got It Bad" and "Chocolate Shake" are all given beautiful treatments), with a 16-piece band and in a septet with Eric Dolphy and Wayne Shorter. This well-rounded and highly recommended showcase shows why Freddie Hubbard was considered the top trumpeter to emerge during the early '60s. — *Scott Yanow*

Breaking Point / May 7, 1964 / Blue Note +++++
This CD reissue (which augments the original five-song program with alternate takes originally issued on 45s of "Blue Frenzy" and "Mirrors") brings back the first recording Hubbard cut with his own working band (as opposed to an all-star studio group). On these selections (particularly the memorable "Breaking Point"), Hubbard and his quintet (James Spaulding on alto and flute, pianist Ronnie Matthews, bassist Eddie Khan and drummer Joe Chambers) play music that falls in between hard bop and the avant-garde, stretching the boundaries of the jazz modern mainstream. Their explorative flights are still quite interesting more than three decades later and Hubbard, having broken away from his earlier Clifford Brown and Lee Morgan influences, really sounds very much like himself. — *Scott Yanow*

Blue Spirits / Feb. 19, 1965–Mar. 5, 1966 / Blue Note ++++
This CD, Freddie Hubbard's last Blue Note release of the 1960s (with the exception of the blowing session *The Night of the Cookers*), adds two numbers to the original LP program and features the great trumpeter in three challenging settings ranging from a sextet to an octet. Hubbard uses such sidemen as altoist James Spaulding, tenors Joe Henderson and Hank Mobley, the euphonium of Kiane Zawadi, pianists Harold Mabern, McCoy Tyner and Herbie Hancock, bassists Larry Ridley, Bob Cranshaw and Reggie Workman, drummers Clifford Jarvis, Pete La Roca and Elvin Jones, the congas of Big Black and, on one song, bassoonist Hosea Taylor. The set comprises seven diverse Hubbard originals and, even though none of the songs caught on to become standards, the music is quite challenging and fairly memorable. — *Scott Yanow*

The Night of the Cookers: Vols. 1 & 2 / Apr. 9, 1965–Apr. 10, 1965 / Blue Note ++
This double CD reissues the two LP volumes titled *The Night of the Cookers*. Since these performances (four lengthy workouts ranging from 19-24 minutes apiece) were taken from a club date that matched together the trumpets of Freddie Hubbard and Lee Morgan (along with James Spaulding on alto and flute, pianist Harold Mabern, bassist Larry Ridley, drummer Pete La Roca and the congas of Big Black), this should have been a classic. However, Morgan sounds quite subpar, the recording quality is just passable, the individual solos are stretched out far too long and the overall results are a major disappointment. — *Scott Yanow*

Backlash / Oct. 19, 1966+Oct. 24, 1966 / Atlantic ++++
Trumpeter Freddie Hubbard led a particularly fine quintet in the mid-'60s that has long been underrated. The edition heard on this Atlantic LP features James Spaulding on alto and flute, pianist Albert Dailey, bassist Bob Cunningham and drummer Otis Ray Appleton. This studio recording is most notable for debuting Hubbard's "Little Sunflower" and also has a good remake of "Up Jumped Spring" along with four other obscure pieces. The music straddles the boundaries between hard bop, soul and the avant-garde and has plenty of unpredictable moments. This is the strongest of Freddie Hubbard's three Atlantic records of the period. — *Scott Yanow*

High Blues Pressure / Nov. 1967 / Atlantic +++
For this studio album, Freddie Hubbard expanded his quintet by adding tenor saxophonist Bennie Maupin, Kiane Zawadi on euphonium and the tuba of Howard Johnson. The music is complex but swinging with fine solos from the trumpeter/leader, altoist James Spaulding, Maupin and pianist Kenny Barron. This LP (which has not yet been reissued on CD) will be hard to find. — *Scott Yanow*

The Black Angel / 1969 / Atlantic +++
The most obscure and the last of Freddie Hubbard's three Atlantic LPs of the 1960s (none of which have reappeared yet on CD), features the trumpeter right before he found some commercial success on CTI. He performs three of his originals, Walter Bishop, Jr.'s "Coral Keys" and Kenny Barron's "The Black Angel" with an excel-

lent sextet that includes James Spaulding on alto and flute, Kenny Barron on keyboards, bassist Reggie Workman, drummer Louis Hayes and percussionist Patato Valdes. Although not essential, the music is quite advanced, hard-swinging and explorative. *—Scott Yanow*

The Hub of Hubbard / Dec. 9, 1969 / MPS ✦✦✦✦
Trumpeter Freddie Hubbard, whose Atlantic recordings had straddled the boundary between hard bop and the avant-garde, sticks to bebop on this excellent recording. Performing in a quintet with tenor saxophonist Eddie Daniels (no clarinet this time), pianist Roland Hanna, bassist Richard Davis and drummer Louis Hayes, Hubbard is in top form on four selections: "Without a Song," a ridiculously uptempo "Just One of Those Things," "Blues for Duane" and a ballad rendition of "The Things We Did Last Summer." *—Scott Yanow*

A Soul Experiment / 1969 / Atlantic ✦✦
☆ **Red Clay** / Jan. 27, 1970–Jan. 29, 1970 / CTI ✦✦✦✦✦
Freddie Hubbard has long considered this recording to be his best, and with good reason. The trumpeter is heard at the peak of his powers performing five originals (one, "Cold Turkey," was released for the first time on this CD reissue) in a quintet with tenor saxophonist Joe Henderson, keyboardist Herbie Hancock, bassist Ron Carter and drummer Lenny White. "Red Clay" is a classic and the other selections ("The Intreprid Fox," "Suite Sioux" and "Delphia") all feature Hubbard taking colorful solos in a style that blends together hard bop with subtle funky rhythms. Classic music of the early 1970s. *—Scott Yanow*

★ **Straight Life** / Nov. 16, 1970 / CTI ✦✦✦✦✦
Recorded between trumpeter Freddie Hubbard's better-known classics *Red Clay* and *First Light, Straight Life* is actually arguably Hubbard's greatest recording, and it hasn't been reissued on CD yet. Hubbard, joined by an all-star group that includes tenor saxophonist Joe Henderson, keyboardist Herbie Hancock, guitarist George Benson, bassist Ron Carter and drummer Jack DeJohnette, is frequently astounding on "Straight Life" (check out that introduction!) and "Mr. Clean," constructing classic solos. The very memorable set is rounded off by the trumpeter's duet with Benson on a lyrical version of the ballad "Here's That Rainy Day." This exciting LP is essential for all serious jazz collections. *—Scott Yanow*

Sing Me a Song of Songmy / Jan. 21, 1971 / Atlantic ✦✦
This is a strange LP. Trumpeter Freddie Hubbard and his quintet (which consisted of tenor saxophonist Junior Cook, pianist Kenny Barron, bassist Art Booth and drummer Louis Hayes) is joined by a chorus, a string orchestra, several reciters, an organist and a variety of processed sounds emanating from tapes. The thoughts expressed in the music (topical and anti-war messages) are quite sincere but the abstract sounds will only be enjoyed by a limited audience; jazz fans should look elsewhere. *—Scott Yanow*

First Light / Sep. 1971 / CTI ✦✦✦✦
The third of Freddie Hubbard's "big three" recordings for CTI (it was preceded by *Red Clay* and *Straight Life*), *First Light* was probably the trumpeter's most popular album. The first of his recordings to utilize the string and woodwind arrangements of Don Sebesky, Hubbard sounds quite inspired by his accompaniment and plays at his best throughout, particularly on "First Light" and "Uncle Albert/Admiral Halsey." The CD reissue by Columbia adds one previously unissued selection ("Fantasy in D") to the original program. *—Scott Yanow*

Sky Dive / Oct. 1972 / CTI ✦✦✦✦
Freddie Hubbard's fourth CTI recording (and the second one with Don Sebesky arrangements) certainly has a diverse repertoire. In addition to his originals "Povo" and "Sky Dive" (both of which are superior jam tunes), the trumpeter stretches out on the theme from *The Godfather* and Bix Beiderbecke's "In a Mist." The charts for the brass and woodwinds are colorful, there is a fine supporting cast that includes guitarist George Benson, Keith Jarrett on keyboards and flutist Hubert Laws and Hubbard takes several outstanding trumpet solos. This LP (not yet reissued on CD) is worth searching for. *—Scott Yanow*

In Concert, Vols. 1 & 2 / Mar. 3, 1973 / CTI ✦✦✦✦
The CTI All-Stars are featured on this enjoyable CD, which presents highlights originally released on two LPs. Trumpeter Freddie Hubbard and tenor saxophonist Stanley Turrentine always made for a potent team and, with the assistance of an all-star rhythm section (guitarist Eric Gale, keyboardist Herbie Hancock, bassist

Ron Carter and drummer Jack DeJohnette), the very individual stylists sound in fine form, particularly on "Povo" and "Gibraltar." *—Scott Yanow*

Keep Your Soul Together / Oct. 1973 / CTI ✦✦✦✦
Trumpeter Freddie Hubbard's CTI recordings have long been underrated and a bit downgraded by writers who get them confused with his much commercial output for Columbia. For this LP (not yet reissued on CD) Hubbard is heard in fine form on four of his originals (highlighted by "Spirits of Trane") with a septet that includes tenor saxophonist Junior Cook, keyboardist George Cables, guitarist Aurell Ray, either Kent Brinkley or Ron Carter on bass, drummer Ralph Penland and Juno Lewis on percussion. The music is sometimes funky but definitely creative jazz, with Hubbard heard during his prime period. *—Scott Yanow*

Polar AC / 1974 / CTI ✦✦✦
Trumpeter Freddie Hubbard's sixth and final CTI studio recording has its moments although it is not on the same level as his first three. Hubbard, backed on four of the five songs by a string section arranged by either Don Sebesky or Bob James, is assisted on songs such as "People Make the World Go Round" and "Betcha By Golly, Wow" by flutist Hubert Laws and guitarist George Benson. "Son of Sky Dive" showcases his trumpet with a sextet including Laws and tenor saxophonist Junior Cook. The music is enjoyable but not essential and this LP has yet to appear on CD. *—Scott Yanow*

High Energy / Apr. 29, 1974–May 2, 1974 / CTI ✦✦✦
One of Freddie Hubbard's few decent efforts during his very commercial period with Columbia, this LP found his quintet (with tenor saxophonist Junior Cook and keyboardist George Cables) joined by a small orchestra and a string section on a set of potentially dismal material. Fortunately, these six performances (particularly "Crisis," "Ebony Moonbeams" and Stevie Wonder's "Too High") are given fairly creative treatment. The leader/trumpeter is in good form and there is solo space given to Ernie Watts (on bass flute, soprano and flute) and tenorman Pete Christlieb in addition to the quintet members. *—Scott Yanow*

Liquid Love / 1975 / Columbia ✦✦
Imagine hearing trumpeter Freddie Hubbard sing! Truth be told he only joins in on the group vocal of "Put It in the Pocket," but that is about the only historic aspect to this wasteful release. While Hubbard's CTI recordings had perfectly balanced both the artistic and commercial, much of his Columbia output sounds as if it was recorded strictly for the money. None of the six selections heard on this LP stayed in Hubbard's repertoire long (when was the last time that he performed "Midnight at the Oasis" and "Liquid Love"?) and the funky rhythms do little to uplift the music. George Cables, who plays keyboards on this album and was responsible for some of the arrangements, has his name misspelled "Gables" on the album jacket; was he trying to hide his identity? *—Scott Yanow*

Gleam / Mar. 17, 1975 / Sony ✦✦✦✦
In contrast to his rather commercial Columbia albums of the period, this live double LP from Japanese Sony finds trumpeter Freddie Hubbard really digging into the material, even on such songs as "Put It in the Pocket," "Midnight at the Oasis" and a memorable version of the Stevie Wonder-associated "Too High." Hubbard and his working group of the time (which consisted of tenor saxophonist Carl Randall, keyboardist George Cables, bassist Henry Franklin, drummer Carl Burnett and Buck Clark on congas) are in particularly creative form, especially on "Kuntu" and "Spirits of Trane." *—Scott Yanow*

Windjammer / 1976 / Columbia ✦
This LP is (along with his *Splash* album on Fantasy) probably trumpeter Freddie Hubbard's worst recording. Hubbard, who is joined by a string section, five vocalists and an oversized orchestra, sounds like a parody of himself on these meaningless funk tracks. Why jazz's top trumpeter of the 1970s would allow himself to get sucked into this trashy Bob James production is debatable, but there is no debate as to the merit of this fortunately out-of-print LP. This is insincere music that was dated before it was even released. *—Scott Yanow*

Bundle of Joy / 1977 / Columbia ✦✦
Freddie Hubbard's string of commercial albums for Columbia in the mid-to-late '70s ruined the trumpeter's reputation. This particular LP is not as bad as some (at least his duet with harpist Dorothy Ashby on "Portrait of Jenny" is pretty and Ernie Watts

gets a good tenor solo on "Rahsaan") but it is not one of his finer moments either. With an oversized funky rhythm section, a string section and five "background" vocalists, Hubbard had little to do. Skip this and get his CTI and Blue Note albums instead. — *Scott Yanow*

Super Blue / 1978 / Columbia ◆◆◆
After several terrible sellout albums for Columbia, Freddie Hubbard attempted to rekindle some of the magic from his CTI years on this small group date. With such CTI alumni as flutist Hubert Laws, tenorman Joe Henderson, and even guitarist George Benson (on one selection) helping out, Hubbard shows that he still had the chops (if not necessarily the creativity) to continue being a major jazz trumpeter. Unfortunately, his career has been pretty aimless ever since. — *Scott Yanow*

The Love Connection / Feb. 1979–Mar. 1979 / Columbia ◆◆

Skagly / Dec. 1979 / Columbia ◆◆◆
In general, Freddie Hubbard's Columbia recordings (none of which have been reissued on CD) can be skipped by serious jazz fans because, with the exception of *Super Blue* and to a lesser extent this album, they are overtly commercial and rather insincere efforts. This particular record at least uses the trumpeter's regular quintet of the period (with Hadley Caliman on tenor and flute, the up-and-coming keyboardist Billy Childs, bassist Larry Klein and drummer Carl Burnett) although the title cut has three guests (including keyboardist George Duke) whose role seemed to be to make the music more funky. With the exception of the standard "Theme from *Summer of '42*," none of the other songs (all group originals) caught on, but Hubbard takes some good solos during these modern mainstream performances. — *Scott Yanow*

Live at the North Sea Jazz Festival / Jul. 12, 1980 / Pablo ◆◆◆◆
Trumpeter Freddie Hubbard's recording career was rather aimless by 1980 but, as shown by his playing on this live double LP, he was still in prime form. Hubbard and his quintet (which consisted of tenor saxophonist David Schnitter, keyboardist Billy Childs, bassist Larry Klein and drummer Sinclair Lott) play extended versions of five of his compositions plus "The Summer Knows" and "Impressions." Although these renditions of "First Light" and "Red Clay" will not make listeners forget the original versions, it is gratifying to hear the trumpeter really pushing himself. His reputation had been soiled by his Columbia funk albums, but this two-fer shows that in 1980 Hubbard had few competitors among trumpeters. It's well worth searching for. — *Scott Yanow*

Outpost / Mar. 16, 1981–Mar. 17, 1981 / Enja ◆◆◆◆
This little-known CD is actually a special outing for Freddie Hubbard. Pianist Kenny Barron, bassist Buster Williams and drummer Al Foster are quite complementary on the diverse material, which includes "You Don't Know What Love Is," two Hubbard originals, Williams' "Dual Force" and Eric Dolphy's "Loss." Throughout, Hubbard is heard in prime form. — *Scott Yanow*

Rollin' / May 2, 1981 / MPS ◆◆◆
Trumpeter Freddie Hubbard and his 1981 quintet (which included Dave Schnitter on tenor and soprano, keyboardist Billy Childs, bassist Larry Klein and drummer Carl Burnett) are in fine form on this live set originally recorded for MPS. The LP consists of seven songs Hubbard often performed during that period including "One of Another Kind," "Here's That Rainy Day," "Up Jumped Spring" and his heated blues "Byrdlike." Although few surprises occur, the largely straight-ahead music is quite enjoyable and Hubbard's fans may want to search for this fairly rare item. — *Scott Yanow*

Keystone Bop: Sunday Night / Nov. 29, 1981 / Prestige ◆◆◆
This CD reissues an LP and a half's worth of material recorded by Freddie Hubbard and his sextet (with tenor saxophonist Joe Henderson, pianist Billy Childs, vibraphonist Bobby Hutcherson, bassist Larry Klein and drummer Steve Houghton) at the legendary San Francisco club Keystone Korner one night in 1981. The great trumpeter is in excellent form on remakes of three of his compositions ("Birdlike," "Sky Dive" and "The Intrepid Fox"), Hutcherson's "The Littlest One of All" and "Body and Soul." Although few surprises occur, Hubbard fans can be assured that this set finds him in excellent form on a good night. — *Scott Yanow*

Born to Be Blue / Dec. 14, 1981 / Original Jazz Classics ◆◆◆◆
Trumpeter Freddie Hubbard teams up with veteran tenor saxophonist Harold Land and Hubbard's regular rhythm section of the

period (keyboardist Billy Childs, bassist Larry Klein, drummer Steve Houghton and percussionist Buck Clark) on this fine modern hard bop CD, a straight reissue of the original Pablo LP. Hubbard had hurt his reputation with his very commercial Columbia recordings of the mid-to-late '70s so, in 1981, he was doing his best to return to his brand of straight-ahead jazz. This date is highlighted by "Gibraltar," Clifford Brown's "Joy Spring" and a revisit to Hubbard's "Up Jumped Spring." — *Scott Yanow*

Splash / 1981 / Fantasy ◆

Face to Face / May 24, 1982 / Pablo ◆◆◆◆◆
Trumpeter Freddie Hubbard met the Pablo All-Stars for this unique and frequently exciting set. Inspired by the presence of pianist Oscar Peterson, guitarist Joe Pass, bassist Niels-Henning Orsted Pedersen and drummer Martin Drew, Hubbard stretches out on five numbers, which include "All Blues," his own "Thermo" and "Portrait Of Jenny." A combative player, Hubbard both challenges and is challenged by the remarkable pianist; pity they did not record together more often. This stimulating CD is a reissue of the original LP. — *Scott Yanow*

Back to Birdland / Aug. 1982 / Real Time ◆◆◆◆
This well-recorded outing (which has been reissued on CD by Drive Archive) was trumpeter Freddie Hubbard's first worthwhile studio recording (with the exception of *Super Blue*) since the mid-'70s. Essentially a bebop date, Hubbard is teamed with a sextet comprised of altoist Richie Cole, trombonist Ashley Alexander, pianist George Cables, bassist Andy Simpkins and drummer John Dentz; altoist Med Flory sits in on "Byrdlike." Hubbard shows on such standards as "Shaw Nuff," "Star Eyes" and "Lover Man" that he could still play straight-ahead jazz with the best of them, Alexander is featured on "Stella by Starlight" and Cole is also in excellent form. — *Scott Yanow*

Sweet Return / Jun. 13, 1983–Jun. 14, 1983 / Atlantic ◆◆◆◆
One of Freddie Hubbard's best albums since the early '70's, this quintet date finds him joined by quite an all-star lineup: Lew Tabackin on tenor and flute, pianist Joanne Brackeen (who has many fine solos throughout the album), bassist Eddie Gomez and drummer Roy Haynes. Highpoints include Hubbard's tender version of "Misty" (at the time he had a particularly lovely tone on fluegelhorn), Brackeen's "Heidi-B" and the quintet's rendition of the standard "The Night Has a Thousand Eyes." — *Scott Yanow*

Freddie Hubbard & Woody Shaw Sessions / Nov. 21, 1985–Jun. 12, 1987 / Blue Note ◆◆◆

Life Flight / Jan. 23, 1987–Jan. 24, 1987 / Blue Note ◆◆◆◆
This CD captures the great trumpeter Freddie Hubbard at the age of 48 just before he began to decline. Hubbard is heard in excellent shape on two selections apiece with two separate bands. One group, a sextet with tenor saxophonist Stanley Turrentine and guitarist George Benson, recalls the trumpeter's glory days on CTI although the material ("Battlescar Galorica" and "A Saint's Homecoming Song") was of recent vintage. The other band, a quintet with tenor saxophonist Ralph Moore, looks back toward his earlier Blue Note and Atlantic days; they perform two Hubbard originals ("The Melting Pot" and "Life Flight"). Overall this set (from an era when the veteran trumpeter was being overshadowed by Wynton Marsalis) gives listeners one of the last opportunities to hear Freddie Hubbard in peak form. — *Scott Yanow*

Topsy: Standard Book / Oct. 10, 1989–Oct. 11, 1989 / Evidence ◆◆◆
It was the producer's idea for this CD that Freddie Hubbard play all of the nine standards with a mute in his trumpet. Hubbard was not happy with the restriction but does his best on the quartet/quintet session with pianist Benny Green, bassist Rufus Reid, drummer Carl Allen and, on three numbers, altoist Kenny Garrett. While it is interesting to hear Freddie Hubbard tackle such material as "Topsy," "As Time Goes By," "Cherokee" and "Love Me or Leave Me," the music is often more mellow (even when uptempo) then one might hope. It's a pleasing but not essential release from the Japanese label Alfa/Compose. — *Scott Yanow*

Bolivia / Dec. 13, 1990–Jan. 14, 1991 / Music Masters ◆◆◆
Freddie Hubbard is in decent, but not quite prime, form on this CD; his tone was starting to decline ever so gradually. His sidemen were quite strong (Ralph Moore on tenor, altoist Vincent Herring, pianist Cedar Walton, bassist David Williams and drummer Billy Higgins), the material is superior (highlighted by

"Bolivia," Hubbard's "Dear John" and a few of his recent Latin-flavored originals) and overall the music is satisfying enough to make this a recommended disc to fans of the modern mainstream. —*Scott Yanow*

Live at Fat Tuesday / Dec. 6, 1991–Dec. 7, 1991 / Music Masters ✦✦
This live double CD is a bit odd. Trumpeter Freddie Hubbard's once beautiful tone was definitely on the decline by this point, which is particularly noticeable on high notes they often sound painful) and the lone ballad "But Beautiful." Tenor saxophonist Javon Jackson seems content to imitate Joe Henderson while pianist Benny Green, who normally sounds like a mixture of Bobby Timmons, Gene Harris and Oscar Peterson, here adopts the heavy tone and chord voicings of McCoy Tyner. Bassist Christian McBride and drummer Tony Reedus play fine in support but these often-lengthy performances are not at all memorable,. Better to pick up Freddie Hubbard's earlier sessions instead. —*Scott Yanow*

Monk, Miles, Trane & Cannon / Aug. 19, 1994–Jan. 1995 / Music Masters ✦✦

Peanuts Hucko (Michael Andrew Hucko)

b. Apr. 7, 1918, Syracuse, NY
Clarinet / Swing, Dixieland
Peanuts Hucko has long had a sound on clarinet that is nearly identical to that of Benny Goodman. A fine tenor player in his early days (although he largely gave up the instrument after the 1940s), Hucko's clarinet is an attractive addition to any Dixieland or swing combo. He started out as a tenor saxophonist playing in the big bands of Will Bradley (1939–41), Charlie Spivak (1941–42) and Bob Chester. Hucko was a member of Glenn Miller's Army Air Force Band where he was a star clarinet soloist. After being discharged from the military and playing with Benny Goodman (1945–46) and Ray McKinley (1946–47), Hucko started an on-and-off association with Eddie Condon. He worked in the studios in the 1950s, visited Europe with Jack Teagarden and Earl Hines in 1957, toured the world with Louis Armstrong's All-Stars (1958–60) and, in the 1960s, often led his own Dixie/swing band. In the 1970s for a period he was the leader of the Glenn Miller ghost orchestra, and in recent times Hucko has often headed groups featuring his wife, vocalist Louise Tobin. —*Scott Yanow*

Tribute to Louis Armstrong with Benny Goodman / Oct. 24, 1983 / Timeless ✦✦✦

● **Swing That Music** / 1992 / Starline ✦✦✦
Peanuts Hucko, one of the few swing clarinetists still active in the 1990s, heads a fine octet for this spirited set of standards. With solo contributions made from trumpeter Randy Sandke, Danny Moss on tenor, trombonist Roy Williams, pianist Johnny Varro and vibraphonist Lars Erstrand (not to mention singer Louise Tobin), this set should easily satisfy Benny Goodman fans. Highlights include "Swing That Music," an exciting "Stealin' Apples" and "One O'Clock Jump"; Hucko has a rare vocal on "When You're Smiling." —*Scott Yanow*

Spike Hughes (Patrick Cairns Hughes)

b. Oct. 19, 1908, London, England, **d.** Feb. 2, 1987, London, England
Bass, Composer / Classic Jazz
Spike Hughes, as a bassist (one of the best in the early '30s), arranger and bandleader made an important (if little-known) contribution to jazz. He arranged for British dance bands of the late '20s before beginning an excellent series of jazz records in 1930 with his Decca-Dents and Three Blind Mice. Among his sidemen were some of England's top jazz musicians, many of whom rarely had such a good opportunity to get away from playing commercial music; one session found Hughes and his rhythm section backing Jimmy Dorsey. In 1933 Hughes came to New York and recorded with an all-star group whose nucleus was the Benny Carter Orchestra. These recordings featured such greats as Carter, Coleman Hawkins, Chu Berry, Red Allen, Dickie Wells, flutist Wayman Carver and Sid Catlett playing Hughes' colorful arrangements. A multi-talented individual, Spike Hughes unfortunately chose to leave jazz altogether in 1934 to concentrate on classical music and being a journalist. —*Scott Yanow*

● **Vols. 1 & 2** / Mar. 12, 1930–Nov. 5, 1930 / Kings Cross ✦✦✦✦
● **Vols. 3 & 4** / Nov. 19, 1930–Nov. 18, 1932 / Kings Cross ✦✦✦✦

Helen Humes

b. Jun. 23, 1913, Louisville, KY, **d.** Sep. 9, 1981, Santa Monica, CA
Vocals / Swing, Blues
Helen Humes was a versatile singer equally skilled on blues, swing standards and ballads. Her cheerful style was always a joy to hear. As a child she played piano and organ in church and made her first recordings (ten blues in 1927) when she was only 13 and 14. In the 1930s she worked with Stuff Smith and Al Sears, recording with Harry James in 1937–38. In 1938 Humes joined Count Basie's Orchestra for three years. Since Jimmy Rushing specialized in blues, Helen Humes mostly got stuck singing pop ballads, but she did a fine job. After freelancing in New York (1941–43) and touring with Clarence Love (1943–44), Humes moved to Los Angeles. She began to record as a leader and had a hit in "Be-ba-ba-le-ba"; her 1950 original "Million Dollar Secret" is a classic. Humes sometimes performed with Jazz at the Philharmonic but was mostly a single in the 1950s. She recorded three superb albums for Contemporary during 1959-61 and had tours with Red Norvo. She moved to Australia in 1964, returning to the U.S. in 1967 to take care of her ailing mother. Humes was out of the music business for several years but made a full comeback in 1973 and stayed busy up until her death. Throughout her career Helen Humes recorded for such labels as Savoy, Aladdin, Mercury, Decca, Dootone, Contemporary, Classic Jazz, Black & Blue, Black Lion, Jazzology, Columbia and Muse. —*Scott Yanow*

E-Baba-Le-Ba / Nov. 20, 1944–Nov. 20, 1950 / Savoy ✦✦✦
The rhythm and blues years. 1986 reissue of 1944 and 1950 sessions. Stomping, lusty cuts with Humes at her most down-and-dirty. Though she said she didn't sing blues, this is sure close to it. —*Ron Wynn*

Tain't Nobody's Bizness If I Do / Jan. 5, 1959–Feb. 10, 1959 / Original Jazz Classics ✦✦✦✦
This Helen Humes date will lock in one's mind—because she was one of the immediately identifiable jazz stylists and because it was an excellent example, perhaps one of the best post Count Basie days examples, of her work. Emotion, open, warm and swinging is what you've got here. —*Bob Rusch, Cadence*

★ **Songs I Like to Sing** / Sep. 6, 1960–Sep. 8, 1960 / Original Jazz Classics ✦✦✦✦
Nice, classy set from vocalist Helen Humes, who enjoyed success throughout her career singing everything from classic blues to jazz and gospel to rock. She sticks to jazz on this '60 date, doing both scat and sophisticated ballads. —*Ron Wynn*

Swingin' with Humes / Jul. 27, 1961–Jul. 29, 1961 / Original Jazz Classics ✦✦✦
A solid early '60s set by vocalist Helen Humes, doing a program of standards with a fine combo sparked by tenor saxophonist Teddy Edwards and trumpeter Joe Gordon. The four-member rhythm section includes pianist Wynton Kelly, guitarist Al Viola, bassist Leroy Vinnegar, and drummer Frank Butler. —*Ron Wynn*

Let the Good Times Roll / Aug. 1, 1973 / Classic Jazz ✦✦✦
Triumphant, but sometimes ragged, mid-'70s performances featuring Humes doing new versions of prior hits she made during her stint with Count Basie and in the '40s and '50s. She's backed by a group that includes Arnett Cobb, Jay McShann, Gatemouth Brown, Milt Buckner, and Major Holley, among others, but they don't always hit on all cylinders. This, originally cut for the Black and Blue label, has been reissued on CD. —*Ron Wynn*

Sneakin' Around / Mar. 16, 1974 / Classic Jazz ✦✦✦
Helen Humes did both bawdy, double-entendre-laden blues and R&B, and more sophisticated, jazz-tinged numbers during her career. This date with Gerald Badini, Gerry Wiggins, Major Holley, and Ed Thigpen, had a little of both, and was spiced up by Humes, singing with equal parts sass and grace. It was originally done for the Black and Blue label and was recently on CD. —*Ron Wynn*

On the Sunny Side of The Street / Jul. 2, 1974 / Black Lion ✦✦✦
A booming, authoritative live date from the Montreux Festival. —*Ron Wynn*

The Incomparable / Sep. 1974 / Jazzology ✦✦✦✦

Helen Humes: Talk of the Town / Feb. 18, 1975 / Columbia ✦✦✦✦

Helen Humes and the Muse All Stars / Oct. 5, 1979+Oct. 8, 1978 / Muse ✦✦✦✦✦

Helen Humes' return to an active singing career was one of the happier events in jazz of the late '70s. Able to give great feeling and sensitivity to ballads but also a superb lowdown blues singer, Humes flourished musically during her last years. On this excellent release (the CD reissue adds two alternate takes to the original program), Humes matches wits with altoist/singer Eddie "Cleanhead" Vinson on "I'm Gonna Move to the Outskirts of Town" and is in top form throughout. Tenors Arnett Cobb and Buddy Tate (along with a fine rhythm section led by pianist Gerald Wiggins) don't hurt either. An enthusiastic "Loud Talking Woman" and "My Old Flame" are highpoints. —Scott Yanow

Helen / Jun. 17, 1980+Jun. 19, 1980 / Muse ✦✦✦✦✦

Helen Humes was one of the most appealing jazz singers of the late '30s, and of the late '70s. Her comeback in her last few years was a happy event and all of her recordings for Muse are recommended. This one finds her backed by a veteran sextet including tenorman Buddy Tate, trumpeter Joe Wilder and pianist Norman Simmons. Her versions of "There'll Be Some Changes Made," "Easy Living" and "Draggin' My Heart Around" are particularly memorable. —Scott Yanow

Alberta Hunter

b. Apr. 1, 1895, Memphis, TN, d. Oct. 17, 1984, New York, NY
Vocals / Blues, Standards

An early blues vocalist in the 1920s, a sophisticated supper club singer in the 1930s and a survivor in the '80s, Alberta Hunter had quite a career. Hunter actually debuted in clubs as a singer as early as 1912, starting out in Chicago. She made her first recording in 1921, wrote "Down Hearted Blues" (which became Bessie Smith's first hit) and used such sidemen on her recordings in the 1920s as Fletcher Henderson, Eubie Blake, Fats Waller, Louis Armstrong and Sidney Bechet. She starred in Showboat with Paul Robeson at the London Palladium (1928–29), worked in Paris and recorded straight ballads with John Jackson's Orchestra. After returning to the U.S., Hunter worked for the USO during World War II and Korea, singing overseas. She retired in 1956 to become a nurse (she was 61 at the time) and continued in that field (other than a 1961 recording) until she was forced to retire in 1977 when it was believed she was 65; actually Hunter was 82! She then made a startling comeback in jazz, singing regularly at the Cookery in New York until she was 89, writing the music for the 1978 film Remember My Name and recording for Columbia. After the 1920s, Alberta Hunter recorded on an infrequent basis but her dates from 1935, 1939, 1940 and 1950 have been mostly reissued by Stash, her Bluesville album (1961) is out in the OJC series and her Columbia sets are still available. —Scott Yanow

The Twenties / 1921–1929 / Stash ✦✦✦✦✦

The Legendary Alberta Hunter: '34 London Sessions / Sep. 24, 1934–Nov. 2, 1934 / DRG ✦✦

Classic Alberta Hunter / 1935–1950 / Stash ✦✦✦✦

Songs We Taught Your Mother / Aug. 16, 1961 / Original Blues Classics ✦✦✦✦

Blues Serenaders / Sep. 1, 1961 / Original Blues Classics ✦✦✦✦

Remember My Name / 1977 / CBS ✦✦✦✦

★ Amtrack Blues / 1978 / Columbia ✦✦✦✦✦

Glory of Alberta Hunter / 1981 / CBS ✦✦✦✦✦

Look for the Silver Lining / 1982 / CBS ✦✦✦✦

Charlie Hunter

b. 1968, Rhode Island
Guitar / Post-Bop

Charlie Hunter, who plays an eight-string guitar, provides his own basslines and leads an otherwise bassless guitar-sax-drums trio. He grew up in Berkeley, CA, and began playing guitar when he was 12. Hunter played in rock bands until forming his trio with tenor saxophonist Dave Ellis and drummer Jay Lane. Although very much a jazz group, the group also displays their interests in funk and rock. In addition to recording for Blue Note with his trio, Hunter works with T.J. Kirk, a band playing the music of

Thelonious Monk, James Brown and Rahsaan Roland Kirk that has recorded for Warner Bros. —Scott Yanow

Charlie Hunter Trio / 1993 / Mammoth ✦✦✦✦

● Bing, Bing, Bing! / 1995 / Blue Note ✦✦✦✦✦

It is difficult not to be impressed with the playing of guitarist Charlie Hunter. By using an extra string, Hunter is able to create his own basslines and have a very self-sufficient bassless (and keyboardless) trio with tenor saxophonist Dave Ellis and drummer Jay Lane that has all of the parts covered. The music on this CD (all originals) crosses over between straight-ahead jamming to '70s retro funk (a la Eddie Harris) that is infectious enough to fit into an acid jazz setting. However, even at its funkiest, the rhythms are subtle and the improvising reasonably creative, making this a potentially popular group that should still interest jazz listeners. —Scott Yanow

Chris Hunter

b. Feb. 21, 1957, London, England
Flute, Alto Saxophone / Crossover, Post-Bop

Closely inspired by David Sanborn (who he often sounds like on alto), Chris Hunter is best-known in the U.S. for his work with Gil Evans. He started playing music when he was 12 and toured with the National Youth Jazz Orchestra at 19. After playing with Mike Westbrook (1978–79), Hunter became a studio musician in Europe. He first played with Evans in 1983, which led to him moving to New York. In 1984 he toured with Evans, played with the Michel Camilo sextet and began working with Mike Gibbs. He has since recorded as a leader for the Japanese Paddle Wheel label. —Scott Yanow

Chris Hunter / May 1986–Jun. 1986 / Atlantic ✦✦✦✦

Robert Hurst III

b. Oct. 4, 1964, Detroit, MI
Bass / Hard Bop

Robert Hurst came to fame for his work with Wynton and Branford Marsalis. He was originally a guitarist but instead became an important bassist in the Detroit jazz scene of the late '70s. He recorded with Out of the Blue (1985) and has since recorded with Tony Williams, Mulgrew Miller, Harry Connick, Jr., Geri Allen, Russell Malone and Steve Coleman among others. Hurst was with Wynton Marsalis' group during 1986–91, switched over to Branford's band and became a member of the Tonight Show Orchestra. Robert Hurst, a very supportive bassist, debuted as a leader in 1993 with a release on DIW/Columbia. —Scott Yanow

● Robert Hurst Presents: Robert Hurst / Aug. 20, 1992–Aug. 23, 1992 / DIW/Columbia ✦✦✦

This set finds bassist Robert Hurst leading The Tonight Show All-Stars (with Branford Marsalis on various reeds and pianist Kenny Kirkland) plus trumpeter Marcus Belgrave and guest Ralph Miles Jones III (on bass clarinet and bassoon) through 11 of his originals and a solo bass version of Thelonious Monk's "Evidence." The music is complex and hard-driving, but the improvisations are rather cold and sometimes boring. Hurst, a superior bassist, is not a superior composer and his compositions at best set moods. Of the supporting cast, the most distinctive voices are Belgrave and Jones; the latter has a colorful bass clarinet solo on "The Snake Charmer." This is a decent effort but not all that essential. —Scott Yanow

One For Namesake / Nov. 18, 1993–Nov. 19, 1993 / Columbia ✦✦✦

Bobby Hutcherson

b. Jan. 27, 1941, Los Angeles
Marimbas, Vibes / Hard Bop, Post-Bop

When he first came up, vibraphonist Bobby Hutcherson was associated with the avant-garde, he has since settled down into being "merely" a brilliant stylist, whose playing falls between hard bop and post bop, rather than an innovator. Hutcherson originally studied piano and then started concentrating on vibes as a teenager. He worked in the L.A. area with Curtis Amy and Charles Lloyd before joining the Al Grey-Billy Mitchell Quintet. Hutcherson moved to New York in 1961, made a big impression with his playing on Eric Dolphy's Out to Lunch (1964) and worked with everyone from Jackie McLean, Hank Mobley and Grachan Moncur III to Hank Mobley, Herbie Hancock, Andrew Hill, McCoy Tyner and

Grant Green. Whenever an advanced vibraphonist was needed for a recording, Hutcherson got the call. He recorded a long series of albums as a leader for Blue Note (1965–77), co-led a quintet with Harold Land (1967–71) and has headed his own groups ever since, other than his dates with the Timeless All Stars in the 1980s. In addition to Blue Note, Bobby Hutcherson has recorded as a leader for Cadet, Columbia, Timeless, Evidence, Contemporary and Landmark. — *Scott Yanow*

☆ **Dialogue** / Apr. 3, 1965 / Blue Note ✦✦✦✦✦
An album that was a landmark work in its time, this still has an edgy, avant-garde feeling, thanks to Sam Rivers (ts) and Andrew Hill (p). — *Ron Wynn*

Spiral / Apr. 3, 1965+Nov. 25, 1968 / Blue Note ✦✦✦

Components / Jun. 10, 1965 / Blue Note ✦✦✦✦✦
This CD reissue spans a wide variety of styles, from hard bop (Bobby Hutcherson's attractive "Little B's Poem") to mostly atonal sound explorations ("Air"). There are four compositions apiece by the vibraphonist/leader and drummer Joe Chambers, with Chambers tending to be freer and more avant-garde. The talented young musicians (trumpeter Freddie Hubbard, James Spaulding on alto and flute, pianist Herbie Hancock, bassist Ron Carter, Chambers and Hutcherson) are up to the challenge and the results are always stimulating. Open-eared listeners are advised to pick up this CD, taken from a period when the versatile Bobby Hutcherson was considered one of the brightest new voices of what was called "the New Thing." — *Scott Yanow*

Happenings / Feb. 8, 1966 / Blue Note ✦✦✦✦
This is an excellent showcase for Bobby Hutcherson, who plays vibes and marimba in a quartet with pianist Herbie Hancock, bassist Bob Cranshaw and drummer Joe Chambers. On the straight CD reissue of the original LP, Hutcherson performs six of his diverse originals (which range from advanced hard bop to the nearly free form "The Omen") plus Hancock's "Maiden Voyage." Hutcherson's outings on marimba are particularly interesting since they show the influence of modern classical music. His own style would become more conservative and predictable through the years, making Bobby Hutcherson's earlier records the ones to get for adventurous listeners. — *Scott Yanow*

Stick Up! / Jul. 14, 1966 / Blue Note ✦✦✦✦✦

Total Eclipse / Jul. 12, 1967 / Blue Note ✦✦✦✦
Although thought of as an avant-garde vibraphonist when he first emerged, Bobby Hutcherson eventually became an important part of the modern mainstream. This set, with its modal originals, is somewhere in between where Hutcherson had been and where he was going. Joined by tenor saxophonist Harold Land (with whom he had just started co-leading a quintet) and the up-and-coming pianist Chick Corea, Hutcherson is in excellent form on four of his originals and Corea's "Matrix." — *Scott Yanow*

Patterns / Mar. 14, 1968 / Blue Note ✦✦✦
Bobby Hutcherson was one of the last viable jazz artists to be associated with the original Blue Note label. His *Patterns* from 1968 has concise but searching solos from the leader, James Spaulding (a major but underrated talent) on alto and flute and pianist Stanley Cowell; drummer Joe Chambers contributed four of the six tunes. The music is complex but coherent and surprisingly accessible due to the lightly funky rhythms and some long melody statements. — *Scott Yanow*

Medina / Aug. 11, 1969 / Blue Note ✦✦✦✦
The Bobby Hutcherson-Harold Land Quintet was one of the main unsung groups of this era. Not avant-garde enough to be grouped with the free jazz innovators and owing nothing to fusion, vibraphonist Hutcherson and tenor saxophonist Land seemed to fall between the cracks, as bandleaders if not as solo musicians. This 1969 recording, not released until 1980, teams the co-leaders with pianist Stanley Cowell, bassist Reggie Johnson and drummer Joe Chambers for a variety of complex originals; two apiece by Hutcherson, Cowell and Chambers. The modal music is between hard bop and the avant-garde but can simply be called explorative and unpredictable. — *Scott Yanow*

Now / 1969 / Blue Note ✦✦✦
Prime Hutcherson/Harold Land quintet material. — *Ron Wynn*

San Francisco / Jul. 15, 1970 / Blue Note ✦✦✦✦✦
This CD reissue is an exact duplicate of the original LP. Vibraphonist Bobby Hutcherson and tenor saxophonist Harold Land co-led a quintet on the West Coast for quite a few years. The

remainder of the personnel was often open to change and on this particular release the duo is augmented by keyboardist Joe Sample (normally with The Jazz Crusaders at the time), bassist John Williams and drummer Mickey Roker. The music is often quite advanced yet more accessible than one would expect. There are hints of rock rhythms on a few tracks along with modal melodies influenced by John Coltrane and plenty of rewarding solos from the co-leaders. — *Scott Yanow*

Natural Illusions / Mar. 2, 1972+Mar. 3, 1972 / Blue Note ✦✦

Live at Montreux / Jul. 5, 1973 / Blue Note ✦✦✦✦✦
By 1973 Blue Note was pretty well a dead label, and this often-brilliant advanced hard bop set was only released at the time in Europe and Japan. Now with the CD reissue, Americans can finally hear the mutually inspiring performance of vibraphonist Bobby Hutcherson and trumpeter Woody Shaw. Joined by a fine rhythm section, they create fiery solos on modal originals with Shaw, in particular, in prime form. Highly recommended. — *Scott Yanow*

Cirrus / Apr. 17, 1974+Apr. 18, 1974 / Blue Note ✦✦✦

Linger Lane / 1974 / Blue Note ✦✦

The View from the Inside / Aug. 4, 1976–Aug. 6, 1976 / Blue Note ✦✦✦

Knucklebean / 1977 / Blue Note ✦✦✦✦
This little-known gem is from the declining days of Blue Note. Vibraphonist Bobby Hutcherson welcomed his friend, trumpeter Freddie Hubbard, to his date and Hubbard (who is heard on four of the six selections) almost stole the show. It is particularly nice to hear Hubbard (whose recordings from this era are horrible) playing jazz again. In addition to the leader (who also doubles on marimbas), solo space is given to keyboardist George Cables and the reed players Manny Boyd and Hadley Caliman. This LP is worth searching for since it may be awhile before it returns on CD. — *Scott Yanow*

Highway One / May 1978–Jun. 23, 1978 / Columbia ✦✦✦
With keyboardist George Cables and vibraphonist Bobby Hutcherson contributing all of the compositions, it is not too surprising that this LP has plenty of strong melodies. Hutcherson is heard backed by string and horn sections on one selection apiece, but they add to, rather than detract from, the melodic but not simplistic music. Freddie Hubbard drops by for a cameo on one ballad and flutist Hubert Laws is heard from in spots. A fine (if not overly adventurous) outing. — *Scott Yanow*

Conception: The Gift of Love / Mar. 15, 1979+Mar. 16, 1979 / Columbia ✦✦✦

Un Poco Loco / 1979 / Columbia ✦✦✦✦
Fine Hutcherson exchanges with George Cables (p). — *Ron Wynn*

Solo / Quartet / Sep. 28, 1981–Mar. 1, 1982 / Original Jazz Classics ✦✦✦✦✦
This is one of vibraphonist Bobby Hutcherson's most unusual and interesting releases. The first half of the set features Hutcherson all by himself although, by utilizing overdubbing, he almost sounds like Max Roach's M'Boom ensemble. Hutcherson is heard on vibes, marimbas, bass marimba, chimes, xylophone and bells and these three selections are quite fun and energetic. The second half is more conventional, with Hutcherson welcoming pianist McCoy Tyner (in his first sideman appearance in a decade), bassist Herbie Lewis and drummer Billy Higgins for two standards and a pair of the vibist's originals. The quartet set is excellent, but it is Bobby Hutcherson's solo performances that are most memorable and unique. — *Scott Yanow*

Farewell to Keystone / Jul. 10, 1982–Jul. 11, 1982 / Evidence ✦✦✦✦
Vibist Bobby Hutcherson paid the storied Keystone Korner a wonderful tribute by cutting one of the last live dates done there in July of 1982; the club closed almost exactly a year later. Hutcherson's swinging, joyous phrases and bluesy riffs were nicely buttressed by the hard driving tenor sax of Harold Land, plus excellent rhythm section assistance and textures from pianist Cedar Walton, bassist Buster Williams, and drummer Billy Higgins. Trumpeter Oscar Brashear added competent solos and meshed smoothly in the ensembles. — *Ron Wynn*

Four Seasons / Dec. 11, 1983 / Timeless ✦✦✦

Good Bait / Aug. 9, 1984–Aug. 10, 1984 / Landmark ✦✦✦✦
An excellent date with the cream of old and new players. Branford Marsalis (ts) is in top form. — *Ron Wynn*

Color Schemes / Oct. 1985 / Landmark ✦✦✦✦
On *Color Schemes*, Bobby Hutcherson (vibes) is backed by a top-notch rhythm section for a set of jazz standards and originals. Every selection has its worthwhile points, with the standouts being a bossa nova-flavored version of Joe Henderson's "Recorda-Me." The leader dueted with pianist Mulgrew Miller (who continued to move forward as an impressive soloist, gradually discarding the McCoy Tyner influence) on his ballad "Rosemary, Rosemary," an uptempo rendition of "Remember" and on a colorful overdubbed duet with percussionist Airto Moreira ("Color Scheme") that found Hutcherson blending together vibes, marimba and orchestra bells. This is an easily recommended album of high-quality, if conservative, music. — *Scott Yanow*

● **In the Vanguard** / Dec. 5, 1986+Dec. 6, 1986 / Landmark ✦✦✦✦✦
Vibraphonist Bobby Hutcherson was once associated with the avant-garde to a certain extent, but by the 1970s it was clear he had found his voice in the modern mainstream of jazz. This live set from the Village Vanguard features him on both vibes and marimbas with stellar sidemen: pianist Kenny Barron, bassist Buster Williams and drummer Al Foster. Their repertoire (in addition to Hutcherson's "I Wanna Stand over There") is comprised of five standards and the results are high-quality modern bebop. The communication between the players is quite impressive. — *Scott Yanow*

Cruisin' the Bird / Apr. 15, 1988+Apr. 16, 1988 / Landmark ✦✦✦✦

Ambos Mundos / Aug. 1989–Sep. 1989 / Landmark ✦✦✦✦
A fine venture into Afro-Latin and Latin jazz. Hutcherson is tops on vibes and marimba, joined here by three percussionists. — *Ron Wynn*

Mirage / Feb. 15, 1991+Feb. 18, 1991 / Landmark ✦✦✦

Landmarks / Feb. 12, 1992 / Landmark ✦✦✦

Acoustic Masters II / Mar. 1993 / Atlantic ✦✦✦✦

Dick Hyman

b. Mar. 8, 1927, New York City
Piano / Swing, Stride, Classic Jazz
A very versatile virtuoso, Dick Hyman once recorded an album on which he played "A Child Is Born" in the styles of 11 different pianists from Scott Joplin to Cecil Taylor. Hyman can clearly play anything he wants to and during the past two decades he has mostly concentrated on pre-bop swing and stride styles. Hyman worked with Red Norvo (1949–50) and Benny Goodman (1950) and then spent much of the 1950s and '60s as a studio musician. He appears on the one known sound film of Charlie Parker (*Hot House* from 1952), recorded honky tonk under pseudonyms, played organ and early synthesizers in addition to piano, was Arthur Godfrey's music director (1959–62), collaborated with Leonard Feather on some History of Jazz concerts (doubling on clarinet) and even performed rock and free jazz, but all of this was a prelude to his present-day work. In the 1970s Hyman played with the New York Jazz Repertory Company, formed the Perfect Jazz Repertory Quintet (1976) and started writing soundtracks for Woody Allen films. He has recorded frequently during the past 20 years (sometimes in duets with Ruby Braff) for Concord, Music Masters and Reference and ranks at the top of the classic jazz field. — *Scott Yanow*

★ **Jelly and James: Music of "Jelly Roll" Morton and James P. Johnson** / 1973 / Sony ✦✦✦✦✦

Charleston / Apr. 29, 1975–May 29, 1975 / Columbia ✦✦✦✦✦
Dick Hyman is a modern day wonder, a pianist who can seemingly recreate the style of practically any jazz keyboardist. Since his favorite era is pre-swing, he has in recent years mostly concentrated on the jazz pioneers. This well-rounded set looks into the music of James P. Johnson, the king of stride pianists and an eminent composer of the 1920s. Hyman casts Johnson's music in several different settings. He takes "Caprice Rag" as a piano solo, joins in on three duets with cornetist Ruby Braff (including one outing on organ), uses a fairly straight dance band and an even less adventurous theater orchestra on some tracks, and for three selections features a jazz band that includes Braff, Bob Wilber on soprano and trombonist Vic Dickenson. Although there is not a great deal of improvisation on this program, the expert transcriptions and colorful arrangements pay a glorious tribute to the great James P. Johnson. — *Scott Yanow*

Themes and Variations on "A Child Is Born" / Oct. 11, 1977–Oct. 12, 1977 / Chiaroscuro ✦✦✦✦✦
Dick Hyman took "A Child Is Born" and beat it to death by playing it not only in his style, but also in the style of 11 other pianists (Scott Joplin, Jelly Roll Morton, James P. Johnson, Fats Waller, Earl Hines, Teddy Wilson, Erroll Garner, George Shearing, Cecil Taylor, Art Tatum and Bill Evans). — *Bob Rusch, Cadence*

★ **Music of Jelly Roll Morton** / Feb. 26, 1978 / Smithsonian ✦✦✦✦✦
Of all the Jelly Roll Morton tribute albums that have been recorded through the years, Dick Hyman's is one of the most rewarding. He utilizes a very suitable septet (with clarinetist Bob Wilber, trumpeter Warren Vache, trombonist Jack Gale, Marty Grosz on guitar and banjo, Major Holley doubling on bass and tuba, and Morton alumnus Tommy Benford on drums) on nine of Morton's best tunes, including two ("King Porter Stomp" and "Wolverine Blues") not recorded by Morton in this format. In addition, there is a close re-creation of the quartet piece "Mournful Serenade," a couple of trios with Wilber And Benford, and two piano solos ("Fingerbreaker" and "The Pearls") that give Hyman an opportunity to do his Jelly Roll Mortons impressions. This LP should satisfy all traditional jazz fans. — *Scott Yanow*

Live At Michael's Pub / Jul. 24, 1981–Jul. 25, 1981 / JazzMania ✦✦✦✦
In addition to being piano virtuosos with a mastery of a wide variety of styles ranging from bop and stride to classical music, Dick Hyman and Roger Kellaway both have outrageous sense of humors. During the two live concerts heard on this CD, Hyman and Kellaway play piano duet versions of four jazz standards plus Kellaway's theme from *All in the Family* ("Remembering You"), the "Woody Woodpecker Song" and "Chopsticks." Their treatments of these songs are quite adventurous with plenty of emotional and atonal outbursts while always keeping the melody in clear sight. The ensembles are often dense but the two pianists listen very closely to each other. In fact, when one changes keys, the other one goes right along and extends the idea. The episodic "Chopsticks" (which is really torn apart) is worth the price of this recording by itself. — *Scott Yanow*

Kitten on the Keys / 1983 / RCA ✦✦✦✦

Runnin' Ragged / Sep. 1985 / Pro Arte ✦✦✦

At Chung's Chinese Restaurant / Sep. 26, 1985 / Musical Heritage Society ✦✦✦✦

Manhattan Jazz / 1987 / Music Masters ✦✦✦✦

The Kingdom of Swing & The Republic of Oop Bop Sh'bam / Jul. 30, 1987 / Music Masters ✦✦✦

Face the Music: A Century of Irving Berlin / Dec. 8, 1987–Dec. 9, 1987 / Music Masters ✦✦✦✦

Live from Toronto's Cafe Des Copains / 1988 / Music & Arts ✦✦✦✦✦

Plays Fats Waller / Dec. 1988 / Reference ✦✦✦✦
Pianist Dick Hyman has mastered reproducing classic songs by jazz masters without losing his identity. That was the case on this Fats Waller tribute done directly to disc. Hyman neatly, respectfully, and flawlessly plays such songs as "Honeysuckle Rose" and "Ain't Misbehavin'," captures and reproduces the rhythms and spirit, and injects enough personal twists and phrases to show he understands that he's not Fats Waller, just someone who loves his music and wants to convey its importance to the listener. — *Ron Wynn*

Live at Maybeck Recital Hall, Vol. 3: Music of 1937 / Feb. 14, 1989 / Concord Jazz ✦✦✦✦✦

Harold Arlen Songs / Apr. 13, 1989–Apr. 14, 1989 / Music Masters ✦✦✦✦

All Through the Night / 1991 / Music Masters ✦✦✦✦

Plays Duke Ellington / Aug. 23, 1992 / Reference ✦✦✦✦
Hyman's most recent foray into repertory is done with the same ferocity, attention to detail, and reverential qualities as his Fats Waller project, and once more was recorded direct to disc on the amazing Bosendorfer 275SE Reproducing Piano. The instrument's clarity, tuning, and precise pitch make Hyman's solos even more striking, and though he doesn't always capture Ellington's stride manner, he's got the pacing and rhythms down. The 14 numbers were wisely chosen; several, like "Jubilee Stomp" and "Come Sunday," are piano showcases, while such others as "Echoes Of Harlem" and "Prelude To A Kiss" are wonderful works worthy of inclusion on any Ellington set. — *Ron Wynn*

The Gershwin Songbook: Jazz Variations / Sep. 15, 1992–Sep. 16, 1992 / Music Masters ✦✦✦

In 1932 George Gershwin published variations of 18 of his songs, turning some of his classics into more challenging workouts. Sixty years later Dick Hyman recorded the 18 pieces in two versions apiece: first a straight rendition of the original sheet music and then his own versions, based partly on Gershwin's 1932 songbook. It would have been interesting to hear Hyman perform Gershwin's variations, for one can only guess how much his own improvisations are taken from the composer's embellishments. The flavor of Gershwin is strong throughout this date, but Hyman does feel free to insert some obvious departures such as his hot stride on "Fascinating Rhythm," a bit of Tatum and Tristano on "Strike up the Band," hints of Bix on "Do, Do, Do" and some Errol Garnerisms on "Clap Yo' Hands." Although a tad gimmicky, this CD has its fascinating moments and plenty of typically brilliant playing from Dick Hyman. —*Scott Yanow*

● **Dick Hyman/Ralph Sutton** / 1993 / Concord ✦✦✦✦✦

The two top living stride pianists, Dick Hyman and Ralph Sutton, are teamed up for an exciting live duo session recorded at Maybeck Recital Hall. Hearing the two masters explore jazz standards (moslty from the pre-1940 era) is analogous to seeing Fats Waller and James P. Johnson sharing the same stage in the 1930s. Somehow Hyman and Sutton leave just enough room for the other one to slip in, and the ensembles, although sometimes bursting at the seams, are never overcrowded. Sutton has "Everything Happens to Me" as his ballad feature while Hyman tears into "Old Man River" by himself, but it is the stomps by the duo (such as "Sunday," "Dinah," "The World Is Waiting for the Sunrise" and "I'm Sorry I Made You Cry") that make the session so memorable. This historic encounter is a gem. —*Scott Yanow*

I

Abdullah (Dollar Brand) Ibrahim
(Adolph Johannes Brand)

b. Oct. 9, 1934, Cape Town, South Africa
Piano, Leader / Post-Bop, African Folk Music
A highly individual pianist/composer whose music is influenced by Duke Ellington, Thelonious Monk and especially his own South African heritage, Abdullah Ibrahim (who until the 1970s was known as Dollar Brand) performs explorative originals that are full of strong melodies and spirituality. He started on piano when he was seven and was a member of the Jazz Epistles, recording South Africa's first jazz album in 1960. Ibrahim and his future wife, singer Sathima Bea Benjamin, went into self-imposed exile from the apartheid system in 1962, going to Zurich. Duke Ellington heard them perform and arranged for recording sessions. Ibrahim was also sponsored by Ellington at the 1965 Newport Jazz Festival and even got to sub for him with his orchestra during a tour. In 1966 Ibrahim worked with Elvin Jones, but otherwise he has generally been a bandleader. He has recorded for many labels in settings ranging from a piano soloist and head of a large band to his septet Ekaya including numerous sessions for Enja. Ibrahim, who visited South Africa in 1976, has returned home several times since its liberation from apartheid. —*Scott Yanow*

★ **Anatomy of a South African Village** / Jan. 30, 1965 / Black Lion ✦✦✦✦✦
A sublime, transcendent date. Trio live at Cafe Montmartre in Copenhagen. Rare. —*Michael G. Nastos*

The Dream / Jan. 30, 1965 / Freedom ✦✦✦✦

Reflections / Mar. 16, 1965 / Black Lion ✦✦✦✦✦

African Piano / Oct. 22, 1969 / ECM ✦✦✦✦
A 1989 reissue of some fine live playing from a 1969 concert in Copenhagen. —*Ron Wynn*

Fats Duke and the Monk / Feb. 18, 1973 / Sackville ✦✦✦✦

Sangoma / Feb. 18, 1973 / Sackville ✦✦✦✦✦
The great South African musician Abdullah Ibrahim (then going by his original name of Dollar Brand) performs a six-song suite dedicated to his main influences "Fats, Duke and the Monk," along with a couple of three-part originals: "The Aloe and the Wild Rose" and "Ancient Africa." Ibrahim's distinctive percussive style with its emphasis on folk melodies was very much in evidence at this relatively early stage. —*Scott Yanow*

African Portraits / Feb. 18, 1973 / Sackville ✦✦✦✦

African Space Program / Nov. 7, 1973 / Enja ✦✦✦
Poorly recorded, but a great 12-piece group date. —*Ron Wynn*

Good News from Africa / Dec. 10, 1973 / Enja ✦✦✦✦

Ode to Duke Ellington / Dec. 12, 1973 / Inner City ✦✦✦✦

The Banyana: Children of Africa / Jan. 27, 1976 / Enja ✦✦✦
Abdullah Ibrahim sings and plays soprano on "Ishmael," but otherwise sticks to piano on this trio set with bassist Cecil McBee and drummer Roy Brooks. As usual, Ibrahim's folkish melodies (this CD has six of his originals plus a previously alternate take of "Ishmael") pay tribute to his South African heritage and Islam religion without becoming esoteric or inaccessible. Some of the unpredictable music gets a bit intense (Ibrahim is in consistently adventurous form), but his flights always return back to earth and have an air of optimism. An above average effort from a true individualist. —*Scott Yanow*

Journey / Sep. 1977 / Chiaroscuro ✦✦✦
An excellent nonette with Hamiet Bluiett (baritone sax) and Don Cherry (tpt). —*Ron Wynn*

Autobiography / Jun. 18, 1978 / Planisphere ✦✦✦✦

Africa: Tears and Laughter / Mar. 11, 1979–Mar. 12, 1979 / Enja ✦✦✦
Featured on this 1990 reissue is the quartet with some vocals by Ibrahim and saxophonist Talib Qadr for variety. —*Myles Boisen*

Echoes from Africa / Sep. 7, 1979 / Enja ✦✦✦
This is a rather emotional duet set by pianist Abdullah Ibrahim and bassist Johnny Dyani, two masterful musicians from South Africa. Their often introspective music includes three originals (with one piece dedicated to McCoy Tyner) plus a nearly 17-minute improvisation based on a folk melody that also allows one to hear the voices of the two musicians. This moody music has an almost sacred credibility and is quite personal. —*Scott Yanow*

African Marketplace / Dec. 1979 / Elektra ✦✦✦✦✦

★ **Live at Montreux** / Jul. 18, 1980 / Enja ✦✦✦✦✦
A 1990 reissue of a tremendous concert done in 1980. Carlos Ward and Craig Harris star alongside Ibrahim. —*Ron Wynn*

African Dawn / Jun. 7, 1982 / Enja ✦✦✦✦
These are solo versions of his greatest originals, plus Monk tributes. —*Myles Boisen*

Zimbabwe / May 29, 1983 / Enja ✦✦✦✦
This was a nicely blended, somewhat mellow and seemingly quite finished recording by Abdullah Ibrahim with Carlos Ward (alto sax, flute), Essiet Okun Essiet (bass) and Don Mumford (drums) called *Zimbabwe*. Interspaced with non-originals were four Ibrahim compositions, most of which were inspired by the imagery from Ibrahim's South African roots. —*Bob Rusch, Cadence*

Live at Sweet Basil, Vol. 1 / Oct. 3, 1983 / Ekapa ✦✦✦✦

☆ **Ekaya** / Nov. 17, 1983 / Ekapa ✦✦✦✦✦
This studio date with septet is a must-buy. Extraordinary ensemble music. —*Michael G. Nastos*

★ **Water from an Ancient Well** / Oct. 1985 / Tiptoe ✦✦✦✦✦
Also made available domestically at one time by the defunct Black-Hawk label, this superior Abdullah Ibrahim recording features the pianist/composer with a very strong septet. Such superior musicians as tenor saxophonist Ricky Ford, altoist Carlos Ward, baritonist Charles Davis and trombonist Dick Griffin are heard at their most creative and emotional on these eight Ibrahim originals. Many of the melodies (particularly "Mandela," "Song for Sathima," "Water from an Ancient Well" and the beautiful "The Wedding") are among Ibrahim's finest compositions. —*Scott Yanow*

South Africa / Jul. 1986 / Enja ✦✦✦✦
Abdullah Ibrahim's spiritual and very melodic South African folk music is always worth hearing and his individuality remains quite impressive. This set, recorded live at the Montreux Jazz Festival, features the pianist (who also plays a bit of soprano and adds his emotional voice to the proceedings) with his longtime altoist Carlos Ward, bassist Essiet Okun Essiet, drummer Don Mumford and vocalist Johnny Classens. The music, dealing with themes related to South African life, is quite personal, unique and surprisingly accessible. —*Scott Yanow*

Mindif / Mar. 7, 1988–Mar. 8, 1988 / Enja ✦✦✦
Soundtrack recordings expose his favorite themes with top-notch backing U.S. jazz musicians. —*Myles Boisen*

African River / Jun. 1, 1989 / Enja ✦✦✦✦
Seamless, breathtaking blend of jazz and traditional African rhythms featuring Ibrahim and his group, Ekaya. —*Ron Wynn*

Mantra Mode / Jan. 1991 / Enja ✦✦✦✦
This was a very special recording for pianist/composer Abdullah Ibrahim because, after nearly 30 years of exile, he was back in Cape Town, South Africa performing with local musicians. The musicianship is surprisingly high and the African septet does a fine job of interpreting eight of Ibrahim's newer folk melodies. — *Scott Yanow*

Desert Flowers / Dec. 18, 1991 / Enja ✦✦✦
Release by pianist and bandleader Abdullah Ibrahim, combining the sweeping township jive rhythms of his native South Africa, swing and gospel piano riffs and hard-hitting bop solos and progressions. —*Ron Wynn*

Keith Ingham

b. Feb. 5, 1942, London, England
Piano / Swing, Dixieland
A fine swing pianist, Keith Ingham's recent recordings of 1930s vintage songs for the Jump label are quite enjoyable. He started playing professionally in 1964 and worked with Sandy Brown, Bruce Turner and Wally Fawkes (among others) in England during the next decade. In 1974 Ingham recorded with Bob Wilber and Bud Freeman and, in 1978, settled in New York. He had the opportunity to play with Benny Goodman and the World's Greatest Jazz Band and became the musical director and pianist for Susannah McCorkle. Keith Ingham also recorded three albums with Maxine Sullivan, worked with Marty Grosz and Harry Allen, toured with the Eddie Condon Memorial Band and has led sessions for Sackville and Progressive in addition to Jump. —*Scott Yanow*

Fred Astaire Collection / May 21, 1989–May 23, 1989 / Jump ✦✦✦✦

Music Of Victor Young / May 21, 1989–May 23, 1989 / Jump ✦✦✦✦

Out of the Past / Dec. 1990 / Sackville ✦✦✦

Donaldson Redux / Nov. 1991 / Stomp Off ✦✦✦✦

Music From The Mauve Decades / Apr. 20, 1993–Apr. 21, 1993 / Sackville ✦✦✦✦✦

● **The Keith Ingham New York 9, Vol. 1** / May 9, 1994–May 17, 1994 / Jump ✦✦✦✦✦

● **The Keith Ingham New York 9, Vol. 2** / May 9, 1994–May 17, 1994 / Jump ✦✦✦✦✦

International Sweethearts of Rhythm

b. 1939, **d.** 1949
Big Band / Swing
Probably the finest all-female jazz group, the International Sweethearts of Rhythm was formed in 1939 at the Piney Woods Country Life School in Mississippi. The 17-piece swing group, which was led by singer Anna Mae Winburn, included such fine soloists as tenor saxophonist Vi Burnside and trumpeter Tiny Davis. Eddie Durham and Jesse Stone were among the arrangers. The Sweethearts gradually became popular in the 1940s, appearing on radio broadcasts, touring the U.S. and visiting Europe (1945). The orchestra only made a few records before its breakup in 1949, but a couple of its broadcasts from 1945–46 were released on a Rosetta LP. —*Scott Yanow*

★ **International Sweethearts of Rhythm** / 1945-1946/ Rosetta ✦✦✦✦✦

Irakere

b. 1973
Group / Afro-Cuban Jazz
Many of the top Cuban jazz musicians have played in Irakere during the past 23 years including altoist Paquito D'Rivera and trumpeter Arturo Sandoval (before both individually defected). Pianist Chucho Valdes has been the orchestra's longtime leader and its music ranges from Latin-jazz and bop to Cuban folk melodies with an emphasis on infectious rhythms and advanced improvisations. Several of Irakere's records have been made available domestically (including sets for Columbia and more recently Jazz House), but the exciting band has never been allowed to visit the U.S. —*Scott Yanow*

Irakere / May 1979 / CBS ✦✦✦✦✦

Chekere Son / Sep. 1982 / Milestone ✦✦✦

El Coco / Apr. 1983 / Milestone ✦✦✦

★ **Live at Ronnie Scott's** / Sep. 1991 / World Pacific ✦✦✦✦✦
In Irakere's earlier days, this premiere Cuban group often had to disguise the fact that they were playing imperialistic music from the West (i.e. jazz). Maybe now the masquerade is no longer necessary for the music on this definitive CD would never be mistaken for anything else. Heavily influenced both by Dizzy Gillespie and the rhythms of Cuba and South America, the 11-piece group is in top form interpreting the compositions of its pianist/leader Chuco Valdes (who has a memorable workout on "Mr. Bruce"). Five of the six selections are primaily features for individual players. Throughout this memorable set, the ensemble work is clean and loose, the percussionists keep the proceedings fiery and the soloists are excellent. —*Scott Yanow*

Chuck Israels

b. Aug. 10, 1936, New York, NY
Bass / Cool, Post-Bop
Chuck Israels is still best-known for his work with the Bill Evans Trio (1961–66), but he has been an important educator since the 1970s. A tasteful and supportive bassist, Israels' first recording was the 1958 meeting between John Coltrane and Cecil Taylor. He played with George Russell's sextet (1959–61), was briefly with Eric Dolphy's band and then joined Bill Evans. During the Evans years, Israels also appeared on records led by J.J. Johnson, Herbie Hancock, Gary Burton and Stan Getz. He founded and headed the National Jazz Ensemble (1973–78), a top repertory band that recorded two albums for Chiaroscuro. Since then Israels has been less active as a player but he did record with the Kronos String Quartet (1984) and Rosemary Clooney (1985) in addition to heading an obscure session for Anima (1991). —*Scott Yanow*

● **National Jazz Ensemble** / 1976 / Chiaroscuro ✦✦✦✦

David Izenon

b. May 17, 1932, Pittsburgh, PA, **d.** Oct. 8, 1979, New York, NY
Bass / Free Jazz, Avant-Garde
A brilliant bassist who was an expert with the bow, David Izenzon's playing in the mid-'60s Ornette Coleman Trio was outstanding. He did not start playing bass until he was already 24. Izenzon worked locally in Pittsburgh until moving to New York in 1961. He played with Paul Bley, Archie Shepp, Sonny Rollins and Bill Dixon and first joined Ornette's group in October 1961. Izenzon freelanced after Coleman's 1962 Town Hall concert and then played regularly with the innovative altoist during 1965–68. He taught at Bronx Community College (1968–71), played with Perry Robinson and Paul Motian, gained a Ph.D. in psychotherapy (1973) and worked again with Coleman and Motian in 1977 before his early death. —*Scott Yanow*

J

Jackie & Roy

Vocal Group / Standards, Bop

Singer Jackie Cain (b. May 22, 1928, Milwaukee, WI) and singer/pianist Roy Kral (b. Oct. 10, 1921, Chicago, IL) first joined forces in 1946 and in 1996 they are celebrating their 50th anniversary as a vocal duo. Jackie and Roy were with Charlie Ventura's band during 1948–49 (which gave them a great deal of recognition); Lou Stein's "East of Suez" was an unusual feature for their voices. Shortly after leaving Ventura in June 1949, they were married and have worked together on a regular basis ever since. Jackie and Roy had their own television show in Chicago in the early '50s, worked in Las Vegas during 1957-60, settled in New York in 1963 and appeared on some television commercials. They have recorded many spirited jazz performances for a variety of labels through the decades and still perform in the mid-'90s. Roy is the brother of the late singer Irene Kral. —*Scott Yanow*

Star Sounds / Oct. 1979 / Concord Jazz ✦✦✦

A Stephen Sondheim Collection / Jul. 24, 1982 / DRG ✦✦✦✦
Jackie Cain & Roy Kral. An excellent live date with solid vocals throughout. Excellent interpretations of Sondheim's stage music by Jackie And Roy. —*Ron Wynn*

● **We've Got It** / 1984 / Discovery ✦✦✦✦✦

Full Circle / Jan. 14, 1992 / Contemporary ✦✦✦✦

Cliff Jackson

b. Jul. 19, 1902, Culpepper, WI, d. May 24, 1970, New York, NY
Piano / Stride

One of the most powerful stride pianists, Cliff Jackson never became all that famous in the jazz world despite his talent. In 1923 he moved to New York where he played with Lionel Howard's Musical Aces in 1924 and freelanced. Jackson recorded in 1927 with Bob Fuller and Elmer Snowden and then formed a big band (the Krazy Kats) that made some exuberant recordings in 1930 including "Horse Feathers," and "The Terror." After that band broke up, Jackson mostly worked as a soloist in New York clubs. He recorded with Sidney Bechet during 1940–41, cut some solos and Dixieland sides for Black & White (1944–45), made three solos for Disc (1945), led a band for a Swingville session (1961) and recorded solo for Black Lion, Ri-Disc, Jazzology and Master Jazz (1969). Cliff Jackson is also documented in 1966 playing at a festival (on Jazzology) with his wife, Maxine Sullivan. —*Scott Yanow*

Carolina Shout / Dec. 30, 1961+Jan. 16, 1962 / Black Lion ✦✦✦✦
Cliff Jackson was one of the top stride pianists to emerge in the 1920s so this solo piano disc promises a great deal. Although Jackson plays these standards and stride classics well enough, his metronomic left hand gets a bit tiring after awhile. He keeps time so perfectly that Jackson often fails to let much life and feeling into his improvisations. However, taken in small doses, these 15 performances (which include an unreleased version of "Squeeze Me" and three "new" alternate takes) do showcase his impressive talents during a period when he did not record very often. —*Scott Yanow*

Franz Jackson

b. Nov. 1, 1912, Rock Island, IL
Tenor Saxophone, Clarinet / Dixieland, Swing

One of the last survivors of the pre-swing era, Franz Jackson (a fine tenorman and clarinetist) is still active as of this writing in 1996, having recorded recently for Parkwood with Marcus Belgrave. He worked in the Chicago area starting in 1926 includ-ing with Albert Ammons, Carroll Dickerson (1932 and 1934–36), Jimmie Noone (1934), Roy Eldridge (1937) and Fletcher Henderson's Orchestra (1937-38). Jackson travelled to New York with Eldridge (1938–39), played in California with Earl Hines' Orchestra (1940–41) and then worked with Fats Waller (1941) and the Cootie Williams big band (1942). Stints with Frankie Newton (1942–43) and Wilbur DeParis (1944–45) followed and he played in the Pacific on several USO tours. In the mid-'50s after return-ing to Chicago, Franz Jackson formed his Original Jazz All Stars, a group that lasted for around 20 years. He recorded for Riverside in 1961, Delmark and for his own label Pinnacle; Jackson also recorded with Art Hodes in 1974. He has continued playing regu-larly in the Chicago area up to the present time. —*Scott Yanow*

Chicago: The Living Legends, Feat. Bob Shoffner / Sep. 5, 1961 / Original Jazz Classics ✦✦✦✦✦

Snag It / Aug. 1990 / Delmark ✦✦✦✦
With Jim Beebe's Chicago Jazz Band. Fourteen swing-era-styled songs, with Jackson's reed work and vocals shown. Beebe plays trombone with sextet. Excellent sound of band and recording. About time we heard Jackson on a recording—he's 80! —*Michael G. Nastos*

● **Live At Windsor Jazz Festival III.** / Jul. 9, 1994 / Parkwood ✦✦✦✦✦
Eighty-two at the time of this 1994 concert, Franz Jackson (a gruff-toned tenor influenced by the style of Coleman Hawkins) was still playing in his prime. The octogenarian is matched with trumpeter Marcus Belgrave and a fine Detroit-based rhythm section that includes veteran drummer Frank Isola for nine standards and a closing blues. Belgrave, a very versatile player capable of playing much more advanced styles of jazz, fits in perfectly in the swing-oriented format, trading off with the older tenor and taking spir-ited solos. The music is highlighted by "Chicago," "Perdido," a double-time version of "Body and Soul" and "After You've Gone," showing that even in the mid-'90s small-group swing lives. —*Scott Yanow*

Javon Jackson

b. Jun. 16, 1965, Carthage, MI
Tenor Saxophone / Hard Bop

A fine tenor saxophonist influenced by Joe Henderson, Javon Jackson helps to keep the legacy of Art Blakey and hard bop alive. He grew up in Cleveland and Denver and studied at Berklee (1984–86). Jackson was with the last version of the Jazz Messengers (1987–90) and, since Blakey's death, he has worked with the Harper Brothers, Benny Green, Freddie Hubbard and Elvin Jones. Javon Jackson has recorded as a leader for Criss Cross and Blue Note. —*Scott Yanow*

● **Me and Mr. Jones** / Dec. 16, 1991 / Criss Cross ✦✦✦✦✦

When the Time Is Right / Sep. 7, 1993–Oct. 1, 1993 / Blue Note ✦✦✦✦
Former Messenger Javon Jackson does his best to break the generic trap that burdens so many hard bop-oriented jazz releas-es in the 1990s. His recent Blue Note CD includes three originals enriched by his passionate tenor sax solos and Jacky Terrasson's rich piano phrases. These are the set's most spirited songs, although Jackson includes four expertly done standards and a bop anthem ("Love Walked In") featuring intense exchanges with alto saxophonist Kenny Garrett. Dianne Reeves' guest vocal on "I Waited For You" is warmly phrased and delivered. It's a testimo-

nial to Jackson that several tunes are more than simple blowing exercises. —*Ron Wynn*

For One Who Knows / Jan. 18, 1995–Jan. 19, 1995 / Blue Note ♦♦♦

This CD only has one fault but it is a major one. It seems that no matter what he plays (whether it be obscure songs by Wayne Shorter, Herbie Hancock, Sonny Rollins and Antonio Carlos Jobim or one of his two originals), Javon Jackson sounds too close for comfort to Joe Henderson; in fact, there are times when the tenor saxophonist sounds identical. That is a real pity for Jackson consistently shows the ability to take chances successfully and his supporting cast (particularly pianist Jacky Terrasson and acoustic guitarist Fareed Haque) is quite strong. The music, essentially advanced hard bop with hints of the avant-garde, is stimulating and generally unpredictable. Now if only Javon Jackson would put away his Joe Henderson records for a few years. —*Scott Yanow*

Milt Jackson

b. Jan. 1, 1923, Detroit, MI
Vibes / Bop, Hard Bop

Before Milt Jackson there were only two major vibraphonists: Lionel Hampton and Red Norvo. Jackson soon surpassed both of them in significance and, despite the rise of other players (including Bobby Hutcherson and Gary Burton), still wins the popularity polls. Jackson (or Bags as he has long been called) has been at the top of his field for 50 years, playing bop, blues and ballads with equal skill and sensitivity.

Milt Jackson started on guitar when he was seven and piano at 11; a few years later he switched to vibes. He actually made his professional debut singing in a touring gospel quartet. After Dizzy Gillespie discovered him playing in Detroit, he offered him a job with his sextet and (shortly after) his innovative big band (1946). Jackson recorded with Dizzy and was soon in great demand. During 1948–49 he worked with Charlie Parker, Thelonious Monk, Howard McGhee and the Woody Herman Orchestra. After playing with Gillespie's sextet (1950–52) which, at one point, included John Coltrane, Jackson recorded with a quartet comprised of John Lewis, Percy Heath and Kenny Clarke (1952) which soon became a regular group called the Modern Jazz Quartet. Although he recorded regularly as a leader (including dates in the 1950s with Miles Davis and/or Thelonious Monk, Coleman Hawkins, John Coltrane and Ray Charles), Milt Jackson stayed with the MJQ through 1974, becoming an indispensable part of their sound. By the mid-'50s Lewis became the musical director and some felt that Bags was restricted by the format but it actually served him well, giving him some challenging settings. And he always had an opportunity to jam on some blues including his "Bags' Groove." However, in 1974 Jackson felt frustrated by the MJQ (particularly financially) and broke up the group. He recorded frequently for Pablo in many all-star settings in the 1970s and, after a seven-year vacation, the MJQ came back in 1981. In addition to the MJQ recordings, Milt Jackson cut records as a leader throughout his career for many labels including Savoy, Blue Note (1952), Prestige, Atlantic, United Artists, Impulse, Riverside, Limelight, Verve, CTI, Pablo, Music Masters and Qwest. —*Scott Yanow*

In the Beginning / Apr. 1948 / Original Jazz Classics ♦♦♦

This is a very interesting CD, particularly for bop collectors, since it contains very rare early performances by altoist Sonny Stitt and vibraphonist Milt Jackson; some of the titles were originally under trumpeter Russell Jacquet's name. There are eight songs by a quintet with Stitt, Jacquet and pianist Sir Charles Thompson, which could be considered the first Modern Jazz Quartet records (actually a quintet with Milt Jackson, pianist John Lewis, drummer Kenny Clarke, bassist Al Jackson and Chano Pozo on congas) and five songs from a septet with Jacquet, Stitt, trombonist J.J. Johnson and baritonist Leo Parker. Recorded in Detroit for the tiny Galaxy label, these performances are not essential, but they do give listeners an early glimpse at the future stars. —*Scott Yanow*

Bluesology / Jan. 25, 1949–Feb. 23, 1949 / Savoy ♦♦♦♦

This valuable LP collects together a session led by vibraphonist Milt Jackson for Savoy in 1949 (featuring a septet that includes the pioneering jazz french horn of Julius Watkins and tenor saxophonist Billy Mitchell), a sextet set led by drummer Kenny Clarke that has similar personnel (including Watkins, Mitchell and the addition of trumpeter Kenny Dorham) and two songs from a date led by singer Wini Brown. Throughout, Jackson shows why he

was considered the first important vibraphonist to emerge after Lionel Hampton and Red Norvo. This LP from 1980 is much more coherent (consisting of complete sessions and two alternate takes) than the more recent Savoy CD reissues. —*Scott Yanow*

The First Q / Aug. 24, 1951–Apr. 1952 / Savoy ♦♦♦♦

The early evolution of The Modern Jazz Quartet is traced on this perfectly done LP (far superior to the more recent Savoy CD reissue series). Three four-song sessions that were originally released under vibraphonist Milt Jackson's name are included and these only predate The MJQ by less than a year. Pianist John Lewis is on all of the titles, bassist Ray Brown and drummer Al Jones appear on four apiece and original members bassist Percy Heath and drummer Kenny Clarke are on the other eight. Despite the similarity in personnel, these boppish jams are very much Jackson's dates rather than a co-op although some of the songs (particularly "Bluesology" and "Softly as in a Morning Sunrise") would soon enter The MJQ's repertoire. —*Scott Yanow*

A Date in New York / Mar. 7, 1954 / Inner City ♦♦♦♦

This European bop session was actually led by pianist Henri Renaud. Milt Jackson has a generous amount of vibraphone solos and is also heard playing piano on three selections; he even takes a vocal on "The More I See You." Tenor saxophonist Al Cohn pops up on four of the performances but the most impressive soloist throughout this out-of-print LP is the great trombonist J.J. Johnson who often steals the show. —*Scott Yanow*

Milt Jackson Quartet / May 20, 1955 / Original Jazz Classics ♦♦♦

The music on this quartet date (which features vibraphonist Milt Jackson, pianist Horace Silver, bassist Percy Heath and drummer Connie Kay) is excellent, but the playing time (31 minutes) is pretty disgraceful, particularly when one considers that Jackson did a lot of recording for Prestige; certainly more selections could have been added to make this CD have a decent amount of music. Even the old two-LP set *Opus De Funk* added four selections to the album containing this otherwise enjoyable straight-ahead set. Quantity aside, Bags and Silver make for a good combination on five standards and Jackson's "Stonewall." —*Scott Yanow*

Opus De Jazz / Oct. 28, 1955 / Savoy ♦♦♦

This Savoy CD is a duplicate of the original LP although it lacks the fine liner notes included on the Arista/Savoy 1978 LP. The four selections (which unfortunately total under 34 minutes) are excellent, particularly a fun version of Horace Silver's blues "Opus De Funk" in which vibraphonist Milt Jackson, flutist Frank Wess and pianist Hank Jones have a long tradeoff. The quintet (which also includes bassist Eddie Jones and drummer Kenny Clarke) swings nicely throughout the three blues and lone ballad ("You Leave Me Breathless"). This is not essential but easily enjoyable music. —*Scott Yanow*

The Jazz Skyline / Jan. 23, 1956 / Savoy Jazz ♦♦♦♦

This session has interest as an example of Milt Jackson's mid-'50s work in a non-Modern Jazz Quartet context. And despite the many critical assertions that the vibist was restrained by pianist John Lewis' direction, his playing here revealed no marked change. The overall feel of the group (Lucky Thompson, tenor sax; Hank Jones, piano; Wendell Marshall; bass, Kenny Clarke, drums; Jackson, vibes), however, was somewhat more dynamic than that of The MJQ, as Clarke and Jones generally achieved a greater sense of forward momentum than Connie Kay or Lewis. —*Bob Rusch, Cadence*

Soul Brothers / Sep. 12, 1957 / Atlantic ♦♦♦♦♦

It is surprising that this set has not yet been issued on CD for it is a real historical curiosity. Not only does vibraphonist Milt Jackson double here on piano but he plays guitar (for the only time on record) during "Bags' Guitar Blues." In addition, Ray Charles is heard in a purely instrumental role on piano and, during two songs, on alto sax! Charles' fine playing makes one wonder why he so rarely picked up the horn in later years. Billy Mitchell contributes some fine tenor solos on this boppish/blues material and guitarist Skeeter Best, bassist Oscar Pettiford and drummer Connie Kay offer stellar support. —*Scott Yanow*

Bean Bags / Sep. 12, 1958 / Atlantic ♦♦♦♦

Many of vibraphonist Milt Jackson's Atlantic recordings are long overdue to appear on CD and that certainly includes this album, a meeting with the great tenor Coleman Hawkins. Assisted by a top-notch quartet (pianist Tommy Flanagan, guitarist Kenny Burrell, bassist Eddie Jones and drummer Connie Kay), Bean and Bags romp through "Stuffy," "Get Happy," a pair of Jackson originals and two fine ballads with "Don't Take Your Love from Me" being particularly memorable. —*Scott Yanow*

Bags' Opus / Dec. 28, 1958–Dec. 29, 1958 / Blue Note ✦✦✦✦✦
Vibraphonist Milt Jackson welcomes the two future co-leaders of The Jazztet (trumpeter Art Farmer and tenor saxophonist Benny Golson) along with a fine rhythm section (pianist Tommy Flanagan, bassist Paul Chambers and drummer Connie Kay) on this CD reissue. The repertoire (which includes early versions of Golson's "Whisper Not" and "I Remember Clifford" in addition to two standards, a Milt Jackson blues and John Lewis' "Afternoon in Paris") is very much in The Jazztet hard bop vein, and Jackson fits in very well with the two lyrical horn soloists. A successful outing by some of the greats. —*Scott Yanow*

☆ **Bags and Trane** / Jan. 15, 1959 / Atlantic ✦✦✦✦✦
Vibraphonist Milt Jackson and tenor saxophonist John Coltrane make for a surprisingly complementary team on this 1959 studio session, their only joint recording. With fine backup by pianist Hank Jones, bassist Paul Chambers and drummer Connie Kay, Bags and Trane stretch out on two of Jackson's originals (including "The Late Late Blues") and three standards: a romping "Three Little Words," "The Night We Called It a Day" and the rapid "Be-Bop." This enjoyable music has been included as part of Rhino's *Complete Coltrane on Atlantic* box. —*Scott Yanow*

Statements / Dec. 14, 1961–Aug. 6, 1964 / Impulse! ✦✦✦
Vibraphonist Milt Jackson has been so consistent throughout his lenghty career that his excellence can be taken for granted. This CD reissue of an Impulse LP features Bags with a quartet (including pianist Hank Jones) from 1961 and leading a quintet (with tenor saxophonist Jimmy Heath and pianist Tommy Flanagan) in 1964; the latter was originally half of the LP *Jazz 'N' Samba*. In addition, there is a feature for Flanagan in a trio without the vibraphonist that was originally on an Impulse! sampler. The blues, ballads, standards and originals are typical of Jackson's recordings as is the high-quality of the swinging music. Nothing too unusual occurs, but the results are pleasing. —*Scott Yanow*

Bags Meets Wes / Dec. 18, 1961+Dec. 19, 1961 / Original Jazz Classics ✦✦✦✦
His Riverside debut album was a stunner. Wonderful Wes Montgomery Guitar. —*Ron Wynn*

Big Bags / Jun. 19, 1962–Jul. 1962 / Original Jazz Classics ✦✦✦✦
Vibraphonist Milt Jackson is backed by a big band for this change-of-pace release, reissued on CD along with two alternate takes. The Ernie Wilkins and Tadd Dameron arrangements fit the high-quality standards well and Jackson (who contributed two originals) is in top form. There are short solos for cornetist Nat Adderley, trombonist Jimmy Cleveland and the tenors of James Moody and Jimmy Heath, but Milt Jackson is the main voice throughout this melodic and always-swinging set. —*Scott Yanow*

Invitation / Aug. 30, 1962–Nov. 7, 1962 / Original Jazz Classics ✦✦✦
Six of the eight selections on this CD (plus two previously unreleased alternate takes) showcase vibraphonist Milt Jackson in an all-star sextet with trumpeter Kenny Dorham, tenor saxophonist Jimmy Heath, pianist Tommy Flanagan, bassist Ron Carter and drummer Connie Kay; the two remaining selections substitute Virgil Jones for Heath, giving the band two trumpets. The music swings (as one would expect from a Milt Jackson date) and the repertoire (three standards, Thelonious Monk's classic ballad "Ruby, My Dear," the obscure "Ruby" and three group originals) gives the set enough variety to hold one's interest throughout. It's not essential, but Milt Jackson fans will enjoy this music. —*Scott Yanow*

For Someone I Love / 1963 / Original Jazz Classics ✦✦✦✦✦
The main reasons for this CD reissue's success are Melba Liston's inventive and unpredictable arrangements for the brass orchestra. Vibraphonist Milt Jackson has nearly all the solos (although trumpeter Clark Terry, trombonist Quentin Jackson, Julius Watkins on French horn and Major Holley on tuba do make their presence known) and seems understandably inspired by the backup orchestra, which consists of four or five trumpets, three trombones, three or four French horns, Holley's tuba and a rhythm section. The well-conceived set (which includes such songs as "Days of Wine and Roses," "Save Your Love for Me," some Duke Ellington ballads and "Bossa Bags") is consistently excellent, making this a highly recommended set. —*Scott Yanow*

Live at the Village Gate / Dec. 9, 1963 / Original Jazz Classics ✦✦✦✦
Vibraphonist Milt Jackson's own sessions outside of The Modern Jazz Quartet tend to be hard-swinging jams through attractive chord changes, a mixture of boppish romps and thoughtful ballad statements. Jackson has frequently worked with tenors and Jimmy Heath, who is well-featured throughout this set (a CD reissue that brings back an earlier LP plus two "new" selections) became an occasional associate. With fine work by pianist Hank Jones, bassist Bob Cranshaw and drummer Al "Tootie" Heath, Milt Jackson is in typically swinging form on some blues, standards, ballads and Jimmy Heath's "Gemini." —*Scott Yanow*

Jazz 'n Samba / Aug. 6, 1964–Aug. 7, 1964 / Impulse! ✦✦✦
This is an odd LP. The first session is a conventional one with vibraphonist Milt Jackson, tenor saxophonist Jimmy Heath, pianist Tommy Flanagan, bassist Richard Davis and drummer Connie Kay performing Heath's recent "Gingerbread Boy," Duke Ellington's "I Got It Bad" and a pair of Jackson originals. The flip side substitutes two guitars for Flanagan's piano and uses bossa nova rhythms in hopes of getting a hit. Milt does play well on "I Love You" and Lillian Clark's vocal on "Jazz 'N' Samba" is fine but "The Oo-Oo Bossa Noova" is strictly for those listeners who are nostalgic for *Car 54, Where Are You*. —*Scott Yanow*

Sunflower / Dec. 12, 1972–Dec. 13, 1972 / Columbia ✦✦✦✦✦
Vibraphonist Milt Jackson recorded three albums for CTI in the early '70s; this LP is the best of the trio. The Don Sebesky arrangements for the strings showcase Jackson well, trumpeter Freddie Hubbard and pianist Herbie Hancock make impressions the four songs (highlighted by Hubbard's "Sunflower") receive fine treatment. —*Scott Yanow*

Montreux '75 / Jul. 17, 1975 / Pablo ✦✦✦✦
Vibraphonist Milt Jackson teams up with pianist Oscar Peterson, bassist Niels Pedersen and drummer Mickey Roker for a particularly appealing set, one of the few Pablo sessions by the vibist which has not yet been reissued on CD. Pity, for there are many exciting performances (particularly Blue Mitchell's "Funji Mama," "Speed Ball" and "Mack the Knife") and some emotional ballad statements ("Everything Must Change" and "Like Someone like Love"). Bags and O.P. always bring out the best in each other and this well-conceived set is no exception. —*Scott Yanow*

★ **The Big 3** / Aug. 25, 1975 / Pablo ✦✦✦✦✦
This CD (a straight reissue of the original LP) features a rather notable pianoless combo: vibraphonist Milt Jackson, guitarist Joe Pass and bassist Ray Brown. During the Pablo years, these three masterful players recorded together in many settings, but only this once as a trio. The colorful repertoire (which ranges from "The Pink Panther" and "Blue Bossa" to "Nuages" and "Come Sunday") acts as a device for the musicians to construct some brilliant bop-based solos. —*Scott Yanow*

Feelings / Apr. 12, 1976–Apr. 14, 1976 / Original Jazz Classics ✦✦

Soul Fusion / Jun. 1, 1977–Jun. 2, 1977 / Original Jazz Classics ✦✦✦✦✦
Pianist Monty Alexander had first appeared on a Milt Jackson record in 1969. Eight years later the great vibraphonist used Alexander's trio (which included bassist John Clayton and drummer Jeff Hamilton, future big band co-leaders) for this spirited Pablo session, which has been reissued on CD. Much of the material is obscure (including Jackson's three originals) with Stevie Wonder's "Isn't She Lovely" being the only standard. The music, however, is as straight-ahead as one would expect from these fine musicians and can be easily recommended to their fans. —*Scott Yanow*

Montreux '77 / Jul. 13, 1977 / Original Jazz Classics ✦✦✦✦
This set from the 1977 Montreux Jazz Festival was very much a spontaneous jam session. Flugelhornist Clark Terry (who happened to be in town early) was added to vibraphonist Milt Jackson's group at the last moment. When players of the caliber of Terry, tenor saxophonist Eddie "Lockjaw" Davis, pianist Monty Alexander, bassist Ray Brown, drummer Jimmie Smith and Jackson get together, one does not have to worry about the lack of rehearsal time. The sextet romps happily through Brown's "Slippery," "A Beautiful Friendship," "Mean to Me," "You Are My Sunshine," the CD's bonus cut "That's The Way It Is" and "C.M.I." On the latter, both Terry and Jackson have humorous vocals. —*Scott Yanow*

Milt Jackson, Count Basie & The Big Band, Vol. 1 / Jan. 18, 1978 / Original Jazz Classics ✦✦

Milt Jackson, Count Basie & The Big Band, Vol. 2 / Jan. 18, 1978 / Original Jazz Classics ✦✦

Soul Believer / Jan. 20, 1978–Sep. 19, 1978 / Original Jazz Classics ✦✦✦

As vibraphonist Milt Jackson relates in the liner notes of this CD, he was a singer before he ever played vibes. This is one of his very few vocal albums and Jackson (who also takes some solos) is reasonably effective, displaying a personable voice and a gentle swing in his style. The backup utilizes synthesizers on three of the ten selections (a very unusual event at Pablo), but otherwise the lineup for these ballads and jump tunes is comprised of old musical friends, most notably pianist Cedar Walton. —*Scott Yanow*

Bag's Bag / 1979 / Pablo ✦✦✦✦

Vibraphonist Milt Jackson teams up with pianist Cedar Walton, bassist Ray Brown and (on six of the eight songs) either Billy Higgins or Frank Severino on drums. Together they play group originals and (on the two drumless pieces) a pair of standards. Although the material was largely new, the swinging style is timeless and Milt Jackson typically sounds in top form; has he ever made an indifferent recording? —*Scott Yanow*

All Too Soon: the Duke Ellington Album / Jan. 1980 / Original Jazz Classics ✦✦✦✦

Outstanding tribute by classy band of pros. —*Ron Wynn*

Night Mist / Apr. 14, 1980 / Original Jazz Classics ✦✦✦✦✦

Most of vibraphonist Milt Jackson's recordings as a leader have been at the head of a quartet or quintet. This spirited set has a variety of "near blues" material being interpreted by an all-star septet featuring such unique voices as trumpeter Harry "Sweets" Edison, the tenor of Eddie "Lockjaw" Davis and altoist Eddie "Cleanhead" Vinson in addition to Jackson, pianist Art Hillery, bassist Ray Brown and drummer Larance Marable. There are plenty of magical moments created on this set by these classic jazzmen. —*Scott Yanow*

Big Mouth / Feb. 26, 1981–Feb. 27, 1981 / Original Jazz Classics ✦✦✦

It is to vibraphonist Milt Jackson's credit that he is able to "overcome" his backing on this CD and play some typically swinging music. Jackson is joined by electric keyboards and electric bass on most selections, in addition to a couple of Latin percussionists and as many as four singers. Yet even with the many studio musicians, Jackson's basic bebop approach is unchanged and the repertoire includes several standards (such as "Bags' Groove," "The Days of Wine and Roses" and "I'm Getting Sentimental over You") that he has performed a countless number of times. —*Scott Yanow*

Ain't But a Few of Us Left / Nov. 30, 1981 / Original Jazz Classics ✦✦✦✦

Despite the pessimistic title, all of the members of this particular quartet (vibraphonist Milt Jackson, pianist Oscar Peterson, bassist Ray Brown and drummer Grady Tate) were still active into the mid-'90s. The music is unsurprising but still quite enjoyable and virtuosic as Bags and Co. perform blues, standards and ballads with their usual swing and bop-based creativity. Highlights include the title cut, "Stuffy," "What Am I Here For" and a vibes-piano duo version of "A Time for Love." —*Scott Yanow*

A London Bridge / Apr. 23, 1982–Apr. 24, 1982 / Pablo ✦✦✦✦✦

One of three albums of material recorded by the Milt Jackson Quartet (which consisted of pianist Monty Alexander, bassist Ray Brown and drummer Mickey Roker) during a stay at Ronnie Scott's Club in London, this excellent set features the veterans playing in their usual style (bop, blues and ballad) but with a fresher repertoire than usual including "Impressions," "Good Bait" and Alexander's "Reggae/Later." The pianist often steals the show on this fine set; all three records from this gig are easily recommended. —*Scott Yanow*

★ **Mostly Duke** / Apr. 23, 1982–Apr. 24, 1982 / Pablo ✦✦✦✦✦

The third of three sets released by Pablo from Milt Jackson's engagement at Ronnie Scott's Club in London in 1982 (this CD first came out in 1991) lives up to its title. The great vibraphonist, pianist Monty Alexander, bassist Ray Brown and drummer Mickey Roker play two standards, the leader's "Used to Be Jackson" and six songs associated with Duke Ellington. The music swings hard, Alexander competes with Bags for solo honors and the music should please all straight-ahead jazz fans. —*Scott Yanow*

Memories of Thelonious Sphere Monk / Apr. 28, 1982 / Original Jazz Classics ✦✦✦✦

Milt Jackson and his quartet of 1982 (with pianist Monty Alexander, bassist Ray Brown and drummer Mickey Roker) recorded three albums of material during an engagement at Ronnie Scott's Club in London. Pianist/composer Thelonious Monk had passed away two months earlier and Jackson decided to pay tribute to his old associate. The vibraphonist is in excellent form on four of Monk's standards in addition to a lengthy "Django," his own "Think Positive" and Ray Brown's "Blues for Groundhog." —*Scott Yanow*

Jackson, Johnson, Brown & Company / May 25, 1983–May 26, 1983 / Pablo ✦✦✦✦

The interplay between vibraphonist Milt Jackson and trombonist J.J. Johnson is the main reason to acquire this set. With fine backup from pianist Tom Ranier, guitarist John Collins, bassist Ray Brown and drummer Roy McCurdy, Bags and Johnson are in top form on a variety of bop standards including Johnson's "Lament," "Our Delight," "Bags Groove" and "My One and Only Love." Happy and consistently swinging music from some of the best. —*Scott Yanow*

Soul Route / Nov. 30, 1983–Dec. 1, 1983 / Original Jazz Classics ✦✦✦✦

Vibraphonist Milt Jackson recorded quite extensively during his decade with Norman Granz's Pablo label. This particular release (which has been reissued on CD) is most notable for helping launch the comeback of pianist Gene Harris who had been in obscurity ever since he ended his days with The Three Sounds. Harris' soulful style and expertise with blues fit in perfectly with Milt Jackson's approach and (with fine backup from bassist Ray Brown and drummer Mickey Roker) they play some typically joyful music on some blues, standards and ballads. —*Scott Yanow*

It Don't Mean a Thing If You Can't Tap Your Foot to It / Jul. 1984 / Original Jazz Classics ✦✦✦✦

Vibraphonist Milt Jackson's recording career has been remarkably consistent, and his Pablo recordings of 1975-85 are uniformly excellent. This particular set features his 1984 quartet (a group consisting of pianist Cedar Walton, bassist Ray Brown and drummer Mickey Roker) performing four obscure group originals and three standards with swing, subtle creativity and soul. This CD is a good example of Milt Jackson's easily enjoyable music. —*Scott Yanow*

Brother Jim / May 17, 1985 / Pablo ✦✦✦✦

Milt Jackson recorded a couple of dozen albums for Pablo during 1975-85; this CD reissue was the final one before the label drastically slowed down. The vibraphonist's quartet of the period (with pianist Cedar Walton, bassist Bob Cranshaw and drummer Mickey Roker) is augmented by Jimmy Heath and Harold Vick (who both double on soprano and tenor) and, on one song, guitarist Joe Pass. The stimulating instrumentation is sometimes a bit unusual (the two sopranos even get to trade off) but the highpoint is actually Jackson's unaccompanied version of "Lullaby of the Leaves." Easily enjoyable swinging, straight-ahead jazz. —*Scott Yanow*

Bebop / 1988 / East West ✦✦✦

The music on this East-West CD (made available through Atlantic) certainly lives up to its title. Vibraphonist Milt Jackson welcomes some of his best musical friends including both veterans and a couple of younger greats: trumpeter Jon Faddis, trombonist J.J. Johnson, Jimmy Heath on tenor, pianist Cedar Walton, bassist John Clayton and drummer Mickey Roker. Together they perform nine classic songs from the bop era with the emphasis on medium and uptempo workouts. Few surprises occur, but the hard-swinging music largely comes up to one's expectations. —*Scott Yanow*

The Harem / Dec. 10, 1990–Dec. 11, 1990 / Music Masters ✦✦✦✦

The phrase that can be used to describe a typical recording by vibraphonist Milt Jackson is "predictably excellent." There are no unexpected revelations revealed during this outfit set with flutist James Moody, Jimmy Heath (on soprano and tenor), pianist Cedar Walton, bassist Bob Cranshaw and drummer Kenny Washington (although the soprano-flute blend works very well), but there are also no weak moments. The group performs three standards and two originals apiece by Jackson, Heath and Walton and the music should please fans of those fine veterans. —*Scott Yanow*

Reverence and Compassion / 1993 / Qwest ✦✦✦✦

Vibraphonist Milt Jackson is joined by a top-notch rhythm section (pianist Cedar Walton, bassist John Clayton and drummer Billy Higgins), a six-piece horn section and a large string section on various selections but, despite the potential distractions and competition, Bags' vibes are the stars throughout. The music on this CD is mostly standards along with four Jackson bluish originals and a song apiece from Clayton and Walton. Milt Jackson's style has not changed since the 1950s, but he has retained his enthusiasm and creativity and remained a potent force in jazz. —Scott Yanow

The Prophet Speaks / 1994 / Qwest/Reprise ✦✦✦✦✦
Forty-eight years after he first made a major impression on a Dizzy Gillespie recording date, vibraphonist Milt Jackson proves that he was still at the top of his form on this CD. The happy straight-ahead date finds his quartet (with pianist Cedar Walton, bassist John Clayton and drummer Billy Higgins) welcoming guests Joshua Redman (whose tenor is on six of the dozen selections) and singer Joe Williams who helps out on three songs. Redman easily fits into the role that other tenors (such as Teddy Edwards and Jimmy Heath) have had with Jackson, taking concise solos while allowing the great vibist to be the lead in most of the ensembles. Joe Williams is fine during his three spots, but it is the apparently ageless Milt Jackson who is the main star during this enjoyable set. —Scott Yanow

Burnin' In The Woodhouse / 1995 / Qwest/Warner Brothers ✦✦✦✦

Quentin Jackson

b. Jan. 13, 1909, Springfield, OH, d. Oct. 2, 1976, New York, NY
Trombone / Swing
A fixture with Duke Ellington's Orchestra in the 1950s, Quentin Jackson was Duke's best "wa-wa" trombonist (an expert with the plunger mute) since Tricky Sam Nanton. His brother-in-law Claude Jones (who played with McKinney's Cotton Pickers) taught him trombone. Jackson played with Zack Whyte (1930), McKinney's Cotton Pickers (1931), Don Redman's Orchestra (1932-40), Cab Calloway (1940-48) and Lucky Millinder. He took occasional solos with those groups and in the early days was a ballad singer. But most important were his contributions to Duke Ellington's music (1949-60), both as a soloist and in the ensembles. After leaving Duke, he toured Europe with Quincy Jones (1960), played with Count Basie (1961-62), recorded with Charles Mingus (1962), returned to Ellington (1963) and worked with the big bands of Louie Bellson and Gerald Wilson. Quentin Jackson was with the Thad Jones/Mel Lewis Orchestra (1971-75) near the end of his life. His only session as a leader resulted in four titles in 1959 that were reissued by Swing. —Scott Yanow

Ronald Shannon Jackson

b. Jan. 12, 1940, Fort Worth, TX
Free Funk
Drummer Ronald Shannon Jackson and his Decoding Society of the 1980s learned from the example of Ornette Coleman's Prime Time and are a logical extension of the group. They featured colorful and noisy ensembles, were not afraid of the influence of rock and their rhythms were funky, loud and unpredictable. Jackson played professionally in Texas with James Clay when he was 15. He moved to New York in 1966 where he worked with Byard Lancaster, Charles Mingus, Betty Carter, Stanley Turrentine, Jackie McLean, McCoy Tyner, Kenny Dorham and most significantly Albert Ayler (1966-67) among others. He took time off the scene and then joined Ornette Coleman's Prime Time (1975-79). Jackson also worked with Cecil Taylor (1978-79) and James "Blood" Ulmer (1979-80). The Decoding Society (formed in 1979) through the years featured many talented and advanced improvisers with the best-known ones being Vernon Reid, Zane Massey, Billy Bang and Byard Lancaster. Jackson also played with the explosive group Last Exit (starting in 1986) and in the early '90s with Power Tools. Ronald Shannon Jackson's music is not for easy-to-offend ears! —Scott Yanow

★ **Eye on You** / 1980 / About Time ✦✦✦✦✦
Drummer Roland Shannon Jackson's Decoding Society on this About Time LP is comprised of quite an all-star lineup: violinist Billy Bang, altoist Byard Lancaster, tenor saxophonist Charles Brackeen, Vernon Reid and Bern Nix on guitars, bassist Melvin Gibbs and percussionist Erasto Vasconcelos. The Decoding Society plays what could be called "free funk," a combination of loud funky rhythms with free jazz and the harmolodics pioneered by Ornette Coleman's Prime Time. Everyone solos together constant-

ly, leading to dense and exciting ensembles that are overflowing with passion. Although this style of jazz (a forerunner of Steve Coleman's groups) never really caught on, the music is quite stimulating and a logical extension of '70s fusion. —Scott Yanow

Nasty / Mar. 1981 / Moers ✦✦✦✦
Street Priest / Jun. 13, 1981–Jun. 16, 1981 / Moers ✦✦✦✦
Mandance / Jun. 1982 / Antilles ✦✦✦✦✦
The ensemble-oriented "free funk" music of drummer Roland Shannon Jackson's Decoding Society never can be accused of being overly mellow or lacking in excitement. The 1982 version of his band features trumpeter Henry Scott, Zane Massey on reeds, guitarist Vernon Reid and both Melvin Gibbs and Bruce Johnson on electric basses. The frenetic and intense ensembles (essentially everyone solos at once) would not be classified as relaxing background music. —Scott Yanow

Barbeque Dog / Mar. 1983 / Antilles ✦✦✦✦
Erratic, powerful and explosive. —Ron Wynn

Pulse / Jan. 1984 / Celluloid ✦✦✦✦
Furious, classic jazz-rock in the absolute sense of the term, plus some free and R&B influences filtered through the compositions as well. Drummer Ronald Shannon Jackson has played with Ornette Coleman and Cecil Taylor and led his own Decoding Society band. His music rips and roars, while seamlessly moving through multiple idioms, sometimes blurring and combining them as he goes along. —Ron Wynn

Decode Yourself / 1984–1985 / Island ✦✦✦
When Colors Play / Sep. 12, 1986–Sep. 13, 1986 / Caravan Of Dreams ✦✦✦
Live at the Caravan of Dreams / 1986 / Caravan Of Dreams ✦✦✦✦
Red Warrior / 1990 / Axiom ✦✦✦
Sprawling drums and guitar highlight this recent session. Produced by Bill Laswell. —Ron Wynn

Taboo / 1990 / Venture ✦✦✦
Some dynamic adventures with Vernon Reid (g) venturing outside Living Colour arena. —Ron Wynn

Ron Jackson

Guitar / Hard Bop
A fine bop guitarist, Ron Jackson has thus far recorded two albums as a leader for Muse. Born in the Philippines (his father was in the military), Jackson grew up near Boston. He attended Berklee starting in 1982 and played electric bass in Paris during 1985-87 (including with Bobby Few, Hal Singer and Leo Wright). Jackson returned to both the U.S. and the guitar in 1987, working with James Spaulding, Jimmy McGriff and with his own groups. He has strong potential for the future. —Scott Yanow

✳ **A Guitar Thing** / Jul. 1991 / Muse ✦✦✦✦✦
Guitarist Ron Jackson's debut as a leader is an impressive outing with pianist Benny Green, bassist Lonnie Plaxico and drummer Cecil Brooks III. Very much a straight-ahead date, Jackson (who describes himself as a "modern traditionalist") performs standards and originals (of which "On the Edge" is most memorable) with a reasonably original voice. His music always swings. —Scott Yanow

Willis Jackson

b. Apr. 25, 1932, Miami, FL, d. Oct. 25, 1987, New York, NY
Tenor Saxophone / Early R&B, Hard Bop, Soul Jazz
An exciting tenor saxophonist whose honking and squeals (although influenced by Illinois Jacquet) were quite distinctive, Willis Jackson was also a strong improviser who sounded perfectly at home with organ groups. He played locally in Florida early on until joining Cootie Williams (on and off during 1948-55). His two-sided honking feature "Gator Tail" with Cootie (which earned him a lifelong nickname) was a hit in 1948 and he started recording as a leader in 1950. Jackson was married to singer Ruth Brown for eight years and often appeared on her recordings during this era. His extensive series of Prestige recordings (1959-64) made him a big attraction on the organ circuit. Although generally overlooked by critics, Willis Jackson continued working steadily in the 1970s and '80s. In 1977 he recorded one of the finest albums of his career for Muse, *Bar Wars*. —Scott Yanow

★ **Call of the Gators** / Dec. 21, 1949–May 2, 1949 / Delmark
✦✦✦✦

Please Mr. Jackson / May 25, 1959 / Original Jazz Classics
✦✦✦✦

Headed and Gutted / May 16, 1974 / Muse ✦✦✦✦
Brilliant soul-jazz date. —*Ron Wynn*

In the Alley / 1976 / Muse ✦✦✦
Solid soul-jazz from a tenor sax master of the style. Willis Jackson never tried to play intricate or elaborate solos; he relied on intensity, blues feeling and simplicity to communicate his soulful messages. —*Ron Wynn*

The Gator Horn / Mar. 8, 1977 / Muse ✦✦✦

☆ **Bar Wars** / Dec. 21, 1977 / Muse ✦✦✦✦✦
Willis Jackson, a veteran of the jazz-oriented R&B music of the late '40s, was a powerful tenor in the tradition of Gene Ammons. This is a particularly exciting release with Charles Earland pumping away at the organ, guitarist Pat Martino offering a contrasting solo voice and Jackson in top form, wailing away on the uptempo pieces. The CD reissue of the original LP adds two alternate takes to the program. The chord changes might be fairly basic, but Willis Jackson plays with such enthusiasm and exuberance that it almost sounds as if he had discovered the joy of playing music. —*Scott Yanow*

Single Action / Apr. 26, 1978 / Muse ✦✦✦✦
Willis Jackson was a tough-toned tenor who came to fame as a honker and screamer with Cootie Williams' big band in the late '40s. Although he calmed down his style a bit through the years, he always has a passionate sound and an accessible style best heard on blues, ballads and standards. This is a CD reissue of a 1978 session that features Jackson with guitarist Pat Martino, organist Carl Wilson and a supportive rhythm section. Although the Barbara Streisand-associated "Evergreen" (heard in two versions) and "You Are the Sunshine of My Life" may not seem like the best material for the tenor, he uplifts the songs. But best are a pair of hard-driving blues and a warm rendition of "Makin' Whoopee." Joe Fields accurately states in the liner notes that Willis Jackson's best recording was his prior Muse release *Bar Wars*, but *Single Action* does give one a good example of Jackson playing in a tenor style that (other than Houston Person and now Joshua Redman) is quickly disappearing. —*Scott Yanow*

Illinois Jacquet (Jean Baptiste Illinois Jacquet)

b. Oct. 31, 1922, Boussard, LA
Tenor Saxophone, Alto Saxophone / Bop, Swing, Early R&B
One of the great tenors, Illinois Jacquet's 1942 "Flying Home" solo is considered the first R&B sax solo and spawned a full generation of younger tenors (including Joe Houston and Big Jay McNeely) who built their careers from his style and practically from that one song!

Jacquet, whose older brother Russell (1917–1990) was a trumpeter who sometimes played in his bands, grew up in Houston and his tough-toned and emotional sound defined the Texas tenor school. After playing locally, he moved to Los Angeles where, in 1941, he played with Floyd Ray. He was the star of Lionel Hampton's 1942 big band ("Flying Home" became a signature song for Jacquet, Hampton and even Illinois' successor Arnett Cobb) and also was with Cab Calloway (1943–44) and well-featured with Count Basie (1945–46). Jacquet's playing at the first Jazz at the Philharmonic concert (1944) included a screaming solo on "Blues" that found him biting on his reed to achieve high register effects; the crowd went wild. He repeated the idea during his appearance in the 1944 film short *Jammin' the Blues*. In 1945 Jacquet put together his own band and both his recordings and live performances were quite exciting. He appeared with JATP on several tours in the 1950s, recorded steadily and never really lost his popularity. In the 1960s he sometimes doubled on bassoon (usually for a slow number such as "'Round Midnight") and it was an effective contrast to his stomping tenor. In the late '80s Jacquet started leading an exciting part-time big band that thus far has only recorded one album, an Atlantic date from 1988. Through the years Illinois Jacquet (whose occasional features on alto are quite influenced by Charlie Parker) has recorded as a leader for such labels as Apollo, Savoy, Aladdin, RCA, Verve, Mercury, Roulette, Epic, Argo, Prestige, Black Lion, Black & Blue, JRC and Atlantic. —*Scott Yanow*

★ **The Black Velvet Band** / Dec. 18, 1947–Jul. 1967 / Bluebird
✦✦✦✦✦

Flies Again / Nov. 8, 1959 / Roulette ✦✦✦✦
1991 reissue. Incendiary set. Explosive Jacquet. —*Ron Wynn*

Illinois Jacquet / Feb. 5, 1962–May 21, 1962 / Epic/Legacy ✦✦✦
This CD reissue, which adds five alternate takes to the original LP program, finds tenor great Illinois Jacquet totally dominating the proceedings. Jacquet is heard in prime form on a few heated romps, is warm on the ballads, does a close imitation of Lester Young on "Pucker Up," and is quite effective during his appearances on alto, especially on "Indiana." The rhythm section, led by pianist Sir Charles Thompson, is very much in the Basie tradition, and the other horns, playing Jimmy Mundy's arrangements, get to riff a lot behind the distinctive leader. The brevity of the performances (only one song exceeds 4 1/2 minutes) and the small amount of solo space given combative trumpeter Roy Eldridge, who would have been an ideal partner for Jacquet, are slight disappointments, but this set is worth picking up. —*Scott Yanow*

Bottoms Up / Mar. 26, 1968 / Original Jazz Classics ✦✦✦✦
Even in 1968 when the jazz avant-garde was becoming quite influential, tenor saxophonist Illinois Jacquet played in his own timeless style, performing in an idiom little changed during the past 20 years. With the assistance of pianist Barry Harris, bassist Ben Tucker and drummer Alan Dawson, Jacquet is heard throughout this CD reissue (which adds a previously unissued "Don't Blame Me" to the original program) swinging hard and generally expressing himself in a typically extroverted fashion. "Bottoms Up" (a relative of "Flying Home"), "Jivin' with Jack the Bellboy" and Jacquet's excellent original ballad "You Left Me All Alone" are most memorable. —*Scott Yanow*

The King / Aug. 20, 1968 / Original Jazz Classics ✦✦✦
Tenor saxophonist Illinois Jacquet has never made an indifferent record, and this CD reissue of a Prestige date from 1968 has its strong moments. High points include the rousing, if overly brief "The King," a warm "Blue and Sentimental," and an atmospheric feature on "Caravan" for Jacquet's bassoon. On the other hand, this version of "How High the Moon" does not live up to its potential, and the two other songs ("A Haunting Melody" and "I Wish I Knew How It Would Feel to Be Free") are a bit dated. Two previously unissued alternate takes are included on the still rather brief (41 minutes) CD, which also has worthwhile contributions from trumpeter Joe Newman, pianist Milt Buckner and guitarist Billy Butler. Enjoyable music but not all that essential. —*Scott Yanow*

The Soul Explosion / Mar. 25, 1969 / Original Jazz Classics
✦✦✦✦
The great tenor Illinois Jacquet is joined by a ten-piece group that includes trumpeter Joe Newman and Milt Buckner on piano and organ for this 1969 Prestige studio session, which has been reissued on CD by the OJC series. Jacquet is in prime form, particularly on "The Soul Explosion" (which benefits from a Jimmy Mundy arrangement), a definitive "After Hours" and a previously unissued version of "Still King." This blues-based set is full of soul, but often swings quite hard with the focus on Jacquet's exciting tenor throughout. —*Scott Yanow*

★ **The Blues: That's Me!** / Sep. 16, 1969 / Original Jazz Classics
✦✦✦✦✦
Tenor saxophonist Illinois Jacquet is heard in top form throughout this quintet set with pianist Wynton Kelly, guitarist Tiny Grimes, bassist Buster Williams and drummer Oliver Jackson. The music, which falls between swing, bop and early rhythm & blues, is generally quite exciting, especially "Still King," "Everyday I Have the Blues" and the lengthy title cut. A particular surprise is a moody version of "Round Midnight" which features some surprisingly effective Illinois Jacquet, on bassoon. This CD reissue is highly recommended. —*Scott Yanow*

The Comeback / Apr. 13, 1971–Apr. 14, 1971 / Black Lion ✦✦✦✦

On Jacquet's Street / Jul. 16, 1976 / Classic Jazz ✦✦✦✦

Jacquet's Got It! / 1988 / Atlantic ✦✦✦✦✦

Ahmad Jamal

b. Jul. 2, 1930, Pittsburgh, PA
Piano / Post-Bop, Cool
One of the few pianists in the 1950s who did not sound like a close copy of Bud Powell, Ahmad Jamal's use of space, ability to gradually increase or decrease the volume with his trio and bril-

liant use of tension and release were quite original. He greatly impressed Miles Davis (who borrowed from his repertoire and insisted that Red Garland try to sound like him) and Jamal also cut some very popular records without altering his style.

Jamal began playing professionally in Pittsbrugh when he was 11. In the late '40s he joined George Hudson's Orchestra. In 1951 he formed his first trio, the Three Strings, a group with guitarist Ray Crawford and bassist Eddie Calhoun. Israel Crosby took Calhoun's place in 1955. One of Jamal's recordings from that year was a version of "Pavanne" that at one point states the melody from John Coltrane's "Impressions," five years before Trane "wrote" the song! In 1956 Jamal switched to a piano-bass-drums trio with Walter Perkins replacing Crawford. With Vernell Fournier on drums by 1958, Jamal recorded his most popular album, *Ahmad Jamal at the Pershing*, and his version of "Poinciana" is still famous. The trio broke up in 1962, but Jamal continued growing as a pianist (sometimes doubling on electric piano in the 1970s) and he remains one of the most distinctive (and indirectly influential) pianists in jazz. Ahmad Jamal recorded through the years for Epic, Argo/Cadet, Impulse, Catalyst, 20th Century, Atlantic and Telarc. *—Scott Yanow*

Poinciana / Oct. 25, 1951–Oct. 25, 1955 / Portrait ✦✦✦✦✦

Chamber Music of New Jazz / May 23, 1955 / Argo ✦✦✦✦✦

Ahmad Jamal Trio / Oct. 25, 1955 / Epic ✦✦✦✦✦

★ **Ahmad Jamal at the Pershing, Vol. 1** / Jan. 16, 1958–Jan. 17, 1958 / Argo ✦✦✦✦✦

Ahmad Jamal Trio, Vol. 4 / Sep. 5, 1958–Sep. 6, 1958 / Argo ✦✦✦✦

Poinciana / Sep. 5, 1958–Sep. 6, 1958 / Chess ✦✦✦✦✦

Ahmad's Blues / Sep. 6, 1958 / Chess ✦✦✦✦✦

Ahmad Jamal at the Penthouse / Feb. 27, 1959–Feb. 28, 1959 / Argo ✦✦✦

All of You / Jun. 1961 / Argo ✦✦✦✦

Ahmad Jamal's Alhambra / Jun. 1961 / Argo ✦✦✦✦

The Awakening / Feb. 3, 1970 / MCA ✦✦✦
This is a 1986 reissue of some of his most beloved trio performances. *—Ron Wynn*

Live at Bubba's / Mar. 20, 1980 / Who's Who In Jazz ✦✦✦

Live in Concert / Jan. 26, 1981 / Chiaroscuro ✦✦✦✦

Live at the Montreux Jazz Festival / 1985 / Atlantic ✦✦✦✦✦
Shimmering, attacking style at times. Still the master of space and pauses. *—Ron Wynn*

Digital Works / 1985 / Atlantic ✦✦✦
Later Jamal, experimenting with digital sound electronics. He remains a gripping player. *—Ron Wynn*

Rossiter Road / Feb. 1, 1986–Feb. 2, 1986 / Atlantic ✦✦✦

Crystal / 1987 / Atlantic ✦✦✦

Pittsburgh / 1989 / Atlantic ✦✦✦✦

Live in Paris '92 / Apr. 3, 1992–Apr. 4, 1992 / Verve ✦✦✦

Chicago Revisited: Live at Joe / Nov. 13, 1992–Nov. 14, 1992 / Telarc ✦✦✦✦✦

I Remember Duke, Hoagy & Strayhorn / Jun. 2, 1994–Jun. 3, 1994 / Telarc ✦✦✦✦
Ahmad Jamal, in paying tribute to Duke Ellington, Billy Strayhorn and Hoagy Carmichael, performs nearly every selection on this CD at a very slow tempo. Or at least his sidemen do, since the pianist often plays doubletime lines, witty quotes from other songs and occasional violent outbursts. In general the music is quite thoughtful and subtle with plenty of surprising ideas and unusual turns. Carmichael gets stiffed a bit (just two songs counting the "Stardust"-inspired "I Remember Hoagy") and a couple of numbers are departures from the theme (including "My Flower," "Never Let Me Go" and "Goodbye"), but most of the melodies come from the Ellington/Strayhorn songbook. Throughout, Ahmad Jamal (with the assistance of bassist Ephriam Wolfolk and drummer Arti Dixson) shows that he can sound relaxed, alert and swinging at the slowest of paces, making this a set deserving (and perhaps needing) several listens to fully appreciate. *—Scott Yanow*

Khan Jamal

b. Jul. 23, 1946, Jacksonville, FL
Vibes / Post-Bop, Avant-Garde
A talented if underrated vibraphonist, Khan Jamal took up the

vibes in 1964 and worked early on with the Cosmic Forces and with Byard Lancaster. After further study, Jamal played with Sunny Murray in the late '70s and in the 1980s was with Ronald Shannon Jackson's Decoding Society, the bands of Joe Bonner and Billy Bang and his own groups. He has led sessions for Philly Jazz, Stash, Gazell/Storyville and most notably SteepleChase. *—Scott Yanow*

Infinity / Dec. 7, 1982–Mar. 14, 1984 / Stash ✦✦✦✦

● **Don't Take No** / Dec. 7, 1982–1989 / Vintage Jazz ✦✦✦✦✦

Dark Warrior / Sep. 30, 1984 / SteepleChase ✦✦✦✦

Three / Oct. 1984 / SteepleChase ✦✦✦✦

The Traveller / Oct. 31, 1985 / SteepleChase ✦✦✦✦

Thinking of You / Oct. 1986 / Storyville ✦✦✦

Speak Easy / Sep. 2, 1988 / Gazell ✦✦✦

Bob James

b. Dec. 25, 1939, Marshall, MO
Composer, Arranger, Keyboards / Instrumental Pop, Crossover
Bob James' recordings have practically defined pop/jazz and crossover during the past two decades. Very influenced by pop and movie music, James has often featured R&Bish soloists (most notably Grover Washington, Jr.) who add a jazz touch to what is essentially an instrumental pop set. He actually started out music going in a much different direction. In 1962 Bob James recorded a boppish trio set for Mercury and three years later his album for ESP was quite avant-garde, with electronic tapes used for effects. After a period with Sarah Vaughan (1965-68), he became a studio musician and by 1973 was arranging and working as a producer for CTI. In 1974 James recorded his first purely commercial effort as a leader; he later made big-selling albums for his own Tappan Zee label, Columbia and Warner Bros. including collborations with Earl Klugh and David Sanborn. Listeners who prefer challenging jazz to background dance music will be consistently disappointed by Bob James' post-1965 albums. *—Scott Yanow*

Bold Conceptions / Aug. 13, 1962–Aug. 15, 1962 / Mercury ✦✦✦

Explosions / May 10, 1965 / ESP ✦✦✦
Early and very different Bob James material from his pop-oriented, heavily-arranged instrumental funk and fusion albums of the '70s and '80s. Here, he's playing in a trio and going far outside conventional structure, at times showing the influence of Cecil Taylor, although not that much into the avant-garde. *—Ron Wynn*

One / Apr. 1974 / Warner Brothers/Tappan Zee ✦✦✦
Bob James' first recording for his Tappan Zee label, which has been reissued on CD along with virtually James' entire output by Warner Bros., is typically lightweight. Although Grover Washington, Jr., has two spots on soprano and trumpeter Jon Faddis is in the brass section, James' dated Fender Rhodes keyboard is the lead voice throughout the six pieces, which include two adaptations of classical works. Only a lightly funky version of "Feel Like Making Love" rises above the level of pleasant background music. *—Scott Yanow*

Two / 1975 / Warner Brothers/Tappan Zee ✦✦
Bob James largely defined pop/jazz crossover in the 1970s. This CD, reissued by Warner Brothers, is typical of his output. Mixing together aspects of pop, R&B and classical with just a touch of jazz, James (heard throughout on electric keyboards) put the emphasis on catchy melodies and lightly funky rhythms. The results range from insipid to pleasant, with a brass section, a string section and vocalists (including Patti Austin) utilized to create what is essentially background music. *—Scott Yanow*

Three / 1976 / Warner Brothers/Tappan Zee ✦✦
Virtually all of keyboardist/arranger Bob James' Tappan Zee catalog has been reissued by Warner Bros. on CD. Unfortunately, the lightweight crossover music has not dated well. James' keyboards often sound gimmicky, the arrangements are danceable but mundane and, despite two spots for Grover Washington, Jr.'s tenor, little of significance occurs. *—Scott Yanow*

Four / 1977 / CTI ✦✦

Lucky Seven / 1979 / Warner Brothers/Tappan Zee ✦✦✦✦
Successful fusion album by a superstar in the genre. James made an art form of short solos, pop-tinged instrumentals, multi-tracked vocals by guest stars and unchallenging tracks. This album utilized all those elements. *—Ron Wynn*

Sign of the Times / 1979 / Warner Brothers/Tappan Zee ✦✦✦
Another among several hit albums for pianist and composer Bob

James during the '70s. The album contained miminal solo space, tightly arranged, cleverly constructed songs with electronic backgrounds and double-tracked backup vocalists and some orchestrated numbers. It didn't do quite as well as some other James albums, but still managed respectable sales. —*Ron Wynn*

● **Grand Piano Canyon** / 1990 / Warner Brothers ✦✦✦✦
James displays his forgotten jazz roots. —*Ron Wynn*

Harry James

b. Mar. 15, 1916, Albany, GA, **d.** Jul. 5, 1983, Las Vegas, NV
Trumpet, Leader / Swing
Harry James was the most famous trumpeter of the swing era and his big band was the most popular in the world during 1942–46 (after Glenn Miller went in the Army). A household name even today, James was a talented player with a wide range and impressive technique whose heart was always in jazz even when playing schmaltzy versions of pop melodies or flashy versions of classical themes.

James gained early experience working with his father's circus band, building up his endurance and technique. After playing locally, he made his recording debut while with Ben Pollack's big band (1935–36). Harry James was a star from the time he first joined Benny Goodman's Orchestra (1937–39) and he greatly overshadowed the band's former soloist Ziggy Elman. He had a few record sessions of his own while still with BG and when he formed his own big band in 1939 it was with Goodman's blessing.

The Harry James Orchestra struggled for a time, but in 1941 they had their first huge hit with an instrumental version of "You Made Me Love You." Other big sellers followed including "Strictly Instrumental," "Sleepy Lagoon," "I'll Get By," "I Had the Craziest Dream" (one of many Helen Forrest vocals) and the classic "It's Been a Long Long Time"; James' repertoire also always included his theme "Ciribiribin" and "Two O'Clock Jump." A celebrity who had speaking parts in several movies, Harry James married Betty Grable, added a string section to his band for a few years and was flying high. Even with the end of the big-band era, James was able to keep his orchestra together (although he dropped the strings after 1947). With altoist Willie Smith and tenor saxophonist Corky Corcoran as key soloists, James' postwar bands played a large share of jazz and there was even a period in the late '40s when James sounded open to bop; his solo on "Tuxedo Junction" in 1947 shows that he was well aware of Dizzy Gillespie.

Despite such drummers as Louis Bellson and Buddy Rich, by the 1950s Harry James seemed happy to have his band sound like Count Basie's (helped out by Ernie Wilkins' arrangements) and to often revisit the past. He remained a popular attraction into the early '80s, but failed to advance any further. Perhaps he did not really need to, for no one played Harry James' music better than Harry James! Far too few of his prime Columbia recordings (1941–55) have been reissued on CD. —*Scott Yanow*

And His Great Vocalists / Jan. 5, 1938–May 12, 1952 / Columbia/Legacy ✦✦✦✦
This CD puts the emphasis on Harry James' vocal hits. Such fine singers as Dick Haymes, Helen Forrest, Helen Humes, Kitty Kallen, Art Lund, Rosemary Clooney and even Willie Smith and Betty Grable (among others) are heard from. Among the more famous recordings are "I'll Get By," "I Don't Want to Walk Without You," "I Had the Craziest Dream," "I've Heard That Song Before" and "It's Been a Long Long Time." There are some spots for James' trumpet on these popular numbers, but the jazz content is not that strong. When is Columbia going to do a much more complete reissue of Harry James valuable recordings? —*Scott Yanow*

● **Bandstand Memories 1938 To 1948** / Apr. 2, 1938–Nov. 30, 1948 / Hindsight ✦✦✦✦✦
This very interesting three-CD set features trumpeter Harry James' Orchestra on a variety of previously unreleased radio broadcast performances. While there are many vocals from Frank Sinatra (in his pre-Tommy Dorsey days), Helen Forrest and Kitty Kallen, it is the instrumentals that are of greatest interest, particularly the earliest tracks which date from the period before James really hit it big. Many of these songs were not recorded commercially by the trumpeter and this strong jazz-oriented set is highly recommended to swing fans. —*Scott Yanow*

Best of Big Bands / Jan. 8, 1941–Nov. 13, 1946 / Columbia ✦✦✦✦
Harry James and Dick Haymes / 1941 / Circle ✦✦✦
The Uncollected Harry James & His Orchestra, Vol. 1 (1943–1946) / 1943–1946 / Hindsight ✦✦✦✦
The Uncollected Harry James & His Orchestra, Vol. 2 (1943–1946) / 1943–1946 / Hindsight ✦✦✦✦
The Uncollected Harry James & His Orchestra, Vol. 4 (1943–1946) / 1943–1946 / Hindsight ✦✦✦✦
The Uncollected Harry James & His Orchestra, Vol. 5 (1943–1953) / 1943–1953 / Hindsight ✦✦✦✦
The Uncollected Harry James & His Orchestra, Vol. 6 (1947–1949) / 1947–1949 / Hindsight ✦✦✦✦
The Uncollected Harry James & His Orchestra, Vol. 3 (1948–1949) / 1948–1949 / Hindsight ✦✦✦✦
Trumpet Blues / Mar. 1955–Apr. 1955 / Drive Archive ✦✦✦
This CD contains previously unreleased performances from Harry James' Orchestra caught live (in stereo) at the Hollywood Palladium in 1955. No real surprises occur, but the trumpeter/bandleader is in good form on his usual repertoire with highlights including "Roll 'Em," "Don't Be That Way," "Trumpet Blues" and "You Made Me Love You." —*Scott Yanow*

Harry James in Hi-Fi / Jul. 20, 1955–Jul. 25, 1955 / Capitol ✦✦✦
More Harry James in Hi-Fi / Nov. 1955–Jan. 1956 / Pausa ✦✦✦
Harry's Choice / Jun. 1958 / Capitol ✦✦✦✦
Double Dixie / Jul. 20, 1962 / MGM ✦✦✦✦
The Golden Trumpet of Harry James / Apr. 1968 / London ✦✦✦
Mr. Trumpet / Jan. 6, 1972–Jan. 8, 1972 / Hindsight ✦✦✦
Considering its opening number, a strong Dixielandish version of "The Sheik of Araby," this CD starts out quite promising, but its extreme brevity (just 29 minutes) and some sticky muzaky strings on the ballads result in a lower rating. Trumpeter Harry James is in good form, whether it be on a relaxed "Indiana," a recreation of Benny Goodman's version of "Don't Be That Way" or a swinging "Hot Lips," but every song on this set would have benefited from being twice as long. —*Scott Yanow*

The King James Version / Jul. 29, 1976–Jul. 30, 1976 / Sheffield Lab ✦✦
Comin' from a Good Place / Jul. 29, 1976–Jul. 30, 1976 / Sheffield Lab ✦✦
Still Harry After All These Years / May 26, 1979–May 30, 1979 / Sheffield Lab ✦✦

Jon Jang

Piano, Composer, Leader / Avant-Garde
An important force in the San Francisco Bay Area with his Pan Asian Arkestra and small-group concerts, Jon Jang has had David Murray and James Newton among his sidemen. A leader in the Asian Improv movement (playing inside/outside music influenced by both Charles Mingus and his Chinese heritage), Jang has recorded stirring sets for the RPM (1982), AIR and Soul Note labels and composed adventurous and ambitious works. —*Scott Yanow*

Never Give Up! / 1989 / AsianImprov ✦✦✦✦
Self Defense! / 1991 / Soul Note ✦✦✦✦
★ **Tiananmen!** / Feb. 1993 / Soul Note ✦✦✦✦✦

Joseph Jarman

b. Sep. 14, 1937, Pine Bluff, Arkansas
Reeds / Avant-Garde, Free Jazz
A longtime member of the Art Ensemble of Chicago, Joseph Jarman's playing has always been adventurous and utterly unpredictable. He grew up in Chicago, played drums in high school and started on saxophones and clarinet while in the Army. He was in Muhal Richard Abrams' Experimental Band and in 1965 he joined the AACM. Jarman's first album as a leader, 1966's *Song For*, was a very radical statement with an unusual utilization of sound and silence. Although he would record occasional records as a leader for Delmark, India Navigation and Black Saint (including *The Magic Triangle* with Don Pullen and Don Moye), Jarman's main vehicle has been the Art Ensemble of Chicago where his theatrical performances keep the music from ever getting too conservative or comfortable. —*Scott Yanow*

● **Song For** / Oct. 20, 1966–Dec. 1, 1966 / Delmark ✦✦✦✦✦
This was one of the early classics of the AACM. Altoist Joseph Jarman, who would become a permanent member of The Art Ensemble of Chicago shortly after this recording, is heard in a sextet with trumpeter William Brimfield, the legendary tenor Fred Anderson, pianist Christopher Gaddy, bassist Charles Clark and either Steve McCall or Thurman Barker on drums. The four very diverse improvisations include a Jarman recitation, a dirge, the intense "Little Fox Run" and the title cut, which contrasts sounds and a creative use of silence. Overall this music was the next step in jazz after the high-energy passions of the earlier wave of the avant-garde started to run out of fresh ideas. It's recommended for open-eared listeners. —*Scott Yanow*

As If It Were the Seasons / 1967–1968 / Delmark ✦✦✦✦
A textbook '60s Chicago free jazz album from a founding member of the AACA, multi-instrumentalist Joseph Jarman. He employs his full array of horns and is joined by several mainstays, among them pianist Muhal Richard Abrams, bassist Charles Clark, drummer Thurman Barker and tenor saxophonist John Stubblefield. This is not compromising material; the songs are long, and everything from bells to whistles to shakers to energized sax screaming comprises the music. —*Ron Wynn*

Together Alone / Dec. 1971 / Delmark ✦✦✦

Egwu-Anwu / Jan. 8, 1978 / India Navigation ✦✦✦

☆ **Magic Triangle** / Jul. 24, 1979–Jul. 26, 1979 / Black Saint ✦✦✦✦✦

Black Paladins / Dec. 1979 / Black Saint ✦✦✦✦

Earth Passage Density / Feb. 16, 1981–Feb. 17, 1981 / Black Saint ✦✦✦✦

Calypso's Smile / Mar. 22, 1984+Dec. 1984 / AECO ✦✦✦

Keith Jarrett

b. May 8, 1945, Allentown, PA
Piano, Leader / Post-Bop
One of the most significant pianists to emerge since the 1960s, Keith Jarrett's career has gone through several phases. He gained international fame for his solo concerts, which found him spontaneously improvising all of the music without any prior planning, but he has also led a couple of dynamic quartets/quintets, performed classical music and recently been playing explorative versions of standards with his longtime trio. Although his tendency to "sing along" with his piano now and then is distracting, Jarrett continues to grow as a powerful improviser after 30 years of important accomplishments.

Keith Jarrett started on the piano when he was three and by the time he was seven he had already played a recital. A child prodigy, Jarrett was a professional while still in grade school. In 1962 he studied at Berklee and then started working in the Boston area with his trio. He moved to New York in 1965 and spent four months with Art Blakey's Jazz Messengers. As a member of the very popular Charles Lloyd Quartet (1966–69), Jarrett traveled the world and became well-known; he also began doubling occasionally on soprano (which he would utilize through the 1970s). During 1969–71 he was with Miles Davis' fusion group, playing organ and electric keyboards; Chick Corea was also in the band for the first year. Jarrett can be heard "battling" Corea throughout Davis' *Live at the Fillmore*, but is in more creative form on *Live/Evil*.

Upon leaving Miles Davis, Keith Jarrett permanently swore off electric keyboards. He had cut sessions as a leader for Vortex (1967–69) and Atlantic (1971), but starting in November 1971 he recorded extensively for ECM (in addition to some sessions in the 1970's for ABC/Impulse!, an association that continues to the present day. In the 1970s Jarrett led two groups, an exciting unit with Dewey Redman, Charlie Haden, Paul Motian and occasional percussionists (often Guilherme Franco) and a European group with Jan Garbarek, Palle Danielsson and Jon Christensen that recorded the popular "My Song." In addition, starting in 1972 Jarrett began his famous series of improvised concerts, which resulted in such popular recordings as *Solo Concerts, Koln Concert* and the mammoth *Sun Bear Concerts*. By the 1980s Jarrett was performing classical music as much as jazz, but in the 1990s he has recorded extensively (including a six-CD live set) with his "standards trio" that includes Gary Peacock and Jack DeJohnette. Although initially influenced by Bill Evans, Keith Jarrett has had an original and influential style of his own since the early '70s and remains a vital force in jazz. —*Scott Yanow*

Somewhere Before / Oct. 30, 1968–Oct. 31, 1968 / Atlantic ✦✦✦✦
A 1968 live trio recording at Shelly's Manne Hole in Hollywood, with Charlie Haden (b), Paul Motian (d). Rare and excellent. —*Michael G. Nastos*

Foundations / 1968–1971 / Rhino/Atlantic ✦✦✦✦
This two-disc anthology presents formative Jarrett material from the late '60s and early '70s; it doesn't have the depth, emotional intensity, imagination or charm of his Impulse! or ECM releases, but still contains some fine tracks. These include two superb songs with Gary Burton, plus a cut with Blakey's Messengers and some odds and ends from unrelated dates. The second disc includes three 1971 tunes by the Jarrett unit with Haden, Motian and Redman. At this time, the foursome wasn't fully comfortable or used to each other, and there are uncertain, tentative stretches balanced by other periods with all four interacting smoothly. Jarrett is regarded now as an enigma by some and a genius by others; these songs are reminders of a less assured, but in some ways less predictable and wary pianist. —*Ron Wynn*

The Mourning of a Star / Jul. 9, 1971 / Atlantic ✦✦✦
This LP gives one an interesting look at the early Keith Jarrett, who was already an album of the Charles Lloyd Quartet and Miles Davis' early fusion band. He had not yet fully developed his style but he was clearly on his way. These trio performances (with bassist Charlie Haden and drummer Paul Motian) are impressive for the period but the best was yet to come. —*Scott Yanow*

Birth / Jul. 15, 1971–Jul. 16, 1971 / Atlantic ✦✦✦
Very early example of his quirky style, technique. Jarrett is an excellent pianist, but a horrible recorder/soprano saxist. W/ first-rate personnel: Charlie Haden (b), Paul Motian (d) and Dewey Redman (ts). —*Ron Wynn*

Expectations / Oct. 1971 / Columbia ✦✦✦✦
Two-record set with lots of experimental, high energy moments. 1991 reissue. —*Ron Wynn*

● **Facing You** / Nov. 10, 1971 / ECM ✦✦✦✦✦
Keith Jarrett's first solo acoustic piano recording remains one of his best. At this point in late 1971, Jarrett had just started improvising completely freely. That does not mean that his solos were necessarily atonal, but simply that they were not planned in any way in advance. The music on these eight improvisations are often quite melodic, very rhythmic and bluesy. This set makes for a perfect introduction to Jarrett's many solo piano recordings. —*Scott Yanow*

Rutya and Daitya / Mar. 1972 / ECM ✦✦✦
Piercing duets with Jack DeJohnette (d). —*Ron Wynn*

Fort Yawuh / Feb. 24, 1973 / MCA ✦✦✦✦
This live set features pianist Keith Jarrett's finest regular band; all of their recordings are heartily recommended. Jarrett, joined by tenor saxophonist Dewey Redman, bassist Charlie Haden, drummer Paul Motian and percussionist Danny Johnson, performs four diverse originals. The two ballads in particular work well (this group from the start had its own sound) although Redman's playing on Chinese musette might take a bit of getting used to. —*Scott Yanow*

★ **Solo Concerts: Bremen and Lausanne** / Mar. 20, 1973+Jul. 1, 1973 / ECM ✦✦✦✦✦
These are the recordings that made Keith Jarrett famous. Originally released as a three-LP set, the two solo piano recitals feature Jarrett freely improvising and never seeming to run out of ideas. A simple figure often develops through repetition and subtle variations into a rather complex sequence and eventually evolves into a new figure. One of the improvisations lasts for three LP sides (64 minutes), while the second concert has two long solos for 30 and 35 minutes respectively. Despite the length, the music never loses one's interest, making this an essential recording for all jazz collections. —*Scott Yanow*

Treasure Island / Feb. 27, 1974–Feb. 28, 1974 / MCA/Impulse! ✦✦✦✦
Originally an Impulse! LP that surfaced on MCA as a straight reissue on CD, this fine recording features pianist Keith Jarrett's best regular group. Dewey Redman is heard from on tenor, bassist Charlie Haden, drummer Paul Motian and percussionists Guilherme Franco and Danny Johnson are superb in ensembles and guitarist Sam Brown guests on two selections. The emphasis is on the band's sound and Jarrett's rich melodies; he contributed eight originals to this enjoyable modern set. —*Scott Yanow*

Belonging / Apr. 1974 / ECM ✦✦✦✦✦
This quartet album is a fine first collaboration between Jarrett and Jan Garbarek (ts). —*Michael G. Nastos*

Luminessence / Apr. 1974 / ECM ✦✦✦✦

Death & The Flower / Oct. 1974 / GRP ✦✦✦
This set by the Keith Jarrett Quintet (with the leader on piano, soprano and flute, tenor saxophonist Dewey Redman, bassist Charlie Haden, drummer Paul Motian and percussionist Guilherme Franco) contains three of Jarrett's originals. The main selection, the 21-minute "Death and the Flower," develops logically from atmospheric sounds to intense group improvising and back again; it is the main reason to acquire this CD. —*Scott Yanow*

Backhand / Oct. 9, 1974–Oct. 10, 1974 / Impulse! ✦✦✦✦✦
Landmark quintet with Dewey Redman (ts), Charlie Haden (b), Paul Motian (d), Guilherme Franco (per). Any recording by this band is worthwhile. —*Michael G. Nastos*

Personal Mountains / 1974 / ECM ✦✦✦✦
W/ Jan Garbarek & Danielsson. Classic ECM chamber-jazz date. —*Ron Wynn*

Shades / 1975 / Impulse! ✦✦✦✦
Pianist Keith Jarrett's mid-'70s quintet was the strongest regular group that he ever led and all of its recordings (even some that ramble a bit) are worth picking up. Thanks to its strong start, *Shades* is one of this unit's most rewarding recordings. "Shades of Jazz" has a memorable melody and logical (if unpredictable) improvisations by Jarrett and tenor saxophonist Dewey Redman. The momentum slows down a bit with the gospellish "Southern Smiles" and "Rose Petals," but picks up again with the final number, the rather intense "Diatribe," an excellent vehicle for this classic group. Throughout, bassist Charlie Haden, drummer Paul Motian and percussionist Guilherme Franco keep the band's juices flowing. —*Scott Yanow*

★ **The Koln Concert** / Jan. 24, 1975 / ECM ✦✦✦✦✦
Many critics consider this to be Keith Jarrett's most rewarding solo recording although *Solo Concerts* from the previous year is on the same level. Originally released as a two-LP set, this music is best suited for CD because, while the first 26-minute improvisation fits on one LP side, the second of the two solos (which totals 41 minutes) was programmed over the remaining 11 LPs, with side four being only seven minutes long. Logistics aside, the music is quite brilliant with Jarrett (who was improvising freely without any prior planning) developing the most interesting and occasionally startling ideas. The strong fresh melodies and his bluesy feel make this a very enjoyable outing. —*Scott Yanow*

Arbour Zena / Oct. 1975 / ECM ✦✦✦

Mysteries / 1975 / ABC/Impulse! ✦✦✦✦

☆ **The Survivor's Suite** / Apr. 1976 / ECM ✦✦✦✦✦
This is one of the finest recordings by pianist Keith Jarrett's mid-'70s group. Jarrett (on piano, soprano and bass recorder), tenor saxophonist Dewey Redman, bassist Charlie Haden and drummer Paul Motian (no percussionist this time) by 1976 were thinking alike during the ensemble's improvisations. "The Survivor's Suite," a 49-minute two-part work, finds the group continually building up and then releasing tension together. There are strong individual solos, but it is the interplay between the bandmembers that makes this a particularly memorable outing. —*Scott Yanow*

Eyes of the Heart / May 1976 / ECM ✦✦✦
Excellent music from a great quartet. Dewey Redman (ts) challenges Jarrett for solo honors. —*Ron Wynn*

Staircase / May 1976 / ECM ✦✦✦✦

Hymns / Spheres / Sep. 1976 / ECM ✦✦

Sun Bear Concerts / Nov. 5, 1976–Nov. 18, 1976 / ECM ✦✦✦✦

Silence / Sep. 9, 1977 / ECM ✦✦✦✦
Tremendous mid-'70s quartet session headed by pianist Keith Jarrett. Jarrett was in the midst of an impressive recording and touring string with this group, which included tenor saxophonist Dewey Redman, bassist Charlie Haden and drummer Paul Motian. Almost every release they issued was superb; this one was no different. It has been reissued on CD. —*Ron Wynn*

Bop-Be / Nov. 1, 1977 / Impulse! ✦✦✦✦

My Song / Nov. 1977 / ECM ✦✦✦✦✦
In addition to his solo piano concerts and the American group he led that featured tenor saxophonist Dewey Redman, Keith Jarrett

was also busy in the mid-'70s with his European band, a quartet comprised of Jan Garbarek on tenor and soprano, bassist Palle Danielsson and drummer Jon Christensen. Due to the popularity of the haunting "My Song," this album is the best-known of the Jarrett-Garbarek collaborations and it actually is their most rewarding meeting on records. Jarrett contributed all six compositions and the results are relaxed and introspective yet full of inner tension. —*Scott Yanow*

Byablue / 1977 / ABC/Impulse! ✦✦✦✦

Nude Ants / May 1979 / ECM ✦✦✦✦✦
There is a lot of music on this set, including the 30-minute "Oasis." This is a *Live at the Village Vanguard* recording by pianist Keith Jarrett and his European quartet (Jan Garbarek on soprano and tenor, bassist Palle Danielsson and drummer Jon Christensen). The pianist very much dominates the music, but Garbarek's unique floating tone on his instruments and the subtle accompaniment by Danielsson and Christensen are also noteworthy. —*Scott Yanow*

Concerts / May 28, 1981–Jun. 2, 1981 / ECM ✦✦✦

Changes / Jan. 1983 / ECM ✦✦✦✦
Unlike the other two Keith Jarrett trio recordings from January 1983, this collaboration with bassist Gary Peacock and drummer Jack DeJohnette does not feature standards. The trio performs the 30-minute "Flying" and a 6-minute "Prism," both of them Jarrett originals. "Flying," which has several sections, keeps one's interest througout while the more concise "Prism" has a beautiful melody. It is a nice change to hear Jarrett (who normally plays unaccompanied) interacting with a trio of superb players. —*Scott Yanow*

Standards, Vol. 1 / Jan. 1983 / ECM ✦✦✦✦
In January of 1983, Keith Jarrett returned to the trio format and his collaboration with bassist Gary Peacock and drummer Jack DeJohnette resulted in three albums. The first release finds the trio digging into five standards with "God Bless the Child" being dragged out (although not unmercifully) for 15 minutes. The performances, which usually do not swing in a conventional sense, do have a momentum of their own. Jarrett is generous in allocating solo space to Peacock and it is obvious that the three musicians were listening very closely to each other. —*Scott Yanow*

Standards, Vol. 2 / Jan. 1983 / ECM ✦✦✦✦
One of three trio albums that pianist Keith Jarrett recorded with bassist Gary Peacock and drummer Jack DeJohnette during the same month, this second volume of *Standards* gets the edge over the first due to its slightly more challenging material. Jarrett, who has often taken himself a bit too seriously, is surprisingly playful at times in this format. In addition to Jarrett's "So Tender," there are such superior songs explored on this date as Alec Wilder's "Moon and Sand," "If I Should Lose You" and "I Fall in Love Too Easily." Bassist Gary Peacock and drummer Jack DeJohnette listen closely to Jarrett and no matter what direction the pianist turns, they are already there waiting for him. —*Scott Yanow*

Standards Live / Jul. 2, 1985 / ECM ✦✦✦✦
Standards Live, from 1987, continued at the same high level of previous *Standards Vol. 1 & 2* with pianist Keith Jarrett often recalling his early influence, Bill Evans. The well-integrated trio (Gary Peacock, bass; Jack DeJohnette, drums) plays three frequently performed tunes and three obscurities. The interplay between the players was constantly impressive. —*Scott Yanow*

Still Live / Jul. 13, 1986 / ECM ✦✦✦

Changeless / Oct. 9, 1987–Oct. 14, 1987 / ECM ✦✦✦✦

Tribute / Oct. 15, 1989 / ECM ✦✦✦✦✦

The Cure / Apr. 21, 1990 / ECM ✦✦✦✦

Paris Concert / 1990 / ECM ✦✦✦✦

Vienna Concert / Jul. 13, 1991 / ECM ✦✦✦✦
The pianist has come under increasing fire for the sameness of his material and his tendency to sing underneath his piano playing on album. He doesn't do that this time out, and the piano solos are intense and frequently striking, while ECM's glittering production puts the piano squarely in the spotlight. —*Ron Wynn*

Bye Bye Blackbird / Oct. 1991 / ECM ✦✦✦✦✦

At the Deer Head Inn / Sep. 1992 / ECM ✦✦✦✦
Keith Jarrett returns to his roots, both musically and physically, on this CD. His first significant jazz gig was at the Deer Head Inn in Allentown, PA (his hometown) and 30 years later Jarrett agreed to perform at the venue again. With the assistance of bassist Gary

Peacock and drummer Paul Motian, Jarrett plays six jazz standards (several of which were associated with Miles Davis) plus Jaki Byard's medium-tempo blues, "Chandra." The inventive interpretations give listeners plenty of surprises and variety, making this a very enjoyable outing. *—Scott Yanow*

☆ **Keith Jarrett at the Blue Note: The Complete Recordings** / Jun. 3, 1994–Jun. 5, 1994 / ECM ♦♦♦♦♦
The six-CD box set *Keith Jarrett at the Blue Note* fully documents three nights (six complete sets from June 3–5, 1994) by his trio with bassist Gary Peacock and drummer Jack DeJohnette. Never mind that this same group has already had ten separate releases since 1983; this box is still well worth getting! The repertoire emphasizes (but is not exclusively) standards with such songs as "In Your Own Sweet Way," "Now's The Time" "Oleo," "Days Of Wine And Roses" and "My Romance" given colorful and at times surprising explorations. Some of the selections are quite lengthy (including a 26 1/2 minute version of "Autumn Leaves") and Jarrett's occasional originals are quite welcome; his 28 1/2 minute "Desert Sun" reminds one of the pianist's fully improvised "Solo Concerts of the 1970s." Throughout the three nights at the Blue Note, the interplay between the musicians is consistently outstanding. Those listeners concerned about Jarrett's tendency to "sing along" with his piano have little to fear for, other than occasional shouts and sighs, he wisely lets his piano do the talking. *—Scott Yanow*

Standards In Norway / Oct. 7, 1989 / ECM ♦♦♦♦
Keith Jarrett has recorded quite a few albums with his "Standards Trio," which also features bassist Gary Peacock and drummer Jack DeJohnette, and virtually all of their releases are enjoyable. The music that they create is in some ways an update of the type of interplay that took place between Bill Evans and his sidemen, where all three musicians often act as equals (although Jarrett, like Evans, has most of the solo space). An uptempo "Love Is a Many-Splendored Thing" is a surprising highpoint of this disc but also quite memorable are "All of You," "Old Folks" and "How About You?"; none of the eight performances from the concert appearance are throwaways. Jarrett's vocal sounds are more restrained than usual while his piano playing is in peak form. *—Scott Yanow*

Bobby Jaspar

b. Feb. 20, 1926, Liege, Belgium, d. Feb. 28, 1963, New York, NY
Flute, Tenor Saxophone / Hard Bop, Cool
A fine bop-oriented soloist equally skilled on his cool-toned tenor and flute, Bobby Jaspar's early death from a heart ailment was a tragic loss. As a teenager he played tenor in a Dixieland group with Toots Thielemans in Belgium. He recorded with Henri Renaud (1951 and 1953) and played with touring Americans including Jimmy Raney, Chet Baker (1955) and his future wife Blossom Dearie. In 1956 Jaspar moved to New York where he worked with J.J. Johnson, was briefly with Miles Davis (1957) and Donald Byrd. He mostly freelanced during the remainder of his career. Bobby Jaspar recorded for Swing, Vogue and Barclay while in Paris and led dates for Prestige, Riverside in the U.S. during 1957. *—Scott Yanow*

● **Bobby Jaspar in Paris** / Dec. 27, 1955+Dec. 29, 1955 / Disques Swing ♦♦♦♦♦
Wonderful 1986 reissue of prime Jaspar small-combo dates from mid 50's. Tommy Flanagan (p), Elvin Jones (d), Milt Hinton (b) among the crew. *—Ron Wynn*

Memory of Dick / Dec. 27, 1955+Dec. 29, 1955 / EmArcy ♦♦♦♦

Tenor & Flute / May 23, 1957 / Riverside ♦♦♦♦

With George Wallington, Idrees Sulieman / May 23, 1957+May 28, 1957 / Original Jazz Classics ♦♦♦♦
Bobby Jaspar was one of Europe's top jazzmen of the 1950s. This CD reissue (which adds one track to the original six-song LP program) features him on both tenor and flute in a quintet with trumpeter Idrees Sulieman, pianist George Wallington, bassist Wilbur Little and drummer Elvin Jones. The music is strictly straight-ahead bop/cool jazz with many fine solos from Jaspar, Sulieman and Wallington. Nothing all that surprising occurs as the quintet jams on a variety of attractive chord changes, but this set serves as a fine example of the somewhat forgotten Bobby Jaspar's talents. *—Scott Yanow*

Jazz at the Philharmonic

All-Star Groups / Bop, Swing
In 1944 producer Norman Granz organized a concert billed as

"Jazz at the Philharmonic" (also JATP) as a fundraiser in Los Angeles. The event, which was recorded, featured Illinois Jacquet, Jack McVea, J.J. Johnson, Shorty Sherock and a rhythm section with Nat King Cole and Les Paul; Jacquet's playing in particular caused a bit of a sensation. After a few more similar events, Granz in 1946 began organizing extensive annual tours using classic swing and bop musicians in a jam-session setting. Although some critics often complained that these events encouraged grandstanding (R&B honking was getting popular during the era), a great deal of rewarding and exciting music resulted and Granz recorded (and later released) much of it on his Verve label. He paid his musicians very well and did his best to fight racism every bit of the way. Among JATP's stars through the years were tenors Flip Phillips (whose solo on "Perdido" became famous), Jacquet, Coleman Hawkins, Lester Young, Ben Webster and Stan Getz; trumpeters Roy Eldridge, Charlie Shavers, Dizzy Gillespie and Harry "Sweets" Edison; trombonists Bill Harris and Tommy Turk; altoists Charlie Parker, Willie Smith and Benny Carter; pianists Hank Jones and Oscar Peterson; a variety of bassists (often Ray Brown); and drummers Louie Bellson, Gene Krupa and Buddy Rich. Ella Fitzgerald started touring with JATP early on, usually having her own separate set and joining in on a finale, and later tours often also included performances by regular groups such as the Oscar Peterson Trio, Gene Krupa's combo, Stuff Smith or Lester Young. After 1957 the annual tours stopped although there was an attempt to revive JATP in 1967 and Granz kept the spirit of Jazz at the Philharmonic alive on his many jam session-type records for Pablo in the 1970s. *—Scott Yanow*

The First Concert / Jul. 2, 1944 / Verve ♦♦♦♦♦
This single CD contains the seven documented selections from the very first performance of Norman Granz's travelling jam session, Jazz at the Philharmonic. A pretty colorful cast of characters is heard from: trumpeter Shorty Sherock (on the last three numbers), trombonist J.J. Johnson (who is on the first four selections), Illinois Jacquet and Jack McVea on tenors and a strong rhythm section that includes pianist Nat King Cole and guitarist Les Paul. Together they perform six standards and a blues with five of the seven numbers over nine-minutes long. Jacquet's screaming solos (he was the first real R&B tenor player) and the humorous and rather remarkable tradeoff between Cole And Paul on the "Blues" are the highpoints of this historically significant and very enjoyable release which ranges from touches of Dixieland through swing, bop and early R&B. *—Scott Yanow*

Jazz at the Philharmonic/Bird And Pres: The '46 Concerts / Jan. 1946–Apr. 22, 1946 / Verve ♦♦♦♦
This double LP, which was released by Verve in 1977, contains nine lengthy performances, all taken from 1946 Jazz at the Philharmonic concerts. Altoist Charlie Parker is on all but the first two selections and those seven numbers have been reissued on CD. The main problem with these recordings is that the rhythm section (particularly Lee Young's drumming) is over-recorded and very repetitive and sometimes the mixture of bop and swing stylists (especially on the two numbers without Parker) leads to some uncomfortable ensembles. However, this version of "Lady Be Good" is a classic (especially the solos of pianist Arnold Ross and Bird), and there are some good moments on the other selections by the likes of tenors Lester Young, Coleman Hawkins and Charlie Ventura, altoist Willie Smith, trumpeters Dizzy Gillespie, Howard McGhee, Buck Clayton and Al Killian and pianists Mel Powell and Ken Kersey. *—Scott Yanow*

Jazz at the Philharmonic: The Rarest Concerts / Apr. 23, 1946–1953 / Verve ♦♦♦♦
In 1983 Polygram came out with ten LPs that document a variety of concerts by Norman Granz's traveling jam session, which he dubbed Jazz at the Philharmonic. This particular album has three rare performances. "I Found a New Baby" and "I Can't Get Started" are taken from the 1946 tour and feature trumpeter Buck Clayton, the tenors of Coleman Hawkins and Lester Young, pianist Ken Kersey and (on the former song) altoist Willie Smith. However, the reason to search for this LP is for the 22-minute "Concert Blues" which has excellent solos from altoists Willie Smith and Benny Carter, the tenors of Flip Phillips and Ben Webster, trombonist Bill Harris and trumpeters Charlie Shavers and Roy Eldridge; the Oscar Peterson trio and drummer Gene Krupa really drive the horns. *—Scott Yanow*

★ **Jazz at the Philharmonic: Bird & Pres** / Sep. 18, 1949 / Verve ♦♦♦♦♦
Of all the ten JATP LPs released by Verve in the early '80s, this

one has the most essential music and happily its contents have since been reissued on CD. For those who do not have the latest reissue and run across this album, don't let it get away. Not only does this set feature altoist Charlie Parker and the tenors of Flip Phillips and Lester Young but trumpeter Roy Eldridge, the forgotten but brilliant trombonist Tommy Turk, pianist Hank Jones, bassist Ray Brown and drummer Buddy Rich. "The Opener" and "Lester Leaps In" (both over 12 minutes long) are quite exciting but it is Charlie Parker's remarkable solo on "Embraceable You" that takes honors. The concluding blues (rightfully called "The Closer") is also quite memorable, for after Eldridge and Rich have a tradeoff, the performance ends temporarily until it is remembered that Bird had not had a chance to play yet. His second breath (which has a countless number of perfectly placed notes) cuts everyone. —*Scott Yanow*

Jazz at the Philharmonic: Norgran Blues 1950 / Sep. 16, 1950 / Verve ✦✦✦
The 1950 version of Norman Granz's traveling jam session JATP is featured on this LP, one of ten released by Polygram Classics in 1983. Four fairly basic chord changes ("Norgran Blues," "Lady Be Good," "Ghost of a Chance" and "Indiana") are explored by the all-star lineup (trumpeter Harry "Sweets" Edison, trombonist Bill Harris, the tenors of Flip Phillips and Lester Young, pianist Hank Jones, bassist Ray Brown and drummer Buddy Rich). Due to the absence of JATP regular trumpeter Roy Eldridge, there are less fireworks than usual but the music is still quite enjoyable with Young in fine form and Phillips pleasing the enthusiastic audience. —*Scott Yanow*

Jazz at the Philharmonic: The Trumpet Battle 1952 / Sep. 13, 1952 / Verve ✦✦✦✦✦
In 1983 Polygram Classics came out with ten LPs featuring various concerts by Jazz at the Philharmonic, producer Norman Granz's all-star groups. This album is one of the more exciting sets since it features trumpeters Roy Eldridge and Charlie Shavers on a "Jam Session Blues," taking their turns on a five-song ballad medley and most notably participating in "The Trumpet Battle." In addition, altoist Benny Carter (who seems inspired by the jam-session setting) and the tenors of Flip Phillips and Lester Young (along with the Oscar Peterson Trio and drummer Buddy Rich) are not to be overlooked. This classic and memorable music has yet to be reissued on CD. —*Scott Yanow*

Jazz at the Philharmonic: Gene Krupa & Buddy Rich / Oct. 11, 1952+Sep. 17, 1954 / Verve ✦✦✦
Drum battles are always much better live than on record. For this Jazz at the Philharmonic LP, the emphasis is on the soloing of both Buddy Rich and Gene Krupa. Rich is heard in 1954 driving an all-star group (with clarinetist Buddy DeFranco, vibraphonist Lionel Hampton and the Oscar Peterson Trio), which climaxes with Hampton apparently jumping on his own set of drums. Gene Krupa in 1952 plays "Drum Boogie" in a trio with altoist Willie Smith and pianist Hank Jones and at the same concert Rich has a solo on "Cottontail" that is preceded by short spots from trumpeters Roy Eldridge and Charlie Shavers, altoist Benny Carter and the tenors of Lester Young and Flip Phillips. Krupa joins the band on second drums during a brief version of "Perdido" that is a feature for Phillips' honking and the two drummers have the stage to themselves on a mercifully brief piece accurately titled "The Drum Battle." Of the ten JATP releases, this is the least significant, but it still has its fun moments. —*Scott Yanow*

Jazz at the Philharmonic in Tokyo: Live at The ... / 1953 / Pablo ✦✦✦✦✦
This two-CD set (originally out as three LPs) features the contents of a single Jazz at the Philharmonic concert held in Tokyo. There are minisets by the Oscar Peterson Trio with guitarist Herb Ellis and bassist Ray Brown (which is highlighted by "Tenderly" and "Swingin' Till the Girls Come Home") and Gene Krupa (in a trio with altoist Benny Carter and Peterson) along with ten numbers that feature Ella Fitgerald (who scats wildly on "Lady Be Good," "How High the Moon" and the closing "Perdido"). But the real reason to get this set is for the Jazz at the Philharmonic All-Stars (trumpeters Roy Eldridge and Charlie Shavers, trombonist Bill Harris, altoists Willie Smith and Benny Carter, tenors Ben Webster and Flip Phillips, the Oscar Peterson Trio and drummer J.C. Heard) who, in addition to a seven-song ballad medley and a drum feature, stretch out on "Tokyo Blues" and "Cotton Tail." The latter has a witty and explosive trumpet battle by Shavers and Eldridge; Shavers comes out on top. This reissue is highly

recommened as a fine example of the excitement of JATP in the mid-'50s. —*Scott Yanow*

Jazz at the Philharmonic: Hartford, 1953 / May 1953 / Pablo ✦✦✦✦
This CD has some typically exciting performances from Norman Granz's traveling jam session Jazz at the Philharmonic. Actually the JATP All-Stars (trumpeters Charlie Shavers and Roy Eldridge, trombonist Bill Harris, Ben Webster and Flip Phillips on tenors, altoists Benny Carter and Willie Smith, the Oscar Peterson Trio and drummer Gene Krupa) only appear on one song, an enjoyable 15-minute version of "Cotton Tail." The Oscar Peterson Quartet (with guitarist Herb Ellis, bassist Ray Brown and drummer J.C. Heard) are in excellent form on four selections (including a burning "7 Come 11") and tenor-great Lester Young (accompanied by Peterson's group) shows on three numbers that he was still very much in his prime in 1953. Fans of swinging jazz will want this colorful music, which was released for the first time in 1984 on Pablo (and does not duplicate any of the Verve sets). —*Scott Yanow*

Jazz at the Philharmonic: One O'Clock Jump 1953 / Sep. 19, 1953 / Verve ✦✦✦✦✦
In 1983 Polygram Classics released ten LPs taken from Jazz at the Philharmonic concerts. This album is particularly enjoyable due to the remarkable all-star lineup: trumpeters Roy Eldridge and Charlie Shavers, trombonist Bill Harris, altoists Benny Carter and Willie Smith, the tenors of Flip Phillips, Ben Webster and (on "One O'Clock Jump") Lester Young, the Oscar Peterson Trio plus drummer J.C. Heard. Together they play a 25-minute version of "Cool Blues" (the excitable Eldridge as usual climaxes the proceedings), "The Challenges" (which has a fiery trumpet battle) and "One O'Clock Jump"; the latter two performances are over 13 minutes apiece. This is passionate and competitive music that deserves to be reissued on CD. —*Scott Yanow*

Jazz at the Philharmonic: The Challenges / Sep. 17, 1954 / Verve ✦✦✦✦✦
1954 was Dizzy Gillespie's first year with Jazz at the Philharmonic and Norman Granz's decision to team the trumpeter with the competitive Roy Eldridge (his former idol) was both inspired and logical. On this LP (one of ten released by Polygram Classics in 1983), the sparks really fly as Diz and Eldridge are joined by the tenors of Ben Webster and Flip Phillips, trombonist Bill Harris, the Oscar Peterson Trio and drummer Louie Bellson; no weak spots in that lineup. Their 16-minute "Jazz Concert Blues" is quite exciting and a lengthy five-song ballad medley has its moments (Gillespie's abstract "Stardust" takes honors) but it is the trumpet battle on "The Challenge" that is most memorable. Until the timeless music is reissued on CD, this hard-to-find LP (JATP at its height) is essential. —*Scott Yanow*

● **Stockholm '55–The Exciting Battle** / Feb. 2, 1955 / Pablo ✦✦✦✦✦

Jazz at the Philharmonic: Blues In Chicago 1955 / Oct. 2, 1955 / Verve ✦✦✦✦
This LP, one of ten released by Polygram in 1983 (and whose contents are not yet available on CD) has its moments of interest. The 20-minute "Blues" features enjoyable solos by five classic horn players: Flip Phillips, Lester Young and Illinois Jacquet on tenors and trumpeters Roy Eldridge and Dizzy Gillespie. In addition Diz and Young are teamed up in "The Modern Set" while "The Swing Set" features Eldridge, Flip and Jacquet and there is a tasteful five-song ballad medley. Fans of these talented players will want to search for this out-of-print album. —*Scott Yanow*

Jazz at the Philharmonic in Europe, Vol. 3 / Nov. 21, 1957 / Verve ✦✦✦✦
By 1957 the once-popular all-star traveling jam session, Jazz at the Philharmonic, was primarily performing in Europe, but fortunately producer Norman Granz documented some of the concerts. This out-of-print LP matches together trumpeter Roy Eldridge, altoist Benny Carter and the complementary but contrasintg tenors of Coleman Hawkins and Don Byas with pianist Lalo Schifrin, bassist Art Davis and drummer Jo Jones. There are some fireworks on lengthy versions of "Take the 'A' Train," "Indiana" and a blues that is wittily titled "A Jazz Portrait of Brigitte Bardot" along with a four-song ballad medley. Everyone plays up to par and, considering the talent involved, that is saying a lot. —*Scott Yanow*

Jazz at the Philharmonic In Europe / 1958 / Verve ✦✦✦✦
This double LP draws its music from one of the final tours of

Norman Granz's Jazz at the Philharmonic. Three different all-star groups are heard from, including a septet with trumpeter Dizzy Gillespie, trombonist J.J. Johnson and altoists Benny Carter and Cannonball Adderley (in probably the two altos' only joint recording) for spirited versions of "Bernie's Tune" and "Swedish Jam." There is also a collaboration between Gillespie's group of the era (with altoist Leo Wright and pianist Lalo Schifrin), Johnson and Stan Getz. However, the most memorable selection is a rendition of "All the Things You Are" that, in addition to trumpeter Roy Eldridge, matches together the tenors of Getz, Coleman Hawkins and Don Byas. This generally exciting music has not yet been reissued on CD. —Scott Yanow

Jazz at the Philharmonic: London (1969) / Mar. 1969 / Pablo ✦✦✦✦✦

By 1969 producer Norman Granz's Jazz at the Philharmonic was largely a thing of the past in the U.S., but he put together occasional European tours that resulted in the very interesting and consistently enjoyable music heard on this double CD. Trumpeters Dizzy Gillespie and Clark Terry, tenors Zoot Sims and James Moody, pianist Teddy Wilson, bassist Bob Cranshaw and drummer Louis Bellson form the core group and play two jams and a four-song ballad medley in addition to accompanying blues singer/guitarist T-Bone Walker on three numbers. Teddy Wilson's Trio with Cranshaw and Bellson is in typically flawless form on a few songs and then comes the biggest surprise of the two-fer. The great veteran tenor Coleman Hawkins was in sad shape during the last few years of his life (he would pass away two months after this concert) yet he manages to almost sound as if he were still in his prime, far exceeding any of his post-1965 recordings on "Blue Lou" and three ballads including a partly unaccompanied "September Song" and an emotional rendition of "Body and Soul." Altoist Benny Carter is also heard from and all of the horns join in for a finale, "What Is This Thing Called Love?" This is historic and frequently exciting music. —Scott Yanow

Jazz at the Philharmonic: at The Montreux Jazz... / Jul. 16, 1975 / Pablo ✦✦✦✦

Norman Granz and Pablo Records took over a large segment of the 1975 Montreux Jazz Festival and many recordings resulted. This particular CD is a colorful reissue featuring trumpeters Roy Eldridge and Clark Terry, Zoot Sims on tenor, altoist Benny Carter, guitarist Joe Pass, pianist Tommy Flanagan, bassist Keter Betts and drummer Bobby Durham performing four fairly lengthy renditions of standards. Everyone is in fine form, but it is the joyful playing of the two complementary but contrasting trumpeters (both of whom can be immediately recognized in a note or two) that makes this a recommended set for fans of straight-ahead jazz. —Scott Yanow

Jazz at the Philharmonic: Tokyo—Return to Happiness / 1983 / Pablo ✦✦✦✦

To commemorate the 30th anniversary of JATP's first visit to Japan, producer Norman Granz put together a new Jazz at the Philharmonic show in 1983. Many of the earlier players were either no longer around or unavailable but Granz was able to gather a pretty strong all-star crew (Harry "Sweets" Edison and Clark Terry on trumpets, Zoot Sims and Eddie "Lockjaw" Davis on tenors, trombonists J.J. Johnson and Al Grey, pianist Oscar Peterson, guitarist Joe Pass, bassist Niels Pedersen and drummer Louie Bellson) for what would be JATP's final tour. This two-CD set starts off with the all-stars jamming on three lengthy tunes. Each of the horns are also showcased on two short ballads apiece (which by itself totals 33 minutes). The Oscar Peterson Quartet and Ella Fitzgerald both have fine mini-sets and the proceedings conclude with Fitzgerald scatting with the horns on "Flying Home." Although the music does not reach the heights of JATP's '50s performances, this is a well-conceived, enjoyable and now somewhat nostalgic set. —Scott Yanow

Jazz Futures

Group / Hard Bop

This short-lived all-star group toured during part of 1991 and showcased in an intelligent and coherent fashion some of the top young lions of the era: trumpeters Roy Hargrove and Marlon Jordan, altoist Antonio Hart, Tim Warfield on tenor, guitarist Mark Whitfield, pianist Benny Green, bassist Christian McBride and drummer Carl Allen. They recorded one fine album for Novus before the future bandleaders all went their separate ways. —Scott Yanow

Live in Concert / Jul. 18, 1991+Aug. 18, 1991 / Novus ✦✦✦

When one considers the lineup of talented young musicians (trumpeters Roy Hargrove and Marlon Jordan, altoist Antonio Hart, Tim Warfield on tenor, guitarist Mark Whitfield, pianist Benny Green, bassist Christian McBride and drummer Carl Allen), this CD should have been a classic; instead it is merely good. There is a ballad feature apiece for each of the hornmen, spirited showcases for Green and Whitfield and three group jams. Unfortunately, the ballads are disappointing with none of the horns adding anything new to their interpratons of standards. Hargroves fares well on "You Don't Know What Love Is," but Jordan falters a bit on "Stardust." The pianist really romps in an Oscar Peterson groove on "Picadilly Square" and Whitfield is memorable on "Medgar Evers Blues," but the tradeoffs on the closing jam, "Public Eye," are self-indulgent and a bit silly. So overall the results are quite mixed. —Scott Yanow

Jazz Passengers

Group / Post-Bop

A versatile and often-humorous outfit co-led by trombonist Curtis Fowlkes and Roy Nathanson (doubling on tenor and alto) that was an outgrowth of the Lounge Lizards, the Jazz Passengers' music ranges from Charles Mingus-type ensembles and hints at swing and Dixieland to freer explorations. Marc Ribot (doubling on guitar and E-flat horn but unfortunately leaving the group in the early '90s), vibraphonist Bill Ware, violinist Jim Nolet, bassist Brad Jones and drummer E.J. Rodriguez all contribute to the band's unique ensembles. They have recorded for such labels as Les Disques Du Crepuscule (based in Belgium), New World Records, Knitting Factory and an unusual vocal date on High Street. —Scott Yanow

Implement Yourself / 1990 / New World ✦✦✦✦

Arguably the best group to emerge on the new music/avant-garde scene in many years, Roy Nathanson's Jazz Passengers suffer from both audience ignorance about their talents and meager album distribution due to being on a small label. But they make fine, constantly changing music that's reminiscent of The Art Ensemble in its early days. —Ron Wynn

● **Live at the Knitting Factory** / 1991 / Knitting Factory ✦✦✦✦✦

The Jazz Passengers blend collective improvisation, outside arrangements, free playing and cohesive intragroup interplay better than most hard bop and mainstream jazz groups. They also include other non-jazz elements into their music, from funk to rock and blues. This melange of styles and idioms was on display throughout the 1991 concert captured on this CD. Whether it was the African/Arabic flavor of "Jazz Passengers In Egypt Overture" or the offbeat pace of "Prozak" and "Tikkun," The Passengers don't content themselves with merely executing chord changes and ripping out solos. They take their followers on trips that seldom proceed smoothly, but always result in rewarding experiences. —Ron Wynn

Plain Old Joe / 1993 / Knitting Factory ✦✦✦

The Jazz Passengers (which is comprised of Roy Nathanson on alto, tenor and soprano, trombonist Curtis Fowlkes, violinist Jim Nolet who doubles on guitar, vibraphonist Bill Ware, bassist Brad Jones and drummer E.J. Rodriguez) is an eccentric group with a nutty sense of humor. On this somewhat odd CD the Jazz Passengers use a great deal of bizarre humor along with interesting combinations of instruments, references to earlier eras of jazz, spoken interludes, vocals by would-be crooner Curtis Fowlkes, noisy sound explorations and some swinging solos. Their version of "If I Were a Bell" is quite silly and "Inzane" lives up to its title. Not everything works but *Plain Old Joe* is certainly not run-of-the-mill music or forgettable. —Scott Yanow

In Love / 1994 / Windham Hill ✦✦✦

Eddie Jefferson (Edgar Jefferson)

b. Aug. 3, 1918, Pittsburgh, PA, d. May 9, 1979, Detroit, MI
Vocals, Lyricist / Vocalese, Bop

The founder of vocalese (putting recorded solos to words), Eddie Jefferson did not have a great voice, but he was one of the top jazz singers, getting the maximum out of what he had. He started out working as a tapdancer but by the late '40s was singing and writing lyrics. A live session from 1949 (released on Spotlite) finds him pioneering vocalese by singing his lyrics to "Parker's Mood" and Lester Young's solo on "I Cover the Waterfront." However, his classic lyrics to "Moody's Mood for Love" was recorded first by

King Pleasure (1952), who also had a big hit with his version of "Parker's Mood." Jefferson had his first studio recording that year (which included Coleman Hawkins' solo on "Body and Soul") before working with James Moody (1953–57). Although he recorded on an occasional basis in the 1950s and '60s, his contributions to the idiom seemed to be mostly overlooked until the 1970s. Jefferson worked with Moody again (1968–73) and during his last few years often performed with Richie Cole. He was shot to death outside of a Detroit club in 1979. Eddie Jefferson, who also wrote memorable lyrics to "Jeannine," "Lady Be Good," "So What," "Freedom Jazz Dance" and even "Bitches' Brew," recorded for Savoy, Prestige, a single for Checker, Inner City and Muse. — *Scott Yanow*

The Jazz Singer / Jan. 19, 1959–Feb. 5, 1959 / Evidence ◆◆◆◆◆

★ **Letter from Home** / Dec. 18, 1961–Feb. 8, 1962 / Original Jazz Classics ◆◆◆◆◆
This CD (which augments the original LP program with two alternate takes) is a fine showcase for the vocalese master Eddie Jefferson. Backed by either a tentet or a quintet which gives solo space to altoist James Moody and the tenor of Johnny Griffin, Jefferson sings his lyrics to such numbers as "Take the 'A' Train," "Billie's Bounce," "I Cover the Waterfront," "Parker's Mood" (the latter differs from the famous lines immortalized by King Pleasure), "A Night in Tunisia" and "Body and Soul" among others. Jefferson is in prime form and these boppish renditions as a whole form a near-classic. — *Scott Yanow*

Body and Soul / 1968 / Original Jazz Classics ◆◆◆◆◆
Eddie Jefferson had not been on record in quite a few years when he recorded this excellent set (reissued on CD) for Prestige. A few of the songs ("Mercy, Mercy, Mercy," "Psychedelic Sally" and "See If You Can Git to That") were attempts to update the singer's style in the mod idiom of the late '60s, but the most memorable selections are "So What" (on which Jefferson recreates Miles Davis' famous solo), "Body and Soul", "Now's the Time," "Oh Gee" and "Filthy McNasty"; the latter has very effective lyrics by writer Ira Gitler. Tenorman James Moody, trumpeter Dave Burns and pianist Barry Harris are in the supporting cast of this excellent set. — *Scott Yanow*

Come Along with Me / Aug. 12, 1969 / Original Jazz Classics ◆◆◆◆
Vocalist Eddie Jefferson (the founder of vocalese) is in top form throughout this outstanding set, a CD reissue of the original LP. There is a liberal amount of solo space for trumpeter Bill Hardman, altoist Charles McPherson and pianist Barry Harris, but it is Jefferson's singing and his witty lyrics to such songs as Horace Silver's "The Preacher," "Yardbird Suite," "Dexter Digs In," "Baby Girl" (based on "These Foolish Things") and even "When You're Smiling" that are the main reasons to acquire this very enjoyable disc. — *Scott Yanow*

Things Are Getting Better / Mar. 5, 1974 / Muse ◆◆◆◆

Godfather of Vocalese / Mar. 17, 1976 / Muse ◆◆◆◆◆
The innovative scat singer and vocalese lyricist was having a comeback during his final years, teaming up with altoist Richie Cole for spirited performances. The set features Cole, trumpeter Wayman Reed and a fine four-piece rhythm section, but the emphasis is naturally on the singer. Jefferson performs such classics as "I Got the Blues" and "Ornithology," teams up with vocalist Betsy Fersmire on "Keep Walkin' " and "Pinetop's Boogie," and even tackles Herbie Hancock's "Chameleon." — *Scott Yanow*

The Live-Liest / Mar. 26, 1976–Mar. 27, 1976 / Muse ◆◆◆◆

Main Man / Oct. 9, 1977 / Inner City ◆◆◆◆◆
Eddie Jefferson's final recording (cut less than two years before his murder) has many highpoints. This LP includes classic versions of his funny "Benny's from Heaven," "Moody's Mood for Love" (with the talented singer Janet Lawson helping out), "Body and Soul" (which Jefferson turned into a tribute for Coleman Hawkins), "Jeannine" and the complex "Freedom Jazz Dance." Well worth searching for, hopefully this music will eventually be reissued on CD. — *Scott Yanow*

Herb Jeffries

b. Sep. 24, 1916, Detroit, MI
Vocals / Ballads, Standards
Although not really a jazz singer, Herb Jeffries is the last surviving member of the 1940 Duke Ellington Orchestra and a fine interpreter of swing songs and ballads. He performed with

Erskine Tate in the early '30s, Earl Hines (1931–34) and Blanche Calloway before becoming the first Black cowboy actor in a series of 1930s Westerns. He gained his greatest fame while with Ellington (1940–42), having a big hit in "Flamingo." Jeffries, who recorded with Sidney Bechet in 1940, has worked as a single since leaving Duke in 1942, recording on an occasional basis and remaining active into the mid-'90s. — *Scott Yanow*

● **A Brief History Of Herb Jeffries (The Bronze Buckaroo)** / 1934–1995 / Warner Western ◆◆◆◆
Herb Jeffries, who in 1995 was the only survivor of the 1940 Duke Ellington Orchestra, is heard on 14 selections on this CD, which covers a six-decade period. There are two tracks from the likable singer's cowboy films of 1938, appearances with Earl Hines' Orchestra in 1934 and Sidney Bechet, four numbers with Ellington (including the hit "Flamingo" and "Jump for Joy"), guest shots with Joe Liggins' Honeydrippers, one song taken from a live concert at the Apollo in 1954 and two numbers (including "I'm a Happy Cowboy") from a 1995 session. Throughout, Jeffries is in surprisingly consistent form, displaying a warm baritone. Although not a jazz singer himself, Herb Jeffries sounds quite at home in these diverse settings. A recommended set. — *Scott Yanow*

The Bronze Buckaroo (Rides Again) / 1995 / Warner Brothers ◆◆

John Jenkins

b. Jan. 3, 1931, Chicago, IL
Alto Saxophone / Hard Bop
John Jenkins, who had a similar sound to Jackie McLean, was most active in 1957, but dropped out of music by the mid-'60s. In 1955 he worked with Art Farmer, led his own group and freelanced around Chicago. Jenkins moved to New York in 1957, played with Charles Mingus, led two albums of his own (on New Jazz and Blue Note) and recorded as a sideman with Donald Byrd, Hank Mobley, Paul Quinichette, Clifford Jordan, Sahib Shihab and Wilbur Ware. Not much has been heard from him since. — *Scott Yanow*

● **Jenkins, Jordan and Timmons** / Jul. 26, 1957 / Original Jazz Classics ◆◆◆◆
1987 reissue of prototype jam session/blowing date with Clifford Jordan (ts), John Jenkins, Bobby Timmons (p). — *Ron Wynn*

John Jenkins / Aug. 11, 1957 / Blue Note ◆◆◆

Leroy Jenkins

b. Mar. 11, 1932, Chicago, IL
Violin / Avant-Garde, Free Jazz
Free jazz's leading violinist, Leroy Jenkins has greatly expanded the options and range of sounds and possibilities for stringed instruments in free music. His techniques have included sawing, string bending and plucking. Jenkins plays adventurous phrases and distorted solos, while including elements of blues, bebop and classical in his approach. Jenkins' often lists as influences a diverse group of violinists (Eddie South and Jascha Heifetz) and other instrumentalists (Charlie Parker, Ornette Coleman and John Coltrane among others). Jenkins began playing violin at eight, often at church in Chicago. He was another student of Walter Dyett at Du Sable High, where he also played alto sax. Jenkins graduated from Florida A&M, where he dropped alto and concentrated on violin. He spent about four years teaching stringed instruments in Mobile, Alabama. Jenkins returned to Chicago in the mid-'60s and divided his time from 1965 to 1969 between teaching in the Chicago public school system and working with the Association for the Advancement of Creative Musicians (AACM). Jenkins was among the AACM musicians who left Chicago for Europe in the late '60s. While in Paris, Jenkins, Anthony Braxton, Leo Smith and Steve McCall founded The Creative Construction Company. He also played with Ornette Coleman there. Jenkins returned to Chicago in 1970 and moved to New York with Braxton shortly after, living and studying at Coleman's New York home for three months. After working briefly with Cecil Taylor and Braxton, Jenkins played with Archie Shepp, Alice Coltrane and Rahsaan Roland Kirk. But more importantly, in 1971 Jenkins, Sirone and Jerome Cooper founded The Revolutionary Ensemble, one of the decade's great trios. They were truly a co-operative venture, with each musician contributing compositions and their performances often resembling works in progress. All three played several instruments during their con-

certs. The Ensemble maintained its integrity while making albums that were aesthetic triumphs and commercial flops for six years on various labels. After the trio disbanded, Jenkins made several tours of Europe, led a quintet and a trio featuring Anthony Davis and Andrew Cyrille. During the mid-'80s, he served on the board of directors of the Composers' Forum and was a member of Cecil Taylor's quintet in 1987. Jenkins has presented many free music performances and written numerous pieces for soloists, small groups and large ensembles. A few of his Black Saint and India Navigation sessions are available on CD. —*Ron Wynn*

For Players Only / Jan. 30, 1975 / JCOA ✦✦✦✦

★ **Solo Concert** / Jan. 11, 1977 / India Navigation ✦✦✦✦✦
About as adventurous and experimental as violin playing gets. Despite far-out tendencies, Jenkins knows when to come back in and how. —*Ron Wynn*

Lifelong Ambitions / Mar. 11, 1977 / Black Saint ✦✦✦✦✦
Leroy Jenkins, free jazz's greatest violinist, has always worked best in intimate situations with equally talented partners. He certainly had the optimum conditions on this duet date pairing him with outstanding pianist, composer, arranger and conductor Muhal Richard Abrams. The duo played six Jenkins compositions for the session, which was recorded live. Abrams and Jenkins frequently alternated roles, letting each other set the pace, never colliding and forging a highly effective musical partnership. Jenkins' whiplash lines, percussive effects and seamless blend of free and blues influences was capably contrasted by Abrams' driving, soulful piano phrases and solos. —*Ron Wynn*

The Legend of Ai Glatson / Jul. 1978 / Black Saint ✦✦✦✦
Excellent session by dynamic violinist Leroy Jenkins, once part of the wonderful avant-garde trio The Revolutionary Ensemble. Jenkins cut this session in 1978, shortly after the trio's demise, and it's loaded with great violin solos, as well as some unusual, intriguing arrangements and compositions. —*Ron Wynn*

Space Minds / New Worlds / Survival America / Aug. 1978–Sep. 1978 / Tomato ✦✦✦
Music that is dynamic and invigorating, far from hard bop, swing, or traditional styles. —*Ron Wynn*

Mixed Quintet / Mar. 22, 1979–Mar. 23, 1979 / Black Saint ✦✦✦✦✦

Urban Blues / Jan. 2, 1984 / Black Saint ✦✦✦✦
Violinist Leroy Jenkins was at the helm of Sting, which played funky and free, did originals and vintage spirituals and would shift from stretches of collective improvisation to challenging solo exchanges. They were a unique, intriguing group, but sadly didn't last. This 1984 album, reissued on CD, presented them at their best, displaying the breadth of influences, genres, sources and styles that converged and resulted in the work of a great band. —*Ron Wynn*

Leroy Jenkins Live! / Mar. 15, 1992 / Black Saint ✦✦✦
Two CDs that give an overview of Jenkins' earlier tune-oriented and later free playing. Muhal Richard Abrams is a composer who has served as an important musical, spiritual and social influence as president of the AACM (Association for the Advancement of Creative Musicians) founded in Chicago in 1965, by members of his earlier group The Experimental Band. His own work may be heard on "Blu Nlu Blu" (Black Saint 1991) and "Family Talk" (Black Saint 1993) in excellent performances that reach out to the listener. Abrams' recent and daring work, the masterpiece "Duet for Pianos #1" has yet to be recorded. —*Blue Gene Tyranny*

Santa Fe / 1994 / Lovely Music ✦✦✦
A magnificent CD of violin and viola solos showing the dynamic "pure music" side of this great composer/performer who worked with the AACM in Chicago in the '60s, moved to New York City and founded The Revolutionary Ensemble (they recorded five albums). He has composed many large works played by the Brooklyn Philharmonic, the Cleveland Chamber Symphony, the Albany Symphony, Kronos Quartet and was included in the Kennedy Center's American Composer series; he recently premiered his opera-for-dance "The Mother of Three Sons" commissioned by the Munich Biennale, and his "Off-Duty Dryad" (1990) was played by The Soldier String Quartet with dancers. He is currently at work on a new opera, which includes three rappers as characters and a work about the recently uncovered Negro Graveyard in Manhattan. He is a totally engaging performer who keeps the listener on the seat's edge waiting for the next surprising variation and invention. —*Blue Gene Tyranny*

Themes & Improvisations / 1995 / CRI ✦✦✦✦

Ingrid Jensen

Trumpet / Hard Bop
A talented young trumpeter, Ingrid Jensen made a strong impression during 1994–95, recording her first solo album (*Vernal Fields* on Enja) and taking fine solos with the big band Diva. —*Scott Yanow*

● **Vernal Fields** / Oct. 11, 1994–Oct. 12, 1994 / Enja ✦✦✦✦
Although trumpeter Ingrid Jensen has a wide range and a potentially fiery style, she holds a great deal in reserve on her debut recording, letting one peek at her emotional intensity now and then, but mostly making lyrical statements. Her supporting cast (altoist Steve Wilson, George Garzone on tenor, pianist Bruce Barth, bassist Larry Grenadier and drummer Lenny White) is quite impressive and adds a great deal to the CD without taking the spotlight away from the leader. Ingrid Jensen sounds particularly strong on "Marsh Blues" and the standards "Ev'rytime We Say Goodbye," "I Love You" and an ironic "By Myself," but all nine selections have their moments. The music is basically advanced hard bop with Jensen (when she is playing open) sounding like a logical successor to Freddie Hubbard and Woody Shaw while resembling her teacher Art Farmer a bit when utilizing a mute. This is an impressive beginning to what should be an important career. —*Scott Yanow*

Papa Bue Jensen

b. May 8, 1930, Copenhagen, Denmark
Trombone, leader / Dixieland
Leader of the Viking Jazz Band since 1956, Papa Bue Jensen is an excellent Dixieland trombonist who has been active for decades in Denmark. He had recorded with Chris Barber before forming his group (which during 1956–58 was known simply as the New Orleans Jazz Band). Through the years, the band has recorded (sometimes for Storyville or Timeless) with such American guests as George Lewis, Wingy Manone, Wild Bill Davison, Edmond Hall, Champion Jack Dupree, Albert Nicholas and Art Hodes. —*Scott Yanow*

● **A Tribute to Wingy Manone** / 1967 12 / Storyville ✦✦✦✦✦

Live in Dresden / 1971 01 / Storyville ✦✦✦✦

On Stage / 1982 04 + 1982 09 / Timeless ✦✦✦✦

Antonio Carlos Jobim

b. Jan. 25, 1927, Rio de Janeiro, Brazil, **d.** Dec. 8, 1994, New York, NY
Composer, Guitar, Piano, Vocals / Bossa Nova
Without question one of the greatest 20th Century popular music composers in any idiom, Antonio Carlos Brasileiro de Almeida Jobim has an unprecedented impact on Brazilian and American and world music. His music mixes the romantic and the ugly, is alternately lyrical, urbane, harmonically and rhythmically sophisticated, as well as melodically rich and striking. Above all, it's extraordinarily beautiful. His style avoids jarring effects and mixes simple, evocative lyrics with syncopated melodic figures and subtle chord progressions. Jobim persuaded Odeon Records, where he was music director, to record Joao Gilberto performing his composition "Chega de Saudade." The recording helped launch a reshaping of the samba into the bossa nova. This was popularized in America by Stan Getz and Charlie Byrd with their album *Jazz Samba* in 1962. The album included Jobim's composition "Desafinado," which was later recorded by Coleman Hawkins. Jobim And Gilberto later appeared with Getz, Byrd and Dizzy Gillespie at a Carnegie Hall concert in 1962. Astrud Gilberto's recording of his composition "The Girl from Ipanema" with Stan Getz on tenor sax later was a number one pop hit. The bossa nova was enormously popular in the '60s, and many other jazz musicians recorded in the style. Jobim recorded as a leader for Verve and A&M in the '60s, CTI, Discovery and Columbia in the '70s, Warner Bros., Verve and Polydor in the '80s and Verve in the '90s. His list of hit compositions includes "Wave," "Corcovado," "Aguas de Marco," "Felicidade," "Once I Loved," "Dindi," "One Note Samba" and "Triste." Vocalist, pianist and arranger Tom Ze has emerged as one of Jobim's finest interpreters, but many others–from Frank Sinatra to Wayne Shorter–have recorded his compositions. Jobim's also done albums with Sinatra, Nelson Riddle and

Claus Ogerman's orchestras, Gal Costa and Elis Regina among others. —*Ron Wynn and Terri Hinte*

The Composer of 'Desafinado' Plays / 1963 / Verve ✦✦✦✦

Wave / May 22, 1967–Jun. 1, 1967 / A&M ✦✦✦

★ **Elis and Tom** / 1974 / Verve ✦✦✦✦✦
A perfect record: Brazil's beloved cantora Elis Regina singing an all-Jobim program, accompanied by the composer, who also joins her for several duets, notably his masterpiece "Aguas de Marco." —*Terri Hinte*

Urubu / Nov. 1976 / Warner Brothers ✦✦✦✦
This beautiful 1976 session features Claus Ogerman's incomparable string arrangements. In fact, half the album is orchestral-only; on the other half, Jobim sings such gems as "Correnteza," co-written by Bonf. —*Terri Hinte*

Terra Brasilis / 1980 / Warner Brothers ✦✦✦✦
Once again teaming with arranger Claus Ogerman on this 1980 double album, Jobim reworks many of his classic compositions, including "Dindi," "One Note Samba," and, of course, "The Girl from Ipanema." —*Terri Hinte*

The Art of / Verve ✦✦✦
Recent release covering Jobim material issued on Verve's import label. It includes lush ballads, more celebratory tunes and his romantic, poetic love material. —*Ron Wynn*

Girl from Ipanema: The Antonio Carlos Jobim Songbook / Verve ✦✦✦

Man From Ipanema / Verve ✦✦✦

Budd Johnson (Albert J. Johnson)

b. Dec. 14, 1910, Dallax, TX, d. Oct. 20, 1984, Kansas City, MO
Tenor Saxophone, Soprano Saxophone, Arranger / Swing, Bop
Budd Johnson was a talented and valuable jazz musician for many decades, a behind-the-scenes player and writer who uplifted a countless number of sessions from the 1930s into the '80s. Johnson started off playing in Kansas City in the late '20s including with the bands of Terrence Holder, Jesse Stone and George E. Lee. He made his recording debut while with Louis Armstrong's big band (1932–33) and gained attention for his work as tenor soloist and arranger during three stints with the Earl Hines Orchestra (1932–42). One of the first tenor saxophonists to be influenced by Lester Young (although by the 1940s he had a distinctive tone of his own), Johnson had brief stints with Gus Arnheim (1937) and the bands of Fletcher and Horace Henderson (1938) between his periods with Hines. He contributed arrangements to several big bands including those of Woody Herman, Buddy Rich, Boyd Raeburn and Billy Eckstine and was partly responsible for Hines hiring young modernists during 1942–43. He recorded with Coleman Hawkins on the first bebop session (1944), worked with Dizzy Gillespie and Sy Oliver (1947) and in the 1950s led his own groups in addition to touring with Snub Mosley (1952) and Benny Goodman (1957). Johnson was with the big bands of Quincy Jones (1960) and Count Basie (1961–62) before renewing ties with Earl Hines, who he played with on and off again starting in 1964. He formed the JPJ Quartet, which worked on an occasional basis during 1969–75, held his own at the 1971 Newport in New York jam sessions, became a jazz educator and recorded an excellent album with Phil Woods eight months before his death. Budd Johnson led some obscure sessions during 1947–56 in addition to notable albums for Felsted (1958), Riverside, Swingville, Argo, Black & Blue, Master Jazz, Dragon and Uptown. —*Scott Yanow*

Blues a La Mode / Feb. 11, 1958–Feb. 14, 1958 / Affinity ✦✦✦✦
Rare Johnson septet date. —*Ron Wynn*

And the Four Brass Giants / Sep. 22, 1960+Sep. 6, 1960 / Original Jazz Classics ✦✦✦✦✦
This was one of Budd Johnson's finest leadership moments; he not only wrote charts, which did a marvelous job of setting up his gems, but he also made particularly clever use of four distinctive trumpeters. Cannonball Adderley produced this date. —*Bob Rusch, Cadence*

★ **Let's Swing** / Dec. 2, 1960 / Original Jazz Classics ✦✦✦✦✦
Stout, robust vehicle with standard Johnson solos. —*Ron Wynn*

In Memory of a Very Dear Friend / Mar. 23, 1978 / Dragon ✦✦✦✦

The Ole Dude and the Fundance Kid / Feb. 4, 1984 / Uptown ✦✦✦✦
The veteran tenor saxophonist Budd Johnson (who first emerged

50 years before this recording) was still in fine form when he met up with altoist Phil Woods for this frequently heated quintet session. During what would be his final recording date (he died later in 1984), Johnson is excellent on the ballads, but even better on the faster material where his interplay and tradeoffs with Woods are a constant joy. There is a lot of spirit on this happy set; the mutual love and respect felt by the saxophonists is obvious. —*Scott Yanow*

Bunk Johnson (William Geary Johnson)

b. Dec. 27, 1889, New Orleans, d. Jul. 7, 1949, New Orleans, LA
Trumpet / New Orleans Jazz
Due to the difference of opinion between his followers (who claimed he was a brilliant stylist) and his detractors (who felt than his playing was worthless), Bunk Johnson was a controversial figure in the mid-'40s when he made a most unlikely comeback. The truth is somewhere in between.

Bunk Johnson, who tended to exaggerate, claimed that he was born in 1879 and that he played with Buddy Bolden in New Orleans, but it was discovered that he was actually a decade younger. He did have a pretty tone and, although not an influence on Louis Armstrong (as he often stated), he was a major player in New Orleans starting around 1910 when he joined the Eagle Band. Johnson was active in the South until the early '30s, but did not record during that era. Discovered in the latter part of the decade by Bill Russell and Fred Ramsey, he was profiled in the 1939 book *Jazzmen*. A collection was taken up to get Bunk new teeth and a horn. In 1942 he privately recorded in New Orleans and the next year he was in San Francisco playing with the wartime edition of the Yerba Buena Jazz Band. An alcoholic, Johnson's playing tended to be erratic and when Sidney Bechet recruited him for a band in 1945, he essentially drank himself out of the group. In 1946 Bunk led a group that included the nucleus of the ensemble George Lewis would make famous a few years later, but Johnson disliked the playing of the primitive New Orleans musicians. He was more comfortable the following year heading a unit filled with skilled swing players and his final album (Columbia's *The Last Testament of a Great Jazzman*) was one of his best recordings. In 1948 the trumpeter (who was only 59 but seemed much older) returned to Louisiana and retired. Many of Bunk Johnson's better recordings have been reissued on CD by Good Time Jazz and American Music. —*Scott Yanow*

Bunk and Lu / Dec. 19, 1941–Feb. 1944 / Good Time Jazz ✦✦✦✦✦
This put together two sessions. The first was from Dec. 19, 1941 and was recorded on Watters' 30th birthday at a gathering with Bob Scobey (cornet), Turk Murphy (trombone), Ellis Horne (clarinet), Wally Rose (piano), Clancy Hayes, Russ Bennett (banjo), Dick Lammi (tuba) and Bill Dart (drums) to play and pay tribute to the traditional jazz of the "past." ... The other session here was from Spring of 1944 and featured Bunk Johnson's spirited, sometimes sour, but strong 66-year-old trumpet with Hayes, Murphy, Horn, Pat Patton (bass), Squire Girsback (bass) and Sister Lottie Peavey (vocal on two cuts) on eight tracks. —*Bob Rusch, Cadence*

Bunk Johnson and His Superior Jazz Band / Jun. 11, 1942 / Good Time Jazz ✦✦✦
'91 reissue of magnificent early '40s traditional jazz album with the great New Orleans trumpeter Bunk Johnson. Johnson didn't make many records, and this was among his greatest. The supporting lineup included two other Crescent City greats, Jim Robinson and George Lewis. —*Ron Wynn*

Bunk Johnson in San Francisco / Sep. 1943–Jan. 1944 / American Music ✦✦✦

1944 [2nd Masters] / Jul. 29, 1944–Aug. 1944 / American Music ✦✦✦✦✦

King of the Blues / Jul. 1944–Aug. 1944 / American Music ✦✦✦✦

Bunk Plays the Blues: The Spirituals / Aug. 2, 1944 / American Music ✦✦✦✦✦

Bunk's Brass Band And Dance Band 1945 / May 14, 1945–May 18, 1945 / American Music ✦✦✦

New York 1945 / Nov. 21, 1945–Jan. 6, 1946 / Folklyric ✦✦✦✦✦
Early Crescent City trumpeter Johnson was a major figure of The Revival, both revered and denigrated to excess. As only the True Believer's ear could ignore, most of his 1940s recordings were pretty bad. But not all of them—and this album contains most of the exceptions: a wonderful "Tishomingo Blues," a revelatory

"Alexander's Ragtime Band," outstanding versions of several other standards. For once, everything worked: Johnson's drive edged with poignancy, Lewis' birdsong clarinet, Robinson, Johnson and pianist Alton Purnell all playing at the style's plain-man best. — *John Storm Roberts*

Bunk Johnson & Mutt Carey In New York / Oct. 3, 1947–Oct. 24, 1947 / American Music ✦✦✦

★ **Last Testament of a Great Jazzman** / Dec. 23, 1947–Dec. 26, 1947 / Columbia ✦✦✦✦✦
Venerable New Orleans jazz legend Bunk Johnson teamed with a group of mostly swing era veterans in the mid- and late '40s for several controversial albums. Rather than cutting strictly traditional material, Johnson's band blended rags, spirituals, blues, swing and some traditional numbers. The music was largely successful, but the band didn't attract a wide enough audience to make it fiscally worthwhile. The 14 cuts on this CD reissue were done in 1947, the band's final year and originally released on Columbia. Johnson, clarinetist Garvin Bushnell, trombonist Eddie Cuffee, guitarist Danny Barker, bassist Wellman Braud and drummer Alphonse Steele meshed and played with fire, precision and fervor. — *Ron Wynn*

Charlie Johnson

b. Nov. 21, 1891, Philadelphia, PA, **d.** Dec. 13, 1959, New York, NY
Leader, Piano / Classic Jazz
A decent pianist who rarely soloed, Charlie Johnson is of greatest significance for leading his Paradise Ten, an orchestra that had five excellent recording sessions during 1925–29 and played at Smalls' Paradise during 1925–35. Among the sidemen who appear on Johnson's records are trumpeters Jabbo Smith, Thomas Morris, Leonard Davis and Sidney DeParis, trombonists Charlie Irvis and Jimmy Harrison, altoists Benny Carter (who made his recording debut with Johnson in 1927) and Edgar Sampson and tenor saxophonist Benny Waters. In general, their recordings live up to the great potential. Charlie Johnson led his band until 1938 and freelanced until ill health forced his retirement in the 1950s. — *Scott Yanow*

★ **The Complete Charlie Johnson Sessions** / Oct. 1925–May 8, 1925 / Hot & Sweet ✦✦✦✦✦

Freddy Johnson

b. Mar. 12, 1904, New York, NY, **d.** Mar. 24, 1961, New York, NY
Piano / Swing
An excellent swing-based pianist in the 1930s, Freddy Johnson's peak years were spent in Europe. He worked with Elmer Snowden (1925) and Noble Sissle then first visited Europe in 1928 with Sam Wooding. In 1929 he moved to Paris, leading his own band, working with Arthur Briggs and recording during 1933–34. Johnson spent time in Belgium and Amsterdam, performed often with Coleman Hawkins and Willie Lewis and had a final record session in 1939. Unfortunately, he chose to ignore the dominance of the Nazis, was arrested and spent 1941–44 in a prison camp. After being released and returned to the U.S., Johnson played with Garvin Bushell and mostly worked as a piano teacher in the 1950s. His sessions as a leader are available on a Classics CD. — *Scott Yanow*

● **1933–1939** / Jul. 8, 1933–Jun. 30, 1939 / Classics ✦✦✦✦✦
Freddy Johnson was a talented swing-oriented pianist who spent the 1930s playing in Europe. This Classics CD contains all five of his sessions, a song ("Wo Ist Der Mann?") on which his band accompanies Marlene Dietrich plus a date with trumpeter Louis Bacon's septet. In addition to Johnson's many piano solos, the top players are trumpeter Arthur Briggs, Big Boy Goudie on tenor, trombonist Herb Flemming, tenorman Alix Combelle and Bacon. Four songs recorded in 1934 with a Dutch band have delightful vocals from the completely obscure Rosie Poindexter. This CD is a must for collectors of small-group swing. — *Scott Yanow*

Henry Johnson

b. Jan. 28, 1954, Chicago, IL
Guitar / Soul Jazz
A guitarist heavily influenced by his idol Wes Montgomery, Henry Johnson is a fine player with an appealing tone. He has played with the groups of Jack McDuff (1976–77), Sonny Stitt, Hank Crawford, Ramsey Lewis (1979–83) and Joe Williams in addition to recording three albums as a leader for MCA/Impulse! during 1987–90. — *Scott Yanow*

● **You're the One** / Apr. 1987 / MCA ✦✦✦
Slick, but sometimes soulful, '87 date by New Orleans pianist Henry Johnson. He's got a good voice, but is an even better instrumentalist. Sometimes he'll explode out of the tight format, laying down some funky licks or spinning a bluesy solo. At other times, he sticks to the melody and the songs are pleasant, but forgettable. — *Ron Wynn*

Never Too Much / 1990 / MCA ✦✦
Recent contemporary set bogged down by feeble material. — *Ron Wynn*

Missing You / 1993 / Heads Up ✦✦
Guitarist Henry Johnson, a talented Wes Montgomery clone, performs easy-listening pop jazz on his Heads Up CD. His solos are pleasant but without adventure, and each selection fades out as the performance nears five minutes. The melodic music is enjoyable enough, but Henry Johnson is capable of producing much more valuable improvisations than is heard during this set of high-quality background music. — *Scott Yanow*

Howard Johnson

b. Aug. 7, 1941, Montgomery, AL
Tuba, Baritone Saxophone / Post-Bop
One of the top tuba soloists of the 1970s and '80s, Howard Johnson is a very versatile player who not only plays tuba and baritone but other reeds and trumpet. He moved to New York in 1963 where he worked with Charles Mingus (1964–66), Hank Crawford and Archie Shepp. In 1966 he started a 20-year off-and-on association with Gil Evans. Johnson's four-tuba group, Substructure, performed with Taj Mahal and in the late '70s he had a different tuba band called Gravity. Howard Johnson has recorded with Crawford (1983–84), Jack DeJohnette's Special Edition, Jimmy Heath, Bob Moses, George Gruntz's Concert Jazz Band and frequently with Evans' Orchestra among others. — *Scott Yanow*

J.J. Johnson (James Louis Johnson)

b. Jan. 22, 1924, Indianapolis, IN
Trombone, Composer, Arranger / Bop, Hard Bop
Considered by many to be the finest jazz trombonist of all time, J.J. Johnson somehow transferred the innovations of Charlie Parker and Dizzy Gillespie to his more awkward instrument, playing with such speed and deceptive ease that at one time some listeners assumed he was playing valve (rather than slide) trombone! Johnson toured with the territory bands of Clarence Love and Snookum Russell during 1941–42 and then spent 1942–45 with Benny Carter's big band. He made his recording debut with Carter (taking a solo on "Love for Sale" in 1943) and played at the first JATP concert (1944). Johnson also had plenty of solo space during his stay with Count Basie's Orchestra (1945–46). During 1946–50 he played with all of the top bop musicians including Charlie Parker (with whom he recorded in 1947), the Dizzy Gillespie big band, Illinois Jacquet (1947–49) and the Miles Davis Birth of the Cool nonet. His own recordings from the era included such sidemen as Bud Powell and a young Sonny Rollins. J.J., who also recorded with the Metronome All-Stars, played with Oscar Pettiford (1951) and Miles Davis (1952) but then was outside of music, working as a blueprint inspector for two years (1952–54). His fortunes changed when, in August 1954, he formed a two-trombone quintet with Kai Winding that became known as Jay and Kai and was quite popular during its two years.

After J.J. and Kai went their separate ways (they would later have a few reunions), Johnson led a quintet that often included Bobby Jaspar. He began to compose ambitious works starting with 1956's "Poem for Brass" and including "El Camino Real" and a feature for Dizzy Gillespie, "Perceptions"; his "Lament" became a standard. Johnson worked with Miles Davis during part of 1961–62, led some more small groups of his own and, by the late '60s, was kept busy writing television and film scores. J.J. Johnson was so famous in the jazz world that he kept on winning *Downbeat* polls in the 1970s even though he was not playing at all! However, starting with a Japanese tour in 1977, J.J. gradually returned to a busy performance schedule, leading a quintet in the 1980s that often featured Ralph Moore. In the mid-'90s he remains at the top of his field. J.J. Johnson has recorded as a leader for Savoy, Prestige, Blue Note, RCA, Bethlehem, Columbia, Impulse, Verve, A&M, Pablo, Milestone, Concord and Antilles. — *Scott Yanow*

Mad Bebop / Jun. 26, 1946–Aug. 26, 1954 / Savoy ✦✦✦✦✦
The great trombonist J.J. Johnson is heard in several different settings on this out-of-print but valuable two-LP set. Johnson is featured on three dates from 1946–49 that are greatly expanded by the inclusion of alternate takes; among the sidemen are pianists Bud Powell, John Lewis and Hank Jones, altoist Cecil Payne, baritonist Leo Parker, tenorman Sonny Rollins and drummer Max Roach. In contrast to those early bop sides are eight performances co-led by J.J. Johnson and fellow trombonist Kai Winding in 1954 in a pair of quintets, also including either guitarist Billy Bauer or pianist Wally Cirillo, bassist Charles Mingus (whose presence is definitely felt) and drummer Kenny Clarke. Those selections, highlighted by "What Is This Thing Called Love," "Blues for Trombones" and "Lament," would lead to the popular Jay and Kai group. Overall, excellent music that deserves to be reissued in complete fashion on CD. —*Scott Yanow*

Jay and Kai / Dec. 24, 1947–Aug. 26, 1954 / Savoy Jazz ✦✦✦
The music on this Savoy CD is excellent, but the packaging is rather dumb. Rather than reissue all 12 selections from a pair of 1954 sessions that led to the birth of the J.J. Johnson-Kai Winding two-trombone quintet (renditions that also include either pianist Wally Cirillo or guitarist Billy Bauer along with bassist Charles Mingus and drummer Kenny Clarke), there are just eight on this CD along with a Johnson track from 1947 ("Yesterdays") and three of the four Winding performances (in a quintet with pianist Lou Stein) from 1952. Sure to frustrate completists, this reissue is still worth picking up if found at a budget price, for the music contains plenty of worthy trombone solos. —*Scott Yanow*

Trombone by Three / May 26, 1949–Oct. 5, 1951 / Original Jazz Classics ✦✦✦✦✦

Early Bones / May 26, 1949–1955 / Prestige ✦✦✦✦✦
This two-LP set features three different trombonists in a variety of settings. On the first album, J.J. Johnson is heard leading a sextet in 1949 with the young tenor saxophonist Sonny Rollins and trumpeter Kenny Dorham, Kai Winding heads a group with tenorman Brew Moore and baritonist Gerry Mulligan (although trumpeter Jerry Lloyd, who is listed in the personnel, is not on the date) and Bennie Green in 1951 jams with a high-powered septet that also includes baritonist Rudy Williams and the tough tenors of Eddie "Lockjaw" Davis and Big Nick Nicholas. Green is also heard with a sextet in 1955 that matches his personable sound with that of tenor saxophonist Charlie Rouse, but the bulk of the second is taken up by the first official recordings of the popular J.J. Johnson-Kai Winding quintet. Throughout this two-fer, there are many memorable performances, especially by the trio of talented trombonists. —*Scott Yanow*

The Eminent Jay Jay Johnson, Vol. 1 / Jun. 22, 1953 / Blue Note ✦✦✦✦✦
The CD reissue of the two volumes titled *The Eminent Jay Jay Johnson* straighten out his three Blue Note sessions of 1953–55 and add alternate takes. This particular CD concentrates exclusively on the trombonist's 1953 sextet date with the great trumpeter Clifford Brown, Jimmy Heath (who doubles on tenor and baritone), pianist John Lewis, bassist Percy Heath and drummer Kenny Clarke. The six titles (plus three alternates) are highlighted by "It Could Happen to You," "Turnpike" and a classic rendition of "Get Happy." Although Johnson has a couple of features, Clifford Brown largely steals the show. This CD is well worth getting by listeners who do not have the music on Brownie's own *Complete* Blue Note set. —*Scott Yanow*

Four Trombones: The Debut Recordings / Sep. 18, 1953 / Original Jazz Classics ✦✦✦✦
W/ Kai Winding (tb), Bennie Green (tb). Outstanding 1990 reissue of superb 1953 four-trombone summit. —*Ron Wynn*

The Eminent Jay Jay Johnson, Vol. 2 / Sep. 24, 1954+Jun. 6, 1955 / Blue Note ✦✦✦✦✦
The second of two Blue Note CDs (which differ in their content from the similarly titled LPs) contains two complete sessions that showcase trombonist J.J. Johnson. The first six titles (highlighted by "Old Devil Moon" and "Too Marvelous for Words") feature Johnson in a quintet with pianist Wynton Kelly, bassist Charles Mingus, drummer Kenny Clarke and the congas of Sabu. For the later session, there are also six titles (including "Pennies from Heaven" and "Portrait of Jennie") plus three alternate takes; Johnson is joined by Hank Mobley on tenor, pianist Horace Silver, bassist Paul Chambers and drummer Kenny Clarke. Both of these

dates offer listeners excellent examples of the talents of the great trombonist who always played his instrument with the fluidity of a trumpet. Recommended. —*Scott Yanow*

The Finest Of / Jan. 25, 1955–Jan. 27, 1955 / Bethlehem ✦✦✦✦
It may not be the "finest," but this LP does feature one of the most popular jazz groups of the mid-'50s, the two-trombone quintet co-led by J.J. Johnson and Kai Winding. Both of the players (who are joined by pianist Dick Katz, Milt Hinton or Wendell Marshall on bass and drummer Al Harewood) had similar but generally distinctive styles. On tunes ranging from "Out of This World," "Lover" and "It's All Right with Me" to "Mad About the Boy" and even "Yes Sir, That's My Baby," the unusual band's sound consistently uplifts the themes and the co-leaders' improvising talents keep the music from becoming merely easy-listening. —*Scott Yanow*

Trombone Master / Apr. 26, 1957–Dec. 22, 1960 / Columbia ✦✦✦
Although released in the usually consistent *Columbia Jazz Masterpieces* series, this LP is a mere sampler of trombonist J.J. Johnson's 1957–60 recordings. The nine selections are drawn from four albums, and although there are some fine moments (most notably on "Misterioso," "Blue Trombone" and "What Is This Thing Called Love"), it is unfortunate that all four of the LPs, three of which showcase Johnson in quartets, remain out of print. —*Scott Yanow*

J.J. Inc. / Aug. 1, 1960+Aug. 3, 1960 / Columbia ✦✦✦✦
Trombonist J.J. Johnson's 1960 sextet is featured on this Columbia reissue LP. Most notable among the sidemen is a rather young trumpeter named Freddie Hubbard on one of his first sessions; also helping out are tenor saxophonist Clifford Jordan, pianist Cedar Walton, bassist Arthur Harper and drummer Albert "Tootie" Heath. All six compositions are Johnson's and, although none caught on, "Mohawk," "In Walked Horace" and "Fatback" are all fairly memorable. A fine, straight-ahead date from the premiere trombonist, but, as with all of his Columbia recordings of the period, this music has not yet been reissued on CD. —*Scott Yanow*

The Great Kai and J.J. / Nov. 4, 1960–Nov. 9, 1960 / MCA/Impulse! ✦✦✦✦✦
This Impulse! set (which was given the catalog number of A-1 when it first came out) was the first recorded reunion of trombonists J.J. Johnson and Kai Winding. Given a straight reissue on CD (the original liner notes are reproduced so small as to be largely unreadable), the music still sounds fresh and lively. With pianist Bill Evans, either Paul Chambers or Tommy Williams on bass and Roy Haynes or Art Taylor on drums, the two trombonists are in melodic and witty form on such tunes as "This Could Be the Start of Something Big," "Blue Monk," "Side by Side" and the "Theme from Picnic." Recommended. —*Scott Yanow*

Proof Positive / May 1, 1964 / GRP/Impulse! ✦✦✦✦✦
This CD reissue finds trombonist J.J. Johnson in prime form. In fact, his melancholy minor-toned explorations often recall Miles Davis, whose group he had played with the year before. Backed on six of the seven tracks by pianist Harold Mabern, who at the time was heavily influenced by McCoy Tyner, bassist Arthur Harper and drummer Frank Gant, Johnson gets to really stretch out on "Neo," "Minor Blues" and "Blues Waltz"; "Gloria" was previously available only on an Impulse! sampler. Manny Albam's "Lullaby of Jazzland," on which Johnson is joined by guitarist Toots Thielemans, pianist McCoy Tyner, bassist Richard Davis and drummer Elvin Jones, rounds out the excellent set. —*Scott Yanow*

Say When / Dec. 7, 1964–Dec. 5, 1966 / Bluebird ✦✦✦✦
Most of two of trombonist J.J. Johnson's Victor big-band dates (seven of nine numbers from a 1964 album and eight of the nine selections on Johnson's *The Total* LP from 1966) are included on this Bluebird single CD from 1987. In addition to his typically brilliant trombone playing, Johnson did virtually all of the arranging, except for Oliver Nelson's work on his own "Stolen Moments," and contributed nine of the compositions. The emphasis is on the writing with J.J. Johnson and pianist Hank Jones generally being the main soloists; Johnson's reworkings of George Russell's challenging "Stratusphunk" and Miles Davis' "Swing Spring" are among the highlights. —*Scott Yanow*

Israel / Feb. 19, 1968–Apr. 16, 1968 / A&M ✦✦
Trombonists J.J. Johnson and Kai Winding had two reunions on A&M LPs in 1968; they had led a very popular two-trombone quintet during 1954–56 before going their separate ways. This date is a bit commercial with a small string section and woodwinds utilized on five of the nine numbers. Still, the beautiful

tones of the co-leaders make this a worthwhile set with the highlights including "My Funny Valentine," "Israel," "St. James Infirmary" and "Django." —*Scott Yanow*

Yokohama Concert / Apr. 20, 1977 / Pablo ✦✦✦
Trombonist J.J. Johnson's first recording in eight years (he had spent much of the 1965–76 period working nearly full-time as an arranger/composer) is a live double-LP set with a quintet also including cornetist Nat Adderley, keyboardist Billy Childs, bassist Tony Dumas and drummer Kevin Johnson. Of the 11 songs, only four could be considered standards with "Walkin'" being the only piece not written by Johnson, Adderley or Dumas. The music is challenging and well-played if not overly exciting, but it did result in J.J. Johnson returning to a much busier schedule as a trombonist again. —*Scott Yanow*

Pinnacles / Sep. 17, 1979–Sep. 10, 1979 / Milestone ✦✦✦
After seven years off recording (1970–76), during which he worked full-time writing in the studios, trombonist J.J. Johnson began a successful "comeback" showing that he had lost none of his power or creativity through the years. For this LP (not yet reissued on CD), Johnson teams up on some selections with trumpeter Oscar Brashear and tenor saxophonist Joe Henderson, pianist Tommy Flanagan (who surprisingly plays electric keyboards on half of the selections), bassist Ron Carter and drummer Billy Higgins. Although not quite an essential set, J.J. Johnson is in excellent form on this date, and he contributes four originals; ironically "See See Rider" and "Mr. Clean" are actually the most memorable selections. —*Scott Yanow*

Concepts in Blue / Sep. 23, 1980–Sep. 26, 1980 / Original Jazz Classics ✦✦✦✦
This is a fun set of straight-ahead jazz. The colorful frontline (trombonist J.J. Johnson, fluegelhornist Clark Terry, and Ernie Watts on tenor and alto) obviously enjoyed playing the blues-oriented repertoire and the solos are consistently rewarding. Nothing all that innovative occurs, but the results are pleasing. —*Scott Yanow*

★ **Things Are Getting Better All the Time** / Nov. 28, 1983–Nov. 29, 1983 / Original Jazz Classics ✦✦✦✦✦
J.J. Johnson teams up with fellow trombonist Al Grey for a variety of superior standards and obscurities in a quintet with pianist Kenny Barron, bassist Ray Brown and drummer Mickey Roker. Reissued on CD, this session has many joyful moments, and the interaction between the two very different-sounding trombonists (Grey is hot, while Johnson is cool) on such tunes as "Soft Winds," "It's Only a Paper Moon," "Boy Meets Horn" and the title cut is consistently memorable and enjoyable. Recommended. —*Scott Yanow*

● **Quintergy: Live** / Jul. 1988 / Antilles ✦✦✦✦✦
Trombonist J.J. Johnson, 64 at the time, is heard in top form on this "Live at the Village Vanguard" set. His quintet, which includes Ralph Moore on tenor and soprano, pianist Stanley Cowell, bassist Rufus Reid and drummer Victor Lewis, is perfectly suited to interpret the spirited set of advanced bop. Highlights include Johson's feature on "You've Changed," "Coppin' the Bop," "Lament" and his unaccompanied playing on "It's All Right with Me." Excellent music. Another Antilles CD, *Standards*, comes from the same sessions. —*Scott Yanow*

● **Standards: Live at the Village** / Jul. 1988 / Antilles ✦✦✦✦✦
The second of two CDs coming from the same engagement at the Village Vanguard (the first was *Quintergy*), this set features trombonist J.J. Johnson's quintet with Ralph Moore on tenor and soprano, pianist Stanley Cowell, bassist Rufus Reid and drummer Victor Lewis jamming on nine standards, plus the leader's "Shortcake." Johnson is in top form, particularly on "My Funny Valentine," "Just Friends," "Misterioso" and "Autumn Leaves." A good example of the ageless trombonist's talents. —*Scott Yanow*

Vivian / Jun. 2, 1992–Jun. 3, 1992 / Concord Jazz ✦✦✦
The great trombonist J.J. Johnson sticks exclusively to ballads on this ten-song set. Accompanied by pianist Rob Schneiderman, guitarist Ted Dunbar, bassist Rufus Reid and drummer Akira Tana, Johnson's tone sounds at its warmest throughout the CD, which is dedicated to his late wife. Highlights include "Alone Together," "I Thought About You," "How Deep Is the Ocean" and "There Will Never Be Another You," but all of the numbers are rewarding. Due to the lack of variety in tempos and moods, this set is not quite definitive, but collectors will find much to enjoy. —*Scott Yanow*

Let's Hang Out / Dec. 1992 / Verve ✦✦✦✦
Forty-nine years after his recording debut, trombonist J.J. Johnson still sounds in peak form on this disc. Most of the numbers on his Verve CD find him accompanied by either Stanley Cowell or Renee Roenes on piano, bassist Rufus Reid and Victor Lewis or Lewis Nash on drums with occasional contributions from trumpeter Terence Blanchard (whose chops sound a little off) and Ralph Moore on tenor and soprano. In addition, tenor saxophonist Jimmy Heath makes a couple of guest appearances and "Beautiful Love" is taken by Johnson as an unaccompanied solo. Despite the strong supporting cast, the great trombonist is the star throughout, particularly on "It Never Entered My Mind," his "Kenya," "It's You or No One" and a tasteful quartet rendition of "I Got It Bad." Excellent music. —*Scott Yanow*

Tangence / Jul. 13, 1994–Jul. 15, 1994 / Gitanes ✦✦✦✦
Trombonist J.J. Johnson is joined by a string orchestra arranged by Robert Farnon for most of the performances on this CD. Farnon's sweeping scores can sometimes come closer to movie music and muzak than jazz, but the high quality of the songs and a few surprising departures make this CD recommended. Wynton Marsalis has three guest appearances (including a spirited unaccompanied duet with Johnson on the old Jimmy Lunceford hit "For Dancers Only"), Johnson takes his blues "Opus De Focus" as a duet with bassist Chris Laurence and the trombonist is in particularly fine form on such numbers as "The Meaning of the Blues," "Dinner for One, Please, James," "The Very Thought of You" and his own "Lament." —*Scott Yanow*

James P. Johnson

b. Feb. 1, 1894, New Brunswick, NJ, **d.** Nov. 17, 1955, New York, NY

Piano, Composer / Stride, Classic Jazz
One of the great jazz pianists of all time, James P. Johnson was the king of stride pianists in the 1920s. He began working in New York clubs as early as 1913 and was quickly recognized as the pacesetter. In 1917 Johnson began making piano rolls. Duke Ellington learned from these (by slowing them down to half-speed) and a few years later Johnson became Fats Waller's teacher and inspiration. During the 1920s (starting in 1921), James P. Johnson began to record, he was the nightly star at Harlem rent parties (accompanied by Waller and Willie "The Lion" Smith) and he wrote some of his most famous compositions. For the 1923 Broadway show *Running Wild* (one of his dozen scores), James P. composed "The Charleston" and "Old Fashioned Love," his earlier piano feature "Carolina Shout" became the test piece for other pianists and some of his other songs included "If I Could Be with You One Hour Tonight" and "A Porter's Love Song to a Chambermaid."

Ironically, James P. Johnson, the most sophisticated pianist of the 1920s, was also an expert accompanist for blues singers and he starred on several memorable Bessie Smith and Ethel Waters recordings. In addition to his solo recordings, Johnson led some hot combos on records and guested with Perry Bradford and Clarence Williams; he also shared the spotlight with Fats Waller on a few occasions. Because he was very interested in writing longer works, Johnson (who had composed "Yamekraw" in 1927) spent much of the 1930s working on such pieces as "Harlem Symphony," "Symphony in Brown" and a blues opera. Unfortunately, much of this music has been lost through the years. Johnson, who was only semiactive as a pianist throughout much of the 1930s, started recording again in 1939, often sat in with Eddie Condon and was active in the 1940s despite some minor strokes. A major stroke in 1951 finished off his career. Most of his recordings have been reissued on CD. —*Scott Yanow*

Carolina Shout / May 1917–Jun. 1925 / Biograph ✦✦✦
This CD contains 14 of James P. Johnson's piano rolls (cut during an eight-year period) mostly for the QRS company. Although piano rolls generally sound somewhat mechanical (particularly rhythmically), this set is not without interest. There is a version of "Carolina Shout" that originally inspired Duke Ellington and a highlight is a song that few remember that Johnson wrote and he never otherwise recorded, "The Charleston." —*Scott Yanow*

Yamekraw and Other Selections / Jan. 1921-1945 / Smithsonian/Folkways ✦✦✦
This is an odd but very interesting LP. The great pianist James P. Johnson is heard performing his lengthy "Yamekraw" in 1945, an orchestral work that he interprets here as an episodic solo piano

performance. On the flip side of the album there are four early recordings that singer/hustler Perry Bradford had something to do with. He sings "Sam Jones Done Snagged His Britches" (probably from the mid-'30s) and "Georgia's Always on My Mind" with the Gulf Coast Seven in 1928; in addition there are two early instrumentals ("That Thing Called Love" and "Shim-Me King's Blues") by Mamie Smith's Jazz Hounds from 1921. This LP is worth getting primarily for the rare James P. Johnson performance. —*Scott Yanow*

★ **Harlem Stride Piano** / Aug. 1921–Nov. 18, 1929 / Hot 'N Sweet ✦✦✦✦✦

This European import consists of the first 24 recordings led by the great stride pianist James P. Johnson plus the piano roll version of his hit "The Charleston." Many of these performances have been formerly issued in haphazard or incomplete fashion but this exciting CD has all of Johnson's dates up until his 1930 solos. There are three early band sides from 1921 (including Johnson's "Carolina Shout"), 13 piano solos ("Snowy Morning Blues," "Riffs" and "Feeling Blue" are particularly memorable) and hot combos that feature such sidemen as cornetists/trumpeters Louis Metcalfe, Cootie Williams and King Oliver and (on two songs) fellow pianist Fats Waller. The somewhat obscure CD is the perfect way to accumulate these historic performances. —*Scott Yanow*

Father of the Stride Piano / Oct. 18, 1921–Jun. 15, 1939 / Columbia ✦✦✦

This LP gives one a good all-round introduction into pianist James P. Johnson's music although it does not list the recording dates. There are piano solos from 1921, 1923, 1927 and 1939, a humorous vocal/piano duet with Clarence Williams ("How Could I Be Blue") and four selections from a 1939 septet session with trumpeter Red Allen and trombonist J.C. Higginbottham. Most of this music has since been reissued in more complete fashion on CD. —*Scott Yanow*

Giants of Jazz / Oct. 18, 1921–Apr. 1945 / Time Life ✦✦✦✦✦

This three-LP box set serves as a near-perfect retrospective of the music of the great stride pianist James P. Johnson. There are two piano solos from 1921 (including his famous "Carolina Shout"), numbers on which the pianist accompanied Bessie Smith and Ethel Waters, some heated combo sides, more classic piano solos (including "Riffs," "What Is This Thing Called Love?" and "Jingles"), jams with clarinetist Pee Wee Russell and trumpeter Frankie Newton and a generous amount of Johnson's 1943–45 performances. The accompanying booklet is definitive, making this a highly recommended set even for collectors who already have the majority of these exciting performances. —*Scott Yanow*

Watch Me Go / Nov. 1921–Oct. 22, 1941 / IAJRC ✦✦✦

This is a perfect LP for collectors for it features the great stride pianist James P. Johnson as an accompanist. Virtually all of the 18 recordings are obscure with the pianist heard backing such singers as Lavinia Turner, Sadie Jackson, Rosa Henderson, Clara Smith, Perry Bradford, Roy Evans, Chick Bullock, Clarence Williams (in 1941) and The Great Day New Orleans Singers. The music is not essential (particularly since Johnson is mostly confined to the background), but veteran collectors of '20s music will love this now-rare LP. —*Scott Yanow*

James P. Johnson & Perry Bradford / Dec. 5, 1921–Mar. 5, 1929 / Arcadia ✦✦✦✦✦

This collector's LP contains 16 consistently heated recordings from the 1920s. The masterful stride pianist James P. Johnson leads his "Harmony Eight" on two numbers from 1921 and is heard on all of his band sides from 1927–29; a special highpoint is his playing (along with fellow pianist Fats Waller) on "What's the Use of Being Alone?" from a session led by cornetist Johnny Dunn. Rounding out the rather exciting album are six selections that feature vocals by Perry Bradford, two of which offer early examples of the great cornetist Jabbo Smith. 1920s collectors should go out of their way to acquire this set. —*Scott Yanow*

James P. Johnson 1928–1931 / Mar. 27, 1928–Mar. 25, 1931 / Swaggie ✦✦✦✦

This very enjoyable LP from the Australian Swaggie label has more than its share of classic recordings. Pianist James P. Johnson combines with Fats Waller (on organ), cornetist Jabbo Smith and Garvin Bushell (who switches between clarinet, alto and bassoon) for four melodic selections that were released under the name of The Louisiana Sugar Babes. In addition Johnson has two piano solos, duets with fellow pianist Clarence Williams on "I've Found

a New Baby" and leads a variety of bands that feature vocals from Perry Bradford, Andy Razaf and the "Keep Shufflin' Trio"; among the soloists are trumpeters Cootie Williams, Ward Pinkett, Louis Metcalf and King Oliver. This is timeless music that is essential in one form or another; fortunately, much of it has already been reissued on CD. —*Scott Yanow*

★ **Snowy Morning Blues** / Jan. 21, 1930–Sep. 22, 1944 / GRP ✦✦✦✦✦

James P. Johnson was one of the greatest jazz pianists of all time and in the 1920s was considered the "king of the stride piano." This Decca reissue CD contains a great deal of valuable music. Johnson is first heard on four classic piano solos from 1930 ("You've Got to Be Modernistic" and "Jingles" are particularly memorable) and then on eight Fats Waller-associated tunes in duets with drummer Eddie Dougherty from 1944; the latter performances differ from the eight identical Waller songs that Johnson had recorded earlier in the same year as solos. Since Waller (who had passed away in 1943) was his close friend and former student, there is a lot of emotion in the tributes but also much joy. This highly recommended CD concludes with James P. Johnson romping on eight of his own timeless compositions including "Carolina Shout," "Old Fashioned Love" and "If I Could Be with You." —*Scott Yanow*

Original James P. Johnson / 1943–1945 / Smithsonian/Folkways ✦✦✦✦

The great stride pianist James P. Johnson is heard on 14 of the 16 selections included on this LP, taking memorable piano solos; two of the selections ("Memphis Blues" and the first take of "Sweet Lorraine") are actually by an uncredited Cliff Jackson. Despite that error, the music is recommended because Johnson is in top form throughout, particularly on such numbers as "Daintiness Rag," "Snowy Morning Blues," "Liza" and "The Dream." This LP will be a hard one to find. —*Scott Yanow*

Ain'tcha Got Music / Jun. 17, 1944–Aug. 1949 / Pumpkin ✦✦✦✦

Previously unreleased until this LP came out in 1986, these performances feature pianist James P. Johnson during his final period. Johnson takes the title cut unaccompanied, is heard as a guest at Eddie Condon concerts from 1944–47 and (best of all) has five lengthy selections as either solos or duets with drummer Danny Alvin in 1949, shortly before a major stroke put him permanently out of action. Historic value aside, Johnson is heard in prime form on such numbers as "If Dreams Come True," "Over the Waves" and the closing "Liza." This increasingly hard-to-find LP should be of great interest to fans of the innovative stride pianist. —*Scott Yanow*

Victory Stride / Feb. 1992+Jan. 1994 / Music Masters ✦✦✦

James P. Johnson passed away in 1955 and, although he gained fame as the top stride pianist of the 1920s, his ambitious major works were rarely ever performed. During the two years covered by this CD, several of Johnson's most extended suites (much of which was feared to have been lost) were recorded for the first time: "Victory Stride," the four-part "Harlem Symphony," "Concerto Jazz A Mine," the "American Symphonic Suite" and "Drums—A Symphonic Poem"; in addition, The Concordia Orchestra and pianist Leslie Stifelman play an extended version of Johnson's "The Charleston." The music, although technically outside of jazz, should greatly interest jazz collectors for these colorful performances cast new light on the talents of James P. Johnson. —*Scott Yanow*

Lonnie Johnson (Alonzo Johnson)

b. Feb. 8, 1889, New Orleans, LA, d. Jun. 16, 1970 Toronto, Canada

Guitar, Vocals / Blues, Classic Jazz

Lonnie Johnson spent most of his long career as a solo blues vocalist/guitarist, but in his early days he showed that, if he wanted to pursue it, he could have been one of the top jazz guitarists. Born in New Orleans, he played guitar and violin in Storyville. Johnson went up north by 1920, playing with Charlie Creath's band (with whom he would record in 1925) in St. Louis. In the 1920s in addition to his own solo recordings (which occasionally included some hot instrumentals), Johnson made notable appearances on records by Louis Armstrong's Hot Five and big band ("Hotter than That" finds him battling Armstrong), Duke Ellington, McKinney's Cotton Pickers, King Oliver and duets with his jazz counterpart (and only real competitor technique-wise) Eddie Lang who used the pseudonym Blind Willie Dunn.

However, by the 1930s Johnson was mostly sticking to the blues, emphasizing his smooth vocals. All of his many recordings (which include a Dixieland date in 1965 with Jimmy McHarg's Metro Stompers) are of interest to jazz listeners, but his work in the 1920s in particular makes one wonder "what if?" —*Scott Yanow*

★ **Steppin' on the Blues** / Nov. 4, 1925–Aug. 12, 1932 / Columbia/Legacy ✦✦✦✦✦
A fine collection of nineteen blues, ragtime and pop songs from one of the best guitarists, vocalists and composers around. —*Barry Lee Pearson*

He's a Jelly Roll Baker / Nov. 2, 1939–Dec. 14, 1944 / Bluebird ✦✦✦✦✦
This 20-song collection covers 1930s and '40s material in which Johnson primarily performs blues tunes, doing salty, sassy, mournful and suggestive numbers in a distinctive, memorable fashion. His vocals on "Rambler's Blues," "In Love Again," the title cut and several others are framed by brilliant, creative playing and excellent support from such pianists as Blind John Davis, Lil Hardin Armstrong and Joshua Altheimer. This is tight, intuitive music in which Johnson set the tone and dominated the songs. If you're unaware of Lonnie Johnson's brilliant blues material, here's an excellent introduction. —*Ron Wynn*

Blues By Lonnie / Mar. 8, 1960 / Original Blues Classics ✦✦✦✦

Blues & Ballads / Apr. 5, 1960 / Original Blues Classics ✦✦✦✦✦
Later Johnson, doing blues and ballads with jazz guitarist Elmer Snowden. Johnson's vocals are refined and sensitive. It is hard to hear him sing his own composition "I Found a Dream" and remain unmoved. Such a lovely album. —*Michael Erlewine*

● **Blues, Ballads & Jumpin' Jazz** / Apr. 5, 1960 / Original Blues Classics ✦✦✦✦✦
This is an unusual CD. In 1960 guitarists Lonnie Johnson and Elmer Snowden (along with bassist Wendell Marshall) teamed up for *Blues and Ballads*, which was primarily a showcase for Johnson's blues vocals. This previously unreleased set from the same session has six instrumentals and just four vocals with Snowden generally in the lead. The two guitarists are heard good-naturedly suggesting songs before launching into spontaneous improvisations and the results sound like an intimate concert. Highlights of this fun outing include "Lester Leaps In," "C-Jam Blues" and "Careless Love." —*Scott Yanow*

Idle Hours / Jul. 1961 / Original Blues Classics ✦✦✦✦

Another Night to Cry / Apr. 6, 1962 / Original Blues Classics ✦✦✦✦

Stompin' At The Penny / Nov. 1965 / Columbia/Legacy ✦✦✦✦

Marc Johnson

b. Oct. 21, 1953, Omaha, NE
Bass / Post-Bop
Marc Johnson gained his initial reputation as a member of Bill Evans' last rhythm section and his work with Bass Desires (a group featuring both Bill Frisell and John Scofield on guitars) showed off his versatility. While at North Texas State University, Johnson played with a group that included Lyle Mays. He was with Woody Herman's Orchestra (1977), Bill Evans (1978–80), Stan Getz (1981–82) and John Abercrombie (1983) before forming Bass Desires (1985). The latter group recorded two intriguing albums for ECM. In 1989 Marc Johnson made a series of duets with various all-stars for EmArcy and in 1993 he led the group Right Brain Patrol, a trio with guitarist Ben Monder and percussionist Arto Tunçboyaciyan that recorded for JMT. —*Scott Yanow*

★ **Bass Desires** / May 1985 / ECM ✦✦✦✦✦
Prime contemporary fusion with guitarists Bill Frisell and John Scofield. A worthy purchase. —*Michael G. Nastos*

Second Sight / Mar. 1987 / ECM ✦✦✦✦
Fine release from Bass Desires. A top modern unit that blends improvisatory, pop and rock components. —*Ron Wynn*

2 by 4 / Apr. 17, 1989–Apr. 18, 1989 / Verve ✦✦✦✦✦
Better than average tunes, excellent playing from Gary Burton (vib), Toots Thielemans (harmonica). —*Ron Wynn*

Right Brain Patrol / Sep. 1991–Nov. 1991 / JMT ✦✦✦

Pete Johnson

b. Mar. 25, 1904, Kansas City, MO, d. Mar. 23, 1967, Buffalo, NY
Piano / Boogie-Woogie, Blues
Pete Johnson was one of the three great boogie-woogie pianists

(along with Albert Ammons and Meade Lux Lewis) whose sudden prominence in the late '30s helped make the style very popular. Originally a drummer, Johnson switched to piano in 1922. He was part of the Kansas City scene in the 1920s and '30s, often accompanying singer Big Joe Turner. Producer John Hammond discovered him in 1936 and got him to play at the Famous Door in New York. After taking part at Hammond's 1938 *Spirituals to Swing* Carnegie Hall concert in 1938, Johnson started recording regularly and appeared on an occasional basis with Ammons and Lewis as the Boogie Woogie Trio. He also backed Turner on some classic records. Johnson recorded often in the 1940s and spent much of 1947–49 based in Los Angeles. He moved to Buffalo in 1950 and, other than an appearance at the 1958 Newport Jazz Festival, he was in obscurity for much of the decade. A stroke later in 1958 left him partly paralyzed. Johnson made one final appearance at John Hammond's January 1967 *Spirituals to Swing* concert, playing the right hand on a version of "Roll 'Em Pete" two months before his death. —*Scott Yanow*

● **Pete Johnson 1938–1939** / Dec. 30, 1938–Dec. 1939 / Classics ✦✦✦✦✦

☆ **The Pete Johnson/Earl Hines/Teddy Bunn Blue Note Sessions** / Jul. 29, 1939–Mar. 28, 1940 / Mosaic ✦✦✦✦✦

Central Avenue Boogie / Apr. 18, 1947–Nov. 29, 1947 / Delmark ✦✦✦
Boogie-woogie pianist Pete Johnson is in excellent form on these selections, but this complete reissue of his Apollo recordings does not have much meat. Johnson only cut eight sides for the label so three alternate takes are included plus two titles (and an alternate) from pianist Arnold Wiley's only Apollo session. The results are enjoyable (particularly Johnson's versions of "Margie" and "Swanee River") although few surprises or real highpoints occur. —*Scott Yanow*

Plas Johnson (John Johnson, Jr.)

b. Jul. 21, 1931, Donaldsonville, LA
Tenor Saxophone / Soul Jazz, Hard Bop
Plas Johnson's seductive tenor sound has been utilized on many studio sessions including most notably in the *Pink Panther* film (1963). A more versatile player than one might think, Johnson sounds equally at home in blues, R&Bish and hard bop settings. He recorded a single in New Orleans (1950), moved to Los Angeles and was quickly established as a popular studio musician. Johnson worked with Johnny Otis and Charles Brown, recorded dates as a leader for Tampa (1956–57), Score, Capitol (1958–60), Ava (1964) and Concord (1975–76), worked with the Capp-Pierce Juggernaut and toured with the Gene Harris Superband in 1990. —*Scott Yanow*

Bop Me Daddy / 1956–1957 / VSOP ✦✦✦
This LP (originally on the Tampa label) is subtitled "Rock 'N Roll Instrumentals," but is actually an R&B-flavored jazz album. Plas Johnson, whose tenor would be featured anonymously on many hit rock & roll and pop records, is joined by pianist Ray Johnson, bassist Duke Harris and drummer Sharky Hall for a variety of fairly basic melodies. Johnson plays quite melodically and with soul on such numbers as "Makin' Whoopee," "Blue Jean Shuffle" and "Last Call." The music on this LP is pleasing, if not all that essential. —*Scott Yanow*

● **The Blues** / Sep. 1975 / Concord Jazz ✦✦✦✦✦
Here is the veteran honking sax star in more conventional jazz setting. —*Ron Wynn*

Positively / May 1976 / Concord Jazz ✦✦✦✦
Good mainstream date with soul-jazz feel. —*Ron Wynn*

L.A. (1955) / 1983 / Carell Music ✦✦✦

Pete Jolly (Peter A. Ceragioli)

b. Jun. 5, 1932, New Haven, CT
Piano / Bop, Cool
A powerful pianist who came to fame on the West Coast in the 1950s, Pete Jolly has been a fixture in Los Angeles for over 40 years. He started on accordion when he was three and began piano when he was eight. He played his first jobs when he was 12. In 1946 his family moved to Phoenix and the following year he joined the Musicians Union and started working extensively in clubs. During a visit to Los Angeles in 1954, Jolly sat in the Lighthouse, which led to him joining Shorty Rogers' Giants (1954–56). He recorded three albums as a leader for Victor in 1956

(taking rare jazz accordion solos on a few tracks), worked with Buddy DeFranco, Terry Gibbs, Richie Kamuca, Chet Baker and Art Pepper among others in the late '50s and had a surprise hit with "Little Bird" in 1963. Jolly became a busy studio musician in the 1960s, but has led his trio with bassist Chuck Berghofer and drummer Nick Martinis regularly in local clubs for over 30 years. In addition to RCA, Pete Jolly has recorded for Metrojazz, MGM, Ava, Charlie Parker Records, Columbia, A&M, Atlas, Holt and VSOP as a leader. — *Scott Yanow*

The Red Chimney And Sherry's Bar Recordings / Oct. 11, 1960–Feb. 27, 1965 / VSOP ✦✦✦
Released for the first time in 1994, these straight-ahead performances are the earliest live recordings by the Pete Jolly Trio. With either Ralph Pena or Chuck Berghofer on bass and drummer Nick Martinis playing on most of the selections, Jolly is in typically exuberant form on a variety of jazz standards including "Oleo," a lengthy "Falling in Love with Love," a humorous "Blues in the Closet" and even "Whistle While You Work." The one flaw to this set is that the noise from the crowd is occasionally distracting, making it advisable to acquire some of Pete Jolly's studio recordings first. — *Scott Yanow*

Little Bird / Nov. 1962+Jan. 1963 / VSOP ✦✦✦
This LP reissue of a release from the obsolete Ava label brings back a hit record. Pianist Pete Jolly, his trio (with bassist Chuck Berghofer and drummer Larry Bunker) and guests (guitarist Howard Roberts and percussionist Kenny Hume) play mostly standards, but it is Jolly's version of the catchy "Little Bird" that caught on. This is a fine all-around straight-ahead session (highlighted by "Never Never Land," "Spring Can Really Hang You Up the Most" and "Falling in Love with Love") that deserves to be reissued on CD eventually. — *Scott Yanow*

Pete Jolly Trio and Friends / Nov. 1962–Aug. 1964 / VSOP ✦✦✦
This CD contains selections taken from pianist Pete Jolly's three mid-'60s LPs for Ava. Although it would have been preferable to have all of the music complete, this is a fine all-round sampler. The talented bop-based pianist is joined by bassist Chuck Berghofer, guitarist Howard Roberts, either Larry Bunker or Nick Martinis on drums and, on seven of the 16 selections, a string orchestra. All but five of the performances are under 3 1/2 minutes and, although those are enjoyable enough, it is Jolly's longer explorations ("Falling in Love with Love," "Alone Together," "No Other Love," "Can't We Be Friends" and "I'm Beginning to See the Light") that are most memorable. This CD serves as a good introduction to Pete Jolly's fine playing. — *Scott Yanow*

Gems / 1990 / Holt ✦✦✦

● **Yours Truly** / 1993 / Bainbridge ✦✦✦✦
Pete Jolly and his longtime sidemen (Chuck Berghofer has been his regular bassist since the late '50s while drummer Nick Martinis joined up in 1964) perform 11 standards plus his old hit "Little Bird" on this fine outing. The virtuosic pianist dominates the ensembles, but the contributions of Berghofer And Martinis (who have to think fast to keep up with him) should not be overlooked. Jolly's total command of the piano and infectious enthusiasm, which can result in some explosive outbursts, do not overshadow his good taste and the self-restraint that he shows on the ballads. — *Scott Yanow*

Bobby Jones

b. Oct. 30, 1928, Louisville, KY, d. Mar. 6, 1980, Munich, Germany
Flute, Tenor Saxophone / Hard Bop
A minor figure best-known for his association with Charles Mingus in the early '70s, Bobby Jones was a talented tenor saxophonist with a versatile style. He struggled in the musical minor leagues for a long time, playing with the Glenn Miller ghost band (1959), a few months with Woody Herman (1963) and for a short while clarinet with Jack Teagarden. Jones played well with Mingus (1970–72) and recorded albums as a leader for Cobblestone (1972) and Enja (1974), doubling on tenor and clarinet for the latter. He settled in Munich but his emphysema forced him to stop playing and concentrate on arranging before cutting short his life. — *Scott Yanow*

● **Legacy of Bobby Jones** / Jul. 12, 1972 / Muse ✦✦✦✦
Hill Country Suite / Aug. 30, 1974 / Enja ✦✦✦
A solid, underrated saxophonist throughout his career, Bobby Jones didn't make a lot of records, but this was a fine one. It's a simple hard bop and mainstream session from '72, with Jones

playing furiously on tenor and occasionally flute, while driving a competent band that deferred to him on this date. — *Ron Wynn*

Carmell Jones (William Carmell Jones)

b. Jul. 19, 1936, Kansas City, KS
Trumpet / Hard Bop
An excellent hard bop trumpeter, Carmell Jones would probably be much better-known today if he had not moved to Europe in the mid-'60s at the height of his career. After military service and two years at the University of Kansas, Carmell Jones led a band in Kansas City (1959). The next year he moved to Los Angeles where he recorded a couple of albums as a leader for Pacific Jazz and made records with Bud Shank, Harold Land, Curtis Amy and, most significantly, Gerald Wilson's Orchestra (1961–63). Jones toured with Horace Silver for a year (1964–65), recording the original version of "Song for My Father" with Silver before moving to Berlin. Although quite active in Europe, Carmell Jones was largely forgotten by the time he moved back to Kansas City in 1980, although a 1982 album for Revelation helped remind a few listeners how good he still was. — *Scott Yanow*

● **The Remarkable Carmell Jones** / Jun. 1961 / Pacific Jazz ✦✦✦✦✦
The Remarkable Carmell Jones was the debut for this trumpeter and found him in the strong company of Harold Land (tenor sax), Frank Strazzeri (piano), Gary Peacock (bass) and Leon Pettis (drums) for six tracks. This was an unspectacular whole with some very nice parts in its program and solos. — *Bob Rusch, Cadence*

Dill Jones

b. Aug. 19, 1923, Newcastle Emlyn, Wales, d. Jan. 22, 1984, New York, NY
Piano / Stride
An excellent if now somewhat forgotten stride pianist, Dill Jones was born in Wales, studied piano in London and played with Humphrey Lyttelton (1947–48). He led his own trio and worked in the studios and on radio in London during the 1950s. In 1961 Jones moved to New York where he played regularly at Condon's, Ryan's and the Metropole with such players as Yank Lawson, Max Kaminsky, Roy Eldridge, Bob Wilber, Jimmy McPartland and Gene Krupa, fitting right in with the Condon gang. Jones teamed up with Budd Johnson in the JPJ Quartet (1969–74), recorded a solo tribute to Bix Beiderbecke for Chiaroscuro (1972) and worked with the Countsmen and the Harlem Blues and Jazz Band. — *Scott Yanow*

Elvin Jones

b. Sep. 9, 1927, Pontiac, MI
Drums / Avant-Garde, Post-Bop, Hard Bop
Elvin Jones will always be best-known for his association with the classic John Coltrane Quartet (1960–65), but he has also had a notable career as a bandleader and has continued being a major influence during the past 30 years. One of the all-time great drummers (bridging the gap between advanced hard bop and the avant-garde), Elvin is the younger brother of a remarkable musical family that also includes Hank and Thad Jones. After spending time in the Army (1946–49), he was a part of the very fertile Detroit jazz scene of the early '50s. He moved to New York in 1955, worked with Teddy Charles and the Bud Powell Trio and recorded with Miles Davis and Sonny Rollins (the latter at his famous Village Vanguard session). After stints with J.J. Johnson (1956–57), Donald Byrd (1958), Tyree Glenn and Harry "Sweets" Edison, Elvin Jones became an important member of John Coltrane's Quartet, pushing the innovative saxophonist to remarkable heights and appearing on most of his best recordings. When Coltrane added Rashied Ali to his band in late 1965 as second drummer, Jones was not pleased and he soon departed. He went on a European tour with the Duke Ellington Orchestra and then started leading his own groups, which, in the 1990s, became known as Elvin Jones' Jazz Machine. Among his sidemen have been saxophonists Frank Foster, Joe Farrell, George Coleman, Pepper Adams, Dave Liebman, Pat LaBarbera, Steve Grossman, Andrew White, Ravi Coltrane and Sonny Fortune, trumpeter Nicholas Payton, pianists Dollar Brand and Willie Pickens, keyboardist Jan Hammer and bassists Richard Davis, Jimmy Garrison, Wilbur Little and Gene Perla among others. Elvin Jones has recorded as a leader for many labels including Atlantic, Riverside, Impulse, Blue Note, Enja, PM, Vanguard, Honey Dew, Denon, Storyville, Evidence and Landmark. — *Scott Yanow*

Elvin! / Jul. 11, 1961–Jan. 3, 1962 / Original Jazz Classics ✦✦✦✦
Drummer Elvin Jones' first full-length album as a leader (reissued on CD in the OJC series) is different than one would expect when it is taken into consideration that he was a member of the fiery John Coltrane Quartet at the time. This sextet session, which also includes his brothers Thad and Hank on cornet and piano in addition to flutist Frank Wess, Frank Foster on tenor and bassist Art Davis, is straight-ahead with a strong Count Basie feel. Elvin is still recognizable on the fairly obscure material (only "You Are Too Beautiful" qualifies as a standard) and shows that he can cook in the fairly conventional setting. All of the musicians are in fine form and two selections feature the rhythm section as a trio. —*Scott Yanow*

Illumination / Aug. 8, 1963 / Impulse! ✦✦✦✦✦
Sextet with Jimmy Garrison (b), Prince Lasha (as), Sonny Simmons (as), Charles Davis (bar sax) and McCoy Tyner (p). All originals in progressive stance. A jewel. —*Michael G. Nastos*

Dear John C. / Feb. 1965 / GRP/Impulse! ✦✦✦
Drummer Elvin Jones may have been breaking down new rhythmic boundaries at the time with John Coltrane's Quartet, but his own sessions as a leader were not all that innovative. This quartet set with altoist Charlie Mariano, bassist Richard Davis and either Roland Hanna or Hank Jones on piano is an example of how the avant-garde of the era was starting to influence the more mainstream players. The music is, in general, safe but enjoyable with the virtuosic bassist Richard Davis often taking solo honors on what was in reality a modern bop date. —*Scott Yanow*

Heavy Sounds / 1968 / MCA/Impulse! ✦✦✦
One of Elvin Jones lesser-touted albums. A good session co-led by strong bassist Richard Davis. —*Ron Wynn*

Puttin' It Together / Apr. 8, 1968 / Blue Note ✦✦✦✦
Solid pianoless trio date, Joe Farrell handles heavy reed load. Jimmy Garrison on bass. —*Ron Wynn*

The Ultimate Elvin Jones / Sep. 6, 1968 / Blue Note ✦✦✦✦✦
This is one of Joe Farrell's finest recordings. Switching between tenor, soprano and flute, Farrell had to be good because he was joined in the pianoless trio by bassist Jimmy Garrison and drummer Elvin Jones. The group performs two standards, three Garrison originals and one by Farrell; it is a tossup as to who takes honors. Farrell is in consistently creative form, but Garrison's occasional solos and Jones' polyrhythmic accompaniment are also noteworthy. This LP is long overdue to reappear on CD. —*Scott Yanow*

The Prime Element / Mar. 14, 1969–Jul. 26, 1973 / Blue Note ✦✦✦✦
This two-LP set consists of a pair of unrelated Elvin Jones Blue Note sessions that had not been previously released. The earlier date features Jones in a septet with the tenors of George Coleman and Joe Farrell along with trumpeter Lee Morgan, while the 1973 album has an 11-piece group that includes a large rhythm section, baritonist Pepper Adams and the tenors of Steve Grossman and Frank Foster. The challenging modal material (an extension of John Coltrane's music of the early '60s) and diverse soloists make this two-fer into a rather stimulating listen. —*Scott Yanow*

Poly-Currents / Sep. 26, 1969 / Blue Note ✦✦✦✦
1986 reissue of Blue Note release. W/ horn players Joe Farrell, Pepper Adams, George Coleman. Farrell plays English horn on one cut. —*Ron Wynn*

Mr. Jones / Sep. 26, 1969–Jul. 13, 1972 / Blue Note ✦✦✦✦

Coalition / Jul. 17, 1970 / Blue Note ✦✦✦✦

Merry-Go-Round / Dec. 15, 1971 / Blue Note ✦✦✦
A big 11-piece dynamic sound. —*Ron Wynn*

Genesis / 1971 / Blue Note ✦✦✦✦
Often magnificent; three-horn frontline. —*Michael G. Nastos*

★ **Live at the Lighthouse, Vol. 1** / Sep. 9, 1972 / Blue Note ✦✦✦✦✦
Originally solid twin-record set reissued in separate versions. Strong quartet with saxmen Steve Grossman, Dave Liebman. CD has two bonus cuts. —*Ron Wynn*

☆ **Live at the Lighthouse, Vol. 2** / Sep. 9, 1972 / Blue Note ✦✦✦✦✦
Second volume of dynamic Lighthouse set. CD has three bonus cuts. —*Ron Wynn*

New Agenda / 1975 / Vanguard ✦✦✦

Elvin Jones Is on the Mountain / 1975 / PM ✦✦✦

Elvin Jones Live at the Town Hall / May 1976 / PM ✦✦✦✦
Elvin Jones Live was taken from a John Coltrane Memorial

Concert performed at New York's Town Hall, Sept. 12, 1971 and featured his group at that time, Frank Foster on soprano and tenor saxes, Chick Corea's piano, Joe Farrell's sax and flute and Gene Perla's bass on two extended compositions...This was five strong individual artists giving exceptionally of themselves, bringing forth a record where the dynamics of the whole were equal to the sum of the parts, making for an exceptional and truly beautiful record. —*Bob Rusch, Cadence*

Summit Meeting / Nov. 18, 1976 / Vanguard ✦✦✦✦
These are some top-shelf sessions w/ James Moody (sax), Clark Terry (tpt). —*Ron Wynn*

Time Capsule / 1977 / Vanguard ✦✦✦

Remembrance / Feb. 3, 1978–Feb. 5, 1978 / MPS ✦✦✦✦
The Elvin Jones Jazz Machine has frequently featured hard-toned tenors who improvise in a style influenced by John Coltrane, modal originals and high-powered performances in which the drummer/leader can push his sidemen. This MPS set is no exception. Pat LaBarbera and Michael Stuart double on tenors and sopranos, guitarist Roland Prince offers a contrasting solo voice and all of the material is obscure with four of the seven songs penned by LaBarbera. It's an excellent if somewhat lesser-known outing. —*Scott Yanow*

Very R.A.R.E. / Apr. 1978–Jun. 20, 1978 / Evidence ✦✦✦
Dynamic drummer Elvin Jones led two different units on the eight selections featured on this disc of late '70s material. The first six were done in New York during 1978 and include Jones spearheading a great band with Art Pepper on three selections, backed by outstanding bassist Richard Davis and fine pianist Roland Hanna. This is first-rate quartet material with Pepper surging and the trio challenging him, then contrasting and complementing his solos with their own great work. The other two cuts were recorded in Tokyo and issued on a previous release. They include a turbulent, often evocative version of "A Love Supreme," a 26-minute-plus tribute with Jones driving the band. The music is not as special as the title indicates, but is well worth hearing. —*Ron Wynn*

Heart to Heart / Aug. 1980 / Denon ✦✦✦✦
Exemplary material, superb Tommy Flanagan (p). —*Ron Wynn*

Earth Jones / Feb. 10, 1982 / Palo Alto ✦✦✦
An early '80s album by drummer Elvin Jones for the now defunct Palo Alto label. The album's highlights are some relentless, spiraling solos from Jones; otherwise, it's a routine, straight-ahead date with decent but basic arrangements and compositions. —*Ron Wynn*

Reunited / 1982 / Blackhawk ✦✦✦✦
McCoy Tyner (p) and Elvin together again; Pharoah Sanders (sax) plus intriguing guitar from Jean-Paul Bourelly. —*Ron Wynn*

The Elvin Jones Jazz Machine in Europe / Jun. 23, 1991 / Enja ✦✦✦✦✦

Youngblood / 1992 / Enja ✦✦✦✦✦

★ **It Don't Mean A Thing** / Oct. 18, 1993–Oct. 19, 1993 / Enja ✦✦✦✦✦
Elvin Jones has participated in many recording sessions through the years, but this CD is one of the most well-rounded sets he has ever led. The lineup of musicians is very impressive: trumpeter Nicholas Payton, Sonny Fortune on tenor and flute, trombonist Delfeayo Marsalis, pianist Willie Pickens, bassist Cecil McBee and vocalist Kevin Mahogany. Everyone plays up to their potential and the material has plenty of variety, ranging from Monk, Ellington and Strayhorn to a traditional Japanese folk song arranged by Elvin's wife Keiko ("A Lullaby of Itsugo Village"), two features for Mahogany (a touching version of "Lush Life" and his scat-filled "Bopsy") and some authentic-sounding R&B (Sam Cooke's "A Change Is Gonna Come"). Payton, Marsalis And Fortune are not on every selection, but each have their chance to shine while pianist Willie Pickens is showcased with the trio on a medley of "A Flower Is a Lovesome Thing" and "Ask Me Now." And as for the drummer, there is still no one around who has captured the sound and spirit of Elvin Jones. —*Scott Yanow*

Etta Jones

b. Nov. 25, 1928, Aiken, SC
Vocals / Standards
An excellent singer who is always worth hearing, Etta Jones grew up in New York and at 16 toured with Buddy Johnson. She debuted on record with Barney Bigard's pickup band (1944) for

Black & White, singing four Leonard Feather songs, three of which (including "Evil Gal Blues") were hits for Dinah Washington. She recorded other songs during 1946-47 for RCA and worked with Earl Hines (1949-52). Jones' version of "Don't Go to Strangers" (1960) was a hit and she made many albums for Prestige during 1960-65. Jones toured Japan with Art Blakey (1970), but was largely off record during 1966-75. However, starting in 1976 Etta Jones began recording regularly for Muse, often with her husband, the fine tenor saxophonist Houston Person. —*Scott Yanow*

● **Don't Go to Strangers** / Jun. 21, 1960 / Original Jazz Classics ◆◆◆◆◆
Etta Jones had been on the jazz scene for over a decade when she recorded this Prestige set (which has been reissued on CD in the OJC series), but it was this album that gave her a breakthrough, specifically the memorable song "Don't Go to Strangers." Actually, Jones is in superb form throughout the other nine songs too, mixing together the dramatic ability of Abbey Lincoln and some of the expressive qualities of Billie Holiday in the 1950s. With perfectly suitable accompaniment from Frank Wess (doubling on flute and tenor), pianist Richard Wyands, guitarist Skeeter Best, bassist George Duvivier and drummer Roy Haynes, Etta Jones is heard at her early peak on "Yes Sir, That's My Baby" (a warhorse that she greatly uplifts), "Fine and Mellow," "If I Had You" and "Bye Bye Blackbird." —*Scott Yanow*

Something Nice / Sep. 16, 1960-Mar. 30, 1961 / Original Jazz Classics ◆◆◆◆
An excellent reissue of some prime cuts with Oliver Nelson (reeds) and Roy Haynes (drums) from 1960 and 1961. —*Ron Wynn*

Lonely and Blue / Apr. 6, 1962-May 4, 1962 / Original Jazz Classics ◆◆◆
Singer Etta Jones often recalls late-period Billie Holiday and Dinah Washington on her CD reissue. The first 11 songs find her accompanied by tenor saxophonist Budd Johnson on four of the songs, guitarist Wally Richardson on seven and the Patti Bown Trio throughout; the final three numbers (bonus tracks), are actually from a date led by tenor-great Gene Ammons and are among the highlights of this set. But overall, despite some fine performances (particularly "You Don't Know My Mind" and "Trav'lin Light"), Jones' lack of individuality at that point in time makes this CD of less importance than her later sets for Muse. —*Scott Yanow*

Ms. Jones to You / Jan. 7, 1976 / Muse ◆◆◆◆
My Mother's Eyes / Jun. 23, 1977 / Muse ◆◆◆◆
Fine and Mellow / 1987 / Muse ◆◆◆◆
With fine sax from Houston Person. —*Ron Wynn*
I'll Be Seeing You / Sep. 1987 / Muse ◆◆◆◆
W/ good Houston Person tenor sax cuts. Originally recorded on September 23, 1987. —*Ron Wynn*
Sugar / Oct. 18, 1989+Oct. 30, 1989 / Muse ◆◆◆
Nice (though limited) soul-jazz and light-swing cuts. Recorded in October, 1989. —*Ron Wynn*
Reverse the Charges / Sep. 19, 1991-Jan. 1991 / Muse ◆◆◆◆
At Last / Apr. 21, 1995+Feb. 1995 / Muse ◆◆◆◆

Hank Jones

b. Jul. 31, 1918, Vicksburg, MS
Piano / Bop, Swing
The oldest of the three illustrious Jones brothers (which include Thad and Elvin), Hank Jones was also the first of the great Detroit pianists (including Tommy Flanagan, Barry Harris and Roland Hanna) to emerge after World War II although by then he had long since left town. Jones played in territory bands while a teenager and in 1944 he moved to New York to play with Hot Lips Page. He had stints with John Kirby, Howard McGhee, Coleman Hawkins, Andy Kirk and Billy Eckstine. Influenced by Teddy Wilson and Art Tatum, Jones' style was also open to bebop and his accessible playing was flexible enough to fit into many genres. He was on several Jazz at the Philharmonic tours (starting in 1947), worked as accompanist for Ella Fitzgerald (1948-53) and recorded with Charlie Parker. In the 1950s Jones performed in Artie Shaw, Benny Goodman, Lester Young, Cannonball Adderley and many others. He was on the staff of CBS during 1959-1976 but always remained active in jazz. In the late '70s Jones was the pianist in the Broadway musical *Ain't Misbehavin'* and he record-

ed with a pickup unit dubbed the Great Jazz Trio which, at various times, includes Ron Carter, Buster Williams or Eddie Gomez on bass and Tony Williams, Al Foster or Jimmy Cobb on drums. Among the many labels that Hank Jones has recorded for as a leader are Verve, Savoy, Epic, Golden Crest, Capitol, Argo, ABC-Paramount, Impulse, Concord, East Wind, Muse, Galaxy, Black & Blue, MPS, Inner City and Chiaroscuro. —*Scott Yanow*

Bluebird / Nov. 1, 1955-Dec. 20, 1955 / Savoy ◆◆◆◆
These relaxed cool jazz performances feature pianist Hank Jones in a variety of settings. In addition to drummer Kenny Clarke and either Eddie Jones or Wendell Marshall on bass, "Hank's Pranks" has both Donald Byrd and Manny Dice on trumpets, trumpeter Joe Wilder and flutist Herbie Mann are on a song apiece and Jerome Richardson (doubling on flute and tenor) drops by for two. It's a tasteful set of melodic bop. —*Scott Yanow*

Jones-Brown-Smith / 1974 / Concord Jazz ◆◆◆

Hanky Panky / Jul. 14, 1975-Jul. 15, 1975 / Inner City ◆◆◆
Mid-'70s session from an extremely busy period in pianist Hank Jones' career. He was juggling recording dates at four studios, working with various bassists and drummers and making immaculate trio dates like this one. Everything, from the nicely crafted openings and transitions to his skillful solos and pace, is the work of a genuine master. —*Ron Wynn*

● **Solo Piano** / Jan. 24, 1976 / All Art Jazz ◆◆◆◆◆
One of Hank Jones' finest solo sessions, this date (recorded in Tokyo but recently reissued on CD through an association with the Jazz Alliance label) finds the veteran pianist performing seven Duke Ellington ballads and seven other fairly well-known standards. The music is melodic, sometimes exquisite and full of subtle twists and turns. It is worth picking up as an example of Hank Jones' tasteful and very musical style. —*Scott Yanow*

Bop Redux / Jan. 18, 1977-Jan. 19, 1977 / Muse ◆◆◆◆
Veteran pianist Hank Jones teams up with bassist George Duvivier and drummer Ben Riley for a set of high-quality explorations of eight bop standards; four apiece by Charlie Parker and Thelonious Monk. Jones is sensitive on the ballads and lightly but firmly swinging on the more uptempo material. Typically tasteful performances come from one of the greats. —*Scott Yanow*

Great Jazz Trio at the Village Vanguard / Feb. 19, 1977+Feb. 20, 1977 / Inner City ◆◆◆◆◆
The name "Great Jazz Trio" is not an overstatement when being applied to a group comprised of pianist Hank Jones, bassist Ron Carter and drummer Tony Williams. The all-stars really dig into "Moose the Mooche," "Naima," Claus Ogerman's "Favors" and the Ron Carter blues "12+12." It is a pleasure to hear Williams pushing Jones to come up with some of his most fiery recent playing. —*Scott Yanow*

Just for Fun / Jun. 27, 1977-Jun. 28, 1977 / Original Jazz Classics ◆◆◆◆
Includes some good working by this always-insightful, creative soloist. —*Michael G. Nastos*

Tiptoe Tapdance / Jun. 29, 1977-Jan. 21, 1978 / Original Jazz Classics ◆◆◆
Originally on the Galaxy label, this CD reissue is a rare solo outing by pianist Hank Jones. The emphasis is on ballads and his treatments of these songs (which include three religious pieces) are respectful, melodic and lightly swinging. There is not much variety here, but the music (within its limitations) is enjoyable. —*Scott Yanow*

Have You Met This Jones? / Aug. 1, 1977-Aug. 2, 1977 / MPS ◆◆◆

Groovin' High / Jan. 25, 1978 / Muse ◆◆◆◆
Nicely phrased and played, mellow and memorable. —*Ron Wynn*

I Remember You / Jul. 28, 1978 / Black & Blue ◆◆◆◆
Bluesette / Jul. 1978+Jul. 1979 / Black & Blue ◆◆◆
Ain't Misbehavin' / Aug. 5, 1978-Aug. 6, 1978 / Galaxy ◆◆◆
Hank Jones paying his tribute to Waller. —*Ron Wynn*
In Japan / May 2, 1979 / All Art Jazz ◆◆◆◆
1991 reissue of excellent live trio take. —*Michael G. Nastos*
The Oracle / Mar. 1989 / EmArcy ◆◆◆◆◆
With Dave Holland, Billy Higgins. Includes three different generations of jazzmen. A very nice album. —*Michael G. Nastos*
Lazy Afternoon / Jul. 1989 / Concord Jazz ◆◆◆◆
Strong mainstream date, some spry Jones solos. —*Ron Wynn*

★ **Live at Maybeck Recital Hall, Vol. 16** / Nov. 11, 1991 / Concord Jazz ✦✦✦✦✦
A high point in the career of distinguished pianist Hank Jones was being among the artists tabbed for a solo release in the Maybeck series. While he's always been known as a great accompanist and good trio contributor, his solo skills have sometimes been undervalued. But after hearing him work in this unaccompanied setting, there should be no doubt that Hank Jones is a superb soloist, along with all his other talents. *—Ron Wynn*

Rockin' in Rhythm / Mar. 6, 1992 / Concord Jazz ✦✦✦✦
Superb trio music despite a conservative menu. *—Ron Wynn*

Handful of Keys / Apr. 28, 1992–Apr. 29, 1992 / Verve ✦✦✦✦
There are a playfulness and charm underneath Jones' solos that repeatedly surface throughout his excellent renditions on this disc dedicated to Fats Waller's music. While 10 of the 16 songs are Waller compositions, those that aren't, like "How Come You Do Me Like You Do" and "Your Feet's Too Big," are closely identified with him. Jones' flourishes, expert handling of stride rhythms and delicate but skillful reworkings not only capture the flavor Waller brought to such songs as "Ain't Misbehavin'," "Honeysuckle Rose" and the title track, but add his character to them with tricky phrases, quick melodies and nimble lines. *—Ron Wynn*

Isham Jones

b. Jan. 31, 1894, Coalton, IA, d. Oct. 19, 1956, Hollywood, FL
Composer, Leader / Classic Jazz, Standards
Isham Jones led and broke up several bands during the 1920s and '30s, but his greatest legacy is as a songwriter, having composed "It Had to Be You," "On the Alamo," "I'll See You in My Dreams," "The One I Love Belongs to Somebody Else" and "There Is No Greater Love" among others. Although he was originally a saxophonist and pianist, Isham Jones did not take any real solos with his bands. In the early '20s his outfit featured trumpeter Louis Panico, a pretty good soloist for 1921. Jones recorded prolifically during 1920–27 with most selections being jazz-oriented dance band performances. While his 1929–32 recordings are more commercial, the musicianship is high and the melodic renditions are not without interest. Jones' 1932–36 big band became the nucleus of the first Woody Herman Orchestra when Isham Jones decided to temporarily retire. He had another band in 1937 and recorded as late as 1947, but it is for his songs that he will always be remembered. *—Scott Yanow*

Jimmy Jones

b. Dec. 30, 1918, Memphis, TN, d. Apr. 29, 1982, Burbank, CA
Piano, Arranger / Swing
An unusual piano stylist (who sometimes played complex block chords) and a masterful accompanist for singers, Jimmy Jones had his first important job playing and recording with Stuff Smith (1943–45). After working with J.C. Heard (1946–47) he was Sarah Vaughan's pianist (1947–52 and 1954–58) with a two-year illness separating his two long stints. Jones recorded often throughout the 1950s including "How Hi the Fi" (1954) with Buck Clayton. He worked with Duke Ellington on the 1963 show *My People*, accompanied Ella Fitzgerald (1967–68) and wrote for the studios. In addition to obscure dates as a leader for Sesion, HRS, Wax, Swing and GNP and sessions with Stuff Smith, J.C. Heard, Sarah Vaughan and Ella, Jimmy Jones appeared as a sideman on recordings led by many swing all-stars including Don Byas, Coleman Hawkins, Ben Webster, Johnny Hodges, Clark Terry and Paul Gonsalves. *—Scott Yanow*

Jo Jones

b. Oct. 7, 1911, Chicago, IL, d. Sep. 3, 1985, New York, NY
Drums / Swing
Jo Jones shifted the timekeeping role of the drums from the bass drum to the hi-hat cymbal, greatly influencing all swing and bop drummers. Buddy Rich and Louie Bellson were just two who learned from his light but forceful playing, as Jones swung the Count Basie Orchestra with just the right accents and sounds. After growing up in Alabama, Jones worked as a drummer and tap-dancer with carnival shows. He joined Walter Page's Blue Devils in Oklahoma City in the late '20s. After a period with Lloyd Hunter's band in Nebraska, Jones moved to Kansas City in 1933, joining Count Basie's band the following year. He went with Basie to New York in 1936 and with Count, Freddie Green and Walter Page he formed one of the great rhythm sections. Jones was with

the Basie band (other than 1944–46 when he was in the military) until 1948 and in later years he participated in many reunions with Basie alumni. He was on some Jazz at the Philharmonic tours and recorded in the 1950s with Illinois Jacquet, Billie Holiday, Teddy Wilson, Lester Young, Art Tatum and Duke Ellington among others; Jones appeared at the 1957 Newport Jazz Festival with both Basie and the Coleman Hawkins-Roy Eldridge Sextet. Jo Jones led sessions for Vanguard (1955 and 1959) and Everest (1959–60), a date for Jazz Odyssey on which he reminisced and played drum solos (1970) and mid-'70s sessions for Pablo and Denon. In later years, he was known as "Papa" Jo Jones and thought of as a wise, if brutally frank, elder statesman. *—Scott Yanow*

★ **The Essential Jo Jones** / Aug. 11, 1955–Apr. 30, 1958 / Vanguard ✦✦✦✦✦

Jo Jones Trio / 1959 / Fresh Sound ✦✦✦✦

The Main Man / Nov. 29, 1976–Nov. 30, 1976 / Original Jazz Classics ✦✦✦✦
This date with Harry Edison (tpt), Roy Eldridge (tpt), Vic Dickerson (tb) and others is sterling silver. *—Michael G. Nastos*

Our Man Papa Jo! / Dec. 12, 1977 / Denon ✦✦✦
The final session for a jazz legend. Drummer Jo Jones was nearing the end when he got together with his old friends, pianist Hank Jones and bassist Major Holley, for this 1982 session. He still managed to play with some degree of authority and anchor the rhythm section, while saxophonist Jimmy Oliver and Jones took care of solo responsibilites. This has been reissued on CD. *—Ron Wynn*

Jonah Jones (Robert Elliott Jones)

b. Dec. 31, 1909, Louisville, KY
Trumpet / Swing, Dixieland
A talented and flashy trumpeter, Jonah Jones hit upon a formula in 1955 that made him a major attraction for a decade; playing concise versions of melodic swing standards and show tunes muted with a quartet. But although the nonjazz audience discovered Jones during the late '50s, he had already been a very vital trumpeter for two decades. Jonah Jones started out playing on a Mississippi riverboat in the 1920s. He freelanced in the Midwest (including with Horace Henderson), was briefly with Jimmie Lunceford (1931), had an early stint with Stuff Smith (1932–34) and then spent time with Lil Armstrong's short-lived orchestra and the declining McKinney's Cotton Pickers. Jones became famous for his playing with Stuff Smith's Onyx club band (1936–40), recording many exciting solos. He gigged with Benny Carter and Fletcher Henderson and became a star soloist with Cab Calloway (1941–52), staying with the singer even after his big band became a combo. Jones played Dixieland with Earl Hines (1952–53), toured Europe in 1954 (including a brilliant recording session with Sidney Bechet) and then led his quartet at the Embers (1955), hitting upon his very successful formula. His shuffle version of "On the Street Where You Live" was the first of many hits, and he recorded a long series of popular albums for Capitol during 1957–63, switching to Decca for a few more quartet albums in 1965–67. Jonah Jones recorded a fine date with Earl Hines for Chiaroscuro (1972) and still played on an occasional basis in the 1980s and early '90s. *—Scott Yanow*

★ **With Dave Pochoney and His All Stars** / Jul. 1, 1954–Jul. 7, 1954 / Swing ✦✦✦✦✦

Jonah Jones Sextet / Dec. 9, 1954 / Bethlehem ✦✦✦✦

● **Jonah Jones at the Embers** / Feb. 14, 1956–Feb. 29, 1956 / Groove ✦✦✦✦✦

Muted Jazz / Feb. 22, 1957–Feb. 25, 1957 / Capitol ✦✦✦✦✦

Swingin' on Broadway / Dec. 1957 / Capitol ✦✦✦✦

Jumpin' with Jonah / Jan. 26, 1958–Apr. 26, 1958 / Capitol ✦✦✦✦

Swingin' at the Cinema / Jun. 1958–Jul. 1958 / Capitol ✦✦✦✦

Jonah Jumps Again / Sep. 1958 / Capitol ✦✦✦

Swingin' 'round the World / 1958 / Capitol ✦✦✦

Jonah Jones / Glen Gray / Sep. 1962 / Capitol ✦✦✦

Oliver Jones

b. Sep. 11, 1934, Montreal, Quebec
Piano / Bop
Oliver Jones was already in his 50s when he was discovered by

the Jazz world. He had started playing piano when he was seven, and at nine he studied with Oscar Peterson's sister Daisy; the Peterson influence is still felt in his style. Jones played with show bands and worked with pop singer Ken Hamilton (1963–80), much of the time in Puerto Rico. It was not until he returned to Montreal in 1980 that he committed himself to playing jazz full-time. Since the mid-'80s, Oliver Jones has recorded extensively for Justin Time and established himself as a major modern mainstream player with impressive technique and a hard-swinging style. —Scott Yanow

The Many Moods of Oliver Jones / Feb. 1984–Mar. 1984 / Justin Time ✦✦✦✦✦

The Lights of Burgandy / Apr. 1985 / Justin Time ✦✦✦✦✦

Speak Low Swing Hard / Jul. 1985–Sep. 1985 / Justin Time ✦✦✦✦

Requestfully Yours / Nov. 1985 / Justin Time ✦✦✦✦

★ **Cookin' at Sweet Basil** / Sep. 3, 1987 / Justin Time ✦✦✦✦✦
This brilliant Canadian pianist caught live. Excellent. —Michael G. Nastos

Just Friends / Jan. 1989 / Justin Time ✦✦✦✦

Northern Summit / Jun. 1990–Sep. 1990 / Justin Time ✦✦✦✦✦

☆ **A Class Act** / Mar. 1991–May 1991 / Justin Time ✦✦✦✦✦
'91 trio date featuring Canadian pianist Oliver Jones, with bassist Steve Wallace and drummer Ed Thigpen. It's well done and ranks as his best record to date on the strength of his originals "Mark My Time" and "Peaceful Time," plus other material and a good rendition of a Bill Evans number. —Ron Wynn

Just 88 / Oct. 19, 1992 / Justin Time ✦✦✦✦✦

Yuletide Swing / May 1994 / Justin Time ✦✦✦✦

From Lush To Lively / May 31, 1995–Jun. 1, 1995 / Justin Time ✦✦✦

Philly Joe Jones

b. Jul. 15, 1923, Philadelphia, PA, **d.** Aug. 30, 1985, Philadelphia, PA

Drums / Hard Bop

A fiery drummer and a masterful accompanist, Philly Joe Jones came to fame as a key member with the first classic Miles Davis Quintet. After serving in the Army, he moved to New York in 1947, became the house drummer at Cafe Society and played with the who's who of bop (including Charlie Parker, Dizzy Gillespie and Fats Navarro). He worked regularly with Ben Webster, Joe Morris, Tiny Grimes, Lionel Hampton and Tadd Dameron (1953). Jones was with Miles Davis during 1955–58 including the quintet years (1955–56) with John Coltrane, Red Garland and Paul Chambers and the beginnings of the super sextet that also included Cannonball Adderley (recording the classic *Milestones* album). In 1958 he started leading his own groups, recording for Riverside (1958–59) and Atlantic (1960). Jones lived in London and Paris during 1967–72 (performing and recording with some avant-garde players including Archie Shepp). He eventually returned to Philadelphia where he led a fusion group Le Grand Prix, toured with Bill Evans during 1976, recorded for Galaxy in 1977 and 1979 and worked with Red Garland. Starting in 1981 he led the group Dameronia, which revived Tadd Dameron's music. But in reality everything that Philly Joe Jones did after Miles Davis was anti-climatic. —Scott Yanow

Blues for Dracula / Sep. 17, 1958 / Original Jazz Classics ✦✦✦✦
The program opened with the title track and a too long and unamusing monologue by the leader spoken in the style of Bela Lugosi and largely borrowed from Lenny Bruce. This, of course, made the record memorable, but not good. Over the program, each member of the sextet (Nat Adderley, Julian Priester, Johnny Griffin, Tommy Flanagan, Jimmy Garrison) all had their moments (and this was a prime period for Griffin, arguably one of the most distinct and strongest bop tenors in the late '50s). —Bob Rusch, Cadence

Drums Around the World / May 28, 1959–May 29, 1959 / Original Jazz Classics ✦✦✦
Drummer Philly Joe Jones takes a lot of solo space (including an unaccompanied "The Tribal Message") throughout this CD reissue. He utilizes an all-star group with such soloists as trumpeter Lee Morgan and Blue Mitchell, trombonist Curtis Fuller, Herbie Mann on flute and piccolo, altoist Cannonball Adderley, Benny

Golson on tenor, baritonist Sahib Shihab, pianist Wynton Kelly and either Sam Jones or Jimmy Garrison on bass. The music is supposed to showcase styles from around the world including Latin America and the Far East, but, in general, those references are somewhat superficial (including "Cherokee") and come out sounding like hard bop. There is some strong playing, but this set is primarily recommended to fans of Philly Joe Jones' drum solos. —Scott Yanow

Showcase / Nov. 17, 1959 / Original Jazz Classics ✦✦✦✦
Fine sextet and septet material. —Ron Wynn

Mean What You Say / Apr. 6, 1977–Apr. 7, 1977 / Sonet ✦✦✦✦✦
Philly Joe Jones led a quartet (pianist Mickey Tucker, Charles Bowen on soprano and tenor saxes, bassist Mickey Bass) and quintet (add trumpeter Tommy Turrentine) on an April 1977 date called *Mean What You Say*. This was a nice blowing date for Bowen, who at the time had an R&B background and had never before recorded a jazz album…Mickey Tucker was very strong on this set and, at times, almost seemed to be the leader with Jones seemingly pushing to assert his position. Still, this was an enjoyable recording with just that little extra added personality to give it an extra edge. —Bob Rusch, Cadence

Philly Mignon / Nov. 29, 1977–Dec. 1, 1977 / Galaxy ✦✦✦✦

● **Drum Song** / Oct. 10, 1978–Oct. 12, 1978 / Galaxy ✦✦✦✦✦
Hard bop is spoken here on this straight-ahead set. Drummer Philly Joe Jones is the leader, but the main emphasis is on such soloists as trumpeter Blue Mitchell (heard in one of his last recordings), the tenors of Harold Land and Charles Bowen, pianist Cedar Walton and trombonist Slide Hampton who arranged the four full-band numbers. Hampton (who also contributed two originals) gets "I Wait for You" as his feature while Bowen is showcased on "High Fly." In addition, these versions of "Our Delight" and "Two Bass Hit" have their heated moments. —Scott Yanow

Advance! / Oct. 10, 1979–Oct. 12, 1979 / Galaxy ✦✦✦✦
Steady and consistently high caliber. —Ron Wynn

Look Stop and Listen / Jul. 11, 1983 / Uptown ✦✦✦✦✦
Tadd Dameron was arguably the top composer/arranger of the early bebop years. Drummer Philly Joe Jones put together the group Dameronia specifically to perform Dameron's music and this was their second and final album before Jones' death. The lineup of this band was very impressive (trumpeters Don Sickler and Virgil Jones, trombonist Benny Powell, altoist Frank Wess, Charles Davis on tenor, baritonist Cecil Payne, pianist Walter Davis Jr, bassist Larry Ridley and Jones on drums) and, when one adds in guest soloist Johnny Griffin on tenor and Sickler's accurate transcriptions of the seven Dameron compositions (plus Benny Golson's "Killer Joe"), the result is an album that is significant both historically and musically. In other words, get this one. —Scott Yanow

Quincy Jones

b. Mar. 14, 1933, Chicago, IL

Arranger, Composer, Leader / Bop, Swing, Crossover, Pop

Quincy Jones has had several very successful careers, largely leaving jazz altogether by the early '70s to make his money out of producing pop, R&B and even rap records. His earlier years were much more significant to improvised music. He grew up in Seattle and his first important job was playing trumpet and arranging for Lionel Hampton's Orchestra (1951–53), sitting in a trumpet section with Clifford Brown and Art Farmer. During the 1950s, he started freelancing as an arranger, writing memorable charts for sessions led by Oscar Pettiford, Brown, Farmer, Gigi Gryce, Count Basie, Tommy Dorsey, Cannonball Adderley and Dinah Washington among others. He toured with Dizzy Gillespie's big band (1956), started recording as a leader for ABC-Paramount in 1956 and worked in Paris (1957–58) for the Barclay label as an arranger and producer. In 1959 Jones toured Europe with his all-star big band, which was originally put together to play for Harold Arlen's show Free and Easy. He kept the orchestra together through 1960, recording for Mercury. In 1961 Jones returned to New York and became the head of Mercury's A&R department, becoming a vice-president in 1964. Although he kept on recording throughout the 1960s, Jones' focus shifted to writing for films and television. During 1969–81, he worked for A&M, founding Qwest Records in 1980, a label that has become more active in the 1990s. Among his best jazz compositions have been "Stockholm Sweetnin'," "For Lena and Lennie," "Quintessence,"

"Jessica's Day" and "The Midnight Sun Never Sets." Although he deserves credit for talking Miles Davis into performing Gil Evans arrangements at the 1991 Montreux Jazz Festival and for signing such artists as Milt Jackson and Sonny Simmons to his Qwest label in the 1990s, very little that Quincy Jones has accomplished during the past 25 years is of any real relevance to jazz. —*Scott Yanow*

★ **This Is How I Feel About Jazz** / Sep. 14, 1956–Feb. 1956 / GRP ✦✦✦✦✦
Arranger Quincy Jones made many excellent straight jazz records in the '50s and '60s before he began gravitating toward pop and R&B. He assembled a strong cast and made his arrangements the focal point for *This Is How I Feel About Jazz*, which serves as a yardstick for directions that the music was heading at the time. —*Ron Wynn*

Swiss Radio Days Jazz Series, Vol. 1 / Jun. 27, 1960 / TCB ✦✦✦✦
Quincy Jones led one of his finest orchestras in 1960. This spirited CD is taken from a live concert (and radio broadcast) from Switzerland. With such soloists as trumpeter Benny Bailey, trombonist Jimmy Cleveland, altoist Phil Woods, Jerome Richardson on tenor and baritonist Sahib Shihab (among others), the repertoire mostly sticks to bebop. Surprisingly enough, not all of the arrangements heard on the CD are Jones'; there are also swinging charts from Ernie Wilkins, Billy Byers, Melba Liston, Phil Woods and Al Cohn. This well-recorded and previously unissued performance (which came out for the first time in 1994) makes one wish that Quincy Jones would return to jazz someday. —*Scott Yanow*

Walking in Space / Jun. 1969 / A&M ✦✦✦✦
A Grammy-winning work that marked the beginning of Jones' shift into R&B and pop. —*Ron Wynn*

Gula Matari / Mar. 25, 1970–May 1, 1970 / A&M ✦✦✦✦

Smackwater Jack / 1971 / Mobile Fidelity ✦✦

Mellow Madness / 1972 / A&M ✦✦

Body Heat / 1974 / A&M ✦✦

Back on the Block / 1990 / Qwest ✦✦
Big hit urban/pop release, with virtually no jazz content. —*Ron Wynn*

Q's Jook Joint / 1995 / Qwest/Warner Brothers ✦✦
The multi-talented Quincy Jones has excelled at idiomatic combinations in his albums since the '60s, when his mix-and-match soundtracks for television and films alerted everyone he'd switched from a pure jazz mode to a populist trend. *Q's Jook Joint* blends the latest in hip-hop-flavored productions with sleek urban ballads, vintage standards and derivative pieces; everything's superbly crafted, though few songs are as exciting in their performance or daring in their conception as such past Jones epics like *Gula Matari* or the score from *Roots*. Still, you can't fault Jones for his choice of musical collaborators; everyone from newcomer Tamia to longtime stars like Ray Charles, rappers, instrumentalists, male and female vocalists, percussionists and toasters. The CD really conveys the seamless quality one gets from attending a juke joint, though it lacks the dirt-floor grit or blues fervor of traditional Southern and chitlin' circuit hangouts. —*Ron Wynn*

Richard M. Jones

b. June 13, 1892, Donalsonville, LA, **d.** Dec. 8, 1945, Chicago, IL
Piano, leader / Classic Jazz, Blues
The composer of "Trouble in Mind," Richard M. Jones' main significance to jazz was as the leader of an interesting series of recording dates. He played alto horn and cornet with the Eureka Brass Band as early as 1902 and worked as a pianist in New Orleans during 1980–17. After playing with Oscar Celestin (1918), Jones moved to Chicago where he worked for Clarence Williams' publishing company. He recorded as a piano soloist in 1923, accompanies Blanche Calloway and Chippie Hill on record dates (1925–26) and led his Jazz Wizards on sessions of his own during 1925–29; Jones' sidemen included Albert Nicholas, Jonny St. Cyr, Ikey Robinson, Roy Palmer, Omer Simeon and some lesser-known musicians. Richard M. Jones sayed in Chicago for the rest of his life, leading further sessions during 1935–36 and working as a talent scout for Mercury in the 1940s. All of his records as a leader have been reissued on two Classic CDs. —*Scott Yanow*

● **1923–1927** / 1923 06 01-1927 07 20 / Classics ✦✦✦✦
Richard M. Jones was more important as a talent scout and an

organizer of bands than as a pianist. This Classics CD features Jones as a soloist on two numbers from 1923 ("Jazzin' Babies Blues: and "12th Street Rag"), with the Chicago Hottentots, backing the mediocre singer Lillie Delk Christian, playing with Nelson's Paramount Serenaders and Willie Hightower's Night Hawks and leading his own Jazz Wizards. Among the other players are clarinetist Albert Nicholas, Banjoist Johnny St. Cyr, cornetist Shirley Clay and trombonist Preston Jackson. Although the music is generally not all that classic, this formerly rare material has its strong moments and gives one a good example of middle-of-the-road Chicago jazz of the mid-'20s. —*Scott Yanow*

Sam Jones

b. Nov. 12, 1924, Jacksonville, FL, **d.** Dec. 15, 1981, New York, NY
Bass, Cello / Hard Bop
Sam Jones, a greatly in-demand bassist who often teamed with drummer Louis Hayes, was also a talented jazz cello soloist. He always took advantage of the fairly rare opportunities he had to lead sessions to create memorable music. He played with Tiny Bradshaw (1953–55), moved to New York in 1955 and worked with the groups of Kenny Dorham, Cannonball Adderley (1957), Dizzy Gillespie (1958–59) and Thelonious Monk among others. While a member of Cannonball Adderley's very successful quintet (1959–65), Jones wrote such originals as "Unit 7" and "Del Sasser" and led three highly recommended albums for Riverside during 1960–62 (all have been reissued in the OJC series) that featured some of his finest cello playing. Sam Jones was with the Oscar Peterson Trio (as Ray Brown's first replacement) during 1966–70 and then freelanced for the remainder of his life, making many recordings including albums of his own for East Wind (1974), Xanadu, Muse, Inner City, Steeplechase, Interplay and SeaBreeze. —*Scott Yanow*

★ **The Soul Society** / Mar. 8, 1960+Mar. 10, 1960 / Original Jazz Classics ✦✦✦✦✦
Bassist Sam Jones' debut as a leader resulted in one of his finest recordings. On four of the eight selections on the CD reissue of his Riverside set, Jones is well-featured on bass while the other four numbers find him playing very effective cello. The uncredited arrangements for the groups are uniformly excellent and there is solo space for cornetist Nat Adderley, trumpeter Blue Mitchell, Jimmy Heath on tenor, baritonist Charles Davis and pianist Bobby Timmons. The repertoire is superior too with highlights including the debut of Adderley's "The Old Country," a fine jam on "Just Friends," Keter Betts' "Some Kinda Mean," Jones' bowing on "Home" and Bobby Timmons' "So Tired." Actually, all eight selections are memorable on this highly recommended disc. —*Scott Yanow*

The Chant / Jan. 13, 1961+Jan. 26, 1961 / Original Jazz Classics ✦✦✦✦✦
Bassist Sam Jones' Riverside recordings have long been underrated. This CD reissue features Jones on bass and cello for four songs apiece with a particularly strong supporting cast including cornetist Nat Adderley, trumpeter Blue Mitchell, trombonist Melba Liston, altoist Cannonball Adderley (who only takes one solo) and Jimmy Heath on tenor; Victor Feldman and Heath provided the colorful arrangments. Highlights include "Four," "Sonny Boy," Jones' "In Walked Ray" and "Over the Rainbow," but all eight selections in this straight-ahead set are rewarding. —*Scott Yanow*

Down Home / Aug. 15, 1962–Aug. 16, 1962 / Original Jazz Classics ✦✦✦✦
Bassist Sam Jones, always best known for being a sideman (most notably with Cannonball Adderley's Quintet), recorded three superior Riverside albums as a leader during 1960–62 that have all been reissued on CD in the OJC series. This particular one, the third, features Jones on bass and cello in several settings. Four selections (including Horace Silver's "Strollin'" and "Unit Seven") are with an all star nonet/tentet while four others showcase Jones' cello in quintets with either Les Spann or Frank Strozier on flute and Israel Crosby or Ron Carter on bass. This is excellent hard bop-based music, but it would be another 12 years before Jones had his next opportunity to be a leader! —*Scott Yanow*

Cello Again / Jan. 5, 1976 / Xanadu ✦✦✦✦
Bassist Sam Jones, who had not recorded on cello in 14 years at the time of this session, sticks exclusively to that instrument throughout the easily enjoyable boppish set. Altoist Charles McPherson helps out (and almost steals the show) on three of the seven selections, but the rhythm section (pianist Barry Harris,

bassist David Williams and drummer Billy Higgins) is happily subservient to Jones who takes cello solos on each selection. — *Scott Yanow*

Something in Common / Sep. 13, 1977 / Muse ✦✦✦✦
A fine sextet plus Cedar Walton on piano and Billy Higgins on drums. —*Ron Wynn*

Changes & Things / Sep. 14, 1977 / Xanadu ✦✦✦✦
Louis Hayes on drums shakes the rafters. Excellent Jones on bass. —*Ron Wynn*

Visitation / Mar. 1978 / SteepleChase ✦✦✦

The Bassist / Jan. 3, 1979 / Interplay ✦✦✦
Sam Jones—The Bassist was a reissue of a session originally released on Interplay, although I don't remember the record actually existing. This was an outing for a snappy trio. Jones, Kenny Barron (keyboards) and Keith Copeland (drums) produced music of subtle but quite unrelenting drive. Even on the slower tempoed "Lily", the bass and drum work pushed close up to maintain the swing tension, which so marked the entire date. Everybody had some fine moments in a set of demanding protein jazz. Two points of interest; "Rhythm-A-Ning" (5:30) was taken at breakneck tempo and almost seemed to get away from the trio, who managed not to stumble, but instead pushed home an exciting foray into Thelonious Monk-land. "Hymn Of Scorpio" utilized electric piano and was one of those rare times when it worked well (Hank Jones and Tommy Flanagan are two other "traditional" pianists who have succeeded here as well). This was very nice. —*Bob Rusch, Cadence*

Something New / Jun. 4, 1979 / Sea Breeze ✦✦✦✦
An intense 12-piece session. —*Ron Wynn*

Thad Jones (Thaddeus Joseph Jones)

b. Mar. 28, 1923, Pontiac, MI, d. Aug. 20, 1986, Copenhagen, Denmark
Trumpet, Cornet, Arranger, Leader, Composer / Bop, Hard Bop
A harmonically advanced trumpeter/cornetist with a distinctive sound and a talented arranger/composer, Thad Jones (the younger brother of Hank and older brother of Elvin) had a very productive career. Self-taught on trumpet, he started playing professionally when he was 16 with Hank Jones and Sonny Stitt. After serving in the military (1943–46), Jones worked in territory bands in the Midwest. During 1950–53, he performed regularly with Billy Mitchell's quintet in Detroit and he made a few recordings with Charles Mingus (1954–55). Jones became well-known during his long period (1954–63) with Count Basie's Orchestra, taking a "Pop Goes the Weasel" chorus on "April in Paris" and sharing solo duties with Joe Newman. While with Basie, Jones had the opportunity to write some arrangements and he became a busy freelance writer after 1963. He joined the staff of CBS, co-led a quintet with Pepper Adams and near the end of 1965 organized a big band with drummer Mel Lewis that from February 1966 on played Monday nights at the Village Vanguard. During the next decade, the orchestra (although always a part-time affair) became famous and gave Jones an outlet for his writing. He composed one standard ("A Child Is Born") along with many fine pieces including "Fingers," "Little Pixie" and "Tiptoe." Among the sidemen in the Thad Jones-Mel Lewis Orchestra (which started out as an all-star group and later on featured younger players) were trumpeters Bill Berry, Danny Stiles, Richard Williams, Marvin Stamm, Snooky Young and Jon Faddis, trombonists Bob Brookmeyer, Jimmy Knepper and Quentin Jackson, the reeds of Jerome Richardson, Jerry Dodgion, Eddie Daniels, Joe Farrell, Pepper Adams and Billy Harper, pianists Hank Jones and Roland Hanna and bassists Richard Davis and George Mraz. In 1978 Jones surprised Lewis by suddenly leaving the band and moving to Denmark, an action he never explained. He wrote for a radio orchestra and led his own group called Eclipse. In late 1984 Jones took over the leadership of the Count Basie Orchestra, but within a year bad health forced him to retire. Thad Jones recorded as a leader for Debut (1954–55), Blue Note, Period, United Artists, Roulette, Milestone, Artists House and Metronome, and many of the Thad Jones-Mel Lewis Orchestra's best recordings have been reissued on a five-CD Mosaic box set. —*Scott Yanow*

Lust For Life / Mar. 7, 1954–Nov. 4, 1957 / Drive Archive ✦✦✦
The material on this CD had frequently appeared on Everest back in the LP era. Best are three selections featuring the great tenor saxophonist Sonny Rollins ("Sonnymoon for Two," "Like Someone

in Love" and the "Theme from Tchaikovsky's Symphony Pathetique"). Also on this fine budget set are a selection apiece from trombonists J.J. Johnson and Kai Winding and performances from several mid-'50s sessions by cornetist Thad Jones including two numbers with bassist Charles Mingus, a quintet set with tenor saxophonist Frank Foster and "The Jones Bash," which features six unrelated musicians all of whom have Jones as their last name! This bop sampler has its strong moments. —*Scott Yanow*

Fabulous Thad Jones / Aug. 11, 1954–Mar. 10, 1955 / Original Jazz Classics ✦✦✦✦✦
A 1991 reissue of super cuts from Debut label. —*Ron Wynn*

Detroit-New York Junction / Mar. 13, 1956 / Blue Note ✦✦✦✦

★ **Magnificent Thad Jones** / Jul. 14, 1956 / Blue Note ✦✦✦✦✦
An excellent reissue. Subtle, harmonic ensemble jazz. —*Michael G. Nastos*

After Hours / Jun. 21, 1957 / Original Jazz Classics ✦✦✦✦

Mean What You Say / Apr. 26, 1966–May 9, 1966 / Original Jazz Classics ✦✦✦✦✦
A topflight date co-led by Pepper Adams (bar sax). —*Ron Wynn*

☆ **The Complete Solid State Recordings Of The Thad Jones/Mel Lewis Big Band** / May 4, 1966–May 25, 1970 / Mosaic ✦✦✦✦✦
The Thad Jones/Mel Lewis big band was one of the finest jazz orchestras of the late '60s, but its Solid State LPs had been long out-of-print for decades before Mosaic wisely reissued all of the music (plus seven previously unissued performances) on this deluxe but limited-edition five-CD set. With Jones' colorful and distinctive arrangements, such soloists as trumpeters Danny Stiles, Marvin Stamm and Richard Williams, trombonists Bob Brookmeyer and Jimmy Knepper, the reeds of Jerome Richardson, Jerry Dodgion, Joe Farrell, Billy Harper, Eddie Daniels and Pepper Adams and pianists Hank Jones and Roland Hanna, plus a rhythm section driven by bassist Richard Davis and drummer Mel Lewis, this was a classic band. Highlights among the 42 performances include "Mean What You Say," "Don't Git Sassy," "Tiptoe," "Fingers," "Central Park North" and the original version of "A Child Is Born," but nearly every selection is memorable. —*Scott Yanow*

Suite for Pops / Jan. 25, 1972–Sep. 1, 1972 / Horizon ✦✦
Despite the sincerity involved, this tribute to Louis Armstrong really does not come off. Thad Jones, in his compositions and arrangements, never quotes or borrows (either directly or abstractly) from Louis Armstrong's music, making this homage little more than namedropping. None of the seven originals or performances are by themselves memorable, despite the all-star nature of this band. There are many much more worthy recordings by The Thad Jones-Mel Lewis Orchestra than this later effort. — *Scott Yanow*

New Life: Dedicated to Max Gordon / Dec. 16, 1975–Dec. 17, 1975 / A&M/Horizon ✦✦✦

Live in Munich / Sep. 9, 1976 / A&M/Horizon ✦✦✦
This was not a solo Thad Jones album, but was one of many outstanding releases featuring The Thad Jones/Mel Lewis orchestra, an 18-piece band that the two co-founded back in 1965. Jones was the band's principal arranger during the bulk of its tenure and supplied several charts for this fine session, their second for the Horizon label. —*Ron Wynn*

★ **Thad Jones/The Mel Lewis Quartet** / Sep. 24, 1977 / A&M ✦✦✦✦✦
This is one of the finest small-group sessions of cornetist Thad Jones' career. With strong and very alert assistance from drummer Mel Lewis (his co-leader in their celebrated big band), pianist Harold Danko and bassist Rufus Reid, Jones plays at his peak on six standards, two of which were issued for the initial time on this CD reissue. Four of the songs are at least nine minutes long (two are over 15 minutes) yet Thad never loses his momentum. The musicians constantly surprise each other and there are many spontaneous moments during this often-brilliant outing. —*Scott Yanow*

Scott Joplin

b. Nov. 24, 1868, Texarkana, TX d. Apr. 1, 1917, New York, NY
Composer, Piano / Ragtime
Ragtime was jazz's direct predecessor (differing from jazz in the absence of blues and improvisation) and Scott Joplin was ragtime's greatest composer. Joplin lived in St. Louis during 1885–93, playing in local bars and clubs. In 1894 he led a band at the

Chicago World's Fair and formed the Texas Medley Quartet, which played in vaudeville shows. Relocating to Sedalia, MO, Joplin began having pieces published as early as 1895 and in 1899 his "Maple Leaf Rag" (published by his supporter John Stark) became ragtime's most popular number, selling over 75,000 copies of sheet music during its first year. Joplin soon had many other rags published that helped to make ragtime the pop music of its day, but the tragedy of his life was that his goals were beyond ragtime. He staged a ballet (*The Ragtime Dance*) and two ragtime operas (*The Guest of Honor* and *Treemonisha*), but none were successful, a fact that continually frustrated him. By 1910 Joplin was becoming ill with syphilis and at his death in 1917, ragtime was in the process of being replaced by jazz. Ironically, 57 years after his death, Scott Joplin finally became a household name because his music (most notably "The Entertainer") was used by Marvin Hamlisch in his score for the popular film *The Sting*. Although he never recorded, Scott Joplin's music has been fully documented with "Maple Leaf Rag" becoming a Dixieland jazz standard and pianist Richard Zimmerman (on an excellent five-LP set for Murray Hill) recording everything that Joplin ever wrote. —*Scott Yanow*

● **The Elite Syncopations: Classic Ragtime from Rare** / 1910 / Biograph ✦✦✦✦
If you want to hear exactly how ragtime should be played, here's the real thing from a founding father. These vintage Scott Joplin rags were transferred to digital from piano rolls and are the way he wanted his rags to sound. —*Ron Wynn*

Joplin, Scott: 1916 (Classic Solos from Piano Rolls) / Apr. 16, 1916–May 1917 / Biograph ✦✦✦
More vintage ragtime taken from piano rolls. Scott Joplin was incensed whenever he heard someone playing his rags too fast, so he tried to put them down on piano rolls himself to keep them from being speeded up. These were transferred digitally from rolls. —*Ron Wynn*

Clifford Jordan

b. Sep. 2, 1931, Chicago, IL, d. Mar. 27, 1993, New York, NY
Tenor Saxophone / Post-Bop, Hard Bop
Clifford Jordan was a fine inside/outside player who somehow held his own with Eric Dolphy in the 1964 Charles Mingus Sextet. Jordan had his own sound on tenor almost from the start. He gigged around Chicago with Max Roach, Sonny Stitt and some R&B groups before moving to New York in 1957. Jordan immediately made a strong impression, leading three albums for Blue Note (including a meeting with fellow tenor John Gilmore) and touring with Horace Silver (1957–58), J.J. Johnson (1959–60), Kenny Dorham (1961–62) and Max Roach (1962–64). After performing in Europe with Mingus and Dolphy, Jordan worked mostly as a leader but tended to be overlooked since he was not overly influential or a pacesetter in the avant-garde. A reliable player, Clifford Jordan toured Europe several times, was in a quartet headed by Cedar Walton in 1974–75 and during his last years led a big band. He recorded as a leader for Blue Note, Riverside, Jazzland, Atlantic (a little-known album of Leadbelly tunes), Vortex, Strata-East, Muse, SteepleChase, Criss Cross, Bee Hive, DIW, Milestone and Mapleshade. —*Scott Yanow*

★ **Blowing in from Chicago** / Mar. 3, 1957 / Blue Note ✦✦✦✦✦

Spellbound / Aug. 10, 1960 / Original Jazz Classics ✦✦✦✦
Tenor saxophonist Clifford Jordan was sponsored by Cannonball Adderley on this set for Riverside, which has been reissued on CD in the OJC series. Jordan did not, at this point, quite have the distinctive sound that he would develop by his period with Charles Mingus, but he was already a strong hard bop stylist. Assisted by pianist Cedar Walton, bassist Spanky DeBrest and drummer Albert "Tootie" Heath, Jordan performs four originals (including "Toy" is best known), an unusual waltz version of "Lush Life," the ballad "Last Night When We Were Young" and the romping Charlie Parker blues "Au Privave." It's an excellent, straight-ahead outing. —*Scott Yanow*

Bearcat / Oct. 1961–1962 / Original Jazz Classics ✦✦✦

These Are My Roots / Feb. 1, 1965–Feb. 17, 1965 / Atlantic ✦✦✦✦
An intriguing concept: Jordan arranging and doing Leadbelly songs. —*Ron Wynn*

Night of the Mark 7 / Mar. 26, 1975 / Muse ✦✦✦✦

On Stage, Vol. 1 / Mar. 29, 1975 / SteepleChase ✦✦✦

On Stage, Vol. 2 / Mar. 29, 1975 / SteepleChase ✦✦✦

Firm Roots / Apr. 18, 1975 / SteepleChase ✦✦✦✦
One of Jordan's best releases with The Magic Triangle ensemble

of Cedar Walton (p), Sam Jones (b) and Billy Higgins (d). —*Ron Wynn*

The Highest Mountain / Apr. 18, 1975 / Muse ✦✦✦✦
Although not an innovator himself, tenor saxophonist Clifford Jordan had a distinctive tone and an adventurous style almost from the start of his career. Overlooked a bit throughout his career, Jordan was always a consistent performer who could be counted on to bring some excitement to whatever music he played. On this CD, Jordan is joined by a superior rhythm section (pianist Cedar Walton, bassist Sam Jones and drummer Billy Higgins) for "Blue Monk," three group originals (including his own complex "Highest Mountain") and Bill Lee's "John Coltrane," which has a bit of chanting by the players. —*Scott Yanow*

Remembering Me-Me / May 18, 1976 / Muse ✦✦✦✦

Inward Fire / Apr. 5, 1977 / Muse ✦✦✦✦

On Stage, Vol. 2 / Jan. 1978 / SteepleChase ✦✦✦

The Adventurer / Feb. 9, 1978 / Muse ✦✦✦✦
Steady, with consistently interesting and gripping solos. —*Ron Wynn*

Repetition / Feb. 9, 1984 / Soul Note ✦✦✦✦
Strong leads and good compositions. —*Ron Wynn*

Dr. Chicago / Aug. 3, 1984 / Bee Hive ✦✦✦✦

Two Tenor Winner! / Oct. 1984 / Criss Cross ✦✦✦✦✦

Royal Ballads / Dec. 23, 1986 / Criss Cross ✦✦✦✦

Live at Ethell's / Oct. 16, 1987–Oct. 18, 1987 / Mapleshade ✦✦✦✦✦
The passing of Clifford Jordan was another in the recent series of irreplaceable jazz greats departing. Jordan was among the finest straight-ahead soloists, an exceptional ballad interpreter and combative uptempo player who excelled in any situation. This live date, done in 1987 in Baltimore at the club Ethell, was a quartet session, with Jordan handling the frontline and repeatedly showing how to craft, develop and then conclude a solo. He never rushes things or relies on gimmicks or repetition, knowing when and how to end a line or wrap up an idea. —*Ron Wynn*

Four Play / 1990 / DIW ✦✦✦✦✦
Simply magical 1990 quartet date done for a Japanese label. Veteran tenor saxophonist Clifford Jordan teamed with another veteran and two young players for the kind of no-frills, dynamic jazz album that seldom gets made anymore by American major labels. Pianist James Williams and drummer Ronnie Burrage brought youthful excitement; bassist Richard Davis and Jordan, seasoning and experience. —*Ron Wynn*

Live at Condon's, New York/Down through the Years / Oct. 7, 1991 / Milestone ✦✦✦✦

Duke Jordan (Irving Sidney Jordan)

b. Apr. 1, 1922, New York, NY
Piano / Bop, Hard Bop
Although he has had a long career, Duke Jordan will always be best-known for being pianist with Charlie Parker's classic 1947 quintet. A little earlier he had worked with the Savoy Sultans, Coleman Hawkins and the Roy Eldridge big band (1946). After his year with Parker, (his piano introductions to such songs as "Embraceable You" were classic), Jordan worked with the Sonny Stitt-Gene Ammons Quintet (1950–51) and Stan Getz (1949 and 1952–53). He started recording as a leader in 1954, debuting his most famous composition "Jordu" the following year. Although he worked steadily during the next few decades (writing part of the soundtrack for the French film *Les Liaisons Dangereuses*), Jordan was in obscurity until he began recording on a regular basis for SteepleChase in 1973. Duke Jordan, who was married for a time to the talented jazz singer Sheila Jordan, has lived in Denmark since 1978 and has recorded through the years for Prestige, Savoy, Blue Note, Charlie Parker Records, Muse, Spotlite and Steeplechase. Still possessing an unchanged bop style, Jordan remains active in the mid-'90s. —*Scott Yanow*

★ **Flight to Jordan** / Aug. 4, 1960 / Blue Note ✦✦✦✦✦
Duke Jordan, who played regularly with the Charlie Parker Quintet in 1947, has long been known as a superior bebop player whose style was touched by the genius of Bud Powell's innovations. This quintet album (which also features trumpeter Dizzy Reece and the young tenor Stanley Turrentine) gave Jordan an opportunity to record six of his originals and, although none

became as well-known as his "Jordu," the music has plenty of strong melodies and variety. This is one of Duke Jordan's better recordings and is quite enjoyable. *—Scott Yanow*

Brooklyn Brothers / Mar. 16, 1973 / Muse ✦✦✦✦
A nice session with fellow reed player Cecil Payne. *—Ron Wynn*

The Murray Hill Caper / Apr. 7, 1973–Apr. 23, 1973 / Spotlite ✦✦✦

Two Loves / Nov. 25, 1973+Dec. 12, 1973 / SteepleChase ✦✦✦✦

Flight to Denmark / Nov. 25, 1973–Dec. 2, 1973 / SteepleChase ✦✦✦✦
Aggressive, dynamic solos. *—Ron Wynn*

Duke's Delight / Nov. 18, 1975 / SteepleChase ✦✦✦✦✦
Lovely ballads and fine uptempo pieces. *—Ron Wynn*

Osaka Concert, Vol. 1 / Sep. 20, 1976 / SteepleChase ✦✦✦✦

Osaka Concert, Vol. 2 / Sep. 20, 1976 / SteepleChase ✦✦✦✦

Duke's Artistry / Jun. 30, 1978 / SteepleChase ✦✦✦✦

The Great Session / Jun. 30, 1978 / SteepleChase ✦✦✦
Aptly titled—wonderful Jordan playing. *—Ron Wynn*

Change a Pace / Oct. 29, 1979 / SteepleChase ✦✦✦

Thinking of You / Oct. 1979 / SteepleChase ✦✦✦✦
The Duke Jordan set (pianist Jordan, bassist Niels-Henning Orstead Pedersen, drummer Billy Hart) swings nicely in an underplayed fashion. "Foxie Cakes" was taken solo and was interesting for its mix of piano techniques like Thelonious Monk; one begun to hear a more pronounced stride element in his playing. *—Bob Rusch, Cadence*

Midnight Moonlight / 1979 / SteepleChase ✦✦✦

● **Tivoli One** / Oct. 1984 / SteepleChase ✦✦✦✦✦
This is a fine, all-around trio date for veteran pianist Duke Jordan. Possessor of a rather pure bop style, Jordan (accompanied by bassist Wilbur Little and drummer Dannie Richmond) is in fine form on four of his originals (including a brief rendition of his famous "Jordu," which he uses as a closing theme) and three familiar standards. Bop fans should enjoy this one, along with virtually all of Jordan's SteepleChase recordings. *—Scott Yanow*

● **Tivoli Two** / Oct. 1984 / SteepleChase ✦✦✦✦✦
The second of two recordings, this set also finds the classic bop pianist Duke Jordan being joined by bassist Wilbur Little and drummer Dannie Richmond, live from the Tivoli Gardens in Copenhagen. This time around Jordan interprets three originals (a lengthy "No Problem," a blues and "Jordu," which functions as a closing theme) along with three standards. Jordan is heard at the top of his game during these swinging and probing performances. *—Scott Yanow*

As Time Goes By / Jul. 1985 / SteepleChase ✦✦✦✦

Kent Jordan

b. Oct. 28, 1958, New Orleans, LA
Flute / Hard Bop, Crossover
The son of saxophonist Kidd Jordan and the older brother of trumpeter Marlon Jordan, Kent Jordan's early venture into commercialism on his first two Columbia albums almost ruined his reputation in the jazz world before he had a chance to mature. He had studied at the Eastman School of Music and New Orleans' Center for the Creative Arts, inspired at the latter by Ellis Marsalis (with whom he recorded). Jordan played and recorded with the groups Jasmine and the Improvisational Arts Quartet before cutting his two Columbia albums (1984 and 1986). His third Columbia album (1988's *Essence*) is much stronger from a jazz standpoint and since that time Jordan has toured with Elvin Jones and shown the jazz world that he can indeed play creative music. *—Scott Yanow*

Essence / 1988 / Columbia ✦✦✦

Louis Jordan

b. Jul. 8, 1908, Brinkley, AR, d. Feb. 4, 1975, Los Angeles, CA
Alto Saxophone, Vocals, Leader / Swing, Early R&B
One of the most beloved of all musicians, Louis Jordan was an excellent altoist, a talented singer and a memorable performer. His Tympani Five bridged the gap between swing and R&B and during 1941-53 had dozens of hit records. Unlike many of the blacks who made it big during the segregated years in show biz and movies, Jordan never felt compelled to play an Uncle Tom or

a loser; in fact his character always came out ahead, finding ways to outsmart any possible trouble and thoroughly enjoy life.

Jordan was taught to play reeds by his father who led the Rabbit Foot Minstrels; Louis' first professional job was touring with that group. He worked in territory bands and played with Charlie Gaines (1933-35) and Leroy Smith (1935-36) before spending a period as a member of the Chick Webb Orchestra (1936-38). While with Webb, Jordan was mostly featured as a ballad singer, not getting any significant solo space. Brief stints with the groups of Fats Waller and Kaiser Marshall still found Jordan to be quite obscure, but that quickly changed. In 1939 he formed the Tympani Five and soon began having such hits as "Choo Choo Ch-Boogie," "Saturday Night Fish Fry," "Caldonia," "I'm Gonna Move to the Outskirts of Town," "Ain't Nobody Here but Us Chickens," "Five Guys Named Moe" and "Is You Is or Is You Ain't My Baby." Louis Jordan appeared in several films (most of them low-budget items made for the black market, but *Follow the Boys* with George Murphy was an exception). Many of his best film appearances have been collected on a video issued by Vintage Jazz Classics. He also recorded duets with Louis Armstrong, Ella Fitzgerald and Bing Crosby. In 1951 he broke up his group to form a big band, but within a short period Jordan's string of hits came to an end. He was still in his musical prime, but the rise of rock & roll and the end of his Decca contract found him suddenly out of style. Louis Jordan kept working up until the end of his life (including some tours with Chris Barber) and ironically is more popular after his death (as witness the 1992 Broadway play *Five Guys Named Moe*) than he was during his leaner years. His recordings have been reissued constantly during the past 20 years. *—Scott Yanow*

At the Swing Cats' Ball / Jan. 15, 1937–Nov. 1937 / JSP ✦✦✦✦

☆ **Let the Good Times Roll: The Complete Decca Recordings 1938–54** / Dec. 20, 1938–Jan. 4, 1954 / Bear Family ✦✦✦✦✦

★ **The Best of Louis Jordan** / 1939 / MCA ✦✦✦✦✦
This is the best domestic collection of seminal Jordan cuts. In many ways, it's foundation music for the creation of R&B and can be linked to rap as well. Funny lyrics, superior arrangements, amazing material from the '40s and '50s. *—Ron Wynn*

Louis Jordan 1940–1941 / Mar. 13, 1940–Nov. 1940 / Classics ✦✦✦✦✦

1941–43 / Nov. 15, 1941–Nov. 1943 / Classics ✦✦✦✦✦

Five Guys Named Moe: Original Decca Recordings, Vol. 2 / Jul. 21, 1942–May 8, 1952 / Decca ✦✦✦✦
Since this is the second CD taken from Louis Jordan's Decca recordings, there are fewer hits and more obscurities included, making it of greater value to veteran collectors. In addition to such familiar (but still) songs as "Five Guys Named Moe," "Is You Is or Is You Ain't My Baby," "G.I. Jive" and "Look Out," highpoints include such lesser-known numbers as "Life Is So Peculiar" (which co-stars Louis Armstrong), "Boogie Woogie Blue Plate," "Jordan for President" and "Pettin' and Pokin'. " This CD is recommended to listeners who want a good sampling of Louis Jordan's many recordings. *—Scott Yanow*

Just Say Moe! Mo' Best of Louis / Jul. 21, 1942–1973 / Rhino ✦✦✦✦
Rhino's *Just Say Moe!* covers Jordan's entire career, including some material from his peak years at Decca and a song from the Broadway musical, *Five Guys Named Moe*, based on his life. It's a good compliment to MCA's *Best of Louis Jordan*. *—AMG*

One Guy Named Louis / 1954 / Blue Note ✦✦✦
It is a strange fact that as rock & roll began to catch on, one of the artists who helped influence its birth was dropping rapidly in popularity. Singer/altoist Louis Jordan, who had had dozens of hits with his Tympani Five while on Decca, recorded 21 songs for Aladdin in 1954 (all of which are included on this CD) and none of them sold well. The strange part is that there is nothing wrong with the music. It compares quite well artistically with his earlier performances; it was just out of style. That fact should not trouble latter-day Jordan fans, for the formerly rare music on this set is witty, swinging and eternally hip. *—Scott Yanow*

I Believe in Music / Nov. 6, 1973 / Evidence ✦✦✦✦✦
Nice early '70s date with alto saxophonist and vocalist Louis Jordan doing more conventional blues and jazz material and very few comedy routines. As he became a celebrity, Jordan's instrumental prowess took a back seat to his quips and monologues. But this time, the music reigned. *—Ron Wynn*

Marlon Jordan

b. Aug. 21, 1970, New Orleans, LA
Trumpet / Hard Bop

The younger brother of flutist Kent Jordan and the son of avant-garde saxophonist Kidd Jordan, Marlon Jordan gained a great deal of attention early in his career, recording as a leader for Columbia when he was 19, before he had an original sound of his own. He started playing trumpet in the fourth grade and knew Wynton Marsalis (a major influence) and Terence Blanchard when he was a child. Jordan was a featured soloist with the New Orleans Symphony when he was 15, studied at the now-legendary New Orleans Center for Creative Arts and recorded as a sideman with his brother Kent (1987) and Dennis Gonzalez (1988). He cut three albums as a leader for Columbia, toured with Jazz Futures (1991) alongside Roy Hargrove and showed potential. Whether he will someday develop into a jazz giant is not known at this time, but Marlon Jordan certainly has the technical skills, if not yet the musical individuality. *—Scott Yanow*

For You Only / Dec. 1988 / Columbia ✦✦✦
An erratic but worthy 1990 release of this latest New Orleans prodigy's debut. *—Ron Wynn*

● Learson's Return / 1991 / Columbia ✦✦✦✦
Quintet. A more confident, stronger release. *—Ron Wynn*

The Undaunted / Jan. 11, 1992–Jan. 12, 1992 / Columbia ✦✦✦

The Undaunted / 1993 / Columbia ✦✦✦
This date includes longer pieces and more substantial and creative playing and unveiled Jordan's newest group. Tenor saxophonist Tim Warfield, Jr. is also an impressive player, while the rhythm section of pianist Eric Reed, bassist Tarus Mateen and drummer Troy Davis is solid, if sometimes a bit derivative. Reed has the strongest solos, while Reed And Mateen team effectively. Although still firmly in a hard bop mode, Jordan and his comrades show that they're starting to find their own voices and directions. *—Ron Wynn*

Sheila Jordan

b. Nov. 18, 1928, Detroit, MI
Vocals / Bop, Post-Bop

One of the most consistently creative of all jazz singers, Sheila Jordan has a relatively small voice, but has done the maximum with her instrument. She is one of the few vocalists who can improvise logical lyrics (which often rhyme!), she is a superb scat singer and is also an emotional interpreter of ballads. Yet despite her talents, Jordan spent much of the 1960s and '70s working at a conventional day job! She studied piano when she was 11 and early on sang vocalese in a vocal group. Jordan moved to New York in the 1950s, was married to Duke Jordan (1952–62), studied with Lennie Tristano and worked in New York clubs. George Russell used her on an unusual recording of "You Are My Sunshine" and she became one of the few singers to lead her own Blue Note album (1962). However, it would be a decade before she appeared on records again, working with Carla Bley, Roswell Rudd and co-leading a group with Steve Kuhn in the late '70s. Jordan recorded a memorable duet album with bassist Arild Andersen for SteepleChase in 1977 and has since teamed up with bassist Harvie Swartz on many occasions. By the 1980s Sheila Jordan was finally performing jazz on a full-time basis and gaining the recognition she deserved 20 years earlier. She has recorded as a leader (in addition to the Blue Note session) for East Wind, Grapevine, SteepleChase, Palo Alto, Blackhawk and Muse. *—Scott Yanow*

Looking Out / 1961 / Wave ✦✦✦

★ Portrait of Sheila Jordan / Sep. 19, 1962+Oct. 12, 1962 / Blue Note ✦✦✦✦✦
This innovative date with Barry Galbraith (g), Steve Swallow (b) and Denzil Best (d) is the one to get *—Richard Lieberson*

Confirmation / Jul. 12, 1975–Jul. 13, 1975 / Eastwind ✦✦✦✦

Sheila / Aug. 27, 1977–Aug. 28, 1977 / SteepleChase ✦✦✦✦✦
This was a breakthrough recording for Sheila Jordan. She recorded a superb album for Blue Note in 1962 and then was off records (and only working in jazz on a part-time basis) up until the mid-'70s. She cut two albums for tiny labels and then came this, the first of her vocal-bass duet recordings. While in later years bassist Harvie Swartz would be her frequent musical partner, Jordan's SteepleChase set features the talented Arild Andersen on bass.

The communication between the two often borders on the miraculous and it is a pleasure to hear Sheila Jordan's fresh and original interpretations of such songs as "Lush Life," "On Green Dolphin Street," "Don't Explain" and "Better than Anything." *—Scott Yanow*

Playground / Jul. 1979 / ECM ✦✦✦✦
A studio date with the Steve Kuhn Trio. The most distinctive voice in modern jazz. *—Michael G. Nastos*

Last Year's Waltz / 1981 / ECM ✦✦✦✦✦
Live at Fat Tuesdays in NYC with the Steve Kuhn Trio. Sheila at her best. *—Michael G. Nastos*

Old Time Feeling / Oct. 15, 1982 / Muse ✦✦✦✦
Good duo date with Harvie Swartz (b). *—Ron Wynn*

The Crossing / Oct. 1, 1984–Oct. 2, 1984 / Blackhawk ✦✦✦✦✦
Outstanding sessions with brilliant—often breathtaking—lead vocals. *—Ron Wynn*

Songs From Within / Mar. 1989 / MA ✦✦✦✦
Sheila Jordan is one of the few singers to record duets frequently with just a string bass, usually Harvie Swartz. Jordan and Swartz interpret a wide variety of standards on their CD along with two originals. Although the always-inventive singer is clearly the lead voice, Swartz is not restricted to merely an accompanying role; he often shares center stage in close interplay with Jordan and his lines are almost as unpredictable as Sheila's. Their versions of such veteran songs as "Waltz for Debbie," "St. Thomas," "My Shining Hour" and "In a Sentimental Mood" sound quite original and fresh. As is the custom with M-A, this CD concludes with a selection taken from another release on the label, a melancholy showcase for Marty Krystall's bass clarinet. *—Scott Yanow*

Lost and Found / Sep. 28, 1989–Sep. 29, 1989 / Muse ✦✦✦✦✦

★ One for Junior / Sep. 1991 / Muse ✦✦✦✦✦
This CD is a real gem. Singers Sheila Jordan and Mark Murphy both possess unusual and immediately recognizable voices and are among the top jazz improvisers around. On a typically intelligent and chancetaking program there are many highlights including a humorous conversation between hipsters on "Where or When," a couple of ballad medleys and Jordan's witty lyrics on "The Bird." Assisted by pianist Kenny Barron, bassist Harvie Swartz, drummer Ben Riley and Bill Mays on occasional synthesizer, the two vocalists sound mutually inspired. *—Scott Yanow*

Heart Strings / Mar. 5, 1993–Mar. 6, 1993 / Muse ✦✦✦✦
Although sparsely recorded during much of her career, Sheila Jordan has been one of the top jazz singers since 1960. In addition to loving the words she sings (a la Billie Holiday), Jordan constantly improvises (few can scat with her sensitivity and swing) and also has the remarkable ability of being able to make up lyrics on the spot that are not only logical but rhyme. Jordan realized a lifelong dream on this Muse CD for she had always wanted to record with a string quartet. Fortunately, the group was given colorful arrangements by pianist Alan Broadbent; in addition, there are two songs with a standard trio that includes Jordan's longtime bassist Harvie Swartz and a duet with Broadbent. The emphasis is on ballads but typically Sheila Jordan makes each of the songs sound like they must have been written specifically for her, even "Look for the Silver Lining" and "Inch Worm." This is a highly recommended gem. *—Scott Yanow*

Stanley Jordan

b. Jul. 31, 1959, Chicago, IL
Guitar / Bop, Pop

Stanley Jordan's discovery in the early '80s rightfully earned a lot of headlines in the jazz world for he came up with a new way of playing guitar. Although he was not the first to use tapping, Jordan's extensive expertise gave him the ability to play two completely independent lines on the guitar (as if it were a keyboard) or, when he wanted, two guitars at a time. He had originally studied piano, although he switched to guitar when he was 11. After graduating from Princeton in 1981, Jordan played for a time on the streets of New York. Soon he was discovered, had the opportunity to play with Benny Carter and Dizzy Gillespie and, after recording a solo album for his own Tangent label, signed with Blue Note. Since then his career has been surprisingly aimless. Stanley Jordan can play amazing jazz, but he often wastes his talent on lesser material, so one has to be picky in deciding which of his recordings to acquire. *—Scott Yanow*

Touch Sensitive / 1982 / Tangent ✦✦✦✦
He first featured the two-handed touch style, which he has perfected on this rare independent release. —*Paul Kohler*

Magic Touch / 1985 / Blue Note ✦✦✦✦✦

Standards, Vol. 1 / 1986 / Blue Note ✦✦✦✦✦
A stunning collection of jazz standards, it's done to perfection by a superb guitarist. —*Paul Kohler*

Flying Home / 1988 / EMI ✦✦✦
Album from a contemporary guitar hero who sometimes justifies his reputation, particularly when he stretches out on standards or jazz anthems and showcases his unique way of playing guitar. Jordan's strumming technique enables him to present unusual chords, phrases and statements and, when done in a non-gimmicky manner, offers a genuine alternative to the traditional and fusion guitar vocabulary. —*Ron Wynn*

Street Talk / 1990 / EMI ✦✦

● **Stolen Moments** / Nov. 7, 1990–Nov. 9, 1990 / Somethin' Else ✦✦✦✦✦
Guitarist Stanley Jordan's acclaimed technique, in which he roams over the fretboard strumming and gliding rather than picking, has earned him both plaudits and brickbats. His albums have been inconsistent affairs, but he quieted critics with this '91 session. He took standards and anthems that had been done to death and made them sound fresh through invigorating, explosive guitar solos. —*Ron Wynn*

Bolero / Feb. 15, 1994 / Arista ✦✦

Taft Jordan (James Jordan)

b. Feb. 15, 1915, Florence, SC, **d.** Dec. 1, 1981, New York, NY
Trumpet / Swing
A fine trumpeter, Taft Jordan was known early in his career (when he joined Chick Webb) as a Louis Armstrong soundalike both on trumpet and vocals. In fact, his recording of "On the Sunny Side of the Street" was so close to Armstrong's live show that when Louis got around to documenting it the following year, some listeners thought he was copying Jordan! Taft Jordan had played and recorded with the Washboard Rhythm Kings before starting his long stint with Webb (1933–42), which continued after the drummer's death when the band was fronted by Ella Fitzgerald. Jordan

was (along with Bobby Stark) Webb's main trumpet soloist throughout the 1930s and he gradually developed an original sound of his own. He gained a lot of attention during his period with Duke Ellington (1943–47), although Jordan maintained a lower profile during his last 24 years. He worked at the Savannah Club in New York with Lucille Dixon (1949–53), toured with Benny Goodman (1958), played in show bands and the New York Jazz Repertory Company and had his own group. Taft Jordan recorded four titles as a leader in 1935 and one album apiece for Mercury, Aamco and Moodsville during 1960–61. —*Scott Yanow*

Mood Indigo / Jun. 30, 1961 / Moodsville ✦✦✦✦

Vic Juris

b. 1953
Guitar / Post-Bop
Guitarist Vic Juris is best-known for his association with Richie Cole. He made his recording debut with Eric Kloss (1975), gigged with Barry Miles' fusion group and started his off-and-on association with Cole in 1976, appearing on some of the altoist's finest recordings. In addition to recording with Don Patterson, Mel Tormé and Bireli Lagrene, Juris (a fine hard bop-oriented improviser) has played duets with Larry Coryell, been a member of groups led by Dave Liebman and Gary Peacock and recorded as a leader for Muse and SteepleChase. —*Scott Yanow*

Roadsong / Sep. 19, 1977–Sep. 21, 1977 / Muse ✦✦✦✦

Horizon Drive / Jun. 19, 1979 / Muse ✦✦✦

Bleecker Street / Jul. 14, 1981–Jul. 15, 1981 / Muse ✦✦✦

● **Night Tripper** / Apr. 1994 / SteepleChase ✦✦✦✦✦
During some of the selections on his SteepleChase CD, guitarist Vic Juris displays an echoey tone reminiscent of John Scofield while on a few other numbers he has a drier and subtle acoustic sound. Juris' improvising is on a high level, performing "Estate," "Falling in Love with Love," two obscurities and six group originals (four of which are his) with creativity. His sidemen (pianist Phil Markowitz, basssist Steve LaSpina and drummer Jeff Hirshfield) are alert and have quick reactions. Two highpoints are the eccentric "Dekooning" and a tasteful bossa nova rendition of "Estate," numbers that best show off Juris' impressive flexibility. —*Scott Yanow*

K

Max Kaminsky

b. Sep. 7, 1908, Brockton, MA, **d.** Sept. 6, 1994
Trumpet / Dixieland

Max Kaminsky was a reliable Dixieland player who was featured on many sessions with Eddie Condon's gang in the 1940s and '50s. He played early on in Boston and was a veteran of 1920s Chicago where he gigged with Bud Freeman, Frank Teschemacher and Condon. Moving to New York in 1929, Kaminsky had a short stint with Red Nichols and then worked in commercial bands although he did have opportunities to record with Condon, Benny Carter (1933) and Mezz Mezzrow (1933–34). Kaminsky gained some fame for his work with Tommy Dorsey's Orchestra (1936) including broadcasts with an early version of the Clambake Seven. He was with Artie Shaw briefly in 1938, returned to TD and then was perfectly at home in Bud Freeman's freewheeling Summa Cum Laude Orchestra (1939–40). After periods with Tony Pastor (1940–41) and Artie Shaw's 1942 orchestra, Kaminsky went in the military where he played with Shaw's Navy band throughout the Pacific. Maxie was a star at Eddie Condon's legendary Town Hall concerts (1944–45) and began recording as a leader for Commodore (1944). He alternated between Condon's bands and his own groups, wrote one of the great memoirs (*Jazz Band: My Life in Jazz*), kept an open mind toward newer styles (even jamming with Charlie Parker) while not altering his straightforward approach and toured the Far East with Jack Teagarden (1959). He was a fixture at Jimmy Ryan's for decades and at his death (after a decade of semi-retirement) one of the last surviving Condonites. Max Kaminsky recorded as a leader for Commodore, MGM, Victor (1954), Jazztone, Winchester, United Artists, Chiaroscuro (1977) and Fat Cat Jazz. —*Scott Yanow*

Two for Tea / Dec. 6, 1975–Dec. 5, 1976 / Fat Cat ✦✦✦✦
When Summer Is Gone / Nov. 1, 1977–Nov. 3, 1977 / Chioroscuro ✦✦✦✦✦

Richie Kamuca

b. Jul. 23, 1930, Philadelphia, PA, **d.** Jul. 22, 1977, Los Angeles, CA
Tenor Saxophone / Cool

An excellent cool-toned tenor who found his own voice in the Lester Young-influenced "Four Brothers" sound, Richie Kamuca tended to be overshadowed by those who came first (such as Stan Getz, Zoot Sims and Al Cohn), but musicians knew how good he was. Kamuca was a soloist with the orchestras of Stan Kenton (1952–53) and Woody Herman (1954–56) and then worked steadily on the West Coast with such groups as those led by Chet Baker, Maynard Ferguson, the Lighthouse All-Stars (1957–58), Shorty Rogers and Shelly Manne (1959–61). He recorded one album apiece as a leader for Liberty, Mode and Hi Fi (1956–57); the latter two have been reissued by VSOP. Moving to New York in 1962, Kamuca played with Gerry Mulligan, Gary McFarland and Roy Eldridge (1966–71), but was fairly obscure. In 1972 he moved back to Los Angeles to work in the studios, but he also played jazz locally with small groups and with Bill Berry's L.A. Big Band. In his later years (1977) before his death from cancer (the day before his 47th birthday), Richie Kamuca recorded three wonderful albums for Concord. —*Scott Yanow*

Richie Kamuca Quartet / Jun. 1957 / VSOP ✦✦✦
Considering his talent, it is very surprising that tenor saxophonist Richie Kamuca led so few record dates throughout his career—

just three during 1956–58 and three for Concord in 1977. This quartet set (a MOD LP reissued by VSOP on CD) features the excellent cool-toned tenor in a quartet with pianist Carl Perkins, bassist Leroy Vinnegar and drummer Stan Levey. Only the brief playing time (just over 30 minutes) keeps this set from getting a higher rating, for Kamuca is in prime form. Highlights include "Just Friends," "What's New" and "Cherokee." —*Scott Yanow*

West Coast Jazz in Hi Fi / 1959 / Original Jazz Classics ✦✦✦✦
Originally recorded for the Hi Fi label, this CD reissue features tenor saxophonist Richie Kamuca as the main soloist on a variety of standards and basic material arranged by Bill Holman who plays baritone with the octet. Also heard from are trumpeters Conte Candoli and Ed Leddy, trombonist Frank Rosolino, pianist Vince Guaraldi, bassist Monty Budwig and drummer Stan Levey. The music, although based on the West Coast, is not as cool-toned or as laidback as one might expect. Highpoints of the consistently swinging session include "Blue Jazz" (a Kamuca blues), "Star Eyes," "Linger Awhile" and "Indiana." —*Scott Yanow*

★ **Richie** / 1977 / Concord Jazz ✦✦✦✦✦
Richie Kamuca, a hard-swinging but cool-toned tenorman, did not lead any record sessions after 1958 until he recorded three albums for Concord in early 1977, ironically just months before his death at age 47 from cancer. This particular set may very well have been Kamuca's most rewarding. Accompanied by guitarist Mundell Lowe, bassist Monty Budwig and drummer Nick Ceroli, Kamuca is quite lyrical on the eight superior standards, taking a surprisingly effective vocal on " 'Tis Autumn" and coming up with memorable melodic statements on the other songs. —*Scott Yanow*

Charlie / 1977 / Concord Jazz ✦✦✦✦
Richie Kamuca's death from cancer at age 47 just months after this final session was a major loss to jazz. One of the top proponents of The Four Brothers sound on tenor, Kamuca always swung and his tone was quite attractive. This particular set is a tribute to Charlie Parker featuring Kamuca's quintet (which includes trumpeter Blue Mitchell, pianist Jimmy Rowles, bassist Ray Brown and drummer Donald Bailey). Most unusual is the fact that Kamuca decided to play alto instead of tenor throughout this set and, although this was clearly not his strongest ax, he solos quite well on this date. The music (bop standards and blues) receives favorable and swinging treatment from the talented veterans. —*Scott Yanow*

Drop Me off in Harlem / Feb. 2, 1977 / Concord Jazz ✦✦✦✦✦

Connie Kay

b. Apr. 27, 1927, Tuckahoe, NY, **d.** Nov. 30, 1994
Drums / Cool

For two months shy of 40 years (including seven years in which it was on "vacation"), Connie Kay was the drummer/percussionist with the Modern Jazz Quartet. His subtle contributions (showing both restraint and swing) were an invaluable asset to the group. Self-taught on the drums, Kay played in the mid-'40s with Sir Charles Thompson, Miles Davis and Cat Anderson. He was in Lester Young's quintet off and on during 1949–55, a period in which Kay also worked with Beryl Booker, Stan Getz, Coleman Hawkins and Charlie Parker among others. In February 1955 he joined the MJQ, traveling the world with the band up until it called it "quits" in 1974. During that era, he also appeared as a guest on small group dates by Chet Baker, Cannonball Adderley, Jimmy Heath and Paul Desmond/Jim Hall. During 1975–81 Kay worked with Tommy Flanagan, Soprano Summit, Benny Goodman (including his 40th-anniversary Carnegie Hall Concert) and was the house drummer at Eddie Condon's club. He spent his last 13 years back with the MJQ; Mickey Roker filled in when he was ill and Albert "Tootie" Heath took over the drum slot after Connie Kay's death. *—Scott Yanow*

Geoff Keezer

b. Nov. 21, 1970, Eau Claire, WI
Piano / Hard Bop
Geoff Keezer was only 17 when he became the last pianist in Art Blakey's Jazz Messengers (1988–90), a perfect gig for the talented hard bop musician who fit right in with the Horace Silver-Bobby Timmons-Cedar Walton-James Williams-Benny Green tradition. Since Blakey's death, Keezer has recorded steadily as a leader for Sunnyside, Blue Note, DIW/Columbia and Sackville and played on records led by Art Farmer, Roy Hargrove and Antonio Hart among others. *—Scott Yanow*

Waiting in the Wings / Sep. 16, 1988–Sep. 17, 1988 / Sunnyside ✦✦✦✦
The impressive debut for acclaimed young pianist Geoff Keezer, whose name had been mentioned in New York jazz circles for many months before this release was issued in 1988. He quickly justified the advance notices; his facility, solo flair and harmonic knowledge were quite impressive. He played with a strong band that included vibist Steve Nelson, tenor saxophonist Billy Pierce and bassist Rufus Reid. *—Ron Wynn*

Curveball / Jun. 22, 1989 / Sunnyside ✦✦✦
★ **Here and Now** / Oct. 3, 1990–Oct. 4, 1990 / Blue Note ✦✦✦✦✦
With Steve Nelson on vibes. Excellent version of Harold Mabern's "There but for the Grace of..." *—Michael G. Nastos*

Live At Maybeck Recital Hall, Vol. 11 / Mar. 10, 1991 / Concord ✦✦✦✦✦

World Music / Jan. 5, 1992 / Columbia ✦✦✦✦
Despite the title, there's as much American hard bop as anything, but the set also shows Keezer's knowledge of Afro-Latin rhythms and pulse. He's working with a new group featuring James Genus, Tony Reedus and Rudy Bird. *—Ron Wynn*

Roger Kellaway

b. Nov. 1, 1939, Newton, MA
Piano / Bop, Hard Bop
A virtuosic pianist whose phenomenal technique rivals Dick Hyman's, Roger Kellaway's work in commercial settings prior to the 1980s led to him being initially overlooked in the jazz world. He played piano and bass at the New England Conservatory (1957–59) and actually left school to play bass with Jimmy McPartland. Switching permanently to piano, Kellaway picked up experience working with Kai Winding, Al Cohn/Zoot Sims and Clark Terry/Bob Brookmeyer (1963–65). He recorded with many players including Ben Webster, Maynard Ferguson, Wes Montgomery and Sonny Rollins and, in 1966, moved to Los Angeles where he played with Don Ellis' innovative orchestra. Kellaway became Bobby Darin's musical director, worked in the studios (his piano is heard playing the theme of *All in the Family*), wrote film scores, experimented with electric keyboards, played with Tom Scott and recorded with his popular (but mostly non-jazz) Cello Quartet. Although he gigged locally with Zoot Sims and Harry "Sweets" Edison, it was not until the mid-'80s that Kellaway started playing jazz nearly fulltime. His many records since then (for Concord, All Art, Stash and Chiaroscuro) attest to his impressive talents. *—Scott Yanow*

Cello Quartet / Jul. 1971 / A&M ✦✦✦
Keyboardist Roger Kellaway has specialized in both classic pre-jazz and pop music and has also done some classical arrangements and conducting. This early '70s record featured Kellaway serving as arranger/conductor for a cello quartet and is not a jazz date. It's also out of print. *—Ron Wynn*

Ain't Misbehavin' / Feb. 1986 / Choice ✦✦✦✦
Kellaway showed off his command of the piano on a medium-tempo "How Deep Is the Ocean?" and although "Blue in Green" wanders a bit, "Skylark" is very explorative, almost atonal in spots. Despite its weak beginning, *Almost Misbehavin'* is one of Kellaway's best jazz records to date. *—Scott Yanow*

In Japan / Jun. 5, 1986–Jun. 6, 1986 / All Art Jazz ✦✦✦✦
Alone Together / Jul. 1988 / Dragon ✦✦✦✦
That Was That / Jan. 1991 / Dragon ✦✦✦✦
★ **Live at Maybeck Recital Hall, Vol. 11** / Mar. 10, 1991 / Concord Jazz ✦✦✦✦✦
A recent view of Kellaway's style, it's melodic yet driving with a strong stride-piano influence. *—Hank Davis*

Roger Kellaway Meets Gene Bertoncini and Michael... / Feb. 27, 1992–Feb. 28, 1992 / Chiaroscuro ✦✦✦✦

Concord Duo Series, Vol. 1 (Life's a Take) / May 31, 1992 / Concord Jazz ✦✦✦✦

Sue Keller

b. Jul. 7, 1952, Allentown, PA
Piano / Ragtime, Classic Jazz
A talented ragtime pianist and occasional vocalist who has thus far put out four CDs on her HVR label, Sue Keller started playing piano when she was four. She also studied flute and took voice lessons, played guitar and sang in some school operas. After a wide variety of musical jobs (including playing rock), she started concentrating on vintage jazz and ragtime. In 1992 Sue Keller established Ragtime Press to publish rags by little-known composers and the HVR label to document her music. *—Scott Yanow*

Kellerized / 1992 / Ragtime Press ✦✦✦✦
● **Ol' Muddy** / 1993 / Ragtime Press ✦✦✦✦✦
Nola / 1993 / Ragtime Press ✦✦✦✦
Although essentially a ragtime pianist, Sue Keller usually alters the classic compositions a bit, infusing her performances with her own appealing musical personality. Keller has emerged in recent years as an important force not only in keeping ragtime alive but in mixing together both early and recent compositions. Her third CD has many rewarding moments as she sticks mostly to lesser-known material including "Agitation Rag," "Crazy Bone Rag," two Zez Confrey numbers plus four newer rags from the 1970s and '80s. Her singing on a few tracks (closer to Broadway cabaret in style than to jazz) is okay but of lesser importance next to her sparkling and frequently superb piano playing. *—Scott Yanow*

Ragtime Sue / 1994 / Ragtime Press ✦✦✦✦
Sue Keller's fourth release for Ragtime Press finds the pianist not only playing classic rags but popular songs of the early days (including "Alexander's Ragtime Band" and "St. Louis Blues") and, most significantly, five rags written since 1975. She also sings a few of the non-ragtime pieces with a decent and spirited voice. However, the emphasis is on her piano playing and Keller manages to bring life to the veteran selections by varying the tempos. This CD contains fresh and enthusiastic renditions that keep ragtime from being just a museum piece. *—Scott Yanow*

Peck Kelley

b. Oct. 22, 1898, Houston, TX, **d.** Dec. 26, 1980, Houston, TX
Piano / Classic Jazz
For a brief while before the end of the LP era, it was possible for there to be a Peck Kelley section in the jazz section of some record stores. Considering that Kelley avoided leaving Houston throughout his life and went out of his way not to be recorded, it is miraculous that any documentation exists. In the 1920s Kelley led Peck's Bad Boys in Texas, which featured a young Jack Teagarden and Pee Wee Russell. A talented pianist considered advanced at the time, Kelley was supposed to join Russell, Bix Beiderbecke and Frankie Trumbauer at a gig in St. Louis, but union problems prevented that and Kelley used the excuse to stay home. He was constantly offered jobs up North by major bandleaders and celebrities (including Bing Crosby) but turned them all down. In 1983 (a couple years after his death) a double-LP was released by Commodore featuring Kelley in 1957 near the end of his career playing with a sextet. Shortly after, the collector's label Arcadia came out with privately recorded solo and duet performances from 1951 and 1953. On a whole, these rough but very interesting recordings prove that Kelley was advancing with the times, holding onto his roots in stride while showing that he was quite familiar with Lennie Tristano. *—Scott Yanow*

★ **Jam** / Jun. 9, 1957–Jun. 16, 1957 / Columbia ✦✦✦✦✦

Julie Kelly

b. Oct. 28, 1947, Oakland, CA
Vocals / Standards
A fine singer based in Los Angeles, Julie Kelly studied classical

guitar and attended Oakland City College. She lived in Brazil during 1970 and then started seriously performing in 1973. She freelanced in San Francisco (including with John Handy's group), moved to Los Angeles in 1980 and has recorded for Pausa and CMG. Julie Kelly teaches and performs regularly in L.A. —*Scott Yanow*

Never Let Me Go / 1986 / PA/USA ♦♦♦

● **Some Other Time** / Aug. 13, 1988–Aug. 14, 1988 / Chase Music Group ♦♦♦♦♦

Stories To Tell / 1993 / Chase Music Group ♦♦♦

We're on Our Way / 1985 / Pausa ♦♦♦♦

Wynton Kelly

b. Dec. 2, 1931, Jamaica, **d.** Apr. 12, 1971, Toronto, Canada
Piano / Hard Bop
A superb accompanist loved by Miles Davis and Cannonball Adderley, Wynton Kelly was also a distinctive soloist who decades later would be a strong influence on Benny Green. He grew up in Brooklyn and early on played in R&B bands led by Eddie "Cleanhead" Vinson, Hal Singer and Eddie "Lockjaw" Davis. Kelly, who recorded 14 titles for Blue Note in a trio (1951), worked with Dinah Washington, Dizzy Gillespie and Lester Young during 1951–52. After serving in the military, he made a strong impression with Washington (1955–57), Charles Mingus (1956–57) and the Dizzy Gillespie big band (1957), but he would be most famous for his stint with Miles Davis (1959–63), recording such albums with Miles as *Kind of Blue, At the Blackhawk* and *Someday My Prince Will Come*. When he left Davis, Kelly took the rest of the rhythm section (bassist Paul Chambers and drummer Jimmy Cobb) with him to form his trio. The group actually sounded at its best backing Wes Montgomery. Before his early death, Kelly recorded as a leader for Blue Note, Riverside, Vee-Jay, Verve and Milestone. —*Scott Yanow*

Piano Interpretations / Jul. 25, 1951–Aug. 1, 1951 / Blue Note ♦♦♦♦
Recorded at WOR Studios, NYC. Trio. His first solo recording sessions. Even the uptempo pieces have a gentle quality. Very nice mainstream jazz. —*Michael Erlewine*

Wynton Kelly / Jan. 31, 1958 / Original Jazz Classics ♦♦♦♦♦
With the exception of an album for Blue Note in 1951, this was pianist Wynton Kelly's first opportunity to record as a leader. At the time he was still a relative unknown but would soon get a certain amount of fame as Miles Davis' favorite accompanist. With guitarist Kenny Burrell, bassist Paul Chambers and (on four of the seven selections) drummer Philly Joe Jones, Kelly performs four jazz standards, Oscar Brown, Jr.'s "Strong Man" and two of his originals. Kelly became a major influence on pianists of the 1960s and '70s and one can hear the genesis of many other players in these swinging performances. —*Scott Yanow*

Kelly Blue / Feb. 19, 1959–Mar. 10, 1959 / Original Jazz Classics ♦♦♦♦
Classic Kelly. Bluesy, bright, nice. There is magic in this album. —*Michael Erlewine*

Kelly Great / Aug. 12, 1959 / Vee-Jay ♦♦♦
This presents pianist Wynton Kelly from Feb. 19, 1959 and Mar. 10, 1959 with trumpeter Nat Adderley, saxophonists Bobby Jaspar and Benny Golson, bassist Paul Chambers and drummers Jimmy Cobb. Adderley, Jaspar and Golson played only on the Feb. 19, 1959 tracks (two) and Kelly was accompanied by just the rhythm trio on the remaining four cuts. The sides with horns were best; Nat Adderley was in especially good form. The trio sides were solid, if not particularly explosive or individualistic. The entire LP was also issued as part of a two-fer. —*Bob Rusch, Cadence*

Kelly at Midnight / Apr. 27, 1960 / Vee-Jay ♦♦♦
The problem with this CD reissue is simply that at just over 32 minutes there is not enough of it. The influential pianist Wynton Kelly swings hard and creatively within the bebop tradition with the assistance of bassist Paul Chambers and drummer Philly Joe Jones. Although all three musicians were alumni of Miles Davis' Quintet, Jones had departed before Kelly joined up. However, their familiarity with each other's playing is obvious on this brief but enjoyable set. —*Scott Yanow*

★ **Someday My Prince Will Come** / Sep. 20, 1961–Sep. 21, 1961 / Vee-Jay ♦♦♦♦♦
Pianist Wynton Kelly is heard on this CD reissue (the ten songs

from the original LP plus five "new" alternate takes) with either bassist Sam Jones and drummer Jimmy Cobb or bassist Paul Chambers and drummer Philly Joe Jones. His light touch and perfect taste are very much present, along with a steady stream of purposeful single-note lines that are full of surprising twists. Trumpeter Lee Morgan and tenor saxophonist Wayne Shorter drop by for one song (the blues "Wrinkles"), but otherwise this recommended set (a definitive Wynton Kelly release) showcases magical trio performances. —*Scott Yanow*

Blues on Purpose / Jun. 25, 1965–Aug. 17, 1965 / Xanadu ♦♦♦♦
Fidelity may not be as high as some may wish on this mono disk, but the level of playing *is*, and the sound is quite good enough to document the bristling excitement these three soulmates could generate, whether playing the blues at various tempos or giving Tadd Dameron's "If You Could See Me Now" an elegantly burnished treatment. —*Bob Rusch, Cadence*

Smokin' at the Half Note / Jun. 1965+Sep. 22, 1965 / Verve ♦♦♦♦♦
Some recorded Sept 22, 1965, at Englewood Cliffs, NJ. Wynton Kelly Trio w/ Wes Montgomery (g). Slow to mid-tempos—very listenable. Both Wynton and Wes are in fine form. A rare chance to hear Montgomery in a small-group setting. —*Michael Erlewine*

Full View / 1967 / Milestone ♦♦♦
Trio work; solid and authoritative. —*Ron Wynn*

Last Trio Session / Aug. 4, 1968 / Delmark ♦♦♦
An album of mostly pop tunes, "Light My Fire," "Say a Little Prayer for Me," plus a nice blues by Kelly. Great players working off lighter material, but there are plenty of fine moments. Or, just nice listening. —*Michael Erlewine*

Stan Kenton

b. Dec. 15, 1911, Wichita, KS, **d.** Aug. 25, 1979, Los Angeles, CA
Piano, Leader, Arranger, Composer / Progressive Jazz
There have been few jazz musicians as consistently controversial as Stan Kenton. Dismissed by purists of various genres while loved by many others, Kenton ranks up there with Chet Baker and Sun Ra as jazz's top cult figure. He led a succession of highly original bands that often emphasized emotion, power and advanced harmonies over swing, and this upset listeners who felt that all big bands should aim to sound like Count Basie. Kenton always had a different vision.

Stan Kenton played in the 1930s in the dance bands of Vido Musso and Gus Arnheim but he was born to be a leader. In 1941 he formed his first orchestra, which later was named after his theme song "Artistry in Rhythm." A decent Earl Hines-influenced pianist, Kenton was much more important in the early days as an arranger and inspiration for his loyal sidemen. Although there were no major names in his first band (bassist Howard Rumsey and trumpeter Chico Alvarez come the closest), Kenton spent the summer of 1941 playing regularly before a very appreciative audience at the Rendezvous Ballroom in Balboa Beach, CA. Influenced by Jimmie Lunceford (who, like Kenton, enjoyed high-note trumpeters and thick-toned tenors), the Stan Kenton Orchestra struggled a bit after its initial success. Its Decca recordings were not big sellers and a stint as Bob Hope's backup radio band was an unhappy experience; Les Brown permanently took Kenton's place.

By late 1943 with a Capitol contract, a popular record in "Eager Beaver" and growing recognition, the Stan Kenton Orchestra was gradually catching on. Its soloists during the war years included Art Pepper, briefly Stan Getz, altoist Boots Mussulli and singer Anita O'Day. By 1945 the band had evolved quite a bit. Pete Rugolo became the chief arranger (extending Kenton's ideas), Bob Cooper and Vido Musso offered very different tenor styles and June Christy was Kenton's new singer; her popular hits (including "Tampico" and "Across the Alley from the Alamo") made it possible for Kenton to finance his more ambitious projects. Calling his music "Progressive Jazz," Kenton sought to lead a concert orchestra as opposed to a dance band at a time when most big bands were starting to break up. By 1947 Kai Winding was greatly influencing the sound of Kenton's trombonists, the trumpet section included such screamers as Buddy Childers, Ray Wetzel and Al Porcino, Jack Costanzo's bongos were bringing Latin rhythms into Kenton's sound and a riotous version of "The Peanut Vendor" contrasted with the somber "Elegy for Alto." Kenton had succeeded in forming a radical and very original band that gained its own audience.

In 1949 Stan Kenton took a year off. In 1950 he put together his most advanced band, the 39-piece Innovations in Modern Music orchestra that included 16 strings, a woodwind section and two French horns. Its music ranged from the unique and very dense modern classical charts of Bob Graettinger to works that somehow swung despite the weight. Such major players as Maynard Ferguson (whose high-note acrobatics set new standards), Shorty Rogers, Milt Bernhart, John Graas, Art Pepper, Bud Shank, Bob Cooper, Laurindo Almeida, Shelly Manne and June Christy were part of this remarkable project but, from a commercial standpoint, it was really impossible. Kenton managed two tours during 1950–51, but soon reverted to his usual 19-piece line-up. Then quite unexpectedly, Stan Kenton went through a swinging period. The charts of such arrangers as Shorty Rogers, Gerry Mulligan, Lennie Niehaus, Marty Paich, Johnny Richards and particularly Bill Holman and Bill Russo began to dominate the repertoire. Such talented players (in addition to the ones already named) as Lee Konitz, Conte Candoli, Sal Salvador, Stan Levey, Frank Rosolino, Richie Kamuca, Zoot Sims, Sam Noto, Bill Perkins, Charlie Mariano, Mel Lewis, Pete Candoli, Lucky Thompson, Carl Fontana, Pepper Adams and Jack Sheldon made strong contributions. The music was never predictable and could get quite bombastic, but it managed to swing while still keeping the Kenton sound.

Stan Kenton's last successful experiment was his mellophonium band of 1960–63. Despite the difficulties in keeping the four mellophoniums (which formed their own separate section) in tune, this particular Kenton Orchestra had its exciting moments. However, from 1963 on, the flavor of the Kenton big band began to change. Rather than using talented soloists, Kenton emphasized relatively inexpensive youth at the cost of originality. While the arrangements (including those of Hank Levy) continued to be quite challenging, after Gabe Baltazar's "graduation" in 1965, there were few new important Kenton alumni (other than Peter Erskine and Tim Hagans). For many of the young players, touring with Stan Kenton would be the highpoint of their careers rather than just an important early step. *Kenton Plays Wagner* (1964) was an important project, but by then the bandleader's attention was on jazz education. By conducting a countless number of clinics and making his charts available to college and high-school stage bands, Kenton ensured that there would be many bands that sounded like his, and the inverse result was that his own young orchestra sounded like a professional college band! Kenton continued leading and touring with his big band up until his death in 1979.

Stan Kenton recorded for Capitol for 25 years (1943–68) and in the 1970s formed his Creative World label to reissue most of his Capitol output and record his current band. In recent times, Capitol has begun reissuing Kenton's legacy on CD and there have been two impressive Mosaic box sets. — *Scott Yanow*

Kenton Era / Nov. 1, 1940–Sep. 18, 1953 / Creative World ✦✦✦✦✦
This four-LP set contains a great deal of extraordinary music from Stan Kenton, most of it recorded live in concert or taken from radio transcriptions. Kenton is heard reminiscing about his first 15 years in the business, there are some selections taken from his famous 1941 stint at the Rendezvous Ballroom in Balboa, CA, numbers from rehearsals in 1944, radio airchecks dating from 1944–48, some startling performances by Kenton's Innovations orchestra of 1950–51 and a few swinging numbers from his 1952–53 big band. Virtually all of the music is rare, making this an essential acquisition for collectors. — *Scott Yanow*

The Uncollected Stan Kenton & His Orchestra, Vol. 1 (1941) / 1941 / Hindsight ✦✦✦
Hindsight has released six Stan Kenton LPs originating from noncommercial sources. The first volume, taken from various radio transcriptions cut during 1941, gives one an interesting look at the early Kenton orchestra including performances of many songs that were not otherwise recorded by the innovative bandleader. Red Norris (who takes the tenor solos and has two vocals) was Kenton's first star and trumpeter Chico Alvarez has a few good spots on trumpet, but it is the unusual arrangements that gave this orchestra its own unique personality. — *Scott Yanow*

The Uncollected Stan Kenton & His Orchestra, Vol. 2 (1941) / 1941 / Hindsight ✦✦✦
The second of the six Hindsight Stan Kenton LPs covers the same early period as the first. tenor saxophonist Red Dorris and trumpeter Chico Alvarez are the main soloists while Kenton's arrange-

ments (including the four part "Suite for Saxophones") are the main reason that this orchestra gained such a loyal following. No other big band sounded like it and, although its sound would evolve and change (the emphasis in the early days was on the saxophone section led by altoist Jack Ordean), the performances by Stan Kenton's first orchestra can easily be enjoyed by the fans of his later bands. These formerly rare performances are taken from radio transcriptions and contain many songs not otherwise recorded by Kenton. — *Scott Yanow*

The Formative Years / Sep. 11, 1941+Feb. 13, 1942 / Creative World ✦✦✦
It is easy to believe that Stan Kenton's first recordings took place when he signed with Capitol in 1943, but this LP contains his nine earlier performances for Decca. None of the songs were hits even though the band had caused a sensation in 1941 with their engagement in Balboa, CA. With tenor saxophonist Red Dorris and trumpeter Chico Alvarez as the main soloists and altoist Jack Ordean leading the saxophone section (which in the early days was more important to Kenton's sound than the trumpets), this orchestra already stood out from its contemporaries. Highlights among the nine performances on this necessarily brief album (only 27 minutes) are "Gambler's Blues," "Reed Rapture" and "Concerto for Doghouse." This set is essential for all true Stan Kenton fans. — *Scott Yanow*

Milestones / Nov. 19, 1943–Dec. 22, 1947 / Creative World ✦✦✦✦
This LP from Creative World has the original version of Stan Kenton's theme song, "Artistry in Rhythm," his first hit "Eager Beaver," "Artistry Jumps" and eight of his most popular recordings from the 1946–47 period including "Intermission Riff," "Concerto to End All Concertos" and "The Peanut Vendor." This music is essential in one form or another and virtually all of it is available in the four-CD Kenton set *Retrospective*. These performances are still exciting a half-century later. — *Scott Yanow*

By Request, Vol. 3 (1943–1951) / Nov. 19, 1943–Mar. 28, 1951 / Creative World ✦✦✦✦
The third volume in Creative World's *By Request* series mostly sticks to the 1946–47 period with three numbers from 1943–45 and three dating from 1950–51. Highlights include "Harlem Folk Dance," "Southern Scandal," "Unison Riff" and "Dynaflow" and among the soloists are altoist Art Pepper (heard from in two different periods), the tenor of Vido Musso, trumpeter Chico Alvarez and trombonist Kai Winding; in addition, there are two vocal tracks for The Pastels and Anita O'Day sings "Gotta Be Gettin'." This diverse LP fills some important gaps since many of the selections are not reissued that often; most importantly the music is consistently enjoyable. — *Scott Yanow*

★ **Retrospective** / Nov. 19, 1943–Jul. 18, 1968 / Capitol ✦✦✦✦✦
This four-CD set has virtually all of Stan Kenton's most significant recordings from his prime years. Although Kenton completists will prefer to pick up dozens of his individual Creative World releases instead, all other jazz collectors are well-advised to get this very well-conceived release. Starting with the original version of "Artistry in Rhythm" from 1943 and continuing through all of the different editions of Kenton's orchestras up to 1968's "How Are Things in Glocca Morra," this set includes not only all of the band's most popular recordings but some of its most inventive and esoteric ones too. Whether it be "Tampico," "Concerto to End All Concertos," "Jolly Rogers," "Art Pepper," "Orange Colored Sky" (with guest Nat King Cole), "All About Ronnie," "Peanut Vendor," and "Maria" or a section of "City of Glass" and a number from the Kenton/Wagner album, the remarkable career of Stan Kenton is covered definitively on this package. It's highly recommended for all jazz collections. — *Scott Yanow*

The Uncollected Stan Kenton & His Orchestra, Vol. 3 (1943–1944) / 1943–1944 / Hindsight ✦✦✦
The Stan Kenton Orchestra, after some initial success, was struggling a bit during the period covered by this Hindsight LP, the third of six volumes. The material performed on these radio broadcasts is certainly eclectic, ranging from such current pop hits as "Paper Doll," "Hit That Jive, Jack" and "Begin the Beguine" to "Eager Beaver" and "In a Little Spanish Town." However, the Kenton Orchestra (which was then in a transitional stage) was already quite unique and among the many soloists are a young Stan Getz on tenor (taking a spot on "I Got Rhythm"), veteran tenor Red Dorris and trumpeter Karl George (well featured on "Liza"). Anita O'Day (who was only with the band a brief time)

has three vocals and Dolly Mitchell is heard on "Shoo Shoo Baby."
—*Scott Yanow*

Lighter Side / May 20, 1944–Jan. 25, 1955 / Creative World ✦✦✦✦
When one thinks of Stan Kenton's music, humor is not the first
word that comes to mind. But the innovative bandleader did
record some humorous numbers through the years and 11 are
included on this memorable LP. "The Hot Canary" (which features
some ridiculous high-note trumpet from Maynard Ferguson) and
"Blues in Burlesque" (a hilarious satire of rhythm & blues with a
remarkable vocal by Shelly Manne) are classics of a sort but all of
these performances stick in one's mind. —*Scott Yanow*

By Request, Vol. 1 (1944–1952) / Dec. 15, 1944–Mar. 20, 1952 /
Creative World ✦✦✦✦
Other than three early selections ("Balboa Bash," "Machito" and
"Harlem Holiday"), this LP concentrates on the more swinging
performances from Stan Kenton's orchestras of 1950-52.
Highlights include two charts by Shorty Rogers ("Jolly Rogers"
and "Round Robin"), "Blues in Riff" and "Love for Sale." Many
notable names have solo space including trombonist Kai Winding,
tenor great Bob Cooper, altoist Art Pepper, Shorty Rogers and
Maynard Ferguson on trumpets and altoist Bud Shank. It's a
strong introduction to the music of Stan Kenton. —*Scott Yanow*

**The Uncollected Stan Kenton & His Orchestra, Vol. 4
(1944–1945)** / 1944–1945 / Hindsight ✦✦✦
This LP is the fourth in Hindsight's series of Stan Kenton material originally recorded for the C.P. MacGregor radio transcription
service and leased to radio stations for air play only. These performances (which were never available commercially before) feature two different editions of the Stan Kenton Orchestra along
with vocal features for Anita O'Day and her successor June
Christy. The music is quite distinctive, standing apart from the
swing and bop idioms and highlighted by the arrangements of
Pete Rugolo and Gene Roland. Stan Kenton fans will want all six
LPs in this enjoyable series. —*Scott Yanow*

Some Women I've Known / Jan. 16, 1945–Sep. 11, 1963 /
Creative World ✦✦✦
This fine LP contains 12 performances, two apiece from these six
singers with Stan Kenton's Orchestra: Anita O'Day, June Christy,
Chris Connor, Jerri Winters, Ann Richards and Jean Turner. With
the exception of Connor's "All About Ronnie," none of the recordings are all that familiar and five were actually issued for the first
time on this album. Fans of swing-oriented singers will enjoy the
valuable set. —*Scott Yanow*

Christy Years / May 4, 1945–Dec. 21, 1947 / Creative World
✦✦✦✦✦
Of all the vocalists who worked with Stan Kenton's Orchestra, June
Christy was the most popular and fit the group's music the best. In
fact her popularity indirectly helped Kenton finance his more adventurous projects. This LP from Creative World has a dozen of Christy's
best recordings including such hits as "Tampico," "Across the Alley
from the Alamo," "Shoo Fly Pie and Apple Pan Dowdy" and "How
High the Moon." Such soloists as Vido Musso on tenor, trombonist
Kai Winding and trumpeter Chico Alvarez also have spots while
altoist Art Pepper pops up on "How High the Moon." —*Scott Yanow*

Encores / Oct. 30, 1945–Dec. 22, 1947 / Creative World ✦✦✦
This LP contains 11 fairly rare and diverse performances from the
1945-47 edition of Stan Kenton's Orchestra. June Christy sings
"He's Funny That Way" and such soloists as Vido Musso on tenor,
trumpeter Chico Alvarez, trombonist Kai Winding, Bob Cooper on
tenor and altoist Art Pepper have spots. None of the selections are
considered classics, but most (particularly "Painted Rhythm,"
"Capitol Punishment" and "Abstraction") should delight Kenton
collectors. —*Scott Yanow*

Artistry in Rhythm / Oct. 30, 1945–Sep. 4, 1950 / Creative ✦✦✦✦
This sampler from the Creative World catalog consists of 12 per-
formances by Stan Kenton's Orchestra, mostly from 1945-46.
There are four June Christy vocals (including "Just A-Sittin' And
A-Rockin' "), a pair of features for guest tenor Vido Musso ("Come
Back to Sorrento" and "Santa Lucia") and six other pieces (all
Kenton and Pete Rugolo arrangements) of which the highlights
include "Safranski," "Artisrty in Bolero" and "Opus in Pastels." It's
a fine sampling of Stan Kenton's mid-'40s orchestra. —*Scott
Yanow*

Stan Kenton and His Orchestra, Vol. 5 / 1945–1947 / Hindsight
✦✦✦
It was during the period covered by this Hindsight LP that Stan

Kenton caught on and became a household name. These radio
performances mostly feature arrangements by Pete Rugolo and
Gene Roland, although Boots Mussulli contributed a memorable
rendition of "I Surrender Dear" and Kenton himself wrote the
chart for "Begin the Beguine." Singer June Christy, tenor Vido
Musso, trombonist Kai Winding, trumpeter Buddy Childers are
the main stars, but it is the ensembles and the distinctive arrangements that gave this edition of the Stan Kenton Orchestra its own
personality. All of the well-recorded sets in this valuable
Hindsight series are recommended to Kenton fans. —*Scott Yanow*

A Concert in Progressive Jazz / Sep. 24, 1947–Sep. 20, 1951 /
Creative World ✦✦✦✦✦
This is a fascinating collection of very advanced music. All but
two numbers from 1951 ("Theme for Alto" and June Christy's
vocal feature on "Come Rain or Come Shine") are from 1947 and
all of the charts except for Bob Graettinger's somewhat amazing
"Thermopolae" are by Pete Rugolo. This LP contains some of
Rugolo's most interesting work (highlighted by "Elegy for Alto,"
"Monotony," "Lonely Woman," "Cuban Carnival" and "Theme for
Alto") and finds Stan Kenton realizing his goal of leading a concert orchestra rather than a dance band. The unique performances
(many of which helped Stan Kenton become a cult hero) reward
repeated listenings. —*Scott Yanow*

☆ **City of Glass** / Dec. 6, 1947–May 28, 1953 / Capitol ✦✦✦✦✦
Bob Graettinger was arguably the most radical arranger to ever
work in jazz. In fact, it is doubtful if any other big-band leader
other than Stan Kenton (who always encouraged adventurous
writers) would have used his very complex charts during this era.
Graettinger's works, which were influenced by aspects of modern
classical music (but were not at all derivative) are all included on
this fascinating, if difficult, CD reissue. The four-part "City of
Glass," the pieces that comprised "This Modern World" and a variety of shorter works (including the remarkably dense
"Thermopylae") make for some very stimulating listening! This is
avant-garde music that still sounds futuristic 45 years later. —
Scott Yanow

Innovations in Modern Music / Feb. 3, 1950–Feb. 4, 1950 /
Creative World ✦✦✦✦✦
In 1950 Stan Kenton led his most radical band, a 37-piece orches-
tra with 14 strings and such sidemen as altoists Art Pepper and
Bud Shank, Bob Cooper on tenor, trumpeters Shorty Rogers,
Chico Alvarez and Maynard Ferguson, trombonist Milt Bernhart,
two French horns, a tuba, guitarist Laurindo Almeida, drummer
Shelly Manne, Carlos Vidal on congas and singer June Christy.
This LP contains some very advanced writing by Pete Rugolo
("Conflict" and "Mirage"), Bill Russo ("Solitaire") and particularly
Bob Graettinger ("Incident in Jazz") in addition to features for
Kenton's piano ("Theme for Sunday"), June Christy ("Lonesome
Road") and Carlos Vidal ("Cuban Episode"). The music is often
quite fascinating and very advanced; most of it is has not yet been
reissued on CD. —*Scott Yanow*

Kenton Presents / Feb. 3, 1950–Aug. 24, 1950 / Creative World
✦✦✦✦✦
Stan Kenton's most ambitious orchestra was his huge 1950 band.
This LP, which mostly contains material not yet reissued on CD,
has self-titled showcases for "Art Pepper," "Maynard Ferguson,"
"June Christy" and "Shelly Manne" in addition to such pieces as
"Halls of Brass," "House of Strings" and "Soliloquy." The soloists
(which also include trombonist Milt Bernhardt) are very impressive, but it is the writing (by Shorty Rogers, Bill Russo, Frank
Marks, Johnny Richards and Kenton himself) that is most startling, combining together aspects of modern classical music with
the most advanced forms of jazz. Although Kenton's Innovations
orchestra was a short-lived project and did not influence the
future of jazz, its recordings still sound very adventurous over
four decades later. —*Scott Yanow*

☆ **Complete Capitol Recordings of the Bill Holman and Bill
Russo** / Feb. 3, 1950–Sep. 11, 1963 / Mosaic ✦✦✦✦
This limited-edition box set is a bit unusual for, rather than reis-
suing the complete output of a particular artist during a certain
era as Mosaic usually does, these four CDs contain all of Stan
Kenton's recordings of arrangements by either Bill Holman or Bill
Russo. There are three selections from The Innovations band of
1950-51, many recordings from the more swinging 1952-55 peri-
od (featuring such soloists as trumpeters Maynard Ferguson and
Conte Candoli, trombonist Frank Rosolino, altoists Lee Konitz and
Charlie Mariano, tenors Zoot Sims and Bill Perkins and singer

Chris Connor) and Holman's three charts for Kenton's mellophonium band of 1961 in addition to less significant vocal features for Ann Richards and Jean Turner. Kenton completists will already have much of this material (only an early version of "All About Ronnie" was previously unissued), but this attractive box (which is overflowing with classics) will still be treasured by true Kentonites. —*Scott Yanow*

By Request, Vol. 4 (1950–1952) / Sep. 12, 1950–Sep. 11, 1952 / Creative World ✦✦✦
Stan Kenton's 1951–52 orchestra is well-featured on the dozen somewhat obscure studio recordings included on this LP. With solo space allocated to altoist Art Pepper, trombonists Frank Rosolino and Milt Bernhardt, trumpeter Conte Candoli and Maynard Ferguson, guitarist Laurindo Almeida and altoist Lee Konitz (there are also three vocals by the forgotten Jay Johnson and June Christy sings "Daddy"), bop fans should be interested in searching for this now-rare collection. The music is not essential and there are no classics here, but the set has its strong moments and most of it has not been reissued on CD yet. —*Scott Yanow*

Collector's Choice / Sep. 12, 1950–Feb. 11, 1956 / Creative World ✦✦✦
The emphasis is on standards and melodic material on this enjoyable LP from Creative World. Quite a few of the performances by Stan Kenton's Orchestra are features for talented individuals including the dramatic tenor of Vido Musso ("Santa Lucia" and "Pagliacci"), trumpeter Ray Wetzel ("September Song"), trombonist Milt Bernhart ("Artistry in Tango"), trombonist Carl Fontana ("Sunset Tower" and "Southern Scandal"), trumpeter Chico Alvarez ("Laura") and Maynard Ferguson ("What's New") although Shorty Rogers' "Viva Prado" is probably the best-known recording. A worthy collection mostly dating from 1950–51. —*Scott Yanow*

Summer of '51 / Dec. 21, 1950 / Garland ✦✦✦✦

Stan Kenton and His Innovations Orchestra / 1950–1951 / Laserlight ✦✦✦✦✦
The total amount of time (a little over 38 minutes) is quite brief for this CD, but the release is selling for a budget price and the previously unreleased performances are quite valuable. Stan Kenton's Innovations Orchestra (39 members strong counting 16 strings) was the bandleader's most ambitious project with the many brilliant soloists (including altoists Bud Shank and Art Pepper, Bob Cooper on tenor, trumpeters Conte Candoli and Maynard Ferguson) being challenged by the very complex arrangements of Bill Russo, Shorty Rogers and Bob Graettinger among others. This recommended set is highlighted by four selections named after their stars ("Shelly Manne," "Conte Candoli," "Art Pepper" and "Bob Cooper"), Bill Russo's "Improvisation" and Bob Graettinger's dense "Reflections." —*Scott Yanow*

Live (1951) / Mar. 1951 / Band Stand ✦✦✦✦
This collector's CD is a bit unusual for it features Stan Kenton's Innovations Orchestra without its string section. Actually, the big band mostly sticks to its repertoire of the 1940s on these radio broadcasts, playing fairly straight-ahead charts that give such players as trumpeters Maynard Ferguson and Shorty Rogers, altoists Art Pepper and Bud Shank, tenor saxophonist Bob Cooper and trombonist Milt Bernhart an opportunity to be featured. Fans of Stan Kenton's earlier groups will find these updated and often re-arranged versions of such songs as "Peanut Vendor," "Eager Beaver," "Southern Scandal," "Intermission Riff" and "Round Robin" quite interesting. —*Scott Yanow*

Portraits on Standards / Sep. 20, 1951–May 6, 1954 / Creative World ✦✦✦✦
While most of Stan Kenton's recordings in the 1950s tend to be complex and sometimes bombastic, his versions of standards could often be sentimental and very melodic. This LP from the Creative World catalog (music originally released by Capitol) alternates between ballads and boppish romps, mostly featuring the 1953–54 orchestra, a band that could often swing hard. With such major soloists as altoist Art Pepper (featured on "Street of Dreams"), trumpeter Conte Candoli, Zoot Sims on tenor, altoist Lee Konitz and trombonist Frank Rosolino, Kenton's orchestra could hold its own with any big band of the period. The arrangements (all by either Bill Russo or Kenton) showcase these talents at their best. —*Scott Yanow*

Live At Cornell University, 1951 / Oct. 14, 1951 / Jazz Unlimited ✦✦✦
This 1993 CD of previously unreleased material features the most

adventurous and controversial of Stan Kenton's bands, his Innovations orchestra. Heard in the middle of their second (and sadly final) tour, the 40-piece orchestra (which includes 17 strings) plays such material as "Opus In Pastels," "Dance Before the Mirror" (which is taken from Bob Graettinger's "City of Glass Suite"), "Halls of Brass" and the self-titled pieces "Shelly Manne," "John Graas," "Maynard Ferguson," "Art Pepper" and "Bob Cooper." With such soloists as the screaming trumpeter Maynard Ferguson, Bud Shank (mostly on flute), altoist Art Pepper, John Graas on French horn, tenorman Bob Cooper and trumpeter Conte Candoli, the huge aggregation was top heavy with talent. However, it was the very advanced arrangements and the innovative use of strings that made this a unique, if short-lived, orchestra. This concert recording has decent sound and some inspired playing that ranks at the level of the band's studio sessions. Highly recommended to Stan Kenton fans. —*Scott Yanow*

23 Degrees North, 82 / Sep. 2, 1952–Apr. 23, 1953 / Natasha ✦✦✦
This CD features Stan Kenton's Orchestra on five separate radio broadcasts from 1952–53. Unfortunately, the first seven songs (all taken from April 2, 1953) have a distracting hum, but otherwise the music is consistently enjoyable. Kenton's band of 1953 was one of his most swinging, featuring a strong rhythm section propelled by drummer Stan Levey and such soloists as tenorman Richie Kamuca, trumpeter Conte Candoli, trombonist Frank Rosolino and altoist Lee Konitz in addition to singer Chris Connor. Konitz in particular is well-featured on this CD, which puts the emphasis on standards and hard-swinging. —*Scott Yanow*

● **New Concepts of Artistry in Rhythm** / Sep. 8, 1952–Sep. 16, 1952 / Capitol ✦✦✦✦✦
Stan Kenton's 1952 Orchestra was a very interesting transitional band, still performing some of the complex works of the prior Innovations orchestra but also starting to emphasize swing. This CD contains the rather pompous "Prologue" and Bill Holman's complex "Invention for Guitar and Trumpet" (starring guitarist Sal Salvador and trumpeter Maynard Ferguson) but also Gerry Mulligan's boppish "Young Blood" and Bill Russo's features for trumpeter Conte Candoli ("Portrait of a Count"), trombonist Frank Rosolino ("Frank Speaking") and altoist Lee Konitz ("My Lady"). —*Scott Yanow*

Spotlight on Konitz and Connor / Dec. 11, 1952–Apr. 30, 1953 / Nata ✦✦✦✦
This CD contains selections taken from radio broadcasts by one of Stan Kenton's finest orchestras. With such soloists as altoist Lee Konitz (who has many features), trombonist Frank Rosolino and trumpeter Conte Candoli, in addition to five warm vocals by Chris Connor, the Kenton Orchestra uplifts the many standards it interprets, making this one of the more accessible Stan Kenton releases. —*Scott Yanow*

Sketches on Standards / Jan. 28, 1953–Jan. 25, 1955 / Creative World ✦✦✦
This LP contains six Bill Russo arrangements, five from Stan Kenton and one by Lennie Niehaus. The repertoire features many songs not associated with Kenton (such as "Sophisticated Lady," "Pennies from Heaven" and "Over the Rainbow"), but the inventive yet melodic treatments certainly sound like the Kenton band. The main soloists are altoist Lee Konitz, guitarist Sal Salvador, trumpeter Conte Canoli and trombonist Frank Rosolino and, although these concise interpretations (none of the dozen performances are much over three minutes) are not essential, the music is quite pleasing. This collection is a change of pace for the Stan Kenton Orchestra. —*Scott Yanow*

By Request, Vol. 5 (1953–1960) / Feb. 11, 1953–Sep. 19, 1960 / Creative World ✦✦✦
It is doubtful that anyone would have requested any of the dozen performances heard on this LP because they are among the more obscure recordings by Stan Kenton's Orchestra. There are no classics here, but fans of Kenton's music will be interested in this rare material. Highlights include Chris Connor's vocal on "If I Should Lose You," Lennie Niehaus' alto solo on "I'm Glad There Is You" and three features for Kenton's piano. —*Scott Yanow*

The Definitive Kenton / Jun. 9, 1953–Nov. 18, 1955 / Artistry ✦✦✦✦
This double LP from the Artistry label is particularly special because it contains three songs apiece on which Charlie Parker and Dizzy Gillespie guest with the Stan Kenton Orchestra. Although those performances took place on the same day (Feb.

28, 1954), unfortunately Diz and Bird appear separately; Gillespie fares best. However, this two-fer would be worth acquiring anyway due to the many swinging concert performances and the consistently exciting solos by such Kenton sidemen as altoist Lee Konitz, trombonist Frank Rosolino, trumpeter Conte Candoli and tenor saxophonist Zoot Sims among others. With Bill Holman and Bill Russo contributing most of the arrangements and drummer Stan Levey driving the band, this is one of the better Stan Kenton collections from the 1950s. —*Scott Yanow*

Kenton '53–Concert In Weisbaden / Sep. 9, 1953 / Astral Jazz ✦✦✦✦

The Stan Kenton Orchestra, on a 1953 tour of Europe, arrived in Weisbaden, Germany exhausted and a bit late. However, the music quickly revived the bandmembers and the results can be heard on this small-label CD. The recording quality is quite good, allowing listeners to sample a typical Kenton program from the era. No major new works were premiered, but such talented players as altoist Lee Konitz, tenor saxophonist Zoot Sims and trombonist Frank Rosolino are well featured; trumpeter Conte Candoli, altoist Dave Shildkraut and trombonist Bob Burgess are also heard from. June Christy, back with the band after a three-year absence, has five happy vocals. The enthusiastic crowd obviously inspired the musicians and this set should please all Kenton fans. —*Scott Yanow*

The European Tour: 1953 / Sep. 16, 1953 / Artistry ✦✦✦✦✦

This CD features Stan Kenton's 1953 Orchestra live during a concert from Munich, Germany. This was a particularly strong band with such soloists as trumpeter Conte Candoli, tenor saxophonist Zoot Sims, altoist Lee Konitz and trombonist Frank Rosolino; arrangers Bill Russo and Bill Holman also played in the orchestra (on trombone and tenor) and first trumpeter Buddy Childers and drummer Stan Levey were particularly important assets. There are many highlights to this well-recorded and consistently exciting performance, including a six-song mini-set by singer June Christy who rejoined Kenton for the historic tour. It's highly recommended. —*Scott Yanow*

By Request, Vol. 2 (1953–1960) / Nov. 30, 1953–Sep. 20, 1960 / Creative World ✦✦✦

This enjoyable LP from the Creative World catalog has selections taken from a seven-year period with the emphasis on the 1954–56 bands. Highlights include "Lover Man" (a feature for altoist Lee Konitz), "Opus in Chartreuse," "Opus in Turquoise" and "Lazy Afternoon." Since this program has performances from several Kenton Orchestras, a wide variety of soloists are heard from including guitarist Laurindo Almeida, tenor saxophonist Bill Perkins, trumpeter Sam Noto, altoist Charlie Mariano and veteran tenor Sam Donahue. The arrangements (by Bill Russo, Bill Holman, Gene Roland and Kenton among others) are generally colorful and the rarity of some of this material makes this set of particular interest to Kenton collectors. —*Scott Yanow*

Duet / May 5, 1955–May 9, 1955 / Capitol ✦✦✦✦✦

Kenton in Stereo / Feb. 11, 1956–Feb. 12, 1956 / Capitol ✦✦✦

In the mid-to-late '50s, many of the surviving big bands (some of which were thrown together just for the occasion) were rerecording their hits in stereo or hi fi. Stan Kenton was no exception. This set is comprised of remakes of a dozen of his earlier recordings. Veteran tenor Vido Musso returned to Kenton for the album and he is the chief soloist although there are also spots for trombonist Milt Bernhart, trumpeters Sam Noto and Pete Candoli and altoist Lennie Niehaus. Among the selections are "Intermission Riff," "The Peanut Vendor," "Eager Beaver" and "Concerto to End All Concertos." —*Scott Yanow*

Cuban Fire / May 22, 1956–May 24, 1956 / Capitol ✦✦✦✦✦

This CD contains one of the classic Stan Kenton albums, a six-part suite composed and arranged by Johnny Richards. The Kenton orchestra was expanded to 27 pieces for these dates including six percussionists, two French horns and six trumpets. With such soloists as tenor-great Lucky Thompson (on "Fuego Cubano," trombonist Carl Fontana, altoist Lennie Niehaus, Bill Perkins on tenor and trumpeters Sam Noto and Vinnie Tanno and plenty of raging ensembles, this is one of Stan Kenton's more memorable concept albums of the 1950s. —*Scott Yanow*

Kenton '56 / Nov. 5, 1956 / Artistry ✦✦✦✦

The Artistry label has released several live sets by Stan Kenton's Orchestra from the 1950s and all of these well-recorded sets are highly recommended to Stan Kenton fans. This particular LP originates from a club appearance in San Francisco and finds the 20-piece big band performing arrangements by Bill Holman and Gerry Mulligan along with one by Johnny Richards. At the time, Kenton had an all-star saxophone section comprised of Bill Perkins and Richie Kamuca on tenors, altoist Lennie Niehaus and baritonist Pepper Adams; all have solo space on this set with Adams showcased on "My Funny Valentine." The other horn players are not as well-known, but also do well in their spots during the swinging bop-oriented material. The rhythm section (driven by drummer Mel Lewis) really pushes the oversized band to play at its best. —*Scott Yanow*

Kenton with Voices / Jan. 17, 1957–Mar. 4, 1957 / Capitol ✦✦

Rendezvous with Kenton / Oct. 8, 1957–Sep. 10, 1957 / Creative World ✦✦

This LP is one of the less essential Stan Kenton recordings. The 18-piece orchestra is featured playing Joe Coccia's dance arrangements of melodic standards. None of the dozen performances are as long as four minutes (two clock in under two minutes) and the solos generally stick close to the themes. There are some brief spots for trumpeter Sam Noto, altoist Lennie Niehaus, trombonist Kent Larson and the tenor of Bill Perkins but no real excitement occurs. The music is pleasant but not up to the fiery level one would expect of the Stan Kenton Orchestra. —*Scott Yanow*

Back to Balboa / 1958 / Capitol ✦✦✦

For this LP, Stan Kenton's Orchestra performs seven Johnny Richards arrangements and two from Marty Paich along with Bill Holman's "Royal Blue." The 1958 Kenton big band had several excellent soloists and there is a generous amount of individual space for tenor saxophonist Bill Perkins, altoist Lennie Niehaus, trumpeter Sam Noto and trombonist Archie LeCoque among others during a set dominated by modern versions of standards. Well-played if not quite essential music. —*Scott Yanow*

By Request, Vol. 6 (1958–1962) / May 15, 1958–Sep. 28, 1962 / Creative World ✦✦

With the exception of one earlier track, the 11 performances on this LP feature Stan Kenton's 1961–62 Mellophonium Band. Actually, many of these numbers are a bit lightweight with three Jean Turner vocals, a group "singalong" on "Beside Balboa Bay" and a couple of melodic standards that have Kenton's piano in the lead. There are a few stronger charts (mostly by Gene Roland) and although this is not one of the essential Stan Kenton albums (who "requested" these songs?), any recording by what was Kenton's last great orchestra is worth hearing. —*Scott Yanow*

Lush Interlude / Jul. 14, 1958 / Creative World ✦✦

A 1958 selection with the Kenton Orchestra doing mostly soft, sentimental pieces instead of the surging, frenetic brass works that they were making famous during this period. —*Ron Wynn*

The Stage Door Swings / Sep. 22, 1958 / Capitol ✦✦

Several of Stan Kenton's late-'50s studio recordings do not live up to the potential of his talented orchestra. This is a pleasant set that features Lennie Niehaus' concise (mostly under three minutes) arrangements of then-current show tunes such as "The Party's Over," "Whatever Lola Wants," "Younger than Springtime" and "I Love Paris." Soloists include trumpeter Jack Sheldon, trombonist Ken Larson, Bill Perkins on tenor and Niehaus himself on alto but little exciting happens on what was really a dance-oriented set. — *Scott Yanow*

Kenton Touch / Dec. 23, 1958 / Creative World ✦✦

A 1958 Kenton album that's pretty straightforward and less ambitious than many during that period. The arrangements are standard, the brass section plays with more restraint and less volume, and it's among his best conventional jazz releases. Bill Holman's charts are excellent. —*Ron Wynn*

Kenton Live from the Las Vegas Tropicana / Feb. 2, 1959 / Creative World ✦✦✦

The 1959 Stan Kenton Orchestra, which boasted such soloists as trumpeter Jack Sheldon, altoist Lennie Niehaus, Richie Kamuca and Bill Trujillo on tenors and trombonist Ken Larsen, is heard in spirited form on this live LP. Performing arrangements mostly by Gene Roland along with one apiece by Johnny Richards, Niehaus and Kenton, the band plays some surprising material (such as "Tuxedo Junction" and "Street Scene") but mostly comes up with creative, fresh and concise statements. This is admittedly not one of the classic Stan Kenton recordings, but is generally superior to his studio recordings of the period. —*Scott Yanow*

Standards in Silhouette / Sep. 21, 1959–Sep. 22, 1959 / Capitol ◆◆◆
This LP is a ballad date by Stan Kenton's 1959 orchestra. Although many of Kenton's top sidemen of a few years earlier had departed, a few of the youngsters in their place included future greats such as trumpeters Rolf Ericson and Bill Chase, trombonist Don Sebesky and baritonist Jack Nimitz. Best known among the soloists is altoist Charlie Mariano. The music (all Bill Mathieu arrangements) is not all that innovative, but the treatments given such songs as "The Meaning of the Blues," "Django" and "I Get Along Without You Very Well" are pleasing and reasonably enjoyable on this relaxed session. —*Scott Yanow*

Viva Kenton / Sep. 22, 1959–Sep. 23, 1959 / Creative World ◆◆◆◆
Stan Kenton added three Latin percussionists to his 18-piece orchestra for this happy program. Gene Roland wrote all of the arrangements and composed each of the Latin-flavored tunes except "Adios" and "Artistry in Rhythm." Altoist Charlie Mariano, trombonist Don Sebesky and trumpeter Rolf Ericson are among the soloists and the results as heard on this LP from the Creative World catalog are potentially gimmicky, but surprisingly successful. —*Scott Yanow*

West Side Story / Mar. 15, 1961–Apr. 11, 1961 / Creative World ◆◆◆◆◆
When the producers of the film *West Side Story* heard a sampling of what the Stan Kenton Orchestra had done to their score, they were disappointed that they had not thought to ask the band to play on the soundtrack. Johnny Richards' arrangements of ten of the famous play's melodies are alternately dramatic and tender with plenty of the passion displayed by the characters in the story. Soloists include altoist Gabe Baltazar, veteran tenor Sam Donahue and trumpeter Conte Candoli, but it is the raging ensembles that are most memorable about the classic recording. This CD reissue is highly recommended. —*Scott Yanow*

Adventures In Blues / Dec. 7, 1961–Dec. 13, 1961 / Creative World ◆◆◆◆
Arranger Gene Roland composed nine blues based originals for this LP, featuring himself on soprano and mellophonium along with altoist Gabe Baltazar and trumpeter Marvin Stamm. This is one of the finer recordings by The Mellophonium Band, arguably Stan Kenton's last great orchestra. With the use of 20 horns, Roland was able to get a surprising amount of variety out of the material, making this a Kenton recording well worth investigating. —*Scott Yanow*

Adventures in Jazz / Dec. 11, 1961–Dec. 14, 1961 / Creative World ◆◆◆◆
This excellent outing by the 1961 edition of Stan Kenton's orchestra has one classic (Bill Holman's arrangement of "Malaguena"), a superior solo by altoist Gabe Baltazar on "Stairway to the Stars," a feature for Ray Starling's mellophonium ("Misty"), a good workout by veteran tenor Sam Donahue on "Body and Soul," Holman's reworking of "Limehouse Blues" and two colorful Dee Barton composition-arrangements. This well-rounded LP (which also has some solos by trumpeter Marvin Stamm) is one of Kenton's best of the era. —*Scott Yanow*

The Uncollected Stan Kenton & His Orchestra, Vol. 6 (1962) / 1962 / Hindsight ◆◆◆◆
The sixth of Hindsight's six Stan Kenton LPs features his Mellophonium Orchestra, a 22-piece ensemble with 19 horns including a four-piece mellophonium section. These noncommercial recordings (cut strictly for radio airplay) include charts by several arrangers (with Gene Roland and Ray Starling represented the most) and excellent solos from trumpeter Marvin Stamm and especially altoist Gabe Baltazar, who was arguably the last major graduate from Stan Kenton's Orchestras. Highpoints include "Four of a Kind," Lennie Niehaus' arrangement of "Between the Devil and the Deep Blue Sea," a remake of "The Peanut Vendor," "Mellophobia" and Bill Holman's fresh version of "Limehouse Blues." —*Scott Yanow*

Adventures In Time / Sep. 1962 / Capitol ◆◆◆
This LP is comprised of eight compositions by arranger Johnny Richards that feature Stan Kenton's Mellophonium Orchestra in a variety of time signatures, quite often 5/4 and 7/4. The soloists (altoist Gabe Baltazar, trumpeter Marvin Stamm, Don Menza on tenor and Ray Starling on mellophonium) do their best even if none of the songs are all that memorable by themselves. This

worthwhile if not particuarly essential release is a bit of a historical curiosity. —*Scott Yanow*

Kenton / Wagner / Sep. 1964 / Creative World ◆◆◆◆◆
This unique album is a surprising artistic success. Stan Kenton and a large studio orchestra filled with many of his alumni perform his adaptations of eight themes from the classical works of Richard Wagner. Somehow, Kenton turns Wagner's music into jazz, capturing the intense emotion, pomposity and drama with daring ideas. Not for all tastes, this LP was one of Stan Kenton's last innovative recordings. —*Scott Yanow*

Stan Kenton Conducts the Los Angeles Neophonic Orchestra / Jan. 4, 1965 / Capitol ◆◆
For a relatively brief period, The Los Angeles Neophonic orchestra was the world's only permanent resident orchestra devoted to contemporary music. This LP, conducted by the orchestra's inspiration, Stan Kenton, contains music by Hugo Montenegro, Johnny Williams, Allyn Ferguson, Jimmy Knight and Russ Garcia that attempts to combine together aspects of classical with jazz. Much of the time the results are somewhat pompous and stiff, although there are several features for altoist Bud Shank; other soloists include Bob Cooper on oboe, trumpeter Gary Barone, vibraphonist Emil Richards and the tenor of Bill Perkins. The music, like the project, had good intentions, but is uneven. —*Scott Yanow*

The Compositions of Dee Barton / Dec. 19, 1967–Dec. 20, 1967 / Capitol ◆◆◆
Up until the breakup of his Mellophonium Orchestra in 1963, all of Stan Kenton's big bands had major soloists and future stars. But during his final decade, his orchestras would mostly consist of younger (and one would expect inexpensive) players, few of whom went on to greater heights. This LP consists of seven Dee Barton charts of his originals. Barton was the band's drummer and, along with tenor saxophonist Kim Richmond (who would later develop into a top arranger himself), is about the graduate of this particular group to have a significant jazz career. The music is well-played but not overly memorable, sort of like this edition of the Stan Kenton Orchestra. —*Scott Yanow*

Live at Redlands University / Oct. 1970 / Creative World ◆◆◆
This double LP is pretty definitive of Stan Kenton's later orchestras. Few of the musicians ever became even minor names; not counting veteran saxophonist Willie Maiden, trumpeters Mike Vax and Warren Gale, trombonist Dick Shearer and drummer John Von Ohlen are the only recognizable players. The arrangements are generally workmanlike and sometimes dramatic, but rarely memorable (those of Bill Holman and Willie Maiden excepted), and the old favorite "Peanut Vendor" (here renamed "More Peanut Vendor") gets the most spirited performance. By this point Stan Kenton had so influenced the college stage band movement (and was largely forced economically to use younger musicians) that his orchestra itself sounded like one of the faceless college orchestras. Still, these versions of "Artistry in Rhythm" and "Granada" make up in emotion for the general lack of creative spontaneity and should satisfy fans of those anonymous student big bands. —*Scott Yanow*

Live at Brigham Young University / Aug. 13, 1971 / Creative World ◆◆
Stan Kenton's young "no-name" big band of the 1970s performs ambitious works by Ken Hanna, Hank Levy, Willie Maiden and Bill Holman on this live double LP. The musicianship is impressive and some of the arrangements are quite dramatic, but not all that much originality is shown. A lot of soloists are heard from, but few of them would have significant jazz careers after their period with Kenton ended; the main exceptions are veteran saxophonist Willie Maiden, trumpeter Mike Vax, trombone Dick Shearer and drummer John Von Ohlen. This set is well-played but forgettable. —*Scott Yanow*

Stan Kenton Today / 1972 / Phase 4 ◆◆
This double LP in its long liner notes does not give a complete listing of the personnel of Stan Kenton's 1972 orchestra: an unintentional but ironically understandable omission because Kenton's young band had few original personalities at this point. Other than veteran Willie Maiden (heard here on baritone), the soloists are at best semiobscure. However, the musicianship is flawless and the repertoire for this "Live in London" set is dominated by old classics including "Malaguena," "Intermission Riff," "Interlude," "Artistry in Percussion" and naturally "The Peanut Vendor." Fans of college stage bands should enjoy this spirited music. —*Scott Yanow*

National Anthems of the World / Aug. 1972 / Creative ✦

Birthday in Britain / Feb. 19, 1973+Feb. 23, 1973 / Creative World ✦✦✦

The Stan Kenton Orchestra of the 1970s featured high musicianship, dramatic arrangements, forceful ensembles and workmanlike solos. The 19-piece band heard on this LP is mostly filled with forgotten youngsters; the exceptions are veteran saxophonist Willie Maiden, trombonist Dick Shearer and the then-unknown drummer Peter Erskine. The arrangements are by Hank Levy, Bill Holman (one of his two is "Happy Birthday to You") and Maiden. Well-played and sometimes exciting, this music is rarely memorable. —*Scott Yanow*

7.5 on the Richter Scale / Aug. 17, 1973–Aug. 18, 1973 / Creative World ✦✦✦

Solo: Stan Kenton without His Orchestra / Dec. 1973 / Creative World ✦✦

This LP was Stan Kenton's only solo piano record of his career, and it's a disappointment. Kenton was never a virtuoso, but he had an Earl Hines-inspired style and was capable of much better than this introspective and wandering outing. There are some moments of interest as Kenton explores songs one is used to hearing played by his orchestra, but the limited amount of emotions expressed (and the lack of any real swinging) makes this set easily passable. —*Scott Yanow*

Stan Kenton Plays Chicago / Jun. 4, 1974 / Creative World ✦✦

Fire, Fury and Fun / Sep. 26, 1974–Sep. 27, 1974 / Creative World ✦✦✦

Kenton '76 / Dec. 3, 1975–Dec. 5, 1975 / Creative World ✦✦✦

This reasonably enjoyable LP features the Stan Kenton Orchestra during its final period. The ensemble sound remained impressive but among the sidemen only trumpeter Tim Hagans (and to a lesser extent bassist Dave Stone) would go on to greater heights although baritonist Greg Smith is impressive on his feature "A Smith Named Greg." Hank Levy contributed three of the charts, "Tiburon" is Bill Holman's and Kenton's piano is featured on the two ballads "Send in the Clowns" and "My Funny Valentine." This is not one of the major Stan Kenton albums, but the set will be enjoyed by fans of college stage bands. —*Scott Yanow*

Journey into Capricorn / Aug. 16, 1976–Aug. 18, 1976 / Creative World ✦✦✦

Stan Kenton's final studio recording features his young no-name crew (only trumpeter Tim Hagans among the soloists is notable today) showing enthusiasm and impressive musicianship on charts by Hank Levy, Mark Taylor and Alan Yankee. Highlights include Yankee's adaptation of Chick Corea's "Celebration Suite," Levy's "Pegasus" and Hagan's solos. The leader's piano is featured on Stevie Wonder's "Too Shy to Say." This decent LP closed Stan Kenton's rather remarkable career. —*Scott Yanow*

★ **50th Anniversary Celebration** / May 30, 1991–Jun. 2, 1991 / Mama Foundation ✦✦✦✦✦

During the 50th anniversary of Stan Kenton's debut at the Rendezvous Ballroom on Balboa Island in California (an engagement that served as a spectacular beginning to his career), a four-day convention was held to celebrate the late bandleader's legacy, filled with music by his alumni and very interesting panel discussions. The MAMA Foundation put out many of the highlights on this very impressive five-CD set. The first two CDs have 29 selections by an all-star orchestra (which includes among others, trumpeters Conte and Pete Candoli and saxophonists Bob Cooper, Gabe Baltazar, Bud Shank, Bill Perkins and Jack Nimitz) and such guests as Anita O'Day, Maynard Ferguson and Chris Connor; the original arrangers conducted their own work. The next two discs have individual selections for Bob Florence's Limited Edition (a particularly touching medley of "Artistry in Rhythm" and "All the Things You Are"), Maynard Ferguson's Big Bop Nouveau Band, the Lighthouse All-Stars, big bands led by Shorty Rogers, Buddy Childers, Bill Holman, Tom Talbert and Mark Masters and combos headed by Lee Konitz, Bob Cooper, Gabe Baltazar, Bill Perkins and Bud Shank along with The CSULB Vocal Jazz Ensemble. The performances are quite satisfying and pretty well cover Kenton's entire career. The final disc actually has over two hours taken from the informative, humorous and often-touching panel discussions; one hour is heard in each speaker simultaneously so one side has to be turned off at a time. This valuable set is essential for all listeners having at least a slight interest in Stan Kenton's music. —*Scott Yanow*

Freddie Keppard

b. Feb. 27, 1890, New Orleans, LA, d. Jul. 15, 1933, Chicago, IL

Cornet / Classic New Orleans Jazz

One of the New Orleans cornet "kings" (succeeding Buddy Bolden and preceding King Oliver), Freddie Keppard was one of the few innovators of the 1910 era who had a chance to record later on, giving listeners a glimpse of his abilities. Keppard was active from around 1906, leading the Olympia Orchestra and freelancing in New Orleans. In 1914 he helped bring jazz to Los Angeles with his Original Creole Band. After settling in Chicago in the early '20s, Keppard worked with Doc Cook's Dreamland Orchestra (with whom he recorded on several occasions), Erskine Tate, Ollie Powers and Charles Elgar. He could have been the first jazz musician to record (back in 1916), but passed on the opportunity because he was afraid that competitors would steal his ideas. Keppard did record between 1923–27 (his best sides were with his own Jazz Cardinals, particularly "Stock Yard Strut") and those performances feature him using a staccato phrasing influenced by brass bands and displaying a spirited tone. Unfortunately, Keppard was an alcoholic by the mid-'20s and was soon in a decline just when he should have been entering his prime. He died of tuberculosis in 1933 at the age of 43. All of his recordings are currently available on a single CD put out by the European King Jazz label. —*Scott Yanow*

● **The Complete Freddie Keppard 1923/27** / Jun. 23, 1923–Jan. 1927 / King Jazz ✦✦✦✦✦

Barney Kessel

b. Oct. 17, 1923, Muskogee, OK

Guitar / Bop, Cool

One of the finest guitarists to emerge after the death of Charlie Christian, Barney Kessel was a reliable bop soloist throughout his career. He played with a big band fronted by Chico Marx (1943), was fortunate enough to appear in the classic jazz short "Jammin' the Blues" (1944) and then worked with the big bands of Charlie Barnet (1944–45) and Artie Shaw (1945); he also recorded with Shaw's Gramercy Five. Kessel became a busy studio musician in Los Angeles, but was always in demand for jazz records. He toured with the Oscar Peterson Trio for one year (1952–53) and then, starting in 1953, led an impressive series of records for Contemporary that lasted until 1961 (including several with Ray Brown and Shelly Manne in a trio accurately called "The Poll Winners"). After touring Europe with George Wein's Newport All-Stars (1968), Kessel lived in London for a time (1969–70). In 1973 he began touring and recording with the Great Guitars, a group also including Herb Ellis and Charlie Byrd. A serious stroke in 1992 put Barney Kessel permanently out of action, but many of his records (which include dates for Onyx, Black Lion, Sonet and Concord in addition to many of the Contemporaries) are currently available along with several video collections put out by Vestapol. —*Scott Yanow*

Easy Like / Nov. 14, 1953–Feb. 23, 1956 / Original Jazz Classics ✦✦✦✦

This presents the first two sessions guitarist Barney Kessel recorded for Contemporary: Nov. 14, 1953 and Dec. 19, 1953. These were pleasant, somewhat easy swinging dates with backing from Bud Shank (alto sax, flute), Arnold Ross (piano), Harry Babasin (bass) and Shelly Manne (drums). They were originally released as a 10-incher. They blend well with the Feb. 23, 1956 date that fills out the 12-inch LP. —*Bob Rusch, Cadence*

Kessel Plays Standards / Jun. 4, 1954–Sep. 12, 1954 / Original Jazz Classics ✦✦✦✦

Guitarist Barney Kessel and the great American standard were the program on *Plays Standards*, the ringer being "Barney's Blues," the one Kessel original. Recorded between June 4, 1954 and Sept. 12, 1955 in three sessions, the cumulative personnel included Bob Cooper, Claude Williamson, Monty Budwig, Shelly Manne, Hampton Hawes, Red Mitchell and Chuck Thompson. —*Bob Rusch, Cadence*

★ **Barney Kessel, Vol. 3: To Swing or Not to Swing** / Mar. 28, 1955–Jun. 26, 1956 / Original Jazz Classics ✦✦✦✦✦

Music to Listen to Barney Kessel By / Aug. 6, 1956–Dec. 4, 1956 / Original Jazz Classics ✦✦✦✦

Featured is Kessel's guitar with five woodwinds and a rhythm section. 12 songs were recorded with Buddy Collette (fl), Andre

Previn (p), Shelly Manne (d), Jimmy Rowles (p), Red Mitchell (b), Buddy Clark (b) and others. —AMG

The Poll Winners with Ray Brown and Shelly Manne / Mar. 18, 1957–Mar. 19, 1957 / Original Jazz Classics ++++
Because guitarist Barney Kessel, bassist Ray Brown and drummer Shelly Manne all won the *Downbeat*, *Metronome* and *Playboy* jazz polls of 1956, it was decided to team the trio together for this and a few other future recordings. Kessel is generally the lead voice of the pianoless group although Brown and Manne also have plenty of solo space. Together they perform swinging yet quiet versions of a variety of standards (in addition to the guitarist's "Minor Mood") in a relaxed and thoughtful set, reissued on this CD. —*Scott Yanow*

Let's Cook / Aug. 6, 1957+Nov. 11, 1957 / Contemporary ++++
Two cuts with Ben Webster (ts). —*Ron Wynn*

The Poll Winners Ride Again / Aug. 19, 1958+Aug. 21, 1958 / Original Jazz Classics ++++
Guitarist Barney Kessel, bassist Ray Brown and drummer Shelly Manne were dubbed "the Poll Winners" when they swept the *Downbeat*, *Metronome* and *Playboy* polls during 1956-57. They recorded several albums together and this CD reissue features the pianoless trio playing a variety of material, some of it a little odd (including "Volare," "Custard Puff," "When the Red, Red Robin Comes Bob, Bob Bobbin' Along" and "The Merry Go Round Broke Down"). This is a good outing, particularly for bop guitarist Barney Kessel. —*Scott Yanow*

Barney Kessel Plays "Carmen" / Dec. 19, 1958+Dec. 23, 1958 / Original Jazz Classics +++

Some Like It Hot / Mar. 30, 1959–Apr. 3, 1959 / Original Jazz Classics +++++
Here was one of two sessions guitarist Barney Kessel recorded in the middle of his ten-year exclusive Contemporary period ('53-'62). It was a 1959 (Mar. 30, 31, Apr. 3) date, which included Art Pepper (clarinet, alto saxophone), Joe Gordon (trumpet), Jimmy Rowles (piano), Jack Marshall (rhythm guitar), Monty Budwig (bass) and Shelly Manne (drums). It was somewhat contained by ten air-play length cuts. —*Bob Rusch, Cadence*

Poll Winners Three! / Nov. 1959 / Original Jazz Classics ++++
'91 reissue of superb 1959 release by a topflight trio with guitarist Barney Kessel, bassist Ray Brown and drummer Shelly Manne. It was a followup to their two previous outstanding records and the third of four they cut for the Contemporary Records family. —*Ron Wynn*

Barney Kessel's Swingin' Party at Contemporary / Jul. 19, 1960 / Contemporary +++

The Poll Winners • Exploring the Scene / Aug. 1960–Sep. 1960 / Contemporary ++++
Includes Ornette Coleman's "The Blessing." With Ray Brown (b) and Shelly Manne (d). —*Michael G. Nastos*

Workin' Out / Jan. 9, 1961–Jan. 10, 1961 / Contemporary +++

Feeling Free / Mar. 12, 1969 / Original Jazz Classics +++++
This was the last date (Feb. 13, 1969) guitarist Barney Kessel led for Contemporary Records. It was recorded 13 long years after his initial sessions for the company and featured a quartet with Bobby Hutcherson, Chuck Domanico and Elvin Jones stretching out over six tracks. The title, *Feeling Free*, of the LP could be arguably interpreted in different ways, but would seem to mainly deal with Kessel's decision to abandon the studio work on the West Coast and move to England. But it was also obvious that the guitarist kept in touch with post Charlie Parker music (I hear some Wes Montgomery influence at this time, also), and while he was still in honest touch with the blues he now took so many more chances, digging in and challenging the listener and the quartet. A great deal of credit must go to Elvin Jones (drums), his support, base and encouragement were brilliant. Bobby Hutcherson offered an interesting soft contrasting coloring to the often locked sounds of Kessel and Jones. This group, though brought together just for this session, was obviously hot to play—even the two standards quickly shed their themes to open up to hard working creative interpretations. —*Bob Rusch, Cadence*

★ **Limehouse Blues** / Jun. 24, 1969 / Black Lion +++++

Two Way Conversation / Jun. 5, 1973–Oct. 2, 1973 / Jzm Sonet +++

Just Friends / Sep. 27, 1973 / Sonet +++

Barney Plays Kessel / Apr. 1975 / Concord Jazz +++
A good, career-summation, retrospective vehicle. —*Ron Wynn*

● **The Poll Winners Straight Ahead** / Jul. 12, 1975 / Original Jazz Classics +++++
15 years after their last joint recordings, The Poll Winners (a trio with guitarist Barney Kessel, bassist Ray Brown and drummer Shelly Manne) had a reunion for this excellent session, which has been reissued on CD. All three players had grown quite a bit musically since the 1950s, and Kessel, in particular, is heard in excellent form on the three standards and three swinging originals. Overall this is the best all-around recording by The Poll Winners and is easily recommended to bop fans. —*Scott Yanow*

Soaring / Aug. 25, 1976 / Concord Jazz +++

Poor Butterfly / 1976 / Concord Jazz ++
Fine playing but a low energy level. —*Ron Wynn*

Jellybeans / Apr. 1981 / Concord Jazz +++
Supple solos and straightforward accompaniment. —*Ron Wynn*

Solo / Apr. 1981 / Concord Jazz +++

Spontaneous Combustion / Feb. 20, 1987–Feb. 22, 1987 / Contemporary ++++
Excellent piano from Monty Alexander. —*Ron Wynn*

Red Hot and Blues / Mar. 15, 1988–Mar. 17, 1988 / Contemporary ++++
One of guitarist Barney Kessel's final recordings before a stroke put him out of action, this is an excellent quintet session with vibraphonist Bobby Hutcherson, pianist Kenny Barron, bassist Rufus Reid and drummer Ben Riley. Three of Kessel's originals (a pair of blues and a bossa nova) alternate with four standards and Laurindo Almeida's dedication to the guitarist ("Barniana") on this well-paced and consistently swinging set; the uptempo version of "By Myself" is a highpoint. —*Scott Yanow*

Steve Khan

b. Apr. 28, 1947, Los Angeles, CA
Guitar / Fusion, Post-Bop
The son of lyricist Sammy Cahn, Steve Khan is best-known for his fusion records, but has proven, on a few occasions, that he can also play more straight-ahead. He originally played piano and drums, not starting on guitar until he was 20. After graduating from UCLA in 1969, Khan moved to New York and worked steadily in jazz, pop and R&B settings including with Maynard Ferguson, Buddy Rich, the Brecker Brothers, Joe Zawinul's Weather Update and with fellow guitarist Larry Coryell. In 1981 he formed the quartet Eyewitness, which worked on an occasional basis throughout the 1980s. Steve Khan's most intriguing recordings are a 1980 solo exploration of Thelonious Monk tunes for Novus and a trio outing for Bluemoon named *Let's Call This* (1991). —*Scott Yanow*

Tightrope / 1977 / Columbia +++

The Blue Man / Feb. 1978 / Columbia +++
This LP features Steve Khan in his fusion period during which his guitar tone was usually a bit distorted and he tended to improvise over funky rhythms. This particular outing features such players as altoist David Sanborn, tenor saxophonist Michael Brecker, trumpeter Randy Breckner and a large rhythm section with the likes of keyboardists Don Grolnick and Bob James and drummer Steve Gadd. The music is not overly memorable, but certainly has spirit and power. —*Scott Yanow*

Arrows / 1979 / Columbia ++

● **Evidence** / Jul. 1980 / Novus +++++

Eyewitness / Nov. 7, 1981–Nov. 8, 1981 / Antilles +++++
Unlike his previous all-star sets, guitarist Steve Khan features his regular group on this album and the results are quite superior. Whether one calls this music fusion or modern funk, the interplay between Khan, electric bassist Anthony Jackson, drummer Steve Jordan and percussionist Manolo Badrena is quite impressive; in fact, the four of them share composer credits on three of the five originals. It's one of Steve Khan's best fusion-oriented efforts of the 1980s. —*Scott Yanow*

Blades / Aug. 3, 1982–Aug. 4, 1982 / Passport +++

Local Colour / Apr. 1983–May 1987 / Denon +++
Good '87 duo session, in which session and studio ace guitarist Steve Khan went against his reputation and did an album of duets

with keyboardist and vocalist Rob Mounsey that weren't just funk and fusion, but mostly jazz-tinged instrumentals. —*Ron Wynn*

Casa Loco / May 21, 1983–May 22, 1983 / Antilles ✦✦✦
Mid-'80s session that blends funk, fusion and occasional mainstream work by guitarist Steve Khan. Nice production, decent arrangements and generally fine playing by Khan, although he does few solos. —*Ron Wynn*

Public Access / Jan. 1989 / GRP ✦✦✦

Let's Call This / Jan. 19, 1991–Jan. 20, 1991 / Blue Moon ✦✦✦✦✦
Best-known for his fusion recordings, Steve Khan (ten years after recording the purely acoustic solo date Evidence) stretches out on this pure jazz date. Accompanied by bassist Ron Carter and drummer Al Foster, Khan explores a variety of superior jazz standards (including songs by Thelonious Monk, Wayne Shorter, Larry Young, Freddie Hubbard and Lee Morgan) along with his own "Buddy System." This is one of Steve Khan's finest recordings to date and is highly recommended to those listeners not familiar with this side of his musical personality. —*Scott Yanow*

Headline / 1992 / Blue Room ✦✦✦✦

Crossings / Dec. 28, 1993–Dec. 30, 1993 / Verve Forecast ✦✦✦✦

Franklin Kiermyer

b. Jul. 21, 1956, Montreal Canada
Drums / Avant-Garde, Free Jazz
Franklin Kiermyer, a fairly obscure drummer, burst on the scene in 1994 with his Evidence CD *Solomon's Daughter*, a remarkably intense quartet date that features Pharoah Sanders at his most ferocious. Kiermyer keeps up with the passion, making one wonder why he was not known before that date. —*Scott Yanow*

★ **Solomon's Daughter** / 1994 / Evidence ✦✦✦✦✦
Drummer Franklin Kiermyer may not be a well-known name but his Evidence CD is a real gem. tenor saxophonist Pharoah Sanders, a powerful screamer who added a lot of fire and intensity to John Coltrane's 1966 quintet, had, during the 1980s, become much mellower and more melodic both in concert and on records, but this extremely powerful set restored one's faith in his uniqueness. Sanders is heard at the peak of his powers, playing miraculous solos full of screams, shrieks, overtone manipulation and pure emotion. Kiermyer (who wrote all six of the compositions) has the power of an Elvin Jones or a Rashied Ali without really copying their styles; his explosive playing fits in very well with Sanders. Pianist John Esposito and bassist Drew Gress cannot help being overshadowed by the dominant duo, but they play quite well and make their contributions felt during the quieter pieces such as "Peace on Earth" and "Birds of the Niles," during which Sanders is quite lyrical and tender. But it is the lengthy blowouts on "If I Die Before I Wake" and "Three Jewels" that really make this set very memorable. "Blowing up a Storm" does not even begin to describe the ferocious music. —*Scott Yanow*

John Kirby

b. Dec. 31, 1908, Baltimore, MD, d. Jun. 14, 1952, Hollywood, CA
Bass, Tuba, Leader / Swing
John Kirby led a most unusual group during the height of the big-band era, a sextet comprised of trumpeter Charlie Shavers, clarinetist Buster Bailey, altoist Russell Procope, pianist Billy Kyle, drummer O'Neil Spencer and his own bass. Although Shavers and Bailey could be quite extroverted, the tightly arranged ensembles tended to be very cool-toned and introverted yet virtuosic. Kirby, originally a tuba player, switched to bass in 1930 when he joined Fletcher Henderson's Orchestra. He was one of the better bassists of the 1930s, playing with Henderson (1930–33 and 1935–36) and Chick Webb's big band (1933–35). By 1937 Kirby had his own group at the Onyx Club; Frankie Newton and Pete Brown passed through the band before the personnel was set. With Maxine Sullivan (Kirby's wife at the time) offering occasional vocals, the John Kirby Sextet was quite popular during 1938–42. Shavers' "Undecided" became a hit and the band's abilities to "swing the classics" caught on. The sextet gradually declined in the 1940s. Spencer became ill and was replaced by Specs Powell and later Bill Beason, Kyle was drafted and Procope was replaced by George Johnson. By 1945 (with Shavers' departure to join Tommy

Dorsey), the only original members still in the group were Bailey and Kirby himself. The following year the band disbanded and despite some attempts by the bassist to form another similar sextet (including a poorly attended Carnegie Hall reunion in 1950), John Kirby was never able to duplicate his earlier successes. Classics has reissued all of Kirby's prime recordings. —*Scott Yanow*

Boss of the Bass / Dec. 3, 1930–Jan. 15, 1941 / Columbia ✦✦✦✦
John Kirby was never actually the "boss of the bass," even back in the 1930s, but he was an important bandleader. The second half of this admirable two-LP set features his unique group on 14 of their more rewarding recordings from 1939–41. The complex yet tight arrangements and concise solos by the virtosi (trumpeter Charlie Shavers, bassist Buster Bailey, altoist Russell Procope, pianist Billy Kyle, drummer O'Neil Spencer and Kirby on bass) gave the John Kirby Sextet a unique sound of its own. The first of these two LPs contains 14 selections featuring Kirby as a sideman with such groups as the Chocolate Dandies, Fletcher Henderson, Chick Webb, Putney Dandridge, Teddy Wilson, Charlie Barnet and Lucky Millinder along with backup work with early versions of his sextet behind singers Midge Williams, Maxine Sullivan and Mildred Bailey. A well-conceived reissue, it contains more than its share of exciting swing performances. —*Scott Yanow*

★ **John Kirby 1938–1939** / Oct. 28, 1938–Oct. 12, 1939 / Classics ✦✦✦✦✦

★ **John Kirby 1939–1941** / Oct. 12, 1939–Jan. 15, 1941 / Classics ✦✦✦✦✦

1941 / 1941 / Circle ✦✦✦

★ **1941–1943** / Jan. 2, 1941–Dec. 1943 / Classics ✦✦✦✦
The third John Kirby CD from the European Classics label has 21 performances that trace Kirby's unique sextet from the peak of its popularity in 1941 through the war years. In addition to a dozen songs originally released by Victor, this set has nine rarer numbers that appeared on V-Discs. With trumpeter Charlie Shavers, clarinetist Buster Bailey and altoist Russell Procope, (along with pianist Billy Kyle and drummer O'Neil Spencer), Kirby was able to form an unusual and very distinctive group sound that, although comprised of swing virtuosoes, looked toward cool jazz of the 1950s. By the later tracks of this CD, the band was starting to come apart a bit with first Specs Powell and then Bill Beason replacing the late Spencer, George Johnson ably filling in for Procope and Shavers departing before the final number; the group sound, however, remained intact and among the many highlights of this CD are "Coquette," "Royal Garden Blues," "Night Whispers," "St. Louis Blues" and "9:20 Special." —*Scott Yanow*

Andy Kirk

b. May 28, 1898, Newport, KY, d. Dec. 11, 1992, New York, NY
Leader, Bass, Bass Saxophone / Swing
Andy Kirk was never a major musician (in fact he never really soloed), arranger or personality yet he was a successful big bandleader in the 1930s and '40s. He started playing bass sax and tuba in Denver with George Morrison's band in 1918. In 1925 he moved to Dallas where he played with Terrence Holder's Dark Clouds of Joy. In 1929 he took over leadership of the band (which was renamed Andy Kirk's Twelve Clouds of Joy) and moved to Kansas City. During 1929–30 they recorded some excellent hot performances with such players as pianist/arranger Mary Lou Williams, violinist Claude Williams and trumpeter Edgar "Puddinghead" Battle. Surprisingly, Kirk's Orchestra was off records entirely during 1931–35, but in 1936 (the year it relocated to New York) it immediately had a pop hit in "Until the Real Thing Comes Along" featuring the high voice of singer Pha Terrell. In future years such fine soloists as tenor saxophonist Dick Wilson, the early electric guitarist Floyd Smith, Don Byas, Harold "Shorty" Baker, Howard McGhee (1942–43), Jimmy Forrest and even Fats Navarro and (briefly) Charlie Parker would be among Kirk's sidemen. However, Mary Lou Williams was the most important musician in the band, both as a soloist and as an arranger. In 1948 Andy Kirk broke up the band (which had recorded mostly for Decca) and in later years ran a hotel and served as an official in the Musicians' Union. A lone "reunion" date in 1956 featured the classic charts, but almost none of the original sidemen. —*Scott Yanow*

Lady Who Swings the Band / Mar. 2, 1936–Feb. 8, 1938 / MCA ✦✦✦✦

Imstrumentally Speaking / Mar. 2, 1936–Jul. 14, 1942 / Decca ✦✦✦✦

● **1936** / Mar. 1936–Dec. 1936 / Classics ✦✦✦✦✦

● **1937** / Feb. 1937–Dec. 1937 / Classics ✦✦✦✦✦

● **1938** / 1937–1938 / Classics ✦✦✦✦✦

Andy Kirk (1944) / 1944 / Hindsight ✦✦✦

Rahsaan Roland Kirk (Ronald T. Kirk)

b. May 15, 1936, Columbus, Ohio, **d.** Dec. 5, 1977, Bloomington, IN

Tenor Saxophone, Stritch, Manzello, Flute, Clarinet / Bop, Hard Bop, R&B, Swing, Avant-Garde, New Orleans Jazz

Sometimes musicians have used flamboyance to mask talent deficiencies. But in other cases, a willingness to have a good time results in talented players skills being downplayed. That was the case with Rahsaan Roland Kirk, who loved clowning, telling outrageous jokes and enjoying himself in concert. That, coupled with his penchant for playing three horns at once and homemade instruments, convinced some individuals he was more sideshow than legitimately superb soloist. But Kirk's playing three horns was done through skillful use of false fingerings. He modified the keys of his tenor, using the left hand to cover the tenor's range and his right to play the manzello and stritch. It was an incredible combination of musical knowledge and physical dexterity, made even more amazing by the fact the individual doing it had been blind since two. Kirk was a master of circular breathing, another practice that led him to be accused of gimmickry. He could hold and sustain notes for what seemed like hours. Kirk used a siren whistle to punctuate key moments in his solos. He discovered the long forgotten manzello and stritch, a pair of saxophones used in turn-of-the-century Spanish marching bands, in a music store. He made alterations to them with rubber bands and tape, turning them into part of his performing arsenal. Rahsaan Roland Kirk was an amazing musician and personality, who could play lightning fast bebop, outrageous free solos, heartfelt 12-bar blues and any and everything in between. He played over 40 instruments, many of his own making. At his concerts it seemed he'd raided a music store, there were so many horns, flutes and devices on stage. His homemade instruments included the trumpophone (trumpet with soprano sax mouthpiece), slidesophone (miniature trombone resembling Snub Mosley's slide saxophone), black puzzle flute and black mystery pipes. He used flutes like microphones, speaking and sending messages with them. Kirk was one of the funniest people of all time on or back stage, but he didn't find anything humorous about the music business or the treatment jazz musicians received from the general media. He was the leader of the early '70s Jazz and People's Movement, another of those worthy causes that later degenerates into a mutually unproductive series of confrontations. Kirk and Lee Morgan got nationwide press, little of it favorable, in 1970 when they disrupted the taping of a "Merv Griffin" show protesting the lack of African-American musicians and absence of black music and compositions from most radio and television shows. The Jazz and People's Movement had a legitimate beef; unfortunately, they were bogged down by publicity-seeking ringers in the ranks and their tactic of disrupting television tapings cost them points with many of the people they were trying to reach. That was probably the low point of Kirk's great career. He began playing bugle and trumpet as a child, later starting on clarinet and C-melody saxophone. He was a professional at 15, working in R&B bands. He moved from Louisville to Chicago in 1960. Ira Sullivan played on Kirk's second album. Kirk toured Germany in the early '60s and later played briefly with Charles Mingus. Then he led his own bands exclusively, playing a wide variety of styles and mainly originals while fronting his "Vibration Society." Kirk made his first album for King in 1956, then moved to Argo. He recorded in the '60s and '70s for Argo/Cadet, Prestige, Mercury, Verve, Atlantic and Warner Bros. Before becoming a leader, Kirk played with Brother Jack McDuff and Jaki Byard. He took the name "Rahsaan" after having a vision during a dream. Such albums as *Volunteered Slavery*, *Natural Black Inventions* and *Bright Moments* packed musical and philosophical/political punch. Kirk worked on such guests on his albums as Horace Parlan, Quincy Jones, Al Hibbler and Leon Thomas. He suffered a stroke in 1975, but continued playing two more years. Kirk founded the Vibration School of

Music in 1977 to help saxophonists. It was one of his final acts. Mercury issued a two-record compilation of his early '60s work immediately after his death, then did Kirk justice with a boxed set compilation of his sessions *The Complete Roland Kirk on Mercury*. —*Ron Wynn*

Early Roots / Nov. 9, 1956 / Bethlehem ✦✦✦

Rahsaan Roland Kirk's first recording predated his second by four years and would be a real obscurity until its reissue in the mid-'70s. Kirk at 20 already had a recognizable sound on tenor and, although he had not yet mastered the art of playing two or three horns at once, he did overdub his manzello and stritch on three of the selections released on his debut, hinting at the exciting innovations to come. The music is mostly blues and ballads with a touch of R&B thrown in, a good beginning to a unique career. —*Scott Yanow*

Introducing Roland Kirk / Jun. 7, 1960 / Chess ✦✦✦

Roland Kirk's second recording was his first to get noticed. Playing three horns at once got him some attention, but those who listened closely realized that Kirk was a truly masterful player. Teamed with Ira Sullivan (who himself switched between trumpet and tenor) and a Chicago-based rhythm section, Kirk is in good form on these bop-oriented selections although his great sessions were in the near future. This CD is a straight reissue of the original LP outfitted with newer liner notes. —*Scott Yanow*

★ **Kirk's Work** / Jul. 11, 1961 / Original Jazz Classics ✦✦✦✦✦

Roland Kirk is in excellent form on this CD reissue of a typically varied (and occasionally amazing) set with organist Jack McDuff, bassist Joe Benjamin and drummer Art Taylor. Kirk mostly sticks to playing tenor and manzello (with highlights including "Three for Dizzy" and "Makin' Whoopee"), but takes "Funk Underneath" as a flute feature and tears into the ancient "Skater's Waltz" on both stritch and manzello. McDuff plays well, but Roland Kirk dominates the set, displaying an encyclopedic knowledge of music and swinging up a storm. —*Scott Yanow*

Pre Rahsaan / Jul. 11, 1961+Sep. 17, 1968 / Prestige ✦✦✦✦

This out-of-print two-LP set combines together a pair of Prestige sessions that feature the amazing Rahsaan Roland Kirk in the days before he added the "Rahsaan" to his name. The earlier date (which has since been reissued on CD) matches Kirk (on tenor, flute, stritch, manzello and even siren) with organist Jack McDuff, bassist Joe Benjamin and drummer Art Taylor for a wide-ranging set highlighted by "Three for Dizzy," "Makin' Whoopee" and "Skater's Waltz." However, it is the 1968 session with pianist Jaki Byard (who was actually the date's leader), bassist Richard Davis and drummer Alan Dawson that is most memorable. "Memories of You" is a classic Kirk-Byard duet (they both had mastered every jazz style), "Parisian Thoroughfare" really roars and the versions of Thelonious Monk's "Evidence" and "Teach Me Tonight" bring fresh life to those songs. —*Scott Yanow*

We Free Kings / Aug. 16, 1961–Aug. 17, 1961 / Mercury ✦✦✦✦✦

This CD is one of Roland Kirk's finer recordings from his Mercury period. Accompanied by a rhythm section led by pianist Richard Wyands, Kirk on tenor, manzello and stritch (sometimes all three at once) and flute plays some typically miraculous music. Highlights include "Three for the Festival," "Moon Song," "Blues for Alice" and "We Free Kings," but all of the selections contain plenty of Kirk's magic. Twenty years after his death there is still no one around to replace Roland Kirk. This release is recommended to those listeners who do not already have his ten-CD complete Mercury set. —*Scott Yanow*

★ **Complete Recordings of Roland Kirk** / Aug. 16, 1961–Nov. 17, 1965 / Mercury ✦✦✦✦✦

This ten-CD set not only contains all of the music from Roland Kirk's nine albums for Mercury and Limelight and his guest appearances with Quincy Jones, Tubby Hayes and on one song with organist Eddie Baccus, but quite a few previously unreleased selections (especially from the *Kirk in Copenhagen* sessions). Roland Kirk was a unique performer, not only able to play a variety of reed instruments at the same time (including the tenor, flute, clarinet, manzello and stritch) and 20-minute one-breath solos (via circular breathing) but a master of virtually every jazz style from bop and New Orleans to free. Some of his greatest recordings are on this remarkable set, including the entire albums originally titled *We Free Kings*, *Domino*, *Reeds and Deeds*, *Gifts and Messages*, *I Talk with the Spirits* and *Rip, Rig & Panic*. Such pianists as Richard Wyands, Wynton Kelly, Andrew Hill (including a previously unreleased three-song set from the 1962 Newport Jazz Festival), Harold Mabern, Tete Montoliu, Horace Parlan and Jaki Byard are heard from and the Tubby Hayes date matches together the three reeds of Kirk, Hayes and James Moody in memorable fashion. Although more general collectors may want to start off with a smaller Roland Kirk set, those in-the-know will go out of their way to grab this one before it disappears. — *Scott Yanow*

● **Does Your House Have Lions: The Rahsaan Roland Kirk Anthology** / Nov. 6, 1961–Mar. 1976 / Rhino ✦✦✦✦
Any listener who feels that Rahsaan Roland Kirk's ability to play three horns simultaneously was a gimmick and that he was a primitive improviser should be forced to listen to this two-CD set. A well-conceived sampler that has highlights from Kirk's Atlantic period (dating from 1965–76 plus an earlier selection from his brief period with Charles Mingus), this anthology is most highly recommended to listeners not familiar with Kirk's musical miracles; more serious collectors will want to get the complete sessions (although there is a previously unavailable version of "Three for the Festival" from 1970 included). In addition to tenor, manzello and stritch, he shows mastery of the baritone, bass sax, the flexaphone, clarinet, flute, nose flute, piccolo, trumpet, English horn, the black mystery pipes, harmonica and various percussion instruments. Although the selections are unfortunately not programmed in chronological order, producer Joel Dorn did a fine job of picking out most of the classic cuts including Kirk's close imitation of both Miles Davis and John Coltrane on "Bye Bye Blackbird," his live versions of "If I Loved You," "The Old Rugged Cross" (complete with a monologue), Kirk's remarkable simultaneous playing of the melodies of "Sentimental Journey" and "Going Home," etc. Not a flawless set (a medley of two unrelated excerpts is a frivolity and "Bright Moments" is unaccountably missing), this two-fer is fine for beginners. — *Scott Yanow*

Domino / Apr. 17, 1962–Sep. 6, 1962 / Mercury ✦✦✦✦✦
Early '60s Kirk vehicle in which his inspired blend of show business, hard bop and multi-horn/multiphonic solos hadn't yet jelled. It's conventional, straight-ahead material, well played but not as imaginative or as transcendent as Kirk's music would become in the '70s. — *Ron Wynn*

Reeds & Deeds / Feb. 25, 1963–Feb. 26, 1963 / Mercury ✦✦✦✦✦
Roland Kirk Meets the Benny Golson Orchestra / Jun. 11, 1963–Jun. 12, 1963 / Mercury ✦✦✦✦
Kirk in Copenhagen / Oct. 1963 / Mercury ✦✦✦✦✦
I Talk to the Spirits / Sep. 16, 1964–Sep. 17, 1964 / Limelight ✦✦✦✦
Gifts and Messages / Nov. 1964 / Mercury ✦✦✦✦
Rip, Rig and Panic / Now Please Don't ... / Jan. 13, 1965+Apr. 1, 1967 / EmArcy ✦✦✦✦
Two of Roland Kirk's albums are combined together on this CD. *Rip, Rig & Panic* is one of the remarkable multi-instrumentalist's greatest recordings for it matches him with pianist Jaki Byard (along with bassist Richard Davis and drummer Elvin Jones) who also has the ability to play in virtually every jazz style. With such titles as "No Tonic Pres," "Once in a While", "From Bechet, Byas and Fats" and the electronic "Slippery, Hippery, Flippery," obviously this is an eclectic (and unique) set. While that session has also been included in the ten-CD complete Mercury box, *Now Please Don't You Cry, Beautiful Edith* is a lesser-known recording (originally on Verve) that has Kirk backed up by pianist Lonnie Smith, bassist Ronald Boykins and drummer Grady Tate. Highlights inclue "Stompin' Ground," "It's a Grand Night for Swinging," "Alfie" and the title cut. — *Scott Yanow*

Slightly Latin / Nov. 16, 1965–Nov. 17, 1965 / Limelight ✦✦✦✦
Here Comes the Whistleman / 1966 / Atlantic ✦✦✦✦
Now Please Don't You Cry, Beautiful Edith / Apr. 1967 / Verve ✦✦✦✦
This April 1967 recording with Lonnie Smith (piano), Ronnie Boykins (bass) and Grady Tate (drums) presented a solid display of Rahsaan Roland Kirk's talents on tenor, manzello, whistle, stritch and flute in what was perhaps typical of the cornucopia of musical roots and messages that became part of his statements from the '60s up until his death. — *Bob Rusch, Cadence*

The Inflated Tear / Nov. 27, 1967+Nov. 30, 1967 / Atlantic ✦✦✦✦✦
This is a fine all-around set by the remarkable Rahsaan Roland Kirk, which has yet to be fully reissued on CD. The LP, from the

Atlantic *Jazzlore* reissue series of the early '80s, features Kirk on tenor, manzello, stritch, clarinet, flute, English horn, flexafone and whistle performing a wide variety of colorful originals along with Duke Ellington's "Creole Love Call." Highlights include the memorable "The Black and Crazy Blues," "The Inflated Tear" and "A Handful of Fives." It's one of Kirk's better Atlantic sets. — *Scott Yanow*

Left and Right / Jun. 18, 1968 / Atlantic ✦✦✦✦
This LP features two different sides of the unique Rahsaan Roland Kirk. While the first half of the program is dominated by his nine-part suite "Expansions" (a variety of melodies he had written in the 1950s) and features Rahsaan's intense playing with a variety of guest artists (including Alice Coltrane on harp, baritonist Pepper Adams and trumpeter Richard Williams), the second side generally showcases Kirk on one horn at a time performing six ballads while backed by a string section; he plays beautifully and with melodic creativity. — *Scott Yanow*

Volunteered Slavery / Jul. 7, 1969–Jul. 23, 1969 / Rhino ✦✦✦✦
This straight CD reissue of an Atlantic LP has plenty of variety. Rahsaan Kirk (on tenor, flutes, manzello, stritch and even gong) performs three melodic originals (including the title cut) along with two pop tunes during which he is assisted by "the Roland Kirk Spirit Choir" on background vocals. However, it is his performance at the 1969 Newport Jazz Festival (near-riotous versions of "One Ton" and "Three for the Festival" plus a remarkable John Coltrane three-song medley) that is most memorable. — *Scott Yanow*

Rahsaan / Rahsaan / May 11, 1970–May 12, 1970 / Atlantic ✦✦✦✦✦
On this very interesting set, the unique Rahsaan Roland Kirk performs a musical miracle or two. A 17-minute "The Seeker" goes through several musical styles including bop and New Orleans jazz. In addition there are several unusual shorter pieces, but it is during a medley that Kirk performs some real magic. At one point he plays two completely different melodies ("Going Home" and "Sentimental Journey") on two different horns at the same time, splitting his lobes so to speak. Topping off that medley is Kirk's perfectly harmonized rendition of "Lover" as played spontaneously by Kirk on three horns at once. — *Scott Yanow*

Natural Black Inventions: Root Strata / Jan. 26, 1971–Jan. 28, 1971 / Atlantic ✦✦✦✦
This is a rather unusual solo LP (not yet available on CD). Other than a couple of percussionists (and piano accompaniment on "Day Dream" by Sonelius Smith), all of the music was created by Rahsaan Roland Kirk without overdubs or edits. He plays tenor, stritch, manzello, clarinets, flutes, black mystery pipes, percussion and various sound effects, often two or three instruments simultaneously. The performances are episodic and colorful with plenty of humor and adventurous moments, worthy of repeated listenings and amazement. — *Scott Yanow*

Blacknuss / Aug. 1971–Sep. 1971 / Atlantic ✦✦✦
The list of songs interpreted by Rahsaan Roland Kirk on this CD (which include such pop/R&B hits as "Ain't No Sunshine," "What's Going On," "Mercy Mercy Me" and "Never Can Say Goodbye") may make this reissue look like a commercial effort but in reality Kirk's versions of these songs are often quite hilarious. The many riotous performances and Princess Patience Burton's crazy vocal on "One Nation" are often crackups. Kirk uplifts, alters, distorts, satirizes and sometimes tears apart these familiar melodies. — *Scott Yanow*

A Meeting of the Times / Mar. 30, 1972–Mar. 31, 1972 / Atlantic ✦✦✦
On first glance, this LP combines together a pair of unlikely musical partners; the unique multi-instrumentalist Rahsaan Roland Kirk and Duke Ellington's former ballad singer Al Hibbler. However Rahsaan was very well acquainted with Ellington's music and he plays respectfully behind Hibbler on many of the standards, taking the wild "Carney and Bigard Place" as an instrumental. Hibbler (who did not record much this late in his career) is in good voice and phrases as eccentrically as ever on such songs as "Do Nothin' Till You Hear from Me," "Don't Get Around Much Anymore" and "I Didn't Know About You." One leftover selection from Rahsaan's session with singer Leon Thomas ("Dream") rounds out this surprising set. — *Scott Yanow*

★ **Bright Moments** / Jun. 8, 1973–Jun. 9, 1973 / Rhino ✦✦✦✦✦
This Rhino two-CD set (a straight reissue of an Atlantic two-LP

release) is the closest one can come nowadays to hearing what it would be like to see Rahsaan Roland Kirk perform in a club. Kirk, who is joined by a fine four-piece rhythm section for this appearance at San Francisco's legendary Keystone Korner, has colorful (and sometimes very humorous) monologues between the songs and shows off his remarkable virtuosity. Whether it be his emotional renditions of "Prelude to a Kiss" and "If I Loved You," his demonstration of nose flutes on "Fly Town Nose Blues," some authentic New Orleans clarinet playing on "Dem Red Beans and Rice" or a memorable version of his theme "Bright Moments," the music is exciting and unpredictable. This is the definitive Rahsaan Roland Kirk recording of the 1970s and is essential for any serious jazz collection. —*Scott Yanow*

Prepare Thyself to Deal with a Miracle / Oct. 1973 / Atlantic ✦✦✦✦
Although the title of this LP (not yet reissued on CD) is a bit immodest, much of the music lives up to its billing. Not all of the material on side one is all that memorable but how could Rahsaan Roland Kirk play both nose flute and a regular flute simultaneously on "Seasons"? The most remarkable selection is the 21-minute "Saxophone Concerto," which mostly consists of a nonstop one-breath tenor solo overflowing with creative ideas. There is still no one around in Rahsaan's league. —*Scott Yanow*

The Man Who Cried Fire / 1973–1977 / Night ✦✦✦✦
The best of the releases put out on Joel Dorn's Night Records, this CD has previously unreleased live performances by the amazing Rahsaan Roland Kirk. A few of the numbers are unfortunately just excerpts (including a potentially amazing encounter with The Olympia Brass Band), but there are plenty of highlights. Kirk imitates both Miles Davis and John Coltrane effectively on "Bye Bye Blackbird," performs "Multi-Horn Variations" unaccompanied on three horns, yells humorously through his flute on "You Did It, You Did It," jams in an R&B vein on "Night Train," trades off with singer Jon Hendricks on "Mr. P.C." and is heard making humorous yet insightful comments to the audience. The final selection ("A Visit from the Blues") was Kirk's last recording, an outing on flute just two months before his death. Fans are advised to pick up this valuable and consistently enjoyable CD before it disappears altogether. —*Scott Yanow*

The Case of the 3 Sided Dream in Audio Color / Nov. 1975 / Atlantic ✦✦
The music on this two-LP set (the fourth side except for an odd phone conversation placed near its end) is rather self-indulgent and erratic. Rahsaan Roland Kirk, one of the most talented saxophonists in jazz history, constructed an odd sound collage with dream sequences, some straightforward performances and too many throwaway pieces. On "Bye Bye Blackbird" first he does an excellent imitation of Miles Davis on trumpet and then, switching to tenor, he emulates John Coltrane; unfortunately, the power of this performance is greatly lessened by having this cut divided into two sections and placed on different sides. Overall this release is a misfire with only a few moments of interest. —*Scott Yanow*

Kirkatron / 1976 / Warner Brothers ✦✦✦
Shortly after Rahsaan Roland Kirk finished his first album for Warner Brothers, he suffered a major stroke that put him out of action and greatly shortened his life. His second LP for the label was actually comprised of leftovers from the earlier session plus three songs taken from an appearance at the Montreux Jazz Festival; the latter has been reissued on CD in a sampler but the other selections (which include "Serenade to a Cuckoo," his cover of "This Masquerade," "Sugar," "The Christmas Song" and "Bright Moments") remain out of print. This LP (which finds him mostly sticking to tenor), Kirk's next-to-last album, has enough highlights to make it worth searching for. —*Scott Yanow*

The Return of the 5000 Lb. Man / 1976 / Warner Brothers ✦✦✦
Rahsaan Roland Kirk's first Warner Bros. album was recorded shortly before he had a serious stroke and is one of the final examples of the unique musician being at full strength. The first portion of this LP ("Theme for the Eulipions," a lighthearted "Sweet Georgia Brown" and a passionate "I'll Be Seeing You") has since been reissued on CD, but the interesting second half (Minnie Riperton's "Loving You," vocal versions of "Goodbye Pork Pie Hat" and "Giant Steps" and an excellent version of "There Will Never Be Another You") remains out of print. Kirk (mostly heard on tenor but also playing a bit of flute, harmonica and stritch) puts on a typically remarkable show. —*Scott Yanow*

Simmer, Reduce, Garnish & Serve / 1976–1977 / Warner Archives ✦✦✦✦
This single CD has selections from Rahsaan Roland Kirk's final three albums. His work on his last record *Boogie-Woogie String Along for Real* was quite heroic and miraculous because he had suffered a major stroke that greatly limited his abilities; in fact Kirk had the use of only one of his hands so his playing was sadly restricted. There is a remarkable amount of variety plus a liberal dose of Kirk's humor on this retrospective, ranging from a "Bagpipe Medley" and "Sweet Georgia Brown" (complete with a whistler and Freddie Moore's washboard) to a warm "I'll Be Seeing You" and a tribute to Johnny Griffin, the main influence on Rahssan's tenor sound. For those listeners who do not already have the three LPs, this is a strong best-of sampler of the saxophonist's final period although his earlier recordings are recommended first. This CD concludes with an emotional and rather touching collage that pays tribute to Kirk's genius and mourns his premature death. —*Scott Yanow*

Boogie Woogie String Along for Real / 1977 / Warner Brothers ✦✦
Rahsaan Roland Kirk's final recording is a bit melancholy. Kirk, making a comeback after a serious stroke, only performs on tenor on this date along with a little clarinet (on "Make Me a Pallet on the Floor") and harmonica; even he could not play more than one horn at a time with just the use of one hand. Four songs are performed with a veteran rhythm section that includes pianist Sammy Price and guitarist Tiny Grimes, the title cut has Kirk backed by strings and the remainder of the album features pianist Hilton Ruiz and trombonist Steve Turre in the backup group. The music is generally joyful although obviously not on the same powerful level as his pre-stroke recordings. But unlike Richard Nixon (who is "saluted" here on "Watergate Blues"), Rahsaan Roland Kirk was never a quitter and he fought gamely until the end. —*Scott Yanow*

Kenny Kirkland

b. Sep. 28, 1955, Newport, NY
Piano, Keyboards / Post-Bop
Closely associated at times with Wynton and Branford Marsalis, Kenny Kirkland has surprisingly only led one CD of his own as of this writing. He started playing piano at age six and later studied at the Manhattan School of Music. Among his early jobs were playing with Michal Urbaniak (on electric keyboards) during 1977, Miroslav Vitous (1979), Terumasa Hino and Elvin Jones. Influenced by Herbie Hancock, Kirkland was well-featured while with Wynton Marsalis' band (1981–85), but his departure in 1985 to play pop music with Sting (along with Branford Marsalis) greatly upset Wynton. After leaving Sting in 1986, Kirkland became a session musician and in the early '90s he joined the Tonight Show band (under the direction of Branford Marsalis); his only album as a leader is for GRP (1991). —*Scott Yanow*

● **Kenny Kirkland** / 1991 / GRP ✦✦✦✦✦
This is a good set with Afro-Latin and hard-bop influences mixed. —*Ron Wynn*

Randy Klein

b. Sept. 9, 1949, Jersey City, NJ
Vocals, Lyricist / Hard Bop
A fine pianist and a talented lyricist, Randy Klein made a strong impression in 1994 for the song lyrics he contributed to his Jazzheads CD. In 1995 he recorded a sensitive set of duets that showcased the sound of bassist Harvie Swartz. Otherwise he has worked extensively as a composer for films, television and theater. —*Scott Yanow*

Jazzheads / 1993 / Jazzheads ✦✦✦✦
With the release of this CD, pianist/vocalist Randy Klein takes his place as one of the better jazz lyricists. Six of the eight originals feature his singing and scatting and they deal with such subject matters as avoiding negativity, not wanting to get out of bed to go to work, the need to live in the present, being buried by an excess of information and his love for coffee. The two instrumentals are sensitive duets featuring Klein's piano and bassist Harvie Swartz while the other selections utilize a standard quartet with the tenor of Michael Migliore. On the minus side, the music is not as memorable as the lyrics and therefore it is doubtful if any of these

songs will be covered by other musicians. Perhaps for next time Randy Klein should get a musical partner to match his witty words to catchier melodies. — *Scott Yanow*

John Klemmer

b. Jul. 3, 1946, Chicago, IL
Tenor Saxophone / Hard Bop, Post-Bop, Crossover
An innovator on the electrified saxophone (using echo effects quite effectively), John Klemmer was also a very strong Coltrane-inspired acoustic tenor saxophonist. He started on tenor when he was 11 in Chicago, toured as a teenager with Ted Weems and made his first recording as a leader in 1967. Klemmer was a key soloist with Don Ellis' innovative big band (1968-70), started electrifying his horn (using an echoplex) and worked on the West Coast. His easy-listening recordings for ABC in the mid-'70s were quite popular, particularly 1975's *Touch*, which found him playing melodies fairly simply. Klemmer alternated the more pop-oriented projects with fiery efforts; his finest jazz album was the two-LP set *Nexus* (mostly reissued on CD), a set of duets and trios with drums and occasional bass. He recorded with Roy Haynes in 1977, cut a few impressive unaccompanied solo saxophone records and then in 1981 dropped out of music altogether due to physical and mental problems. Other than an erratic MCA album in 1989, little has been heard from John Klemmer since. His many recordings for Cadet, ABC/Impulse, ABC, MCA and Elektra are mostly out-of-print. — *Scott Yanow*

Involvement / 1967 / Cadet ✦✦✦
Blowin' Gold / Feb. 1969 / Cadet ✦✦✦
Decent late '60s set by tenor saxophonist John Klemmer, not as focused nor as exciting as his early '70s sessions. Klemmer at this point was still finding his own sound and searching for comfortable middle ground between rock, pop and jazz. — *Ron Wynn*

All the Children Cried / Sep. 26, 1969 / Cadet ✦✦✦
Eruptions / Aug. 25, 1970 / Cadet ✦✦✦✦
Constant Throb / Aug. 12, 1971 / Impulse! ✦✦✦✦✦
Waterfalls / Jun. 17, 1972–Jun. 22, 1972 / Impulse! ✦✦✦✦✦
A stunning, explosive date. By far his best material. — *Ron Wynn*

Intensity / Feb. 23, 1973 / Impulse! ✦✦✦✦
Magic and Movement / Jul. 6, 1973 / Impulse! ✦✦✦
Barefoot Ballet / Apr. 1976–May 1976 / MCA ✦✦✦✦
Touch / 1976 / MCA ✦✦✦✦
Better solos and higher energy level than most of Klemmer's albums. This is the best-sounding version. — *Ron Wynn*

Arabesque / 1977 / MCA ✦✦✦
Lifestyle / 1977 / MCA ✦✦
Hush / 1978 / Elektra ✦✦✦

★ Nexus for Duo and Trio / 1979 / Novus ✦✦✦✦✦
At a period of time when John Klemmer had a pop hit with "Touch" and was becoming well-known for his electrified renditions of simple melodies, this double LP must have shocked some of his unsuspecting fans. The tenor saxophonist is heard on five jazz standards with bassist Bob Magnusson and drummer Carl Burnett, and on four often-stunning tenor-drums duets with Burnett; four of the performances are over ten minutes long. Quite possibly John Klemmer's finest hour (or really two hours) on record, five of the nine performances have been reissued on CD by Bluebird but, if you can, get the double LP (and the entire program) instead. — *Scott Yanow*

★ Nexus One (for Trane) / 1979 / Bluebird ✦✦✦✦✦
This CD reissues five of the nine selections from what was arguably tenor saxophonist John Klemmer's greatest recording session. In addition to forceful versions of "Mr. P.C." and "My One and Only Love" that feature Klemmer joined by bassist Bob Magnusson and drummer Carl Burnett, there are three lengthy explorations (of "Softly as in a Morning Sunrise," "Impressions" and his original "Nexus") that are taken as tenor-drums duets. The music is so powerful that listeners should search for the original double LP, which includes three additional trios and a duet on "Four." Klemmer, who was becoming very popular as a melodic pop saxophonist, must have surprised many of his fans with this very explorative document. — *Scott Yanow*

Brazilia / 1979 / MCA ✦✦✦
Finesse / Dec. 10, 1980 / Elektra ✦✦
Solo Saxophone II: Life / 1981 / Elektra ✦✦✦✦
Music / Mar. 1989 / MCA ✦

Eric Kloss

b. Apr. 3, 1949, Greenville, PA
Alto Saxophone / Hard Bop, Post Bop
Eric Kloss, a talented high-powered altoist with an open mind toward funk and certain aspects of pop music, recorded a long series of fine albums for Prestige and Muse from the mid-'60s into the late '70s. Blind since birth, Kloss began playing professionally in Pittsburgh in the early '60s. He worked with Pat Martino in 1965, the same year he started recording as a 16-year old for Prestige. Through the years Kloss used such players on his records as Martino, organist Don Patterson, Jaki Byard, Richard Davis, Alan Dawson, Cedar Walton, Jimmy Owens, Kenny Barron, Jack DeJohnette, Booker Ervin, Chick Corea and Barry Miles in addition to collaborations with Richie Cole and duets with Gil Goldstein. But Eric Kloss seemed to disappear after his 1981 Omnisound album and has not been heard from by the jazz world in quite some time. — *Scott Yanow*

Introducing Eric Kloss / Sep. 1, 1965 / Prestige ✦✦✦
Love and All That Jazz / Mar. 14, 1966–Apr. 11, 1966 / Prestige ✦✦✦
Grits and Gravy / Dec. 21, 1966–Dec. 22, 1966 / Prestige ✦✦✦✦
Soul-jazz and funk from alto saxophonist Eric Kloss on one of his early works. The influence of Cannonball Adderley and Hank Crawford comes across in Kloss' solos, especially on the uptempo numbers. — *Ron Wynn*

First Class Kloss / Jul. 14, 1967 / Prestige ✦✦✦✦
Life Force / Sep. 18, 1967 / Prestige ✦✦✦✦
We're Goin' Up / Dec. 22, 1967 / Prestige ✦✦✦
Sky Shadows / Aug. 3, 1968 / Prestige ✦✦✦✦
In the Land of the Giants / Feb. 2, 1969 / Prestige ✦✦✦✦✦
To Hear Is to See / Jul. 22, 1969 / Prestige ✦✦✦✦

★ Eric Kloss & The Rhythm Section / Jul. 22, 1969+Jan. 6, 1970 / Fantasy ✦✦✦✦✦
Whatever happened to Eric Kloss? A brilliant player by the time he was 20, Kloss has largely disappeared from the jazz scene since his string of excellent recordings for Prestige and Muse stopped in 1976. This particular CD reissue has two complete albums (*To Hear Is to See* and *Consciousness*) that feature Kloss with the Miles Davis rhythm section of the period (keyboardist Chick Corea, electric bassist Dave Holland and drummer Jack DeJohnette; the second session also has the innovative guitarist Pat Martino. It is to Eric Kloss' great credit that he keeps up with his more famous sidemen on the adventurous program which is comprised of his seven originals and one song apiece by Pat Martino, Joni Mitchell and Donovan ("Sunshine Superman"). The music blends together aspects of the avant-garde and fusion and rewards repeated listenings. — *Scott Yanow*

Consciousness! / Jan. 6, 1970 / Prestige ✦✦✦✦✦
One, Two, Free / Aug. 28, 1972 / Muse ✦✦✦✦
The best album to date from alto saxophonist Eric Koss, thanks in part to the guest stars, guitarist Pat Martino and bassist Dave Holland, plus his own explosive playing and better-than-usual compositions. — *Ron Wynn*

Essence / Dec. 14, 1973 / Muse ✦✦✦
Bodies' Warmth / Jun. 24, 1975–Jun. 25, 1975 / Muse ✦✦✦
Battle of the Saxes / Mar. 26, 1976–Mar. 27, 1976 / Muse ✦✦✦✦
Together / Jul. 19, 1976–Jul. 20, 1976 / Muse ✦✦✦
Now / Jan. 4, 1978 / Muse ✦✦✦
Energetic, surging alto sax solos from Eric Kloss that sometimes allows him to rise above generally average material. — *Ron Wynn*

Celebration / Jan. 6, 1979–Jan. 7, 1979 / Muse ✦✦✦
Good, sometimes strong alto sax solos by Eric Kloss are the lure for this otherwise routine blend of fusion, soul-jazz and funk with decent production, arrangements and compositions. — *Ron Wynn*

Sharing / Jun. 30, 1981 / Omnisound ✦✦✦✦

Earl Klugh

b. Sep. 16, 1954, Detroit, MI
Guitar / Instrumental Pop, Crossover
An acoustic guitarist with a very pretty tone, Earl Klugh does not

consider himself a jazz player and thinks of Chet Atkins as being his most important influence. Klugh played on a Yusef Lateef album when he was 15 and gained recognition in 1971 for his contributions to George Benson's *White Rabbit* record. He played regularly with Benson in 1973, was a member of Return to Forever briefly in 1974 and then, in the mid-'70s, began recording as a leader. Klugh's popular recordings (for Blue Note, Capitol, Manhattan and Warner Bros.) tend to use light funk beats, stick closely to the melody and put the emphasis on his sound; little surprising ever occurs. —*Scott Yanow*

Magic in Your Eyes / 1976 / Liberty ◆◆◆
Nice, pleasant melodies and delicate, sentimental playing by acoustic guitarist Earl Klugh. The jazz content is minimal, but the moods and colors are lush and the arrangements are generally enticing. —*Ron Wynn*

Earl Klugh / 1976 / EMI ◆◆◆◆
The session that portended his light-touch, fusion-pop approach. —*Ron Wynn*

Finger Paintings / Feb. 1977 / Blue Note ◆◆
Acoustic guitarist Earl Klugh has always had an appealing sound, but so many of his recordings are sleepy affairs that do not raise themselves above the level of background music. This early session definitely falls into that category and its reissue as a Blue Note CD reminds one of the swift decline of that label in the 1970s. The melodic music that Klugh creates is quite pleasant but little more than that and the accompaniment by fellow guitarist Lee Ritenour, an anonymous-sounding rhythm section and occasional horns and strings gives listeners no real reason to wake up. —*Scott Yanow*

Two of a Kind / 1982 / EMI ◆◆
Keyboardist Bob James and acoustic guitarist Earl Klugh struck gold with this session, recently reissued on CD. The formula hasn't changed much in succeeding years. Both Klugh and James are capable musicians; they demonstrated on this collection of light, innocuous melodies and occasionally interesting backbeats a high degree of professionalism. Klugh is a first-rate guitarist whose solos are concise and nicely delivered, but frequently sound thin. James' piano and electric keyboard playing is a puzzling combination of flawlessness and lifelessness. —*Ron Wynn*

Wishful Thinking / 1983 / EMI ◆◆◆
With some heavyweight sidemen mixed in, the sound is light, relaxing, jazz-space music. Pleasant stuff. —*Michael Erlewine*

Soda Fountain Shuffle / 1984 / Warner Brothers ◆◆◆
Synthesizer, drum machine backgrounds. Easy-listening programmed light jazz with a touch of space music. One of his most popular. —*Michael Erlewine*

Life Stories / 1986 / Warner Brothers ◆◆◆

Midnight in San Juan / Mar. 1989–Apr. 1990 / Warner Brothers ◆◆◆

● **Solo Guitar** / 1989 / Warner Brothers ◆◆◆◆
Earl Klugh's long-awaited solo album showcased his pretty sound on the acoustic guitar, giving two-to-three-three minute melodic readings of superior standards. Some of the pieces (notably "I'm Confessin' ") found Klugh playing a relaxed "stride" similiar to some of the guitarists of the '30s. —*Scott Yanow*

Whispers and Promises / 1989 / Warner Brothers ◆◆◆
Standard fusion. Pleasant, lightweight material. —*Ron Wynn*

Move / 1993 / Warner Bros. ◆◆
This is a typical set of safe background music by acoustic guitarist Earl Klugh. Klugh has always had an attractive sound, but he remains content to record lightweight, poppish material with bland sidemen. There is nothing memorable or distinctive about these innocuous performances. —*Scott Yanow*

Jimmy Knepper

b. Nov. 22, 1927, Los Angeles, CA
Trombone / Hard Bop
A fine soloist with a distinctive sound not overly influenced by J.J. Johnson, Jimmy Knepper's improvisations are full of subtle surprises. He began on trombone when he was nine, started playing professionally when he was 15 and worked in the big bands of Freddie Slack (1947), Roy Porter (1948–49), Charlie Spivak (1950–51), Charlie Barnet (1951), Woody Herman and Claude Thornhill. Knepper gained fame for his versatile and inventive playing with several of Charles Mingus' groups (1957–62). He also

worked with Stan Kenton (1959), Herbie Mann (a 1960 tour of Africa), Gil Evans, Benny Goodman (the 1962 tour of the Soviet Union) and the Thad Jones-Mel Lewis Orchestra (1968–74) in addition to playing in the 1970s with the Lee Konitz Nonet and Mingus Dynasty. Knepper's reputation in the jazz world has remained quite strong although he has not recorded that often as a leader, cutting sessions for Debut, Bethlehem (both in 1957), SteepleChase (1976), Inner City and Blackhawk. —*Scott Yanow*

Idol of the Flies / Sep. 1957 / Bethlehem ◆◆◆◆
Other than a few titles for Debut, this was trombonist Jimmy Knepper's only record date as a leader until 1976. The music is essentially cool-toned bop with six standards and three Knepper originals all given swinging treatment. Six of the songs feature the trombonist in a quintet with altoist Gene Quill and the young pianist Bill Evans, while the other three titles also star trumpeter Gene Roland (who takes a rare vocal on "Gee Baby, Ain't I Good to You") and pianist Bob Hammer. —*Scott Yanow*

● **Cunningbird** / Nov. 8, 1976 / SteepleChase ◆◆◆◆◆
Quintet w/ Al Cohn (ts), Sir Roland Hanna (p), George Mraz (b), Dannie Richmond (d). A tremendous date. —*Ron Wynn*

Jimmy Knepper in L.A. / Sep. 8, 1977–Sep. 9, 1977 / Inner City ◆◆◆◆◆
For this blowing session, trombonist Jimmy Knepper performs with an all-star quintet comprised of Lew Tabackin on tenor and a touch of flute, pianist Roger Kellaway, bassist Monty Budwig and drummer Shelly Manne. These veterans have little difficulty coming up with fresh statements on the six familiar chord changes that they interpret. The hard-charging Tabackin matches very well with Knepper's sly trombone; they should have a rematch someday. —*Scott Yanow*

Primrose Path / Nov. 19, 1980 / Hep ◆◆◆◆

First Place / Feb. 1982 / Blackhawk ◆◆◆◆

I Dream Too Much / Feb. 1984–Mar. 1984 / Soul Note ◆◆◆◆
With John Clark (french horn), John Eckert (tpt). All brass front line. Includes three Knepper compositions, two standards, one by Hanna. —*Michael G. Nastos*

Dream Dancing / Apr. 1986 / Criss Cross ◆◆◆◆◆

Lee Konitz

b. Oct. 13, 1927, Chicago, IL
Alto Saxophone, Soprano Saxophone / Cool, Post Bop
One of the most individual of all altoists (and one of the few in the 1950s who did not sound like a cousin of Charlie Parker), the cool-toned Lee Konitz has always had a strong musical curiosity that has led him to consistently take chances and stretch himself, usually quite successfully. Early on he studied clarinet, switched to alto and played with Jerry Wald. Konitz gained some attention for his solos with Claude Thornhill's Orchestra (1947). He began studying with Lennie Tristano, who had a big influence on his conception and approach to improvising. Konitz was with Miles Davis' Birth of the Cool nonet during their one gig and their Capitol recordings (1948–50) and recorded with Lennie Tristano's innovative sextet (1949) including the first two free improvisations ever documented. Konitz blended very well with Warne Marsh's tenor (their unisons on "Wow" are miraculous) and would have several reunions with both Tristano and Marsh through the years but he was also interested in finding his own way; by the early '50s he started breaking away from the Tristano school. Konitz toured Scandinavia (1951) where his cool sound was influential and he fit in surprisingly well with Stan Kenton's Orchestra (1952–54), being featured on many charts by Bill Holman and Bill Russo. Konitz was primarily a leader from that point on. He almost retired from music in the early '60s, but re-emerged a few years later. His recordings have ranged from cool bop to thoughtful free improvisations and his Milestone set of *Duets* (1967) is a classic. In the late '70s Konitz led a notable Nonet and in 1992 he won the prestigious Jazzpar Prize. He has recorded on soprano and tenor but has mostly stuck to his distinctive alto. Lee Konitz has led consistently stimulating sessions for many labels including Prestige, Dragon, Pacific Jazz, Vogue, Storyville, Atlantic, Verve, Wave, Milestone, MPS, Polydor, Bellaphon, SteepleChase, Sonet, Groove Merchant, Roulette, Progressive, Choice, IAI, Chiaroscuro, Circle, Black Lion, Soul Note, Storyville, Evidence and Philogy. —*Scott Yanow*

● **Subconscious–Lee** / Jan. 11, 1949–Apr. 7, 1950 / Original Jazz Classics ◆◆◆◆◆
This very interesting CD has altoist Lee Konitz's first recordings

as a leader, taken from a period of time when he was very much under the musical influence of pianist Lennie Tristano. In fact the program starts off with a quintet date from Jan. 1949 that was actually originally headed by Tristano but features the young altoist. The latter two sessions match Konitz with his fellow Tristano students (including tenor saxophonist Warne Marsh, guitarist Billy Bauer and Tristano-soundalike Sal Mosca on piano). The original style developed by Tristano, Konitz and the others (which was different than bop and cool jazz) still sounds fresh today. —Scott Yanow

Ezz-Thetic / Mar. 8, 1951+Sep. 18, 1953 / Prestige ✦✦✦✦
This LP contains important early music from altoist Lee Konitz. There are four little-known selections that team Konitz in a sextet with trumpeter Miles Davis in 1951 (along with such Tritanoites as pianist Sal Mosca and guitarist Billy Bauer); most notable is George Russell's "Ezz-thetic" and Konitz's "Hi Beck." The remainder of this album features the altoist with a quintet in France in 1953 performing four standards, which are augmented by four alternate takes. Early examples of cool-toned bop. —Scott Yanow

Sax Of A Kind / Nov. 19, 1951+Aug. 22, 1953 / Dragon ✦✦✦✦
This is a set that Lee Konitz collectors will definitely want. The distinctive cool-toned altoist is heard in Stockholm in 1951 performing with a variety of fine Swedish players; best known is pianist Bengt Hallberg. The set is rounded off by a version of "Lover Man" that showcases the altoist with Stan Kenton's orchestra in 1953. The recording quality of these radio broadcasts are quite good and Konitz is in top form for the period. —Scott Yanow

Konitz Meets Mulligan / Jan. 30, 1953 / Pacific Jazz ✦✦✦✦✦
W/ Gerry Mulligan Quartet. A simply wonderful pairing of idiosyncratic talents. —Ron Wynn

Lee Konitz/Bob Brookmeyer In Paris / Sep. 17, 1953+Jun. 5, 1954 / Vogue ✦✦✦
Two unrelated quintet sessions led by altoist Lee Konitz and valve trombonist Bob Brookmeyer are reissued in full on this Vogue CD. The Konitz set (with guitarist Jimmy Gourley, pianist Henri Renaud, bassist Don Bagley and drummer Stan Levey) has 11 performances of four standards including five of "I'll Remember April." The cool-toned altoist is in fine form for his set as is Bob Brookmeyer who plays one version apiece of four songs with Gourley, Renaud, bassist Red Mitchell and drummer Frank Isola. Bop fans will want this fine straight-ahead set. —Scott Yanow

Jazz at Storyville / Jan. 5, 1954 / Black Lion ✦✦✦✦✦
This excellent CD gives one a definitive look at altoist Lee Konitz at a period of time when he was breaking away from being a sideman and a student of Lennie Tristano and asserting himself as a leader. With pianist Ronnie Ball, bassist Percy Heath and drummer Alan Levitt, Konitz explores a variety of his favorite chord changes, some of which were disguised by newer melodies such as "Hi Beck," "Subconscious Lee" and "Sound Lee." Among the other highpoints of this well-recorded set are "Foolin' Myself" and a lengthy exploration of "If I Had You." —Scott Yanow

Konitz / Aug. 6, 1954 / Black Lion ✦✦✦✦✦
The 1954 Lee Konitz Quartet did not last long, but they did record some worthwhile performances that still sound fresh over 40 years later. In addition to eight selections (highlighted by "Bop Goes the Leesel," "Mean to Me," "I'll Remember April" and "Limehouse Blues"), there are six previously unissued alternate takes included on this attractive 1989 CD. Altoist Konitz is ably assisted by pianist Ronnie Ball, bassist Peter Ind and drummer Jeff Morton on cool/bop performances which give one a good sampling of how Konitz sounded in his early prime. —Scott Yanow

Jazzlore: Lee Konitz / Warne Marsh / Jun. 14, 1955 / Atlantic ✦✦✦✦
Altoist Lee Konitz and tenor saxophonist Warne Marsh always made for a perfect team. Even by the mid-'50s when they were not as influenced by Lennie Tristano as previously (particularly Konitz), their long melodic lines and unusual tones caused them to stand out from the crowd. On this LP reissue Konitz and Marsh co-lead a particularly strong group that also includes pianist Sal Mosca, guitarist Billy Bauer, bassist Oscar Pettiford and drummer Kenny Clarke. Their renditions of "originals" based on common chord changes along with versions of "Topsy," "There Will Never Be Another You" and "Donna Lee" are quite enjoyable and swing hard yet fall into the category of cool jazz. This set is worth searching for, as are all of the Konitz-Marsh collaborations. —Scott Yanow

Lee Konitz / Jan. 17, 1956+Jan. 21, 1956 / Swingtime ✦✦✦✦
These somewhat rare recordings were made in 1956 when altoist Lee Konitz went on tour with the great Swedish baritonist Lars Gullin. Konitz, who also plays tenor on one tune and baritone on two others, works well with this complementary group, which includes the tenor of Hans Koller, a second baritonist and a German rhythm section. Pianist Roland Kovac contributed three of the originals, Konitz brought in three others, Gullin contributed "Late Summer" and the group stretches out on the lone standard "I'm Getting Sentimental over You." The fresh material and interesting combination of saxophonists make this European import LP of above average interest to bop and cool jazz fans. —Scott Yanow

Inside Hi-Fi / Sep. 26, 1956+Sep. 16, 1956 / Atlantic ✦✦✦✦
This excellent Atlantic reissue LP (part of their 1987 Jazzlore series) features altoist Lee Konitz with two separate quartets during 1956. Either guitarist Billy Bauer or pianist Sal Mosca are the main supporting voices in groups also including either Arnold Fishkind or Peter Ind on bass and Dick Scott on drums. The most unusual aspect to the set is that on the four selections with Mosca, Konitz switches to tenor, playing quite effectively in a recognizable cool style. The overall highlights of this enjoyable LP are "Everything Happens to Me," "All of Me" and "Star Eyes," but all eight performances are well played and swinging. —Scott Yanow

The Real Lee Konitz / Feb. 15, 1957 / Atlantic ✦✦✦✦
Tranquility / Oct. 22, 1957 / Verve ✦✦✦✦
An Image: Lee Konitz with Strings / Feb. 6, 1958 / Verve ✦✦✦
★ **Live at the Half Note** / Feb. 24, 1959+Mar. 3, 1959 / Verve ✦✦✦✦✦
The music on this two-CD set has a strange history. Pianist Lennie Tristano had a rare reunion with altoist Lee Konitz and tenor saxophonist Warne Marsh (his two greatest "students") during an extended stay at the Half Note in 1959. Tristano took Tuesday nights off to teach and Bill Evans was his substitute, but the pianist had a couple of those performances recorded for posterity. Years later while listening to his tapes he was so impressed with Marsh's playing that he sent edited versions (comprised entirely of the tenor's solos) to Marsh and somehow they ended up being released in that form by the Revelation label. Finally, in 1994, the unedited music was issued by Verve; the consistently exciting playing by Konitz, Marsh and Evans (with backup by bassist Jimmy Garrison and drummer Paul Motian) makes one wonder what took so long. They perform a dozen extended standards (or "originals" based on the chord changes of familiar tunes) with creativity and inspiration. In fact, of all the Konitz-Marsh recordings, this set ranks near the top. —Scott Yanow

Lee Konitz Meets Jimmy Giuffre / May 12, 1959–May 13, 1959 / Verve ✦✦✦

Motion / Aug. 29, 1961 / Verve ✦✦✦✦
This very spontaneous LP (altoist Lee Konitz had never played before in a trio with bassist Sonny Dallas and drummer Elvin Jones) is quite successful and easily enjoyable. Konitz and his trio perform five familiar standards, stretching out on such tunes as "I Remember You," "All of Me" and "You'd Be So Nice to Come Home To." The music is searching but melodic, explorative yet accessible. This is one of Konitz's better albums from the era and is long overdue to be reissued on CD. —Scott Yanow

★ **The Lee Konitz Duets** / Sep. 25, 1967 / Original Jazz Classics ✦✦✦✦✦
This CD brings back one of altoist Lee Konitz's greatest sessions. In 1967 he recorded a series of very diverse duets, all of which succeed on their own terms. Konitz is matched with valve trombonist Marshall Brown on a delightful version of "Struttin' with Some Barbecue," matches wits with the tenor of Joe Henderson on "You Don't Know What Love Is," plays "Checkerboard" with pianist Dick Katz, "Erb" with guitarist Jim Hall, "Tickle Toe" with the tenor of Richie Kamuca (Konitz switches to tenor on that cut) and an adventurous and fairly free "Duplexity" with violinist Ray Nance, has three different duets on "Alone Together" and, on "Alphanumeric," welcomes practically everyone back for a final blowout. The music ranges from Dixieland to bop and free and is consistently fascinating. —Scott Yanow

Alto Summit / Jun. 2, 1968–Jun. 3, 1968 / Verve ✦✦✦
This unusual album teams together the altos of Lee Konitz, Pony Poindexter, Phil Woods and Leo Wright (along with pianist Steve Kuhn, bassist Palle Danielsson and drummer Jon Christensen) on

a variety of challenging material. There are four pieces for the full septet (including one that pays tribute to both Bach and Bird), a pair of quintet performances and a ballad medley that ends in a complete fiasco (it has to be heard to be believed). Despite the latter, everyone fares well on this summit meeting. —*Scott Yanow*

Peacemeal / Mar. 20, 1969–Mar. 21, 1969 / Milestone ✦✦✦✦✦
This Lee Konitz recording is of even greater interest than usual. Altoist Konitz, in a quintet with valve trombonist Marshall Brown, pianist Dick Katz, bassist Eddie Gomez and drummer Jack DeJohnette, performs jazz adaptations of three Bela Bartok piano compositions, a trio of Dick Katz originals, two of his own pieces (including "Subconscious-Lee") and versions of "Lester Leaps In" and "Body and Soul" that include transcriptions of recorded solos by, respectively, Lester Young and Roy Eldridge. A thought-provoking and consistently enjoyable set of music. —*Scott Yanow*

Spirits / Feb. 1971 / Milestone ✦✦✦✦
Altoist Lee Konitz revisits his roots in pianist Lennie Tristano's music on this enjoyable LP from 1971. Four of the nine songs are duets with pianist Sal Mosca (who always sounded a lot like Tristano) while the five other pieces add bassist Ron Carter and drummer Mousie Alexander to the group. Konitz performs three of his own compositions, five by Tristano and one from tenor saxophonist Warne Marsh; typically all of these originals are based closely on the chord changes (and sometimes the melodies) of familiar standards. Despite that lack of originality, this is excellent music and finds altoist Lee Konitz in creative form. —*Scott Yanow*

Jazz a Juan / Jul. 26, 1974 / SteepleChase ✦✦✦

I Concentrate on You / Jul. 30, 1974 / SteepleChase ✦✦✦
A nice duo with Red Mitchell (b). —*Ron Wynn*

Lone-Lee / Aug. 15, 1974 / SteepleChase ✦✦✦✦
This is an unusual release, for it features altoist Lee Konitz playing unaccompanied. He performs lengthy versions of "The Song Is You" (over 19 minutes long) and "Cherokee" (nearly 18 minutes) in swinging but relaxed and fairly free fashion. The improvisations are quite thoughtful and logical yet avoid being predictable and hold onto one's interest throughout. —*Scott Yanow*

Satori / Sep. 30, 1974 / Milestone ✦✦✦✦
This is an excellent release that is fairly typical of a Lee Konitz program from the 1970s and '80s. There are a few standards (such as "Just Friends," "Green Dolphin Street" and "What's New"), a few fairly advanced pieces ("Satori" and "Free Blues"), thoughtful improvisations and a bit of hard-swinging. Inspired by the presence of pianist Martial Solal, bassist David Holland and drummer Jack DeJohnette, Konitz stretches himself as usual and comes up with consistently fresh statements while generally playing at a low introspective volume. This thought-provoking music was last available on this Milestone LP and deserves to be reissued on CD. —*Scott Yanow*

Oleo / Jan. 1975 / Sonet ✦✦✦
The strong interplay between Lee Konitz (who doubles here on alto and soprano), pianist Dick Katz and bassist Wilbur Little is the main reason to search for this Sonet LP. Together they perform eight standards including "I Want a Little Girl," "Oleo," "St. Thomas" and "There Is No Greater Love." In general the improvisations are quite relaxed and thoughtful and, although the results are not all that essential (since there are a lot of Lee Konitz recordings currently available), the altoist's fans will find much to enjoy during these fine performances. —*Scott Yanow*

Chicago 'n All That Jazz / May 6, 1975 / Denon ✦✦✦
This CD is better than it initially appears. Altoist Lee Konitz and his augmented nonet perform eight numbers from the musical *Chicago*, all songs that have been long forgotten ever since. However Konitz (switching between alto and soprano) and his sidemen (who include trumpeter Richard Hurwitz, Dick Katz and Michael Longo on keyboards and bassist Major Holley who also takes a couple of vocals) play with enthusiasm and melodic creativity; some of the themes are quite catchy. The playing time (around 30 minutes) is quite brief and the music is far from essential, but the performances are surprisingly pleasing, making this a worthy purchase if found at a budget price. —*Scott Yanow*

Windows / Nov. 6, 1975 / SteepleChase ✦✦✦
Another good duo, this time with Hal Galper (p). —*Ron Wynn*

Lee Konitz Meets Warne Marsh Again / May 24, 1976 / PA/USA ✦✦✦✦
Recorded in London, this quartet date with bassist Peter Ind and

drummer Al Levitt is a reunion between the very complementary stylists Lee Konitz on alto and tenor saxophonist Warne Marsh. Their repertoire (common chord changes) and cool jazz styles are not that surprising, but both of the saxophonists sound quite inspired to be in each other's presence; they always brought out the best in each other. The melodic and boppish improvisations reward repeated listenings. —*Scott Yanow*

★ **The Lee Konitz Nonet** / Oct. 13, 1976+Oct. 18, 1976 / Roulette ✦✦✦✦✦
This is a group that should have been able to stay together but it was formed a few years too soon, at the height of the fusion era. Altoist Lee Konitz's nonet (featuring trumpeter Burt Collins, trombonist Jimmy Knepper and keyboardist Andy Laverne among others) reflected its leader's interest in a wide variety of jazz. The music on this out-of-print but valuable LP ranges from swing classics ("If Dreams Come True" and "A Pretty Girl Is like a Melody") and bop ("Without a Song") to Wayne Shorter's "Nefertiti" and a pair of Chick Corea tunes ("Matrix" and "Times Lie"). Sy Johnson wrote most of the arrangements (including a full orchestration of six choruses from Chick Corea's piano solo on "Matrix"). This album is well worth a long search since it is one of Lee Konitz's finest recordings of the 1970s. —*Scott Yanow*

Figure and Spirit / Oct. 20, 1976 / Progressive ✦✦✦✦
Altoist Lee Konitz (who doubles on this CD on soprano) teams up with tenor saxophonist Ted Brown, pianist Albert Dailey, bassist Rufus Reid and drummer Joe Chambers for this session. The six songs (originals based on standards by Konitz, Brown and Lennie Tristano) were all performed in one take and although there are a few minor mistakes, the music is quite exciting and spontaneous. Brown was the best possible substitute for Wayne Marsh (Konitz's original choice for the record) and sounds in prime form. It's worth acquiring by fans of straight-ahead jazz, Lennie Tristano and Lee Konitz. —*Scott Yanow*

Tenorlee / Jan. 1977+Jul. 1977 / Choice ✦✦✦✦✦
This is one of Lee Konitz's more swing-oriented sessions. Switching exclusively from his customary alto to tenor, Konitz (in a trio with pianist Jimmy Rowles and bassist Michael Moore) sticks to standards and sounds in prime form on such tunes as "I Remember You," "Thanks for the Memory," "Autumn Nocturne" and "Lady Be Good"; the brief title cut features Konitz unaccompanied. This LP from the Choice label should delight fans of straight-ahead jazz. —*Scott Yanow*

Pyramid / Jun. 11, 1977 / Improvising Artists ✦✦
Reissued on CD by the Black Saint/Soul Note labels, this entry from Paul Bley's IAI label features fairly free playing from an unusual trio comprised of Lee Konitz (on alto and soprano), keyboardist Bley and Bill Connors on electric and acoustic guitars. Actually, due to the free nature of the pieces, the music is less exciting than one might hope. Everyone takes chances in their solos, but several of the pieces wander on much too long. Overall this session does not reach the heights one might expect from these great players. —*Scott Yanow*

The Lee Konitz Nonet / Sep. 20, 1977–Sep. 21, 1977 / Chiaroscuro ✦✦✦✦✦
The Lee Konitz Nonet was never able to prosper but fortunately they recorded several excellent albums. With such top players as fluegelhornist John Eckert, trombonist Jimmy Knepper and baritonist Ronnie Cuber in the group and colorful arrangements provided by Sy Johnson, this band's repertoire was as wide as one would expect from a Konitz band. Whether it be the Louis Armstrong-associated "Struttin' with Some Barbeque," a Lester Young-inspired "Sometimes I'm Happy," Charlie Parker's "Chi-Chi," "Giant Steps" or some newer originals, the results are frequently superb. This subtle but swinging set deserves to be reissued. —*Scott Yanow*

Lee Konitz Quintet / Sep. 1977 / Chiaroscuro ✦✦✦
This frequently heated session teams together the great veteran altoist Lee Konitz with the much younger alto saxophonist Bob Mover, who, at that point in time, sounded like Konitz's clone. Accompanied by pianist Ben Aranov, bassist Mike Moore and drummer Jim Madison, the two very complementary saxophonists take explorative solos on eight appealing chord changes, constantly challenging each other. Bob Mover would become much more individual within a few years, but on this album it is very much like listening to a teacher and his prize student. —*Scott Yanow*

● **Yes, Yes, Nonet** / Apr. 17, 1979 / SteepleChase ✦✦✦✦✦
It was a tragedy that Lee Konitz's versatile nonet was not able to succeed commercially. Just like its leader, the group was able to stretch from swing standards, bop and cool jazz to freer improvisations and challenging originals. This SteepleChase release (featuring the nonet when it was comprised of such fine players as trumpeters Tom Harrell and John Eckert, trombonists Jimmy Knepper and Sam Burtis, baritonist Ronnie Cuber, pianist Harold Danko, bassist Buster Williams and drummer Billy Hart in addition to Konitz on alto and soprano) features the group at its best on such pieces as "Footprints," "Stardust," "My Buddy" and four songs by Jimmy Knepper. It's an excellent outing from a somewhat neglected group. —*Scott Yanow*

Live at Laren / Aug. 12, 1979 / Soul Note ✦✦✦
1979 version of his nonet. Extended examples of Corea's "Matrix" and "Times Lie". —*Michael G. Nastos*

Seasons Change / Oct. 29, 1979 / Circle ✦✦✦
Duets with vibist Karl Berger. —*Michael G. Nastos*

Heroes / Jan. 11, 1980–Jan. 12, 1980 / Verve ✦✦
This CD (and its follow-up *Anti-Heroes*) features the rather odd duo of Lee Konitz (on alto and soprano) and pianist Gil Evans. Since Evans was far from a virtuoso and at best played "arranger's piano" (particularly at this late stage in his life), his accompaniment behind Konitz is quite sparse. The repertoire includes standards, Konitz's "Aprilling," an adaptation of some Chopin and a medley of Evans' "Blues Improvisation" and "Zee Zee." But frankly overall this is a rather uneventful and often dull release that can easily be passed by. —*Scott Yanow*

Anti-Heroes / Jan. 11, 1980–Jan. 12, 1980 / Verve ✦✦
This Verve CD (and its predecessor from the same gigs, *Heroes*) contains duos featuring Lee Konitz on alto and soprano and pianist Gil Evans (just four months before the latter's death). Actually, the music is rather disappointing; although Konitz plays fairly well on the mixture of standards and obscurities, Evans often wanders and his backing of the saxophonist is sparse and erratic. The results are more important historically than musically. —*Scott Yanow*

Live at the Berlin Jazz Days / Oct. 30, 1980 / MPS ✦✦✦
This Pausa LP contains the music performed at a Lennie Tristano memorial, duets by altoist Lee Konitz (Tristano's greatest student) and pianist Martial Solal. Although the repertoire certainly pays tribute to Tristano's legacy (including such songs as "No. 317 East 32nd Street," "Star Eyes" and Konitz's "Subconsciously"), the altoist had grown quite a bit as an improviser during the previous 30 years and Solal is a major stylist in his own right. Their explorative and spontaneous music covers a wide area of styles from swing and cool-toned bop to freer explorations and lives up to one's expectations. —*Scott Yanow*

Dovetail / Feb. 25, 1983+Feb. 27, 1983 / Sunnyside ✦✦✦✦
Billed as the "Lee Konitz Terzet" (without ever defining what "Terzet" is), this fine trio set features Konitz on alto, tenor, soprano and even a vocal, pianist Harold Danko and bassist Jay Leonhart. Konitz in the liner notes states that "we played in a club for one week and found a way to create nice instant arrangements on familiar tunes...." That pretty well describes this music for even the so-called originals by the trio have a close relationship to a familiar standard. The repertoire is certainly a bit offbeat for these modernists, particularly such songs as "I Want to Be Happy," "Sweet Georgia Brown" and "Penthouse Serenade," but the musicians come up with fresh statements on all of the tunes. A continually interesting set, like most of Lee Konitz's recordings. —*Scott Yanow*

Glad, Koonix! / Nov. 5, 1983 / Dragon ✦✦✦✦
Ever since 1951, altoist Lee Konitz has performed and recorded often in Sweden where his cool-toned sound has long been popular and influential. On this excellent release from the Swedish label Dragon, Konitz is teamed with the fine trumpeter Jan Allan and a good veteran rhythm section from Sweden. There are two originals by pianist Utsava Goran Strandberg and otherwise the tunes are familiar standards including "Lover Man" (taken as a waltz), "A Child Is Born" (a feature for Allan), Konitz's "Hi Beck," "Cherokee" and "Body and Soul." Somehow Lee Konitz never sounds stale and his solos (even on tunes he had been playing for over 30 years) still have a strong amount of curiosity and wonderment in them. His fans will enjoy this fine straight-ahead session. —*Scott Yanow*

Dedicated to Lee / Nov. 7, 1983-Nov. 8, 1983 / Dragon ✦✦✦✦✦
Despite its title (a name of a song from 1953), this set from the Swedish Dragon label is actually a tribute to the music of the late baritonist Lars Gullin rather than to Lee Konitz. Most of the selections (all Gullin compositions) feature altoist Konitz with an octet comprised of talented (but fairly obscure) Swedish players. Best known among the sidemen is trumpeter Jan Allan who is featured on "Peter of April" in a quintet including Konitz; the altoist has "Happy Again" as his feature. Considering that all of the music is obscure outside of Sweden ("Danny's Dream" is the best-known song) and that the quality is quite high, this set is easily recommended to musicians who are looking for a fresher bop-based repertoire and to listeners who enjoy discovering "new" material. —*Scott Yanow*

Ideal Scene / Jul. 22, 1986–Jul. 23, 1986 / Soul Note ✦✦✦✦
This Soul Note release features Lee Konitz with his 1986 quartet, a unit that also includes pianist Harold Danko, bassist Rufus Reid and drummer Al Harewood. Konitz, listed as playing soprano on the album but actually sticking exclusively to alto, not only interprets three veteran standards ("Ezz-thetic," "If You Could See Me Now" and "Stella by Starlight"), but also three of Danko's thenrecent originals and his own "Chick Came Around." The subtle but swinging music is harmonically advanced and full of surprising twists; no predictable bebop here! More than most members of his musical generation, Lee Konitz has continued to keep his music and improvising style fresh and imaginative while retaining his own original musical personality through the years. —*Scott Yanow*

Round and Round / 1988 / Music Masters ✦✦✦
The most unusual aspect to this outing by altoist Lee Konitz is that all nine selections are performed in 3/4 time. "Someday My Prince Will Come" and Sonny Rollins' "Valse Hot" were originally waltzes, but "Lover Man," "Bluesette" and particularly "Giant Steps" were never recorded in that time signature before. With the assistance of pianist Fred Hersch, bassist Mike Richmond and drummer Adam Nussbaum, Konitz manages to uplift this session above the level of a potential gimmick and finds unexpected beauty in these standards and originals. —*Scott Yanow*

Lee Konitz in Rio / 1989 / M·A Music ✦✦
Lee Konitz (on alto and soprano) plays well enough on this set, but the original material (all composed and arranged by Allan Botschinsky) is somewhat forgettable, the accompaniment (by a Brazilian rhythm section and on some songs a full string section) sounds quite anonymous and little happens in the way of development or surprises. In fact, the only unusual aspect to this date is that Konitz was unsuccessful at uplifting the lightweight (if reasonably enjoyable) music. Considering how many more viable Lee Konitz recordings are currently available, this is one of the lesser efforts. —*Scott Yanow*

Zounds / May 23, 1990–May 24, 1990 / Soul Note ✦✦✦
This is a very interesting if occasionally unsettling CD. Lee Konitz (doubling on alto and soprano) and his 1990 quartet (which is comprised of Kenny Werner on piano and occasional synthesizer, bassist Ron McClure and drummer Bill Stewart) emphasize freely improvised performances throughout the date. Two standards ("Prelude to a Kiss" and "Taking a Chance on Love") are interpreted pretty freely while all of the other selections are group originals; Konitz even takes an unplanned "vocal" (more an example of sound explorations then an attempt at conventional singing) on "Synthesthetics." This is a consistently stimulating and rather unpredictable outing by the talented group. —*Scott Yanow*

Lullaby of Birdland / Sep. 6, 1991–Sep. 7, 1991 / Candid ✦✦✦✦

Lunasea / 1992 / Soul Note ✦✦✦✦
Altoist Lee Konitz certainly covers a lot of ground on this Soul Note CD. Performing with his recent discovery Peggy Stern on piano, guitarist Vic Juris, bassist Harvie Swartz, drummer Jeff Williams and percussionist Guilherme Franco, Konitz and his players perform everything from jams in the Lennie Tristano tradition and Brazilian pieces that are almost pop-oriented to free improvisations. Stern is quite impressive throughout the date. Classically trained, she proves from the start that she has a real talent at improvisation and is not afraid to take chances. Konitz sounds inspired by her presence and their interplay makes this an easily recommended set for adventurous listeners. —*Scott Yanow*

And The Jazzpar All Star Nonet / Mar. 27, 1992-Mar. 29, 1992 / Storyville ✦✦✦✦✦
On this diverse and highly enjoyable set, altoist Lee Konitz is

heard in a variety of settings. Five songs (four of them recently composed) feature Konitz interacting with a fine Danish nonet and on "Subconscious Lee" he is showcased in a quintet with fluegelhornist Allan Botchinsky and pianist Peggy Stern. However, it is his six duets (with Stern, Botchinsky, bassist Jesper Lundgaard and fellow altoist Jens Sondergaard) that are most notable. Konitz, who can play as freely as any avant-gardist, somehow always sounds relaxed and thoughtful, turning these duets into comfortable dialogues. — *Scott Yanow*

Jazz Nocturne / Oct. 5, 1992 / Evidence ✦✦✦✦✦
Although never a poll winner, altoist Lee Konitz has had a more productive and consistently stimulating career than most of his contemporaries, never afraid to improvise fairly freely in his relaxed style. For this Evidence CD, Konitz digs into seven standards with an impressive rhythm section (pianist Kenny Barron, bassist James Genus and drummer Kenny Washington) and constantly comes up with interesting ideas and new twists. There are no phony disguises of familiar tunes with new titles on this date; just creative blowing. Konitz uplifts such often-overplayed material as "You'd Be So Nice to Come Home To," "Misty," "Alone Together," "Body and Soul" and "My Funny Valentine" without ever becoming predictable; Kenny Barron is in excellent form, too. This CD is recommended as a strong example of Lee Konitz's playing in the 1990s. — *Scott Yanow*

The Jobim Collection / Jan. 6, 1993–Jan. 10, 1993 / Philogy ✦✦✦✦
Altoist Lee Konitz and pianist Peggy Stern (who also plays synthesizer on a few of the tracks) sound like they really enjoyed themselves during this set of 14 Antonio Carlos Jobim songs. The emphasis is very much on melodic improvising (one can hear Jobim's themes throughout these performances), but Konitz, as usual, sounds very much like himself and Stern is consistently inventive both in reharmonizing some of the songs and in her subtle solos. The results are quite delightful and this CD is easily recommended to fans of both bossa nova and Lee Konitz. — *Scott Yanow*

Rhapsody / Jun. 20, 1993–Jul. 14, 1993 / Evidence ✦✦
Lee Konitz's Evidence release has seven selections from the veteran altoist that utilize different all-star personnel. The performances all have a similar commitment to relaxed and melodic freedom but some work better than others. "I Hear a Rhapsody" (featuring a haunting vocal by Helen Merrill) precedes a more abstract "Rhapsody" (titled "Lo-Ko-Mo-And Frizz"), which has wandering interplay by Konitz (on alto, soprano and tenor), Joe Lovano (switching between tenor, alto clarinet and soprano), guitarist Bill Frisell and drummer Paul Motian. Jay Clayton's beautiful voice and adventurous style is well displayed on "The Aerie" and baritone great Gerry Mulligan sounds reasonably comfortable on a free improvisation with Konitz and pianist Peggy Stern, but a fairly straightforward vocal by Judy Niemack on "All the Things You Are" is followed by an overlong (19-minute) exploration of the same chord changes (renamed "Exposition") by the quartet of Konitz, clarinetist Jimmy Giuffre, pianist Paul Bley and bassist Gary Peacock; their different approaches never really mesh together and this selection is a bit of a bore. The final performance, an extroverted duet by Konitz (on soprano) and fluegelhornist Clark Terry (titled "Flyin'—Mumbles and Jumbles") adds some badly needed humor to the set. While one can admire Lee Konitz for still challenging himself after all this time, some of the drier material on the CD (especially the two quartet numbers) should have been performed again; maybe the next versions would have been more inspired. — *Scott Yanow*

Diana Krall

b. Nanaimo, Canada
Piano, Vocals / Bop, Swing
Skilled as both a pianist and a vocalist, Diana Krall began playing piano when she was four. She attended Berklee (1982–85), studied in Los Angeles with Jimmie Rowles and in 1990 moved to New York. Krall debuted on record in a 1993 trio date for Justin Time with Ray Brown and Jeff Hamilton and has since recorded for GRP and Impulse, the latter a 1995 tribute to Nat King Cole. — *Scott Yanow*

Stepping Out / 1993 / Justin Time ✦✦✦
Diana Krall's debut recording was a good start for the singer/pianist although at that point she did not stand out from

the crowd. A pleasing vocalist a bit in the Ernestine Anderson vein who sings with detached coolness, Krall is also a fine modern mainstream pianist. On this session she is joined by bassist John Clayton and drummer Jeff Hamilton so it is not too surprising that the music swings. Krall sticks mostly to standards and ballads (including her original "Jimmie" and a rather downbeat version of "42nd Street") and shows a lot of potential for the future. — *Scott Yanow*

● **Only Trust Your Heart** / Sep. 13, 1994–Sep. 16, 1994 / GRP ✦✦✦✦✦

Carl Kress

b. Oct. 20, 1907, Newark, NJ, **d.** Jun. 10, 1965, Reno, NV
Guitar / Swing
One of the great guitarists of the 1930s, Carl Kress had a very sophisticated chordal style on acoustic guitar. He originally played banjo before gradually shifting to guitar. Kress played with Paul Whiteman in 1926 and then became a very busy studio musician, recording with all of the top white musicians (including Bix Beiderbecke, Red Nichols' Five Pennies and two classic duets with Eddie Lang) in those segregated days. Kress often teamed up with fellow guitarist Dick McDonough in the 1930s, he co-owned the Onyx Club on 52nd Street for a time and continued working in the studios into the 1960s, playing during his last years in a duo with George Barnes. Most of Carl Kress' solo and duet (with McDonough) recordings from the 1930s are long overdue to be reissued. — *Scott Yanow*

● **Two Guitars (And a Horn)** / 1962 / Vintage Jazz ✦✦✦✦✦

Ernie Krivda

b. Feb. 6, 1945, Cleveland, OH
Tenor Saxophone / Post-Bop
A brilliant tenor saxophonist with a forceful sound and an original attack that sometimes utilizes staccato phrases, Ernie Krivda has recorded stimulating sessions for Inner City, North Coast Jazz, Cadence and Koch without gaining much fame. He originally played clarinet, switching to alto in high school and later tenor. In 1964 he played for a few months with the Jimmy Dorsey ghost band and he spent the late '60s playing locally in Cleveland, recording with Bill Dobbins for the Advent label (1969); they co-led a quintet for a few years. Krivda played in Los Angeles with Quincy Jones (1973) and then lived in New York for a period (1976–79). But, in general, Ernie Krivda (who deserves much greater recognition) has spent the bulk of his career as a vital part of Cleveland's jazz scene. — *Scott Yanow*

Satanic / 1977 / Inner City ✦✦✦✦
The Alchemist / Jan. 1978 / Inner City ✦✦✦✦✦
The Glory Strut / Dec. 1979 / Inner City ✦✦✦✦
Quartet. Original music from Cleveland's innovative, relentless post-Coltrane disciple. Pretty melodies forcefully maneuvered. A solid album. — *Michael G. Nastos*

Fireside Sessions / Oct. 1983+Jan. 1984 / North Coast Jazz ✦✦✦✦

★ **Tough Tenor, Red Hot** / Nov. 24, 1985 / Cadence ✦✦✦✦✦
Live date at Cleveland State University. Originals and standards from this brilliant tenor saxophonist. — *Michael G. Nastos*

Ernie Krivda / Jan. 1991–Aug. 1991 / Cadence ✦✦✦✦
The Art of the Ballad / Jun. 1993 / Koch ✦✦✦✦

Karin Krog

b. May 15, 1937, Oslo, Norway
Vocals / Post Bop, Avant-Garde
An adventurous singer who is quite versatile, Karin Krog is able to sing anything from standards to fairly free improvisations. She made her recording debut in 1964, appeared at many jazz festivals in Europe in the mid-'60s and in 1967 came to the U.S., performing and recording with the Don Ellis Orchestra and Clare Fischer's trio. A world traveler based in Europe, Karin Krog has recorded fairly steadily through the years, using such sidemen as Kenny Drew, Niels-Henning Orsted Pedersen, Jan Garbarek, Ted Curson, Dexter Gordon, Palle Mikkelborg, Steve Kuhn, Steve Swallow, Archie Shepp, Bengt Hallberg and John Surman; she has made records for Philips, Sonet, Polydor and other European labels. — *Scott Yanow*

Jazz Moments / Nov. 11, 1966–Nov. 12, 1966 / Sonet ++++
Joy / Jul. 6, 1968–Oct. 2, 1968 / Sonet ++++
★ **Some Other Spring** / May 10, 1970 / Storyville +++++
Hi-Fly / Jun. 23, 1976 / Compendium +++++
A recording of this most unique vocalist with Archie Shepp (sax). All standards interpreted innovatively. —*Michael G. Nastos*

A Song for You / Jul. 18, 1977–Jul. 19, 1977 / Phontastic ++++

Kronos Quartet

Group / Avant-Garde, Classical
The Kronos String Quartet is not a jazz group since they do not improvise at all, but they deserve to be listed in this guide because they recorded tribute albums to Thelonious Monk (1984) and Bill Evans (1985) for Landmark. Ron Carter, Chuck Israels and drummer Eddie Marshall are strong assets on selective cuts for the Monk date while Eddie Gomez and Jim Hall help out on the Evans program. Kronos, which preceded the Turtle Island String Quartet (which is a jazz group), was innovative in its expansion of the repertoire of a classical string quartet to include pieces from jazz, world music and rock. —*Scott Yanow*

Monk Suite / 1984 / Landmark ++++
The Kronos Quartet, a very open-minded classical string quartet, caused a lot of eyebrows to be raised with this unusual set. They perform eight Thelonious Monk compositions and two Duke Ellington pieces that Monk had recorded. All of the notes played by the strings were written out in advance by arranger Tom Darter, but the improvising bassist Ron Carter is a major asset on five of the selections, which are placed in a "Monk Suite." In addition, the two Ellington numbers have The Kronos Quartet joined by bassist Chuck Israels and drummer Eddie Marshall. Fortunately, the string arrangements are very much in Monk's style, with many of the lines taken directly off of the pianist's recordings. This unique set is worth checking out. —*Scott Yanow*

● **Music of Bill Evans** / 1985 / Landmark +++++
Eclectic string quartet, which operates from a classical base, then expands to include everything else from jazz to rock. They pay tribute to Bill Evans with some spirited remakes of his classics. They don't swing (much), but they do communicate a good sense of his brilliance. —*Ron Wynn*

Gene Krupa

b. Jan. 15, 1909, Chicago, IL, d. Oct. 16, 1973, Yonkers, NY
Drums, Leader / Swing, Dixieland
The first drummer to be a superstar, Gene Krupa may not have been the most advanced drummer of the 1930s, but he was in some ways the most significant. Prior to Krupa, drum solos were a real rarity and the drums were thought of as a merely supportive instrument. Krupa, who with his good lucks and colorful playing became a matinee idol, changed the image of drummers forever.

Gene Krupa made history with his first record. For a session in 1927 with the McKenzie-Condon Chicagoans, he became the first musician to use a full drum set on records. He was part of the Chicago jazz scene of the 1920s before moving to New York and worked in the studios during the early years of the Depression. In December 1934 he joined Benny Goodman's new orchestra and for the next three years he was an important part of BG's pace-setting big band. Krupa, whose use of the bass drum was never too subtle, starred in Goodman's Trio and Quartet and his lengthy drum feature "Sing, Sing, Sing" in 1937 was historic. After he nearly stole the show at BG's 1938 Carnegie Hall Concert, Krupa and Goodman had a personality conflict and Gene soon departed to form his own orchestra. It took the drummer a while to realize with his band that drum solos were not required on every song! Such fine players as Vido Musso, Milt Raskin, Floyd O'Brien, Sam Donahue, Shorty Sherock and the excellent singer Irene Daye were assets to Krupa's Orchestra and "Drum Boogie" was a popular number, but it was not until 1941 when he had Anita O'Day and Roy Eldridge that Krupa's big band really took off. Among his hits from 1941–42 were "Let Me Off Uptown," "After You've Gone," "Rockin' Chair" and "Thanks for the Boogie Ride." Unfortunately, Krupa was arrested on a trumped-up drug charge in 1943, resulting in bad publicity, a short jail sentence and the breakup of his orchestra.

In September 1943 he had an emotional reunion with Benny Goodman (who happily welcomed him back to the music world).

Krupa also worked briefly with Tommy Dorsey before putting together another big band in mid-1944, one that had a string section. The strings only lasted a short time but Krupa was able to keep his band working into 1951. tenor saxophonist Charlie Ventura and pianist Teddy Napoleon had a trio hit in "Dark Eyes" (1945), Anita O'Day returned for a time in 1945 (scoring with "Opus No. 1") and, although his own style was unchanged (being a Dixieland drummer at heart), Krupa was one of the first swing bandleaders to welcome the influence of bebop into his group's arrangements, some of which were written by Gerry Mulligan (most notably "Disc Jockey Jump"). Among the soloists in the second Krupa Orchestra were Don Fagerquist, Red Rodney, Ventura, altoist Charlie Kennedy, tenorman Buddy Wise and in 1949 Roy Eldridge.

After breaking up his band in 1951, Krupa generally worked with trios or quartets (including such sidemen as Ventura, Napoleon, Eddie Shu, Bobby Scott, Dave McKenna, Eddie Wasserman, Ronnie Ball, Dave Frishberg and John Bunch), toured with Jazz at the Philharmonic, ran a drum school with Cozy Cole and had occasional reunions with Benny Goodman. Gradually worsening health in the 1960s resulted in his semi-retirement, but Krupa remained a major name up until his death. Ironically his final recording was led by the same person who headed his first appearance on records, Eddie Condon. Gene Krupa's pre-war big-band records are gradually being released by the Classics label. —*Scott Yanow*

● **Gene Krupa 1935–1938** / Nov. 19, 1935–Jun. 18, 1938 / Classics +++++

Gene Krupa 1938 / Jul. 19, 1938–Dec. 12, 1938 / Classics ++++
Gene Krupa 1939 / Feb. 26, 1939–Jul. 25, 1939 / Classics ++++
The European label's third Gene Krupa set reissues all of the recordings made by the drummer's big band during a five-month period in 1939. Although working steadily, Krupa's Orchestra had not broken through yet (it was still two years away from its prime period). With Irene Daye contributing ten pleasing vocals among the 22 selections and such soloists as trumpeter Nate Kazebier, trombonist Floyd O'Brien, tenor saxophonist Sam Donahue and pianist Milt Raskin (along with the drummer/leader), the group was starting to show some strong potential, particularly on the instrumentals such as "The Madam Swings It" and "Hodge Podge." Well-played if not overly distinctive swing music. —*Scott Yanow*

Drum Boogie / Jan. 2, 1940–Jan. 17, 1941 / Columbia +++++
Leave Us Leap / Mar. 30, 1945–1948 / Vintage Jazz Classics +++
Gene Krupa & Buddy Rich / May 16, 1955–Nov. 1, 1955 / Verve ++++
With studio recordings from each drummer, there are also several joint appearances. The small-group titles are better than the big-band selections, featuring as they do the likes of horn giants Flip Phillips, Illinois Jacquet, Dizzy Gillespie and Roy Eldridge. —*Bob Porter*

Drummer Man / Feb. 15, 1956 / Verve +++
Roy Eldrige (trumpet) got the featured billing (along with vocalist Anita O'Day) he deserved on *Drummer Man*, a Feb. 12, 1956 date featuring Gene Krupa fronting a big band. This was a reunion of sorts, but one that worked well, better in some cases than the original. The title's a bit misleading, for although Krupa's propulsions were clearly heard, his soloing was limited to a few features. Still, any drummer or fan of drumming will respond to the ambiance of this date. —*Bob Rusch, Cadence*

★ **Uptown** / 1941–42 / Columbia +++++

Marty Krystall

Tenor Saxophone, Bass Clarinet / Post-Bop
An intense tenor saxophonist influenced a bit by the sound of Ben Webster but open to adventurous improvisations, Marty Krystall has appeared in several of Buell Neidlinger's groups through the years. He has worked as a studio musician in Los Angeles since the late '70s, helped run the K2B2 label and has recorded with Neidlinger in Krystall Klear and the Buells, Buellgrass (later renamed String Jazz), the group Thelonious and a recent tribute to Herbie Nichols. —*Scott Yanow*

Ready for the 1990s / 1960–1989 / K2B2 +++++
1980 release with this progressive-edge saxophonist leading the way. Very well-done music for special tastes. Featuring Buell Neidlinger (b), Cecil Taylor (p) and Warren Gale. —*Michael G. Nastos*

Our Night Together / May 14, 1981 / K2B2 ++++

● **Seeing Unknown Colors** / May 1990 / M-A Recordings +++++

Joachim Kuhn

b. Mar. 15, 1944, Leipzig, Germany
Piano / Avant-Garde, Post-Bop
The younger brother of clarinetist Rolf Kuhn, Joachim Kuhn has mostly worked in Europe but gained a reputation in the U.S. for his adventurous playing. He has led his own trios since 1962, sometimes worked with his brother and had stints with Jean-Luc Ponty (1971-72), Tony Oxley's quintet in the 1980s and Mike Gibbs. Kuhn has recorded for several labels (sometimes on electric keyboards) including MPS, Atlantic and CMP. —*Scott Yanow*

Springfever / Apr. 1976 / Atlantic ++++

Sunshower / Feb. 1978-Mar. 1978 / Atlantic +++

I'm Not Dreaming / Mar. 1983 / CMP ++++
An early '80s quintet work that juggles free, contemporary classical and mainstream jazz elements. Pianist Kuhn plays with more rhythmic energy than on his solo works and is less concerned with texture and mood. The band includes trombonist George Lewis, cellist Ottomar Borwitzky (who adds a distinctly different sound), plus percussionists Herbert Forsch and Mark Nauseef, who doubles on piccolo and tenor sax. —*Ron Wynn*

Distance / May 1984 / CMP +++++
Fine, expressive solo piano by Joachim Kuhn from '84, with lots of shimmering melodies, sweeping phrases and strong rhythms. The album is also superbly recorded and gives Kuhn's accomplished technique a great aural portrait. —*Ron Wynn*

From Time to Time Free / Apr. 1988 / CMP ++++
Has intense improvisations from the German veteran pianist. Kuhn evokes images of Monk, Nichols, Taylor and Tyner. J.F. Jenny Clarke is on bass, Daniel Humair on drums. This trio knows each other well. Standouts are "Spy vs. Spy" and "Para." Also a nice version of Coltrane's "India." —*Michael G. Nastos*

Live (1989) / Nov. 27, 1989 / CMP +++
Recorded live in Paris, this album includes two standards and four Kuhn originals. —*Michael G. Nastos*

Let's Be Generous / Aug. 1990 / CMP +++

● **Dynamics** / 1992 / CMP +++++
Release by fine European pianist Joachim Kuhn, with his usual outstanding solos and keyboard explorations. The songs are generally good, and the production and arrangements, as usual, are first-rate. —*Ron Wynn*

Rolf Kuhn

b. Sep. 29, 1929, Cologne, Germany
Clarinet / Post-Bop, Swing
Rolf Kuhn's style has evolved through the years. The clarinetist started out playing in German dance bands in the late '40s. He worked with radio orchestras starting in 1952 and moved to the U.S. in 1956. Kuhn subbed for Benny Goodman on a few occasions during 1957-58, played in the Tommy Dorsey ghost band (1958) and worked in a big band led by Urbie Green (1958-60). In 1962 Kuhn returned to Germany where he has explored more adventurous styles of jazz (including dates with his younger brother, keyboardist Joachim Kuhn), but still occasionally shows off his ties to swing. Kuhn recorded with an all-star group called "Winner's Circle" (1957), Toshiko Akiyoshi (1958) and as a leader starting in 1953 including a 1956 New York quartet date for Vanguard. —*Scott Yanow*

Streamline / Nov. 26, 1956-Nov. 27, 1956 / Vanguard ++++

Impressions of New York / 1967 / Impulse! +++++

The Day After / 1972 / MPS +++

As Time Goes By / Apr. 1989 / Blue Flame +++
Intriguing, but sometimes ragged, session matching clarinet and synthesizer player Rolf Kuhn with his pianist brother Joachim, plus bassist Detlev Beier. Kuhn sometimes takes his music in a quasi-traditional jazz vein and at other times soars and approaches avant-garde; Joachim Kuhn is effective in any style, as is Beier. —*Ron Wynn*

Big Band Connection / 1993 / Miramar ++
As noted in the brief liner notes, clarinetist Rolf Kuhn utilizes the same instrumentation on this CD as the 1938 Benny Goodman big band (except for the lack of a rhythm guitar), but the orchestra (arranged by Rob Pronk and Barry Ross) actually sounds much closer to Count Basie's in the 1960s than to Goodman's. Kuhn draws his players from The NDR Big Band. Unfortunately, except for short spots (most notably on "Sister Sadie"), little is heard from his sidemen except in anonymous ensembles; altoist Herb Geller pops up just twice while pianist Fritz Pauer and trombonist Joe Gallardo make stronger impressions. Rolf Kuhn is a talented bop-oriented soloist and has several fine solos, but overall these swinging renditions of tunes such as "Sweet Georgia Brown," "Autumn Leaves" and "Satin Doll" are very safe, middle-of-the-road and without any real surprises. —*Scott Yanow*

Steve Kuhn

b. Mar. 24, 1938, Brooklyn
Piano / Post-Bop
Steve Kuhn has had an interesting career. A talented jazz pianist, he has worked in many types of settings through the years. He began classical piano lessons when he was five, studied with Madame Chaloff and accompanied her son, baritonist Serge Chaloff, on some gigs when the pianist was 14. He freelanced in Boston as a teenager, graduated from Harvard and moved to New York where he worked with Kenny Dorham's group (1959-60). Kuhn was the original pianist in John Coltrane's Quartet, playing for two months before McCoy Tyner succeeded him. He was with the bands of Stan Getz (1961-63) and Art Farmer (1964-66), lived in Europe (1967-70) and then returned to the U.S. in 1971. Kuhn doubled on electric piano in the 1970s, recorded for ECM and co-led a group with Sheila Jordan in the latter part of the decade. After a period playing commercial music, he formed an acoustic trio in the mid-'80s which has been his main vehicle ever since. Steve Kuhn has recorded as a leader for Impulse! (1966), Contact, MPS, BYG, Muse, ECM, Black Hawk, New World, Owl, Concord and Postcards. —*Scott Yanow*

Raindrops (Steve Kuhn Live in New York) / Nov. 1972 / Muse +++
A good quartet date from 1984, cut live in New York. Pianist Steve Kuhn's greatest attributes are his steady, sometimes impressive phrasing and interpretative ability; his weak links are a less than intense rhythmic capability and a derivative style. That's overcome on this session mainly because he's playing with a sympathetic rhythm section, and bassist George Mraz in particular helps push the music and increase the energy level. —*Ron Wynn*

Trance / Nov. 11, 1974-Nov. 12, 1974 / ECM ++++

Ecstasy / Nov. 1974 / ECM +++++

Motility / Jan. 1977 / ECM ++++

Non-Fiction / Apr. 1978 / ECM ++++

Playground / Jul. 1979 / ECM +++++
With Sheila Jordan (v), Harvie Swartz (b), Bob Moses (d). Intense group interplay with Jordan's deep tones. Very emotional music, especially "The Zoo" and "Deep Tango." A record for the ages. —*Michael G. Nastos*

Last Year's Waltz / Apr. 1981 / ECM +++

Mostly Ballads / Jan. 3, 1984 / New World ++++
The title says it all; pianist Steve Kuhn's menu of mostly standards and ballads, with the occasional original, is well played and recorded. Kuhn is a good, lyrical soloist who isn't among the more intense or aggressive players, instead relying on his harmonic and interpretative skills. —*Ron Wynn*

Life's Magic / Mar. 28, 1986-Mar. 30, 1986 / +++++
Live at New York City's Village Vanguard. With Ron Carter (b), Al Foster (d). Four Kuhn originals, three standards. Pristine quality of Kuhn's playing shines. —*Michael G. Nastos*

Oceans in the Sky / Sep. 20, 1989-Sep. 21, 1989 / Owl ++++

Looking Back / Oct. 1990 / Concord Jazz ++++

Live at Maybeck Recital Hall, Vol. 13 / Nov. 18, 1990 / Concord Jazz +++++

Years Later / Sep. 1992 / Concord Jazz ++++

● **Seasons Of Romance** / Apr. 12, 1995-Apr. 13, 1995 / Postcards +++++

Bill Kyle

b. Jul. 14, 1914, Philadelphia, PA
d. Feb. 23, 1966, Youngstown, OH
Piano / Swing
A fluent pianist with a light touch, Billy Kyle never achieved much

fame but he always worked steadily. A professional from the time he was 18, Kyle played in the big bands of Tiny Bradshaw and Lucky Millinder and then became an important part of the John Kirby Sextet (1938–42), a perfect vehicle for his style. He was forced to leave the band when he was drafted and, after three years in the military (1942–45), Kyle freelanced, working fairly often with Sy Oliver. He joined Louis Armstrong's All-Stars in 1953 and was there for nearly 13 years until his death. His playing with Armstrong, although appealing, tended to be very predictable. Billy Kyle had very few opportunities to record as a leader and none during his Armstrong years; just some octet and septet sides in 1937, two songs with a quartet in 1939, and outings in 1946 with a trio and an octet, 17 songs in all! —*Scott Yanow*

L

Pat LaBarbera (Pascel Labarbera)

b. April 7, 1944, Warsaw, NY
Tenor Saxophone, Soprano Saxophone / Hard Bop
The older brother of Joe LaBarbera (drummer with Bill Evans during 1978–80) and arranger/trumpeter John LaBarbera, Pat has been a fixture in Toronto since moving to Canada in 1974. He played in a family band early on, attended Berklee (1964–67) and gained recognition for his exciting solos with Buddy Rich's big band (1967–73). After settling in Toronto (where he has done quite a bit of studio work), LaBarbera toured with Elvin Jones (1975–78). He has recorded as a leader for PM, Sackville and Justin Time. —*Scott Yanow*

Pass It On / Jan. 19, 1976–Jun. 1976 / PM ◆◆◆◆

● **Virgo Dance** / Apr. 1987 / Justin Time ◆◆◆◆◆

JMOG / Dec. 28, 1992–Dec. 29, 1992 / Sackville ◆◆◆◆
"JMOG" stands for "Jazz Man on the Go" since each of the musicians on this CD are talented enough to be constantly in great demand. tenor saxophonist Pat LaBarbera, pianist Don Thompson, bassist Neil Swainson and drummer Joe LaBarbera team up on their Sackville release for a set of originals (two apiece from the saxophonist and Swainson and three by Thompson). The music is generally modal-based, with Pat LaBarbera showing the influence of John Coltrane. In fact, were it not for the sophistication of Swainson's bass playing, much of this session could have taken place in the late '60s instead of 1992. Despite their conflicting schedules, the quartet meshes together quite well with the impressive interplay between Thompson and Swainson, the alert support by Joe LaBarbera and the passionate playing of his older brother giving the band a strong identity. The compositions of Pat LaBarbera and Swainson tend to be quite serious, so Thompson's "Elk the Mooche" (an abstract "Moose the Mooche") is a welcome change of pace. —*Scott Yanow*

Steve Lacy

b. Jul. 23, 1934, New York, NY
Soprano Saxophone / Avant-Garde, Post Bop, Free Jazz
One of the great soprano saxophonists of all time (ranking up there with Sidney Bechet and John Coltrane), Steve Lacy's career was fascinating to watch develop. He originally doubled on clarinet and soprano (dropping the former by the mid-'50s), inspired by Bechet and playing Dixieland in New York with Rex Stewart, Cecil Scott, Red Allen and other older musicians during 1952–55. He debuted on record in a modernized Dixieland format with Dick Sutton in 1954. However Lacy soon jumped over several styles to play free jazz with Cecil Taylor during 1955–57. They recorded together and performed at the 1957 Newport Jazz Festival. Lacy recorded with Gil Evans in 1957 (they would work together on an irregular basis into the 1980s), was with Thelonious Monk's quintet in 1960 for four months and then formed a quartet with Roswell Rudd (1961–64) that exclusively played Monk's music; only one live set (for Emanem in 1963) resulted from that very interesting group.
Steve Lacy, who is considered the first "modern" musician to specialize on soprano (an instrument that was completely neglected during the bop era), began to turn toward avant-garde jazz in 1965. He had a quartet with Enrico Rava that spent eight months in South America. After a year back in New York, he permanently moved to Europe in 1967 with three years in Italy preceding a move to Paris. Lacy's music evolved from free form to improvis-

ing off of his scalar originals. By 1977 he had a regular group that is still together in the mid-'90s, featuring Steve Potts on alto and soprano, Lacy's wife, violinist/singer Irene Aebi, bassist Kent Carter (later succeeded by Jean-Jacques Avenel) and drummer Oliver Johnson; pianist Bobby Few joined the group in the 1980s. Lacy, who has also worked on special projects with Gil Evans, Mal Waldron and Misha Mengelberg, among others, and in situations ranging from solo soprano concerts, many Monk tributes, big bands and setting poetry to music, has recorded a countless number of sessions for almost as many labels. His early dates (1957–61) were for Prestige, New Jazz and Candid and later on he appeared most notably on sessions for Hat Art, Black Saint/Soul Note and Novus. —*Scott Yanow*

The Complete Steve Lacy / Aug. 8, 1954–Nov. 24, 1954 / Fresco ◆◆◆
Two-fer of "progressive" Dixieland with Dick Sutton sextet. Lacy on soprano and clarinet. Interesting, considering where Lacy's music was headed. —*Michael G. Nastos*

Soprano Saxophone / Nov. 1, 1957 / Original Jazz Classics ◆◆◆◆◆
A brilliant set. Lacy stakes out his claim as king of soprano sax, years before Coltrane popularizes it. —*Ron Wynn*

Reflections: Steve Lacy Plays Thelonious Monk / Oct. 17, 1958 / Original Jazz Classics ◆◆◆◆◆
Enamored of Thelonious Monk, Lacy stretches out on challenging harmonic material with the Mal Waldron trio. —*Michael G. Nastos*

★ **The Straight Horn of Steve Lacy** / Sep. 1960 / Candid ◆◆◆◆◆
Some of soprano saxophonist Steve Lacy's most interesting recordings are his earliest ones. After spending periods of time playing with Dixieland groups and then with Cecil Taylor (which was quite a jump), Lacy made several recordings that displayed his love of Thelonious Monk's music plus his varied experiences. On this particular set, Lacy's soprano contrasts well with Charles Davis' baritone (they are backed by bassist John Ore and drummer Roy Haynes) on three of the most difficult Monk tunes ("Introspection," "Played Twice" and "Criss Cross") plus two Cecil Taylor compositions and Charlie Parker's (or is it Miles Davis'?) "Donna Lee." —*Scott Yanow*

Evidence / Nov. 14, 1961 / Original Jazz Classics ◆◆◆◆◆
This early Steve Lacy album teams the great soprano saxophonist with trumpeter Don Cherry, bassist Carl Brown and drummer Billy Higgins for four Thelonious Monk songs, an obscurity by Duke Ellington ("The Mystery Song") and Billy Strayhorn's "Something to Live For." It is quite unusual to hear Cherry during a period when he was regularly performing with Ornette Coleman's Quartet, playing this kind of standard material. Lacy and Cherry approach these standards from a different angle, bringing new life and opening up new possibilities for these songs. Although the playing time of this CD is brief (under 34 minutes), the quality is quite high. —*Scott Yanow*

School Days / Mar. 1963 / Emanem ◆◆◆◆

Disposability / Dec. 21, 1965–Dec. 22, 1965 / RCA ◆◆◆◆

Forest and the Zoo / Oct. 8, 1966 / ESP ◆◆◆

Solo / Aug. 7, 1972–Aug. 8, 1972 / In Situ ◆◆◆◆

Scraps / Feb. 18, 1974+Feb. 21, 1974 / Sravah ◆◆◆◆◆

Saxophone Special / Dec. 19, 1974 / Emanem ◆◆◆◆

Stabs / Apr. 1, 1975 / FMP ◆◆◆

Trickles / Mar. 11, 1976+Mar. 14, 1976 / Black Saint ◆◆◆◆
The Reunion with trombonist Roswell Rudd. —*Ron Wynn*

Sidelines / Sep. 1, 1976 / Improvising Artists ◆◆◆
Soprano saxophonist Steve Lacy and the obscure pianist Michael Smith performed seven of their originals (five by Lacy and two from Smith) for this Improvising Artists set, which has recently been reissued on CD. The music is explorative, thoughtful and a bit dry. It may take listeners a few listens to get into these deliberate collaborations. —*Scott Yanow*

Raps / Jan. 29, 1977 / Adelphi ◆◆◆◆
This is a quirky, explosive date with co-conspirator Steve Potts (as). —*Ron Wynn*

Follies / Apr. 11, 1977 / FMP ◆◆◆◆◆

Clinkers / Jun. 9, 1977 / Hat Hut ◆◆◆◆

Stamps / Aug. 27, 1977–Feb. 22, 1978 / Hat Hut ◆◆◆◆◆
Steve Lacy and his quintet are well featured on this double LP, which documents two appearances at European festivals. In addition to the soprano/leader, altoist Steve Potts has long been a commanding improviser in his own right and offers a contrasting yet complementary solo voice. Bassist Kent Carter and drummer Oliver Johnson are always alert during this complex music (seven Lacy scalar originals) while Irene Aebi (on cello, violin and occasional background vocal) is more of an acquired taste. Overall this set gives one a good example of Steve Lacy's late-'70s group and its distinctive music. —*Scott Yanow*

High, Low and Order / Dec. 1977 / Hat Art ◆◆◆◆

The Way / Jan. 23, 1979 / Hat Hut ◆◆◆◆

● **Troubles** / May 24, 1979–May 25, 1979 / Black Saint ◆◆◆◆◆
Lacy and Steve Potts (as) at their best and most frenetic. —*Ron Wynn*

Capers / Dec. 29, 1979 / Hat Hut ◆◆◆◆

Ballets / Dec. 18, 1980 / Hat Art ◆◆◆◆

Songs / Jan. 28, 1981–Jan. 29, 1981 / Hat Art ◆◆◆

Snake Out / Aug. 14, 1981 / Hat Music ◆◆◆◆

The Flame / Jan. 18, 1982–Jan. 19, 1982 / Soul Note ◆◆◆◆◆
The Flame was recorded in January 1982. This Steve Lacy conversation brought together Bobby Few (piano) and Dennis Charles (drums). "Wet Spot" was a solo spot for Few and "Gusts" and "Licks" were solo outings for Lacy (soprano sax). Lacy is a great conversationalist. I find his overall style appealing, but on this record I didn't find all that he had to say very interesting and on repeated listenings things began to drag, particularly through "Licks" and "Flames," tracks that comprised the whole of side two. Of course, this was relative to a Lacy standard. I admit I entered into this listening relationship with expectations perhaps higher than normal—such are the burdens of being a master. I could recommend one track, "The Match," a very powerful performance with both the group and individuals within the group moving/playing in-out, out-in and exchanging leading roles with a naturalness and freedom which transcended a leadership position. This one track presented a strong statement out of proportion with the rest of the music. —*Bob Rusch*

Prospectus / Nov. 1, 1982–Nov. 2, 1982 / Hat Art ◆◆◆◆

★ **Regeneration** / 1982 / Soul Note ◆◆◆◆◆
The consensus album of the year in 1983, it includes one side of Monk and the other of Herbie Nichols' music. Includes Roswell Rudd (tb), Misha Mengleberg (p), Kent Carter (b) and Hans Bennik (d). —*Michael G. Nastos*

Blinks / Feb. 12, 1983 / Hat Art ◆◆◆◆

Change of Season / Jul. 2, 1984–Jul. 3, 1984 / Soul Note ◆◆◆◆◆
This is the follow-up to *Regeneration,* featuring George Lewis (tb) and Anjen Garter (b). All material by Herbie Nichols. —*Michael G. Nastos*

Futurities / Nov. 1984+Jan. 1985 / Hat Art ◆◆◆◆

Deadline / Mar. 1985 / Sound Aspects ◆◆◆◆

The Condor / Jun. 20, 1985–Jun. 24, 1985 / Soul Note ◆◆◆◆
A good sextet date. —*Ron Wynn*

Chirps / Jul. 1985 / FMP ◆◆◆◆

Morning Joy: Live at Sunset Paris / Feb. 16, 1986 / Hat Art ◆◆◆◆

Sempre Amore / Feb. 1986 / Soul Note ◆◆◆◆
Lacy turns to Ellington and Strayhorn. —*Ron Wynn*

Only Monk / Jul. 29, 1986–Jul. 31, 1986 / Soul Note ◆◆◆◆
Lacy mines Monk's lode with a vengeance. —*Ron Wynn*

★ **Momentum** / May 20, 1987–May 22, 1987 / Novus ◆◆◆◆◆
On Steve Lacy's first album for an American label in over a decade, his sextet is heard on four extensive originals by the great soprano saxophonist. The music is complex yet often melodic and, although Irene Aebi takes typically eccentric vocals on two of the songs, the main reasons to acquire this album are for the thoughtful yet unpredictable solos of Lacy and altoist Steve Potts. —*Scott Yanow*

The Window / Jul. 1987 / Soul Note ◆◆◆◆

The Super Quartet Live at Sweet Basil / Aug. 28, 1987–Aug. 29, 1987 / Evidence ◆◆◆
Mal Waldron and Steve Lacy reunited on this four-track set recorded live at Sweet Basil's in 1987. The usually undulating, highly unorthodox Lacy sounds at times almost self-effacing, although his playing retains its sharpness and harmonic edge. But he has played looser, more quirky versions of "Evidence" and "Let's Call This." He seems more in a commemorative than freewheeling mood. Waldron's snaking, ripping chords and angular piano solos are more aggressive, while bassist Reggie Workman and drummer Eddie Moore alternate between providing concise support and taking their own strong solos. It is a fine date, just not as electrifying as some of Lacy's studio and independent sessions. —*Ron Wynn*

The Door / Jul. 4, 1988–Jul. 5, 1988 / Novus ◆◆◆◆

Anthem / 1989 / Novus ◆◆◆◆

More Monk / Apr. 18, 1989–Apr. 19, 1989 / Soul Note ◆◆◆◆◆

Hot House / Jul. 12, 1990–Jul. 13, 1990 / Novus ◆◆◆
With Mal Waldron. A 1991 reissue of some fine duets. —*Ron Wynn*

Itinerary / Nov. 26, 1990–Nov. 28, 1990 / Hat Art ◆◆◆◆

Remains / Apr. 29, 1991–Apr. 30, 1991 / Hat Art ◆◆◆◆

★ **Live at Sweet Basil** / Jul. 6, 1991+Jul. 7, 1991 / Novus ◆◆◆◆◆
Recorded live in a New York club with a sextet. Includes many familiar themes. Soprano saxophonist with regular working band: Steve Potts on alto and soprano sax, Irene Aebi on violin and vocal, Jean Jacques Avenel on bass, Bobby Few on piano and John Betsch on drums. —*Michael G. Nastos*

We See / Sep. 1, 1992–Sep. 2, 1992 / Hat Art ◆◆◆◆

Vespers / Jul. 1993 / Soul Note ◆◆◆◆
Steve Lacy's tributes to several recently deceased musical and visual arts giants feature his octet in a session that is both poignant and rampaging. Besides Lacy and his characteristic squealing, swaying soprano sax, the octet includes tenor saxophonist Ricky Ford offering some of his strongest, most intense tenor playing in ages and equally fiery alto and soprano solos from longtime Lacy contributor Steve Potts. This date fulfills its objective of commemorating artistic achievement while also spotlighting Steve Lacy's continuing musical mastery. —*Ron Wynn*

Tommy Ladnier

b. May 28, 1900, Florence, LA, **d.** Jun. 4, 1939, Geneva, NY
Trumpet / Classic Jazz
An exciting trumpeter who can be seen as a bridge stylewise between King Oliver and Louis Armstrong, Tommy Ladnier played early in life in New Orleans and in 1917 moved to Chicago. He worked for a period in St. Louis with Charlie Creath and was part of the Chicago scene in the early '20s, playing with Ollie Powers (1923), Fate Marable and King Oliver (1924–25). He also recorded with a variety of blues singers and Lovie Austin's Blues Serenaders. In 1925 Ladnier visited Europe with Sam Wooding and then became a star soloist with Fletcher Henderson's Orchestra (1926–27), making many excellent records. He returned to Europe with Wooding (1928–29) and worked with Benny Peyton and Noble Sissle (1930–31). Ladnier teamed up with Sidney Bechet on a memorable recording session as the New Orleans Feetwarmers (1932) but work was slow and the duo ran a tailor shop (1933–34) that was more notable for its jam sessions than for its alterations! Ladnier largely dropped out of sight for a few years, leading groups in New Jersey and Connecticut, but was rediscovered in 1938. He recorded the "Panassie Sessions" with Bechet and his new friend Mezz Mezzrow but died suddenly in 1939 from a heart attack. Tommy Ladnier never led any recording sessions of his own but most of his work as a sideman has been reissued. —*Scott Yanow*

Scott LaFaro

b. Apr. 3, 1936, Newark, NJ
d. Jul. 6, 1961, Geneva, NY
Bass / Post-Bop
During his tragically short life, Scott LaFaro quickly developed into one of the most advanced bassists around, competing with Charlie Haden and Charles Mingus. He emphasized high notes, could play with great speed and his interplay with Bill Evans in their trio was mutually stimulating and influential. LaFaro originally played clarinet and tenor before settling on bass while in college. He was with Buddy Morrow's band (1955–56), toured with Chet Baker (1956–57) and worked during the next few years with Ira Sullivan, Barney Kessel, Cal Tjader and Benny Goodman among others. LaFaro joined the Bill Evans Trio in 1959 and, although he would record with Ornette Coleman (including *Free Jazz*) and gig with Stan Getz, the bassist is best remembered for his association with Evans, particularly their Village Vanguard recordings of 1961. The 25-year-old Scott LaFaro's death in a car accident shortly after was a major shock to the jazz world. — *Scott Yanow*

Bireli Lagrene

b. Sept. 4, 1966, Saverene, France
Guitar / Swing, Fusion, Post Bop
When Bireli Lagrene first emerged in 1980 as a 13-year-old who sounded exactly like Django Reinhardt, he was considered a marvel. Born (like Django) to a Gypsy family, he had been playing guitar since he was four. After a few years and several recordings, Lagrene purposely got away from the Reinhardt influence, playing high-powered rock-oriented fusion and recording with Jaco Pastorius in 1986. He sounded more original but much less interesting during this period. The guitarist has since returned to a quieter form of jazz, playing hard bop versions of standards with hints of his earlier interests in Django and fusion. Bireli Lagrene has recorded thus far for Antilles, Jazzpoint and Blue Note. — *Scott Yanow*

★ **Routes to Django: Live** / May 29, 1980–May 30, 1980 / Antilles ✦✦✦✦✦
Guitarist Lagrene turns in a stunning live performance on this recording which, as the title implies, is a homage to the late great guitarist Django Reinhardt. Perhaps the most extraordinary thing about this recording is the fact that Lagrene is a mere 13 years old! — *Paul Kohler*

Swing '81 / Apr. 1981 / Jazz Point ✦✦✦✦

Fifteen / Feb. 1982 / Antilles ✦✦✦✦✦
An early, inconsistent album by guitarist Bireli Lagrene that, despite its problems, still showed his enormous potential. At this stage, Lagrene was so intent on displaying his complete arsenal that he roamed all over the fretboard on every song, throwing in extraneous lines and elaborate licks where they weren't necessary. But the album presented an early portrait of a player who's gone on to fulfill his promise. — *Ron Wynn*

Bireli Lagrene Ensemble Live Featuring Vic Juris / Jun. 1, 1985–Jun. 2, 1985 / Jazzpoint ✦✦✦
Five years after *Routes to Django*, the 18-year-old Lagrene is joined by jazz-fusion guitarist Vic Juris, who more than holds his own. Included on this excellent live recording are a few jazz standards and a few Django tunes as well. — *Paul Kohler*

Stuttgart Aria / Mar. 1986 / Jazzpoint ✦✦✦

Inferno / 1988 / Blue Note ✦✦
This album marks the next phase in young Lagrene's career. On this album he makes an about face by turning to the electric guitar instead of the acoustic guitar that made him so well known. Many of the tunes contain grooves and rhythms derived from rock music, but are treated with a jazz feel. A force to be reckoned with! — *Paul Kohler*

Foreign Affairs / Aug. 10, 1988 Aug. 13, 1988 / Blue Note ✦✦✦
Guitarist Bireli Lagrene, who started out as a young teenager very influenced by Django Reinhardt, has made a strong attempt to get away from the Reinhardt gypsy image. On this set, his guitar is often very rock-oriented and, although there are some acoustic moments, the emphasis is on fusion originals. The music is spirited and fun but not performed with a great deal of subtlety. Bireli Lagrene's future development (which direction will he head in next?) should be well worth watching. — *Scott Yanow*

Acoustic Moments / Jul. 1990 / Blue Note ✦✦
Bireli Lagrene, a guitarist who first came up as a remarkable Django Reinhardt clone before getting interested in rock, switches back and forth throughout this CD. He plays some songs acoustically in a classical vein, swings a bit on a couple of standards and then finishes the set with a brief blowout on "Metal Earthquake." Most of the so-called acoustic pieces have electric keyboards and/or synthesizers provided by Koono (there is no actual bass on this set) and one gets the impression that at this point in his career Bireli Lagrene was unsure what direction to go in. The results are interesting but sometimes almost incoherent. — *Scott Yanow*

● **Standards** / Jun. 1992 / Blue Note ✦✦✦✦✦
This is one of guitarist Bireli Lagrene's better jazz albums of the 1990s. By this time he had pretty much discarded his original Django Reinhardt influence (even on "Nuages" he sounds nothing like Reinhardt) and he took time off from playing rock to perform a dozen familiar standards with bassist Niels Pedersen and drummer Andre Ceccarelli. Lagrene's technique had been admirable from the start and on this studio session his own musical personality was allowed to come to the surface. Highlights include "Softly as in a Morning Sunrise," "Autumn Leaves," "Donna Lee" and "Ornithology." — *Scott Yanow*

My Favorite Django / 1994 / Dreyfus ✦✦✦

Oliver Lake

b. Sept. 14, 1942, Marianna, AR
Flute, Alto Saxophone, Soprano Saxophone / Reggae, Avant-Garde
A expressive, energetic alto, tenor and soprano saxophonist and flutist who's led free, hard bop and reggae bands, Oliver Lake has been a consistently outstanding soloist, composer and bandleader since the early '70s. His solos, especially on alto, have a pungent, bluesy edge reflecting Lake's bebop and R&B background. He's accomplished on tenor, soprano and flute, but alto is his best instrument. Lake began playing drums as a child, then turned to alto sax at 18 and later flute. He graduated from Lincoln University in 1968, then taught for a while in public schools and played in R&B bands around the St. Louis area, while also serving as a leader in the Black Artists Group (BAG). Lake played in Paris with a quintet of BAG members from 1972 to 1974. He then moved to New York, where he played both free jazz and classical music with combos and as a soloist. He was a founding member with Hamiett Bluiett, David Murray and Julius Hemphill of The World Saxophone Quartet in 1976, playing in a New Orleans concert. That same year Lake began a trio with Michael Gregory Jackson and Pheeroan Ak Laff. He staged the theatrical presentation "The Life Dance of Is," for which he also wrote the music and poetry, in 1977. Lake presented a program of compositions for string quartet at Carnegie Hall in 1979. Then he switched gears in the early '80s, forming a reggae/funk/fusion unit Jump Up. They played into the mid-'80s and recorded for Gramavision. Lake recorded in Italy in 1984 and 1985 and performed in New York with a free jazz band that included Kevin Eubanks and Ak Laff. He recorded with Fred Hopkins, Geri Allen, AkLaff and Rasul Sidik on Gramavision in 1987 and did another session in '88. Lake began recording as a leader in the '70s and has done sessions for Arista, Sackville, Black Saint, Gramavision, Blue Heron and Gazell. — *Ron Wynn*

Ntu: The Point from Which Freedom Begins / 1971 / Freedom ✦✦✦✦
Altoist Oliver Lake's debut recording features him with a ten-piece unit in St. Louis. The performances are quite avant-garde, often very loose and influenced by The Art Ensemble of Chicago; Don Moye sits in on congas. In addition to Lake, the other notable players include trumpeter Baikida E.J. Carroll, trombonist Joseph Bowie and drummer Bobo Shaw. Much of this music is hit and miss but it has its successful moments. — *Scott Yanow*

Heavy Spirits / Jan. 31, 1975–Feb. 5, 1975 / Freedom ✦✦✦✦✦
This will be one of the least accessible of altoist Oliver Lake's recordings for most people, but repeated listenings reveal a great deal of beauty. The avant-garde master is backed by three violinists on a trio of intense pieces, takes "Lonely Blacks" unaccompanied and performs "Rocket" in an unusual trio with trombonist Joseph Bowie and drummer Bobo Shaw. The other three selections have a more conventional instrumentation (a quintet with trumpeter Olu Dara and pianist Donald Smith) but are almost as

challenging. It's worth investigating but listeners will have to have patience in order to fully appreciate this music. —*Scott Yanow*

Holding Together / Mar. 1976 / Black Saint ✦✦✦✦
Driving solos, surging pieces. —*Ron Wynn*

Life Dance of Is / Feb. 16, 1978 / Novus ✦✦✦✦

Buster Bee / Mar. 1, 1978 / Sackville ✦✦✦

Shine / Oct. 30, 1978–Oct. 31, 1978 / Novus ✦✦✦

Zaki / Sep. 1, 1979 / Hat Art ✦✦✦✦

Prophet / Aug. 11, 1980–Aug. 12, 1980 / Black Saint ✦✦✦✦

Jump Up / 1981 / Gramavision ✦✦
Lake steps back to dance music with mixed results. —*Ron Wynn*

Plug It / 1982 / Gramavision ✦✦
This is Lake's least ambitious album conceptually, but it has some good blues and honking R&B-type solos. —*Ron Wynn*

★ **Expendable Language** / Sep. 17, 1984+Sep. 20, 1984 / Black Saint ✦✦✦✦✦
This freebop session (which is often quite free but often has a strong pulse) is one of altoist Oliver Lake's more rewarding sessions. Guitarist Kevin Eubanks sometimes seems a bit out of place (generally he plays in more conservative settings) but pianist Geri Allen, bassist Fred Hopkins and drummer Pheeroan AkLaff are quite comfortable thinking on their feet during these spirited performances. —*Scott Yanow*

Dancevision / 1986 / Blue Heron ✦✦
Oliver Lake makes a daring attempt to link basic R&T, reggae and jazz into a seamless mix. It works in some places, but fails in others. —*Ron Wynn*

Gallery / Jul. 1986 / Gramavision ✦✦✦✦

Impala / 1988 / Gramavision ✦✦✦

Boston Duets / 1989 / Music & Arts ✦✦✦✦✦
The brilliant avant-garde explorer Oliver Lake (here playing alto, soprano and flute) and the classical pianist Donal Leonellis Fox might seem at first glance to be an odd combination, but this set of duets easily exceeds one's expectations. Fox is fortunately a strong improviser and he not only sets a strong foundation for Lake's flights but often challenges and inspires the saxophonist. Together they play a variety of moody originals plus Thelonious Monk's "Rhythm-a-Ning." This set is a surprise success. —*Scott Yanow*

Again and Again / Apr. 1991 / Gramavision ✦✦✦✦
Altoist Oliver Lake (who also plays a bit of soprano on this session) performs eight of his complex but generally accessible ballads with pianist John Hicks, bassist Reggie Workman and drummer Pheeroan AkLaff. Although none of these originals are destined to become standards, they inspire Lake to come up with some of his more lyrical solos. —*Scott Yanow*

Virtual Reality: Total Escapism / Oct. 9, 1991 / Gazell ✦✦✦

Edge-ing / Jun. 28, 1993–Jun. 29, 1993 / Soul Note ✦✦✦✦

Dave Lambert

b. Jun. 19, 1917, Boston, MA, d. Oct. 3, 1966, Westport, CT
Vocals / Bop, Vocalese
Best-known for being the "Lambert" in the premiere jazz vocal group Lambert, Hendricks & Ross, Dave Lambert was already a veteran singer when that ensemble was formed in 1957. Originally a drummer, Lambert sang with Johnny Long's big band for a year. He was with Gene Krupa's Orchestra (1944–45) and when he sang "What's This" with Buddy Stewart, it was considered the first vocal version of a bop line. On an infrequent basis during the late '40s and early '50s, Lambert led a group of singers. He appeared with Charlie Parker on a Royal Roost broadcast (1949) and his singers backed Bird on his 1953 recordings of "Old Folks" and "In the Still of the Night"; renditions that are somewhat bizarre. Lambert recorded a few numbers with his vocal group for Capitol in 1949 and teamed up with John Hendricks (along with two other singers) for the first time in 1955 for an obscure version of "Four Brothers." After Lambert, Hendricks & Ross became popular in 1957, that group dominated his activities although Lambert did record a solo album for United Artists in 1959. He stayed with the ensemble after it became Lambert, Hendricks & Bavan in 1962 (when Annie Ross was succeeded by Yolande Bavan) until its breakup in 1964. The warm-voiced singer's last recording was a scat-filled version of "Donna Lee" performed at a 1965 Charlie Parker memorial concert. Dave Lambert died tragically in 1966, hit by a car while changing a tire. —*Scott Yanow*

Dave Lambert Sings and Swings Alone / 1958–1959 / United Artists ✦✦✦✦✦

Donald Lambert

b. 1904, Princeton, NJ, d. May 8, 1962, Newark, NJ
Piano / Stride
Donald Lambert ranks in jazz history as one of the great unknown stride pianists. In the late '20s he was a top pianist appearing regularly at rent parties and clubs in Harlem. However by the 1930s he preferred to stay in New Jersey, playing in out-of-the-way clubs. He recorded four brilliant solos for Bluebird in 1941 in which he strided various classical themes. Other than privately recorded sets from 1960-62 that were released decades later by Solo Art, IAJRC and two on Pumpkin, that is all the documentation that exists of Donald Lambert. But even with the low quantity, his brilliant technique and appealing ideas come through and one can understand why he was held in such high esteem by his contemporaries (if not why he avoided New York). —*Scott Yanow*

● **Giant Stride** / Mar. 1, 1961 / Solo Art ✦✦✦✦✦

Lambert, Hendricks & Ross

Vocal Group / Bop, Vocalese
Arguably the greatest jazz vocal group of all time, Lambert, Hendricks & Ross comprised three masterful bop singers who specialized in vocalese: Dave Lambert (1917–1966), John Hendricks (1921–) and Annie Ross (1930–). Originally Lambert and Hendricks tried to record recreations of classic Count Basie performances, but they had difficulty coming up with enough talented singers to fill in for all of the horns. However, once they discovered Ross, it was decided to just use the three of them and overdub the parts; the result was the classic *Sing a Song of Basie*. Lambert, Hendricks & Ross immediately became a very popular group and during the next few years they recorded several notable albums including a real collaboration with Basie and a collection of Duke Ellington songs. Bad health caused Ross to drop out of the group in 1962 and her replacement, Yolande Bavan (the group was renamed Lambert, Hendricks & Bavan), was better in ensembles than as a soloist. When Bavan and Lambert both left the band in 1964, the classic group was history. Lambert, Hendricks & Ross recorded for Impulse, World Pacific and Columbia while Lambert, Hendricks & Bavan made a few albums for RCA. Their influence is still felt in the singing of Manhattan Transfer, the work of the Hendricks Family and in nearly every jazz vocal group formed during the past 30 years. —*Scott Yanow*

★ **Sing a Song of Basie** / Aug. 26, 1957–Nov. 26, 1957 / GRP/Impulse! ✦✦✦✦✦
Arguably the best and most influential of the Lambert, Hendricks & Ross recordings. Hendricks writes lyrics for strings and solos. —*Ron Wynn*

★ **Sing Along with Basie** / 1958 / Roulette ✦✦✦✦✦
A wonderful follow-up to *Sing a Song of Basie*. This time the trio cut with the full Basie Orchestra. —*Ron Wynn*

The Swingers! / 1959 / Pacific Jazz ✦✦✦✦✦

Everybody's Boppin' / Aug. 6, 1959–Nov. 4, 1959 / Columbia ✦✦✦✦✦

The Hottest New Group in Jazz / Mar. 1960 / Columbia ✦✦✦✦✦

Sings Ellington / May 9, 1960–Aug. 18, 1960 / Sony Special Products ✦✦✦✦
Nice release from the great vocal jazz trio who had previously done their own unique twist on Count Basie's music. This time they tackled Duke Ellington's and did the same superb job, both on the ballads and the faster material. No trio ever had better timing and interaction than this threesome, and Annie Ross was at her peak. —*Ron Wynn*

Lambert, Hendricks and Ross / Mar. 13, 1961 / Columbia ✦✦✦✦✦

Swingin' Til the Girls Come Home / Sep. 6, 1962–Dec. 21, 1963 / Bluebird ✦✦✦✦

Byard Lancaster (William Byard Lancaster)

b. Aug. 6, 1942, Philadelphia, PA
Flute, Alto Saxophone / Avant-Garde, Post-Bop
A lesser-known avant-gardist who has been based much of his

career in Philadelphia, Byard Lancaster is an advanced improviser who is not shy about showing the influence of blues and soul in his solos. He played with Sunny Murray starting in 1965 and worked with Bill Dixon (1966–67), Sun Ra (off and on between 1968–71) and McCoy Tyner (1971–77). Lancaster played for a bit with Memphis Slim in Paris but has mostly performed jazz locally. All of his own recordings were for obscure labels (including Vortex, Dogtown, Palm, Philly Jazz and Bellows) but his 1966 ESP date with Sunny Murray has been reissued on CD. —*Scott Yanow*

● **It's Not Up to Us** / Dec. 19, 1966 / Vortex ✦✦✦✦✦
A rare recording. Two standards, six originals. —*Michael G. Nastos*

Worlds / 1993 / Gazell ✦✦✦✦

Harold Land

b. Dec. 18, 1928, Houston, TX
Tenor Saxophone / Hard Bop
Harold Land is an underrated tenor saxophonist whose tone has hardened with time and whose improvising style after the 1960s became influenced by (but not a copy of) John Coltrane's. He grew up in San Diego and started playing tenor when he was 16. After working locally and making his recording debut for Savoy (1949), Land had his first high-profile gig in 1954 when he joined the Clifford Brown-Max Roach Quintet. Land performed and recorded with the group until late 1955, when due to family problems he had to return home to Los Angeles (where he has been based ever since). He played with Curtis Counce's band (1956–58), recorded a pair of memorable albums for Contemporary (1958–59), led his own groups in the 1960s and co-led groups with Bobby Hutcherson (1967–71) and Blue Mitchell (1975–78). Harold Land has continued freelancing around Los Angeles up to the present time and has recorded as a leader (in addition to Savoy and Contemporary) for such labels as Jazzland, Blue Note, Imperial, Atlantic, Cadet, Mainstream, Concord, Muse and Postcards. His son Harold Land, Jr. has occasionally played piano with his groups. —*Scott Yanow*

● **Harold in the Land of Jazz** / Jan. 13, 1958–Jan. 14, 1958 / Original Jazz Classics ✦✦✦✦✦

The Fox / Aug. 1959 / Original Jazz Classics ✦✦✦✦
Due to his decision to settle in Los Angeles, tenor saxophonist Harold Land has long been underrated. A strong bop stylist who later on would be influenced a great deal by John Coltrane, Land in 1959 had a sound closer to Sonny Rollins. For this excellent straight-ahead quintet set with trumpeter Dupree Bolton and pianist Elmo Hope, Land performs four of Hope's superior but little-known compositions along with two of his own. This is high-quality hard bop, easily recommended to fans of straight-ahead jazz. —*Scott Yanow*

West Coast Blues! / May 17, 1960–May 18, 1960 / Original Jazz Classics ✦✦✦✦
Recorded with Wes Montgomery (g), this is another of many excellent Land albums. —*Michael G. Nastos*

Eastward Ho! Harold Land in New York / Jul. 5, 1960–Jul. 8, 1960 / Original Jazz Classics ✦✦✦✦
An exemplary date, w/ Kenny Dorham (tpt) in top form. —*Ron Wynn*

Mapenzi / Apr. 14, 1977 / Concord Jazz ✦✦✦✦✦
With Kirk Lightsey (p), Blue Mitchell (tpt). Near essential album. —*Michael G. Nastos*

Xocia's Dance (Sue-Sha's Dance) / Oct. 22, 1981 / Muse ✦✦✦✦
An early '80s reunion between tenor saxophonist Harold Land and vibist Bobby Hutcherson, who co-led some vital West Coast combos in the late '60s and early '70s. Their cohesion and interaction remains intact, as does their solo prowess. Pianist George Cables and drummer Billy Higgins are also terrific. —*Ron Wynn*

A Lazy Afternoon / Dec. 28, 1994–Dec. 31, 1994 / Postcards ✦✦✦✦
Harold Land, a long underrated tenor giant based in Los Angeles, is quite melodic yet subtly explorative on this surprising disc. Backed by a string orchestra arranged and conducted by Ray Ellis and a rhythm section led by pianist Bill Henderson, Land explores dozen standards that are highlighted by "Nature Boy," Invitation" and "You've Changed." He treats the melodies with respect and taste yet doesn't hesitate to stretch the music when called for. Harold Land plays beautifully throughout this memorable release. —*Scott Yanow*

Eddie Lang (Blind Willie Massaro)

b. Oct. 25, 1902, Philadelphia, PA, d. Mar. 26, 1933, New York, NY
Guitar / Classic Jazz
The first jazz guitar virtuoso, Eddie Lang was everywhere in the late '20s; all of his fellow musicians knew that he was the best. A boyhood friend of Joe Venuti, Lang took violin lessons for 11 years but switched to guitar before he turned professional. In 1924 he debuted with the Mound City Blue Blowers and was soon in great demand for recording dates, both in the jazz world and in commercial settings. His sophisticated chord patterns made him a superior accompanist who uplifted everyone else's music, and Lang was also a fine single-note soloist. He often teamed up with violinist Venuti (including some classic duets) and played with Red Nichols' Five Pennies, Frankie Trumbauer and Bix Beiderbecke (most memorably on "Singing the Blues"), the orchestras of Roger Wolfe Kahn, Jean Goldkette and Paul Whiteman (appearing on one short number with Venuti in Whiteman's 1930 film *The King of Jazz*) and anyone else who could hire him. A measure of Lang's versatility and talents is that he mostly played the chordal parts on a series of duets with Lonnie Johnson (during which he used the pseudonym Blind Willie Dunn) yet on his two duets with Carl Kress (whose chord voicings were an advancement on Lang's), he played the single-note leads. Eddie Lang, who led some dates of his own during 1927–29, worked regularly with Bing Crosby during the early '30s in addition to recording many sessions with Venuti. Tragically his premature death was caused by a botched operation on a tonsillectomy. —*Scott Yanow*

★ **Stringing the Blues** / Nov. 8, 1926–May 8, 1933 / Columbia ✦✦✦✦
This two-LP set (which is long overdue to be reissued on CD) contains a definitive cross-section of the recordings of violinist Joe Venuti and guitarist Eddie Lang. The 32 performances include everything from duets and a few of Lang's meetings with fellow guitarist Lonnie Johnson to examples of Venuti's Blue Four and guest appearances with singer Annette Hanshaw, Clarence Williams, Tommy Dorsey (on trumpet!) and Bing Crosby (on a hot "Some of these Days"). Virtually all of these recordings are superb, with solos also heard from bass saxophonist Adrian Rollini, Don Murray (on clarinet and baritone), cornetist King Oliver, the C-melody sax of Frankie Trumbauer and Jimmy Dorsey (switching between clarinet, alto and cornet). Highly recommended for all collections. —*Scott Yanow*

Handful of Riffs / Apr. 1, 1927–Sep. 27, 1928 / ASV/Living Era ✦✦✦✦

★ **Jazz Guitar** / Apr. 1, 1927–Jan. 15, 1932 / Yazoo ✦✦✦✦✦
Lang's solo features are here, plus duets with guitarists Lonnie Johnson and Carl Kress. To get the complete picture of Lang, this recording should be heard in conjunction with the Joe Venuti/Eddie Lang duets. —*Richard Lieberson*

Michael Lang

b. Dec. 10, 1941, Los Angeles, CA
Piano / Hard Bop
Due to his busy schedule in the studios, Michael Lang did not record his first solo album until 1994, after more than 30 years as a professional pianist. He graduated from the University of Michigan in 1963, played with Paul Horn (1964–65) and then moved to Los Angeles and started working in the studios. Lang worked with Stan Kenton's Neophonic Orchestra (1966), Don Ellis (1967) and Tom Scott (1968) and recorded with John Klemmer, Milt Jackson, Ella Fitzgerald, Lee Konitz, Art Pepper, Sarah Vaughan and many others, mostly outside of jazz. Mike Lang always played jazz locally on an occasional basis and finally in 1994 came out with his own album, jazz treatments of Henry Mancini songs for Varese Sarabande. —*Scott Yanow*

● **Days Of Wine And Roses** / Sep. 3, 1994+Sep. 15, 1994 / Varese Sarabande ✦✦✦✦
Michael Lang has worked as a studio pianist for over 30 years but, despite his obvious talent, he had never led a jazz record date until the release of this CD. The theme of the album (which is subtitled "The Classic Songs of Henry Mancini") is certainly a challenging one for, other than "Days of Wine and Roses" (which Lang takes as the leadoff tune), none of Mancini's compositions became jazz standards; after all, these songs were written specifically for the movies and not for the improvising musician. The

repertoire, other than "Charade" and "Moon River," is dominated by obscurities such as "Whistling Away the Dark" (from *Darling Lili*), "Tom's Theme" (used in the *Glass Menagerie*) and "The Sweetheart Tree" (from *The Great Race*). Six of the songs are taken as piano solos while the other pieces have either Chuck Domanico or Dave Carpenter on bass and Harvey Mason or Joel Taylor on drums assisting Lang. Among the better transformations are turning "Dear Heart" into a soulful ballad, making a hard swinger out of "It's Easy to Say" (from *10*), giving "Charade" a Latin feel and creating an introspective treatment to "Moon River." Some of the melodies are less interesting than others and there are more moody ballads than romps, but in general Michael Lang uplifts the material and turns it successfully into jazz. *—Scott Yanow*

Don Lanphere

b. Jun. 26, 1928, Wenatchee, WA

Soprano Saxophone, Tenor Saxophone / Bop, Post Bop

Don Lanphere's career can easily be divided into two periods with a long interlude in between. He came to New York when he was 19 and made some impressive recordings with Fats Navarro in 1949, keeping up with the fiery trumpeter. Lanphere played with Woody Herman's Second Herd (1949), Artie Shaw and the big bands of Claude Thornhill, Charlie Barnet and Billy May. Unfortunately drug use soon resulted in his arrest and much of 1951–81 found Lanphere either in prison or running the family music store in Washington. An exception was his stint with Woody Herman during 1959–61. However Don Lanphere beat the odds, kicked drugs and made a full comeback starting in 1982. He has since recorded regularly for Hep, developed his style (doubling on soprano) and become a major if somewhat underrated improviser. *—Scott Yanow*

From Out of Nowhere / Jun. 1982 / Hep ✦✦✦✦

Into Somewhere / Dec. 1983 / Hep ✦✦✦✦

Don Loved Midge / Oct. 21, 1984–Oct. 24, 1984 / Hep ✦✦✦✦

Don Lanphere / Larry Coryell / Apr. 11, 1990–Apr. 12, 1990 / Hep ✦✦✦✦✦

● **Lopin'** / Dec. 1992 / Hep ✦✦✦✦✦

Don Lanphere, a veteran of the late '40s, really came into his own in the 1980s as can be heard on his recordings for the Scottish Hep label. An unimaginative player who has not forgotten (or felt restricted by) his bop roots, Lanphere is matched with baritonist Denney Goodhew and alto-great Bud Shank on this sextet date. They perform an original apiece from Lanphere and Miller, four by pianist Marc Seales (who leads the fine rhythm section) and three standards. Shank is consistently passionate (really showing emotion on "A Time for Love"), Lanphere is featured on an abstract ballad version of "Have You Met Miss Jones" and Goodhew plays strong enough not to be overshadowed by the better-known saxophonists. This superior modern mainstream release has fresh material and several surprising moments. *—Scott Yanow*

Jazz Worship/A Closer Walk / 1993 / DGL ✦✦✦

John LaPorta

b. Apr. 1, 1920, Philadelphia, PA

Clarinet, Alto Saxophone, Tenor Saxophone / Big Band, Bop, Cool, Swing, Hard Bop

At one point in time John LaPorta looked he was going to be one of the leading clarinetists in modern jazz. His cool tone and very advanced style (influenced by Lennie Tristano) seemed to be making him the Lee Konitz of the clarinet. He had played with the big bands of Bob Chester (1942–44) and Woody Herman (1944–46) but more importantly recorded with Lennie Tristano in 1947. LaPorta studied with Tristano and six years later was part of the Jazz Composers' Workshop with Charles Mingus and Teo Macero, seeking to bring elements of classical music into jazz. The clarinetist recorded with Mingus in 1954 before the bassist changed directions and LaPorta led sessions for Debut, Fantasy and Everest during 1954–58. However John LaPorta chose to pursue a career as a teacher (at the Manhattan School of Music and Berklee) and has performed very infrequently during the past 40 years although he does appear on a mid-'90s GM CD. *—Scott Yanow*

Ellis Larkins

b. May 15, 1923, Baltimore, MD

Piano / Swing

Few have attained as much fame for accompaniment as pianist

Ellis Larkins, the player of choice for numerous singers. Blessed with an impeccable ear and ability to provide absolutely perfect support for any vocalist, Larkins has done numerous recordings and sessions. Larkins' father was a janitor and part-time violinist who played in a local Baltimore orchestra. Larkins studied at the Peabody Conservatory and Juilliard andworked in New York clubs in the '40s and '50s. He debuted in a trio led by Billy Moore at Cafe Society in New York. Larkins worked sporadically in New York at The Blue Angel in the '40s and '50s andplayed at Cafe Society in Edmond Hall's sextet in the mid-'40s. He accompanied Mildred Bailey on a Majestic recording session, then worked with Coleman Hawkins and Dickey Wells at Signature. He accompanied Joe Williams, Larry Adler andChris Connor in the '50s, as well as Ruby Braff on sessions for Vanguard and Bethlehem. Larkins began recording for Decca, but took time off from performing to concentrate on studio duties. He returned in the '70s doing several dates on Antilles, Chiaroscuro, Classic Jazz andConcord. He also recorded with Braff, Sylvia Sims andElla Fitzgerald. Larkins performed at Town Hall in 1973 andtoured South America with Marian McPartland, Teddy Wilson and Earl Hines in 1973 and 1974. Larkins worked in the late '70s and through the '80s at New York clubs, among them Gregory's, Michael's Pub, the Cookery and Carnegie Tavern. Larkins was featured in Concord's acclaimed Live At Maybeck Hall Series in 1992. *—Ron Wynn*

Blues in the Night / Jun. 21, 1951–Jan. 9, 1952 / Decca ✦✦✦✦

Stomping blues, charming ballads anddazzling interpretations of standards by pianist Ellis Larkins, one of the most underrated players from the swing era still active. *—Ron Wynn*

A Smooth One / Jul. 21, 1977 / Black & Blue ✦✦✦✦✦

● **Live at Maybeck Recital Hall, Vol. 22** / Mar. 29, 1992 / Concord Jazz ✦✦✦✦✦

Pete LaRoca (Peter Sims)

b. Apr. 7, 1938, New York, NY

Drums / Latin Jazz, Hard Bop

Pete LaRoca's decision to leave music in 1968 and become an attorney (under his original name of Pete Sims) cut short a productive career. He started his career playing timbales in Latin bands, changing his name to Pete LaRoca at the time. He played drums with Sonny Rollins (1957–early 1959) and had associations with Jackie McLean, Slide Hampton, the John Coltrane Quartet (where he was the original drummer in 1960) and Marian McPartland. LaRoca led his own group (1961–62), was the house drummer at the Jazz Workshop in Boston (1963–64) and worked with Art Farmer (1964–65), Freddie Hubbard, Mose Allison, Charles Lloyd (1966), Paul Bley and Steve Kuhn among others. He led two impressive albums: the classic Blue Note record *Basra* with Joe Henderson and *Bliss,* a Douglas session (reissued on Muse) featuring Chick Corea and John Gilmore. LaRoca started playing jazz again in 1979 and has performed on an occasional basis up to the present time. *—Scott Yanow*

● **Basra** / May 19, 1965 / Blue Note ✦✦✦✦✦

It is strange to realize that drummer Pete La Roca only led two albums in his career, for this CD reissue of his initial date is a classic. La Roca's three originals ("Basra" which holds one's interest despite staying on one chord throughout, the blues "Candu" and the complex "Tears Come from Heaven") are stimulating but it is the other three songs that really bring out the best playing in the quartet (which is comprised of tenor saxophonist Joe Henderson, pianist Steve Kuhn and bassist Steve Swallow in addition to La Roca). "Malaguena" is given a great deal of passion, Swallow's "Eiderdown" (heard in its initial recording) receives definitive treatment and the ballad "Lazy Afternoon" is both haunting and very memorable; Henderson's tone perfectly fits that piece. *—Scott Yanow*

Bliss! / May 25, 1967 / Muse ✦✦✦✦

Prince Lasha (William B. Lawsha)

b. Sep. 10, 1929, Fort Worth, TX

Flute / Avant-Garde, Free Jazz

A survivor of the 1960s who has not been heard from in some time, Prince Lasha was an inventive avant-garde flutist who occasionally played alto and clarinet. He played in Texas in an early '50s band that also included Ornette Coleman. In 1954 Lasha moved to California, where he was pretty much in obscurity until the 1960s. He recorded two Contemporary albums with Sonny Simmons (1962 and 1967), a 1966 session for British Columbia and as a sideman with Eric Dolphy and the Elvin Jones/Jimmy Garrison Sextet (both of the latter in 1963). After a few more records for small labels (the last one around 1983), Lasha disappeared from the jazz scene. Considering the major comeback that Sonny Simmons had in 1994 after a decade of silence, hopefully Prince Lasha's story will have the same happy ending. —*Scott Yanow*

The Cry / Nov. 21, 1962 / Contemporary ◆◆◆◆◆

★ **Firebirds** / Sep. 28, 1967–Sep. 29, 1967 / Original Jazz Classics ◆◆◆◆◆

The alto saxophone duo of Prince Lasha and Sonny Simmons teamed during the late '60s, operating in roughly the same territory as the John Coltrane/Eric Dolphy tandem. They explored both inside and outside music andSimmons doubled on English horn, while Lasha also played alto clarinet and flute. The group did torrid free dates as well as hard bop-influenced material; their songs were seldom predictable and often inspired. The band recorded *Firebirds* in 1967. The most intense piece is the ten-minute title track, with the Simmons/Lasha team swapping furious solos; other songs are more demure and gentle. —*Ron Wynn*

Yusef Lateef (William Evans)

b. Oct. 9, 1920, Chatanooga, TN

Tenor Saxophone, Flute, Oboe / New Age, Hard Bop

Yusef Lateef has long had an inquisitive spirit and he was never just a bop or hard bop soloist. Lateef, who does not care much for the name "jazz," has consistently created music that has stretched (and even broke through) boundaries. A superior tenor saxophonist with a soulful sound and impressive technique, Lateef by the 1950s was one of the top flutists around. He also developed into the best jazz soloist to date on oboe, was an occasional bassoonist and introduced such instruments as the argol (a double clarinet that resembles a bassoon), shanai (a type of oboe) and different types of flutes. Lateef played "world music" before it had a name and his output was much more creative than much of the pop and folk music that passes under that label in the 1990s.

Yusef Lateef grew up in Detroit and began on tenor when he was 17. He played with Lucky Millinder (1946), Hot Lips Page, Roy Eldridge and Dizzy Gillespie's big band (1949–50). He was a fixture on the Detroit jazz scene of the 1950s, where he studied flute at Wayne State University. Lateef began recording as a leader in 1955 for Savoy (and later Riverside and Prestige) although he did not move to New York until 1959. By then he already had a strong reputation for his versatility and for his willingness to utilize "miscellaneous instruments." Lateef played with Charles Mingus in 1960, gigged with Donald Byrd and was well-featured with the Cannonball Adderley Sextet (1962–64). As a leader his string of Impulse! recordings (1963–66) were among the finest of his career although Lateef's varied Atlantic sessions (1967–76) usually also had some strong moments. He spent some time in the 1980s teaching in Nigeria. His Atlantic records of the late '80s were closer to mood music (or new age) than jazz but in the 1990s (for his own YAL label) Yusef Lateef has recorded a wide variety of music (all originals) including some strong improvised music with the likes of Ricky Ford, Archie Shepp and Von Freeman. —*Scott Yanow*

Every Village Has A Song / May 6, 1949–Mar. 1976 / Rhino/Atlantic ◆◆◆◆

This good two-disc set covers Lateef's tenure at Atlantic as well as featuring formative material from early sessions for Transition, Prestige/Moodsville, Riverside, Impulse, Blue Note and Savoy. The discs show Lateef honing a thick, bluesy, expressive tenor tone in the beginning, evolving into a superior straight jazz player, then expanding his repertoire and choice of instruments and contexts. His flute playing became arguably superior to his tenor, while his solos on oboe, shenai and other previously little-known instruments enabled Lateef to create arresting, fresh and ultimately significant music. While the sampler approach can't fully document his contributions, it's a solid introduction for those unfamiliar with his output. —*Ron Wynn*

Morning / Apr. 5, 1957–Apr. 9, 1957 / Savoy ◆◆◆◆◆

Yusef Lateef's first two sessions as a leader (which were originally released on three LPs) are included in full on this two-LP set. Although he had played with Dizzy Gillespie's big band in the late '40s, Lateef spent a long period in the 1950s studying in Detroit.

By the time he emerged with these recordings, he had a fully formed sound not only on tenor but on flute, where his style was definitely touched by Eastern music. With a group of fellow Detroiters (trombonist Curtis Fuller, pianist Hugh Lawson, bassist Ernie Farrow, drummer Louis Hayes and Doug Watkins, a fine bassist who here plays percussion) Lateef performs 13 of his originals, which range from riffing stomps to modal pieces. —*Scott Yanow*

Gong / Oct. 9, 1957–Oct. 10, 1957 / Savoy ◆◆◆◆

Other Sounds / Oct. 11, 1957 / Original Jazz Classics ◆◆◆◆

These recordings are among his early African/Middle Eastern fusion efforts, with many exotic instruments. —*Myles Boisen*

Yusef Lateef / Oct. 11, 1957–Dec. 29, 1961 / Prestige ◆◆◆◆

This excellent two-LP set combines together material taken from three Yusef Lateef LPs; all of Lateef's Prestige and New Jazz recordings were very effectively reissued in Prestige's admirable two-fer series. Lateef, one of the first jazz musicians to integrate aspects of Middle Eastern music into his playing, not only performs on tenor and flute during these sessions but also oboe (he was probably jazz music's greatest oboeist ever) and the argol. These performances (with such sidemen as fluegelhornist Wilbur Hardin, trumpeter Lonnie Hillyer and pianists Hugh Lawson and Barry Harris) range from atmospheric modal ballads to straight-ahead stomping. This two-fer is a fine example of Yusef Lateef at his best. —*Scott Yanow*

Yusef at Cranbrook / Apr. 8, 1958 / Argo ◆◆◆

The Dreamer / Jun. 11, 1959 / Savoy ◆◆◆◆

The Fabric of Jazz / Jun. 11, 1959 / Savoy ◆◆◆◆

★ **Cry! / Tender** / Oct. 16, 1959 / Original Jazz Classics ◆◆◆◆◆

First-rate '50s works cover a diversity of jazz standards, European folk andblues, with Yusef on tenor, flute andoboe fronting a mid-sized group. —*Myles Boisen*

★ **The Three Faces of Yusef Lateef** / May 9, 1960 / Original Jazz Classics ◆◆◆◆

Lateef's first album as a multi-instrumental player after his move from Detroit to New York City. With Ron Carter (b, cello), Hugh Lawson (p), Herman Wright (b) and Lex Humphries (d). This is an early attempt at fusion—mixing jazz with Eastern motifs and classical flavors. —*Michael Erlewine*

Centaur and the Phoenix / Oct. 4, 1960–Oct. 6, 1960 / Original Jazz Classics ◆◆◆◆

Lost in Sound / Oct. 22, 1960 / Charlie Parker ◆◆◆

★ **Eastern Sounds** / Sep. 5, 1961 / Original Jazz Classics ◆◆◆◆◆

Asian sounds abound here, as well as a couple of movie themes, with accompaniment by Barry Harris on piano and bass and drums. —*Myles Boisen*

★ **Into Something** / Dec. 29, 1961 / Original Jazz Classics ◆◆◆◆◆

Lateef at his pre-international best. —*Ron Wynn*

Jazz Around the World / Dec. 19, 1963–Dec. 20, 1963 / Impulse! ◆◆◆◆

Re-Evaluations: The Impulse Years / Dec. 19, 1963–Jun. 16, 1966 / Impulse! ◆◆◆◆

Multi-instrumentalist Yusef Lateef recorded eight albums for the Impulse! label during the 1963–66 period. All are worth acquiring, but as a sampler this two-LP set (which draws its 18 selections from six of the albums) gives one a fine all-around picture of Lateef's many talents. He is heard on his highly appealing tenor, playing flute, jamming "Exactly like You" and an emotional "Trouble in Mind" on oboe, utilzing the exotic shannas and theremin (the latter being an early electronic instrument) and even having a few rare outings on alto. The music ranges from bop and ballads to some avant-garde explorations and mood pieces. —*Scott Yanow*

★ **Live at Pep's** / Jun. 29, 1964 / Impulse! ◆◆◆◆◆

This mid-'60s concert was one of Lateef's finest, as it perfectly displayed his multiple influences and interests. There were hard bop originals, covers of jazz classics like Oscar Pettiford's "Oscarlypso" (a CD bonus track) and Leonard Feather's "Twelve Tone Blues," as well as an unorthodox but effective version of Ma Rainey's "See See Rider." On "Sister Mamie," "Number 7" and drummer James Black's "The Magnolia Triangle," Lateef moved away from strict jazz, although he retained his improvisational flair. Lateef played meaty tenor sax solos, entrancing flute and bamboo flute offerings andalso had impressive stints on oboe, shenai and argol. This was a pivotal date in his career, and those unaware of it will get a treat with this disc. —*Ron Wynn*

1984 / Feb. 24, 1965 / Impulse! ✦✦✦✦✦

Psychicemotus / Jul. 21, 1965–Jul. 22, 1965 / Impulse! ✦✦✦✦

A Flat, G Flat and C / Mar. 8, 1966–Mar. 9, 1966 / Impulse! ✦✦✦✦
Quintet. Mid-'60s date with Hugh Lawson Trio. —*Michael G. Nastos*

The Golden Flute / Jun. 15, 1966–Jun. 16, 1966 / Impulse! ✦✦✦✦✦

The Complete Yusef Lateef / May 31, 1967 / Atlantic ✦✦✦✦

The Blue Yusef Lateef / Apr. 23, 1968–Apr. 24, 1968 / Atlantic ✦✦✦

Yusef Lateef's Detroit / May 19, 1969–May 20, 1969 / Atlantic ✦✦

The Diverse Yusef Lateef/Suite 16 / Jan. 15, 1970–Nov. 2, 1970 / Atlantic ✦✦✦✦
For this single CD Rhino combined together two complete LPs from Yusef Lateef's period on Atlantic. Although there are some period trappings and the use of a vocal group on a few selections, the music sounds fairly fresh and its diversity (ranging from exotic vamps to the adventurous seven-movement "Symphonic Blues Suite") is a major strength. Earl Klugh's solo guitar rendition of "Michelle" is pleasant if out of place, and there are some forgettable tracks, but Lateef's willingness to take chances, his highly individual sound on his instruments (tenor, flute, oboe and a rare outing on soprano) and the impressive amount of variety make this a recommended set. —*Scott Yanow*

Part of the Search / Sep. 1, 1971–Dec. 26, 1973 / Atlantic ✦✦✦
This mid-'70s session (recently reissued on CD by Rhino) marked Yusef Lateef's brief return to mainstream sounds before turning almost exclusively to African and Asian instruments and styles. *Part of the Search* featured robust interpretations of pop standards like "Gettin' Sentimental," Ray Charles' R&B stomper "Rockhouse" and the doo-wop anthem "In The Still Of The Night." The album employed a host of guest musicians, backing vocalists andeven string players, with their impact ranging from effective to disturbing. This wasn't among Lateef's greatest Atlantic releases, but it contained some entertaining sections. —*Ron Wynn*

The Gentle Giant / Jul. 5, 1974–Jul. 6, 1974 / Atlantic ✦✦✦
An overlooked date, with Kenny Barron (p). —*Ron Wynn*

Ten Years Hence / 1975 / Atlantic ✦✦✦

Doctor Is In & Out / Mar. 1, 1976 / Atlantic ✦✦

In Nigeria / Aug. 1983 / Landmark ✦✦✦
In this 1983 session, Lateef plays with more vigor and fire than on most of his recent sessions. —*Ron Wynn*

Concerto for Yusef Lateef / 1986 / Atlantic ✦✦

Yusef Lateef's Little Symphony / Jun. 1987 / Atlantic ✦✦

Nocturnes / Feb. 1989 / Atlantic ✦✦

Meditations / Feb. 1990 / Atlantic ✦✦

Tenors Of Yusef Lateef And Von Freeman / Jul. 1992 / YAL ✦✦✦✦

Yusef Lateef Plays Ballads / 1993 / YAL ✦✦✦

Yusef Lateef Tenors Featuring Rene McLean / May 1993 / YAL ✦✦✦✦

Woodwinds / Jul. 1993 / YAL ✦✦✦

Metamorphosis / Dec. 1993 / YAL ✦✦

Claiming Open Spaces / 1994 / YAL ✦✦

Tenors of Yusef Lateef & Ricky Ford / 1994 / YAL ✦✦✦✦
Veteran tenors Yusef Lateef and Ricky Ford team up for this frequently explosive set. Their seven originals all pay tribute to various tenormen (James Moody, Stanley Turrentine, Sonny Rollins, Jimmy Heath, Wayne Shorter, Joe Henderson and Lateef himself) and the two lead voices, while not copying their inspirations, occasionally insert some of their trademark phrases. Electric bassist Avery Sharpe and drummer Kamal Sabir offer fairly accessible and often-funky backings, but one's main focus is on the intense playing of the two great tenors, who battle it out in fiery fashion. —*Scott Yanow*

Cantata / May 1994 / YAL ✦✦

Suite Life / Dec. 1994 / YAL ✦✦

Andy Laverne

b. Dec. 4, 1947, New York, NY
Piano, Keyboards / Post Bop
A fine keyboardist who has ranged in styles from Bill Evans to

Chick Corea and fusion, Andy LaVerne has managed to avoid predictability throughout his career. He began studying as a classical piano student at Juilliard when he was eight. After discovering jazz, Laverne had some important lessons from Bill Evans. He toured with Woody Herman's big band (1973–75), played with John Abercrombie and Miroslav Vitous and was with Stan Getz's group during 1977–80, often playing electric piano. In the 1980s he performed with the Brubeck-LaVerne Trio (which also featured Chris and Dan Brubeck), recorded a tribute to Chick Corea for DMP and became a busy jazz educator. In the 1990s LaVerne has concentrated on acoustic piano, recording a solo concert at Maybeck Recital Hall. Through the years Andy LaVerne has recorded as a leader for Storyville (1977), Jazzline, SteepleChase, DMP, Triloka, Concord and some smaller labels. —*Scott Yanow*

Another World / Sep. 1977 / SteepleChase ✦✦✦

Plays the Music of Chick Corea / 1981–1986 / Jazzline ✦✦✦✦
Assisted by John Abercrombie (g), Danny Gottlieb (d), Mark Egan (b) and Marc Johnson (b), pianist Laverne pays tribute to keyboardist/composer Chick Corea. A beautifully executed album, one track features Laverne and Corea playing piano together. —*Paul Kohler*

Liquid Silver / Oct. 1984–Nov. 3, 1984 / DMP ✦✦✦✦

● **Jazz Piano Lineage** / 1988 / DMP ✦✦✦✦✦
A superbly remastered, nicely played tribute date by pianist Andy Laverne. He runs through songs from Thelonious Monk, Dave Brubeck and Bill Evans, among others, playing them well but adding little to what they've already injected into the composition. Still, he's an accomplished player and picks consistently top-notch songs to cover. —*Ron Wynn*

Frozen Music / Apr. 1989 / SteepleChase ✦✦✦✦
This album features Rick Margitza (ts, ss), Marc Johnson (b), Danny Gottlieb (d). With excellent compositions and playing throughout, it's a must! —*Paul Kohler*

Fountainhead / Jun. 1989 / SteepleChase ✦✦✦✦

Severe Clear / 1990 / SteepleChase ✦✦✦✦
Augmented by trumpeter Tim Hagans, this recording finds Laverne in top gear playing some of the most incredible chord voicings. Rick Margitza (ts) is also prominently featured. —*Paul Kohler*

Standard Eyes / Oct. 1990 / SteepleChase ✦✦✦✦

Pleasure Seekers / Jan. 10, 1991–Jan. 12, 1991 / Triloka ✦✦✦✦
For his debut release on Triloka Records, a label founded by Walter Becker of Steely Dan fame, Laverne puts Bob Sheppard (s, c, f), John Patitucci (b) and Dave Weckl (d) through the paces by setting up some great progressions for the band to solo over. —*Paul Kohler*

Double Standard / Jan. 1993 / Triloka ✦✦✦
Pianist Andy Laverne's idea behind this CD was to play six standards and then six "originals" based on the older tunes, but reharmonized and given new melodies. Unfortunately the programming makes little sense, with only one of the newer songs actually following its original source and, because Laverne also reharmonizes the standards, there is less of a contrast between the two pairs of songs than one might expect. The music (quartet performances with Billy Drewes on tenor and soprano, bassist Steve LaSpina and drummer Greg Hutchinson) is generally satisfying with the influence of Bill Evans (and to a lesser extent Chick Corea) felt in the piano solos while Drewes comes across as a light-toned Coltranite. This is overall a good recording that falls short of being special. —*Scott Yanow*

● **Live at Maybeck Recital Hall, Vol. 28 (Andy Laverne at Maybeck)** / Apr. 1993 / Concord Jazz ✦✦✦✦✦
The Maybeck Recital Hall series has given many post-bop pianists a rare opportunity to record solo. Andy LaVerne, who is normally heard with trios, sounds surprisingly comfortable in the solo setting. His performances on this date are rhapsodic and occasionally wandering as he performs nine standards, Chick Corea's "Impressions for Piano" and his own "Stan Getz in Chappaqua." LaVerne reharmonizes the better-known songs and, by often adding vamps, he makes some of the music dark and faintly disturbing; even "Melancholy Baby" and "When You Wish Upon a Star." This is an interesting set of creative jazz. —*Scott Yanow*

Time Well Spent / Dec. 15, 1994–Dec. 16, 1994 / Concord Jazz ✦✦✦✦

Azar Lawrence

b. Nov. 3, 1953, Los Angeles, CA
Soprano Saxophone, Tenor Saxophone / Post Bop
Azar Lawrence showed a great deal of potential during his period with McCoy Tyner's Quartet (1973–77) but has not made that strong an impression since. A fine tenor and soprano saxophonist (which he took up in 1970 and 1972 after a few years playing alto), Lawrence performed with Horace Tapscott in Los Angeles. He toured Europe with Clark Terry in 1970 and in 1973 joined Elvin Jones' band. After three months Lawrence decided to switch to Tyner's group and he recorded several impressive albums (on Milestone) while a sideman with the great pianist. Azar Lawrence also recorded three albums as a leader for Prestige during 1974–76 (the last one rather commercial) but has not had further opportunities to head sessions and has maintained a low profile ever since. —*Scott Yanow*

● **Bridge into the New Age** / May 1974+Sep. 1974 / Prestige ✦✦✦✦
Summer Solstice / Mar. 29, 1975+May 1, 1975 / Prestige ✦✦✦
People Moving / Mar. 1976 / Prestige ✦✦

Elliot Lawrence (Elliott Lawrence Broza)

b. Feb. 14, 1925, Philadelphia, PA
Piano, Leader / Post Bop
If he had been born ten years earlier, Elliot Lawrence might have been one of the more significant bandleaders of the swing era. As it worked out he was a bit of a prodigy, leading a strong dance band when he was only 20, but by then (1945) the swing era was ending. Lawrence did record steadily as a leader during 1946–60 (for Columbia, Decca, King, Fantasy, Vik and Sesac), sometimes using Gerry Mulligan arrangements, but he mostly worked in the studios. After 1960 Lawrence stopped recording jazz altogether to compose, arrange and conduct for television, films and the theater. Few of his jazz-oriented sessions are currently available but his hard-to-find music is worth exploring. —*Scott Yanow*

The Uncollected Elliot Lawrence & His Orchestra (1946) / 1946 / Hindsight ✦✦✦✦

● **Elliot Lawrence Band Plays Gerry Mulligan Arrangements** / Mar. 4, 1955–Jul. 5, 1955 / Original Jazz Classics ✦✦✦✦
Music of Elliot Lawrence / 1956–1957 / Mobile Fidelity ✦✦✦
This Audiophile CD release is comprised of 22 brief performances (generally 2–2 1/2 minutes apiece) that were originally recorded as radio transcriptions (rather than commercial records). Altoist Gene Quill and tenorman Al Cohn (one of the main arrangers) are the main soloists on the big-band selections, while Lawrence (on piano) is also featured in a sextet with guitarist Mary Osborne and Tyree Glenn (who doubles on trombone and vibes). The music ranges from middle-of-the-road instrumental pop and swing to hints of bop and Dixieland. Although not a major release, this CD does have enjoyable performances and is one of the few Elliot Lawrence recordings currently available. —*Scott Yanow*

Hubert Laws

b. Nov. 10, 1939, Houston, TX
Flute / Hard Bop, Crossover, Classical, Instrumental Pop
A talented flutist whose musical interest was never exclusively straight-ahead jazz, Hubert Laws exceeded Herbie Mann in popularity in the 1970s when he recorded for CTI. He was a member of the early Jazz Crusaders while in Texas (1954–60) and he also played classical music during those years. In the 1960s Laws made his first recordings as a leader (Atlantic dates from 1964–66) and gigged with Mongo Santamaria, Benny Golson, Jim Hall, James Moody and Clark Terry among many others. His CTI recordings from the first half of the 1970s made Laws famous and were a highpoint, particularly compared to his generally wretched Columbia dates from the late '70s. He was less active in the 1980s but has come back with a pair of fine Music Masters sessions in the 1990s. Hubert Laws has the ability to play anything well but not always the desire to perform creative jazz. —*Scott Yanow*

The Laws of Jazz / Apr. 2, 1964+Apr. 22, 1964 / Atlantic ✦✦✦✦
Flute By-Laws / Aug. 25, 1965–Feb. 22, 1966 / Atlantic ✦✦✦✦
★ **Afro Classic** / Dec. 1970 / CTI ✦✦✦✦✦
This is by far the best solo work Laws has on record. He sets the standard for classical-influenced modern jazz. —*Ron Wynn*

Crying Song / 1970 / CTI ✦✦✦
The Rite of Spring / Jun. 1971 / CTI ✦✦✦✦✦
A good follow-up to *Afro Classic.* —*Ron Wynn*
Morning Star / Sep. 1972–Oct. 1972 / CTI ✦✦✦✦
Carnegie Hall / Jan. 12, 1973 / CTI ✦✦✦✦
★ **In the Beginning** / Feb. 1974 / CTI ✦✦✦✦✦
This double LP features flutist Hubert Laws at his finest. The music ranges from classical-oriented pieces to straight-ahead jazz with touches of '70s funk included in the mix. The supporting cast includes keyboardist Bob James on most tracks, guitarist Gene Bertoncini, bassist Ron Carter, drummer Steve Gadd, three strings and Hubert's brother Ronnie on tenor (his solo on John Coltrane's "Moment's Notice" is arguably Ronnie's best ever on record). Whether it be works by Satie or Sonny Rollins, this recording is one of the most rewarding of Hubert Laws' career. —*Scott Yanow*
Chicago Theme / Feb. 1975–Apr. 1975 / CTI ✦✦✦
The San Francisco Concert / Oct. 4, 1975 / Columbia ✦✦✦
Solid playing, but an otherwise humdrum release, though with occasional moments of glory. —*Ron Wynn*
Romeo and Juliet / 1976 / Columbia ✦✦
Light jazz (with strings, keyboards, voices, etc.) and a classical/Eastern flavor. —*Michael Erlewine*
Land of Passion / 1978 / Columbia ✦✦
How to Beat the High Cost of Living / 1980 / Columbia ✦✦✦
My Time Will Come / 1990–1992 / Music Masters ✦✦
This is a streaky affair, Hubert Laws' first recording as a leader in quite a few years. The great flutist has a reunion with Don Sebesky on a version of "Malaguena" that becomes an imitation of Chick Corea's "Spain," a few of the selections are forgettable funk and "Moonlight Sonata" is ruined by an unbearable rhythm. However there are some fine performances that feature excellent soloing by Laws and pianist John Beasley. Still, only Hubert Laws' most loyal fans will want this release. —*Scott Yanow*
Storm Then The Calm / 1994 / Music Masters ✦✦✦✦

Ronnie Laws

b. Oct. 3, 1950, Houston, TX
Tenor Saxophone / Instrumental Pop
The younger brother of Hubert Laws, Ronnie Laws has a nice soulful sound on tenor but has never seriously pursued playing jazz. Throughout his career, which includes early-'70s gigs with Quincy Jones, his brother, Ramsey Lewis and Earth, Wind and Fire, Laws has been essentially an R&B player. He has led his own albums since 1975 but recorded very little of interest to the jazz world although he is often listed on *Billboard*'s nonsensical "contemporary jazz" chart. —*Scott Yanow*
Pressure Sensitive / Mar. 1975–Apr. 1975 / Blue Note ✦✦
Ronnie Laws has always been an R&B-oriented saxophonist miscast in the jazz world, starting with his early association with the rapidly declining Blue Note label. His debut album (reissued on CD) has a couple of decent melodies (the opening "Always There" is the most memorable), some soulful tenor and soprano playing by the leader in a style heavily influenced by Grover Washington, Jr. and vocals on only one of the eight selections; Laws' attempts to make it as a singer were still in the future. However this obviously commercial effort (every song fades out before it hits the five-minute mark) can only be recommended in comparison to Ronnie Laws' later more inferior recordings. —*Scott Yanow*
Fever / Jan. 19, 1976–Mar. 1976/ Blue Note ✦✦✦
True Spirit / 1991 / Par ✦✦
● **Deep Soul** / 1992 / Par ✦✦✦
Few of saxophonist Ronnie Laws' recordings are of much interest to jazz fans and, as with his previous sessions, this Par CD is essentially R&Bish dance music. However this time around vocalists are only utilized on two tracks, the funky rhythms are generally surprisingly subtle and on a few occasions Laws actually wanders a bit from the melody. The results are still essentially fluff but for Ronnie Laws about as good as it gets. —*Scott Yanow*

Hugh Lawson (Richard Hugh Jerome Lawson)

b. Mar. 12, 1935, Detroit, MI
Piano / Hard Bop
One of many talented Detroit pianists of the 1950s (although one of the lesser-known players), the Bud Powell-inspired Hugh

Lawson first gained recognition for his work with Yusef Lateef during the late '50s. He recorded with Harry "Sweets" Edison (1962), Roy Brooks and Lateef on several occasions in the 1960s. In 1972 he was with the Piano Choir (a group with seven pianists!). Lawson went on tours with Charles Mingus in 1975 and 1977 and made recordings with Charlie Rouse (1977), George Adams and as a leader for Storyville and Soul Note. —*Scott Yanow*

● **Colours** / Jan. 1983 / Soul Note ✦✦✦✦

Janet Lawson

b. Nov. 13, 1940, Baltimore, MD
Vocals / Post Bop
A brilliant singer who spent a long period off the scene, Janet Lawson is long overdue for much greater recognition. She performed on the radio and regional television as a child. In 1960 she moved to New York where she worked with Art Farmer, Ron Carter, Duke Pearson, Chick Corea and others during the decade. Lawson appeared regularly on Steve Allen's television show (1968-69), worked in theater and in 1976 formed a quintet. She recorded two superb albums in 1980 and 1983 for Inner City and Omnisound. Lawson (an inventive and expressive scat singer with a very wide range) also appeared on records by Eddie Jefferson (1977) and David Lahm (1982). Her father's long-term illness resulted in her leaving music for much of the second half of the 1980s but in recent years Janet Lawson has worked as a jazz educator and been gigging on the East Coast. —*Scott Yanow*

★ **Janet Lawson Quintet** / Mar. 28, 1980 / Columbia ✦✦✦✦✦
Features the same band as *Dreams Can Be*. Tunes are by Fats Waller, Bob Dorough, Thelonious Monk, Blossom Dearie and Sam Brown. Lawson's creative voice comes through and the band mates are locked in. This is artistry on such a high level that it may take some getting used to. —*Michael G. Nastos*

Dreams Can Be / May 1983 / Omnisound ✦✦✦✦
Lawson, called "the dream jazz voice," is a wise and wondrous improviser. She can scat, whir and whisper with inventive and singular purpose. Non-compromising. —*Michael G. Nastos*

Yank Lawson (John Rhea Lawson)

b. May 3, 1911, Trenton, MO, **d.** Feb. 18, 1995
Trumpet / Dixieland, Swing
An exciting Dixieland trumpeter with an appealing tone and strong melodic ideas, Yank Lawson was a popular attraction on the Dixieland scene for decades. He was with Ben Pollack's band during 1933-35 and when it broke up he was one of the many sidemen who became founding members of the Bob Crosby Orchestra. Lawson was featured on many records both with the big band and Bob Crosby's Bobcats during 1935-38. He was with Tommy Dorsey during 1938-39 and had plenty of solo space with TD's Clambake Seven. After a period back with Crosby (1941-42) and with Benny Goodman (1942), Lawson became a studio musician and started leading his own Dixieland sessions. He recorded extensively with Bob Haggart in the Lawson-Haggart band during the 1950s, had reunions with Crosby, played the musical part of King Oliver on Louis Armstrong's *A Musical Autobiography* and had sessions with Eddie Condon, playing at Condon's club regularly during 1964-66. In 1968 he and Haggart put together the World's Greatest Jazz Band, an all-star Dixieland group that was together for ten years. He continued playing with Haggart and other top Dixieland players at festivals and jazz parties up until his death at age 83. Yank Lawson recorded as a leader through the years for Bob Thiele's various labels (including Signature), Decca, Everest, ABC-Paramount, Project 3, Atlantic, World Jazz Records, Audiophile and Jazzology. —*Scott Yanow*

Best of Broadway / 1959 / Signature ✦✦✦✦

● **Big Yank Is Here** / Mar. 29, 1965+Mar. 30, 1965 / ABC ✦✦✦✦
Ole Dixie / May 2, 1966-May 19, 1966 / ABC ✦✦✦✦

Barbara Lea

b. Detroit, MI
Vocals / Swing, Dixieland
An excellent singer who has been associated with swing and Dixieland, Barbara Lea has never broken through with the general public but she has recorded quite a few worthy albums. She

sang with Detroit dance orchestras while in school, performed with the college jazz band (the Crimson Stompers) at Harvard and worked on the East Coast in the 1950s. She recorded for Riverside (1955) and Prestige (1956-57), using such sidemen as trumpeter Johnny Windhurst and pianists Billy Taylor and Dick Hyman. In the 1960s Lea worked as a stage actress and taught. In the 1970s she sang with Dick Sudhalter and Ed Polcer and recorded in the 1980s for Audiophile, including a tribute to her idol and influence Lee Wiley. —*Scott Yanow*

● **Barbara Lea** / Oct. 18, 1956-Oct. 19, 1956 / Original Jazz Classics ✦✦✦✦✦

Lea in Love / Apr. 19, 1957-May 1, 1957 / Original Jazz Classics ✦✦✦✦✦
Singer Barbara Lea often recalls her idol and friend Lee Wiley on this set of love songs. The backup is uniformly tasteful but changes from song to song with such impressive stylists as trumpeter Johnny Windhurst, baritonist Ernie Caceres, Garvin Bushell (on oboe and bassoon), Dick Cary (the arranger on piano and alto horn), guitarist Jimmy Raney and (on a beautiful version of "True Love") harpist Adele Girard making memorable appearances. Lea's straightforward and heartfelt delivery is heard at its best on such songs as "You'd Be So Nice to Come Home To," "Mountain Greenery," "More than You Know" and "Autumn Leaves" (which is partly taken in French). These interpretations are often touching. —*Scott Yanow*

Jeanne Lee

b. Jan. 29, 1939, New York, NY
Vocals / Avant-Garde, Free Jazz
Jeanne Lee combines acrobatic vocal maneuvers with a deeply moving sound and quality that allows her to alternate between soaring, upper register flights and piercing, emotive interpretations. She's extremely precise and flexible and moves from a song or solo's top end to its middle and bottom, accompanying an instrument with a stunning ease. Though many critics have cited Lee as creating free jazz's most innovative vocal approach, she's done very little recording, almost none of it as a leader and even less on American labels. She's best known for her many sessions with Gunther Hampel. Lee studied dance rather than music at Bard College, but while a student there she met Ran Blake. They formed a duo, and she did her first recordings with him, which excited many critics. They toured Europe in 1963. Lee moved to California in 1964 and worked with Ian Underwood and sound poet David Hazelton, whom she later married. She and Hampel established their musical relationship while Lee was in Europe in 1967. Lee recorded with Archie Shepp, Sunny Murray and Hampel in the late '60s and with Marion Brown, Anthony Braxton, Enrico Rava and Andrew Cyrille in the '70s, while also working with Cecil Taylor. She began composing extensively in the '80s and has concentrated in recent years on performing her original material, which frequently includes poetic and dance components. Most of her recordings have either been done for European labels or small independents. —*Ron Wynn*

★ **Legendary Duets** / Nov. 15, 1961-Dec. 7, 1961 / Bluebird ✦✦✦✦✦
With Ran Blake. It's an appropriate title. A must-buy for creative music listeners. Jeanne Lee does vocals; Ran Blake is on piano. —*Ron Wynn*

Julia Lee

b. Oct. 31, 1902, Boonville, MO, **d.** Dec. 8, 1958, San Diego, CA
Piano, Vocals / Early R&B, Blues, Swing
A popular entertainer who recorded frequently for Capitol during 1944-50, Julia Lee's double-entendre songs and rocking piano made her a major attraction in Kansas City. She played piano and sang in her brother George E. Lee's orchestra during 1920-34, recording with him in 1927 and 1929 (including "If I Could Be with You One Hour Tonight") and cutting two titles of her own in 1929 ("He's Tall, He's Dark and He's Handsome" and "Won't You Come Over to My House"). Lee worked regularly as a single in Kansas City after her brother's band broke up. In 1944 she started recording for Capitol and among her sidemen on some sessions were Jay McShann, Vic Dickenson, Benny Carter, Red Norvo and Red Nichols, along with many local players. After 1952 Julia Lee only recorded four further songs but she was active up until her death. —*Scott Yanow*

★ **Kansas City Star [box]** / Nov. 1, 1944–Jul. 9, 1952 / Bear Family ✦✦✦✦✦

● **Jazz Origin: Julia Lee and Her Boy Friends** / Aug. 23, 1946–Jul. 9, 1952 / PA/USA ✦✦✦✦✦

Peggy Lee
b. May 26, 1920, Jamestown, OH
Vocals / Swing, Pop

Peggy Lee only had a small voice and she never improvised much but her singing often crossed over into jazz and she always swung. She came to fame with Benny Goodman (1941–43) although she was so scared at her first recording session ("Elmer's Tune") that John Hammond urged Goodman to fire her. BG knew better and she had a big hit within a year with "Why Don't You Do Right." After marrying Dave Barbour in 1943, Lee retired briefly but was soon a major recording artist for Capitol and during the 1940s and '50s she had quite a few popular records including "It's a Good Day," "Black Coffee," "Manana" and "Fever"; she also proved to be a talented songwriter. Lee appeared in the Dixieland movie *Pete Kelly's Blues* and recorded *Beauty and the Beat* (1959) with the George Shearing Quintet, but then moved farther away from jazz in the 1960s. Peggy Lee's often-atmospheric records from her prime years can be easily enjoyed by jazz fans. —*Scott Yanow*

Black Coffee / Apr. 3, 1952–Jun. 8, 1956 / MCA/Decca ✦✦✦✦
This attractive two-CD set is an anthology of Peggy Lee's 1952–1956 period with Decca. Much of the music is outside of jazz and more in the genre of period pop and novelties but Lee sounds cheerful about the whole thing and swings lightly throughout. Some of the later material does give her a chance to show off her jazz chops and among the highlights are "Lover," a duet with Bing Crosby ("Watermelon Weather") and the hit title cut, but jazz listeners will want to be selective. —*Scott Yanow*

Songs from "Pete Kelly's Blues" / May 6, 1955+May 10, 1955 / Decca ✦✦✦✦

● **Beauty and the Beat** / Apr. 28, 1959 / Capitol ✦✦✦✦✦

Basin Street East / Feb. 9, 1961+Mar. 8, 1961 / Blue Note ✦✦
This is a lesser Peggy Lee release. Originally it was planned that the singer (at the height of her popularity) would record a live set at Basin Street East in New York. Unfortunately, she caught a cold and her voice was a bit hoarse, so some of the numbers were re-recorded in the studio the following month and spliced quite effectively into the set. However, whether in concert or not, the performances on this CD reissue are rather routine, with no chances taken (the dozen sidemen do not get a single solo), and everything sounds pretty well planned in advance. Lee, who is best here on the ballads, never wanders at all from the melodies, and these renditions of her usual repertoire have nothing unique or unusual to offer except perhaps an overly rapid version of "Fever." —*Scott Yanow*

Legends Of Jazz
Group / New Orleans Jazz

Formed and led by drummer Barry Martyn, this New Orleans jazz band featured a variety of ancient players on occasional tours and recordings. The title of their 1978 show (*1000 Years of Jazz*) was not much of an exaggeration! With trumpeter Andrew Blakeney, trombonist Louis Nelson, clarinetist Joe Darensbourg, pianist Alton Purnell, bassist Ed Garland and Martyn forming the original sextet, the Legends recorded two albums for the Crescent Jazz label during 1973–74; the relative youngster Barney Bigard was a guest on the second date. The personnel in future years included trombonist Clyde Bernhardt and bassist Chester Zardis along with lesser-known players, and the erratic but spirited group had successful tours of South America and Australia before fading out in the late '80s. —*Scott Yanow*

● **The Legends of Jazz** / 1973 / Crescent Jazz Productions ✦✦✦✦✦
In the early '70s, English drummer Barry Martyn (who was then 32) gathered together a sextet comprised of New Orleans jazz veterans, billed them as "The Legends of Jazz" and took them on several tours. This LP, the first release by the Crescent Jazz Productions label, contains some good playing from trumpeter Andrew Blakeney, trombonist Louis Nelson and clarinetist Joe Darensbourg; the rhythm section (comprised of pianist Alton Purnell, Martyn and the 88-year-old bassist Edward "Montudi" Garland) also works together quite well. Although the band plays

a couple of warhorses, there is also some lesser-known material on the set (including Mike Delay's "Conti Street Parade" and A.J. Piron's "Red Man Blues"), and overall, this joyful album is much better than expected. —*Scott Yanow*

Michel Legrand
b. Feb. 24, 1932, Paris, France
Arranger, Composer, Piano / Pop, Hard Bop

Michel Legrand has made his fame and fortune from writing for films but he has done significant work in jazz on an occasional basis. In 1957 he arranged a set of Dixieland and swing standards for a French orchestra (recorded on Phillips), in 1958 he used three different all-star groups for the classic *Legrand Jazz* (with such sidemen as Miles Davis, John Coltrane, Phil Woods, Herbie Mann, Bill Evans, Ben Webster, Art Farmer and others), in 1968 he recorded a strictly jazz set with a trio and Legrand has written for albums led by Stan Getz (1971), Sarah Vaughan (1972) and on several occasions Phil Woods. Several of his songs (such as "What Are You Doing the Rest of Your Life," "Watch What Happens" and "The Summer Knows") have been recorded many times by jazz musicians. —*Scott Yanow*

★ **Legrand Jazz** / Jun. 25, 1958–Jun. 30, 1958 / Philips ✦✦✦✦✦
Michel Legrand has spent most of his life as a composer in the studios and for films but this release is a jazz classic. Legrand took 11 famous jazz compositions and arranged them for three different groups. Tenor-great Ben Webster, flutist Herbie Mann, four trombonists and a rhythm section perform pieces by Duke Ellington, Earl Hines, Django Reinhardt ("Nuages") and the Count Basie-associated "Blue and Sentimental." A big band with trumpeters Art Farmer and Donald Byrd and altoist Phil Woods plays "Stompin' at the Savoy," "A Night in Tunisia" and Bix Beiderbecke's "In a Mist." The most famous session has Miles Davis, John Coltrane, Phil Woods, Herbie Mann, pianist Bill Evans, harp, vibes, baritone and a rhythm section performing music by Thelonious Monk, John Lewis, Jelly Roll Morton ("Wild Man Blues") and Fats Waller's "Jitterbug Waltz." Throughout this superlative album, the arrangements are colorful and unusual, making one wish that Legrand had recorded more jazz albums through the years. —*Scott Yanow*

Michel LeGrand at Shelly Manne's Hole / Jan. 1968 / Verve ✦✦✦✦✦
A good upbeat mainstream session. Legrand shines as an improviser. —*Ron Wynn*

Jazz Grand / Mar. 1978 / Gryphon ✦✦✦
Michel Legrand has spent much of his career doing commercial writing for the studios, so whenever he emerges to record a jazz album, it is a special event. For this Gryphon LP, Legrand uses a big band (plus as soloists trumpeter Jon Faddis, altoist Phil Woods and baritonist Gerry Mulligan) to perform a 23-minute jazz suite based on his soundtrack from the film *Les Routes De La Sud*. In addition, there are individual features for the three horns, with a septet that includes Legrand himself on piano. Although this set falls short of being overly memorable, the music is well played and there are some exciting moments from the soloists. —*Scott Yanow*

After the Rain / May 28, 1982 / Original Jazz Classics ✦✦✦✦

Legrand/Grappelli / May 25, 1992–May 27, 1992 / Verve ✦✦✦

Michel Plays Legrand / Sep. 27, 1993–Sep. 28, 1993 / Laserlight ✦✦
Michel Legrand's Laserlight CD boasts quite an all-star band (trumpeter Arturo Sandoval, trombonist Bill Watrous, altoist Bud Shank, Buddy Collette and Hubert Laws on flutes, guitarist John Pisano, bassist Brian Bromberg, drummer Peter Erskine and the leader/pianist) but is surprisingly (and disappointingly) relaxed. The emphasis is on ballads, Legrand sings two dramatic pieces that are outside of jazz and none of the solos are all that memorable. Sandoval is overly restrained and, even with some strong moments from Watrous and Laws, this session does not reach the heights one would expect from this cast of musical personalities. —*Scott Yanow*

Peter Leitch
b. 1944, Ottawa, Canada
Guitar / Hard Bop

Peter Leitch has long been one of the top straight-ahead guitarists in jazz, a fine hard bop-based improviser with a swinging style and an appealing quiet tone. He grew up in Montreal, lived in Toronto during 1977–81, recorded with Oscar Peterson, the Al Grey-Jimmy Forrest Quintet and Sadik Hakim, and debuted as a leader in 1981 on the Jazz House label. Since moving to New York in 1983, Leitch has been a busy freelancer and has recorded as a leader for Uptown, Criss Cross, Concord and most frequently for Reservoir. In addition, he has been an occasional and insightful jazz journalist. —Scott Yanow

Jump Street / Feb. 9, 1981–Feb. 10, 1981 / PA/USA ✦✦✦
Good program of standards, an occasional original and ballads by guitarist Peter Leitch. He plays in a huge-toned, open style similar to Kenny Burrell or Joe Pass, although he hasn't yet developed either an original conception or his compositional skills. —Ron Wynn

★ **Red Zone** / Nov. 17, 1984–Jul. 20, 1988 / Reservoir ✦✦✦✦✦
Quartet. With Kirk Lightsey Trio. Two originals, great rendition of Thelonious Monk's "Off Minor." Two by Wayne Shorter. A fine effort by all involved. —Michael G. Nastos

Exhilaration / Nov. 17, 1984–Dec. 6, 1988 / Reservoir ✦✦✦✦
With Pepper Adams (bar sax). Leitch and Thelonious Monk share compositions. Formidable John Hicks Trio as backing. No-frills bop and hard, swinging music. —Michael G. Nastos

On a Misty Night / Nov. 2, 1986 / Criss Cross ✦✦✦✦✦

Mean What You Say / Jan. 1990 / Concord Jazz ✦✦✦✦✦
Quartet. A nice mainstream date. Very conservative in tone and style. CD version has a bonus cut. —Ron Wynn

Trio/Quartet '91 / Feb. 23, 1991–Feb. 24, 1991 / Concord Jazz ✦✦✦✦

From Another Perspective / Jun. 10, 1992 / Concord Jazz ✦✦✦✦

A Special Rapport / Jul. 1, 1993 / Reservoir ✦✦✦✦✦

Duality / Jun. 1, 1994–Jun. 2, 1994 / Reservoir ✦✦✦✦

John Leitham

b. Philadelphia, PA
Bass / Hard Bop
A talented bassist who has been based in the Los Angeles area since 1983, John Leitham has toured with Woody Herman, George Shearing and Mel Tormé. His two USA albums (1989 and 1992) feature him in trio and quintet settings with pianist Tom Ranier and are strong examples of straight-ahead jazz. —Scott Yanow

Leitham Up / May 29, 1989–May 31, 1989 / USA Music Group ✦✦✦✦

● **The Southpaw** / Sep. 8, 1992–Sep. 10, 1992 / USA ✦✦✦✦✦

Stan Levey

b. Apr. 5, 1925, Philadelphia, PA
Drums / Cool, Bop
Stan Levey, one of the early bop drummers, was greatly in demand in the jazz world of the 1950s. He played with Dizzy Gillespie for the first time in Philadelphia in 1942. Two years later he moved to New York and worked with Charlie Parker, Coleman Hawkins (when his group included Thelonious Monk) and Ben Webster. He toured with Woody Herman in 1945 and was in the Gillespie-Parker Quintet (1945–46). Levey proved to be a superior big band drummer during his stints with Charlie Ventura, Georgie Auld and Freddie Slack, gaining his greatest recognition while with Stan Kenton's Orchestra (1952–54). Settling in Los Angeles, Levey was with the Lighthouse All-Stars (1954–58) and worked for the next decade as a studio musician. In 1973 he permanently retired from music to run a photography business. Stan Levey led three dates for Bethlehem (1954–56) and one apiece for Liberty and Mode in 1957. —Scott Yanow

Plays Bob Cooper, Bill Holman, Jimmy Giuffre / Dec. 6, 1954 / Bethlehem ✦✦✦✦

Stanley the Steamer / Dec. 1954–Sep. 1955 / Affinity ✦✦✦✦

This Time the Drum's on Me / Sep. 27, 1955–Sep. 28, 1955 / Bethlehem ✦✦✦✦

Grand Stan / Nov. 1956 / Bethlehem ✦✦✦✦

● **Stan Levey 5** / Jun. 1957 / VSOP ✦✦✦✦✦
The excellent bop drummer Stan Levey, who retired from playing in the 1960s to become a full-time photographer, led five record dates during 1954–57 of which this set for MOD (which has been reissued on CD by the VSOP label) was the last one. Levey gath-

ered together quite an impressive lineup (trumpeter Conte Candoli, Richie Kamuca on tenor, pianist Lou Levy and bassist Monty Budwig) to perform two of Kamuca's originals, three standards and the rarely played "Ole Man Rebop." All of the musicians are in prime form, displaying contrasting but complementary styles. This swinging date is easily recommended. —Scott Yanow

Milcho Leviev

b. Dec. 19, 1937, Plovdiv, Bulgaria
Keyboards, Piano / Post Bop
Milcho Leviev is a virtuosic pianist whose ability to play effortlessly in complex time signatures is quite impressive. He worked early on in Bulgaria, directing the national radio and television big band and leading the quartet Jazz Focus (1965–69) before defecting to the West in 1970, working with Albert Mangelsdorff in Germany. Leviev moved to Los Angeles the following year, becoming a key part of the Don Ellis Orchestra (1971–77) where his ability to play in odd meters was a major asset. He worked with Willie Bobo, John Klemmer, Billy Cobham, Airto Moreira, Art Pepper and Manhattan Transfer before helping to found Free Flight (1980–83). Leviev has freelanced in the L.A. area ever since, recording in recent times for the M-A label. —Scott Yanow

Blues for the Fisherman / Jun. 27, 1980–Jun. 29, 1980 / Mole ✦✦✦✦

Plays the Music of Irving Berlin / Sep. 9, 1982 / Discovery ✦✦✦✦
An outstanding early '80s tribute to the songwriting genius by pianist Milcho Leviev. His solos are clear and striking and his ensemble work is sophisticated without sounding stiff or derivative. —Ron Wynn

★ **Up And Down** / Sep. 15, 1987 / M-A Recordings ✦✦✦✦✦
Originating from a Japanese concert, this CD from M-A teams together pianist Milcho Leviev in duets with the superb bassist Dave Holland. The music ranges from variations of standards to more introspective interplay and stimulating originals by the duo. Highpoints include versions of Leviev's "Up and Down" and Holland's challenging and rather exciting "Jumpin' In." Although the bassist has a fair share of solo space, Leviev's command of the keyboard constantly grabs one's attention; he has long been one of Los Angeles' unheralded treasures. This recommended disc concludes (as do all of M-A's discs) with a selection taken from another CD, a fine performance by pianist Todd Garfinkle. —Scott Yanow

Bulgarian Piano Blues / Apr. 1989 / M-A Recordings ✦✦✦✦✦

Lou Levy

b. Mar. 5, 1928, Chicago, IL
Piano / Bop
A superior bop-based pianist who has worked with a countless number of top jazz artists, Lou Levy started on piano when he was 12. He played with Georgie Auld (1947), Sarah Vaughan, Chubby Jackson (1947–48), Boyd Raeburn, Woody Herman's Second Herd (1949–50), Tommy Dorsey (1950), Auld again and Flip Phillips. Levy was outside of music for a few years (1952–54) and then gained a strong reputation as a fine accompanist to singers, working with Peggy Lee (on and off during 1955–73), Ella Fitzgerald (1957–62), June Christy, Anita O'Day and more recently Pinky Winters. Levy also played with Shorty Rogers, Stan Getz, Terry Gibbs, Benny Goodman, Supersax and most of the major West Coast players. Lou Levy has recorded as a leader for Nocturne (1954), RCA, Jubilee, Philips, Interplay (1977) and Verve. —Scott Yanow

● **Lunacy** / Feb. 1992 / Verve ✦✦✦✦✦

Ya Know / Mar. 30, 1993–Apr. 1, 1993 / Verve ✦✦✦✦
This is a rather unusual outing for veteran pianist Lou Levy, since eight of the ten selections have both Eric Von Essen, who doubles on cello and Pierre Michelot on basses, along with drummer Alvin Queen. The large number of bass solos make this set of more limited interest than expected, but Levy's fine bop-based playing and some excellent originals uplift what could have been a lesser effort. Worth investigating. —Scott Yanow

George Lewis

b. Jul. 13, 1900, New Orleans, LA, **d.** Dec. 31, 1968, New Orleans, LA
Clarinet / New Orleans Jazz
George Lewis never tried to be a virtuoso soloist. He loved to play

melodic ensembles where his distinctive clarinet was free to improvise as simply as he desired. When Lewis was inspired and in tune, he could hold his own with any of his contemporaries in New Orleans and he always sounded beautiful playing his "Burgundy Street Blues." To everyone's surprise (including himself), he became one of the most popular figures of the New Orleans revival movement of the 1950s.

It took Lewis a long time to achieve fame. He taught himself clarinet when he was 18 and worked in the 1920s with the Black Eagle Band, Buddy Petit, the Eureka Brass Band, Chris Kelly, Kid Rena, the Olympia Orchestra and other New Orleans groups. He played with Bunk Johnson in Evan Thomas' group in the early '30s but had a day job throughout most of the decade. When Bunk was discovered in 1942, Lewis became part of his band, playing with him on and off through 1945 and getting opportunities to lead his own sessions during 1943–45. However Johnson was difficult to get along with and a homesick Lewis returned to New Orleans by 1946. He played locally with his own group (featuring trombonist Jim Robinson) and in 1950 was portrayed in an article for *Look*. That exposure led to him recording regularly and by 1952 Lewis was in such great demand that he was soon working before crowds in California and touring Europe and Japan. In addition to Robinson, Lewis' band in its prime years often featured trumpeter Kid Howard, pianist Alton Purnell, banjoist Lawrence Marrero, bassist Alcide "Slow Drag" Pavageau and drummer Joe Watkins. George Lewis, who recorded for many labels (a Mosaic box set of his Blue Note sessions is one of the best reissues), became a symbol of what was right and wrong about the New Orleans revival movement, overpraised by his fans and overcritized by his detractors. At his best he was well worth hearing. —*Scott Yanow*

★ **Complete Blue Note Recordings** / May 15, 1943–Apr. 11, 1955 / Mosaic ◆◆◆◆◆
A centerpiece for the dedicated New Orleans collector, it begins with Lewis' "Climax" session in 1943 and ranges through a variety of studio and concert performances over a twelve-year period—definitely some of the clarinetist's best work (1943–1944, 1954–1955). —*Bruce Raeburn*

George Lewis with Kid Shots Madison / Jul. 31, 1944–Aug. 5, 1944 / American Music ◆◆◆

George Lewis of New Orleans / Feb. 26, 1946–Feb. 27, 1946 / Original Jazz Classics ◆◆◆◆
Some great New Orleans standards appear from The Original Zenith Brass Band and The Eclipse Alley Five, featuring Lewis in good company—Isidore Barbarin (Paul's father), Peter Bocage, Jim Robinson, Baby Dodds and others. —*Bruce Raeburn*

Jazz in the Classic New Orleans Tradition / Aug. 19, 1951–Sept. 1953/ Original Jazz Classics ◆◆◆◆◆

The Beverly Caverns Sessions / May 26, 1953–May 27, 1953 / Good Time Jazz ◆◆◆◆◆
Clarinetist George Lewis and his usual band of this period (which consisted of trumpeter Kid Howard, trombonist Jim Robinson, pianist Alton Purnell, Lawrence Marrero on banjo, bassist Slow Drag Pavageau and drummer Joe Watkins) are in better-than-average form on this well-recorded live set. Lewis and his group emphasize ensembles on the dozen New Orleans standards and the clarinetist/leader is in surprisingly extroverted form, easily the most impressive soloist. Fans of traditional jazz should go out of their way to pick up this CD. These performances were released for the first time in 1994. —*Scott Yanow*

★ **Hot Creole Jazz: 1953** / Oct. 26, 1953 / DCC ◆◆◆◆◆

George Lewis at Club Hangover, Vol. 1 / Nov. 7, 1953+Nov. 14, 1953 / Storyville ◆◆◆

Club Hangover, Vol. 3 / Nov. 21, 1953–Nov. 28, 1953 / Storyville ◆◆◆

The Sounds of New Orleans, Vol. 7 / Dec. 27, 1953+Jan. 2, 1954 / Storyville ◆◆◆
George Lewis' New Orleans Jazz Band is featured on two well-recorded radio broadcasts on this CD. The clarinetist/leader is generally in fine form, as is trombonist Jim Robinson, while trumpeter Kid Howard is typically erratic; Howard, drummer Joe Watkins and bassist Alcide Pavageau have spirited (if not necessarily musical) vocals and guest Lizzie Miles sings "Bill Bailey" and "Darktown Strutters' Ball" in both English and Creole. Fans of George Lewis' band will want this release, but more general collectors can find better sets to acquire first. —*Scott Yanow*

George Lewis / Paul Barbarin / Jan. 1, 1954–Jun. 17, 1954 / Storyville ◆◆◆◆

Jazz at Vespers / Feb. 21, 1954 / Original Jazz Classics ◆◆◆◆

George Lewis & His Ragtime Band / May 28, 1954 / Storyville ◆◆◆

George Lewis and Turk Murphy at Newport / Jul. 4, 1957 / Verve ◆◆◆◆

Jazz at Preservation Hall / Jul. 6, 1962–Jul. 7, 1962 / Atlantic ◆◆◆◆◆

Reunion with Don Ewell / Jun. 5, 1966 / Delmark ◆◆◆◆

George Lewis

b. Jul. 14, 1952, Chicago, IL
Trombone, Electronics / Avant-Garde
George Lewis has really had two overlapping careers, being both an avant-garde jazz trombonist and an experimenter with electronics whose work in the latter field is closer to modern classical music. He started on trombone when he was nine, attended Yale and played while still in college with Anthony Davis' sextet. He studied at the AACM school in the early '70s and developed quickly as a player. After two months with Count Basie's Orchestra (1976) he joined Anthony Braxton's exciting quartet, where his trombone fit in perfectly with Braxton's reeds; their interplay could often be quite witty. Since then Lewis has played with most of the top avant-garde players (including Roscoe Mitchell, Barry Altschul, Derek Bailey, Evan Parker and Lester Bowie) while simultaneously working on advanced music outside of jazz. His collaboration with John Zorn and Bill Frisell on 1987's *News for Lulu* (for Hat Art) gives one a good example of his trombone playing. George Lewis has also led sessions for Sackville and Black Saint. —*Scott Yanow*

Solo Trombone Album / Nov. 21, 1976 / Sackville ◆◆◆◆

Shadowgraph / 1977 / Black Saint ◆◆◆
Trombonist George Lewis ranks among the more inspired artists working in improvisational circles. He doesn't restrict himself to hard bop and jazz standards; he uses both electric and acoustic instruments, and his compositions are often intricate, yet also allow maximum improvisational freedom. This date, reissued on CD, mixes pieces for large and small groups. The combo pieces are more interesting; the larger pieces are tightly structured and expertly presented, but lack color and tension, despite the fine playing. Lewis limits his own solo space, which is a shame, for he's one of the finest trombonists of his generation. *Shadowgraph, 5* has its flaws, but when it works, it's a reminder of George Lewis' special gifts as a composer and improviser. —*Ron Wynn*

George Lewis/ Douglas Ewart / 1978 / Black Saint ◆◆◆

★ **Homage to Charles Parker** / 1979 / Black Saint ◆◆◆◆◆
Both of Lewis' compositions on this album are for an ensemble with Anthony Davis, piano; Douglas Ewart, bass clarinet; George Lewis, tenor trombone and electronics; and Richard Teitelbaum, Polymoog, Multimoog and Micromoog synthesizers. "Blues" (1977) is a "collective orchestration" that builds in a fragmentary style of changing timbres and a happy to Tibetan-meditation spirit from material arranged in four basically diatonic choruses, using the essential harmonic sequence of the classic blues form as a starting point... but don't expect to hear a traditional "blues" because this music goes to the spirit behind the tune, rather than playing the tune. In the "Homage to Charles Parker" (1978) "the iconography (of the first section)... represents the life of Charles Parker—what is known, what is thought to be known, what is dreamed, heard and said—and his 'reality,' i.e. birth and death" and the second part is based on the traditional solo with the chordal accompaniment form that Charles Parker "brought to a rare level of perfection" and "makes loving inferences as to Parker's afterlife and points to a new appraisal of world music after his life—one in which Afro-American creative music decisively affirms its place as a living, growing, vital part of world culture". —*Blue Gene Tyranny*

Voyager / 1993 / Avant ◆◆◆
This features Lewis in a collaborative affair with Art Ensemble of Chicago saxophonist and composer Roscoe Mitchell, an integral part of Lewis' eight-part composition "Voyager," which encompasses all but the disc's final selection. The piece features computerized, synthesized backing designed to replicate that of an orchestra or ensemble. Lewis has programmed the computers to

respond instantaneously to Mitchell's lines and solos, creating a variety of musical responses that Mitchell then reacts to on alto or soprano. Lewis' trombone solos are also linked to this interplay. While this is hardly what's normally called "jazz" in any setting, the results are intriguing, if sometimes jarring, featuring everything from choppy, jagged dialogues to tranquil sequences. The experiments of Lewis and a few others are worth hearing and can be as rewarding as standard improvisational material. —*Ron Wynn*

Changing With The Times / 1993 / New World ✦✦
Innovative pieces, each with a speaker, poet, or singer reflecting on modern living. Titles include "Chicago Dadagram," "So You Say," "The View From Skates In Berkeley," "Airplane," "Epilogue." —*Blue Gene Tyranny*

John Lewis

b. May 3, 1920, La Grange, IL
Piano, Leader, Composer / Bop, Cool, Third Stream
The musical director of the Modern Jazz Quartet for its entire history, John Lewis found the perfect outlet for his interest in bop, blues and Bach. Possessor of a "cool" piano style that (like Count Basie) makes every note count, Lewis with the MJQ has long helped make jazz look respectable to the classical music community without watering down his performances.

After serving in the military, Lewis was in the Dizzy Gillespie big band (1946-48). He recorded with Charlie Parker during 1947-48 (including "Parker's Mood") and played with Miles Davis' Birth of the Cool Nonet, arranging "Move" and "Rouge." He worked with Illinois Jacquet (1948-49) and Lester Young (1950-51) and appeared on many recordings during the era. In 1951 Lewis recorded with the Milt Jackson Quartet, which by 1952 became the Modern Jazz Quartet. Lewis' musical vision was fulfilled with the MJQ and he composed many pieces, with "Django" being the best-known. In addition to constantly touring with the MJQ during 1952-74, Lewis wrote the film scores to *Odds Against Tomorrow, No Sun in Venice* and *A Milanese Story,* recorded as a leader (including the 1956 cool classic "Two Degrees East, Three Degrees West," collaborations with Gunther Schuller and records with Svend Asmussen and Albert Mangelsdorff) and worked with Orchestra U.S.A. in the mid-'60s. When the MJQ broke up in 1974, Lewis worked as an educator and occasionally recorded as a leader. With the MJQ's rebirth in 1981, he has resumed his former role as its guiding spirit. Most of John Lewis' own projects were recorded for Atlantic. —*Scott Yanow*

★ **Grand Encounter** / Feb. 10, 1956 / Pacific Jazz ✦✦✦✦✦
The John Lewis Piano / Jul. 30, 1956-Feb. 21, 1957 / Atlantic ✦✦✦✦✦
Afternoon in Paris / Dec. 4, 1956-Dec. 7, 1956 / Atlantic ✦✦✦✦
European Windows / Feb. 20, 1958-Feb. 21, 1958 / RCA ✦✦✦
Improvised Meditations and Excursions / May 7, 1959-May 8, 1959 / Atlantic ✦✦✦✦
Odds Against Tomorrow / Jul. 16, 1959 / United Artists ✦✦✦
The Golden Striker / Feb. 12, 1960-Feb. 16, 1960 / Atlantic ✦✦✦
★ **Wonderful World of Jazz** / Jul. 29, 1960-Sep. 9, 1960 / Atlantic ✦✦✦✦✦
Jazz Abstractions / Dec. 19, 1960-Dec. 20, 1960 / Atlantic ✦✦✦✦✦
Original Sin / Mar. 28, 1961-Mar. 31, 1961 / Atlantic ✦✦
A Milanese Story / Jan. 17, 1962 / Atlantic ✦✦✦✦
Essence / May 25, 1962-Oct. 5, 1962 / Atlantic ✦✦✦
European Encounter / Jul. 2, 1962-Jul. 3, 1962 / Atlantic ✦✦✦✦
A 1986 reissue of a sublime meeting between Lewis and violinist Svend Asmussen. —*Ron Wynn*
Animal Dance / Jul. 30, 1962 / Atlantic ✦✦✦✦
Evening with Two Grand Pianos / Jan. 25, 1979-Feb. 9, 1979 / Little David ✦✦✦
Kansas City Breaks / May 25, 1982-May 26, 1982 / DRG ✦✦✦✦
Has the interesting instrumentation of a flute, violin, guitar and piano trio. All selections are Lewis originals, including the especially famous "Django," "Milano," and "Sacha's Mardi." A sweet session. —*Michael G. Nastos*

The Garden of Delight / Oct. 1987 / EmArcy ✦✦✦✦
● **Midnight in Paris** / Dec. 1988 / EmArcy ✦✦✦✦✦
Private Concert / Oct. 23, 1991 / EmArcy ✦✦✦✦

Meade "Lux" Lewis

b. Sep. 4, 1905, Chicago, IL, d. Jun. 7, 1964, Minneapolis, MN
Piano / Boogie-Woogie
One of the three great boogie-woogie pianists (along with Albert Ammons and Pete Johnson) whose appearance at John Hammond's 1938 *Spirituals to Swing* concert helped start the boogie-woogie craze, Meade "Lux" Lewis was a powerful if somewhat limited player. He played regularly in Chicago in the late '20s and his one solo record of the time "Honky Tonk Train Blues" (1927) was considered a classic. However, other than a few sides backing little-known blues singers, Lewis gained little extra work and slipped into obscurity. John Hammond heard Lewis' record in 1935 and after a search found Lewis washing cars for a living in Chicago. Soon Meade Lux Lewis was back on records and after the 1938 concert he was able to work steadily, sometimes in duets or trios with Ammons and Johnson. He became the first jazz pianist to double on celeste (starting in 1936) and was featured on that instrument in a Blue Note quartet date with Edmond Hall and Charlie Christian; he also played harpsichord on a few records in 1941. After the boogie-woogie craze ended, Lewis continued working in Chicago and California, recording as late as 1962 although by then he was pretty much forgotten. Meade Lux Lewis led sessions through the years that have come out on MCA, Victor, Blue Note, Solo Art, Euphonic, Stinson, Atlantic, Storyville, Verve, Tops, ABC-Paramount, Riverside and Philips. —*Scott Yanow*

1939-1954 / Feb. 1939-Sep. 25, 1954 / Story Of Blues ✦✦✦✦✦
Vintage recordings from a premier boogie-woogie stylist detailing the evolution and fruition of his approach. It features recordings done in the '30s, '40s and '50s with sessions for various labels, solos, duets with Albert Ammons and some combo dates. —*Ron Wynn*

● **The Blues Piano Artistry of Meade Lux Lewis** / Nov. 1, 1961 / Original Jazz Classics ✦✦✦✦✦
Boogie-woogie pianist Meade Lux Lewis' next-to-last record was his first recording in five years and his final opportunity to stretch out unaccompanied. This solo Riverside set (reissued by OJC on CD) as usual finds Lewis generally sticking to the blues (with "You Were Meant for Me" and "Fate" being exceptions), mostly performing originals. On a few of the songs Lewis switches effectively to celeste. It apparently only took Meade Lux Lewis two hours to record the full set, and the results are quite spontaneous yet well organized, a fine all-around portrait of the veteran pianist in his later period. —*Scott Yanow*

Mel Lewis (Melvin Sokoloff)

b. May 10, 1929, Buffalo, NY, d. Feb. 2, 1990, New York, NY
Drums, Leader / Bop, Post Bop
Although he was generally reluctant to solo, Mel Lewis was considered one of the definitive big-band drummers, a musician who was best at driving an orchestra but could also play quite well with smaller units. He started playing professionally when he was 15 and worked with the big bands of Boyd Raeburn (1948), Alvino Rey, Ray Anthony and Tex Beneke. Lewis gained a great deal of recognition in the jazz world for his work with Stan Kenton (1954-57), making the large ensemble swing hard. In 1957 he settled in Los Angeles, became a studio drummer and worked with the big bands of Terry Gibbs and Gerald Wilson. Lewis went to New York to play with Gerry Mulligan's Concert Jazz Band in 1960 and he toured Europe with Dizzy Gillespie (1961) and the Soviet Union with Benny Goodman (1962). In 1965 Lewis formed an orchestra in New York with Thad Jones, which grew to be one of the top big bands in jazz. When Jones surprised everyone by suddenly fleeing to Europe in 1979, Lewis became the orchestra's sole leader, playing regularly each Monday night at the Village Vanguard with the band up until his death. Mel Lewis recorded as a leader in the 1950s for San Francisco Jazz Records, Mode (reissued on VSOP) and Andex and, after Thad Jones left their orchestra, Mel Lewis recorded with his big band for Atlantic, Telarc and Music Masters. —*Scott Yanow*

Mel Lewis Sextet / Jul. 1957 / VSOP ✦✦✦✦
Mel Lewis, formerly with the Stan Kenton Orchestra (and at the

time a busy West Coast studio musician), had a rare opportunity to lead a record date in 1957 when he headed this sextet session for the MOD (Music of the Day) label; it has since been reissued on LP by VSOP With arrangements by Bob Brookmeyer, Marty Paich and Bill Holman, Lewis and his group (which features Charlie Mariano on alto and tenor, Bill Holman doubling on tenor and baritone, trumpeter Jack Sheldon, pianist Marty Paich, bassist Buddy Clark and the leader/drummer) perform originals by the three arrangers and Sheldon, in addition to the standard "You Took Advantage of Me." The enjoyable boppish music is quite colorful and will hopefully be reissued on CD eventually. —*Scott Yanow*

Mel Lewis and Friends / Jun. 18, 1976 / A&M ✦✦✦✦
This was a fine straight-ahead blowing bop date, with the only electricity being that produced by the players themselves. This was trumpeter Freddie Hubbard's best recorded effort in nearly five years and he deserved support for his work here…The trio also shined on "Wind Flower," a John Lewis-type loper by Sarah Cassey on which the horns sat out; Hank Jones, Ron Carter and Lewis all had outstanding feature spots…This was a faultless date with many high moments of musical substance. —*Bob Rusch, Cadence*

Naturally / Mar. 20, 1979–Mar. 21, 1979 / Telarc ✦✦✦✦
Topnotch recording with Lewis on the case as leader and drummer. —*Ron Wynn*

Live at Village Vanguard / Apr. 1980 / Gryphon ✦✦✦✦
A 1991 reissue of prime sessions, with Lewis at the helm of his longtime big band. High-octane solos and energetic compositions. —*Ron Wynn*

Mel Lewis Plays Herbie Hancock / Jul. 16, 1980 / Pausa ✦✦✦✦
Live at Montreux. A first-rate big-band date. —*Ron Wynn*

Mellifuous / Mar. 31, 1981 / Landmark ✦✦✦
Mel Lewis & The Jazz Orchestra / Jan. 7, 1982–Jan. 11, 1982 / Red Baron ✦✦✦✦✦
Recorded live at the Village Vanguard, the Mel Lewis big band (which at the time was in the process of finding its own sound) performs arrangements by Bob Brookmeyer. While letting the band swing and leaving space for such soloists as fluegelhornist Tom Harrell, altoist Dick Oatts, Joe Lovano's tenor, pianist Jim McNeely and altoist Kenny Garrett, Brookmeyer (who sits in on valve trombone during "Goodbye World") nevertheless constructs difficult charts that are more than a little inspired by modern classical music; this version of "My Funny Valentine" is quite eerie. Somehow the Mel Lewis Orchestra sounds relaxed on this rather complex music and the overall results are rewarding. —*Scott Yanow*

20 Years at the Village Vanguard / Mar. 20, 1985–Mar. 22, 1985 / Atlantic ✦✦✦✦
A portrait of his orchestra with fresh faces and sounds. —*Ron Wynn*

● **Definitive Thad Jones, Vol. 1** / Feb. 11, 1988–Feb. 15, 1988 / Music Masters ✦✦✦✦
The band playing from the book of longtime co-leader Thad Jones. —*Ron Wynn*

Definitive Thad Jones, Vol. 2 / Feb. 11, 1988–Feb. 15, 1988 / Music Masters ✦✦✦✦✦
A continuation of the series dedicated to Thad Jones' repertory. —*Ron Wynn*

Soft Lights and Hot Music / Feb. 11, 1988–Feb. 15, 1988 / Music Masters ✦✦✦✦
The Lost Art / Apr. 11, 1989–Apr. 12, 1989 / Music Masters ✦✦✦✦
To You: A Tribute to Mel Lewis / Sep. 10, 1990–Sep. 12, 1990 / Music Masters ✦✦✦✦

Ramsey Lewis
b. May 27, 1935, Chicago, IL
Piano, Keyboards / Instrumental Pop, Soul Jazz, Crossover
Ramsey Lewis has long straddled the boundary between bop-oriented jazz and pop music. Most of his recordings (particularly by the mid-'60s) were very accessible and attracted a large nonjazz audience. In 1956 he formed a trio with bassist Eldee Young and drummer Red Holt. From the start (1958) their records for Argo/Cadet were popular, although in the early days they had a strong jazz content. In 1958 Lewis also recorded with Max Roach and Lem Winchester. On the 1965 albums *The In Crowd* and

Hang On, Ramsey made the pianist into a major attraction and from that point on his records became much more predictable and pop-oriented. In 1966 his trio's personnel changed with bassist Cleveland Eaton and drummer Maurice White (later the founder of Earth, Wind and Fire) joining Lewis. In the 1970s Lewis often played electric piano although by later in the decade he was sticking to acoustic and hiring an additional keyboardist. He can still play melodic jazz when he wants to but Ramsey Lewis has mostly stuck to easy-listening pop music during the past 30 years. —*Scott Yanow*

Ramsey Lewis and the Gentlemen of Jazz / Feb. 9, 1958 / Argo ✦✦✦✦
Lem Winchester and the Ramsey Lewis Trio / Oct. 1958 / Argo ✦✦✦✦
Down to Earth / Nov. 6, 1958–Dec. 4, 1958 / Mercury ✦✦✦✦
Stretchin' Out / Feb. 23, 1960–Feb. 24, 1960 / Cadet ✦✦✦✦
Ramsey Lewis Trio in Chicago / Apr. 30, 1960 / Argo ✦✦✦✦
More Music from Soul / Feb. 16, 1961–Feb. 17, 1961 / Cadet ✦✦✦
Never on Sunday / Aug. 10, 1961–Aug. 11, 1961 / Cadet ✦✦✦
Bach to the Blues / Jan. 31, 1964 / Cadet ✦✦✦
The Ramsey Lewis Trio at the Bohemian Caverns / Jun. 4, 1964–Jun. 6, 1964 / Argo ✦✦✦✦
★ **The In Crowd** / May 13, 1965–May 14, 1965 / Chess ✦✦✦✦✦
The In Crowd was the Ramsey Lewis Trio's big hit of the time. The title track typified part of the Lewis style, but helped commercially lock it in to a narrow style. Recorded in May 1965 at the once hip Bohemian Caverns in Washington, D.C., it remains a pleasant easy listen. —*Bob Rusch, Cadence*

Hang on Ramsey / Oct. 14, 1965–Oct. 17, 1965 / Cadet ✦✦✦
Sun Goddess / 1974 / Columbia ✦✦
Tequila Mocking Bird / 1977 / Columbia ✦✦
Routes / 1980 / Columbia ✦✦✦
Standard Ramsey Lewis vehicle; good-to-routine pop-flavored and soulful material with some rousing piano solos and some not so energetic. Lewis was in the middle of another impressive run, making one hit album after another. —*Ron Wynn*

We Meet Again / 1990 / CBS ✦✦✦✦
Billy Taylor (p) takes the date, but Lewis shows chops he seldom taps these days. —*Ron Wynn*

Ivory Pyramid / Nov. 4, 1992 / GRP ✦✦
Sky Islands / 1993 / GRP ✦✦
Ramsey Lewis has long been content to record lightweight pop/R&B grooves. Occasionally on this set the acoustic pianist (whose backup crew includes guitarist Henry Johnson and keyboardist Michael Logan) sounds like he would like to break away a bit from the predictable but he keeps the impulse in check. There is little to distinguish this CD from his previous few. —*Scott Yanow*

David Liebman
b. Sep. 4, 1946, New York, NY
Flute, Soprano Saxophone, Tenor Saxophone / Avant-Garde, Post Bop
Dave Liebman has developed through time to become one of the top soprano saxophonists in jazz. A highly individual and explorative (yet versatile) improviser who can stretch from bop to free, Liebman studied early on with Lennie Tristano and Charles Lloyd. He gained important experience playing with Ten Wheel Drive (1970), Elvin Jones (1971–73) and Miles Davis' fusion group (1973–74). Liebman formed Lookout Farm in 1974, the first of several groups (including Quest in the 1980s) that teamed his reeds with pianist Richie Beirach. By the late '80s he had largely dropped the tenor to concentrate on soprano and occasionally flute although he made a rare recording on tenor for Double-Time in 1995. Dave Liebman, who is very active in jazz education and has written several books, has recorded for a countless number of labels through the years as a leader, including PM, ECM, Horizon, Timeless, Palo Alto, Impulse, Soul Note, Heads Up, Storyville, Owl, CMP, Red and Candid. —*Scott Yanow*

Open Sky / May 1, 1972–Jun. 10, 1972 / PM ✦✦✦✦
Adventurous pieces. A triumphant exhibition of multi-reed versatility. Tremendous work in a small-combo format. —*Ron Wynn*

Lookout Farm / Oct. 10, 1973–Oct. 11, 1973 / ECM ✦✦✦✦✦
Liebman at the top-of-the-heap as an unabashed improviser. A

high-water mark for this period. Completely original post-Tristano piano of Richard Beirach. —*Michael G. Nastos*

Drum Ode / May 1974 / ECM ✦✦✦

Sweet Hands / Jul. 25, 1975–Jul. 30, 1975 / Horizon ✦✦

Forgotten Fantasies / Nov. 18, 1975–Nov. 20, 1975 / Horizon ✦✦✦✦

Light'n up Please! / May 19, 1976–Sept., 1976/ Horizon ✦✦

Pendulum / Feb. 4, 1978–Feb. 5, 1978 / Artists House ✦✦✦✦✦

Dedications / Sep. 1979 / CMP ✦✦✦✦
'79 septet performances led by saxophonist David Liebman. These mix standards, originals, blues and ballads, with strong, intense solos from Liebman, fine arrangements and ensemble interaction and standout contributions from pianist Richie Beiarch and bassist Eddie Gomez. —*Ron Wynn*

What It Is / 1980 / Columbia ✦✦✦

If Only They Knew / Jul. 14, 1980 / Impulse! ✦✦✦

Quest / Dec. 28, 1981–Dec. 29, 1981 / Palo Alto ✦✦✦✦
Quartet with Liebman, Beirach (p), George Mraz (b) and Al Foster (d). They hit hard and heavy, or at times mournfully wistful. An excellent document of this group. —*Michael G. Nastos*

Sweet Fury / Mar. 23, 1984–Mar. 24, 1984 / From Bebop To Now ✦✦✦✦
Mid-'80s blues, funk and straight-ahead sessions featuring tenor saxophonist David Liebman. A fine soloist and underrated composer, Liebman can make standard blues seem intense and loosen up rigid funk material, while stretching out on tenor or soprano and adding some punch to routine mainstream numbers. —*Ron Wynn*

The Loneliness of a Long-Distance Runner / Nov. 1985–Dec. 1985 / CMP ✦✦✦✦
David Liebman did it alone (solo and ensemble multi-dubbing) on *The Loneliness of a Long Distance Runner*. The "distance" on this very personal program conception was one of one's life span, with Liebman viewing the importance of the race being not the finality but the process of the experience. Included with this work are notes by the artist, which may or may not help the listener relate to the music by the suggested imagery of the notes or titles. The multi overdubs were particularly well integrated, giving much of this a WSQ (World Saxophone Quartet)-like texture under Liebman's bluesy Ornette Coleman-like lines (a lonely woman-like phrase recurs throughout)…The overdubbing adds a great textural emotion and conveys the involvement and harmony one expects from a group. Over this the soprano saxman involves himself in some outstanding improvisations, maintaining a tension, passion and involvement which is unfaltering. —*Bob Rusch*

Quest II / Apr. 17, 1986 / Storyville ✦✦✦✦
Quartet set with Liebman, Richie Beirach (p), Ron McClure (b) and Billy Hart (d). —*Ron Wynn*

★ **Homage to John Coltrane** / Jan. 27, 1987–Jan. 28, 1987 / Owl ✦✦✦✦✦
1991 reissue. An intense tribute to one of Liebman's prime influences. —*Ron Wynn*

Midpoint / Apr. 21, 1987–Apr. 22, 1987 / Storyville ✦✦✦✦

The Energy of the Chance / 1988 / Heads Up ✦✦✦

Trio + One / May 1, 1988–May 2, 1988 / Owl ✦✦✦✦✦
Soprano master doing variation of familiar themes and out-and-out original material. With Dave Holland (b) and Jack DeJohnette (d). Very worthwhile new music. —*Michael G. Nastos*

Quest / Natural Selection / Jun. 1988 / Pathfinder ✦✦✦✦

Chant / Jul. 1989 / CMP ✦✦✦✦

★ **The Tree** / Apr. 24, 1990 / Soul Note ✦✦✦✦✦
This rather interesting set of solo soprano saxophone explorations by David Liebman (one of the greats on that instrument) has an odd concept that works. Liebman plays a six-part suite that has titles of "Roots," "Trunk," "Limbs," "Branches," "Twigs" and "Leaves" and then does a second version, playing the sections in the opposite order. The sections farthest from the "Roots" are the most advanced, although all of these movements are fairly free. It's well worth several listens. —*Scott Yanow*

● **West Side Story Today** / Oct. 13, 1990–Oct. 17, 1990 / Owl ✦✦✦✦✦

Classic Ballads / Dec. 1990–Jan. 1991 / Candid ✦✦✦✦
Outstanding straight-ahead and mainstream date by veteran sax-

ophonist Dave Liebman, dedicated to Natalie Visentin. Liebman is great in any style, but this time sounds more convincing and passionate than on any recent traditional set he's done. It's a trio setting, with pianist Vic Juris and drummer Steve Gilmore. —*Ron Wynn*

Joy / Mar. 19, 1992–Mar. 20, 1992 / Candid ✦✦✦✦✦
David Liebman has recorded several tributes to John Coltrane through the years (even though he really doesn't sound like him) and his Candid CD is one of his most rewarding. Utilizing a strong college orchestra, some guests and (on "After the Rain") the 17 flutes and five bass clarinets of the JMU Flute Choir, Liebman performs six of Coltrane's top compositions from the 1961–66 period. He sticks to soprano except for some Indian flute on "India" and pays tribute to Coltrane's creative spirit rather than just imitating his solos. "Alabama" and "Naima" are passionate ballads, "India" sounds exotic and the medley of "Joy" and "Selflessness" are free and intense. There are strong individual moments from pianist Butch Taylor and trumpeter John D'Earth, although Liebman is the main soloist throughout. He tackles Coltrane's music on its own terms and the results are fresh and often quite exciting. —*Scott Yanow*

Setting the Standard / May 1992 / Red ✦✦✦✦

Seasons / Dec. 27, 1992–Jan. 19, 1993 / Soul Note ✦✦✦✦
David Liebman is at his best in pastoral, ethereal situations. This trio session, recorded in 1992 and '93, contains both lengthy tunes and shorter works in which Liebman's intense soprano sax and flute and more robust tenor solos are nicely supported by Billy Hart's sensitive yet assertive drumming and Cecil McBee's bass work, which provides whatever is necessary, from interaction to competition. The three never become detached or predictable and don't allow the music to lose its edge. The songs don't have a propulsive rhythmic quality, but never lack appeal or distinction. —*Ron Wynn*

Songs For My Daughter / May 1994 / Soul Note ✦✦✦✦

Lighthouse All Stars

Group / Bop, Cool
Bassist Howard Rumsey initiated a jazz policy at the Lighthouse Cafe in Hermosa Beach, CA, in 1949. His Lighthouse All-Stars performed on a nightly basis and on Sundays there was traditionally a 12-hour jam session. The Contemporary label recorded Rumsey's groups on a fairly regular basis during 1952–57 and such major players as Shorty Rogers, Maynard Ferguson, Rolf Ericson, Stu Williamson, Conte Candoli, Milt Bernhart, Bob Enevoldsen, Frank Rosolino, Jimmy Giuffre, Bob Cooper, Bud Shank, Hampton Hawes, Marty Paich, Claude Williamson, Sonny Clark, Shelly Manne, Max Roach, Stan Levey and guests Miles Davis and Chet Baker were among the participants. The music was essentially bebop with some cooler-toned performances, particularly the ones starring Cooper on oboe or English horn and Shank on flute. The Lighthouse All-Stars only made one record after 1957 (an outing for Philips during 1961–62) before passing into history. In the 1980s the group was revived for some appearances and further Contemporary recordings; the last version featured Shorty Rogers, Cooper, Shank, Bill Perkins, Pete Jolly, Monty Budwig and Larance Marable. —*Scott Yanow*

Sunday Jazz á la Lighthouse / Feb. 21, 1953 / Original Jazz Classics ✦✦✦✦✦
Lots of Jimmy Giuffre (reeds) and Shorty Rogers (tpt). Frank Patchen on piano. Ten-piece all-stars. Live at The Lighthouse in Hermosa Beach. Top-notch version of group. —*Michael G. Nastos*

In the Solo Spotlight / Aug. 17, 1954–Mar. 12, 1957 / Original Jazz Classics ✦✦✦✦✦

★ **Music for Lighthousekeeping** / Oct. 2, 1956–Dec. 16, 1956 / Original Jazz Classics ✦✦✦✦✦
Sextet with Bob Cooper's tenor sax and Bill Holman's music (four selections) dominating. Excellent "Taxi War Dance" and Sonny Clark's "I-Deal." Also features Conte Candoli and Frank Rosolino. —*Michael G. Nastos*

Kirk Lightsey

b. Feb. 15, 1937, Detroit, MI
Piano / Hard Bop, Post Bop
A pianist who is not a trendsetter but is consistently excellent,

Kirk Lightsey long ago developed his own sound within the hard bop tradition. He started playing piano when he was five, although he also played clarinet while in high school. Lightsey worked in Detroit and California in the early '60s, often accompanying singers. He gained some attention in 1965 when he recorded with Sonny Stitt and was on five Prestige records with Chet Baker. However Lightsey mostly had low-profile gigs until he toured with Dexter Gordon (1979–83) and became part of the Leaders (starting in the late '80s). Kirk Lightsey has recorded with Jimmy Raney, Clifford Jordan, Woody Shaw, David Murray and Harold Land among others and has led his own sessions for Criss Cross and Sunnyside, including piano duets with Harold Danko. —*Scott Yanow*

Lightsey 1 / Sep. 22, 1982+Oct. 5, 1982 / Sunnyside ✦✦✦✦✦

Lightsey 2 / Sep. 22, 1982+Aug. 19, 1983 / Sunnyside ✦✦✦✦✦

Isotope / Feb. 1983 / Criss Cross ✦✦✦✦

★ **Shorter by Two** / Jul. 19, 1983+Jul. 21, 1983 / Sunnyside ✦✦✦✦✦

Everything Happens to Me / 1983 / Timeless ✦✦✦✦

Lightsey Live / Jun. 28, 1985 / Sunnyside ✦✦✦✦
For this solo concert Lightsey played one original along with works by Tony Williams, Thelonious Monk, Rodgers & Hart, Wayne Shorter and Cole Porter, a rather distinct group of composers. Even so, all the music here became a collaboration with the pianist whose individual style composes itself on the music as well. —*Bob Rusch*

Everything Is Changed / Jun. 4, 1986–Jun. 5, 1986 / Sunnyside ✦✦✦✦
This excellent album finds pianist Kirk Lightsey exploring five standards and his bassist Santi Wilson Debriano's "Nandi" with a solid quartet. Drummer Eddie Gladden is an asset, but trumpeter Jerry Gonzales (whose muted statements on four of the six selections recall the lyricism of Miles Davis) often comes close to stealing the show. Lightsey, who sounds particularly strong on the ballads, is the obvious leader, and his tasteful yet swinging piano is a joy to hear. *Scott Yanow*

● **From Kirk to Nat** / Nov. 1990 / Criss Cross ✦✦✦✦✦
One of the main reasons why this tribute to the Nat King Cole Trio by Kirk Lightsey is a success is that Lightsey (who is from a much later bop-influenced generation) sounds nothing like Cole. Featured in a trio with guitarist Kevin Eubanks and bassist Rufus Reid, Lightsey performs a set of music reminiscent of Cole but several of the songs (including his original "Kirk's Blues," "Never Let Me Go" and "Close Enough for Love") were never actually recorded by Cole; Lightsey takes surprisingly effective vocals on the latter two songs. —*Scott Yanow*

Abbey Lincoln (Anna Marie Woolridge)

b. Aug. 6, 1930, Chicago, IL
Vocals / Avant-Garde, Post Bop, Standards
As with her hero Billie Holiday, Abbey Lincoln always means the lyrics she sings. A dramatic performer whose interpretations are full of truth and insight, Lincoln actually began her career as a fairly lightweight supper-club singer. She went through several name changes (including Anna Marie, Gaby Lee and Gaby Woolridge) before settling on Abbey Lincoln. She recorded with Benny Carter in 1956 and performed a number in the 1957 Hollywood film *The Girl Can't Help It*. Lincoln's first of three albums for Riverside (1957–59) had Max Roach on drums and he was a major influence on her; she began to be choosy about the songs she sang and to give words the proper emotional intensity. Lincoln held her own on her early dates with such sidemen as Kenny Dorham, Sonny Rollins, Wynton Kelly, Curtis Fuller and Benny Golson. She was quite memorable on Roach's *Freedom Now Suite*, showing some very uninhibited emotions. Lincoln's Candid date *Straight Ahead* (1961) had among its players Roach, Booker Little, Eric Dolphy and Coleman Hawkins and she made some important appearances on Roach's Impulse! album *Percussion Bitter Suite*.

Abbey Lincoln and Max Roach were married in 1962, an association that lasted until 1970. They worked together for a while but Lincoln (who found it harder to get work in jazz due to the political nature of some of her music) became involved in acting and did not record as a leader during 1962–72. She finally recorded for Inner City in 1973 and gradually became more active in jazz. Her two Billie Holiday tribute albums for Enja (1987) showed

listeners that the singer was still in her prime and she has recorded several excellent sets for Verve in the 1990s. Because she puts so much thought into each of her recordings, it is not an understatement to say that every Abbey Lincoln set is well worth owning. —*Scott Yanow*

Affair / 1956 / Liberty ✦✦✦
This CD reissues the music from Abbey Lincoln's first LP along with two slightly earlier numbers originally available as a single. Lincoln was at the time making the transition from a potential sex symbol and lounge singer to becoming a dramatic jazz interpreter. Her voice was recognizable even at this early stage but some of the ballads are more lightweight than the ones she would be performing in the near future. Backed by anonymous orchestras arranged by Benny Carter, Jack Montrose and Marty Paich, Abbey Lincoln's straightforward delivery was already impressive and pleasing. —*Scott Yanow*

★ **That's Him** / Oct. 28, 1957 / Original Jazz Classics ✦✦✦✦✦
Striking cuts from the late '50s. Sonny Rollins (ts) is a dynamic guest star. —*Ron Wynn*

★ **It's Magic** / Aug. 23, 1958 / Original Jazz Classics ✦✦✦✦✦

Abbey Is Blue / Mar. 25, 1959–Mar. 26, 1959 / Original Jazz Classics ✦✦✦✦✦

★ **Freedom Now Suite** / 1960 / Candid ✦✦✦✦✦
Definitive social protest and jazz. Lincoln and her then-husband Max Roach were a great team. —*Ron Wynn*

★ **Straight Ahead** / Feb. 22, 1961 / Candid ✦✦✦✦✦
Reissued several times since it originally came out on a Candid LP, this is one of Abbey Lincoln's greatest recordings. It is a testament to the credibility of her very honest music (and her talents) that Abbey's sidemen on this date include the immortal tenor saxophonist Coleman Hawkins (who takes a memorable solo on "Blue Monk"), Eric Dolphy on flute and alto, trumpeter Booker Little (whose melancholy tone is very important in the ensembles), pianist Mal Waldron and drummer Max Roach. Highpoints include "When Malindy Sings," "Blue Monk," Billie Holiday's "Left Alone" and "African Lady." —*Scott Yanow*

People in Me / Jun. 23, 1973–Jun. 27, 1973 / Inner City ✦✦✦✦
As good as she gets on this recording. A perennial favorite for many. With David Liebman (soprano/tenor and flute), Al Foster (d), Mtume (per) and two Japanese musicians. "Living Room," "Africa," "Naturally," and the title track stand out. Proud music. —*Michael G. Nastos*

Golden Lady / 1981 / Inner City ✦✦✦✦✦
Early '80s material by neglected vocalist Abbey Lincoln. Her intonation, delivery, phrasing and style are unique and sometimes so distinctive they seem wrong for a song. But Lincoln makes every number come alive, giving even overly familiar lyrics fresh, vibrant treatments. —*Ron Wynn*

Abbey Sings Billie, Vol. 1 / Nov. 6, 1987–Nov. 7, 1987 / Enja ✦✦✦✦

Talking to the Sun / Nov. 1983 / Enja ✦✦✦✦
A 1990 release of a session with Lincoln singing and accompanied by some prime young lions. —*Ron Wynn*

Abbey Sings Billie, Vol. 2 / Nov. 6, 1987+Nov. 7, 1987 / Enja ✦✦✦✦✦
Abbey Lincoln is the perfect person to pay tribute to Billie Holiday. She knew Lady Day during her last years and, like Holiday, Lincoln has always lived the words she sings and chosen to only interpret lyrics that have great meaning to her. Her expressive powers have been quite strong throughout her career and there are plenty of dramatic moments on this disc, along with its first volume. tenor saxophonist Harold Vick, who would die suddenly within days of these sessions, is quite effective, as is the supportive rhythm section. Abbey Lincoln shows off her versatility in such diverse numbers as "Gimme a Pigfoot," "Don't Explain" and "Please Don't Talk About Me When I'm Gone." —*Scott Yanow*

The World Is Falling Down / Feb. 21, 1990–Feb. 27, 1990 / Verve ✦✦✦✦

You Gotta Pay the Band / Feb. 25, 1991–Feb. 26, 1991 / Verve ✦✦✦✦
Studio date featuring Stan Getz one last time and Hank Jones Trio. Maxine Roach on viola for two cuts. Six cuts feature either words and/or music written by Moseka. She has lost absolutely none of her brilliance or passion for singing, interpreting and creating. —*Michael G. Nastos*

Devil's Got Your Tongue / Feb. 24, 1992–Feb. 25, 1992 / Verve ✦✦✦✦

When There Is Love / Oct. 4, 1992–Oct. 6, 1992 / Verve ✦✦✦✦

A Turtle's Dream / May 19, 1994–Nov. 1994 / Verve ✦✦✦✦

John Lindberg

b. Mar. 16, 1959, Royal Oak, MI
Bass / Avant-Garde
A steady, sympathetic accompanist and solid soloist, bassist John Lindberg's best known for his work in The String Trio of New York. Lindberg studied music in Ann Arbor, Michigan, before moving to New York in 1977. He played and recorded in The Human Arts Ensemble with Joseph Bowie and Bobo Shaw in the late '70s and worked with Anthony Braxton from 1978 to 1985. They performed in both Europe and America. Lindberg was a founding member of The String Trio of New York in 1979 and currently remains with the ensemble. He also worked in a trio with Jimmy Lyons and Sunny Murray in 1980. Lindberg lived and worked in Paris from 1980 to 1983, leading small combos, playing solo and working in a group led by Murray that also featured John Tchicai. Lindberg has recorded as a leader for Cecma, Black Saint, West Wind, ITM and Sound Aspects. —*Ron Wynn*

Give and Take / Nov. 1982 / Black Saint ✦✦✦✦

The East Side Suite / Jul. 1983 / Sound Aspects ✦✦✦✦

★ **Dodging Bullets** / Jun. 8, 1992–Jun. 9, 1992 / Black Saint ✦✦✦✦✦

Quartet Afterstorm / Mar. 18, 1994–Mar. 20, 1994 / Black Saint ✦✦✦✦✦

Paul Lingle

b. Dec. 3, 1902, Denver, CO **d.** Oct. 30, 1962, Honolulu, HI
Piano / Dixieland, Ragtime
Paul Lingle was a local legend in San Francisco during the 1940s. A talented stride pianist who also played ragtime, Lingle was a fan of Jelly Roll Morton. He started playing piano when he was six and first worked professionally in San Francisco in the 1920s. Lingle was Al Jolson's accompanist in the late '20s, recording the soundtrack of some of his first sound films. He spent the 1930s working in radio and with Al Zohn's jazz band in San Francisco. During the Dixieland revival of the 1940s, Lingle at first was a piano tuner in Santa Cruz but by 1944 was playing in San Francisco clubs, generally solo. When Leadbelly and Bunk Johnson passed through town, they both asked for him. In 1952 Lingle moved to Honolulu, where he continued playing up until his death. Unfortunately he was reluctant to record throughout his career and his only studio session resulted in just eight songs cut for Good Time Jazz in 1952. However 3 1/2 albums of private tapes from 1951–52 were released posthumously on the Euphonic label that allow listeners to get a fuller picture of Paul Lingle's talent. —*Scott Yanow*

Ray Linn

b. Oct. 20, 1920, Chicago, IL
Trumpet / Bop, Dixieland
A versatile trumpeter, Ray Linn started out as a modernist and has ended up as a revivalist. Linn began his professional career playing with the orchestras of Tommy Dorsey (1938–41) and Woody Herman (1941–42); he would rejoin Herman on three occasions (1945, 1947 and 1955–59). Linn also worked on and off with Jimmy Dorsey (1942–45), Benny Goodman (1943 and 1947), Artie Shaw (1944–46) and Boyd Raeburn (1946). While with Raeburn his solos were quite advanced for the period. Linn became a studio musician after moving to Los Angeles in 1945 but had the opportunity to work with Bob Crosby (1950–51) and many of the top West Coast jazz players in the 1950s in addition to Woody Herman. From the 1960s on he mostly worked in television. Although his sessions as a leader in 1946 (which resulted in eight songs) had such titles as "The Mad Monk" and "Blop Blah," Ray Linn's later albums for Trend (1978) and Discovery (1980) were Dixieland-oriented. —*Scott Yanow*

Chicago Jazz / Sep. 28, 1978 / Trend ✦✦✦
Although Ray Linn had had a diverse career with stints with a variety of swing bands (Boyd Raeburn, the Sauter-Finegan Orchestra and Bill Holman), by the 1970s he was mostly playing Dixieland. This spirited direct-to-disc LP matches Linn's trumpet with Henry Cuesta (doubling on clarinet and baritone), tenor great Eddie Miller, trombonist Bob Havens, pianist Dave

Frishberg, bassist Richard Maloof and drummer Jack Davenport on six veteran swing and Dixieland standards, a pair of his originals (including "Bix's Bugle") and Frishberg's "North Hollywood Rotary Parade." Although not essential, the music on this tasteful set is quite enjoyable. —*Scott Yanow*

● **Empty Suit Blues** / Sep. 26, 1980 / Discovery ✦✦✦✦

Jeff Linsky

b. 1952, Los Angeles, CA
Guitar / Bop, Brazilian Jazz
An appealing guitarist who specializes in Brazilian and Latin jazz, Jeff Linsky was primarily self-taught, although he studied briefly with Spanish guitarist Vicente Gomez and Joe Pass. He lived in Hawaii during 1972–88 before moving to the San Francisco Bay Area. Linsky has thus far recorded easily enjoyable albums for Kamei (1991–92), GSP (1992) and Concord (1988 and 1994). —*Scott Yanow*

Up Late / 1988 / Concord Jazz ✦✦✦✦

Simpatico / 1991 / Kamei ✦✦✦✦

● **Solo** / 1992 / GSP ✦✦✦✦✦

Rendezvous / 1992 / Kamei ✦✦✦✦

Angel's Serenade / 1994 / Concord Picante ✦✦✦✦✦

Melba Liston

b. Jan. 13, 1926, Kansas City, MO
Trombone, Arranger / Bop, Hard Bop
A fine section trombonist, Melba Liston achieved her greatest fame as an arranger, particularly for her projects with Randy Weston. She grew up in California and played with Gerald Wilson's Orchestra starting in 1943. Her most notable recording as a soloist was with Dexter Gordon in 1947. Liston worked with Count Basie (1948–49) Dizzy Gillespie's big band (1949–50) and backed Billie Holiday, but then spent a few years outside of music. She toured with and wrote for Dizzy Gillespie's orchestra (1956–57) and visited Europe with Quincy Jones' big band (1959), staying with that orchestra into 1961. Liston then became a freelance arranger, working on sessions led by Weston, Johnny Griffin and Milt Jackson, writing for the studios, teaching and occasionally playing. A serious stroke has confined her to a wheelchair since 1985 but Melba Liston has written for several recent Randy Weston projects. —*Scott Yanow*

And Her Bones / Dec. 22, 1958–Dec. 24, 1958 / Metrojazz ✦✦✦✦

Booker Little

b. Apr. 2, 1938, Memphis, TN, **d.** Oct. 5, 1961, New York, NY
Trumpet / Post Bop
The first trumpeter emerging after Clifford Brown's death to gain his own sound, Booker Little had a tremendous amount of potential before his premature death. He began on trumpet when he was 12 and played with Johnny Griffin and the MJT + 3 while attending Chicago Conservatory. Little was with Max Roach (1958–59) and then freelanced in New York. He recorded with Roach and Abbey Lincoln, was on John Coltrane's *Africa/Brass* album and was well-documented during a July 1961 gig at the Five Spot with Eric Dolphy. Little had a memorable melancholy sound and his interval jumps looked toward the avant-garde, but he also swung like a hard bopper. Booker Little led four sessions (one album apiece for United Artists, Time, Candid and Bethlehem) but died of uremia at the age of 23, a particularly tragic loss. —*Scott Yanow*

Booker Little 4 and Max Roach / Oct. 1958 / Blue Note ✦✦✦✦✦
A tremendous showcase of early-'60s sessions that has exceptional musicians and wonderful compositions. Everyone from Phineas and Calvin Newborn to George Coleman and Max Roach. —*Ron Wynn*

Booker Little / Apr. 13, 1960–Apr. 15, 1960 / Bainbridge ✦✦✦✦
A session with the excellent trumpeter Booker Little playing in a slightly more relaxed fashion than usual. But the casual atmosphere didn't prevent him from contributing some extraordinary solos, or coaxing similar performances from his group that included pianists Tommy Flanagan or Wynton Kelly, bassist Scott LaFaro and drummer Roy Haynes. This session has been reissued. —*Ron Wynn*

★ **Out Front** / Mar. 17, 1961–Apr. 4, 1961 / Candid ✦✦✦✦✦
Booker Little was the first trumpet soloist to emerge in jazz after the death of Clifford Brown to have his own sound. His tragically brief life (he died at age 23 later in 1961) cut short what would have certainly been a major career. Little, on this sextet date with multireedist Eric Dolphy, trombonist Julian Priester and drummer Max Roach, shows that his playing was really beyond bebop. His seven now-obscure originals (several of which deserve to be revived) are challenging for the soloists and there are many strong moments during these consistently challenging and satisfying performances. — *Scott Yanow*

★ **Victory and Sorrow** / Aug. 1961–Sep. 1961 / Bethlehem ✦✦✦✦✦
Although he only lived to be 23 and recorded for just a little over three years, Booker Little proved to be one of the top young trumpeters of his era. *Victory and Sorrow* was his fourth and final recording as a leader. Little's melancholy tone is heartbreaking on the date's lone standard "If I Should Lose You" and he contributed all of the other six selections. With fine playing from tenor saxophonist George Coleman, trombonist Julian Priester, pianist Don Friedman, bassist Reggie Workman and drummer Pete LaRoca, this advanced session has many touching and hard-swinging moments. — *Scott Yanow*

Charles Lloyd

b. Mar. 15, 1938, Memphis, TN
Flute, Tenor Saxophone / Hard Bop, Crossover
During 1966–69 Charles Lloyd led one of the most popular groups in jazz, a unit that played at the rock palace Fillmore West in San Francisco and toured the U.S.S.R. Lloyd's music, although generally a bit melodic, was not watered-down and managed to catch on for several years during a time when jazz was at its low point in popularity.

Lloyd played locally in Memphis (including with B.B. King and Bobby Blue Bland) and then in the mid-'50s moved to Los Angeles to attend USC. During his six years in L.A., he gigged around town and played alto with Gerald Wilson's Orchestra. In 1961 he joined the Chico Hamilton Quintet on flute and tenor, making his recording debut and gaining a strong reputation. During 1964–65 he was with the Cannonball Adderley Sextet and then in mid-1965 formed his own group. By 1966 the Charles Lloyd Quartet included Keith Jarrett, Cecil McBee (who was later succeeded by Ron McClure) and Jack DeJohnette and the band was the hit of the 1966 Monterey Jazz Festival, recorded steadily, toured Europe six times and was remarkably popular. Lloyd, whose most famous composition is "Forest Flower," played tenor in a soft-toned version of John Coltrane, while his lyrical flute playing is more original. After his group changed personnel in 1969, Lloyd gradually faded out of music, becoming a teacher of transcendental meditation. The few records he made in the 1970s were quite spiritual and bordered on New Age. However, pianist Michel Petrucciani looked Lloyd up in the early '80s and persuaded him to return to active playing. For a period Petrucciani was in his quartet. By the late '80s Lloyd had a new group with pianist Bobo Stenson, bassist Palle Danielsson and drummer Jon Christensen that regularly recorded for ECM. Charles Lloyd, whose style remains virtually unchanged from the 1960s, has recorded as a leader for Columbia, Atlantic, Kapp, A&M, Blue Note and ECM. — *Scott Yanow*

Discovery! The Charles Lloyd Quartet / May 27, 1964+May 29, 1964 / Columbia ✦✦✦✦

Of Course, of Course / Mar. 8, 1965+May 1965 / Columbia ✦✦✦✦

Dream Weaver / Mar. 20, 1966 / Atlantic ✦✦✦✦✦
Sweeping flute, craggy tenor sax solos and fine piano by Keith Jarrett. — *Ron Wynn*

★ **Forest Flower** / Sep. 8, 1966+Sep. 18, 1966 / Atlantic ✦✦✦✦✦
Live at Monterey. With Keith Jarrett. Definitive Lloyd. — *Michael G. Nastos*

Charles Lloyd in Europe / Oct. 29, 1966 / Atlantic ✦✦✦✦✦

Live at the Fillmore in San Francisco / Jan. 27, 1967 / Atlantic ✦✦✦✦
An album where the menu is uneven, but the tenor sax solos are entrancing. — *Ron Wynn*

Charles Lloyd in the Soviet Union / May 14, 1967 / Atlantic ✦✦✦✦✦
The Charles Lloyd Quartet was (along with Cannonball Adderley's

band) the most popular group in jazz during the latter half of the 1960s. Lloyd somehow managed this feat without watering down his music or adopting a pop repertoire. A measure of the band's popularity is that Lloyd and his sidemen (pianist Keith Jarrett, bassist Ron McClure and drummer Jack DeJohnette) were able to have a very successful tour of the Soviet Union during a period when jazz was still being discouraged by the communists. This well-received festival appearance has four lengthy performances, including an 18-minute version of "Sweet Georgia Bright" and Lloyd (who has always had a soft-toned Coltrane-influenced tenor style and a more distinctive voice on flute) is in top form. — *Scott Yanow*

Warm Waters / Jan. 1971 / Kapp ✦✦

Waves / 1972 / A&M ✦✦

Big Sur Tapestry / 1979 / Pacific Arts ✦

Montreux (1982) / Jul. 1982 / Elektra ✦✦✦✦
A live recording with Michel Petrucciani (p). — *Ron Wynn*

Night in Copenhagen / 1983 / Blue Note ✦✦✦✦
On this mid-'80s set, Lloyd played with the brashness and rough edge that characterized his late-'60s dates, although his tenor was not as assertive or animated. Indeed, it is Lloyd's solos on flute and the Chinese oboe that are the real eye-openers. He is more energized on those, as he strains and struggles to extend his solo beyond simple lines and statements and ends up challenging the musicians through his own struggles. Special guest Bobby McFerrin (then still a struggling "jazz" vocalist) chimes in nicely on "Third Floor Richard." Lloyd's days in the spotlight were pretty much over by 1969, but the caliber of this session shows that he was foolish to waste his time on the sidelines. — *Ron Wynn*

Fish out of Water / Jul. 1989 / ECM ✦✦✦
This new release offers quasi-mystical themes, shimmering horn riffs and flute melodies, plus fine keyboard contributions from Bob Stenson and decent, though hardly aggressive, rhythm section work by bassist Palle Danielsson and drummer Jon Christensen. — *Ron Wynn*

Notes from Big Sur / Nov. 1991 / ECM ✦✦✦✦

The Call / Jul. 1993 / ECM ✦✦✦✦

Acoustic Masters I / Jul. 1993 / Atlantic ✦✦✦✦✦

All My Relations / 1995 / ECM ✦✦✦✦✦
This CD by the Charles Lloyd Quartet avoids fitting into any of the stereotypes that one might have about ECM's recordings. Pianist Bobo Stenson has carved his own identity out of the styles of Bill Evans and Keith Jarrett, drummer Billy Hart is stimulating in support and Anders Jormin provides a walking bass on many of the tracks; a rarity for ECM sessions. As one might expect, the main focus is on Charles Lloyd, whose playing during the past decade has been some of the finest of his career. He mostly sticks to tenor (just playing flute on "Little Peace" and Chinese oboe on the very brief "Milarepa"), and although traces of John Coltrane's sound will always be in his tone, Lloyd comes up with quite a few original ideas. He is best on "Thelonious Theonnlyus" (which has a slight calypso feel to it), the episodic "Cape to Cairo Suite" (a tribute to Nelson Mandela), a long tenor/drums duet on "All My Relations" (which is a mix between "Chasin' the 'Trane" and "Bessie's Blues") and the brooding spiritual "Hymn to the Mother." A strong effort. — *Scott Yanow*

Didier Lockwood

b. Feb. 11, 1956, Calais, France
Violin / Post Bop, Fusion
Didier Lockwood has had a diverse career, ranging from fusion to swing and advanced hard bop. In the 1980s he was considered the next in a line of great French violinists after Stephane Grappelli and Jean-Luc Ponty, but he has maintained a fairly low profile in the 1990s. Lockwood began studying violin when he was six. Ten years later he stopped his formal training and joined a rock group. He played in Paris with Aldo Romano and Daniel Humair among others, met Grappelli and toured with him. He had a fusion group called Surya and recorded with Tony Williams around the same period of time (1979). Didier Lockwood played in the United States on several occasions in the 1980s and recorded an acoustic album in 1986 with fellow violinists John Blake and Michal Urbaniak. — *Scott Yanow*

New World / Feb. 20, 1979–Feb. 22, 1979 / PA/USA ✦✦✦
● **Surya** / 1980 / Inner City ✦✦✦✦✦
Didier Lockwood Group / Dec. 1983+Jan. 1984 / Gramavision ✦✦✦✦
Out of the Blue / Apr. 1985 / Gramavision ✦✦✦✦
1 2 3 4 / 1987 / Nova ✦✦
Phoenix 90 / Jun. 1990–Jul. 1990 / Gramavision ✦✦
Lockwood Didier Group. Lockwood makes a slight comeback as a player, but the material is still light. —*Ron Wynn*

Mike Longo

b. Mar. 19, 1939, Cincinnati, OH
Piano / Bop
Mike Longo is best-known as a reliable and versatile player who was the pianist with Dizzy Gillespie during 1966–73. He started taking piano lessons when he was three, played professionally when he was 15 and while in high school in Ft. Lauderdale he had the opportunity to play with Cannonball Adderley. In 1960 Longo worked at the Metropole in New York with Red Allen and Coleman Hawkins, he spent 1961 living in Toronto (where he studied with Oscar Peterson) and then returned to New York where he accompanied some singers. Mike Longo recorded with Gillespie during his period with the great trumpeter and led a few of his own sessions for Mainstream, Pablo (1976) and Consolidated Artists (1981), but has not been heard from much since. —*Scott Yanow*
● **Talk with the Spirits** / Jan. 1976 / Pablo ✦✦✦
Solo Recital / Jun. 1982 / Consolidated Artists ✦✦✦

Eddy Louiss

b. May 12, 1941, Paris, France
Organ / Hard Bop
Eddy Louiss has spent most of his career leading his own group in France, but twice has made particularly notable recordings, both on organ. He had sung as a member of the Double Six (1961–63), played piano with Johnny Griffin in the mid-'60s and worked at times with Kenny Clarke and Jean-Luc Ponty. But he is best-known for recording *Dynasty* with Stan Getz (1971) and for his recent duet set with pianist Michel Petrucciani (1994) on Dreyfus. —*Scott Yanow*
★ **Eddy Louiss/Michael Petrucciani** / Jun. 14, 1994–Jun. 16, 1994 / Dreyfus ✦✦✦✦✦
Organ-piano duet recordings are quite rare in jazz history, making this successful collaboration rather historical in its own way, It is particularly interesting to hear pianist Michel Petrucciani, who usually dominates his own recordings, being matched up with and inspired by an equal. Organist Eddy Louiss proved to be the perfect choice for this date. The duo performs originals that are often quite boppish along with three standards. Louiss' comping and basslines really push the pianist while Petrucciani (who gets to show off his expert skills as an accompanist) constantly sets a fire under Louiss during this live date. The interplay between the pair is quite exciting and they have plenty of torrid tradeoffs. It's a highly recommended disc. —*Scott Yanow*

Joe Lovano

b. Dec. 29, 1952, Cleveland, OH
Tenor Saxophone / Post Bop, Hard Bop
One of the top saxophonists of the 1990s, Joe Lovano still seems to be improving! His tenor tone is based in the tradition but is fairly original and his chancetaking improvisations are both stimulating and refreshing. His father, Tony "Big T" Lovano was a fine tenorman who played in Cleveland. Joe originally started on alto when he was six, switching to tenor five years later. He attended Berklee and then worked with Jack McDuff and Lonnie Smith. After three years touring with Woody Herman's Orchestra (1976–79), Lovano moved to New York, playing regularly with Mel Lewis' Big Band, Paul Motian's various groups (since 1981), Charlie Haden's Liberation Music Orchestra and (in the early '90s) John Scofield in addition to touring Europe with Elvin Jones (1987). Joe Lovano has recorded as a leader for Soul Note, Jazz Club, Label Bleu (reissued by Evidence), Enja, JSL (a date with his father) and a long string of very impressive outings for Blue Note. His 1995 Blue Note set *Rush Hour* features Joe Lovano and his wife, singer Judi Silvano in top form collaborating with Gunther Schuller on a challenging set of music. —*Scott Yanow*

Tones, Shapes and Colors / Nov. 21, 1985 / Soul Note ✦✦✦✦
One Time Out / Sep. 1987 / Soul Note ✦✦✦✦
Village Rhythm / Jun. 7, 1988–Jun. 9, 1988 / Soul Note ✦✦✦✦
Worlds / May 5, 1989 / Evidence ✦✦✦✦✦
Landmarks / Aug. 13, 1990–Aug. 14, 1990 / Blue Note ✦✦✦✦✦
Although the title of this CD makes it sound as if tenor saxophonist Joe Lovano was performing veteran jazz classics on this date, all but one of the ten songs played by his quintet are actually Lovano originals. With strong assistance provided by guitarist John Abercrombie, pianist Ken Werner, bassist Marc Johnson and drummer Bill Stewart, Lovano often sounds like a mixture of Dewey Redman and early John Coltrane on his enjoyable set. His music has enough variety to hold one's interest, Abercrombie is in particularly strong form and Lovano is consistently creative during the modern mainstream music. —*Scott Yanow*
Sounds of Joy / Jan. 1991 / Enja ✦✦✦✦
From the Soul / Dec. 28, 1991 / Blue Note ✦✦✦✦
Joe Lovano heads a lineup with pianist Michel Petrucciani, bassist Dave Holland and late drummer Ed Blackwell. It's hard-edged, explosive playing all around, with Blackwell laying down his patented bombs while Petrucciani and Holland converge behind Lovano's dynamic solos. —*Ron Wynn*
Universal Language / Jun. 26, 1992–Jun. 28, 1992 / Blue Note ✦✦✦✦✦
Tenor Legacy / Jun. 18, 1993 / Blue Note ✦✦✦✦
Joe Lovano welcomes Joshua Redman to his sextet set (which also features pianist Mulgrew Miller, bassist Christian McBride, bassist Lewis Nash and percussionist Don Alias) and, rather than jam on standards, Joe Lovano composed five new originals, revived three obscurities and only chose to perform two familiar pieces. By varying the styles and instrumentation (for example "Bread and Wine" does not have piano or bass), Lovano has created a set with a great deal of variety and some surprising moments. The two tenors (who have distinctive sounds) work together fine and some chances are taken. This matchup works well. —*Scott Yanow*
★ **Live At Village Vanguard** / Mar. 12, 1994–Jan. 22, 1995 / Blue Note ✦✦✦✦✦
★ **Rush Hour** / Apr. 6, 1994–Jun. 12, 1994 / Blue Note ✦✦✦✦✦
This is one of the most exciting jazz releases of 1995. Joe Lovano is showcased on four songs backed by a string section, is accompanied by a stringless big band filled with woodwinds and brass during four other pieces, performs Ornette Coleman's "Kathline Gray" with a chamber group, takes two songs as duets with his wife Judi Silvano (who contributes wordless vocals), plays his own "Wildcat" as an overdubbed feature for his tenor and drums and does a straightforward version of "Chelsea Bridge" unaccompanied. Gunther Schuller's arrangements for the larger pieces (which include three of his own colorful originals: "Rush Hour on 23rd Street," "Lament for M" and "Headin' out, Movin' In") expertly blend together Gil Evans-type orchestrations with aspects of modern classical music and freer forms of jazz while allowing the music to swing. Silvano's voice is also an asset on three of the orchestra performances and trumpeter Jack Walrath briefly makes his presence felt. However this very well-conceived release would not have succeeded were it not for the talent, versatility and risk-taking of Joe Lovano. His improvisations (mostly on tenor) push the boundaries of this already adventurous music, Lovano's sound (which occasionally hints a little at Clifford Jordan) is quite original and, on the basis of this date alone, he must rank as one of the top tenors of the 1990s. —*Scott Yanow*

Frank Lowe

b. Jun. 24, 1943, Memphis, TN
Tenor Saxophone / Avant-Garde, Free Jazz
Another saxophonist forging an alliance of R&B, soul and free music, Frank Lowe's high-energy style has been heard on '60s and '70s sessions. Though his tone sometimes seems to flatten out, his array of screams, shrieks, octave leaps and bursts is always attention grabbing, if occasionally chaotic. Lowe began on tenor at 12, then studied briefly at the University of Kansas and with Donald Garrett in San Francisco. He played with Sun Ra in New York during the late '60s, returned to study classical music at San Francisco Conservatory, then played with Alice Coltrane, Rashied Ali, Archie Shepp, Milford Graves and Don Cherry in New York in the early '70s. He's been a leader since the mid-'70s, recording

on Survival, ESP, Cadence Jazz, Musicworks and Soul Note among others. Lowe has played with Lester Bowie, Bobo Shaw, Joseph Bowie, Anthony Braxton and many others. —*Ron Wynn*

● **Fresh** / Sep. 1974–Mar. 7, 1975 / Freedom ✦✦✦✦✦
The emphasis is on color and sound on this spirited avant-garde album. Four of the five selections feature the adventurous tenor of Frank Lowe with trumpeter Lester Bowie, trombonist Joseph Bowie, cellist Abdul Wadud and either Steve Reid or Bob Shaw on drums. They perform two Lowe originals and two pieces by Thelonious Monk; these renditions are full of surprises and contrasts. In addition, Lowe is heard with an unknown group of local musicians called "the Memphis Four" on "Chu's Blues" in 1974. Open-eared listeners should find this set to be quite stimulating. —*Scott Yanow*

The Flam / Oct. 1975 / Black Saint ✦✦✦✦✦
On this free jazz date the powerful tenor Frank Lowe teams up with trumpeter Leo Smith, trombonist Joseph Bowie, bassist Alex Blake and drummer Charles Bobo Shaw for five group originals including the collaboration "Third St. Stomp." The very explorative and rather emotional music holds one's interest throughout. These often heated performances are better heard than described. —*Scott Yanow*

Doctor Too Much / Nov. 1978 / Kharma ✦✦✦

Lowe and Behold / Dec. 1979 / Musicworks ✦✦✦

Exotic Heartbreak / Nov. 1982 / Soul Note ✦✦✦

Skizoke / Nov. 1982 / Cadence ✦✦✦✦

Decision in Paradise / Sep. 24, 1984+Sep. 28, 1984 / Soul Note ✦✦✦✦
The all-star lineup (tenor saxophonist Frank Lowe, trumpeter Don Cherry, trombonist Grachan Moncur III, pianist Geri Allen, bassist Charnette Moffett and drummer Charles Moffett) practically guarantees that this music will be worth hearing. Although a touch more conservative than one might expect (more of an open-minded straight-ahead set than music emphasizing sound explorations), all six group originals are of interest, including Lowe's unaccompanied performance on Butch Morris' "I'll Whistle Your Name" and Moncur's whimsical "You Dig!" —*Scott Yanow*

Mundell Lowe (James Mundell Lowe)
b. Apr. 21, 1922, Laurel, MS
Guitar / Cool, Swing
A reliable cool toned guitarist who was on many sessions through the years despite never becoming a household name, Mundell Lowe picked up early experience during 1936–40 playing Dixieland in New Orleans and country music in Nashville. He toured with Jan Savitt (1942), Ray McKinley (1945–47), Mary Lou Williams (1947–49), Red Norvo and Ellis Larkins. In 1950 he became a staff musician at NBC, although he always played jazz on the side. Lowe was with the Sauter-Finegan Orchestra (1952–53), worked with Benny Goodman on an occasional basis and recorded as a leader for RCA, Riverside, Camden and Charlie Parker Records. In 1965 Lowe moved to California and worked as a composer for films and television, teaching film composition during 1979–85. He played locally in Los Angeles, often with Richie Kamuca and Benny Carter. Mundell Lowe (who is married to singer Betty Bennett) recorded sets for Famous Door (1974), Dobre (1976) and Jazz Alliance (1992). —*Scott Yanow*

Mundell Lowe Quartet / Aug. 27, 1955+Oct. 4, 1955 / Original Jazz Classics ✦✦✦✦
Most of this set is essentially straight-ahead bebop, with guitarist Mundell Lowe heard in top form on such numbers as "Will You Still Be Mine," "I'll Never Be the Same," "All of You" and "Cheek to Cheek." The wild card here is Dick Hyman who, in addition to piano and some celeste on "The Night We Called It a Day," mostly plays organ. His tone is thin and restrained, almost as if he were playing a cheap electric piano; Jimmy Smith would not make his presence known for another year. However Lowe is the main voice throughout this fairly colorful Riverside quartet date (also including supportive playing by bassist Trigger Alpert and drummer Ed Shaughnessy), which has been reissued on CD in the OJC series. —*Scott Yanow*

California Guitar / 1974 / Famous Door ✦✦✦✦

● **Souvenirs** / Nov. 10, 1977+Feb. 27, 1992 / Jazz Alliance ✦✦✦✦
Nick Ceroli also plays on the album, along with saxophonist Bob Magnusson and drummer Mike Wofford. The mood is both cool

and cagey, with no one trying to take the spotlight, but yet contributing some fervent solos when in the spotlight. —*Ron Wynn*

Jimmie Lunceford
b. Jun. 6, 1902, Fulton, MS, **d.** Jul. 12, 1947, Seaside, OR
Leader / Swing
The Jimmie Lunceford Orchestra has always been a bit difficult to evaluate. Contemporary observers rated Lunceford's big band at the top with Duke Ellington and Count Basie but, when judging the music solely on their records (and not taking into account their visual show, appearance and showmanship), Lunceford's ensemble has to be placed on the second tier. His orchestra lacked any really classic soloists (altoist Willie Smith and trombonist Trummy Young came the closest) and a large portion of the band's repertoire either featured the dated vocals of Dan Grissom or were pleasant novelties. And yet, the well-rehearsed ensembles were very impressive, some of the arrangements (particularly those of Sy Oliver) were quite original and the use of glee-club vocalists and short concise solos were pleasing and often memorable. Plus Lunceford's was the first orchestra to feature high-note trumpeters (starting with Tommy Stevenson in 1934) and had a strong influence on the early Stan Kenton Orchestra.

Although he was trained on several instruments and was featured on flute on "Liza" in the 1940s, Jimmie Lunceford was much more significant as a bandleader than as a musician. While teaching music at Manassa High School in Memphis in 1927, Lunceford organized a student band called the Chickasaw Syncopators, recording two songs that year and a pair in 1930. After leaving Memphis, the band (known by then as the Jimmie Lunceford Orchestra) played in Cleveland and Buffalo and cut two songs in 1933 that were not issued until decades later. 1934 was the breakthrough year. The orchestra made a strong impression playing at New York's Cotton Club, waxed a few notable songs for Victor and then started recording regularly for Decca. Their tight ensembles and colorful shows made them a major attraction throughout the remainder of the swing era. Among their many hits were "Rhythm Is Our Business," "Four or Five Times," "Swanee River," "Charmaine," "My Blue Heaven," "Organ Grinder's Swing," "Ain't She Sweet," "For Dancers Only," "'Tain't What You Do, It's the Way That Cha Do It," "Uptown Blues" and "Lunceford Special." The stars of the band included arranger Sy Oliver (on trumpet and vocals), Willie Smith, Trummy Young (who had a hit with "Margie") and tenor saxophonist Joe Thomas.

In 1939 it was a major blow when Tommy Dorsey lured Sy Oliver away (although trumpeters Gerald Wilson and Snooky Young were important new additions). Unfortunately Lunceford underpaid most of his sidemen and, not thinking to reward them for their loyalty in the lean years. In 1942 Willie Smith was one of several key players who left for better-paying jobs elsewhere and the orchestra gradually declined. Jimmie Lunceford was still a popular bandleader in 1947 when he suddenly collapsed; rumors have persisted that he was poisoned by a racist restaurant owner who was very reluctant about feeding his band. After Lunceford's death, pianist/arranger Ed Wilcox and Joe Thomas tried to keep the orchestra together but in 1949 the band permanently broke up. —*Scott Yanow*

★ **Jimmie Lunceford** / Dec. 13, 1927–Sep. 4, 1934 / Masters of Jazz ✦✦✦✦✦

Jimmie Lunceford (1930–1934) / Jun. 6, 1930–Nov. 7, 1934 / Classics ✦✦✦✦

● **Stomp It Off** / Sep. 4, 1934–May 29, 1935 / Decca ✦✦✦✦✦

★ **Vol. 2 1934** / Sep. 5, 1934–Dec. 17, 1934 / Masters Of Jazz ✦✦✦✦✦

Jimmie Lunceford (1934–1935) / Nov. 1934–Sep. 1935 / Classics ✦✦✦✦

Jimmie Lunceford (1935–1937) / Sep. 1935–Jun. 1937 / Classics ✦✦✦✦

For Dancers Only / Oct. 26, 1936–Nov. 5, 1937 / Decca ✦✦✦

Hollywood '36—Culver City '46—New York '48 / 1936–1948 / Jazz Up ✦✦
This CD features the Jimmie Lunceford orchestra on three separate occasions. The band is heard on a soundtrack from a short film in 1936 (including "Rhythm Is Our Business") and on radio broadcasts from Los Angeles in 1946 (during which they revisit some of their earlier hits) and in New York in 1948 a year after its leader's death; the band's style during the latter is unchanged. Frankly nothing that unique occurs on any of these performances

and the recording quality is a bit streaky at times, making this CD of greatest interest to Lunceford completists. —*Scott Yanow*

Jimmie Lunceford (1937–1939) / Jun. 1937–Jan. 1939 / Classics ++++

Jimmie Lunceford (1939) / Jan. 1939–Sep. 1939 / Classics ++++

Jimmie Lunceford (1939–1940) / Dec. 1939–Jun. 1940 / Classics ++++

Jimmie Lunceford (1940–1941) / Jul. 1940–Dec. 1941 / Classics ++++

Margie / Apr. 25, 1946–May 1947 / Savoy ++++

Carmen Lundy

b. Nov. 1, 1954, Miami, FL
Vocals / Bop, Standards, Post Bop
The sister of bassist Curtis Lundy, Carmen is a talented singer who is also a composer (writing a good portion of her repertoire), actor and painter. After studying at Miami University, she moved to New York in 1978 where she worked with Ray Barretto and formed her own trio in 1980, using such pianists as John Hicks and Onaje Gumbs. Lundy recorded for Blackhawk (1987) and Sony (1988) and appeared in the plays *Sophisticated Ladies* and *They Were All Gardenias*, portraying Billie Holiday in the latter. In 1991 she moved to Los Angeles and has since recorded for Arabesque (1992) and JVC. Although open to the influences of folk, R&B and pop, Carmen Lundy (who seems on the brink of much greater recognition in the mid-'90s) is a strong improviser. —*Scott Yanow*

Good Morning Kiss / Jan. 1985+Aug. 1985 / Blackhawk ++++

Moment to Moment / Apr. 10, 1991–Apr. 18, 1991 / Arabesque ++++

● **Self Portait** / Nov. 1994 / JVC +++++
Today's jazz singers have a great deal of difficulty in building a fresh repertoire, because so many of the current pop songs are not really transferable to creative music. Carmen Lundy solves the problem on this CD by writing six of her own songs, both lyrics and music. Her talents in that area are impressive and it would not be surprising if a few future standards came out of her repertoire. Lundy's memorable deep voice, which has a wide range, can go very low (as heard on Jobim's "Triste") and on "Firefly" she overdubs a second part, making the performance sound like a male-female duet. A tasteful string section is used on some selections, but most songs utilize the core of a strong rhythm section (pianist Cedar Walton, John Clayton or Nathan East on bass and drummer Ralph Penland) plus occasional guests Ernie Watts and Gary Herbig on reeds. Whether interpreting ballads, singing more heated pieces or floating over a funky vamp, Carmen Lundy pays close attention to the lyrics and mood of each song but feels free to improvise spontaneously. This is one of her strongest recordings to date with the highpoints including "Spring Can Really Hang You up the Most," "Firefly," "Forgive Me" and "My Ship." —*Scott Yanow*

Brian Lynch

b. Milwaukee, WI
Trumpet / Hard Bop
A fine hard bop trumpeter with a crackling sound, Brian Lynch started out played locally in Milwaukee from age 16. After graduating from the Wisconsin Conservatory, he spent much of 1980 in San Diego, where he played with Charles McPherson. Relocating to New York in 1981, Lynch worked with George Russell, Horace Silver (1982–85) and the Toshiko Akiyoshi Jazz Orchestra in addition to freelancing. In 1987 he was with Frank Wess' Quintet and started playing with Eddie Palmieri. Lunch was the last trumpeter to be a member of Art Blakey's Jazz Messengers (Dec. 1988–Oct. 1990) and

he has been in the Phil Woods Quintet since 1992. Brian Lynch has thus far recorded as a leader for Ken and Criss Cross. —*Scott Yanow*

Peer Pressure / Dec. 1986 / Criss Cross ++++
Lynch wrote three of the six tracks. Horace Silver (p), T. Turrentine wrote the others. A solid date from a promising musician. One to look for. —*Michael G. Nastos*

Back Room Blues / Dec. 30, 1989 / Criss Cross ++++

● **In Progress** / 1991 / Ken Music +++++

Jimmy Lyons

b. Dec. 1, 1933, Jersey City, NJ, **d.** May 19, 1986, New York, NY
Alto Saxophone, Soprano Saxophone / Free Jazz
Jimmy Lyons worked with Cecil Taylor from 1960 until his death in 1986. Although initially influenced by Charlie Parker, Lyons found a niche for his alto in Taylor's dense and passionate music, becoming an indispensable part of the Cecil Taylor Unit for 26 years. He grew up in Harlem and started playing alto when he was 15, being largely self-taught. A relative unknown when he joined Taylor, Jimmy Lyons was from then on always associated with the innovative pianist although he did have opportunities to lead sessions for BYG (1969), Hat Art and Black Saint, often utilizing bassoonist Karen Borca. It is not surprising that for his own dates, Lyons never used a pianist! —*Scott Yanow*

Other Afternoons / Aug. 15, 1969 / Affinity +++++
Because he spent virtually his entire career as Cecil Taylor's altoist, Jimmy Lyons had relatively few chances to record as a leader. This Affinity LP was his first opportunity to head a session and Lyons picked a particularly superior group of sidemen: trumpeter Lester Bowie, bassist Alan Silva and drummer Andrew Cyrille. Rather than sounding like The Art Ensemble of Chicago (Bowie's group) or Taylor's Unit, the all-star band comes closer at times to seeming like an updated version of Ornette Coleman's Quartet. The renditions of four originals are quite adventurous and passionate, yet thoughtful and logical. An excellent outing that has not yet reappeared on CD. —*Scott Yanow*

● **Jump Up / What to Do About** / Aug. 30, 1980 / Hat Hut +++++

Something in Return / Feb. 13, 1981 / Black Saint ++++

Burnt Offering / May 15, 1982 / Black Saint ++++

Wee Sneezawee / Sep. 26, 1983–Sep. 27, 1983 / Black Saint ++++

Give It Up / Mar. 1985 / Black Saint ++++

Humphrey Lyttelton

b. May 23, 1921, Eton, England
Clarinet, Trumpet / Dixieland, Swing
One of the leaders of England's revivalist movement of the late '40s, Humphrey Lyttelton's music gradually evolved into small-group swing and he has alternated between the two idioms throughout his productive career. After serving in the military, Lyttelton played with George Webb's Dixielanders in 1947 and formed his own group the following year. His band (which usually featured clarinetist Wally Fawkes) was one of the pacesetters throughout the 1950s, sometimes growing in size to include two or three saxophonists (including Tony Coe and Joe Temperley). Lyttelton recorded with Sidney Bechet in 1949 and on a few occasions in the early '60s he collaborated with Buck Clayton. Of his many recordings, Lyttelton's dates for Black Lion and a set for Sackville are the easiest to find in the U.S. Humphrey Lyttelton, who doubles quite effectively on clarinet, founded his own label in the 1980s (Calligraph) and has written several very informative books on jazz. —*Scott Yanow*

● **Rent Party** / Aug. 10, 1991–Jan. 4, 1992 / Stomp Off +++++

M

M'Boom

Group / Post-Bop

In 1970 Max Roach first organized M'Boom, a ten-piece unit composed entirely of percussionists. By utilizing such instruments as marimba, xylophone, tympani, vibes, bells, gongs, drum sets and even a musical saw, Roach leads a very colorful and self-sufficient group. Originally a septet comprising Roach, Warren Smith, Freddie Waits, Omar Clay, Joe Chambers, Roy Brooks and Ray Mantilla, the group grew to ten pieces in later years. A part-time project, M'Boom has recorded for Baystate (1973), Columbia (1979), Soul Note (1984) and Blue Moon (1992) and appeared at the 1994 Monterey Jazz Festival. *—Scott Yanow*

M'Boom / Jul. 25, 1979–Jul. 27, 1979 / Columbia ✦✦✦✦✦
Max Roach's percussion sextet. *—Michael G. Nastos*

Collage / Oct. 16, 1984–Oct. 18, 1984 / Soul Note ✦✦✦✦

● **Live at S.O.B.'s New** / 1992 / Blue Moon ✦✦✦✦✦
Exciting percussion duels, multiple rhythms, and teeming arrangements and performances by the conglomeration of drummers known as M'Boom. This recent release included founding member Max Roach, plus Roy Brooks, Joe Chambers, Omar Clay, Fred King, Ray Mantilla, Warren Smith and Freddy Waits performing live at the celebrated New York club S.O.B.'s. *—Ron Wynn*

Harold Mabern

b. Mar. 20, 1936, Memphis, TN
Piano / Hard Bop

One of several excellent hard bop pianists from the Memphis area, Harold Mabern has led relatively few dates through the years, but he has always been respected by his contemporaries. He played in Chicago with MJT + 3 in the late '50s and then moved to New York in 1959. Mabern worked with Jimmy Forrest, Lionel Hampton, the Jazztet (1961–62), Donald Byrd, Miles Davis (1963), J.J. Johnson (1963–65), Sonny Rollins, Freddie Hubbard, Wes Montgomery, Joe Williams (1966–67) and Sarah Vaughan. During 1968–70 Mabern led four albums for Prestige; he was with Lee Morgan in the early '70s, and in 1972 he recorded with Stanley Cowell's Piano Choir. In more recent times Harold Mabern recorded as a a leader for DIW/Columbia and Sackville and toured with the Contemporary Piano Ensemble (1993–95). *—Scott Yanow*

Rakin' & Scrapin' / Dec. 23, 1968 / Prestige ✦✦✦✦

Wailin' / Jun. 30, 1969+Jan. 26, 1970 / Prestige ✦✦✦✦✦
This CD reissue combines together two sessions (*'Workin' & Wailin'* and *Greasy Kid Stuff*) led by pianist Harold Mabern during 1969–70. The first date utilizes trumpeter Virgil Jones, tenor saxophonist George Coleman, bassist Buster Williams and drummer Idris Muhammad on four challenging Mabern originals and Johnny Mandel's "A Time for Love." However it is the second session that is most memorable for, in addition to Mabern, Williams and Muhammad, it features trumpeter Lee Morgan and flutist Hubert Laws; the latter mostly plays some surprisingly passionate tenor that makes one wish he had performed on tenor more through the years. Excellent advanced hard bop music that hints at fusion. *—Scott Yanow*

Live at Cafe Des Copains / Apr. 25, 1984+Jan. 9, 1985 / Sackville ✦✦✦✦✦
Outstanding piano solos, sturdy compositions. *—Ron Wynn*

Philadelphia Bound / Apr. 15, 1991+Feb. 29, 1992 / Sackville ✦✦✦✦

★ **The Leading Man** / Nov. 9, 1992–Apr. 12, 1993 / Columbia ✦✦✦✦✦
A brilliant pianist who continues to develop and has found his own voice in the modern mainstream, Harold Mabern chose consistently superior tunes for his Columbia CD, ranging from Wes Montgomery's "Full House" (featuring guitarist Kevin Eubanks in a duet with the leader) and songs by Wayne Shorter, Coltrane and Bird, to his own "B&B" (a ballad dedicated to Clifford Brown and Booker Little) and the pop tune "Save the Best for Last." Although one can hear aspects of McCoy Tyner's chord voicings in some of Mabern's solos, he has plenty of very individual ideas; check out his near-miraculous playing on "Moment's Notice." With strong support from drummer Jack DeJohnette and either Christian McBride or Ron Carter on bass (in addition to two appearances by trumpeter Bill Mobley), this is one of Harold Mabern's most impressive outings to date, and it is highly recommended. *—Scott Yanow*

Teo Macero

b. Oct. 30, 1925, Glens Falls, NY
Tenor Saxophone / Avant-Garde, Third Stream

Teo Macero is best-known for being a busy jazz producer at Columbia from 1957 until the late '80s, most noticeably for producing Miles Davis' records. However he has also been an occasional tenor saxophonist who has been involved in some adventurous sessions. After serving in the Navy, Macero came to New York in 1948 where he attended Julliard until he graduated in 1953. That year he became a member of Charles Mingus' Jazz Composer's Workshop. He made several records with Mingus during 1953–55, recorded with Teddy Charles (1956) and led three albums of his own for Debut, Columbia and Prestige (1953–57). Macero's dry tones on tenor and baritone and advanced choice of notes sometimes put him closer to modern classical music than to jazz. In the late '50s he wrote some atonal classical works but by then he was working fulltime as a producer. Teo Macero played on a very infrequent basis during the 1960s and '70s but in 1983 returned as a player to record a tribute to Charles Mingus on Palo Alto; in 1985 he played on one number during a Doctor Jazz date that he fronted. Some of Macero's earlier recordings as a saxophonist have been reissued on a Stash collection. *—Scott Yanow*

The Best of Teo Macero / Dec. 5, 1953–1979 / Stash ✦✦✦✦✦
Interesting anthology with super-producer Teo Macero presented during his playing days in various lineups. Guests include Art Farmer, Bill Evans, Lee Konitz, Ed Shaughnessy, Mal Waldron, Al Cohn and Charles Mingus. *—Ron Wynn*

● **Teo Macero with the Prestige Jazz Quartet** / Apr. 27, 1957 / Original Jazz Classics ✦✦✦✦✦

Time + 7 / 1963–1965 / Finnadar ✦✦✦✦
This album was way ahead of its time. A reissue with Art Farmer (tpt), John La Porta (reeds), Ed Shaughnessy (d) and Mal Waldron (p). *—Michael G. Nastos*

Impressions of Charles Mingus / 1983 / Palo Alto ✦✦✦
An early '80s recording putting longtime producer Teo Macero back in the studio for sessions with him playing tenor sax and leading a band doing Charles Mingus compositions. It resembled a Mingus Dynasty session, but was more subdued and restrained. *—Ron Wynn*

Acoustical Suspension / 1984 / Doctor Jazz ✦✦✦✦
Teo Macero, best known as a producer, has only recorded as a tenor saxophonist on a very infrequent basis through the decades. This unusual album has four very different groups performing Macero's originals. Vibraphonist Lionel Hampton and tenor saxophonist Gato Barbieri (an odd couple) are heard on five numbers along with a saxophone section, two keyboards, two guitars and a rhythm section. "Summer Rain" matches together flutist Dave Valentin and soprano saxophonist Dave Liebman while "Silent Summer" is a piano duet for Mike Nock and Mal Waldron. Macero only pops up on one number, teaming up with Liebman, altoist Carlos Ward, bassist Cecil McBee and Orlando Digirolamo on accordian; quite a quintet. In general the writing is not as strong as the solos but this somewhat eccentric album certainly stands out in the crowd. —*Scott Yanow*

Machito (Frank Grillo)

b. Feb. 16, 1912, Havana, Cuba, **d.** Apr. 15, 1984, London, England
Vocals, Leader / Afro-Cuban Jazz
An institution in Latin jazz and international music, Machito (Frank Raul Grillo) was a fixture from the early '40s till the mid-'80s. His bands, thanks to the innovations of brother-in-law and longtime musical director Mario Bauza, blended excellent jazz arrangements with frenetic Cuban rhythms, creating a sound that was fresh and intriguing. Bauza called it Afro-Cuban music, while others labeled it "Cubop." Machito was the leader, vocalist and maracas player. The son of a cigar manufacturer, he sang and danced with his father's employees as a child and later sang in the group Jovenes de Rendicion. He worked with several Cuban bands in the late '20s and '30s before coming to America in 1937 as a vocalist with the group La Estrella Habanera. Machito recorded with Alfredito Valdez, El Quarteto Caney, El Conjunto Moderno and La Orchestra Hatuey while working with other groups in the late '30s. He and Bauza formed a band, but shortly disbanded it. Machito worked with The Orchestra Siboney and recorded with Xavier Cugat before forming The Afro-Cubans in 1940. The next year Bauza joined this band and remained until they had another conflict in 1976, one that couldn't be resolved. The band made its first recordings for Decca. Machito's sister Graciela was bandleader while he was in the Army in the mid-'40s. The Afro-Cubans became immensely popular. They appeared with Stan Kenton's big band in the late '40s and played several concerts with jazz groups. Bauza's idea that they employ top non-Latin jazz stars as special guests led to such players as Charlie Parker, Dizzy Gillespie, Flip Phillips, Howard McGhee, Brew Moore, Buddy Rich, Harry Edison, Cannonball Adderley, Curtis Fuller, Herbie Mann, Johnny Griffin, Eddie Bert and Aaron Sachs working and recording with the band from the late '40s through the '60s. They maintained their popularity through the mambo era of the '50s and early '60s and were a staple when salsa surged in popularity during the '70s and 80s. The Afro-Cubans kept busy on both the jazz and salsa circuits, and they were featured in Carlos Ortiz's documentary film "Machito: A Jazz Legacy" in 1987. They recorded for Verve, Roulette, Trip, Tico, Secco, Forum, Coral, RCA, Pablo and Timeless. Machito's 1982 LP *Machito And His Salsa Big Band* won a Grammy. He was still working when he suffered a fatal stroke at Ronnie Scott's club in 1984. —*Ron Wynn and Michael G. Nastos*

★ **Mucho Macho Machito** / 1948 / Pablo ✦✦✦✦✦
Finally on CD, Pablo's old compilation includes some of Machito's finest Cubop classics, by what was perhaps the finest of all his bands. "Asia Minor," "Babarabatiri," "Tea for Two," "St. Louis Blues," even "Donkey Serenade" are among the featured tracks. This great release has fine notes and great old photos. —*John Storm Roberts*

Afro-Cubop / Mar. 26, 1949–May 7, 1949 / Spotlite ✦✦✦✦

★ **Afro-Cuban Jazz Moods** / Jun. 4, 1975–Jun. 5, 1975 / Original Jazz Classics ✦✦✦✦✦

Machito & His Salsa Big Band / Feb. 6, 1982–Feb. 7, 1982 / Impulse ✦✦✦✦
A dynamite band with Chocolate Armenteros in the trumpet section and Macho's daughter as lead female vocalist, it also has a fine mix of well-known and less-familiar numbers including "El Manicero" and a Machito warhorse, "Quimbombo." —*John Storm Roberts*

Live at North Sea / Jul. 18, 1982 / Timeless ✦✦✦✦
Powerful, great live sessions. —*Ron Wynn*

1982 / Timeless ✦✦✦✦
This double cassette consists of Machito's last band, after the split with Bauza and Graciela. It has two albums' worth of the driving big-band sound this group's ancestor created back in the 1940s. There's roof-raising ensembles, good solos and fine singing, of course. —*John Storm Roberts, Original Music*

Fraser MacPherson (John Fraser MacPherson)

b. Apr. 10, 1928, Winnipeg, Canada,   Sept. 28, 1993, Vancouver, Canada
Tenor Saxophone / Swing, Cool
Fraser MacPherson, who took an awful long time before he was discovered by Americans, was one of the top cool-toned tenors (in the "Four Brothers" style) still active in the 1980s. A professional since 1951, he spent over 25 years in Canada playing in the studios and local dance bands. Although he recorded for the CBC between 1962–72 on a few occasions, it was not until a 1975 session for the small West End label was picked up by Concord that MacPherson began to be known outside of Vancouver. He made several records for Concord and Sackville, often teaming up with the equally cool-sounding guitarist Oliver Gannon. Fraser MacPherson toured the Soviet Union four times but ironically rarely had the opportunity to perform in the U.S. —*Scott Yanow*

Live at the Planetarium / Dec. 16, 1975 / Concord Jazz ✦✦✦✦✦

Indian Summer / Jun. 1983 / Concord Jazz ✦✦✦✦

● **Jazz Prose** / Aug. 1984 / Concord Jazz ✦✦✦✦✦

Honey and Spice / Mar. 1987 / JustIn Time ✦✦✦✦

Encore / 1990 / JustIn Time ✦✦✦✦

In the Tradition / Nov. 15, 1991–Nov. 16, 1991 / Concord Jazz ✦✦✦✦
Steady Canadian tenor saxophonist heads a good quintet in this session with MacPherson showing his roots in cool-style, introspective soloing on a menu of mostly standards and ballads. He's backed by Ian McDougall, Oliver Gannon, Steve Wallace and John Sumner. —*Ron Wynn*

Mahavishnu Orchestra

Group / Fusion
One of the premiere fusion groups, the Mahavishnu Orchestra was considered by most observers during its prime to be a rock band but its sophisticated improvisations actually put its high-powered music between rock and jazz. Founder and leader John McLaughlin had recently played with Miles Davis and Tony Williams' Lifetime. The original lineup of the group was McLaughlin on electric guitar, violinist Jerry Goodman, keyboardist Jan Hammer, electric bassist Rick Laird and drummer Billy Cobham. They recorded three intense albums for Columbia during 1971–73, and then the personnel changed completely for the second version of the group. In 1974 the band consisted of violinist Jean-Luc Ponty, Gayle Moran on keyboards and vocals, electric bassist Ralphe Armstrong and drummer Michael Warden; by 1975 Stu Goldberg had replaced Moran and Ponty had left. John McLaughlin's dual interests in Eastern religion and playing acoustic guitar resulted in the band breaking up in 1975. Surprisingly an attempt to revive the Mahavishnu Orchestra in 1984 (using Cobham, saxophonist Bill Evans, keyboardist Mitchell Forman and electric bassist Jonas Hellborg and percussionist Danny Gottlieb) was unsuccessful; one Warner Bros. album resulted. However when one thinks of the Mahavishnu Orchestra, it is of the original lineup which was very influential throughout the 1970s. —*Scott Yanow*

★ **Inner Mounting Flame** / Aug. 14, 1971 / Columbia ✦✦✦✦✦
Classic first album. Definitive fusion. —*Michael G. Nastos*

★ **Birds of Fire** / 1972 / Columbia ✦✦✦✦✦
Classic second album. More definitive fusion. —*Michael G. Nastos*

Between Nothingness & Eternity / Aug. 1973 / Columbia ✦✦✦✦
Fine early '70s jazz-rock session from a pioneering group in this genre. The Mahavishnu Orchestra were among a handful of artists who really did achieve a fusion between rock energy and jazz improvisation. This was their last great album, with blistering solos all around and intelligent, captivating compositions. —*Ron Wynn*

Apocalypse / Mar. 1974 / Columbia ✦✦

Visions of the Emerald Beyond / Dec. 4, 1974–Dec. 14, 1974 / Columbia ✦✦✦
Orchestral concepts in ensemble format. —*Michael G. Nastos*

Inner Worlds / 1975 / Sony ✦✦✦
Mahavishnu / Apr. 1984–May 1984 / Warner Brothers ✦✦✦

Kevin Mahogany

b. Jul. 30, 1958, Kansas City, MO
Vocals / Standards, Bop
Kevin Mahogany's sudden prominence in the mid-'90s was a relief to many who felt that male jazz singers under the age of 60 were non-existent. His swinging style is reminiscent but not derivative of Joe Williams. Mahogany played piano, clarinet and various saxophones while growing up before deciding to specialize in singing. Mahogany attended Baker University in Kansas and sang locally in some R&B groups. In the early '90s he dedicated himself to jazz and has thus far led two albums for Enja and also recorded as a guest on dates by Elvin Jones and arranger Frank Mantooth. —*Scott Yanow*

● Songs And Moments / 1994 / Enja ✦✦✦✦✦
In the 1990s there has been a serious shortage of male jazz singers under the age of 60, making Kevin Mahogany's "arrival" in his second Enja release quite noteworthy. A strong improviser who can not only scat creatively but uplift lyrics, Mahogany may very well end up as a future pollwinner. He is joined on this CD by a six-piece rhythm section and a strong rhythm section (pianist John Hicks, bassist Ray Drummond and drummer Marvin "Smitty" Smith); plus there are guest appearances by altoist Arthur Blythe and guitarist Kevin Eubanks. The material (which includes Cedar Walton's "Night Flight," "Caravan," "When I Fall in Love" and the title cut by Milton Nascimento) is challenging and diverse. —*Scott Yanow*

You Got What It Takes / Mar. 19, 1995 / Enja ✦✦✦✦

Mike Mainieri

b. Jul. 24, 1938, New York, NY
Leader, Vibes / Post-Bop, Crossover, Fusion
Mike Mainieri, a talented and distinctive vibraphonist, has had a productive and diverse career. He first played vibes professionally when he was 14, touring with Paul Whiteman in a jazz trio called Two Kings and a Queen. He played with Buddy Rich's bands for a long period (1956–63) and then became a busy studio musician, appearing on many pop records. Mainieri had opportunities to work with Benny Goodman, Coleman Hawkins and Wes Montgomery (1967–68) among many others and played in the early fusion band Jeremy and the Satyrs. During 1969–72 he led a 20-piece rehearsal group called White Elephant that included the Brecker Brothers and other studio players. In 1979 he formed Steps (which later became Steps Ahead), an all-star jazz-oriented R&B/fusion band that originally included such players as Mike Brecker, Don Grolnick, Eddie Gomez and Steve Gadd in its original lineup. Mainieri has revived the group several times since with such musicians as saxophonist Bendik, Warren Bernhardt, Eliane Elias, Rachel Z, Mike Stern, Tony Levin, Victor Bailey, Peter Erskine and Steve Smith making strong contributions. In 1992 Mainieri founded the NYC label, in recent times recording the adventurous *An American Diary*. Prior to NYC, Mike Mainieri had recorded as a leader for such labels as Argo (1962), Solid State, Arista, Artists House, Warner Bros and Elektra. —*Scott Yanow*

Insight / 1967 / Solid State ✦✦✦✦
Free Smiles / Jul. 22, 1978 / Novus ✦✦✦
Wanderlust / Feb. 25, 1981–Feb. 26, 1981 / NYC ✦✦✦

● An American Diary / Oct. 1, 1994–Oct. 2, 1994 / NYC ✦✦✦✦✦
In addition to a few group originals, vibraphonist Mike Mainieri performs some unusual pieces with his quartet (Joe Lovano on tenor, soprano and alto clarinet, bassist Eddie Gomez and drummer Peter Erskine) on this CD including two folk songs and selections by Leonard Bernstein ("Somewhere"), Frank Zappa ("King Kong"), Aaron Copland ("Piano Sonata"), Roger Sessions ("Piano Sonata No. 1") and Samuel Barber ("Overture to the School for Scandal"). The pianoless quartet (which displays a lot of versatility by Joe Lovano) turns all of the music into creative jazz. The most interesting aspect to this thought-provoking disc is how difficult it is to tell which compositions are taken from classical music and which are new. There is a surprising unity to the potentially difficult material; the performances on the rather moody outing reward repeated listenings. —*Scott Yanow*

Adam Makowicz (Adam Matyszkowicz)

b. Aug. 18, 1940, Cesky Tesin, Czech.
Piano / Bop, Swing
Adam Makowicz made a strong impression when he first came to the U.S., and at the time he was often compared to Art Tatum. Although his technique is nearly on Tatum's level, Makowicz has long had his own style, mixing together different aspects of jazz ranging from swing to hard bop. He started playing jazz in the late '50s, and with Tomasz Stanko formed one of the first European free jazz groups, the Jazz Darings. He led his own groups in Warsaw from 1965 on and in 1970 played electric piano in Michal Urbaniak's band. Makowicz also worked with Urszula Dudziak and recorded several albums in Poland before coming to the United States in 1977. Although the initial publicity (when he was championed by John Hammond) has long since died down, Makowicz has if anything continued to improve as a pianist. He has recorded many records as a leader for such labels as Columbia, Stash, Choice, Sheffield Lab, Novus and Concord. —*Scott Yanow*

Adam / 1977 / Columbia ✦✦✦✦✦
Classic Jazz Duets / 1979 / Stash ✦✦✦✦
The Name is Makowicz (Ma-Ko-Vitch) / Apr. 25, 1983–Apr. 29, 1983 / Sheffield Lab ✦✦✦
Naughty Baby / Jul. 25, 1987–Jul. 27, 1987 / Novus ✦✦✦✦
An all-Gershwin program with two bassists, Dave Holland and Charlie Haden. —*Michael G. Nastos*

Plays Irving Berlin / Sep. 22, 1991–Sep. 23, 1991 / VWC Productions ✦✦✦✦
The flamboyant, gifted pianist brought plenty of harmonic flair and spirit to these interpretations. There have been numerous Irving Berlin repertory projects, and this one wasn't very different from the standpoints of song selection, respectful attitude, etc. But as a showcase for Makowicz's pianistic brilliance, it was ideal. —*Ron Wynn*

★ Live at Maybeck Recital Hall / Jul. 19, 1992 / Concord Jazz ✦✦✦✦✦

The Music of Jerome Kern / Sep. 1992 / Concord Jazz ✦✦✦✦✦
Adam Makowicz interprets 11 well-known Jerome Kern compositions on his trio date with bassist George Mraz and drummer Alan Dawson. The pianist's arrangements are full of surprising turns and twists, and his unpredictable flights result in some of the familiar songs being given unusual treatments. Stimulating and occasionally exciting music. —*Scott Yanow*

Adam Makowicz /George Mraz / May 22, 1993 / Concord Jazz ✦✦✦✦
The fifth volume in the Concord Duo Series matches pianist Adam Makowciz and bassist George Mraz in a concert at the Maybeck Recital Hall; both musicians are virtuosoes originally from Eastern Europe who found fame in the U.S. On what is very much a duo set, Mraz gets nearly as much solo space as Makowciz. Their repertoire mixes together six fresh renditions of standards with four of the pianist's complex originals, and the harmonically advanced music (which features plenty of close interplay) has enough variety to continually hold one's interest. —*Scott Yanow*

My Favorite Things:The Music Of Richard Rodgers / Sep. 7, 1993–Sep. 8, 1993 / Concord Jazz ✦✦✦✦✦

Russell Malone

b. Nov. 8, 1963, Albany GA
Guitar / Bop, Swing
A fine guitarist who has made a stir with his Columbia records of the early-to-mid-'90s, Russell Malone started playing music when he was five. He was with Jimmy Smith's band for two years in the late '80s and since 1989 has often toured with Harry Connick, Jr. Malone's influences range from swing to R&B, and he has an appealing bop-oriented approach that often pays tribute to earlier styles. —*Scott Yanow*

Russell Malone / Aug. 19, 1991–Mar. 25, 1992 / Columbia ✦✦✦✦

● Black Butterfly / Mar. 18, 1993–Apr. 29, 1993 / Columbia ✦✦✦✦✦
Guitarist Russell Malone displayed a solid sense of swing and good rhythmic skills on his debut CD as a leader, but precious little flair or spark. Malone was more impressive as a contributor in various studio and session dates, but this release did highlight some impressive influences (most notably Wes Montgomery). He

covered Duke Ellington, Cole Porter and Burt Bacharach/Hal David songs, plus his own material and compositions by contemporary jazz players like Enrico Pieranuzi. The CD performed its main function, introducing Russell Malone as a player with potential. —*Ron Wynn*

Junior Mance (Julian Clifford Mance, Jr.)

b. Oct. 10, 1928, Chicago, IL
Piano / Bop, Soul Jazz
Junior Mance is well-known for his soulful bluesy style, but he is also expert at playing bop standards. He started playing professionally when he was ten. Mance worked with Gene Ammons in Chicago during 1947–49, played with Lester Young (1950) and was with the Ammons-Sonny Stitt group until he was drafted. He was the house pianist at Chicago's Bee Hive (1953–54), worked as Dinah Washington's accompanist (1954–55), was in the first Cannonball Adderley Quintet (1956–57) and then spent two years touring with Dizzy Gillespie (1958–60). After a few months with the Eddie "Lockjaw" Davis-Johnny Griffin group, Mance formed his own trio and has mostly been a leader ever since. He has led sessions for Verve, Jazzland, Riverside, Capitol, Atlantic, Milestone, Polydor, Inner City, JSP, Nilva, Sackville and Bee Hive among other labels. —*Scott Yanow*

Junior Mance Trio at the Village Vanguard / Feb. 22, 1961–Feb. 23, 1961 / Original Jazz Classics ◆◆◆◆
Pianist Junior Mance has long been typecast as a soulful blues player so, as if to confuse listeners, he starts off this live set with an uptempo "Looptown" on which he displays technique worthy of Oscar Peterson. Mance's many fans have no reason to despair though for, in addition to a boppish rendition of "Girl of My Dreams," the pianist does perform a generous amount of blues and soulful pieces. Bassist Larry Gales and drummer Ben Riley help out on this reissue LP which has yet to come out on CD. It's a strong outing. —*Scott Yanow*

For Dancers Only / Jul. 3, 1983 / Sackville ◆◆◆◆
Outstanding sets that includes some of Mance's flashiest recent playing. —*Ron Wynn*

Truckin' & Trakin' / Dec. 13, 1983 / Bee Hive ◆◆◆◆
Recorded by a quartet with pianist Mance and saxophonist David Newman. The group really comes together for the blues/jazz legend. —*Michael G. Nastos*

● **Mance's Special** / Sep. 14, 1986+Nov. 30, 1988 / Sackville ◆◆◆◆◆
Fine '86 set with pianist Junior Mance running through romping blues, intricate originals, moving standards and ballads in a solo set. While he's best at blues-tinged material, Mance shows the versatility necessary to do other material, and doesn't substitute cliches and gimmicks for ideas and substance. —*Ron Wynn*

Here 'Tis / 1992 / Sackville ◆◆◆◆

Softly As In a Morning Sunrise / Jul. 21, 1994 / Enja ◆◆◆◆

Albert Mangelsdorff

b. Sep. 5, 1928, Frankfurt, Germany
Trombone / Avant-Garde, Free Jazz
The master of multiphonics (playing more than one note at a time on a horn), Mangelsdorff has been a giant of the European avant-garde for the past 30 years. He originally studied violin and worked as a jazz guitarist before taking up the trombone in 1948. He played bop in the 1950s including with Hans Koller and local orchestras. In 1958 Mangelsdorff visited the United States to play with Marshall Brown's International Youth Band at the Newport Jazz Festival, but his stays in America have always been fairly brief. By the time he recorded an album with John Lewis in 1962, Mangelsdorff was starting to lean toward the avant-garde. He has since recorded unaccompanied solo albums, been documented at a concert with Jaco Pastorius, led trios and worked with the Globe Unity Orchestra and the United Jazz & Rock Ensemble. Of his many records, the John Lewis set and his valuable MPS albums will be difficult to find, but Albert Mangelsdorff's work for Enja and Sackville can be acquired. —*Scott Yanow*

Live in Tokyo / Feb. 15, 1971 / Enja ◆◆◆◆

★ **Tromboneliness** / Jan. 1976+Mar. 1976 / Sackville ◆◆◆◆◆
A full album of unaccompanied solo trombone might seem a bit tedious, but Albert Mangelsdorff is on a different level than most trombonists. For one thing he is a master of multiphonics (playing chords on a horn), and his use of a wa-wa mute is also quite

expert. Although an avant-garde master, Mangelsdorff's version of "Creole Love Call" on this solo album is brilliant, as are his seven diverse originals. In addition, there is plenty of humor on these rambunctious performances. —*Scott Yanow*

Trilogue / Nov. 6, 1976 / PA/USA ◆◆◆◆◆
Live trio recording for virtuoso German trombonist. Startling sounds. With Jaco Pastorius (b). —*Michael G. Nastos*

Chuck Mangione

b. Nov. 29, 1940, Rochester, NY
Trumpet, Fluegelhorn / Bop, Instrumental Pop
Throughout the 1970s, Chuck Mangione was a celebrity. His purposely lightweight music was melodic pop that was upbeat, optimistic and sometimes uplifting. Mangione's records were big sellers yet few of his fans from the era knew that his original goal was to be a bebopper. His father had often taken Chuck and his older brother Gap (a keyboardist) out to see jazz concerts, and Dizzy Gillespie was a family friend. While Chuck studied at the Eastman School, the two Mangiones co-led a bop quintet called the Jazz Brothers that recorded several albums for Jazzland, often with Sal Nistico on tenor. Chuck Mangione played with the big bands of Woody Herman and Maynard Ferguson (both in 1965) and Art Blakey's Jazz Messengers (1965–67). In 1968, now sticking mostly to his soft-toned fluegelhorn, Mangione formed a quartet that also featured Gerry Niewood on tenor and soprano. They cut a fine set for Mercury in 1972, but otherwise Mangione's recordings in the 1970s generally used large orchestras and vocalists (including Esther Satterfield), putting the emphasis on lightweight melodies such as "Hill Where the Lord Hides," "Land of Make Believe," "Chase the Clouds Away" and the huge 1977 hit (featuring guitarist Grant Geissman) "Feels So Good." After a recorded 1978 Hollywood Bowl concert that summed up his pop years and a 1980 two-LP set that alternated pop and bop (with guest Dizzy Gillespie), Mangione gradually faded out of the music scene. In the 1970s Chuck Mangione recorded for Mercury and A&M; in the 1980s he had a couple of very forgettable Columbia albums and has not been heard from much in the '90s. —*Scott Yanow*

Spring Fever / Nov. 1961 / Original Jazz Classics ◆◆◆
The third and final recording originally released as "the Jazz Brothers" features trumpeter Chuck Mangione, pianist Gap Mangione and tenor saxophonist Sal Nistico in a 1961 hard bop quintet. The music is strictly straight-ahead with four group originals and versions of "What's New" and "Softly as in a Morning Sunrise" being given winning treatments. Even if the overall results are not all that memorable (none of the musicians had distinctive voices yet), the music should please fans of 1950s jazz. —*Scott Yanow*

Recuerdo / Jul. 31, 1962 / Original Jazz Classics ◆◆◆◆
With Wynton Kelly (p), Sam Jones (b), Lou Hayes (d) and Joe Romano (fl, as). —*Michael G. Nastos*

Friends and Love . . . a Chuck Mangione Concert / May 9, 1971 / Mercury ◆◆

● **Chuck Mangione Quartet** / Mar. 1972 / Mercury ◆◆◆◆◆

● **Alive!** / Aug. 1972 / Mercury ◆◆◆◆◆

Land of Make Believe / 1973 / Mercury ◆◆

Bellavia / 1975 / A&M ◆◆◆

Chase the Clouds Away / 1975 / A&M ◆◆◆

Main Squeeze / 1976 / A&M ◆◆

Feels So Good / 1977 / A&M ◆◆◆
Recorded at Kendun Recorders, Burbank, CA. Small group. Pop/jazz yes, but it is too pretty to not enjoy. Platinum album. —*Michael Erlewine*

An Evening of Magic, Live at the Hollywood Bowl / Jul. 16, 1978 / A&M ◆◆◆

Children of Sanchez / 1978 / A&M ◆◆

Fun and Games / 1979 / A&M ◆◆

Tarantella / Dec. 27, 1980 / A&M ◆◆◆◆

Love Notes / 1982 / Columbia ◆◆

Disguise / 1984 / Columbia ◆

Live at the Village Gate / 1987 / Feels So Good ◆◆◆

Manhattan Transfer

Vocal Group / Bop, Pop
The Manhattan Transfer has never stuck exclusively to perform-

ing jazz (other than their classic 1985 album *Vocalese*), but they rank as the top jazz vocal group since Lambert, Hendricks and Ross. Tim Hauser put together the first version of the band in 1969, and by 1972 he was joined by Alan Paul, Janis Siegel and Laurel Masse; in 1979 Cheryl Bentyne took Masse's place. The four singers are versatile, blend together well, and each have their own distinct personalities. Whether it be doo wop, recent pop tunes or swing standards, the Manhattan Transfer has long been at the top of its field. Since 1975 they have recorded for Atlantic. —*Scott Yanow*

Jukin' / Apr. 8, 1969–Jan. 25, 1971 / Capitol ✦✦

The Manhattan Transfer / 1975 / Atlantic ✦✦✦✦✦

The Best of Manhattan Transfer / 1975–1981 / Atlantic ✦✦✦

Coming Out / 1976 / Atlantic ✦✦

Pastiche / Dec. 1976 Sep. 1977 / Atlantic ✦✦✦

Extensions / 1979 / Atlantic ✦✦✦

Mecca for Moderns / 1981 / Atlantic ✦✦✦✦✦

Bodies and Souls / 1983 / Atlantic ✦✦✦
'83 release that saw Manhattan Transfer at their popular peak, doing some jazz-influenced harmonizing but more mood music and light pop. They sing with energy and style here but had moved away from the strict jazz formalism of their early material. —*Ron Wynn*

★ **Vocalese** / 1985 / Atlantic ✦✦✦✦✦

Bop Doo Wopp / 1985 / Atlantic ✦✦✦✦

Brasil / 1987 / Atlantic ✦✦✦
Worth hearing. Milton Nascimento (v) and Stan Getz (ts) are on the date. Afro-Latin flavor. —*Ron Wynn*

Herbie Mann (Herbert Jay Solomon)

b. Apr. 16, 1930, New York, NY
Flute, Leader / Crossover, Instrumental Pop, Bop, Soul Jazz
Herbie Mann has played a wide variety of music throughout his career. He became quite popular in the 1960s, but in the '70s became so immersed in pop and various types of world music that he seemed lost to jazz. Fortunately Mann has never lost his ability to improvise creatively as he has shown in recent times.
   Herbie Mann began on clarinet when he was nine but was soon also playing flute and tenor. After serving in the Army, he was with Mat Mathews' Quintet (1953–54) and then started working and recording as a leader. During 1954–58 Mann stuck mostly to playing bop, sometimes collaborating with such players as Phil Woods, Buddy Collette, Sam Most, Bobby Jaspar and Charlie Rouse. He doubled on cool-toned tenor and was one of the few jazz musicians in the 1950s who recorded on bass clarinet; he also recorded in 1957 a full album (for Savoy) of unaccompanied flute.
   After spending time playing and writing music for television, in 1959 Mann formed his Afro-Jazz Sextet, a group using several percussionists, vibes (either Johnny Rae, Hagood Hardy or Dave Pike) and the leader's flute. He toured Africa (1960) and Brazil (1961), had a hit with "Comin' Home Baby" and recorded with Bill Evans. The most popular jazz flutist during the era, Mann explored bossa nova (even recording in Brazil in 1962), incorporated music from many cultures (plus current pop tunes) into his repertoire and had among his sidemen such top young musicians as Willie Bobo, Chick Corea (1965), Attila Zoller and Roy Ayers; at the 1972 Newport Festival his sextet included David Newman and Sonny Sharrock. By then Mann had been a producer at Embryo (a subsidiary of Atlantic) for three years and was frequently stretching his music outside of jazz. As the 1970s advanced, Mann became much more involved in rock, pop, reggae and even disco. After leaving Atlantic at the end of the 1970s, Mann had his own label for awhile and gradually came back to jazz. He recorded for Chesky, made a record with Dave Valentin and in the 1990s founded the Kokopelli label on which he is free to pursue his wide range of musical interests. Through the years Herbie Mann has recorded as a leader for Bethlehem, Prestige, Epic, Riverside, Savoy, Mode, New Jazz, Chesky, Kokopelli and most significantly Atlantic. —*Scott Yanow*

Herbie Mann Plays / Dec. 1954 / Bethlehem ✦✦✦✦
Flutist Herbie Mann's first recording as a leader (seven selections from 1954, originally on a 10-inch LP, plus four others cut in 1956) has been reissued on CD with three alternate takes added on. Even back in 1954 Mann (who doubles here on flute and alto flute) had his own sound. The music (featuring either Benny

Weeks or Joe Puma on guitar in a pianoless quartet) is essentially straight-ahead bop and finds Mann playing quite melodically and with swing. This set is a good example of Herbie Mann's early style before he started exploring various types of world music. —*Scott Yanow*

The Mann with the Most / Oct. 12, 1955+Oct. 17, 1955 / Bethlehem ✦✦✦✦
This out-of-print Bethlehem LP, reissued in 1977, matches together flutists Herbie Mann and Sam Most in a fine bop program with guitarist Joe Puma, bassist Jimmy Gannon and drummer Lee Kleinman. The music consistently swings lightly, and other than an original apiece from Puma and Most, the selections are all standards; highlights include "Fascinating Rhythm," "Let's Get Away from It All" and "Seven Come Eleven." Most often takes honors, but Mann is also in fine form on these Russ Garcia arrangements. Worth searching for. —*Scott Yanow*

● **Flute Souffle** / Mar. 21, 1957 / Original Jazz Classics ✦✦✦✦
At the time of this Prestige set (reissued on CD), Herbie Mann was a flutist who occasionally played tenor and Bobby Jaspar a tenor saxophonist who doubled on flute. Two of the four songs find them switching back and forth while the other two are strictly flute features. With pianist Tommy Flanagan, guitarist Joe Puma, bassist Wendell Marshall and drummer Bobby Donaldson contributing quiet support, the two lead voices constantly interact and trade off during this enjoyable performance. Highpoints are the haunting "Tel Aviv" and a delightful version of "Chasing the Bird." —*Scott Yanow*

Let Me Tell You / Mar. 21, 1957–Apr. 8, 1957 / Milestone ✦✦✦✦
This excellent double-LP from 1973 has all of the contents from flutist Herbie Mann's Sultry Serenade and Flute Souffle albums plus one cut that was on a similar session. At the time Mann was very much into playing cool-toned bop, and he started out near the top of his field. The first half of the two-fer features Mann leading a sextet with trombonist Urbie Green, Jack Nimitz (doubling on baritone and bass clarinet) and guitarist Joe Puma; "When the Sun Comes Out," "Little Man, You've Had a Busy Day" and "Swing Till the Girls Come Home" are most memorable. The second set is actually the superior of the two, for Mann is teamed with fellow flutist Bobby Jaspar in a sextet also including Puma and pianist Tommy Flanagan. On "Somewhere Else" both Mann and Jaspar switch to tenors (Jasper also plays tenor on "Tel Aviv") but best is their flute "battle" on "Chasin' the Bird." Fortunately the latter session has been reissued on CD in the Original Jazz Classics series. —*Scott Yanow*

When Lights Are Low / Apr. 18, 1957+Apr. 29, 1957 / Portrait ✦✦✦✦
This Portrait LP (a 1988 reissue of an Epic album titled *Salute to the Flute*) found flutist Herbie Mann accompanied for the first time by a big band on five of the nine selections. Prior to 1959, virtually all of Mann's recordings were bop-oriented, and this one is no exception. Whether it be "Little Niles," "When Lights Are Low," "Beautiful Love" or even "Old Honky Tonk Piano Roll Blues," Mann proves to be an excellent bop soloist; other important players on this date include trumpeter Joe Wilder, altoist Anthony Ortega, pianist Hank Jones, guitarist Joe Puma and bassist Oscar Pettiford. This LP will be a difficult one to find. —*Scott Yanow*

Yardbird Suite / May 14, 1957 / Savoy ✦✦✦✦
Although flutist Herbie Mann's reputation suffered in the jazz world in later years due to his interest in other styles of music, during the 1954–58 period he stuck mostly to cool bebop and held his own with the best. This Savoy LP finds him matching ideas with the great altoist Phil Woods, along with vibraphonist Eddie Costa, guitarist Joe Puma, bassist Wendell Marshall and drummer Bobby Donaldson, and the results are quite enjoyable. In addition to his flute flights on three group originals and "Yardbird Suite," Mann fares quite well on tenor during the two other pieces. This hard-to-find album, which has not yet been reissued on CD, is easily recommended to bop fans. —*Scott Yanow*

Great Ideas of Western Mann / Jul. 3, 1957 / Riverside ✦✦✦
This LP contains a slightly unusual and somewhat obscure session. Flutist Herbie Mann decided to record a full album (five standards and his own "A Stella Performance") on the rarely utilized bass clarinet; this was two years before Eric Dolphy rose to fame. Mann essentially plays bop on the bass clarinet while assisted by trumpeter Jack Sheldon, pianist Jimmy Rowles, bassist Buddy

Clark and drummer Mel Lewis. High points include "The Theme," "Get Out of Town" and "Is It True What They Say About Dixie." This enjoyable set is long overdue to be reissued in the OJC series. —*Scott Yanow*

Flute Fraternity / Jul. 1957 / VSOP ◆◆◆
In the 1950s, Herbie Mann frequently shared the spotlight on record dates with other flutists. This VSOP LP, a reissue of a set originally for Mode and also out for awhile on Premier, matches Mann (who here also plays piccolo, clarinet and tenor) with Buddy Collette (switching between flute, clarinet, tenor and alto) in a quintet with pianist Jimmy Rowles, bassist Buddy Clark and drummer Mel Lewis. The results are generally pleasing, if somewhat lightweight, with such obscure tunes as "Here's Buddy," Rowles' "Pop Melody," "Here's Pete" and Mann's "Theme From" alternating with three standards and Chico Hamilton's "Morning After." The most interesting aspect to this lightly swinging music is the constant switching around of the lead voices on their various horns. —*Scott Yanow*

Hi Flutin' / Jul. 1957 / Mode ◆◆◆◆
The music on this LP has been reissued several times (including on Premier and on CD by Drive Archive). Herbie Mann (flute, alto flute, clarinet and tenor) and Buddy Collette (flute, alto flute, clarinet, tenor and alto) constantly switch instruments on the fairly basic material which mixes together recent works with originals and a couple of standards. With the assistance of pianist Jimmy Rowles, bassist Buddy Clark and drummer Mel Lewis, Mann and Collette "battle" to a tie, creating light but substantial music. —*Scott Yanow*

Flute, Brass, Vibes and Percussion / 1960 / Verve ◆◆◆◆◆
In 1960, flutist Herbie Mann put together a very interesting band that was in its brief existence (before Mann's interests shifted elsewhere) one of the top in Afro-Cuban jazz. Utilizing four trumpets (including Doc Cheatham), up to three percussionists and a flute-vibes-bass-drums quartet, Mann performs four standards (including "Dearly Beloved," "I'll Remember April" and "Autumn Leaves") and two originals in a style that was beyond bop and much more African- and Cuban-oriented. This LP (long deserving of being reissued on CD) is quite underrated and is one of the finest of Mann's long career. —*Scott Yanow*

Herbie Mann Anthology / Aug. 3, 1960–Apr. 18, 1992 / Rhino ◆◆
Rhino Records' two-CD retrospective of flutist Herbie Mann's career (subtitled "The Evolution of Mann") is put in a typically attractive box and has fine liner notes but is somewhat flawed. There are no selections included from Mann's bop years (1954–58) and far too many cuts from the 1970s when his output was much less significant; in fact several of the numbers on the second disc are so dated as to be practically unlistenable. This two-fer does have some of the highpoints of Mann's career (including "Comin' Home Baby," "Memphis Underground" and "Hold on, I'm Comin'"), but it is better to get the original sessions instead. —*Scott Yanow*

Herbie Mann Returns to the Village Gate / Apr. 26, 1961+Nov. 17, 1961 / Atlantic ◆◆◆
By 1961, flutist Herbie Mann was really starting to catch on with the general public. This LP, a follow-up to his hit *At the Village Gate* (two songs are from the same gig while three others actually date from seven months earlier), features Mann in an active group with either Hagood Henry or Dave Pike on vibes, Ahmed Abdul-Malik or Nabil Totah on bass, drummer Rudy Collins and two percussionists. Mann really cooks on four of his own originals, plus "Bags' Groove," blending in the influence of African, Afro-Cuban and even Brazilian jazz. Worth searching for. —*Scott Yanow*

● **At the Village Gate** / Nov. 17, 1961 / Atlantic ◆◆◆◆◆
Remarkably few of flutist Herbie Mann's recordings are available on CD, but fortunately, this one did get reissued. Mann's hit version of "Comin' Home Baby" from this live set became his first big hit. The composer, Ben Tucker, plays second bass on that cut, and Mann's other sidemen include vibraphonist Hagood Hardy, bassist Ahmed Abdul-Malik, drummer Rudy Collins and Chief Bey and Ray Mantilla on percussion. In addition to "Comin' Home Baby," Mann and his men perform memorable versions of "Summertime" and "It Ain't Necessarily So;" the latter is 20 minutes long. Recommended. —*Scott Yanow*

Nirvana / Dec. 8, 1961–May 4, 1962 / Atlantic ◆◆◆◆

Brazil Blues / 1961–1962 / United Artists ◆◆◆◆
A slightly expanded version of flutist Herbie Mann's 1961–62

group performs African-, Cuban- and Brazilian-influenced jazz on this appealing LP. With guitarist Billy Bean, vibraphonist Hagood Hardy, Dave Pike on marimba and four percussionists in the backup group, Mann's flute is well featured on tunes ranging from his own "B.N. Blues" and the standard "Brazil" to "One Note Samba." This album will be difficult to find but is worth the search. —*Scott Yanow*

Do the Bossa Nova with Herbie Mann / Oct. 16, 1962–Oct. 19, 1962 / Atlantic ◆◆◆◆
Rather than play a watered-down version of bossa nova in New York studios (which was becoming quite common as the bossa nova fad hit its peak in 1962), flutist Herbie Mann went down to Brazil and recorded with some of the top players of the style. Guitarist Baden Powell and the group of then-unknown pianist Sergio Mendes, which included drummer Dom Um Romao, formed the nucleus for this generally delightful album. Antonio Carlos Jobim himself dropped by to sing two of his compositions, including "One Note Samba," and even on the token jazz standard "Blues Walk," the music is as much Brazilian as it is jazz. This "fusion" works quite well; pity that the performances last appeared on this out-of-print LP. —*Scott Yanow*

Herbie Mann Live at Newport / Jul. 7, 1963 / Atlantic ◆◆◆

Standing Ovation at Newport / Jul. 3, 1965 / Atlantic ◆◆◆◆

● **New Mann at Newport** / Mar. 10, 1966+Jul. 10, 1966 / Atlantic ◆◆◆◆◆
A follow-up to his well-received *Standing Ovation at Newport* from 1965, this out-of-print LP features the popular flutist at the 1966 Festival (except for "All Blues," which is from four months earlier) jamming some heated grooves with trumpeter Jimmy Owens, trombonists Joe Orange and Jack Hitchcock, bassist Reggie Workman, drummer Bruno Carr and percussionist Patato Valdes. The material is stronger than was often the case on Mann's albums from this period, with Jimmy Heath's "Project S," Wayne Henderson's "Scratch" and "All Blues" being among the high points. Herbie Mann's 1960s recordings, which are generally superior to what he would be playing a decade later, tend to be underrated because he had become quite popular. This fine date is worth searching for. —*Scott Yanow*

Glory of Love / Jul. 26, 1967–Oct. 6, 1967 / A&M ◆◆
Flutist Herbie Mann is backed by a large rhythm section and a small horn section on this Creed Taylor-produced A&M set (which has been reissued on CD). Actually the most interesting aspect of the R&B-oriented date (which includes such songs as "Hold on, I'm Comin'," "House of the Risin' Sun" and "Unchain My Heart") is that the up-and-coming flutist Hubert Laws is matched with Mann on several tracks. —*Scott Yanow*

Live at the Whisky / 1968 / Atlantic ◆◆◆◆
Flutist Herbie Mann had a particularly strong group in the late '60s, a sextet also including vibraphonist Roy Ayers, Steve Marcus on tenor, guitarist Sonny Sharrock, bassist Miroslav Vitous and drummer Bruno Carr. Although this LP is long out-of-print, and its total length is under a half-hour, the group's sidelong jams on "Ooh Baby" and "Philly Dog" are danceable, funky and spontaneous, making this one of Herbie Mann's better sets of the era. —*Scott Yanow*

Memphis Underground / 1969 / Atlantic ◆◆◆
Herbie Mann has always been open to new trends in his music. For this 1969 studio session, he and three other top soloists (vibraphonist Roy Ayers and guitarists Larry Coryell and Sonny Sharrock) went down to Memphis and combined their talents with a top-notch local rhythm section. The music effectively mixes R&B and country rhythms with the lead jazz voices, although the material, which includes "Memphis Underground," "Hold On, I'm Comin'" and "Chain of Fools," is rather weak. —*Scott Yanow*

Push Push / Jul. 1, 1971 / Embroyo ◆◆◆◆
Flutist Herbie Mann opened up his music on this date (and during the era) toward R&B, rock and funk music. The results were generally appealing, melodic and danceable. On such songs as "What's Going On," "Never Can Say Goodbye," "What'd I Say" and the title cut, Mann utilizes an impressive crew of musicians, which include guitarist Duane Allman and keyboardist Richard Tee. This out-of-print LP is worth picking up. —*Scott Yanow*

● **Hold on I'm Coming** / Jun. 25, 1972–Jul. 8, 1972 / Atlantic ◆◆◆◆◆
This is one of the best Herbie Mann recordings and arguably his most rewarding of the 1970s. This long out-of-print LP features

the leader/flutist, David Newman (on tenor and flute), the avant-garde guitarist Sonny Sharrock and a fine backup rhythm section (electric pianist Pat Rebillot, bassist Andy Muson and drummer Reggie Ferguson) stretching out on a variety of R&Bish material including "Respect Yourself," "Memphis Underground" and "Hold on I'm Comin." The high quality of the solos and the spirited ensembles (which were inspired by the audience at the 1972 New York Jazz Festival) make this a generally memorable session. — *Scott Yanow*

Reggae / 1974 / Atlantic ✦✦✦
Despite its title, most of the music on this out-of-print LP is not actually reggae but a mixture of jazz, R&B and pop. Flutist Herbie Mann, guitarists Mick Taylor and Albert Lee and keyboardist Pat Rebillot combine with the eight-piece Tommy McCook band to create some spirited and danceable (if a bit dated) music. Together they jam on The Beatles' "Ob-La-Di, Ob-La-Da," the traditional "Rivers of Babylon," Moe Koffman's old hit "Swingin' Shepherd Blues" and an 18-minute version of "My Girl." The results are fun if not all that substantial. — *Scott Yanow*

Discotheque / 1974–1975 / Atlantic ✦✦

Water Bed / 1975 / Atlantic ✦✦

Bird in a Silver Cage / 1976 / Atlantic ✦✦

Brazil: Once Again / 1978 / Atlantic ✦✦
More than 15 years earlier Herbie Mann was among the first Americans to record in Brazil with local musicians and really explore bossa nova at its roots. In 1978 for this LP he performed music of contemporary Brazil with a bigger accent on its pop music than on its jazz. With Pat Rebillot contributing arrangements and his keyboard work, the music is listenable but somewhat forgettable. — *Scott Yanow*

Astral Island / 1983 / Atlantic ✦✦
Although Herbie Mann's flute is typically melodic and lively, the music on this out-of-print Atlantic album is generally pretty routine. Mann uses a "contemporary" electric rhythm section on a variety of then-recent Brazilian tunes, his own "Gold Rush" and even the "Theme from Tootsie;" the results were dated within a year of this record's release! — *Scott Yanow*

Opalescence / Dec. 1988–Jan. 1989 / Kokopelli ✦✦
This release by flutist Herbie Mann for his Kokopelli label is a disappointment. With a few exceptions (a remake of "Comin' Home Baby" and the bossa nova "Sir Charles Duke"), most of the Brazilian-based originals are rather forgettable, and the interpretations by Mann and his five piece rhythm section often border on easy-listening music. The musicianship is high, but the creative level is only so-so. — *Scott Yanow*

Caminho De Casa / Mar. 14, 1990–Mar. 16, 1990 / Chesky ✦✦✦
Flutist Herbie Mann and his group of the time (Jasil Brazz) perform contemporary Brazilian music on this CD, including three numbers by Ivan Lins. Some of the treatments are strictly easy listening or close to bossa nova, while others would fit into the "contemporary jazz" category. On a whole, this is a pleasing set, both as background music and for close listenings—one of Mann's better ones from the past 20 years. — *Scott Yanow*

Deep Pocket / Apr. 28, 1992–May 26, 1992 / Kokopelli ✦✦✦
This is a decent set that could have been a great one. Flutist Herbie Mann had a reunion in 1992 with many of his former sidemen (tenorman David "Fathead" Newman, guitarist Cornell Dupree and keyboardist Richard Tee) along with his contemporary pianist-vocalist Les McCann, and they play a wide ranging program of music (highlighted by "Moanin'," "Papa Was a Rolling Stone," "Sunny," "Mercy, Mercy, Mercy" and "Amazing Grace"). But somehow, once one gets beyond the nostalgia, the performances seem workmanlike and surprisingly uninspired, unlike Herbie Mann's live concerts with this group during the period. There are a few worthwhile moments, but this set is recommended mostly for Mann's greatest fans; get his earlier Atlantics instead. — *Scott Yanow*

Peace Pieces / Mar. 15, 1995–Jul. 16, 1995 / Kokopelli ✦✦✦✦

Shelly Manne

b. Jun. 11, 1920, New York, NY, d. Sep. 26, 1984, Los Angeles, CA
Drums, Leader / Hard Bop, Cool
Shelly Manne made a countless number of records from the 1940s into the 1980s but is best-known as a good-humored bandleader who never hogged the spotlight. Originally a saxophonist,

Manne switched to drums when he was 18 and started working almost immediately. He was with Joe Marsala's band (making his recording debut in 1941), played briefly in the big bands of Will Bradley, Raymond Scott and Les Brown and was on drums for Coleman Hawkins' classic "The Man I Love" session of late 1943. Manne worked on and off with Stan Kenton during 1946–52, also touring with Jazz at the Philharmonic (1948–49) and gigging with Woody Herman (1949). After leaving Kenton, Manne moved to Los Angeles where he became the most in-demand of all jazz drummers. He began recording as a leader (his first session was cut in Chicago in 1951) on a regular basis starting in 1953 when he first put together the quintet Shelly Manne and His Men. Among the sidemen who were in his band during their long string of Contemporary recordings (1955–62) were Stu Williamson, Conte Candoli, Joe Gordan, Bob Enevoldsen, Joe Maini, Charlie Mariano, Herb Geller, Bill Holman, Jimmy Giuffre, Richie Kamuca, Victor Feldman, Russ Freeman, Ralph Pena, Leroy Vinnegar and Monty Budwig. Manne, who had the good fortune to be the leader of a date by the Andre Previn Trio that resulted in a major seller (jazz versions of tunes from *My Fair Lady*), always had an open musical mind, and he recorded some fairly free pieces on *The Three and the Two* (trios with Shorty Rogers and Jimmy Giuffre that did not have a piano or bass, along with duets with Russ Freeman) and enjoyed playing on an early session with Ornette Coleman. In addition to his jazz work, Manne appeared on many film soundtracks and even acted in *The Man with the Golden Arm.* He ran the popular club Shelly's Manne-Hole during 1960–74, kept his music open to freer sounds (featuring trumpeter Gary Barone and tenor saxophonist John Gross during 1969–72), played with the L.A. Four in the mid-'70s and was very active up until his death. Throughout his career Shelly Manne recorded as a leader for Savoy, Interlude, Contemporary, Jazz Groove, Impulse, Verve, Capitol, Atlantic, Concord, Mainstream, Flying Dutchman, Discovery, Galaxy, Pausa, Trend and Jazziz in addition to a few Japanese labels. — *Scott Yanow*

Shelly Manne & His Friends, Vol. 1 / Jan. 22, 1944–May 26, 1944 / Doctor Jazz ✦✦✦✦
Although this LP has drummer Shelly Manne as the leader, in reality the 23-year old was just a sideman on these three four-song sessions; one of the main connecting threads. Manne is heard with clarinetist Barney Bigard and pianist Eddie Heywood in a trio (including five versions of "Tea for Two," and Bigard's originals "Step Steps Up" and "Step Steps Down"), in another trio with the great altoist Johnny Hodges and Heywood (including a memorable version of "On the Sunny Side of the Street") and on four rare titles with an Eddie Heywood group that includes Ray Nance on trumpet and violin, clarinetist Aaron Sachs, Don Byas on tenor and bassist John Simmons. These small-group swing performances are quite enjoyable but unfortunately out-of-print. — *Scott Yanow*

Hot Skins / 1952 / VSOP ✦✦✦
This reissue LP of a session originally for the long defunct Interlude label contains one of drummer Shelly Manne's more obscure dates. Manne teams up with the congas of Carlos Vidal and the bongos of Mike Pacheco in an oversized rhythm section of fairly unknown players; guitarist Tony Rizzi comes the closest to being a household name, and pianist Robert Gil, who contributed four of the originals, never became famous. The accent is on Latin polyrhythms, and the performances are generally quite likable and accessible if not all that essential. — *Scott Yanow*

★ **Vol. 1: the West Coast Sound** / Apr. 6, 1953–Sep. 13, 1955 / Original Jazz Classics ✦✦✦✦✦
Drummer Shelly Manne's first sessions for Contemporary contain plenty of definitive examples of West Coast jazz. This CD has four titles apiece from a 1953 septet date with altoist Art Pepper, Bob Cooper on tenor, baritonist Jimmy Giuffre and valve trombonist Bob Enevoldsen, four from a few months later with Bud Shank in Pepper's place and four other songs from 1955 when Manne headed a septet with altoist Joe Maini and Bill Holman on tenor in addition to Giuffre and Enevoldsen. With arrangements by Marty Paich (who plays piano on the first two dates), Giuffre, Shorty Rogers, Bill Russo, Holman and Enevoldsen, the music has plenty of variety yet defines the era, ranging from Bill Russo's "Sweets" (a tribute to trumpeter Harry "Sweets" Edison), Giuffre's "Fugue," the Latin folk tune "La Mucura" and updated charts on older swing tunes. Highly recommended and proof (if any is really needed) that West Coast Jazz was far from bloodless. — *Scott Yanow*

The Three and "The Two" / Sep. 10, 1954 / Original Jazz Classics ✦✦✦✦✦

These two sets for the Contemporary label (reissued on CD in the OJC label) are two of the more unusual sessions led by drummer Shelly Manne in the 1950s. *"The Three"* features trumpeter Shorty Rogers, Jimmy Giuffre alternating on clarinet, tenor and baritone, and Manne; no piano or bass! Some of the six performances (particularly the four originals) are quite free, particularly the completely improvised "Abstract No. 1." Although these selections were not influential, they rank second in chronological order (behind Lennie Tristano's performances of 1949) among free jazz records. The remainder of this set (*"The Two"*) is a duet between pianist Russ Freeman and Manne and is also quite advanced in spots, although in general it is a more swinging session while still being unpredictable. Overall, a very interesting reissue! —*Scott Yanow*

Swinging Sounds, Vol. 4 / Jan. 19, 1956–Feb. 2, 1956 / Original Jazz Classics ✦✦✦✦

This early edition of "Shelly Manne & His Men" is a well-integrated unit featuring the light-toned trumpet of Stu Williamson, the cool but hard-driving altoist Charlie Mariano, pianist Russ Freeman and bassist Leroy Vinnegar in addition to the drummer/leader. The excellent quintet plays one original apiece from each musician except Vinnegar in addition to Bud Powell's "Un Poco Loco," Sonny Rollins' "Doxy," the standard "Bernie's Tune" and their closing theme, Bill Holman's "A Gem from Tiffany." A consistently swinging and well-rounded LP that is overdue to be reissued on CD. —*Scott Yanow*

Shelly Manne & His Friends / Feb. 11, 1956 / Original Jazz Classics ✦✦✦✦

In addition to his regular quintet recordings with "His Men," drummer Shelly Manne recorded a series of trio dates with "His Friends" which generally included pianist Andre Previn and bassist Leroy Vinnegar; eventually Red Mitchell would take over the bass spot. This initial release from the group, as with all of the later sets, is really a showcase for the remarkable piano playing of Previn who was not even 27 yet but already had a dozen years of major league experience behind him. The trio largely sticks to standards and jazz tunes on this date with "Tangerine," Johnny Hodges' "Squatty Roo" and "Girl Friend" being among the highlights. —*Scott Yanow*

More Swinging Sounds / Jul. 16, 1956–Aug. 16, 1956 / Original Jazz Classics ✦✦✦✦

Drummer Shelly Manne and his 1956 quintet (with trumpeter Stu Williamson, altoist Charlie Mariano, pianist Russ Freeman and bassist Leroy Vinnegar) perform some challenging material on this CD reissue. The longest piece is Bill Holman's 15-1/2 minute four-part suite "Quartet" which, despite its potential complexity, actually swings pretty well. In addition, Manne & His Men interpret Johnny Mandel's obscure "Tommyhawk," a Mariano blues number, Charlie Parker's "Moose the Mooche" and Russ Freeman's "The Wind." Shelly Manne deserves great credit for being continually open to new directions and fresh material while staying on his own singular path. —*Scott Yanow*

★ **My Fair Lady** / Aug. 17, 1956 / Original Jazz Classics ✦✦✦✦✦

This trio set by "Shelly Manne & His Friends" (which consists of the drummer/leader, pianist Andre Previn and bassist Leroy Vinnegar) was a surprise best-seller and is now considered a classic. Previn (who is really the main voice) leads the group through eight themes from the famous play including "Get Me to the Church on Time," "I've Grown Accustomed to Her Face," "I Could Have Danced All Night" and "On the Street Where You Live." A very appealing set that is easily recommended; an audiophile version has also been released on CD by DCC Jazz. —*Scott Yanow*

Li'l Abner / Feb. 6, 1957–Feb. 23, 1957 / Contemporary ✦✦✦

In a follow-up to their hit recording of music from *My Fair Lady,* Shelly Manne and his Friends (a trio with pianist Andre Previn, bassist Leroy Vinnegar and the drummer/leader) recorded nine songs from the play *Li'l Abner.* Although Johnny Mercer and Gene DePaul wrote the score, none of the songs caught on except for the ballad "Namely You", and this LP (whose music has not been reissued yet on CD) was not a best-seller. The musicians are in fine form, but the melodies are not too memorable (when was the last time anyone played "If I Had My Druthers" or "Progress Is the Root of All Evil"?). Actually the main reason to search for this album is for the hilarious photo on the cover! —*Scott Yanow*

Bells Are Ringing / Apr. 15, 1958–Jul. 22, 1958 / Contemporary ✦✦✦

When Shelly Manne & His Friends (a trio starring pianist Andre Previn) had a surprise hit with their interpretations of melodies from *My Fair Lady,* it started a trend toward recording jazz versions of scores from plays. For this LP, Manne's trio (with Previn and bassist Red Mitchell) performs nine songs from the play *Bells Are Ringing.* Although seven of the pieces remained obscure, "The Party's Over" (which is heard twice) and particularly "Just in Time" caught on. As is always the case with this group, Previn's piano is the lead voice, and his virtuosity, good taste, melodic improvising and solid sense of swing are chiefly responsible for the music's success. —*Scott Yanow*

Shelly Manne Plays Peter Gunn / Jan. 19, 1959+Jan. 20, 1959 / Contemporary ✦✦✦

Son of Gunn!! / May 21, 1959–May 26, 1959 / Contemporary ✦✦✦

At The Black Hawk, Vol. 1 / Sep. 23, 1959–Sep. 24, 1959 / Original Jazz Classics ✦✦✦✦

Shelly Manne's Quintet was recorded extensively at San Francisco's Black Hawk club for three nights in 1959. Although not the most significant group that the drummer led, this edition (with trumpeter Joe Gordon, tenor saxophonist Richie Kamuca, pianist Victor Feldman and bassist Monty Budwig) was certainly capable of playing high-quality bebop. Originally their output was released on four LPs; the reissue expanded the music to five CDs. The first volume adds an alternate take of Frank Rosolino's "Blue Daniel" to a set that includes swinging version of "Blue Daniel," "Poinciana," "Our Delight" and "Summertime." The extended performances are easily recommended to straight-ahead jazz fans. —*Scott Yanow*

At The Black Hawk, Vol. 2 / Sep. 23, 1959+Sep. 24, 1959 / Original Jazz Classics ✦✦✦✦

Vol. 2 of the five CDs that document drummer Shelly Manne's Quintet at the Black Hawk club in San Francisco during a three-day period adds a new alternate take of Charlie Mariano's "Step Lightly" to the original program ("Step Lightly," "What's New," "Vamp's Blues"). These lengthy performances ("Vamp's Blues" is over 19 minutes long) give trumpeter Joe Gordon, the cool-toned tenor saxophonist Richie Kamuca, pianist Victor Feldman, bassist Monty Budwig and the leader/drummer a chance to really stretch out. Fine 1950s bebop. —*Scott Yanow*

At The Black Hawk, Vol. 3 / Sep. 23, 1959–Sep. 24, 1959 / Original Jazz Classics ✦✦✦✦

Originally released as four LPs, the Shelly Manne's Quintet's three days at San Francisco's Black Hawk club is now documented on five CDs. The third volume adds a second (and longer) version of "Whisper Not" to the original rendition, Cole Porter's "I Am in Love" and the spontaneous 18-minute "Black Hawk Blues." Considering how much music was documented, it is fortunate that trumpeter Joe Gordon, tenorman Richie Kamuca, pianist Victor Feldman, bassist Monty Budwig and drummer Shelly Manne were in top form for this enjoyable gig. The music is high-quality straightforward and uncomplicated bebop. —*Scott Yanow*

At The Black Hawk, Vol. 4 / Sep. 23, 1959+Sep. 24, 1959 / Original Jazz Classics ✦✦✦✦

Shelly Manne's 1959 Quintet (with trumpeter Joe Gordon, tenor saxophonist Richie Kamuca, pianist Victor Feldman, bassist Montyu Budwig, and the drummer/leader) was not his most important, but it was a hard-swinging unit well versed in bebop. Their three days at the Black Hawk (a popular San Francisco jazz club during this era) were almost completely documented, originally on four LPs and now expanded to five CDs. As with the first three sets, the fourth volume adds an alternate take (of "Cabu") to the original program ("Cabu," "Just Squeeze Me," "Nightingale" and a full-length version of their theme "A Gem from Tiffany"). The lengthy solos are consistently excellent, making this entire series recommended to straight-ahead fans. —*Scott Yanow*

Shelly Manne & His Men at the Blackhawk, Vol. 5 / Sep. 23, 1959+Sep. 24, 1959 / Contemporary ✦✦✦✦

Unlike the first four volumes of this series, which included three or four selections previously released plus a "new" alternate take, the final CD of the extensive documentation of the Shelly Manne Quintet's stint at the Black Hawk club consists entirely of previously unreleased material. Fortunately the performances by trumpeter Joe Gordon, tenor saxophonist Richie Kamuca, pianist Russ

Freeman, bassist Monty Budwig and the drummer/leader are the same high level as on the more familiar material. They perform obscure songs by Horace Silver (has anyone else ever recorded his "How Deep Are the Roots?") and Victor Feldman, in addition to a trio feature on "Wonder Why," the ballad "This Is Always" and a new version of the band's theme song "A Gem from Tiffany." — *Scott Yanow*

● **At the Manne-Hole, Vol. 1** / Mar. 3, 1961–Mar. 5, 1961 / Original Jazz Classics ✦✦✦✦✦
On the first of two CDs (both of which are straight reissues of the original LPs), Shelly Manne and His Men are heard in prime form performing live at their home base, Shelly's Manne-Hole. Trumpeter Conte Candoli was in particularly strong form throughout the stint, showing self-restraint yet playing with power. Tenor saxophonist Richie Kamuca made for a complementary partner while pianist Russ Freeman and bassist Chuck Berghofer formed an excellent rhythm section with the leader/drummer. For *Vol. 1* they play "Love for Sale," Duke Ellington's fairly obscure "How Could It Happen to a Dream," "Softly as in a Morning Sunrise" and Dizzy Gillespie's uptempo blues "The Champ." This classic music falls between cool jazz and hard bop. —*Scott Yanow*

At the Manne-Hole, Vol. 2 / Mar. 3, 1961–Mar. 5, 1961 / Original Jazz Classics ✦✦✦✦✦
The second of two CDs (originally an LP for Contemporary) features Shelly Manne's Quintet in superior form at the legendary Shelly's Manne-Hole club in Hollywood. Trumpeter Conte Candoli (in top form) and the cool-toned tenor Richie Kamuca work together very well while the contributions of the rhythm section (pianist Russ Freeman, bassist Chuck Berghofer and the drummer/leader) should not be overlooked. Together they perform four standards (highlighted by "On Green Dolphin Street" and "If I Were a Bell") plus their closing theme "A Gem from Tiffany." Both of the volumes are easily recommended. —*Scott Yanow*

Checkmate / Oct. 17, 1961–Oct. 24, 1961 / Contemporary ✦✦✦
This LP from Shelly Manne is a bit different than his other recordings of scores. In the past, it was his trio with pianist Andre Previn that performed music from hit plays (most notably *My Fair Lady*). For this date it is Manne's regular quintet (with trumpeter Conte Candoli, tenor saxophonist Richie Kamuca, pianist Russ Freeman and bassist Chuck Berghofer) that play seven themes from a now-forgotten television series (*Checkmate*) composed by Johnny Williams. None of the melodies caught on, but at least they gave these fine musicians some fresh material to improvise on. However, this album is not essential despite some strong solos. — *Scott Yanow*

Sounds Unheard Of! / 1962 / Contemporary ✦✦
In the early days of stereo, there were quite a few demonstration and sound effects records released that were designed to show consumers the wide variety of sounds that could be accurately captured on record. Most of those releases are quite dispensable, and that includes this duet set by guitarist Jack Marshall and drummer Shelly Manne. On a dozen standards, Marshall's playing serves as interludes between the percussion displays of Manne; the liners give a full description of every device he hits. The music is fairly routine even if the sound is excellent for the period. It is of little surprise that this set has not been reissued yet on CD. — *Scott Yanow*

2-3-4 / Feb. 5, 1962 / Impulse ✦✦✦✦
This unusual CD reissue has five selections from a date featuring the great tenor Coleman Hawkins, pianist Hank Jones, bassist George Duvivier and drummer Shelly Manne. Both "Take the 'A' Train" and "Cherokee" find the group at times playing two tempos at once (Manne sticks to doubletime throughout "Cherokee") and showing that they had heard some of the avant-garde players. The most swinging piece, "Avalon," was previously available only on a sampler while "Me and Some Drums" features Hawkins and Manne in a very effective duet with the veteran tenor making his only recorded appearance on piano during the first half. This CD is rounded off by a pair of trio features for Eddie Costa (with Duvivier and Manne); one song apiece on vibes and drums. A very interesting set with more than its share of surprises. — *Scott Yanow*

My Son the Jazz Drummer / Dec. 17, 1962–Dec. 20, 1962 / Contemporary ✦✦✦
This album is a real rarity. For his final Contemprary LP of this

era, drummer Shelly Manne and a sextet (with fluegelhornist Shorty Rogers, Teddy Edwards on tenor, Victor Feldman doubling on piano and vibes, guitarist Al Viola and bassist Monty Budwig) perform jazz versions of ten Jewish and Israeli-based melodies. Best known are such tunes as "Hava Nagila," "Bei Mir Bist Du Shein" and "Exodus." The arrangements by Rogers, Feldman, Edwards and Lennie Niehaus turn the music into modern mainstream jazz circa 1962, looking toward hard bop and the funky soul jazz that was popular during the era. This long out-of-print historical curiosity is more successful than one might expect. — *Scott Yanow*

Manne, That's Gershwin / Feb. 24, 1965–Feb. 26, 1965 / Discovery ✦✦✦
On this Discovery LP (which reissues a set originally on Capitol), drummer Shelly Manne heads a big band (arranged by John Williams) on seven selections and his usual quintet of the era (with trumpeter Conte Candoli, altoist Frank Strozier, pianist Russ Freeman and bassist Monty Budwig) on the three remaining songs. The Gershwin program includes some of the typical familiar standards but also versions of the lesser-known "By Strauss," "The Real American Folk Song," "Prelude #2" and "Theme from Concert in F." Although not all that memorable, this music generally swings, leaves space for concise solos and is fairly fresh. — *Scott Yanow*

Perk Up / Jun. 19, 1967–Jun. 20, 1967 / Concord Jazz ✦✦✦✦
This CD reissue brings back one of the oldest recordings ever issued by the Concord label, a set that was already nine years old when it debuted. Drummer Shelly Manne heads a strong quintet comprising trumpeter Conte Candoli, altoist Frank Strozier (who doubles on flute), pianist Mike Wofford and bassist Monty Budwig. Although the musicians are all associated with the West Coast hard bop tradition, there are plenty of moments during this stimulating set when they make it obvious that they had been listening with some interest to some of the avant-garde players, allowing the new innovations to open up their styles a bit. The fresh material (two standards and a pair of originals apiece by Strozier, Wofford and pianist Jimmy Rowles) inspire the soloists, and the music is not at all predictable. Worth investigating. — *Scott Yanow*

Outside / Dec. 11, 1969–Dec. 12, 1969 / Contemporary ✦✦✦

Alive in London / Jul. 30, 1970–Jul. 31, 1970 / Original Jazz Classics ✦✦✦
This CD reissue is taken from drummer Shelly Manne's brief avant-garde period. Actually Manne does not play much different than usual, but his sextet (trumpeter Gary Barone, John Gross on tenor, keyboardist Mike Wofford, guitarist John Morell and bassist Roland Haynes) was open to much freer improvising than one would have heard in Manne's more famous groups of the 1950s. John Gross is easily the most impressive soloist, but in general the well-intentioned music is not all that memorable. —*Scott Yanow*

Mannekind / 1972 / Mainstream ✦✦
One of the least interesting groups that drummer Shelly Manne led can be heard on this long out-of-print Mainstream LP. Manne tried hard to keep his mind open to the avant-garde and free jazz during this era, but his septet (comprising trumpeter Gary Barone, John Gross on tenor, pianist Mike Wofford, guitarist John Morell, bassist Jeffry Castleman and percussionist Brian Moffatt) only had one distinctive soloist (Wofford), and the group originals (by Wofford and Morell) are uncomfortable and immediately forgettable. Despite a few good solos, this is one of the weaker Shelly Manne albums. —*Scott Yanow*

Hot Coles / 1975 / Flying Dutchman ✦✦✦
This is an interesting, if often-eccentric LP. Drummer Shelly Manne and a variety of L.A.-based musicians of the mid-'70s (including pianist Mike Wofford, bassist Chuck Domanico, Tom Scott on flute and soprano, guitarist Tommy Tedesco, trumpeter Oscar Brashear and Victor Feldman on vibes and piano) perform unusual versions of eight veteran Cole Porter standards. The somewhat spontaneous arrangements are full of unpredictable moments, and even if everything does not work, the surprising nature of the performances holds one's interest throughout. — *Scott Yanow*

Plays Richard Rodgers' Musical "Rex" / May 6, 1976 / Discovery ✦✦
Drummer Shelly Manne, who first started the trend of jazz musicians recording scores from plays with *My Fair Lady* in 1956, 20

years later failed to hit pay dirt with his interpretations of eight forgettable songs from Richard Rodgers' Broadway musical *Rex*. There are some good solos from his sidemen (which include Lew Tabackin on tenor and flute, keyboardist Mike Wofford and bassist Chuck Domanico), but in general, this is a so-so effort with the musicians being defeated by the material. — *Scott Yanow*

Essence / Jul. 5, 1977–Jul. 6, 1977 / Galaxy ✦✦✦✦

French Concert / 1977 / Galaxy ✦✦✦✦
This is an excellent LP long overdue to be reissued on CD. Drummer Shelly Manne features pianist Mike Wofford (and bassist Chuck Domanico) on two standards ("Softly, As in a Morning Sunrise" and "Body and Soul") before welcoming the great altoist Lee Konitz to the group for four others (highlighted by "What Is This Thing Called Love" and "Take the Coltrane"). This combination of jazzmen works quite well, resulting in music that is both swinging and explorative. — *Scott Yanow*

Double Piano Jazz Quartet at Carmelo's, Vol. 2 / Sep. 12, 1980–Sep. 13, 1980 / Trend ✦✦✦

Double Piano Jazz Quartet at Carmelo's, Vol. 1 / Sep. 12, 1980–Sep. 13, 1980 / Trend ✦✦✦
An unusual 1980 session with drummer Shelly Manne heading a group that includes pianists Bill May and Alan Broadbent and bassist Chuck Domanico, but no brass, reeds, or woodwinds. Manne's crisp, steady drumming teams with Domanico's consistent bass to set the rhythmic foundation, while pianists Mays and Broadbent alternate solos and interact, complement, or contrast with Manne and Domanico. — *Ron Wynn*

In Zurich / Feb. 1984 / Contemporary ✦✦✦✦
Seven months before his death, drummer Shelly Manne was still in apparently good health for this trio outing with pianist Frank Collett and bassist Monty Budwig, Manne's next-to-last record. Collett has long been an underrated pianist and the LP is a fine outing for him. Highlights of the straight-ahead set include Miles Davis' "Solar," "Good Bait," "All of You" and a "French Medley" comprising "Where Is Your Heart" (from "Moulin Rouge") and "La Vie En Rose." Tasteful and swinging music. — *Scott Yanow*

Remember / May 4, 1984–Jan. 15, 1985 / Jazzizz ✦✦✦✦
When Shelly Manne died of a heart attack on September 26, 1984, at age 64, it was a major surprise, for he had been in apparently good health. This rather obscure LP from the Jazzizz label (no connection to the similarly-titled magazine) is the drummer's final recording, and it features his last working group, an excellent trio with pianist Frank Collett and bassist Monty Budwig. Highlights of the live set (Manne's final recording) include "Speak Low," "My Romance" and "Hi-Fly." In addition, Collett and Budwig on January 15, 1985, performed Collett's original "Remember" in tribute to the late drummer. Worth searching for. — *Scott Yanow*

Wingy Manone (Joseph Matthews Manone)

b. Feb. 13, 1900, New Orleans, LA., **d.** Jul. 9, 1982, Las Vegas, NV
Trumpet, Vocals / Dixieland
Wingy Manone was an excellent Dixieland trumpeter whose jivey vocals were popular and somewhat reminiscent of his contemporary Louis Prima. He had lost his right arm in a streetcar accident when he was ten, but Manone (who Joe Venuti once gave one cuff link for a Christmas present!) never appeared to be handicapped in public (effectively using an artificial arm). He played trumpet in riverboats starting when he was 17, was with the Crescent City Jazzers (which later became the Arcadian Serenaders) in Alabama and made his recording debut with the group in the mid-'20s. He worked in many territory bands throughout the era before recording as a leader in 1927 in New Orleans. By the following year Manone was in Chicago and soon relocated to New York, touring with theatre companies. His "Tar Paper Stomp" in 1930 used a riff that later became the basis for "In the Mood." In 1934 Manone began recording on a regular basis, and after he had a hit with "The Isle of Capri" in 1935, he became a very popular attraction. Among his sidemen on his 1935-41 recordings were Matty Matlock, Eddie Miller, Bud Freeman, Jack Teagarden, Joe Marsala, George Brunies, Brad Gowans and Chu Berry. In 1940 Manone appeared in the Bing Crosby movie *Rhythm on the River*, he soon wrote his humorous memoirs *Trumpet on the Wing* (1948), and he would later appear on many of Crosby's radio shows. Wingy Manone lived in Las Vegas from 1954 up until his death, and he stayed active until near the end although he only recorded one full album (for Storyville in 1966) after 1960. — *Scott Yanow*

● **The Wingy Manone Collection, Vol. 1 (1927–1930)** / Apr. 11, 1927–Sep. 19, 1930 / Collector's Classics ✦✦✦✦

● **The Wingy Manone Collection, Vol. 2** / May 2, 1934–Sep. 26, 1934 / Collector's Classics ✦✦✦✦✦

● **The Wingy Manone Collection, Vol. 3** / Oct. 3, 1934–May 3, 1935 / Collector's Classics ✦✦✦✦✦

● **Wingy Manone Collection, Vol. 4 1935–36** / May 27, 1935–Jan. 28, 1936 / Collector's Classics ✦✦✦✦✦
Trumpeter Wingy Manone recorded pretty frequently during the year covered by this CD, and his sextet/septet includes such top soloists (at one time or another) as clarinetists Matty Matlock and Joe Marsala, tenors Eddie Miller and Bud Freeman and trombonist George Brunies; plus trombone great Jack Teagarden is aboard for one session. With Manone taking spirited vocals on every selection, these Dixielandish performances gained an audience of their own during this early year in the swing era. Highlights of the fourth volume in this highly recommended series (which is reissuing all of Manone's recordings in chronological order) include "Lulu's Back in Town," "I'm Shooting High" and "The Music Goes 'Round and 'Round." — *Scott Yanow*

Wingy Monone and Sidney Bechet: Together at Town Hall / Oct. 11, 1947 / Jazz Archives ✦✦✦✦

Wingy Manone / Papa Bue's Viking Jazzband / Oct. 11, 1966 / Storyville ✦✦✦✦

Michael Mantler

b. Aug. 10, 1943, Vienna, Austria
Trumpet / Avant-Garde
Michael Mantler has been equally prominent in the performing and business ends of the improvisational world. He was part of the original group that formed the Jazz Composer's Guild hoping to improve the lot of jazz musicians. This was the forerunner to The Jazz Composers Orchestra and Jazz Composers Orchestra Association (JCOA), a nonprofit cooperative conceived to commission, perform and record original compositions for jazz orchestras in the '60s. The JCOA eventually started a record company, JCOA records, and distribution outlet, the New Music Distribution Service (NMDS). Mantler and Carla Bley, whom he later married, also formed Watt Works and Watt Records, a publishing company to issue their compositions and a recording label in 1973. As a trumpeter Mantler's a steady, occasionally outstanding,but not innovative or influential player. He's better known for his compositions and collaborations with Bley, which have often been recorded by either the JCOA or its members. Mantler began playing trumpet at 12 and attended the Akademie in Vienna. He studied trumpet and musicology before moving to America in 1962, settling in Boston. He studied at Berklee, then moved in 1964 to New York, working with Lowell Davidson. They played such places as the Cellar Cafe and Town Hall. Mantler also played trumpet with Cecil Taylor's group. After meeting Bley, the two became involved in various JCOA groups and organizations. They traveled to Europe in 1965, where they formed the quintet Jazz Realities with Steve Lacy and toured Germany and Austria.

Upon their return to America in 1966, Mantler composed a number of rather bleak orchestral works noteworthy for their slow tempos. He played trumpet on Bley's "A Genuine Tong Funeral" composition for Gary Burton's album with orchestra, then did his own double album on the JCOA label in 1968, working with Taylor, Don Cherry, Rosewell Rudd, Pharoah Sanders and many others. The album won several international awards including the Grand Prix, Academie, Charles Cros, France. Mantler joined Charlie Haden's Liberation Music Orchestra in 1969 and recorded with it for Impulse. He also conducted performances of his originals by the orchestra and soloists at The Electric Circus in New York. Mantler co-ordinated with Bley the recording of her *Escalator Over The Hill* in 1970 and 1971, and worked on a JCOA triple album with guest soloists Jack Bruce, John McLaughlin, Linda Ronstadt, Gato Barbieri and Cherry. He started The NMDS in 1972, and then he and Bley began Watt Works and Records in 1973. Mantler built a recording studio near Woodstock, New York in 1975 and received composition grants from the Creative Artists Program Service and National Endowment For The Arts. These and a Ford Foundation grant enabled Mantler to record *13*, a work for two orchestra and piano. He later recorded six more albums of his originals featuring Bley, Jack DeJohnettte, Steve Swallow, Ron McClure, Larry Coryell and

Terje Rypdal. Mantler eventually became JCOA/NMDS executive director and later worked, performed and recorded with Bley's big band. In the '80s Mantler's new orchestral suite "Twenty Five" was premiered in Cologne by The West German Radio Orchestra. He also continued recording on Watt, which secured a distribution deal with ECM, through the '80s. —*Ron Wynn*

No Answer / Jul. 1973–Nov. 1973 / Watt ✦✦✦
Music by Mantler, Don Cherry, Carla Bley and Jack Bruce with words from Samuel Beckett. —*Michael G. Nastos*

Silence / Jan. 11, 1977 / Watt ✦✦✦

Movies / Aug. 1979+Mar. 1980 / Watt ✦✦✦✦

More Movies / Aug. 1979–Mar. 1980 / Watt ✦✦✦✦

Something There / Feb. 1982–Jul. 1982 / Watt ✦✦✦

Alien / Mar. 1985–Jul. 7, 1985 / ECM ✦✦
Ambitious four-part composition that works at times and bombs at others. —*Ron Wynn*

● **Live** / Feb. 1987 / ECM ✦✦✦✦✦
Performance art at its heights, with Jack Bruce (b), Don Preston (synth) and Pink Floyd drummer Nick Mason. —*Michael G. Nastos*

Many Have No Speech / Apr. 1987–Dec. 1987 / ECM ✦✦
An intriguing concept with 42-piece Danish Radio Concert Orchestra, rockers and jazz elements. Not for all tastes. —*Ron Wynn*

Steve Marcus
b. Sep. 18, 1939, New York, NY
Soprano Saxophone, Tenor Saxophone / Hard Bop
A fine saxophonist who is often a bit overlooked, Steve Marcus has led relatively few sessions throughout his career. After attending Berklee he played with Stan Kenton in 1963. He recorded with Gary Burton (1966) and the Jazz Composer's Orchestra and had stints with Herbie Mann (1967–70) and Woody Herman. He led an early fusion group (the Count's Rock Band) and then gained some attention when he played with Larry Coryell's Eleventh House (1971–73). In 1975 Marcus joined Buddy Rich's Orchestra where he was a star soloist and an important lieutenant up until Rich's death in 1987. Steve Marcus has recorded as a leader for Vortex (1967–69), Storyville (1970) and much more recently Red Baron (1992). —*Scott Yanow*

Steve Marcus and 201 / 1992 / Red Baron ✦✦✦✦

● **Smile** / Feb. 16, 1993 / Red Baron ✦✦✦✦✦
This is one of Steve Marcus' best all-around recordings to date. Alternating barnburning version of "Oleo," "Confirmation" and "Woody 'n You" with ballads, Marcus tends to play the slower pieces on his lyrical soprano, saving the romps for his passionate tenor. Backed by pianist John Hicks, bassist Christian McBride and drummer Marvin "Smitty" Smith, Marcus is consistently brilliant within the bebop tradition although McBride's bowed bass solo on "Confirmation" almost steals the show. —*Scott Yanow*

Kitty Margolis
b. Nov. 7, 1955, San Mateo, CA
Vocals / Bop
One of the most talented of the female jazz singers of the 1990s, Kitty Margolis made a strong impression with her appearances at the Monterey Jazz Festival (starting in 1989). A chancetaking scat singer and a constant improviser, Margolis played guitar for ten years starting when she was 12, performing in folk rock groups in high school. She attended Harvard (during which she sang in a Western swing band) and San Francisco State University. In 1978 she began to perform as a jazz singer and often collaborated in the early '80s with guitarist/singer Joyce Cooling; among her sidemen were Eddie Henderson and Pee Wee Ellis. By 1986 Kitty Margolis was working regularly in the San Francisco Bay area with her trio, and she has visited Europe on a regular basis. Her two Mad-Kat records hint strongly at her great potential. —*Scott Yanow*

Live at the Jazz Workshop / 1989 / Madkat ✦✦✦✦✦
This CD (which adds "Too Marvelous for Words" to the original seven-song LP program) was the recording debut of Kitty Margolis, a talented bop-based singer who is both an expert scatter and a constant improviser. With fine backup from pianist Al Plank, bassist Scott Steed and drummer Vince Lateano, Margolis is in excellent early form on a set of high-quality standards with

the highpoints including "I Concentrate on You," "All Blues" and "All the Things You Are." —*Scott Yanow*

● **Evolution** / 1993 / Mad Kat ✦✦✦✦✦
Kitty Margolis is a brilliant scat singer who is also expert at interpreting lyrics and shows a great deal of enthusiasm in her performances. Her second release for her Mad Kat label is a wide-ranging set encompassing everything from Brazilian music, blues and Margolis' new lyrics to Wayne Shorter's "Footprints" and Cedar Walton's "Firm Roots," to some standards, ballads and hot scatting ("Anthropology"). The backup crew is pretty impressive too with Joe Henderson's tenor present on half of the selections, guitarist Joe Louis Walker adding fire to the blues numbers and pianist Dick Hindman offering sympathetic support throughout. This versatile set is a perfect introduction to one of the most exciting jazz singers of the 1990s. —*Scott Yanow*

Tania Maria (Correa Reis Maria)
b. May 9, 1948, Sao Luis, Brazil
Vocals, Piano / Latin Jazz, Pop
An enthusiastic performer who has the occasional tendency to ramble on too long, Tania Maria has been popular in the U.S. ever since she started recording for Concord in 1980. She studied classical music, moved to Paris in 1974 and relocated to New York in 1981. A spirited singer and a rhythmic pianist, Tania Maria has recorded for Barclay (1978), Accord (1978–79), Concord, Manhattan and World Pacific. —*Scott Yanow*

Piquant / Dec. 1980 / Concord Jazz ✦✦✦✦

Taurus / Sep. 1981 / Concord Jazz ✦✦✦✦✦

★ **Come with Me** / Aug. 1982 / Concord Jazz ✦✦✦✦✦

Love Explosion / Sep. 1983–Oct. 1983 / Concord Jazz ✦✦✦

The Wild / Sep. 1984 / Concord Jazz ✦✦✦

Made in New York / 1985 / Manhattan ✦✦✦

Bela Vista / 1990 / World Pacific ✦✦✦

Forbidden Colors / Nov. 8, 1991 / Manhattan ✦✦✦✦

Outrageous / Apr. 1993 / Concord Picante ✦✦
Tania Maria sticks to Brazilian pop music on her concise but unremarkable program. The entire focus is on her vocals, and there is little or no improvising over the repetitious vamps. The closer one listens to the admittedly danceable music, the more tedious it sounds. —*Scott Yanow*

Charlie Mariano
b. Nov. 12, 1923, Boston, MA
Alto Saxophone, Soprano Saxophone / World Music, Bop
Charlie Mariano's career can easily be divided into two. Early on he was a fixture in Boston, playing with Shorty Sherock (1948), Nat Pierce (1949–50) and his own groups. After gigging with a band co-led by Chubby Jackson and Bill Harris, Mariano toured with Stan Kenton's Orchestra (1953–55) which gave him a strong reputation. He moved to Los Angeles in 1956 (working with Shelly Manne and other West Coast jazz stars), returned to Boston to teach in 1958 at Berklee and the following year had a return stint with Kenton. After marrying Toshiko Akiyoshi, Mariano co-led a group with the pianist on and off up to 1967, living in Japan during part of the time and also working with Charles Mingus (1962–63).

The second career began with the formation of his early fusion group Osmosis in 1967. Known at the time as a strong bop altoist with a sound of his own developed out of the Charlie Parker style, Mariano began to open his music up to the influences of folk music from other cultures, pop and rock. He taught again at Berklee, traveled to India and the Far East and in the early '70s settled in Europe. Among the groups Mariano has worked with have been Pork Pie (which also featured Philip Catherine), the United Jazz and Rock Ensemble and Eberhard Weber's Colours. Charlie Mariano's airy tones on soprano and the nadaswaram (an Indian instrument a little like an oboe) fit right in on some new agey ECM sessions, and he also recorded as a leader through the years for Imperial, Prestige, Bethlehem, World Pacific, Candid (with Toshiko Akiyoshi in 1960), Regina, Atlantic, Catalyst, MPS, CMP, Leo and Calig. —*Scott Yanow*

★ **Boston All Stars** / Dec. 1951–Jan. 27, 1953 / Original Jazz Classics ✦✦✦✦✦
Altoist Charlie Mariano plays very much in a Charlie Parker style on these early recordings from Boston (eight from 1951 and six

from 1953), but his arrangements for the octet (six of the pieces from the former session) are quite original and unpredictable; only trumpeter Joe Gordon among the otherwise obscure personnel ever gained much recognition. The later six selections match Mariano with trumpeter Herb Pomeroy and the brilliant pianist Dick Twardzik in a quintet; Twardzik, with his odd mixture of Bud Powell and Lennie Tristano, consistently steals the show. A historical and generally enjoyable set, it's recommended to bop fans. —*Scott Yanow*

Charlie Mariano Sextet / Mar. 1953 / Fantasy ✦✦✦✦

The Bethlehem Years / Dec. 21, 1953–Jul. 11, 1954 / Fresh Sound ✦✦✦✦✦

Reflections / Mar. 14, 1974–Mar. 15, 1974 / Catalyst ✦✦✦
With Finnish musicians, including saxophonist Eero Koivistoinen. —*Michael G. Nastos*

Helen Twelve Trees / May 6, 1976–May 8, 1976 / BASF ✦✦✦✦

October / Oct. 5, 1977–Oct. 7, 1977 / Inner City ✦✦✦
A '77 session with onetime Charlie Parker imitator Charlie Mariano now as immersed in Asian and Indian music as he ever was in bop. He's working with a European rhythm section that includes keyboardist Rainer Bruninghaus and bassist Barre Phillips. There are some compositions that reflect Mariano's jazz background, while others have everything from classical strains to Asian scales and instruments. —*Ron Wynn*

Innuendo / Jul. 1991–Sep. 1991 / Lipstick ✦✦

Eric Marienthal

b. Sacramento, CA
Alto Saxophone / Crossover
Every once in a while (generally when he appears as a sideman) Eric Marienthal shows listeners that he can break away from playing crossover and is capable of being a creative improviser. He attended Berklee for two years, went on tour for seven months with Al Hirt, worked in the studios (including being on the staff at Disney) and in 1986 he met Chick Corea. Soon he was in Corea's Elektric Band and started recording his own dates for GRP. Eric Marienthal has also toured with David Benoit and Lee Ritenour in addition to recording with the GRP All-Star Big Band. —*Scott Yanow*

Voices of the Heart / Dec. 1987–Jan. 1988 / GRP ✦✦✦✦
Including Frank Gambale on a track, the solo debut from this Chick Corea Elektric Band saxophonist has nice compositions. —*Paul Kohler*

Round Trip / 1989 / GRP ✦✦✦
His second offering has former Chick Corea Elektric Band mates. —*Paul Kohler*

Crossroads / 1990 / GRP ✦✦✦✦✦

Oasis / 1991 / GRP ✦✦✦

One Touch / 1993 / GRP ✦✦✦

Street Dance / 1994 / GRP ✦✦
Altoist Eric Marienthal plays well enough in parts of this CD, but the material is generally poppish, a bit anonymous and forgettable. Since Marienthal co-wrote many of the songs with producer/keyboardist Jeff Lorber, he inadvertently proves that he is a stronger saxophonist than he is a composer. Vibraphonist Gary Burton makes an unimportant cameo on one song. Marienthal has sounded better elsewhere. —*Scott Yanow*

Dodo Marmarosa (Michael Marmarosa)

b. Dec. 12, 1925, Pittsburgh, PA
Piano / Bop
One of the finest pianists of the bop era, Dodo Marmarosa's career was cut short by mental illness. He played locally at first and then made strong contributions to the orchestras of Gene Krupa (1942–43), Tommy Dorsey (1944), Charlie Barnet (taking the opening piano solo on the hit "Skyliner") and Artie Shaw (playing with the Gramercy Five). Marmarosa was often teamed with Barney Kessel (with whom he had been with Barnet and Shaw) and both settled in Los Angeles by 1946. Marmarosa recorded with Boyd Raeburn and Lester Young, became the house pianist for the Atomic label, made an important session with Charlie Parker in 1947 (which resulted in "Relaxin' in Camarillo") and worked with his trio. But after a Savoy date in 1950, nothing was heard from him for a decade. Marmarosa resurfaced in Chicago

during 1961–62 to record two trio outings and a session with Gene Ammons (for Argo and Prestige) but then disappeared, permanently retiring in Pittsburgh. Dodo Marmarosa's 1946–47 recordings have been partially reissued by Onyx and Dial while live dates surfaced on Jazz Showcase, Swing House and Phoenix. —*Scott Yanow*

Dodo's Back / May 9, 1961–May 10, 1961 / Argo ✦✦✦✦
The Chicago Sessions / May 1962 / Affinity ✦✦✦✦

Joe Marsala

b. Jan. 7, 1907, Chicago, IL, d. Mar. 4, 1978, Santa Barbara, CA
Clarinet / Swing, Dixieland
An excellent swing clarinetist who could fit into Dixieland settings yet welcomed Dizzy Gillespie to a memorable session in 1945, Joe Marsala was the older brother of trumpeter Marty Marsala (1909–75) and the husband of the great jazz harpist Adele Girard (1913–1993). He freelanced around Chicago starting in the late '20s including with Wingy Manone and Ben Pollack. He recorded with Manone in the mid-'30s, playing with Wingy on 52nd Street during 1935–36. Marsala soon became a leader himself, and during the next ten years (much of which was spent playing at the Hickory House), he featured such sidemen as Adele Girard (who he married in 1937), Buddy Rich (his first important job), Red Allen, Eddie Condon, Joe Bushkin, Dave Tough, Shelly Manne, Max Kaminsky and his brother Marty among others. He retired from full-time playing in 1948, working instead in music publishing. However Joe Marsala continued playing on an occasional basis into the 1960s. His studio recordings from 1936–42 are all collected on a Classics CD. Other sessions have been released on IAJRC, Aircheck, Jazzology, Savoy, Black & White, Musicraft and a 1957 album for Stereo-O-Craft. —*Scott Yanow*

Joe Marsala 1936–1942 / Jan. 17, 1936–Jul. 6, 1942 / Classics ✦✦✦✦✦
Greenwich Village Sound / Nov. 29, 1944–Jan. 12, 1945 / Pickwick ✦✦✦✦✦

Branford Marsalis

b. Aug. 26, 1960, Breaux Bridge, LA
Alto Saxophone, Soprano Saxophone, Tenor Saxophone / Post-Bop, Hard Bop
The oldest of the four musical Marsalis brothers, Branford Marsalis has already had an impressive career. After studying at Southern University and Berklee, Branford toured Europe with the Art Blakey big band in the summer of 1980 (playing baritone), played three months with Clark Terry and then spent five months playing alto with Art Blakey's Jazz Messengers (1981). He mostly played tenor and soprano while with Wynton Marsalis' influential group (1982–85), at first sounding most influenced by Wayne Shorter but leaning more toward John Coltrane at the end. The musical telepathy between the two brothers (who helped to revive the sound of the mid-'60s Miles Davis Quintet) was sometimes astounding. Branford toured with Herbie Hancock's VSOP II. in 1983 and recorded with Miles Davis (1984's *Decoy*). In 1985 when he left Wynton to join Sting's pop/rock group, it caused a major (if temporary) rift with his brother that made headlines. Marsalis enjoyed playing with Sting but did not let the association cause him to forget his musical priorities. By 1986 he was leading his own group which eventually consisted of pianist Kenny Kirkland, bassist Bob Hurst and drummer Jeff "Tain" Watts; sometimes the band was a pianoless trio that really allowed Marsalis to stretch out. After a couple of film appearances (in *School Daze* and *Throw Mama from the Train*), Branford Marsalis became even more of a celebrity when he joined Jay Leno's Tonight Show as the musical director in 1992. However being cast in the role of Leno's sidekick rubbed against Marsalis' temperament, and after two years he had had enough. Branford Marsalis, who attempted to mix together hip-hop and jazz in his erratic *Buckshot LeFonque* project, has recorded steadily for Columbia ever since 1983 (including a classical set) and still seems to be searching for his niche. —*Scott Yanow*

Scenes in the City / Apr. 18, 1983–Nov. 29, 1983 / Columbia ✦✦✦✦✦
Branford Marsalis' debut as a leader is ambitious yet consistently successful. On "Scenes of the City," his narrative is in the same spirit of some of Charles Mingus' recordings of the 1950s. Otherwise the music is in the modern mainstream vein with

Marsalis (on tenor and soprano) hinting strongly at Wayne Shorter and John Coltrane, along with a touch of Sonny Rollins. The backup crew includes such notable young lions as pianist Mulgrew Miller and Kenny Kirkland, bassist Charnett Moffett and drummers Jeff "Tain" Watts and Marvin "Smitty" Smith in addition to bassist Ron Carter. It's an impressive start to a notable career. —*Scott Yanow*

Royal Garden Blues / Mar. 18, 1986–Jul. 2, 1986 / Columbia ++++
Quartet sessions that feature some outstanding piano by Kenny Kirkland. —*Ron Wynn*

Renaissance / Dec. 31, 1986–Jan. 28, 1987 / Columbia +++++
Marsalis' best ensemble with Kenny Kirkland (p), Bob Hurst and Tony Williams (d). Four standards, two of Williams' originals and one of Branford's. A very solid album. —*Michael G. Nastos*

Random Abstract / Aug. 1987 / Columbia ++++
First-rate quartet performances and excellent solos. —*Ron Wynn*

● **Trio Jeepy** / Jan. 3, 1988–Jan. 4, 1988 / Columbia +++++

Crazy People Music / Jan. 10, 1990–Mar. 1, 1990 / Columbia ++++

The Beautyful Ones Are Not Yet Born / May 16, 1991–May 18, 1991 / Columbia +++++

Bloomington / Sep. 23, 1991 / Columbia ++
This live set (part of which was included in the performance film *The Music Tells You*) features Branford Marsalis and his longtime trio (bassist Robert Hurst and drummer Jeff "Tain" Watts) really stretching out on six pieces. Most of the playing is unfortunately very long-winded and rather dull. Marsalis seems content to play the part of a chameleon, doing his impressions of late-period Coltrane, Sonny Rollins and (when he switches to soprano) Ornette Coleman. Also, the music lacks variety and Marsalis is off-mic part of the time. Although the final two selections give this set a much needed dose of humor, it is too little too late. —*Scott Yanow*

I Heard You Twice the First Time / 1992 / Columbia +++
A first-rate recent release by tenor saxophonist Branford Marsalis. This was his "blues" date and included songs and/or performances by B.B. King, Joe Louis Walker, Linda Hopkins and John Lee Hooker, plus a guest stint by Wynton Marsalis and contributions from Kenny Kirkland, Jeff Watts, Robert Hurst III and, of course, Branford Marsalis on tenor and soprano. He and the rest of the cast fill their roles well, but it's the least self-conscious performers, like vocalist Linda Hopkins, who steal the show. —*Ron Wynn*

Delfeayo Marsalis

b. 1965
Trombone / Bop
Imagine being the younger brother of Wynton and Branford Marsalis! It is little surprise that Delfeayo Marsalis took a while before making his debut on records. The son of Ellis Marsalis and the older brother of drummer Jason (1976–), Delfeayo was always interested in engineering, and he started off as a busy record producer, studying both trombone and studio production at Berklee. In addition to his producing, Delfeayo has written some of the most absurd liner notes ever seen, raving about his brothers while trying to pretend that he is an impartial observer! More importantly, Delfeayo Marsalis is a fine J.J. Johnson-inspired trombonist who toured with Ray Charles, Art Blakey's Jazz Messengers and Abdullah Ibrahim before recording his first album as a leader in 1992. He is long overdue for a follow-up. —*Scott Yanow*

● **Pontius Pilate's Dec** / 1992 / Novus +++++
The debut major label project by longtime producer and trombonist Delfeayo Marsalis. It's a concept work based on an instrumental interpretation about events behind Christ being crucified. Marsalis plays some long and harmonically impressive trombone solos and is joined by his brothers Wynton, Branford and the newest prodigy, Jason, plus pianists Kenny Kirkland and Marcus Roberts. —*Ron Wynn*

Ellis Marsalis

b. Nov. 14, 1934, New Orleans, LA
Piano / Post-Bop, Hard Bop
It is a bit ironic that Ellis Marsalis had to wait for sons Wynton and Branford to get famous before he was able to record on a reg-

ular basis, but Ellis has finally received his long-overdue recognition. The father of six sons (including Wynton, Branford, Delfeayo and Jason), Ellis Marsalis' main importance to jazz may very well be as a jazz educator; his former pupils (in addition to his sons) include Terence Blanchard, Donald Harrison, Harry Connick, Jr., Nicholas Payton and Kent and Marlon Jordan among others. He started out as a tenor saxophonist, switching to piano while in high school. Marsalis was one of the few New Orleans musicians of the era who did not specialize in Dixieland or rhythm & blues. He played with fellow modernists (including Ed Blackwell) in the late '50s with AFO, recorded with Cannonball and Nat Adderley in the 1960s, played with Al Hirt (1967–70) and was busy as a teacher. Marsalis freelanced in New Orleans during the 1970s and taught at the New Orleans Center for Creative Arts. He recorded with Wynton and Branford on *Father and Sons* in 1982, an album that they shared with Chico and Von Freeman. Since then Marsalis has recorded for ELM, Spindletop (a duet session with Eddie Harris), Rounder, Blue Note and Columbia. —*Scott Yanow*

The Classic Ellis Marsalis / Jan. 1963–Mar. 1963 / AFO ++++

Syndrome / 1983 / Elm ++++

Piano in E-Solo Piano / Jul. 24, 1986 / Rounder +++++
Ellis Marsalis got his time in the spotlight with this fine solo piano session. His mix of swing, Afro-Latin, classical and bebop was spotlighted on superbly crafted versions of Horace Silver's "Nica's Dream" and John Lewis' "Django," as well as Bud Powell's "Hallucinations" and Fats Waller's "Jitterbug Waltz." Marsalis' own originals, "Fourth Autumn" and "Zee Blues" were also expertly written, with charming melodies and smooth, relaxed, yet impressive solos. While he'll probably never get as much publicity as sons Wynton and Branford, Ellis Marsalis certainly deserves high praise for his formidable piano skills. —*Ron Wynn*

A Night in Snug Harbor, New Orleans / Apr. 30, 1989 / Evidence ++++

Ellis Marsalis Trio / Mar. 18, 1990 / Blue Note ++++

● **Heart of Gold** / Feb. 1991–Jun. 1991 / Columbia +++++
Pianist Ellis Marsalis' inspired mix of New Orleans and bebop influences has seldom been presented more effectively than on this session, nicely mixing stunning covers and excellent originals. Marsalis' touch, spinning phrases, surging lines and clever voicings were impressive on such standards as "Spring Can Really Hang You Up The Most" and "Love For Sale." He also conveyed the sense of longing and loss inherent in "Do You Know What It Means To Miss New Orleans," while his own "El-Ray Blues" was alternately funky and vibrant. —*Ron Wynn*

Whistle Stop / Mar. 20, 1993–Jun. 6, 1993 / Columbia +++++
For this CD, veteran pianist Ellis Marsalis performs songs composed by some of the top modern New Orleans players of the 1960s including drummer James Black, tenor saxophonist Nat Perrilliat, clarinetist Alvin Batiste, saxophonist Harold Battiste and himself. With the exception of Alvin Batiste's tunes (based on "Cherokee" and a Dixielandish blues), the originals have strong melodies, slightly tricky chord structures and sound quite fresh today. Marsalis utilizes his son Branford on tenor and soprano, bassist Robert Hurst and drummer Jeff "Tain" Watts; the young Jason Marsalis sits in on drums during two numbers. Ellis Marsalis is in particularly inventive form on this unusually obscure material. —*Scott Yanow*

Loved Ones / Aug. 14, 1995–Sep. 11, 1995 / Columbia ++++

Wynton Marsalis

b. Oct. 18, 1961, New Orleans, LA
Trumpet, Leader, Composer, Arranger / Post-Bop, New Orleans Jazz, Swing, Bop, Classical
The most famous jazz musician since 1980, Wynton Marsalis made a major impact on jazz almost from the start. In the early '80s it was major news that a young and very talented Black musician would choose to make a living playing acoustic jazz rather than fusion, funk or R&B. Marsalis' arrival on the scene started the "Young Lions" movement and resulted in major labels (most of whom had shown no interest in jazz during the previous decade) suddenly signing and promoting young players. There had been a major shortage of new trumpeters since 1970, but Marsalis' sudden prominence inspired an entire new crop of brass players. The music of the mid-'60s Miles Davis Quintet had been somewhat overshadowed when it was new, but Marsalis' Quintet focused on extending the group's legacy, and soon other "Young

Lion" units were using Davis' late acoustic work as their starting point.

During the past 15 years Wynton Marsalis has managed to be a controversial figure despite his obvious abilities. His selective knowledge of jazz history (considering post-1965 avant-garde playing to be outside of jazz and 1970s fusion to be barren) is unfortunately influenced by the somewhat eccentric beliefs of Stanley Crouch, and his hiring policies as musical director of the Lincoln Center Jazz Orchestra led to exaggerated charges of ageism and racism from local writers. However, more than balancing all of this out is Marsalis' inspiring work with youngsters, many of whom he has introduced to jazz; a few young musicians, such as Roy Hargrove, have been directly helped by Marsalis.

Wynton Marsalis' trumpet playing has been both overcriticized and (at least early on) overpraised. When he first arrived on the scene with the Jazz Messengers, his original inspiration was Freddie Hubbard. However by the time he began leading his own group, Marsalis often sounded very close to Miles Davis (particularly when holding a long tone) although a version of Miles with virtuosic technique. He was so widely praised by the jazz press at the time (due to their relief that the future of jazz finally seemed safe) that there was an inevitable backlash. Marsalis' sometimes inaccurate statements about jazz of the 1970s and the avant-garde in general made some observers angry, and his rather derivative tone at the time made it seem as if there was always going to have to be an asterisk by his name when evaluating his talents. Some listeners formed permanent impressions of Marsalis as a Miles Davis imitator, but they failed to take into account that he was still improving and developing. With the 1990 recording *Tune in Tomorrow,* Marsalis at last sounded like himself. He had found his own voice by exploring earlier styles of jazz (such as Louis Armstrong's playing), mastering the wa-wa mute and studying Duke Ellington. From that point on, even when playing a Miles Davis standard, Marsalis has had his own sound and has finally taken his place as one of jazz's greats.

The son of pianist Ellis Marsalis, the younger brother of Branford and the older brother of Delfeayo and Jason (the Marsalis clan as a whole can be accurately called "The First Family of Jazz"), Wynton (who was named after pianist Wynton Kelly) received his first trumpet at age six from Ellis' employer Al Hirt. He studied both classical and jazz and played in local marching bands, funk groups and classical orchestras. Marsalis played first trumpet in the New Orleans Civic Orchestra while in high school. He went to Juilliard when he was 18, and in 1980 he made his first recordings with the Art Blakey Big Band and joined the Jazz Messengers.

By 1981 the young trumpeter was the talk of the jazz world. He toured with Herbie Hancock (a double-LP resulted), continued working with Blakey, signed with Columbia and recorded his first album as a leader. In 1982 Marsalis not only formed his own quintet (featuring brother Branford and soon Kenny Kirkland, Charnett Moffett and Jeff "Tain" Watts) but recorded his first classical album; he was immediately ranked as one of the top classical trumpeters of all time. His quintet with Branford lasted until late 1985 although a rift developed between the brothers (fortunately temporary) when Branford finally quit the band to tour with Sting's pop group. By that time Wynton was a superstar, winning a countless number of awards and polls.

Marsalis' next group featured pianist Marcus Roberts, bassist Robert Hurst and drummer Watts. Over time the group grew to become a four-horn septet with trombonist Wycliffe Gordon, altoist Wes Anderson, Todd Williams on tenor, bassist Reginald Veal, drummer Herlin Riley and (by the early '90s) pianist Eric Reed. Marsalis has really developed his writing during the past decade (being influenced by Duke Ellington), and the septet proved to be a perfect outlet for his arranging. Although Wynton Marsalis broke up the band by 1995, many of the musicians still appear in his special projects or with the Lincoln Center Jazz Orchestra.

With the passing of so many jazz giants during the past few years, Wynton Marsalis' importance (as a trumpeter, leader, writer and spokesman for jazz) continues to grow. —*Scott Yanow*

All American Hero / Oct. 11, 1980 / Who's Who In Jazz ✦✦✦✦
Along with the other Who's Who album which was simply called *Wynton Marsalis,* this LP features some of the trumpeter's earliest recordings although in reality it is a live performance by Art Blakey's Jazz Messengers. At the time the drummer/leader had a particularly strong sextet with altoist Bobby Watson, Billy Pierce

on tenor, pianist James Williams and bassist Charles Fambrough. Together with the trumpeter (who was then not quite 19), the group performs a particularly strong set highlighted by "One by One," "My Funny Valentine (Marsalis' feature) and "ETA." It is interesting to note that his main influence at the beginning of his career was Freddie Hubbard, not Miles Davis. Both of the Who's Who albums contain excellent music. —*Scott Yanow*

Wynton / Oct. 11, 1980 / Who's Who In Jazz ✦✦✦✦

Wynton Marsalis / Aug. 1981 / Columbia ✦✦✦✦✦
Trumpeter Wynton Marsalis' debut on Columbia, recorded when he was only 19, made it clear from the start that he was going to be a major force in jazz. At the time Marsalis (who was originally a bit influenced by Freddie Hubbard) was starting to closely emulate Miles Davis of the mid-'60s and his slightly older brother Branford took Wayne Shorter as his role model. The inclusion of Davis' rhythm section from that era (pianist Herbie Hancock, bassist Ron Carter, and drummer Tony Williams) on four of the seven selections reinforced the image. The three other numbers feature such up-and-coming talents as pianist Kenny Kirkland, Charles Fambrough or Clarence Seay on bass and drummer Jeff "Tain" Watts, helping to launch the rise of The Young Lions. But although not overly original, there is a great deal of outstanding playing on this set, including a definitive version of Tony Williams' "Sister Cheryl" and the long tradeoff between Wynton and Branford on "Hesitation." —*Scott Yanow*

Think of One / 1983 / Columbia ✦✦✦✦✦
Wynton Marsalis' second Columbia recording as a leader features his working band of 1983: brother Branford on tenor and soprano, pianist Kenny Kirkland, either Phil Bowler or Ray Drummond on bass and drummer Jeff "Tain" Watts. They perform the ballad "My Ideal," Duke Ellington's "Melancholia" and Thelonious Monk's "Think of One" along with some group originals. Wynton was deep in his Miles Davis period while Branford (who was still most influenced by Wayne Shorter) was just beginning to come into his own. Of course Wynton was already a remarkable virtuoso a few years earlier. All of his recordings are worth getting, and this early document has more than its share of brilliant playing. —*Scott Yanow*

Hot House Flowers / May 30, 1984–May 31, 1984 / Columbia ✦✦✦✦
Wynton Marsalis, very much in his Miles Davis period, plays quite melodically throughout this ballad-dominated outing with strings. Branford Marsalis (on tenor and soprano), flutist Kent Jordan, pianist Kenny Kirkland, bassist Ron Carter and drummer Jeff Watts are strong assets, but it is Wynton's subtle creativity on such songs as "Stardust," "When You Wish Upon a Star," Duke Ellington's "Melancholia" and "I'm Confessin'" that makes this recording special. The arrangements by Robert Freedman generally keep the strings from sounding too sticky, and Wynton's tone is consistently beautiful. —*Scott Yanow*

★ **Black Codes (from the Underground)** / Jan. 11, 1985+Jan. 14, 1985 / Columbia ✦✦✦✦✦
This is probably the best Wynton Marsalis recording from his Miles Davis period. With his brother Branford (who doubles here on tenor and soprano) often closely emulating Wayne Shorter and the rhythm section (pianist Kenny Kirkland, bassist Charnett Moffett and drummer Jeff Watts) sounding a bit like the famous Herbie Hancock-Ron Carter-Tony Williams trio, Wynton is heard at the head of what was essentially an updated version of the mid-to-late-'60s Miles Davis Quintet (despite Stanley Crouch's pronouncements in his typically absurd liner notes about Marsalis' individuality). The music is brilliantly played and displays what the "Young Lions" movement was really about: young musicians choosing to explore acoustic jazz and to extend the innovations of the pre-fusion modern mainstream style. Marsalis would develop his own sound a few years later, but even at age 23 he had few close competitors. —*Scott Yanow*

J Mood / Dec. 17, 1985–Dec. 20, 1985 / Columbia ✦✦✦✦✦
When Branford Marsalis and Kenny Kirkland chose to leave Wynton Marsalis' group to make money with Sting, Wynton had to regroup fast. For this quartet recording with bassist Robert Hurst III and drummer Jeff "Tain" Watts, the trumpeter met up with pianist Marcus Roberts for the first time, performing originals by Wynton, Roberts, Ellis Marsalis and Donald Brown. Marsalis was still very much under Miles Davis' influence at the time, but at age 24 he had rather remarkable technique. He

stretches out in explorative and consistently creative fashion on these seven straight-ahead and generally unpredictable selections. —*Scott Yanow*

Standard Time, Vol. 1 / May 29, 1986–Sep. 25, 1986 / Columbia ✦✦✦✦
On the first of three volumes, Wynton Marsalis explores ten standards plus two of his originals with his quartet of the period (which consists of pianist Marcus Roberts, bassist Robert Hurst III and drummer Jeff "Tain" Watts). Marsalis' tone is quite beautiful on the well-balanced set; even the ballads have their unpredictable moments. Among the more memorable performances are his treatments of "Caravan," "April in Paris," "New Orleans," "Memories of You" and two versions of "Cherokee." —*Scott Yanow*

The Live at Blues Alley / Dec. 19, 1986–Dec. 20, 1986 / Columbia ✦✦✦✦✦
This double LP features the great trumpeter Wynton Marsalis and his 1986 quartet, a unit featuring pianist Marcus Roberts, bassist Robert Hurst and drummer Jeff "Tain" Watts. Although Marsalis during this period still hinted strongly at Miles Davis, his own musical personality was starting to finally shine through. With the versatile Marcus Roberts (who thus far has been the most significant graduate from Marsalis' groups), Wynton Marsalis was beginning to explore older material, including on this set "Just Friends," and "Do You Know What It Means to Miss New Orleans?" other highlights include lengthy workouts on "Au Privave" and Kenny Kirkland's "Chambers of Tain." This two-fer is recommended, as are virtually all of Wynton Marsalis' recordings. —*Scott Yanow*

Carnival / 1987 / Columbia ✦✦✦✦✦
Although this is not a jazz album, it should be of interest to jazz collectors. Wynton Marsalis switches to cornet and performs virtuosic pieces written for marching bands and wind ensembles, mostly from the 1890–1920 period. Marsalis makes the impossible sound somewhat effortless on such workouts as "Carnival of Venice," "Flight of the Bumblebee" and a couple of Herbert L. Clarke pieces. In addition, he brings out the beauty in some traditional folk songs (including "Sometimes I Feel like a Motherless Child") and wrestles successfully with Paganini's "Moto Perpetuo, Op. II." —*Scott Yanow*

Standard Time, Vol. 2: Intimacy Calling / Sep. 1987–Aug. 1990 / Columbia ✦✦✦✦
Wynton Marsalis' second of three standard albums was actually released after the third volume. On most of the selections the brilliant trumpeter is heard in excellent form with his quartet (composed of pianist Marcus Roberts, bassist Reginald Veal or Robert Hurst and either Herlin Riley or Jeff Watts on drums); tenorman Todd Williams helps out on "I'll Remember April," and altoist Wes Anderson is also added to "Crepuscule with Nellie." Marsalis' tone really makes the ballads worth hearing, and his unusual choice (and placement) of notes keeps the music stimulating. This mostly bop-oriented set is rounded off by a happy version of "Bourbon Street Parade." —*Scott Yanow*

Thick in the South: Soul Gestures in Southern Blue, Vol. 1 / 1988 / Columbia ✦✦✦✦
The three volumes that Wynton Marsalis subtitled "Soul Gestures in Southern Blue" (of which this CD is the first) are overall rather disappointing. This initial CD is the strongest of the three due to the inclusion of tenor saxophonist Joe Henderson and (on two of the five numbers) drummer Elvin Jones, but overall Marsalis (who was in the final section of his Miles Davis period), although playing quite well, seemed to have hit a dead-end. His five compositions lack any memorable melodies and his own virtuosic solos do not have any distinctive qualities; pianist Marcus Roberts occasionally emerges as the top soloist. However, once he had gotten his three-part tribute to the blues out of the way, Marsalis would once again make some giant leaps forward. —*Scott Yanow*

Uptown Ruler: Soul Gestures in Southern Blue, Vol. 2 / 1988 / Columbia ✦✦✦
The second of the three-part "Soul Gestures in Southern Blue" finds Wynton Marsalis at a transitional spot in his career. While his pianist, Marcus Roberts, had largely found his own style, the trumpeter was still searching and had not yet thrown off the dominant Miles Davis influence. This quintet outing (which also features the tenor of Todd Williams, bassist Reginald Veal and drummer Herlin Riley) lacks any memorable melodies although the

playing is fine. But overall the music is much more forgettable than Stanley Crouch's rather incredible liner notes. This CD can be safely passed by in favor of Marsalis' more recent projects. —*Scott Yanow*

Levee Low Moan: Soul Gestures in Southern Blue, Vol. 3 / 1988 / Columbia ✦✦✦
Wynton Marsalis' three-part "Soul Gestures in Southern Blue" (of which this CD is the final section) is a disappointment. None of the themes are particularly memorable, and although the individual solos are fine, not much really happens; overall it is a rather weird tribute to the blues. Actually the main significance to this particular set is that the trumpeter had for the first time put together the nucleus to his septet. Although there was no trombonist yet, altoist Wessell Anderson, tenor saxophonist Todd Williams, bassist Reginald Veal and drummer Herlin Riley were already in place while pianist Marcus Roberts was still a part of Marsalis' group. But musically this trilogy can be bypassed; get his more recent recordings instead. —*Scott Yanow*

The Majesty of the Blues / Oct. 27, 1988–Oct. 28, 1988 / Columbia ✦✦✦
This is a good album that should have been a great one. Two lengthy originals ("The Majesty of the Blues" and "Hickory Dickory Dock") find Wynton Marsalis displaying his rapidly developing writing skills which were happily being touched at the time by Duke Ellington and Charles Mingus. His sextet with pianist Marcus Roberts, tenorman Todd Williams and altoist Wes Anderson is in outstanding form on these performances. However the three-part "New Orleans Function" has two fatal flaws. Marsalis returned to his New Orleans heritage by welcoming the erratic clarinetist Dr. Michael White, veteran banjoist Danny Barker, trombonist Freddie Lonzo and trumpeter Teddy Riley as guests. Unfortunately an endless "Sermon" about jazz that was written by Stanley Crouch and is narrated by Reverend Jeremiah Wright, Jr., drones on for 16 minutes and is unspeakably pompous, killing the momentum for the record. In addition, the closing Dixieland blues is led by the frequently faltering Teddy Riley (while Marsalis plays second trumpet) and is much too ragged to have been released. So, the main reason to acquire this album is for the first two pieces. —*Scott Yanow*

Original Soundtrack from "Tune in Tomorrow" / 1989 / Columbia ✦✦✦✦✦
This soundtrack recording is very significant in the career of Wynton Marsalis. For the first time the trumpeter displayed a sound of his own; the Miles Davis influence was finally gone. In addition Marsalis not only debuted with his septet (which consisted of trombonist Wycliffe Gordon, altoist Wes Anderson, Todd Williams on tenor, soprano and clarinet, pianist Marcus Roberts, bassist Reginald Veal and drummer Herlin Riley), but in writing this score, Marsalis showed how talented an arranger he was; very much in the Duke Ellington tradition but without resorting to copying. The 16 selections are sometimes a bit fragmented (a few use extra personnel including clarinetist Michael White on six tracks and vocals by Shirley Horn and Johnny Adams), but they hold up very well apart from the movie and have plenty of spirit and humor. —*Scott Yanow*

Standard Time, Vol. 3 / 1990 / Columbia ✦✦✦
On the third of his three standards albums, trumpeter Wynton Marsalis meets up with his father, pianist Ellis Marsalis (along with bassist Reginald Veal and drummer Herlin Riley), for 17 standards and three of his originals (including "In the Court of King Oliver"). Wynton, perhaps because of his father's presence, is very respectful of the melodies, sometimes overly so. The result is that this set is not as adventurous as one would like although Marsalis' beautiful tone makes the music worth hearing. —*Scott Yanow*

Blue Interlude / 1991 / Columbia ✦✦✦✦✦
Wynton Marsalis' septet was the perfect outlet both for his playing and his writing. The impressive young personnel (pianist Marcus Roberts, altoist Wessell Anderson, Todd Williams on tenor, soprano and clarinet, trombonist Wycliffe Gordon, bassist Reginald Veal and drummer Herlin Riley) were flexible enough to sound like a New Orleans parade band or the David Murray Octet and Wynton's writing also made them occasionally appear to be a small group from the Duke Ellington Orchestra. On this CD the music is quite strong as are the solos, and the colorful group is heard at their best on a wide variety of challenging material. —*Scott Yanow*

★ **In This House, on This Morning** / May 28, 1992–Mar. 21, 1993 / Columbia ✦✦✦✦✦
For this double CD trumpeter Wynton Marsalis musically depicts in three parts a lengthy Sunday church service with program music composed for each of the traditional activities. The set does take quite awhile to get going with much of the first two parts consisting of introductions and transitions to themes that never seem to arrive. There are some exceptions, particularly Marsalis' violent trumpet distortions on "Call to Prayer," a spirited New Orleans blues and Todd Williams' tenor solo on another blues. However it is the third section that is most notable. The 28-minute "In the Sweet Embrace of Life" instrumentally portrays a preacher giving a heated sermon, building up to a very feverish level. Marsalis' model in his writing is clearly Duke Ellington. Trombonist Wycliffe Gordon is an expert with mutes, and Todd Williams is able to hint at both Paul Gonsalves on tenor and Dixieland clarinetists on soprano while altoist Wes Anderson and pianist Eric Reed are also major assets to the septet. Due to the memorable final section, this lengthy work is one of the highpoints of his career thus far. — *Scott Yanow*

★ **Citi Movement** / Jul. 27, 1992–Jul. 28, 1992 / Columbia ✦✦✦✦✦
This double CD contains Wynton Marsalis' score for the modern ballet *Griot New York*. Even more than his trumpet playing, his writing skills had developed quickly during the five years prior to this set. Marsalis' superb septet (which included trombonist Wycliffe Gordon, altoist Wes Anderson, Todd Williams on tenor and soprano, pianist Eric Reed, bassist Reginald Veal and drummer Herlin Riley) performs the complex and consistently colorful music, which goes through a wide variety of styles (including New Orleans jazz, swing, bop, modal music and even some sections bordering on the avant-garde). The results are unpredictable, exciting and quite enjoyable. This is one of Wynton Marsalis' finest recordings to date. — *Scott Yanow*

Joe Cool's Blues / Apr. 12, 1994–Aug. 25, 1994 / Columbia ✦✦✦✦
For this CD Wynton and Ellis Marsalis perform music both old and new that is heard on the *Peanuts* television specials. Wynton's septet (altoist Wessell Anderson, Victor Goines on tenor, trombonist Wycliffe Gordon, pianist Eric Reed, bassist Benjamin Wolfe and drummer Herlin Riley in addition to the trumpeter-leader) jam on eight of Marsalis' compositions and the perennial "Linus & Lucy," Ellis Marsalis' trio performs four of Vince Guaraldi's themes and, on "Little Birdie," an all-star group (including three of the Marsalises but not Wynton) back Germaine Bazzle's vocal. The music is reasonably enjoyable but not too substantial, worth getting even if it is not one of Wynton's more significant albums. — *Scott Yanow*

Warne Marsh

b. Oct. 26, 1927, Los Angeles, CA, d. Dec. 18, 1987, Hollywood, CA
Tenor Saxophone / Cool
Along with Lee Konitz, Warne Marsh was the most successful "pupil" of Lennie Tristano, and unlike Konitz, Marsh spent most of his career exploring chordal improvisation the Tristano way. The cool-toned tenor played with Hoagy Carmichael's Teenagers during 1944–45, and then after the Army he was with Buddy Rich (1948) before working with Lennie Tristano (1949–52). His recordings with Tristano and Konitz still sound remarkable today with unisons that make the two horns sound like one. Marsh had occasional reunions with Konitz and Tristano through the years, spent periods outside of music and stayed true to his musical goals. He moved to Los Angeles in 1966 and worked with Supersax during 1972–77, also filling in time teaching. Marsh, who collapsed and died on stage at the legendary Donte's club in 1987 while playing "Out of Nowhere," is now considered legendary. He recorded as a leader for Xanadu, Imperial, Kapp, Mode (reissued on VSOP), Atlantic, Wave, Storyville, Revelation, Interplay, Criss Cross and Hot Club. — *Scott Yanow*

Live in Hollywood / Dec. 23, 1952 / Xanadu ✦✦✦✦
This privately recorded club appearance (from the Haig in Los Angeles) features the vastly underrated tenor saxophonist Warne Marsh in excellent form. His long melodic lines contrast well with the Bud Powell-inspired playing of pianist Hampton Hawes. Bassist Joe Mondragon and drummer Shelly Manne complete the quartet which performs seven bop standards. Since Warne Marsh was sparsely recorded during this era, this is a valuable document of his playing. — *Scott Yanow*

Music for Prancing / Sep. 1957 / VSOP ✦✦✦✦
The Art of Improvising / 1959 / Revelation ✦✦
Ne Plus Ultra / Sep. 14, 1969–Oct. 25, 1969 / Hat Hut ✦✦✦✦
Report of the 1st Annual Symposium on Relaxed Improvisation / May 9, 1972 / Revelation ✦✦✦
Warne Marsh and Lee Konitz, Vol. 3 / Dec. 3, 1975–Dec. 5, 1975 / Storyville ✦✦✦✦✦
All Music / Feb. 21, 1976 / Nessa ✦✦✦✦
Tenor Gladness / Oct. 13, 1976–Oct. 14, 1976 / Disco-Mate ✦✦✦
It features brilliant and lively interplay between Marsh and the underrated Lew Tabackin (sax). — *David Szatmary*
How Deep, How High / Apr. 25, 1977–Aug. 8, 1979 / Discovery ✦✦✦✦
Warne Out / May 15, 1977–Jun. 5, 1977 / Interplay ✦✦✦✦
An album where wit and inventiveness are the theme, from the title to the leads. — *Ron Wynn*
★ **Star Highs** / Aug. 14, 1982 / Criss Cross ✦✦✦✦✦
A Ballad Album / Apr. 7, 1983 / Criss Cross ✦✦✦✦✦
Nicely played quartet session done in 1983 by Lennie Tristano disciple Warne Marsh. His exacting passages, winding solos and slow, intricately constructed phrases show how much Marsh was affected by Tristano's "cool" conception. His backing band of pianist Lou Levy, bassist Jesper Lundgaard and drummer James Martin falls in behind Marsh smartly, with Levy also taking a few nice solos. — *Ron Wynn*
Newly Warne / Mar. 15, 1985 / Storyville ✦✦✦✦
Two Days in the Life Of . . . / Jun. 4, 1987–Jun. 5, 1987 / Interplay ✦✦✦✦

Wendell Marshall

b. Oct. 24, 1920, St. Louis, MO
Bass / Swing
Best-known for his excellent work as a supportive bassist with Duke Ellington (1948–55), Wendell Marshall was the cousin of Jimmy Blanton. After attending Lincoln University and serving in the Army, he worked for a few months with Stuff Smith. In 1948 he moved to New York and joined Mercer Ellington. Soon he was with Duke, and his seven years touring with Ellington gave him a strong reputation. Marshall freelanced after 1955 (including recordings with Mary Lou Williams, Art Blakey, Donald Byrd, Milt Jackson and Hank Jones among many others) and eventually was working steadily in Broadway pit bands. He retired from music in 1968. — *Scott Yanow*

Mel Martin

b. Sacramento, CA
Alto Saxophone, Tenor Saxophone, Soprano Saxophone / Bop, Post-Bop
The leader of Bebop and Beyond and a versatile bop-based reed player with an open-minded style, Mel Martin has been a fixture in San Francisco since the 1970s. He had his first gig when he was 14, and after attending San Francisco State he dropped out to become a professional musician. Among his early associations were such rock groups as Santana, Azteca, Cold Blood, Boz Scaggs and Van Morrison in addition to working in the studios. During 1977–78 he led an adventurous fusion band Listen, a group that recorded two albums for Inner City and included among its sidemen steel drum wizard Andy Narell. In 1983, after recording a duet album (for Catero) with guitarist Randy Vincent, Martin formed Bebop and Beyond, a band that has since recorded for Concord and Bluemoon including tribute albums to Thelonious Monk and Dizzy Gillespie; Dizzy participated on the latter. Among Bebop and Beyond's sidemen have been Vincent, George Cables, Eddie Marshall and Warren Gale with such guests on their albums as John Handy and Howard Johnson. In addition to recently performing music from the Charles Mingus songbook with Bebop and Beyond, Martin has recorded a solo Enja set of Benny Carter tunes. — *Scott Yanow*

● **Bebop and Beyond** / Feb. 1984 / Concord Jazz ✦✦✦✦✦
Plays Benny Carter / Mar. 2, 1994–Apr. 30, 1994 / Enja ✦✦✦✦✦

Pat Martino (Pat Azzara)

b. Aug. 25, 1944, Philadelphia, PA
Guitar / Post-Bop
One of the most original of the jazz-based guitarists to emerge in

the 1960s, Pat Martino made a remarkable comeback after brain surgery in 1980 to correct an aneurysm caused him to lose his memory and completely forget how to play. It took years, but he regained his ability, partly by listening to his older records!

Martino began playing professionally when he was 15. He worked early on with groups led by Willis Jackson, Red Holloway and a series of organists including Don Patterson, Jimmy Smith, Jack McDuff, Richard "Groove" Holmes and Jimmy McGriff. After playing with John Handy (1966), he started leading his own bands and heading sessions for Prestige, Muse and Warner Bros. that found him welcoming the influences of avant-garde jazz, rock, pop and world music into his advanced hard bop style. After the operation, Martino did not resume playing until 1984. Although not as active as earlier, Pat Martino has regained his earlier form, recording again for Muse and Evidence. —*Scott Yanow*

El Hombre / May 1967 / Original Jazz Classics ✦✦✦

Strings! / Oct. 2, 1967 / Original Jazz Classics ✦✦✦✦
Guitarist Pat Martino's second recording as a leader (which has been reissued on CD) finds him essentially playing advanced bop. His quintet (with Joe Farrell on tenor and flute, pianist Cedar Walton, bassist Ben Tucker and drummer Walter Perkins) really roars on an uptempo version of "Minority" and is diverse enough to come up with meaningful statements on four of Martino's originals. —*Scott Yanow*

● **East!** / Jan. 8, 1968 / Original Jazz Classics ✦✦✦✦✦
Despite the title and the cover of this CD reissue (which makes it appear that the performances are greatly influenced by music of the Far East), the style played by guitarist Pat Martino's quartet is very much in the hard bop tradition. Martino was already developing his own sound and is in excellent form with pianist Eddie Green, drummer Lenny McBrowne and either Ben Tucker or Tyrone Brown on bass during two group originals, Benny Golson's "Park Avenue Petite," John Coltrane's "Lazy Bird" and the standard "Close Your Eyes." It's a good example of Pat Martino's playing in his early period. —*Scott Yanow*

Baiyina (The Clear Evidence) / Jun. 11, 1968 / Original Jazz Classics ✦✦✦✦

Desperado / Mar. 1970 / Original Jazz Classics ✦✦✦✦

Footprints / Mar. 24, 1972 / Muse ✦✦✦✦✦

Live! / Sep. 7, 1972 / Muse ✦✦✦✦✦

★ **Consciousness** / Oct. 7, 1974 / Muse ✦✦✦✦✦
Martino on the way up. Mostly quartet recordings for the brilliant guitarist. "Willow" is a dark, understated gem. Contains seven tracks, three by Martino, three standards and Joni Mitchell's "Both Sides Now." Guitar students should study this one. —*Michael G. Nastos*

Exit / Feb. 10, 1976 / Muse ✦✦✦✦

We'll Be Together Again / Feb. 13, 1976–Feb. 17, 1976 / Muse ✦✦✦✦

Starbright / Jul. 1976 / Warner Brothers ✦✦✦

Joyous Lake / Jun. 1977 / Warner Brothers ✦✦✦

The Return / Feb. 1987 / Muse ✦✦✦
Facile guitarist on a comeback with this live recording. —*Michael G. Nastos*

Interchange / Mar. 1, 1994 / Muse ✦✦✦✦

● **The Maker** / Sep. 11, 1994 / Evidence ✦✦✦✦✦

Steve Masakowski

b. Sept. 2, 1954, New Orleans, LA
Guitar / Post-Bop
A fine New Orleans guitarist whose advanced improvisations display the influence of his native city's early jazz and R&B scenes (at least rhythmically), Steve Masakowski attended Berklee in 1974. He invented a key tar in 1978, an early guitar synthesizer. In 1982 he recorded for his own private Prescriptions label, and he has since made albums as a leader for Blue Note and appeared as a sideman on dates led by Rick Margitza, Mose Allison, Red Tyler, Tony Dagradi and Johnny Adams among others. In recent times Steve Masakowski has toured with Dianne Reeves. —*Scott Yanow*

What It Was / Apr. 1993 / Blue Note ✦✦✦✦
Guitar Steve Masakowski has a guitar sound that falls somewhere between Jim Hall and John Scofield. His laidback music (ten of

the dozen songs on his Blue Note CD are his originals) is generally unpredictable, moody and full of strong solos. Masakowski's guitar largely dominates his CD, but there are a few good spots for Rick Margitza's tenor. Frankly, Masakowski at this point was a stronger player than composer, but several of the selections (particularly the mysterious "Budapest" and a couple of bossa novas) stick in one's mind. —*Scott Yanow*

● **Direct AXEcess** / Sep. 1994 / Blue Note ✦✦✦✦✦
Steve Masakowski dedicates his Blue Note CD to Joe Pass, and his unaccompanied renditions of "Monk's Mood" and "Emily" would have pleased the late guitarist. Masakowski, who is influenced by Pat Martino and to a lesser extent Jim Hall, also pays tribute to Wes Montgomery, Emily Remler and (on a melodic if unadventurous duet version of "New Orleans" with Hank Mackie) Danny Barker. The guitarists playing is in the modern mainstream idiom, and even if Masakowski's basic sound is not at this point instantly recognizable, his solos are inventive, swinging and versatile. Bassist James Singleton, drummer Brian Blade and (on six of the songs) pianist David Torkanowsky are excellent in support. —*Scott Yanow*

George Masso

b. Nov. 17, 1926, Cranston, RI
Trombone / Swing, Dixieland
An excellent trombonist who currently records for Arbors, George Masso has had a long if somewhat underrated career. Other than some early gigs (including a 1948 association with Jimmy Dorsey), Masso made his living from teaching in schools up until 1973. However he always played trombone on the side, and soon after becoming a full-time musician, he toured with the Benny Goodman Sextet (1973). Masso worked with Bobby Hackett, Bobby Rosengarden and the World's Greatest Jazz Band (the latter starting in 1975) and recorded with Scott Hamilton, Warren Vache and Woody Herman. He led sessions for Famous Door, World Jazz and Dreamstreet during 1978–83, frequently sharing the frontline with tenor saxophonist Al Klink and trumpeter Glenn Zottola. Since then George Masso has recorded for Sackville and Arbors and become a reliable fixture at jazz parties and classic jazz festivals. —*Scott Yanow*

Just For A Thrill / Aug. 1990 / Sackville ✦✦✦✦

● **Let's Be Buddies** / Jul. 14, 1993–Jul. 15, 1993 / Arbors ✦✦✦✦✦

Mark Masters

b. 1958
Arranger, Leader / Post-Bop
One of the finer arrangers in the Los Angeles area, Mark Masters worked for Stan Kenton's Creative World in the 1980s and has led his Jazz Composers Orchestra since the early '80s. His big band has recorded for Sea Breeze (1984 and 1986), Capri (1990) and Focus (1993); the latter a set of Jimmy Knepper compositions. —*Scott Yanow*

Early Start / Jan. 17, 1984–Mar. 27, 1984 / Sea Breeze ✦✦✦✦

Priestess / Dec. 1990 / Capri ✦✦✦✦

● **Jimmy Knepper Songbook** / Feb. 22, 1993–Feb. 23, 1993 / Focus ✦✦✦✦✦
This recording is a bit of a surprise for it features the Mark Masters Jazz Orchestra performing eight Jimmy Knepper compositions. Knepper is much better-known for his individual bop-based trombone style than for his writing. However Masters' colorful arrangements for his 14-piece big band show that Knepper is a talented composer too. In general the melodies are fresher than the chord changes (one can often guess the original sources), but the charts have their unpredictable moments on this continually interesting CD. In addition to such fine soloists as trumpeter Johnny Coles, tenor saxophonist Jerry Pinter, pianist Tommy Gill, Jr., altoist Gary Foster and baritonist Danny House (who is powerful on the blues "Who You"), Knepper himself is a major force throughout the program, soloing on all but two numbers and sounding very much in his prime. A highly recommended straight-ahead set. —*Scott Yanow*

The Mastersounds

Group / Cool
Vibraphonist Buddy Montgomery (1930–) and electric bassist Monk Montgomery (1921–82) came together to form the Mastersounds with pianist Richie Crabtree and drummer Benny

Barth in 1957, a melodic bop group. The band caught on for a few years, cutting ten records in four years for Pacific Jazz, World Pacific and Fantasy. Wes Montgomery appeared on one of their 1958 albums, a set of songs from the play *Kismet*. After the group disbanded in 1961, they had a brief reunion in 1965. The two Montgomery brothers had numerous opportunities to play with their more famous sibling under Wes' leadership throughout the 1960s. *—Scott Yanow*

Jazz Showcase Introducing the Mastersounds / Sep. 12, 1957 / World Pacific ✦✦✦✦
This is the debut of the lightly swinging quartet distinguished by vibist Buddy Montgomery. It appeals to fans of The Modern Jazz Quartet. *—David Szatmary*

The King and I / Sep. 19, 1957 / World Pacific ✦✦✦
The first of many dates (Kismet, Flower Drum Song) that use showtunes as points of departure. *—David Szatmary*

● **Kismet** / Apr. 22, 1958 / World Pacific ✦✦✦✦✦

Flower Drum Song / Dec. 4, 1958 / World Pacific ✦✦✦✦

Ballads and Blues / Jan. 7, 1959 / World Pacific ✦✦✦✦
This is an excellent showcase for the quartet's soft swing. *—David Szatmary*

The Mastersounds in Concert / Apr. 11, 1959 / World Pacific ✦✦✦✦

The Mastersounds Play Horace Silver / 1959–1960 / World Pacific ✦✦✦✦✦

Happy Holidays from Many Lands / 1960 / World Pacific ✦✦✦

Swingin' with the Mastersounds / 1961 / Original Jazz Classics ✦✦✦✦
Exquisite, precise swinging jazz, it delivers a light, unique sound. *—David Szatmary*

Date with the Mastersounds / 1961 / Fantasy ✦✦✦✦

Matty Matlock (Julian Clifton Matlock)

b. Apr. 27, 1907, Paducah, KY, d. Jun. 14, 1978, Los Angeles, CA
Clarinet / Dixieland, Swing
A fine clarinetist, Matty Matlock also gained a lot of work in the 1950s as an arranger for Dixieland-flavored sessions. He started playing clarinet when he was 12 and performed in a variety of little-known bands including one led by Jimmy Joy. He was with Ben Pollack's group during 1929–34, and when the orchestra became Bob Crosby's, Matlock stayed on. He became busy as an arranger but continued playing with Crosby off and on until 1942. At that point he moved to Los Angeles and worked in the studios. Matlock worked with Red Nichols and Pollack again and participated in the music for the film and the television series *Pete Kelly's Blues*. Matty Matlock led the Rampart Street Paraders in the 1950s, had many reunions with Bob Crosby and continued playing into the mid-'70s. Unfortunately his recordings as a leader for the X, Columbia, Tops and Warner Bros. labels during 1954–60 are all long out of print. *—Scott Yanow*

Pete Kelly's Blues / Jun. 7, 1955–Jun. 9, 1955 / Columbia ✦✦✦✦

Pete Kelly at Home / 1957 / RCA ✦✦✦✦

● **And They Called It Dixieland** / Oct. 22, 1958–Nov. 5, 1958 / Warner Brothers ✦✦✦✦✦

Bennie Maupin

b. Aug. 29, 1940, Detroit, MI
Flute, Bass Clarinet, Soprano Saxophone, Tenor Saxophone / Post Bop, Hard Bop, Fusion
Bennie Maupin is best-known for his association with Herbie Hancock and his atmospheric bass clarinet playing on Miles Davis' classic *Bitches Brew* album. Maupin started playing tenor in high school and attended the Detroit Institute for Musical Arts, playing locally in Detroit. He moved to New York in 1963, freelancing with many groups including ones led by Marion Brown and Pharoah Sanders. Maupin played regularly with Roy Haynes (1966–68) and Horace Silver (1968–69), recording with McCoy Tyner (1968), Lee Morgan (1970) and Woody Shaw. After recording with Miles, he joined the Herbie Hancock Sextet. When Hancock broke up his group to form the more commercial Headhunters in 1973, Maupin was the only holdover. He led dates for ECM (1974) and a commercial one for Mercury (1976–77) but failed to catch on as a bandleader and has maintained a low profile during the past 15 years. *—Scott Yanow*

Almanac / 1967 / Improvising Artists ✦✦✦
Hard-edged swing and improvisations with Mike Nock, Cecil McBee and Eddie Marshall. *—Michael G. Nastos*

● **The Jewel in the Lotus** / Mar. 1974 / ECM ✦✦✦✦✦
Detroit multi-instrumentalist with other members of Herbie Hancock's Mwandishi. Early-period progressive fusion. *—Michael G. Nastos*

Slow Traffic to the Right / 1976 1977 / Mercury ✦✦

Bill Mays

b. Feb. 5, 1944, Sacramento, CA
Piano / Post Bop
A fine pianist, Bill Mays has often worked behind the scenes, leading to him being a somewhat overlooked jazz improviser. Mays worked in Los Angeles as a studio musician from the late '60s on, accompanying Sarah Vaughan (1972–73) and Al Jarreau (1975) but mostly doing session work. In the early '80s he began to record jazz as a sideman with Howard Roberts, Bud Shank, Bobby Shew, Road Work Ahead and Mark Murphy. He recorded a duet date with Red Mitchell for ITI (1982) and led a quintet album for Trend (1983). In 1984 Mays moved to New York, and since then he has worked with Murphy, Gerry Mulligan, Ron Carter, James Moody, Sonny Stitt, Art Pepper and the Mel Lewis Orchestra among others. Bill Mays has recorded fairly regularly for DMP (duet records with Ray Drummond) and especially Concord. *—Scott Yanow*

Two of a Mind / Oct. 1982 / ITI ✦✦✦✦

Tha's Delights / Jan. 24, 1983 / Trend ✦✦✦✦

Kaleidoscope / Oct. 1989 / Jazz Alliance ✦✦✦
Recent release by pianist Bill Mays, pairing him with frequent partner Dick Oatts, plus Peter Sprague, Havie Swartz and Jeff Hirschfield for a contemporary jazz, fusion and mainstream set. Mays takes solo honors, but there's no real outstanding individual player or composition. *—Ron Wynn*

One to One, Vol. 1 / Dec. 4, 1989–Dec. 5, 1989 / DMP ✦✦✦✦

One to One, Vol. 2 / Dec. 19, 1990–Dec. 20, 1990 / DMP ✦✦✦✦

● **Live at Maybeck Recital Hall, Vol. 26** / Sep. 1992 / Concord Jazz ✦✦✦✦✦
Bill Mays gets a rare opportunity to record a full CD unaccompanied on his entry in the renowned *Maybeck Recital Hall* series. He mixes together swing standards with a few more recent selections. Mays' brilliant rendition of "A Nightingale Sang in Berkeley Square" (which starts and ends with a very impressionistic fantasy, making one wonder if its swinging middle section was indeed a dream) is most memorable. Also fun are his renditions of "Stompin' at the Savoy," "I'm Confessin'" and a boogie-woogie filled "Jitterbug Waltz." *—Scott Yanow*

An Ellington Affair / Jul. 22, 1994 / Concord Jazz ✦✦✦✦

Lyle Mays

b. Nov. 27, 1953, Wausaukee, WI
Keyboards, Piano / Post Bop
Lyle Mays' style is difficult to describe, more atmospheric (with plenty of unique colors) than swinging and an invaluable part of the sound of the Pat Metheny Group. Mays played and composed for the North Texas State University Lab Band in the mid-1970's. He met Metheny in 1975, toured with Woody Herman's Orchestra (1975–76) and then joined Metheny's band, continuing to play with the guitarist's group up to the present time. Lyle Mays (who is also an excellent acoustic pianist) has recorded two albums as a leader for Geffen (1986 and 1988). *—Scott Yanow*

Lyle Mays / 1985 / Geffen ✦✦✦✦

Street Dreams / 1988 / Geffen ✦✦✦
This is more to the fusion side but has lots of exceptional playing. *—Ron Wynn*

● **Fictionary** / Apr. 23, 1992 / Geffen ✦✦✦✦✦
Lyle Mays, who came to fame for his electric collaborations with Pat Metheny, surprised many with this superior outing in an acoustic trio setting. On the liner jacket Mays thanks Herbie Hancock, Keith Jarrett and Paul Bley for their inspiration. If one adds in Chick Corea and especially Bill Evans, that should give listeners an idea what to expect. However to his credit (and with the assistance of bassist Marc Johnson and drummer Jack Dejohnette)

Mays avoids performing overly played standards and sticks mostly to originals (including two free improvisations). There is no coasting on this excellent set. —*Scott Yanow*

Cecil McBee

b. May 19, 1935, Tulsa, OK
Bass / Post Bop, Avant-Garde
A masterful bassist with an authoritative sound and a thoughtful but adventurous style, Cecil McBee uplifts every session he is on. After playing clarinet in his early years, he switched to bass when he was 17. After college McBee played with Dinah Washington in 1959 before going in the military. After his discharge in 1962 he moved to Detroit where he played with Paul Winter (1963–64). Relocating to New York in 1964, McBee worked and recorded with many top advanced players including Jackie McLean, Wayne Shorter, Charles Tolliver, the Charles Lloyd Quartet (1966), Yusef Lateef, Sam Rivers, Pharoah Sanders, Alice Coltrane, Abdullah Ibrahim, Sonny Rollins and Chico Freeman among many others. Among his associations in the 1980s were McCoy Tyner, James Newton, Joanne Brackeen and (from 1984) the Leaders. Cecil McBee has led his own sessions for Strata East (1974), Enja and India Navigation. —*Scott Yanow*

Music from the Source / Aug. 2, 1977 / Enja ✦✦✦✦✦
Compassion / Aug. 8, 1977 / Enja ✦✦✦✦✦
Fine late '70s sextet date led by outstanding bassist Cecil McBee and including a great lineup with tenor saxophonist Chico Freeman and dual percussionists in The Art Ensemble's Don Moye and the late Steve McCall. —*Ron Wynn*

Alternate Spaces / 1979 / India Navigation ✦✦✦
● **Flying Out** / 1982 / India Navigation ✦✦✦✦✦

Christian McBride

b. May 21, 1972, Philadelphia, PA
Bass / Hard Bop
Everyone's favorite young acoustic bassist of the 1990s, Christian McBride's large sound and expertise both with plucked and bowed solos recall Ray Brown and particularly Paul Chambers. He actually started on electric bass when he was eight and took R&B gigs in high school, but by then he was getting more interested in jazz and playing the acoustic bass. McBride studied at Juilliard (starting in 1989) and then played briefly in the bands of Bobby Watson, Benny Golson, Roy Hargrove and Freddie Hubbard. He toured with the Benny Green Trio, played duets with Ray Brown at the 1994 Monterey Jazz Festival and recorded his debut as a leader for Verve before touring with his own group in 1995. —*Scott Yanow*

Gettin' To It / Aug. 30, 1994–Sep. 1, 1994 / Verve ✦✦✦✦

Steve McCall

b. Sept. 20, 1933, Chicago, IL, d. May 24, 1989
Drums / Avant-Garde
One of the finest drummers in free jazz, Steve McCall was a subtle improviser who could keep a pulse going without actually stating the beat. He played early on with Lucky Carmichael, a blues singer. McCall met Muhal Richard Abrams in 1961 and became a founding member of the AACM in 1965. Based in Chicago, McCall played with hard bop groups but made more of an impact performing with top avant-garde players including Anthony Braxton, Leroy Jenkins, Joseph Jarman, Roscoe Mitchell and Leo Smith. McCall was in Paris during 1967–70, playing and recording with Braxton, Marion Brown and Gunter Hampel. He returned to Chicago in 1970, was on a session with Dexter Gordon and Gene Ammons and was in the trio Reflection with Henry Threadgill and Fred Hopkins. After another year in Europe, McCall went to New York in 1975 where he reunited with Threadgill and Hopkins, and they formed the successful avant-garde group Air. McCall was with Air until the early '80s, also recording with Chico Freeman, Arthur Blythe and David Murray. McCall played with Cecil Taylor's Unit in 1985 and performed regularly with Roscoe Mitchell's Quartet up until his death from a stroke. Although he was on a lot of important sessions (including dates with Joseph Jarman, Fred Anderson and Murray's octet), Steve McCall never led an album of his own. —*Scott Yanow*

Paul McCandless

b. Mar. 24, 1947, Indiana, PA
English Horn, Oboe, Soprano Saxophone / New Age, Post Bop
A talented multi-instrumentalist, Paul McCandless is best-known for his longtime association with Oregon and for the floating and meditative sounds that he achieves out of his unusual combination of instruments. McCandless played in Paul Winter's band the Winter Consort (1968–73), and then (with Ralph Towner, Glen Moore and Collin Walcott) he left the group to form Oregon. McCandless is still primarily associated with Oregon (which is operating on a part-time basis in the 1990s) although he has also played and recorded with Gallery and Eberhard Weber and has led sessions of his own for Elektra, Landslide and Windham Hill. —*Scott Yanow*

All the Mornings Bring / Jan. 1979 / Elektra ✦✦✦✦
With strings and horns. Quite enjoyable. —*Michael G. Nastos*

Navigator / Feb. 1981 / Landslide ✦✦✦✦✦
Group includes McCandless (on his usual soprano sax, English horn, oboe, bass clarinet), vocalist Jay Clayton and vibist David Samuels plus Traut and Rodby. —*Michael G. Nastos*

Heresay / 1988 / Windham Hill ✦✦✦
This is a studio date with Art Lande (p) and Trilok Gurtu (per). Atmospheric without being dissipated. Very good record. —*Michael G. Nastos*

Premonition / Oct. 1991–Dec. 1991 / Windham Hill ✦✦✦

Les McCann

b. Sep. 23, 1935, Lexington, KY
Piano, Vocals / Soul Jazz, Hard Bop
Les McCann reached the peak of his career at the 1968 Montreux Jazz Festival, recording "Compared to What" and "Cold Duck Time" for Atlantic (*Swiss Movement*) with Eddie Harris and Benny Bailey. Although he has done some worthwhile work since then, much of it has been anti-climatic.

Les McCann first gained some fame in 1956 when he won a talent contest in the Navy as a singer that resulted in an appearance on television on *The Ed Sullivan Show*. After being discharged, he formed a trio in Los Angeles. McCann turned down an invitation to join the Cannonball Adderley Quintet so he could work on his own music. He signed a contract with Pacific Jazz and in 1960 gained some fame with his albums *Les McCann Plays the Truth* and *The Shout*. His soulful funk style on piano was influential, and McCann's singing was largely secondary until the mid-'60s. He recorded many albums for Pacific Jazz during 1960–64, mostly with his trio but also featuring Ben Webster, Richard "Groove" Holmes, Blue Mitchell, Stanley Turrentine, Joe Pass, the Jazz Crusaders and the Gerald Wilson Orchestra. McCann switched to Limelight during 1965–67 and then signed with Atlantic in 1968. After the success of *Swiss Movement*, McCann emphasized his singing at the expense of his playing, and he began to utilize electric keyboards. His recordings became less interesting from that point on, and after his Atlantic contract ran out in 1976, McCann appeared on records much less often. However he stayed popular, and a 1994 reunion tour with Eddie Harris was quite successful. —*Scott Yanow*

● **Les McCann Anthology: Relationships** / Feb. 1960–Nov. 1972 / Rhino/Atlantic ✦✦✦✦✦
Keyboardist/vocalist Les McCann ranked among jazz's more successful populists, injecting healthy doses of blues, soul and R&B vocals and feeling into his work without neglecting the improvisational end. McCann made hits but didn't plug into any formula, moving back and forth between short, pop-centered arrangements and longer, looser funk jams. The 21 tracks on this twin-CD set range from trio works to complex, multi-artist suites and include two songs from his tenure with Eddie Harris, plus collaborations with The Jazz Crusaders, Groove Holmes, Ben Webster, the Gerald Wilson orchestra, Stanley Turrentine and Lou Rawls. —*Ron Wynn*

The Shout / Jan. 1960 / Pacific Jazz ✦✦✦
Les McCann in San Francisco / Dec. 1960 / Pacific Jazz ✦✦✦✦
Les McCann Plays the Truth / 1960 / Pacific Jazz ✦✦✦✦
● **Les McCann Ltd. in New York** / 12 / Pacific Jazz ✦✦✦✦✦
1989 reissue; w/ hot tenor from Stanley Turrentine. —*Ron Wynn*
Les McCann Sings / Aug. 1961 / Pacific Jazz ✦✦✦✦
A super set with Ben Webster (ts) and Groove Holmes on organ. Soul-jazz and blues at their best. —*Ron Wynn*

Les McCann Plays the Shampoo at the Village / Dec. 28, 1961 / Pacific Jazz ✦✦✦

Pretty Lady / 1961 / Pacific Jazz ✦✦✦✦

Les McCann on Time / Jul. 1962–Aug. 1962 / Pacific Jazz ✦✦✦✦

The Gospel Truth / 1963 / Pacific Jazz ✦✦✦

Jazz Waltz / 1963 / Pacific Jazz ✦✦✦

Soul Hits / 1963 / Pacific Jazz ✦✦✦✦

But Not Really / Dec. 1964 / Limelight ✦✦✦✦

McCanna / 1964 / Pacific Jazz ✦✦✦

Spanish Onions / 1964 / Pacific Jazz ✦✦✦✦

Live at Shelly's Manne-Hole / Dec. 31, 1965 / Limelight ✦✦✦✦

Les McCann Plays the Hits / Sep. 9, 1966–Dec. 28, 1966 / Limelight ✦✦✦

Bucket of Grease / Dec. 27, 1966–Dec. 28, 1966 / Limelight ✦✦✦

Les is More / 1967 / Night ✦✦

Les McCann Live at the Bohemian Caverns / 1967 / Limelight ✦✦✦✦

★ **Much Les** / Jul. 22, 1968–Jul. 24, 1968 / Atlantic ✦✦✦✦✦
This straight CD reissue of an Atlantic LP offers one a pretty definitive look at Les McCann in his prime. The pianist/singer develops long funky vamps that swing, sings "With These Hands," and even with a string section added to four of the six numbers and three also having two percussionists, the emphasis is on McCann's trio with bassist Leroy Vinnegar and drummer Donald Dean. This is high-quality and intelligent groove music. —*Scott Yanow*

★ **Swiss Movement** / Jun. 22, 1969 / Atlantic ✦✦✦✦✦

Comment / Aug. 19, 1969–Oct. 22, 1969 / Atlantic ✦✦✦

Invitation to Openness / 1971 / Atlantic ✦✦✦✦

Talk to the People / May 1972 / Atlantic ✦✦

Live at Montreux / Jun. 24, 1972 / Atlantic ✦✦✦✦
A good two-disc date, with two hot stints by Rahsaan Roland Kirk (reeds). —*Ron Wynn*

Layers / Nov. 1972 / Atlantic ✦✦
On this studio session, Les McCann augments his piano with various keyboards and synthesizers, showing the influence of Miles Davis' music of the period. McCann sets solid grooves with his trio (plus two percussionists) but dilutes his sound to a large extent. The music is set up as two lengthy suites but unfortunately lacks any really catchy melodies. McCann does his best to stretch himself and there are moments of interest, but this Rhino CD reissue of an Atlantic LP is not all that essential. —*Scott Yanow*

Another Beginning / 1974 / Atlantic ✦✦

Hustle to Survive / 1975 / Atlantic ✦✦

River High, River Low / 1976 / Atlantic ✦✦

Les McCann the Mann / 1978 / A&M ✦✦

Music Box / 1984 / Jam ✦✦✦

On The Soul Side / Jan. 1994 / Music Masters ✦✦✦✦

Rob McConnell

b. Feb. 14, 1935, London, Ontario
Trombone, Arranger, Leader / Bop, Swing
Although it has always been a part-time venture (working maybe 30 days a year counting an annual recording), Rob McConnell's Boss Brass has been one of the finest big bands since the mid-'70s. An excellent soloist, McConnell has played valve trombone in Toronto (both in the studios and in jazz settings) for nearly four decades. During 1965–69 he was in Nimmons 'n' Nine Plus Six (led by Phil Nimmons) and in 1968 formed the Boss Brass. Originally the group was composed entirely of brass instruments plus a rhythm section and emphasized pop music. Although it added a saxophone section in 1971, the Boss Brass did not record much jazz until 1976. Comprising many of Toronto's top musicians (including Sam Noto, Guido Basso, Ian McDougall, Moe Koffman, Eugene Amaro, Rick Wilkins, Ed Bickert, Don Thompson and Terry Clarke among others), the orchestra mostly plays McConnell's swinging but surprising charts. For a period in the late '80s McConnell moved to Los Angeles, and the group broke up, but by 1991 it was back together again. Rob McConnell, who has also cut a few small-group dates for Concord, has record-ed with his Boss Brass for Pausa, MPS, Dark Orchid, Innovation and Concord. —*Scott Yanow*

The Jazz Album / 1976 / Pausa ✦✦✦✦

Big Band Jazz / 1977 / Umbrella ✦✦✦✦

The Boss Brass Again! / 1978 / Umbrella ✦✦✦✦

Present Perfect / Oct. 29, 1979–Oct. 31, 1979 / PA/USA ✦✦✦

Live in Digital / Dec. 1, 1980–Dec. 3, 1980 / Sea Breeze ✦✦✦

All In Good Time / 1982 / Sea Breeze ✦✦✦✦

Old Friends, New Music / May 17, 1984+May 25, 1984 / Unisson ✦✦✦✦

Boss Brass & Woods / Mar. 11, 1985–Mar. 12, 1985 / MCA ✦✦✦✦✦
Potent solos by Phil Woods (as), excellent playing by Canada's premier big band. Four standards, one each by saxophonist Rick Wilkins, Quincy Jones, two by leader. 23 pieces working as one. Great solos from Guido Basso, Jan McDougal and Ed Bickert. —*Michael G. Nastos*

The Jive 5 / Aug. 1990 / Concord Jazz ✦✦✦✦✦

● **The Brass is Back** / Jan. 28, 1991–Jan. 29, 1991 / Concord Jazz ✦✦✦✦✦
More emphasis on post-bop from composers Silver and Kai Winding. Tunes from Don Thompson, R. Wilkins, Roger Kellaway and McConnell. Two standards. —*Michael G. Nastos*

Brassy and Sassy / 1992 / Concord Jazz ✦✦✦✦✦
Bandleader Rob McConnell and his Boss Brass band blast through big band stompers, mellow ballads, and fiery standards and originals on this '92 session. —*Ron Wynn*

★ **Our 25th Year** / Mar. 1993 / Concord Jazz ✦✦✦✦✦
Rob McConnell's Boss Brass has produced 25 years of solid music making, most of in the swinging bebop tradition. The music on this Concord CD has more than its share of surprises such as a bar of 3/4 put in one chorus of "4 B.C.," phrases "borrowed" from Bob Florence and inserted in "Riffs I Have Known" and an inventive version of "Flying Home." Among the other highpoints are trumpeter Guido Basso's feature on "Imagination," Eugene Amaro's tenor on "What Am I Here For" and a driving "Broadway." This solid effort is recommended to big band fans. —*Scott Yanow*

Trio Sketches / May 20, 1993–May 21, 1993 / Concord ✦✦✦✦
The trio of valve trombonist Rob McConnell, guitarist Ed Bickert and bassist Neil Swainson creates mellow and melodic bop-based music. While Bickert has one of the quietest guitar sounds around and Swainson is often content to play softly in the background, McConnell's cool tone and accessible style are often in the lead. The results are predictably swinging with plenty of subtle interplay. —*Scott Yanow*

Overtime / 1994 / Concord Jazz ✦✦✦✦✦

Susannah McCorkle

b. Jan. 1, 1946, Berkeley, CA
Vocals / Standards
One of the finest interpreters of lyrics active in the jazz world during the 1980s and '90s, Susannah McCorkle does not improvise all that much, but she brings the proper emotional intensity to the words she sings—a lyricist's dream! She moved to England in 1971 where she worked with Dick Sudhalter and Keith Ingham among others, performing at concerts with such visiting Americans as Bobby Hackett, Ben Webster and Dexter Gordon. McCorkle sang at the Riverboat jazz room in Manhattan during 1975 (gaining a lot of attention) and recorded two albums in England (tributes to Harry Warren and Johnny Mercer) that were released domestically by Inner City. By 1980 she was back in the U.S., recording a Yip Harburg set and a fourth album for Inner City. After that label folded, McCorkle switched over to Pausa but by the late '80s was recording regularly for Concord. She has expanded her pre-bop repertoire to include Brazilian songs and blues, and in the mid-'90s Susannah McCorkle is at the top of her field. —*Scott Yanow*

The Songs of Johnny Mercer / Sep. 19, 1977–Oct. 3, 1977 / Inner City ✦✦✦✦✦
A first-rate interpretative and standards vocalist tackles classic songs written by a compositional master. The results are just what you'd expect: magical and outstanding. McCorkle's timing, instincts and lyric readings are exceptional, as are her choices of Mercer material. —*Ron Wynn*

Over the Rainbow / Jan. 11, 1980–Feb. 19, 1980 / Inner City ✦✦✦✦✦
More classy standards and pre-rock pop from jazz vocalist Susannah McCorkle, whose rendition of the title track wisely doesn't try to imitate other, higher-pitched vocalists, but instead works off her strengths: pacing, enunciation, dramatic tension and delivery. —*Ron Wynn*

Thanks for the Memory (Songs of Leo Robin) / Dec. 1983–Jan. 1984 / PA/USA ✦✦✦✦
While several of these songs aren't strictly jazz or even necessarily pop, Susannah McCorkle makes them all worth hearing. That's because she's a marvelous lyric interpreter, who also has an easy, swinging style and excellent delivery. She makes you pay attention to whatever she's singing, whether you understand it or not (or even care about it). —*Ron Wynn*

How Do You Keep the Music Playing? / Jun. 1985 / PA/USA ✦✦✦✦
The lightweight title song aside, here's another expertly done album showcasing the swinging skills of jazz vocalist Susannah McCorkle, among the finest contemporary singers around. Her timing, delivery and sound, even on disposable fodder, is consistently impressive, and she's an outstanding lyric interpreter as well. —*Ron Wynn*

★ **No More Blues** / Oct. 1988 / Concord Jazz ✦✦✦✦✦

Sabia / Feb. 1990 / Concord Jazz ✦✦✦

● **I'll Take Romance** / Sep. 15, 1991–Sep. 17, 1991 / Concord Jazz ✦✦✦✦✦

From Bessie to Brazil / Feb. 1993 / Concord Jazz ✦✦✦✦✦

From Broadway To Bebop / 1994 / Concord Jazz ✦✦✦✦

Dick McDonough

b. 1904, d. May 25, 1938, New York, NY
Guitar / Classic Jazz, Swing
With the premature death of Eddie Lang in 1933, Dick McDonough and Carl Kress were considered his likely successors both on jazz dates and in the studios. McDonough was already a very busy player. He had started out in 1927 as a banjoist with Red Nichols, had switched over to guitar and appeared on hundreds of sessions including with the Dorsey Brothers, the Boswell Sisters, Joe Venuti and in more commercial music. His work accelerated with Lang's passing; he occasionally teamed up with Kress, and during 1936–37 McDonough led a notable series of medium-size group recordings, few of which have ever been reissued. McDonough also recorded with Glenn Miller's unsuccessful big band of 1937 and made a notable appearance on an all-star date with Fats Waller, Tommy Dorsey, Bunny Berigan and George Wettling that was issued as "A Jam Session at Victor." A strong acoustic guitarist who emphasized chords in his solos (influencing Marty Grosz decades later), Dick McDonough's alcoholism cut short his life much too early. —*Scott Yanow*

Jack McDuff (Eugene McDuffy)

b. Sep. 17, 1926, Champaign, IL
Organ / Soul Jazz, Hard Bop
A marvelous bandleader and organist as well as capable arranger, "Brother" Jack McDuff has one of the funkiest, most soulful styles of all time on the Hammond B-3. His rock-solid bass lines and blues-drenched solos are balanced by clever, almost pianistic melodies and interesting progressions and phrases. McDuff began as a bassist playing with Denny Zeitlin and Joe Farrell. He studied privately in Cincinnati and worked with Johnny Griffin in Chicago. He taught himself organ and piano in the mid-'50s and began gaining attention working with Willis Jackson in the late '50s and early '60s, cutting high caliber soul jazz dates for Prestige. McDuff made his recording debut as a leader for Prestige in 1960, playing in a studio pickup band with Jimmy Forrest. They made a pair of outstanding albums, *Tough Duff* and *The Honeydripper*. McDuff organized his own band the next year, featuring Harold Vick and drummer Joe Dukes. Things took off when McDuff hired a young guitarist named George Benson. They were among the most popular combos of the mid-'60s and made several excellent albums. McDuff's later groups at Atlantic and Cadet didn't equal the level of the Benson band, while later dates for Verve and Cadet were uneven, though generally good. McDuff experimented with electronic keyboards and fusion during the '70s, then in the '80s got back in the groove with the Muse

session *Cap'n Jack*. Other musicians McDuff played with in the '60s and '70s include Joe Henderson, Pat Martino, Jimmy Witherspoon, David "Fathead" Newman, Rahsaan Roland Kirk, Sonny Stitt and Gene Ammons. There are only a few McDuff sessions available on CD, though they include the fine sessions with Forrest. His work with Benson has also been reissued on CD. —*Ron Wynn and Bob Porter*

Brother Jack / Jan. 25, 1960 / Prestige ✦✦✦

Tough 'Duff / Jul. 12, 1960 / Original Jazz Classics ✦✦✦✦✦
McDuff's second lead session for Prestige. Good small-group Hammond organ funk—provided you like vibes, which is not a usual funk instrument. The title cut is excellent. Jimmy Forrest (ts) is in top form here. W/ Lem Winchester (vib). —*Michael Erlewine*

The Honeydripper / Feb. 3, 1961 / Original Jazz Classics ✦✦✦✦✦
Soul jazz-funk. This is first-rate jazz-funk, perhaps a little more bluesy than average—which is nice. His third album, w/ Grant Green (g). Excellent. —*Michael Erlewine*

On with It / Dec. 1, 1961 / Prestige ✦✦✦

● **Brother Jack Meets the Boss** / Jan. 23, 1962 / Original Jazz Classics ✦✦✦✦✦
Straight-ahead bop with some funky organ. Early McDuff, recorded within months of the start of his rise to fame. —*Michael Erlewine*

Crash! / Jan. 8, 1963+Feb. 26, 1963 / Prestige ✦✦✦✦✦
Organist Jack McDuff has long had a powerful style, and the two former LPs that are combined on this single CD offer some strong examples of his accessible playing. In both cases McDuff is joined by guitarist Kenny Burrell (in fact one of the two sets was originally under Burrell's name), drummer Joe Dukes and occasionally Ray Barretto on congas. In addition Harold Vick is on tenor for most selections, and Eric Dixon guests on tenor and flute during three songs. Highlights include a driving "How High the Moon," "Love Walked In" and a pair of original blues: "Smut" and "Our Miss Brooks." McDuff and Burrell work together quite well. This 76-minute CD is easily recommended to fans of the jazz organ. —*Scott Yanow*

★ **Live!** / Jan. 26, 1963+Jun. 5, 1963 / Prestige ✦✦✦✦✦
Good as organist Jack McDuff's studio recordings are from the early '60s, it is his live sets that are truly exciting. This single CD combines together two former in-concert LPs and find McDuff leading a very strong group that features the young guitarist George Benson, tenorman Red Holloway, drummer Joe Dukes and on a few numbers the second tenor of Harold Vick. The material (cooking blues, standards, Latin numbers and originals) has plenty of variety and drive, McDuff really pushes Benson and Holloway, and the music is both accessible and creative —*Scott Yanow*

Live at the Jazz Workshop / Oct. 3, 1963 / Prestige ✦✦✦
Organist Jack McDuff enjoyed some pop recognition in 1963, when his combo recorded at The Jazz Workshop featured a young, blazing guitarist influenced by Wes Montgomery. George Benson's torrid licks and blues fills make this among his hottest albums, along with McDuff's always-smoking, relentless organ accompaniment, transitional lines and solos. —*Ron Wynn*

Hot Barbeque / Oct. 19, 1965 / Prestige ✦✦✦

Do It Now! / Dec. 15, 1966–May 23, 1967 / Atlantic ✦✦✦

The Re-Entry / Mar. 1988 / Muse ✦✦✦✦
A late-'80s return to the sound of earlier recordings, it features Houston Person (ts). Not inspired, it's still a solid performance all around. —*Bob Porter*

Another Real Good'un / Mar. 1, 1989+Jul. 18, 1990 / Muse ✦✦✦✦

Color Me Blue / May 1991+Mar. 1992 / Concord Jazz ✦✦✦✦✦
Recent cuts showing that organist Jack McDuff can still stomp through bluesy wailers, pound the bass pedals and lead a hot combo through funky exuberant numbers. He's heading a group with former band members like guitarist George Benson and drummer Joe Dukes, plus saxophonist Red Holloway, guitarist Ron Eschete and Phil Upchurch, among others. —*Ron Wynn*

Write On, Capt'n / 1993 / Concord Jazz ✦✦✦
This date doesn't pack the same punch as McDuff's 1960s classics but is mostly enjoyable despite some annoying trumpet from Joey DeFrancesco (a fine organist and McDuff fan) and McDuff's own arrangements for the large band backing him. Sometimes the

JACK MCDUFF

ALL MUSIC GUIDE TO JAZZ

two-trumpet/two-sax/trombone frontline seems more of a burden than a help. They are good players, but they aren't given enough to do to be exciting and sometimes just seem in the way. While it's great to hear McDuff back on the Hammond B-3, this will not make anyone forget his Prestige dates with George Benson. —*Ron Wynn*

Gary McFarland

b. Oct. 23, 1933, Los Angeles, CA, d. Nov. 3, 1971, New York, NY
Vibes, Arranger, Composer / Post Bop, Hard Bop
Gary McFarland displayed a great deal of promise as a composer/arranger by the mid-'60s, but his career became aimless before his premature death. He attended Oregon State University and learned vibes while in the Army. He went to Berklee during 1959-60, moved to New York and quickly found work as a writer. Gerry Mulligan recorded two of his originals in 1961, and McFarland was soon working on album projects by Anita O'Day, Stan Getz and John Lewis. He started leading sessions of his own in 1961, and his finest moment was a Philharmonic Hall concert in 1966 that was released on Impulse. However McFarland's later albums (mostly for his own Skye label) were an uncomfortable mixture of social comment, pop music and jazz. Gary McFarland, who also recorded for Verve, did not live long enough to create truly significant music. —*Scott Yanow*

How to Succeed in Business without Really Trying / Nov. 14, 1961+Nov. 8, 1961 / Verve ✦✦✦✦

Point of Departure / Sep. 5, 1963–Sep. 6, 1963 / Impulse ✦✦✦✦✦
Brilliant arrangements, intriguing compositions. —*Ron Wynn*

Tijuana Jazz / Oct. 1965 / Impulse ✦✦✦
A nice incorporation of Latin themes and influences into the jazz-arranging mode. —*Ron Wynn*

● Profiles / Feb. 6, 1966 / Impulse ✦✦✦✦✦

America the Beautiful / Oct. 1968 / DCC ✦✦

Bobby McFerrin

b. Mar. 11, 1950, New York, NY
Vocals / Bop, Post-Bop, Pop
A truly remarkable singer, Bobby McFerrin's ability to make rhythmic sounds while inhaling makes his vocals into nonstop flights of constant creativity. By alternating falsetto quickly with deep bass notes (and somehow not getting lost!), McFerrin can sound like two or three singers at once. His quick reactions and wide knowledge of musical styles plus a strong wit make his solo performances not only remarkable but hugely entertaining.

Despite all of that, Bobby McFerrin's career has not yet lived up to his enormous potential. The son of opera signers, McFerrin was trained as a pianist, but by 1977 he had shifted to singing. He worked for a time with Jon Hendricks and then recorded his debut for Elektra Musician in 1982. In 1983 he started doing concerts featuring his unaccompanied solos, and his 1984 release *The Voice* is still his finest recording. In 1988 McFerrin had a fluke hit with "Don't Worry, Be Happy" (which was actually on one of his weaker albums), and he seemed somewhat embarassed by his unexpected commercial success. He maintained a much lower profile, conducting classical orchestras (why?), forming a thus far unrecorded "Voicestra" with other singers and recording on only an infrequent basis for EMI and Blue Note; a joke-filled encounter with Chick Corea was often closer to performance art than to jazz. Bobby McFerrin is still a major name but not the influential force (and poll-winner) that he should be. —*Scott Yanow*

Bobby McFerrin / 1982 / Elektra ✦✦✦✦

★ The Voice / Mar. 17, 1984–Mar. 26, 1984 / Elektra ✦✦✦✦✦
The Voice was a milestone in jazz history; it was the first time a jazz singer had recorded an entire album solo, without accompaniment or overdubbing, for a major label. Bobby McFerrin's amazing ability to switch back and forth between bass notes and falsetto, along with his talent for jumping octaves made this record quite a virtuoso showcase. For those interested in the potential of the human voices and in an important jazz talent, *The Voice* is recommended without reservations. —*Scott Yanow*

Spontaneous Inventions / 1985 / Blue Note ✦✦✦✦✦
More superb vocal gymnastics are included, on everyone from The Beatles to Dizzy Gillespie. —*Hank Davis*

Simple Pleasures / 1988 / EMI ✦✦✦✦
The breakthrough platinum album contains the mega hit "Don't

Worry, Be Happy" and other gems like "Drive My Car." —*Hank Davis*

Medicine Man / 1990 / EMI ✦✦

Play / Jun. 23, 1990 / Blue Note ✦✦✦

Bang! Zoom / 1995 / Blue Note ✦✦

Howard McGhee

b. Mar. 6, 1918, Tulsa, OK, d. Jul. 17, 1987, New York, NY
Trumpet / Bop, Hard Bop
During 1945-49 Howard McGhee was one of the finest trumpeters in jazz, an exciting performer with a sound of his own who among the young bop players ranked at the top with Dizzy Gillespie and Fats Navarro. The "missing link" between Roy Eldridge and Fats Navarro (Navarro influenced Clifford Brown who influenced most of the post-1955 trumpeters), McGhee originally played clarinet and tenor, not taking up trumpet until he was 17. He worked in territory bands, was with Lionel Hampton in 1941 and then joined Andy Kirk (1941-42), being featured on "McGhee Special." McGhee participated in the fabled bop sessions at Minton's Playhouse and Monroe's Uptown House, modernizing his style away from Roy Eldridge and toward Dizzy Gillespie. He was with Charlie Barnet (1942-43), returned to Kirk (where he sat next to Fats Navarro in the trumpet section) and had brief stints with Georgie Auld and Count Basie before traveling to California with Coleman Hawkins in 1945; their concise recordings of swing-to-bop transitional music (including "Stuffy," "Rifftide" and "Hollywood Stampede") are classic. McGhee stayed in California into 1947, playing with Jazz at the Philharmonic, recording and gigging with Charlie Parker (including the ill-fated "Lover Man" date) and having an influence on young players out on the Coast. His Dial sessions were among the most exciting recordings of his career, and back in New York he recorded for Savoy and had a historic meeting on record with Navarro (1948 on Blue Note).

However, drugs began to adversely affect Howard McGhee's career. He traveled on a USO tour during the Korean War, recording in Guam. McGhee also had sessions for Bethlehem (1955-56) but was inactive during much of the 1950s. He recorded some strong dates for Felsted, Bethlehem, Contemporary and Black Lion during 1960-61 and a quartet recordings for United Artists (1962) but (with the exception of a Hep big band date in 1966) was largely off records again until 1976. He had a final burst of activity during 1976-79 for Sonet, SteepleChase, Jazzcraft, Zim and Storyville, but by then Howard McGhee was largely forgotten, and few knew about his link to Fats Navarro and Clifford Brown. —*Scott Yanow*

★ Trumpet at Tempo / Jul. 29, 1946–Dec. 3, 1947 / Spolite ✦✦✦✦✦

Sextet with Milt Jackson / Feb. 1948 / Savoy ✦✦✦✦

South Pacific Jazz / Jan. 17, 1952 / Savoy ✦✦✦
Originally half of a Savoy two-LP set, this single CD features trumpeter Howard McGhee and a potentially interesting sextet (with trombonist J.J. Johnson and Rudy Williams on tenor) at concerts performed in Guam. After a rather slapdash history-of-jazz segment, the band digs into more familiar music with some hard-swinging results. The lack of a piano leaves a large gap in the ensembles (despite the presence of guitarist Clifton Best), and it is strange to hear Rudy Williams (formerly a swing altoist) as an R&Bish tenor. Although not essential, Howard McGhee fans will want to pick this up if they do not already own the LP two-fer. —*Scott Yanow*

The Return of Howard McGhee / Oct. 22, 1955 / Bethlehem ✦✦✦✦

● Maggie's Back in Town / Jun. 26, 1961 / Original Jazz Classics ✦✦✦✦✦
Trumpeter Howard McGhee's date was a rather common outing made interesting because of the quality of the individuals. Maggie (McGhee) was in good command; his rumpled style of playing always seemed to have direction and purpose and rarely dipped into predictable phrasing. Bassist Leroy Vinnegar and drummer Shelly Manne were as you would expect—solid. The added plus was pianist Phineas Newborn, whose quixotic playing provided a strong second voice adding unexpected zing. —*Bob Rusch, Cadence*

Sharp Edge / Dec. 8, 1961 / Black Lion ✦✦✦✦

Cookin' Time / Sep. 22, 1966 / Hep ✦✦✦✦
Fine big-band arrangements and playing. —*Ron Wynn*

488

Just Be There / Dec. 9, 1976 / SteepleChase ✦✦✦

Jazz Brothers / Oct. 19, 1977 / Storyville ✦✦✦✦
Charlie Rouse (ts) equals his stints with Monk. —*Ron Wynn*

Live at Emerson's / Mar. 10, 1978–Mar. 11, 1978 / Zim ✦✦✦
Triple-threat bop with tenors Rouse and Frank Wess. —*Ron Wynn*

Home Run / Oct. 11, 1978 / Jazzcraft ✦✦✦✦
Expatriate Benny Bailey (tpt) blows up the rafters. —*Ron Wynn*

Wise in Time / Oct. 4, 1979–Oct. 6, 1979 / Storyville ✦✦

Young at Heart / Oct. 4, 1979–Oct. 6, 1979 / Storyville ✦✦✦
A welcome appearance by Teddy Edwards (ts). —*Ron Wynn*

Chris McGregor

b. Dec. 24, 1936, Umtata, South Africa, **d.** May 26, 1990, Ager, France

Piano, Leader / Avant-Garde
A revered and respected bandleader and pianist, South African Chris McGregor's life was changed forever hearing the hymns of the Xhosa poeple in his father's Church of Scotland mission. He'd eventually depart his South African homeland in protest against apartheid and lead several seminal ensembles of expatriate South Africans. McGregor selected several great players at the 1962 Johannesburg Jazz Festival, among them Mongezi Fesa, Dudu Pukwana and Johnny Dyani to be in a new band. The Blue Notes as an integrated band were anathema in '60s South Africa, which was ruled by strict apartheid. They left the country in the early '60s on a European tour and never returned. They remained in Switzerland for a year, then moved to London. McGregor led at various times the Chris McGregor Group and the Brotherhood of Breath. This was an an African version of Sun Ra's Arkestra or Cecil Taylor's large orchestra, mixing free and avant-garde arrangements with township jive and other African styles. They developed out of a series of big band concerts McGregor had been presenting weekly at Ronnie Scott's club. McGregor moved to France in the mid-'70s and did solo dates but periodically revived The Brotherhood of Breath. Its ranks at one time included Pukwana, Fezi, Dyani and Louis Moholo. McGregor died in 1990 of lung cancer. —*Ron Wynn*

★ **And the Brotherhood of Breath** / Oct. 1970 / Neon ✦✦✦✦✦

Live at Willisau / Jan. 27, 1973 / Ogun ✦✦✦✦✦
The pianist/leader with an 11-piece band of South African expatriates and English free-jazz men. Explosive. —*Michael G. Nastos*

Blue Notes for Mongezi / 1975 / Ogun ✦✦✦✦

Country Cooking / Jan. 1988 / Venture ✦✦✦✦
A rare domestic release from a great Afro jazz big band. —*Ron Wynn*

Jimmy McGriff

b. Apr. 3, 1936, Philadelphia, PA
Organ / Soul Jazz, Hard Bop
The finest blues soloist among organists, Jimmy McGriff can also play superb soul jazz though he's turned in dreary performances on fusion and pop dates in the '70s. McGriff studied bass, drums, tenor sax and vibes in his teens and attended Combe College of Music in Philadelphia and Juilliard. McGriff later studied electric organ with Jimmy Smith, Milt Buckner and Groove Holmes. His debut record *I Got A Woman* put him at No. 20 Top 20 hit in 1962, and he followed it with *All About My Girl* and *Kiko* in 1963 and 1964. McGriff began a long relationship with producer Sonny Lester in 1966, when he joined Solid State Records. The two later teamed at Blue Note, Capitol, Groove Merchant and LRC. McGriff recorded many fine organ combo sides while also cutting R&B-tinged work during the '60s. He had a huge hit with "The Worm" in '68/'69 but also made the LP *The Big Band*, a stirring tribute to Count Basie. During the '70s McGriff made more solid small combo jazz dates, including some organ battles with Groove Holmes. But he also did trendy material utilizing multiple electronic keyboards. He didn't distinguish himself on several later LRC sessions. McGriff's earlier Groove Merchant recordings were his best in this period. McGriff, like Hank Crawford, got back to basics when he signed with Milestone in 1980. He's done several dates with Hank Crawford and played with Al Grey. McGriff's early '90s Headfirst sessions mix electronic fusion material with organ jazz. —*Ron Wynn and Bob Porter*

● **Movin' Upside the Blues** / Dec. 19, 1980–Jan. 24, 1981 / Jazz America ✦✦✦✦✦
There are few better combinations for producing after hours funk

than organist Jimmy McGriff and guitarist Jimmy Ponder. Irrepressibly swinging McGriff is always in spitting distance of those down home or South Side blues. Ponder compliments with a lightness that brings an appealing optimism to the realities...If you haven't had a taste yet, start here; if you have had a taste and have room for more in your diet, this is a tasty dish. —*Bob Rusch, Cadence*

Countdown / Apr. 27, 1983–Apr. 28, 1983 / Milestone ✦✦✦✦

Skywalk / Mar. 19, 1984–Mar. 20, 1984 / Milestone ✦✦✦
McGriff sometimes veers away from his soul-jazz strength, but it's still a fine set overall. —*Ron Wynn*

State of the Art / May 13, 1985–Jun. 11, 1985 / Milestone ✦✦✦✦

The Starting Five / Oct. 14, 1986–Oct. 15, 1986 / Milestone ✦✦✦✦✦

Blue to the Bone / Jul. 19, 1988–Jul. 20, 1988 / Milestone ✦✦✦✦

You Ought to Think / 1990 / Headfirst ✦✦✦
Outstanding players, less-than-stellar results. —*Ron Wynn*

On the Blue Side / May 1990 / Milestone ✦✦✦✦
An updated version of the vintage McGriff formula: bluesy, soulful organ fare with a balance struck between jazz sensibility and a funk/R&B groove. —*Ron Wynn*

In a Blue Mood / 1991 / K-Tel ✦✦
Jimmy McGriff's 1991 release *In A Blue Mood* ranked as one of his most controversial. McGriff, certainly among the finest wailing and soul-jazz organists ever, spent as much time playing the Kurzweil 1200 synthesizer as he did the Hammond (and it was B-5 rather than the classic B-3), was joined by then-Prince saxophonist Eric Leeds and also backed on two cuts by vocalists. It was far from late-night soul-jazz at its best; still, McGriff did play a couple of nice solos when he did turn to the organ. "Blue Juice," "The Bird," and "Charlotte" are strong McGriff vehicles; the others were done with style but often lacked substance. —*Ron Wynn*

● **Right Turn On Blues** / Jan. 22, 1994–Jan. 23, 1994 / Telarc ✦✦✦✦✦
There was virtually no prior planning for this meeting between organist Jimmy McGriff and altoist Hank Crawford, but none was needed. The veterans had already recorded four prior albums together so they simply jammed through blues, ballads and a few basic originals without any difficulty; Crawford could play this material blindfolded. McGriff sets the grooves expertly with his foot-pedal basswork with assistance from guitarist Rodney Jones and drummer Jesse Hameen. The overall result is a happy and enthusiastic session of foot-tapping music. No real surprises occur, but lovers of hard-swinging organ combos have nothing to complain about. —*Scott Yanow*

Blues Groove / Jul. 21, 1995–Jul. 22, 1995 / Telarc ✦✦✦✦✦

Kalaparusha Maurice McIntyre
(Maurice McIntyre)

b. Mar. 24, 1936
Tenor Saxophone / Free Jazz
An intense tenor saxophonist who often plays quite freely, Kalaparusha Maurice McIntyre is a natural extension of the high-energy tenors of the mid-'60s. He was a founding member of the AACM and recorded on Roscoe Mitchell's groundbreaking *Sound* album. He played with other members of the AACM and moved back and forth between Chicago and New York without gaining much fame. McIntyre worked with Jerome Cooper and Muhal Richard Abrams in addition to some of Chicago's blues musicians. In the 1980s he was a member of Kahil El Zabar's Ethnic Heritage Ensemble. Kalaparusha Maurice McIntyre has recorded as a leader for Delmark (1969–70), Black Saint (1979) and Cadence (1981). —*Scott Yanow*

● **Humility in the Light of the Creator** / Feb. 5, 1969–Feb. 15, 1969 / Delmark ✦✦✦✦✦
Superb album by multi-instrumentalist McIntyre, one of the lesser-known Chicago musicians who helped form the AACM and has participated in the city's avant-garde jazz movement since its inception. This was his finest album, a work with sweeping, complex, yet also invigorating and visceral compositions. It also has dazzling playing from McIntyre and his associates. —*Ron Wynn*

Peace and Blessings / Jun. 18, 1979 / Black Saint ✦✦✦✦

Ram's Run / Mar. 6, 1981 / Cadence ✦✦✦
This album (taken from a live concert) has an unusual instru-

mentation: tenor (Kalaparusha Maurice McIntyre), alto (Julius Hemphill), trumpet (Malachi Thompson) and drums (J.R. Mitchell). The music, five McIntyre compositions, contains plenty of intense moments, but the lack of a bass or a chordal instrument is a difficult handicap to overcome. The complex performances will certainly challenge listeners who expect all jazz to swing conventionally. —*Scott Yanow*

Ken McIntyre

b. Sep. 7, 1931, Boston, MA

Flute, Tenor Saxophone, Oboe, Bassoon, Bass Clarinet / Avant-Garde, Post-Bop

A versatile player with a thoughtful style who can play quite freely, Ken McIntyre has never been a major name in jazz despite his talents. After serving in the military and graduating from the Boston Conservatory, he arrived in New York in 1960 and made a strong impression. He recorded two albums for New Jazz that year including one in which he held his own against Eric Dolphy. McIntyre also led two now-scarce records for United Artists during 1962-63 (including one titled *Way Way Out*) but became involved in education, teaching in the public schools starting in 1961. He continued playing on a part-time basis (recording with Cecil Taylor in 1966). McIntyre led five albums for SteepleChase during 1974-78 including his definitive set Hindsight (which finds him spotlighting each of his five horns in a quartet). He also recorded with Craig Harris in 1983 and put together an Eric Dolphy tribute set for Serene in 1991, but Ken McIntyre has never achieved the recognition he deserved. —*Scott Yanow*

● **Stone Blues** / May 31, 1960 / Original Jazz Classics ✦✦✦✦✦
This early effort by Ken McIntyre (who doubles here on alto and flute) grows in interest with each listen. On a couple of his six originals (including a song called "Cornballs"), McIntyre slides humorously between notes, but other selections are much more serious. McIntyre's sidemen are now somewhat obscure (trombonist John Mancebo Lewis, pianist Dizzy Sal, bassist Paul Morrison and drummer Bobby Ward), but they fit well into his conception which at this early stage was essentially advanced bop slightly influenced by the "new thing" music of Ornette Coleman. This interesting set has been reissued on CD. —*Scott Yanow*

Looking Ahead / Jun. 28, 1960 / Original Jazz Classics ✦✦✦✦✦
Eric Dolphy (alto sax, bass clarinet, flute) had a featured role on Ken McIntyre's date *Looking Ahead* which also included Walter Bishop (piano), Sam Jones (bass) and Art Taylor (drums). McIntyre's alto playing was marked by an original tone (sort of an unresolved thrust which seemed bent on trailing away into the outward bounds). —*Bob Rusch, Cadence*

Year of the Iron Sheep / Jun. 1962 / United Artists ✦✦✦✦

Way Way Out / 1963 / United Artists ✦✦✦✦

★ **Hindsight** / Jan. 13, 1974 / SteepleChase ✦✦✦✦✦
Ken McIntyre had not recorded as a leader in 11 years when he cut this quartet set for SteepleChase, but he was more than ready. The well-rounded program (which on the CD reissue includes a second version of "Body and Soul") features McIntyre on separate features for his alto, flute, bassoon, oboe and bass clarinet. Although often compared to Eric Dolphy early in his career, McIntyre actually has a style of his own, open to the innovations of the avant-garde but not shy to embrace melodies. With the assistance of pianist Kenny Drew, bassist Bo Stief and drummer Alex Riel, McIntyre is consistently brilliant form with the highlights being "Lush Life" (on bassoon), "Body and Soul" (taken on bass clarinet) and "Naima" (for his oboe) and a heated alto workout on "Sunnymoon for Two." —*Scott Yanow*

Home / Jun. 23, 1975 / SteepleChase ✦✦✦✦✦

Open Horizon / Nov. 19, 1975 / SteepleChase ✦✦✦✦

Introducing the Vibrations / Oct. 30, 1976 / SteepleChase ✦✦✦

Chasing the Sun / Jul. 1978 / SteepleChase ✦✦✦✦

Tribute / 1991 / Serene ✦✦✦
A welcome set from an extremely underrated multi-sax performer. —*Ron Wynn*

Dave McKenna

b. May 30, 1930, Woonsocket, RI

Piano / Swing

One of the top swing-based pianists of the past 25 years, Dave McKenna's hard-driving bass lines give momentum to uptempo pieces, and his vast knowledge of superior songs from the 1930s has resulted in many rewarding albums of traditional but fresh music. Although talented from the start, McKenna did not achieve that much recognition until he was already in his 40s. He joined the Musicians' Union when he was 15 and picked up early experience playing with Boots Mussulli (1947), Charlie Ventura (1949) and Woody Herman's Orchestra (1950-51). After two years in the military, McKenna had a second stint with Ventura (1953-54) and then worked with a variety of top swing and Dixieland players including Gene Krupa, Stan Getz, Zoot Sims, Al Cohn, Eddie Condon, Bobby Hackett and Bob Wilber (in the late '70s) and was a soloist at piano bars in Massachusetts. McKenna had recorded for ABC-Paramount (1956), Epic (1958), Bethlehem (a two-piano date shared with Hall Overton in 1960) and Realm (1963), but in 1973 McKenna's talents finally began to be more fully documented. He led sets for Halycon, Shiah, Famous Door, Inner City (with vocalist Teddi King) and four for Chiaroscuro. Then in 1979 with *No Bass Hit* (a trio date with Scott Hamilton and Jake Hanna), McKenna debuted with Concord, finding his home. He has made many sessions for Concord ever since, some as a sideman or with small groups but the best ones being unaccompanied recitals. In the mid-'90s Dave McKenna is at the top of his field. —*Scott Yanow*

This is the Moment / Jul. 22, 1958–Jul. 23, 1958 / Portrait ✦✦✦✦

Solo Piano / Feb. 24, 1973 / Chiaroscuro ✦✦✦
Prior to 1973, pianist Dave McKenna had not recorded as a leader in a decade, and it was this particular album (now available on CD with two additional songs and a few alternate takes) that helped McKenna gain recognition for his brilliant playing; it would be followed by two other Chiaroscuro dates and a countless number of sets for Concord. A couple of attempts at uplifting current material aside ("Norwegian Wood" and "My Cherie Amour" do not fit McKenna's sound), this solo performance finds McKenna displaying his fully formed swing style on a variety of superior tunes, (including a three-part "Have You Met Miss Jones Sequence." —*Scott Yanow*

Cookin' at Michael's Pub / Feb. 28, 1973 / Halcyon ✦✦✦✦
A fine '73 album that was issued on Marian McPartland's Halcyon label. Pianist Dave McKenna mixes stride, light boogie and blues, plus his own devices, and has a style that is both unorthodox and compelling. His odd rhythmic lines, phrasing and swinging approach were well documented on this one. —*Ron Wynn*

Dave McKenna Quartet Featuring Zoot Sims / Oct. 1974 / Chiaroscuro ✦✦✦✦✦
With Zoot Sims. Quartet. A 1990 reissue of a delightful date that's hotter than usual, thanks to Zoot Sims (ts) and Major Holley (b). —*Ron Wynn*

★ **No Bass Hit** / Mar. 1979 / Concord Jazz ✦✦✦✦✦
The bass-less trio with Scott Hamilton on tenor sax and Jake Hanna on drums was a nice idea. All selections are early-period standards. McKenna is an undisputed master. —*Michael G. Nastos*

Giant Strides / May 1979 / Concord Jazz ✦✦✦✦✦

Left Handed Compliment / Dec. 1979 / Concord Jazz ✦✦✦✦
Dave McKenna is one of the great swing pianists of modern times. His exciting left-hand bassline really propels his faster performances while his encyclopediac knowledge of early American popular songs and general good taste make his ballad performances memorable. This solo outing finds McKenna playing superior tunes with swing and subtle creativity, as usual. —*Scott Yanow*

Piano Mover / Apr. 1980 / Concord Jazz ✦✦✦✦
Pianist Dave McKenna teams up with bassist Bob Maize, drummer Jake Hanna and what is called "the Dick Johnson reed section" for a set of standards both fresh and obscure. Johnson, switching between clarinet, alto and flute, works well with McKenna on this small-group swing set; highlights include "Cottontail," "Star Eyes" and Clare Fischer's "Morning." —*Scott Yanow*

Dave McKenna Trio Plays Music of Harry Warren / Aug. 1981 / Concord Jazz ✦✦✦✦✦

Celebration of Hoagy Carmichael / May 1983 / Concord Jazz ✦✦✦✦✦

● **The Keyman** / Aug. 1984 / Concord Jazz ✦✦✦✦✦
The best way to hear pianist Dave McKenna is solo. His joyous left-hand basslines are always enjoyable, as his knack for per-

forming rarely heard but superior songs. On this solo set, McKenna not only revives the Bix Beiderbecke-associated "Singing the Blues" but "I'll Be a Friend with Pleasure" and "Louisiana" too, along with some tender ballads and even a Michael Franks song ("Don't Be Blue"). This fine all-around recording offers many fine examples of Dave McKenna's magical swing piano. —*Scott Yanow*

★ **Dancing in the Dark** / Aug. 1985 / Concord Jazz ✦✦✦✦
The great swing pianist Dave McKenna performs 11 selections written by Arthur Schwartz, one of the lesser-known (but very talented) songwriters of the golden age of American popular music. Among the pieces that McKenna joyfully revives are "By Myself," "A Shine on Your Shoes," "I Guess I'll Have to Change My Plan" and "Dancing in the Dark." Happy melodic treatments of classic music. —*Scott Yanow*

My Friend the Piano / Aug. 1986 / Concord Jazz ✦✦✦
Pianist Dave McKenna fills *My Friend the Piano* with constant surprises; rhythm, tempo and key changes that somehow seem logical after the fact. There is a slight emphasis on ballads, but one's attention rarely wanders for the music, although tasteful, is never entirely predictable. —*Scott Yanow*

No More Ouzo for Puzo / Jun. 1988 / Concord Jazz ✦✦✦✦
Recorded by a quartet with guitarist Gray Sargent. The title piece was written by McKenna, the rest are all standards treated with tender loving care. —*Michael G. Nastos*

★ **Live at Maybeck Recital Hall, Vol. 2** / Nov. 1989 / Concord Jazz ✦✦✦✦✦

Shadows 'N Dreams / Mar. 1990 / Concord Jazz ✦✦✦✦
A Handful of Stars / Jun. 15, 1992 / Concord Jazz ✦✦✦✦
Concord Duo Series, Vol. 2 / Dec. 16, 1992 / Concord Jazz ✦✦✦
Easy Street / 1995 / Concord Jazz ✦✦✦

Red McKenzie

b. Oct. 14, 1899, St. Louis, MO, d. Feb. 7, 1948, New York, NY
Vocals, Comb / Classic Jazz
Red McKenzie was virtually jazz's only comb player, putting tissue paper on a comb and making sounds on his "instrument" similar to a kazoo. McKenzie was quite effective playing his "ax," often more so than when he sang sentimental ballads. In 1924 he formed the Mound City Blue Blowers, a trio with Jack Bland on banjo or guitar and Dick Slevin on kazoo. The group was quite popular for a few years, recording a dozen titles (two with guest Frankie Trumbauer and the last six with Eddie Lang making the group a quartet) during 1924-25. McKenzie also recorded under his own name (as leader of the Candy Kids, the exact same quartet!) during 1924-25. The Blue Blowers was used for two classic titles ("Hello Lola" and "One Hour") in 1929 featuring Coleman Hawkins, Pee Wee Russell and Glenn Miller along with the leader's comb; further Blue Blowers titles were cut during 1931 (featuring Hawkins, Jimmy Dorsey and Muggsy Spanier) and 1935-36 (often with Bunny Berigan). McKenzie, who recorded as a straight singer in 1931 and was with Paul Whiteman the following year, never did become a major name, but he did front the Spirits of Rhythm (1934) and the Farley-Riley group (1935) on record dates. He was retired during 1939-43 but came back for a brief while, appearing on some of Eddie Condon's Town Hall concerts and recording a few titles during 1944-47; by then the comb was sadly just a memory. —*Scott Yanow*

● **Red McKenzie** / Jul. 12, 1935-Nov. 16, 1937 / Timeless ✦✦✦✦✦

Ray McKinley

b. Jun. 18, 1910, Fort Worth, TX, d. May 7, 1995
Drums, Vocals, Leader / Swing
A top drummer during the swing era and a likable and personable singer who always displayed good humor, Ray McKinley was most significant in the 1940s in several settings. He played at the start of his career in territory bands, with Smith Ballew and then the Dorsey Brothers Orchestra, staying with Jimmy after the battling Dorseys went their separate ways. In 1939 McKinley became the co-leader (in reality if not in its name) of the new Will Bradley Orchestra. His vocals and the boogie-woogie piano playing of Freddie Slack made the band a hit with such numbers as "Beat Me Daddy, Eight to the Bar" and "Celery Stalks at Midnight." By 1942 trombonist Bradley had gotten sick of the repertoire (which also included "Rock-A-Bye the Boogie," "Scrub Me Mama with a

Boogie Beat," "I Boogied When I Should Have Woogied," "Boogie Woogie Conga," "Bounce Me Brother with a Solid Four," "Booglie Wooglie Piggy" and "Fry Me Cookie with a Can of Lard"), and the group broke up. McKinley led a short-lived big band and then went in the military, playing in Europe with Glenn Miller's Army Air Force Orchestra and a small group also including Peanuts Hucko and Mel Powell. After Miller's death, McKinley was one of the band's co-leaders. In 1946 he put together his own orchestra which used some very modern arrangements by Eddie Sauter, was open to the influence of bop and yet had a Dixieland flavor at times. Not too surprisingly it failed to catch on (although a Savoy LP shows how strong the band could be). Ray McKinley led the Glenn Miller ghost band during 1956-66 and freelanced with small groups and headed another Glenn Miller-type orchestra until drifting into semi-retirement. —*Scott Yanow*

★ **The Most Versatile Band in the Land** / Mar. 7, 1946-1947 / Savoy ✦✦✦✦✦
A recent reissue of material that Ray McKinley's band cut for Savoy in the late '40s featuring innovative arrangements provided by Eddie Sauter. His charts featured a more intricate, yet swinging style and was more energetic and intense than what McKinley had done on his own. —*Ron Wynn*

Class of '49 / 1949 / Hep ✦✦✦

McKinney's Cotton Pickers

Big Band / Swing, Classic Jazz
William McKinney was a drummer who by 1923 had retired from playing in favor of conducting and managing a big band. In 1926 his outfit became known as McKinney's Cotton Pickers, and the following year they scored a major coup by hiring arranger-/altoist/vocalist Don Redman away from Fletcher Henderson. As the band's musical director, Redman put together an outfit that competed successfully with Henderson and the up-and-coming Duke Ellington. The lineup of musicians by the time they started recording in 1928 included Langston Curl, Claude Jones, George Thomas and Dave Wilborn, but it was the advanced arrangements, the tight ensembles and the high musicianship of the orchestra on a whole that was most impressive. There were a few special all-star sessions with such players as Joe Smith, Sidney DeParis, Coleman Hawkins, Fats Waller, Lonnie Johnson making appearances, and James P. Johnson sat in on one date. Among the more rewarding recordings overall were "Four or Five Times," "It's Tight like That," "It's a Precious Little Thing Called Love" and four future standards that Redman introduced: "Gee Baby Ain't I Good to You," "Baby Won't You Please Come Home," "I Want a Little Girl" and "Cherry."

It was a major blow in 1931 when Don Redman departed to form his own band. Benny Carter took over as musical director, but despite the presence of such fine players as Doc Cheatham, Hilton Jefferson and holdovers Quentin Jackson, Rex Stewart and Prince Robinson, there would only be one final recording session. The Depression eventually did the band in, and after much turnover, in 1934 the classic group broke up. McKinney organized later versions of the Cotton Pickers but without making an impression. —*Scott Yanow*

McKinney's Cotton Pickers (1928-1929) / Jun. 1928-Nov. 1929 / Classics ✦✦✦✦

● **The Band Don Redman Built** / Jul. 11, 1928-Nov. 3, 1930 / Bluebird ✦✦✦✦
McKinney's Cotton Pickers were among the most forward-looking big jazz bands of the late '20s, clearly anticipating the swing era that arrived in the mid '30s. These recordings, some of which feature Benny Carter, Coleman Hawkins and Fats Waller, show the band emerging from a Dixieland style into what can only be called swing. —*William Ruhlmann*

McKinney's Cotton Pickers (1929-1930) / Nov. 1929-Nov. 1930 / Classics ✦✦✦✦

Hal McKusick

b. Jun. 1, 1924, Medford, MA
Alto Saxophone, Clarinet / Cool
A fine cool-toned altoist and an occasional clarinetist, Hal McKusick worked with the big bands of Les Brown, Woody Herman (1943), Boyd Raeburn (1944-45), Alvino Rey (1946), Buddy Rich and Claude Thornhill (1948-49). In the 1950s, in addition to his work with Terry Gibbs and Elliot Lawrence, he was a

busy and versatile studio musician. During 1955-58 McKusick recorded nine albums of material as a leader for Jubilee, Bethlehem, Victor, Coral, New Jazz, Prestige and Decca. Those small group recordings, although basically cool bop, sometimes used very advanced arrangements including charts by George Handy, Manny Albam, Gil Evans, Al Cohn, Jimmy Giuffre and particularly George Russell. After 1958 McKusick led no further jazz dates, and he has since retired. —Scott Yanow

Hal McKusick Quartet / Feb. 17, 1955 / Fresh Sound ✦✦✦✦
Hal McKusick was a fine journeyman cool-toned bop-based altoist and clarinetist on this 1955 Bethlehem studio date (reissued on CD by Fresh Sound) that is accompanied by guitarist Barry Galbraith, bassist Milt Hinton and drummer Osie Johnson on a variety of straight-ahead tunes including seven originals by arranger Manny Albam. The music is pleasing, light and swinging. —Scott Yanow

● **Hal McKusick: Jazz Workshop** / Mar. 3, 1956–Dec. 31, 1956 / Victor ✦✦✦✦✦

Now's the Time / Feb. 4, 1957–Sep. 7, 1958 / Decca ✦✦✦✦

Triple Exposure / Dec. 27, 1957 / Original Jazz Classics ✦✦✦
Two talented but forgotten bop-based improvisers are featured on this quintet set: Hal McKusick (who switches between his Paul Desmond-inspired alto, tenor and cool-toned clarinet) and trombonist Billy Byers. Accompanied by pianist Eddie Costa, bassist Paul Chambers and drummer Charlie Persip, the two horns get rare opportunities to stretch out on material ranging from "Saturday Night" and an early version of Dizzy Gillespie's "Con Alma" to "I'm Glad There Is You" and three McKusick originals. This obscure Prestige session (reissued on CD in the OJC series) should interest straight-ahead jazz fans. —Scott Yanow

John McLaughlin

b. Jan. 4, 1942, Yorkshire, England
Guitar, Leader / Fusion, World Music, Post Bop
A household name since the early '70s, John McLaughlin was an innovative fusion guitarist when he led the Mahavishnu Orchestra and has continued living up to his reputation as a phenomenal and consistently inquisitive player through the years. He started on guitar when he was 11 and was initially inspired by blues and swing players. McLaughlin worked with Alexis Korner, Graham Bond, Ginger Baker and others in the 1960s and played free jazz with Gunter Hampel for six months. His first album was a classic (1969's *Extrapolation*) and was followed by an obscurity for the Dawns label with John Surman, a quintet set with Larry Young (*Devotion*) and *My Goals Beyond* in 1970 which was half acoustic solos and half jams involving Indian musicians.

In 1969 McLaughlin moved to New York to play with Tony Williams' Lifetime, and he appeared on two classic Miles Davis records: *In a Silent Way* and *Bitches Brew*. In 1971 McLaughlin formed the Mahavishnu Orchestra, a very powerful group often thought of as rock but having the sophisticated improvisations of jazz. After three influential albums (*The Inner Mounting Flame, Birds of Fire* and *Between Nothingness and Eternity*), the group broke up in 1973. McLaughlin, who recorded a powerful spiritual album with Carlos Santana that was influenced by John Coltrane, put together a new Mahavishnu Orchestra in 1974 that, despite the inclusion of Jean-Luc Ponty, failed to catch on and broke up by 1975. McLaughlin then surprised the music world by radically shifting directions, switching to acoustic guitar and playing Indian music with his group Shakti. They made a strong impact on the world music scene (which was in its infancy) during their three years. Since then McLaughlin has gone back and forth between electric and acoustic guitars, leading the One Truth Band, playing in trios with Al DiMeola and Paco De Lucia, popping up on some mid-'80s Miles Davis records, forming a short-lived third version of the Mahavishnu Orchestra (with saxophonist Bill Evans), recording an introspective tribute to pianist Bill Evans and in 1993 touring with a rollicking jazz trio featuring Joey DeFrancesco and drummer Dennis Chambers. Throughout his productive career John McLaughlin has recorded as a leader for Marmalade, Dawns, Douglas Int, Columbia, Warner Bros. and Verve. —Scott Yanow

Extrapolation / Jan. 18, 1969 / Polydor ✦✦✦
John McLaughlin's first recording as a leader features the future innovator playing guitar in an English quartet. Although McLaughlin contributed all ten pieces, baritonist John Surman actually dominates this music, often swinging quite hard. The his-

torically significant set, although a lesser-known item in McLaughlin's discography, is quite musical and enjoyable in its own right. —Scott Yanow

Devotion / 1970 / Restless ✦✦✦✦
This often-exciting set, John McLaughlin's third as a leader and predating The Mahavishnu Orchestra by just a year, is actually more in the style of Tony Williams' Lifetime than McLaughlin's later groups. That fact is not all that surprising when one considers that Lifetime's organist Larry Young is an integral of this rockish but explorative set. None of the individual songs (which also feature bassist Billy Rich and drummer Buddy Miles) caught on, but McLaughlin's guitar style was already becoming distinctive. —Scott Yanow

★ **My Goals Beyond** / 1970 / Rykodisc ✦✦✦✦✦
My Goals Beyond ranked among John McLaughlin's finest acoustic guitar projects; it mixed stunning remakes of jazz classics with piercing originals that blended rock energy, jazz technique and Asian rhythmic patterns. Billy Cobham and Jerry Goodman were later part of the original Mahavishnu Orchestra, and here they demonstrated the empathy they shared with McLaughlin. Dave Liebman's swirling soprano punctuates McLaughlin's brilliant lines on "Peace One" and "Peace Two," while Airto, Badal Roy and Mahalakshmi found a comfortable meeting place for their Afro-Latin and Indian colorations and beats. —Ron Wynn

Love, Devotion and Surrender / 1972 / Columbia ✦✦✦✦✦

Shakti with John McLaughlin / Jul. 5, 1975 / Columbia ✦✦✦✦
Ragas meet jazz. Extraordinary energy. —Michael G. Nastos

Natural Elements / Jul. 1977 / Columbia ✦✦✦

Electric Dreams / Nov. 1978–Dec. 1978 / Columbia ✦✦✦

Electric Guitarist / 1979 / Columbia ✦✦✦✦
1990 reissue of a date with Carlos Santana (g), Chick Corea (k) and Jack Bruce (b). —Ron Wynn

● **Friday Night in San Francisco** / Dec. 5, 1980 / Columbia ✦✦✦✦✦

Belo Horizonte / 1981 / Warner Brothers ✦✦✦

Passion, Grace and Fire / Oct. 1982–Nov. 1982 / Columbia ✦✦✦✦
Two years after they recorded *Friday Night in San Francisco*, John McLaughlin, Al DiMeola and Paco De Lucia reunited for another set of acoustic guitar trios. If this can be considered a guitar "battle" (some of the playing is ferocious, and these speed demons do not let up too often), then the result is a three-way tie. This guitar summit lives up to its title. —Scott Yanow

Music Spoken Here / May 1983 / Warner Brothers ✦✦✦

Adventures in Radioland / 1987 / Relativity ✦✦✦✦

Live at the Royal Festival Hall / Nov. 27, 1989 / JMT ✦✦✦✦
Trio recording with Kai Eckhart (b) and Trilok Gurtu (per). —Michael G. Nastos

Que Alegria / Nov. 29, 1991–Dec. 3, 1991 / Verve ✦✦✦✦
McLaughlin's band for the '90s currently includes Indian percussionist Trilok Gurtu and bassist Dominique Dipiazza. Covering as many jazz facets as possible, McLaughlin employs his nylon-string classical guitar outfitted with a MIDI guitar synthesizer pickup to create some of the most beautiful sounds imaginable. —Paul Kohler

Time Remembered: John McLaughlin Plays Bill Evans / Mar. 25, 1993–Mar. 28, 1993 / Verve ✦✦
Pianist Bill Evans was one of guitarist John McLaughlin's early heroes so this Evans tribute seemed like a logical idea. Sticking to acoustic guitar, McLaughlin is joined by four other guitarists (along with the acoustic bass guitar of Yan Maresz) to create an unusual instrumentation that often sounds as full as a keyboard. The leader arranged ten of Evans' compositions and his own "Homage" for a largely introverted set of music that has a strong classical feel. McLaughlin lets loose a few times, but more mood and tempo variations would have kept this from being such a sleepy and overly respectful session. —Scott Yanow

Tokyo Live / Dec. 16, 1993+Dec. 18, 1993 / Verve ✦✦✦✦
Although it is tempting to think that The Free Spirits (the trio featured on this CD), due to the similarity of the instrumentation (guitarist John McLaughlin, organist Joey DeFrancesco and drummer Dennis Chambers), would be an updating of Tony Williams' groundbreaking fusion group Lifetime, the reality is somewhat different. McLaughlin may get top billing, but this music sounds very much like a Joey DeFrancesco-led Jimmy Smith revival date

with most of the selections being blues-based. There are some introspective moments for the guitarist (who plays strictly electric here), but DeFrancesco dominates the ensembles and takes the lion's share of the solo space. The music is enjoyable enough although none of the compositions (all but Miles Davis' "No Blues" are by McLaughlin) are all that memorable. —*Scott Yanow*

Promise / 1995 / Verve ✦✦✦✦✦

Jackie McLean

b. May 17, 1932, New York, NY
Alto Saxophone / Post Bop, Hard Bop
Jackie McLean has long had his own sound, played slightly sharp and with great intensity; he is recognizable within two notes. McLean was one of the few bop-oriented players of the early '50s who explored free jazz in the 1960s, widening his emotional range and drawing from the new music qualities that fit his musical personality.

The son of guitarist John McLean (who played guitar with Tiny Bradshaw), Jackie started on alto when he was 15. As a teenager he was friends with such neighbors as Bud Powell, Thelonious Monk and Sonny Rollins. He made his recording debut with Miles Davis in 1951, and the rest of the decade could be considered his apprenticeship. McLean worked with George Wallington, Charles Mingus and Art Blakey's Jazz Messengers (1956-58). He also participated on a string of jam session-flavored records for Prestige and New Jazz which, due to the abysmal pay and his developing style, he has since disowned. Actually they are not bad but pale compared to McLean's classic series of 21 Blue Note albums (1959-67). On sessions such as *One Step Beyond* and *Destination Out*, McLean really stretches and challenges himself; this music is quite original and intense yet logical. McLean also appeared as a sideman on some sessions for Blue Note, acted in the stage play *The Connection* (1959-61) and led his own groups on a regular basis. By 1968 however he was moving into the jazz education field, and other than some SteepleChase records from 1972-74 (including two meetings with his early idol Dexter Gordon) and an unfortunate commercial outing for RCA (1978-79), McLean was less active as a player during the 1970s. However in the 1980s Jackie McLean returned to a more active playing schedule (sometimes with his son Rene McLean on tenor), recording for Triloka and most recently Antilles with all of the intensity and passion of his earlier days. —*Scott Yanow*

The Jackie McLean Quintet / Oct. 21, 1955 / Ad Lib ✦✦✦

Lights Out / Jan. 27, 1956 / Original Jazz Classics ✦✦✦✦
Altoist Jackie McLean's second session as a leader is reissued on this CD. The music that he makes with trumpeter Donald Byrd, pianist Elmo Hope, bassist Doug Watkins and drummer Art Taylor is essentially hard bop with fairly simple (or in some cases nonexistent) melody statements preceding two romps through the "I Got Rhythm" chord changes, a pair of blues, a thinly disguised "Embraceable You" and a straightforward version of "A Foggy Day." Enjoyable if not really essential music from the up-and-coming altoist. —*Scott Yanow*

4, 5 and 6 / Jul. 1956 / Prestige ✦✦✦✦
This is a well-rounded CD reissue that brings back altoist Jackie McLean's third recording as a leader. McLean has several fine ballad features ("Sentimental Journey," "Why Was I Born," "When I Fall in Love" and Mal Waldron's "Abstraction") welcomes trumpeter Donald Byrd to Kenny Drew's "Contour" and jams on a lengthy version of Charlie Parker's "Confirmation" with a sextet that includes Byrd and tenor saxophonist Hank Mobley. With pianist Waldron, bassist Doug Watkins and drummer Art Taylor offering fine support, this is a strong hard bop set that is tied to the tradition of bebop while looking forward. —*Scott Yanow*

Jackie's Pal / Aug. 31, 1956 / Original Jazz Classics ✦✦✦
The "pal" of altoist Jackie McLean is trumpeter Bill Hardman, a fine hard bop soloist who would be best-known for his association with Art Blakey's Jazz Messengers. This CD reissue is very much in the style of Blakey with the two horns joined by pianist Mal Waldron, bassist Paul Chambers and drummer Philly Joe Jones. Four of the six selections are group originals (by McLean, Hardman or Waldron), and the set is rounded off by Charlie Parker's "Steeplechase" and the standard "It Could Happen to You;" the latter is a showcase for Hardman. Although not overly memorable, this is a good early outing for McLean and Hardman and will be enjoyed by straight-ahead jazz fans. —*Scott Yanow*

McLean's Scene / Dec. 4, 1956-Feb. 15, 1957 / Original Jazz Classics ✦✦✦✦
Altoist Jackie McLean tends to downgrade his Prestige recordings due to the low pay, the little prior preparation and the jam session feel of the music. Although all of the above is true, the music (while not on a par with his Blue Notes of the 1960s) is still pretty worthy, particularly when compared to the output of his contemporaries. McLean never really copied Charlie Parker and was one of the first in his generation to develop his own sound. Three of the six selections on this CD reissue (a pair of standards and a blues) feature McLean with trumpeter Bill Hardman, pianist Red Garland, bassist Paul Chambers and drummer Art Taylor. The remainder of the set is from a marathon quartet set with pianist Mal Waldron, bassist Arthur Phipps and drummer Taylor that would result in material that was used as part of five separate albums! McLean is in lyrical form on "Our Love Is Here to Stay" and "Old Folks" while playing with great intensity on his accurately-titled original "Outburst." —*Scott Yanow*

Jackie McLean and Co. / Feb. 8, 1957 / Original Jazz Classics ✦✦✦
Although altoist Jackie McLean's Prestige recordings of the 1950s are not as significant as his Blue Notes from the '60s, he did record quite a bit of enjoyable hard bop material during this era. This CD is unusual for, in addition to a conventional quintet (with trumpeter Bill Hardman, pianist Mal Waldron, bassist Doug Watkins and drummer Art Taylor), the young tuba player Ray Draper is heard on three of the five group originals. Draper played his instrument as part of the frontline rather than in the rhythm section, and even if he was not on the level of McLean and Hardman, he gives some needed color to this set. Waldron, who contributed two of the five selections (the others are by McLean, Watkins or Draper) really sets the melancholy mood for much of the music and is an important force behind the scenes. An interesting CD. —*Scott Yanow*

Strange Blues / Feb. 15, 1957-Aug. 30, 1957 / Prestige ✦✦✦✦
The last of the Jackie McLean Prestige sessions, this CD reissue has material from two different sets, but fortunately, the music is on a higher level than one might expect of "leftovers." "Strange Blues" is from a marathon quartet set that McLean had with pianist Mal Waldron, bassist Arthur Phipps and drummer Art Taylor as is a rendition of "What's New" that is an alternate version to the one included on *Makin' the Changes*. In addition, "Disciples Love Affair" and "Millie's Pad" match McLean with the tuba of Ray Draper (who contributed both songs), trumpeter Webster Young, pianist John Meyers, bassist Bill Salter and drummer Larry Ritchie, while the incomplete "Not So Strange Blues" is all McLean on an explosive blues with the rhythm section. A generally strong set chiefly recommended to Jackie McLean completists. —*Scott Yanow*

Alto Madness / May 3, 1957 / Original Jazz Classics ✦✦✦
Altoists Jackie McLean and John Jenkins pay tribute to Charlie Parker throughout this session, not just on Parker's blues "Bird Feathers" but in practically every phrase they play. McLean became much more individual within a few years while Jenkins would fade from the scene altogether. This likable jam session also features a fine boppish rhythm section (pianist Wade Legge, bassist Doug Watkins and drummer Art Taylor) and plenty of tradeoffs by the two altoists. —*Scott Yanow*

A Long Drink of the Blues / Aug. 30, 1957 / Original Jazz Classics ✦✦✦✦
This CD reissue begins with what is titled "Take 1" of "A Long Drink of the Blues." After a false start, the musicians argue for two minutes about the tempo; why was this ever released? "Take 2" is a much more successful 20-minute jam featuring Jackie McLean (doubling on alto and tenor), trombonist Curtis Fuller, trumpeter Webster Young, pianist Gil Coggins, bassist Paul Chambers and drummer Louis Hayes. The second half of this reissue is from a quartet session that showcases McLean on three standard ballads with pianist Mal Waldron, bassist Arthur Phipps and drummer Art Taylor. Although not quite as intense as McLean's later Blue Note dates, the ballad renditions show just how mature and original a soloist he was even at this early stage. Despite "Take 1," this CD is worth getting. —*Scott Yanow*

Makin' the Changes / Aug. 30, 1957 / New Jazz ✦✦✦✦
This CD reissue of a Jackie McLean LP features the altoist in two different settings. On three selections—a rollicking "Bean and the Boys," an uptempo "I Never Knew" and "I Hear a Rhapsody"—

McLean teams up with pianist Mal Waldron in a quartet with bassist Arthur Phipps and drummer Art Taylor. The other three numbers ("What's New," "Chasin' the Bird" and McLean's original "Jackie's Ghost") have more of a jam session feel and feature McLean in a sextet with trumpeter Webster Young, trombonist Curtis Fuller, pianist Gil Coggins, bassist Paul Chambers and drummer Louis Hayes. In general, the hard bop music is swinging and fairly advanced, a step above the usual jam sessions of the time. —*Scott Yanow*

Jackie McLean Plays Fat Jazz / Dec. 27, 1957 / Jubilee ✦✦✦

Jackie's Bag / Jan. 18, 1959–Sep. 1, 1960 / Blue Note ✦✦✦✦✦
This very interesting LP was a giant step forward for altoist Jackie McLean, although it was originally released after a couple of his other Blue Note albums. For the first time, McLean shows some of the influence of Ornette Coleman—not in his sound but in his improvising approach—and his freer style bridged the gap between hard bop and the avant-garde. Three of the songs, highlighted by "Quadrangle" and "Fidel," match McLean in 1959 with trumpeter Donald Byrd, pianist Sonny Clark, bassist Paul Chambers and drummer Philly Joe Jones while the other numbers, which include "Appointment in Ghana," showcase McLean in a sextet with trumpeter Blue Mitchell, Tina Brooks on tenor, pianist Kenny Drew, Chambers and drummer Art Taylor. Jackie McLean's Blue Note albums were the most significant of his career, and this LP is well worth searching for. —*Scott Yanow*

New Soil / May 2, 1959 / Blue Note ✦✦✦✦
This CD reissue adds "Formidable," which was first released on the 1980 LP *Vertigo*, to the original program. A quintet date with trumpeter Donald Byrd, pianist Walter Davis, Jr., bassist Paul Chambers and drummer Pete La Roca, this music is far superior to the jam session-oriented sets that altoist Jackie McLean made for Prestige a few years earlier. Rehearsal time gave the musicians an opportunity to learn the two McLean originals and the four songs contributed by Davis; the latter's "Davis Cup" is the best-known of the pieces. The music is funky but adventurous, beyond hard bop but still tied to chordal improvisation. Stimulating listening. —*Scott Yanow*

Vertigo / May 2, 1959–Feb. 11, 1963 / Blue Note ✦✦✦✦
This 1980 LP released for the first time "Formidable" from a 1959 session and five numbers from a 1963 McLean set. While "Formidable" has a strong quintet (with altoist Jackie McLean, trumpeter Donald Byrd, pianist Walter Davis, bassist Paul Chambers and drummer Pete La Roca), the 1963 session has the recording debut of drummer Tony Williams along with strong contributions from Byrd, pianist Herbie Hancock (then also near the beginning of his career) and bassist Butch Warren. The latter unit sticks to group originals by Byrd, Hancock and McLean, and the music ranges from catchy funk and hard bop to strong hints of the avant-garde. The later session has yet to appear on CD, making this LP worth searching for by Jackie McLean collectors. —*Scott Yanow*

Swing Swang Swingin / Oct. 2, 1959 / Blue Note ✦✦✦✦

Capuchin Swing / Apr. 17, 1960 / Blue Note ✦✦✦✦

Bluesnik / Jan. 8, 1961 / Blue Note ✦✦✦✦✦
This is one of the most accessible of altoist Jackie McLean's Blue Note sessions, for the six songs, which have been augmented on the CD reissue by "new" alternate versions of "Goin' Way Blues" and "Torchin'," are all blues. McLean teams up with the fiery young trumpeter Freddie Hubbard, pianist Kenny Drew, bassist Doug Watkins and drummer Pete La Roca for diverse originals by the leader, Drew and Hubbard that all have the feeling (if not always the exact structure) of the blues. The variety of tempos, moods and styles make this a highly recommended set. —*Scott Yanow*

A Fickle Sonance / Oct. 26, 1961 / Blue Note ✦✦✦✦✦
A remarkable merger of new-time/avant-garde leanings and hard-bop fluidity and feelings. —*Ron Wynn*

★ **Let Freedom Ring** / Mar. 19, 1962 / Blue Note ✦✦✦✦✦
This is one of altoist Jackie McLean's most significant recordings. A veteran of the hard bop scene of the 1950s, McLean was one of the few musicians from his generation to embrace aspects of the avant-garde without losing his own musical personality. McLean kept his own intense sound but opened up his playing to the point where he could improvise without using chord structures or even a steady tempo. His emotional style is heard at its prime on the four selections included on this CD reissue, a quartet date with

pianist Walter Davis, bassist Herbie Lewis and drummer Billy Higgins. Although the music is not quite as free as Ornette Coleman's, it is nearly as innovative, particularly when one considers the expanded vocabulary that McLean uses (with screams and honks being integrated logically into his solos). Even on Bud Powell's ballad "I'll Keep Loving You," McLean's playing is very advanced, and in its own way, free. This is a gem that still sounds quite modern. —*Scott Yanow*

Hipnosis / Jun. 14, 1962 / Blue Note ✦✦✦✦
This valuable and attractive two-LP set from 1978 issued for the first time a couple of sessions by altoist Jackie McLean that had been lost in the vaults. The 1962 date is fairly boppish with McLean being teamed up with trumpeter Kenny Dorham, pianist Sonny Clark, bassist Butch Warren and drummer Billy Higgins. The emphasis is on blues and straight-ahead swinging, but even here McLean sounds like he is pushing the boundaries a bit. The later session features McLean, trombonist Grachan Moncur, pianist Lamont Johnson, bassist Scotty Holt and Higgins. Despite some soulful moments, the music sounds ten (rather than five) years more advanced and is strongly influenced (but not derivative) of the avant-garde players. Despite being overlooked, the music on both of these dates is up to the high level of Jackie McLean's better-known Blue Note dates and is easily recommended to fans of the innovative altoist. —*Scott Yanow*

Tippin' the Scales / Sep. 28, 1962 / Blue Note ✦✦✦✦
This fairly straight-ahead LP by altoist Jackie McLean was released for the first time in 1984. Due to its boppish nature, as opposed to his more adventurous recordings of the period, it languished in the vaults for over 20 years, but the music is actually quite enjoyable. With assistance from pianist Sonny Clark, bassist Butch Warren and drummer Art Taylor, McLean is in excellent form on two of his originals, three by Clark (including "Nursery Blues" and "Nicely") and the standard ballad "Cabin in the Sky." A fine hard bop session. —*Scott Yanow*

★ **One Step Beyond** / Apr. 30, 1963 / Blue Note ✦✦✦✦✦
One of the great Jackie McLean records, this album features the innovative altoist performing two of his originals plus a pair by trombonist Grachan Moncur, III. With vibraphonist Bobby Hutcherson (on one of his earliest recordings), bassist Eddie Khan and drummer Tony Williams (McLean's discovery) completing the quintet, this was a group that could play the most advanced material with creativity and improvise freely when it fit the music. The solos and ensembles on the "difficult" material are quite memorable, and it is to Jackie McLean's credit that he was not satisfied to spend his entire career playing hard bop; his musical curiosity led him to listening closely to the music of Ornette Coleman and to adapting aspects of free jazz that fit his distinctive sound. —*Scott Yanow*

● **Destination Out** / Sep. 20, 1963 / Blue Note ✦✦✦✦✦
Five very talented and versatile jazzmen (altoist Jackie McLean, trombonist Grachan Moncur III, vibraphonist Bobby Hutcherson, bassist Larry Ridley and drummer Roy Haynes) explore three of Moncur's originals plus McLean's "Kahlil the Prophet" on this CD reissue of their 1963 Blue Note album. McLean was one of the few players of his generation to be influenced by the free jazz movement yet he never lost his musical personality or his distinctive sound. The improvisations by these musicians are both thoughtful and passionate, making expert use of space, tricky time changes and emotional intensity. —*Scott Yanow*

It's Time / Aug. 5, 1964 / Blue Note ✦✦✦✦
Altoist Jackie McLean and his sidemen on this excellent quintet set (which also features trumpeter Charles Tolliver, pianist Herbie Hancock, bassist Cecil McBee and drummer Roy Haynes) explore aspects of free jazz (particularly on "Cancellation") without letting go completely of the concepts of chordal improvisation. Strange as it seems, McLean's sound and highly expressive vocabulary are more advanced than his actual notes while Tolliver's notes are more unpredictable than his Clifford Brown-inspired tone. Ranging from "Cancellation" to the funky "Das' Dat," this is a stimulating LP that has been reissued as part of Mosaic's four-CD Jackie McLean box set. —*Scott Yanow*

★ **Complete Blue Note 1964–1966** / Aug. 5, 1964–Apr. 18, 1966 / Mosaic ✦✦✦✦✦
Altoist Jackie McLean has recorded so many fine albums throughout his career, particularly in the 1960s for Blue Note, that Mosaic could have reissued his complete output without any loss of qual-

ity. This four-CD limited-edition box set contains six complete LPs worth of material plus one "new" alternate take. The music (which also features trumpeters Charles Tolliver and Lee Morgan, pianists Herbie Hancock, Larry Willis and Harold Mabern, vibraphonist Bobby Hutcherson, bassists Cecil McBee, Bob Cranshaw, Larry Ridley, Herbie Lewis and Don Moore and drummers Roy Haynes, Billy Higgins, Clifford Jarvis, Jack DeJohnette and Billy Higgins) is explorative (showing the influence of Ornette Coleman) but without totally disgarding McLean's bebop roots. The performances straddle the boundaries between advanced hard bop and free jazz with Jackie McLean consistently emerging as the main star; his solos are consistently exciting and full of unexpected twists and turns. —Scott Yanow

Action / Sep. 16, 1964 / Blue Note ◆◆◆◆
This LP, whose music has been reissued as part of a Mosaic Jackie McLean box set, has several selections that are quite fascinating. McLean (along with trumpeter Charles Tolliver, vibraphonist Bobby Hutcherson, bassist Cecil McBee and drummer Billy Higgins) plays quite free on "Action" (which does not have a specific set of chord changes to follow), a pair of Tolliver ballads ("Plight" is best known) and even the standard "I Hear a Rhapsody" (McLean's feature). Only the bluesy "Hootman" is a bit more conventional, although those solos are also far from predictable. This album is full of exciting music that has long been overshadowed. —Scott Yanow

Right Now / Jan. 26, 1965 / Blue Note ◆◆◆◆◆
With the exception of a beautiful ballad version of Larry Willis' "Poor Eric," the music on this CD (which is also available in Mosaic's four-CD Jackie McLean box set) is hard-charging, intense and fairly free. Altoist McLean was at the peak of his powers during this period, and inspired by the versatile rhythm section (pianist Larry Willis, bassist Bob Cranshaw and drummer Clifford Jarvis), he plays explorative versions of his own "Eco," Willis' "Christel's Time" and Charles Tolliver's "Right Now;" an alternate version of the latter is added on for the CD reissue. This CD offers listeners a particularly strong example of Jackie McLean's unique inside/outside music of the 1960s. —Scott Yanow

Consequences / Dec. 3, 1965 / Blue Note ◆◆◆◆
Unreleased until 1979 but fortunately currently available in a Mosaic Jackie McLean CD box set, this superior outing features altoist McLean and trumpeter Lee Morgan as equals in a quintet that also includes pianist Harold Mabern, bassist Herbie Lewis and drummer Billy Higgins. The music is more straight-ahead than on the altoist's better-known gems of the period but is never predictable. Morgan really challenges McLean on "Bluesanova," and other highlights include McLean's "Consequence" and the calypso feel of "Tolypso." —Scott Yanow

Jacknife / Apr. 12, 1966 / Blue Note ◆◆◆◆◆
The dynamic music on this two-LP set was released for the first time in 1975, although it has since been reissued as part of Mosaic's four-CD Jackie McLean box set. It is surprising that the music was originally overlooked for both of these sessions have more than their share of brilliant moments. Altoist McLean teams up with trumpeters Lee Morgan and Charles Tolliver (the brassmen play two songs apiece and are both on "Soft Blue") along with pianist Larry Willis, bassist Larry Ridley and drummer Jack Dejohnette on the earlier date. Most memorable is Tolliver's atmospheric "On the Nile," but all of the selections (essentially modal hard bop with some influences from the avant-garde) are quite notable. However it is the later session, a quartet outing with Willis, Dejohnette and bassist Don Moore, that really finds McLean playing at the peak of his expressive powers. His open style makes occasional shrieks, screams and honks fit in logically as part of his improvisations, and his solos (check out the lengthy "High Frequency") are quite adventurous yet logical. This important music is essential, in one form or another, for all followers of advanced jazz. —Scott Yanow

Dr. Jackle / Dec. 18, 1966 / SteepleChase ◆◆◆◆
Jackie McLean was one of the few hard bop stars (John Coltrane was another) who was greatly affected by the avant-garde innovations of the 1960s. His sound did not change, but his solos became freer and much more emotional. By the time he played in Baltimore for the 1966 concert released on this CD, he had greatly opened up his style and had reconciled his roots with free jazz. With the strong assistance of pianist Lamont Johnson, bassist Scotty Holt and drummer Billy Higgins, McLean stretches out on five numbers (including a previously unreleased "Jossa Bossa")

which clock in between 8 and over 14-1/2 minutes. From the start the music is quite intense, and it may take listeners a few moments to get used to the altoist's abrasive and sharp tone. However his creative ideas and constant originality win one over fast, and by the time he finished the set with a blues ("Closing"), the logic of Jackie McLean's improvisations is more apparent. The recording quality is sometimes a little distorted, but the power, color and pure courage of the music is memorable. —Scott Yanow

Tune Up / Dec. 18, 1966 / SteepleChase ◆◆◆◆
From the same "live in Baltimore" session that resulted in Dr. Jackle, altoist Jackie McLean and his regular quartet of the period (composed of pianist Lamont Johnson, bassist Scotty Holt and drummer Billy Higgins) explore lengthy versions of three standards ("Tune Up," "I Remember You" and a passionate "Smile") along with McLean's original "Jack's Tune." As well as the altoist plays, it is the solos of the underrated and underrecorded pianist, LaMont Johnson, that make this explorative hard bop release most notable. —Scott Yanow

New and Old Gospel / Mar. 24, 1967 / Blue Note ◆◆◆◆
With Ornette Coleman on trumpet. —Michael G. Nastos

Bout Soul / Sep. 8, 1967 / Blue Note ◆◆◆◆

Demon's Dance / Dec. 22, 1967 / Blue Note ◆◆◆◆◆
Altoist Jackie McLean's final Blue Note album preceded four and a half years of silence as he withdrew from the New York scene and started working as an educator. McLean was still very much in top form at the time of this hard-to-find LP. Teaming up with trumpeter Woody Shaw, pianist LaMont Johnson, bassist Scott Holt and drummer Jack Dejohnette, McLean is quite passionate and typically intense on two of his originals plus a couple songs apiece from Cal Massey (including "Message from Trane") and Shaw. The modal-oriented music fit the styles of these advanced jazzmen, and the results are quite stimulating and adventurous. —Scott Yanow

Live at Montmartre / Aug. 5, 1972 / SteepleChase ◆◆◆◆
Altoist Jackie McLean's first recording in five years found him exploring two Charlie Parker tunes, Charlie Chaplin's "Smile" and his own "Das Dat." All but the 9 minute "Confirmation" are over 15 minutes long yet McLean's lengthy solos hold one's interest, as does the playing of pianist Kenny Drew, bassist Bo Stief and drummer Alex Riel. Although not as advanced as some of his Blue Note classics of the 1960s, McLean is in top form and quite explorative during these performances; his sound is certainly instantly recognizable. —Scott Yanow

Ode to Super / Jul. 17, 1973 / SteepleChase ◆◆◆
This matchup between altoists Jackie McLean and Gary Bartz has always been a bit of a disappointment with the solos much stronger than the material. The title cut, "Ode to Super," (which has vocals from the two co-leaders) is taken from a play, and the originals by McLean, Bartz and pianist Thomas Clausen are not too memorable. Only a torrid jam on Charlie Parker's "Red Cross" really works. A more suitable encore by the two greats is long overdue! —Scott Yanow

A Ghetto Lullaby / Jul. 18, 1973 / Inner City ◆◆◆
Within a five day period in 1973, altoist Jackie McLean, who had only made one album (a live set) between 1968–72, cut enough material for five records! This worthy set features his intense style in a quartet with pianist Kenny Drew, bassist Niels Pedersen and drummer Alex Riel, recorded live at Montmartre in Copenhagen. Although the material—Drew's "Callin'," the ballad "Where Is Love," a pair of William Gault songs and McLean's "Jack's Tune"— is not all that memorable, the altoist's passionate solos and very distinctive sound uplift the music and make this an advanced hard bop set worth acquiring. —Scott Yanow

The Meeting / Jul. 20, 1973–Jul. 21, 1973 / SteepleChase ◆◆◆
Altoist Jackie McLean met with up his idol, tenor saxophonist Dexter Gordon for a couple of club dates, and the result is a pair of hard-swinging if somewhat loose albums; the accompanying set is The Source. The pair of saxophonists (along with pianist Kenny Drew, bassist Niels Pedersen and drummer Alex Riel) give four pieces ("On the Trail" and three obscure originals) lengthy renditions with Dexter's "All Clean" being over 17 minutes long. The music falls short of being classic but is quite spirited and recommended to fans of both Dexter Gordon and Jackie McLean. —Scott Yanow

The Source / Jul. 20, 1973–Jul. 21, 1973 / SteepleChase ◆◆◆
Veteran tenor Dexter Gordon and altoist Jackie McLean teamed

up for a few club dates in 1973, and the results have been released on two SteepleChase albums; the other one is *The Meeting*. Unlike the earlier release which focused on lesser-known material, *The Source* features the saxophonists on three jazz standards (Miles Davis's "Half Nelson," "I Can't Get Started" and Charlie Parker's "Another Hair-Do") in addition to reviving Dexter Gordon's 1947 composition "Dexter Digs In." The music is a bit loose and long-winded ("Half Nelson" is over 18 minutes long) but recommended to straight-ahead jazz fans. —*Scott Yanow*

Antiquity / Aug. 1974 / SteepleChase ✦✦✦

New York Calling / Oct. 30, 1974 / SteepleChase ✦✦✦
A wonderful session that helped introduce McLean's then-26-year-old son Rene to the jazz audience. —*Ron Wynn*

New Wine in Old Bottles / Apr. 6, 1978–Apr. 7, 1978 / Inner City ✦✦✦✦
This out-of-print LP (originally put out by the East Wind label in Tokyo) is a bit different than it appears. Although its title makes it seem as if altoist Jackie McLean is bringing back a variety of older standards, only three of the songs ("It Never Entered My Mind," "'Round Midnight" and "Confirmation") fit into that category. In addition, McLean and his all-star quartet (pianist Hank Jones, bassist Ron Carter and drummer Tony Williams) perform "Bein' Green" and two of the altoist's tunes: "Appointment in Ghana" and "Little Melonae." The music is essentially hard bop with McLean's unique tone indeed giving new life to this swinging yet often introspective music. —*Scott Yanow*

Monuments / Nov. 19, 1978-Jan. 1979 / RCA ✦
It seems as if nearly every major jazz musician has a dud or two in their discography. This out-of-print LP is the only major flaw in altoist Jackie McLean's long career, a set of electronic rhythms, dumb vocals ("Doctor Jackyll and Mister Funk!") and unadventurous playing that is instantly forgettable. It would be quite a few years before Jackie McLean reappeared on records again after this artistic (and commercial) fiasco. —*Scott Yanow*

★ **Dynasty** / Nov. 5, 1988 / Triloka ✦✦✦✦✦
This is one of the great Jackie McLean albums. After nearly a decade off of records, the veteran altoist teamed up with his son Rene (who triples on tenor, soprano and flute), pianist Hotep Idris Galeta, bassist Nat Reeves and drummer Carl Allen for a very passionate and high-powered live set. Whether it be originals by Rene McLean (including "J. Mac's Dynasty") or Galeta, a very intense version of "A House Is Not a Home" or Jackie's "Bird Lives," this is dynamic and consistently exciting music. The go-for-broke solos (which transcend any easy categories) and Jackie's unique sharp tone make this an essential CD, one of the top recordings to be released in 1990. —*Scott Yanow*

Rites of Passage / Jan. 29, 1991-Jan. 30, 1991 / Triloka ✦✦✦✦✦
Recorded over two years after his "comeback" album, *Dynasty*, but using the same personnel, altoist Jackie McLean once again sounds in prime form. His intensity and passion had not declined through the years, and his sometimes-abrasive tone had, if anything, become even more distinctive. With this particularly strong group (which has son Rene on tenor, alto and soprano, pianist Hotep Idris Galeta, bassist Nat Reeves and drummer Carl Allen), McLean pours his heart out on two of his originals plus pieces by Rene and Galeta. Outstanding no-holds-barred music. —*Scott Yanow*

The Jackie Mac Attack Live / Apr. 1991 / Verve ✦✦✦✦
Veteran altoist Jackie McLean is in top form on this live quartet session with pianist Hotep Idris Galeta, bassist Nat Reeves and drummer Carl Allen. He performs two originals by Galeta, Rene McLean's "Dance Little Mandissa," "'Round Midnight" and his own "Minor March" and "Five." The amount of passion and intensity that McLean puts into his improvisations is quite impressive, and 40 years after his recording debut, he remains in prime form. This strong, advanced hard bop date gives listeners a good example of his abilities. —*Scott Yanow*

Rhythm of the Earth / Mar. 12, 1992–Mar. 13, 1992 / Antilles ✦✦✦✦
The music on this CD is dedicated to the Dogon people of Mali in West Africa. The originals (by altoist Jackie McLean, trombonist Steve Davis and pianist Alan Palmer) are challenging but swinging, and inspire the members of the septet, which also include trumpeter Roy Hargrove, vibraphonist Steve Nelson, bassist Nat Reeves and drummer Eric McPherson. The sound of the group (with trombone and vibes) is a throwback of sorts to

McLean's mid-'60s recordings on Blue Note, although the music is not quite as explorative. Jackie McLean is in fine form, and it is good to hear Hargrove playing in this advanced setting. Worth checking out. —*Scott Yanow*

Rene McLean

b. 1947, New York, NY
Flute, Tenor Saxophone, Alto Saxophone / Hard Bop
The son of altoist Jackie McLean, Rene studied alto with his father and Sonny Rollins from the age of nine. He played baritone and later alto with Tito Puente for three years in the early '70s and also worked with Sam Rivers, Lionel Hampton and with his father in the Cosmic Brotherhood. McLean played in the mid-'70s in a quintet with Woody Shaw and Louis Hayes, started touring with Hugh Masekela in 1978, settled in South Africa in 1985, led his own group and in the late '80s recorded with his father for Triloka. Rene McLean has also led his own albums for SteepleChase (1975) and Triloka (1993). —*Scott Yanow*

● **Watch Out** / Jul. 9, 1975 / Steeplechase ✦✦✦✦✦
This session was Rene McLean's debut as a leader, and it found the 28 year old switching between alto, soprano, tenor and flute. The son of Jackie McLean, Rene did not yet have a distinctive voice, but he showed much potential for the future. His sextet (with trumpeter Danny Coleman, pianist Hubert Eaves and guitarist Nathan Page) hints at the innovations of the avant-garde while remaining closer to the style of Art Blakey's Jazz Messengers. It's a worthwhile if not overly memorable effort. —*Scott Yanow*

In African Eyes / 1993 / Triloka ✦✦✦

Jimmy McPartland

b. Mar. 15, 1907, Chicago, IL., **d.** Mar. 13, 1991, Port Washington, NY
Cornet / Dixieland
A solid Dixieland cornetist with his own lyrical sound (influenced by Bix Beiderbecke initially), Jimmy McPartland played the music he loved for over 60 years. The younger brother of guitarist Dick McPartland (1905–1957), Jimmy was a member of the legendary Austin High School Gang in the 1920s. He was Bix Beiderbecke's replacement with the Wolverines during 1925, joined Ben Pollack's band in 1927 and recorded with the McKenzie and Condon Chicagoans during their famous session. McPartland was one of the main soloists (along with Benny Goodman) with Pollack, and he stayed with the band into 1929. He then moved to Chicago, working steadily through the 1930s. While stationed overseas during World War II (1942–44) he met his future wife, the English pianist Marian Turner. McPartland freelanced at Dixieland sessions during the next four decades, working with Eddie Condon, Art Hodes and other Chicago jazz veterans and often leading his own band. Although eventually divorced from Marian McPartland, they were still close friends and occasionally played together, remarrying just a few weeks before Jimmy McPartland's death two days short of his 84th birthday. Many of his best early recordings were collected on an MCA two-LP set in the 1970s. In addition, he recorded as a leader for Harmony, Prestige, MGM, Grand Award, Jazztone, Epic, Mercury, RCA, Design, Jazzology, Halcyon (Marian's label) and Riff. —*Scott Yanow*

★ **Shades of Bix** / Apr. 24, 1936–Feb. 2, 1956 / Brunswick ✦✦✦✦✦
This double LP is long overdue to be reissued on CD. Trumpeter Jimmy McPartland originally succeeded the legendary Bix Beiderbecke with the Wolverines back in 1925. Decades later, although still influenced a bit by Beiderbecke's sound, McPartland had long developed his own musical personality. The first twelve selections on this set (eight from 1953 and the other four from 1956) feature McPartland paying tribute to Beiderbecke by performing a variety of songs associated with him. Such players as trombonist Lou McGarity, clarinetist Peanuts Hucko, tenorman Bud Freeman and baritonist Ernie Caceres help out on some of the numbers, and pianist Marian McPartland is aboard for the later sides. Highpoint is an emotional version of "In a Mist" that utilizes oboe and bassoon in the arrangement. In addition, this twofer includes McPartland's sessions of 1936 and 1939, superior Dixieland performances that, on four selections, are highlighted by rare solos from altoist Boyce Brown. This highly recommended set is rounded out by eight superior ballads from 1943 and

1946 featuring the mellow cornet of Bobby Hackett. —*Scott Yanow*

Jimmy McPartland's Dixieland / Feb. 2, 1957+Mar. 5, 1957 / Epic ++++

Meet Me in Chicago / May 7, 1959 / Mercury +++++

Ambiance / 1970 / Halcyon ++++

McPartlands Live at the Monticello / Nov. 1972 / Halcyon ++++

Marian McPartland

b. Mar. 20, 1920, Windsor, England

Piano / Bop, Swing

Marian McPartland has become famous for hosting her *Piano Jazz* radio program since 1978, but she was a well-respected pianist decades before. She played in a four-piano vaudeville act in England and performed on the European continent for the troops during World War II. In Belgium in 1944 she met cornetist Jimmy McPartland, and they soon married. Marian moved with her husband to the United States in 1946, where she sometimes played with him even though her style was more modern than his Dixieland-oriented groups. McPartland eventually had her own trio at the Embers (1950) and the Hickory House (1952-60) which until 1957 included drummer Joe Morello. She recorded regularly for Savoy and Capitol during the 1950s and also made sessions for Argo (1958), Time (1960 and 1963), Sesac and Dot. Although divorced eventually from Jimmy, they remained close friends, sometimes played together and remarried just weeks before his death. She formed her own Halcyon label and recorded several fine albums between 1969-77. McPartland also made three albums for Tony Bennett's Improv label during 1976-77 before signing with Concord where she has been since 1978. The Jazz Alliance label has made available on over a couple dozen CDs quite a few episodes of Marian McPartland's *Piano Jazz* show. — *Scott Yanow*

Marian McPartland / 1963 / Bainbridge ++++

Interplay / 1969 / Halcyon ++++

A Delicate Balance / 1971 1972 / Halcyon +++

A Sentimental Journey / 1972-1973 / Jazz Alliance ++++
Marian McPartland (famous as a modern pianist and for her *Piano Jazz* radio show) was initially introduced to the jazz major leagues through her husband, the late Jimmy McPartland, who was a talented Dixieland-oriented cornetist. During 1972-73 The McPartlands recorded two of their concerts which were later released on Marian's Halcyon label. This CD reissue contains 12 of the 14 selections, and these are among Jimmy McPartland's best live recordings. With frontlines that include either trombonist Vic Dickenson and tenorman Buddy Tate or trombonist Hank Berger and clarinetist Jack Maheu, the cornetist performs Dixieland and swing standards with enthusiasm and power, taking an occasional vocal and clearly having a good time. It's recommended for traditional fans. —*Scott Yanow*

Plays the Music of Alec Wilder / Jun. 20, 1973-Jun. 21, 1973 / Jazz Alliance +++

Maestro and Friend / Jul. 1973 / Halcyon ++++
Violinist Joe Venuti teams up with pianist Marian McPartland for a set of duets, mostly on standards. The music is quite melodic but has some exciting moments; there are not that many violin-piano duet versions of "That's a Plenty." A tasteful outing by two masterful players. —*Scott Yanow*

Solo Concert at Haverford / Apr. 12, 1974 / Halcyon +++
The emphasis is on ballads during this solo piano recital by Marian McPartland. She performs swing standards, a couple of medleys (including one of "Yesterdays" and "Yesterday"), a blues, Alec Wilder's "I'll Be Around" and her own "Afterglow." Nothing that memorable occurs, but this subtle easy-listening set put out on her private label Halcyon is enjoyable enough and recommended to McPartland's fans. —*Scott Yanow*

Concert in Argentina / Nov. 1974 / Jazz Alliance ++++
This Buenos Aires concert, originally released as a two-LP set, features four different but complementary pianists in solo performances: Marian McPartland, Teddy Wilson, Ellis Larkins and Earl Hines. The Jazz Alliance CD reissue unfortunately leaves out a selection or two apiece by each of the keyboardists (it should have come out as a double CD) so the LP version is the more highly recommended format. McPartland shows off her versatility on a Duke Ellington medley, Wilson swings impeccably, Larkins is typ-

ically subtle on his ballads, and Hines is the most reckless (and exciting) improviser. —*Scott Yanow*

Now's the Time / Jun. 30, 1977 / Halcyon +++

Marian McPartland's Piano Jazz with Guest Mary Lou Williams / Oct. 8, 1978 / Jazz Alliance ++
This CD is composed of the very first *Piano Jazz* radio show, and although interesting to hear once, it does not invite repeated listenings. Marian McPartland sounds nervous, and she constantly interrupts Mary Lou Williams' talking while Williams seems quite uptight in spots. There is some good playing by Williams (mostly duets with bassist Ronnie Boykins with McPartland occasionally joining in), but overall this set is mostly a historical curiosity. Fortunately Marian McPartland would improve quickly as a host, and most of the other CDs in this valuable series are more easily recommended than this debut effort. —*Scott Yanow*

★ **Piano Jazz: McPartland/Evans** / Nov. 6, 1978 / Jazz Alliance +++++

From This Moment on / Dec. 1978 / Concord Jazz +++

★ **At the Festival** / 1979 / Concord Jazz +++++
This nice small-group session accents McPartland's fortes: touch, delicacy and melodic interpretation. —*Ron Wynn*

Portrait of Marian McPartland / May 1979 / Concord Jazz ++++

Live at the Carlyle / Sep. 10, 1979 / Halcyon ++++

● **Piano Jazz: McPartland/Blake** / Dec. 15, 1979 / Jazz Alliance +++++

Piano Jazz: McPartland/Peterson / Jun. 2, 1980 / Jazz Alliance ++++

Piano Jazz: McPartland/Cowell / Jun. 26, 1981 / Jazz Alliance +++

Piano Jazz: McPartland/Wellstood / Jun. 27, 1981 / Jazz Alliance +++++

Piano Jazz: McPartland/Stacy / Dec. 1, 1981 / Jazz Alliance +++++
This is one of the most valuable of the *Piano Jazz* episodes for the great swing pianist Jess Stacy, who had been semiretired since the late '50s, made his final commercial recording in 1977. After stumbling a bit on "Dancing Fool," he is quite modest while discussing his own playing, but he gets stronger as the hour progresses. Although Stacy has four unaccompanied solos, and Marian McPartland is fine on her feature "Heavy Hearted Blues," it is their three joyous duets ("Keepin' out of Mischief Now," "I Would Do Anything for You" and "St. Louis Blues") along with the priceless reminiscing that makes this CD highly recommended to swing collectors. —*Scott Yanow*

Piano Jazz: McPartland/Coltrane / Dec. 4, 1981 / Jazz Alliance ++++

Personal Choice / Jun. 1982 / Concord Jazz ++++

Piano Jazz: McPartland/Wilson / 1985 / Jazz Alliance ++++

Marian Mc Partland's Piano Jazz with Guest Dizzy Gillespie / Jan. 1985 / Jazz Alliance ++

● **Willow Creek and Other Ballads** / Jan. 1985 / Concord Jazz +++++
The exemplary solo playing on this album helped embellish her new-star status won through her "Piano Jazz" series on National Public Radio. —*Ron Wynn*

Marian McPartland's Piano Jazz with Henry Mancini / Mar. 14, 1985 / Jazz Alliance ++++
Henry Mancini saw his role in music as a film and television composer rather than as a songwriter. During his interesting hour on Marian McPartland's *Piano Jazz* radio show, Mancini discusses his life with good humor and modesty. He takes two brief melody choruses (on "Two for the Road" and "Meggie's Theme"), duets with McPartland on several songs (including "The Pink Panther" and a touching version of "Days of Wine and Roses") and enjoys hearing McPartland interpret "Mr. Lucky" and "Charade." Although only one of his songs ("Days of Wine and Roses") really became a jazz standard, Mancini enjoyed jazz and loved to hear improvising musicians develop his themes. This is an enjoyable set worth a few listens. —*Scott Yanow*

Piano Jazz: McPartland/Short / Nov. 10, 1986 / Jazz Alliance +++

The Music of Billy Strayhorn / Mar. 1987 / Concord Jazz ++++
This is a solid tribute to Strayhorn, whose compositions are a perfect fit for McPartland. —*Ron Wynn*

Piano Jazz: McPartland/Hampton / Jan. 11, 1989 / Jazz Alliance ✦✦✦✦

Piano Jazz: McPartland/Carter / Feb. 20, 1989 / Jazz Alliance ✦✦
This particular episode of Marian McPartland's famed radio series *Piano Jazz* features the great altoist Benny Carter as her special guest, and it should have been a classic. The interview and verbal interplay is interesting, but unfortunately Carter chose (for unrevealed reasons) to stick exclusively to playing piano. Since piano is about his fifth best instrument (he sticks mostly to melody statements), the duets between McPartland and Carter are of much less interest than expected. McPartland does take three songs as a solo (the program sticks exclusively to her guest's compositions), but this CD can be easily skipped without much regret. —*Scott Yanow*

Piano Jazz: McPartland/Brubeck / 1990 / Jazz Alliance ✦✦✦✦

● **Marian McPartland Plays the Benny Carter Songbook** / Jan. 1990 / Concord Jazz ✦✦✦✦✦
This is McPartland's finest work in quite some time and includes wonderful interpretations of great compositions by Benny Carter—a spry, exciting alto soloist, in his eighth decade as a player! Good support comes from John Clayton and Harold Jones. —*Ron Wynn*

Piano Jazz: McPartland/Carroll / Jan. 30, 1990 / Jazz Alliance ✦✦✦

Piano Jazz: McPartland/Hyman / Dec. 7, 1990 / Jazz Alliance ✦✦✦✦

Piano Jazz: McPartland/J.Williams / 1991 / Jazz Alliance ✦✦✦✦

Live at Maybeck Recital Hall / Jan. 20, 1991 / Concord Jazz ✦✦✦✦✦
Great solos, with strong rhythmic work and phrasing. —*Ron Wynn*

● **Piano Jam: McPartland Hinton** / Aug. 15, 1991 / Jazz Alliance ✦✦✦✦✦
This is one of the stronger entries in the numerous releases taken from Marian McPartland's *Piano Jazz* radio series. The octogenarian bassist Milt Hinton is a talented storyteller, he takes his autobiographical "Milt's Rap" and "Joshua" (the latter demonstrates his timeless slapping technique) unaccompanied, and he plays six enjoyable duets with the pianist/host. McPartland also has a feature solo ("Stranger in a Dream"), and her love and respect for the veteran bassist is obvious. —*Scott Yanow*

Piano Jazz: McPartland/Myers / Aug. 29, 1991 / Jazz Alliance ✦✦✦

★ **Piano Jazz: McPartland/Konitz** / Sep. 6, 1991 / Jazz Alliance ✦✦✦✦✦

Piano Jazz: McPartland/Clooney / Oct. 14, 1991 / Jazz Alliance ✦✦✦✦

Piano Jazz: McPartland/Richards / Oct. 16, 1991 / Jazz Alliance ✦✦✦

Piano Jazz: McPartland/DeJohnette / Dec. 11, 1992 / Jazz Alliance ✦✦✦
This entry from Marian McPartland's Piano Jazz radio series is a bit surprising for drummer Jack DeJohnette switches to piano for all but two selections, and bassist Christian McBride makes the duos into trios. Also, most of the music consists of jazz standards from the 1950s, so (with the exception of DeJohnette's "Silver Hollow") there are no examples of his own more advanced compositions. However the mutual respect felt by McPartland and DeJohnette is obvious, and some of the verbal conversations are quite interesting; in addition the two pianos work together quite well. —*Scott Yanow*

In My Life / Jan. 1993 / Concord Jazz ✦✦✦✦✦
Pianist Marian McPartland displays her versatility throughout this reflective and generally thoughtful CD on such selections as The Beatles "In My Life," John Coltrane's "Red Planet," Ivan Lins' "Velas" and Ornette Coleman's "Ramblin'." Despite the diverse repertoire, McPartland's own flexible style shines through, and her individual musical personality is felt in each song. Altoist Chris Potter makes the trio a quartet on half of the selections, and he uplifts the session a bit. McPartland's closing wistful solo piano version of "Singin' the Blues" (dedicated to her late husband cornetist Jimmy McPartland) should not be missed. —*Scott Yanow*

Piano Jazz: McPartland/Burrell / Apr. 15, 1993 / Jazz Alliance ✦✦✦
This is the 21st of Marian McPartland's *Piano Jazz* radio shows to

be issued on CD. The pianist welcomes guitarist Kenny Burrell for an hour of talk (covering briefly his early days, the legacy of Duke Ellington and his current activities) and music. With the exception of the closing "Raincheck," all of the typically tasteful playing emphasizes slower tempos with two Burrell solos, one McPartland feature ("All Too Soon") and five duets. The biggest surprises are on "Listen to the Dawn" (during which Burrell plays piano in duet with McPartland) and the guitarist's effective vocal on "I'm Just a Lucky So and So." —*Scott Yanow*

Piano Jazz: McPartland/Terry / Sep. 21, 1993 / Jazz Alliance ✦✦✦✦

Piano Jazz: McPartland/Ellington / Jan. 24, 1994 / Jazz Alliance ✦✦

Piano Jazz: McPartland/McKenna / May 19, 1994 / Jazz Alliance ✦✦✦
For this edition of Marian McPartland's radio show Piano Jazz, she welcomes Dave McKenna. The mutual respect they feel toward each other is obvious. The music is at its best when the two pianists duet on older material ("Let's Get Away from It All" and "Struttin' with Some Barbeque") and a bit trivial when they take turns on a Stevie Wonder medley. The results overall are not essential but worth hearing once or twice. —*Scott Yanow*

Joe McPhee

b. Nov. 3, 1939, Miami, FL
Soprano Saxophone, Tenor Saxophone, Trumpet / Avant-Garde
A multi-instrumentalist who plays adventurous solos on both tenor and trumpet, Joe McPhee began on trumpet when he was eight. After serving in the military, he made his recording debut with Clifford Thornton (1967). By 1969 he was doubling on reeds, and he cut his first date as a leader. In 1975 the Hat Hut label was started largely to document McPhee's passionate music, and with the exception of a fine Sackville date with Bill Smith (1983), Hat Hut and its successors (Hat Art and Hat Musics) have continued exclusively recording Joe McPhee's highly original music. —*Scott Yanow*

Black Magic Man / Dec. 12, 1970 / Hat Hut ✦✦✦

The Willisau Concert / Oct. 11, 1975 / Hat Hut ✦✦✦✦

Variations on a Blue Line 'ound Midnight / Oct. 11, 1977 / Hat Hut ✦✦✦✦✦

Old Eyes and Mysteries / May 30, 1979 / Hat Art ✦✦✦✦

Oleo & A Future Retrospective / Aug. 2, 1982 / Hat Hut ✦✦✦✦✦

● **Visitation** / Nov. 6, 1983 / Sackville ✦✦✦✦✦
The versatile Joe McPhee (who on this set plays fluegelhorn, pocket trumpet, tenor and soprano) teams up with Bill Smith's Ensemble (Smith on soprano, sopranino and alto, violinist David Prentice and bassist David Lee) plus drummer Richard Bannard for a stimulating set of avant-garde music. The interplay between these masterful improvisers on group originals and Albert Ayler's classic "Ghosts" is consistently impressive and worthy of a close investigation by the more open-eared segment of the jazz audience. —*Scott Yanow*

Po Music: Oleo / Mar. 24, 1984–Mar. 25, 1984 / Hat Music ✦✦✦✦✦

Po Music: A Future Retrospective / May 1987 / Hat Art ✦✦✦

Linear B / Jan. 9, 1990–Jan. 12, 1990 / Hat Art ✦✦✦

Charles McPherson

b. Jul. 24, 1939, Joplin, MO
Alto Saxophone / Bop, Hard Bop
A Charlie Parker disciple who brings his own lyricism to the bebop language, Charles McPherson has been a reliable figure in modern mainstream jazz for the past 35 years. He played in the Detroit jazz scene of the mid-'50s, moved to New York in 1959 and within a year was working with Charles Mingus. McPherson and his friend Lonnie Hillyer succeeded Eric Dolphy and Ted Curson as regular members of Mingus' band in 1961, and he worked with the bassist off and on up until 1972. Although he and Hillyer had a short-lived quintet in 1966, McPherson was not a fulltime leader until 1972. In 1978 he moved to San Diego which has been his home ever since, and sometimes he uses his son Chuck McPherson on drums. Charles McPherson, who helped out on the film *Bird* by playing some of the parts not taken from Charlie Parker records, has led dates through the years for

Prestige (1964–69), Mainstream, Xanadu, Discovery and Arabesque. —*Scott Yanow*

● **Be-Bop Revisited** / Nov. 20, 1964 / Original Jazz Classics ◆◆◆◆◆
Bebop is the thing on this excellent outing as altoist Charles McPherson and pianist Barry Harris do their interpretations of Charlie Parker and Bud Powell. With trumpeter Carmell Jones, bassist Nelson Boyd and drummer Al "Tootie" Heath completing the quintet, the band romps through such bop classics as "Hot House," "Nostalgia," "Wail" and "Si Si" along with an original blues and "Embraceable You." A previously unissued "If I Love You" is added to the CD reissue. McPherson and Jones make for a potent frontline on these spirited performances, easily recommended to fans of straight-ahead jazz. —*Scott Yanow*

Con Alma / Aug. 6, 1965 / Original Jazz Classics ◆◆◆◆
Altoist Charles McPherson teams up with distinctive tenor Clifford Jordan, pianist Barry Harris, bassist George Tucker and drummer Alan Dawson for jazz classics by Thelonious Monk, Duke Ellington, Charlie Parker, Dizzy Gillespie (a mysterious version of "Con Alma") and Dexter Gordon in addition to an original McPherson blues, "I Don't Know," which closely recalls "Parker's Mood." McPherson and Harris both have their share of fine solos, but Jordan generally takes honors on this set; he is the only musician who was looking beyond bop and playing in a more original style. —*Scott Yanow*

The Charles McPherson Quintet Live! / Oct. 13, 1966 / Original Jazz Classics ◆◆◆◆
Altoist Charles McPherson and pianist Barry Harris are the stars of this live bop-oriented session. Trumpeter Lonnie Hillyer does his best although he stumbles a bit on the rapid "Shaw 'Nuff," drummer Billy Higgins and the forgotten bassist Ray McKinney are fine in support, and the repertoire (ranging from the funky "The Viper" and "I Can't Get Started" to "Here's That Rainy Day" and the recent "Never Let Me Go") is diverse and challenging. It's an excellent CD overall. —*Scott Yanow*

Siku Ya Bibi / 1972 / Mainstream ◆◆◆
A CD reissue of a 1972 tribute album to Billie Holiday suffers a bit from overproduction and glossy orchestrations, but alto saxophonist Charles McPherson's passionate playing, along with that of pianist Barry Harris and trumpeter Lonnie Hillyer, helps overcome the sappiness and at least brings home the point of Holiday's poignancy as a vocalist. —*Ron Wynn*

★ **Live in Tokyo** / Apr. 14, 1976 / Xanadu ◆◆◆◆◆
Altoist Charles McPherson, who developed his own sound out of the Charlie Parker style, plays a couple of blues and four standards on this frequently exciting session. With the strong assistance of pianist Barry Harris, bassist Sam Jones and drummer Leroy Williams, McPherson is in top form with the highlights being his feature on "East of the Sun" and a heated "Bouncing with Bud." —*Scott Yanow*

New Horizons / Sep. 28, 1977 / Xanadu ◆◆◆◆

Free Bop! / Oct. 23, 1978 / Xanadu ◆◆◆◆◆
Entertaining hard-bop workout. This is perhaps his fiercest, most exciting playing as a leader. —*Ron Wynn*

The Prophet / May 14, 1983 / Discovery ◆◆◆
Early '80s bop and hard bop session from veteran alto saxophonist Charles McPherson. This has a more relaxed, stately quality, not as animated nor as much in debt to mentor Charlie Parker as some past releases. McPherson has been one of the less frenzied, mellower bop players, and this quality emerges throughout his solos. —*Ron Wynn*

First Flight Out / Jan. 25, 1994–Jan. 26, 1994 / Arabesque ◆◆◆◆

Beautiful / 1995 / Xanadu

Come Play With Me / Mar. 2, 1995 / Arabesque Jazz ◆◆◆◆
Charles McPherson, who will always be best-known for his roots in Charlie Parker's style and his period with Charles Mingus, proves on this CD to still be in his musical prime decades later. Although he had rarely played with any of the sidemen heard on his Arabesque release before, the quartet presents a unified sound, as if they were a regularly working group. McPherson performs three veteran standards and six originals with most of the latter being closely related to the blues; "Pretty Girl Blues" sounds like a mixture of a couple of Bird lines, and "Fun House" is based on "Limehouse Blues" while the best of the new compositions is the hard bop boogaloo "Marionette." But no matter what the vehicle, McPherson is in top form throughout this fine date, and he sounds

clearly inspired by the presence of pianist Mulgrew Miller, bassist Santi Debriano and drummer Lewis Nash. —*Scott Yanow*

Carmen McRae

b. Apr. 8, 1920, New York NY, **d.** Nov. 10, 1994
Vocals / Bop, Standards
Carmen McRae always had a nice voice (if not on the impossible level of an Ella Fitzgerald or Sarah Vaughan), but it was her behind-the-beat phrasing and ironic interpretations of lyrics that made her most memorable. She studied piano early on and had her first important job singing with Benny Carter's big band (1944), but it would be another decade before her career really had much momentum. McRae married and divorced Kenny Clarke in the 1940s, worked with Count Basie (briefly) and Mercer Ellington (1946–47) and became the intermission singer and pianist at several New York clubs. In 1954 she began to record as a leader, and by then she had absorbed the influences of Billie Holiday and bebop into her own style. McRae would record pretty steadily up to 1989, and although her voice was higher in the 1950s, and her phrasing would be even more laidback in later years, her general style and approach did not change much through the decades. Championed in the 1950s by Ralph Gleason, Carmen McRae was fairly popular throughout her career. Among her most interesting recording projects were participating in Dave Brubeck's the Real Ambassadors with Louis Armstrong, cutting an album of live duets with Betty Carter, being accompanied by Dave Brubeck and George Shearing and closing her career with brilliant tributes to Thelonious Monk and Sarah Vaughan. Carmen McRae, who refused to quit smoking, was forced to retire in 1991 due to emphysema. She recorded for many labels including Bethlehem, Decca (1954–58), Kapp, Columbia, Mainstream, Focus, Atlantic (1967–70), Black Lion, Groove Merchant, Catalyst, Blue Note, Buddah, Concord and Novus. —*Scott Yanow*

I'll Be Seeing You / Jun. 14, 1955–Mar. 10, 1959 / Decca ◆◆◆◆
This two-CD set mostly brings back material from singer Carmen McRae's Decca years that had been bypassed by other reissues. The oversized box, after a memorable version of "Something to Live For" (in which McRae is accompanied by the song's composer Billy Strayhorn), has many orchestra tracks that are weighed down by middle-of-the-road arrangements more suitable to Doris Day than to McRae; only "Whatever Lola Wants" is memorable among the routine ballads of 1955–56. However, things start improving with "Skyliner," and a March 1957 set with just a rhythm section is quite enjoyable; McRae herself contributes some effective piano on swinging renditions of "Perdido" and "Exactly like You." The majority of the later selections use orchestras, but the charts are more jazz-oriented, and McRae (who was in her mid-to-late 30s during the period) had clearly grown as a singer; tenor saxophonist Ben Webster helps out on "Bye Bye Blackbird" and "Flamingo." Overall this set is worth picking up for fans of Carmen McRae's early years, giving one a fine overview of her talents in the 1950s. —*Scott Yanow*

Here to Stay / Jun. 14, 1955–Nov. 12, 1959 / GRP ◆◆◆◆◆
A '92 anthology covering prime Carmen McRae material from her early years on Decca. These are the songs that established her reputation as an improvising singer and include backing from great veterans like Kenny Clarke, Billy Strayhorn, Herbie Mann and many others. It also was the period when she actually had some songs on the charts. —*Ron Wynn*

Carmen McRae Sings Great American Songwriters / Jun. 16, 1955–Mar. 4, 1959 / GRP ◆◆◆◆

Song Time / 1963–1969 / Hindsight ◆◆◆
In the 1960s Carmen McRae did several sessions for a public-service radio series called *The Navy Swings*. They were 15-minute shows, with Navy recruiting spiels between songs, so the performances are miniatures two or three minutes long. The repertoire is familiar from her LPs of the time (when her voice was in its prime), but the intimate setting of the piano trio rather than the orchestral backdrop makes the rediscovery of these tapes especially welcome. —*Les Line*

Live: Take Five / 1964 / Columbia Special Products ◆◆◆◆
A very good meeting of the minds. Dave Brubeck (p) gets comfortable behind McRae. —*Ron Wynn*

Woman Talk / 1964 / Mainstream ◆◆
This is a compilation from sessions done for the Mainstream label featuring the rich, striking McRae vocals backed by a large

orchestra conducted by either Peter Matz or Don Sebesky. Her interpretations and delivery are masterful, but these albums lack the intimacy of her small combo works and are more pop-centered than the Atlantic dates. It has been reissued on CD. —*Ron Wynn*

★ **The Great American Songbook** / 1970 / Atlantic ✦✦✦✦✦
A wonderful two-disc set, with McRae showing her complete music vocabulary and interpretive talents. —*Ron Wynn*

It Takes a Lot of Human Feelings / Feb. 1973 / Groove ✦✦✦

I Am Music / Apr. 1975 / Blue Note ✦✦

Can't Hide Love / May 3, 1976–May 12, 1976 / Blue Note ✦
This is the type of session that killed Blue Note the first time around. Carmen McRae gamely tries to interpret unsuitable and inferior pop tunes ("The Man I Love" and "A Child Is Born" are the only exceptions) and is backed by an all-star but faceless orchestra that is given nothing to do. The trumpet section (which includes Buddy Childers, Bobby Shew, Al Aarons, Snooky Young, Oscar Brashear and Blue Mitchell) is not given a single solo. The title cut is quite ludicrous, and songs such as "Only Women Bleed" and "I Wish You Well" do not fit McRae's style at all. Pass on this one and get her earlier Deccas or her later Novus releases instead. —*Scott Yanow*

Live at Bubba's / Jan. 17, 1981 / Who's Who In Jazz ✦✦✦
A fine, rather informal set from Lionel Hampton's label. —*Ron Wynn*

Heat Wave / Jan. 1982 / Concord Jazz ✦✦✦✦

You're Lookin' at Me (A Collection of Nat King Cole Songs) / Nov. 1983 / Concord Jazz ✦✦✦✦✦
Carmen McRae's tribute to Nat King Cole (which predated the late-'80s revival of Cole's music) has its strong and weak points. She wisely adds Cole's former guitarist John Collins to her regular trio and picked some fine material (including "I'm an Errand Girl for Rhythm," "I Can't See for Lookin'" and "Just You, Just Me"). However McRae's phrasing is much different than Cole's, and why did she sing "Sweet Lorraine" without changing any of the words? Despite those reservations, this set has enough strong moments to justify its purchase. —*Scott Yanow*

● **For Lady Day** / Dec. 31, 1983 / Novus/RCA ✦✦✦✦✦
Carmen McRae always considered Billie Holiday to be the most important influence not only on her singing but on her life. Six years before she recorded her monumental tributes to Thelonious Monk and Sarah Vaughan, McRae performed a Billie Holiday set at New York's Blue Note Club that was broadcast over the radio, on the first of two volumes McRae, who talks movingly about Lady Day at the beginning of the set and accompanies herself on piano on "I'm Pulling Through," is heard in prime form, combining the power and range of her earlier years with the emotional depth and behind-the-beat phrasing of her last period. Accompanied by her rhythm section of the time (pianist Marshall Otwell, bassist John Leftwich and drummer Donald Bailey) and occasionally the tenor of Zoot Sims, McRae really digs into the material, interpreting the songs in her own style but with a knowing nod toward Holiday. This wonderful set is far superior to most of the Billie Holiday tribute albums of recent years and reminds us how much Carmen McRae is missed. —*Scott Yanow*

Carmen McRae-Betty Carter Duets / Jan. 30, 1987–Feb. 1, 1987 / Great American Music Hall ✦✦✦✦

Fine and Mellow: Live at Birdland West / Dec. 1987 / Concord Jazz ✦✦✦✦
An excellent live set. McRae handles uptempo and ballads with ease. CD has one bonus cut. —*Ron Wynn*

★ **Carmen Sings Monk** / Jan. 30, 1988–Feb. 1, 1988 / Novus ✦✦✦✦✦

Sarah: Dedicated to You / Oct. 12, 1990–Oct. 14, 1990 / Novus ✦✦✦✦✦

Jay McShann

b. Jan. 12, 1916, Muskogee, OK
Piano / Swing, Blues
The great veteran pianist Jay McShann (also known as Hootie) has had a long career, and it is unfair to primarily think of him as merely the leader of an orchestra that featured a young Charlie Parker. He was mostly self-taught as a pianist, worked with Don Byas as early as 1931 and played throughout the Midwest before settling in Kansas City in 1936. McShann formed his own sextet

the following year and by 1939 had his own big band. In 1940 at a radio station in Wichita, KS, McShann and an octet out of his orchestra recorded eight songs that were not released commercially until the 1970s; those rank among the earliest of all Charlie Parker records (he is brilliant on "Honeysuckle Rose" and "Lady Be Good") and also feature the strong rhythm-section team McShann had with bassist Gene Ramey and drummer Gus Johnson. The full orchestra recorded for Decca on two occasions during 1941–42, but they were typecast as a blues band and did not get to record many of their more challenging charts (although very rare broadcasts have since surfaced and been released on CD by Vintage Jazz Classics). In addition to Bird (who had a few short solos), the main stars were trumpeter Bernard Anderson, the rhythm section and singer Walter Brown. McShann and his band arrived in New York in February 1942 and made a strong impression, but World War II made it difficult for any new orchestras to catch on. There was a final session in December 1943 without Parker, but McShann was soon drafted, and the band broke up. After being discharged later in 1944, McShann briefly reformed his group but soon moved to Los Angeles where he led combos for the next few years; his main attraction was the young singer Jimmy Witherspoon.

McShann was in obscurity for the next two decades, making few records and mostly playing in Kansas City. In 1969 he was rediscovered and McShann (who had first sung on records in 1966) was soon a popular pianist/vocalist. Sometimes featuring violinist Claude Williams, he has toured constantly, recorded frequently and appeared at many jazz festivals since then, being active into the mid-'90s. Jay McShann, who has recorded through the years for Onyx (the 1940 radio transcriptions), Decca, Capitol, Aladdin, Mercury, Black Lion, EmArcy, Vee Jay, Black & Blue, Master Jazz, Sackville, Sonet, Storyville, Atlantic, Swingtime and Music Masters among others, is a vital pianist and an effective blues vocalist who keeps a classic style alive. —*Scott Yanow*

★ **Blues from Kansas City** / Apr. 30, 1941–Dec. 1, 1943 / GRP ✦✦✦✦✦
Fine '92 reissue of vintage Kansas City swing featuring groups led by pianist Jay McShann in the early '40s, some of which included alto saxophonist Charlie Parker. These have been available before in either bare-bones domestic or more comprehensive import packages. This is the first time parent label MCA has taken care to sequence, remaster and annotate this vital music in the manner it deserves. —*Ron Wynn*

★ **The Jazz Heritage: Early Bird Charlie Parker (1941–1943)** / Apr. 30, 1941–Dec. 1, 1943 / Spotlite ✦✦✦✦✦
1940-1943 air-checks. With Charley Parker (as), Paul Quinichette and Gus Johnson. —*Michael Erlewine*

McShann's Piano / Aug. 1966 / Capitol ✦✦✦✦

Confessin' the Blues / Mar. 28, 1969 / Classic Jazz ✦✦✦
Pianist Jay McShann sticks to the blues on this enjoyable release, not only welcoming bassist Roland Lobligeois and drummer Paul Gunther but, in a rare (and purely instrumental role) as a sideman, guitarist T-Bone Walker. McShann takes vocals on several of the selections and contributes his accessible brand of blues piano. The results are enjoyable if not essential.A bit more imagination could have gone into picking out a more inventive repertoire. —*Scott Yanow*

Going to Kansas City / Mar. 6, 1972 / New World ✦✦✦✦

Man from Muskogee / Jun. 24, 1972 / Sackville ✦✦✦✦✦
One of McShann's finest recordings. With Claude Williams (violin). —*Michael Erlewine*

Kansas City Memories / Jul. 18, 1973+Jul. 31, 1973 / Black & Blue ✦✦✦

Vine Street Boogie / Jul. 2, 1974 / Black Lion ✦✦✦✦

Crazy Legs and Friday Strut / Jul. 1, 1976 / Sackville ✦✦✦✦✦
On this recording pianist Jay McShann's playing was closer in many ways to Earl Hines and Teddy Wilson than to what I know as McShann. McShann was even a little Erroll Garnerish on "Crazylegs" with touches of Randy Weston and Mal Waldron. Certainly McShann's work on "Crazylegs" will fascinate his fans. With further listenings I began to detect a detachment between saxophonist Buddy Tate and the rest of the group (McShann). This was least noticeable on "Melancholy Baby" and the Ellington medley ("I Got It Bad and That Ain't Good," "Sentimental Mood," "Sophisticated Lady") where they both seemed to be listening to each other, more so McShann, but on the majority of these tracks

Tate seemed quite apart, playing as a soloist in a larger group, not as part of a duo with its special demands. —*Bob Rusch, Cadence*

The Last of the Blue Devils / Jun. 29, 1977–Jul. 1, 1977 / Atlantic ✦✦

Kansas City Hustle / Jun. 20, 1978–Jun. 21, 1978 / Sackville ✦✦✦✦

A Tribute to Fats Waller / Jun. 20, 1978–Jun. 21, 1978 / Sackville ✦✦✦

● **The Big Apple Bash** / Aug. 3, 1978–Aug. 1, 1978 / New World ✦✦✦✦✦

Pianist Jay McShann has spent much of his career being classified as a blues pianist when in fact he is a flexible swing stylist. On this excellent release, McShann appears with two groups of all-stars. His original "Crazy Legs and Friday Strut" and "Georgia on My Mind" find him joined by Herbie Mann (on flute and tenor), baritonist Gerry Mulligan and a rhythm section that includes guitarist John Scofield. The other selections (two standards, Duke Ellington's "Blue Feeling" and McShann's own "Jumpin' the Blues") are performed by an octet also featuring Mann, altoist Earle Warren, trumpeter Doc Cheatham, trombonist Dicky Wells and Scofield. The unusual grouping of swing, bop and modern stylists is successful (the material is pretty basic), and Janis Siegel's guest appearance for a vocal duet with McShann on "Ain't Misbehavin'" works. —*Scott Yanow*

Tuxedo Junction / Aug. 24, 1980 / Sackville ✦✦✦

Swingmatism / Oct. 20, 1982–Oct. 21, 1982 / Sackville ✦✦✦✦

At Cafe Des Copains / Aug. 17, 1983–Sep. 27, 1989 / Sackville ✦✦✦

Airmail Special / Aug. 1985 / Sackville ✦✦✦

● **Paris All-Star Blues: A Tribute** / Jun. 13, 1989 / Music Masters ✦✦✦✦✦

A '91 tribute album (recorded in '89) to Charlie Parker by a great cast of veteran and recent jazz musicians under leadership of pianist Jay McShann, who conducted the band that gave Parker his start. The lineup runs from Benny Carter, Al Grey and James Moody to Terence Blanchard. *Ron Wynn*

Hootie & Hicks/Missouri Connec / Sep. 14, 1992–Sep. 15, 1992 / Reservoir ✦✦✦

Myra Melford

b. 1957, Glencoe, IL
Piano, Composer / Avant-Garde
A powerful pianist and a very original composer, Myra Melford studied with Art Lande at Evergreen State College in Washington and with Henry Threadgill in New York. She worked with Leroy Jenkins, co-led a group with flutist Marion Brandis (recording some cassettes for the Nisus label) and made a few albums for Enemy and an outstanding quintet set for Hat Art in 1994. —*Scott Yanow*

● **Even The Sounds Shine** / May 5, 1994–May 6, 1994 / Hat Art ✦✦✦✦✦

Pianist Myra Melford is one of the leaders of the avant-garde of the 1990s. Her lengthy compositions are episodic yet logical, building up logically to passionate levels yet leaving room for quieter moments; she is a master of dynamics. Her melodies are strong, but her sideman also have the option to improvise pretty freely within the context of the music. On this CD Melford is fortunate to have such versatile players as the powerful trumpeter Dave Douglas, the very impressive Marty Ehrlich on alto, clarinet and bass clarinet, bassist Lindsey Horner and drummer Reggie Nicholson. Despite their presence, Myra Melford is consistently the most interesting improviser, and her accompaniment behind the horn solos constantly drives and pushes her musicians to play at their maximum creativity. Overall this is a memorable set of innovative jazz well deserving of several listens. —*Scott Yanow*

Misha Mengelberg

b. Jun. 5, 1935, Kiev, USSR
Piano / Avant-Garde, Post-Bop
One of Europe's top jazz pianists, Misha Mengelberg (although born in the Ukraine) is actually Dutch. He studied in the Netherlands and was on Eric Dolphy's famous *Last Date* album in 1964. In 1967 Mengelberg was a founder of the Instant Composers Pool (which sponsors performances by the Dutch avant-garde) and formed a duo with Han Bennink. He has since

worked with the ICP Orchestra, the Berlin Contemporary Jazz Orchestra and his own groups, and he has recorded adventurous tributes to Thelonious Monk and Herbie Nichols with Steve Lacy. —*Scott Yanow*

★ **Change of Season** / Jul. 2, 1984–Jul. 23, 1984 / Soul Note ✦✦✦✦✦

Don Menza

b. Apr. 22, 1936, Buffalo, NY
Tenor Saxophone, Arranger / Hard Bop, Bop
Don Menza is a powerful tenor saxophonist who, although able effectively to imitate most of the top stylists (from Coleman Hawkins to John Coltrane), has a distinctive sound of his own. Menza started playing tenor when he was 13. After getting out of the Army he was with Maynard Ferguson's Orchestra (1960–62) as both a soloist and an arranger. A short stint with Stan Kenton and a year leading a quintet in Buffalo preceded a period living in Germany (1964–68). After returning to the U.S. he was with Buddy Rich's big band in 1968, recording a famous solo on "Channel One Suite" that utilized circular breathing and was quite classic. He settled in California and has worked with Elvin Jones (1969), Louie Bellson, as an educator and in the studios. Don Menza, who has made far too few records, recorded as a leader for Saba (1965) in Germany, Discwasher (1979), Realtime and Palo Alto (the latter two in 1981). —*Scott Yanow*

● **Horn of Plenty** / May 1, 1979–May 2, 1979 / Voss ✦✦✦✦✦
With sextet. Excellent mainstream jazz. —*Michael G. Nastos*

Hip Pocket / Oct. 2, 1981–Oct. 3, 1981 / Palo Alto ✦✦✦✦✦

Burnin' / 1981 / Real Time ✦✦✦

Johnny Mercer

b. Nov. 18, 1909, Savannah, GA, d. Jun. 25, 1976, Los Angeles, CA
Vocals, Lyricist / Standards
A marvelous lyricist and multi-faceted composer, talent scout and recording artist, Johnny Mercer truly did it all. He wrote or co-wrote more than 1,000 songs, and his compositions have been played and sung by numerous jazz greats and many pop stars. Mercer as a vocalist, despite lacking great technique or tools, had many hits from the late '30s into the early '50s done in a relaxed, easygoing style. He teamed with Bing Crosby on Decca from 1938 to 1940, then had 25 hits on Capitol over a 10-year period, including chart toppers "Candy" with Jo Stafford, "Ac-Cent-Tchu-Ate The Positive" and "On The Atchinson, Topeka and The Santa Fe." Mercer won multiple Oscars, co-founded Capitol Records and signed Nat King Cole and Peggy Lee, was a co-founder and President of the Songwriters Hall of Fame and a director of ASCAP in 1940 and 1941. His lyrics were unfailingly upbeat and optimistic; by today's cynical standards he'd be deemed not just a hopeless romantic but a foolish one. Mercer gems include "I'm An Old Cowhand," "Dream (When You're Feelin' Blue)," "That Old Black Magic," "One For My Baby," "Lazy Bones" and numerous others. He collaborated on masterpieces with Henry Mancini, Harold Arlen, Hoagy Carmichael, Harry Warren, Billy Strayhorn and Duke Ellington, Ralph Burns, Jerome Kern, Gordon Jenkins and Rube Bloom among others. Mercer sang with Benny Goodman on radio, hosted his own shows with Paul Whiteman serving as music director, contributed to films and plays and recorded duets with Bobby Darin. There's almost no facet of American popular entertainment Mercer didn't affect positively. Compilations of various singers doing his compositions have recently been issued on Rhino and are available on other labels like RCA. Mercer's vocals are featured on CD compilations by Capitol, Hindsight and other labels. —*Ron Wynn and Kenneth M. Cassidy*

● **Johnny Mercer Sings Johnny Mercer** / Apr. 6, 1942–Dec. 13, 1944 / Capitol ✦✦✦✦✦

The Uncollected Johnny Mercer (1944) / 1944 / Hindsight ✦✦✦✦
A collection of radio transcripts, they were recorded in 1944 with the Paul Weston Orchestra. —*Kenneth M. Cassidy*

Helen Merrill (Helen Milcetic)

b. Jul. 21, 1930, New York, NY
Vocals / Bop, Post Bop
A fine singer with a warm expressive voice, Helen Merrill's infrequent recordings tend to be quite special with plenty of surprises and chancetaking. She started singing in public in 1944 and was

with the Reggie Childs Orchestra during 1946–47. Merrill, who was married for a period to clarinetist Aaron Sachs, had opportunities to sit in with some of the top modernists of the time including Charlie Parker, Miles Davis and Bud Powell. She was with Earl Hines in 1952 and started recording regularly for EmArcy in 1954. Her collaboration with Clifford Brown was her first classic. She made several notable EmArcy albums during 1954–58 (including one in 1956 that helped bring Gil Evans out of retirement); all have been reissued in a large box. After recording for Atco and Metrojazz in 1959, she moved to Italy for the next four years, touring often in Europe and Japan. Back in the U.S., Merrill teamed with pianist/arranger Dick Katz for a pair of notable and unpredictable Milestone dates (1967–68) and then moved to Japan where she was quite popular. Helen Merrill returned to the United States in the mid-'70s and has since recorded for Inner City, Owl, EmArcy (including a reunion date with Gil Evans) and Antilles. — *Scott Yanow*

★ **Complete Helen Merrill on Mercury (1954–1958)** / Feb. 1954–Feb. 21, 1958 / Mercury ✦✦✦✦✦
1954–1958. For Helen Merrill fans, here is an exhaustive 4-disc set. —*Ron Wynn*

● **Helen Merrill with Clifford Brown** / Dec. 22, 1954–Dec. 24, 1954 / EmArcy ✦✦✦✦✦
This has arrangements by Quincy Jones and trumpet by Clifford Brown. It was a wonderfully emotive session, perfect for Merrill's serenely confident tones. All are standards. —*Michael G. Nastos*

Dream of You / Jul. 26, 1956–Jul. 29, 1956 / EmArcy ✦✦✦

Merrill at Midnight / 1957 / EmArcy ✦✦✦✦

The Nearness of You / Dec. 18, 1957–Feb. 21, 1958 / EmArcy ✦✦✦✦
With small-ensemble accompaniment. Sidemen include Bill Evans (p), Oscar Pettiford (b), George Russel (g), Jo Jones (d) and John Frigo (b). —*Michael G. Nastos*

You've Got a Date with the Blues / 1959 / Verve ✦✦✦✦✦

American Country Songs / May 25, 1959–Jun. 11, 1959 / Atco ✦✦

The Artistry of Helen Merrill / Mar. 1964–Aug. 1964 / Mainstream ✦✦✦✦

The Feeling Is Mutual / 1967 / Milestone ✦✦✦✦✦

A Shade of Difference / Jul. 1968 / Landmark ✦✦✦✦✦

Sposin' / Oct. 21, 1971–Oct. 25, 1971 / Storyville ✦✦✦✦

Helen Merrill / John Lewis / May 17, 1976+Sep. 8, 1976 / Mercury ✦✦✦

Chasin' the Bird / Mar. 6, 1979+Mar. 9, 1979 / Inner City ✦✦✦✦

Casa Forte / Apr. 11, 1980–May 27, 1980 / Inner City ✦✦✦✦

No Tears, No Goodbyes / Nov. 1, 1984–Nov. 3, 1984 / Owl ✦✦✦

Music Makers / Mar. 1984 / Owl ✦✦✦

★ **Collaboration** / Aug. 18, 1987–Aug. 26, 1987 / EmArcy ✦✦✦✦✦
Arranged by Gil Evans, this work includes Jimmy Knepper, Steve Lacy, Joe Beck, Buster Williams and Mel Lewis. —*AMG*

Duets / Dec. 8, 1988–Dec. 9, 1988 / EmArcy ✦✦✦✦
Ron Carter's dense, sparkling bass accompaniment lifts and caresses Merrill's vocals. —*Ron Wynn*

Just Friends / Jun. 11, 1989–Jul. 5, 1989 / EmArcy ✦✦✦✦

This Is My Night to Cry / Sep. 1989 / EmArcy ✦✦✦✦

Clear out of This World / Jul. 31, 1991–Sep. 3, 1991 / Antilles ✦✦✦✦
A '92 session with jazz vocalist Helen Merrill's smoky, sometimes sensual, sometimes piercing singing supported by a group including pianist Roger Kellaway, bassist Red Mitchell and drummer Terry Clarke. The songs are carefully crafted, finely executed standards and ballads for adult audiences. —*Ron Wynn*

Louis Metcalf

b. Feb. 28, 1905, Webster Groves, MO, **d.** Oct. 27, 1981, New York, NY
Trumpet / Classic Jazz
Louis Metcalf seemed to be everywhere in the 1920s but was largely forgotten once the Depression hit despite remaining active into the late '60s. He played with Charlie Creath in St. Louis in the early '20s, moved to New York, backed a variety of classic blues singers and worked with Willie "The Lion" Smith, Sidney

Bechet, Elmer Snowden, Charlie Johnson and Sam Wooding. His most important association was with Duke Ellington, recording with Duke in 1926 and being a regular member of his orchestra during 1927–28. Metcalf's solo style was a contrast to the wa-wa playing of Bubber Miley. He also played with Jelly Roll Morton, King Oliver and Luis Russell and recorded with Bessie Smith in 1931. But after that he stopped recording, leading a band in Montreal and working in the Midwest. Metcalf was back in New York for a few years in the late 1930's and spent 1946–52 leading the International Band in Montreal. He recorded obscure sides as a leader for Franwill (1954–55), Stereo-O-Craft (1958) and Pickwick (1963); an excellent album for Spivey (1966) finds the trumpeter to have been influenced by bop and playing in a surprisingly modern style. But Louis Metcalf will always be best-remembered for his short stint with Duke Ellington forty years earlier. —*Scott Yanow*

At the Ali Baba / Apr. 1966 / Spivey ✦✦✦✦

Mike Metheny

b. 1949, Lee's Summit, MO
Trumpet / Crossover, Hard Bop
The older brother of Pat Metheny, Mike Metheny started off as a classical trumpeter. After graduating from the University of Missouri and serving in the Army, he was encouraged by his brother to play jazz. Already 25, Metheny attended Berklee and soon became a member of the faculty. He switched to fluegelhorn which he felt best suited his soft tone and mellow style and has recorded five albums as a leader thus far for Headfirst (1982), MCA/Impulse and Altenburgh (1995). Based in Kansas City, Metheny (who sometimes utilizes the EVI) has also recorded with Karrin Allyson and is a freelance music journalist. —*Scott Yanow*

● **Blue Jay Sessions** / Nov. 1982 / Headfirst ✦✦✦✦✦

Day in—Night Out / 1986 / Impulse ✦✦✦

From Then 'til Now / Jul. 1989–Aug. 1990 / Altenburgh ✦✦✦

Street Of Dreams / 1995 / Altenburgh ✦✦✦✦

Pat Metheny

b. Aug. 2, 1954, Lee's Summit, MO
Guitar, Leader, Composer / Avant-Garde, Post-Bop, Crossover
One of the most original guitarists of the past 20 years (he is instantly recognizable), Pat Metheny is a chancetaking player who has gained great popularity but also taken some wild left turns. His records with the Pat Metheny Group are difficult to describe (folk-jazz? mood music?) but managed to be both accessible and original, stretching the boundaries of jazz and making Metheny famous enough so he could perform whatever type of music he wants without losing his audience.

Metheny (whose older brother is the trumpeter Mike Metheny) started on guitar when he was 13. He developed quickly, taught at both the University of Miami and Berklee while he was a teenager and made his recording debut with Paul Bley and Jaco Pastorius in 1974. He spent an important period (1974–77) with Gary Burton's group, met keyboardist Lyle Mays and in 1978 formed his Group which originally featured Mays, bassist Mark Egan and drummer Dan Gottlieb. Within a short period he was ECM's top artist and one of the most popular of all jazzmen, selling out stadiums. Metheny mostly avoided playing predictable music, and his freelance projects were always quite interesting. His 1980 album *80/81* featured Dewey Redman and Mike Brecker in a post bop quintet, he teamed up with Charlie Haden and Billy Higgins on a trio date in 1983 and two years later recorded the very outside *Song X* with Ornette Coleman. Among Metheny's other projects away from the Group were a sideman recording with Sonny Rollins, a 1990 tour with Herbie Hancock in a quartet, a trio album with Dave Holland and Roy Haynes and a collaboration (and tour) with Joshua Redman. Although his *Zero Tolerance for Silence* in 1994 was largely a waste (40 minutes of feedback), Pat Metheny has retained his popularity and remained a consistently creative performer. He has recorded as a leader for ECM (starting in 1975) and Geffen. —*Scott Yanow*

Bright Size Life / Dec. 1975 / ECM ✦✦✦✦✦
First album, with Jaco Pastorius (b) and Bob Moses (d). Excellent original material. —*Michael G. Nastos*

Watercolours / Feb. 1977 / ECM ✦✦✦
The group's second album; important since it shows Metheny

breaking away from the style he'd honed with Gary Burton. — *Ron Wynn*

★ **Pat Metheny Group** / Jan. 1978 / ECM ✦✦✦✦✦
The first recording by Pat Metheny's "Group" features the innovative guitarist along with keyboardist Lyle Mays, bassist Mark Egan and drummer Dan Gottlieb. The music is quite distinctive, floating rather than swinging, electric but not rockish and full of folkish melodies. The best known of these six Metheny-Mays originals are "Phase Dance" and "Jaco." This music grows in interest with each listen. — *Scott Yanow*

New Chautauqua / Apr. 1979 / ECM ✦✦✦
Among his formative albums: he was still trying to find the right blend of rock, pop, fusion and jazz elements. — *Ron Wynn*

American Garage / Jun. 1979 / ECM ✦✦✦✦✦
This is the session that marked Metheny's coming of age; better songs, more intense playing and more variety in arrangements. — *Ron Wynn*

● **1980–1981** / May 26, 1980–May 29, 1980 / ECM ✦✦✦✦✦
The album that showed jazz purists Metheny's guitar chops extended beyond fusion rock. Extensive crisp performances. The CD issue contains two bonus cuts. — *Ron Wynn*

As Wichita Falls So Falls Wichita / Sep. 1980 / ECM ✦✦✦
Intelligent, thoughtful compositions, with excellent solos and ensemble work. — *Ron Wynn*

Offramp / Oct. 1981 / ECM ✦✦✦✦
This 1982 date is the successor to *Wichita Falls* but lacks that album's charm and flair. — *Ron Wynn*

Travels / Jul. 19, 1982–Nov. 1982 / ECM ✦✦✦✦

● **Rejoicing** / Nov. 29, 1983–Nov. 30, 1983 / ECM ✦✦✦✦✦
Pat Metheny takes a vacation from his "Group" and performs advanced material with bassist Charlie Haden and drummer Billy Higgins. In addition to Horace Silver's "Lonely Woman," Haden's "Blues for Pat" and three Ornette Coleman tunes, the guitarist plays three of his originals including "The Calling," a lengthy exploration of sounds with his guitar synthesizer. Throughout this excellent set, Metheny and his sidemen engage in close communication and create memorable and unpredictable music. — *Scott Yanow*

First Circle / Feb. 15, 1984–Feb. 19, 1984 / ECM ✦✦✦✦

The Falcon and the Snowman / 1984 / EMI ✦✦✦

Song X / Dec. 1985 / Geffen ✦✦✦✦✦
With Ornette Coleman. Metheny pays tribute to a surprising influence, teaming with Ornette Coleman in a collaboration that shocked everyone with its musical effectiveness. — *Ron Wynn*

Still Life (Talking) / 1987 / Geffen ✦✦✦✦

Letter from Home / Mar. 1989 / Geffen ✦✦✦✦
Continuing in the steps of his previous release, *Still Life Talking*, Metheny's band continues to explore the use of Brazilian rhythms in their music with excellent results. — *Paul Kohler*

● **Question and Answer** / Dec. 21, 1989 / Geffen ✦✦✦✦✦
A great trio. Metheny stretches out. This is highly recommended. — *Michael G. Nastos*

Secret Story / Jul. 1992 / Geffen ✦✦✦
Assisted by The London Symphony Orchestra on several selections, guitarist/composer Metheny displays a true understanding of life's joys and sorrows by letting his music tell the tale of a deep love relationship between a man and a woman. This record is without a doubt his most sensitive and sincere work to date. Compositionally this record will set new standards. — *Paul Kohler*

Zero Tolerance for Silence / Dec. 16, 1992 / Geffen ✦

Secret Storm / 1993 / Geffen ✦✦✦
Metheny mixes his always enchanting chordal flurries with orchestrations from The London Symphony and combines jazz, Latin American and contemporary instrumental elements. The 14 songs are all Metheny originals, and he not only plays acoustic and electric guitar but acoustic and electric keyboards, guitar and standard synthesizer, bass and percussion devices. Far from simply displaying his virtuosity, Metheny's various instrumental forays are more variations in texture and color. His expressive, fleeting lines, delicate phrasing and overall control register throughout this session, as well as some amazing mastering and production, ensuring a sound that's staggering in scope and dimension. — *Ron Wynn*

I Can See Your House From Here / 1993 / Blue Note ✦✦✦✦
Guitar giants John Scofield and Pat Metheny teamed up for the first time on records for this CD. The collaboration does take awhile to get going, and it is not until the fourth cut, the bluish "Everybody's Party," that the sparks begin to fly; fortunately the momentum does not let up much throughout the remainder of the CD. All of the selections (including two blues) are originals by either of the guitarists, and with the accompaniment of bassist Steve Swallow and drummer Bill Stewart, this varied set generally lives up to expectations. — *Scott Yanow*

Road To You–live In Europe / 1993 / Geffen ✦✦✦✦

● **We Live Here** / 1994 / Geffen ✦✦✦✦✦
The first Pat Metheny Group recording in five years is a bit unusual in two ways. The band uses "contemporary" pop rhythms on many of their selections but in creative ways and without watering down the popular group's musical identity. In addition Metheny for the first time in his recording career sounds a bit like his early influence, Wes Montgomery, on a few of the songs. With his longtime sidemen (keyboardist Lyle Mays, bassist Steve Rodby and drummer Paul Wertico) all in top form, Metheny successfully reconciles his quartet's sound with that of the pop music world, using modern technology to expand the possibilities of his own unusual vision of creative improvised music. As a bonus, some of the melodies are catchy. — *Scott Yanow*

The Metronome All Stars

All-Star Groups / Bop, Swing
Metronome Magazine had an annual poll during 1939–61 that picked who their readers considered the top jazz instrumentalists on each instrument for that year. Unlike with other magazine polls, *Metronome* actually recorded the all-stars (trying for the actual winners but usually also including a few runner-ups) on a fairly regular basis with sessions gathering the victors of the 1939–42, 1945–50, 1953 and 1956 contests. In most cases the group recorded two songs, and there were short solos (generally one chorus) from practically all of the participants. The early groups were swing-oriented while the later ones were filled with top bop players, but sometimes the combination of players was unusual. Highlights included Benny Goodman playing with many of his alumni in 1940 (including Harry James, Jess Stacy and Gene Krupa), Nat King Cole and June Christy sharing the vocal mic on "Nat Meets June" (1946), Dizzy Gillespie, Fats Navarro and Miles Davis trading off in 1949 and Billy Eckstine scatting quite effectively in 1953. A jam on "Billie's Bounce" in 1956 wrapped up the valuable series which was recorded for labels now owned by Columbia, RCA and Capitol. — *Scott Yanow*

Metronome All-Stars 1956 / Jun. 26, 1956–Jul. 18, 1956 / Verve ✦✦✦✦✦
This LP features a variety of great jazz players (the 1956 Metronome All-Stars) performing together. Count Basie's Orchestra plays their hit "April in Paris" with Ella Fitzgerald in what was the first meeting on records between Basie and Fitzgerald. "Everyday I Have the Blues" not only has the duo but Joe Williams, the orchestra goes solo on "Basie's Back in Town," and on "Party Blues" Basie and the two singers have fun with a small group taken from the big band. In addition George Wallington performs a piano solo ("Lady Fair"), and a 21-minute "Billie's Bounce" has solos by an impressive assortment of individualists: trumpeter Thad Jones, altoist Lee Konitz, Al Cohn and Zoot Sims on tenors, clarinetist Tony Scott, baritonist Serge Chaloff, trombonist Eddie Bert, vibraphonist Teddy Cohen, guitarist Tal Farlow, pianist Billy Taylor, bassist Charles Mingus and drummer Art Blakey. This would be the final recording by The Metronome All-Stars (a series that started in the late '30s), and the music on this LP still sounds exciting and joyful. — *Scott Yanow*

Hendrik Meurkens

b. 1957, Hamburg, Germany
Harmonica / Bop, Latin Jazz
Ever since he started taking harmonica solos in the mid-'50s, Toots Thielemans has been without any close competition on his instrument, at least until Hendrik Meurkens arrived on the scene. Born in Germany to Dutch parents, Meurkens began as a vibraphonist, not playing harmonica until he heard Thielemans when he was 19. He traveled to the U.S. to study at Berklee and spent time in Brazil in the early '80s during which he immersed himself in Brazilian jazz. Back in Berlin, Meurkens worked in the stu-

dios but also recorded with the Danish Radio Orchestra and had his own jazz group. He made a record in Brazil for the Bellaphon label (1989) and since 1991 has recorded several sets for Concord and Concord Picante as a leader in addition to appearing on records as a sideman with Charlie Byrd. —*Scott Yanow*

Samba Importado / Oct. 1989 / Optimism ✦✦✦

Sambahia / Oct. 1990–Dec. 1990 / Concord Jazz ✦✦✦✦
A nice Afro-Latin date that includes alto sax solos from Pacquito D'Rivera.—*Ron Wynn*

Clear of Clouds / 1992 / Concord Jazz ✦✦✦✦

● **A View from Manhattan** / Jul. 26, 1993–Aug. 4, 1993 / Concord Jazz ✦✦✦✦
Hendrik Meurkens secures his position as the second-best jazz harmonica player (behind Toots Thielemans) with this fine release. Unlike his two earlier Concord recordings, Meurkens sticks to straight-ahead jazz (rather than Brazilian music) on this set, tackling a variety of challenging material (four of the 11 pieces are his originals) with apparent ease. He comes up with fresh statements on such veteran songs as "Whisper Not," "Naima," "Body and Soul" and "Moment's Notice" and his supporting cast (which includes saxophonist Dick Oatts, trombonist Jay Ashby and pianist Mark Soskin) is consistently strong. This CD gives one an excellent example of Hendrik Meurkens' talents. —*Scott Yanow*

Slidin / 1994 / Concord Jazz ✦✦✦✦
Most of Hendrik Meurkens' previous recordings have a strong emphasis on Brazilian rhythms, but this CD is more of a modern bop date. With pianists Dado Moroni and Mark Soskin trading off, David Finck and Harvie Swartz sharing the bass spot and guitarist Peter Bernstein and drummer Tim Horner present on most selections, the impressive harmonica player Meurkens improvises pretty freely on material ranging from standards such as "Have You Met Miss Jones" and "All of You" to four of his own straight-ahead originals. The music is moody yet swinging, demonstrating Hendrik Meurkens' continued growth from his earlier discs. —*Scott Yanow*

October Colors / 1995 / Concord Picante ✦✦✦✦

Mezz Mezzrow (Milton Mesirow)
b. Oct. 9, 1899, Chicago, IL, d. Aug. 5, 1972, Paris, France
Clarinet, Tenor Saxophone / Dixieland
Mezz Mezzrow occupies an odd and unique place in jazz history. Although an enthusiastic clarinetist, he was never much of a player, sounding best on the blues. A passionate propagandist for Chicago and New Orleans jazz and the rights of Blacks (he meant well but tended to overstate his case), Mezzrow was actually most significant for writing his colorful and somewhat fanciful memoirs *Really the Blues* and for being a reliable supplier of marijuana in the 1930s and '40s. In the 1920s he was part of the Chicago jazz scene, at first helping the young White players and then annoying them with his inflexible musical opinions. Mezzrow recorded with the Jungle Kings, the Chicago Rhythm Kings and Eddie Condon during 1927-28, often on tenor. In the 1930s he led a few swing-oriented dates that featured all-star integrated bands in 1933-34 and 1936-37. The French critic Hugues Panassie was always a big supporter of Mezzrow's playing, and Mezz was well-featured on sessions in 1938 with Tommy Ladnier and Sidney Bechet; "Really the Blues" is a near-classic. Mezzrow had his own King Jazz label during 1945-47, mostly documenting ensemble-oriented blues jams with Bechet and occasionally Hot Lips Page. After appearing at the 1948 Nice Jazz festival, Mezzrow eventually moved to France where he recorded fairly regularly during 1951-55 (including with Lee Collins and Buck Clayton) along with a final album in 1959. —*Scott Yanow*

● **Mezz Mezzrow 1928–1936** / Apr. 6, 1928–Mar. 12, 1936 / Classics ✦✦✦✦✦

King Jazz Story, Vol. 1: Out of the Gallion / Mar. 27, 1945–Dec. 20, 1947 / Storyville ✦✦✦✦
On five CDs (the four volumes in this series and a Sidney Bechet set) the entire output of clarinetist Mezz Mezzrow's King Jazz label has been reissued although (due to the many alternate takes and the similar sessions), the reissue producers decided not to program the material in strict chronological order. The first volume has three piano solos from Sammy Price, four numbers from a heated septet date with the great soprano Sidney Bechet and trumpeter Hot Lips Page and 15 selections by various quintets fea-

turing Mezzrow and Bechet. On five instances Mezzrow (years later) is heard telling the story behind certain performances. There is a certain sameness to much of the material, but some selections stand out, particularly "Evil Gal Blues" (featuring the vocal of Coot Grant), a two-part "The Blues and Freud," "Ole Miss," "Blues of the Roaring Twenties," "The Sheik of Araby" and the happy "Perdido Street Stomp." —*Scott Yanow*

King Jazz Story, Vol. 2: Really the Blues / Mar. 27, 1945–Dec. 20, 1947 / Storyville ✦✦✦✦
On the second of five CDs (the four sets in this series plus a single Sidney Bechet release) all of the recordings made for Mezz Mezzrow's King Jazz label have been reissued although unfortunately not in chronological order. This CD contains three piano solos by Sammy Price, five selections from the Mezzrow-Bechet septet (featuring trumpeter Hot Lips Page) plus 14 blues-oriented performances that feature clarinetist Mezz and the great soprano Sidney Bechet in a quintet; Mezzrow also introduces five of the numbers. A pair of two-part jams ("Really the Blues" and "Revolutionary Blues") stand out from the 74 minutes of fairly similar material; Bechet is in typically explosive form throughout. —*Scott Yanow*

King Jazz Story, Vol. 3: Gone Away the Blues / Mar. 27, 1945–Dec. 20, 1947 / Storyville ✦✦✦✦
The third of four CDs in this series from the European Storyville label (along with a single Sidney Bechet set) continues the complete documentation of Mezz Mezzrow's King Jazz label, a company dedicated to "the real jazz" according to its clarinetist and president; namely ensemble and blues-oriented jams matching the erratic Mezzrow with the great soprano saxophonist Sidney Bechet. Since it is not programmed in strict chronological order, this reissue has selections from each of the King Jazz sessions including piano solos from Sammy Price (in addition to a Price duet with drummer Sid Catlett), a vocal from Pleasant Joe, jams from an all-star septet with trumpeter Hot Lips Page, lots of performances from the Mezzrow-Bechet quintet and an oddity, a feature on "Caravan" for an unidentified harmonica player. Mezzrow (in segments obviously recorded quite a few years later) introduces some of the selections with an anecdote. All in all, this series is quite enjoyable (even if a bit repetitive) and easily recommended to Dixieland and Bechet fans. —*Scott Yanow*

King Jazz Story, Vol. 4: Revolutionary Blues / Mar. 27, 1945–Dec. 20, 1947 / Storyville ✦✦✦✦
For the fourth of four CD volumes that (along with a single Sidney Bechet release) reissues every recording made by Mezz Mezzrow's King Jazz label, the erratic clarinetist is once again matched with the great soprano saxophonist Sidney Bechet. Not programmed in strict chronological order (unfortunately), this enjoyable CD has three piano solos from Sammy Price, a vocal by Pleasant Joe and many jams (mostly blues) by groups featuring Bechet, Mezzrow and (on two numbers) trumpeter Hot Lips Page; Mezz verbally introduces five of the songs. Much of the basic material (Mezz loved ensemble-oriented blues) is rather similar, but Bechet generally makes the results quite exciting. —*Scott Yanow*

Masters of Jazz: Sidney Bechet / Jul. 1945–Dec. 1947 / Storyville ✦✦✦✦

Mezz Mezzrow / May 20, 1955 / Disques Swing ✦✦✦✦

Pierre Michelot
b. Mar. 3, 1928, Saint Denis, France
Bass / Bop, Hard Bop
For decades Pierre Michelot has been the bassist of choice for Americans traveling through France. His supportive playing was always up-to-par with the American bassists of the 1950s and '60s. Michelot started on bass when he was 16 and through the years played with Rex Stewart (1948), Coleman Hawkins, Django Reinhardt, Stephane Grappelli, Don Byas, Thelonious Monk, Lester Young, Dexter Gordon, Stan Getz, Bud Powell (in a trio with Kenny Clarke), Zoot Sims, Dizzy Gillespie, Miles Davis, Chet Baker, etc. He even appeared in the movie 'Round Midnight about American jazz musicians living in Paris. —*Scott Yanow*

● **Bass and Bosses** / Dec. 10, 1989–Dec. 11, 1989 / EmArcy ✦✦✦✦✦
Veteran French bassist Pierre Michelot has had very few chances throughout his career to lead record sessions so this CD is a real rarity. Michelot teams up with the great harmonica player Toots Thielemans, violinist Pierre Blanchard, pianist Maurice Vander

and drummer Billy Higgins for a well-rounded program high-lighted by Jimmy Rowles' "The Peacocks," "Jitterbug Waltz," "A Child Is Born" and the bassist's feature "Blues in the Closet." Everyone plays well, and the unusual combination of instruments make these standards sound quite fresh. —*Scott Yanow*

Palle Mikkelborg

b. Mar. 6, 1941, Copenhagen, Denmark
Trumpet, Composer / Post Bop, Avant-Garde
Palle Mikkelborg is a fine trumpeter who is best-known stateside for his *Aura* suite which in 1984 featured Miles Davis. Self-taught on trumpet, Mikkelborg started working professionally in 1960. He joined the Danish Radio Jazz Group in 1963 and led it during 1967–72. Mikkelborg performed at the 1968 Newport Jazz Festival in a quintet and worked through the years with such players as Thomas Clausen, Niels-Henning Orsted Pedersen, Terje Rypdal, Abdullah Ibrahim, Jan Garbarek, George Russell, Dexter Gordon, Gil Evans, Karin Krog and George Gruntz's Concert Jazz Band. He has recorded as a leader for Debut, Metronome, Sonet and ECM. —*Scott Yanow*

Heart to Heart / 1986 / Storyville ✦✦✦✦

Butch Miles

b. Jul. 4, 1944, Ironton, OH
Drums / Swing
A colorful soloist and an impressive technician in the tradition of Buddy Rich and Gene Krupa, Butch Miles graduated from West Virginia State College in 1966 and worked locally in West Virginia. He toured with Mel Tormé (1972–74) and made a strong impression propelling Count Basie's Orchestra (1975–79). After a few months with Dave Brubeck (recording *Back Home* for Concord in 1979) and a year with Tony Bennett, Miles became a busy freelance musician. He has played at many jazz parties and festivals with a countless number of musicians including most notably Gerry Mulligan, Zoot Sims, Woody Herman, Wild Bill Davison, Clark Terry, Scott Hamilton, Warren Vache and Bob Wilber's Bechet Legacy. Butch Miles led five fine albums for Famous Door (1977–82) that featured swing standards and a vocal date for Dreamstreet (1978). —*Scott Yanow*

Lizzie Miles (Elizabeth Mary Pajaud)

b. Mar. 31, 1895, New Orleans, LA., **d.** Mar. 17, 1963, New Orleans, LA.
Vocals / Blues, Dixieland
Lizzie Miles was a fine classic blues singer from the 1920s who survived to have a full comeback in the 1950s. She started out singing in New Orleans during 1909–11 with such musicians as King Oliver, Kid Ory and Bunk Johnson. Miles spent several years touring the South in minstrel shows and playing in theaters. She was in Chicago during 1918–20 and then moved to New York in 1921, making her recording debut the following year. Her recordings from the 1922–30 period mostly used lesser-known players, but Louis Metcalf and King Oliver were on two songs apiece, and she recorded a pair of duets with Jelly Roll Morton in 1929. Miles sang with A.J. Piron and Sam Wooding, toured Europe during 1924–25 and was active in New York during 1926–31. Illness knocked her out of action for a period, but by 1935 she was performing with Paul Barbarin, she sang with Fats Waller in 1938 and recorded a session in 1939. Lizzie Miles spent 1943–49 outside of music but in 1950 began a comeback, she often performed with Bob Scobey or George Lewis during her final decade. —*Scott Yanow*

Moans and Blues / 1954 / Cook ✦✦✦✦

● **Queen Mother of the Rue Royale** / 1955 / Cook ✦✦✦✦✦
An unjustly forgotten name in classic blues annals. Lizzie Miles was a great entertainer and versatile song stylist who could handle everything from vaudeville to classic blues to traditional New Orleans jazz. She had passed her prime by these recordings but was still able to retain her grit and intensity while relying on experience rather than power. —*Ron Wynn*

Hot Songs My Mother Taught Me / 1955 / Cook ✦✦✦✦

Bubber Miley

b. Apr. 3, 1903, Aiken SC, **d.** May 20, 1932, New York, NY
Trumpet / Classic Jazz
One of the great trumpeters of the 1920s, Bubber Miley was a

master with the plunger mute, distorting his sound quite color-fully. He was largely responsible for Duke Ellington's early suc-cess and was the most prominent voice in Duke's Jungle Band of 1926–28, teaming up with trombonist Tricky Sam Nanton; Cootie Williams and Ray Nance would follow in the tradition of Miley. He grew up in New York and played professionally starting in 1920. Miley was with Elmer Snowden's Washingtonians as early as 1923 and freelanced on recordings during 1924–26. He was influenced a bit by King Oliver and Johnny Dunn but was quite distinctive by 1926 and an innovator in his own way. Miley co-wrote "East St. Louis Toodle-oo" and "Black and Tan Fantasy" and starred on the majority of Ellington's recordings during 1926–28. Unfortunately, he was an alcoholic and by early 1929 was becom-ing increasingly unreliable, leading to Duke reluctantly firing him. Miley worked in France with Noble Sissle, played in the U.S. with society bandleader Leo Reisman (taking a memorable solo on "What Is This Thing Called Love") and formed his own band in 1930, recording six titles. Bubber Miley played in a few shows in 1931 but died the following year of tuberculosis at the age of 29. —*Scott Yanow*

Bobby Militello

b. Mar. 25, 1950, Buffalo, NY
Alto Saxophone / Hard Bop
An excellent reed player who has thus far been underrated, Bobby Militello brings back the spirit of Paul Desmond when he performs with the Dave Brubeck Quartet. After playing locally in Buffalo, he toured with Maynard Ferguson (1975–79). Militello freelanced in Buffalo (1981–84) and Los Angeles (1984–92), playing with the Bill Holman and Bob Florence Orchestras. Bobby Militello, who has recorded with Holman, Florence, Ferguson and Charlie Shoemake among others, has played on and off with Brubeck since 1983 (usually alternating with Bill Smith) and has led several of his own albums for Positive. —*Scott Yanow*

● **Easy To Love** / Nov. 9, 1993–Nov. 12, 1993 / Positive ✦✦✦✦✦
Bobby Militello, on both alto and flute, has an opportunity to stretch out during this CD, playing bebop, '60s-type funky jazz and R&Bish ballads; he even takes an enthusiastic vocal on "I Thought About You." Organist Bobby Jones actually dominates the ensembles, contributing strong solos, heated accompaniment of Militello and four of the ten selections. With drummer Bob Leatherbarrow providing driving rhythms and trumpeter Jeff Jarvis helping out on a few numbers, the set has the feel of a clas-sic hard bop organ combo, inspiring Bobby Militello to play at his best. —*Scott Yanow*

Straight Ahead / 1995 / Positive Music ✦✦✦✦

Eddie Miller

b. Jun. 23, 1911, New Orleans, LA., **d.** Apr. 1, 1991, Van Nuys, CA
Clarinet, Tenor Saxophone / Dixieland, Swing
Eddie Miller had a beautiful tone on his tenor, similar to Bud Freeman although his style was much less angular. Miller was a solidly swinging player who fit easily into Dixieland and swing settings. He worked professionally in New Orleans at the age of 16 and in 1930 made his recording debut with Julie Wintz. He was well-featured with Ben Pollack's Orchestra (1930–34), and when Bob Crosby took over the ensemble, Miller became one of its main stars. In addition to his many solos with Crosby's Orchestra and the Bobcats, Miller was a superior clarinetist who took a famous solo on "South Rampart Street Parade." In addition he composed the haunting "Slow Mood." When Crosby broke up the band in 1942, Eddie Miller put together a short-lived orchestra of his own before being drafted. He was discharged from the mili-tary early due to illness and settled in Los Angeles in 1945, becoming a studio musician and appearing on many soundtracks for 20th Century-Fox. Miller participated in nearly all of the Bob Crosby reunions and was on many jazz dates in the 1950s. During 1967–76 he worked in New Orleans with Pete Fountain, and he was active at jazz parties and festivals into the mid-'80s. Eddie Miller recorded as a leader for Capitol, Jump, Decca, Tops, Southland, Coral, Blue Angel Jazz Club, 77, Famous Door and Magna Graphic Jazz. —*Scott Yanow*

The Uncollected Eddie Miller & His Orchestra (1944–1945) / 1943–1945 / Hindsight ◆◆◆◆
● **Eddie Miller-George Van Eps** / Mar. 21, 1946–Mar. 8, 1949 / Jump ◆◆◆◆◆
Portrait of Eddie / 1971 / Blue Angel ◆◆◆◆◆
It's Miller Time / 1979 / Famous Door ◆◆◆◆

Glenn Miller (Alton Glenn Miller)

b. Mar. 1, 1904, Clarinda, IA, d. Dec. 15, 1944, English Channel
Trombone, Leader / Swing

Glenn Miller led the most popular band in the world during 1939–42 and the most beloved of all the swing-era orchestras. His big band played a wide variety of melodic music (including swing, vocal ballads and novelties) and had tremendous success in every area. Jazz was only part of their music, and Miller (like Stan Kenton) was just not interested in swinging like Count Basie. He employed some good horn soloists along the way but was most concerned in displaying strong musicianship, well-rehearsed ensembles, danceable tempos and putting together an enjoyable and well-rounded show.

Miller grew up in Colorado, attended college for a short time and in 1926 joined Ben Pollack's new band. He was with the group for two years, contributing arrangements and taking some trombone solos but, after Jack Teagarden was discovered and signed up, Miller took the hint and quit. In 1928 he was a free-lance arranger in New York, and he would work most prominently during the next few years with Red Nichols in pit orchestras, as Smith Ballew's musical director and with the Dorsey Brothers. In 1935 he helped organize Ray Noble's American Orchestra and led his first session, but even by 1937, Glenn Miller was still obscure. He was inspired by the success of many new big bands, and he put together an orchestra of his own. That venture started out promising with some fine recordings, but it soon failed, partly because it did not have a personality of its own. In mid-1938 Miller tried again, and although he had a recording contract with Bluebird, the first year was mostly a struggle. However this time around, by having a clarinet double the melody of the saxophones an octave higher, he had his own trademark. An engagement at Glen Island Casino in the summer of 1939 earned the orchestra a regular radio broadcast, their recordings of "Moonlight Serenade" (Miller's theme), "Sunrise Serenade" and particularly "Little Brown Jug" became hits. By the end of the year Glenn Miller was a household name, and his band was considered a sensation. During 1939–42 there were many additional hits including "In the Mood," "At Last," "Stairway to the Stars," "Tuxedo Junction," "Pennsylvania 6-5000," "Chattanooga Choo Choo," "A String of Pearls," "Elmer's Tune," "Don't Sit Under the Apple Tree," "American Patrol," "I've Got a Gal in Kalamazoo," "Serenade in Blue" and "Jukebox Saturday Night." There was simply no competition!

From the jazz standpoint, Miller's best soloists were trumpeters Clyde Hurley, Johnny Best and (by 1942) Bobby Hackett. Tex Beneke, who was more famous for his good-natured vocals, was a decent tenor saxophonist who had a lot of short solos. Less tolerable to jazz listeners were the many ballad vocals of Ray Eberle (who often sounded as if he were straining) and the lightweight but cheerful contributions of singer Marion Hutton.

Only Glenn Miller's decision to enlist in the Army stopped his orchestra's success. He did the near-impossible and organized the finest military jazz band ever heard, his Army Air Force Band. By 1944, when it had relocated to London, it featured clarinetist Peanuts Hucko, pianist Mel Powell, drummer/singer Ray McKinley, trumpeter Bobby Nichols and sometimes a string section and a vocal group. Their version of "St. Louis Blues March" became famous, and this group's broadcasts and radio transcriptions are well worth searching for. Glenn Miller flew across the English Channel in December 1944 with plans of setting up engagements on the Continent. His plane was shot down (quite possibly in error by the Allies) and lost.

The Army Air Force Band stayed together through 1945. There have been many Glenn Miller ghost orchestras since, but all have been stuck in the role of recreating the past including note-for-note duplications of the recorded solos. The oddest case is Tex Beneke who has spent the past 50 years essentially performing over and over again the same routines that he had done with Miller during a three-year period!

All of Glenn Miller's Bluebird recordings (from 1938–42) have been reissued a countless number of times including in "complete" sets. His band appears quite prominently in two Hollywood movies of the 1940s (*Sun Valley Serenade* and *Orchestra Wives*) that are recommended viewing. —*Scott Yanow*

His Complete Recordings On Columbia Records / Nov. 21, 1928–May 23, 1938 / Everest ◆◆◆◆
This five-LP box set is rather unusual in that, although listed under Glenn Miller's name, the first three albums actually feature Miller as a sideman, mostly playing in the ensembles since he was never a major soloist. There are 25 selections from The Dorsey Brothers Orchestra of 1928–31 and 1934, dance-band performances with a variety of vocalists (including Bing Crosby) and some fine solos from trombonist Tommy Dorsey (who is also heard a little on trumpet), Jimmy Dorsey on clarinet and alto and (on one session) the great trumpeter Bunny Berigan. Miller is also heard with Clark Randall's Orchestra in 1935 (the singer's backup group is really the early Bob Crosby band). The final two discs feature Miller leading a studio group in 1935 (Berigan has a memorable solo on "Solo Hop") and heading his own unsuccessful big band of 1937–38. Although not essential, this appealing set has a great deal of valuable and historic music and will fill some gaps for swing collectors who might have wondered what Glenn Miller did before he hit it big in 1939. —*Scott Yanow*

Best of the Big Bands: Evolution of a Band / Apr. 25, 1935–May 23, 1938 / Columbia ◆◆◆
The majority of Glenn Miller's early recordings as a bandleader are included on this CD which is subtitled "Evolution of a Band." Miller heads a studio group (which includes trumpeter Bunny Berigan) on two numbers from 1935 (why weren't all four from that date included?) and on three complete sessions from 1937–38; if the liner notes are to be believed, the final four performances are previously unissued alternate takes. All of the selections from 1937–38 are taken from a period when Miller was struggling to find his sound, and even by the time of "Dippermouth Blues" (from May 23, 1938), he had not found it yet. But although these recordings are not that distinctive, there are some good moments; the vocals by Kathleen Lane and Gail Reese are excellent. —*Scott Yanow*

On The Air / Jun. 25, 1938–Nov. 29, 1941 / RCA Victor ◆◆◆◆
Three LPs (which were originally available separately) are combined in this box set. The performances by Glenn Miller's Orchestra (dance music, vocal features and a bit of jazz) are taken from radio broadcasts and over half of the selections were not recorded by the band commercially. Since most of this music (released for the first time in 1963 and kept in-print for many years afterward) has not reappeared on CD, this is a set that Glenn Miller collectors will want to go out of their way to acquire although more general listeners should get the studio recordings first. —*Scott Yanow*

The Complete Glenn Miller, Vol. 1 / Sep. 27, 1938–Jun. 2, 1939 / Bluebird ◆◆◆◆
In 1975 the Bluebird reissue series initiated a "complete Glenn Miller" program of double LPs; it would be completed in 1980 with *Vol. IX*, and all of the music has since appeared in a comprehensive set on CD. This first two-fer is particularly interesting for it has two sessions (from Sept. 27, 1938 and Feb. 6, 1939) that predate the beginning of Glenn Miller's phenomenal success. "King Porter Stomp" and a two-part version of "By the Waters of Minnetonka" are from the early days while the later dates on this set are highlighted by the original versions of "Moonlight Serenade" and "Little Brown Jug." —*Scott Yanow*

★ **Complete Glenn Miller, Vols. 1–13** / Sep. 27, 1938–Jul. 16, 1942 / Bluebird ◆◆◆◆◆
This 13-CD set (which is enclosed in an attractive and compact black box) completely reissues the contents of the nine double-LP series of the same name, all 277 studio recordings (including 20 alternate takes which have been placed on the 13th disc) that were made by Glenn Miller's extremely popular orchestra. In addition to all of the hits and the occasional jazz performances, the misses (and the many Ray Eberle vocals) are also on this set so general collectors just wanting a taste of Glenn Miller's music would be better off getting a less expensive greatest-hits set. However, true Glenn Miller fans should consider this remarkable reissue to be essential; it's all here. —*Scott Yanow*

● **Spirit is Willing** / Sep. 27, 1938–Jul. 16, 1942 / Bluebird ◆◆◆◆◆
This single CD looks at the jazz side of Glenn Miller, reissuing 22

Music Map

Miscellaneous Instruments

A few of the more famous examples of "miscellaneous instruments" being utilized in jazz:

Bagpipes
Rufus Harley

Bass Saxophone
Adrian Rollini
Spencer Clark
Joe Rushton (with Red Nichols in the 1950s')
Charlie Ventura

Celeste
Meade Lux Lewis

C-Melody Sax
Frankie Trumbauer

Conch Shells
Steve Turre

Contrabass Clarinet
Anthony Braxton • James Carter

English Horn
Bob Cooper • Paul McCandless

Goofus and Hot Fountain Pen
Adrian Rollini

Harpsichord
Johnny Guarnieri (with Artie Shaw's Gramercy Five)

Mandolin
Dave Grisman • John Abercrombie

Marimba
Dave Samuels

Mellophone
Dudley Fosdick (in 1920s with Red Nichols)
Hot Lips Page
Don Elliot

Mellophonium
Gene Roland
Ray Starling

Nagaswaram
Charlie Mariano

Piccolo
Alphonse Picou (famous "High Society" solo
later transferred to clarinet)

Puccolo (whistling)
Ron McCroby

Reed Trumpet
Eddie Harris

Sarussophone
Sidney Bechet
(1924 recording of "Mandy Make Up Your Mind")

Siren
Firehouse Five Plus Two
Rahsaan Roland Kirk

Sitar
Collin Walcott

Slide Saxophone
Snub Mosley

Steel Drums
Andy Narell

Tympani
Vic Berton • Max Roach

In His Own Category
Rahsaan Roland Kirk (Stritch, Manzello, trumpophone,
slidesophone, black puzzle flute, black mystery pipes,
claviette, flexafone)

instrumentals from his prime years. Although Miller did not have a great jazz band, his orchestra was capable of swinging and at one time or another had such fine soloists as trumpeters Clyde Hurley, Billy May and Johnny Best, tenor saxophonist Al Klink and clarinetist Ernie Caceres. This is an interesting set even if it offers nothing that is not available elsewhere. — *Scott Yanow*

Pennsylvania 6-5000, Vol. 1: The Sustaining Remotes / Dec. 30, 1938–Oct. 7, 1940 / Vintage Jazz Classics ✦✦✦
On the first of three Glenn Miller CDs put out by the Vintage Jazz Classics label, there are three previously unreleased (and complete) radio broadcasts featuring Miller's Orchestra. The first aircheck is of greatest interest for it is from Dec. 30, 1938, when Glenn Miller's band was still quite unknown. With the exception of the opening theme, none of the nine selections were ever recorded commercially by Miller. The other broadcasts (from Aug. 10, 1939 and Oct. 7, 1940) are more conventional but will be enjoyed by Glenn Miller's many fans. — *Scott Yanow*

Memorial 1944–1969 / Apr. 4, 1939–Jul. 15, 1942 / RCA Victor ✦✦✦✦✦
Before the CD era, this two-LP set was the definitive Glenn Miller greatest-hits package. All 30 selections were big-sellers (there are no duds included), and none of Miller's most popular songs are missing. Programmed in chronological order, the music starts with "Moonlight Serenade" and continues up to "St. Louis Blues March" (which was actually from Miller's Army Air Force Band). Highlights include "Little Brown Jug," "In the Mood," "Pennsylvania Six-Five Thousand," "Anvil Chorus," "Chattanooga Choo Choo," "A String of Pearls" and "Serenade in Blue;" in fact every song. — *Scott Yanow*

★ **The Popular Recordings (1938–1942)** / Apr. 4, 1939–Jul. 15, 1942 / Bluebird ✦✦✦✦✦
Of the many compilations of Glenn Miller hits, this three-disc set strikes the best balance between comprehensiveness and economy. More casual listeners might want to try *Pure Gold*, while true scholars will have to have the *Complete Glenn Miller*, but this 60-track collection contains the best of the most popular bandleader of the last part of the swing era. — *William Ruhlmann*

★ **Legendary Performer** / May 17, 1939–Sep. 24, 1942 / Bluebird ✦✦✦✦✦
On first glance, this CD may appear to be a greatest-hits package since many of the songs were recorded by Glenn Miller's Orchestra in the studios, but actually the set contains (in chronological order) many of Miller's most historic radio performances. Starting with his theme "Moonlight Serenade" from the band's opening appearance at the Glen Island Casino (when they were unknown), one can experience from song-to-song the quick rush to success, a New Year's Eve version of "In the Mood," and a classic rendition of "Chattanooga Choo Choo" (with Miller being awarded the first Gold record in history), all the way up to the announcement of Miller's entry into the Army, a surprise guest appearance by Harry James and Glenn Miller's emotional farewell to the audience. This is an essential release for anyone with an interest in Glenn Miller's music and life. — *Scott Yanow*

Little Brown Jug, Vol. 3 / Jun. 20, 1939–Dec. 7, 1939 / Vintage Jazz Classics ✦✦✦
The third of three Glenn Miller CDs put out by the VJC label has three previously unreleased radio broadcasts from 1939, the period when Miller began to make it big. With Clyde Hurley contributing some trumpet solos and both Tex Beneke and Al Klink heard on tenors, this well-rounded set has a stronger dose of jazz than usual along with the usual vocals of Ray Eberle and Marian Hutton. It's a nice set of solid swing from a legendary orchestra. — *Scott Yanow*

The Complete Glenn Miller, Vol. 2 (1939) / Jun. 22, 1939–Oct. 3, 1939 / Bluebird ✦✦✦✦
The second of nine double LPs put out by Bluebird in the mid-'70s that reissue the complete studio output of the Glenn Miller Orchestra finds the big band enjoying (and probably very surprised about) its big success. The 33 selections were recorded in just over a three-month period, and although few of the songs were hits, the program does include the original version of "In the Mood" and a fair amount of hot Clyde Hurley trumpet solos. — *Scott Yanow*

The Complete Glenn Miller, Vol. 9 (1939–1942) / Jun. 27, 1939–Jul. 16, 1942 / Bluebird ✦✦✦✦
The ninth and final Glenn Miller double LP released by Bluebird

in the late '70s finishes the complete reissuance of his studio recordings for Victor. The two-fer starts off with 18 alternate takes from the 1939–42 period and then features Miller's civilian band's last 14 recordings (including "That Old Black Magic," "Juke Box Saturday Night" and "Rhapsody in Blue"). Glenn Miller completists are advised to either pick up the 13-CD box set that is currently available or search for these nine attractive LP sets; the music and packaging is exactly the same. — *Scott Yanow*

Tuxedo Junction (1939–1940) / Jul. 20, 1939–Apr. 5, 1940 / Vintage Jazz Classics ✦✦✦
The second of three Glenn Miller CDs put out by the VJC label, like the other two in this series, contains three complete (and previously unreleased) radio broadcasts. The performances from Glen Island Casino and the Hotel Pennsylvania are fairly typical for the Miller band of the period with sweet vocals by Ray Eberle, spirited ones from Marion Hutton, a bit of jazz and a lot of dance music. Glenn Miller fans will want all three of the VJC CDs. — *Scott Yanow*

The Complete Glenn Miller, Vol. 3 (1939–1940) / Oct. 9, 1939–Jan. 29, 1940 / Bluebird ✦✦✦✦
The third of nine double LPs reissuing all of Glenn Miller's studio recordings for Victor has 32 selections from a four-month period. Despite the busy activity, the closest that Miller came to a hit out of these largely forgotten tunes is "Johnson Rag." Fans of Miller's music will want all of the two-fers (or better yet, the 13-CD set that is currently available), but more general collectors should stick to samplers because many of these numbers (particularly those with Ray Eberle vocals) are quite forgettable. — *Scott Yanow*

The Glenn Miller Carnegie Hall Concert / Dec. 6, 1939 / RCA ✦✦✦✦
The Glenn Miller Orchestra's appearance at Carnegie Hall does not contain any unusual material, sticking to the band's regular repertoire. However this was an auspicious occasion (showing that after years of struggle Miller had finally arrived), and there are plenty of highlights. Excellent versions of such songs as "Running Wild," "Little Brown Jug," "One O'Clock Jump" and "In the Mood" are the highlights, and there are also two vocals by Ray Eberle and three from Marion Hutton. A good all-around showcase for the band, it is surprising that the music on this LP has yet to be reissued on CD. — *Scott Yanow*

The Complete Glenn Miller, Vol. 4 (1940) / Feb. 5, 1940–Jun. 13, 1940 / Bluebird ✦✦✦✦
With the exception of two titles, all of the music reissued on this two-fer (the fourth volume out of nine) was recorded within a three-month period, a measure of the great commercial success that Glenn Miller was experiencing in 1940. The hits of the two-fer are "Tuxedo Junction" (heard in two versions) and "Pennsylvania 6–5000," but generally even the lesser-known titles (at least the ones without Ray Eberle's vocals) are enjoyable. Glenn Miller fanatics in particular will want this set (or the currently available 13-CD box) although those just hoping to acquire his most popular numbers will probably be better off with a sampler instead. — *Scott Yanow*

The Complete Glenn Miller, Vol. 5 (1940) / Jun. 13, 1940–Nov. 22, 1940 / Bluebird ✦✦✦✦
Although one thinks of the Glenn Miller Orchestra (the most popular big band in the world during 1939–42) as having one hit record after another, this two-LP set (which covers a five-month period in 1940) does not contain a single one of his best-sellers; "Blueberry Hill" and "A Nightingale Sang in Berkeley Square" come the closest. As usual, the band plays a mixture of dance music, pop vocals and swing-oriented jazz. This two-LP set (the fifth of nine) is definitely for completists who do not have Miller's 13-CD box set. — *Scott Yanow*

On The Alamo / Jun. 13, 1940–Nov. 3, 1941 / Drive Archive ✦✦✦
The songs might be familiar, but these renditions are a little different than usual because this Glenn Miller CD is composed of excerpts from radio broadcasts. The music mostly emphasizes the jazz side of Miller; only four of the 14 selections have vocals, and only two are by their ballad singer Ray Eberle. With Johnny Best contributing some fine trumpet solos, Tex Beneke getting a few good spots for his tenor and such songs being performed as "Everybody Loves My Baby," "Down for the Count" and "Limehouse Blues" (along with "new" versions of some of Miller's hits), this is a fine all-around release by the still very popular bandleader. — *Scott Yanow*

The Complete Glenn Miller, Vol. 6 (1940–1941) / Nov. 22, 1940–May 28, 1941 / Bluebird ✦✦✦✦
The sixth two-LP set in the admirable complete Glenn Miller series, unlike *Vol. 5* (which had virtually no hits), finds the orchestra introducing several of their best-loved numbers. Highlights include "Anvil Chorus," "Song of the Volga Boatmen," "Sun Valley Jump," "Perfidia" and "Chattanooga Choo Choo." Miller's repertoire included pop vocals, novelties and jazz, all of it quite danceable and melodic, and this two-fer finds his big band in peak form. —*Scott Yanow*

Glenn Miller in Hollywood / Mar. 1941–May 1942 / Mercury ✦✦✦✦
The Glenn Miller Orchestra appeared in two Hollywood movies during 1941–42: *Sun Valley Serenade* and *Orchestra Wives*. Their performances recorded for both the films (including songs not used in the pictures) are included on this rather brief (64 minute) two-LP set. The former movie, in addition to featuring fine versions of "In the Mood" and "Sun Valley Jump," introduced the two hits "I Know Why" and "Chattanooga Choo Choo." *Orchestra Wives* was most notable for "I've Got a Gal in Kalamazoo" and "American Patrol." The easily enjoyable music makes for an interesting contrast to Glenn Miller's more familiar studio recordings of these songs. —*Scott Yanow*

The Complete Glenn Miller, Vol. 7 (1941) / May 28, 1941–Nov. 24, 1941 / Bluebird ✦✦✦✦
The seventh of nine Glenn Miller two-LP sets released by Bluebird during the 1975–80 period has all of the music recorded by the popular bandleader during a six-month period in 1941, 32 selections in all. Highlights include "It Happened in Sun Valley," "Elmer's Tune" and "A String of Pearls." Although this series (or its replacement, a 13-CD box set) is not essential for more general swing collectors, Glenn Miller completists will want this perfectly done series. —*Scott Yanow*

The Complete Glenn Miller, Vol. 8 (1941–1942) / Dec. 8, 1941–Jun. 17, 1942 / Bluebird ✦✦✦✦
This two-LP set, the eighth of nine Glenn Miller two-fers to be released by Bluebird in the late '70s, continues the complete reissuance of Miller's Victor recordings. Highlights include "Moonlight Cocktail," "Keep 'Em Flying," "Don't Sit Under the Apple Tree," "American Patrol," "I've Got a Gal in Kalamazoo" and "Serenade in Blue." The mixture of dance music, pop vocals, novelties and swing worked very well for Miller, whose orchestra was the most popular in the world during 1939–42. A more recent 13-CD set also has all of the music in this valuable series. —*Scott Yanow*

Glenn Miller Army Air Force Band / Jul. 17, 1943–Jun. 1944 / RCA Victor ✦✦✦✦✦
Glenn Miller's greatest orchestra was the one he led while in the Army, a 30-piece outfit (not counting vocalists) with ten strings that was capable of playing everything from hard-swinging jazz to mood music. This excellent five-LP set features some of the band's finest recorded performances with such soloists as trumpeters Bernie Privin and Bobby Nichols, clarinetist Peanuts Hucko, Hank Freeman on tenor, altoist Vince Carbone and pianist Mel Powell; the vocalists include the Crew Chiefs, Johnny Desmond and drummer Ray McKinley. Highpoints of this hard-to-find but well-worth-the-search box include "Tail-End Charlie," "Anvil Chorus," "In the Mood," "Everybody Loves My Baby," "Sun Valley Jump," "St. Louis Blues March," "Flying Home" and a few medleys. —*Scott Yanow*

★ **Major Glenn Miller & the Army Air Force Band (1943–1944)** / Oct. 29, 1943–Apr. 22, 1944 / Bluebird ✦✦✦✦✦
During the two years of its existence the Glenn Miller Army Air Force Band (the greatest orchestra he ever led) performed and recorded frequently although most of its sessions have been difficult to find ever since. The group was filled with talented jazz soloists (including trumpeters Bobby Nichols and Bernie Privin, clarinetist Peanuts Hucko and pianist Mel Powell), had fine singers in Ray McKinley, Johnny Desmond and the Crew Chiefs and even an occasional 21-piece string section. This CD has many of the best performances by the huge band including "St. Louis Blues March," "Tail-End Charlie," "Anvil Chorus," "Everybody Loves My Baby" and "It Must Be Jelly", and it is highly recommended to swing fans and jazz historians. —*Scott Yanow*

The Glenn Miller V-Disc Sessions: Vol. 1 / Oct. 29, 1943–May 13, 1944 / Mr. Music ✦✦✦✦
Glenn Miller's Army Air Force Band was the finest group that he

ever led. Although it did not make any commercially available recordings, the huge outfit did perform 43 songs for V-Discs that were sent to servicemen overseas. The earliest 22 are included on this first of two rewarding CDs. Mood pieces and novelty vocals alternate with some fine jazz, showing the wide variety of music that this impressive group (which often had a full string section) could generate. Highlights include "St. Louis Blues March," "Tail End Charlie," "G.I. Jive," "Stealin' Apples" and "Here We Go Again." Although the exact personnel is not given, clarinetist Peanuts Hucko, pianist Mel Powell and trumpeter Bobby Nichols are all heard from. —*Scott Yanow*

The Glenn Miller V-Disc Sessions: Vol. 2 / May 20, 1944–Nov. 17, 1945 / Mister Music ✦✦✦✦
The second of two Mister Music CDs that reissue all of the Glenn Miller Army Air Force Band's V-Disc recordings gets the edge over the first due to its stronger jazz content. With top soloists in trumpeter Bobby Nichols, clarinetist Peanuts Hucko and pianist Mel Powell along with singer Johnny Desmond and the Crew Chiefs, Miller's huge orchestra performs such numbers as "Everybody Loves My Baby," "Poinciana," "I Hear You Screamin'," "Sun Valley Jump" and "Holiday for Strings" in addition to worthy remakes of "Little Brown Jug" and "Chattanooga Choo Choo." This CD concludes with five numbers from October–November 1945, long after Glenn Miller's plane went down over the English channel. One can hear the influence of bebop on the group during "Passage Interdit" and "7-0-5," making one wonder what direction Glenn Miller's music would have gone in if he had lived. Recommended. —*Scott Yanow*

War Broadcast / Sep. 15, 1944–Nov. 1944 / Laserlight ✦✦
This rather brief (just 35 minutes) CD features the Glenn Miller Army Air Force Band on a radio show that was broadcast in Nazi Germany. Miller and an interpreter talk in German about the virtues of America and jazz, and the orchestra plays a few of Miller's hits (including "In the Mood," "Tuxedo Junction" and "A String of Pearls") along with two vocal features for Johnny Desmond and a Ray McKinley feature on "Is You Is or Is You Ain't My Baby." This is a budget release, but the extreme brevity of the otherwise interesting program is unfortunate. —*Scott Yanow*

A Tribute To Glenn Miller / Jun. 5, 1945 / Metronome ✦
This two-LP set features a lengthy broadcast that is supposed to be paying tribute to the late Glenn Miller. Unfortunately many of the guests (which include comedians, show-biz types and musicians) had little or nothing to do with Miller, and no one ever bothers to explain (or even seem to know) what was so significant about the bandleader. There are some good moments, particularly from Count Basie, Louis Prima, Cab Calloway and an emotional Tex Beneke, but so many of the appearances are obviously self-serving, and the comedy routines (especially from an obnoxious Milton Berle who does not even mention his work with Glenn Miller in the movie *Sun Valley Serenade*) are poorly dated, that this two-fer is only interesting from a historical standpoint. —*Scott Yanow*

Original Reunion / Apr. 17, 1954 / GNP ✦✦✦✦
Most recordings by the Glenn Miller ghost band are rather stale and predictable recreations, but this concert is surprisingly effective. In 1954 after the successful release of *The Glenn Miller Story*, producer Gene Norman gathered together a big band that was mostly filled with alumni from Miller's Orchestra. Although there was already a ghost band, this was apparently the first time that many of the former members had had a reunion. Although sticking mostly to the old Miller songs and the original arrangements, the players felt free to improvise fresh new solos, and the results are better than expected. With strong contributions made by clarinetist Willie Schwartz, tenors Babe Russin and Eddie Miller (both of whom were ringers) and trumpeters Clyde Hurley and Johnny Best, this well-recorded and nostalgic reunion (which also has a medley from a vocal group) was a success; the CD reissue is worth picking up. —*Scott Yanow*

In the Digital Mood / 1983 / GNP ✦✦

Marcus Miller

b. Jun. 14, 1959, New York, NY
Bass / Funk, Pop, Crossover, Post Bop
Marcus Miller has spent much of his career as an R&B producer, but he is also one of the most talented electric bassists around. He played R&B as a youth and had stints with Bobbi Humphrey (1977) and Lenny White before becoming a studio musician.

Miller was an important part of Miles Davis' band during 1981–82, and he collaborated with the trumpeter on several later projects including *Tutu* and the *Music from Siesta*. He also worked on some David Sanborn albums and appeared on the McCoy Tyner/Jackie McLean record *It's About Time* (1985). After Miles Davis' death, Marcus Miller put together his own group which performs many songs in the style of Davis' later band; they have recorded for the PRA label. —*Scott Yanow*

The Sun Don't Lie / 1993 / PRA ◆◆◆

● **Tales** / 1994 / PRA ◆◆◆◆
It is obvious from the music of his group that Marcus Miller badly misses Miles Davis. The funky grooves he uses on this CD sound like a continuation of Davis' later band, Michael "Patches" Stewart contributes muted trumpet in Davis' style, altoist Kenny Garrett is among Miller's sidemen and Miles Davis himself (along with the voices of several other notables in very brief moments) pops up twice on Miller's release. Marcus Miller's electric bass is a major force throughout the music. Samples are used intelligently, a tribute is paid to the late guitarist Eric Gale (Hiram Bullock starts off his solo sounding uncannily like Gale), "Strange Fruit" (a feature for Miller's bass clarinet) gets a revamping, and all of the music is both danceable and full of development. A few songs (especially later in the program) ramble on a bit, and one wishes that Marcus Miller would drop the funk now and then for variety's sake, but in general his set holds one's interest. —*Scott Yanow*

Mulgrew Miller

b. Aug. 13, 1955, Greenwood, MS
Piano / Post Bop, Hard Bop
An excellent pianist who plays in a style influenced by McCoy Tyner, Mulgrew Miller has been quite consistent throughout his career. He was with Mercer Ellington's big band in the late '70s and had important stints with Betty Carter (1980), Woody Shaw (1981–83) and Art Blakey's Jazz Messengers (1983–86). For a long period he was a member of the Tony Williams Quintet (1986–94). In addition, Mulgrew Miller has led his own sessions for Landmark (starting in 1985) and Novus. —*Scott Yanow*

Keys to the City / Jun. 28, 1985 / Landmark ◆◆◆
Trio session. Marvin "Smitty" Smith's drumming and Miller's solos give this one some clout. —*Ron Wynn*

Work / Apr. 23, 1986–Apr. 24, 1986 / Landmark ◆◆◆◆
Memphis pianist Miller with trio (Teri Lyne Carrington on drums). Excellent. —*Michael G. Nastos*

Wingspan / May 11, 1987 / Landmark ◆◆◆◆◆
Fine group jazz, with saxophonist Kenny Garrett. —*Michael G. Nastos*

The Countdown / Aug. 15, 1988–Aug. 16, 1988 / Landmark ◆◆◆◆
A sparkling release that boasts standout writing and exacting interaction between Joe Henderson (ts), Ron Carter (b) and Tony Williams (d). —*Ron Wynn*

From Day to Day / Mar. 14, 1990–Mar. 15, 1990 / Landmark ◆◆◆◆
Miller takes center stage and shows his Memphis roots in blues and gospel throughout, plus a good touch on the occasional standard. —*Ron Wynn*

Time and Again / Aug. 19, 1991+Aug. 21, 1991 / Landmark ◆◆◆◆
A release by pianist Mulgrew Miller, this time featuring him in a trio format playing primarily his own compositions from '91. He's backed by bassist Peter Washington and drummer Tony Reedus, and this constitutes his most intimate, distinctive set as a leader. —*Ron Wynn*

Hand In Hand / Dec. 16, 1992–Dec. 18, 1992 / Novus ◆◆◆◆◆
Mulgrew Miller, a talented McCoy Tyner-influenced pianist, leads an all-star septet on much of this date. The main stars, however, are Miller's nine diverse originals which range from modal to Monkish. With tenor saxophonist Joe Henderson appearing on five selections, trumpeter Eddie Henderson on six and altoist Kenny Garrett heard throughout the full CD, Miller has a perfect frontline to interpret his tricky but logical originals. Vibraphonist Steve Nelson, bassist Christian McBride and drummer Lewis Nash do not exactly get overshadowed either. —*Scott Yanow*

● **With Our Own Eyes** / Dec. 1993 / Novus ◆◆◆◆◆
The consistent pianist Mulgrew Miller leads his trio (which includes bassist Richie Good and drummer Tony Reedus) through a set dominated by his originals but also including "Body and Soul" and Michel Legran's "Summer Me, Winter Me." The McCoy Tyner influence will probably always remain a significant part of Miller's style, but he is such a powerful player in his own right that one really does not mind. His originals on this set range from the modal 6/4 piece "Somewhere Else" and the thoughtful "Dreamin'" to the melancholy "Carousel." As with all of Mulgrew Miller's releases thus far, this one is well worth picking up. —*Scott Yanow*

Getting To Know You / 1995 / Novus ◆◆◆◆

Punch Miller (Ernest Miller)

b. Jun. 10, 1894, Raceland, LA, **d.** Dec. 2, 1971
Trumpet / Dixieland
A solid New Orleans trumpeter who never really made it big, Punch Miller worked in New Orleans until moving to Chicago in 1926. He played with Al Wynn, Tiny Parham, Freddie Keppard and Jelly Roll Morton in the 1920s and worked with low-profile jazz and blues groups in Chicago until returning to New Orleans in 1956. He recorded a few numbers for Atlantic in 1962 and toured Japan with George Lewis in 1963. Punch Miller's 1920s recordings as a sideman have been gathered together and reissued on a CD by the RST label. —*Scott Yanow*

Mills Blue Rhythm Band

Big Band / Swing
This fine big band was originally formed by drummer Willie Lynch as the Blue Rhythm Band in 1930, and as the Coconut Grove Orchestra it backed Louis Armstrong on some records. In 1931 Irving Mills became its manager, and it was renamed the Mills Blue Rhythm Band. Lynch's departure later that year resulted in Baron Lee fronting the band until Lucky Millinder took over in 1934. The big band recorded frequently during 1931–37 (all of its recordings have been reissued on five Classics CDs), and although the orchestra never really caught on or developed its own personality, its recordings did document many fine performances. Among the sidemen were pianist Edgar Hayes, altoist Charlie Holmes, Joe Garland on tenor, drummer O'Neil Spencer and by 1934 trumpeter Red Allen, trombonist J.C. Higginbotham and clarinetist Benny Bailey; later editions included altoist Tab Smith, pianist Billy Kyle and trumpeters Charlie Shavers and Harry "Sweets" Edison. When it broke up in 1938, Lucky Millinder formed his own big band. —*Scott Yanow*

Blue Rhythm / Jan. 1931–Jun. 1931 / Hep ◆◆◆◆

Rhythm Spasm / Aug. 1931–Aug. 1932 / Hep ◆◆◆◆

● **Mills Blue Rhythm Band 1933–1934** / Mar. 1, 1933–Dec. 11, 1934 / Classics ◆◆◆◆◆

Mills Blue Rhythm Band 1934–1935 / Dec. 19, 1934–May 20, 1936 / Classics ◆◆◆◆◆

Mills Blue Rhythm Band 1936–1937 / May 20, 1936–Jul. 1, 1937 / Classics ◆◆◆◆◆

Mills Brothers

Vocal Group / Swing, Classic Jazz, Pop
The Mills Brothers became so popular as a middle-of-the-road pop vocal group that one forgets just how innovative they were in the 1930s. Billed as "Four Boys and a Guitar," they were experts at imitating instruments including trumpet, trombone, tuba and string bass. With the backing of just a guitar, they simulated a full band and amazed listeners. The Mills Brothers (Herbert, Harry, Donald and John Jr.) started out singing in vaudeville and tent shows, were featured on a radio show for ten months in Cincinnati, arrived in New York and by the end of 1931 were an instant hit. They recorded frequently throughout the decade, made appearances in many films (including 1932's *Big Broadcast*) and recorded with Bing Crosby, the Boswell Sisters and Duke Ellington. John Jr.'s death in 1935 was a tragic loss although John Sr. effectively took his place. However by 1942 with their hit "Paper Doll," the old sound gave way to a more conventional pop setting. Fortunately the English JSP label has reissued on six CDs all of the Mills Brothers' early recordings (1931–39), and these feature the group at the peak of their creativity. —*Scott Yanow*

★ **Chronological, Vol. 1** / Oct. 1931-Apr. 14, 1932 / JSP ◆◆◆◆◆

Chronological, Vol. 2 / May 1932-Feb. 24, 1934 / JSP ◆◆◆◆◆

Chronological, Vol. 5 (1937–38) / Feb. 2, 1933-Aug. 23, 1938 / JSP ◆◆◆◆◆

Chronological, Vol. 3 / Mar. 29, 1934-Feb. 20, 1935 / JSP ◆◆◆◆◆

Chronological, Vol. 6 / May 30, 1935-Aug. 23, 1939 / JSP ◆◆◆◆◆

Chronological, Vol. 4 / Oct. 28, 1935-Jun. 29, 1937 / JSP ◆◆◆◆◆

★ **Anthology** / MCA ◆◆◆◆◆
The Mills Brothers: The Anthology is a comprehensive 48-song overview of the vocal group's career, spanning their entire career and featuring 32 of their biggest hits. Most of their most famous songs—including "Paper Doll," "Glow-Worm," "Lazy River," and "Rockin' Chair"—are included on this double disc set, and the sound is the best it has ever been. In short, it is the definitive retrospective of this ground-breaking vocal quartet. —*Stephen Thomas Erlewine*

Irving Mills

b. Jan. 16, 1884, New York, NY, d. Apr. 21, 1985, Palm Springs, CA
Vocals / Classic Jazz
Irving Mills did a great deal to help jazz, making himself a great deal of money in the process. He is most famous for his work as manager for Duke Ellington during 1926-39, helping Duke gain his job at the Cotton Club in addition to securing numerous recording sessions and important engagements; he also wrote the lyrics to some of Ellington's songs including "It Don't Mean a Thing If It Ain't Got That Swing," "Mood Indigo" and "Sophisticated Lady." He had earlier worked with his brother Jack in establishing a music publishing business that became Mills Music, Inc. Mills also promoted Cab Calloway, Benny Carter, Fletcher Henderson, Jimmie Lunceford and Don Redman and appeared as a singer on many sessions (including some with Ellington). He put together all-star recording groups under the names of the Whoopee Makers and Irving Mills' Hotsy Totsy Gang (1928-30) and in 1931 became the manager for an orchestra which he renamed the Mills Blue Rhythm Band. After breaking with Ellington in 1939, Irving Mills maintained a lower profile but stayed active in management and music publishing into the 1960s. —*Scott Yanow*

● **Irving Mills and His Hotsy Totsy Gang, Vol. 1** / Jul. 27, 1928–Jul. 31, 1929 / Retrieval ◆◆◆◆◆

Irving Mills and His Hotsy Totsy Gang, Vol. 2 / Jul. 31, 1929–Jan. 6, 1930 / Retrieval ◆◆◆◆◆

Irving Mills and His Hotsy Totsy Gang, Vol. 3 / Feb. 6, 1930–May 3, 1931 / Retrieval ◆◆◆◆◆

Pete Minger

b. Orangeburg, SC
Trumpet, Fluegelhorn / Bop
A talented bop-based trumpeter, Pete Minger has an attractive sound and a strong improvising style. After attending Tennessee State College and Berklee, Minger spent ten years with Count Basie's Orchestra (1970-80) as a featured soloist. Minger settled in Miami in the early '80s and has freelanced in the area ever since. He has led superior quartet sessions for Spinnster (1983, later reissued on Concord) and Concord (1992). —*Scott Yanow*

Straight from the Source / Oct. 31, 1983 / Spinster ◆◆◆◆◆

★ **Minger Paintings** / 1991 / Jazz Alliance ◆◆◆◆◆
Originals and reworked standards are on the menu for Pete Minger on this '91 release, which matches him with various bassists and drummers in an introspective, well-played, low-key session. —*Ron Wynn*

Look to the Sky / Aug. 1992 / Concord Jazz ◆◆◆◆
Fluegelhornist Pete Minger had one of his rare chances to lead a record date for this Concord session, and he used it to play quiet but spirited bebop in a quartet with pianist John Campbell, bassist Kiyoshi Kitagawa and drummer Ben Riley. While Campbell's solos show the influence of Bud Powell, and the bass-drums team is quite supportive, Minger's soft-toned but fluid fluegelhorn is well featured. He is not afraid to push himself, and to his credit his occasional mistakes are left on the record. Pete Minger proves to be a master of the bop vocabulary and is in generally excellent

form on nine melodic standards along with his title cut. Bop lovers will not be disapointed by this fine CD. —*Scott Yanow*

Mingus Big Band

Group / Post-Bop
A major expansion on Mingus Dynasty, the Mingus Big Band (which often uses more than 20 musicians) has since 1991 explored the great bassist's music at least once a week. They play regularly at the Time Spot Cafe in New York, and their two recordings for Dreyfus are often rather remarkable. The huge group performs some of Mingus' most complex works with spirit, virtuosity and plenty of color. Such musicians as Randy Brecker, Ryan Kisor, Lew Soloff, Jack Walrath, Philip Harper, Art Baron, Frank Lacy, Ronnie Cuber, Alex Foster, Craig Handy, Chris Potter, Steve Slagle, John Stubblefield, James Carter, Kenny Drew, Jr., Michael Formanek and Marvin "Smitty" Smith are among the many involved in this worthy and exciting project. —*Scott Yanow*

★ **Mingus Big Band 93: Nostalgia in Times Square** / Mar. 1993 / Dreyfus ◆◆◆◆◆
There have been many attempts to revisit the music of Charles Mingus ever since his death in 1979 (with several of the groups being called Mingus Dynasty), but this is by far the most successful of all the Mingus tribute albums. The 20-piece Mingus Big Band is an all-star unit composed of mostly younger musicians who have spent several years really studying and getting inside the great bassist's music. Their debut CD has such spirited soloists as baritonist Ronnie Cuber (who introduces "Nostalgia in Times Square" with a memorable story of his first encounter with Mingus), trumpeters Randy Brecker, Ryan Kisor and Jack Walrath, trombonists Art Baron, Frank Lacy and Dave Taylor, altoist Steve Slagle, tenors Chris Potter, Craig Handy and John Stubblefield and pianist Kenny Drew Jr. among others. The ten Mingus compositions are all given memorable treatments, particularly "Moanin'," the witty and somewhat nutty "Don't Be Afraid, the Clown's Afraid Too" and "Weird Nightmare." The new arrangements by Sy Johnson, Jack Walrath and Ronnie Cuber are quite crowded and very much in the spirit of Mingus. This was one of the top recordings to be released in 1994 and is essential for all serious jazz collections. —*Scott Yanow*

Gun Slinging Bird / 1995 / Dreyfus ◆◆◆◆◆

Mingus Dynasty

Group / Post Bop
Started shortly after bassist/leader Charles Mingus' death in 1979, Mingus Dynasty has featured many of his top alumni in spirited concerts and recordings. Not all of the records come up to the level of Mingus' best performances (the bassist is clearly missed), but many recapture his spirit. The group expanded for a 1988 concert to temporarily become "Big Band Charlie Mingus." Among the musicians who have participated in the Mingus Dynasty project (which has resulted in recordings for Elektra, Atlantic, Soul Note and Storyville) were Jimmy Owens, Randy Brecker, Richard Williams, Jon Faddis, Jimmy Knepper, John Handy, Joe Farrell, Ricky Ford, George Adams, David Murray, Clifford Jordan, Nick Brignola, Don Pullen, Sir Roland Hanna, Jaki Byard, Dannie Richmond, Billy Hart, Kenny Washington and bassists Charlie Haden, Aladar Pege, Mike Richmond, Reggie Johnson, Reggie Workman and Richard Davis. Mingus Dynasty has been eclipsed in recent years by the remarkable Mingus Big Band. —*Scott Yanow*

● **Chair in the Sky** / Jul. 9, 1979–1979 / Elektra ◆◆◆◆◆

Live at Montreax / Jul. 18, 1980 / Atlantic ◆◆◆◆

Reincarnation / Apr. 5, 1982–Apr. 7, 1982 / Soul Note ◆◆◆

Live at the Village Vanguard / 1984 / Storyville ◆◆◆

Mingus' Sounds of Love / Sep. 29, 1987–Sep. 30, 1991 / Soul Note ◆◆◆◆
One of the better Mingus Dynasty projects, it's possibly Dannie Richmond's last recording session. Long-time Mingus sideman Knepper has taken a number of tunes that Mingus wrote for the women in his life and fashioned a coherent session. —*Stuart Kremsky*

Next Generation Performs Charles Mingus Band New Compositions / Nov. 13, 1991 / Columbia ◆◆◆

Charles Mingus

b. Apr. 22, 1922, Nogales, AZ, d. Jan. 5, 1979, Cuernavaca, MX
Bass, Piano, Leader, Composer / Avant-Garde, Bop, Post-Bop
Charles Mingus' accomplishments and stature merit their own

category. He was an awesome bassist, phenomenal composer and irascible, beloved, hated and celebrated personality. His music combined numerous influences: gospel, blues, traditional New Orleans, swing, bebop, Afro-Latin and symphonic. He turned the bass into a percussive, harmonic, melodic, rhythm and lead instrument. Only Ellington and Monk rivaled his creativity; his use of shifting tempos, alternating meters and trombones, tuba and baritone sax in his arrangements was inspired. He insisted on individuality among his players but would also assign parts and time improvisations in rehearsals. Mingus' knowledge of and ability on the piano led him at one point to hire separate bassists and play piano himself at Jazz Workshop concerts.

His legendary temper caused many confrontations on and off the bandstand and often lead to musicians being fired in mid-performance, or concerts halted so reprimands could be immediately given. His ire would even extend to audiences he felt were inattentive.

Mingus' sisters studied classical violin and piano, but his stepmother only allowed religious music in the house. She took the young Mingus to church meetings, where the moans, groans and hollers, as well as pastor/congregation interaction proved ultimately influential. He studied trombone and cello, then switched to bass partly due to exasperation at poor teachers but also because classmate Buddy Collette informed him the high school band needed a bassist. Others in this band included Chico Hamilton, Dexter Gordon and Ernie Royal. Mingus later studied with Joe Comfort and Red Callender, plus classical player H. Reinschagen and took composition lessons with Lloyd Reese. Mingus wrote "What Love" in 1939 and "Half-Mast Inhibitions" in 1940 while working with Reese, and these were recorded in the '60s.

He played in Barney Bigard's band in 1942 along with Kid Ory, then joined Louis Armstrong in 1943. While in this band, some transcription sessions for broadcast became his first recordings. Mingus briefly replaced Callender in Lee Young's band. There were stints with Howard McGhee, Illinois Jacquet, Dinah Washington and Ivie Anderson, plus a few engagements heading groups. Mingus worked in 1946 and 1947 with Lionel Hampton and made jazz and R&B recordings, becoming known as "Baron Von Mingus." But his major jazz attention came in the early '50s. Mingus left a Post Office gig to join Red Norvo's trio with Tal Farlow. He exited the ensemble a year later after an incident in which he was temporarily displaced by a white bassist for a New York television show. This ugliness was caused by a combination of union and racial politics. Mingus worked with Billy Taylor, Lennie Tristano, Duke Ellington, Stan Getz, Art Tatum and Bud Powell in the early and mid-'50s.

His stint with Ellington ended on a downbeat; his legendary temper erupted during a dispute with trombonist Juan Tizol, and he joined the short list of musicians openly fired by Duke. Mingus participated in the landmark 1953 Massey Hall concert in Canada with Charlie Parker, Dizzy Gillespie, Bud Powell and Max Roach. He began his own record company, Debut, in partnership with Roach in 1952. It lasted until 1955, issuing recordings by Teo Macero, Kenny Dorham, Paul Bley, John La Porta and Sam Most among others. One Debut release, Four Trombones, led to Mingus cutting a Savoy session with J.J. Johnson and Kai Winding. He also worked with Thad Jones, Eddie Bert, Willie Jones, George Barrow and many others.

From 1953 to 1955, he was one of several musicians who contributed pieces to a Jazz Composers' Workshop. Mingus founded his own Jazz Workshop in 1955, turning it into a top repertory company. He'd present his pieces to musicians partly by dictating them their lines. The personnel ranged from a low of four to a high of 11 and included over the years Eric Dolphy, Booker Ervin, Jackie McLean, Shafi Hadi, John Handy, Rahsaan Roland Kirk, Jaki Byard, Jimmy Knepper and longtime drummer Dannie Richmond. Mingus' unprecedented compositional skills flourished from the mid-'50s through the '60s. He wrote extended suites, open-ended jams, "free" selections, songs with collectively improvised sections colliding with chaotic dialogues, works for large orchestra, tributes, socio-political anthems and songs with Afro-Latin and African rhythms. The list of brilliant compositions included "My Jelly Roll Soul," "Jelly Roll," "Fables of Faubus," "Orange Was The Color of Her Dress," "Goodbye Pork Pie Hat," "Meditations on Integration" and "Wednesday Night Prayer Meeting." There were others like "Epitaph" that were never completely performed or perfected during his lifetime.

This proved an equally productive period for albums. Seminal works issued included Pithecanthropus Erectus, The Clown, East Coasting, Scenes In The City, Tijuana Moods and Wonderland. There were also remarkable dates for Columbia with Mingus leading a superb 8–10 piece unit and cutting unforgettable versions of "Goodbye Pork Pie Hat" and "Fables Of Faubus." His early '60s groups with Dolphy may have been his finest; they were certainly among his most dynamic performance bands. There were artistic triumphs but sales failures for Candid, ambitious dates for Impulse, including one where he played unaccompanied solo piano throughout, and more successful financially successful works for Atlantic. His acclaimed early and mid-'60s European tours with The Dolphy group were later issued on Atlantic and Prestige recordings.

Earlier in his career, Mingus had expressed outrage over the treatment and inequities musicians faced. He'd tried to change things before with his record label. He tried again in 1960, organizing a series of concerts to compete with the Newport Jazz Festival. This effort led to the formation of the short-lived Jazz Artists Guild, an organization that was conceived to assist musicians in promoting and controlling their work. Unfortunately, it collapsed in a wave of rancor and discord, and a financially disastrous 1962 Town Hall concert virtually ended his promotional ventures. Mingus tried to start another record company, but the Charles Mingus label issued few titles and made even less money in its brief existence during 1964 and 1965. He stormed off the Monterey Festival stage in 1965 and eventually withdrew from performing, broke and embittered. A 1968 film "Mingus" directed by Thomas Reichman got lots of attention for showing Mingus being booted out of his New York apartment.

Mingus resumed his performing career in 1969. Fantasy purchased the Debut masters and provided him vital funds. Early '70s albums on Columbia and Atlantic, including a live sold-out date at Avery Fisher Hall, rekindled public attention. He received a well-deserved Guggenheim fellowship in composition. Mingus' controversial autobiography "Beneath The Underdog," which had been rejected for publication nearly 10 years earlier, was published and triggered widespread discussion and evaluation (though many raised doubts about various chapters and incidents).

Sadly, Mingus' health was fading; he had developed amyotrophic lateral sclerosis, better known as Lou Gehrig's disease. He composed more big band music, including the wonderful Cumbia and Jazz Fusion in 1977 and led one last great combo before becoming physically unable to play. This group with tenor saxophonist George Adams, trumpeter Jack Walrath, pianist Don Pullen and drummer Dannie Richmond issued superb albums Mingus Moves, Changes One and Changes Two in the early '70s. Mingus collaborated on an album with folk and rock vocalist Joni Mitchell and directed his bands from a wheelchair. His last session came in January of 1978, though he did live long enough to be recognized at the White House by President Carter, a truly poignant moment.

Charles Mingus' work lives on via reissues galore. Mosaic has reissued both his Candid output and his amazing 1959 Columbia releases. Prestige has issued the complete Debut masters. Atlantic in 1993 issued the Mingus anthology Thirteen Pictures and reissued Mingus Moves, Changes One & Two. His piano album and other Impulses are being reissued by MCA. England's Affinity has reissued some of his great late '50s albums. "Epitaph" was finally performed by an orchestra in 1991, and an album featuring it has also been released. The Mingus Dynasty repertory band has recorded and toured in various editions. Brian Priestly's fine 1982 book, "Mingus," has provided a scholarly and comprehensive view of his achievements. —Ron Wynn and Mike Katz

The Young Rebel / May 6, 1946–Oct. 16, 1952 / Swingtime ✦✦✦✦

This collector's LP features bassist Charles Mingus in his early days on a variety of mostly very rare recordings. Four advanced selections are by "Baron Mingus" in 1946 and 1949, four are with Earl Hines (although three of those have vocals by Wini Brown) in 1947, and the remaining six tracks include two by Mingus with Lee Konitz in 1952 and an interesting quartet date led by bassist Oscar Pettiford who is heard here exclusively on cello. A bit of a hodgepodge set ranging from swing/bop to more adventurous sounds, this valuable LP should fill some gaps in Mingus collections. —Scott Yanow

★ **The Complete Debut Recordings** / Apr. 1951–1958 / Debut ♦♦♦♦♦

This mammoth 12-CD box set may not contain Charles Mingus' most significant recordings (those would take place shortly after these sessions), but there is a remarkable amount of exciting and somewhat innovative music in this reissue of all of the dates recorded for Mingus' label Debut. There are duets and trios with pianist Spaulding Givens, a variety of odd third-stream originals (some with vocalist Jackie Paris and altoist Lee Konitz), the famous Massey Hall concert with Charlie Parker and Dizzy Gillespie (heard in two versions, one with Mingus' overdubbed bass), a four-trombone date with J.J. Johnson, Kai Winding, Bennie Green and Willie Dennis, trio sets with pianists Paul Bley, Hazel Scott and the obscure John Dennis, a quintet with trumpeter Thad Jones and Frank Wess on tenor and flute, Miles Davis' "Alone Together" session, a date led by trombonist Jimmy Knepper, a completely unissued 1957 sextet session and, most importantly, a greatly expanded live session with trombonist Eddie Bert and tenor saxophonist George Barrow which found Mingus finally finding himself musically. Many of these performances are now also available in smaller sets, but this attractive box (which has 64 previously unissued tracks among the 169 selections) is the best way to acquire this valuable music. —*Scott Yanow*

Thirteen Pictures: the Charles Mingus Anthology / 1952–1977 / Rhino ♦♦

Even on a loving two-disc anthology, it's impossible to accurately or fully convey the accomplishments of Charles Mingus, arguably jazz's finest modern bassist/composer. *Thirteen Pictures* tries to outline his career achievements by spotlighting his most famous works and also showcase his abilities. But the sequencing is odd, with songs hopping from decade to decade and the older things coming near the end rather than beginning. Still, there are many essential Mingus pieces here, from the sprawling "Cumbia & Jazz Fusion" to the seminal "Goodbye Pork Pie Hat," "Pithecanthropus Erectus," and "Better Git It In Your Soul." The absence of "Fables of Faubus" is puzzling, and the inclusion of only one track featuring Eric Dolphy is bizarre, but for the Mingus newcomer to whom this set was obviously directed, it fulfills its basic goal of introducing a genius' work. —*Ron Wynn*

Jazz Composers Workshop / Oct. 31, 1954–Jan. 30, 1955 / Savoy ♦♦♦

The complex music on this LP finds bassist Charles Mingus looking toward contemporary classical music in some of the rather cool-toned arrangements. It was not until later in 1955 that he found the right combination of influences in which to express himself best, but these slightly earlier performances have their moments. Four of the selections feature tenor saxophonist Teo Macero, pianist Wally Cirillo, drummer Kenny Clarke and Mingus in a quartet while the other five tracks showcase a sextet with Macero, George Barrow on tenor and baritone and clarinetist-/altoist John La Porta. —*Scott Yanow*

Intrusions / Dec. 1954 / Drive Archive ♦♦♦

Bassist Charles Mingus was at a transitional point in his career when he recorded this music (which was formerly out on Everest). He was about ready to chuck his explorations with modern classical music devices and add a strong emotional feel to his music. For these five selections the unique voices of trumpeter Thad Jones, altoist John LaPorta, Teo Macero on tenor and baritone, cellist Jackson Wiley and drummer Clem DeRosa are mixed together with Mingus' bass and occasional piano to create music tied to bop but utilizing some simultaneous soloing and unusual combinations of sound. The results are not quite essential, but they are often fascinating. —*Scott Yanow*

Mingus at the Bohemia / Dec. 23, 1955 / Original Jazz Classics ♦♦♦♦♦

A live performance at the Club Bohemia in New York, this is the first Mingus recording to feature mostly his own compositions. Some are his future standards. Here are his first attempts at future techniques such as combining two songs into one. His bass playing really stands out. —*Michael Katz*

★ **Pithecanthropus Erectus** / Jan. 30, 1956 / Atlantic ♦♦♦♦♦

This Atlantic set has the first truly classic Charles Mingus performance, the lengthy title cut which attempts to depict musically the rise and fall of man. Altoist Jackie McLean, tenor saxophonist J.R. Monterose, pianist Mal Waldron and drummer Willie Jones join the bassist/leader for some stirring music with the humorous "A Foggy Day," (complete with sirens and horns honking like

automobiles), "Profile of Jackie" and "Love Chant" completing the particularly strong program. —*Scott Yanow*

The Clown / Feb. 13, 1957–Mar. 12, 1957 / Atlantic ♦♦♦♦♦

All of Charles Mingus' Atlantic sessions are well worth picking up, including this LP. "Haitian Fight Song" is a classic, "Reincarnation of a Lovebird" is close, "Blue Cee" gives the principals (which include trombonist Jimmy Knepper and Shafi Hadi on alto and tenor) a chance to stretch out, and Jean Shepherd verbally improvises a memorable story on "The Clown." —*Scott Yanow*

Tonight at Noon / Mar. 12, 1957+Nov. 6, 1961 / Atlantic ♦♦♦♦

Mingus Three / Jul. 9, 1957 / FSR ♦♦♦

A rather conventional Charles Mingus recording, this trio set mostly features pianist Hampton Hawes (along with drummer Danny Richmond) performing jazz standards and blues along with Mingus' "Dizzy Moods." The music is high-quality bop as one would expect from the talented pianist, and this LPs contents have been reissued several times since. —*Scott Yanow*

★ **New Tijuana Moods** / Jul. 18, 1957–Aug. 6, 1957 / Bluebird ♦♦♦♦♦

One of the great Charles Mingus recordings, *Tijuana Moods* found the bassist really inspiring his sidemen (trombonist Jimmy Knepper, altoist Shafi Hadi, trumpeter Clarence Shaw, pianist Bill Triglia and drummer Danny Richmond) to play above their heads. The music, inspired by a trip to Mexico, is intense yet quite accessible, and all five selections are memorable. This two-LP set is actually two sets in one, the original program plus a full LP of alternate takes, all longer than the original masters. The music never loses one's interest and is quite innovative for the period. —*Scott Yanow*

East Coasting / Aug. 16, 1957 / Bethlehem ♦♦♦♦

One of Charles Mingus' lesser-known band sessions, this set of five of his originals (plus the standard "Memories of You") features his usual sidemen of the period (trombonist Jimmy Knepper, trumpeter Clarence Shaw, Shafi Hadi on tenor and alto and drummer Danny Richmond) along with pianist Bill Evans. The music stretches the boundaries of bop, is never predictable, and even if this is not one of Mingus' more acclaimed dates, it is well worth acquiring for the playing is quite stimulating. —*Scott Yanow*

Scenes In The City / Oct. 1957 / Affinity ♦♦♦♦

A lesser effort but still with more than its share of memorable moments, this Mingus set (a reissue of a date for Bethlehem) has plenty of fine solos by trombonist Jimmy Knepper and tenor saxophonist Shafi Hadi, appearances by trumpeters Bill Hardman and Clarence Shaw and a narration by Melvin Stewart on the interesting "Scenes in the City," one of the better "jazz and poetry" efforts. —*Scott Yanow*

Jazz Portraits / Jan. 16, 1959 / United Artists ♦♦♦♦

This CD, a straight reissue of *Wonderland*, finds bassist/leader Charles Mingus really pushing altoist John Handy and tenor saxophonist Booker Ervin on four lengthy selections, highlighted by "Nostalgia in Times Square" and "No Private Income Blues." The music is advanced bop that looks toward the upcoming innovations of the avant-garde and is frequently quite exciting. —*Scott Yanow*

★ **Blues and Roots** / Feb. 4, 1959 / Atlantic ♦♦♦♦♦

One of Charles Mingus' finest studio albums, this date finds the bassist utilizing a nonet (including altoists Jackie McLean and John Handy, Booker Ervin on tenor, baritonist Pepper Adams and the trombones of Jimmy Knepper and Willie Dennis) on six diverse but consistently stimulating originals. Highlights including "Wednesday Night Prayer Meeting," "Cryin' Blues," "E's Flat Ah's Flat Too" and especially "Moanin'." Although "My Jelly Roll Soul" does not really work, the other numbers find Mingus successfully looking both backwards (with group improvising, stop-time breaks and church-like harmonies) and forward (with advanced improvisations and a wider use of emotions than was being utilized in bop). —*Scott Yanow*

★ **Mingus Ah Um** / May 5, 1959–May 12, 1959 / Columbia ♦♦♦♦♦

This LP from 1959 is one of Charles Mingus' classics, highlighted by the original versions of "Better Git It in Your Soul," "Goodbye Pork Pie Hat," "Boogie Stop Shuffle" and "Fables of Faubus." Well deserving of reissue on CD, such top-notch musicians as altoist John Handy, tenors Booker Ervin and Shafi Hadi, trombonists Jimmy Knepper and Willie Dennis, pianist Roland Hanna and drummer Danny Richmond gave bassist Mingus one of his strongest units. —*Scott Yanow*

Complete 1959 CBS Charles Mingus Sessions / May 5, 1959–Nov. 13, 1959 / Mosaic ✦✦✦✦✦
In 1959 Charles Mingus recorded two tightly edited LPs for Columbia titled *Mingus Ah Um* and *Mingus Dynasty*. Both of those albums are recommended in their original form as is this limited edition four-LP set which restores solos originally cut out and adds numerous alternate takes to these fascinating sessions. Such players as altoist John Handy, tenor saxophonists Booker Ervin and Shafi Hadi, trombonists Jimmy Knepper and Willie Dennis and trumpeters Richard Williams and Don Ellis and pianist Roland Hanna and Horace Parlan are heard on this deluxe set which is highlighted by the original versions of "Better Git It in Your Soul,," "Fables of Faubus,," "Boogie Stop Shuffle," "Goodbye Pork Pie Hat," and "Song with Orange." —*Scott Yanow*

Mingus Dynasty / Nov. 1, 1959–Nov. 13, 1959 / Columbia ✦✦✦✦✦
This CD is a straight reissue of the original LP and finds bassist Charles Mingus leading two overlapping but different nine and ten piece groups. Much of the music was written for soundtracks of the time, but they easily stand out on their own with fine solos from trombonist Jimmy Knepper, Booker Ervin on tenor, altoist John Handy and pianist Roland Hanna uplifting such songs as "Slop," "Song with Orange," "Far Wells, Mill Valley" and two Duke Ellington-associated numbers. The music can also be heard in unedited form (with many solos added back in) on a Mosaic box set. —*Scott Yanow*

Mingus Revisited / May 24, 1960+May 25, 1960 / EmArcy ✦✦✦✦
This is an LP reissue of a set that was originally titled *Pre Bird* because it features some of the advanced originals that Charles Mingus wrote prior to hearing Charlie Parker. The bassist leads an undisciplined but colorful 25-piece orchestra on three titles including an Eric Dolphy feature on "Bemonable Lady" while the other five tracks are by a ten-piece (including two pianos) band; Lorraine Cousins sings "Eclipse" and "Weird Nightmare." It's an interesting set of typically unconventional music by Mingus. —*Scott Yanow*

★ **Mingus at Antibes** / Jul. 13, 1960 / Atlantic ✦✦✦✦✦
During 1960 bassist Charles Mingus led one of his finest bands, a pianoless quartet with Eric Dolphy (on alto, flute and bass clarinet), trumpeter Ted Curson and drummer Danny Richmond. For this live concert, the band is augmented by the great tenor Booker Ervin for some stirring music. All of the music is memorable: "Wednesday Night Prayer Meeting," "Prayer for Passive Resistance," "What Love," "Folk Forms I." and "Better Git It in Your Soul." The immortal pianist Bud Powell sits in on a fine version of "I'll Remember April," and Dolphy and Ervin in particular generate a great deal of heat during some of their solos. —*Scott Yanow*

Charles Mingus Presents Charles Mingus / Oct. 20, 1960 / Candid ✦✦✦✦✦
This quartet date is probably among the very finest jazz records ever made. Dolphy and Curson make a great front line, and Mingus and Richmond seem to share one mind between them. The absence of a piano keeps everyone on their toes. All first takes recorded in one afternoon, the session is presented as if it were a nightclub set of the period, complete with Mingus' spoken introduction. —*Stuart Kremsky*

★ **Complete Candid Recordings** / Oct. 20, 1960–Nov. 11, 1960 / Mosaic ✦✦✦✦✦
Bassist/leader Charles Mingus cut some of his most exciting and rewarding recordings for Candid in 1960, and this superb four-LP set (which unfortunately is a limited edition) contains all of the music except for a couple of alternate takes that showed up later on. Five selections feature the brilliant pianoless quartet of Eric Dolphy (on alto, bass clarinet and flute), trumpeter Ted Curson, Mingus and drummer Dannie Richmond, and these are highlighted by the bass clarinet-bass conversation on "What Love" and the interplay between the four musicians on the very memorable "Folk Forms No. 1." Other musicians are added to six other selections (including the 19-minute jam "MDM"), and five other numbers feature trumpeter Roy Eldridge who is teamed with altoist Dolphy on three of the songs; those pieces originally appeared on The Newport Rebels LP. This is a highly recommended set that promises to be hard to find in the future. —*Scott Yanow*

Mysterious Blues / Oct. 20, 1960–Nov. 11, 1960 / Candid ✦✦✦✦
Although a Mosaic box set claims to have all of Charles Mingus'

Candid recordings, this CD, in addition to four duplications from the box, contains three alternate takes not included elsewhere: "Body and Soul" (featuring trumpeter Roy Eldridge and altoist Eric Dolphy), the Dannie Richmond drum solo "Melody from the Drums" and a septet runthrough on "Reincarnation of a Love Bird." A fine introduction into the music of Charles Mingus, this set still cannot compare to the Mosaic box which has the Mingus' pianoless quartet with Dolphy, Richmond and trumpeter Ted Curson, but completists will have to acquire both releases. —*Scott Yanow*

★ **Oh Yeah** / Nov. 6, 1961 / Atlantic ✦✦✦✦✦
One of the great Charles Mingus LPs, this Atlantic release (which finds Mingus sticking exclusively to piano and vocal shouts throughout) not only features tenor saxophonist Booker Ervin, trombonist Jimmy Knepper, bassist Doug Watkins and drummer Dannie Richmond but the amazing Rahsaan Roland Kirk on tenor, manzello, stritch, flute and siren. The music is quite emotional and passionate with "Hog Callin' Blues," "Wham Bam Thank You Ma'am" and the explosive "Ecclusiastics" being particularly memorable. —*Scott Yanow*

Town Hall Concert / Oct. 12, 1962 / United Artists ✦
What a mess. Charles Mingus' Town Hall concert in 1962 (which was to utilize a large band) found him totally unprepared, with writers literally copying out parts on tables during the performance itself. Mingus' volatile personality did not help matters at all, and while the band was jamming the final number, stagehands closed the curtain. Just as well. This LP seeks to preserve some of the highlights of this fiasco, but there is not much of value here other than glimpses of Mingus' mammoth work, "Epitaph." —*Scott Yanow*

Complete Town Hall Concert / Oct. 12, 1962 / Bllue Note ✦✦✦
Charles Mingus' Town Hall Concert has long been considered a famous fiasco, and the original United Artists LP (which contained just 36 minutes of music and did not bother identifying the personnel) made matters worse. But this Blue Note CD (released in 1994) does its best to clean up the mess. It contains over a half-hour of previously unreleased music and programs the selections largely in the same order as the concert. There are still confusing moments, inconclusive performances and songs cut off prematurely; Mingus was not in a good temper that day. A highlight among the "new" material is an Eric Dolphy alto solo on the second version of "Epitaph." Blue Note is to be congratulated for doing what they could with what they had, but there are still at least a couple dozen Mingus recordings that would be recommended before this one. —*Scott Yanow*

The Black Saint and the Sinner Lady / Jan. 20, 1963 / Impulse ✦✦✦✦✦
One of Charles Mingus' most successful longer suites, the six-part "Black Saint and the Sinner Lady" is full of surprising moments with the 11-piece band exploring a wide variety of moods and colors. Of particular note are Quentin Jackson's wa-wa trombone (which lets Mingus hint strongly at Duke Ellington) and Charlie Mariano's passionate alto. —*Scott Yanow*

Mingus, Mingus, Mingus, Mingus, Mingus / Jan. 20, 1963+Sep. 20, 1963 / Impulse ✦✦✦✦✦
This CD features two separate recording sessions with such top players as trumpeter Richard Williams, trombonists Quentin Jackson and Britt Woodman, Dick Hafer and Booker Ervin on tenors, the many reeds of Eric Dolphy and Jerome Richardson, altoist Charles Mariano and pianist Jaki Byard. Of the seven selections (all of which are memorable), highpoints include "Mood Indigo," the fiery "Hora Decubitus" and the definitive version of "Better Get Hit in Yo' Soul." —*Scott Yanow*

Mingus Plays Piano / Jul. 30, 1963 / Mobile Fidelity ✦✦✦✦
Bassist Charles Mingus would never qualify as a virtuoso on the piano, but his technique was reasonably impressive, and his imagination quite brilliant. This unique solo piano CD (a reissue of a date for Impulse) has a few standards ("Body and Soul," "Memories of You" and "I'm Getting Sentimental over You") along with some freely improvised originals, most of which are quite fascinating to hear, as if one were listening to Mingus think aloud. —*Scott Yanow*

Concertgebouw Amsterdam, Vol. 1 / Apr. 10, 1964 / Ulysse Musique ✦✦✦✦
Charles Mingus' 1964 sextet was one of his most exciting bands, featuring Eric Dolphy (on alto, bass clarinet and flute) at his very

best (just months before his premature death) along with tenor saxophonist Clifford Jordan, trumpeter Johnny Coles, the remarkably versatile pianist Jaki Byard, drummer Dannie Richmond and the bassist/leader. This first of two CDs taken from early in the band's European tour features lengthy versions of "Ow" (which was also called "Parkeriana" by Mingus), "So Long Eric" and "Orange Was the Color of Her Dress Then Blue Silk." Fascinating music; all of this classic group's live recordings are well worth searching for. —*Scott Yanow*

Concertgebouw Amsterdam, Vol. 2 / Apr. 10, 1964 / Ulysse Musique ✦✦✦✦
The second of two CDs taken from an Amsterdam concert features Charles Mingus' remarkable 1964 sextet (which included Eric Dolphy, Clifford Jordan, Jaki Byard and Johnny Coles) on a half-hour version of "Fables of Faubus," a nearly 23-minute rendition of "Meditation on a Pair of Wire Cutters" and a more concise bass feature on "Sophisticated Lady." The music is quite explorative, episodic, unpredictable and exciting. —*Scott Yanow*

Live in Oslo / Apr. 13, 1964 / Jazz Up ✦✦✦✦
It is very fortunate that Charles Mingus' 1964 sextet was so extensively recorded during its European tour for the great Eric Dolphy (who would pass away only a few months later) rarely sounded better, and this was one of the strongest groups the volatile bassist ever led. This particular CD was taken from a television broadcast that is miraculously now also available on video. The very talented band really digs into "Fables of Faubus" and "Orange Was the Color of Her Dress," and after Mingus stops "Ow" prematurely, the group swings hard on "Take the 'A' Train." —*Scott Yanow*

Astral Weeks / Apr. 14, 1964 / Moon ✦✦✦✦
The Charles Mingus sextet of 1964 was arguably the bassist's finest group, featuring the remarkable Eric Dolphy on alto, bass clarinet and flute, tenor saxophonist Clifford Jordan, trumpeter Johnny Coles, pianist Jaki Byard, drummer Dannie Richmond and the bassist/leader. Their European tour was well documented with many radio broadcasts later released on CD. This particular set has long versions of "Meditations on Integration" and "Fables of Faubus," although the latter is nearly 34 minutes long, its episodic and unpredictable nature and colorful solos hold one's interest throughout. All of the group's recordings are quite exciting, and this Italian import is a good place to start in exploring this important band's innovative music. —*Scott Yanow*

★ **The Great Concert of Charles Mingus** / Apr. 17, 1964–Apr. 19, 1964 / Prestige ✦✦✦✦✦
This three-LP set is the finest recording by one of Charles Mingus' greatest bands, his sextet with Eric Dolphy (on alto, bass clarinet and flute), tenor saxophonist Clifford Jordan, trumpeter Johnny Coles, pianist Jaki Byard and drummer Dannie Richmond. Taken from their somewhat tumultuous but very musical tour of Europe, most of these rather lengthy workouts actually just feature a quintet because Coles took sick (he is only heard on "So Long Eric" which here is mistitled "Goodbye Pork Pie Hat"), but the playing is at such a high level that the trumpeter is not really missed. "Orange Was the Color of Her Dress" is given definitive treatment, and the nearly 29-minute "Fables of Faubus" and Mingus' relatively brief feature on "Sophisticated Lady" are impressive, but it is the passionate "Meditations on Integration" (an utterly fascinating performance) and "Parkeriana" (a tribute to Charlie Parker that features some stride piano from Byard and what may very well have been Eric Dolphy's greatest alto solo) that make this gem truly essential in all jazz collections. —*Scott Yanow*

Mingus in Europe / Apr. 26, 1964 / Enja ✦✦✦✦
This CD reissues three selections originally on the LP *Mingus in Europe, Vol. 2* ("Orange Was the Color of Her Dress Then Blue Silk," "Sophisticated Lady" and "AT-FW-YOU") and also includes two performances ("Peggy's Blue Sky Light" and the nearly 23-minute "So Long Eric") that do not seem to have been issued previously. The 1964 Charles Mingus Quintet (trumpeter Johnny Coles had departed a few days earlier due to illness) teamed together the unique multi-instrumentalist Eric Dolphy, tenor saxophonist Clifford Jordan, pianist Jaki Byard, drummer Dannie Richmond and the bassist/leader in one of the great bands of the 1960s. There are many recordings currently available from their European tour, and all are worth acquiring including this excellent Enja set (at least by Mingus fans not already owning *Vol. 2*). —*Scott Yanow*

In Europe, Vol. 1 / Apr. 26, 1964 / Enja ✦✦✦
A rare legitimate issue from the much-bootlegged 1964 tour of

Europe, Enja released this (and *Volume 2*) with the full cooperation of his widow, Sue Mingus. Besides a lengthy version of the perennial Mingus favorite, "Fables of Faubus" (unfortunately split into two parts on the LP release), this set features a real treat in a seven-minute Mingus/Dolphy (on flute) duet on the changes to "I Can't Get Started." —*Stuart Kremsky*

Right Now: Live at the Jazz Workshop / Jun. 2, 1964–Jun. 3, 1964 / Original Jazz Classics ✦✦✦✦
Soon after Charles Mingus finished touring Europe with his band (the unit that featured Eric Dolphy), he recorded this CD, performed live at The Jazz Workshop in San Francisco. With tenor saxophonist Clifford Jordan and drummer Danny Richmond still in the group but Jane Getz replacing pianist Jaki Byard and altoist John Handy filling in for Dolphy on one song, the band performs excellent versions of "Meditations on Integration" and "New Fables," both of which are over 23 minutes long. Although not up to the passionate level of the Mingus-Dolphy Quintet, this underrated unit holds its own. —*Scott Yanow*

Mingus at Monterey / Sep. 20, 1964 / VDJ ✦✦✦✦✦
One of the highpoints of Charles Mingus' career was his appearance at the 1964 Monterey Jazz Festival. This long out-of-print double LP contains the entire set: a lengthy Duke Ellington medley, "Orange Was the Color of Her Dress Then Blue Silk" and a stunning version of "Meditations on Integration" as performed by a 12-piece group featuring such players as altoist Charles McPherson, John Handy (on tenor), trumpeter Lonnie Hillyer and pianist Jaki Byard. This music is well deserving of eventual reissue on CD for it showcases the bassist/composer/bandleader at the peak of his powers. —*Scott Yanow*

Music Written For Monterey, 1965 / Sep. 25, 1965 / JWS ✦✦✦
Following his big success at the 1964 Monterey Jazz Festival, Charles Mingus' appearance the following year was a major disappointment; he walked off after a half-hour when he sensed that his time slot was anticlimactic and that the audience was not paying attention. A week later he performed the full program he had originally planned for Monterey at UCLA, and this two-LP set (released privately by his East Coasting Records) preserves that concert. Most of the originals use a nine-piece group although Mingus at one point expels many of the musicians because he felt they had not learned his music well enough; that verbal confrontation is included on the record. There are some strong moments on this set (which often features trumpeter Lonnie Hillyer and altoist Charles McPherson), but this is an erratic if colorful effort. —*Scott Yanow*

Reincarnation of a Lovebird / Nov. 30, 1970–Nov. 31, 1970 / Prestige ✦✦✦✦
This excellent two-LP set features Charles Mingus and his 1970 sextet (with trumpeter Eddie Preston, altoist Charles McPherson, tenor saxophonist Bobby Jones, pianist Jaki Byard and drummer Dannie Richmond) stretching out on three of the bassist/leader's standards along with his more recent "Love Is a Dangerous Necessity," a version of "I Left My Heart in San Francisco" and a 17-minute version of "Blue Bird" (a Charlie Parker blues). Practically Mingus' only studio recordings of 1965–71, these performances find the great bassist in fine form, pushing his sidemen to make original statements on the distinctive originals. —*Scott Yanow*

With Orchestra / Jan. 14, 1971 / Denon ✦✦
This obscure session found bassist Charles Mingus along with two of his sidemen (tenor saxophonist Bobby Jones and trumpeter Eddie Preston) performing three of the bassist's compositions in Japan with Toshiyuki Miyama and His New Herd, a fine big band. Little all that memorable occurs and there is only around 32 minutes of music so this CD is not all that essential, but Mingus completists will want to pick up this rarity. —*Scott Yanow*

Let My Children Hear Music / Sep. 23, 1971–Nov. 18, 1971 / Columbia ✦✦✦
The CD reissue of the original LP adds one selection ("Taurus in the Arena of Life") to the program of original music. Mingus' unique compositions (mostly recent although one was written back in 1939) receive sympathetic treatment by a partly unidentified large orchestra and are full of interesting textures, sound explorations and surprises. It makes for a stimulating listen. —*Scott Yanow*

Charles Mingus And Friends In Concert / Feb. 4, 1972 / Columbia ✦✦✦
Most of Charles Mingus' larger-group recordings, particularly in

the later part of his career, tended to be unruly and somewhat undisciplined. This two-LP set, which celebrated Mingus' return to jazz after six years of little activity, allowed such great jazzmen as baritonist Gerry Mulligan, tenor saxophonist Gene Ammons, altoist Lee Konitz, pianist Randy Weston, James Moody (heard on flute) and a variety of Mingus regulars a chance to play with the great bassist; even fellow bassist Milt Hinton and Bill Cosby (taking a humorous scat vocal) join in. Most of the music is overly loose, but the overcrowded "E's Flat, Ah's Flat Too" and particularly the "Little Royal Suite" are memorable. The "Little Royal Suite," in addition to Ammons, Konitz, Mulligan, Charles McPherson and Bobby Jones, features an 18-year old Jon Faddis (who was sitting in for an ailing Roy Eldridge) stealing the show. —*Scott Yanow*

Mingus Moves / 1973 / Atlantic ✦✦✦✦
On this Atlantic LP, Charles Mingus introduced his new group which at the time included trumpeter Ronald Hampton, tenor saxophonist George Adams, pianist Don Pullen and his longtime drummer Dannie Richmond. Together this excellent quintet performed seven recent compositions including one ("Moves") that features the vocals of Honey Gordon and Doug Hammond. Only three of the pieces are by Mingus, but all of the music is greatly influenced by his searching and unpredictable style. This out-of-print LP is worth searching for. —*Scott Yanow*

Mingus at Carnegie Hall / Jan. 19, 1974 / Atlantic ✦✦✦✦✦
Although Charles Mingus is the leader on this date, it is actually a jam session featuring an all-star cast (the amazing Rahsaan Roland Kirk, trumpeter Jon Faddis, John Handy on alto and tenor, altoist Charles McPherson, tenor saxophonist George Adams, baritonist Hamiet Bluiett, pianist Don Pullen, drummer Dannie Richmond and the bassist-leader) playing rather long versions of "C Jam Blues" and "Perdido." Of the many soloists, Handy shows off his high note alto on "Perdido," and Faddis (who was then 20) plays some of his favorite Dizzy Gillespie licks, but Rahsaan Roland Kirk (who at one point imitates George Adams) cuts everyone. This CD is a straight reissue of the original LP and is often quite exciting. —*Scott Yanow*

Changes One / Dec. 27, 1974–Dec. 30, 1974 / Atlantic ✦✦✦✦✦
Charles Mingus' finest recordings of his later period are *Changes One* and *Changes Two,* two Atlantic LPs that have been reissued on CD by Rhino. The first volume features four stimulating Mingus originals ("Remember Rockefeller at Attica," "Sue's Changes," "Devil Blues" and "Duke Ellington's Sound of Love") performed by a particularly talented quintet (tenor saxophonist George Adams who also sings "Devil Blues," trumpeter Jack Walrath, pianist Don Pullen, drummer Dannie Richmond and the leader/bassist). The band has the adventurous spirit and chance-taking approach of Charles Mingus' best groups, making this an easily recommended example of the great bandleader's music. —*Scott Yanow*

Changes Two / Dec. 27, 1974–Dec. 30, 1974 / Atlantic ✦✦✦✦✦
Along with *Changes One* (both Atlantic LPs have been reissued on CD by Rhino), this set is one of Charles Mingus' most rewarding of his later period. Mingus' band (trumpeter Jack Walrath, tenor saxophonist George Adams, pianist Don Pullen and drummer Dannie Richmond) was particularly strong. This set is highlighted by a 17-minute version of "Orange Was the Color of Her Dress," then "Silk Blue," Sy Johnson's "For Harry Carney" and Jackie Paris' vocal on "Duke Ellington's Sound of Love." —*Scott Yanow*

Cumbia and Jazz Fusion / Mar. 31, 1976–Mar. 10, 1977 / Atlantic ✦✦✦✦
As Charles Mingus' career (and life) moved into its final phase, his recordings exclusively featured large (and often potentially unruly) ensembles. This CD, which contains two rather long performances originally recorded as soundtracks for films, is better than most of what followed. "Cumbia & Jazz Fusion" has a large percussion section and quite a few woodwinds along with trumpeter Jack Walrath, tenor saxophonist Ricky Ford and trombonist Jimmy Knepper while "Music for 'Todo Modo'" adds five horns to Mingus' Quintet. The music is episodic but generally holds its own away from the film. —*Scott Yanow*

Three or Four Shades of Blues / Mar. 9, 1977 / Atlantic ✦✦✦
During Charles Mingus' last year of recording, it seemed that much of the jazz world wanted to play with the bassist. This particular LP includes such major stylists as tenor saxophonists

George Coleman and Ricky Ford, trumpeter Jack Walrath, guitarists Philip Catherine, John Scofield and Larry Coryell, pianist Jimmy Rowles and even bassists George Mraz and Ron Carter. The music, two remakes and three newer pieces, is occasionally exciting but not as coherent and purposeful as Mingus' best work, which is understandable because the guests were not as familiar with the great bassist's unique music as his regular group. It still makes for some interesting listening though. —*Scott Yanow*

Lionel Hampton Presents Music of Charles Mingus / Nov. 6, 1977 / Who's Who In Jazz ✦✦✦
Charles Mingus' final recording as a player (before serious illness struck) is a fun session in which his last quintet (with trumpeter Jack Walrath, tenor saxophonist Ricky Ford, pianist Bob Nelums and drummer Dannie Richmond) is joined by vibraphonist Lionel Hampton, baritonist Gerry Mulligan, trumpeter Woody Shaw, Paul Jeffrey (who arranged the music) on tenor and the French horn of Peter Matt. A bit of a jam session, this group performs seven of Mingus' compositions including versions of such songs as "Peggy's Blue Skylight," "Fables of Faubus" and "Duke Ellington's Sound of Love." Nothing that unusual occurs, but good spirits dominate this final effort. —*Scott Yanow*

Something Like a Bird / Jan. 18, 1978–Jan. 23, 1978 / Atlantic ✦✦✦
Although confined to a wheelchair and less than a year from his death, Charles Mingus supervised the recording sessions that resulted in this LP and its companion *Me Myself An Eye.* The music on this set utilizes a 27-piece band (including 11 saxophones and four guitars) on the 31-minute "Something like a Bird" and a smaller 21-piece orchestra (only nine saxes and three guitars) for "Farewell Farwell." It seems that everyone wanted to play with (or at least for) Mingus during his last few years, and such musicians as Lee Konitz, Charles McPherson, George Coleman, Mike Brecker, Ricky Ford, Pepper Adams, Randy Brecker, Jack Walrath, Slide Hampton, Jimmy Knepper, Larry Coryell and bassists Eddie Gomez and George Mraz help out on this spirited if overcrowded music. It's not essential but certainly colorful. —*Scott Yanow*

Me, Myself an Eye / Jan. 19, 1978–Jan. 23, 1978 / Atlantic ✦✦✦
The companion to *Something like a Bird,* this LP also finds Charles Mingus (who was confined to a wheelchair and only a year away from his death) supervising large orchestras (in this case 23 and 25 pieces) on some of his compositions. "Devil Woman," "Wednesday Night Prayer Meeting" and "Carolyn 'Keki' Mingus" are fairly concise, but "Three Worlds of Drums" is over a half-hour long and has its rambling sections. The music is colorful and spirited but not as memorable as one might hope. Still, these loose sessions have their moments. —*Scott Yanow*

Epitaph / 1990 / Columbia ✦✦✦
This double CD is a posthumous recording of a long multisectioned work by Charles Mingus that was only hinted at during his ill-fated Town Hall Concert of 1962. Gunther Schuller conducted and reconstructed this massive work which utilizes 30 musicians including many all-stars; the trumpet section alone is composed of Wynton Marsalis, Jack Walrath, Randy Brecker, Lew Soloff, Joe Wilder and Snooky Young. "Epitaph" has some strong moments (including sections in which the band performs "Better Get It in Your Soul," "Monk, Bunk & Vice Versa," "Peggy's Blue Skylight," "Wolverine Blues" and "Freedom"), but on a whole the music is somewhat unsatisfying and inconclusive. Still, there are enough moments of interest to make this set recommended even if the presence of Mingus is missed. —*Scott Yanow*

Passions of a Man (Anthology of His Atlantic Recordings) / Atlantic ✦✦✦
A generous sampling of Mingus material is drawn from his two periods of residency at Atlantic. The earlier work was done during the 1950s; the last quarter of this set is drawn from 1974–1977. Virtually all of the '50s work is important, and this compilation should make you want to run out and find the five albums this is taken from (*Tonight at Noon, Pithecanthropus Erectus, Blues and Roots, Oh Yeah!* and *The Clown*). The '70s performances are not as crucial, though there is that marvelous pair of *Changes One and Two.* It's a valuable introduction, but don't stop here. —*Stuart Kremsky*

Bob Mintzer

b. Jan. 27, 1953, New Rochelle, NY
Tenor Saxophone, Bass Clarinet / Post-Bop
A versatile soloist influenced by Michael Brecker on tenor, Bob Mintzer gained experience playing with Deodato, Tito Puente

(1974), Buddy Rich, Hubert Laws and the Thad Jones-Mel Lewis Orchestra (1977). In addition to leading his own bands starting in 1978, Mintzer worked with Jaco Pastorius, Mike Mainieri, Louie Bellson, Bob Moses and the American Saxophone Quartet. He has guested with several Philharmonic Orchestras and led a fine big band in New York since the mid-'80s. Mintzer, a member of the Yellowjackets since 1991 (where his bass clarinet in particular adds a great deal of color to the group), has recorded regularly for DMP for the past decade. —*Scott Yanow*

Incredible Journey / Feb. 1985–Apr. 1985 / DMP ✦✦✦

Camouflage / Jun. 1986 / DMP ✦✦✦✦
Good '86 big band set led by tenor saxophonist and bass clarinetist Bob Mintzer, a fine player and arranger. These recordings are in a conventional format, with polished ensemble sections and good, occasionally great solos. They are well produced and mastered, but the material and style tend to be conservative. —*Ron Wynn*

● **Spectrum** / Jan. 1988 / DMP ✦✦✦✦✦
Included is an all-star lineup of R. Brecker, P. Erstine, D. Grolnick, B. Malach, L. Gaines, and 14 other players. This is big-band jazz at its finest. The recording was made live to two-track digital, and the music, exceptional from start to finish, deserves it. —*Paul Kohler*

Urban Contours / Feb. 24, 1989–Mar. 5, 1989 / DMP ✦✦✦✦
This set mixes small and big-band sessions. —*Ron Wynn*

Art of the Big Band / Sep. 22, 1990–Sep. 23, 1990 / DMP ✦✦✦
A great technical recording, with good sidemen, but unadventurous music. —*Ron Wynn*

I Remember Jaco / Mar. 6, 1991–Mar. 7, 1991 / Novus ✦✦✦✦
Nice tribute to the late bassist by tenor saxophonist and bass clarinetist Bob Mintzer. Instead of his usual big band, Mintzer heads a small combo, which provides space for both himself and other soloists, like pianist Joey Calderazzo. —*Ron Wynn*

Departure / Sep. 11, 1991–Sep. 17, 1991 / DMP ✦✦✦✦

One Music / 1991 / DMP ✦✦✦✦✦
This saxophonist's best small-group work, with fellow Yellow Jackets. The best cuts are the title and "Look Around." Ventures funky and creative into neo-bop modes. —*Michael G. Nastos*

Only In New York / Nov. 20, 1993–Nov. 21, 1993 / DMP ✦✦✦

Billy Mitchell

b. Nov. 3, 1926, Kansas City, MO
Tenor Saxophone / Hard Bop
A hard-swinging tenor saxophonist (who is no relation to the crossover keyboardist of the same name), Billy Mitchell made his mark in several settings. He worked in Detroit with Nat Towles band, and in the late '40s he played with Lucky Millinder's Orchestra in New York. In 1949 Mitchell recorded with Milt Jackson, worked in the big bands of Milt Buckner and Gil Fuller and toured with Woody Herman's Second Herd for two months. He spent the first half of the 1950s playing locally in Detroit and then was with Dizzy Gillespie's big band during 1956–57, taking a memorable solo on "Cool Breeze" at the 1957 Newport Jazz Festival. Mitchell was with Count Basie's Orchestra during 1957–61 and in the early '60s led a sextet with Al Grey that featured a young Bobby Hutcherson. He played again with Basie during 1966–67, worked as an educator and recorded frequently on Xanadu in the late '70s but has been less prominent since then. Billy Mitchell cut sessions as a leader for Dee Gee, Jubilee, Smash, Catalyst and Xanadu. —*Scott Yanow*

Now's the Time / 1976 / Catalyst ✦✦✦✦

● **Colossus of Detroit** / Apr. 18, 1978 / Xanadu ✦✦✦✦✦
Veteran tenor saxophonist Billy Mitchell could not ask for a better rhythm section than he has here (pianist Barry Jones, bassist Sam Jones and drummer Walter Bolden). Mitchell was careful to pick out a superior program of songs highlighted by a few classic ballads (including "Unforgettable" which in 1978 had been largely forgotten) and Joe Henderson's "Recordame." The results are quite boppish and one of Mitchell's better recordings of the past 20 years. —*Scott Yanow*

Night Flight to Dakar / Mar. 14, 1980–Mar. 19, 1980 / Xanadu ✦✦✦✦

De Lawd's Blues / Jun. 26, 1980 / Xanadu ✦✦✦✦
Rare appearance from expatriate trumpeter Benny Bailey and declarative tenor sax by Mitchell. —*Ron Wynn*

Blue Mitchell (Richard Allen Mitchell)

b. Mar. 13, 1930, Miami, FL, d. May 21, 1979, Los Angeles, CA
Trumpet / Hard Bop
A wonderful hard bop, blues and ballad player, Blue Mitchell was the kind of hard working, consistent player who gets overlooked because he's not a star or innovator. Mitchell's lyrical sound and luminous timbre were superbly presented in some fine groups and as a leader in his own combos. He began playing trumpet in high school, acquiring both a good reputation and his nickname. Mitchell toured with the R&B bands of Paul Williams, Earl Bostic and Chuck Willis in the early '50s. He returned to his Miami hometown off the road in the late '50s, and Cannonball Adderley heard him playing at a club. Adderley took Mitchell with him to New York, and they recorded for Riverside in 1958. Mitchell joined Horace Silver's quintet that same year and remained until 1964, participating in some invigorating dates. When Silver disbanded the ensemble, its members stayed together. The original band was Mitchell, Junior Cook, Gene Taylor and Roy Brooks. Later Chick Corea and Al Foster replaced Taylor and Brooks, with Mitchell and Cook dividing leadership duties. Later Harold Mabern and Billy Higgins replaced Corea and Foster. Mitchell became a prolific pop and soul session player in the late '60s, recording instrumental pop LPs, touring with Ray Charles and John Mayall. During the mid-'70s, Mitchell did various dates in Los Angeles, while often serving as principal soloist for Tony Bennett and Lena Horne. He played in the big bands of Louis Bellson, Bill Holman and Bill Berry and worked in several bebop bands, including a quintet with Richie Kamauca. Mitchell was also in a quintet with Harold Land, from 1975 until 1978, while cutting more instrumental pop and disco albums in the late '70s. His career was cut short by his death of cancer at 49. —*Ron Wynn*

★ **Big Six** / Jul. 2, 1958–Jul. 3, 1958 / Original Jazz Classics ✦✦✦✦✦
Trumpeter Blue Mitchell was a virtual unknown when he recorded this Riverside album, his first as a leader. Now reissued on CD in the *OJC* series, Mitchell is heard in excellent form in an all-star sextet with trombonist Curtis Fuller, tenor-great Johnny Griffin, pianist Wynton Kelly, bassist Wilbur Ware and drummer Philly Joe Jones. In addition to some group originals, obscurities and the standard "There Will Never Be Another You," the group also plays the earliest recorded version of Benny Golson's "Blues March," predating Art Blakey's famous recording. —*Scott Yanow*

Out of the Blue / Jan. 1959 / Original Jazz Classics ✦✦✦✦✦
This early recording by Blue Mitchell finds the distinctive trumpeter in excellent form in a quintet also featuring tenor-saxophonist Benny Golson (who contributed "Blues on My Mind"), either Wynton Kelly or Cedar Walton on piano, Paul Chambers or Sam Jones on bass and drummer Art Blakey. The consistently swinging repertoire includes a surprisingly effective version of "When the Saints Go Marching In." "Studio B," recorded in the same period, but formerly available only in a sampler, has been added to the program. It's an easily enjoyable date of high-quality hard bop. —*Scott Yanow*

Blue Soul / Sep. 1959 / Original Jazz Classics ✦✦✦✦✦
This CD reissue brings back one of trumpeter Blue Mitchell's better sessions from his early period, his third recording as a leader for Riverside. Six of the selections also feature trombonist Curtis Fuller (in excellent form) and the tenor of Jimmy Heath in a sextet with pianist Wynton Kelly, bassist Sam Jones and drummer Philly Joe Jones; the arrangements were provided by Heath and Benny Golson. The other three numbers are more informal and showcase Mitchell in a quartet with Kelly and the two Joneses. Excellent hard bop with the repertoire consisting of "The Way You Look Tonight," "Polka Dots and Moonbeams," "Nica's Dream" and two originals apiece from Golson, Heath and Mitchell. —*Scott Yanow*

Blue's Moods / Aug. 24, 1960–Aug. 25, 1960 / Original Jazz Classics ✦✦✦✦
Smooth 1060 session that blends romantic pieces, soul-jazz and mainstream. —*Ron Wynn*

Smooth As the Wind / Dec. 27, 1960–Mar. 30, 1961 / Riverside ✦✦✦

A Sure Thing / Mar. 7, 1962–Mar. 28, 1962 / Original Jazz Classics ✦✦✦✦
Trumpeter Blue Mitchell is well featured on this CD reissue with a nonet arranged by Jimmy Heath. The music is straight-ahead but, thanks to Heath's arrangements, sometimes unpredictable.

Best is Mitchell's solo on "I Can't Get Started," "Hootie's Blues" and a quintet workout (with Heath, pianist Wynton Kelly bassist Sam Jones and drummer Albert "Tootie" Heath) on "Gone with the Wind." — *Scott Yanow*

Cup Bearers / Apr. 11, 1963 / Original Jazz Classics ✦✦✦✦✦
Trumpeter Blue Mitchell and four-fifths of the Horace Silver Quintet (with Cedar Walton in Silver's place) perform a variety of superior songs on this CD reissue including Walton's "Turquoise," Tom McIntosh's "Cup Bearers," Thad Jones' "Tiger Lily" and a couple of standards. The music swings hard, mostly avoids sounding like a Horace Silver group, and has particularly strong solos from Mitchell, tenor saxophonist Junior Cook and Walton; excellent hard bop. — *Scott Yanow*

Step Lightly / Aug. 13, 1963 / Blue Note ✦✦✦✦

★ **The Thing to Do** / Jul. 30, 1964 / Blue Note ✦✦✦✦✦
With Chick Corea, Jr. Cook (ts) and Al Foster (d). Recommended for jazz/trumpet lovers. — *Michael G. Nastos*

Down with It / Jul. 14, 1965 / Blue Note ✦✦✦✦
One of Mitchell's least-recognized sessions, this has some fervent trumpet pieces, plus nice piano from a then still-emerging Chick Corea. — *Ron Wynn*

Bring It on Home to Me / Jan. 6, 1966 / Blue Note ✦✦✦✦

Boss Horn / Nov. 17, 1966 / Blue Note ✦✦✦✦

Heads Up / Nov. 17, 1967 / Blue Note ✦✦✦

Collision in Black / Sep. 11, 1968–Sep. 12, 1968 / Blue Note ✦✦✦

Bantu Village / May 22, 1969–May 23, 1969 / Blue Note ✦✦✦

Blue's Blues / 1972–1974 / Mainstream ✦✦✦
A fine mainstream/bop date that includes some arresting Mitchell trumpet work on ballads. — *Ron Wynn*

Graffiti Blues / 1973–1974 / Mainstream ✦✦
A new reissue of a 1973 mainstream session that was part funk, part pop and far too tame. — *Ron Wynn*

Many Shades of Blue / 1974 / Mainstream ✦✦

Stratosonic Nuances / 1975 / RCA ✦✦

Red Mitchell (Keith Moore Mitchell)

b. Sep. 20, 1927, New York, NY, **d.** Nov. 8, 1992, Salem, OR
Bass / Cool, Hard Bop
A talented bassist who was always in great demand, Red Mitchell was originally a pianist, and he doubled on piano on an occasional basis throughout his career. He switched to bass when he was a member of an Army band in Germany. Mitchell played with Jackie Paris (1947-48), Mundell Lowe, Chubby Jackson's big band and Charlie Ventura (1949), toured with Woody Herman's Orchestra (1949-51) and was a member of the popular Red Norvo Trio (1952-54). He played with the Gerry Mulligan Quartet (1954) and then settled in Los Angeles where during 1954-68 he played with nearly everyone, from West Coast jazz stars (particularly Hampton Hawes) to recording with Ornette Coleman (1959) and being a member of the studio orchestra of MGM. He also co-led a quintet with Harold Land during 1961-62 that recorded for Atlantic. In 1968 Mitchell moved to Stockholm where he led groups, played with European jazzmen and accompanied visiting Americans including Dizzy Gillespie and Phil Woods. Mitchell made occasional visits to the U.S., and shortly before he died he moved to Oregon. In addition to the Atlantic date, Red Mitchell led albums for Bethlehem (1955), Contemporary, Pacific Jazz, Mercury, SteepleChase, Caprice, Gryphon, Phontastic, Enja and Capri in addition to a few smaller European labels. — *Scott Yanow*

Presenting Red Mitchell / Mar. 26, 1957 / Original Jazz Classics ✦✦✦✦
One of the earliest sessions for this bassist, pianist and singer from New York City; it helped launch his career. — *Ron Wynn*

● **Hear Ye!** / Oct. 14, 1961 / Atlantic ✦✦✦✦✦

Talking / Jan. 10, 1989–Jan. 11, 1989 / Capri ✦✦✦✦✦
This Capri CD has trio playing of the highest order. Bassist Red Mitchell welcomes pianist Kenny Barron and drummer Ben Riley and surprisingly only performs three standards along with Thelonious Monk's "Locomotive;" the remainder of the program comprises a Kenny Barron song and five originals from the multitalented Mitchell. The close communication between these three players is quite impressive and the music always swings. — *Scott Yanow*

Roscoe Mitchell

b. Aug. 3, 1940, Chicago, IL
Multiple Reeds, Alto Saxophone, Tenor Saxophone / Avant-Garde, Free Jazz
One of the top saxophonists to come out of Chicago's AACM movement of the mid-'60s, Roscoe Mitchell is a particularly strong and consistently adventurous improviser long associated with the Art Ensemble of Chicago. After getting out of the military, Mitchell led a hard bop sextet in Chicago (1961) which gradually became much freer. He was a member of Muhal Richard Abrams' Experimental Band and a founding member of the AACM in 1965. Mitchell's monumental *Sound* album (1966) introduced a new way of freely improvising, utilizing silence as well as high energy and "little instruments" as well as conventional horns. Lester Bowie and Malachi Favors were on that date and Mitchell's 1967 follow-up *Old/Quartet*. With the addition of Joseph Jarman and Philip Wilson (who was later succeeded by Don Moye), the Art Ensemble of Chicago was born. The colorful unit was one of the most popular groups in the jazz avant-garde, and Mitchell was an integral part of the band. Roscoe Mitchell (who, in addition to his main horns, plays clarinet, flute, piccolo, oboe, baritone and bass saxophones) also was involved in individual projects through the years and has recorded as a leader for Delmark, Nessa, Sackville, Moers Music, 1750 Arch, Black Saint, Cecma and Silkheart in settings ranging from large ensembles to unaccompanied solo concerts. — *Scott Yanow*

★ **Sound** / Aug. 11, 1966+Sep. 18, 1966 / Delmark ✦✦✦✦✦
Mitchell's first significant statement as a leader has ambitious pieces, amazing solos and unorthodox arrangements. — *Ron Wynn*

Old / Quartet / May 18, 1967–May 25, 1967 / Nessa ✦✦✦✦✦

The Roscoe Mitchell Solo Saxophone Concerts / Oct. 22, 1973–Jul. 12, 1974 / Sackville ✦✦✦✦✦
Roscoe Mitchell is a founding member of The Art Ensemble of Chicago and has only had occasional dates as a leader through the years. This is one of his most rewarding although listeners accustomed to full rhythm sections and conventional swinging might find this one hard to get into. Mitchell proves to be a brilliant architect of sound, frequently building up a simple idea to unimagined heights of complexity. Performing on soprano, alto, tenor and bass saxophones at the three festivals at which this music is taken from, Roscoe Mitchell demonstrates why he is considered one of the masters of avant-garde jazz. This solo set is only topped by his 1976-77 Nessa recording *Nonaah*. — *Scott Yanow*

Quartet / Oct. 4, 1975–Oct. 5, 1975 / Sackville ✦✦✦
With pianist Muhal Abrahms, trombonist George Lewis and guitarist A. Spencer Barefield. Very challenging listening. — *Michael G. Nastos*

★ **Nonaah** / Aug. 23, 1976–Feb. 22, 1977 / Nessa ✦✦✦✦✦
1976-1977. This is arguably Mitchell's best solo statement. It includes a full-side treatment of the title cut, solo works, duos and an incredible alto number with Mitchell, Henry Threadgill (as), Joseph Jarman (reeds) and the undervalued Wallace McMillan (b). — *Ron Wynn*

Duets with Anthony Braxton / Dec. 13, 1977 / Sackville ✦✦✦✦

L-R-G / The Maze / SII Examples / Jul. 27, 1978–Aug. 17, 1978 / Nessa ✦✦✦✦
Free improvisation. Definitive statement from Art Ensemble saxophonist and composer. One piece is all horns, another all percussion, and one is solo. This one is for open ears only. — *Michael G. Nastos*

Snurdy Mcgurdy and Her Dancin' Shoes / Dec. 11, 1980+Dec. 12, 1980 / Nessa ✦✦✦✦
This album is more upbeat and humorous, less dense and intense than some past Mitchell dates, but the music's just as ferocious. — *Ron Wynn*

3x4 Eye / Feb. 18, 1981–Feb. 19, 1981 / Black Saint ✦✦✦
Roscoe Mitchell has continued to head his Sound Ensemble, and this 1981 session presented them doing two extensive numbers and two shorter pieces. The longer works had fiery solos and intricate unison sections, while "JoJar" featured Mitchell's group in a looser, more relaxed posture, and "Variations On A Folk Song" alternated between jagged, flamboyant solos and simple statements. This wasn't among his most intense or combative dates,

but Mitchell and the Sound Ensemble were still well worth hearing. —*Ron Wynn*

And the Sound and Space Ensembles / Jun. 2, 1983–Jun. 3, 1983 / Black Saint ✦✦✦✦

The Flow of Things, the / Jun. 29, 1986–Sep. 7, 1986 / Black Saint ✦✦✦✦✦

Live at the Knitting Factory / Nov. 1987 / Black Saint ✦✦✦✦

After Fallen Leaves / Oct. 1989 / Silkheart ✦✦✦✦

Duets & Solos / Mar. 1990 / Black Saint ✦✦✦✦

This Dance Is for Steve Mc Call / May 1992 / Black Saint ✦✦✦✦

● **Hey Donald** / May 23, 1994–May 25, 1994 / Delmark ✦✦✦✦✦
Since Roscoe Mitchell (who on this set made his return to the Delmark label after 28 years) is best known as a free jazz pioneer and a longtime member of The Art Ensemble of Chicago, the straight-ahead nature of a few of the selections will surprise some of his followers. "Walking in the Moonlight" is a sly and witty strut, "Jeremy" a melodic ballad for the leader's flute and "Hey Donald" could have come from the Sonny Rollins songbook. But Mitchell has not forsaken his innovative style. On "Dragons" his soprano playing (with its circular breathing) sounds very African, there are four free duets with bassist Malachi Favors, and the blowouts on "Song for Rwanda" and "See You at the Fair" are pretty adventurous. In general Mitchell (who is joined by a versatile rhythm section composed of pianist Jodie Christian, bassist Favors and drummer Tootie Heath) saves the more boppish pieces for his tenor while on soprano his intense sound creates a drone effect reminiscent a bit of bagpipes. In all his release for Delmark should keep listeners guessing. —*Scott Yanow*

Hank Mobley

b. Jul. 7, 1930, Eastman, GA, d. May 30, 1986, Philadelphia, PA
Tenor Saxophone / Hard Bop
Accurately described by critic Leonard Feather as "the middleweight champion of the tenor" due to his sound (not as light as Lester Young's or as heavy as Sonny Rollins), Hank Mobley tended to be taken for granted during his career but recorded a long string of valuable albums for Blue Note. He first gained attention for his work with Max Roach (on and off during 1951–53) and Dizzy Gillespie (1954). An original member of the Jazz Messengers (1954–56), Mobley joined Horace Silver when the pianist broke away from Art Blakey to form his own group (1956–57). Mobley was back with Blakey for a bit in 1959 and spent an unhappy period with Miles Davis (1961–62) but mostly worked as a leader in the 1960s. He was in Europe during much of 1968–70 and recorded with Cedar Walton in 1972 but by the mid-'70s was largely retired due to bad health. Hank Mobley led isolated dates for Savoy, Prestige and Roulette, but it is for his 25 Blue Note albums (recorded during 1955–70) with the who's who of hard bop (including such sidemen as Horace Silver, Art Blakey, Lee Morgan, Milt Jackson, Art Farmer, Donald Byrd, Bobby Timmons, Sonny Clark, Kenny Dorham, Pepper Adams, Wynton Kelly, Freddie Hubbard, Grant Green, Philly Joe Jones, Herbie Hancock, Andrew Hill, Barry Harris, Curtis Fuller, McCoy Tyner, Billy Higgins, James Spaulding, Jackie McLean, Blue Mitchell, Cedar Walton, Ron Carter and Woody Shaw) that he will be best-remembered. —*Scott Yanow*

Hank Mobley Quartet / Mar. 27, 1955 / Blue Note ✦✦✦✦
This debut of Mobley on Blue Note includes Horace Silver on piano and Doug Watkins on bass, plus someone named Art Blakey on drums. —*Ron Wynn*

The Jazz Message of Hank Mobley, Vol. 1 / Jan. 30, 1956–Feb. 8, 1956 / Savoy ✦✦✦
Other than a Blue Note date from the previous year, this CD contains tenor saxophonist Hank Mobley's first two sessions as a leader. With trumpeter Donald Byrd, either Hank Jones or Ronnie Ball on piano, Wendell Marshall or Doug Watkins on bass, drummer Kenny Clarke and (on three numbers) the unusual altoist John LaPorta, Mobley performs a mixture of originals and standards. The results (highlighted by "There'll Never Be Another You," "When I Fall in Love" and "Budo") are a swinging hard bop date. Nothing all that unusual occurs, and the CD clocks in at an average LP's length, but the swinging music is easily recommended to straight-ahead jazz fans, and (unlike many of Denon's Savoy reissues) these two sessions are brought back complete. —*Scott Yanow*

Messages / Jul. 20, 1956+Jul. 27, 1956 / Prestige ✦✦✦✦
With the exception of Hank Mobley's original "Alternating Current," which was left out due to lack of space, this single CD has all of the music from the two Prestige LPs. *Mobley's Message* and *Hank Mobley's Second Message*, a two-LP set from 1976 which had the same *Messages* title and catalog number but also the complete program is actually the preferred acquisition but will be difficult to locate. The first session mostly features the fine tenor Hank Mobley jamming on four superior bop standards, including "Bouncing with Bud," "52nd Street Theme" and "Au Privavem" and his own "Minor Disturbance" in a quintet with trumpeter Donald Byrd, pianist Barry Harris, bassist Doug Watkins and drummer Art Taylor; altoist Jackie McLean has a strong cameo on "Au Privave." The second set, recorded a week later, is less of a jam session, with Mobley, trumpeter Kenny Dorham, pianist Walter Bishop, bassist Doug Watkins and drummer Art Taylor essaying three of Mobley's now-obscure compositions, Benny Harris' "Crazeology" and the standards "These Are the Things I Love" and "I Should Care." The two dates give one a good example of Hank Mobley's playing prior to becoming a regular Blue Note artist, where he would create his greatest work. —*Scott Yanow*

The Jazz Message of Hank Mobley, Vol. 2 / Jul. 23, 1956+Nov. 7, 1956 / Savoy ✦✦✦✦

Hank Mobley Sextet / Nov. 25, 1956 / Blue Noe ✦✦✦

Hank Mobley and His All-Stars / Jan. 13, 1957 / Blue Note ✦✦✦✦
This is great Mobley with Milt Jackson (vib) and Horace Silver (p). —*David Szatmary*

Hank Mobley Quintet / Mar. 9, 1957 / Blue Note ✦✦✦✦✦
Tenor saxophonist Hank Mobley teamed up with a couple of his more notable employers (pianist Horace Silver and drummer Art Blakey) plus trumpeter Art Farmer and bassist Doug Watkins for this superior Blue Note album which has been reissued (along with two alternate takes) on CD. Mobley's "Funk in Deep Freeze" is the most memorable selection, but on a whole the six compositions (all Mobley originals) display his underrated writing talents. It is a particular joy to hear the inspired playing of Silver and Blakey on this lesser-known but consistently stimulating hard bop set. —*Scott Yanow*

Hank / Apr. 21, 1957 / Blue Note ✦✦✦✦

Hank Mobley / Jun. 23, 1957 / Blue Note ✦✦✦

Curtain Call / Aug. 18, 1957 / Blue Note ✦✦✦

Poppin' / Oct. 20, 1957 / Blue Note ✦✦✦✦

Peckin' Time / Feb. 9, 1958 / Blue Note ✦✦✦✦✦
Tenor saxophonist Hank Mobley, who throughout his career was overshadowed by more influential tenors such as Sonny Rollins and John Coltrane, was himself a talented and fairly original player and a fine composer; many of his originals deserve to be revived. For this Blue Note session, which in its CD reissue includes three alternate takes, Mobley, trumpeter Lee Morgan, pianist Wynton Kelly, bassist Paul Chambers and drummer Charlie Persip interpret four of the tenor's songs, including "High and Flighty" and the 12-minute "Gil-Go Blues," along with the standard "Speak Low." The results are high-quality hard bop, the modern mainstream of the era. —*Scott Yanow*

Another Monday Night at Birdland / Apr. 21, 1958 / Roulette ✦✦✦

★ **Soul Station** / Feb. 7, 1960 / Blue Note ✦✦✦✦✦
Other than his 1955 debut for Blue Note, this set (reissued on CD) was tenor saxophonist Hank Mobley's first opportunity to record as leader of a quartet without any other competing horns. With the stimulating support of pianist Wynton Kelly, bassist Paul Chambers and drummer Art Blakey, Mobley is in peak form on four of his originals (of which "This I Dig of You" is best-known), "Remember" and the ballad "If I Should Lose You." Mobley's improvisations are melodic and thoughtful, yet always swinging and full of inner fire. This CD serves as a perfect introduction to the playing and writing abilities of this underrated talent. —*Scott Yanow*

Roll Call / Nov. 13, 1960 / Blue Note ✦✦✦✦
This set, reissued on CD, differs from tenor saxophonist Hank Mobley's *Soul Station* release of nine months earlier in that although he uses the same impressive rhythm section (pianist Wynton Kelly, bassist Paul Chambers and drummer Art Blakey),

Mobley also welcomes young trumpeter Freddie Hubbard. Hubbard actually steals the show on a few of the numbers, but since five of the pieces are Mobley originals, including such forgotten gems as "Roll Call," "My Groove Your Move" and "A Baptist Beat," the tenorman obviously set up this date partly as a way of featuring the fiery Hubbard. Art Blakey took note of the trumpeter's talents and hired him to replace Lee Morgan with the Jazz Messengers a year later. Overall, this is an excellent hard bop date, and as is true of all of Hank Mobley's Blue Note albums, it is easily recommended to fans of straight-ahead jazz. —*Scott Yanow*

● **Workout** / Mar. 26, 1961 / Blue Note ✦✦✦✦✦
This is one of the best-known Hank Mobley recordings and for good reason. Although none of his four originals ("Workout," "Uh Huh," "Smokin'," "Greasin' Easy") caught on, the fine saxophonist is in top form. He jams on four tunes, plus "The Best Things in Life Are Free," with an all-star quintet of young modernists—guitarist Grant Green, pianist Wynton Kelly, bassist Paul Chambers and drummer Philly Joe Jones—and shows that he was a much stronger player than his then-current boss Miles Davis seemed to think. This recommended CD reissue adds a version of "Three Coins in the Fountain" from the same date, originally released on *Another Workout*, to the original LP program. —*Scott Yanow*

Another Workout / Mar. 26, 1961+Dec. 5, 1961 / Blue Note ✦✦✦✦
This LP has material from 1961 that for no real reason went unreleased until 1985. One song, "Three Coins in a Fountain," is from the same session that resulted in tenor saxophonist Hank Mobley's famous *Workout* session with guitarist Grant Green, pianist Wynton Kelly, bassist Paul Chambers and drummer Philly Joe Jones. The other five numbers—three obscure Mobley originals, plus "I Should Care" and "Hello Young Lovers"—are from the previously unheard December 5, 1961 session with the same personnel except for Green. Hank Mobley was in a prime period around this time, and all of his Blue Note recordings are well worth picking up. —*Scott Yanow*

No Room for Squares / Mar. 7, 1963+Oct. 2, 1963 / Blue Note ✦✦✦✦
By 1963, Hank Mobley, whose tenor tone perfectly fit the hard bop modern mainstream music of the late '50s and early '60s, had altered his sound slightly to get a harder tone, influenced to an extent by John Coltrane. This CD reissue differs quite a bit from the original LP program, adding alternate takes of "No Room for Squares" and "Carolyn," along with two previously unissued selections ("Comin' Back" and "Syrup and Biscuits") while dropping two songs from the LP which were cut at a slightly earlier session. Mobley leads a top-notch quintet with trumpeter Lee Morgan, pianist Andrew Hill, bassist John Ore and drummer Philly Joe Jones through a set of high-quality, if obscure, originals written by either the leader or Morgan. The music is as satisfying and adventurous, as one would expect. —*Scott Yanow*

The Turnaround / Mar. 7, 1963+Feb. 5, 1965 / Blue Note ✦✦✦✦
The CD reissue of Hank Mobley's *The Turnaround* is different from the original LP in that two songs from a March 7, 1963 date were dropped, while two previously unissued ones from February 4, 1965 were added. Most intriguing about this quintet set with trumpeter Freddie Hubbard, pianist Barry Harris, bassist Paul Chambers and drummer Billy Higgins are the six likable but complex Mobley compositions. A very underrated writer, many of Hank Mobley's originals deserve to be revived, including these six ("Pat 'N Chat," "Third Time Around," "Hank's Waltz," "The Turnaround," "Straight Ahead" and "My Sin"). Rather than stick to the standard 32-bar format heard on most pre-1970 songs, Mobley's pieces utilize choruses of 44, 20 and 50 bars while still sounding logical. All of the musicians play up to par on these advanced hard bop tunes. —*Scott Yanow*

Dippin' / Jun. 18, 1965 / Blue Note ✦✦✦✦
All of tenor saxophonist Hank Mobley's Blue Note recordings are recommended for his harmonically advanced, tricky, yet logical originals, in addition to consistently fine soloing from some of the top modern mainstream players of the era; these albums helped define the Blue Note sound of the 1960s. For this date, a straight CD reissue of the original LP, Mobley, trumpeter Lee Morgan, pianist Harold Mabern, bassist Larry Ridley and drummer Billy Higgins perform four of the tenorman's originals, the highly appealing "Recado Bossa Nova" and the standard ballad "I See

Your Face Before Me." An excellent outing, even if no "hits" resulted. —*Scott Yanow*

A Caddy for Daddy / Dec. 18, 1965 / Blue Note ✦✦✦✦
Hank Mobley was a perfect artist for Blue Note in the 1960s. A distinctive but not dominant soloist, Mobley was also a very talented writer whose compositions avoided the predictable, yet could often be quite melodic and soulful; his tricky originals consistently inspired the young all-stars in Blue Note's stable. For this CD, which is a straight reissue of a 1965 session, Mobley is joined by trumpeter Lee Morgan, trombonist Curtis Fuller, pianist McCoy Tyner, bassist Bob Cranshaw and drummer Billy Higgins (a typically remarkable Blue Note lineup) for the infectious title cut, three other lesser-known but superior originals, plus Wayne Shorter's "Venus Di Mildew." Recommended. —*Scott Yanow*

A Slice of the Top / Mar. 18, 1966 / Blue Note ✦✦✦✦✦
This is one of tenor saxophonist Hank Mobley's more intriguing sessions, for the talented composer had an opportunity to have four of his originals, plus the standard "There's a Lull in My Life," performed by an octet in the cool-toned style of Miles Davis' "Birth of the Cool" nonet, arranged by Duke Pearson. Although recorded in 1966, this date was not released until 1979 and unfortunately has not yet been reissued on CD. Mobley, who continued to evolve into a more advanced player throughout the 1960s, fits right in with such adventurous players as altoist James Spaulding, trumpeter Lee Morgan (with whom Mobley recorded frequently), pianist McCoy Tyner, bassist Reggie Workman and drummer Billy Higgins. The inclusion of Kiane Zawadi on euphonium and Howard Johnson on tuba adds a lot of color to this memorable outing. —*Scott Yanow*

Hi Voltage / 1967 / Blue Note ✦✦✦✦
This is a typically enjoyable Hank Mobley date from the last great year of music from Blue Note, 1967. The talented tenor, who contributed all six compositions, is teamed with trumpeter Blue Mitchell, altoist Jackie McLean, pianist John Hicks, bassist Bob Cranshaw and drummer Billy Higgins (all Blue Note veterans except Hicks), and everyone plays up to par. The music sticks to advanced hard bop with hints of funk, bossa nova and modal tunes. Strange that none of these selections, which include the ballad "No More Goodbys," "Bossa De Luxe" and "Flirty Gerty," caught on. —*Scott Yanow*

Third Season / Feb. 24, 1967 / Blue Note ✦✦✦✦
Tenor saxophonist Hank Mobley recorded frequently for Blue Note in the 1960s (six albums from 1967–70), and although overshadowed by the flashier and more avant-garde players, Mobley's output was consistently rewarding. For this overlooked session, which was not issued until 1980 and has yet to resurface on CD, a regular contingent of top Blue Note artists (Mobley, trumpeter Lee Morgan, altoist James Spaulding, pianist Cedar Walton, bassist Walter Booker and drummer Billy Higgins) are joined by a wild card, guitarist Sonny Greenwich. The music is mostly in the hard bop vein, with hints of modality and the gospellish piece "Give Me That Feelin'," but Greenwich's three solos are a bonus, and the performances of five Mobley originals and one by Morgan are up to the usual caliber of Blue Note's releases. Pity that this one has been lost in the shuffle; it is one to search for by Hank Mobley fans. —*Scott Yanow*

Far Away Lands / Mar. 26, 1967 / Blue Note ✦✦✦✦
Of all the Blue Note artists of the 1960s, tenor saxophonist Hank Mobley may very well be the most underrated. A consistent player whose style evolved throughout the decade, Mobley wrote a series of inventive and challenging compositions that inspired the all-stars he used on his recordings while remaining in the genre of hard bop. For this lesser-known outing, Mobley teams up with trumpeter Donald Byrd, pianist Cedar Walton, bassist Ron Carter and drummer Billy Higgins for four of his songs (given such colorful titles as "A Dab of This and That," "No Argument," "The Hippity Hop" and "Bossa for Baby"), along with a song apiece from Byrd and Jimmy Heath. An excellent outing, fairly late in the productive career of Hank Mobley. —*Scott Yanow*

Reach Out / Jan. 19, 1968 / Blue Note ✦✦✦

The Flip / Jul. 12, 1969 / Blue Note ✦✦✦

Thinking of Home / Jul. 13, 1970 / Blue Note ✦✦✦✦✦
For what would be his final of over 20 Blue Note albums, tenor saxophonist Hank Mobley uses a sextet that also includes trumpeter Woody Shaw, the obscure guitarist Eddie Diehl, pianist Cedar Walton, bassist Mickey Bass and drummer Leroy Williams

for a typically challenging set of advanced hard bop music. For the first and only time in his career, Mobley recorded a "Suite" (consisting of "Thinking of Home," "The Flight" and "Home at Last"); the remainder of the set has three of his other attractive originals plus Mickey Bass' "Gayle's Groove." This music was not released for the first time until 1980 and has not popped up yet on CD. It is only fitting that Hank Mobley would record one of the last worthwhile Blue Note albums before its artistic collapse (it would not be revived until the 1980s) for his consistent output helped define the label's sound in the 1960s. Mobley's excellent playing and the adventurous solos of Woody Shaw make this hard-to-find LP (his last as a leader) one to hunt for. —*Scott Yanow*

The Modern Jazz Quartet

Group / Cool, Third Stream

Pianist John Lewis, vibraphonist Milt Jackson, bassist Ray Brown and drummer Kenny Clarke first came together as the rhythm section of the 1946 Dizzy Gillespie Orchestra, and they had occasional features that gave the overworked brass players a well-deserved rest. They next came together in 1951, recording as the Milt Jackson Quartet. In 1952 with Percy Heath taking Brown's place, the Modern Jazz Quartet (MJQ) became a permanent group. Other than Connie Kay suceeding Clarke in 1955, the band's personnel was set. In the early days Jackson and Lewis both were equally responsible for the group's musical direction, but the pianist eventually took over as musical director. The MJQ has long displayed John Lewis' musical vision, making jazz seem respectable by occasionally interacting with classical ensembles and playing concerts at prestigious venues but always leaving plenty of space for bluesy and swinging improvising. Their repertoire, in addition to including veteran bop and swing pieces, introduced such originals as Lewis' "Django" and Jackson's "Bags' Groove." The group recorded for Prestige (1952–55), Atlantic (1956–74), Verve (1957), United Artists (1959) and Apple (1967–69), and in addition to the many quartet outings, they welcomed such guests as Jimmy Giuffre, Sonny Rollins, the Beaux Arts String Quartet, a symphony orchestra conducted by Gunther Schuller, singer Diahann Carroll (on one piece), Laurindo Almeida, a big band and the Swingle Singers. Although the musicians all had opportunities to pursue individual projects, in 1974 Milt Jackson tired of the constant touring and the limitations on his improvising, and he quit the group, causing the MJQ to have a final tour and break up. In 1981 Jackson relented, and the Modern Jazz Quartet (which has recorded further albums for Pablo and Atlantic) became active again although on a more part-time basis. Connie Kay's health began to fade in the early '90s (Mickey Roker often filled in for him), and after his death in 1995, Albert "Tootie" Heath became his replacement. —*Scott Yanow*

MJQ: 40 years [Boxed Set] / Dec. 22, 1952–Feb. 3, 1988 / Atlantic ✦✦✦✦✦

To celebrate The Modern Jazz Quartet's 40th anniversary as a group, Atlantic came out with an attractive four-CD box set that has selections (programmed in chronological order) that cover the group's long career. Most of the selections come from the Atlantic catalog although they have leased a few numbers owned by other labels, and with the exception of four songs from a Japanese concert and one previously unissued performance, all of the music is readily available elsewhere. But this well-conceived set serves as a perfect introduction for new listeners and as a fine retrospective of this important group's legacy. All of the best-known compositions are included, and they find vibraphonist Milt Jackson, pianist John Lewis, bassist Percy Heath and drummer Connie Kay (along with a few notable guests) playing at their peak. —*Scott Yanow*

MJQ / Dec. 22, 1952+Jun. 16, 1954 / Original Jazz Classics ✦✦✦✦

Two different groups are heard from on this CD reissue. The original Modern Jazz Quartet (with vibraphonist Milt Jackson, pianist John Lewis, bassist Percy Heath and drummer Kenny Clarke) performs four numbers at the first recording session of The MJQ. In addition there are four selections from a pickup group led by Jackson that also includes pianist Horace Silver and trumpeter Henry Boozier; the latter date introduced Silver's "Opus De Funk." Overall this somewhat brief CD has swinging music that bop fans will want to get. —*Scott Yanow*

★ **Django** / Jun. 25, 1953–Jan. 9, 1955 / Original Jazz Classics ✦✦✦✦✦

Although it had recorded one prior session, The Modern Jazz

Quartet really came into its own during the three dates that comprise this CD reissue. Highlights include the original versions of John Lewis' "Django," "Milano," "Delauney's Dilemma" and the four-part "La Ronde Suite." In addition to vibraphonist Milt Jackson, pianist John Lewis and bassist Percy Heath, these performances have the last studio appearances of drummer Kenny Clarke with the group. —*Scott Yanow*

Concorde / Jul. 2, 1955 / Original Jazz Classics ✦✦✦✦

This CD reissue is most significant for having the first recordings of drummer Connie Kay as a regular member of The Modern Jazz Quartet. His subtle style fit in perfectly with vibraphonist Milt Jackson, bassist Percy Heath and pianist John Lewis. Highlights of this rather brief (around 33 minutes) CD are a four-song "Gershwin Medley," "Softly as in a Morning Sunrise" and "Ralph's New Blues." Excellent and somewhat historic music although the brevity of this set makes one wish that it were combined on CD with Prestige's other MJQ sessions. —*Scott Yanow*

Fontessa / Jan. 22, 1956+Feb. 14, 1956 / Atlantic ✦✦✦✦✦

This LP has a particularly strong all-around set by The Modern Jazz Quartet. While John Lewis' "Versailles" and an 11-minute "Fontessa" show the seriousness of the group (and the influence of Western classical music), other pieces (such as "Bluesology," "Woody 'n You" and a pair of ballads) look toward the group's roots in bop and permit the band to swing hard. As with most of The MJQ's many Atlantic LPs, this one is long overdue to be reissued on CD. —*Scott Yanow*

Modern Jazz Quartet at Music Inn / Aug. 28, 1956 / Atlantic ✦✦✦✦

The first of two albums The Modern Jazz Quartet recorded at the Music Inn in Lenox, MS, this LP (reissued as part of Atlantic's *Jazzlore* series in 1982) is highlighted by "Oh Bess, Oh Where's My Bess," "Two Degrees East, Three Degrees West," "A Morning in Paris" and "England's Carol" which is The MJQ's reworking of "God Rest Ye Merry, Gentlemen." Clarinetist Jimmy Giuffre sits in with the group successfully on three numbers; best is "Fun." This is a worthwhile outing that has not yet been reissued on CD. —*Scott Yanow*

One Never Knows / Apr. 4, 1957 / Atlantic ✦✦✦

This LP has six John Lewis compositions that were used in the French film *No Sun in Venice*. The music is quite complex and disciplined, making this set of lesser interest to fans who prefer to hear Milt Jackson playing bebop-oriented blues. However the versatile group was perfect for this type of music, and these thought-provoking performances reward repeated listenings.—*Scott Yanow*

The Modern Jazz Quartet / Apr. 5, 1957 / Mobile Fidelity ✦✦✦✦

The audiophile label Mobile Fidelity in 1994 came out with a rare LP, a reissue of a 1957 Modern Jazz Quartet session originally on Atlantic. The emphasis is very much on The MJQ's bebop roots, and vibraphonist Milt Jackson stars on a five-song ballad medley and several standards including "Night in Tunisia" and his own "Bags' Groove." Fine straight-ahead music; this group could always swing. —*Scott Yanow*

Third Stream Music / Aug. 23, 1957–Jan. 15, 1960 / Atlantic ✦✦✦✦

This Atlantic LP has some unusual performances by The Modern Jazz Quartet. Two selections ("Da Capo" and "Fine") combine The MJQ (which comprises vibraphonist Milt Jackson, pianist John Lewis, bassist Percy Heath and drummer Connie Kay) with the Jimmy Giuffre Three (Giuffre on clarinet and tenor, guitarist Jim Hall and bassist Ralph Pena), on "Exposure" six chamber classical musicians add color, and a pair of other numbers ("Conversation" and the very successful "Sketch") match The MJQ with the Beaux Arts String Quartet. There is plenty of thought-provoking music on this out-of-print album even if the idea of creating a "Third Stream" between jazz and classical music never came to pass. —*Scott Yanow*

Modern Jazz Quartet and Oscar Peterson Trio at the Opera / Oct. 19, 1957 / Verve ✦✦✦✦

This frequently exciting LP has three lightly swinging performances by The Modern Jazz Quartet ("Now's the Time," "'Round Midnight" and "D & E Blues") and five from the Oscar Peterson Trio (which at the time consisted of the pianist/leader, guitarist Herb Ellis and bassist Ray Brown). While the MJQ sounds much more introverted than the more exuberant O.P. Trio, the two popular groups have more similarities than differences. Polygram has reissued the Peterson material on CD but not yet the songs from The Modern Jazz Quartet. —*Scott Yanow*

The Historic Donaueschingen Jazz Concert / Oct. 27, 1957 / Pausa ✦✦✦
Although given top billing, The Modern Jazz Quartet is actually only featured on half of this reissue LP of material from the MPS label. The MJQ performs three complex John Lewis originals composed for the French film *No Sun in Venice* along with the more straightforward "J.B. Blues." Arranger Eddie Sauter leads a German orchestra on three pieces that are influenced by contemporary classical music, utilize quite a few percussive devices and feature the tenor of Hans Koller. In addition, writer Andre Hodeir directs a smaller group through his complicated "Paradoxe II" and Duke Jordan's "Jordu." Overall this set is not all that essential (the move toward a "Third Stream" between jazz and classical music never really caught on) but has its interesting moments. —*Scott Yanow*

At Music Inn, Vol. 2 / Aug. 3, 1958+Sep. 3, 1958 / Mobile Fidelity ✦✦✦✦
This Mobile Fidelity CD reissues an Atlantic album by The Modern Jazz Quartet. Vibraphonist Milt Jackson, pianist John Lewis, bassist Percy Heath and drummer Connie Kay perform a pair of Lewis originals (the rather dry "Midsommer" and "Festival Sketch"), Charlie Parker's "Yardbird Suite" and a three-song ballad medley; the latter features Milt Jackson exclusively. The most unusual aspect to this set is that the great tenor Sonny Rollins joins the quartet for "Bags' Groove" (during which he is quite witty) and "Night in Tunisia." Rollins is quite creative and fits in naturally with the group. This very well-recorded reissue from the audiophile Mobile Fidelity label is worth picking up. —*Scott Yanow*

Pyramid / Aug. 22, 1959+Jan. 15, 1960 / Atlantic ✦✦✦✦✦
This is a strong LP from The Modern Jazz Quartet with inventive versions of John Lewis' "Vendome," Ray Brown's "Pyramid," Jim Hall's "Romaine," Lewis' famous "Django" and happy jams on "How High the Moon" and "It Don't Mean a Thing." The MJQ had become a jazz institution by this time, but they never lost their creative edge, and their performances (even on the remakes) are quite stimulating, enthusiastic and fresh. —*Scott Yanow*

Odds Against Tomorrow / Oct. 9, 1959 / Blue Note ✦✦✦✦✦
The Modern Jazz Quartet never actually recorded for Blue Note, but their United Artists date was reissued on this Blue Note CD. The MJQ (vibraphonist Milt Jackson, pianist John Lewis, bassist Percy Heath and drummer Connie Kay) perform six of Lewis' compositions which were used in the film *Odds Against Tomorrow*. Best known is "Skating in Central Park," but all of the selections have their memorable moments, and it is good to hear this classic unit playing such fresh material. —*Scott Yanow*

European Concert / Apr. 11, 1960–Apr. 13, 1960 / Atlantic ✦✦✦✦✦
This live double LP does an excellent job of summing up the first eight years of The Modern Jazz Quartet. Vibraphonist Milt Jackson, pianist John Lewis, bassist Percy Heath and drummer Connie Kay perform remakes of 15 high-quality songs that were permanent parts of their repertoire, everything from the inevitable hits ("Django," "Bluesology" and "Bags' Groove") to "La Ronde," "Vendome," "Odds Against Tomorrow" and "Skating in Central Park." Needless to say the solos are not close duplicates of the original versions even if some of the frameworks are similar; the audience is understandably enthusiastic. This is a definitive set that is long overdue to be reissued in full on CD. —*Scott Yanow*

Dedicated to Connie / May 27, 1960 / Atlantic Jazz ✦✦✦✦✦

The Modern Jazz Quartet and Orchestra / Jun. 3, 1960+Jun. 4, 1960 / Atlantic ✦✦✦

The Comedy / Oct. 20, 1960–Jan. 24, 1962 / Atlantic ✦✦
This is the type of album that led many bop purists to criticize The Modern Jazz Quartet (and John Lewis in particular) for being overly influenced by Western classical music. The LP has seven of Lewis' compositions, episodic works arranged in a suite that portrays characters from a fictional Italian comedy based in the 1500s; singer Diahann Carroll guests fairly effectively on "La Cantatrice." Despite being tied to a story, there are some strong improvisations from pianist Lewis and vibraphonist Milt Jackson on this unusual material. The release is not that essential, but it is quite interesting. —*Scott Yanow*

Lonely Woman / Jan. 24, 1962–Feb. 2, 1962 / Atlantic ✦✦✦
This LP (last put out by Atlantic in 1987 as part of their *Jazzlore* reissue series) is best known for having one of the first "covers" of an Ornette Coleman tune, a fine adaptation of "Lonely Woman." Otherwise the set is less significant with six lesser-known John Lewis originals and Gary McFarland's "Why Are You Blue?" being given uplifting but not overly memorable treatments by The MJQ. —*Scott Yanow*

A Quartet is a Quartet is a Quartet / May 17, 1963 / Atlantic ✦✦✦

Collaboration with Almeida / Jul. 21, 1964 / Atlantic ✦✦✦✦✦
When Atlantic gets around to reissuing their many Modern Jazz Quartet records on CD, this should be one of the first to come back. The MJQ (vibraphonist Milt Jackson, pianist John Lewis, bassist Percy Heath and drummer Connie Kay) were joined for this 1964 session by the great acoustic guitarist Laurindo Almeida, and the music is very memorable. Their version of "One Note Samba" (which starts out with Almeida playing unaccompanied) is a classic, the guitarist fits into the four John Lewis compositions quite comfortably, and "Concierto De Aranjuez" is given lengthy and inventive treatment. —*Scott Yanow*

Plays George Gershwin's "Porgy and Bess" / Jul. 23, 1964–Jul. 26, 1964 / Atlantic ✦✦✦✦
This is one of the lesser-known Modern Jazz Quartet recordings. The MJQ (pianist John Lewis, vibraphonist Milt Jackson, bassist Percy Heath and drummer Connie Kay) interpret seven themes from Gershwin's *Porgy & Bess*, and the results are predictably excellent. The ballads (especially "My Man's Gone Now," "I Loves You Porgy" and "Oh Bess, Oh Where's My Bess") are the most memorable selections on this pleasing and respectful LP. —*Scott Yanow*

Jazz Dialogue / May 25, 1965 / Atlantic ✦✦✦
This is an unusual record in The Modern Jazz Quartet's discography for it matches The MJQ (vibraphonist Milt Jackson, pianist John Lewis, bassist Percy Heath and drummer Connie Kay) with an all-star big band that comprises a dozen horns and guitarist Howard Collins. Unfortunately the orchestra (which has a pretty impressive lineup) is used exclusively for backup of the rhythm section, and none of the horns have any solos. The music, which is highlighted by new versions of such standbys as "Django," "Ralph's New Blues" and "The Golden Striker," is enjoyable enough although this LP does not live up to its potential. —*Scott Yanow*

Blues at Carnegie Hall / Apr. 27, 1966 / Mobile Fidelity ✦✦✦✦
On this Mobile Fidelity CD reissue of a live Atlantic set from 1966, The Modern Jazz Quartet performs eight blues-based compositions. In addition to such familiar pieces as the inevitable "Bags' Groove," "Ralph's New Blues" (dedicated to jazz critic Ralph Gleason) and "The Cylinder," there are a few newer pieces (including "Home" which is similar to Lee Morgan's hit "The Sidewinder") included for variety. This predictable but consistently swinging set is particularly recommended to fans of vibraphonist Milt Jackson. —*Scott Yanow*

Place Vendôme / Sep. 27, 1966–Oct. 30, 1966 / PolyGram ✦✦✦
With The Swingle Singers. This is a good departure for MJQ. Swingle Singers are a fine unit. —*Ron Wynn*

Live at the Lighthouse / Mar. 1967 / Atlantic ✦✦✦✦
This fairly obscure LP by The Modern Jazz Quartet features fresh material and improvisations that are both swinging and creative. Pianist John Lewis' "The Spiritual" and "Baseball" along with vibraphonist Milt Jackson's "Novamo" and "For Someone I Love" comprise half the program; there are also excellent ballad renditions of "The Shadow of Your Smile" and "What's New." The MJQ plays up to its usual level, and really none of the classic group's recordings should be passed by. It is a pity that few of The MJQ's Atlantic LPs have been reissued on CD yet. —*Scott Yanow*

Under the Jasmine Tree / Dec. 12, 1967 / Apple ✦✦✦

Space / 1969 / Apple ✦✦✦
The Modern Jazz Quartet took a hiatus from Atlantic Records to record two LPs for The Beatles' Apple label. Despite the switch, The MJQ's music remained unchanged; it was too classic to alter. This out-of-print album has among its selections a pair of obscure John Lewis originals ("Visitor from Venus" and "Visitor from Mars"), vibraphonist Milt Jackson's ballad feature on "Here's That Rainy Day" and the lengthy "Adagio from Concierto De Aranjuez."

Overall this is an average but worthy outing from a group whose excellence could always be taken for granted. —*Scott Yanow*

Plastic Dreams / May 1971 / Atlantic ✦✦✦
This is a streaky LP. The low points are the rather repetitious "Variations on a Christmas Theme" and "England's Carol" (the latter is based on "God Rest Ye Merry Gentleman"). However "Walkin' Stomp" is quite memorable as is the tango "Plastic Dreams" and "Trav'lin." Two selections add a five-piece brass section to the classic group (John Lewis on piano and harpsichord, vibraphonist Milt Jackson, bassist Percy Heath and drummer Connie Kay). Despite its faults, this generally enjoyable album deserves to be reissued on CD. —*Scott Yanow*

Legendary Profile / 1972 / Atlantic ✦✦✦
The Modern Jazz Quartet had been together 20 years at the time of this lesser-known Atlantic LP. Vibraphonist Milt Jackson and pianist John Lewis introduced two new songs apiece for this date, and the quartet (with bassist Percy Heath and drummer Connie Kay) also performs Tim Harden's "Misty Roses" and the pop song "What Now My Love." Nothing all that unusual happens except that Lewis for the first time with The MJQ doubles on two songs on electric piano. Despite that, the classic sound was still intact, and the style remained unchanged. —*Scott Yanow*

Blues on Bach / 1973 / Atlantic ✦✦✦✦
This LP has an interesting concept, alternating four original blues with five adaptations of melodies from classical works by Bach. The Modern Jazz Quartet had long been quite adept in both areas, and despite a certain lack of variety on this set (alternating back and forth between the two styles somewhat predictably), the music is largely enjoyable. Vibraphonist Milt Jackson, pianist John Lewis (doubling here on harpsichord), bassist Percy Heath and drummer Connie Kay were still all very much in their musical prime during the 21st year of The MJQ's existence. —*Scott Yanow*

In Memoriam / Nov. 5, 1973–Nov. 6, 1973 / Little David ✦✦
The Modern Jazz Quartet's last studio album before their breakup (which fortunately ended up just being a hiatus) in some ways shows why the group fell apart. All of the music on this LP (two works by John Lewis and a remake of "Adagio from the Guitar Concerto: Concierto De Aranjuez") is classically oriented. One can imagine that vibraphonist Milt Jackson (who usually preferred playing bebop) was getting a bit bored. The MJQ is accompanied by an orchestra conducted by Maurice Peress, and despite some stimulating moments, the music is often quite dry. It's one of the classic group's lesser releases. —*Scott Yanow*

★ **The Last Concert** / Nov. 25, 1974 / Atlantic ✦✦✦✦✦
The Modern Jazz Quartet broke up after the concert documented on this double CD. It would be nearly seven years before the group got back together again, but it certainly went out on top. Mostly revisiting their greatest hits, the MJQ is heard on this offer playing inspired versions of such songs as "Softly as in a Morning Sunrise," "Bags' Groove," "Skating in Central Park," "Confirmation," for "The Golden Striker" and of course, "Django." This set is a real gem (the music is essential for all serious jazz collections), featuring vibraphonist Milt Jackson, pianist John Lewis, bassist Percy Heath and drummer Connie Kay at their very best. —*Scott Yanow*

Reunion at Budokan / Oct. 19, 1981–Oct. 20, 1981 / Pablo ✦✦✦
After a seven-year "vacation," The Modern Jazz Quartet came back together in 1981 for a special reunion that ended up beginning another 14 plus years of playing together on at least a part-time basis. It is somehow fitting that on this Pablo LP (which has music taken from a Japanese concert) seven of the eight selections (all but John Lewis' "Odds Against Tomorrow") were remakes of songs that The MJQ had played in 1974 at their *Last Concert*. The revivals of "Softly as in a Morning Sunrise" and the group's two biggest "hits," "Bags' Groove" and "Django" are among the highlights of this excellent release. —*Scott Yanow*

Together Again at Montreux Jazz / Jul. 25, 1982 / Pablo ✦✦✦
This CD reissue features the revived Modern Jazz Quartet during their 30th year (counting a seven-year "vacation"), playing some of their usual repertoire (such as "Django," "The Cylinder" and "Bags' Groove" which for some reason was renamed "Bags' New Groove") before a happy audience at the 1982 Montreux Jazz Festival. In reality this release adds little to The MJQ's legacy (since all of the songs but vibraphonist Milt Jackson's "Monterey Mist" had been recorded before, some of them many times), but it does show that the band still had its enthusiasm and the abili-

ty to make the veteran material sound fresh and swinging. —*Scott Yanow*

Echoes / Together Again 1984 / Mar. 6, 1984 / Pablo ✦✦✦✦✦
If proof were needed that The Modern Jazz Quartet was back together permanently after a seven-year hiatus (1974–81), it is this CD for the six selections were all fairly new (as opposed to more runthroughs of their earlier hits). Pianist John Lewis contributed three compositions (including the appealing "That Slavic Smile" and "Sacha's March"), vibraphonist Milt Jackson wrote two, and bassist Percy Heath brought in his lighthearted "Watergate Blues." With drummer Connie Kay as usual rounding out the group, The MJQ's return was one of the happiest events in jazz of the 1980s. —*Scott Yanow*

Topsy: This One's for Basie / Jun. 3, 1985–Jun. 4, 1985 / Pablo ✦✦✦✦
Despite the title of this CD, the music on this 1985 studio set from The Modern Jazz Quartet is not a program of Count Basie tunes (with the exception of "Topsy") although Basie apparently liked the John Lewis composition "D and E." The other unrelated music is highlighted by an unaccompanied feature for vibraphonist Milt Jackson ("Nature Boy"), "Reunion Blues" and three more complex pieces from pianist John Lewis. Overall this CD gives listeners a fine example of the music of The MJQ during the 1980s. —*Scott Yanow*

Three Windows / Mar. 16, 1987–Mar. 20, 1987 / Atlantic ✦✦✦
The New York Chamber Symphony accompanies The Modern Jazz Quartet on this fine orchestral set. As usual the writing of John Lewis (who contributed all five compositions) dominates in this type of setting. The material includes three fairly recent originals plus "Three Windows" (which blends together three themes from Lewis' score for the French film *No Sun in Venice*) and the perennial "Django." Nice music overall although this is not one of the most essential MJQ releases. —*Scott Yanow*

For Ellington / Feb. 1, 1988–Feb. 3, 1988 / East West ✦✦✦✦
This is a tribute album that works quite well. The Modern Jazz Quartet is heard at their best on such Duke Ellington tunes as "Rockin' in Rhythm," "Jack the Bear" and "Ko-Ko." Also quite noteworthy are their two newer pieces, John Lewis' "For Ellington" and Milt Jackson's "Maestro E.K.E." which perfectly capture the spirit of Ellington's music. The ballads sometimes get a little sleepy, but on a whole this is a very enjoyable release. —*Scott Yanow*

● **Celebration** / Jun. 17, 1992–Jul. 16, 1993 / Atlantic ✦✦✦✦✦
As part of their 40th anniversary, The Modern Jazz Quartet welcomed ten guest artists to their CD: Bobby McFerrin (brilliant on "Billie's Bounce"), Take Six, Phil Woods, Wynton Marsalis (who gets to show off his technique on "Cherokee"), Illinois Jacquet, Harry "Sweets" Edison, Branford Marsalis, Jimmy Heath, Freddie Hubbard and Nina Tempo. As usual vibraphonist Milt Jackson and pianist John Lewis also have plenty of solo space, and bassist Percy Heath is perfect in support. Since drummer Connie Kay was ailing in 1992 (but back in action the following year), Mickey Roker fills in on seven of the 13 selections. With the exception of "Django" (which features Phil Woods) and "Bags' Groove," the music sticks to bop standards rather than MJQ standbys. It's an enjoyable and varied set. —*Scott Yanow*

Charles Moffett

b. Sept. 6, 1929, Fort Worth, TX
Drums / Avant-Garde
Charles Moffett is most significant for being the drummer with Ornette Coleman's 1965-67 trio and for being the father of a remarkable musical family that includes bassist Charnett, drummer Codaryl, vocalist Charisse, trumpeter Mondre and tenor saxophonist Charles, Jr.!

Charles Moffett, Sr. actually started out as a trumpeter, playing with Jimmy Witherspoon and other groups as a teenager. He switched to drums while in college. Moffett worked as a high school teacher in Texas (1953-61) but also played with jazz and R&B bands on the side. He first joined Ornette Coleman in 1961, but the altoist soon went into retirement for three years. Moffett worked with Sonny Rollins in 1963, recorded with Archie Shepp (*Four for Trane*) and led his own group which included Pharoah Sanders and Carla Bley. When Coleman began playing again, Moffett was a part of his classic trio which also included bassist David Izenzon; a couple of Blue Note records resulted. In 1970 he moved to Oakland where he directed a music school and played locally with Steve Turre and Prince Lasha. He later played with Frank Lowe in New York and continued teaching. Charles Moffett has recorded two albums as a leader: a Savoy set in 1969 that featured him also playing trumpet and vibes and a 1974 outing for LRS with his children. — *Scott Yanow*

The Gift / 1969 / Savoy ✦✦✦✦

Charnett Moffett

b. Jun. 10, 1967, New York, NY
Bass / Post-Bop, R&B
A virtuosic bassist who is equally skilled on acoustic and electric, Charnett Moffett has thus far been a better sideman than leader. His own recordings (for Manhattan, Blue Note and Evidence) to this point have had an excess of bass features while failing to develop a group sound. The son of drummer Charles Moffett, Sr. and the younger brother of drummer Codaryl, singer Charisse, trumpeter Mondre and tenor saxophonist Charles, Jr. (all of whom have guested on his records), Charnett started on bass early and appeared at age eight on a family record in 1974 for LRS. He later studied at Julliard and was in Wynton Marsalis' quintet when he was 16, playing with the trumpeter regularly during 1983–85. Moffett, who appeared on 17 records before he turned 20, has worked with Tony Williams, Slide Hampton, Mulgrew Miller, Monty Alexander, Sonny Sharrock, Stanley Jordan, David Sanborn, Arturo Sandoval, Diane Reeves among many others and played regularly with Ornette Coleman during 1993–95. —*Scott Yanow*

Net Man / 1986 / Blue Note ✦✦✦

Beauty Within / 1987 / Blue Note ✦✦✦
This is the second album from this offspring of a famous jazz musician and shows potential in places. —*Ron Wynn*

Nettwork / 1991 / Manhattan ✦✦✦
This recent Moffett has better songs than its predecessors but is still not completely satisfying. Guest appearances from his father and sister. —*Ron Wynn*

● **Planet Home** / Nov. 26, 1994–Nov. 27, 1994 / Evidence ✦✦✦✦✦

Miff Mole (Irving Milfred Mole)

b. Mar. 11, 1898, Roosevelt, NY, **d.** Apr. 29, 1961, New York, NY
Trombone / Classic Jazz, Dixieland
For a period in the 1920s, Miff Mole was (prior to the emergence of Jack Teagarden) the most advanced trombonist in jazz. He had gained a strong reputation playing with the Original Memphis Five (starting in 1922), and his many recordings with Red Nichols during 1926–27 found him taking unusual interval jumps with staccato phrasing that perfectly fit Nichols' style. However in 1927 he started working as a studio musician, and Mole concentrated less on jazz during the next couple of decades. He played with Paul Whiteman during 1938–40 and was with Benny Goodman in 1943. By the time he returned to small-group jazz in the mid-'40s (working with Eddie Condon and leading a band at Nick's), Mole sounded like a disciple of Teagarden, and his style was no longer unique although his record of "Peg of My Heart" was popular. Miff Mole's health was erratic by the 1950s, and he was largely forgotten by the greater jazz world by the time he died in 1961. His best recordings as a leader were when he led his Molers during 1927–30 although there was a four-song session in 1937 and later albums released by Jazzology, Commodore, Storyville and Argo. —*Scott Yanow*

● **Miff Mole Aboard the Dixie Hi-Flyer** / Jun. 25, 1959 / Stepheny ✦✦✦✦

Grachan Moncur III

b. Jun. 3, 1937, New York, NY
Trombone / Avant-Garde
One of the first trombonists to explore free jazz, Grachan Moncur III is still best-known for his pair of innovative Blue Note albums (1963–64) which also featured Lee Morgan and Jackie McLean on the first session and Wayne Shorter and Herbie Hancock on the later date. The son of bassist Grachan Moncur II who played with the Savoy Sultans during 1937–45, Grachan III started on trombone when he was 11. He toured with Ray Charles (1959–62) was with the Jazztet (1962) and in 1963 played advanced jazz with Jackie McLean. Moncur toured with Sonny Rollins (1964) and played and recorded with Marion Brown, Joe Henderson and Archie Shepp, matching up with fellow trombonist Roswell Rudd in the latter group. He also was part of the cooperative band 360 Degree Music Experience with Beaver Harris. Grachan Moncur,

who has also recorded as a leader for BYG (1969) and JCOA (1974), has continued playing challenging music up to the present day and has been an educator. Some of his more recent associations have been with Frank Lowe (1984–85), Cassandra Wilson (1985) and the Paris Reunion Band. —*Scott Yanow*

● **Evolution** / Nov. 21, 1963 / Blue Note ✦✦✦✦✦
Easily recommended Blue Note date from the '60s with Lee Morgan (tpt) and Jackie McLean (as). —*Michael G. Nastos*

★ **Some Other Stuff** / Jul. 6, 1964 / Blue Note ✦✦✦✦✦

New Africa / Aug. 11, 1969 / Actuel ✦✦✦✦
The trombonist in a modal setting with Archie Shepp (sax), Roscoe Mitchell (reeds) and Dave Burrell (p) in a Paris studio. —*Michael G. Nastos*

Echoes of Prayer / Apr. 11, 1974 / JCOA ✦✦✦✦
The 1974 *Melody Maker* Jazz Album of the Year. Progressive and thought-provoking. A legendary recording, with The Jazz Composers Orchestra. —*Michael G. Nastos*

T.S. Monk

b. 1951, New York, NY
Drums, Leader / Hard Bop
Although it took him a while before he decided to dedicate himself to playing jazz, T.S. Monk (Thelonious Monk, Jr.) has already accomplished a lot. He started out playing trumpet and piano before switching to drums when he was 13, taking some lessons from Max Roach. His first public performance was with his father Thelonious Monk on a television show in 1970. He toured with his father's quartet during 1970–71 and then played with the fusion band Natural Essence, the Paul Jeffrey Big Band and had an R&B group called T.S. Monk that had a few hits. In 1986 he established the Thelonious Monk Institute of Jazz, an organization that not only celebrates Monk, Sr.'s music but has an annual competition that has resulted in fame for some of its winners. His work with the Institute inspired the drummer to return to jazz. He played in Clifford Jordan's big band and with Walter Davis before putting together his own sextet which has had stable personnel since the late '80s. Monk's group often performs obscure jazz originals from the 1960s hard bop era with accurate transcriptions contributed by its trumpeter/arranger Don Sickler. Monk himself is an excellent drummer who sounds a little reminiscent of Tony Williams. —*Scott Yanow*

Take One / Oct. 16, 1991 / Blue Note ✦✦✦✦
The son of piano great Thelonious Monk, drummer T.S. Monk heads a contemporary hard bop band with some solid soloists, like saxophonist Willie Williams and pianist Ronnie Matthews. A surprise is trumpeter Don Sickler, better known in recent years for arrangements and production. —*Ron Wynn*

Changing of the Guard / 1993 / Blue Note ✦✦✦✦
Drummer T.S. Monk's sextet has quickly become one of the top repertory bands of hard bop. They revive quite a few obscurities on their Blue Note CD, including such forgotten compositions as J.J. Johnson's "Kelo," Clifford Jordan's "Middle of the Block," and Idrees Sulieman's "Doublemint," songs that are not exactly performed every day. They also perform more recent compositions by the likes of James Williams, Bobby Watson, Donald Brown and some of the bandmembers. Trumpeter Don Sickler's arrangements and transcriptions insure that the band plays the songs properly. With consistently inventive solos from Sickler, altoist Bobby Porcelli (who often takes honors), Willie Williams on teno-rand soprano and bassist Scott Colley, there is no weak link to this excellent sextet. The band adds to rather than merely copies the tradition. —*Scott Yanow*

● **The Charm** / 1995 / Blue Note ✦✦✦✦✦
T.S. Monk, by successfully keeping his sextet together as a regularly working outfit for several years, has been able to form a recognizable group sound in the hard bop tradition. Trumpeter Don Sickler's skills at transcribing charts from records has been a major asset, and the band's emphasis of obscurities has resulted in a very fresh repertoire; certainly Buddy Montgomery's "Budini," Melba Liston's "Just Waiting" and even Walter Davis, Jr.'s "Gypsy Folk Tales" would never qualify as standards. In addition to the older material (which includes an offbeat version of Thelonious Monk's "Bolivar Blues"), pianist Ronnie Mathews and altoist Bobby Porcelli have contributed newer pieces that fit the group's style. Although sometimes overlooked, T.S. Monk's sextet (which also includes Willie Williams on tenor and soprano and bassist

Scott Colley) has no weak links and is one of the most consistently satisfying jazz groups around in the mid-'90s. Their fine disc is easily recommended. — *Scott Yanow*

Thelonious Monk

b. Oct. 10, 1917, Rocky Mount, NC, **d.** Feb. 17, 1982, Weehawken, NJ

Piano, Composer, Leader / Bop, Post-Bop

The most important jazz musicians are the ones who are successful in creating their own original world of music with its own rules, logic and surprises. Thelonious Monk, who was criticized by observers who failed to listen to his music on its own terms, suffered through a decade of neglect before he was suddenly acclaimed as a genius; his music had not changed one bit in the interim. In fact, one of the more remarkable aspects of Monk's music was that it was fully formed by 1947, and he saw no need to alter his playing or compositional style in the slightest during the next 25 years.

Thelonious Monk grew up in New York, started playing piano when he was around five and had his first job touring as an accompanist to an evangelist. He was inspired by the Harlem stride pianists (James P. Johnson was a neighbor), and vestiges of that idiom can be heard in his later unaccompanied solos. However when he was playing in the house band of Minton's Playhouse during 1940-43, Monk was searching for his own individual style. Private recordings from the period find him sometimes resembling Teddy Wilson but starting to use more advanced rhythms and harmonies. He worked with Lucky Millinder a bit in 1942 and was with the Cootie Williams Orchestra briefly in 1944 (Williams recorded Monk's "Epistrophy" in 1942 and in 1944 was the first to record "'Round Midnight"), but it was when he became Coleman Hawkins' regular pianist that Monk was initially noticed. He cut a few titles with Hawkins (his recording debut), and although some of Hawkins' fans complained about the eccentric pianist, the veteran tenor could sense the pianist's greatness.

The 1945-54 period was very difficult for Thelonious Monk. Because he left a lot of space in his rhythmic solos and had an unusual technique, many people thought that he was an inferior pianist. His compositions were so advanced that the lazier bebop players (although not Dizzy Gillespie and Charlie Parker) assumed that he was crazy, and Thelonious Monk's name, appearance (he liked funny hats) and personality (an occasionally uncommunicative introvert) helped to brand him as some kind of nut. Fortunately Alfred Lion of Blue Note believed in him and recorded Monk extensively during 1947-48 and 1951-52. He also recorded for Prestige during 1952-54, had a solo set for Vogue in 1954 during a visit to Paris and appeared on a Verve date with Bird and Diz. But work was very sporadic during this era, and Monk had to struggle to make ends meet.

His fortunes slowly began to improve. In 1955 he signed with Riverside and producer Orrin Keepnews persuaded him to record an album of Duke Ellington tunes and one of standards so his music would appear to be more accessible to the average jazz fan. In 1956 came the classic *Brilliant Corners* album, but it was the following year when the situation permanently changed. Monk was booked into the Five Spot for a long engagement, and he used a quartet that featured tenor saxophonist John Coltrane. Finally the critics and then the jazz public recognized Thelonious Monk's greatness during this important gig. The fact that he was unique was a disadvantage a few years earlier when all modern jazz pianists were expected to sound like Bud Powell (who was ironically a close friend), but by 1957 the jazz public was looking for a new approach. Suddenly Monk was a celebrity, and his status would not change for the remainder of his career. In 1958 his quartet featured the tenor of Johnny Griffin (who was even more compatible than Coltrane), in 1959 he appeared with an orchestra at Town Hall (with arrangements by Hall Overton), in 1962 he signed with Columbia and two years later was on the cover of *Time*. A second orchestra concert in 1963 was even better than the first, and Monk toured constantly throughout the 1960s with his quartet which featured the reliable tenor of Charlie Rouse. He played with the Giants of Jazz during 1971-72 but then in 1973 suddenly retired. Monk was suffering from mental illness, and other than a few special appearances during the mid-'70s, he lived the rest of his life in seclusion. After his death it seemed as if everyone was doing Thelonious Monk tributes. There were so many versions of "'Round Midnight" that it was practically a pop hit! But despite the posthumous acclaim and attempts by pianists

ranging from Marcus Roberts to Tommy Flanagan to recreate his style, there was no replacement for the original.

Some of Thelonious Monk's songs became standards early on, most notably "'Round Midnight," "Straight No Chaser," "52nd Street Theme" and "Blue Monk." Many of his other compositions have by now been figured out by other jazz musicians and are occasionally performed including "Ruby My Dear," "Well You Needn't," "Off Minor," "In Walked Bud," "Misterioso," "Epistrophy," "I Mean You," "Four in One," "Criss Cross," "Ask Me Now," "Little Rootie Tootie," "Monk's Dream," "Bemsha Swing," "Think of One," "Friday the 13th," "Hackensack," "Nutty," "Brilliant Corners," "Crepuscule with Nellie," "Evidence" and "Rhythm-a-Ning." Virtually all of Monk's recordings (for Blue Note, Prestige, Vogue, Riverside, Columbia and Black Lion) have been reissued, and among his sidemen through the years were Idrees Sulieman, Art Blakey, Milt Jackson, Lou Donaldson, Lucky Thompson, Max Roach, Julius Watkins, Sonny Rollins, Clark Terry, Gerry Mulligan, John Coltrane, Wilbur Ware, Shadow Wilson, Johnny Griffin, Donald Byrd, Phil Woods, Thad Jones and Charlie Rouse. His son Thelonious Monk, Jr. (T.S. Monk) has helped keep the hard bop tradition alive with his quintet and has headed the Thelonious Monk Institute whose yearly competitions succeed in publicizing talented young players. — *Scott Yanow*

★ **Complete Blue Note Recordings** / Oct. 15, 1947–Apr. 14, 1957 / Blue Note ♦♦♦♦♦

Shortly after Mosaic's limited-edition four-LP box set of pianist/composer Thelonious Monk's Blue Note recordings ran out of stock, Blue Note reissued Monk's entire output plus his recently discovered 1958 live performance with John Coltrane on this four-CD package. The music is unique, highly influential and timeless. Monk did not record all that often for Blue Note during 1947-52 (six sessions), but the number of classics is quite impressive: "Ruby My Dear," "Well You Needn't," "Off Minor," "In Walked Bud," "'Round Midnight," "Evidence," "Misterioso," "Epistrophy," "I Mean You," "Four in One," "Criss Cross," "Straight No Chaser," and "Ask Me Now." Add to that his two appearances on a 1957 Sonny Rollins date along with the remarkable Coltrane session and the result is a set that should be in every jazz collection. — *Scott Yanow*

The Vibes Are On / Feb. 16, 1948–Nov. 15, 1952 / Chazzer ♦♦♦

Although Thelonious Monk is now considered one of the giants of jazz, up until his breakthrough in 1957 Monk's music was considered far too advanced and eccentric even for followers of bop. Therefore there are relatively few recordings of the pianist/composer during his early years outside of his Blue Note studio sides. This bootleg LP contains a rare broadcast from 1948 that finds him in a quartet with trumpeter Idrees Sulieman, bassist Curly Russell and drummer Art Blakey performing three songs in his unique style. In addition, this set has ten fine solos from pianist Art Tatum during the 1950-51 period and a rare version of "Blue 'N' Boogie" performed on Nov. 15, 1952 by an octet starring altoist Charlie Parker and trumpeter Dizzy Gillespie. This obscure release is well worth going out of one's way to acquire. — *Scott Yanow*

Thelonious Monk / Herbie Nichols / Mar. 6, 1952–Oct. 15, 1955 / Savoy ♦♦♦

This was a gap filler when it first came out. Thelonious Monk is heard on four selections from a 1955 quartet date with altoist Gigi Gryce, bassist Percy Heath and drummer Art Blakey. Check out Monk's songtitles: "Brake's Sake," "Shuffle Boil" and "Gallop's Gallop." Herbie Nichols, who only recorded three other albums of material as a leader, is heard on a comparatively light session with guitarist Danny Barker, bassist Chocolate Williams and drummer Shadow Wilson in 1952; Williams sings two of the blues. Although these dates are not essential, Monk and Nichols collectors will find this LP quite valuable. — *Scott Yanow*

Thelonious Monk And Joe Turner In Paris / Mar. 1952+Jun. 7, 1954 / Vogue ♦♦♦♦

This French Vogue reissue CD combines together two unrelated solo piano sets. The nine performances by Thelonious Monk are a bit familiar since these renditions (which are highlighted by "'Round Midnight," "Well You Needn't," "We See" and "Hackensack") had been previously reissued by GNP/Crescendo and Mosaic. However the 13 selections (including three alternate takes) by Joe Turner (no relation to singer Big Joe Turner) are much rarer. Turner, a talented American stride pianist who spent most of his life living in France, had only recorded ten songs as a leader prior to this 1952 session and is in top form for such numbers as "Hallelujah," "Between the Devil and the Deep Blue Sea," "Wedding Boogie" and three versions of "Tea for Two." This CD is easily recommended to jazz piano collectors who do not already have the Monk selections. —*Scott Yanow*

Thelonious Monk Trio / Oct. 15, 1952+Dec. 18, 1952 / Original Jazz Classics ✦✦✦✦
1952 & 1954. Wonderful trio recordings. The difference between the Max Roach (d) and Art Blakey (d) cuts is quite instructive. These are some of Monk's more captivating solos from the 50s. —*Ron Wynn*

Thelonious Monk / Oct. 15, 1952–Sep. 22, 1954 / Prestige ✦✦✦✦✦
This two-LP set contains all 19 of pianist/composer Thelonious Monk's Prestige recordings. Although he was unhappy with the treatment he received while with the label during 1952–54 (a period when he was in undeserved obscurity), Monk's playing on these trio and quintet sides (some of which feature either Sonny Rollins or Frank Foster on tenor, trumpeter Ray Copeland and the great French horn player Julius Watkins) find him in particularly strong and creative form. Such tunes as "Little Rootie Tootie," "Bye-ya," "Trinkle Trinkle," "Bemsha Swing," "Friday the 13th" and "Hackensack" are heard in their earliest recordings. —*Scott Yanow*

Monk / Oct. 15, 1952–Sep. 22, 1954 / Original Jazz Classics ✦✦✦✦

Thelonious Monk and Sonny Rollins / Nov. 13, 1953–Sep. 22, 1954 / Original Jazz Classics ✦✦✦✦✦
This date contained "The Way You Look Tonight" from the *Moving Out* session, plus titles from Nov. 13, 1953 and Sept. 22, 1954. The latter two were pianist Thelonious Monk's dates with tenor saxophonist Sonny Rollins, Julius Watkins (French horn), Percy Heath (bass) and Willie Jones (drums) or Heath and Art Blakey (drums on the Sept. 22, 1954 cuts). For me, the standout here was the wonderfully effervescent handling of "The Way You Look Tonight." Rollins attacked it with a *major* spirit and played with a euphoria rarely matched in recorded jazz. —*Bob Rusch, Cadence*

★ **Complete Black Lion and Vogue** / Jun. 7, 1954–Nov. 15, 1971 / Mosaic ✦✦✦✦✦
This four-LP limited-edition box set from Mosaic contains the nine piano solos recorded by Thelonious Monk while in Paris on June 7, 1954 (most of which have also been issued by GNP Crescendo) and, more importantly, his complete marathon London session of Nov. 15, 1971. The latter, split between solo and trio performances (with bassist Al McKibbon and drummer Art Blakey) was (other than a record with the Giants of Jazz) Monk's final recording and found the unique pianist in brilliant form, really romping on some of his solos. Although the majority of the songs are his originals, the emphasis on this essential music is on the piano playing. Those critics and listeners who feel that Monk was a limited musician should give these final performances a very close listen. —*Scott Yanow*

Plays Duke Ellington / Jul. 21, 1955+Jul. 27, 1955 / Original Jazz Classics ✦✦✦✦
One genius tackles the music of another. Superb trio recordings spiced by Oscar Pettiford (b) and Kenny Clarke (d). —*Ron Wynn*

Riverside Trios / Jul. 21, 1955–Apr. 3, 1956 / Milestone ✦✦✦✦✦
When Thelonious Monk first signed with Riverside Records in 1955, producer Orrin Keepnews thought that it would be a good idea for the unrecognized giant to record an album of Duke Ellington compositions and follow it up with a set of standards so as to discount his eccentric and forbidding image. The results were quite satisfying, trio performances with bassist Oscar Pettiford and either Kenny Clarke or Art Blakey on drums that made Monk's playing seem more accessible to the regular jazz audience without watering down his style. This two-LP set contains both albums (the program of Ellington's music is particularly unique) and is very enjoyable. —*Scott Yanow*

★ **The Complete Riverside Recordings** / Jul. 21, 1955–Apr. 21, 1961 / Riverside ✦✦✦✦✦
Although this 15-CD box set is not inexpensive, this is the most essential of all of Thelonious Monk's releases. It was during his years with Riverside that Monk achieved the fame he had long deserved. Producer Orrin Keepnews was wise enough to feature the unique pianist/composer in a wide variety of settings, and they are all here: separate trio sessions comprising Duke

Ellington songs and standards, meetings on record with Sonny Rollins (including "Brilliant Corners"), John Coltrane, Coleman Hawkins, Gerry Mulligan and Johnny Griffin, the beginnings of Monk's Quartet with Charlie Rouse, a truncated (and previously unissued) session with Shelly Manne, Monk's famous Town Hall concert of 1959 and a full date of unaccompanied piano solos. Most of this music has also been made available on Milestone two-LP sets and single CDs, but this is the best (and most complete) way to acquire these classics. —*Scott Yanow*

The Unique Thelonious Monk / Mar. 17, 1956+Apr. 3, 1956 / Original Jazz Classics ✦✦✦✦
The trio with Oscar Pettiford (b) and Blakey (d) plays standards, no originals. —*Hank Davis*

Straight No Chaser: Thelonius Monk / Sep. 1956–1968 / Columbia ✦✦✦✦
This LP, taken from the soundtrack of the fascinating film *Straight No Chaser*, contains a great deal of previously unissued material by Thelonious Monk. Three songs were released before, but the other eight numbers (two solos from 1956 and the remainder from 1967–68) are "new," including rehearsal and club performances and two numbers from Monk's otherwise forgotten octet of 1967. It's a real bonus for collectors and a fine complement to the highly recommended film. —*Scott Yanow*

● **Brilliant Corners** / Dec. 17, 1956–Dec. 23, 1956 / Original Jazz Classics ✦✦✦✦✦
A recording feat features an excellent version of the title tune. Clark Terry (tpt), Sonny Rollins (ts) and Max Roach (d) guest. —*Hank Davis*

Thelonious Himself / Apr. 5, 1957–Apr. 16, 1957 / Original Jazz Classics ✦✦✦✦✦
These are mostly solo; with one cut Coltrane (ts) and Wilbur Ware (b). —*Ron Wynn*

Thelonious Monk & John Coltrane / Apr. 16, 1957–1957 / Milestone ✦✦✦✦✦
Much of the music on this two-LP set is quite essential for any serious jazz library (all of it is also included in Monk's giant 15-CD box set *The Complete Riverside Recordings*). Although Thelonious Monk and John Coltrane played together for several months in 1957, until the discovery of a live tape (which has been issued on Blue Note), the music on this two-fer (which includes several tracks with a larger group that also features Coleman Hawkins, "Monk's Mood" by a trio with bassist Wilbur Ware and three outstanding tracks with a quartet) was all that existed of their historic collaboration. Coltrane developed rapidly during his period with Monk, and he is heard in brilliant form on "Trinkle, Tinkle" and "Nutty." —*Scott Yanow*

Art Blakey's Jazz Messengers with Thelonious Monk / May 19, 1957 / Atlantic ✦✦✦✦✦
Thelonious Monk rarely performed or recorded as a sideman, making this Atlantic LP on which he shares co-billing with drummer Art Blakey a rare event. Monk sounds quite comfortable sitting in with the 1957 version of The Jazz Messengers; in fact tenor saxophonist Johnny Griffin would soon join his own quartet. The Messengers (which also includes trumpeter Bill Hardman and bassist Spanky DeBrest) perform fine versions of five Monk compositions and Griffin's "Purple Shades." This set deserves to be reissued on CD. —*Scott Yanow*

● **Thelonious with John Coltrane** / Jun. 25, 1957–1958 / Original Jazz Classics ✦✦✦✦✦
Tenor saxophonist John Coltrane was present on a spring of '58 date as part of the Thelonious Monk quartet on a session which made up half of *Thelonious Monk With John Coltrane*. The remainder was a June 12, 1957 date with Trane, Coleman Hawkins, Gigi Gryce, Ray Copeland, Ware and Art Blakey, and Monk solo piano on "Functional." The material has been scattered around; most of it was on a previous two-fer. It was great music— Trane, Hawk, Blakey... This presented classic encounters and lasting music. —*Bob Rusch, Cadence*

★ **Discovery! at the Five Spot** / 1958 / Blue Note ✦✦✦✦✦
The collaboration between pianist Thelonious Monk and tenor saxophonist John Coltrane was considered (along with the 1943 Earl Hines big band with Charlie Parker and Dizzy Gillespie and the music of the pioneering jazz cornetist Buddy Bolden) to be one of the three lost wonders of jazz history. Although they recorded a trio of quartet numbers in the studios (which are included in various Milestone and Riverside reissues), there was

apparently no documentation of their lengthy gig at the Five Spot in 1957, until a tape that Coltrane's wife had recorded was recently discovered. This CD has the happy results, five songs performed by Monk, Coltrane, bassist Ahmed Abdul-Malik and drummer Roy Haynes at the Five Spot. Highpoints of this somewhat miraculous find include "Trinkle Tinkle," "In Walked Bud" and "I Mean You;" there are also shorter versions of "Epistrophy": and "Crepuscule With Nellie." —Scott Yanow

Blues Five Spot / Feb. 25, 1958–Apr. 18, 1961 / Milestone ✦✦✦✦
This LP contains eight performances that were being released for the first time in 1984. Thelonious Monk is heard on several numberswith his 1958 Quartet that featured tenor saxophonist Johnny Griffin and on a selection apiece with a sextet (with Griffin, trumpeter Donald Byrd and baritonist Pepper Adams), quintet (featuring his longtime tenor Charlie Rouse and cornetist Thad Jones), quartet ("Crepescule with Nellie") and solo ("Body and Soul"). A strong all-round set it certainly deserved to be released. —Scott Yanow

Thelonious in Action: Recorded at the Five Spot Cafe / Aug. 7, 1958 / Original Jazz Classics ✦✦✦✦✦

● **Misterioso** / Aug. 7, 1958 / Milestone ✦✦✦✦✦
One of Thelonious Monk's finest bands was the quartet he led in 1958 that featured tenor saxophonist Johnny Griffin. Griffin sounded quite comfortable playing Monk's music, and his fiery style really inspired the pianist/composer. This two-LP set (whose contents are also available on Monk's massive CD box *The Complete Riverside Recordings*) has many great moments including "In Walked Bud," "Nutty," and "Let's Cool One" and makes one regret that this band did not stay together for a much longer period. —Scott Yanow

★ **The Thelonious Monk Orchestra at Town Hall, the** / Feb. 28, 1959 / Original Jazz Classics ✦✦✦✦✦
Thelonious Monk Orchestra. A great orchestral showpiece for Monk the composer, one of his best live dates. —Ron Wynn

In Person / Feb. 28, 1959 / Milestone ✦✦✦✦✦
Prior to Fantasy reissuing all of Thelonious Monk's Riverside dates on the 15-CD box set *The Complete Riverside Recordings*, it repackaged most of his music on a series of attractive two-LP sets. The first half of *In Person* contains the pianist/composer's famous Town Hall concert of 1959 in which he performed his compositions as part of a ten-piece group also featuring trumpeter Donald Byrd, altoist Phil Woods, Charlie Rouse on tenor and baritonist Pepper Adams; Hall Overton's arrangement of Monk's recorded piano solo for the full band on "Little Rootie Tootie" is a highpoint. The second half of this two-fer finds Monk leading a strong sextet with trumpeter Joe Gordon and tenors Rouse and Harold Land live at the Blackhawk in 1960 for four of his originals and "I'm Getting Sentimental over You." —Scott Yanow

Evidence / Feb. 28, 1959–Apr. 29, 1960 / Milestone ✦✦✦✦
This single LP complements the two-fer *In Person* by offering additional music from both of the sessions: the Town Hall concert of 1959 (all but a brief "Thelonious" were actually performances by his quartet) and a sextet gig from 1960 with trumpeter Joe Gordon and the tenors of Charlie Rouse and Harold Land. Although not essential (and this music has since been reissued on CD), these are excellent recordings by the unique pianist/composer. —Scott Yanow

Five by Monk by Five / Jun. 1, 1959–Jun. 2, 1959 / Original Jazz Classics ✦✦✦
Quintet. The music proves as intriguing as the title. Excellent trumpet solos from Thad Jones. —Ron Wynn

Alone in San Francisco / Oct. 21, 1959+Oct. 22, 1959 / Original Jazz Classics ✦✦✦✦✦
Solo piano. Exacting, distinctive renditions of such Monk classics as "Blue Monk," "Pannonica," and "Reflections." —Ron Wynn

At the Blackhawk / Apr. 29, 1960 / Original Jazz Classics ✦✦✦
Special guests Harold Land (ts) and Joe Gordon (tpt) make this a great sextet. Monk's playing is daring and energized. —Ron Wynn

Made in France / Apr. 18, 1961 / Original Jazz Classics ✦✦✦
The pianist/leader and tenor saxophonist Charlie Rouse are in fine form even if the solos by bassist John Ore and drummer Frankie Dunlop are somewhat pedestrian. This is good but not essential music with lengthy runthroughs on seven Monk originals (plus three standards). —Scott Yanow

Thelonious Monk in Italy / Apr. 21, 1961 / Original Jazz Classics ✦✦✦
A good quartet date, with tremendous work from Charlie Rouse (ts) and Monk. —Ron Wynn

Live in Stockholm (1961) / May 16, 1961 / Dragon ✦✦✦
This two-LP set from the Swedish label Dragon features the Thelonious Monk Quartet just prior to the pianist signing with Columbia. Taken from a radio broadcast, these performances feature ten Monk compositions plus "I'm Getting Sentimental over You" and brief piano solos on "Just a Gigolo" and "Body and Soul." As with the other Monk European recordings from this tour, the solos of bassist John Ore and drummer Frankie Dunlop are run of the mill, but Monk and tenor saxophonist Charlie Rouse are in excellent form. —Scott Yanow

Monk's Dream / Oct. 31, 1962–Nov. 6, 1962 / Columbia ✦✦✦✦
Most of Thelonious Monk's recordings for Columbia featured his regular working quartet which at the time of his debut consisted of tenor saxophonist Charlie Rouse, bassist John Ore and drummer Frankie Dunlop. The music on this LP is fairly typical of his repertoire of the period, five originals (only "Bright Mississippi" had not been recorded before) and three standards, two of which are taken as brief piano solos. However despite a certain amount of predictability, the playing is consistently excellent and enthusiastic; even if the jazz world was starting to catch up to Monk, his highly original music stood on its own merits. —Scott Yanow

Always Know / Nov. 2, 1962–Feb. 14, 1968 / Columbia ✦✦✦✦
Thelonious Monk fans in particular are advised to search for this valuable two-LP set for it contains a variety of unissued material from the pianist/composer's six-year period with Columbia. Monk is heard on three piano solos, with his regular working quartet, heading a trio on "Easy Street" and at his renowned Lincoln Center concert with a nonet on "Light Blue" and "Bye Ya." The music on this two-fer is at the same consistent high level as his Columbia recordings of the 1960s and contains some surprising moments. —Scott Yanow

Criss-Cross / Nov. 6, 1962–Mar. 29, 1963 / Columbia/Legacy ✦✦✦✦✦
This CD reissue of the Columbia LP adds a previously unissued version of "Pannonica" to the original program along with updated liner notes. The high-quality repertoire (which includes "Hackensack," "Tea for Two," "Criss-Cross" and "Rhythm-A-Ning") and some consistent solos from the leader/pianist and tenor saxophonist Charlie Rouse make this a CD worth picking up. —Scott Yanow

The Composer / Nov. 6, 1962–Nov. 20, 1968 / Columbia ✦✦✦
This CD contains a fine cross section of Thelonious Monk's performances of his own originals during the 1960s, drawing its material from five separate sessions. All of the music (even a then-previously unreleased version of "Blue Monk") is currently available elsewhere but, for listeners just beginning to explore Monk's music, this set (which contains 11 of his compositions performed solo, by his quartet that included tenor saxophonist Charlie Rouse or with Oliver Nelson's orchestra) can serve as a fine introduction to the unique innovator. —Scott Yanow

Tokyo Concerts / May 21, 1963 / Columbia ✦✦✦✦
This two-LP set of material (all but "Evidence" was only previously out in Japan) features the Thelonious Monk Quartet (with tenor saxophonist Charlie Rouse, bassist Butch Warren and drummer Frankie Dunlop) romping through Monk's usual repertoire (eight familiar originals, a brief piano solo on "Just a Gigolo" and the standard "I'm Gettin' Sentimental over You"). The solos are fresh, and even if no real surprises occur, the enthusiasm and joy of this music makes it recommended even to Monk collectors who already have most of his recordings. —Scott Yanow

Misterioso / May 1963–Mar. 2, 1965 / Columbia ✦✦✦✦
This LP contains music taken from a variety of sources dating from 1963–65. Pianist/composer Thelonious Monk and tenor saxophonist Charlie Rouse are a constant while bassist Butch Warren and drummer Frank Dunlop are succeeded on a few tracks by bassist Larry Gales and drummer Ben Riley. Not many surprises occur although it is good to hear this band playing "All the Things You Are" and "Honeysuckle Rose" in addition to their usual repertoire. Worth picking up, this music should be reissued on CD eventually. —Scott Yanow

Monterey Jazz Festival '63 / Sep. 21, 1963–Sep. 22, 1963 / Storyville ✦✦✦✦
This double-CD contains pianist/composer Thelonious Monk's

two sets at the 1963 Monterey Jazz Festival, music that was unreleased until 1994. Monk plays with tenor saxophonist Charlie Rouse, bassist John Ore and drummer Frank Dunlop perform lengthy versions of two standards ("I'm Getting Sentimental over You" and a nearly 19-minute "Sweet and Lovely") and seven of Thelonious's originals. Nothing all that unusual occurs (outside of the two-beat feel that Ore gives "I Mean You"), but Monk and Rouse have plenty of fine solos. An above-average effort. —*Scott Yanow*

Live at the Village Gate / Nov. 12, 1963 / Xanadu ++++

★ **Big Band and Quartet in Concert** / Dec. 30, 1963 / Columbia +++++

It's Monk's Time / Jan. 30, 1964–Mar. 9, 1964 / Columbia ++++

Solo Monk / Oct. 31, 1964 / Columbia ++++
A 1965 session with superb and quirky unaccompanied piano. —*Hank Davis*

Straight, No Chaser / Nov. 14, 1966–Jan. 10, 1967 / Columbia ++++
Charlie Rouse (ts) and Monk's magic is the highlight of this 1966 set. —*Ron Wynn*

Nonet: Live! / Nov. 3, 1967 / Le Jazz ++++
Pianist/composer Thelonious Monk led a quartet throughout the 1960s, but on a European tour in 1967 his group was expanded with the addition of several top horn players. This CD, which contains all of the music from a Paris concert, features Monk with his regular tenor Charlie Rouse, bassist Larry Gales and drummer Ben Riley on a couple of songs, adds trumpeter Ray Copeland to make the band a quintet, and for a few numbers they are joined by trombonist Jimmy Cleveland, altoist Phil Woods and tenor saxophonist Johnny Griffin; in addition fluegelhornist Clark Terry sits in and stars on "Blue Monk." Monk had only recorded with this large a group on two prior occasions, making this rare recording a historical curiosity; more importantly the music (six of his originals) is excellent. —*Scott Yanow*

Underground / Dec. 14, 1967–Feb. 14, 1968 / Columbia +++++
An excellent latter-period Monk group. "Green Chimneys" is a prime cut. Charlie Rouse is on tenor sax. —*Michael G. Nastos*

Monk's Blues / Nov. 19, 1968 / Columbia +++

The London Collection, Vol. 1 / Nov. 15, 1971 / Black Lion +++++

The London Collection, Vol. 2 / Nov. 15, 1971 / Black Lion +++++

The London Collection, Vol. 3 / Nov. 15, 1971 / Black Lion +++++

J.R. Monterose (Frank Anthony Monterose, Jr.)

b. Jan. 19, 1927, Detriot, MI, d. Sept. 16, 1993, Utica, NY
Tenor Saxophone / Hard Bop
J.R. Monterose (not to be confused with fellow tenor Jack Montrose) is most famous for a gig that he personally did not enjoy, playing with Charles Mingus in 1956 and recording on Mingus' breakthrough album *Pithecanthropus Erectus*. He grew up in Utica, NY, played in territory bands in the Midwest and then moved to New York City in the early '50s. Monterose played with Buddy Rich (1952) and Claude Thornhill and recorded with (among others) Teddy Charles, Jon Eardley and Eddie Bert. After leaving Mingus (who he did not get along with), Monterose played with Kenny Dorham's Jazz Prophets and recorded a strong set for Blue Note as a leader. Although he performed into the 1980s (doubling on soprano in later years), Monterose never really became famous. In addition to his Blue Note date he led sets for Jaro (a 1959 session later reissued by Xanadu), Studio 4 (which was reissued by VSOP), a very obscure 1969 outing for the Dutch label Heavy Soul Music (1969) and during 1979–81 albums for Progressive, Cadence and two for Uptown. —*Scott Yanow*

● **J. R. Monterose** / Oct. 21, 1956 / Blue Note +++++

Straight Ahead / Nov. 24, 1959 / Xanadu +++++
Even though the music was magnificent, it wouldn't matter to Monterose fanatics. The added treat were the liner notes which filled us up on where Monterose had been (Europe) and what he was into (playing sax and guitar). This record was a reissue of the phantom Jaro disc, *The Message*, recorded on Nov. 24, 1959... Throughout this set Monterose played with great ease and authority. Certainly there was never a played out quality in the improvised work, which came with an ease of breath, nor did the impro-

vising become static. It was always inventive and warm. —*Bob Rusch, Cadence*

In Action with the Joe Abodeely Trio / Nov. 1964 / Bainbridge ++++
The LP that launched the VSOP label is a reissue of a real rarity by the obscure but talented tenor J.R. Monterose, originally cut for Studio 4. With good backing from pianist Dale Oehler, bassist Gary Allen and drummer Joe Abodeely, Monterose displays a unique tone and the ability to play creatively within the advanced hard bop idiom. Considering how well he plays on this set (which has not yet been reissued on CD), it is surprising to realize that this was one of only two sessions (with the other set being even less known) led by J.R. Monterose during a 20-year period. Worth a search. —*Scott Yanow*

Live in Albany / May 8, 1979 / Uptown +++

A Little Pleasure / Apr. 6, 1981–Apr. 7, 1981 / Uptown ++++

Buddy Montgomery (Charles F. Montgomery)

b. Jan. 30, 1930, Indianapolis, IN
Piano, Vibes / Hard Bop
The youngest of the three Montgomery Brothers, Buddy Montgomery has long been a reliable if underrated vibraphonist and pianist. He became a professional in 1948 and the following year toured with Big Joe Turner. He played piano with Slide Hampton in his native Indianapolis, served in the Army and then was a member (on vibes) of the popular Mastersounds with his brother Monk. Buddy had a brief stint with Miles Davis (playing vibes) in 1960 and frequently played with brothers Wes and Monk (under the guitarist's leadership) in the 1960s. He moved to Milwaukee in 1969, becoming a local fixture and an educator. In the early '80s Montgomery moved to Oakland where he has recorded for producer Orrin Keepnews on Landmark and with the Riverside Reunion Band. Buddy Montgomery's earlier dates as a leader were for World Pacific (1957), Fantasy, Riverside, Milestone and Impulse (1969). —*Scott Yanow*

The Two-Sided Album / Feb. 28, 1968 / Milestone +++

This Rather Than That / Sep. 10, 1969+Jan. 1971 / Impulse +++

Ties of Love / 1986 / Landmark ++++

● **So Why Not?** / 1988 / Landmark +++++
Rare record as a leader. Well-done, with some contemporary touches. —*Michael G. Nastos*

Live at Maybeck Recital Hall, Vol. 15 / Jul. 14, 1991 / Concord Jazz ++++

Monk Montgomery
(William Howard Montgomery)

b. Oct. 10, 1921, Indianapolis, IN, d. May 20, 1982, Las Vegas, NV
Bass / Hard Bop, Crossover
The oldest of the three Montgomery brothers, Monk Montgomery has the distinction of being the first significant jazz electric bassist, starting on the instrument in 1953. He actually did not start playing bass until he was already 30 but was soon strong enough to play with Lionel Hampton's Orchestra (1951–53). He played in the Montgomery-Johnson Quintet in Indianapolis with his brothers Wes and Buddy (along with tenor saxophonist Alonzo Johnson and drummer Robert Johnson) during 1955–56. Monk moved to Seattle, was joined by Buddy, and they formed the Mastersounds, a popular quartet (1957–60). He played occasionally with his brothers in the 1960s (including a short-lived group called the Montgomery Brothers), freelanced, was with Cal Tjader in 1966 and in 1970 settled in Las Vegas. Montgomery played locally (including with Red Norvo's trio during 1970–72), was a disc jockey and led obscure sessions for the Chiss (1971) and Philadelphia Int. (1974) labels. During his last years he was active as the founder of the Las Vegas Jazz Society. —*Scott Yanow*

Reality / 1974 / Philadelphia International +++

Wes Montgomery (John Leslie Montgomery)

b. Mar. 6, 1925, Indianapolis, IN, d. Jun. 15, 1968, Indianapolis, IN
Guitar / Hard Bop, Crossover
Wes Montgomery was one of the great jazz guitarists, a natural extension of Charlie Christian whose appealing use of octaves became influential and his trademark. He achieved great commercial success during his last few years, only to die prematurely.

It had taken Wes a long time to become an overnight success. He started to teach himself guitar in 1943 (using his thumb rather than a pick) and toured with Lionel Hampton during 1948-50; he can be heard on a few broadcasts from the period. But then Montgomery returned to Indianapolis where he was in obscurity during much of the 1950s, working a day job and playing at clubs most nights. He recorded with his brothers vibraphonist Buddy and electric bassist Monk during 1957-59 and made his first Riverside album (1959) in a trio with organist Melvin Rhyne. In 1960 the release of his album *The Incredible Jazz Guitar of Wes Montgomery* made him famous in the jazz world. Other than a brief time playing with the John Coltrane Sextet (which also included Eric Dolphy) later in the year, Wes would be a leader for the rest of his life.

Montgomery's recordings can be easily divided into three periods. His Riverside dates (1959-63) are his most spontaneous jazz outings, small-group sessions with such sidemen as Tommy Flanagan, James Clay, Victor Feldman, Hank Jones, Johnny Griffin and Mel Rhyne. The one exception was the ironically titled *Fusion*, a ballad date with a string section. All of the Riverside recordings have been reissued in a massive 12-CD box set. With the collapse of Riverside, Montgomery moved over to Verve where during 1964-66 he recorded an interesting series of mostly orchestral dates with arranger Don Sebesky and producer Creed Taylor. These records were generally a good balance between jazz and accessibility, even if the best performances were small-group outings with either the Wynton Kelly Trio or Jimmy Smith. In 1967 Wes signed with Creed Taylor at A&M, and during 1967-68 he recorded three best-selling albums that found him merely stating simple pop melodies while backed by strings and woodwinds. His jazz fans were upset, but Montgomery's albums were played on AM radio during the period, he helped introduce listeners to jazz, and his live performances were as freewheeling as his earlier Riverside dates. Unfortunately, at the height of his success, he died of a heart attack. However Wes Montgomery's influence is still felt on many young guitarists. *—Scott Yanow*

Far Wes / Apr. 18, 1958-Oct. 1959 / Pacific Jazz ✦✦✦✦✦
This historical CD contains some of guitarist Wes Montgomery's first recordings; in fact only three small-group songs predate these performances. The then-obscure guitarist is heard in two different quintets, both of which include his brothers Buddy (on piano) and Monk (playing electric bass). The earlier set has Harold Land's tenor as a lead voice while altoist Pony Poindexter takes his place on the later date, Wes' sound was already quite recognizable, and he contributes six originals which alternate with Harold Land's "Hymn for Carl" and four standards. *—Scott Yanow*

Guitar on the Go / Oct. 5, 1959+Nov. 27, 1963 / Original Jazz Classics ✦✦✦
The final Riverside release of Wes Montgomery material (before the important label went completely bankrupt) was similar to his debut four years earlier; a trio with organist Melvin Rhyne and an obscure drummer (this time George Brown). The CD reissue even includes one leftover track from the earliest session ("Missile Blues") along with newer jams and a pair of "bonus tracks": an alternate take of "The Way You Look Tonight" and a brief "Unidentified Solo Guitar" piece. In general the music swings hard (particularly the two versions of "The Way You Look Tonight") and is a worthy if not essential addition to Wes Montgomery's discography. He would have a few straight-ahead dates for Verve, but this release was really the end of an era. *—Scott Yanow*

Wes Montgomery Trio / Oct. 5, 1959-Oct. 6, 1959 / Original Jazz Classics ✦✦✦✦
Wes Montgomery's first of many sessions for Riverside matched his guitar with organist Melvin Rhyne and drummer Paul Parker for some straight-ahead swinging. Highlights include "Yesterdays," "'Round Midnight" and Montgomery's originals "Missile Blues" and "Jingles." This CD reissue adds two alternate takes to the original program. *—Scott Yanow*

★ **The Complete Riverside Recordings [Box Set]** / Oct. 5, 1959-Nov. 27, 1963 / Riverside ✦✦✦✦✦
Wes Montgomery recorded exclusively for the Riverside label during the four years covered by this massive 12-CD box set, and although his later albums for Verve and particularly the pop/jazz A&M dates sold many more copies, it is for his Riverside dates that his legacy was primarily formed. Virtually unknown at the time of his debut on Riverside, Montgomery soon became a major

influence whose style is still copied in the 1990s. The guitarist is heard in quite a few different settings on this box including in trios with organist Melvin Rhyne, a quartet with pianist Tommy Flanagan, as a sideman on different sessions with Nat Adderley, Harold Land and Cannonball Adderley, performing with his brothers Buddy and Monk, holding his own with pianist George Shearing, vibraphonist Milt Jackson and tenor great Johnny Griffin and (for an album ironically titled *Fusion*) playing with strings for the first time. All in all there are a tremendous amount of rewarding performances included in this essential set, most of which show why Wes Montgomery is still considered one of the all-time great jazz guitarists. *—Scott Yanow*

★ **The Incredible Jazz Guitar of Wes Montgomery** / Jan. 26, 1960+Jan. 28, 1960 / Original Jazz Classics ✦✦✦✦✦
This is one of Wes Montgomery's greatest recordings, a classic that really alerted the world about the talents of the guitarist. In a quartet with pianist Tommy Flanagan, bassist Percy Heath and drummer Albert Heath, Wes introduced his originals "West Coast Blues," "Four on Six," and "D-Natural Blues," performed his "Mister Walker" and stretched out on "Airegin," the ballad "Polka Dots and Moonbeams," "In Your Own Sweet Way" and "Gone with the Wind." All of the unique qualities of Wes Montgomery's style are on display on this essential CD reissue which is also available as part of his 12-CD Riverside boxed set. *—Scott Yanow*

Groove Brothers / Jul. 1960-Dec. 1961 / Milestone ✦✦✦✦
It always seemed strange (considering their popularity) that guitarist Wes Montgomery and the group The Mastersounds (which featured his brothers Buddy and Monk) were never able to successfully (on a commercial basis) combine forces. This two-LP set consists of Wes' recordings with his brothers' group: the full album titled *Groove Yard* and half of two other Fantasy records. With Buddy on piano and vibes, Monk on bass and alternating drummers, the music is consistently excellent with the emphasis on attractive chord changes (including two originals apiece by Buddy and Wes) and solid swinging. Most of this rewarding music has since been reissued on CD. *—Scott Yanow*

Movin' Along / Oct. 11, 1960 / Original Jazz Classics ✦✦✦✦✦
Because it was recorded between two of Wes Montgomery's best-known albums (*Incredible Jazz Guitar* and *So Much Guitar*), this particular CD is a bit underrated. The great guitarist is teamed with flutist James Clay (who switches to tenor on Wes' "So Do It"), pianist Victor Feldman, bassist Sam Jones and drummer Louis Hayes for four standards (highlighted by Clifford Brown's "Sandu!!" and "Body and Soul"), Sam Jones' "Says You" and two Montgomery originals. The reissue also adds a pair of alternate takes to the fine program. Wes Montgomery made many of his finest jazz recordings originally for Riverside, and this is an often-overlooked gem. *—Scott Yanow*

The Alternative Wes Montgomery / Oct. 12, 1960-Nov. 27, 1963 / Milestone ✦✦✦✦
This CD has 12 "alternate" versions of songs recorded in a variety of settings by guitarist Wes Montgomery during his period with Riverside. Montgomery's sidemen include tenor saxophonist Johnny Griffin, organist Mel Rhyne, vibraphonist Milt Jackson, the flute of James Clay, pianists Wynton Kelly, Buddy Montgomery and Victor Feldman and (on "Tune Up") a string section. The two-LP set that this succeeded actually had two additional selections; all of the material is also available in more definitive form on Wes Montgomery's 12-CD boxed set. In any case, the mistakes and flaws (such as they are) are minor on these performances, and this CD gives one a good introduction into Montgomery's early recordings. *—Scott Yanow*

Wes' Best / 1960-1961 / Fantasy ✦✦✦
(1960-1961). Selections from *The Montgomery Brothers* and *The Montgomery Brothers in Canada*. *—Michael Erlewine*

● **So Much Guitar** / Aug. 4, 1961 / Original Jazz Classics ✦✦✦✦✦
This CD contains one of Wes Montgomery's finest recordings, a Riverside date that showcases the influential guitarist in a quintet with pianist Hank Jones, bassist Ron Carter, drummer Lex Humphries and the congas of Ray Barretto. All eight performances are memorable in their own way with "Cottontail," "I'm Just a Lucky So and So" and a brief unaccompanied "While We're Young" being highpoints. *—Scott Yanow*

Recorded Live At Jorgies Jazz Club / Aug. 19, 1961 / VGM ✦✦✦✦
The tiny VGM label came out with two valuable Wes

Montgomery LPs back in the 1980s. This first volume features the influential guitarist stretching out on four pieces in a quartet with brothers Buddy (on piano and vibes) and Monk (bass) along with drummer Billy Hart. These versions of "All of You," Milt Jackson's "Heartstrings," "Summertime" and Wes' "Bock to Bock" range from six to 14 minutes, are reasonably well-recorded and contain stirring improvisations that have not yet surfaced on CD. Fans of the guitarist should go out of their way to find this one. —*Scott Yanow*

Live At Jorgies And More / Aug. 19, 1961–1968 / VGM ♦♦♦
The second of the tiny VGM label's two Wes Montgomery LPs picks up where the first one left off, with a pair of performances (an unknown original "Starlight" and an incomplete version of "'Round Midnight") from a live date in 1961. In addition this LP is filled out by two numbers from a 1968 TV appearance and a pair of lengthy interviews that actually take up more than half of the record. This interesting but not really essential set is strictly for Wes Montgomery's greatest fans. —*Scott Yanow*

Wes and Friends / Oct. 9, 1961–Dec. 19, 1961 / Milestone ♦♦♦♦
Two complementary albums are combined on this attractive two-LP set from the mid-'70s. The great guitarist Wes Montgomery meets up with vibraphonist Milt Jackson, pianist Wynton Kelly, bassist Sam Jones and drummer Philly Joe Jones for some soulful and swinging numbers (including two previously unissued performances) and then essentially becomes part of the George Shearing Quintet for 11 other songs. The latter date also has vibraphonist Buddy Montgomery and electric bassist Monk Montgomery joining Shearing, drummer Walter Perkins and two Latin percussionists for some enjoyable if overly polite jamming. This music has since been reissued on CD. —*Scott Yanow*

● **Full House** / Jun. 25, 1962 / Original Jazz Classics ♦♦♦♦♦
Tenor saxophonist Johnny Griffin lit a fire under guitarist Wes Montgomery during this live set, and the result is quite a bit of memorable playing, not only by the principals but by pianist Wynton Kelly, bassist Paul Chambers and drummer Jimmy Cobb. Montgomery is heard in the prime of his straight-ahead Riverside period. Highlights include such numbers as "Blue 'N' Boogie," "Cariba" and "S.O.S." This CD reissue adds two alternate takes and a version of "Born to Be Blue" to the original program. —*Scott Yanow*

Fusion! Wes Montgomery with Strings / Apr. 18, 1963–Apr. 19, 1963 / Original Jazz Classics ♦♦♦♦
Although most Wes Montgomery fans associate his playing with strings with his later A&M and Verve recordings, the influential guitarist actually fronted a string section for the first time on this Riverside date from 1963 which had the ironic name of *Fusion*. As with his later albums, Montgomery's guitar solos here are brief and melodic, but the jazz content is fairly high even if the emphasis is (with the exception of "Tune-Up") on ballads. This CD has three additional performances than the original LP and is worth picking up; the music is quite pretty and pleasing. —*Scott Yanow*

Boss Guitar / Apr. 22, 1963 / Original Jazz Classics ♦♦♦
Guitarist Wes Montgomery's string of brilliant straight-ahead jazz recordings for the Riverside label was near its end when he recorded this trio outing with organist Mel Rhyne and drummer Jimmy Cobb. The music swings hard and is highlighted by "Besame Mucho," "Days of Wine and Roses," "Canadian Sunset" and "The Breeze and I." This CD from the *Original Jazz Classics* series adds two alternate takes to the eight LP performances. Enjoyable if not essential. —*Scott Yanow*

Portrait of Wes / Oct. 10, 1963 / Original Jazz Classics ♦♦♦♦
Wes Montgomery's first recordings for Riverside were in a trio with organist Mel Rhyne, and ironically his final albums for the struggling (and soon to be bankrupt) label were with Rhyne again. The brilliant guitarist is in fine form on these appealing tunes with the highlights including "Freddie the Freeloader," "Blues Riff" and "Moanin'." As is true with most of Montgomery's CD reissues, there are a couple of "bonus" cuts (alternates of "Blues Riff" and "Moanin'") added to bring the playing time up a bit. All of this music is also available as part of Wes Montgomery's 12-CD Riverside box set.
—*Scott Yanow*

Movin' Wes / Nov. 11, 1964+Nov. 16, 1964 / Verve ♦♦♦
Wes Montgomery's debut for Verve, although better from a jazz standpoint than his later A&M releases, is certainly in the same vein. The emphasis is on his tone, his distinctive octaves and

melody statements. Some of the material (such as "People" and "Matchmaker") are pop tunes of the era, and the brass orchestra (arranged by Johnny Pate) is purely in the background, but there are some worthy performances; chiefly the two-part "Movin' Wes," "Born to Be Blue" and "West Coast Blues." —*Scott Yanow*

Bumpin' / May 1965 / Verve ♦♦♦♦♦
Wes Montgomery's second Verve album was the best of his orchestral performances. With arrangements by Don Sebesky, Montgomery had opportunities to stretch out on a couple of the selections (most notably on the title cut and "Here's That Rainy Day"), and even though the jazz is not up to the level of his free-wheeling Riverside performances, this set is a good compromise between the demands of the jazz and pop worlds. Plus some of the melodies are quite memorable. —*Scott Yanow*

Small Group Recordings / May 1965–Sep. 28, 1966 / Verve ♦♦♦♦♦
This double LP contains the very best recordings that guitarist Wes Montgomery recorded for Verve. Actually most of these performances originally came out with woodwinds and brass arranged by Claus Ogerman added so as to make the music more commercial, but fortunately the overdubs were tossed out for this reissue. For nearly the last time in his career, Montgomery got a chance to stretch out with a very complementary trio (pianist Wynton Kelly, bassist Paul Chambers and drummer Jimmy Cobb), and he really digs into the nine standards (which include his "Four on Six"). This record stands as proof that Wes Montgomery never did decline as a jazz improviser even while his recordings became much more pop-oriented. The two-fer is rounded out by two worthwhile numbers ("James and Wes" and "Mellow Mood") left over from the guitarist's collaboration with organist Jimmy Smith. This music is highly recommended either on this set or on CD. —*Scott Yanow*

Willow Weep for Me / Aug. 1965 / Verve ♦♦♦
Recorded at the Half Note Club in NYC in the Summer and Autumn of 1965. With Wynton Kelly (p), Paul Chambers (b) and Jimmy Cobb (d). Includes brass and woodwinds arrangements by Claus Ogerman on three cuts. —*Michael Erlewine*

Goin' out of My Head / Dec. 7, 1965–Dec. 22, 1965 / Verve ♦♦
Guitarist Wes Montgomery had a hit with this version of "Goin' out of My Head," but musically it is little more than a pleasant melody statement. Accompanied by a wasted all-star big band given dull arrangements by Oliver Nelson, Montgomery mostly sticks to playing themes, even those as dull as "Chim Chim Cheree" and "It Was a Very Good Year." Recordings like this one disheartened the jazz world but made him a household name and a staple on AM radio. Heard three decades later, the recording is at its best when serving as innocuous background music. —*Scott Yanow*

Tequila / Mar. 17, 1966–May 18, 1966 / Verve ♦♦♦
Wes Montgomery on two of the songs included on this LP ("Tequila" and "The Thumb") had an opportunity to jam a bit while backed by just bassist Ron Carter, drummer Grady Tate and the congas of Ray Barretto. The other six selections utilize a string section arranged by Claus Ogerman but, even with a throwaway version of "What the World Needs Now Is Love," there are memorable renditions of "Bumpin' on Sunset" and "How Insensitive" that uplift this album quite a bit beyond the guitarist's later A&M recordings. —*Scott Yanow*

California Dreaming / Sep. 14, 1966–Sep. 16, 1966 / Verve ♦♦
Wes Montgomery's last album for Verve (other than an exciting collaboration with Jimmy Smith) is a so-so orchestral album featuring arrangements by Don Sebesky. The material (which includes "Sunny" and "California Dreaming") is strictly pop fluff of the era, and the great guitarist had little opportunity to do much other than state the melody in his trademark octaves. This record was perfect for AM radio of the period. —*Scott Yanow*

Futher Adventure of J. Smith and W. Montgomery / Sep. 21, 1966 / Verve ♦♦♦

A Day in the Life / Jun. 6, 1967–Jun. 26, 1967 / A&M ♦♦♦
By the time Wes Montgomery recorded this album (his debut for A&M), he was a major name in the pop world. Montgomery's melodic renditions of current pop hits caught on and were played regularly on Top 40 radio. In most cases the guitarist did little more than play the melody, using his distinctive octaves, and it was enough to make him saleable. Of his three A&M recordings, *A Day in the Life* (the first one) was by far the best, and although

the jazz content is almost nil, the results are pleasing as background music. "Windy" was a bit of a hit; the other selections (which find Montgomery backed by muzaky strings arranged by Don Sebesky) include "Watch What Happens," "California Nights," "Eleanor Rigby" and the title cut. —*Scott Yanow*

Down Here on the Ground / Dec. 20, 1967–Jan. 26, 1968 / A&M ♦♦

Guitarist Wes Montgomery's three A&M records (of which this was the second) are strictly dated pop music. He sticks to melody statements (with a liberal use of his trademark octaves) on such songs as ""I Say a Little Prayer for You," "Georgia on My Mind," a couple of Lalo Schifrin movie themes and The Tijuana Brass' "Wind Song." At least Montgomery was able to make a good living during his last few years, but jazz fans are advised to avoid this one altogether. —*Scott Yanow*

Road Song / May 7, 1968–May 9, 1968 / A&M ♦
Wes Montgomery's final record (before his death from a heart attack at age 45) is, as with his two previous A&M releases, pure pop. The great guitarist sticks to simple melody statements (with a lot of octaves thrown in) while backed by Don Sebesky's unimaginative arrangements for an orchestra; commercially the combination was a big success. Unless one really has the desire to hear such songs as "Greensleeves," "Fly Me to the Moon," "Yesterday" and "Scarborough Fair" played perfectly straight, this strictly for-the-money effort can be safely passed by. —*Scott Yanow*

Tete Montoliu (Vincente Montoliu)

b. Mar. 28, 1933, Barcelona, Spain
Piano / Hard Bop
An outstanding veteran pianist from Spain, Tete Montoliu was born blind. He learned to read music in Braille when he was seven and developed impressive technique on piano. He recorded with Lionel Hampton in 1956, had his first session as a leader in 1958 and played with the touring Roland Kirk in 1963. Through the years he also worked with such visiting Americans as Kenny Dorham, Dexter Gordon, Ben Webster, Lucky Thompson and even Anthony Braxton. Tete Montoliu's visits to the U.S. have been very infrequent, but his SteepleChase albums (starting in 1971) are generally available; he also cut one date for Contemporary in 1979. —*Scott Yanow*

That's All / Sep. 25, 1971 / SteepleChase ♦♦♦♦♦
The virtuosic Spanish pianist Tete Montoliu is usually heard from in trio settings, making this rare solo outing particularly special. Montoliu digs into eight familiar standards (including "You Go to My Head," "'Round Midnight," "A Child Is Born" and "Giant Steps") and to his credit comes up with fresh new variations. Montoliu's style has Bud Powell's bop approach as its foundation but also incorporates the more modern chord voicings of McCoy Tyner and Bill Evans. This album is a fine example of his talents. —*Scott Yanow*

Lush Life / Sep. 25, 1971 / SteepleChase ♦♦♦♦

Body and Soul / 1971 / Enja ♦♦♦♦

Music for Perla / May 26, 1974 / Inner City ♦♦♦

Catalonian Fire / May 26, 1974 / SteepleChase ♦♦♦♦

Tete! / May 28, 1974 / SteepleChase ♦♦♦♦♦
The great Spanish pianist Tete Montoliu has recorded many rewarding sessions for SteepleChase. This trio outing (with bassist Niels Pedersen and drummer Albert "Tootie" Heath) is a typically excellent date. In addition to the lesser-known "Theme for Ernie," Montoliu performs five well-known jazz standards in his own modern jazz style, combining together aspects of Bud Powell, McCoy Tyner and Bill Evans. —*Scott Yanow*

Tete a Tete / Feb. 15, 1976–Feb. 16, 1976 / SteepleChase ♦♦♦

Tootie's Tempo / Feb. 1976 / SteepleChase ♦♦♦♦

Lunch in L.A. / Oct. 2, 1979 / Contemporary ♦♦♦♦♦
Fine two-piano set from the early '80s, with flamboyant Spanish pianist Tete Montliu dueting with fellow pianist Chick Corea. Their exchanges, sometimes combative, sometimes complementary and always engaging and gripping, are brilliant. —*Ron Wynn*

Catalonian Nights, Vol. 1 / May 30, 1980 / SteepleChase ♦♦♦♦

The Music I Like to Play, Vol. 2 / Dec. 1, 1986 / Soul Note ♦♦♦♦

The Music I Like to Play, Vol. 1 / Dec. 1, 1986 / Soul Note ♦♦♦♦
The first in a four-part series that featured pianist Tete Montliu

doing his favorite material, much of it standards, but also bop and mainstream pieces, ballads and an occasional blues. —*Ron Wynn*

The Music I Like to Play, Vol. 4 / 1990 / Soul Note ♦♦♦♦

The Music I Like To Play, Vol. 3 / Jan. 28, 1990 / Soul Note ♦♦♦♦

● **A Spanish Treasure** / Jun. 27, 1991 / Concord Jazz ♦♦♦♦♦

Jack Montrose

b. Dec. 30, 1928, Detroit, MI
Saxophone / Cool
Jack Montrose has long been a fine tenor saxophonist, and in the 1950s he was an important arranger in West Coast jazz. After graduating from Los Angeles State College (1953) he worked with Jerry Gray, Art Pepper (who he collaborated with on some memorable sessions), Red Norvo, Shorty Rogers, Mel Tormé and others in L.A. Montrose recorded with Clifford Brown in 1954 (providing the arrangements) and led some excellent albums for Atlantic, World Pacific and RCA during 1955-57. However the 1960s found him out of fashion. Montrose played at strip joints in Los Angeles, did studio work and then moved to Nevada in 1966, working with show bands. In 1986 he made a recording for Slingshot with Pete Jolly and Jack Montrose has resurfaced on an occasional basis since, playing in a similar cool-toned style to how he sounded in the 1950s. —*Scott Yanow*

With Bob Gordon / Mar. 11, 1955+Mar. 12, 1955 / Atlantic ♦♦♦♦

● **Jack Montrose Sextet** / Jun. 24, 1955–Jul. 6, 1955 / Pacific Jazz ♦♦♦♦♦

The Horn's Full / Sep. 10, 1957–Sep. 11, 1957 / RCA ♦♦♦♦♦

Better Late than Never / 1986 / Slingshot ♦♦♦

Let's Do It / Sep. 10, 1990–Sep. 11, 1990 / Holt ♦♦♦♦

James Moody

b. Mar. 26, 1925, Savannah, GA
Flute, Alto Saxophone, Tenor Saxophone / Bop, Hard Bop
James Moody has been an institution in jazz since the late '40s, whether on tenor, flute, occasional alto or yodelling his way through his "Moody's Mood for Love."

After serving in the Air Force (1943-46), he joined Dizzy Gillespie's bebop orchestra and began a lifelong friendship with the trumpeter. Moody toured Europe with Gillespie and then stayed overseas for several years, working with Miles Davis, Max Roach and top European players. His 1949 recording of "I'm in the Mood for Love" in 1952 became a hit under the title of "Moody's Mood for Love" with classic vocalese lyrics written by Eddie Jefferson and a best-selling recording by King Pleasure. After returning to the U.S., Moody formed a septet that lasted for five years, recorded extensively for Prestige and Argo, took up the flute and then from 1963-68 was a member of Dizzy Gillespie's quintet. He worked in Las Vegas show bands during much of the 1970s before returning to jazz, playing occasionally with Dizzy, mostly working as a leader and recording with Lionel Hampton's Golden Men of Jazz. Moody, who has alternated between tenor (which he prefers) and alto throughout his career, has an original sound on both horns. He is also one of the best flutists in jazz. James Moody has recorded as a leader for Blue Note, Xanadu, Vogue, Prestige, EmArcy, Mercury, Argo, DJM, Milestone, Perception, MPS, Muse, Vanguard and Novus. —*Scott Yanow*

Hi-Fi Party / Aug. 23, 1955–Aug. 24, 1955 / Original Jazz Classics ♦♦♦♦♦
For a period in the mid-'50s tenor saxophonist James Moody (who doubled on alto) was able to keep together a swinging septet that played bop in a fairly accessible way. On this CD reissue of two 1955 sessions, Moody and his group (which includes the fine trumpeter Dave Burns, trombonist William Shepherd, baritonist Pee Wee Moore, pianist Jimmy Boyd, bassist John Lathan and drummer Clarence Johnson) perform swinging versions of fairly obscure originals including the lengthy "Jammin' with James" (which has a long tradeoff between Moody and Burns), Benny Golson's "Big Ben" and "There Will Never Be Another You." The highpoint is Eddie Jefferson's one appearance, singing his alternate lyrics to Charlie Parker's famous solo on "Lady Be Good" which he renamed "Disappointed." —*Scott Yanow*

Wail, Moody, Wail / Dec. 12, 1955 / Original Jazz Classics ♦♦♦♦
James Moody's mid-'50s band was a septet featuring four horns including the leader's tenor and alto. The bop-based group had

plenty of spirit (as best shown here on the 14-minute title cut) if not necessarily a strong personality of its own. This CD (a straight reissue of the original LP plus two additional titles from the same session) is accessible, melodic and swinging; trumpeter Dave Burns is the best soloist among the sidemen. —*Scott Yanow*

Flute 'N The Blues / Aug. 22, 1956 / Chess ◆◆◆◆

Moody's Mood for Love / Dec. 14, 1956+Jan. 13, 1957 / Argo ◆◆◆◆
A strong version of the "Moody's Mood for Love", with a vocal by the late Eddie Jefferson (v). —*Ron Wynn*

● **Last Train from Overbrook** / Sep. 13, 1958–Sep. 16, 1958 / Argo ◆◆◆◆◆

James Moody / Aug. 1959 / Argo ◆◆◆

Hey! It's James Moody / Dec. 29, 1959 / Argo ◆◆◆

Moody and the Brass Figures / 1967 / Milestone ◆◆◆◆

Don't Look Away Now / Feb. 14, 1969 / Prestige ◆◆◆◆◆

The Blues and Other Colors, the / 1969 / Milestone ◆◆◆◆

Never Again / Jun. 8, 1972 / Muse ◆◆◆◆◆

Feelin' it Together / Jan. 15, 1973 / Muse ◆◆◆◆

Something Special / Jul. 1986 / Novus ◆◆◆◆

Moving Forward / Nov. 10, 1987+Nov. 18, 1987 / Novus ◆◆◆◆
Excellent Kenny Barron piano. —*Ron Wynn*

Sweet and Lovely / Mar. 11, 1989+Mar. 13, 1989 / Novus ◆◆◆◆
Saxophone veteran James Moody stages an impromptu reunion with his longtime friend and onetime leader Dizzy Gillespie on this '89 session. Their interaction hasn't been dulled by their time apart; they still anticipate each other and mesh effectively. Moody's own solos are mellow, well-constructed and superbly played. The backing band wisely defers to the giants, although keyboardist Marc Cohen has a few good passages. —*Ron Wynn*

Honey / Oct. 4, 1990–Oct. 15, 1990 / Novus ◆◆◆
The selections on this recent album are eratic, but he and veteran Kenny Barron (p) uphold things. It is certainly not a classic but is worth having. —*Ron Wynn*

Brew Moore (Milton Aubrey Moore, Jr.)

b. Mar. 26, 1924, Indianola, MS, **d.** Aug. 19, 1973, Copenhagen
Tenor Saxophone / Cool
Brew Moore once said that "Anyone who doesn't play like Lester Young is wrong," a philosophy he followed throughout his career. In the early '50s he recorded on a session with fellow tenors Stan Getz, Al Cohn, Zoot Sims and Allan Eager; at the time they all sounded identical. Moore was the only one of the five who did not change his sound through the years. During 1942–48 he worked with local bands in New Orleans and Memphis, moving to New York in 1948 and playing with Claude Thornhill's Orchestra (1948–49). During the next few years he freelanced, working with Machito, Kai Winding and Gerry Mulligan among others. In 1954 he moved to San Francisco where he led his own groups and played with Cal Tjader. Moore, whose cool sound became out of fashion, moved to Copenhagen in 1961, and other than three years in New York (1967–70), stayed overseas until his death. He recorded as a leader for Savoy (1948–49), Fantasy (1955–57), Jazz Mark, Debut, SteepleChase, Sonet and Storyville. —*Scott Yanow*

● **Brew Moore Quintet** / Aug. 1955–Feb. 22, 1956 / Original Jazz Classics ◆◆◆◆◆
Unsung tenor saxophonist with pianist and composer John Marabuto. A good bet. —*Michael G. Nastos*

Brew Moore / Nov. 5, 1957–1958 / Original Jazz Classics ◆◆◆◆
A good late-50s hard-blowing session from an underrated saxophonist. —*Ron Wynn*

● **Svinget 14** / Sep. 26, 1962 / Black Lion ◆◆◆◆◆
A more upbeat and hard-edged date than usual for undervalued tenor saxophonist Brew Moore. He plays with two other challenging, strong musicians in a three-horn frontline. Baritone saxophonist Lars Gullin rivals John Surman as the best foreign stylist on his instrument, while Sahib Shihab (normally on baritone) shows his prowess on alto for this date. The three saxes, plus vibist Louis Hjulmand and pianist Bent Axen, carry the instrumental load, while bassist Niels-Henning Orsted Pedersen and drummer William Schioppfe handle rhythm responsibilities. —*Ron Wynn*

If I Had You / Apr. 15, 1965 / SteepleChase ◆◆◆◆

I Should Care / Apr. 29, 1965 / SteepleChase ◆◆◆

No More Brew / Feb. 25, 1971 / Storyville ◆◆◆◆
Brew Moore was a very underrated, capable tenor saxophonist who made good, consistent albums playing in a style that merged cool and blues elements into a breezy, mellow personalized concept. He was backed on this '71 date by a decent Swedish rhythm section, but it's his expressive tenor licks that carry the date. —*Ron Wynn*

Brew's Stockholm Dew / Feb. 25, 1971 / Sonet ◆◆◆

Glen Moore

b. Oct. 28, 1941, Portland, OR
Bass / New Age, Post-Bop
One of the longtime members of Oregon, Glen Moore's playing tends to be on the introspective side, thoughtful and melodic improvisations that are open to the influence of folk, classical and ethnic music. He started on bass when he was 13 and freelanced in New York in the mid-'60s. Moore recorded with Nick Brignola in 1967, played part-time with the Paul Bley Synthesizer Show during 1969–71, was with Paul Winter's Consort in 1970 and then left to help form Oregon. In addition to his work with the eclectic group, Glen Moore recorded with Annette Peacock, Larry Coryell, Ralph Towner and Zbigniew Seifert plus some nonjazz dates. He has also led dates for Enja, Elektra and Audioquest. —*Scott Yanow*

Introducing Glen Moore / Feb. 1980 / Elektra ◆◆◆

Oscar Moore

b. Dec. 25, 1912, Austin, TX, **d.** Oct. 8, 1981, Las Vegas, NV
Guitar / Swing
An excellent guitarist influenced after 1939 by Charlie Christian, Oscar Moore was an invaluable part of the Nat King Cole Trio during 1937–47, appearing on virtually all of Cole's records during the period. He also recorded with Lionel Hampton, Art Tatum (1941), the Capitol Jazzmen and Lester Young. Unfortunately, Moore's post-Cole career was not that successful. He played with his brother Johnny Moore in the Three Blazers from 1947 to the mid-'50s (the group declined in popularity after pianist/singer Charles Brown left), and he recorded three records for Verve and Tampa during 1953–54 but then was largely outside of music with the exception of a 1965 Nat Cole tribute album. —*Scott Yanow*

Oscar Moore Quartet with Carl Perkins / 1954 / VSOP ◆◆◆
Guitarist Oscar Moore, who will always be best-known for his years with the Nat King Cole Trio, had a couple of opportunities to record as a leader in the mid-'50s, but despite the worthy music, his solo career never caught on. This CD reissue of a Tampa LP matches the swing guitarist with pianist Carl Perkins, bassist Joe Comfort and drummer Lee Young for a brief easy-listening set of standards and basic originals. Nice music. —*Scott Yanow*

● **Oscar Moore Quartet** / 1954 / VSOP ◆◆◆◆
Although he was a pioneering electric guitarist and gained a certain amount of fame playing with the original Nat King Cole Trio, Oscar Moore had relatively few opportunities to record in the 1950s. This CD reissue of a set originally cut for Tampa features Moore in a quartet with pianist Carl Perkins, bassist Joe Comfort and Mike Pacheco on bongos. Sticking mostly to standards (including the "Samson and Delilah Theme," Moore is in fine form for this set of melodic and easy-listening music that always swings. —*Scott Yanow*

We'll Remember You, Nat / Mar. 1966 / Surrey ◆◆◆◆

Ralph Moore

b. Dec. 24, 1956, London, England
Tenor Saxophone / Hard Bop
Ralph Moore, who has lived in the U.S. since 1970, is a fine tenor saxophonist influenced by John Coltrane but possessing a slightly softer tone. He attended Berklee (during that period he had opportunities to play with James Williams and Kevin Eubanks), moved to New York in 1981 and worked with many veteran players including Horace Silver (1981–85), Roy Haynes, Dizzy Gillespie, Freddie Hubbard, Jimmy Knepper, Bobby Hutcherson and Kenny Barron. Ralph Moore debuted on record as a leader in 1985 for Reservoir, recorded several fine albums for Landmark, Criss Cross, Savoy and Mons (with the L.A. Jazz Summit), toured

extensively with J.J. Johnson and since 1995 has been a member of the Tonight Show Orchestra in Los Angeles. —*Scott Yanow*

Round Trip / Dec. 21, 1985 / Reservoir ✦✦✦✦
First date from British tenor saxophonist. Some great playing here, in the mainstream bag with Brian Lynch (tpt). —*Michael G. Nastos*

623 C Street / Feb. 27, 1987+Dec. 31, 1987 / Criss Cross ✦✦✦✦

Rejuvenate / Feb. 19, 1988 / Criss Cross ✦✦✦✦✦
Strong, tough playing by tenor saxophonist Ralph Moore, who once lived in England but has been a familiar face on the West Coast jazz scene since the late '80s. This group was exceptionally deep, with trombonist Steve Turre and pianist Mulgrew Miller both superb as either soloists or accompanists, while bassist Peter Washington and drummer Marvin "Smitty" Smith were equally gifted at both supporting and driving a group and stepping out front and making their own statements. —*Ron Wynn*

Images / Dec. 15, 1988+Dec. 17, 1988 / Landmark ✦✦✦✦
This is a well-done 1988 set with Terence Blanchard (tpt) and Benny Green (tb). —*Ron Wynn*

● **Furthermore** / Mar. 3, 1990+Mar. 5, 1990 / Landmark ✦✦✦✦✦
One of the best among the "Young Lion" tenor saxophonists makes an aggressive, explosive statement. —*Ron Wynn*

Who It Is You Are / Apr. 5, 1993–Apr. 6, 1993 / Savoy ✦✦✦✦
For this fairly relaxed modern mainstream session, Ralph Moore sheds some of the influence of John Coltrane that he displayed on earlier dates. He features his attractive tone and melodic ideas on a set of superior material, mostly underplayed standards. The rhythm section (pianist Benny Green, bassist Peter Washington and drummer Billy Higgins) is as supportive and tasteful as one would expect with Green occasionally taking solo honors. Whether it be classic ballads such as "Skylark" and "Some Other Time," the pianist's memorable gospel/jazz number "Testifyin'" or the danceable Latin stomp "Esmeralda," this is an easily enjoyable set of middle-of-the-road modern jazz. —*Scott Yanow*

Airto Moreira

b. Aug. 5, 1941, Itaiopolis, Brazil
Vocals / Crossover, Latin Jazz
The most high-profile percussionist of the 1970s and still among the most famous, Airto Moreira (often simply known by his first name) helped make percussion an essential part of many modern jazz groups; his tambourine solos can border on the amazing! Airto originally studied guitar and piano before becoming a percussionist. He played locally in Brazil, collected and studied over 120 different percussion instruments and in 1968 moved to the U.S. with his wife, singer Flora Purim. Airto played with Miles Davis during part of 1969–70, appearing on several records (most notably *Live Evil*). He worked with Lee Morgan for a bit in 1971, was an original member of Weather Report and in 1972 was part of Chick Corea's initial version of Return to Forever with Flora Purim; he and Corea also recorded the classic *Captain Marvel* with Stan Getz. By 1973 Airto was famous enough to have his own group, signed to CTI and appearing on Purim's sessions. Since then he has stayed busy, mostly co-leading bands with his wife and recording as a leader for many labels including Buddah, CTI, Arista, Warner Bros, Caroline, Rykodisc, In & Out and B&W. Not all of his music as a leader would be called jazz, but Airto remains a very impressive player. —*Scott Yanow*

● **Free** / Apr. 1972–May 1972 / CTI ✦✦✦✦✦
This great album includes the first version of "Return to Forever." With Chick Corea (k), Keith Jarrett (p), Stanley Clarke (b) and Joe Farrell (ts). —*Michael G. Nastos*

Fingers / Apr. 1973 / CTI ✦✦✦✦
Vocals by Flora Purim. Potent, uplifting music. Many familiar themes. —*Michael G. Nastos*

Virgin Land / 1974 / CTI ✦✦✦

Identity / 1975 / Arista ✦✦✦

Promises of the Sun / 1976 / Arista ✦✦

I'm Fine / 1977 / Warner Brothers ✦✦

Three-way Mirror / May 1985 / Reference ✦✦✦✦
Few vocal/instrumental teams have ever worked more smoothly than the unit of singer Flora Purim, saxophonist and flutist Joe Farrell and percussionist Airto Moreira. They initially clicked on the first edition of Return to Forever in the early '70s, and they

worked together often until Farrell's death in the mid-'80s. The eight songs featured on *Three-Way Mirror* were Farrell's last sessions, but his saxes and flute retained their drive, range and authority throughout, punctuated as always by Moreira's array of sounds and Purim's floating, ethereal lead vocals. —*Ron Wynn*

The Other Side of This / Aug. 21, 1992 / Rykodisc ✦✦✦

Joe Morello

b. Jul. 17, 1928, Springfield, MA
Drums / Hard Bop, Cool
A brilliant drummer, Joe Morello played early on with Phil Woods and Sal Salvador. He had short stints during 1952–53 with Johnny Smith, Stan Kenton's Orchestra and Gil Melle but really gained a strong reputation for his work with the Marian McPartland trio (1953–56); he also played during the period with Tal Farlow and Jimmy Raney. Morello gained fame as a member of the Dave Brubeck Quartet during 1956–67, making it possible for Brubeck to experiment with unusual time signatures. Due to his failing eyesight (he went blind in 1976) Morello has mostly worked as a drum instructor since (Danny Gottlieb was a student) but still plays and participated in reunions with Brubeck and McPartland. He has led sessions for Score (1956), RCA (1961–62), Ovation (1969) and DMP (1993–94). —*Scott Yanow*

● **Joe Morello** / Jun. 6, 1961+Nov. 13, 1962 / Bluebird ✦✦✦✦✦
It's About Time features ten songs with the word "time" in their title. Of these, five of the six quintet selections (starring Phil Woods and a young Gary Burton) and two of the four other songs (which has the quintet augmented by a brass section) are on this along with a totally unreleased big-band session from the following year. With Manny Albam contributing the arrangements, *It's About Time* is a happy surprise, a hard-driving set of swinging music. —*Scott Yanow*

Going Places / 1993 / DMP ✦✦✦✦
Drummer Joe Morello is in prime form for this rare opportunity to record as a leader. Morello (who takes a drum solo on the "Mission: Impossible Theme" and shares a duet with bassist Gary Mazzaroppi on "Autumn Leaves") propels the solid rhythm section (which includes pianist Greg Kogan) while Ralph Lalama contributes tenor solos very much in the vein of 1950s Sonny Rollins. The strong repertoire and a certain amount of variety make this CD into an easily enjoyable bop date. —*Scott Yanow*

Morello Standard Time / 1994 / DMP ✦✦✦✦

Frank Morgan

b. Dec. 23, 1933, Minneapolis, MN
Alto Saxophone / Bop, Hard Bop
It is a real rarity for a jazz musician to have his career interrupted for a 30-year period and then be able to make a complete comeback. Frank Morgan showed a great deal of promise in his early days, but it was a long time before he could fulfill his potential. The son of guitarist Stanley Morgan (who played with the Ink Spots), he took up clarinet and alto early on. Morgan moved with his family to Los Angeles in 1947 and won a talent contest, leading to him recording a solo with Freddie Martin. Morgan worked on the bop scene of early-'50s Los Angeles, recording with Teddy Charles (1953) and Kenny Clarke (1954) and leading his own album for GNP in 1955. But then 30 years of darkness intruded. A heroin addict (following in the footsteps of his idol Charlie Parker), Morgan was arrested for possession of drugs and was in and out of jails for decades. He performed locally on an occasional basis, but it was not until 1985 when he had an opportunity to lead his second date. Morgan managed to permanently kick drugs, and after an initial period during which he sounded very close to Charlie Parker, he developed his own bop-based style. Frank Morgan has recorded a string of excellent sets for Contemporary and Antilles and has become an inspiring figure in the jazz world. —*Scott Yanow*

Frank Morgan / 1955 / GNP ✦✦✦✦✦
In 1955 when altoist Frank Morgan recorded his debut as a leader, he was being hyped as "the new bird." Unfortunately he followed in Charlie Parker's footsteps mostly by becoming an irresponsible drug addict. Thirty years passed before he cut his second album and seriously began his successful comeback. The GNP album features Morgan back at the beginning, performing four numbers with Machito's rhythm section and six other songs with a septet that also includes tenor saxophonist Wardell Gray (heard on his

final recordings). Trumpeter Conte Candoli is a major asset on both of these boppish dates while Frank Morgan shows why he was rated so high at this point in his career. —*Scott Yanow*

Easy Living / Jun. 1985 / Original Jazz Classics ✦✦✦✦✦
Solid hard bop, blues and ballads from a great veteran. —*Ron Wynn*

Lament / Apr. 1986 / Contemporary ✦✦✦✦
A fine, if unambitious, 1986 quartet date. Bonus cut on CD version. With Cedar Walton, Buster WIlliams and Billy Higgins. —*Ron Wynn*

Double Image / May 21, 1986–May 22, 1986 / Contemporary ✦✦✦✦
With George Cables. An excellent collaboration, pairing a great old veteran and a relatively youthful one on piano in Cables. —*Ron Wynn*

Bebop Lives! / Dec. 14, 1986+Dec. 15, 1986 / Contemporary ✦✦✦✦✦
Live date at the Village Vanguard in NYC, with this veteran alto saxophonist on top of things. Prime bop, not to be missed. —*Michael G. Nastos*

Quiet Fire / Mar. 26, 1987–Mar. 28, 1987 / Contemporary ✦✦✦✦

Major Changes / Apr. 1987 / Contemporary ✦✦✦✦

★ **Yardbird Suite** / Jan. 10, 1988+Jan. 11, 1988 / Contemporary ✦✦✦✦✦
Excellent piano from Mulgrew Miller, bass from Ron Carter and drums from Al Foster. Morgan is sharp and authoritative as a leader and player. —*Ron Wynn*

Reflections / Jan. 11, 1988+Jan. 12, 1988 / Contemporary ✦✦✦✦
Studio date with Joe Henderson (sax). Recommended. —*Michael G. Nastos*

Mood Indigo / 1989 / Antilles ✦✦✦✦

A Lonesome Thing / Sep. 5, 1990–Sep. 6, 1990 / Antilles ✦✦✦
Displays the other side of Morgan's personality, as he turns to sentimental numbers and old favorites like "When You Wish Upon A Star" and "Ten Cents A Dance." There's also the demanding "Pannonica," where Morgan gets to stretch out a bit more, but mostly he's doing light, impressionistic fare here, albeit doing it with his customary flair and fire.—*Ron Wynn*

You Must Believe in Spring / Mar. 10, 1992–Mar. 11, 1992 / Antilles ✦✦✦✦
A '92 release by marvelous alto saxophonist Frank Morgan, whose life story and triumph over heroin addiction and imprisonment was one of the '80s' great success tales. Morgan's biting, yet sensitive and rich alto has rightly been traced to Charlie Parker, but Morgan long ago rid his style of any imitative excesses. He was excellently supported on this program of duets by an amazing lineup of rotating pianists: Kenny Barron, Tommy Flanagan, Barry Harris, Roland Hanna and Hank Jones. —*Ron Wynn*

Listen To The Dawn / Apr. 19, 1993–Nov. 27, 1993 / Antilles ✦✦✦✦

● **Love, Lost & Found** / Mar. 7, 1995–Mar. 9, 1995 / Telarc Jazz ✦✦✦✦✦

Lanny Morgan (Harold Lansford Morgan)

b. Mar. 30, 1934, Des Moines, IA
Alto Saxophone / Bop
A superb altoist who is a bit underrated due to living in Los Angeles and not leading that many sessions of his own, Lanny Morgan grew up in L.A. He worked (starting in 1954) in the big bands of Charlie Barnet, Si Zenter, Terry Gibbs and Bob Florence, served in the military (which prevented him from joining Stan Kenton) and then spent the 1960–65 period playing with Maynard Ferguson's Orchestra. After freelancing in New York, he returned to Los Angeles in 1969. Morgan became a busy studio musician, a permanent member of Supersax and a reliable soloist in big bands led by Bill Berry, Bob Florence and Bill Holman. He has thus far led just two albums, a 1981 record for Palo Alto and a 1993 quartet set for VSOP and he has few peers on "Cherokee!" —*Scott Yanow*

It's About Time / Sep. 7, 1981–Sep. 8, 1981 / Palo Alto ✦✦✦✦

★ **The Lanny Morgan Quartet** / Jun. 11, 1993+Jun. 13, 1993 / VSOP ✦✦✦✦✦
Altoist Lanny Morgan, despite being a very talented bop-based

improviser and a greatly in-demand sideman, has had relatively few opportunities to record as a leader through the years; only two! This quartet set with pianist Tom Ranier, bassist Bob Maize and drummer Frankie Capp is his definitive recording. Morgan is in particularly creative and fiery form on such songs as "Subconscious Lee," "Bloomdido," "After You've Gone" and a song he practically owns, "Cherokee." None of the nine tunes (eight jazz standards plus Tom Garvin's "Flash") are throwaways, and this is a CD highly recommended to bop fans. —*Scott Yanow*

Lee Morgan

b. Jul. 10, 1938, Philadelphia, PA, d. Feb. 19, 1972, New York, NY
Trumpet / Hard Bop
One of the great jazz trumpeters of the 1960s, Lee Morgan was the natural successor to Clifford Brown, making an impact on the scene shortly after Brownie's death and at first playing in a very similar style. He was a bit of a prodigy, working professionally in Philadelphia when he was 15 and joining Dizzy Gillespie's orchestra when he was barely 18. Morgan led his first Blue Note session later that year, and he would record his first two classic albums for the label during 1957-58: *The Cooker* and *Candy.* Morgan was with Gillespie's band into 1958 when he became a member of Art Blakey's Jazz Messengers (1958–61), touring and recording extensively with the group and sharing the frontline with Benny Golson, Hank Mobley and finally Wayne Shorter. Drug problems resulted in him quitting the band in 1961 and maintaining a low profile in Philadelphia until 1963. When Morgan came back, his first recording was his biggest hit, "The Sidewinder." He entered his greatest period, recording one memorable album after another, writing "Ceora" and "Speedball" and spending a second period with Blakey (1964–65). Morgan's playing became more adventurous, and by the end of the decade he was exploring modal music, using some avant-garde elements and opening his playing to the influence of funk. On February 19, 1972 he was fatally shot by a girlfriend, ending his life at the age of 33. Lee Morgan recorded many records throughout his career as a sideman, and he led 25 albums for Blue Note (coincidentally the same number as Hank Mobley) plus sessions for Vee-Jay, Roulette, Jazzland and Trip. —*Scott Yanow*

Presenting Lee Morgan / Nov. 4, 1956 / Blue Note ✦✦✦
Trumpeter Lee Morgan's debut as a leader finds him sounding surprisingly mature at the age of 18. On this LP, Morgan welcomes his fellow Philadelphian altoist Clarence Sharpe and an allstar rhythm section (pianist Horace Silver, bassist Wilbur Ware and drummer Philly Joe Jones) for six hard bop selections; best known among the compositions are Benny Golson's "Reggie of Chester" and Donald Byrd's "Little T." Although at this point Morgan was heavily influenced by Clifford Brown (who had died only a few months earlier), his playing was already quite impressive. —*Scott Yanow*

A-1 / Nov. 5, 1956–Nov. 7, 1956 / Savoy ✦✦✦
Trumpeter Lee Morgan, then 18 and at the beginning of his career (his recording debut as a leader resulted in a Blue Note album the day before his brief stint with Savoy began), co-led this session with tenor saxophonist Hank Mobley. Pianist Hank Jones, bassist Doug Watkins and drummer Art Taylor form a tasteful rhythm section behind the lead voices who are in fine form on Fats Navarro's "Nostalgia," originals by Mobley and Watkins and a four-song ballad medley. Although not essential, this hard bop-oriented LP gives one a good early look at Lee Morgan when he was just 18. —*Scott Yanow*

Lee Morgan, Vol. 2 / Dec. 2, 1956 / Blue Note ✦✦✦

Dizzy Atmosphere / Feb. 1957 / Original Jazz Classics ✦✦✦✦
This is an excellent match between Lee Morgan and Wynton Kelly (p), plus stirring tenor from Bill Mitchell and rollicking trombone from Al Grey. Bonus cuts on CD. —*Ron Wynn*

Lee Morgan, Vol. 3 / Mar. 24, 1957 / Blue Note ✦✦✦✦
Although trumpeter Lee Morgan (then only 18) was the nominal leader of this set, tenor saxophonist Benny Golson contributed all five of the compositions and did the arrangements for the sextet (which also includes altoist Gigi Gryce, pianist Wynton Kelly, bassist Paul Chambers and drummer Charlie Persip). Most notable among the songs is the original version of "I Remember Clifford;" Morgan was the perfect trumpeter to play the tribute to Clifford Brown, who had died in a car crash a year earlier. This CD reissue (a fine hard bop date) adds an alternate take of "Tip-Toeing" to the original program. —*Scott Yanow*

City Lights / Aug. 25, 1957 / Blue Note ✦✦✦✦

The Cooker / Sep. 29, 1957 / Blue Note ✦✦✦✦✦
The trumpeter, then just 19, teams up with baritonist Pepper Adams, pianist Bobby Timmons, bassist Paul Chambers and drummer Philly Joe Jones for a particularly strong set that is highlighted by a lengthy and fiery "Night in Tunisia," "Lover Man" and a rapid rendition of "Just One of Those Things." Morgan plays remarkably well for his age (already ranking just below Dizzy Gillespie and Miles Davis), making this an essential acquisition. — *Scott Yanow*

★ **Candy** / Nov. 18, 1957 / Blue Note ✦✦✦✦✦
Lee Morgan's only quartet album is one of his best. Although only 19 at the time, Morgan already had a mature style, a sound influenced by Clifford Brown and a near-complete mastery of the bop vocabulary. With the strong assistance of pianist Sonny Clark, bassist Doug Watkins and drummer Art Taylor, Morgan is very expressive and creative on this CD reissue, particularly on such songs as "Candy," "Since I Fell for You," "All the Way" and even "Personality." — *Scott Yanow*

Here's Lee Morgan / Feb. 2, 1960–Feb. 8, 1960 / Vee-Jay ✦✦✦✦
This CD reissue has its original six songs expanded to 11 with the inclusion of five alternate takes. The music is good solid hard bop that finds Lee Morgan (already a veteran at age 21) coming out of the Clifford Brown tradition to display his own rapidly developing style. Matched with Clifford Jordan on tenor, pianist Wynton Kelly, bassist Paul Chambers and drummer Art Blakey, Morgan's album could pass for a Jazz Messengers set. — *Scott Yanow*

Leeway / Apr. 28, 1960 / Blue Note ✦✦✦✦
This date was one of trumpeter Lee Morgan's more obscure Blue Note sessions, but fortunately it has been reissued on CD. Matched with altoist Jackie McLean, pianist Bobby Timmons, bassist Paul Chambers and drummer Art Blakey, Morgan interprets two of Calvin Massey's compositions, McLean's "Midtown Blues" and his own blues "The Lion and the Wolf." The music is essentially hard bop with a strong dose of soul; the very distinctive styles of the principals is the main reason to acquire this easily enjoyable music. — *Scott Yanow*

Minor Strain / May 12, 1960+Jul. 1960 / Roulette ✦✦✦
Lee Morgan shares this CD reissue with fellow trumpeter Thad Jones. Morgan's three selections feature a quintet with tenor saxophonist Wayne Shorter, pianist Bobby Timmons, bassist Jimmy Rosar and drummer Art Taylor. While that hard bop group democratically performs one original apiece from Morgan, Timmons and Shorter, Thad Jones' date has four of his songs plus a previously unissued alternate take of "Subtle Rebuttal," best-known is "Tip Toe" which was later recorded by The Thad Jones/Mel Lewis Orchestra. Jones' septet is filled with Count Basie sidemen (trombonist Al Grey and tenors Billy Mitchell and Frank Wess) along with a fine rhythm section (pianist Hank Jones, bassist Richard Davis and drummer Osie Johnson) and is more swing-oriented than The Morgan group, but the two sets are equally rewarding. — *Scott Yanow*

Expoobident / Oct. 14, 1960 / Vee-Jay ✦✦✦
Trumpeter Lee Morgan is heard on this CD reissue (which augments the original LP with four additional alternate takes) when he was 22 and near the end of his first stint with Art Blakey's Jazz Messengers. Morgan heads a first-class hard bop quintet that also includes tenor saxophonist Clifford Jordan, pianist Eddie Higgins, bassist Art Davis and drummer Blakey and together they perform two standards and five originals. The results are not as essential as Morgan's best Blue Note albums, but this set swings and should please fans of hard bop. — *Scott Yanow*

Take Twelve / Jan. 24, 1962 / Original Jazz Classics ✦✦✦✦
This CD reissue (which adds an alternate take of "Second's Best" to the original LP program) was trumpeter Lee Morgan's only recording during an off-period that lasted from mid-1961 to late 1963. Morgan (who sounds in fine form) leads a quintet with tenor saxophonist Clifford Jordan, pianist Barry Harris, bassist Bob Cranshaw and drummer Louis Hayes through four of his originals, Jordan's "Little Spain" and the title cut, an Elmo Hope composition. The superior material uplifts the set from being a mere "blowing" date, but it generally has the spontaneity of a jam session. It's one of Lee Morgan's lesser-known dates. — *Scott Yanow*

★ **The Sidewinder** / Dec. 21, 1963 / Blue Note ✦✦✦✦✦
This album is trumpeter Lee Morgan's best-known recording; the

catchy title cut became a hit, launched the boogaloo fad and is still performed decades later. The CD reissue (which adds an alternate take of "Totem Pole" to the original set) finds Morgan at the peak of his powers (where he would remain for the next four or five years) as the leading trumpeter in hard bop. The young (and already immediately recognizable) tenor Joe Henderson, pianist Barry Harris, bassist Bob Cranshaw and drummer Billy Higgins also make strong contributions to this well-rounded program which includes four other memorable Morgan originals: "Totem Pole," "Gary's Notebook," "Boy, What a Night" and "Hocus-Pocus." — *Scott Yanow*

★ **Search for the New Land** / Feb. 15, 1964 / Blue Note ✦✦✦✦✦
This set (the CD reissue is a duplicate of the original LP) is one of the finest Lee Morgan records. The great trumpeter contributes five challenging compositions ("Search for the New Land," "The Joker," "Mr. Kenyatta," "Melancholee" and "Morgan the Pirate"); songs that deserve to be revived. Morgan, tenor saxophonist Wayne Shorter, guitarist Grant Green, pianist Herbie Hancock, bassist Reggie Workman and drummer Billy Higgins are all in particularly creative form on the fresh material, and they stretch the boundaries of hard bop (the modern mainstream jazz of the period). The result is a consistently stimulating set that rewards repeated listenings. — *Scott Yanow*

Tom Cat / Aug. 11, 1964 / Blue Note ✦✦✦✦
It seems strange that the music on this CD was not released initially until 1980. Trumpeter Lee Morgan had had an unexpected hit with "The Sidewinder" so his more challenging recordings were temporarily put aside. As it turns out, this was one of Morgan's better sets from the 1960s, and he had gathered together quite an all-star cast: altoist Jackie McLean, trombonist Curtis Fuller, pianist McCoy Tyner, bassist Bob Cranshaw and drummer Art Blakey. They perform "Rigormortis," McCoy Tyner's "Twilight Mist" and three of the trumpeter's originals including the title cut. The advanced hard bop music still sounds fresh decades later despite its initial neglect. — *Scott Yanow*

Rumproller / Apr. 21, 1965 / Blue Note ✦✦✦
To follow up on his unexpected boogaloo hit "The Sidewinder," Lee Morgan recorded Andrew Hill's somewhat similar "The Rumproller," but this time the commercial magic was not there. However, the trumpeter, tenor saxophonist Joe Henderson, pianist Ronnie Mathews, bassist Victor Sproles and drummer Billy Higgins all play quite well on the title cut, two of Morgan's songs (the bossa nova "Eclipso" is somewhat memorable), a ballad tribute to Billie Holiday and Wayne Shorter's "Edda." This LP (not yet reissued on CD) is worth picking up, but it is not essential. — *Scott Yanow*

The Gigolo / Jun. 25, 1965+Jul. 1, 1965 / Blue Note ✦✦✦✦✦
Lee Morgan was the leading trumpeter in hard bop during the 1960s, and he recorded quite a few classic albums for Blue Note. This is one of them. The CD reissue (which adds an alternate take of the title cut to the original five-song program) features Morgan at his best, whether playing his memorable blues "Speed Ball," an explorative ballad version of "You Go to My Head," a lengthy "The Gigolo" or his other two originals ("Yes I Can, No You Can't" and "Trapped"). There are no weak selections on this set, and the playing by the leader, Wayne Shorter on tenor, pianist Harold Mabern, bassist Bob Cranshaw and drummer Billy Higgins is beyond any serious criticism. — *Scott Yanow*

★ **Cornbread** / Sep. 8, 1965 / Blue Note ✦✦✦✦✦
This session (reissued on CD by Blue Note) is best known for introducing Lee Morgan's beautiful ballad "Ceora," but actually all five selections (which include Morgan's "Cornbread," "Our Man Higgins," "Most like Lee" and the standard "Ill Wind") are quite memorable. The trumpeter/leader performs with a perfectly complementary group of open-minded and talented hard bop stylists (altoist Jackie McLean, Hank Mobley on tenor, pianist Herbie Hancock, bassist Larry Ridley and drummer Billy Higgins) and creates a Blue Note classic that is heartily recommended. — *Scott Yanow*

Infinity / Nov. 16, 1965 / Blue Note ✦✦✦✦
Although recorded in 1965, this excellent Lee Morgan Quintet session (which features the trumpeter with altoist Jackie McLean, pianist Larry Willis, bassist Reggie Workman and drummer Billy Higgins) was not released until 1980 on this LP and then went quickly out of print. It deserved much better fate. The music, although tied to the hard bop tradition, is challenging and (with

the exception of the closing uptempo blues "Zip Code") tricky, really challenging the talented players. This is an album worth searching for (and one that Blue Note should reissue). —*Scott Yanow*

Delightfulee / Apr. 8, 1966+May 27, 1966 / Blue Note ✦✦✦✦✦
This classic set by trumpeter Lee Morgan was reissued on LP in 1984 but has not yet appeared on CD. Of the four quintet numbers with tenor saxophonist Joe Henderson, pianist McCoy Tyner, bassist Bob Cranshaw and drummer Billy Higgins, the instantly likable "Ca-Lee-So" is the most memorable although the other three Morgan originals ("Zambia," "Nite Flite" and "The Delightful Deggie") also find the trumpeter in excellent form. An unusual aspect to this collection is that there are also two ballads ("Yesterday" and "Sunrise Sunset") that have a nonet playing Oliver Nelson arrangements behind Morgan's lyrical horn; Tyner and tenor saxophonist Wayne Shorter have opportunities to take concise solos. —*Scott Yanow*

Charisma / Sep. 29, 1966 / Blue Note ✦✦✦✦

The Rajah / Nov. 29, 1966 / Blue Note ✦✦✦
This long-lost Lee Morgan session was not released for the first time until it was discovered in the Blue Note vaults by Michael Cuscuna in 1984; it has still not been reissued on CD. Originals by Cal Massey, Duke Pearson ("Is That So") and Walter Davis, in addition to a couple of surprising pop tunes ("What Not My Love" and "Once in My Lifetime") and Morgan's title cut, are well-played by the quintet (which includes the trumpeter/leader, Hank Mobley on tenor, pianist Cedar Walton, bassist Paul Chambers and drummer Billy Higgins). Much of the music is reminiscent of The Jazz Messengers, and that may have been the reason that it was lost in the shuffle for Morgan was soon investigating modal-oriented tunes. Despite its neglect, this is a fine session that Lee Morgan and hard bop fans will want. —*Scott Yanow*

Sonic Boom / Apr. 14, 1967 / Blue Note ✦✦✦✦
This well-rounded LP was not released until 1979 and then remained in print only for a brief time. In addition to the great trumpeter Lee Morgan and a fine rhythm section (pianist Cedar Walton, bassist Ron Carter and drummer Billy Higgins), the set is a bit special for it allows the often R&B-associated tenor David "Fathead" Newman an opportunity to stretch out in a more challenging setting than usual. Highlights include the funky "Fathead," the complex "Sneaky Pete," Morgan's lyricism on "I'll Never Be The Same" and the infectious rhythms on "Mumbo Jumbo." This is an undeservedly obscure session. —*Scott Yanow*

The Procrastinator / Jul. 14, 1967 / Blue Note ✦✦✦✦✦
This out-of-print double LP from 1978 released for the first time a pair of "lost" Lee Morgan albums. The music (from 1967 and 1969) falls into the category of advanced hard bop with the influence of the avant-garde and modal jazz mixing in with the trumpeter's roots in Art Blakey's brand of hard bop. The earlier date has a particularly impressive lineup of talent (tenor saxophonist Wayne Shorter, vibraphonist Bobby Hutcherson, pianist Herbie Hancock, bassist Ron Carter and drummer Billy Higgins) while the later album is not exactly a throwaway since it features trombonist Julian Priester, George Coleman on tenor, pianist Harold Mabern, bassist Walter Booker and drummer Mickey Roker. There are many highlights to this enjoyable (but now difficult-to-locate) two-fer as Morgan and his contemporaries perform 12 group originals plus the lone standard "Stormy Weather." —*Scott Yanow*

The Sixth Sense / Nov. 10, 1967 / Blue Note ✦✦✦
For this lesser-known Lee Morgan LP, the trumpeter was starting to stretch beyond hard bop into more modal areas while retaining his easily recognizable sound. None of Morgan's originals (which are performed along with pianist Cedar Walton's "Afreaka" and Cal Massey's "The Cry of My People") caught on, but the music is creatively performed by the trumpeter, altoist Jackie McLean (who was always a perfect musical partner), the obscure tenor Frank Mitchell, Walton, bassist Victor Sproles and drummer Billy Higgins. —*Scott Yanow*

Taru / Feb. 15, 1968 / Blue Note ✦✦✦✦
Trumpeter Lee Morgan performs two funky boogaloos, a ballad and three complex group originals on this out-of-print LP whose music was first released in 1980. This is a transitional date with the hard bop stylist leaning in the direction of modal music and even anticipating aspects of fusion. His sextet (which includes Bennie Maupin on tenor, guitarist George Benson, pianist John Hicks, bassist Reggie Workman and drummer Billy Higgins) is

quite advanced for the period and inspires Morgan to some fiery and explorative playing. —*Scott Yanow*

Caramba / May 3, 1968 / Blue Note ✦✦✦

Live at the Lighthouse / Jul. 10, 1970–Jul. 12, 1970 / Blue Note ✦✦✦✦
This double LP, which was trumpeter Lee Morgan's next-to-last recording, contains four lengthy side-long explorations by the trumpeter's regular quintet of the period (with Bennie Maupin on tenor, flute and bass clarinet, pianist Harold Mabern, bassist Jymie Merritt and drummer Mickey Roker). The music is very modal-oriented and probably disappointed many of Morgan's longtime fans, but he had gotten tired of playing the same hard bop-styled music that he had excelled at during the past decade and was searching for newer sounds. The influence of the avant-garde and early fusion is also felt in spots, but the trumpeter's sound was still very much intact, and he takes some fiery solos that still sound lively decades later. —*Scott Yanow*

Speedball / Jul. 10, 1970–Jul. 12, 1970 / Trip ✦✦✦

Lee Morgan / Sep. 17, 1971–Sep. 18, 1971 / Blue Note ✦✦
The final recording by Lee Morgan, this double LP has its moments but is somewhat erratic with some modal-oriented selections that ramble on too long and a forgettable debut (on "Croquet Ballet") for the trumpeter's discovery, flutist Bobbi Humphrey. Morgan (who was still just 33) is in generally good form, and his band (with Billy Harper on tenor, keyboardist Harold Mabern, Jymie Merritt or Reggie Workman on bass and drummer Freddie Waits) is quite stimulating, but the music has an uncomfortable and incomplete feel to it. It does leave one wondering what Lee Morgan would have done next had he lived. —*Scott Yanow*

Butch Morris (Lawrence Morris)

b. 1947, Long Beach, CA
Cornet, Conductor / Avant-Garde
In recent years, Butch Morris has worked on what he calls "conduction." By utilizing a vast array of hand signals, he is able to push an improvising ensemble in any direction he wants without actually playing an instrument. Morris is actually a fine mellow-toned cornetist although his playing has often taken second place behind his writing. The brother of bassist Wilber Morris, Morris played with Horace Tapscott, Bobby Bradford and Frank Lowe in California in the early '70s, worked in New York in 1975 with Charles Tyler, Hamiet Bluiett and David Murray, lived in Paris during 1976–77 (recording with Steve Lacy) and returned to the U.S. Morris has been closely associated with David Murray during the past 20 years, playing in his octet and conducting his big band. Butch Morris has led sessions for Kharma, Sund Aspects and New World including a recent ten-CD set of his "Conductions." —*Scott Yanow*

Current Trends in Racism in Modern America / Feb. 1985 / Sound Aspects ✦✦✦✦✦

★ **Dust to Dust** / Nov. 18, 1990–Nov. 20, 1990 / New World ✦✦✦✦✦
A fine large-group recording. The ensemble has several top players, including Wayne Horvitz (k), Marty Ehrlich (reeds) and John Purcell (reeds). Morris conducts and supervises with his usual skill. —*Ron Wynn*

Jelly Roll Morton (Ferdinand Joseph Lemott)

b. Oct. 20, 1890, New Orleans, LA, **d.** Jul. 10, 1941, Los Angeles, CA
Piano, Composer, Leader / Classic New Orleans Jazz
One of the very first giants of jazz, Jelly Roll Morton did himself a lot of harm posthumously by exaggerating his worth, claiming to have invented jazz in 1902. Morton's accomplishments as an early innovator are so vast that he did not really need to stretch the truth.

Morton was jazz's first great composer, writing such songs as "King Porter Stomp," "Grandpa's Spells," "Wolverine Blues," "The Pearls," "Mr. Jelly Roll," "Shreveport Stomp," "Milenburg Joys," "Black Bottom Stomp," "The Chant," "Original Jelly Roll Blues," "Doctor Jazz," "Wild Man Blues," "Winin' Boy Blues," "I Thought I Heard Buddy Bolden Say," "Don't You Leave Me Here," and "Sweet Substitute." He was a talented arranger (1926's "Black Bottom Stomp" is remarkable), getting the most out of the three-minute limitations of the 78 record by emphasizing changing instrumentation, concise solos and dynamics. He was a greatly underrated pianist who had his own individual style. Although he only took one vocal on records in the 1920s ("Doctor Jazz"), Morton in his late-'30s recordings proved to be an effective vocalist, and he was a true character.

Jelly Roll Morton's pre-1923 activities are shrouded in legend. He started playing piano when he was ten, worked in the bordellos of Storyville while a teenager (for which some of his relatives disowned him) and by 1904 was traveling throughout the South. He spent time in other professions (as a gambler, pool player, vaudeville comedian and even a pimp) but always returned to music. The chances are good that in 1915 Morton had few competitors among pianists. He was an important transition figure between ragtime and early jazz. He played in Los Angeles during 1917–22 and then moved to Chicago where for the next six years he was at his peak. Morton's 1923–24 recordings of piano solos introduced his style, repertoire and brilliance. Although his earliest band sides were quite primitve, his 1926–27 recordings for Victor with his Red Hot Peppers are among the most exciting of his career. With such sidemen as cornetist George Mitchell, Kid Ory or Gerald Reeves on trombone, clarinetists Omer Simeon, Barney Bigard, Darnell Howard or Johnny Dodds, occasionally Stomp Evans on C-melody, Johnny St. Cyr or Bud Scott on banjo, bassist John Lindsay and either Andrew Hilaire or Baby Dodds on drums, Morton had the perfect ensembles for his ideas. He also recorded some exciting trios with Johnny and Baby Dodds.

With the center of jazz shifting to New York by 1928, Morton relocated. His bragging ways unfortunately hurt his career, and he was not able to always get the sidemen he wanted. His Victor recordings continued through 1930, and although some of the performances are sloppy or erratic, there were also a few more classics. Among the musicians Morton was able to use on his New York records were trumpeters Ward Pinkett, Red Allen and Bubber Miley, trombonists Geechie Fields, Charles Irvis and J.C. Higginbotham, clarinetists Omer Simeon, Albert Nicholas and Barney Bigard, banjoist Lee Blair, guitarist Bernard Addison, Bill Benford on tuba, bassist Pops Foster and drummers Tommy Benford, Paul Barbarin and Zutty Singleton.

But with the rise of the Depression, Jelly Roll Morton drifted into obscurity. He had made few friends in New York, his music was considered old-fashioned, and he did not have the temperament to work as a sideman. During 1931–37 his only appearance on records was on a little-known Wingy Manone date. He ended up playing in a Washington D.C. dive for patrons who had little idea of his contributions. Ironically Morton's "King Porter Stomp" became one of the most popular songs of the swing era, but few knew that he wrote it. However in 1938 Alan Lomax recorded him in an extensive and fascinating series of musical interviews for the Library of Congress. Morton's storytelling was colorful, and his piano playing in generally fine form as he reminisced about old New Orleans and demonstrated the other piano styles of the era. A decade later the results would finally be released on albums.

Morton arrived in New York in 1939 determined to make a comeback. He did lead a few band sessions with such sidemen as Sidney Bechet, Red Allen and Albert Nicholas and recorded some wonderful solo sides, but none of those were big sellers. In late 1940 an ailing Morton decided to head out to Los Angeles but, when he died at the age of 50, he seemed like an old man. Ironically his music soon became popular again as the New Orleans jazz revivalist movement caught fire, and if he had lived just a few more years, the chances are good that he would have been restored to his former prominence (as was Kid Ory).

Jelly Roll Morton's early piano solos and classic Victor recordings (along with nearly every record he made) have been reissued on CD. —Scott Yanow

★ **Jelly Roll Morton** / Jun. 9, 1923–Feb. 2, 1926 / Milestone ✦✦✦✦✦
The legendary Jelly Roll Morton recorded many of his finest piano solos for Gennett and Paramount during 1923–24 and all 20 (counting a second version of "New Orleans Joys") are on this essential CD; highpoints include the original versions of "King Porter Stomp," "Grandpa's Spells," "Wolverine Blues" and "The Pearls." In addition, there are four early (and surprisingly primitive) band performances (including a version of "Mr. Jelly Lord" from 1926) and two piano-cornet duets with King Oliver. This single CD differs from the earlier two-LP set in that it leaves out a few of Morton's less significant 1924 band sides but includes the Oliver duets and the second "New Orleans Joys." —Scott Yanow

The Piano Solos (1923–1924) / Jul. 1923–Jun. 1924 / Fountain ✦✦✦✦✦

Rarities, Vol. 2 / Oct. 19, 1923–Aug. 1934 / Rhapsody ✦✦✦✦
This LP gives Jelly Roll Morton collectors some of the odds and ends that they might have missed in only acquiring the Victor and Milestone releases. The legendary pianist/composer is heard in 1923 on two primitive numbers with a quintet, on the obscure "Soap Suds" in 1926, performing four hot numbers with cornetist Johnny Dunn's band in 1928, participating in his only recordings from the 1931–37 period (two songs with Wingy Manone in 1934), playing four superb piano solos in 1926 (including a definitive version of "King Porter Stomp") and leading groups behind singers Edmonia Henderson in 1926 and Frances Hereford in 1928. This highly enjoyable set has more than its share of gems. —Scott Yanow

Jelly Roll Morton / Sep. 1924–Dec. 1924 / Everest ✦✦✦
This budget LP has Jelly Roll Morton's 11 piano rolls, music that has also been issued on Biograph. Although these are not actually recordings of Morton live, his spirit does come through on the reproductions, particularly on "Grandpa's Spells," "King Porter Stomp" and "Mr. Jelly Lord." It is particularly interesting to hear these versions of "Sweet Man" and "Tin Roof Blues" for Morton never otherwise recorded those songs. —Scott Yanow

Jelly Roll Morton (1924–1926) / Sep. 1924–Dec. 1926 / Classics ✦✦✦✦

1926–1934 / Sep. 15, 1926–Aug. 15, 1934 / ABC ✦✦✦
This CD, using Robert Parker's innovative enginneering, brings 16 of pianist Jelly Roll Morton's better Victor recordings to life. This is a good sampling of Morton's sessions although it is not recommended to completists. Highlights include "Black Bottom Stomp," "Grandpa's Spells," "Beale Street Blues" and "You Need Some Loving," the latter with cornetist Johnny Dunn's band. —Scott Yanow

★ **Jelly Roll Morton Centennial: His Complete Victor Recording** / Sep. 15, 1926–Sep. 28, 1939 / Bluebird ✦✦✦✦✦
This five-CD set contains the very best band recordings of Jelly Roll Morton's career. There are 111 performances in this reissue including all of the alternate takes. Bypassed are the pianist's recordings with the vaudevillian clarinetist Wilton Crawley, singers Lizzie Miles and Billie Young and two songs he performed on a radio broadcast in 1940; otherwise all of his Victor recordings are here. The classics (most from the 1926–28 period) include the remarkable "Black Bottom Stomp," "Grandpa's Spells," "The Pearls," "Wolverine Blues" (a trio with clarinetist Johnny Dodds and drummer Baby Dodds), "Shreveport Stomp," "Low Gravy," "Strokin' Away" and "I Thought I Heard Buddy Bolden Say", but listeners will each have their own favorites. In general this is New Orleans jazz at its best with Jelly Roll Morton (as with the best jazz composer/bandleaders) creating his own world of music. —Scott Yanow

Jelly Roll Morton (1926–1928) / Dec. 1926–Jun. 1928 / Classics ✦✦✦✦✦

Jelly Roll Morton (1928–1929) / Dec. 1928–Dec. 1929 / Classics ✦✦✦✦✦

● **Kansas City Stomp: the Library of Congress Recordings, Vol. 1** / May 23, 1938–Jun. 7, 1938 / Rounder ✦✦✦✦✦
Pianist/composer Jelly Roll Morton, one of the pioneers of New Orleans jazz, was down and out in 1938 when Alan Lomax found him playing in a Washington D.C. dive. Lomax, realizing that Morton had seen and heard many timeless incidents that would otherwise be forgotten, started interviewing him for the Library of Congress on a wire recorder. Released originally on eight LPs, these discussions found Morton talking about the old days and peppering his talk with piano solos. Rounder has reissued all of the music (and done a fine job of correcting the speed) on four CDs but unfortunately decided to leave out Morton's often-fascinating monologues. This first CD has many strong moments including Morton's demonstration of the piano styles of many forgotten players, his depiction of a New Orleans funeral, his famous demonstration of how "Tiger Rag" evolved from being a quadrille into becoming jazz and comparisons of "Maple Leaf Rag" as played as ragtime and the way Morton preferred it. —Scott Yanow

● **Anamule Dance** / May 23, 1938–Jun. 7, 1938 / Rounder ✦✦✦✦✦
The second of four CDs that reissue the music (but not the verbal monologues) that pianist/composer Jelly Roll Morton recorded for the Library of Congress is, like the other volumes, filled with memorable performances that are sometimes (due to time limita-

tions) incomplete or heard in excerpts. The most interesting selections on this disc are the lengthy "Winin' Boy Blues," Morton's playful "The Anamule Dance," "Mr. Jelly Lord" and a lengthy (and somewhat filthy) version of "Make Me a Pallet on the Floor." — *Scott Yanow*

● **The Pearls** / May 23, 1938–Jun. 7, 1938 / Rounder ✦✦✦✦✦
The third of four CDs taken from pianist Jelly Roll Morton's Library of Congress recordings is highlighted by the nearly half-hour "Murder Ballad" (a sexual fantasy by Morton about women's prisons), "King Porter Stomp," a two-part "Wolverine Blues and a seven-minute version of "The Pearls." All four of these releases are recommended to collectors of early jazz although the LP equivalent (which runs to eight volumes) also includes all of his storytelling. — *Scott Yanow*

● **Winin Boy Blues** / Jun. 7, 1938–Dec. 14, 1938 / Rounder ✦✦✦✦✦
The fourth and final CD in Rounder's Library of Congress series has the later recordings from this extensive program, including two numbers from six months after the original discussions had concluded. Morton, who is heard very briefly on guitar on "L'il Liza Jane," takes fine piano solos on such numbers as "Freakish," "Pep," "Ain't Misbehavin'" and a medley of "Spanish tinge" songs including "The Crave." This facinating series (which Rounder pitch corrected) is recommended to collectors of early jazz. — *Scott Yanow*

1938–1940 / 1938–May 1940 / Alamac ✦✦
This Alamac LP is primarily for the Jelly Roll Morton completist. Most of the album consists of privately recorded club appearances from Baltimore in 1938. The legendary pianist/composer is matched up with mediocre local musicians in a quintet, and although Morton has some solos and even sings "I Ain't Got Nobody," the music is just barely listenable. This LP concludes with his final recording, excellent versions of "Winin' Boy Blues" and "King Porter Stomp" taken from a radio broadcast in 1940; the aircheck is fortunately available elsewhere. — *Scott Yanow*

New Orleans Memories Plus Two / Dec. 14, 1939–Jan. 23, 1940 / Commodore ✦✦✦✦✦
This two-LP set (whose contents have been reissued in Mosaic's massive *Complete Commodore Jazz Recordings* series) contains New Orleans pioneer Jelly Roll Morton's final commercial recordings. Best are his ten piano solos, some of which he sings; "Winin' Boy Blues," "Don't You Leave Me Here," "The Crave" and "King Porter Stomp" are particularly memorable. The second half of this set has some interesting but nonessential band performances that also feature trumpeter Red Allen and clarinetist Albert Nicholas. Only the lone standard "Panama" and "Sweet Substitute" (the only one of the 11 Morton originals to catch on) are really that worthwhile. But this two-fer is worth picking up for the solo recordings. — *Scott Yanow*

Bob Moses

b. Jan. 28, 1948, New York, NY
Composer, Drums / Avant-Garde, Post-Bop
A fine drummer, Bob Moses has received his strongest recognition as a colorful and adventurous arranger/composer for large ensembles. He played as a teenager with Rahsaan Roland Kirk (1964–65), formed the early fusion group Free Spirits with Larry Coryell (1966) and toured with Gary Burton's quartet (1967–69). Moses collaborated with Dave Liebman in the trio Open Sky, recorded with Gary Burton in the mid-'70s and worked with Jack DeJohnette's Compost, Pat Metheny (recording *Bright Size Life*), Mike Gibbs, Hal Galper, Gil Goldstein, Steve Swallow, the Steve Kuhn-Sheila Jordan group (1979–82), George Gruntz's Concert Jazz Band and Emily Remler (1983–84). He recorded as a composer for his own Mozown label in 1975, but Moses' reputation as a writer rests primarily with his three Gramavision releases *When Elephants Dream of Music* (1982), *Visit with the Great Spirit* (1983) and 1994's *Time Stood Still*. — *Scott Yanow*

★ **When Elephants Dream of Music** / Apr. 11, 1982–Apr. 12, 1982 / Gramavision ✦✦✦✦✦
With Teramasa Hino, Howard Johnson, Jeremy Steig, Lyle Mays, David Friedman, Steve Swallow, Nana Vasconcelos, Sheila Jordan and Jeanne Lee. — *Michael Erlewine*

Visit with the Great Spirit / 1983 / Gramavision ✦✦✦✦
Bob Moses, formerly known as a tasteful and flexible drummer, really came into his own as a composer/arranger during his period with Gramavision. This ambitious effort has seven of his diverse and colorful originals. Such distinctive voices as trumpeter

Tiger Okoshi, soprano saxophonist David Liebman, tenorman Bob Mintzer, altoist David Sanborn, guitarists Bill Frisell and John Scofield and tuba player Howard Johnson (not to mention various percussionists and background singers) are utilized by Moses in imaginative ways. *When Elephants Dream of Music*, Moses' previous release, is still his definitive recording, but this album comes close, making one wish that Bob Moses could record in this type of setting on at least an annual basis. — *Scott Yanow*

The Story of Moses / 1987 / Gramavision ✦✦✦✦

Michael Mossman

b. Oct. 12, 1959, Philadelphia, PA
Trumpet / Hard Bop
A fine hard bop trumpeter with a wide range, Michael Mossman has proven to be an asset to many swinging sessions. A flexible player, he toured Europe in 1978 with an orchestra led by Anthony Braxton and played on two tours with Roscoe Mitchell. But Mossman was in more logical surroundings when he was with Lionel Hampton (1984) and during the one month he played with Art Blakey's Jazz Messengers. He played with Machito and Gerry Mulligan in 1985 and then toured and recorded with Out of the Blue (OTB). Mossman played lead trumpet with Toshiko Akiyoshi's Jazz Orchestra, was in Horace Silver's group (1989–91) and was a member of Gerry Mulligan's Rebirth of the Cool Band (1992). In addition he toured with Dizzy Gillespie's United Nation Orchestra, the Philip Morris Superband and Slide Hampton's Jazz Masters Orchestra. He has also played with the Latin bands of Michel Camilo and Mario Bauza. Michael Mossman co-led sessions for EGT and Red and had a 1995 release on Claves. — *Scott Yanow*

Granulate / Apr. 1990 / Red ✦✦✦✦

Abe Most

b. Feb. 27, 1920, New York, NY
Clarinet / Swing
A superior swing clarinetist who has spent much of his career either in the studios or recreating the work of Artie Shaw and Benny Goodman, Abe Most is the older brother of flutist Sam Most. He joined Les Brown in 1939, spent 1942–45 in the military and was briefly with Tommy Dorsey in 1946. He moved to Los Angeles in the late '40s where he has worked steadily as a studio musician. Abe Most frequently plays in local clubs (sometimes with his brother) and classic jazz festivals but despite his talent has recorded as a leader much too infrequently. He led obscure sessions for Superior (1946), Trend (1954), Annunciata (1978) and Canard (1984). — *Scott Yanow*

The Most (Abe, That Is) / 1978 / Camard ✦✦✦✦

● **Swing Low Sweet Clarinet** / Sep. 21, 1984 / Camard ✦✦✦✦✦

Sam Most

b. Dec. 16, 1930, Atlantic City, NJ
Flute, Tenor Saxophone / Bop, Cool
One of the first great jazz flutists, a cool-toned tenor and a fine (if infrequent) clarinetist, Sam Most is the younger brother of clarinetist Abe Most. He picked up early experience playing with the orchestras of Tommy Dorsey (1948), Boyd Raeburn and Don Redman. By the time he led his first session (1953), Most was a brilliant flutist (among the first to sing through his flute), and he briefly had the jazz field to himself. Most recorded fine sessions for Prestige, Debut (reissued on Xanadu), Vanguard and Bethlehem during 1953–58, doubling on clarinet. He also worked in different settings with Chris Connor, Paul Quinichette and Teddy Wilson. After playing with Buddy Rich's Orchestra (1959–61), he moved to Los Angeles and became a studio musician. Sam Most worked with Red Norvo and Louie Bellson, gained some new prominence with his Xanadu recordings of 1976–79 and became a local fixture in Los Angeles, sometimes playing in clubs with his brother. — *Scott Yanow*

But Beautiful / 1976 / Catalyst ✦✦✦✦
Although he was one of the pioneers of the jazz flute and remained one of its finest exponents, Sam Most did not have an opportunity to record as a leader after 1958 until this Catalyst session. The enjoyable LP also includes fine work from pianist George Muribus, bassist Putter Smith and drummer Will Bradley, Jr., although Most is easily the main star. He plays his cool-toned tenor on two tracks, but it his flute that is most individual; check out his interpretation of "I've Grown Accustomed to Your Face" on this LP, if you can find it. — *Scott Yanow*

★ **Mostly Flute** / May 27, 1976 / Xanadu ✦✦✦✦✦
With Duke Jordan Trio and Tal Farlow on guitar. Two Sam Most originals, five standards. Great interplay between Most and Farlow. —*Michael G. Nastos*

Flute Flight / Dec. 28, 1976 / Xanadu ✦✦✦✦✦
Sam Most, one of a handful of truly great flute players, is in fine form on this quartet session with pianist Lou Levy, bassist Monty Budwig and drummer Donald Bailey. He has a classic duet with Levy on "It Might as Well Be Spring," plays beautifully on "Last Night When We Were Young," switches to clarinet for "Am I Blue," demonstrates his ability to sing along with his flute on "The Humming Blues" and really cooks during "Flying Down to Rio." A fine all-round showcase for Sam Most's underrated talents. —*Scott Yanow*

From the Attic of My Mind / Apr. 25, 1978 / Xanadu ✦✦✦✦
Flutist Sam Most contributed eight of the compositions to this easily enjoyable quintet date. With tasteful support from pianist Kenny Barron, bassist George Mraz, drummer Walter Bolden and percussionist Warren Smith, Most could have easily taken the laidback approach often favored by flutists, but instead he digs in and comes up with some fiery statements. None of the originals (which includes blues, ballads and blowing devices) caught on elsewhere, but they work well on this set. —*Scott Yanow*

Flute Talk / Jan. 23, 1979–Jan. 24, 1979 / Xanadu ✦✦✦✦
Essentially a blowing session, the flutes of Sam Most and Joe Farrell are in the forefront of this enjoyable straight-ahead date. Pianist Mike Wofford, bassist Bob Magnusson, drummer Roy McCurdy and percussionist Jerry Steinholtz are quite supportive of the flutes. Most and Farrell play a few numbers including a creative version of "When You Wish upon a Star"), some straightforward originals, and on "Leaves" they freely improvise around each other in an interesting (if overly brief) duet. —*Scott Yanow*

Bennie Moten

b. Nov. 13, 1894, Kansas City, MO, **d.** Apr. 2, 1935, Kansas City, MO
Piano, Leader / Classic Jazz
Bennie Moten is today best-remembered as the leader of a band that partly became the nucleus of the original Count Basie Orchestra, but Moten deserves better. He was a fine ragtime-oriented pianist who led the top territory band of the 1920s, an orchestra that really set the standard for Kansas City jazz. In fact it was so dominant that Moten was able to swallow up some of his competitors' groups including Walter Page's Blue Devils, most of whom eventually became members of Moten's big band. Moten formed his group (originally a sextet) in 1922, and the following year they made their first recordings. Among Moten's 1923-25 sides for Okeh was the original version of his greatest hit "South." During 1926-32 Moten's Orchestra recorded for Victor, and although none of his original musicians became famous, the later additions included his brother Buster on occasional jazz accordion, Harlan Leonard, Jack Washington, Eddie Durham, Jimmy Rushing, Hot Lips Page and (starting in 1929) Count Basie. So impressed was Moten by Basie's playing that Count assumed the piano chair for recordings from that point on (although in clubs Moten would generally play a feature or two). The most famous Bennie Moten recording session was also his last, ten songs cut on December 13, 1932 that find the ensemble strongly resembling Basie's five years later. In addition to Hot Lips Page, Durham, Washington and Basie, the band at that point also starred Ben Webster, Eddie Barefield and Walter Page and one of the highpoints was the debut of "Moten Swing."
Tragically Bennie Moten died in 1935 from a botched tonsillectomy operation. Buster Moten briefly took over the band, but many of its top members (along with some important additions like Lester Young) eventually gravitated toward Count Basie. —*Scott Yanow*

Bennie Moten (1923—1927) / Sep. 1923-Jun. 1927 / Classics ✦✦✦✦✦

South (1926-1929) / Dec. 13, 1926-Jul. 17, 1929 / Bluebird ✦✦✦✦✦

Bennie Moten (1927—1929) / Jun. 1927-Jun. 1929 / Classics ✦✦✦✦✦

Bennie Moten (1929—1930) / Jul. 1929-Oct. 1930 / Classics ✦✦✦✦✦

★ **Basie Beginnings (1929-1932)** / Oct. 23, 1929-Dec. 13, 1932 / Bluebird ✦✦✦✦✦
Bennie Moten's orchestra, arguably the top territory band at the

time Count Basie joined as second pianist in 1929, had been reasonably well-represented on records since 1923. This does have the cream of Moten's 1929 and 1930 sessions, plus seven of the ten songs cut at their superb Dec. 13, 1932 date. Moten himself never again appeared on records after Basie joined. —*Scott Yanow*

Bennie Moten (1930—1932) / 1930-Dec. 13, 1932 / Classics ✦✦✦✦✦

Paul Motian (Stephen Paul Motian)

b. Mar. 25, 1931, Philadelphia, PA
Leader, Drums / Avant-Garde, Post-Bop
Paul Motian is a subtle drummer who is equally important as the leader of several rather stimulating bands and quite a few colorful recording sessions. Born in Philadelphia, Motian grew up in Providence, RI. After moving to New York in 1955 he played with many top jazz musicians from a wide variety of styles including Tony Scott, Gil Evans, Art Farmer, Lee Konitz, George Russell, Stan Getz, Lennie Tristano, Thelonious Monk, Coleman Hawkins and Roy Eldridge. As a member of Bill Evans' most famous trio (the one with Scott LaFaro), Motian helped define the role of the modern drummer in that type of intimate setting. He remained with Evans after LaFaro's death (Chuck Israels took over as bassist) until 1963. Motian then played with Paul Bley's Trio (1963–64), and he later had a longterm musical relationship with Keith Jarrett, starting in 1966 and including work with Jarrett's quintet in the 1970s. Motian also freelanced and among the many musicians that he worked with were Mose Allison, Charles Lloyd, Charlie Haden's Liberation Music Ensemble and Carla Bley. Motian began leading his own groups in 1977 and these included a trio with Joe Lovano and Bill Frisell and the Electric Bebop Band in the 1990's with Joshua Redman and two guitarists. He has recorded many albums as a leader (starting in 1972) for ECM, GM, Soul Note and JMT including collaborations with Lee Konitz. —*Scott Yanow*

Conception Vessel / Nov. 25, 1972-Nov. 26, 1972 / ECM ✦✦✦✦
This is Motian's debut as a leader. It includes ambitious cuts with guitarist Sam Brown and also features pianist Keith Jarrett. —*Ron Wynn*

Tribute / May 1974 / ECM ✦✦✦✦
Quintet with guitarist Sam Brown, Charlie Haden (b), early work of saxophonist Carlos Ward. Coleman's "War Orphans" and Haden's immortal "Song for Che" are included. —*Michael G. Nastos*

Dance / Sep. 1977 / ECM ✦✦✦✦✦
Excellent solos by saxophonist Charles Brackeen and above-average writing and ensemble work —*Ron Wynn*

Le Voyage / Mar. 1979 / ECM ✦✦✦✦

● **Psalm** / Dec. 1981 / ECM ✦✦✦✦✦
A pianoless session by drummer Paul Motian, this time leading a band with two saxophonists, guitar and bass. While Joe Lovano provides his normal exemplary tenor sax solos, Billy Drewes on alto and tenor has to both match Lovano and complement him—not an easy task. Guitarist Bill Frisell mixes the straight with the bizarre, while bassist Ed Schuller and Motian hold everything together. —*Ron Wynn*

The Story of Maryam, the / Jul. 27, 1983-Jul. 28, 1983 / Soul Note ✦✦✦✦

Jack of Clubs / Mar. 26, 1984-Mar. 28, 1984 / Soul Note ✦✦✦✦
A quintet with Jim Pepper (ts), Joe Lovano (ts), Bill Frisell (g) and Ed Schuller (b) plays seven pieces, all by Motian. This is very intense yet lyrical. Pepper and Lovano are excellent sax foils. —*Michael G. Nastos*

It Should Have Happened a Long Time Ago / Jul. 1984 / ECM ✦✦✦✦

Circle the Line / Jun. 1986 / GM ✦✦✦✦

One Time Out / Sep. 21, 1987-Sep. 22, 1987 / Soul Note ✦✦✦✦✦
Drummer Paul Motian never makes predictable or conventional albums, and this mid- and late '80s date proves no different. The trio lineup, with Motian, tenor saxophonist Joe Lovano, and guitarist and synthesizer player Bill Frisell, offers some unusual voicings, solos and harmonies, filling in the space that would normally be completed by a pianist, bassist, or second horn. It's not hard bop, fusion, or free, but a mix of all three and more. —*Ron Wynn*

★ **Monk in Motian** / Mar. 1988 / JMT ✦✦✦✦✦
A top tribute, with sterling work by Frisell (g) and Dewey Redman (ts). —*Ron Wynn*

★ **Paul Motian on Broadway, Vol. 1 (with Bill Frisell, Charlie Haden, Joe Lovano & Paul M** / Nov. 1988 / JMT ✦✦✦✦✦

● **Paul Motian on Broadway, Vol. 2** / Sep. 1989 / JMT ✦✦✦✦✦

Bill Evans: Tribute to the Great Post-Bop Pianist / May 1990 / JMT ✦✦✦✦✦
An excellent quartet date featuring sensational guitar by Bill Frisell and nice tenor sax from Joe Lovano. —*Ron Wynn*

Motian in Tokyo / 1992 / JMT ✦✦✦✦

Paul Motian & The Electric Bebop Band / Apr. 1992 / JMT ✦✦✦✦

On Broadway, Vol. 3 / Apr. 20, 1993 / JMT ✦✦✦✦✦

Trio I SM / Jun. 1993 / JMT ✦✦✦✦

Alphonse Mouzon

b. Nov. 21, 1948, Charleston, SC
Drums / Fusion, Crossover, Post Bop
A talented drummer whose music stretches from jazz to fusion, rock, funk and pop, Alphonse Mouzon made his first record date in 1969 with Gil Evans. After freelancing in New York, Mouzon was with Roy Ayers during 1970-71, was the original drummer with Weather Report (1971-72), played with McCoy Tyner and then during 1973-75 was with Larry Coryell's Eleventh House. He has since freelanced, worked with Al DiMeola, George Benson, Herbie Hancock (1979-82) and led his own groups, leading dates for Blue Note, MPS, Optimism and Pausa plus his own Tenacious label. —*Scott Yanow*

The Essence of Mystery / 1972-1973 / Blue Note ✦✦✦
Some frenetic drumming and good jazz/rock arrangments. —*Ron Wynn*

● **Funky Snakefoot** / Dec. 10, 1973-Dec. 12, 1973 / Blue Note ✦✦✦✦
One of the few intelligent uses of funk and soul in a '70s instrumental setting (at least from a fusion standpoint). After this album, he became more pop oriented. —*Ron Wynn*

Mind Transplant / Dec. 4, 1974-Dec. 10, 1974 / Blue Note ✦✦✦

The Man Incognito / Dec. 1975+Jan. 1976 / Blue Note ✦✦

Virtue / Nov. 1976 / PA/USA ✦✦✦

Back to Jazz / 1986 / PA/USA ✦✦✦✦

Love, Fantasy / 1991 / Optimism ✦✦

The Survivor / 1992 / Tenacious ✦✦✦

Early Spring / 1993 / Optimism ✦✦✦

Bob Mover

b. Mar. 22, 1952, Boston, MA
Alto Saxophone, Soprano Saxophone / Hard Bop
When Bob Mover had his highest visibility in the late '70s, he played in a style very similar to Lee Konitz (with whom he recorded in 1977). Mover worked with Ira Sullivan when he was 16 and after moving to New York in 1969 freelanced in the local scene. Mover played with Charles Mingus briefly in 1973, was with Chet Baker during 1973-75 and started leading his own group in 1976. He had two recording sessions in 1977 (one apiece for Choice and Vanguard) and two for Xanadu in 1981; the latter dates found him beginning to develop his own individuality. —*Scott Yanow*

Bob Mover / May 1979 / Vanguard ✦✦✦✦

● **In the True Tradition** / Jun. 23, 1981 / Xanadu ✦✦✦✦✦
Altoist Bob Mover, who originally sounded quite a bit like Lee Konitz, fully displays his individuality on this passionate trio set. Accompanied by bassist Rufus Reid and drummer Bobby Ward, Mover is free to be as explorative as he likes on the high-quality material which includes two originals, a pair of ballads, "Poinciana" and Thelonious Monk's "Evidence." This is one of Mover's finest recordings to date. —*Scott Yanow*

Things Unseen! / Jun. 23, 1981-Dec. 21, 1982 / Xanadu ✦✦✦✦
One selection on this album is a song leftover from Mover's Xanadu debut *In the True Tradition*; the altoist is heard jamming with bassist Rufus Reid and drummer Bobby Ward on "Jimmy Garrison's Blues." Otherwise this album mostly features Mover with pianist Albert Dailey, bassist Ray Drummond and drummer Ward on a variety of standards. Tenor saxophonist Steve Hall sits in on "Twardzik" during which Mover switches to soprano. A highpoint on the album is the duet between Dailey and Mover on

a lengthy rendition of "Yesterdays." Overall this set offers high-quality modern bebop. —*Scott Yanow*

Famoudou Don Moye

b. May 23, 1946, Rochester, NY
Percussion, Drums / Avant-Garde, Free Jazz
When Don Moye joined the Art Ensemble of Chicago in 1970, he filled the gap that had been there since Philip Wilson left the group a couple years earlier to tour with the Butterfield Blues Band. Moye fit in perfectly, never just functioning as a timekeeper or an accompanist but becoming an equal partner in the innovative avant-garde quintet. He had studied at Wayne State University, toured Europe with the group Detroit Free Jazz and played with Steve Lacy before joining the Art Ensemble in Paris. In addition to his activities with the band, Moye has recorded with the Black Artists Group, performed with Randy Weston, recorded with Joseph Jarman, Don Pullen, Cecil McBee, Hamiet Bluiett, Julius Hemphill, Chico Freeman and Lester Bowie's Brass Fantasy (among others) and since 1984 has been a member of the Leaders. He also recorded an unaccompanied percussion date for the Art Ensemble label AECO in 1975. —*Scott Yanow*

Sun Percussion / Mar. 27, 1975 / AECO ✦✦✦✦
Quintessential solo recording (all percussion) from an Art Ensemble standout. —*Michael G. Nastos*

● **Black Paladins** / 1981 / Black Saint ✦✦✦✦✦
Adventurous concept pieces, excellent percussive foundations and adept playing. —*Ron Wynn*

George Mraz

b. Sept. 9, 1944, Czechoslovakia
Bass / Hard Bop
George Mraz has been a greatly in-demand bassist for straightahead dates ever since he emigrated to the United States in 1968. After a brief time playing violin and alto, Mraz studied bass at the Prague Conservatory and gigged at a club in Munich for a year. In 1968 he attended Berklee, and he soon toured with Oscar Peterson (1970-72). After moving to New York, Mraz became a member of the Thad Jones-Mel Lewis Orchestra (1973-76), worked with Stan Getz (1974-75) and has since played with most of the top jazz players including Walter Norris, Pepper Adams, Roland Hanna, Zoot Sims, Tommy Flanagan, John Abercrombie, Carmen McRae, Jimmy Rowles, Stephane Grappelli and countless others. Other than an obscure duo date with Roland Hanna for Trio in 1976, George Mraz has surprisingly not led any record sessions of his own. —*Scott Yanow*

Idris Muhammad (Leo Morris)

b. Nov. 13, 1939, New Orleans, LA.
Drums / Post-Bop, Crossover
An excellent drummer who has appeared in many types of settings, Idris Muhammad became a professional when he was 16. He played primarily soul and R&B during 1962-64 and then spent 1965-67 as a member of Lou Donaldson's band. He was the house drummer at Prestige Records (1970-72), appearing on many albums as a sideman. Of his later jazz associations, Muhammad played with Johnny Griffin (1978-79), Pharoah Sanders in the 1980s, George Coleman and the Paris Reunion Band (1986-88). He has recorded everything from post bop to dance music as a leader for such labels as Prestige, Kudu, Fantasy, Theresa and Lipstick. —*Scott Yanow*

Black Rhythm Revolution / Nov. 2, 1970 / Prestige ✦✦✦
The well-known session drummer steps out front with a funk and soul-jazz oriented session. There's minimal solo space, but some expert production and competent playing. —*Ron Wynn*

Peace & Rhythm / Sep. 13, 1971-Sep. 20, 1971 / Prestige ✦✦
Competent funk and soul-jazz outing by the onetime house drummer for Prestige. Things are tightly supervised, with minimal solo space, but there are some enjoyable moments. Arrangements and production were aimed at achieving maximum crossover attention and appeal. —*Ron Wynn*

Power of Soul / Nov. 1974 / Kudu ✦✦✦

● **Kabsha** / 1980 / Theresa ✦✦✦✦✦
Much more jazz-oriented than some of the session drummer's releases, this '81 date included a guest stint by Pharoah Sanders and had Muhammad anchoring the date and playing far more aggressively. —*Ron Wynn*

My Turn / 1993 / Lipstick ✦✦✦
Included are strong instrumental tunes with great contributions
by well-known guest stars. The vocal tunes, including "Free" with
vocals by Hiram Bullock, might not be to everyone's taste. Idris
plays with a sideman attitude—he does not dominate the band
but delivers a solid groove which serves the music. Overall, the
album is a strange mixture between jazz and pop tunes. —*Alex
Merck*

Gerry Mulligan

b. Apr. 6, 1927, New York, NY, **d.** Jan. 19, 1996
Baritone Saxophone, Arranger, Composer, Leader, Piano / Cool
The most famous and probably greatest jazz baritonist of all time,
Gerry Mulligan was a giant. A flexible soloist who was always
ready to jam with anyone from Dixielanders to the most
advanced boppers, Mulligan brought a somewhat revolutionary
light sound to his potentially awkward and brutal horn and
played with the speed and dexterity of an altoist.

Mulligan started on the piano before learning clarinet and the
various saxophones. His initial reputation was as an arranger. In
1944 he wrote charts for Johnny Warrington's radio band and
soon was making contributions to the books of Tommy Tucker
and George Paxton. He moved to New York in 1946 and joined
Gene Krupa's Orchestra as a staff arranger; his most notable chart
was "Disc Jockey Jump." The rare times he played with Krupa's
band was on alto, and the same situation existed when he was
with Claude Thornhill in 1948.

Gerry Mulligan's first notable recorded work on baritone was
with Miles Davis' *Birth of the Cool* nonet (1948-50), but once
again his arrangements ("Godchild," "Darn That Dream" and
three of his originals "Jeru," "Rocker" and "Venus De Milo") were
more significant than his short solos. Mulligan spent much of
1949 writing for Elliot Lawrence's orchestra and playing anonymously in the saxophone section. It was not until 1951 that he
began to get a bit of attention for his work on baritone. Mulligan
recorded with his own nones for Prestige, displaying an already
recognizable sound. After he traveled to Los Angeles, he wrote
some arrangements for Stan Kenton (including "Youngblood,"
"Swing House" and "Walking Shoes"), worked at the Lighthouse
and then gained a regular Monday night engagement at the Haig.
Around this time Mulligan realized that he enjoyed the extra freedom of soloing without a pianist. He jammed with trumpeter Chet
Baker, and soon their magical rapport was featured in his pianoless quartet. The group caught on quickly in 1952 and made both
Mulligan and Baker into stars.

A drug bust put Mulligan out of action and ended that
Quartet but, when he was released from jail in 1954, Mulligan
began a new musical partnership with valve trombonist Bob
Brookmeyer that was just as successful. Trumpeter Jon Eardley
and Zoot Sims on tenor occasionally made the group a sextet,
and in 1958 trumpeter Art Farmer was featured in Mulligan's
Quartet. Being a very flexible player with respect for other stylists, Mulligan went out of his way to record with some of the
great musicians he admired. At the 1958 Newport Jazz Fetival
he traded off with baritonist Harry Carney on "Prima Bara
Dubla" while backed by the Duke Ellington Orchestra, and during 1957-60 he recorded separate albums with Thelonious
Monk, Paul Desmond, Stan Getz, Ben Webster and Johnny
Hodges. Mulligan played on the classic *Sound of Jazz* television
special in 1958 and appeared in the movies *I Want to Live* and
The Subterraneans.

During 1960-64 Mulligan led his Concert Jazz Band which
gave him an opporunity to write, play baritone and occasionally
double on piano. The orchestra at times included Brookmeyer,
Sims, Clark Terry and Mel Lewis. Mulligan was a little less active
after the big band broke up, but he toured extensively with the
Dave Brubeck Quartet (1968-72), had a part-time big band in the
1970s (the Age of Steam), doubled on soprano for a period, led a
mid-'70s sextet that included vibraphonist Dave Samuels and in
1986 jammed on a record with Scott Hamilton. In the 1990s he
toured the world with his excellent "no-name" quartet and led a
"Rebirth of the Cool Band" that performed and recorded remakes
of the Miles Davis Nonet classics. Up until the end, Gerry
Mulligan was always eager to play.

Among Mulligan's compositions were "Walkin' Shoes," "Line
for Lyons," "Bark for Barksdale," "Nights at the Turntable," "Utter
Chaos," "Soft Shoe," "Bernie's Tune," "Blueport," "Song for
Strayhorn," "Song for an Unifinished Woman" and "I Never Was a

Young Man" (which he often sang). He recorded extensively
through the years for such labels as Prestige, Pacific Jazz, Capitol,
Vogue, EmArcy, Columbia, Verve, Milestone, United Artists,
Philips, Limelight, A&M, CTI, Chiaroscuro, Who's Who, DRG,
Concord and GRP. —*Scott Yanow*

The Arranger / May 21, 1946–Apr. 20, 1957 / Columbia ✦✦✦✦
This LP includes some of Gerry Mulligan's charts for the orches-
tras of Gene Krupa ("How High the Moon" and "Disc Jockey
Jump") and Elliot Lawrence ("Between the Devil and the Deep
Blue Sea" and "Elevation") in addition to featuring his own 1957
big band ("Thruway," "All the Things You Are," "Mullenium" and
"Motel"). The Krupa performances are near-classic, the forgotten
Lawrence band is in top form, and Jeru's specially assembled
orchestra features solos from baritonist Mulligan, trumpeters
Jerry Lloyd and Don Joseph, trombonist Bob Brookmeyer, tenor
saxophonist Zoot Sims and altoist Lee Konitz. Excellent music
although most of it has since been reissued on CD. —*Scott Yanow*

Walking Shoes / Nov. 28, 1947–Jan. 29, 1953 / Capitol ✦✦✦✦
The Gerry Mulligan Tentette (which features Chet Baker's trumpet and the leader's baritone) is heard on eight selections in 1953.
In addition, although Mulligan's name heads this LP (which is
subtitled *Capitol Jazz Classics Vol. 4*), the other numbers are
unrelated but classic in their own way. The bop clarinetist Stan
Hasselgard is heard at his peak on four numbers with a sextet
that includes vibraphonist Red Norvo and guitarist Barney Kessel
while the Red Norvo Septet of 1947 (with a young Dexter Gordon
on tenor) performs "Bop!" and a memorable version of "I'll Follow
You." —*Scott Yanow*

Mulligan—Baker / Aug. 1951–1965 / Prestige ✦✦✦✦
This double LP is full of valuable recordings. The classic Gerry
Mulligan pianoless quartet with trumpeter Chet Baker is heard on
eight gems including "Line for Lyons," "Lady Is a Tramp" and
their hit version of "My Funny Valentine." In addition, Gerry
Mulligan performs with his unusual tentette of 1951 (which featured two baritones and maracas), and Jeru and Allen Eager head
a sextet on a 17-minute version of his original "Mulligan's Too."
This two-fer concludes with four numbers taken from Chet
Baker's many quintet sessions of 1965 with tenor saxophonist
George Coleman and pianist Kirk Lightsey. Most of this music has
since appeared on CD, but this was a well-packaged set and does
not duplicate Mulligan's remarkable Mosaic box. —*Scott Yanow*

Mulligan Plays Mulligan / Sep. 27, 1951 / Original Jazz Classics
✦✦✦✦
A standout date, with Mulligan doing his own songs and top-ech-
elon playing by Allen Eager (ts). —*Ron Wynn*

★ **Pacific Jazz and Capitol Recordings** / Jun. 10, 1952–Jun. 10,
1953 / Mosaic ✦✦✦✦✦
This five-LP box set, as its title states, contains all of the Gerry
Mulligan Quartet's recordings for Pacific Jazz and Capitol, everything that that classic group ever recorded other than the material issued by Prestige and a half-record recorded for
GNP/Crescendo. Unfortunately, this is a limited-edition set that is
now out of print, but it is well worth bidding on in auctions, for
not only does it have all of the Mulligan Quartet's other recordings but also 15 previously unissued performances, all of the sides
on which altoist Lee Konitz sat in with the quartet and the eight
recordings by the 1953 Gerry Mulligan Tentette. These highly
influential performances set the standard for West Coast cool jazz,
made trumpeter Chet Baker a star and remain some of the highpoints of Gerry Mulligan's very productive career. —*Scott Yanow*

Gerry Mulligan Quartet with Chet Baker / May 7, 1953–Jun.
1953 / GNP ✦✦✦
The first side of this LP has the six rarest studio performances by
the Gerry Mulligan quartet, excellent music that does not duplicate the Mosaic box or Jeru's Prestige output. The quartet with
trumpeter Chet Baker sounds at the top of its form on such songs
as "Varsity Drag," "Speak Low," "Half Nelson," "Lady Bird," "Love
Me or Leave Me" and "Swing House." The second half of this set
is not on the same level, finding the Buddy DeFranco quartet of
1953 hampered by The Herman McCoy Swing Choir on six numbers, all of which have "Star" in its title. This budget set inexcusably leaves off any personnel or date listing but is worth picking
up for the Mulligan performances. —*Scott Yanow*

Gerry Mulligan In Paris, Vol. 1 / Jun. 1, 1954+Jun. 3, 1954 /
Vogue ✦✦✦✦✦
Formerly available in piecemeal fashion, this CD (and *Vol. 2*) has

all of the music recorded at baritonist Gerry Mulligan's Paris concerts of June 1954. This particular unit (with valve trombonist Bob Brookmeyer, bassist Red Mitchell and drummer Frank Isola) was one of Jeru's finest for his own wit, swing and cool-toned creativity were matched by Brookmeyer. Highpoints include "Walkin' Shoes," "Love Me or Leave Me," "My Funny Valentine" and "Five Brothers", but every selection is quite enjoyable. The audience is rightfully enthusiastic. —*Scott Yanow*

Gerry Mulligan In Paris, Vol. 2 / Jun. 3, 1954–Jun. 7, 1954 / Vogue ◆◆◆◆◆
In June 1954 the Gerry Mulligan Quartet (with the leader/baritonist, valve trombonist Bob Brookmeyer, bassist Red Mitchell and drummer Frank Isola) performed at five all-star concerts, four of which were recorded. Only previously available in fragmented form, the very accessible yet chancetaking music has now been reissued in full on two CDs by the French Vogue label. The second volume is highlighted by "Laura," "Five Brothers," "Love Me or Leave Me," "Line for Lyons" and "Motel" but it is no exaggeration to say that every performance is well worth hearing. Both sets are highly recommended for this cool-toned but witty and hard-swinging music is very easy to enjoy. —*Scott Yanow*

California Concerts, Vol. 1 / Nov. 12, 1954 / Pacific Jazz ◆◆◆◆◆
This CD documents a concert by Gerry Mulligan's Quartet when the baritonist's group featured trumpeter Jon Eardley, bassist Red Mitchell and drummer Chico Hamilton. Half of these ten selections were either previously unissued or only available as part of obscure samplers. The music, comprising standards, some blues and a few Mulligan originals, is quite enjoyable, swinging lightly and with plenty of interplay between the horns. —*Scott Yanow*

California Concerts, Vol. 2 / Dec. 14, 1954 / Pacific Jazz ◆◆◆◆◆
The second of two CDs in this series mostly consists of previously unissued material taken from a high school concert featuring the Gerry Mulligan Quartet (which at the time featured trumpeter Jon Eardley) plus two guests (valve trombonist Bob Brookmeyer and tenor saxophonist Zoot Sims). This swinging and often-witty cool bop music is quite enjoyable and highly recommended. —*Scott Yanow*

Mainstream, Vol. 2 / Sep. 21, 1955–Sep. 22, 1955 / EmArcy ◆◆◆◆
The Gerry Mulligan Sextet of 1955-56 only released three LPs at the time, but decades later the revived EmArcy label came up with two more albums of material, alternate takes that feature completely different solos than the more familiar versions. Mulligan's band at the time of the second volume included trumpeter Jon Eardley, valve trombonist Bob Brookmeyer and Zoot Sims on tenor in addition to bassist Peck Morrison and drummer Dave Bailey. This happy set is highlighted by "The Lady Is a Tramp," "Broadway," and "Bernie's Tune," all of the music previously unissued. —*Scott Yanow*

Presenting the Gerry Mulligan Sextet / Sep. 21, 1955–Oct. 31, 1955 / EmArcy ◆◆◆◆
The short-lived Gerry Mulligan sextet of 1955-56 recorded three albums before disbanding. This particular out-of-print LP features baritonist Mulligan, trumpeter Jon Eardley, valve trombonist Bob Brookmeyer and Zoot Sims on tenor performing such songs as "Nights at the Turntable," "Broadway," "The Lady Is a Tramp" and "Bernie's Tune." Fun swinging music that is still quite accessible. —*Scott Yanow*

A Profile of Gerry Mulligan / Sep. 21, 1955–Sep. 26, 1956 / Mercury ◆◆◆◆
The second of three LPs recorded by the 1955-56 Gerry Mulligan sextet before it broke up, this fine out-of-print set features such excellent players as baritonist Mulligan, valve trombonist Bob Brookmeyer, Zoot Sims on tenor and either Jon Eardley or Don Ferrara on trumpet. Highlights include "Makin' Whoopie," a Duke Ellington medley and "Westward Walk." Excellent music from one of the top "West Coast Jazz" groups; this band was actually based in New York! —*Scott Yanow*

Mainstream of Jazz / Sep. 22, 1955–Sep. 26, 1956 / EmArcy ◆◆◆◆
One of three LPs recorded by the Gerry Mulligan Sextet of 1955-56, this set includes plenty of lesser-known songs including "Mainstream," "Igloo" and "Lollypop." With such strong soloists as baritonist Mulligan, the always swinging tenor of Zoot Sims, valve trombonist Bob Brookmeyer and trumpeter Jon Eardley, this was a classic West Coast style jazz band, and each of its recordings are worth acquiring. —*Scott Yanow*

Mainstream, Vol. 3 / Oct. 31, 1955–Jan. 25, 1956 / EmArcy ◆◆◆◆
Gerry Mulligan's 1955-56 Sextet recorded three LPs that were released at the time. Nearly three decades later two additional albums (*Mainstream, Vols. 2 and 3*) were issued that included previously unknown alternate takes. Naturally the solos by the talented players (which include baritone-saxophonist Mulligan, Zoot Sims on tenor, valve trombonist Bob Brookmeyer and trumpeter Jon Eardley) are different than on the master takes. The music (highlighted by "Broadway," "The Lady Is a Tramp" and "Westwood Walk") is quite enjoyable. All of this band's recordings are recommended; hopefully they will appear on CD eventually. —*Scott Yanow*

At Storyville / Dec. 6, 1956 / Pacific Jazz ◆◆◆◆◆
This live concert from the Storyville Club in Boston features Gerry Mulligan's Quartet in late 1956. Baritonist Mulligan had found a perfect partner in valve trombonist Bob Brookmeyer, and (with the sympathetic support of bassist Bill Crow and drummer Dave Bailey) they romp through a variety of standards and group originals including such odd titles as "Bweebida Bwobbida," "Utter Chaos" (their theme song) and "Bike up the Strand." A fine all-round performance from this cool-toned bop unit. —*Scott Yanow*

Mulligan Meets Monk / Aug. 12, 1957–Aug. 13, 1957 / Riverside ◆◆◆◆

Mulligan and Getz and Desmond / Aug. 1957–Oct. 22, 1957 / Verve ◆◆◆◆
Baritone-saxophonist Gerry Mulligan had opportunities to record sessions with many of the top saxophonists of his time. This double LP includes his meetings with altoist Paul Desmond (which by itself would be rated best) and Stan Getz (merely a good). The Mulligan-Getz encounter is a bit odd in that on three of the eight selections they switch horns, with Getz playing baritone and Mulligan tenor. One really hears the similarity and overlapping of their styles on those performances, but they lower the general quality of the date. On the other hand, the Mulligan-Desmond matchup is wonderful with many swinging and witty moments between the two greats, particularly on "Line for Lyons" and "Battle Hymn of the Republican." —*Scott Yanow*

Gerry Mulligan Meets Stan Getz / Oct. 22, 1957 / Verve ◆◆◆

The Mulligan Songbook / Dec. 4, 1957–Dec. 5, 1957 / Pacific Jazz ◆◆◆◆

Reunion / Dec. 4, 1957–Dec. 17, 1957 / Pacicific Jazz ◆◆◆◆
I Want to Live / May 24, 1958 / United Artists ◆◆◆◆
Baritonist Gerry Mulligan and a group of West Coast all-stars were heard throughout the soundtrack of The Susan Hayward movie *I Want to Live*. Although not a soundtrack, this LP features six themes from the movie (all composed by Johnny Mandel) performed by the same musicians, who this time around get an opportunity to really stretch out. Since the band is composed of Mulligan, trumpeter Art Farmer, altoist Bud Shank, trombonist Frank Rossolino, pianist Pete Jolly, bassist Red Mitchell and drummer Shelly Manne, virtually all of the music is quite interesting with plenty of fine solos and hard-swinging. —*Scott Yanow*

★ **What is There to Say** / Dec. 17, 1958–Jan. 15, 1959 / Columbia ◆◆◆◆◆
The last of the pianoless quartet albums that Gerry Mulligan recorded in the 1950s is one of the best, featuring the complementary trumpet of Art Farmer, bassist Bill Crow and drummer Dave Bailey along with the baritonist/leader. This CD reissue of the LP is a little skimpy on playing time but makes every moment count. Virtually every selection is memorable with "What Is There to Say," "Just in Time," "Festive Minor," "My Funny Valentine" and "Utter Chaos" being the highpoints. Highly recommended both to Mulligan collectors and to jazz listeners who are just discovering the great baritonist. —*Scott Yanow*

Gerry Mulligan Meets Ben Webster / Nov. 3, 1959–Dec. 2, 1959 / Verve ◆◆◆◆◆
Baritone-saxophonist Gerry Mulligan, a modern who loved to jam with the older musicians, always had a flexible style. He had the opportunity (due to his popularity) to record with several of the major active saxophonists of the 1950s and '60s. This CD finds him sharing the spotlight with the great veteran tenor Ben Webster. Their original six-song LP program is, on this reissue, augmented by five additional selections that were previously unissued but are played at the same high quality. The nearly 77-minute program (during which Mulligan and Webster are joined

by pianist Jimmy Rowles, bassist Leroy Vinnegar and drummer Mel Lewis) is full of solid swing, some witty improvising and a few beautiful ballads. —Scott Yanow

A Night in Rome, Vol. 2 / 1959 / Fini Jazz ✦✦✦
The baritone-saxophonist, a modern who loved to jam with the older musicians, always had a flexible style. He had the opportunity (due to his popularity) to record with several of the major saxophonists who were active in the 1950s and '60s. This CD finds him sharing the spotlight with the great veteran tenor Ben Webster. Their original six-song LP program is, on this reissue, augmented by five additional selections that were previously unissued but are played at the same high quality. The nearly 77-minute program (during which Mulligan and Webster are joined by pianist Jimmy Rowles, bassist Leroy Vinnegar and drummer Mel Lewis) is full of solid swing, some witty improvising and a few beautiful ballads. —Scott Yanow

Gerry Mulligan and the Concert Jazz Band / May 28, 1960–Jul. 27, 1960 / Verve ✦✦✦✦
For the third record by his Concert Jazz Band, baritonist Gerry Mulligan recorded concert works by the likes of George Russell ("All About Rosie"), Gary McFarland ("Weep" and "Chuggin'") and Johnny Carisi ("Israel") in addition to two of his own compositions. With strong solos from Mulligan, valve trombonist Bob Brookmeyer, Don Ferrara and Nick Travis on trumpets and altoist Gene Quill, this LP offers a set of excellent music from the legendary big band. —Scott Yanow

Gerry Mulligan Meets Johnny Hodges / Jul. 1960 / Verve ✦✦✦✦
Another one of Gerry Mulligan's encounters with fellow saxophonists, this LP matches the flexible baritonist with the impeccable alto of Johnny Hodges. They contributed three originals apiece to this relaxed date, and their tones proved to be quite complementary. Accompanied by pianist Claude Williamson, bassist Buddy Clark and drummer Mel Lewis, Mulligan and Hodges make for a very potent team. —Scott Yanow

The Gerry Mulligan Concert Jazz Band on Tour / Nov. 1960 / Verve ✦✦✦✦

★ **Gerry Mulligan and the Concert Jazz Band at the Village Vanguard** / Dec. 1960 / Verve ✦✦✦✦✦
Of all the recordings made by Gerry Mulligan's Concert Jazz Band in the 1960s, this is the definitive one. There are many highpoints including "Body and Soul" (which has fine solos from the baritonist-leader and valve trombonist Bob Brookmeyer), "Come Rain or Come Shine" and the swinging "Let My People Be," but "Blueport" takes honors. On the latter, after hot solos by Mulligan, trombonist Willie Dennis and Jim Reider on tenor, Mulligan and trumpeter Clark Terry have a lengthy trade-off that is quite hilarious with a countless number of quotes from different songs; at one point they trade off cities. Not yet out on CD, this music is essential. —Scott Yanow

Holiday with Mulligan / Apr. 10, 1961–Apr. 17, 1961 / DRG ✦✦
Baritone-saxophonist Gerry Mulligan and actress Judy Holliday were an "item" around the time of this recording. Their one meeting on record features Holliday doing some effective singing on eleven songs, mostly lesser-known standards plus four songs cowritten by the two leaders. Unfortunately, Mulligan's Concert Jazz Band is largely wasted, being restricted to anonymous accompaniment of Holliday, making this CD of greater historical value than of interest to jazz listeners. —Scott Yanow

Presents a Concert in Jazz / Jul. 10, 1961–Jul. 11, 1961 / Verve ✦✦✦✦

Jeru / Jun. 30, 1962 / RCA ✦✦✦
While Gerry Mulligan was famous in the 1950s for leading piano-less quartets, he never had anything against pianists; in fact he often played one himself. This 1962 quintet session finds Jeru utilizing the strong talents of pianist Tommy Flanagan along with bassist Ben Tucker, drummer Dave Bailey and the congas of Alec Dorsey to play seven songs (all but "Get out of Town" are somewhat obscure). Mulligan is in fine form, and even if the music on this LP is not all that essential, it is quite enjoyable. —Scott Yanow

And His Quartet / Oct. 6, 1962 / RTE ✦✦✦
Originally broadcast over French radio and released for the first time in 1994, this performance from 1962 finds Gerry Mulligan and his sidemen (valve trombonist Bob Brookmeyer, bassist Bill Crow and drummer Gus Johnson) generally sounding inspired throughout their spirited set. Mulligan is first heard taking a fine blues solo on piano during "Spring Is Sprung" before Brookmeyer

enters to make the trio a quartet; Jeru also plays piano on "Darn That Dream" while Brookmeyer accompanies the baritonist on "Subterranean Blues." The one disappointment to the set is that the two horns only interact on "Five Brothers" and "Blueport" (other than the brief closing theme "Utter Chaos"), but even on the piano pieces there is enough creativity, wit and charm to continually hold one's interest, and the tradeoff on "Blueport" is a highpoint. —Scott Yanow

Gerry Mulligan (1963) / Dec. 18, 1962–Dec. 21, 1962 / Verve ✦✦✦
The final recording by Gerry Mulligan's Concert Jazz Band before he had to break it up is one of its lesser efforts but still quite worthwhile. With originals by Bob Brookmeyer, Gary McFarland and the baritonist/leader (in addition to the standards "Little Rock Getaway" and "My Kind of Love"), this is a high-quality if rather brief program. Trumpeter Clark Terry and guitarist Jim Hall costar with Mulligan in the solo department. It is a pity that this orchestra could not prosper; all five of its recordings are worth getting. —Scott Yanow

Night Lights / Sep. 12, 1963–Oct. 3, 1963 / Verve ✦✦✦
This is a rather relaxed LP featuring baritonist Gerry Mulligan and some of his top alumni (trumpeter Art Farmer, trombonist Bob Brookmeyer, guitarist Jim Hall, bassist Bill Crow and drummer Dave Bailey) exploring three of his own songs (including "Festive Minor"), Chopin's "Prelude in E Minor," "Wee Small Hours" and "Morning of the Carnival" (from Black Orpheus). The emphasis is on ballads, and nothing too innovative occurs, but the results are pleasing and laidback. —Scott Yanow

If You Can't Beat 'em, Join 'em / Jul. 22, 1965–Jul. 28, 1965 / Limelight ✦✦

Feelin' Good / Oct. 10, 1965–Oct. 22, 1965 / Limelight ✦✦

Something Borrowed, Something Blue / Jul. 19, 1966 / Limelight ✦✦✦
This unusual quintet set finds Gerry Mulligan playing alto rather than baritone on four of the six selections. Tenor saxophonist Zoot Sims co-stars, and with the assistance of a fine rhythm section (pianist Warren Bernhardt, bassist Eddie Gomez and drummer Dave Bailey), the complementary horns explore Bix Beiderbecke's "Davenport Blues," the standard "New Orleans," "Sometime Ago" and three obscure but worthwhile Mulligan originals. This forgotten collector's item (the LP has not been available for decades) features swinging music with plenty of fine moments. —Scott Yanow

Jazz Fest Masters / Jun. 1969 / Scotti Bros. ✦✦✦✦✦
This is an easy CD to miss since it was part of the Scotti Bros. Jazzfest Masters, a series probably destined for complete obscurity. Recorded at the 1969 New Orleans Jazz Festival, this set is highlighted by three wonderful chance-taking performances by a quartet comprising baritonist Gerry Mulligan, altoist Paul Desmond, bassist Milt Hinton and drummer Alan Dawson, a brilliant unit that otherwise never recorded. Their version of "Line for Lyons" is classic. Two other songs (including a brief "Take Five") have pianist Jaki Byard making the group a quintet, and there are a pair of features for Mulligan with the University of Illinois Orchestra. The final selection showcases altoist Al Belleto With The Loyola University Jazz Band on "What's New." But the reason to acquire this CD is for the unique Mulligan-Desmond quartet. —Scott Yanow

Age of Steam / Feb. 1971–Sep. 1971 / A&M ✦✦✦✦✦
During the 1952–65 period baritonist Gerry Mulligan was one of the most famous musicians in jazz, but he spent the following five years at a lower profile, recording relatively little and not leading any significant bands. Age of Steam was a comeback record of sorts (although he had never declined), giving Jeru the opportunity to lead a big band again. The ensemble performs eight of his recent originals (the best known is "K4 Pacific"), featuring solos by Mulligan (who was now doubling on soprano), Tom Scott on tenor and soprano, Bud Shank on alto and flute, valve trombonist Bob Brookmeyer and trumpeter Harry "Sweets" Edison. The highly enjoyable music (last available on this A&M LP) still sounds fresh and spirited. —Scott Yanow

Carnegie Hall Concert / Nov. 24, 1974 / CTI ✦✦✦✦
At this 1974 concert baritonist Gerry Mulligan and trumpeter Chet Baker had one of their very rare reunions; it would be only the second and final time that they recorded together after Mulligan's original quartet broke up in 1953. Oddly enough, a fairly contemporary rhythm section was used (keyboardist Bob James,

vibraphonist Dave Samuels, bassist Ron Carter, drummer Harvey Mason and, in one of his first recordings, guitarist John Scofield. However, some of the old magic was still there between the horns, and in addition to two of Mulligan's newer tunes, this set (the first of two LP volumes) also includes fresh versions of "Line for Lyons" and "My Funny Valentine." —*Scott Yanow*

Carnegie Hall Concert, Vol. 2 / Nov. 24, 1974 / CTI ✦✦✦✦
On the second of two LP volumes, Gerry Mulligan and Chet Baker renew ties for only the second and final time since Mulligan's classic quartet disbanded in 1953. In addition to "Bernie's Tune" and the standard "There Will Never Be Another You," Baker, Mulligan and a young rhythm section (which includes guitarist John Scofield and keyboardist Bob James) perform two newer songs by Jeru. This is is a historically significant and musical set by a pair of masters who should have had more reunions. —*Scott Yanow*

Gerry Mulligan Meets Enrico Intra / Oct. 16, 1975–Oct. 17, 1975 / PA/USA ✦✦✦
An unusual entry in baritonist Gerry Mulligan's discography, this LP (recorded in Italy during a two year stay) finds Mulligan teaming up with pianist Enrico Intra, the reeds of Giancarlo Barigozzi and an Italian rhythm section to play four new compositions, one of his and the other three by Intra. Jeru (who also plays some soprano in addition to his customary baritone) sounds quite creative stretching out on these obscure but rewarding originals. —*Scott Yanow*

Idol Gossip / Nov. 1976 / Chiaroscuro ✦✦✦✦
This somewhat forgotten studio session finds Gerry Mulligan, 25 years after he first acheived fame with his quartet, playing six of his fairly recent compositions along with a version of "Waltzing Mathilda." With vibraphonist Dave Samuels and a four-piece rhythm section accompanying him, Mulligan performs such songs as "Walk on the Water," "Idol Gossip" and "Strayhorn 2;" the latter a reworking of his "Song for Strayhorn." Jeru proves to still be in prime form and plays a bit of soprano sax on this date along with his distinctive baritone. —*Scott Yanow*

Lionel Hampton Presents Gerry Mulligan / Oct. 29, 1977 / Who's Who In Jazz ✦✦✦✦

Walk on the Water / Sep. 1980 / DRG ✦✦✦✦
Baritonist Gerry Mulligan has had few opportunities to record with a big band since his Concert Jazz Band broke up in 1963, a real pity considering how talented a composer and arranger he has been. This DRG LP features a strong orchestra (with such soloists as trumpeter Tom Harrell, altoist Gerry Niewood, pianist Mitchel Forman among others) performing several of Jeru's compositions (including "For an Unfinished Woman," "Song for Strayhorn" and "Walk on the Water"), Forman's "Angelica" and Duke Ellington's "Across the Track Blues" along with the standard "I'm Getting Sentimental over You." —*Scott Yanow*

La Menace / 1982 / DRG ✦✦

Little Big Horn / 1983 / GRP ✦✦✦
On one of the first relatively straight-ahead sessions for GRP, baritonist Gerry Mulligan (accompanied by a rhythm section led by Dave Grusin's keyboards with an occasional horn section) performs six of his then-recent compositions including the title cut. Strangely enough, the most memorable selection is "I Never Was a Young Man" which has a rare but very effective Mulligan vocal. Otherwise the music is good but not classic. —*Scott Yanow*

● **Soft Lights and Sweet Music** / Jan. 1986 / Concord Jazz ✦✦✦✦✦
Starting in the late '50s, Gerry Mulligan recorded a series of encounters with fellow saxophonists that included such immortals as Stan Getz, Paul Desmond, Johnny Hodges and Ben Webster. In 1986 he resumed the practice for this one date on which his baritone is matched with the tenor of the young great Scott Hamilton. The music, which includes warm ballads and fairly hot romps (five of the seven songs are Mulligan originals), consistently swing and are quite enjoyable. —*Scott Yanow*

Symphonic Dreams / Feb. 6, 1987–Feb. 7, 1987 / Intersound ✦✦✦
Gerry Mulligan meets a symphony orchestra on this unusual CD. The Houston Symphony (under the direction of Erich Kunzel) performs the seven sections of "The Sax Chronicles" (compositions of Harry Freedman based on Mulligan themes written in the style of a variety of classical composers), two shorter pieces by the classic jazzman ("Song for Strayhorn" and "K-4 Pacific") and a classical work written by Jeru: "Entente for Baritone Sax and Orchestra."

The music fits the category of third stream and could be called jazzy classical music. It's worth a close listen. —*Scott Yanow*

Lonesome Boulevard / Mar. 1989–Sep. 1989 / A&M ✦✦✦✦✦
The 1989 Gerry Mulligan Quartet (with pianist Bill Charlap, bassist Dean Johnson and drummer Richie De Rosa) is well featured on this enjoyable set, performing "Splendor in the Grass" and nine recent Gerry Mulligan compositions including "Lonesome Boulevard," "The Flying Scotsman" and "Good Neighbor Thelonious." Baritonist Mulligan deserves great credit for the consistency of his recordings during the previous 40 years. This CD is easily recommended for the leader remained very much in his prime. —*Scott Yanow*

● **Re-Birth of the Cool** / Jan. 29, 1992–Jan. 31, 1992 / GRP ✦✦✦✦✦
In the summer of 1991 Gerry Mulligan decided to revisit Miles Davis' *Birth of the Cool* recordings. He discussed it with Miles Davis himself who said he might be interested in participating, but sadly, Davis died a few months later. With Wallace Roney (the perfect sound-alike) in the trumpeter's place, baritonist Mulligan got the band's original pianist and tuba player (John Lewis and Bill Barber), used his own bassist (Dean Johnson) and drummer (Ron Vincent), and found able substitutes in altoist Phil Woods (unfortunately Lee Konitz was unavailable to play his old parts), trombonist Dave Bargeron and John Clark on French horn. This GRP CD brings back the dozen *Birth of the Cool* recordings of 1949–50 with Mel Tormé taking Pancho Hagood's vocal on "Darn That Dream." Although the charts are the same (and it is a particular pleasure to listen to them with the improved recording quality), the solos are all different and in many cases have been lengthened; no need to stick to only three minutes apiece. This fascinating disc is most highly recommended to veteran jazz collectors who know the original *Birth of the Cool* records. —*Scott Yanow*

Paraiso-Jazz Brazil / Jul. 5, 1993–Jul. 7, 1993 / Telarc ✦✦✦✦

Dream A Little Dream / 1994 / Telarc ✦✦✦✦
Baritonist Gerry Mulligan had at the time of this recording been a jazz giant for 45 years. His slightly bubbly baritone sound has always been distinctive, and he never had difficulty jamming with anyone. In the 1990s Mulligan's regular trio has been composed of pianist Ted Rosenthal, bassist Dean Johnson and drummer Ron Vincent. The sidemen work together very well on this quartet date (Bill Mays fills in for Rosenthal on two songs) and form a solid foundation for Mulligan to float over. The baritonist performs a variety of superior standards such as "Home," "They Say It's Wonderful" and "My Shining Hour," revives "My Funny Valentine" and revisits a few of his originals (including "Walking Shoes" and "Song for Strayhorn"). This is a fine example of Gerry Mulligan's playing. —*Scott Yanow*

Jimmy Mundy

b. Jun. 28, 1907, Cincinnati, OH, **d.** Apr. 24, 1983, New York, NY
Arranger / Swing
One of the finer arrangers of the swing era, Jimmy Mundy never became a big name to the general public, but musicians of the era certainly knew who he was. He played tenor in various local bands, and when he was hired by Earl Hines in 1932, he originally played in the orchestra. However it was his charts (including his original "Cavernism," "Everything Depends on You" and "Copenhagen") that gave him a strong reputation. In 1936 he became a staff arranger for Benny Goodman, writing arrangements for such pieces as "Bugle Call Rag," "Jumpin' at the Woodside," "Swingtime in the Rockies," "Solo Flight" and "Sing, Sing, Sing." He also wrote charts for Count Basie, Gene Krupa, Paul Whiteman, Dizzy Gillespie (1949) and Harry James among many others and remained active into the 1970s. Jimmy Mundy led relatively few sessions: a small-group date in 1937, four songs by his short-lived orchestra in 1939, there are a few existing broadcasts of his 1946 Los Angeles band, and he led two obscure Epic albums during 1958–59. —*Scott Yanow*

Mark Murphy

b. Mar. 14, 1932, Syracuse, NY
Vocals / Post-Bop
A creative singer who has spent his entire career dedicated to jazz, Mark Murphy's wilder flights do not always succeed (sometimes his scatting in live performances can get a bit out of control), but they are never dull or predictable. Murphy began performing when he was 16, recorded his first album (for Capitol) in the late '50s, appeared on some television shows and then spent 1963–72

overseas, performing on radio and television and recording in Europe. Since returning to the U.S., Murphy has recorded a steady string of stimulating sets for Muse, even incorporating the stories and beat poetry of Jack Kerouac quite effectively on his *Bop for Kerouac* album. Mark Murphy has recorded throughout his career for Capitol, Riverside, Fontana, Saba, Audiophile and Muse. — *Scott Yanow*

This Could Be the Start of Something / May 28, 1959 / Capitol ✦✦✦

Playing the Field / 1960 / Capitol ✦✦✦

● **Rah** / Sep. 1961–Nov. 1961 / Original Jazz Classics ✦✦✦✦✦

That's How I Love the Blues / Oct. 1, 1962–Dec. 28, 1962 / Original Jazz Classics ✦✦✦✦✦

Bridging a Gap / Oct. 1973 / Muse ✦✦✦✦
The celebrated bop, ballads, standards and scat vocalist sings with customary verve, clarity and confidence, backed by a combo featuring Mike and Randy Brecker, Ron Carter and more. — *Ron Wynn*

Mark 2 / May 1975 / Muse ✦✦✦
Strong, individualistic material featuring Murphy doing scat, interpretations and reworkings of jazz and pre-rock pop tunes with his vivid delivery and dynamic manner. This was his second album for Muse under a unique arrangement that saw him cut several sessions for straight fee rather than royalties in exchange for complete artistic freedom. — *Ron Wynn*

● **Mark Murphy Sings** / Aug. 1976 / Muse ✦✦✦✦✦
Strong mid-'70s Murphy session, with particularly solid uptempo numbers, emphatic ballads and mid-tempo pieces. Murphy is backed by a group that includes alto saxophonist Dave Sanborn playing in different setting, with more subtlety and passion than on his hit recordings. — *Ron Wynn*

★ **Satisfaction Guaranteed** / Nov. 21, 1979 / Muse ✦✦✦✦✦
Good '79 session with vocalist Mark Murphy putting his stamp on old standards and new tunes, scatting, vocalizing and extending them in his fiery, dynamic way. His backing band included veteran trombonist Slide Hampton, plus alto saxophonist Richie Cole and baritone saxophonist Ronnie Cuber. — *Ron Wynn*

Bop for Kerouac / Mar. 12, 1981 / Muse ✦✦✦✦✦
This is an unusual recording. Singer Mark Murphy teams up with a fine sextet (featuring altoist Richie Cole and guitarist Bruce Forman) and alternating bop standards with readings from Jack Kerouac books. Since Kerouac was a big jazz fan in the 1950s and his interest in the music influenced the rhythms of his writing, this "poetry and jazz" set works surprisingly well. It also helps that Mark Murphy is heard at the peak of his powers. — *Scott Yanow*

The Artistry of Mark Murphy / Apr. 2, 1982–Apr. 3, 1982 / Muse ✦✦✦✦
Includes a stunning medley of "Babe's Blue/Little Niles/Dat Dere." Recorded with Tom Harrell (tpt) and Gene Bertoncini (g) and Ben Aranov (p) in a larger-group setting. — *Michael G. Nastos*

Brazil Song (Cancoes Do Brazil) / Aug. 2, 1983–Mar. 22, 1984 / Muse ✦✦✦

Beauty and the Beast / Sep. 10, 1985–Nov. 23, 1986 / Muse ✦✦✦✦✦
This is really good Murphy, arranged by Bill Mays. McCoy Tyner's "Effendi" is a highlight, as is "Doxy" and "I Can't Get Started." — *Michael G. Nastos*

September Ballads / Sep. 15, 1987–Nov. 22, 1987 / Milestone ✦✦✦✦
Includes some beautiful playing from Larry Coryell (g), Art Farmer (tpt). — *Ron Wynn*

What a Way to Go / Sep. 1990 / Muse ✦✦✦

I'll Close My Eyes / Dec. 16, 1991–Dec. 17, 1991 / Muse ✦✦✦✦

Night Mood / Dec. 31, 1991 / Milestone ✦✦✦

Stolen Moments / Jan. 24, 1992 / Muse ✦✦✦✦

Turk Murphy (Melvin Edward Alton Murphy)

b. Dec. 16, 1915, Palermo, CA, d. May 30, 1987, San Francisco, CA
Trombone, Leader / Dixieland
Turk Murphy led one of the most popular bands of the San Francisco Dixieland movement. After playing with various big

bands (including Mal Hallett and Will Osborne), Murphy first gained fame for his work with Lu Watters' highly influential Yerba Buena Jazz Band (1940–47). He formed his own group in 1947, and in 1960 the group found a permanent home at Earthquake McGoon's; it also toured occasionally. Although not thought of as a virtuoso trombone soloist and his occasional singing was just passable, Murphy's ensemble work was superior, he put together a stimulating repertoire filled with obscurities and favorites from the 1920s (along with some newer originals), and his bands were always very musical; among his sidemen through the years were trumpeters Don Kinch, Bob Short and Leon Oakley, clarinetist Bob Helm, pianists Wally Rose, Pete Clute and Ray Skjelbred and singer Pat Yankee. Turk Murphy and his beloved group made many records for such labels as Good Time Jazz, Fairmont, Columbia (1953–56), Verve, Dawn Club, Roulette, RCA, Motherlode, Atlantic, GHB, MPS, Stomp Off and Merry Makers. — *Scott Yanow*

★ **Turk Murphy's Jazz Band Favorites, Vol. 1** / May 31, 1949–Apr. 11, 1952 / Good Time Jazz ✦✦✦✦✦
More Bay Area revival sounds appear from Murphy, this time with Bill Napier, Don Kinch, Wally Rose and George Bruns among the sidemen on "St. James Infirmary," "Canal Street Blues," "Down by the Riverside," and more. — *Bruce Raeburn*

★ **Turk Murphy's Jazz Band Favorites, Vol. 2** / Dec. 31, 1947–Apr. 11, 1952 / Good Time Jazz ✦✦✦✦✦

At The Italian Village / Jan. 6, 1952–1953 / Merry Makers ✦✦✦✦
After the breakup of Lu Watters' Yerba Buena Jazz Band in late 1950, San Francisco had a lot more talent in the traditional jazz area than it did actual employment. Fortunately a Sunday afternoon concert held Jan. 6, 1952 at the Italian Village night club that featured trombonist Turk Murphy was so successful that the venue became a haven for classic jazz for the next two years. The music, never before released, debuted on this very enjoyable CD. Not only was Murphy reunited with such Watters alumni as pianist Wally Rose and clarinetist Bob Helm, but this date was one of the earliest performances of a housewife turned singer Claire Austin who would have a successful career through the rest of the decade. Murphy's septet (with trumpeter Don Kinch) performs a dozen hot jazz selections (four with powerful vocals by Austin in the Bessie Smith tradition), and the CD is rounded out by nine numbers from 1953 featuring a trumpetless quintet with Murphy, Helm and Rose. This very spirted CD is highly recommended for Dixieland fans. *Scott Yanow*

Barrelhouse Jazz / Aug. 12, 1953 / Columbia ✦✦✦✦

When the Saints Go Marching In / Aug. 30, 1953–Dec. 14, 1953 / Columbia ✦✦✦✦

Music of Jelly Roll Morton / Aug. 31, 1953–Sep. 14, 1953 / Columbia ✦✦✦✦✦

The Many Faces of Ragtime / 1972 / Atlantic ✦✦✦✦
Traditional jazz bandleader tackles another style close to his heart, vintage ragtime tunes, on this early '70s date. He doesn't necessarily adhere to ragtime's strict time but does communicate the spirit and style of the early form. — *Ron Wynn*

David Murray

b. Feb. 19, 1955, Berkeley, CA
Tenor Saxophone, Bass Clarinet / Avant-Garde, Post-Bop, Free Jazz
A giant of the avant-garde, David Murray has long had a distinctive tone on tenor and the willingness to play anything from completely free improvisations to bop. Among the most recorded of all jazzmen, Murray's trademark is his sudden leaps into the upper register of his horn.

He started on alto when he was nine and played tenor in a soul group that he led as a teenager. In Southern California Murray often gigged with Bobby Bradford and Arthur Blythe, and in 1975 he moved to New York. He was an original member of the World Saxophone Quartet in 1976 and worked as a sideman with Sunny Murray, James "Blood" Ulmer, Jack DeJohnette's Special Edition and Clarinet Summit, playing bass clarinet in the latter. However Murray is best-known as a leader whose groups have ranged from freewheeling quartets to a spirited big band and an acclaimed octet. He started recording as a leader in 1976 and has since made sessions for Adelphi, India Navigation, Circle, Marge, Red, Horo, Palm, Cadillac, Black Saint, Hat Hut, Cecma, Enja,

Portrait, Red Baron and DIW. In 1991 David Murray was award-ed the prestigious Danish Jazzpar prize. —*Scott Yanow*

Low Class Conspiracy / May 14, 1976–Jun. 29, 1976 / Adelphi ✦✦✦✦
This is one of his earliest albums to make an impact on the gen-eral jazz audience. Fred Hopkins (b) and Phillip Wilson (d) excel. —*Ron Wynn*

Flowers for Albert / Jun. 16, 1976 / India Navigation ✦✦✦✦✦
David Murray, who was 21 at the time, shows a lot of promise on this early recording. The explorative tenor saxophonist joins with trumpeter Olu Dara, bassist Fred Hopkins and drummer Phillip Wilson for two adventurous pieces (including the title cut which is dedicated to Albert Ayler). In addition, Murray duets with Hopkins on "Ballad for a Decomposed Beauty" and collaborates with Wilson on their duet "Roscoe." The music is often quite free, but it also takes its time, showing high energy in well-chosen spots. Since this period David Murray has lived up to his great potential. —*Scott Yanow*

Live at the Lower Manhattan Ocean Club, Vols. 1 & 2 / Dec. 31, 1977 / India Navigation ✦✦✦
This double CD, which packages together the two original LPs, captures David Murray's quartet (trumpeter Lester Bowie, bassist Fred Hopkins and drummer Phillip Wilson) in high spirits. The six selections (four are over ten minutes, and "For Walter Norris" exceeds 21) are full of spirit, looseness, humor, screams and screeches. Some of it rambles on too long (and Murray's soprano on "Bechet's Bounce" is quite silly), but it generally holds on to one's attention. —*Scott Yanow*

Interboogieology / Feb. 1978 / Black Saint ✦✦✦
For this fairly early recording, avant-garde tenor saxophonist David Murray teams up with cornetist Butch Morris, bassist Johnny Dyani and drummer Oliver Johnson for some fairly free improvisations, with the originals written by either Murray or Morris. Two of the numbers also utilize the adventurous voice of Marta Contreras. The results are stimulating if not essential; a lesser but still interesting effort. —*Scott Yanow*

Murray's 3d Family / Sep. 3, 1978 / Hat Art ✦✦✦✦✦

Sweet Lovely / Dec. 4, 1979–Dec. 5, 1979 / Black Saint ✦✦✦✦

★ **Ming** / Jul. 25, 1980+Jul. 28, 1980 / Black Saint ✦✦✦✦✦

Home / Oct. 31, 1981+Nov. 1, 1981 / Black Saint ✦✦✦✦✦
Tenor saxophonist David Murray regrouped the same octet that recorded *Ming* and released *Home*....There was not a weak solo moment on the set, and it was that combination of arrangements and ensemble strength which made this more than just another date. —*Bob Rusch, Cadence*

★ **Murray's Steps** / Jul. 14, 1982–Jul. 19, 1982 / Black Saint ✦✦✦✦✦
The octet is the perfect vehicle for David Murray as an outlet for his writing, a showcase for his compositions and as an inspiring vehicle for his tenor and bass clarinet solos. For the third octet album (all are highly recommended) Murray meets up with altoist Henry Threadgill, trumpeter Bobby Bradford, cornetist Butch Morris, trombonist Craig Harris, pianist Curtis Clark, bassist Wilber Morris and drummer Steve McCall; quite a talented group of individuals. Their interpretations of four of Murray's originals ("Murray's Steps," "Sweet Lovely," "Sing Song" and "Flowers for Albert") are emotional, adventurous and exquisite; sometimes all three at the same time. —*Scott Yanow*

Morning Song / Sep. 25, 1983–Sep. 30, 1983 / Black Saint ✦✦✦✦
Tenor saxophonist and bass clarinetist David Murray has seldom recorded a bad album, no matter what the label or the configura-tion. This was a straight-ahead quartet set, with lengthy, tartly played originals and some high-register wailing by Murray on tenor and bass clarinet. —*Ron Wynn*

Live at Sweet Basil, Vol. 1 / Aug. 24, 1984–Aug. 26, 1984 / Black Saint ✦✦✦

Live at Sweet Basil, Vol. 2 / Aug. 24, 1984–Aug. 26, 1984 / Black Saint ✦✦✦
The second of two marvelous big band dates featuring the Murray Big Band recorded at Sweet Basil's. The band included the cream of '70s and '80s jazz, with Murray roaring and spearheading things on tenor and bass clarinet and Butch Morris conducting. —*Ron Wynn*

Children / Oct. 1984–Nov. 1984 / Black Saint ✦✦✦✦

I Want to Talk About You / Mar. 1, 1986 / Black Saint ✦✦✦✦✦
An exceptional quartet set from 1986 with tenor saxophonist and

bass clarinetist David Murray, pianist John Hicks, bassist Ray Drummond and drummer Ralph Peterson, Jr. going through mostly standards, plus the occasional original. The title cut ranks among Murray's finest recorded ballads. —*Ron Wynn*

In Our Style / Sep. 3, 1986–Sep. 4, 1986 / FTC ✦✦✦✦
David Murray, doubling on tenor and bass clarinet, interacts with drummer Jack Dejohnette and (on two of the seven selections) bassist Fred Hopkins for a set of originals by Murray, DeJohnette and Butch Morris. The duo/trio explore a variety of moods with Murray's extroverted and advanced solos generally serving as the lead voice. Although an avant-garde set, this Japanese import has its mellow and melodic moments before the fire takes over again. —*Scott Yanow*

The Hill / Nov. 1986 / Black Saint ✦✦✦✦

Hope Scope / May 12, 1987 / Black Saint ✦✦✦✦✦
The perfect setting for the innovative David Murray is the octet that he leads on an irregular basis. This spirited set has tributes to Ben Webster and Lester Young but is at its best when the full ensemble (trumpeters Hugh Ragin and Rasul Siddik, trombonist Craig Harris, altoist James Spaulding, pianist Dave Burrell, bassist Wilber Morris and drummer Ralph Peterson, Jr., along with the leader on tenor and bass clarinet) get to improvise together. This is one of their strongest all-round recordings with "Hope Scope" being a particular highpoint. —*Scott Yanow*

The Healers / Sep. 26, 1987 / Black Saint ✦✦✦✦
A stirring duo, with Randy Weston striking on piano. —*Ron Wynn*

Spirituals / Jan. 1988 / DIW ✦✦✦
David Murray mostly sticks to spirituals on this Japanese import, a quartet outing with pianist Dave Burrell, bassist Fred Hopkins and drummer Ralph Peterson, but that does not mean that all of the improvising is mellow and melodic. There are some peaceful moments on tunes such as "Amazing Grace" and a spirited "Down by the Riverside," but Murray's playing is so violent on "Abel's Blissed Out Blues" as to be almost satirical. A mixed success from the masterful tenor. —*Scott Yanow*

Ming's Samba / Jul. 20, 1988 / Portrait ✦✦✦
Recorded at CBS Studios in NYC, this album is named after David Murray's wife Ming. It includes some nice work, in particular the very lovely cut "Spooning." —*Michael Erlewine*

New Life / 1988 / Black Saint ✦✦✦✦

★ **Special Quartet** / Mar. 26, 1990 / Columbia ✦✦✦✦✦
A simply magnificent Murray quartet session from '90, issued under a joint Columbia/DIW deal. His roaring tenor sax was the focal point for some excellent compositions, which were punctu-ated by pianist McCoy Tyner, bassist Fred Hopkins and drummer Elvin Jones. Here's one group that most definitely should record again. —*Ron Wynn*

Shakill's Warrior / Mar. 1, 1991–Mar. 2, 1991 / Columbia ✦✦✦✦
Tenor saxophonist David Murray has recorded so many CDs dur-ing the past 20 years that it is difficult to keep up with them. This one finds him in mostly restrained form, updating the tenor/organ soul jazz tradition with Don Pullen (who sticks exclu-sively to organ), guitarist Stanley Franks and drummer Andrew Cyrille. The music, with the exception of some typical Murray out-bursts into the extreme upper register, is generally respectful and soulful, one of Murray's mellower efforts. Unfortunately, Columbia has since ended its association with DIW so this release will be a difficult one to find. —*Scott Yanow*

David Murray Big Band, Conducted by Lawrence "Butch" Morris / Mar. 5, 1991–Mar. 6, 1991 / Columbia ✦✦✦✦✦
The David Murray big band, which can be undisciplined and even a bit out-of-control, is never dull. This generally brilliant effort has quite a few highpoints. "Paul Gonsalves" recreates the tenor's famous 1956 Newport Jazz Festival solo and has some heated playing from the ensemble. While "Lester" does not really capture the style of Lester Young, "Ben" does bring back the spirit of Ben Webster. "Calling Steve McCall" is a heartfelt tribute to the late drummer (although the poetry does not need to be heard twice!) and trombonist Craig Harris' singing on "Let the Music Take You" is so-so, but the colorful "David's Tune" and the eerie "Instanbul" are more memorable. This disc is easily recommended to listen-ers with open ears. —*Scott Yanow*

Jazzpar Prize / Mar. 16, 1991–Mar. 17, 1991 / Enja ✦✦✦✦✦

Black and Black / Oct. 7, 1991 / Red Baron ✦✦✦✦
A powerhouse '92 session by the prolific tenor saxophonist and

bass clarinetist David Murray. He heads a strong quintet, with trumpeter Marcus Belgrave, pianist Kirk Lightsey, bassist Santi Debriano and drummer Roy Haynes, through some bristling uptempo originals, mixed with a couple of nice mid-tempo and ballad pieces for contrast. —*Ron Wynn*

Fast Life / Oct. 16, 1991–Oct. 17, 1991 / DIW/Columbia ✦✦
This CD is a bit of a mixed bag. The great tenor David Murray is joined by pianist John Hicks, bassist Ray Drummond and drummer Idris Muhammad and is heard at his best on two relatively straight-ahead pieces, "Luminous" and "Off Season." But Branford Marsalis guests on two other selections, and those are much more erratic with rambling solos by the two tenors and a lot of aimless high energy. Wrapping up this set are a calypso and the lightweight "Intuitively," making the net results less than one might hope. —*Scott Yanow*

Body and Soul / Feb. 11, 1993–Feb. 12, 1993 / Black Saint ✦✦✦✦✦
No matter how many albums Murray issues, he never coasts or goes through the motions. This is mainly a quartet date, although Murray shows on the title track his ability to back a singer as Taana Running gives a moving vocal, complete with her original lyrics. Otherwise, these are either spirited uptempo numbers or equally energized ballads. Murray's sweeping tenor sound remains a marvel, and few can match him in controlling drive, pitch and volume. Drummer Rashied Ali has not lost the rippling intensity from his days with John Coltrane; he and Murray conclude things in a dazzling duo performance on "Cuttin' Corners" deliberately intended to evoke memories of the Coltrane/Ali album *Interstellar Space*. —*Ron Wynn*

Jazzosaurus Rex / Aug. 18, 1993 / Red Baron ✦✦✦
Two songtitles on this CD ("Jazzosaurus Rex" and "Dinosaur Park Blues") try to make a connection between David Murray's music and the recent movie *Jurassic Park* but, despite that dubious attempt at commercialism, this is actually a fairly typical Murray modern mainstream outing. Accompanied by pianist John Hicks, bassist Ray Drummond and drummer Andrew Cyrille, Murray's playing is consistently exciting whether tearing into the rhythm changes of "The Eternal Triangle," playing ferocious doubletime lines on his "Mingus in the Poconos" or showing off his huge tone on "Chelsea Bridge." The poet G'ar's narration on a blues "Now He's Miles Away" (a tribute to Miles Davis) is a bit trivial but only a minor flaw for this worthwhile David Murray set. —*Scott Yanow*

Saxmen / Aug. 19, 1993 / Red Baron ✦✦
On this Red Baron CD tenor saxophonist David Murray allegedly pays homage to six saxophonists (Lester Young, Sonny Rollins, Charlie Parker, Charlie Rouse, Sonny Stitt and John Coltrane), but much of the time he does not even seem to realize who he is paying tribute to. Not only does Murray not imitate or emulate his predecessors, he often ignores the outlines of the songs themselves. On "Lester Leaps In" his ferocious solo (with its sudden upper-register outbursts) is unintentionally humorous. He is a bit more involved with Thelonious Monk's "Bright Mississippi" and "Broadway," but on the only ballad of the day "Central Park West," Murray's solo gets downright silly during its second half, ruining the peaceful meditative mood of the song with some self-indulgent upper-register ramblings. The rhythm section (pianist John Hicks, bassist Ray Drummond and drummer Andrew Cyrille) largely ignores the tenor's improvisations, making this one of David Murray's more forgettable recordings. —*Scott Yanow*

Sunny Murray (James Marcellus Arthur Murray)

b. Sep. 21, 1937, Idabel, OK
Drums / Free Jazz, Avant-Garde
An important early free drummer, Sunny Murray was one of the first to play without keeping a steady rhythm or pulse (interacting directly with the lead voices) although he was always perfectly capable of playing more conventionally. He started on drums

when he was nine and in 1956 moved to New York. Murray picked up early experience gigging with Red Allen, Willie "The Lion" Smith, Jackie McLean and Ted Curson. He made a giant stylistic leap when he started playing with Cecil Taylor (1959–64) and was the perfect "accompanist" for Albert Ayler (1964–67). Murray also worked with Don Cherry, Ornette Coleman and John Tchicai during the period. He spent 1968–71 in France, playing and recording with Archie Shepp and freelancing. In the 1970s Murray moved to Philadelphia and led bands usually called the Untouchable Factor. For a time in the 1980s his quintet included Steve Coleman, Grachan Moncur III., pianist Curtis Clark and bassist William Parker, and he had a recorded reunion with Taylor in 1980. Sunny Murray has led dates for Jihad (a 1965 session with Albert Ayler as a sideman), ESP, Shandar, Pathe, BYG, Kharma, Philly Jazz, Marge, Moers Music and Circle although he has maintained a lower profile during the past decade. —*Scott Yanow*

Sunny's Time Now / Nov. 1965 / Jihad ✦✦✦
● **Sunny Murray Quintet** / Jul. 23, 1966 / ESP ✦✦✦✦✦
Dynamic, slashing, left-field jazz, both free-form and more traditional hard bop. —*Ron Wynn*

Live at the Moers Festival / Jun. 3, 1979 / Moers ✦✦✦

Amina Claudine Myers

b. Mar., 1943, Blackwell, AR
Organ, Piano, Vocals / Avant-Garde
A very original pianist who displays her gospel roots when she plays organ or sings, Amina Claudine Myers started studying music when she was seven. She sang with gospel groups in school. After moving to Chicago Myers taught in the public schools, played with Gene Ammons and Sonny Stitt and joined the AACM. She moved to New York in 1976 (where she would record with Lester Bowie and Muhal Richard Abrams), formed her own group, spent a few years in the early '80s in Europe and toured with Charlie Haden's Liberation Music Orchestra in 1985. Amina Claudine Myers has recorded a diverse variety of music as a leader for Sweet Earth, Leo, Black Saint, Minor Music and Novus. —*Scott Yanow*

Poems for Piano: The Piano Music of Marion Brown / Jul. 26, 1979 / Sweet Earth ✦✦✦✦

Song for Mother Earth / Oct. 9, 1979 / Leo ✦✦✦✦✦
Duets with percussionist Pheeroan Aklaff. Sounds like a bigger group. Excellent. *Michael G. Nastos*

★ **Salutes Bessie Smith** / Jun. 19, 1980–Jun. 22, 1980 / Leo ✦✦✦✦✦
Vocal perfection and landmark recording for this keyboardist and singer. Desert-island music. —*Michael G. Nastos*

The Circle of Time / Feb. 3, 1983–Feb. 4, 1983 / Black Saint ✦✦✦✦

Jumping in the Sugar Bowl / Mar. 29, 1984–Mar. 30, 1984 / Minor Music ✦✦✦✦
Intense, provocative mixture of outside and inside sensibilities. Myers at times ranges and attacks the keyboard, then will change direction and display a soulful, gospel-influenced style. The constantly shifting session keeps things interesting, and there are some fine solos as well. —*Ron Wynn*

Country Girl / Apr. 1986 / Minor Music ✦✦✦

Amina / Nov. 1987 / Novus ✦✦✦

In Touch / 1988 / Novus ✦✦
An album that surprised some fans when it was issued in 1984, due to the reputations of everyone involved. Myers has been a fierce soloist and adventurous composer and worked in experimental, on-the-edge contexts for much of her career but turned to fusion and light pop on this date, playing more synthesizer than anything else. It was well produced and effectively played, but guitarist Jerome Harris had a larger role than Myers. —*Ron Wynn*

N

Najee

b. New York, NY

Soprano Saxophone, Tenor Saxophone / Instrumental Pop, Crossover

A popular multi-instrumentalist whose style is very similiar to Kenny G, Dave Koz and George Howard. His releases feature heavily produced, tightly arranged covers of urban contemporary songs, often include appearances by R&B vocalists and have very limited solos and improvisational space. A saxophonist, flutist and occasional keyboardist, Najee makes no claims to being a jazz musician, but his releases are marketed as "contemporary" jazz, and he's aired on lite jazz stations. He's recorded several sessions for EMI and Manhattan; all are available on CD. —*Ron Wynn*

Najee's Theme / 1987 / EMI ✦✦

Day by Day / 1988 / EMI ✦✦

Tokyo Blue / 1990 / EMI ✦✦✦✦

Just an Illusion / 1992 / EMI ✦✦

Share My World / 1994 / EMI ✦✦✦

● **Songs From the Key of Life** / 1995 / EMI ✦✦✦✦

Ray Nance

b. Dec. 10, 1913, Chicago, IL, **d.** Jan. 28, 1976, New York, NY

Violin, Cornet, Vocals / Swing

Ray Nance was a multi-talented individual. He was a fine trumpeter who not only replaced Cootie Williams with Duke Ellington's Orchestra, but gave the "plunger" position in Duke's band his own personality. In addition, Nance was one of the finest jazz violinists of the 1940s, an excellent jazz singer and even a dancer. He studied piano, took lessons on violin and was self-taught on trumpet. After leading a small group in Chicago (1932-37) spending periods with the orchestras of Earl Hines (1937-38) and Horace Henderson (1939-40) and a few months as a solo act, Nance joined Duke Ellington's Orchestra. His very first night on the job was fully documented as the band's legendary Fargo concert. A very valuable sideman, Nance played a famous trumpet solo on the original version of "Take the 'A' Train" and proved to be a fine wa-wa player; his violin added color to the suite "Black, Brown and Beige" (in addition to being showcased on numerous songs), and his singing on numbers such as "A Slip of a Lip Will Sink a Ship" and "Tulip or Turnip" was an added feature. Nance was with Ellington with few interruptions until 1963; by then, the returning Cootie Williams had taken some of his glory. The remainder of Nance's career was relatively insignificant with occasional small group dates, gigs with Brooks Kerr and Chris Barber (touring England in 1974) and a few surprisingly advanced sideman recordings with Jaki Byard and Chico Hamilton. —*Scott Yanow*

● **Body and Soul** / May 1969 / Solid State ✦✦✦✦✦

Tricky Sam Nanton

b. Feb. 1, 1904, New York, NY, **d.** Jul. 20, 1946, San Francisco, CA

Trombone / Classic Jazz, Swing

One of the most colorful trombonists of all time, Tricky Sam Nanton's expertise with the plunger mute (emitting a large assortment of growls and colorful tones) was a major part of Duke Ellington's original sound and has rarely been duplicated since (although Quentin Jackson sometimes came close). He gained early experience playing with bands led by Cliff Jackson and Elmer Snowden and recorded with Thomas Morris, but after mid-1926 Nanton was only heard with Duke Ellington's Orchestra and small groups; he never led a record date of his own. Nanton made for a perfect team with trumpeter Bubber Miley and, when Miley was replaced by Cootie Williams in 1929, Nanton helped to inspire the younger trumpeter to build on Miley's role. He was well-featured on many classic recordings (including "East St. Louis Toodle-oo" and "Black and Tan Fantasy") and was a major attraction with Ellington up until his premature death in 1946. —*Scott Yanow*

Marty Napoleon (Matthew Napoli Napoleon)

b. Jun. 2, 1921, New York, NY

Piano / Swing

Pianist Marty Napoleon actually preferred bebop to traditional jazz, but because of his famous uncle (Phil Napoleon), he was always placed in the early camp. Napoleon had good touch, fine phrasing and range, and displayed flexibility and fluidity in his solos. He effectively moved back and forth between the two styles. Napoleon started as a trumpeter, but a heart attack caused him to switch to piano. He worked in the big bands of Chico Marx, Joe Venuti, Lee Castle and Charlie Barnet in the early '40s, then replaced his brother Teddy in Gene Krupa's band in 1945. He joined his uncle's Memphis Five band in 1950, where he got his traditional jazz initiation. The next year, Napoleon played in Charlie Ventura's Big Four. He later worked with Louis Armstrong's All Stars, then co-led a quartet with his brother. Napoleon ended the '50s working with Coleman Hawkins and Charlie Shavers, then, in the '60s, led his own trios and played solo. Napoleon would periodically reunite with Armstrong in the late '60s. He continued working into the '80s, recording with Peanuts Hucko in 1983 and appearing at an Armstrong memorial concert in New York in 1986. Napoleon recorded with Ventura, Krupa, Armstrong, Ruby Braff, and Red Allen among others on Manor, Columbia, Clef, Decca, Concert Hall, RCA, Mercury and Brunswick. He has no albums listed under his name as a leader on CD. —*Ron Wynn*

Phil Napoleon

b. Sep. 2, 1901, Boston, MA, **d.** Sep. 30, 1990, Miami, FL

Trumpet / Classic Jazz, Dixieland

Although it is often overlooked, Phil Napoleon was one of the top trumpeters to be active in New York during 1921-25. At a time when most so-called hot players in the Big Apple were still playing staccato and halting lines (not up to the level of their Chicago counterparts), Napoleon's warm sound and legato phrasing swung (before the word had been coined). Classically trained, Napoleon decided to play popular music. By 1921 he was recording frequently with many overlapping groups (most notably the Original Memphis Five, Ladd's Black Aces, the Carolina Cotton Pickers and later on the Charleston Chasers), appearing on literally hundreds of excellent melodic jazz records where his appealing tone and solid lead were a major asset. Although a slight influence on Red Nichols and Bix Beiderbecke (as much for his professionalism and consistency as for his tone), Napoleon never did become a big name. He worked in the studios during the 1930s and '40s, leading his own big band briefly in 1938 and spending part of 1943 with Jimmy Dorsey. In 1949 he emerged with a new version of the Original Memphis Five, playing Dixieland for seven years at Nick's. Napoleon eventually moved to Miami, opened a club called Napoleon's Retreat and played regularly during his declining years. —*Scott Yanow*

Phil Napoleon and the Memphis Five / Oct. 1959 / Capitol ✦✦✦✦

Andy Narell

b. Mar. 18, 1954, New York, NY
Steel Drums / World Fusion, Crossover, Post Bop
Andy Narell introduced the steel drums to jazz as a solo instrument, playing not only Caribbean and Latin melodies but R&B, funk and some straight-ahead jazz. After graduating from Berkeley in 1973, he formed the Hip Pocket label and has led his group ever since, recording on a regular basis both as a leader and as a sideman. In 1995 Narell teamed up with Paquito D'Rivera and Dave Samuels in a colorful band called the Caribbean Jazz Project. —*Scott Yanow*

Hidden Treasure / Jan. 1979 / Inner City ✦✦✦
Narrell is among the rare steel drummers active in jazz as well as traditional Caribbean music. He manages to find ways to blend the two, and also injects elements of pop, rock, and fusion into his albums. These intriguing compositional touches and different musical elements take some weight off the songs, which are mostly routine. —*Ron Wynn*

Stickman / Jun. 1980–Jul. 1980 / Hip Pocket ✦✦✦✦
An '89 CD reissue of an early '80s album in which steel drummer and percussionist Andy Narell expanded his vision and made his songs more rhythmically vigorous and harmonically complex, while integrating Caribbean flavoring (via his steel drums), Afro-Latin, jazz, and fusion touches. —*Ron Wynn*

Light in Your Eyes / Jan. 1983–Mar. 1980 / Hip Pocket ✦✦✦✦
An '89 CD reissue of an album steel drummer Andy Narrell recorded for Windham Hill during the late '70s, which is another mix of Caribbean, jazz, pop, fusion, and rock elements. There are some involved sections and others with straight backbeats and light solos. —*Ron Wynn*

Slow Motion / Jan. 1985–Mar. 1985 / Hip Pocket ✦✦✦✦
A 1985 recording from steel drummer Andy Narrell for a small independent label that has more of a funk and R&B flavor than his earlier material. Narell also includes reggae and traditional music of Trinidad in the musical mix. —*Ron Wynn*

● **The Hammer** / 1987 / Windham Hill ✦✦✦✦✦
Narell's finest album and one of the most imaginative ever done using steel drums in both pop and jazz settings. Music included calypso, pop, and mainstream originals, and was expertly produced, arranged, and mastered. —*Ron Wynn*

Little Secrets / 1989 / Windham Hill ✦✦✦
A 1989 release by steel drummer Andy Narell that's mostly distinguished by Narrell's playing, which helps override the facts that the compositions are routine and the music has been overproduced. —*Ron Wynn*

Down the Road / 1992 / Windham Hill ✦✦✦✦
Narell, a first-rate steel drummer in both traditional pan and jazz settings, demonstrates the instrument's flexibility and versatility. While some tunes aren't very complex, Narell's alternately dreamy and aggressive playing proves intriguing. —*Ron Wynn*

Fats Navarro (Theodore Navarro)

b. Sep. 24, 1923, Key West, FL, d. Jul. 7, 1958, New York, NY
Trumpet / Bop
One of the greatest jazz trumpeters of all time, Fats Navarro had a tragically brief career yet his influence is still being felt. His fat sound combined aspects of Howard McGhee, Roy Eldridge and Dizzy Gillespie, became the main inspiration for Clifford Brown and, through Brownie, greatly affected the tones and styles of Lee Morgan, Freddie Hubbard and Woody Shaw.

Navarro originally played piano and tenor before switching to trumpet. He started gigging with dance bands when he was 17, was with Andy Kirk during 1943–44 and replaced Dizzy Gillespie with the Billy Eckstine big band during 1945–46. During the next three years, Fats was second to only Dizzy among bop trumpeters. Navarro recorded with Kenny Clarke's Bebop Boys, Coleman Hawkins, Eddie "Lockjaw" Davis, Illinois Jacquet, and most significantly Tadd Dameron during 1946–47. He had short stints with the big bands of Lionel Hampton and Benny Goodman, continued working with Dameron, made classic recordings with Bud Powell (in a quintet with a young Sonny Rollins) and the Metronome All-Stars, and a 1950 Birdland appearance with Charlie Parker was

privately recorded. However, Navarro was a heroin addict and that affliction certainly did not help him in what would be a fatal bout with tuberculosis that ended his life at age 26. He was well-documented during the 1946–49 period and most of his sessions are currently available on CD, but Fats Navarro (who would have turned 72 in 1995) could have done so much more! —*Scott Yanow*

Fat Girl-The Savoy Sessions / Sep. 6, 1946–Dec. 5, 1947 / Savoy ✦✦✦✦✦
Landmark Navarro Savoy sessions with Howard McGhee (tp), Ernie Henry (as), and others. —*Ron Wynn*

★ **Fats Navarro and Tadd Dameron** / Sep. 26, 1947–Aug. 8, 1949 / Blue Note ✦✦✦✦✦
Many valuable performances from the height of the bop era are included on this double CD. Subtitled "The Complete Blue Note and Capitol Recordings" and comprised of 23 songs and 13 alternate takes, the reissue features the great trumpeter Fats Navarro in peak form with three groups headed by pianist/arranger Tadd Dameron, in trumpet battles with one of his major influences, Howard McGhee, and on a remarkable all-star quintet with pianist Bud Powell and the young tenor Sonny Rollins; among the other sidemen are altoist Ernie Henry, tenors Charlie Rouse, Allen Eager, Wardell Gray and Dexter Gordon and vibraphonist Milt Jackson. In addition to such gems as "Our Delight," "Lady Bird," "Double Talk," "Bouncing with Bud," "Dance of the Infidels" and "52nd Street Theme," Fats is heard with the 1948 Benny Goodman septet ("Stealin' Apples") and Dameron leads a group with the 22-year old Miles Davis. On a whole, this double CD has more than its share of essential music that belongs in all historical jazz collections. —*Scott Yanow*

Fats Navarro with Tadd Dameron / 1948 / Milestone ✦✦✦✦✦
1989 reissue. Simply sublime sessions spotlighting the radical innovations of the great Fats Navarro, plus Tadd Dameron's creative arrangements. —*Ron Wynn*

Buell Neidlinger

b. Mar. 2, 1936, New York, NY
Bass, Cello / Avant-Garde, Post Bop, Free Jazz
Bassist Buell Neidlinger has played with distinction in free-jazz, traditional jazz, and bluegrass bands. He studied piano, trumpet, and cello as a child, then, in his early professional years, played traditional and mainstream jazz in New York with Rex Stewart, Eddie Condon, and Vic Dickenson, among others. During the '50s, he was part of Cecil Taylor's explosive group and worked with him from 1955-1960. In fact, the great album *New York City R&B* was actually a Neidlinger session for Candid that wasn't issued until 11 years after it was recorded, and then under Taylor's name. Neidlinger also worked in the '50s with Steve Lacy, then later did session work on electric as an R&B player. He switched styles again in 1960, spending two years playing part-time with The Houston Symphony Orchestra while also doing some club work playing soul jazz with Arnett Cobb. Then came rock sessions and dates with Frank Zappa and jazz-rock/fusion with Jean-Luc Ponty. He eventually formed his own K2B2 label and made jazz and contemporary music recordings, while doing freelance bluegrass and classical work. In recent times, Neidlinger has made a record of Monk tunes with Anthony Braxton and recorded a brilliant (and rather unusual) tribute to Herbie Nichols on the K2B2 label, *Blue Chopsticks.* —*Ron Wynn*

Ready for the '90s / Jan. 9, 1961+1980 / K2B2 ✦✦✦✦

New York City R&B / Jan. 9, 1961–Jan. 10, 1961 / Candid ✦✦✦✦
W/ Cecil Taylor. This is actually Neidlinger's date. It is currently issued under Cecil Taylor's name. —*Ron Wynn*

Rear View Mirror / Sep. 6, 1979–Nov. 1986 / K2B2 ✦✦✦✦

Buellgrass (Swingrass) / Aug. 23, 1981 / KZBZ ✦✦✦✦

★ **Locomotive** / Jun. 24, 1987–Jun. 25, 1987 / Soul Note ✦✦✦✦✦
Virtuoso bassist and Marty Krystall on tenor sax. Fine music written by Monk and Ellington. —*Michael G. Nastos*

Big Drum / Jun. 6, 1990 / K2B2 ✦✦✦✦

★ **Blue Chopsticks** / Jul. 6, 1994–Jul. 7, 1994 / K2B2 ✦✦✦✦✦

Oliver Nelson

b. Jun. 4, 1932, St. Louis, MO, d. Oct. 27, 1975, Los Angeles, CA
Alto Saxophone, Tenor Saxophone, Arranger, Composer, Leader / Post Bop, Hard Bop
Oliver Nelson was a distinctive soloist on alto, tenor and even soprano, but his writing eventually overshadowed his playing

skills. He became a professional early on in 1947, playing with the Jeter-Pillars Orchestra and with St. Louis big bands headed by George Hudson and Nat Towles. In 1951 he arranged and played second alto for Louis Jordan's big band and followed with a period in the Navy and four years at a university. After moving to New York, Nelson worked briefly with Erskine Hawkins, Wild Bill Davis and Louie Bellson (the latter on the West Coast). In addition to playing with Quincy Jones' Orchestra (1960–61), between 1959–61 Nelson recorded six small-group albums and a big-band date; those gave him a lot of recognition and respect in the jazz world. *Blues and the Abstract Truth* (from 1961) is considered a classic and helped to popularize a song that Nelson had included on a slightly earlier Eddie "Lockjaw" Davis session, "Stolen Moments." He also fearlessly matched wits effectively with the explosive Eric Dolphy on a pair of quintet sessions. But good as his playing was, Nelson was in greater demand as an arranger, writing for big-band dates of Jimmy Smith, Wes Montgomery and Billy Taylor among others. By 1967 when he moved to Los Angeles, Nelson was working hard in the studios, writing for television and movies. He occasionally appeared with a big band, wrote a few ambitious works and recorded jazz on an infrequent basis, but Oliver Nelson was largely lost to jazz a few years before his unexpected death at age 43 from a heart attack. —*Scott Yanow*

Meet Oliver Nelson / Oct. 30, 1959 / Original Jazz Classics ◆◆◆◆
This dynamic session pairs Nelson with Kenny Dorham (tpt), Art Taylor (d), and others. —*Ron Wynn*

● **Takin' Care of Business** / Mar. 22, 1960 / Original Jazz Classics ◆◆◆◆◆
Oliver Nelson would gain his greatest fame later in his short life as an arranger/composer, but this superior session puts the emphasis on his distinctive tenor and alto playing. In a slightly unusual group (with vibraphonist Lem Winchester, organist Johnny "Hammond" Smith, bassist George Tucker and drummer Roy Haynes), Nelson improvises a variety of well-constructed but spontaneous solos; his unaccompanied spots on "All the Way" and his hard-charging playing on the medium-tempo blues "Groove" are two of the many highpoints. Nelson remains a vastly underrated saxophonist and all six performances on this recommended CD reissue (four of them his originals) are excellent. —*Scott Yanow*

Screamin' the Blues / May 27, 1960 / Original Jazz Classics ◆◆◆◆
Oliver Nelson and Eric Dolphy (alto sax, bass clarinet, flute) collaborated on some classic material and while *Screamin' the Blues* may not be classic, it did have bite, and excellent solos from a band that also included Richard Williams (once again producing stronger trumpet work as a sideman than he did as a leader), Richard Wyands (piano), George Duvivier (bass), and Roy Haynes (drums). —*Bob Rusch, Cadence*

Nocturne / Aug. 23, 1960 / Prestige ◆◆◆
This relaxed set (originally on the Prestige subsidiary Moodsville) puts the emphasis on ballads and slower material. Nelson (switching between alto and tenor) is joined by vibraphonist Lem Winchester, pianist Richard Wyands, bassist George Duvivier and drummer Roy Haynes for four standards and three of his originals (including the swinging "Bob's Blues"). Everyone plays well, but the intentional lack of mood variation keeps this release from being all that essential. —*Scott Yanow*

Soul Battle / Sep. 9, 1960 / Original Jazz Classics ◆◆◆◆
Recorded at Englewood Cliffs, NJ. Oliver Nelson with King Curtis and Jimmy Forrest...called a *Soul Battle*, but it's really just a straight-ahead blowing date by three saxmen with distinct styles representative of different eras and/or genres. None of the saxes concede or compromise. This is King Curtis' most compelling jazz work...and makes one wonder just how big his talent was. —*Bob Rusch, Cadence*

★ **Blues and the Abstract Truth** / 1961 / Impulse! ◆◆◆◆◆
This was Oliver Nelson's finest recording and one of the top jazz albums of 1961, a true classic. The lineup is an inspired one: Nelson on tenor and alto, Eric Dolphy doubling on alto and flute, a young trumpeter named Freddie Hubbard, baritonist George Barrow for section parts, pianist Bill Evans, bassist Paul Chambers and drummer Roy Haynes. The contrasting voices of the soloists really uplift these superior compositions, which are highlighted by "Stolen Moments" (a future standard), the fun "Hoe-Down" and "Yearnin'." Dolphy cuts everyone, but Nelson and Hubbard are also in top form. —*Scott Yanow*

Straight Ahead / Mar. 1, 1961 / Original Jazz Classics ◆◆◆◆
Oliver Nelson and Eric Dolphy were a formidable pair...This date was also issued on another two-fer...Maybe it was too *straight ahead* rather than letting the muses go where they might naturally take themselves at this point in time. However, as usual, Dolphy's playing was rewarding. The program had Richard Wyands (piano), George Duvivier (bass) and Roy Haynes (drums) as the rhythm section. —*Bob Rusch, Cadence*

Main Stem / Aug. 25, 1961 / Original Jazz Classics ◆◆◆◆
Unlike most of Oliver Nelson's recordings, this one has the feel of a jam session. A CD reissue of a Prestige set, Nelson (on tenor and alto) teams up with trumpeter Joe Newman (in exciting form), pianist Hank Jones, bassist George Duvivier, drummer Charlie Persip and Ray Barretto on congas for two superior standards ("Mainstem" and "Tangerine") plus four of Nelson's more basic originals. The spirited solos of Nelson and Newman are strong reasons to get this happy session. —*Scott Yanow*

Afro-American Sketches / Sep. 1961–Nov. 10, 1961 / Original Jazz Classics ◆◆◆◆◆
Oliver Nelson merged the rhythmic fervor of Africa and Black America with the organizational flair of Europe on this release. The often spectacular work, which sounds even more dynamic and impressive in its newly remastered digital fashion on CD, features the orchestra sometimes whooping and clashing in the backdrop and other times doing soulful statements or converging in a blues setting. While Nelson combined Afro-Latin rhythmic support from Ray Barretto with crisp jazz drumming from Ed Shaughnessy, he also contributed his own soaring alto and tenor sax solos and conducted the orchestra. It was a monumental job, and the results can now be enjoyed again by both jazz and classical fans. —*Ron Wynn*

Fantabulous / Mar. 17, 1964 / Argo ◆◆◆◆

More Blues & Abstract Truth / Nov. 10, 1964–Nov. 11, 1964 / Impulse! ◆◆◆
More Blues and the Abstract Truth was an excellent blues-oriented date that included plenty of bright moments, both from the colorful charts and the soloists, especially Adams And Roger Kellaway. —*Scott Yanow*

Sound Pieces / Sep. 27, 1966–Sep. 28, 1966 / Impulse! ◆◆◆◆

● **Black, Brown and Beautiful** / Mar. 17, 1970–Mar. 19, 1970 / Bluebird ◆◆◆◆◆
An exciting set. The reissue has three bonus cuts. —*Ron Wynn*

Live in Berlin / Nov. 5, 1970 / Flying Dutchman ◆◆◆◆
Leon Thomas makes a soaring, impressive vocal contribution. Nelson's alto sax solos sizzle. —*Ron Wynn*

Swiss Suite / Jun. 18, 1971 / Flying Dutchman ◆◆◆◆◆
Gato Barbieri (ts) almost steals the show on tenor; Eddie "Cleanhead" Vinson (sax) also sparkles in a guest stint. —*Ron Wynn*

Stolen Moments / Mar. 6, 1975 / Inner City ◆◆◆◆

Steve Nelson

b. 1955, Pittsburgh, PA
Vibes / Hard Bop

Steve Nelson developed in the 1990s into one of the most promising of the vibraphonists around, influenced by Milt Jackson but gradually developing his own sound. After gigging with Grant Green in the early '70s, Nelson picked up important experience playing with Kenny Barron, James Spaulding, Bobby Watson and David "Fathead" Newman and has played in a countless number of settings in recent times. Nelson has recorded as a leader thus far for Criss Cross, Red and Sunnyside. —*Scott Yanow*

Communications / Dec. 30, 1987 / Criss Cross ◆◆◆◆

Live Session, Vol. 1 / Jul. 1989 / Red ◆◆◆

Live Session, Vol. 2 / Jul. 1989 / Red ◆◆◆

● **Full Nelson** / Aug. 8, 1989 / Sunnyside ◆◆◆◆◆

Roger Neumann

b. Minot, ND
Arranger, Tenor Saxophone, Leader / Bop

A colorful arranger, Roger Neumann has released only two albums by his "Rather Large Band" (one in 1983 and the other in 1994, both for SeaBreeze), but they are both memorable. A jazz educator based in Los Angeles with experience playing tenor with

Woody Herman (1967), Bob Crosby and Anita O'Day, Neumann has contributed arrangements for his wife-singer Madeline Vergari, Buddy Rich, Count Basie, Ray Brown and even the Beach Boys! —*Scott Yanow*

★ **Introducing Roger Neumann's Rather Large Band** / Apr. 1983–Jun. 1983 / Sea Breeze ✦✦✦✦✦

Instant Heat / Nov. 22, 1993–Nov. 24, 1993 / Sea Breeze ✦✦✦✦✦
It is very surprising that this SeaBreeze CD was Roger Neumann's first release since 1983 for his arrangements are colorful, fairly original and hard-swinging. In addition to all of the charts, he wrote eight of the new set's dozen compositions, plays some fine tenor and is very generous in allocating solo space to his 17 sidemen; in fact every musician (including the six subs) gets at least one chance to be heard. The fresh versions of "Good Bait," "Stompin' At The Savoy," "For Heaven's Sake" and Chick Corea's "Children's Song, No. 2" alternate with Neumann's unpredictable originals and the music is consistently enjoyable. This CD is highly recommended to big-band fans as was the earlier SeaBreeze recording *Introducing Roger Neumann's Rather Large Band*. —*Scott Yanow*

New Orleans Owls

Group / Classic Jazz
The New Orleans Owls, an excellent if now obscure band, recorded 18 spirited sides during 1925–27. Although none of its sidemen (other than banjoist Nappy Lamare who is on the final two songs) became famous, the band (which grew from seven to ten pieces) effectively bridged the gap between the New Orleans Rhythm Kings and late-'20s dance bands. All of their enjoyable recordings were made available recently on a Frog CD from England. —*Scott Yanow*

★ **The Owls' Hoot** / Mar. 26, 1925–Oct. 26, 1927 / Frog ✦✦✦✦✦
The New Orleans Owls were a spirited seven-to-nine piece band whose hot jazz and interesting arrangements made it a legendary group to early jazz collectors. Its entire output, 18 selections from five sessions, is reissued on this highly enjoyable CD from the English label Frog. The Owls did not have any famous musicians (other than guitarist Nappy Lamare on the final date), but its versions of such songs as "Stomp Off, Let's Go," "Tampeekoe," "White Ghost Shivers" and "Brotherly Love" in particular are memorable. In addition to those classic sides, The New Orleans Rhythm Kings' final recordings (two takes apiece of "She's Cryin' for Me" and "Everybody Loves Somebody Blues") and the recordings of John Hyman's Bayou Stompers (two versions apiece of a pair of songs that, in addition to the standard instrumentation, includes the harmonica of Alvin Gautreaux) wrap up this thoroughly enjoyable disc. —*Scott Yanow*

New Orleans Rhythm Kings

Group / Classic Jazz
The New Orleans Rhythm Kings (NORK) were the finest jazz group to be on record in 1922 and the white band has served as proof that, even that early, blacks were not the only ones that could play jazz with individuality and integrity. The key members of the group (leader-cornetist Paul Mares, trombonist George Brunis and clarinetist Leon Roppolo) were childhood friends from New Orleans. In 1922 they started a 17-month residency at the Friar's Inn Nightclub in Chicago and, in August, they made their first recordings. Although Mares (unlike Nick LaRocca of the Original Dixieland Jazz Band) was modest about his own playing, saying that he was very influenced by King Oliver, he actually sounded quite a bit different and had a voice of his own. Roppolo was the first significant soloist on record, while Brunis would have a long career playing Dixieland. The changing rhythm sections sometimes included the first great jazz bassist Steve Brown (although largely inaudible on his early session), drummer Ben Pollack (a future bandleader) and, on a pair of memorable sessions in 1923, pianist Jelly Roll Morton. Among the future standards introduced by the NORK were "Farewell Blues," "Panama," "That's a Plenty" and "Tin Roof Blues"; the latter included a famous Brunis trombone solo. The band broke up in 1924 when Mares and Roppolo returned to New Orleans. With Santo Pecora on trombone they regrouped for a fine session on January 1925, but Roppolo was already suffering from mental problems; the group's final date two months later was without Roppolo, who would soon be institutionalized for the remainder of his life. Mares came back for one further session in 1935, but seemed

happy in retirement, leaving the legacy of the NORK to history. — *Scott Yanow*

★ **New Orleans Rhythm Kings and Jelly Roll Morton** / Aug. 29, 1922–Jul. 17, 1923 / Milestone ✦✦✦✦✦

Phineas Newborn

b. Dec. 14, 1931, Whiteville, TN, **d.** May 26, 1989, Memphis, TN
Piano / Hard Bop
Despite having severe personal and mental problems most of his career, Phineas Newborn, Jr. was one of jazz's most accomplished, technically brilliant pianists. Many compared his incredible speed, harmonic knowledge, dexterity and rhythmic facility with that of Tatum and Bud Powell. But a combination of being repeatedly off the scene due to illness and spending much of his life in the South rather than on the East or West Coast prevented Newborn from attaining his rightful place in jazz history during his lifetime. He studied piano, theory, alto sax and various brass instruments while in high school. Both his father and brother were musicians, and Newborn played in various Memphis bands during the '40s until he joined Lionel Hampton in the early '50s. He played with Hampton in 1950 and 1952. Newborn was in the service during 1953, '54 and '55, then moved to New York in 1956. He had a duo with Charles Mingus in 1958, and toured Europe in '58 and '59. Newborn made some highly praised records for Atlantic, RCA and United Artists in the late '50s, gaining enormous respect from critics and musicians alike. He continued recording on Prestige and Roulette through the late '50s, doing a trio date with Roy Haynes and Paul Chambers for Prestige. He moved to Los Angeles in 1960, and made more outstanding trio sessions for Contemporary in the '60s. But his illness, coupled with a hand injury, led to infrequent appearances at best and long absences from playing, touring or recordings. Newborn was hospitalized in Memphis for a time. He returned to a limited schedule of performances and recordings in the early and mid-'70s. His album *Solo Piano* for Atlantic was a brilliant exposition of gospel and blues-tinged modern playing. Newborn made an acclaimed appearance at a 1975 concert sponsored by the World Jazz Association in Los Angeles. There were other sessions for Pablo and some foreign labels. During the '80s, Newborn was a familiar sight at Memphis clubs, and he recorded sonatas by Alexander Scriabin for VSOP in 1987. Newborn died in Memphis in 1989. There are several Newborn '50s and '60s dates that have been reissued within the last couple of years on CD. —*Ron Wynn*

Piano Artistry of / May 3, 1956–May 4, 1956 / Atlantic ✦✦✦✦✦

Phineas' Rainbow / Oct. 16, 1956–Oct. 22, 1956 / Victor ✦✦✦✦

While My Lady Sleeps / Apr. 23, 1957–Apr. 3, 1958 / Bluebird ✦✦✦✦
Some late '50s cuts by piano great Phineas Newborn, then at the peak of his powers. Newborn could totally pick apart and rework any standard, while his own works were often so full of tricky phrases and dazzling devices that they astonished even other great players. —*Ron Wynn*

Phineas Newborn Plays Jamaica / Sep. 7, 1957–Sep. 9, 1957 / RCA ✦✦✦

Piano Portraits / Jun. 17, 1959–Jun. 18, 1959 / Roulette ✦✦✦✦

I Love a Piano / Oct. 26, 1959–Oct. 29, 1959 / Roulette ✦✦✦✦✦

★ **The World of Piano** / Oct. 16, 1961–Nov. 21, 1961 / Original Jazz Classics ✦✦✦✦✦

★ **The Great Jazz Piano of Phineas Newborn Jr.** / Nov. 21, 1961–Sep. 12, 1962 / Original Jazz Classics ✦✦✦✦✦
This recording lives up to its title. Phineas Newborn at his prime had phenomenal technique (on the level of an Oscar Peterson), a creative imagination and plenty of energy. These trio sessions (with Leroy Vinnegar or Sam Jones on bass and either Milt Turner or Louis Hayes on drums) feature Newborn displaying plenty of heat and fresh ideas on compositions by Bud Powell, Bobby Timmons, Benny Golson, Duke Ellington, Thelonious Monk, Sonny Rollins and Miles Davis, and two of his own. This is piano jazz at its highest level. —*Scott Yanow*

Newborn Touch / Apr. 1, 1964 / Original Jazz Classics ✦✦✦✦✦
Pianist Phineas Newborn, Jr. was a keyboard genius; his remarkable forays with independent movements occuring octaves apart in each hand were a marvel to keyboardists and other instrumentalists alike. This mid-'60s trio date, reissued on CD with

three bonus cuts, features Newborn covering compositions by Art Pepper, Ornette Coleman, Benny Carter and Hampton Hawes, among others. Each becomes a rousing, personalized treatment, with Newborn's consistently unpredictable touch, fleeting solos and uncanny phrasing. This session only reaffirms how much Newborn's insights and skills are missed. —*Ron Wynn*

Harlem Blues / Feb. 12, 1969–Feb. 13, 1969 / Original Jazz Classics ✦✦✦✦
The superb trio (pianist Phineas Newborn, bassist Ray Brown and drummer Elvin Jones) had never played together before, but it didn't matter. They had little trouble finding common ground. The piano virtuoso (still in peak form) leads the way on such pieces as his "Harlem Blues," "Ray's Idea" (composed decades earlier by Brown) and Horace Silver's "Cookin' at the Continental." —*Scott Yanow*

Please Send Me Someone to Love / Feb. 12, 1969–Feb. 13, 1969 / Contemporary ✦✦✦✦
Fabulous piano technique by the late Phineas Newborn, one of jazz's finest pure soloists. His amazing harmonic knowledge and masterful playing were ideal for the standards he performed on this album, especially the title track. —*Ron Wynn*

Solo Piano / 1974 / Atlantic ✦✦✦✦

Back Home / Sep. 17, 1976–Sep. 18, 1976 / Contemporary ✦✦✦✦
Trio. A stunning date with Ray Brown (b) and Elvin Jones (d). —*Ron Wynn*

Look Out: Phineas Is Back / Dec. 7, 1976–Dec. 8, 1976 / Original Jazz Classics ✦✦✦✦

David "Fathead" Newman

b. Feb. 24, 1933, Dallas, TX
Flute, Tenor Saxophone, Alto Saxophone / Soul Jazz, Hard Bop
A first-rate soul jazz, blues, R&B and funk saxophonist and flutist, David "Fathead" Newman has been a star in seminal bands, issued excellent recordings and been featured on several fine sessions. He can certainly play bebop and has shown surprising chops when so inclined, but that's not his strength. Hearing the gorgeous, huge Newman tenor sax tones filling the space left by a singer laying out, ripping through a 12-bar blues, interacting with an organist or guitarist, or just embellishing a melody, is one of jazz and popular music's great pleasures. His taste has sometimes deserted him, but when working in the right arena Newman's a wonderful player and bandleader. He got his "Fathead" nickname from a music teacher as a child. He began playing with local bands in Dallas, and later toured with Lowell Fulson and T-Bone Walker. Newman became a star while working with Ray Charles. He stayed with Charles a full decade in the '50s and '60s, and was a pivotal part of many landmark R&B dates. The sounds he made with Charles still guide Newman's music. He later worked with King Curtis in the mid-'60s. Newman began recording as a leader for Atlantic in the late '50s. He did several small combo dates, then later worked with larger bands. Newman played with Blue Mitchell, Roy Ayers, Dr. John, and Ron Carter among others. Things began to go astray in the mid-'70s; there were some experiments with overdubbed strings and horns. But Newman returned to soul jazz and blues basics on Prestige, Muse and Atlantic in the '80s. He's recorded for Milestone in the late '80s and '90s, still doing reliable blues and soul jazz, with an occasional bebop date. He's also recorded for Candid and Timeless, and worked with Cornell Dupree and Ellis Marsalis on a fine session for Amazing Records. Newman has a fair number of titles available on CD. Rhino issued a CD anthology of some earlier Atlantic dates in '93. —*Ron Wynn*

★ **House of David Newman: David "Fathead" Anthology** / 1952 / Rhino ✦✦✦✦✦
There have not been many saxophonists and flutists more naturally soulful than David "Fathead" Newman. This two-disc set captures Newman at his best. He never really was an album artist; each LP has had its nuggets, and that's what this captures. It has Newman wailing the blues, then stretching out in the Ray Charles band. He covers a Beatles tune, then an Aaron Neville number. He backs Aretha Franklin and pays homage to the great Buster Cooper. This is one anthology that can be recommended without hesitation, because there aren't going to be many complete Newman albums coming down the reissue pike. —*Ron Wynn*

Fathead: Ray Charles Presents David Newman / Nov. 5, 1958 / Atlantic ✦✦✦✦

Straight Ahead / Dec. 21, 1960 / Atlantic ✦✦✦✦

Bigger & Better (The Many Facets of David Newman) / Mar. 5, 1968–Feb. 11, 1969 / Rhino/Atlantic ✦✦
The packaging on this Rhino CD (which is a reissue of two complete Atlantic LPs) is excellent, but these sets are among tenor saxophonist David "Fathead" Newman's more commercial efforts. The sessions that resulted in *Bigger & Better* feature Newman with a string section and studio musicians for forgettable versions of two Beatles songs, a pair of Sam Cooke R&B pieces and a couple of lesser items. *The Many Facets of David Newman* is less poppish and more blues-oriented with the lengthy "Children of Abraham" showing some passion, but overall the material is rather weak and has not aged very well. Skip this set in favor of Newman's more recent efforts. —*Scott Yanow*

Captain Buckles / Nov. 3, 1970–Nov. 5, 1970 / Atlantic ✦✦✦✦

Lonely Avenue / Nov. 2, 1971–Nov. 4, 1971 / Atlantic ✦✦✦
Textbook soul-jazz; fine vibes from Roy Ayers. —*Ron Wynn*

Back to Basics / May 1977–Nov. 1977 / Milestone ✦✦✦✦
A '91 CD reissue of a late '70s session by tenor saxophonist and flutist David Newman, which emphasized his patented soul jazz and blues while matching Newman with different players on various tracks, rather than having a fixed rhythm section. The top guest stars included keyboardists Hilton Ruiz and George Cables and guitarist Lee Ritenour. —*Ron Wynn*

Concrete Jungle / Nov. 1977 / Prestige ✦✦

Resurgence / Sep. 23, 1980 / Muse ✦✦✦✦
Newman shows bop talents heading a fine ensemble and supported by Cedar Walton on piano. —*Ron Wynn*

Still Hard Times / Apr. 1982 / Muse ✦✦✦✦✦
Saxophonist in his prime. Tuneful and exuberant. —*Michael G. Nastos*

Fire! Live at the Village Vanguard / Dec. 22, 1988–Dec. 23, 1988 / Atlantic ✦✦✦✦
A nice outing that matches Newman with Stanley Turrentine (ts) and Hank Crawford (as). —*Ron Wynn*

Blue Head / Sep. 3, 1989 / Candid ✦✦✦✦✦
An excellent '90 session by tenor saxophonist and flutist David Newman, done without fanfare or flash. Newman plays a big-toned, bluesy tenor and more introspective flute. He's backed by some top players, including guitarist Ted Dunbar, tenor saxophonist Clifford Jordan, and Buddy Montgomery on piano. —*Ron Wynn*

● **Return to the Wide Open Spaces** / 1990 / Amazing ✦✦✦✦✦
Texas tenor saxophonists David Newman and James Clay recorded a first-rate album in 1960, which seamlessly fused blues, soul, swing-tinged jazz and honking R&B styles. Some 30 years later, Newman and Clay reunited for a sequel, joined by pianist Ellis Marsalis. The resulting release was both timely and delightful, as Newman and Clay showed they hadn't lost any energy or facility. Their gutbucket licks, robust exchanges and alternately soulful, moving, and swaggering solos on a great collection of tunes by everyone from Billy Strayhorn to Buster Smith was entertaining and distinctive. It was one red-hot night at the Caravan of Dreams, and this CD fully captured the night's flavor. —*Ron Wynn*

● **Mr. Gentle Mr. Cool** / 1994 / Kokopelli ✦✦✦✦✦
David "Fathead" Newman is in excellent form on this tasteful program of 11 Duke Ellington compositions. Performing in a sextet with trombonist Jim Pugh, pianist David Leonhardt, bassist Peter Washington, Ron Carter on piccolo bass and drummer Lewis Nash, Newman splits his time between tenor and alto and takes a flute solo on "Azure." The music contains few real surprises (other than the utilization of both bass and piccolo bass), but swings nicely and has fine melodic solos. —*Scott Yanow*

Joe Newman

b. Sep. 7, 1922, New Orleans, LA, d. Jul. 4, 1992, New York, NY
Trumpet / Swing
Joe Newman was a superb, exciting trumpeter whose style echoed the best of Harry Edison, Dizzy Gillespie and Thad Jones, seasoned with his own flavoring. He was among a select corps who not only enjoyed playing, but communicated that joy and exuberance in every solo. He provided high note and upper register antics, but functioned best doing soft, enticing melodies or engag-

ing in mildly combative jam sessions. He was also an accomplished player in the traditional New Orleans style. Newman began his professional career with Lionel Hampton in 1942 and 1943, joining him after touring with the Alabama State Teachers College band. Newman became a member of the Count Basie orchestra in 1943, remaining until 1947. He co-led groups with Illinois Jacquet and J.C. Heard, before returning to The Basie band for a great run from 1952 to 1961. During that time, there were periodic outside recording sessions. Newman did sessions for Savoy, Vanguard and RCA in the '50s, most of them small-combo and tasteful, enjoyable outings. The 1956 album *Salute To Satch* was with a big band. *The Happy Cats* was a sextet date. There was a quintet session with Zoot Sims on Roulette and another Roulette recording with an 11-piece band. Newman toured Europe with the Basie band in 1954. During the early '60s, he continued recording and touring with Basie and making other sides on his own. These included sessions with Tommy Flanagan for Prestige and a quartet set for Stash. There was a 1962 Russian tour with Benny Goodman. Newman became involved with Jazz Interaction, an organization promoting awareness and jazz education in the early '60s, and soon became a tireless advocate. He assumed the organization's presidency in 1967. Newman also wrote compositions for their organization. He began playing with The New York Repertory Orchestra in 1974, and toured Europe and the Soviet Union with them in 1975. During the '70s, '80s and '90s, Newman juggled educating, recording, and doing an infrequent reunion with The Basie orchestra. He made nice sessions with Ruby Braff and Jimmy Rowles in the '70s and Joe Wilder and Hank Jones in the '80s. —*Ron Wynn*

★ **The Complete Joe Newman** / Feb. 8, 1955–1956 / RCA ✦✦✦✦✦
Trumpeter Joe Newman, best-known for his playing with Count Basie's Orchestra, led four albums for RCA during 1955–56. This generous two-CD set reissues all the music from these dates and has plenty of swinging performances. The first disc puts the focus on Newman and tenor saxophonist Al Cohn in a pair of octets with arrangements by Ernie Wilkins, Manny Albam and Cohn. The second disc starts out with a tribute to Louis Armstrong, a dozen of Satch's songs modernized for a big band; Newman takes a few rare vocals. The final session matches Newman with flutist Frank Wess in a two-guitar septet arranged by Wilkins. While most of the other two-fers in this French RCA Jazz Tribune series are reissues of earlier two-LP sets, this one was newly compiled and has 48 splendid examples of Basie-ish swing. Highly recommended. —*Scott Yanow*

Locking Horns / Apr. 10, 1957 / Roulette ✦✦✦✦

Jive at Five / May 4, 1960 / Original Jazz Classics ✦✦✦

Good 'N Groovy / Mar. 17, 1961 / Original Jazz Classics ✦✦✦✦
This was the second of Joe Newman's three dates he led under the Swingville banner. For this session, he was in the very fine company of Frank Foster (tenor sax), Tommy Flanagan (piano), Eddie Jones (bass) and Bill English (drums). —*Bob Rusch, Cadence*

Hangin' Out / May 1984 / Concord Jazz ✦✦✦
This relaxed, jovial session is co-led by Joe Wilder (tpt). "Smitty" Smith adds fire on drums. —*Ron Wynn*

Frankie Newton (William Frank Newton)

b. Jan. 4, 1906, Emory, VA, d. Mar. 11, 1954, NYC
Trumpet / Swing
Trumpeter Frankie Newton, whose mellow and thoughtful style sometimes seemed somewhat out-of-place in the swing era, had a relatively brief but artistically rewarding career. He had stints with Lloyd Scott (1927–29), Cecil Scott (1929–30), Chick Webb, Elmer Snowden, Charlie Johnson and Sam Wooding, and appeared on Bessie Smith's final recording session in 1933. Newton worked with Charlie Garnet's short-lived integrated band in 1936 and Teddy Hill before briefly becoming closely associated with bassist John Kirby and his associates. The eventual John Kirby Sextet would have been the logical place for the trumpeter, but a falling out in 1937 ended up with the younger Charlie Shavers getting the spot in the commercially successful group. Newton instead played for Mezz Mezzrow and Lucky Millinder, led a few record dates (including participating in a set for Hugues Panassie) and worked at Cafe Society, accompanying Billie Holiday on several of her records (most notably "Strange Fruit"). As the 1940s progressed, Newton became less interested in music and gradually faded from the scene, painting more than playing, dying a forgotten and underutilized talent. —*Scott Yanow*

At the Onyx Club / Mar. 5, 1937–Apr. 12, 1939 / Tax ✦✦✦✦
The lyrical trumpeter Frankie Newton offered a contrast to the blazing solos of Roy Eldridge. Newton could play high notes, but much of the time he was more interested in expressing himself gently and with intelligent subtlety. This LP contains eight selections from recording sessions led by Newton (these have since been reissued on a Classics CD) and some of his backup work with singers Maxine Sullivan and Midge Williams when he was associated with John Kirby's early group. There are a few inferior vocals on Newton's own recordings, but also such fine performances as "Who's Sorry Now," "Frankie's Jump" and "Jam Fever;" altoists Pete Brown and Tab Smith (on different dates) are the most memorable of Newton's sidemen. Other highpoints of these swing dates include Maxine Sullivan's "Loch Lomond" (a major hit) and Midge Williams' version of "The Lady Is a Tramp." —*Scott Yanow*

James Newton

b. May 1, 1953, Los Angeles, CA
Flute / Avant-Garde
James Newton comes closest of any contemporary flutist to invoking the spirit of Eric Dolphy. His soaring, beautiful tones have that same evocative, bird-like quality, and he's nearly as accomplished with his armada of trills, vocal effects, swirling phrases, flutter tonguing, humming, glissandos and overblowing. Newton once played alto and tenor saxophones, but gave them up to concentrate on flute. He has a classical timbre, but a jazz musician's heart and that's enabled him to execute solos that are astonishing in their harmonic brillance and performed with what seems a minimum of effort. Newton played electric bass, alto and tenor sax, bass clarinet and flute in high school, oddly picking up flute last. He attended a California junior college, majoring in music, and studied under Buddy Collette. Newton played flute and sax in a funk band, and performed with Arthur Blythe, David Murray and others in Stanley Crouch's Black Music Infinity in the early '70s. He became a flutist exclusively in the late '70s, and joined the exodus of West Coast musicians to New York. He co-led an ensemble with Anthony Davis, and performed in a trio with a Japanese koto player, a flute quartet with Frank Wess and a woodwind quintet. He began recording as a leader on India Navigation in the late '70s, and continued on Circle, ECM, Gramavision, Bvhaast, Celestial Harmonies and Blue Note in the '80s. James Newton, who has long since retuned to California, is an innovative virtuoso active in many areas from straight ahead to free form and World Music. In the 1990's he remains at the top of his field, leading the way for other flutists. —*Ron Wynn and Scott Yanow*

Solomon's Sons / Jan. 16, 1977 / Circle ✦✦✦

From Inside / Jul. 27, 1978–Jul. 29, 1978 / BVHaast ✦✦✦✦

Crystal Texts / Nov. 27, 1978 / Moers ✦✦✦

Paseo Del Mar / 1978 / India Navigation ✦✦✦✦

Mystery School / 1979 / India Navigation ✦✦✦✦✦
James Newton explores many moods and tone colors with this unusual album. The instrumentation (flutist Newton, clarinetist John Carter, bassoonist John Nunez, Charles Owens on oboe and English horn and the veteran Red Callender on tuba) by itself would give Newton's originals a sound of its own, but the complex arrangements (which give more than adequate space for improvisations) display the influences of both modern classical music and jazz. —*Scott Yanow*

Axum / Aug. 1981 / ECM ✦✦✦
This thrilling solo flute extends the instrument's scope and range beyond expected frontiers. —*Ron Wynn*

James Newton / Oct. 1982 / Gramavision ✦✦✦✦✦
Features three Newton originals for pianists Anthony Davis and Billy Strayhorn. With Jay Hoggard (vib) and Slide Hampton (tb). Excellent, creative music. —*Michael G. Nastos*

Portraits / 1982 / India Navigation ✦✦✦✦✦

Luella / 1983 / Gramavision ✦✦✦✦✦
An ambitious, intricately composed and structured album from flutist James Newton that blends improvised and set pieces played by eight-piece group. The lineup includes vibist Jay Hoggard, pianist Kenny Kirkland, violinists John Blake and Gayle Dixon, cellist Abdul Wadud, bassist Cecil McBee, and drummer Billy Hart. —*Ron Wynn*

Echo Canyon / Sep. 5, 1984–Sep. 7, 1984 / Celestial Harmonies
✦✦✦
Excellent playing of Newton's compositions for solo flute. —*Ron Wynn*

Water Mystery / Jan. 1985 / Gramavision ✦✦✦✦✦
Some soothing, some entrancing, and some astonishing flute performances from James Newton on this album, one of his finest ever from both a performance and compositional standpoint. —*Ron Wynn*

★ **The African Flower** / Jun. 24, 1985–Jun. 25, 1985 / Blue Note
✦✦✦✦✦
On *The African Flower,* flutist James Newton explored the music of Billy Strayhorn and his mentor Duke Ellington; the results were a fresh reappraisal of timeless music. —*Scott Yanow*

● **Romance and Revolution** / Aug. 20, 1986–Aug. 21, 1986 / Blue Note ✦✦✦✦✦
Flutist James Newton's brilliantly written and performed pieces for octet were featured on this '87 session. Trombonists Steve Turre and Robin Eubanks, vibist Jay Hoggard, and pianist Geri Allen, along with Newton, were among the solo stars. —*Ron Wynn*

Albert Nicholas

b. May 27, 1900, New Orleans, LA, **d.** Sep. 3, 1973, Basle, Switzerland
Clarinet / New Orleans Jazz
A superb clarinetist with an attractive mellow tone, Albert Nicholas had a long and diverse career, but his playing was always consistently rewarding. He studied with Lorenzo Tio, Jr. in New Orleans and played with cornet legends Buddy Petit, King Oliver and Manuel Perez while in his teens. After three years in the Merchant Marine, he joined King Oliver in Chicago for much of 1925–7, recording with Oliver's Dixie Syncopators. He spent a year in the Far East and Egypt, arriving in New York in 1928 to join Luis Russell for five years. Nicholas, who had recorded in several settings in the 1920s, sounded perfectly at home with Russell, taking his solos alongside Red Allen, J.C. Higginbottham and Charlie Holmes. He would later rejoin Russell when the pianist had the backup orchestra for Louis Armstrong a few years later and Nicholas also worked with Jelly Roll Morton in 1939 (he had recorded with Morton previously in 1929). Things slowed down for a time in the early '40s, but the New Orleans revival got him working in France later in the mid-'40s with Art Hodes, Bunk Johnson and Kid Ory; by 1948 the clarinetist was playing regularly with Ralph Sutton's trio at Jimmy Ryan's. In 1953 Nicholas followed Sidney Bechet's example and moved to France where, other than returning to the U.S. for recording sessions in 1959 and 1960, he happily remained for his final 20 years. —*Scott Yanow*

Albert Nicholas Quartet / Jul. 19, 1959+Jul. 27, 1959 / Delmark
✦✦✦✦✦
Like Sidney Bechet, clarinetist Albert Nicholas moved permanently to France later in his career. Although he was there 20 years (1953 until his death in 1973), Nicholas never received Bechet's fame but he seemed to prosper overseas, no longer having to be concerned with the lack of interest of Americans in traditional jazz. This particular album, one of two cut by Nicholas during a rare 1959 visit to the States, teams the melodic clarinetist with the great pianist Art Hodes, bassist Earl Murphy and drummer Freddy Kohlman. They jam happily through a set of standards and blues and the results are easily enjoyable. —*Scott Yanow*

● **All Star Stompers** / Jul. 30, 1959–Jul. 31, 1959 / Delmark ✦✦✦✦✦
A Tribute to Jelly Roll Morton / Aug. 1970 / Storyville ✦✦✦✦

Herbie Nichols

b. Jan. 3, 1919, New York, NY, **d.** Apr. 12, 1963, New York, NY
Piano, Composer / Post Bop
Few jazz musicians have had as frustrating a career as Herbie Nichols. A very original composer and pianist, Nichols' music was largely unknown not only during his lifetime but still up to the present day. After serving in the Army during 1941–43, he played with many different groups including those led by Herman Autrey, Hal Singer, Illinois Jacquet and John Kirby (1948–49). Although he recorded his originals in trios for Blue Note and Bethlehem during 1955–57, those records were largely overlooked. Nichols spent most of his career making his living not in

bop bands but with Dixieland groups, playing music that was unchallenging but sometimes paid the rent. He was just beginning to gain a following with younger musicians (including Roswell Rudd, Archie Shepp, Steve Swallow and Bill Watrous) when Nichols was fatally stricken with leukemia. Decades later, Mosaic released all of his Blue Note recordings (including many previously unissued) in a box set. A chapter in A.B. Spellman's *Four Lives in The Bebop Business* in definitive fashion tells the Herbie Nichols story, and there have been recent tribute albums by Misha Mengelberg and Buell Neidlinger (the latter's *Blue Chopsticks* interpreted Nichols' originals with two reeds, violin, viola and cello!). But with the exception of "Lady Sings the Blues" (which Billie Holiday had recorded), Herbie Nichols' music is still pretty obscure. —*Scott Yanow*

★ **Complete Blue Note** / May 6, 1955–Apr. 19, 1956 / Mosaic
✦✦✦✦✦
This limited-edition, five-LP box set from Mosaic salutes one of the unknown greats of jazz and gives him the treatment he never received while he was alive. Pianist/composer Herbie Nichols had a very original style in the 1950s, but was unable to find work of any kind with modern jazz players; instead he spent nights playing anonymous piano in Dixieland bands before his premature death in 1963. Nichols only recorded three full albums, two on Blue Note and one for Bethlehem. The former's 22 performances have been expanded to 48 (24 never issued before) by Mosaic and they give listeners as full a picture of Herbie Nichols as is possible. Heard exclusively in trios (with either Al McKibbon or Teddy Kotick on bass and Art Blakey or Max Roach on drums), Herbie Nichols plays his unique music and now, finally, these rare performances can be heard and savored. —*Scott Yanow*

● **The Bethlehem Session** / Nov. 1957 / Affinity ✦✦✦✦✦
Herbie Nichols was one of the tragedies of jazz, a very original pianist and composer who could not find regular employment for his thought-provoking music and ended up playing in anonymous Dixieland bands. He only recorded three complete albums as a leader and his *Bethlehem* date was his last. With perfectly suitable accompaniment from bassist George Duvivier and bassist Danny Richmond, Nichols introduces nine of his originals in addition to performing the standard "Too Close for Comfort." —*Scott Yanow*

Red Nichols (Ernest Loring Nichols)

b. May 8, 1905, Ogden, UT, **d.** Jun. 28, 1965, Las Vegas, NV
Cornet, Leader / Dixieland, Classic Jazz
Overrated in Europe in the early 1930's when his records (but not those of his black contemporaries) were widely available, then later underrated and often unfairly called a Bix imitator, Red Nichols was actually one of the finest cornetists to emerge from the 1920s. An expert improviser whose emotional depth did not reach as deep as Bix or Louis Armstrong, Nichols was in many ways a hustler, participating in as many recording sessions (often under pseudonyms) as any other horn player of the era, cutting sessions as Red Nichols and his Five Pennies, the Arkansas Travelers, the Red Heads, the Louisiana Rhythm Kings and the Charleston Chasers among others, usually with similar personnel! Nichols studied cornet with his father, a college music teacher. After moving from Utah to New York in 1923 Nichols, an excellent sightreader who could always be relied upon to add a bit of jazz to a dance band recording, quickly became in great demand. His own sessions at first featured trombonist Miff Mole and Jimmy Dorsey on alto and clarinet, playing advanced music that utilized unusual intervals, whole tone scales and often the tympani of Vic Berton along with hot ensembles. Later on in the decade, his sidemen included such young greats as Benny Goodman, Glenn Miller, Jack Teagarden, Pee Wee Russell, Joe Venuti, Eddie Lang, Adrian Rollini, Gene Krupa and the wonderful mellophone specialist Dudley Fosdick among others; their version of "Ida" was a surprise hit. Although still using the main name of The Five Pennies, Nichols' bands were often quite a bit larger and, by 1929, he was alternating sessions featuring bigger commercial orchestras with small combos. At first Nichols weathered the Depression well with work in shows, but by 1932 his long string of recordings came to an end. He headed a so-so swing band up until 1942, left music for a couple of years and for a few months in 1944 was with Glen Gray's Casa Loma orchestra. Later that year he reformed The Five Pennies as a Dixieland sextet and, particularly after bass saxophonist Joe Rushton became a permanent member, it was one of the finer traditional jazz bands of the

next 20 years. Nichols recorded several memorable hot versions of "Battle Hymn Of the Republic," the best in 1959. That same year that a highly enjoyable if rather fictional Hollywood movie called *The Five Pennies* (and featuring Nichols' cornet solos and Danny Kaye's acting) made Red into a national celebrity at the twilight of his long career. Nichols' earlier sessions are just now being reissued on CD in piecemeal fashion, but none of his later albums are in print yet. —*Scott Yanow*

Red Nichols, Vol. 1 / 1926 / Classic Jazz ✦✦✦✦✦
Red Nichols, Vol. 2 / Jun. 20, 1927–Mar. 2, 1928 / Classic Jazz ✦✦✦✦✦
Red Nichols, Vol. 3 / Mar. 2, 1928–May 31, 1928 / Classic Jazz ✦✦✦✦✦
Red Nichols, Vol. 4 / Jun. 1, 1928–Jan. 1929 / Classic Jazz ✦✦✦✦✦
Red Nichols, Vol. 5 / Feb. 1, 1929–Apr. 1929 / Classic Jazz ✦✦✦✦✦

● **Syncopated Chamber Music** / Feb. 8, 1953–Feb. 9, 1953 / Audiophile ✦✦✦✦✦

Parade of the Pennies / Nov. 1958 / Capitol ✦✦✦✦
For part of this LP, cornetist Red Nichols (with the assistance of clarinetist Heinie Beau's arrangements) revisited his earlier "hits" with successful remakes of such songs as "Buddy's Habits," "Japanese Sandman," "Avalon" and "Washboard Blues." In addition, there are three newer songs co-written by Nichols and Beau. Red's Five Pennies are augmented by Jackie Coon's mellophone, a couple of reeds and the percussion (including tympani) of Ralph Hansell. This is an excellent album well deserving (along with most of Nichols' hard-to-find Capitol LPs) of being reissued on CD. —*Scott Yanow*

Red Nichols and the Five Pennies at Marineland / Jun. 11, 1959 / Capitol ✦✦✦

Lennie Niehaus

b. Jun. 11, 1929, St. Louis, MO
Alto Saxophone, Arranger / Cool, Bop
An excellent altoist and jazz arranger in the 1950s (most notably for Stan Kenton), Lennie Niehaus in more recent times has won fame for his work scoring the music for Clint Eastwood films. After graduating from college, Niehaus played alto and occasionally wrote for Kenton (1951–52) before being drafted for the Army (1952–54). Upon his discharge, Kenton welcomed Niehaus back and he worked for the bandleader on and off for the rest of the decade. Niehaus, who led and played alto on six albums between 1954–57 (five for Contemporary), had a cool tone a bit reminiscent of Lee Konitz. By the 1960s his playing had gone by the wayside as Niehaus concentrated on writing for films. Although he largely left jazz at that time, his work on *Play Misty for Me* and particularly *Bird* for Clint Eastwood allowed one to once again admire his jazz writing. —*Scott Yanow*

★ **The Lennie Niehaus, Vol. 1: The Quintet** / Jul. 2, 1954–Jul. 9, 1954 / Original Jazz Classics ✦✦✦✦✦
Lennie Niehaus, Vol. 2: The Octet, Pt. 1 / Aug. 23, 1954 / Original Jazz Classics ✦✦✦✦
The Lennie Niehaus, Vol. 3: The Octet, Pt. 2 / Jan. 11, 1955–Feb. 15, 1955 / Original Jazz Classics ✦✦✦✦
★ **Lennie Niehaus, Vol. 4: The Quintets and Strings** / Mar. 16, 1955–Apr. 25, 1955 / Original Jazz Classics ✦✦✦✦
This CD reissue brings back one of Lennie Niehaus' finest recordings of the 1950s. His alto is featured throughout the dozen selections and the varied settings (Niehaus is backed by a string quartet, a standard rhythm section and sometimes two other saxophonists in addition to performing four numbers with a standard quintet) gives him an opportunity to show off his writing abilities. Niehaus varies tempos a lot (the strings are often heard on faster material), there is solo space for the tenor of Bill Perkins, baritonist Bob Gordon and Stu Williamson on trumpet and valve trombone, and the leader's boppish alto is heard at the peak of his playing powers. Bop collectors can consider this disc to be essential. —*Scott Yanow*

Lennie Niehaus, Vol. 5: The Sextet / Jan. 9, 1956–Jan. 12, 1956 / Contemporary ✦✦✦✦

Sal Nistico

b. Apr. 2, 1948, Syracuse, NY, **d.** Mar. 3, 1991, Berne, Switzerland
Tenor Saxophone / Bop, Hard Bop
Sal Nistico's explosive tenor solos with Woody Herman in the

mid-'60s helped make that edition of Herman's Herds into a success. Originally an altoist, Nistico switched to tenor in 1956 and played with R&B bands for three years. He gigged with and made his recording debut in 1959–60 with the Jazz Brothers, a band also including Chuck and Gap Mangione. But it was while with Herman in 1962–65 that Nistico made history. In 1965 he spent five months with Count Basie. He returned to Count in 1967 and to Herman on several occasions (1968–70, 1971, 1981–82) although without the impact of the first stint. Otherwise the tenor freelanced throughout his career, playing with Don Ellis and Buddy Rich, but mostly working with pickup groups. Nistico recorded for several labels as a leader including Riverside, Red and Beehive. —*Scott Yanow*

Heavyweights / Dec. 20, 1961 / Jazzland ✦✦✦✦
Neo Nistico / Nov. 3, 1978 / Bee Hive ✦✦✦✦
● **Empty Room** / 1988 / Red ✦✦✦✦✦

Jimmie Noone

b. Apr. 23, 1895, New Orleans, LA, **d.** Apr. 19, 1944, Los Angeles, CA
Clarinet / Classic New Orleans Jazz
Considered one of the three top New Orleans clarinetists of the 1920s (with Johnny Dodds and Sidney Bechet), Jimmie Noone had a smoother tone than his contemporaries that appealed to players of the swing era (including Benny Goodman). He played guitar as a child and at age 15 took clarinet lessons from Lorenzo Tio, Jr. and Sidney Bechet (the latter was only 13!). Noone developed quickly and he played with Freddie Keppard (1913–14), Buddy Petit and the Young Olympia Band (1916), which he led. In 1917 he went to Chicago to join Keppard's Creole Band. After it broke up the following year, he became a member of King Oliver's band, staying until he joined Doc Cook's Dreamland Orchestra (1920–26). Although Noone recorded with Cook, it was when he started leading a band at the Apex Club that he hit his stirde. By 1928 he had pianist Earl Hines and altoist Joe Poston in the unusual quintet (Poston stuck to playing melodies behind Noone) and was recording for Vocalion, creating classic music including an early version of "Sweet Lorraine" (his theme song) and "Four or Five Times." Noone worked steadily in Chicago throughout the 1930s (although he received less attention from the jazz world), he used Charlie Shavers on some of his late-'30s recordings and welcomed the young singer Joe Williams to the bandstand; unfortunately, they never recorded together. In 1944 Noone was in Kid Ory's band on the West Coast and seemed on the brink of greater fame when he died unexpectedly. Thanks to European reissue series, Jimmie Noone's recordings are readily available on CD. His son Jimmie Noone, Jr. suddenly emerged out of obscurity in the 1980's to play clarinet and tenor with the Cheathams. —*Scott Yanow*

Complete Recordings, Vol. 1 / Jun. 1926–Jun. 1930 / Affinity ✦✦✦✦
★ **Apex Blues** / May 16, 1928–Jul. 1, 1930 / Decca ✦✦✦✦✦
Jimmie Noone ranked among the finest traditional jazz clarinetists. He had immaculate tone, a wonderful sound, and the facility to execute tricky phrases, fast runs, and clever lines. He was matched on several of this disc's cuts with another early jazz giant, pianist Earl Hines. His imagination, rhythmic verve and harmonic dexterity made him an ideal partner for Noone; he was neither too combative to support Noone nor so compliant that he posed no challenge. Their efforts, both joint and separate, are the disc's highlights. Pivotal, often delightful and always musically demanding early jazz, performed by two of its masters. —*Ron Wynn*

Jimmie Noone 1930–1934 / May 16, 1930–Nov. 23, 1934 / Classics ✦✦✦✦✦

Walter Norris

b. Dec. 27, 1931, Little Rock, AR
Piano / Post Bop
Walter Norris is a brilliant pianist, a virtuoso whose improvisations can be both very complex harmonically yet often remain melodic. He would be better-known in the U.S. if he had not spent so much time in Germany. Norris worked with Howard Williams in Arkansas (1944–50) as a teenager, was in Houston with Jimmy Ford (1952–53), led his own trio in Las Vegas (1953–54) and then settled in Los Angeles. He was on quite a few sessions during the

latter half of the 1950s, most notably with Jack Sheldon, Frank Rosolino and Herb Geller in addition to Ornette Coleman's first record (1958); he did his best to fit into the latter setting but (other than Paul Bley at the Hillcrest Club) it was the last time for decades that Coleman would use a pianist! The music director of the Playboy Club during 1963-70, Norris was with the Thad Jones-Mel Lewis Orchestra during 1974-76. After a stay in Scandinavia and a brief stint with Charles Mingus, Norris moved to Berlin in 1977 where he has taught and been performing ever since. In the 1990s Walter Norris visited the U.S. several times, recording dates for Concord and displaying his impressive musical growth of the past 20 years. —*Scott Yanow*

Drifting / Aug. 1974–May 1978 / Enja ✦✦✦✦
A '92 reissue of an excellent mid-'70s session by pianist Walter Norris, who's made few records, all of which are worth having. He's a slashing, more unorthodox player with both free and hard bop ties. His patterns, solos, and phrases aren't among the easiest to follow, but bassist George Mraz and drummer Aladar Page manage to find a comfort zone after some early problems. —*Ron Wynn*

Synchronicity / May 5, 1978 / Enja ✦✦✦✦✦

Stepping on Cracks / Jul. 17, 1978 / Progressive ✦✦✦✦
A late '70s date with some energetic, if at times nearly chaotic, piano solos from Walter Norris. Norris blends blues, gospel, free, and hard bop elements in his playing, which is filled with crackling runs and unorthodox lines. He's backed by his favorite bassist, George Mraz, and drummer Ronnie Bedford. —*Ron Wynn*

Winter Rose / Jun. 18, 1980–Sep. 1980 / Enja ✦✦✦✦✦

● **Lush Life** / 1990 / Concord Jazz ✦✦✦✦✦
A fine trio date, with a particularly good version of the title cut. CD version has two bonus cuts. —*Ron Wynn*

Live at Maybeck Recital Hall, Vol. 4 / Apr. 1990 / Concord Jazz ✦✦✦✦✦
Norris is an under-recorded, daring pianist who also writes distinctive pieces and is good on standards as well. —*Ron Wynn*

Sunburst / Aug. 13, 1991–Aug. 14, 1991 / Concord Jazz ✦✦✦✦✦
After struggling for years to get some exposure, when pianist Walter Norris made a critically acclaimed solo release for Concord, he was suddenly in demand. This date has the added bonus of superb tenor solos from the great Joe Henderson. He and Norris threaten, but don't totally overwhelm, bassist Larry Grenadier and drummer Mike Heyman. —*Ron Wynn*

Love Every Moment / Sep. 30, 1992–Oct. 1, 1992 / Concord Jazz ✦✦✦

Red Norvo (Kenneth Norville)
b. Mar. 31, 1908, Beardstown, IL
Vibes, Leader / Cool, Swing
Red Norvo was an unusual star during the swing era, playing jazz xylophone. After he switched to vibes in 1943, Norvo had a quieter yet no less fluent style than Lionel Hampton. Although no match for Hamp popularity-wise, Norvo and his wife, singer Mildred Bailey, did become known as Mr. and Mrs. Swing!

Red Norvo started on marimba when he was 14 and soon switched to xylophone. Active in vaudeville in the late '20s as a tap dancer, Norvo joined Paul Whiteman's Orchestra in the early '30s (meeting and marrying Mildred Bailey). He recorded some sides in the early-to-mid-'30s that showed off his virtuosity and imagination; two numbers (the atmospheric "Dance of the Octopus" and "In a Mist") had Benny Goodman playing bass clarinet! Norvo led his own bands during 1936-44, which, with its Eddie Sauter arrangements (particularly in the early days), had an ensemble sound that made it possible for one to hear the leader's xylophone. In 1944 Norvo (who by then had switched permanently to vibes) broke up his band and joined Benny Goodman's Sextet. Norvo welcomed Charlie Parker and Dizzy Gillespie to a 1945 record date, was part of Woody Herman's riotous first Herd in 1946 and recorded with Stan Hasselgard in 1948. At the beginning of the 1950s, Norvo put together an unusual trio with guitarist Tal Farlow (later Jimmy Raney) and bassist Charles Mingus (later Red Mitchell). The light yet often speedy unisons and telepathic interplay by the musicians was quite memorable. Norvo led larger groups later in the decade, had reunions with Benny Goodman and made many fine recordings. The 1960s found Red Norvo adopting a lower profile after he had a serious ear operation in 1961. He worked with the Newport All-Stars later in the decade and from the mid-'70s to the mid-'80s was once again

quite active, making several excellent recordings. However, his hearing worsened and a stroke put Red Norvo out of action altogether after 55 years of music. —*Scott Yanow*

Red Norvo / Apr. 8, 1933–Jan. 18, 1957 / Time/Life ✦✦✦✦
Red Norvo had a lengthy and diverse career, which is perfectly summed up in the 40 performances included on this three-LP Time/Life box set. Starting with his brilliant xylophone showcase on 1933's "Knockin' on Wood" and his early all-star recordings through the small groups he led at the beginning of the swing era, Norvo's unique big band (which featured the vocals of his wife Mildred Bailey), all of the music from a particularly memorable Teddy Wilson quartet session (with Harry James and bassist John Simmons) through the war years, collaborations with the Benny Goodman Sextet and Woody Herman and his brilliant trios in the 1950s before concluding with 1957's "Just a Mood," this definitive set certainly covers a lot of ground although it leaves off the music from Norvo's last 25 years on record! Its attractive booklet is another reason to acquire this valuable set, even listeners who already have the majority of the recordings. —*Scott Yanow*

★ **Dance of the Octopus** / Apr. 18, 1933–Mar. 16, 1936 / Hep ✦✦✦✦✦
The first 26 selections that xylophonist Red Norvo ever led are on this essential (and generous) CD. Among the many illustrious sidemen are future bandleaders Benny Goodman (heard on bass clarinet during memorable versions of "In a Mist" and "Dance of the Octopus"), Jimmy Dorsey, Artie Shaw, Jack Jenney, Charlie Barnet and Bunny Berigan in addition to Chu Berry, Teddy Wilson and Gene Krupa. While the first half of the program features all-star groups, the later tracks are prime examples of small-group swing with arranger Eddie Sauter's mellophone, trumpeter Stew Pletcher and Herbie Haymer's tenor playing key roles. This readily available CD from the Scottish label Hep contains more than its share of classic performances and is essential. —*Scott Yanow*

Red Norvo and His Big Band Featuring Mildred Bailey / Aug. 1936–Mar. 1942 / Sounds Of Swing ✦✦✦✦
This collector's LP contains 16 big-band performances from Red Norvo's impressive band, all but 1942's "Jersey Bounce" are from 1936-39. Mildred Bailey has five vocals and the sidemen include trumpeters Stew Fletcher and Jimmy Blake, clarinetist Hank D'Amico and tenors Herbie Haymer and Jerry Jerome. Since quite a few of these titles have not been reissued much since (a complete Red Norvo big-band series is needed on CD), this sampler is well worth picking up since it does contain some of the highlights of this often-overlooked band. —*Scott Yanow*

Red Norvo, Featuring Mildred Bailey / Mar. 22, 1937–Jul. 28, 1958 / Columbia ✦✦✦✦
This CD reissue by Columbia in their Legacy series is a bit of a hodgepodge, covering a 2-1/2 year period in the bandleading career of xylophonist Red Norvo. Unfortunately, the music is not programmed in chronological order, but since most of these largely enjoyable 18 titles (including two never previously released) have rarely been reissued, this sampler will have to do until a more "complete" session comes along. Norvo's band during this period not only featured the occasional vocals of his wife, Mildred Bailey, but fine solo work from the tenor of Herbie Haymer, clarinetist Hank D'Amico and trumpeter Stew Pletcher in addition to the leader. The biggest key in Norvo's orchestra achieving a sound of its own, however, were the distinctive and inventive arrangements of Eddie Sauter. This CD contains great music that deserves to be reissued more coherently. —*Scott Yanow*

Red Norvo and Mildred Bailey / 1938 / Circle ✦✦✦
This LP of radio transcriptions features Red Norvo's 1938 big band. The Eddie Sauter arrangements are consistently inventive and allow the orchestra to play quite quietly at times so its leader's xylophone could be heard not only as a solo instrument but in the ensembles. Mildred Bailey and Terry Allen contribute occasional vocals while the most impressive soloist next to Norvo is clarinetist Hank D'Amico. The band's distinctive sound and ability to swing hard at a light volume makes its music quite delightful and accessible. —*Scott Yanow*

Red Norvo Orchestra Live from the Blue Gardens / Jan. 4, 1942 / Music Masters ✦✦✦✦
Red Norvo's 1942 big band only recorded two songs and was otherwise completely undocumented. However, a tape of a radio broadcast was saved by trombonist Eddie Bert through the years and released on CD in 1992 by Music Masters. Although, other than Bert and singer Helen Ward, Norvo's sidemen are quite

obscure, he had a very interesting band throughout this period; the largest he ever led. Norvo (who plays xylophone here, but would switch to vibraphone the next year) leads an orchestra of three trumpets, three trombones, five reeds (including Sam Spumberg who tripled on tenor, oboe and English horn), a standard rhythm section and up to four vocalists. With colorful arrangements provided by Johnny Thompson, Norvo and his quietly powerful crew perform standards from the era plus five originals by the leader. This appealing and rather historical set is easily recommended to swing collectors. —*Scott Yanow*

Volume 1 / Oct. 28, 1943–May 17, 1944 / Vintage Jazz Classics ✦✦✦✦
This CD from the VJC label features vibraphonist Red Norvo's V-Disc sessions of 1943–44. Most of the music (which includes some breakdowns and alternate takes) finds Norvo leading an octet that includes trumpeter Dale Pearce, trombonist Dick Taylor, clarinetist Aaron Sachs and the tenor of Flip Phillips; Carol Bruce has three vocals and Helen Ward takes two, but the high points are instrumental versions of "1-2-3-4 Jump," "Seven Come Eleven" and "Flyin' Home." The last three titles (from 1944) feature Norvo leading a quintet with clarinetist Aaron Sachs. Overall, this CD contains plenty of fine examples of late swing, just before the influence of bop began to be felt on the principal's styles. Recommended to fans of the era. —*Scott Yanow*

● **Volume Two: The Norvo-Mingus-Farlow Trio** / Oct. 28, 1943–1950 / Vintage Jazz Classics ✦✦✦✦✦
With the exception of two titles and an alternate take featuring singer Helen Ward that were left over from Red Norvo's V-Disc sessions of 1943 (which were otherwise reissued in full on *Volume One*), this CD comprises 30 concise performances by Red Norvo's brilliant 1949–50 trio, which also includes guitarist Tal Farlow and bassist Charles Mingus. These radio transcriptions (which do not duplicate the group's studio recordings) contain melodic but often-speedy versions of standards. The near-telepathic communication among the three brilliant players and the appealing sound of the group make this a recommended disc for lovers of straight-ahead jazz and vibes. —*Scott Yanow*

Improvisations on Keynote / Jul. 27, 1944–Oct. 10, 1944 / Mercury ✦✦✦✦
As nice a cross-section of mid-'40s Norvo cuts as is available. It was culled from the massive Keynote box. —*Ron Wynn*

Time in His Hands / May 28, 1945–Aug. 22, 1945 / Xanadu ✦✦✦✦
Three of vibraphonist Red Norvo's more obscure studio sessions are released in full on this excellent Xanadu LP. A dozen of the selections (taken from two dates) feature Norvo with the great singing bassist Slam Stewart, pianist Johnny Guarnieri (who does a funny Fats Waller vocal imitation on "Honeysuckle Rose"), drummer Morey Feld and either Bill DeArango or Chuck Wayne on guitar. The quintet performances show the influence of bop while remaining advanced swing. The remaining four numbers find Norvo with a conventional rhythm section that welcomes baritonist Harry Carney, Charlie Ventura on tenor and both Johnny Bothwell and Otto Hardwick on altos. A spontaneous session, these Duke Ellington-flavored performances are also enjoyable. —*Scott Yanow*

Fabulous Jam Session / Jun. 6, 1945 / Stash ✦✦✦✦✦
This is a famous recording session that deserves the very complete treatment it receives on this CD from the Stash label. On June 6, 1945, vibraphonist Red Norvo and an all-star swing rhythm section (pianist Teddy Wilson, bassist Slam Stewart and either Specs Powell or J.C. Heard on drums) joined the jump tenor Flip Phillips and the two bop innovators, altoist Charlie Parker and trumpeter Dizzy Gillespie. This mixture of swing and bop stylists recorded four songs ("Hallelujah," "Get Happy," "Slam Slam Blues" and "Congo Blues") and those recordings plus eight alternate takes are included on this exciting album. The performances point out the evolutionary (as opposed to revolutionary) nature of bop from swing, but also its differences. It is fascinating to hear and rewards repeated listenings. —*Scott Yanow*

Norvo / May 29, 1947–Dec. 18, 1947 / Pausa ✦✦✦✦✦
This Pausa LP (which contains recordings originally issued by Capitol) features Red Norvo in several very interesting settings. The first three selections have the vibraphonist with an all-star group that includes altoist Benny Carter, trumpeter Charlie Shavers and his old boss Benny Goodman; the band was dubbed The Hollywood Hucksters. In addition to two straightforward performances, on "Happy Blues" Benny Goodman and Stan Kenton

have hilarious vocals. Norvo also performs with notable players including tenors Jimmy Dorsey and Dexter Gordon (on a very memorable version of "I'll Follow You" and "Bop") and with Benny Carter and tenor Eddie Miller on two other songs. A special event occurs when Norvo switches back to the xylophone (his original instrument) for six selections that utilize oboe, flute, french horns, bass clarinet and bassoon; their version of "Twelfth Street Rag" is unique! Worth searching for. —*Scott Yanow*

★ **Red Norvo Trio with Tal Farlow and Charles Mingus at the Savoy** / May 3, 1950–Apr. 13, 1951 / Savoy ✦✦✦✦✦
Although vibraphonist Red Norvo had been on records for nearly 20 years and had been a pacesetter in both swing and bop, it was when he formed his trio with guitarist Tal Farlow and bassist Charles Mingus in 1950 that he found the perfect setting for his vibes. The interplay between the three masterful musicians on the 25 performances included on this Savoy double-LP (issued by Arista in 1976) is quite memorable with many classic performances. Highlights include "Little White Lies," "Swedish Pastry," "Godchild," "Move" and "Deed I Do," among many others. This two-fer is highly recommended particularly since Savoy has not yet released all of the music on CD. —*Scott Yanow*

The Red Norvo Trios / Sep. 1953–Oct. 1955 / Prestige ✦✦✦✦✦
Although the most famous of Red Norvo's vibes/guitar/bass trios featured guitarist Tal Farlow and bassist Charles Mingus, he continued the appealing format for a few years after his sidemen departed. This CD features Norvo with guitarist Jimmy Raney and bassist Red Mitchell on 15 enjoyable performances from 1953–54 and is rounded off by four songs from 1955 when Farlow rejoined Norvo and Mitchell. —*Scott Yanow*

With Jimmy Raney and Red Mitchel / Mar. 1954 / Original Jazz Classics ✦✦✦✦
This CD reissues an album by the 1954 version of the Red Norvo Trio vibraphonist Red Norvo, guitarist Jimmy Raney and bassist Red Mitchell. Although not quite reaching the heights of the earlier version with Tal Farlow and Charles Mingus, the close interplay between the musicians on cool-toned bop versions of such songs as "Just One of Those Things," "Crazy Rhythm" and "Bernie's Tune" is consistently hard-swinging yet light, adventurous yet accessible. An enjoyable set. —*Scott Yanow*

● **Just a Mood** / Sep. 17, 1954–Jan. 18, 1957 / Bluebird ✦✦✦✦✦
Red Norvo was among the most flexible of improvisers from his generation. On this Bluebird CD, Norvo is heard with three different groups. He interacts with trumpeter Harry "Sweets" Edison, tenor saxophonist Ben Webster and pianist Jimmy Rowles in a swing-oriented sextet; their performances are highlighted by the memorable "Just a Mood." In addition, Norvo plays four songs that have the word "Blue" in their titles with a quintet that is an outgrowth of his trio of a few years earlier (this group consists of flutist Buddy Collette, guitarist Tal Farlow, Monty Budwig or Red Callender on bass and drummer Chico Hamilton) and four "Rose" songs with the who's who of West Coast Jazz: trumpeter Shorty Rogers, clarinetist Jimmy Giuffre, pianist Pete Jolly, Farlow, Callender and drummer Larry Bunker. No matter what the setting, Norvo fits in comfortably, and the quality of the formerly rare music makes this a recommended set to bop collectors. —*Scott Yanow*

Music to Listen to Red Norvo By / Jan. 26, 1957–Mar. 2, 1957 / Contemporary ✦✦✦
Although vibraphonist Red Norvo is the leader of this sextet date, clarinetist Bill Smith (who contributed the 20-minute, four-movement "Divertimento") often sets the tone for the music. His work has classical elements, but the five shorter pieces (by Jack Montrose, Barney Kessel, Lennie Niehaus, Duane Tatro and Norvo) are more jazz-oriented. Norvo's light-toned sextet (which consists of his vibes, flutist Buddy Collette, clarinetist Bill Smith, guitarist Barney Kessel, bassist Red Mitchell and drummer Shelly Manne) was not a regularly working unit, but it sounds well-integrated and tight during the complex but swinging music, which has not yet been reissued on CD. —*Scott Yanow*

Hi Five / Jan. 29, 1957–Feb. 2, 1957 / RCA ✦✦✦
This is one of the most obscure Red Norvo LPs and this quintet (with the leader's vibes, Bob Drasnin on flute, clarinet and alto, guitarist Jimmy Wyble, bassist Bob Carter and drummer Bill Douglass) has long-been forgotten. However, their version of cool jazz (reminiscent of the Chico Hamilton Quintet in atmosphere) always swings and features subtle creativity and fine solos from the lead voices. Maybe someday RCA will get around to reissuing the music and rescuing it from their vaults. —*Scott Yanow*

Norvo . . . Naturally / Mar. 2, 1957 / VSOP ✦✦✦✦
Originally released on the obscure Rave label and later reissued
by VSOP on this LP, this enjoyable set from vibraphonist Red
Norvo features his 1957 quintet: Bob Drasnin on flute and alto,
guitarist Jim Wyble, bassist Buddy Clark and drummer Bill
Douglass. The music is essentially cool-toned bop that swings
hard but lightly; an excellent setting for Norvo's vibes. In addition
to two of Red's originals ("Spiders' Web" and "Scorpion's Nest"),
the band performs six superior (if somewhat overplayed) standards. The results make one wonder why Jimmy Wyble and Bob
Drasnin never became much better known. —*Scott Yanow*

The Forward Look / Dec. 31, 1957 / Reference ✦✦✦✦
The music on this CD, taken from a New Year's Eve concert, had
never been issued prior to the release of this CD by Reference in
1991. With Jerry Dodgion (mostly on alto and flute), guitarist
Jimmy Wyble, bassist Red Wooten and drummer John Markham
being his sidemen, this was a well-integrated group despite the
lack of major names. Norvo's vibe playing was in its prime and
he is in excellent form during a wide-ranging set that ranges from
"My Funny Valentine" and "When You're Smiling" to Quincy
Jones' "For Lena and Lennie" and "How's Your Mother in Law";
the repertoire includes quite a few obscurities. This surprisingly
well-recorded CD is well worth picking up as an example of Red
Norvo's playing in the latter half of the 1950s. —*Scott Yanow*

Windjammer City Style / 1958 / Dot ✦✦
Here is a real historical curiosity. Red Norvo and his group perform nine songs from what was billed as a "history-making film"
but is, in reality, a long-forgotten movie called *Windjammer*. The
ensemble—consisting of Norvo's vibes, Jerry Dodgion on alto and
flute, Marvin Koral switching between alto, flute and clarinet, guitarist Jimmy Wyble, pianist Bernie Nierow, bassist Red Wooten
and drummer Karl Kiffe—uplifts the folkish melodies as best they
can, but fails to make any of them memorable. This LP, therefore,
is of interest only to Red Norvo completists. —*Scott Yanow*

Red Norvo Quintet / 1962 / Studio West ✦✦✦
This CD, taken from radio transcriptions cut for the radio show
titled "The Navy Swings," features vibraphonist Red Norvo's group
in 1962, which by itself is notable for Norvo made no other
recordings as a leader during 1960–68. Red's quintet (which also
includes guitarist Al Viola, pianist Jack Wilson, bassist Jimmy
Bond and drummer Bill Goodwin) plays in the cool-toned but
often-heated style of his earlier trios. Mavis Rivers and Ella Mae
Morse take a total of three vocals, but it is the 11 instrumentals
(counting four alternate takes) that are particularly memorable,
most notably "Spider's Web," "Lena and Lennie" and "Rhee, 0,
Rhee." Easily enjoyable music. —*Scott Yanow*

Swing That Music / Oct. 22, 1969 / Affinity ✦✦✦✦

Vibes à la Red / 1974 1975 / Famous Door ✦✦✦

The Second Time Around / 1975 / Famous Door ✦✦✦✦
After making only one recording as a leader between 1960–73,
vibraphonist Red Norvo cut three albums for Famous Door during 1975–77, launching a bit of a comeback. This LP, his second
Famous Door release, is an excellent effort. The veteran vibraphonist plays seven swing standards plus his own blues "A Long
One for Santa Monica" with pianist Dave McKenna, bassist Milt
Hinton, drummer Mousey Alexander and (on four of the seven
numbers) Kenny Davern on soprano. These small-group swing
performances (which some would call "mainstream") are enjoyable, but because the Famous Door label is obsolete, this LP will
be difficult to find. —*Scott Yanow*

Red in New York / 1977 / Famous Door ✦✦✦✦
Red Norvo's third and final recording as a leader for the short-
lived Famous Door label is most notable for being one of the earliest recordings of tenor saxophonist Scott Hamilton. In addition,
vibraphonist Norvo was happy to once again have the services of
his favorite pianist of the era (Dave McKenna) along with bassist
Richard Davis and drummer Connie Kay. Together they perform
seven swing standards, ranging from "Hindustan" and "All of Me"
to "Undecided." Everyone plays up-to-par and Red Norvo, 46 years
after his recording debut, sounds in his musical prime. This LP
will be hard to find but is worth the search. —*Scott Yanow*

Live at Rick's Cafe Americain / 1978 / Flying Fish ✦✦✦
This jam session was supposed to be led by violinist Joe Venuti, but
his unexpected death led to vibraphonist Red Norvo (in view of his
seniority) becoming the nominal leader. The all-star group (which
also includes Buddy Tate on tenor, trombonist Urbie Green, pianist

Dave McKenna, bassist Steve LaSpina and drummer Barrett
Deems) plays loosely but coherently on lengthy versions of "Green
Dolphin Street," "Undecided" and "Just Friends" in addition to a
more concise "Here's That Rainy Day" and a two-song ballad medley. Nothing all that historic occurs, but there are many fine solos
from the principals during these informal jams. —*Scott Yanow*

Red and Ross / Jan. 1979 / Concord Jazz ✦✦✦✦
Red Norvo, 48 years after his first recording, sounds in fine form on
this live set with pianist Ross Tompkins, bassist John Williams and
drummer Jake Hanna. Tompkins, who takes the opening "Whisper
Not" as his feature, fits in well with the masterful vibist and their
two-chorus duets in the middle of "The One I Love" and "All of Me"
(during which the bass and drums drop out) are the high points of
a spirited and consistently swinging session. —*Scott Yanow*

Just Friends / Aug. 8, 1983–Aug. 9, 1983 / Stash ✦✦✦✦
For what was one of vibraphonist Red Norvo's final recordings
(his recording debut was in 1931, 52 years earlier!), Norvo teams
up quite effectively with guitarist Buck Pizzarelli (an old friend),
pianist Russ Kassoff and bassist Jerry Bruno. The seven standards
plus John Pizzarelli's "Blues for Red" make for a well-rounded
session, balancing ballads such as "My Old Flame" and "I Thought
About You" with stomps including "Just Friends" and "Sweet
Georgia Brown." Although hearing problems and a stroke would
end Red Norvo's career, this record is proof that the great vibraphonist didn't decline before his forced retirement. —*Scott Yanow*

Sam Noto

b. Apr. 17, 1930, Buffalo, NY
Trumpet, Fluegelhorn / Bop
An excellent bop soloist, Sam Noto's late-'70s recordings for Xanadu
briefly gave him a high profile in the U.S. Best-known in his early
days as a big-band player, Noto was with Stan Kenton (1955–58),
Louie Bellson (1959), back with Kenton (1960) and twice with
Count Basie during 1964–67. He spent much of 1969–75 working in
Las Vegas where he became acquainted with Red Rodney. Rodney
used Noto on a 1974 recording, and although he moved to Toronto
in 1975 (where he worked in the studios and with Rob McConnell's
Boss Brass into the early '80s), Noto gained some fame for his
recordings with Xanadu. Although appearing on records less since
then, Sam Noto is active in Toronto. —*Scott Yanow*

● **Entrance!** / Mar. 1975 / Xanadu ✦✦✦✦✦

Act One / Dec. 1, 1975 / Xanadu ✦✦✦

Notes to You / May 18, 1977 / Xanadu ✦✦✦✦

Noto-Riety / Oct. 17, 1978 / Xanadu ✦✦✦✦
The Canadian trumpeter Sam Noto and flutist Sam Most make for
a surprisingly effective blend during this enjoyable straight-ahead
date. Noto contributed all six selections and they cover a variety
of tempos and grooves in the bebop tradition. With a rhythm section of pianist Dolo Coker, bassist Monty Budwig and drummer
Frank Butler, the music is guaranteed to swing. —*Scott Yanow*

2-4-5 / Nov. 2, 1986–Jun. 12, 1987 / Unisson ✦✦✦✦

Adam Nussbaum

b. Nov. 29, 1955, New York, NY
Drums / Post Bop
Both a prolific contributor and fiery drummer, Adam Nussbaum's
one of the most in-demand percussionists active. He's a fiery
soloist and ideal accompanist, able to play with combos, trios, or
large bands, and contribute in hard bop, free, swing, jazz-rock or
even New Age/contemporary instrumental contexts. Nussbaum
studied drumming with Charlie Persip and worked at New York
clubs with Monty Waters, Albert Dailey and Nina Sheldon in the
mid-'70s. He also worked with David Liebman in Washington.
Nussbaum played with John Scofield in the late '70s and early
'80s, performing and recording with him in both America and
Europe. He also did sessions with Hal Galper. Nussbaum and
Scofield played and recorded with Liebman and with Steve
Swallow in the early '80s. He played with the Gil Evans orchestra
through the '80s, touring Europe and Japan in 1985. Nussbaum
also recorded with Bill Evans (saxophonist), Bobby Watson and
Art Farmer in the mid-'80s, and worked with Eddie Gomez and
Gary Burton. Nussbaum's extensive list of late '80s and '90s ses-
sions include dates with Jerry Bergonzini, Mike Brecker, Richie
Bierarch, Joey Calderazzo, Eddie Daniels, Christian Minh Doky,
Marc Ducret, Evans, Lee Konitz, Rick Margitza, Ron McClure,
Mark Murphy, Mike Richmond, and Glenn Wilson. —*Ron Wynn*

O

Jimmy O'Bryant

b. 1896, Arkansas, **d.** Jun. 24, 1928, Chicago, IL
Clarinet / Classic Jazz, Blues
Of all the clarinetists in the 1920s, Jimmy O'Bryant probably came closest to duplicating the sound (if not the genius) of Johnny Dodds. O'Bryant worked with the Tennessee Ten (1920–21), in a group co-led by Jelly Roll Morton and W.C. Handy (1923) and briefly with King Oliver (1924), but he is best remembered for his recordings with Lovie Austin's Blues Serenaders and his own Washboard Band; all of the latter have been reissued on two RST CDs. Jimmy O'Bryant's early death robbed him of any chance of gaining lasting fame, but his fine (if sometimes primitively recorded) performances as a leader give one a good idea as to his abilities. — *Scott Yanow*

Jimmy O'Bryant (Vol. 2) & Vance Dixon (1923–1931) / Oct. 3, 1923–Jun. 12, 1931 / RST ✦✦✦
The second of two Jimmy O'Bryant CDs released by the Austrian RST label features the early and long-obscure clarinetist (who sometimes sounded a bit like Johnny Dodds) on the last nine recordings made by his ironically titled "Famous Original Washboard Band." These trio performances feature O'Bryant, pianist Jimmy Blythe and either Jasper Taylor or W.E. Buddy Burton on washboard; Burton plays effective banjo on "Sugar Babe" and other highlights include "Milenberg Joys," "My Man Rocks Me" and "Shake That Thing." The latter half of this set has recordings by clarinetist and altoist Vance Dixon (who makes O'Bryant seem famous in comparison!) with Deppe's Serenaders in 1923 ("Congaine" also features pianist Earl Hines), in duos and trios from 1926–27, backing blues singer Hattie McDaniels (the future actress) on two numbers in 1929 and leading his own group on four novelties from 1931 (including "Laughing Stomp"). Although not as essential as the more significant 1920s recordings, this CD (along with *Jimmy O'Bryant—Vol. 1*) is certainly worth exploring by fans of the era. — *Scott Yanow*

● **Vol. 1 (1924–1925)** / Nov. 1924–Jul. 1925 / RST ✦✦✦
On the first of two CDs released by the Austrian RST label, clarinetist Jimmy O'Bryant, a long-forgotten, but talented, player who died in 1928, is featured with his ironically titled "Famous Original Washboard Band" (a trio/quartet with pianist Jimmy Blythe, Jasper Taylor on washboard and guest cornetist Bob Shoffner) on 19 selections. In addition, O'Bryant and Blythe accompany singer Sodarisa Miller during two songs and O'Bryant, cornetist Tommy Ladnier and pianist Lovie Austin assist blues singer Julia Davis on two others. O'Bryant, who in his best moments sounds close to the great Johnny Dodds, was not a major soloist although he might have grown into a stronger talent were it not for his premature death. The primitive recording quality of these early performances may put some off, but O'Bryant plays quite well and many of his originals have not been revived and are worth investigating. 1920s jazz fans will want this CD along with the second volume. — *Scott Yanow*

Anita O'Day (Anita Belle Colton)

b. Dec. 18, 1913, Chicago, IL
Vocals / Bop, Swing
One of the finest singers to emerge from the swing era, Anita O'Day at her prime was a masterful scat singer and a true improviser whose interpretations of standards uplifted and altered even the most familiar songs. After struggling through dance marathons and discovering that she could sing, O'Day picked up valuable experience performing with Max Miller's group in Chicago. Her big break was hooking with the Gene Krupa Orchestra. During her two years with the drummer's big band (1941–43), O'Day had hits in "Let Me Off Uptown," "Thanks for the Boogie Ride," and "Bolero at the Savoy." She was with Stan Kenton for a year (1944–45), scoring with "And Her Tears Flowed like Wine." When she decided that Kenton's progressive jazz did not suit her, she recommended June Christy as her successor; Christy, Chris Connor and Helen Merrill would all spend the early parts of their careers trying to emulate O'Day.

After a period back with Krupa (during which she recorded popular versions of "Opus No. 1" and "Boogie Blues"), O'Day went out on her own. She recorded for Signature in 1947 and London in 1950, but did not appear on records on a regular basis on records until she began her association with Verve in 1952. The singer's finest recordings were for Verve during 1952–63, both with big bands and small groups. Very open to the innovations of bebop, O'Day was one of the top singers of the decade, captured at the peak of her powers at the 1958 Newport Jazz Festival in the film *Jazz on a Summer's Day*, during which she performed memorable renditions of "Sweet Georgia Brown" and a scat-filled "Tea for Two." She also appeared briefly in *The Gene Krupa Story*. However, heroin addiction (which she fully outlined in her 1981 memoirs *High Times Hard Times*) took its toll and, after 1963, O'Day's life was quite erratic. In 1970 she made a strong comeback at the Berlin Jazz Festival and by the mid-'70s was recording regularly for her Emily label. O'Day's voice has gradually deteriorated through the years, particularly after the mid-'80s, but her prime recordings from the 1950s are quite enjoyable and rank with the best of the era. — *Scott Yanow*

Hi Ho Trailus Boot Whip / 1947 / Flying Dutchman ✦✦✦
The music on this LP has been circulating on Bob Thiele's various labels for decades. Comprised of the first ten selections recorded by Anita O'Day as a leader, these diverse selections find O'Day (when she was 27) singing in several different settings. Two songs (including the atmospheric "Ace in the Hole") are performed with Alvy West's Little Band (a sextet including an accordion player), while the other eight numbers (highlighted by the eccentric title cut, a multi-tempoed "What Is This Thing Called Love" and "How High the Moon") have the singer joined by larger orchestras arranged by either Sy Oliver or Ralph Burns. Highly enjoyable music. — *Scott Yanow*

Anita O'Day 1949–1950 / Sep. 11, 1949–Dec. 27, 1950 / Tono ✦✦✦
This is an interesting LP for it has 15 formerly rare Anita O'Day recordings from 1949–50, material originally cut for the Gem and London labels (prior to her signing with Verve). O'Day, who was 29 and 30 during this period, handles the wide variety of songs (ranging from bop and dated novelties to a calypso and "Tennessee Waltz") with humor and swing, mostly uplifting the occasionally indifferent material. Most of the musicians in the four backup bands are obscure or not featured, but there are short spots for guitarist George Barnes and trombonist Will Bradley. Although not essential, this LP is a must for Anita O'Day collectors. — *Scott Yanow*

Anita O'Day Swings Cole Porter with Billy May / Jan. 22, 1952–Aug. 17, 1960 / Verve ✦✦✦
Most of this CD reissue is taken from sessions in April 1959 on which Anita O'Day interprets Cole Porter songs while accompa-

nied by some rather rambunctious big-band arrangements from Billy May. While her emotional range is wider than Ella Fitzgerald's (who had previously recorded her much better-known *Cole Porter Songbook*), strangely enough O'Day's voice does not sound as strong on the Billy May set as it does on the six "bonus" cuts, which are Cole Porter songs she recorded on other occasions (from 1952-60). Still, this CD does have its moments with highlights including "I Get a Kick out of You," "All of You," "It's Delovely," "You're the Top" and two versions of "Love for Sale." —*Scott Yanow*

An Evening with Anita O'Day / Apr. 15, 1954–Aug. 11, 1955 / Verve ✦✦✦✦

● **Anita** / Dec. 6, 1955–Dec. 8, 1955 / Verve ✦✦✦✦✦
This CD is a straight reissue of the original LP with singer Anita O'Day heard in prime form. Accompanied by an orchestra conducted and arranged by Buddy Bregman, O'Day is heard near the peak of her powers on such songs as "You're the Top," "Honeysuckle Rose," an emotional rendition of "A Nightingale Sang in Berkeley Square" and "As Long as I Live." One of her better recordings, this CD is recommended. —*Scott Yanow*

Pick Yourself up with Anita O'Day / Dec. 15, 1956+Dec. 17, 1956 / Verve ✦✦✦✦✦
For this well-rounded CD reissue that adds nine cuts to the original program, Anita O'Day, in her prime period, is mostly heard accompanied by Buddy Bregman's Orchestra, but there are also a few tracks on which she is joined by a jazz combo featuring trumpeter Harry "Sweets" Edison. Highlights include "Don't Be That Way," "Stompin' at the Savoy," "Pick Yourself Up," "Sweet Georgia Brown" and "I Won't Dance." Virtually all of Anita O'Day's 1950s recordings are recommended, for her drug use had not yet affected her voice and her creativity was generally at its height. —*Scott Yanow*

★ **Anita Sings the Most** / Jan. 31, 1957 / Verve ✦✦✦✦✦
Anita O'Day recorded many rewarding albums in the 1950s when her voice was at its strongest, and this collaboration with the Oscar Peterson Quartet (comprised of pianist Peterson, guitarist Herb Ellis, bassist Ray Brown and drummer John Poole) may very well be her best. Not only is the backup swinging, giving a *Jazz at the Philharmonic* feel to some of the songs, but O'Day proves that she could keep up with Peterson. "Them There Eyes" is taken successfully at a ridiculously fast tempo, yet the singer displays a great deal of warmth on such ballads as "We'll Be Together Again" and "Bewitched, Bothered and Bewildered." While Peterson and Ellis have some solos, O'Day is never overshadowed (which is saying a lot!) and is clearly inspired by their presence. The very brief playing time (just 33 minutes) is unfortunate on this straight CD reissue of the original LP, but the high quality definitely makes up for the lack of quantity. A gem. —*Scott Yanow*

Anita O'Day Sings the Winners / Sep. 1958 / Verve ✦✦✦✦✦
For this CD, which is greatly expanded from the original LP, Anita O'Day sings standards associated with other musicians, including "Four" (Miles Davis), "Early Autumn" (Stan Getz), "Four Brothers" (Woody Herman), "Sing, Sing, Sing" (Benny Goodman and Gene Krupa) and "Peanut Vendor" (Stan Kenton). Some of the material is unusual for a singer to interpret, but O'Day, one of the top jazz vocalists of the decade, improvises when the lyrics are not that strong (or barely exist!). The backup by the Russ Garcia Orchestra is not all that memorable, but the focus is entirely on the vocalist, and O'Day really comes through. —*Scott Yanow*

Cool Heat / Apr. 6, 1959–Apr. 8, 1959 / Verve ✦✦✦✦✦
This LP, which ought to be reissued on CD, finds Anita O'Day's swinging singing backed by cool-toned arrangements from Jimmy Giuffre. Although the orchestra is surprisingly anonymous, the ensembles fit O'Day's voice well on tunes such as "Mack the Knife," "Gone with the Wind," "Come Rain or Come Shine," "The Way You Look Tonight" and even "Hooray for Hollywood." All of O'Day's recordings in the 1950s are recommended, and this out-of-print set is no exception. —*Scott Yanow*

Once upon a Summertime / Jun. 1963–Mar. 19, 1976 / Glendale ✦✦✦
This LP is definitely a transitional one for Anita O'Day. Four of the dozen performances are taken from June 1963. Her trio joins the singer on four of her "hits" ("Sweet Georgia Brown," "Boogie Blues," "Tea for Two" and "A Nightingale Sang in Berkeley Square"), which were O'Day's final recordings until 1970 due to personal problems. The remainder of this set is from 1975-76, with several trios backing O'Day on a repertoire dominated by swing standards. Although her voice was not as young, O'Day was

still in good form at that point, making this album a worthwhile acquisition for her fans. —*Scott Yanow*

Recorded Live at the Berlin Jazz Festival / Nov. 7, 1970 / MPS ✦✦✦
Singer Anita O'Day's first recording in seven years finds her still possessing a decent voice at 50 and the ability to swing and improvise creatively. Backed by pianist George Arvanitas, bassist Jacky Samson and drummer Charles Saudrais, O'Day is at her best on "Honeysuckle Rose," a medley of "Yesterday" and "Yesterdays," and "Street of Dreams," although some of the more recent material (her own "Soon It's Gonna Rain" and "Sunny") is of lesser interest. —*Scott Yanow*

I Get a Kick Out of You / Apr. 25, 1975 / Evidence ✦✦✦✦
At 55 Anita O'Day was having a bit of a renaissance, having kicked drugs and become more active in the 1970s. This live in Japan set (reissued on CD by Evidence) finds the singer stretching out on nine numbers ("Gone with the Wind" is nearly 11 minutes long) and carefully choosing a tune or two from each of six decades (1920s to the '70s). Of the latter "What Are You Doing the Rest of Your Life" and Leon Russell's "A Song for You" (given a definitive treatment) are effective; other highlights include "Undecided," "I Get a Kick out of You" and "Opus One." This is one of O'Day's best recordings of the 1970s. —*Scott Yanow*

Anita O'Day Live / Sep. 1976 / Star Line ✦✦✦✦✦
Anita O'Day is heard in excellent form on this 1976 concert, released for the first time in 1993. Highlights of this CD include a version of "Tea for Two" that finds O'Day trading one-bar phrases with three of her sidemen, a touching rendition of "A Nightingale Sang in Berkeley Square," a jubilant rendering of "Honeysuckle Rose" and versions of "A Song for You" and "You Are the Sunshine of My Life" that actually top the original recordings. In addition, the late tenor Fraser MacPherson proves to be a perfect foil for O'Day's chancetaking vocal flights. With the exception of pianist Al Wold having trouble with the rapid tempo of "S' Wonderful," the rhythm section also plays quite well. This is one of the best Anita O'Day CDs available. —*Scott Yanow*

Mello Day / 1978 / GNP Crescendo ✦✦✦
For this studio set, Anita O'Day performs with the Lou Levy trio and guests Ernie Watts on reeds, percussionist Paulinho Da Costa and either Laurindo Almeida or Joe Diorio on guitar. She mostly sticks to fresher material, some of it of more recent vintage than usual. High points include "Lost in the Stars," "You're My Everything," "Them There Eyes," "Limehouse Blues" and several bossa nova pieces. This LP, although not essential, is worth picking up. —*Scott Yanow*

Anita O'Day, Live at the City / Sep. 29, 1979–Sep. 30, 1979 / Emily ✦✦
This LP documents a typical live performance by Anita O'Day, who was 59 at the time. Although there is some good music (her renditions of Johnny Mandel's "Hershey Bar," "Emily" and "Four Brothers"), there is also a lot of loose chit-chat and filler. Although Nat Hentoff raves about O'Day's performance, this hard-to-find LP, which also features pianist Norman Simmons, bassist Rob Fisher, drummer John Poole and Greg Smith on baritone and flute, is a historical curiosity rather than an essential acquisition. —*Scott Yanow*

In a Mellow Tone / Mar. 13, 1989–Mar. 15, 1989 / DRG ✦✦✦
Anita O'Day's voice was slipping by the time this studio album was made; she was already 69. However, the backup group, with Gordon Brisker on tenor and flute, harpist Corky Hale, pianist Pete Jolly, bassist Brian Bromberg and drummer Frank Capp, is strong, the material (11 veteran standards, plus "Anita's Blues") is excellent, and O'Day's swinging style compensates for her declining voice. This may very well be her last good recording. —*Scott Yanow*

At Vine St.: Live / Aug. 2, 1991–Aug. 3, 1991 / DRG ✦✦
At age 71, Anita O'Day was way past her prime when she performed this live date at the now-defunct Vine St. club. The songs had all been recorded earlier by O'Day in versions more rewarding than these, although she tries her best. Gordon Brisker on tenor and flute leads the backing quintet, which also includes pianist Pete Jolly and does what it can to hold O'Day up. At least she didn't feel compelled to record "Let Me Off Uptown" this late in her career. —*Scott Yanow*

Rules of the Road / 1993 / Pablo ✦
This CD should not have been released. Anita O'Day, at age 73, had no voice left. Although the backup group (a big band led by Jack Sheldon) is excellent and the arrangements by Buddy Bregman (with the exception of a corny interpretation of

"Shaking the Blues Away") are fine, but the ambitious program is sunk by O'Day's wavering voice, which is out of tune more often than not. Jack Sheldon's trumpet solos (and participation in a vocal with O'Day on "I Told Ya I Love Ya, Now Get Out") are the only highlights of this unfortunate effort. —*Scott Yanow*

Chico O'Farrill (Arturo O'Farrill)
b. Oct. 28, 1921, Havana, Cuba
Arranger / Bop, Latin Jazz
A pivotal composer, arranger and trumpeter who was highly visible during the Afro-Latin and Latin jazz revolution of the '40s and '50s as a writer and bandleader. Chico O'Farrill's compositions were recorded by Benny Goodman, Stan Kenton, Machito and Dizzy Gillespie. They include "Undercurrent Blues" and "Shishka-Bop" for Goodman and "Cuban Suite" for Kenton. He provided other arrangements of "Cuban Suite" for Machito and various bands. O'Farrill studied composition in Havana and played with Armando Romeu's band as well as his own group in the '40s. He moved to New York in 1948, and began writing compositions for Goodman, Kenton, Machito, Gillespie and Charlie Parker. O'Farrill formed his own band in 1950, appearing at Birdland and recording for Clef. He moved to Mexico City at the end of the '50s, and perfomed concerts there in the early '60s. O'Farrill returned to New York in the mid-'60s, and worked as an arranger and music director on the CBS show "Festival of the Lively Arts." Gillespie, Count Basie, Gerry Mulligan and Stan Getz were some of the musicians who participated in the program. He wrote arrangements of pop tunes for Basie in the mid-'60s, and composed songs for Gato Barbieri, Kenton and a band co-led by Gillespie and Machito in the '70s. O'Farrill tunes were included on a Candido LP in the '70s, as well as a Frank Wess date. He also had a symphony premiered in Mexico City in 1972. O'Farrill's own albums are scarce, but include sessions for Verve and Impulse, as well as Clef. O'Farrill was profiled in Ira Gitler's *From Swing To Bop* book in the mid-'80s. —*Ron Wynn and Michael G. Nastos*

Nine Flags / Nov. 10, 1966–Nov. 14, 1966 / Impulse! ✦✦✦
● **Pure Emotion** / Feb. 1995 / Milestone ✦✦✦✦

Tiger Okoshi (Toru Okoshi)
b. Mar. 21, 1950, Ashita, Japan
Trumpet / Fusion, Hard Bop
Tiger Okoshi is a versatile trumpeter who has played both fusion and fairly straight-ahead jazz. A resident of the U.S. since 1972, Okoshi first gained attention playing with Gary Burton; he also had a stint with George Russell's Living Time Orchestra in the early '90s and recorded with Bob Moses. Okoshi has recorded regularly as a leader for JVC including an unusual Louis Armstrong tribute album, *Echoes of a Note*, on which he drastically modernized some Dixieland standards. —*Scott Yanow*

Tiger's Baku / 1981 / JVC ✦✦✦✦
Face to Face / 1989 / JVC ✦✦✦

That Was Then, This Is Now / Aug. 1990 / JVC ✦✦✦
Fusion, funk, some mainstream, and light bop are the ingredients for this recent release by Japanese trumpeter Tiger Okoshi. He plays in a high-note, piercing style similar to Terusuma Hino, but lacks his harmonic command. The arrangements, production, and mastering are fine, as would be expected. —*Ron Wynn*

Echoes of a Note (A Tribute to Louis "Pops" Armstrong) / Mar. 1993 / JVC ✦✦✦
● **Two Sides To Every Story** / Jun. 21, 1994–Jun. 22, 1994 / JVC ✦✦✦✦✦
This set is a rare straight-ahead outing for trumpeter Tiger Okoshi. Some of the Post Bop music is reminscent of the mid-'60s Miles Davis Quintet although Okoshi (who does hint at Davis here and there) is also influenced by Kenny Dorham and Freddie Hubbard. The rhythm section of pianist Gil Goldstein, bassist Dave Holland and drummer Jack DeJohnette is quite strong (swinging but advanced) and guitarist Mike Stern is more restrained than usual. The group blends together well and Okoshi (on two standards and a variety of originals) is in excellent form. —*Scott Yanow*

Old and New Dreams
Group / Post Bop, Free Jazz
Though they didn't make many records, the quartet of Old And New Dreams was one of the late '80s finest. The lineup included trumpeter Don Cherry, tenor saxophonist Dewey Redman, bassist Charlie Haden and drummer Edward Blackwell. They were veterans of Ornette Coleman bands, and united to celebrate his music.

Music Map

Oboe

Rare Instances of the Oboe in a Jazz Setting
Don Redman
(Early 1920s, Fletcher Henderson Orchestra)
Mitch Miller
(1949, Charlie Parker recording of "Just Friends")

1950s
Bob Cooper (first jazz soloist)

First Jazz Virtuoso
Yusef Lateef

Avant-Garde
Ken McIntyre
Marshall Allen (with Sun Ra)

Other Oboeists
Andrew White
(1971, on Weather Report's "I Sing The Body Electric")
Paul McCandless (with Oregon)

They made their first album for ECM in 1978, a self-titled release. They followed it with another wonderful ECM session *Playing*, in 1980. The group reunited for a third album for Black Saint, *One For Blackwell*, in 1987, seven years later. The first two albums were superbly produced and engineered, with ECM's customary high-quality sound making their interactions and solos even more resplendent. As with Coleman's groups, this was a co-operative venture. Redman soloed on both tenor and musette, while Cherry played more conventional trumpet and didn't have any intonation problems on either album. The quartet regrouped in 1987 at a Blackwell festival in Atlanta. Though not in the best of health, Blackwell provided fiery rhythmic support, mixing New Orleans marching band beats with African talking drum rhythms and multiple accents and textures. Cherry and Redman were excellent again, as was Haden. Why this band only recorded three albums is anyone's guess, but they joined The Mingus Dynasty, Sphere and Dameronia as bands that weren't simply repertory units, but evolving groups using a great composer's material as a starting point for their own peerless interpretations. —*Ron Wynn*

● **Old and New Dreams** / Oct. 1976 / ECM ✦✦✦✦✦
A wonderful album that qualifies as an Ornette Coleman repertory release. Trumpeter Don Cherry, tenor saxophonist Dewey Redman, bassist Charlie Haden, and drummer Ed Blackwell all played with Coleman extensively, and they take his compositions and brilliantly put their own twists on them. —*Ron Wynn*

Old and New Dreams / Aug. 1979 / ECM ✦✦✦✦✦
Playing / Jun. 1980 / ECM ✦✦✦
One for Blackwell / Nov. 7, 1987 / Black Saint ✦✦✦✦

King Oliver (Joe Oliver)
b. May 11, 1885, New Orleans, LA, **d.** Apr. 8, 1938, Savannah, GA
Cornet / Classic New Orleans Jazz
Joe "King" Oliver was one of the great New Orleans legends, an

early giant whose legacy is only partly on records. In 1923 he led one of the classic New Orleans jazz bands, the last significant group to emphasize collective improvisation over solos, but ironically his second cornetist (Louis Armstrong) would soon permanently change jazz. And while Armstrong never tired of praising his idol, he actually sounded very little like Oliver; the King's influence was more deeply felt by Muggsy Spanier and Tommy Ladnier.

Although originally a trombonist, by 1905 Oliver was playing cornet regularly with various New Orleans bands. Gradually he rose to the top of the crowded local scene and, in 1917, he was being billed "King" by bandleader Kid Ory. A master of mutes, Oliver was able to get a wide variety of sounds out of his horn; Bubber Miley would later on be inspired by Oliver's expertise. In 1919 Oliver left New Orleans to join Bill Johnson's band at the Dreamland Ballroom in Chicago. By 1920 he was a leader himself and, after an unsuccessful year in California, King Oliver started playing regularly with his Creole Jazz Band at the Lincoln Gardens in Chicago. He soon sent for his protégé Louis Armstrong and with clarinetist Johnny Dodds, trombonist Honore Dutrey, pianist Lil Harden and drummer Baby Dodds as a core, Oliver had a remarkable band whose brilliance was only hinted at on records. As it is, the group's 1923 sessions far exceeded any jazz previously recorded; Oliver's three chorus solo on "Dippermouth Blues" has since been memorized by virtually every Dixieland trumpeter.

Unfortunately, the Creole Jazz Band gradually broke up in 1924. Oliver recorded a pair of duets with pianist Jelly Roll Morton, but otherwise was off records that year. He took over Dave Peyton's band in 1925 and renamed it the Dixie Syncopators; Barney Bigard and Albert Nicholas were among the members. New recordings resulted (including "Snag It," which has a famous eight-bar passage by Oliver) but when the cornetist moved to New York in 1927, his music was behind the times and he made some bad business decisions (including turning down a chance to play regularly at the Cotton Club). Worse yet, his dental problems (caused partly by an early liking of sugar sandwiches) made playing cornet increasingly painful and, on many of his later recordings, Oliver is barely present (although he did a heroic job on 1929's "Too Late"). Pianist Luis Russell took over the Dixie Syncopators in 1929 and, although Oliver's last recordings (from 1931) are superior examples of hot dance music, he was quickly becoming a forgotten name. Unsuccessful tours in the South eventually left Oliver stranded there, working as a janitor in a poolroom before his death at age 52. — *Scott Yanow*

★ **Louis Armstrong/King Oliver** / Apr. 6, 1923–Dec. 22, 1924 / Milestone ✦✦✦✦✦
Classic renditions (1923–24) of "Snake Rag," "Dippermouth Blues," and "Canal Street Blues" come from the hottest band of its day—Oliver's Creole Jazz Band. — *Bruce Raeburn*

★ **Okeh Sessions** / Jun. 22, 1923–Oct. 26, 1923 / EMI ✦✦✦✦✦
This LP contains performances by the pacesetting group of 1923, King Oliver's Creole Jazz Band, that do not duplicate The Gennetts reissued by Milestone. The band introduced the cornets of King Oliver and Louis Armstrong, clarinetist Johnny Dodds and drummer Baby Dodds to records and was the most influential New Orleans jazz group of its era. The highly enjoyable LP features particularly memorable versions of "Snake Rag," "Sobbin' Blues," "Dippermouth Blues," "Jazzin' Babies Blues" and "Buddy's Habits." This particular set may be hard to find, but these recordings belong in every jazz library in one form or another. — *Scott Yanow*

Sugar Foot Stomp / Mar. 11, 1926–Jun. 11, 1928 / GRP ✦✦✦✦✦
This Decca reissue CD put out by GRP is a fine sampler of King Oliver's 1926–28 recordings with his Dixie Syncopators. The hot jazz dance music is highlighted by several classics ("Too Bad," "Snag It," Jackass Blues," "Sobbin' Blues," "Farewell Blues" and two versions of "Snag It"). With such sidemen as trombonist Kid Ory, clarinetists Albert Nicholas and Omer Simeon and Barney Bigard on tenor and clarinet, Oliver's suppporting cast is quite strong. The cornetist was himself starting to fade during this period, but do take a few heated solos and his break on "Snag It" remains quite famous. True King Oliver collectors, though, will want to bypass this one and instead acquire the entries in one of the more comprehensive European complete series. — *Scott Yanow*

King Oliver (1926–1928) / Mar. 1926–Jun. 1928 / Classics ✦✦✦✦✦

King Oliver (1928–1930) / Jun. 1928–Mar. 1930 / Classics ✦✦✦✦✦

★ **King Oliver** / Jan. 16, 1929–Sep. 19, 1930 / RCA ✦✦✦✦✦
This double-CD set (part of the French RCA *Jazz Tribune* series) includes all of King Oliver's Victor recordings of 1929–30 except for a few alternate takes. The 32 selections are better than one might expect considering that Oliver's playing abilities were rapidly fading (due to serious gum problems). The cornetist in fact takes a few memorable solos, particularly on "Too Late" and "Struggle Buggy." But it is the high musicianship of his sidemen, which include trumpeters Dave Nelson, Red Allen and Bubber Miley (who is outstanding on "St. James Infirmary"), trombonists J.C. Higginbottham and Jimmy Archey, clarinetist Omer Simeon, altoist Charlie Holmes and, filling in for Oliver, cornetists Louis Metcalf and Punch Miller, that makes this set so enjoyable. — *Scott Yanow*

New York Sessions (1929–1930) / Oct. 8, 1929–Sep. 19, 1930 / Bluebird ✦✦✦✦✦
Rather than reissue all of the Victor recordings released under King Oliver's name, this CD has the 22 recordings that best show off the cornetist's playing during his final period on records, including several alternate takes. Oliver was plagued with dental problems by 1928 but is in generally good form on these late recordings, taking a dramatic solo on "Too Late" and sounding surprisingly strong on "Struggle Buggy." Otherwise the music would still be well worth getting for Oliver's sidemen alone since together they form a high-quality dance band. This CD is recommended to all 1920s collectors except King Oliver completists, and even they might be forced to acquire this due to the inclusion of a few very rare alterante takes including the previously unreleased first take of "Olga." — *Scott Yanow*

King Oliver (1930–1931) / Apr. 19, 1930–Apr. 1931 / Classics ✦✦✦✦✦

Sy Oliver (Melvin James Oliver)

b. Dec. 17, 1910, Battle Creek, MI, **d.** May 28, 1988, NYC
Arranger, Trumpet, Vocals / Swing
Sy Oliver's melodic yet sophisticated arrangements helped define the Jimmy Lunceford sound in the 1930s and modernized Tommy Dorsey's band in the '40s. A fine trumpeter (excellent with a mute) and a likable vocalist, Oliver made his recording debut with Zack Whyte's Chocolate Beau Brummels in the late '20s and also worked with Alphonse Trent. Joining Lunceford in 1933, Oliver was responsible for such memorable charts as "My Blue Heaven," "Ain't She Sweet," "Organ Grinder's Swing," and "'Tain't What You Do" among many. It was a major blow to Lunceford when Oliver jumped at the chance to make a lot more money arranging and occasionally singing for Tommy Dorsey. The hiring of Sy Oliver was a major help for TD in getting Buddy Rich to join his band. Oliver's arrangement of "On the Sunny Side of the Street" was his biggest hit for Dorsey. After a brief attempt at leading his own orchestra in 1946, Oliver became a freelance arranger and producer for the remainder of his long career. As late as 1975–80 he was regularly leading a band, but Sy Oliver will always be bestknown for his classic Lunceford charts. — *Scott Yanow*

Oliver's Twist & Easy Walker / Jul. 7, 1960+Oct. 18, 1962 / Mobile Fidelity ✦✦✦✦
During the 1950s and '60s, arranger Sy Oliver's groups reflected its leader's loyalty to the swing era and lack of interest in newer jazz styles. This audiophile CD from Mobile Fidelity reissues two rare Oliver albums that were originally recorded as radio transcriptions. The 24 concise performances range from folk melodies such as "Oh, Them Golden Slippers," "I'm a Little Teapot" and "Arkansas Traveler" to swing compositions. Trumpeter Charlie Shavers is the star of the earlier set while the tenor of Budd Johnson takes honors on the second session. Overall the music is a bit lightweight but enjoyable enough. — *Scott Yanow*

Junko Onishi

b. 1967, Kyoto, Japan
Piano / Post Bop
With the release of her 1994 Blue Note debut *Cruisin',* pianist

Junko Onishi has arrived as one of the most promising of Japan-born jazz musicians. Growing up in Tokyo, Onishi received classical piano lessons but became quite interested in jazz. She studied at Berklee and, after three years, she moved to New York. Already a well-developed player, Onishi worked with Joe Henderson, Betty Carter, Kenny Garrett and Mingus Dynasty before recording her debut as a leader. She considers her style to be based on Duke Ellington, Thelonious Monk and Ornette Coleman. — *Scott Yanow*

Cruisin' / Apr. 21, 1993–Apr. 22, 1993 / Blue Note ✦✦✦✦
On her debut, pianist Junko Onishi (who is accompanied by bassist Rodney Whitaker and drummer Billy Higgins) shows a great deal of creativity. She builds up her "Eulogia" gradually and colorfully with impressive use of the piano's lower register. When she tackles Ornette Coleman's "Congeniality," Onishi manages to be both free and melodic and the pianist also comes up with something fresh to say on "Caravan." In general her tricky frameworks, self-restraint, use of space and careful attention to dynamics and pacing are impressive and show quite a bit of maturity. — *Scott Yanow*

★ **Live At The Village Vanguard** / May 6, 1994–May 8, 1994 / Blue Note ✦✦✦✦✦
This is a memorable set. When pianist Junko Onishi performs songs from the likes of Charles Mingus ("So Long Eric"), John Lewis ("Concorde") and Ornette Coleman ("Congeniality"), she interprets each of the tunes as much as possible within the intent and style of its composer. "So Long Eric," although performed by her trio, gives one the impression at times that several horns are soloing together; in addition polyrhythms are utilized part of the time, Ornette's "Congeniality" has a strong bop feel but fairly free improvising while "Concorde" sounds both distinguished and full of blues feeling, like John Lewis himself. Onishi's exploration of "Blue Skies" uplifts the warhorse through the use of colorful vamps and an altered melody, she takes the slow ballad "Darn That Dream" as a medium-tempo stomp and her original "How Long Has This Been Goin' On" is brooding but not downbeat and swings hard without losing its serious nature. There is not a weak selection in the bunch and the interplay between Onishi, bassist Reginald Veal and drummer Herlin Riley is quite impressive. — *Scott Yanow*

Oregon

Group / New Age, Post Bop
Oregon emerged in 1970 as a splinter band from The Paul Winter Consort. Its members each had experience in jazz, classical and a variety of nonwestern musical styles, and were also multi-instrumentalists. Ralph Towner played standard acoustic and 12-string guitar, piano, a variety of electric keyboards, trumpet and fluegelhorn. Paul McCandless' instrumental arsenal included oboe, English horn, soprano sax, bass clarinet, the musette and tin flute. Collin Walcott handled most of the percussion duties on tabla and various African and Latin rhythm instruments plus sitar, dulcimer, clarinet and violin. Glen Moore was the bassist, and also played clarinet, viola, piano and flute. They suffered some snide comments labelling them the "Modern Jazz Quartet of the '70s" or "a white, European imitation of the Art Ensemble of Chicago." In truth, they were an excellent ensemble playing a hybrid style that wasn't exactly jazz, certainly wasn't rock, but liberally quoted and borrowed from free jazz, Asian, African, European and pop music sources. They began on Vanguard, later moved to ECM, and also issued albums on Elektra and Portrait/Columbia.Collin Walcott's death in a car accident in 1984 was a major blow, but he was eventually successfully replaced by percussionist Trilok Gurtu. Oregon has worked at times with some guest players (including Zbigniew Seifert, Nancy King and Elvin Jones). Their Elektra albums have been reissued on Discover CDs while many of their Vanguard and ECM albums have also been reissued on CD. In recent times (due to conflicting schedules) Oregon has been touring as a trio without Gurtu. — *Ron Wynn*

Our First Record / 1970 / Vanguard ✦✦✦✦✦
The acoustic band Oregon shocked and surprised the jazz world when they debuted in 1970. They blended many influences and styles easily, but also had an ambitious improvisational bent that made them tough to characterize. This, in many ways, remains their most intriguing release. — *Ron Wynn*

Music of Another Present Era / 1972 / Vanguard ✦✦✦✦✦
A 1989 reissue of an outstanding release that blows most similar ECM albums out of the water. — *Ron Wynn*

Distant Hills / Jul. 2–5, 1973 / Vanguard ✦✦✦✦✦
This is one of the first releases to click from this group that knows how to make soothing, acoustic fare without becoming boring or wimpy. — *Ron Wynn*

Winter Light / Jul. 16, 1974–Aug. 7, 1974 / Vanguard ✦✦✦✦✦
Here are some simply brilliant, feathery compositions. Marvelous playing. — *Ron Wynn*

In Concert / Apr. 8–09, 1975 / Vanguard ✦✦✦✦

Together / Jan. 1976 / Vanguard ✦✦✦✦

Violin / 1977 / Vanguard ✦✦✦✦✦
Fine late '70s material from the acoustic band Oregon. Despite the title, it's not violin-dominated material, but their standard blend of Asian, European, African, and American elements and influences. — *Ron Wynn*

Out of the Woods / Apr. 1978 / Discovery ✦✦✦✦

Moon and Mind / 1978 / Vanguard ✦✦✦✦

★ **Roots in the Sky** / Apr. 1979 / Discovery ✦✦✦✦✦
A '92 CD reissue of their '79 album, among their only releases ever issued by a major label. It was characteristically free-wheeling and eclectic, with long stretches of classical, Asian, African, and jazz coming together, and the group mixing structured ensemble work with surging free solos. — *Ron Wynn*

In Performance / Nov. 29–30, 1979 / Elektra ✦✦✦✦

Oregon / Feb. 1983 / ECM ✦✦✦✦✦
This is among the more memorable ECM releases, and one of their best from an ensemble-playing standpoint. — *Ron Wynn*

Crossing / Oct. 1984 / ECM ✦✦✦
Ethereal playing with tremendous solos from Ralph Towner (on guitar and piano) and Paul McCandless (oboe/sax). — *Ron Wynn*

Ecotopia / Mar. 1987 / ECM ✦✦✦
New percussionist Trilok Gurtu makes an impact within the group. — *Ron Wynn*

45th Parallel / 1988 / Portrait ✦✦✦
Pastiche of the group's winning acoustic/chamber and music/new age jazz formula. — *Ron Wynn*

Always, Never and Forever / 1992 / Intuition ✦✦✦✦

Original Dixieland Jazz Band

Group / Classic Jazz
The first jazz group to ever record, the Original Dixieland Jazz Band in 1917 made history. They were not the first group to ever play jazz (Buddy Bolden had preceded them by 22 years!), nor was this white quintet necessarily the best band of the time, but during 1917–23 (particularly in their earliest years) they did a great deal to popularize jazz. The musicians learned about jazz from their fellow New Orleans players (including King Oliver) but happened to get their big break first. In 1916 drummer Johay Stein, cornetist Nick LaRocca, trombonist Eddie Edwards, pianist Henry Ragas and clarinetist Alcide "Yellow" Nunez played together in Chicago. With Tony Sbarbaro replacing Stein and Larry Shields taking over for Nunez, the band was booked at Resenweber's restaurant in New York in early 1917. Their exuberant music (which stuck exclusively to ensembles with the only solos being short breaks) caused a major sensation. Columbia recorded the ODJB playing "Darktown Strutters Ball" and "Indiana" but was afraid to put out the records. Victor stepped in and recorded the group playing the novelty "Livery Stable Blues" (which found the horns imitating barnyard animals) and the "Dixie Jass Band One Step" and quickly released the music; "Livery Stable Blues" was a huge hit that really launched the jazz age. During the next few years, the ODJB would introduce such future standards as "Tiger Rag," "At the Jazz Band Ball," "Fidgety Feet," "Sensation," "Clarinet Marmalade," "Margie," "Jazz Me Blues" and "Royal Garden Blues." The group (with J. Russel Robinson taking the place of Ragas who died in the 1919 flu epidemic and trombonist Emile Christian filling in for Edwards) visited London during 1919–20 and they once again caused quite a stir, introducing jazz to Europe. However, upon their return to the U.S., the ODJB was bit out of fashion after the rise of Paul Whiteman and, in 1922, the New Orleans Rhythm Kings (a far superior group). By 1923 when many of the first black jazz giants finally were recorded, the ODJB

was thought of as a historical band and due to internal dissension they soon broke up. In 1936, LaRocca, Shields, Edwards, Robinson and Sbarbaro (the latter the only musician to have a full-time career by then) had a reunion and did a few final recordings together before LaRocca permanently retired. Although the cornetist's arrogant claims that the ODJB had invented jazz are exaggerated and tinged with racism, the Original Dixieland Jazz Band did make a strong contribution to early jazz (most groups that recorded during 1918-21 emulated their style), helped supply the repertoire of many later Dixieland bands and were an influence on Bix Beiderbecke and Red Nichols. — *Scott Yanow*

Sensation! / Feb. 26, 1917–Nov. 24, 1920 / ASV/Living Era ✦✦✦✦
This set reissues 18 of The Original Dixieland Jazz Band's recordings. A cross-section of their output (rather than a complete set), the release starts off with their hit version of "Livery Stable Blues," includes such classics as "Tiger Rag" and "Sensation," reissues some of the superior performances that were cut in London during 1919-1920 including "I've Lost My Heart in Dixieland," and concludes with "Margie." It's a fine introduction to this pioneering jazz band. — *Scott Yanow*

★ **75th Anniversary** / Feb. 26, 1917–Jun. 7, 1921 / Bluebird ✦✦✦✦✦
The Original Dixieland Jazz Band was the first jazz group to record. Although their two earliest titles for Columbia ("Darktown Strutters Ball" and "Indiana") has not been reissued in a long time. All of The ODJB's output for Victor (including "Livery Stable Blues," which was the first jazz recording to ever be released) is on this definitive CD. This colorful group, which stuck exclusively to ensembles with no solos, introduced such standard tunes as "Original Dixieland One Step," "At the Jazz Band," "Fidgety Feet," "Sensation," "Clarinet Marmalade," "Margie," "Jazz Me Blues," "Royal Garden Blues" and "Tiger Rag," all of which are included on this release. It's an essential acquisition for any serious jazz library. — *Scott Yanow*

The Complete Original Dixieland Jazz Band / Feb. 26, 1917–Sep. 25, 1936 / RCA ✦✦✦✦✦
This double CD has all of the Victor recordings of the first jazz group to record, The Original Dixieland Jazz Band. The five-piece New Orleans band, which essentially stuck exclusively to ensembles, set the standard for 1917-21 jazz. Their "Livery Stable Blues" (which found the horns imitating barnyard animals) was a big hit and The ODJB introduced such future Dixieland standards as "Original Dixieland One-Step," "At the Jazz Band Ball," "Fidgety Feet," "Sensation," "Clarinet Marmalade," "Jazz Me Blues," "Royal Garden Blues" and "Tiger Rag." The 23 numbers from 1917-21, which are rounded out by the humorous "Bow Wow Blues (My Mama Treats Me like a Dog)," were reissued in a single CD by Bluebird, but this two-fer also has The ODJB's "comeback" recordings of 1936; six titles by the original five plus eight very rare titles, that find The ODJB forming the nucleus of a musical if not too distinctive big band. Important historical music. — *Scott Yanow*

Original Dixieland Jazz Band / **Louisiana Five** / Aug. 17, 1917–Mar. 1919 / Retrieval ✦✦✦
This English LP has the seven selections that The Original Dixieland Jazz Band cut for Aeolian in 1917 (which do not duplicate their recordings during the same period for Victor) and the first eight sides by The Louisiana Five from 1918-19. The ODJB titles are excellent, particularly these versions of "Barnyard Blues" (a remake of "Livery Stable Blues"), "Tiger Rag" and "Look at 'Em Doing It Now." However, The Louisiana Five, a trumpetless quintet featuring clarinetist Alcide "Yellow" Nunez and trombonist Charles Panelli, is not at the same level and is quite primitive even for the period. The packaging by Retrieval is flawless, but this music is primarily for specialists. — *Scott Yanow*

● **In England** / Sep. 1917–Jan. 21, 1924 / EMI Pathe/Jazztime ✦✦✦✦✦
The original Dixieland Jazz Band's visit to England during 1919-20 caused a sensation and did much to help popularize and even "legitimize" jazz. More importantly for history, The ODJB cut some of their finest recordings while overseas. These very well-recorded documents (some of which are around four rather than three minutes long) feature The ODJB at their best. The performances still do not include any real solos (sticking exclusively to

ensembles), but many of the melodies are quite strong. Of their 17 London recordings (all of which are on this CD), highpoints include "At the Jazz Band Ball," "Tiger Rag," "Tell Me," "I'm Forever Blowing," "Sensation, Bubbles" (one of the first jazz waltzes), "I've Lost My Heart in Dixieland" and "Alice Blue Gown." This CD is rounded out by five real obscurities from English bands cut between 1917-24. Spirited as they are, those groups demonstrate that The ODJB was really the pacesetters for the era. — *Scott Yanow*

1943 / Dec. 3, 1943 / GHB ✦✦✦✦
After a brief comeback the year before, The Original Dixieland Jazz Band was finished by 1937 with cornetist Nick LaRocca's retirement. However, in 1943, multi-instrumentalist Brad Gowans, who had extensively studied their music, gathered together some of The ODJB alumni (trombonist Eddie Daniels, drummer Tony Sbarbaro and one of their later pianists Frank Signorelli) to revisit the old repertoire and frameworks. Gowans, who sticks here to clarinet (coming up with a pretty good imitation of Larry Shields' style), enlisted cornetist Wild Bill Davison who, although he does his best to recreate LaRocca's style, sounds rather restrained as he tries to hide his own extroverted musical personality. The quintet is featured on this LP on a set of radio transcriptions and everything is here (including alternate takes and false starts); ten fine performances resulted from this interesting experiment. — *Scott Yanow*

Original Dixieland Jazz in Hi-Fi / Oct. 3, 1957 / Paramount ✦✦✦
Around 1956-57, trumpeter Don Fowler and clarinetist George Phillips, two musicians from the Pacific Northwest, recreated The Original Dixieland Jazz Band on this rather unique LP. Using trombonist George Phillips, pianist George Ruschka and drummer Darrell Renfro, they perform a dozen ODJB selections note-for-note from the original recordings of 40 years earlier. It must have taken a great deal of work and research to get this down correctly, but somehow the bizarre project works. This LP will be very difficult to find and it is somehow doubtful that it will be reissued in the near future. — *Scott Yanow*

The Original Memphis Five

Group / Classic Jazz
Founded in 1917 by trumpeter Phil Napoleon and pianist Frank Signorelli, this excellent New Orleans jazz quintet made a ton of records between 1921-31, including many under different names (such as Ladd's Black Aces and the Carolina Cotton Pickers). Napoleon, trombonist Miff Mole (who in 1922 was succeeded by Charles Panelli), clarinetist Jimmy Lytell, Signorelli and drummer Jack Roth were regular fixtures in the early days; starting in 1926 the personnel changed fairly frequently with cornetist Red Nichols, drummer Ray Bauduc, Mole and (during one session apiece in 1928, 1929 and 1931), Tommy and Jimmy Dorsey making appearances. The original Memphis Five's music was melodic, swinging and very jazz-oriented. Unfortunately, most of their hundreds of recordings have not been reissued on CD yet. — *Scott Yanow*

★ **Collection, Vol. 1: 1922–1923** / Apr. 22, 1922–Dec. 10, 1923 / Storyville ✦✦✦✦✦
Phil Napoleon was arguably the best trumpeter on record during 1921-22 and one of the first jazz musicians to swing. Possessor of an attractive and clear tone along with impressive technique, Napoleon's melodic lead was heard on a countless number of sides by the original Memphis Five and other groups with similar personnel. Despite its title, this CD actually starts out with the nine selections recorded by Jazzbo's Carolina Serenaders, a quintet with Napoleon, trombonist Miff Mole, several different clarinetists, pianist Frank Signorelli and drummer Jack Roth. The set also has two numbers from The Southland Six (a similar group with Napoleon, trombonist Charles Panelli and clarinetist Jimmy Lytell) in addition to five sessions from the original Memphis Five. Throughout, Napoleon and his musicians sound way ahead, evolution-wise, of the original Dixieland Jazz Band and show the influence of The New Orleans Rhythm Kings, but do not sound like a copy of either. This ensemble-oriented music happily does not include dated vocals, novelties (other than the weak "barking" on "That Barking Dog-Woof! Woof!"), military staccato phrasing or doo-wacka-doo nonsense, and this CD fills an often-overlooked gap in jazz history. — *Scott Yanow*

Kid Ory (Edward Ory)

b. Dec. 25, 1886, La Place, LA, **d.** Jan. 23, 1973, Honolulu, HI
Trombone / Dixieland

Kid Ory was one of the great New Orleans pioneers, an early trombonist who virtually defined the "tailgate" style (using his horn to play rhythmic bass lines in the front line behind the trumpet and clarinet) and who was fortunate enough to last through the lean years so he could make a major comeback in the mid-'40s. Originally a banjoist, Ory soon switched to trombone and by 1911 was leading a popular band in New Orleans. Among his trumpeters during the next eight years were Mutt Carey, King Oliver and a young Louis Armstrong and his clarinetists included Johnny Dodds, Sidney Bechet and Jimmie Noone. In 1919 Ory moved to California, and in 1922 (possibly 1921) recorded the first two titles by a Black New Orleans jazz band ("Ory's Creole Trombone" and "Society Blues") under the band title of "Spike's Seven Pods of Pepper Orchestra." In 1925 he moved to Chicago, played regularly with King Oliver and recorded many classic sides with Oliver, Louis Armstrong (in his Hot Five and Seven) and Jelly Roll Morton among others.

The definitive New Orleans trombonist of the 1920s, Ory (whose "Muskrat Ramble" became a standard) was mostly out of music after 1930, running a chicken ranch with his brother. However, in 1942, he was persuaded to return, and after a stint with Barney Bigard's group, he formed his own band. Ory's group was featured on Orson Welles' radio show in 1944 and the publicity made it possible for the band to catch on. The New Orleans revival was in full swing and Ory (whose group included trumpeter Mutt Carey and clarinetists Omer Simeon or Darnell Howard) was still in prime form. He appeared in the 1946 film *New Orleans* (and later on in *The Benny Goodman Story*) and worked steadily in Los Angeles. After Mutt Carey departed in 1948, Ory used Teddy Buckner, Marty Marsala, Alvin Alcorn (the perfect musician for his group) and Red Allen on trumpets and his Dixieland bands always boasted high musicianship (even with the leader's purposely primitive style) and a consistent level of excitement. They recorded regularly (most notably for Good Time Jazz) up to 1960 by which time Ory (already 73) was cutting back on his activities. He retired altogether in 1966, moving to Hawaii. *—Scott Yanow*

Kid Ory's Creole Jazz Band / Mar. 15, 1944–1945 / Folklyric
◆◆◆

This historically significant LP features Kid Ory's New Orleans-styled jazz band on airchecks from the Orson Welles radio show. It was these performances that resulted in a renaissance in Ory's career after more than a decade of obscurity. The tailgate trombonist shares the frontline with trumpeter Mutt Carey and clarinetist Jimmie Noone on the first five selections. Noone's sudden death resulted in his being replaced first by Wade Whaley and Barney Bigard before Joe Darensburg became the band's permanent clarinetist. The final five numbers on this set originate from a different series of broadcasts in early 1945. Overall, the music on this LP is better than the recording quality, which tends to be a bit shaky and Ory's Good Time Jazz sets from the 1950s are actually his definitive recordings. *—Scott Yanow*

Kid Ory (1944–1945) / Aug. 1944–Nov. 1945 / Good Time Jazz
◆◆◆◆◆

Trombonist Kid Ory led one of the finest and most consistently exciting New Orleans jazz bands of the 1944–60 period. This CD contains 16 selections from 1944–45 when, after a decade out of music, Ory was making what would be a very successful comeback. These studio sides feature veteran trumpeter Mutt Carey and either Omer Simeon or Darnell Howard on clarinet along with a fine rhythm section and Ory's trombone. Highlights include "Blues for Jimmie Noone," "Panama," "Do What Ory Said," "Maryland, My Maryland," "1919 Rag" and "Ory's Creole Trombone." This is fun and often hard-swinging music. *—Scott Yanow*

Kid Ory / Oct. 15, 1946–Jul. 6, 1950 / Columbia ◆◆◆◆

This out-of-print LP features two different versions of trombonist Kid Ory's Creole Jazz Band. The earlier selections (which are highlighted by "Tiger Rag," "Eh, La Bas" and "Bill Bailey") feature trumpeter Mutt Carey and clarinetist Barney Bigard, while the sides from 1950 have solos from the strong trumpet of Teddy Buckner and the reliable clarinetist Joe Darensbourg; their eight recordings include "Savoy Blues," "Mahogany Hall Stomp" and

---

Music Map

Organ

Early Jazz Organ
Fred Longshaw (reed organ in 1925 with Bessie Smith on famous recording of "St. Louis Blues")

Pipe Organ
Fats Waller

Swing Organ
Count Basie
Milt Herth
Glenn Hardman

Pre-Jimmy Smith Pacesetters
Wild Bill Davis
Bill Doggett
Milt Buckner

Innovator
Jimmy Smith

1960s

Charles Earland	Clare Fischer
Groove Holmes	Eddie Louiss
Jack McDuff	Jimmy McGriff
Don Patterson	Big John Patton
Shirley Scott	Johnny Hammond Smith
Lonnie Smith	Sun Ra

Modal Jazz
Larry Young

1980s

Joey DeFrancesco	Barbara Dennerlein
Larry Goldings	Amina Claudine Myers
Jeff Palmer	Don Pullen

"At a Georgia Camp Meeting." Pity that Columbia has kept this enjoyable set unavailable for three decades. *—Scott Yanow*

Kid Ory at The Green Room, Vol. 1 / Feb. 10, 1947 / American Music ◆◆

Recently released for the first time, this is the first of two volumes that documents Kid Ory's 1947 band live during a gig. Recorded without the knowledge of the musicians who include trombonist Ory, trumpeter Mutt Carey and clarinetist Joe Darensbourg), most of the music they played on that particular evening is on these CDs. The first volume is the weaker of the two for the New Orleans jazz band is saddled with requests for swing standards that do not fit their style that well; Ory grudgingly ran through 13 of these tunes as quickly as possible before playing six songs that fit better in his band's repertoire. The music has its moments, but the recording quality is just so-so and it takes awhile for Mutt Carey to get warmed up. The second volume is much better. — *Scott Yanow*

Kid Ory at The Green Room, Vol. 2 / Feb. 10, 1947 / American Music ✦✦✦
Far superior to the first volume, this CD continues the documentation of a 1947 gig for Kid Ory's Creole Jazz Band. At the time, the trombonist's group included trumpeter Mutt Carey (who would leave the band right after this engagement ended) and clarinetist Joe Darensbourg. This group seemed to improve with each song so, by the second half of the night, they were in hot form. The recording quality varies, but is listenable (with the crowd becoming more enthusiastic and probably drunker as the night progressed). The band runs through some of their favorite tunes, including "Do What Ory Said," "Eh, La Bas," "1919 March," "High Society" and "Oh! Didn't He Ramble." Ory fans are advised to pick this one up. — *Scott Yanow*

Edward Kid Ory and His Creole Band at the Dixieland Jubilee / 1948 / GNP ✦✦✦
This LP features a typically consistent performance from Kid Ory's popular New Orleans band. Teddy Buckner contributes some impressive trumpet solos, clarinetist Joe Darensbourg is a strong asset and the audience is quite enthusiastic. Nothing unusual occurs, but this joyous music (highlighted by "Shine," "Tiger Rag," "Muskrat Ramble" and "Maryland, My Maryland") is enjoyable, if not up to the level of Ory's Good Time Jazz studio recordings. — *Scott Yanow*

King of the Tailgate Trombone / 1948-1949 / American Music ✦✦✦✦
Consisting of previously unissued live performances from two editions of Kid Ory's Creole Jazz Bands, these relatively well-recorded jams should satisfy any lover of New Orleans jazz. Clarinetist Joe Darensbourg (who is on all of the selections) is in good form, trumpeter Andrew Blakeney (heard on 11 of the 15 numbers) has rarely sounded better and trumpeter Teddy Buckner (who stars during the last four songs), although not as expert an ensemble player as some of Ory's sidemen have been, takes some outstanding solos. The Dixieland standards that Ory performs include romping versions of "Panama," "Mahogany Hall Stomp," "Sugar Foot Stomp," "High Society" and "Sweet Georgia Brown." — *Scott Yanow*

At The Beverly Cavern / 1951 / Sounds ✦✦✦
This set consists of broadcast versions of ten songs performed by Kid Ory's New Orleans Jazz band featuring the leader's trombone, cornetist Teddy Buckner and either Joe Darensbourg or Pud Brown on clarinet. Unlike many of the other New Orleans revival groups, this ensemble was very consistent and, although this music is not essential, they are in typically fine form on this fairly obscure LP. — *Scott Yanow*

Live at Club Hangover, Vol. 1 / May 9, 1953-May 16, 1953 / Dawn Club ✦✦✦✦
This is the first of several Dawn Club LPs documenting the 1953-54 version of Kid Ory's Creole Jazz Band. Consisting of two broadcasts, this set features trombonist Ory, cornetist Teddy Buckner and clarinetist Joe Darensbourg (along with a fine rhythm section) joyfully jamming on a variety of Dixieland standards. One song on each broadcast features the duet of pianist Meade Lux Lewis and drummer Smoky Stover. It's recommended for New Orleans jazz collectors. — *Scott Yanow*

This Kid's the Greatest! / Jul. 17, 1953-Jun. 18, 1956 / Good Time Jazz ✦✦✦✦✦
This CD features selections from some of Kid Ory's finest New Orleans jazz bands, spanning a three-year period; these studio performances never found their way onto the other Good Time Jazz sets. Such excellent players as the colorful cornetist Teddy Buckner (a superior soloist although not as gifted an ensemble player) and his replacement Alvin Alcorn, clarinetists Pud Brown, Bob McCracken, George Probert and Phil Gomez, pianists Lloyd Glenn, Don Ewell and Cedric Haywood, bassists Ed Garland, Morty Corb and Wellman Braud and drummer Minor Hall all make strong contributions on a variety of Dixieland standards including "Milneberg Joys," "Bill Bailey" and "How Come You Do Me like You Do." Quite spirited and very musical New Orleans jazz. — *Scott Yanow*

Kid Ory Plays the Blues / Oct. 3, 1953-Feb. 5, 1955 / Storyville ✦✦✦✦
During the 1950s, trombonist Kid Ory, who would turn 70 in 1956, led his finest bands. Among the pacesetters in the New Orleans revival, Ory's groups were always in tune and featured both colorful ensembles and strong soloists. This Storyville LP has strong solos from either Teddy Buckner or Alvin Alcorn on trumpet and Bob McCracken, George Probert or Phil Gomez on clarinet. The rhythm section of pianist Don Ewell, bassist Ed Garland and drummer Minor Hall was one of the best in the idiom. Most of the songs in this series of live broadcasts from the Hangover Club in San Francisco are blues (some just have "blues" in the title), but there is enough variety to make this a recommended set. — *Scott Yanow*

Sounds of New Orleans, Vol. 9 / May 8, 1954-Feb. 26, 1955 / Storyville ✦✦✦✦✦
Although trombonist Kid Ory had formerly used the veteran Mutt Carey and the nearly virtuosic Teddy Buckner as his trumpeters, Alvin Alcorn (who joined The Creole Jazz Band in 1954) proved to be his perfect partner. Alcorn's lyrical but passionate tone was well-featured on solos, but it was his ensemble work (building up a song to several climaxes and expertly utilizing dynamics) that made him ideal for this band. This series of broadcasts from Kid Ory's main gig, the Hangover Club in San Francisco, features superior and rather exciting versions of such songs as "Eh, La Bas," "Maryland, My Maryland" "Mahogany Hall Stomp" and "Original Dixieland One-Step." Fans of New Orleans jazz will love this CD. — *Scott Yanow*

★ **Kid Ory's Creole Jazz Band (1954)** / Aug. 9, 1954-Aug. 10, 1954 / Good Time Jazz ✦✦✦✦✦
Although some Kid Ory fans might disagree, the veteran trombonist led his finest bands (at least the ones that recorded) in the 1950s. The one heard on this CD is really quite definitive, featuring the brilliant ensemble player (and distinctive soloist) Alvin Alcorn on trumpet, the talented clarinetist George Probert and an excellent rhythm section (pianist Don Ewell, guitarist Bill Newman, bassist Ed Garland and drummer Minor Hall). Their versions on this set of "That's a Plenty," "Gettysburg March," "Clarinet Marmalade" and even "When the Saints Go Marching In" are true classics of New Orleans jazz. This joyous and exciting music is essential for all serious jazz collections. — *Scott Yanow*

Creole Jazz Band / Nov. 30, 1954-Dec. 2, 1954 / Good Time Jazz ✦✦✦✦✦
Trombonist Kid Ory, already 68 at the time of this recording, was at the peak of his powers in the mid-'50s. This particular version of his Creole Jazz Band was one of the finest, featuring trumpeter Alvin Alcorn and clarinetist George Probert, talented soloists who were also superb group players. Alcorn generated a lot of excitement perfectly placing long notes near the end of each ensemble chorus. This Good Time Jazz CD is almost up to the level of its 1954 and 1956 counterparts, highlighted by torrid versions of "Shake That Thing," "Royal Garden Blues" and "Indiana." — *Scott Yanow*

★ **Legendary Kid** / Nov. 22, 1955-Nov. 25, 1955 / Good Time Jazz ✦✦✦✦✦
One of trombonist Kid Ory's greatest recordings, this consistently exciting CD features trumpeter Alvin Alcorn, clarinetist Phil Gomez and a strong rhythm section that includes bassist Wellman Braud and Ory's longtime drummer Minor Hall. These versions of "Mahogany Hall Stomp," "There'll Be Some Changes Made," "At the Jazz Band Ball" and "Shine" are all gems, giving listeners some of the very best in New Orleans jazz, and showing that the music need not be played haltingly by over-the-hill musicians; one can capture its spirit and joy without sacrificing musicianship. Every jazz collection should have this music. — *Scott Yanow*

Favorites! / Jun. 1956-Jul. 1956 / Good Time Jazz ✦✦✦✦
This single CD contains 15 of the 17 selections performed by Kid Ory's 1956 Creole Jazz Band that were originally issued on a double LP. Trombonist Ory, trumpeter Alvin Alcorn and clarinetist Phil Gomez make for a very tight but spontaneous frontline, featuring strong melodic solos and exciting ensembles that paid close attention to dynamics and gradually building up the excitement level. New Orleans jazz at its best. Highlights include "Do What Ory Says," "Jazz Me Blues," "Original Dixieland One-Step," "Panama," "Maryland, My Maryland," "1919 Rag" and "Bugle Call Rag." — *Scott Yanow*

At The Jazz Band Ball 1959 / Nov. 11, 1959 / Rhapsody ◆◆◆◆
Trombonist Kid Ory (a New Orleans traditionalist) and trumpeter Henry "Red" Allen (New Orleans-born but always looking forward in his playing) make for a frequently explosive combination on this set of Dixieland standards. With clarinetist Bob McCracken and a fine rhythm section helping out, the music on this LP is often quite exciting and heated. —*Scott Yanow*

The Kid Ory Storyville Nights / Dec. 5, 1961 / Verve ◆◆◆

Greg Osby

b. Aug. 3, 1960, St. Louis, MO
Alto Saxophone / Avant-Garde, Free Funk
One of the finest talents to emerge in jazz during the 1980s, Greg Osby's own recordings are often frustrating to listen to. His chance-taking approach is admirable, but mixing rap with jazz (as he occasionally does) is analogous to slabbing bacteria on one's bread! Osby studied jazz at Howard University (1978–80) and attended Berklee. He worked in New York with Woody Shaw, Jon Faddis, Ron Carter, Dizzy Gillespie and most notably Jack DeJohnette's Special Edition (1985). A member of the so-called M-Base scene (essentially an extension of the free funk of Ornette Coleman's Prime Time), Osby has recorded as a leader for JMT and Blue Note, but some of his finest playing can be heard on Andrew Hill's records. —*Scott Yanow*

● **Greg Osby and the Sound Theatre** / Jun. 1987–Jun. 1987 / JMT ◆◆◆◆◆
This is Osby's most-accomplished ensemble, especially with Michele Rosewoman on piano. —*Ron Wynn*

Mind Games / May 1988 / JMT ◆◆
Some torrid solos, but his least successful release artistically. —*Ron Wynn*

Season of Renewal / Jul. 1989 / JMT ◆◆◆◆
Strong cuts, good concept, and excellent Osby solos. —*Ron Wynn*

Man Talk for Moderns, Vol. 10 / Oct. 19, 199091 11 / Blue Note ◆◆
Early album from alto saxophonist who has emerged as a leading figure in the hip-hop/jazz fusion school. Osby's '91 release didn't include much rap or hip-hop, but did reflect its influence with its heavily edited short songs, strutting bravado, and Osby's pungent alto solos. —*Ron Wynn*

3-D Lifestyles / May 4, 1993 / Blue Note ◆
Greg Osby is a hugely talented altoist, but this attempted mixture

of rap and jazz is a disaster. Not only does rap that is filled with meaningless name dropping and profanity plague all but one selection, but Osby's alto sounds like an anemic version of Sadao Watanabe. The monotone delivery of the rappers is extremely annoying to hear, as is the uninspired playing of Osby. —*Scott Yanow*

Jimmy Owens

b. Dec. 9, 1943, New York, NY
Trumpet, Fluegelhorn / Hard Bop
A fine hard bop soloist, Jimmy Owens has never achieved much fame. He started on trumpet when he was ten and later on studied trumpet with Donald Byrd. Owens has played as a sideman with many major players including Lionel Hampton (1963–64), Hank Crawford (1964–65), Charles Mingus, Herbie Mann, Duke Ellington, Gerry Mulligan, Count Basie, the Thad Jones-Mel Lewis Orchestra and the Dizzy Gillespie reunion band (1968). He played on Billy Cobham's *Spectrum* album in 1973, worked extensively in Europe, was one of the founders of the Collective Black Artists, was closely involved with the Jazzmobile in New York and served on several arts commissions. But playing-wise, Jimmy Owens has not lived up to his potential yet. —*Scott Yanow*

Makoto Ozone

b. Mar. 25, 1961, Kobe, Japan
Piano / Post Bop
A premier jazz musician in Japan, Ozone has made a successful transition to America, where he became equally prominent in this nation's improvisational community. He began on organ at four, then took up piano as a teenager. He went to Berklee in 1980 and studied composing and arranging. He was noticed by Gary Burton and later recorded with him and was part of his band. Ozone's striking ability (especially on mid-tempo pieces) and impressive technique made him a big hit at the Kool Jazz Festival. His 1984 debut recording featured Burton and bassist Eddie Gomez. It was a stunning example of complete knowledge and mastery of the full jazz piano spectrum. Ozone later worked with European pianist Michel Petrucciani and spent extensive time studying classical music. —*Ron Wynn*

Makoto Ozone / Jun. 23, 1981–Jun. 24, 1981 / Columbia ◆◆◆
Produced by Gary Burton. Solo piano in light jazz to edges of new age. Bright, but not shining. —*Michael G. Nastos*

After / Oct. 1986 / Columbia ◆◆◆

● **Starlight** / Nov. 1989–Dec. 1989 / JVC ◆◆◆◆

P

Hot Lips Page (Oran Thaddeus Page)

b. Jan. 27, 1908, Dallas, TX, **d.** Nov. 5, 1954, New York, NY
Trumpet, Vocals / Swing, Blues, Dixieland
One of the great swing trumpeters in addition to being a talented blues vocalist, Hot Lips Page's premature passing left a large hole in the jazz world; virtually all musicians (no matter their style) loved him. Page gained early experience in the 1920s performing in Texas, playing in Ma Rainey's backup band. He was with Walter Page's Blue Devils during 1928–31 and then joined Bennie Moten's band in Kansas City in time to take part in a brilliant 1932 recording session. Page freelanced in Kansas City and in 1936 was one of the stars in Count Basie's orchestra but, shortly before Basie was discovered, Joe Glaser signed Hot Lips as a solo artist. Although Page's big band did alright in the late '30s (recording for Victor), if he had come east with Basie he would have become much more famous. Page was one of the top sidemen with Artie Shaw's Orchestra during 1941–42 and then mainly freelanced throughout the remainder of his career, recording with many all-star groups and being a welcome fixture at jam sessions. —*Scott Yanow*

★ **The Chronological Hot Lips Page (1938–1940)** / Mar. 10, 1938–Dec. 3, 1940 / Classics ◆◆◆◆◆

After Hours in Harlem / 1941 / Onyx ◆◆◆◆

Dr. Jazz Series, Vol. 6 / Dec. 21, 1951–Mar. 7, 1952 / Storyville ◆◆◆◆
There are not that many recordings from the later part of Page's career, which makes this CD (comprised of radio broadcasts) of great interest. Page is heard on a variety of Dixieland and swing standards with quite an assortment of all-stars including cornetist Wild Bill Davison, trombonists Lou McGarity and Sandy Williams, clarinetists Pee Wee Russell, Bob Wilber, Eddie Barefield, Cecil Scott and Peanuts Hucko, pianists Red Richards, Dick Cary, Joe Sullivan and Charlie Queener and drummer George Wettling (who was actually the leader of these groups). Page is in exuberant form whether singing tunes such as "When My Sugar Walks down the Street" and a riotous "St. Louis Blues" or leading the ensembles. This is one of his best recordings currently available and is often quite exciting. —*Scott Yanow*

Walter Page

b. Feb. 9, 1900, Gallatin, MS, **d.** Dec. 20, 1957, New York, NY
Bass / Swing
One of the finest bassists of the swing era, Walter Page rarely soloed, but his four-to-the-bar walking behind soloists set the standard for bassists in the 1930s before the rise of Jimmy Blanton. A longtime resident of Kansas City, Page was with Bennie Moten in the early days (1918–23) and then during 1925–31 led the Blue Devils, Moten's main competition. Unfortunately, Page's group only made two recordings and by 1931 Moten had achieved his goal of stealing most of the band's top players, including Page himself. After Moten's death in 1935, Walter Page achieved fame as part of Count Basie's unbeatable rhythm section (along with the pianist/leader, rhythm guitarist Freddie Green and drummer Jo Jones) during 1935–42 and 1946–1949. He spent his remaining years playing with Eddie Condon's Dixieland bands and with his friends from the swing world including Hot Lips Page, Jimmy Rushing and various Basie alumni. Page collapsed on the way to filming *The Sound of Jazz* and died shortly after at the age of 57. —*Scott Yanow*

Marty Paich

b. Jan. 23, 1925, Oakland, CA, **d.** Aug. 12, 1995, Santa Ynez, CA
Piano, Arranger / Bop, Cool
A fine pianist, Marty Paich was much better-known as an arranger, responsible for several famous sessions in the 1950s (most notably Art Pepper's *Modern Jazz Classics*). After serving as arranger for the U.S. Army Air Force Band (1943–46), Paich studied music extensively. Starting in 1952, he became an important fixture in the West Coast jazz scene. Paich worked with Peggy Lee and both the Shelly Manne and Shorty Rogers bands during 1953–54. He led a few dates in the 1950s as a pianist, but it was his arrangements for Pepper, Stan Kenton, the Dave Pell Octet and Mel Tormé (the latter utilizing his ten-piece "Dektette") that gave him fame in the jazz world. After 1960, Marty Paich worked mostly in the studios but in 1988 he put together a new Dektette to accompany Tormé. —*Scott Yanow*

Marty Paich Quartet / Aug. 1956 / VSOP ◆◆◆◆
This CD from VSOP reissues a fairly obscure Tampa LP featuring pianist Marty Paich (better-known as an arranger), altoist Art Pepper, bassist Buddy Clark and drummer Frank Capp; this music has also been issued under Pepper's name. Pepper and Paich would have several notable collaborations during the next few years, but this was their first. Pepper is generally the main star (particularly on such numbers as "You and the Night and the Music," "Over the Rainbow" and "All the Things You Are") while Paich (who has several fine piano solos) contributes three of the eight songs to this cool-toned, but hard-swinging, set. —*Scott Yanow*

Jazz For Relaxation / Aug. 1956–Sep. 1956 / VSOP ◆◆◆
This VSOP CD, a straight reissue of a Marty Paich date for Tampa, repeats the packaging faults of the original LP. Although it is a quintet date, the only personnel listed are the pianist/leader, bassist Joe Mondragon and vibraphonist Larry Bunker; guitarist Howard Roberts and drummer Frank Capp go unacknowledged but certainly not unheard. The scanty liner notes claim that this is music to relax by and that all of the tunes are uptempo; actually the first tune ("Dool's Blues") is quite slow! But overlooking those discrepancies, the unfortunately brief program is actually quite enjoyable, showcasing Paich the pianist (rather than the arranger) in prime form. Roberts And Bunker also have plenty of solos and the boppish repertoire (five standards, two originals and Count Basie's obscure "Jump for Me") continually holds one's interest. —*Scott Yanow*

● **What's New** / Jun. 7, 1957–Jun. 8, 1957 / Discovery ◆◆◆◆◆
Marty Paich Trio / Jun. 1957 / VSOP ◆◆◆
Marty Paich became so well-known as an arranger in the 1950s that his piano playing became secondary. This LP reissue of a session for the Mode label was Paich's only trio set. With the assistance of bassist Red Mitchell and drummer Mel Lewis, Paich plays tasteful versions of three standards, Jack Montrose's "A Dandy Line" and four of his own originals. The music is subtle and quiet, but swinging and reasonably enjoyable. —*Scott Yanow*

New York Scene / Jan. 1959 / Discovery ◆◆◆◆◆
I Get a Boot out of You / Jun. 30, 1959–Jul. 12, 1959 / Warner Brothers ◆◆◆◆
A good showcase for the orchestrations and arrangements of Marty Paich, one of the top arrangers and conductors during the '50s and '60s. —*Ron Wynn*

Joanie Pallatto

Vocals / Bop, Post Bop

An excellent singer, Joanie Pallatto (along with her partner pianist Bradley Parker-Sparrow) has run the Chicago jazz label Southport since 1981. Pallatto has several fine releases of her own with such guests as Bob Dorough, Howard Levy, and Von Freeman. —*Scott Yanow*

● **Passing Tones** / Dec. 1974–May 1995 / Southport ✦✦✦✦

Joanie Pallatto, who (with pianist/producer Bradley Parker-Sparrow) founded and runs Southport (one of the top Midwest jazz record labels), has a versatile and very jazz-oriented style. Her scatting sometimes recalls Sheila Jordan; she has a strong voice for ballads and her adventurous spirit allows her to tackle material ranging from "In a Mellow Tone" (during which she interacts quite successfully with tenor saxophonist Von Freeman), "All Blues," "Blue in Green" (for which she wrote the lyrics) and "Save Your Love for Me" to Bob Dorough's "Nothing Like You." Other highlights include Sparrow's "Live" which, in addition to solos from the composer's thunderous piano (a bit reminiscent of Don Pullen) and trumpeter Brad Goode, has some close harmony and hot scatting by Pallatto and April Alosio, a duet with bassist John Whitfield on a pleading "Get out of Town" and an Ellington tribute "Looking for Duke." With the other musicians including pianist Willie Pickens and drummer Robert Shy, this is a particularly memorable effort. —*Scott Yanow*

Jeff Palmer

b. Jackson Heights, NY
Organ / Hard Bop

A fine organist who has carved out his own voice from the dominant Jimmy Smith influence, Jeff Palmer started out on accordion. He switched to organ when he was around 15 and was completely self-taught, never having been a pianist. Palmer has played with such guitarists as Grant Green, George Benson, John Scofield and John Abercrombie and recorded as a leader for Statiras, Soul Note, AudioQuest and Reservoir. —*Scott Yanow*

Laser Wizard / Jul. 16, 1985 / Statiras ✦✦✦✦

Ease on / Sep. 1992 / Audioquest ✦✦✦✦

● **Shades of the Pine** / Sep. 14, 1994 / Reservoir ✦✦✦✦✦

Jeff Palmer is a talented organist whose style (as with virtually all organists) is influenced by Jimmy Smith. For this CD he performs nine similar blues, all of which are given strong solos by the leader, tenor saxophonist Billy Pierce and guitarist John Abercrombie; drummer Marvin "Smitty" Smith is consistently swinging in support. Despite the sameness of the repertoire (all but Thelonious Monk's "Ba-lue Bolivar Ba-lues-are" are by Palmer), the cooking music holds one's interest and is quite enjoyable. —*Scott Yanow*

Charlie Palmieri

b. 1927, New York, NY, d. 1988, New York, NY
Piano / Latin Jazz

Charlie Palmieri was a child prodigy as a pianist and was among Latin jazz's flashiest, most flamboyant stylists. His playing was alternately aggressive and mellow, percussive, then very supportive and low-key. He began studying piano at seven, and eventually attended Juilliard. Palmieri played dances at 14 and turned professional at 16. He started his group "El Conjunto Pin Pin" in 1948, and played piano for Pupi Campo, Tito Puente, Tito Rodriguez, Bicentico Valdes and Pete Terrace before forming his Charanga Dubonney group in 1958. They recorded in the '60s for United Artists and Alegre. Palmieri helped initiate the charanga (flute and violin band) explosion of the early '60s.

He was music director for The Alegre All Stars on a series of descarga (jam session) albums, working with such stars as Johnny Pacheco, Willie Rosario, and Cheo Feliciano. They spawned a growth industry as other Latin labels like Tico and Fania established their own all-star groups to compete. Palmieri formed The Duboney Orchestra in the mid-'60s, replacing the violin and flute with three trumpets and two trombones. He temporarily moved to RCA from Alegre, but returned and recorded some albums in the the popular R&B/latin "boogaloo" style. One for Atlantic was produced by Herbie Mann. Palmieri survived a near mental breakdown in 1969, and was hired by Tito Puente to be musical director for his "El Mambo De Tito Puente" television program.

Palmieri began a parallel career in the '70s as a cultural historian and lecturer on Latin music and history, and subsequently taught courses at various New York institutions. He added organ to his band in the '70s, and continued recording on Alegre before switching to Coco. There were subsequent albums on Tipica, Cotique, then Alegre again. He was featured on the 1979 British television film "Salsa". Palmieri moved to Puerto Rico in 1980, remaining there until 1983.

He'd planned a concert in Puerto Rico with his brother Eddie, but suffered a severe heart attack and stroke while back in New York organizing the event. After his recovery, Palmieri returned to the Latin music wars with a small combo in 1984. He played with Ralphy Marzan, Joe Quijano and co-led the band Combo Gigante with Jimmy Sabater.

Palmieri made his first trip to England in 1988, but suffered another heart attack upon his return to New York. This time he didn't recover. Charlie Palmieri left a legacy of masterful albums in various Latin pop and jazz styles. Unfortunately most of them aren't available on CD, except through Latin or international music specialty stores. —*Ron Wynn and Max Salazar*

Charanga / 1960 / United Artists ✦✦✦

Pachanga at the Caravana Club / 1961 / Alegre ✦✦✦

Tribute to Noro Morales / 1965 / Alegre ✦✦✦✦✦

Latin Bugalu / 1968 / Atlantic ✦✦✦✦

The Giant of the Keyboard / 1972 / Alegre ✦✦✦✦✦

● **Impulsos** / 1975 / Mpl ✦✦✦✦✦

The late Charlie P. was a greater pianist than his brother, as deeply musical, as universally loved, and with far more sense. He picked musicians by talent not fame, and they blew their hearts out for him. This mid-'70s session has the swing, as hot as EPs but more benign; the jazz solos and tipico ensembles. —*John Storm Roberts*

Perdido / 1977 / Alegre ✦✦✦✦

Eddie Palmieri

b. Dec. 15, 1936, New York, NY
Piano / Latin Jazz

A sometimes dazzling pianist whose technique incorporates bits and pieces of everyone from McCoy Tyner to Herbie Hancock and recycles them through a dynamic Latin groove, Eddie Palmieri has been a Latin jazz and salsa master since the '50s. His approach can be compared to Thelonious Monk's for its unorthodox patterns; odd rhythms, sometimes disjointed phrases and percussive effects, played in a manner that seems frazzled, but is always successfully resolved. It's a free/bebop/Latin blend, with keyboard solos that are never predictable, but always stimulating.

Palmieri started as a vocalist, but his elder brother Charlie influenced him to become a pianist. He began with the neighborhood band of Orlando Marin, then made his professional debut in 1955 with Johnny Sequi's orchestra. Following stints with Vicentico Valdes, Pete Terrace and Tito Rodriguez, Palmieri formed Conjunto La Perfecta in 1962. The group included Barry Rogers, Johnny Pacheco, Manny Oquendo and George Castro. He developed with Rogers a two-trombone/flute frontline that was a variation on the charanga (flute and violin) style that Palmieri dubbed "trombanga." The group initially recorded for Alegre, then switched to Tico. They made several albums in the '60s, including two with Cal Tjader, before disbanding due to money problems in 1968. Palmieri worked with The Tico All-Stars and appeared on The Fania All-Stars debut album. He continued recording, working with such players as Alfredo "Chocolate" Armenteros, Israel "Cachao" Lopez and Justo Betancourt. He made some R&B/Latin "boogaloo" dates, and in the early '70s attracted some R&B and funk interest working with the band Harlem River Drive. Palmieri held concerts at Sing Sing and at the University of Puerto Rico.

He began recording for Coco in the mid-'70s, and eventually amassed five Grammy awards in the '70s and '80s. Palmieri's productions were elaborate combinations of contemporary Latin, pop, rock and soul, jazz improvisation, Spanish vocals and Afro-Latin rhythms. He became so popular even albums he didn't personally like, such as 1976's *Unfinished Masterpiece* on Coco won Grammys. Every album he issued between 1978 and 1987 was nominated for a Grammy. But Palmieri didn't fare as well with record labels. His superb late '70s album *Lucumi Macumba Voodoo*, recorded for Columbia, was a sales flop despite a huge publicity campaign. Palmieri was later quoted saying joining Columbia had been a major mistake. He also said the same thing about his affiliation with Fania, even though he won a fifth Grammy for the album *La Verdad/The Truth*. Palmieri suffered yet another label disappointment with 1989's *Sueno* on Capitol that included special guest Dave Sanborn. But it flopped both sales-wise and aesthically, as Capitol sought some Latin instrumental filler to plug into the Kenny G./Najee urban contemporary/Quiet Storm market. Palmieri eventually issued another album on Fania in 1990, *EP*.

Despite his failure to attain major label success, Eddie Palmieri's artistic triumphs have cemented his place in the Latin jazz, salsa and international arena. He has very few albums on CD available anywhere except the specialist and mail-order route. —*Ron Wynn and Max Salazar*

Mozambique / 1965 / Tico ◆◆◆◆◆
Eddie Palmieri first hit in the '60s with his classic two-trombone sound. This is one of his finest albums; unassuming, joyous, punchy, and sharp, it has the outstanding Ismael Quintana on vocals and Manny Oquendo on timbales. —*John Storm Roberts*

El Sonido Nuevo / Oct. 1966 / Verve ◆◆◆
The meeting of vibist Cal Tjader and pianist Eddie Palmieri yielded a fresh, innovative sound. This date was one of those magical ones in which every cut was masterful, showing how carefully Tjader and Palmieri navigated the line between tasteful pop covers and searing Afro-Latin workouts. The disc has six bonus cuts culled from various Tjader sessions that display his versatility. While they're entertaining, the disc's real meat comes in the nine songs that match Tjader and Palmieri, supported sometimes by a three-trombone/flute frontline with bass and percussion and at other times by an orchestra. The CD also has extensive liner notes and excellent remastering. —*Ron Wynn*

Champagne / 1968 / Tico ◆◆◆◆
Champagne was a transitional album from 1968, one that retained tracks with the two-trombone Perfecta but had others that looked forward—an off-center piano solo here, some blazing solo trumpet, a melody that is "Un Dia…" in embryo, a touch of proto-Latin-funk. —*John Storm Roberts, Original Music*

★ **Sun of Latin Music** / 1973 / Coco ◆◆◆◆◆
This album almost perfectly combines Palmieri's experimentalism with the devastating swing that kept him ahead on the street. The "Un Dia Bonito" suite got most attention, but "Una Rosa Española," a one-cut mini-history of salsa, is enchanting. —*John Storm Roberts*

Paragon Ragtime Orchestra

Group / Ragtime
In 1985 Rick Benjamin stumbled across priceless arrangements of the Arthur Pryor Orchestra, which had been lost for 65 years. After acquiring the vast amount of music, Benjamin formed the 15-piece Paragon Ragtime Orchestra, an ensemble that has, during the past decade, performed works ranging from rags and early popular music to novelties and even satires of classical music. They have thus far recorded three excellent sets for Newport Classic and Dorian Discovery that show that there was always more to ragtime than piano solos! —*Scott Yanow*

★ **On the Boardwalk** / 1986 / Newport Classics ◆◆◆◆◆
Although ragtime is primarily thought of as music played by solo pianists, during the ragtime era there were many orchestras that performed the lively syncopated style using full orchestrations. Educator Rick Benjamin in 1985 accidentally discovered most of the existing library of The Arthur Pryor Orchestra (which was about to be thrown away) and formed The Paragon Ragtime Orchestra so as to bring the music back to life. In addition to a string quintet, the band uses two cornets, a trombone, two clarinets, a flute, tuba, string bass, drums and percussion on this CD, their recording debut. The colorful charts range from Scott Joplin and W.C. Handy to obscurities, pop tunes of the era, a "George M. Cohan medley" and "An Operatic Nightmare: Desecration Rag No. 2." This is delightful and timeless music that was almost permanently lost. —*Scott Yanow*

The Whistler and His Dog / 1988 / Newport Classics ◆◆◆◆◆
The second CD by Rick Benjamin's Paragon Ragtime Orchestra (which is comprised of a string quartet, two cornets, one trombone, two clarinets, flute, bass, drums and percussion) is the equal of the first. Using arrangments originally part of The Arthur Pryor Orchestra, this nonimprovising but very syncopated ensemble performs a wide variety of music from the 1905–1920 period,

everything from "Dynamite Rag" and "Smiles" to "The Whistler and His Dog" and a waltz medley titled "Old Chestnuts." The little-known music should greatly please followers of classic jazz since it is its direct predecessor. —*Scott Yanow*

That Demon Rag / Mar. 2, 1992–Mar. 3, 1992 / Dorian ◆◆◆◆
The Paragon Ragtime Orchestra is one of the premiere bands in the esoteric but very accessible idiom of orchestrated ragtime (as opposed to solo pianists). Consisting of a string quartet, two clarinets, two cornets, one trombone, a flutist doubling on piccolo, a bassist and a versatile drummer, this ensemble is directed by its founder Rick Benjamin. Its third recording has quite a variety of mostly obscure music among its 19 pieces including Arthur Pryor's "A Cakewalk Contest," two of Scott Joplin's lesser-known rags, "Ragtime Travesty on 'Il Trovatore' " (which satirizes classical music), Eubie Blake's "Chevy Chase Foxtrot," the "Spirit of Independence" march and a couple of popular numbers. This prejazz music (which has no improvisation but plenty of syncopation) is colorfully performed and should greatly interest fans of early American music, jazz and ragtime alike. —*Scott Yanow*

Barbara Paris

b. Oct. 2, 1954, Colorado
Vocals / Standards
An excellent jazz vocalist who is able to make even warhorses sound fresh, Barbara Paris has recorded two fine CDs for her Perea label. —*Scott Yanow*

● **Where Butterflies Play** / 1992–1993 / Perea Productions ◆◆◆◆◆
Barbara Paris, who has a lovely sweet voice and a gentle straightfoward style, is based in Boulder, CO. On this CD her singing is featured in three different settings. Paris performs four ballads (including Harold Vick's "Where Butterflies Play" and "Do You Know What It Means to Miss New Orleans") in duets with pianist Joe Bonner, interprets two Jobim songs plus "How Deep Is the Ocean" while accompanied by guitarist Mitchell Long and concludes the set with four songs in which she is joined by the talented pianist Ellyn Rucker, the Stan Getz-inspired Richie Chiaraluce on tenor and bassist Dean Ross. The one fault to this program is that the tempos tend to be similar; only the closing pieces with the quartet ("Star Eyes" and "April in Paris") cook a bit. However, the sincerity and appealing simplicity of Barbara Paris' style easily compensate. —*Scott Yanow*

Happy Talk / Apr. 1994 / Perea ◆◆◆◆
Singer Barbara Paris does the near-impossible on this disc, tackling a set of music dominated by veteran standards and making them sound fresh and alive. Certainly "All of Me," "He May Be Your Man" (which uses some phrases identified with Joe Williams) and "But Not for Me" have not exactly been underrecorded through the years, but Paris' subtle creativity and highly appealing phrasing (along with a strong voice), manages to give new life to these warhorses. The supporting cast (pianist Joe Bonner, bassist Kenny Walker, drummer Mike Whitted And Richie Chiaraluce on tenor, alto and flute), although Bonner is the only one with a national reputation, are some of the best musicians based in Colorado. Highlights of the program include "Everything Happens to Me," "April in Paris," "Whisper Not" and "I Fall in Love Too Easily." This CD is easily recommended to listeners who enjoy swinging bop-based vocalists. —*Scott Yanow*

Charlie Parker

b. Aug. 29, 1920, Kansas City, **d.** Mar. 12, 1955, NYC
Alto Saxophone, Leader, Composer / Bop
One of a handful of musicians who can be said to have permanently changed jazz, Charlie Parker was arguably the greatest saxophonist of all time. He could play remarkably fast lines that, if slowed down to half speed, would reveal that every note made sense. Bird, along with his contemporaries Dizzy Gillespie and Bud Powell, is considered a founder of bebop; in reality he was an intuitive player who simply was expressing himself. Rather than basing his improvisations closely on the melody as was done in swing, he was a master of chordal improvising, creating new melodies that were based on the structure of a song. In fact Bird wrote several future standards (such as "Anthropology," "Ornithology," "Scrapple from the Apple," and "Ko Ko" along with such blues as "Now's the Time" and "Parker's Mood") that "borrowed" and modernized the chord structures of older tunes. Parker's remarkable technique, fairly original sound and ability to come up with harmonically advanced phrases that could be both

logical and whimsical were highly influential. By 1950 it was impossible to play "modern jazz" with credibility without closely studying Charlie Parker.

Born in Kansas City, KS, Charlie Parker grew up in Kansas City, MO. He first played baritone horn before switching to alto. Parker was so enamored of the rich Kansas City music scene that he dropped out of school when he was 14 even though his musicianship at that point was questionable (with his ideas coming out faster than his fingers could play them). After a few humiliations at jam sessions, Bird worked hard woodshedding over one summer, building up his technique and mastery of the fundamentals. By 1937 when he first joined Jay McShann's Orchestra, he was already a long way toward becoming a major player.

Charlie Parker, who was early on influenced by Lester Young and the sound of Buster Smith, visited New York for the first time in 1939, working as a dishwasher at one point so he could hear Art Tatum play on a nightly basis. He made his recording debut with Jay McShann in 1940, creating remarkable solos with a small group from McShann's Orchestra on "Lady Be Good" and "Honeysuckle Rose." When the McShann big band arrived in New York in 1941, Parker had short solos on a few of their studio blues records and his broadcasts with the orchestra greatly impressed (and sometimes scared) other musicians who had never heard his ideas before. Parker, who had met and jammed with Dizzy Gillespie for the first time in 1940, had a short stint with Noble Sissle's band in 1942, played tenor with Earl Hines' sadly unrecorded bop band of 1943 and spent a few months in 1944 with Billy Eckstine's orchestra, leaving before that group made their first records. Gillespie was also in the Hines and Eckstine big bands and the duo became a team starting in late 1944.

Although Charlie Parker recorded with Tiny Grimes' combo in 1944, it was his collaborations with Dizzy Gillespie in 1945 that startled the jazz world. To hear the two virtuosos play rapid unisons on such new songs as "Groovin' High," "Dizzy Atmosphere," "Shaw 'Nuff," "Salt Peanuts" and "Hot House" and then launch into fiery and unpredictable solos could be an upsetting experience for listeners much more familiar with Glenn Miller and Benny Goodman. Although the new music was evolutionary rather than revolutionary, the recording strike of 1943-44 resulted in bebop arriving fully formed on records, seemingly out of nowhere.

Unfortunately, Charlie Parker was a heroin addict ever since he was a teenager and some other musicians who idolized Bird foolishly took up drugs in the hope that it would elevate their playing to his level. When Gillespie and Parker (known as "Diz & Bird") traveled to Los Angeles and were met with a mixture of hostility and indifference (except by younger musicians who listened closely), it was decided to return to New York. Impulsively Parker cashed in his ticket, ended up staying in L.A. and, after some recordings and performances (including a classic version of "Lady Be Good" with Jazz at the Philharmonic), the lack of drugs (which he combatted by drinking an excess of liquor) resulted in a mental breakdown and six months of confinement at the Camarillo State Hospital. Released in January 1947, Parker soon headed back to New York and engaged in some of the most rewarding playing of his career, leading a quintet that included Miles Davis, Duke Jordan, Tommy Potter and Max Roach. Parker, who recorded simultaneously for the Savoy and Dial labels was in peak form during the 1947-51 period, visiting Europe in 1949 and 1950 and realizing a lifelong dream to record with strings starting in 1949 when he switched to Norman Granz's Verve label.

But Charlie Parker, due to his drug addiction and chance-taking personality, enjoyed playing with fire too much. In 1951 his cabaret license was revoked in New York (making it difficult for him to play in clubs) and he became increasingly unreliable. Although he could still play at his best when he was inspired (such as at the 1953 Massey Hall Concert with Gillespie), Bird was heading downhill. In 1954 he twice attempted suicide before spending time in Bellevue. His health, shaken by a very full if brief life of excesses gradually declined and when he died in March 1955 at the age of 34, he could have passed for 64!

Charlie Parker, who was a legendary figure during his lifetime, has if anything grown in stature since his death. Virtually all of his studio recordings are available along with a countless number of radio broadcasts and club appearances. Clint Eastwood put together a well-intentioned if simplified movie about aspects of his life (*Bird*). Parker's influence, after the rise of John Coltrane, has become more indirect than direct, but jazz would sound a

great deal different if Charlie Parker had not existed. The phrase "Bird Lives" (which was scrawled as graffiti after his death) is still very true. —*Scott Yanow*

★ **The Complete "Birth of Bebop"** / May 1940–Dec. 29, 1945 / Stash ✦✦✦✦✦
This is the type of Charlie Parker CD that is essential for Bird collectors but less important to more casual jazz fans. The contents of this set should amaze Parker fanatics: Bird's initial private recording of May 1940 (unaccompanied versions of "Honeysuckle Rose" and "Body and Soul" cut in a private recording booth), four remarkable studio-quality selections from 1942 (including "Cherokee") in which the altoist is just backed by rhythm guitar and quiet drums, rehearsal and jam session numbers from 1943 with Bird on tenor (including an amazing seven-minute version of "Sweet Georgia Brown" by the trio of Parker, trumpeter Dizzy Gillespie and bassist Oscar Pettiford) and three lengthy cuts from a late-1945 broadcast by Diz and Bird with a sextet. These important recordings fill a major gap, giving one many clues as to how Charlie Parker sounded before he emerged fully formed on records in 1945. —*Scott Yanow*

Early Bird (1940–1944) / Aug. 1940-1944 / Stash ✦✦✦✦✦
This Stash CD contains some remarkable performances by the young Charlie Parker with pianist Jay McShann's Orchestra. First Bird is heard at the age of 20 with an octet from McShann's big band playing six standards and a blues; his solos on "Lady Be Good" and particularly "Honeysuckle Rose" are classic. Then, after Parker's early version of "Cherokee" from 1942 with the house band at Monroe's Uptown House, one gets to hear what Bird really sounded like on a typical night with Jay McShann's big band. Parker's studio recordings with McShann's Orchestra were three-minute affairs that generally gave him a chorus at the most but, on this 1942 broadcast, Bird really stretches out on a few of the songs, particularly "I'm Forever Blowing Bubbles," and shows just how advanced a player he was at that early stage. This CD concludes with the 1944 McShann big band (after Bird had departed) in fine form on a radio aircheck and, as a bonus strictly for completists, a very scratchy (and almost unlistenable) version of "I Got Rhythm" from August 1940 by McShann with Bird. —*Scott Yanow*

● **The Charlie Parker Story, Vol. 1** / Nov. 1940–Feb. 26, 1947 / Stash Budget ✦✦✦✦
This budget CD release from Stash has some of the highlights of Charlie Parker's career, tracing in chronological order his evolution during 1940-47. The most interesting of the 13 selections are the first six. "Lady Be Good" from 1940 with a small group from Jay McShann's band, Bird playing "I'm Forever Blowing Bubbles" on the radio with the full McShann orchestra, jam session versions of "Body and Soul," "Cherokee" and "Sweet Georgia Brown" from 1942-43 (the latter song has Parker on tenor with a trio comprised of trumpeter Dizzy Gillespie and bassist Oscar Pettiford!) and a Bird and Diz broadcast version of " 'Shaw Nuff." The remainder of the set is more familiar, drawing from Parker's Dial studio recordings of 1946-47. Overall, this CD (and the second volume) gives listeners an interesting introduction to Charlie Parker's music, although all of these performances are available in more complete form elsewhere. —*Scott Yanow*

★ **Complete Savoy Studio Sessions** / Sep. 15, 1944–Sep. 24, 1948 / Savoy ✦✦✦✦✦
This three-CD box set contains all of the recordings Charlie Parker made for the Savoy label and it is overflowing with gems and an almost countless number of alternate takes. Bird was one of the most important jazzmen of all time and nearly every note he recorded (in the studios if not live) is well worth hearing. This box starts off with his sideman date with Tiny Grimes in 1944, contains Parker's famous "Ko Ko" session of 1945 (with a young Miles Davis on trumpet and highlighted by "Now's the Time" and "Billie's Bounce") and continues through his 1947-48 quintet sessions with a more mature Miles Davis, either Bud Powell, John Lewis or Duke Jordan on piano, bassists Tommy Potter, Curly Russell or Nelson Boyd and drummer Max Roach. Together they recorded such classics as "Donna Lee," "Chasin' the Bird," "Milestones" and "Parker's Mood." Every scrap that the great altoist cut for Savoy is on this box. —*Scott Yanow*

Bird/The Savoy Recordings (Master Takes) / 1944-1948 / Savoy ✦✦✦✦✦
Foundation recordings by alto sax giant Charlie Parker, which have been reissued in many other forms. These are remastered

versions taken directly from the master tapes. Parker was making history at this point, playing with a speed, harmonic brilliance, and creativity that hadn't been imagined before, particularly on alto sax. —*Ron Wynn*

Every Bit of It / Jan. 1945–Dec. 1945 / Spotlite ♦♦♦♦♦
This very interesting double LP from the English Spotlite label contains many of Charlie Parker's lesser-known recordings from 1945. Bird is featured with trumpeter Dizzy Gillespie not only on the five songs recorded by blues singer Rubberlegs Williams but backing trombonist Trummy Young's vocals (real rarities), three numbers featuring Sarah Vaughan and on a session with guitarist/jokester Slim Gaillard; "Slim's Jam" is a classic of its kind. In addition Parker participates on a half-hour broadcast by Cootie Williams' orchestra (although he only solos on the lone sextet number "Floogie Boo") and on four hot titles with pianist Sir Charles Thompson, trumpeter Buck Clayton and tenor saxophonist Dexter Gordon. —*Scott Yanow*

Yardbird in Lotus Land / Dec. 29, 1945–Apr. 1946 / Spotlite ♦♦♦♦
This LP from the fine English label Spotlite contains several remarkable radio broadcasts featuring the immortal altoist Charlie Parker. First Bird is heard with trumpet great Dizzy Gillespie in a quintet (with one number adding vibraphonist Milt Jackson) from Los Angeles on Dec. 29, 1945 during their famous stint at Billy Berg's. These versions of "Shaw 'Nuff," "Groovin' High" and "Dizzy Atmosphere" are four to six minutes long and really let the soloists stretch out. A briefer "Salt Peanuts" is also heard from the same group. Bird then participates on a ballad medley with fellow altoists Willie Smith and Benny Carter, plays "Ornithology" while joined by the Nat King Cole Trio and Buddy Rich, and finally performs five numbers with trumpeter Miles Davis in a quintet; all of these performances took place in Los Angeles before Parker was hospitalized. —*Scott Yanow*

Bebop's Heartbeat / Dec. 29, 1945–Sep. 29, 1947 / Savoy ♦♦♦♦
Half of this LP consists of the odd but famous Slim Gaillard session in which the guitarist/personality was joined by altoist Charlie Parker and trumpeter Dizzy Gillespie for four songs (highlighted by the humorous "Slim's Jam"). The flip side contains more essential music, the appearance by Diz and Bird at Carnegie Hall on Sept. 29, 1947. These renditions of "A Night in Tunisia," "Dizzy Atmosphere," "Groovin' High" and "Ko Ko" (despite the so-so recording quality) are brilliant, but Parker's solo on "Confirmation" really takes honors. —*Scott Yanow*

★ **Bird: Complete on Verve** / Jan. 28, 1946–Dec. 10, 1954 / Verve ♦♦♦♦♦
As a leader, Charlie Parker recorded for Savoy and Dial during 1945–48 and then for Verve exclusively (at least in the studios) during 1949–54. This remarkable ten-CD box set, which adds quite a bit of material to an earlier ten-LP set, has all of these recordings plus Bird's earlier appearances with Jazz at the Philharmonic. The JATP jams are highlighted by Parker's perfect solo on "Lady Be Good," a ferocious improvisation on "The Closer" and a solo on "Embraceable You" that tops his more famous studio recording. In addition, this box has all of the "Bird and Strings" sides, his meetings with Machito's Cuban orchestra, the 1950 session with Dizzy Gillespie and Thelonious Monk, small-group dates (including a 1951 meeting with Miles Davis), odd encounters with voices and studio bands, the famous "Jam Blues" with fellow altoists Johnny Hodges and Benny Carter and his final recordings, a set of Cole Porter tunes. The fact-filled 34 page booklet is also indispensable. Highly recommended. —*Scott Yanow*

★ **Complete Dial Sessions** / Feb. 5, 1946–Dec. 17, 1947 / Stash ♦♦♦♦♦
Charlie Parker recorded for Dial during the same period he was cutting his better-known sides for Savoy. This four-CD set contains his 89 Dial recordings including all of the alternate takes. The innovative altoist is heard with Dizzy Gillespie on "Diggin' Diz," playing definitive versions of "Moose the Mooche," "Yardbird Suite" and "Ornithology" in a septet, struggling during his tragic "Lover Man" date, on excerpts from a poorly recorded live session, backing singer Earl Coleman and interacting with the Erroll Garner Trio, playing his classic "Relaxin' at Camarillo" (four versions), and finally leading several sessions with his classic quintet (which included trumpeter Miles Davis, pianist Duke Jordan, bassist Tommy Potter and drummer Max Roach,) recording such gems as "Dewey Square," "Embraceable You," and "Scrapple from

the Apple," the final session adds the great trombonist J.J. Johnson to the group for more classic music. Essential music, highly recommended for all jazz collections. —*Scott Yanow*

The Charlie Parker Story, Vol. 2 / Mar. 28, 1946–1954 / Stash Budget ♦♦♦♦
The second of two CDs in this budget series has a few of the highlights from Charlie Parker's brief but remarkable career. Six of the 13 selections are taken from his Dial recordings, there is a stunning version of "Ko Ko" from a 1949 Carnegie Hall Concert and a variety of live appearances from the 1949–54 period that are mostly drawn from radio and television broadcasts. All of the music is available in more complete form on a variety of Stash releases, but these two volumes can serve as a good introduction to Bird's music for general collectors who just want a taste of the master's magic. —*Scott Yanow*

The Legendary Dial Masters, Vol. 1 / 1946–1947 / Stash ♦♦♦♦
The recordings alto saxophonist Charlie Parker made for the Dial label in the late '40s are among bop's most storied and vital. He helped establish the genre's vocabulary, playing with the verve, fury, and harmonic excellence that forever altered jazz's course and that of alto saxophonists. Parker worked with Miles Davis, Dizzy Gillespie, Lucky Thompson, and many others while cutting several sessions in California for a label owned by Ross Russell. While they have been reissued on vinyl by England's Spotlite label in nearly complete form, and in a haphazard manner by Warner Bros., this 1989 disc collects 25 seminal master takes from 1946 and 1947. Every solo deserves close scrutiny, as Parker and company turn theory and tradition inside out. —*Ron Wynn*

The Legendary Dial Sessions, Vol. 2 / 1946–1947 / Stash ♦♦♦
The second volume devoted to Charlie Parker's Dial recordings includes 10 master takes from 1947, plus eight numbers from a 1947 jam session at the home of Hollywood studio musician Chuck Kopely done shortly after Parker was released from Camarillo State Hospital, and nine alternate cuts with Parker playing in quartet, quintet, septet, and sextet settings. They are all essential, many brilliant, and even those that contain audible flubs or detail problems in group organization and performance present amazing, frenetic Parker solos. —*Ron Wynn*

Lullaby in Rhythm / Feb. 1, 1947–Sep. 20, 1947 / Spotlite ♦♦♦
This LP contains music from two radio broadcasts that feature a remarkable all-star band: altoist Charlie Parker, trumpeter Dizzy Gillespie, clarinetist John LaPorta, pianist Lennie Tristano, guitarist Billy Bauer, bassist Ray Brown and drummer Max Roach. In addition to playing bop standards of the period, to answer a request the ensemble performs a rather hilarious version of "Tiger Rag." The matchup of Tristano and his sidemen with Bird and Diz does not always work, but it is fascinating to hear. In addition, there are a few excerpts from live sessions featuring poorly recorded but interesting Parker solos. —*Scott Yanow*

The Dean Benedetti Recordings of Charlie Parker / Mar. 1, 1947–Jul. 1, 1948 / Mosaic ♦♦
The packaging is impeccable, this seven-CD box set has a definitive 48-page booklet and the recording quality is as good as possible, so why the "Poor" rating? Dean Benedetti, a fanatical Charlie Parker disciple, recorded Bird extensively during three periods in 1947–48, but did his best to turn off his wire recorder whenever anyone but Parker was soloing. He became legendary, as did his long lost acetates, and Mosaic has done what it could to make the excerpts coherent but the results are still quite unlistenable. None of the performances on this large set are complete; guests such as Thelonious Monk and Carmen McRae are introduced, play or sing two notes and then are cut off. And, although Parker seems to play well, these performances reveal no new secrets and add nothing to his legacy. —*Scott Yanow*

With Dizzy Gillespie & Miles Davis / 1947–1950 / Stash ♦♦
This CD from Stash's budget series has some "new" Charlie Parker performances but, as veteran collectors well know when confronted with Bird discoveries, the main question must always be "What condition is it in?" Unfortunately, the answer in this case is "not good." The great altoist is heard playing with the Dizzy Gillespie big band on ten songs in addition to five selections with his own quintet (when Miles Davis was his trumpeter) and one obscurity from 1950. However, the music (recorded by customers in the audience on low-budget tape recorders) is generally incomplete since the tapes were often turned off at the conclusion of Parker's solos. Although Stash's engineers did what they could to

correct the pitch and clean up the music, the results are still diffi-cult to listen to, at least until one gets used to it. It is very inter-esting to hear Bird with Gillespie's orchestra (a collaboration oth-erwise never recorded) and to listen to Parker playing such unlikely songs as "Things to Come," a fairly lengthy "'Round Midnight," "Good Bait" and "Manteca." But this release is only for true Charlie Parker fanatics. —*Scott Yanow*

The Band That Never Was / Mar. 1948 / Spotlite ✦✦✦
In 1950 arranger Gene Roland briefly ran a huge 25-piece rehearsal band. The orchestra did not last very long, but on April 3 they recorded three numbers plus a lot of excerpts and those are included on this LP. Most notable is the fact that Charlie Parker pops up briefly on these songs, along with trombonist Jimmy Knepper and tenors Al Cohn and Zoot Sims, but the music is mostly of historical interest. Side Two of this LP features the Charlie Parker quintet with trumpeter Miles Davis live from the Three Deuces in March 1948, playing quite well. —*Scott Yanow*

Bird on 52nd Street / Jul. 1948 / Original Jazz Classics ✦✦
An excellent 1948 date, with formative Miles Davis (tpt) solos, good Duke Jordan (p), and brilliant Parker. —*Ron Wynn*

★ **Bird at the Roost: Savoy Years** / Sep. 4, 1948–Jan. 1, 1949 / Savoy ✦✦✦✦✦
Among the most rewarding live recordings of Charlie Parker are his performances on a regular series of broadcasts that emanated from the Royal Roost during 1948–49. Muse, in its Savoy series, released all of this valuable music on two double LPs and a sin-gle album; some of it has since appeared on CD. This first volume has six of these radio airchecks (with Symphony Sid Torin announcing) and finds Parker and his quintet (either Miles Davis or Kenny Dorham on trumpets, Tadd Dameron or Al Haig on piano, Curley Russell or Tommy Potter on bass and Max Roach or Joe Harris on drums) getting the opportunity to stretch out on four- to five-minute versions of such songs as "Groovin' High," "Big Foot," "Ornithology," "Slow Boat to China" and "East of the Sun" among others. A special highlight occurs when Bird answers a request on the December 25 broadcast and does a brilliant reworking of "White Christmas." Highly recommended. —*Scott Yanow*

Sessions Live, Vol. 2 / Dec. 12, 1948–Sep. 26, 1952 / Zeta ✦✦
This CD features Charlie Parker during live appearances from two periods. The first eight selections are taken from his Royal Roost broadcasts of 1948–49, music that is available in more coherent fashion elsewhere but is well worth hearing, featuring Miles Davis on one version of "Hot House" and Kenny Dorham elsewhere. The second half of this disc originated from the Rockland Palace Dance Hall in 1952, is poorly recorded (lots of audience noise) and has been reissued by many labels through the years. Bird is heard with a four-piece rhythm section (with strings added on "Laura") and plays reasonably well. —*Scott Yanow*

Sessions Live, Vol. 1 / 1948–1950 / Zeta ✦✦
An '89 CD reissue of late '40s and early '50s tracks with alto sax great Charlie Parker cut live at two seminal locations, Birdland and the Royal Roost. Some have been previously issued on sepa-rate live recordings from the same places. Miles Davis, Kenny Dorham, Max Roach, Fats Navarro, Art Blakey, Curley Russell, and Bud Powell are among the participants. —*Ron Wynn*

★ **Bird at the Roost: the Savoy Years (Complete Royal Roost Performances), Vol. 2** / Jan. 1, 1949–Feb. 19, 1949 / Savoy ✦✦✦✦✦
This double LP, the second of three volumes, continues the docu-mentation of Charlie Parker's Royal Roost broadcasts, perfor-mances that allowed his quintet (with trumpeter Kenny Dorham, pianist Al Haig, bassist Tommy Potter and usually drummer Max Roach) to stretch out on such songs as "Scrapple from the Apple," "Hot House," "Barbados," "Groovin' High" and "Oop Bop Sh'Bam." The immortal altoist is heard at his peak throughout and is in consistently brilliant form giving one a good idea as to what his live performances from the era must have been like. —*Scott Yanow*

Rara Avis / Feb. 21, 1949–1954 / Stash ✦✦✦✦
This CD released for the first time the soundtrack of two of Charlie Parker's appearances on television. Some of the music and talking is trivial and loose but a few of the performances are quite unique and Bird is heard with a variety of intriguing groups. From 1949 Parker plays a fine version of "Lover" and helps trum-

peter Shorty Sherrock on "I Can't Get Started," but is drowned out by Sidney Bechet on an uptempo blues. From 1952 Bird gets fea-tured on "Anthropology" and participates in a "Bop vs. Dixieland" blues with trumpeters Max Kaminsky and Miles Davis, trombon-ists Kai Winding and Will Bradley and clarinetist Joe Marsala; everyone gets to solo. This interesting CD concludes with Bird in fine form in 1954 with a quintet that also includes trumpeter Herb Pomeroy, material not available elsewhere. —*Scott Yanow*

Bird at the Roost: the Savoy Years (Complete Royal Roost Performances), Vol. 3 / Feb. 26, 1949–Mar. 12, 1949 / Savoy ✦✦✦✦✦
Some of Charlie Parker's finest live recordings were performed at the Royal Roost and broadcast on the radio during 1948–49. Savoy, on two double LPs and this single album, released all of the music in chronological order. Vol. 3 contains the final three broadcasts with Bird's quintet of the period (trumpeter Kenny Dorham, pianist Al Haig, bassist Tommy Potter and drummer Max Roach) being augmented by such special guests as vibra-phonist Milt Jackson, tenor saxophonist Lucky Thompson and bop singers Dave Lambert and Buddy Stewart. Highlights include "Half-Nelson," "Cheryl," "Anthropology" and a six-minute version of "Chasin' the Bird." Highly recommended along with the two earlier volumes. —*Scott Yanow*

Bird in Paris / May 8, 1949–Nov. 1950 / Spotlite ✦✦
During the last five or six years of his life, Charlie Parker's live per-formances were frequently recorded and, later on, many of these ses-sions were released posthumously. This LP documents Charlie Parker's first visit to France and is mostly comprised of a quintet per-formance (with trumpeter Kenny Dorham, pianist Al Haig, bassist Tommy Potter and drummer Max Roach) originally recorded on a portable disc machine; the recording quality is quite erratic and there are breaks in a few of the songs where the fan had to turn the disc over. This LP concludes with part of an overcrowded blues (that is chiefly notable as the only example of a song boasting solos from both Bird and soprano great Sidney Bechet) and a broadcast version of "Ladybird" from the following year that features Parker with a French orchestra. It's a very interesting set from a historical stand-point, but this LP is not at all essential. —*Scott Yanow*

★ **Charlie Parker & Stars of Modern Jazz at Carnegie Hall (Christmas 1949)** / Dec. 25, 1949 / Jass ✦✦✦✦✦
This Carnegie Hall concert can be considered the height of the bebop era. Among the top young modernists heard near their early peaks are pianist Bud Powell, trumpeter Miles Davis, bari-tonist Serge Chaloff, altoist Sonny Stitt, trombonist Kai Winding, tenor saxophonists Stan Getz and Warne Marsh, pianist Lennie Tristano, altoist Lee Konitz and Sarah Vaughan. But while their performances are consistently outsanding, Charlie Parker and his quintet (which includes trumpeter Red Rodney, pianist Al Haig, bassist Tommy Potter and drummer Roy Haynes) steals the show. Bird and Rodney rarely sounded more fiery than on their five songs, and Parker's incredible solo on this version of "Ko Ko" might very well be his best. This CD is highly recommended for all collections. —*Scott Yanow*

One Night in Chicago / 1950 / Savoy ✦✦
Another LP primarily for Charlie Parker fanatics, this live perfor-mance finds Bird playing with some top Chicago musicians (the obscure Claude McLin on tenor, guitarist George Freeman, pianist Chris Anderson, bassist Leroy Jackson and drummer Bruz Freeman). Most of the selections are not quite complete although they offer a rare chance to hear Bird play songs not in his reper-toire (including "There's a Small Hotel," "These Foolish Things" and "Keen and Peachy") but the recording quality is much worse than one would hope. It's interesting music but not really worth hearing more than once or twice. —*Scott Yanow*

Live at Birdland (1950) / Feb. 14, 1950 / EPM ✦
A major disappointment, this CD from its outside looks like a promising sextet session with Charlie Parker, trumpeter Red Rodney and trombonist J.J. Johnson, but whoever recorded these bootlegs shut off their machine whenever Bird was finished solo-ing, cutting off Rodney and Johnson after a few notes and virtu-ally ruining the performances. In addition, the recording quality is pretty shaky and Bird really does not say anytything all that new. This should not have been released. —*Scott Yanow*

Bird at St. Nick's / Feb. 18, 1950 / Original Jazz Classics ✦✦
In this top-shelf session, Red Rodney shines on trumpet and Al Haig stars on piano. —*Ron Wynn*

Bird & Diz / Jun. 6, 1950 / Verve ✦✦✦✦✦
This session features quite a group: Charlie Parker on alto, trumpeter Dizzy Gillespie, pianist Thelonious Monk, bassist Curly Russell and drummer Buddy Rich. They perform five Bird originals along with "My Melancholy Baby" and there are also seven alternate takes included on this CD. This music is available as part of the Verve ten-CD box, but this particular release is quite enjoyable by itself. Bird and Monk never recorded together otherwise. —*Scott Yanow*

One Night at Birdland / Jun. 30, 1950 / Columbia ✦✦✦✦
The recording date may be suspect (trumpeter Fats Navarro died of tuberculosis only a week later) and the recording quality is not state of the art but the music on this two-LP set is often quite brilliant. Charlie Parker is teamed with Navarro, pianist Bud Powell, bassist Curley Russell and drummer Art Blakey for extended (usually six- to ten-minute) versions of 13 songs including "'Round Midnight" (the only time that Bird ever recorded a Thelonious Monk tune), "Move," "Out of Nowhere" and "Ornithology." The all-star lineup clearly inspired each other, making this two-fer well worth searching for. —*Scott Yanow*

Apartment Sessions / Jun. 1950 / Spotlite ✦✦
This LP is strictly for Charlie Parker collectors because the music was privately recorded, the technical quality is streaky and Bird's solos were nearly all that was documented at these two jam sessions from 1950. Parker was in fine form on those days, but there are many more essential Bird recordings available. —*Scott Yanow*

Bird with Strings / Aug. 23, 1950–Nov. 14, 1952 / Columbia ✦✦✦
During 1949–54, Charlie Parker often recorded and performed with a string section. This LP contains a cross section of Bird's live performances from 1950–52 and, although the string arrangements are the same as for the studio recordings, Parker's solos are quite a bit different. Pity there's no live version of "Just Friends," his most successful string recording. It's not quite essential music, but worth picking up. —*Scott Yanow*

The Bird You Never Heard / Aug. 28, 1950–Jan. 18, 1954 / Stash ✦✦
This CD features Charlie Parker caught live in 1954 with a quintet including Herb Pomeroy, as part of an unknown group in 1950, with pianist Bud Powell, bassist Charles Mingus, drummer Art Taylor and Candido on congas on two songs from 1953 and sitting in with the Chet Baker Quartet in 1953 (although only Bird's solos from the latter were recorded). The recording quality is streaky and these leftover performances from routine gigs are recommended only for Charlie Parker completists. —*Scott Yanow*

In Sweden / Nov. 24, 1950 / Alamac ✦✦
This LP from the budget label Alamac finds Charlie Parker in brilliant form playing with a small group filled with talented young Swedish players (including trumpeter Rolf Ericson). Unfortunately, the poor recording quality of this live performance lowers the rating quite a bit although listeners who really love Bird will want this one. —*Scott Yanow*

Summit Meeting at Birdland / Mar. 31, 1951–May 9, 1953 / Columbia ✦✦✦✦✦
This LP features the quintet of altoist Charlie Parker, trumpeter Dizzy Gillespie, pianist Bud Powell, bassist Tommy Potter and drummer Roy Haynes performing stirring versions of four bebop standards; "Blue 'N Boogie" and "Anthropology" receive definitive and very exciting treatment. The flip side features Bird on "Groovin' High" with Milt Buckner's trio (the only time that Parker recorded with an organist) and on a few songs with pianist John Lewis, bassist Curly Russell, drummer Kenny Clarke; percussionist Candido sits in for "Broadway." The recording quality is acceptable and Bird's playing is exceptional. This recommended music should be reissued on CD. —*Scott Yanow*

The Happy Bird / Apr. 12, 1951 / Charlie Parker ✦✦✦
The weak recording quality hurts this LP a bit, but it does offer extended performances of "Scapple from the Apple" (over 15 minutes), "I Remember April" and "Lullaby in Rhythm" (mislabelled "I May Be Wrong") in addition to a short blues. These jam sessions, in addition to altoist Charlie Parker, feature solos from tenor saxophonist Wardell Gray, pianist Dick Twardzik and trumpeter Benny Harris; bassist Charles Mingus and drummer Roy Haynes are fine in support. Not essential music, but recommended if seen at a budget price. —*Scott Yanow*

Live: Boston, Brooklyn . . . 1951 / Apr. 1951–Jun. 1951 / EPM ✦✦
Some of Charlie Parker's more fanatical fans followed him around

constantly, taping his live performances, but usually turning off their recorders whenever Bird's sidemen soloed. The results are poorly recorded excerpts from often-routine gigs. This CD, which features Parker on three separate occasions in 1951, is better than some of the bootleg releases in this idiom, but of very limited interest except to Charlie Parker completists who have to have every note of his that has survived. —*Scott Yanow*

Bird With The Herd: 1951 / Aug. 1951 / Alamac ✦✦✦
As is often the case with Charlie Parker's live recordings from the 1950s, this rare performance has erratic sound and bad balance. Still this session, which finds Bird sitting in with Woody Herman's Third Herd, is quite unique. Parker is the main soloist throughout the budget LP, getting a chance to play some fresh material like "The Goof and I," "Four Brothers," and "Lemon Drop" and to interact with a big band. —*Scott Yanow*

Inglewood Jam / Jun. 16, 1952 / Time Is ✦✦✦
This CD's historic value outweighs the below-par recording quality. Trumpeter Chet Baker is heard shortly before he joined Gerry Mulligan's quartet participating on a jam session with altos Charlie Parker and Sonny Criss. They play lengthy versions of four songs and there are plenty of heated moments on this bop set. It's recommended to listeners who do not demand state-of-the-art sound. —*Scott Yanow*

One Night in Washington / 1953 / Elektra ✦✦✦✦
Charlie Parker had a rare chance to play with a big band during this Washington, D.C., concert. Appearing without any rehearsal or even with music in front of him, Bird performed eight numbers with the orchestra, anticipating where the arrangements would go and not missing a cue. His brilliant playing on this out-of-print LP demonstrates to all listeners why he was considered one of the giants of jazz. The recommended set concludes with Red Rodney in the early '80s reminiscing a bit about his time with Charlie Parker. —*Scott Yanow*

Charlie Parker at Storyville / Mar. 10, 1953–Sep. 22, 1953 / Blue Note ✦✦✦
This LP contains two broadcasts featuring Charlie Parker at Boston's Storyville club in 1953. One set finds him accompanied by the Red Garland Trio (two years before Garland became famous playing with Miles Davis) while the other one also features trumpeter Herb Pomeroy and a trio led by pianist Sir Charles Thompson. The recording quality is just so-so, but Bird was in fine form for these sessions, playing hot versions of his usual repertoire. —*Scott Yanow*

Yardbird: DC-53 / Mar. 1953–Apr. 1953 / VGM ✦✦✦
This LP contains a couple of live sessions from late in Charlie Parker's career. He is heard on three selections with a fairly large big band that probably includes Zoot Sims on tenor and guitarist Charlie Byrd along with four numbers performed with a trio. Bird is in better form than the recording quality, making this set of primary interest to his long-time collectors. —*Scott Yanow*

★ **Jazz at Massey Hall** / May 15, 1953 / Original Jazz Classics ✦✦✦✦✦
The music on this CD features the famous Massey Hall Concert, which teamed together (for the last time on records) the unbeatable team of altoist Charlie Parker and trumpeter Dizzy Gillespie along with pianist Bud Powell, bassist Charles Mingus and drummer Max Roach. The full quintet performs six of their standards; listen to Bird burn on "Salt Peanuts" as a reaction to Gillespie's clowning. This is timeless and highly recommended music. —*Scott Yanow*

Bird at The Hi-Hat / Dec. 18, 1953–Jan. 24, 1954 / Blue Note ✦✦✦✦
One of the better examples of late-period Charlie Parker, this CD contains performances by Bird with a Boston-based quintet (featuring trumpeter Herbie Williams). The repertoire was already largely eight years old, but Parker still played such standbys as "Ornithology," "Groovin' High" and "Out of Nowhere" with enthusiasm and creativity. Previously out as a pair of Phoenix LPs, this set should delight Bird's fans. —*Scott Yanow*

Bird / 1988 / Columbia ✦✦✦
This set has the soundtrack of Clint Eastwood's film *Bird*. Arranger Lennie Niehaus managed to isolate Charlie Parker's original alto solos (some from studio sessions and a few from rarer club appearances) and re-recorded them with contemporary bop-based musicians. The effect is rather eerie and generally works, allowing such musicians as pianists Monty Alexander,

Barry Harris and Walter Davis, Jr., bassists Ray Brown, Chuck Berghofer and Ron Carter, drummer John Guerin and trumpeters Jon Faddis and Red Rodney to play with Bird. Worth acquiring if only for the novelty value since this setting did not allow Parker the opportunity to react to the other musicians. —*Scott Yanow*

Errol Parker

b. 1930, Oran, Algeria
Piano, Drums, Leader / Avant-Garde
Errol Parker's music, though largely overlooked by the jazz establishment, is quite fresh and original. Utilizing polytonality (playing in two keys at once), simultaneous soloing and his own drumming (which achieves an African sound by substituting a conga for the snare drum), Parker's tentet sounds unlike any other group. Mostly self-taught on piano, he moved to Paris in 1947 to study sculpture, but was soon playing jazz. Parker (under his original name Raph Schecroun) recorded on sessions led by Kenny Clarke, James Moody and Django Reinhardt and played off and on with Don Byas during 1956-58. He recorded some commercial music on organ in 1960 and then, to escape from an exclusive contract so as to record jazz versions of Top 40 material on piano, he used the pseudonym Errol Parker. The latter records sold so well that he permanently changed his name. A car accident in 1963 cut short his commercial success and forced Parker to change his style.

After moving to New York in 1968, he formed the Errol Parker Experience, which featured two horns. Because he was not satisfied with any other drummers, he began doubling on drums himself, and the first few records for his Sahara label had Parker playing (via overdubbing) both piano and drums. In 1982 while teaching at the Williamsburg Music Center, he formed a big band that eventually became his tentet. Due to the eight horns he utilizes, Parker stopped playing piano except for solo engagements and stuck to drums. His recordings (which include a solo piano tribute to Thelonious Monk) have utilized such sidemen as Robin Eubanks, Wallace Roney, Donald Harrison, Steve Coleman, Graham Haynes, Philip Harper, Byard Lancaster and Jimmy Owens among others. —*Scott Yanow*

Doodles / 1979 / Sahara ✦✦✦✦

★ **Tentet** / Apr. 26, 1982 / Sahara ✦✦✦✦✦
Algerian-born pianist/percussionist in an original mode. Extraordinary creative music, live in 'rehearsal' at the Williamsburg Music Center in Brooklyn. —*Michael G. Nastos*

● **Tribute to Thelonius Monk** / May 4, 1982 / Sahara ✦✦✦✦✦

Compelling Forces / 1985 / Cadence ✦✦✦✦

A Night in Tunisia / Apr. 1991 / Sahara ✦✦✦✦
Tentet plays six Parker originals and two standards. Teamwork in playing leader's quirky Monk-like themes is most evident. A fine outing. —*Michael G. Nastos*

Remembering Billy Strayhorn / Sep. 7, 1994+Sep. 28, 1994 / Sahara ✦✦✦✦

Evan Parker

b. Apr. 5, 1944, Bristol, England
Soprano Saxophone, Tenor Saxophone / Avant-Garde, Free Jazz
Among Europe's most innovative and intriguing saxophonists, Evan Parker's solos and playing style are distinguished by his creative use of circular breathing and false fingering. Parker can generate furious bursts, screeches, bleats, honks and spiraling lines and phrases and his solo sax work isn't for the squeamish. He's one of the few players not only willing but anxious to demonstrate his affinity for late-period John Coltrane. Parker worked with a Coltrane-influenced quartet in Birmingham in the early '60s.

Upon resettling in London in 1965, Parker began playing with Spontaneous Music Ensemble. He joined them in 1967 and remained until 1969. Parker met guitarist Derek Bailey while in the group, and the duo formed The Music Improvisation Company in 1968. Parker played with them until 1971, and also began working with the Tony Oxley Sextet in the late '60s. Parker started playing extensively with other European free music groups in the '70s, notably The Globe Unity Orchestra as well as its founder Alexander von Schlippenbach's trio and quartet. Parker, Bailey and Oxley co-formed Incus Records in 1970 and continued operating it through the '80s.

Parker also played with Chris McGregor's Brotherhood of

Breath and other groups with Bailey and did duet sessions with John Stevens and Paul Lytton as well as giving several solo concerts. Parker's albums as a leader and his collaborations are all for various foreign labels; they can be obtained through diligent effort and mail order catalogs. —*Ron Wynn*

Collective Calls / Apr. 15, 1972-Apr. 16, 1972 / Incus ✦✦✦✦

★ **Saxophone Solos** / Jun. 17, 1975-Dec. 9, 1975 / Incus ✦✦✦✦✦

Monoceros / Apr. 30, 1978 / Incus ✦✦✦✦✦

Six of One / Jun. 18, 1980 / Incus ✦✦✦✦✦

Incision / Mar. 1981 / FMP ✦✦✦

Hook, Drift and Shuffle / Feb. 4, 1983 / Incus ✦✦✦

Conic Sections / Jun. 21, 1989 / Ah Um ✦✦✦✦✦

Hall of Mirrors / Feb. 1990 / MM&T ✦✦✦

Process and Reality / 1991 / FMP ✦✦✦✦

Leo Parker

b. Apr. 18, 1925, Washington, D.C., **d.** Feb. 11, 1962, New York, NY
Baritone Saxophone / Bop, Hard Bop
One of the most soulful, as well as skilled, jazz baritonists Leo Parker unfortunately didn't make many albums and didn't have a lengthy career. But he displayed a sustained excellence and intensity that made his baritone solos memorable. Parker blended the flamboyance and downhome simplicity of blues and R&B with the sophistication of bebop. He initially recorded on alto sax with Coleman Hawkins in 1944. While playing with Billy Eckstine's orchestra in 1944, '45 and '46, Parker switched to baritone. He worked in a group led by Dizzy Gillespie on 52nd Street in 1946, and played briefly in Gillespie's big band. A 1947 recording with Sir Charles Thompson "Mad Lad," brought Parker some fame and notoriety. He played with Fats Navarro and in Illinois Jacquet's group from 1947 into the '50s, while making his recording debut as a leader for Savoy in 1947. He was most famous for his late '50s Blue Note albums, but also did sessions for Columbia and Chess. Parker died of a heart attack in 1962 at 37. There's actually quite a bit of Parker's output available on CD, considering the brevity of his career. —*Ron Wynn*

The Baritone Great (1951-1953) / Jul. 7, 1951-Aug. 10, 1953 / Chess ✦✦✦✦
His best, with Sahib Shihab (fl/sax) and Red Saunders. One to seek. —*Michael G. Nastos*

Let Me Tell You 'Bout It / Sep. 9, 1961 / Blue Note ✦✦✦✦
A good 1990 release that provides notable Leo Parker baritone sax. —*Ron Wynn*

● **Rollin' with Leo** / Oct. 12, 1961+Oct. 20, 1961 / Blue Note ✦✦✦✦✦
Baritonist Leo Parker was in the early stages of a comeback when he recorded this, his second Blue Note album of 1961. Tragically, he died just four months later at the age of 37. Performing with a fairly obscure cast (trumpeter Dave Burns is the best known of his sidemen), the full-toned baritonist (who was most influenced by Illinois Jacquet and Charlie Parker) is in excellent form on these basic blues, ballads and jump tunes. —*Scott Yanow*

Horace Parlan

b. Jan. 19, 1931, Pittsburgh, PA
Piano / Hard Bop
Horace Parlan has overcome physical disability and thrived as a pianist despite it. His right hand was partially crippled by polio in his childhood, but Parlan's made frenetic, highly rhythmic right-hand phrases part of his characteristic style, contrasting them with striking left hand chords. He's also infused blues and R&B influences into his style, playing in a stark, sometimes somber fashion. Parlan has always cited Ahmad Jamal and Bud Powell as prime influences.

He began playing in R&B bands during the '50s, joining Charles Mingus' group from 1957 to 1959 following a move from Pittsburgh to New York. Mingus aided his career enormously, both through his recordings and his influence. Parlan played with Booker Ervin in 1960 and 1961, then in the Eddie "Lockjaw" Davis-Johnny Griffin quintet in 1962. Parlan played with Rahsaan Roland Kirk from 1963 to 1966, and had a strong series of Blue Note recordings in the '60s. He left America for Copenhagen in 1973, and gained international recognition for some stunning albums on Steeplechase, including a pair of superb duet sessions with Archie Shepp. He also recorded with Dexter Gordon, Red Mitchell, and in the '80s Frank Foster and Michael Urbaniak. He's done sessions in the '80s on Enja and Timeless. —*Ron Wynn*

Movin' and Groovin' / Feb. 29, 1960 / Blue Note ✦✦✦✦
An album of wonderful trio work with Sam Jones (b), Al Harewood (d). —*Ron Wynn*

Us Three / Apr. 20, 1960 / Blue Note ✦✦✦✦

Speakin' My Piece / Jul. 16, 1960 / Blue Note ✦✦✦✦✦

Headin' South / Dec. 4, 1960 / Blue Note ✦✦✦✦

On the Spur of the Moment / Mar. 18, 1961 / Blue Note ✦✦✦✦

Up and Down / Jun. 18, 1961 / Blue Note ✦✦✦✦✦
Tremendous solos from Booker Ervin (ts) and Grant Green (g), with dynamic and bluesy Parlan piano. —*Ron Wynn*

Happy Frame of Mind / Feb. 15, 1963 / Blue Note ✦✦✦✦✦
Expatriate pianist on a reissue of one of his best albums, with Booker Ervin (ts). Search for others. —*Michael G. Nastos*

Arrival / Dec. 21, 1973–Dec. 22, 1973 / SteepleChase ✦✦✦✦✦

No Blues / Dec. 10, 1975 / SteepleChase ✦✦✦✦
A sparkling trio date. —*Ron Wynn*

Frankly Speaking / Feb. 5, 1977 / SteepleChase ✦✦✦✦

Blue Parlan / Nov. 13, 1977 / SteepleChase ✦✦✦✦
Parlan gets down in this striking trio outing. —*Ron Wynn*

The Maestro / Nov. 26, 1979 / SteepleChase ✦✦✦

Musically Yours / Nov. 26, 1979 / SteepleChase ✦✦✦

● **Pannonica** / Feb. 11, 1981 / Enja ✦✦✦✦✦
Good early '80s trio session with pianist Horace Parlan working alongside bassist Reggie Johnson and drummer Alvin Queen. The material, mostly standards with some originals and ballads, isn't overly ambitious, but Parlan's dense, strong blues-influenced solos and good interaction among the three principals keeps things moving. —*Ron Wynn*

Like Someone in Love / Mar. 1983 / SteepleChase ✦✦✦✦

Glad I Found You / Jul. 30, 1984 / SteepleChase ✦✦✦✦✦
Straight-ahead blowing date. Eddie Harris (ts) almost outdoes Parlan. —*Ron Wynn*

Little Esther / Mar. 1987 / SteepleChase ✦✦✦

Joe Pass (Joseph Anthony Passalaqua)

b. Jan. 13, 1929, New Brunswick, NJ, d. May 23, 1994
Guitar / Bop
Joe Pass did the near-impossible. He was able to play uptempo versions of bop tunes such as "Cherokee" and "How High the Moon" unaccompanied on the guitar. Unlike Stanley Jordan, Pass used conventional (but superb) technique, and his *Virtuoso* series on Pablo still sounds remarkable two decades later.

Joe Pass had a false start in his career. He played in a few swing bands (including Tony Pastor's) before graduating from high school and was with Charlie Barnet for a time in 1947. But after serving in the military, Pass became a drug addict, serving time in prison and essentially wasting a decade. He emerged in 1962 with a record cut at Synanon, made a bit of a stir with his *For Django* set, recorded several other albums for Pacific Jazz and World Pacific and performed with Gerald Wilson, Les McCann, George Shearing and Benny Goodman (1973).

However, in general, Pass maintained a low profile in Los Angeles until he was signed by Norman Granz to his Pablo label. 1973's *Virtuoso* made him a star and he recorded very prolifically for Pablo, unaccompanied, with small groups, on duo albums with Ella Fitzgerald and with such masters as Count Basie, Duke Ellington, Oscar Peterson, Milt Jackson and Dizzy Gillespie. Pass remained very active up until his death from cancer. —*Scott Yanow*

● **The Complete "Catch Me!" Sessions** / 1963 / Blue Note ✦✦✦✦✦

Great Movie Themes / 1963 / World Pacific ✦✦

Joy Spring / Feb. 6, 1964 / Blue Note ✦✦✦✦

★ **For Django** / Oct. 1964 / Pacific Jazz ✦✦✦✦✦

A Sign of the Times / 1965 / World Pacific ✦✦

The Stones Jazz / 1966 / World Pacific ✦✦

Simplicity / 1967 / Pacific Jazz ✦✦✦
An aptly titled release, as guitarist Joe Pass offers smooth, fluent songs, crisp, polished solos, and sentimental material, and does everything with a modicum of effort and intensity. —*Ron Wynn*

Living Legends / Aug. 20, 1969 / Discovery ✦✦✦

Virtuoso, Vol. 4 / Nov. 1973 / Pablo ✦✦✦✦✦
The fourth in the series that gave guitarist Joe Pass a forum to show things that weren't always evident on his many studio dates. Everything, from the elaborate and complicated solos to his choices of material, reflected his commitment to excellence, and every release he made for the line was superb. —*Ron Wynn*

★ **Virtuoso, Vol. 1** / Dec. 1973 / Pablo ✦✦✦✦✦

Portraits of Duke Ellington / Jun. 21, 1974 / Pablo ✦✦✦✦✦
A tremendous set, with Pass paying homage to Ellington. —*Ron Wynn*

Live at Dante's / Dec. 8, 1974+Dec. 9, 1974 / Pablo ✦✦✦✦
During a period when he was receiving renown as an unaccompanied solo guitarist, the release of this double LP reminded listeners that Joe Pass could also swing hard in a trio setting. Accompanied by the electric bass of Jim Hughart and drummer Frank Severino, Pass mostly explores standards including a few ("What Have They Done to My Song," "A Time for Love" and "You Are the Sunshine of My Life") that were fairly recent at the time. The performances are as excellent as one would expect. In fact, considering how many albums he did for Pablo (a few dozen), it is remarkable to realize that every one of them are quite rewarding. —*Scott Yanow*

Montreux '75 / Jul. 17, 1975–Jul. 18, 1975 / Original Jazz Classics ✦✦✦✦✦
Outstanding solo guitar by Joe Pass, done at the '75 Montreux Festival to an appreciative audience. Pass plays with more energy than on his studio works, doing the usual standards, ballads, and mainstream fare, but also demonstrating an exuberance and joyful flair that's more understated on most occasions. —*Ron Wynn*

Virtuoso, Vol. 2 / Sep. 14, 1976+Oct. 26, 1976 / Pablo ✦✦✦✦✦
The second of Joe Pass' solo guitar albums for Pablo finds the remarkable Pass exploring more recent standards than one might expect. In addition to a few warhorses, there is also "Feelings" (which he somehow manages to make tolerable), "If," two Chick Corea songs ("Five Hundred Miles High" and "Windows") and even "Giant Steps." Pass' mastery of the guitar is obvious throughout this enjoyable set. —*Scott Yanow*

Quadrant / Feb. 2, 1977 / Original Jazz Classics ✦✦✦✦
There's a bit more intensity here, thanks to the presence of Milt Jackson (vib), Ray Brown (b), and Mickey Roker (d). —*Ron Wynn*

Virtuoso, Vol. 3 / May 27, 1977+Jun. 1, 1977 / Original Jazz Classics ✦✦✦✦✦
A '92 CD reissue of the third in a series recorded in 1977. Guitarist Joe Pass, whose talent is often taken for granted due to the introspective, relaxed nature of his sessions, displayed his full range and technical skills on a three-volume set designed to highlight those abilities. This third volume was no less a standout than the previous two. —*Ron Wynn*

Montreux '77: Live! / Jul. 15, 1977 / Original Jazz Classics ✦✦✦✦
An '89 CD reissue of a '77 release that was originally included in the Pablo Live series. The digital remastering accents the shadings, voicings, and melodic counterpoint that are Pass' strong points. He's doing familiar material, but adding twists and turns that the receptive, aware audience greatly appreciated. —*Ron Wynn*

Guitar Interludes / 1977 / Discovery ✦✦✦
Exquisite melodies, refrains, solos, and choruses from guitarist Joe Pass, a master at playing elegant, refined, delightful music, whether using an electric or acoustic instrument. —*Ron Wynn*

Tudo Bem! / May 8, 1978 / Original Jazz Classics ✦✦✦
Afro-Latin and Brazilian material done by guitarist Joe Pass, as he shows his fluency in this idiom. The songs are mostly solid, and even on those that are less than impressive, Pass' steady playing and fluid sound makes them tolerable. —*Ron Wynn*

Chops / Nov. 19, 1978 / Original Jazz Classics ✦✦✦✦✦

I Remember Charlie Parker / Feb. 17, 1979 / Original Jazz Classics ✦✦✦✦

Northsea Nights / Jul. 1979 / Pablo ✦✦✦✦
Guitarist Joe Pass and bassist Niels Pedersen, a pair of talented virtuosi, are typically outstanding on this live set of standards. With the exception of their ad-lib "Blues for the Hague," all of the material would qualify as overdone through the years (such as " 'Round Midnight" and "Stella by Starlight"), but the duo makes these veteran pieces sound fresh and new again. —*Scott Yanow*

All Too Soon / Feb. 21, 1980 / Original Jazz Classics ✦✦✦✦
Solid, nicely played standards, originals, blues, and ballads by guitarist Joe Pass. He seldom plays in an exuberant fashion, preferring a smooth, relaxed, yet also intricately crafted solo approach. His full notes and elaborate voicings are technically impressive, although sometimes a lack of thematic variety results in his albums all sounding the same. —*Ron Wynn*

Checkmate / Jan. 12, 1981 / Pablo ✦✦✦✦

George, Ira & Joe (Joe Pass Loves Gershwin) / Nov. 23, 1981 / Pablo ✦✦✦✦
There aren't many better matches than the lush, innocent songs of George Gershwin and Joe Pass' equally sentimental, spinning guitar phrases embellishing Gershwin's music. Certainly these songs have been done by countless jazz greats, and Pass doesn't necessarily add anything new. But his takes are wonderfully played, and his choices of material are first-rate. —*Ron Wynn*

Eximious / May 25, 1982-Jul. 8, 1982 / Pablo ✦✦✦✦

● **We'll Be Together Again** / Oct. 23, 1983 / Pablo ✦✦✦✦✦

Live at Long Bay Beach College / Jan. 20, 1984 / Pablo ✦✦✦✦
During the '80s, the Pablo label instituted a series of live albums by their prime stars. This one featured guitarist Joe Pass, and like several Pass dates done in concert, there was more energized playing. Pass' big, sustained tones, carefully constructed solos, and generally impressive technique were demonstrated with a minimum of flair. —*Ron Wynn*

Whitestone / Feb. 28, 1985-Mar. 1, 1985 / Pablo ✦✦✦

Joe Pass at Akron University / Mar. 1986 / Pablo ✦✦✦✦
Most of the material on this concert was familiar, but remained fresh. Of the newer work, "Bridgework" was a blues with a bridge, "Tarde" a Milton Nascimento ballad and "Time In," a key-switching blues.... Joe Pass retains his position as one of the masters of the jazz guitar with this album. —*Scott Yanow*

Blues for Fred / Feb. 2, 1988-Feb. 3, 1988 / Pablo ✦✦✦✦

One for My Baby / Dec. 28, 1988 / Pablo ✦✦✦✦

Summer Nights / Dec. 1989 / Pablo ✦✦✦✦

Appassionato / Aug. 9, 1990-Aug. 11, 1990 / Pablo ✦✦✦✦
Guitarist Joe Pass reunited with the same musicians he had used on his classic 1963 album *For Django* for this relaxed exploration of a dozen jazz standards: rhythm guitarist John Pisano, bassist Jim Hughart and drummer Colin Bailcy. Alternating romps with ballads, Pass is in typically fine form throughout with "Relaxin' at Camarillo," "Red Door" and "That's Earl, Brother" receiving rare revivals. This CD is one of literally dozens of worthy Joe Pass Pablo recordings. —*Scott Yanow*

Virtuoso: Live! / Sep. 13, 1991-Sep. 15, 1991 / Pablo ✦✦✦✦✦
This continuation of the virtuoso series spotlighting guitarist Joe Pass' skills differed from the others in that this time he was recorded live. The extra ingredient seemed to make Pass play with even more brilliance; he executed difficult runs, octave jumps, and phrases with verve, while his interpretations of standards and harmonic maneuvers were often amazing. —*Ron Wynn*

Joe Pass & Co. / Jan. 1992 / Pablo ✦✦✦✦

Live at Yoshi's / Jan. 30, 1992-Feb. 1, 1992 / Pablo ✦✦✦✦
An inspired and exciting set by jazz's guitarist nonpareil, it ranges from a blistering race through Sonny Rollins' "Oleo" to the gentle duet with Pass' longtime partner Pisano on "Alone Together." "Swingin' Till the Girls Come Home" is a feature for Budwig, the great West Coast bass player who died shortly after this set. It's one of the best of the many Joe Pass albums. —*Les Line*

Six String Santa / Feb. 4, 1992 / Laserlight ✦✦✦

Songs For Ellen / Aug. 7, 1992-Aug. 20, 1992 / Pablo ✦✦✦

My Song / Feb. 1993 / Telarc ✦✦✦✦
During his last years, guitarist Joe Pass often used the same unit on a regular basis that he had utilized to record his classic *For Django*, back in 1963. For this pleasing effort, John Pisano offers some suitable rhythm guitar while bassist Jim Hughart and drummer Colin Bailey are typically tasteful in support. Tom Ranier is an important addition to the quartet, having one outing apiece on tenor, clarinet and soprano while playing piano on the remaining tracks. Joe Pass naturally emerges as the main star, interpreting the nine standards and two of his originals with taste, hard-driving swing and creativity within the bop tradition. Pass made so many recordings during the 20 years preceding this date that it is

difficult to call any one of them "definitive," but this is an excellent group effort. —*Scott Yanow*

Roy Clark & Joe Pass Play Hank Williams / 1994 / Buster Ann Music ✦✦✦✦

Jaco Pastorius (John Francis Pastorius)

b. Dec. 1, 1951, Norristown, PA, **d.** Sep. 21, 1987, Fort Lauderdale, FL
Bass / Fusion, Post Bop
The Jaco Pastorius story is a tragedy in a music littered with far too many of them, each frustrating and maddening. Pastorius was simply the greatest electric bassist of the jazz-rock/fusion era, an incredibly fast, imaginative and brilliant musician and technician, who not only conceived possibilities on the instrument no one else considered but executed them flawlessy. He considered the electric bass a bass guitar and lead rather than rhythm/support instrument; even as an accompanist his lines and phrases had so much depth and form they stood out within the arrangement. His solos were adventures, performed with a fluidity and harmonic elan that remain unbelievable no matter how many times they're heard. Pastorius also knew how good he was, and his personality, coupled with repeated drug and alcohol problems, no doubt hastened his demise. "I'm Jaco f-ing Pastorius," was heard far too often at his concerts or in response to quesions from admiring fans about his facility. But there was no faulting his tone or talents.

Pastorius accompanied visiting R&B and pop musicians who came to his native Fort Lauderdale while in his teens. He quickly emerged as a major electric bassist by the mid-'70s, and his work with Pat Metheny attracted so much notice he was tabbed to join Weather Report in 1976. That long-term role, plus many other sessions, cemented Pastorius' stature within the jazz and rock/pop world. He played with Blood, Sweat & Tears in 1975 and their drummer, Bobby Colomby, helped arrange the session that led to Pastorius' Epic debut as a leader. Pastorius recorded with Ira Sullivan, Paul Bley, Joni Mitchell, Metheny and Bireli Lagrene in the '70s and '80s in addition to his Weather Report duties. He toured with his own group, Word of Mouth, from 1980 to 1983, recording in 1980 with various jazz musicians and, in 1982, with a big band. Pastorius recorded an album in 1983 and 1984 with Brian Melvin.

Then he suffered a series of personal reversals and problems that were as monumental as their musical talents. There were repeated rumors of sightings in drug-infested inner city hangouts. Pastorius died as a result of injuries suffered during a brawl at the Midnight Club in Fort Lauderdale in 1987. Many later Pastorius live performances from his post-Weather Report days have been released posthumously. Bill Milkowski's definitive biography, *Jaco*, traces the innovative bassist's rise and fall and is well worth picking up. —*Ron Wynn*

Jaco / Jun. 16, 1974 / Improvising Artists ✦✦✦✦
This live recording is quite historic for it has the earliest documentation of both electric bassist Jaco Pastorius and guitarist Pat Metheny. Recorded by keyboardist Paul Bley for his Improvising Artists label (without the knowledge of his sidemen which also included drummer Bruce Ditmas), this CD reissues the same relatively brief program as was on the LP. Metheny is actually a minor figure on this date (the recording quality keeps him from sounding distinctive), but Pastorius' raging solos and heated accompaniment inspired Bley to make him the leader of this date. The program consists (with one exception) of songs by either Paul or Carla Bley and generally holds one's interest. —*Scott Yanow*

★ **Jaco Pastorius** / Aug. 1976 / Epic ✦✦✦✦✦
Studio group date and first album from this late/great electric bass guitar genius. A must-buy. —*Michael G. Nastos*

Word of Mouth / Dec. 1981 / Warner Brothers ✦✦✦✦
Bassist Jaco Pastorius' Word of Mouth orchestra was an unfulfilled dream, a worthy concept that did not last long enough to live up to its potential. Its debut album was released without a listing of the personnel, so here it is: Wayne Shorter, Michael Brecker and Tom Scott on reeds, trumpeter Chuck Findley, the easily recognizable Toots Thielemans on harmonica, Howard Johnson on tuba, drummers Jack DeJohnette and Peter Erskine and percussionist Don Alias. The music ranges from The Beatles' "Blackbird" and some Bach to Jaco originals that cover straight-ahead jazz, Coltranish vamps and fusion. Next to the bassist/leader,

Thielemans emerges as the main voice. It's worth checking out but not essential. *—Scott Yanow*

Invitation / 1983 / Warner Brothers ✦✦✦✦

Honestly: Solo Live / Mar. 1986 / Big World ✦✦✦✦
Bassist Jaco Pastorius' throbbing, booming electric bass lines made him both a celebrity and a marked man during his lifetime. This Italian date caught Pastorius in peak form; both his speed and facility were unequaled, and he truly approached his instrument like a lead guitar, strumming, zipping through passages, and executing incredible runs. *—Ron Wynn*

Live in Italy / Mar. 1986 / Jazzpoint ✦✦✦
While this bears Pastorius' name as a leader, guitarist Bireli Lagrene comes close to making it his own work. The usually dominating Pastorius takes a more supportive position, while Lagrene ranges, roams, and soars, ripping off swinging solos that reflect his debt to Django Reinhardt. Drummer Thomas Borocz, although playing sensitively and with power, almost gets left behind by the Lagrene/Pastorius team. *—Ron Wynn*

John Patitucci

b. Dec. 22, 1959, Brooklyn, NY
Bass / Fusion, Post Bop
One of the top bassists of the 1990s (on both acoustic and electric), Patitucci's speed, very clear tone and versatility are quite impressive. He started playing bass when he was 11, grew up in Northern California and in 1978 moved south near Los Angeles. He played with Gap Mangione (1979) while going to college and during 1982–85 worked in Los Angeles with Tom Scott, Robben Ford, Stan Getz, Larry Carlton, Dave Grusin, Ernie Watts, Freddie Hubbard and others in addition to becoming a studio musician. In 1985 he gained a high profile when he joined Chick Corea as a regular member of both the Elektric and Akoustic bands. Patitucci toured and recorded extensively with Corea and has made a series of his own diverse sessions for GRP and Stretch (although he is not as strong a composer as he is a bassist). John Patitucci left the Elektric Band in the early '90s, but has continued working with Corea on an occasional basis. *—Scott Yanow*

John Patitucci / Dec. 1987 / GRP ✦✦

On the Corner / 1989 / GRP ✦✦

Sketchbook / 1990 / GRP ✦✦✦

● **Heart of the Bass** / 1991 / Stretch ✦✦✦✦✦
Fusion standout John Patitucci flashes the speed, facility, and flash that's made him the darling of the contemporary jazz set. He's joined by the man whose band has showcased him, pianist Chick Corea, plus percussionist Alex Acuna and other guest stars. The songs are pretty routine, but Patitucci and Corea's performances elevate them. *—Ron Wynn*

Another World / 1993 / GRP ✦✦✦✦
John Patitucci has quickly developed into one of the world's great bassists, both on acoustic and electric. He is not on the same level as a composer, but is steadily improving as witness the music on ths fine release. There are many bass solos as one would expect (Patitucci's high-note flights often sound like a guitar) but he does leave space for his sidemen, most notably keyboardist John Beasley (who has two numbers without the bassist), trumpeter Jeff Beal and one selection apiece for the steel drums of Andy Narell and Mike Brecker's tenor. A few tracks are throwaway funk, but there are enough surprise twists and unusual improvisations to make this a recommended disc even for adventurous listeners. *— Scott Yanow*

Mistura Fina / Jun. 23, 1994–Aug. 20, 1994 / GRP ✦✦✦
John Patitucci, a brilliant bassist best known for his fusion playing with Chick Corea's Elektric Band, leans strongly in the direction of Brazilian pop music on this CD. Most of the selections have vocals and, although Patitucci takes a lot of excellent acoustic bass solos (and there are occasional solo spots for keyboardist John Beasley and saxophonist Steve Tavaglione), this CD is more in the world music than fusion vein. The vocalists include Joao Bosco, Dori Caymmi, Kleber Jorge, Ivan Lins, Cathy Brandolino and Kevyn Lettau. *—Scott Yanow*

Pat Patrick

b. Nov. 1929, d. Dec. 31, 1991
Baritone Sax, Flute / Avant-Garde
Pat Patrick, like John Gilmore, spent virtually his entire career

with Sun Ra's Arkestra, leading to him being somewhat underrated. Patrick had a particularly appealing sound on baritone and, although he did not lead any recording sessions of his own, he was one of the better baritonists of the 1950s and '60s. As a child he studied piano, drums and trumpet before switching to saxophone. At Du Sable High School in Chicago he first met John Gilmore. Patrick did record with John Coltrane (*Africa Brass*), play briefly with Duke Ellington, was a member of a little-known version of Thelonious Monk's quartet (1970) and in 1974 he recorded with the Jazz Composer's Orchestra. But otherwise Pat Patrick from 1954 on and off through his death was closely associated with Sun Ra where he was a reliable sideman. *—Scott Yanow*

Don Patterson

b. Jul. 22, 1936, Columbus, OH, d. Feb. 10, 1988, Philadelphia, PA
Organ / Soul Jazz, Hard Bop
A solid soul jazz, blues and hard bop organist with a pianistic background, Don Patterson didn't utilize the pedals or play with as much rhythmic drive as some other stylists, but developed a satisfactory alternative approach. Patterson's organ solos were smartly played, and more melodic than explosive. He switched from piano after hearing Jimmy Smith. Patterson made his organ debut in 1959, and worked with Sonny Stitt, Eddie "Lockjaw" Davis, Gene Ammons and Wes Montgomery in the early '60s. He recorded with Ammons, Stitt and Eric Kloss in the early and mid-'60s. Patterson worked often in a duo with Billy James and made several recordings in the '60s and '70s as a leader. He and Al Grey worked together extensively in the '80s. Patterson recorded as a leader for Prestige and Muse. He has one session available on CD. *—Ron Wynn and Michael G. Nastos*

● **Dem New York Blues** / Jun. 5, 1968+Jun. 2, 1969 / Prestige ✦✦✦✦✦
Despite claims to the contrary, organist Don Patterson was very much of the Jimmy Smith school, a hard-driving player with fine improvising skills but lacking a distinctive sound of his own. This CD (which reissues two complete Lp's) features Patterson in prime form in a quintet with trumpeter Blue Mitchell, Junior Cook on tenor and guitarist Pat Martino, and with a separate group that features trumpeter Virgil Jones and both George Coleman and Houston Person on tenors. Although "Oh Happy Day" is a throwaway, Patterson's spirited renditions of the blues and standards make this a fairly definitive example of his talents. *—Scott Yanow*

The Return Of... / Oct. 30, 1972 / Muse ✦✦✦✦
Quartet with Eddie Daniels (ts), Ted Dunbar (g), and Freddie Waits (d). Any Don Patterson album is worthwhile. *—Michael G. Nastos*

These Are Soulful Days / Sep. 17, 1973 / Muse ✦✦✦✦✦
Quartet with this great Hammond B-3 organist, Jimmy Heath (sax), Pat Martino (g) and A. Heath (d). *—Michael G. Nastos*

Movin' Up / Jan. 31, 1977 / Muse ✦✦✦✦
Competent, sometimes animated soul-jazz from organist Don Patterson. Although not as blues-oriented as Jimmy McGriff or Jack McDuff, nor as ambitious as Charles Earland, Patterson plays catchy, clever tunes with good solos and interesting rhythm hooks. *—Ron Wynn*

Why Not / Jan. 26, 1978 / Muse ✦✦✦

Big John Patton

b. Jul. 12, 1935, Kansas City, MO
Organ / Hard Bop, Soul Jazz
A first-rate soul jazz and blues organist, Big John Patton's dates are among the most danceable, funky and exuberant ever done at Blue Note. He wasn't as adventurous as Larry Young, but matched any organist for sheer energy and rousing fervor. Patton played piano in the late '40s, and toured with Lloyd Price in the mid and late '50s. He began playing organ in the '60s, and recorded with Lou Donaldson from 1962 to 1964. Patton also did sessions with Harold Vick, Johnny Griffin, Grant Green and Clifford Jordan in the '60s, while doing his own dates with a trio. At various times Clifford Jarvis and James "Blood" Ulmer were members of Patton's trio. Bobby Hutcherson, Junior Cook, Blue Mitchell and Richard Williams as well as Vick served as special guests on different sessions. Patton recorded with Johnny Lytle in 1977 and 1983. In obscurity during the 1970s when the Hammond organ was overshadowed by electric pianos and synthesizers, Patton's career was revived in the 1980s thanks in part to John Zorn

singing his praises and using him on some recordings. —*Ron Wynn and Scott Yanow*

Along Came John / Apr. 5, 1963 / Blue Note ✦✦✦

Blue John / Jul. 11, 1963–Aug. 2, 1963 / Blue Note ✦✦✦✦✦
Recording from "Big John," another Hammond heavyweight. With George Braithwaite (sax) , Grant Green (g), and Tommy Turrentine (tpt). —*Michael G. Nastos*

The Way I Feel / Jun. 19, 1964 / Blue Note ✦✦✦

Oh Baby / Mar. 8, 1965 / Blue Note ✦✦✦

● **Let 'em Roll** / Dec. 11, 1965 / Blue Note ✦✦✦✦✦
Organist Big John Patton was never an innovator, but he created some enjoyable funky jazz during his Blue Note years. This CD reissue has plenty of boogaloos and energetic vamping, is enjoyable enough as background or party music. Guitarist Grant Green, vibraphonist Bobby Hutcherson and drummer Otis Finch help out but Patton's organ dominates these blues-oriented jams. —*Scott Yanow*

Got a Good Thing Goin' / Apr. 29, 1966 / Blue Note ✦✦✦✦

That Certain Feeling / Mar. 8, 1968 / Blue Note ✦✦✦✦

Boogaloo / Aug. 9, 1968 / Blue Note ✦✦✦
The main reason to purchase this previously unissued set from the declining years of Blue Note is not for the trivial rhythmic themes (which use fairly basic chord sequences) or even the solos of organist John Patton (who never does escape entirely from the shadow of Jimmy Smith), but for the somewhat out-of-place avant-garde outbursts by Harold Alexander (on tenor and flute) who often takes improvisations that go completely outside; his squeals on "Boogaloo Boogie" are a real surprise and he may very well be the reason that this music was not put out at the time. Otherwise this is a routine and now-dated set of commercial late-'60s jazz/funk. —*Scott Yanow*

Understanding / Oct. 25, 1968 / Blue Note ✦✦
Organist John Patton is featured on this CD (a straight reissue of the original LP) in a stripped-down trio with Harold Alexander (on tenor and flute) and drummer Hugh Walker. Patton's one-chord funky vamps are fine in small doses, but the endless repetitions on these rather simplistic originals may drive alert listeners batty after awhile. —*Scott Yanow*

Accent on the Blues / Aug. 15, 1969 / Blue Note ✦✦✦

Soul Connection / Jun. 7, 1983 / Nilva ✦✦✦

Blue Planet Man / Apr. 12, 1993–Apr. 13, 1993 / Evidence ✦✦✦

Memphis to New York Spirit / 1969–1970 / Blue Note ✦✦✦
Although it was scheduled for release two times, *Memphis to New York Spirit* didn't appear until 1996, over 25 years after it was recorded. The album comprises the contents of two separate sessions—one recorded in 1970 with guitarist James "Blood" Ulmer, drummer Leroy Williams and saxophonist/flautist Marvin Cabell; the other recorded in 1969 with Cabell, Williams, and saxophonist George Coleman—that were very similiar in concept and execution. Patton leads his combo through a selection of originals and covers that range from Wayne Shorter and McCoy Tyner to the Meters. Though the group is rooted in soul-jazz, they stretch the limits of the genre on these sessions, showing a willingness to experiment, while still dipping into the more traditional blues and funk reserves. Consequently, *Memphis to New York Spirit* doesn't have a consistent groove like some other Patton records, but when it does click, the results are remarkable; it's a non-essential but worthy addition to a funky soul-jazz collection. —*Stephen Thomas Erlewine*

Cecil Payne

b. Dec. 14, 1922, Brooklyn
Flute, Baritone Saxophone / Bop, Hard Bop
A fluid, soulful and excellent baritone saxophonist, Cecil Payne has been a top player since the '40s, when his work in Dizzy Gillespie's big band established his credentials. He has a softer, lighter sound than on his earlier recordings, but hasn't sacrificed any power or authority. Payne's emotional intensity and natural bluesy qualities enabled him to do some R&B and rock and roll dates in the '50s, and his rumbling baritone navigates a steady middle ground between carthiness and a smooth, polished approach.

Payne initially played guitar and then alto sax, playing clarinet in Army bands from 1943 to 1946. He began on baritone while

in Clarence Biggs' big band in 1946. Payne made his recording debut on alto sax that same year with J.J. Johnson on Savoy. After a brief stint with Roy Eldridge, Payne played in Gillespie's big band from 1946 until 1949. He worked for Tadd Dameron and James Moody in New York, before becoming a freelancer from 1949 until 1952, and also doing some Atlantic sessions. Payne toured with Illinois Jacquet from 1952 to 1954, while doing numerous recording dates with such players as Duke Jordan and Randy Weston. Payne played on Tadd Dameron's *Fontainebleau* and John Coltrane's *Dakar,* while doing two albums with Jordan on Savoy.

He temporarily left the music world in the '50s, then returned to both act and write songs for Jack Gelber's play "The Connection" in 1961 and 1962. Payne again teamed with Jordan for two sessions on Charlie Parker Records in 1961 and 1962. He was a soloist in Machito's band, The Afro-Cubans, in 1963 and 1964, while also playing in Lucky Thompson's octet and touring Europe with Lionel Hampton in 1964. He once more worked with Jordan on a 1966 date for Spotlite. Payne left music again in the mid-'60s, returning to work with Weston, Woody Herman and Gillespie in the late '60s. He played with Count Basie in 1969, 1970 and 1971, and also led a quartet. Payne recorded with Kenny Dorham in 1969 for Strata-East, and headed a combo. He recorded in the '70s on Muse and Spotlite, with Nick Brignola and also Jordan again, and played with Bill Hardman and Richard Wyands' trio in 1986. There's only a few Payne sessions available on CD. —*Ron Wynn*

Patterns / May 19, 1956–May 22, 1956 / Savoy ✦✦✦✦
Fine late-'50s hard bop session featuring baritone saxophonist Cecil Payne. This was one of two strong albums that matched Payne with pianist Duke Jordan, who was then establishing his own reputation as an aggressive soloist and good accompanist. These are mostly short, tartly played, and well-written and arranged pieces. —*Ron Wynn*

Night at the Five Spot / Aug. 12, 1957 / Signal ✦✦✦✦

Brooklyn Brothers / Mar. 16, 1973 / Muse ✦✦✦✦✦
With Duke Jordan (p) & Trio. Excellent mainstream jazz. —*Michael G. Nastos*

● **Bird Gets the Worm** / Feb. 2, 1976 / Muse ✦✦✦✦✦
Some of Payne's most vibrant, expressive playing. Good ensemble and compositions. —*Ron Wynn*

Bright Moments / Jul. 19, 1979+Jul. 20, 1979 / Spotlite ✦✦✦

Nicholas Payton

b. 1973, New Orleans, LA
Trumpet / Hard Bop, New Orleans Jazz
One of the brightest new trumpet stars of the 1990s, Nicholas Payton combines references to his New Orleans heritage with the young lions' brand of hard bop and a warm sound. His father Walter Payton, a top bassist, and his mother (a classical pianist) encouraged his interest in music, and he received his first trumpet when he was four. Payton developed quickly and, at age nine, he had opportunities to sit in with the Young Tuxedo Brass Band. One day when Payton was 12, Wynton Marsalis called to speak to his father; Nicholas spontaneously played his trumpet over the phone, impressing Marsalis who, in the future, would recommend him to other bandleaders. Payton worked steadily in New Orleans while in high school, he graduated from the New Orleans Center for Creative Arts and studied with Ellis Marsalis. In 1992 he toured with Marcus Roberts, in 1994 he toured Europe with Jazz Futures II and, in addition, Payton toured with Elvin Jones and worked with the Jazz at Lincoln Center program. He has recorded with Jones, as a leader on Verve and with the New Orleans Collective on Evidence. —*Scott Yanow*

● **From This Moment** / Sep. 11, 1994–Sep. 12, 1994 / Verve ✦✦✦✦
The young trumpeter Nicholas Payton is featured on this CD as the only horn in a sextet also including guitarist Mark Whitfield, pianist Mulgrew Miller and vibraphonist Monte Croft. Best are Payton's melodic and very mature statements on the veteran standards "You Stepped out of a Dream," "It Could Happen to You," "From This Moment On" and "Taking a Chance on Love." His six originals are less memorable, but overall this is a pleasing date that finds the trumpeter showing a great deal of potential. Payton's tone, mixing together aspects of Freddie Hubbard, Wynton Marsalis and New Orleans jazz in a postbop setting, is quite appealing. —*Scott Yanow*

Gary Peacock

b. May 12, 1935, Burley, ID
Bass / Post Bop

A subtle but adventurous bassist, Gary Peacock's flexibility and consistently creative ideas have been an asset to several important groups. He was originally a pianist, playing in an Army band while stationed in Germany in the late '50s. Peacock switched to bass in 1956, staying on in Germany after his discharge to play with Hans Koller, Attila Zoller, Tony Scott and Bud Shank. In 1958 he moved to Los Angeles where he performed with Barney Kessel, Don Ellis, Terry Gibbs and Shorty Rogers and (most importantly) Paul Bley among others. After moving to New York in 1962, Peacock worked with Bill Evans (1962-63), the Paul Bley trio, Jimmy Giuffre, Roland Kirk and George Russell. In 1964, after a brief stint with Miles Davis, Peacock started an association with Albert Ayler in Europe, also playing with Roswell Rudd and Steve Lacy. Peacock alternated between Ayler and Paul Bley for a time and returned briefly to Miles Davis in the late '60s. After a period in Japan (1969-72), Peacock studied biology (1972-76), worked with Bley, and off and on from the late '70s has played (and recorded) in a trio with Keith Jarrett and Jack DeJohnette. — *Scott Yanow*

Tales of Another / Feb. 1977 / ECM ✦✦✦✦
Bassist Gary Peacock contributed all six originals to this set, which also features pianist Keith Jarrett and drummer Jack DeJohnette. These musicians (who are equals) have played together many times through the years and their support of each other and close communication during these advanced improvisations is quite impressive. It's a good example of Peacock's music. — *Scott Yanow*

December Poems / Dec. 1977 / ECM ✦✦✦

Shift in the Wind / Feb. 1980 / ECM ✦✦✦✦
Bassist Gary Peacock teams up with the underrated pianist Art Lande and drummer Eliot Zigmund for a set of group originals that emphasize close communication between the trio members, really an extension on the innovations of Bill Evans. The interplay between these masterful musicians is more significant than the actual compositions and rewards repeats listenings. — *Scott Yanow*

Paradigm / Aug. 1981 / ECM ✦✦✦

Guamba / Mar. 1987 / ECM ✦✦✦✦
Good late-'80s session with bassist Gary Peacock heading a group that has saxophonist Jan Garbarek and trumpeter Palle Mikkleborg taking the lead and Peacock working with drummer Peter Erskine in the rhythm section. The only defect comes from ECM's occasional tendency to introduce New Age themes and production values into the mix. — *Ron Wynn*

Partners / Dec. 1989 / Owl ✦✦✦✦

Cosi Lontano ... Quasi Dentro / Jan. 25, 1991 / ECM ✦✦✦

Tethered Moon / Nov. 1991 / Evidence ✦✦✦✦

● **Oracle** / May 1993 / ECM ✦✦✦✦✦
This set of duets by bassist Gary Peacock and guitarist Ralph Towner, as one might expect from an ECM album, makes expert use of space and has its quiet moments. But there is a surprising amount of ferocious interplay between the two musicians. They may play at a consistently low volume, but the set of originals has a few rather passionate grooves and a little more energy than one would have predicted. — *Scott Yanow*

Duke Pearson (Columbus Calvin Pearson, Jr.)

b. Aug. 17, 1932, Atlanta, GA, d. Aug. 4, 1980, Atlanta, GA
Piano, Arranger / Hard Bop

A good pianist who later became a producer and A&R assistant, Duke Pearson was a fine bebop player during the '50s and early '60s, providing nicely constructed solos on many dates. He was a crafty rather than dazzling player, as well as a fine composer and arranger. Jordan studied piano and several brass instruments in his youth, then chose piano because problems with his teeth eliminated the trumpet.

He worked in the South as a pianist during the mid and late '50s, then moved to New York. Pearson worked regularly with Donald Byrd and Pepper Adams, and Byrd recorded Pearson's seminal compositions "Cristo Redentor" and "Jeannine." He was briefly in The Jazztet in 1960, and served as Nancy Wilson's accompanist in 1961. Pearson produced many sessions for Blue

Note from 1963 to 1970, and co-formed a big band with Byrd. He soon had sole leadership duties, and the Duke Pearson Big Band dueled the Thad Jones—Mel Lewis Orchestra from the late '60s until 1970. Adams, Lew Tabackin, Randy Brecker, Joe Shepley and Garnett Brown were regular members, and the band provided a forum for Pearson's compositions. He taught at Clark in 1971, then reformed the big band in 1972. Pearson toured with Carmen McRae in 1972 and 1973; he battled multiple sclerosis in the late '70s, which severely limited his playing. The former husband of jazz vocalist Sheila Jordan, Pearson also accompanied Dakota Staton and Joe Williams. He recorded for Prestige, Polydor, and Atlantic in addition to Blue Note. — *Ron Wynn and Michael G. Nastos*

Dedication / Aug. 2, 1961 / Prestige ✦✦✦✦✦
This is among Pearson's finest '60s sessions. Includes sterling solos by Freddie Hubbard (tpt) and Pepper Adams (sax). — *Ron Wynn*

Hush! / Jan. 12, 1962 / Jazzline ✦✦✦✦

● **Wahoo** / Nov. 24, 1964 / Blue Note ✦✦✦✦✦

Sweet Honey Bee / Dec. 7, 1966 / Blue Note ✦✦✦✦
Pianist/composer Duke Pearson leads an all-star group on this runthrough of seven of his compositions. The musicians (trumpeter Freddie Hubbard, altoist James Spaulding, tenorman Joe Henderson on tenor, bassist Ron Carter, drummer Mickey Roker and the pianist/leader) are actually more impressive than many of the compositions, although the swinging minor-toned "Big Bertha" deserved to become a standard. The frameworks are quite intelligent, with everyone not soloing on each selection, and the improvisations are concise and clearly related to each tune's melody and mood. Although not quite essential, this CD reissue has some rewarding music. — *Scott Yanow*

★ **The Right Touch** / Sep. 13, 1967 / Blue Note ✦✦✦✦✦
Duke Pearson rises to the challenge of writing for an all-star octet (with trumpeter Freddie Hubbard, trombonist Garnett Brown, altoist James Spaulding, Jerry Dodgion on alto and flute, Stanley Turrentine heard on tenor, bassist Gene Taylor, drummer Grady Tate and the leader/pianist), contributing colorful frameworks and consistently challenging compositions. The set is full of diverse melodies (the CD reissue has a previously unissued take of "Los Malos Hombres") played by a variety of distinctive soloists; many of these songs deserve to be revived. This is one of the finest recordings of Duke Pearson's career. — *Scott Yanow*

Introducing Duke Pearson's Big Band / Dec. 1967 / Blue Note ✦✦✦✦

It Could Only Happen with You / Mar. 13, 1970–Jan. 10, 1971 / Blue Note ✦✦✦

I Don't Care Who Knows It / Mar. 5, 1996 / Blue Note ✦✦
The sessions that comprise *I Don't Care Who Knows It* date from 1969 and 1970 (with one stray track from a 1968 session with Bobby Hutcherson), when Duke Pearson was experimenting with Latin jazz, soul-jazz and funk; they are also the second-to-last dates the pianist ever recorded for Blue Note. Working with a fairly large group that included bassist Ron Carter, drummer Micey Roker, saxophonists Jerry Dodgion, Frank Foster, Lew Tabackin, trumpeter Burt Collins, trombonist Kenny Rupp and occasionally vocalist Andy Bey, Pearson plays the electric piano throughout the majority of the album. As expected, the music swings with an understated funk, with the band alternating between standard hard-bop and mellow, soulful grooves. On the whole, *I Don't Care Who Knows It* is fairly uneven—the sessions don't set well together, but work well as individual sets. Nevertheless, there is enough good material here to make it worthwhile for soul-jazz, Latin-jazz and, especially, Pearson afficianados. — *Stephen Thomas Erlewine*

Niels-Henning Orsted Pedersen

b. May 27, 1946, Osted, Denmark
Bass / Bop, Hard Bop

A virtuoso who mostly has played in bop-oriented settings, Niels Pedersen has been in great demand since he was a teenager. One of many superb European bassists to emerge during the 1960s, Pedersen originally studied piano before starting to play bass with Danish groups when he was 14. He had to reluctantly turn down Count Basie's offer to join his orchestra when he was just 17, but worked steadily as the house bassist at the Club Montmartre and as a member of the Danish Radio Orchestra.

Whenever American jazzmen passed through Scandinavia,

they asked for Pederson; during the 1960s he played with Sonny Rollins, Bill Evans, Roland Kirk, Dexter Gordon, Bud Powell and even Albert Ayler (although the latter's session was not too successful). In the 1970s Pedersen was featured in a duo with Kenny Drew. Starting in the mid-'70s, he was an occasional member of the Oscar Peterson Trio and he recorded several dates as a leader for SteepleChase. Pedersen also recorded in many different settings for Pablo Records during the era. He has remained very active up to the current time. —*Scott Yanow*

Jaywalkin' / Sep. 9, 1975+Dec. 10, 1975 / SteepleChase ✦✦✦✦

Live at Montmartre, Vol. 1 / Oct. 2, 1977–Oct. 3, 1977 / SteepleChase ✦✦✦

Live at Montmartre, Vol. 2 / Oct. 1977 / SteepleChase ✦✦✦

● **Dancing on the Tables** / Jul. 1979+Aug. 1979 / SteepleChase ✦✦✦✦✦

The Viking / May 1983 / Pablo ✦✦✦✦

Klaus Suonsaari, Niels-Henning Orsted Pedersen & Niels Lan Doky Play the Music of Tom Harrell / Jul. 1989 / Jazz Alliance ✦✦✦✦

Ken Peplowski

b. May 23, 1959, Cleveland, OH

Clarinet, Tenor Saxophone / Dixieland, Swing

One of the top clarinetists of the 1990s and a very talented tenor player, Ken Peplowski has helped keep the tradition of small-group swing (and occasionally Dixieland) alive. He made his professional debut at ten and played locally in Cleveland. After spending 1978–80 touring with the Tommy Dorsey ghost orchestra (directed by Buddy Morrow), Peplowski settled in New York, freelanced in a variety of settings and played with Benny Goodman. By 1987 he was a Concord artist and has since recorded frequently for that label, backing Mel Tormé and Rosemary Clooney and leading his own sets including brilliant duets with guitarist Howard Alden. —*Scott Yanow*

Double Exposure / Dec. 1987 / Concord Jazz ✦✦✦✦

Good swing-influenced, small-combo set by alto/tenor saxophonist and clarinetist Ken Peplowski. While Peplowski's solos are conservative in their range and style, they're well played and done with good taste. He's backed by a group whose members all reflect his values in their own playing—guitarist Ed Bickert, pianist John Bunch, bassist John Goldsby and drummer Terry Clarke. —*Ron Wynn*

Sonny Side / Apr. 1989 / Concord Jazz ✦✦✦✦✦

● **Mr. Gentle and Mr. Cool** / Feb. 1990 / Concord Jazz ✦✦✦✦✦

Quintet. This tasty swing/mainstream date has exciting piano by Hank Jones and excellent drumming from Alan Dawson. —*Ron Wynn*

Illuminations / Nov. 20, 1990–Nov. 21, 1990 / Concord Jazz ✦✦✦✦

Quintet. A conservative but well-played small-combo set with swing influences. Junior Mance brings some blues fervor on piano. The CD has two bonus cuts. —*Ron Wynn*

The Natural Touch / Jan. 14, 1992–Jan. 15, 1992 / Concord Jazz ✦✦✦✦✦

A '92 session done in saxophonist Ken Peplowski's usually restrained, sophisticated fashion. His material, solo approach, and ensemble style can either be called conservative or derivative, depending on one's slant. He picks supporting players who also don't get overly aggressive or animated in either their solos or their responses. The CD has three bonus cuts. —*Ron Wynn*

★ **Concord Duo Series, Vol.** / Dec. 1992 / Concord Jazz ✦✦✦✦✦

Steppin' with Peps / Mar. 1993 / Concord Jazz ✦✦✦✦✦

Ken Peplowski is in top form on this consistently exciting swing-based release. Whether playing clarinet (where his Benny Goodman influence is touched by the coolness of Tony Scott) or romping on tenor (mixing together Don Byas with touches of Paul Gonsalves), Peplowski excels throughout this well-planned yet spontaneous session. The dozen performances have many highlights including the interplay of Peplowski and guitarist Howard Alden on "The Courtship," a very beautiful version of "Lotus Blossom" (with Joe Wilder's lyrical trumpet), a hot version of "The Lady's in Love with You" and a reasonably "free" version of Ornette Coleman's "Turn Around." Trumpeters Randy Sandke and Joe Wilder appear on several numbers and the rhythm section (with Alden, pianist Ben Aronov, bassist John Goldsby and drum-

mer Alan Dawson) is excellent, but Ken Peplowski emerges as the main star on this memorable set. —*Scott Yanow*

Live / 1994 / Concord Jazz ✦✦✦✦

It's a Lonesome Old Town / 1995 / Concord Jazz ✦✦✦✦

Art Pepper

b. Sep. 1, 1925, Gardenia, CA, d. Jun. 1, 1982, Panorama, CA

Alto Saxophone / Cool, Post Bop, Bop

Despite a remarkably colorful and difficult life, Art Pepper was quite consistent in the recording studios; virtually every recording he made is well worth getting. In the 1950s he was one of the few altoists (along with Lee Konitz and Paul Desmond) that was able to develop his own sound despite the dominant influence of Charlie Parker. During his last years, Pepper seemed to put all of his life's experiences into his music and he played with startling emotional intensity.

After a brief stint with Gus Arnheim, Pepper played with mostly black groups on Central Avenue in Los Angeles. He spent a little time in the Benny Carter and Stan Kenton orchestras before serving time in the military (1944–46). Some of Pepper's happiest days were during his years with Stan Kenton (1947–52), although he became a heroin addict in that period. The 1950s found the altoist recording frequently both as a leader and a sideman resulting in at least two classics (*Plays Modern Jazz Classics* and *Meets the Rhythm Section*), but he also spent two periods in jail due to drug offenses during 1953–56. Pepper was in top form during his Contemporary recordings of 1957–60, but the first half of his career ended abruptly with long prison sentences that dominated the 1960s. His occasional gigs between jail terms found him adopting a harder tone influenced by John Coltrane that disturbed some of his longtime followers. He recorded with Buddy Rich in 1968 before getting seriously ill and rehabilitating at Synanon (1969–71).

Art Pepper began his serious comeback in 1975 and the unthinkable happened. Under the guidance and inspiration of his wife Laurie, Pepper not only recovered his former form but topped himself with intense solos that were quite unique; he also enjoyed occasionally playing clarinet. His recordings for Contemporary and Galaxy rank with the greatest work of his career. Pepper's autobiography *Straight Life* (written with his wife) is a brutally honest book that details his sometimes-horrifying life. When Art Pepper died at the age of 57, he had attained his goal of becoming the world's great altoist. —*Scott Yanow*

Surf Ride / Feb. 7, 1952–Dec. 24, 1953 / Savoy Jazz ✦✦✦

The music on this Savoy CD (put out by Nippon Columbia) is quite brilliant, but the packaging leaves a lot to be desired. The recording dates are all incorrect, there are only 12 performances included (around 37 minutes) and none of the sessions are reissued in complete form. Two of the dates, quartet outings with either Russ Freeman or Hampton Hawes on piano, have just three of their four numbers reissued while only six of the eight songs from the altoist's classic session with tenor saxophonist Jack Montrose are here. Even if the four missing selections had been included, the program would have totaled around 49 minutes. The somewhat random nature of this set is unfortunate, for Pepper is in superior form throughout with highlights including "Tickle Toe," "The Way You Look Tonight" and his earliest recordings of such originals as "Susie the Poodle," "Straight Life" and "Surf Ride." Get the more definitive LP sets instead. —*Scott Yanow*

The Early Show: A Night at the Surf Club, Vol. 1 / Feb. 12, 1952 / Xanadu ✦✦✦✦

Altoist Art Pepper was 26 when he led the quartet heard on this Xanadu LP at the Surf Club in Hollywood. The earliest documentation of Pepper as a bandleader is this album and its follow-up, *The Late Show*. Even at this early stage, Pepper largely had his own sound (he never chose to copy Charlie Parker) and he was a creative improviser. The sound quality of these tapes is not state-of-the-art, but the performances by Pepper (who also plays some effective clarinet on "Rose Room"), pianist Hampton Hawes, bassist Joe Mondragon and Larry Bunker on drums and vibes are consistently excellent. The repertoire, standards and Pepper "originals" based on fairly common chord changes, is typical of the era, but Pepper's often-brilliant solos already put him near the top of his field. —*Scott Yanow*

The Late Show: A Night at the Surf Club, Vol. 2 / Feb. 1952 / Xanadu ✦✦✦✦

The follow-up to *The Early Show,* this Xanadu LP is quite valuable for it continues the documentation of Art Pepper's earliest recording as a bandleader. Saved on an amateur tape recorder from the audience at Los Angeles' Surf Club, these performances have erratic recording quality, but the music is quite exciting. Pepper, joined by pianist Hampton Hawes, bassist Joe Mondragon and Larry Bunker on drums and vibes, performs bop standards and a variety of his originals that were based on the chord changes of familiar tunes. Even at this early stage, Art Pepper's talents and individuality were obvious. —*Scott Yanow*

● **Discoveries** / Oct. 8, 1952–Aug. 25, 1954 / Savoy ✦✦✦✦✦
This double-LP reissues two of altoist Art Pepper's earliest studio dates as a leader. On four songs he is joined by pianist Russ Freeman, bassist Bob Whitlock and drummer Bobby White, a quiet trio that allows Pepper to dominate such songs as "Everything Happens to Me" and "Tickle Toe." In addition, Pepper matches harmonies and wits with tenor saxophonist Jack Montrose (along with pianist Claude Williamson, bassist Monty Budwig and drummer Larry Bunker) on eight exuberant numbers including the earliest recording of Art's famous "Straight Life." But that is not all, for the second of these two LPs contains previously unissued alternate takes of all but one of the 11 pieces! Because Pepper and Montrose were in very good form during the performances, they are well worth hearing twice. In fact, a slightly later LP (titled *Rediscoveries*) would add 14 more versions to the legacy of these two exciting sessions. Unfortunately, this highly enjoyable music has only been reissued on CD thus far in random fashion. —*Scott Yanow*

Rediscoveries / Oct. 8, 1952–Aug. 25, 1954 / Savoy ✦✦✦✦
This valuable Savoy LP, put out by Muse in 1986, has 14 previously unissued alternate takes taken from two Art Pepper sessions. The great altoist is heard with a quiet West Coast trio (pianist Russ Freeman, bassist Bob Whitlock and drummer Bobby White) and with a quintet co-starring tenor saxophonist Jack Montrose. The Pepper-Montrose matchup is particularly exciting, but Pepper is actually in fine form on all of the performances; it is difficult to believe that these were all rejected takes! The remainder of the two productive sessions were released on a two-LP set around the same period titled *Discoveries*, and most of this music (particularly the alternate takes) has not been reissued on CD yet. —*Scott Yanow*

Art Pepper Quartet, Vol. 1, with the Sonny Clark Trio / May 31, 1953 / Time Is ✦✦✦
This CD contains a live performance from early in altoist Art Pepper's career in which he is joined by pianist Sonny Clark, Harry Babasin on bass and cello, and drummer Bobby White. Recorded at the legendary Lighthouse, the music is better than the recording quality. Pepper and Clark have many fine solos on the six standards and Art's "Brown Gold" (based on "I Got Rhythm"), but this CD (there never was a Vol. 2!) is strictly for collectors. —*Scott Yanow*

Mucho Calor / 1956 / VSOP ✦✦✦
This VSOP LP brings back an obscure session from the long defunct Andex label that was probably recorded around 1956. The emphasis is on Latin jazz with altoist Art Pepper, trumpeter Conte Candoli and tenor saxophonist Bill Perkins, pianist Russ Freeman, bassist Ben Tucker and drummer Chuck Flores interacting with the percussion of Jack Costanza and Mike Pacheko. With arrangements by Bill Holman, Johnny Mandel, Benny Carter and Pepper, the music is quite jazz-oriented if a touch lightweight. Worth investigating by fans of the idiom. —*Scott Yanow*

★ **The Complete Pacific Jazz Small Group Recordings of Art Pepper** / Jul. 26, 1956–Aug. 12, 1957 / Mosaic ✦✦✦✦
This superior three-LP box set reissues all of altoist Art Pepper's small-group dates for the Pacific Jazz label. Virtually all of the music has since been reissued on CD (part of it as *The Artistry of Pepper* and part of it under trumpeter Chet Baker's name), but the Mosaic box, which has an attractive booklet, is the definitive treatment of this chapter in Pepper's musical story. The great altoist is heard in a sextet with Baker and tenor saxophonist Richie Kamuca, on a version of "Tenderly" with Chet Baker's big band, with Baker and tenor Phil Urso in a different sextet, sharing the spotlight with tenor saxophonist Bill Perkins in a quintet and heading a nonet playing arrangements by Shorty Rogers. The music is very much in the cool/bop tradition, but Art Pepper is instantly recognizable (he never sounded that much like Charlie Parker) and even at this early stage, he was at the top of his form. All 26 performances are quite enjoyable and swinging, making this hard-to-find set worth the search. —*Scott Yanow*

The Art Pepper Quartet / Aug. 1956 / VSOP ✦✦✦
Originally released on the defunct Tampa label and then on CD by the small VSOP label, this straight reissue in the OJC series features the great altoist Art Pepper with pianist Russ Freeman, bassist Ben Tucker and drummer Gary Frommer. Despite the inclusion of five alternate takes, there is still only around 41 minutes of music but the quality is high; even with his erratic lifestyle, Pepper never made a bad record. Highlights include Art's original "Diane," "Besame Mucho" and "Pepper Pot." Fine music, but not essential when one considers how many gems Art Pepper recorded during his rather hectic life. —*Scott Yanow*

Val's Pal / Nov. 23, 1956 / VSOP ✦✦✦
The music on this VSOP CD, which originally came out on the obsolete Tampa label in the 1950s, has since been reissued by Fantasy in its OJC series. Altoist Art Pepper, who is assisted by pianist Russ Freeman, bassist Ben Tucker and drummer Gary Frommer, is in excellent form during the 41 or so minutes. The seven selections are augmented by five alternate takes. Although not an essential release, these versions of "Diane," "Pepper Pot" and "Besame Mucho" (the latter a song that Art would perform frequently in the late '70s) are somewhat memorable. —*Scott Yanow*

The Way It Was / Nov. 26, 1956–Nov. 23, 1960 / Original Jazz Classics ✦✦✦✦
Despite his erratic lifestyle, altoist Art Pepper never made a bad record. This collection is better than most. The first four titles team together Pepper with tenor saxophonist Warne Marsh, pianist Ronnie Ball, bassist Ben Tucker and drummer Gary Frommer for generally intriguing explorations of four standards. One can feel the influence of Lennie Tristano (with Pepper in Lee Konitz's place) although Pepper had his own sound and a more hard-swinging style. The success of the Pepper-Marsh frontline makes one wish that they had recorded together again. The other three selections are leftovers from a trio of classic Pepper albums and all are quite worthwhile. Pepper is heard backed by three separate rhythm sections, which include pianists Red Garland, Dolo Coker or Wynton Kelly, either Paul Chambers or Jimmy Bond on bass and Philly Joe Jones, Frank Butler or Jimmie Cobb on drums. Overall, this album sticks to bop standards and finds Art Pepper in top form. —*Scott Yanow*

● **The Artistry of Pepper** / Dec. 11, 1956–Aug. 12, 1957 / Pacific Jazz ✦✦✦✦
This CD starts off with four selections from a date led by tenor saxophonist Bill Perkins that features altoist Art Pepper; the remainder of the quintet is comprised of pianist Jimmy Rowles, bassist Ben Tucker and Mel Lewis. While they perform boppish versions of two standards and a pair of Pepper originals, the remainder of the CD has a particularly strong set that showcases Pepper in a nonet arranged by Shorty Rogers. The music in the latter date are all Rogers originals and there are alternate takes of "Diablo's Dance " and "Popo" to round out the program. The other soloists include trumpeter Don Fagerquist, Bill Holman on tenor, baritonist Bud Shank, valve trombonist Stu Williamson and pianist Russ Freeman. Highly recommended to fans of Art Pepper and West Coast jazz. —*Scott Yanow*

★ **Meets the Rhythm Section** / Jan. 19, 1957 / Original Jazz Classics ✦✦✦✦
This Contemporary album is one of Art Pepper's greatest recordings. Although he was reportedly nervous to be playing with Miles Davis' rhythm section (pianist Red Garland, bassist Paul Chambers and drummer Philly Joe Jones), the altoist is quite inspired on the nine high-quality tunes. In addition to some bop standards, this album introduced Pepper's "Straight Life," recast the Dixieland tune "Jazz Me Blues" in a modern setting and also includes Pepper's "Waltz Me Blues." The combination of musicians worked very well, making this one of the top jazz albums of a great jazz year, 1957. —*Scott Yanow*

Omega Alpha / Apr. 1, 1957 / Blue Note ✦✦✦✦
The music on this Blue Note LP has always been somewhat obscure. Originally released by Omegatape only on pre-recorded tapes, it did not make its debut on an American LP until this 1980 album came out. It was a strange twist of fate, for the music for altoist Art Pepper (who was in one of his prime periods) was in top form throughout the date, playing "Surf Ride," "Webb City" and five familiar standards with pianist Carl Perkins, bassist Ben Tucker and drummer Chuck Flores. Highlights include "Surf Ride," "Fascinatin' Rhythm" and "Body and Soul." —*Scott Yanow*

★ **Art Pepper + Eleven: Modern Jazz Classics** / Mar. 14, 1959–May 11, 1959 / Original Jazz Classics ✦✦✦✦
This is a true classic. Altoist Art Pepper is joined by an 11-piece band playing Marty Paich arrangements of a dozen jazz standards from the bop and cool jazz era. Trumpeter Jack Sheldon has a few solos, but the focus is very much on the altoist who is in peak form for this period. The CD reissue adds two additional versions of "Walkin' " and one of "Donna Lee" to the original program. Throughout, Pepper sounds quite inspired by Paich's charts, which feature the band as an active part of the music rather than just in the background. Highlights of this highly enjoyable set include "Move," "Four Brothers," "Shaw Nuff," "Anthropology" and "Donna Lee," but there is not a single throwaway track to be heard. Essential music for all serious jazz collections. —*Scott Yanow*

Gettin' Together / Feb. 29, 1960 / Original Jazz Classics ✦✦✦✦✦
As a sort of follow-up to Art Pepper's matchup with Miles Davis' trio in the 1957 classic *Art Pepper Meets the Rhythm Section*, Pepper utilizes Davis' sidemen on this 1960 near-classic. In addition to pianist Wynton Kelly, bassist Paul Chambers and drummer Jimmy Cobb, trumpeter Conte Candoli makes the group a quintet on four of the eight numbers. The CD reissue adds "The Way You Look Tonight" (formerly only available on another LP) and an alternate take of the title cut to the original repertoire. This time around, rather than emphasizing standards, Pepper performs just three ("Softly, As in a Morning Sunrise," Thelonious Monk's "Rhythm-A-Ning" and "The Way You Look Tonight") and includes three originals of his own: "Diane," "Bijou the Poodle" and "Gettin' Together." The music is all very straight-ahead and bop-oriented, but as usual, Pepper brings something very personal and unique to his playing; he sounds like no one else. —*Scott Yanow*

Smack Up / Oct. 24, 1960–Oct. 25, 1960 / Original Jazz Classics ✦✦✦✦✦
The title of this recording (which has been reissued on CD with two takes of the otherwise unknown "Solid Citizens" added) is ironic and inadvertently truthful. Within a short period, Art Pepper would begin spending many years in jail due to his heroin addiction; this was his next-to-last album of this period. Despite the bleak future, the great altoist (who never seemed to make an uninspired record during his unstable life) is in excellent form in a quintet with trumpeter Jack Sheldon, pianist Pete Jolly, bassist Jimmy Bond and drummer Frank Butler. Highlights of this fine album include Harold Land's title cut, the 5/4 blues "Las Cuevas De Mario" and Ornette Coleman's "Tears Inside." —*Scott Yanow*

Intensity / Nov. 23, 1960–Nov. 25, 1960 / Original Jazz Classics ✦✦✦✦✦
This album, reissued on CD with an additional song, "Fine Points," was altoist Art Pepper's final one of his early period and was released when he was already serving a long prison sentence due to his addiction to heroin. Assisted by pianist Dolo Coker, bassist Jimmy Bond and drummer Frank Butler, Pepper was just starting to show the influence of John Coltrane and Ornette Coleman in his style, freeing up his playing and displaying a greater intensity during his improvisations. Ironically, Pepper sticks to swinging standards such as "I Can't Believe That You're in Love with Me," "Gone with the Wind" and "I Wished on the Moon" as points of departure on the interesting and largely enjoyable set. Excluding a 1973 recording with Mike Vax's big band, it would be 15 years before Art Pepper led another record date in the studios. —*Scott Yanow*

Art Pepper Quartet in San Francisco (1964) / May 8, 1964–Jun. 1964 / Fresh Sound ✦✦✦
For altoist Art Pepper, the 1960s were largely a waste with long periods spent in prison due to his narcotics addiction. He spent most of 1964 between prison terms and even tried to make a musical comeback. This CD from the Spanish Fresh Sound label features Pepper with pianist Frank Strazzeri, bassist Hersh Hamel and drummer Bill Goodwin playing a few originals on a television show (Pepper is interviewed briefly by Ralph Gleason) and performing two lengthy numbers at The Jazz Workshop in San Francisco. Many of the altoist's longtime fans were disappointed by his playing during this period for Pepper had become very influenced by John Coltrane and fearful that, if he did not sound like 'Trane, he would be regarded as old fashioned. Actually, Art Pepper, who plays with more intensity here than he often did in the 1950s, sounds pretty good during these sets, although the recording quality is not always the greatest, and his fans (along

Music Map

Percussion

Prior to the bop era, percussionists were not utilized in jazz.

Pioneers
Chano Pozo (with Dizzy Gillespie 1947-48)
Jack Costanzo
(with Stan Kenton and Nat King Cole Trio 1947-5)

Giants of Latin Jazz
Machito
Cal Tjader (bongos early in his career)
Mongo Santamaria
Willie Bobo
Tito Puente
Poncho Sanchez

Brazilian
Airto Moreira   Guilherme Franco
Paulhino Da Casto   Dom Um Ramao
Nana Vasconcelos

Other Important Percussionists
Ray Barretto
Carlos Vidal
Babatunde Olatunji
Big Black
Candido
Armando Peraza
(regular guest with George Shearing Quintet)
Sabu Martinez
Potato Valdez
Ralph MacDonald
Mtume
Don Alias
Alex Acuna
Kahil El'Zabar (Ethnic Heritage Ensemble)
Mino Cinelu
Marilyn Mazur
Don Moye
Badal Roy

Tabla and Other Percussion with Oregon
Collin Walcott
Trilok Gurtu

Two Important Percussion-oriented Groups
Fort Apache Band (Jerry Gonzalez)
Max Roach's M'Boom
(nine percussionists including Roach, Roy Brooks, Joe Chambers, Ray Mantilla and Warren Smith)

with jazz historians) will find these rare performances quite interesting. —*Scott Yanow*

I'll Remember April: Live at Foothill College / Feb. 14, 1975 / Storyville ✦✦✦✦
Altoist Art Pepper was at the beginning of his successful (if relatively brief) seven-year renaissance when he performed at the concert documented on this Storyville CD. Recorded six months before his first official comeback record (*Living Legend*), the great altoist is heard playing with a quartet comp of Tommy Gumina on polychord (an organ-sounding accordion), bassist Fred Atwood and drummer Jimmie Smith. Pepper is in excellent form on lengthy versions of his "Foothill Blues," "I'll Remember April" and "Cherokee" and is quite passionate on a four-and-a-half-minute version of "Here's That Rainy Day." Gumina mostly stays out of the way, and the audience sounds quite happy to get an opportunity to hear the legendary altoist sounding so strong. —*Scott Yanow*

Living Legend / Aug. 9, 1975 / Original Jazz Classics ✦✦✦✦
Art Pepper, one of the major bop altoists to emerge during the 1950s, started his comeback with this excellent set. After 15 years filled with prison time and spent fighting drug addiction, Pepper was finally ready to return to jazz. Accompanied by three of his old friends (pianist Hampton Hawes, bassist Charlie Haden and drummer Shelly Manne), Pepper displays a more explorative and darker style than he had had previously. He also shows a greater emotional depth in his improvisations and was open to some of the innovations of the avant-garde in his search for greater self-expression. Although this recording would be topped by the ones to come, the music (five Pepper originals and an intense version of "Here's That Rainy Day") is quite rewarding. —*Scott Yanow*

● **The Trip** / Sep. 15, 1976+Sep. 16, 1976 / Original Jazz Classics ✦✦✦✦✦
Although some listeners prefer altoist Art Pepper's playing of the 1950s, when he re-emerged in 1975, there was a much greater emotional intensity to his improvisations, and his solos used a wider vocabulary with nonmusical and emotional sounds being added to his ideas as punctuations. This strong quartet date (with pianist George Cables, bassist David Williams and drummer Elvin Jones) finds Pepper performing Michel Legrand's "The Summer Knows," lesser-known tunes by Woody Shaw and Joe Gordon and three originals of his own; the CD reissue also has an alternate take of "The Trip." Powerful music. —*Scott Yanow*

A Night in Tunisia / Jan. 23, 1977 / Storyville ✦✦✦✦
Altoist Art Pepper was nearing the turning point in his career at the time that he performed at the concert at Half Moon Bay, CA, that is included on this Storyville CD. He had been back on the scene for two years and had not quite broken through to the wider jazz audience yet, but major successes were in the near future. It is obvious from his talking to the audience that Pepper was still unsure about his future, but his playing on this date (with a pickup group comprised of pianist Smith Dobson, bassist Jim Nichols and drummer Brad Bilhorn) finds him in top form, creating emotional versions of "A Night in Tunisia" and his three originals "Mr. Yohe," "The Trip" and "Lost Life." Since there are only 40 minutes of music on the CD and this was not one of Pepper's strongest groups, the release is not essential, but fans of the unique altoist will want to pick up these interesting performances. —*Scott Yanow*

No Limit / Mar. 26, 1977 / Original Jazz Classics ✦✦✦✦✦
Art Pepper's third recording in his comeback years was recorded in a studio, but has the emotional intensity and chance-taking improvisations of his live concerts of the period. Joined by his regular group (pianist George Cables, bassist Tony Dumas and drummer Carl Burnett), Pepper performs lengthy versions of three of his originals (including the modal "My Laurie") and "Ballad of the Sad Young Men." "Mambo de la Pinta" is a little unusual because Pepper overdubbed himself on tenor to join his alto in the ensembles. Throughout this album (and during his final ten years), Art Pepper played every note as if it might be his last one. The passion displayed on this particular album is enough of a reason by itself to acquire it. —*Scott Yanow*

Tokyo Debut / Apr. 5, 1977 / Galaxy ✦✦✦✦✦
After Art Pepper returned to the scene in 1975, it took him two years to get noticed outside of Los Angeles. His initial visit to Japan was a major turning point, and music from one of the very well-received concerts was released for the first time on this 1995

CD. Pepper performs four numbers—"Cherokee," his original "The Spirit Is Here," a passionate "Here's That Rainy Day" and a speedy workout on "Straight Life"—with a quintet comprised of Clare Fischer (who unfortunately sticks exclusively to electric piano), bassist Rob Fisher, drummer Peter Riso and percussionist Poncho Sanchez. For the final three numbers—"Manteca," "Manha De Carnaval" and "Felicidade"—the group is joined by vibraphonist Cal Tjader (this is the only time he ever recorded with Pepper) and guitarist Bob Redfield. The unexpected enthusiasm of the crowd really got to Pepper and his improvisations (even though he is not playing with his regular group) are quite inspired. Memorable music. —*Scott Yanow*

Thursday Night at the Village Vanguard / Jul. 28, 1977 / Original Jazz Classics ✦✦✦✦✦
Art Pepper's appearances at the Village Vanguard in 1977 were a major success, making the brilliance of the West Coast-based altoist obvious to the New York critics. His historical stint at the Vanguard was originally made available on four LPs (all reissued as CDs with one additional selection added on each disc) and more recently in more expanded form as a nine-CD boxed set. The single CD reissue of the Thursday night portion features the great altoist on lengthy versions of "Valse Triste," a particularly passionate version of "Goodbye," "Blues for Les," "My Friend John" and "Blues for Heard." In addition to Pepper, his trio—pianist George Cables, bassist George Mraz and drummer Elvin Jones—is also in top form, and the music is consistently stimulating and emotional. —*Scott Yanow*

More for Less / Jul. 28, 1977–Jul. 30, 1977 / Original Jazz Classics ✦✦✦✦✦
The fourth of four CD reissues taken from Art Pepper's three nights at the Village Vanguard in July 1977, as with the other releases, adds one selection ("Scrapple from the Apple") to the music of the original LP; all of the performances on this and the other sets have since been made available as part of a massive nine-CD box set. The great altoist was clearly excited to be playing at the famous New York club, and his rhythm section—pianist George Cables, bassist George Mraz and drummer Elvin Jones—consistently stimulates his imagination. This release has more variety than usual, for in addition to his alto playing (including a memorable unaccompanied solo on "Over the Rainbow"), Pepper switches to clarinet for the lengthy "More for Les" and interprets the ballad "These Foolish Things" on tenor. The nine-CD set is essential for Art Pepper fanatics, but those just wanting a taste of the great altoist's talents will be satisfied with this release. —*Scott Yanow*

★ **The Complete Village Vanguard Sessions** / Jul. 28, 1977–Jul. 30, 1977 / Contemporary ✦✦✦✦✦

Friday Night at the Village Vanguard / Jul. 29, 1977 / Original Jazz Classics ✦✦✦✦✦
The second of four releases taken from altoist Art Pepper's very successful stint at the Village Vanguard in July 1977 has been reissued on CD with one extra track, "A Night in Tunisia." Pepper, who is greatly assisted by a highly sympathetic rhythm section (pianist George Cables, bassist George Mraz and drummer Elvin Jones) is at his best on "Caravan," which finds him doubling on tenor, and on an intense rendition of "But Beautiful." All of this music is currently available as part of a massive nine-CD box set that really documents the historic engagement. —*Scott Yanow*

Saturday Night at the Village Vanguard / Jul. 30, 1977 / Original Jazz Classics ✦✦✦✦
The CD reissue of this release, the third of four single sets that document Art Pepper's well-received engagement at the Village Vanguard, adds "For Freddie" to the original three-song program. The other selections, which feature pianist George Cables, bassist George Mraz and drummer Elvin Jones in addition to the altoist/leader, are intense interpretations of "You Go to My Head," Pepper's "The Trip" and a 16-minute version of "Cherokee." The altoist was entering his peak period and the entire gig has also been fully documented on a massive nine-CD box set. —*Scott Yanow*

Live in Japan, Vol. 1 / Mar. 14, 1978 / Storyville ✦✦✦✦
Art Pepper concluded a very successful tour of Japan with a concert in Yamagata that was recorded and released on two Storyville CDs. The first CD has just 38 minutes of music, but the quality is quite high. Pepper (with pianist Milcho Leviev, bassist Bob Magnusson and drummer Carl Burnett) performs lengthy ver-

sions of two originals ("Ophelia," "My Laurie") and "Besame Mucho"; the latter was a request from his Japanese friends that was very well received and became a permanent part of his repertoire. The recording quality is excellent and Pepper is in explorative and somewhat inspired form. —*Scott Yanow*

Live in Japan, Vol. 2 / Mar. 14, 1978 / Storyville ✦✦✦
The second of two CDs taken from the final night of Art Pepper's 1978 Japanese tour features the great altoist (along with pianist Milcho Leviev, bassist Bob Magnusson and drummer Carl Burnett) exploring two of his originals ("The Trip," and "Red Car"), a lyrical version of Michel Legrand's "The Summer Knows" and an intense rendition of "Caravan." None of the Storyville sets have been reissued elsewhere, and each adds to the remarkable legacy of Art Pepper whose second career (covering 1975–82) was arguably even greater than his first. —*Scott Yanow*

Among Friends / Sep. 2, 1978 / Discovery ✦✦✦✦
Art Pepper mostly sticks to standards on this Discovery LP, but he brings out new life in the veteran songs, particularly on such ballads as "Round Midnight," "What's New" and "Besame Mucho." With the assistance of pianist Russ Freeman, bassist Bob Magnusson and drummer Frank Butler, the great altoist (who is heard just prior to signing an exclusive contract with the Galaxy label) is also in top form on such pieces as "What Is This Thing Called Love" and "I'll Remember April." An excellent (if not quite essential) release. —*Scott Yanow*

Art Pepper Today / Dec. 1, 1978+Dec. 2, 1978 / Original Jazz Classics ✦✦✦✦
Altoist Art Pepper, in the midst of a successful comeback, recorded this excellent set (also included in full in his massive Galaxy box set) for Galaxy. With pianist Stanley Cowell, bassist Cecil McBee and drummer Roy Haynes, Pepper performs a definitive version of his intense ballad "Patricia"; other highlights include "Miss Who," "Lover Come Back to Me" and "Chris' Blues." The CD reissue also has a second alternate version of "These Foolish Things." —*Scott Yanow*

★ **Complete Galaxy Recordings** / Dec. 1, 1978–Apr. 14, 1982 / Galaxy ✦✦✦✦✦
Altoist Art Pepper was at the height of his career during his final five years. A brilliant improviser in the 1950s, by the late '70s the many dark experiences he had had in life were reflected in a deep emotional intensity in his playing. He played each solo as if it might be his last and his passion was brutally honest. This giant 16-CD Galaxy set features Pepper at the peak of his powers. Most of the performances are in a quartet setting although there is a session with strings, five unaccompanied alto solos (he also plays clarinet on a few tracks) and a pair of CDs in which Pepper duets with pianist George Cables. Although more general collectors may want to acquire some of the individual sessions first (most of which are available separately on CD), the more dedicated jazz fans are advised to save their money and acquire this essential package. —*Scott Yanow*

Laurie's Choice / 1978–1981 / Laserlight ✦✦✦✦
Although it has come out on a budget label, these four performances (taken from concert appearances in 1978, 1980 and 1981) had never previously been released before. With support from either George Cables or Milcho Leviev on piano, David Williams or Bob Magnusson on bass and drummer Carl Burnett, the great altoist Art Pepper is in excellent form on an emotional "Kobe Blues," an intense version of "Patricia" and hard-swinging renditions of "Allen's Alley" and his own "Straight Life." —*Scott Yanow*

So in Love / Feb. 23, 1979–May 26, 1979 / Artists House ✦✦✦✦
This deluxe release from the classy (but long defunct) Artists House label, as with all of Art Pepper's recordings of his comeback years, is easily recommended. Actually, all of this music has been reissued in greatly expanded form in Pepper's massive 16-CD Galaxy box set. The original LP has lengthy versions of "So in Love," "Stardust," "Straight No Chaser" and two Pepper originals ("Diane" and "Blues for Blanche"). Assisted by two equally talented rhythm sections (pianists Hank Jones and George Cables, bassists Ron Carter and Charlie Haden, and drummers Al Foster and Billy Higgins), Pepper is in excellent form throughout the album, giving these songs heartwrenching interpretations. —*Scott Yanow*

Artworks / May 25, 1979–May 26, 1979 / Galaxy ✦✦✦
The performances on this Galaxy LP are essentially outtakes and leftovers from Art Pepper's 1979 sessions for Artists House.

However, the quality is quite high, making one wonder why this material was not released until 1984. "Body and Soul" and "You Go to My Head" are particularly special, for they are unaccompanied alto solos, and on "Anthropology," Pepper has a rare outing on clarinet. The remaining numbers—"Desafinado," "Donna Lee" and "Blues for Blanche"—feature the great altoist with pianist George Cables, bassist Charlie Haden and drummer Billy Higgins. All of the highly enjoyable and bop-based but explorative music has since been reissued on CD in Pepper's 16-CD Galaxy box set. —*Scott Yanow*

Landscape / Jul. 1979 / Original Jazz Classics ✦✦✦✦✦
Altoist Art Pepper was in inspired form during this Tokyo concert, which has also been reissued as part of a huge "complete" Galaxy box set. This particular single-CD features Pepper (along with pianist George Cables, bassist Tony Dumas and drummer Billy Higgins) on memorable versions of "True Blues," "Sometime" (during which Pepper switches to clarinet), "Landscape," "Avalon," "Over the Rainbow," "Straight Life" and the CD "bonus" cut "Mambo De La Pinta." Throughout, Pepper's intensity and go-for-broke style are exhilarating. —*Scott Yanow*

★ **Straight Life** / Sep. 21, 1979 / Original Jazz Classics ✦✦✦✦✦
Altoist Art Pepper recorded many albums for the Galaxy label during 1979–82, all of which have been reissued in a massive 16-CD "complete" box set. This single CD is pretty definitive and serves as a perfect introduction to Pepper's second (and most rewarding) period. Not only is there a superior version of Pepper's famous title cut, but very emotional (and explorative) renditions of "September Song" and "Nature Boy." Filling out this quartet set (which also features pianist Tommy Flanagan, bassist Red Mitchell and drummer Billy Higgins) are "Surf Ride," "Make a List" and "Long Ago and Far Away." Brilliant music. —*Scott Yanow*

Winter Moon / Sep. 3, 1980–Sep. 4, 1980 / Galaxy ✦✦✦✦
Ever since Artie Shaw and Charlie Parker, most jazz musicians have had a desire to record at least once in their lives with strings, often considering it a prestigious honor. Altoist Art Pepper finally had his chance on this album and, fortunately, the string arrangements (by Bill Holman and Jimmy Bond) do not weigh down the proceedings. Pepper sounds quite inspired performing seven strong compositions highlighted by Hoagy Carmichael's "Winter Moon," "When the Sun Comes Out" and a clarinet feature on "Blues in the Night." This material (plus four alternate takes and two other songs from the same sessions) is included in the massive Art Pepper Galaxy box set. —*Scott Yanow*

One September Afternoon / Sep. 5, 1980 / Original Jazz Classics ✦✦✦
This is one of the lesser-known Art Pepper Galaxy sessions. In addition to pianist Stanley Cowell, bassist Cecil McBee and drummer Carl Burnett, guitarist Howard Roberts helps out on two songs. Three alternate takes are added to the original six-tune program, which is highlighted by "There Will Never Be Another You" and a passionate rendition of "Brazil." —*Scott Yanow*

Arthur's Blues / 1981 / Galaxy ✦✦✦✦
A '92 CD reissue of another sparkling late-'80s session from alto saxophonist Art Pepper, this one a quartet date with a blues theme. Pepper's jagged, turbulent solos expressed the rage and despair he felt knowing he was nearing the end and still had many things he wanted to say. He's backed by what had become his regular band: pianist George Cables, bassist David Williams, and drummer Carl Burnett. —*Ron Wynn*

Art Lives / Aug. 13, 1981–Aug. 15, 1981 / Galaxy ✦✦✦✦
The music on this LP is from altoist Art Pepper's well-documented engagement at the Maiden Voyage club in Los Angeles in 1981. All of the music has since been reissued on CD as part of his giant 16-CD set. Pepper, pianist George Cables, bassist David Williams and drummer Carl Burnett are heard at their best on "Allen's Alley," and "Samba Mom Mom." A special highlight is a passionate duet by Pepper and Cables on "But Beautiful." —*Scott Yanow*

● **Roadgame** / Aug. 15, 1981 / Original Jazz Classics ✦✦✦✦
Altoist Art Pepper's 1981 appearances at Los Angeles' now-obsolete Maiden Voyage club were fully documented, resulting in three LPs and a greatly expanded program that is included on Pepper's massive "complete" Galaxy box set. This particular release, the only one thus far to be made available as a single CD, has Pepper and his quartet (with pianist George Cables, bassist David Williams and drummer Carl Burnett) performing

"Roadgame" (an alternate take has been added to the CD reissue), "Road Waltz," an intense "Everything Happens to Me" and "When You're Smiling"; on the latter, Pepper switches to clarinet. Although only a year away from his death, the great Art Pepper was still very much in his prime for this memorable outing. — *Scott Yanow*

Art 'N' Zoot / Sep. 27, 1981 / Pablo ✦✦✦✦

Goin' Home / May 11, 1982–May 12, 1982 / Original Jazz Classics ✦✦✦✦✦

Art Pepper's final recording sessions were comprised of duets with pianist George Cables. Pepper, who splits his time almost evenly here between alto and clarinet, is in surprisingly strong form considering that he only had a month left to live. He is heard at his best on "Goin' Home," "Don't Let the Sun Catch You Cryin'," "Isn't She Lovely" and "Lover Man," really pouring out his emotions into the ballads. Two alternate takes were added to the CD reissue, although for the complete picture, one has to acquire Art Pepper's 16-CD Galaxy box set, which contains plenty of otherwise unissued performances. — *Scott Yanow*

Tete-A-Tete / May 11, 1982–May 12, 1982 / Galaxy ✦✦✦✦

Altoist Art Pepper's final recordings resulted in two albums worth of duets with pianist George Cables; the music was reissued in expanded form on Pepper's 16-CD Galaxy box set, but otherwise, this LP is out of print. Highlights of these relaxed but passionate encounters include "Over the Rainbow," "Body and Soul," "The Way You Look Tonight" and "You Go to My Head." Pepper never did decline on record, and although he died in June 1982 (just a month after the last of these duets), he is prime form throughout the emotional performances. — *Scott Yanow*

Darn That Dream / May 23, 1982 / Real Time ✦✦✦

Altoist Art Pepper and tenor saxophonist Joe Farrell teamed up for the first and only time on this Real Time LP, most of which has been reissued on CD by Drive Archives. With pianist George Cables, bassist Tony Dumas and drummer John Dentz also participating, Pepper and Farrell are in good form. They interact on a blues, "Sweet Lorraine," "Mode for Joe" and "Who Can I Turn To," but the highpoints are their two individual features; Farrell has "Someday My Prince Will Come" and Pepper really tears into "Darn That Dream." — *Scott Yanow*

Tokyo Encore / Jul. 16, 1979–Jul. 23, 1979 / Dreyfus ✦✦✦✦✦

It is not obvious looking at the outside of this CD, but the music from this live performance is also included in Art Pepper's 16-CD Galaxy box set. However, those Pepper fans unable to afford the larger box are advised to acquire this Dreyfus single CD for the altoist is heard in superb form. Accompanied (and inspired) by pianist George Cables, bassist Tony Dumas and drummer Billy Higgins, Pepper stretches out on six superior pieces that are highlighted by "Besame Mucho," "Straight Life" and one of the greatest versions ever recorded of "Over the Rainbow." — *Scott Yanow*

Ivo Perelman

b. Jan. 12, 1961, Sao Paulo, Brazil
Tenor Saxophone / Avant-Garde

The intense Brazilian tenor player Ivo Perelman combines together the emotional fire of an Albert Ayler with a strong respect for melodies. Originally a classical guitar player, Perleman also played cello, piano, trombone and clarinet before settling on tenor. His passionate style made it difficult for him to catch on at first but Perelman has recorded successful albums for K2B2 and GM with such players as Airto, Flora Purim, Eliane Elias, Buell Neidlinger and Joanne Brackeen in the supporting cast. — *Scott Yanow*

● **Ivo** / Apr. 24, 1990 / ✦✦✦✦✦

The Children of Ibeji / May 22, 1991–Jul. 10, 1991 / Enja ✦✦✦✦

Soccer Land / 1994 / Ibeji ✦✦✦✦

Man Of The Forest / Jan. 3, 1994–Jan. 4, 1994 / GM ✦✦✦✦✦

Ivo Perelman, who has been thought of as a Brazilian Albert Ayler (although that is a simplification and a denial of his originality), fuses together Brazilian music (the playing of his percussionists) with creative jazz in this unusual tribute to the compositions of the Brazilian classical composer Heitor Villa-Lobos. Actually, Perelman just uses Villa-Lobos' motifs as a point of departure, but one could call the results world fusion since Perelman's mixture creates some startling jazz. Pianist Joanne Brackeen makes her presence felt during her three appearances (including the modal

waltz "Veleiro" and the ballad "Rasga O Coracao") while the interaction between the tenor, the accordion of Dom Salvador and the percussionists on "Cantiga Caico" is delightful. Ivo Perelman has an intense sound, complete control of his instrument and an emotional style a little like Archie Shepp in his prime. His passionate music deserves close attention. — *Scott Yanow*

Danilo Perez

b. 1966, Panama
Piano / Post Bop

A brilliant pianist who has combined the bebop tradition with his Panamanian heritage, African elements and a willingness to take chances, Danilo Perez's improvisations are fascinating to watch develop. In concert he has been known to have his quartet improvising in four different time signatures simultaneously with surprisingly coherent results and his originals tend to develop as they go along with surprising results. Perez started playing piano in Panama at age eight and, in 1985, moved to Boston to study at Berklee. He played with Jon Hendricks (1987) and Claudio Roditi (1988) and has had a longtime association with Paquito D'Rivera. Danilo Perez gigged and recorded with Dizzy Gillespie during the trumpeter's last years and has headed several sessions as a leader for Novus. — *Scott Yanow*

Danilo Perez / Sep. 1992 / Novus ✦✦✦✦✦

★ **The Journey** / Dec. 1993 / Novus ✦✦✦✦✦

Bill Perkins (William Reese Perkins)

b. Jul. 22, 1924, San Francisco, CA
Tenor Saxophone, Baritone Saxophone, Soprano Saxophone / Cool, Post Bop, Hard Bop

Among the "coolest" of the West Coast tenor players of the 1950s, Bill Perkins in later years became a bit influenced by John Coltrane and modernized his style in a personal way. A flexible and versatile musician who also plays baritone, alto, soprano and flute, Perkins is best-known for his work on tenor. Born in San Francisco, he grew up in Santa Barbara and served in the military in World War II. After studying music and engineering, he played in the big bands of Jerry Wald, Woody Herman (1951–53 and 1954) and Stan Kenton (1953–54 and 1955–58). Perk started recording as a leader in 1956 (most notably *Grand Encounter* with John Lewis) including sets with Art Pepper and Richie Kamuca. During the 1960s, he had a dual career as a studio musician and a recording engineer, and during 1970–92 he was a member of the Tonight Show band. In recent years, Perkins has played baritone and tenor with the Lighthouse All-Stars and been a member of the Bud Shank Sextet in addition to heading his own sessions for a variety of labels. — *Scott Yanow*

★ **Jazz Origin: 2 Degrees East, 3 Degrees West** / Feb. 10, 1956 / PA/USA ✦✦✦✦✦

Tenors Head-On / Jul. 1956–Oct. 29, 1956 / Pacific Jazz ✦✦✦✦✦

Quietly There / Nov. 23, 1966–Nov. 30, 1966 / Original Jazz Classics ✦✦✦✦

This set by multi-reedist Bill Perkins (who switches between tenor, baritone, bass clarinet and flute) has been reissued on CD with one extra selection. On what was one of the earliest tributes to film composer Johnny Mandel, Perkins was careful to not only perform ballads such as "Emily," "A Time for Love" and "The Shadow of Your Smile," but to add some variety by also playing a few of Mandel's more obscure medium-tempo numbers. Still, the results are generally pretty relaxed and tasteful on a quintet set with pianist Victor Feldman (who also plays some cheesy-sounding organ and vibes), guitarist John Pisano, bassist Red Mitchell and drummer Larry Bunker. — *Scott Yanow*

Front Line / Nov. 20, 1978 / Storyville ✦✦✦

Many Ways to Go / Mar. 1980 / Sea Breeze ✦✦✦

Journey to the East / Nov. 19, 1984–Nov. 24, 1984 / Contemporary ✦✦✦✦

I Wished on the Moon / Nov. 23, 1989+Apr. 25, 1990 / Candid ✦✦✦✦✦

Remembrance of Dino's / May 21, 1990 / Interplay ✦✦✦✦

Our Man Woody / Jan. 8, 1991–Sep. 1991 / Jazz Mark ✦✦✦✦

● **Frame Of Mind** / May 20, 1993–May 21, 1993 / Interplay ✦✦✦✦✦

It is typical of Bill Perkins' adventurous spirit that on his Interplay CD, a session on which he had complete control (including repertoire and sidemen), Perk would perform ten challenging pieces: four Frank Strazzeri originals and compositions by Mike Stern, Duke Pearson, Jimmy Heath, Thelonious Monk, Billy Strayhorn and trumpeter Clay Jenkins. A couple of the pieces are blues but, due to the tricky frameworks, this was far from a routine jam session. Perkins' tenor (he switches to baritone on "You Know I Care") blends in well with Jenkins while the rhythm seciton (pianist Strazzeri, either Tom Warrington or Ken Filiano on bass and drummer Bill Berg) benefits from the inclusion of vibraphonist Bob Leatherbarrow on four of the selections. A wide variety of moods are covered on a rather modern set that serves as an excellent showcase for Bill Perkins. — *Scott Yanow*

Carl Perkins

b. Aug. 16, 1928, Indianapolis, IN, d. Mar. 17, 1958, Los Angeles, CA
Piano / Hard Bop
A fine bop-oriented pianist who overcame a slightly crippled left hand (due to polio), Carl Perkins was a victim of his drug problems, passing away when he was just 29. After stints with Tiny Bradshaw and Big Jay McNeely, he became a fixture on the West Coast. Perkins was with Oscar Moore's trio (1953–54) and briefly played with an early version of the Max Roach-Clifford Brown quintet (1954), but is best-known for his association with Curtis Counce (1956–58). Perkins, who composed one jazz standard ("Grooveyard"), recorded with Counce, Chet Baker, Jim Hall, Art Pepper and as a leader for Savoy (1949), Dootone (1956) and Pacific Jazz (1957), but did not live long enough to realize his potential. — *Scott Yanow*

Introducing Carl Perkins / Apr. 4, 1956 / Dootone ✦✦✦✦
Recorded two years before legendary West Coast pianist's death. With Leroy Vinnegar (b), Lawrence Marable (d). Six Perkins originals make this an important document. He was an important sideman. Here as a leader he shows his true worth. A must find/buy. — *Michael G. Nastos*

Tom Peron

Trumpet / Hard Bop
A fixture in Northern California, trumpeter Tom Peron in 1982 became a member of pianist Jessica Williams' quartet. A bop-oriented player with a wide range, Peron recorded two albums for his own Tomcat label, teamed up with drummer Bud Spangler for a Monarch release and has appeared on records by Joe Gilman and Kitty Margolis. — *Scott Yanow*

● **Interplay** / 1994 / Monarch ✦✦✦✦
Trumpeter Tom Peron, who co-leads this quartet set with drummer Bud Spangler, is a fine bop-based improviser whose first important early musical association was with the great pianist Jessica Williams. Williams is also on this date (along with bassist John Wiitala) and occasionally steals solo honors. However, the main significance to the CD is the excellent playing of Peron, who contributes two originals and really digs into the five standards. Whether taking solo flights open or muted á la Miles Davis, Tom Peron displays a lot of potential for the future. Highlights include the tricky "Trumpeter's Revenge," "Oleo," an uptempo "We See" and a lengthy investigation of "Summertime." — *Scott Yanow*

Rich Perry

b. Cleveland, OH
Guitar / Post Bop
A fine young veteran tenor player, Rich Perry went on the road in 1975 with the Glenn Miller ghost band. In 1976 he moved to New York and joined the Thad Jones/Mel Lewis Orchestra. Since then he has played with a wide variety of top players including Chet Baker, Machito, Bob Moses, Jack McDuff, Billy Hart, Eddie Gomez, Tom Harrell, the Mel Lewis big band and Harold Danko. Rich Perry recorded in 1993 as a leader for SteepleChase. — *Scott Yanow*

● **To Start Again** / Apr 1993 / Steeplechase ✦✦✦✦✦
On his debut as a leader, Rich Perry (a longtime member of the Mel Lewis Orchestra) often recalls Warne Marsh, playing harmonically advanced lines that are full of unusual twists. Occasionally he also sounds a little like Eddie Harris and Stan Getz but, in general, his dry yet fairly colorful improvisations are quite original. With strong assistance from pianist Harold Danko, bassist Scott Colley and drummer Jeff Hirshfield, Perry is in top form on a set dominated by obscure material including two Thad

Jones songs, Antonio Carlos Jobim's attractive "Retrato Em Braco E Preto" and originals by Maria Schneider, Danko and himself. This modern mainstream jazz contains plenty of fire along with a variety of moods. — *Scott Yanow*

Beautiful Love / 1994 / SteepleChase ✦✦✦✦

Charli Persip

b. Jul. 26, 1929, Morristown, NJ
Drums / Hard Bop
An excellent drummer both in big bands and combos, Charli Persip changed his name from Charlie in the early '80s. He had early experience playing locally in New Jersey and with Tadd Dameron (1953) but gained his initial recognition for his work with Dizzy Gillespie's big band and quintet (1953–58). In 1959 he formed his own group, the Jazz Statesmen, which featured a young Freddie Hubbard. Persip appeared on many record sessions in the 1950s and '60s with such players as Lee Morgan, Dinah Washington, Red Garland, Gil Evans, Don Ellis, Eric Dolphy, Roland Kirk, Gene Ammons and Archie Shepp among others. He was with Billy Eckstine during 1966–73, was the main drum instructor for the Jazzmobile in the mid-'70s and has led his Superband (a part-time big band) since the early '80s, recording several dates. — *Scott Yanow*

Superband / 1980 / Stash ✦✦✦✦✦

In Case You Missed It / Sep. 12, 1984–Sep. 13, 1984 / Soul Note ✦✦✦

No Dummies Allowed / Nov. 19, 1987+Nov. 25, 1987 / Soul Note ✦✦✦✦

Houston Person

b. Nov. 10, 1934, Florence, SC
Tenor Saxophone / Soul Jazz, Hard Bop
In the 1990s Houston Person has kept the soulful, thick-toned tenor tradition of Gene Ammons alive, particularly in his work with organists. After learning piano as a youth, Person switched to tenor. While stationed in Germany with the Army, he played in groups that also included Eddie Harris, Lanny Morgan, Leo Wright and Cedar Walton. Person picked up valuable experience as a member of Johnny Hammond's group (1963–66) and has been a bandleader ever since, often working with his wife, singer Etta Jones. A duo recording with Ran Blake was a nice change of pace, but most of Houston Person's playing has been done in blues-oriented organ groups. He has recorded a consistently excellent series of albums for Muse. — *Scott Yanow*

Goodness! / Aug. 25, 1969 / Original Jazz Classics ✦✦✦✦
Tenor saxophonist Houston Person was still a relatively new name at the time he recorded this set, his sixth session for Prestige. The funky music (which includes the hit title song) emphasizes boogaloos, danceable rhythms and repetitious vamps set down by the rhythm section (organist Sonny Phillips, guitarist Billy Butler, electric bassist Bob Bushnell, drummer Frankie Jones and Buddy Caldwell on congas), but it is primarily Person's passionate tenor solos that will come the closest to holding on to the attention of jazz listeners. The music is generally quite commercial and is certainly not recommended to bebop purists, although it has some strong moments. But overall these performances succeed more as background music than as creative jazz. — *Scott Yanow*

The Truth! / Feb. 23, 1970 / Prestige ✦✦✦

Stolen Sweets / Apr. 29, 1976 / Muse ✦✦✦✦✦
First-rate soul jazz, funk, blues, and ballads by tenor saxophonist Houston Person. Vocalist Etta Jones wasn't on this session, so things were mostly uptempo and cooking, with plenty of robust tenor from Person, tasty guitar by Jimmy Ponder, swirling organ riffs and support from Sonny Phillips, and percussion and rhythmic assistance from Frankie Jones and Buddy Caldwell. — *Ron Wynn*

The Big Horn / May 20, 1976 / Muse ✦✦✦✦
Reliable soul jazz, nicely played ballads, and good standards are tenor saxophonist Houston Person's forte. He demonstrates that repeatedly on this '76 quintet set. Pianist Cedar Walton is the type of no-nonsense, consistent player whose skills are often taken for granted, while bassist Buster Williams and drummer Grady Tate are equally unassuming veterans. — *Ron Wynn*

Wildflower / Sep. 12, 1977 / Muse ✦✦✦✦
Not everything tenor saxophonist Houston Person does depends

on funky, raw, upbeat arrangements and grooves. This session from '77 did have some of that, but it also had some straight-ahead hard bop and mainstream cuts. Trumpeter Bill Hardman, who wasn't making many albums by this point, was a most welcome addition, while Sonny Phillips on organ and guitarist Jimmy Ponder were familiar Person session men at this time. —*Ron Wynn*

The Nearness of Houston Person / Nov. 1977 / Muse ✦✦✦
Intimate, nicely played late '70s session by tenor saxophonist Houston Person that balances robust soul jazz and blues with stately ballads and standards featuring vocalist Etta Jones. When things heat up, organist Charles Earland helps punctuate Pearson's solos. Then, when Jones steps out front, it's Person who puts the accents behind her singing. —*Ron Wynn*

Suspicions / Apr. 24, 1980 / Muse ✦✦✦
Some robust funk and fine soul licks, plus solid mainstream fare. —*Ron Wynn*

Very Personal / Aug. 29, 1980 / Muse ✦✦✦✦✦
A departure for tenor saxophonist Houston Person, normally a soul jazz, blues, funk, and ballads player. This is more mainstream jazz and hard bop, with Person working alongside pianist Cedar Walton, trombonist Curtis Fuller, bassist Buster Williams, and drumer Vernell Fournier. All those who felt that Person couldn't play bop changes were left looking silly when this came out in 1980. —*Ron Wynn*

Heavy Juice / 1982 / Muse ✦✦✦

Always on My Mind / 1985 / Muse ✦✦✦

The Talk of the Town / Jan. 23, 1987 / Muse ✦✦✦
Marvelous standards and ballads, with excellent trumpet solos by Cecil Bridgewater. —*Ron Wynn*

● **Basics** / Oct. 12, 1987 / Muse ✦✦✦✦✦
A good session, with blues and bop leanings. —*Ron Wynn*

Something in Common / Feb. 23, 1989 / Muse ✦✦✦
Person shows his more-adventurous side in duels with bass great Ron Carter. —*Ron Wynn*

The Party / Nov. 14, 1989 / Muse ✦✦✦✦✦
Good soul jazz and blues session, with young lion organist Joey DeFrancesco providing the funky undercurrent to tenor saxophonist Houston Person's thick, authoritative solos and Randy Johnston and Bertell Knox filling the spaces on bass and drums, plus Sammy Figueroa adding some Afro-Latin fiber for additional support. —*Ron Wynn*

Now's the Time / Jan. 1990 / Muse ✦✦✦✦

● **Why Not!** / Oct. 5, 1990 / Muse ✦✦✦✦✦
Organ-tenor-trumpet session. Person's album includes hot contributions by young lions Harper Brothers plus Joey DeFrancesco on the Hammond Organ. —*Ron Wynn*

Lion and His Pride / Sep. 13, 1991 / Muse ✦✦✦✦

Hannibal Marvin Peterson

b. Nov. 11, 1948, Smithville, TX
Trumpet / Avant-Garde
One of the more intriguing avant-garde trumpeters, Marvin Peterson is also able to play very credible hard bop. After playing trumpet in the North Texas State University band, he moved to New York in 1970. Among his most important associations were with Rahsaan Roland Kirk, Gil Evans (1973–1980), Pharoah Sanders, Elvin Jones and his own bands. Although he has never received the recognition he deserves, the performances of Marvin "Hannibal" Peterson are always stimulating and unpredictable. —*Scott Yanow*

In Antibes / Jul. 20, 1977 / Inner City ✦✦✦
This live blowout features trumpeter Marvin "Hannibal" Peterson, George Adams on tenor and flute, cellist Diedre Murray, bassist Steve Neil and drummer Makaya Ntshoko stretching out on two 19- to 21-minute jams. "Ro" has some of Adams' intense tenor although he switches to his less impressive flute on "Swing Low Sweet Chariot." There are some strong moments on this set but also lots of rambling. This music was probably better experienced live than on this LP. —*Scott Yanow*

● **The Angels of Atlanta** / Feb. 15, 1981+Feb. 19, 1981 / Enja ✦✦✦✦✦
Although the Harlem Boys Choir is occasionally utilized and Pat Peterson takes a soulful vocal on "The Inner Voice," this CD is

very much trumpeter Marvin "Hannibal" Peterson's date. The explorative trumpeter is heard at his absolute peak, taking lengthy and fiery improvisations that show off not only his virtuosity but his emotional range. The superlative band (tenor- saxophonist George Adams, pianst Kenny Barron, cellist Diedre Murray, bassist Cecil McBee and drummer Dannie Richmond) really inspires Peterson who stretches the boundaries of his music toward gospel and soul without watering down the jazz content. This well-balanced set is one of Hannibal's finest recordings. —*Scott Yanow*

Visions of a New World / 1989 / Atlantic ✦✦✦
High-note hijinks, verbal forays, superb percussion, and alternately gripping and confusing lyrics combine to keep things unpredictable, intense, and sometimes infuriating. — *Ron Wynn*

Oscar Peterson

b. Aug. 15, 1925, Montreal, Quebec
Piano, Leader / Bop, Swing
Thanks to Norman Granz, Oscar Peterson ranks among the most extensively recorded jazz pianists in history. He's also been more harshly criticized than many who aren't nearly as gifted a stylist. Peterson's technique comes close, though isn't as awesome as Art Tatum's; his phrasing, facility, speed, harmonic knowledge, ideas and style are dazzling. But he's been accused of lacking soul, being unable to play the blues (questionable) and making too many records that sound the same (fair criticism). His early work reflected the influence of Teddy Wilson, Earl Hines and Nat "King" Cole, but he's long since developed his own recognizable, compelling approach. The elegant lines, flashy, yet intricate phrases and teeming solos represent the work of a genuine piano master, though he does recycle overly familiar standards and ballads. He works best in a trio setting, where he gets the space to create freely.

Peterson studied classical piano at the age of six, and won a local talent contest in Montreal at 14. He was a regular on a weekly radio program during his late teens, and played with The Johnny Holmes Orchestra throughout the mid-'40s. Granz invited him to appear at a 1949 Carnegie Hall Jazz at the Philharmonic concert, and shortly after became his manager. When Granz founded Verve in the '50s, Peterson became their house pianist. The same was true for subsidiaries Norgran, Clef and Mercury, and again in the '70s, when Granz formed Pablo. The bulk of Peterson's nearly 100 albums as a leader have been made on Granz labels. While on Verve, Peterson recorded with Billie Holiday, Lester Young, Louis Armstrong, Ella Fitzgerald, Coleman Hawkins, Fred Astaire, Benny Carter, Roy Eldridge, Buddy DeFranco, Nelson Riddle and Milt Jackson. He traveled with the JATP revue through the early '50s, and formed a trio patterned after The Cole ensemble; guitar, piano and bass. From 1953 until 1958, the Oscar Peterson Trio with guitarist Herb Ellis and bassist Ray Brown was a popular attraction. When Ellis left, drummer Ed Thigpen replaced him, and this trio stayed intact from 1959 until 1965.

Peterson, Brown, Thigpen and Phil Nimmons established the Advanced School of Contemporary Music in Toronto in 1960. Peterson kept things going for three years. He recorded for the MPS/BASF label in the late '60s and early '70s. He rejoined Granz on Pablo in the '70s, and decided to concentrate on solo recordings, issuing a number of often astonishing, if thematically similar, releases. Peterson began branching out by mid-decade, working with orchestras and playing with veterans like Gillespie, Terry, Joe Pass, Eddie "Lockjaw" Davis, Count Basie and Niels-Henning Orsted Pedersen. Peterson has continued his steady touring and recording in the '80s and '90s, making mainly trio but some dates for independent labels like Telarc. Prestige has reissued many of the Pablo's and several Verve dates are also available. Gene Lees biography *Oscar Peterson: The Will To Swing* was published in 1988 and is must reading for Peterson fans. —*Ron Wynn and Michael Erlewine*

● **The Complete Young Oscar Peterson** / Apr. 30, 1945–Nov. 14, 1949 / RCA ✦✦✦✦✦
This double CD reissues the complete contents of two valuable LPs, the first 32 studio recordings of the great pianist Oscar Peterson. Recorded in Montreal, Canada, with local musicians during 1945–49 before his fame spread worldwide, these trio performances let one hear how Peterson sounded before he fully discovered bop and formed his own distinctive sound; the pianist

already had his remarkable virtuosity along with a taste for boo-gie-woogie that he later lost. Sticking mostly to swing standards and rollicking blues, Peterson sounds more touched by the style of Teddy Wilson than he would later on. Fascinating and easily enjoyable music, highly recommended for all serious jazz collections. —*Scott Yanow*

1951 / 1951 / Just A Memory ✦✦✦✦

The Trio Set / Sep. 13, 1952+Sep. 19, 1953 / Verve ✦✦✦✦
This LP features two versions of the Oscar Peterson Trio, heard during a pair of Jazz at the Philharmonic Carnegie Hall concerts. The 1952 performance has five jazz standards including a famous version of "Tenderly"; guitarist Barney Kessel and bassist Ray Brown somehow manage to keep up with Peterson on heated renditions of "C Jam Blues" and "Seven Come Eleven." The second trio, with Herb Ellis in Kessel's place, features complex arrangements and spontaneous improvising on such songs as "Swingin' on a Star" and "Swingin' Till the Girls Come Home"; the concert was the latter unit's earliest recording. This LP gives one a definitive look at these two classic groups. —*Scott Yanow*

★ **At Zardis'** / Nov. 8, 1955 / Pablo ✦✦✦✦✦
The group that Oscar Peterson led between 1953-58 with guitarist Herb Ellis and bassist Ray Brown was one of the great piano trios of all time. It was never so much a matter of Peterson having two other musicians accompany him as it was that they could meet the pianist as near-equals and consistently inspire him. And unlike most trios, O.P.'s had many arranged sections that constantly needed rehearsals and were often quite dazzling. This live double CD from 1955 has previously unreleased (and unknown) performances of 31 songs (28 standards plus three of Peterson's originals) that were released for the first time in 1994. The pianist is often in typically miraculous form, Ellis (whether playing harmonies, offering short solos or getting his guitar to sound like a conga by tapping it percussively) proves to be a perfect partner, and Brown's subtle but sometimes telepathic contributions should not be overlooked either. —*Scott Yanow*

● **Oscar Peterson Plays Count Basie** / Dec. 27, 1955 / Clef ✦✦✦✦✦
On the face of it, pianist Oscar Peterson (whose virtuosity always allowed him to play an infinite amount of notes) and Count Basie (who made inventive use of silence and space by emphasizing single rhythmic sounds) would seem to have had little in common. However, they both swung and there was a definite overlapping in their repertoire. Peterson's Basie tribute is a near masterpiece. With guitarist Herb Ellis, bassist Ray Brown and guest drummer Buddy Rich all playing quite sympathetically, O.P.'s arrangements make the nine Basie-associated songs (along with Peterson's original "Blues for Basie") all sound quite fresh and lightly swinging. Quite a few of these renditions (particularly "Easy Does It," "9:20 Special," "Broadway" and "One O'Clock Jump") are instantly memorable. This CD reissue is highly recommended. —*Scott Yanow*

★ **At the Stratford Shakesperean Festival** / Aug. 8, 1956 / Verve ✦✦✦✦✦
This CD contains what is considered by most listeners to be the finest recording of the Oscar Peterson-Herb Ellis-Ray Brown trio, a group that lasted from 1953-58. Although the soloing was always quite passionate and spontaneous, it was the very complex arrangements that really made this unit sound unique. The live CD adds two selections ("Nuages" and the 13-minute "Daisy's Dream") to the original program and contains particularly memorable renditions of "Falling in Love with Love," "How About You," "Swinging on a Star," "How High the Moon" and "52nd Street Theme." Essential music from a classic band. —*Scott Yanow*

★ **At The Concertgebouw** / Sep. 29, 1957+Oct. 9, 1957 / Verve ✦✦✦✦✦
Although the music on this CD was originally said to be recorded in Europe, it actually comes from a Chicago concert, and the five additional selections (last issued on an LP shared with The Modern Jazz Quartet, supposedly performed in Chicago, are from an appearance in Los Angeles. But, despite the geographical mix-ups, the music is consistently brilliant and often wondrous. The Oscar Peterson-Herb Ellis-Ray Brown Trio had been together for over four years and would be among their last (and finest) recordings. The very tricky arrangements sandwiched remarkable solos with pianist Peterson sounding especially inspired. Together with their *Stratford Shakespearean* CD of the previous year, this set features the Trio at the peak of their powers. Highlights

include "The Lady Is a Tramp," "Budo," "Daahoud," "Indiana" and "Joy Spring." —*Scott Yanow*

Oscar Peterson Plays the Jerome Kern Songbook / Jul. 21, 1959–Aug. 1, 1959 / Verve ✦✦✦
Within a one-month period, the Oscar Peterson Trio (with bassist Ray Brown and their new drummer Ed Thigpen) recorded nine different *Songbooks*, 108 selections in all. Not too surprisingly, this music had a minimum of prior planning and few arranged passages, making it on a lower level than the typical music played by Peterson's prior trio with guitarist Herb Ellis. The 12 numbers performed for the *Jerome Kern* LP (which has not yet been reissued on CD) are given melodic and consistently swinging treatments with such songs as "I Won't Dance," "The Song Is You" and "Pick Yourself Up" among the better selections heard on this pleasing program. —*Scott Yanow*

Oscar Peterson Plays the Harry Warren Songbook / Jul. 1959–Aug. 1959 / Verve ✦✦✦
This LP is one of nine different *Songbook* LPs recorded by the Oscar Peterson Trio (with bassist Ray Brown and drummer Ed Thigpen) within one month. Peterson performs six songs apiece by Harry Warren (including "Lullaby of Broadway," and "I Only Have Eyes for You") and Vincent Youmans (highlighted by "More than You Know" and "Without a Song") with his usual swinging approach. Very much an ad-lib, one-take set, the music is given respectful melodic treatment while being updated to the late '50s. The results are not essential, but the pianist's many fans will enjoy his songbooks. —*Scott Yanow*

Oscar Peterson Plays Porgy and Bess / Oct. 12, 1959 / Verve ✦✦✦✦
Oscar Peterson and his trio (with bassist Ray Brown and drummer Ed Thigpen) explore ten of the stronger themes from George Gershwin's *Porgy and Bess* on this CD reissue. It is true that Peterson's version of "Summertime" will not make one forget the classic rendition by Miles Davis with Gil Evans but, as is true with all of these performances, Peterson makes the melodies sound like his own. "It Ain't Necessarily So" and "I Got Plenty O' Nuttin'" are among the more memorable selections. —*Scott Yanow*

The Trio / Sep. 1961–Oct. 1961 / Verve ✦✦✦✦
Oscar Peterson's Trio with bassist Ray Brown and drummer Ed Thigpen lacked the competitiveness of his earlier group with Brown and guitarist Herb Ellis and the later daring of his solo performances, but the pianist is in generally peak form during this era. He sticks to standards on this live CD (a good example of the Trio's playing), stretching out "Sometimes I'm Happy" creatively for over 11 minutes and uplifting such songs as "In the Wee Small Hours of the Morning," "Chicago" and "The Night We Called It a Day." Few surprises occur, but Peterson plays at such a consistently high level that one doesn't mind. —*Scott Yanow*

Very Tall / Dec. 1961 / Verve ✦✦✦✦✦
Pianist Oscar Peterson and vibraphonist Milt Jackson met up for the first time on record during this studio session, which has been reissued on CD. Peterson here is often content to let Jackson be the main voice during many of the ensembles, although he also works at pushing the vibist to play at his most swinging. With the assistance of bassist Ray Brown and drummer Ed Thigpen, Peterson and Jackson are sensitive on the two ballads and really romp throughout "Green Dolphin Street," "Work Song," "John Brown's Body" and "Reunion Blues." —*Scott Yanow*

West Side Story / Jan. 24, 1962–Jan. 25, 1962 / Verve ✦✦✦
The Oscar Peterson Trio (comprised of pianist Peterson, bassist Ray Brown and drummer Ed Thigpen) do a fine job of interpreting six melodies from *West Side Story* in addition to a closing reprise of the themes. Originally recorded for Verve, this well-recorded reissue is brief on time (31 minutes) and not all that essential, but it swings nicely and is quite enjoyable. —*Scott Yanow*

Bursting out with the All Star Big Band / Jun. 13, 1962-Jun. 14, 1962 / Verve ✦✦✦✦
Pianist Oscar Peterson has a rare outing with a big band on this excellent CD reissue. In addition to his usual bassist Ray Brown and drummer Ed Thigpen, Peterson is joined by a particularly strong big band arranged by Ernie Wilkins; there are short solos for several of the sidemen including altoist Norris Turney, James Moody on tenor and altoist Cannonball Adderley. However, the main focus is on Peterson and he is in excellent form on such songs as "West Coast Blues," "Here's That Rainy Day," "Tricotism"

and "Manteca," blending in very well with the orchestra. —*Scott Yanow*

Affinity / Sep. 25, 1962–Sep. 27, 1962 / Verve ✦✦✦
This is a fairly typical date from the Oscar Peterson Trio (which features the pianist-leader, bassist Ray Brown and drummer Ed Thigpen). Many of the songs on this LP are associated with other musicians (such as "Waltz for Debbie," "This Could Be the Start of Something Big" and "Six and Four"), but Peterson has little difficulty swinging them in his usual fashion; a highlight is the original version of Ray Brown's "Gravy Waltz." —*Scott Yanow*

Live At The London House / Sep. 27, 1962 / Verve ✦✦✦
Two former LPs are combined on this CD reissue: *Something Warm* and *Put on a Happy Face*. All of the music was recorded at the London House in Chicago in 1962 by the Oscar Peterson Trio (with the pianist/leader, bassist Ray Brown and drummer Ed Thigpen) and the emphasis is on swinging versions of standards, although Oscar also contributes three originals among the 13 selections. Few surprises occur, but no disappointments either. Peterson has long been among the most consistent of pianists and whether it be "There Is No Greater Love," "Autumn Leaves," "Old Folks" or even "Put on a Happy Face," he usually finds something fresh and swinging to play. —*Scott Yanow*

Night Train, Vol. 1 / Dec. 15, 1962–Dec. 16, 1962 / Verve ✦✦✦✦
Although the repertoire on this CD reissue by the Oscar Peterson Trio (with bassist Ray Brown and drummer Ed Thigpen) is fairly typical (with such veteran standards as "C Jam Blues," "Bags' Groove," "Easy Does It" and "I Got It Bad"), Peterson and his sidemen sound fairly inspired. Actually, the highpoints are the final two selections: Duke Ellington's "Band Call" and the original version of O.P.'s "Hymn to Freedom." This CD gives one a definitive look at the 1960s Oscar Peterson Trio. —*Scott Yanow*

★ **Exclusively for My Friends [Box Set]** / 1963–Apr. 1968 / Verve ✦✦✦✦✦
Oscar Peterson has stated that he feels his MPS recordings are his finest. That is quite a statement considering the huge amount of records that the pianist has produced through the past 50 years. This four-CD set reissues the music from six of his MPS LPs: *Action, Girl Talk, The Way I Really Play, My Favorite Instrument, Mellow Mood* and *Travelin' On*. While some of the performances feature the 1963 trio he had with bassist Ray Brown and drummer Ed Thigpen, most of the music dates from 1967-68 and matches O.P. with bassist Sam Jones and either Louis Hayes or Bobby Durham on drums. A special treat is Oscar Peterson's first unaccompanied solo album, which fills up the final CD. Peterson's many fans know what to expect in this set, while other listeners need to discover him to realize what all of the fuss was about. Quite simply, Oscar Peterson has long been one of the greatest pianists the world has ever known; this reissue offers plenty of proof. —*Scott Yanow*

★ **Oscar Peterson Trio + One** / Aug. 17, 1964 / Verve ✦✦✦✦✦
This is a true classic. Flugelhornist Clark Terry, who long has had the happiest sound in jazz, performs ten enthusiastic and generally hard-swinging songs with the Oscar Peterson Trio (which at the time included bassist Ray Brown and drummer Ed Thigpen). Terry is quite exuberant on such pieces as "Brotherhood of Man" and "Mack the Knife" and even the ballads ("They Didn't Believe Me" and "I Want a Little Girl" among them) are full of excitement. This session, though, is best known for having introduced Clark Terry's humorous "Mumbles" vocals, which can be heard on that piece and "Incoherent Blues." This delightful and essential release has fortunately been reissued on CD. —*Scott Yanow*

Canadian Suite / Sep. 9, 1964 / Limelight ✦✦✦✦
The remarkable pianist Oscar Peterson had never been thought of that much as a composer, making this set of eight of his compositions a bit of a surprise when it was originally released. Now available on CD, Peterson's tribute to his native Canada includes several noteworthy pieces of which "Hogtown Blues" and "Wheatland" are best known. With his 1964 trio (featuring bassist Ray Brown and drummer Ed Thigpen), Peterson swings hard but often with sensitivity throughout the enjoyable set. —*Scott Yanow*

We Get Requests / Oct. 19, 1964–Oct. 20, 1964 / Verve ✦✦
Pianist Oscar Peterson has long been such a consistent performer that none of his records are throwaways, but this particular CD reissue is weaker than most. Since several of the songs are the type that in the mid-'60s would get requested (such as "People," "The Girl from Ipanema" and "The Days of Wine and Roses"), the

program would not seem to have much potential, but Peterson mostly uplifts the material (although not much could be done with "People") and adds a few songs (such as his own "Goodbye J.D." and John Lewis' "D. & E.") that probably no one asked for. Overall, this is an average although reasonably enjoyable Oscar Peterson session, featuring bassist Ray Brown and drummer Ed Thigpen. —*Scott Yanow*

Eloquence / May 29, 1965 / Limelight ✦✦✦
This was the last album that pianist Oscar Peterson and bassist Ray Brown recorded with Ed Thigpen before the drummer departed from O.P.'s trio after six years of steady work. The music heard during this "live from Copenhagen" concert is excellent although, discounting brief selections at the beginning and end of the program, the six songs only total around 37 minutes for the CD reissue. Peterson is in particularly strong form on "Misty," "Django," a cooking "Autumn Leaves" and "Moanin'." —*Scott Yanow*

The Canadian Concert Of Oscar Peterson / Aug. 25, 1965 / Can-Am ✦✦✦✦
Drummer Louis Hayes (who replaced Ed Thigpen) made his recording debut with the Oscar Peterson Trio on the radio broadcast, which has been released on this LP. The program (highlighted by "My One and Only Love," "Hallelujah Time," "Corcovado" and "Younger than Springtime") is typical for Peterson during the era, and the music is very well-played and consistently swinging. —*Scott Yanow*

With Respect to Nat / Oct. 28, 1965 / Limelight ✦✦✦✦✦
This LP (which is long overdue to be reissued on CD) is quite unusual. Recorded shortly after Nat King Cole's death, pianist Oscar Peterson takes vocals on all but one of the dozen selections, sounding almost exactly like Cole. Peterson, who rarely ever sang, is very effective on the well-rounded program whether backed by a big band (arranged by Manny Albam) on half of the selections, or recreating both the spirit of the Nat King Cole Trio and his own group of the late '50s during a reunion with guitarist Herb Ellis and bassist Ray Brown. —*Scott Yanow*

Blues Etude / Dec. 3, 1965+May 4, 1966 / Verve ✦✦✦✦
This CD reissue finds pianist Oscar Peterson at a transitional point in his career. Louis Hayes was the new drummer in his trio and, although veteran Ray Brown is on bass during the earlier of the two sessions, by 1966 he would depart after 15 years and be replaced by Sam Jones. However, the basic sound of the Oscar Peterson Trio remained unchanged (O.P. was the dominant voice anyway) and the personality of the group remained intact. Peterson contributed three originals (including the hard-swinging title cut) to this program and also sounds typically fine on "Let's Fall in Love," "The Shadow of Your Smile," "If I Were a Bell" and a definitive version of "Stella by Starlight." —*Scott Yanow*

★ **My Favorite Instrument** / Apr. 1968 / Verve ✦✦✦✦✦
Oscar Peterson recorded a remarkable amount of albums during his career but, surprisingly, this was his first full record of unaccompanied piano solos. Some observers consider his MPS recordings to be his best (quite a few are collected in the four-CD reissue *Exclusively for My Friends* including this one). The solo LP features Peterson (freed from the constraints of his trio) stretching out on nine standards, really tearing into a few of them including "Perdido," "Bye Bye Blackbird," "Lulu's Back in Town" while giving "Little Girl Blue" a beautiful lyrical treatment. A prelude to his outstanding Pablo recordings, *My Favourite Instrument* is one of Peterson's top albums of the 1960s. —*Scott Yanow*

Hello, Herbie / Nov. 5, 1969–Nov. 6, 1969 / MPS ✦✦✦✦✦
Guitarist Herb Ellis still considers this to be one of his personal favorite recordings. Ellis was reunited with his old boss Oscar Peterson and, with the assistance of O.P.'s trio of the period (with bassist Sam Jones and drummer Bobby Durham), the two lead voices often romp on the jam session-flavored set. Most of the chord changes are fairly basic (including three blues and "Seven Come Eleven") and Peterson is clearly inspired by Ellis' presence (and vice versa). This frequently exciting LP has been reissued several times, but not yet on CD. —*Scott Yanow*

Tristeza on Piano / 1970 / Verve ✦✦✦
At the beginning of this set, Oscar Peterson so overwhelms the normally gentle "Tristeza" that it almost becomes a parody. Fortunately, the remainder of the bossa nova-flavored CD reissue is more tasteful and, even if Peterson is overly hyper in spots, he is able to bring out the beauty of such songs as George

Gershwin's "Porgy," Antonio Carlos Jobim's "Trieste" and "Watch What Happens" in addition to stomping through the straight-ahead "You Stepped out of a Dream." *—Scott Yanow*

★ **Tracks** / Nov. 1970 / Verve ✦✦✦✦
Pianist Oscar Peterson is frequently astounding on this solo set. After nearly 20 years of mostly performing with trios, O.P. sounds quite liberated in this setting, throwing in some hot stride, unexpected changes in tempos and keys, and surprises whenever he thinks of it. "Give Me the Simple Life," "Honeysuckle Rose" and the ironically titled "A Little Jazz Exercise" are quite remarkable, yet Peterson also leaves space for some sensitive ballads. This LP, one of Oscar Peterson's finest recordings, is long overdue to show up on CD. *—Scott Yanow*

Oscar's Choice / Nov. 1970 / MPS ✦✦✦✦
Pianist Oscar Peterson is in his usual hard-swinging form on this LP, which features one of his more obscure trios (with bassist George Mraz and drummer Ray Price). In addition to such standards as "I'm Old Fashioned," "All the Things You Are" and "Too Close for Comfort," Peterson explores "Greensleeves," Johnny Griffin's "The Jams Are Coming" and (the biggest surprise) James P. Johnson's "Carolina Shout," which actually sounds much closer to "Little Rock Getaway." *—Scott Yanow*

Reunion Blues / Jul. 1971 / MPS ✦✦✦
Pianist Oscar Peterson joins up with his old friends vibraphonist Milt Jackson and bassist Ray Brown, in addition to his drummer of the period Louis Hayes, for a particularly enjoyable outing. After a throwaway version of The Rolling Stones' "I Can't Get No Satisfaction," the all-star quartet performs Jackson's title cut, Benny Carter's ballad "Dream of You" and four standards. Although not up to the excitement of Peterson's best Pablo recordings of the 1970s, this is an easily enjoyable LP. *—Scott Yanow*

Great Connection / Oct. 1971 / Verve ✦✦✦✦
This matchup between pianist Oscar Peterson, bassist Niels Pedersen and drummer Louis Hayes directly precedes Peterson's recordings for Pablo. The pianist is in typically brilliant form on the LP, performing six standards (including "Soft Winds" and "On the Trail") along with his own "Wheatland." It is not too surprising that Peterson would want to record frequently with Pedersen in future years. *—Scott Yanow*

History of an Artist, Vol. 1 / Dec. 27, 1972 / Pablo ✦✦✦✦✦
It was only fitting that Oscar Peterson's first of his many recordings for Norman Granz's Pablo label would revisit the instrumental combinations he had utilized in the past. This two-CD set has all of the music originally included on three LPs (a two-album set plus a single record) and showcases the great pianist in duets with bassist Ray Brown, in trios that also include guitarists Irving Ashby, Barney Kessel and Herb Ellis and with other trios that feature such alumni as bassists Sam Jones, George Mraz and Niels-Henning Orsted Pedersen, guitarist Joe Pass and drummers Bobby Durham and Louis Hayes. The only fault with this consistently inventive and hard-swinging program is that the formats (particularly those on the second disc) are not in strictly chronological order. But the music (which also features Peterson taking "Lady of the Lavender Mist" as an unaccompanied solo) is superb. *—Scott Yanow*

Oscar Peterson Featuring Stephane Grappelli / Feb. 22, 1973+Feb. 23, 1973 / Prestige ✦✦✦✦✦
This two-LP set, whose music has not yet resurfaced on CD, teams together pianist Oscar Peterson with violinist Stephane Grappelli, bassist Niels Pedersen and drummer Kenny Clarke. It is an understatement to say that there are no weak spots in that quartet. The brilliant musicians perform a dozen swing standards plus their original "Blues for Musidisc" and the music is often quite exciting; Peterson sounds thrilled to be playing with Grappelli and vice versa. *—Scott Yanow*

The Good Life / May 16, 1973–May 19, 1973 / Original Jazz Classics ✦✦✦✦
Taken from the same live sessions that resulted in *The Trio*, this CD reissue of a Pablo album features three remarkable virtuosos: pianist Oscar Peterson, guitarist Joe Pass and bassist Niels-Henning Orsted Pedersen. Although not quite reaching the heights of the other set, this CD features some typically extraordinary solos and interplay from these musicians. Highlights include Peterson's "Wheatland," the blues "For Count" (which is referred to in the liner notes as "Miles") and "The Good Life." *—Scott Yanow*

★ **The Trio** / May 16, 1973–May 19, 1973 / Pablo ✦✦✦✦✦
Guitarist Joe Pass and bassist Niels Pedersen both play well on these live performances, but the reason to acquire this set is for the remarkable Oscar Peterson. The pianist investigates several jazz styles brilliantly on "Blues Etude" (including stride and boogie-woogie), plays exciting versions of his "Chicago Blues" and "Easy Listening Blues," tears into "Secret Love" and shows honest emotion on "Come Sunday." Peterson really flourished during his years with Norman Granz's Pablo label, and this was one of his finest recordings of the period. *—Scott Yanow*

In Russia / Nov. 17, 1974 / Pablo ✦✦✦✦
Although the music of this two-LP set took place at a concert in the Soviet Union, it is a fairly typical recital by pianist Oscar Peterson with no obvious reference to the exotic location. Peterson takes five selections unaccompanied, performs four others as duets with bassist Niels Pedersen and adds drummer Jake Hanna to the nine remaining numbers. Other than three originals, all of the music is comprised of veteran standards and, although no real surprises occur, the results are what one would expect from the great Oscar Peterson, who alternates hard swingers with sensitive ballad renditions. *—Scott Yanow*

Oscar Peterson and Dizzy Gillespie / Nov. 28, 1974–Nov. 29, 1974 / Pablo ✦✦✦✦✦
This album was the first of five projects in which pianist Oscar Peterson dueted with a trumpeter. Now reissued on CD, the encounter finds Dizzy Gillespie (then 57) in good form for the period, interacting with Peterson on such pieces as "Caravan," "Autumn Leaves," "Blues for Bird" and two of Gillespie's originals that have become standards: "Dizzy Atmosphere" and "Con Alma." It's a worthy acquisition for fans of Peterson and Gillespie. *—Scott Yanow*

Jousts / Nov. 28, 1974–Jun. 5, 1975 / Original Jazz Classics ✦✦✦✦
This LP contains nine previously unissued performances from the sessions that resulted in Oscar Peterson's five duet albums with great trumpeters. Clark Terry, Roy Eldridge, Dizzy Gillespie and Harry "Sweets" Edison are heard on two songs apiece while Jon Faddis pops up on one duet. Eldridge's combative "Crazy Rhythm" and Faddis' "Oakland Blues" are highpoints, although fans of this interesting series will want all of this often-heated music. *—Scott Yanow*

Satch and Josh / Dec. 2, 1974 / Pablo ✦✦✦✦

The Giants / Dec. 7, 1974 / Original Jazz Classics ✦✦✦✦

Oscar Peterson and Roy Eldridge / Dec. 8, 1974 / Original Jazz Classics ✦✦✦✦✦

Oscar Peterson & Harry Edison / Dec. 21, 1974 / Original Jazz Classics ✦✦✦✦✦
The third of Oscar Peterson's five duet albums with great trumpeters (the other encounters feature Dizzy Gillespie, Roy Eldridge, Clark Terry and Jon Faddis) teams the masterful pianist with the great swing stylist Harry "Sweets" Edison. The trumpeter, who uses repetition to great degree and had pared his style down to a relatively few notes, matches well with the virtuosic Peterson on these seven standards and their two simple originals "Basie" and "Signify." Together, Edison and O.P. give the impression that their chancetaking improvisations are completely logical and a lot easier to play than they really are. *—Scott Yanow*

★ **Oscar Peterson Et Joe Pass A Salle Pleyel** / Mar. 17, 1975 / Pablo ✦✦✦✦✦
This double LP (whose contents have not yet been reissued on CD) has more than its share of remarkable music. Pianist Oscar Peterson takes seven performances (including a five-song Duke Ellington medley and racehorse renditions of "Indiana" and "Sweet Georgia Brown") unaccompanied, and guitarist Joe Pass follows with five solo selections of his own. But it is when Peterson and Pass team together for the final six numbers that the sparks really fly, particularly on "Honeysuckle Rose" and "Blues for Bise"; the results are often quite wondrous. This is essential music from two of the best. *—Scott Yanow*

Oscar Peterson and Clark Terry / May 18, 1975 / Original Jazz Classics ✦✦✦✦✦

● **Oscar Peterson & Jon Faddis** / Jun. 5, 1975 / Original Jazz Classics ✦✦✦✦✦

Porgy and Bess / Jan. 26, 1976 / Original Jazz Classics ✦✦
This is a strange duet album (a Pablo LP reissued on CD in the OJC series). For a set of ten melodies taken from George

Gershwin's famous *Porgy and Bess*, Joe Pass sticks to acoustic guitar while the great pianist Oscar Peterson for the first and only time in his career records exclusively on the clavichord, an instrument from the 1600s that preceded the piano! The clavichord comes across as a mix between a harpsichord and a primitive stringed instrument, and apparently, it cannot be played all that fast. The results are novel at first but rather limited on the whole, making one wonder whose bright idea this was! — *Scott Yanow*

Jam Montreux (1977) / Jul. 14, 1977 / Original Jazz Classics ✦✦✦✦
One of many Pablo albums taken from the 1977 Montreux Jazz Festival, this outing teams together pianist Oscar Peterson, bassist Niels Pedersen and drummer Bobby Durham with tenorman Eddie "Lockjaw" Davis and trumpeters Clark Terry and Dizzy Gillespie. The talented (and very competitive) players really dig into the opening uptempo blues ("Ali and Frazier") and they continue cooking on "If I Were a Bell," "Bye Bye Blues" (which has been added to the CD reissue), "Things Ain't What They Used to Be" and "Just in Time." As often happens in this type of situation, the musicians mutually inspire each other; this is one of Dizzy Gillespie's better sessions of the 1970s. There are no losers during these battles. — *Scott Yanow*

Live-Montreux '77 / Jul. 15, 1977 / Original Jazz Classics ✦✦✦✦
This is an interesting CD, one of many taken from the concerts sponsored by Pablo Records at the 1977 Montreux Jazz Festival. Pianist Oscar Peterson is teamed in an unusual trio with both Ray Brown and Niels Pedersen on basses. Sticking to standards and two blues on the boppish set, Peterson allows both of his sidemen plenty of solo space, permitting listeners to compare the large tone of Brown with the speedy fingers of Pedersen. — *Scott Yanow*

Satch & Josh Again / Sep. 20, 1977 / Pablo ✦✦✦✦

Time Keepers / 1978 / Pablo ✦✦✦✦
The pairing of pianists Count Basie and Oscar Peterson might seem unlikely, given their stylistic differences. Basie's notoriety resulted from his ability to say a lot with a little, while Peterson has been celebrated as a modern technical master, whose solos were full of riveting phrases, lines, and statements. Yet the duo made effective partners on this reissued 1978 session and often played against their reputations. Basie has several solos where he demonstrates impressive technique, while Peterson, often accused of overkill, shows he can utilize restraint and delicacy with as much flair as bombast and flash. — *Ron Wynn*

The Paris Concert / Oct. 5, 1978 / Pablo ✦✦✦✦
Pianist Oscar Peterson made so many recordings for Norman Granz's Pablo label (and was so consistent) that while all of his records are recommended, it is difficult to pick out any one as the definitive or essential release. This two-CD set (a straight reissue of the original two-LP release) features Peterson with an all-star trio, a unit comprised of guitarist Joe Pass and bassist Niels Pedersen. Just 16 days later Peterson would record *The London Concert* with a different trio. This time around he mostly sticks to standards but includes three songs associated with Benny Goodman (including the riff-filled "Benny's Bugle"), features Pass (who contributed his original "Gentle Tears") unaccompanied on "Lover Man" and really romps with his fellow virtuosoes on such numbers as "Ornithology," "Donna Lee" and "Sweet Georgia Brown." — *Scott Yanow*

The London Concert / Oct. 21, 1978 / Pablo ✦✦✦✦
This two-CD set, which reissues a Pablo two-LP release, features pianist Oscar Peterson in a strong and supportive trio with bassist John Heard and drummer Louis Bellson. Although his sidemen get some solo space, the focus is primarily on the remarkable pianist on a variety of standards, his own "Hogtown Blues" and a six-song Duke Ellington medley. Whether it be on rapid stomps or sensitive ballads, this trio (which was in reality an all-star pickup group) sounds as if they had worked together regularly for years. — *Scott Yanow*

The Silent Partner / Mar. 14, 1979 / Original Jazz Classics ✦✦✦
This fairly obscure Oscar Peterson LP is unusual for the all-star septet (which includes altoist Benny Carter, fluegelhornist Clark Terry, Zoot Sims on tenor, vibraphonist Milt Jackson, bassist John Heard and drummer Grady Tate) plays pianist Peterson's score from the film *The Silent Partner*. Although none of the eight themes caught on independently, the rather distinctive playing of the great stylists (along with the swinging rhythm section) makes the music stand alone from the movie. — *Scott Yanow*

Night Child / Apr. 11, 1979–Apr. 12, 1979 / Pablo ✦✦✦
This is a most unusual album for Oscar Peterson because the pianist not only performs six of his own compositions but he plays the great majority of time on electric piano. With the assistance of guitarist Joe Pass, bassist Niels Pederson and drummer Louie Bellson, he keeps his own musical personality despite the change in "axes" and, although the results are not essential, this setting does cast a fresh light on Peterson's creativity. — *Scott Yanow*

Skol / Jul. 6, 1979 / Pablo ✦✦✦✦
Pianist Oscar Peterson and violinist Stephane Grappelli meet up on this Scandinavian concert. The "backup" crew (guitarist Joe Pass, bassist Niels Pedersen and drummer Mickey Roker) is not too bad either. In addition to a closing blues (which is highlighted by tradeoffs from Peterson and Grappelli), the quintet performs five veteran standards with creativity and swing. This CD, a straight reissue of a Pablo LP, contains plenty of fine music. — *Scott Yanow*

Digital at Montreux / Jul. 16, 1979 / Pablo ✦✦✦
The title is pretty generic but this duet set from pianist Oscar Peterson and bassist Niels Pedersen has plenty of excellent music from two of the best. Peterson and Pedersen perform six standards and a well-conceived five-song Duke Ellington medley. Few real surprises occur, but the duo plays up to one's high expectations. — *Scott Yanow*

The Personal Touch / Jan. 28, 1980–Feb. 19, 1980 / Pablo ✦✦✦
This is a somewhat unusual Oscar Peterson record (a CD reissue) in a number of ways. Peterson (along with fluegelhornist Clark Terry, bassist Dave Young, drummer Jerry Fuller and either Peter Leitch or Ed Bickert on guitar) performs 13 songs either written or popularized by Canadians. In addition, he sings the majority of the tunes in his Nat King Cole-influenced voice and contributes two new songs of his own. The repertoire includes some familiar standards ("Some of These Days," "I'll Never Smile Again," "The World Is Waiting for the Sunrise" and "Sweethearts on Parade"), jazz versions of a few pop tunes (including "Spinning Wheel") and a few obscurities. — *Scott Yanow*

Live at the Northsea Jazz Festival / Jul. 13, 1980 / Pablo ✦✦✦✦✦
This double LP matches and mixes together four masterful musicians: pianist Oscar Peterson, guitarist Joe Pass, bassist Niels Pedersen and harmonica great Toots Thielemans. Together they perform O.P.'s "City Lights" and ten veteran standards with creativity and solid swing. There are a few miraculous moments as one would expect from musicians of this caliber and the results are generally quite memorable. Recommended. although this music has not yet surfaced on CD. — *Scott Yanow*

A Royal Wedding Suite / Apr. 15, 1981–Apr. 25, 1981 / Pablo ✦✦✦
To celebrate the marriage of Prince Charles and Lady Di of England, Oscar Peterson composed a ten-song suite that he performs on this LP while accompanied by an unidentified string orchestra arranged by Rick Wilkins. Not too surprisingly Peterson (who doubles here on electric piano) proves to be a talented composer and, even if none of the individual pieces caught on (or was ever apparently recorded again by the pianist), the music on a whole is quite satisfying. — *Scott Yanow*

Nigerian Marketplace / Jul. 16, 1981 / Pablo ✦✦✦✦
For this trio set with bassist Niels Pedersen and drummer Terry Clarke, the great pianist Oscar Peterson (appearing at the 1981 Montreux Jazz Festival) performs a medley of "Misty" and "Waltz for Debby," three standards, his own "Cakewalk" and the debut of "Nigerian Marketplace," the first section of an extended suite not yet completed at the time. This is a well-rounded set (reissued on CD) that finds the remarkable Oscar Peterson in typically swinging and prime form. — *Scott Yanow*

The Oscar Peterson Big 4 In Japan '82 / Feb. 20, 1982–Feb. 21, 1982 / Pablo ✦✦✦✦
For this two-LP set, pianist Oscar Peterson teams up with guitarist Joe Pass, bassist Niels Pedersen and drummer Martin Drew for a strong program comprised of 11 standards, six Peterson originals and Pedersen's "Future Child." The music is essentially straight-ahead bop with some impressionistic moments and with the rapid pieces being outnumbered by the sensitive ballads. Highlights include "'Round Midnight," "Move," "Nigerian Marketplace" and a medley of Peterson's "Hymn to Freedom" and "The Fallen Warrior." — *Scott Yanow*

Face to Face / May 24, 1982 / Pablo ++++

Two of the Few / Jan. 20, 1983 / Original Jazz Classics ++++
This CD reissue brings back a unique duet recording featuring pianist Oscar Peterson and vibraphonist Milt Jackson. One would expect the instrumentation to feature mostly ballads, but the opposite is true as O.P. and Bags romp through quite a few uptempo pieces. Highlights include "Lady Be Good," "Limehouse Blues," "Reunion Blues" and "Just You, Just Me." This is a successful and highly enjoyable outing. —Scott Yanow

Tribute to My Friends / Nov. 8, 1983 / Pablo ++++
Pianist Oscar Peterson recorded so many albums for Pablo during 1972-83 that it must have been rather difficult for him to come up with fresh material and ideas for records. However, this LP, which features songs associated with nine of his associates (ranging from Louis Armstrong and Billie Holiday to Dizzy Gillespie, Ella Fitzgerald and Lester Young) features a variety of tunes that Peterson had not played that much through the years. With the assistance of guitarist Joe Pass, bassist Niels Pedersen and drummer Martin Drew, Peterson sounds inspired on such themes as "Blueberry Hill," "Stuffy," "Cottontail" and even "A Tisket, a Tasket." This album is long overdue to be reissued on CD. —Scott Yanow

If You Could See Me Now / Nov. 9, 1983 / Pablo ++++
Oscar Peterson recorded a countless number of albums for Norman Granz's Pablo label during 1972-83 before Granz decided to call a halt (which was temporary) to his company's operations. This set was the pianist's last before a three-year hiatus and it finds his quartet of the period (with guitarist Joe Pass, bassist Niels Pedersen and drummer Martin Drew) in typically swinging form on Miles Davis' "Weird Blues," a pair of Peterson originals, two veteran ballads and a ridiculously rapid "Limehouse Blues," which is taken as a Peterson-Pass duet. —Scott Yanow

Edison / **Vinson** / Nov. 12, 1986 / Pablo +++++
During Nov. 12-14, 1986, pianist Oscar Peterson recorded three albums worth of material for Norman Granz's Pablo label. This particular CD features the great pianist with his quartet (bassist Dave Young, drummer Martin Drew and guest guitarist Joe Pass) along with trumpeter Harry "Sweets" Edison and altoist Eddie "Cleanhead" Vinson. The strictly instrumental set has many fine solos on appealing tunes such as "Stuffy," "Broadway" and the lengthy blues "Slooow Drag." This boppish session gave Vinson a rare chance to really stretch out and he was up for the challenge. —Scott Yanow

Live / Nov. 12, 1986+Nov. 14, 1986 / Pablo ++++
Pianist Oscar Peterson's stint at the Westwood Playhouse in Los Angeles in Nov. 1986 resulted in two CDs' worth of material. Peterson's quartet (with guitarist Joe Pass, bassist David Young and drummer Martin Drew) performs an interesting medley of "Perdido" and "Caravan," plays sensitively on "If You Only Knew," explores the pianist's "City Lights" and performs a three-part "The Bach Suite," which is climaxed by "Bach's Blues." Easily enjoyable music, it's recommended to Peterson's many fans. —Scott Yanow

Time After Time / Nov. 12, 1986+Nov. 14, 1986 / Pablo ++++
Pianist Oscar Peterson's final Pablo album (after a countless amount of appearances as both a leader and a sideman) features his quartet (which at the time included guitarist Joe Pass, bassist David Young and drummer Martin Drew) on the second of two CDs (along with Oscar Peterson Live) recorded during an engagement at Los Angeles' Westwood Playhouse in Nov. 1986. For the well-rounded set, Peterson performs two of his originals, the blues "Soft Winds," a solo ballad medley and, as a climax, a burning version of "On the Trail." —Scott Yanow

The Legendary Oscar Peterson Trio Live at the Blue Note / Mar. 16, 1990 / Telarc ++++
Pianist Oscar Peterson had a reunion with guitarist Herb Ellis and bassist Ray Brown at a well-publicized get-together at New York's Blue Note in March 1990. The trio (his regular group of the late '50s) was augmented by Peterson's late '60s drummer Bobby Durham for spirited performances. Rather than using their complex arrangements of the past, the pianist and his alumni simply jammed through the performances and the results are quite rewarding. On the first of four CDs released by Telarc, the quartet performs "Honeysuckle Rose," a ballad medley, three of the pianist's originals and "Sweet Georgia Brown." As this and the other CDs in the series show, the magic was still there. —Scott Yanow

Last Call / Mar. 16, 1990-Mar. 17, 1990 / Telarc ++++
The third of four Telarc CDs to be released from an Oscar Peterson reunion engagement at New York's Blue Note Club matches together the great pianist with guitarist Herb Ellis, bassist Ray Brown and drummer Bobby Durham. Although the veterans did not rehearse together beforehand, the repertoire is quite fresh with five standards being balanced by five Peterson originals including "Bach's Blues," "Wheatland" and "Blues Etude." The performance is as strong as one would expect, although the inclusion of Durham's drums makes the music less exciting and risky than the late-'50s trio recordings. It's worth picking up as are the other Oscar Peterson Telarc releases from this now-legendary engagement. —Scott Yanow

Encore at the Blue Note / Mar. 16, 1990-Mar. 17, 1990 / Telarc ++++
The fourth CD taken from a reunion engagement at the Blue Note by pianist Oscar Peterson, guitarist Herb Ellis, bassist Ray Brown and drummer Bobby Durham, this set is up to the same level as the other three. The O.P. Trio of the late '50s (along with Peterson's drummer of a decade later) happily jam through five standards (including a heated "Falling in Love with Love") and four of Peterson's originals highlighted by a medley of his "Goodbye Old Girl" and "He Has Gone." —Scott Yanow

Saturday Night at the Blue Note / Mar. 17, 1990 / Telarc ++++
Oscar Peterson reunited with guitarist Herb Ellis and bassist Ray Brown for this well-recorded engagement, which has resulted in four CDs being released by Telarc. The inclusion of drummer Bobby Durham did make the music a bit safer (and less risky) and, rather than revisit their classic complex arrangements, the ensemble jammed the songs so one does not hear the startling octaves that were present in the Trio's work of the late '50s. However, the repertoire on this CD (which includes two standards, Milt Jackson's "Reunion Blues" and five of Peterson's originals) is fresh and fairly challenging. Easily enjoyable music, it's recommended to the pianist's fans. —Scott Yanow

The More I See You / Jan. 15, 1995-Jan. 16, 1995 / Telarc ++++
After Oscar Peterson suffered a severe stroke in the spring of 1993, it was feared that he would never again play on a professional level, but two years of intense therapy resulted in the masterful pianist returning to what sounds on this Telarc CD like near-prime form. For the all-star date, Peterson tears into seven standards and two blues and outswings all potential competitors. Altoist Benny Carter at 87 sounds like he is 47 (if Carter had retired back in 1940 he would still be a legend) and fluegelhornist Clark Terry (now 74) proves to be not only (along with the remarkable 90-year-old Doc Cheatham) the finest trumpeter over 70, but one of the top brassmen of any age. The cool-toned guitarist Lorne Lofsky and drummer Lewis Nash are also strong assets while bassist Ray Brown (a year younger than Peterson at a mere 68) displays his typical limitless energy. On appealing tunes such as "In a Mellow Tone," "When My Dream Boat Comes Home" and a medium-up version of "For All We Know," the musicians all play up to their usual high level, making this a joyous comeback album for the great Oscar Peterson. —Scott Yanow

Ralph Peterson

b. May 20, 1962, Pleasantville, NJ
Drums, Leader / Post Bop, Hard Bop
During his relatively brief period in the spotlight, Ralph Peterson has already distinguished himself not only as a superior drummer but as an important bandleader, too. It was natural that Peterson would be a drummer for four of his uncles and a grandfather played drums. He started at age three and, after attending Rutgers and settling in New York, he became a constantly working drummer. In addition to sessions with OTB, David Murray and the Terence Blanchard-Donald Harrison group, Peterson has led several diverse and adventurous sessions for Blue Note. —Scott Yanow

V / Apr. 1988 / Blue Note ++++
Some tremendous hard bop and modern jazz material from a session led by drummer Ralph Peterson, featuring trumpeter Terence Blanchard, pianist Geri Allen, and bassist Phil Bowler. —Ron Wynn

Triangular / Aug. 20, 1988-Aug. 22, 1988 / Blue Note +++++

Volition / Feb. 27, 1989-Feb. 28, 1989 / Blue Note ++++
Quintet. Excellent session; wondrous lineup. Pianist Geri Allen and trumpeter Terence Blanchard are masterly. —Ron Wynn

Ralph Peterson Introduces the Fo'tet / Dec. 22, 1989–Dec. 23, 1989 / Blue Note ✦✦✦✦✦
An album where this tremendous young drummer unveils a strong lineup of contemporary talent and turns it loose on a hard-bop menu. —*Ron Wynn*

● **Fo'tet Ornettology** / Aug. 7, 1990–Aug. 9, 1990 / Somethin' Else ✦✦✦✦✦
An outstanding hard bop session by drummer Ralph Peterson, heading a band that includes many top modern players, among them Don Byron on clarinet, plus Melissa Slocum and Bryan Carroll. The compositions are mostly originals, and, although arranged in a vintage style, have a contemporary flavor. —*Ron Wynn*

Art / Mar. 18, 1992–Mar. 20, 1992 / Blue Note ✦✦✦✦

The Reclamation Project / Nov. 28, 1994–Nov. 29, 1994 / Evidence ✦✦✦✦

Michel Petrucciani

b. Dec. 28, 1962, Orange, France
Piano / Post Bop
Michel Petrucciani has overcome the effects of osteogenesis imperfecta (a bone disease that greatly stunted his growth) to become a powerful pianist. Originally greatly influenced by Bill Evans and to a lesser extent Keith Jarrett, Petrucciani has since developed his own individual voice. He started by playing in the family band with his guitarist father and bassist brother. At the age of 15 he had the opportunity to play with Kenny Clarke and Clark Terry, and at 17 he made his first recording. Petrucciani toured France with Lee Konitz in a duo (1980) and moved to the U.S. in 1982. At that time he coaxed Charles Lloyd out of retirement and toured with his quartet, a mutually beneficial relationship. Since then, Petrucciani has been a strong attraction in the U.S., usually playing with a quartet (sometimes featuring Adam Holzman's synthesizer for color) or as a soloist; in 1986 he recorded at Montreux with Jim Hall and Wayne Shorter. Although Petrucciani's ability to overcome his affliction is admirable, his impressive playing stands by itself. —*Scott Yanow*

Michel Petrucciani / Apr. 3, 1981–Apr. 4, 1981 / Owl ✦✦✦

Toot Sweet / May 25, 1982 / Owl ✦✦✦

Oracle's Destiny / Oct. 18, 1982 / Owl ✦✦✦✦

★ **100 Hearts** / Jun. 1983 / George Wein Collection ✦✦✦✦✦
If it were not for Michel Petrucciani's good taste, it is likely that his very impressive technique would dominate his solos. As it is, the pianist has been able to use his technique in surprising ways, avoiding the obvious and showing self-restraint while coming up with ingenious ideas in his improvisations. This solo album, his first for an American label, finds Petrucciani exploring pieces by Ornette Coleman, Charlie Haden and Sonny Rollins in addition to two of his own songs and a lengthy wandering medley that somehow incorporates "Someday My Prince Will Come," "All the Things You Are," "A Child Is Born" and Bill Evans' "Very Early" into a collage. A very impressive outing. —*Scott Yanow*

Live at the Village Vanguard / Mar. 16, 1984 / Concord ✦✦✦✦
This double LP finds pianist Michel Petrucciani often showing the influence of Bill Evans. His interplay with bassist Palle Danielsson and drummer Eliot Zigmund (an Evans alumnus) is consistently impressive and these eight performances (all but two are between eight and 12 minutes long) never lose their momentum. It's recommended for lovers of piano trios. —*Scott Yanow*

Note 'n' Notes / Oct. 5, 1984 / Owl ✦✦✦✦

Cold Blues / Jan. 11, 1985 / Owl ✦✦✦✦
A '91 CD reissue featuring outstanding pianist Michel Petrucciani in duets with bassist Ron McClure. While some accuse Petrucciani of too much flash and not enough soul, his expressive phrasing and often dazzling solos reflect a complete knowledge and mastery of the keyboard, while bassist McClure adds enough depth and bottom to keep things from getting too spacy. —*Ron Wynn*

Pianism / Dec. 20, 1985 / Blue Note ✦✦✦✦✦
The virtuosic pianist Michel Petrucciani was at his best throughout this dazzling set. Although frequently recorded in recent years, *Pianism* rankes among Petrucciani's most satisfying releases because he emphasizes emotion over his remarkable technique. —*Scott Yanow*

Power of Three / Jul. 14, 1986 / Blue Note ✦✦✦✦✦
It was logical that Michel Petrucciani (piano) and Jim Hall (guitar) would eventually play together. Both are masters of chordal improvisation and possessors of harmonically rich and introverted styles. At the 1986 Montreux Jazz Festival, the pair worked together perfectly, sounding as one on the altered blues "Careful" (where their comping behind each other's solos was exquisite) and on a lengthy and well-constructed version of "In a Sentimental Mood." —*Scott Yanow*

Michel Plays Petrucciani / Sep. 24, 1987–Dec. 10, 1987 / Blue Note ✦✦✦✦
The frequently arresting player tackles his own work. His solos outstrip his writing. —*Ron Wynn*

Music / 1989 / Blue Note ✦✦✦

Playground / 1991 / Blue Note ✦✦✦✦
In his most recent set, he dominates as soloist. Omar Hakim provides welcome energy on drums. —*Ron Wynn*

Live / 1992 / Blue Note ✦✦✦

Promenade With Duke / 1993 / Blue Note ✦✦✦

Marvellous / 1994 / Dreyfus ✦✦✦

Oscar Pettiford

b. Sep. 30, 1922, Okmulgee, OK, **d.** Sep. 8, 1960, Copenhagen
Bass, Cello / Bop
Oscar Pettiford was (along with Charles Mingus) the top bassist of the 1945-60 period and the successor to the late Jimmy Blanton. In addition, he was the first major jazz soloist on the cello. A bop pioneer, it would have been very interesting to hear what Pettiford would have done during the avant-garde '60s if he had not died unexpectedly in 1960. After starting on piano, Pettiford switched to bass when he was 14 and played in a family band. He played with Charlie Barnet's band in 1942 as one of two bassists (the other was Chubby Jackson) and then hit the big time in 1943 participating on Coleman Hawkins' famous "The Man I Love" session; he also recorded with Earl Hines and Ben Webster during this period. Pettiford co-led an early bop group with Dizzy Gillespie in 1944 and in 1945 went with Coleman Hawkins to the West Coast, appearing on one song in the film *The Crimson Canary* with Hawkins and Howard McGhee. Pettiford was part of Duke Ellington's Orchestra during much of 1945-48 (fulfilling his role as the next step beyond Jimmy Blanton) and worked with Woody Herman in 1949. Throughout the 1950s he worked mostly as a leader (on bass and occasional cello) although he appeared on many records both as a sideman and a leader, including with Thelonious Monk in 1955-56. After going to Europe in 1958, he settled in Copenhagen where he worked with local musicians plus Stan Getz, Bud Powell and Kenny Clarke. Among Pettiford's better-known compositions are "Tricotism," "Laverne Walk," "Bohemia After Dark" and "Swingin' Till the Girls Come Home." —*Scott Yanow*

Discoveries / Oct. 21, 1952–Oct. 1957 / Savoy ✦✦✦✦✦
A stunning early work by the bass and cello great. Has some duets with Charles Mingus (b), plus other examples of his stirring cello technique. —*Ron Wynn*

The Oscar Pettiford Memorial Album / Dec. 29, 1953–Mar. 13, 1954 / Prestige ✦✦✦✦
Stunning bass and cello playing from Oscar Pettiford showing his technical prowess both with bow and plucked. Phenomenal showcase for Pettiford's work and for bass and cello in general. —*Ron Wynn*

Oscar Pettiford Modern Quintet / Sep. 1954 / Bethlehem ✦✦✦✦

Basically Duke / Dec. 17, 1954 / Bethlehem ✦✦✦✦

Another One / Aug. 12, 1955 / Bethlehem ✦✦✦✦

★ **Deep Passion** / Jun. 11, 1956–Aug. 23, 1957 / Impulse! ✦✦✦✦✦

Oscar Pettiford and his Birdland Band / May 26, 1957 / Spotlite ✦✦✦✦

Vienna Blues: The Complete Sessions / Jan. 9, 1959+Jan. 12, 1959 / Black Lion ✦✦✦✦✦
Tremendous sessions featuring bass and cello giant Oscar Pettiford heading an unusual group with tenor saxophonist Hans Koller, guitarist Atilla Zoller, and drummer Jimmy Pratt. These were recorded near the end of Pettiford's career, but were first-rate, especially Pettiford's cello solos and Koller's tenor. —*Ron Wynn*

Montmartre Blues / Aug. 22, 1959–Jul. 6, 1960 / Black Lion
✦✦✦✦

Flip Phillips (Joseph Edward Filipelli)

b. Feb. 26, 1915, Brooklyn, NY
Tenor Saxophone / Bop, Swing
Flip Phillips, who angered some critics early on because he gained
riotous applause for his exciting solos during Jazz at the
Philharmonic concerts, has, for over 50 years, been an excellent
tenor saxophonist equally gifted on stomps, ballads and standards.
He played clarinet regularly in a Brooklyn restaurant during
1934–39, was in Frankie Newton's group (1940–41) and spent
time in the bands of Benny Goodman, Wingy Manone and Red
Norvo. However, it was in 1944 that he had his breakthrough. As
a well-featured soloist with Woody Herman's Herd (1944–46),
Phillips became a big star. His warm tenor was most influenced
by Ben Webster, but sounded distinctive even at that early stage.
He toured regularly with Jazz at the Philharmonic during
1946–57, scoring a bit of a sensation with his honking solo on
"Perdido" and holding his own with heavy competition (including
Charlie Parker and Lester Young). He occasionally co-led a group
with Bill Harris and that band was the nucleus of the ensemble
that Benny Goodman used in 1959. Phillips then retired to Florida
for 15 years, playing on just an occasional basis, taking up the
bass clarinet as a double and making only a sporadic record date.
But by 1975 he was back in music full-time making quite a few
records and playing at festivals and jazz parties. Even as he
passed his 80th birthday, Flip Phillips has lost none of the enthusiasm or ability that he had a half-century earlier. —*Scott Yanow*

★ **A Melody from the Sky** / Sep. 1944–Nov. 1945 / Doctor Jazz
✦✦✦✦✦
This CD is a straight reissue of a Flying Dutchman LP and has all
four of tenor saxophonist Flip Phillips' recording sessions as a
leader prior to 1949. At the time he was a key member of Woody
Herman's First Herd and these performances have short solos
from other Herman sidemen (including trombonist Bill Harris
and Neal Hefti on trumpet) although Phillips is the main star. His
jumping tenor was already quite distinctive whether on romps or
ballads. "Sweet and Lovely" and "Stompin' at the Savoy" are highpoints of this definitive early Flip Phillips set. —*Scott Yanow*

Flip in Florida / May 1963 / Onyx ✦✦✦✦
Tenor saxophonist Flip Phillips' only session as a leader during
1955–74 was this obscurity, which was originally released on a
tiny label and reissued by Onyx a decade after the fact. Phillips,
who enjoyed having a much lower profile than previously, had
relocated to Florida by 1954. Fortunately, his powers were still in
peak form for this quartet set, which finds him accompanied by
local musicians for a set, dominated by standards. Phillips makes
his debut playing bass clarinet on "Satin Doll," "The Girl from
Ipanema" and "Just Say I Love Her" while featuring his stomping
warm tenor to the other pieces. —*Scott Yanow*

Phillips' Head / Aug. 1975 / Choice ✦✦✦
● **Flipenstein** / Jul. 20, 1981 / Progressive ✦✦✦✦✦
The Claw: Live at the Floating Jazz Festival / 1986 / Chiaroscuro
✦✦✦✦✦
Veteran tenor Flip Phillips is heard leading a jam session during
what was dubbed the 1986 Floating Jazz Festival since the music
took place on the S.S. Norway somewhere in the Caribbean Sea.
Phillips and his fellow tenors Buddy Tate, Al Cohn and Scott
Hamilton (along with pianist John Bunch, guitarist Chris Flory,
bassist Major Holley and drummer Chuck Riggs) clearly had a
good time stretching out on the five pieces (which all sport fairly
basic chord changes); fluegelhornist Clark Terry dropped by and
joins in on three of the pieces. Unfortunately, the liner notes do
not tell who solos when, but veteran collectors should be able to
tell the tenors apart. The only minus to this CD is a surprisingly
boring monologue by Phillips (one of Chiaroscuro's few unsuccessful "Jamsspeaks") at the conclusion of this disc. However, his
nine minutes of talking is preceded by 64 minutes of hot jamming, making this CD easily recommended to fans of Jazz at the
Philharmonic and straight-ahead jazz. —*Scott Yanow*

Live At The 1993 Floating Jazz Festival / Nov. 1, 1993+Nov. 3,
1993 / Chiaroscuro ✦✦✦✦
Flip Phillips was 79 at the time of this live performance but
proves to still be very much in his musical prime. Joined by a
rhythm section comprised of fellow veterans (pianist Derek

Smith, guitarist Bucky Pizzarelli, bassist Milt Hinton and drummer Ray Mosca), Phillips gives standards and riff tunes warm and
often hard-swinging treatment. Other than a few tasteless (if
humorous) jokes, this is a flawless release that serves as a definitive portrait of Flip Phillips in his later years. —*Scott Yanow*

Pieces of a Dream

Group / R&B, Crossover
Comprised of bassist Cedric Napoleon, drummer Curtis Harmon
and keyboardist James Lloyd, Pieces of a Dream was founded in
1975 in Philadelphia when the principal members were all
teenagers. Originally somewhat jazz-oriented, Pieces of a Dream
has mostly emphasized R&B although they usually include a few
jazz numbers in their performances. Grover Washington, Jr., produced their first three albums (all for Elektra during 1981–83);
they have since recorded for Manhattan. Saxophonist Ron Kerber
became a member in the 1990s. —*Scott Yanow*

In Flight / Jun. 1, 1993 / Manhattan ✦✦✦
Pieces of a Dream can always be counted on to offer lightweight
jazz-influenced R&B that is pleasing as long as one does not listen too closely or have overly high expectations. This set has several forgettable vocals, some sax solos by Ron Kerber and Marian
Meadows that attempt to sound like Grover Washington, Jr., and
consistently danceable rhythms. —*Scott Yanow*

● **Goodbye Manhattan** / 1994 / Manhattan ✦✦✦✦✦
This is one of Pieces of a Dream's better efforts. Saxophonist Ron
Kerber looks toward Grover Washington, Jr., (on soprano) and
David Sanborn (during his alto spots) for inspiration and the keyboardists recall Ramsey Lewis but, even with the inclusion of a
few throwaway rhythm tracks and some Eva Cassidy pop vocals,
some of these selections do contain strong improvising within the
R&B genre. Nothing too innovative occurs but the results are
mostly quite listenable and always danceable. —*Scott Yanow*

Bill Pierce

b. Sep. 25, 1948, Hampton, VA
Tenor Saxophone / Hard Bop
Bill Pierce is an excellent saxophonist who also works as an educator. He started off his career in Boston playing R&B with such
stars as Stevie Wonder and Marvin Gaye. However, he is essentially a hard bop player as he showed during stints with James
Williams (1979–80 and 1984–85) and a high-profile association
with Art Blakey's Jazz Messengers (1980–82); with the latter he
shared the front line with Wynton Marsalis and Bobby Watson.
From 1986–94 Pierce was a regular member of Tony Williams'
Quintet, somehow making himself heard over the leader's very
loud drumming! He has led several of his own dates for
Sunnyside. —*Scott Yanow*

● **William the Conqueror** / May 29, 1985–May 30, 1985 /
Sunnyside ✦✦✦✦✦
It is the powerful tenor of Billy Pierce that makes this a highly
recommended album. —*Scott Yanow*

Give and Take / Jun. 6, 1987+Oct. 24, 1987 / Sunnyside ✦✦✦
Equilateral / Jan. 2, 1988 / Sunnyside ✦✦✦
One for Chuck / Apr. 6, 1991–Apr. 7, 1991 / Sunnyside ✦✦✦✦
Rio / May 25, 1994–May 26, 1994 / Sunnyside ✦✦✦✦

Dave Pike

b. Mar. 23, 1938, Detroit, MI
Vibes / Hard Bop
Dave Pike has been a consistent vibraphonist through the years
without gaining much fame. He originally played drums and is
self-taught on vibes. Pike moved with his family to Los Angeles
in 1954 and played with Curtis Counce, Harold Land, Elmo Hope,
Dexter Gordon, Carl Perkins and Paul Bley among others. After
moving to New York in 1960 he put an amplifier on his vibes.
Pike toured with Herbie Mann during 1961–64, spent 1968–73 in
Germany (recording with the Kenny Clarke-Francy Boland big
band) and then resettled in Los Angeles, playing locally and
recording for Timeless and Criss Cross. —*Scott Yanow*

Dave Pike / Nov. 1961 / Portrait ✦✦✦✦
Jazz for the Jet Set / Oct. 26, 1965–Nov. 2, 1965 / Atlantic ✦✦✦
Times out of Mind / Oct. 13, 1975–Oct. 14, 1975 / Muse ✦✦✦
Some of vibist Dave Pike's best playing makes this an enjoyable
album, even if the compositions are ordinary and the arrange-

ments frequently only competent. But his solos are nicely played, and often render at least enjoyable some otherwise routine material. —*Ron Wynn*

On a Gentle Note / Nov. 1, 1977 / Muse ✦✦✦✦
Let the Minstrels Play on / Mar. 22, 1978–Mar. 23, 1978 / Muse ✦✦✦
Some Afro-Latin, some fusion and things in between from vibist Dave Pike. Pike is a good player, but sometimes his arrangements bog down between pop and jazz. His style is more reminiscent of Red Norvo, with its lighter, less aggressive and flowing lines. —*Ron Wynn*

Moon Bird / 1981 / Muse ✦✦✦
● **Pike's Groove** / Feb. 5, 1986 / Criss Cross ✦✦✦✦✦
Bluebird / Oct. 1988–Nov. 1988 / Timeless ✦✦

Courtney Pine
b. Mar. 18, 1964, London, England
Soprano Saxophone, Tenor Saxophone / Post Bop
For a while, Courtney Pine appeared as if he were going to be the next Wynton Marsalis. While Marsalis in the mid-'80s was doing close impressions of mid-'60s Miles Davis, Pine's impressive playing was nearly identical to John Coltrane's of the same era. Since then Pine has received less publicity (at least in the U.S.) and his importance has diminished a bit. He played with reggae and funk bands while in school and has always had a strong interest in several forms of music outside of jazz. He played with John Stevens in the early '80s, formed the Jazz Warriors (an open-minded big band) a few years later and started leading his own small groups. In 1986 he toured with George Russell's Orchestra and sat in with Art Blakey's Jazz Messengers, but since then, despite some fine records for Antilles, Pine's career has seemed a bit directionless. —*Scott Yanow*

● **Journey to the Urge Within** / Jul. 21, 1986–Jul. 23, 1986 / Antilles ✦✦✦✦✦
This early Courtney Pine recording (the tenor saxophonist was 22 at the time), features some of the most promising black English jazz musicians of the time including Pine (who also plays some bass clarinet and soprano), singer Cleveland Watkiss (who often is reminiscent of Bobby McFerrin), vibraphonist Orphy Robinson and pianist Julian Joseph. While most of these players have not yet lived up to their potential (Pine remains an expert Coltrane imitator), this disc has its share of strong music. The emphasis is on Courtney Pine's originals, which cover a wide span of emotions and grooves. —*Scott Yanow*

Destiny's Song and the Image of Pursuance / Jul. 29, 1987–Aug. 1, 1987 / Antilles ✦✦✦✦
The Vision's Tale / Jan. 17, 1989–Jan. 19, 1989 / Antilles ✦✦✦
The Vision's Tale / 1990 / Antilles ✦✦
Within the Realms of Our Dream / Jan. 20, 1990–Jan. 21, 1990 / Antilles ✦✦✦✦✦
Closer to Home / 1992 / Antilles ✦✦✦
A '92 release by British saxophonist Courtney Pine, who with each album moves more toward the musical center. He's working with pop, rock, and reggae compositions and musicians, but at the same time still playing forceful, frequently dynamic tenor and soprano solos. It's not really fusion, nor is it the kind of uncompromising jazz that he once championed. —*Ron Wynn*

Jon Pisano
b. Feb. 6, 1931, New York, NY
Guitar / Bop
There have been few jazz musicians as modest and self-effacing as John Pisano, an excellent guitarist who has often been quite happy to be in the background. He started playing guitar when he was 14 and, after performing in an Air Force band (1952–55), he gained some recognition as Jim Hall's replacement in the popular Chico Hamilton Quintet (1956–58). Pisano settled in Los Angeles and became a well-respected studio musician who, among other assignments, recorded duets with Billy Bean, played in the Joe Pass Quartet (recording the legendary *For Django* album), worked with Peggy Lee (1960–69) and was a member of Herb Alpert's Tijuana Brass (1965–69). Pisano had a reunion with Joe Pass (touring with him from 1989 until Pass' death in 1994), sticking almost exclusively to rhythm guitar. A collection of collaborations with various associates (*Among Friends*) was released on Pablo in

1995. Recently he has been performing with singer Jeanne Pisano (his wife) in a group called the Flying Pisanos. —*Scott Yanow*

John Pizzarelli
b. Apr. 6, 1960, Paterson, NJ
Guitar, Vocals / Swing
The son of the fine guitarist Bucky Pizzarelli, John is not at his level instrumentally, but has blossomed into a charming (if limited) vocalist. Taught guitar by his father, John Pizzarelli sat in with Bucky and Zoot Sims at a 1980 concert and has played with duets with the older Pizzarelli on an occasional basis ever since. He worked with Tony Monte's trio in 1986 and in 1990 started his solo career, recording as a leader for Chesky, Stash and Novus. His voice is not all that strong, but to his credit John Pizzarelli does not take himself too seriously. —*Scott Yanow*

My Blue Heaven / Feb. 6, 1990–Feb. 7, 1990 / Chesky ✦✦✦
This son of a guitar legend has good technique. He's a tasteful player and picks good songs. —*Ron Wynn*

All of Me / 1991 / Novus ✦✦✦✦
A family guitar showcase with guitarists Bucky Pizzarelli and John, Jr. playing jazz standards, light Afro-Latin, and some sentimental ballads. They're joined by a group with clarinetist Phil Bodner, Walt Levinsky, John Frosk, and Paul Faulice. It's nice, well done, soothing music. —*Ron Wynn*

Naturally / 1993 / Novus ✦✦✦✦
New Standards / 1994 / Novus ✦✦✦
Dear Mr. Cole / 1994 / Novus ✦✦✦✦
John Pizzarelli's tribute to Nat King Cole features him in a drumless trio with pianist Benny Green and bassist Christian McBride on all but one selection. Pizzarelli is fine as a rhythm guitarist but since he sings on most of the selections and his voice is merely average, this session (which includes 18 selections, most of which were originally associated with Cole) is of less interest than one might hope. At least Pizzarelli has a cheerful style and does not seem to take himself too seriously. Green has many forceful solos, but the leader's limited vocal abilities keep this recording from being too essential. —*Scott Yanow*

● **After Hours** / 1995 / Novus ✦✦✦✦✦
I'm Hip / May 1983 / Stash ✦✦✦

John "Bucky" Pizzarelli
b. Jan. 9, 1926, Paterson, NJ
Guitar / Swing
A superior guitarist who swing musicians in particular appreciate, Bucky Pizzarelli has been a fixture in jazz and the studios since the early '50s. Self-taught, Pizzarelli has long been a master of the seven-string guitar. He toured with Vaughn Monroe before and after a stint in the military. In 1952 Pizzarelli joined the staff of NBC and 12 years later he switched to ABC; in addition he worked with the Three Sounds (1956–57) and had several tours with Benny Goodman. In the 1970s he was more active in jazz, co-leading a duo with George Barnes and working with Zoot Sims, Bud Freeman and Stephane Grappelli among many others. Pizzarelli has since kept up a busy recording schedule and plays often at jazz parties. Bucky has also recorded with his son John Pizzarelli on an occasional basis since the early '80s. —*Scott Yanow*

Plays Bix Beiderbecke Arrangements by Bill Challis / May 3, 1972–Jun. 30, 1972 / Monmouth ✦✦✦✦✦
Solo Flight / 1981 / Stash ✦✦✦
Cafe Pierre Trio / Aug. 25, 1982–Aug. 26, 1982 / Monmouth ✦✦✦✦
● **Complete Guitar Duos** / Mar. 19, 1984–Apr. 1984 / Stash ✦✦✦✦✦
Fine guitar vehicle for Bucky Pizzarelli and John, Jr. They team on both uptempo and slow tunes, with some originals, but mostly interpretations of both jazz and non-jazz items. This is wonderful for guitar devotees; others may have problems with the lack of variety and generally sedate production and sound. —*Ron Wynn*

Lonnie Plaxico
b. Sep. 4, 1960, Chicago, IL
Bass / Post Bop
Although he became associated for a time with the M-Base musicians, Lonnie Plaxico has been a very flexible bassist throughout his career. Early on he played with Chet Baker, Sonny Stitt and

Junior Cook. After spending time in Wynton Marsalis' band (1982), Plaxico worked with Dexter Gordon and Hank Jones before joining Art Blakey's Jazz Messengers in the mid-'80s. He recorded with Dizzy Gillespie and David Murray and led his own sessions for Muse starting in the late '80s. In recent times, Lonnie Plaxico has performed with everyone from Steve Coleman and Greg Osby to Bud Shank, Cassandra Wilson and Don Byron. —*Scott Yanow*

● **Plaxico** / Sep. 13, 1989 / Muse ✦✦✦✦✦

Iridescence / Dec. 13, 1990 / Muse ✦✦✦

Short Takes / May 4, 1992–Jun. 6, 1992 / Muse ✦✦✦

With All Your Heart / 1995 / Muse ✦✦✦✦

King Pleasure (Clarence Beeks)

b. Mar. 24, 1922, Oakdale, TN, d. Mar. 21, 1981, Los Angeles, CA
Vocals / Vocalese, Bop
Whether Eddie Jefferson or King Pleasure invented "vocalese," the art of putting lyrics to jazz solos, Pleasure (AKA Clarence Beeks) had the first huge hit. His version of "Moody's Mood For Love" on Prestige with Jefferson's lyrics did so well in 1952 that it landed Pleasure a label deal. He also had success with "Red Top" and "Parker's Mood." But Pleasure did not enjoy sustained success, though he continued recording for Prestige, Jubilee and Aladdin, as well as HiFi Jazz and United Artists. His style influenced the team of Lambert, Hendricks and Ross as well as more contemporary performers like Al Jarreau and the Manhattan Transfer. He And Ross, as well as Hendricks, subsequently recorded together. Several vintage Pleasure sessions have been reissued. —*Ron Wynn and Bob Porter*

★ **King Pleasure Sings with Annie Ross** / Feb. 19, 1952–Dec. 24, 1953 / Original Jazz Classics ✦✦✦✦✦
1950–1952. Undoubtedly the best. A must-buy. —*Michael G. Nastos*

● **Moody's Mood for Love** / 195509 05 / Blue Note ✦✦✦✦✦

Golden Days / Jun. 14, 1960 / Original Jazz Classics ✦✦✦
The always-entertaining King Pleasure does vocalize, scat, and vocals with humor, warmth, and comic ease. W/ Teddy Edwards (ts) and Harold Land (ts). —*Ron Wynn*

Paul Plimley

b. 1953, Vancouver, British Columbia, Canada
Piano / Avant-Garde
One of Canada's finest musicians, pianist Paul Plimley has built a fresh style that was originally influenced by Cecil Taylor. In 1977 he became a member of the New Orchestra Quintet, he studied with Cecil Taylor in 1979 and was often teamed with bassist Lisle Ellis until Ellis moved in the 1990s to the Bay Area. Plimley has recorded for several labels (including Nine Winds and Hat Art) and remains a vital force in Canada. —*Scott Yanow*

Both Sides of the Same Mirror / Nov. 1989 / Nine Winds ✦✦✦

Paul Plimley/Lisle Ellis/Andrew Cyrille Trio / Nov. 3, 1990 / Music & Arts ✦✦✦✦✦

● **When Silence Pulls** / 1992 / Music & Arts ✦✦✦✦✦

Kaleidoscopes / Apr. 8, 1992–Apr. 9, 1992 / Hat Art ✦✦✦✦
This is a very interesting concept that is partly successful. Pianist Paul Plimley and bassist Lisle Ellis perform ten Ornette Coleman tunes (including two versions of the title cut); never mind that Coleman never used a piano. However, because the duo's interpretations are very free and sometimes only refer to the themes in an abstract way, these performances are not as exciting as they would have been if the melodies had been used as the basis for the improvisations. —*Scott Yanow*

Jean Luc Ponty

b. Sep. 29, 1942, Avranches, France
Violin / Post Bop, Fusion, Crossover
A wide-ranging violinist and one of the finest soloists in the instrument's history, French musician Jean-Luc Ponty helped popularize the use of electronics among string players and developed a style that mixed swing, bebop, free and modal jazz, as well as jazz-rock and pop. He sometimes plays dynamic, intricately constructed, harmonically surprising solos; other times offers simple, bluesy statements with a prominent rhythmic focus. Ponty moved from amplifying an acoustic violin to exclusively using electric violins. He also began playing an violectra (an electric instrument tuned an octave below the violin). Ponty creatively utilized wa wa

pedals, fuzztone, echoplex and phase shifters, sometimes using an electronic device with a conventional mute. He later began using a five-string electric violin, with the lowest string tuned to C. Ponty alternated between acoustic and electric in his '70s bands and added synthesizer.

Ponty's father was a violin teacher, and director of the music school in Avranches, while his mother taught piano. Ponty began playing piano and violin at five, and clarinet at 11. He left school at 13, opting to become a concert violinist. He studied two years at the Paris Conservatory, winning the Premier prix at 17. Ponty played three years with The Concerts Lamoureux orchestra, where he was introduced to jazz. He started improvising on clarinet and tenor sax, and doing violin duets with Jef Gilson. Ponty was in the Army during the early '60s, then turned to jazz exclusively. He appeared at the 1964 Antibes-Juan-les-Pins Jazz Festival leading a quartet. Ponty played and recorded in quartets and trios with Eddy Louiss and Daniel Humair in the '60s, also heading a quartet with Wolfgang Dauner, Niels-Henning Orsted Pedersen and Humair. Ponty paid his first visit to America in the late '60s, playing at a violin workshop at the Monterey Jazz Festival. His quartet went to England in February of 1969. Ponty went to Los Angeles in March where he played and recorded with Frank Zappa, cutting the album *King Kong*. Later that year he joined George Duke's trio.

Ponty returned to France and lead a free jazz band, the Jean-Luc Ponty Experience, in the early '70s. He returned to America in 1973, and toured with Zappa's Mothers of Invention band. He worked in 1974 and 1975 with the second edition of The Mahavishnu Orchestra. Ponty began heading his own bands in 1975. He started recording for European labels in the mid-'60s, cutting sessions for Palm, Phillips, Saba/Pausa and Electrola, before making his American recording debut on Pacific Jazz with Duke in 1969. Ponty has subsequently recorded for Blue Note, Pausa, MPS/BASF, Inner City, Atlantic, Columbia, Prestige and Verve in the '70s and '80s. He's recorded with George Benson, Chick Corea and Giorgio Gaslini, while doing a violin summit LP with Stuff Smith, Svend Asmussen and Stephane Grappelli. Ponty has also included solo tracks on several albums. He has several titles, most of them Atlantic dates from the '70s, currently available on CD. —*Ron Wynn and Michael G. Nastos*

Violin Summit / Sep. 30, 1966 / Verve ✦✦✦✦✦
Violin Summit featured Stuff Smith, Stephane Grappelli, Svend Asmussen and Jean Luc-Ponty (with pianist Kenny Drew, bassist Niels-Henning Orsted Pedersen, drummer Alex Riel) in concert (Sept. 30, 1966)...The music came off quite well, in large part probably because the four violinists were paired in different sets with all four actually featured together on only one take, "It Don't Mean a Thing If It Ain't Got That Swing." —*Bob Rusch, Cadence*

Sunday Walk / Jun. 1967 / BASF ✦✦✦✦

Electric Connection / Mar. 3, 1969–Mar. 4, 1969 / Pacific Jazz ✦✦✦

King Kong: Ponty Plays Zappa / Mar. 14, 1969–Mar. 15, 1969 / World Pacific ✦✦✦✦

Canteloupe Island / Mar. 1969 / Blue Note ✦✦✦

★ **Experience** / Sep. 1969 / Pacific Jazz ✦✦✦✦✦

● **Live at Dontes** / Nov. 19, 196969 12 / Blue Note ✦✦✦✦✦

Open Strings / Dec. 1971 / BASF ✦✦✦✦

● **Upon the Wings of Music** / Jan. 1975 / Atlantic ✦✦✦✦✦
Jean-Luc Ponty, who at the time was still with the second version of The Mahavishnu Orchestra, is heard playing his own brand of fusion on this excellent recording, which set the standard for his music of the next decade. With keyboardist Patrice Rushen, Dan Sawyer or Ray Parker on guitars, bassist Ralphe Armstrong and drummer Ndugu, the violinist performs eight of his highly arranged but spirited originals. His early Atlantic recordings (of which this is the first) remain underrated for their important contributions to the history of fusion. —*Scott Yanow*

Aurora / Dec. 1975 / Atlantic ✦✦✦✦

Imaginary Voyage / Jul. 1976–Aug. 1976 / Atlantic ✦✦✦

Enigmatic Ocean / Jun. 1977–Jul. 1977 / Atlantic ✦✦✦
A terrific jazz-fusion album performed by violinist Ponty, it also features Allan Holdsworth (g), Steve Smith (d), and Daryl Steurmer (g). This album was and still is in many ways ahead of its time in terms of musicality. —*Paul Kohler*

Cosmic Messenger / 1978 / Atlantic ✦✦✦

A Taste for Passion / Jun. 1979–Jul. 1979 / Atlantic ✦✦

Live / 1979 / Atlantic ✦✦✦✦

Civilized Evil / Jul. 6, 1980 / Atlantic ✦✦✦

Mystical Adventures / Aug. 1981–Sep. 1981 / Atlantic ✦✦✦

Individual Choice / Mar. 1983–May 1983 / Atlantic ✦✦

A turning point in Ponty's career, this record finds the violinist/composer using computer-based sequences and synthesizers to create several backdrops for his violin playing. It is a nice mixture of acoustic instruments and modern technology. —*Paul Kohler*

Open Mind / Jul. 5, 1984 / Atlantic ✦✦

Fables / Jul. 1985–Aug. 1985 / Atlantic ✦✦✦

Continuing in his use of keyboard synthesizers, Ponty never takes a back seat to technology. Augmented by guitarist Scott Henderson, Ponty blends the instruments into a tasty set of jazz-fusion material. —*Paul Kohler*

The Gift of Time / 1987 / Columbia ✦✦

Storytelling / 1989 / Columbia ✦✦

Tchokola / 1991 / Epic ✦✦✦

Odeon Pope

b. Oct. 24, 1938, Ninety Six, SC
Tenor Saxophone / Post Bop

A dynamic, hard-driving tenor sax soloist noted for his work with Max Roach, Odean Pope's among the most fiery of contemporary players. His muscular tone, thrusts, honks and vocal cries make every Pope solo memorable. Pope learned saxophone and harmony from Ray Bryant while growing up in Philadelphia. Jymie Merrit introduced him to Roach, and Pope toured Europe with his quartet in the late '60s, and also accompanied Vi Redd during a London recording session. He formed Catalyst in 1971, a band that made four good jazz-rock and hard bop albums in the early '70s. Pope organized The Saxophone Choir in 1977, a band featuring eight saxes and a rhythm section. He headed the group until 1979, when he rejoined Roach for another European tour. Although he has led The Saxophone Choir on an occasional basis and recorded as a leader heading a funky trio (for Moers Music), Pope is best-known for being with the Max Roach Quartet for the past 17 years. —*Ron Wynn*

Almost Like Me / Aug. 25, 1982 / Moers ✦✦✦✦

★ The Saxophone Shop / Sep. 30, 1985–Oct. 1, 1985 / Soul Note ✦✦✦✦✦

Odeon Pope's "Saxophone Choir" is well titled. The tenor saxophonist is joined by three altos and three tenors (along with a standard rhythm section) for six of his originals and two other songs that he arranged. The saxophonists primarily function as "background singers," making their voices heard mostly as accompanists for the leader. It's an interesting concept. —*Scott Yanow*

The Ponderer / Mar. 12, 1990 / Soul Note ✦✦✦✦

Out for a Walk / Oct. 1990 / Moers ✦✦✦✦

Epitome / Oct. 4, 1993–Oct. 14, 1993 / Soul Note ✦✦✦✦

Chris Potter

b. Jan. 1, 1971, Chicago, IL
Alto Saxophone, Tenor Saxophone / Post Bop

Although often overlooked in popularity polls, the talented and often adventurous Chris Potter shows a great deal of potential. His first instrument was the piano, but when he was ten he began playing tenor and alto. At 18 he moved to New York and spent four years playing with Red Rodney's Quintet, mostly alto but impressing listeners with an occasional piano feature. Since then he has performed with the Mingus Big Band, Paul Motian, Marian McPartland and John Patitucci among others and led his own dates for Criss Cross and Concord. —*Scott Yanow*

Presenting Chris Potter / Dec. 29, 1992 / Criss Cross ✦✦✦✦

● Concentric Circles / Dec. 1993 / Concord ✦✦✦✦✦

Only 23 at the time of this Concord CD, Chris Potter shows a great deal of originality in his explorative styles on alto and soprano while on tenor he alternates between sounding like John Coltrane (his "Dusk" is not all that different than "Naima") and Dewey Redman. All but two songs on this set are his originals

and on some pieces Potter utilizes some overdubbing. Essentially a quintet session, this CD also contains some fine chancetaking solos from pianist Kenny Werner and guitarist John Hart with the music ranging from modal to freebop. —*Scott Yanow*

Pure / Jun. 14, 1994–Jun. 15, 1994 / Concord Jazz ✦✦✦✦

Bud Powell (Earl Powell)

b. Sep. 27, 1924, New York, NY, d. Jul. 31, 1966, New York, NY
Piano, Composer / Bop

One of the giants of the jazz piano, Bud Powell changed the way that virtually all post-swing pianists play their instruments. He did away with the left hand striding that had been considered essential earlier and used his left hand to state chords on an irregular basis. His right often played speedy single-note lines, essentially transforming Charlie Parker's vocabulary to the piano (although he developed parallel to Bird).

Tragically, Bud Powell was a seriously ill genius. After being encouraged and tutored to an extent by his friend Thelonious Monk at jam sessions in the early '40s, Powell was with Cootie Williams' orchestra during 1943–45. In a racial incident he was beaten on the head by police; Powell never fully recovered and would suffer from bad headaches and mental breakdowns throughout the remainder of his life. Despite this, he recorded some true gems during 1947–51 for Roost, Blue Note and Verve, composing such major works as "Dance of the Infidels," "Hallucinations" (also known as "Budo"), "Un Poco Loco," "Bouncing with Bud," and "Tempus Fugit." Even early in his erratic behavior also resulted in lost opportunities (Charlie Parker supposedly told Miles Davis that he would not hire Powell because "he's even crazier than me!"), but Powell's playing during this period was often miraculous.

A breakdown in 1951 and hospitalization that resulted in electroshock treatments weakened him but Powell was still capable of playing at his best now and then, most notably at the 1953 Massey Hall Concert. Generally in the 1950s, his Blue Notes find him in excellent form while he is much more erratic on his Verve recordings. His warm welcome and lengthy stay in Paris (1959–64) extended his life a bit, but even here Powell spent part of 1962–63 in the hospital. He returned to New York in 1964, disappeared after a few concerts and did not live through 1966.

In later years Bud Powell's recordings and performances could be so intense as to be scary, but other times he sounded quite sad. However, his influence on jazz (particularly up until the rise of McCoy Tyner and Bill Evans in the 1960s) was very strong and he remains one of the greatest jazz pianists of all time. —*Scott Yanow*

● Early Years of a Genius (1944–1948) / Jan. 1944–Dec. 19, 1948 / Mythic Sound ✦✦✦✦✦

This set is the first of ten CDs of privately recorded Bud Powell recordings owned by his friend Francis Paudras. All of the releases will be wanted by Powell's greatest fans, but some are better than others. *Vol. 1* is the most historic, for ten selections feature the innovative pianist at age 20 in 1944 as a sideman with trumpeter Cootie Williams' Orchestra and there are some unique moments. Powell plays a duet with Williams on "West End Blues," joins in with Williams' sextet (which also includes altoist Eddie "Cleanhead" Vinson and tenorman Eddie "Lockjaw" Davis) on "Smack Me" and backs guest Ella Fitzgerald on two numbers in addition to playing six songs with the full big band. This valuable set concludes with versions of "Perdido" and "Indiana" that Powell performed at the Royal Roost on Dec. 19, 1948 with an all-star group including trumpeter Benny Harris, trombonist J.J. Johnson, altoist Lee Konitz and clarinetist Buddy DeFranco among others. Bop collectors will have to get this one. —*Scott Yanow*

Bud Powell Trio Plays / Jan. 10, 1947+1953 / Roulette ✦✦✦✦✦

All of the music on this single CD is included in the Blue Note four-CD, "complete" set (the best way to acquire these important performances); however, listeners who do not have the larger reissue will not go wrong by getting this CD. The first eight selections (which find the pianist joined by bassist Curley Russell and drummer Max Roach) are from Bud Powell's first trio date and he is in prime form on such numbers as "I'll Remember April," "Someboy Loves Me" and "Bud's Bubble." The second session (with bassist George Duvivier and drummer Art Taylor in 1953) does not quite reach the same heights, but it does contain some fine playing from the founder of bop piano. —*Scott Yanow*

★ **Complete Blue Note and Roost Recordings** / Jan. 10, 1947–Dec. 29, 1958 / Blue Note ✦✦✦✦✦
Although pianist Bud Powell recorded some great albums elsewhere (most notably his first couple of sessions for Verve), on a whole his Blue Note records were his most significant and definitive. This four-CD set has all of the music from his five Blue Note albums, his two sessions for the Roost label and all known alternate takes. Powell literally changed the way that the piano is played in jazz and this magnificent set has more than its share of classics. In addition to the many trio performances, trombonist Curtis Fuller sits in on three numbers, there are a few solo cuts and one date features Powell at the head of a quintet with trumpeter Fats Navarro and the young tenor Sonny Rollins. Although there are a few faltering moments in the later dates, this essential release (unlike the similar Verve reissue) is quite consistent. — *Scott Yanow*

New York All Star Sessions / Dec. 19, 1948–1957 / Bandstand ✦✦✦✦
This LP contains a variety of live recordings featuring pianist Bud Powell, mostly during his prime years. Three of the selections (from a Christmas 1949 Carnegie Hall Concert) have been reissued on CD by Jass, but otherwise the performances are quite rare. Highlights include a version of "Dance of the Infidels" from 1953 with Charlie Parker, "Woody 'n You" from the same year with Dizzy Gillespie and two songs from a Dec. 1948 all-star group that includes trumpeter Benny Harris, trombonist J.J. Johnson, clarinetist Buddy DeFranco and altoist Lee Konitz. Although not essential, this collector's LP should greatly interest bop fans. — *Scott Yanow*

Complete Bud Powell On Verve / Jan. 1949–Sep. 13, 1956 / Verve ✦✦✦✦✦
This five-CD deluxe set contains an impressive 150-page booklet and reissues every scrap of music that the innovative pianist Bud Powell recorded for Verve. The first disc has the best music, four truly outstanding sessions from 1949–51. The other performances (trio sides from 1954–56) are much more erratic, particularly the alternate takes, with gems followed by completely lost solos. Bop fans will want this set, but more general collectors are advised to pick up The Blue Notes first. — *Scott Yanow*

★ **The Amazing Bud Powell, Vol. 1** / Aug. 8, 1949–May 1, 1951 / Blue Note ✦✦✦✦✦
The CD reissue of the two LPs titled *The Amazing Bud Powell* puts the important recordings in chronological order (which it wasn't in the LP version) and adds some alternate takes; all of the music has also been included in a definitive four-CD box set. Although the latter is the best way to acquire the important performances, this CD gives one a strong sampling of pianist Bud Powell at his best. Powell is heard on a classic session with trumpeter Fats Navarro and tenor saxophonist Sonny Rollins (which is highlighted by exciting versions of "Dance of the Infidels," "52nd Street Theme" and "Bouncing with Bud") and in a trio for "Over the Rainbow" and three versions of his intense "Un Poco Loco." — *Scott Yanow*

The Complete Bud Powell Blue Note Recordings (1949–1958) / Aug. 8, 1949–Dec. 29, 1958 / Mosaic ✦✦✦✦✦
The Amazing Bud Powell, Vol. 2 / May 1, 1951–Aug. 14, 1953 / Blue Note ✦✦✦✦
These two CD volumes (all of the music has also been reissued on a definitive "complete" Blue Note Bud Powell four-CD set) differ from the original two LPs in that, in addition to the inclusion of some alternate takes, they are programmed in strict chronological order. The influential bebop pioneer (who not only set the standard for bop pianists but largely invented the style) is heard on fine trio performances from 1951 (with bassist Curly Russell and drummer Max Roach) and 1953 (during which he is matched with bassist George Duvivier and drummer Art Taylor). Highlights include "A Night in Tunisia," "Reets and I," "I Want to Be Happy" and "Glass Enclosure." — *Scott Yanow*

Inner Fires / Apr. 5, 1953 / Elektra ✦✦✦✦
This LP features two performances by pianist Bud Powell, bassist Charles Mingus and drummer Roy Haynes that were recorded live at a Washington, D.C., club; they were released for the first time in 1982. Powell is in consistently exciting form (this was one of his good nights) and the musicians sound inspired and creative during the set of bop-oriented standards. This now-out-of-print LP concludes with a couple of excerpts from Bud Powell interviews held in 1963, giving listeners a rare chance to hear his voice. — *Scott Yanow*

Jazz at Massey Hall, Vol. 2 / May 15, 1953 / Original Jazz Classics ✦✦✦✦
This is the less famous half of the May 15, 1953 Massey Hall concert. These are the trio (Charles Mingus, bass; Max Roach, drums) sides that were also on a prior Prestige two-fer…On the record as a whole, the brilliance comes overwhelmingly from Powell. — *Bob Rusch, Cadence*

Burning in the USA (1953–1955) / 1953–Sep. 1955 / Mythic Sound ✦✦✦
The second of ten CDs of previously unknown and privately recorded Bud Powell performances released by his friend Francis Paudras has a variety of rewarding and fairly exciting renditions. Most of the selections (from 1953 and 1955) are with trios (often matching the pianist with bassist Oscar Pettiford and Art Blakey or Roy Haynes on drums), but there is a rare outing with a big band ("Big Band Blues") and two selections ("Woody 'n You" and "Salt Peanuts") with trumpeter Dizzy Gillespie, bassist Charles Mingus and drummer Max Roach that are listed as being recorded at the famous Massey Hall concert in 1953; the year is right but the location is probably wrong since that concert was fully documented by the Debut label. Bud Powell fanatics are advised to search for all ten of the Mythic Sound releases, although more general listeners should pick and choose; this is not one of the most essential ones. — *Scott Yanow*

Strictly Powell / Oct. 5, 1956 / RCA ✦✦✦
Time Was / Oct. 5, 1956+Feb. 11, 1957 / Bluebird ✦✦✦
Pianist Bud Powell's two recording sessions for Victor during 1956–57 resulted in 22 selections; this CD contains 18 of them. Powell was not in the best of shape during this period and he is erratic in these trio outings with bassist George Duvivier and drummer Art Taylor. Quite frequently a brilliant chorus is followed by one in which Powell gets lost, making the performances very interesting, to say the least. — *Scott Yanow*

Swingin' with Bud / Feb. 11, 1957 / RCA ✦✦✦
The Amazing Bud Powell, Vol. 3 / Aug. 3, 1957 / Blue Note ✦✦✦✦✦
Bud Powell's playing in the late '50s (just prior to his move to Paris) found the troubled pianist in erratic form, often struggling to make it through songs he had written. However, his three Blue Note recordings from the era (which include the slightly later *Time Waits* and *The Scene Changes*) feature Powell in surprisingly inspired form; all of the releases have since been reissued on a comprehensive CD set. *Bud!* (which is subtitled *The Amazing Bud Powell, Vol. 3*) has five trio performances with bassist Paul Chambers and drummer Art Taylor (highlighted by "Bud on Bach" and "Some Soul") and three standards on which the group is joined by trombonist Curtis Fuller. This strong bop set is well worth getting. — *Scott Yanow*

Cookin' at Saint Germain (1957–1959) / 1957–1959 / Mythic Sound ✦✦✦✦
For the third of ten CDs taken from tapes donated by Francis Paudras, pianist Bud Powell is heard in generally excellent form. Most of his performances (all of which were recorded in Paris in 1957 or 1959) feature the bebop innovator in a trio with bassist Pierre Michelot and drummer Kenny Clarke; four of the songs add the always-joyous trumpet of Clark Terry and three of those pieces also feature Barney Wilen on tenor. The sound quality is decent and Bud Powell was definitely "on" for these jams. — *Scott Yanow*

Groovin' at the Blue Note (1959–1961) / 1957–Dec. 17, 1961 / Mythic Sound ✦✦✦✦
The fifth of ten Bud Powell CDs taken from the private tapes of Francis Paudras features the innovative pianist in fine form. Best are three selections (over half of the music) on which Powell, bassist Pierre Michelot and drummer Kenny Clarke are joined by the always-swinging tenor Zoot Sims. All of the music on this release was recorded at the Blue Note club in Paris including a version of "How High the Moon" from 1957 that has trumpeter Dizzy Gillespie and Barney Wilen on tenor making Powell's trio a quintet. This is one of the better releases in the valuable series. — *Scott Yanow*

Time Waits / May 25, 1958 / Blue Note ✦✦✦✦
This set from pianist Bud Powell (which has been reissued on CD in a "complete" four-CD set) is most notable for having the debut versions of seven of Powell's compositions; most memorable are "Time Waits," "Monopoly" and especially "John's Abbey." With

bassist Sam Jones and drummer Philly Joe Jones completing the trio, Powell is in surprisingly fine form throughout the enjoyable session, creating music that is far superior to his later Verve recordings. —*Scott Yanow*

The Scene Changes / Dec. 29, 1958 / Blue Note ✦✦✦✦
This CD reissue of pianist Bud Powell's final Blue Note session (the music is also available in a definitive four-CD set) adds an alternate take of "Comin' Up" to the original nine-song program; all are Powell originals. While none of the tunes caught on as standards, most (particularly "Cleopatra's Dream," "Crossin' the Channel" and "The Scene Changes") are memorable. All of Bud Powell's Blue Note records (including this trio outing with bassist Paul Chambers and drummer Art Taylor) feature the innovative pianist in top form. —*Scott Yanow*

Bud in Paris / Dec. 12, 1959–Oct. 14, 1960 / Xanadu ✦✦✦
Pianist Bud Powell's move to France in 1959 helped revive his career, getting him away from the pressures and temptations of New York and probably lengthening his life by a few years. This Xanadu LP features some privately recorded performances with his trio (which includes bassist Pierre Michelot and drummer Kenny Clarke), a pair of heated duets ("Idaho" and "Perdido") with tenor great Johnny Griffin and four quartets with the tenor of Barney Wilen (along with Michelot and Clarke). The recording quality is decent if not of studio quality, but the passion in the playing generally comes through and Powell's fans will want to search for this one. —*Scott Yanow*

● **The Complete Essen Jazz Festival Concert** / Apr. 2, 1960 / Black Lion ✦✦✦✦✦
Pianist Bud Powell is heard in top form throughout this CD, playing six selections with his all-star trio (which also includes bassist Oscar Pettiford and drummer Kenny Clarke) and three songs on which the trio is joined by the great tenor Coleman Hawkins. There is plenty of classic bebop throughout the concert performance with Powell mostly sticking to standards (along with his original "John's Abbey"); Hawkins is best on "Stuffy." This release is recommended as a fine example of the playing of these classic masters. —*Scott Yanow*

A Portrait of Thelonious / Dec. 17, 1961 / Sony France ✦✦✦✦
This LP is one of the most rewarding Bud Powell recordings to come from his period in France. Powell (along with bassist Pierre Michelot and drummer Kenny Clarke) explores four of Thelonious Monk's tunes, Earl Bostic's "No Name Blues" and the standard "There Will Never Be Another Day," but it is the final two numbers ("I Ain't Foolin' " and "Squatty") that really find the bop master at his most spirited and swinging. This is a superior release long overdue to be reissued on CD. —*Scott Yanow*

Relaxin' at Home (1961–1964) / 1961–1964 / Mythic Sound ✦✦
The fourth of ten CDs in the Mythic Sound series of privately recorded Bud Powell performances is the least significant. Powell is heard playing solo piano quite loosely at Francis Paudras' home, the recording quality is erratic and (despite some creative outbursts) some of the selections are throwaways. From a historic standpoint there are a few unique renditions including Powell playing (and singing) "The Christmas Song" and a brief version of "La Marseillaise." But overall, this CD is strictly for Bud Powell completists. —*Scott Yanow*

Round Midnight At The Blue Note / 1962 / Dreyfus ✦✦✦
The music on this CD (released for the first time in 1994) features a group accurately dubbed "the Three Bosses." Comprised of pianist Bud Powell, bassist Pierre Michelot and drummer Kenny Clarke, this was a tight trio that lived up to its potential. The innovative pianist is in excellent form, performing four Thelonious Monk tunes along with four jazz standards. Highpoints include "Shaw Nuff" and "Night in Tunisia." The only problem is the brevity of this CD, which, at 35 minutes, should have been twice as long. —*Scott Yanow*

Bouncing with Bud / Apr. 26, 1962 / Delmark ✦✦✦✦
This Delmark LP is an excellent set by the great pianist Bud Powell in a trio with the teenage bassist Niels Pederson and drummer William Shiopffe. Recored in Copenhagen, the session features Powell exploring seven bop standards (including his own "Bouncing with Bud") and "The Best Thing for You." All eight selections (which put the emphasis on faster material other than "I Remember Clifford") showcase Bud Powell during his European renaissance period, giving pianists a definitive lesson in playing bop. —*Scott Yanow*

Writin' for Duke (1963) / Feb. 1963 / Mythic Sound ✦✦✦
In Feb. 1963 Duke Ellington sponsored a Reprise recording date by Bud Powell (in a trio with bassist Gilbert Rovere and drummer Kansas Fields) that resulted in the album *Bud in Paris*. This set, released as part of Mythic Sound's ten-CD series of privately recorded sessions featuring the innovative bop pianist, is comprised of outtakes and previously unreleased songs from that studio date. There are many highlights to the excellent session including performances of some of Powell's lesser-known originals ("Bud's Blue Bossa," "Tune for Duke," "For My Friends," "Get It Back," "Trapped," "Free" and "Rue De Clichy"), a few of which deserve to be revived. Also memorable are an emotional "I Got It Bad" and a strong version of "Dear Old Stockholm." —*Scott Yanow*

Bud Powell in Paris / Feb. 1963 / Reprise ✦✦✦✦
Considering how late it was in his career, Bud Powell was in surprisingly good spirits at this live session with bassist Gilbert Rovere and drummer Kansas Fields. The innovative pianist stretches out on nine bop standards including two he had written ("Reets and I" and "Parisian Thoroughfare"); in addition, there are previously unreleased versions of "Indiana" and "B-Flat Blues." Far superior to most of his 1955–58 sessions, this was one of Powell's best late-period recordings; he is in near-prime form throughout. —*Scott Yanow*

Strictly Confidential / 1963–1964 / Black Lion ✦✦
These informal performances find the great but ill-fated pianist Bud Powell playing a series of relaxed solos in Francis Paudras' apartment in Paris. The recording quality is just ok, and there are some missteps in Powell's solos, but there are also moments of interest, particularly his striding on a few of the numbers. This CD is particularly recommended to Bud Powell collectors, although more general listeners should pick up his Blue Notes first. —*Scott Yanow*

The Invisible Cage / Jul. 31, 1964 / Black Lion ✦✦✦
This rather late Bud Powell session is better than expected and probably his last worthwhile recording. Performed shortly before he returned to New York and only two years prior to his death, Powell is at his best on the uptempo material and at his most erratic on the intense ballads. Accompanied ably by bassist Michel Gaudry and drummer Art Taylor, the innovative pianist (even with a few missteps) is mostly in excellent form, particularly on "Like Someone in Love," "Blues for Bouffemont" and his calypso "Una Noche con Francis." —*Scott Yanow*

Blues for Bouffemont / Jul. 1964–Aug. 1964 / Black Lion ✦✦✦
Teeming, sometimes ragged but always blistering piano tracks from Bud Powell, recorded in 1964. These were done in recognition of Powell's stint at the Bouffemont facility following his near breakdown. He and drummer Art Taylor are the dominant musicians, while either Michel Gaudray or Guy Hayat on bass and other drummer Jacques Gervais are competent, but not in Powell's or Taylor's class. —*Ron Wynn*

Salt Peanuts / Aug. 1964 / Black Lion ✦✦✦
In Aug. 1964 pianist Bud Powell and his friend/guardian Francis Paudras went on vacation to Edenville on the coast of France. Powell played at a small club each night in a very relaxed atmosphere. This CD contains some of the performances, four songs with a trio (that includes bassist Guy Hayat and drummer Jacques Gervais) and, best of all, three hot numbers that feature tenor great Johnny Griffin, who makes the group a quartet. The recording quality is a little erratic on this set, but Powell often sounds quite inspired. —*Scott Yanow*

Holidays in Edenville (1964) / Aug. 10, 1964–Aug. 12, 1964 / Mythic Sound ✦✦✦
On the eighth of ten CDs in Mythic Sound's valuable series of privately recorded Bud Powell performances, the masterful pianist is heard playing informally in a small club on the coast of France shortly before he made the fatal decision to return to the United States. These previously unreleased selections feature Powell with a young trio (bassist Guy Hayat and drummer Jacques Gervais) and (on two of the ten songs including a 17-minute version of "Hot House") joyfully welcoming the great tenor Johnny Griffin to the bandstand. The recording quality is sometimes a little erratic, but Powell is in suprisingly strong form this late in his career; this set should be checked out by bop collectors. —*Scott Yanow*

Award at Birdland (1964) / Oct. 1, 1964 / Mythic Sound ✦✦✦
When pianist Bud Powell returned to the United States after five

Music Map

Piano

Ragtime
Scott Joplin
Tony Jackson
Eubie Blake

New Orleans Jazz Innovator
Jelly Roll Morton

Stride Piano
James P. Johnson   Fats Waller   Luckey Roberts
Donald Lambert   Cliff Jackson   Herman Chittison

Stride Pianists Who Later Became Modern
Duke Ellington   Mary Lou Williams

Boogie-Woogie
Jimmy Yancey   Albert Ammons
Pete Johnson   Meade Lux Lewis

Unclassifiable Innovators
Earl Hines   Art Tatum

Swing
Teddy Wilson   Joe Sullivan   Jess Stacy
Bob Zurke   Count Basie   Billy Kyle
Nat King Cole   Mel Powell   Eddie Heywood
Jay McShann   Johnny Guarnieri

Founder of Bop Piano
Bud Powell

Bop
George Wallington   Al Haig   Duke Jordan
Dodo Marmarosa   Hampton Hawes   Joe Albany

Very Individual Pianists Beyond Bop
Thelonious Monk   Erroll Garner
Lennie Tristano   Oscar Peterson

1950s
Dave Brubeck   John Lewis
George Shearing   Hank Jones
Barry Harris   Tommy Flanagan
Roland Hanna   Billy Taylor
Lou Levy   Russ Freeman
Claude Williamson   Pete Jolly
Jimmy Rowles   Marian McPartland
Ellis Larkins   Elmo Hope
Walter Bishop Jr   Walter Davis
Kenny Drew   Red Garland
Wynton Kelly   Sonny Clark
Phineas Newborn   Gerald Wiggins
Ray Bryant   Mal Waldron
Randy Weston   Martial Solal
Ahmad Jamal

Funky Hard Bop
Horace Silver   Bobby Timmons
Les McCann   Ramsey Lewis
Junior Mance   Gene Harris

Revival
Art Hodes   Wally Rose
Ralph Sutton   Dick Wellstood
Dick Hyman   Johnny Varro
Dave McKenna   Dave Frisberg
James Dapogny   Judy Carmichael
Reginald Robinson

Avant-Garde
Cecil Taylor   Herbie Nichols
Paul Bley   Sun Ra
Andrew Hill   Ran Blake
Horace Tapscott   Muhal Richard Abrams
Dave Burrell   Don Pullen
Misha Mengelberg   Anthony Davis
Amina Claudine Myers   Vyacheslav Ganelin
Giorgio Gaslini   Irene Schweizer
Yosuke Yamashita   Marilyn Crispell
Myra Melford   Alexander Von Schlippenbach

Post Bop
Herbie Hancock   Chick Corea
Keith Jarrett   Cedar Walton
Kenny Barron   Jaki Byard
Monty Alexander   Walter Norris
Toshiko Akiyoshi   Steve Kuhn
Roger Kellaway   Horace Parlan
Clare Fischer   Mike Garson
Abdullah Ibrahim   Kirk Lightsey
Tete Montoliu   Alan Broadbent
Joanne Brackeen   Richie Beirach
Adam Makowicz   Hal Galper
George Cables   James Williams
Donald Brown   Larry Willis
Harold Mabern   Stanley Cowell
John Hicks   Michel Petrucciani
Mulgrew Miller   Hilton Ruiz
Danilo Perez   Geri Allen
Michele Rosewoman   Billy Childs
Bill Cunliffe   Fred Hersch
Kenny Kirkland   Benny Green
Geoff Keezer   Marcus Roberts
Jim McNeely   Renee Rosnes
Cyrus Chestnut   Stephen Scott
Jacky Terasson   Kenny Drew, Jr.
Gonzalo Rubalcaba

relatively happy years in France, he played a successful engagement at Birdland and then had a quick decline before passing away in 1966. This CD from the Mythic Sound label was Powell's last hurrah (he would only record one more studio album in his career) and it features him playing in a trio with bassist John Ore and drummer J.C. Moses at Birdland. The set begins with Powell receiving an obscure award (and saying a few words) before he performs a dozen numbers; all are standards except for his own "Monopoly." Although not the strongest Bud Powell set available (and the recording quality is quite erratic), this interesting release hints at what might have been and shows that Powell could still play well this late in his troubled life. —Scott Yanow

Ups and Downs / 1964–1965 / Mainstream ✦✦
This CD reissue of the Mainstream LP states in Nat Hentoff's liner notes that the performances are from the mid-'50s and that pianist Bud Powell is heard at the peak of his powers. Wrong on both counts. Actually, this set is comprised of Powell's final recordings, dating from late 1964 to early 1965, shortly following his return to New York after several years of relative security in Paris. The great bop innovator had declined greatly since his prime days, but actually plays better than one might expect. The bassist and drummer have never been identified. This set is important historically, but obviously there are many more rewarding Bud Powell recordings to acquire first. —Scott Yanow

Mel Powell (Melvin Epstein)

b. Feb. 12, 1923, New York, NY
Piano, Arranger / Swing
One of the finest swing pianists and a prodigy, Mel Powell was playing piano and writing important arrangements for Benny Goodman by the time he was 18. He had previously played with Bobby Hackett, George Brunis and Zutty Singleton (1939), was the intermission pianist at Nick's and worked in the short-lived Muggsy Spanier big band. During his stay with BG, when he and the clarinetist struck up a lifelong friendship; among his arrangements for Goodman were "The Earl," "Mission to Moscow," "Clarinade" and "Jersey Bounce."

After a period working for the CBS orchestra under Raymond Scott (1942), Powell was one of the stars of the Glenn Miller Army Air Force Band. Powell, whose style was reminiscent of Teddy Wilson's, recorded with Goodman during 1945–47, led a few record dates (his first one was in 1942) and worked in the studios. However, after studying with Paul Hindemith at Yale (1952), he switched his career and became a classical composer. Powell did record some superior jazz dates for Vanguard during 1953–55 and sat in with Bobby Hackett in the mid-'60s, but was otherwise occupied completely outside of jazz. After decades of work as a well-respected serial composer, Mel Powell returned to jazz for cruises in 1986 and 1987 that were recorded by Chiaroscuro. However, a muscular disease in his legs has since knocked him out of action. —Scott Yanow

● **Unavailable Mel Powell** / Dec. 10, 1947–Dec. 31, 1947 / PA/USA ✦✦✦✦✦
Return of Mel Powell / Oct. 21, 1987 / Chiaroscuro ✦✦✦✦

Chano Pozo

b. Jan. 7, 1915, Havana, Cuba, **d.** Dec. 2, 1948, New York, NY
Percussion / Afro-Cuban Jazz
Chano Pozo played a major role in the founding of Latin-jazz which was essentially a mixture of bebop and Cuban folk music. He gained his musical background from Cuban religious cults. After moving to New York in 1947, he met Dizzy Gillespie who enthusiastically added him to his bebop big band. Among his features with Dizzy were "Cubana Be, Cubana Bop," "Tin Tin Deo" and "Manteca"; Pozo co-wrote the latter two. Unfortunately, Chano Pozo had a hot temper and he was killed in a Harlem bar a month shy of his 34th birthday. —Scott Yanow

Andre Previn (Andreas Ludwig Priwin)

b. Apr. 6, 1929, Berlin, Germany
Piano / Cool
A conductor and classical pianist of immense standing, Andre Previn has also amassed some impressive jazz credentials. While not among the most spectacular or dazzling stylists and certainly not a great soloist, Previn has nonetheless made many creditable recordings and enjoyed major crossover successes.

He started piano lessons as a child in his native Berlin, and

later was booted out of the Conservatory in a blatant anti-Semitic incident. His family immediately went to Paris, and then to Los Angeles after they received their visas. Previn played piano and did the score for a Jose Iturbi film at 16. He split time between classical, film and jazz material until he was drafted in the early '50s, and stationed in San Francisco. Previn scored numerous films in the '50s, '60s and early '70s, among them Oscar winners *Gigi, Porgy and Bess, Irma La Douce,* and *My Fair Lady.* During the '40s, '50s and '60s, Previn made over 20 trio albums ranging from Fats Waller material to jazz versions of Broadway shows. The trio of Previn, Leroy Vinnegar and Shelly Manne struck commercial gold with *My Fair Lady,* in 1956. Previn had a string of albums make the charts in the '60s, among them *Like Love, A Touch of Elegance, Andre Previn in Hollywood,* and a remake of *My Fair Lady.*

He concentrated on conducting and classical music during much of the mid and late '60s and through the '70s. But Previn returned to jazz in the early '80s, working with Manne and Monty Budwig, cutting an album of rags with Itzhak Perlman, and working in a quintet with Perlmann, Red Mitchell, Manne and Jim Hall on the session *A Different Kind of Blue* that again resulted in a Previn date making the pop charts. This group did another album in 1981, and Previn recorded with Ella Fitzgerald and Niels-Henning Orsted Pedersen in 1983. He teamed with Ray Brown and Mundell Lowe for a jazz date and with Thomas Stevens for a repertory set of pre-rock standards in the '90s. Previn has many dates available on CD. —*Ron Wynn and Michael G. Nastos*

★ **Previn At Sunset** / Oct. 13, 1945–May 31, 1946 / Black Lion ✦✦✦✦✦
Andre Previn Plays Fats Waller / Jun. 24, 1953 / Tops ✦✦✦
Li'l Abner / Feb. 6, 1957 / Contemporary ✦✦✦
Double Play! / Apr. 30, 1957+May 11, 1957 / Original Jazz Classics ✦✦✦✦
Pianists Andre Previn and Russ Freeman team up with drummer Shelly Manne in a trio to play eight of their originals (along with the standard "Take Me out to the Ball Game"), all given titles having to do with baseball. This was advertised as the first time that two pianists recorded what was then modern jazz together. Previn and Freeman had very complementary styles, making it difficult to know who was playing when, although a complete play-by-play is included. —*Scott Yanow*

Pal Joey / Oct. 28, 1957–Oct. 29, 1957 / Original Jazz Classics ✦✦✦✦
Gigi / Apr. 7, 1958–Apr. 8, 1958 / Original Jazz Classics ✦✦✦
Andre Previn Plays Vernon Duke / Aug. 12, 1958–Aug. 30, 1958 / Contemporary ✦✦✦✦

● **Jazz: King Size** / Nov. 26, 1958 / Original Jazz Classics ✦✦✦✦✦
The multitalented Andre Previn is heard on this straight CD reissue of a Contemporary LP as the leader of a trio with bassist Red Mitchell and drummer Frankie Capp. Previn always had his own swing/bop piano style and he is in top form on two of his originals (including the bluish "Much Too Late") and four superior standards. This fine release gives one an excellent example of Previn's skills as a jazz pianist. —*Scott Yanow*

Andre Previn Plays Jerome Kern / Feb. 26, 1959+Mar. 10, 1959 / Original Jazz Classics ✦✦✦✦✦
For this solo piano session (a Contemporary date which has been reissued on CD), the remarkably versatile Andre Previn interprets ten Jerome Kern songs including several ("Sure Thing," "WhipPoor-Will," "Go Little Boat" and "Put Me to the Test") that are quite obscure. Sometimes he treats the melodies with great respect while other performances find him stretching the themes and coming up with fresh variations; "They Didn't Believe Me" is a highpoint. This is a well-rounded set with plenty of surprises along with consistently tasteful playing, one of Previn's better jazz efforts. —*Scott Yanow*

West Side Story / Aug. 24, 1959–Aug. 25, 1959 / Original Jazz Classics ✦✦✦✦
Like Previn! / Feb. 20, 1960–Mar. 1, 1960 / Original Jazz Classics ✦✦✦✦
This trio set for Contemporary (reissued on CD in the OJC series) differs from other Andre Previn sessions in that all eight of the selections were composed by the pianist. With fine assistance from bassist Red Mitchell and drummer Frankie Capp, Previn is in con-

sistently swinging form on his originals and, even if none of the songs caught on, they make for a solid and varied set of bop-oriented music. —*Scott Yanow*

Andre Previn Plays Harold Arlen / May 4, 1960–May 5, 1960 / Original Jazz Classics ✦✦✦
This solo piano set from Andre Previn is a bit unusual for he recasts ten Harold Arlen compositions (all but "For Every Man There's a Woman" and "Cocoanut Sweet" are quite well-known) by reharmonizing the chords and modernizing the melodies. Most of the songs are taken at slow tempos and the set (which has been reissued on CD) has a consistently melancholy and thoughtful mood throughout. —*Scott Yanow*

A Touch of Elegance / Nov. 9, 1960–Dec. 18, 1962 / Columbia/Legacy ✦✦✦
This CD draws its material from five of pianist Andre Previn's Columbia albums of the 1961–62 period. Three of the five albums (13 of the 18 selections on this sampler) feature Previn's piano backed by string orchestras on well-played but easy-listening music that rarely wanders from the melody. Two other songs are taken from a quartet set with trombonist J.J. Johnson while three pieces feature guitarist Herb Ellis. These are more adventurous, but overall the music on this CD is overly safe; tasteful but predictable. —*Scott Yanow*

Uptown / Mar. 9, 1990–Mar. 10, 1990 / Telarc ✦✦✦✦

Old Friends / Aug. 24, 1991 / Telarc ✦✦✦✦
Superb trio recordings that marked the return of well-known classical conductor Andre Previn to intimate jazz recording. He teamed with bassist Ray Brown and guitarist Mundell Lowe, and the three complemented each other expertly, while their solos were tasteful and concise. —*Ron Wynn*

What Headphones? / Oct. 5, 1993 / Angel ✦✦✦

Plays Show Boat / 1995 / Deutsche Grammophon ✦✦✦✦
Performing in a style a bit reminiscent of Oscar Peterson, pianist Andre Previn plays eight selections from the play *Show Boat*, six of which are standards plus the obscure "Life on the Wicked Stage" and "I Might Fall Back on You." In addition Previn contributed three newer pieces with the uptempo blues "Lickety Split" having his most impressive solo. Although the partly bitonal treatment given the usually sweet "Make Believe" takes a bit away from the memorable melody, Previn's interpretations of the other pieces are melodic, respectful and swinging. Guitarist Mundell Lowe has an occasional solo and bassist Ray Brown and drummer Grady Tate are typically excellent in support. This fine bop oriented date shows that Andre Previn (who has spent most of the past three decades in the classical music world) is still the top part-time jazz pianist around! —*Scott Yanow*

Bobby Previte

b. Jul. 16, 1957, Niagara Falls, NY
Drums / Avant-Garde
An adventurous drummer and bandleader, Bobby Previte's open-minded approach has resulted in some consistently stimulating (if unpredictable) music with some of New York's finest including John Zorn, Bill Frisell and Wayne Horvitz. His 1990 set of music for the Moscow Circus is particularly memorable. Previte has recorded as a leader for Gramavision, Sound Aspects and Enja, heading such groups as Empty Suits and Weather Clear, Track Fast. —*Scott Yanow*

Bump the Renaissance / Jun. 1985 / Sound Aspects ✦✦✦✦

Claude's Late Morning / 1988 / Gramavision ✦✦✦✦✦

Empty Suits / May 1990 / Gramavision ✦✦✦✦

Weather Clear Track Fast / Jan. 7, 1991–Jan. 8, 1991 / Enja ✦✦✦✦✦

● **Music of the Moscow Circus** / Aug. 1991 / Gramavision ✦✦✦✦✦

Hue & Cry / Dec. 1993 / Enja ✦✦✦✦

Ruth Price

b. Apr. 27, 1938, Phoenixville, PA
Vocals / Standards
A talented singer whose wide expressive qualities do justice to any lyrics that she chooses to interpret, Ruth Price has made relatively few recordings throughout her career. Originally a dancer, she attended ballet school in 1952. However, by 1954 she was singing with Charlie Ventura and, after freelancing in

Philadelphia, she worked as a singer and dancer in New York. Price moved to Hollywood in 1957, recorded a fine album with Shelly Manne (which has been reissued in the Original Jazz Classics series) but did not cut her second album as a leader until 1983 (for ITI). She toured with Harry James (1964–65), but in recent years has become best-known for running one of Los Angeles' top jazz clubs, the Jazz Bakery. —*Scott Yanow*

● **Ruth Price with Shelly Manne at the Manne-Hole** / Mar. 3, 1961–Mar. 5, 1961 / Original Jazz Classics ✦✦✦✦✦
Singer Ruth Price on this early set falls somewhere between swinging jazz, middle-of-the-road pop and cabaret. She does not improvise much, but her strong and very appealing voice uplifts the diverse material that she interprets (including "Dearly Beloved," "Shadrack," "Crazy He Calls Me" and "Look for the Silver Lining") and she brings great sincerity to Leonard Bernstein's "Who Am I." Backed by Shelly Manne's Quintet (with plenty heard from pianist Russ Freeman, but just guest spots by Richie Kamuca on tenor and one lone appearance by trumpeter Conte Candoli), Price is in fine form for her debut recording as a leader, which has been reissued on CD in the *OJC* series. —*Scott Yanow*

Lucky to Be Me / Jan. 1983 / ITI ✦✦✦✦

Sammy Price

b. Oct. 6, 1980, Honey Grove, TX, d. Apr. 14, 1992, New York, NY
Piano / Blues, Boogie-Woogie, Swing, Early R&B
Sammy Price had a long and productive career as a flexible blues and boogie-woogie-based pianist. He studied piano in Dallas and was a singer and dancer with Alphonso Trent's band during 1927–30. In 1929 he recorded one solitary side under the title of "Sammy Price and his Four Quarters." After a few years in Kansas City, he spent time in Chicago and Detroit. In 1938 Price became the house pianist for Decca in New York and appeared on many blues sides with such singers as Trixie Smith and Sister Rosetta Tharpe. He led his own band on records in the early '40s, which included (on one memorable session) Lester Young. Price worked steadily on 52nd Street, in 1948 played at the Nice Festival with Mezz Mezzrow, spent time back in Texas and then a decade with Red Allen; he was also heard on many rock & roll-type sessions in the 1950s. In later years he recorded with Doc Cheatham, and Sammy Price was active until near his death, 63 years after his recording debut. —*Scott Yanow*

● **Sam Price 1929–1941** / Sep. 29, 1929–Dec. 10, 1941 / Classics ✦✦✦✦

Rib Joint/Roots of Rock & Roll / Oct. 17, 1956–Mar. 24, 1959 / Savoy ✦✦✦✦
Great mid-'50s instrumental R&B with Price's 88s abetted by King Curtis on sax and guitarist Mickey Baker. —*Bill Dahl*

Barrelhouse and Blues / Dec. 4, 1969 / Black Lion ✦✦✦

Sweet Substitute / Nov. 1, 1979 / Sackville ✦✦✦✦

Paradise Valley Duets / Feb. 26, 1988–Feb. 28, 1988 / Parkwood ✦✦✦✦✦
Recorded live in Windsor, this album features J.C. Heard (d), George Benson (g), and Marcus Belgrave (tpt) playing nine standards and one blues from Price and Belgrave. This is a delight. One whole side features Price and the legendary drummer Heard. Precious Texas piano stomps & jazz. —*Michael G. Nastos*

Julian Priester

b. Jun. 29, 1935, Chicago
Trombone / Avant-Garde, Hard Bop
Julian Priester has long been a flexible and adventurous trombonist who has not yet achieved the fame he deserved. He originally studied piano, baritone horn and finally trombone. Prior to moving to New York in 1958 he worked with Muddy Waters, Bo Diddley, Sun Ra (1954–56), Lionel Hampton and Dinah Washington (1957). Priester gained recognition for his playing with Max Roach (1958–61) during a period when the drummer often used Booker Little and Eric Dolphy. He played in a wide variety of settings throughout the 1960s including six months with Duke Ellington (1969–70). Priester's highest profile gig was with Herbie Hancock's sextet during 1970–73 with whom he toured and recorded. Moving to San Francisco in the mid-'70s, he experimented with electronic music while still playing trombone, recording with Stanley Cowell and Red Garland. Most of the first half of the 1990s was spent with Dave Holland's quintet and, later in the decade, he worked with George Gruntz and Sun Ra. —*Scott Yanow*

● **Keep Swinging** / Jan. 11, 1960 / Original Jazz Classics ✦✦✦✦
Trombonist Julian Priester sounds very much under the influence
of J.J. Johnson during his debut as a leader, a Riverside date reissued on CD in the Original Jazz Classic series. The repertoire is
comprised of four Priester originals, one apiece by Jimmy Heath
(whose tenor makes the group a quintet on five of the eight songs)
and baritonist Charles Davis, and two standards. Priester is heard
in his early prime on a warm version of "Once in a While" and
plays solid hard bop with pianist Tommy Flanagan, bassist Sam
Jones, drummer Elvin Jones and sometimes Heath on this swinging modern mainstream session. —*Scott Yanow*

Love, Love / Jun. 28, 1974–Sep. 12, 1974 / ECM ✦✦✦

Polarization / Jan. 1977 / ECM ✦✦✦

Louis Prima

b. Dec. 7, 1911, New Orleans, LA, d. Aug. 24, 1978, New Orleans,
LA
Trumpet, Vocals / Dixieland, Swing, Early R&B
Louis Prima became very famous in the 1950s with an infectious
Las Vegas act co-starring his wife (singer Keely Smith) that mixed
together R&B (particularly the honking tenor of Sam Butera),
early rock & roll, comedy and Dixieland. Always a colorful personality, Prima was leading a band in New Orleans when he was
just 11. In 1934 he began recording as a leader with a Dixieland-
oriented unit and soon he was a major attraction on 52nd Street.
His early records often featured George Brunies and Eddie
Miller, and Pee Wee Russell was a regular member of his groups
during 1935–36. Prima, who composed "Sing, Sing, Sing" (which
for a period was his theme song), recorded steadily through the
swing era, had a big band in the 1940s and achieved hits in
"Angelina" and "Robin Hood." In 1954 he began having great success in his latter-day group (their recordings on Capitol were big-
sellers and still sound joyous today), emphasizing vocals and
Butera's tenor, but he still took spirited trumpet solos. Although he
eventually broke up with Keely Smith, Louis Prima (who played a
character in Walt Disney's animated film *The Jungle Book* in 1966)
remained a popular attraction into the 1970s. —*Scott Yanow*

Play Pretty for the People / 1940 / Savoy ✦✦✦✦

★ **Capitol Collectors Series** / Apr. 19, 1956–Feb. 23, 1962 / Capitol ✦✦✦✦✦

Wildest / Jan. 1957 / Capitol ✦✦✦✦✦

The Call of the Wildest / Jul. 1957 / Capitol ✦✦✦✦✦

Wildest show at Tahoe / Jan. 1958 / Capitol ✦✦✦✦

Las Vegas Prima Style / Jun. 1958 / Capitol ✦✦✦✦

Louis and Keely! / 1959 / Dot ✦✦✦

Russell Procope

b. Aug. 11, 1908, New York, NY, d. Jan. 21, 1981, New York, NY
Clarinet, Alto Saxophone / Swing
An excellent altoist, Russell Procope became much better-known
as a New Orleans-style clarinetist during his Duke Ellington
years. He studied violin for eight years before switching to clarinet and alto. Procope recorded with Jelly Roll Morton in 1928 and
had important stints with the big bands of Benny Carter (1929),
Chick Webb (1929–31), Fletcher Henderson (1931–34), Tiny
Bradshaw (1934–35), Teddy Hill (1935–37) and Willie Bryant.
However, it was as a member of the John Kirby Sextet (1938–43)
during which he exclusively played alto that Russell Procope did
his finest work, playing brilliant solos with a distinctive tone that
perfectly fit the music. After a period in the Army and a reunion
with Kirby (1945), Procope became a member of the Duke
Ellington Orchestra in 1946, staying (except for a short period in
1961 with Wilbur DeParis) until Ellington's death 28 years later
in 1974. Because of Johnny Hodges' presence, Procope had very
few alto solos, serving instead as a section player and occasional
clarinet soloist whose warm tone contrasted with that of the cooler Jimmy Hamilton; Procope was underutilized but secure and
happy during his Ellington years. Later, in the 1970s, he played
with Brooks Kerr's group. —*Scott Yanow*

The Persuasive Sax of Russell Procope / 1956 / Dot ✦✦✦✦

Arthur Prysock

b. Jan. 2, 1929
Vocals / Standards
Arthur Prysock's commanding, robust, and deep baritone voice

have made a huge impression through smash R&B, blues, and
jazz-flavored recordings, as well as commercials and radio spots.
Arthur Prysock became famous in Buddy Johnson's band in
1944–1952, having a number of big R&B hits. He gained even
more notoriety as a romantic ballad specialist in the '50s and '60s.
During the '70s, Prysock did mainly club dates, but resurfaced as
a recording artist in 1985 with super recording. —*Ron Wynn*

● **Rockin' Good Way** / Jul. 29, 1985–Aug. 2, 1985 / Milestone ✦✦✦✦
Great comeback on records that helped reestablish Prysock
among some who'd forgotten his '50s & '60s material. —*Ron Wynn*

This Guy's in Love with You / Aug. 1986 / Milestone ✦✦✦

Today's Love Songs Tomorrow's / 1987–1988 / Milestone ✦✦✦✦
1988 release of some lush 1987 and 1988 sessions. Arthur Prysock
sings wonderful ballads, backed by brother Red's good band. —
Ron Wynn

Tito Puente

b. Apr. 20, 1923, New York, NY
Percussion, Leader / Latin Jazz
Mario Bauza's death in 1993 leaves Tito Puente as the elder, reigning leader of Latin jazz, salsa and Afro-Cuban/Afro-Latin music. A
magnificent timbales player, great bandleader, flamboyant entertainer, underrated vibes soloist, and competent saxophonist,
pianist, conga and bongos player, Puente has done everything in
Latin music.
His original intention was to be a dancer, but that was ruined
by a torn ankle tendon he suffered in an accident. Puente got
early lessons in composition from Charlie Spivak, whom he met
aboard the USS Santee in World War II. Puente later got formal
training at Juilliard, which he attended after his discharge. He
worked in the bands of Noro Morales, Machito and Pupi Campo
before forming The Piccadilly Boys in the late '40s; they eventually became the Tito Puente Orchestra. With lead vocalist
Vincentico Valdes, Puente's group made its recording debut on
Secco.
Puente was the first signee on Tico, then a new Latin label, in
the late '40s. He made several albums for them in the late '40s
and '50s, and helped popularize the "mambo" rage. His hit
"Abaniquito" was a crossover smash, and RCA lured Puente from
Tico for a string of albums in the '50s that mixed spicy dance
beats and red-hot jam sessions. His single "Para los Rumberos"
was later covered by Santana and his late '50s singles and albums
were prominent in the rise of the chachacha sound. Puente took
vintage Cuban chachacha songs and transferred them from the
violin/flute charanga format to a brass and reeds, big band context. His '50s bands included several major stars like Ray Barretto,
Mongo Santamaria, Willie Bobo and Johnny Pacheco.
Puente enjoyed more crossover success in the early '60s for
GNP, with albums combining Latin interpretations of Broadway
shows, bossa nova and big band dates. He returned to Tico and
stayed there until the '80s, cutting numerous records in the Latin
jazz, Afro-Cuban and Afro-latin vein. Puente recorded with
Santamaria, Bobo and Carlos "Patato" Valdez, did a live date in
Puerto Rico, played with The Tico All Stars and Fania All Stars,
backed such vocalists as Manny Roman, Rolando Le Series and
Celia Cruz, did "boogaloo" and pop dates, and recorded salsa and
big band albums. Santana enjoyed a huge hit with a cover of his
single "Oye Como Va," and Puente's bands and albums were the
place to hear the greatest Latin musicians and vocalists throughout the '70s.
Puente was one of the artists featured in Jeremy Marre's television film "Salsa '79" and he made several tours of Europe with
The Latin Percussion Jazz Ensemble. They became an octet in the
early '80s, and the album *Tito Puente And His Latin Ensemble On
Broadway* won a Grammy in 1983 and gained credibility and
exposure for Concord's Picante Latin line. Puente has continued
recording for Concord/Picante, winning another Grammy in 1985
for the album *Mambo Diablo* that included special guest George
Shearing on "Lullaby Of Birdland." Puente also did guest stints
with Cal Tjader and Ray Barretto for '70s albums on Fantasy and
Atlantic, and another guest stint with Barretto on an '81 CTI
album. He's also recorded for Timeless, and was featured in the
1992 film "The Mambo Kings." Some of his classic RCA dates are
being reissued on CD by RCA/Bluebird, while his recent Concord
and Timeless material is also available on CD. Several of his

numerous Tico releases are also available on CD from Latin music stores. —*Ron Wynn and Michael G. Nastos*

Puente Goes Jazz / 1956 / RCA ✦✦✦
Birdland series. Orchestra plays jazz and Latin music. Includes a great "What Is This Thing Called Love?" and "Birdland After Dark." —*Michael G. Nastos*

Top Percussion / 1957 / BMG ✦✦✦✦✦
A stunner from Puente's golden age, this 1957 recording brought together Tito, Mongo, Willie Bobo, Aguabella, and Julito Collazo on percussion with vocalists that included Mercedita Valdez, in seven wonderful cuts of traditional and (then) contemporary Afro-Cuban skin-on-skin. Then as an unexpected gift, there is a seven-minute Latin-jazz suite featuring Puente's considerable jazz-arranger head and a powerful band with Doc Severinson on lead trumpet. —*John Storm Roberts*

● **Dance Mania** / 1958 / BMG ✦✦✦✦✦
Many have long despaired of finding anything from the days of Puente's young prime, and here's one of his two best albums reissued in CD. This was Puente's big band at the height of its powers, one of the great documents of New York Latin music and the sort of thing that established the man's claim to be one of the creators of big-band mambo. —*John Storm Roberts*

New Cha Cha/Mambo Herd / 1958 / Laserlight ✦✦✦✦
Tito Puente and Woody Herman teamed in the late '50s with spectacular results. Puente's blazing timbales and splendid Afro-Latin rhythms were easily adapted into the Herman swing mode. Puente, Ray Barretto, Gilbert Lopez, Ray Rodriquez and/or Willie Rodriquez simply laid down a barrage of beats, rhythmic patterns and textures, while Herman and his band did their solos and unison arrangements directly over them, easing into the intervals and letting the grooves direct them. Herman himself was still wailing away on clarinet and alto sax, teaming with Puente to ensure that the beat never clashed with the frontline. Laserlight's remastering is fine, and they have used the original 1958 liner notes. A pivotal event in jazz and Afro-Latin music. —*Ron Wynn*

On Broadway / Jul. 1982 / Concord Picante ✦✦✦✦✦
The great Latin bandleader Tito Puente has long been one of the pioneers in fusing bebop with very danceable Latin music. On this Concord disc, Puente plays vibes and timbales and utilizes an 11-piece band featuring trumpeter Jimmy Frisaura, Mario Rivera on tenor, soprano and flute, pianist Jorge Dalto and an infectious rhythm section. Jazz standards (including "Sophisticated Lady," "Bluesette" and even Freddie Hubbard's "First Light") alternate with Latin numbers. —*Scott Yanow*

★ **El Rey** / May 1984 / Concord Picante ✦✦✦✦
This is '80s Puente, with the Latin-jazz ensemble that has brought him back into the limelight, and back to the small-group New York sound that was one of the finest of all crossover styles. This album includes the great reed-player, Mario Rivera. *El Rey* has the late Jorge (Dalto) on piano. It contains a mix of jazz and Latin numbers, and includes "Oye Como Va," "Ran Kan Kan," "Autumn Leaves" (which Puente first recorded back in the 1950s) Coltrane's "Giant Steps" and "Equinox." —*John Storm Roberts, Original Music*

Mambo Diablo / May 1985 / Concord Picante ✦✦✦

Sensacion / 1987 / Concord Picante ✦✦✦
It includes "Jordu" and "Round Midnight" as well as a "Guajira for Cal" (Tjader). Terry Gibbs is a guest artist on two cuts. —*John Storm Roberts, Original Music*

Un Poco Loco / Jan. 1987 / Concord Picante ✦✦✦✦✦
One of his best for the label. Puente's playing in both large and small contexts. —*Ron Wynn*

● **Salsa Meets Jazz** / Jan. 1988 / Concord Picante ✦✦✦✦✦
& Latin Ensemble. Excellent, maybe his best on the label. Phil Woods (as) joins the party and soars. —*Ron Wynn*

Goza Me Timbal / Jul. 31, 1989–Aug. 1, 1989 / Concord Picante ✦✦✦✦
The songs mix Sonny Rollins and Miles Davis landmarks with topical Puente numbers, extending both bop and Latin horizons. —*Ron Wynn*

Out of This World / Dec. 1990 / Concord Picante ✦✦✦

The Mambo King / 1991 / RMM ✦✦✦✦
Puente's 100th album is a celebration of that fact, with a procession of vocalists, most of whom—like Celia Cruz—were professionally associated with him at one time or another. That doesn't

make for a very tight concept, but recordings by musicians of his generation didn't have concepts, they had music. So does this one, including a minor riot with Celia Cruz riding a big, burly mambo arrangement by a band full of just everybody, and a wonderful "El Bribon del Aguacero" with Chocolate Armenteros on trumpet. —*John Storm Roberts*

Mambo of the Times / Dec. 1991 / Concord Picante ✦✦✦✦
A '92 CD session showing that the great Afro-Latin and Latin jazz master Tito Puente continues to churn out tremendous music. This is his current band, and they're all first-rate jazz players and execute the tricky Latin clave beat easily. —*Ron Wynn*

● **Live at the Village Gate** / Apr. 27, 1992 / Sony Discos ✦✦✦✦✦

Tito Puente & His Latin Jazz All Stars / 1993 / Concord Picante ✦✦✦✦
This Concord Puente date offers a frenetic mix of furious Latin jazz and danceable cuts, among them "Vaya Puente" and "Master Timbalero," as well as the more ambitious "Nostalgia In Times Square" and "Espresso Por Favor." Puente not only plays vibes, marimba, timbales and percussion, but drives a band that has three sterling rhythmic contributors in Johnny Rodriquez, Jose Madera and Jose Rodriguez, as well as superior saxophonists Mario Rivera and Bobby Porcelli, and capable pianist Sonny Bravo. The band plays straight dance music, intricate bop or big band swing. The ageless Puente continues issuing versatile, first-rate sessions, and this disc adds another chapter to his remarkable legacy. —*Ron Wynn*

In Session / 1993 / Bellaphon ✦✦✦✦✦
This outing from Tito Puente is a throwback to Latin-jazz of the 1950s and '60s. Very much a jazz session, most of the selections feature fine solos from trumpeter Charlie Sepulveda, the muscular tenor of Mario Rivera, flutist Dave Valentin and pianist Hilton Ruiz. Drummer Ignacio Berroa and three percussionists really push the ensembles and Puente (on timbales and vibes) has plenty of fine spots. As a bonus, James Moody drops by to do a lively version of his "Moody's Mood for Love" (complete with yodeling). It's an excellent Latin-jazz set. —*Scott Yanow*

● **Royal T** / Jan. 18, 1993+Jan. 19, 1993 / Concord Picante ✦✦✦✦✦
Tito Puente has long championed Latin-jazz, a combination of Latin percussion and rhythms with bebop-oriented jazz. This release from the Concord Picante label serves as a perfect introduction to his music. For this date, Puente (who performs on timbales and marimba) uses six horns, piano, bass, synthesizer and three other percussionists to play everything from "Donna Lee" and "Stompin' at the Savoy" to his own exotic originals. Soloists include the many reeds (including piccolo) of Mario Rivera, trumpeter Tony Lujan, trombonist Art Velasco and of course the percussion section. One of Tito Puente's better recordings of recent times. —*Scott Yanow*

Master Timbalero / Sep. 20, 1993–Sep. 21, 1993 / Concord Picante ✦✦✦✦

Dudu Pukwana

b. Jul. 18, 1938, Port Elizabeth, South Africa, d. Jun. 28, 1990, London, England
Alto Saxophone / Avant-Garde
A fiery, inspirational alto saxophonist, Dudu Pukwana's wailing leads and indomitable spirit brilliantly fused township jive, free music and honking R&B. Pukwana actually began on piano, taking lessons from his father at 10. He joined Tete Mbambisa's Four Yanks as a teen in the late '50s after the family moved from Port Elizabeth to Cape Town, South Africa. He also started learning saxophone from Nick Moyake, and listening to imported American jazz and R&B records. Chris McGregor invited Pukwana to join The Blue Notes, an integrated band in the early '60s. He'd eventually depart his homeland with the rest of the band, settle temporarily in Switzerland then later in London. Pukwana stayed with McGregor's groups until 1969, when he joined Hugh Masekela's Union of South Africa in America.

After they disbanded in 1970, Pukwana returned to England and formed his own band. They were initially Spear, and later Assegai. Pukwana also worked with Keith Tippett's Centipede, Jonas Gwangwa, Traffic, the Incredible String Band, Gwigwi Mrwebi, Sebothane Bahula's Jabula, Harry Miller's Isipingo and the Louis Moholo Unit. Pukwana recorded with Mrwebi in 1970, and made two albums with Assegai before founding a new edition of Spear in 1972. He also played that year on Masekela's *Home Is Where The Music Is* Chisa session. The new Spear, which included Mongezi Feza, Moholo and Miller, plus Bixo Mngqikana made some excellent albums, among them *In The Townships* and *Flute Music* before they disbanded in 1978. Pukwana formed the big band Zila, recorded with them, and continued heading the group until his death of liver failure in 1990. Sadly, none of Pukwana's sessions are available in America on CD. *—Ron Wynn*

In the Townships / Aug. 25, 1973–Nov. 10, 1973 / Earthworks ◆◆◆
An excellent recording with Feza, Louis Moholo, and Harry Miller. *—Michael G. Nastos*

● **Diamond Express** / 1975 / Freedom ◆◆◆◆◆
An early-'70s recording of this saxophonist, with the late trumpeter Mongezi Feza, in their last meeting before Feza died of pneumonia. Squeaky sax and ensemble in an unabashed mood. South African free jazz. *—Michael G. Nastos*

Zila / 1981 / JIKA ◆◆◆◆
A live date at the 100 Club in London, with a larger ensemble and great soloists. *—Michael G. Nastos*

Don Pullen

b. Dec. 25, 1941, Roanoke, VA, d. Apr. 22, 1995
Organ, Piano / Avant-Garde, Post Bop
Don Pullen rivals Cecil Taylor in his percussive approach to the piano. He incorporates free, blues and bebop elements into his solos, featuring tone clusters, funk and R&B backbeats and rhythms, glissandos and dense, rigorous right-hand lines. Pullen's also an accomplished organist; his bass pedal work, accompaniment and soulful melodies and riffs are remniscent of classic soul jazz combo dates.

Pullen began playing gospel in church and R&B in clubs in his youth. He turned to jazz in his teens. Pullen played in Muhal Richard Abrams' Experimental Band during the mid-'60s in Chicago, and Giuseppi Logan's quartet in New York. He also played on R&B sessions backing Big Maybelle, Ruth Brown and Arthur Prysock and on organ with soul jazz groups. Pullen led a group in the '60s and early '70s that included Roland Prince, Tina Brooks and Al Dreares. He worked in a duo with Milford Graves in the mid-'60s. Pullen was in Charles Mingus' last great '70s combo along with George Adams and Dannie Richmond. After that experience, he went solo. Pullen worked with Sam Rivers, David Murray, Hamiett Bluiett and various Art Ensemble of Chicago members before co-forming a quartet in the '70s with Adams that also included Richmond and Cameron Brown. The Don Pullen/George Adams quartet was a super band whose only failing was recording their finest work for an independent label, thus never enjoying the exposure available only through a conglommerate's publicity machine. Pullen also played with Beaver Harris' 360 Degree Music Experience and in The Mingus Dynasty.

Since the quartet disbanded, Pullen has led his own bands and currently records for Blue Note. His recent *Ode To Life* has been highly praised in the mainstream jazz press, hip-hop magazines like "Vibe," and even international publications such as "Latin Beat." Pullen has recorded for Atlantic, Horo, Timeless, Black Saint, Sackville, and DIW, among others. He's played with Eddie Gomez, Nina Simone, Bobby Battle, Fred Hopkins, Olu Dara, Donald Harrison, Alex Blake, Gary Peacock, Tony Williams and Chico Freeman among others. *—Ron Wynn*

Solo Piano Album / Feb. 5, 1975 / Sackville ◆◆◆◆

Capricorn Rising / Oct. 16, 1975–Oct. 17, 1975 / Black Saint ◆◆◆◆◆

Healing Force / Apr. 1976 / Black Saint ◆◆◆◆

Tomorrow's Promises / 1976–1977 / Atlantic ◆◆◆◆◆
Long overdue to be reissued on CD, this early Don Pullen LP helped introduce him to jazz listeners. The pianist is heard in a variety of settings including a duet with multireedist George Adams on "Last Year's Lies and Tomorrow's Promises," and in two groups with Adams and trumpeter Hannibal Marvin Peterson. Actually, the most accessible and memorable piece is the rollicking "Big Alice," which also features violinist Michal Urbaniak and trumpeter Randy Brecker. Pullen, a very rhythmic avant-gardist who can play inside or outside, was well-served by this release. *— Scott Yanow*

Montreux Concert / Jul. 12, 1977 / Atlantic ◆◆◆

Warriors / Apr. 1978 / Black Saint ◆◆◆◆

The Magic Triangle / Jul. 24, 1979–Jul. 26, 1979 / Black Saint ◆◆◆◆◆

Evidence of Things Unseen / Sep. 28, 1983–Sep. 29, 1983 / Black Saint ◆◆◆◆

The Sixth Sense / Jun. 1985 / Black Saint ◆◆◆◆◆
Studio date with quintet. Another great Pullen album. *—Michael G. Nastos*

Breakthrough / Apr. 30, 1986 / Blue Note ◆◆◆◆◆
With George Adams Quartet. Pianist Don Pullen and sax/flute/vocalist George Adams (both ex-Mingus players) with drummer Dan Richmond at their creative zenith. *—Michael G. Nastos*

New Beginnings / Dec. 1988 / Blue Note ◆◆◆◆

Random Thoughts / Mar. 23, 1990 / Blue Note ◆◆◆◆◆

● **Kele Mou Bana** / Sep. 25, 1991+Sep. 26, 1991 / Blue Note ◆◆◆◆◆
This CD features pianist Don Pullen's "African-Brazilian Connection." Always a very percussive player, Pullen gets to romp with two percussionists on this date while altoist Carlos Ward flies over the top and bassist Nilson Matta keeps the foundation solid. The repertoire is comprised of originals and, even in its freer moments, the rhythms keep the music quite accessible. *—Scott Yanow*

Ode to Life / Jun. 29, 1993 / Blue Note ◆◆◆
Pianist Don Pullen's second recording by his African-Brazilian Connection (which includes bassist Nilson Matta, two percussionists and altoist Carlos Ward) is dedicated to the memory of the late tenor saxophonist George Adams. The music is more subdued than is usual on a Pullen disc, with the harmonies being less dissonant and the mood often melancholy and reflective but occasionally joyous. This is one of Pullen's more accessible and introspective sessions. *—Scott Yanow*

Sacred Common Ground / 1994 / Blue Note ◆◆

Flora Purim

b. Mar. 6, 1942, Rio de Janeiro, Brazil
Guitar, Percussion, Vocals / Fusion, Brazilian Jazz
Since her husband, Airto Moreira, ranks as Brazil's most famous percussionist, it's only fitting Flora Purim qualify as that nation's most celebrated jazz vocalist, though she's never had a huge hit like Astrud Gilberto's "The Girl From Impanema." While Purim's thunder has been stolen in the '80s and '90s by newer, more invigorating, progressive types like Margareth Menezes and Tania Maria, Purim was a revelation in the '70s. With a voice that at one time could range over six octaves, a soothing, alluring sound and superb timing and delivery, she thrilled audiences with her vocals on the debut Return To Forever album and as a leader.

The daughter of professional musicians, Purim studied piano and guitar, and performed in Sao Paulo and Rio de Janeiro with Moreira. They moved to Los Angeles in the late '60s, then to New York. While Moreira worked with Miles Davis, Purim joined Stan Getz's band. She recorded with Duke Pearson, then with Return to Forever and Moreira. The duo left Return to Forever in the mid-'70s to form their own band, but Purim's career was derailed by an arrest for cocaine possession. She was imprisoned in 1974 and 1975, then resumed her career. Purim's records in the late '70s were more pop and light jazz oriented.

She started her own band in 1978, as her career and Moreira's seemed headed in opposite stylistic directions. But they reteamed in the mid-'80s, and are still working together. Purim recorded in the '70s for Milestone, then for Concord/Crossover, Sobocode, Venture, and Reference with Mickey Hart in the '80s. She's recorded for Fantasy in the '90s. Most of Purim's sessions are available on CD, both her dates and those with Airto. *—Ron Wynn*

★ **Butterfly Dreams** / Dec. 1973 / Original Jazz Classics ◆◆◆◆◆
A wonderful release that she's seldom equalled since. Joe Henderson (sax), George Duke (p), and Airto (per). *—Ron Wynn*

Stories to Tell / May 1974–Jul. 1974 / Original Jazz Classics ◆◆◆◆

500 Miles High / Jul. 6, 1974 / Milestone ◆◆◆◆◆
Fine album by Purim from the period when she was a dominant Afro-Latin vocalist. She cut this with husband Airto; it's a blend of light romantic songs, Afro-Latin tunes, and easy-listening instru-

mentals. Purim's singing, which grew in range, depth, and impact during this period, keeps things interesting, as does presence of Milton Nascimento. *—Ron Wynn*

Open Your Eyes / 1976 / Milestone ✦✦✦
Purim's finest hour includes the title track that is Flora at her soaring, swooping best. There is great instrumental backing from George Duke (p) and friends. *—Michael G. Nastos*

Encounter / Apr. 1976–Feb. 1977 / Original Jazz Classics ✦✦✦✦
Purim teamed with fellow Afro-Latin vocalist and instrumentalist Hermeto Pascoal, as well as Airto, on this album. It had more interesting rhythmic elements due to Pascoal's presence; the vocal contrast was also intriguing. *—Ron Wynn*

Nothing Will Be as It Was . . . Tomorrow / 1976 / Milestone ✦✦✦
With lots of string, synth, and vocal arrangements, this includes classics such as the title track, "You Love Me Only," and "Bridges" (written by Milton Nascimiento). Support comes from keyboardists Patrice Rushen and George Duke, and Airto (per). *—Michael G. Nastos*

That's What She Said / 1977 / Milestone ✦✦✦
One of Latin vocalist Flora Purim's final albums for Milestone in an impressive mid- and late-'60s release series. She was mixing light pop, fusion, and more conventional Latin and Afro-Latin material into her albums, while working with her husband Airto, bassist Ron Carter, and trumpeter Oscar Brashear. Despite some overproduction, Purim's voice is still strong and impressive on this release. *—Ron Wynn*

Everyday, Everynight / Sep. 1978 / Warner Brothers ✦✦

Humble People / 1985 / Concord ✦✦✦✦
An all-star band supports Flora and Airto Moreira (per) through jazz, funk, and Latin pop. Guests include David Sanborn (as), Joe Farrell (ts), Milton Cardona (per), and Jerry Gonzalez (per). This is one of Purim's better later-period albums. *—Michael G. Nastos*

The Magicians / Mar. 1986–Apr. 1986 / Crossover ✦✦✦

The Sun Is Out / 1987 / Crossover ✦✦

Q

Ike Quebec

b. Aug. 17, 1918, Newark, NJ, **d.** Jan. 16, 1963, New York, NY
Tenor Saxophone / Swing, Early R&B

A magnificent "populist" saxophonist whose abilities were undervalued by many critics during his lifetime, Ike Quebec showed simple, compelling music need not be played in a simplistic manner. He had a pronounced swing bent in his style and tone, particularly the sound of Coleman Hawkins. But Quebec didn't simply parrot Hawkins; he displayed a huge, bluesy tone, swooping, jubilant phrases and played joyous uptempo tunes and evocative, slow blues and ballads. There were no false fingerings, or anything intricate; it was just direct, heartfelt solos. Quebec was once a pianist and part-time soft shoe artist, but switched to tenor in the '40s, playing with The Barons of Rhythm. He worked with several New York bands, among them groups led by Kenny Clarke, Benny Carter and Roy Eldridge. He co-wrote the song "Mop Mop" with Clarke, which was later recorded by Coleman Hawkins during one of the earliest bebop sessions. Quebec played from the mid-40s into the early '50s with Cab Calloway's orchestra and also his spinoff unit, The Cab Jivers. Quebec cut one of Blue Note's rare 78 albums in the '40s, and also recorded for Savoy. His song "Blue Harlem" became a huge hit. Quebec also worked with Lucky Millinder and recorded with Calloway. Alfred Lion made Quebec Blue Note's A&R man in the late '40s, after Quebec repeatedly informed him about talented prospective signees. Quebec doubled for a while as a bandleader, but concentrated until the late '50s on recording and finding acts for the label. Some of the people he brought Lion included Thelonious Monk and Bud Powell. Quebec wrote "Suburban Eyes" for Monk's label debut. He began playing again in the late '50s, doing Blue Note sessions with Sonny Clark, Jimmy Smith, singer Dodo Green, and Stanley Turrentine, plus his own dates. Just as he was attracting renewed attention and some appreciation from critics who'd previously dismissed him as another honking R&B type, Quebec died of lung cancer in 1963. Mosaic has issued some superb Quebec boxed sets, *The Complete Blue Note Forties Recordings of Ike Quebec and John Hardee* and *The Complete Blue Note 45 Sessions. —Ron Wynn*

★ **Complete Blue Note Recordings** / Jul. 18, 1944–Sep. 23, 1946 / Mosaic ✦✦✦✦✦
This is an essential compilation of virtually all the early Quebec jazz dates. —*Ron Wynn*

★ **Complete Blue Note 45 Sessions** / Jul. 1, 1959–Feb. 13, 1962 / Mosaic ✦✦✦✦✦
A wonderful three-disc collection of Quebec's 1959–1962 songs that packed jazz punch, had R&B appeal, and were originally recorded for and designed as singles for jukeboxes. —*Ron Wynn*

Heavy Soul / Nov. 26, 1961 / Blue Note ✦✦✦✦
The thick-toned tenor Ike Quebec is in excellent form on this CD reissue of a 1961 Blue Note date. His ballad statements are quite warm and he swings nicely on a variety of medium-tempo material. Unfortunately, organist Freddie Roach has a rather dated sound which weakens this session a bit; bassist Milt Hinton and drummer Al Harewood are typically fine in support. Originals alternate with standards with "Just One More Chance," "The Man I Love" and "Nature Boy" (the latter an emotional tenor-bass duet) being among the highlights. —*Scott Yanow*

It Might As Well Be Spring / Dec. 9, 1961 / Blue Note ✦✦✦

● **Blue and Sentimental** / Dec. 16, 1961+Dec. 23, 1961 / Blue Note ✦✦✦✦✦
Hot, lusty, and wonderful. Quebec was a rare jazz musician who never lost his appeal in the R&B community. W/ Sonny Clark (p), Grant Green (g), Paul Chambers (b), Philly Joe Jones (d). —*Ron Wynn*

Congo Lament / Jan. 20, 1962 / Blue Note ✦✦✦

Easy Living / Jan. 20, 1962 / Blue Note ✦✦✦✦✦
This CD reissue (which adds three songs to the original LP) is really two sets in one. The first five selections are a blues-oriented jam session that matches together the contrasting tenors of Ike Quebec and Stanley Turrentine with trombonist Bennie Green, pianist Sonny Clark, bassist Milt Hinton and drummer Art Blakey. However, it is the last three numbers ("I've Got a Crush on You," "Nancy with the Laughing Face" and "Easy Living") that are most memorable; ballad features for Quebec's warm tenor. All in all, this set gives one a definitive look at late-period Ike Quebec. —*Scott Yanow*

With a Song in My Heart / Feb. 5, 1962+Feb. 13, 1962 / Blue Note ✦✦✦

Soul Samba / Nov. 5, 1962 / Blue Note ✦✦✦

Alvin Queen

b. Aug. 16, 1950, New York, NY
Drums / Hard Bop

A crisp, powerful and swinging drummer, Alvin Queen hasn't recorded as often as his talents merit, but what he's done is consistently engaging and demanding. Queen worked with George Benson and Stanley Turrentine, then traveled to Europe with Charles Tolliver's quartet. During the '70s he worked with the group Music Inc. co-led by Tolliver and Stanley Cowell. Queen departed America in 1979 for Switzerland, and established Nilva Records. Queen toured France with Plas Johnson and Harry Edison and recorded with John Collins and Junior Mance in the '80s, while working in Zurich with a trio led by Wild Bill Davis and recording with another led by Lonnie Smith. He also did his own dates. Queen has no sessions currently available on CD, but can be heard on reissues by Music Inc. —*Ron Wynn and Michael G. Nastos*

In Europe / Feb. 8, 1980 / Nilva ✦✦✦✦

Glidin' and Stridin' / Jul. 29, 1982 / Nilva ✦✦✦

● **A Day in Holland** / Mar. 23, 1983 / Nilva ✦✦✦✦✦

Gene Quill (Daniel Eugene Quill)

b. Dec. 15, 1927, Atlantic City, NJ, **d.** Jan. 1989, Atlantic City, NJ
Alto Saxophone / Bop, Cool

A consistent alto saxophonist whose style changed from straight bebop to a milder, more mellow sound, Gene Quill initially played with fire and exacting fluidity. He gradually smoothed the edges off his solos, and opted for a relaxed, introspective approach. Quill started on saxophone in his childhood, and was a professional at 13. He worked in big bands during the '50s and '60s, playing and recording with Buddy DeFranco, Claude Thornhill, Gene Krupa, Quincy Jones, Johnny Richards, Manny Albam, Johnny Carisi, Bill Potts and Gerry Mulligan. Quill also played in the combos of Mundell Lowe and Jimmy Knepper, led his own bands, and memorably teamed with Phil Woods; they were known as Phil and Quill. He did some session work, but his career was tragically cut short, as he suffered partial paralysis following brain damage. Quill's sessions with Woods for Prestige and RCA have been reissued on CD, but not their Epic dates. His own dates for such labels as Dawn and Roost haven't been reissued on CD. —*Ron Wynn*

Three Bones and a Quill / 1958 / Fresh Sound ✦✦✦✦

Paul Quinichette

b. May 17, 1916, Denver, CO, **d.** May 25, 1983, New York, NY
Tenor Saxophone / Swing

Paul Quinichette was known throughout his career as the "Vice Prez" because he sounded so similar to Lester Young. While most of Young's other followers emulated his 1930's style, Quinichette sounded like Lester Young of the then-present day (the 1950's). After getting experience with Nat Towles, Lloyd Sherock and Ernie Fields, Quinichette was featured with Jay McShann during 1942–44. He played on the West Coast with Johnny Otis (1945–47), traveled to New York with Louis Jordan and performed with Lucky Millinder (1948–49), Red Allen and Hot Lips Page. Quinichette was with Count Basie during 1952–53 (when Basie had reformed his orchestra), worked with Benny Goodman in 1955, recorded with Billie Holiday and held his own on a session with John Coltrane. Otherwise Quinichette mostly led his own group in the 1950s, recording several excellent (if obviously derivative) records. He left music in the late '50s to become an electrical engineer, returning to jazz briefly in the early-to-mid-'70s, playing with Sammy Price, Brooks Kerr and Buddy Tate before being forced to retire due to bad health. —*Scott Yanow*

Kid from Denver / Jul. 16, 1956 / Biograph ✦✦✦

A nice, animated late '50s session with tenor saxophonist Paul Quinichette leading a combo featuring trumpeters Joe Newman and Thad Jones, plus other big band veterans like Nat Pierce and Bill Graham. —*Ron Wynn*

On the Sunny Side / May 10, 1957 / Original Jazz Classics ✦✦✦✦✦

A standout late '50s blowing date led by tenor saxophonist Paul Quinichette with trombonist Curtis Fuller, alto saxophonists John Jenkins and Sonny Red, pianist Mal Waldrons, bassist Doug Watkins, and drummer Ed Thigpen. This was simply straight-ahead blues, ballads, and standards, with Jenkins in particular taking some torrid solos. —*Ron Wynn*

● **Cattin'** / May 17, 1953–1957 / Mobile Fidelity ✦✦✦✦✦

The Chase Is on / Aug. 29, 1957+Sep. 8, 1957 / Bethlehem ✦✦✦

With fellow tenor Charlie Rouse, and the Wynton Kelly Trio, this is a nice mix of standards, tunes by Rouse and Carmen McRae. Two tracks are with Hank Jones (p) and Freddie Green (g). —*Michael G. Nastos*

For Basie / Oct. 18, 1957 / Prestige ✦✦✦✦

Like Who? / Mar. 20, 1959 / United Artists ✦✦✦✦

R

Boyd Raeburn (Boyde Albert Raeburn)
b. Oct. 27, 1913, Faith, SD, d. Aug. 2, 1966, Lafayette, LA
Bass Saxophone, Leader / Bop

Boyd Raeburn was never much of a soloist, but his short-lived big bands in the mid-'40s featured some of the most advanced arrangements of the time, particularly those of George Handy. Raeburn actually started out leading commercial orchestras in the 1930s, and it was not until 1944 that his music became relevant to jazz. That year he had a forward-looking swing band that included, at various times, such players as Benny Harris, the Johnny Hodges-influenced Johnny Bothwell, Serge Chaloff, Roy Eldridge, Trummy Young and Handy on piano that played charts from George Williams, Eddie Finckel and Handy. The group overall was influenced by Count Basie, but they were also the first to record Dizzy Gillespie's "Night in Tunisia"; Dizzy even guested with the band.

By 1945 Raeburn's music became much more radical with George Handy's charts (which were sometimes influenced by modern classical music) dominating the repertoire. Vocalists David Allyn and Ginnie Powell (Raeburn's wife) cheerfully sang while all types of dissonant events occurred behind them! Even though it was a constant struggle to keep the orchestra together, Raeburn's band actually grew in size during 1946 with reed players doubling on woodwinds and the addition of French horns and a harp. Such players as Lucky Thompson, Dodo Marmarosa, Ray Linn and Buddy DeFranco were among the many who passed through the band. Johnny Richards was the key arranger in 1947, but by the end of the year the band was no longer recording, and Raeburn soon went back to performing dance music. His pleasant Columbia records of 1956-57 are of little interest, but Boyd Raeburn's earlier bands are represented on sessions for Savoy and broadcasts released by IAJRC and Hep. —*Scott Yanow*

Boyd Raeburn and His Orchestra 1944 / Jun. 13, 1944–Jan. 17, 1945 / Circle ✦✦✦

Experiments in Big Band Jazz / Jan. 26, 1945–May 13, 1945 / Musicraft ✦✦✦✦

● **Jewells** / Oct. 15, 1945–Sep. 19, 1949 / Savoy ✦✦✦✦✦

Dance Spectacular / Feb. 28, 1956–Jul. 19, 1956 / Columbia ✦✦

Doug Raney
b. Aug. 29, 1956
Guitar / Cool

The son of legendary guitarist Jimmy Raney, Doug has understandably been heavily influenced by his father. He's an impressive soloist and utilizes almost identical full tones, crisp chording and fluid voicings. He made his first recording with his father and Al Haig in the mid-'70s, then did duo dates with his dad in the late '70s. Raney recorded for SteepleChase in the '70s and '80s and Criss Cross in the '80s. He's recorded with Chet Baker and Bernt Rosegren and played in Horace Parlan's band. Raney has a couple of sessions available on CD. —*Ron Wynn*

Meeting the Tenors / Apr. 29, 1983 / Criss Cross ✦✦✦✦

Everything We Love / Aug. 17, 1983–Aug. 18, 1983 / Hot Club ✦✦✦

Blue and White / Apr. 29, 1984 / SteepleChase ✦✦✦✦

Lazy Bird / Nov. 1, 1984 / SteepleChase ✦✦✦✦✦

● **The Doug Raney Quintet** / Aug. 1988 / SteepleChase ✦✦✦✦✦

Jimmy Raney
b. Aug. 20, 1927, Louisville, KY, d. May 10, 1995
Guitar / Cool

Jimmy Raney was the definitive cool jazz guitarist, a fluid bop soloist with a quiet sound who had a great deal of inner fire. He worked with local groups in Chicago before spending nine months with Woody Herman in 1948. From then on he was in the major leagues, having associations with Al Haig, Buddy DeFranco, Artie Shaw and Terry Gibbs. His work with Stan Getz (1951-52) was historic as the pair made for a classic musical partnership. Raney was also very much at home in the Red Norvo Trio (1953-54) before spending six years primarily working in a supper club with pianist Jimmy Lyon (1954-60). After playing with Getz during 1962-63, he returned to Louisville and was outside of music until resurfacing in the early '70s. During the 1970s Raney recorded often for Xanadu. He worked frequently with his son Doug Raney (who has a very similar sound on guitar) and was less active in the late '80s and '90s up until his 1995 death. —*Scott Yanow*

Too Marvelous for Words / Feb. 10, 1954 / Biograph ✦✦✦
Intimate, tasteful mid-'50s recordings from guitarist Jimmy Raney. His delicate, fluid voicings were also featured during this period with the Red Norvo trio, and Raney's solos are carefully paced and developed, marked by understated technique and a light, expressive sound. —*Ron Wynn*

Jimmy Raney / May 28, 1954–Feb. 18, 1955 / Original Jazz Classics ✦✦✦✦✦

Two Jims and Zoot / May 1964 / Mobile Fidelity ✦✦✦✦
With Jim Hall (g). Steamy exchanges between Raney and Zoot Sims (ts). —*Ron Wynn*

The Influence / Sep. 2, 1975 / Xanadu ✦✦✦✦

★ **Live in Tokyo** / Apr. 12, 1976+Apr. 14, 1976 / Xanadu ✦✦✦✦✦
This album features the great guitarist Jimmy Raney in a trio with bassist Sam Jones and drummer Leroy Williams, all regulars for the Xanadu label in the 1970s. The boppish performances (which Raney considers among his very best) are subtle with lots of interplay between the players. Highpoints include "Anthropology," "A Burning Cherokee" and Raney's unaccompanied playing on "Stella by Starlight." —*Scott Yanow*

Solo / Dec. 20, 1976 / Xanadu ✦✦✦✦

Stolen Moments / Apr. 19, 1979 / SteepleChase ✦✦✦✦

Duets / Apr. 21, 1979 / SteepleChase ✦✦✦✦

Here's That Raney Day / Jul. 21, 1980 / Black & Blue ✦✦✦✦

● **Raney (1981)** / Feb. 27, 1981 / Criss Cross ✦✦✦✦✦
This was the first release by Criss Cross, one of the top bop-based labels in Europe. The CD reissue adds six alternate takes to the original seven-song program. The cool-toned guitarist Jimmy Raney is teamed with his son Doug (who has a very similar style on guitar) along with bassist Jesper Lundgaard and drummer Eric Ineke. Together they perform one original and six standards in light but forcefully swinging style. The interplay between the two guitarists is a major plus. —*Scott Yanow*

The Master / Feb. 16, 1983 / Criss Cross ✦✦✦
A nice mid-'80s session with the relaxed, fluid guitar of Jimmy Raney playing such standards as "The Song Is You" and "Tangerine." He's supported with style by pianist Kirk Lightsey, who emerges as the date's other dominant solo voice. The other musicians, bassist Jesper Lundgaarad and drummer Eddie Gladden, are complementary figures and do their jobs competently. —*Ron Wynn*

Nardis / Mar. 7, 1983 / SteepleChase ✦✦✦
Wisteria / Dec. 30, 1985 / Criss Cross ✦✦✦✦
But Beautiful / Dec. 5, 1990 / Criss Cross ✦✦✦

Nelson Rangell

b. Denver, CO
Alto Saxophone, Flute / Instrumental Pop, Crossover
Nelson Rangell has primarily played pop/jazz throughout his career, although he did a credible job playing some soulful alto with the straight-ahead GRP Big Band. He started on the flute at 15, studied at the Interlochen Arts Academy and the New England Conservatory of Music and in 1984 moved to New York. His records for Gaia and GRP made him into a popular attraction in the David Sanborn tradition. —*Scott Yanow*

Playing for Keeps / 1989 / GRP ✦✦✦
● **Nelson Rangell** / 1990 / GRP ✦✦✦✦
In Every Moment / 1992 / GRP ✦✦
Yes Then Yes / 1993 / GRP ✦✦
Nelson Rangell plays with plenty of energy throughout his R&Bish set and sounds fine on flute and piccolo during two tracks, but his alto playing can barely be told apart from David Sanborn; the lack of individuality can be a serious problem, even in instrumental pop music. Essentially, this is a set of background dance music that stays quite predictable and obvious. Nelson Rangell is capable of better. —*Scott Yanow*

Destiny / 1995 / GRP ✦✦

Kenny Rankin

Vocals / Pop, Standards
Although he has spent most of his career as a pop singer, Kenny Rankin, in the mid-'90s, started emphasizing veteran standards in his performances and using jazz accompaniment. He is an unusual jazz singer, sticking to the lyrics of songs but improvising and constantly altering the notes. His Private Music set *Professional Dreamer* finds him reshaping such tunes as "The Very Thought of You" and "More than You Know." *Scott Yanow*

● **Professional Dreamer** / 1994 / Private Music ✦✦✦✦✦
Kenny Rankin sings like Chet Baker would have if Baker had had a voice. His tone is high (Rankin's speaking voice is actually fairly low), and he has a subtle cool style. It is a bit of a surprise, but Rankin (whose previous output has been in pop music) is actually a fine jazz singer. He always sticks to the lyrics when performing veteran standards (there is no scatting) but changes many of the notes, even during the melody statements, and he is definitely improvising. Rankin's concept is kind of strange ("At Last" and "The Very Thought of You" are radically changed) but successful, and he has a strong and likable voice. An all-star acoustic trio (consisting of pianist Mike Wofford, bassist Brian Bromberg and drummer Roy McCurdy) backs the singer on most of the tracks, Tom Scott (on tenor and alto) and trombonist Bill Watrous add melodic bop solos to three songs apiece, "It Had to Be You" is taken as a romping duet with pianist Alan Broadbent, and the remarkable singer Sue Raney interacts with Rankin on "I've Got a Crush on You." This surprising CD is highly recommended. —*Scott Yanow*

Enrico Rava

b. Aug. 20, 1943, Trieste, Italy
Trumpet, Fluegelhorn / Avant-Garde
One of Italy's finest jazz trumpeters, Enrico Rava has been recording stimulating music for 25 years. He started on trombone before taking up the trumpet and fluegelhorn. Rava was with Gato Barbieri in 1964, played with Steve Lacy during 1965-68 in several countries and spent much of 1969-72 with Roswell Rudd's groups. By 1975 he had a band with John Abercrombie and was soon recording for ECM. Other than stints with Gil Evans (1982) and Cecil Taylor (1984), he has generally been a bandleader ever since. Rava often plays quite free but, due to his mellow tone, his music is fairly accessible. He has releases easily available on ECM and Soul Note. —*Scott Yanow*

● **The Pilgrim and the Stars** / Jun. 1975 / ECM ✦✦✦✦✦
The trumpet of Enrico Rava perfectly fits into the ECM sound. He never gets all that heated, has a healthy respect for the value of space and recalls Miles Davis a bit in spots. Joined by a sparse trio (guitarist John Abercrombie, bassist Palle Danielsson and drummer Jon Christensen), Rava explores seven of his moody originals and creates thoughtful and introspective music. —*Scott Yanow*

The Plot / Aug. 1976 / ECM ✦✦✦✦
Italian trumpeter with quartet. Original ideas and compositions. With guitarist John Abercrombie. —*Michael G. Nastos*

Quartet / Mar. 1978 / ECM ✦✦✦✦
Opening Night / Dec. 1981 / ECM ✦✦✦
Rava String Band / Apr. 11, 1984–Apr. 12, 1984 / Soul Note ✦✦✦
This release ranges from moments of reflective, ambient serenity to periods with more intense activity, although there's seldom any real instrumental ardor or passion exhibited. Trumpeter Enrico Rava's glorious tone and Nana Vasconcelos' percussive dexterity on berimbau and gongs are the closest anyone gets to displaying some fire, but all the participants are expert musicians and nicely demonstrate their proficiency. This finely crafted mood music seems more up ECM's alley than Soul Note's, but Rava and company showed that they could play the same game to perfection. —*Ron Wynn*

Secrets / Jul. 1986 / Soul Note ✦✦✦✦

Real Group

Vocal Group / Bop
The Real Group is an a cappella quintet from Stockholm, Sweden consisting of three men and two women. Inspired by Bobby McFerrin, the unit brilliantly performs bop, vocalese and a few originals on their Town Crier debut, leading Jon Hendricks himself to say "I wish I was in this group!" —*Scott Yanow*

● **Unreal!** / 1991–1994 / Town Crier ✦✦✦✦✦
The Real Group is a three-male, two-female Swedish a cappella quintet that, on the basis of their debut recording, ranks near the top of their field. Their CD for Town Crier is highlighted by Neal Hefti's "Flight of the Foobirds," "Walkin'," a heated "I've Found a New Baby" and "It Don't Mean a Thing." Although the ballads (including "A Child Is Born" and "Body and Soul") are sometimes a bit too respectful, this disc continually holds on to one's interest. In addition to the jazz standards, there are also a few originals (of which "A Cappella in Acapulco" is most memorable), adaptations of two Swedish folk songs and a version of The Beatles' "Come Together." This release is worth searching for. —*Scott Yanow*

Sonny Red (Sylvester Kyner)

b. Dec. 17, 1932, Detroit, MI. **d.** Mar. 20, 1981, Detroit, MI
Alto Saxophone / Hard Bop
Sonny Red was a good, but not great, altoist who was somewhat lost in the shuffle in the 1960s and '70s. He worked in Detroit with Barry Harris (1949–52), in 1954 temporarily switched to tenor while with Frank Rosolino and later that year joined Art Blakely briefly. In 1957 with his arrival in New York he gained some recognition, recording with Curtis Fuller and Paul Quinichette in addition to having several dates as a leader (1958–62) for Savoy, Blue Note and particularly Jazzland. Despite some freelancing and recording with Clifford Jordan, Pony Poindexter, Donald Byrd, Kenny Dorham and Yusef Lateef among others in the 1960s, Red was in obscurity by the 1970s. —*Scott Yanow*

Out of the Blue / Dec. 5, 1959–Jan. 23, 1960 / Blue Note ✦✦✦
With Wynton Kelly (p) and Paul Chambers (b). —*Michael G. Nastos*

Breezing / Nov. 3, 1960 / Jazzland ✦✦✦✦
The Mode / May 29, 1961–Dec. 14, 1991 / Jazzland ✦✦✦✦
● **Images** / Jul. 1962 / Original Jazz Classics ✦✦✦✦✦
The leader, Sonny Red Kyner (alto), never really became the individual strong player that his playing hinted he might develop into. Basically, he was in the Charlie Parker-Jackie McLean tradition, and the material here had that spirit, but little punch. Others involved were Grant Green (guitar), Barry Harris (piano), George Tucker, (bass), Lex Humphries or Jimmy Cobb (drums). Trumpeter Blue Mitchell was also featured on three cuts. —*Bob Rusch, Cadence*

Freddie Redd

b. May 29, 1928, New York, NY
Piano, Composer / Hard Bop
Freddie Redd has blended the rough, furious rhythmic pace of early blues and barrelhouse playing with bebop's voicings and

structures. The results are a sound that's both dense and sprawling, energetic, yet never cliched or simplistic. Redd's largely a self-taught player. He began working in New York and Syracuse clubs after his discharge from the Army in 1949. He was in a small group led by Johnny Miller, then recorded in the early '50s with Tiny Grimes and toured the South with Cootie Williams. Redd returned to New York in 1952 and worked for a brief period with Oscar Pettiford and Charlies Mingus in 1953. Redd played in The Jive Bombers and recorded with Art Farmer and Gigi Gryce's quintet, plus the Gene Ammons all-stars. He toured Sweden with Ernestine Anderson and Rolf Ericson in 1956, recording with Ericson and Tommy Potter and cutting trio sessions. He moved to San Francisco when he returned to America, working for a short time at the Black Hawk club with Mingus and serving as house pianist at Bop City.

Redd wrote most of the music for Jack Gelber's play "The Connection" and participated in the New York performances in 1959 and 1960 and in London and Paris in 1961. Redd also played on the soundtrack for the film version. He lived and performed in Europe during the '60s and early '70s, working and playing in Paris, Denmark and the Netherlands. Redd returned to America in 1974, settling in Los Angeles. He recorded a new trio album in 1977 and did more work in the '80s but didn't maintain a hectic schedule. He recorded new sessions for Triloka in 1988 and Milestone in 1990. —*Ron Wynn*

San Francisco Suite for Jazz Trio / Oct. 2, 1957 / Original Jazz Classics ✦✦✦✦

Music from "The Connection" / 1960 / Blue Note ✦✦✦✦✦

★ **The Complete Blue Note Freddie Redd** / Feb. 15, 1960–Jan. 17, 1961 / Mosaic ✦✦✦✦✦
Available in a box set as either three LPs or two CDs, this limited-edition release has all of the music recorded at pianist Freddie Redd's three Blue Note sessions. In addition to the selections originally included on the LPs *Music from the Connection* and *Shades of Redd*, there is a completely unissued date that adds to the fairly slim Freddie Redd discography. Altoist Jackie McLean (who is on all three sets) and tenor saxophonist Tina Brooks (a key soloist on two) co-star with the pianist; trumpeter Benny Bailey is also heard from on the later date. The music is comprised mostly of Redd's originals (including seven songs written for the stage play *The Connection*) and fits into the style of the mainstream hard bop of the day although with a few personal touches. Straight-ahead fans and Blue Note collectors can consider this set to be essential. —*Scott Yanow*

Straight Ahead! / Dec. 3, 1977 / Interplay ✦✦✦

Lonely City / Jan. 18, 1985–Jan. 19, 1985 / Uptown ✦✦✦✦
Freddie Redd, an aggressive, emphatic hard bop pianist, has had an erratic recording career due to personal and drug problems that forced him off the scene. He shows on this session the swinging style, distinctive phrasing and consistently impressive solo skills that made his Blue Note and Prestige dates so popular during the late '50s. —*Ron Wynn*

● **Live at the Studio Grill** / May 19, 1988+May 26, 1988 / Triloka ✦✦✦✦✦
An enchanting session with Al McKibbon (b) and Billy Higgins (d). —*Ron Wynn*

Everybody Loves a Winner / Oct. 9, 1990+Oct. 10, 1990 / Milestone ✦✦✦✦
Pianist Freddie Redd has not recorded all that much during his 45-year career, but most of his records have been special events. This particular set has eight of Redd's tightly arranged compositions performed by a fine sextet that also features tenor saxophonist Teddy Edwards, altoist Curtis Peagler and trombonist Phil Ranelin. —*Scott Yanow*

Dewey Redman (Walter Dewey Redman)

b. May 17, 1931, Fort Worth, Texas
Tenor Saxophone / Post Bop, Free Jazz
One of the great avant-garde tenors, Dewey Redman has never received anywhere near the acclaim that his son Joshua Redman gained in the 1990s, but ironically Dewey is much more of an innovative player. He began on clarinet when he was 13 and played in his high school marching band, a group that also included Ornette Coleman, Charles Moffett and Prince Lasha. Redman was a public school teacher during 1956–59 but, after getting his master's degree in education from North Texas State, moved to

San Francisco where he freelanced as a musician for seven years; Pharoah Sanders was among his sidemen.

All of this was a prelude to his impressive association with the Ornette Coleman Quartet (1967–74) during which Redman's tenor playing was a perfect match for Ornette's alto. Redman could play as free as the leader, but his appealing tone made the music seem a little more accessible. He also worked with Charlie Haden's Liberation Music Orchestra and was an important part of Keith Jarrett's greatest group, his quintet of the mid-'70s. Redman guested on Pat Metheny's notable *80/81* album and teamed up with Don Cherry, Charlie Haden and Ed Blackwell in the Ornette Coleman reunion band called Old and New Dreams. Despite all of this activity and plenty of recordings (including occasional ones as a leader), Dewey Redman has yet to be fully recognized for his innovative talents. —*Scott Yanow*

Look for the Black Star / Jan. 4, 1966 / Freedom ✦✦✦✦✦
Although always a bit under-recognized and overshadowed by his contemporaries, tenor saxophonist Dewey Redman has long been one of the giants of avant-garde and free bop. This early recording finds Redman discovering his own individual voice on five of his frequently emotional originals. Assisted by pianist Jym Young, bassist Donald Raphael Gareet and drummer Eddie Moore, this San Francisco date is quite adventurous and holds one's interest throughout. —*Scott Yanow*

Tarik / Oct. 1, 1969 / Affinity ✦✦✦

The Ear of the Behearer / Jan. 1974 / Impulse! ✦✦✦✦
This is an excellent set that has free leanings and smashing Redman. —*Ron Wynn*

Coincide / Sep. 9, 1974–Sep. 10, 1974 / Impulse! ✦✦✦
Debut for this exciting saxophonist in a progressive setting, leaning toward avant-garde. —*Michael G. Nastos*

Musics / Oct. 17, 1978–Oct. 19, 1978 / Galaxy ✦✦✦✦
This is one of tenor saxophonist Dewey Redman's more accessible sessions. With the assistance of pianist Fred Simmons, bassist Mark Helias and drummer Eddie Moore, Redman is heard on the lyrical ballad "Alone Again (Naturally)," a bossa nova, jamming over parade rhythms and performing originals that sometimes are advanced bop. The music is excellent although not as explorative as most of Redman's other recordings. —*Scott Yanow*

Redman and Blackwell in Willisau / Aug. 31, 1980 / Black Saint ✦✦✦

● **The Struggle Continues** / Jan. 1982 / ECM ✦✦✦✦✦
His best shows great teamwork from bassist Mark Helias, drummer Ed Blackwell and pianist Charles Eubanks. It's a record to make you say "wow." "Turn over Baby" is a good boogie and "Joie de Vivre" one of Redman's best vehicles for improv. —*Michael G. Nastos*

● **Living on the Edge** / Sep. 13, 1989–Sep. 14, 1989 / Black Saint ✦✦✦✦✦
A first-rate, late-'80s date by tenor saxophonist Dewey Redman. He's working alongside excellent pianist Geri Allen, and the compositions are rigorously played. Redman, as the only horn player, gets extensive space and offers his patented twisting, slashing solos. Bassist Cameron Brown and drummer Eddie Moore prove equally adept at adjusting to the Redman/Allen team. —*Ron Wynn*

Choices / Jul. 29, 1992–Jul. 30, 1992 / Enja ✦✦✦

African Venus / Dec. 11, 1992 / Evidence ✦✦✦✦

Don Redman

b. Jul. 29, 1900, Piedmont, WV, d. Nov. 30, 1964, New York, NY
Clarinet, Alto Saxophone, Leader, Composer, Arranger / Swing, Classic Jazz
The first great arranger in jazz history, Don Redman's innovations as a writer essentially invented the jazz-oriented big band with arrangements that developed yet left room for solo improvisations.

After graduating from college at the age of 20 with a music degree, Redman played for a year with Billy Paige's Broadway Syncopators and then met up with Fletcher Henderson. Redman became Henderson's chief arranger (although Fletcher was often later on mistakenly given credit for the innovative charts) in addition to playing clarinet, alto and (on at least one occasion) oboe. Redman, whose largely spoken vocals were charming, recorded the first ever scat vocal on "My Papa Doesn't Two Time" in early

1924, predating Louis Armstrong. Although his early arrangements were futuristic, they could be a bit stiff, and it was not until Armstrong joined Henderson's Orchestra that Redman (learning from the brilliant cornetist) began to really swing in his writing; "Sugar Foot Stomp" and "The Stampede" are two of his many classic charts.

It was a shock to Fletcher Henderson when Redman was persuaded in 1927 by Jean Goldkette to direct McKinney's Cotton Pickers. Redman soon turned the previously unknown group into a strong competitor of Henderson's, composing such future standards as "Gee Baby, Ain't I Good to You" and "Cherry." He sang more, emphasized his alto over his more primitive-sounding clarinet (guesting on some famous recordings with Louis Armstrong's Savoy Ballroom Five in 1928) and made a strong series of memorable records. In 1931 Redman put together his own big band which lasted (if not prospered) up until 1941. After that he freelanced as an arranger for the remainder of the swing era, led an all-star orchestra in 1946 that became the first band to visit postwar Europe and eventually became Pearl Bailey's musical director. Although he recorded a few sessions in the late '50s, Don Redman's main significance is for his influential work of the 1920s and '30s. —*Scott Yanow*

Shakin' the African / Sep. 24, 1931–Sep. 19, 1932 / Hep ◆◆◆◆

● **Don Redman, 1931–1933** / Sep. 24, 1931–Feb. 2, 1933 / Classics ◆◆◆◆◆

Doin' the New Low Down / Sep. 16, 1932–Apr. 26, 1933 / Hep ◆◆◆◆

● **Don Redman, 1933–1936** / Feb. 2, 1933–May 7, 1936 / Classics ◆◆◆◆◆

● **Don Redman, 1936–1939** / May 7, 1936–Mar. 23, 1939 / Classics ◆◆◆◆◆

For Europeans Only / Sep. 15, 1946 / SteepleChase ◆◆

Don Redman's Park Ave. Patter / Apr. 11, 1957+1957 / Golden Crest ◆◆

Dixieland in High Society / Mar. 16, 1959–Mar. 19, 1959 / Roulette ◆◆◆

Joshua Redman

b. Feb. 1, 1969, Berkeley, CA
Tenor Sax / Post-Bop, Hard Bop
Every few years it seems as if the jazz media goes out of its way to hype one young artist, overpraising him to such an extent that it is easy to tear him down when the next season arrives. In the early '90s Joshua Redman briefly became a media darling, but in his case he largely deserved the attention. A talented loop-based tenorman, Redman (who will probably never be an innovator) is a throwback to the styles of Red Holloway and Gene Ammons but also has an inquisitive spirit and can play intriguing music when inspired.

The son of the great tenor saxophonist Dewey Redman, Joshua graduated from Harvard, and (after debating about whether to become a doctor) he seemed headed toward studying law at Yale. However, Redman came in first place at the 1991 Thelonious Monk competition, landed a recording contract with Warner Bros. and was soon on the cover of most jazz magazines. Pat Metheny was a guest on one of his albums (the Redman-Metheny interplay during their engagements was quite memorable), and although Redman has had success constantly touring with his own group, it is a pity that his apprentice period as a sideman was so brief. —*Scott Yanow*

Joshua Redman / May 27, 1992–Sep. 15, 1992 / Warner Brothers ◆◆◆◆

★ **Wish** / 1993 / Warner Brothers ◆◆◆◆◆
Joshua Redman may be the person to unite warring sects, since he is neither a committed neobop conservative nor a jazz/hip-hopper or "acid" player. He is one of the few young lions that has made great music from day one. Redman's soaring tone, intelligently constructed solos, control and ability to play riveting uptempo, midtempo, or slow works has justifiably made him a sensation. When the lineup includes Pat Metheny offering marvelous solos on electric and acoustic and Charlie Haden and Billy Higgins being their customary masterful selves on bass and drums, you have the kind of great, uncompromising jazz work you seldom get from a major label in the 1990s. —*Ron Wynn*

Moodswing / Mar. 8, 1994–Mar. 10, 1994 / Warner Brothers ◆◆◆◆◆

Spirit of the Moment: Live at the Village Vanguard / 1995 / Warner Brothers ◆◆◆◆◆

Dizzy Reece (Alphonso Son Reece)

b. Jan. 5, 1931, Kingston, Jamaica
Trumpet / Hard Bop
Dizzy Reece is a fine hard-loop trumpeter who has been overshadowed by the innovators of the style. He started on trumpet when he was 14 and moved to Europe in 1949. It was while he was based in England (1954–59) that he achieved some recognition through a series of recordings with top English musicians plus a 1958 date with Donald Byrd. He moved to New York in 1959 but, after a few notable recordings and a bit of publicity, Reece seemed to largely fade away despite remaining active. He was with the Dizzy Gillespie's Orchestra in 1968 and the Paris Reunion Band in 1985. —*Scott Yanow*

Blues in Trinity / Aug. 24, 1958 / Blue Note ◆◆◆◆

Star Bright / Nov. 9, 1959 / Blue Note ◆◆◆◆◆

Soundin' Off / May 12, 1960 / Blue Note ◆◆◆◆

● **Asia Minor** / Mar. 13, 1962 / Original Jazz Classics ◆◆◆◆◆
This is one of trumpeter Dizzy Reece's finest recordings, a well-planned sextet date (reissued on CD) with baritonist Cecil Payne, Joe Farrell on tenor and flute, pianist Hank Jones, bassist Ron Carter and drummer Charlie Persip that is on the level of a Blue Note album. Reece (who contributed three diverse originals) performs mostly minor-toned songs that seem to really inspire the musicians. The solos tend to be concise, but quite meaningful, and overall this hard bop but occasionally surprising session is quite memorable. Strange that Reece would not get another opportunity to lead a record date until 1970. —*Scott Yanow*

Manhattan Project / Jan. 17, 1978 / Bee Hive ◆◆◆◆

Blowin' Away / Jun. 9, 1978 / Interplay ◆◆◆

Eric Reed

b. Philadelphia, PA
Piano / Post-Bop
A superior pianist who is growing in stature year-by-year, Eric Reed began playing piano when he was two and in his childhood often performed in his father's church. He started classical lessons when he was seven, moved with his family to Los Angeles when he was 11 and first met Wynton Marsalis when he was 14, impressing the trumpeter. Reed played in L.A. with John Clayton and the Gerald Wilson Orchestra, toured with Marsalis when he was 18, worked with Freddie Hubbard and Joe Henderson and in the early '90s became a regular member of Wynton Marsalis' group, replacing Marcus Roberts. Eric Reed has recorded with Marsalis and led a couple of fine sessions for the Mojazz label. —*Scott Yanow*

Soldier's Hymn / Nov. 7, 1990 / Candid ◆◆◆◆
Youthful pianist Eric Reed, who at the time of this recording was debuting as Marcus Roberts' replacement in the Wynton Marsalis band, plays carefully and sometimes tentatively on his first release as a leader. It's a trio affair, and although Reed doesn't throw many challenges toward bassist Dwayne Burno or drummer Gregory Hutchinson, he's certainly a solid player with the potential to become a great one. —*Ron Wynn*

● **It's All Right to Swing** / Apr. 1993 / Mojazz ◆◆◆◆◆

The Swing and I / Aug. 9, 1994–Aug. 11, 1994 / Mojazz ◆◆◆◆

Waymon Reed

b. Jan. 10, 1940, Fayetteville, NC, **d.** Nov. 25, 1983, Nashville, TN
Trumpet, Fluegelhorn / Hard Bop
A journeyman jazz trumpeter, Reed was a reliable bop-oriented soloist. After attending the Eastman School of Music and gaining experience playing with R&B groups and with Ira Sullivan in Miami, Reed was a member of James Brown's group during 1965–69 and then was with Count Basie (1969–73). Short stints with the Frank Foster and Thad Jones-Mel Lewis big bands preceded another tour of duty with Basie (1977–78). Reed was married for a time to Sarah Vaughan, and he worked with her during much of 1978–80 before their marriage broke up, and he was stricken with cancer. —*Scott Yanow*

46th & 8th / May 25, 1977 / Artists House ✦✦✦✦
Trumpeter Waymon Reed was considered a reliable bop-influenced soloist and a fine section player in big bands. This was his only opportunity to lead a record date, and the results are pleasingly straight-ahead. Reed is heard on one original (the title cut which is a blues) and four standards along with tenor saxophonist Jimmy Foster, pianist Tommy Flanagan, bassist Keeter Betts and drummer Bobby Durham. Nothing surprising occurs but Reed (particularly on a warm version of the ballad "But Beautiful") is in fine form. —*Scott Yanow*

Dianne Reeves

b. 1956, Detroit, MI
Vocals / R&B, Hard Bop, Pop
Dianne Reeves has thus far had a rather confusing and aimless career. Blessed with a very attractive voice and the ability to be the premiere jazz singer of this era, Reeves seems reluctant to stick to jazz. Her recordings are often rather schizophrenic affairs, rarely reaching the heights of her exciting live performances. Reeves sang (and recorded) with her high school band and was encouraged by Clark Terry, performing with him while a college student at the Univesity of Colorado. She did session work in Los Angeles starting in 1976, toured with Sergio Mendes (1981) and Harry Belafonte (1984) and first started recording as a solo artist in 1982, soon becoming a familiar name on the festival circuit. Many of Reeves' records are long out-of-print although her Blue Note sets (of which *Quiet After The Storm* is the most satisfying thus far) are available. Why Dianne Reeves seems so unwilling to commit herself to jazz (or to any specific idiom) as she nears 40 remains a mystery. —*Scott Yanow*

Welcome to My Love / 1982 / Palo Alto ✦✦

For Every Heart / 1984 / Palo Alto ✦✦

Better Days / 1987 / Blue Note ✦✦✦
Title track was a huge hit. Fluctuates from R&B to jazz. —*Ron Wynn*

I Remember / Apr. 27, 1988–Sep. 11, 1990 / Blue Note ✦✦✦✦
Her best and most complete jazz statement. Top-flight instrumental cast. —*Ron Wynn*

Never Too Far / 1990 / EMI ✦✦✦
Well-sung pop/R&B release. —*Ron Wynn*

● **Quiet After The Storm** / 1994 / Blue Note ✦✦✦✦✦
Dianne Reeves, who has always had a beautiful voice and the potential for greatness in jazz, has conducted a rather directionless career, performing many concerts filled with spontaneity while at the same time recording erratic albums that usually feature both veteran jazz ballads and newer material that is closer to pop and folk music. There are some strong jazz moments on this CD. "Comes Love" has an inventive arrangement that uses a riff from the Miles Davis version of "'Round Midnight" and a familiar rhythmic phrase from "Star Eyes" in surprising ways. "Detour Ahead" is fine and "The Benediction" ("Country Preacher" with Reeves' lyrics) is a sincere tribute to Cannonball Adderley (who makes a brief appearance on soprano via sampling), but on some of the other pieces Reeves wanders far away from jazz. She sings a couple of folk songs with guitarist Dori Caymmi, introduces the heartwarming if poppish original "Nine" and performs a very straight version of Joni Mitchell's "When Morning Comes" that makes the song sound like a Broadway show tune. Perhaps Dianne Reeves' eventual niche will be as a jazz-influenced folk-pop singer; someday she should probably make up her mind. —*Scott Yanow*

Reuben Reeves

b. Oct. 25, 1905, Evansville, IN, **d.** Sep. 1975, New York, NY
Trumpet / Classic Jazz
At one point in the late '20s, Reuben Reeves was one of the more exciting trumpeters in jazz although his star soon faded. After playing locally in the Midwest, he moved to New York in 1924. The following year Reeves relocated to Chicago, and in 1926 he became a member of Erskine Tate's Orchestra. He recorded with Fess Williams and worked with Dave Peyton during 1928–30 but most importantly led a series of record dates in 1929 with his Tributaries and his River Boys; sidemen included his brother Gerald Reeves on trombone and the great clarinetist Omer Simeon. Reuben Reeves had a wild extroverted style that was a little bit like Roy Eldridge would develop a few years later. Reeves

was with Cab Calloway's Orchestra during 1931–32 and then in 1933 returned to Chicago and organized his River Boys for one final session. He toured with his own group during 1933–35, freelanced for a few years, served with the Army during World War II (leading an Army band) and then joined Harry Dial's Blusicians in 1946. His last few years were largely spent outside of music. An RST CD has all of Reuben Reeves' recordings as a leader. —*Scott Yanow*

● **Reuben 'River' Reeves and His River Boys** / May 22, 1929–Dec. 14, 1933 / RST ✦✦✦✦✦

Rufus Reid

b. Feb. 10, 1944, Sacramento, CA
Bass / Post-Bop
A prolific bassist who's seemingly always in the recording studio, Rufus Reid's name appears on countless hard bop, bebop, swing, and even some pop sessions. His restrained, yet emphatic and pungent tone, time, harmonic sensibility and discernible, if understated, swing are welcome on any session. Trumpet was Reid's first love, but he switched to bass while in the Air Force. He played with Buddy Montgomery in Sacramento, then studied music in Seattle and Chicago in the late '60s and early '70s. Reid worked in Chicago with Sonny Stitt, James Moody, Milt Jackson, Curtis Fuller and Dizzy Gillespie and recorded with Kenny Dorham, Dexter Gordon, Lee Konitz and Howard McGhee in 1970. He toured internationally several times with the Bobby Hutcherson—Harold Land quintet, Freddie Hubbard, Nancy Wilson, Eddie Harris and Gordon through the '70s. Reid moved to New York in 1976, playing and recording with a quartet co-led by Thad Jones and Mel Lewis and taught at Williams Paterson College in Wayne, New Jersey starting in 1979. He recorded with Konitz, Ricky Ford, Jack DeJohnette's Special Edition with Kenny Burrell, with a quintet co-led by Frank Wess and Art Farmer and in duos with Kenny Burrell and Harold Danko in the '80s. Reid also did sessions with Art Farmer and Jimmy Heath. He has co-led a group with drummer and longtime musical confidant Akira Tana in the late '80s and '90s. Reid has recorded as a leader for Theresa and Sunnyside. He has some dates available as a leader. —*Ron Wynn*

Perpetual Stroll / Jan. 27, 1980 / Theresa ✦✦✦✦
Bassist Rufus Reid, pianist Kirk Lightsey and drummer Eddie Gladden (all three of whom worked together for awhile as Dexter Gordon's rhythm section) are in fine form on this trio set. Reid contributed two of the songs, Lightsey brought one to the date, and in addition the musicians play a rapid version of Herbie Hancock's "One Finger Snap" while Oscar Pettiford's classic "Tricrotism" becomes a solo bass feature for Reid. Since all three musicians have tended to be underrated through the years, this recording served as a excellent showcase for their often overlooked talents. —*Scott Yanow*

Seven Minds / Nov. 25, 1984 / Sunnyside ✦✦✦✦✦
Premier bassist Reid with pianist Jim McNeely and drummer Teri Lyne Carrington. Extraordinary playing, approaching telepathic. —*Michael G. Nastos*

Corridor to the Limits / Mar. 5, 1989 / Sunnyside ✦✦✦✦

● **Yours and Mine** / Sep. 1990 / Concord Jazz ✦✦✦✦✦
Rufus Reid (b) and Akira Tana (d). Effective session with strong help from young lions Ralph Moore (ts), Jesse Davis (as). 1991 release. —*Ron Wynn*

Django Reinhardt (Jean Baptiste Reinhardt)

b. Jan. 23, 1910, Liverchies, Belgium, **d.** May 16, 1953, Fontainebleau, France
Guitar / Swing
Europe's first influential jazz figure, Django Reinhardt's melodic and harmonic ideas, solo style and general technique have been recycled, absorbed and spread by generations of jazz and blues guitarists. A 1928 fire cost him two fingers on his fret hand. Reinhardt developed a new fingering system and switched from banjo to guitar. He was a spectacular soloist, able to play with furious intensity or incredible sensitivity and a remarkable accompanist who could compliment and support any musician. His switch to electric guitar in the '40s made him even more influential, as he tackled and mastered issues of amplification and volume. Reinhardt wandered through Belgium and France as a gypsy, playing mostly violin and banjo, plus a little guitar. He was

already an adult and professional musician when he discovered jazz. Working with vocalist Jean Sablon, Reinhardt synthesized jazz and traditional gypsy music, developing an approach that borrowed from both but wasn't totally defined by either.

He formed The Hot Club of France in 1934 with violinist Stephane Grappelli plus two other guitarists and a bassist. One original guitarist was his brother Joseph. The Hot Club recorded over 200 songs and were a sensation on both sides of the Atlantic. Such Reinhardt compositions as "Love's Melody," "Stomping At Decca," "Djangology" and "Nocturne" became an established part of the jazz vocabulary. Reinhardt recorded with Coleman Hawkins, Benny Carter, Dicky Wells, Rex Stewart and Barney Bigard between 1937 and 1939, then the quintet recorded in London in 1939. Reinhardt's "Nuages" was a fan favorite during World War II. He began experiments with a big band, while also forming a quintet with clarinetist Hubert Rostaing. The Nazis banned jazz in France and murdered 500,000 gypsies, but Reinhardt continued playing.

The quintet was recreated for a 1946 recording session, and Reinhardt arranged the music for the film "Le Village De La Colere" with Andre Hodeir. Later that year Reinhardt journeyed to America to tour with Duke Ellington. But the tour was unsuccessful, in part due to Reinhardt's penchant for disappearing. He began to appreciate, then play bop and adapt its lines on guitar. There were occasional reunions with Grappelli before Reinhardt died of a stroke in 1953. A documentary film about his life was made by Paul Paviot in 1958. Django Reinhardt remains a highly influential force and can be thought of not only as a top European jazz artist but as the world's top jazz guitarist (along with Charlie Christian) of 1933–53. —*Ron Wynn and Dan Morgenstern*

Djangologie 1 / Mar. 15, 1928–May 4, 1936 / EMI ✦✦✦✦
This 20-LP series by EMI features guitarist Django Reinhardt and violinist Stephane Grappelli on recordings not duplicated by the various GNP/Crescendo reissues. In fact, the first 11 selections on the first volume (which has sideman appearances with pianist Garnet Clark, tenor saxophonist Coleman Hawkins, violinist Michel Warlop and three early recordings including one song that features Django on banjo in 1928), are not on the massive EMI ten-CD set Djangology. —*Scott Yanow*

★ **Djangologie/USA, Vols. 1–7** / Mar. 15, 1928–Oct. 1, 1940 / Swing ✦✦✦✦✦
This seven LP box set, made available domestically by DRG, mostly features the remarkable guitarist Django Reinhardt with The Quintet of the Hot Club of France during 1936–39, showing that not only could Europeans play swinging jazz as far back as the 1930s, but they could be pacesetters and innovators too. Violinist Stephane Grappelli also stars throughout this set, which includes appearances with bands led by Benny Carter, Coleman Hawkins, Rex Stewart, harmonica wizard Larry Adler, trumpeter Philippe Brun, trumpeter Bill Coleman, violinist Eddie South and trombonist Dicky Wells along with many performances by the Quintet. The first album is in some ways the most interesting for it features Django as a sideman with a wide variety of French groups including two very early appearances on banjo. A book included in the box has a complete discography of Django Reinhardt's career. Highly recommended, it's superior to the CD reissues of some of this material. —*Scott Yanow*

The Versatile Giant / Aug. 1934–Feb. 10, 1951 / Inner City ✦✦✦✦
This hard-to-find LP contains a variety of collectors items that nearly span guitarist Django Reinhardt's entire career. He is heard on three very early recordings (two with violinist Stephane Grappelli), playing four songs taken from his erratic 1946 tour with Duke Ellington (Ellington's orchestra unfortunately is very much in the background), on a few rarities with his 1947 sextet and in 1951 performing two numbers recorded live at the Club Saint Germain in Paris. Reinhardt collectors will have to be patient searching for this one. —*Scott Yanow*

Django Reinhardt (1935) / 1935 / GNP ✦✦✦
Of the dozen selections on this LP, six feature The Quintet of the Hot Club of France, either tenor saxophonist Alix Combelle or multi-instrumentalist Frank "Big Boy" Goudie (heard on trumpet, tenor and clarinet) sit in on four other numbers and two songs find guitarist Django Reinhardt and violinist Stephane Grappelli welcoming three trumpeters and a trombonist to the Quintet. Highlights include "Djangology," "Smoke Rings," "Cloudsof" and "The Sheik of Araby." All of the GNP Django LPs are recom-

mended and they generally do not duplicate other reissue series. —*Scott Yanow*

Parisian Swing / Apr. 1935–Aug. 25, 1939 / GNP ✦✦✦✦
Over a period of time, GNP/Crescendo released seven LPs featuring guitarist Django Reinhardt, violinist Stephane Grappelli and The Quintet of the Hot Club of France. This particular set has four titles from 1935 and the remainder from 1938–39. Of the latter, four songs actually find Reinhardt and Grappelli playing duets (Stephane is on piano on three of those cuts). Highpoints of this enjoyable LP include "Undecided," "Djangology," "Nocturne" and "I've Got My Love to Keep Me Warm." —*Scott Yanow*

Django '35–'39 / Sep. 30, 1935–Mar. 21, 1939 / GNP ✦✦✦✦
Although it would have been preferable for GNP/Crescendo in their seven LPs of Django Reinhardt recordings to reissue his music in strict chronological order, each of these sets are well worth acquiring. Guitarist Reinhardt and violinist Stephane Grappelli are in superb form on the 14 selections that comprise this particular LP, performances taken from four different recording sessions. Such numbers as "Limehouse Blues," "I Found a New Baby," "It Don't Mean a Thing" and "Swing '39" are among the highlights of this consistently swinging set. —*Scott Yanow*

★ **Djangology** / May 4, 1936–Mar. 10, 1948 / EMI ✦✦✦✦✦
This massive ten-CD set of Django Reinhardt's recordings covers some of the same ground as the earlier 20-LP Djangology EMI series, duplicating the music on Vols. 2–15 along with three tracks from the first LP and ten from Vol. 16. However, there are 34 additional selections that were formerly overlooked (on some of those songs Reinhardt only plays a minor role). This essential box contains 243 performances taken from a twelve-year period, tracing Reinhardt's career from his performances with The Quintet of the Hot Club of France (which co-starred violinist Stephane Grappelli) through the war years (with the guitarist heard in a wide variety of settings) and the formation of his postwar quintet with clarinetist Hubert Rostaing before concluding with a reunion with Grappelli. Recommended to all serious Django Reinhardt collectors. —*Scott Yanow*

Django Reinhardt & Stephane Grappelli / Jan. 31, 1938–Feb. 1, 1946 / GNP Crescendo ✦✦✦✦✦
Of the seven LPs of Django Reinhardt's recordings reissued by GNP/Crescendo, this is the most consistently exciting set. Guitarist Reinhardt and violinist Stephane Grappelli are heard teaming up in their 1938–39 quintet and on a reunion session in 1946. They are in particularly superb form on "Honcysuckle Rose," "Liza," "Nuages" and "Sweet Georgia Brown"; actually all 14 performances are quite rewarding. —*Scott Yanow*

Vol. 3 / Mar. 14, 1938–May 17, 1939 / JSP ✦✦✦✦✦
This CD from the English label JSP will fill some major gaps even for veteran Django Reinhardt collectors for the 24 selections (which include five alternate takes) are among the rarest in Django's discography. The remarkable guitarist is teamed with violinist Stephane Grappelli and The Quintet of the Hot Club of France for consistently exciting and heated swing performances. Highlights include "Swing from Paris," "Swing '39," "Tea for Two" and "My Melancholy Baby." —*Scott Yanow*

Django's Music / Feb. 22, 1940–Jul. 7, 1943 / Hep ✦✦✦✦

Paris 1945 / 1945 / Columbia ✦✦✦✦
This French Columbia LP will be difficult to find but contains a variety of valuable music from postwar Paris. Guitarist Django Reinhardt is heard jamming on four selections with an American sextet that also features trumpeter Bernie Privin, Peanuts Hucko on tenor and pianist Mel Powell. Hucko (on clarinet) is featured on four other songs in a trio and Powell gets a few unaccompanied piano solos including "Hommage a Fats Waller" and "Hommage a Debussy." High-quality late swing music that has not been reissued in recent times. —*Scott Yanow*

Swing Guitar / Oct. 26, 1945–Mar. 1946 / Jass ✦✦✦✦
In late 1945 the great guitarist Django Reinhardt had an opportunity to broadcast regularly with The ATC (Air Transport Command) Orchestra, a big band filled with talented but now-forgotten American servicemen. Reinhardt is the main soloist throughout, whether with the full orchestra or with small groups out of the band; he also takes "Improvisation No. 6" unaccompanied. In addition, The ATC band is heard on six selections without the guitarist. All in all, this is a surprising and consistently interesting release. —*Scott Yanow*

★ **Peche a La Mouche** / Apr. 16, 1947–Mar. 10, 1953 / Verve ✦✦✦✦✦
Legend has it that guitarist Django Reinhardt was at his absolute
peak in the 1930s during his recordings with violinist Stephane
Grappelli and that when he switched from acoustic to electric guitar after World War II, he lost a bit of his musical personality.
Wrong on both counts. This double CD documents his Blue Star
recordings of 1947 and 1953 and Reinhardt (on electric guitar)
takes inventive boppish solos that put him at the top of the list of
jazz guitarists who were active during the era. Most of the earlier
tracks feature Reinhardt in The Quintet of the Hot Club of France
with clarinetist Hubert Rostaing, but it is the eight later selections
in which he is backed by a standard rhythm section that are most
interesting. These well-recorded performances hint at what
Django Reinhardt might have accomplished in the 1950s had he
lived longer. Highly recommended. —Scott Yanow

Legendary Django / Sep. 7, 1947–Nov. 8, 1947 / GNP ✦✦✦
This GNP/Crescendo LP (which lists neither dates nor personnel)
is drawn from several session from 1947, a year when guitarist
Django Reinhardt recorded quite a bit. He is heard with violinist
Stephane Grappelli on four standards (including interesting
remakes of "Tiger Rag" and "Dinah") and with quintets featuring
either Hubert Rostaing or Gerald Leveque on clarinets. This is one
of seven Reinhardt albums put out by GNP/Crescendo, and all are
recommended. —Scott Yanow

The Immortal Django Reinhardt / Sep. 7, 1947–Nov. 21, 1947 /
GNP ✦✦✦
On this GNP/Crescendo LP (one of seven Django Reinhardt
albums the label has released), the guitarist is featured in two settings. He joins violinist Stephane Grappelli for a 1947 reunion
that swings fairly well and is also heard with his quintet (featuring clarinetist Hubert Rostaing) for ten other numbers from the
same period. The recording dates are unfortunately not listed in
the liner notes, but the music (which shows the influence of bop)
is timeless. —Scott Yanow

Djangologie 16 / Nov. 14, 1947–Jan. 1949 / EMI ✦✦✦✦
All 14 selections on this 16th volume of EMI's twenty-LP Django
Reinhardt series reunite the great guitarist with violinist Stephane
Grappelli. They teamed up on Nov. 14, 1947, March 10, 1948 and
then, starting with the final four selections, for an extensive series
of recordings in Jan. and Feb. 1949. Although there are a few stan-
dards included, there are also a surprising number of originals.
The old magic was still there. —Scott Yanow

Django Reinhardt/Sidney Bechet—Deux Geants Du Jazz /
1947–Jun. 26, 1957 / Vogue ✦✦✦
Despite the title, unfortunately guitarist Django Reinhardt and
soprano saxophonist Sidney Bechet do not actually play together.
Instead they are heard on alternating tracks. Reinhardt's performances (taken from radio broadcasts) feature him in 1947 with
his Quintet (starring clarinetist Maurice Meurnier) and are fine,
but it is the Bechet selections (which originated from a variety of
sources between 1952–57) that are most exciting, particularly
"Roses of Picardy," "Down by the Old Stream" and his hit "Petite
Fleur." It's worth picking up as an introduction to these two classic jazzmen. —Scott Yanow

Djangologie 17 / Jan. 1949–Feb. 1949 / EMI ✦✦✦✦
Unlike the first 16 LPs in this 20-volume series, the final four
albums were not reissued as part of EMI's ten-CD box set. Vol. 17
has 14 of the many selections recorded at some marathon sessions in Italy during Jan. and Feb. 1949, the final recorded reunion
of guitarist Django Reinhardt and violinist Stephane Grappelli.
Eleven of the songs on this album (including Reinhardt's
"Nuages") are standards, but the two principals (backed by a standard rhythm section) come up with consistently fresh and swinging statements. —Scott Yanow

Djangologie 20 / Jan. 1949–Feb. 1949 / EMI ✦✦✦✦
The 20th and final volume in this giant EMI Django Reinhardt
series sticks to the Django Reinhardt-Stephane Grappelli reunion
of 1949, their final meeting on records. The guitarist proves to be
much more influenced by bop (and more modern) than the violinist, but they clearly inspired and brought out the best in each
other. —Scott Yanow

● **Djangology 49** / Jan. 1949–Feb. 1949 / Bluebird ✦✦✦✦✦
In 1949, guitarist Django Reinhardt and violinist Stephane
Grappelli met up in Italy, playing several engagements with
Italian rhythm sections and recording an extensive series of songs.
This Bluebird CD contains 20 of the best performances, and even

if the rhythm section is fairly irrelevant, Django and Grappelli
constantly challenge each other to play at their most creative.
These recordings do not duplicate the ones reissued by EMI. —
Scott Yanow

Djangologie 18 / Jan. 1949–1950 / EMI ✦✦✦✦
In addition to three numbers from his 1949 reunion with violinist Stephane Grappelli, guitarist Django Reinhardt is heard on this
LP with the 1950 version of his Quintet of the Hot Club of France,
which at the time also featured altoist Andre Ekyan. The hot
album of updated swing (the 18th in a series of 20) concludes
with unaccompanied guitar performances of "Belleville" and
"Nuages." This classic music has not yet appeared on CD. —Scott
Yanow

Djangologie 19 / Jan. 1949–May 1950 / EMI ✦✦✦✦
The 19th of 20 LPs in EMI's very valuable Django Reinhardt
series contains more timeless music that is not yet available on
CD. Six selections date from the extensive (and final) musical
reunion with violinist Stephane Grappelli in 1949. It is interesting
to hear them interpret such songs as "The Peanut Vendor" and "It
Might as Well Be Spring." The remainder of this set is from April
and May 1950 and finds altoist Andre Ekyan co-starring as a
member of Reinhardt's Quintet of the Hot Club of France. Five of
the seven songs that they perform are Reinhardt originals. It's a
well-rounded and highly enjoyable album. —Scott Yanow

At Club St. Germain / Feb. 1951 / Honeysuckle Rose ✦✦✦✦
This collector's LP contains music privately recorded at two live
engagements in 1951 that feature the great guitarist Django
Reinhardt just two years before his death. Performing with a quintet and a sextet that also includes altoist Hubert Fol and sometimes trumpeter Bernard Hulin, Reinhardt is in fine form on the
mixture of standards and originals, playing in a boppish style that
shows that he was continuing to evolve. —Scott Yanow

Emily Remler

b. Sep. 18, 1957, New York, NY, **d.** May 4, 1990, Sydney, Australia
Guitar / Hard Bop
Emily Remler's death at age 32 from a heart attack (certainly not
helped by her frequent use of heroin) was a shock to the jazz
world and a sad waste. She was just beginning to emerge from
the Wes Montgomery influence and develop her own voice.
Remler began playing guitar when she was ten, attended Berklee
(1976–79) and recorded as a leader for the first time in 1980. She
played with the L.A. version of the show *Sophisticated Ladies*
(1981–82) and in 1985 had a duo with Larry Coryell but otherwise mostly worked as a leader with her own small groups. After
recording bop-oriented dates for Concord, she had a "contemporary" set for Justice and toured with David Benoit before her sudden death. —Scott Yanow

Firefly / Apr. 1981 / Concord Jazz ✦✦✦✦

Retrospective, Vol. 2 / 1981–1988 / Concord Jazz ✦✦✦

● **Take Two** / Jun. 1982 / Concord Jazz ✦✦✦✦✦

Transitions / Oct. 1983 / Concord Jazz ✦✦✦✦✦

Catwalk / Aug. 1984 / Concord Jazz ✦✦✦✦✦
Guitarist Emily Remler's fourth Concord recording makes one
regret even more her premature death at age 32. While her earlier dates were very much in the bop mainstream, this one (in a
quartet with trumpeter John D'Earth, bassist Eddie Gomez and
drummer Bob Moses) finds her looking ahead and partly finding
her own voice on her seven diverse originals. Although she never
became an innovator, Remler certainly had a lot to offer the jazz
world, and this fairly adventurous effort was one of the finest
recordings of her short career. —Scott Yanow

East to West / May 1988 / Concord Jazz ✦✦✦✦
With the Hank Jones Trio. —Michael G. Nastos

This Is Me / 1990 / Justice ✦✦✦

Revolutionary Ensemble

Group / Avant-Garde
One of the most radical jazz groups of 1971–77, the Revolutionary
Ensemble was comprised of violinist Leroy Jenkins, bassist Sirone
and drummer Frank Clayton (who was replaced by Jerome
Cooper in September 1971). Their music emphasized group
improvisations, made strong use of space and "miscellaneous
instruments" (following in the tradition of the AACM and the Art
Ensemble of Chicago) and was quite original if not at all accessi-

ble. The group recorded for ESP, India Navigation, Horizon and Enja before disbanding. —*Scott Yanow*

Manhattan Cycles / Dec. 31, 1972 / India Navigation ✦✦✦✦

Vietnam / 1972 / ESP ✦✦✦✦

★ **The People's Republic** / Dec. 4, 1975–Dec. 6, 1975 / A&M ✦✦✦✦✦
Definitive statement from the all-time best avant-garde band (next to The Art Ensemble). Open listeners only. This album is a must-buy. —*Michael G. Nastos*

Mel Rhyne

b. Oct. 12, 1936, Indianapolis, IN
Organ / Hard Bop
Organist who was a major foil for Wes Montgomery. The bridge between Jimmy Smith and Larry Young. Still plays in the Milwaukee area but was originally from the legendary Indianapolis conclave. —*Michael G. Nastos*

Organizing / Mar. 31, 1960 / Jazzland ✦✦✦✦
With Johnny Griffin on tenor sax and Blue Mitchell on trumpet. —*Michael G. Nastos*

The Legend / Dec. 30, 1991 / Criss Cross ✦✦✦✦

● **Boss Organ** / Jan. 6, 1993 / Criss Cross ✦✦✦✦✦
Mel Rhyne, best known for his association in the 1960s with Wes Montgomery, re-emerged with this Criss Cross CD as one of the finest jazz organists around. He is matched with guitarist Peter Bernstein, drummer Kenny Washington and the young tenor great Joshua Redman for a set of good-natured and often hard-swinging performances. In addition to superior versions of "All God's Chillun Got Rhythm" and "Jeannine," the quartet explores lesser-known songs such as Hubert Laws' "Shades of Light," Stevie Wonder's "You and I" and Mel Tormé's "Born to Be Blue." The music is consistently stimulating and swinging. —*Scott Yanow*

Buddy Rich (Bernard Rich)

b. Sep. 30, 1917, New York, NY, d. Apr. 2, 1987, Los Angeles, CA
Drums, Leader / Bop, Swing
When it came to technique, speed, power and the ability to put together incredible drum solos, Buddy Rich lived up to the billing of "the world's greatest drummer." Although some other drummers were more innovative, in reality none were in his league even during the early days. A genius, Buddy Rich started playing drums in vaudeville as "Traps, the Drum Wonder" when he was only 18 months old; he was completely self-taught. Rich performed in vaudeville throughout his childhood and developed into a decent singer and a fine tap dancer. But drumming was his purpose in life, and by 1938 he had discovered jazz and was playing with Joe Marsala's combo. Rich was soon propelling Bunny Berigan's Orchestra, he spent most of 1939 with Artie Shaw (at a time when the clarinetist had the most popular band in swing), and then from 1939–45 (except for a stint in the military) he was making history with Tommy Dorsey. During this era, it became obvious that Buddy Rich was the king of drummers, easily dethroning his friend Gene Krupa. Rich had a boppish band during 1945–47 that did not catch on, toured with Jazz at the Philharmonic, recorded with a countless number of All-Stars in the 1950s for Verve (including Charlie Parker, Lester Young, Art Tatum and Lionel Hampton) and worked with Les Brown, Charlie Ventura, Tommy Dorsey (1954–55) and Harry James (off and on during 1953–66). A heart attack in 1959 only slowed him down briefly, and although he contemplated becoming a fulltime vocalist, Rich never gave up the drums.
In 1966 Buddy Rich beat the odds and put together a successful big band that would be his main outlet for his final 20 years. His heart began giving him trouble starting in 1983, but Rich never gave his music less than 100 percent and was still pushing himself at the end. A perfectionist who expected the same from his sidemen (some of whom he treated cruelly), Buddy Rich is definitively documented in Mel Tormé's book *Traps the Drum Wonder*. His incredible playing can be viewed on several readily available videotapes although surprisingly few of his later big-band albums have been made available yet on CD. —*Scott Yanow*

And His Legendary '47–'48 Orchestra / Oct. 1946–Sep. 1948 / Hep ✦✦✦✦

This One's for Basie / Aug. 24, 1956–Aug. 25, 1956 / Verve ✦✦✦✦✦
Marty Paich, Buddy and top Los Angeles studio musicians play Basie. —*Buz Overbeck*

Rich Versus Roach / Apr. 1959 / Mercury ✦✦✦✦
Definitive battle of the drummers from 1959. CD has four bonus cuts. —*Ron Wynn*

Swingin' New Big Band / Sep. 29, 1966–Oct. 10, 1966 / Pacific Jazz ✦✦✦✦

Big Swing Face / Feb. 22, 1967–Mar. 14, 1967 / Pacific Jazz ✦✦✦
A mid-'60s session with swing great Buddy Rich and his big band trying to find some comfortable middle ground between pop and jazz. This had some decent stompers and some not-so-good pop and rock covers. But there are a couple of high-energy Buddy Rich drum solos included, so his legions won't be disappointed. —*Ron Wynn*

The New One / Jun. 15, 1967–Nov. 30, 1967 / Pacific Jazz ✦✦✦✦

★ **Mercy, Mercy** / Jul. 10, 1968 / World Pacific ✦✦✦✦✦

Buddy & Soul / Jan. 3, 1969–Jun. 22, 1969 / PA/USA ✦✦✦✦

Keep the Customer Satisfied / Feb. 1970 / Liberty ✦✦✦

Different Drummer / Jul. 14, 1971–Aug. 16, 1971 / RCA ✦✦✦✦

● **Time Being** / Aug. 13, 1971–Aug. 10, 1972 / Bluebird ✦✦✦✦✦

● **Rich in London** / Dec. 6, 1971–Dec. 8, 1971 / RCA ✦✦✦✦✦

The Roar of '74 / Oct. 1973 / Groove Merchant ✦✦✦✦
Mid-'70s big band tracks featuring the Buddy Rich orchestra doing a mixture of straight swing, pop, rock and even a little soul jazz and blues on this set. It was originally issued on the now-defunct Groove Merchant label and included some high-voltage Rich drum solos as well. —*Ron Wynn*

Very Live at Buddy's Place / May 1974 / Groove Merchant ✦✦✦✦

The Last Blues Album, Vol. 1 / Nov. 1974 / Groove Merchant ✦✦✦

Big Band Machine / 1975 / Groove Merchant ✦✦✦✦

Speak No Evil / Feb. 1976 / RCA ✦✦✦

Buddy Rich Plays and Plays and Plays / Feb. 2, 1977 / RCA ✦✦✦✦

Lionel Hampton Presents Buddy Rich / Jul. 1977 / Who's Who In Jazz ✦✦✦✦
One in the series of albums Hampton produced and issued on the Who's Who label in the '70s, this one featured Buddy Rich's late-'70s orchestra. It was a well-polished, cohesive group, although it lacked dynamic soloists other than tenor saxophonist Steve Marcus. Still, Rich drove them hard and provided his own excitement with powerhouse drumming. —*Ron Wynn*

Best Band I Ever Had / Oct. 1977 / DCC ✦✦✦✦✦

Live at King Street Cafe / Apr. 3, 1985 / Cafe ✦✦✦✦

Jerome Richardson

b. Nov. 15, 1920, Sealy, TX
Flute, Soprano Saxophone, Soprano Saxophone / Cool, Hard Bop
Jerome Richardson was once a notable, versatile jazz saxophonist. He remains quite versatile, but his visibility has been limited for years due to his heavy studio output. Since the early '70s, Richardson's often robust saxophone and tart flute have been heard mostly on film and television soundtracks. Richardson began playing alto at eight and was a professional at 14. He worked with Texas dance bands until 1941, then was briefly in Jimmie Lunceford's band before joining the Navy. He worked in a band led by Marshall Royal in the service. Richardson toured with Lionel Hampton after his discharge in the late '40s, then played with Earl Hines in the early '50s. Richardson moved to New York in 1953, led his own band at Minton's and worked with Oscar Pettiford in 1956 and 1957. He did sessions with Lucky Millinder, Cootie Williams, Chico Hamilton, Johnny Richards, Gerry Mulligan and Gerald Wilson, then joined Quincy Jones' orchestra in 1959. He was part of the band for the show "Free and Easy," which toured Europe and performed in Paris.
Richardson played in bands backing several singers in the '60s, among them Peggy Lee, Billy Eckstine, Brook Benton and Julie London. He was a founding member of the Thad Jones–Mel Lewis orchestra in the mid-'60s and was its lead alto saxophonist until 1970. Then Richardson moved to Hollywood and has since frequently collaborated with Jones, doing albums and touring Japan three times together. He toured Europe with Nat Adderley in 1980. Richardson recorded in the '60s as a leader for New Jazz and United Artists, among others. He currently has no sesssions available as a leader but can be heard on CD reissues by Jones and the Thad Jones–Mel Lewis orchestra. —*Ron Wynn*

● **Midnight Oil** / Nov. 10, 1958 / Original Jazz Classics ✦✦✦✦✦
Flutist Jerome Richardson (who switches to tenor on one of the five selections on this CD reissue) has long been underrated and has had relatively few opportunities to lead his own record dates, only four up to the present time of which *Midnight Oil* was the first. The music (three of Richardson's originals plus Artie Shaw's "Lyric" and the standard "Caravan") is performed in swinging fashion by Richardson, trombonist Jimmy Cleveland (the unusual flute-trombone blend heard on three of the songs is quite pleasing), pianist Hank Jones, guitarist Kenny Burrell, bassist Joe Benjamin and drummer Charlie Persip. This set offers cool-toned bop that, although brief in playing time (just over 35 minutes), is easy to enjoy. —*Scott Yanow*

Roamin' with Richardson / Oct. 21, 1959 / Original Jazz Classics ✦✦✦✦
Jerome Richardson has long been one of the most versatile of jazzmen, able to get a personal sound and to swing on flute, tenor, alto, soprano and baritone. For his quartet date with pianist Richard Wyands (who at this point often sounded like Red Garland), bassist George Tucker and drummer Charlie Persip, Richardson plays baritone on three songs (in a deep tone a little reminiscent of Pepper Adams and Leo Parker), two on tenor and one on flute. The CD reissue (the second of only four sessions that the reedman has had as a leader) finds Richardson in excellent form, swinging through three group originals, "I Never Knew," "Poinciana" and a strong version (on baritone) of Duke Ellington's "Warm Valley." —*Scott Yanow*

Going to the Movies / Apr. 1962 / United Artists ✦✦✦
Groove Merchant / Oct. 13, 1967+Oct. 17, 1967 / Verve ✦✦

Dannie Richmond (Charles D. Richmond)

b. Dec. 15, 1935, New York City, d. Mar. 15, 1988, New York City
Drums / Post-Bop
Closely associated with Charles Mingus, Dannie Richmond was on most of his sessions from 1955-78, showing impressive versatility. Richmond and Mingus made for a very potent team, shifting rhythms, tempos and grooves together, hinting at New Orleans jazz now and then while sometimes playing very freely. Richmond was originally a tenor saxophonist who as a teenager played R&B, touring with Paul Williams. He took up the drums in 1955 and six months later joined Charles Mingus when he proved that he could play at very fast tempos. During Mingus' off periods, Richmond freelanced with Chet Baker, the group Mark-Almond, Joe Cocker and even Elton John. After Mingus' death, Richmond played with Mingus Dynasty and then became a member of the George Adams-Don Pullen Quartet (1980-85), occasionally leading his own groups. —*Scott Yanow*

In Jazz for the Culture Set / 1965 / Impulse! ✦✦✦✦
With pianist Jaki Byard and harmonicist Toots Thielemans. Andy Warhol soup-can cover art. Great record. —*Michael G. Nastos*

Ode to Mingus / Nov. 23, 1979–Nov. 24, 1979 / Soul Note ✦✦✦✦✦
A super tribute to his longtime employer and musical comrade. The set should have made the jazz world notice Bill Saxton on tenor sax. —*Ron Wynn*

Plays Charles Mingus / Aug. 16, 1980 / Timeless ✦✦✦✦

● **Quintet** / Sep. 24, 1980 / Gatemouth ✦✦✦✦✦
Mingus drummer with bandmates trumpeter Jack Walrath, saxophonist Ricky Ford. Great 21-1/2-minute version of "Cumbia & Jazz Fusion." —*Michael G. Nastos*

Dionysius / May 30, 1983 / Red Record ✦✦✦✦
An album played by ex-Mingusites, this is one side originals and one side of Charles Mingus' music. Features Jack Walrath (tpt), Ricky Ford (ts), Bob Neloms (p), and Cameron Brown (b). —*Michael G. Nastos*

Gentleman's Agreement / 1983 / Soul Note ✦✦✦
Sizzling cuts, with old pros Jimmy Knepper on trombone and Hugh Lawson on piano taking care of business. —*Ron Wynn*

Larry Ridley

b. Sept. 3, 1937, Indianapolis, IN
Bass / Hard Bop
A consistently propulsive, aggressive player, bassist Larry Ridley's among the more energized players in bebop and hard bop circles. His tone isn't as pronounced as some others, but he compensates with strong support and a steady rhythmic intensity. Ridley began

on violin as a child, then later turned to bass. He worked with longtime friend Freddie Hubbard in Indianapolis as a teen, then got his first professional job with Wes Montgomery. Ridley changed from violin to bass studies at Indiana University and later was tutored by Percy Heath at the Lenox School of Jazz. He worked briefly with Hubbard in New York in 1959, then toured the next year with Slide Hampton. Ridley worked with Max Roach, Philly Joe Jones, Roy Haynes and Horace Silver in the '60s, then recorded in Europe with George Wein's Newport All-Stars in 1969. He toured with Thelonious Monk in 1970 and played with him until 1973. After obtaining a degree in music education from New York University in 1971, Ridley eventually became head of the jazz program and chairman of the music department at Livingston College (Rutgers). He was in Jones' group Dameronia in the '80s and served on the executive committee of the National Jazz Service Organization. Ridley recorded as a leader for Strata East in the '70s and with Hampton, Lee Morgan, Silver, Stephane Grappelli and Joe Venuti, James Moody and Teddy Edwards in the '60s and '70s. His lone album has not been reissued on CD, but he can be heard on reissues by Morgan, Silver and others. —*Ron Wynn*

Ben Riley

b. Jul. 17, 1933, Savannah, GA
Drums / Hard Bop
An excellent drummer whose strong support has helped a variety of advanced bop sessions, Ben Riley is best-known for his association with Thelonious Monk's Quartet even though he was only a member for three years. Prior to playing with Monk, Riley performed with many combos including those led by Randy Weston, Sonny Stitt, Stan Getz, Junior Mance, Kenny Burrell, Eddie "Lockjaw" Davis-Johnny Griffin (1960-62), Ahmad Jamal, Billy Taylor and Ray Bryant. His well-documented stint with Monk (1964-67) was followed by associations with Alice Coltrane (on and off during 1968-75), the New York Quartet (throughout the 1970s and '80s), Ron Carter (1975-77), Jim Hall (1981) and the group Sphere. In addition, Riley has toured extensively with Abdullah Ibrahim. —*Scott Yanow*

The Rippingtons

Group / Instrumental Pop, Crossover
One of the most popular groups in what is loosely termed "contemporary jazz," the Rippingtons were formed (and have been led ever since) by guitarist/keyboardist Russ Freeman (no relation to the veteran West Coast bop pianist of the same name). Freeman (born Feb. 11, 1960 in Nashville) studied at Cal Arts and UCLA and recorded *Nocturnal Playground* as a leader in 1985 for the Brainchild label, a one-man project. In 1987 he was approached to record for the Japanese Alfa label and came up with the Rippingtons name for the all-star group he used on the disc (*Moonlighting*), an ensemble featuring David Benoit, Kenny G. and Brandon Fields. Their album was released domestically by Passport and became a hit. Freeman soon formed a regular touring band (usually including saxophonist Jeff Kashiwa, bassist Kim Stone, drummer Tony Morales and percussionist Steve Reid), cut a second disc for Passport, and the group has since recorded regularly for GRP. Russ Freeman writes all of the music for the Rippingtons, much of which falls in the pop/R&B genre. —*Scott Yanow*

Kilimanjaro / 1988 / GRP ✦✦✦
Tourist in Paradise / 1989 / GRP ✦✦✦
Welcome to the St. James' Club / 1990 / GRP ✦✦✦
Curves Ahead / 1991 / GRP ✦✦
Weekend in Monaco / 1992 / GRP ✦✦
● **Live in L.A.** / Sep. 1992 / GRP ✦✦✦✦✦

Lee Ritenour

b. Nov. 1, 1952, Hollywood, CA
Guitar / Instrumental Pop, Crossover
Lee Ritenour has long been the perfect studio musician, one who can melt into the background without making any impact. While he possesses impressive technique, Ritenour has mostly played instrumental pop throughout his career, sometimes with a Brazilian flavor. His few jazz efforts have found him essentially imitating Wes Montgomery, but despite that he has been consistently popular since the mid-'70s. After touring with Sergio

Mendes' Brasil '77 in 1973, Ritenour became a very busy studio guitarist in Los Angeles, taking time off for occasional tours with his groups and in the mid-'90s with Bob James in Fourplay. He has recorded many albums as a leader, most recently for GRP. — *Scott Yanow*

First Course / 1976 / Epic ♦♦

Gentle Thoughts / May 1977 / JVC ♦♦♦

Sugarloaf Express / Sep. 1977 / JVC ♦♦♦

Captain Fingers / 1977 / Epic ♦♦

Captain's Journey / Dec. 13, 1978 / Elektra ♦♦♦
Guitarist Lee Ritenour had just switched from Epic to Elektra when he cut *Captain's Journey*. It was a followup to the successful crossover work *Captain Fingers* and used a similar strategy: tight, hook-laden arrangements, polished production and minimal solo space. What individual things it has are dominated by Ritenour, a supremely talented guitarist who doesn't display that much of it with these arrangements. — *Ron Wynn*

Rio / Aug. 1979–Sep. 1979 / GRP ♦♦♦♦
Ritenour on acoustic. Very nice music. — *Michael Erlewine*

Feel the Night / 1979 / Elektra ♦♦
One of the albums that established the guitarist. — *Michael Erlewine*

Banded Together / 1984 / Elektra ♦♦

Earth Run / Apr. 1986 / GRP ♦♦

Portrait / Jan. 1987 / GRP ♦♦♦

Festival / May 1988 / GRP ♦♦♦

Color Rit / Mar. 1989 / GRP ♦♦♦

Stolen Moments / 1990 / GRP ♦♦♦♦

Wes Bound / Sep. 1992–Oct. 1992 / GRP ♦♦♦♦
Lee Ritenour, a superior studio guitarist, has recorded very few jazz albums throughout his career, preferring to play melodic pop and light funk. On the rare occasions when he has had an urge to perform jazz, Ritenour has been more than happy to show off the influence of Wes Montgomery; therefore this tribute is a logical move even if the results are not all that exciting. Ritenour mostly plays pieces from the later (and more commercial) half of Montgomery's career along with four of his own originals that are sort of in the tradition. He also hedges his bet a little by throwing in a Bob Marley reggae tune. For jazz listeners who wish to sample some Lee Ritenour, this is one of his better recordings, but why purchase *Wes Bound* when there are so many more signifi cant Wes Montgomery albums currently in print? — *Scott Yanow*

● **Larry & Lee** / Jun. 1994–Jan. 1995 / GRP ♦♦♦♦♦
Larry Carlton and Lee Ritenour have had parallel careers, but this CD is their first joint meeting on record. The two guitarists complement each other well, and there are hints of Wes Montgomery along with a tribute to Joe Pass ("Remembering J.P."), but the songs (all of them their originals) are little more than rhythmic grooves most of the time with the usual fadeouts. The consistently lightweight music is reasonably pleasing but never too stimulating. — *Scott Yanow*

Sam Rivers

b. Sep. 25, 1930, El Reno, OK
Flute, Soprano Saxophone, Tenor Saxophone / Avant-Garde, Post-Bop
Although often overlooked, Sam Rivers has long been one of the most original voices of the avant-garde, equally skilled on tenor, soprano and flute. Music ran in his family for his grandfather published a book of hymns and black folk songs in 1882, his mother played piano, and his father sang with the Fisk Jubilee Singers. Rivers' musical interests, however, were in a different direction. He started on piano when he was five and then learned violin, alto, soprano and finally tenor. He played regularly in Boston from 1947 when he went to the Boston Conservatory, and during 1955–57 he was freelancing in Florida. By 1950 Rivers was back in Boston with the Herb Pomeroy big band, and in the early '60s he was leading a band that backed R&B and blues singers (including a tour with T-Bone Walker). Rivers, who by then had become very interested in the music of Cecil Taylor and Ornette Coleman, was still pretty obscure as a Boston legend.

In 1964 Tony Williams (who had played with Rivers when he was a young teenager) recommended him for the tenor opening with Miles Davis' Quintet. Although Rivers' playing was too

advanced for Davis at the time, he did last through a tour of Japan that was recorded. Rivers made a few records for Blue Note before becoming a member of Cecil Taylor's Unit during 1968–73. With his wife Bea, he opened Studio Rivbea as a jazz loft in New York in 1971 and became involved in teaching in addition to presenting concerts. Other than a late-'80s association with Dizzy Gillespie (where he good-naturedly played bebop and even took an occasional scat vocal), Rivers has mostly been a leader during the past two decades in duets with Dave Holland or heading a large orchestra. He has recorded mostly for many European labels. — *Scott Yanow*

Fuschia Swing Song / Dec. 11, 1964 / Blue Note ♦♦♦♦♦

★ **Contours** / May 21, 1965 / Blue Note ♦♦♦♦♦
Excellent, with Herbie Hancock (p), Freddie Hubbard (tpt). — *Michael G. Nastos*

A New Conception / Oct. 11, 1966 / Blue Note ♦♦♦♦

Dimensions and Extensions / Mar. 17, 1967 / Blue Note ♦♦♦♦♦
Stinging, expansive solos with one foot in avant-garde, one in hard bop. — *Ron Wynn*

Hues / Feb. 13, 1971–Nov. 10, 1973 / Impulse! ♦♦♦

Streams: Live at Montreux / Jul. 6, 1973 / Impulse! ♦♦♦♦
Streams featured Sam Rivers as the lead voice on the album-long "Streams," a lengthy multisectioned free improvisation recorded at the Montreux Jazz Festival (July 6, 1973). With support from the brilliant bassist Cecil McBee and subtle drumming from the pre-disco Norman Connors, Rivers took a powerful solo on tenor, sung through his flute, rambled a bit on piano and concluded with a strong dosage of his soprano.... *Streams* remains one of Sam Rivers' strongest recordings. — *Scott Yanow*

Crystals / 1974 / Impulse! ♦♦♦♦♦
Creative orchestra music. Out of this world. — *Michael G. Nastos*

Sizzle / 1975 / Impulse! ♦♦♦♦
Trio with Barry Altschul (d) and Dave Holland (b). Funky with electric touches. Fierce. — *Michael G. Nastos*

Sam Rivers/Dave Holland, Vol. 1 / Feb. 18, 1976 / Improvising Artists ♦♦♦♦

Sam Rivers/Dave Holland, Vol. 2 / Feb. 18, 1976 / Improvising Artists ♦♦♦
When Sam Rivers met up with bassist Dave Holland for a set of duets, he decided to record two LPs and play a different instrument on each of the sidelong pieces. While Rivers performs on tenor and soprano during the first volume, the second recording finds him playing "Ripples" on flute and switching to piano for "Deluge"; both performances are over 23 minutes long. Since tenor is easily Rivers' strongest ax, this set (which has now been reissued on CD) is of somewhat limited interest, yet is generally successful. The flute piece has several different sections that keep both the musicians and listeners interested, while Rivers' piano feature is quite intense; he leaves few notes unplayed. Still, the first volume should be acquired. — *Scott Yanow*

The Quest / Mar. 12, 1976–Mar. 13, 1976 / Red ♦♦♦♦

Waves / Aug. 1978 / Tomato ♦♦♦♦
An explosive late '70s set with underrated composer, multi-instrumentalist and arranger Sam Rivers leading a strong quartet. While bassist and cellist Dave Holland and percussionist Thurman Barker merged to form a strong, challenging rhythm section, Rivers and Joe Daley, playing tuba and baritone horn, worked together to create instrumental dialogues in sequence. Their array of contrasting voicings, with Rivers on tenor and soprano sax and flute, makes for compelling listening. — *Ron Wynn*

Contrasts / Dec. 1979 / ECM ♦♦♦♦

Colours / Sep. 13, 1982 / Black Saint ♦♦♦
Stomping, swinging arrangements. Exuberant 11-piece orchestra supervised and spurred by Rivers. — *Ron Wynn*

Max Roach

b. Jan. 10, 1924, New Land, NC
Drums, Leader / Avant-Garde, Bop, Post-Bop, Hard Bop
On the basis of his persistence, adaptability and symbolic importance Max Roach would merit inclusion in jazz's pantheon of special performers. But he's done more than outlive many of his contemporaries; He, along with Kenny Clarke, changed the direction of drummers in the bop revolution. He shifted the rhythmic focus

from the bass drum to the ride cymbal, a move that gave drummers more freedom. He emerged as arguably bebop's greatest drum soloist. Roach didn't simply drop bombs and blast away. He told a complete story, varying his pitch, tuning, patterns and volume. He was a brilliant brush player and could push, redirect or break up the beat. Roach has never stood still musically, though the links between what he played in the '40s and today aren't that far apart. He's worked with pianoless trios, played with symphony orchestras, done duos with free and avant-garde musicians, backed gospel choirs, even played with a rapper long before the jazz/hip-hop thing became a media event. He was outspoken about social injustices in the pre-civil rights era and recorded powerful, undiluted protest material.

His mother sang gospel, and Roach began playing drums in gospel bands at 10. He had formal studies at the Manhattan School of Music, then started playing with Charlie Parker, Dizzy Gillespie and others at Minton's Playhouse in 1942. He was house drummer and a frequent participant in after-hours jam sessions. One of the other participants was Kenny Clarke. Roach had brief stints with Benny Carter and Duke Ellington's band, then joined Gillespie's quintet in 1943 and was in Parker-led bands in 1945, 1947 to 1949 and 1951 to 1953. He made his recording debut with Coleman Hawkins in 1943, then recorded with Miles Davis and Parker in the late '40s. Roach traveled to Paris with Parker in 1949 and recorded there with him and others including Kenny Dorham. He also played with Louis Jordan, Red Allen and Coleman Hawkins and participated in the Birth of the Cool sessions in 1948–1950.

During the early '50s, Roach toured with The Jazz At The Philharmonic revue, played at Massey Hall in an all-star concert with Parker, Gillespie, Charles Mingus and Bud Powell and recorded with Howard Rumsey's Lighthouse All-Stars. During the mid-'50s, he co-lead the Max Roach/Clifford Brown orchestra, with Powell's brother Richie on piano and saxophonists Harold Land and Sonny Rollins. His frenetic, yet precise drumming laid the foundation for Brown's amazing trumpet solos. This group made some landmark records in its short tenure, among them *Study In Brown* and *At Basin Street*. After Brown and Powell were tragically killed in a car crash in 1956, Roach tried to keep the group going using Dorham and Rollins. He became involved in a record label partnership with Charles Mingus as well, forming Debut Records in the mid-'50s. Later Roach led another influential band, this time with trumpeters Dorham or Booker Little, tenor saxophonist George Coleman, trombonist Julian Priester and sometimes Ray Draper on tuba. They cut seminal dates for Riverside and EmArcy, among them *On The Chicago Scene* and *Deeds Not Words*. The Max Roach +4 became a prototype hard bop unit.

Then Roach made another change during the early '60s, composing multi-faceted suites and writing openly political, confrontational material featuring his wife Abbey Lincoln criticizing American racial injustices. He dispensed with the piano on occasion and experimented with solo drum compositions as wholly independent pieces. There were more albums for Atlantic and Impulse. The list included *Freedom Now Suite, Percussion Bitter Sweet, It's Time, Speak, Brother, Speak. The Legendary Hassan, Lift Every Voice and Sing* and *Members, Don't Get Weary*. There was also the brilliant *Drums Unlimited*, in 1965. The *Freedom Now Suite* was made into a film by Gianni Amici in 1966, but Roach and Lincoln maintain they suffered severe career reprisals as a result.

During the '70s Roach continued recording prolifically for various labels, though most were for import companies like Denon and Soul Note. Roach founded M'Boom Re: Percussion in 1970, a co-operative group of 10 percussionists performing works written for them. The group still records and performs 23 years later. He recorded with Cecil Taylor, Anthony Braxton, Archie Shepp and Abdullah Ibrahim, while maintaining his own bands. Roach also began a career in education, becoming a professor at the University of Massachusetts at Amherst and later holding a position at the Lennox School of Jazz. He's continued in the '80s and '90s, leading at various times a regular quartet, Double Quartet (an acoustic and string quartet together) and M'Boom, while continuing to lecture, perform and exemplify the real meaning of jazz. —*Ron Wynn*

The Max Roach Quartet, Featuring Hank Mobley / Apr. 10, 1953–Apr. 21, 1953 / Original Jazz Classics ✦✦✦
Drummer Max Roach's first studio session as a leader falls style-

wise between bop and hard bop. The earlier set, which has four group originals played by a septet that also includes trumpeter Idrees Sulieman, trombonist Leon Comegys, altoist Gigi Gryce, Hank Mobley on tenor, pianist Walter Davis, Jr. and bassist Frank Skeete, was the recording debut for both Mobley and Davis. The other session (two standards, two originals by Roach including his solo "Drum Conversation," Mobley's "Kismet" and Charlie Parker's "Chi Chi") features the same rhythm section, with Mobley as the only horn. The music is enjoyable although not as essential as the great drummer's later dates. This CD reissue adds "Drum Conversation Part 2" to the original LP program. —*Scott Yanow*

Max Roach Plus Four / Oct. 12, 1956 / EmArcy ✦✦✦✦✦
After the tragic deaths of trumpeter Clifford Brown and pianist Richie Powell in a car accident a few months earlier, drummer Max Roach regrouped with trumpeter Kenny Dorham and pianist Ray Bryant filling in the unfillable holes; tenor great Sonny Rollins and bassist George Morrow remained from the earlier band. This EmArcy CD finds Roach taking plenty of solo space including almost all of "Dr. Free-zee" and the climaxes of "Just One of Those Things" and "Woody 'n You." The horns have plenty of good spots and other highlights of this worthy set includes George Russell's "Ezz-thetic" and a warm rendition of "Body and Soul." —*Scott Yanow*

Jazz in 3/4 Time / Mar. 18, 1957–Mar. 21, 1957 / Mercury ✦✦✦✦
The post-Clifford Brown quintet that drummer Max Roach led tends to get overlooked, but it actually ranked up there with the Jazz Messengers and the Horace Silver Quintet in the late '50s. With tenor saxophonist Sonny Rollins becoming a stronger soloist month-by-month (he was arguably the top tenor in jazz at the time) and veteran trumpeter Kenny Dorham in prime form, Roach was able to stretch himself; the obscure pianist Billy Wallace and bassist George Morrow completed the group. On this LP, Roach explores six songs in waltz time, an innovation for the period (predating Dave Brubeck's recording of "Take Five" by two years). Roach contributed two originals and the group played 3/4 versions of three standards, but it was Rollins' "Valse Hot" (which clocks in on this EmArcy album at 14:15) that was the hit of the date. These excellent performances show that jazz does not always have to be in 4/4 time in order to swing. —*Scott Yanow*

Max Roach 4 Plays Charlie Parker / Dec. 23, 1957 / EmArcy ✦✦✦✦
The music on this CD finds drummer Max Roach for the first time dropping the piano out of his quintet and performing with a pianoless quartet. With the departure of Sonny Rollins (who is replaced on three songs apiece by either Hank Mobley or George Coleman), Roach's group (which also featured trumpeter Kenny Dorham and either George Morrow or Nelson Boyd on bass) was temporarily without any major innovators (outside of the leader). So it was perfectly fitting that Roach would look backwards and perform six of Charlie Parker's compositions. Highlighted by "Yardbird Suite," "Confirmation" and "Ko Ko," this set is generally fine although the lack of a piano is really felt on some of this material. —*Scott Yanow*

Percussion Discussion / 1957–Jan. 4, 1958 / Chess ✦✦✦✦
This double-LP from Chess combines together unrelated sessions led by drummer Max Roach and Art Blakey, both of which were originally made for the Cadet label. Blakey features the 1957 version of his Jazz Messengers (which includes altoist Jackie McLean, trumpeter Bill Hardman, pianist Sam Dockery and bassist Spanky DeBrest) on a pair of Duke Jordan songs (including "Flight to Jordan"), a selection apiece from Blakey and altoist Gigi Gryce and a brief four-song "Gershwin Medley." The Roach selections are most significant for featuring a young pianist named Ramsey Lewis in a straight-ahead setting; the other musicians are trumpeter Kenny Dorham, Hank Mobley on tenor and bassist George Morrow, and the music is dominated by group originals. Overall, neither of the two sets are essential or overly innovative, but they helped to define what hard bop sounded like in the late '50s and will be savored by straight-ahead jazz fans. —*Scott Yanow*

Max / Jan. 4, 1958 / Argo ✦✦✦

Max Roach Plus Four on the Chicago Scene / Jun. 1958 / EmArcy ✦✦✦✦
Drummer Max Roach's abilities as a talent scout have often been overlooked through the years, but quite a few musicians (from Hank Mobley and Clifford Brown to Stanley Turrentine and Odeon Pope) have benefitted greatly from their association with

Roach. An ill-fated trumpeter who the drummer helped introduce was Booker Little who made his recording debut at the age of 20 on this excellent LP. With George Coleman on tenor, pianist Eddie Baker and bassist Bob Cranshaw also in the quintet, this album might be brief (only around 31 minutes), but it has plenty of fine playing. Little's feature on "My Old Flame" is a highpoint, Coleman sounds fine on "Stompin' at the Savoy," the uptempo blues "Memo to Maurice" and "Stella by Starlight" are both quite enjoyable, and Roach has several typically well-constructed solos. Recommended, as are all the mostly hard-to-find Roach-Little sessions. —*Scott Yanow*

Max Roach Plus Four at Newport / Jul. 6, 1958 / EmArcy ✦✦✦✦
The main reason to search for this out-of-print LP is for the playing of the great, if short-lived, trumpeter Booker Little who was the first on his instrument to emerge from the shadow of Clifford Brown and start to develop his own voice. With tenor saxophonist George Coleman, Ray Draper on tuba, bassist Art Davis and the drummer/leader (then 33 but already considered a giant for over a decade), the quintet performs six consistently enjoyable and hard-swinging numbers; highlights include "Night in Tunisia," "Tune-Up," Little's "Minor Mode" and "Love for Sale." —*Scott Yanow*

Deeds, Not Words / Sep. 4, 1958 / Original Jazz Classics ✦✦✦✦
This CD reissue of a Max Roach Riverside date is notable for featuring the great young trumpeter Booker Little and for utilizing Ray Draper's tuba as a melody instrument; tenor saxophonist George Coleman and bassist Art Davis complete the excellent quintet. Highlights include "It's You or No One," "You Stepped out of a Dream" and Roach's unaccompanied drum piece "Conversation." This is fine music from a group that was trying to stretch themselves beyond hard bop. —*Scott Yanow*

The Many Sides of Max / Oct. 1959 / Mercury ✦✦✦
This album (although listed in some discographies as 1959) was probably recorded in 1961. A reunion of Max Roach's sidemen, it features a particularly strong group comprised of the great trumpeter Booker Little, George Coleman on tenor, trombonist Julian Priester, pianist Ray Bryant and bassist Bob Boswell. Among the many highpoints of this LP (which was reissued on a Trip album but is not yet on CD) include Roach's tympani work on "Tympanalli," "Bemsha Swing" and "There's No You," but all seven selections on the admittedly brief album (around 31 minutes) are worth hearing. —*Scott Yanow*

Max Roach / Nov. 25, 1959 / Bainbridge ✦✦✦✦
Any session that drummer Max Roach had in which he used Booker Little (who died at age 23 in 1961) is quite valuable, for Little was the first trumpeter since the death of Clifford Brown to develop his own personal voice. This set, which also features George Coleman on tenor, bassist Art Davis and the young tuba player Ray Draper, has its stimulating moments although it is not quite up to the level of the group's best recordings. The musicians do stretch themselves on five group originals plus John Lewis' "Milano" and the standard "Old Folks" so, even though this LP is not essential, it is worth checking out. —*Scott Yanow*

Quiet As It's Kept / Jan. 1960 / Mercury ✦✦✦

Long As You're Living / Feb. 5, 1960 / Enja ✦✦✦
The most obscure group that drummer Max Roach led actually recorded four albums in 1960; a quintet with tenor saxophonist Stanley Turrentine (then a complete unknown), his brother Tommy on trumpet, trombonist Julian Priester and bassist Bobby Boswell. Strange that this Enja release is the only one of their recordings thus far to appear on CD. Although the playing of The Turrentines is not at the same innovative level as Roach's prior group with Booker Little and George Coleman, they come up with consistently fresh statements during the well-rounded set, and the tenorman was already instantly recognizable. Highlights include a couple of Roach drum features, two Kenny Dorham compositions ("Lotus Blossom," "The Villa") and "Night in Tunisia." —*Scott Yanow*

Parisian Sketches / Mar. 1, 1960 / Mercury ✦✦✦

Drum Conversation / Mar. 1960 / Enja ✦✦✦

★ **Freedom Now Suite** / Aug. 31, 1960+Sep. 6, 1960 / Columbia ✦✦✦✦✦
This is a classic. At a time when the civil rights movement was starting to heat up, drummer Max Roach performed and recorded a seven-part suite dealing with Black history (particularly slavery) and racism. "Driva' Man" has a powerful statement by veter-

an tenor Coleman Hawkins, and there is valuable solo space elsewhere for trumpeter Booker Little and trombonist Julian Priester, but it is the overall performance of Abbey Lincoln that is most notable. Formerly a nightclub singer, Lincoln really came into her own under Roach's tutelage, and she is a strong force throughout this intense set. On "Tryptich: Prayer/Protest/Peace," Lincoln is heard in duets with the drummer, and her wrenching screams of rage are quite memorable. This timeless protest record is a gem. —*Scott Yanow*

Moon Faced and Starry-Eyed / Oct. 1960 / Mercury ✦✦✦

★ **Percussion Bitter Sweet** / Aug. 1961 / Impulse! ✦✦✦✦✦
This CD reissue brings back a classic album, one of the finest of drummer Max Roach's very productive career. The illustrious sidemen (trumpeter Booker Little, trombonist Julian Priester, Eric Dolphy on alto, bass clarinet and flute, tenorman Clifford Jordan, pianist Mal Waldron and bassist Art Davis in addition to some guest percussionists) all have opportunitites to make strong contributions, and Dolphy's pleading alto solo on "Mendacity" is particularly memorable. Abbey Lincoln has two emotional and very effective vocals, but it is the overall sound of the ensembles and the political nature of the music that make this set (along with Roach's *Freedom Now Suite*) quite unique in jazz history. —*Scott Yanow*

It's Time / 1961–1962 / Impulse! ✦✦✦✦

Speak Brother Speak / Oct. 4, 1962 / Original Jazz Classics ✦✦✦
This reissue CD of a live set originally put out on Debut has two very lengthy tracks (the 25-minute "Speak, Brother, Speak" and the 22-1/2 minute "A Variation") featuring solos by tenor saxophonist Clifford Jordan, pianist Mal Waldron, bassist Eddie Khan and drummer Max Roach (who wrote both of the pieces). The music is somewhere between hard bop and the avant-garde, and the musicians really push each other, although the results are not quite essential. Clifford Jordan fans in particular will find this to be an interesting set. —*Scott Yanow*

The Max Roach Trio, Featuring the Legendary Hasaan / Dec. 4, 1964+Dec. 7, 1964 / Atlantic ✦✦✦✦✦
Pianist Hasaan Ibn Ali only made one recording in his life, this trio set with drummer Max Roach and bassist Art Davis. A very advanced player whose style fell somewhere between Thelonious Monk and Cecil Taylor (with hints of Herbie Nichols), Hasaan actually had a rather original sound. His performances of his seven originals on this set (a straight CD reissue of a long out-of-print LP) are intense, somewhat virtuosic and rhythmic, yet often melodic in a quirky way. This is a classic of its kind, and it is fortunate that it was made, but it is a tragedy that Hasaan would not record again and that he would soon sink back into obscurity. —*Scott Yanow*

Drums Unlimited / Oct. 14, 1965–Apr. 25, 1966 / Atlantic ✦✦✦✦
Other than a trio set with the legendary pianist Hasaan Ibn Ali, this set was Max Roach's only recording as a leader during 1963-67. Three of the six numbers ("Nommo," "St. Louis Blues" and "In the Red") find Roach heading a group that includes trumpeter Freddie Hubbard, altoist James Spaulding, pianist Ronnie Mathews, bassist Jymie Merritt, and on "St. Louis Blues," Roland Alexander on soprano. Their music is essentially advanced hard-bop with a generous amount of space taken up by Roach's drum solos. The other three selections ("The Drum Also Waltzes," "Drums Unlimited" and "For Big Sid") are unaccompanied features for Max Roach, and because of the melodic and logically-planned nature of his improvisations, they continually hold on to one's attention. —*Scott Yanow*

Members, Don't Git Weary / Jun. 25, 1968–Jul. 1968 / Atlantic ✦✦✦

Lift Every Voice and Sing / Apr. 7, 1971+Apr. 8, 1971 / Atlantic ✦✦✦

Force: Sweet Mao—Suid Africa '76 / Jul. 1976 / BASE ✦✦✦✦
Duets with Archie Shepp (sax). Extended pieces from two virtuosos. Quintessential. —*Michael G. Nastos*

Live in Tokyo / Jan. 21, 1977 / Denon ✦✦✦✦

The Loadstar / Jul. 27, 1977 / Horo ✦✦✦✦
Quartet two-fer (one piece per album) with Billy Harper (ts), Cecil Bridgewater (tpt), Reggie Workman (b). This is powerful music. —*Michael G. Nastos*

Birth and Rebirth / Sep. 1978 / Black Saint ✦✦✦✦✦
The first of drummer Max Roach's two duet sets with multireedist

Anthony Braxton consists of seven fairly free improvisations that they created in the studio. Each of the selections (particularly "Birth," which builds gradually in intensity to a ferocious level, the waltz time of "Magic and Music," the atmospheric "Tropical Forest" and "Softshoe") have their own plot and purpose. Braxton (who performs on alto, soprano, sopranino and clarinet) and Roach continually inspire each other, which is probably why they would record a second set the following year. Stimulating avant-garde music. *—Scott Yanow*

The Long March / Aug. 30, 1979 / Hat Hut ✦✦✦✦

★ **One in Two, Two in One** / Aug. 31, 1979 / Hat Hut ✦✦✦✦✦
The second of two duet albums by drummer Max Roach and multireedist Anthony Braxton was recorded live and released on this two-LP set; this is the more interesting of the two projects since it is a nearly 78-minute continual improvisation. Braxton gets to stretch out on alto, soprano, sopranino, contra bass clarinet (which really gets a monstrous sound), clarinet and flute. With Roach pushing Braxton, the results are quite adventurous, yet full of joy. Followers of avant-garde jazz can consider this set to be essential. *—Scott Yanow*

Pictures in a Frame / Sep. 10, 1979–Sep. 17, 1979 / Soul Note ✦✦✦✦
Although drummer Max Roach has been engaged in many special projects during the past 20 years, his main group has been his regular quartet. On this Soul Note LP from 1979, trumpeter Cecil Bridgewater, Odean Pope (on tenor, flute and oboe) and bassist Calvin Hill (who would later be succeeded by Tyrone Brown) join Roach for concise interpretations of eight group originals (everyone contributes at least one song) along with Clifford Jordan's "Japanese Dream." Although the group would continue to grow and evolve, it was already a pretty impressive unit by 1979. As usual with Max Roach's bands, this group filled the gap between hard bop and the avant-garde. *—Scott Yanow*

Historic Concerts / Dec. 15, 1979 / Soul Note ✦✦✦✦
Drummer Max Roach met up with the intense avant-garde pianist Cecil Taylor for a 1979 concert that resulted in this double CD. After Roach and Taylor play separate five-minute solos (Taylor's is surprisingly melodic and bluesy), they interact during a two-part 78-minute encounter that finds Roach not shy to occasionally take control. The passionate music is quite atonal but coherent with Taylor displaying an impressive amount of energy and the two masters (who had not rehearsed or ever played together before) communicating pretty well. This set is weakened a bit by a 17-minute radio interview that includes excerpts from the concert one just heard (!) although some of the anecdotes are interesting. No revelations really occur in the music, but it certainly holds one's interest! *—Scott Yanow*

Chattahoochee Red / 1981 / Columbia ✦✦✦✦
For this quartet outing, Max Roach performs seven group originals plus tributes to Clifford Brown ("I Remember Clifford"), Thelonious Monk ("'Round Midnight") and John Coltrane ("Giant Steps"). Roach's regular band (with trumpeter Cecil Bridgewater, Odean Pope on tenor, flute and oboe, bassist Calvin Hill and on "Wefe," guest pianist Walter Bishop, Jr.) is in excellent form on this spirited outing; pity that this LP has been out of print for quite some time. *—Scott Yanow*

Swish / Feb. 26, 1982 / New Artists ✦✦✦

In the Light / Jul. 1982 / Soul Note ✦✦✦
An early '80s date with drummer Max Roach's regular quartet. There was talk that Roach was starting to run out of steam during this period, but his drumming doesn't lack energy or pace. True, some of the compositions weren't as good as in the past, but the quartet's earnest ensemble lines and solos compensated for any weaknesses in material. *—Ron Wynn*

Live at Vielharmonie Munich / Nov. 1983 / Soul Note ✦✦✦

Scott Free / May 31, 1984 / Soul Note ✦✦✦✦✦
This strong set from the Max Roach Quartet (one of the finest regular bands of the 1980s) finds the group performing a 40-minute version of trumpeter Cecil Bridgewater's "Scott Free." Because the piece has plenty of solo space (two lengthy improvisations apiece for Bridgewater, tenor saxophonist Odean Pope, bassist Tyrone Brown and drummer Roach, with a medium-tempo section, a rapid segment and some free interludes), there is more variety on this lengthy work than one might expect. This is excellent music, easily recommended as an example of the underrated but consistently brilliant Max Roach Quartet. *—Scott Yanow*

It's Christmas Time Again / Jun. 2, 1984–Jun. 26, 1984 / Soul Note ✦
Poetry and jazz rarely mix, with jazz generally delegated to the background. That is the case with this disappointing set, which finds the poems of Bruce McMarion Wright accompanied by rather anonymous blues playing from Max Roach's quartet. One of the two lengthy tracks also has playing from guests altoist Lee Konitz and clarinetist Tony Scott, but they are subservient to the routine storytelling. *—Scott Yanow*

Survivors / Oct. 19, 1984–Oct. 21, 1984 / Soul Note ✦✦✦✦
Drummer Max Roach kept his string of excellent small combo sessions alive with this mid-'80s effort. Trumpeter Cecil Bridgewater and tenor saxophonist Odean Pope were the ideal players for Roach's taut, clipped and mostly uptempo pieces. They were both solid soloists and also were able to execute difficult chord changes or switch tempos quickly. Max Roach also played with his customary drive and expressiveness. *—Ron Wynn*

Easy Winners / Jan. 1985 / Soul Note ✦✦✦✦✦
The Max Roach Double Quartet, which combined the drummer's regular group (comprised of trumpeter Cecil Bridgewater, tenor saxophonist Odean Pope and electric bassist Tyrone Brown) with The Uptown String Quartet, was a perfect match, and its few recordings are all quite enjoyable and occasionally wondrous. In addition to a transcription of Scott Joplin's "Easy Winners" for the strings, this superior release has colorfully arranged versions of works by Bridgewater ("Birds Says"), Pope ("Sis") and Roach ("A Little Booker"). The wide variety of colors and the consistently-strong improvisations make this a highly recommended set of stirring music. *—Scott Yanow*

Bright Moments / Oct. 1, 1986–Oct. 2, 1986 / Soul Note ✦✦✦✦
The combination of drummer Max Roach's regular group (which includes trumpeter Cecil Bridgewater, tenor saxophonist Odean Pope and electric bassist Tyrone Brown) with The Uptown String Quartet to form his Double Quartet works extremely well. Because the strings get to improvise and are not restricted to the background, the interplay between the two groups is a special highlight of this particularly strong outing. In addition to works by Pope and Brown (the latter contributed "Tribute to Duke and Mingus"), The Double Quartet interprets Steve Turre's "Double Delight," Randy Weston's "Hi Fly" and Roland Kirk's happy "Bright Moments." A frequently exquisite yet adventurous album, highly recommended. *—Scott Yanow*

Max & Dizzy: Paris 1989 / Mar. 23, 1989 / A&M ✦
This double-CD set was a big mistake. Teaming drummer Max Roach and trumpeter Dizzy Gillespie together as a duo might have worked had it taken place 20 years earlier when Dizzy was still in his musical prime. However the immortal players did not even discuss what they were going to play beforehand, and the result is a series of rambling sketches, essentially a long drum solo with occasional trumpet interludes that are full of clams. The closing 32-1/2 minute "Interview" also wanders and could have been cut in half. *—Scott Yanow*

★ **To the Max** / Sep. 15, 1990–Jun. 25, 1991 / Blue Moon ✦✦✦✦✦
Max Roach is heard in a variety of settings on this colorful and varied double CD. The three-part "Ghost Dance" features the innovative drummer with a vocal choir and his percussion group, M'Boom. M'Boom also pops up on two other selections, the Max Roach Quartet (with trumpeter Cecil Bridgewater, Odean Pope on tenor and electric bassist Tyrone Brown) has four features, Roach takes two unaccompanied drum solos, and the Quartet joins up with The Uptown String Quartet to form Roach's Double Quartet on a 21-minute version of "A Little Booker." The music, which crosses quite a few boundaries, is consistently fascinating and forms a definitive portrait of the ageless drummer's wide musical interests in the early '90s. *—Scott Yanow*

Hank Roberts

Cello / Avant-Garde
Hank Roberts, through his association with Bill Frisell's groups and his own JMT recordings, has for the past decade been arguably the most stimulating jazz cellist around. *—Scott Yanow*

● **Black Pastels** / Nov. 1987–Dec. 1987 / JMT ✦✦✦✦✦

Birds of Prey / Jan. 1990–Feb. 1990 / JMT ✦✦✦✦
This music crosses pop/funk/jazz/Third World parameters. Roberts is an excellent cellist. The music is progressive at times

and too commercial at others. His best work lies ahead. —*Michael G. Nastos*

Little Motor People / Dec. 1992 / JMT ++++

Howard Roberts

b. Oct. 2, 1929, Phoenix, AZ, **d.** Jun. 28, 1992, Seattle, WA
Guitar / Pop, Cool
Howard Roberts was a talented guitarist on the level of a Barney Kessel or Herb Ellis who spent most of his career playing commercial music in the studios. Shortly after he moved to Los Angeles in 1950, Roberts was firmly established in the studios although on occasion he recorded jazz (most notably twice for Verve during 1956-59, a Concord session from 1977 and one for Discovery in 1979); however, most of his other output (particularly for Capitol in the 1960's) is of lesser interest. The co-founder of the Guitar Institute of Technology in Hollywood, Roberts was an enthusiastic and talented educator and wrote a regular instructional column for *Guitar Player*. —*Scott Yanow*

Mr. Roberts Plays Guitar / 1956 / Norgran +++++

H.R. Is a Dirty Guitar Player / Jun. 3, 1963–Jun. 16, 1963 / Capitol ++++
This is classic Roberts. A very nice album to have around. —*Michael Erlewine*

● **The Real Howard Roberts** / Aug. 26, 1977 / Concord Jazz +++++
Nice, tasteful swing-inspired music. —*Ron Wynn*

Turning to Spring / Nov. 6, 1979 / Discovery +++

Luckey Roberts (Charles Luckeyeth Roberts)

b. Aug. 7, 1887, Philadelphia, PA, **d.** Feb. 5, 1968, New York, NY
Piano / Stride
Luckey Roberts was considered one of the all-time great stride pianists, but he unfortunately left very few records behind and none from his early years. Roberts actually pre-dated stride, publishing "Pork and Beans" and "Junk Man Rag" as early as 1913. He spent most of his career leading society bands and writing for musical comedies; his "Ripples of the Nile" became a hit for Glenn Miller in 1941 as "Moonlight Cocktail." Although much of his career was actually at the fringe of jazz, Roberts showed on his 1946 record session (which resulted in six stunning solos) and a couple of dates in 1958 that he deserved his legendary status. —*Scott Yanow*

★ **Luckey Roberts & Ralph Sutton** / May 21, 1946–Jun. 11, 1952 / Solo Art +++++
Luckey Roberts, considered one of the big three of 1920s stride piano (along with James P. Johnson and Fats Waller), was by far the most obscure of the trio, running a successful society band for decades but leading only three record sessions during his long career. This Solo Art CD brings back the six songs from his earliest (1946) date and is quite impressive. Roberts' virtuosity and total command of the piano is remarkable, and he really tears into his originals, which include "Ripples of the Nile" (turned by Glenn Miller into the pop hit "Moonlight Cocktail"), "Pork & Beans" and "Music Box Rag." Also on this valuable CD are pianist Ralph Sutton's four performances (plus an alternate take) from his debut as a leader in 1949 and eight exciting stride-filled duets with drummer George Wettling from 1952. While Sutton shows the influences of Bob Zurke and Joe Sullivan on the earlier titles, by 1952 he had found his own voice within the classic idiom. A highly recommended disc. —*Scott Yanow*

Happy Go Lucky / 1958 / Period +++

Luckey Roberts and Willie The Lion Smith / Mar. 18, 1958 / Good Time Jazz +++++

Marcus Roberts

b. Aug. 7, 1963, Jacksonville, FL
Piano / Post-Bop, Hard Bop, Stride
Marcus Roberts has begun to get some of the attacks normally reserved for Wynton Marsalis and others regarded as reactionaries by some members of the jazz press. Roberts' seeming obsession with vintage styles, notably stride, and his willingness to speak openly and voice his disdain of contemporary music has not been well accepted in some circles. A notorious *Down Beat* blindfold test in which Roberts casually ripped some major play-

ers for an alleged lack of swing also generated heated replies via letters to the editor. But Roberts must be credited with going his own way; he's one of the few contemporary pianists with little or no ties to McCoy Tyner, Ahmad Jamal, or Bill Evans. He has some Thelonious Monk influence, especially in his phrasing, but Roberts' models, at least in the last few years, have been Jelly Roll Morton and Fats Waller.

While his earlier work reflected pronounced gospel and blues ties, mixed with bebop, Roberts has now devoted himself to stride and ragtime, a tactical decision wide open to intense scrutiny and second guessing. He hasn't mastered either form but continues cutting solo piano albums featuring these styles. Roberts studied piano at Florida State after beginning on the instrument in his youth. He won several competitions in the mid-'80s, then joined Wynton Marsalis' band as his first regular pianist since Kenny Kirkland. Roberts emerged as the Marsalis band's second prime soloist and the hub of its rhythm section. His swing kept the group focused and prevented Marsalis' music from getting too stiff or introspective. Roberts' own late '80s and '90s albums for RCA/Novus, particularly the 1990 release *Alone with Three Giants* detail his commitment to classic music. Whether that makes him a dedicated preservationist or hopeless nostalgia buff remains open to debate. —*Ron Wynn*

The Truth Is Spoken Here / Jul. 26, 1988–Jul. 27, 1988 / Novus +++

Deep in the Shed / Aug. 9, 1989–Dec. 10, 1989 / Novus ++++
His second solo project accents the blues, with nicely arranged compositions and a full band that sometimes swells to include alto and tenor sax, trumpet and trombone, plus bass and drums. —*Ron Wynn*

Alone with Three Giants / Jun. 3, 1990–Sep. 22, 1990 / Novus ++++
Fifteen tracks of solo piano from young, blind pianist from Jacksonville, FL. Repertoire of Monk, Ellingson and Jelly Roll Morton. Fares best on the Monk, and there are five of them. —*Michael G. Nastos*

● **As Serenity Approaches** / Jun. 1991–Nov. 1991 / Novus +++++
Every one of pianist Marcus Roberts' recordings thus far are recommended. This outing has 11 impressive solo performances and eight duets with trumpeters Scotty Barnhart, Nicholas Payton and Wynton Marsalis (the latter on a fun version of Jelly Roll Morton's "King Porter Stomp"), Todd Williams on clarinet and tenor and trombonist Ronald Westray in addition to two meetings with fellow pianist Ellis Marsalis. This music finds Roberts using techniques of the past (especially stride and old-time breaks) in both his new originals and revivals of classic tunes. However, he never resorts to mere copying and feels free to update elements of the music or to throw in eccentric ideas. There is a great deal for listeners to investigate on this thoroughly fascinating recital. —*Scott Yanow*

If I Could Be with You / 1993 / Novus ++++

Gershwin For Lovers / 1994 / Sony +++

Plays Ellington / 1995 / Novus ++++

Ikey Robinson

b. Jul. 28, 1904, Dublin, VA, **d.** Oct. 25, 1990, Chicago, IL
Banjo, Guitar, Vocals / Classic Jazz, Blues
Ikey Robinson was an excellent banjoist and singer who was versatile enough to record both jazz and blues from the late '20s into the late '30s. Unfortunately he spent long periods off records after the swing era, leading to him being less known than he should be. After working locally, Robinson moved to Chicago in 1926, playing and recording with Jelly Roll Morton, Clarence Williams and (most importantly) Jabbo Smith during 1928-29. He led his own recording sessions in 1929, 1931, 1933 and 1935 (all have been reissued on a CD from the Austrian label RST). Robinson played with Wilbur Sweatman, Noble Sissle, Carroll Dickerson and Erskine Tate in the 1930s, recorded with Clarence Williams and led small groups from the 1940s on. In the early '60s he was with Franz Jackson, and in the 1970s (when he was rediscovered) he had an opportunity to tour Europe and be reunited with Jabbo Smith. —*Scott Yanow*

● **"Banjo" Ikey Robinson** / Jan. 4, 1929–May 19, 1937 / RST +++++
It would not be an understatement to call this CD definitive of Ikey Robinson's work since it includes every selection (except for

two songs that have Half Pint Jaxon vocals) ever led by the banjoist/vocalist. The diversity is impressive, for Robinson is heard (on "Got Butter on It" and "Ready Hokum") with a hot group featuring cornetist Jabbo Smith, singing the blues, performing with The Hokum Trio and The Pods of Pepper (both good-time bands), backing singer Charlie Slocum and heading his own Windy City Five (a fine swing group) in 1935; he even plays clarinet on one song. This consistently enjoyable Austrian import is well worth searching for. —*Scott Yanow*

Orphy Robinson

b. Oct. 13, 1960, London, England
Vibes / Post-Bop
Orphy Robinson was one of the many young British jazz musicians who was discovered by Americans in the mid-'80s. Inspired originally by Roy Ayers, Robinson played funk, pop and avant-garde music before joining Courtney Pine's Jazz Warriors. An open-minded player who has worked with Pine's small group, Andy Sheppard and his own band, Robinson has recorded for Blue Note but has not really had a breakthrough in the U.S. yet; his style is quite eclectic. —*Scott Yanow*

● **When Tomorrow Comes** / Oct. 11, 1991–Oct. 13, 1991 / Blue Note ◆◆◆◆
English vibraphonist Orphy Robinson's Blue Note CD features original compositions that use repetition, funky rhythms and long vamps a great deal but lack any particularly memorable melodies. The solos by Robinson and his rhythm section are fine, and the inclusion of Tunde Jegede's kora and cello (the former sounds like an upper register guitar) adds color to the ensembles, but the music makes no lasting impression. —*Scott Yanow*

The Vibes Describes / 1994 / Blue Note ◆
This effort from English vibraphonist Orphy Robinson is appallingly dull, the type of recording that Alfred Lion would never have allowed to be released on his label. Most of the ten pieces feature a lazy funk bass, background long tones from the synthesizer and Robinson's speedy but directionless vibes on top. The musicianship is good, but the material is instantly forgettable. When Leroy Osbourne on one song sings about the need of "making a change," one wonders if he means adding a chord change to uplift the monotonous vamp. —*Scott Yanow*

Perry Robinson

b. Sep. 17, 1938, New York, NY
Clarinet / Avant-Garde, Free Jazz
Throughout his career, Perry Robinson has sought to do the near-impossible: establish himself as an avant-garde leader on an instrument still closely associated with the swing era. After extensive formal study (including the Lenox School of Jazz in 1959), Robinson played with such advanced musicians as Paul Bley, Archie Shepp and Bill Dixon. He was with Roswell Rudd's quintet in 1968, appeared on several works by the Jazz Composers' Orchestra and in 1972 worked with Gunter Hampel. In a change of pace, Robinson was with Dave Brubeck's Two Generations of Brubeck band in 1973, but he has continued recording and performing avant-garde jazz up to the present time. —*Scott Yanow*

● **Funk Dumpling** / 1962 / Savoy ◆◆◆◆◆
With Kenny Barron (p). Creative, loose, straight-ahead. —*Michael G. Nastos*

Perry Robinson / 1965 / ESP ◆◆◆

Kundalini / Feb. 2, 1978+Feb. 9, 1978 / Improvising Artists ◆◆
With Badal Roy on tabla and Nana Vasconcelos on percussion. Captivating world fusion. —*Michael G. Nastos*

The Traveler / 1978 / Chiaroscuro ◆◆◆◆

Reginald R. Robinson

b. 1973, Chicago, IL
Piano / Ragtime
Reginald Robinson certainly stands out in his generation for this young man performs ragtime piano; in addition, he has composed dozens of rags. He started on piano at 13 and dropped out of school the following year to devote himself to his music, memorizing rags by ear because he had not yet learned to read music! Robinson began serious lessons the following year and gradually gained a reputation. Reginald Robinson has thus far recorded two

solo piano albums for Delmark, the first cut when he was 20. All but three of the 41 songs he has recorded are his own, and they fit squarely into the classic rag tradition. —*Scott Yanow*

● **Sounds In Silhouette** / 1994 / Delmark ◆◆◆◆◆
Ragtime, which had largely died with Scott Joplin in 1917, did not begin a renaissance until Marvin Hamlisch used some of Joplin's compositions as the basis of his soundtrack to *The Sting* in 1973. Reginald R. Robinson, who coincidentally was born in 1973, quickly emerged not only as one of ragtime's top practioners of the mid-'90s but (along with David Thomas Roberts) as its top contemporary composer. On his second Delmark release he performs 19 selections including Scott Joplin's "Peacherine Rag," a medley of turn-of-the-century pieces by Charles Johnson and 17 of his own compositions. Robinson does not feel the need to "update" ragtime, but he does infuse it with many fresh new melodies and his enthusiasm. He also plays a bit of boogie and stride on this set but, since improvising is not his main forte, the emphasis fortunately is on extending the legacy of Scott Joplin. Ragtime fans should go out of their way to discover Robinson's music. —*Scott Yanow*

Spike Robinson

b. Jan. 16, 1930, Kenosha, WI
Tenor Saxophone / Cool
Spike Robinson in the mid-'90s is just about the last major tenor stylist who plays in the Four Brothers cool-toned style popularized by Stan Getz, Zoot Sims and Al Cohn. The remarkable part is that Robinson seemed to emerge fully-formed in 1981 when he was already past 50. Originally he started on alto when he was 12, and after being in the military, in 1950 Spike played with some of England's top bop musicians, recording with them. However, after he returned to the U.S., Robinson got a degree in engineering and had a day job in Colorado for the next 30 years, just gigging on a part-time basis in local clubs on tenor. When he began playing music fulltime in 1981, Robinson initially created a bit of a sensation. Spike Robinson has continued swinging (often sounding close to Stan Getz) up to the present day, and he has recorded many excellent sets for Discovery, Capri, Concord and particularly Hep. —*Scott Yanow*

● **Plays Harry Warren** / Dec. 18, 1981–Aug. 18, 1993 / Hep ◆◆◆◆◆

At Chester's, Vol. 2 / Jul. 26, 1984 / Hep ◆◆◆◆

At Chester's, Vol. 1 / Jul. 26, 1984 / Hep ◆◆◆◆

London Reprise / Aug. 9, 1984 / Capri ◆◆◆◆◆
Relaxed, fluid, swing-tinged quartet session with tenor saxophonist Spike Robinson doing familiar material backed by Martin Taylor, Dave Green and Spike Wells. Nothing out of the ordinary, but the quartet's easy interaction and the good set of tunes make it palatable. —*Ron Wynn*

Spring Can Really Hang You Up the Most / Jul. 17, 1985 / Capri ◆◆◆◆
Spike Robinson's sessions are usually pleasant, casually swinging and musically proficient, and this quartet outing isn't any different. Robinson explores ballads, mid-tempo standards and originals with a steady, big tone and full sound. He doesn't try anything too intricate, sticking close to the melody and then adding some embellishments and slight alterations. The backing group featuring Ted Beament, Peter Ind and Bill Eyden follow the same formula. —*Ron Wynn*

It's a Wonderful World / Jul. 21, 1985 / Capri ◆◆◆◆

In Town / Oct. 1986 / Hep ◆◆◆

Henry B. Meets Alvin G. Once in a Wild / Jun. 17, 1987 / Capri ◆◆◆◆◆

Odd Couple / Aug. 11, 1988 / Capri ◆◆◆◆

Just a Bit O' Blues, Vol. 1 / Sep. 19, 1988 / Capri ◆◆◆◆
Dazzling swing/traditional jazz coalition. —*Ron Wynn*

Just a Bit O' Blues, Vol. 2 / Sep. 21, 1988 / Capri ◆◆◆◆
This second of two CDs once again teams together the hard swinging but cool-toned tenor of Spike Robinson with veteran trumpeter Harry "Sweets" Edison. Accompanied by pianist Ross Tompkins, bassist Monty Budwig and drummer Paul Humphrey, the two complementary horn soloists are in fine form on a variety of standards and blues. The music always swings, and even if no surprises occur, the chemistry makes this set (along with its first volume) worth picking up. —*Scott Yanow*

Three for the Road / Jul. 1989 / Hep ✦✦✦✦✦
Stairway to the Stars / Oct. 1990 / Hep ✦✦✦✦
Reminiscin / Dec. 12, 1991–Dec. 15, 1991 / Capri ✦✦✦✦✦

Betty Roche (Mary Elizabeth Roche)

b. Jan. 9, 1920, Wilmington, DE
Vocals / Standards

Betty Roche had an oddly episodic career with its highpoints being two separate moments with Duke Ellington's Orchestra. She sang and recorded with the Savoy Sultans (1941–42) and had short stints with Hot Lips Page and Lester Young. Roche had the misfortune of being with Duke Ellington in 1943, a year when the recording strike kept all bands off records. However, at Duke's premiere Carnegie Hall concert she sang the celebrated "Blues" section of his "Black, Brown & Beige Suite"; four decades later this was finally released by Prestige. After a period with Earl Hines, Roche spent time outside of music, but she rejoined Ellington in 1952 and recorded a classic version of "Take the 'A' Train" that was later adopted by Ray Nance. She recorded three solo albums during 1956–61 but then went back into obscurity, having made her brief mark on jazz history. — *Scott Yanow*

Take the 'A' Train / Mar. 1956 / Bethlehem ✦✦✦
Singin' & Swingin' / Jun. 1960 / Original Jazz Classics ✦✦✦✦
★ **Lightly and Politely** / Jan. 24, 1961 / Original Jazz Classics ✦✦✦✦✦

It is ironic that what is arguably singer Betty Roche's finest all-around recording was also her last. For this session, which has been reissued in the *OJC* series on CD, Roche (backed by pianist Jimmy Neeley, guitarist Wally Richardson, bassist Michel Mulia and drummer Rudy Lawless) improvises constantly and uplifts a variety of superior standards including "Someone to Watch over Me," "Polka Dots and Moonbeams," "I Had the Craziest Dream" and three songs by her former boss Duke Ellington. It's recommended, particularly to jazz fans not aware of Betty Roche's musical talents. — *Scott Yanow*

Claudio Roditi

b. May 28, 1946, Rio de Janeiro, Brazil
Trumpet / Latin Jazz, Hard Bop

A superior if sometimes overlooked trumpeter (the Kenny Dorham of the 1990s), Claudio Roditi is a frequently exciting hard bop player. He came to the U.S. to study at Berklee (1970–71) and gigged around the Boston area until moving to New York in 1976. Roditi played with Charlie Rouse and Herbie Mann, and most importantly, in the early '80s he started working regularly with Paquito D'Rivera. The reliable trumpeter has been on many straight-ahead recording sessions since, in addition to being a member of Dizzy Gillespie's United Nation Orchestra. Roditi has recorded as a leader for Green Street (an obscure date in 1984), Uptown, Candid and most recently Reservoir. — *Scott Yanow*

Claudio / 1985 / Uptown ✦✦✦✦

The quintet showcases this straight-ahead trumpeter from Brazil on six standards played with bop flavor (Dorham, Stiff and J.J. Johnson wrote three.) Slide Hampton plays trombone. This is a good, upbeat band. — *Michael G. Nastos*

Gemini Man / Mar. 7, 1988–Mar. 22, 1988 / Milestone ✦✦✦✦
Slow Fire / 1989 / Milestone ✦✦✦
Two of Swords / Sep. 24, 1990–Sep. 25, 1990 / Candid ✦✦✦✦

A solid, although conservative in arrangements and direction, release by trumpeter Claudio Roditi. His pungent melodies and clipped, striking solos are among the disc's positive points. Another is a good crop of supporting musicians, including Edward Simon, Jay Ashby, Duke Fonseca, and Danilo Perez. — *Ron Wynn*

● **Milestones** / Nov. 13, 1990–Nov. 14, 1990 / Candid ✦✦✦✦✦

There aren't many trumpeters around more animated and energetic than Claudio Roditi. His searing solos and equally fiery accompaniment have been featured in several bands, and he takes center stage on *Milestones*. Besides his solos, the disc has some first-rate songs and an even better group. Alto saxophonist Paquito D'Rivera, pianist Kenny Barron, bassist Ray Drummond and drummer Ben Riley would constitute a great band by themselves and are no less playing with Roditi. — *Ron Wynn*

Free Wheelin': The Music Of Lee Morgan / Jul. 29, 1994 / Reservoir ✦✦✦✦✦

Red Rodney (Robert Chudnick)

b. Sep. 27, 1927, Philadelphia, PA, **d.** May 27, 1994
Trumpet / Bop, Hard Bop

Red Rodney's comeback in the late '70s was quite inspiring and found the veteran bebop trumpeter playing even better than he had during his legendary period with Charlie Parker. He started his professional career by performing with Jerry Wald's orchestra when he was 15, and he passed through a lot of big bands including those of Jimmy Dorsey (during which Rodney closely emulated his early idol Harry James), Elliot Lawrence, Georgie Auld, Benny Goodman and Les Brown.

He totally changed his style after hearing Dizzy Gillespie and Charlie Parker, becoming one of the brighter young voices in bebop. Rodney made strong contributions to the bands of Gene Krupa (1946), Claude Thornhill and Woody Herman's Second Herd (1948–49). Off and on during 1949–51, Rodney was a regular member of the Charlie Parker Quintet, playing brilliantly at Bird's recorded Carnegie Hall Concert of 1949. But drugs cut short that association and Rodney spent most of the 1950s in and out of jail. After he kicked heroin, almost as damaging to his jazz chops was a long period playing for shows in Las Vegas.

When he returned to New York in 1972, it took Rodney several years to regain his former form. However, he hooked up with multi-instrumentalist Ira Sullivan in 1980, and the musical partnership benefitted both of the veterans; Sullivan's inquisitive style inspired Rodney to play post-bop music (rather than continually stick to bop), and sometimes their quintet (which also featured Garry Dial) sounded like the Ornette Coleman Quartet! After Sullivan went back to Florida a few years later, Rodney continued leading his own quintet, which in later years featured the talented young saxophonist Chris Potter. Red Rodney, who was portrayed quite sympathetically in the Clint Eastwood film *Bird* (during which he played his own solos), stands as proof that for the most open-minded veterans there is life beyond bop. — *Scott Yanow*

The New Sounds: Red Rodney / Sep. 9, 1951 / Prestige ✦✦✦✦
Modern Music from Chicago / Jun. 20, 1955 / Original Jazz Classics ✦✦✦✦
★ **The Red Arrow** / Nov. 22, 1957–Nov. 24, 1957 / Onyx ✦✦✦✦✦

With Ira Sullivan (tpt/sax) and Tommy Flanagan Trio. Historic early meeting between Rodney and Sullivan. Two by Rodney, one by bassist Oscar Pettiford, three standards. — *Michael G. Nastos*

Red Rodney Returns / 1959 / Argo ✦✦✦
Bird Lives! / Jul. 9, 1973 / Muse ✦✦✦

Quintet with Roy Brooks (d), Charles McPherson (as), Barry Harris (p), Sam Jones (b). Three Bird compositions, Monk's rousing "52nd St. Theme," "'Round Midnight" and one standard. — *Michael G. Nastos*

Superbop / Mar. 26, 1974 / Muse ✦✦✦✦
Red Tornado / Sep. 30, 1975+Oct. 2, 1975 / Muse ✦✦✦✦

Nicely played mid-'70s bop, one in a series that marked the return of trumpeter Red Rodney to the jazz scene after a lengthy absence. His solos are solidly executed, and ensemble interaction, production and arrangements are conservative but well done. — *Ron Wynn*

Red, White & Blues / May 11, 1976–May 12, 1976 / Muse ✦✦✦

Plenty of straight bop and blues, plus some ballads and standards from trumpeter Red Rodney. This one features some aggressive, energized solos on bop and uptempo pieces, plus nice interpretations on the slower material. — *Ron Wynn*

Home Free / Dec. 19, 1977 / Muse ✦✦✦✦

Good, consistently played mainstream fare by trumpeter Red Rodney. This '77 date was one among many he did for the Muse label that followed the same pattern. They minimized the length and extent of Rodney's solos, had him doing anthems and unexacting originals and got the best takes of him and his group, smoothly executing the hard bop and mainstream formulas. — *Ron Wynn*

The Three R's / Mar. 13, 1979–Mar. 14, 1979 / Muse ✦✦✦✦✦
Hi Jinx (at the Vanguard) / May 5, 1980–Jul. 5, 1980 / Muse ✦✦✦✦
Alive in New York / May 8, 1980–Jul. 5, 1980 / Muse ✦✦✦✦✦

Red Rodney, a veteran from bop's early days, has some ardent fans and some just as vocal detractors. The range and tone have slipped some over the years, but he has compensated by playing more middle- and lower-register material and not constantly doing uptempo items. This was a good live set done in '86, with Rodney backed by, among others, the multi-instrumentalist Ira Sullivan and Gary Dial. —*Ron Wynn*

Live at the Village Vanguard / May 8, 1980–Jul. 7, 1980 / Muse ✦✦✦✦✦
With Ira Sullivan (tpt/sax) and quintet. Three Jack Walrath originals, three standouts. This is one of the most together jazz bands of the '80s. A perfect vehicle for both of them to blow. Sullivan plays saxs, flute and fluegelhorn. —*Michael G. Nastos*

Night and Day / Jun. 15, 1981–Jun. 16, 1981 / Muse ✦✦✦✦✦
Trumpeter Red Rodney has worked with multi-instrumentalist Ira Sullivan since the '50s. Their friendship carries over into their musical relationship. This '81 date sometimes has Rodney dominating a song with Sullivan supporting him; then they switch roles, and sometimes they duel or complement each other. They carry the album, for everything else, from backing musicians to songs and production, is competent and nothing more. —*Ron Wynn*

★ **Spirit Within** / Sep. 21, 1981–Sep. 24, 1981 / Elektra ✦✦✦✦
The first of two early '80s albums reuniting frequent collaborators Red Rodney and multi-instrumentalist Ira Sullivan. Sullivan plays second trumpet and a variety of saxophones and provides a challenging and complementary presence to Rodney, who sometimes plays in a restrained, easy fashion, then other times turns up his own playing a notch in response to Sullivan. —*Ron Wynn*

★ **Sprint** / Nov. 3, 1982–Nov. 4, 1982 / Elektra ✦✦✦✦✦
No Turn on Red / Aug. 10, 1986–Aug. 11, 1986 / Denon ✦✦✦
Red Giant / Apr. 1988 / SteepleChase ✦✦✦
One for Bird / Jul. 1988 / SteepleChase ✦✦✦
Red Snapper / Jul. 1988 / SteepleChase ✦✦✦
Red Alert! / Oct. 1990–Nov. 1990 / Continuum ✦✦✦
Quintet. A delightful workout, with excellent Rodney solos. —*Ron Wynn*

Then and Now / 1992 / Chesky ✦✦✦✦
A '92 session in which trumpeter Red Rodney gets back to his bop roots and plays in a quartet with Gary Dial, Jay Anderson and Jimmy Madison. He does both fresh originals and classics from the '40s and '50s. —*Ron Wynn*

Shorty Rogers (Milton M. Rajonsky)

b. Apr. 14, 1924, Great Barrington, MA, **d.** Nov. 7, 1994
Trumpet, Arranger, Leader / Cool
A fine middle-register trumpeter whose style seemed to practically define "cool jazz," Shorty Rogers was actually more significant for his arranging, both in jazz and in the movie studios. After gaining early experience with Will Bradley and Red Norvo and serving in the military, Rogers rose to fame as a member of Woody Herman's First and Second Herds (1945–46 and 1947–49), and somehow he managed to bring some swing to the Stan Kenton Innovations Orchestra (1950–51), clearly enjoying writing for the stratospheric flights of Maynard Ferguson.
After that association ran its course, Rogers settled in Los Angeles where he led his Giants (which ranged from a quintet to a nonet and a big band) on a series of rewarding West Coast-styled recordings and wrote for the studios, helping greatly to bring jazz into the movies; his scores for *The Wild One* and *The Man with the Golden Arm* are particularly memorable. After 1962, Rogers stuck almost exclusively to writing for television and films, but in 1982 he began a comeback in jazz. Rogers reorganized and headed the Lighthouse All-Stars, and although his own playing was not quite as strong as previously, he remained a welcome presence both in clubs and recordings. —*Scott Yanow*

★ **The Complete Atlantic and EMI Jazz Recordings** / Oct. 8, 1951–Mar. 30, 1956 / Mosaic ✦✦✦✦✦
Another exhaustive Mosaic boxed set, this one devoted to the complete material trumpeter Shorty Rogers cut for EMI and Atlantic in the '50s, including both cool-influenced material and concept "Martians" albums. Art Pepper is featured on some cuts on alto sax, along with Shelly Manne, Jimmy Giuffre, and Curtis Counce. —*Ron Wynn*

Popo / Dec. 27, 1951 / Xanadu ✦✦✦✦
● **Short Stops** / Jan. 12, 1953–Mar. 3, 1954 / Bluebird ✦✦✦✦✦
1953–1954. A thorough 2-LP reissue that covers his first three

RCA albums. For some strange reason, the CD only has 20 of 32 cuts. —*Ron Wynn*

Big Band, Vol. 1 / Jul. 11, 1953 / Time Is ✦✦✦
Fine big band doing West Coast material. —*Ron Wynn*

Collaboration / Mar. 30, 1954–Jun. 14, 1954 / Fresh Sound ✦✦✦✦
The Swinging Mr. Rogers / Oct. 21, 1955–Nov. 3, 1955 / Atlantic ✦✦✦✦✦
Trumpeter Shorty Rogers switched labels in the mid-'50s, moving to Atlantic from RCA. This was his Atlantic debut and was an intimate quartet date featuring Rogers alongside clarinetist and saxophonist Jimmy Giuffre, bassist Curtis Counce and drummer Shelly Manne. The single "Martians Go Home" proved so popular that it eventually spawned its own album, *Martians Come Back!* —*Ron Wynn*

Shorty Rogers Plays Richard Rodgers / Jan. 30, 1957–Feb. 3, 1957 / Fresh Sound ✦✦✦✦
Portrait of Shorty / Jul. 15, 1957+Aug. 11, 1957 / RCA ✦✦✦
Gigi in Jazz / Jan. 27, 1958+Jan. 30, 1958 / Fresh Sound ✦✦✦
Chances Are It Swings / Dec. 8, 1958–Dec. 20, 1958 / Fresh Sound ✦✦✦✦
Swings / Dec. 9, 1958–Feb. 5, 1959 / Bluebird ✦✦✦✦
The Wizard of Oz and Other Harold Arlen Songs / Feb. 3, 1959+Feb. 10, 1959 / RCA ✦✦✦✦✦
The Shorty Rogers Quintet / 1962 / Studio West ✦✦✦
The first of four CDs taken from radio transcriptions used in the show "The Navy Swings" features trumpeter/fluegelhornist Shorty Rogers playing with two versions of his quintets in 1962, just prior to him greatly de-emphasizing his playing in favor of full-time writing for the studios. The 13 selections generally clock in around three minutes, so the cool bop performances are quite concise. Jeri Southern has three warm vocals and Rogers shares the frontline with either Harold Land or Gary Lefebvre on tenors. The results are not quite essential but will be enjoyed by Shorty's fans; highlights include "Paul's Pal," "Martian's Go Home," "Popo" and two versions of "What Is This Thing Called Love." —*Scott Yanow*

Bossa Nova / Jun. 12, 1962–Jun. 14, 1962 / Reprise ✦✦
Yesterday, Today and Forever / Jun. 1983 / Concord Jazz ✦✦✦✦
This quintet, with Bud Shank on flute and alto sax, plays three Shorty tunes and four standards. They perform fine readings of Tiny Kahn's "TNT" and Bud Powell's "Budo." —*Michael G. Nastos*

Back Again / May 2, 1984 / Choice ✦✦✦✦
Lighthouse All Stars / 1991 / Candid ✦✦✦✦
America the Beautiful / Aug. 4, 1991–Aug. 5, 1991 / Candid ✦✦✦✦

Sonny Rollins (Theodore Walter [Newk] Rollins)

b. Sep. 7, 1930, New York City
Tenor Saxophone / Bop, Hard Bop, Post Bop
For over 40 years, Sonny Rollins has been one of the true jazz giants, ranking up there with Coleman Hawkins, Lester Young and John Coltrane as one of the all time great tenor saxophonists. He started on piano, took up the alto and then permanently switched to tenor in 1946. After making his recording debut with Babs Gonzales in 1949, Rollins made a major impact on dates with J.J. Johnson and Bud Powell the same year; the latter session also matched him with Fats Navarro. Rollins' abilities were obvious to the jazz world from the start, and he started recording with Miles Davis in 1951 and with Thelonious Monk in 1953. After a period out of music, Rollins joined the Max Roach-Clifford Brown Quintet in late 1955, continuing after Brownie's death until 1957. From then on he was always a leader.
Sonny Rollins' series of brilliant recordings for Prestige, Blue Note, Contemporary and Riverside in the 1950s found him in peak form, and he was acclaimed the top tenor saxophonist of the time, at least until John Coltrane rose to prominence. Therefore Rollins' decision to drop out of music from 1959–61 shocked the jazz world. When he came back in 1961 with a quartet featuring Jim Hall, his style was largely unchanged, but he soon became a much freer player who was well aware of Ornette Coleman's innovations; he even used Ornette's cornetist Don Cherry for a time. Although his playing was a bit more eccentric than previously, Rollins was a major force until he again decided to retire in 1968.
Upon his return in 1971, Sonny Rollins was more open to the

influence of R&B rhythms and pop music, and his recordings since then have not always been essential (often using sidemen not up to his level), but Rollins remains a very vital soloist. His skill at turning unlikely material into jazz, his unaccompanied flights and his rhythmic freedom and tonal distortions have kept Sonny Rollins one of the masters of jazz into the mid-'90s. He has literally dozens of superior recordings currently available. —*Scott Yanow*

★ **The Complete Prestige Recordings** / May 26, 1949–Dec. 7, 1956 / Prestige ✦✦✦✦✦

This seven-CD box set lives up to its title, reissuing in chronological order all of tenor saxophonist Sonny Rollins' recordings for Prestige. Dating mostly from 1951–56, these valuable performances find Rollins developing from a promising player to a potential giant; many of his best recordings would take place a year or two after this program ends. In addition to his own sessions, Rollins is featured with trombonist J.J. Johnson, on four dates with Miles Davis and on sessions led by Thelonious Monk and trumpeter Art Farmer. Among the other musicians participating are trumpeters Kenny Dorham and Clifford Brown, pianists John Lewis, Kenny Drew, Horace Silver, Elmo Hope, Ray Bryant, Red Garland and Tommy Flanagan, drummers Max Roach, Roy Haynes, Art Blakey and Philly Joe Jones, the Modern Jazz Quartet, Julius Watkins on french horn, altoist Jackie McLean and even Charlie Parker. Among the many highlights are the original versions of Rollins' compositions "Airegin," "Oleo," "Doxy," "St. Thomas" and "Blue 7" and his one recorded meeting with John Coltrane ("Tenor Madness"). Essential music that is treated as it should be. The attractive booklet is a major plus, too. —*Scott Yanow*

Sonny Rollins with the Modern Jazz Quartet / Jan. 17, 1951–Oct. 7, 1953 / Original Jazz Classics ✦✦✦✦

Moving Out / Aug. 18, 1954–Oct. 25, 1954 / Original Jazz Classics ✦✦✦✦

Work Time / Dec. 2, 1955 / Original Jazz Classics ✦✦✦✦✦

Work Time presents an entire Sonny Rollins session from Dec. 2, 1955 with pianist Ray Bryant, drummer Max Roach and bassist George Morrow. There was nothing tentative about this performance, and fans of Rollins and Roach should find many joyful encounters with it. —*Bob Rusch, Cadence*

Sonny Rollins Plus 4 / Mar. 22, 1956 / Original Jazz Classics ✦✦✦✦✦

In 1956 Sonny Rollins used the Clifford Brown-Max Roach Quintet (of which he was a member) as his sidemen for this Prestige set. The highpoints of this particularly strong hard bop set include "Valse Hot" (an early jazz waltz), a rapid rendition of "I Feel a Song Coming On" and Rollins' classic "Pent-Up House." Trumpeter Brown (heard on one of his final sessions) is in excellent form as is the strong rhythm section and the young tenor-leader himself. This excellent music is also included as part of Rollins' seven-CD box set for Prestige. —*Scott Yanow*

Tenor Madness / May 24, 1956 / Original Jazz Classics ✦✦✦✦✦

This CD (whose contents have since been reissued many times) is highlighted by the one meeting on records between Sonny Rollins and John Coltrane, an exciting battle on "Tenor Madness." Otherwise, this is a more conventional but no less worthy Rollins quartet session with him turning such odd material as "My Reverie" and "The Most Beautiful Girl in the World" into creative jazz. —*Scott Yanow*

★ **Saxophone Colossus and More** / Jun. 22, 1956 / Original Jazz Classics ✦✦✦✦✦

Plays for Bird / Oct. 5, 1956 / Original Jazz Classics ✦✦✦✦

Quintet. This is an emphatic tribute to one of his idols, influences and mentors. —*Ron Wynn*

Sonny Boy / Oct. 5, 1956 / Original Jazz Classics ✦✦✦✦

This includes impressive stints by Kenny Dorham (tpt), Kenny Drew (p) and Max Roach (p) (among others). —*Ron Wynn*

Tour De Force / Dec. 7, 1956 / Original Jazz Classics ✦✦✦✦

A fine session with Kenny Drew (p) setting the rhythm section pace on piano. —*Ron Wynn*

Sonny Rollins, Vol. 1 / Dec. 16, 1956 / Blue Note ✦✦✦

Compared to Sonny Rollins' other classics of this era, this Blue Note LP usually gets lost in the shuffle, but the music is actually quite good. The great tenor is teamed with trumpeter Donald Byrd, pianist Wynton Kelly, bassist Gene Ramey and drummer

Max Roach for four of his originals (none of which caught on) and an interesting transformation of "How Are Things in Glocca Morra?" —*Scott Yanow*

★ **Way out West** / Mar. 7, 1957 / Original Jazz Classics ✦✦✦✦✦

This timeless recording established Sonny Rollins as jazz's top tenor saxophonist (at least until John Coltrane surpassed him the following year). Joined by bassist Ray Brown and drummer Shelly Manne, Rollins is heard at one of his peaks on such pieces as "I'm an Old Cowhand," his own "Way out West," "There Is No Greater Love" and "Come, Gone" (a fast stomp based on "After You've Gone"). The William Claxton photo of Rollins wearing Western gear (and holding his tenor) in the desert is also a classic. —*Scott Yanow*

Alternate Takes / Mar. 7, 1957–Oct. 22, 1958 / Riverside ✦✦✦✦✦

This LP contains alternate versions of selections from two famous Sonny Rollins albums: *Way out West* and *Sonny Rollins and the Contemporary Leaders*. These "new" renditions of "I'm an Old Cowhand," "Come, Gone," "Way out West," "The Song Is You," "You" and "I've Found a New Baby" (released for the first time in the mid-'80s) hold their own against the classic versions. Rollins is heard with bassist Ray Brown and drummer Shelly Manne on the first session and is joined by a four-piece rhythm section (including pianist Hampton Hawes and guitarist Barney Kessel) on the later date. In any case, the music is often hard-swinging and is frequently superb. —*Scott Yanow*

Sonny Rollins, Vol. 2 / Apr. 14, 1957 / Blue Note ✦✦✦

Compared to his Prestige, Riverside and Contemporary recordings of the 1950s, some of Rollins' appearances on Blue Note seemed anticlimactic, but none should be overlooked. This unusual LP mostly has Rollins in an all-star quintet with trombonist J.J. Johnson, pianist Horace Silver, bassist Paul Chambers and drummer Art Blakey, but Thelonious Monk sits in on his ballad "Reflections," and on "Misterioso" both Silver and Monk get to take contrasting solos. Of the other selections, Rollins' two originals ("Why Don't I" and "Wail March") are worth reviving, and he finds something new to say on "Poor Butterfly" and an uptempo "You Stepped out of a Dream." —*Scott Yanow*

The Sound of Sonny / Jun. 11, 1957–Jun. 19, 1957 / Original Jazz Classics ✦✦✦✦

Wonderful standards and originals, with funky, inventive piano from Sonny Clark (p). —*Ron Wynn*

Newk's Time / Sep. 22, 1957 / Blue Note ✦✦✦✦

This fairly conventional but frequently exciting quartet session finds Sonny Rollins in top form on material ranging from "Tune Up" and "The Surrey with the Fringe on Top" to his own "Blues for Philly Joe." With pianist Wynton Kelly, bassist Doug Watkins and drummer Philly Joe Jones, Rollins shows on the CD that even his less-acclaimed sessions from this era are brilliant. —*Scott Yanow*

More from the Vanguard / Nov. 3, 1957 / Blue Note ✦✦✦✦✦

This double LP added ten more performances to Sonny Rollins' famous night at the Village Vanguard, and the music is at the same level as the original set. With bassist Wilbur Ware and drummer Elvin Jones (on one song bassist Donald Bailey and drummer Pete La Roca take their places), Rollins was inspired to come up with some of his best extended improvisations, sticking to standards but making fresh and unpredictable statements. —*Scott Yanow*

★ **A Night at the Village Vanguard** / Nov. 3, 1957 / Blue Note ✦✦✦✦✦

This CD is often magical. Sonny Rollins, one of jazz's great tenors, is heard at his peak with a pair of pianoless trios (either Wilbur Ware or Donald Bailey on bass and Elvin Jones or Pete La Roca on drums) stretching out on particularly creative versions of "Old Devil Moon," "Softly As In A Morning Sunrise," "Sonnymoon For Two" and "A Night In Tunisia" among others. Not only did Rollins have a very distinctive sound, but his use of time, his sly wit and his boppish but unpredictable style were completely his own by 1957. —*Scott Yanow*

Sonny Rollins / Dec. 12, 1957–Nov. 4, 1957 / Everest ✦✦✦

The material included on this budget LP has been bouncing around for years, turning up on many records. The great tenor Sonny Rollins is heard in a quintet with trombonist Jimmy Cleveland in 1957 performing his "Sonnymoon for Two," the ballad "Like Someone in Love" and strangely enough the "Theme from Tchaikovsky's Symphony Pathetique." In addition, cornetist

Thad Jones performs two of his originals ("Lust for Life" and "I Got It Thad") and a ballad medley with a variety of modern swing players, many from Count Basie's Orchestra. Nowhere on this set does it mention that Rollins is absent on half of the selections and that he never does play with Thad Jones (who is simply listed as "Guest Artist"). The music is better than the crummy packaging. —*Scott Yanow*

European Concerts / 1957–1958 / Bandstand ✦✦✦
Freedom Suite / Feb. 11, 1958+Mar. 7, 1958 / Original Jazz Classics ✦✦✦✦✦
By the time *Freedom Suite* was recorded, Sonny Rollins' influences were well integrated into a mature, individual style. The *Freedom Suite* was much heralded, and the title can arguably be interpreted both musically and socially. An extended piece not yet usual for jazz recordings, it held up well over its entire run. This was a tribute not only to Rollins technical and imaginative powe, but also to Oscar Pettiford (bass) and Max Roach (drums), who completed the trio and were "up" for the entire 19 minutes. —*Bob Rusch, Cadence*

Brass & Trio / Jul. 10, 1958–Jul. 11, 1958 / Verve ✦✦✦✦✦
In 1958 Sonny Rollins split an LP between two very different settings. On four selections he is backed by a big band arranged by Ernie Wilkins (Rollins' appearances with big bands have been quite rare through the years) including Gershwin's "Who Cares?" The flip side showcases the great tenor in a trio with bassist Henry Grimes and drummer Charles Wright including "Manhattan," one of the very few jazz versions of "If You Were the Only Girl in the World" and a brilliant unaccompanied performance of a song often associated with his idol Coleman Hawkins, "Body and Soul." Rollins excels in both of these settings, making this an easily recommended set. —*Scott Yanow*

Sonny Rollins and the Contemporary Leaders / Oct. 20, 1958–Oct. 22, 1958 / Contemporary ✦✦✦✦✦
The last of the classic Sonny Rollins albums prior to his unexpected three-year retirement features the great tenor with pianist Hampton Hawes, guitarist Barney Kessell bassist Leroy Vinnegar and drummer Shelly Manne (all bandleaders for Contemporary Records during this era) on an unusual but inspired list of standards. Rollins creates explorative and often witty improvisations on such songs as "Rock-A-Bye Your Baby with a Dixie Melody," "You," "In the Chapel in the Moonlight" and roaring versions of "I've Found a New Baby" and "The Song Is You." Great music. —*Scott Yanow*

In Stockholm (1959) / Mar. 4, 1959 / Dragon ✦✦✦✦
This radio broadcast is taken from one of Sonny Rollins' final concerts before going into an unexpected three-year retirement. Joined by bassist Henry Grimes and drummer Pete LaRoca, Rollins explores seven songs that he had previously recorded including "St. Thomas," "There Will Never Be Another You," "Oleo" and "Paul's Pal." The music is quite enjoyable and sometimes pretty adventurous, making one very sorry that Rollins decided to drop out of music altogether during some key years. —*Scott Yanow*

Aix-En-Provence / Mar. 11, 1959 / Royal Jazz ✦✦✦
This broadcast from a French concert was Sonny Rollins' last recording before his surprising retirement; he would not resurface until late 1961. Along with John Coltrane, Rollins was the most important tenor saxophonist of the period, and during the trio set with bassist Henry Grimes and drummer Kenny Clarke heard on this CD, Rollins really stretches out on "Woody 'n You," "But Not for Me" and "Lady Bird"; the individual selections range in time from 15:50 to 18:35. Although not as essential as his studio recordings of the period, this decently recorded concert performance will be savored by Sonny Rollins collectors. —*Scott Yanow*

★ **The Bridge** / Jan. 30, 1962–Feb. 13, 1962 / Bluebird ✦✦✦✦✦
One of the more important Sonny Rollins recordings, this set was his first after a highly publicized three-year retirement. The great tenor, joined by guitarist Jim Hall, bassist Bob Cranshaw and drummer Ben Riley, is in particularly strong form on this session even if his style was not changed much from 1959. Advanced bop that hints a bit at the avant-garde. —*Scott Yanow*

Alternatives / May 14, 1962–Apr. 14, 1964 / Bluebird ✦✦✦✦✦
Sonny Rollins' RCA recordings of 1962–64 found him really stretching out his style, listening to and learning from Ornette Coleman without losing his own musical personality. This CD, in addition to two numbers with bassist Bob Cranshaw and the con-

gos of Candido ("Jungoso" and "Bluesongo") that were originally on the album *What's New*, has four selections from *Now's the Time* along with four very different alternate takes. For example, the original version of "52nd Street Theme" was four minutes long, but the alternate is 14. The personnel also differs much of the time with cornetist Thad Jones and pianist Herbie Hancock making appearances, but the emphasis is on the exciting improvisations of Rollins, one of the great tenor saxophonists of all time. —*Scott Yanow*

On the Outside / Jul. 27, 1962–Feb. 20, 1963 / Bluebird ✦✦✦✦✦
A very interesting CD of material from Sonny Rollins. It reissues the complete *Our Man in Jazz* (three lengthy performances including a 25-minute version of "Oleo") along with three briefer selections previously on a sampler. These are among Rollins' most avant-garde improvisations, for he seems inspired by trumpeter Don Cherry's presence (although Cherry clearly could not keep up with the great tenor). Rollins really digs into "Oleo" and the 15-minute "Doxy" and plays some remarkable music. —*Scott Yanow*

All the Things You Are / Jul. 15, 1963–Jul. 2, 1964 / Bluebird ✦✦✦✦
Half of this CD contains the famous session on which Sonny Rollins teamed up with his idol, the great tenor Coleman Hawkins. Actually the competitive Rollins did everything he could during these performances to throw Hawk off with plenty of sound explorations and free playing, but Hawkins keeps from getting lost and battles Rollins to a tie; pianist Paul Bley plays well too. The remainder of this CD (three selections apiece from the former LPs *Now's the Time* and *The Standard Sonny Rollins*) is more conventional but has its moments of interest. The young Herbie Hancock is on piano for all of these tracks, and guitarist Jim Hall helps on "Trav'lin Light." Rollins' RCA recordings of the 1960s are all worth picking up even though they are currently being reissued in piecemeal fashion. —*Scott Yanow*

Stuttgart (1963) / Nov. 1963 / Jazz Anthology ✦✦✦
Sonny Rollins and his 1963 Quartet (with trumpeter Don Cherry, bassist Henry Grimes and drummer Billy Higgins) play very long versions of "Green Dolphin Street" (18 minutes) and "Sonnymoon for Two" (over 22 minutes) with some of the improvising being very free. The solos generally hold one's interest (Rollins' always do), but the so-so recording quality and some aimless sections lower this LP's rating a little. It's still worth picking up. —*Scott Yanow*

Sonny Rollins & Co. 1964 / Jan. 24, 1964–Jul. 9, 1964 / Bluebird ✦✦✦✦
This CD from the Bluebird reissue series fills a lot of gaps in Sonny Rollins' discography. The 13 selections are taken from six different sessions from 1964. The personnel changes from date to date with either Ron Carter or Bob Cranshaw on bass and Roy McCurdy or Mickey Roker on drums, along with pianist Herbie Hancock (on five songs) and guitarist Jim Hall on three others. Some of the music is actually alternate takes, and in contrast to a rambling 16-minute version of "Now's the Time," a few of the briefer songs (seven are under 31 minutes) shut down prematurely. However, the great tenor's improvisations are consistently fascinating as he reconciles his avant-garde flights to the standards he is performing; "Autumn Nocturne" is a highpoint. —*Scott Yanow*

There Will Never Be Another You / Jun. 17, 1965 / Impulse! ✦✦
This LP features Sonny Rollins and a quintet (pianist Tommy Flanagan, bassist Bob Cranshaw and both Billy Higgins and Mickey Roker on drums) playing an outdoor concert in the rain. Rollins was in a strolling mood, and he wanders all over the stage, which means that he is off-mike much of the time. His playing on these five standards (which includes a 16-minute version of the title tune) is fine, but the erratic recording quality makes this one of the lesser Rollins albums. —*Scott Yanow*

Sonny Rollins on Impulse! / Jul. 8, 1965 / Impulse! ✦✦✦✦
The first of three studio albums that tenor saxophonist Sonny Rollins recorded for Impulse! contains the joyous calypso "Hold 'Em Joe" and four unusual versions of standards in which the rhythms he plays are more important than the actual melodies. Joined by pianist Ray Bryant, bassist Walter Booker and drummer Mickey Roker, Rollins sounds quite distinctive on this brief but enjoyable set. —*Scott Yanow*

Alfie / Jan. 26, 1966 / Impulse! ✦✦✦✦✦
Sonny Rollins compositions for the film *Alfie* (which benefited

greatly from Oliver Nelson's arrangements) are heard on this CD as played by Rollins and a nine-piece band. The music easily stands by itself without the movie, and Rollins is in fine form on these generally memorable themes, particularly "On Impulse" and "Alfie's Theme." — *Scott Yanow*

★ **East Broadway Run Down** / May 9, 1966 / Impulse! ♦♦♦♦♦
Sonny Rollins' last recording before taking another long retirement (this time six years) is a real gem, one of his top albums of the 1960s. This CD includes the 20-minute title cut (which has some rather free moments but always remains quite coherent), the tenor's memorable original "Blessing in Disguise" and his glorious ballad statement on "We Kiss in a Shadow." Trumpeter Freddie Hubbard helps out on "East Broadway Run Down," but otherwise this excellent set showcases Rollins in a trio with bassist Jimmy Garrison and drummer Elvin Jones. — *Scott Yanow*

● **Next Album** / Jul. 1972 / Original Jazz Classics ♦♦♦♦♦
Sonny Rollins first album after ending his six-year retirement is a particularly strong effort. The highpoint is a ten-minute version of "Skylark" that has a long unaccompanied section by the great tenor. Other memorable selections include "The Everywhere Calypso" and "Playing in the Yard." Rollins plays soprano on "Poinciana" and is heard using electronics (George Cables' electric piano) for the first time, but this music is not all that different from what he was playing prior to his retirement. — *Scott Yanow*

Horn Culture / Jun. 1973–Jul. 1973 / Original Jazz Classics ♦♦♦
This decent effort from Sonny Rollins finds the classic tenorsaxophonist at his best on "Good Morning Heartache" and "God Bless the Child" although some of his own originals seem a touch lightweight. His backup band (which includes keyboardist Walter Davis, Jr., and guitarist Masuo) is supportive but somewhat anonymous. Nothing too essential occurs, but the music is generally enjoyable. — *Scott Yanow*

The Cutting Edge / Jul. 6, 1974 / Original Jazz Classics ♦♦♦♦
Sonny Rollins' 1974 appearance at the Montreux Jazz Festival was warmly received. Joined by his usual band of the period (pianist Stanley Cowell, guitarist Masuo, electric bassist Bob Cranshaw, drummer David Lee and percussionist Mtume), Rollins manages to turn such unlikely material as "To a Wild Rose" and "A House Is Not a Home" into jazz. The world's only jazz bagpipe player (Rufus Harley) makes his presence felt on "Swing Low, Sweet Chariot." — *Scott Yanow*

Nucleus / Sep. 2, 1975–Sep. 5, 1975 / Original Jazz Classics ♦♦♦
It has long been a disappointment to many longtime followers that Rollins' recordings of the 1970s and '80s were generally not at the same level as his earlier sessions. Nucleus is a case in point. This funky date (which also includes trombonist Raul DeSouza, Bennie Maupin on reeds and keyboardist George Duke) has its moments (including an updated version of "My Reverie") but falls far short of hinting at any new innovations — *Scott Yanow*

The Way I Feel / Aug. 1976–Oct. 1976 / Original Jazz Classics ♦♦♦
A '91 reissue of '76 sessions with tenor saxophonist Sonny Rollins playing alongside session musicians and guest stars. The roster includes keyboardist Patrice Rushen, trumpeter Oscar Brashear, trombonist George Bohannon, drummer Billy Cobham and guitarist Lee Ritenour. — *Ron Wynn*

Easy Living / Aug. 3, 1977–Aug. 6, 1977 / Milestone ♦♦♦♦
One of Sonny Rollins' better recordings of the 1970s, this spirited set finds the veteran tenor adopting a thicker and raunchier R&Bish tone. Although sticking close to the melody, he really tears into Stevie Wonder's "Isn't She Lovely" and finds interesting new variations to play on "My One and Only Love" (on soprano) and "Easy Living." The fine backup group includes keyboardist George Duke and drummer Tony Williams. — *Scott Yanow*

Don't Stop the Carnival / Apr. 13, 1978–Apr. 15, 1978 / Milestone ♦♦♦
This set (recorded live over a three-day period at the Great American Music Hall in San Francisco in 1978) finds the great tenor Sonny Rollins welcoming trumpeter Donald Byrd to half of the selections; Byrd was beginning his comeback but sounds rusty and is only in so-so form. The four-piece rhythm section includes drummer Tony Williams and these versions of "Don't Stop the Carnival" and "Autumn Nocturne" are memorable, but most of the rest of the set, although spirited, is a bit lightweight; when was the last time anyone performed "Camel," "President Hayes" or "Sais"? — *Scott Yanow*

Milestone Jazzstars in Concert / Sep. 1978–Oct. 1978 / Milestone ♦♦♦♦
In 1978 a tour was set up that would feature three of the top jazz stars of Milestone Records (tenor saxophonist Sonny Rollins, pianist McCoy Tyner and bassist Ron Carter) in a quartet with drummer Al Foster. The resulting recording has many strong moments including Rollins' unaccompanied solo on "Continuum," his duet with Tyner on "In a Sentimental Mood," Tyner's showcases on "A Little Pianissimo" and "Alone Together" (the latter a duet with Carter) and the bassist's lengthy reworking of "Willow Weep for Me." The quartet pieces generally work well too, with these compatible but very individual stylists blending together much better than one might expect. — *Scott Yanow*

Don't Ask / May 15, 1979–May 18, 1979 / Milestone ♦♦♦
The main reasons to acquire this release are for the Sonny Rollins-Larry Coryell duets on "The File" and particularly "My Ideal." Less worthwhile is a song given the hideous title of "Disco Monk" and Rollins' attempt to forge a personality on the lyricon on "Tai Chi." A bit erratic, this LP is still worth acquiring for its stronger moments. — *Scott Yanow*

Love at First Sight / May 9, 1980–May 12, 1980 / Milestone ♦♦♦
Sonny Rollins has an all-star backup band on this 1980 release: keyboardist George Duke, bassist Stanley Clarke, drummer Al Foster and on some selections percussionist Bill Summers. The music ranges from "The Very Thought of You" and a remake of "Strode Rode" to some more lightweight group originals. Decent music but nothing that memorable occurs. — *Scott Yanow*

No Problem / Dec. 9, 1981–Dec. 15, 1981 / Milestone ♦♦♦
An average effort from the great tenor saxophonist Sonny Rollins, No Problem also features guitarist Bobby Broom, vibraphonist Bobby Hutcherson, electric bassist Bob Cranshaw and drummer Tony Williams. Rollins is in generally fine form, but none of the compositions are all that inspiring, and for these fine players this session sounds too safe and routine. — *Scott Yanow*

Reel Life / Aug. 17, 1982–Aug. 22, 1982 / Milestone ♦♦
As is often the case on Sonny Rollins' recordings of the '80s, he sounds best on a ballad (in this case Billy Strayhorn's "My Little Brown Book") yet often coasts on his own originals. The backup band (guitarists Bobby Broom and Yoshiaki Masuo, electric bassist Bob Cranshaw and drummer Jack DeJohnette) does little to uplift this decent but somewhat forgettable effort. — *Scott Yanow*

Sunny Days, Starry Nights / Jan. 23, 1984–Jan. 27, 1984 / Milestone ♦♦♦
By 1984 it was a common complaint that Sonny Rollins' live appearances were much more exciting than his studio recordings. Although none of the latter were throwaways (and virtually all of the Milestone sessions have their moments of interest), few were real gems. Sunny Days, Starry Nights as usual finds the great tenor at his best on the two ballads ("I'm Old Fashioned" and Noel Coward's "I'll See You Again") while the other four originals have been largely forgotten. His backup crew features trombonist Clifton Anderson and keyboardist Mark Soskin. — *Scott Yanow*

The Solo Album / Jul. 19, 1985 / Milestone ♦
One of the few complete duds of Sonny Rollins' career, this rambling live session is a major disappointment. His unaccompanied explorations (which in the past usually clocked in at around three minutes) gave one the impression that he would be heard best in a solo setting where he could fly freely without having to be concerned about his accompanists. Perhaps that is true, but for this concert he apparently planned nothing in advance, resulting in 56 minutes of wandering around, throwing in occasional song quotes but managing to not play anything of real value. In other words, it sounds as if Rollins were merely warming up, playing whatever came into his mind without any thought of developing a coherent statement. — *Scott Yanow*

G-Man / Aug. 16, 1986 / Milestone ♦♦♦♦
The soundtrack to the performance film Saxophone Colossus features long Sonny Rollins tenor solos on "G-Man" and "Don't Stop the Carnival" and a briefer one during "Kim." Joined by his usual quintet of the era (trombonist Clifton Anderson, pianist Mark Soskin, electric bassist Bob Cranshaw and drummer Marvin "Smitty" Smith), Rollins is in good form, saying little that it is new but delivering passionate messages with his typical spirit; the video is worth getting too. — *Scott Yanow*

Dancing in the Dark / Sep. 15, 1987–Sep. 25, 1987 / Milestone
✦✦✦

The better-than-usual repertoire (including the calypso "Duke or Iron," "Dancing in the Dark" and The Warren & Dubin number "I'll String Along with You") makes this outing by Sonny Rollins' usual band (with trombonist Clifton Anderson, keyboardist Mark Soskin, electric bassist Jerome Harris and drummer Marvin "Smitty" Smith) one of the more interesting Rollins albums of recent times. Although not up to the level of his best live performances, this studio album is quite enjoyable and gives one a clear idea as to how Sonny Rollins sounded in the 1980s. —*Scott Yanow*

Falling in Love with Jazz / Jun. 3, 1989–Sep. 9, 1989 / Milestone
✦✦✦

This average effort from Sonny Rollins and his regular sextet is most notable for two numbers ("For All We Know" and "I Should Care") that find Branford Marsalis joining Rollins in a quintet with pianist Tommy Flanagan. Unfortunately, Marsalis makes the fatal error of trying to imitate Rollins (instead of playing in his own musical personality), and he gets slaughtered. Much better are Rollins' romps on "Tennessee Waltz" and "Falling in Love with Love." —*Scott Yanow*

Here's to the People / Aug. 10, 1991–Aug. 27, 1991 / Milestone
✦✦✦

Sonny Rollins' usual sextet (with trombonist Clifton Anderson, pianist Mark Soskin, guitarist Jerome Harris, electric bassist Bob Cranshaw and drummer Steve Jordan) welcomes guest drummers Jack DeJohnette and Al Foster and, most importantly, trumpeter Roy Hargrove on two selections. Hargrove sounds fine on "I Wish I Knew" and "Young Roy" while Rollins is in good form on such songs as "Why Was I Born," "Someone to Watch over Me" and "Long Ago and Far Away." Nothing very innovative occurs, but the music is quite pleasing. —*Scott Yanow*

Old Flames / 1993 / Milestone ✦✦✦✦
Sonny Rollins mostly sticks to standard ballads on this excellent CD that finds him joined by trombonist Clifton Anderson, pianist Tommy Flanagan, bassist Bob Cranshaw, drummer Jack DeJohnette and, on two selections, a five-piece brass choir arranged by Jimmy Heath. Comfortable and occasionally passionate music by one of the classic tenor saxophonists. —*Scott Yanow*

Wallace Roney

b. May 25, 1960, Philadelphia, PA
Trumpet / Post-Bop, Hard Bop
Listening to Wallace Roney can be a frustrating experience for, despite his obvious technical skills, virtually all of his solos sound like an imitation of Miles Davis circa 1965–70. It is not that he is copying phrases so much, but his sound, phrasing and approach are nearly identical, and now that he is in his mid-30s, one wonders if he is ever going to develop his own voice.

Roney joined Abdullah Ibrahim's Big Band in 1979 and was with Art Blakey's Jazz Messengers in 1981 (subbing for Wynton Marsalis when he was touring with Herbie Hancock). Since that time he has spent a long period with the Tony Williams Quintet, assisted Miles Davis at the 1991 Montreux Jazz Fesitval (in which Davis revisited for one last time the arrangements of Gil Evans), played as a substitute Miles in both Gerry Mulligan's Rebirth of the Cool and Herbie Hancock's Tribute to Miles Davis quintet and recorded steadily as a leader. His own records tend to be modal-based, and they all contain strong (if derivative) trumpet playing. —*Scott Yanow*

Verses / Feb. 19, 1987 / Muse ✦✦✦✦
Aggressive, attacking material with fiery exchanges between Gary Thomas (reeds) and Roney. Top front line of young talent, Roney and Gary Thomas. —*Ron Wynn*

Intuition / Jan. 6, 1988 / Muse ✦✦✦✦
This is a stirring set from one of the best "Young Lion" trumpeters. Very dynamic hard-bop line with superior alto and tenor sax by Kenny Garret (as/ts) and Gary Thomas (ts). —*Ron Wynn*

The Standard Bearer / Mar. 3, 1989 / Muse ✦✦✦✦✦
Obsession / Sep. 7, 1990 / Muse ✦✦✦✦
The latest from this trumpet whiz boasts excellent songs supplied by both Roney and pianist Donald Brown. —*Ron Wynn*

Seth Air / Sep. 28, 1991 / Muse ✦✦✦✦
Trumpeter Wallace Roney, 32 at the time of this recording, has yet to escape from the shadow of Miles Davis. However, he is one of

the stronger brassmen in jazz of the 1990s and plays quite well on this set, which includes three numbers by younger brother Antoine Roney (who is heard on this CD on tenor), two from Roney's pianist Jacky Terasson and three odd standards: "People," Gershwin's "Gone" and Burt Bacharach's "Wives & Lovers." The music is straight-ahead but occasionally as unpredictable as the repertoire. —*Scott Yanow*

● **Crunchin'** / Jul. 30, 1993 / Muse ✦✦✦✦✦
Trumpeter Wallace Roney sounds poignant and fabulous throughout the eight tracks on his latest release. His lines on "What's New" and "You Stepped Out Of A Dream" are full and gorgeous, while his soloing on "Woody 'n You" and "Time After Time" has warmth, intensity and edge. Alto saxophonist Antonio Hart chimes in with equal facility and spark, while Geri Allen shows that she is just as outstanding as an accompanist on standards and hard bop as in trios or as a leader. —*Ron Wynn*

Misterioso / 1994 / Warner Brothers ✦✦✦✦
Trumpeter Wallace Roney avoids the standard repertoire altogether on this CD, playing pieces by Pat Metheny, the Beatles, Egberto Gismonti, Jaco Pastorius and even Dolly Parton among others but, try as hard as he may, he still sounds like Miles Davis every time he hits a long tone or plays a doubletime passage. Backed by a small orchestra that mostly interprets Gil Goldstein arrangements, Roney is the main soloist throughout this interesting ballad-dominated set. —*Scott Yanow*

Wallace Roney Quintet / Feb. 20, 1995–Feb. 22, 1995 / Warner Brothers ✦✦✦✦

Michele Rosewoman

b. 1953, Oakland, CA
Piano / Avant-Garde
An exciting, ambitious pianist particularly effective with Afro-Latin rhythms, Michele Rosewoman has been in the forefront of jazz composers and performers anxious to find new frontiers. But instead of fusion or hip-hop, Rosewoman chose Afro-Cuban music. With parents who owned a record store in Oakland and an older brother who's a musician, Rosewoman began playing piano at six and took lessons at 17 from Edwin Kelly. She studied Cuban percussion with Orlando Rios as well as traditional Shona and Yoruba African music. Rosewoman later worked with members of both the Black Artists Group and Association for the Advancement of Creative Musicians. She moved to New York in 1978 and played with Oliver Lake at a Carnegie Hall concert. Rosewoman worked with Billy Bang in the early '80s and also recorded with Los Kimy, a contemporary Cuban band. She formed the 15-piece New Yor-Uba in the mid-'80s and later premiered the production "New Yor-Uba: A Music Celebration of Cuba in America" at the Public Theatre. Rosewoman began recording as a leader for Soul Note in the mid-'80s and formed the quintet Quintessence in 1986. She toured with Carlos Ward in the early '90s and later did a trio date with Rufus Reid and Ralph Peterson, Jr. —*Ron Wynn and Michael G. Nastos*

The Source / Dec. 1984 / Soul Note ✦✦✦
Quintessence / Jan. 27, 1987–Jan. 28, 1987 / Enja ✦✦✦✦
Pianist Michele Rosewoman makes a strong showing on this '87 release, leading a group with alto saxophonist Steve Coleman, alto and soprano saxophonist Greg Osby, bassist Anthony Cox and drummer Terri Lyne Carrington. The material is mainly originals and mixed Afro-Latin, hard bop, and animated arrangements with some free influences. —*Ron Wynn*

● **Contrast High** / Jul. 1988 / Enja ✦✦✦✦✦
With Quintessence. Pianist with intriguing compositions. —*Michael G. Nastos*

Occasion to Rise / Sep. 13, 1990–Sep. 15, 1990 / Evidence ✦✦✦✦
Pianist Michele Rosewoman shows tremendous rhythmic drive, fine harmonic skills and outstanding phrasing and playing throughout the 10 cuts on this 1990 set. With drummer Ralph Peterson briskly outlining the rhythmic direction and bassist Rufus Reid proving the link between his piercing rhythms and Rosewoman's energetic playing, this is not polite or casual piano fare. It is fiery, sometimes slashing ("The Sweet Eye of Hurricane Sally") and sometimes sentimental ("Prelude To A Kiss" and "We Are"). —*Ron Wynn*

Renee Rosnes

b. 1962, Regina, Saskatchewan, Canada
Piano / Hard Bop, Post Bop
Renee Rosnes, who plays in an advanced and flexible hard bop

style, seems on the brink of great success. A native of Canada, she began piano lessons at age three and violin when she was five. She worked throughout Canada, performing on CBC Jazz Radio Canada shows, gigging with her trio regularly at a hotel and playing on the S.S. Rotterdam Cruise Liner. Rosnes moved to New York in 1985 and has played and/or recorded with a wide variety of artists including Joe Henderson, Wayne Shorter, J.J. Johnson, Jon Faddis, James Moody, the group Out of the Blue, Gary Thomas and Robin Eubanks. In addition she has recorded a couple of her own sessions for Blue Note. —*Scott Yanow*

Renee Rosnes / Apr. 18, 1988–Feb. 4, 1989 / Blue Note ✦✦✦✦
High-caliber duet and quartet sessions. Rosnes proves captivating in any context. Guests include Wayne Shorter (sax) and Branford Marsalis (sax). —*Ron Wynn*

For the Moment / Feb. 15, 1990–Feb. 16, 1990 / Blue Note ✦✦✦✦
Four Rosnes originals, four others from Monk, Woody Shaw, Walt Weiskopf and the Warren/Dubin team. Joe Henderson featured on seven of the eight cuts. —*Michael G. Nastos*

● **Without Words** / Jan. 8, 1992–Jan. 9, 1992 / Blue Note ✦✦✦✦✦

Frank Rosolino

b. Aug. 20, 1926, Detroit, MI, **d.** Nov. 26, 1978, Los Angeles, CA
Trombone / Bop
The horrible way that Frank Rosolino's life ended (killing himself after shooting his two sons) has largely overshadowed his earlier musical accomplishments. One of the top trombonists of the 1950s, Rosolino's fluid and often-humorous style put him near the top of his field for awhile.

He was a guitarist when he was ten but switched to trombone as a teenager. After serving in the military, Rosolino played with the big bands of Bob Chester, Glen Gray, Gene Krupa (1948–49), Tony Pastor, Herbie Fields and Georgie Auld. However all of those experiences were just preludes to his high profile association with Stan Kenton (1952–54), which gave him fame. Rosolino recorded frequently in Los Angeles as a member of the Lighthouse All-Stars (1954–60), a freelancer and as a studio musician. His song "Blue Daniel" became a jazz standard, and Rosolino was a popular attraction as a brilliant trombonist and a comical singer. He was with Supersax for a period in the 1970s. Rosolino's shocking ending was a surprise to even his closest associates. —*Scott Yanow*

Kenton Presents Jazz: Frank Rosolino / Mar. 12, 1954–Nov. 6, 1954 / Capitol ✦✦✦

● **Frankly Speaking** / May 4, 1955–May 5, 1955 / Affinity ✦✦✦✦✦
Perhaps his greatest album as a leader. Immaculate trombone solos. —*Ron Wynn*

I Play Trombone / May 1956 / Bethlehem ✦✦✦✦

Frank Rosolino Quartet / Jun. 1957 / VSOP ✦✦✦✦✦
This matchup works out quite well. Trombonist Frank Rosolino and tenor saxophonist Richie Kamuca make for a potent frontline and are accompanied quite ably by pianist Vince Guaraldi, bassist Monty Budwig and drummer Stan Levey. This 1957 studio session, originally put out on the long-defunct Mode label, has been reissued on CD by VSOP and is well worth picking up. Rosolino contributes three originals, Bill Holman arranged some of the ensembles, and the solos are consistently enjoyable and swinging. —*Scott Yanow*

Free for All / Dec. 22, 1958 / Specialty ✦✦✦✦
This CD reissue expands upon the original eight-song program by adding three alternate takes. The fine bop trombonist Frank Rosolino teams up with tenor saxophonist Harold Land and a West Coast rhythm section (pianist Victor Feldman, bassist Leroy Vinnegar and drummer Stan Levey) for a set of standards and melodic group originals. Originally cut for Specialty, the formerly rare session has its strong moments although it is not really all that essential, but fans of Rosolino and Land will want to get it. —*Scott Yanow*

Thinking About You / Apr. 21, 1976–Apr. 23, 1976 / Sackville ✦✦✦
Recorded live at Bourbon Street in Toronto with Ed Bickert (g), Don Thompson (b), and Terry Clarke (d), this album includes four long standards. With room to stretch, the whole band is up to the task. This is on the mellow side. —*Michael G. Nastos*

Annie Ross (Annabelle Lynch)

b. Jul. 25, 1930, Surrey, England
Vocals / Vocalese, Bop
Although she has had a long career as an actress in England, Annie Ross will always be best-remembered for being part of the premiere jazz vocal group Lambert, Hendricks and Ross. At the age of three she moved in with her aunt Ella Logan (a fine singer) in Los Angeles and for a time was a successful child film actress. After working in Europe singing in cabarets during 1947–50, Ross returned to the U.S. and came to prominence with her vocalese versions of "Twisted," "Farmer's Market" and "Jackie" during 1952–53. She visited Europe with Lionel Hampton's big band in 1953 and stayed for a few years. Back in New York, her singing was heard at its prime during 1956–62 with Lambert, Hendricks and Ross (the three very talented yet diverse singers blended together quite well and constantly challenged each other) and on her own solo records. However, the constant travelling and work caused Ross to have to leave the group in 1962 due to ill health. She returned to England, recovered and worked locally. Ross eventually became better-known as an actress, and her recent returns to jazz have been more nostalgic than musical since age has taken its toll on her voice. However, for jazz fans, Annie Ross will always be eternally youthful and part of L, H & Ross. —*Scott Yanow*

★ **Annie Ross Sings a Song of Mulligan** / Feb. 11, 1958+Sep. 25, 1958 / Pacific Jazz ✦✦✦✦✦
With Gerry Mulligan (sax). Expertly done all-around, a wonderful collaboration. —*Ron Wynn*

Gypsy / 1958–1959 / Pacific Jazz ✦✦✦

● **Gasser!** / Feb. 1959–Mar. 1959 / World Pacific ✦✦✦✦✦
1988 reissue, another tremendous joint effort between Ross and a top saxophonist, this time Zoot Sims. —*Ron Wynn*

Annie Ross Sings A Handful of Songs / Jun. 26, 1963–Jul. 1, 1963 / Fresh Sound ✦✦✦✦

Charlie Rouse

b. Apr. 6, 1924, Washington, D.C., **d.** Nov. 30, 1988, Seattle, WA
Tenor Saxophone / Hard Bop
Possessor of a distinctive tone and a fluid bop-oriented style, Charlie Rouse was in Thelonious Monk's Quartet for over a decade (1959–70) and, although somewhat taken for granted, was an important ingredient in Monk's music. Rouse was always a modern player, and he worked with Billy Eckstine's orchestra (1944) and the first Dizzy Gillespie big band (1945), making his recording debut with Tadd Dameron in 1947. Rouse popped up in a lot of important groups including Duke Ellington's Orchestra (1949–50), Count Basie's octet (1980), on sessions with Clifford Brown in 1953 and with Oscar Pettiford's sextet (1955). He co-led the Jazz Modes with Julius Watkins (1956–59) and then joined Monk for a decade of extensive touring and recordings. In the 1970s he recorded a few albums as a leader, and in 1979 he became a member of Sphere. Charlie Rouse's unique sound began to finally get some recognition during the 1980s. He participated on Carmen McRae's classic *Carmen Sings Monk* album, and his last recording was at a Monk tribute concert. —*Scott Yanow*

The Chase Is on / 1957 / Bethlehem ✦✦✦
This relaxed set matches together the very different tenor tones of Charlie Rouse and Paul Quinichette with a fine rhythm section (Wynton Kelly or Hank Jones on piano, bassist Wendell Marshall and drummer Ed Thigpen). The music includes a few forgotten songs of the era (including "You're Cheating Yourself," "Tender Trap" and Carmen McRae's "Last Time for Love") and has competent if generally polite playing from the tenors. However, the boppish music (which contains no real surprises) is enjoyable overall. —*Scott Yanow*

Takin' Care of Business / May 11, 1960 / Original Jazz Classics ✦✦✦✦
Quintet with Blue Mitchell (tpt) and the Walter Bishop (p) Trio plays two numbers penned by Randy Weston, one apiece by Kenny Drew and Rouse and two standards. This is a supremely confident group that plays strong music in a somewhat cool mood. —*Michael G. Nastos*

Unsung Hero / Dec. 20, 1960–Jul. 13, 1961 / Epic ✦✦✦✦✦

Cinnamon Flower / 1976 / Rykodisc ✦✦✦

Moment's Notice / Oct. 20, 1977 / Storyville ✦✦✦✦
This quartet features pianist Hugh Lawson, bassist Bob Cranshaw and drummer Ben Riley. —*Michael G. Nastos*

The Upper Manhattan Jazz Society / 1981 / Enja ✦✦✦
A fine early '80s album with tenor saxophonist Charlie Rouse leading a group featuring bassist Buster Williams, pianist Al Dailey, trumpeter Benny Bailey and drummer Keith Copeland. This contains some of Rouse's strongest post-Monk playing and compositions. —*Ron Wynn*

Social Call / Jan. 21, 1984–Jan. 22, 1984 / Uptown ✦✦✦
This studio session with Red Rodney and the Albert Dailey Trio consisted of all post-bop standards save Rouse's "Little Chico." Arrangements were by Don Sickler. —*Michael G. Nastos*

● **Epistrophy** / Oct. 10, 1988 / Landmark ✦✦✦✦✦
An adventurous late-'80s date, with Rouse stepping out and handling the challenge posed by Don Cherry (cnt), Buddy Montgomery (p), and George Cables (p). —*Ron Wynn*

ROVA Saxophone Quartet

Group / Modern Creative, Avant-Garde
The most advanced of the saxophone quartets, ROVA (consisting of Jon Raskin, Larry Ochs, Andrew Voigt and Bruce Ackley) was formed in 1977. Since then, this adventurous unit has recorded extensively for many labels (including Metalanguage, Moers, Ictus, New Albion, Sound Aspects, Hat Art and Black Saint), visited Europe and the Soviet Union (the latter twice) and put out sets of Steve Lacy and Anthony Braxton tunes in addition to many originals. In 1988 Steve Adams took Voigt's place. —*Scott Yanow*

Cinema Rovate / Jul. 25, 1978+Aug. 2, 1978 / Metalanguage ✦✦✦✦
This debut album of open-ended compositions was a response to the groups' perceived lack of discipline in contemporary free jazz. —*Myles Boisen*

Daredevils / Mar. 11, 1979 / Metalanguage ✦✦✦
An early collaboration with guitarist Henry Kaiser. —*Myles Boisen*

This, This, This, This / Aug. 7, 1979–Aug. 24, 1979 / Moers ✦✦✦✦

Invisible Frames / May 15, 1980–Oct. 4, 1981 / Fore ✦✦✦

As Was / Apr. 1981 / Metalanguage ✦✦✦✦

Saxophone Diplomacy / Jun. 1983 / Hat Art ✦✦✦✦✦
The least heralded saxophone ensemble on the scene, but ROVA's music is just as emphatic and frenetic as The World Sax Quartet's, even if no one is a compositional match for David Murray or Hamiett Bluiett. They make dynamic, hard-hitting, free-wheeling music that never degenerates into chaos. —*Ron Wynn*

Favorite Street / Nov. 15, 1983–Nov. 17, 1983 / Black Saint ✦✦✦✦✦
ROVA plays (and deconstructs) the music of saxophonist Steve Lacy—a triumph of structural improv and a personal favorite. —*Myles Boisen*

The Crowd / Jun. 20, 1985–Jun. 23, 1985 / Hat Art ✦✦✦✦✦

Beat Kennel / Apr. 1987 / Black Saint ✦✦✦✦
A late-'80s session with The ROVA sax quartet. The lineup at this time included Jon Raskin, Larry Ochs, Andrew Voigt, and Bruce Akley. They did mostly originals in an energized, explosive manner. —*Ron Wynn*

Electric Rags II / Sep. 1989 / New Albion ✦✦✦

★ **This Time We Are Both** / Nov. 1989 / New Albion ✦✦✦✦✦
Featuring live recordings from their second USSR tour in 1989, this is a definitive statement from the second version of ROVA with Adams—gorgeous sound and stunning scores. —*Myles Boisen*

★ **The Aggregate** / Dec. 1991 / Sound Aspects ✦✦✦✦✦
This superb live set with Anthony Braxton (sax) as a fifth member was one of the last recordings with Voight. —*Myles Boisen*

Long on Logic / Dec. 1991 / Sound Aspects ✦✦✦✦
With music by ROVA, Henry Kaiser (g), and Fred Frith, this was an outgrowth of a successful local concert series. It's one of the few sax quartet albums that utilizes studio and sampling technology as an artistic tool. —*Myles Boisen*

From the Bureau of Both / Feb. 1992 / Black Saint ✦✦✦✦

Jimmy Rowles

b. Aug. 19, 1918, Spokane, WA
Piano / Bop, Swing
Long known for his expertise in coming up with the perfect chord for the perfect situation, the subtle Jimmy Rowles has been in demand for decades as an accompanist while being underrated as a soloist. After playing in local groups in Seattle, Rowles moved to Los Angeles in 1940 and worked with Slim Gaillard, Lester Young, Benny Goodman and Woody Herman. After serving in the military he returned to Herman (in time to play with the first Herd), recorded with Benny Goodman and also had stints with Les Brown and Tommy Dorsey. Working as a studio musician, Rowles appeared in a countless number of settings in the 1950s and '60s but was best-known for his playing behind Billie Holiday and Peggy Lee. In 1973 he moved to New York where he recorded more extensively in jazz situations (including duets with Stan Getz), but after touring with Ella Fitzgerald during 1981–83 he returned to California. His song "The Peacocks" has become a standard, and Rowles has recorded for many labels including recently with his daughter, fluegelhornist Stacy Rowles. —*Scott Yanow*

Weather in a Jazz Vane / 1958 / VSOP ✦✦✦
The focus is on Jimmy Rowles' piano throughout this relaxed and well-rounded LP reissue of an Andex session. Rowles is joined by trumpeter Lee Katzman, valve trombonist Bob Envoldsen, Bill Holman on tenor, altoist Herb Geller, bassist Monty Budwig and drummer Mel Lewis for renditions of nine superior standards, all of which have references to seasons, weather or the sun in their titles. Highlights include "With the Wind and the Rain in Your Hair," "When the Sun Comes Out," "Some Other Spring" and Rowles' spontaneous vocal (his first on record) on "Too Hot for Words." —*Scott Yanow*

Let's Get Acquainted with Jazz (For People Who Hate Jazz) / Jun. 20, 1958 / VSOP ✦✦✦
The drawing on the cover and the liner notes, such as they are, are rather silly, but the music on this brief, but enjoyable, CD reissue features some fine playing from a variety of top West Coast-based musicians. Pianist Jimmy Rowles is the leader and is assisted by guitarist Barney Kessel, bassist Red Mitchell, drummer Mel Lewis, sometimes vibraphonist Larry Bunker and either tenor saxophonist Harold Land or trumpeter Pete Candoli. They perform six standards, "The Blues" and three obscurities that one assumes are Rowles originals. Tasteful and lightly swinging music. —*Scott Yanow*

The Special Magic of Jimmy Rowles / Apr. 7, 1974 / Halcyon ✦✦✦✦✦
This album includes duets with Rusty Gilder on bass. Solo, Rowles shows he can do it alone, and with Gilder, sparks occasionally fly. Mostly, this is laidback. They play lots of Duke Ellington. There is a good version of Carl Perkin's "Grooveyard." —*Michael G. Nastos*

Grandpaws / Mar. 1976 / Choice ✦✦✦✦
The trio for this pianist includes Buster Williams on bass and Billy Hart on drums. They play two by Rowles, the others are standards. They do an exquisite medley of "Lush Life/A Train/I Love You/I Hadn't Anyone 'Till You/Margie/Chicago/Desert Fire." Rowles shows his ballad skills best. —*Michael G. Nastos*

Paws That Refresh / Mar. 1976 / Choice ✦✦✦
Nice, casually swinging set by pianist Jimmy Rowles. Rowles plays in an easy, relaxed manner with a pace that's neither hurried nor slow; he doesn't offer waves of notes or blistering rhythms, yet crams more ideas into his solos than many players who take more time and rip off barrages of chords and fancy phrases. —*Ron Wynn*

Music's the Only Thing That's on My Mind / Dec. 22, 1976 / Progressive ✦✦✦

● **The Peacocks** / 1977 / Columbia ✦✦✦✦✦

We Could Make Such Beautiful Music Together / Apr. 4, 1978 / Xanadu ✦✦✦✦
Solo, trio and quartet performances by pianist Jimmy Rowles from the late '70s. These were originally issued on the Xanadu label, then reissued on CD in '89 for EPM. Rowles plays with bassists Sam Jones or George Mraz, drummers Leroy Williams or Freddie Waits, and trumpeter Sam Noto. His prickly, sometimes humorous and sometimes poignant piano playing provides the disc's high points. —*Ron Wynn*

Isfahan / May 1978 / Sonet ✦✦✦

Plays Ellington and Billy Strayhorn / Jun. 1981 / Columbia ✦✦✦✦✦

With the Red Mitchell Trio / Mar. 18, 1985–Mar. 19, 1985 / Contemporary ✦✦✦✦
With Red Mitchell. Excellent date; splendid Rowles trio material. —*Ron Wynn*

Jimmy Rowles, Vol. 2 / 1985 / Contemporary ✦✦✦✦
Rowles, Red Mitchell (b), Rowles' daughter Stacey and Colin Bailey (d). —*Ron Wynn*

Looking Back / Jun. 8, 1988 / Delos ✦✦✦✦

Trio / Aug. 11, 1988–Aug. 12, 1988 / Capri ✦✦✦

Plus 2, Plus 3, Plus 4 / Dec. 16, 1988–Dec. 20, 1988 / JVC ✦✦✦✦

Lilac Time / 1994 / Kokopelli ✦✦✦✦

Stacy Rowles

b. Sep. 11, 1955
Trumpet, Fluegelhorn / Bop, Swing
A mellow-toned fluegelhornist who emphasizes ballads, Stacy Rowles (the daughter of veteran pianist Jimmy Rowles) has recorded for Concord and Delos and become a fixture in the L.A. area with her work in the group Jazz Birds. —*Scott Yanow*

● **Tell It Like It Is** / Mar. 1984 / Concord Jazz ✦✦✦✦
On trumpeter Stacy Rowles' only album as a leader to date, she teams up with her father (veteran pianist Jimmy Rowles) for a set of generally exquisite music. With the assistance of Herman Riley on tenor and flute, bassist Chuck Berghofer and drummer Donald Bailey, the two Rowles play a variety of lyrical material including a moving duet on "Lotus Blossom." Stacy, who has emphasized ballads throughout her career, is in fine form on this set although one wonders when she will get around to recording an encore. —*Scott Yanow*

Gonzalo Rubalcaba

b. May 27, 1963, Havana, Cuba
Piano / Post-Bop, Afro-Cuban Jazz
One of the great Cuban jazz musicians, only in recent times has Gonzalo Rubalcaba been able to freely travel in the United States. He studied classical piano from 1971–83, toured France and Africa with the Orquesta Aragon in 1983 and formed the Grupo Proyecto in 1985, touring Europe frequently. In 1986 he met Charlie Haden who sang his praises and helped arrange his appearances at the Montreal and Montreux festivals. By 1990 Gonzalo Rubalcaba had been discovered by the jazz world, and his records began to be released on Blue Note. An advanced improviser with a dense style, Rubalcaba has unlimited potential. —*Scott Yanow*

Live in Havana / Feb. 1986 / Messidor ✦✦✦✦
Many consider Rubalcaba the next dominant Afro-Latin pianist, while others criticize what they see as too much flash and not enough substance. There's plenty of fire on this live session and also some impressive, percussive solos from a keyboard dynamo. —*Ron Wynn*

Mi Gran Pasion / Jul. 1987 / Messidor ✦✦✦✦✦
Cuba's most celebrated musical prodigy, Rubalcaba, is presently busy becoming a major jazz pianist, having expanded his activities well outside Cuba. This album, recorded in Germany with a Cuban band, is a masterpiece: his salute to danzon, the music Rubalcaba's father (Guillermo Rubalcaba) still plays in Havana. Modernist and at the same time an elegant essay on how to play this most decorous of musical forms. —*Ned Sublette*

Giraldilla / Apr. 1990 / Rounder ✦✦✦
Rubalcaba's follow-up to *Mi Gran Pasion* couldn't have been more unlike its predecessor. Musicians from a country where the phones don't work are set down in a high-tech German studio. It's strident, sprawling and brilliant. World music? This is it. Dissonant counterpoint worthy of an Austrian, percussion that only a Cuban could play—and the excitement of a young world-class pianist still learning to control his power. —*Ned Sublette*

● **Discovery: Live at Montreux** / Jul. 15, 1990 / Blue Note ✦✦✦✦✦

★ **The Blessing** / May 12, 1991–May 15, 1991 / Blue Note ✦✦✦✦✦
The virtuosic Cuban pianist Gonzalo Rubalcaba's first recording to be issued in the U.S. is still one of his best. With strong accompaniment from bassist Charlie Haden (one of his early champions) and drummer Jack DeJohnette, Rubalcaba is in frequently exciting form throughout these performances. Highlights include an outstanding investigation of "Besame Mucho," "Giant Steps," Ornette Coleman's beautiful "The Blessing" and an unusual treatment given Bill Evans' "Blue in Green." —*Scott Yanow*

Images: Live at Mt. Fuji / Aug. 24, 1991–Aug. 25, 1991 / Blue Note ✦✦✦✦
A powerhouse live session from dynamic Cuban pianist Gonzalo

Rubalcaba. It was recorded live for Blue Note and is a trio date with bassist John Patitucci and drummer Jack DeJohnette. Patitucci, normally heard in either a fusion or an instrumental pop setting, shows his facility and versatilty as he smoothly adjusts to Rubalcaba's upbeat, unorthodox style and meshes with DeJohnette. —*Ron Wynn*

Suite 4 Y 20 / May 7, 1992–May 12, 1992 / Blue Note ✦✦✦✦
Recorded in Spain, this excellent set by the remarkable Cuban pianist Gonzalo Rubalcaba features his working group (trumpeter Reynaldo Melian, electric bassist Felipe Cabrera and drummer Julio Barreto) along with guest bassist Charlie Haden on four songs. The repertoire includes several pieces by Cuban composers, five of Rubalcaba's originals, "Perfidia," "Love Letters," Haden's "Our Spanish Love Song" and The Beatles' "Here, There and Everywhere." Gonzalo Rubalcaba shows maturity and self-restraint throughout much of this disc, performing a well-rounded set of advanced music. —*Scott Yanow*

Rapsodia / Nov. 15, 1992–Nov. 21, 1992 / Blue Note ✦✦✦✦✦
Pianist Gonzalo Rubalcaba has such impressive technique that he has the potential of completely overwhelming any song he plays, but Rubalcaba shows admirable restraint throughout much of this quartet date. Influenced to a degree by Chick Corea and Herbie Hancock, Rubalcaba still shows a fresh personality when he utilizes an electric keyboard on a few of the selections. His quartet (which includes trumpeter Reynaldo Melian, bassist Felipe Cabrera and drummer Julio Barreto), in addition to fine support, offers a contrasting solo voice in its virtuosic trumpeter. This is a well-rounded set of complex but fairly accessible music. —*Scott Yanow*

Imagine / May 14, 1993–Jun. 24, 1994 / Blue Note ✦✦✦

Diz / Dec. 14, 1993–Dec. 15, 1993 / Blue Note ✦✦✦
Although one might assume that having the title of "Diz" means that this set would be a tribute to Dizzy Gillespie, only four of the nine selections were actually associated with the great trumpeter; the other numbers range from Bird and Bud Powell to Benny Golson and Charles Mingus ("Smooch"). Gonzalo Rubalcaba makes each of the jazz standards his own by reharmonizing chord structures, playing in his own dense style and coming up with fresh new statements rather than just recreating bebop. He is quite lyrical and somber on the ballads, makes "Donna Lee" unrecognizable and (with the assistance of bassist Ron Carter and drummer Julio Barreto) modernizes all of the potential warhorses. This is a very interesting workout. —*Scott Yanow*

Vanessa Rubin

b. Cleveland, Ohio
Vocals / Standards
An appealing singer who does not improvise much, Vanessa Rubin has recorded several fine albums for Novus. She studied classical music but switched to jazz early on. Rubin sang with and managed the Blackshaw Brothers (an organ quartet from Cleveland). After working with several groups locally (and recording with the Cleveland Jazz All-Stars) in 1982 Rubin moved to New York. She worked with Pharoah Sanders, Frank Foster's Loud Minority and the big bands of Mercer Ellington and Lionel Hampton and studied with Barry Harris in addition to teaching in the NYC public school system. In 1992 she signed with Novus and has thus far had four releases including a fine tribute to Carmen McRae. —*Scott Yanow*

Soul Eyes / 1991 / Novus ✦✦✦✦
Contemporary jazz vocalist Vanessa Rubin displays her ability to handle vintage pre-rock standards and jazz classics. She does a good job, even though she's still developing her technique. Rubin is backed by a great lineup that includes pianist Kirk Lightsey, drummer Lewis Nash and bassist Cecil McBee. —*Ron Wynn*

● **Pastiche** / 1993 / Novus ✦✦✦✦
Throughout this well-planned date, Vanessa Rubin sounds like an able successor to the more jazz-oriented sides of Nancy Wilson, Lorez Alexandria and Ernestine Anderson. Rubin's soulful voice and subtle variations blend in well with the solos of the various horns even if she is not really an improviser herself. Assisted by a fine rhythm section and such sidemen as trumpeters E.J. Allen and Cecil Bridgewater, trombonist Steve Turre and (on one song) tenorman Houston Person, Rubin expertly interprets the lyrics with both honest emotion and swing, occasionally scatting in unison or in counterpoint with the horns. This disc offers a good example of her talents. —*Scott Yanow*

I'm Glad There Is You / May 1994 / Novus ✦✦✦✦
This Vanessa Rubin release is a tribute to Carmen McRae. Although she cites McRae as a major influence, Rubin actually does not sound much like her and leans as much toward middle-of-the-road music as jazz. Also, not all of these songs are really identified with McRae (most notably "Send in the Clowns," which was largely owned by Sarah Vaughan). The ballad-dominated set does have a reasonable amount of variety, Rubin gets off some fine scatting on "Yardbird Suite," and she introduces an excellent original in "No Strings Attached." A variety of guests (including Grover Washington, Jr., Frank Foster, Antonio Hart, Cecil Bridgewater, Kenny Burrell and Monty Alexander) only appear on one or two songs apiece and do not make that much of an impression. However Vanessa Rubin's attractive voice is strong enough to carry the music, and this release is a step forward for her. —*Scott Yanow*

Vanessa Rubin Sings / 1995 / Novus ✦✦✦
Vanessa Rubin has a lovely voice but rarely wanders much from the melody. Since many of the songs that she performs on this Novus CD have already been done definitively dozens of times by others (such as "Our Love Is Here to Stay," "My Ship," "Morning" and even "Being Green"), the value of the release is not as high as it should be. Rubin does contribute new lyrics to Wayne Shorter's "Speak No Evil" (renamed "All for One"), her singing is heartfelt on "His Eye Is on the Sparrow," and Steve Turre's four appearances (on trombone and conch shells) are a major asset. But why revive "Black Coffee" (another song that has already been done perfectly) with its self-pitying attitude and dated references to cigarettes? —*Scott Yanow*

Ellyn Rucker

b. Jul. 29, 1937, Des Moines, Iowa
Piano, Vocals / Bop, Hard Bop
A talented loop-based pianist and a highly appealing and sensuous singer, Ellyn Rucker has long been a fixture in the Denver area. Although she started playing piano when she was eight, discovered jazz at 13 and studied classical piano at Drake University, she did not decide to become a fulltime musician until 1979. Rucker has toured Europe several times (with and without Spike Robinson), recorded several albums for Capri, has a full-length video on Leisure Jazz and performed at many festivals. Perhaps if Ellyn Rucker had taken up music fulltime 20 years earlier or lived in a larger area than Denver she would be a bigger name. However, her talent has long been in the major leagues, and her recordings are all quite appealing and powerful. —*Scott Yanow*

Ellyn / Sep. 2, 1987–Sep. 3, 1987 / Capri ✦✦✦✦
★ **This Heart of Mine** / Aug. 18, 1988–Aug. 19, 1988 / Capri ✦✦✦✦✦
Effective, professionally performed standards, ballads and pre-rock from Ellyn Rucker. She sings in an energetic, sometimes charming fashion, although she's not among the more dynamic or aggressive interpreters. The production, arrangements and mastering are tremendous. —*Ron Wynn*

Nice Work! / Jan. 18, 1989–Jan. 19, 1989 / Capri ✦✦✦✦✦

Roswell Rudd

b. Nov. 17, 1935, Sharon, CT
Trombone / Free Jazz, Avant-Garde
One of the pioneer trombonists in free jazz, Roswell Rudd's extroverted style was heard at its best in the mid-'60s matching wits with Archie Shepp. He studied French horn from age 11 and during 1954–59 played Dixieland trombone with a variety of groups including Eli's Chosen Six (with whom he recorded). After recording with Cecil Taylor in 1960 and working (but not recording) with Herbie Nichols, Rudd teamed up with another former Dixielander, Steve Lacy, to have a quartet that exclusively played the music of Thelonious Monk. He was with Bill Dixon in 1962 and then was a member of the New York Art Quartet with John Tchicai in 1964. 1965–67 was spent mostly with Archie Shepp although Rudd also recorded a couple albums of his own. He played with Robin Kenyatta in 1968 and Charlie Haden's Liberation Music Orchestra in 1969; there were also recordings with Gato Barbieri, Beaver Harris, Lonnie Liston Smith, the Jazz Composers' Orchestra, Enrico Rava, Misha Mengelberg and more as a leader. Rudd taught at Bard College and the University of Maine and by the 1990s was playing in obscurity in the Catskills, forgotten but apparently still in prime form. —*Scott Yanow*

Everywhere / Sep. 1966 / Impulse! ✦✦✦✦
With legendary flutist/bass clarinettist Giuseppi Logan and two bass players. All originals. —*Michael G. Nastos*

Numatik Swing Band / Jul. 6, 1973 / JCOA ✦✦✦✦
With The Jazz Composers Orchestra. —*Michael G. Nastos*

Flexible Flyer / Mar. 1974 / Freedom ✦✦✦✦✦
Date for creative trombonist who fell in the cracks when Ray Anderson arrived. A solid album, with Sheila Jordan (v). —*Michael G. Nastos*

Inside Job / May 21, 1976 / Arista ✦✦✦
Solid quintet date with intense Dave Burrell on piano. —*Ron Wynn*

★ **Regeneration** / Jun. 25, 1982–Jun. 26, 1982 / Soul Note ✦✦✦✦✦
One of many intriguing collaborations pairing Rudd and Steve Lacy (sop sax). —*Ron Wynn*

Hilton Ruiz

b. May 29, 1952, New York City
Piano / Bop, Latin Jazz
One of the finest pianists in Afro-Cuban jazz, Hilton Ruiz is also an expert bop player. A child prodigy who appeared at Carnegie Recital Hall when he was eight, Ruiz gigged with Latin bands as a teenager and gained early experience playing with Joe Newman, Frank Foster, Freddie Hubbard. He studied with Mary Lou Williams and had an important association with Rahsaan Roland Kirk (1973–77). After touring with George Coleman (1978–79) he recorded with Charles Mingus, Betty Carter, Archie Shepp, Clark Terry and Chico Freeman among others. Hilton Ruiz has mostly led his own groups since the early '80s, and fortunately he has recorded quite a few rewarding discs. —*Scott Yanow*

Piano Man / Jul. 10, 1975 / SteepleChase ✦✦✦✦
Steppin' Into Beauty / Feb. 7, 1977–Feb. 8, 1977 / SteepleChase ✦✦✦✦
New York Hilton / Feb. 8, 1977 / SteepleChase ✦✦✦✦
Cross Currents / Nov. 1984 / Stash ✦✦✦✦✦
Something Grand / Oct. 14, 1986–Oct. 15, 1986 / Novus ✦✦✦✦
Fine Afro-Latin jazz excursion by this solid pianist. Sensational trombone by Steve Turre. Sam Rivers (sax) is also in the ensemble. —*Ron Wynn*

● **El Camino [The Road]** / Jun. 1988 / Novus ✦✦✦✦✦
An ambitious, often dazzling set from '86 with pianist Hilton Ruiz. He's heading an outstanding band that includes some great players who seldom ever recorded on major label sessions. Trombonist Dick Griffin, saxophonist Sam Rivers and guitarist Rodney Jones are dynamite, while trumpeter Lew Soloff and Ruiz are dependable and entertaining during their solos and more explosive in their exchanges with Griffin, Rivers and Jones. —*Ron Wynn*

Strut / Nov. 30, 1988–Dec. 1, 1988 / Novus ✦✦✦✦
Funky and brassy, plus great arrangements, make this date a success. —*Ron Wynn*

Doin' It Right / Nov. 9, 1989–Nov. 11, 1989 / Novus ✦✦✦✦
Strong '89 release by Afro-Latin and jazz pianist Hilton Ruiz. His fiery, exciting solos spark a group that includes trumpeter Don Cherry, bassists Jimmy Ronson and Ruben Rodriguez, drummer Steve Berrior and percussionist Daniel Ponce. The music ranges from frenetic Latin jams to a nice reworking of "I Didn't Know What Time It Was." —*Ron Wynn*

A Moment's Notice / Feb. 25, 1991–Mar. 12, 1991 / Novus ✦✦✦✦✦
Pianist Hilton Ruiz mixes Afro-Latin, Latin jazz and bop on this '91 session. Flutist Dave Valentin has stronger, more dynamic solos here than on his own records, while saxophonists George Coleman and Kenny Garrett are hot and consistently outstanding. —*Ron Wynn*

Excitation / Feb. 7, 1992 / SteepleChase ✦✦✦
Manhattan Mambo / Apr. 28, 1992 / Telarc ✦✦✦✦
Pianist Hilton Ruiz is heard with a superior group of musicians adept at playing both bebop and Latin-jazz. With a frontline of trumpeter Charlie Sepulveda, David Sanchez on tenor and trombonist Papo Vazquez in addition to four percussionists, Ruiz's nonet displays plenty of fire on a set of originals, Perez Prado's "Mambo Numero Cinco" and John Coltrane's "Impressions." —*Scott Yanow*

Live At Birdland / Jun. 24, 1992–Jun. 25, 1992 / Candid ✦✦✦
Heroes / Nov. 8, 1993–Nov. 9, 1993 / Telarc ✦✦✦

Howard Rumsey

b. Nov. 7, 1917, Brawley, CA
Bass, Leader / Cool, Bop
Although a good enough bassist to play with Stan Kenton's big band, Howard Rumsey's main importance is as the organizer of the Lighthouse All-Stars and manager of the Lighthouse. Originally a drummer, Rumsey switched to bass while at college. He played with Vido Musso in the late '30s, and when Stan Kenton formed his first band in 1941, Rumsey became its bassist. A year later he started freelancing in the Los Angeles area. In 1949 Rumsey brought jazz into the Lighthouse in Hermosa Beach, CA. Within a few years the jam sessions featured some of the top jazz-oriented studio players in the area, and the bassist was heading "the Lighthouse All-Stars," which recorded frequently for Contemporary in the 1950s, starring such players as Shorty Rogers, Jimmy Giuffre, Bob Cooper, Bud Shank and Bill Perkins. In the 1960s Rumsey quit playing to devote fulltime to running the Lighthouse, and after he sold the establishment, for a time he ran the nearby club Concerts by the Sea. *—Scott Yanow*

Howard Rumsey's Lighthouse All-Stars, Vol. 3 / Jul. 22, 1952–Aug. 2, 1956 / Original Jazz Classics ✦✦✦✦
This was a set of three dates put together by entrepreneur and bassist Howard Rumsey. The July 22, 1952 session on four tracks boasted crowded arrangements and not very distinct solos...(On the Oct. 20, 1953 date) there was a heavy Latin tinge to some of this music, but, overall, it was largely undistinguished. The last date opened things up a bit more with a smaller group on three tracks and had the most extended blowing and clearest projection along with some nice solos from Shank and Rosolino in particular. *—Bob Rusch, Cadence*

Sunday Jazz á la Jazzhouse / Feb. 21, 1953 / Original Jazz Classics ✦✦✦✦
Rumsey made numerous LPs for Contemporary in the '50s and this was the first. This was live and captured the hip jams that took place every Sunday from noon till night. People would sit in and drop out, and the changing personnel reflected that. The playing was intense and enthusiastic though imperfect, and at times ill-constructed; the frontier ambiance came through. *—Bob Rusch, Cadence*

Howard Rumsey's Lighthouse All-Stars / May 15, 1953 / Contemporary ✦✦✦✦

Oboe/Flute / Feb. 25, 1954–Sep. 25, 1956 / Original Jazz Classics ✦✦✦✦

★ **In the Solo Spotlight** / Aug. 17, 1954–Mar. 12, 1957 / Original Jazz Classics ✦✦✦✦✦
Lighthouse All-Stars. 1954 & 1957. This large-group date has its moments but not enough to make it fully successful. *—Ron Wynn*

Howard Rumsey's Lighthouse All-Stars, Vol. 6 / Dec. 3, 1954–Mar. 1, 1955 / Original Jazz Classics ✦✦✦✦

Lighthouse at Laguna / Jun. 20, 1955 / Original Jazz Classics ✦✦✦

In the Solo Spotlight, Vol. 5 / Mar. 12, 1956 / Contemporary ✦✦✦✦✦

Music for Lighthousekeeping / Oct. 2, 1956–Oct. 16, 1956 / Original Jazz Classics ✦✦✦✦✦

Double or Nothin' / Feb. 14, 1957–Feb. 27, 1957 / Liberty ✦✦✦

Jazz Rolls-Royce / Oct. 28, 1957 / Lighthouse ✦✦✦

Jazz Structures / 1961–1962 / Philips ✦✦✦

Jazz Invention / Feb. 12, 1989 / Contemporary ✦✦✦✦✦
To celebrate the 40th anniversary of the first music played at the legendary club the Lighthouse, The Lighthouse All-Stars were reunited for a special concert. Some of the personnel were a little different than in the old days. Howard Rumsey no longer played bass, and both trombonist Frank Rosolino and drummer Shelly Manne were no longer around, but the group was still filled with plenty of great talent: Tenorman Bob Cooper, altoist Bud Shank, trumpeter Conte Candoli, valve trombonist Bob Enevoldsen, pianist Claude Williamson, bassist Monty Budwig and drummer John Guerin. Together they perform eight songs from the period with spirit and creativity within the genre of cool jazz. As a result of this successful reunion, Shorty Rogers would be heading the group for the next few years. *—Scott Yanow*

Jimmy Rushing

b. Aug. 26, 1903, Oklahoma City, OK, **d.** Jun. 8, 1972, New York
Vocals / Swing, Blues
A huge, striking artist, Jimmy Rushing defined and transcended jazz-based blues shouting. His huge voice was dominating and intricately linked to the beat. He could maintain his intonation regardless of volume and could sing sensitively one moment, then bellow and yell in almost frightening fashion the next, making both styles sound convincing. Rushing's parents were musicians, and he studied music theory in high school. He attended Wilberforce University but dropped out. He moved to the West Coast and did odd jobs while sometimes singing at house parties. Composer and pianist Jelly Roll Morton was among the people he met while making these appearances. Rushing joined Walter Page's Blue Devils in the late '20s. He left them to work in his father's cafe in Oklahoma City but returned to Page's group in 1928. He made his first records with them in 1929.

Rushing toured with Bennie Moten from 1929–1935, recording with Moten in 1931, then joined Count Basie in 1936. Basie has credited Rushing with helping hold things together when times got tough. At an early 1936 session with John Hammond producing things came together. This marked Lester Young's debut with the band. The songs "Boogie-Woogie" (better known as "I May Be Wrong") and "Evenin'" were instant classics. Rushing's booming voice and The Basie orchestra proved a perfect fit until 1950; they recorded for Columbia and RCA, cutting everything from steamy blues to joyous stomps and novelty tunes like "Did You See Jackie Robinson Hit that Ball." When Basie disbanded the orchestra in 1950, Rushing briefly tried retirement. He ended it a short time later, forming his own band. He'd made some solo recordings in 1945, and continued in the mid-'50s and early '60s, this time for Vanguard. Rushing recreated Basie classics, worked with some of his sidemen and even accompanied himself on piano. He cut other sessions with Buck Clayton, Dave Brubeck, and Earl Hines and frequently had reunions with Basie and/or his sidemen. Rushing appeared in both film shorts and features, among them "Take Me Back, Baby," "Air Mail Special," "Choo Choo Swing" and "Funzapoppin'" between 1941 and 1943. He participated in the historic 1957 television show "The Sound Of Jazz," and was featured on the sixth episode of a 13-part series "The Subject Is Jazz" in 1958. He was also in the 1973 film "Monterey Jazz," which profiled the '70 festival. Rushing also had a singing and acting role in the '69 film "The Learning Tree." He died three years later. *—Ron Wynn and Bob Porter*

★ **The Essential Jimmy Rushing** / Dec. 1, 1954–Mar. 5, 1957 / Vanguard ✦✦✦✦✦
Fine anthology collecting material done by the great blues shouter for Vanguard during the mid-'50s. Songs included a remake of "Going To Chicago," plus other combo dates, and he was backed by such Basie comrades as Jo Jones and Buddy Tate. This has been reissued on CD. *—Ron Wynn*

Dave Brubeck and Jimmy Rushing / Jan. 29, 1960–Aug. 4, 1960 / Columbia ✦✦✦✦
Pairing of divergent styles proves effective session. *—Ron Wynn*

Everyday I Have the Blues / Feb. 9, 1967–Feb. 10, 1967 / Bluesway ✦✦✦✦✦
A CD reissue of the great blues shouter Jimmy Rushing singing recreated versions of his classics with the Basie band. This originally came out in the mid-'50s, when Rushing had left Basie and was heading his own band. While these versions aren't the definitive ones, they're far from bad. *—Ron Wynn*

Gee, Baby, Ain't I Good to You / Oct. 30, 1967 / Master Jazz ✦✦
This is a decent session that, considering the lineup, does not live up to its potential. At what was essentially a jazz party held in a recording studio, the musicians (trumpeter Buck Clayton, trombonist Dickie Wells, tenor saxophonist Julian Dash, pianist Sir Charles Thompson, bassist Gene Ramey and drummer Jo Jones) are all veterans of the famous series of Buck Clayton jam sessions held in the 1950s, and along with singer Jimmy Rushing, the majority are alumni of the Count Basie Orchestra. The problem is that their rendition of the blues and swing standards are often quite loose, there are a generous amount of missteps, and although Clayton is heroic under the circumstances (this was one of his final recordings before ill health caused his retirement), most of the musicians would have benefited from running through the songs an additional time. It's recommended only to completists. *—Scott Yanow*

Livin' the Blues / Oct. 1968 / Bluesway ✦✦✦✦
The You and Me That Used to Be / 1971 / RCA ✦✦✦✦✦

George Russell

b. Jun. 23, 1923, Cincinnati, OH
Piano, Arranger, Composer, Leader / Avant-Garde, Post Bop
George Russell's "Lydian Concept," which he began working on in
the '40s, has evolved into one of jazz's major advances. Russell,
whose father was a professor of music at Oberlin, derived a system that graded intervals by how far their pitches were from a
central note. This theory provided musicians with a wider choice
of notes by making the tonal center of a piece also its center of
gravity. He linked the ancient Lydian mode with modern uses of
chromaticism. Russell developed this into the "Lydian Chromatic
concept of Tonal Organization," and his work was hailed as a historical breakthrough. He was among the first to combine Afro-
Latin influences and jazz elements with "Cubana Be/Cubana Bop"
and Russell studied composition with Stefan Wolpe. He taught at
the Lenox School of Jazz, Lund Unversity in Sweden and at the
New England Conservatory. Russell also published several papers
and two volumes on the Lydian Chromatic Concept.

He began playing drums in Cincinnati clubs while attending
Wilberforce University High School, where he'd won a scholarship. Russell played briefly in Benny Carter's band but was
replaced by Max Roach and turned to composing and arranging.
He sold his first big band arrangement to Carter and Dizzy
Gillespie in the mid-'40s. Russell later wrote for Earl Hines. He
moved to New York and wanted to play drums in Charlie Parker's
group but became ill. Russell worked on his Lydian theories during a lengthy recovery period in the mid-'40s. Later, he wrote several pieces for Dizzy Gillespie, including "Cubana Be/Cubana
Bop" and compositions for Buddy DeFranco and Lee Konitz. He
also wrote for Charlie Ventura, Artie Shaw, and Claude Thornhill.
Besides his teaching stints in the '50s, Russell made his recording
debut as a leader on RCA and Decca. He turned to piano and
formed a group in the early '60s. Its members included Don Ellis,
Eric Dolphy, Chuck Israels and Steve Swallow. There were sessions for Riverside, Decca, MPS and Flying Dutchman. He also
played at the landmark 1962 Washington D.C. Jazz Festival.

Russell moved to Europe in the mid-'60s and spent six years
there teaching at various institutions and recording before returning to America in 1969, where he joined the faculty at the New
England Conservatory. During the '70s and '80s he recorded for
Soul Note, Blue Note and ECM. Russell stopped composing in the
mid-'70s to finish the second volume of the "Lydian Chromatic
Concept." He recorded albums in the late '70s and '80s with The
Swedish Radiojazzgruppen and big bands in New York. Russell's
compositions have earned him many honors, among them composer awards from *Metronome* and *Down Beat* magazine, a pair
of Guggenheim fellowships, the National Music Award, three
grants from the National Education Association and the Oscar du
Disque de Jazz. Among his discoveries were vocalist Shelia Jordan,
and he was also an early champion of European saxophonist Jan
Garbarek. His *African Game* album in 1985 was one of the first
issued on the revived Blue Note label and included Russell's compositions inspired by African drum choirs. He toured England in
the late '80s and worked with Courtney Pine and Kenny Wheeler
as well as other British jazz and rock musicians. —*Ron Wynn*

● Jazz Workshop / Mar. 31, 1956–Dec. 21, 1956 / Bluebird ✦✦✦✦✦
A CD reissue of an intriguing release from 1956 by George
Russell. This was a superb album, marked by brilliant playing and
provocative compositions. Russell spearheads everything and
occasionally helps out on piano. The band includes another brilliant player in pianist Bill Evans, plus Hal McKusick on alto sax
and flute, Art Farmer on trumpet, guitarist Barry Galbraith,
bassists Milt Hinton and Teddy Kotick and Joe Harris, Osie
Johnson or Paul Motian on drums. —*Ron Wynn*

● New York, New York / Sep. 12, 1958–Mar. 25, 1959 / MCA
✦✦✦✦✦
This is a landmark of conceptual, arranging, production and play-
ing magnificence. John Coltrane (ts), Max Roach (d), Bill Evans (p),
Jon Hendricks (v) all soar. —*Ron Wynn*

Jazz in the Space Age / May 1960 / Decca ✦✦✦✦
George Russell at the Five Spot / Sep. 20, 1960 / Decca ✦✦✦✦
Stratusphunk / Oct. 18, 1960 / Original Jazz Classics ✦✦✦✦
★ Ezz-Thetic / May 8, 1961 / Original Jazz Classics ✦✦✦✦✦
This is a true classic. Composer/pianist George Russell gathered

together a very versatile group of talents (trumpeter Don Ellis,
trombonist Dave Baker, Eric Dolphy on alto and bass clarinet,
bassist Steve Swallow and drummer Joe Hunt) to explore three of
his originals, "'Round Midnight" (which is given an extraordinary
treatment by Dolphy), Miles Davis' "Nardis" and David Baker's
"Honesty." The music is post-bop, and although using ideas from
avant-garde jazz, it does not fall into any simple category. The
improvising is at a very high level, and the frameworks (which
include free and stoptime sections) really inspire the players.
Highly recommended. —*Scott Yanow*

The Stratus Seekers / Jan. 31, 1962 / Original Jazz Classics
✦✦✦✦✦
Septet. Fine example of Russell's inside/outside arranging style.
Dave Baker (tb) is impressive. —*Ron Wynn*

The Outer View / Aug. 27, 1962 / Original Jazz Classics ✦✦✦✦✦
Composer George Russell's early-'60s Riverside recordings are
among his most accessible. For this set (the CD reissue adds an
alternate take of the title cut to the original program), Russell and
his very impressive sextet (which is comprised of trumpeter Don
Ellis, trombonist Garnett Brown, Paul Plummer on tenor, bassist
Steve Swallow and drummer Pete La Roca) are challenged by the
complex material; even Charlie Parker's blues "Au Privave" is
transformed into something new. It is particularly interesting to
hear Don Ellis this early in his career. The most famous selection,
a very haunting version of "You Are My Sunshine," was singer
Sheila Jordan's debut on records. —*Scott Yanow*

At Beethoven Hall / Aug. 31, 1965 / German ✦✦✦✦
The Essence Of . . . / Sep. 16, 1966–Nov. 4, 1968 / Soul Note ✦✦✦
Othello Ballet Suite and Electronic Sotana No.1 / Nov. 3,
1967–Oct. 1, 1968 / Flying Dutchman ✦✦✦
An uneven but compelling work by George Russell that combines
jazz, classical and Shakespeare. The results range from magnificent to chaotic; there's a large band that includes mostly obscure
foreign musicians. It was one of the first times that Norway's Jan
Garbarek appeared playing tenor sax on a major label. This has
been reissued on CD. —*Ron Wynn*

Trip to Prillargui / Mar. 1970 / Soul Note ✦✦✦
Listen to the Silence / Jun. 1971 / Concept ✦✦✦✦
Vertical Form 6 / Mar. 10, 1977 / Soul Note ✦✦✦✦
A magnificent and critically acclaimed large band recording with
arrangements by George Russell, who also conducted. His compositions, with their intricate, unpredictable and keenly structured
pace, textures and layers, are expertly played by an international
orchestra. This '77 release was unfortunately poorly distributed in
America, since it was on a foreign label. —*Ron Wynn*

New York Big Band / Aug. 16, 1978 / Soul Note ✦✦✦✦✦
★ Electronic Sonata for Souls Loved by Nature 1980 / Mar. 9,
1980–Jun. 10, 1980 / Strata East ✦✦✦✦✦
Composer, theorist, arranger and pianist George Russell debuted
his 14-part master composition "Electronic Sonata For Souls Loved
By Nature" on April 28, 1969 at a concert in Norway. The ambitious,
elaborate work blended bebop, free, Asian and blues elements, as
well as electronic effects and mixed live performance with tape and
vocal segments. It was a testimony to the prowess of trumpeter
Manfred Schoof, tenor saxophonist Jan Garbarek, guitarist Terje
Rypdal, bassist Red Mitchell and drummer John Christensen that
they weren't overwhelmed by the sheer weight of the experience.
The digital mastering enables listeners to fully hear the disparate
styles converging and understand just how advanced Russell's concepts were, particularly for the time. While not everything worked,
the composition ranks alongside Ornette Coleman's "Free Jazz" as
one of jazz's finest, most adventurous pieces. —*Ron Wynn*

American Time Spiral / Jul. 30, 1982–Jul. 31, 1982 / Soul Note
✦✦✦
African Game / Jun. 18, 1983 / Blue Note ✦✦
Electronic Sonata: 1968 / 1985 / Soul Note ✦✦✦✦
London Concert, Vol. 1 / Aug. 28, 1989 / Stash ✦✦✦
London Concert, Vol. 2 / Aug. 31, 1989 / Stash ✦✦✦✦

Hal Russell

b. 1926, Detroit, MI, d. 1992
*Piano, Tenor Saxophone, Trumpet, Drums, Soprano Saxophone /
Avant-Garde*
Composer and instrumentalist Hal Russell was an ardent free

music booster and participant, though he also played everything else from traditional jazz to blues. Russell's NRG Ensemble, which he assembled in the late 70s was the ideal forum for his songs, which ranged from comedic and simple to intricate and intense. Russell's prime instruments were drums and vibes, though he also played trumpet, C-melody and tenor sax, cornet and various percussion devices. He moved to Chicago from Detroit as a teen and majored in trumpet at the University of Illinois. He played with Woody Herman and Boyd Raeburn in the '40s. Russell once sat in with Duke Ellington and a Benny Goodman combo and played with Miles Davis, Sonny Rollins and Stan Getz in Chicago clubs. He played in a band led by Joe Daley in the '50s, then turned to free music in the early '60s. Russell later rejoined Daley in a trio with Russell Thorne. They recorded an album for RCA in 1963. During the '70s Russell led various experimental and free groups in Chicago, among them The Chemical Feast before finally assembling his NRG Ensemble in 1978. He led different editions of it until his death, recording occasionally for Nessa. The final Russell album, *Hal's Bells*, issued in 1992, is available on CD. —*Ron Wynn*

NRG Ensemble / May 11, 1981 / Nessa ✦✦✦✦

Eftsoons / Aug. 21, 1981 / Nessa ✦✦✦

Conserving Nrg / Mar. 15, 1984–Mar. 16, 1984 / Principally Jazz ✦✦✦✦✦

Hal Russell, a Chicago legend, switches between tenor, cornet, vibes and drums on this fascinating avant-garde session. Together with saxophonist Chuck Burdelik, Brian Sandstrom (who plays trumpet, guitar and bass), bassist Curt Bley and drummer Steve Hunt, Russell explores seven diverse and consistently colorful group originals that are more accessible than expected. This highly expressive music (which has plenty of variety) is worth checking out although this small label release will be difficult to locate. —*Scott Yanow*

The Finnish/Swiss Tour / Nov. 1990 / ECM ✦✦✦

Naked Colours / Dec. 17, 1991 / Silkheart ✦✦✦✦

● **Hal's Bells** / May 1992 / ECM ✦✦✦✦✦

Luis Russell

b. Aug. 6, 1902, Panama, **d.** Dec. 11, 1963, NYC
Piano, Leader, Arranger / Swing, Classic Jazz
Luis Russell led one of the great early big bands, an orchestra that during 1929–31 could hold its own with nearly all of its competitors. Unfortunately, his period in the spotlight was fairly brief, and ironically Russell fell into obscurity just as the big-band era really took hold. Russell studied guitar, violin and piano in his native Panama. After winning $3000 in a lottery, he moved with his mother and sister to the United States where he began to make a living as a pianist in New Orleans. In 1925 Russell moved to Chicago to join Doc Cook's Orchestra and then became the pianist in King Oliver's band. He was with Oliver when the cornetist relocated to New York before leading his own band at the Nest Club in 1927. Russell had recorded seven songs as a leader in 1926 with his Hot Six and Heebie Jeebie Stompers.
By 1929 his ten-piece band (which included several former Oliver sidemen) boasted four major soloists in trumpeter Red Allen, trombonist J.C. Higginbotham, altoist Charlie Holmes and clarinetist Albert Nicholas; the other trumpeter, Bill Coleman, ended up leaving because of the lack of solo space! In addition, Russell, a decent but not particularly distinctive pianist, was part of one of the top rhythm sections of the era along with guitarist Will Johnson, the powerful bassist Pops Foster and drummer Paul Barbarin. During the next couple of years, Luis Russell's band recorded a couple dozen sides that (thanks to the leader's arrangements) combined the solos and drive of New Orleans jazz with the riffs and ensembles of swing; some of these performances are now considered classics.
The band also backed Louis Armstrong on a few of his early orchestra recordings. But after a few commercial sides in 1931, Luis Russell only had one more opportunity to record his band (a so-so session in 1934) before Louis Armstrong took it over altogether in 1935. For eight years the nucleus of Russell's orchestra primarily functioned as background for the great trumpeter/vocalist, a role that robbed it of its personality and significance. From 1943–48 Russell led a new band that played the Savoy and made a few obscure recordings for Apollo before quietly breaking up. He spent his last 15 years before dying of can-

cer in 1963 largely outside of music, running at first a candy shop and then a toy store. Fortunately most of Russell's early recordings have been made available on CD by European labels. —*Scott Yanow*

★ **Luis Russell and His Louisiana Swing Orchestra** / Nov. 17, 1926–Aug. 8, 1934 / Columbia ✦✦✦✦✦
Pianist Luis Russell led one of the finest jazz bands between 1929–31, a unit that featured such talented soloists as trumpeter Red Allen, trombonist J.C. Higginbottham, altoist Charlie Holmes and clarinetist Albert Nicholas in addition to one of the top rhythm sections of the era (with bassist Pops Foster and drummer Paul Barbarin). This two-LP set includes almost all of their recordings (leaving out just three lesser sessions) and has very enjoyable (and frequently exciting) music that serves as a transition between New Orleans jazz and swing. In addition there are two earlier dates (including one with Nicholas, trumpeter Bob Shoffner and Barney Bigard who ranks as one of the top tenor players of the era) and Russell's complete session of 1934, which features cornetist Rex Stewart. There are a few minor mistakes in the personnel listing, and the dates are not included, but otherwise this is a definitive release of a somewhat forgotten classic band. —*Scott Yanow*

The Luis Russell Collection (1926–1934) / 1926–Aug. 8, 1934 / Collector's Classics ✦✦✦✦✦
Bandleader Luis Russell's most successful recordings were during 1929–30 when his brilliant orchestra featured such soloists as trumpeter Red Allen, trombonist J.C. Higginbotham, clarinetist Albert Nicholas and altoist Charlie Holmes along with what was arguably (thanks to bassist Pops Foster and drummer Paul Barbarin) the top rhythm section of the period. This CD from Collector's Classics, (which is made available through Storyville) only has one session from the prime period (two songs plus a previously unissued version of "The Way He Loves Is Just Too Bad") but has all of Russell's earlier and slightly later recordings. Best are the initial two sessions, six titles plus an alternate take that feature hot jazz in 1926 from such fine players as George Mitchell or Bob Shoffner on cornet, Kid Ory or Preston Jackson on trombone, Nicholas or Darnell Howard on clarinet, pianist Russell and Johnny St. Cyr on banjo. However, the most impressive soloist is clarinetist Barney Bigard, who sticks exclusively to tenor and stakes out his claim as the number two tenor player (behind Coleman Hawkins) of the period. In addition, three rare sessions from 1930–31 hint at the band's former greatness (trumpeter Red Allen stars, but there are also some indifferent vocals), and this CD closes with the six titles from Russell's 1934 date (highlighted by Rex Stewart's dynamic cornet on "Ol' Man River"). Collectors will want this one. —*Scott Yanow*

Savoy Shout / Jan. 1929–Dec. 1930 / JSP ✦✦✦✦✦

Pee Wee Russell (Charles Ellsworth Russell)

b. Mar. 27, 1906, St. Louis, MO, **d.** Feb. 15, 1969, Alexandria, VA
Clarinet / Dixieland
Pee Wee Russell, although never a virtuoso, was one of the giants of jazz. A highly expressive and unpredictable clarinetist, Russell was usually grouped in Dixieland-type groups throughout his career, but his advanced and spontaneous solos (which often sounded as if he were thinking aloud) defied classification.
A professional by the time he was 15, Pee Wee Russell played in Texas with Peck Kelley's group (meeting Jack Teagarden), and then in 1925 he was in St. Louis jamming with Bix Beiderbecke. Russell moved to New York in 1927 and gained some attention for his playing with Red Nichols' Five Pennies. Russell freelanced during the era, making some notable records with Billy Banks in 1932 that matched him with Red Allen. He played clarinet and tenor with Louis Prima during 1935–37, appearing on many records and enjoying the association. After leaving Prima, he started working with Eddie Condon's freewheeling groups and would remain in Condon's orbit on and off for the next 30 years. Pee Wee's recordings with Condon in 1938 made him a star in the trad Chicago jazz world. Russell was featured (but often the butt of jokes) on Condon's Town Hall Concerts.
Heavy drinking almost killed him in 1950, but Pee Wee Russell made an unlikely comeback and became more assertive in running his career. He started leading his own groups (which were more swing- than Dixieland-oriented), was a star on the 1957 television special *The Sound of Jazz* and by the early '60s was playing in a pianoless quartet with valve trombonist Marshall Brown,

whose repertoire included tunes by John Coltrane and Ornette Coleman; he even sat in with Thelonious Monk at the 1963 Newport Jazz Festival and took up abstract painting. But after the death of his wife in 1967, Pee Wee Russell accelerated his drinking and went quickly downhill, passing away less than two years later. —*Scott Yanow*

Giants of Jazz / Aug. 15, 1927–Nov. 12, 1962 / Time Life ✦✦✦✦✦
This three-LP box set is regrettably out-of-print, for it serves as a fine introduction to the unique clarinetist Pee Wee Russell. The 40 selections included here span a 35-year period and are highlighted by early sides with Red Nichols, many encounters with Eddie Condon's bands (including some real classic performances), a few numbers from Russell's mid-'30s association with Louis Prima and later recordings with his own pickup groups. Along with an excellent booklet, this box is an excellent tribute to a truly individual stylist. —*Scott Yanow*

A Chronological Remembrance / Sep. 6, 1927–Sep. 4, 1965 / IAJRC ✦✦✦✦✦
IAJRC, the superb collector's label, issued this single LP, full of rare studio recordings and concert performances from a wide assortment of groups, all of them featuring the distinctive clarinet of Pee Wee Russell. Whether heard with The Charleston Chasers in 1927, with Red McKenzie, Louis Prima, Bobby Hackett, Teddy Wilson or "in concert" with Eddie Condon, Russell is in fine form. An extra bonus is an ad-lib blues from the 1964 Monterey Jazz Festival shared with baritonist Gerry Mulligan. —*Scott Yanow*

★ **Jack Teagarden / Pee Wee Russell** / Aug. 31, 1938–Dec. 15, 1940 / Original Jazz Classics ✦✦✦✦✦
This classic set reissues a couple of important sessions that were made for the H.R.S. label and later acquired by Riverside. The great trombonist Jack Teagarden is heard in 1940 with an octet dominated by Duke Ellington sidemen (including cornetist Rex Stewart, clarinetist Barney Bigard and tenor saxophonist Ben Webster). Recorded during a period when Teagarden was struggling with his big band, it was a rare treat for him to stretch out with a combo, and the results (which include a superior version of "St. James Infirmary") are memorable. In addition, clarinetist Pee Wee Russell is heard with an all-star octet of his own that co-stars trumpeter Max Kaminsky, trombonist Dicky Wells and pianist James P. Johnson in 1938; the final two numbers feature the unique trio of Russell, Johnson and drummer Zutty Singleton. The musicians seem quite inspired, and both trad and swing fans are advised to get this excellent reissue. —*Scott Yanow*

The Pied Piper of Jazz / Sep. 30, 1944 / Commodore ✦✦✦✦
Now here's some cooking music. I'd recommend this record just for the seven trio tracks; the added quartet tracks are a good bonus but clearly of a more common cloth, though Pee Wee Russell was never really common—as in average. Surprisingly, to me, these sessions were rather overlooked by annotations of Russell's music, but then again Zutty Singleton (drums) and Joe Sullivan (piano) are often overlooked in favor of derivative or lesser talent. Sullivan was a great two-fisted pianist and Singleton, along with Baby Dodds, a great stylist and father of traditional jazz whose influence could probably be traced right up to Ed Blackwell through Gene Krupa and Art Blakey. And it was absolutely fitting that he be the drummer on this trio date, because with Singleton at the drums you really never need a bass. On this record, one gets to hear some prime playing from the clarinetist but pay attention to the rhythm, particularly Sullivan and Singleton. —*Bob Rusch, Cadence*

The Individualism of Pee Wee Russell / Jan. 27, 1952 / Savoy ✦✦✦✦
In December 1950, Russell nearly died from the effects of years of excessive drinking and limited eating. By the time of the Boston engagement that resulted in this double LP, he was 90 percent recovered. Leading a strong sextet that boasted fine solos from trombonist Eph Resnick and the great young trumpeter Ruby Braff, Russell performs mostly veteran, Dixieland standards during these extended workouts, avoiding cliches and playing his typically unique ideas with spirit and enthusiasm. —*Scott Yanow*

Clarinet Strut / Jan. 27, 1952–Feb. 19, 1958 / Drive Archive ✦✦✦
The unique clarinetist Pee Wee Russell is heard on this CD at two separate key points in his career. Five selections are taken from his first recordings after recovering from a near fatal illness in 1951. Russell jams in better-than-expected form with a sextet that includes the great young cornetist Ruby Braff. The other eight

numbers date from 1958 when Russell was beginning to escape from the confines of Dixieland and playing more modern swing-oriented standards. Pianist Nat Pierce contributed the arrangements for a septet that also features Braff, tenor saxophonist Bud Freeman and trombonist Vic Dickenson. The music is uniformly excellent, although virtually all of the performances from these two sessions are available in more complete form elsewhere. —*Scott Yanow*

We're in the Money / 1953–Oct. 2, 1954 / Black Lion ✦✦✦✦
His unique clarinet style is featured on this CD with two overlapping groups, both of which include trombonist Vic Dickenson and pianist George Wein. One band has Russell matching wits with the brilliant trumpet of Wild Bill Davison, while the other date showcases the more mellow horn of Doc Cheatham, heard in a rare solo spot in the mid-'50s. This music mostly avoids the old warhorses and features superior swing standards by some of the top Condonites. —*Scott Yanow*

A Portrait of Pee Wee / Feb. 18, 1958–Feb. 19, 1958 / Dunhill ✦✦✦
Issued originally on Counterpoint and reissued many times since by budget labels like Everest, this CD version has superior sound. From 1958, this set matches the great clarinetist Pee Wee Pussell with an all-star horn section (trumpeter Ruby Braff, trombonist Vic Dickenson and tenor saxophonist Bud Freeman) on a program of swing standards along with "Pee Wee Blues." Russell, a bit weary of playing Dixieland by this time, was starting to look toward more modern eras of music, although in reality his own playing was always beyond categorization. —*Scott Yanow*

Over the Rainbow / Feb. 18, 1958–1965 / Xanadu ✦✦✦✦
With the exception of a 1965 version of "I'm in the Market for You," which has a few notes at its close by cornetist Bobby Hackett, this LP finds Russell (normally heard in Dixieland bands) showcased as the only horn. The other selections (taken from two sessions in 1958) feature him and one of two rhythm sections playing some of his favorite songs, including "I Would Do Anything for You," "I'd Climb the Highest Mountain" and "If I Had You." Russell, always a modern player although usually confined to more traditional settings, is really heard at his most lyrical throughout this very interesting set. Three of these performances are also included on *Portrait of Pee Wee*. —*Scott Yanow*

Salute to Newport / Feb. 23, 1959–Oct. 12, 1962 / ABC/Impulse! ✦✦✦✦
This out-of-print double LP reissues Pee Wee Russell's 1959 Dot album with trumpeter Buck Clayton, trombonist Vic Dickenson and veteran tenor Bud Freemen along with a particularly hot session from Impulse! by George Wein's Newport All-Stars (which also includes Freeman along with cornetist Ruby Braff and trombonist Marshall Brown) from 1962. The earlier record is fine, but The Newport All-Stars (whose exciting performance is highlighted by such tunes as "At the Jazz Band Ball," Freeman's feature on "Crazy Rhythm" and Russell's "The Bends Blues") is the reason to search for this set. —*Scott Yanow*

Memorial Album / Mar. 29, 1960 / Prestige ✦✦✦✦
Teaming together trumpeter Buck Clayton with clarinetist Pee Wee Russell in 1960 was a logical move. Both of these individual stylists had been stuck often in Dixieland settings in the 1950s, yet they were really highly distinctive swing soloists, Joined by a modern rhythm section led by pianist Tommy Flanagan, Clayton and Russell are in top form on six fine standards, making one wish that they had teamed up in this type of setting more often. —*Scott Yanow*

Jazz Reunion / Feb. 23, 1961–Mar. 8, 1961 / Candid ✦✦✦✦
The reunion that took place in this 1961 session was between Russell and tenor-great Coleman Hawkins; they had first recorded one of the songs, ("If I Could Be with You") back in 1929. Both Hawk and Russell had remained modern soloists, and on this unusual but very satisfying date (which also features trumpeter Emmett Berry and trombonist Bob Brookmeyer) they explore such numers as a pair of Ellington classics ("All Too Soon" and "What Am I Here For?"), two Russell originals and even the boppish "Tin Tin Deo." —*Scott Yanow*

New Groove / Nov. 12, 1962–Jan. 19, 1963 / Columbia ✦✦✦✦

Hot Licorice / 1964 / Honey Dew ✦✦✦
In 1964, the clarinet great was caught live jamming through some Dixieland standards with a pickup group of New England musicians. Only trombonist Porky Cohen (who later played with

Roomful of Blues) is slightly known, although trumpeter Tony Tomasso acquits himself well on this decent outing. Russell fans will want to search for this now-rare LP, the first of two Honeydews from this gig. —*Scott Yanow*

Gumbo / 1964 / Honey Dew ✦✦✦
The second of two LPs taken from a pickup date in 1964, this album finds Russell jamming Dixieland standards with some local musicians from New England; trumpeter Tony Tomasso and trombonist Porky Cohen keep up with Russell on this happy if somewhat predictable session. —*Scott Yanow*

★ **Ask Me Now!** / 1965 / Impulse! ✦✦✦✦✦
After a lifetime spent playing unusual and unpredictable clarinet solos in Dixieland settings, Russell late in life broke out of the stereotype and played in more modern settings. This Impulse! LP (begging to be reissued on CD) has his clarinet placed in a piano-less quartet with valve-trombonist Marshall Brown, playing tunes by John Coltrane, Thelonious Monk and Ornette Coleman, along with some classic ballads. It is a remarkable and very lyrical date that briefly rejuvenated the career of this veteran individualist. —*Scott Yanow*

College Concert of Pee Wee Russell and Henry Red / Apr. 17, 1966 / Impulse! ✦✦✦✦
Although trumpeter Red Allen (heard in his final recording) and Russell had recorded back in 1932, their paths only crossed on an infrequent basis through the years. For this LP, the two veteran modernists (who spent much of their careers in Dixieland settings) are joined by a young rhythm-section pianist Steve Kuhn, bassist Charlie Haden and drummer Marty Morell). The music is generally relaxed with an emphasis on blues and a fine feature for Allen on "Body and Soul." —*Scott Yanow*

The Spirit of '67 / Feb. 14, 1967–Feb. 15, 1967 / Impulse! ✦✦✦
Pee Wee Russell's final recording found the veteran clarinetist joined by a big band arranged by Oliver Nelson. The tunes range from the recent "The Shadow of Your Smile" to such classics from Pee Wee's career as "Love Is Just Around the Corner," "Pee Wee's Blues" and "Ja-Da." In general, the charts are colorful and complement Russell well during what would be his swansong. —*Scott Yanow*

Marc Russo

Alto Saxophone / Crossover
Altoist Marc Russo was a key member of the Yellowjackets during 1982–90. Although an R&B-oriented player, Russo's solos pushed the popular group in a stronger jazz direction than it had been earlier with guitarist Robben Ford. Growing up in the San Francisco Bay area, Russo worked locally in clubs and as a studio musician, showing impressive control of his horn. He was with Tower of Power during most of 1981–85 (overlapping with his Yellowjackets years). After leaving the Jackets, Russo led a set for JVC. —*Scott Yanow*

The Window / 1993 / JVC ✦✦✦
Marc Russo's first recording since leaving The Yellowjackets showcases his alto backed by sparse funk-oriented rhythms provided by a variety of anonymous-sounding rhythm sections. Russo draws his inspiration from David Sanborn although some of his own personality comes through in his fiery solos. Most of the originals on this effort (with the exception of "School") are not too memorable, but Russo can certainly blow, and with better writers, he should have a worthwhile solo career. —*Scott Yanow*

● **Instrumental Christmas** / MM Productions ✦✦✦✦

Paul Rutherford

b. Feb. 29, 1940, London, England
Trombone / Avant-Garde
An experimental, unpredictable player who also has a good sense of humor, English trombonist Paul Rutherford's worked in many seminal free bands since the '60s. He started on saxophone in the mid-'50s, then switched to trombone and played that instrument in Royal Air Force bands from 1958 to 1963. He met John Stevens and Trevor Watts in the RAF, and they co-formed The Spontaneous Music Ensemble in 1965. Rutherford studied days at the Guildhall School of Music in London and played free sessions at night during the mid- and late-'60s. He began working regularly with Mike Westbrook in 1967 and formed his own group, Iskra 1903, with Derek Bailey and Barry Guy in the early '70s. Rutherford also played with the London Jazz Composers

Orchestra, Globe Unity Orchestra and Tony Oxley septet, as well as Evan Parker and Paul Lovens. He began developing an unusual trombone language in the mid-'70s, mixing electronics, vocal effects, traditional jazz devices and intriguing sounds and voicings. Rutherford issued some compelling solo sessions in the '70s, then formed a new edition of Iskra 1903 with Guy and Phil Wachsmann in the '80s. He also continued working with The London Jazz Composers Orchestra, played in The Free Jazz Quartet and recorded duos with George Haslam. Rutherford currently has no sessions available on CD in America. —*Ron Wynn*

● **Gentle Harm of the Bourgeoisie** / Jul. 2, 1974–Dec. 17, 1974 / Emanem ✦✦✦✦
Recording of solo trombone. One of the most revered avant-garde statements. —*Michael G. Nastos*

Ali Ryerson

b. 1952, New York, NY
Flute / Hard Bop
A fine bop-oriented flutist, Ali Ryerson is the daughter of guitarist Art Ryerson. She started on flute at age eight and had extensive classical training, graduating from Hart College. However, Ryerson developed a strong interest in jazz and has maintained a versatile career, playing both classical and jazz. Ryerson spent three years freelancing in Belgium and then became a top studio player in New York. She performed with Art Farmer, Lou Donaldson, Maxine Sullivan and Stephane Grappelli among others and has recorded two sets as a leader for Bob Thiele's Red Baron label. —*Scott Yanow*

Blue Flute / Dec. 9, 1991 / Red Baron ✦✦✦
Good '92 set with underrecorded flutist Ali Ryerson doing both sweeping, gentle melodies and more aggressive, emphatic uptempo tunes. The lineup includes three great veterans in Red Rodney, Roy Haynes, and Kenny Barron, plus an emerging player in bassist Santi Debriano. —*Ron Wynn*

I'll Be Back / Jul. 28, 1993 / Red Baron ✦✦✦✦
It is a testament to flutist Ali Ryerson that on her second release she is not overshadowed by her all-star rhythm section (pianist Kenny Barron, bassist Cecil McBee and drummer Danny Gottlieb) and that her sidemen sound happy to be playing with her. The music on this CD ranges from Bobby Jaspar's blues "Bobby's Minor" to a memorable version of Horace Silver's "Peace" and an emotional "That's All." Nothing that innovative occurs, but Ryerson's very pleasing flute sounds perfectly at home in this modern mainstream setting. Recommended for straight-ahead jazz fans. —*Scott Yanow*

Portraits In Silver / Sep. 12, 1994–Sep. 13, 1994 / Concord Jazz ✦✦✦✦

● **In Her Own Sweet Way** / Sep. 18, 1995–Sep. 19, 1995 / Concord Jazz ✦✦✦✦✦

Terje Rypdal

b. Aug. 23, 1947, Oslo, Norway
Guitar / Avant-Garde, Fusion, Post Bop
A flexible Norwegian guitarist and composer, Terje Rypdal's blended rock and jazz elements as well as contemporary classical and even New Age ingredients into his solos. He's added an unusual touch, sometimes playing electric guitar with a violin bow, and he utilizes synthesizers and electronic attachments. Rydal's a self-taught guitarist who studied classical piano, attended Oslo University and took composition with Finn Mortensen and learned the Lydian chromatic concept from its creator George Russell. Rypdal worked with Jan Garbarek from the late '60s into the '70s and gained significant attention for his performance at the 1969 New Jazz Meeting in Baden-Baden, Germany. He formed the group Oydessy in the early '70s and visited London and America with them. Rypdal recorded with Palle Mikkelborg at the Festpill in Norway in 1978. He led a trio with Audun Kleive and Bjorn Kjellemyr that toured Eastern Europe and England in the mid-'80s. Rypdal played in a duo with Mikkelborg in 1986. He's recorded often as a leader for ECM in the '70s, '80s and '90s. Rypdal has several sessions available on CD as a leader. —*Ron Wynn*

Whenever I seem to be Far Away / 1974 / ECM ✦✦

● **Odyssey** / Aug. 1975 / ECM ✦✦✦✦✦
A magnificent effort that combines crushingly powerful rock/jazz ("Over Bierkerot" is a killer) with long, brooding electric rumina-

tions, it was originally a double album; one track has been left off the CD. —*Michael P. Dawson*

After the Rain / Aug. 1976 / ECM ✦✦

Waves / Sep. 1977 / ECM ✦✦✦✦
This contains some of Rypdal's jazziest music—"Per Ulv" even verges on bebop, despite its chattering rhythm box—alongside the more characteristic free-fall rhapsodies. —*Michael P. Dawson*

Rypdal, Vitous, DeJohnette / Jun. 1978 / ECM ✦✦✦
Recorded with Miroslav Vitous & Jack Dejohnette, Rypdal gets spacy but muscular support from two of the superstars of '70s jazz on this 1978 session. —*Michael P. Dawson*

Descendre / Mar. 1979 / ECM ✦✦✦✦
The unusual trio form of guitar, trumpet and drums makes for some gorgeous floating sounds. —*Michael P. Dawson*

To Be Continued / Jan. 1981 / ECM ✦✦✦

Eos / May 1983 / ECM ✦✦✦
Probably Rypdal's most experimental release, it's a set of heavily electronic duets with cellist David Darling. —*Michael P. Dawson*

Chaser / May 1985 / ECM ✦✦✦✦
This 1985 release finds Rypdal working in a hard-hitting power-trio format with his new group, The Chasers. —*Michael P. Dawson*

Blue / Nov. 1986 / ECM ✦✦✦✦
The second album with the rock-oriented Chasers adds keyboards to the mixture. —*Michael P. Dawson*

The Singles Collection / Aug. 1988 / ECM ✦✦✦✦
The title is a joke: this is actually the third album by The Chasers. Inspirational song title: "There is a Hot Lady in My Bedroom and I Need a Drink." —*Michael P. Dawson*

Undisonus / 1990 / ECM ✦✦✦
None of Rypdal's haunting guitar here: this is an album of his purely orchestral compositions. —*Michael P. Dawson*

S

Eddie Safranski

b. Dec. 25, 1913, Pittsburgh, PA, **d.** Jan. 10, 1974, Los Angeles, CA
Bass / Bop
A very effective bassist in either swing or bebop, Eddie Safranski was known for very precisely articulated lines, a good tone and aggressively swinging sound that served him well both with Stan Kenton and in other bands. He studied violin in his childhood, then played bass in high school. Safranski joined Hal McIntyre in the early '40s, playing with him until 1945 and also writing arrangements. He later worked with Miff Mole, Kenton and Charlie Barnet in the late '40s. Safranski moved to New York and became a staff musician at NBC in the early '50s. He worked with Benny Goodman in 1951 and 1952. Safranski did studio work until the late '60s, then became a representative for a bass company. He also gave workshops and taught, while playing traditional jazz and bebop with various Los Angeles groups. Safranski recorded for Atlantic and Savoy as a leader, but these are not currently available on CD. He can be heard on CD reissues by Kenton, Goodman and Don Byas. —*Ron Wynn*

Johnny St. Cyr

b. Apr. 17, 1890, New Orleans, LA, **d.** Jun. 17, 1966, Los Angeles, CA
Banjo, Guitar / New Orleans Jazz
A fine rhythmic banjoist and guitarist, Johnny St. Cyr was a New Orleans pioneer who was greatly in demand in the 1920s. Self-taught, St. Cyr had his own trio as far back as 1905. He played in New Orleans with A.J. Piron, the Superior, Olympia and Tuxedo bands and with Kid Ory (when King Oliver was the cornetist) in addition to Fate Marable's riverboat band. After moving to Chicago in 1923, St. Cyr made his place in history by recording with King Oliver, Jelly Roll Morton and Louis Armstrong (as a key member of Armstrong's Hot Five and Hot Seven) while performing nightly with Doc Cook's Dreamland Orchestra. In 1930 he returned to New Orleans where he made his living outside of music but still played with local groups (including with Paul Barbarin and Alphonse Picou). In 1955 St. Cyr moved to Los Angeles and returned to music fulltime, leading the Young Men from New Orleans at Disneyland from 1961 until his death in 1966. —*Scott Yanow*

Johnny St. Cyr and His Hot Five: Paul Barbarin and His ... / May 13, 1954 / Southland ✦✦✦✦

Sal Salvador

b. Nov. 21, 1925, Monson, MA
Guitar / Bop, Cool
A versatile guitarist and recent head of the guitar department at the University of Bridgeport, Sal Salvador has been a capable soloist and accompanist since the late '40s. His single string style, shaped by his early interest in the music of Charlie Christian, has been augmented by extensive studies of guitar technique. Salvador's years of research, playing and analysis eventually led to his writing guitar methodology books, among them "Sal Salvador's Chord Method for Guitar" and "Sal Salvador's Single String Studies for Guitar" in the '50s and '60s. He became interested in jazz during his teens and began playing professionally in Springfield, Mass in 1945. He worked with Terry Gibbs and Mundell Lowe in New York at the end of the '40s, then joined Stan Kenton's orchestra in 1952. Salvador worked with Kenton

until the end of 1953 and appeared on the *New Concepts of Artistry in Rhythm* album. He led bebop bands featuring Eddie Costa and Phil Woods. Salvador was featured in the film "Jazz On A Summer's Day" and headed a big band in the late '50s and early '60s. He worked in a guitar duo with Alan Hanlon in the early '70s and began recording again as a leader later in the decade. He reformed his big band in the '80s and was named to his position at the University of Bridgeport. Salvador has recorded for Bee Hive and Stash among others. He currently has a few sessions available on CD as a leader. —*Ron Wynn*

Sal Salvador Quintet / Dec. 24, 1953 / Blue Note ✦✦✦
Starfingers / Mar. 24, 1978 / Bee Hive ✦✦✦✦
Juicy Lucy / Sep. 5, 1978 / Bee Hive ✦✦✦✦
World's Greatest Jazz Standards / Nov. 1983 / Stash ✦✦✦
These 11 songs might not be the world's greatest jazz standards, but they are certainly all familiar songs. Veteran guitarist Sal Salvador, along with vibraphonist Paul Johnson, bassist Gary Mazzaroppi and drummer Butch Miles give the warhorses fairly straightforward treatments, and there are few surprises with all but one of the performances being between three and five minutes. The music is pleasing but somewhat predictable. —*Scott Yanow*

● **Sal Salvador and Crystal Image /** 1989 / Stash ✦✦✦✦✦
Guitarist Sal Salvador started his two-guitar quartet, Crystal Image, with the idea of reviving the group he had had with Mundell Lowe in the early '50s. This CD adds another element to the music, the voice of Barbara Oakes, which is often used as if it were a third guitar. With guitarist Mike Giordano, bassist Phil Bowler and drummer Greg Burrows completing the group, the arrangements of Salvador and Hank Levy on these complex originals and a few standards (plus Chick Corea's "Got a Match?") give Crystal Image its own fresh group sound. Worth investigating. —*Scott Yanow*

The Way Of The Wind / 1994 / JazzMania ✦✦✦✦

Sergio Salvatore

b. Mar. 3, 1981, Ringwood, NJ
Piano / Post-Bop
Sergio Salvatore certainly qualifies as a prodigy, having recorded two albums for GRP by the time he was 13. His father is a music teacher while his mother is a singer. Sergio began taking serious piano lessons at age four, and amazingly enough his first two recordings give no hint as to his youth. Salvatore, who is influenced by Keith Jarrett and Chick Corea among others, held his own with the all-star casts (which include Dave Samuels, Bob Mintzer, Randy Brecker and even Corea), quite an impressive start to what should be a lengthy career. —*Scott Yanow*

Sergio Salvatore / 1993 / GRP ✦✦✦✦✦
The youngest of the "Young Lions," pianist Sergio Salvatore was 11 at the time of this recording. However, one quickly forgets his age for he plays with surprising maturity, starting off his debut with a thoughtful unaccompanied version of "Like Someone in Love" that sounds like Keith Jarrett in spots; other selections hint more at Chick Corea. Salvatore has good technique, but it's his self-restraint on the ballads that is most impressive. The selections (seven of the pianist's originals plus three standards) are both funky and straight-ahead, and there are solos from vibraphonist Dave Samuels and (on three cuts) Bob Mintzer on tenor, but the

remarkable Sergio Salvatore is the main reason to acquire this disc. —*Scott Yanow*

● **Tune Up** / GRP ✦✦✦✦✦
Pianist Sergio Salvatore was only 13 at the time of this recording, his second release. But despite his extreme youth, one forgets Salvatore's age by the third song. He certainly gets the star treatment on the date, playing quartets with Gary Burton, interacting with The Brecker Brothers and even duetting with Chick Corea on "Sea Journey." But Salvatore somehow manages to keep up with his illustrious sidemen and the fairly complex music (which includes three of his impressive originals) rewards repeated listenings. It will be very interesting to see how Sergio Salvatore sounds ten years from now. —*Scott Yanow*

Joe Sample

b. Feb. 1, 1939, Houston, TX
Piano / Hard Bop, Soul Jazz, Crossover
Pianist Sample formed a group with some Texas comrades in the late '50s that played an aggressive brand of funky blues, instrumental R&B with jazz touches that they called the "Gulf Coast Sound." When the group moved to Los Angeles in 1960 they changed their name to The Jazz Crusaders. Though he also worked with some other musicians in the '60s, among them Tom Scott and the Harold Land/Bobby Hutcherson group, the main unit (Sample on keyboards, Wayne Henderson on trombone, Wilton Felder on tenor sax and Stix Hooper on drums) were unparalled at playing R&B-infused soul-jazz. The group dropped the Jazz surname in the '70s, became The Crusaders and gradually began doing less ambitious, markedly lighter material without the strong blues and R&B backing. Sample got more involved in the production in '70s and '80s, and his most recent releases have been heavy on studio touches, weaker on content. —*Ron Wynn*

Fancy Dance / Apr. 20, 1969 / Gazell ✦✦✦✦
A different and rather strong session for keyboardist Joe Sample from '69. Rather than the fusion, blues and funky instrumentals he's done both with and without his fellow Crusaders, this is a mainstream trio session with Sample, bassist Red Mitchell and drummer J.C. Moses. While there are two spry blues pieces, there are also some demanding standards and bop in which Sample shows he can execute the chord changes and perform conventional jazz with conviction, even if it's not what he does today. —*Ron Wynn*

The Three / Nov. 28, 1975 / Inner City ✦✦✦✦
Rainbow Seeker / 1978 / MCA ✦✦✦✦✦
Swing Street Cafe / Nov. 29, 1978–Nov. 30, 1978 / MCA ✦✦✦✦
● **Carmel** / 1978 / MCA ✦✦✦✦✦
Voices in the Rain / 1980 / MCA ✦✦✦
The Hunter / 1982 / MCA ✦✦✦
Roles / 1987 / MCA ✦✦
Spellbound / 1989 / Warner Brothers ✦✦✦
Ashes to Ashes / 1990 / Warner Brothers ✦✦✦✦
Invitation / 1993 / Warner Brothers ✦✦✦✦
● **Did You Feel That?** / 1994 / Warner Brothers ✦✦✦✦✦
Fans of The Crusaders of the early '70s will want this set. Joe Sample utilizes a Fender Rhodes keyboard much of the time, and a two-horn frontline (with trumpeter Oscar Brashear and tenorman Joel Peskin) is reminiscent of his former group; even guitarist Arthur Adams returns. This is intelligent and lightly funky soulful jazz-oriented dance music that is very easy to enjoy. —*Scott Yanow*

Edgar Sampson

b. Aug. 31, 1907, New York, NY, d. Jan. 16, 1973, Englewood, NJ
Violin, Alto Saxophone, Arranger / Swing
While he was a first-rate violinist and versatile saxophonist, Edgar Sampson's greatness came as a composer and arranger. His greatest works include "Stompin' At The Savoy," "Don't Be That Way," "Blue Minor," "If Dreams Come True," "Blue Lou," "Lullaby In Rhythm" and many others, plus numerous arrangements. He began playing violin as a child, then alto sax as a teen. He started his professional career with Joe Coleman in 1924, then worked with Duke Ellington in 1925. Later came stints with Bingie Madison, Billy Fowler, Arthur Gibbs, Charlie Johnson and Alex

Jackson. Sampson joined Fletcher Henderson in 1931, remaining until 1933. He played with Chick Webb from '33 until '37, and began writing arrangements with Rex Stewart while in Webb's band. Sampson was a prolific freelance arranger during the swing era's heyday, providing them for Webb, Benny Goodman, Artie Shaw, Red Norvo and Teddy Wilson. He played baritone sax with Lionel Hampton in 1938, then became Ella Fitzgerald's music director in 1939. Sampson played alto and baritone sax for Al Sears in 1943, then started his own bands. During the late '40s and '50s, Sampson played in many Afro-Latin bands, including those of Marcellino Guerra, Tito Puente and Tito Rodriquez. He continued heading bands through the '60s and died in 1973. —*Ron Wynn*

Sampson Swings Again / Apr. 2, 1956–Apr. 4, 1956 / MCA ✦✦✦✦

Dave Samuels

b. Oct. 9, 1948, Waukegan IL
Vibes / Post-Bop, Crossover
A vibist and marimba player whose records run the gamut from exacting and ambitious to impressionistic and tedious, Dave Samuels can sometimes be more technically impressive than musically enticing. He studied with Gary Burton at Berklee and later became an instructor there himself in jazz improvisation and percussion. Samuels moved to New York in 1974 and recorded for three years with Gerry Mulligan while also touring internationally. Samuels played and recorded with Carla Bley and Gerry Niewood. He formed a duo with fellow vibist, marimba player and percussionist Dave Friedman. They recorded with Harvie Swartz and Hubert Laws under Friedman's name in 1975, then called themselves Double Image for sessions with Michael Di Pasqua and Swartz from 1977 to 1980. Double Image toured Europe, taught at workshops and were on the faculty at the Manhattan School of Music for a time. Samuels worked and recorded with Double Image in 1985 and also played with the group Gallery. He'd begun working with Spyro Gyra in 1979 and continued playing with them until he joined full time in 1986. Samuels recorded with Paul McCandless, Art Lande, Anthony Davis and Bobby McFerrin in the late '70s and '80s and did a solo date in 1981. In recent times Dave Samuels has left Spyro Gyra and has been working on special projects and his own solo records. Unfortunately, the latter have continued in the same lightweight vein as his later dates with Spyro Gyra, rarely rising above the level of superior background music. —*Ron Wynn and Scott Yanow*

● **Double Image** / Jun. 1977 / Enja ✦✦✦✦✦
Ten Degrees North / 1989 / MCA ✦✦✦
Natural Selection / 1991 / GRP ✦✦✦✦
Del Sol / 1992 / GRP ✦✦✦
Vibraphonist Dave Samuels plays quite well on this CD, but he is often overshadowed by his sidemen, especially pianist Danilo Perez, flutist Dave Valentin, guitarist Jorge Strunz and (on two numbers) steel drummer Andy Narell. The easy-listening music is pleasing, and due to the utilization of several groupings of players, there is a certain amount of variety. However, the lack of any memorable melodies and real climaxes in the improvisations mean that this recording falls into the lightweight pop/jazz vein. A decent effort that could have been stronger. —*Scott Yanow*

David Sanborn

b. Jul. 30, 1945, Tampa, FL
Alto Saxophone, Crossover, Soul Jazz
David Sanborn has been the most influential saxophonist on pop, R&B and crossover players of the past 20 years. Most of his recordings have been in the dance music/R&B vein although Sanborn is a capable jazz player. His greatest contributions to music have been his passionate sound (with its crying and squealing high notes) and his emotional interpretations of melodies, which generally uplift any record he is on. Unlike his countless number of imitators, Sanborn is immediately recognizable within two notes. While growing up in St. Louis, Sanborn played with many Chicago blues greats (including Albert King) and became a skilled alto saxophonist despite battling polio in his youth. After important stints with Paul Butterfield (he played with the Butterfield Blues Band at Woodstock), Gil Evans, Stevie Wonder, David Bowie and the Brecker Brothers, Sanborn began recording as a leader in the mid-'70s, and he racked up a string of pop suc-

cesses. Over the years he has worked with many pop players, but he has made his biggest impact leading his own danceable bands. Occasionally Sanborn throws the music world a curve his eccentric but rewarding *Another Hand,* a guest stint with avant-gardist Tim Berne on a 1993 album featuring the compositions of Julius Hemphill and a set of ballads (*Pearls*) on which he is accompanied by a string orchestra arranged by Johnny Mandel. For a couple years in the early '90s, Sanborn was the host of the syndicated television series *Night Music,* which had a very eclectic lineup of musicians (from Sonny Rollins and Sun Ra to James Taylor and heavy metal players), most of whom were given the unique opportunity to play together. It displayed David Sanborn's wide interest and musical curiosity even if many of his own recordings remain quite predictable. —*Scott Yanow*

Taking Off / 1975 / Warner Brothers ✦✦✦
Altoist David Sanborn has long been one of the leaders of what could be called rhythm & jazz (R&B-oriented jazz). His debut for Warner Brothers was a major commercial success and helped make him into a major name. The music is fairly commercial but certainly danceable and melodic. Even at that point in time, Sanborn's alto cries were immediately recognizable; The Brecker Brothers, guitarist Steve Khan and Howard Johnson on baritone and tuba are prominent in support. —*Scott Yanow*

Sanborn / 1976 / Warner Brothers ✦✦✦
Heart to Heart / Jan. 1978 / Warner Brothers ✦✦✦✦
Hideaway / 1979 / Warner Brothers ✦✦✦✦
Voyeur / 1980 / Warner Brothers ✦✦✦✦✦
As We Speak / 1981 / Warner Brothers ✦✦✦
Backstreet / 1982 / Warner Brothers ✦✦✦
Straight from the Heart / 1984 / Warner Brothers ✦✦✦✦✦
Double Vision / 1986 / Warner Brothers ✦✦✦✦
Change of Heart / 1987 / Warner Brothers ✦✦✦
Close-Up / 1988 / Reprise ✦✦✦
● **Another Hand** / 1991 / Elektra ✦✦✦✦✦
Upfront / 1992 / Elektra ✦✦✦✦
Despite an array of session musicians and some heavily arranged material, alto saxophonist Dave Sanborn cuts long with his most expressive, joyous playing in many years. That's partly due to Marcus Miller's bass work, which is fluid and backbeat-oriented, while others, like trumpeter Herb Robertson and organist Richard Tee, lay in some perfect riffs in support of Sanborn's earnest solos. —*Ron Wynn*

Hearsay / 1994 / Elektra ✦✦✦
● **Pearls** / 1995 / Elektra ✦✦✦✦✦
David Sanborn is joined on this CD by an orchestra arranged by Johnny Mandel for a set of music dominated by melodic versions of standards. Sanborn does not get all that far away from the themes (which include "Try a Little Tenderness," "Smoke Gets in Your Eyes," "For All We Know," "This Masquerade" and a very emotional "Everything Must Change" in addition to a few newer songs), but his sound is so soulful and full of passion that he does not really need to improvise much to make his point. It's a fine change of pace for the highly influential altoist. —*Scott Yanow*

David Sanchez

b. 1968, Guaynabo, Puerto Rico
Tenor Saxophone / Post-Bop, Latin Jazz
David Sanchez took up the conga when he was eight and started playing tenor at age 12. He graduated from a performing arts high school in 1986, spent a year studying psychology and then moved to New York City in 1988, having decided to become a musician. Sanchez attended Rutgers University, studying with Kenny Barron, Ted Dunbar and John Purcell. After a period freelancing in New York with many top Latin players (including Paquito D'Rivera and Claudio Roditi), Sanchez joined Dizzy Gillespie's United Nation Orchestra in 1990, also getting the opportunity to play with Dizzy's small group. Since then he has toured with the Philip Morris SuperBand, recorded with Slide Hampton's Jazz Masters, Charlie Sepulveda, Kenny Drew, Jr., Rayan Kisor, Danilo Perez, Rachel Z and Hilton Ruiz (among others) and headed his own sessions for Columbia. David Sanchez is an up-and-coming tenor player whose music mixes together Afro-Cuban rhythms with advanced bebop. —*Scott Yanow*

● **Sketches Of Dreams** / Dec. 7, 1994–Dec. 9, 1994 / Columbia ✦✦✦✦
David Sanchez, who has an appealing tone on the tenor (at times hinting at Joe Henderson and Stanley Turrentine), matches well with trumpeter Roy Hargrove and the creative Latin percussionists during the first two numbers, However, at that point Hargrove disappears (only popping up on "Sketches of Dreams"), and the percussionists are often de-emphasized in favor of more straight-ahead music; three numbers are played with just a standard rhythm section. Pianists David Kikoski and Danilo Perez both have plenty of solo space with Perez's complex yet accessible style sometimes coming close at times to stealing honors. But Sanchez's warm sound (which is quite appealing on the ballad "Tu Y Mi Cancion" and a tender "It's Easy to Remember") eventually emerges as the main star. Perhaps in the future he should do a full Latin album or an entire set of ballads. This sampler CD (which includes two outings on soprano) is a good example of his talents. —*Scott Yanow*

Poncho Sanchez

b. Oct. 30, 1951, Laredo, Texas
Percussion, Leader / Latin Jazz
Ever since he led his first record date in 1982, Poncho Sanchez has headed one of the most popular and influential Latin-jazz bands around. The youngest of 11 children, Sanchez taught himself to play guitar, flute, drums and timbales before settling on the congas. After a period playing with local bands, he joined Cal Tjader's band in 1975 and was an important part of Tjader's pacesetting group until his idol's death in 1982. Shortly after he formed his own band and has since recorded on a regular basis for Concord Picante. Sanchez's group is very active, playing in clubs, concerts and festivals on a regular basis. —*Scott Yanow*

Poncho / Jan. 10, 1979 / Discovery ✦✦✦✦
A fine '79 date matching percussionist Poncho Sanchez with pianist and bandleader Clare Fischer, who also did the arrangements and conducted the band. This was among the last things the two did together, because Sanchez soon left and formed his own band. Excellent arrangements, plus some exciting ensemble work and good solos. —*Ron Wynn*

Straight Ahead / Mar. 12, 1980 / Discovery ✦✦✦✦
Another collaboration between pianist/bandleader Clare Fischer and conga player Poncho Sanchez. This one was tailored more toward mainstream jazz than Afro-Latin and Latin material, although it also included some effective Latin songs. The Fischer and Sanchez collaboration lasted into the early '80s and was mutually beneficial. —*Ron Wynn*

Sonando / Aug. 1982 / Concord Picante ✦✦✦
Good, sometimes entrancing Afro-Latin jazz and salsa by a consistently effective conguero and bandleader. Sanchez is just notch below Mongo Santamaria and Ray Barretto as a pure percussionist, while his bands are never spectacular but always energetic and entertaining. —*Ron Wynn*

Bien Sabroso / Nov. 1983 / Concord Picante ✦✦✦✦
Steady, frequently frenetic Latin jazz session from Concord recording artist Sanchez. Each album has a good blend of upbeat, driving tunes and more relaxed, dance-oriented pieces. Sanchez is a high-level player and expert accompanist and can become a stunning soloist when given the spotlight. —*Ron Wynn*

El Conguero / May 1985 / Concord Picante ✦✦✦✦
A mid-'80s date by Afro-Latin/Latin jazz bandleader and conga player Poncho Sanchez, one of several he's made for Concord. They're all good, although pretty similar. There are one or two standards and a number of originals that feature a good band comprised of session pros and Latin jazz types. Sanchez belongs in the same class as Daniel Ponce, Candido, or Ralph McDonald—just a step below greats like Chano Pozo, Mongo Santamaria, or Ray Barretto. —*Ron Wynn*

★ **Papa Gato** / Oct. 1986 / Concord Picante ✦✦✦✦✦
Percussionist Poncho Sanchez has long led one of the top Latin-jazz groups, succeeding his former boss, the late Cal Tjader. On this easily enjoyable release, Sanchez features plenty of solos from Justo Almario (on alto, tenor and flute), trumpeter Sal Cracchiolo and trombonist Art Velasco and the three percussionists have many opportunities to romp. The jazz content is pretty high with such songs as "Jumpin' with Symphony Sid," "Senor Blues" and "Manteca" alternating with group originals. A fine introduction to the accessible Latin-jazz of Poncho Sanchez. —*Scott Yanow*

Fuerte / Nov. 1987 / Concord Picante ✦✦✦✦✦
Features an octet with standout pianist/composer Charlie Otwell,
who wrote the title track and two other cookers. Saxophonist Ken
Goldberg wrote two others. Because of these two, this stands as a
prime Sanchez album, aside from the group's hot playing. —
Michael G. Nastos

La Familia / Nov. 1988 / Concord Picante ✦✦✦✦

Chile Con Soul / Nov. 1989 / Concord Picante ✦✦✦✦✦

Cambios / Oct. 15, 1990–Oct. 17, 1990 / Concord Picante ✦✦✦

A Night with Poncho Sanchez Live: Bailar / Dec. 1990 /
Concord Picante ✦✦✦
Poncho Sanchez leads his band through a solid live set recorded at Kimball's. The accent is on galvanizing Afro-Latin rhythms
and duels between Sanchez on congas, Ramon Banda on timbales and Jose Rodriquez on bongos. His band has decent trumpeters and saxophonists, but it's the rhythm section that carries
the weight throughout the date. That's fine, because Sanchez has
emerged enough to put himself in the neighborhood of superstar congueros Ray Barretto, Candido and Mongo Santamaria.
Those who question that contention should listen closely to
Sanchez's patterns, array of beats and solos on "Sonando" or "La
Familiar." Poncho Sanchez is making Afro-Latin music equal or
superior to any coming from bigger names in the '90s. —*Ron
Wynn*

A Night at Kimball's East / Dec. 8, 1990 / Concord Picante ✦✦✦
This concert performance (which is also available on video) features spirited Latin-jazz from Poncho Sanchez's octet. There are
some strong contributions from trumpeter Sal Cracchiolo, trombonist Art Velasco and saxophonist Gene Burkert along with the
percussionists. The excessive amount of group vocals and the
often-routine (if infectious) material keep this set from being
essential, but Sanchez's many fans should enjoy it. —*Scott Yanow*

El Mejor / Apr. 18, 1992–Apr. 9, 1992 / Concord Picante ✦✦✦✦
A '92 session with bandleader Poncho Sanchez spearheading his
group through his latest collection of Afro-Latin jams, originals
and the occasional standard. The band includes the dynamic Justo
Almario, who provides some welcome intensity, plus Sanchez's
driving, steady rhythms. —*Ron Wynn*

Para Todos / Oct. 25, 1993–Oct. 26, 1993 / Concord Picante
✦✦✦✦✦
Everyone plays flawlessly, and Sanchez's conga work provides an
array of expertly placed accents, multiple rhythms and support.
The songs are uniformly excellent, and Sanchez's group smoothly
handles standards, hard bop and Afro-Latin numbers. —*Ron
Wynn*

Soul Sauce: Memories of Cal Tjader / Mar. 7, 1995–Mar. 8, 1995
/ Concord Picante ✦✦✦✦✦

Pharoah Sanders (Farrell Sanders)
b. Oct. 13, 1940, Little Rock, AR
Tenor Saxophone / Avant-Garde, Hard Bop, Free Jazz
Pharoah Sanders has had a rather unique career. He came to fame
when he made the John Coltrane Quartet a Quintet, taking ferocious, emotional and atonal solos that started where Coltrane's left
off. After Coltrane's death, for a period Sanders came close to
making the avant-garde popular as his alternately intense and
peaceful solos proved to be a perfect team with singer Leon
Thomas ("The Creator Has a Master Plan"). Unfortunately, most of
Sanders' output since the late '70s has been quite derivative of
Coltrane's hard bop-oriented music circa 1959, years before
Sanders joined 'Trane. After graduating high school, Pharoah
Sanders freelanced in San Francisco. He moved to New York in
1962, struggled in obscurity for two years, then made his recording debut on ESP. He came to the attention of John Coltrane, and
from mid-1965 until 'Trane's death in 1967 he was usually a part
of Coltrane's controversial group with his role being largely to create violent sound explorations. Sanders' most rewarding recordings took place during the late '60s/early '70s for Impulse! with
and without Leon Thomas. However, by the mid-'70s his sessions
had become predictable, and Sanders' career never seemed to
regain its earlier momentum. Pharoah Sanders' decision in the
early '80s to explore standards melodically pleased the bebop
purists but resulted in many of his followers being disappointed
by the absence of his own musical personality. Since that time
Sanders (now a legend) has largely continued in that direction
although occasionally (such as on drummer Franklin Kiermyer's

very intense Evidence CD) the real Pharoah Sanders shows up
and reminds the jazz world of his significance! —*Scott Yanow*

Pharoah's First Album / Sep. 10, 1964 / ESP ✦✦✦✦✦

Tauhid / Nov. 15, 1966 / Impulse! ✦✦✦✦
This was Pharoah Sanders' first recording on Impulse! as a leader,
but it is a surprisingly weak effort. It takes quite awhile for the
16-minute "Upper Egypt and Lower Egypt" to get going. That
piece sets a spiritual mood, but Sanders does not really play tenor
until the music had already been meandering for 12 minutes. The
mercifully brief "Japan" mostly focuses on the leader's off-key
chant-like singing, so virtually the only interesting performance is
a long medley that spotlights guitarist Sonny Sharrock. This CD
can safely be skipped by all but Pharoah Sanders completists. —
Scott Yanow

Izipho Zam / Jan. 14, 1969 / Strata East ✦✦✦✦
Wild, crazy and frenzied. Sanders and Sonny Sharrock (g) explore.
—*Ron Wynn*

★ **Karma** / Feb. 14, 1969–Feb. 19, 1969 / Impulse! ✦✦✦✦✦
Karma was a real rarity, an avant-garde "hit." One could almost
call it "free jazz for the masses." Pharoah Sanders, who in 1966
would have easily won a poll for "least likely to succeed commercially" by 1969 was out on his own featuring his Jekyll-and-
Hyde tenor (alternately peaceful and screaming) over rhythmic
vamps. With Leon Thomas singing and yodelling, the 33-minute
atmospheric "The Creator Has a Master Plan" caught on and
received quite a bit of airplay on jazz stations at the time. —*Scott
Yanow*

Jewels of Thought / Oct. 20, 1969 / Impulse! ✦✦✦✦✦

Deaf Dumb Blind / Jul. 1, 1970 / Impulse! ✦✦✦✦

Thembi / Nov. 25, 1970–Jan. 12, 1971 / MCA ✦✦✦✦✦

Black Unity / Dec. 8, 1971 / Impulse! ✦✦✦
Powerhouse solos, dense compositions, two bassists, drummers. —
Ron Wynn

Live at the East / 1971 / Impulse! ✦✦✦✦

Village of the Pharoahs / Nov. 22, 1972–Sep. 14, 1973 / Impulse!
✦✦✦

Elevation / Sep. 7, 1973–Sep. 13, 1973 / Impulse! ✦✦✦

Love in Us All / Sep. 14, 1973 / Impulse! ✦✦✦
With two extended tracks. Includes the revered "Love Is
Everywhere." —*Michael G. Nastos*

Love Will Find a Way / 1977 / Arista ✦✦

Beyond a Dream / Jul. 22, 1978 / Arista ✦✦✦

Journey to the One / 1980 / Evidence ✦✦✦✦✦
Formerly a Theresa double LP, this single CD contains all ten of
Pharoah Sanders' performances from the sessions. As usual,
Sanders shifts between spiritual peace and violent outbursts in his
tenor solos. The backup group changes from track to track but
often includes pianist John Hicks, bassist Ray Drummond and
drummer Idris Muhammad. Sanders really recalls his former
boss John Coltrane on "After the Rain" (taken as a duet with
pianist Joe Bonner) and a romantic "Easy to Remember"; other
highpoints include "You've Got to Have Freedom" (which has
Bobby McFerrin as one of the background singers) and the exotic "Kazuko" on which Sanders is accompanied by kato, harmonium and wind chimes. —*Scott Yanow*

Rejoice / 1981 / Evidence ✦✦✦✦
Pharoah Sanders again offered something new on this album.
"Nigerian JuJu HiLife" was a presentation of a quasi-African pop
song, although more pop than African, and while "Lights Are
Low" and "Farah" were mellow, reflective numbers, "Rejoice" was
a celebratory outing. But on "Central Park West" and "Origin,"
Sanders played with the ferocity, vocal effects and intensity that
marks his finest work. He enlisted some outstanding musicians,
including vibist Bobby Hutcherson, drummer Elvin Jones, trombonist Steve Turre, bassist Art Davis, drummer Billy Higgins and
pianist John Hicks, among others. —*Ron Wynn*

Heart Is a Melody / Jan. 23, 1982 / Evidence ✦✦✦
This Evidence CD is a reissue of a Theresa LP, adding two songs
("Naima" and "Rise 'N' Shine") to the original program. Pharoah
Sanders is heard at his best on a 22-minute version of "Ole"
where the tenor really gets a chance to stretch out. His "vocal" on
"Goin' to Africa" is spirited, but otherwise most of his solos are
very much in the tradition of John Coltrane. There are some fiery

moments but few surprises on this date chiefly recommended to Sanderss fans. —*Scott Yanow*

Live / Nov. 19, 1982–Nov. 20, 1982 / Theresa ✦✦✦

Shukuru / 1985 / Evidence ✦✦✦
A mid-'80s session reuniting a great team from the '70s—vocalist Leon Thomas and tenor saxophonist Pharoah Sanders. They don't take things as far outside as they did then but still soar and glide while pianist William Henderson, bassist Ray Drummond and drummer Idris Muhammad fill in underneath them. —*Ron Wynn*

Oh Lord, Let Me Do No Wrong / Jul. 13, 1987 / Doctor Jazz ✦✦✦

Welcome to Love / Jul. 17, 1990–Jul. 19, 1990 / Evidence ✦✦✦✦

Crescent with Love / Oct. 19, 1992–Oct. 20, 1992 / Evidence ✦✦✦✦
This two CD set from the Evidence label features tenor saxophonist Pharoah Sanders accompanied by a supportive rhythm section (pianist William Henderson, bassist Charles Fambrough and drummer Sherman Ferguson). Although there are some passionate moments, this is actually one of his mellower sessions, and he explores such songs as "Misty," "In a Sentimental Mood," "Too Young to Go Steady," "Body and Soul," "Naima" and "After the Rain" in a ballad style not that different than John Coltrane's of the early '60s. There are some heated moments on some of the other selections (such as "Wise One" and "Crescent") but Sanders' trademark screeches are at a minimum this time around. —*Scott Yanow*

Randy Sandke

b. 1949, Chicago, IL
Trumpet / Swing, Classic Jazz
Since his emergence in the mid-'80s, Randy Sandke has been one of the top swing-oriented trumpeters in jazz. His older brother Jordan (himself a fine trumpeter) introduced Randy to the many styles of jazz. In 1968 he formed a rock band with Michael Brecker that featured a horn section, and they played at the Notre Dame Jazz Festival. However, Sandke had to turn down the opportunity to join Janis Joplin's band due to a hernia in his throat. Although an operation corrected the problem, Sandke's loss of confidence resulted in him deciding to take up the guitar, and he worked in New York as a guitarist for the next decade. Finally he was persuaded to take up the trumpet again, and Sandke spent five years with Vince Giordano's Nighthawks, worked regularly with Bob Wilber, and he was a part of Benny Goodman's last band during 1985–86. Since that time Sandke has worked and recorded with Buck Clayton, Michael Brecker, the Newport All Stars, Jon Hendricks, Ralph Sutton, Kenny Davern, Benny Carter, Dizzy Gillespie, the World's Greatest Jazz Band, Mel Tormé and Joe Williams among many others, touring Europe over 20 times. In addition he has recorded several impressive albums as a leader for Concord. —*Scott Yanow*

The Sandke Brothers / May 30, 1985–Jun. 12, 1985 / Stash ✦✦✦✦

Stampede / Dec. 4, 1990+Dec. 6, 1990 / Jazzology ✦✦✦✦✦

Wild Cats / Jul. 9, 1992+Jul. 13, 1992 / Jazzology ✦✦✦✦✦

★ **I Hear Music** / Feb. 1993 / Concord Jazz ✦✦✦✦✦

Get Happy / Sep. 1993 / Concord Jazz ✦✦✦

Chase / Aug. 3, 1994–Aug. 4, 1994 / Concord Jazz ✦✦✦✦
Because Randy Sandke is best known as a swing trumpeter, this CD (which features such highly individual modernists as the outrageous trombonist Ray Anderson, tenor great Michael Brecker, altoist Chris Potter and multi-instrumentalist Scott Robinson, who is heard on the selections in which he appears sticking to tenor) is a bit of a surprise. As it turns out Sandke had gone to school with Anderson and Brecker and is a much more flexible trumpeter than one might have thought. Joined by a talented rhythm section comprised of pianist Ted Rosenthal, bassist John Goldsby and drummer Marvin "Smitty" Smith, Sandke leads his unusual group through a variety of material ranging from a remake of "Lullaby of Broadway" that often simulates a traffic jam, a cooking "Jordu" and four of his originals to the Bix Beiderbecke-associated "Oh Miss Hannah." This set is full of surprises (check out the baroque beginning of "Jordu"), and there is plenty of space for each of Sandke's sidemen. Despite all of the potential competition, it is to his credit that Randy Sandke is not all overshadowed on his stimulating set from Concord. —*Scott Yanow*

Arturo Sandoval

b. Nov. 6, 1949, Artemisa, Cuba
Trumpet / Bop, Afro-Cuban Jazz
An energetic, often exciting trumpeter whose flashing phrases, high-note acrobatics and dynamic, charismatic playing style was first noticed in the group Irakere. Arturo Sandoval hasn't made the great records as a leader that many anticipated but displays such potential as a soloist it seems only a matter of time before his definitive recording will be issued. His time, range, timbre and approach are solid, as are his ballad skills. The only thing lacking has been consistency, particularly on record. Sandoval was one of the founding members in The Orquesta Cubana de Musica Moderna in Havana during the '70s, along with Paquito D'Rivera. Various members of this band later formed Irakere. The group recorded with David Amram in 1977. Sandoval left the group in 1981 and toured internationally with his own band and recorded in Cuba. He met his idol Dizzy Gillespie in the '70s and played with him in Cuba, America, Puerto Rico and England, recording together in Finland for Pablo in the early '80s. Sandoval defected to America during the '80s and has since recorded for Messidor and GRP. He and D'Rivera played together on a recent Messidor release. In the 1990s his regular Afro-Cuban group reflects his high-energy virtuosic approach, giving Sandoval an opportunity not only to display his remarkable range (his high notes rival Jon Faddis'!) and warm trumpet sound but his skills on timbales, piano and as a vocalist. —*Ron Wynn and Scott Yanow*

● **To a Finland Station** / Sep. 9, 1982 / Original Jazz Classics ✦✦✦✦✦
With Dizzy Gillespie (tpt) in Helsinki. Excellent interplay. Lots of good feeling on this session. —*Michael G. Nastos*

Tumbaito / 1986 / Messidor ✦✦✦✦
A tremendous session with dynamic trumpeter Arturo Sandoval mixing things up with an all-star lineup. It was originally only available overseas but has now been issued in America through Messidor. —*Ron Wynn*

★ **Straight Ahead** / Aug. 1988 / Ronnie Scott's Jazz House ✦✦✦✦✦
With his remarkable range and phenomenal technique, Arturo Sandoval is one of the world's great trumpeters; he can do virtually anything he wants on his instrument. Some detractors have claimed that he has too much technique (is such a thing possible?) and that his recordings thus far for GRP are a bit erratic. The latter criticism cannot be applied to this 1988 release. Sandoval is heard with a standard quartet comprised of the great pianist Chucho Valdes (the leader of Irakere), bassist Ron Matthewson and drummer Martin Drew. Recorded in England before Sandoval broke ties with Cuba, Arturo is in near miraculous form on some blues, a lyrical "My Funny Valentine" and a few basic originals. Just listen to him tear through "Blue Monk," playing in the low register with the speed of an Al Hirt before jumping into the stratosphere like Maynard Ferguson. This CD serves as an excellent introduction for the bop lover to the very talented Arturo Sandoval. —*Scott Yanow*

Flight to Freedom / 1991 / GRP ✦✦✦✦

I Remember Clifford / 1992 / GRP ✦✦✦✦✦
Arturo Sandoval's high-note explosions, racing lines, expressive tone and charismatic playing style were ideal for the songs of Clifford Brown, a certified jazz legend. Sandoval's exploits were more than matched by a marvelous group that included pianist Kenny Kirkland, saxophonist Ernie Watts and bassist Charnett Moffett, plus drummer Kenny Washington. —*Ron Wynn*

Dreams Come True / 1993 / GRP ✦✦✦✦
This is one of trumpeter Arturo Sandoval's more restrained sessions, but he cuts loose effectively in some spots. Accompanied by one of two orchestras arranged and conducted by Michel Legrand on most of the selections, Sandoval displays his warm tone and infuses songs such as "Little Sunflower," "Once Upon a Summertime" and "To Diz with Love" with lots of feeling; his duet with Legrand on Dizzy Gillespie's "Con Alma" is touching. The ten-minute "Dahomey Dance" (which also has solos from tenor saxophonist Ernie Watts and trombonist Bill Watrous) and a hyper "Giant Steps" are among the many highlights of this recommended disc. —*Scott Yanow*

Danzon (Dance On) / Oct. 10, 1993–Nov. 24, 1993 / GRP ✦✦✦✦
Trumpeter Arturo Sandoval comes close on *Danzon* to cutting the Afro-Cuban masterpiece everyone's awaited since his glorious sound first surfaced. From the animated solos on "Africa," "Tres

Palabras," and "Conjunto" to the flowing, crisply articulated lines on "Groovin' High," Sandoval plays with imagination, verve and flair, displaying a more original and distinctive concept than on any of his GRP albums to date. He's joined by many top Latin musicians, plus special guest ringers like Vikki Carr, Bill Cosby, and Gloria Estefan, but there's no pandering or stylistic compromises to integrate them into the proceedings. For those who've longed for Sandoval to cut loose, here's the evidence that justifies his reputation. —*Ron Wynn*

Arturo Sandoval & the Latin Train / 1995 / GRP ✦✦✦✦✦

Mongo Santamaria

b. Apr. 7, 1922, Jesus Maria, Havana, Cuba
Percussion / Latin Jazz

Arguably the greatest Cuban percussionist of his generation, and outside of Chano Pozo, the most influential in jazz history, Mongo Santamaria's astonishing ability as a player remains ever impressive, even when's he is featured on albums far below his abilities. No one's been more dominant on congas and bongos for as long as Santamaria, who's played in bebop, hard bop, big bands, Latin jazz combos, dance bands and pop groups. He's recorded for major labels, independents and tiny Latin companies. There aren't many musicians more intense, nor as blazing fast, as Santamaria doing a conga solo.

He originally studied violin, but then switched to drums. Santamaria dropped out of school in Cuba to become a professional conguero. He was an established star in Havana prior to Castro's takeover. Santamaria left Cuba for Mexico City with his cousin Armanda Peraza in 1948. They arrived in New York City in 1950 and were billed as The Black Cuban Diamonds. Santamaria made his American debut with Perez Prado; he played with him three years, then spent seven fabulous years with Tito Puente. Their multiple percussion barrages and rhythmic assaults were historic in Latin jazz and jazz circles. Santamaria made several first-rate albums of traditional African and Afro-Cuban music in the early '50s, taking the music directly from Cuban religous practices and ceremonies.

He began playing Latin jazz with George Shearing in the early '50s; the group also included Willie Bobo on timbales, Peraza on bongos and Cal Tjader on vibes. Santamaria and Bobo later joined Tjader's group in 1958. Santamaria made several fine albums with him for three years, then played with Dizzy Gillespie and Brother Jack McDuff. He began recording for Fantasy in the late '50s. Santamaria's '60s and early '70s releases blended pop, fusion, rock, jazz and R&B with Latin arrangements and rhythms. He had a Top 10 hit with his cover of Herbie Hancock's "Watermelon Man" in 1963 and employed such jazz stars as Chick Corea and Hubert Laws in various bands. Santamaria's LPs on the Battle and Riverside labels were extremely popular and eventually led to a contract with Columbia. Santamaria issued several albums on Columbia between 1965 and 1970, several of which made the pop LP charts. His cover of The Temptations "Cloud Nine" single also made the Top 40. Santamaria made "boogaloo" recordings and crossover releases as *Soul Bag, Stone Soul, La Bamba* and *Workin' On A Groovy Thing*. He continued cutting fusion material in the early '70s for Atlantic, though his band at this time included Israel "Cachao" Lopez and Peraza. But he soon returned to more traditional Latin music. The LP *Up From The Roots* blended Afro-Cuban and conjunto.

He signed with Vaya in the early '70s and shared a Yankee Stadium bill with The Fania All Stars, as well as doing a guest stint with them. Santamaria cut a Latin jazz date live at Montreux for Pablo in the '80s with Dizzy Gillespie and Toots Thielemans. There were also sessions for Roulette, Tropical Buddah and a reunion date with The Fania All Stars. Santamaria was featured in the documentary film "Salsa" and teamed with Charlie Palmieri on a sensational late '80s session for Concord Picante, one of Palmieri's final albums. Santamaria has continued into the '90s, recording a new album of Latin music for Chesky in 1993. Several classic Santamaria sessions have been reissued on CD, and he also has current releases available. His recordings on Latin labels can be obtained from specialty stores. —*Ron Wynn*

Afro-Roots / Dec. 1958–May 1959 / Prestige ✦✦✦✦✦
Mongo Santamaria made a pair of superb Latin jazz albums for Fantasy in the late '50s. These were subsequently reissued on a two-record set on vinyl in the '70s, then repackaged again for CD. The disc contains the full albums *Yambu* and *Mongo,* each one brilliant. —*Ron Wynn*

Sabroso / May 1959 / Original Jazz Classics ✦✦✦✦
1987 reissue of a wonderful album with Willie Bobo (per) and Pete Escovedo. —*Ron Wynn*

At The Black Hawk / 1962 / Fantasy ✦✦✦✦✦
This CD, which includes the contents of two former Mongo Santamaria LPs, is a fine showcase for his Latin-jazz band of the early '60s. The first set is more jazz-oriented with plenty of solo space for the Stan Getz-inspired tenor of Jose Silva while the second date has a stronger role for a violinist and has some group vocals that show where Poncho Sanchez came from. With Santamaria and Wilie Bobo leading the four-member percussion section, such songs as "Tenderly," "All the Things You Are" and "Body and Soul" are successfully Latinized; in addition there are many group originals including three by pianist Joao Donato. —*Scott Yanow*

★ **Skins** / Jul. 9, 1962–1964 / Milestone ✦✦✦✦✦
This CD (originally *So Mongo* and *Mongo Explodes* on Riverside) includes many compositions by trumpeter Marty Sheller. Guests include Hubert Laws, Chick Corea and Jimmy Cobb. Every track is vital. —*Michael G. Nastos*

Mongo at the Village Gate / Sep. 2, 1963 / Original Jazz Classics ✦✦✦✦
This is a nonet with Pat Patrick, Bobby Capers, Marty Sheller and Chihuahua Martinez—a latin, jazz and soul combo. MC'd by Symphony Sid, it is startlingly fresh for its era. It still sounds fresh. —*Michael G. Nastos*

Mighty Mongo / 1964 / Fantasy ✦✦✦

Red Hot / 1979 / Columbia ✦✦✦

Summertime / Jul. 19, 1980 / Original Jazz Classics ✦✦

Soy Yo / Apr. 1987 / Concord Jazz ✦✦✦✦✦
Outstanding sessions by Mongo's nine-piece band. —*Ron Wynn*

Soca Me Nice / May 1988 / Concord Jazz ✦✦✦✦

Ole Ola / May 1989 / Concord Jazz ✦✦✦✦

Live at Jazz Alley / Mar. 1990 / Concord Jazz ✦✦✦✦✦

Mambo Mongo / Mar. 30, 1992–Mar. 31, 1992 / Chesky Gold ✦✦✦

Mongo Returns / Jun. 28, 1995–Jun. 29, 1995 / Milestone ✦✦✦✦

Our Man in Havana / Fantasy ✦✦✦
Our man, of course, is Mongo (or was, in early 1960). And what a lineup this one boasts, including the great tres player Nino Rivera (wonderful solos on "Miss Patti Cha Cha") and a couple of the finest lucumi-oriented singers ever, Mercedita Valdes and Carlos Embales, plus a raft of other fine players (great flutist) identified irritatingly only by first names. —*John Storm Roberts, Original Music*

Saheb Sarbib

b. 1944
Bass / Avant-Garde

Raised in Europe, bassist Saheb Sarbib came to New York around 1977–78, and although he has received little publicity since, he has recorded several notable records as a leader both with a big band and a quartet; Sarbib's albums have come out on the Cadence and Soul Mote labels. Although a fine bassist, Sarbib's main significance thus far has been as an underrated but important avant-garde bandleader. —*Scott Yanow*

● **UfO! Live on Tour** / Mar. 1, 1979–Mar. 21, 1979 / Cadence ✦✦✦✦✦

Live at the Public Theater / Oct. 17, 1980 / Cadence ✦✦✦✦

Aisha / Jul. 1981–Aug. 1981 / Cadence ✦✦✦✦✦

Seasons / Nov. 5, 1981 / Soul Note ✦✦✦✦
Although Saheb Sarbib switches between bass and piano and contributed all but one of the eight selections heard on this disc (every piece but Ornette Coleman's "Round Trip"), this live set is most notable for the saxophone solos of Mel Ellison (on alto, soprano and tenor) and altoist Mark Whitecage. With the support of drummer Paul Motian, Sarbib lays down a solid foundation for the adventurous horns. The music is quite coherent but often free, making for a stimulating listen. —*Scott Yanow*

Jancin' at Jazzmania / 1982 / Jazzmania ✦✦✦✦

It Couldn't Happen without You / Jan. 1984–Feb. 1984 / Soul Note ✦✦✦✦

Gray Sargent

Guitar / Swing
Guitarist Gray Sargent, based in New England, has worked with

Illinois Jacquet, Ruby Braff and George Wein's Newport All-Stars but gained national recognition for his recordings with Dave McKenna and Scott Hamilton. A talented swing/bop player, Sargent's 1993 Concord release *Shades of Gray* was his debut as a leader. —*Scott Yanow*

● **Shades of Gray** / Feb. 1993 / Concord Jazz ✦✦✦✦✦
Throughout this enjoyable set, guitarist Gray Sargent is the epitome of cool, unhurried and relaxed no matter what the tempo. Sargent is accompanied by bassist Marshall Wood and drummer Ray Mosca, and on half of the set, the great pianist Dave McKenna. The music falls between swing and bop, sounding both spontaneous and fully under control. Sargent, who has a very appealing sound, uplifts each of the standards, and some of them (particularly the ones with McKenna) swing quite hard. —*Scott Yanow*

Lalo Schifrin

b. Jun. 21, 1932, Buenos Aires, Argentina
Piano, composer/Bop, Film Music
Lalo Schifrin has spent much of his career outside of jazz but he has made his contributions to creative music. He studied at the Paris Conservatoire and was equally versed in classical band in Argentina. In 1958, he moved to New York and gained fame for playing with Dizzy Gillespie's Quintet (1960-62); Dizzy recorded his lengthy works "Billespiana" and "the new Continent." After 1962, Schifrin mostly worked as a composer and arranger for films although his 1965 Jazz Mass received good notices and he recorded a quintet date for Palo Alto in 1982. In the early '90s his Jazz Meets the Symphony Series featured tributes to many of his jazz idols, emphasizing lengthy medleys. Schifrin on an occasional basis returns to jazz to demonstrate how strong a pianist he remains. —Scott Yanow

Ins and Outs 1982 / Mar. 29-30, 1982 / Palo Alto ✦✦✦✦

● **Jazz Meets the Symphony** / Nov. 1992 / Atlantic ✦✦✦✦✦

More Jazz Meets the Symphony /Dec. 1993 / Atlantic ✦✦✦✦✦

Alex Schlippenbach

b. Apr. 7, 1938, Berlin, Germany
Piano, Leader / Avant-Garde
One of Europe's premier free jazz bandleaders and pianist, Alexander von Schlippenbach's music mixes free and contemporary classical elements, with his slashing solos often the link between the two in his compositions. Schlippenbach formed The Globe Unity Orchestra in 1966 to perform the piece "Globe Unity," which had been commissioned by the Berliner Jazztage. He remained involved with the orchestra into the '80s, with the exception of one period from 1971 to 1972. Schlippenbach began taking lessons at eight and studied at the Staatliche Hochschule for Musik in Cologne with composers Bernd Alois Zimmermann and Rudolf Petzold. He played with Gunther Hampel in 1963 and was in Manfred Schoof's quintet from 1964 to 1967. Schlippenbach began heading various bands after 1967, among the m a 1970 trio with Evan Parker and Paul Lovens, and a duo with drummer/vocalist Sven-Ake Johansson, which they co-formed in 1976. Schlippenbach has also given many solos performances. He's recorded for the FMP, Japo, Saba and Po Torch labels, both as a leader and with The Globe Unity Orchestra. These CDs can be obtained through diligent searches and mail order. —*Ron Wynn*

★ **Globe Unity** / 1966 / Saba ✦✦✦✦✦

Anticlockwise / Jul. 1984 / FMP ✦✦✦

Maria Schneider

b. Nov. 27, 1960, Windom, MN
Piano, Composer, Arranger, Leader / Avant-Garde, Post-Bop
In the mid-'90s, Maria Schneider is widely thought of as a potentially great arranger who is following in the footsteps of Gil Evans (her main inspiration), George Russell and Bob Brookmeyer. After extensive musical study, Schneider moved to New York in 1985 and from 1985-88 was an assistant to Gil Evans. She has since conducted her music with a variety of European radio orchestras, written for the Mel Lewis big band and received many commissions. Schneider's highly original music often falls between avant-garde jazz and modern classical. —*Scott Yanow*

● **Evanescence** / Sep. 1992 / Enja ✦✦✦✦✦
Maria Schneider's debut as a leader is quite impressive. Her com-

plex arrangements of her nine originals are most influenced by Gil Evans and Bob Brookmeyer although her own musical personality shines through. There are strong solos from tenors Rick Margitza and Rich Perry, trumpeter Tim Hagan, altoist Tim Ries and particularly pianist Kenny Werner, but it is the moody ensembles that most stick in one's mind. Schneider's arrangements are often dense, a bit esoteric and thoughtprovoking; this music may need several listens for one to grasp all that is going on. —*Scott Yanow*

David Schnitter

b. Mar. 19, 1948, Newark, NJ
Tenor Saxophone / Hard Bop
If someone were to suggest an example of a textbook hard bop player, they wouldn't go far wrong naming Dave Schnitter. Here's one saxophonist who's most certainly not an eclectic; the fierce, driving, big-toned Schnitter sound's definitely in the hard bop camp. He studied clarinet as a child, then switched to tenor sax at 15. Schnitter worked in rock bands and played at weddings before forming his own group in the early '70s. He worked with Ted Dunbar in 1973, then played with Art Blakey's Jazz Messengers from 1974 to 1979. Schnitter worked with Freddie Hubbard from 1979 to 1981, recording in '80 and '81. Schnitter played with Frank Foster, Charles Earland, Groove Holmes and Johnny Lytle in the '80s. He recorded with Sonny Stitt and Blakey in the '70s, and did several sessions for Muse in the late '70s as a leader. None of Schnitter's dates are currently available on CD. —*Ron Wynn and Michael G. Nastos*

Invitation / 1976 / Muse ✦✦✦✦
Recording debut from East Coast tenor saxophonist. Top-notch. —*Michael G. Nastos*

Goliath / Oct. 29, 1977 / Muse ✦✦✦
Good hard bop and mainstream material from an aggressive, fiery tenor saxophonist. Schnitter has never been a star, but he plays with passion, doesn't take forever to make his points and fuels his combo effectively. —*Ron Wynn*

Thundering / Sep. 13, 1978 / Muse ✦✦✦✦

● **Glowing** / Dec. 1981 / Muse ✦✦✦✦✦

Loren Schoenberg

b. 1949, Fair Lawn, NJ
Tenor Sax / Swing
Loren Schoenberg took piano lessons from the age of four, and early on he became a jazz historian, working at the New York Jazz Museum. In 1974 he began playing tenor and within two years was playing professionally. Schoenberg worked with a variety of swing greats (including Benny Goodman) and started leading a regular big band in 1980. Since then the increasingly distinctive soloist (and prolific liner note writer) has recorded a series of excellent swing-oriented records for Aviva and Music Masters, both with his big band and with a combo. —*Scott Yanow*

That's the Way It Goes / Jul. 19, 1984-Jul. 20, 1984 / Aviva ✦✦✦

Time Waits for No One / 1987 / Music Masters ✦✦✦✦

Solid Ground / Aug. 8, 1988-Aug. 9, 1988 / Music Masters ✦✦✦✦

Just A-Settin' and A-Rockin' / 1990 / Music Masters ✦✦✦✦✦

S'posin' / Jun. 21, 1990-Jun. 22, 1990 / Music Masters ✦✦✦✦✦

● **Manhattan Work Song** / Apr. 21, 1992-Apr. 22, 1992 / Jazz Heritage ✦✦✦✦✦
Loren Schoenberg's Jazz Orchestra (which has been around for over a decade) is a top-notch modern swing band with a fresh repertoire, mostly new arrangements and a lot of colorful soloists who are able to make the most of their short spots. This CD, their fifth recording, is one of their most rewarding. Such arrangers as Schoenberg, Mark Lopeman, James Chirillo, John Carisi (his last work, a new version of his advanced "Springville"), Bill Finegan, Nat Pierce and Benny Carter contributed charts. Four lesser-known Ellington pieces are among the highpoints while solo-wise Schoenberg's full-toned tenor often takes honors although there are also features for baritonist Danny Bank and Ken Peplowski. It would be nice to hear the musicians get more opportunities to stretch out beyond the usual three- to five-minute time limit, but this is a satifying effort. —*Scott Yanow*

Gunther Schuller

b. Nov. 11, 1925, Jackson Heights, NY

French Horn, Arranger, Composer / Ragtime, Third Stream

Gunther Schuller has made major inroads in jazz and classical music as a theorist, author and performer. The son of a former New York Philharmonic violinist, Schuller helped popularize the term "Third Stream," a hybrid of symphonic and improvisational strains.

He wrote several compositions in this format, organized concerts and performances of Third Stream material and was among the founders of the Lenox School of Jazz in Massachusetts. He was president of the New England Conservatory for over a decade, wrote for such magazines as *Jazz Review* and did comprehensive research on early jazz, the works of Rollins and Monk and Third Stream among other things. Schuller played with the American Ballet Theatre and Cincinnati Symphony Orchestra in the early and mid-'40s, then with The Metropolitan Opera from 1945 to 1959. He was lecturing at Brandeis when he first used the term "Third Stream." Schuller composed such works as "Transformation," "Concertino" and "Abstraction" for jazz ensemble, quartet and orchestra respectively, and later wrote a piece for 13 instruments, which Ornette Coleman, Eric Dolphy and Bill Evans recorded.

Schuller played French horn on the Miles Davis' Birth of the Cool sessions in 1949 and 1950. Schuller recorded on Columbia and Verve in the '50s. He and John Lewis formed a close bond, and The Modern Jazz Quartet performed and recorded several Schuller pieces in the late '50s and early '60s, even doing an album titled *Third Stream Music.* His ballet "Variants" was choreographed in 1961 by George Balanchine, and he participated in the Montreux festivals in 1959 and 1961 and presented the first jazz concert held at Tanglewood in 1963. Schuller, Lewis and Harold Farberman led Orchestra U.S.A. from 1962 to 1965, and Lewis assisted in establishing the Lennox School. Schuller was an instructor there and in the mid '60s toured Eastern Europe lecturing for the State Department. While at the New England Conservatory, Schuller prepared editions, did transcriptions and gave performances of works by Scott Joplin, Jelly Roll Morton, Paul Whiteman and Duke Ellington.

As a performer, he formed The New England Conservatory's Ragtime Ensemble, which had a hit album; *Scott Joplin: The Red Back Book*, made it to 65 on the pop charts in '73, and the arrangements were later incorporated into the film *The Sting.* Schuller also began The New England Conservatory Jazz Repertory Orchestra, which played vintage early jazz pieces. He started the firms Margun Music and Gunmar Music in the '70s to publish works by Charles Mingus, George Russell, Johnny Carisi, Ran Blake and Jimmy Giuffre and founded the GM record label in 1980. GM releases have included previously unissued Eric Dolphy recordings and big band sessions of Schuller compositions from the '40s to the '60s that had never been recorded. Schuller's seminal books, particularly *Early Jazz* and *The Swing Era* remain in print. *—Ron Wynn*

★ **Jazz Abstractions** / Dec. 19, 1960–Dec. 20, 1960 / Atlantic ✦✦✦✦✦

★ **Jumpin' in the Future** / Mar. 26, 1988–May 1, 1988 / GM ✦✦✦✦✦
A historic big band session led by composer/conductor Gunther Schuller. The ensemble performed Schuller compositions that had never been recorded, covering the years 1947–1966. The band included such musicians as Howard Johnson. *—Ron Wynn*

Art of the Rag / Jan. 3, 1989–Jan. 4, 1989 / GM ✦✦✦✦

Diane Schuur

b. 1953, Seattle, WA

Piano, Vocals / Pop, Standards

Diane Schuur, who has thus far been on the periphery of jazz, has the potential to be an important jazz singer although her screeching in the upper register and her desire to include an over-abundance of pop material in her repertoire has resulted in her significance being much less than originally expected. Blinded at birth due to a hospital accident, Schuur (who would later be nicknamed "Deedles") imitated singers as a child. She had her first gig at a Holiday Inn when just ten and originally sang country music. The turning point in her career occurred when she sang "Amazing Grace" at the 1979 Monterey Jazz Festival, greatly impressing Stan

Getz. After Getz featured her singing at a televised concert from the White House in 1982, Schuur was signed to GRP and began recording regularly. Although her 1987 collaboration with the Count Basie Orchestra was a highpoint, Diane Schuur's recordings tend to be a mixed success from the jazz standpoint; hopefully her best work is still in the future. *—Scott Yanow*

Deedles / 1984 / GRP ✦✦✦

Schuur Thing / 1985 / GRP ✦✦✦

Timeless / 1986 / GRP ✦✦✦✦

● **And the Count Basie Orchestra** / 1987 / GRP ✦✦✦✦✦

Talkin' 'bout You / 1988 / GRP ✦✦✦

Pure Schuur / 1991 / GRP ✦✦✦

In Tribute / 1992 / GRP ✦✦✦✦

Love Songs / 1993 / GRP ✦✦✦✦✦
The jazz content on this CD from singer Diane Schuur is rather slight, but this is actually one of her finest recordings. Schuur (who has a lovely voice) sings straightforward versions of ten veteran ballads while accompanied by one of two string orchestras. Tom Scott on reeds and trumpeter Jack Sheldon have short spots, but this is very much Schuur's show. She really excels in the restrained setting, making this a superior middle-of-the-road pop recording. *—Scott Yanow*

Heart to Heart / 1994 / GRP ✦✦
B.B. King's recent recordings have been thoroughly professional, occasionally engaging albums that showcase his still striking vocal skills and add infrequent examples of his fabulous guitar skills. This one includes a partner in the stylish pop-jazz singer Dianne Schuur (she actually gets first billing, but this is really King's LP). King's guitar solos are expertly articulated but restrained, while Schuur is also careful not to oversing or allow any excesses to ruin their chemistry. Indeed, they seem so attuned and in sync that there is little tension or edge to the performances. They're well done and enjoyable, but this CD sounds more like a recital between old friends than a genuine exchange or dialogue. *—Ron Wynn*

Bob Scobey

b. Dec. 9, 1916, Tucumcari, NM, **d.** Jun. 12, 1963, Montreal, Canada

Trumpet, Leader / Dixieland

Throughout his prime years, Bob Scobey was one of the more popular trumpeters in Dixieland. After many low-profile jobs in dance bands in the 1930s, in 1938 Scobey met trumpeter Lu Watters. As a member of Watter's Yerba Buena Jazz Band in San Francisco during 1940–49 (with much of 1942-46 spent in the military), Scobey participated in one of the most influential bands of the Dixieland revival movement. In 1949 he left to form his own Frisco Jazz Band, recording frequently (most notably for Good Time Jazz) and often featuring Clancy Hayes or appearing with Lizzie Miles. In 1959 Scobey opened his Club Bourbon Street in Chicago, but four years later he died at the age of 46 from cancer. Many of Bob Scobey's Good Time Jazz dates have been reissued on CD, and they still contain stirring and joyful music. *— Scott Yanow*

● **Scobey Story** / Apr. 29, 1950–Nov. 6, 1951 / Good Time Jazz ✦✦✦✦✦
This rather brief CD (just 35 minutes), a straight reissue of an LP) gives listeners a good example of the playing of trumpeter Bob Scobey. Taken from his earliest period as a bandleader, these Dixieland performances also feature trombonist Jack Buck, either Darnell Howard, Albert Nicholas or George Probert on clarinet, pianists Burt Bales or Wally Rose and banjoist Clancy Hayes who also takes a few vocals. Excellent goodtime music. *— Scott Yanow*

● **The Scobey Story, Vol. 2** / Apr. 12, 1952–Nov. 10, 1953 / Good Time Jazz ✦✦✦✦
The second of two CDs (both clock in around 35 minutes and are reissues of original LPs) continues the documentation of trumpeter Bob Scobey's earliest performances as a bandleader. With trombonist Jack Buck, clarinetist George Propert, pianist Wally Rose, bassist Dick Lammi and drummer Fred Higuera, Scobey had a hot and easily enjoyable band. In Clancy Hayes, the trumpeter was fortunate to have a major attraction who played banjo, set the standard for singing in this format and contributed a minor hit "Huggin' & A-Chalkin'" which is heard here in its orig-

inal version. Other highpoints include "Big Butter and Egg Man," "Silver Dollar," "Ace in the Hole" and "Hindustan." —*Scott Yanow*

Vocals by Clancy Hayes / Jan. 17, 1955–Jan. 21, 1955 / Good Time Jazz ✦✦✦✦

Scobey and Clancy / Jul. 6, 1955–Jul. 7, 1955 / Good Time Jazz ✦✦✦✦✦

Direct from San Francisco / Mar. 13, 1956–Mar. 15, 1956 / Good Time Jazz ✦✦✦✦

Swingin' on the Golden Gate / Jan. 21, 1957–Jan. 22, 1957 / RCA ✦✦✦✦

College "Classics" / Dec. 12, 1957–Dec. 14, 1967 / RCA ✦✦✦

Raid the Juke Box / Jan. 19, 1958–Jan. 20, 1958 / Good Time Jazz ✦✦✦

John Scofield

b. Dec. 26, 1951, Dayton, OH
Guitar, Leader / Post-Bop
One of the "big three" of current jazz guitarists (along with Pat Metheny and Bill Frisell), Scofield's influence has been growing in recent years. Possessor of a very distinctive rock-oriented sound that is often a bit distorted, Scofield is a masterful jazz improviser whose music generally falls somewhere between post bop, fusion and soul jazz. He started on guitar while at high school in Connecticut, and from 1970–73 Scofield studied at Berklee and played in the Boston area. After recording with Gerry Mulligan and Chet Baker at Carnegie Hall, Scofield was a member of the Billy Cobham-George Duke band for two years. In 1977 he recorded with Charles Mingus and later joined the Gary Burton quartet and Dave Liebman's quintet. His own early sessions as a leader were funk-oriented. During 1982–85 Scofield toured the world and recorded with Miles Davis. Since that time he has led his own groups, played with Bass Desires and recorded frequently as a leader for Gramavision and Blue Note, using such major players as Charlie Haden, Jack DeJohnette, Joe Lovano and Eddie Harris. —*Scott Yanow*

East Meets West / Aug. 12, 1977 / Blackhawk ✦✦✦

John Scofield Live / Nov. 4, 1977 / Enja ✦✦✦✦

Rough House / Nov. 27, 1978 / Enja ✦✦✦

Who's Who? / 1979 / Novus ✦✦

Bar Talk / Aug. 1980 / Novus ✦✦✦

Shinola / Dec. 12, 1981–Dec. 13, 1981 / Enja ✦✦✦✦
Trio set reissued in 1991. Dense, prickly and lots of space for guitar work. —*Ron Wynn*

Out Like a Light / Dec. 14, 1981 / Enja ✦✦✦✦
Fine trio date from '81, with guitarist John Scofield stretching out in multiple directions and showing his facility with the swing style, mainstream and jazz-rock genres. Besides his fluid, inventive solos, Scofield works well with bassist Steve Swallow, who approaches his instrument like a second guitar and drummer Adam Nussbaum. —*Ron Wynn*

Electric Outlet / Apr. 1984–May 1984 / Gramavision ✦✦✦

Still Warm / Jun. 1986 / Gramavision ✦✦✦

Blue Matter / Sep. 1986 / Gramavision ✦✦✦✦

Pick Hits Live / Oct. 7, 1987 / Gramavision ✦✦✦✦

Loud Jazz / Dec. 1987 / Gramavision ✦✦✦

Flat Out / Dec. 1988 / Gramavision ✦✦✦✦

Time on My Hands / Nov. 19, 1989–Nov. 21, 1989 / Blue Note ✦✦✦✦✦

Meant to Be / Dec. 1990 / Blue Note ✦✦✦✦

Grace under Pressure / Dec. 1991 / Blue Note ✦✦✦✦✦
Guitarist John Scofield leads a top-notch group on this '91 session. It's a pianoless band, with Scofield's nimble guitar lines contrasted by those of second guitarist Bill Frisell. They team with trombonist Jim Pugh, bassist Charlie Haden and drummer Joey Baron, plus Randy Brecker on fluegelhorn and John Clark on French horn. —*Ron Wynn*

What We Do / May 1992 / Blue Note ✦✦✦✦✦

★ **Hand Jive** / Oct. 1993 / Blue Note ✦✦✦✦✦
Guitarist John Scofield and tenor saxophonist Eddie Harris make a very complementary team on this upbeat set of funky jazz for both have immediately identifiable sounds and adventurous spirits. Along with a fine rhythm section that includes Larry Goldings

on piano and organ, Scofield and Harris interact joyfully on ten of the guitarist's originals. —*Scott Yanow*

● **Groove Elation** / 1995 / Blue Note ✦✦✦✦✦

Shirley Scott

b. Mar. 14, 1934, Philadelphia, PA
Organ / Hard Bop, Soul Jazz
Shirley Scott surprised many people in 1992 when she appeared on Bill Cosby's reprise of The Groucho Marx game and personality show "You Bet Your Life." Not that he'd picked her to be his music director, but that she was playing piano. Her reputation was cemented during the '60s on several superb, soulful organ/soul jazz dates where she demonstrated an aggressive, highly rhythmic attack blending intricate bebop harmonies with bluesy melodies and a gospel influence, punctuating everything with great use of the bass pedals. But Scott demonstrated an equal flair and facility on piano, many days incorporating snatches of anthemic jazz compositions while noodling in the background. The show was a bore, but it was great to see Scott back in the spotlight.

She began playing piano as a child, then trumpet in high school. Scott was working a club date in the mid-'50s in Philadelphia when the owner rented her a Hammond B-3. She learned quickly and was soon leading both popular and artistically superior trios featuring either Eddie "Lockjaw" Davis or then husband Stanley Turrentine on tenor sax. The Scott/Turrentine union lasted until the early '70s, and their musical collaborations in the '60s were among the finest in the field. Scott continued recording in the '70s, working with Harold Vick and Jimmy Forrest and then in the early '80s Dexter Gordon. She also made a lot of appearances on television in New York and Philadelphia. Scott recorded prolifically for Prestige in the '50s and '60s, then for Impulse! in the mid-'60s and Atlantic in the late '60s. She moved to Chess/Cadet in the early '70s and also did sessions for Strata-East. In recent years Scott has recorded for Muse and Candid. Her later material wasn't as consistent as her best work for Prestige and Impulse. —*Ron Wynn and Bob Porter*

Great Scott! / May 27, 1958 / Prestige ✦✦✦

Workin' / May 27, 1958–Mar. 24, 1960 / Prestige ✦✦✦
One of several trio and/or combo works that organist Shirley Scott recorded for Prestige in the late '50s and early '60s. Her swirling, driving lines, intense bass pedal support, and bluesy fervor were ideal for the soul jazz format, and this is a typical example. —*Ron Wynn*

Soul Sisters / Jun. 23, 1960 / Prestige ✦✦✦

Like Cozy / Sep. 27, 1960 / Moodsville ✦✦

Satin Doll / Mar. 7, 1961 / Prestige ✦✦✦

Hip Soul / Jun. 2, 1961 / Prestige ✦✦✦✦✦

Blue Seven / Aug. 22, 1961 / Prestige ✦✦✦
A quintet with Roy Brooks (d), Oliver Nelson (ts) and Joe Newman (tpt) plays one Scott original, the title song by Sonny Rollins and an excellent "Wagon Wheels." —*Michael G. Nastos*

Hip Twist / Nov. 17, 1961 / Prestige ✦✦✦

Happy Talk / Dec. 5, 1962 / Prestige ✦✦✦

★ **Sweet Soul** / Dec. 5, 1962 / Prestige ✦✦✦✦✦
Reissued from the "Happy Talk" session this features Earl May on bass and Roy Brooks on drums. It includes a nice "Jitterbug Waltz." All are standards. —*Michael G. Nastos*

Soul Is Willing / Jan. 10, 1963 / Prestige ✦✦✦✦✦
This is a good album that shows the husband and wife team of Shirley Scott and Stanley Turrentine in excellent form. This is a fine example of the small organ combo playing soul jazz. now part of the Prestige two-fer called *Soul Shoutin'*. —*Michael Erlewine*

★ **Soul Shoutin'** / Jan. 10, 1963+Oct. 15, 1963 / Prestige ✦✦✦✦✦
Organist Shirley Scott and her then-husband tenor great Stanley Turrentine always made potent music together. This CD, which combines together the former Prestige LPs *The Soul Is Willing* and *Soul Shoutin'*, finds "Mr. T." at his early peak, playing some intense yet always soulful solos on such pieces as Sy Oliver's "Yes Indeed," "Secret Love" and his memorable originals "The Soul Is Willing" and "Deep Down Soul." Scott, who found her own niche within the dominant Jimmy Smith style, swings hard throughout the set, and (together with drummer Crassella Oliphant and either Major Holley or Earl May on bass) the lead voices play with such

consistent enthusiasm that one would think these were club performances. Highly recommended. —*Scott Yanow*

★ **Great Scott! / For Members Only** / Aug. 22, 1963–May 20, 1964 / MCA ✦✦✦✦✦
Compilation blends two prime Scott albums, some cuts arranged and conducted by Oliver Nelson. —*Ron Wynn*

Blue Flames / Mar. 31, 1964 / Original Jazz Classics ✦✦✦✦✦
Recorded in Englewood Cliffs, N.J. with Turrentine and Stanley. This is exactly the kind of straight-ahead funky music you would expect from the Scott/Turrentine combination. No disappointments. Now available on CD. —*Michael Erlewine*

The Great Live Sessions / Sep. 23, 1964 / ABC/Impulse! ✦✦✦✦✦
Recorded live at the Front Room in Newark, N.J., the album includes ten tracks with a quartet including Stanley Turrentine (ts). On a rare night for music, the band delivered on all counts. You can't go wrong here. —*Michael G. Nastos*

Queen of the Organ / Sep. 23, 1964 / Impulse! ✦✦✦✦
A steamy, hot mid-'60s soul jazz session with soulful, bluesy organist Shirley Scott providing some booming, funky solos. This was one of several combo works she cut, usually with saxophonist Stanley Turrentine, who was her husband at the time. Anything Scott recorded from this period is worth hearing. —*Ron Wynn*

Roll 'em / Apr. 15, 1966–Apr. 19, 1966 / Impulse! ✦✦✦

Girl Talk / 1967 / Impulse! ✦✦✦
Trio. Album includes one Scott original. The rest, including the classic title track, are standards. A bit sweet. —*Michael G. Nastos*

Shirley Scott and the Soul Saxes / Jul. 9, 1969 / Atlantic ✦✦✦
Steamy workout with Scott, Hank Crawford (as), King Curtis (ts), and David Neuman (ts). —*Ron Wynn*

One for Me / Nov. 1974 / Strata East ✦✦✦✦✦
The record is a beauty with Harold Vick, perhaps the most suited and sensitive horn player Ms. Scott has worked with ... (a) thoroughly enjoyable album of bop stream music, and while it is nothing overly heavy or deep, it's thoughtfully and sensitively produced and of its kind an almost perfect album. —*Bob Rusch, Cadence*

Oasis / Aug. 28, 1989 / Muse ✦✦✦✦✦
A sophisticated bop outing. Some nice mid-sized band music here. —*Michael Erlewine*

Blues Everywhere / Nov. 23, 1991 / Candid ✦✦✦✦

Skylark / 1995 / Candid ✦✦✦✦

Tom Scott

b. May 19, 1948, Los Angeles, CA
Reeds, Alto Saxophone, Tenor Saxophone / Instrumental Pop, Crossover
Since he was a teenager Tom Scott has been consistent, a talented multireedist with little or no interest in playing creative jazz. His mother was a pianist and father a composer. Scott early on became a studio musician and arranger. Able to play most reeds with little difficulty, Scott performed with the Don Ellis and Oliver Nelson bands, and his L.A. Express became one of the most successful pop-jazz groups of the 1970s. Associations with Joni Mitchell, Carole King and George Harrison were just a few of his successful assignments in the pop world, and although his 1992 GRP release *Born Again* was surprisingly inventive, it was a one-time departure from crossover. —*Scott Yanow*

Tom Scott & LA Express / Aug. 19, 197373 09 / Ode ✦✦✦✦

Great Scott / 1973 / A&M ✦✦✦✦✦

Tom Cat / 1974 / Ode ✦✦✦

Blow It Out / 1976 / Epic ✦✦

Apple Juice / Jan. 15, 1981–Jan. 17, 1981 / Columbia ✦✦✦

Desire / Jul. 23, 1982–Jul. 24, 1982 / Elektra ✦✦

Target / Jul. 23, 1983–Jul. 24, 1983 / Atlantic ✦✦✦

Night Creatures / Aug. 22, 1984–Oct. 17, 1984 / GRP ✦
Granted that this Tom Scott CD (as with many of his) is not really a jazz set but, even when rating this music as R&B or funk, its lack of originality is appalling. Four songs are dominated by anonymous vocalists (Phil Perry and Philip Ingram, who are among the dozen or so singers, are capable of much better), and the other tracks misuse electronic percussion. Scott mostly sticks to passionate but mundane melodies that he could play in his

sleep. Even in pop music individuality is a must, and there is really nothing to distinguish this strictly-for-the-money release. —*Scott Yanow*

One Night/One Day / 1986 / Soundwings ✦✦✦

Streamlines / Jul. 1987 / GRP ✦✦

Flashpoint / 1988 / GRP ✦✦

Them Changes / 1990 / GRP ✦✦

Keep This Love Alive / 1991 / GRP ✦✦

● **Born Again** / 1992 / GRP ✦✦✦✦✦
Longtime session and studio saxophonist Tom Scott surprised many inside and outside the jazz community in '92 when he made this non-fusion, mainstream and straight-ahead session. It showed he could still play strong, undiluted tenor sax solos and also fit in with a group that included such distinguished players as pianist Kenny Kirkland, trumpeter Randy Brecker and trombonist George Bohannon. Bassist John Patitucci and drummer Will Kennedy were the fusion stars who rounded out the date. —*Ron Wynn*

Reed My Lips / 1993 / GRP ✦✦
Saxophonist Tom Scott sticks to R&Bish pop music on his release with electronic rhythms, two throwaway vocal tracks and cliches dominating an utterly forgettable program. The presence of Grover Washington, Jr., on the title track is largely wasted, and Scott succeeds in hiding his individuality on this strictly-for-the-money release. At best, these performances can function as routine background music. —*Scott Yanow*

Tony Scott

b. Jun. 17, 1921, Morristown, NJ
Clarinet / Cool, Post-Bop, New Age
Since leaving New York in 1959, Tony Scott (a top bebop-oriented clarinetist) has been an eager world traveler who enjoys exploring the folk music of other countries. Unfortunately, his post-1959 recordings have been few, far between, difficult-to-locate and sometimes erratic, but Scott was an unheralded pioneer in both world music and new age.

Tony Scott attended Julliard during 1940–42, played at Minton's Playhouse, and then after three years in the military he became one of the few clarinetists to play bop. His cool tone (heard at its best on a 1950 Sarah Vaughan session that also includes Miles Davis) stood out from the more hard-driving playing of Buddy DeFranco. Scott worked with a wide variety of major players (including Ben Webster, Trummy Young, Earl Bostic, Charlie Ventura, Claude Thornhill, Buddy Rich and Billie Holiday), led his own record dates (among his sidemen were Dizzy Gillespie and a young Bill Evans), which ranged from bop and cool to free improvsations (all are currently difficult to locate) and ranked with DeFranco at the top of his field.

Unfortunately, the clarinet was not exactly a popular instrument in the 1950s (as opposed to during the swing era), and Tony Scott remained an obscure name outside of jazz circles. In 1959 he gave up on the U.S. and began extensive tours of the Far East. He played Eastern classical music, recorded meditation music for Verve and other than some brief visits to the U.S, has lived in Italy since the 1970s where he has sometimes experimented with electronics. —*Scott Yanow*

The Touch of Tony Scott / Jul. 2, 1956+Jul. 3, 1956 / Victor ✦✦✦✦

The Complete Tony Scott / Dec. 11, 1956–Feb. 6, 1957 / RCA Victor ✦✦✦✦✦
Best from series of mid-'50s recordings showcasing Scott in quartet, big band and combo situations. —*Ron Wynn*

The Modern Art of Jazz / 1957 / Seeco ✦✦✦✦✦
Beautiful, accomplished and distinctive solos from Scott. Very hard to find. —*Ron Wynn*

● **Golden Moments** / Aug. 1, 1959 Aug. 9, 1959 / Muse ✦✦✦✦✦
Tony Scott was one of the major jazz clarinetists of the 1950s, but his decision to become a world traveller in 1960 has resulted in him becoming rather obscure. This valuable Muse release features the clarinetist in top form on an original blues and four standards (including 12 minute versions of "Walkin'" and "Melancholy Baby") in a quartet that also includes the up-and-coming pianist Bill Evans (who had just left Miles Davis' Sextet), bassist Jimmy Garrison and drummer Pete LaRoca. The bop-oriented improvisations hold one's interest and make one wish that Scott had

stayed in New York throughout the '60s; he had much more to say. —*Scott Yanow*

I'll Remember / Aug. 1, 1959+Aug. 9, 1959 / Muse ✦✦✦✦
A second-time-around for same lineup proves equally rewarding. —*Ron Wynn*

Sung Heroes / Oct. 28, 1959–Oct. 29, 1959 / Sunnyside ✦✦✦

Music For Zen Meditation (and Other Joys) / Feb. 1964 / Verve ✦✦✦
This elegant, contemplative set of pieces was conceived during one of the jazz artist's trips to Japan when Scott had the opportunity to record with a shakuhachi flutist and a koto player. Though ears unaccustomed to oriental styles might assume it's a performance of traditional Japanese music, the album is actually a set of finely wrought improvisations merging Eastern and Western sensibilities. —*Linda Kohanov*

African Bird: Come Back! Mother Africa / 1981–1984 / Soul Note ✦✦✦
Clarinetist as a world music pacemaker. Removed from his early jazz and meditative phases, while combining aspects of both with African rhythms and Charlie Parker inflections. "African Bird Suite" is a modal stunner. —*Michael G. Nastos*

Al Sears

b. Feb. 21, 1910, Macomb, IL, d. Mar. 23, 1990, New York, NY
Tenor Saxophone / Early R&B, Swing
It is ironic that tenor saxophonist Al Sears' one hit," Castle Rock," was recorded under Johnny Hodges' name (the altoist is virtually absent on the record!), denying Sears his one chance at fame. Sears had actually had his first important job in 1928 replacing Hodges with the Chick Webb band. However, despite associations with Elmer Snowden (1931-2), Andy Kirk (1941–42), Lionel Hampton (1943–4) and with his own groups (most of 1933–41), it was not until Sears joined Duke Ellington's Orchestra in 1944 that he began to get much attention. His distinctive tone, R&Bish phrasing and abiltiy to build up exciting solos made him one of Ellington's most colorful soloists during the next five years although his period was overshadowed by both his predecessor (Ben Webster) and his successor (Paul Gonsalves). Among Sears' many recordings with Ellington are notable versions of "I Ain't Got Nothing but the Blues" and a 1945 remake of "It Don't Mean a Thing." Sears worked with Johnny Hodges' group during 1951–52, recorded a variety of R&B-oriented material in the 1950s and cut two excellent albums for Swingville in 1960 before going into semi-retirement —*Scott Yanow*

● **Swing's the Thing** / Nov. 29, 1960 / Original Jazz Classics ✦✦✦✦✦
Al Sears had the misfortune of having his one hit "Castle Rock" released under the leadership of Johnny Hodges, cheating him of his one chance at fame. A fine swing-based tenor who could stomp and honk with the best of them (although he rarely screamed), Sears had relatively few opportunities to record as a leader, and this CD (which reissues a 1960 LP) was one of his last. Sears (along with pianist Don Abney, guitarist Wally Richardson, bassist Wendell Marshall and drummer Joe Marshall) sticks to basic originals, blues and standards and is in top form on these swinging and generally accessible performances. —*Scott Yanow*

Cathy Segal-Garcia

b. May 28, 1953, Boston, MA
Vocals / Bop, Post-Bop
One of the top jazz singers based in Los Angeles in the 1990s, Cathy Segal-Garcia has a beautiful voice and is an adventurous improviser, even when interpreting a well-known standard. After singing on the East Coast from the age of 12, she moved to L.A. in 1976, recorded CDs for her CSG label and the Japanese Koyo Sounds company and has performed often in Japan and Europe. —*Scott Yanow*

Point Of View / 1985 / CSG ✦✦✦✦

● **Song Of The Heart** / Sep. 1992 / Koyo Sounds ✦✦✦✦✦

Doc Severinsen

b. Jul. 7, 1927, Arlington, OR
Trumpet / Swing, Pop
Trumpeter Doc Severinsen is a perfect example of a very talented player who cared much more about making a living than playing creative jazz. Although he had stints in the late '40s with Tommy Dorsey and Charlie Barnet (in the latter band the trumpet section also included Maynard Ferguson, Rolf Ericson and Ray Wetzel),

Severinsen joined the staff of NBC in 1949 and stuck to studio work. In 1962 he became the assistant leader of the Tonight Show Orchestra and in 1967 he succeeded Skitch Henderson. Famous for his silly wardrobe and occasional wisecracks with Johnny Carson, Severinsen was heard five nights a week by millions of people until Carson's retirement in 1992 resulted in the band being changed.

A talented high-note trumpeter whose heroes included Bunny Berigan and Harry James, Severinsen recorded a variety of commercial swing albums in the 1960s but did not get around to recording the Tonight Show band (for Amherst) until it was near the end of the Carson years. He has frequently appeared with classical and pops orchestras, occasionally led a fusion band (Xebron) and toured the U.S. in 1993 with the Tonight Show band. Still, one would have expected Doc Severinsen to have done so much more with his talent. —*Scott Yanow*

Night Journey / 1975 / Epic ✦✦

Tonight Show Band with Doc Severinsen / Aug. 5, 1986+Aug. 7, 1986 / Amherst ✦✦✦✦

The Tonight Show Band, Vol. 2 / Feb. 1987 / Amherst ✦✦✦✦

● **Once More, with Feeling!** / 1991 / Amherst ✦✦✦✦✦

Bud Shank (Clifford Everett Shank, Jr.)

b. May 27, 1926, Dayton, OH
Flute, Alto Saxophone / Cool, Hard Bop
Alto saxophonist and flutist Bud Shank was a major player in '50s West Coast circles and has continued as an active contributor into the '90s. His light, steady, yet confident and assured style has been featured on bebop, cool, big band and Latin dates, and Shank was among the earliest, most accomplished jazz flutists.

He studied clarinet, alto, tenor saxes and flute and attended the University of North Carolina as a freshman. Shank studied with Shorty Rogers on the West Coast in 1947. He began to specialize on alto in the late '40s, playing with Charlie Barnet, then added flute while with Stan Kenton in 1950 and 1951. Shank played and recorded with Howard Rumsey's Lighthouse All-Stars, Laurindo Almeida and Bob Cooper in the '50s, as well as with Kenton, Rogers, Jimmy Giuffre, Gerald Wilson and many others. Shank also recorded extensively for World Pacific as a leader in the '50s and '60s, most of the time working with a combo. He appeared at several festivals in Europe and South America in the '60s.

Shank became mainly a studio musician during the '60s, playing on such film scores and soundtracks as *Slippery When Wet, Barefoot Adventure, War Hunt, Assault On A Queen* and *The Thomas Crown Affair*. He recorded with Sergio Mendes for Capitol in 1965 and with Chet Baker on World Pacific a year later. Their album *Michelle* reached number 56 on the pop charts. Shank formed The L.A. Four along with Almeida, Ray Brown and Chuck Flores in 1974. Flores was later replaced by Shelly Manne, then by Jeff Hamilton. Starting in the mid-1980s Shank dropped the flute to concentrate exclusively on the alto. His tone has become harder, his style more adventurous, and Shank has continued to grow in importance through time. He has recorded extensively (most notably for Concord, Contemporary and Candid) and in addition to reunions with Shorty Rogers' Lighthouse All-Stars has generally led his own stimulating quartet in addition to a pianoless sextet. —*Ron Wynn and Scott Yanow*

Live at the Haig / Jan. 1956 / Bainbridge ✦✦✦✦
An '85 CD reissue of a strong Shank set done in the mid-'50s at the Haig. This was among his earliest stereo sessions and also features some superb piano solos by Claude Williamson. He was finding a comfortable middle ground between swing, cool and bop, and growing stronger and more individualistic as an alto saxophonist. —*Ron Wynn*

Bud Shank and the Sax Section / Dec. 1966 / Pacific Jazz ✦✦✦

Sunshine Express / Jan. 1976 / Concord Jazz ✦✦✦✦
A '91 reissue of a Shank quintet series and a title in the Concord label's new collector's line. Alto saxophonist Shank was hitting his stride at this point in the late '70s; he decided to begin doing solo sessions after years of session work and was also returning to alto, virtually discarding the flute. This was the first among several dates he cut from '76 to '80; this one included Mike Wofford, Bobby Shew, Larry Bunker and Fred Atwood. —*Ron Wynn*

Heritage / Dec. 19, 1978 / Concord Jazz ✦✦✦✦
Some torrid, energetic alto sax solos by Bud Shank in the midst
of a busy late-'70s stretch that saw him re-establish himself on alto
after many years of playing mostly flute. He was working with
what was his regular band at the time, with pianist Billy Mays
providing both an occasional composition and some strong support as the second soloist. —*Ron Wynn*

Crystal Comments / Oct. 1979 / Concord Jazz ✦✦✦

Explorations 1980 / 1980 / Concord Jazz ✦✦✦

This Bud's for You / Nov. 14, 1984 / Muse ✦✦✦✦✦
Arguably his best quartet date ever and certainly among the top
three. Alto saxophonist Bud Shank took a page from Art Pepper's
book and decided to work with a set rhythm section. Bassist Ron
Carter, pianist Kenny Barron and drummer Al Foster kicked into
gear on the opening song and never faltered. Shank soared, playing more aggressively and showing more conviction in his solos
than at any time since the '50s. —*Ron Wynn*

California Concert / May 19, 1985 / Contemporary ✦✦✦✦

★ **That Old Feeling** / Feb. 17, 1986+Feb. 18, 1986 / Contemporary
✦✦✦✦✦
After many years of studio work and a period co-leading The L.A.
Four, Bud Shank permanently put away his flute and started concentrating exclusively on alto. This modern bop set with pianist
George Cables, bassist John Heard and drummer Tootie Heath
finds Shank at his most passionate and creative, stretching out on
jazz standards and an eccentric blues. He shows listeners just how
much he has grown as an improviser since gaining his initial
fame in the 1950s. —*Scott Yanow*

At Jazz Alley / Oct. 16, 1986–Oct. 18, 1986 / Contemporary ✦✦✦✦

Serious Swingers / Dec. 2, 1986–Dec. 4, 1986 / Contemporary
✦✦✦✦✦

Tomorrow's Rainbow / Sep. 2, 1988–Sep. 3, 1988 /
Contemporary ✦✦✦✦

Plays Tales of the Pilot: The Music of David Peck / Dec. 2,
1989–Dec. 3, 1989 / Capri ✦✦✦

Drifting Timelessly / 1990 / Capri ✦✦✦

● **The Doctor Is In** / Sep. 9, 1991–Sep. 10, 1991 / Candid ✦✦✦✦✦
Good '91 session featuring the steady cool and bop-tinged alto sax
solos of Bud Shank in a combo setting. He's backed by pianist
Mike Wofford, bassist Bob Magnusson and drummer Sherman
Ferguson. They tackle familiar standards and a few originals and
make satisfying, if unchallenging, music. —*Ron Wynn*

I Told You So / Jun. 26, 1992–Jun. 27, 1992 / Candid ✦✦✦✦

Avery Sharpe

Bass / Post-Bop
A strong bassist with a compelling tone and fine technique, Avery
Sharpe has been featured prominently with McCoy Tyner for several years. Sharpe began recording with Tyner in the mid-'80s and
has remained with him through the '90s. He can be heard on several Tyner CDs that are currently available. —*Ron Wynn*

● **Unspoken Words** / Jan. 1988 / Sunnyside ✦✦✦✦

Extended Family / Feb. 1993 / JKNM ✦✦✦

Sonny Sharrock (Warren Harding Sharrock)

b. Aug. 27, 1940, Ossining, NY, **d.** May 25, 1994
Guitar / Avant-Garde, Free Jazz
Along with Derek Bailey (whose free-form explorations went in a
different direction), Sonny Sharrock was the top avant-garde guitarist. His sonic explorations mixed together Jimi Hendrix with
Pharoah Sanders and were often quite ferocious. From 1953–60
Sharrock was a singer in a doo wop group then in 1960 he started playing guitar. He studied composition at Berklee in 1961
(although he was thrown out of the guitar class!). Sharrock
worked with Byard Lancaster (1966), was with Pharoah Sanders
during 1967–68, participated (uncredited) on Miles Davis' *Jack
Johnson* album and had his most high-profile job as a member of
Herbie Mann's popular group where his adventurous guitar con-
trasted with Mann's flute and David Newman's soulful tenor.
   A long period of obscurity occurred after leaving Mann, but by
the 1980s Sharrock was being rediscovered, recording with
Material in 1982 and Last Exit (a quartet with saxophonist Peter
Brotzmann) later in the decade. 1991's *Ask the Ages* teamed
Sharrock with Sanders, bassist Charnett Moffett and Elvin Jones.

But just when he seemed on the brink of a potential commercial
breakthrough, Sonny Sharrock died unexpectedly at the age of 53.
—*Scott Yanow*

Guitar / 1986 / Enemy ✦✦✦✦✦

Last Exit / 1986 / Enemy ✦✦✦✦

Seize the Rainbow / May 1987 / Enemy ✦✦✦✦✦
Some powerful and at times chaotic playing from a plugged-in
and turned-on lineup headed by adventurous guitarist Sonny
Sharrock. His splintering, rambunctious licks are matched by
bassists Melvin Gibbs and Bill Laswell and drummers Abe Speller
and Pheeroan akLaff. —*Ron Wynn*

Live in New York / Aug. 1989 / Enemy ✦✦✦✦

Faith Moves / 1989 / CMP ✦✦✦

Highlife / Oct. 1990 / Enemy ✦✦✦

★ **Ask the Ages** / 1991 / Axiom ✦✦✦✦✦
Sonny Sharrock was often thought of as the "Pharoah Sanders of
the guitar," so it was quite fitting that one of his finest recordings
is this matchup with Sanders, bassist Charnett Moffett and drummer Elvin Jones. This fiery outing was also very good for Sanders
who, after many years of recording more lyrical material in the
John Coltrane vein, returned to his prime early form with ferocious solos that match the intensity of Sharrock's. —*Scott Yanow*

Charlie Shavers

b. Aug. 3, 1917, New York, NY, **d.** Jul. 8, 1971, New York, NY
Trumpet / Swing
Charlie Shavers was one of the great trumpeters to emerge during the swing era, a virtuoso with an open-minded and extroverted style along with a strong sense of humor. He originally played
piano and banjo before switching to trumpet, and he developed
very quickly. In 1935 he was with Tiny Bradshaw's band, and two
years later he joined Lucky Millinder's big band. Soon afterward
he became a key member of John Kirby's Sextet where he showed
his versatility by mostly playing crisp solos while muted. Shavers
was in demand for recording sessions and participated on notable
dates with New Orleans pioneers Johnny Dodds, Jimmy Noone
and Sidney Bechet. He also had many opportunities to write
arrangements for Kirby and had a major hit with his composition
"Undecided."
   After leaving Kirby in 1944, Charlie Shavers worked for a year
with Raymond Scott's CBS staff orchestra and then was an important part of Tommy Dorsey's Orchestra from 1945 until past TD's
death in 1956. Although well-featured, this association kept
Shavers out of the spotlight of jazz, but fortunately he did have
occasional vacations in which he recorded with the Metronome
All-Stars and toured with Jazz at the Philharmonic; at the latter's
concerts in 1953 Shaver's trumpet battles with Roy Eldridge were
quite exciting. After Dorsey's death, Shavers often led his own
quartet although he came back to the ghost band from time to
time. During the 1960s his range and technique gradually faded,
and Charlie Shavers died from throat cancer in 1971 at the age of
53. —*Scott Yanow*

Finest of Charlie Shavers: The Most Intimate / 1955 /
Bethlehem ✦✦

● **Like Charlie** / Oct. 1960–Nov. 1960 / Everest ✦✦✦✦✦

Charlie Shavers at Le Crazy Horse / Jun. 1964 / Everest ✦✦✦

Live / Feb. 7, 1970–Feb. 8, 1970 / Black & Blue ✦✦✦✦

Artie Shaw (Arthur Jacob Arshawsky)

b. May 23, 1910, New York, NY
Clarinet, Leader / Swing
One of jazz's finest clarinetists, Artie Shaw never seemed fully satisfied with his musical life, constantly breaking up successful
bands and running away from success. While Count Basie and
Duke Ellington were satisfied to lead just one orchestra during
the swing era, and Benny Goodman (due to illness) had two,
Shaw led five, all of them distinctive and memorable. After growing up in New Haven, Connecticut and playing clarinet and alto
locally, Shaw spent part of 1925 with Johnny Cavallaro's dance
band and then played off and on with Austin Wylie's band in
Cleveland during 1927–29 before joining Irving Aaronson's
Commanders. After moving to New York, Shaw became a close
associate of Willie "the Lion" Smith at jam sessions and by 1931
was a busy studio musician.
   He retired from music for the first time in 1934 in hopes of

Music Map

Alto Saxophone

Pioneers
Benny Krueger (1920-21, recorded with Original
Dixieland Jazz Band)
Don Redman (recorded with Fletcher Henderson
starting in 1921)
Jimmy Dorsey (1926, first recorded with Red Nichols)

Most Significant Altoists of the Swing Era
Johnny Hodges • Benny Carter • Willie Smith

Other Top Swing Altoists
Charlie Holmes (1929-31, with Luis Russell)
Hilton Jefferson
Pete Brown
Tab Smith
Don Stovall
Russell Procope (with John Kirby Sextet)
Woody Herman

Superior Section Players
Toots Mondello (1934–35 and 1939-40,
with Benny Goodman)
Earle Warren (1937-45, with Count Basie)
Marshall Royal (1951-70, with Count Basie)

Early R&B Stars
Louis Jordan • Earl Bostic

Creator of Bop
Charlie Parker

Other Important Bop-Based Altoists
Sonny Stitt	Sonny Criss
Charlie Mariano	Herb Geller
Gigi Gryce	Lou Donaldson
Phil Woods	Richie Cole
Cannonball Adderley	Charles McPherson

Cool Jazz Innovators
Lee Konitz • Art Pepper • Paul Desmond

Hard Bop to Modern Mainstream
Jackie McLean	Sonny Red
Oliver Nelson	James Spaulding
Gary Bartz	Bud Shank
Frank Morgan	Bobby Watson
Paquito D'Rivera	Kenny Garrett
Antonio Hart	Vincent Herring

Free Jazz/Avant-Garde Innovators
Ornette Coleman • Eric Dolphy • Anthony Braxton

Other Top Avant-Garde Altoists
Jimmy Lyons (with Cecil Taylor 1960-86)
Ken McIntyre
Marion Brown
John Tchicai (later switched to tenor)
Roscoe Mitchell (founder of Art Ensemble Of Chicago)
Joseph Jarman (founder of Art Ensemble Of Chicago)
Sonny Simmons
Henry Threadgill
Julins Hemphill
Marshall Allen (1951-93 with Sun Ra)
Oliver Lake
Arthur Blythe
John Zorn
Tim Berne
Free Funk Players
Steve Coleman
Greg Osby

Crossover
Hank Crawford
David Sanborn
Sadao Watanabe
Marc Russo (of the Yellowjackets)

writing a book, but when his money started running out, Shaw returned to New York. A major turning point occurred when he performed at an all-star big band concert at the Imperial Theatre in May 1936, surprising the audience by performing with a string quartet and a rhythm section. He used a similar concept in putting together his first orchestra, adding a Dixieland-type frontline and a vocalist while retaining the strings. Despite some fine recordings, that particular band disbanded in early 1937, and then Shaw put together a more conventional big band. The surprise success of his 1938 recording of "Begin The Beguine" made the clarinetist

into a superstar and his orchestra (which featured the tenor of Georgie Auld, vocals by Helen Forrest and Tony Pastor and by 1939, Buddy Rich's drumming) into one of the most popular in the world. Billie Holiday was with the band for a few months although only one recording ("Any Old Time") resulted.

Shaw found the pressure of the band business difficult to deal with, and in November 1939 he suddenly left the bandstand and moved to Mexico for two months. When Shaw returned his first session, one utilizing a large string section, resulted in another major hit "Frenesi"; it seemed that no matter what he did he could not escape from success! Shaw's third regular orchestra, which had a string section and such star soloists as trumpeter Billy Butterfield and pianist Johnny Guarnieri, was one of his finest, waxing perhaps the greatest version of "Stardust" along with the memorable "Concerto For Clarinet." The Gramercy five, a small group out of the band (using Guarnieri on harpsichord), also scored with the million selling "Summit Ridge Drive."

Despite all this, Shaw broke up the orchestra in 1941, only to reform an even larger one later in the year. The latter group featured Hot Lips Page along with Auld and Guarnieri. After Pearl Harbor Shaw enlisted and would lead a Navy band before getting a medical discharge in Feb. 1944. Later in the year his new orchestra featured Roy Eldridge, Dodo Marmarosa and Barney Kessel and found Shaw's own style becoming quite modern, almost boppish. But, with the end of the swing era, Shaw again broke up his band in early 1946 and was semi-retired for several years, playing classical music as much as jazz. His latest attempt at a big band was a short-lived one, a boppish unit that lasted for a few months in 1949 and included Zoot Sims, Al Cohn and Don Fagerquist; its modern music was a commercial flop.

After a few years of only limited musical activity, Shaw returned one last time, recording extensively with a version of The Gramercy Five that featured Tal Farlow or Joe Puma on guitar along with Hank Jones. Then in 1955 Artie Shaw permanently gave up the clarinet to pursue his dreams of being a writer. Although he served as frontman (with Dick Johnson playing the clarinet solos) for a reorganized Artie Shaw orchestra in 1983, Shaw never played again. Although he received plenty of publicity for his six marriages (including to Lana Turner, Ava Gardner and Evelyn Keyes) and his odd autobiography The Trouble With Cinderella (which barely touches on the music business or his wives!), the still outspoken Artie Shaw deserves to be best remembered as one of the great clarinetists. His recordings are available in piecemeal fashion on Bluebird. — Scott Yanow

One Night Stand With Artie Shaw at The Steel Pier / Apr. 8, 1936–Apr. 8, 1945 / Joyce ✦✦✦✦
Half of this LP from the collector's label Joyce features the 1941 Artie Shaw Orchestra during a broadcast that is highlighted by "Frenesi" and Hot Lips Page singing and playing on a Bill Challis arrangement of "Blues in the Night." Also included on this set are a few numbers from Shaw's orchestra in 1940 and two cuts from 1945 (featuring trumpeter Roy Eldridge on "Little Jazz"), but the most significant selection is the earliest: Artie Shaw's historic 1936 performance of "Interlude" (here mistitled "Blues in B Flat") with a string quartet. The acclaim received from the latter inspired the clarinetist to form his first big band. Overall this is a varied and continually interesting set. — Scott Yanow

Best of the Big Bands / Jun. 11, 1936–Oct. 30, 1936 / Columbia ✦✦✦✦
Artie Shaw's first big band was quite unusual, originally comprised of four horns, a string quartet and a four-piece rhythm section. This unimaginatively titled CD (whose chatty liner notes unfortunately do not include personnel and date information) has the first 16 recordings by this fine orchestra, featuring vocals by the forgettable Wesley Vaughn, Peg LaCentra and the young Tony Pastor but more importantly, successfully matching together the horns with the strings on such enjoyable numbers as "Japanese Sandman," "Sugar Foot Stomp" and "The Skeleton in the Closet." Pity that this potentially great orchestra did not catch on. — Scott Yanow

Early Artie Shaw, Vol. 3 / Feb. 15, 1937–Jul. 22, 1937 / Ajaz ✦✦✦
Clarinetist Artie Shaw's first orchestra (heard on the opening two numbers in the third volume of this five-LP series) was an admirable but commercially unsuccessful venture that incorporated a string quartet as part of a swing band. When that folded, Shaw returned with a more conventional and louder orchestra, a band that would soon be a major success (perhaps because it was less unusual). This LP contains that orchestra's first dozen recordings, and although it had not caught on yet, one can hear (in Tony Pastor's vocals, Shaw's superb clarinet and the tightness of the ensembles) the beginnings of his "Begin the Beguine" band. Most of this material has not yet been reissued on CD. — Scott Yanow

Artie Shaw and The Rhythmakers, Vol. 1 / Feb. 19, 1937–Apr. 29, 1937 / Swingdom ✦✦✦✦✦
During 1937–38, Artie Shaw and two of his orchestras participated in six marathon recording sessions during which they cut 127 selections for radio transcriptions. Swingdom, on a pair of two-LP

sets and a four-LP box, has released these well-recorded performances in complete chronological order. The first two-fer is among the most interesting, for it captures the clarinetist's first orchestra (which, in addition to five horns and a four-piece rhythm section, featured a string quartet) a few days after its final regular recording session, and his second band shortly before its first record date; the only holdovers were Tony Pastor (on tenor and vocals), bassist Ben Ginsberg and Shaw himself! The first band deserved to succeed (it had a unique new sound of its own) but could not compete with the much more powerful ensembles of his competitors. The second orchestra, which a year later would be a surprise sensation, was more conventional but no less musical. Artie Shaw collectors in particular will have to acquire this valuable series. — Scott Yanow

Artie Shaw and the Rhythmakers, Vol. 2 / Apr. 29, 1937–Jul. 13, 1937 / Swingdom ✦✦✦✦✦
This second of three LP sets taken from Artie Shaw's recordings made for radio transcriptions features his second orchestra in its very early days. In fact, the earlier of the two sessions included on this two-LP set was actually cut before that particular band even had a regular recording date! Although heard here a year or so before his orchestra hit it big with "Begin the Beguine," Shaw's band already had an easily recognizable sound at the time of these transcriptions. Singers Dorothy Howe and Peg LaCentra would not last, and surprisingly, Tony Pastor sticks to playing tenor, but otherwise the orchestra's style was quickly being formed. Artie Shaw fans should particularly enjoy hearing these rare sides for many of the selections were not otherwise recorded by the great clarinetist. — Scott Yanow

Early Artie Shaw, Vol. 5 / Apr. 29, 1937–Dec. 30, 1937 / Ajaz ✦✦✦✦
The fifth and final LP in this collector's series concludes the documentation of the pre-"Begin the Beguine" Artie Shaw Orchestra. In addition to four numbers taken from broadcasts, the final ten selections cut by Shaw in 1937 are included with "Just You, Just Me," "Free for All" and "Non-Stop Flight" being the hottest numbers. A struggle still lay ahead for Artie Shaw because it would be over seven months before his orchestra entered the recording studio again, but from then on he would be a household name. This valuable early music has not yet appeared on CD. — Scott Yanow

Artie Shaw and The Rhythmakers, Vols. 5–8 / Jul. 13, 1937–Feb. 15, 1938 / Swingdom ✦✦✦✦
During 1937–38 the then-fairly-unknown Artie Shaw Orchestra participated in six marathon recording sessions in which they cut 127 selections for radio transcriptions.. — Scott Yanow

The Early Artie Shaw, Vol. 4 / Aug. 4, 1937–Oct. 18, 1937 / Ajazz ✦✦✦✦
The fourth of five LPs in this collector's series traces the studio recordings of the Artie Shaw orchestra during August–October 1937, a year before Shaw's band hit it big with "Begin the Beguine." The orchestra's sound was already recognizable and such selections as "The Chant," the two-part "Blues" and "Free Wheeling" find this band at its early best. The unique Leo Watson takes two vocals and a special highpoint is the original recording of Shaw's theme "Nightmare." Most of this material has not been made available yet on CD. — Scott Yanow

The Complete Artie Shaw, Vol. 1: 1938–39 / Jul. 24, 1938–Jan. 23, 1939 / Bluebird ✦✦✦✦✦
The Artie Shaw success story really began in 1938 with his signing to Victor. Between then and 1945, Shaw would lead and break up four separate orchestras, but his artistic and commercial success would be consistently phenomenal. Fortunately, RCA, in its Bluebird series of two-LP sets, released every Shaw recording in its vaults on eight volumes; unfortunately, much of this music (outside of the better-known hits) has not yet appeared in coherent fashion on CD, so I would advise searching for (and treasuring) the LPs. The first volume finds Shaw debuting on Victor with his giant hit "Begin the Beguine" and continuing with such classics as "Back Bay Shuffle," "Any Old Time" (Billie Holiday's only recording with Shaw), his theme "Nightmare," "Softly, As in a Morning Sunrise," if "They Say" (featuring Helen Forrest's vocal) and "Carioca," among many others. It is no wonder that by 1939 Artie Shaw led the most popular big band in jazz and popular music. — Scott Yanow

● **Begin the Beguine** / Jul. 24, 1938–Jul. 23, 1941 / Bluebird ✦✦✦✦
Since Artie Shaw's Victor recordings have not been reissued in

full on CD, this sampler serves as a fine place for swing beginners to start. Featured are many of the more popular recordings of his second and third orchestras including the title cut, "Frenesi," "Star Dust" and "Summit Ridge Drive," giving one a good idea as to why Artie Shaw was so popular and still remains highly rated as a clarinetist today, decades after his retirement. — *Scott Yanow*

Personal Best / Jul. 24, 1938–Jul. 19, 1945 / Bluebird ✦✦✦
This is a rather odd but intriguing collection of Artie Shaw recordings. Shaw himself picked out these performances as his personal favorites, and they include both familiar studio recordings and lesser-known broadcasts. Most Shaw collectors will already have "Any Old Time," the magnificent "Concerto for Clarinet" and "Lover, Come Back to Me" but may not possess copies of the seven broadcast performances. This hodgepodge set is actually more highly recommended for the clarinetist's lengthy quotes in the liner notes than for the music; the broadcasts should be released in the future separately from the studio sides. — *Scott Yanow*

Traffic Jam / 1938 / Natasha ✦✦✦✦
Of all of Artie Shaw's orchestras (not counting his Army band, he had six significant ones), his second was by far the most popular. During 1938–39, Shaw's ensemble was way ahead of the competition, dethroning Benny Goodman's orchestra and not fully surpassed by Glenn Miller until the clarinetist's sudden decision to flee to Mexico to escape the pressure. *Traffic Jam* contains lively radio performances from this era with many fine moments from Tony Pastor, tenor saxophonist Georgie Auld, singer Helen Forrest, a young but powerful Buddy Rich and the leader/clarinetist. An excellent sampling of Artie Shaw's most famous band. — *Scott Yanow*

22 Original Hits / 1938 / Hindsight ✦✦✦✦
Hindsight specializes in reissuing radio broadcast performances and transcriptions from most of the main swing bands. This fine CD features Shaw's most famous orchestra, his 1938–39 band with tenor Georgie Auld, Tony Pastor, singer Helen Forrest and (in 1939) Buddy Rich. There is no version of "Begin the Beguine" (their big hit) on this CD, but there are many superior examples of the band's music with solos always differing from their studio records. — *Scott Yanow*

Complete Artie Shaw, Vol. 2 (1939) / Jan. 31, 1939–Jun. 22, 1939 / Bluebird ✦✦✦✦✦
The second of seven two-LP sets released by RCA Bluebird in the late '70s (still the best Artie Shaw series ever) traces his orchestra throughout 1939, the year they were the most popular in the land. Among the 32 studio sides are "Deep Purple," "One Night Stand" and "Traffic Jam." In addition to the leader/clarinetist, the main soloists include Georgie Auld on tenor, trumpeter Bernie Privin and pianist Bob Kitsis while Helen Forrest and Tony Pastor provide vocals on half of the songs. Shaw would lead stronger orchestras, but this band remains the best loved. — *Scott Yanow*

Complete Artie Shaw, Vol. 7 (1939–1945) / Jun. 12, 1939–Aug. 2, 1945 / RCA ✦✦✦✦
The final volume in this definitive series of two-LP sets covers Artie Shaw's 1945 orchestra, a band that boasted the playing of trumpeter Roy Eldridge, pianist Dodo Marmarosa and guitarist Barney Kessel; all three joined Shaw and the rhythm section in his Gramercy Five class. The band often hints strongly at bop and has moments of excitement, but the end of the swing era brought its demise. All seven volumes in this series should be acquired if they can still be found. — *Scott Yanow*

Complete Artie Shaw, Vol. 3 (1939–1940) / Aug. 27, 1939–Sep. 3, 1940 / Bluebird ✦✦✦✦✦
The third of seven two-LP sets in Bluebird's definitive series consists of the last 18 recordings by Shaw's very popular 1939 orchestra (riding on the success of "Begin the Beguine"), his two orchestral sessions of 1940 (recorded after the clarinetist's return from his celebrated flight to Mexico) and three of the four selections performed by his new small group, The Gramercy Five in September 1940. The 1939 orchestra (featuring Georgie Auld's tenor, Buddy Rich's drums and vocals from Helen Forrest and Tony Pastor) is at its best on "Lady Be Good" and "I Surrender Dear." Artie Shaw's first session after his return yielded his second biggest hit ("Freseni") and some fascinating classical-influenced pieces with a full string section. The initial Gramercy Five date included yet another major best-seller in "Summit Ridge Drive." Shaw just could not avoid success at this time despite his best efforts. — *Scott Yanow*

Complete Artie Shaw, Vol. 4 (1940–1941) / Sep. 3, 1940–Mar. 20, 1941 / Bluebird ✦✦✦✦✦
Of the six main orchestras that Shaw formed and broke up during 1936–49 his third, the "Stardust" band was arguably his greatest. He had a strong variety of soloists in trumpeter Billy Butterfield, trombonist Jack Jenney, tenor saxophonist Jerry Jerome and pianist Johnny Guarnieri, in addition to a string section. Such arrangers as William Grant Still, Lennie Hayton, Jerry Gray and Ray Coniff were employed, and the writing was as creative as the solos, with the string section really uplifting the music instead of weighing it down. The results, as heard on this two-fer, include such classics as "Temptation," "Prelude in C Major," "Moonglow," "Love of My Life" and particularly "Concerto for Clarinet" and the best-ever version of "Stardust." As a bonus, this set also has five of the eight recordings made by Shaw's original Gramercy Five (with Johnny Guarnieri heard on harpsichord). — *Scott Yanow*

★ **The Complete Gramercy Five Sessions** / Sep. 3, 1940–Aug. 2, 1945 / Bluebird ✦✦✦✦✦
Many swing big-band leaders featured small groups out of their orchestra as added attractions, particularly Benny Goodman, Tommy Dorsey with his Clambake Seven and Bob Crosby's Bobcats. In contrast, Artie Shaw recorded relatively few sides with his Gramercy Five. His original unit from 1940 found the great pianist Johnny Guarnieri playing harpsichord exclusively and matched Shaw's clarinet with trumpeter Billy Butterfield. Their eight recordings include "My Blue Heaven," "Smoke Gets in Your Eyes" and a million-seller, "Summit Ridge Drive." The remainder of this CD is from 1945 and features Shaw, trumpeter Roy Eldridge and the two young modernists pianist Dodo Marmarosa (on piano!) and guitarist Barney Kessel. Shaw would lead a few other Gramercy Fives in the future, but these are his two most famous. The music is consistently brilliant with every note counting. — *Scott Yanow*

Artie Shaw at The Hollywood Palladium / Oct. 26, 1940–Sep. 6, 1941 / Hep ✦✦✦✦
Although there are many releases featuring radio broadcasts from Artie Shaw's very popular 1939 orchestra, relatively few exist from his next two bands, the outfits from 1940 and 1941. This particular LP shows just how creative the writing was for his string orchestras. Billy Butterfield, Hot Lips Page, Jack Jenney and Georgie Auld are among the many soloists, and there is one rare small-group live version of "Dr. Livingstone I Presume." — *Scott Yanow*

Complete Artie Shaw, Vol. 5 (1941–1942) / Mar. 20, 1941–Jan. 20, 1942 / Bluebird ✦✦✦✦✦
Despite his success with his "Stardust" band, Shaw broke up the orchestra and took time off in early 1941. This fifth in a highly recommended (but increasingly hard to find) series of two-LP sets documents his activity during the remainder of 1941. The clarinetist led a very successful, if unusual, orchestral session with such guests as trumpeter Red Allen, trombonist J.C. Higginbotham, altoist Benny Carter and singer Lena Horne, and then later in the year formed his fourth big band. The new orchestra had an even larger string section than its predecessor and such alumni as trombonist Jack Jenney, Georgie Auld on tenor and pianist Johnny Guarnieri in addition to the great trumpeter/singer Hot Lips Page. Unfortunately, Shaw impulsively broke it up shortly after Pearl Harbor but, as can be heard on this very enjoyable set, it also had a personality of its own. Highpoints include "Blues in the Night," "Beyond the Blue Horizon" "St. James Infirmary Blues" and several classical-oriented pieces. Fascinating if relatively obscure recordings from another of Shaw's great orchestras. — *Scott Yanow*

Blues in the Night / Sep. 2, 1941–Jul. 26, 1945 / Bluebird ✦✦✦
While Bluebird in the late '70s released all of Shaw's recordings in chronological order on a series of two-LP sets, its CD reissues have thus far been samplers. *Blues in the Night* has ten selections from the 1941 string orchestra that featured trumpeter/singer Hot Lips Page in addition to 11 by the 1945 big band that showcased trumpeter Roy Eldridge. Filled with such memorable performances as "Blues in the Night," "St. James Infirmary," "Lady Day," "Little Jazz" and a classic Eddie Sauter arrangement of "Summertime," this excellent CD is recommended to those not already possessing the two-fers. — *Scott Yanow*

Complete Artie Shaw, Vol. 6 (1942–1945) / Jan. 21, 1942–Jul. 3, 1945 / Bluebird ✦✦✦✦✦
The sixth in a seven volume of two-fer LPs that reissue all of clar-

inetist Artie Shaw's recordings for Victor during 1938–45, after including the last session by his fourth orchestra, concentrates on his fifth big band, a modern swing outfit from 1944–45 that featured trumpeter Roy Eldridge, pianist Dodo Marmarosa and guitarist Barney Kessel among others. Quite a few of the arrangements are memorable; among the classics are Jimmy Mundy's "Lady Day," Eddie Sauter's "Summertime," Buster Harding's "Little Jazz" and Ray Coniff's "'S Wonderful." it is difficult to believe that, with one brief exception, this was Shaw's last regularly working big band. —*Scott Yanow*

The Indispensable Artie Shaw, Vols. 5 & 6 / Nov. 23, 1944–Aug. 1, 1945 / RCA ✦✦✦✦
This two-CD set, a straight reissue of the original French RCA two-LP release, has most of the highlights from clarinetist Artie Shaw's final year with the Victor label. Not a "complete" series but more of a "best of," the two-fer features exciting solos from the clarinetist/leader, trumpeter Roy Eldridge, guitarist Barney Kessel and pianist Dodo Marmarosa with the more memorable selections including "Lady Day," "'S Wonderful," "The Grabtown Grapple," "Little Jazz," "Summertime," "Love Walked In," "Dancing on the Ceiling" and "Scuttlebutt." The set is well worth picking up by collectors who do not already have the complete LP series of Artie Shaw recordings reissued in the late '70s. —*Scott Yanow*

Spotlight on Artie Shaw: 1945 / Sep. 12, 1945–Sep. 26, 1945 / Joyce ✦✦✦
This collector's LP contains three rare broadcasts from September 1945 by Shaw's fifth big band, a unit featuring trumpeter Roy Eldridge. Three performances by Shaw's Gramercy Five and two vocals from Imogene Lynn add variety to this fine set, recorded shortly before the clarinetist gave up the big-band business altogether. —*Scott Yanow*

With Strings / Nov. 14, 1945–Jun. 19, 1946 / Musicraft ✦✦✦
By the end of 1945, Shaw was ready to leave the big-band business and become semi-retired musically. He recorded his fifth big band (which by this time no longer had trumpeter Roy Eldridge) and then broke it up. This Musicraft LP, the first of two, features Shaw with his modern swing band of 1945 (Ray Linn takes the trumpet solos) and then on some less significant dance sides from 1946. A young Mel Tormé sings two numbers, his Mel-Tones romp on "I Got the Sun in the Morning," and the clarinetist himself is in generally good form, but one senses by the later sessions that his heart was not always in the music anymore. —*Scott Yanow*

For You, for Me, Forever / Apr. 30, 1946–Oct. 18, 1946 / Musicraft ✦✦✦
On the second of two LPs of Shaw's recordings for Musicraft, the great clarinetist is heard with studio musicians playing superior standards and obscurities in 1946. Mel Tormé and/or his Mel-Tones are actually the stars on nine of these 15 selections, including a spirited "What Is This Thing Called Love?" The clarinetist plays well enough but often sounds as if his heart was not really in the music; at this point it was just a day's work for him. —*Scott Yanow*

Later Artie Shaw, Vol. 1 / May 31, 1949–Apr. 4, 1950 / Ajazz ✦✦✦✦
Shaw's recordings of 1949–52 remain his rarest, last issued on this collector's LP series. Having largely given up the band business by mid-1946, the clarinetist came out of semiretirement in 1949 to lead his sixth and final regularly working orchestra, but that modern bop group was a quick flop and left few recordings. *Volume 1* (out of seven) in the *Later Artie Shaw* series has a wide variety of recordings, including two with a studio orchestra, a pair of intriguing items in which the clarinetist fronts a quartet consisting of cello, piano, bass and drums, six titles with his short-lived orchestra and two with a new Gramercy Five (featuring vocalist Mary Ann McCall and trumpeter Don Fagerquist). Although Shaw's career had become directionless, his playing remained in its prime. This "lost" music deserves to be reissued on CD. —*Scott Yanow*

Pied Piper / Dec. 1949 / First Heard ✦✦✦✦
In 1949 Shaw put together what would be his last regularly working orchestra, a modern outfit featuring such younger players as trumpeter Don Fagerquist, the tenors of Al Cohn and Zoot Sims, pianist Dodo Marmarosa and guitarist Jimmy Raney. Striking a balance between his earlier swing hits and the new bop music,

Artie Shaw's new orchestra had a great deal of potential and seemed like a perfect outlet for his always-modern playing. But it stood little chance in 1949 when the big-band era was gone, and his older fans wanted Shaw to put on a nostalgic show. The orchestra flopped commercially. This LP of live performances shows that the music of his last big band was excellent, swinging and well worth remembering. —*Scott Yanow*

● **1949** / 1949 / Music Masters ✦✦✦✦✦
In 1949 the swing era was already in the past, and the public's enthusiasm for bebop was quickly receding. No matter, Artie Shaw decided that it was time to put together a modern big band. The venture only lasted three months, but the largely forgotten music that it performed was quite rewarding. This Musicmasters CD consists of private recordings of the barely documented orchestra, valuable performances that feature the always-modern clarinetist with an outfit that included trumpeter Don Fagerquist, a great saxophone section with the tenors of Al Cohn and Zoot Sims and guitarist Jimmy Raney. It is a real pleasure to hear Artie Shaw stretching out in this setting and a real pity that this band could not have lasted. —*Scott Yanow*

Later Artie Shaw, Vol. 2 / Apr. 4, 1950–Jul. 19, 1950 / Ajazz ✦✦✦
With the collapse of his short-lived bop big band in early 1950, Shaw went back into semiretirement. His recordings, heard on this LP (the second in a valuable seven-volume series), finds him with studio groups ranging from a standard big band to ballads with string sections and two jazz performances with a new Gramercy Five (this time featuring Lee Castle's trumpet and Don Lanphere's tenor). Most of these performances, however, have Shaw merely backing up commercial vocalists including Dick Haymes, Don Cherry (no relation to the trumpeter) and The Chelsea Three. —*Scott Yanow*

Later Artie Shaw, Vol. 3 / Sep. 14, 1950–Jul. 2, 1953 / Ajazz ✦✦✦
The third volume in this seven-LP series by the collector's label (a subsidiary of Joyce) has some real rarities, taken from a period of time when Shaw was barely active in music. He is heard with studio big bands on such songs as "Jingle Bells," "White Christmas" and "In the Still of the Night," backing singer Trudy Richards and with two versions of The Gramercy Five (but somewhat confined to accompanying vocals by June Hutton and Connie Boswell). True Artie Shaw collectors will have to get this intriguing set, but more general listeners are advised to acquire his earlier recordings instead. —*Scott Yanow*

Later Artie Shaw, Vol. 4 / Jul. 2, 1953–Feb. 1, 1954 / Ajazz ✦✦✦✦
The fourth in a seven-LP series documenting Artie Shaw's little-known "later" recordings has six selections featuring the clarinetist with a studio orchestra and strings and seven more rewarding performances with his final Gramercy Five, a sextet featuring pianist Hank Jones, guitarist Tal Farlow and vibraphonist Joe Roland. Shaw had listened closely to bebop and had subtly modernized his style; now he was fully prepared to stretch out with younger players. Most of this material has not been reissued on CD. —*Scott Yanow*

Later Artie Shaw, Vol. 5 / Feb. 1954 / Ajazz ✦✦✦
The fifth of seven LPs in this collector's series of recordings from the post-swing era features seven lengthy performances from the clarinetist's last Gramercy Five, a boppish unit with guitarist Tal Farlow, pianist Hank Jones and vibraphonist Joe Roland that served as a perfect outlet for Shaw's creativity. It is a real shame that he did not have the will power to keep similar groups in existence for the remainder of the decade, instead choosing to quit altogether the following year. —*Scott Yanow*

Later Artie Shaw, Vol. 6 / Feb. 1954 / Ajazz ✦✦✦✦
The sixth in a valuable seven-LP series put out by the collector's label Ajazz focuses on Shaw's final working band, a version of The Gramercy Five that also boasts solos by pianist Hank Jones, guitarist Tal Farlow and vibraphonist Joe Roland. On such songs as "Besame Mucho," "The Grabtown Grapple," "Stop and Go Mambo" and "Love of My Life," Artie Shaw shows that he never did decline and that there was no musical reason (except his own boredom) why he chose to quit playing clarinet entirely shortly after this band broke up. All of the entries in this series are worth searching for. —*Scott Yanow*

★ **The Last Recordings, Vol. 1: Rare and Unreleased** / Feb. 1954–Jun. 1954 / Music Masters ✦✦✦✦✦
The first of two double-CD sets contains a healthy share of the recordings the clarinetist made with his final Gramercy Five, a

unit that included pianist Hank Jones, either Tal Farlow or Joe Puma on guitar and usually Joe Roland's vibes. Unlike his long-time competitor Benny Goodman, Shaw felt perfectly comfortable with younger modernists. In fact his own clarinet playing had evolved through the years, and sometimes he hints strongly at Buddy DeFranco without losing his own musical personality during these 20 performances. This is very rewarding music that makes one especially regret that Artie Shaw chose to give up the clarinet after this band ran its course. —*Scott Yanow*

More Last Recordings / Feb. 1954–Jun. 1954 / Music Masters ◆◆◆◆◆

The second two-CD set of recordings by Shaw's final Gramercy Five is comparable to the first. He would give up his clarinet permanently shortly after this band broke up, but the musical evidence shows that he was still very much in his prime and growing as an improviser, making his retirement a tragedy for jazz. With pianist Hank Jones, vibraphonist Joe Roland and guitarist Tal Farlow contributing strong solos and inspiration for Shaw, this cool bop music (which even has updated performances of "Begin the Beguine," "Frenesi" and "Stardust" that owe surprisingly little to the original hit versions) is quite enjoyable and creative. —*Scott Yanow*

Later Artie Shaw, Vol. 7 / Jun. 1954–Nov. 21, 1955 / Ajazz ◆◆◆◆

The seventh and final volume in this valuable LP series completes the Artie Shaw story only 19 years after his first recording session as a leader. There are five lengthy performances with his final Gramercy Five in June 1954 (featuring solos from pianist Hank Jones and guitarist Joe Puma) and three final performances with a string orchestra in November 1955. Shaw then became one of the very few major jazz figures to retire at his prime, a major loss to the music. This LP does show that he pretty much went out on top, still sounding quite modern. —*Scott Yanow*

Woody Shaw

b. Dec. 24, 1944, Laurinburg, NC, **d.** May 10, 1989, New York, NY
Trumpet / Hard Bop, Post Bop
Woody Shaw was one of the top trumpeters of the 1970s and '80s, a major soloist influenced by Freddie Hubbard but more advanced harmonically, who bridged the gap between hard bop and the avant-garde. Unfortunately, he never broke through to greater stardom (due partly to "personal problems" and failing eyesight) and his premature death from injuries incurred after being hit by a train was a major loss.

Woody Shaw grew up in Newark, NJ, where his father was a member of the Diamond Jubilee Singers. After starting on bugle, he switched to the trumpet when he was 11. Shaw left town for a tour with Rufus Jones when he was 18 and then joined Willie Bobo at a time when Bobo's band included Chick Corea. Shaw played and recorded with Eric Dolphy, and after being invited by Dolphy, he travelled to Paris in 1964 just a little too late to join the late saxophonist's band. After a period in Europe playing with (among others) Bud Powell, Shaw spent periods in the groups of Horace Silver (1965–66), Max Roach (1968–69) and Art Blakey (1973) in addition to making many recordings (some as a sideman for Blue Note) with such players as Jackie McLean, Andrew Hill and McCoy Tyner. Other than playing with Dexter Gordon in 1976, Shaw was primarily a leader from this point on, recording for Columbia (important sessions reissued in a Mosaic box set), Red, Enja, Elektra, Muse and Timeless plus two Blue Note dates co-led with Freddie Hubbard. But overshadowed throughout his career by Hubbard, Miles Davis, Dizzy Gillespie and later on Wynton Marsalis, Woody Shaw would never find much fame or fortune. —*Scott Yanow*

In the Beginning... / Dec. 1965 / Muse ◆◆◆◆
Some interesting, uneven, but worthwhile '65 material from trumpeter Woody Shaw. He was still fresh on the jazz scene and had only recently recovered from the death of mentor Eric Dolphy. Shaw teamed with tenor saxophonist Joe Henderson, pianist Herbie Hancock and bassists Ron Carter or Paul Chambers on these cuts. His potential certainly emerges, as does the fact he was a tentative, unsure soloist at this juncture. —*Ron Wynn*

★ **Blackstone Legacy** / Dec. 8, 1970–Dec. 9, 1970 / Contemporary ◆◆◆◆◆
Stunning two-record set marking Shaw's debut as leader. Affirmative solos from Gary Bartz (sax), Bennie Maupin (sax), and twin basses on several cuts. —*Ron Wynn*

Song of Songs / Sep. 15, 1972+Sep. 18, 1972 / Original Jazz Classics ◆◆◆◆

The Moontrane / Dec. 11, 1974+Dec. 18, 1974 / Muse ◆◆◆◆◆

Love Dance / Nov. 1975 / Muse ◆◆◆◆

● **Little Red's Fantasy** / Jun. 29, 1976 / Muse ◆◆◆◆◆
Woody Shaw was one of the great trumpeters of the 1970s. Although influenced soundwise by Freddie Hubbard, Shaw's more advanced improvisations on his modal originals were quite original and fiery. This Muse set has three of his compositions (including "In Case You Haven't Heard") and a song apiece from pianist Ronnie Mathews and bassist Stafford James; altoist Frank Strozier and drummer Eddie Moore complete the quintet. The varied originals give the musicians strong foundations for their freewheeling and spontaneous solos, making this one of Woody Shaw's better recordings. —*Scott Yanow*

Woody Shaw Concert Ensemble at the Berliner Jazztage / Nov. 6, 1976 / Muse ◆◆◆◆◆
The Woody Shaw Quintet (featuring the trumpeter/leader, altoist Rene McLean, pianist Ronnie Mathews, bassist Stafford James and drummer Louis Hayes) were joined by tenor saxophonist Frank Foster and trombonist Slide Hampton for this frequently exciting and often quite advanced Berlin concert. The obscure originals are given lengthy treatment (Joe Chambers' "Hello to the Wind" is nearly 17 minutes long), and yet there are no slow moments. The solos are uniformly creative and often quite explorative. —*Scott Yanow*

The Iron Men / Apr. 6, 1977+Apr. 13, 1977 / Muse ◆◆◆◆

★ **Rosewood** / Dec. 15, 1977–Dec. 19, 1977 / CBS ◆◆◆◆◆
This album, Woody Shaw's first for a major label, has been reissued as part of his Mosaic box set. Shaw, one of the top trumpeters of the late '60s and throughout the next decade, is heard with a sextet (either Joe Henderson or Carter Jefferson on tenor, pianist Onaje Allan Gumbs, bassist Clint Houston and drummer Victor Lewis) on two numbers and with a "concert ensemble" (which reaches as many as 14 pieces) on the other four selections. Shaw is in top form throughout, particularly on "Rosewood," "Rahsaan's Run" and "Theme for Maxine." This modal music ranks with his best work, making the Mosaic box particularly essential. —*Scott Yanow*

★ **The Complete CBS Studio Recordings of Woody Shaw** / Dec. 15, 1977–Mar. 17, 1981 / Mosaic ◆◆◆◆◆
Between late 1977 and early 1981 trumpeter Woody Shaw recorded four albums for Columbia. This Mosaic three-CD set reissues those LPs plus one previously unissued selection. Shaw was one of the great hard bop trumpeters, able to improvise comfortably and with creativity over difficult modal progressions, and although he had a sound that was similar to Freddie Hubbard's, he was a more advanced soloist. These performances feature him in a variety of settings ranging from a 15-piece group to a quintet. The strong supporting cast includes such fine players as tenors Joe Henderson and Carter Jefferson, altoists Gary Bartz and James Spaulding, trombonists Steve Turre and Curtis Fuller and pianists Mulgrew Miller, Larry Willis, George Cables and Onaje Allan Gumbs. Shaw wrote the majority of the compositions but also jams on a couple of standards. This important reissue finds him at the peak of his powers. —*Scott Yanow*

Lotus Flower / Jan. 7, 1982 / Enja ◆◆◆◆◆

Master of the Art / Feb. 25, 1982 / Elektra ◆◆◆◆
A nice early '80s set Shaw cut for the defunct Musician/Elektra label that seems to have dropped off the face of the earth. It has not been reissued and wasn't heavily publicized at the time. But it was first-rate, with Shaw playing gorgeous ballads, fiery originals and some masterful interpretations of standards. —*Ron Wynn*

Night Music / Feb. 25, 1982 / Elektra ◆◆◆
This out-of-print Elektra LP features the great trumpeter Woody Shaw with one of his final regular groups, a quintet with trombonist Steve Turre, pianist Mulgrew Miller, bassist Stafford James, drummer Tony Reedus and guest vibraphonist Bobby Hutcherson. Recorded at the same session that resulted in Shaw's prior Elektra release *Master of the Art*, the set features three uptempo pieces and a slightly slower "All the Things You Are." There are plenty of fine solos from the principles on this enjoyable if not quite essential outing. —*Scott Yanow*

Time is Right / Jan. 1, 1983 / Red ✦✦✦✦

● **Setting Standards** / Dec. 1, 1983 / Muse ✦✦✦✦✦
Despite restrictive menu, some brilliant solos. —*Ron Wynn*

Woody Shaw with the Tone Jansa Quartet / Apr. 1985 / Timeless ✦✦✦✦

Solid / Mar. 1986 / Muse ✦✦✦✦
A consistently well-played, steady late '80s date on Muse by the Woody Shaw group. This album helped introduce alto saxophonist Kenny Garrett and also boasted quietly effective, yet often stunning, rhythm section work by pianist Kenny Barron and drummer Victor Jones. Shaw played with his usual urgent, fiery fury. —*Ron Wynn*

In My Own Sweet Way / Feb. 1987 / In + Out ✦✦✦✦✦

Imagination / Jun. 24, 1987 / Muse ✦✦✦✦

George Shearing

b. Aug. 13, 1919, London, England
Piano, Leader / Bop, Cool, Latin Jazz
Pianist George Shearing, who was influenced by Errol Garner, popularized a unique jazz sound in 1949, with a quintet that featured piano, vibes, guitar, bass and drums. Shearing used a block chord approach that combined techniques dating back to Milt Buckner that he's probably gotten through Lennie Tristano. He mixed this with the chordal playing style of the Glenn Miller orchestra, whose records he'd closely examined. His sound and touch have been greatly admired by various musicians. Shearing's ensemble sound, especially the piano/vibes interplay, attracted widespread attention. He later began performing classical concertos with orchestras during his concerts, including orchestrations featuring his quintet. Such talents as Cal Tjader, Gary Burton, Toots Thielemans, Joe Pass, Israel Crosby and Vernel Fournier passed through the Shearing group.
Shearing began playing piano at three but had only limited musical training at the Linden Lodge School for the Blind in London, which he attended from 12 to 16. He absorbed the techniques and influence of Fats Waller, Teddy Wilson and Art Tatum among others, as well as boogie woogie and blues pianists through records. He played on British Broadcasting Company broadcasts, including appearances with Ambrose. An accomplished jazz accordionist as well as a fine boogie woogie player, Shearing once played for the King of England. He began recording in 1936, then came to America in 1947 with Leonard Feather's assistance, settling in New York where he immersed himself in bebop.
Shearing replaced Erroll Garner in the Oscar Pettiford trio, then led a quartet with Buddy DeFranco in 1948, before forming his famous quintet in 1949. The original members included Marjorie Hyams on vibes, Chuck Wayne on guitar, John Levy on bass and Denzil Best on drums. Shearing compositions "Conception" (which was recorded by Miles Davis as "Deception") and "Consternation" were eventually recorded by one of his idols, Bud Powell. Shearing recorded for Discovery, Savoy, and MGM in the late '40s and early '50s. He wrote "Lullaby of Birdland" in 1952 as a theme for both the club and radio shows being broadcast there. He switched to Capitol and remained with that label into the early '70s, enjoying substantial chart succes in the late '50s and early '60s. Shearing made albums with Peggy Lee, Nancy Wilson, Dakota Staton and Nat King Cole, later with Stephane Grappelli and the Robert Farnon Orchestra.
He started his own label, Sheba records, for a brief period, then in the '70s signed with Concord. He earned critical plaudits and Grammy awards for dates with Mel Tormé. Shearing also worked with Carmen McRae, Jim Hall and Marian McPartland among others in the '70s and '80s. He's currently recording for the Telarc label. Such pianists as Bill Evans and Herbie Hancock are among the many who've been influenced by Shearing. His material from the late '40s to the '90s is available on CD. —*Ron Wynn*

● **The London Years 1939–1943** / Mar. 2, 1939–Dec. 21, 1943 / Hep ✦✦✦✦✦
Most of pianist George Shearing's earliest recordings are included on this easily enjoyable swing-oriented CD. During the war years when he was in his early 20s, Shearing was most influenced by Teddy Wilson, Earl Hines and Art Tatum, but even at that early stage he was developing his own musical personality. A virtuoso from the start, Shearing is in consistently brilliant form on these standards, originals and a few interesting boogie-woogie stomps.

Of the 25 selections, 22 are piano solos, two are duets with drummer Carlo Krahmer and one song ("Squeezin' the Blues") is a rare outing for Shearing on accordion; his backup group consists of Krahmer and Leonard Feather on piano. Highly recommended. —*Scott Yanow*

So Rare / Feb. 12, 1947–Jan. 31, 1949 / Savoy ✦✦✦✦
This excellent LP is a must for George Shearing fans for it has the pianist's first recordings cut in the United States (eight trio sides from 1947 with either Gene Ramey or Curly Russell on bass and Cozy Cole or Denzil Best on drums) and his earliest quintet sides, eight numbers cut for the Discovery label in early 1949. Less than three weeks later Shearing's quintet would hit it big on their first MGM session with "September in the Rain." The Discovery date, which has the same personnel (vibraphonist Margie Hyams, guitarist Chuck Wayne, bassist John Levy and drummer Denzil Best), is quite appealing and the real birth of this classic group. Two songs ("Cherokee" and "Four Bars Short") are rare examples of Shearing playing jazz accordion. This album is recommended; hopefully Savoy will get around to reissuing the valuable material on CD eventually. —*Scott Yanow*

Lullaby of Birdland / Feb. 17, 1949–Mar. 28, 1954 / Verve ✦✦✦✦✦
This double LP from 1986, although not "complete," does a fine job of summing up the MGM recordings of the George Shearing Quintet. The popular group is heard at its best on such songs as "September in the Rain," "East of the Sun," "Conception," "Tenderly," "Pick Yourself Up" and the original version of "Lullaby of Birdland." With such sidemen as Marjorie Hyams, Don Elliott, Joe Roland, Cal Tjader or George Devins on vibes, and Chuck Wayne, Dick Evans or Toots Thielemans on guitar (and assistance on the final three of the 28 selections by either Candido or Armando Peraza on bongos), Shearing's groups were quite exciting during this era, showing stronger solo strength than they would in the 1960s although the pianist/leader was clearly the main star. This definitive collection will hopefully resurface on CD eventually. —*Scott Yanow*

The Shearing Spell / 1955 / Capitol ✦✦✦✦
This was the first recording that George Shearing and his Quintet made for Capitol, an association that lasted up until 1969 and would result in quite a few enjoyable but now long-out-of-print LPs that have not been reissued since. At the time Shearing's popular group consisted of the leader/pianist, vibraphonist Johnny Rae, guitarist Toots Thielemans, bassist Al McKibbon, drummer Bill Clark and on some selections Armando Peraza and Willie Bobo on percussion. Their easy-listening brand of bop-based music is heard at its best on this LP on "Autumn in New York," "Out of This World," "Moonray" and "Cuban Fantasy." —*Scott Yanow*

Latin Escapade / Nov. 25, 1956 / Capitol ✦✦✦
George Shearing's popular Quintet (with vibraphonist Emil Richards, guitarist Toots Thielemans, bassist Al McKibbon and drummer Percy Brice) is joined by the congas of Armando Peraza for a variety of melodic and rhythmic pieces. Highlights of this easy-listening but enjoyable LP include "Perfidia," "Mambo with Me," "Old Devil Moon," "Cuban Love Song" and even "Poodle Mambo." —*Scott Yanow*

Shearing Piano / Nov. 1956–Sep. 1957 / Capitol ✦✦
This Capitol LP is a bit unusual for it features George Shearing (who always played with his Quintet during this period) performing a set of solo piano. Actually the results are a bit disappointing for Shearing mostly sticks to dreamy versions of ballads with the results generally closer to mood music than jazz. The music is pleasing for what it is, but it could have been much more considering Shearing's technique and improvising skills. —*Scott Yanow*

● **The Complete Capitol Live Recordings** / Mar. 8, 1958–Jul. 6, 1963 / Mosaic ✦✦✦✦✦
Pianist George Shearing, whose vibes-guitar-piano-bass-drums quintet was one of the most popular in jazz throughout the 1950s and '60s, seemed to have had a dual career while signed to Capitol. While his studio recordings often found his quintet augmented with strings, voices, brass and/or Latin percussion in performances closer to mood music (or even muzak) than jazz, his live engagements were definitely in the cool/bop vein. This Mosaic five-CD limited-edition box set brings back his five in-concert recordings, two of which are now double in length thanks to the inclusion of 13 previously unissued selections. There is more variety than expected to this program with the full quintet featured on most numbers but space also set aside for showcases by

the trio, Shearing's solo piano and his regular "guest" Armando Peraza on congas. Although the sidemen include such fine players as vibraphonist Gary Burton, Emil Richards and Warren Chiasson, guitarists Toots Thielemans (who plays harmonica on "Caravan"), Dick Garcia, John Gray and Ron Anthony, bassists Al McKibbon, Ralph Pena, Bill Yancey and Gene Cherico and drummers Percy Brice and Vernel Fournier, Shearing is the star throughout. His funny comments to the audience have also been included and the result is a classy show filled with accessible but surprisingly inventive bop-based music. — *Scott Yanow*

Latin Lace / Mar. 1958 / Capitol ◆◆◆
The second of pianist George Shearing's full-length Latin albums once again finds his quintet (with vibraphonist Emil Richards, guitarist Toots Thielemans, bassist Al McKibbon and drummer Percy Brice) being joined by the exciting congas of Armando Peraza. Most of the easy-listening melodies are from south of the border, but even the ones that aren't (such as "The Story of Love," "The Moon Was Yellow" and "It's Not for Me to Say") are given a Latinized treatment. This is nice (if rather safe) music, but the LP is long out of print. — *Scott Yanow*

Latin Affair / Dec. 1958 / Capitol ◆◆◆
Pianist George Shearing's third Latin LP for Capitol is similar to his first two. Although the personnel in his popular Quintet had changed a bit (this album has vibraphonist Warren Chasen, guitarist Toots Thielemans, bassist Carl Pruitt and drummer Roy Haynes), Shearing and his guest Armando Peraza on congas remain the main soloists. The music on their melodic set includes South American melodies and swing standards; in both cases the easy-listening music is Latinized yet still influenced by bop. This enjoyable LP will be difficult to find. — *Scott Yanow*

Satin Brass / Oct. 1959 / Capitol ◆◆◆
The George Shearing Quintet (comprised of piano, vibes, guitar, bass and drums) is joined by four trumpets, four trombones, two French horns and a tuba for a dozen easy-listening performances on this Capitol LP. The pianist/leader arranged the majority of the selections, which include a few standards and several obscurities. Although the instrumentation might lead one to believe that this LP will contain shouting performances, actually the playing is often quite mellow and restrained with the Quintet very much in the lead throughout. Nice music but not too essential. — *Scott Yanow*

● **The Swingin's Mutual** / Jun. 29, 1960–Jan. 7, 1961 / Capitol ◆◆◆◆◆
The music on this set, a dozen selections featuring the George Shearing Quintet including six that have vocals by a young Nancy Wilson, has been reissued on CD by Capitol with five additional tracks. This was one of Wilson's most jazz oriented dates (even if she was never a jazz singer) and is highlighted by her vocals on "The Nearness of You" and "The Things We Did Last Summer" along with instrumental versions of "Oh! Look at Me Now," "Blue Lou" and "Lullaby of Birdland." — *Scott Yanow*

Mood Latino / 1961 / Capitol ◆◆◆
During his Capitol years, pianist George Shearing recorded several Latin-flavored albums, which generally found his popular piano-vibes-guitar-bass-drums Quintet augmented by the congas of Armando Peraza. For this particular album not only is Peraza added to the group but so are a couple of other percussionists and an unidentified flutist. The Quintet sound is still quite dominant during the rhythmic easy-listening set with the music ranging from "Blue Moon" and "You and the Night and the Music" to "Jackie's Mambo" and "Say 'Si Si'." The performances on this LP have not yet been reissued on CD. — *Scott Yanow*

George Shearing and the Montgomery Bros. / Oct. 9, 1961 / Original Jazz Classics ◆◆◆◆
Pianist George Shearing meets up with guitarist Wes, vibraphonist Buddy and bassist Monk Montgomery on this enjoyable if slightly lightweight outing. The performances are a bit too concise at times, but the CD reissue does add three extra takes to the original 11-song program and has some fine soloing by the principals. Highlights include "Love Walked In," "Love for Sale" and "The Lamp Is Low." — *Scott Yanow*

Jazz Moments / Jun. 20, 1962–Jun. 21, 1962 / Blue Note ◆◆◆◆
This fairly rare LP freed pianist George Shearing from the confines of his popular Quintet and showcases him in a trio with Ahmad Jamal's former sidemen (bassist Israel Crosby and drummer Vernel Fournier). Crosby, heard in his final recording, is in

excellent form during these performances and receives some rare opportunities to solo. The main star as usual is the pianist, whose style was perfectly suited to the material heard on this album. Highlights include "Makin' Whoopee," "Like Someone in Love," "Symphony," "When Sunny Gets Blue" and "It Could Happen to You." This date, which was reissued on LP by Pausa in 1985, is worth searching for. — *Scott Yanow*

As Requested / 1972 / Sheba ◆◆◆
After pianist George Shearing's longtime association with Capitol ended in 1969, he formed his own Sheba label and started to gradually de-emphasize his quintet. On the fifth of Sheba's seven LPs (none of which have been reissued on CD yet), the George Shearing Quintet (with the exception of a specially assembled group gathered for an MPS record in 1974) is heard on records for the final time. The music is typically easy-listening with three- to five-minute versions of such songs as "I'll Never Smile Again," "Over the Rainbow," "Moon Ray" and current pop songs "Close to You" and "We've Only Just Begun" among others. With vibraphonist Charlie Shoemake and guitarist Ron Anthony in the group, the Quintet was not without interest, but it was clearly running out of gas. — *Scott Yanow*

My Ship / Jun. 25, 1974 / Polydor ◆◆◆◆
This solo piano set by George Shearing (which has been reissued on CD through Polygram) is quite eccentric and unpredictable. Shearing, freed from the constraints of his popular Quintet, lets his imagination loose on songs ranging from "My Ship," "Happy Days Are Here Again," "The Entertainer" (which after a raggish beginning is turned into jazz) "Londonberry Air," and unfortunately "Send in the Clowns" (on which he makes the mistake of singing). Some of the classical allusions are a bit too cute, but Shearing's wit and charm eventually win one over. — *Scott Yanow*

Light Airy and Swinging / Jul. 23, 1974–Jul. 24, 1974 / MPS ◆◆◆◆
George Shearing, after over two decades as leader of his popular Quintet, was largely taken for granted as a pianist. His trio recordings for MPS in the mid-'70s did a lot to salvage and restore his former reputation as a virtuoso and a distinctive player. On this trio set with bassist Andy Simpkins and drummer Stix Hooper, Shearing fully investigates a variety of superior standards, particularly "Speak Low," Johnny Mandel's "Emily" and "Beautiful Friendship," which are given the most extensive explorations of the eight songs; only "Love Walked In" is a holdover from the quintet days. This enjoyable LP is long overdue to be reissued on CD. — *Scott Yanow*

The Reunion / Apr. 11, 1976 / PA/USA ◆◆◆◆◆
A wonderful duo release from '76 with pianist George Shearing collaborating with violinist Stephane Grappelli. Shearing's sessions are usually more introspective and light than upbeat and hot, but Grappelli's soaring, exuberant violin solos seem to put a charge into Shearing, who responds with some of his hottest playing in many years. — *Ron Wynn*

Getting In The Swing Of Things / Sep. 19, 1979–Sep. 21, 1979 / Pausa ◆◆◆◆
This particular George Shearing Trio (with guitarist Louis Stewart and bassist Niels Pedersen) recorded three albums for MPS during 1977–79 and provided an excellent outlet for the brilliant pianist just prior to his association with the Concord label. The Pausa reissue LP has the trio's renditions of five standards and four obscure originals including two ("Consternation" and "G & G") by Shearing. His renditions of "Don't Get Around Much Anymore" and "This Can't Be Love" are most memorable among these generally swinging tracks. — *Scott Yanow*

● **Blues Alley and Jazz** / Oct. 2, 1979–Oct. 7, 1979 / Concord Jazz ◆◆◆◆◆
Pianist George Shearing started a productive ten-year association with the Concord label with this live set, a duo outing matching him with the brilliant bassist Brian Torff. Their performances are virtuosic, intuitive, full of sly wit and always swinging; it is surprising that Torff did not become more famous. The close interaction between the two masterful musicians on such numbers as Billy Taylor's "One for the Woofer," "The Masquerade Is Over" and a humorous "Lazy River" are quite impressive as is Shearing's surprisingly effective vocal on "This Couldn't Be the Real Thing." This CD is recommended. — *Scott Yanow*

On a Clear Day / Aug. 1980 / Concord Jazz ◆◆◆◆◆
George Shearing's second Concord album, which like the previous

Blues Alley Jazz is a set of duets with bassist Brian Torff, is the equal of the first. The close communication between the duo and their ability to think fast and immediately react to each other makes it possible for them to uplift such songs as "Love For Sale," "On a Clear Day," "Lullaby of Birdland," and even "Happy Days Are Here Again." Brilliant music. —*Scott Yanow*

Alone Together / Mar. 1981 / Concord Jazz ✦✦✦
Pianists George Shearing and Marian McPartland, both originally from England, teamed up for this polite but swinging affair. In addition to an original apiece and a collaboration, the duo is heard on seven standards, and the results are quite tasteful, as one would expect from these fine players. Few surprises occur, but the results are pleasing. —*Scott Yanow*

First Edition / Sep. 1981 / Concord Jazz ✦✦✦✦
This tasteful set matches together pianist George Shearing and guitarist Jim Hall in a program of duets. The fresh material (two originals apiece by Shearing and Hall, the obscure "I See Nothing to Laugh About" and just three standards challenge the pair and their quiet and subtle styles match together well. The pianist's tributes to Antonio Carlos Jobim and Tommy Flanagan are among the more memorable pieces in this interesting and somewhat unexpected musical collaboration. —*Scott Yanow*

Top Drawer / Mar. 1983 / Concord Jazz ✦✦✦✦✦
A year after their first meeting on record, pianist George Shearing and singer Mel Tormé (this time with Don Thompson on bass) had an equally successful joint recording. The material is often a bit offbeat (including the obscure swing song "Shine on Your Shoes," "How Do You Say Auf Wiedersehen" and the early bop vocal "What's This"), but there are also inventive remakes of "Stardust" and "Hi Fly" along with two instrumentals: "Oleo" and a Shearing piano solo on "Away in the Manger." Obviously this CD is full of surprises; all of the Tormé-Shearing Concord sessions (which bring out the best in both of the principals) are well worth acquiring. —*Scott Yanow*

Live at the Cafe Carlyle / Jan. 1984 / Concord Jazz ✦✦✦✦
Don Thompson spent several years as George Shearing's bassist, and this album is his best recording with the veteran pianist. Thompson, who plays second piano on Herbie Hancock's "Tell Me a Bedtime Story," jams with strong intuition and consistent swing, easily picking up on Shearing's musical directions during such songs as "Pent up House," "The Shadow of Your Smile," "Cheryl" and a couple of originals. Shearing, who takes "I Cover the Waterfront" as a piano solo, had his career rejuvenated during his years on Concord through stimulating musical encounters such as this one. Fine music. —*Scott Yanow*

Elegant Evening / 1985 / Concord Jazz ✦✦✦

Grand Piano / May 1985 / Concord Jazz ✦✦✦
George Shearing recorded frequently while on Concord, but this was his first full-length session of unaccompanied solos for the label. Most of the ten selections are interpreted as ballads (Shearing takes an effective vocal on his original "Imitations"), but he does cook a bit on "Nobody Else but Me" and "Easy to Love." However, the emphasis is on slow thoughtful tempos and introspective improvising. —*Scott Yanow*

Plays Music of Cole Porter / Jan. 1986 / Concord Jazz ✦✦✦
Released as part of Concord's Concerto subsidiary, this unusual release matches together pianist George Shearing with the classical French horn player Barry Tuckwell for a set of 11 Cole Porter songs. Five selections use a full string section, two are performed with a quartet, and four others are duets by Shearing and Tuckwell. In general Tuckwell does not improvise, but Shearing's arrangements give a jazz feel to all of the performances and make the music accessible (if not really essential) to both classical and jazz listeners. —*Scott Yanow*

More Grand Piano / Oct. 1986 / Concord Jazz ✦✦✦✦
This was a very spontaneous session. For his second solo piano date for Concord, George Shearing picked out ten songs while he was at the studio and without any real prior planning, simply played. The results are consistently enjoyable as Shearing performs some of his favorite songs. A few of the tunes (such as "You Don't Know What Love Is" and "East of the Sun") had long been part of his repertoire, but some of the other songs (such as "My Silent Love," an unusual reworking of "Change Partners" and "Dream") are full of surprises. An excellent outing. —*Scott Yanow*

Breakin' Out / May 1987 / Concord Jazz ✦✦✦✦
Most of George Shearing's recordings for Concord feature the pianist with his regular duo or trio. This release is different for the great pianist is matched up with bassist Ray Brown (who he had first played with in 1948) and drummer Marvin "Smitty" Smith. The nine songs they perform include four by Duke Ellington, Leonard Feather's "Twelve Tone Blues," Bud Powell's exciting "Hallucinations," two standards and Shearing's own down home "Break out the Blues." The music is as rewarding and swinging as one would expect from this lineup. —*Scott Yanow*

Dexterity / Nov. 1987 / Concord Jazz ✦✦✦✦✦
For his first tour of Japan in 24 years, pianist George Shearing worked for the initial time with bassist Neil Swainson who soon afterward became a regular member of his duo. This Concord CD features Shearing and Swainson performing a variety of material including Charlie Parker's "Dexterity," "You Must Believe in Spring," a traditional Japanese melody and a couple of ballads. In addition, singer Ernestine Anderson sits in with the group on "As Long As I Live" and a typically soulful "Please Send Me Someone to Love" before the duo concludes the show (recorded at the second annual Fujitsu-Concord Jazz Festival) with a five-song Duke Ellington medley. A well-rounded and consistently enjoyable program. —*Scott Yanow*

The Spirit of 1776 / Mar. 1988 / Concord Jazz ✦✦✦✦
George Shearing and Hank Jones have always been very well-rounded pianists fully capable of playing unaccompanied solos. Their unique matchup as a two-piano duo on this Concord release works surprisingly well for the two pianists manage to stay out of each other's way, and the ensembles are not overcrowded. The pianist's tackle colorful material including "Angel Eyes," Thelonious Monk's "I Mean You," an original apiece, Mary Lou Williams' "Lonely Moments," "Star Eyes" and "Confirmation," and the results are swinging and tasteful. This somewhat obscure Concord CD is worth investigating. —*Scott Yanow*

Perfect Match / May 1988 / Concord Jazz ✦✦✦✦
Pianist George Shearing and singer Ernestine Anderson (who had teamed up briefly at the 1987 Fujitsu-Concord Jazz Festival) collaborated on this full-length Concord release. With strong assistance from bassist Neil Swainson and drummer Jeff Hamilton, Shearing and Anderson mostly stick to standards, and their versions uplift the veteran songs. "Body and Soul" is taken as a vocal-piano duet while "The Best Thing for You" is given an instrumental treatment. Other highlights include Anderson's vocals on "I'll Take Romance," a heartfelt "I Remember Clifford," "On the Sunny Side of the Street" and "Some Other Time." An excellent outing for all concerned. —*Scott Yanow*

George Shearing in Dixieland / Feb. 1989 / Concord Jazz ✦✦
This promising effort is a major disappointment. Pianist George Shearing planned to revisit his roots in Dixieland and swing, but he hedged his bets. Despite having an impressive septet with such players as cornetist Warren Vache, Ken Peplowski on tenor, trombonist George Masso and clarinetist Kenny Davern, Shearing wrote out most of the ensembles, taking away from the spontaneity and potential excitement of the music. Despite the interesting repertoire (ranging from "Truckin'," "Honeysuckle Rose" and "Jazz Me Blues" to "Take Five," "Desafinado" and even a Dixiefied "Lullaby Of Birdland"), this date falls far short of its potential. —*Scott Yanow*

Piano / May 1989 / Concord Jazz ✦✦✦
This relaxed solo set features the great pianist George Shearing playing 14 songs; some of them (such as Mel Tormé's "Daisy," "Thinking of You," "Miss Invisible" and two of Shearing's originals) are quite obscure. The emphasis is on slower tempos and relaxed improvising, but Shearing's distinctive solos and subtle creativity hold on to one's interest throughout. A tasteful set. —*Scott Yanow*

I Hear a Rhapsody: Live at the Blue Note / Feb. 27, 1992–Feb. 29, 1992 / Telarc ✦✦✦✦✦
This excellent trio set by George Shearing with bassist Neil Swainson and drummer Grady Tate finds the veteran pianist still in prime form. The repertoire mostly consists of challenging material and tunes not overplayed by Shearing throughout the years. The musical communication between the players on such tunes as "Bird Feathers," "The End of a Love Affair," "The Duke," "The Masquerade Is Over" and an original apiece by Shearing and Swainson is very impressive, and the pianist's solos are typically distinctive. This CD (Shearing's debut on the Telarc label) is a fine example of George Shearing's still-viable playing as he neared his mid-70s. —*Scott Yanow*

● **Walkin'-Live At The Blue Note** / Feb. 27, 1992–Feb. 29, 1992 / Telarc ✦✦✦✦✦

Shearing is often in joyous form on the uptempo tracks of this well-paced trio date. Highlights include such bop classics as "That's Earl, Brother," Bud Powell's "Celia" and "Subconscious Lee" along with a couple of familiar blues. In contrast the ballads are generally rather melancholy affairs with the pianist wringing as much emotion as possible out of each note. Neil Swainson contributes fluid bass solos and alert accompaniment while Grady Tate plays supportive drums. Shearing (in his early 70s at the time of this recording) is heard near his creative peak throughout this consistently enjoyable live set. — *Scott Yanow*

That Shearing Sound / Feb. 14, 1994–Feb. 16, 1994 / Telarc ✦✦✦✦

This was pianist George Shearing's first recording in a piano-vibes-guitar-bass-drums quintet since he broke up his original group in 1978 after 30 years of steady work; Shearing sounds surprisingly inspired throughout. With guitarist Louis Stewart, vibraphonist Steve Nelson, bassist Neil Swainson and drummer Dennis Mackrel, Shearing explores such vintage Quintet standards as "East of the Sun" and "I'll Never Smile Again" along with two Horace Silver compositions, a pair of his own songs ("Conception" and his biggest hit "Lullaby of Birdland") and a variety of other suitable material. The music ranges from easy-listening to hard-driving bebop. The sound of the George Shearing Quintet remains as appealing as ever. — *Scott Yanow*

Jack Sheldon

b. Nov. 30, 1931, Jacksonville, FL
Trumpet / Bop

One of the great jokesters in jazz (whose spontaneous monologues are as hilarious as they are tasteless), Jack Sheldon's personality has sometimes overshadowed his excellent trumpet playing and effective vocals. Sheldon started playing professionally at age 13. He moved to Los Angeles in 1947, joined the Air Force and played in military bands. After his discharge, Sheldon became a popular figure on the West Coast, playing and recording with many top musicians including Jimmy Giuffre, Herb Geller, Wardell Gray, Stan Kenton, Benny Goodman, Curtis Counce and Art Pepper. He worked as an actor in the 1960s (including starring in the short-lived television series *Run Buddy Run*), was seen nightly on *The Merv Griffin Show* and in the 1970s and '80s he performed with Benny Goodman, Bill Berry's big band, in the studios and with his own groups. Into the mid-'90s Jack Sheldon (who often uses a big band arranged by Tom Kubis) remains quite active in the Los Angeles area, recording regularly for Concord and his Butterfly label. — *Scott Yanow*

Jack Sheldon and His All Star Band / Jul. 19, 195759 05 / GNP ✦✦✦✦

Jack Sheldon Presents The Entertainers / Mar. 1964+Mar. 1, 1965 / VSOP ✦✦✦

The recording quality of the two concerts that comprise this CD is far from optimal, but there is enough good music and nutty humor to make it worth acquiring. Trumpeter Jack Sheldon has four vocals (including "Born to Lose," which has a mostly humorous monologue), trombonist Frank Rosolino scats and yodels briefly on a speedy "Pennies from Heaven," Johnny Mercer drops by to sing an original blues about the band and "Charade," all three take their turns on "How Long, How Long Blues," and there are four instrumentals that also feature guitarist Howard Roberts. None of the boppish music is all that essential, and there are some overly loose moments, but the happy spirit of the date (which also includes bassist Joe Mondragon, either Shelly Manne or Stan Levey on drums and rhythm guitarist Jack Marshall) generally overcomes the recording quality. — *Scott Yanow*

Playin' It Straight / Nov. 13, 1980–Nov. 14, 1980 / Real Time ✦✦✦✦

★ **Stand by for Jack Sheldon** / Mar. 1983 / Concord Jazz ✦✦✦✦✦
This is one of Jack Sheldon's better recordings. His trumpet solos (accompanied by pianist Ross Tompkins, bassist Ray Brown and drummer Jake Hanna) are consistently excellent, and his five vocals, although not containing the humor one generally hears in his live performances, are also well-done. The ten standards and ballads are given swinging and melodic treatment, making this a fine all round showcase for Sheldon. — *Scott Yanow*

Blues in the Night / Aug. 3, 1984–Aug. 4, 1984 / Phontastic ✦✦✦✦

Hollywood Heroes / Sep. 1987 / Concord Jazz ✦✦✦✦✦
A quintet of fairly undistinguished sidemen provides good support for Sheldon. Mostly they play early-period swing-era music bordering on bop. — *Michael G. Nastos*

On My Own / Sep. 12, 1991 / Concord Jazz ✦✦✦✦✦

Archie Shepp

b. May 24, 1937, Fort Lauderdale, FL
Tenor Saxophone, Soprano Saxophone / Avant-Garde, Free Jazz, Hard Bop

Archie Shepp has been at various times a feared firebrand and radical, soulful throwback and contemplative veteran. He was viewed in the '60s as perhaps the most articulate and disturbing member of the free generation, a published playwright willing to speak on the record in unsparing, explict fashion about social injustice and the anger and rage he felt. His tenor sax solos were searing, harsh and unrelenting, played with a vivid intensity. But in the '70s, Shepp employed a fatback/swing-based R&B approach, and in the '80s he mixed straight bebop, ballads and blues pieces displaying little of the fury and fire from his earlier days.

Shepp studied dramatic literature at Goddard College, earning his degree in 1959. He played alto sax in dance bands and sought theatrical work in New York. But Shepp switched to tenor, playing in several free jazz bands. He worked with Cecil Taylor, co-led groups with Bill Dixon and played in The New York Contemporary Five with Don Cherry and John Tchicai. He led his own bands in the mid-'60s with Roswell Rudd, Bobby Hutcherson, Beaver Harris and Grachan Moncur III. His Impulse! albums included poetry readings and quotes from James Baldwin and Malcolm X. Shepp's releases sought to paint an aural picture of African-American life and included compositions based on incidents like Attica or folk sayings.

He also produced plays in New York among them "The Communist" in 1965 and "Lady Day: A Musical Tragedy" in 1972 with trumpeter/composer Cal Massey. But starting in the late '60s, the rhetoric was toned down, and the anger began to disappear from Shepp's albums. He substituted a more celebratory and at times reflective attitude. Shepp turned to academia in the late '60s, teaching at SUNY in Buffalo, then the University of Massachusetts. He was named an associate professor there in 1978. Shepp toured and recorded extensively in Europe during the '80s, cutting some fine albums with Horace Parlan, Niels-Henning Orsted Pedersen and Jasper van't Hof. He has recorded extensively for Impulse, Byg, Arista/Freedom, Phonogram, SteepleChase, Denon, Enja, EPM and Soul Note among others over the years.Unfortunately, his tone declined from the mid-1980's on (his highly original sound was his most important contribution to jazz), and Archie Shepp is a less significant figure in the 1990's than one might hope. — *Ron Wynn and Scott Yanow*

Archie Shepp—Bill Dixon Quartet / Oct. 1962 / Savoy ✦✦✦✦

The New York Contemporary Five / Nov. 11, 1963 / Storyville ✦✦✦✦✦
This historically significant CD has ten of the 11 selections recorded by The New York Contemporary Five (and originally issued on two separate LPs) on November 11, 1963. The short-lived group, which consists of cornetist Don Cherry, altoist John Tchicai, Archie Shepp on tenor, bassist Don Moore and drummer J.C. Moses, was avant-garde for the period, influenced most by Ornette Coleman's Quartet; the participation of Coleman's cornetist certainly helped! However, Tchicai (although sometimes hinting at Coleman) had a different approach than Ornette Coleman, and it was obvious that Shepp had already developed his own original voice and was the group's most passionate soloist. Together this very interesting quintet (which would soon break up) performs pieces by Ornette Coleman, Thelonious Monk (short melodic renditions of "Monk's Mood" and "Crepescule with Nellie"), Bill Dixon, Tchicai, Shepp and Cherry. — *Scott Yanow*

● **Archie Shepp in Europe** / Nov. 15, 1963 / Delmark ✦✦✦✦✦
The New York Contemporary Five was a co-op band in 1963 featured such up-and-coming talent as tenor saxophonist Archie Shepp (who had previously been with Cecil Taylor), altoist John Tchicai, cornetist Don Cherry (well-known due to his association with Ornette Coleman), bassist Don Moore and drummer J.C. Moses. Their music was a bridge between the innovations of Ornette Coleman's Quartet and the avant-garde explosion of 1965. The performances of originals by Cherry, Coleman, Shepp and Tchicai, in addition to Thelonious Monk's "Crepuscule with

Nellie," are not flawless but are generally quite fascinating as these young talents did what they could to break through the "rules" of bebop and create new music and sounds. A historic set. —*Scott Yanow*

The House I Live In / Nov. 21, 1963 / SteepleChase ✦✦✦✦
This is a fascinating release. Tenor saxophonist Archie Shepp would not burst upon the U.S. avant-garde scene until 1964–65, but here he is featured at a Danish concert with the great coolbop baritonist Lars Gullin and a top-notch straight-ahead rhythm section (pianist Tete Montoliu, bassist Niels Pedersen and drummer Alex Riel). The quintet stretches out on four lengthy standards (including "Sweet Georgia Brown" and a 19-minute rendition of "You Stepped out of a Dream"), and it is particularly interesting to hear the reactions of the other musicians to Shepp's rather free flights; at a couple of points Gullin tries to copy him! An important historical release. —*Scott Yanow*

★ **Four for Trane** / Aug. 10, 1964 / Impulse! ✦✦✦✦✦
Tenor saxophonist Archie Shepp's debut for Impulse! is a classic. This LP (not yet reissued on CD) features the avant-garde innovator playing four of John Coltrane's compositions, including "Cousin Mary" and "Naima," along with his own "Rufus." To his great credit, Shepp never sounded like Coltrane—his raspy tone was much closer to a free version of Ben Webster—and he is heard in top form on this studio date with a sextet also including fluegelhornist Alan Shorter, trombonist Roswell Rudd, altoist John Tchicai, bassist Reggie Workman and drummer Charles Moffett. Shepp's interpretations of the Coltrane tunes are quite fresh and original. Highly recommended to open-eared listeners. —*Scott Yanow*

Archie Shepp / Aug. 10, 1964 / Impulse! ✦✦✦

Fire Music / Feb. 16, 1965+Mar. 28, 1965 / Impulse! ✦✦✦✦
This particular early Archie Shepp recording (reissued on CD) has its strong moments, although it is a bit erratic. Four selections utilize an advanced sextet. Of these songs, "Hambone" has overly repetitive and rather monotonous riffing by the horns behind the soloists, and Shepp's bizarre exploration of "The Girl from Ipanema" gets tedious, but the episodic "Los Olvidaos" is quite colorful, and the tenorman sounds fine on a spacey rendition of "Prelude to a Kiss." "Malcolm, Malcolm-Semper Malcolm" has Shepp reading a brief poem for the fallen Malcolm X before he jams effectively on tenor in a trio with bassist David Izenzon and drummer J.C. Moses. The CD is rounded out by a "bonus" cut not on the original LP—a live version of "Hambone" that is much more interesting than the earlier rendition. Overall, this set, even with its faults, is recommended. —*Scott Yanow*

● **On This Night** / Mar. 9, 1965+Aug. 12, 1965 / GRP ✦✦✦✦✦
Tenor saxophonist Archie Shepp made his mark early in his career and reached heights that he had trouble attaining later on. This Impulse! reissue gathers together all of Shepp's recordings from two dates, some of which were originally scattered on a variety of LPs. Highlights include the three very different versions of the explosive "The Chased," a reworking of "In a Sentimental Mood" and "The Original Mr. Sonny Boy Williamson." Shepp's quintet also features vibraphonist Bobby Hutcherson who is heard early in his career. This passionate music is not for the fainthearted. —*Scott Yanow*

Three for a Quarter: One for a Dime / Feb. 19, 1966 / Impulse! ✦✦✦✦✦
This is an LP long overdue to be reissued on CD. Archie Shepp's main contributions to jazz were an adventurous spirit and the introduction of a forceful, raspy sound that, even with its debt to Ben Webster, was quite original—unlike many of his contemporaries in the avant-garde, he owed nothing to John Coltrane. Shepp and his regular quintet of 1966, which also includes trombonist Roswell Rudd, drummer Beaver Harris, and bassists Donald Garrett and Lewis Worrell, really stretch out on this live blowout, playing continuously for nearly 33 minutes. There is some solo space for his sidemen, but Shepp dominates the performance, and his emotional style and endurance are in peak form. Intense and rewarding music. —*Scott Yanow*

Live in San Francisco / Feb. 19, 1966 / Impulse! ✦✦✦✦
This out-of-print Impulse! LP features the fiery tenor Archie Shepp with his regularly working group of the period, a quintet also featuring trombonist Roswell Rudd, drummer Beaver Harris and both Donald Garrett and Lewis Worrell on basses. Although two pieces (Shepp's workout on piano on the ballad "Sylvia" and his

recitation on "The Wedding") are departures, the quintet sounds particularly strong on Herbie Nichols' "The Lady Sings the Blues" and "Wherever June Bugs Go" while Shepp's ballad statement on "In a Sentimental Mood" is both reverential and eccentric. —*Scott Yanow*

Mama Too Tight / Aug. 1966 / Impulse! ✦✦✦✦✦
Tenor saxophonist Archie Shepp's Impulse! recordings, most of which have not been reissued on CD yet, are among the most rewarding of his career. This LP matches his raspy, explorative tenor with trumpeter Tommy Turrentine, trombonists Roswell Rudd and Grachan Moncur, clarinetist Perry Robinson, Howard Johnson on tuba, bassist Charlie Haden and drummer Beaver Harris. Although three of the four songs (including the nearly 19-minute "A Portrait of Robert Thompson," which uses a section of "Prelude to a Kiss") are eulogies for fallen heroes, the music goes through a wide variety of emotions, makes strong use of the blues, and is both adventurous and often surprisingly accessible. —*Scott Yanow*

Magic of Ju–Ju / Apr. 26, 1967 / Impulse! ✦✦✦✦✦
For this Impulse! LP (not yet reissued on CD), innovative avant-garde tenor Archie Shepp is well-featured on his four originals, including the 18-1/2 minute sidelong title cut. Assisted by the trumpets of Martin Banks and Michael Zwerin, bassist Reggie Workman and five drummer/percussionists (Beaver Harris, Norman Connors, Ed Blackwell, Frank Charles and Dennis Charles), Shepp is heard in peak form throughout the album, hinting at the past while often playing with great intensity. —*Scott Yanow*

★ **Live at the Donaueschingen Music Festival** / Oct. 21, 1967 / MPS ✦✦✦✦✦
This is an exciting album. The important tenor Archie Shepp and his 1967 group—with both Roswell Rudd and Grachan Moncur on trombones, bassist Jimmy Garrison and drummer Beaver Harris—romp through the continuous 43-1/2 minute "One for the Trane" before an enthusiastic audience at a German music festival. Although he improvises very freely and with great intensity, Shepp surprised the crowd by suddenly bursting into a spaced-out version of "The Shadow of Your Smile" near the end of this memorable performance. On the whole, this very spirited set represents avant-garde jazz at its peak and Archie Shepp at his finest. —*Scott Yanow*

The Way Ahead / Jan. 29, 1968 / Impulse! ✦✦✦✦

Live at the Pan-African Festival / Jul. 29, 1969–Jul. 30, 1969 / Affinity ✦✦✦✦
Archie Shepp probably led more BYG recordings than anyone else. The first of his BYG's has been reissued as *Live at the Pan African Festival*. The Pan African Festival in Algiers served as a great realization of art and culture for many of the participants and on this recording we heard Shepp, Clifford Thornton, and Grachan Moncur III in an impromptu jam ("Brotherhood at Ketcha") with various native Algerian percussionists and "horn" men…Any study of Shepp makes listening to all of his BYG recordings essential. —*Bob Rusch, Cadence*

Yasmina: A Black Woman / Aug. 12, 1969 / Affinity ✦✦✦
There is some intriguing music on this out-of-print Affinity LP. Tenor saxophonist Archie Shepp met up with members of the Chicago avant-garde school for the first time, including Art Ensemble of Chicago members Lester Bowie, Roscoe Mitchell and Malachi Favors, on the lengthy "Yasmina," a track that also includes drummers Philly Joe Jones, Art Taylor and Sunny Murray. On "Sonny's Back," there is an unlikely tenor tradeoff between Shepp and Hank Mobley, while "Body and Soul" gives Shepp a showcase opportunity. Although this set is not essential, it is unique enough to be recommended to avant-garde collectors fortunate enough to find it. —*Scott Yanow*

Poem For Malcolm / Aug. 14, 1969 / Affinity ✦✦✦
This LP from the English Affinity LP is a mixed bag. Best is "Rain Forest" on which tenor saxophonist Archie Shepp, in a collaboration with trombonist Granchar Moncur III, pianist Vince Benedetti, bassist Malachi Favors and drummer Philly Joe Jones performs some stirring free jazz; the interplay between Shepp and Jones is particularly exciting. On a 4-1/2 minute "Oleo," Shepp "battles" some bebop with fellow tenor Hank Mobley, but the other two tracks, a workout for the leader's erratic soprano on "Mama Rose" and his emotional recitation on "Poem for Malcolm," are much less interesting, making this a less than essential release despite "Rain Forest." —*Scott Yanow*

Blase / Aug. 16, 1969 / Affinity ◆◆◆
Experimental quality, often raging solos. —*Ron Wynn*

Black Gypsy / Nov. 9, 1969 / Prestige ◆◆◆

Archie Shepp & Philly Joe Jones / Nov. 1969–Dec. 1969 / Fantasy ◆◆
This intriguing LP does not live up to its potential. Three generations of jazzmen were involved in this 1969 project, with veteran drummer Philly Joe Jones and the great avant-garde tenor Archie Shepp meeting up with two of the top "new jazz" players (altoist Anthony Braxton and violinist Leroy Jenkins). Unfortunately, both of the sidelong pieces have recitations, the performances are overly long, and there is quite a bit of rambling. This is a lesser effort that has been long out-of-print. —*Scott Yanow*

Live at Antibes / Jul. 18, 1970 / BYG ◆◆◆

Things Have Got to Change / May 17, 1971 / Impulse! ◆◆◆

Attica Blues / Jan. 24, 1972–Jan. 26, 1972 / Impulse! ◆◆◆

The Cry of My People / Sep. 25, 1972–Sep. 27, 1972 / ABC/Impulse! ◆◆◆

Coral Rock / Oct. 1973 / Prestige ◆◆◆

There's a Trumpet in My Soul / Apr. 12, 1975 / Freedom ◆◆◆
Raspy avant-garde tenor saxophonist Archie Shepp (who unfortunately also plays some soprano on this date) is the lead voice in a group that sometimes grows to 13 pieces, including four brass players, two keyboards and two percussionists, on this reissue. Two vocals and a poem recitation weigh down the music a bit, although Shepp gets in some good licks. The overall results are not essential, but Archie Shepp was still in his musical prime at the time. —*Scott Yanow*

Montreux, Vol. 2 / Jul. 18, 1975 / Freedom ◆◆◆◆
Tenor saxophonist Archie Shepp was at a turning point of sorts in 1975. He was near the end of his free jazz phase and would soon be exploring melodies from both the jazz tradition and the early 20th century; in addition his tone would begin to decline within a decade. However, that is not in evidence during this fairly rousing live appearance at the Montreux Jazz Festival with his quintet (which also includes trombonist Charles Greenlee, pianist Dave Burrell, bassist Cameron Brown and drummer Beaver Harris). This second of two CDs is the better of the pair and a good outing for Archie Shepp. —*Scott Yanow*

Montreux, Vol. 1 / Jul. 18, 1975 / Arista/Freedom ◆◆◆◆
The first of two CDs that resulted from the great tenor Archie Shepp's appearance at the 1975 Montreux Jazz Festival features the important avant-garde player in a quintet with trombonist Charles Greenlee, pianist Dave Burrell, bassist Cameron Brown and drummer Beaver Harris. Shepp, who was nearing the end of his free jazz period (soon he would be exploring hymns and traditional melodies) puts a lot of emotion into "Lush Life" and sounds fine on originals by Burrell and Greenlee in addition to his own "U-jamsa." A worthy effort. —*Scott Yanow*

A Sea of Faces / Aug. 4, 1975–Aug. 5, 1975 / Black Saint ◆◆◆

Steam / May 14, 1976 / Enja ◆◆◆◆
This colorful live LP features Archie Shepp on tenor, and a bit of his more basic piano, playing three lengthy compositions (Duke Ellington's "Solitude," Cal Massey's "A Message from Trane" and Shepp's own "Steam") in a sparse trio with bassist Cameron Brown and drummer Beaver Harris. The avant-garde innovator Shepp still sounds pretty strong at what was for him a fairly late period, displaying his distinctive raspy tone and what were for him some typically emotional ideas. —*Scott Yanow*

The Rising Sun Collection / Apr. 12, 1977 / Just A Memory ◆◆◆
This 1994 CD released for the first time a live set from 1977 by tenor saxophonist Archie Shepp from the Rising Sun Celebrity Jazz Club in Montreal. Shepp starts quite strong with his original "Ujaama" and a forceful statement on "Sonny's Back" (balancing the jazz tradition with his own distinctive raspy sound and avant-garde explorations). His outings on soprano are quite a bit weaker despite the presence of a fine rhythm section (pianist Dave Burrell, bassist Cameron Brown and drummer Charlie Persip) but, after a few uneven tracks, Shepp finishes with memorable versions of Burrell's "Crucificado" and Charlie Parker's "Confirmation." The good outweighs the bad, making this CD one that Archie Shepp fans will want. —*Scott Yanow*

Ballads for Trane / May 7, 1977 / Denon ◆◆◆◆

Day Dream / Jun. 3, 1977 / Denon ◆◆◆◆

On Green Dolphin Street / Nov. 28, 1977 / Denon ◆◆◆

Duet with Dollar Brand / Jun. 5, 1978 / Denon ◆◆◆◆
Excellent duos with traces of Afro-pop and free-jazz. —*Ron Wynn*

Live in Tokyo / Jun. 6, 1978 / Denon ◆◆◆

Lady Bird / Dec. 7, 1978 / Denon ◆◆◆◆

● **Trouble in Mind** / Feb. 6, 1980 / SteepleChase ◆◆◆◆◆
The second set of duets by Archie Shepp (doubling on tenor and soprano) and pianist Horace Parlan (the earlier SteepleChase set is *Goin' Home*) features the duo on a dozen blues-oriented pieces from the 1920s, two of which were released for the first time on this CD reissue. It is particularly interesting to hear Shepp, best known for his ferocious free jazz performances of the mid-to-late '60s, adjusting his sound and giving such songs as "Trouble in Mind," Earl Hines' "Blues in Thirds" and "St. James Infirmary" tasteful and respectful yet emotional treatment. Recommended. —*Scott Yanow*

Looking at Bird / Feb. 7, 1980 / SteepleChase ◆◆◆◆◆
Avant-garde tenor saxophonist Archie Shepp created a stir in 1977 when he recorded a set of hymns and folk melodies in melodic duets with pianist Horace Parlan. On February 6, 1980, he reunited with Parlan for a set of blues associated with Bessie Smith, and the following day, as a sort of sequel, Shepp played eight songs associated with Charlie Parker in collaboration with bassist Niels-Henning Orsted Pedersen. Although never a bebopper, Shepp does surprisingly well on such tunes as "Moose the Mooche," "Ornithology," "Yardbird Suite" and "Confirmation," even if he makes the mistake of doubling on his erratic soprano during a few numbers. Archie Shepp pays tribute to Bird not by copying him, but by being creative and playing Parker's repertoire in his own sound. Recommended. —*Scott Yanow*

I Know About the Life / Feb. 11, 1981 / Sackville ◆◆◆◆
By the time tenor saxophonist Archie Shepp recorded this Sackville date, which has been reissued on CD, he had shifted his focus from free-form improvisations to exploring standards. Joined by pianist Ken Werner, bassist Santi Debriano and drummer John Betsch, Shepp stretches out on "Giant Steps," "'Round Midnight" and "Well You Needn't," in addition to his own "I Know About the Life." Shepp's sound was not as strong as it had been previously, and would continue to get more erratic as the decade progressed, but he comes up with consistently inventive ideas, showing listeners that he did indeed know how to "play changes." A worthy effort. —*Scott Yanow*

Mama Rose / Feb. 5, 1982 / SteepleChase ◆◆◆

Soul Song / Dec. 1, 1982 / Enja ◆◆
This is one of Archie Shepp's more erratic sets. On the 15-1/2 minute "Mama Rose," the great tenor (who is joined by pianist Ken Werner, bassist Santi DeBriano and drummer Marvin "Smitty" Smith) unfortunately plays his out-of-tune soprano and takes an eccentric vocal. Additionally, Werner's brief "Soul Song" tends to wander without much direction. Much better is the 18-1/2 minute "Geechee," a lengthy workout for Shepp's emotional tenor, but due to this release's weak first half, it can be safely passed by. —*Scott Yanow*

The Good Life / 1984 / Varrick ◆◆
Archie Shepp's most rewarding recordings were mostly in the 1960s, when he was at his most fiery and innovative, and in the '70s, when he began exploring older standards and his tone was still in its prime. By the 1980s, Shepp was recording too frequently, spending more time than he should on his generally out-of-tune soprano and taking an excess of shouting vocals; worst of all, his tenor playing was losing some of its power. On this quartet session with pianist Kenny Werner, bassist Avery Sharpe and drummer Marvin "Smitty" Smith, Shepp plays three bop standards as best he can, although the recording quality has an exaggerated echo, then makes the mistake of singing "The Good Life" and plays his unfortunate soprano on two originals. An erratic and lesser effort. —*Scott Yanow*

California Meeting / May 22, 1985 / Soul Note ◆◆◆
Archie Shepp recordings in the 1980s are hit and miss; this is one of the more interesting ones. Shepp does make the mistake of playing soprano on "A Night in Tunisia" (his abilities on that instrument pale next to his tenor) and having a guest singer (Royal Blue) brought out of the audience to sing "St. James

Infirmary." But Shepp's tenor playing is excellent on a roaring "Giant Steps" and the ballad "My Romance," and his sidemen (pianist George Cables, bassist Herbie Lewis and drummer Eddie Marshall) are flexible and versatile enough for the diverse music. Not essential, but this CD is worth picking up by Archie Shepp's fans. —*Scott Yanow*

Little Red Moon / Dec. 11, 1985–Dec. 13, 1985 / Soul Note ✦✦
By 1985 Archie Shepp's tone on tenor had declined quite a bit from just a few years earlier. This should have been a strong set for the sidemen (trumpeter Enrico Rava, keyboardist Siegfried Kessler, bassist Wilbur Little and drummer Clifford Jarvis) are excellent and the repertoire is both diverse and challenging. However, Shepp fouls up "Naima" by playing his out-of-tune soprano, talks and sings on the 18-minute "Little Red Moon" more than he plays tenor and his sax sounds quite sloppy on "Whisper Not" and "Sweet Georgia Brown." Despite some good moments from the supporting cast, this is one to skip. —*Scott Yanow*

The Fifth of May / May 7, 1987–May 8, 1987 / Optimism ✦✦✦
This is an unusual CD with Archie Shepp, mostly playing tenor but also contributing a couple of vocals and a bit of soprano, performing duets with the keyboards and synthesizer of Jasper Van't Hof. The music (originals by Shepp or Van't Hof, along with John Coltrane's "Naima") ranges from danceable tracks and mood pieces to explorative works, and generally holds one's interest. A good couple of days for Archie Shepp, who could be quite erratic in the 1980s. —*Scott Yanow*

In Memory of / Mar. 13, 1988–Mar. 14, 1988 / Optimism ✦✦
This is one of the odder releases of the 1980s. For the first and only times, trumpeter Chet Baker and tenor saxophonist Archie Shepp teamed up for a pair of concerts in a quintet, which also included pianist Horace Parlan, bassist Herman Wright and drummer Clifford Jarvis. The fact that Shepp is an emotional avant-gardist and Baker a cool-toned lyrical trumpeter and that both have radically different singing styles (they take a vocal apiece) results in the obvious: these two individualists do not blend together very well. Other than Shepp's "Dedication to Bessie Smith's Blues," the repertoire is all standards. Baker plays pretty, while Shepp sounds sloppy and heavy. This CD is definitely a historical curiosity, but does not need to be listened to more than once. —*Scott Yanow*

Swing Low / Sep. 27, 1991–Sep. 28, 1991 / Plainisphare ✦✦✦✦
Tenor saxophonist Archie Shepp and pianist Horace Parlan had teamed up for a series of well-received SteepleChase studio duet albums that found the former avant-garde tenor exploring melodic and emotional renditions of traditional folk songs and blues. For this fairly rare Plainisphare CD, Shepp (who plays effective alto on two of the eight songs) is once again matched with Parlan although this time in a club. They mix together such tunes as "Swing Low, Sweet Chariot," "See See Rider" and "Go Down Moses" with a couple of standards ("Embraceable You" and Duke Ellington's "I Didn't Know About You") and Parlan's original "Billie's Bossa." Although Shepp's three vocals are an acquired taste, this set features some of his finest playing of the 1990s. —*Scott Yanow*

Andy Sheppard

b. Jan. 20, 1957, Warminster, Wilshire, England
Flute, Tenor Saxophone, Soprano Saxophone / Post-Bop, Crossover
One of the more intriguing and versatile British musicians, Andy Sheppard has on occasion made a big impression in the United States. He did not start playing music until he was 19 and planning to go to art college; a listen to John Coltrane's recordings changed the direction of his life. Within three weeks Sheppard was playing in public, but quite a few years of scuffling followed as he learned his craft and developed his own sound. In 1986 Andy Sheppard won a jazz competition and was signed to the Antilles label, which served as his breakthrough. Among his activities since then has been work with Gil Evans in France (1987), George Russell and Carla Bley. Although he has led his own group, Sheppard's highest profile thus far has been his involvement in a trio recording (*Songs with Legs*) with Carla Bley and Steve Swallow. —*Scott Yanow*

Andy Sheppard / 1988 / Antilles ✦✦✦✦
Young British star, with Randy Brecker (tpt) making guest appearance. —*Ron Wynn*

Introductions in the Dark / 1989 / Antilles ✦✦✦✦
Contemporary date. Yes, there are synthesizers galore and relatively simple rhythms. Still, Sheppard's sax solos are meaty and cleverly executed, despite an occasional indulgence for post-Coltrane theatrics. —*Ron Wynn*

● **Soft on the Inside** / Nov. 6, 1989–Nov. 9, 1989 / Antilles ✦✦✦✦✦

In Co-Motion / Feb. 1991 / Antilles ✦✦✦
British jazz-rock pianist Andy Sheppard leads a combo with Claude Deppa, Steve Lodder, Sylvan Richardson, Jr., and Dave Addams. They run through everything from rock and reggae to straight-ahead jazz and fusion, playing it with style and energy, although the solos sometimes lack ideas. —*Ron Wynn*

Rhythm Method / May 21, 1993–Jun. 12, 1993 / Blue Note ✦✦✦
Andy Sheppard, a fine tenor and soprano saxophonist, is heard here on an above-average fusion date. While Sheppard's solos are good enough, his rhythm section is somewhat anonymous and the six originals (all but one being over nine minutes long) do little other than set up grooves for Sheppard's fairly basic improvisations. Not a bad release but not all that memorable either. —*Scott Yanow*

Bobby Shew (Robert Joratz)

b. Mar. 4, 1941, Albuquerque, NM
Trumpet / Hard Bop
A fine technical trumpeter, Bobby Shew works well in brass sections and big bands. As a soloist, his soft tone and striking, but derivative style don't always result in memorable statements. But he's a highly competent player, with good facility and command of the horn. Shew began working professionally at 13 at dances in New Mexico. He played in bands during his years in the service, then joined the Tommy Dorsey Orchestra under Sam Donahue in the mid-'60s. Later came stints with Woody Herman and Buddy Rich. Shew was Rich's lead trumpeter during one stretch. He worked nine years in Las Vegas backing singers, playing in show bands and on film and television shows during the '60s and '70s.

Shew moved to Los Angeles in the '70s, and divided his time between studio work and jazz dates. He played with the Akiyoshi-Tabackin big band in the late '70s, and worked in bands led by Don Menza, Frank Capp, Nat Pierce and Louis Bellson. Shew moved from big bands to small combos in the '80s, recording and performing, heading a quintet, and playing in bands led by Art Pepper and Bud Shank. He's done workshops nationally and internationally. Shew's recorded for Delos, Pausa and Inner City. He has some dates available on CD. —*Ron Wynn and Michael G. Nastos*

Outstanding in His Field / Dec. 18, 1978–Jul. 3, 1979 / Inner City ✦✦✦
Studio veteran Bobby Shew plays with a confidence and technical mastery developed from years of session work. He's a steady, never flashy or gimmicky player who sometimes delivers powerhouse solos. These songs are very traditional West Coast jazz, and both Shew and his band perform them smoothly and professionally. —*Ron Wynn*

Class Reunion / 1980 / Sutra ✦✦✦✦

Play Song / May 20, 1981–May 21, 1981 / Jazzhounds ✦✦✦✦✦

Shewhorn / Jun. 1982–Jul. 1983 / PA/USA ✦✦✦✦

Breakfast Wine / Sep. 1983 / PA/USA ✦✦✦✦✦

Round Midnight / Dec. 17, 1984–Dec. 19, 1984 / Mo Pro ✦✦✦✦✦
All standards, all vital, from this trumpeter and the Steve Schmidt Trio. —*Michael G. Nastos*

Metropole Orchestra / Dec. 16, 1986–Nov. 24, 1988 / Mons ✦✦✦✦

Tribute To The Masters / Mar. 19, 1995–Mar. 20, 1995 / Double-Time ✦✦✦✦
Trumpeter Bobby Shew, a long underrated but talented bop-oriented trumpeter, helped to launch the new Double-Time label with this fine release. Shew teams up with saxophonist Jamey Aebersold (world renowned for his series of play-along instructional recordings) in a quintet with pianist Steve Schmidt, bassist Tyrone Wheeler and drummer Ed Soph for a set of music paying tribute to a variety of jazz composers (Horace Silver, Benny Golson, Thelonious Monk, Dave Brubeck, Charlie Parker, Clifford Brown, Duke Ellington, Hank Mobley and Dizzy Gillespie). Nothing all that surprising occurs (the standards are given con-

ventional and respectful treatment), but the solos are of a consistently high level and the music always swings. Bop fans will enjoy this CD. —*Scott Yanow*

● **Heavyweights** / Sep. 20, 1995–Sep. 21, 1995 / MMF ✦✦✦✦✦

Travis Shook

b. 1969, Oroville, Ca
Piano / Post-Bop
Travis Shook's career got off to a fast start although it has stalled somewhat since then. He started on piano at seven, spent some time playing heavy metal guitar and then came back to the piano. While at William Paterson College in New Jersey, he had the chance to play with such musicians as Benny Golson and Branford Marsalis. Shook won several contests (most notably the 1991 Great American Jazz Piano Competition at the Jacksonville Jazz Festival) and in 1993 he made his recording debut on his self-titled Columbia CD in a quartet that included Tony Williams and Bunky Green. His future musical directions should be worth watching. —*Scott Yanow*

● **Travis Shook** / 1993 / Columbia ✦✦✦✦✦
Travis Shook's debut as a leader features four standards and four lesser-known pieces and finds the 22-year old pianist displaying very impressive technique and (almost as importantly) plenty of self-restraint. His style shows slight echoes of McCoy Tyner and Herbie Hancock but also builds and releases tension in a colorful fashion reminiscent of Ahmad Jamal. Shook acquits himself well in the trio outing with bassist Ira Coleman and drummer Tony Williams and even maintains the spotlight during the two intense appearances by veteran altoist Bunky Green. Shook's solo version of "My Foolish Heart" is a highpoint. —*Scott Yanow*

Wayne Shorter

b. Aug. 25, 1933, Newark, NJ
Soprano Saxophone, Tenor Saxophone, Composer / Fusion, Post-Bop, Hard Bop
It's possible to measure some fans' tenures following jazz and popular music by how they recognize Wayne Shorter. There are many who remember him only as the soprano saxophonist in Miles Davis' jazz-rock bands, and co-leader of Weather Report. Those with longer memories harken back to his days as a young lion on Vee-Jay and with Art Blakey. Shorter has perfected on tenor and soprano sax the same evolving, eclectic approach as longtime friend and musical comrade Herbie Hancock on piano. He's combined hard bop and modal elements in his solos, playing with an intense and original style that includes a biting, terse attack and soulfulness. His soprano has one of the most elastic, wondrous tones ever; it's beauty and lyricism is unparalled. Shorter's better known for soprano than tenor since 1969, and during The Weather Report era played it about twice as often as he did tenor. He's also an excellent composer who was once Blakey's music director and provided such compositions to Miles Davis as "E.S.P.," "Pinocchio," "Nefertiti" and "Sanctuary." His writing was altered and simplified for Weather Report, consisting mainly of lyrical melodies and heavily syncopated funk backbeats.

Shorter began playing clarinet at 16, then switched to tenor sax. He studied music at New York University in the '50s, graduating in 1956. After working in a local band, Shorter joined Horace Silver for a short time before being drafted. Upon his discharge, he joined Maynard Ferguson in 1958, meeting Joe Zawinul while in this group. Shorter began working with Art Blakey in 1959, and was in The Messengers until 1963. He made his recording debut as a leader on Vee Jay, and made several recordings for Blue Note in the mid-'60s working with many top musicians, including his latter day Miles Davis comrades as well as Freddie Hubbard, James Spaulding and others. Shorter joined Davis' band in 1964, finally filling the seat and vacuum from John Coltrane's departure.

He stayed with the band until 1970, playing in two critical eras; the looser, freer work of the mid-'60s and the jazz-rock of the late '60s and early '70s, during which time Shorter began playing soprano. He recorded in the late '60s and '70s with Davis' comrade John McLaughlin, Sonny Sharrock, Miroslav Vitous, and others like Chick Corea and Jack DeJohnette who had also played jazz-rock with Davis. Shorter experimented with Latin and rock on such Blue Note albums as *Super Nova* and *Odyssey Of Iska*.

Shorter and Zawinul co-founded Weather Report in 1970, which they continued until 1985. The band began as a jazz-rock group, but gradually enjoyed so much success as a funk/rock/fusion out-

fit they grew stagnant churning out albums filled with conservative, trendy material and less open-ended, aggressive playing. Shorter was relatively inactive in the '70s outside of working with Weather Report, just recording a Brazilian album (*Native Dancer*) with Milton Nascimento early in the decade that made the Billboard charts. He toured with Hancock and other Davis' alumni on The VSOP acoustic jazz tour in the late '70s, also recording for Columbia. Shorter did sessions with Joni Mitchell and Steely Dan. He and Zawinul disbanded Weather Report in 1985.

Shorter started a new group in 1986 but overloaded it with electronics and generic compositions and arrangements. The results were poorly received albums such as *Atlantis* and *Phantom Navigator*, although the band's tours were more successful in terms of audience response and reaction. Shorter presented in his group a promising discovery, drummer Terri Lyne Carrington. She parlayed the exposure into a contract with talk show host Arsenio Hall's first "posse" and her own album deal. Shorter performed in the film "Round Midnight" in 1986, and played on the *Power Of Three* album with Michel Petrucciani and Jim Hall. He co-led a Latin jazz-rock group with Carlos Santana in 1988, touring internationally with them. His '88 Columbia album *Joy Ryder* didn't recapture past glories. But Wayne Shorter's list of achievements are such fans anxiously anticipate new developments in the '90s. —*Ron Wynn*

Blues á la Carte / Nov. 10, 1959 / Vee-Jay ✦✦✦✦✦
Wonderous early cuts. —*Ron Wynn*

Second Genesis / Oct. 11, 1960 / Vee-Jay ✦✦✦✦

Wayning Moments Plus / 1962 / Vee-Jay ✦✦✦✦
Wayne Shorter's third and final recording for Vee-Jay is reissued on this CD which augments the original eight songs with seven additional alternate takes. Shorter already had an original sound by this time, and with a young and fiery Freddie Hubbard joining him in the frontline and a fine rhythm section (pianist Eddie Higgins, bassist Jymie Merritt and drummer Marshall Thompson), the young tenor is heard in his early prime. There are some fine chancetaking solos on this hard bop date; "Black Orpheus," "Moon of Manakoora" and "All or Nothing at All" are among the highlights. —*Scott Yanow*

Night Dreamer / Apr. 29, 1964 / Blue Note ✦✦✦✦✦
1988 reissue of prime 60s lineup: Lee Morgan (tpt), McCoy Tyner (p), Reggie Workman (b), Elvin Jones (d). —*Ron Wynn*

★ **Juju** / Aug. 3, 1964 / Blue Note ✦✦✦✦✦

★ **Speak No Evil** / Dec. 24, 1964 / Blue Note ✦✦✦✦✦

The Soothsayer / Mar. 4, 1965 / Blue Note ✦✦✦✦✦

Etcetera / Jun. 14, 1965 / Blue Note ✦✦✦✦✦
It is strange that this classic Blue Note album was not released for the first time until 1980 for it finds tenor saxophonist Wayne Shorter in prime form, his four originals (along with Gil Evans' "Barracudas") are quite inventive and the rhythm section (pianist Herbie Hancock, bassist Cecil McBee and drummer Joe Chambers) is state of the art for 1965. These challenging performances find the musicians really listening closely to each other and pushing themselves. Although advanced, the music should not be labelled "avant-garde" or "free jazz" as much as just simply being called "original." —*Scott Yanow*

The All Seeing Eye / Oct. 15, 1965 / Blue Note ✦✦✦✦

★ **Adam's Apple** / Feb. 3, 1966 / Blue Note ✦✦✦✦✦

Schizophrenia / Mar. 20, 1967 / Blue Note ✦✦✦✦✦

Super Nova / Aug. 29, 1969+Sep. 2, 1969 / Blue Note ✦✦✦✦
1988 reissue of careening, eventful date; has Chick Corea (k), John McLaughlin (g), Jack DeJohnette (d). —*Ron Wynn*

Moto Grosso Feio / Aug. 26, 1970 / Blue Note ✦✦✦

Odyssey of Iska / Aug. 26, 1970 / Blue Note ✦✦✦

Native Dancer / Sep. 12, 1974 / Columbia ✦✦✦✦
Wayne Shorter surprised the jazz world with this exotic excursion into Brazilian music in 1975. Milton Nascimento, who accompanies Shorter, wrote five of the nine compositions on this album. Reminiscent of the best of the jazz-samba fusion recordings of Stan Getz, *Native Dance* is every bit as lush and rich. This is an inspired recording of the first water and in a word: lovely. —*Michael Erlewine*

Atlantis / 1985 / Columbia ✦✦

Phantom Navigator / Jun. 1987 / Columbia ✦✦

Joy Ryder / 1987 / Columbia ✦✦
Spotlights more jazz/rock/fusion lineup and material. —*Ron Wynn*

High Life / 1994-1995 / Verve ✦✦✦✦
Wayne Shorter's debut for Verve was his first release as a leader in quite a long time and his most rewarding recording since the prime years of Weather Report, 15 years before. Shorter and keyboardist Rachel Z. spent a year working on developing and orchestrating his ideas and the results are these nine originals. Although use was made of orchestral horns and strings, most of the backing in these often-dense ensembles is by a standard rhythm section (which includes Marcus Miller on electric bass and bass clarinet) and Rachel Z's synthesizers. The pieces set moods rather than state singable melodies, are not afraid to utilize electronic rhythms now and then in an unpredictable fashion, and are both intelligent and largely danceable. However, Wayne Shorter's playing (not only on soprano and tenor but a bit of alto and baritone) is always distinctive and he sounds very much as if he is pushing himself. In fact his emotional statements and the complexity of the ensembles push this music way above virtually all of the so-called "contemporary jazz" (which is often merely a synonym for jazzy pop) into the idiom of creative music. It helps for listeners to have a liking for the sound of Weather Report (even though this group is not a copy), but even Shorter's older fans will find his playing here to be quite stimulating. *—Scott Yanow*

Horace Silver

b. Sep. 2, 1928, Norwalk, CT
Piano, Composer, Leader / Hard Bop, Soul Jazz
The leading composer and hard bop pioneer, Horace Silver's piano solos have been a jazz force since the early '50s. He blended vintage R&B, bebop, gospel, blues and Caribbean elements into jazz in an inspired manner, writing and playing works that were rhythmically and melodically simple, yet gripping and compelling. His work has harmonic sophistication but seldom loses its earthiness and grit. He's been among the rare jazz musicians who've composed the bulk of their material. He's written for combos and vocalists equally well, even on many occasions providing lyrics to accompany his instrumental pieces.

Silver was a founding member of the original Jazz Messengers with Art Blakey and his ensembles have helped introduce and/or nurture quite a few careers including Blue Mitchell, Junior Cook, Donald Byrd, Art Farmer, Joe Henderson, Woody Shaw, Tom Harrell, Michael Brecker and Randy Brecker. Silver began studying saxophone and piano in high school, listening heavily to the blues and boogie woogie. He later mixed that with the Cape Verdean folk music he'd heard as a child. Silver worked in 1950 on a date with Stan Getz, who'd come to make a guest apearance in Hartford. Getz tabbed Silver to work with him, and Silver stayed for a year. Getz cut three of his compositions, "Penny," "Potter's Luck" and "Split Kick."

The next year Silver moved to New York, where he worked with Coleman Hawkins, Lester Young, Oscar Pettiford and then Art Blakey. He recorded with Lou Donaldson for Blue Note in 1954, and subsequently cut his own trio sessions for the label shortly afterward, working with bassists Gene Ramey, Percy Heath or Curley Russell and Blakey on drums. This began an association with Blue Note that lasted nearly 30 years. Silver was co-leader from 1953 to 1955 of a band with Blakey known as the Jazz Messengers. When Silver departed in 1956, Blakey took over the leadership role. Silver's groups became quite popular in the '50s and '60s. Such numbers as "The Preacher," "Doodlin'," "Sister Sadie" and "Song For My Father" became jazz classics, and Silver's albums often crossed over to R&B, soul and blues audiences. Ray Charles covered "Doodlin'" and Silver band members Mitchell, Joe Henderson, Kenny Dorham, Clifford Jordan and Hank Mobley went on to lead their own bands. Silver's forays into hard bop, soul jazz and funk made Blue Note both an artistic and commercial juggernaut. "Song For My Father" and "Cape Verdean Blues" both charted in the mid-'60s. Silver began to experiment with concept albums in the '70s, doing a trilogy he called "The United States Of Mind." The jazz content of some of this was miminal, but he experimented with strings, African and Indian percussion and multiple vocalists.

Silver left Blue Note at the end of the '70s, forming his own label and issuing recordings he called "Holistic Metaphysical Music." Much of Silver's late '70s and early '80s material was in a quasi-religious bent, but he also established Emerald, a subsidary of Silveto, and issued vintage dates like *Horace Silver—Live 1964*, which had unreleased versions of "Senor Blues" and "Filthy McNasty." A new Silver album was released in 1993 by Columbia,

It's Got To Be Funky. There's plenty of classic Silver sessions available on CD. *—Ron Wynn*

The Trio Sides / Oct. 9, 1952-Mar. 25, 1968 / Blue Note ✦✦✦✦✦
This double LP includes all of Horace Silver's trio recordings for Blue Note including 14 selections from 1952-53 and nine other performances dating from 1956-68 when he normally recorded with his quintet. Silver, a highly individual composer and pianist whose funky style became very influential by the late '50s, is sometimes overlooked as a keyboard soloist so this hard-to-find set (which includes early versions of "Ecaroh" and "Opus de Funk") sheds new light on his versatile talents. Well worth searching for. *—Scott Yanow*

Horace Silver Trio, Vol. 1: Spotlight on Drums / Oct. 23, 1952 / Blue Note ✦✦✦✦
Most Silver albums are with a combo (quintet, etc.). It is refreshing and clarifying to listen to his trio work. Includes the classic "Opus De Funk." *—Michael Erlewine*

★ **Horace Silver and the Jazz Messengers** / Nov. 13, 1954-Feb. 6, 1955 / Blue Note ✦✦✦✦✦
A true classic, this CD found pianist Horace Silver and drummer Art Blakey co-leading the Jazz Messengers; Silver would leave a year later to form his own group. Also featuring trumpeter Kenny Dorham, Hank Mobley on tenor and bassist Doug Watkins, this set is most notable for the original versions of Silver's "The Preacher" and "Doodlin'," funky standards that helped launch hard bop and both the Jazz Messengers and Silver's quintet. Essential music. *—Scott Yanow*

Silver's Blue / Jul. 2, 1956-Jul. 17, 1956 / Portrait ✦✦✦✦
This LP documents the birth of the Horace Silver Quintet, recorded shortly after he left The Jazz Messengers along with some of the other original members. The seven selections (three of which are Silver compositions) feature either Joe Gordan or Donald Byrd on trumpets, tenor saxophonist Hank Mobley, bassist Doug Watkins and either Kenny Clarke or Art Taylor on drums. Although Silver's piano style was already largely formed, his group did not yet have the distinctive sound it would develop. However, this hard bop music is still quite enjoyable and very historical. *—Scott Yanow*

Six Pieces of Silver / Nov. 10, 1956 / Blue Note ✦✦✦✦✦
The first classic album by the Horace Silver Quintet, this CD is highlighted by "Senor Blues" (heard in three versions including a later vocal rendition by Bill Henderson) and "Cool Eyes." The early Silver quintet was essentially The Jazz Messengers of the year before (with trumpeter Donald Byrd, tenor saxophonist Hank Mobley and bassist Doug Watkins while drummer Louis Hayes was in Blakey's place), but already the band was starting to develop a sound of its own. "Senor Blues" officially put Horace Silver on the map. *—Scott Yanow*

Sterling Silver / Nov. 10, 1956-Jan. 28, 1964 / Blue Note ✦✦✦
This very interesting collector's LP is comprised of versions of "Senor Blues" and "Tippin" that were originally part of a 45, along with seven previously unissued performances from a variety of sets by the Horace Silver Quintet (in addition to a trio rendition of "Que Pasa"). General collectors should get the pianist/composer's regular Blue Note releases first, but Silver's longtime fans will find this fresh music fascinating and quite enjoyable. *—Scott Yanow*

The Stylings of Silver / May 8, 1957 / Blue Note ✦✦✦✦
The 1957 Horace Silver Quintet (featuring trumpeter Art Farmer and tenor saxophonist Hank Mobley) is in top form on this date, particularly on "My One and Only Love" and their famous version of "Home Cookin'." All of Silver's Blue Note quintet recordings are consistently superb and swinging, and although not essential, this is a very enjoyable set. *—Scott Yanow*

Further Explorations by the Horace Silver Quintet / Jan. 3, 1958 / Blue Note ✦✦✦✦
With trumpeter Art Farmer and tenor saxophonist Clifford Jordan as key members of his quintet, it is not surprising that pianist Horace Silver sounds inspired throughout this set. His increasingly distinctive hard bop group performed five Silver compositions (none of which became standards despite these versions) and the standard "Ill Wind" for this excellent session. *—Scott Yanow*

★ **Finger Poppin' with the Horace Silver Quintet** / Feb. 1, 1959 / Blue Note ✦✦✦✦✦
The first recording by the most famous version of the Horace Silver Quintet is also one of the highpoints of the pianist/com-

poser's career. Among the more memorable tracks of this classic set are "Juicy Lucy" (the epitome of funky jazz), "Cookin' at the Continental" and "Come on Home," but all eight performances are superlative. With trumpeter Blue Mitchell, Junior Cook's tenor, bassist Eugene Taylor and drummer Louis Hayes, Horace Silver had found the perfect forum for his piano and his highly accessible songs. Essential music. —*Scott Yanow*

Blowin' the Blues Away / Aug. 10, 1959 / Blue Note ✦✦✦✦✦
The second recording by the classic version of the Horace Silver Quintet (with trumpeter Blue Mitchell, tenor saxophonist Junior Cook, bassist Eugene Taylor and drummer Louis Hayes) introduced Silver's compositions "Sister Sadie" and "Peace" (both of which became jazz standards) in addition to the title track. No jazz library is complete without at least three or four Horace Silver albums. —*Scott Yanow*

Horace-Scope / Jul. 9, 1960 / Blue Note ✦✦✦✦
The most famous version of the Horace Silver Quintet lasted five years (1959-64) and resulted in six albums of which *Horace Scope* was the third. "Strollin'" is the best known of the new Silver compositions introduced on this set although his "Nica's Dream" (which was already a few years old) is the only standard. With trumpeter Blue Mitchell, tenor saxophonist Junior Cook, bassist Gene Taylor and his new drummer Roy Brooks, this was the perfect group for Horace Silver's music. —*Scott Yanow*

Doin' the Thing (At the Village Gate) / May 19, 1961–May 20, 1961 / Blue Note ✦✦✦✦✦
This live set (recorded at the Village Gate) finds pianist/composer Horace Silver and his most acclaimed quintet (the one with trumpeter Blue Mitchell, tenor saxophonist Junior Cook, bassist Gene Taylor and drummer Roy Brooks) stretching out on four selections including his new song "Filthy McNasty." Two shorter performances were added to the CD version of this easily enjoyable and always funky hard bop session. —*Scott Yanow*

The Tokyo Blues / Jul. 13, 1962–Jul. 14, 1962 / Blue Note ✦✦✦✦
Pianist/composer Horace Silver was inspired by a successful tour of Japan to write these four originals (the best known of which was the title cut) for this fine set, which also includes Ronnell Bright's "Cherry Blossom." Although the material is now somewhat obscure, the funky music still communicates very well and the solos of trumpeter Blue Mitchell, tenor saxophonist Junior Cook and Silver himself are always worth hearing. —*Scott Yanow*

Silver's Serenade / Apr. 11, 1963–Apr. 12, 1963 / Blue Note ✦✦✦✦
The sixth and final recording session by the most famous of Horace Silver's quintets (the version with trumpeter Blue Mitchell and tenor saxophonist Junior Cook) did not introduce any new classic tunes ("Silver's Serenade" is the best known) but, as with the previous sets, the results are swinging, funky and quite creative within the idiom. All of Silver's Blue Note quintet recordings are quite enjoyable. —*Scott Yanow*

Horace Silver Live: 1964 / Jun. 6, 1964 / Emerald ✦✦✦✦
Released by Horace Silver's own label, this LP contains "new" versions of "Filthy McNasty," "The Tokyo Blues," "Senor Blues" and the lesser-known "Skinney Minnie," as played by his quintet with tenorman Joe Henderson and trumpeter Carmell Jones. These renditions make for an interesting comparison with the earlier versions cut by Silver with Junior Cook and Blue Mitchell and they are reasonably well-recorded. Recommended. —*Scott Yanow*

★ **Song for My Father** / Oct. 26, 1964 / Blue Note ✦✦✦✦✦
Horace Silver's most famous album includes the memorable title cut, four of his other recent compositions (including "Calcutta Cutie" and "Lonely Woman") and Joe Henderson's "The Kicker." Although trumpeter Blue Mitchell and tenor saxophonist Junior Cook reunited for "Calcutta Cutie," the remainder of this classic set features Henderson's tenor and trumpeter Carmell Jones. Funky hard bop at its best, this is essential music for any jazz collection. —*Scott Yanow*

Natives Are Restless Tonight / Apr. 16, 1965–Feb. 18, 1966 / Emerald ✦✦✦✦✦
Taken from three concerts performed during 1965-66 and released by Horace Silver's own record label decades later, this valuable CD features tenor saxophonist Joe Henderson and either Carmell Jones or Woody Shaw on trumpet playing fresh versions of four of Silver's compositions including a "new" "Song for My Father," "Que Pasa," two versions of "The African Queen" and the title cut. Since the great Silver has tended to record on an annual basis through the years, mostly sticking to new material, this live

Music Map

Baritone Saxophone

Pre-Bop Style Baritonists
Harry Carney (1926-74 with Duke Ellington)
Jack Washington (1927-35 with Bennie Moten,
1936-43 with Count Basie)
Ernie Caceres (in Eddie Condon's Chicago Jazz groups)
Haywood Henry (with Erskine Hawkins)
Charlie Fowlkes
Joe Temperley

Bop Soloists
Serge Chaloff   Cecil Payne
Leo Parker   Sahib Shihab

R&B
Paul "Hucklebuck" Williams

Cool Jazz
Gerry Mulligan
Lars Gullin
Bob Gordon

Hard Bop to Modern Mainstream
Pepper Adams   Jack Nimitz
Charles Davis   Bruce Johnston
Ronnie Ross   Ronnie Cuber
Nick Brignola   Gary Smulyan

Avant-Garde
Pat Patrick
John Surman
Hamiett Bluiett

set gives one a rare opportunity to hear his quintet stretching out on songs that were more familiar to them. —*Scott Yanow*

Cape Verdean Blues / Oct. 1, 1965–Oct. 22, 1965 / Blue Note ✦✦✦✦✦
By late 1965 Horace Silver's Quintet featured trumpeter Woody Shaw and tenor saxophonist Joe Henderson and on half of this set, the great trombonist J.J. Johnson sits in. "The Cape Verdean Blues," "Pretty Eyes" and Henderson's "Mo' Joe" are among the highlights of this high-quality set of funky hard bop by one of the pacesetting groups. —*Scott Yanow*

The Jody Grind / Nov. 2, 1966–Nov. 23, 1966 / Blue Note ✦✦✦✦
This excellent set finds Horace Silver fronting a particularly advanced edition of his quintet. This band featured trumpeter Woody Shaw, tenor saxophonist Tyrone Washington and on half of the six tracks (all Silver compositions) the alto and flute of James Spaulding. "The Jody Grind" and "Dimples" are the closest any of these songs came to becoming standards, but Silver fans will find much to enjoy here. —*Scott Yanow*

Serenade to a Soul Sister / Mar. 25, 1968–Mar. 25, 1968 / Blue Note ✦✦✦✦✦
One of the final classic albums by the Horace Silver Quintet, this set finds Silver using such sidemen as trumpeter Charles Tolliver,

either Stanley Turrentine or Bennie Maupin on tenors and on half of the tracks, the young drummer Billy Cobham. The six Silver compositions include "Psychedelic Sally" and "Serenade to a Soul Sister." This music is both timeless and very much of the period. —*Scott Yanow*

You Gotta Take a Little Love / Jan. 10, 1969 / Blue Note ✦✦✦✦
One of the final Horace Silver Quintet Blue Note albums, this somewhat forgotten LP, dedicated to "The Brotherhood of Men," is an instrumental set that introduced six new compositions by the pianist/leader (none of which caught on as standards) along with Bennie Maupin's "Lovely's Daughter." Maupin (on tenor and flute), trumpeter Randy Brecker, bassist John Williams and drummer Billy Cobham comprise Silver's excellent late-'60s hard bop group. —*Scott Yanow*

That Healin' Feelin' / Apr. 8, 1970–Jun. 18, 1970 / Blue Note ✦✦✦
Lyrics a bit to the pretentious side; music overcomes it. —*Ron Wynn*

Total Response / Nov. 15, 1970+Jan. 29, 1971 / Blue Note ✦✦

In Pursuit of the 27th Man / 1970+Nov. 10, 1972 / Blue Note ✦✦✦✦
This obscure Horace Silver LP features two separate sessions by the pianist/composer. On three selections he is joined by trumpeter Randy Brecker, tenor great Michael Brecker, Bob Cranshaw on electric bass and drummer Mickey Roker. The other four numbers feature vibraphonist David Friedman in a quartet with Silver, Cranshaw and Roker, a very unusual sound for a Horace Silver set. But no matter what the instrumentation, the style is pure Silver, hard-driving and melodic hard bop with a strong dose of funky soul. —*Scott Yanow*

All (Phase III) / Jan. 17, 1972+Feb. 14, 1972 / Blue Note ✦✦

Silver 'n Brass / Jan. 10, 1975+Jan. 17, 1975 / Blue Note ✦✦✦
The first of five LPs that feature Horace Silver's Quintet being augmented by other instrumentalists, this set finds trumpeter Tom Harrell, tenor saxophonist Bob Berg, either Ron Carter or Bob Cranshaw on bass and either Al Foster or Bernard Purdie on drums joined by five brass players and two reed specialists. Although there are tributes to Tadd Dameron ("Dameron's Dance") and Duke Ellington ("The Sophisticated Hippie"), the music is recognizably Silver—funky hard bop. —*Scott Yanow*

Silver 'n Wood / Nov. 7, 1975–Jan. 3, 1976 / Blue Note ✦✦✦
The second of five LPs that find Horace Silver's Quintet (which by 1976 featured trumpeter Tom Harrell and tenor saxophonist Bob Berg) augmented by a group of other players, this set has six reeds and two trombones, giving Silver more tone colors to work with than usual. The two sidelong works ("The Tranquilizer Suite" and "The Process of Creation Suite") are not all that memorable, but the music overall (helped out by strong solos) is typical Silver hard bop. —*Scott Yanow*

Silver 'n Voices / Sep. 24, 1976–Oct. 1, 1976 / Blue Note ✦✦
Horace Silver, a brilliant composer of funky melodies, was never that strong a lyricist despite his good intentions. For this set (following the *Silver 'N Brass* and *Silver 'N Wood* sessions), the pianist's quintet (featuring trumpeter Tom Harrell and tenorman Bob Berg) is joined by six voices under the direction of Alan Copeland. The self-help lyrics get a bit cloying and the voices simply weigh down the music, but there are some good solos along the way. —*Scott Yanow*

Silver 'n Percussion / Nov. 12, 1977–Nov. 17, 1977 / Blue Note ✦✦✦
Following sessions that featured Horace Silver's Quintet being augmented respectively by brass, reeds and voices, percussion was the logical next step. Silver's 1977 band starred trumpeter Tom Harrell and tenor saxophonist Larry Schneider and on this record they are joined by one or two percussionists, and seven voices. The pianist/leader pays tribute to his African heritage and to the American Indians' spiritual beliefs in two separate sidelong suites but, even with the "plot," the music has its funky moments. —*Scott Yanow*

Silver 'n Strings Play the Music of the Spheres / Nov. 3, 1978–Nov. 2, 1979 / Blue Note ✦✦
Horace Silver's final Blue Note record (after over 25 years on the label) is a double LP that augments his quintet (featuring fluegelhornist Tom Harrell and tenor saxophonist Larry Schneider) with 14 strings and a harp. In addition, there are four vocalists (including Gregory Hines) singing lyrics that reflect Silver's self-help and

spiritual beliefs. He was never as strong a lyricist as he was a composer and pianist so the vocals weigh down the music a bit. The song titles probably kept a few of these pieces from becoming better-known. Who ever heard of such songs as "Negative Patterns of the Subconscious", "Progress Through Dedication and Discipline" and "We Expect Positive Results"? —*Scott Yanow*

Spiritualizing the Senses / Jan. 19, 1983 / Silveto ✦✦✦

There's No Need to Struggle / Aug. 25, 1983–Sep. 1, 1983 / Silveto ✦✦✦

Continuity of Spirit / Mar. 25, 1985 / Silveto ✦✦
After the original Blue Note label eventually left jazz and then collapsed, pianist Horace Silver (who was with the company for over 25 years) formed his own private label, Silveto (using the Emerald subsidiary to issue older concert performances). The *Continuity of Spirit* finds Silver (along with The Los Angeles Modern String Orchestra, four woodwinds, fluegelhornist Carl Saunders and three vocalists) paying tribute to Duke Ellington, W.C. Handy and Scott Joplin. The idea of using disc jockey Chuck Niles as "the spirit of Duke Ellington" is pretty hokey and the original music owes little to Ellington, Handy or Joplin; everything is in Horace Silver's own style. But there are some swinging moments on this well-intentioned set. —*Scott Yanow*

Music to Ease Your Disease / Mar. 31, 1988 / Silveto ✦✦✦
Horace Silver has long been a believer in the self-help holistic movement and this has been reflected in the lyrics he has written during the past decade. Andy Bey interprets such songs on this LP as "What Is the Sinus-Minus," "The Respiratory Story" and the title cut, none of which seem destined to be covered by other artists. However, there are plenty of strong instrumental moments from an all-star quintet that includes pianist Silver, fluegelhornist Clark Terry, tenor saxophonist Junior Cook, bassist Ray Drummond and drummer Billy Hart, and for that reason this is the strongest release on Silveto to date. —*Scott Yanow*

It's Got to Be Funky / Feb. 1993 / Columbia ✦✦✦✦
After a 13-year period in which he mostly recorded for his private Silveto label, pianist/composer Horace Silver was rediscovered by Columbia for this session. Rather than featuring a standard quintet as he did throughout his career, the funky pianist is heard with his trio, a six-piece brass ensemble and guest tenors Red Holloway, Eddie Harris and Branford Marsalis; Andy Bey contributes four vocals. All of the music (except for a remake of "Song for My Father") was new and served as proof that the master of jazz-funk had not lost his stuff. —*Scott Yanow*

Pencil Packin' Papa / 1994 / Columbia ✦✦✦✦
This CD's main assets are the many new compositions by Horace Silver and his colorful arrangements for the six-piece brass section. Although not enough is heard from the brass players on an individual basis (the greatly underrated trumpeter Oscar Brashear and trombonist George Bohanon get just one solo apiece), this is partly alleviated by the guest tenors. Red Holloway solos on seven songs while James Moody, Eddie Harris and Rickey Woodard each pop up twice. In addition, O.C. Smith does a fine job on his four vocals although Silver's abilities as a lyricist are still open to question. However, his piano solos are typically exciting and inventive and Silver has obviously lost none of his enthusiasm even after four decades of music making. —*Scott Yanow*

Omer Simeon

b. Jul. 21, 1902, New Orleans, LA, d. Sep. 17, 1959, New York, NY
Clarinet, Tenor Saxophone / New Orleans Jazz, Swing
Omer Simeon was Jelly Roll Morton's favorite clarinetist, but he was versatile enough to hold down a longtime position in Earl Hines' big band during the swing era. Simeon began to play clarinet when his family moved from New Orleans to Chicago in 1914. Lorenzo Tio, Jr. gave him lessons from 1918 to 1920. Simeon played in his brother Al's band briefly, then worked with Charlie Elgar's Creole Orchestra in Chicago and Milwaukee in the mid and late '20s. He recorded with Jelly Roll Morton in 1926, and was featured on "Black Bottom Stomp." Simeon joined King Oliver in 1927, touring with him in St. Louis and New York. He also worked with Luis Russell in New York and recorded with Morton again in 1928.

Simeon worked in Chicago with Erskine Tate in the late '20s and early '30s, then with Earl Hines in the early and mid-'30s, Horace Henderson in 1938, Walter Fuller in 1940 and Coleman Hawkins in 1941. He became a member of Jimmie Lunceford's orchestra in 1942. Simeon also recorded with Kid Ory in 1944 and 1945 in Hollywood. He stayed with The Lunceford band after the leader's death until 1950, then worked in New York the remainder of his life. Omer Simeon played and recorded with Wilbur de Paris' New New Orleans Jazz Band from 1951 up until his death in 1959 and is today remembered as one of the most technically skilled clarinetists of the 1920s. —*Ron Wynn and Scott Yanow*

Omer Simeon Trio with James P. Johnson / Disc ✦✦✦✦

Sonny Simmons (Huey Simmons)

b. Aug. 4, 1933, Sicily Island, LA
Alto Saxophone / Avant-Garde, Free Jazz
Altoist Sonny Simmons made a strong impression in the 1960s as one of the most promising avant-garde players. He grew up in Oakland, CA, started playing English horn and then at 16 took up the alto. Stints with Lowell Fulsom and Amos Milburn and some time spent playing bebop preceded Simmons finding his own sound in free jazz. In 1961 he spent some time with Charles Mingus and then in 1962 he formed a group with flutist Prince Lasha. After they recorded *The Cry*, Simmons moved to New York, recorded with Elvin Jones and Eric Dolphy and then in 1965 he returned to the Bay Area. Simmons met and married the powerful trumpeter Barbara Donald, recorded for ESP and the duo performed and recorded in several settings. However, by the mid-'70s Simmons largely dropped out of music, the marriage broke up and the altoist was forgotten for nearly 20 years. In 1994 Sonny Simmons (who had apparently played on the streets and been scuffling) suddenly re-emerged in peak form and as adventurous as ever, recording a brilliant trio album (*Ancient Ritual*) for Qwest/Warner Bros that earned him long overdue recognition and launched the beginning of his second career. —*Scott Yanow*

Staying on the Watch / Aug. 30, 1966 / ESP ✦✦✦✦
Music from the Spheres / Dec. 1966 / ESP ✦✦✦✦✦
Free-jazz gem from this saxophonist with trumpeter Barbara Donald. —*Michael G. Nastos*

Manhattan Egos / Feb. 10, 1969 / Arhoolie ✦✦✦✦✦
Rumasuma / Jul. 31, 1969–Aug. 1, 1969 / Contemporary ✦✦✦
Burning Spirits / Nov. 24, 1970 / Contemporary ✦✦✦✦
A two-fer with Barbara Donald (tpt), Cecil McBee (b) and Richard Davis (d). —*Michael G. Nastos*

Backwoods Suite / Jan. 1982 / West Wind ✦✦✦✦✦
★ **Ancient Ritual** / Dec. 7, 1992–Dec. 8, 1992 / Warner Brothers ✦✦✦✦✦

Nina Simone

b. Feb. 21, 1933, Tryon, NC
Vocals, Piano / Standards
Of all the major singers of the late 20th century, Nina Simone is one of the hardest to classify. She's recorded extensively in the soul, jazz, and pop idioms, often over the course of the same album; she's also comfortable with blues, gospel, and Broadway. It's perhaps most accurate to label her as a "soul" singer in terms of emotion, rather than form. Like, say, Aretha Franklin, or Dusty Springfield, Simone is an eclectic, who brings soulful qualities to whatever material she interprets. These qualities are among her strongest virtues; paradoxically, they also may have kept her from attaining a truly mass audience. The same could be said of her stage persona; admired for her forthright honesty and individualism, she's also known for feisty feuding with audiences and promoters alike.

If Simone has a chip on her shoulder, it probably arose from the formidable obstacles she had to overcome to establish herself as a popular singer. Raised in a family of eight children, she originally harbored hopes of becoming a classical pianist, studying at New York's prestigious Juilliard School of Music—a rare position for an African-American woman in the 1950s. Needing to support herself while she studied, she generated income by working as an accompanist and giving piano lessons. Auditioning for a job as a pianist in an Atlantic City nightclub, she was told she had the spot if she would sing as well as play. Almost by accident, she began to carve a reputation as a singer of secular material, though her skills at the piano would serve her well throughout her career.

In the late '50s, Simone began recording for the small Bethlehem label (a subsidiary of the vastly important early R&B/rock & roll King label). In 1959, her version of George Gershwin's "I Loves You Porgy" gave her a Top 20 hit—which would, amazingly, prove to be the only Top 40 entry of her career.

Nina wouldn't need hit singles for survival, however, establishing herself not with the rock & roll/R&B crowd but with the adult/nightclub/album market. In the early '60s, she recorded no less than nine albums for the Candix label, about half of them live. These unveiled her as a performer of nearly unsurpassed eclecticism, encompassing everything from Ellingtonian jazz and Israeli folk songs to spirituals and movie themes.

Simone's best recorded work was issued on Philips during the mid-'60s. Here, as on Candix, she was arguably over-exposed, issuing seven albums within a three-year period. These records can be breathtakingly erratic, moving from warm ballad interpretations of Jacques Brel and Billie Holiday and instrumental piano workouts to brassy pop and angry political statements in a heartbeat. There's a great deal of fine music to be found on these, however. Simone's moody-yet-elegant vocals are like no one else's, presenting a fiercely independent soul who harbors enormous (if somewhat hard-bitten) tenderness.

Like many African-American entertainers of the mid-'60s, Simone was deeply affected by the civil rights movement and burgeoning Black pride. Some (though by no means most) of her best material from this time addressed these concerns in a fashion more forthright than almost any other singer. "Old Jim Crow" and, more particularly, the classic "Mississippi Goddam" were especially notable self-penned efforts in this vein, making one wish that Nina had written more of her own material instead of turning to outside sources for most of her repertoire.

Not that this repertoire wasn't well-chosen. Several of her covers from the mid-'60s, indeed, were classics: her revision of Weill-Brecht's "Pirate Jenny" to reflect the bitter elements of African-American experience, for instance, or her mournful interpretation of Brel's "Ne Me Quitte Pas." Other highlights were her versions of "Don't Let Me Be Misunderstood," covered by the Animals for a rock hit; "I Put a Spell on You," which influenced the vocal line on the Beatles' "Michelle"; and the buzzing, jazzy "See Line Woman."

Simone was not as well-served by her tenure with RCA in the late '60s and early '70s, another prolific period that saw the release of nine albums. These explored a less eclectic range, with a considerably heavier pop-soul base to both the material and arrangements. One bonafide classic did come out of this period: "Young, Gifted & Black," written by Simone and Weldon Irvine, Jr., would be successfully covered by both Aretha Franklin and Donny Hathaway. She did have a couple of Top Five British hits in the late '60s with "Ain't Got No" (from the musical *Hair*) and a cover of the Bee Gees' "To Love Somebody," neither of which rank among her career highlights.

Simone fell on turbulent times in the 1970s, divorcing her husband/manager Andy Stroud, encountering serious financial problems, and becoming something of a nomad, settling at various points in Switzerland, Liberia, Barbados, France, and Britain. After leaving RCA, she recorded rarely, although she did make the critically well-received *Baltimore* in 1978 for the small CTI label. She had an unpredictable resurgence in 1987, when an early track, "My Baby Just Cares for Me," became a big British hit after being used in a Chanel perfume television commercial. 1993's *A Single Woman* marked her return to an American major label, and her profile was also boosted when several of her songs were featured in the film *Point of No Return*. She published her biography, *I Put a Spell on You*, in 1991. —*Richie Unterberger*

★ **Nina at Town Hall** / Sep. 12, 1959 / Colpix ✦✦✦✦
★ **Best Of The Colpix Years** / 1959–1963 / Roulette ✦✦✦✦
19 tracks from her Colpix label recordings. Dating from 1959 to 1963, this mix of studio and live material is considerably more weighted toward jazz and standards by the likes of Ellington, Cole Porter, Rodgers/Hammerstein, and Irving Berlin than the more eclectic albums she would later cut in the '60s and '70s for Philips and RCA. The highlights are when she steps out of the soulful supper club style into more earthier settings, as on "House Of The Rising Sun," "Forbidden Fruit," "Gin House Blues," "Work Song," and her own "Children Go Where I Send You" (all of which she would considerably rework over the years). Includes three previously unreleased tracks in a traditional jazz style with minimal arrangements. Note: the version of "(I Loves You) Porgy," her sole Top 20 entry, is not her 1959 hit single but a live 1960 version. —*Richie Unterberger*

Nina Simone at Newport / Jun. 30, 1960 / Colpix ✦✦✦✦
Nina Simone at the Village Gate / 1961 / Roulette ✦✦✦✦✦
Nina Simone in Concert / Mar. 21, 1964–Apr. 6, 1964 / Philips ✦✦✦✦✦
This is probably the most personal album that Simone issued dur-

ing her stay on Philips in the mid-'60s. On most of her studio sessions, she worked with orchestration that either enhanced her material tastefully or smothered her, and she tackled an astonishingly wide range of material that, while admirably eclectic, made for uneven listening. Here, the singer and pianist is backed by a spare, jazzy quartet, and some of the songs rank among her most socially conscious declarations of African-American pride: "Old Jim Crow," "Pirate Jenny," "Go Limp," and especially "Mississippi Goddam" were some of the most forthright musical reflections of the civil rights movement to be found at the time. In a more traditional vein, she also reprises her hit "I Loves You, Porgy," and the jazz ballad "Don't Smoke In Bed." This LP was combined with the 1965 album *I Put A Spell On You* on a CD reissue. —*Richie Unterberger*

Pastel Blues / May 19, 1965–May 20, 1965 / Mercury ✦✦✦
If this is blues, it's blues in the Billie Holiday sense, not the Muddy Waters one. This is one of Nina's more subdued mid-'60s LPs, putting the emphasis on her piano rather than band arrangements. It's rather slanted toward torch-blues ballads like "Strange Fruit," "Trouble In Mind," Billie Holiday's own composition "Tell Me More And More And Then Some," and "Nobody Knows You When You're Down And Out." Simone's then-husband, Andy Stroud, "wrote" "Be My Husband," an effective adaptation of a traditional blues chant. By far the most impressive track is her frantic ten-minute rendition of the traditional "Sinnerman," an explosive tour de force that dwarfs everything else on the album. *Pastel Blues* has been combined with the 1966 LP *Let It Out* onto a single-disc CD reissue. —*Richie Unterberger*

Nina Simone Sings the Blues / Dec. 19, 1966–Jan. 5, 1967 / RCA ✦✦✦✦✦

Essential, Vol. 2 / 1967–1971 / RCA ✦✦
Simone's stint with RCA in the late '60s and early '70s was not her most fruitful. Whether of her own volition or RCA's, she pursued a more consciously pop/soul direction. While her vocal skills remained intact, the arrangements and material were not among her best. *Essential, Vol. 2* collects 16 tracks from 1967–71, many of them inappropriate pop or rock covers. "Here Comes the Sun" and "Just like a Woman" are great songs, but these are not great versions. "Angel of the Morning," "Everyone's Gone to the Moon," and "Cherish" aren't bad mainstream pop songs, but they will not be remembered as the best ones that Simone was given to sing. Simone herself wrote none of this material (except "Revolution"), and her considerable jazz inclinations are virtually absent. She's most effective when singing with nothing except a piano, as she does on "The Human Touch," "Another Spring," and "The Desperate Ones." —*Richie Unterberger*

The Essential Nina Simone / 1967–1972 / RCA ✦✦
Nina Simone has penned unforgettable protest material, covered jazz, folk, rock, and pop with equal flair, and created a body of work that's kept her popularity high. While this title is hardly accurate, since it only covers RCA material from 1967–1972, there's plenty of anthemic fare among the CD's 16 selections. These include "Mr. Bojangles," "To Be Young, Gifted, And Black," "Seems I'm Never Tired Lovin' You," and "Since I Fell For You." While the absence of "Baltimore," "I Wish I Knew How It Feels To Be Free," and "Here Comes The Sun" (to name only three) is sizable, and the weighting of this compilation toward well-known rock types (Bob Dylan, Randy Newman, Jimmy Webb, George Harrison, two Bee Gees cuts) debatable, there's still no way it can be dismissed. —*Ron Wynn*

Baltimore / Jan. 1978 / CTI ✦

Live At Ronnie Scott's / Nov. 17, 1984 / DRG ✦✦✦✦

A Single Woman / 1993 / Asylum ✦✦✦
Vocalist, composer and pianist Nina Simone returned from a lengthy self-imposed exile in 1993 with an autobiography and outstanding CD highlighting her still impressive singing and interpretative skills in an intriguing context, surrounded by strings and guitars. While the backdrops were lush and occasionally corny, Simone's deep, penetrating voice, careful pacing and dramatic delivery kept the songs from becoming sappy. While she's always been a great protest and political singer, Simone is also a superb romantic/love song stylist. Simone remains among America's premier performers, and this CD was a welcome addition to her sparkling legacy. —*Ron Wynn*

Zoot Sims (John Haley Sims)

b. Oct. 29, 1925, Inglewood, CA, **d.** Mar. 23, 1985, New York, NY
Tenor Saxophone / Bop, Cool
Zoot Sims was a tenor sax stylist associated with the cool era whose sound had an exuberant, swinging energy and bluesy zeal, though it maintained a smooth, relaxed feel. Sims was particularly outstanding in a combo setting, though he could also soar in jam sessions, with a large orchestra or accompanying vocalists. Though inspired by Lester Young, Sims was far from a slavish imitator. Indeed, near the final portion of his careeer, Sims had reverted back to playing in a Ben Webster mode rather than either a Lester Young or a bop-influenced approach.

Sims' family were vaudeville artists, and he began playing drums and clarinet as a child, then moved to tenor sax at 13. He was a professional two years later, and began touring in dance bands. He played with Bobby Sherwood in the early '40s before joining Benny Goodman in 1943, beginning an association that would remain prominent into the '70s. Sims played at Cafe Society in New York during 1944 with Bill Harris, recording with the group under Joe Bushkin's leadership.

Then he went to California, performing with Big Sid Catlett. Following Army service, Sims worked again with Goodman in 1946 and 1947, and with Gene Roland. He played in Woody Herman's big band from 1947 to 1949, and it was Roland's compositions for four saxes that led to the creation of The Four Brothers section. Sims played with Stan Getz, Jimmy Giuffre and Herbie Steward. Upon leaving Herman, there was a brief period with Buddy Rich, another stint with Goodman in 1950 and an even shorter stay with Chubby Jackson. He then worked with Elliot Lawrence in 1951. Sims debuted as a leader on Prestige in the early '50s, and played in Stan Kenton's group for a while in 1953.

He toured Europe and played in Gerry Mulligan's bands from 1954 to 1956, and later was a soloist in Mulligan's Concert Band. Sims began a long-term musical collaboration with Al Cohn in the '50s; the two had a friendly, yet mildly combative relationship and made some marvelous twin sax recordings. They toured Scandanavia and Japan in the '70s. Some sessions Sims did in a quintet with Bob Brookmeyer eventually found their way to five different labels. He recorded on United Artists, Riverside and ABC-Paramount in the '50s.

Sims visited England and Europe with Jazz at the Philharmonic in 1967 and 1975 and performed at the Grande Parade du Jazz in Nice with various ensembles. He also toured the Soviet Union with Goodman in the early '60s, and played with John Coltrane, Sonny Rollins and Coleman Hawkins at a 1966 Titans of The Tenor concert in New York City. Sims began playing soprano sax in the '70s, and recorded an excellent Pablo album playing soprano exclusively. He remained busy in the '60s and '70s, recording for Pumpkin, Impulse, Sonet, Argo, RCA, Pacific Jazz, Colpix, Famous Door, Choice, Groove Merchant, Ahead and Pablo. He continued into the mid '80s, mostly on Pablo. There's lots of Sims available, many sessions featuring his groups, and others matching him with Cohn, Brookmeyer, Harry Edison, Jimmy Rowles and Joe Pass. —*Ron Wynn and Dan Morgenstern*

Brother in Swing / Jun. 16, 1950 / Inner City ✦✦✦✦
With the exception of five songs recorded in Sweden two months earlier, the music on this out-of-print Inner City LP (material licensed from the French Vogue label) is from the first recording session led by tenor saxophonist Zoot Sims. Sims, heard in a quartet with pianist Gerry Wiggins, bassist Pierre Michelot and drummer Kenny Clarke, performs eight selections plus is heard on five alternate takes. Twenty-five at the time, a veteran of Woody Herman's "Four Brothers" band and currently touring Europe with Benny Goodman's Sextet, Zoot Sims was more influenced by Lester Young than he would be a few years later, but he was already a hard-swinger. Historic and enjoyable music. —*Scott Yanow*

Zoot Sims in Paris / Jun. 26, 1950–Nov. 18, 1953 / Vogue ✦✦✦✦
This reissue CD from Vogue (made available domestically through BMG) has all of the music that the constantly swinging tenor Zoot Sims recorded at two Paris sessions. He is heard on seven titles (plus six alternate takes) in 1950 with a quiet but firm quartet comprised of pianist Gerald Wiggins, bassist Pierre Michelot and drummer Kenny Clarke; "Night and Day," "I Understand" and "Zoot and Zoot" are among the highpoints. The final six selections feature Sims with trombonist Frank Rosolino,

pianist Henri Renaud, guitarist Jimmy Gourley, bassist Don Bagley and drummer Jean-Louis Viale for some cool bop in the same basic style as the earlier set. —*Scott Yanow*

Quartets / Sep. 16, 1950+Aug. 14, 1951 / Original Jazz Classics ◆◆◆◆
This CD reissue features the great tenor saxophonist Zoot Sims (who was then 25) leading his first American recording dates. He is heard with two quartets, the team of pianist John Lewis, bassist Curly Russell and drummer Don Lamond and with pianist Harry Biss, bassist Clyde Lombardi and drummer Art Blakey. All but two numbers clock in around the three-minute mark: an over eight-minute alternate version of "Zoot Swings the Blues" and an 11-minute "East of the Sun." Sims is in fine form throughout these cool-toned but hard-swinging sets. —*Scott Yanow*

One to Blow on / Jan. 11, 1956+Jan. 18, 1956 / Biograph ◆◆◆◆
This 1979 Biograph LP (seven of the eight numbers have since been reissued by the label on CD) features some exciting if "cool" performances by tenorman Zoot Sims and valve trombonist Bob Brookmeyer in a quintet with pianist John Williams, bassist Milt Hinton and drummer Gus Johnson. Highlights include "September in the Rain," "Them There Eyes" and several of Sims' fairly basic originals including the medium-tempo blues "One to Blow On." The LP is filled with swinging music that features some exciting jammed ensembles. —*Scott Yanow*

The Rare Dawn Sessions / Jan. 11, 1956–Aug. 10, 1956 / Biograph ◆◆◆
This CD is a bit of a disappointment, not for the music but for the packaging. During 1979–1980, Biograph came out with two Zoot Sims L Ps (*One to Blow On* and *The Big Stampede*) that contained 16 selections in all. But this CD just has ten of the songs, seven of the eight tunes from the first album (why did they leave out "September in the Rain"?) and three of the eight numbers from the second date. The incomplete nature of this reissue series is a pity for the music is excellent. Sims' tenor fits in very well with the valve trombone of Bob Brookmeyer during the earlier quintet date and also blends nicely with the cool-toned trumpet of Jerry Lloyd on the final three numbers. The music is swinging with Sims already starting to show an original musical personality built out of the sound of Lester Young. But the CD is only recommended to those listeners unable to find the two earlier LPs. —*Scott Yanow*

● **Tonite's Music Today** / Jan. 31, 1956 / Black Lion ◆◆◆◆◆
Valve trombonist Bob Brookmeyer's musical partnerships in the 1950s with Stan Getz and especially Gerry Mulligan were celebrated, but he also recorded three fine albums with tenor saxophonist Zoot Sims in 1956 that are quite enjoyable, feature colorful jammed ensembles and hard-swinging yet cool-toned solos that owe as much to the swing tradition as to the innovations of bebop. This Storyville CD finds Zoot and Brookmeyer accompanied by pianist Hank Jones, bassist Wyatt Reuther and drummer Gus Johnson. Highlights include "I Hear a Rhapsody," "Blue Skies" and Sims' first ever recorded vocal on a "Blues." This release is easily recommended as is its companion Storyville CD Morning Fun. —*Scott Yanow*

● **Morning Fun** / Feb. 1956 / Black Lion ◆◆◆◆◆
Although it claims on the back of this CD that the music was recorded in August 1956, discographies state February and that seems more logical since valve trombonist Bob Brookmeyer and tenor saxophonist Zoot Sims did not team up for a very long period (although three records resulted from their valuable collaboration). With assistance from pianist John Williams, bassist Bill Crow and drummer Jo Jones, Sims and Brookmeyer are in fine form on such selections as a rollicking "The King," "Lullaby of the Leaves," a brief two-song ballad medley and Brookmeyer's "Whooeeeee!" Sims takes a rare (and fairly effective) vocal on "I Can't Get Started." Recommended, as is the other Black Lion Zoot Sims CD from the same period, *Tonite's Music Today*. —*Scott Yanow*

The Big Stampede / Aug. 10, 1956–Sep. 1956 / Biograph ◆◆◆◆
This LP features tenor saxophonist Zoot Sims in a quintet with trumpeter Jerry Lloyd (a fine if somewhat forgotten cool-toned bopper), pianist John Williams, Bill Anthony or Knobby Totah on bass and drummer Gus Johnson. The band plays a rare version of Thelonious Monk's "Bye Ya" (one of the first by a non-Monk group), three standards and originals by Jerry Lloyd, John Williams and Al Cohn ("Jerry's Jaunt"). Although nothing all that

surprising occurs, Sims blends in well with Lloyd and the solos by the principals are up to par. Straightahead jazz collectors will want this LP, which has only partly (three out of the eight songs) been reissued on CD. —*Scott Yanow*

Zoot! / Dec. 13, 1956+Dec. 18, 1956 / Original Jazz Classics ◆◆◆
For a little while in the mid-'50s, Zoot Sims occasionally doubled on alto although he soon switched back exclusively to tenor where he had a stronger musical personality. On this CD reissue of a Riverside set from 1956, Sims plays alto on two of the seven tracks and works well with trumpeter Nick Travis. Actually pianist George Handy, who contributed four originals (two standards and drummer Osie Johnson's "Osmosis" complete the program) and did all of the arranging, comes across as the key supporting player; bassist Wilbur Ware and Johnson are fine in quiet support. Although Handy's arrangements are a bit modern, this is still a typically hard-swinging and melodic Zoot Sims date. —*Scott Yanow*

Zoot Sims Plays Four Altos / Jan. 11, 1957 / ABC/Paramount ◆◆
This brief LP (under 33 minutes) is a bit of a novelty since Zoot Sims, normally a tenor player, overdubbed his playing on four altos (with support from pianist John Williams, bassist Knobby Totah and drummer Gus Johnson). The obvious question "why?" is never answered and the music (arranged and composed by George Handy) is nothing that unique or special. Zoot Sims completists will want to get these obscure but swinging solos, but this experimental date was ultimately rather pointless. —*Scott Yanow*

Happy Over There / 1957–1958 / Jass ◆◆◆
There is less than a half-hour of music on this date and the liner graphics are dumb, but there are some fine moments to be heard from the boppish players. Pianist Elliott Lawrence actually organized the date (which was not released until this LP came out in 1987) and Bill Elton wrote the colorful arrangements. In addition to tenor saxophonist Zoot Sims, the other musicians include Al Cohn (sticking to baritone), trumpeter Nick Travis, trombonist Jimmy Cleveland, bassist Milt Hinton and drummer Osie Johnson. Together they perform eight of Hoagy Carmichael's best-known compositions including "Skylark," "The Nearness of You," "Georgia on My Mind" and "Stardust." The playing is fine although, due to the set's brevity, this LP is only recommended to those listeners who can find it at a budget price. —*Scott Yanow*

Down Home / Jul. 1960 / Bethlehem ◆◆◆◆
Tenor saxophonist Zoot Sims recorded on a regular basis as a leader for most of 45 years and virtually all of his many sessions are worth acquiring. Sims' Bethlehem date also gives one a look at the great pianist Dave McKenna in his early days, along with bassist George Tucker and drummer Danny Richmond. Sims mostly explores standards from the swing era (including a rare version of "Bill Bailey") on this easily enjoyable and consistently swinging set. —*Scott Yanow*

Either Way / Feb. 1961 / Evidence ◆◆◆◆
This formerly obscure set (reissued on CD by Evidence) matches together the always complementary (and sometimes identical-sounding) tenors of Zoot Sims and Al Cohn. A special treat to the spirited quintet date (with Mose Allison on piano, bassist Bill Crow and drummer Gus Johnson) are the three excellent vocals from the long-forgotten singer Cecil "Kid Haffey" Collier. Based on his swinging version of "Nagasaki" and fine renditions of "Sweet Lorraine" and "I Like It Like That," he certainly did not deserve his obscurity. It is fun to hear Sims and Cohn work with a vocalist, jamming behind him and launching into their solos. The five instrumentals, which include the riffing "P-Town," the only ballad of the date ("Autumn Leaves") and the heated blues "Morning Fun," are excellent too, making this a set well worth picking up. —*Scott Yanow*

Two Jims and Zoot / May 1964 / Mainstream ◆◆◆
This slightly unusual date features tenor saxophonist Zoot Sims interacting with two guitarists (Jimmy Raney and Jim Hall) while given subtle support by bassist Steve Swallow and drummer Osie Johnson. Although the eight selections (none of which caught on as standards) had all been written recently and sometimes display the influence of bossa nova, the quiet performances could pass for 1954 rather than 1964. The cool-toned improvisations and boppish playing have a timeless quality about them although for the time period aspects of this music already sounded a bit old-fashioned. —*Scott Yanow*

Suitably Zoot / Oct. 29, 1965+Nov. 26, 1965 / Pumpkin ◆◆◆◆
It is strange to think that Zoot Sims, who made many records in

the 1950s and the '70s, only had one studio date as a leader between 1964-1971 (not counting this Pumpkin LP). On this album Zoot Sims is teamed with fellow tenors Al Cohn and Richie Kamuca (along with pianist Dave Frishberg, bassist Tommy Potter and drummer Mel Lewis) for lengthy versions of "Tickle Toe" and "Broadway"; Cohn takes solo honors. In addition Sims has a reunion with valve trombonist Bob Brookmeyer (they had played together regularly during part of 1956) and (with fine work from pianist Roger Kellaway, bassist Bill Crow and drummer Dave Bailey), their versions of "On the Alamo" and "The King", are hard-swinging and enjoyable. This collector's LP (whose music has not yet been reissued on CD) is highly recommended for Zoot Sims and bebop fans. —*Scott Yanow*

Nirvana / 1972 / Groove Merchant ✦✦✦✦

Zoot at Ease / May 1973–Aug. 1973 / Mobile Fidelity ✦✦✦✦
A good mid-'70s date by Zoot Sims. Label head Norman Granz kept Sims busy cutting an array of standards, blues, mainstream, bop, and cool tunes, then issuing them whenever he felt the time was right. This isn't bad music; in fact, much of the time it's very good. It's just not original or much different from any other Sims album issued during the period. —*Ron Wynn*

Zoot Sims Party / Apr. 1974 / Choice ✦✦✦✦
Just prior to starting his longtime association with Norman Granz's Pablo label, Zoot Sims recorded this relaxed set for Choice. Sims, who switches between tenor and soprano, swings lightly with pianist Jimmy Rowles, bassist Bob Cranshaw and drummer Mickey Roker on six standards, three of which ("Fred," "Restless" and "Dream Dancing") are somewhat obscure. The results are tasteful, informal and typically swinging. —*Scott Yanow*

★ **Zoot Sims and the Gershwin Brothers** / Jun. 6, 1975 / Original Jazz Classics ✦✦✦✦✦
Along with his album with Count Basie (*Basie and Zoot*) during the same period, this is one of Sims' most exciting recordings of his career. Greatly assisted by pianist Oscar Peterson, guitarist Joe Pass, bassist George Mraz and drummer Grady Tate, he explores ten songs written by George and Ira Gershwin. Somehow the magic was definitely present, and whether it's stomps such as "The Man I Love," "Lady Be Good" and "I Got Rhythm" or warm ballads (including "I've Got a Crush on You" and "Embraceable You"), Zoot Sims is heard at the peak of his powers. A true gem that has been reissued on CD. —*Scott Yanow*

Zoot Plays Soprano / Jan. 8, 1976–Jan. 9, 1976 / Pablo ✦✦✦✦✦
Zoot Sims, known throughout his career as a hard-swinging tenor saxophonist, started doubling successfully on soprano in 1973 and managed to become one of the best by simply playing in his own musical personality. This particular LP (not yet available on CD) was his only full-length set on soprano, but it is a rewarding one. Assisted by pianist Ray Bryant, bassist George Mraz and drummer Grady Tate, Sims is in top form on such songs as "Someday Sweetheart," "Wrap Your Troubles in Dreams," "Ghost of a Chance" and two of his originals. A delightful set of swinging jazz, it's a surprise success. —*Scott Yanow*

Zoot Sims with Bucky Pizzarelli / Aug. 1976 / Classic Jazz ✦✦✦
Tenor saxophonist Zoot Sims' "friend" on this LP is guitarist Bucky Pizzarelli and together they perform eight highly enjoyable duets although, at under 32 minutes, this album is overly brief. However, what is here is excellent with the highlights including "What Is This Thing Called Love," "Take Ten" and "There Will Never Be Another You." This music has not yet been reissued on CD. —*Scott Yanow*

Hawthorne Nights / Sep. 20, 1976–Sep. 21, 1976 / Original Jazz Classics ✦✦✦✦
Unlike most of his Pablo sessions, this Zoot Sims CD is not a quartet outing but an opportunity for his tenor to be showcased while joined by a nine-piece group that includes six horns (three reeds among them). Bill Holman's inventive arrangements are a large part as to why the date is successful but Sims' playing on the five standards, two Holman pieces and his own "Dark Cloud" should not be overlooked. Fortunately there is also some solo space saved for the talented sidemen (who include Oscar Brashear and Snooky Young on trumpets, trombonist Frank Rosolino and the woodwinds and reeds of Jerome Richardson, Richie Kamuca and Bill Hood). A well-rounded set of swinging jazz. —*Scott Yanow*

If I'm Lucky / Oct. 27, 1977–Oct. 28, 1977 / Original Jazz Classics ✦✦✦✦
Tenor saxophonist Zoot Sims recorded quite a few albums with pianist Jimmy Rowles during his Pablo years; all are recommended. Rowles assisted Sims in coming up with obscurities to interpret and this CD reissue is highlighted by such little-performed songs as "If I'm Lucky," "Shadow Waltz," "Gypsy Sweetheart" and "I Wonder Where Our Love Has Gone." The lead voices are backed ably by bassist George Mraz and drummer Mousey Alexander on this easily enjoyable straight-ahead date. —*Scott Yanow*

For Lady Day / Apr. 10, 1978–Apr. 11, 1978 / Pablo ✦✦✦✦
It is strange that this album was not released until the CD came out in 1990 because tenor saxophonist Zoot Sims and pianist Jimmy Rowles' tribute to Billie Holiday is melodic, tasteful and largely memorable. Together with bassist George Mraz and drummer Jackie Williams back in 1978, they perform 11 songs associated with Billie Holiday including quite a few that would have been lost in obscurity if Lady Day had not uplifted them with her recordings. Highlights include "Easy Living," "Some Other Spring," "I Cried for You," "Body and Soul" and "You're My Thrill." A lyrical and heartfelt tribute. —*Scott Yanow*

Warm Tenor / Sep. 18, 1978–Sep. 19, 1978 / Pablo ✦✦✦✦
The Pablo label was a perfect home for Zoot Sims during the second half of the 1970s for the cool-toned tenor always sounded at his best in informal settings with small groups where he had the opportunity to stretch out. This quartet set with pianist Jimmy Rowles, bassist George Mraz and drummer Mousey Alexander (which has been reissued on CD) gives Zoot a chance to interpret a variety of mostly underplayed standards along with a duet with Mraz on an ad-lib "Blues for Louise." Highlights include "Old Devil Moon," "You Go to My Head," "Blue Prelude" and "You're My Thrill." —*Scott Yanow*

I Wish I Were Twins / Jul. 6, 1981 / Pablo ✦✦✦✦
Zoot Sims (doubling on tenor and soprano) teams up once again with pianist Jimmy Rowles; this time bassist Frank Tate and drummer Akira Tana are the supporting cast. Rowles is a master not only at accompanying soloists (he always seems to come up with the perfect chord) but in picking up superior obscurities to perform. In addition to "Georgia on My Mind" and "The Touch of Your Lips," this LP contains such tunes as "I Wish I Were Twins," "Changes" and Johnny Mercer's "You Go Your Way"; Sims contributed "The Fish Horn" to feature his soprano. A fine swinging date filled with thoughtful improvisations. —*Scott Yanow*

Blues for Two / Mar. 6, 1982+Jun. 23, 1982 / Original Jazz Classics ✦✦✦✦✦
Although guitarist Joe Pass recorded many unaccompanied solo albums, he made relatively few dates as part of a duo. This CD reissue of a session with tenor saxophonist Joe Pass works quite well because Zoot Sims was a natural swinger who did not need a full rhythm section to push him. His playing on the selections (mainly standards including "Dindi," "Poor Butterfly," "Pennies From Heaven" and "I Hadn't Anyone Till You") is as heated and lyrical as usual. Pass also warms up quickly to the situation (Sims must have been easy to accompany) and takes many fine solos of his own. The pair collaborated on the opening "Blues for 2" and "Takeoff," which wraps up the highly enjoyable set. —*Scott Yanow*

Innocent Years / Mar. 9, 1982 / Original Jazz Classics ✦✦✦
For this Pablo album, the great tenor Zoot Sims (who doubles on soprano) interprets five pretty melodies plus his own "Pomme Au Four" with a quartet comprised of pianist Richard Wyands, bassist Frank Tate and drummer Akira Tana. All of the selections are highlights so they are worth mentioning: "I Hear a Rhapsody," "Over the Rainbow" (which Sims plays for nearly 11 minutes), "The Very Thought of You," "If You Were Mine" and "Indian Summer." This ballad-oriented set is successful both as background music and for close listening. —*Scott Yanow*

Zoot Case / Jun. 8, 1982 / Sonet ✦✦✦✦✦
During a 30-year period the very complementary tenors Zoot Sims and Al Cohn teamed up on an irregular but always consistently satisfying basis. This club date from Stockholm, one of their final joint recordings, features the pair backed by pianist Claes Croona, bassist Palle Danielsson and drummer Petur Ostlund. Both Zoot and Cohn sound quite inspired and they really push each other on "Exactly like You," "After You've Gone" (which features Sims on soprano) and even a surprisingly heated version of

"The Girl from Ipanema." Al Cohn's tone had deepened during the years, and although they sounded nearly identical in the 1950s, it is quite easy to tell the two tenors apart during this encounter. The CD (available through the Swedish Sonet label) is highly recommended for fans of the saxophonists and for bop collectors in general. —*Scott Yanow*

On the Korner / Mar. 20, 1983 / Pablo ✦✦✦✦✦
Just two years and three days away from his death at age 59, the great tenor Zoot Sims is heard in prime form on this live session from San Francisco's legendary club Keystone Korner. The music was not initially released until this 1994 CD, but it was worth the wait. The hard-swinging tenor (who plays equally effective soprano on Duke Ellington's "Tonight I Shall Sleep" and "Pennies from Heaven") is ably supported by the fine pianist Frank Collett, bassist Monty Budwig and drummer Shelly Manne. Sims plays his usual repertoire from the period (including "I Hear a Rhapsody," "If You Could See Me Now" and "Dream Dancing") but, although he had previously recorded virtually all of these selections, the "new" versions are well worth hearing. This late date gives one a definitive look into Zoot Sims' playing of his last decade, when he interpreted standards in a timeless style that had grown but not really changed since the 1950s. Recommended. —*Scott Yanow*

Suddenly It's Spring / May 26, 1983 / Original Jazz Classics ✦✦✦✦
This CD reissue of one of tenor saxophonist Zoot Sims' final recordings adds a version of "Emaline" to the original program. Pianist Jimmy Rowles often co-stars on the date (with bassist George Mraz and drummer Akira Tana offering solid support). The lyrical repertoire emphasizes ballads and pretty melodies with the highpoints including such offbeat material as Woody Guthrie's "So Long," Sims' "Brahms…I Think," "In the Middle of a Kiss" and the more familiar "Never Let Me Go" and "Suddenly It's Spring." The melodic performances are quite warm, romantic and enjoyable, fine examples of subtle creativity. —*Scott Yanow*

Quietly There: Zoot Sims Plays Johnny Mandel / Mar. 20, 1984 Mar. 21, 1984 / Original Jazz Classics ✦✦✦✦
For his final Pablo session and next-to-last recording (just a year before his death), tenor saxophonist Zoot Sims shows that, on record at least, he never did decline. With tasteful accompaniment provided by pianist Mike Wofford, bassist Chuck Berghofer, drummer Nick Ceroli and Victor Feldman on percussion, the great tenor performs seven of Johnny Mandel's compositions. The emphasis is on ballads but, other than "A Time for Love" and "Emily," the material is somewhat obscure and therefore quite fresh. A special highlight is a song that Mandel wrote for Sims that is aptly titled "Zoot." Overall this is a tasteful and typically swinging session that finds Zoot Sims exiting on top while still in his musical prime. —*Scott Yanow*

In a Sentimental Mood / Nov. 21, 1984 / Sonet ✦✦✦✦

Frank Sinatra

b. Dec. 12, 1915, Hoboken, NJ
Vocals / Swing, Middle-of-the-Road Pop
A certified American music legend, Francis Albert Sinatra represents the ultimate male romantic vocalist to many people. A huge argument starter as the 20th century ends is who's America's premier singer; Armstrong, Holiday, Sinatra or Presley. Aside from the fact several others could legitimately be named, a serious case can be made for Sinatra.

As a relaxed, yet swinging stylist, he was magnificent in his prime, and this quality has slipped more dramatically than anything else in his arsenal. Though not a good scatter nor great vocal improviser, Sinatra helped expand Crosby's breakthroughs with microphone singing, achieving a wide range of dynamics and displaying a delivery and crystal-clear enunciation that projected any and every possible nuance or emotional shade in a lyric. Until age turned his act into a parody, Sinatra was among the most convincing singers ever; the sincerity he expressed frequently fooled people into thinking his offstage character was as innocent and good-natured as the onstage personna. Indeed, Sinatra's rocky personal life, while not plagued with public drug incidents outside of alcohol, nevertheless makes many jazz and popular music bad boys (and girls) look like candidates for sainthood. Still, Sinatra's had enormous impact on pre-rock era vocalists, and has never hesitated to say how much Billie Holiday influenced his style.

Sinatra's parents were Italian immigrants, and he quit school at age 16 to sing anywhere he could get an audience. He was in The Hoboken Four singing group when they won the Major Bowes Amateur Hour talent show on radio in 1935. This quartet toured with Bowes and had the dubious distinction of being caught on film performing as blackface ministrels. They sang from 1937 to 1939 at the Rustic Cabin roadhouse in New Jersey, with Sinatra doubling as head waiter. He started singing sans fee on a WNEW radio program "Dance Parade" in 1939.

Harry James was starting a band after leaving Benny Goodman and quickly contacted Sinatra. A song that Sinatra recorded with James in the summer of 1939 "All or Nothing at All" sold 8,000 copies when initally issued with Sinatra uncredited; it topped the charts when Columbia reissued it in 1943. On the recommendation of a Columbia executive, Tommy Dorsey went to hear Sinatra sing. James let Sinatra leave to join Dorsey and his ascension to icon status began. He recorded with Dorsey in 1940, backed by a vocal quartet including Jo Stafford and Connie Hines called The Pied Pipers. Sinatra made his first film appearance in 1940 with the band; *Las Vegas Nights* didn't win anyone any Oscars. But Sinatra soon became a commercial juggernaut; "I'll Never Smile Again," "Delores," "There are Such Things" and "In the Blue of the Evening" all topped the charts between 1940 and 1943.

Sinatra bought out his contract with Dorsey in 1942. He appeared for a month at the Paramount Theatre in 1942 with Benny Goodman, and the screams and yells from girls (some rumored to be paid for their trouble) are considered the beginning of modern pop idolatry and/or groupies. A Sinatra return engagement in 1944 resulted in 25,000 teenagers blocking the streets. He cut his first solo dates for Columbia in 1943, and had 86 hit records for them from 1943–1952, 33 in the Top Ten. Sinatra began to appear frequently in films, and gossip columns after he left his wife Nancy to marry actress Ava Gardner in 1951. He was even targeted for accusations of communism. His support of Franklin D. Roosevelt and winning of a special Oscar in 1946 for his efforts on behalf of religious and racial tolerance established Sinatra's reputation as a liberal, progressive-minded individual (at least in public). He held it well into the '60s, before switching party allegiances to the Republicans.

Sinatra rebounded from a slump in the mid-'50s, winning an Oscar for his film role in *From Here to Eternity* in 1954. He cut several tremendous records for Capitol with arrangements from top arrangers like Billy May and Nelson Riddle. He was successfully remarketed as a seasoned vocalist singing adult love songs for older audiences. He made 13 enormously profitable albums for Capitol from 1954 to 1961. Some, like *Songs for Swingin' Lovers* in 1956, creatively used big band arrangements and support; others such as *In the Wee Small Hours* in 1955 featured him doing songs around a singular concept or developing themes and moods with related tunes throughout an album.

Sinatra reaffirmed his jazz credentials in the '60s, with albums that had arrangements from Don Costa and Neal Hefti, plus collaborations with Count Basie and albums featuring Quincy Jones arrangements. He even tackled the bossa nova. But decline and exhaustion began to set in, and there were unfortunate flirtations with dubious material like Rod McKuen poetry. Sinatra did land another number one hit in 1966, "Strangers in the Night," but the '60s established the fact that he now needed the right material, producers and arrangers. No longer could he survive just by being Sinatra, at least not in the creative arena. The '70s would clearly prove that.

He'd retired for a while, but the 1973 comeback album *Ol' Blue Eyes Is Back* reached the number 15 spot on the charts. He remained in the Top 40 with the next album, *Sinatra—The Main Event* even though the two-record set was littered with painful material. Sinatra returned to the charts in 1980 with *Trilogy: Past, Present, Future*, thanks to arrangements from May, Riddle and others. Jones arranged and released on his own label *L.A. Is My Lady* in 1984. Sinatra kept touring and performing into the '90s, issuing an album of duets featuring collaborations with U2's Bono, Tony Bennett and Aretha Franklin among others, in the fall of 1993. It also topped the charts and closed out 1993 among the Top Ten sellers among pop releases.

The list of horrendous Sinatra marriages, ugly affairs, hotel and nightclub incidents, rumors of reprisals against club owners, performers, critics and managers, and supposed gangster links filled several magazines long before Kitty Kelley's infamous biography. But none of that deserves equal billing with Frank Sinatra's achievements. Even if you feel some Sinatra boosters think he invented music, there's no denying he earned his spurs many years ago. —*Ron Wynn and John Floyd*

The Frank Sinatra Story in Music / Dec. 3, 1944–Apr. 7, 1946 / Sony ✦✦✦✦✦

This is a stunning two-disc collection of Sinatra's early years. His nickname at the time was "The Voice," and you can hear why: if you could "hear" velvet, it would sound like Sinatra's vocals on "I Concentrate on You" and "I've Got a Crush on You." —*John Floyd*

★ **In the Wee Small Hours** / Mar. 1, 1954–Mar. 4, 1955 / Capitol ✦✦✦✦✦

Expanding on the concept of Songs for Young Lovers, *In the Wee Small Hours* was a collection of ballads arranged by Nelson Riddle. The first 12-inch album recorded by Sinatra, *Wee Small Hours* was more focused and concentrated than his two earlier concept records. It's a blue, melancholy album, built around a spare rhythm section featuring a rhythm guitar, celesta, and Bill Miller's piano, with gently aching strings added every once and a while. Within that melancholy mood, is one of Sinatra's most jazz-oriented performances—he restructures the melody and Miller's playing is bold throughout the record. Where *Songs for Young Lovers* emphasized the romantic aspects of the songs, Sinatra sounds like a lonely, broken man on *In the Wee Small Hours*. Beginning with the newly-written title song, the singer goes through a series of standards that are lonely and desolate. In many ways, the album is a personal reflection of the heartbreak of his doomed love affair with actress Ava Gardner, and the standards that he sings form their own story when collected together. Sinatra's voice had deepened and worn to the point were his delivery seems ravished and heartfelt, as if he were living the songs. —*Stephen Thomas Erlewine*

★ **Songs for Young Lovers/Swing Easy** / 1955 / Capitol ✦✦✦✦✦

Combining Frank Sinatra's first two 10-inch albums for Capitol, the compact disc *Songs for Young Lovers/Swing Easy* not only contains some of the best music Sinatra recorded, it captures a turning point in popular music. *Songs for Young Lovers* was the first album Frank Sinatra recorded for Capitol, as well as his first collaboration with Nelson Riddle. It was also one of the first—arguably the very first—concept album. Sinatra, Riddle, and producer Voyle Gilmore decided that the new album format should be a special event, featuring a number of songs that are arranged around a specific theme; in addition, the new format was capable of producing a more detailed sound, which gave Riddle more freedom in his arrangements and orchestrations. *Songs for Young Lovers* is a perfect example of this. Supported by a small orchestra, Sinatra and Riddle create an intimate, romantic atmosphere on the record, breathing new life to standards like "My Funny Valentine," "They Can't Take That Away From Me," "I Get A Kick Out of You," and "A Foggy Day." Sinatra sounds revived. No longer does he have to sing the lightweight pop drivel that was forced on him during his latter days at Columbia—he is given weighty songs, and he tears into them. There is a breezy confidence to his singing, as he inhabits each song as if he were living the emotions. Riddle's arrangements are light but jazzy and are more complex than they intially appear. Sinatra and Riddle expanded this approach on his second Capitol album, *Swing Easy!* As the title implies, the record concentrates on up-tempo swingers. Again, the songs were all standards—"Just One of Those Things," "Wrap Your Troubles In Dreams," "All of Me"—that benefitted from the new thematic setting, the new arrangements and, of course, Sinatra's increasingly playful and textured vocals. Sinatra plays around with the melodies without leaving them behind, delivering each line with precision. It ranks as one of his most jazzy performances, as well as one of his most fun and carefree records. —*Stephen Thomas Erlewine*

★ **Songs for Swingin' Lovers!** / Oct. 17, 1955–Jan. 16, 1956 / Capitol ✦✦✦✦✦

After the ballad-heavy *In The Wee Small Hours*, Frank Sinatra and Nelson Riddle returned to uptempo, swing material with *Songs for Swingin' Lovers*, arguably the vocalist's greatest swing set. Like Sinatra's previous Capitol albums, *Songs for Swingin' Lovers* consists of reinterpreted pop standards, ranging from the ten-year old "You Make Me Feel So Young" to the 20-year old "Pennies From Heaven" and "I've Got You Under My Skin." Sinatra is supremely confident throughout the album, singing with authority and joy. That joy is replicated in Riddle's arrangements, which manage to rethink these standards in fresh yet rev-

erent ways. Working with a core rhythm section and a full string orchestra, Riddle writes scores that are surprisingly subtle. "I've Got You Under My Skin," with its breathtaking middle section, is a perfect example of how Sinatra works with the band. Both swing hard, stretching out the rhythms and melodies but never losing sight of the original song. *Songs For Swingin' Lovers* never loses momentum. The great songs keep coming and the performances are all stellar, resulting in one of Sinatra's true classics. — *Stephen Thomas Erlewine*

★ **Where Are You** / 1957 / Capitol ✦✦✦✦✦

Following the hard-driving *A Swingin' Affair*, Frank Sinatra released another all-ballads record, *Where Are You* The album was the first he recorded at Capitol without Nelson Riddle, as well as the first he recorded in stereo. Where Nelson Riddle's downbeat albums are stately and sullen, Jenkins favors lush, melancholy arrangements played by large, string-dominated orchestras. Jenkins' arrangements suggested classical textures, although the tempos alluded to Billie Holiday's ballad style. *Where Are You?* primarily consists of torch songs, including "The Night We Called It A Day," "I Cover the Waterfront," and "Lonely Town." Throughout the record, Sinatra blends with Jenkins' sumptuous strings, making his voice sound rich, relaxed and regretful. It doesn't have the stark despair of *In the Wee Small Hours*, but its luxurious sadness makes *Where Are You?* a majestic experience of its own. —*Stephen Thomas Erlewine*

★ **A Swingin' Affair!** / 1957 / Capitol ✦✦✦✦✦

In some ways, *A Swingin' Affair* is *Songs for Swingin' Lovers, Pt. 2*, following the same formula of Sinatra's hit album of the previous year. Beneath the surface, there are enough variations on *A Swingin' Affair* to make it a distinctive, and equally enjoyable listen. The most noticeable difference between the two records is their basic approach. Where *Songs for Swingin' Lovers* swung hard but managed to stay rather light, *A Swingin' Affair* is a forceful, brassy album—it exudes a self-assured, confident aura. It is a hard, jazzy album However, the attack is more brash, —*Stephen Thomas Erlewine*

Close to You / 1957 / Capitol ✦✦✦✦

Close to You is one of Frank Sinatra's most gentle and intimate albums, and that is due in no small part to the Hollywood String Quartet, which forms the core of the album's instrumental support. It also was one of the most difficult to record, taking eight months and five different sessions. Certainly, it is one of the most unusual and special of Sinatra's albums, featuring subdued and detailed performances that accentuate both the romantic longing and understated humor of the numbers, which are mainly torch songs. With the Quartet's support, the album comes closer to sounding like a classical album, like a pop variation on chamber music. Where the intimacy of *In the Wee Small Hours* sounded confessional and heart-broken, *Close to You* has a delicate, lovely quality; it may not be seductive, but it is charming and romantic. —*Stephen Thomas Erlewine*

★ **Come Fly with Me** / Oct. 1, 1957–Oct. 8, 1957 / Capitol ✦✦✦✦✦

Constructed around a light-hearted travel theme, *Come Fly with Me*, Frank Sinatra' first project with arranger Billy May, was a breezy change of pace from the somber *Where Are You*. From the first swinging notes of Sammy Cahn and Jimmy Van Heusen's "Come Fly With Me"—which is written at Sinatra's request—it's clear that the music on the collection is intended to be fun. Over the course of the album, Sinatra and May travel around the world in song, performing standards like "Moonlight In Vermont" and "April In Paris," as well as humorous tunes like "Isle of Capri" and "On the Road to Mandalay." May's signature bold, brassy arrangements give these songs a playful, carefree, nearly sarcastic feel, but never is the approach less than affectionate. In fact, *Come Fly with Me* is filled with varying moods and textures, as it moves from boisterous swing numbers to romantic ballads, and hitting any number of emotions in between. There may be greater albums in Sinatra's catalog, but few are quite as fun as *Come Fly with Me*. —*Stephen Thomas Erlewine*

★ **Sings for Only the Lonely** / 1958 / Capitol ✦✦✦✦✦

Originally, Frank Sinatra had planned to record *Only the Lonely* with Gordon Jenkins, who had arranged his previous all-ballads album, *Where Are You*. Jenkins was unavailable at the time of the sessions, which led Sinatra back to his original arranger at Capitol, Nelson Riddle. The result is arguably his greatest ballads album. *Only the Lonely* follows the same formula as his previous down albums, but the tone is considerably bleaker and more desperate. Riddle used a larger orchestra for the album than he had in the past, which lends the album a stately, nearly classical atmosphere. At its core, however, the album is a set of brooding saloon songs, highlighted by two of Sinatra's tour de forces—"Angel Eyes" and "One for My Baby." Sinatra never forces emotion out of the lyric, he lets everything flow naturally, with grace. It's a heartbreaking record, the ideal late-night album. *—Stephen Thomas Erlewine*

★ **Come Dance with Me!** / Dec. 9, 1958–Dec. 23, 1958 / Capitol ✦✦✦✦✦

Working with Billy May again, Frank Sinatra recorded his hardest swing album ever with *Come Dance With Me!* Driven by an intensely swinging horn section, the album has a fair share of slower numbers, but the songs that make the biggest impression are the uptempo cuts. With May's charts careening wildly all over the place, Sinatra relies on his macho swagger; as a result, *Come Dance with Me!* is an intoxicating rush of invigorating dance songs. *—Stephen Thomas Erlewine*

No One Cares / 1959 / Capitol ✦✦✦✦✦

Frank Sinatra's second set of torch songs recorded with Gordon Jenkins, *No One Cares* was nearly as good as its predecessor, *Where Are You.* Expanding the melancholy tone of the duo's previous collaboration, *No One Cares* consists of nothing but brooding, lonely songs. Jenkins gives the songs a subtlely tragic treatment, and Sinatra responds with a wrenching performance. It lacks the grandiose melancholy of *Only the Lonely*, and isn't as lush as *Where Are You*, but in its slow, bluesly tempos and heartbreaking little flourishes, it is every bit moving. *—Stephen Thomas Erlewine*

★ **Nice 'n' Easy** / 1960 / Capitol ✦✦✦✦✦

Breaking slightly from his pattern of a swing album following the release of ballads set, Frank Sinatra followed *No One Cares* with *Nice 'n' Easy*, a breezy collection of midtempo numbers arranged by Nelson Riddle. Not only is it the lightest set that he recorded for Capitol, it is the one with the loosest theme. Sinatra selected a collection of songs he had sang early in his career, having Riddle rearrange the tunes with warm, cheery textures. Unlike his previous ballads albums, *Nice 'N' Easy* doesn't have a touch of brooding sorrow—it rolls along steadily, charming everyone in its path. *—Stephen Thomas Erlewine*

Sinatra's Swingin' Session!!! (& More) / 1961 / Capitol ✦✦✦✦✦

Sinatra's Swingin' Session is a fast, driving album, the speediest and hardest swing collection Frank Sinatra ever recorded. The majority of the album is a re-recording of six of the eight songs from his first LP, *Sing and Dance With Frank Sinatra*, as rearranged by Nelson Riddle. Sinatra performed the songs twice as fast as was expected; consequently, it's one of his jazziest swing sets, with the musicians spitting out energetic, forceful solos and providing tough, gutsy support. Not only do the uptempo numbers speed by, the ballads are sprightly. It doesn't have the brassy verve of *A Swingin' Affair*, but *Sinatra's Swingin' Session* does have a confident, swaggering flavor of its own that makes it nearly as enjoyable. *—Stephen Thomas Erlewine*

Come Swing with Me / 1961 / Capitol ✦✦✦

Arranged by Billy May, *Come Swing with Me* was Frank Sinatra's final swing session for Capitol Records. The album falls somewhere between the carefree *Come Fly with Me* and the hard-swinging *Come Dance with Me*, borrowing elements of the humor of *Fly* and the intense, driving rhythms of *Dance*. Recorded without strings or saxes, the brass-heavy sound of the album was noticeable, but it wasn't nearly as distinctive as the ping-ponging, stereo effects of the album. With its extreme stereo separation, *Come Swing with Me* has a bizzare, off-kilter feel that is accentuated by Sinatra's restless vocals. At the time of recording the album, Sinatra was also recording *I Remember Tommy* for Reprise and his affections were with his new label. That doesn't mean he sounds careless on *Come Swing with Me*—in fact, his intense, speedy energy gives the album an edge that distinguishes the record. The album might not be as special as his two previous May collaborations, but it does have enough genuine gems to make it necessary. *—Stephen Thomas Erlewine*

All the Way / 1961 / Capitol ✦✦✦

All the Way is an entertaining collection of Sinatra singles that have since been collected as bonus tracks on compact disc editions of the singer's original albums. *—Stephen Thomas Erlewine*

Ring a Ding Ding / 1961 / Reprise ✦✦✦

Ring a Ding Ding, Frank Sinatra's first album for his own record

label, broke somewhat from the strict concepts of his Capitol Records; in the process, it set a kind of template for the rest of his '60s Reprise albums. Instead of following a theme, the record captures the atmosphere of Sinatra in 1961—a time when he was running the Rat Pack, so it's no coincidence that the album is named after one of his favorite phrases of the era. The title track was written especially for Sinatra by Sammy Cahn and Jimmy Van Heusen. And that song reflects the brassy, swaggering feeling of the record—even the ballads are arrogant and self-confident. *—Stephen Thomas Erlewine*

Sinatra Swings / 1961 / Reprise ✦✦✦

Recorded with Billy May, *Sinatra Swings* was Frank Sinatra's first straight swing album for Reprise Records. In terms of content and approach, the record is remarkably similar to his final Capitol swing effort, *Come Swing with Me*. In fact, Capitol thought the album, originally titled *Swing Along with Me*, was so close in its sound and title that they sued Sinatra. The record label won the suit and the singer had to change the name of his Reprise album to *Sinatra Swings*. Of course, that didn't change the actual content of the record. Even though the tone was similar, there were some differences from *Come Swing with Me*—the ballads have strings, there are saxophones on the record, and the material is more lighthearted on *Sinatra Swings*, much like the songs on *Come Fly with Me*. The restored sense of humor makes *Sinatra Swings* preferable to *Come Swing with Me*, even if it doesn't have the concentrated precision of the first two Sinatra/May sets. *—Stephen Thomas Erlewine*

I Remember Tommy / May 1, 1961–May 4, 1961 / Reprise ✦✦✦

As the title suggests, *I Remember Tommy* is an affectionate tribute to Tommy Dorsey, the legendary band leader that helped elevate Frank Sinatra to stardom. Arranged by Sy Oliver, who also gained attention through Dorsey, the album contains a number of songs that were part of the Sinatra/Dorsey repertoire, given slightly new readings. Though the intentions were good, the new versions pale in comparision to the originals. Nevertheless, there are a handful of gems included on the record, making it worthwhile for dedicated Sinatra afficionados. *—Stephen Thomas Erlewine*

Point of No Return / Nov. 11, 1961 / Capitol ✦✦✦

At the time he recorded his final Capitol album, *Point of No Return*, Frank Sinatra was no longer interested in giving his record label first-rate material, preferring to save that for his new label, Reprise. However, someone persuaded the singer to make the album a special occasion by reuniting with Axel Stordahl, the arranger/conductor who helped Sinatra rise to stardom in the '40s; he also arranged the vocalist's first Capitol session, so his presence gave a nice sense of closure to the Capitol era. Even though The Voice gave a more heartfelt, dedicated performance than expected, the project was rushed along, necessitating the use of a ghost-arranger, Heinie Beau, for several tracks. *Point of No Return* remains a touching farewell, consisting of moving renditions of standards like "September Song," "There Will Never Be Another You," "I'll Remember April," and "These Foolish Things," with only three charts replications of their previous work ("I'll Be Seeing You," "September Song," "These Foolish Things"). Sinatra would never sing these standards with such detailed, ornate orchestrations and, as such, the album has a feeling of an elegy. [The compact disc edition includes the first Sinatra/Stordahl sessions for Capitol.] *—Stephen Thomas Erlewine*

Sinatra Sings Great Songs From Great Britain / 1962 / Warner Brothers ✦✦

Sinatra Sings Great Songs From Great Britain is one of the oddest albums in Sinatra's catalog. Recorded in the summer of 1962 and available only in the UK for a number of years, the album consists of songs by British composers, performed with British musicians, and recorded in Britain, while Sinatra was on tour. As it happened, Sinatra was tired and worn out during the sessions and arranger/conductor Robert Farnon had written a set of charts that were ambitious, lush, ornate, and sweeping. Although the arrangements are provocative—occasionally they are more interesting than the actual songs—Sinatra was simply not in good shape for the sessions, which is clear by his thin, straining singing. As such, *Great Songs From Great Britain* isn't much more than a curiousity. *—Stephen Thomas Erlewine*

Sinatra / Basie / 1962 / Reprise ✦✦✦✦✦

The pairing of Frank Sinatra and Count Basie always promised more rewards than it actually yielded. *Sinatra/Basie* was the first of their three collaborations and it is the most successful studio album they recorded as a pair. Sinatra isn't in particularly fine voice, and Basie doesn't shine, but the two come up with enough fine moments to make it worthwhile for devoted listeners. — *Stephen Thomas Erlewine*

Sinatra & Sextet: Live in Paris / 1962 / Reprise ♦♦♦♦♦
If you've cringed at the quality of recent Sinatra projects, this 1962 session will remind you of his glorious past. The 26 cuts include many Sinatra signature pieces ("I've Got You Under My Skin," "The Second Time Around," "Night And Day," "Moonlight In Vermont") with backing from an intimate small band that provides lush, supportive frameworks around which Sinatra can build and create his inimitable charm. The session also shows Sinatra at his most loutish, with some crude (even for the time) commentary during the beginning of "One For My Baby," and borderline racist cracks at the end of "Ol' Man River" and start of "The Lady Is A Tramp." But Sinatra's vocal excellence often overcame his idiocy and bad manners, and it does on this fine set. — *Ron Wynn*

Sinatra and Strings / Jan. 1962 / Reprise ♦♦♦
Sinatra and Strings, Frank Sinatra's first album with arranger Don Costa, is an exquisite, romantic collection of ballads and is one of his most sensual records. Costa has given the songs, which consist entirely of standards, (the CD version added two newer songs) exceedingly lush, heavily orchestrated arrangements that sound like updated, contemporary versions of Axel Stordahl's ornate charts. Sinatra responds with smooth, nuanced yet powerful vocals that make these traditional songs sound fresh. The pair take some chances with their arrangements—"Stardust" never reaches the chorus, for instance—but *Sinatra and Strings* remains a definitive ballads album, complete with impassioned readings and endlessly rich, detailed arrangements. — *Stephen Thomas Erlewine*

All Alone / Jan. 15, 1962–Jan. 17, 1962 / Reprise ♦♦♦
Originally, *All Alone* was going to called *Come Waltz with Me*. Though the title and the accompanying specially-written title song were dropped before the album's release, the record remained a stately collection of waltzes, arranged and conducted by Gordon Jenkins. Out of all the arrangers Sinatra regularly worked with, Jenkins had the most overt classical influences in his writing, making him the perfect choice for the project. Nevertheless, *All Alone* is an uneven album, even as it is one of the most intriguing records Sinatra recorded. Divided between standards and relatively recent tunes, the most distinctive element of the album are the rich, neo-classical arrangements by Jenkins. Sinatra doesn't strictly follow Jenkins' intentions. Instead of playing close to the vest, he wrenches the emotions out of the songs. Most of the time, the results are quite moving, especially on the opening and closing Irving Berlin ballads, "All Alone" and "The Song Is Ended." When the results aren't quite as successful, they are still interesting and the elegant, ruminating music makes *All Alone* a necessary listen for dedicated Sinatra fans. — *Stephen Thomas Erlewine*

Sinatra and Swingin' Brass / Apr. 10, 1962–Apr. 11, 1962 / Reprise ♦♦♦
Sinatra and Swingin' Brass, a collection of brash, bold uptempo numbers, followed the all-ballads effort, *Sinatra & Strings*. Again working with Billy May, Sinatra turned in a robust, energetic performance, which was infectious even when his voice was showing signs of wear—he was suffering from a cold during the sessions. The record captures the spirit of the Rat Pack era nearly as well as *Ring a Ding Ding*. — *Stephen Thomas Erlewine*

The Concert Sinatra / Feb. 18, 1963–Feb. 21, 1963 / Reprise ♦♦♦
The Concert Sinatra is one of Frank Sinatra's best records of the early '60s, an album that successfuly rearranges a selection of show tunes, primarily those composed by Richard Rodgers, for the concert stage. Nelson Riddle arranged and conducted one of the largest orchestras that had ever supported Frank Sinatra and his work is light and delicate. Despite the large number of musicians, the music is never over-bearing—instead, it is grand and sweeping, providing appropriately epic settings for songs like "Lost In the Stars," "You'll Never Walk Alone," and the stunning "Soliloquy." Sinatra is given the opportunity to demonstrate his full emotional range, from the melodrama of "Ol' Man River" to the tender romanticisim of "Bewitched," which helps make *The Concert Sinatra* one of his most fulfilling albums of the era. — *Stephen Thomas Erlewine*

Sinatra's Sinatra / Apr. 1963 / Reprise ♦♦♦
In the early '60s, Columbia and Capitol were issuing collections of Frank Sinatra's biggest hits, which tended to sell quite well. *Sinatra's Sinatra* was the singer's attempt to get a piece of that action for his new record label, Reprise. Arranged and conducted by Nelson Riddle, the album is a collection of re-recorded versions of 12 of his favorite songs, including two new charts ("Nancy" and "Oh What It Seemed to Be"). Some of his biggest hits and most famous songs are included in his picks, including "I've Got You Under My Skin" and "Young At Heart," and while many of the performances are quite enjoyable, they tend to pale in direct comparison to the originals. Nevertheless, *Sinatra's Sinatra* is successful on its own terms—it's entertaining, if inconsequential. — *Stephen Thomas Erlewine*

America, I Hear You Singing / 1964 / Reprise ♦♦
America, I Hear You Singing is a minor entry in Frank Sinatra's catalog. Recorded with Bing Crosby and Fred Waring's glee club, the record is a collection of patriotic songs that were recorded as a tribute to the assassinated President John F. Kennedy. Although the sentiment is respectable, the album isn't an engaging, suffering from hackneyed arrangements and dull songs. —*Stephen Thomas Erlewine*

Sings Days of Wine and Roses, Moon River & Other Academy Award Winners / 1964 / Reprise ♦♦♦
Featuring a selection of Oscar-winning standards, ranging from 1934's "The Continental" to 1962's "Days of Wine and Roses," *Academy Award Winners* is a professional and stylish album, but it only yields a handful of true gems. That isn't the fault of either Frank Sinatra or arranger/conductor Nelson Riddle. Although their performances aren't quite as distinguished as their past collaborations, they are nevertheless highly enjoyable. Sinatra is charming and lively, even if he doesn't demonstarte the full range of his technique on each track, while Riddle's charts are light and entertaining. The main problem with the record is how it plays as a series of individual moments, not as a cohesive collection. Granted, some of the moments are first-rate—"The Way You Look Tonight" is one of Sinatra's classic performances, and "Three Coins in the Fountain" and "All the Way" are nearly as good—but the moments never form a whole, which makes the album an occasionally frustrating listen. —*Stephen Thomas Erlewine*

Softly, as I Leave You / Feb. 14, 1964 / Reprise ♦♦♦
Softly, as I Leave You was Frank Sinatra's first tentative attempt to come to terms with the rock & roll revolution, even if it was hardly a rock & roll album. In fact, it wasn't much of an album, to begin with. The highlight of the record was the hit title song, which featured a subdued but forceful steady backbeat. The rhythm itself was indicative of Sinatra's effort to accept the new popular music. Arranged by Ernie Freeman, "Softly, as I Leave You," "Then Suddenly Love," and "Available" are definitely stabs at incorporating rock & roll into Sinatra's middle-of-the-road pop, featuring drum kits, backing vocals, and keyboards. As pop singles, they were well-constructed and deservedly successful. The rest of the album is pieced together from leftovers from various early '60s sessions, giving the record a decidedly uneven tone. Some of the songs work well as individual moments, particularly the Nelson Riddle-arranged "Emily," but the varying tone is too distracting to make the album a satisfying listen. —*Stephen Thomas Erlewine*

It Might As Well Be Swing / Dec. 1964 / Reprise ♦♦♦
Frank Sinatra and Count Basie's second collaboration, *It Might As Well Be Swing*, was a more structured, swing-oriented set than *Sinatra/Basie* and in many ways the superior album. The album consists of recently written songs, arranged as if they were swing numbers. The results work splendidly, not just because arranger/conductor Quincy Jones found the core of each of the songs, but because Basie and his band were flexible. Adding a string section to their core band, Basie plays a more standard swing than he did on *Sinatra/Basie*, but that doesn't mean *It Might As Well Be Swing* is devoid of jazz. Both Basie and Sinatra manage to play with the melodies and the beat, even though the album never loses sight of its purpose as a swing album. However, what makes *It Might As Well Be Swing* more successful is the consistently high level of the performances. On their previous collaboration, both Sinatra and Basie sounded a bit worn out, but throughout this record they play with energy and vigor. — *Stephen Thomas Erlewine*

Sinatra '65 / 1965 / Reprise ✦✦
An uneven, pop-oriented record, *Sinatra '65* is an odds-and-ends collection of various singles and sessions, highlighted by the hits "Anytime At All," "Somewhere In Your Heart," "Stay With Me," and "Tell Her (You Love Her Each Day)." —*Stephen Thomas Erlewine*

My Kind of Broadway / 1965 / Reprise ✦✦✦
Pieced together from a variety of sessions and soundtracks, *My Kind of Broadway* is an uneven record, featuring a handful of gems among a bunch of competent, but undistinguished, peformances. Most of the songs—from "Luck Be A Lady" and "Hello, Dolly!" to "I'll Only Miss Her When I Think of Her," "They Can't Take That Away From Me," "Yesterdays," and "Nice Work If You Can Get It"—are classics, but the arrangements and performances frequently are nothing more than competent. When Sinatra delivers, as he does on the show-stopper "Luck Be A Lady," the results are pretty spectacular, but the majority of the album is merely pleasant. —*Stephen Thomas Erlewine*

★ **September of My Years** / Apr. 13, 1965–May 27, 1965 / Reprise ✦✦✦✦✦
September of My Years is one of Frank Sinatra's triumphs of the '60s, an album that consolidated his strengths while moving him into new territory, primarily in terms of tone. More than the double disc set *A Man and His Music*—which was released a year after this album—*September of My Years* captures how Sinatra was at the time of his 50th birthday. Gordon Jenkins rich, stately and melancholy arrangements give the album an appropriate reflective atmosphere. Most of the songs are new or relatively recent numbers; every cut fits into a loose theme of aging, reflection and regret. Sinatra, however, doesn't seem stuck in his ways—though the songs are rooted in traditional pop, they touch on folk and contemporary pop. As such, the album offered a perfect summary, as well as suggesting future routes for the singer. —*Stephen Thomas Erlewine*

Moonlight Sinatra / Nov. 1965 / Reprise ✦✦✦
Driven by a set of lush, sparkling Nelson Riddle arrangements, *Moonlight Sinatra* is a low-key, charming collection. Although the basic concept is somewhat nebulous—all of the songs have the word "moon" in the title—Riddle wrote a series of charts that suggest a warm, lovely evening with a variety of tones and moods, from light Latin rhythms to sweet ballads. While the album is a minor entry in Sinatra's catalog, it is nevertheless an enjoyable, romantic listen. Half of the songs on *Moonlight Sinatra* were originally associated with Sinatra's idol Bing Crosby, making the album somewhat of a loose tribute — *Stephen Thomas Erlewine*

A Man and His Music / Dec. 1965 / Reprise ✦✦✦
Released around his 50th birthday, *A Man and His Music* is an ambitious, double-album set that provides a brief history of Frank Sinatra's career. Though the concept sounds quite promising in theory, the execution is somewhat lacking. Instead of using the original recordings—which were made for RCA, Columbia, and Capitol, not his then-current label, Reprise—Sinatra re-recorded the majority of the albums songs. That in itself isn't bad. Many of the new versions are quite enjoyable, with lively, inspired vocals. However, there is also an intrusive narration from Sinatra that runs throughout the album. Although it does offer some amusing anecdotes and gives a sense of his long, complex history, the narration prevents the album from being a consistently engaging listen. —*Stephen Thomas Erlewine*

Strangers in the Night / 1966 / Reprise ✦✦✦
Strangers in the Night marked Frank Sinatra's return to the top of the pop charts in the mid-'60s and it consolidated the comeback he started in 1965. Although he later claimed he disliked the title track, the album was an inventive, rich effort from Sinatra, one that established him as a still-viable star to a wide, mainstream audience without losing the core of his sound. Combining pop hits ("Downtown," "On A Clear Day (You Can See Forever)," "Call Me") with show tunes and standards, the album creates a delicate but comfortable balance between big band and pop instrumentation. Using strings, horns, and an organ, Riddle constructed an easy, deceptively swinging sound that appealed to both Sinatra's dedicated fans and pop radio. And Sinatra's singing is relaxed, confident, and surprisingly jazzy, as he plays with the melody "The Most Beautiful Girl In The World" and delivers a knockout punch with the assured, breathtaking "Summer Wind." Although he would not record another album with Riddle again, Sinatra would

expand the approach of *Strangers in the Night* for the rest of the decade. —*Stephen Thomas Erlewine*

That's Life / 1966 / Reprise ✦✦✦
Following the across-the-boards success of *Strangers in the Night*, *That's Life* continued Frank Sinatra's streak of commercially successful albums that straddled the line between traditional and contemporary pop music. Adding more pop music techniques to his repertoire of show tunes, *That's Life* straddled the line between pop concessions and satisfying Sinatra's own taste for weightier, more respected material. Although it was a pop-oriented record, Sinatra had not begun to rely on rock-influenced productions; instead, arranger/conductor Ernie Freeman contributed charts that alternated between bluesy, brassy swingers and mildy schmaltzy string arrangements, supported by an overbearing backing chorus. While the title track was the hardest blues Sinatra ever attempted, that approach wasn't attempted for the entire album. A few tracks—particularly a rearrangement of the New Vaudeville Orchestra's campy "Winchester Cathedral" and the static version of "The Impossible Dream"—fall flat, but the album works when Sinatra is either tearing into the song (like "That's Life") or coaxing life out of mid-level ballads like "You're Gonna Hear From Me" —*Stephen Thomas Erlewine*

Sinatra at the Sands / Jan. 1966–Feb. 1966 / Reprise ✦✦✦✦
In many ways, *Sinatra at the Sands* is the definitive portrait of Frank Sinatra in the '60s. Recorded in April of 1966, *At the Sands* is the first commercially released, live Frank Sinatra album, recorded at a relaxed Las Vegas club show. For these dates at the Sands, Sinatra worked with Count Basie and his Orchestra, which was conducted by Quincy Jones. Like any of his concerts, the material was fairly predictable, with his standard show numbers punctuated by some nice surprises. Throughout the show, Sinatra is in fine voice, turning in a particularly affecting version of "Angel Eyes." He is also in fine humor, constantly joking with the audience and the band, as well as delivering an entertaining, if rambling, monologue halfway through the album. Some of the humor has dated poorly, appearing insensitive, but that sentiment cannot be applied to the music. Basie and the orchestra are swinging and dynamic, inspiring a textured, dramatic and thoroughly enjoyable performance from Sinatra. —*Stephen Thomas Erlewine*

Frank Sinatra and the World We Knew / 1967 / Reprise ✦✦
More of a singles collection than a proper album, *The World We Knew* illustrates just how heavily Frank Sinatra was courting the pop charts of the late '60s. Much of the material on the record is given a rock-oriented pop production, complete with fuzz guitars, reverb, folky acoustic guitars, wailing harmonicas, drum kits, organs, and brass and string charts that punctuate the songs rather than provide the driving force. Indeed, many of the songs recall the music Nancy Sinatra was making at the time, which the presence of the hit father-daughter duet "Somethin' Stupid" emphasizes. But the songs that Sinatra tackles with a variety of arrangers—everyone from Nancy's hitmaker Lee Hazelwood, Billy Strange, Ernie Freeman, and H.B. Barnum to Don Costas, Gordon Jenkins, and Claus Ogerman—are more ambitious than most mid-dle-of-the-road, adult-oriented soft-rock of the late '60s. "The World We Knew" has an odd, deep winding melody supported by the toughest approximated rock arrangement Sinatra ever used. Similarly, "This Town" is quite bluesy, with pounding brass and harmonica. Even the least successful pop numbers have something enjoyable as far as '60s pop-craftmanship is concerned— "Don't Sleep in the Subway" may be burdened by a histrionic female backing chorus, but the rest of the track is well-layered and as well-constructed as the Petula Clark original. Sinatra doesn't sound engaged with all of the material—"Some Enchanted Evening," with Barnum's ridiculously bombastic arrangement and a tossed-off vocal from the singer, is easily one of the worst versions of the tune recorded—but he generally turns in a fine performance throughout the record. However, there is one true gem on *The World We Knew*. Buried mid-way through the album, Johnny Mercer's ballad "Drinking Again" is given an exceptional treatment, with Sinatra squeezing out every nuance in the lyric; the song ranks as one of the best he recorded in the late '60s. — *Stephen Thomas Erlewine*

Francis Albert Sinatra and Antonio Carlos Jobim / Jan. 30, 1967–Feb. 1, 1967 / Reprise ✦✦✦✦✦
By 1967, bossa nova had become quite popular within jazz and traditional pop audiences, yet Frank Sinatra hadn't attempted any Brazil-influenced material. Sinatra decided to record a full-fledged

bossa nova album with the genre's leading composer, Antonio Carlos Jobim. Arranged by Claus Ogerman and featuring Jobim on guitar and backing vocals, *Francis Albert Sinatra and Antonio Carlos Jobim* concentrated on Jobim's originals, adding three American classics—"Baubles, Bangles and Beads," "Change Partners," and "I Concentrate On You"—that were rearranged to suit bossa nova conventions. The result was a subdued, quiet album that used the Latin rhythms as a foundation, not as a focal point. Supported by a relaxed, sympathetic arrangement of muted brass, simmering percussion, soft strings, and Jobim's lilting guitar, Sinatra turns in an especially noteworthy performance—he has never sounded so subtle, underplaying every line he delivers and showcasing vocal techniques that he never had displayed before. *Francis Albert Sinatra and Antonio Carlos Jobim* doesn't reveal its pleasures immediately; the album is too textured and understated to be fully appreciated within one listen. After a few plays, the album begins to slowly work its way underneath a listener's skin and it emerges as one of his most rewarding albums of the '60s. — *Stephen Thomas Erlewine*

Francis A. Sinatra & Edward K. Ellington / 1968 / Reprise ✦✦✦✦✦

The much-anticipated collaboration between Frank Sinatra and Duke Ellington, *Francis A. & Edward K.* didn't quite match its high expectations. At the time of recording, the Ellington band were no longer at its peak and Sinatra was concentrating on contemporary pop material, not standards. For the album, it was decided that the record would be a mixture of standards and new material; as it happened, only one Ellington number, "I Like the Sunrise," was included. Due to a mild cold, Sinatra was not at his best during the sessions and his performance is consequently uneven on the record, varying between robust, expressive performances and thin singing. Similarly, Ellington and his band are hot and cold, occasionally turning in inspired performances and just as frequently walking through the numbers. That doesn't mean there is nothing to reccommend on *Francis A. & Edward K.* On the contrary, the best moments on the album fulfill all of the duo's promise. All eight songs are slow numbers, which brings out Sinatra's romantic side. "Indian Summer" is a particular standout, with a sensual vocal and a breathtaking solo from saxophonist Johnny Hodges. Much of the material on the album doesn't gel quite as well, but devoted Sinatra and Ellington fans will find enough to treasure on the record to make it a worthwhile listen. — *Stephen Thomas Erlewine*

Frank Sinatra's Greatest Hits! / 1968 / Reprise ✦✦✦✦✦

Frank Sinatra's Greatest Hits concentrates on the Chairman of the Board's pop hits from the mid- and late-'60s, several of which were single-only releases or only available on movie soundtracks. Appropriately, it begins with his biggest solo hit of the '60s, "Strangers in the Night," and then vascillates between adult contemporary pop songs and ballads. Much of the production has dated, with its guitars, reverb, and arrangements bearing all the hallmarks '60s pop. While some of the songs rank among Sinatra's finest moments, particularly "Summer Wind" and "It Was A Very Good Year," most of these songs are guilty pleasures. They might not have the emotional resonance of his finest ballad and swing albums, but fluff like the Nancy Sinatra duet "Somethin' Stupid," the fuzz guitar-tinged "The World We Knew (Over and Over)" and the bluesy "This Town" are enjoyable as pop singles. As such, *Frank Sinatra's Greatest Hits* isn't a good introduction to his music, as it isn't even a representative chronicle of his '60s Reprise recordings. Instead, it's a fun and effective portrait of Sinatra as he was in the late '60s, illustrating how he was struggling to come to terms with contemporary pop music. — *Stephen Thomas Erlewine*

Cycles / 1968 / Reprise ✦✦

Cycles was Frank Sinatra's first fully-fledged pop/rock-oriented album, concentrating on a more orchestrated variation on the popular folk-rock of the late '60s. The foundation of the arrangements on *Cycles* are guitars, bass, and drum kits, all played gently and unobtrusively; the strings are layered on top of the pop rhythm section. Appropriately, Sinatra sang a variety of material associated with folk-rock, particularly Joni Mitchell's "Both Sides Now" and Glen Campbell's "Gentle On My Mind" and "By the Time I Get To Phoenix." Sinatra responds to the softer material by phasing out most of the edginess in his phrasing. He doesn't sing with the nuanced textures of his Jobim albums—he is simply restrained. That doesn't result in an embarrassing album, yet

Cycles isn't the successful rock and traditional pop fusion that it might've been. Some of the material isn't well-suited for Sinatra— neither "Little Green Apples" or "Pretty Colors" sound convincing—but the main problem is with Don Costa's arrangements and production. There simply isn't enough variety to sustain interest throughout the course of the short, ten-song album. Certain sections work well, particularly the Glen Campbell numbers, but there isn't anything distinctive about the record, which makes it one of the weakest albums Sinatra ever released. — *Stephen Erlewine*

My Way / 1969 / Reprise ✦✦✦

Although it follows the same patterns and approach as *Cycles*, *My Way* is a stronger album, with a better, more varied selection of material and a more focused, gutsy performance from Sinatra. Built around the hit single "My Way," the album again alternates between rock covers ("Yesterday," "Hallelujah, I Love Her So," "For Once In My LIfe," "Didn't We," "Mrs. Robinson"), a couple of adapted French songs, and a handful of standards. This time out, Don Costa has written more engaging charts than the previous *Cycles*. The Beatles' "Yesterday" is given an affecting, melancholy treatment that brings out the best in Sinatra, as does the new arrangment of "All My Tomorrows," which is lush and aching. If Sinatra doesn't quite pull off the R&B of "Hallelujah, I Love Her So," he does sing the light Latin stylings of "A Day in the Life Of a Fool" beautifully and he has fun with Paul Simon's "Mrs. Robinson," changing the lyrics dramatically so they become a tongue-in-cheek, swinging hipster tribute. For that matter, most of the record is successful in creating a middle ground between the traditional pop Sinatra loves and the contemporary pop/rock that dominated the charts in the late '60s. *My Way* doesn't have the macho swagger of his prime Rat Pack records, but its reflective, knowing arrangements show that Sinatra could come to terms with rock & roll at some level. — *Stephen Thomas Erlewine*

A Man Alone & Other Songs of Rod McKuen / Mar. 19, 1969–Mar. 21, 1969 / Reprise ✦✦

After making a successful mainstream, contemporary pop album with *My Way*, Frank Sinatra branched out with *A Man Alone*, subtitled *The Words & Music of McKuen*. Unlike most poets, Rod McKuen was extremely popular and successful, selling over a million copies of his books in the late '60s. After meeting at a party, the singer decided to record an entire album of the poet's verse and music. McKuen wrote a selection of new songs and poems for Sinatra; that material became *A Man Alone*. McKuen's musical contributions amount to tone poems more than songs. Six of the pieces are actual songs, with the remaining tracks being spoken word pieces with instrumental backdrops, including one number that is half-sung, half-spoken without any instrumental accompaniment at all. Certainly, with all this emphasis on words, *A Man Alone* was intended to be a serious statement, but much of it comes off as embarrassing posturing. McKuen's compositions are lyrically slight and musically insubstantial, but what saves *A Man Alone* from being a total failure is the conviction of Sinatra's performance, as well as Don Costa's skillful arrangements. Although he's not able to recite the poetry convincingly, Sinatra's singing is textured and passionate, drawing more emotion from the lyrics than are actually there. Similarly, Costa's charts are lush without being sentimental and very sympathetic to Sinatra's vocals, easily masking the compositional weakness. Sinatra and Costa pull so much out of so little on *A Man Alone*, it makes the listener wish they applied their talents and ambitions to a simliar, but more substantial set of songs. As it stands, the album is an intriguing listen but ultimately a failure. — *Stephen Thomas Erlewine*

Watertown / 1970 / Reprise ✦✦✦

Watertown is Frank Sinatra's most ambitious concept album, as well as his most difficult record. Not only does it tell a full-fledged story, it is his most explicit attempt at rock-oriented pop. Since the main composer of *Watertown* is Bob Gaudio, the author of the Four Seasons' hits "Can't Take My Eyes Off of You," "Walk Like A Man," and "Big Girls Don't Cry," that doesn't come as a surprise. With Jake Holmes, Gaudio created a song cycle concerning a middle-aged, small-town man whose wife had left him with the kids. Constructed as a series of brief lyrical snapshots that read like letters or soliloquies, the culminating effect of the songs is an atmosphere of loneliness—and it is a loneliness without much hope or romance—it is the sound of a broken man. Producer Charles Calello arranged musical backdrops that conveyed the despair of the lyrics. Weaving together prominent electric guitars, keyboards, drum kits, and light strings, Calello uses pop/rock instrumentations and production techniques, but that doesn't prevent Sinatra from warming to the material. In fact, he turns in a wonderful performance, drawing out every emotion from the lyrics, giving the album's character depth. —*Stephen Thomas Erlewine*

Sinatra & Company / 1971 / Warner Brothers ✦✦✦
In 1969, Frank Sinatra recorded a second album with Antonio Carlos Jobim. For unknown reasons, Reprise decided not to release *Sinatra-Jobim*, but seven of the ten songs intended for the record did appear on the first side of 1971's *Sinatra & Company*. The selections from *Sinatra-Jobim* have a decidedly different flavor than the material on *Francis Albert Sinatra and Antonio Carlos Jobim*, largely due to the charts of arranger Eumir Deodato. Where Claus Ogerman's arrangements were quite subdued and understated, Deodato's charts are looser and more relaxed; consequently, the music is lighter, more immediate, and arguably more fun. Sinatra responds to the arrangements with more forceful singing than on the previous Jobim collaboration, but his phrasing is still more nuanced than even his soft pop/rock-oriented material. Nevertheless, that subtle phrasing carries over into the second side of *Sinatra & Company*, a collection of pop-oriented tracks. Although the music on the second half of the album is neither as adventerous or as compelling as that on the first, it is still highly entertaining. The seven songs were arranged by Don Costas, who keeps the material shiny and commerically-oriented. In the case of "Close To You," "Leaving On A Jet Plane," "I Will Drink the Wine," "Bein' Green," and "Sunrise In the Morning," that isn't bad—this is material that demands to be delivered in slick, polished arrangements. Under Costas' direction, these songs are given arrangements that feature both strings and gentle folk-rock underpinnings, particularly strummed acoustic guitars. Taken on its own terms, the second half of *Sinatra & Company* ranks as some of his best soft rock-influenced material of the late '60s, even if it doesn't sit comfortably with the excellent bossa nova that comprises the first side of the record. —*Stephen Thomas Erlewine*

Greatest Hits, Vol. 2 / 1972 / Reprise ✦✦✦
Much like its predecessor, *Frank Sinatra's Greatest Hits, Vol. 2* is more effective as a portrait of Sinatra at a particular stage in his career than as a comprehensive collection. Like *Greatest Hits*, the album mainly consists of pop hits and songs pulled from movie soundtracks, adding in a pair of pop/rock hits for good measure. Although "My Way" became Sinatra's signature song of the '70s and '80s—primarily because his spectacular performance rescues the cliched song—none of these tracks were particularly big hits; several of the cuts are album tracks, while the highest-charting single was "Cycles," which peaked at number 23. While the 11 tracks might not all be hits, they are fairly representative of the sound of Sinatra's music in the late '60s. There's a couple of forgotten gems, particularly the wonderfully moving "What's Now Is Now" and a gorgeous arrangement of George Harrison's "Something," but there is also more dross than the previous *Greatest Hits* collection. Even with a handful of mediocre tracks, *Greatest Hits, Vol. 2* remains an enjoyable sampler, containing several classic Sinatra performances ("My Way," "The September of My Years"). —*Stephen Thomas Erlewine*

Ol' Blue Eyes Is Back / 1973 / Reprise ✦✦
Frank Sinatra returned from his brief retirement in 1973 with the appropriately titled *Ol' Blue Eyes Is Back*. Released amidst a whirlwind of publicity, the album was a commercial success, earning a gold album and nearly climbing its way into the Top 10, but it wasn't a return to form. Produced by Don Costa, the album doesn't follow the sound of Sinatra's last handful of albums (*Sinatra & Company, Watertown, A Man Alone, My Way*), jettisoning recent pop hits for selections by upcoming songwriters, particularly Joe Raposo, as well as several current film and Broadway numbers. Much of the material is unmemorable, featuring slight melodies and cliched, underdeveloped lyrics. The noticeable exceptions are "Send in the Clowns" and the moving "There Used to Be a Ballpark," both featuring sublime, subtle arrangements from Gordon Jenkins and outstanding singing by Sinatra. However, Jenkins' arrangements are undercut by the lethargic, uneventful production by Costa. Not that Jenkins' arrangements are all perfect—on "Noah," one of the worst songs Sinatra ever recorded, his writing actually accentuates the banality of Raposo's tune. Much of the material is indicative of the lack of songwriting ingenuity in the early '70s; straddling the line between rock-inflected pop and traditionalist pop, most of the songs wind up making a small impression, if they make one at all. Apart from "Send in the Clowns" and "There Used to Be A

Ballpark," there's little on *Ol' Blue Eyes Is Back* that's rewarding, and Sinatra recorded better versions of both of those songs. —*Stephen Thomas Erlewine*

The Main Event—Live / 1974 / Reprise ✦✦
Some Nice Things I've Missed / 1974 / Reprise ✦✦
After returning to the spotlight with *Ol' Blue Eyes Is Back*, Frank

---

Music Map

Soprano Saxophone

Pioneer and First Innovator
Sidney Bechet

Other Pre-Bop Sopranos
Johnny Hodges
Charlie Barnet

Later Swing and Trad Stylists
Bob Wilber
Kenny Davern
Woody Herman
George Probert (with Firehouse Five Plus Two)

Bop-Based Saxophonists Doubling on Soprano

Lucky Thompson	Zoot Sims
Budd Johnson	Jerome Richardson
Oliver Nelson	Cannonball Adderley

Avant-Garde Innovators
John Coltrane
Steve Lacy
Evan Parker

Also Very Influential
Wayne Shorter

Other Important Stylists

Dave Liebman	Jane Ira Bloom
Jane Bunnett	Bruce Ackley (of ROVA)
John Surman	Jan Garbarek
Joseph Jarman	Roscoe Mitchell
Oliver Lake	Julius Hemphill
Greg Osby	Steve Grossman
Gerry Niewood	Gary Bartz
Branford Marsalis	

Crossover and Instrumental Pop

Grover Washington, Jr.	Ronnie Laws
George Howard	Kenny G.
Bill Evans	

Sinatra continued his comeback with *Some Nice Things I've Missed*. As the title suggests, the bulk of the album consists of songs that became popular during Sinatra's brief retirement, including hits by Stevie Wonder, Neil Diamond, Jim Croce, Bread, and Tony Orlando & Dawn; the two tracks that weren't hits, "I'm Gonna Make It All the Way" and "Satisfy Me One More Time," were written by Floyd Huddleston, best known for contributing several songs to Disney cartoons. By and large, the material is adapted for big bands, with a couple of tracks featuring slight contemporary touches, like folky acoustic guitar. The majority of the album is arranged and produced by Don Costa, who must bear some of the blame for the failure of the record. Most of the songs he had to work with were too simple to withstand substantial orchestration and rearrangement, but Costa's charts are overwhelmingly trite and unimaginative, underscoring how unsuited the material is for Sinatra. With the exception of the breezily swinging "You Are the Sunshine of My Life," the arrangements are forced and awkward, trying to inject swing where there isn't any in "Sweet Caroline" and "Bad, Bad Leroy Brown." Although they occasionally border on muzak, the slower numbers are more effective, with "What Are You Doing the Rest of Your Life?" leading the way among Costa's efforts, but none of his numbers equal Gordon Jenkins' subtle arrangements of "The Summer Knows" and "If," which nevertheless aren't among his most memorable work. Even though the music doesn't provide a good foundation for Sinatra, the vocalist doesn't make an effort to save the material. Throughout the album, he sounds bored, even irritated, with the songs. There are a couple of exceptions to the rule—he brings some life "You Are the Sunshine of My Life," "What Are You Doing the Rest of Your Life," "The Summer Knows," "You Turned My World Around"—but Sinatra sounds disinterested in the project, as if he can't wait to leave the studio. And given the insipidness of "I'm Gonna Make It All the Way," "Satisfy Me One More Time," and "Tie A Yellow Ribbon Round the Ole Oak Tree," who could blame him? *—Stephen Thomas Erlewine*

Trilogy / Jul. 1980 / Reprise ✦✦
By the time the triple-record set *Trilogy* was released, Frank Sinatra had become somewhat of a recluse from the recording studio. For six years, the Chairman of the Board had spent as little time as possible in the studio, preferring to tour. He had recorded some tracks, with a few of the cuts appearing on singles, but he hadn't made an album since 1974's disappointing *Some Nice Things I've Missed*. *Trilogy* was an audacious, ambitious way to stage a comeback. Each of the album's three records are conceived as an individual work, with the first covering "The Past," the second "The Present," and the third "The Future." Each record was arranged by one of Sinatra's major collaborators—Billy May ("The Past"), Don Costa ("The Present"), and Gordon Jenkins ("The Future"). The concept was intended to tie together the diverse strands of Sinatra's music, sum up his career while pointing toward his future. As a concept, *Trilogy* certainly has its flaws, as does some of the music on the lengthy set. However, the best moments are triumphant, proving that the Voice was still vital in his fourth decade of recording. "The Past" is easily the best record on the album. For the first time since the early '60s, Sinatra recorded a record of standards ("The Song Is You," "It Had to Be You," "All of You"), which is the material best suited for his talents. "The Present" isn't quite as accomplished. Featuring a selection of material from the post-rock era, the record concentrates on pop hits like "Love Me Tender," "Something," "Song Sung Blue," "MacArthur Park," and "Just the Way You Are." Some of the material is mediocre, but Don Costa's arrangements are lovely, as is Sinatra's singing. Together, they make mid-level songs like "Theme From New York, New York" into anthems. However good the first two records are, "The Future" is an unqualified mess. Written by Jenkins, the songs on "The Future" are ambitious, experimental, and self-referential—in fact, it's more of a free-form suite than a set of songs. Most of the record is devoid of melody and while the arrangements and orchestration is certainly interesting, it's not very effective. Singing cliched, trite lyrics about peace, space travel, and his past, Sinatra sounds lost in the murky atmospheric music of "The Future." It might be an anti-climatic way to end an otherwise enjoyable set, but "The Future" doesn't ruin the pleasures of *Trilogy*, it just puts them into greater perspective. *—Stephen Thomas Erlewine*

She Shot Me Down / 1981 / Reprise ✦✦✦
She Shot Me Down is Frank Sinatra's last great album, a dark, brooding record of saloon songs delivered with an understated authority by Sinatra. Arranged and conducted by Gordon Jenkins and produced by Don Costa, the record largely consists of contemporary material, including five that were basically tailored for Sinatra. It's a dense, moody record that works spectacularly—Sinatra's vocals are more alive and rich in detail than on *Trilogy*, and the concept is more concise and well-executed. *She Shot Me Down* might not consist of the classic saloon songs, but it has that feeling more than any of his other albums. *—Stephen Thomas Erlewine*

L.A. Is My Lady / Apr. 13, 1984–May 17, 1984 / Qwest ✦✦
Frank Sinatra's final studio album of the '80s—arguably the last true original album Sinatra recorded—was an uneven but surprisingly enjoyable set that tried to adapt the singer's style to contemporary pop standards. Under the direction of arranger/producer Quincy Jones, the album incorporated more synthesizers and slick production techniques than any previous Sinatra album, but the result usually doesn't sound forced, especially on the hit title song. When the album does fail, it is because Jones' overly-ambitious and commercial production—such as the insistent dance beat of "How Do You Keep the Music Playing"—prevents the song from taking root. Nevertheless, everyone involved, from Sinatra and Jones to the band themselves, sounds like they're having fun and that sense of joy effortlessly translates to the listener. *—Stephen Thomas Erlewine*

★ **The Voice: The Columbia Years (1943–1952)** / 1986 / Columbia ✦✦✦✦✦
Divided into six separate thematically-oriented records—covering saloon songs, standards, swing, Broadway, Hollywood, and love songs—this six-LP/four-CD set provides an excellent retrospective of Frank Sinatra's years at Columbia. Sinatra sounds vigorous and Axel Stordahl's arrangements, while sounding somewhat dated, remain breathtaking in their lush, romantic detail. *The Voice* has been superseded by the four-disc *The Best of the Columbia Years*, but it remains an excellent introduction to one of Sinatra's prime periods. *—Stephen Thomas Erlewine*

The Capitol Years / 1990 / Capitol ✦✦✦✦✦
Released to coincide with Frank Sinatra's 75th birthday, the three-disc set *The Capitol Years* has an abundance of classic Sinatra performances—however, it isn't the best place to hear most of these cuts. Sinatra's Capitol albums were designed as cohesive works and it is disconcerting to hear all of the different moods jammed together on one collection, with a handful of singles used as breathers. There is certainly plenty of wonderful music here, and the box is somewhat of an effective sampler, but to really appreciate what the singer achieved during the '50s, it is necessary to listen to the original albums. *—Stephen Thomas Erlewine*

The Reprise Collection / 1990 / Reprise ✦✦✦✦✦
Like *The Capitol Years*, the four-disc box set *The Reprise Collection* was released to celebrate Frank Sinatra's 75th anniversary. However, it works as a better sampler than the Capitol set, partially because Sinatra released so many albums on Reprise that it is necessary to have an introduction to such a large body of work. Also, his Reprise records, while still being concept albums, were more inconsistent and therefore easier to anthologize. Many highlights, as well as most of his biggest hits from the era, are included on *The Reprise Collection*, along with a handful of rarities that are nearly as enjoyable. It's a dynamite collection and proves that the '60s and '70s were a surprisingly diverse, rewarding time for Sinatra. *—Stephen Thomas Erlewine*

The Capitol Collectors Series / 1990 / Capitol ✦✦✦✦✦
Capitol Collectors Series collects a selection of Frank Sinatra's biggest hit singles from the '50s, making for a scattershot but entertaining sampler, even if it is in no way a definitive retrospective of the era. *—Stephen Thomas Erlewine*

★ **Sinatra Reprise: the Very Good Years** / Mar. 26, 1991 / Warner Brothers ✦✦✦✦✦
Sinatra Reprise: The Very Good Years is an excellent single-disc retrospective of Sinatra's career at Reprise, including most of his signature songs from the '60s, '70s, and '80s. Hits like "My Way," "That's Life," "Summer Wind," "Strangers in the Night," "It Was A Very Good Year" and "New York, New York" are present, as are songs that were never singles but were extremely popular, like "Luck Be A Lady," "Fly Me to the Moon," "Love and Marriage," and "The Way You Look Tonight." For many casual fans, this disc captures the essence of Sinatra as an icon and provides a perfect introduction to the singer. *—Stephen Thomas Erlewine*

★ **Sinatra** / 1992 / Reprise ✦✦✦✦✦
This is the two-disc soundtrack to a 1992 television mini-series about the life of Frank Sinatra. There is no musical scoring, and there are no re-recordings. Rather, this is a collection of 30 songs recorded between 1931 and 1979, most by Sinatra, although Bing Crosby, Benny Goodman, and Billie Holiday also make appearances. What is notable about the set is that it is the only album to combine tracks from Sinatra's recordings on Columbia, RCA Victor, Capitol, and Reprise, and thus the only one offering the breadth of his work over a period of 40 years. Of course, it remains a sampler, and there's far more great Sinatra material, but the unique circumstances make this an excellent compilation for the beginner. — *William Ruhlmann*

The Columbia Years (1943–1952) the Complete Recordings / 1993 / Columbia ✦✦✦✦✦
For serious students of popular singing, this 12-disc box set is indispensable. During his early years at Columbia, Sinatra defined what popular singing was, and these 285 songs show why he was so revolutionary. For many, 12 discs is too much music, but for collectors, the set is essential. — *Stephen Thomas Erlewine*

Duets / Oct. 25, 1993 / Capitol ✦
As a marketing concept, Frank Sinatra's comeback album *Duets* was a complete success. A collection of Sinatra standards produced by Phil Ramone, the record wasn't a duets album in the conventional sense—Sinatra never recorded in the studio with his partners. Instead, the other singers recorded their tracks separately, sometimes in different studios, and the two tracks were pasted together to create the illusion of a duet. Certainly, this recording method prevented any spontaneous interaction between the singers, and it also limited the emotional impact of the songs. Since neither vocalist could construct an effective single performance, sustaining a mood throughout the course of the song, each singer sounds restrained. In the case of several duet partners, including Bono and Barbara Streisand, this means they rely on camp as a way of making their performance interesting. Sinatra, meanwhile, is oblivious to all of the vocal grandstanding on the part of his duet partners, simply because he recorded his track well in advance of their contributions. The result is a mess: the vocalists never mesh, and the orchestrations are ham-fisted and overblown, relying more on bombast than showmanship. Furthermore, Sinatra's performance is uneven; occasionally, his voice is remarkable, but just as often, it is thin and worn. Nevertheless, *Duets* was a gigantic hit, selling over two million copies and becoming Sinatra's single most commercially successful record. None of its commercial success had anything to do with the album's artistic merit—the album is easily the worst Sinatra released during his lengthy career. Instead, *Duets* rose to number two on the pop charts because of its masterful marketing strategy. The album was promoted as a piece of nostalgia, primarily to baby boomers but also to Generation X as a piece of kitsch. Both approaches ignore the emotional core of Sinatra's music, which is evident on only one track—"One for My Baby," which was essentially a solo performance introduced by an instrumental from saxophonist Kenny G. Perhaps if *Duets* remained true to the essence of Sinatra's music, it would have been more effective, but as it stands, the album is only admirable as a piece of product, not a piece of music. — *Stephen Thomas Erlewine*

The V-discs: Columbia Years: 1943–45 / 1994 / Sony ✦✦✦
Sinatra's earliest wartime recordings are finally collected on this lovingly assembled two-disc set, which is essential for his serious fans. Sinatra's style isn't as smooth as his recordings with Tommy Dorsey or his Captiol records, but his developing style is very exciting in its own right. — *Stephen Thomas Erlewine*

Duets II / 1994 / Capitol ✦
Following the mult-platinum success of *Duets*, Capitol Records assembled *Duets II*, a sequel that followed the blueprint of its predecessor to the letter. Assembled from leftover tracks from the first album, *Duets II* is a somewhat more consistent album than the original. Looking the superstar names of the first (Tony Bennett, Julio Iglesias, Kenny G, Barbara Streisand, Bono, Aretha Franklin), the artist roster on the sequel generally consists of either faded stars (Neil Diamond, Willie Nelson, Gladys Knight) or mid-level singers (Luis Miguel, Lorrie Morgan) that are popular within their genre but fail to command the attention of the general public. However, there are standouts like Lena Horne and Carlos Jobim, that help lift *Duets II* to a higher level than *Duets*. But that's a minor distinction, actually. The nature of the elec-

tronic duet prohibits the album from having any sort of emotional resonance, even on tracks that feature strong vocals by Sinatra or his partner. It might be nice to hear Horne and Sinatra together on "Embraceable You," but the song doesn't rise above anything more than a technical marvel. The real tragedy is, their performance hints that the album could have been so much more. — *Stephen Thomas Erlewine*

★ **I'll Be Seeing You** / 1995 / RCA/Bluebird ✦✦✦✦✦
Containing many seminal Sinatra performances, *I'll Be Seeing You* distills the highlights from the extensive five-disc *The Song Is You* box set, giving listeners an effective portrait of Sinatra at the beginning of his career. — *Stephen Thomas Erlewine*

The Complete Reprise Studio Recordings / Oct. 17, 1995 / Warner Brothers ✦✦✦✦✦
Encased in a small, leather-bound trunk and comprising a grand total of 20 discs, Frank Sinatra's *The Complete Reprise Studio Recordings* is easily the most lavish box set ever assembled. In addition to the 20 compact discs, the set comes with an hardcover book containing insightful essays by respected Sinatra scholars like Will Friedwald; the only drawback to the book is every photograph, including the reproduced album covers, is in color-tinted black and white. Nevertheless, the main attraction of *The Complete Reprise Studio Recordings* is the music. Sinatra founded Reprise Records in 1961, and he continued to record for his label over the next two decades, completing nearly 500 songs. Every recording that Sinatra made for Reprise, including several previously unreleased tracks and a handful of cuts that have never appeared on compact disc, is included in the set. By and large, the recordings are sequenced according to session order; the only exception are concept albums like *September of My Years* or the *Future* section of the triple album *Trilogy*. (Strangely, the song cycle *Watertown*, which tells a story with its songs, is presented out of order.) Frequently, the sequencing of the original studio albums is more effective than the set's strict chronological presentation, but that's not to say there aren't immense rewards in any one of these long discs. Throughout the 20-disc set, Sinatra comes to grips with rock and contemporary pop music, eventually recording material from songwriters like Jimmy Webb, George Harrison, Neil Diamond, and Billy Joel, as well as occasionally performing arrangements that had more in common with soft rock and easy listening pop than swinging big bands or the lush orchestrations of Nelson Riddle and Gordon Jenkins. While the quality of his voice does decline during the two decades documented on the box set, much of the music is compelling; althought they might not match the consistently brilliant efforts on Columbia and Capitol, the Reprise recordings are rich in variety and drama. The chronological sequencing is effective in portraying Sinatra's evolution, even if the presentation is a bit academic and intimidating for some listeners. Then again, the casual fan isn't going to spend five hundred dollars on a box set. For listeners willing to spend that much money, *The Complete Reprise Studio Recordings* will be endlessly enjoyable and fascinating. — *Stephen Thomas Erlewine*

★ **The Best of the Columbia Years: 1943–1952** / Oct. 31, 1995 / Sony ✦✦✦✦✦
A four-disc distillation of the mammoth 12-disc box *The Columbia Years (1943–1952): The Complete Recordings, The Best of the Columbia Years 1944–52* provides everything most listeners need to know about Frank Sinatra's early career. Nearly all of his classic performances of the era are included in these 100 tracks, which are sequenced chronologically. Completists will need the 12-disc set, but *The Best of the Columbia Years* will satisfy the needs of most fans. — *Stephen Thomas Erlewine*

Sinatra 80th—All The Best / Nov. 1995 / Capitol ✦✦✦✦
Released to coincide with Frank Sinatra's 80th Birthday, *Sinatra 80th—All the Best* is a double-disc set that draws from his classic Capitol concept albums, as well as singles from the '50s and a couple of rarities, which aren't particularly compelling. The main strength of the package is as an introduction, since it recaps most of his essential recordings of the '50s and gives a sense of his accomplishments. Nevertheless, the set is only a teaser, since most of Sinatra's Capitol records—both the original albums and single compilations—are better-sequenced and more rewarding. — *Stephen Thomas Erlewine*

Sinatra 80th—Live / Nov. 28, 1995 / Capitol ✦✦
Culled from a number of different live performances recorded during the '80s (as well as an awkward outtake from the *Duets*

sessions: a version of "My Way" recorded with Luciano Pavarotti), *80th Live* is a suprisingly moving document of Frank Sinatra in the final stages of his career. By the time this material was recorded, Sinatra's voice had eroded somewhat, as his range had decreased and his voice had become reedier. Nevertheless, his singing was still impressive, as he re-interprets many of his classics in a new light, bringing a fresh emotional slant to many of the songs. Not all of the performances are comparable to some of his previously recorded version, but all of the songs offer definitive proof that Sinatra was still capable of producing fine music in his 70s. —*Stephen Thomas Erlewine*

Hal "Cornbread" Singer

b. Oct. 8, 1919, Tulsa, OK
Tenor Saxophone / Swing, Early R&B
It was the great irony of Hal Singer's career that his lifetime goal, to play tenor with Duke Ellington's Orchestra, was cut short when his first recording as a leader ("Cornbread") became a major hit. The acclaim that this R&B song received forced Singer to reluctantly pursue a solo career; no future hits resulted! Hal Singer first played violin before learning clarinet and alto. By 1938 he was playing tenor with Ernie Fields, associations with other territory bands (including Lloyd Hunter, Nat Towles and Tommy Douglas) followed and then Singer came to New York with the Jay McShann Orchestra. He performed with many top swing stars including Hot Lips Page, Roy Eldridge, Don Byas, Red Allen, Sid Catlett and Lucky Millinder before joining Duke Ellington in 1948. After "Cornbread" became a hit, Singer led his own band through 1958 and then spent three years in the Metropole house band. In 1965 Singer moved to Paris and he remained active both in clubs and on recordings in to the 1980s. A flexible soloist who could play both swing and R&B, Hal Singer has long been underrated; his Savoy recordings have been reissued on CD by Denon. —*Scott Yanow*

● **Rent Party** / Jun. 1948–May 3, 1956 / Savoy ✦✦✦✦✦

Blue Stompin' / Feb. 20, 1959 / Original Jazz Classics ✦✦✦✦✦
This is a fun set of heated swing with early R&B overtones. The title cut is a real romp with tenor saxophonist Hal Singer and trumpeter Charlie Shavers not only constructing exciting solos but riffing behind each other. With the exception of the standard "With a Song in My Heart," Singer and Shavers wrote the remainder of the repertoire, and with the assistance of a particularly strong rhythm section (pianist Ray Bryant, bassist Wendell Marshall and drummer Osie Johnson), there are many fine moments on this easily enjoyable set. Recommended. —*Scott Yanow*

Sirone

b. Sep. 28, 1940, Atlanta, GA
Bass / Avant-Garde
An excellent technician and underrated composer, Sirone was part of the great Revolutionary Ensemble trio in the '70s, and has also worked with many other free bandleaders and groups. His prominent tone and decisive playing expertly meshed with Leroy Jenkins and Jerome Cooper's on Ensemble recordings and in concert. Sirone worked in Atlanta with a band called The Group in the late '50s and early '60s. George Adams was among the players in this ensemble. Sirone moved to New York in the mid-'60s, and helped form the Untraditional Jazz Improvisational Team with Dave Burrell. He did sessions with Marion Brown, Gato Barbieri, Pharoah Sanders, Noah Howard and Sonny Sharrock in the late '60s, and also played with Sunny Murray, Albert Ayler, Archie Shepp, Sun Ra and many others. Sirone spent six years with The Revolutionary Ensemble, originally forming it with Jenkins and Frank Clayton (later replaced by Cooper). He recorded with Clifford Thornton, Roswell Rudd, Dewey Redman, Cecil Taylor and Walt Dickerson in the '70s and early '80s. The trio date with Sirone, Dickerson and Andrew Cyrille is available on CD, as are some earlier dates featuring him with Taylor, Redman and others. —*Ron Wynn*

Artistry / Jul. 5, 1978 / Of The Cosmos ✦✦✦✦
Revolutionary Ensemble bassist with flutist James Newton. Very enjoyable. —*Michael G. Nastos*

● **Live** / Jul. 11, 1980 / Serious ✦✦✦✦✦
Trio at NYC's Public Theatre. Potent, creative music. —*Michael G. Nastos*

Noble Sissle

b. Jul. 10, 1889, Indianapolis, IN, **d.** Dec. 17, 1975, Tampa, FL
Vocals, Leader / Classic Jazz, Pop
Noble Sissle was one of the nation's premier composers and bandleaders, particularly in the early days of American popular song and theatre. He worked in a band with Eubie Blake in Baltimore as early as 1915; Luckey Roberts sometimes played piano. The Sissle/Blake team scored an early hit with "It's All Your Fault," which Sophie Tucker performed in her act. Sissle later teamed with James Europe from 1916 until his death in 1919. They co-wrote and produced with Blake the historic shows *Shuffle Along* and *Chocolate Dandies*. Sissle recorded over 30 vocals during the early and mid-'20s, many times accompanied by Blake. They also appeared in some pioneering sound film shorts in 1930.

Sissle led several bands and visited Europe often; his traveling ways led to a split with Blake, who preferred staying in America. Sissle's circle of friends also included Cole Porter and Fred Waring, while the Prince of Wales was guest drummer at one of his concerts in 1930. When Sissle returned to America, he was featured on a broadcast from the Park Central Hotel in 1931, effectively breaking that establishment's color barrier. Lena Horne sang with his band in the mid-'30s; Nat King Cole was reportedly among the cast of *Shuffle Along* of 1933, which didn't enjoy the success of its predecessor. Sissle's band included Buster Bailey, Tommy Ladnier and Sidney Bechet. His orchestra was a featured attraction at Billy Rose's Diamond Horseshoe club from 1938 to 1950, except for USO tours during World War II.

Sissle succeeded Bill "Bojangles" Robinson as honorary mayor of Harlem in 1950, and played at Eisenhower's inaugural in 1953. He was WMGM's first black disc jockey in 1960, ran his own publishing company and owned a club. But repeated muggings led him to close it and retire to Florida to spend time with his son. The book *Reminiscing With Sissle And Blake* in 1973 detailed his varied experiences. Sissle's music is featured on import CDs and anthologies of early stage, show and popular music. —*Ron Wynn*

Carol Sloane

b. 1937, Providence, RI
Vocals / Bop, Standards
Singer Carol Sloane started singing professionally when she was 14 and at 18 she toured Germany in a musical comedy. She was with the Les and Larry Elgart orchestra during 1958–60, and after appearing at a jazz festival in 1960, she was heard by Jon Hendricks who later sent for her to sub for Annie Ross with Lambert, Hendricks and Ross. Sloane made a big impression at the 1961 Newport Jazz Festival and soon cut two records for Columbia. Unfortunately her career never got going, and except for a live set from 1964 released on Honey Dew, Sloane would not record again until 1977, working as a secretary in North Carolina and singing just now and then locally. However in the mid-'70s she became more active again, caught on in Japan (where she began to record frequently) and her career finally got on more solid footing. Sloane's releases for Audiophile, Choice, Progressive and Contemporary feature a mature bop-based singer with a sound of her own. —*Scott Yanow*

● **Out of the Blue** / Dec. 1961 / Fresh Sound ✦✦✦✦✦

Carol Sloane Live at 30th Street / 1962 / Columbia ✦✦✦

Cotton Tail / Nov. 12, 1978 / Choice ✦✦✦✦✦
Classy late-'70s session by vocalist Carol Sloane. She sings sophisticated ballads, reworks standards, and does pre-rock pop, all of it in a polished, entertaining manner. —*Ron Wynn*

Carol Sings / Oct. 28, 1979–Oct. 29, 1979 / Progressive ✦✦✦✦
One of the first albums by vocalist Carol Sloane to enjoy widespread acclaim and critical praises. She shows her ability to swing without overpowering lyrics or losing the tempo, while her ballads and slow songs are done with a minimum of gimmicks and plenty of real soul and depth. —*Ron Wynn*

As Time Goes By / Aug. 29, 1982 / Eastwind ✦✦✦✦
An early-'80s session highlighted by the clean, confident vocals of Carol Sloane. Although she's more jazz-influenced than anything, her understated delivery and surprising range give her renditions of pre-rock standards and pop flavor, depth, and character. —*Ron Wynn*

Love You Madly / Oct. 6, 1988–Oct. 28, 1988 / Contemporary
✦✦✦✦✦

The Real Thing / May 24, 1990–May 25, 1990 / Contemporary
✦✦✦✦✦

Heart's Desire / Sep. 25, 1991–Sep. 27, 1991 / Concord Jazz ✦✦✦✦
A '92 release from vocalist Carol Sloane in the mode of her previous releases. She's backed by a trio and does the usual uptempo jazz-tinged ballads, pre-rock pop, an occasional original or two, and even some more contemporary material. She sings any- and everything well, displaying the delivery, lyric command, and style that's won critical acclaim. The CD has two bonus cuts. —*Ron Wynn*

Sweet & Slow / Apr. 19, 1993–Apr. 21, 1993 / Concord Jazz ✦✦✦✦

When I Look In Your Eyes / Jun. 16, 1994–Jun. 17, 1994 / Concord Jazz ✦✦✦✦

The Songs Carmen Sang / Mar. 21, 1995–Mar. 22, 1995 / Concord
✦✦✦✦✦

Bessie Smith

b. Apr. 15, 1894, Chattanooga, TN, **d.** Sept. 26, 1937, Clarksdale, MS

Vocals / Blues, Classic Jazz

The first major blues and jazz singer on record and one of the most powerful of all time, Bessie Smith rightly earned the title of "The Empress of the Blues." Even on her first records in 1923, her passionate voice overcame the primitive recording quality of the day and still communicates easily to today's listeners (which is not true of any other singer from that early period). At a time when the blues were in and most vocalists (particularly vaudevillians) were being dubbed "blues singers," Bessie Smith simply had no competition.

Back in 1912, Bessie Smith sang in the same show as Ma Rainey who took her under her wing and coached her. Although Rainey would achieve a measure of fame throughout her career, she was soon surpassed by her protégé. In 1920 Bessie had her own show in Atlantic City and in 1923 she moved to New York. She was soon signed by Columbia and her first recording (Alberta Hunter's "Downhearted Blues") made her famous. Bessie worked and recorded steadily throughout the decade, using many top musicians as sidemen on sessions including Louis Armstrong, Joe Smith (her favorite cornetist), James P. Johnson and Charlie Green. Her summer tent show, Harlem Frolics, was a big success during 1925–27 and Mississippi Days in 1928 kept the momentum going.

However, by 1929 the blues were out of fashion and Bessie Smith's career was declining despite being at the peak of her powers (and still only 35!). She appeared in *St. Louis Blues* that year (a low-budget movie short that contains the only footage of her), but her hit recording of "Nobody Knows You When You're Down and Out" predicted her leaner Depression years. Although she was dropped by Columbia in 1931 and made her final recordings on a four-song session in 1933, Bessie Smith kept on working. She played the Apollo in 1935 and substituted for Billie Holiday in the show *Stars over Broadway*. The chances are very good that she would have made a comeback, starting with a Carnegie Hall appearance at John Hammond's upcoming *From Spirituals to Swing* concert, but she was killed in a car crash in Missouri. Columbia has reissued all of her recordings, first in five two-LP sets and more recently on five two-CD boxes that also contain her five alternate takes, the soundtrack of *St. Louis Blues* and an interview with her niece Ruby Smith. "The Empress of the Blues," based on her recordings, will never have to abdicate her throne! —*Scott Yanow*

★ **Bessie Smith/The Complete Recordings, Vol. 1** / Feb. 16, 1923–Apr. 8, 1924 / Columbia/Legacy ✦✦✦✦✦
In the 1970s Bessie Smith's recordings were reissued on five double LPs. Her CD reissue series also has five volumes (the first four are double-CD sets) with the main difference being that the final volume includes all of her rare alternate takes (which were bypassed on LP). The first set (which, as with all of the CD volumes, is housed in an oversize box that includes an informative booklet) contains her first 38 recordings. During this early era, Bessie Smith had no competitors on record and she was one of the few vocalists who could overcome the primitive recording techniques; her power really comes through. Her very first recording (Alberta Hunter's "Downhearted Blues") was a big hit and is

one of the highlights of this set along with "'Tain't Nobody's Bizness If I Do" (two decades before Billie Holiday), "Jail-House Blues" and "Ticket Agent, Ease Your Window Down." Smith's accompaniment is nothing that special (usually just a pianist and maybe a weak horn or two), but she dominates the music anyway, even on two vocal duets with her rival Clara Smith. All of these volumes reward close listenings and are full of timeless recordings. —*Scott Yanow*

★ **The Complete Recordings, Vol. 2** / Apr. 8, 1924–Nov. 18, 1925 / Columbia/Legacy ✦✦✦✦✦
Bessie Smith, even on the evidence of her earliest recordings, well deserved the title "Empress of the Blues" for in the 1920s there was no one in her league for emotional intensity, honest blues feeling and power. The second of five volumes (the first four are two-CD sets) finds her accompaniment improving rapidly with such sympathetic sidemen as trombonist Charlie Green, cornetist Joe Smith and clarinetist Buster Bailey often helping her out. However, they are overshadowed by Louis Armstrong whose two sessions with Smith (nine songs in all) fall into the time period of this second set; particularly classic are their versions of "St. Louis Blues," "Careless Love Blues" and "I Ain't Goin' to Play Second Fiddle." Other gems on this essential set include "Cake Walkin' Babies from Home," "The Yellow Dog Blues" and "At the Christmas Ball." —*Scott Yanow*

★ **Complete Recordings, Vol. 5** / May 6, 1925–Nov. 24, 1933 / Columbia/Legacy ✦✦✦✦✦

★ **The Complete Recordings, Vol. 3** / Nov. 20, 1925–Feb. 16, 1928 / Columbia/Legacy ✦✦✦✦✦
On the third of five volumes (the first four are double-CD box sets) that reissue all of her recordings, the great Bessie Smith is greatly assisted on some of the 39 selections by a few of her favorite sidemen: cornetist Joe Smith, trombonist Charlie Green and clarinetist Buster Bailey. But the most important of her occasional musicians was pianist James P. Johnson, who makes his first appearance in 1927 and can be heard on four duets with Bessie including the monumental "Back Water Blues." Other highlights of this highly recommended set (all five volumes are essential) include "After You've Gone," "Muddy Water," "There'll Be a Hot Time in the Old Town Tonight," "Trombone Cholly," "Send Me to the 'Lectric Chair" and "Mean Old Bedbug Blues." The power and intensity of Bessie Smith's recordings should be considered required listening; even 70 years later they still communicate. —*Scott Yanow*

★ **The Complete Recordings, Vol. 4** / Feb. 21, 1928–Jun. 11, 1931 / Columbia/Legacy ✦✦✦✦
The fourth of five volumes (the first four are two-CD sets) that reissue all of Bessie Smith's recordings traces her career from a period when her popularity was at its height down to just six songs away from the halt of her recording career. But although her commercial fortunes might have slipped, Bessie Smith never declined and these later recordings are consistently powerful. The two-part "Empty Bed Blues" and "Nobody Knows You When You're down and Out" (hers is the original version) are true classics and none of the other 40 songs (including the double-entendre "Kitchen Man") are throwaways. With strong accompaniment during some performances by trombonist Charlie Green, guitarist Eddie Lang, Clarence Williams' band and on ten songs (eight of which are duets) the masterful pianist James P. Johnson, this volume (like the others) is quite essential. —*Scott Yanow*

Buster Smith (Henry Smith)

b. Aug. 24, 1904, Ennis, TX, **d.** Aug. 10, 1991

Alto Saxophone / Swing

Though he was a good arranger who was credited with "One O'Clock Jump," Buster Smith's influence on Charlie Parker at an early stage in his development was vital. His spry, fluid and warm sound, as well as his phrasing and subtle use of blues inflections certainly influenced Parker's style, though Parker also took them to a different level. Smith played alongside a 17 year old Parker in the late '30s, and served as both playing and general mentor. Some of Smith's techniques, notably his biting tone and crisp articulation, as well as some of his phrases, were particularly influential, as was Smith's method of moving through chord progressions.

He taught himself clarinet, and played in the '20s with local Dallas groups. He began on alto sax in 1925, when he joined Walter Page's Blue Devils. Jimmy Rushing, Hot Lips Page, Count

Basie and Eddie Durham had all joined by 1928, but they soon departed to join Bennie Moten's band. Smith took over The Blue Devils in 1931. The group now included Lester Young, and were called The 13 Original Blue Devils. When they disbanded in 1933, Smith settled in Kansas City and joined Moten's band. When Moten died in 1935 the group disbanded. Smith joined a band Basie was leading with other former Moten players, but he stayed in Kansas City when Basie took the band to New York. Smith played with Claude Hopkins and Andy Kirk, and wrote arrangements for Nat Towles.

He formed a group in 1937 with Jay McShann, Fred Beckett and Parker. Smith took the band to New York the next year but couldn't land engagements as a leader. He became an arranger for Basie, Benny Carter, and Snub Mosley and played with Don Redman. Smith moved to Dallas in 1942, and led groups at clubs and hotels. He stopped playing sax in 1959, but kept going on piano, bass and guitar until he retired in 1980. —*Ron Wynn*

● **The Legendary Buster Smith** / Jun. 17, 1959 / Atlantic ✦✦✦✦

Jabbo Smith (Cladys Smith)

b. Dec. 24, 1908, Pembroke, GA, **d.** Jan. 16, 1991
Trumpet / Classic Jazz
Jabbo Smith had one of the oddest careers in jazz history. A brilliant trumpeter, Jabbo had accomplished virtually all of his most significant work by the time he turned 21, yet lived to be 82. He learned to play trumpet at the legendary Jenkins Orphanage in Charleston, and by the time he was 16 Jabbo showed great promise. During 1925–28 he was with Charlie Johnson's Paradise Ten, a top New York jazz group that made some classic recordings. Jabbo was on a recording session with Duke Ellington in 1927 (resulting in a memorable version of "Black and Tan Fantasy") and played in the show "Keep Shufflin'" with James P. Johnson and Fats Waller. The highpoints of Smith's career were his 1929 recordings with his Rhythm Aces. These superb performances feature Jabbo playing with daring, creativity and a bit of recklessness, displaying an exciting style that hints at Roy Eldridge (who would not burst upon the scene for another six years). But although Jabbo Smith at the time was considered a close competitor of Louis Armstrong, he had hit his peak. His unreliability, excessive drinking and unprofessional attitude resulted in lost jobs, missed opportunities and a steep decline. After playing with one of Claude Hopkins' lesser orchestras during 1936–38, Smith settled in Milwaukee and became a part-time player. Decades passed and when he was rediscovered in the 1970s (when he was picked to perform in the musical show "One Mo' Time"), he was a weak player, a mere shadow of what he could have been. —*Scott Yanow*

★ **Jabbo Smith, Vol. 1** / Mar. 1928–Feb. 22, 1929 / Retrieval ✦✦✦✦✦
★ **Jabbo Smith, Vol. 2** / Mar. 1, 1929–Feb. 1, 1938 / Retrieval ✦✦✦✦✦
Hidden Treasure, Vol. 1 / Jun. 3, 1961+Oct. 15, 1961 / Jazz Art ✦✦
Hidden Treasure, Vol. 2 / Jun. 3, 1961+Oct. 15, 1961 / Jazz Art ✦✦

Jimmy Smith

b. Dec. 8, 1925, Norristown, PA
Organ / Soul Jazz, Hard Bop
Though he never received any exaggerated title like the king of soul jazz, Jimmy Smith certainly ruled the Hammond organ in the '50s and '60s. He revolutionized the instrument, showing it could be used creatively in a jazz context and popularized in the process. His Blue Note sessions from 1956 to 1963 were extremely influential and are highly recommended. Smith turned the organ into almost an ensemble itself. He provided walking bass lines with his feet, left hand chordal accompaniment, solo lines in the right and a booming, funky presence that punctuated every song, particulary the uptempo cuts. Smith turned the fusion of R&B, blues and gospel influences with bebop references and devices into a jubilant, attractive sound that many others immediately absorbed before following in his footsteps.

Smith initially learned piano, both from his parents and on his own. He attended the Hamilton School of Music in 1948, and Ornstein School of Music in 1949 and 1950 in Philadelphia. Smith began playing the Hammond in 1951, and soon earned a great reputation that followed him to New York, where he debuted at

the Cafe Bohemia. A Birdland date and 1957 Newport Jazz Festival appearance launched Smith's career. He toured extensively through the '60s and '70s. His Blue Note recordings included superb collaborations with Kenny Burrell, Lee Morgan, Lou Donaldson, Tina Brooks, Jackie McLean, Ike Quebec and Stanley Turrentine among others. He also did several trio recordings, some which were a little bogged down by the excess length of some selections.

Smith scored more hit albums on Verve from 1963 to 1972, many of them featuring big bands and using fine arrangements from Oliver Nelson. These included the excellent *Walk On The Wild Side*. But Verve went to the well once too often seeking crossover dollars, loading down Smith's late '60s album with hack rock covers. His '70s output was quite spotty, though Smith didn't stop touring, visiting Israel and Europe in 1974 and 1975. He and his wife opened a club in Los Angeles in the mid-'70s. Smith resumed touring in the early '80s, returning to New York in 1982 and 1983. He resigned with Blue Note in 1985, and has done more representative dates for them and Milestone in the '90s. — *Ron Wynn and Bob Porter*

A New Star—A New Sound: Jimmy Smith at the Organ, Vol. 1 / Feb. 13, 1956+Feb. 18, 1956 / Blue Note ✦✦✦✦
The debut of organist Jimmy Smith on records (he was already 30) was a major event, for he introduced a completely new and very influential style on the organ, one that virtually changed the way the instrument is played. This LP, which has not yet appeared on CD, features the already-recognizable organist in a trio with guitarist Thornel Schwartz and Bay Perry on drums. Highlights of this very impressive debut include "The Way You Look Tonight," "Lady Be Good" and Horace Silver's "The Preacher." —*Scott Yanow*

The Champ / Mar. 11, 1956 / Blue Note ✦✦✦✦✦
Recorded in NYC. When first issued, many thought there were two players here, or overdubs. Just early Smith cookin'. —*Michael Erlewine*

Greatest Hits, Vol. 1 / Mar. 27, 1956–Feb. 8, 1963 / Blue Note ✦✦✦✦✦
This double LP, even with its clichéd title, is a real gem. It contains eight of the greatest performances recorded by organist Jimmy Smith during his important period with Blue Note. "The Champ" from his second recording features Smith taking around 50 choruses on a blazing blues, and it set a standard that has still not been surpassed. Also included on this valuable two-fer (some of the material has since been reissued on CD) are "All Day Long," a 20-minute "The Sermon," "Midnight Special," "When Johnny Comes Marching Home," "Can Heat," "Flamingo" and "Prayer Meetin'." In the supporting cast are trumpeter Lee Morgan, altoist Lou Donaldson, Tina Brooks and Stanley Turrentine on tenors, guitarists Kenny Burrell, Thornel Schwartz and Quentin Warren, and drummers Art Blakey and Donald Bailey. This set serves as a perfect introduction to Jimmy Smith's early years and has lots of hard-swinging and soulful jams. —*Scott Yanow*

Jimmy Smith at the Organ, Vol. 3 / Jun. 12, 1956 / Blue Note ✦✦✦✦

The Sounds of Jimmy Smith / Feb. 11, 1957 / Blue Note ✦✦✦
This LP, which has been included as part of a Mosaic Jimmy Smith three-CD box set, features the organist taking a pair of rare unaccompanied solos on "All the Things You Are" and a fairly free "The Fight" and jamming several songs ("Zing Went the Strings of My Heart," "Somebody Loves Me" and "Blue Moon") with his trio. Art Blakey fills in for drummer Donald Bailey on "Zing" while guitarist Eddie McFadden is heard throughout the three selections. Excellent straight-ahead jazz from the innovative organist. —*Scott Yanow*

A Date with Jimmy Smith, Vol. 1 / Feb. 11, 1957–Feb. 12, 1957 / Blue Note ✦✦✦
After cutting five albums with his trio, organist Jimmy Smith on Feb. 11, 1957, recorded with trumpeter Donald Byrd, altoist Lou Donaldson and tenor saxophonist Hank Mobley in a sextet that also included guitarist Eddie McFadden and drummer Art Blakey. Among the five songs recorded that day, two (lengthy versions of "Falling in Love with Love" and "Funk's Oats") are included on this LP along with a shorter trio rendition of "How High the Moon" from two days later with McFadden and drummer Donald Bailey in a trio. All of this music has been reissued by Mosaic on a definitive CD box set. —*Scott Yanow*

A Date with Jimmy Smith, Vol. 2 / Feb. 11, 1957–Feb. 12, 1957 / Blue Note ✦✦✦
This LP is one of five that has been reissued by Mosaic in a three-CD box set. For the jam session date altoist Lou Donaldson has a duet with organist Jimmy Smith on "I'm Getting Sentimental over You," and together they match up forces in a sextet with trumpeter Donald Byrd, Hank Mobley on tenor, guitarist Eddie McFadden and drummer Art Blakey, playing lengthy versions of Mobley's "Groovy Date" and Duke Ellington's "I Let a Song Go out of My Heart." All of the Jimmy Smith jam sessions are easily recommended to fans of straight-ahead jazz; get the Mosaic box! — *Scott Yanow*

★ **The Complete February 1957 Jimmy Smith Blue Note Sessions** / Feb. 11, 1957–Feb. 13, 1957 / Mosaic ✦✦✦✦✦
It would not be an overstatement to say that organist Jimmy Smith was busy during Feb. 11–13, 1957, for he recorded enough material for these three CDs, 21 often-lengthy performances that originally appeared on five LPs plus three others that had been previously unissued. Smith is not only heard early in his career with his regular trio but in a sextet with trumpeter Donald Byrd, altoist Lou Donaldson, tenor saxophonist Hank Mobley and drummer Art Blakey, in duets with Donaldson and with a quartet that also stars guitarist Kenny Burrell. These jam sessions feature plenty of exciting solos over fairly common chord changes, and despite the heavy competition, Jimmy Smith (who is still the king of the jazz organ) is the dominant force. Recommended. — *Scott Yanow*

Jimmy Smith at the Organ, Vol. 1: All Day Long / Feb. 12, 1957 / Blue Note ✦✦✦
There is a fair amount of variety on this jam session LP. Organist Jimmy Smith plays "Summertime" in duet with altoist Lou Donaldson and with guitarist Kenny Burrell and drummer Art Blakey completing the all-star quartet, performs swinging versions of "Yardbird Suite," "There's a Small Hotel" and Burrell's "All Day Long." The music (which has been reissued on CD in a Mosaic box set) will be enjoyed by bop fans even though nothing at all that essential occurs. — *Scott Yanow*

The Best of Jimmy Smith / Feb. 12, 1957–Jan. 3, 1986 / Blue Note ✦✦✦✦✦
1958–1986. Small-group setting. Selections from some of Smith's best Blue Note albums, such as: *The Sermon, Go for Whatcha Know, Midnight Special, Back at the Chicken Shack, A New Sound,* and *At the Organ.* — *Michael Erlewine*

Jimmy Smith at the Organ, Vol. 2 / Feb. 13, 1957 / Blue Note ✦✦✦
Five LPs of material (including this one) that were recorded by organist Jimmy Smith within a three-day period have been reissued on CD by Mosaic. But listeners who do not have that set and run across any of the albums would not go wrong by picking them up. This interesting record features Smith in a duet (titled "The Duel") with drummer Art Blakey, jamming with his trio (which includes guitarist Eddie McFadden and drummer Donald Bailey) on "Buns a Plenty" and "Plum Nellie," and interacting with guitarist Kenny Burrell, drummer Blakey and altoist Lou Donaldson on "Billie's Bounce." Excellent bop-oriented jam sessions. — *Scott Yanow*

Plays Pretty Just for You / May 8, 1957 / Blue Note ✦✦✦

Jimmy Smith Trio with Lou Donaldson / Jul. 4, 1957 / Blue Note ✦✦✦✦

House Party / Aug. 25, 1957 / Blue Note ✦✦✦✦
Music from two different sessions are included on this enjoyable LP. All of organist Jimmy Smith's jam sessions are worth acquiring although several (such as this one) have been long out of print. Lengthy versions of "Au Privave" and "Just Friends" and more concise renditions of "Lover Man" and "Blues After All" match Smith with quite a variety of all-stars: trumpeter Lee Morgan, trombonist Curtis Fuller, Lou Donaldson or George Coleman on altos, Tina Brooks on tenor, guitarists Kenny Burrell or Eddie McFadden and Art Blakey or Donald Bailey on drums. Everyone plays up to par and the passionate solos (and Smith's heated background riffing) keep the proceedings continually exciting. — *Scott Yanow*

Confirmation / Aug. 25, 1957+Feb. 25, 1958 / Blue Note ✦✦✦✦
Organist Jimmy Smith led a series of exciting jam sessions for Blue Note during 1957–60 including the three selections heard on this LP. These performances were not released for the first time

until 1979, but their quality is as strong as Smith's other output from the era. "Confirmation" matches Smith with altoist Lou Donaldson, tenor saxophonist Tina Brooks, trumpeter Lee Morgan, guitarist Kenny Burrell and drummer Art Blakey (talk about all-star groups) while a 15-minute rendition of "What Is This Thing Called Love" and a 20-minute "Cherokee" has Morgan, Burrell, Blakey, trombonist Curtis Fuller and George Coleman on alto. The heated solos are quite enjoyable and the organist keeps the momentum constantly flowing throughout this happy set. — *Scott Yanow*

Groovin' at Small's Paradise, Vol. 1 / Nov. 14, 1957+Nov. 18, 1957 / Blue Note ✦✦✦✦

Groovin' at Small's Paradise, Vol. 2 / Nov. 14, 1957+Nov. 18, 1957 / Blue Note ✦✦✦✦

★ **The Sermon** / Feb. 25, 1958 / Blue Note ✦✦✦✦✦
This CD reissue has two of the three selections (the 20-minute "The Sermon" and "Flamingo") from the original LP, adding five additional selections that are related. With such soloists as trumpeter Lee Morgan, trombonist Curtis Fuller, altoist Lou Donaldson, Tina Brooks on tenor, either Eddie McFadden or Kenny Burrell on guitar and Art Blakey or Donald Bailey on drums, the straight-ahead music is as good as one would expect (with the lengthy title cut being the obvious highpoint), and the CD overall offers listeners a strong dose of Jimmy Smith's Blue Note period. — *Scott Yanow*

Softly As a Summer Breeze / Feb. 26, 1958 / Blue Note ✦✦✦✦

★ **Cool Blues** / Apr. 7, 1958 / Blue Note ✦✦✦✦
This CD should greatly interest all Jimmy Smith collectors, including those who already have the original LP. In addition to four excellent selections (quintets with altoist Lou Donaldson, Tina Brooks on tenor, guitarist Eddie McFadden, either Art Blakey or Donald Bailey on drums and the organist/leader), there are three previously unissued numbers from the same gig, featuring the quartet of Donaldson, Smith, McFadden and Bailey. The repertoire is filled with blues and bop standards and the soloing is at a consistently high and hard-swinging level. Jimmy Smith fans will be pleased. — *Scott Yanow*

Home Cookin' / Jul. 7, 1958–Jun. 16, 1959 / Blue Note ✦✦✦✦
Organist Jimmy Smith and guitarist Kenny Burrell always had a close musical relationship, making each of their joint recordings quite special. This LP features the pair along with drummer Donald Bailey and (on four of the seven songs) the obscure but talented tenor saxophonist Percy France. The emphasis is on blues and basic material including versions of "See See Rider," Ray Charles' "I Got a Woman" and several groups originals, and as usual, the performances are swinging and soulful. — *Scott Yanow*

On the Sunny Side / Jul. 15, 1958–Jun. 16, 1959 / Blue Note ✦✦✦✦
Organist Jimmy Smith recorded quite a bit of material for Blue Note during 1956–63. This 1981 LP released for the first time eight selections cut during four sessions in the late '50s. In all cases, Smith is joined by guitarist Kenny Burrell and drummer Donald Bailey; Stanley Turrentine makes the group a quartet on "The Sunny Side of the Street" while his fellow tenor Percy France does the same on his original "Apostrophe." All of the songs (other than the latter) are standards and the tunes generally clock in around a concise five minutes. The results are predictably swinging and highlights include "On the Sunny Side," "Since I Fell for You," "Bye Bye Blackbird" and "I'm Just a Lucky So and So." Excellent music. — *Scott Yanow*

★ **Crazy! Baby** / Jan. 4, 1960 / Blue Note ✦✦✦✦✦
Unlike most of the Jimmy Smith recordings from the era, this CD reissue (which adds "If I Should Lose You" and "When Lights Are Low" to the original LP program) features organist Jimmy Smith's regular group (rather than an all-star band). With guitarist Quentin Warren and drummer Donald Bailey completing the trio, Smith is heard in peak form on swinging and soulful versions of such tunes as "When Johnny Comes Marching Home," "Makin' Whoopee," "Sonnymoon for Two" and "Mack the Knife." Despite claims and some strong challenges by others, there has never been a jazz organist on the level of Jimmy Smith. — *Scott Yanow*

Open House / Plain Talk / Mar. 22, 1960 / Blue Note ✦✦✦✦✦
Recorded in Hackensack, NJ. Studio session featuring Blue Mitchell (tpt), Ike Quebec (ts), and Jackie McClean (as). This is essentially a jam session without Smith's regular sidemen. More

mainstream than most but very nice tracks—fast and slow. This is an excellent album. —*Michael Erlewine*

Open House / Mar. 22, 1960 / Blue Note ✦✦✦✦

★ **Back at the Chicken Shack** / Apr. 25, 1960 / Blue Note ✦✦✦✦✦
Recorded the same day as *Midnight Special*, this initial meeting on records between organist Jimmy Smith and the soulful tenor of Stanley Turrentine was the first of several perfect matchups. Turrentine would lead organ combos (usually with his wife Shirley Scott) throughout much of the next decade, and his warm tone fit in perfectly with the orchestral instrument. With guitarist Kenny Burrell and drummer Donald Bailey, Smith and Mr. T. play five numbers (four from the original LP plus a version of "On the Sunny Side of the Street" that was not released until it was included during the 1970s in a different album). Highpoints include the title track (a blues) and "When I Grow Too Old to Dream." Jimmy Smith recorded many sets for Blue Note during 1956–63; virtually all are recommended. —*Scott Yanow*

★ **Midnight Special** / Apr. 25, 1960 / Blue Note ✦✦✦✦✦
Recorded in Englewood Cliffs, NJ. Small group with Stanley Turrentine (ts). This was recorded at the same session as *Back at the Chicken Shack*, and it is almost as fine—that is: magical! This is a must-have for jazz organ fans. —*Michael Erlewine*

Prayer Meetin' / Jun. 13, 1960+Feb. 8, 1963 / Blue Note ✦✦✦✦✦
Prayer Meetin' was organist Jimmy Smith's final Blue Note recording until 1986. On this CD reissue two earlier selections featuring Smith, tenor saxophonist Stanley Turrentine, guitarist Quentin Warren, bassist Sam Jones (the only time on Blue Note that Smith used a bassist) and drummer Donald Bailey jam on versions of "Lonesome Road" and the original "Smith Walk"; both selections went unreleased until popping up on a 1984 Japanese CD. The bulk of this set is from February 8, 1963, featuring the same personnel without Jones. Highlights include the title cut, a soulful version of "When the Saints Go Marching In" and the Gene Ammons blues "Red Top." Excellent music. —*Scott Yanow*

Jimmy Smith Plays Fats Waller / Jan. 23, 1962 / Blue Note ✦✦✦✦
Although Fats Waller was the first jazz organist, he mostly played piano throughout his career. Organist Jimmy Smith's tribute to Waller is not imitative at all but a good excuse to interpret seven jazz standards that were associated with Fats. With assistance from his regular trio—guitarist Quentin Warren and drummer Donald Bailey—Smith plays such unlikely numbers as "Everybody Loves My Baby," "I've Found a New Baby" and Waller's two biggest hits ("Ain't Misbehavin'" and "Honeysuckle Rose") with soul and swing. An easily enjoyable outing. —*Scott Yanow*

★ **Bashin'** / Mar. 26, 1962+Mar. 28, 1962 / Verve ✦✦✦✦✦
Although still a regular Blue Note artist (he would make four more albums for the company within the next year), *Bashin'* was organist Jimmy Smith's debut for Verve, a label that he would record extensively for during 1963–72. On the first half of the program (reissued in full on this CD), Smith was for the first time joined by a big band. Oliver Nelson provided the arrangements, trumpeter Joe Newman and altoist Phil Woods have a solo apiece and "Walk on the Wild Side" became Smith's biggest hit up to that point. The final three numbers feature Smith's regular trio with guitarist Quentin Warren and drummer Donald Bailey swinging with soul as usual. The historical set (a bit of a turning point for Jimmy Smith's career) has its strong moments, although it is not all that essential. —*Scott Yanow*

I'm Movin on / Jan. 31, 1963 / Blue Note ✦✦✦
This CD reissue of a formerly rare date has a perfectly suitable title for it is the first of four albums that organist Jimmy Smith made within an eight-day period for Blue Note before permanently leaving the label for Verve. Although notable for matching Smith with guitarist Grant Green in what would be their only joint recording (drummer Donald Bailey completes the trio), the music is fairly typical of a Jimmy Smith session with the repertoire including blues, a couple of standards and ballads. The solos are well-played, but nothing too surprising occurs (except perhaps for the sappiness of "What Kind of Fool Am I"); the original LP program is expanded by the inclusion of two other selections from the same date. —*Scott Yanow*

Bucket! / Feb. 1, 1963 / Blue Note ✦✦✦

Rockin' the Boat / Feb. 2, 1963 / Blue Note ✦✦✦✦
Organist Jimmy Smith's next-to-last LP for Blue Note after a very extensive seven-year period is up to his usual level. With altoist

Lou Donaldson joining Smith's regular group (which included guitarist Quentin Warren and drummer Donald Bailey), the quartet swings with soul on such fine numbers as "When My Dream Boat Comes Home," "Can Heat," "Please Send Me Someone to Love" and "Just a Closer Walk with Thee." With the exception of the closing ballad, "Trust in Me," all seven of the selections are closely related to the blues. This is fine music well deserving of being reissued on CD someday. —*Scott Yanow*

Hobo Flats / Mar. 15, 1963+Mar. 20, 1963 / Verve ✦✦✦

Live at the Village Gate / May 31, 1963 / Metro ✦✦✦✦

Any Number Can Win / Jul. 10, 1963–Jul. 29, 1963 / Verve ✦✦✦
Recorded in NYC. Produced by Creed Taylor. Three sessions. Note: this is Smith with a large group, not the small-combo setting. —*Michael Erlewine*

Blue Bash / Jul. 25, 1963–Jul. 26, 1963 / Verve ✦✦✦

Plays the Blues / 1963–1968 / Verve ✦✦✦
Recorded in NJ/NYC. Selection of Smith's Verve output. Three are big-band numbers with Oliver Nelson. The rest are small-combo efforts—"One for Members" is outstanding. —*Michael Erlewine*

Who's Afraid of Virginia Woolf? / Jan. 20, 1964–Apr. 27, 1964 / Verve ✦✦✦
Big band. Jimmy Smith with Oliver Nelson and his orchestra. —*Michael Erlewine*

The Cat / Apr. 27, 1964–Apr. 29, 1964 / Verve ✦✦✦✦
Compared to his earlier Blue Note recordings, organist Jimmy Smith's outings for Verve are not as strong from a jazz standpoint. Certainly his renditions of the "Theme from *Joy House*," "The Cat" and the "Main Title from *The Carpetbaggers*" are not all that significant. However, this CD has some tasteful arrangements for the big band by Lalo Schifrin and some good playing by the great organist on a variety of other blues-oriented material. Also the combination of organ with a big band is sometimes quite appealing, making this CD worth picking up despite its commercial tracks. —*Scott Yanow*

Monster / Jan. 19, 1965–Jan. 20, 1965 / Verve ✦✦
Due to the material, which includes the two-part "Goldfinger," and the themes from *Bewitched, The Munsters* and *The Man with the Golden Arm*, this is one of organist Jimmy Smith's lesser recordings. The LP does have some reasonably inventive arrangements for the accompanying big band by Oliver Nelson and some spirited organ playing but overall is a rather forgettable and overproduced effort. —*Scott Yanow*

Organ Grinder Swing / Jun. 14, 1965–Jun. 15, 1965 / Verve ✦✦✦✦
Most of organist Jimmy Smith's recordings for Verve during the mid-to-late '60s were with big bands, making this trio outing with guitarist Kenny Burrell and drummer Grady Tate a special treat. This CD reissue is a throwback to Smith's Blue Note sets (which had concluded two years earlier) and gives the organists the opportunity to stretch out on three blues and three standards. This release shows that, even with all of his commercial success during the period, Jimmy Smith was always a masterful jazz player. —*Scott Yanow*

Got My Mojo Workin' / Dec. 16, 1965–Dec. 17, 1965 / Verve ✦✦✦✦
Recorded in Englewood Cliffs, NJ. Smith in his large-band context. With Oliver Nelson and his orchestra. —*Michael Erlewine*

Peter and the Wolf / May 11, 1966–May 12, 1966 / Verve ✦✦✦✦✦
Of all of organist Jimmy Smith's big-band albums recorded for Verve, this is one of the most imaginative ones. Oliver Nelson arranged a variety of themes from Prokofiev's *Peter and the Wolf* into a swinging suite featuring the great organist Jimmy Smith. Although there is no verbal narrative on this LP, Nelson's liner notes tell the story (which can actually be followed through the music) and Smith pays respect to the original melodies while making strong statements of his own. A classic of its kind but long out of print. —*Scott Yanow*

Hoochie Coochie Man / Jun. 14, 1966–Jul. 1966 / Verve ✦✦✦

★ **The Dynamic Duo** / Sep. 21, 1966+Sep. 28, 1966 / Verve ✦✦✦✦✦
This CD—a straight reissue of the original LP—is a classic. Organist Jimmy Smith and guitarist Wes Montgomery, both the main pacesetters on their instruments at the time, make for a perfect team on quartet renditions (with drummer Grady Tate and percussionist Ray Barretto) of "James and Wes" and "Baby, It's Cold Outside." However, it is the three numbers with a big band arranged by Oliver Nelson (particularly "Night Train" and a very memorable version of "Down by the Riverside") that really stick

in one's mind. Although it is unfortunate that the Smith-Wes collaboration was short-lived (just one other album), it is miraculous that they did find each other and created this brilliant music. — *Scott Yanow*

Further Adventures of Jimmy and Wes / Sep. 21, 1966+Sep. 28, 1960 / Verve ✦✦✦✦✦
Organist Wes Montgomery and guitarist Wes Montgomery did all of their recordings together during several sessions in September 1966, but despite the relatively low quantity, the results were consistently memorable. This CD, a follow-up to *The Dynamic Duo*, has one selection ("Milestones") in which the two lead voices are joined by Oliver Nelson's big band and several numbers (including the pop hits "King of the Road" and "Call Me") with a quartet that also includes drummer Grady Tate and percussionist Ray Barretto. Although not reaching the heights of the other set, this CD has more than its share of exciting solos from the immortal co-leaders. — *Scott Yanow*

Respect / Jun. 2, 1967+Jun. 14, 1967 / Verve ✦✦
Organist Jimmy Smith, joined by one of two guitar/bass/drums rhythm sections, mostly sticks to then-current R&B hits on this out-of-print LP. He does what he can with "Mercy, Mercy, Mercy," a brief "Respect" and "Funky Broadway" while contributing his own blues "T-Bone Steak." The 31-minute set has its moments but no real surprises, swinging funkily throughout. — *Scott Yanow*

Stay Loose / Jan. 1968 / Verve ✦✦

Livin' It Up / May 13, 1968–May 14, 1968 / Verve ✦✦

The Boss / Nov. 20, 1968 / Verve ✦✦✦
Recorded at Paschal's La Carousel, Atlanta, GA. Lots of fine solos. George Benson (g) does best soul-jazz work since McDuff days. — *Ron Wynn*

Groove Drops / Oct. 1969 / Verve ✦✦✦

Root Down / Feb. 8, 1972 / Verve ✦✦

Jimmy Smith Jam / Jul. 7, 1972 / Cobblestone ✦✦✦✦

Bluesmith / Sep. 11, 1972 / Verve ✦✦✦✦✦
It is ironic that one of Jimmy Smith's best Verve releases would be his next-to-last for the label. This surprisingly freewheeling but relaxed jam session also features Teddy Edwards on tenor, guitarist Ray Crawford, bassist Leroy Vinnegar, drummer Donald Dean and the congas of Victor Pantoja. Together they perform five of Smith's fairly basic originals and Harvey Siders' "Mournin' Wes," a tribute for Wes Montgomery. Fine straight-ahead music that deserves to be reissued again. — *Scott Yanow*

Portuguese Soul / Feb. 8, 1973–Feb. 9, 1973 / Verve ✦✦
Recorded in NYC. Big band. Smith with large orchestra under the direction of Thad Jones. — *Michael Erlewine*

I'm Gonna Git Myself Together / 1973 / MGM ✦✦

Other Side of Jimmy Smith / 1973 / MGM ✦✦✦
Another big-band outing by Smith. with Johnny Pate and orchestra. — *Michael Erlewine*

Blacksmith / Nov. 1974 / Pride ✦✦

Paid in Full / 1974 / Mojo ✦✦✦

Sit on It! / 1976 / Mercury ✦✦

It's Necessary / Jul. 6, 1977–Jul. 7, 1977 / Mercury ✦✦✦
After his long period with Verve ended in 1972, organist Jimmy Smith, although he still won popularity polls and remained a household name in the jazz world, was in relative obscurity until he re-emerged on the Elektra Musician label in 1982. This live album, recorded at Smith's short-lived North Hollywood supper club, finds the great organist and his quartet (with guitarist Ray Crawford) welcoming such guests as tenors Teddy Edwards and Harold Land and trumpeter Blue Mitchell. The material is OK ("Red Top" and "Sometimes I'm Happy" are stronger than the recent originals) and the recording quality is decent if not state-of-the-art. Superior to his other more commercial sets of the period, this reasonably enjoyable LP does not measure up to the excitement level of Smith's earlier classic Blue Note sessions but is worth picking up for his fans. — *Scott Yanow*

Unfinished Business / Jan. 27, 1978–Feb. 1, 1978 / Mercury ✦✦

The Cat Strikes Again / Jul. 1980 / Laserlight ✦✦✦
Recorded in Hollywood. Big band with Lalo Schifrin and orchestra. — *Michael Erlewine*

Off the Top / Jun. 7, 1982 / Elektra ✦✦✦
It had been nine years since organist Jimmy Smith recorded for a

major label when Bruce Lundvall approached him to make an album for Elektra Musician. Smith plays some unusual material (including Lionel Richie's "Endless Love" and the "Theme from *M.A.S.H.*") on this LP but swings everything and has a particularly strong supporting cast—guitarist George Benson, Stanley Turrentine on tenor, bassist Ron Carter and drummer Grady Tate. A fine comeback date. — *Scott Yanow*

Keep on Comin' / Sep. 3, 1983 / Elektra ✦✦✦✦
Organist Jimmy Smith's second of two LPs for the Elektra Musician label is unusual in a couple of respects. He had never played organ with tenor saxophonist Johnny Griffin before and on one piece, "Piano Solo Medley," Smith has a very rare feature on piano. Otherwise the music, which is comprised of recent originals by Smith, Griffin and guitarist Kenny Burrell who completes the quartet with drummer Mike Baker, is in the soulfully swinging vein that one associates with the great organist. — *Scott Yanow*

Go for Whatcha' Know / Jan. 2, 1986 / Blue Note ✦✦✦✦✦
23 years after leaving the label, organist Jimmy Smith returned to the Blue Note label. In addition to signing up two of his old associates who had been with him on many classic Blue Note albums of the past (guitarist Kenny Burrell and tenor saxophonist Stanley Turrentine), Smith uses such fine payers as guest pianist Monty Alexander (on two songs), bassist Buster Williams and drummer Grady Tate (who takes a warm ballad vocal on "She's out of My Life"). "Fungii Mama" and "Go for Whatcha Know" are the highlights of this enjoyable LP. — *Scott Yanow*

Prime Time / 1989 / Milestone ✦✦✦✦✦
For this Milestone release, organist Jimmy Smith utilized some of the top veterans then residing in Los Angeles, many of whom had been long underrated. With sidemen that include Curtis Peagler on tenor and alto, tenors Herman Riley and Rickey Woodard, either Phil Upchurch or Terry Evans on guitar, bassist Andy Simpkins, Michael Baker or Frank Wilson on drums and Barbara Morrison (who takes a vocal on "Farther on up the Road"), this is a particularly strong band. The fresh material (only "C Jam Blues" and "Honky Tonk" are standards) and spirited solos make this an easily recommended set of swinging jazz. — *Scott Yanow*

Fourmost / Nov. 16, 1990–Nov. 17, 1990 / Milestone ✦✦✦✦✦
Organist Jimmy Smith has a reunion on this CD with his 30-plus-year associates tenor saxophonist Stanley Turrentine and guitarist Kenny Burrell along with drummer Grady Tate. Together they play spirited and creative versions of standards and blues. The highpoints include "Midnight Special," a swinging "Main Stem," Tate's warm vocal on "My Funny Valentine" and a lengthy rendition of "Quiet Nights." Suffice to say that this all-star date reaches its potential and is easily recommended to fans of straight ahead jazz. — *Scott Yanow*

Sum Serious Blues / 1993 / Milestone ✦✦✦
Organist Jimmy Smith performs a spirited set of blues-based material (only "You've Changed" is a change of pace) with a dozen of his Los Angeles-based friends including trumpeter Oscar Brashear, the underrated tenor Herman Riley (who is best among the supporting cast), guitarist Philip Upchurch and singers Marlena Shaw and Bernard Ighner who have two vocals apiece. Nothing that surprising occurs other than Smith's surprisingly effective vocal on "Hurry Change, If You're Comin'," but the swinging music, which was arranged by Johnny Pate, should please Jimmy Smith's fans. — *Scott Yanow*

The Masters / Dec. 24, 1993–Dec. 25, 1993 / Blue Note ✦✦✦
Organist Jimmy Smith, in a trio with guitarist Kenny Burrell and drummer Jimmie Smith (no relation) performs six diverse blues and three familiar standards. Although the music is somewhat predictable, it swings hard and is often rollicking. Burrell sounds inspired and Smith, who largely originated this idiom, shows that he is still an enthusiastic and masterful player. — *Scott Yanow*

Damn! / 1995 / Verve ✦✦✦✦

Johnny "Hammond" Smith

b. Dec. 18, 1933, Louisville, KY
Organ / Soul Jazz, Hard Bop
Johnny "Hammond" Smith is one of the many organists to come to prominence in the 1960s who was greatly influenced by Jimmy Smith. Originally a pianist based in Cleveland, after hearing Wild Bill Davis he switched to the organ. Also known as Johnny Hammond, Smith worked for a period in the late '50s as Nancy

Wilson's accompanist but has spent most of his career as a leader, recording a series of enjoyable albums for Prestige during 1959–70. Although he also utilized synthesizers in the 1970s, Smith in more recent times has stuck exclusively to the organ in a style unchanged from three decades before. —*Scott Yanow*

Talk That Talk / Apr. 22, 1960–Oct. 14, 1960 / Prestige ✦✦✦✦

The Stinger / May 7, 1965 / Prestige ✦✦✦✦
Organist Johnny "Hammond" Smith is a decent soul-jazz player. He plays in short, swirling bursts and uses the bass pedals in a pounding, aggressive manner. These are primarily uptempo and funky jam numbers, particularly the title track. —*Ron Wynn*

● **Soul Talk** / May 19, 1969 / Prestige ✦✦✦✦

Johnny Smith

b. Jun. 25, 1922, Birmingham, AL
Guitar / Cool, Classical
Guitarist Johnny Smith will always be best-remembered for his 1952 hit recording of "Moonlight in Vermont," a mellow ballad that also features Stan Getz. Smith, whose chordal-oriented style is self-taught, originally played trumpet, violin and viola before switching to guitar. A studio musician from 1947 on, Smith's impressive technique and quiet sound made him in great demand even before "Moonlight," and although he never had another hit, he was a popular attraction throughout the 1950s. After moving to Colorado in the 1960s he opened a music store, taught and maintained a lower profile, occasionally recording in New York. —*Scott Yanow*

★ **Moonlight in Vermont** / Mar. 11, 1952–Aug. 1953 / Roulette ✦✦✦✦✦
Guitarist Johnny Smith had his single biggest hit with the title track. It exemplifies his style and the album's direction: pleasantly played, jazz-based material, mostly standards and a few originals. —*Ron Wynn*

Leo Smith

b. Dec. 18, 1941, Leland, MS
Trumpet / Avant-Garde, Free Jazz
While an ambitious, unpredictable composer, Leo Smith's trumpet playing has leaned more toward the reflective, introspective side. His tone, approach and sound emphasize lyricism and a calm, pleasing style rather than an energized, exuberant approach. Smith began on mellophone and French horn before turning to trumpet. He played in R&B bands and in the service following his high school graduation. He became a member of the Association for the Advancement of Creative Musicians (AACM) in 1967, and co-founded The Creative Construction Company with Leroy Jenkins and Anthony Braxton later that year. They played and recorded in Europe and with other AACM members in New York during the late '60s before disbanding in 1970.

Smith teamed with Marion Brown to make the documentary film "See The Music" in 1970, then formed The New Delta Ahkri in New Haven. The group's personnel ranged from two to five members, including at various times Henry Threadgill, Anthony Davis, Oliver Lake and Dwight Andrews. Smith began the Kabell record label in 1971, and studied ethnomusicology in the mid-'70s at Wesleyan. He played with Braxton again in the late '70s, and recorded with Derek Bailey's group Company in London. Smith also led a trio with Peter Kowald and Gunther Sommer. He's recorded for Kabell, Moers, ECM, Nessa, Black Saint and Sackville in the '70s and '80s. Smith has a couple of sessions available on CD. —*Ron Wynn*

The Mass on the World / May 1978 / Moers ✦✦✦✦✦

Budding of a Rose / Jun. 1979 / Moers ✦✦✦✦

Touch the Earth / Nov. 1979 / FMP ✦✦✦

Go in Numbers / Jan. 19, 1980 / Black Saint ✦✦✦✦✦

Spirit Catcher / Nov. 1980 / Nessa ✦✦✦

● **Rastafari** / Jun. 12, 1983 / Sackville ✦✦✦✦✦
Few of trumpeter Leo Smith's recordings are readily available, making this introspective but very interesting collaboration with soprano saxophonist Bill Smith, violinist David Prentice, bassist David Lee and vibraphonist Larry Potter an important release. The playing by these adventurous musicians is advanced and quite free on the four group originals, and all five players share equally in the creation of these fresh explorations. —*Scott Yanow*

Lonnie Liston Smith

b. Dec. 28, 1940, Richmond, VA
Keyboards / Fusion, Post Bop
Pianist Lonnie Liston Smith underwent a great stylistic change during the '70s. At one point he was working with Pharoah Sanders and Gato Barbieri providing keyboard interludes for their highly charged, explosive settings. Then Smith played with Miles Davis, plugging into electric funk. When he formed The Cosmic Echoes with his brother Donald, things were radically different. Smith presented low-key arrangements, with Donald singing psuedo-mystic laments and pontifications, with minimal improvisation and solo space. But these albums put Lonnie Liston Smith on the fusion and crossover map; he enjoyed great sales for a string of releases in this pattern that continued through the '80s and into the '90s. He established himself as one of the more popular acts on the black upper middle class professional circuit, playing college campuses and appearing in several cities with heavy African-American populations and high-profile urban contemporary radio stations. Prior to this, Lonnie Liston Smith had graduated in music education from Morgan State in 1961, then moved to New York. He'd played with Betty Carter, Rahsaan Roland Kirk, Art Blakey, Joe Williams and Sanders. Smith has recorded as a leader for Flying Dutchman, Doctor Jazz and Signature. He has several sessions available on CD. —*Ron Wynn*

Astral Travelling / 1973 / Flying Dutchman ✦✦✦✦

Golden Dreams / 1973–1976 / Bluebird ✦✦✦✦✦

Expansions / 1974 / Flying Dutchman ✦✦✦✦✦
The best of his post-Pharoah Sanders releases. —*Ron Wynn*

Cosmic Funk / 1974 / Flying Dutchman ✦✦✦

★ **Reflections of a Golden Dream** / Sep. 1976 / RCA ✦✦✦✦✦

Loveland / 1978 / Columbia ✦✦✦

Dreams of Tomorrow / 1979 / Doctor Jazz ✦✦

Visions of a New World / 1980 / Flying Dutchman ✦✦✦

Rejuvenation / Feb. 26, 1985–Feb. 27, 1985 / Doctor Jazz ✦✦✦

Make Someone Happy / 1989 / Doctor Jazz ✦✦✦

Magic Lady / 1991 / Startrak ✦✦

Lonnie Smith

Organ / Soul Jazz, Hard Bop
Not to be confused with Lonnie Liston Smith, organist Lonnie Smith has been on the soul jazz and jazz scene since the '60s. He's worked often with Lou Donaldson, and done sessions on his own. He's not a great organist but can play the requisite bluesy licks, work the bass pedal and offer good stomping numbers. He's recorded as a leader for Blue Note, CTI and other labels, and done sessions with Donaldson, George Benson, Hank Crawford and many other notables. —*Ron Wynn*

● **Think** / Jul. 23, 1968 / Blue Note ✦✦✦✦✦
With Lee Morgan (tpt). This is an excellent 1986 reissue of a fine soul-jazz Blue Note date by organist Lonnie Smith. —*Ron Wynn*

Move Your Hand / 1969 / Blue Note ✦✦✦✦
Move Your Hand was recorded live at Club Harlem in Atlantic City on August 9, 1969. Organist Lonnie Smith led a small combo—featuring guitarist Larry McGee, tenor saxist Rudy Jones, bari saxist Ronnie Cuber, and drummer Sylvester Goshay—through a set that alternated originals with two pop covers, the Coasters' "Charlie Brown" and Donovan's "Sunshine Superman." Throughout, the band works a relaxed, bluesy and, above all, funky rhythm; they abandon improvisation and melody for a steady groove, so much that the hooks of the two pop hits aren't recognizable until a few minutes into the track. No one player stands out, but *Move Your Hand* is a thoroughly enjoyable, primarily because the group never lets their momentum sag throughout the session. Though the sound of the record might be somewhat dated, the essential funk of the album remains vital. —*Stephen Thomas Erlewine*

Turning Point / Sep. 1969 / Blue Note ✦✦✦

Drives / Dec. 1970 / Blue Note ✦✦✦
Lonnie Smith had the raw skills, imagination and versatility to play burning originals, bluesy covers of R&B and pop, or skillful adaptions of conventional jazz pieces and show tunes. Why he never established himself as a consistent performer remains a mystery, but this 1970 reissue shows why he excited so many

people during his rise. Smith's solos on "Spinning Wheel" and his own composition, "Psychedelic PI," are fleet and furious, boosting the songs from interesting to arresting. He's also impressive on "Seven Steps To Heaven," while the array of phrases, rhythms and voicings on "Who's Afraid Of Virginia Woolf?" demonstrate a mastery of the organ's pedals and keys rivaling that of the instrument's king, Jimmy Smith. —*Ron Wynn*

Marvin Smith

b. Jun. 24, 1961, Waukegan, IL
Drums / Post-Bop, Hard Bop
A prolific, constantly-in-demand drummer whose sensitive, yet authoritative playing has been heard on dozens of '80s and '90s sessions, Marvin "Smitty" Smith seems to live in the studio. A one-time Berklee student, he played with Jon Hendricks' band in New York during the early '80s, then worked with John Hicks, Bobby Watson, and Slide Hampton. Smith later recorded with Archie Shepp, then with a quintet co-led by Frank Wess and Frank Foster. He did sessions with Hamiett Bluiett, Kevin Eubanks and David Murray, as well as playing with Ray Brown, Dave Holland, Ron Carter, Hank Jones and the Jazztet. Smith made his recording debut as a leader in 1987, and also recorded that year with Sonny Rollins, and toured with Sting. Since then, Smith's been constantly featured on sessions, often paired with Ray Drummond. He has a couple of Concord dates available on CD, and can also be heard on numerous releases by other musicians. —*Ron Wynn*

Keeper of the Drums / Mar. 1987 / Concord Jazz ✦✦✦✦
Drummer Marvin "Smitty" Smith, widely regarded among jazz's premier percussionists and accompanists, got his chance in the spotlight when he made his debut as a leader for Concord. This 1987 session was a brilliant first effort, with Smith heading a wonderful four-horn octet. The group included alto and soprano saxophonist Steve Coleman, tenor saxophonist Ralph Moore, trombonist Robin Eubanks and trumpeter Wallace Roney. The eight songs were not lengthy (none much longer than six minutes) but were structured to allow maximum individual identity and collective performances. It was the perfect blend of traditional setting and contemporary insights, which has been lacking in so much 1990s jazz material. —*Ron Wynn*

Road Less Traveled / Feb. 1989 / Concord Jazz ✦✦✦✦✦
Fine 1989 date with strong piano from James Williams. CD version has two bonus cuts. —*Ron Wynn*

● **Carryin' On** / 1993 / Concord Jazz ✦✦✦✦✦
Good, nicely played date with a harder edge than usual for Concord material. —*Ron Wynn*

Paul Smith

b. Apr. 17, 1922, San Diego, CA
Piano / Bop, Cool, Swing
Paul Smith is a brilliant pianist with technique on the level of an Oscar Peterson but a musician who never really dedicated himself to jazz. After playing early on with Johnny Richards in 1941 and spending a couple years in the military, he worked with Les Paul (1946–47) and Tommy Dorsey (1947–49) before moving to Los Angeles and becoming a studio musician. Smith has recorded frequently both with his trios and as a soloist. In addition to recording with Dizzy Gillespie, Anita O'Day, Buddy DeFranco, Louie Bellson, Steve Allen, Louie Bellson and Stan Kenton (among others) he toured with Ella Fitzgerald off and on during 1956–78. —*Scott Yanow*

● **Fine, Sweet and Tasty** / Nov. 13, 1953 / VSOP ✦✦✦✦✦
This CD reissue of a set originally cut for Tampa is a happy surprise. Pianist Paul Smith, who sometimes overwhelms music with his technique, pays tribute to the Nat King Cole Trio on several of the numbers. The presence of guitarist Tony Rizzi (playing in a Charlie Christian vein) is a major asset while bassist Sam Cheifetz and drummer Irv Cottler are excellent in support. The original program is augmented by five extra alternate takes. Highlights include the delightful "Fine, Sweet & Tasty," "Crazy Rhythm" and "Got a Penny." Overall, this swinging affair is one of the most enjoyable of all of Paul Smith's many recordings. —*Scott Yanow*

Art Tatum Touch, Vol. 1 / 1976–1977 / Outstanding ✦✦✦
It would be easy to dismiss this record as no more than easy listening, if it were not for the honesty and the heavy influences of Teddy Wilson and Art Tatum combined with Smith's own individual, rather elegant style. —*Bob Rusch, Cadence*

The Master Touch / 1976–1977 / Outstanding ✦✦✦✦
Outstanding solos from pianist Paul Smith, whose albums progressively became more spirited during the '70s and '80s. While his swing and stride roots can clearly be detected, Smith's willingness to try different styles and his looser, more unpredictable playing brings some unexpected tension and excitement to this collection. —*Ron Wynn*

Paul Smith Plays Steve Allen / 1984 / PA/USA ✦✦✦

Stuff Smith (Hezekiah Leroy Gordon Smith)

b. Aug. 14, 1909, Portsmouth, OH, d. Sep. 25, 1967, Munich, Germany
Violin / Swing
Stuff Smith was one of the big three of pre-bop violinists along with Joe Venuti and Stephane Grappelli. Many of his fans said that he could outswing all of his competitors and certainly Stuff was a major force on the bandstand. Smith, who cited Louis Armstrong as his main influence, studied music with his father and played with the family band as a child. His first major job and recordings were with Alphonse Trent's territory band in the 1920s but it was not until 1936 that he had his breakthrough. Leading a quintet at the Onyx Club with trumpeter Jonah Jones, Smith's comedy vocals and hard-swinging approach made the group a hit on 52nd Street for several years; his novelty "I'se a Muggin'" became a hit. Smith worked regularly with his trios in the 1940s but was in danger of being forgotten in the '50s when Norman Granz recorded him fairly extensively for Verve; Stuff also participated in Nat King Cole's After Midnight sessions for Capitol. The violinist moved to Copenhagen in 1965 and was active until his death two years later. —*Scott Yanow*

★ **Stuff Smith & His Onyx Club Boys** / Feb. 11, 1936–Dec. 1939 / Classics ✦✦✦✦✦

Stuff Smith-Dizzy Gillespie-Oscar Peterson / Jan. 21, 1957–Apr. 17, 1957 / Verve ✦✦✦✦✦

Violins No End / May 4, 1957 / Pablo ✦✦✦✦

● **Live at the Montmartre** / Mar. 18, 1965 / Storyville ✦✦✦✦✦

Swingin' Stuff / Mar. 23, 1965 / Storyville ✦✦✦✦✦
One of two mid-'60s sessions that violinist Stuff Smith recorded with a mostly foreign band, plus expatriate pianist Kenny Drew. He plays with his characteristic fervor, punctuating his rippling phrases with blues licks, smears, and slurs, plus some dazzling phrases. Bassist Niels-Henning Orsted Pedersen emerges as the dominant rhythm section member besides Drew, while drummer Alex Riel mainly follows their lead. —*Ron Wynn*

Tab Smith

b. Jan. 11, 1909, Kingston, NC, d. Aug. 17, 1971, St. Louis, MO
Alto Saxophone / Swing, Early R&B
Tab Smith's career can easily be divided into two. One of the finest altoists to emerge during the swing era, Smith became a popular attraction in the R&B world of the 1950s due to his record "Because of You." After early experience playing in territory bands during the 1930s, Tab Smith played and recorded with Lucky Millinder's Orchestra (1936–38) and then freelanced with various swing all-stars in New York. He had opportunities to solo with Count Basie's band (1940–42) before returning to Millinder (1942–44) and took honors on a recording of "On the Sunny Side of the Street" with a stunning cadenza that followed statements by Coleman Hawkins, Don Byas and Harry Carney. After leaving Millinder, Smith led his own sessions, which became increasingly R&B-oriented (he never became involved with bop). His string of recordings for United in the 1950s (which are being reissued by Delmark on CD) made him a fairly major name for a time even though he had a relatively mellow sound and avoided honking. In the early '60s Tab Smith retired to St. Louis and later became involed in selling real estate. —*Scott Yanow*

● **Jump Time** / Aug. 22, 1951–Feb. 26, 1952 / Delmark ✦✦✦✦✦
Altoist Tab Smith, who first gained recognition with Count Basie's Orchestra in the mid-'40s, became an unexpected R&B star in the early '50s, thanks in large part to his hit version of "Because of You." Between 1951–57, Smith recorded 90 songs for the United Record Company of which only 48 were issued. Delmark, in their CD reissue series, plans to come out with all of the music in chronological order. This first release has the initial 20 (including the hit) and Tab Smith sounds fine on the sweet ballads, blues and concise jump tunes; the backup crew includes trumpeter Sonny

Cohn, tenor Leon Washington and either Lavern Dillon or Teddy Brannon on piano. — *Scott Yanow*

Ace High / Feb. 26, 1952–Apr. 23, 1953 / Delmark ✦✦✦✦

Willie "The Lion" Smith
(William Henry Joseph Bonaparte Bertholoff Smith)

b. Nov. 25, 1897, Goshen, NY, **d.** Apr. 18, 1973, New York, NY
Piano / Stride, Classic Jazz
Willie "The Lion" Smith in the 1920s was considered one of the big three of stride piano (along with James P. Johnson and Fats Waller) even though he made almost no recordings until the mid-'30s. His mother was an organist and pianist and Smith started playing piano when he was six. He earned a living playing piano as a teenager, gained his nickname "the Lion" for his heroism in World War I and after his discharge he became one of the star attractions at Harlem's nightly rent parties. Although he toured with Mamie Smith (and played piano on her pioneering 1920 blues record "Crazy Blues"), Smith mostly freelanced throughout his life. He was an influence on the young Duke Ellington (who would later write "Portrait of the Lion") and most younger New York-based pianists of the 1920s and '30s.

Although he was a braggart and (with his cigar and trademark derby hat) appeared to be a rough character, Smith was actually more colorful than menacing and a very sophisticated pianist with a light touch. His recordings with his Cubs (starting in 1935) and particularly his 1939 piano solos for Commodore (highlighted by "Echoes of Spring") cemented his place in history. Because he remained very active into the early '70s (writing his memoirs *Music on My Mind* in 1965), for quite a few decades Willie "the Lion" Smith was considered a living link to the glory days of early jazz. — *Scott Yanow*

● Willie "The Lion" Smith 1925–1937 / Nov. 5, 1925–Sep. 15, 1937 / Classics ✦✦✦✦✦

Willie "The Lion" Smith 1937–1938 / Sep. 15, 1937–Nov. 30, 1938 / Classics ✦✦✦

Willie the Lion Smith / Dec. 1, 1949–Jan. 29, 1950 / Inner City ✦✦✦✦
Part of the Jazz Legacy series, these 1949–1950 sessions with Wallace Bishop on drums include some solos and some combo efforts with Buck Clayton on trumpet, Claude Luter on clarinet, and Bishop on drums. Ten Smith numbers and eight standards. Includes Smith's classic "Echoes of Spring." — *Michael G. Nastos*

The Lion of the Piano / 1950 / Commodore ✦✦✦

Echoes of Spring / Dec. 17, 1965 / Milan ✦✦✦✦✦
A '92 reissue featuring stomps, stride, and gutbucket blues numbers played by the remarkable Willie "the Lion" Smith. Smith, a friend and associate of everyone from James P. Johnson to Fats Waller, could rip through songs when inspired but was also a wonderful ballad player and good interpreter. He displayed all these skills on this set, recorded at Milan. — *Ron Wynn*

Pork and Beans / Nov. 8, 1966 / Black Lion ✦✦✦✦✦
Rollicking solo cuts. — *Ron Wynn*

Memoirs of Willie the Lion Smith / Apr. 25, 1968–Apr. 28, 1968 / RCA ✦✦✦✦
This double LP is the equivalent of Jelly Roll Morton's *Library of Congress* recordings. The legendary Willie "The Lion" Smith reminisces about his colorful life, plays some piano and warbles out some vocals. Particularly interesting are his stories of the early days, his medleys of songs associated with Eubie Blake, James P. Johnson, Fats Waller and Duke Ellington, and his performances of eight of his own compositions, some of which are quite obscure. Not everything works and some of the talking rambles on a bit, but overall this is a fascinating historical document that has many interesting moments. — *Scott Yanow*

Relaxin' / 1970–1971 / Chiaroscuro ✦✦✦
Stalwart blues, ballads, and standards. — *Ron Wynn*

Willie Smith

b. Nov. 25, 1910, Charleston, SC, **d.** Mar. 7, 1967, Los Angeles, CA
Clarinet, Alto Saxophone / Swing
The alto saxophone stylist generally considered the finest swing performer after Johnny Hodges and Benny Carter, Willie Smith was an accomplished section leader and soloist in the Lunceford Orchestra in the '20s, '30s and '40s. He also wrote first-rate arrangements of "Sophisticated Lady" and "Rose Room" and

sometimes doubled as a vocalist. Smith attended Fisk University, where Lunceford heard him and invited him to join the orchestra. Smith stayed from 1929 until 1942, then worked in 1942 and 1943 with Charlie Spivak. He played in Harry James' band for two extended tours, from 1944 to 1951 and 1954 to 1964. He briefly replaced Johnny Hodges in the Duke Ellington orchestra, toured with Jazz at the Philharmonic and led R&B and jazz groups in Los Angeles. Unfortunately, Smith had no albums to provide a fuller portrait of his skills, but he can be heard on Lunceford reissues and early '50s Ellington sessions. — *Ron Wynn*

● The Best of Willie Smith / Aug. 13, 1965–Aug. 16, 1965 / GNP Crescendo ✦✦✦✦

Elmer Snowden

b. Oct. 9, 1900, Baltimore, MD, **d.** May 14, 1973, Philadelphia, PA
Banjo, Guitar / Classic Jazz
A fine banjo player, Elmer Snowden was the original leader of the Washingtonians, a group that would become the Duke Ellington Orchestra; a dispute over money in the mid-'20s soon found him "at liberty." Snowden had met Ellington in 1919 and before that he had worked with Eubie Blake in Baltimore. He was quite active in the 1920s as a businessman, agent and musician, running several bands and recording occasionally. But although he worked steadily in the 1930s, '40s and '50s, he was essentially a minor figure during those years. In 1963 Snowden moved to California to teach at Berkeley, he toured Europe with George Wein in 1967 and made a few final recordings. — *Scott Yanow*

● Harlem Banjo / Dec. 9, 1960 / Original Jazz Classics ✦✦✦✦✦
The legendary banjo player, with the Cliff Jackson (p) Trio, plays standards with the emphasis on old time swing, including some Ellington. This is a unique album, one every jazz fan should get to know. — *Michael G. Nastos*

Martial Solal

b. Aug. 23, 1927, Algiers
Piano / Post-Bop
One of the finest European jazz pianists of all time, Martial Solal (a unique stylist) has never received as much recognition in the U.S. as he deserves. Born in Algiers to French parents, Solal has been based in Paris since the late '40s. Although a modernist, he was flexible enough to record an album with Sidney Bechet in 1957 and make other records with Django Reinhardt, Don Byas and Lucky Thompson. Solal has been primarily heard with his own trios through the years although he has recorded several notable albums with Lee Konitz. — *Scott Yanow*

★ Live / Sep. 14, 1956–Feb. 7, 1985 / Stefanotis ✦✦✦✦✦
Comprehensive four-disc set of his material from 1959–1985 in every context. — *Ron Wynn*

Martial Solal at Newport (1963) / Jul. 11, 1963–Jul. 16, 1963 / RCA ✦✦✦✦

● Four Keys / May 1979 / PA/USA ✦✦✦✦✦
An all-star quartet (pianist Martial Solal, altoist Lee Konitz, guitarist John Scofield and bassist Niels Pedersen) explores seven diverse Solal originals that range from chamberlike pieces to fairly free group improvising. The results are often exciting if cool in both tone and volume. Thoughtful yet unpredictable music. — *Scott Yanow*

Lew Soloff

b. Jan. 20, 1944, NYC
Trumpet / Post-Bop, Hard Bop
A brilliant high-note trumpeter long in great demand for big bands and session work, Lew Soloff is also a distinctive soloist and an expert with the plunger mute. After studying at Juilliard he freelanced in New York with Maynard Ferguson, Joe Henderson and Clark Terry among others and then was a part of Blood, Sweat & Tears during 1968–73. Soloff was closely associated with Gil Evans from 1973 on, and also played with George Gruntz's Concert Jazz Band, the Manhattan Jazz Quintet and Carla Bley; he was also teamed with the colorful trombonist Ray Anderson on several often-humorous recordings. — *Scott Yanow*

Yesterdays / Sep. 15, 1986–Sep. 16, 1986 / Pro Jazz ✦✦✦
A stunning album of fusion-treated jazz standards, it includes several original compositions by Soloff and features Mike Stern (g), Charnett Moffett (b), and Elvin Jones (d). Mike Stern's guitar work is featured prominently throughout. — *Paul Kohler*

But Beautiful / Jun. 29, 1987–Jun. 30, 1987 / Evidence ✦✦✦✦
Longtime session and section trumpeter Lew Soloff stepped into the spotlight on this '87 date, his third as a leader. Soloff chose a quartet context with no second reed or brass player, putting the melodic and harmonic focus squarely on himself. The results are good but sometimes a bit subdued. Soloff's tone, phrasing, and attack are solid, but there is also a low-key feeling, as if Soloff would rather gamble on things being too cool than overly intense. As a result, a fantastic rhythm section that includes pianist Kenny Kirkland, bassist Richard Davis, and drummer Elvin Jones lays back rather than surges ahead. If you like overly calm, reflective, and mellow material, this one is for you, but it would have been interesting to hear what might have happened had Soloff stepped things up a bit. —*Ron Wynn*

● **Speak Low** / Jun. 29, 1987–Jun. 30, 1987 / Pro-Arte ✦✦✦✦✦
Veteran NYC studio trumpeter steps out. —*Michael G. Nastos*

Eddie South

b. Nov. 27, 1904, Louisiana, MO, d. Apr. 25, 1962, Chicago, IL
Violin / Swing
Classical training and swing in his soul made Eddie South a jazz giant on violin. South's tremendous technique and riveting, left-hand playing style was supported by strong, aggressive bowing and a commanding approach on either uptempo or slow material. His rich, dreamy tone earned him the nickname the "Dark Angel," and he was hypnotic and moving on ballads. South could also blaze and delight on fast-paced material. He was a child prodigy who was coached in jazz by Darnell Howard. South became music director of Jimmy Wade's Syncopators in the mid-'20s, following his studies, which included time at Chicago Musical College. He played in Europe during the late '20s, touring and studying in Paris and Hungary. South also recorded with his group The Alabamians for HMV in Paris. He returned to Chicago in the early '30s, and co-led a band with Everett Barksdale and Milt Hinton that recorded for Victor. He returned to Paris in the late '30s, and made seminal recordings with Django Reinhardt and Stephane Grappelli. South later worked in New York, Chicago and Los Angeles at the end of the decade. He recorded with a West Coast quintet that included Tommy Benford. South led his own groups through the '40s and '50s, mostly combos but occasionally a big band. He did several radio and television programs, and spent his final years in Chicago. Besides his sessions for HMV and Victor, South also recorded for Okeh, Columbia, and Mercury, and some of his early material was reissued in Europe on Swing. —*Ron Wynn and Michael Erlewine*

Eddie South 1923–1937 / Dec. 1923–Nov. 23, 1937 / Classics ✦✦✦✦✦

In Paris / Mar. 12, 1929–Nov. 25, 1937 / DRG ✦✦✦✦
Rare cuts from the late '30s featuring violinist Eddie South, whose beautiful, swinging solos were unfortunately seldom recorded. These songs were cut when South was living in Paris and playing with such European jazz greats as Django Reinhardt and Stephane Grappelli. —*Ron Wynn*

● **Eddie South 1937–1941** / Nov. 25, 1937–Mar. 12, 1941 / Classics ✦✦✦✦✦

The Distinguished Violin of Eddie South / Jul. 14, 1958–Jul. 15, 1958 / Mercury ✦✦✦✦

Muggsy Spanier (Francis Joseph Spanier)

b. Nov. 9, 1906, Chicago, IL, d. Feb. 12, 1967, Sausalito, CA
Cornet / Dixieland
Muggsy Spanier was a predictable but forceful cornetist who rarely strayed far from the melody. Perfectly at home in Dixieland ensembles, Spanier was also an emotional soloist (equally influenced by King Oliver and Louis Armstrong) who was an expert at using the plunger mute. He started on cornet when he was 13, played with Elmer Schoebel's band in 1921 and first recorded in 1924. Spanier was a fixture in Chicago throughout the decade (appearing on several important early records) before joining Ted Lewis in 1929. Although Lewis was essentially a corny showman, Spanier's solos gave his band some validity during the next seven years.

After a stint with Ben Pollack's orchestra (1936–38), Spanier became seriously ill and was hospitalized for three months. After he recovered, the cornetist formed his famous eight-piece

"Ragtime Band" and recorded 16 Dixieland performances for Bluebird (later dubbed "the Great 16") that virtually defined the music of the Dixieland revival movement. But because his group actually preceded the revival by a couple years, it soon had to break up due to lack of work! Muggsy joined Bob Crosby for a time, had his own short-lived big band, freelanced with Dixieland bands in New York and starting in 1950 he gradually relocated to the West Coast. During 1957–59 Spanier worked with Earl Hines' band and he continued playing up until his retirement in 1964, touring Europe in 1960 and always retaining his popularity in the Dixieland world. —*Scott Yanow*

★ **Muggsy Spanier (1924–1928)** / Feb. 25, 1924–Apr. 5, 1928 / Retrieval ✦✦✦✦✦
This is the type of definitive "complete" release that American labels always seem to leave up to the Europeans to do correctly. The English LP reissues all seven selections by The Bucktown Five, the two numbers from The Stomp Six, Charles Pierce's seven 1928 titles and two titles from The Jungle Kings. The somewhat generic group names mask the fact that these performances include solos from such greats as cornetist Muggsy Spanier, clarinetists Volly de Faut and Frankie Teschemacher, and pianist Joe Sullivan. These early recordings find Spanier gradually developing his own style; his solos on "Why Can't It Be Poor Little Me" and "Nobody's Sweetheart" are classics. 1920s collectors can consider this set to be essential. —*Scott Yanow*

Muggsy Spanier (1931+1939) / Mar. 1931–Dec. 12, 1939 / BBC ✦✦✦
Reissues of super '30s dates with Spanier and Fats Waller (p), Benny Goodman (cl), and Joe Bushkin (p). —*Ron Wynn*

★ **The Ragtime Band Sessions** / Jul. 7, 1939–Dec. 12, 1939 / Bluebird ✦✦✦✦✦
During four sessions in 1939 cornetist Muggsy Spanier performed definitive versions of 16 Dixieland standards that, due to the joy of the music and its huge influence on the future revival movement, would later be dubbed "The Great 16." This CD, which adds eight alternate takes, could have been subtitled "The Great 24." Spanier and his octet (which includes trombonist George Brunies, clarinetist Rod Cless, usually pianist Joe Bushkin and several different tenors) roar their way through such songs as "Big Butter and Egg Man," "That Da Da Strain," "I Wish I Could Shimmy like My Sister Kate," "Dinah" and "Mandy, Make up Your Mind." Classic music. —*Scott Yanow*

● **Muggsy Spanier 1939–1942** / Jul. 7, 1939–Jun. 1, 1942 / Classics ✦✦✦✦✦

Muggsy Spanier / Oct. 17, 1944+Oct. 22, 1945 / Everybody's ✦✦✦✦
This LP contains Dixieland performances originally recorded as V-Discs by cornetist Muggsy Spanier. The two all-star jams also feature solos from trombonist Lou McGarity, clarinetists Pee Wee Russell and Peanuts Hucko, tenors Boomie Richman and Bud Freeman, and pianists Jess Stacy and Dave Bowman. The music is pretty straightforward with few surprises but plenty of heat generated from these masterful players. —*Scott Yanow*

Relaxin' at the Touro / 1952 / Jazzology ✦✦✦✦

Rare Custom 45's / Apr. 1956 / IAJRC ✦✦✦✦

Columbia, the Gem of the Ocean / Jun. 13, 1962–Jun. 14, 1962 / Mobile Fidelity ✦✦✦✦

James Spaulding

b. Jul. 30, 1937, Indianapolis, IN
Flute, Alto Saxophone / Post-Bop, Hard Bop
A tremendous alto sax and flute player with one of jazz's slimmest profiles. Spaulding came to prominence during the '60s and '70s as a stirring alto soloist with one foot in bop and one in the free, expressive style being pioneered by Ornette Coleman. He was also among the best flute players, able to play lengthy lines and swirling solos, play sweetly or with funk and bite. Spaulding recorded quite frequently with Sun Ra's Arkestra in the late '50s and early '60s, then moved to New York in 1962. He began heading his own bands, while also working and recording through the '60s with Freddie Hubbard as well as Max roach, Randy Weston and Art Blakey among others. He did numerous dates in the '70s, playing with Horace Silver, Bobby Hutcherson, Budd Johnson, Milt Jackson and Bob Wilber, while continuing to periodically head his own combos. Spaulding earned his BA from Livingston College, Rutgers in the mid-'70s, but wasn't heard from much dur-

ing the late '70s. He resurfaced on the '81 Alvin Queen LP *Ashanti*, and since then has been featured on both his own dates and other sessions. Spaulding has some '80s and '90s dates available on CD, and can also be heard on Blue Note CD reissues of '60s sessions with Hubbard. —*Ron Wynn*

James Spaulding Plays the Legacy of Duke Ellington / Dec. 1, 1976–Dec. 2, 1976 / Storyville ✦✦✦
James Spaulding has been an underrated soloist since he first emerged in the early '60s, playing fiery alto sax and dashing flute. He demonstrates his solid interpretative skills on this mid-'70s session, playing Ellington songs with verve, conviction, and depth. —*Ron Wynn*

Gotstabe a Better Way / May 31, 1988 / Muse ✦✦✦✦✦
Veteran saxophonist in his best light. —*Michael G. Nastos*

★ **Brilliant Corners** / Nov. 25, 1988 / Muse ✦✦✦✦✦

Songs of Courage / Oct. 1991 / Muse ✦✦✦✦

Blues Nexus / Aug. 8, 1993 / Muse ✦✦✦✦

Victoria Spivey

b. Oct. 15, 1906, Houston, TX, d. Oct. 3, 1976, New York, NY
Vocals / Blues
Although primarily a blues singer, Victoria Spivey often crossed over into jazz during her lengthy career. She learned piano early on and was singing professionally when she was 12. She worked locally (most notably with Blind Lemon Jefferson) and then in 1926 had a major hit with her first recording, "Black Snake Blues." A major attraction for the remainder of the decade, Spivey was one of the stars in the all-black MGM musical *Hallelujah* in 1929. She recorded in the late '20s (among her sidemen were Louis Armstrong and Red Allen) and in the mid-'30s, worked in vaudeville and toured with the *Hellzapoppin'* show in the late '40s although by then her years of fame had passed. However, in the 1960s she started her Spivey label, recorded for several companies (including with Lonnie Johnson) and Victoria Spivey remained a constant force in the blues scene until her death in 1976. —*Scott Yanow*

● **1926–1931** / May 11, 1926–Mar. 20, 1931 / Document ✦✦✦✦
Spivey is in marvelous form throughout. This album features the classics "Steady Grind," "Black Snake Blues," and "Blood Thirsty Blues." —*Cub Koda*

And Her Blues, Vol. 2 / Jun. 10, 1961–Jun. 4, 1972 / Spivey ✦✦✦✦
Victoria Spivey, a classic blues singer of the 1920s, started her own label Spivey in 1961 and kept it going for 15 years. This LP, released posthumously, has three solo performances from 1961 (on which the singer plays either piano or ukulele), a trio rendition of "The Rising Sun" from 1962 with clarinetist Eddie Barefield, four numbers from 1972 in small combos and a loose three-song live performance from 1963 with a guitarist and a kazoo player. Although not essential, the music on this set is enjoyable and should be of interest to jazz historians. —*Scott Yanow*

Woman Blues! / Sep. 21, 1961 / Bluesville ✦✦✦✦

Spyro Gyra

Group / Crossover
Founded in 1975 by altoist Jay Beckenstein, Spyro Gyra has consistently been one of the commercially successful pop-jazz groups of the past 20 years. Although originally a studio group, the band became a fulltime venture in 1979 and has been touring ever since. Critics love to attack this band's lightweight and rarely changing music (which combines R&B and elements of pop with jazz), but its live performances are often stimulating, unlike many of its records, which emphasize the danceable melodies at the expense of the improvising. —*Scott Yanow*

Spyro Gyra / 1976 / MCA ✦✦✦

Morning Dance / Jul. 1979 / MCA ✦✦✦

Catching the Sun / Nov. 1980 / MCA ✦✦✦✦
One among many similar-sounding but highly popular albums by premier fusion ensemble Spyro Gyra. The group's songs usually contained catchy melodies, prominent backbeats, and some room for improvisational expression, although it was limited and required quick bursts rather than expansive statements. They were and still are near the top in the light jazz and fusion field. —*Ron Wynn*

Carnival / 1980 / MCA ✦✦✦✦

Freetime / Oct. 1981 / MCA ✦✦✦

Incognito / Dec. 1982 / MCA ✦✦✦✦✦

City Kids / Aug. 1983 / MCA ✦✦✦✦

Access All Areas / Nov. 17, 1983+Nov. 19, 1983 / MCA ✦✦✦✦✦
An excellent live double album, it includes live versions of songs from early albums. —*Paul Kohler*

Alternating Currents / Oct. 1985 / MCA ✦✦✦✦

Breakout / 1986 / MCA ✦✦✦✦
An album with more mid-tempo jazz-style tunes and nice arrangements, it features Julio Fernandez and synth programming by Eddie Jobson. —*Paul Kohler*

Stories without Words / Jul. 1987 / MCA ✦✦✦
A nice mix of jazz, with tenor and soprano sax melodies that really sing. —*Paul Kohler*

Rites of Summer / 1988 / MCA ✦✦✦

Point of View / Jun. 1989 / MCA ✦✦

Fast Forward / 1990 / GRP ✦✦

Three Wishes / 1992 / GRP ✦✦✦

● **Dreams Beyond Control** / 1993 / GRP ✦✦✦✦✦
Spyro Gyra mostly sticks to their formula of danceable melodic music on this GRP release, but there are a few temporary departures. The harmonica of the talented Howard Levy is used prominently on "Breakfast at Igor's," two different horn sections pop up on a few songs and there are a pair of throwaway pop vocals from Alex Ligertwood. However, longtime Spyro Gyra fans have little to fear for the solos of saxophonist Jay Beckenstein and vibraphonist Dave Samuels are predictably pleasant, the light funk rhythms push the ensembles and the band's sound remains distinctive, familiar and comfortable. —*Scott Yanow*

Love & Other Obsessions / 1995 / GRP ✦✦
This recording has a couple of changes from Spyro Gyra's usual formula with vibraphonist Dave Samuels no longer a regular member of the popular group (although he does guest on a few tracks) and R&B vocalists being utilized on a few of the selections, dominating two of them. Neither of these alterations have affected the group's sound or approach much. Jay Beckenstein (on alto and soprano) is still the lead voice, the danceable funk rhythms are as mindless as ever and the 11 selections (which clock in between 4:32 and 5:52) are clearly designed for radio airplay. One would think Beckenstein would have been bored with this automatic pilot music years ago! —*Scott Yanow*

Jess Stacy (Alexandria Stacy)

b. Aug. 11, 1904, Bird's Point, MO, d. Jan. 5, 1994, Los Angeles, CA
Piano / Swing
One of the great swing pianists, Jess Stacy's greatest moment of fame was an unexpected one when during the latter part of "Sing, Sing, Sing" at Benny Goodman's historic 1938 Carnegie Hall Concert, the clarinetist motioned to Stacy to take a solo (which he never had previously on that song). The pianist constructed a remarkable impressionistic improvisation that stole solo honors and was fortunately documented (and released for the first time in 1950). A mostly self-taught player who performed on riverboats during the early '20s, Stacy was part of the fertile Chicago jazz scene of the 1920s with his style being influenced by both Earl Hines and Bix Beiderbecke.

Still obscure when he joined Goodman's big band in 1935, the pianist soon became well-known as one of BG's top sidemen, working with him through 1939 and on and off during the next five years. Stacy also spent time with the bands of Bob Crosby, Horace Heidt and Tommy Dorsey, recorded with Eddie Condon, did some solo recordings of his own (starting in 1935) had a short-lived marriage to singer Lee Wiley and tried twice to lead big bands of his own. He became fairly obscure after moving to California in 1947 (mostly playing in piano bars) and in 1963 Stacy retired from music altogether, only to return briefly on a few special occasions (and for two Chiaroscuro recordings) over the next 20 years. —*Scott Yanow*

● **Jess Stacy 1935–1939** / Nov. 16, 1935–Nov. 30, 1939 / Classics ✦✦✦✦✦
Pianist Jess Stacy did not lead that many recording sessions during the swing era since he spent long periods playing with the big

Tenor Saxophone

Music Map

Pioneer and First Innovative Tenor	1920s
Coleman Hawkins	Barney Bigard Happy Caldwell

Versatile Genius
Rahsaan Roland Kirk

Second Innovative Tenor
Lester Young

Fourth Innovator and Biggest Influence on Post-1960 Tenors
John Coltrane

Swing Era
Chu Berry	Ben Webster	Charlie Barnet
Gene Sedric	Herschel Evans	Buddy Tate
Dick Wilson	Budd Johnson	Benny Waters

Free Jazz/Avant-Garde
John Gilmore	Archie Shepp
Pharoah Sanders	Albert Ayler
Dewey Redman	Frank Wright
Roscoe Mitchell	Joseph Jarman
Sam Rivers	Charles Tyler
Fred Anderson	Dave Liebman
John Purcell	Von Freeman
Chico Freeman	George Adams
Evan Parker	Jan Garbarek
Willem Breuker	Peter Brotzmann
Vladimir Chekasin	Joe McPhee
David Murray	Charles Gayle
David S. Ware	

Chicago Dixieland
Bud Freeman • Eddie Miller

1940s Stompers - Swing to R&B
Illinois Jacquet	Arnett Cobb
Flip Phillips	Don Byas
Ike Quebec	Georgie Auld
Eddie "Lockjaw" Davis	Al Sears
Charlie Ventura	Hal Singer
Willis "Gator" Jackson	Jimmy Forrest

Modern Swing
Scott Hamilton • Ken Peplowski • Harry Allen

Soul Jazz to Crossover
Stanley Turrentine	David "Fathead" Newman
Eddie Harris	Houston Person
Wilton Felder	John Klemmer
Gato Barbieri	Tom Scott
Grover Washington, Jr.	

1940s Los Angeles Bop
Dexter Gordon	Wardell Gray
Teddy Edwards	Lucky Thompson

Most Influential Tenors of the Past 20 Years
Wayne Shorter • Mike Brecker

Cool School
Stan Getz	Zoot Sims
Al Cohn	Herbie Steward
Brew Moore	Allan Eager
Jimmy Giuffre	Paul Quinichette
Buddy Collette	Bob Cooper
Bill Perkins	Richie Kamuca
Dave Pell	Jack Montrose
Frank Wess	Dick Hafer
Fraser MacPherson	Spike Robinson

1980s/'90s
Lew Tabackin	Don Menza
Pete Christlieb	Benny Wallace
Billy Harper	John Stubblefield
Odean Pope	Ricky Ford
Eddie Daniels	Steve Grossman
Billy Pierce	Ralph Moore
Joe Lovano	Branford Marsalis
David Sanchez	Edward Wilkerson
Bill Evans	Bob Mintzer
Bob Berg	Dob Malach
Javon Jackson	Jean Toussaint
Courtney Pine	Tommy Smith
Don Braden	Ralph Bowen
Todd Williams	Joshua Redman
James Carter	

1950s
Sonny Stitt	Gene Ammons	Paul Gonsalves
Frank Foster	James Moody	Benny Golson
Warne Marsh	J.R. Monterose	Johnny Griffin
Harold Land	Junior Cook	Hank Mobley
Jimmy Heath		

Third Innovative Tenor
Sonny Rollins

1960s
Yusef Lateef	Charlie Rouse	Booker Ervin
Clifford Jordan	Sal Nistico	George Coleman
Joe Henderson	Joe Farrell	Charles Lloyd

bands of Benny Goodman and Bob Crosby. This excellent CD contains his 21 selections as a leader from a four-year period. Stacy's three numbers from 1935 include a solo Bix Beiderbecke medley and two songs with bassist Israel Crosby and drummer Gene Krupa. In addition, this set has Stacy's eight piano solos for Commodore, a duet with Bud Freeman on tenor ("She's Funny That Way") and eight very rare performances (plus an alternate take) cut for Varsity in 1939 that also feature trumpeter Billy Butterfield, tenor saxophonist Eddie Miller and either clarinetist Hank d'Amico or Irving Fazola in an octet. This CD contains more than its share of gems. —*Scott Yanow*

Jess Stacy and Friends / Apr. 30, 1938–Nov. 25, 1944 / Commodore ✦✦✦✦

Blue Notion / Oct. 6, 1944 / Jazzology ✦✦✦✦
A good compilation of tracks from early '40s. —*Ron Wynn*

A Tribute to Benny Goodman / Apr. 15, 1954–Oct. 6, 1955 / Atlantic ✦✦✦
Music made to commemorate the making of the film *The Benny Goodman Story*. Pianist Jess Stacy, who was supposed to appear in the film, walked off when he found out he would only get to do one number. He didn't leave this session, thankfully; his spinning, swinging piano solos set the tone for the date, backed by a group that includes Ziggy Elman on trumpet. There are four masterpieces from a trio of pianist Stacy, with Art Shapiro and Nick Fatool. —*Ron Wynn*

Stacy Still Swinging / Jul. 5, 1974–Jul. 20, 1977 / Chiaroscuro ✦✦✦✦✦

Marvin Stamm

b. May 23, 1939, Memphis, TN
Trumpet / Hard Bop
An excellent bop-based trumpeter and a busy session player during much of his career, Marvin Stamm has long been a flexible player. He started on trumpet when he was 12 and later studied at North Texas State University. Stamm was with Stan Kenton's Mellophonium Orchestra during 1961–63 (getting occasional solos) and played with Woody Herman during 1965–66. He gained some recognition for his playing with the Thad Jones-Mel Lewis Orchestra (1966–72) but spent much of his time during the next two decades in the studios. Stamm, who performed with Benny Goodman during 1974–75 and toured with George Gruntz's Concert Jazz Band in 1987, has in recent years concentrated much more on jazz playing and his Music Masters releases are good examples of his talents. —*Scott Yanow*

Machinations / Apr. 16, 1968–Apr. 24, 1968 / Verve ✦✦✦

Stampede / 1983 / Palo Alto ✦✦✦

Bop Boy / Jan. 5, 1990–Jan. 6, 1990 / Music Masters ✦✦✦✦
This trumpeter's first album in a long time as a leader. Spirited playing. —*Michael G. Nastos*

● **Mystery Man** / Sep. 3, 1992–Sep. 4, 1992 / Music Masters ✦✦✦✦✦
Trumpeter Marvin Stamm, rather than drag out the usual bebop standards, mostly introduces new material on his CD. Four songs are played by Berg's quartet with pianist Bill Charlap, bassist Mike Richmond and drummer Terry Clarke, six add Bob Mintzer's tenor, and of those songs three find Bob Malach (on tenor and soprano) making the band a sextet. Because Stamm paid as much attention to varying tempos and moods as he did to changing the instrumentation, this set holds one's interest throughout, swinging hard in a modern fashion. —*Scott Yanow*

State Street Ramblers

Group / Classic Jazz
The name "State Street Ramblers" was used for four different overlapping groups that recorded in 1928 and 1931. The first session features clarinetist Johnny Dodds, but most of the other performances (which include such musicians as cornetist Natty Dominique, pianist Jimmy Blythe, trombonist Roy Palmer, clarinetist Darnell Howard and either W.E. Burton or Alfred Bell on kazoo and vocals) were more primitive. These good-time sessions are quite spirited and fun; all of their recordings are available on a pair of RST CDs. —*Scott Yanow*

● **Vol. 1** / Aug. 12, 1927–Mar. 19, 1931 / RST ✦✦✦✦
The Austrian RST label has reissued the complete output of The State Street Ramblers on two CDs, a primitive but very spirited series of groups that recorded during 1927–28 and 1931 under

that name. The first set has three selections that feature clarinetist Johnny Dodds and cornetist Natty Dominique in a quartet, Natty is showcased on six other erratic numbers (his solo on "Tack It Down" is hilariously bad), there is a sextet with alto, clarinet and the humorous vocal interjections of W.E. Burton and, for the final selections, three exciting numbers in which trombonist Roy Palmer dominates. Although not essential, fans of early jazz will want these occasionally riotous performances. —*Scott Yanow*

● **Vol. 2/Roy Palmer** / Mar. 19, 1931–Apr. 3, 1936 / RST ✦✦✦✦✦
On the second of two CDs put out by the Austrian RST label, there is a very generous amount (26 songs) of enjoyable vintage music. Nine numbers feature the 1931 version of The State Street Ramblers that grouped the great percussive trombonist Roy Palmer with Darnell Howard (who doubles on alto and clarinet) and has plenty of spirit and drive. In addition, there are 13 songs from The Memphis Nighthawks in 1932 and four by the 1936 Chicago Rhythm Kings; both groups are similar in style and also have plenty of space for Roy Palmer's unique playing. A special treat is a previously unreleased trombone-piano duet "The Trombone Slide." Heartily recommended to collectors of the era. —*Scott Yanow*

Statesmen Of Jazz

Group / Classic Jazz
This remarkable group, put together in 1994 by the American Federation of Jazz Societies, features veteran jazz players, all of whom are at least 65 yet are still in their musical prime. Their one recording hints at the band's potential. Most notable among the personnel are 87-year-old violinist Claude Williams and Benny Waters who, at age 93, is still a powerful altoist. —*Scott Yanow*

★ **Statesmen Of Jazz** / Dec. 20, 1994 / AFJS ✦✦✦✦
This is a rather historic recording for it finds altoist Benny Waters, the oldest active jazz musician at a month shy of 93, in surprisingly fiery form; his feature on "Blue Waters" is easily the highpoint. The other members of The Statesmen of Jazz (a group sponsored by the American Federation of Jazz Societies) are all senior citizens too: Violinist Claude Williams (86), fluegelhornist Clark Terry (74), trumpeter Joe Wilder (72), trombonist Al Grey (69), tenor saxoponist Buddy Tate (79), pianist Jane Jarvis (79), bassist Milt Hinton (84) and drummer Panama Francis (76). Although Tate was a little past his prime and Wilder a bit erratic due to recent dental surgery, this is a particularly happy date of wellplayed swing. Waters, Williams and Terry take solo honors. Recommended. —*Scott Yanow*

Dakota Staton (Aliyah Rabia)

b. Jun. 3, 1932, Pittsburgh, PA
Vocals / Standards
Good jazz and blues singer who made a big impact in the mid-'50s and early '60s. Staton was named by *Down Beat* as most promising newcomer in 1955; her releases, especially *The Late, Late Show*, were both popular and enhanced her reputation as a vocalist who could swing, interpret standards, and sing convincing, pulsating blues tunes. She recorded with George Shearing in 1958, and also did one of the most successful vocal versions of "Misty." She spent time in Europe starting in 1965 (including England and Germany) but came back to the U.S. in the early 1970s. Staton's recent Muse sessions show that she remains in fine form although she never did become a household name. —*Ron Wynn and Scott Yanow*

The Late, Late Show / Feb. 28, 1957+Mar. 2, 1957 / Capitol ✦✦✦✦✦

● **Dakota Staton** / Feb. 7, 1990–Feb. 8, 1990 / Muse ✦✦✦✦✦
A '90 session with vocalist Dakota Station, who has recorded in many styles during her career, going back to the combo jazz she made in the '50s and '60s. Her husky, authoritative voice has gotten stronger and deeper with age. She's backed by tenor saxophonist Houston Person and cuts some fine soul-jazz, blues, and standards. —*Ron Wynn*

Darling Please Save Your Love / Oct. 3, 1991 / Muse ✦✦✦✦

Isn't This a Lovely Day / Dec. 23, 1992 / Muse ✦✦✦✦

Lou Stein

b. Apr. 22, 1922, Philadelphia, PA
Piano / Bop, Swing
Although a swing-oriented pianist, Lou Stein has always been

able to fit comfortably in Dixieland, bop and commercial settings. His first major association was with Ray McKinley's band in 1942. While in the service Stein played domestically with Glenn Miller's Army Air Force Band, although he did not go overseas. He gained recognition for his work with Charlie Ventura (1946–47) and for his most famous composition "East of Suez." After that period ended, Stein became a studio musician but found time to perform and record with the Lawson Haggart band, Benny Goodman, Sarah Vaughan, the Sauter-Finegan orchestra, Louie Bellson, Red Allen, Coleman Hawkins and Lester Young in addition to recording a few albums as a leader. In later years he played with Joe Venuti (1969–72), Flip Phillips and recorded his own 1994 album for Pullen. —*Scott Yanow*

Tribute To Tatum / 1976 / Chiaroscuro ✦✦✦✦✦

Stompin' 'Em Down / 1978 / Chiaroscuro ✦✦✦✦

● **Go Daddy!** / 1994 / Pullen Music ✦✦✦✦✦
Pianist Lou Stein's first record as a leader in quite a few years is an excellent all-around showcase both for his solo and trio playing (with bassists Jeff Fuller or Brian Torff and drummers Joe Cucuzzo or Todd Strait) and for his composing; in addition to ten standards, there are six Stein originals on this fine CD. Although his daughter Elise Stein gets nearly equal billing, she only sings on about a third of the set, leaving the spotlight firmly on the veteran and still very viable pianist. Highlights include "Lullaby of the Leaves," "Deed I Do," "Here's That Rainy Day" and Stein's greatest hit, "East of Suez." A fine outing. —*Scott Yanow*

Steps Ahead

Group / Fusion, Post-Bop
Originally called Steps when it was formed in 1979 by vibraphonist Mike Mainieri, this group at various times has included tenor saxophonist Michael Brecker, keyboardists Don Grolnick, Eliane Elias and Rachel Z, guitarist Mike Stern, bassists Eddie Gomez and Darryl Jones and drummers Peter Erskine and Steve Smith among others. Its music combines advanced jazz, R&B, rock and fusion and is frequently exciting. Steps Ahead was most active during 1979–86 although still existed on a part-time basis in the mid-'90s. —*Scott Yanow*

Step by Step / Dec. 8, 1980–Dec. 10, 1980 / Denon ✦✦✦✦
This killer group consists of Michael Brecker (ts), Steve Gadd (d), Eddie Gomez (b) Don Grolnick (p), and Mike Mainieri (vibes). One of three releases available from Japan only, this excellent recording was recorded in the studio under the name Steps. —*Paul Kohler*

Smokin' in the Pit: Live! / Dec. 14, 1980–Dec. 16, 1980 / Denon ✦✦✦✦✦
Recorded live at the Pitt Inn in Tokyo, Japan this superb double-disc is one of jazz music's finest moments!! It includes the same lineup as *Step by Step*. None of the material on any of these three Japanese CDs is repeated on the other CDs. Buy all three, they're worth every penny! —*Paul Kohler*

Paradox / 1982 / Denon ✦✦✦✦
This great recording shows a different side to Steps' music by showcasing a more avant-garde style. Peter Erskine replaces Steve Gadd on drums. —*Paul Kohler*

Steps Ahead / Jul. 1983 / Elektra ✦✦✦✦
This is one of the early albums from Brecker and Mainieri. —*Michael Erlewine*

● **Modern Times** / Jan. 1984–Feb. 1984 / Elektra ✦✦✦✦✦

Magnetic / 1985–1986 / Elektra ✦✦✦
The last Steps Ahead recording to feature Michael Brecker, this album finds the band exploring the use of electronic instruments and synthesis. Michael Brecker's use of the Akai E.W.I. (electronic wind instrument) is astonishing. —*Paul Kohler*

Live In Tokyo 1986 / Jul. 30, 1986 / NYC ✦✦
This Steps Ahead concert (which has long been available on laser disc) has both good and bad points. Michael Brecker's virtuosic tenor solos show a great deal of passion and creativity within the genre. Also Mike Mainieri's vibes are an attractive part of the ensemble sound, making the R&Bish unit sound like Spyro Gyra with guts. Unfortunately, the rhythm section (which consists of guitarist Mike Stern, bassist Darryl Jones and drummer Steve Smith) is never subtle, the rhythms are bombastic and the electronics (including at one pont a drum machine) are excessive. The solos might be fiery, but the unimaginative backup makes this

potentially super band often sound run of the mill and monotonous. There are much better Steps Ahead concerts to preserve than this one. —*Scott Yanow*

N.Y.C. / 1989 / Intuition ✦✦✦
Decent fusion, jazz-rock, and instrumental pop from the East Coast band whose personnel has fluctuated over the years. This edition didn't include either Brecker and instead revolved around vibist and keyboardist Mike Manieri. The band played the usual pop and fusion compositions with its usual competence. —*Ron Wynn*

Yin-Yang / 1992 / NYC ✦✦✦✦

Vibe / 1994 / NYC ✦✦✦✦

Leni Stern

b. Germany
Guitar / Post-Bop
Leni Stern, who has thus far received more recognition for her composing than for her guitar playing, has managed to carve out her own musical personality despite being married to fellow guitarist Mike Stern (a potential dominant influence). She began classical piano lessons when she was six but was much more inspired a few years later when she discovered a guitar in the attic and taught herself to play jazz. Stern's early years were actually spent as an actress in her native Germany, featured on a national television show. However, she took a summer off in 1977 to enroll at Berklee, and she never returned to acting. Stern lived in Boston until 1980 when she moved to New York and has worked steadily in clubs ever since, recording for Passport (now defunct), Enja and Lipstick. —*Scott Yanow*

Clairvoyant / Dec. 16, 1985–Dec. 17, 1985 / Passport ✦✦✦✦
Sextet with Bill Frisell (g), Bob Berg (ts). A fresh approach, not as acerbic as her husband Mike. Larry Willis (p) Trio, a fine support group—Harvie Swartz (b), Paul Motian (d). Stern plays plaintive electric guitar. —*Michael G. Nastos*

The Next Day / 1987 / Passport ✦✦✦

Secrets / Sep. 24, 1988–Oct. 1, 1988 / Enja ✦✦✦✦
Leni Stern utilizes such impressive sidemen as fellow guitarist Wayne Krantz, tenor saxophonist Bob Berg, Lincoln Goines or Harvie Swartz on bass and drummer Dennis Chambers on eight selections, all but one her originals. The music ranges from a three-guitar jam on "Groundhog" (which adds blucs guitarist Dave Tronzo) to a song dedicated to Jaco Pastorius ("Who Loves You") and the melancholy strut "Maybe." Overall this set of music holds one's interest even if Stern was at this point a stronger composer than guitarist. —*Scott Yanow*

● **Closer to the Light** / Dec. 1989 / Enja ✦✦✦✦✦
Surprising release with David Sanborn (as) showing his real skills; fine arrangements. —*Ron Wynn*

Ten Songs / Oct. 1991 / Lipstick ✦✦✦✦

Like One / 1993 / Lipstick ✦✦✦
It isn't elitism that makes many in the jazz hardcore shudder whenever the word "fusion" is mentioned; it is the attempt to define any and everything instrumental as jazz, regardless of sound, structure, intent and content. Guitarist Leni Stern clearly has improvisational skills, and there are certainly songs on his current session designed in a jazz context. But neither Sting's "Every Breath You Take" nor Joni Mitchell's "Court and Spark" qualify; these are clearly pop covers, done with little or no jazz sensibility. Other songs reveal Stern's penchant for light, finely played voicings and bluesy chords, and includes some fervent blowing from tenor saxophonist Bob Malach. There is a lot on this session that is entertaining and commendable; just don't call the Sting cover jazz. —*Ron Wynn*

Words / 1994–1995 / Lipstick ✦✦✦✦

Mike Stern

b. Jan. 10, 1953, Boston, MA
Guitar / Fusion, Post-Bop
A rocking, experimental guitarist who rose to fame playing in a pair of Miles Davis' bands, Mike Stern's a competent bebop and hard bop player but excellent fusion and jazz-rock musician. He's provided some wondrous riffs, blistering lines, complex voicings and dynamite phrases doing fusion, playing with much more force and vigor than on more conventional jazz. Stern attended Berklee in the early '70s, where he studied with Pat Metheny and

Mick Goodrick. Metheny recommended him for a vacancy with Blood, Sweat and Tears, and Stern played with them two years. He later worked with Billy Cobham, then joined Davis' band in 1981. Stern stayed with him two years, then played with Jaco Pastorius' group "Word Of Mouth." Stern made his recording debut as a leader in 1985; he later toured with Davis again, played with Steps Ahead, and worked in bands led by Mike Brecker and Harvie Swartz. Stern's recorded as a leader for Atlantic in the '80s and '90s. He has several sessions available as a leader. —*Ron Wynn and Michael G. Nastos*

Upside Downside / Mar. 1986–Apr. 1986 / Atlantic ✦✦✦

Time in Place / Dec. 1987 / Atlantic ✦✦✦✦
With Michael Brecker (sax) and Bob Berg (ts). "Gossip" a good opening track. —*Michael G. Nastos*

Jigsaw / Feb. 1989 / Atlantic ✦✦✦✦
High-powered jazz-rock with the emphasis on rock. —*Michael G. Nastos*

Odds or Evens / 1991 / Atlantic ✦✦

● **Standards (and Other Songs)** / 1992 / Atlantic ✦✦✦✦✦
Just as the title implies, this is an album of mostly jazz standards augmented by several of Stern's own original compositions. Also featured are Jay Anderson (b), Randy Brecker (t), and Bob Berg (ts). This is perhaps Stern's finest recording. —*Paul Kohler*

Is What It Is / 1993 / Atlantic ✦✦

Between The Lines / 1995 / Atlantic ✦✦✦✦

Bob Stewart

b. Feb. 3, 1945, Sioux Falls, SD
Tuba / Post Bop
A virtuoso tuba player, Bob Stewart's solos explore its full range and shows its ability to serve as both a lead and support instrument within the jazz ensemble. He rivals Howard Johnson in terms of demonstrating depth, facility and imagination on tuba. Stewart began playing trumpet at 10, and studied trumpet and tuba at the Philadelphia College of the Performing Arts. He taught in the public school system in Pennsylvania, then later played in a traditional jazz band at a Philadelphia club. Stewart moved to New York in the late '60s, and joined the tuba ensemble Gravity. He played with Carla Bley, Frank Foster's Loud Minority, and the orchestras of Sam Rivers and Gil Evans in the late '60s. Stewart was a featured member of Arthur Blythe's mid-'70s band that recorded for Columbia, and also worked with The Globe Unity Orchestra, Charles Mingus and McCoy Tyner. Stewart played with David Murray's Big band, Lester Bowie's Brass Fantasy and Henry Threadgill's orchestra in the '80s and into the '90s. —*Ron Wynn*

● **First Line** / Nov. 1987 / JMT ✦✦✦✦✦

Goin' Home / Dec. 1988 / JMT ✦✦✦✦✦
Premier tuba player Bob Stewart with quintet. One side is originals and the other is standards and traditional fare. Highly recommended. —*Michael G. Nastos*

Rex Stewart (William Stewart, Jr.)

b. Feb. 22, 1907, Philadelphia, PA, d. Sep. 7, 1967, Los Angeles, CA
Cornet / Dixieland, Swing
Rex Stewart achieved his greatest glory in a subsidiary role, playing cornet 11 years in the Duke Ellington Orchestra. His famous "talking" style, and half-valve effects were exploited brilliantly by countless Ellington pieces containing perfect passages tailored to showcase Stewart's sound. He played in a forceful, gripping manner that reflected the influence of Louis Armstrong, Bubber Miley and Bix Beiderbecke, whose solos he once reproduced on record. Stewart played on Potomac riverboats before moving to Philadelphia. He went to New York in 1921.

Stewart worked with Elmer Snowden in 1925, then joined Fletcher Henderson a year later. But he felt his talents were not at the necessary level, and departed Henderson's band, joining his brother Horace's band at Wilberforce College. Stewart returned in 1928. He remained there and contributed many memorable solos. There was also a brief period in McKinney's Cotton Pickers in 1931, a stint heading his own band, and another short stay with Luis Russell before Stewart joined the Ellington Orchestra in 1934. He was a star throughout his tenure, co-writing classics "Boy Meets Horn" and "Morning Glory." He also supervised many outside recording sessions using Ellingtonians.

After leaving, Stewart led various combos, and performed throughout Europe and Australia on an extensive Jazz at the Philharmonic tour from 1947–1951. He lectured at the Paris Conservatory in 1948. Stewart settled in New Jersey to run a farm in the early '50s. He was semi-retired but found new success in the media. He worked in local radio and television, while leading a band part time in Boston. Stewart led the Fletcher Henderson reunion band in 1957 and 1958, and recorded with them. He played at Eddie Condon's club in 1958 and 1959, then moved to the West Coast. Stewart again worked as a disc jockey and became a critic. While he published many excellent pieces, a collection containing many of his best reviews came out posthumously, "Jazz Masters of the Thirties." There's also a Stewart autobiography available. —*Ron Wynn*

Rex Stewart and the Ellingtonians / Jul. 23, 1940–1946 / Original Jazz Classics ✦✦✦✦✦
This brings together three HRS dates: July 23, 1940 with Rex Stewart, Lawrence Brown, Barney Bigard, Billy Kyle, Brick Fleasle, Wellman Bruad and Dave Tough; the fall of '46 with Stewart, Kyle, John Levy and Cozy Cole; and Jan. 10, 1946 with Joe Thomas (trumpet), Lawrence Brown, Otto Hardwick (alto sax), Ted Nash (tenor sax), Harry Carney, Jimmy Jones, Billy Taylor (bass) and Shelly Manne (drums)... The '40 date lacked a depth and bottom to its Dixie-ish feel. The '46 quartet sides did give a full spotlight on Stewart's special trumpet playing, always a pleasure for me, but the group lacked a cohesive intimacy. At times the leader's solo development could transcend that and his challenging bursts of fire and brimstone on "Loopin' Lobi'" please as much as remind me of the potential. The last two tracks were under Jimmy Jones' name and did not include Stewart. —*Bob Rusch, Cadence*

Dixieland Free-For-All / Jun. 1953 / Jazztone ✦✦✦✦

Irrepressible Rex Stewart / 1954 / Jazzology ✦✦✦

The Big Challenge / Apr. 30, 1957+May 6, 1957 / Jazztone ✦✦✦✦✦

★ **The Big Reunion** / Nov. 1957–Dec. 2, 1957 / Fresh Sound ✦✦✦✦✦

Porgy and Bess Revisited / 1958 / Warner Brothers ✦✦✦✦✦
Outstanding release, with Ellingtonians Cootie Williams (tpt), and Laurence Brown (tb). —*Ron Wynn*

Chatter Jazz / Jan. 20, 1959–Jan. 22, 1959 / RCA ✦✦✦

Rendezvous with Rex / Jan. 28, 1959+Jan. 31, 1958 / Felsted ✦✦✦✦
Rendezvous with Rex brought together two Rex Stewart dates: Jan. 28, 1958 and Jan. 31, 1958. Stewart will inevitably be tagged an Ellingtonite, and things will usually be related in some degree relative to that. That is understandable as it was with Ellington where he was most magnificent. That said, then note that this was not a recording in the Ellington genre, except for a little of the harmonic ensemble blending that might suggest that association. —*Bob Rusch, Cadence*

The Happy Jazz of Rex Stewart / Mar. 18, 1960 / Prestige ✦✦✦✦✦

Robert Stewart

Tenor Saxophone / Post Bop
An up-and-coming tenor saxophonist based in California, Robert Stewart (an unhurried but explorative hard bop player) had an impressive debut with 1995's *Judgement*. —*Scott Yanow*

● **Judgement** / 1994 / World Stage ✦✦✦✦✦
On a set of six straight-ahead originals and two standards, tenor saxophonist Robert Stewart sounds remarkably laidback and relaxed, particularly when one considers that this was his recording debut. Even on the uptempo tunes, Stewart is often content to emphasize his warm tone and hold long notes, taking his time to get his message across. Assisted by Eric Reed (who on this CD often emulates McCoy Tyner), bassist Mark Shelby and drummer Billy Higgins, this is a pleasing modern mainstream effort from the L.A.-based tenor. —*Scott Yanow*

Slam Stewart (Leroy Elliot Stewart)

b. Sep. 21, 1914, Englewood, NJ, d. Dec. 10, 1987, Binghamton, NY
Bass / Swing
Slam Stewart was a superior swing-oriented bassist whose ability to bow the bass and hum an octave apart made him famous in the jazz world. He had thought of the idea while studying at Boston Conservatory when he heard Ray Perry singing along with

his violin. In 1936 Stewart was with Peanuts Holland's group and the following year he started playing regularly with guitarist/singer/comedian Slim Gaillard in a group logically dubbed "Slim and Slam." "Flat Foot Floogie" became a huge hit and kept the group working through the early '40s. After leaving Gaillard, Stewart was in great demand. He played with Art Tatum's trio, was featured on records with the Benny Goodman Sextet, Red Norvo (a famous session with Charlie Parker and Dizzy Gillespie) and Lester Young (a classic rendition of "Sometimes I'm Happy"), and led his own group, which for a period featured the up-and-coming pianist Erroll Garner. Stewart performed a couple of stunning duets with tenor saxophonist Don Byas at a 1945 Town Hall concert and later worked with Billy Taylor, Roy Eldridge, Bucky Pizzarelli, the Newport All-Stars and a countless number of other jazz greats. He even recorded two albums with bassist Major Holley (who also bowed and hummed but in unison). Up until the end, Slam Stewart occupied his own unique niche in jazz. —*Scott Yanow*

Two Big Mice / Jul. 14, 1977 / Black & Blue ✦✦✦✦

● **Memorial Album 1914–1987** / 1978 / Stash ✦✦✦✦✦

Shut Yo' Mouth! / Dec. 6, 1981 / Delos ✦✦✦✦
With Major Holley. Two great bassists get together for a good time. Highly recommended. —*Michael G. Nastos*

Sonny Stitt (Edward Stitt)

b. Feb. 2, 1924, Boston, MA, d. Jul. 22, 1982, Washington, DC
Tenor Saxophone, Alto Saxophone / Bop
Charlie Parker has had many admirers and his influence can be detected in numerous styles, but few have been as avid a disciple as Sonny Sitt. There was almost note-for-note imitation in several early Stitt solos, and the closeness remained until Stitt began de-emphasizing the alto in favor of the tenor, on which he artfully combined the influences of Parker and Lester Young.

Stitt gradually developed his own sound and style, though he was never far from Parker on any alto solo. A wonderful blues and ballad player whose approach was one of the influences on John Coltrane, Stitt could rip through an uptempo bebop stanza, then turn around and play a shivering, captivating ballad. He was an alto saxophonist in Tiny Bradshaw's band during the early '40s, then joined Billy Eckstine's seminal big band in 1945, playing alongside other emerging bebop stars like Gene Ammons and Dexter Gordon. Stitt later played in Dizzy Gillespie's big band and sextet.

He began on tenor and baritone in 1949, and at times was in a two-tenor unit with Ammons. He recorded with Bud Powell and J.J. Johnson for Prestige in 1949, then did several albums on Prestige, Argo and Verve in the '50s and '60s. Stitt led many combos in the '50s, and rejoined Gillespie for a short period in the late '50s. After a brief stint with Miles Davis in 1960, he reunited with Ammons and for a while was in a three tenor lineup with James Moody. During the '60s, Stitt also recorded for Atlantic, cutting the transcendent *Stitt Plays Bird* that finally addressed he Parker question in epic fashion.

He continued heading bands, though he joined The Giants of Jazz in the early '70s. This group included Gillespie, Art Blakey, Kai Winding, Thelonious Monk and Al McKibbon. Stitt did more sessions in the '70s for Cobblestone, Muse and others, among them another definitive date, *Tune Up*. He continued playing and recording in the early '80s, recording for Muse, Sonet and Who's Who In Jazz. He suffered a heart attack and died in 1982. —*Ron Wynn and Bob Porter*

Sonny Stitt with Bud Powell and J.J. Johnson / Oct. 17, 1949–Jan. 26, 1950 / Original Jazz Classics ✦✦✦✦✦
This superb CD reissues the complete output of three classic bop sessions including five "new" alternate takes. Sonny Stitt (who plays tenor throughout) is heard in a quintet with trombonist J.J. Johnson, pianist John Lewis, bassist Nelson Boyd and drummer Max Roach (playing three Johnson compositions and the original version of John Lewis' "Afternoon in Paris") and in a quartet with the great pianist Bud Powell, bassist Curly Russell and Max Roach. The latter two sessions are highlighted by rapid versions of "All God's Chillun Got Rhythm," "Strike up the Band" and "Fine and Dandy." Highly recommended music. —*Scott Yanow*

Prestige First Sessions, Vol. 2 / Feb. 17, 1950–Aug. 14, 1951 / Prestige ✦✦✦✦✦
Sonny Stitt is heard in his early prime throughout this CD, stick-

ing to tenor on all but two of the 24 selections. Few could play bebop with Stitt's sincerity, quick reflexes and large vocabulary. He swings hard throughout the performances, most of which feature him as the only soloist. Three dull vocals aside (by the forgotten Teddy Williams And Larry Townsend), this gapfilling CD is highly recommended to fans of classic bebop. —*Scott Yanow*

Kaleidoscope / Oct. 8, 1950–Feb. 25, 1952 / Original Jazz Classics ✦✦✦✦✦
Some of Sonny Stitt's better early sessions are collected together on this excellent CD. Stitt (switching between tenor, alto and on two numbers baritone) is heard with a variety of small groups ranging from quartets to an octet with three trumpeters and is the main star throughout these boppish performances. Highlights include "Cherokee," "Liza," "This Can't Be Love" and "Stitt's It." Recommended. —*Scott Yanow*

Symphony Hall Swing / Nov. 20, 1952 / Savoy ✦✦✦
This collector's LP contains the complete Sonny Stitt quartet session of Nov. 20, 1952 (four songs plus four alternate takes featuring Stitt on tenor with the obscure pianist Fletcher Peck, bassist John Simmons and drummer Jo Jones) and a quartet of "new" alternates from a 1956 Stitt date on which Sonny plays alto while joined by pianist Dolo Coker, bassist Edgar Willis and drummer Kenny Dennis. Nothing all that unusual occurs, but bop fans should enjoy these hard-swinging straight-ahead performances. —*Scott Yanow*

At the Hi-Hat / Feb. 11, 1954 / Roulette ✦✦✦✦
For this Roulette CD, Sonny Stitt is in excellent form. Recorded live at a Boston club, Stitt uses a local rhythm section (pianist Dean Earl, bassist Bernie Griggs and drummer Marquis Foster) as he jams happily through a variety of standards. Stitt mostly switches between alto and tenor, but on "Tri-Horn Blues" he takes solos not only on both of those saxes but also on his rarely heard baritone. This CD gives one a good, all-around sampling of early Sonny Stitt. —*Scott Yanow*

Sonny Stitt Sits in with the Oscar Peterson Trio / Oct. 10, 1957+May 18, 1959 / Verve ✦✦✦✦
This CD combines together a complete session that Sonny Stitt (doubling on alto and tenor) did with the 1959 Oscar Peterson Trio (which includes the pianist/leader, bassist Ray Brown and drummer Ed Thigpen) and three titles from 1957 with Peterson, Brown, guitarist Herb Ellis and drummer Stan Levey. The music very much has the feel of a jam session, and other than a themeless blues, all of the songs are veteran standards. Highlights of this fine effort include "I Can't Give You Anything but Love," "The Gypsy," "Scrapple from the Apple," "Easy Does It" and "I Remember You." Lots of cooking music. —*Scott Yanow*

Sonny Stitt / 1958 / Chess ✦✦✦
Sonny Stitt recorded extensively throughout his career, so frequently that he often could not remember his sessions a year later. This informal session, cut in Chicago in 1958, is one that Stitt apparently forgot about, which is why the personnel (probably a local rhythm section that might include pianist Barry Harris) has never been definitely identified. Stitt, doubling on alto and tenor, plays some songs with unfamiliar titles, but all of the chord changes of the originals (half of them blues) are fairly basic. He is in above-average form, making this CD reissue of interest to bebop collectors. —*Scott Yanow*

★ **Boss Tenors** / Aug. 27, 1961 / Verve ✦✦✦✦✦

Stitt Meets Brother Jack / Feb. 16, 1962 / Original Jazz Classics ✦✦✦✦
Sonny Stitt (who sticks on this CD reissue to tenor) meets up with organist Brother Jack McDuff (along with guitarist Eddie Diehl, drummer Art Taylor and Ray Barretto on congas) for a spirited outing. Two standards ("All of Me" and "Time After Time") are performed with a variety of blues-based originals and the music always swings in a soulful boppish way. Worth picking up although not essential. —*Scott Yanow*

Soul Classics / Feb. 16, 1962–Feb. 15, 1972 / Prestige ✦✦
This CD is a sampler of Sonny Stitt's Prestige recordings. Stitt (mostly heard here on tenor) is accompanied by organists (Brother Jack McDuff, Don Patterson or Gene Ludwig) on all but one selection, but unfortunately half of the performances find him utilizing an electrified Varitone sax that watered down his sound and buried his individuality. This set can be safely passed by. —*Scott Yanow*

Boss Tenors in Orbit / Feb. 1962 / Verve ✦✦✦✦✦

Sonny Stitt and the Top Brass / Jul. 16, 1962–Jul. 17, 1962 / Atlantic ✦✦✦✦✦
This LP (reissued in Atlantic's *Jazzlore* series) features altoist Sonny Stitt accompanied by a nonet playing arrangements by either Tadd Dameron or Jimmy Mundy. The charts give this Stitt album more variety than usual and the superior material (which includes "On a Misty Night," "Poinciana" and Sonny's "Hey Pam") challenges the saxophonist to play at his best; trumpeter Blue Mitchell also has a couple of spots. Recommended. —*Scott Yanow*

Autumn in New York / 1962–Oct. 18, 1967 / Black Lion ✦✦✦
This Black Lion CD combines together four selections from a quintet session featuring altoist Sonny Stitt, trumpeter Howard McGhee, pianist Walter Bishop, bassist Tommy Potter and drummer Kenny Clarke (three boppish blues and a Stitt feature on "Lover Man") with four selections showcasing Stitt with unknown accompaniment from a 1962 date at Birdland. The saxophonist recorded so many sessions that it is not necessary to acquire them all to get a good sampling of his playing (particularly since his style was virtually unchanged after the mid-'50s), but the CD has its heated moments. —*Scott Yanow*

★ **Stitt Plays Bird** / Jan. 29, 1963 / Atlantic ✦✦✦✦✦

Salt and Pepper / Sep. 5, 1963 / Impulse! ✦✦✦✦✦
Here is a classic Impulse! LP long overdue to be reissued on CD. Sonny Stitt (sticking to tenor on four of the five selections) met up with fellow tenor Paul Gonsalves for a happy session that also features pianist Hank Jones, bassist Milt Hinton and drummer Osie Johnson. The two tenors battle it out on "Perdido," the blues "Salt and Pepper" and the little-played "S'Posin'" and try (unsuccessfully) for a hit on "Theme from *Lord of the Flies*." However, the highpoint is a version of "Stardust" on which both Stitt (switching to alto) and Gonsalves make beautiful and unpredictable statements that are quite memorable. Overall this set is a gem. —*Scott Yanow*

● **Soul People** / Aug. 25, 1964–1966 / Prestige ✦✦✦✦✦
There are dozens of Sonny Stitt records available at any particular time; this CD reissue is one of the better ones. Stitt (mostly sticking to tenor) battles fellow tenor Booker Ervin with assistance from the fine organist Don Patterson and drummer Billy James on five selections and a ballad medley from 1964. Because both Stitt and Ervin always had very individual sounds, their tradeoffs are quite exciting and end up a draw. Among the "bonus" cuts of this CD are a feature for Patterson with a trio in 1966 ("There Will Never Be Another You") and a collaboration between Stitt, Patterson, James and guitarist Grant Green on a 1966 version of "Tune Up." Easily enjoyable and generally hard-swinging music. —*Scott Yanow*

Sonny Stitt . . . Pow! / Sep. 10, 1965 / Prestige ✦✦✦✦
Altoist Sonny Stitt and trombonist Benny Green make for a potent team on this spirited quintet set. With the exception of the lone standard "I Want to Be Happy," all of the material is obscure. However, the two distinctive horns (along with pianist Kirk Lightsey, bassist Herman Wright and drummer Roy Brooks) have little difficulty essaying these bop pieces, blues and ballads and their personable styles match well together. This LP has been out of print for quite awhile, so grab it if you see it. —*Scott Yanow*

Stardust / Jul. 28, 1966–Jul. 30, 1966 / Roulette ✦✦
On this Roulette LP, Sonny Stitt became the first musician to record on the Varitone sax, an electrified saxophone that allowed him to play octaves and to manipulate his sound a bit. Unfortunately, the result was that Stitt (who used the instrument on and off for the next five years) lost much of his musical individuality when playing the generic sounding horn, and his fast doubletime runs could sound a bit silly and muddled. For this album, Stitt plays a dozen songs (mostly standards), is assisted by tenor saxophonist Illinois Jacquet on two pieces and welcomes a variety of accompanying musicians including trombonist J.J. Johnson, pianist Ellis Larkins and organist Ernie Hayes. But the net results (thanks to the Varitone) are no big deal. —*Scott Yanow*

Made for Each Other / Jul. 13, 1968 / Delmark ✦✦
Sonny Stitt's regular group of the period (which included organist Don Patterson and drummer Billy James) plays a wide variety of material on this LP, ranging from "The Very Thought of You" and two versions of "Funny" to "Blues for J.J." and some then-current pop tunes. Unfortunately, the set is from the period when Stitt often used a Varitone electronic attachment on his alto and tenor,

which gave him a much more generic sound, lowering the quality of this music despite some strong improvisations. It is an okay set that could have been better. —*Scott Yanow*

★ **Tune-Up!** / Feb. 8, 1972 / Muse ✦✦✦✦✦
Sonny Stitt recorded over 100 albums as a leader and several dozen in a quartet setting in his productive career, but this one ranks at the top. The bebop tenor and alto stylist is very inspired by the top-notch rhythm section (pianist Barry Harris, bassist Sam Jones and drummer Alan Dawson) and has rarely sounded more heated than on "Tune Up," "Idaho," "Just Friends" and "Groovin' High." However, it is his nine-minute jam on "I Got Rhythm" (which finds Stitt taking blazing solos on both tenor and alto) that is the highpoint of this essential set. —*Scott Yanow*

Goin' Down Slow / Feb. 15, 1972 / Prestige ✦✦✦✦
Sonny Stitt is in one of his prime periods during the early '70s and this LP finds him in particularly creative form. Best is the 14-minute "Miss Ann, Lisa, Sue and Sadie," which features Stitt, trumpeter Thad Jones, guitarist Billy Butler and pianist Hank Jones soloing over a small string section; Jones' arrangement is quite memorable. Although the other four selections are not quite at the same level, Stitt is in top form throughout this inventive date. —*Scott Yanow*

★ **Constellation** / Jun. 27, 1972 / Muse ✦✦✦✦✦
Along with the previous *Tune Up!*, this set (which has been reissued by Muse) is one of Sonny Stitt's greatest recordings. The bop master is stunning on most of the eight selections, particularly "Constellation," "Webb City" and "It's Magic," switching between alto and tenor and sounding quite creative. The rhythm section (pianist Barry Harris, bassist Sam Jones and drummer Roy Brooks) is outstanding, and whether it's the ballad "Ghost of a Chance," Tadd Dameron's "Casbah" or "Topsy," this set has more than its share of great moments. —*Scott Yanow*

So Doggone Good / Sep. 13, 1972 / Prestige ✦✦✦
Despite its bragging title, this LP is decent but not essential. Sonny Stitt, who during the same period was recording classics for Cobblestone/Muse, is in above-average form for this set although the material (four fairly basic originals and two ballads) is not quite up to par. Stitt (switching between alto and tenor) is ably accompanied by pianist Hampton Hawes, bassist Reggie Johnson and drummer Lenny McBrowne) and the jam session-style music is reasonably enjoyable although recommended primarily for his greatest fans. —*Scott Yanow*

Sonny Stitt/12! / Dec. 12, 1972 / Muse ✦✦✦✦✦
Sonny Stitt was in prime form in the early '70s when he recorded two classics: *Tune Up!* and *Constellation. 12!* from a year later tends to get overlooked, but this LP is also one of the saxophonist's most rewarding recordings. Assisted by pianist Barry Harris, bassist Sam Jones and drummer Louis Hayes, Stitt (switching between alto and tenor) is in superb form on five standards and two blues; highlights include "I Got It Bad," "Every Tub" and "Our Delight." This LP is worth searching for. —*Scott Yanow*

The Champ / Apr. 18, 1973 / Muse ✦✦✦
Sonny Stitt was in great form in the early '70s and the rhythm section on this release (which has been reissued on CD) is excellent: pianist Duke Jordan, bassist Sam Jones and drummer Roy Brooks. The problem is that trumpeter Joe Newman is not quite up to par and Stitt constantly cuts his own solos short to make room for Newman. While there are some good spots for Stitt's tenor and alto, his truncated improvisations are ultimately frustrating, especially compared to his classic recordings from the era. Get *Tune Up* instead. —*Scott Yanow*

Dumpy Mama / 1975 / Flying Dutchman ✦✦✦
Although Sonny Stitt (sticking to tenor except on "It Might as Well Be Spring" where he plays alto) teams up with a variety of musicians on this LP who he had rarely played with previously (including tenor saxophonist Pee Wee Ellis, altoist Frank Strozier, pianist Mike Wofford, bassist Brian Torff and drummer Shelly Manne), he plays in his usual bebop style. In addition to his alto feature there is a duet with Wofford on a sensitive "Danny Boy for Ben," the funky title cut (penned by Oliver Nelson) and boppish renditions of "Just Friends" and Stitt's original, "Jason." The playing is up to par if not overly memorable; this LP's music has yet to be reissued on CD. —*Scott Yanow*

Mellow / Feb. 14, 1975 / Muse ✦✦✦
Jimmy Heath (switching between tenor, soprano and flute) holds his own with Sonny Stitt (who as usual double on tenor and alto)

for this quintet set with pianist Barry Harris, bassist Richard Davis and drummer Roy Haynes. Stitt sounds fairly relaxed throughout, Heath is a strong and contrasting foil and the repertoire (five mostly underplayed standards plus Stitt's "A Cute One") is fairly fresh. A good session of 1970s bop. —*Scott Yanow*

In Walked Sonny / May 16, 1975 / Sonet ✦✦✦✦✦
Stitt joined Art Blakey's Jazz Messengers for this hardswinging LP, and he fits quite comfortably with the quintet (which includes the leader/drummer, trumpeter Bill Hardman, Dave Schnitter on tenor, pianist Walter Davis, Jr., and bassist Chin Suzuki). In addition to the title cut (a Sonny Stitt original), Stitt is in top form on "Blues March," "It Might as Well Be Spring," Freddie Hubbard's "Birdlike" and "I Can't Get Started"; he sits out on Davis' "Ronnie's a Dynamite Lady." The members of The Messengers sound inspired by Stitt's presence and everyone is in fine form on this excellent hard bop session. —*Scott Yanow*

My Buddy: Stitt Plays for Gene Ammons / Jul. 2, 1975 / Muse ✦✦✦✦
Upon the death of his close friend, fellow tenor Gene Ammons, Sonny Stitt recorded this fine tribute album. In addition to an emotional version of the title cut and an original blues, Stitt (mostly on tenor) performs four songs that Ammons used to play including "Red Top" and "Exactly like You." With fine assistance from pianist Barry Harris, bassist Sam Jones and drummer Leroy Williams, this is a high-quality bop set. —*Scott Yanow*

Forecast: Sonny & Red / Nov. 1975 / Catalyst ✦✦✦✦✦
Sonny Stitt and Red Holloway make a perfect team on this exciting jam session record, which has not yet been reissued on CD. Stitt sticks here to tenor while Holloway alternates between tenor and alto. With fine backup by pianist Art Hillary, bassist Larry Gales and drummer Clarence Johnston, Sonny and Red share a ballad medley and battle it out on the title cut, "The Way You Look Tonight," "Lester Leaps In," "Just Friends" and "All God's Chillun Got Rhythm." Holloway was able to keep up with the combative Stitt and the fireworks are well worth savoring. —*Scott Yanow*

Blues for Duke / Dec. 3, 1975–Dec. 4, 1975 / Muse ✦✦✦
Sonny Stitt (on tenor exclusively except for an alto feature on "I Got It Bad") pays tribute to the recently departed Duke Ellington with renditions of five songs associated with Ellington plus Stitt's title cut. The rhythm section (pianist Barry Harris, bassist Sam Jones and drummer Billy Higgins) is excellent, and although the results are somewhat predictable (with "C Jam Blues" and "Perdido" being the highpoints), the music on this LP can be easily enjoyed by bop fans. —*Scott Yanow*

Stomp Off Let's Go / 1976 / Flying Dutchman ✦✦✦
It would have been intriguing to hear bop altoist and tenor saxophonist Sonny Stitt play the title cut (an obscurity from the 1920s whose use as the album's name is actually irrelevant), but instead he performs the "Theme from *Black Orpheus*," "Duke's Place," "Perdido" and "Little Suede Shoes." Actually the most interesting aspect to this date (which also utilizes Frank Owens on keyboards, guitarist Bucky Pizzarelli, Richard Davis on electric bass, drummer Louie Bellson and percussionist Leopoldo Fleming) is that the two high-note trumpeters Jon Faddis and Lew Soloff are also in the frontline and have a fair amount of solo space. Otherwise this is an average although enjoyable Sonny Stitt bop date. —*Scott Yanow*

I Remember Bird / 1977 / Catalyst ✦✦✦✦
The title refers to the Leonard Feather composition rather than a complete set of Charlie Parker songs. Sonny Stitt, who spent his entire career playing in a style built on Bird's, is in good form during this quintet date which features him on both alto and tenor. With trombonist Frank Rosolino, pianist Dolo Coker, bassist Allen Jackson and drummer Clarence Johnston, Stitt stretches out on the title tune, his own blues "Streamlined Stanley," three standards, Rosolino's "Waltz for Diane" and the traditional hymn "Yes Jesus Loves Me." This good bop date is long out of print. —*Scott Yanow*

Sonny Stitt with Strings / 1977 / Catalyst ✦✦✦
Sonny Stitt (on alto and tenor) is joined by a fine rhythm section featuring pianist Gildo Mahones and an eight-piece string section arranged by Bill Finegan for seven familiar Duke Ellington songs. No real surprises occur although the string charts are a cut above the usual. Stitt is at his most melodic and really romps on a few of these pieces, most notably "Cottontail." —*Scott Yanow*

Moonlight in Vermont / Nov. 23, 1977 / Denon ✦✦✦
Sonny Stitt, doubling on alto and tenor, is in fine form on this quartet session (a Japanese import CD) with either Barry Harris or Walter Davis on piano, bassist Reggie Workman and drummer Tony Williams. The repertoire (bop standards, blues and ballads) is fairly typical and nothing too unusual occurs, but fans of straight-ahead jazz in general and Sonny Stitt in particular will be satisfied with this above-average effort, highlighted by "It Might as Well Be Spring" and "Constellation." —*Scott Yanow*

Sonny Stitt Meets Sadik Hakim / Apr. 25, 1978 / Progressive ✦✦✦
Sadik Hakim (whose original name was Argonne Thornton) played with a few notable names from the bop era (including Charlie Parker) but has long been a somewhat obscure pianist. His "meeting" with Sonny Stitt (who splits his time here evenly between alto and tenor) on this Progressive CD is about as high a profile as he ever had. With bassist Buster Williams and drummer J.R. Mitchell completing the quartet, Stitt is in his usual fine form on five veteran standards, a pair of blues-based originals and Stevie Wonder's "You Are the Sunshine of My Life." The music is not essential but has its heated moments; recommended for bop fans. —*Scott Yanow*

Sonny's Back / Apr. 7, 1980+Jul. 14, 1980 / Muse ✦✦✦✦
Sonny Stitt (sticking to tenor on all but one alto feature) uses one of his favorite rhythm sections on this Muse LP (pianist Barry Harris, bassist George Duvivier and drummer Leroy Williams) and for three of the seven selections he welcomes the much younger tenor Ricky Ford; their tradeoffs are quite interesting and end up being a dead heat. Stitt is in fine form throughout this excellent set, which consists of four standards, two Stitt originals and a remake of Charlie Parker's "Constellation." —*Scott Yanow*

In Style / Mar. 18, 1981 / Muse ✦✦✦
Sonny Stitt (heard on both alto and tenor) is in excellent form for this LP, yet another quartet session; he led over 100 sessions through the years. With pianist Barry Harris, bassist George Duvivier and drummer Jimmy Cobb inspiring him, Stitt is creative within the boundaries of bebop on such songs as "Just You, Just Me," "Is You Is or Is You Ain't My Baby," "Yesterdays" and a pair of his basic originals, which he titled "Western Style" and "Eastern Style." —*Scott Yanow*

The Bubba's Sessions With Eddie "Lockjaw" Davis & Harry "Sweets" Edison / Nov. 11, 1981 / Who's Who ✦✦✦✦
The second of two Who's Who LPs recorded during a club appearance by Sonny Stitt (who doubles here on alto and tenor) has guest appearances by tenor saxophonist Eddie "Lockjaw" Davis and trumpeter Harry "Sweets" Edison in addition to fine backup work from pianist Eddie Higgins, bassist Donn Mast and drummer Duffy Jackson. This may look like a budget album, but the playing (particularly by Stitt) on the blues, standards and ballads is top notch. Until the music is reissued on CD, this LP and the complementary set *Sonny, Sweets & Jaws* are collector's items. —*Scott Yanow*

Battle Of The Saxes / Dec. 1981 / AIM ✦✦✦
This Australian import is a real rarity for it teams together Sonny Stitt (mostly playing tenor) and altoist Richie Cole (along with pianist Jack Wilson, bassist Ed Gaston and drummer Allan Turnbull) for the first and only time. Stitt and Cole inspire each other on the seven boppish selections, and even if little surprising occurs, the heated exchanges make this CD worth searching for. —*Scott Yanow*

Last Stitt Sessions, Vols. 1 & 2 / Jun. 8, 1982–Jun. 9, 1982 / Muse ✦✦✦✦✦
It is difficult to believe after listening to this two-CD set, that Sonny Stitt only had six weeks left in his life; he already had cancer but did not know it. Switching between tenor and alto, Stitt on the first disc is heard in top form with pianist Junior Mance, bassist George Duvivier and drummer Jimmy Cobb while the second CD (recorded the following day) adds trumpeter Bill Hardman and has Walter Davis in Mance's place. As was typical of Stitt's career, the music throughout is high-quality bebop with the saxophonist stretching out creatively over common chord changes. This double CD (a straight reissue of two single LPs) shows that Sonny Stitt went out on top. —*Scott Yanow*

Billy Strayhorn

b. Nov. 29, 1915, Dayton, OH, **d.** May 31, 1967, NYC
Piano, Composer, Arranger / Swing
Billy Strayhorn made collaboration an art form; he combined

with Duke Ellington on more than 200 numbers in the orchestra's book, and enjoyed a creative empathy with him that has been alternately described as spooky, remarkable, and magic.

From the time he submitted a piece to Ellington in 1938 and was contacted three months later, until his death in 1967, Strayhorn fuctioned as co-leader, arranger, pianist, confidant and muse. Among his gems are "Take the "A" Train," "Lush Life," "Something To Live For," "Day Dream," "After All," "Passion Flower," "Lotus Blossom," "Johnny Come Lately," "U.M.M.G.," and "Blood Count." Strayhorn found time to write, arrange and participate in many extra-Ellington sessions with such sidemen as Cootie Williams, Barney Bigard, Johnny Hodges, Louie Bellson, The Coronets and Ellingtonians, Ben Webster and Clark Terry, plus duos and trios with Ellington and an occasional album of his own.

Strayhorn received extensive musical training, and the piece he submitted to Ellington surprised him in its depth and structure. The first Strayhorn number they cut was "Something To Live For," with Jean Eldridge"s vocal in 1939. They did more Strayhorn that year, including "I'm Checkin' Out," "Goo'm Bye," and "Grievin'," which were co-written with Ellington, "Lost In Two Flats" by Barney Bigard, and an Ellington tribute to Strayhorn "Weely (A Portrait of Billy Strayhorn)." He served briefly as pianist in Mercer Ellington's Orchestra before officially becoming Ellington's associate arranger and second pianist. Strayhorn helped with both ambitious pieces and pop material; these included "The Perfume Suite," "A Drum Is A Woman" and "Such Sweet Thunder." He directed the band for Ellington's '63 production "My People."

His final composition "Blood Count" was sent to the band from the hospital where he died of cancer. The Ellington orchestra cut one of its most poignant albums in tribute, *And His Mother Called Him Bill.* Ellington played "Lotus Blossom" solo at the end of the session while the musicians packed their gear. Other Strayhorn tributes have been recorded by several musicians, including Art Farmer and Marian McPartland. Joe Henderson won widespread acclaim for his '92 Strayhorn tribute album, and Strayhorn was a prominent influence on Tadd Dameron. —*Ron Wynn*

Live! / Dec. 28, 1958 / Roulette ✦✦✦✦
● **Cue for Saxophone** / Apr. 14, 1959 / London ✦✦✦✦✦
The Peaceful Side / May 1961 / United Artists ✦✦✦✦
Lush Life / Jan. 14, 1964–Aug. 14, 1965 / Red Baron ✦✦✦✦✦
A '92 reissue of a rare session issued under the name of noted arranger/composer Billy Strayhorn, providing the inspiration and material for a combo with Duke Ellington, trumpeters Cootie Williams and Cat Anderson, drummer Sam Woodyard, etc., and featuring his most famous composition. —*Ron Wynn*

Frank Strazzeri

b. Apr. 24, 1930, Rochester, NY
Piano / Hard Bop
A polished, disciplined and fluid pianist, Frank Strazzeri has been successful playing everything from traditional New Orleans to cool and bebop. Not an exciting soloist, nor dazzling stylist, he can provide unobtrusive accompaniment, plus good, if not great individual contributions. Strazzeri began on tenor and clarinet during the early '40s, and then switched to piano. He studied piano at the Eastman school. During the early '50s, Strazzieri worked with Roy Eldridge, J.J. Johnson and others serving as house pianist for a Rochester club. He eventually played in New Orleans with Sharkey Bonano and Al Hirt, and worked with Charlie Ventura and Woody Herman. Strazzieri moved to the West Coast in the '60s, and became a studio musician. He recorded for several labels and played with Herb Ellis and Carmell Jones among other others, while also touring with Joe Williams, Maynard Ferguson and Howard Rumsey's Lighthouse All-Stars. During the '70s, Strazzieri worked with Les Brown and Cal Tjader, then began heading his own combos. He recorded with Bellson and Tal Farlow in the '80s. Strazzieri has done sessions for Glendale, Fresh Sound, Sea Breeze, and Catalyst. He currently has some sessions available on CD. —*Ron Wynn*

● **Relaxin'** / Jul. 28, 1980 / Sea Breeze ✦✦✦✦✦
The title conveys the album's mood and pace. Pianist Frank Strazzeri breezes through these songs, sometimes playing some engaging solos but mostly just gliding along. He offers a few nice melodies, and from time to time makes an interesting progression

or tempo shift, but it's mainly just well-mannered, technically competent mainstream piano. —*Ron Wynn*
Kat Dancin' / Apr. 2, 1985 / Discovery ✦✦✦
I Remember You / Jan. 31, 1989 / Fresh Sound ✦✦
Little Giant / Nov. 1989 / Fresh Sound ✦✦
The Very Thought of You / 1990 / Discovery ✦✦✦
Frank's Blues / 1992 / Night Life ✦✦✦✦
A '92 release with pianist Frank Strazzeri playing his own and other composers' blues pieces, doing them nicely, with a modicum of passion and energy. He's assisted by a quintet of mostly faceless players, flute and saxophonist Sam Most excepted. —*Ron Wynn*
Somebody Loves Me / Feb. 15, 1994–Feb. 16, 1994 / Fresh Sound ✦✦✦✦✦

String Trio of New York

Group / Avant-Garde, Post-Bop
Billy Bang, James Emery and John Lindberg were the original members of The String Trio Of New York; they were a violinist, guitarist and bassist. They made complementary music and worked as a tight-knit, yet also free-wheeling trio playing music that maximized intra-group harmony but also spotlighted each player's own unusual style. The group began recording in 1979; Bang departed in the late '80s, and was replaced by Charles Burnham. Things changed again in '93, when Regina Carter recorded with holdovers Emery and John Lindberg. They've done sessions for Black Saint, Stash and Arabesque. The String Trio has some sessions available on CD. —*Ron Wynn*

First String / Jun. 1979 / Black Saint ✦✦✦
Area Code 212 / Nov. 25, 1980–Nov. 26, 1980 / Black Saint ✦✦✦✦✦
Common Goal / Nov. 12, 1981–Nov. 13, 1981 / Black Saint ✦✦✦✦
Rebirth of a Feeling / Nov. 25, 1983–Nov. 26, 1983 / Black Saint ✦✦✦✦✦
The String Trio of New York's strongest lineup was arguably the edition that included violinist Billy Bang, guitarist James Emery and bassist John Lindberg. That unit was at its best here; the threesome played adventurous unison lines and offered wide-ranging solos. The best example of their interactive/reactive mode was the 14-minute "Utility Grey," with its array of textures, colors, moods and voicings. Emery wrote two selections, Bang a pair, and Lindberg the finale, but this was a unified effort. The String Trio of New York ranks as a premier outside group of the 1970s and '80s. —*Ron Wynn*
● **Natural Balance** / 1986 / Black Saint ✦✦✦✦✦
As Tears Go By / Dec. 1987 / ITM ✦✦
Time Never Lies / Jun. 24, 1990–Jun. 25, 1990 / Vintage Jazz ✦✦✦✦
Ascendant / Oct. 1991 / Stash ✦✦✦✦
★ **Intermobility** / Jul. 1, 1992–Jul. 2, 1992 / Arabesque ✦✦✦✦✦
Octagon / Nov. 5, 1992–Nov. 6, 1992 / Black Saint ✦✦✦✦

Frank Strozier

b. Jun. 13, 1937, Memphis, TN
Alto Saxophone / Hard Bop
An adventurous alto saxophonist, Frank Strozier became a prominent hard bop player in the late '50s and '60s. He displayed some of the same biting, animated tendencies as fellow altoists James Spaulding and Jackie McLean, with a furious intensity on uptempo tunes and poignant quality on ballads. His style built from the classic Charlie Parker foundation, with some blues elements. Strozier studied piano during his younger days in Memphis, then moved to Chicago in 1954, where he played with fellow transplanted Memphians Harold Mabern, George Coleman and Booker Little. He worked in the group MJT + 3 with Walker Perkins in 1959 and 1960, moving to New York in 1959. Strozier recorded for Vee-Jay in the early '60s, and later played briefly with Miles Davis alongside Mabern And Coleman. He also worked in Roy Haynes' group.

He spent six years in Los Angeles, where his associates included Chet Baker, Shelly Manne and Don Ellis. Strozier returned to New York in the early '70s, joining Keno Duke's Jazz Contemporaries. This group recorded for Strata-East, a black-owned musicians co-operative. Strozier also played in The New York Jazz Repertory Company, and recorded his own albums in the late '70s for mostly independent and/or import labels such as

SteepleChase. He also worked with Horace Parlan. At present, Strozier has no current or vintage titles listed in the Schwann catalog, though two of his early '60s Vee-Jay dates were reissued on CD in 1993. —*Ron Wynn*

● **Fantastic Frank Strozier Plus** / Dec. 9, 1959–Feb. 2, 1960 / Vee-Jay ✦✦✦✦✦
Altoist Frank Strozier's first session as a leader has been reissued on this Vee Jay CD with the original six selections joined by five additional and previously unreleased performances, only one of which is actually an alternate take. The altoist's quintet consists of Miles Davis' rhythm section of the time (pianist Wynton Kelly, bassist Paul Chambers and drummer Jimmy Cobb) along with the late great trumpeter Booker Little. The music, mostly comprised of Strozier originals, is advanced hard bop and the music is both enjoyable and (due to Little's presence) somewhat historic. —*Scott Yanow*

Cool, Calm and Collected / Oct. 13, 1960 / Vee-Jay ✦✦✦✦
This advanced hard bop session from 1960 was previously unreleased until it appeared on a Vee-Jay CD in 1994. Altoist Frank Strozier is heard with a Chicago-based trio comprised of pianist Billy Wallace, bassist Bill Lee and drummer Vernel Fournier. The CD really gives listeners two records in one because of the seven songs, all but one are heard in two versions and two of the pieces are heard three times. Strozier is in fine form, the obscure Billy Wallace (mistakenly called Wallace Williams in the liner notes) plays some fiery solos and the performances are satisfying. Still, due to the duplicate titles, one might not want to consume the whole program in one sitting. —*Scott Yanow*

March of the Siamese Children / Mar. 28, 1962 / Jazzland ✦✦✦✦✦
This outstanding session was recorded with Harold Mabern (p). —*David Szatmary*

Remember Me / Nov. 10, 1976 / SteepleChase ✦✦✦✦
What's Goin' Out / Nov. 5, 1977 / SteepleChase ✦✦✦

John Stubblefield

b. Feb. 4, 1945, Little Rock, AR
Tenor Saxophone / Post-Bop
Not as heralded as some fellow members of the Association for the Advancement of Creative Musicians (AACM), John Stubblefield's nonetheless made some excellent hard bop, bebop and free sessions. He's also an in-demand teacher, having lectured, led seminars, and organized workshops at many universities and colleges, plus worked with The Jazzmobile. Stubblefield joined the AACM after moving to Chicago from Arkansas. He studied with Muhal Richard Abrams and George Coleman, then recorded with Joseph Jarman in 1968.
Stubblefield moved to New York in 1971, and played with the Collective Black Artists big band and Mary Lou Williams. He was also in groups led by Charles Mingus, the Thad Jones-Mel Lewis orchestra and Tito Puente's orchestra. Stubblefield switched gears in 1972, playing a free jazz concert at Town Hall with Anthony Braxton, and was featured with him on an album of the same name. He recorded with Abdullah Ibrahim and worked with Miles Davis in 1973. Stubblefield recorded with McCoy Tyner, Gil Evans, Lester Bowie, Nat Adderley, and Sonny Phillips in the '70s, and Kenny Barron and Teo Macero in the '80s, as well as recording as a leader in the '70s and '80s. Stubblefield's done sessions for Soul Note and Enja among others. He has some dates available on CD. —*Scott Yanow*

Prelude / Dec. 8, 1976–Dec. 9, 1976 / Storyville ✦✦✦✦
Tenor saxophonist John Stubblefield (who switches to soprano for one selection) explores six group originals with trumpeter Cecil Bridgewater, pianist Onaje Allen Gumbs, bassist Cecil McBee, drummer Joe Chambers and percussionist Mtume. For his debut as a leader, Stubblefield and the other musicians play what could be called free-bop, a style falling between the modern mainstream and the avant-garde, with fine results. Little unpredictable occurs but this is a good effort. —*Scott Yanow*

Confessin' / Sep. 18, 1984–Sep. 21, 1984 / Soul Note ✦✦✦✦
● **Bushman Song** / Apr. 22, 1986–Apr. 23, 1986 / Enja ✦✦✦✦✦
Countin' on the Blues / May 27, 1987–May 28, 1987 / Enja ✦✦✦

L. Subramaniam (Lakshiminarayana Subramaniam)

b. Jul. 23, 1947, Madras, India
Violin / World Fusion
An excellent violinist in traditional Asian, jazz or jazz-rock/fusion

circles, L. Subramaniam has been mixing the improvisational concepts of America and India since the '70s. He learned violin and played classical concerts as a child. Subramaniam studied medicine, then came to America to pursue a graduate degree in Western music, which he earned from The California Institute for the Arts. He toured America and Europe with George Harrison and Ravi Shanker in the mid-'70s, then composed for and recorded with Stu Goldberg and also Larry Coryell in 1978, making his recording debut as a leader that same year. Subramaniam was later part of John Handy's group Rainbow with Ali Akbar Khan in the late '70s. During the '80s, he led a group with Coryell, George Duke and Tom Scott, then co-led another band with Stephane Grappelli. Subramaniam's recorded for Milestone in the '80s, and has some sessions available on CD. —*Ron Wynn*

Garland / Apr. 1978 / Storyville ✦✦
Fantasy without Limits / Sep. 26, 1979–Sep. 27, 1979 / Trend ✦✦✦✦
Nice East vs. West concept featuring the great Indian violinist L. Subramaniam with the great bop alto saxophonist Frank Morgan. They have an effective team, and the two sensibilities converge for an interesting, but sometimes uneven dialogue. —*Ron Wynn*

● **Spanish Wave** / 1983 / Milestone ✦✦✦✦✦
The earliest and most satisfying of his classical/jazz fusion albums for Milestone, it features top jazz and Indian musicians mixing it up. —*Myles Boisen*

Conversations / 1984 / Milestone ✦✦✦✦
Recorded with Stephane Grappelli, Subramiam meets the French violin master for a program of jazz, classical, and fusion fun. Grappelli plays a rare piano solo too! —*Myles Boisen*

Indian Express / 1984 / Milestone ✦✦✦
Mani and Co. / 1986 / Milestone ✦✦✦✦
Recorded with Tony Williams (d), Bud Shank (sax), Larry Coryell (g), it features more fusion of jazz and Indian currents. —*Myles Boisen*

Dick Sudhalter

b. Dec. 28, 1938, Boston, MA
Cornet / Swing, Classic Jazz
Dick Sudhalter has had an unusual dual career as a superior trad-oriented cornetist and as a jazz journalist. The crowning achievement of his latter career was the co authorship with Philip Evans and William Dean-Myatt) of the superb Bix Beiderbecke biography *Bix–Man and Legend*. Less known is that Sudhalter has long been a fine improviser himself. He grew up in Boston and played in England during the 1960s (organizing the New Paul Whiteman Orchestra). Since returning to the U.S. Sudhalter has freelanced on the classic jazz scene, played with the New York Jazz Repertory Company and the Classic Jazz Quartet and recorded for several labels including Audiophile and Challenge. —*Scott Yanow*

● **After Awhile** / May 30, 1994–Jun. 7, 1994 / Jazz Challenge ✦✦✦✦✦
Dick Sudhalter, best known as one of the three writers responsible for one of the great jazz biographies (*Bix—Man and Legend*), is also a fine trumpeter who has the influence of Bix Beiderbecke fairly well-buried in his own lyrical style. Sudhalter had lived in England during the 1965-75 period, making this get-together (subtitled "& His London Friends") a musical reunion. Sudhalter and 13 other musicians are heard together in different combinations caressing a set of high-quality swing standards. With Keith Nichols (doubling on piano and trombone), altoist John R.T. Davies and trombonists Roy Williams and Jim Shepherd emerging as the top soloists in the supporting cast, Sudhlater sounds quite inspired. Whether it be "Dream a Little Dream of Me," "Tea for Two," "The Blue Room" or "Rose of Washington Square," this is a delightful and very melodic set. —*Scott Yanow*

Idrees Sulieman

b. Aug. 7, 1923, St. Petersburg, FL
Trombone, Fluegelhorn / Bop
Idress Sulieman was among the earliest trumpeters to fully embrace bebop, and has played it with passion and fire since the '40s. He's not better known due to his leaving America for Sweden in the early '60s. Sulieman played with The Carolina Cotton Pickers in the early and mid-'40s before joining Thelonious Monk in 1947. He worked with Cab Calloway in 1948,

then played with Count Basie, Lionel Hampton and Dizzy Gillespie. Sulieman was in Friedrich Gulda's ensemble of American players in the mid-'50s, then worked with Randy Weston in 1958 and 1959. He toured Europe with a group led by Oscar Dennard, then settled in Stockholm in 1961. He also began playing alto sax. Sulieman was a principal soloist with The Kenny Clarke–Francy Boland big band from the mid-'60s until 1973. He moved to Copenhagen in 1964, and has since played mainly in Denmark, working with The Radioens Big Band since the early '70s. He recorded as a leader for SteepleChase in the mid-'70s, and as a sideman with Monk, Mal Waldron, the Radioens Big Band and Horace Parlan among others. —*Ron Wynn*

Bird's Grass / Dec. 10, 1976 / SteepleChase ✦✦✦✦✦
● Groovin' / Aug. 2, 1985 / SteepleChase ✦✦✦✦✦

Ira Sullivan

b. May 1, 1931, Washington, DC
Flute, Tenor Sax, Trumpet, Alto Saxophone, Soprano Saxophone / Bop, Post-Bop
Ira Sullivan, who is equally skilled on trumpet and a variety of reeds, is one of the great talents in jazz. But due to his desire to be away from the spotlight, his contributions have often been overlooked. His father taught him the trumpet and his mother the saxophone. Sullivan was a key part of the Chicago jazz scene of the 1950s, jamming with visiting all-stars and in 1956 spending some time with Art Blakey's Jazz Messengers. He settled in Florida in the early '60s, and although he has been active locally, he only emerges on the national jazz scene on an irregular basis. His most notable association during the past 20 years was with Red Rodney in a brilliant (and fortunately well-recorded) quintet that also included pianist Garry Dial. Sullivan has retained an open-minded approach to music and has never been afraid to try new things. Virtually all of his recordings offer some surprises. —*Scott Yanow*

Nicky's Tune / Dec. 24, 1958 / Delmark ✦✦✦✦
Some stirring solos by trumpeter and saxophonist Ira Sullivan makes this late '50s session delightful. There's also excellent piano from the sadly neglected pianist Jodie Christian. Sullivan at this juncture was playing with flair and conviction. —*Ron Wynn*

Ira Sullivan Quintet: Blue Stroll / Jul. 26, 1959 / Delmark ✦✦✦✦✦
In Chicago with Johnny Griffin (sax) and Jodie Christian (p). Excellent. —*Michael G. Nastos*

Bird Lives! / Mar. 12, 1962 / Vee-Jay ✦✦✦✦
Ira Sullivan's quintet played at a Charlie Parker Memorial concert in Chicago on Mar. 12, 1962 and the results (six selections) were originally released on a single LP. The release of this double CD greatly expanded the program. The multi-instrumentalist Ira Sullivan sticks to trumpet and fluegelhorn throughout, the legendary tenor Nicky Hill (who made very few recordings) has a rare chance to stretch out on record (combining touches of Coltrane and Booker Ervin with a full tone of his own) and it is interesting to hear some hints of the then-current free jazz movement (particularly in the playing of bassist Don Garrett). Overall, a fine bop set. —*Scott Yanow*

Horizons / Mar. 2, 1967 / Discovery ✦✦✦
The third session as a leader for trumpeter and saxophonist Ira Sullivan. This '67 date had him doing mostly originals and leading a lineup that included trombonist and baritone horn player Lou Norman, pianist and electric harpist Dolphe Castellano, bassist William Fry, and drummer Jose Cigno. Sullivan had picked up the soprano sax in addition to tenor and trumpet, and plays all three with determination and fire. —*Ron Wynn*

Ira Sullivan / Dec. 9, 1975–Mar. 9, 1976 / A&M ✦✦✦
Ira Sullivan has long been a remarkable multi-instrumentalist with a personal sound on each of his horns. On this A&M release, Sullivan mostly sticks to soprano and flute although he plays trumpet briefly on "Old Hundredth" and stretches out on tenor during a lengthy medley of his "Slighty Arched" and the standard "Spring Can Really Hang You Up the Most." His supporting cast includes the talented guitarist Joe Diorio and on one selection an unknown bassist named Jaco (here misspelled Joco) Pastorious. The generally thoughtful music is not as exciting as some of Sullivan's other sessions (particularly the later ones with Red Rodney) but has its strong moments. —*Scott Yanow*

Multimedia / Dec. 5, 1977–Sep. 21, 1978 / Galaxy ✦✦✦✦
Ira Sullivan / Dec. 11, 1977–Dec. 20, 1977 / Flying Fish ✦✦✦✦
Peace / Sep. 20, 1978+Sep. 21, 1978 / Galaxy ✦✦✦✦
● The Incredible / Jun. 1980 / Stash ✦✦✦✦✦
Multi-instrumentalist Ira Sullivan puts on an impressive display of technique as he plays several saxes, plus trumpet and flutes. His facility, solos, and spirit are what make this album interesting. —*Ron Wynn*

Ira Sullivan Does It All / Sep. 14, 1981 / Muse ✦✦✦✦
Some frenetic exchanges, ensemble interaction, and solo work by trumpeter/saxophonist Ira Sullivan heading a combo on this '81 release. He's matched almost note for note by trumpeter Red Rodney, a frequent collaborator. The songs are mostly uptempo, with an occasional ballad or standard. —*Ron Wynn*

Strings Attached / Jan. 1982–Mar. 1983 / PA/USA ✦✦✦
A rare date with trumpeter and saxophonist Ira Sullivan backed by strings. His bop roots come forth on these solos, with Sullivan careful not to compete with the arrangements, but also strong enough to prevent them from overwhelming him. —*Ron Wynn*

Joe Sullivan

b. Nov. 4, 1906, Chicago, IL, d. Oct. 13, 1971, San Francisco, CA
Piano / Dixieland, Swing
One of the great Earl Hines disciples (along with Jess Stacy), Joe Sullivan's style was perfect for the freewheeling jazz of Eddie Condon's bands. Sullivan graduated from the Chicago Conservatory and was an important contributor to the Chicago jazz scene of the 1920s. He was in New York during the next decade and his solo recordings include an original ("Little Rock Getaway") that would become a standard. In 1936 Sullivan joined Bob Crosby's band, but tuberculosis put him in the hospital for ten months and Bob Zurke replaced him (having a hit with "Little Rock Getaway!"). However, Sullivan recovered, led his own record dates and was involved in a lot of jam sessions with the Condon gang in the 1940s. By the 1950s he was largely forgotten, playing solo in San Francisco and drinking much more than he should. Despite an occasional recording and a successful appearance at the Teagarden family reunion at the 1963 Monterey Jazz Festival, Sullivan's prime years were long gone by the time he passed away. —*Scott Yanow*

★ Joe Sullivan 1933–1941 / Sep. 26, 1933–Mar. 28, 1941 / Classics ✦✦✦✦✦
All of pianist Joe Sullivan's early recordings as a leader are on this definitive CD. Sullivan is heard on a dozen solo performances from 1933, 1935 and 1941 (including the two earliest versions of his hit "Little Rock Getaway" along with memorable renditions of "My Little Pride and Joy" and "Honeysuckle Rose"), four selections with "the Three Deuces" (a trio with clarinetist Pee Wee Russell and drummer Zutty Singleton) and eight numbers with an octet featuring the underrated trumpeter Ed Anderson, trombonist Benny Morton, clarinetist Edmond Hall and vocals by Big Joe Turner (who manages to turn "I Can't Give You Anything but Love" into a blues) and Helen Ward. This French import is essential for fans of the great stride pianist. —*Scott Yanow*

New Solos by an Old Master / Aug. 1951 / Riverside ✦✦✦✦
Joe Sullivan / Apr. 29, 1963–Nov. 11, 1963 / Pumpkin ✦✦✦✦

Maxine Sullivan (Marietta Williams)

b. May 13, 1911, Homestead, PA, d. Apr. 7, 1987, New York, NY
Vocals / Swing, Standards
A great singer and engaging performer, Maxine Sullivan parlayed a subtle, yet undeniable sense of swing with distinctive phrasing and excellent interpretative qualities to become a fine jazz, standards and pre-rock pop vocalist. She enjoyed success in the swing era, then repeated that success several eras later. Sullivan sang in clubs in Pittsburgh and on radio broadcasts. Her vocals and Claude Thornhill's arrangment of "Loch Lomond" in 1937 resulted in her first hit. That was followed a series of folk novelty numbers like "Cockles And Mussells," and "If I Had A Rainbow Bow." But Sullivan at least landed a nationwide radio program with then husband John Kirby. "Flow Gently Sweet Rhythm" aired Sunday afternoons in 1940 and was the only coast-to-coast radio show featuring black performers on radio. Sullivan even did some acting, appearing on stage in "Swinging The Dream" and in the films "Goin' Places" and "St. Louis Blues."
She toured with Benny Carter in 1941, then retired in 1942. Sullivan returned in the mid-'40s. After tours of England in 1948

and 1954, and another stage appearance in the 1953 play "Take A Giant Step," Sullivan retired once more. She became a nurse but came back again in 1958, this time both singing and playing valve trombone and fluegelhorn. She appeared at several festivals, then did sessions with The World's Greatest Jazz Band, Earl Hines, Ike Isaacs, Bob Wilber and Dick Hyman. In the 1980s Sullivan recorded swing standards for Concord, often working with Scott Hamilton. By the time she passed away a month shy of her 76th birthday, this subtle yet always lightly swinging and classy singer had completed 50 years in jazz. —*Ron Wynn*

The Biggest Little Band in the Land / Oct. 10, 1940–Jan. 20, 1941 / Circle ◆◆◆◆

This CD contains music recorded for The Lang-Worth Transcriptions by the John Kirby Sextet plus singer Maxine Sullivan. Actually Sullivan is only on five of the 18 songs, singing in her typically light and straightforward manner. The other selections feature the unique sextet (trumpeter Charlie Shavers, clarinetist Buster Bailey, altoist Russell Procope, pianist Billy Kyle, bassist John Kirby and drummer O'Neil Spencer) performing a program heavy on adaptations of classical themes and novel melodies. Shavers in particular comes across well and the set should please Kirby's fans. —*Scott Yanow*

● **Tribute to Andy Razaf** / Aug. 30, 1956 / DCC ◆◆◆◆◆

Maxine Sullivan always had a cheerful and subtly swinging style. This formerly rare release (originally on the Period label) finds her interpreting a dozen numbers that have the lyrics of Andy Razaf including such classics as "Keeping out of Mischief Now," "Stompin' at the Savoy," "Honeysuckle Rose," "Memories of You" and "Ain't Misbehavin'." Joined by a sextet reminiscent of John Kirby's group of 15 years earlier (and featuring such Kirby alumni as trumpeter Charlie Shavers and clarinetist Buster Bailey), Sullivan is in top form on this delightful session. —*Scott Yanow*

Close As Pages in a Book / Jun. 11, 1969+Jun. 13, 1969 / Monmouth ◆◆◆◆◆

Sullivan Shakespeare, Hyman / Jun. 15, 1971–Jun. 22, 1971 / Monmouth ◆◆◆

Maxine / Oct. 12, 1975 / Audiophile ◆◆◆

Maxine Sullivan / Oct. 12, 1975 / Riff ◆◆◆◆

A solid date with Ted Easton's sextet. —*Michael G. Nastos*

With Ike Isaacs Trio / Feb. 10, 1978 / Audiophile ◆◆◆

Good Morning, Life! / Nov. 13, 1983–Nov. 14, 1983 / Audiophile ◆◆◆◆

Nice sessions with Loonis McGlohen quartet. —*Ron Wynn*

It Was Great Fun / 1983 / Audiophile ◆◆◆◆◆

Songs from the Cotton Club / Nov. 6, 1984 Nov. 7, 1984 / Mobile Fidelity ◆◆◆◆◆

Vocalist Maxine Sullivan sings the classic blues, jazz, and stomp tunes that were in vogue at the legendary Cotton Club in Harlem during the '20s, '30s, and '40s. Although well along in her career by this point ('84), she still had a hearty, animated voice and dynamic delivery and put enough punch in her versions to make these ancient tunes both authentic and contemporary. —*Ron Wynn*

Uptown / Jan. 1985 / Concord Jazz ◆◆◆◆◆

Good workout with Scott Hamilton (ts) Quintet. —*Ron Wynn*

★ **Sings the Music of Burton Lane** / May 15, 1985–Jun. 4, 1985 / Stash ◆◆◆◆◆

1986 release. Sullivan makes excellent tribute work. —*Ron Wynn*

Together / Jun. 1986–Jan. 1987 / Atlantic ◆◆◆

1987 release. Fine merger between Sullivan and Keith Ingram's (p) group. —*Ron Wynn*

Spring Isn't Everything / Jul. 26, 1986–Jul. 27, 1986 / Audiophile ◆◆

Swingin' Sweet / Sep. 1986 / Concord Jazz ◆◆◆◆◆

Successful meeting with Scott Hamilton (ts) Quintet. —*Ron Wynn*

Sun Ra (Herman "Sonny" Blount)

b. May 22, 1914, Birmingham, AL, d. May 30, 1993, Birmingham, AL

Piano, Keyboards, Leader / Avant-Garde, Free Jazz

Of all the jazz musicians, Sun Ra was probably the most controversial. He did not make it easy for people to take him seriously for he surrounded his adventurous music with costumes and mythology that both looked backwards toward ancient Egypt and

forwards into science fiction. In addition Ra documented his music in very erratic fashion on his Saturn label, generally not listing recording dates and giving inaccurate personnel information so one could not really tell how advanced some of his innovations were. It has taken a lot of time to sort it all out (although Robert Campbell's Sun Ra discography has done a miraculous job). In addition, while there were times when Sun Ra's aggregation performed brilliantly, on other occasions they were badly out of tune and showcasing absurd vocals. Near the end of his life, Ra was featuring plate twirlers and fire eaters in his colorful show as a sort of Ed Sullivan for the 1980s!

But despite all of the trappings, Sun Ra was a major innovator. Born Sonny Blount in Birmingham, AL (although he used to claim he was from another planet), Ra led his own band for the first time in 1934. He freelanced at a variety of jobs in the Midwest, working as a pianist/arranger with Fletcher Henderson in 1946–47. He appeared on some obscure records as early as 1948 but really got started around 1953. Leading a big band (which he called the Arkestra) in Chicago, Ra started off playing advanced bop but was early on open to the influences of other cultures and experimenting with primitive electric keyboards and playing free long before the avant-garde got established. After moving to New York in 1961, Ra performed some of his most advanced work. In 1970 he relocated his group to Philadelphia and in later years alternated free improvisations and mystical group chants with eccentric versions of swing tunes, sounding like a spaced out Fletcher Henderson Orchestra. Many of his most important sidemen were with him on and off for decades (most notably John Gilmore on tenor, altoist Marshall Allen and baritonist Pat Patrick). Ra, who recorded a pair of fine solo piano albums for JAI, has been well served by Evidence's extensive repackaging of many of his Saturn dates, which have at last been outfitted with correct dates and personnel details. Sun Ra's vast legacy remains both confusing and vast. —*Scott Yanow*

Sound Sun Pleasure / 1953–1960 / Evidence ◆◆◆◆◆

Sun Ra's kaleidoscope of sounds was just taking shape in the 1950s and early '60s when the 13 tracks comprising this CD were recorded. His Astro-Infinity Arkestra included several emerging musicians who would later become major stars, like baritone saxophonist Charles Davis, Bob Northern on fluegelhorn and James Spaulding, who is featured on various reeds. The great jazz violinist Stuff Smith is even along on "Deep Purple," providing a dazzling, bluesy solo right at home in the Ra mix. —*Ron Wynn*

Super-Sonic Jazz / 1956 / Evidence ◆◆◆

Sun Ra had only been heading his Arkestra for a couple of years when they recorded the 12 songs featured on this 1956 session. But while the arrangements, ensemble work, and solos are not as ambitious, expansive, or free-wheeling as they became on later outings, the groundwork was laid on such cuts as "India," "Sunology," and one of the first versions of "Blues At Midnight." Ra's band already had the essential swinging quality and first-class soloists, and he had gradually challenged them with compositions that did not rely on conventional hard bop riffs, chord changes, and structure but demanded a personalized approach and understanding of sound and rhythm far beyond standard thinking. You can hear in Ra's solos and those of John Gilmore, Pat Patrick, Charles Davis and others an emerging freedom and looseness, which would explode in the future. —*Ron Wynn*

Sun Song / Jul. 12, 1956 / Delmark ◆◆◆◆

We Travel the Spaceways / **Bad and Beautiful** / 1956–1960 / Evidence ◆◆◆◆◆

The opening numbers range from the humorous and futuristic bent of "Interplanetary Music" and "We Travel The Spaceways" to the more musically expansive "New Horizons" and "Space Loneliness." Trumpeter Phil Cochran and the superb horn section of Marshall Allen, John Gilmore and Pat Patrick sometimes remain in the maze and sometimes explode with short but peppery solos. The other songs mix bop and swing tunes with more experimental fare like "Ankh" and "Exotic Two," where Patrick, Gilmore, Ra and Allen soar while bassist Ronnie Boykins and drummer Tommy Hunter maintain the rhythmic center. —*Ron Wynn*

Angels & Demons at Play/The Nubians of Plutonia / 1956–1960 / Evidence ◆◆◆◆◆

Sun Ra ambles between vigorous hard bop, ambitious, adventurous free jazz, and African and Afro-Latin material on the 15 selections featured on this set of '50s and early '60s tracks. The first half was recorded in 1956 and 1960 and includes originals from Ronnie Boykins and Julian Priester, plus futuristic organ from Ra on "Music From the World Tomorrow" and hard-blowing solos from John Gilmore and Marshall Allen. The second half consists of rehearsal tapes from 1960 with The Arkestra steadily progressing and moving beyond conventional jazz modes into multiple rhythms, chants, and twisting, roaring arrangements spiced by vividly expressive solos. Plus, like every other disc in the series, it is superbly remastered. —*Ron Wynn*

Sound of Joy / Nov. 1, 1957 / Delmark ✦✦✦✦

Jazz in Silhouette / 1958 / Evidence ✦✦✦

Those who question Sun Ra's compositional mettle should listen closely to the eight cuts on this 1958 session. All are either Ra originals or numbers co-written with the late trumpeter Hobart Dotson. He blends a wealth of influences, from Afro-Latin, bop, and cool to swing, and the eight-member horn section flows as precisely as any more heralded big band and never fails to swing. Longtime Ra contributor John Gilmore offers several stunning tenor solos, while the severely underrated Dobson has some marvelous solos, as do baritone saxophonist Charles Davis and alto saxophonists/flutists James Spaulding and Marshall Allen, with Ra directing, conducting, and agitating on piano. —*Ron Wynn*

Planet Earth/Interstellar Low Ways / 1958–1960 / Evidence ✦✦✦✦✦

Sun Ra's arranging and compositional flair for large orchestra is displayed on the 14 selections culled from two albums originally issued in 1958 and 1960. The first half includes rumbling two-baritone sax duels by Pat Patrick and Charles Davis on "Two Tones" and "Reflections in Blue," plus a forceful tympani solo from Jim Herndon on "Reflections" and consistently energized tenor sax by John Gilmore and trumpet from Art Hoyle. The later selections feature a smaller scale but no less emphatic Arkestra with Patrick, Gilmore, and Marshall Allen holding court, as well as Ronnie Boykins' booming bass, sparkling, crackling trumpet licks by Phil Cohran, and Ra's piano accompaniment, solos, and percussive colorations on gong and chimes. —*Ron Wynn*

Holiday for Soul Dance / 1960 / Evidence ✦✦✦✦✦

Sun Ra never concerned himself with the issues of innovation vs. preservation that seem to be the rage in current jazz circles. Instead, his music was both futuristic and classic, embracing the past and anticipating the future. A prime example is this fine eight-track collection of pre-rock standards done in 1968 and 1969. Of course, Ra didn't simply cover these numbers in a reverential manner; instead, he and The Astro-Infinity Arkestra stomp, romp, twist, strut and cut through a collection ranging from "But Not For Me" to "Early Autumn" and "Body and Soul." —*Ron Wynn*

Fate in a Pleasant Mood/ When the Sun Comes Out / 1960–1963 / Evidence ✦✦✦✦✦

Sun Ra left Chicago for New York in the early '60s, and half the sessions on this disc were done at the Choreographers' Workshop in New York during 1962 and 1963. The first half were done in Chicago with Marshall Allen and John Gilmore in the solo forefront on alto sax, flute, tenor sax, and clarinet. Ra's teeming piano, Ronnie Boykins' fluid, throbbing bass lines, and Jon Hardy's drums were at the rhythmic core as the orchestra executed both short bursts and extensive dialogues. Ra turned even further outside on the second set; his space/futuristic concept was solidifying musically and his keyboard work growing more piercing and ethereal. —*Ron Wynn*

We Are in the Future / Oct. 10, 1961 / Savoy ✦✦✦✦

Cosmic Tones for Mental Therapy / Art Forms Of . . . / 1961 / Evidence ✦✦✦

There has always been some controversy revolving around Sun Ra, but few of his albums ever generated more discussion than *Cosmic Tones for Mental Therapy,* which covers half the 12 numbers on this two-LP, single-disc outing. Ra played "astro space organ," and the array of swirling tones, funky licks and smashing rhythms, aided and abetted by John Gilmore on bass clarinet, Marshall Allen on oboe, and arrangements that sometimes had multiple horns dueling in the upper register and other times pivoting off careening beats, outraged those in the jazz community who thought Eric Dolphy and John Coltrane had already taken things too far. —*Ron Wynn*

★ **Other Planes of There** / 1964 / Evidence ✦✦✦✦✦

Sun Ra's suites and long pieces rank among the most challenging and compelling in jazz history. He would mix and match horn soloists, incorporate extensive polyrhythmic barrages, accents, textures, and sounds and cleverly weave voices, chants, and vocal effects in and out of the mix. The disc's 22-minute title cut was among his finest extended compositions and seems even more astonishing since it was recorded in 1964. The Solar Arkestra keeps surging ahead through bop numbers, light swing, an almost pop piece, and then a return to another long, rewarding final piece. The Evidence Sun Ra collection offers with each release more proof that Ra belongs in the pantheon of master jazz composers alongside Ellington, Monk, and Mingus. —*Ron Wynn*

The Magic City / 1965 / Evidence ✦✦✦✦

It is safe to say that no city ever got the kind of tribute Sun Ra paid his Birmingham, Alabama hometown with this 1965 selection. The 27-minute title cut ambles, clashes, and slides toward completion as Ra's movements, segues, and sections alternate between blistering dialogues and emphatic solos, especially Marshall Allen playing piccolo with the same abandon and spiraling intensity as an alto sax, flute, or oboe. But Ra leads them right back through another intense outing, the nearly 11-minute "The Shadow World." After these two pieces, the band sounds more relaxed on the last two cuts. —*Ron Wynn*

The Heliocentric Worlds of Sun Ra, Vol. 1 / Apr. 20, 1965 / ESP ✦✦✦

The Heliocentric Worlds of Sun Ra, Vol. 2 / Nov. 16, 1965 / ESP ✦✦✦

Monorails and Satellites / 1966 / Evidence ✦✦✦✦

Although he did not record nearly as much solo piano as he should have, the results were memorable whenever Sun Ra did take the keyboard spotlight. That was certainly the case on this 1966 date, with Ra showing the complete range of his styles and influences. There are rumbling boogie progressions and angular bop harmonies, bluesy passages, free sections and even stride and Afro-Latin references. —*Ron Wynn*

Nothing Is / May 1966 / ESP ✦✦✦

● **Atlantis** / 1967 / Saturn ✦✦✦✦✦

Sun Ra was soaring far and wide on these late '60s sessions, most notably the 20-minute-plus title cut. This was one of his earliest dates on nothing but electric keyboards, and his manipulation of sounds, noise, whirling phrases, and rhythms was creative and innovative. The other shorter pieces move from somber, almost morose arrangements on *Mu* to the teaming beats of *Bimini* and the otherworldliness of both the Saturn and Impulse! versions of *Yucatan.* As usual, Ra's band meshes hard bop, bebop, cool, free, and swing elements, with John Gilmore, Marshall Allen, and company alternately wailing, colliding with, and complementing the master's dashing clavinet, synthesizer, and organ journeys. An essential and excellent set. —*Ron Wynn*

Outer Spaceways Incorporated / 1968 / Black Lion ✦✦✦✦

Out There a Minute / 1968 / Blast First ✦✦✦

Spotty sound, outrageous lyrics, inspired music. —*Ron Wynn*

My Brother the Wind, Vol. 2 / 1969 / Evidence ✦✦✦✦✦

Sun Ra's synthesizer, organ and electric keyboard playing were probably the most underrated elements of his arsenal. His piano and electronic keyboard journeys were often viewed as gimmicky, clowning or musically illiterate ramblings. Sadly, this ignorance was the prevailing view for much of his career. Now, in retrospect, Ra's playing is being celebrated. The remarkable phrases, rhythms, progressions, statements and solos he offers throughout this 11-cut late-'60s and early-'70s session are a tribute to his understanding of the Moog synthesizer's possiblities and options. —*Ron Wynn*

Space Is the Place / 1972 / Evidence ✦✦

Here is a genuine bonus—some previously unissued cuts. *Space Is the Place* is the soundtrack to a film that was made but never released, and the tunes are among his most ambitious, unorthodox, compelling compositions. Between June Tyson's declarative vocals, chants and dialogue and Ra's crashing, flailing and emphatic synthesizer and organ fills, and with such songs as "Blackman/Love In Outer Space," "It's After The End of the World" and "I Am the Brother of the Wind," this disc offers aggressive, energized, uncompromising material. —*Ron Wynn*

Live at Montreux / Jul. 1976 / Inner City ✦✦✦✦✦

A Quiet Place In The Universe / 1976 / Leo ✦✦✦

Solo Piano / May 20, 1977 / Improvising Artists ✦✦✦✦

St. Louis Blues / Jul. 3, 1977 / Improvising Artists ✦✦✦✦✦

Visions / Jul. 11, 1978 / SteepleChase ✦✦✦
Just a super duo date with Sun Ra on piano, Walt Dickerson on vibes. —*Ron Wynn*

The Other Side of the Sun / Nov. 1, 1978–Jan. 4, 1979 / Sweet Earth ✦✦✦

Sunrise in Different Dimensions / Feb. 24, 1980 / Hat Hut ✦✦✦

Night in East Berlin/My Brothers the Wind and the Sun / Jun. 28, 1986–1990 / Leo ✦✦

Hours After / Dec. 18, 1986–Dec. 19, 1986 / Black Saint ✦✦✦

Reflections in Blue / Dec. 18, 1986–Dec. 19, 1986 / Black Saint ✦✦✦✦

Blue Delight / Dec. 5, 1988 / A&M ✦✦✦✦
A fabulous '89 date by the legendary Sun Ra, one of the few that he made for a major label. The production and mastering gave the group sound a full, gorgeous quality, while the quirky Ra riffs and solos, coupled with the usual explosive and animated work from The Arkestra members, made this a delight. —*Ron Wynn*

Somewhere Else / Dec. 1988–Nov. 1989 / Rounder ✦✦✦✦
Both small-group and larger Arkestra sessions are included on this recent anthology of late-'80s Sun Ra material. The tune "Priest" includes slashing drum support from Billy Higgins and Buster Smith, twin bass interplay from John Ore and Jerib Shahid, Julian Priester's whiplash trombone and Ra's equally dynamic piano solos. Other numbers include appearances by Don Cherry on pocket trumpet, James Spaulding on alto sax and flute teaming with fellow alto stylist Marshall Allen and tenor saxophonist John Gilmore, plus the vocal cries, swoops and hollers of June Tyson and Ra's delightful piano and swirling synthesizer. These selections show that Ra hadn't exhausted his creative faculties by the late '80s. —*Ron Wynn*

Salute to Walt Disney / May 29, 1989 / Leo ✦✦
This is certainly a happy record. In 1989 avant-garde bandleader Sun Ra frequently played sets of music dominated by songs taken from Walt Disney movies. Since Ra did not believe in having any barriers between musical styles and in his later years he often paid tribute (in his own way) to the past, the unlikely concept somehow seemed logical. The music on this offbeat CD was documented by an audience member with a tape recorder so the balance is not always state-of-the-art although the results are quite listenable. Ra's "Intergalactic Arkestra" had a particularly unusual instrumentation during this European tour with three altoists (tenor great John Gilmore is absent), James Jackson doubling on bassoon and oboe, just one trumpet (the excellent Michael Ray), two trombones and a five piece rhythm section plus occasional vocals by June Tyson. Actually there are group vocals on several of the pieces, which include exuberant versions of "Zip a Dee Doo Dah," "High Ho! High Ho!" and "Whistle While You Work." Although Marshall Allen's alto is overly violent on "Someday My Prince Will Come" and there are some rambling moments (some of the vocals were obviously more fun live than on record) this performance generally holds one's interest. Ra has a few piano interludes and Noel Scott's alto flights are fairly boppish. It helps greatly to have an open mind toward the avant-garde (there are some messy ensembles and out-of-tune passages during the exuberant set) but, even if Walt Disney might not have fully approved (he would have preferred a Dixieland treatment), the crazy results are generally quite memorable. —*Scott Yanow*

Purple Night / Nov. 1989 / A&M ✦✦✦
Don Cherry, Julian Priester, Marshall Allen, James Spaulding, and John Gilmore help out on this recording. —*AMG*

Mayan Temples / Jul. 24, 1990–Jul. 25, 1990 / Black Saint ✦✦

Live at the Hackney Empire / Oct. 28, 1990 / Leo ✦✦

At the Village Vanguard / Nov. 1991 / Rounder ✦✦✦✦
Sun Ra often pulled small units out of the larger Arkestra, and that was the case on this 1991 concert recorded live at the Vanguard. He led a sextet with Chris Anderson on piano, John Gilmore's rugged, soaring tenor sax taking the featured soloist role, and bassist John Ore and Buster Smith completing the rhythm section. Bruce Edwards provided guitar fills and accompaniment, while Ra offered synthesizer coloration, textures and

Music Map

Synthesizer/Electric Keyboards

Pioneers
Duke Ellington (recorded on electric piano in 1955!)
Sun Ra
Gil Melle

Innovator
Joe Zawinul

Pacesetters of Fusion
Chick Corea
Herbie Hancock
Jan Hammer (with Mahavishnu Orchestra)

Avant-Garde
Richard Teitelbaum   Paul Bley
George Lewis   Wayne Horvitz
Pete Levin

Other Important Players
Patrick Gleeson (with Herbie Hancock's Sextet)
Lonnie Liston Smith
Lyle Mays
Russell Ferrante (with Yellowjackets)
John Surman
Django Bates
Mitchel Forman
Adam Holzman

Pianists Occasionally Playing Electric Keyboards
Bill Evans   Cedar Walton
Kenny Barron   Oscar Peterson
Gil Evans   Joe Sample
Dave Grusin   Clare Fischer

Crossover
George Duke
Patrice Rushen
Jeff Lorber
Bob James

swirling support. Ra's lines seem to flag a bit on the opening cut, "Round Midnight," but he's worked out the kinks by the second number, "Sun Ra Blues," and for the remainder of the session adds looping countermelodies and phrases to Anderson's themes and statements. —*Ron Wynn*

Destination Unknown / Mar. 29, 1992 / Enja ✦✦✦

Tribute to Stuff Smith / Sep. 1992 / Soul Note ✦✦✦✦
Forty years before recording this very interesting CD, keyboardist Sun Ra made his debut on records on a duet with violinist Stuff

Smith, playing a haunting version of "Deep Purple." For this CD (one of Ra's final sessions) the quartet workout with violinist Billy Bang finds Ra doing a new version of "Deep Purple" and performing a variety of tunes associated with Smith. Actually Ra was a bit hemmed in by the concept and his conception of time was different than Bang's so there is a certain amount of tension in the music. Also, Billy Bang has a much rougher sound (and a freer style) than Stuff Smith, but the end results are well worth hearing. —*Scott Yanow*

Supersax

Group / Bop
In 1972 Med Flory and Buddy Clark formed a five-sax nonet (usually including a trumpeter) dedicated to playing the harmonized solos of Charlie Parker. Their recordings for Capitol, MPS and Columbia (unlike their live performances) did not contain any individual saxophone solos and found the sax section playing note-for-note Bird improvisations (including the roller-coaster "Ko Ko") with impressive precision. Clark left the band in 1975, but Flory has continued the group on a part-time basis up to the present time, sometimes using the L.A. Voices. Among the top sidemen through the years have been Bill Perkins, Warne Marsh, Jay Migliori, Jack Nimitz, Lanny Morgan, trumpeter Conte Candoli and trombonist Carl Fontana. —*Scott Yanow*

● **Supersax Plays Bird** / 1973 / Capitol ◆◆◆◆◆

Jazz Origin: Salt Peanuts / 1974 / PA/USA ◆◆◆◆◆
Faithful recreations of classic Charlie Parker solos by Supersax. They play well, with fluidity and style. If you enjoy repertory and sax sections, then you'll love Supersax. —*Ron Wynn*

Supersax Plays Bird with Strings / Oct. 1974 / Capitol ◆◆◆

Chasin' the Bird / 1977 / Verve ◆◆◆◆

Dynamite / Apr. 24, 1978–Apr. 28, 1978 / MPS ◆◆◆◆◆
A ten-piece band plays glorified horn chants in the spirit of Charlie Parker. Has good, not great, arrangements but excellent playing. Lanny Morgan (as), Don Menza (ts), and Frank Rosolino (tb) are included. Features seven standards, two by arranger Ned Flory. —*Michael G. Nastos*

Stone Bird / 1988 / Columbia ◆◆◆

John Surman

b. Aug. 30, 1944, Tavistock, England
Bass Clarinet, Baritone Saxophone, Soprano Saxophone, Keyboards / Post-Bop
A marvelous baritone saxophonist and good soprano player who's added electronics and bass clarinet in recent years, John Surman has thrived in free, jazz-rock, big band and varied musical situations since the '60s. His baritone playing has richness and great range. A prominent Coltrane disciple, Surman utilizes a full array of tonal colors, and is equally effective in the instrument's upper and lower registers. He combines smashing intensity and soft lyricism. Surman's mastery of electronics and application of synthesizers and keyboards into his compositions has expanded his options as a songwriter and arranger. He's blended European folk, classical and religious sounds into his music, particularly those of England.

Surman played in jazz workshops while still in high school. He studied at the London College of Music and London University Institute of Education in the mid-'60s. Surman played with Alexis Korner, worked with Mike Westbrook until the late '60s, and recorded with him until the mid-'70s. He was voted best soloist at the 1968 Montreux Festival while heading his band. Surman worked with Graham Collier, Mike Gibbs, Dave Holland, Chris McGregor and John McLaughlin in the '60s and toured Europe with the Kenny Clarke/Francy Boland big band in 1970. Surman toured and recorded with Barre Phillips and Stu Martin in the late '60s and early '70s, and again in the late '70s, adding Albert Mangelsdorff to the group. They called themselves the Trio, then Mumps. Surman played with Mike Osborne and Alan Skidmore in the sax trio SOS in the mid-'70s. He also collaborated with The Carolyn Carlson dance company at the Paris Opera through the mid and late '70s. Surman recorded with Stan Tracey and Karin Krog, while working with Miroslav Vitous and Azimuth.

He led The Brass Project in the early '80s and played in Collier's big band and Gil Evans' British orchestra. Surman toured with Evans again in the late '80s. He began recording as a leader for Pye in the early '70s, and did sessions for Ogun and ECM. Surman

continued recording in the '80s, mostly for ECM. He worked with Terje Rypdal, Jack DeJohnette, Pierre Favre, Bengt Hallberg, Archie Shepp, Warne Marsh and Red Mitchell among others. Surman has made many recordings for ECM, spanning from free form to mood music, and he remains one of the label's most consistently stimulating artists. —*Ron Wynn*

Westering Home / 1972 / Island ◆◆◆◆
Solo work from multifaceted creative saxophonist —*Michael G. Nastos*

Upon Reflection / May 1979 / ECM ◆◆◆◆◆
Some of his best playing for ECM. —*Ron Wynn*

The Amazing Adventures of Simon Simon / Jan. 1981 / ECM ◆◆◆

Such Winters of Memory / Dec. 1982 / ECM ◆◆◆
With vocalist Karin Krog and percussionist Pierre Favre. —*Michael G. Nastos*

Withholding Pattern / Dec. 1984 / ECM ◆◆◆◆
A saxophone workout from '85 by outstanding British player John Surman. While solo sax can be extremely tiring, Surman mixes enough elements of rock, free, blues, and hard bop to keep the songs varied. His aggressive style, especially on baritone, keeps the energy level high. —*Ron Wynn*

● **Private City** / Dec. 1987 / ECM ◆◆◆◆◆

Adventure Playground / Sep. 1991 / ECM ◆◆◆◆

Brass Project / Apr. 1992 / ECM ◆◆◆◆◆
For this ECM project, John Surman (who plays soprano, baritone, clarinet, bass clarinet and piano) and conductor John Warren wrote a full set of original music for Surman's reeds, a seven-piece brass section and a rhythm section to interpret. This episodic set has its share of sound explorations but also contains swinging sections and an impressive amount of excitement. The colorful solos (mostly by Surman) and the unpredictable writing make this a highly recommended disc. —*Scott Yanow*

Stranger Than Fiction / Dec. 1993 / ECM ◆◆◆◆
John Surman's thoughtful solos (which take their time and make a liberal use of space) have long made him the perfect ECM artist. On his quartet set with pianist John Taylor, bassist Chris Laurence and drummer John Marshall, Surman mostly sticks to soprano although there are some short spots for his baritone and bass clarinet. Surman always sounds relaxed, even on the more heated originals. It's an interesting set of generally introverted music. —*Scott Yanow*

Nordic Quartet / Aug. 1994 / ECM ◆◆
This ECM CD is only a mixed success. John Surman is the lead voice most of the way and his playing (particularly on baritone and bass clarinet) is typically atmospheric and emotional. However, singer Karin Krog (who is on around half of the songs) only makes an impression on the closing "Wild Bird"; otherwise her long tones sound out of place. Pianist Vigleik Storaas is mostly used in an accompanying role while guitarist Terje Rypdal's feedback-dominated tone is primarily utilized for color. The group never really meshes their disparate voices together and few of the spacey (and sometimes meandering) group originals other than "Wild Bird" are at all memorable. All of the principals have sounded better elsewhere. —*Scott Yanow*

Ralph Sutton

b. Nov. 4, 1922, Hamburg, MO
Piano / Stride
Ralph Sutton is the greatest stride pianist to emerge since World War II with his only close competitors the late Dick Wellstood and the very versatile Dick Hyman. Nearly alone in his generation, Sutton has kept alive the piano styles of Fats Waller and James P. Johnson, not as mere museum pieces but as devices for exciting improvisations. Although sticking within the boundaries of his predecessors, Sutton has infused the music with his own personality; few can match his powerful left hand. Ralph Sutton played with Jack Teagarden's big band briefly in 1942 before serving in the Army.

After World War II he appeared regularly on Rudi Blesh's *This Is Jazz* radio show and spent eight years as the intermission pianist at Eddie Condon's club, recording frequently. He spent time playing in San Francisco, worked for Bob Scobey, moved to Aspen in the mid-'60s and became an original member of the World's Greatest Jazz Band with Yank Lawson, Bob Haggart and

Bud Freeman. In the 1970s he recorded many exciting but now out-of-print albums for the Chaz label and since then has cut albums for quite a few labels. Sutton has kept a busy schedule through the mid-'90s, playing at jazz parties and festivals. Although he would have received much greater fame if he had been born 20 years earlier and come to maturity during the 1930s rather than the 1950s, Ralph Sutton has earned his place among the top classic jazz pianists of all time. —*Scott Yanow*

Ralph Sutton / Mar. 1950 / Commodore ✦✦✦✦✦
Sutton is one of the last great stride pianists, whose style directly reflects the Fats Waller and James P. Johnson influence. This early '50s date offers marvelous stride solos and rollicking rhythms and was among the best releases in this vein done during the decade. —*Ron Wynn*

Jazz at the Olympics / Dec. 1959 / Omega ✦✦✦

The Ralph Sutton Quartet / May 24, 1977–May 25, 1977 / Storyville ✦✦✦✦
Ralph Sutton, one of the great stride pianists of the past four decades, is in excellent form on this European set. Joined on some selections by guitarist Lars Blach, bassist Hugo Rasmussen and drummer Svend Erik Norregard, Sutton (who takes two of the 12 songs unaccompanied) romps through a program of veteran standards that is highlighted by "Thou Swell" and "Jeepers Creepers." —*Scott Yanow*

★ **Last of the Whorehouse Piano Players** / Mar. 27, 1979–Mar. 28, 1979 / Chiaroscuro ✦✦✦✦✦
Back in 1979 pianists Jay McShann and Ralph Sutton teamed together with bassist Milt Hinton and drummer Gus Johnson for spirited and hard-driving renditions of standards that filled up two LPs for the obscure Chaz label. Not only does this single CD contain all of that music but two previously unissued selections as well. Sutton, an orchestra by himself, leaves enough space for the blues-oriented McShann to share the spotlight and the results are very enjoyable; highly recommended to fans of small-group swing. —*Scott Yanow*

The Other Side of Ralph Sutton / 1980 / Chaz Jazz ✦✦✦✦✦

And Ruby Braff / 1980 / Chaz Jazz ✦✦✦✦✦

And Kenny Davern / 1980 / Chaz Jazz ✦✦✦

Big Noise from Wayzata / Jul. 15, 1981 / Chaz Jazz ✦✦✦✦

The Jazz Band / 1981 / Chaz Jazz ✦✦✦✦✦

We've Got Rhythm / 1981 / Chaz Jazz ✦✦✦✦✦

★ **At Cafe Des Copains** / Jun. 1, 1983–Jan. 28, 1987 / Sackville ✦✦✦✦✦

Partners in Crime / Aug. 25, 1983 / Sackville ✦✦✦✦✦

More Ralph Sutton At Cafe Des Copains / Jan. 27, 1988+Jan. 25, 1989 / Sackville ✦✦✦✦

Live at Maybeck Recital Hall, Vol. 30 (Ralph Sutton) / Aug. 1993 / Concord Jazz ✦✦✦

Easy Street / 1994 / Sackville ✦✦✦✦

Svenska Hotkvintetten

Group / Swing
This little-known Swedish band (its name translated to English is The Swedish Hot Quintet) was closely modeled after the Quintet of the Hot Club of France. With violinist Emil Iwring and guitarists Sven Stiberg (single-string) and Folke Eriskberg (chordal) taking solos, this group was one of the hottest in existence during 1939–41. However, its recordings rarely circulated outside of Sweden, and until the issue of a 1993 Dragon CD, it was one of the great unknown bands in jazz history! —*Scott Yanow*

★ **Swedish Hot** / Apr. 1939–May 1941 / Dragon ✦✦✦✦✦
Here is a group no one has heard of! Starting in 1939 and continuing up through 1941, the Svenska Hotkvintetten was an all-string swing quintet closely inspired by Django Reinhardt and Stephane Grappelli. Prior to the release of most of their recordings on this CD, none of the group's performances had ever been available outside of Sweden. Violinist Emil Iwring was almost Grappelli's equal at the time while Sven Stiberg And Folke Eriksberg split the solo work; a third acoustic guitarist and a bassist completed the group. This CD from the Swedish Dragon label is quite generous with 27 selections, most of it falling into the category of hot swing. This is one that all collectors of prebop jazz should want to acquire. —*Scott Yanow*

Neil Swainson

b. Nov. 15, 1955, Victoria, British Columbia, Canada
Bass / Bop, Hard Bop
Neil Swainson worked for two years in Victoria with Paul Horn. He played with Woody Shaw frequently in the 1980s and also gigged with James Moody, George Coleman and Zoot Sims. A member of Moe Koffman's quintet during 1978–82, Swainson gained his greatest fame when he started working with George Shearing in 1988, an association that has continued into the mid-'90s. The reliable bassist has also recorded with Jay McShann, Ed Bickert and Rob McConnell among others. —*Scott Yanow*

● **49th Parallel** / May 1987 / Concord Jazz ✦✦✦✦

Steve Swallow

b. Oct. 4, 1940, Fair Lawn, NJ
Bass / Post-Bop
Steve Swallow has long been many jazz critics' favorite electric bassist for, rather than playing his instrument in a rock-oriented manner, Swallow emphasizes the high notes and approaches the electric bass to an extent as if it were a guitar. He originally started on piano and trumpet before settling on the acoustic bass as a teenager. Swallow joined the Paul Bley trio in 1960 and with Bley was a part of an avant-garde version of the Jimmy Giuffre 3 during 1960–62. Swallow recorded with George Russell and was a member of Art Farmer's quartet (1962–65), Stan Getz's band (1965–67) and an important edition of Gary Burton's quartet (1967–70). The latter group (starting with the addition of guitarist Larry Coryell) was actually one of the first fusion groups and it was during that time that Swallow began playing electric bass; within a few years he stopped playing acoustic altogether. Swallow spent a few years in the early '70s living in Northern California and mostly played locally. Since the late '70s he has been closely associated with Carla Bley's groups although he occasionally works on other projects (including a reunion of the Jimmy Giuffre 3). Steve Swallow has also proven to be a talented composer with "Eiderdown," "Falling Grace," "General Mojo's Well Laid Plan" and "Hotel Hello" among his better-known pieces. —*Scott Yanow*

Home / Sep. 1979 / ECM ✦✦✦
Interesting concept with poetry from Robert Creeley. —*Ron Wynn*

Carla / 1986–1987 / ECM ✦✦✦✦
This is a sextet with a three-piece string ensemble playing eight cuts with a progressive focus. All are originals by Steve Swallow. —*Michael G. Nastos*

● **Swallow** / Sep. 1991–Nov. 1991 / ECM ✦✦✦✦✦
All nine cuts were written by this premier electric bass guitarist and performed by a sextet with guests Gary Burton (vib) and John Scofield (g). —*Michael G. Nastos*

Real Book / Dec. 1993 / ECM ✦✦✦✦

Harvie Swartz

b. Dec. 6, 1948, Chelsea, MA
Bass / Post-Bop
His duets with the redoubtable Sheila Jordan have been a delight, but bassist Harvie Swartz's skillful accompaniment and propulsive lines aren't limited to that role. He's played in many diverse settings, from bebop to large orchestra, hard bop to cool, jazz and pop vocals. Swartz began playing bass at 19 and worked in Boston with Mose Allison, Chris Connor, and the duo of Al Cohn and Zoot Sims. He moved to New York in 1972 and worked in tandem with Mike Abene backing such vocalists as Jackie Cain and Roy Kral, Jackie Paris and Connor. Swartz recorded with Jackie And Roy in 1973. He also played with the Thad Jones—Mel Lewis and Gil Evans' orchestras. Swartz was a regular at Richard's Lounge in New Jersey during the mid-'70s, sometimes backing Lee Konitz, Jan Hammer and John Abercrombie. He played in Barry Miles' Silverlight from 1974 to 1976, doubling on electric bass. Swartz also worked with different editions of groups led by David Friedman, recording with them from 1975 to 1981. He was in a trio with Eddie Daniels, and also played with Dave Matthews big band. Swartz recorded with Friedman's bands between 1975 and 1978, and worked for four years with Steve Kuhn.

Besides the duo with Jordan, Swartz's groups and collaborations in the '80s have included heading an ensemble of bass, piano, fluegelhorn, cello, percussion and drums. He led the Harvie Swartz String Ensemble in 1982 and 1983. Swartz has recorded as a leader for Gramavision and Bluemoon on his own and with Jordan for Muse. He has sessions available both ways on CD. — *Ron Wynn*

Underneath It All / Mar. 1, 1980–Mar. 2, 1980 / Gramavision ♦♦♦♦♦

This bassist's debut album is with Ben Aranov on piano and John D'Earth on trumpet. This is challenging music, approaching fusion. All selections are Swartz's originals. —*Michael G. Nastos*

Urban Earth / Feb. 1985 / Gramavision ♦♦♦♦

● **Smart Moves** / Feb. 1986 / Gramavision ♦♦♦♦♦

A fine, unjustly overlooked '86 combo session with bassist Harvie Swartz stepping from behind the bandstand to take a leadership role. But while it's listed as his group, the key soloists are alto saxophonist Charlie Mariano and tenor saxophonist John Stubblefield, a superb one-two punch. Guitarist Mike Stern, pianist Ben Aronov, and drummer Victor Lewis mesh with Swartz, and percussionist Mino Cinelu adds some Afro-Latin flavoring and colors. —*Ron Wynn*

Full Moon Dancer / May 17, 1989–May 22, 1989 / Blue Moon ♦♦♦

In a Different Light / 1990 / Blue Moon ♦♦

Arrival / Sep. 5, 1991–Sep. 7, 1991 / Novus ♦♦♦♦

Gabor Szabo

b. Mar. 8, 1936, Budapest, Hungary, **d.** Feb. 26, 1982, Budapest, Hungary

Guitar / Post-Bop, Crossover

Gabor Szabo was one of the most original guitarists to emerge in the 1960s, mixing together his Hungarian folk music heritage and his distinctive sound with advanced jazz settings. He started on guitar when he was 14 and was working in Hungary (composing for films and television), when the Soviet invasion of 1956 inspired him to defect to the U.S. Szabo attended Berklee College (1957–59) and made a major impact during his years (1961–65) with the Chico Hamilton Quartet/Quintet. Szabo performed with Charles Lloyd and Gary McFarland and was at his peak with his 1966–68 group, a unit that also featured the talented Jimmy Stewart on second guitar. In the 1970s Szabo became more involved in studio work, commercial recordings and trying to allow a strong rock influence in his music without losing his musical personality; he headed a fusion group First Circle starting in 1975. But his later years were rather directionless and Gabor Szabo had returned to his homeland when he died prematurely, just short of his 46th birthday. —*Scott Yanow*

Gypsy '66 / Nov. 1965 / Impulse! ♦♦♦♦♦

Spellbinder / May 6, 1966 / Impulse! ♦♦♦♦♦

Jazz Raga / Aug. 4, 1966+Aug. 17, 1966 / Impulse! ♦♦♦

★ **The Sorcerer** / Apr. 14, 1967–Apr. 15, 1967 / Impulse! ♦♦♦♦♦

More Sorcery / Apr. 14, 1967–Apr. 15, 1967 / Impulse! ♦♦♦♦

Wind, Sky and Diamonds / Sep. 12, 1967–Sep. 14, 1967 / Impulse! ♦♦♦

At Monterey / Sep. 17, 1967 / Impulse! ♦♦♦♦

Bacchanal / Feb. 9, 1968 / Skye ♦♦♦♦

Dreams / Aug. 6, 1968–Aug. 9, 1968 / Skye ♦♦♦

Gabor Szabo / 1968 / Skye ♦♦♦

High Contrast / 1970 / Blue Thumb ♦♦♦

Rambler / Sep. 1973 / CTI ♦♦♦♦

Macho / Apr. 1975 / Salvation ♦♦

Nightflight / 1976 / Mercury ♦♦

Szakcsi

b. Hungary

Piano, Keyboards / New Age, Post-Bop

Although he achieved recognition for his work in new age, pianist Szakcsi surprised many listeners with his inventive 1994 GRP release *Straight Ahead*, which found him leading a trio/quartet through a set of acoustic jazz originals. Szakcsi enrolled in the Budapest Secondary School of Music at the age of 12 and had originally planned to be a jazz pianist. In his 20s he played in Europe with Art Farmer, Charlie Mariano and Slide Hampton. Szakcsi eventually became an instrumental pop star, but on his GRP date he showed that possibly there is life after new age! — *Scott Yanow*

● **Straight Ahead** / 1993 / GRP ♦♦♦♦♦

Pianist Szakcsi found his initial fame playing new age, but this GRP CD shows that he was careful not to lose his jazz chops. In a trio with bassist Jay Leonhardt and drummer Marvin "Smitty" Smith (Tim Warfield guests on tenor during two songs), Szakcsi really challenged himself on this date, not only finding something fresh to say on "Body and Soul" and tackling Thelonious Monk's "Brilliant Corners" but coming up with eight new songs, many of them hard-driving and all quite straight-ahead. The excellent release shows that, at least for some of its practioners, there is life after New Age! —*Scott Yanow*

T

Lew Tabackin

b. May 26, 1940, Philadelphia, PA
Flute, Tenor Saxophone / Hard Bop
Lew Tabackin's flute playing is so distinguished his tenor work sometimes gets ignored. His flute solos incorporate both an Asian influence and rich, classical style, while he's a rugged tenor soloist with a smooth, relaxed, yet energetic approach. His tenor style is influenced by both Ben Webster and Sonny Rollins. Tabackin began on flute, then started playing tenor in high school. He attended the Philadelphia Conservatory of Music in the early '60s, while studying privately with composer Vincent Persichetti. He also studied with Julius Baker, the principal flutist for the Philadelphia Symphony Orchestra. After serving in the Army, Tabackin played with Tal Farlow and Don Friedman before moving from New Jersey to New York. He worked in the big bands of Les and Larry Elgart, Cab Calloway, Buddy Morrow, Maynard Ferguson, and Thad Jones and Mel Lewis, while also playing with Clark Terry, Duke Pearson, Chuck Israels and Joe Henderson. He recorded with Ferguson and Pearson. Tabackin led his own trio in Philadelphia in the late '60s, and worked in combos with Elvin Jones, Donald Byrd, Atilla Zoller and Roland Hanna. He worked in Bobby Rosengarden's band in 1969, and worked in The Tonight Show band in both New York and Los Angeles until he voluntarily left and was replaced by Pete Christlieb. Tabackin also played with Dick Cavett's studio band. He was a soloist in Europe with the Hamburg Jazz Workshop, Danish Radiojazzgruppen and International Jazz Quintet. Tabackin played extensively with Toshiko Akiyoshi (whom he also married) in the '70s. They formed a quartet and toured Japan, appearing at the Expo '70 jazz festival. Then they co-led a big band in Los Angeles from 1973 until the mid-80s. Tabackin served as principal soloist, and the band recorded often for RCA and import labels. The duo returned to New York in 1983. Tabackin also played and recorded with the big bands of Louis Bellson and Bill Berry in the late '70s. He recorded for Inner City as a leader in the '70s, and for Concord in the '80s and '90s. — *Ron Wynn*

Tabackin / Dec. 19, 1974 / Inner City ♦♦♦
Recorded in Japan with with bass and drums only, this album includes four standards and one apiece from leader, Toshiko Akiyoshi and Sir Roland Hanna. — *Michael G. Nastos*

Dual Nature / Aug. 31, 1976+Sep. 3, 1976 / Inner City ♦♦♦♦♦
Tabackin on flute (he is unbelievable) and tenor sax, with the Don Friedman Trio. — *Michael G. Nastos*

Tenor Gladness / Oct. 13, 1976–Oct. 14, 1976 / Inner City ♦♦♦♦♦
Dueling tenors with Warne Marsh. Six originals were written by the principals or Toshiko Akiyoshi. A thoroughly satisfying date from the two virtuosos. — *Michael G. Nastos*

Rites of Pan / Sep. 1977 / Inner City ♦♦♦♦
Tabackin here is on flute alone with the Toshiko Trio. — *Michael G. Nastos*

Desert Lady / Dec. 1989 / Concord Jazz ♦♦♦♦
Quartet. Better known as co-leader of Akiyoshi/Tabackin big band; Lew Tabackin (sax) shows he's a fine soloist as well. 1989 session. CD version has two bonus cuts. — *Ron Wynn*

● **I'll Be Seeing You** / 1992 / Concord Jazz ♦♦♦♦♦
Lew Tabackin, whose extroverted tone on tenor (influenced most

by Don Byas and Ben Webster) contrasts with the Eastern sound that he gets on flute, is teamed quite successfully with pianist Benny Green, bassist Peter Washington and drummer Lewis Nash on this Concord CD. The repertoire, mostly lesser-known standards like John Coltrane's "Wise One" and Thelonious Monk's "In Walked Bud," is well treated by these masterful musicians. — *Scott Yanow*

What a Little Moonlight Can Do / 1994 / Concord Jazz ♦♦♦♦

Jamaaladeen Tacuma

b. Jun. 11, 1956, Hempstead, NY
Bass / Free Funk
Since his emergence with Ornette Coleman's Prime Time in the mid-'70s, Jamaaladeen Tacuma has been one of the top electric bassists in a style of music that could be called "free funk." Growing up in Philadelphia, Tacuma (who before he converted to Islam was known as Rudy McDaniel) played with Charles Earland. Only 19 when he joined Ornette in 1975, his ability to combine together funky rhythms with free jazz helped give Prime Time its distinctive (if overcrowded) sound. Tacuma's own solo career has been a bit erratic, alternating great moments with throwaway tracks. He also has played with a wide variety of advanced musicians (including James "Blood" Ulmer, Olu Dara, Julius Hemphill and David Murray) but has yet to fulfill his great potential. — *Scott Yanow*

● **Show Stopper** / 1982–1983 / Gramavision ♦♦♦♦♦
The five-piece electric band shows many positive and eclectic forces rooted in jazz but not stuck in the past. Includes "Bird of Paradise" with the Ebony String Quartet. Title track with Olu Dara and Julius Hemphill is a treat of all-out contempo-bop. Other cameos are by Blood Ulmer on guitar and Cornell Rochester on drums. This is a fun album. — *Michael G. Nastos*

Renaissance Man / 1983–1984 / Gramavision ♦♦♦♦

So Tranquilizin' / Sep. 1984–Jan. 1985 / Gramavision ♦♦

Music World / 1986 / Gramavision ♦♦♦

Jukebox / Oct. 1988 / Gramavision ♦♦♦

Boss of the Bass / 1993 / Gramavision ♦♦

Thomas Talbert

b. Aug. 4, 1924, Crystal Bay, MN
Leader, Arranger, Composer, Piano / Bop, Post-Bop
Tom Talbert has been one of the finest arrangers of the past half-century but remains quite underrated due to the relatively few recordings he has made as a leader. He was inspired to become an arranger while hearing the big bands of the swing era on the radio. He developed his piano-playing skills and in high school organized bands to try out his arrangements. After a period in the military (1943–45), Talbert moved to California and on and off during 1946–49 he led an advanced orchestra that struggled unsuccessfully to survive; fortunately many of their rare recordings from this era (and quite a few previously unreleased) have come out on a SeaBreeze CD. Talbert spent part of 1947 touring with Anita O'Day and in 1950 he moved to New York. As a free-lance writer he arranged for Claude Thornhill, Tony Pastor, Johnny Smith, Oscar Pettiford and Don Elliott among others. In the mid-'50s Talbert recorded an album featuring singer Patty McGovern (*Wednesday's Child*) and a classic of his own (*Bix*

Duke Fats); both have been recently reissued on CD. From the mid-'60s until the early '70s Talbert lived in the Midwest, working with a 12-piece band. In 1975 he relocated to Los Angeles where he has written for the L.A. studios and led a part-time orchestra plus a septet, recording several sets for Sea Breeze. —*Scott Yanow*

★ **Tom Talbert Jazz Orchestra 1946–1949** / Jun. 25, 1946–Nov. 1949 / Sea Breeze ✦✦✦✦
Tom Talbert has long been a fixture in Los Angeles, writing arrangements, recording albums and occasionally appearing with his big band in local clubs. He is known for recording one classic set in the 1950s (*Bix Duke Fats*, which has been reissued by the Modern Concepts label), but even veteran collectors can be forgiven for not being familiar with the historic recordings that are on his Sea Breeze CD since the majority of these valuable performances were previously unissued. Talbert led an orchestra in Los Angeles during the 1946–50 period that was (thanks to his advanced writing) as modern as the big bands of Stan Kenton and Boyd Raeburn without copying either. The first four numbers on this CD feature trumpeter Frank Beach and tenor saxophonist Babe Russin as the chief soloists and "Flight of the Vout Bug" (which is actually from a session led by Lyle Griffin) showcases pianist Dodo Marmarosa and the tenor of Lucky Thompson. However it is the charts from 1949 that are of greatest interest among Talbert's sidemen are altoist Art Pepper, Jack Montrose on tenor and pianist Claude Williamson. The music, with its cool-toned reeds, powerful brass, advanced harmonies and solid swing, still sounds fresh and enthusiastic and the occasional vocals are well done. Artistically this orchestra was quite successful, but the band business was collapsing at the time, and when Stan Kenton reformed his orchestra in 1950, Tom Talbert broke up his group and went back to writing full time. Fans of modern big bands should be quite excited by the long-overdue release of this exciting and historic music on SeaBreeze. Highly recommended. —*Scott Yanow*

★ **Bix Fats Duke Interpreted by Thomas Talbert** / 1956 / Atlantic ✦✦✦✦

Louisiana Suite / Oct. 3, 1977–Oct. 5, 1977 / Sea Breeze ✦✦✦✦

Things As They Are / Aug. 11, 1987–Aug. 12, 1987 / Sea Breeze ✦✦✦

The Warm Cafe / Oct. 10, 1991–Jun. 2, 1992 / Modern Concepts ✦✦✦✦

Duke's Domain / May 18, 1993–May 19, 1993 / Sea Breeze ✦✦✦✦✦

Horace Tapscott

b. Apr. 6, 1934, Houston, TX
Piano, Leader / Avant-Garde, Post-Bop
Horace Tapscott has long been Los Angeles' top undiscovered legend, a brilliant pianist who has thus far only recorded for the tiniest (and most obscure) of labels. A powerful player perfectly able to interpret bop but heard at his best playing his own rhythmic originals with his quartet, Tapscott has had an original style for 30 years, but his music is surprisingly accessible even at its most passionate. He moved with his family to Los Angeles in 1945 and was originally a trombonist; Tapscott caught the tail end of the legendary Central Avenue Scene (his early associates included Eric Dolphy and Don Cherry) and played with Gerald Wilson's Orchestra during 1950–51. While in the Air Force (1953–57) he took up the piano, which was fortunate because after touring with Lionel Hampton (1959–61), an automobile accident forced him to give him up the trombone. Tapscott returned to Los Angeles in 1961, formed the Pan Afrikan Peoples Arkestra and has been a major part of the local jazz community ever since. Among his most famous sidemen have been altoist Arthur Blythe and tenor saxophonist Azar Lawrence. Tapscott wrote the arrangements for the late-'60s Sonny Criss album *Sonny's Dream* and shared a Flying Dutchman album (reissued on CD by Novus as *West Coast Hot*) with the John Carter/Bobby Bradford Quartet. Otherwise his recordings have been made for Nimbus along with a pair of live sessions for Hat Art. Tapscott's longtime quartet with saxophonist Michael Sessions, bassist Roberto Miranda and drummer Fritz Wise remains undocumented. —*Scott Yanow*

West Coast Hot / Apr. 1, 1969–Apr. 3, 1969 / Novus ✦✦✦✦✦
Flight 17 / 1978 / Nimbus ✦✦✦
Songs of the Unsung / Feb. 18, 1978 / Interplay ✦✦✦✦
The Call / Apr. 8, 1978 / Nimbus ✦✦✦
Live at the I.U.C.C. / Feb. 1979–Jun. 1979 / Nimbus ✦✦
At the Crossroads / 1980 / Nimbus ✦✦✦
Dial "B" for Barbara / 1981 / Nimbus ✦✦✦✦✦
Live at Lobero / Nov. 12, 1981 / Nimbus ✦✦✦✦✦
The Tapscott Sessions, Vol. 1 / Jun. 1982 / Nimbus ✦✦✦✦
The Tapscott Sessions, Vol. 4 / Sep. 1982 / Nimbus ✦✦✦✦
The Tapscott Sessions, Vol. 2 / Nov. 1982 / Nimbus ✦✦✦✦
The Tapscott Sessions, Vol. 7 / Feb. 1983 / Nimbus ✦✦✦✦
The Tapscott Sessions, Vol. 3 / Mar. 1983 / Nimbus ✦✦✦✦
The Tapscott Sessions, Vol. 6 / Oct. 1983 / Nimbus ✦✦✦✦
The Tapscott Sessions, Vol. 5 / Jan. 1984 / Nimbus ✦✦✦✦
● **The Dark Tree, Vol. 1** / Dec. 14, 1989–Dec. 17, 1989 / Hat Art ✦✦✦✦✦
Pianist Horace Tapscott has long been Los Angeles' great undiscovered legend. A very original stylist capable of playing bop, free jazz or anything in between, Tapscott does not sound like anyone else. Unfortunately he has made few recordings through the years and thus far none with his regular working band of the past decade, but his two Hat Art CDs partly fill the gap. Tapscott was teamed during a stint at Catalina's in Hollywood with clarinetist John Carter, bassist Cecil McBee and drummer Andrew Cyrille. The lengthy renditions they give three of the pianist's compositions (along with trombonist Thurman Green's "One for Lately") allows listeners outside of L.A. a rare opportunity to hear Tapscott stretching out on records; his playing and that of the all-stars is near peak form. —*Scott Yanow*

● **The Dark Tree, Vol. 2** / Dec. 14, 1989–Dec. 17, 1989 / Hat Art ✦✦✦✦✦
Pianist Horace Tapscott, a greatly under-recognized but very original pianist, is showcased even more on this set than on the first volume, for clarinetist John Carter is only on two of the five selections (four of which are Tapscott originals). With bassist Cecil McBee and drummer Andrew Cyrille propelling the all-star group, Tapscott's percussive yet generally melodic style is well featured. But why doesn't some label record his regular working group? —*Scott Yanow*

Buddy Tate (George Holmes Tate)

b. Feb. 22, 1913, Sherman, TX
Tenor Saxophone, Clarinet / Swing
One of the more individual tenors to emerge from the swing era, the distinctive Buddy Tate came to fame as Herschel Evans' replacement with Count Basie's Orchestra. Earlier he had picked up valuable experience playing with Terrence Holder (1930–33), Count Basie's original Kansas City band (1934), Andy Kirk (1934–35) and Nat Towles (1935–39). With Basie a second time during 1939–48, Tate held his own with such major tenors as Lester Young, Don Byas, Illinois Jacquet, Lucky Thompson and Paul Gonsalves. After a period freelancing with the likes of Hot Lips Page, Lucky Millinder and Jimmy Rushing (1950–52), Tate led his own crowd-pleasing group for 21 years (1953–74) at Harlem's Celebrity Club. During this period Tate also took time out to record in a variety of settings (including with Buck Clayton and Milt Buckner), and he was one of the stars of John Hammond's Spirituals to Swing concert of 1967. Tate has kept busy since the Celebrity Club association ended, recording frequently, co-leading a band with Paul Quinichette in 1975, playing and recording in Canada with Jay McShann and Jim Galloway, visiting Europe many times and performing at jazz parties; he was also a favorite sideman of Benny Goodman's in the late '70s. Although age had taken its toll, in the mid-'90s Buddy Tate played and recorded with both Lionel Hampton and the Statesmen of Jazz. —*Scott Yanow*

Swinging Like Tate / Feb. 12, 1958+Feb. 26, 1958 / Felsted ✦✦✦✦✦
Tate's Date / Dec. 18, 1959 / Swingville ✦✦✦
Tate-A-Tate / Oct. 18, 1960 / Original Jazz Classics ✦✦✦✦
Bubbly modern mainstream was found on *Tate-A-Tate*, a Oct. 18, 1960 date with Buddy Tate leading a group (Clark Terry, trumpet;

Tommy Flanagan, piano; Larry Gates, bass; Art Taylor, drums) over six tracks... Clark Terry was right on the money and sounding '60s fresh. —*Bob Rusch, Cadence*

Groovin' with Buddy Tate / Feb. 17, 1961 / Prestige ✦✦✦✦

Buddy Tate and His Buddies / Jun. 3, 1973 / Chiaroscuro ✦✦✦
Jam sessions featuring swing veterans were not that common an occurence on record during the early '70s, making Hank O'Neal's Chiaroscuro label both ahead of and behind the times. This CD reissue is most notable for having pianist Mary Lou Williams (who rarely was invited to this type of freewheeling session) as one of the key soloists. Also heard from are the tenors of Buddy Tate and Illinois Jacquet and the aging but still exciting trumpeter Roy Eldridge; the backup players are rhythm guitarist Steve Jordan, bassist Milt Hinton and drummer Gus Johnson. Together they jam three group originals, Buck Clayton's "Rockaway" and the standard "Sunday," and although falling short of being a classic, this infectious and consistently swinging music is worth picking up. —*Scott Yanow*

Kansas City Woman / Jul. 3, 1974 / Black Lion ✦✦✦✦

The Texas Twister / Feb. 21, 1975 / New World ✦✦✦✦

Meets Dollar Brand / Aug. 25, 1977 / Chiaroscuro ✦✦✦✦
Most unusual pairing that clicks nicely. —*Ron Wynn*

Sherman Shuffle / Jan. 29, 1978 / Sackville ✦✦✦✦✦
Tenor saxophonist Buddy Tate and Bob Wilber (mostly on alto) make for a potent team on this consistently swinging quartet date with bassist Sam Jones and drummer Leroy Williams. Tate has one appearance apiece on baritone and clarinet (the latter for Wilber's exquisite "Curtains of the Night") while Bob Wilber also plays a bit of soprano and clarinet. A superior repertoire, the variety of lead voices and consistently strong solos make this a set worth picking up. —*Scott Yanow*

★ **Hard Blowin'** / Aug. 25, 1978–Aug. 26, 1978 / Muse ✦✦✦✦✦
Muse has released at least six albums of material recorded at Sandy's Jazz Revival in Massachusetts during a week in 1978. This is veteran tenor Buddy Tate's most rewarding album from the engagement and a fine all-around showcase. Accompanied by pianist Ray Bryant, bassist George Duvivier and drummer Alan Dawson, Tate stretches out on four familiar standards and shows listeners that he really had one of the more distinctive tenor sounds of the swing era. Recommended. —*Scott Yanow*

Live at Sandy's / Aug. 25, 1978–Aug. 26, 1978 / Muse ✦✦✦✦✦
One of the six Muse albums recorded at Sandy's Jazz Revival in Massachusetts during an engagement in 1978, this is essentially tenor veteran Buddy Tate's set although altoist Eddie "Cleanhead" Vinson and tenor Arnett Cobb join in on the closing blues "She's Got It." Tate is in fine form on the other four songs, which include an outing on clarinet for "Blue Creek," a warm version of the ballad "Candy" and two lengthy jams with pianist Ray Bryant, bassist George Duvivier and drummer Alan Dawson. Consistently swinging music and one of the better Buddy Tate recordings currently available. —*Scott Yanow*

The Great Buddy Tate / Mar. 1981 / Concord Jazz ✦✦✦✦
Stalwart 1981 session with Hank Jones outstanding. Versatile outing, with Tate also on baritone and clarinet. —*Ron Wynn*

Ballad Artistry of Buddy Tate / Jun. 12, 1981–Jun. 13, 1981 / Sackville ✦✦✦
The veteran swing tenor Buddy Tate mostly sticks fairly close to the melody throughout these ten ballads, three of which were released for the first time on the CD reissue. The music is enjoyable enough if a bit restrained and guitarist Ed Bickert (who is heard along with bassist Don Thompson and drummer Terry Clarke) often shares solo honors on this tasteful affair. —*Scott Yanow*

Just Jazz / Apr. 28, 1984 / Reservoir ✦✦

Grady Tate

b Jan. 14, 1932, Durham, NC
Drums, Vocals / Hard Bop
Though he could have been a star as a vocalist, Grady Tate has gained as much fame and recognition as a drummer. He's equally effective pushing and driving the beat or providing shading and subdued rhythms. Tate's recorded bebop, hard bop, swing, big band and soul jazz, and his own singing ability makes him the ideal drummer to accompany vocalists. He began playing drums at five, and initially taught himself. Tate later learned more fun-

damentals and nuances while in the air force during the '50s. He returned to his North Carolina home after his discharge, studying literature, theater and psychology at North Carolina College while working part-time as a musician. Tate moved to Washington in 1959, where he played with Wild Bill Davis. He moved to New York two years later, where he played in Quincy Jones' big band and with Jerome Richardson. Tate has subsequently worked with Duke Ellington, Count Basie, Jimmy Smith, Wes Montgomery, Rahsaan Roland Kirk and many others. He's also backed vocalists Peggy Lee, Sarah Vaughan, Ella Fitzgerald, Astrud Gilberto, Chris Connor, Ray Charles, Blossom Dearie and Lena Horne. Tate's albums for Skye, Impluse, Milestone and other labels have emphasized his vocals as much, if not more than his drumming. But his drumming is well represented on sessions. Tate currently has a couple of dates available on CD. —*Ron Wynn*

TNT / 1991 / Milestone ✦✦✦✦

● **Body & Soul** / Oct. 27, 1992–Nov. 2, 1992 / Milestone ✦✦✦✦

Art Tatum

b. Oct. 13, 1909, Toledo, OH, d. Nov. 5, 1956, Los Angeles, CA
Piano / Swing
Art Tatum was among the most extraordinary of all jazz musicians, a pianist with wondrous technique who could not only play ridiculously rapid lines with both hands (his 1933 solo version of "Tiger Rag" sounds as if there were three pianists jamming together!) but was also harmonically 30 years ahead of his time; all pianists have to deal to a certain extent with Tatum's innovations in order to be taken seriously. Able to play stride, swing and boogie-woogie with speed and complexity that could only previously be imagined, Tatum's quick reflexes and boundless imagination kept his improvisations filled with fresh (and sometimes futuristic) ideas that put him way ahead of his contemporaries.

Born nearly blind, Tatum gained some formal piano training at the Toledo School of Music but was largely self-taught. Although influenced a bit by Fats Waller and the semi-classical pianists of the 1920s, there is really no explanation for where Tatum gained his inspiration and ideas from. He first played professionally in Toledo in the mid-'20s and had a radio show during 1929–30. In 1932 Tatum traveled with singer Adelaide Hall to New York and made his recording debut accompanying Hall (as one of two pianists!). But for those who had never heard him in person, it was his solos of 1933 (including "Tiger Rag") that announced the arrival of a truly major talent. In the 1930s Tatum spent periods working in Cleveland, Chicago, New York, Los Angeles and (in 1938) England. Although he led a popular trio with guitarist Tiny Grimes (later Everett Barkedale) and bassist Slam Stewart in the mid-'40s, Tatum spent most of his life as a solo pianist who could always scare the competition. Some observers criticized him for having too much technique (is such a thing possible?), working out and then keeping the same arrangements for particular songs and for using too many notes, but those minor reservations pale when compared to Tatum's reworkings of such tunes as "Yesterdays," "Begin the Beguine" and even "Humoresque." Although he was not a composer, Tatum's rearrangements of standards made even warhorses sound like new compositions.

Art Tatum, who recorded for Decca throughout the 1930s and Capitol in the late '40s, starred at the Esquire Metropolitan Opera House concert of 1944 and appeared briefly in his only film in 1947, *The Fabulous Dorseys* (leading a jam session on a heated blues). He recorded extensively for Norman Granz near the end of his life in the 1950s, both solo and with all-star groups; all of the music has been reissued by Pablo on a seven-CD and a six-CD box set. His premature death from uremia has not resulted in any loss of fame, for Art Tatum's recordings still have the ability to scare modern pianists! —*Scott Yanow*

Masters of Jazz, Vol. 8 / Aug. 1932–Jan. 1946 / Storyville ✦✦✦✦
The Swedish label Storyville's *Masters of Jazz* series released a dozen volumes of mostly rare music by swing-era greats. Tatum's set is primarily comprised of selections cut in 1935 for radio airplay, giving listeners a chance to hear the young genius perform some songs that he never recorded otherwise. In addition, there are two selections from 1945–46, along with his earliest recording: a broadcast version of "Tiger Rag." —*Scott Yanow*

★ **Piano Starts Here** / Mar. 21, 1933+1949 / Columbia/Legacy ✦✦✦✦✦
There are many Art Tatum records currently available, but this is the one to pull out to amaze friends, particularly with Tatum's

wondrous version of "Tiger Rag," during which he sounds like three pianists jamming together. This CD consists of Tatum's first studio session as a leader (which resulted in "Tea for Two," "St. Louis Blues," "Tiger Rag" and "Sophisticated Lady") and a remarkable solo concert performance from the spring of 1949. While "Tiger Rag" dwarfs everything else, the live set is highlighted by a very adventurous, yet seemingly effortless exploration of "Yesterdays," a ridiculously rapid "I Know That You Know," and the hard-cooking "Tatum Pole Boogie." This is an essential set of miraculous music that cannot be praised highly enough. — *Scott Yanow*

● **Art Tatum (1932–1934)** / Mar. 1933–Oct. 1934 / Classics ✦✦✦✦✦
This comprehensive CD contains Art Tatum's very first recording (a broadcast version of "Tiger Rag") four selections in which he accompanies singer Adelaide Hall (along with a second pianist!) and then his first 20 solo sides. To call his virtuosic piano style remarkable would be a major understatement; he has to be heard to be believed. His studio version of "Tiger Rag" may very well be his most incredible recording; he sounds like three pianists at once. — *Scott Yanow*

Pure Genius / Feb. 27, 1934–1945 / Atlantis ✦✦✦✦
This English LP contains some rare solo performances that Tatum fans will want to get. A Cleveland broadcast from 1934 (less than a year after his initial recordings) features Tatum performing some rare material (particularly "Young & Healthy" and "Morning, Noon & Night"); he is also heard in duet with bassist Junior Raglin (1945's "The Man I Love") and on an extensive solo broadcast from the same year. Art Tatum was an amazing pianist and no jazz collection is complete without a few of his recordings. — *Scott Yanow*

Art Tatum (1934–1940) / Oct. 1934–Jul. 1940 / Classics ✦✦✦✦✦

★ **Classic Piano Solos (1934–39)** / 1934–1939 / GRP ✦✦✦✦✦
This excellent CD reissues all of Tatum's early Decca piano solos cut at three sessions in 1934 and one in 1937. He was decades ahead of his contemporaries not only in technique but also in harmonic ideas. Highlights of this very impressive set include "Emaline," "After You've Gone," "The Shout," two versions of "Liza" and "The Sheik of Araby." — *Scott Yanow*

I Got Rhythm: Art Tatum, Vol. 3 (1935–44) / Dec. 21, 1935–Jan. 5, 1944 / GRP ✦✦✦✦✦

Standard Transcriptions / Dec. 1935–1943 / Music & Arts ✦✦✦✦✦
In 1935, 1939 and 1943 Tatum recorded an extensive series of piano solos (163 in all) for radio airplay; these were not available commercially until long after the LP era was underway and then only piecemeal. On this two-CD set, Music & Arts gives listeners all of the remarkable music together for the first time. Fans only familiar with his commercial recordings will find much to marvel at during this recommended set. — *Scott Yanow*

Standards / 1938–1939 / Black Lion ✦✦✦✦
This Black Lion CD features brilliant piano solos originally cut as noncommercial radio transcriptions during 1938-39. Duplicating part of Tatum's Music & Arts double CD, *Standards* features a great deal of magic from the remarkable virtuoso. — *Scott Yanow*

Solos (1940) / Feb. 22, 1940–Jul. 26, 1940 / MCA/Decca ✦✦✦✦✦
MCA's short-lived Decca CD-reissue program put out this gem, all of Tatum's piano solos from 1940, including two versions of the previously unknown "Sweet Emalina, My Gal." Some of the routines on these standards were a bit familiar by now (this "Tiger Rag" pales next to his 1933 version) but are no less exciting and still sound seemingly impossible to play. — *Scott Yanow*

God Is in the House / Nov. 11, 1940–Sep. 16, 1941 / Onyx ✦✦✦✦
A real historical curiosity, this out-of-print LP features Tatum playing in nightclubs and in an apartment sometimes with a bassist. Privately recorded (and not of digital quality), the music is still utterly fascinating, particularly a pair of jams with trumpeter Frankie Newton and bassist Ebbenezer Paul and two surprise blues vocals by Tatum himself. — *Scott Yanow*

The Remarkable Art of Tatum / Jan. 5, 1944 / Audiophile ✦✦✦✦
After years of appearing almost exclusively as a piano soloist, Tatum formed a trio in the mid-'40s with guitarist Tiny Grimes and bassist Slam Stewart. Fortunately Grimes and Stewart were quick thinkers and witty improvisers, for they needed all of their creativity in order to keep up with the astounding pianist. All 11 of the performances (including one alternate take) they cut for

World Broadcasting transcriptions are included on this rather brief (under 27 minutes) LP. Their magical interplay was consistently memorable. — *Scott Yanow*

The V-Discs / Jan. 18, 1944–Jan. 21, 1946 / Black Lion ✦✦✦✦
This Black Lion CD mostly features the phenomenal Tatum playing solo during 1945-46, really digging into a variety of standards. A rare version of "Sweet Lorraine" (with bassist Oscar Pettiford and drummer Sid Catlett in 1944) and two numbers with his 1945 trio (featuring guitarist Tiny Grimes and bassist Slam Stewart) round out this excellent CD. — *Scott Yanow*

● **The Complete Capitol Recordings, Vol. 1** / Jul. 13, 1949–Dec. 20, 1952 / Capitol ✦✦✦✦✦
Tatum recorded 20 piano solos in 1949 and eight selections with his 1952 trio (which included guitarist Everett Barksdale and bassist Slam Stewart) for Capitol. Ten solos and four trios are included on each of the two CDs in this "complete" series; he can be heard here at the height of his powers. (He never did decline, creating miraculous variations of standards that still amaze today's pianists.) — *Scott Yanow*

● **The Complete Capitol Recordings, Vol. 2** / Sep. 29, 1949–Dec. 20, 1952 / Capitol ✦✦✦✦✦
On the second of two CDs, Art Tatum is heard playing solo in 1949 on ten standards and interacting with his 1952 trio (which included guitarist Everett Barksdale and bassist Slam Stewart) during four numbers. Tatum always had the ability to amaze fellow pianists (not to mention fans) and there are plenty of remarkable moments in this fine set. — *Scott Yanow*

In Private / 1949 / Jazz Chronicles ✦✦✦
This collector's LP features the amazing Tatum playing solo piano at a private party. Although the recording quality is not flawless, his melodic interpretations of 11 standards are typically virtuosic and fascinating; he was always well worth hearing. — *Scott Yanow*

Art Tatum at His Piano, Vol. 1 / 1950 / GNP ✦✦✦
On the first of two LPs featuring Tatum live at the Crescendo Club in 1950, the great pianist interprets a dozen standards in familiar but impressive fashion. His routines on some tunes became set pieces but still were quite remarkable as evidenced by this fine performance. — *Scott Yanow*

Art Tatum at His Piano, Vol. 2 / 1950 / GNP ✦✦✦
The second of two LPs taken from a 1950 Los Angeles concert, Tatum performs concise melodic variations on another dozen standards. Although not his most adventurous set, he was definitely in fine form that day. — *Scott Yanow*

The Complete Pablo Solo Masterpieces / Dec. 28, 1953–Jan. 19, 1955 / Pablo ✦✦✦✦
During four marathon recording sessions in 1953-55, Norman Granz recorded Art Tatum playing 119 standards, enough music for a dozen LPs. The results have been recently reissued separately on eight CDs and on this very full seven-CD box set. Frankly, Tatum did no real advance preparation for this massive project, sticking mosty to concise melodic variations of standards, some of them virtual set pieces formed over the past two decades. Since there are few uptempo performances, the music in this series has a certain sameness after a while but, heard in small doses, it is quite enjoyable. A special bonus on this box (and not on the individual volumes) are four numbers taken from a 1956 Hollywood Bowl concert. — *Scott Yanow*

The Tatum Solo Masterpieces, Vol. 1 / Dec. 28, 1953–Jan. 19, 1955 / Pablo ✦✦✦✦
The first of eight CDs reissuing the 119 piano solo performances that Art Tatum recorded for Norman Granz during four marathon record sessions has its moments, although in general this series lacks the excitement of Tatum's earliest recordings. The pianist interprets such standards on this first volume as "Body and Soul," "It's Only a Paper Moon" and "Willow Weep for Me." — *Scott Yanow*

The Art Tatum Solo Masterpieces, Vol. 2 / Dec. 28, 1953–Jan. 19, 1955 / Pablo ✦✦✦✦
The second of eight CDs in this series of solo performances taken from four marathon record sessions has among its highlights "Elegy," "This Can't Be Love" and "Tea for Two," but in general this series lacks the excitement of Tatum's earliest recordings. Excellent but somewhat predictable performances by the classic virtuoso. — *Scott Yanow*

The Art Tatum Solo Masterpieces, Vol. 3 / Dec. 28, 1953–Jan. 19, 1955 / Pablo ✦✦✦✦
The third of eight CDs in the Norman Granz series of Tatum

piano solos is highlighted by "Yesterdays," "Prisoner of Love" and "Begin the Beguine" among others. He did little prior preparation for the four marathon sessions that resulted in a dozen LPs (now reissued as eight CDs), so this series lacks the excitement and adventure of his earliest recordings although it is still enjoyable in its own right. —*Scott Yanow*

The Art Tatum Solo Masterpieces, Vol. 4 / Dec. 28, 1953–Jan. 19, 1955 / Pablo ✦✦✦✦
On the fourth volume in this eight-CD series, Tatum sounds at his best on "Ill Wind" and "The Man I Love." Taken from the 119 piano solos he cut for Norman Granz in four lengthy recording sessions during 1953–55, these performances are concise, relaxed, and surprisingly predictable, if virtuosic. —*Scott Yanow*

The Art Tatum Solo Masterpieces, Vol. 6 / Dec. 28, 1953–Jan. 19, 1955 / Pablo ✦✦✦✦
Volume Six of this eight-CD series features Tatum interpreting such standards as "Night and Day," "Cherokee," "Happy Feet" and "Someone to Watch over Me" with taste and melodic creativity. There are no real barnburners or new revelations on this generally relaxed set, but the music should please Tatum's fans. —*Scott Yanow*

The Art Tatum Solo Masterpieces, Vol. 7 / Dec. 28, 1953–Jan. 19, 1955 / Pablo ✦✦✦✦
The next-to-last volume in this eight CD-series features interpretations of a variety of standards, including "Moon Song," "Japanese Sandman," "Moonlight on the Ganges" and even "Mighty Like a Rose." Taken from the 119 numbers that Tatum recorded for Norman Granz during four marathon sessions, the music is pleasing, if at times a bit too relaxed for those who would like to hear the virtuoso really tear into these pieces. —*Scott Yanow*

The Art Tatum Solo Masterpieces, Vol. 5 / Dec. 29, 1953–Jan. 19, 1955 / Pablo ✦✦✦✦
The fifth volume of this eight CD-series features Tatum interpreting 15 of the 119 standards he recorded during four marathon solo recording sessions for Norman Granz. He sounds typically wondrous in spots even though there are few surprises throughout this generally relaxed set. —*Scott Yanow*

The Art Tatum Solo Masterpieces, Vol. 8 / Dec. 29, 1953–Jan. 19, 1955 / Pablo ✦✦✦✦
The final volume of this eight-CD (and originally 12-LP) series is similar to the first seven in that Tatum melodically improvises on a variety of standards, in this case such tunes as "She's Funny That Way," "I Won't Dance," "Begin the Beguine" and "Humoresque." Few revelations occur (most of the interpretations are in the same relaxed medium tempo), but the music is typically well played and generally quite enjoyable. —*Scott Yanow*

The Tatum Group Masterpieces, Vol. 1 / Jun. 25, 1954 / Pablo ✦✦✦✦
During 1954–56 Norman Granz recorded the remarkable pianist Art Tatum with a variety of classic jazz masters, resulting in quite a bit of musical magic. This first of eight volumes finds Tatum matching wits with the classy alto of Benny Carter and drummer Louie Bellson—the results are both tasteful and frequently hard-swinging. —*Scott Yanow*

★ **The Complete Pablo Group Masterpieces** / Jun. 25, 1954–Sep. 11, 1956 / Pablo ✦✦✦✦✦
Tatum spent most of his career as a solo pianist; in fact it was often said that he was such an unpredictable virtuoso that it would be difficult for other musicians to play with him. Producer Norman Granz sought to prove that the theory was false, so between 1954 and 1956 he extensively recorded Tatum with a variety of other classic jazzmen, resulting originally in nine LPs of material that is now available separately as eight CDs and on this very full six-CD box set. In contrast to the massive solo Tatum sessions that Granz also recorded during this period, the group sides have plenty of variety and exciting moments, which is not too surprising when one considers that Tatum was teamed in a trio with altoist Benny Carter and drummer Louie Bellson with trumpeter Roy Eldridge, with clarinetist Buddy DeFranco and tenor saxophonist Ben Webster in separate quartets, in an explosive trio with vibraphonist Lionel Hampton and drummer Buddy Rich, with a sextet including Hampton, Rich and trumpeter Harry "Sweets" Edison, and on a standard trio session. —*Scott Yanow*

The Tatum Group Masterpieces, Vol. 2 / Mar. 23, 1955–Mar. 29, 1955 / Pablo ✦✦✦✦✦
The second of eight CDs teaming the amazing pianist with a vari-

ety of his contemporaries finds Tatum sharing the stage with trumpeter Roy Eldridge, bassist John Simmons and drummer Alvin Stoller. Eldridge, normally a very combative player, knows better than to directly challenge Tatum and instead is surprisingly restrained and muted on this enjoyable set of swing standards. —*Scott Yanow*

The Tatum Group Masterpieces, Vol. 3 / Aug. 1, 1955 / Pablo ✦✦✦✦✦
The third of eight CDs matching the great pianist with a variety of classic jazzmen is the first of two that finds him in a trio with vibraphonist Lionel Hampton and drummer Buddy Rich; no weak spots in that group! Much of this music really burns. —*Scott Yanow*

The Tatum Group Masterpieces, Vol. 4 / Aug. 1, 1955 / Pablo ✦✦✦✦✦
The fourth of eight CDs featuring the pianist interacting with some of his most notable musical contemporaries is the second to match his virtuosity with that of vibraphonist Lionel Hampton and drummer Buddy Rich. The three immortals really challenge each other during this frequently heated jam session. —*Scott Yanow*

The Tatum Group Masterpieces, Vol. 5 / Sep. 7, 1955 / Pablo ✦✦✦✦✦
The fifth of eight CDs in this recommended series (which is also available complete as a six-CD box set) features the largest band in this program, a sextet with Tatum, vibraphonist Lionel Hampton, trumpeter Harry "Sweets" Edison, guitarist Barney Kessel, bassist Red Callender and drummer Buddy Rich. Their treatment of blues and standards is as exciting as one would expect from this all-star lineup. —*Scott Yanow*

The Tatum Group Masterpieces, Vol. 6 / Jan. 27, 1956 / Pablo ✦✦✦✦
Tatum/Callender/Jones. As with all in the set, immaculate trio works. —*Ron Wynn*

The Tatum Group Masterpieces, Vol. 7 / Feb. 6, 1956 / Pablo ✦✦✦✦
The seventh of eight CDs in this valuable series matches the remarkable pianist in a quartet with clarinetist Buddy DeFranco. DeFranco, no slouch himself, directly challenges Tatum and their uptempo romps are often quite wondrous. —*Scott Yanow*

20th Century Piano Genius / Jul. 3, 1956 / Verve ✦✦✦✦
This double LP was taped at a private party in 1956, featuring the amazing Art Tatum on solo piano. Tatum, who died the following year, never did decline, and he is in prime form throughout this highly enjoyable and frequently exciting set of standards. There are no real romps a la "Tiger Rag," but the 27 performances contain plenty of remarkable moments. —*Scott Yanow*

The Tatum Group Masterpieces, Vol. 8 / Sep. 11, 1956 / Pablo ✦✦✦✦
The final volume in this very worthy series is a comparatively relaxed affair, a quartet set with tenor saxophonist Ben Webster. Webster lets Tatum fill the background with an infinite number of notes while emphasizing his warm tenor tone in the forefront on a variety of melodic ballads and standards. The combination works very well. —*Scott Yanow*

Art Taylor

b. Apr. 6, 1929, New York, NY, d. Feb. 6, 1995
Drums / Bop, Hard Bop
One of the great drummers of the 1950s, Art Taylor was on a countless number of hard bop and jam session-styled sessions. His first important gig was with Howard McGhee in 1948 and this was followed by associations with Coleman Hawkins (1950–51), Buddy DeFranco (1952), Bud Powell (1953 and 1955–57) and George Wallington (1954–56). Taylor seemed to live in Prestige's studios during the second half of the 1950s although he found time to lead his Wailers, visit Europe with Donald Byrd in 1958, gig and record with Miles Davis and play with Thelonious Monk (including his acclaimed Town Hall concert) in 1959. In 1963 Taylor moved to Europe where he spent most of the next 20 years (mostly living in France and Belgium), playing with Europeans and such Americans as Dexter Gordon and Johnny Griffin. He interviewed scores of his colleagues and collected many of the insightful discussions in his very readable book *Notes and Tones* (which was re-released in 1993). After returning to the U.S., Taylor resumed his freelancing and in the early '90s he organized a new

version of the Wailers which, during its short existence prior to his death, temporarily filled the gap left by the end of the Jazz Messengers. — *Scott Yanow*

● **Taylor's Wailers** / Feb. 25, 1956–Mar. 22, 1957 / Original Jazz Classics ✦✦✦✦✦

Five of the six selections on this CD reissue feature drummer Art Taylor in an all-star sextet of mostly young players comprised of trumpeter Donald Byrd, altoist Jackie McLean, Charlie Rouse on tenor, pianist Ray Bryant and bassist Wendell Marshall. Among the high points of the 1957 hard bop date are the original version of Bryant's popular "Cubano Chant" and strong renditions of two Thelonious Monk tunes ("Off Minor" and "Well, You Needn't") cut just prior to the pianist/composer's discovery by the jazz public. Bryant is the most mature of the soloists, but the three horn players were already starting to develop their own highly individual sounds. The remaining track (a version of Jimmy Heath's "C.T.A.") is played by the quartet of Taylor, tenor saxophonist John Coltrane, pianist Red Garland and bassist Paul Chambers (although a good one) from another session. — *Scott Yanow*

Taylor's Tenors / Jun. 3, 1959 / Original Jazz Classics ✦✦✦✦

Drummer Art Taylor heads a quintet for a fine jam-session-flavored session featuring the tenors of Charlie Rouse (about the time he joined Thelonious Monk's Quartet) and Frank Foster (then with Count Basie) along with pianist Walter Davis and bassist Sam Jones. The repertoire on this CD reissue (which was originally recorded for Prestige's New Jazz subsidiary) includes two Monk tunes that are ideal for jamming ("Rhythm-Aning" and "Straight No Chaser"), Jackie McLean's "Fidel" (which is given a memorable performance) and originals by Rouse, Davis and Taylor. All in all this is a loose and easily enjoyable hard bop date. — *Scott Yanow*

Art Taylor's Delight / Aug. 6, 1960 / Blue Note ✦✦✦✦

Early-'60s definitive sides from this drummer and group known as Taylor's Wailers. — *Michael G. Nastos*

Mr. A.T. / 1991 / Enja ✦✦✦✦✦

Drummer Art Taylor, who spent many years in Europe, re-emerged as an important bandleader with this Enja CD. Taylor's group (called "Taylor's Wailers") features four Young Lions: the fine tenor Willie Williams, altoist Abraham Burton (most heavily influenced by his teacher Jackie McLean), pianist Marc Cary and bassist Tyler Mitchell, in addition to the drummer/leader. On a variety of tunes from the 1950s and '60s (highlighted by "Hi-Fly," "Soul Eyes" and "Gingerbread Boy") the musicians play some high-quality modern hard bop. Enjoyable music. — *Scott Yanow*

Wailin' at the Vanguard / Aug. 1992 / Verve ✦✦✦✦

Billy Taylor

b. Jul. 21, 1921, Greenville, NC, **d.** Sep. 2, 1986, Fairfax, VA

Piano / Bop, Hard Bop, Swing

Billy Taylor has been such an articulate spokesman for jazz and his profiles on CBS' Sunday Morning television program (where he has been a regular since 1981) are so successful at introducing jazz to a wider audience that sometimes one can forget how talented a pianist he has been for the past half-century. While not an innovator, Taylor has been flexible enough to play swing, bop and more advanced styles while always retaining his own musical personality. After graduating from Virginia State College in 1942, he moved to New York and played with such major musicians as Ben Webster, Eddie South, Stuff Smith (with whom he recorded in 1944) and Slam Stewart among others. In 1951 he was the house pianist at Birdland and soon afterward Taylor formed his first of many trios. He helped found the Jazzmobile in 1965, in 1969 became the first Black band director for a network television series (*The David Frost Show*), in 1975 he earned his doctorate at the University of Massachusetts and he both founded and served as director for the popular radio program *Jazz Alive*. But despite his activities in jazz education, Taylor has rarely gone long between performances and recordings, always keeping his bop-based style consistently swinging and fresh. — *Scott Yanow*

Billy Taylor Trio / Nov. 18, 1952–Dec. 29, 1953 / Prestige ✦✦✦✦

Two albums by pianist Billy Taylor are combined on this single CD reissue. With fine backing from bassist Earl May and drummer Charlie Smith, Taylor is tasteful, swinging and creative within the boundaries of bop and swing on this early set, among his first dates as a leader and excellent examples of his already individual style. — *Scott Yanow*

Cross Section / May 7, 1953–Jul. 30, 1954 / Original Jazz Classics ✦✦✦✦

With Candido / Sep. 7, 1954 / Original Jazz Classics ✦✦✦✦

This Prestige release (which has been reissued on CD) helped to introduce Candido to a jazz audience. Candido's conga and bongos fit in comfortably with pianist Billy Taylor's trio (which also includes bassist Earl May and drummer Percy Brice). Together they perform four of Taylor's boppish originals ("Bit of Bedlam" is straight from Bud Powell), "Love for Sale" and the highly appealing "Mambo Inn." Both Taylor and Candido have plenty of solo space and even if this CD is quite brief (under 32 minutes), the music is consistently delightful. — *Scott Yanow*

● **My Fair Lady Loves Jazz** / Jan. 8, 1957–Feb. 5, 1957 / Impulse! ✦✦✦✦✦

Pianist Billy Taylor and his trio performed this collection of show tunes with impeccable taste and delightful elan, never losing their sense of swing while maintaining the originals' elegance and spirit. Quincy Jones' arrangements put the trio at the music's forefront, keeping the horns behind them and maintaining an even pace. Taylor's crisp, sophisticated figures, delicate phrasing, and breezy rhythms were ably buttressed by Ed Thigpen's precise drumming and bassist Earl May's thick, big-toned backing, plus guitarist Al Casamenti's subtle underpinning. — *Ron Wynn*

Billy Taylor with Four Flutes / Jul. 20, 1959 / Original Jazz Classics ✦✦✦✦

In the 1950s, pianist Billy Taylor was best known for his work with his trios. For this Riverside set (reissued on CD in the *OJC* series) Taylor tried something different, writing arrangements for four flutists (including Frank Wess, Herbie Mann and Jerome Richardson), his rhythm section and the congas of Chino Pozo. The flutists get their opportunities to solo and the music (which includes "The Song Is Ended," "St. Thomas," "Oh Lady Be Good," "How About You" and four of Taylor's originals) is essentially bop, but the unusual instrumentation gives the set its own personality. Enjoyable music that certainly stands out from the crowd. — *Scott Yanow*

I Wish I Knew How It Would Feel to be Free / 1967 / Tower ✦✦✦✦✦

Recorded with a trio and features Taylor's immortal song bearing the title of the album, several pop and jazz standards, Clare Fischer's "Morning" and "Pensativa," Taylor's "CAG." Bandmates featured are Ben Tucker (b) and Grady Tate (d). — *Michael G. Nastos*

Sleeping Bee / Apr. 1969 / PA/USA ✦✦✦✦

Recorded with Ben Tucker on bass and Grady Tate on drums, this album includes four Taylor originals and four standards. — *Michael G. Nastos*

OK Billy! / 1970 / Bell ✦✦✦

Where've You Been? / Dec. 1980 / Concord Jazz ✦✦✦

White Nights and Jazz in Leningrad / Jun. 13, 1988–Jun. 14, 1988 / Taylor Made ✦✦✦✦✦

Solo / Aug. 1, 1988–Aug. 2, 1988 / Taylor Made ✦✦✦✦✦

Jazzmobile Allstars / Apr. 5, 1989–Apr. 6, 1989 / Taylor Made ✦✦✦

Dr. T / 1993 / GRP ✦✦✦✦✦

It's a Matter of Pride / 1993 / GRP ✦✦✦✦✦

This is a particularly well-constructed session by pianist Billy Taylor who is featured in a combo with bassist Christian McBride, drummer Marvin "Smitty" Smith, the congas of Ray Mantilla, and on three songs, tenor saxophonist Stanley Turrentine; Grady Tate also contributes two warm ballad vocals. All nine songs were composed by Taylor (including three pieces taken from a more extended work in tribute to Martin Luther King) and the results are melodic, boppish and swinging. — *Scott Yanow*

Homage / Oct. 10, 1994–Oct. 11, 1994 / GRP ✦✦✦

Billy Taylor's GRP release is comprised of two of the pianist's suites (which are actually a series of songs) along with a pair of shorter pieces. "Homage" pays tribute to some of Taylor's earlier heroes including violinists Eddie South and Stuff Smith, bassists Slam Stewart and Oscar Pettiford, drummers Sid Catlett and Jo Jones, and pianist Art Tatum. None of those musicians are actually imitated, but the three-part work does feature excellent interplay between Taylor's trio (with bassist Chip Jackson and drummer Steve Johns) and the Turtle Island String Quartet. One misses the strings a bit during the ten-part "Step into My Dream," an episodic work that portrays a walk through Harlem and is designed to be performed in conjunction with the David Parsons Dance Company. Most of the music is straight-ahead in a boppish vein although there is a stride piece, a calypso, a free-form section and even a rap that, although typically obnoxious, is more listenable than usual. Taylor plays quite well throughout the program, concluding the set with a jazz waltz and an encore ("One for Fun") with Turtle Island. Although not essential, there are enough bright moments on the stimulating set to make this a recommended release. —*Scott Yanow*

Cecil Taylor

b. Mar. 15, 1929, New York, NY
Piano, Leader / Avant-Garde, Free Jazz
Soon after he first emerged in the mid-'50s, pianist Cecil Taylor was the most advanced improviser in jazz; four decades later he is still the most radical. Although in his early days he used some standards as vehicles for improvisation, since the early '60s Taylor has stuck exclusively to originals. To simplify describing his style, one could say that Taylor's intense atonal percussive approach involves playing the piano as if it were a set of drums. He generally emphasizes dense clusters of sound played with remarkable technique and endurance, often during marathon performances. Suffice it to say that Cecil Taylor's music is not for everyone!

Taylor started piano lessons from the age of six and attended the New York College of Music and the New England Conservatory. Taylor's early influences included Duke Ellington and Dave Brubeck, but from the start he sounded original. Early gigs included work with groups led by Johnny Hodges and Hot Lips Page but, after forming his quartet in the mid-'50s (which originally included Steve Lacy on soprano, bassist Buell Neidlinger and drummer Dennis Charles), Taylor was never a sideman again. The group played at the Five Spot Cafe in 1956 for six weeks and performed at the 1957 Newport Jazz Festival (which was recorded by Verve) but, despite occasional records, work was scarce. In 1960 Taylor recorded extensively for Candid under Neidlinger's name (by then the quartet featured Archie Shepp on tenor) and the following year he sometimes substituted in the play *The Connection*. By 1962 Taylor's quartet featured his longtime associate Jimmy Lyons on alto and drummer Sunny Murray. He spent six months in Europe (Albert Ayler worked with Taylor's group for a time although no recordings resulted), but upon his return to the U.S. Taylor did not work again for almost a year. Even with the rise of free jazz, his music was considered too advanced. In 1964 Taylor was one of the founders of the Jazz Composer's Guild and in 1968 he was featured on a record by the Jazz Composer's Orchestra. In the mid-'60s Taylor recorded two very advanced sets for Blue Note, but it was generally a lean decade.

Things greatly improved starting in the 1970s. Taylor taught for a time at the University of Wisconsin in Madison, Antioch College and Glassboro State College, he recorded more frequently with his Unit, and European tours became common. After being awarded a Guggenheim Fellowship in 1973, the pianist's financial difficulties were eased a bit; he even performed at the White House (during Jimmy Carter's administration) in 1979. A piano duet concert with Mary Lou Williams was a fiasco, but a collaboration with drummer Max Roach was quite successful. Taylor started incorporating some of his eccentric poetry into his performances, and unlike most musicians, he has not mellowed with age! The death of Jimmy Lyons in 1986 was a major blow, but Cecil Taylor has remained quite active up until the present day, never compromising his musical vision. His forbidding music is still decades ahead of its time. —*Scott Yanow*

Jazz Advance / Dec. 10, 1955 / Blue Note ✦✦✦✦✦
Looking Ahead / Jun. 9, 1958 / Original Jazz Classics ✦✦✦
Coltrane Time / Oct. 13, 1958 / United Artists ✦✦✦
Love for Sale / Apr. 15, 1959 / United Artists ✦✦✦
★ Complete Candid Recordings of Cecil Taylor / Oct. 12, 1960–Jan. 10, 1961 / Mosaic ✦✦✦✦✦
The sessions that comprise the four discs on this first-rate Mosaic boxed set were done in 1960 and 1961 for the short-lived Candid label. Taylor's concept had not yet evolved into a finished package, he wasn't always sure where he was going. There are solos that begin in one direction, break in the middle and conclude in another. Tenor saxophonist Archie Shepp often sounds unsure about what to play and whether to try and interact or establish his own direction. At the same time, there is plenty of exceptional playing from Taylor, Shepp and the drum/bass combination of Buell Neidlinger and Dennis Charles. You cannot honestly say everything works on these four discs, but there is never a dull moment.

It won't please everyone, but listeners ready for a challenge should step right up. —*Ron Wynn*

New York City R&B / Jan. 9, 1961–Jan. 10, 1961 / Candid ✦✦✦✦
The contents of this rather brief CD, originally released under bassist Buell Neidlinger's name, have since been reissued in the Cecil Taylor/Buell Neidlinger Mosaic box set. Two selections feature a trio with pianist Taylor, bassist Neidlinger and drummer Billy Higgins and one performance adds the young tenor Archie Shepp (and has Dennis Charles in Higgins' place). This music is quite advanced for the period although more accessible to the average listener than Taylor's later recordings; at least one can hear (even in abstract form) his connection to the bebop tradition and to Duke Ellington. Speaking of the latter, the most intriguing selection is a version of "Things Ain't What They Used to Be" that not only has Taylor, Neidlinger, Higgins and Shepp but Steve Lacy on soprano, baritonist Charles Davis, trombonist Roswell Rudd and trumpeter Clark Terry, making for a very interesting mixture of styles. —*Scott Yanow*

★ Unit Structures / May 19, 1966 / Blue Note ✦✦✦✦✦
Conquistador / Oct. 6, 1966 / Blue Note ✦✦✦✦✦
Student Studies / Nov. 30, 1966 / Affinity ✦✦✦✦
The music on this two record set was recorded in concert in Paris. As usual, the whole was much larger than the parts and I found there was enough inspired listening here to easily recommend the music. *Student Studies* tells some good tales and was full of the Taylor dynamics and at the same time quite accessible. —*Bob Rusch, Cadence*

Great Paris Concert / Jul. 29, 1969 / Freedom ✦✦✦✦✦
This three-LP set is a real blowout. Pianist Cecil Taylor, altoist Jimmy Lyons, Sam Rivers on tenor and soprano, and drummer Andrew Cyrille (there is no bass, but it couldn't have been heard anyway!) perform a 90-minute work followed by a 20-minute encore. The music is unrelentingly intense and Taylor does not let up for a moment. His fans are advised to pick up this major release, but those listeners new to Taylor's music should investigate his solo piano works first. —*Scott Yanow*

Indent / Mar. 11, 1973 / Freedom ✦✦✦✦
Silent Tongues / Jul. 2, 1974 / Freedom ✦✦✦✦✦
Dark Unto Themselves / Jun. 18, 1976 / Enja ✦✦✦✦✦
Air Above Mountains . . . / Aug. 20, 1976 / Enja ✦✦✦✦
★ Unit / Apr. 3, 1978–Apr. 6, 1978 / New World ✦✦✦✦✦
A sextet, this is as close to as definitive an ensemble as Taylor has launched. With Jimmy Lyons (sax), Raphe Malik (tpt), Ramsey Ameen (violin), Sirone (b), and R. Shannon Jackson (d). This runs 60 minutes on vinyl, including a 30 minute "Holiday en Masque." —*Michael G. Nastos*

Three Phasis / Apr. 1978 / New World ✦✦✦✦
The followup to *Unit*, this is one long piece of improv over two sides (57:12) with the same sextet. —*Michael G. Nastos*

One Too Many Salty Swifty and Not Goodbye / Jun. 4, 1978 / Hat Hut ✦✦✦✦✦
With one of his greatest groups in a powerful performance, this was the Unit at its peak. —*Michael G. Nastos*

Historic Concerts / Dec. 15, 1979 / Soul Note ✦✦✦✦✦
Great duo with Max Roach (d). —*Ron Wynn*

It Is in the Brewing Luminous / Feb. 8, 1980–Feb. 9, 1980 / Hat Art ✦✦✦

Fly, Fly, Fly, Fly, Fly / Sep. 14, 1980 / MPS ✦✦✦✦
A solo piano album that defines Taylor's individuality and does indeed fly. —*Michael G. Nastos*

Garden Pt. 1 / Nov. 16, 1981 / Hat Art ✦✦✦✦✦
Taylor slashing away on Bosendorfer piano. —*Ron Wynn*

Garden Pt. 2 / Nov. 1981 / Hat Art ✦✦✦✦✦
The Eighth / Nov. 1981 / Hat Art ✦✦✦✦
Winged Serpent (Sliding Quadrants) / Oct. 22, 1984–Oct. 24, 1984 / Soul Note ✦✦
For Olim / Apr. 9, 1986 / Soul Note ✦✦✦✦✦
One of his greatest solo works. —*Ron Wynn*

In Florescence / Jun. 8, 1989–Sep. 9, 1989 / A&M ✦✦
Taylor . . . remains as unbowed and unpredictable as ever. This is music as sound, rather than structured patterns, easily discernible melodies, or simple backbeats. The 60-minute plus date sways

between snippets, extensive dialogues and tunes with vocalisms and hollers. — *Ron Wynn*

John Tchicai

b. Apr. 28, 1936, Copenhagen, Denmark
Alto Saxophone / Avant-Garde, Free Jazz
John Tchicai will probably always be remembered for his alto playing on John Coltrane's monumental *Ascension* recording, but he's actually spent most of his life in Europe playing tenor sax. His style during the free period had a dry tone and featured a staccato attack; his later material has had a fuller, more soulful and earthy sound. Tchicai began playing violin at ten, then clarinet and alto sax at 16. He studied saxophone three years at the Royal Conservatory in Copenhagen. Tchicai met Archie Shepp at a festival in Helsinki in 1962. That same year he made his recording debut in Warsaw leading a quintet. Tchicai moved to New York in 1963. He played with Shepp and Don Cherry in the New York Contemporary Five, and with Roswell Rudd and Milford Graves in the New York Art Quartet in 1964 and 1965. Both bands toured Europe and recorded. Tchicai also recorded with the Jazz Composers Guild along with Shepp, John Coltrane and Albert Ayler. He returned to Denmark in 1966, and led the workshop ensemble Cadentia nova danica from 1967 to 1971, performing with them in London in 1968. Tchicai cut back on his playing and began teaching full time in 1972, then resumed active playing in 1977. He joined Pierre Dorge's New Jungle Orchestra in 1982 on tenor and has also played in recent times with Six Winds and with various San Francisco-based ensembles. He settled in Northern California and in 1994 appeared at the Monterey Jazz Festival, still playing in an advanced but relatively thoughtful style. —*Ron Wynn and Scott Yanow*

John Tchicai Solo Plus Albert Mangelsdorff / Feb. 16, 1977 / FMP ♦♦♦♦

● **Real Tchicai** / Mar. 23, 1977 / SteepleChase ♦♦♦♦♦

Darktown Highlights / Mar. 29, 1977 / Storyville ♦♦♦

John Tchicai and the Strange Brothers / Oct. 9, 1977 / FMP ♦♦♦♦

Ball at Louisiana / Nov. 11, 1981 / SteepleChase ♦♦♦

Timo's Message / Feb. 7, 1984 / Black Saint ♦♦♦♦♦

Put Up the Fight / Nov. 10, 1987–Nov. 14, 1987 / Storyville ♦♦♦♦

Jack Teagarden (Weldon Leo Teagarden)

b. Aug. 29, 1905, Vernon, TX, d. Jan. 15, 1964, New Orleans, LA
Trombone, Vocals, Leader / Dixieland, Swing
One of the classic giants of jazz, Jack Teagarden was not only the top pre-bop trombonist (playing his instrument with the ease of a trumpeter) but one of the best jazz singers too. He was such a fine musician that younger brother Charlie (an excellent trumpeter) was always overshadowed. Jack started on piano at age five (his mother Helen was a ragtime pianist), switched to baritone horn and finally took up trombone when he was ten. Teagarden worked in the Southwest in a variety of territory bands (most notably with the legendary pianist Peck Kelley) and then caused a sensation when he came to New York in 1928. His daring solos with Ben Pollack caused Glenn Miller to de-emphasize his own playing with the band and during the late-'20s/early Depression era "Mr. T." recorded frequently with many groups including units headed by Roger Wolfe Kahn, Eddie Condon, Red Nichols and Louis Armstrong ("Knockin' a Jug"); his versions of "Basin Street Blues" and "Beale Street Blues" (songs that would remain in his repertoire for the remainder of his career) were definitive. Teagarden, who was greatly admired by Tommy Dorsey, would have been a logical candidate for fame in the swing era, but he made a strategic error. In late 1933, when it looked as if jazz would never catch on commercially, he signed a five-year contract with Paul Whiteman. Although Whiteman's Orchestra did feature Teagarden now and then (and he had a brief period in 1936 playing with a small group from the band, the Three T's, with his brother Charlie and Frankie Trumbauer), the contract effectively kept Teagarden from going out on his own and becoming a star. It certainly prevented him from leading what would eventually become the Bob Crosby Orchestra.

In 1939 Jack Teagarden was finally "free" and he soon put together a big band that would last until 1946. However it was rather late to be organizing a new orchestra (the competition was fierce), and although there were some good musical moments,

none of the sidemen became famous, the arrangements lacked their own musical personality and by the time it broke up Teagarden was facing bankruptcy. The trombonist however was still a big name (he had fared quite well in the 1940 Bing Crosby film *The Birth of the Blues*) and he had many friends. Crosby helped Teagarden straighten out his financial problems and from 1947–51 he was a star sideman with Louis Armstrong's All-Stars; their collaborations on "Rocking Chair" are classic. After leaving Armstrong, Teagarden was a leader of a steadily working sextet throughout the remainder of his career, playing Dixieland with such talented musicians as brother Charlie, trumpeters Jimmy McPartland, Don Goldie and Max Kaminsky and (during a 1957 European tour) pianist Earl Hines. Teagarden toured the Far East during 1958–59, teamed up one last time with Eddie Condon for a television show/recording session in 1961 and had a heartwarming and (fortunately recorded) musical reunion with Charlie, sister-pianist Norma and his mother at the 1963 Monterey Jazz Festival. He died from a heart attack four months later and has yet to be replaced. —*Scott Yanow*

★ **The Indispensable** / Mar. 14, 1928–Jul. 8, 1957 / RCA ♦♦♦♦♦
Much more complete than the Bluebird CD, this two CD set has trombonist Jack Teagarden featured with Roger Wolfe Kahn's orchestra (two takes of "She's a Great, Great Girl"), Eddie Condon's Hot Shots, the Mound City Blue Blowers, eight numbers with Ben Pollack, his better recordings with Paul Whiteman's Orchestra and a complete session under his own leadership in 1947, in addition to three numbers with Bud Freeman in 1957. This set is highly recommended to those who can locate it. —*Scott Yanow*

That's a Serious Thing / Mar. 14, 1928–Jul. 8, 1957 / Bluebird ♦♦♦♦♦
This readily available Bluebird CD gives one an excellent overview of the talents of trombonist/singer Jack Teagarden. "Mr. T." is featured with Eddie Condon on a pair of classic 1929 selections and also with Roger Wolfe Kahn's orchestra ("She's a Great Great Girl"), Ben Pollack, the Mound City Blue Blowers, Fats Waller, Benny Goodman, Paul Whiteman, the Three T's, the Metronome All-Stars, Louis Armstrong (the exciting "Jack-Armstrong Blues") and with Bud Freeman, in addition to a version of "St. Louis Blues" with Teagarden's group in 1947. Quite a few of these performances are famous, and although this is not a "complete" set, the consistent high quality of these recordings makes this CD highly recommended to all. —*Scott Yanow*

★ **King of the Blues Trombone** / Nov. 27, 1928–Jul. 23, 1940 / Epic ♦♦♦♦♦
This deluxe three-LP set (which will hopefully be reissued on CD eventually) features the great trombonist and vocalist Jack Teagarden in a variety of settings. These often-rare recordings showcase Teagarden as a sideman with Jimmy McHugh's Bostonians, Mills Merry Makers, the Whoopee Makers, Jack Pettis, Goody and His Good Timers, Joe Venuti, Ben Pollack, Benny Goodman, Frankie Trumbauer and Teagarden's own big band; the supporting cast includes Goodman, Jimmy McPartland, Artie Shaw, Jimmy Dorsey, Bud Freeman, Fats Waller and many other classic jazz artists. If you are fortunate enough to run across this collection, don't let it out of your sight. —*Scott Yanow*

1930–1934 / Oct. 1, 1930–Mar. 2, 1934 / Classics ♦♦♦♦
This Classics CD has the first 23 titles ever issued under the leadership of trombonist Jack Teagarden. Many of these selections were formerly rare, particularly the earlier titles on Domino, Banner and Crown. Best is the session that co-starred pianist/vocalist Fats Waller, and while some of the titles are a bit commercial, Teagarden's playing (and that of his better sidemen) uplift the music; "A Hundred Years from Today" is a classic. —*Scott Yanow*

Jack & Charlie Teagarden & Frank Trumbauer / Jan. 12, 1934–Jun. 15, 1936 / Teagarden ♦♦♦♦♦
Trombonist Jack Teagarden spent some of the prime years of the swing era tied to Paul Whiteman's Orchestra because in 1934 he signed a five-year contract. If he had not made that decision, Teagarden might very well have ended up as the leader of the Bob Crosby Orchestra. While with Whiteman, Teagarden was given the opportunity to record with a small group from the big band, one that was called "The Three T's" because of the participation of his brother Charlie Teagarden on trumpet and the great C-melody saxophonist Frankie Trumbauer. All of their recordings (most of which were issued under Trumbauer's name) are on this enjoy-

Music Map

Trombone

New Orleans Jazz Pioneers
Kid Ory
George Brunies

1920s
Honore Dutrey	Charlie Green
Charlie Irvis	Miff Mole
Jimmy Harrison	Roy Palmer
J.C. Higginbottham	

Duke Ellington's Trombonists Through the Years
Tricky Sam Nanton	Juan Tizol
Lawrence Brown	Tyree Glenn
Quentin Jackson	Britt Woodman
Buster Cooper	

Innovator
Jack Teagarden

Swing Era
Tommy Dorsey	Trummy Young
Benny Morton	Dickie Wells
Jack Jenney	Fred Beckett

Dixieland
Vic Dickerson	Lou McGarity
Cutty Cutshall	Jim Robinson
Turk Murphy	Wilbur DeParis
Dan Barrett	

Bop Innovator
J.J. Johnson

1950s/'60s
Kai Winding	Frank Rosolino
Bill Harris	Benny Green
Jimmy Cleveland	Carl Fontana
Urbie Green	Jimmy Knepper
Curtis Fuller	Slide Hampton
Al Grey	Phil Wilson
Wayne Henderson	Julian Priester

Avant-Garde/Free Jazz
Roswell Rudd	Grachan Moncur III
Albert Mangelsdorff	George Lewis
Joseph Bowie	Glenn Ferris
Craig Harris	Eje Thelin
Conrad Bauer	Paul Rutherford
Ray Anderson	

1980s/'90s
Bill Watrous	Steve Turre
Robin Eubanks	Thurman Green
Fred Wesley	Jiggs Whigham
Bruce Fowler	Frank Lacy
Wycliffe Gordon	Delfeayo Marsalis

Valve Trombone
Juan Tizol	Brad Gowans
Bob Brookmeyer	Rob McConnell
Mike Fahn	

able CD, which also includes a few solos from clarinetist Artie Shaw and two Teagarden features with Whiteman. The music, essentially small-group swing, has plenty of solo space for the principles and there are many memorable selections. Highly recommended. —*Scott Yanow*

1934–1939 / Sep. 18, 1934–Jul. 19, 1939 / Classics ♦♦♦♦
The second of three Jack Teagarden Classics CDs contains all of his recordings as a leader during this pivotal period. There are three titles from 1934 with a pickup group also including clarinetist Benny Goodman and Frankie Trumbauer on C-melody sax. But the bulk of this CD is taken up by the first 21 studio performances by Jack Teagarden's ill-fated big band in 1939. The trombonist/leader is easily the most interesting soloist and his vocals are a joy while those of Linda Keene are okay. Teagarden's swing band did not have its own identity, but its recordings are generally enjoyable. —*Scott Yanow*

On The Air / Jan. 12, 1936–Dec. 28, 1938 / Sandy Hook ♦♦♦
Trombonist Jack Teagarden spent most of the 1934–38 period buried in Paul Whiteman's Orchestra, but Whiteman was wise enough to feature "Mr. T" from time to time. This Sandy Hook LP

contains 16 rare performances, all radio airchecks from 1936 and 1938 that put the emphasis on Teagarden's trombone and vocals. Quite a few of the songs are then-current pop tunes, but Teagarden's playing is of a consistent high quality and there are many enjoyable moments. —*Scott Yanow*

Jack Teagarden's Big Eight / Pee Wee Russell's Rhythmakers / Aug. 31, 1938–Dec. 15, 1940 / Original Jazz Classics ♦♦♦♦♦

Birth Of A Band / Jan. 31, 1939–Nov. 1939 / Giants of Jazz ♦♦♦♦
This Giants of Jazz LP is a must for Jack Teagarden collectors due to its historic value. First Teagarden is heard on a radio broadcast with Benny Goodman's Orchestra in which it is announced that he has formed his own big band after five years with Paul Whiteman. Teagarden jams with Benny Goodman on "Basin Street Blues," shares the vocal with Johnny Mercer on "Two Sleepy People" and plays a spirited "Roll 'Em" with the Goodman Orchestra and guest pianist Pete Johnson. The remainder of this album contains the earliest existing broadcast by Teagarden's big band. The trombonist's sidemen are enthusiastic and they swing hard on most of the selections. Although the band's potential was

never realized, they sound full of spirit and power on this excellent set. — *Scott Yanow*

Sincerely Jack Teagarden / Apr. 14, 1939–Jun. 23, 1939 / IAJRC ✦✦✦✦
The collector's label IAJRC reissued 16 of the first 18 selections recorded by the Jack Teagarden Orchestra on this well-conceived LP. With such sidemen as first trumpeter Charlie Spivak, baritonist Ernie Caceres and rhythm guitarist Allan Reuss, the trombonist had a solid foundation for his big band. The orchestra in the long run never caught on (although it lasted seven years) and caused Teagarden many financial headaches, but that cannot be told from these enthusiastic early recordings. Teagarden has vocals on nine of the tracks, Linda Keene is heard from on three and Jean Arnold sings two, so the emphasis is on dance music rather than jazz, but these historic recordings have their memorable moments. — *Scott Yanow*

Rompin' and Stompin' / May 1939–Aug. 1944 / Swing Era ✦✦✦
The Jack Teagarden Orchestra never really caught on during the swing era and eventually the trombonist/leader went bankrupt. However, as these studio recordings show, the band was not without interest. Teagarden was easily the most interesting soloist in what was really a no-name outfit, but the 16 performances (the majority from 1942 and 1944) are full of swing, spirit and strong moments. Kitty Kallen has the vocal on "Swing Without Words" and the leader gets two chances to sing, but the emphasis on this LP is, as the title suggests, on "Rompin' and Stompin'." — *Scott Yanow*

1939–1940 / Aug. 23, 1939–Feb. 1940 / Classics ✦✦✦✦✦
The third in Classics' *Complete* Jack Teagarden series traces the trombonist's big-band recordings during his Columbia period. There were no great soloists among Teagarden's sidemen and some of these tunes (particularly the nine with Kitty Kallen vocals) are throwaways, but Teagarden's own singing on six songs (including "Beale Street Blues" and "If I Could Be with You") and distinctive trombone give listeners strong reasons to acquire this entry in the worthy series. Other highlights include "Peg of My Heart," "Wolverine Blues," "Swinging' on the Teagarden Gate" and "The Blues." — *Scott Yanow*

Varsity Drags / Feb. 19, 1940–Jul. 1940 / Savoy ✦✦✦
Savoy's reissue of Jack Teagarden's 16 recordings for Varsity with his big band is perfectly done, but the music is streaky. When one eliminates the pop vocals of Kitty Kallen, Marianne Dunne and David Allyn, all that is left are five selections: four worthy vocals by the leader and just one instrumental ("The Blues"). Overall the music on this set is decent but generally more commercial than one would hope for a Jack Teagarden recording. — *Scott Yanow*

It's Time for Tea / Jan. 31, 1941–Jun. 1941 / Jass ✦✦✦✦
This is the first of two CDs put out by Jass that reissue all of the Standard Transcriptions recorded by Jack Teagarden's big band for radio airplay. These recordings are generally quite superior to his studio sides of the period. Although the trombonist did not have a great big band, his solos and those of trumpeter Pokey Carriere hold one's interest. A young David Allyn, Lynn Clark and Mr. T. himself have the vocals, but half of the selections are swinging instrumentals. — *Scott Yanow*

Has Anybody Here Seen Jackson? / Oct. 1941–Aug. 22, 1944 / Jass ✦✦✦✦
Jack Teagarden's Standard Transcriptions are reissued on this CD and the previous *It's Time for "Tea"*. Teagarden made few studio recordings with his ill-fated big band during this period, and even with the seven commercial vocals by David Allyn and Kitty Kallen, this music is superior to what was generally available to the public from the trombonist's orchestra at the time. Teagarden and his somewhat obscure sidemen are in consistently fine form on the varied material; pity that the big band never really caught on. — *Scott Yanow*

Big "T" & The Condon Gang / Dec. 2, 1944–Dec. 16, 1944 / Pumpkin ✦✦✦✦✦
Although trombonist Jack Teagarden is listed as the main star, in reality the music on this LP is taken from two of Eddie Condon's famous Town Hall concerts. Teagarden, taking a well-deserved vacation from his struggling big band, is consistently inspired by the presence of such all-stars as trumpeters Max Kaminsky, Bobby Hackett, Billy Butterfield and Wingy Manone, clarinetist Pee Wee Russell, baritonist Ernie Caceres and, on "Christmas at Carnegie," the great soprano Sidney Bechet. The music is freewheeling

Chicago jazz with vocals from the trombonist, Lee Wiley and, on the lengthy "Big T & Wingy Blues," both Teagarden and Manone. Classic performances. — *Scott Yanow*

With His Sextet and Eddie Condon's Chicagoans / Jun. 1947–Oct. 30, 1961 / Pumpkin ✦✦✦✦
Trombonist Jack Teagarden is heard in two very different but equally rewarding settings on this worthy LP. He performs eight numbers with his short-lived sextet in 1947 shortly before he became a regular member of Louis Armstrong's All-Stars. Along with trumpeter Max Kaminsky and clarinetist Peanuts Hucko, Mr. T. is heard in top form on eight standards including several Hoagy Carmichael compositions. In addition, he participates in a reunion of Eddie Condon's Chicagoans in Oct. 1961 even though he was not an original member. Teagarden is heard along with cornetist Jimmy McPartland, clarinetist Pee Wee Russell, tenor saxophonist Bud Freeman, pianist Joe Sullivan, guitarist Eddie Condon, bassist Bob Haggart and drummer Gene Krupa on six selections taken from their appearance on *The Today Show*. The music is essentially spirited Dixieland with McPartland contributing some surprisingly advanced solos. — *Scott Yanow*

Meet Me Where They Play the Blues / Nov. 1954 / Bethlehem ✦✦✦
For this LP, trombonist Jack Teagarden is heard with three different groups on a dozen titles recorded in Nov. 1954. Although the supporting cast on various selections includes trumpeter Jimmy McPartland, clarinetists Edmond Hall and Kenny Davern, and Dick Cary, Norma Teagarden and Leonard Feather on pianos, Teagarden is the main star throughout. His trombone playing was still in prime form and his vocals give spirit to the music. Highpoints of this enjoyable Dixieland set include "Original Dixieland One Step," "Blue Funk," "Eccentric" and "Milenburg Joys." — *Scott Yanow*

This Is Teagarden / Jan. 1956 / Capitol ✦✦✦
Trombonist Jack Teagarden revisits a dozen songs he had recorded previously for this Capitol LP. His trombone solos and vocals are consistently excellent although the arrangements for the larger groups by Van Alexander do not leave any room for the interplay found in New Orleans and Chicago jazz. Teagarden is virtually the whole show, but fortunately he is in fine form. — *Scott Yanow*

Tribute to Teagarden / Jan. 1956–Apr. 1958 / Pausa ✦✦✦
This Pausa LP draws its material from three separate Capitol albums. Seven of the titles were originally released as *This Is Teagarden* and these find the great trombonist/singer revisiting some of his past glories (such as "After You've Gone," The Sheik of Araby" and "Beale Street Blues") while being accompanied by Van Alexander arrangements. "Goin' Home" is taken from a rare album of hymns while the final four numbers, recorded with his 1958 sextet (which features trumpeter Dick Oakley, clarinetist Jerry Fuller and pianist Don Ewell) are much more lively. The spirit behind the latter (the original album was accurately titled *Big T's Dixieland Band*) makes one wish that Capitol would get around to reissuing the entire record. — *Scott Yanow*

Jack Teagarden Sextet / May 3, 1958 / Pumpkin ✦✦✦✦
Trombonist Jack Teagarden led one of his finest regular bands in 1958. With cornetist Dick Oakley, clarinetist Jerry Fuller and pianist Don Ewell co-starring in the sextet, Teagarden had strong sidemen who knew how to sound individual in the Dixieland format. This broadcast (live from Cleveland) finds Teagarden and his band running through his usual repertoire, somehow sounding inspired while playing such warhorses as "Basin Street Blues" and "Muskrat Ramble." — *Scott Yanow*

● **Jack Teagarden and His All Stars** / May 1958 / Jazzology ✦✦✦✦✦
Taken from the same period (but not duplicating the music) of Jack Teagarden's Pumpkin LP, this Jazzology CD finds the trombonist leading one of his strongest groups, a band that also features many fine solos from cornetist Dick Oakley, clarinetist Jerry Fuller and pianist Don Ewell. Even on such tunes as "Someday You'll Be Sorry," "High Society" and "When the Saints Go Marching In," this very enjoyable sextet is able to play with enthusiasm and creativity, coming up with something fresh to say on songs the musicians had performed a countless number of times. — *Scott Yanow*

On Okinawa / Jan. 21, 1959 / IAJRC ✦✦✦✦
Recorded in Okinawa, Japan during an Asian tour, the music on

this set is pure Dixieland. The great trombonist Jack Teagarden, heading a sextet with trumpeter Max Kaminsky, clarinetist Jerry Fuller and pianist Don Ewell, performs lively versions of nine Dixieland standards plus a blues. Everyone plays up to par and comes up with spirited statements on the familiar repertoire. — *Scott Yanow*

Hundred Years from Today / Sep. 20, 1963–Sep. 21, 1963 / Memphis Archives ✦✦✦✦✦
Jack Teagarden's final recording (performed less than four months before his death), finds the trombonist/vocalist in particularly happy spirits at the Monterey Jazz Festival. Mr. T. was reunited not only with his brother (trumpeter Charlie) and sister (pianist Norma) but also his mother who performs a couple of ragtime piano solos! The strong supporting cast, in addition to the many Teagardens, features clarinetist Pee Wee Russell, baritonist Gerry Mulligan and pianist Joe Sullivan. The two sets included on this historical CD are filled with blues, standards and Dixieland, the results of Jack Teagarden's two sets at Monterey. This important and easily enjoyable music is proof that the great trombonist went out on top. — *Scott Yanow*

Joe Temperley

b. Sep. 20, 1929, Fife, Scotland
Baritone Saxophone / Swing
Baritonist Joe Temperley is the perfect musician to fill in for Harry Carney during recreations of Duke Ellington's music, a role that has often overshadowed his own fine voice. Temperley actually started on the alto and recorded on tenor with English bands led by Harry Parry (1949), Jack Parnell, Tony Crombie and Tommy Whittle. He stuck to baritone during a long association with Humphrey Lyttelton's popular band (1958–65). In 1965 Temperley moved to New York, working with a variety of big bands (including Woody Herman, Buddy Rich, Thad Jones-Mel Lewis and Clark Terry). In 1974 he became the first replacement for Harry Carney with the Mercer Ellington Orchestra and has since then freelanced with the who's who of jazz including (starting in 1990) the Lincoln Center Jazz Orchestra under the direction of Wynton Marsalis. Temperley has several fine albums out as a leader, most notably for the Scottish Hep label. — *Scott Yanow*

Nightingale / Apr. 1991 / Hep ✦✦✦✦
★ **Concerto For Joe** / Sep. 22, 1993+Jul. 8, 1994 / Hep ✦✦✦✦✦
Joe Temperley's thick-toned baritone and swing-oriented style is heard at its best on this CD, his definitive release. Temperley's huge sound sometimes makes it seems as if he is playing a bass sax rather than a baritone, yet his fluidity is on the level of an altoist! He performs seven selections (including four Duke Ellington songs) with a talented quartet headed by pianist Brian Lemon, and a six-song suite by the late trumpeter Jimmy Deuchar with an 11-piece group; the latter also features fine solos from altoist Peter King and trumpeter Gerard Presencer. The swinging music is all straight-ahead with appealing chord changes serving as an inspiration for the underrated baritonist. Recommended. — *Scott Yanow*

Jacky Terrasson

b. Nov. 27, 1966, Berlin, Germany
Piano / Post-Bop
One of the most promising pianists of the mid-'90s, Jacky Terrasson grew up in Paris and started studying classical piano when he was five. He switched to jazz as a teenager, attended Berklee in Boston and a few years later was a regular in Paris jazz clubs and at European festivals. After a stint working with Dee Dee Bridgewater, Terrasson moved to New York in 1990, worked and recorded with Art Taylor, Cindy Blackman and Betty Carter, won the 1993 Thelonious Monk Jazz Competition and debuted as a leader for Blue Note. — *Scott Yanow*

Jacky Terrasson / 1994 / Blue Note ✦✦✦✦
Jacky Terrasson delights in turning standards inside out. On his CD he gives odd rhythms to "I Love Paris," purposely speeds up and slows down the tempo on "Bye Bye Blackbird," takes "I Fall in Love Too Easily" very slow, does his best to disguise "Bye Bye Blackbird" and shows a grasp of dynamics worthy of Ahmad Jamal. It is fortunate that bassist Ugonna Okegwo and drummer Leon Parker are very alert (or perhaps well rehearsed) because to the uninitiated listener these eccentric and rather quirky perfor-

mances are often quite unpredictable and occasionally jarring. Well worth checking out. — *Scott Yanow*
● **Reach** / 1995 / Blue Note ✦✦✦✦✦

Clark Terry

b. Dec. 14, 1920, St. Louis, MO
Fluegelhorn, Vocals / Bop, Swing
Possessor of the happiest sound in jazz, fluegelhornist Clark Terry always plays music that is exuberant, swinging and fun. A brilliant (and very distinctive) soloist, C.T. gained fame for his "Mumbles" vocals (which started as a satire of the less intelligible ancient blues singers) and is also an enthusiastic educator. He gained early experience playing trumpet in the viable St. Louis jazz scene of the early '40s (where he was an inspiration for Miles Davis), and after performing in a Navy band during World War II, he gained a strong reputation playing with the big band of Charlie Barnet (1947–48), the orchestra and small groups of Count Basie (1948–51) and particularly with Duke Ellington (1951–59). Terry, a versatile swing/bop soloist who started specializing on fluegelhorn in the mid-'50s, had many features with Ellington (including "Perdido") and started leading his own record dates during that era. He visited Europe with Harold Arlen's unsuccessful *The Free & Easy* show of 1959–60 as part of Quincy Jones' Orchestra and then joined the staff of NBC where he was a regular member of the Tonight Show Orchestra. He recorded regularly in the 1960s including a classic set with the Oscar Peterson Trio and several dates with the quintet he co-led with valve trombonist Bob Brookmeyer. Throughout the 1970s, '80s and '90s C.T. has remained a major force, recording and performing in a wide variety of settings including at the head of his short-lived big band in the mid-'70s, with all-star groups for Pablo and as a guest artist who can be expected to provide happiness in every note he plays. — *Scott Yanow*

Clark Terry / Jan. 3, 1955–Jan. 4, 1955 / EmArcy ✦✦✦✦
With the exception of three songs cut as V-Discs in 1947, this set contains fluegelhornist Clark Terry's first recordings as a leader. Joined by trombonist Jimmy Cleveland, baritonist Cecil Payne, pianist Horace Silver, Oscar Pettiford on cello, bassist Wendell Marshall and drummer Art Blakey, C.T. performs eight obscure songs that are arranged quite expertly by Quincy Jones. Terry sounds much more influenced by Dizzy Gillespie than he would in just a couple of years, but his good-humored musical personality and control of his horn was already obvious. With Pettiford offering occasional cello solos (in addition to playing second bass) and Cleveland in top form, this is an LP long overdue to be reissued on CD. — *Scott Yanow*

Serenade to a Bus Seat / Apr. 1957 / Original Jazz Classics ✦✦✦✦
Why it took so long for Clark Terry to be recognized for his fine stylized trumpet work is hard to understand, as even by the time of this date he had quite well established himself as a capable individual voice. — *Bob Rusch, Cadence*

Duke with a Difference / Jul. 29, 1957+Sep. 6, 1957 / Original Jazz Classics ✦✦✦✦✦
For this CD reissue of a Riverside set, trumpeter Clark Terry and some of the top Ellington sidemen of the period (trombonist Britt Woodman, altoist Johnny Hodges, tenor saxophonist Paul Gonsalves, Tyree Glenn on vibes, bassist Jimmy Woode and drummer Sam Woodyard) perform eight songs associated with Duke but with fresh arrangements. There is plenty of solo space for C.T., Gonsalves and Hodges, and the arrangements by Terry and Mercer Ellington cast a new light on some of the warhorses; highlights include "C-Jam Blues," "Cottontail," "Mood Indigo" and "Come Sunday." — *Scott Yanow*

In Orbit / May 1958 / Original Jazz Classics ✦✦✦✦✦
One of Thelonious Monk's rare appearances as a sideman is on this quartet set led by fluegelhornist Clark Terry. With bassist Sam Jones and drummer Philly Joe Jones, Terry and pianist Monk perform a set that surprisingly only has one Thelonious Monk song ("Let's Cool One"). Among the high points of this happy, boppish date are C.T.'s "Globetrotter," "One Foot in the Gutter" and "Zip Co-Ed." — *Scott Yanow*

Top and Bottom Brass / Feb. 24, 1959+Feb. 26, 1959 / Original Jazz Classics ✦✦✦✦
This lesser-known Clark Terry session (reissued on CD in the *OJC* series) has an unusual lineup with the fluegelhornist joined by Don Butterfield on tuba, pianist Jimmy Jones, bassist Sam Jones

and drummer Art Taylor. Butterfield has nearly as much solo space as C.T. (and is given a prominent role in the ensembles) while Jimmy Jones' chordal solos are somewhat eccentric. Terry is in fine form on a variety of blues, originals and obscurities along with the interesting versions of "My Heart Belongs to Daddy" and "A Sunday Kind of Love," but the results overall are not all that significant. *— Scott Yanow*

Paris (1960) / Jan. 1960–Feb. 1960 / Swing ✦✦✦
This is a slightly unusual album recorded by fluegelhornist Clark Terry while in Europe performing with the Harold Arlen show *Free and Easy*. Terry is featured with a sextet that includes Eric Dixon on flute and tenor, guitarist Elek Bacsik and drummer Kenny Clarke on three numbers (highlighted by Duke Jordan's "No Problem"), jams four other songs with the same sextet, but with trombonist Quentin Jackson in Dixon's place, and performs five of pianist Martial Solal's originals written for the Belgian film *Si Le Vent Te Fait Peur* with a French septet that includes the composer. Although this LP, which benefits from lengthy liner notes by Dan Morgenstern, is not essential, it is worth picking up, if it can be found. *— Scott Yanow*

★ **Color Changes** / Nov. 19, 1960 / Candid ✦✦✦✦✦
This is one of fluegelhornist Clark Terry's finest albums. Terry had complete control over the music, and rather than have the usual jam session, he utilized an octet and arrangements by Yusef Lateef, Budd Johnson and Al Cohn. The lineup of musicians (C.T., trombonist Jimmy Knepper, Julius Watkins on French horn, Yusef Lateef on tenor, flute, oboe and English horn, Seldon Powell doubling on tenor and flute, pianist Tommy Flanagan, bassist Joe Benjamin and drummer Ed Shaughnessy) lives up to its potential, and the charts make good use of the sounds of these very individual stylists. The material, which consists of originals by Terry, Duke Jordan, Lateef and Bob Wilber, is both rare and fresh, and the interpretations always swing. Highly recommended. *— Scott Yanow*

Mellow Moods / Jul. 21, 1961–May 15, 1962 / Prestige ✦✦✦✦
This CD combines together two former LPs by fluegelhornist Clark Terry: *Everything's Mellow* and *All American*. Since those two sessions were cut for the Moodsville label (where all of the sets were supposed to be emphasizing quiet ballads) and the second date has songs from a forgotten musical, this CD would not seem to have much potential. However Terry is highly expressive on the former date (a quartet outing with pianist Junior Mance, bassist Joe Benjamin and drummer Charlie Persip) and does not stick only to ballads, throwing in some blues and obscure melodies. As for the *All American* score, Oliver Nelson was enlisted to write arrangements for Terry's septet (which is comprised of Budd Johnson on tenor, trombonist Lester Robertson, baritonist George Barrow, pianist Eddie Costa in one of his final recordings, bassist Art Davis and drummer Ed Shaughnessy), and except for a couple of purposely corny moments, the music is greatly uplifted; in fact a few of the songs deserve to be revived. C.T. and Budd are in great form throughout. This surprising CD is recommended. *— Scott Yanow*

New York Sessions / Oct. 3, 1961–Oct. 4, 1961 / Fontana ✦✦✦
Exciting '60s date, with Tubby Hayes (ts) immense. *— Ron Wynn*

★ **Tread Ye Lightly** / 1963 / Cameo ✦✦✦✦✦
This is one of Clark Terry's finest records of the 1960s but has yet to be reissued on CD. Possessor of the happiest sound in jazz, the fluegelhornist is particularly exuberant on "Georgia on My Mind," "Misty" and "Lilies of the Field." The colorful supporting cast includes Seldon Powell on tenor, baritone and flute, Buddy Lucas doubling on harmonica and tenor, bassist Major Holley (who sings along with some of his solos) and the mysterious "Homer Fields" on piano, who is actually Ray Bryant. Well worth searching for. *— Scott Yanow*

★ **Oscar Peterson Trio with Clark Terry** / 1964 / Mercury ✦✦✦✦✦
The Oscar Peterson Trio, with bassist Ray Brown and drummer Ed Thigpen, welcomed fluegelhornist Clark Terry to this very memorable studio session. Whether on "Brotherhood of Man," "Mack the Knife" or "They Didn't Believe Me," all of the players are mutually inspired, and the results are not only joyful but also explosively exuberant. However, this album (reissued on CD) will be best remembered for Clark Terry's introduction of his unique vocal style on "Mumbles" and "Incoherent Blues"; those spontaneous performances still sound funny. A gem. *— Scott Yanow*

The Happy Horn of Clark Terry / Mar. 13, 1964 / GRP/Impulse! ✦✦✦✦✦
This all-star LP has plenty of memorable moments. Fluegelhornist Clark Terry teams up with altoist Phil Woods (who doubles on clarinet), tenor great Ben Webster, pianist Roger Kellaway, bassist Milt Hinton and drummer Walter Perkins for a varied program that includes a rollicking version of "Rockin' in Rhythm," Bix Beiderbecke's "In a Mist," a Duke Ellington medley and "Return to Swahili," which is mostly a fluegelhorn-drums duet. The lively music is quite enjoyable. *— Scott Yanow*

Live 1964 / May 8, 1964 / Emerald ✦✦✦
This LP from Horace Silver's Emerald label in 1987 released for the first time this particular live set from fluegelhornist Clark Terry. The 1964 quartet session (which also includes pianist Michael Abene, bassist Jimmy Gannon and drummer John Forte) finds Terry in typically joyful form playing his usual repertoire of the period: "Straight No Chaser," "Stardust," "Perdido," "Misty," "Haig and Haig" and a 12-1/2 minute version of "In a Mellow Tone." While the backup group is supportive without showing much of a personality, Terry makes it obvious from the first note who he is! C.T.'s fans will enjoy this one. *— Scott Yanow*

Quintet / Nov. 23, 1964–Nov. 24, 1964 / Mainstream ✦✦✦
Fluegelhornist Clark Terry and valve trombonist Bob Brookmeyer made for a very complementary pair in their mid-'60s quintet. Both had distinctive but similar sounds, impressive technique, the ability to swing anything and plenty of wit. On this Mainstream LP with pianist Roger Kellaway, bassist Bill Crow and drummer Dave Bailey, C.T. and Brookmeyer explore such songs as Herbie Hancock's "Blindman, Blindman," Charlie Parker's "Hymn," Thelonious Monk's "Straight No Chaser" and a variety of originals. Unfortunately, all ten selections clock in at around three minutes, so there is no real stretching out, but what is here is excellent. *— Scott Yanow*

Spanish Rice / Jul. 18, 1966–Jul. 20, 1966 / Impulse! ✦✦✦
Although Clark Terry (on fluegelhorn and occasional vocal) is the main star of this LP, arranger Chico O'Farrill is most responsible for the band's unusual sound. Utilizing an instrumentation of four trumpets, two guitars, bass, drums and four Latin percussionists, O'Farrill explores some veteran melodies (including "Peanut Vendor," "Mexican Hat Dance" and "Tin Tin Deo"), along with some newer pieces. The performances ("Joonji" is the longest at 3-1/2 minutes) are all quite concise and would have benefited from some more extended playing and perhaps an occasional solo by trumpeters Snooky Young, Joe Newman and Ernie Royal, but the overall results are quite joyful, and C.T. is in typically swinging form. *— Scott Yanow*

Gingerbread Men / 1966 / Mainstream ✦✦✦✦
With Bob Brookmeyer (tb) Quintet. This is a fine set. *— Ron Wynn*

At The Montreux Jazz Festival / Jun. 22, 1969 / Polydor ✦✦✦✦
An impressive big band (mostly comprised of Europeans) was put together by arranger Ernie Wilkins to back fluegelhornist Clark Terry at his 1969 appearance at the Montreux Jazz Festival. While Terry (who sings the humorous "Mumbling in the Alps") is the main soloist, there are also spots for Wilkins on tenor (well featured on "All Too Soon"), vibraphonist Dave Pike, guitarist Louis Stewart and some lesser-known players. This out-of-print LP will be a difficult one to find. *— Scott Yanow*

Clark Terry's Big B-A-D-Band Live at the Wichita Jazz Festival / Apr. 21, 1974 / Vanguard ✦✦✦✦

Clark Terry and His Jolly Giants / 1975 / Vanguard ✦✦✦✦

Big Bad Band Live at Buddy's Place / 1976 / Vanguard ✦✦✦
Fluegelhornist Clark Terry's big band did not last all that long, but it was not from a lack of musicianship or spirit. This live set has such players in its sax section as Frank Wess, Chris Woods, Ernie Wilkins and Charles Davis along with trombonist Eddie Bert and pianist Ronnie Mathews. The results are predictably straight-ahead with Wilkins as the chief arranger and a few Duke Ellington-associated pieces among the highpoints. *— Scott Yanow*

Live at Buddy's Place / 1976 / Vanguard ✦✦✦
The Clark Terry big band has always been a part-time venture, which is a real pity, for the fluegelhornist sounds quite natural in front of a jazz orchestra. This out-of-print Vanguard LP contains a live date by the swinging outfit in 1976. Ernie Wilkins' arrangements give the band its own personality, and there is some solo space for Wilkins' tenor, altoist Chris Woods and pianist Ronnie Mathews, among others, although C.T. is the main star. The less-

er-known material, which includes four Wilkins originals and Jimmy Heath's "Gap Sealer," is an added plus, but this album will be difficult to locate until it is eventually (and rightfully) reissued on CD. — *Scott Yanow*

Live At The Jazz House / 1976 / Pausa ✦✦✦
Although the backup trio, pianist Scott Bradford, drummer Hartwig Bartz and bassist Larry "Gailes" (probably Gales) is fairly anonymous, fluegelhornist Clark Terry is in typically exuberant form, performing five standards, a German folk song and his own "Jazzhouse Blues." The lengthy versions of "Perdido," "On the Trail," "Wham" and "Take the 'A' Train" all find C.T. in prime form, coming up with plenty of creative ideas on songs that he had already performed a countless number of times. This Pausa LP contains music originally put out on the MPS label. — *Scott Yanow*

The Globetrotter / 1977 / Vanguard ✦✦✦✦
For this sextet/septet session, fluegelhornist Clark Terry mostly drew his personnel from the big band that he occasionally fronted during the mid-'70s. Of special interest is getting a chance to hear tenor saxophonist Ernie Wilkins (better known as an arranger) stretching out as a soloist; C.T.'s other sidemen include pianist Ronnie Mathews, bassist Victor Sproeles and drummer Ed Soph with guest spots for pianist Walter Bishop and guitarist Roland Prince. The repertoire is particularly strong with classic ballads such as "Misty" and "Autumn Leaves" alternating with Terry's three colorful originals: "One Foot in the Gutter," "Zip Co-Ed" and "Globetrotter." This excellent LP is long overdue to be reissued on CD. — *Scott Yanow*

Ain't Misbehavin' / Mar. 15, 1979–Mar. 16, 1979 / Pablo ✦✦✦✦
This served as a sprightly showcase for tunes either written or associated with Fats Waller. Outstanding in his role as front-line mate was the under-appreciated alto saxophonist Chris Woods. Clark Terry's unforced humor was evident throughout this session. — *Bob Rusch, Cadence*

Memories of Duke / Mar. 11, 1980 / Original Jazz Classics ✦✦✦✦
Fluegelhornist Clark Terry and a strong quartet (pianist Jack Wilson, guitarist Joe Pass, bassist Ray Brown and drummer Frank Severino) perform nine songs associated with Duke Ellington, including seven of Ellington's compositions, plus a tune apiece from Billy Strayhorn ("Passion Flower") and Mercer Ellington ("Things Ain't What They Used to Be"). Terry knows these songs, which include "Cottontail," "Come Sunday" and "Sophisticated Lady," backward, but he infuses each of his renditions with enthusiasm and melodic creativity. Recommended. — *Scott Yanow*

Yes, the Blues / Jan. 19, 1981 / Original Jazz Classics ✦✦✦✦
This blues-oriented Pablo LP has an ideal matchup: fluegelhornist Clark Terry and altoist Eddie "Cleanhead" Vinson. Both musicians take a good-humored vocal apiece, but the emphasis is on their playing. The complementary stylists, backed by pianist Art Hillery, bassist John Heard and drummer Roy McCurdy, work together very well on their originals, plus "Swingin' the Blues," and create some memorable, if fairly basic, music straddling the boundaries between swing, bop and early R&B. — *Scott Yanow*

To Duke and Basie / Jan. 28, 1986 / Enja ✦✦✦✦✦
This is a delightful set. Fluegelhornist Clark Terry and bassist Red Mitchell play a full program of duets with most of the music being associated with either Count Basie or Duke Ellington. Actually the most remembered selection of the date is C.T.'s "Hey Mr. Mumbles, What Did You Say?" This humorous number has a call-and-response vocal by the two masterful musicians. Overall this is a particularly happy set with plenty of wit being displayed along with the hard swing. — *Scott Yanow*

Metropole Orchestra / May 1988+Nov. 1994 / Mons ✦✦✦
The music on this Mons CD is taken from two different occasions on which fluegelhornist Clark Terry was accompanied by the Metropole orchestra, a large string big band from Holland. Rob Pronk and Lex Jasper provided the arrangements, but C.T. mostly performs his usual repertoire. The music swings despite the large number of musicians and the focus is almost entirely on Terry, who sounds as joyful as usual. — *Scott Yanow*

Jive at Five / Jul. 1988 / Enja ✦✦✦✦

Portraits / Dec. 16, 1988 / Chesky ✦✦✦✦✦
Fluegelhornist Clark Terry recorded quite frequently in the 1980s, and his consistency was very impressive. Terry's good humor, joyful and immediately distinctive sound, and creative, bop-oriented ideas combined to form a very accessible, happy style. This

Chesky CD finds C.T. joined by pianist Don Friedman, bassist Victor Gaskin and drummer Lewis Nash for a variety of superior standards and Terry's lone original "Finger Filibuster." The songs all pay tribute to various trumpeters, and some, such as "Pennies from Heaven," "Little Jazz" and "I Don't Wanna Be Kissed," were not performed by the fluegelhornist all that often; the result is fresher than usual music and is often quite inspired. Recommended. — *Scott Yanow*

★ **The Clark Terry Spacemen** / Feb. 13, 1989 / Chiaroscuro ✦✦✦✦✦
This underrated Chiaroscuro CD is a joy from start to finish. Fluegelhornist Clark Terry is teamed with an unusually talented group of all stars (trumpeter Virgil Jones, trombonists Al Grey and Britt Woodman, altoist Phil Woods, Red Holloway on tenor, baritonist Haywood Henry, pianist John Campbell, bassist Marcus McLaurine and drummer Butch Ballard), which is filled with distinctive and colorful swing stylists. The standards and riff tunes give all of the horn players solo space, and it is a particular joy to hear Britt Woodman and Haywood Henry (the latter near the end of his life) getting some feature spots. Highlights include "Swinging the Blues," "For Dancers Only" and "Just Squeeze Me." After 55 minutes of music Clark Terry is heard on the 19-minute "Jazzspeak," verbally telling informative stories about his lengthy career, some of which are quite humorous. Highly recommended. — *Scott Yanow*

Having Fun / Apr. 11, 1990–Apr. 12, 1990 / Delos ✦✦✦✦
The title of this CD definitely fits not only its music but also Clark Terry's career. The colorful fluegelhornist is teamed with Red Holloway doubling on tenor and alto, bassist Major Holley (who sings along with his bass in his solos), pianist Jon Campbell and drummer Lewis Nash. Since C.T., Holloway and Holley were all humorists, the music is not only swinging but also quite enthusiastic. With titles like "Mumbles," "Meet the Flintstones," "The Snapper" and "Mule's Soft Claw," the humor isn't unexpected. An excellent and consistently swinging date. — *Scott Yanow*

Live from the Village Gate / Nov. 19, 1990–Nov. 20, 1990 / Chesky ✦✦✦✦
Fluegelhornist Clark Terry, three weeks shy of his 70th birthday at the time of this live performance, sounds very much at the peak of his powers throughout the date. Teamed up with old friend Jimmy Heath, who doubles on tenor and soprano, pianist Don Friedman, bassist Marcus McLauren and drummer Kenny Washington (altoist Paquito D'Rivera guests on "Silly Samba"), C.T. performs eight little-known originals. The tunes are all fairly basic, but they inspire these talented musicians to some of their best playing. The hard-swinging music, which includes a trumpet-drums duet on "Brushes & Brass" and some singing from the audience on "Hey Mr. Mumbles," is quite enjoyable, among the most accessible type of jazz. — *Scott Yanow*

Second Set / Nov. 19, 1990–Nov. 20, 1990 / Chesky ✦✦✦✦
Clark Terry has made so many fine records in the 1990s that virtually all of them are recommended; this Chesky CD is no exception. A quintet date with tenor saxophonist Jimmy Heath, pianist Don Friedman, bassist Marcus McLauren and drummer Kenny Washington, Terry plays a variety of original tunes based on the blues and other fairly common chord changes. The good-humored music (which includes such song titles as "One Foot in the Gutter," "Serenade to a Bus Seat" and "Ode to a Fluegelhorn") is quite enjoyable, highlighted by Terry's "Mumbles" vocal on "Juonji," a few creative singalongs and lots of exciting fluegelhorn playing. This fine set is rounded off by ten minutes of storytelling by Terry that covers Count Basie, Duke Ellington, jazz education, Dizzy Gillespie and Miles Davis. — *Scott Yanow*

What a Wonderful World: For Louis / Feb. 1, 1993 / Red Baron ✦✦✦✦✦
Clark Terry at age 72 is in exuberant form throughout this very enjoyable disc. On "Duke's Place" he constructs a frequently hilarious monologue about a fictional dive, extolling its virtues (mostly food and women) for quite some time without losing momentum or stumbling even once despite the obvious spontaneity. The other selections (tributes to Duke Ellington and Louis Armstrong) have many spirited solos from Terry on fluegelhorn and wa-wa trombonist Al Grey. The rhythm section is solid and swinging, violinist Lesa Terry (Terry Clark's cousin) is an asset on two numbers, and even if Bob Thiele (credited with "writing" five of the nine songs) makes out like a bandit (he and Glenn Osser are listed as co-composers of "For Louis and Duke," a themeless blues), the

happy spirits and colorful playing of C.T. and Grey make this disc into a delightful hour of joyous music. — *Scott Yanow*

Shades Of Blues / May 13, 1994 / Challenge ✦✦✦✦
Clark Terry at 74 teams up with the veteran wa-wa trombone of Al Grey, pianist Charles Fox and bassist Marcus McLaurine to interpret 11 blues on this highly enjoyable release. Still very much in his musical prime, fluegelhornist Terry has one of the happiest sounds in jazz and he gives a surprising amount of variety to the otherwise similar material. Terry's humorous vocal on "Whispering the Blues," his quick tradeoffs between his two horns (the fluegelhorn and a muted trumpet) on "Cool Vibes" and his interplay with Al Grey make this an easily recommended CD. — *Scott Yanow*

Remember The Time / Aug. 29, 1994–Aug. 30, 1994 / Mons ✦✦✦✦
The ageless Clark Terry (who although 74 at the time of this recording could pass musically for 44) is teamed up on this CD from the German Mons label with the warm-toned trombonist Mark Nightingale, the talented bopster George Robert on alto, pianist Dado Moroni, bassist Ray Brown and drummer Jeff Hamilton. With the exception of two standards (which are mistakenly credited to Terry) and a throwaway version of a Michael Jackson tune, all of the songs are group originals that utilize fairly basic chord changes that are ideal for swinging. Terry's exuberant fluegelhorn is in prime form (he sounds particularly beautiful on "Gypsy" and "The Story of Love" while taking "Gwen" as a duet with bassist Brown) and has a typically humorous vocal on "Hot Sauce." It's an enjoyable outing. — *Scott Yanow*

With Pee Wee Claybrook & Swing Fever / Jan. 1995 / D' Note ✦✦✦
Trumpeter Clark Terry and tenor saxophonist Pee Wee Claybrook were important players in the St. Louis swing scene of the early '40s. After they were both drafted and played together for a period in the Great Lakes Naval Training Station Band, they went their separate ways in 1944. While C.T. would eventually become famous, Claybrook settled in San Francisco, spent time playing with Earl "Fatha" Hines and had a day job. A member of Swing Fever for ten years, Pee Wee Claybrook was 82 at the time it was suggested that he have a reunion with Terry, and this recording for D' Note is the result. In addition to Claybrook, Swing Fever consists of Howard Dudune on alto, clarinet and tenor, trombonist Bryan Gould, guitarist Jim Putman, bassist Dean Reilly and drummer Harold Jones. With the exception of Louis Jordan's "Lemonade" (which gives Gould an opportunity to sing the blues) and Duke Ellington's "Serenade to Sweden," all ten selections on this session are famous swing standards. C.T. and Gould trade scat vocals on an eccentric version of "Straighten Up and Fly Right," Claybrook shows the influence of Johnny Hodges in his wailing solos (although his Buddy Tate-flavored sound is much heavier), Terry is up to his usual exuberant level and there are plenty of fine spots for the versatile reeds of Dudune and trombonist Gould. In addition, the sparse pianoless rhythm section gives this material a lighter feel than expected. A fun date, easily recommended. — *Scott Yanow*

Frank Teschemacher

b. Mar. 13, 1906, Kansas City, MS, **d.** Feb. 29, 1932, Chicago, IL
Clarinet, Alto Saxophone / Classic Jazz
One of the early jazz legends, Frank Teschemacher was an exciting if erratic clarinetist and altoist who was an important participant in the Chicago jazz scene of the 1920s. A member of the fabled Austin High School Gang of young Chicago jazz musicians, Teschemacher started recording in 1927 (with the McKenzie-Condon Chicagoans) although observers of the period have stated that his records were not as strong as his live performances. A fine musician whose solos are a little reminiscent of his contemporary Pee Wee Russell, Teschemacher recorded in Chicago with a variety of overlapping pickup groups in 1927, spent 1928 in New York (where he played with Ben Pollack, Sam Lanin and Red Nichols) and then returned to Chicago. His life was cut short by a tragic automobile accident, making one wonder how Tesch (a good all-round musician) would have fared in the swing era. All 34 of his recordings plus six others that he might be on are included on a perfectly done Time/Life three-LP box set. — *Scott Yanow*

★ **Frank Teschemacher** / Dec. 9, 1927–Jan. 13, 1932 / Time-Life ✦✦✦✦✦
This perfectly done three-LP set from the Time/Life *Giants of Jazz*

series differs from their other releases in that, instead of being a sampler, it contains every possible recording by its subject, the ill-fated clarinetist and altoist Frankie Teschemacher. Although not a virtuoso and occasionally a bit erratic on records, Teschemacher was a consistently exciting performer who always pushed himself. He is heard on the four groundbreaking recordings of McKenzie and Condon's Chicagoans and with Charles Pierce, the Chicago Rhythm Kings, the Jungle Kings, Miff Mole's Little Molers, Eddie Condon, the Dorsey Brothers, the Big Aces, Wingy Manone, Ted Lewis, Elmer Schoebel, the Cellar Boys and on one lone title ("Jazz Me Blues") issued under his own name. Among the other sidemen are cornetists Jimmy McPartland, Red Nichols, Wingy Manone and Muggsy Spanier, Bud Freeman and Mezz Mezzrow on tenors, pianists Joe Sullivan and Art Hodes and drummers Gene Krupa and George Wettling. In addition to the 34 known recordings where he is obviously present, this set has six other titles (from Lennie Hayton, the Original Wolverines and Howard Thomas' Orchestra) that Tesch might possibly have been on (although it is doubtful). The 48-page booklet is quite definitive, making this very attractive out-of-print set (which can still be found, often at budget prices) essential for collectors of early jazz. — *Scott Yanow*

Toots Thielemans (Jean Baptiste Thielemans)

b. Apr. 29, 1922, Brussels, Belgium
Guitar, Harmonica / Bop, Swing, Brazilian Jazz
Although preceded by Larry Adler (who has actually spent much of his career playing popular and classical music), Toots Thielemans virtually introduced the chromatic harmonica as a jazz instrument. In fact ever since the mid-'50s he has had no close competitors. Toots simply plays the harmonica with the dexterity of a saxophonist and has even successfully traded off with the likes of Oscar Peterson.

Toots Thielemans' first instrument was the accordion, which he started when he was three. Although he started playing the harmonica when he was 17, Thielemans' original reputation was made as a guitarist who was influenced by Django Reinhardt. Very much open to bop, Thielemans played in American GI clubs in Europe, visited the U.S. for the first time in 1947 and shared the bandstand with Charlie Parker at the Paris Jazz Festival of 1949. He toured Europe as a guitarist with the Benny Goodman Sextet in 1950 and the following year moved to the U.S. During 1953–59 Toots was a member of the George Shearing quintet (mostly as a guitarist) and has freelanced ever since. He first recorded his big hit "Bluesette" (which featured his expert whistling and guitar) in 1961 and ever since has been greatly in-demand (particularly for his harmonica and his whistling) on pop records (including many dates with Quincy Jones) and as a jazz soloist. Toots' two-volume *Brasil Project* was popular in the 1990s and found him smoothly interacting on harmonica with top Brazilian musicians. — *Scott Yanow*

Man Bites Harmonica / Dec. 30, 1957+Jan. 7, 1958 / Original Jazz Classics ✦✦✦✦✦
Early period. Definitive harmonicist from Belgium. With Pepper Adams, Kenny Drew, Wilbur Ware, and Art Taylor. — *Michael G. Nastos*

The Soul of Toots Thielemans / Oct. 1959–Nov. 1959 / Doctor Jazz ✦✦✦✦

Toots and Svend / Nov. 22, 1972–Nov. 23, 1972 / Sonet ✦✦✦✦

Live / Apr. 4, 1974 / Polydor ✦✦✦

The Silver Collection / Apr. 4, 1974–Apr. 10, 1975 / Verve ✦✦
Two-disc collection of his Verve cuts. — *Ron Wynn*

Captured Alive / Sep. 1974 / Choice ✦✦✦✦✦

★ **Live in the Netherlands** / Jul. 13, 1980 / Pablo ✦✦✦✦✦

Autumn Leaves / May 1984 / Soul Note ✦✦✦

Do Not Leave Me / Jun. 19, 1986 / Stash ✦✦✦✦✦

Apple Dimple / 1987 / Denon ✦✦✦

Only Trust Your Heart / Apr. 1988–May 1988 / Concord Jazz ✦✦✦
Bit to the sentimental side, good playing. CD version has two prime cuts. — *Ron Wynn*

Footprints / Dec. 19, 1989–Dec. 20, 1989 / EmArcy ✦✦✦✦

For My Lady / 1991 / EmArcy ✦✦✦

The Brasil Project / 1992 / Private Music ✦✦✦

The Brasil Project, Vol. 2 / 1993 / Private Music ✦✦✦✦
Guitarist, harmonica player, and whistler Toots Thielemans' fol-

low-up to the critically acclaimed *Brasil Project* doesn't stray far from its predecessor's path. There are 13 nice Afro-Latin selections with Thielemans backing such top Brazilian vocalists as Milton Nascimento, Gilberto Gil, Ivan Lins, Caetano Veloso, and Dori Caymmi, among others, and guitarists Oscar Castro-Nieves and Lee Ritenour assisting Thielemans with delicate shadings and accompaniment. —*Ron Wynn*

East Coast West Coast / 1994 / Private Music ♦♦
For this set, harmonica great Toots Thielemans recorded with separate all-star lineups in New York and Los Angeles. When one considers that such musicians as trumpeter Terence Blanchard, tenor saxophonist Joshua Redman, violinist Jerry Goodman and Ernie Watts on tenor are heard from, this should have been a classic album. The problem is that, for whatever reason, every performance is overly brief. Other than two of the ballads, none of the selections exceed five minutes and Thielemans's sidemen are restricted to very brief solos. Imagine playing "Groovin' High" with Blanchard and Redman and having the horns only solo for one chorus apiece. Thielemans is in fine form as usual and it is a happy surprise to hear Goodman (most famous for his association with the Mahavishnu orchestra) sounding like a combination of Stephane Grappelli and Papa John Creech during his two appearances. But to have Blanchard's inspired outburst at the beginning of "In Walked Bud" cut off after one chorus is quite frustrating, making this set a missed opportunity. —*Scott Yanow*

Ed Thigpen

b. Dec. 28, 1930, Chicago, IL
Drums / Hard Bop
Ed Thigpen's a highly respected, seasoned drummer and percussionist with great skills in every phase of his craft. Thigpen plays with sensitivity and swing; he uses brushes as expertly as sticks, he can provide a driving, steady beat, vary the pulse, solo with flair or remain anchored in the background. He's also written several books on drumming and led international workshops. Thigpen worked with Cootie Williams, Dinah Washington, Johnny Hodges, Lennie Tristano, Bud Powell, Jutta Hipp and Billy Taylor in the '50s. He played in Oscar Peterson's trio with Ray Brown from 1959 to 1965, then joined Ella Fitzgerald's backup band. He moved to Los Angeles in 1967, and rejoined Fitzgerald from 1968 to 1972. Thigpen relocated to Copenhagen in 1972, and taught at the Malmo Conservatory in Sweden while forming the group Action-re-action. He's worked with numerous players in the '70s and '80s, among them Monty Alexander, the Berlin Contemporary Jazz Orchestra, Kenny Drew, Art Farmer, Dexter Gordon, Lionel Hampton, Boulou and Elios Ferre and Johnny Griffin. Thigpen has recorded as a leader for Verve, GNP Crescendo, Reckless, Timeless and Justin Time. He has a couple of sessions available on CD as a leader. —*Ron Wynn*

Young Men and Old / Nov. 20, 1990–Nov. 21, 1990 / Timeless ♦♦♦♦
● **Mr. Taste** / Apr. 11, 1991–Jul. 19, 1991 / Justin Time ♦♦♦♦

Gary Thomas

b. Jun. 10, 1961, Baltimore, MD
Flute, Tenor Saxophone / Avant-Garde, Post-Bop, Free Funk
As with altoists Steve Coleman and Greg Osby, Gary Thomas has developed his own fresh approach to improvisation, avoiding bop cliches and taking solos that are consistently full of surprising twists and turns. Lots of chances are taken, and even if not everything works (the use of rap on one of his JMT albums is unfortunate), Gary Thomas' music would never be called predictable! In the late '80s Thomas gigged with both Miles Davis and Jack DeJohnette's Special Edition. He has also recorded frequently with Greg Osby, Michele Rosewoman and Wallace Roney in addition to leading his own sessions. —*Scott Yanow*

The Seventh Quadrant / Apr. 3, 1987–Apr. 4, 1987 / Enja ♦♦♦
● **Code Violations** / Jul. 20, 1988–Jul. 25, 1988 / Enja ♦♦♦♦♦
By Any Means Necessary / May 1989 / JMT ♦♦♦♦
Aggressive, "Young Lion"-led session with R&B, electronic elements. Thomas is an explosive, constantly growing improviser. —*Ron Wynn*

While the Gate Is Open / May 1990 / JMT ♦♦♦♦
The Kold Kage / Mar. 1991–Jun. 1991 / JMT ♦♦♦♦
● **Till We Have Faces** / May 8, 1992–May 14, 1992 / JMT/Polydor ♦♦♦♦♦
Exile's Gate / May 19, 1993–May 23, 1993 / JMT ♦♦♦

Joe Thomas

b. Jun. 19, 1909, Uniontown, PA, d. Aug. 3, 1986, Kansas City, MO
Tenor Saxophone / Swing
Joe Thomas will always be best known as the tenor soloist with Jimmy Lunceford's Orchestra. He was originally an altoist playing with Horace Henderson but switched to tenor when he joined Stuff Smith's group. As a star with Lunceford from 1933 until the leader's death in 1947, Thomas had many short but often-memorable solos and took several vocals. After Lunceford's unexpected death, Thomas and pianist Ed Wilcox ran the ghost band for a year. Later Thomas on his own recorded a variety of R&B-oriented sides, he left music in the mid-'50s to run his father's undertaking business and from the 1960s on returned to performing on a part-time basis, cutting a session in 1982 for Uptown. —*Scott Yanow*

● **Raw Meat** / Apr. 3, 1979–Apr. 4, 1979 / Uptown ♦♦♦♦
Blowin' in from K.C. / Dec. 9, 1982–Dec. 10, 1982 / Uptown ♦♦♦♦

Leon Thomas (Amos Leone Thomas, Jr.)

b. Oct. 4, 1937, East St. Louis, IL
Vocals / Post-Bop
Leon Thomas' moment of fame occured when he recorded "The Creator Has a Master Plan" with Pharoah Sanders in 1969. His eccentric yodeling worked well with Sanders' emotional tone, making the performance an unexpected avant-garde "hit." Thomas studied music at Tennessee State and in 1959 moved to New York. After some work with Randy Weston and Mary Lou Williams, Thomas was the regular singer with the Count Basie Orchestra during much of 1961–65, but few recordings (none significant) occurred. He worked often with Pharoah Sanders during 1969–72, recorded a set with Oliver Nelson and Johnny Hodges and made a few recordings on his own, but Thomas has yet to fulfill his potential. —*Scott Yanow*

● **Spirits Known and Unknown** / Oct. 21, 1969–Oct. 22, 1969 / Flying Dutchman ♦♦♦♦♦
In Berlin / Nov. 6, 1970 / Flying Dutchman ♦♦♦♦♦
Leon Thomas Album / 1970 / Flying Dutchman ♦♦♦♦
Blues and the Soulful Truth / 1972 / Flying Dutchman ♦♦♦♦♦
This is his best studio album. Contains many of his best numbers. —*Michael G. Nastos*

Full Circle / 1973 / Flying Dutchman ♦♦♦
Precious Energy / Mar. 6, 1987–Mar. 7, 1987 / Mapleshade ♦♦♦♦
Leon Thomas and Gary Bartz are two tremendously gifted artists who have had problems with direction and taste. Thomas' seminal works with Pharoah Sanders, Lonnie Liston Smith, Santana, and others in the '70s weren't matched by some things he did in the early '80s, while Bartz's tough combo dates also weren't equaled by some pop-oriented recordings he cut later. The two have since gone back to their strengths and made an excellent team on the 1987 session *Precious Energy*. Although he doesn't try the ambitious yodeling and special effects he did with Sanders, Thomas does demonstrate the creamy sound and full force of earlier years, while Bartz's solos are once more fluid, strong and expansive. —*Ron Wynn*

Leon Thomas Blues Band / Jan. 6, 1988 / Portrait ♦♦♦♦

Butch Thompson (Richard Enos Thompson)

b. Nov. 28, 1943, Marine, MN
Clarinet, Piano / Stride, Classic Jazz
One of the top pre-bop pianists to be active during the past 30 years, Butch Thompson's piano playing stretches from Jelly Roll Morton and James P. Johnson to swing; he is also an excellent (if occasional) New Orleans-style clarinetist. In 1962 he joined the Hall Brothers New Orleans Jazz Band in Minneapolis, an association that lasted over 20 years. Thompson has led his own trio since the mid-'60s and during 1974–86 he appeared regularly on Garrison Keillor's very popular radio series *A Prairie Home Companion*. Thompson has recorded extensively for many labels

including Center, Jazzology, GHB, Stomp Off and Daring. —*Scott Yanow*

Butch Thompson Plays Jellyroll Morton, Vol. 1 / 1973 / Biograph ✦✦✦✦

Butch Thompson Plays Jellyroll Morton, Vol. 2 / 1974 / Biograph ✦✦✦✦

A'Solas / Feb. 2, 1982–Apr. 28, 1982 / Stomp Off ✦✦✦✦✦

Thompson's King Oliver Centennial Band / Jul. 13, 1988 / GHB ✦✦✦✦✦
Thompson has succeeded in creating a band that effectively celebrates the spirit of Oliver's Creole Jazz Band without indulging in note-for-note imitation. —*Bruce Raeburn*

Chicago Breakdown / Mar. 1, 1989–Mar. 3, 1989 / Daring ✦✦✦✦
A tribute to Jelly Roll Morton and King Oliver during their Chicago "salad days," Thompson offers a dazzling selection of stomps, tangos and blues ballads—his collaboration with Little Brother Montgomery (p) on "Sunday Rag" is a gem. —*Bruce Raeburn*

Good Old New York / Mar. 1, 1989–Mar. 3, 1989 / Daring ✦✦✦✦
The Harlem stride style is done to perfection. This is a judicious sampling of the work of Fats Waller, James P. Johnson and Eubie Blake, done by a virtuoso. —*Bruce Raeburn*

New Orleans Joys / Mar. 1, 1989–Mar. 3, 1989 / Daring ✦✦✦✦
Thompson's ode to Jelly Roll Morton—masterful renditions of tunes associated with Morton in his early years, such as "The Naked Dance" and "The Crave." His own "Ecuadorian Memories" and "Dink's Blues" complement this compliment to Jelly Roll Morton. —*Bruce Raeburn*

The Butch Thompson Trio / Mar. 16, 1992–Mar. 17, 1992 / Solo Art ✦✦✦✦✦

Minnesota Wonder / May 1992–Jun. 1992 / Daring ✦✦✦

Yulestride / 1994 / Daring ✦✦✦

● **Butch & Doc** / Apr. 1994 / Daring ✦✦✦✦✦

Sir Charles Thompson

b. Mar. 12, 1918, Springfield, OH
Piano, Organ / Bop, Swing
An excellent pianist and organist, Sir Charles Thompson, has been a successful swing and bebop player. His organ-playing style showed that this instrument could effectively play bebop. His style is light and bluesy on either instrument, but his solos aren't clichéd, dependent on gimmicks or bereft of ideas. After working in territory bands, Thompson began playing for Lionel Hampton in 1940. He worked with Coleman Hawkins in the mid-'40s, playing with him on the outstanding *Hollywood Stampede* sessions for Capitol in 1945. Thompson then worked with Illinois Jacquet in 1947 and 1948. His composition "Robbins Nest," a tribute to disc jockey Fred Robbins, became both a huge hit for Jacquet and a jazz anthem. Bob Russell recorded a vocal version titled "Just When We're Falling in Love." Thompson worked often with Buck Clayton in the '50s, appearing on a famous series of jam sessions on Columbia. He recorded as a leader for Vanguard in the '50s, and as a sideman with Clayton and Jimmy Rushing. He later did albums for Black and Blue, Prestige and some tracks for Master Jazz. Thompson toured Europe With Clayton in 1961, and toured America, Canada and Puerto Rico leading groups. After working in Pennsylvania during the early '70s, he had some health problems but bounced back in the mid-70s. His seminal dates with Coleman Hawkins, and some cuts with Charlie Parker, were reissued recently by Delmark. Mosaic has reissued the Clayton jam sessions. A little of some Thompson material on Sackville is also available. —*Ron Wynn*

★ **Takin' Off** / Sep. 4, 1945–Dec. 29, 1947 / Delmark ✦✦✦✦✦
This is a reissue of the classic Apollo series. The 1945 and 1947 sessions feature legendary bands with Charlie Parker, Dexter Gordon, Buck Clayton, Danny Barker, J.C. Heard, Joe Newman, Freddie Green, Pete Brown and Shadow Wilson playing 16 cuts, seven previously unissued. This is prime bop. —*Michael G. Nastos*

Sir Charles Thompson and the Swing Organ / Apr. 1960 / Columbia ✦✦✦

Portrait of a Piano / Mar. 18, 1984 / Sackville ✦✦✦✦

Lucky Thompson

b. Jun. 16, 1924, Columbia, SC
Soprano Saxophone, Tenor Saxophone / Bop, Hard Bop
Lucky Thompson was one of the great tenors to emerge during

the 1940s and one of the first "modern" soprano saxophonists (taking up the instrument prior to John Coltrane and around the same time as Steve Lacy), but he was always a bit overshadowed by more spectacular players. After some local gigs he moved to New York in the early '40s, playing briefly with Lionel Hampton and Don Redman in 1943 and Billy Eckstine and Lucky Millinder in 1944. During 1944–45 he gained some attention with Count Basie (where Thompson had succeeded his main influence, Don Byas). Although his large tone looked toward the swing era, Thompson's advanced improvising fit in well with bop players. He settled on the West Coast after leaving Basie, was hired as "insurance" by Dizzy Gillespie in case Charlie Parker did not show up (he recorded with both) and cut many sessions (his solo on "Just One More Chance" was a personal favorite) during his stay in Los Angeles, performing with Boyd Raeburn and the short-lived Stars of Swing. In 1947 Lucky moved to Detroit and the following year he returned to New York. He led a band regularly at the Savoy during 1951–53 and in 1954 starred on Miles Davis' famous *Walkin'* session. In 1956 Thompson was a top soloist with Stan Kenton (appearing on *Cuban Fire*) and during the next two years he cut many sessions both as a leader and as a sideman. He lived in France during two periods (1957–62 and 1968–71), started doubling on soprano and taught at Dartmouth during 1973–74. And then it all stopped. Lucky Thompson completely dropped out of the music business (despite still being in his musical prime) and, other than a few rumors, has not been heard from since; a major loss to jazz. —*Scott Yanow*

● **The Beginning Years** / Oct. 1945–Jun. 7, 1947 / IAJRC ✦✦✦✦✦

Lucky Thompson And Gigi Gryce In Paris / Sep. 28, 1953–Apr. 17, 1956 / Vogue ✦✦✦✦
This reissue CD from the French Vogue label contains formerly rare performances by tenor saxophonist Lucky Thompson, altoist Gigi Gryce and trumpeter Art Farmer. Thompson performs 12 obscure pieces (ten of them his originals), none of which caught on. Some of Thompson's compositions are based closely on other songs, but his playing (which is featured with a French nonet) is consistently excellent and the arrangements hold one's interest. Gigi Gryce's recordings with trumpeter Clifford Brown in Paris during 1953 are well known and have been reissued many times, but the six selections heard on this CD (Brown is only on one song and does not solo) are much more obscure. The focus is very much on Gryce's playing and he sounds excellent whether with a quartet or with a larger group arranged by Quincy Jones. This CD is rounded out by a pair of selections from the same period ("Strike up the Band" and "Serenade to Sonny") that showcase the young Farmer as the leader of a sextet/septet. Although not essential, overall this is a very worthy set of often overlooked 1950s jazz. —*Scott Yanow*

★ **Tricotism** / Jan. 24, 1956–Dec. 12, 1956 / GRP ✦✦✦✦✦
Thompson created a host of spectacular improvisations on the 16 songs on this wonderful CD reissue. It is comprised of two 1956 sessions; one featured Thompson heading a trio backed by bassist Oscar Pettiford and guitarist Skeeter Best, and the other has him heading either a quartet or quintet that included the great trombonist Jimmy Cleveland. Cleveland's smooth, superbly articulated phrases and statements rank alongside Thompson's gliding lines in their brilliance, and pianist Hank Jones (on three cuts) also sparkles with some marvelous solos. But Lucky Thompson is the star on this date; his elegant, yet robust and exuberant playing demonstrated again what a loss his voluntary departure from the scene constitutes. —*Ron Wynn*

Paris (1956) / Mar. 12, 1956+Mar. 14, 1956 / Swing ✦✦✦✦
Robust statement from a great player in overdrive. —*Ron Wynn*

Brown Rose / Mar. 29, 1956–Apr. 17, 1956 / Xanadu ✦✦✦✦
Both Thompson and Martial Solal (p) burn. —*Ron Wynn*

Happy Days / Mar. 8, 1963+Feb. 16, 1965 / Prestige ✦✦✦✦
This CD has the full contents of two of Lucky Thompson's LPs. The earlier session, since it was originally released on the Prestige subsidiary Moodsville, emphasizes ballads as Thompson interprets eight Jerome Kern melodies (none of the obvious ones) plus his own moody original "No More." One of the first "modern" jazz musicians to start doubling on soprano (actually predating John Coltrane), Lucky Thompson displays a light but forceful tone on both soprano and tenor; his versions of "Look for the Silver Lining," "Who" and "They Didn't Believe Me" are particularly memorable. The second date was a six-song tribute to a new

singer of the period, Barbara Streisand. Other than "People" (this version is harmless enough) and Thompson's "Safari," the other tunes are veteran standards including "Happy Days Are Here Again" and a rare medium-tempo rendition of "As Time Goes By." Overall this CD is full of excellent music by the always underrated Lucky Thompson. —*Scott Yanow*

Lucky Strikes / Sep. 15, 1964 / Original Jazz Classics ✦✦✦✦✦
Lucky Thompson brought along Hank Jones (piano), Richard Davis (bass) and Connie Kay (drums) to back him on two standards and six originals. The program here was quite strong and the leader, on both tenor and soprano, brought a soulful and personal approach to his playing. —*Bob Rusch, Cadence*

Lucky Meets Tommy / 1965 / Fresh Sound ✦✦✦
There are far too few Lucky Thompson records; in part because the legendary sax player had a reputation of being "difficult." These rare 1965 sessions with the great Tommy Flanagan on piano (on all but three tracks) produced 70 minutes of relaxed jazz that are a superb introduction to Thompson's tenor stylings, out of Coleman Hawkins and Don Byas; and his soft, airy sound on the soprano. —*Les Line*

Body and Soul / May 1, 1970–May 2, 1970 / Nessa ✦✦✦
One of his last releases and very valuable. —*Ron Wynn*

Goodbye Yesterday / 1972 / Groove Merchant ✦✦

I Offer You / 1973 / Groove Merchant ✦✦✦

Malachi Thompson

Trumpet / Avant-Garde
A veteran Chicago trumpeter who's worked with many of the city's famous players, Malachi Thompson's never been able to break through himself. He's recorded a number of albums for Delmark. Thompson finally got some attention in the late '80s with an album for Delmark that also featured vocals by Leon Thomas. He made an even better follow up album with Carter Jefferson, Harrison Bankhead and some other solid but lesser known players, displaying a pungent tone, good command in every register and some intriguing solos. Unfortunately, neither release got widespread coverage. Thompson's also been a member of Lester Bowie's Brass Fantasy, the Ra Ensemble and the Association for the Advancement of Creative Musicians (AACM). —*Ron Wynn and Michael G. Nastos*

The Seventh Son / May 1972 / RA ✦✦
Trumpeter Malachi Thompson combines some of the innovations of the avant-garde along with dated electronics on this erratic but interesting LP. Thompson gets in a few good solos although most of his supporting cast is much more anonymous. This low-budget release has good intentions even if the results are mixed. —*Scott Yanow*

Spirit / 1990 / Delmark ✦✦✦
Progressive Chicago trumpeter. Originals. A solid album. —*Michael G. Nastos*

The Jaz Life / Jun. 30, 1991 / Delmark ✦✦✦✦

● **Lift Every Voice** / Aug. 24, 1992–Aug. 25, 1992 / Delmark ✦✦✦✦✦
Trumpeter Malachi Thompson merges hard bop, free, African rhythms and gospel stylings on this release. *Lift Every Voice* is reminiscent of what drummer Max Roach did with his regular band in collaboration with The J.C. White gospel singers in the 1970s (his album was also called *Lift Every Voice*), but Thompson has added some more intriguing personnel and rhythmic elements. He uses four trumpets and trombonists, plus a bassist, drummer, two percussionists and eight singers on the title track. Thompson's ringing solos, crisp lines, declarative themes and bursts are also backed by his Freebop band. Thompson deserves high praise not just for trying something different but succeeding. —*Ron Wynn*

New Standards / Apr. 20, 1993–Apr. 22, 1993 / Delmark ✦✦✦✦

Claude Thornhill

b. Aug. 10, 1909, Terre Haute, IN, d. Jul. 1, 1965, NYC
Piano, Arranger, Leader / Cool
Although some of his recordings were on the peripherery of jazz and his orchestra was at its most popular in the early '40s, Claude Thornhill's main importance to jazz was the influence that his arrangements and orchestra's sound had on cool jazz of the late '40s. After studying at a music conservatory and playing piano in bands based in the Midwest, Thornhill worked for Paul Whiteman

and Benny Goodman in 1934 and for Ray Noble's American band of 1935–36 (for whom he also arranged). He appeared on some Billie Holiday records and his arrangement of "Loch Lomond" was a big hit for Maxine Sullivan. Although he recorded as a leader in 1937, it was in 1940 that Thornhill put together his own orchestra. The band, featuring long tones played by horns that de-emphasized vibrato, had an unusual sound that sometimes backed the leader's tinkling piano. The instrumentation included two French horns and a tuba; sometimes all six of the reeds played clarinets in unison. Although classified by some as a sweet rather than swing band (since the group played a lot of ballads), with the addition in 1941 of Gil Evans as one of the arrangers, the recordings of Thornhill's orchestra attracted a lot of attention in the jazz world. After a period in the military (1942–45), Thornhill put together a new orchestra, retaining the services of Gil Evans (and sometimes using Gerry Mulligan charts as well) and featuring such soloists as altoist Lee Konitz, clarinetist Danny Polo and trumpeter Red Rodney. Some of Evans' boppish arrangements for the group were classic and the Miles Davis Nonet of 1948 was based on many of the cool-toned principles of the Thornhill big band. However by then the pianist's glory days were over. He continued leading bands on a part-time basis up until his death, but Claude Thornhill was largely neglected and forgotten during his final 15 years. —*Scott Yanow*

★ **Tapestries** / Jun. 14, 1937–Dec. 17, 1947 / Affinity ✦✦✦✦✦
A comprehensive, two-disc set of his prime cuts, with 17 arranged by Gil Evans. —*Ron Wynn*

Best of Big Bands / Mar. 10, 1941–Dec. 17, 1947 / Columbia ✦✦✦✦

The Uncollected Claude Thornhill & His Orchestra / 1947 / Hindsight ✦✦✦✦

Claude Thornhill and His Orchestra / 1947 / Hindsight ✦✦✦✦

1948 Transcription Performance / Apr. 1948–Oct. 1948 / Hep ✦✦✦✦✦

Henry Threadgill

b. Feb. 15, 1944, Chicago, IL
Alto Saxophone, Flute / Avant-Garde
Although his music can be somewhat forbidding, Henry Threadgill has been one of the most respected members of the avant-garde for the past 20 years. As an altoist and flutist, he has long had an original tone, but it is his work as an innovative composer that is most impressive. He played percussion in marching bands while a child, learned baritone and clarinet in high school, studied at the American Conservatory of Music and played gospel music for traveling evangelists. In 1962-63 Threadgill was a part of Richard Abrams' Experimental Band and he became a member of the AACM. After a period in the Army, he worked in the house band at a Chicago blues club and recorded with Abrams. In 1971 Threadgill first teamed up with Steve McCall and Fred Hopkins in a trio and in 1975 the group became known as Air. Threadgill recorded and performed extensively with Air (and its successor New Air) and later led several unique ensembles including X-75 (which had four bassists), his Sextet and Very Very Circus. His singing to Sony in 1994 was a big surprise for Threadgill's compositions and improvisations are far from accessible; happily his Sony recordings show no sign of being watered-down. —*Scott Yanow*

X-75, Vol. 1 / Jan. 13, 1979 / Novus ✦✦✦
Four bassists predominate (Hopkins, Rufus Reid, Smith, and Leonard Jones) in this pre-sextet recording. Amina Myers (p) and Joseph Jarmen (reeds) also show. Unrestrained freedom and beauty. —*Michael G. Nastos*

When Was That? / 1982 / About Time ✦✦✦✦✦
The title track is a riot on record. Some extraordinary improvising and spontaneous combustion going on here. Landmark recording. —*Michael G. Nastos*

★ **Just the Facts and Pass the Bucket** / 1983 / About Time ✦✦✦✦✦
Sextet (actually seven pieces). Dynamite open-ended compositions especially surly "Black Blues" and the determined "Man Called Trinity Deliverance." Features Olu Dara, Pheeroan Aklaff, and John Betsch and bassist Fred Hopkins. All pungently original material. —*Michael G. Nastos*

Subject to Change / Dec. 1984 / About Time ✦✦✦
Both blistering ensemble work and dynamic solos. —*Ron Wynn*

You Know the Number / Oct. 12, 1986–Oct. 13, 1986 / Novus ✦✦✦✦
New members include Frank Lacy, Rasul Siddik, and Reggie Nicholson. Retains two drummer back line. "Those Who Eat Cookies" a hot one. —*Michael G. Nastos*

Easily Slip into Another World / Sep. 20, 1987 / Novus ✦✦✦✦

Rag, Bush and All / Dec. 1988 / Novus ✦✦✦✦
Ted Daniel (trumpet), Bill Lowe (bass trombone), and Newman Baker (percussion) are in. "Off the Rag" and "The Devil Is Loose" and "Dance with a Monkey" are on. —*Michael G. Nastos*

Spirit of Nuff . . . Nuff / Nov. 19, 1990–Nov. 21, 1990 / Black Saint ✦✦✦

Too Much Sugar for a Dime / 1993 / Axiom ✦✦✦✦
Imagine writing for an instrumentation of two electric guitars, two tubas, French horn, drums and Henry Threadgill's alto. Threadgill was up to the challenge and his four avant-garde originals utilize the odd combination of tones to great advantage. Two additional songs feature Threadgill, just one tuba, drums, a few exotic instruments and three strings to create some particularly unusual music. It's for the open-eared listener only. —*Scott Yanow*

Song out of My Trees / Aug. 1993 / Black Saint ✦✦✦
Even longtime Threadgill fans may be surprised at the direction and content on his most recent session. The five tunes include three pieces where Threadgill is absent, and one ("Over the River Club") is a nine-minute-plus opus dominated by three guitars colliding, intersecting, and dueling. The title track showcases Threadgill's blues and gospel roots, with some wonderful organ by Amina Claudine Myers. Only "Crea" and "Gateway" are similar to past Threadgill works, with "Crea" featuring the unusual sound of Ted Daniel on hunting horns. Even a champion of the unorthodox like Threadgill may have some people scratching their heads after they hear this, but it's a signal that he'll never settle for doing what's expected. —*Ron Wynn*

Carry The Day / 1994 / Columbia ✦✦✦✦✦
It seems that every five years or so Columbia signs a token avant-garde musician. Arthur Blythe and Tim Berne emerged from their experiences as major-label artists relatively unscathed, and on evidence of Henry Threagill's somewhat forbidding Columbia debut, it would not be surprising if the altoist survived his stint with his priorities straight. There is certainly nothing commercial or watered down about this CD. The music ranges from "Come Carry the Day" (which builds from a group chart to some very dense ensembles) and Threadgill's Dolphyish alto on "Between Orchids" to a couple of very odd vocals and the intense group improv "Jenkins Boys." The group sound (with its accordions, tubas and Mark Taylor's french horn) is attractive in its own way even if the originals do little more than set mysterious moods. This unique music takes several listens to absorb and even then it still might be somewhat incomprehensible. At 37 minutes, it is all over too soon. —*Scott Yanow*

Bobby Timmons

b. Dec. 19, 1935, Philadelphia, PA, d. Mar. 1, 1974, New York, NY
Piano, Composer / Hard Bop, Soul Jazz
Bobby Timmons became so famous for the gospel and funky blues clichés in his solos and compositions that his skills as a Bud Powell-inspired bebop player have been long forgotten. After emerging from the Philadelphia jazz scene, Timmons worked with Kenny Dorham (1956), Chet Baker, Sonny Stitt and the Maynard Ferguson Big Band. He was partly responsible for the commercial success of both Art Blakey's Jazz Messengers and Cannonball Adderley's Quintet. For Blakey (who he was with during 1958–59), Timmons wrote the classic "Moanin'," and after joining Adderley in 1959, his song "This Here" (followed later by "Dat Dere") became a big hit; it is little wonder that Adderley was distressed when Timmons in 1960 decided to return to the Jazz Messengers. "Dat Dere" particularly caught on when Oscar Brown, Jr., wrote and recorded lyrics that colorfully depicted his curious son. Timmons, who was already recording as a leader for Riverside, soon formed his own trio but was never able to gain the commercial success that his former bosses enjoyed. Stereotyped as a funky pianist (although an influence on many players including Les McCann, Ramsey Lewis and much later on Benny Green), Timmons' career gradually declined. He continued working until his death at age 38 from cirrhosis of the liver. —*Scott Yanow*

★ **This Here Is Bobby Timmons** / Jan. 13, 1960–Jan. 14, 1960 / Original Jazz Classics ✦✦✦✦✦
Trio with Sam Jones (b) and Jimmy Cobb (d). This pianist's single best album. —*Michael G. Nastos*

Soul Time / Aug. 12, 1960+Aug. 17, 1960 / Original Jazz Classics ✦✦✦✦✦
Pianist Bobby Timmons, best known for his sanctified and funky playing and composing, is mostly heard in a straight-ahead vein on this CD reissue of a Riverside session. Timmons' four originals ("So Tired" is most memorable) alternate with three standards and are interpreted by a quartet with trumpeter Blue Mitchell, bassist Sam Jones and drummer Art Blakey. The swinging music is well played, making this a good example of Bobby Timmons playing in a boppish (as opposed to funky) setting. —*Scott Yanow*

Easy Does It / Mar. 13, 1961 / Original Jazz Classics ✦✦✦✦
Pianist Bobby Timmons, who became famous for his funky originals and soulful playing, mostly sticks to more bop-oriented jazz on this trio set with bassist Sam Jones and drummer Jimmy Cobb. He provides three originals (none of which really caught on) and is in excellent form on the five standards with highlights including "Old Devil Moon," "I Thought About You" and "Groovin' High." The Riverside CD reissue shows that Timmons was a bit more versatile than his stereotype; in any case the music is excellent. —*Scott Yanow*

In Person / Oct. 1, 1961 / Original Jazz Classics ✦✦✦✦

Workin' Out / Oct. 21, 1964+Jan. 20, 1966 / Prestige ✦✦✦✦✦
This CD reissues the contents of two of pianist Bobby Timmons most advanced recordings of the 1960s. For an example of how the popular pianist had continued to evolve after his early funk hits, listen to his often-bitonal solo on "Bags' Groove" from 1964. That session features Timmons in a quartet with vibraphonist Johnny Lytle, bassist Keter Betts and drummer William "Peppy" Hinnant and is filled with subtle surprises. The second recording is even more interesting, for Timmons is teamed with tenor saxophonist Wayne Shorter, bassist Ron Carter and drummer Jimmy Cobb in 1966. The immediately recognizable Shorter in particular plays very well (this version of his "Tom Thumb" is its earliest recording) and the very modern playing of Carter pushes Timmons to really stretch himself. Both of these generally overlooked sessions (even Shorter's best fans may not know about his collaboration with Timmons) were formerly rare and are quite adventurous, making this a highly recommended acquisition that falls somewhere between hard bop and the early avant-garde. —*Scott Yanow*

Live at the Connecticut Jazz Party / 1981 / Early Bird ✦✦✦
Pianist Bobby Timmons had the good fortune to get visibility with drummer Art Blakey and later with alto saxophonist Cannonball Adderley, and of course as a composer.... These were workmanlike performances that won't waste your time or insult your mind. This was an album of interest. —*Bob Rusch, Cadence*

Cal Tjader

b. Jul. 16, 1925, St. Louis, MO, d. May 5, 1982, Manila, Philippines
Vibes, Leader / Cool, Latin Jazz
The greatest non-Latin bandleader in Latin jazz history, Cal Tjader's early interest in the music blossomed into a lifelong love affair. While he wasn't the fastest vibes player, his style matured to the point he could provide efficient, effective solos while his band maintained the groove. Tjader also played piano and bongos. He studied music at San Francisco State University and began as a drummer with Dave Brubeck's trio in the late '40s and early '50s. He worked with Alvino Rey before beginning his own band. Tjader joined George Shearing in 1953; Shearing's band eventually had Tjader playing vibes and percussion with Willie Bobo, Mongo Santamaria and Armanda Peraza. His bassist Al McKibbon helped stimulate Tjader's love affair with Latin jazz and Afro-Latin music. When Tjader left Shearing, he started his own groups, which mixed Latin jazz, Afro-Cuban and jazz. Bobo and Santamaria joined him later in the '50s, and Tjader led fine bands in the '60s, '70s and '80s. He recorded for Fantasy from the '50s to the mid-'60s, then switched to Verve. Tjader's Verve sessions included Lalo Schifrin, Bobo, Donald Byrd and Kenny Burrell and the albums *Several Shades of Jade*, and *Soul Sauce* made the pop albums chart. He recorded with Eddie Palmieri on Verve and Tico and with Charlie Palmieri on Fantasy. Tjader continued on Fantasy in the '70s, working with Stan Getz, Charlie

Music Map

Trumpet (including cornetists)

Pioneer
Buddy Bolden (formed first band in 1895)

Early New Orleans "Kings"	
Freddie Keppard	Manuel Perez
Buddy Petit	Chris Kelly
King Oliver	

1920-25	
Nick LaRocca	Paul Mares
Phil Napoleon	Johnny Dunn
Joe Smith	

Biggest Influence and Most Important Innovator
Louis Armstrong

1926-30	
Bix Beiderbecke	Red Nichols
Tommy Ladnier	George Mitchell
Jabbo Smith	Bob Shoffner
Leonard Davis	Lee Collins
Bobby Stark	Ed Allen
Red Allen	Natty Dominique
Reuben "River" Reeves	

The Ellington Trumpet Tradition	
Bubber Miley	Louis Metcalf
Arthur Whetsol	Freddie Jenkins
Cootie Williams	Rex Stewart
Ray Nance	Cat Anderson
Taft Jordan	Al Killian
Shorty Baker	Clark Terry
Willie Cook	Bill Berry
Barry Lee Hall	

Swing Era	
Roy Eldridge	Bunny Berigan
Charlie Shavers	Hot Lips Page
Buck Clayton	Shad Collins
Emmett Berry	Harry James
Ziggy Elman	Erskine Hawkins
Dud Bascomb	Bill Coleman
Valaida Snow	Nat Gonella
Phillippe Brun	Herman Autrey
Benny Carter	Jonah Jones
Frankie Newton	Sy Oliver
Snooky Young	Harry "Sweets" Edison

Bebop Innovator
Dizzy Gillespie

Bop Era	
Joe Guy	Freddie Webster
Sonny Berman	Howard McGhee
Fats Navarro	

Innovator in Cool, Hard Bop, Modal, Avant-Garde and Fusion!
Miles Davis

New Orleans Jazz to Dixieland and Mainstream	
Jimmy McPartland	Muggsy Spanier
Louis Prima	Sidney DeParis
Wingy Manone	Yank Lawson
Billy Butterfield	Bobby Hackett
Max Kaminsky	Wild Bill Davison
Johnny Windhurst	Lu Watters
Charlie Teagarden	Bob Scobey
Bunk Johnson	Mutt Carey
Pete Daily	Ken Colyer
Humphrey Lyttelton	Alex Welsh
Johnny Wiggs	Doc Evans
Sharkey Bonano	Punch Miller
Thomas Jefferson	Andrew Blakeney
Teddy Buckner	Dick Cathcart
Al Hirt	Kenny Ball
Ruby Braff	Warren Vache
Glenn Zottola	Tom Pletcher
Brent Persson	Dick Sudhaltar
Randy Sandke	Peter Ecklund
Jim Cullum, Jr.	
Alvin Alcorn (with Kid Ory)	
Danny Alguire (with Firehouse Five Plus Two)	
Frank Assunto (with Dukes Of Dixieland)	

1950s	
Shorty Rogers	Conte Candoli
Chet Baker	Jon Eardley
Don Fagerquist	Tony Fruscella
Art Farmer	Red Rodney
Idrees Sulieman	Joe Newman
Thad Jones	Joe Wilder
Ray Copeland	Joe Gordon

–Continued on next page–

Byrd, Hank Jones and Clare Fischer. He also began recording for Concord in the '70s, cutting both straight jazz sessions with Scott Hamiliton and Jones and Latin dates, one that included Carmen McRae. He won a Grammy for the 1980 release *La Onda Va Bien* and continued on Concord until his death in 1982. Tjader has many sessions available on CD. —*Ron Wynn*

Tjader Plays Mambo / Aug. 1954–Sep. 1954 / Original Jazz Classics ✦✦✦✦
Tjader Plays Mambo and *Mambo with Tjader* feature three Fall 1954 sessions with vibist/pianist Tjader playing two dozen Latinized standards. Four of the tracks found Tjader in the company of a small orchestra for added brass accents. The remainder of the tracks were without the horns and with Verlardi added as a third Latin percussionist. —*Bob Rusch, Cadence*

Mambo with Tjader / Sep. 1954 / Fantasy ✦✦✦
Modern Mambo Quintet. 1987 reissue of super session. —*Ron Wynn*

Plays Tjazz / Dec. 4, 1954–Jun. 6, 1955 / Fantasy ✦✦✦✦✦

Latin Kick / Nov. 1956 / Original Jazz Classics ✦✦✦✦✦
1991 reissue of prime session. First-rate Latin-jazz. —*Ron Wynn*

★ **Black Orchid** / 1956–1959 / Fantasy ✦✦✦✦✦
This CD reissues the complete contents of two former Fantasy LPs: *Cal Tjader Goes Latin* and *Cal Tjader Quintet*. The highly influential vibraphonist/bandleader is heard leading his young groups (which include such notable sidemen as flutist Paul Horn, pianist Vince Guaraldi, bassist Eugene Wright and percussionists Willie Bobo and Mongo Santamaria among others) through sets dominated by Latinized versions of standards. Highlights of this delightful (and somewhat definitive) program of Latin-jazz include "The Lady Is a Tramp," "Undecided," "Flamingo," "Stompin' at the Savoy" and "Lullaby of Birdland." —*Scott Yanow*

Jazz at the Blackhawk / Jan. 20, 1957 / Original Jazz Classics ✦✦✦✦
Vibraphonist Cal Tjader became such an influential force in Latin-jazz that many have forgotten about his abilities to play standard bop. This live set (a CD reissue of the original LP) features Tjader with a conventional but talented quartet (which includes pianist Vince Guaraldi, bassist Eugene Wright and drummer Al Torre) playing in a style similar to Milt Jackson and the Modern Jazz Quartet; in fact one song they perform is a Guaraldi original titled "Thinking of You, MJQ." There are no Latin rhythms on this set and oddly enough the liner notes do not refer at all to Tjader's success in that area. The music is a touch derivative but enjoyable, one of the versatile Cal Tjader's better straight-ahead sets. Recommended. —*Scott Yanow*

The Cal Tjader-Stan Getz Sextet / Feb. 8, 1958 / Original Jazz Classics ✦✦✦✦✦

Latin Concert / Sep. 1958 / Original Jazz Classics ✦✦✦✦✦
This CD reissue gives one a pretty good sampling of vibraphonist Cal Tjader's influential Latin-jazz of the 1950s. With pianist Vince Guaraldi, bassist Al McKibbon, Willie Bobo on timbales and drums and the congas of Mongo Santamaria, Tjader's impressive unit performs four of his catchy originals and two by Santamaria in addition to Latinized versions of "The Continental" and Ray Bryant's "Cubano Chant." This highly rhythmic music is difficult to dislike. —*Scott Yanow*

★ **Monterey Concerts** / Apr. 20, 1959 / Prestige ✦✦✦✦✦

Cal Tjader Goes Latin / 1959 / Fantasy ✦✦✦✦

Latino / 1960 / Fantasy ✦✦✦✦✦
Vibraphonist Cal Tjader is heard leading five different groups throughout this CD, but the identities of the flutists, bassists and pianists are less important than knowing that Tjader, Willie Bobo (on drums and timbales) and the great conga player Mongo Santamaria are on every selection. The music really cooks with torrid percussion, inspired ensembles and occasional solos from the sidemen (which sometimes include pianists Lonnie Hewitt or Vince Guaraldi, bassist Al McKibbon and flutist Paul Horn). Highlights include Latinized versions of "Key Largo" and "September Song," "Night in Tunisia," "The Continental" and a definitive version of Santamaria's "Afro Blue." This is Latin-jazz at its finest. —*Scott Yanow*

Concert on the Campus / 1960 / Original Jazz Classics ✦✦✦✦

Soul Sauce / Nov. 19, 1964–Nov. 20, 1964 / Verve ✦✦✦✦✦
One of his most influential '60s releases with Willie Bobo, Donald Byrd, and Kenny Burrell. —*Ron Wynn*

El Sonid Nuevo (The New Soul Sound) / May 24, 1966–May 26, 1966 / Verve ✦✦✦
This Verve CD reissues the popular collaboration between vibraphonist Cal Tjader and pianist Eddie Palmieri (who provided the arrangements) titled *El Sonido Nuevo* along with six other songs taken from a pair of Tjader's other Verve albums. Despite the claims of greatness expressed in the liners ("a landmark in the history of Latin jazz"), much of the music is actually quite lightweight although enjoyable enough, and the easy-listening melodies and accessible rhythms hold on to one's interest. Despite the changing personnel, Tjader is generally the lead voice, and he is in fine form even if the overall results are not all that memorable or unique. —*Scott Yanow*

Cal Tjader Plugs In / 1969 / Skye ✦✦✦

Primo / 1970 / Original Jazz Classics ✦✦✦✦
The frenetic Charlie Palmieri (k) joins Tjader. —*Ron Wynn*

Descarga / 1971–1972 / Fantasy ✦✦✦
Two of vibraphonist Cal Tjader's LPs (*Agua Dulce* and *Live at the Funky Quarters*) are combined on this single-CD. Due to Tjader's utilization of Al Zulaica on Fender Rhodes and the diverse material, some of the selections are commercial throwaways. However there are some stronger performances (particularly "Invitation," "Cubano Chant" and "Manteca") and the musicianship is generally quite good (the team of bassist John Heard and drummer Dick Berk on the second date works well). Latin-jazz fans with an open mind toward 1970s funk will find this CD of interest. —*Scott Yanow*

Primo / 1973 / Original Jazz Classics ✦✦✦✦✦
Vibist Cal Tjader made enormous contributions to Latin jazz, most notably giving exposure and attention to neglected musicians and composers. *Primo*, one of his finest albums, included superb piano from Charlie Palmieri and a stirring guest appearance by Tito Puente on the Mario Bauza tune "Tanga." This reissue also includes an alternate version of "Bang Bang," which is longer and offers both a stronger vibes solo by Tjader and a more intensive, explosive arrangement. Besides Tjader and Palmieri, other stars on the session include saxophonist Bobby Nelson and excellent percussion and rhythmic support by William Rodriquez on bongos and Luis Rodriquez on congas. —*Ron Wynn*

Amazonas / Jun. 1975 / Original Jazz Classics ✦✦✦
This is an unusual date by vibraphonist Cal Tjader. Rather than playing his usual brand of 1950s Latin-jazz, Tjader is joined by some of the top modern Latin performers of the era including pianist Egberto Gismonti, drummer Robertinho Silva, flutist Hermeto Pascoal and (unfortunately on just one song) trombonist Raul DeSouza along with keyboardist George Duke. In general Tjader fits in pretty well, playing songs by Joao Donata, Airto Moreira (the date's producer), Sergio Mendes and Duke among others. An extra version of "Cahuenga" was added to the CD reissue of this funky set. —*Scott Yanow*

Breathe Easy / Sep. 1977 / Galaxy ✦✦✦✦
More straight jazz with Hank Jones (p). —*Ron Wynn*

La Onda Va Bien / Jul. 1979 / Picante ✦✦✦
It was only fitting that vibraphonist Cal Tjader launched the Concord Picante label with this release, for Tjader did a great deal to popularize Latin-jazz. This was not his strongest effort (the solos of Tjader and flutist Roger Glenn are not all that substantial), but the drumming of Vince Lateano and the percussion of Poncho Sanchez keep the momentum flowing on these likable performances. —*Scott Yanow*

Gozame! Pero Ya / Jun. 1980 / Picante ✦✦✦

The Shining Sea / Mar. 1981 / Picante ✦✦✦✦

A Fuego Vivo / Aug. 1981 / Picante ✦✦✦✦
Mixes Latin and mainstream. —*Ron Wynn*

Heat Wave / Jan. 1982 / Picante ✦✦✦✦
Carmen McRae steals honors on vocals. Sparkling vocals and vibes. —*Ron Wynn*

Charles Tolliver

b. Mar. 6, 1942, Jacksonville, FL
Trumpet / Hard Bop, Post Bop
In the early '70s Charles Tolliver was one of the brightest young trumpeters in jazz. Although he is still playing well, Tolliver never broke through to the top as one might have predicted. He studied at Howard University and then moved to New York in 1964, playing and recording with Jackie McLean. Tolliver was on quite a few

Music Map

Trumpet (including cornetists)
—continued

Hard Bop

Clifford Brown	Lee Morgan
Freddie Hubbard	Woody Shaw
Bill Hardman	Donald Byrd
Blue Mitchell	Kenny Dorham
Sam Noto	Nat Adderley
Tommy Turrentine	Carmell Jones
Johnny Coles	Oscar Brashear
Tom Harrell	Franco Ambrosetti
Dusko Goykovic	Tim Hagans
Valery Ponomarev	Claudio Roditi
Michael Mossman	Brian Lynch

Avant-Garde

Booker Little	Don Ellis
Don Cherry	Bill Dixon
Donald Ayler	Lester Bowie
Bobby Bradford	Leo Smith
Barbara Donald	Kenny Wheeler
Baikida Carroll	Olu Dara
Hugh Ragin	Enrico Rava
Herb Robertson	Tomasz Stanko
Manfred Schoof	Dave Douglas
Malachi Thompson	Ahmed Abdullah
Hannibal Marvin Peterson	Paul Smoker

Greatest 90-Year Old Trumpeter
Doc Cheatham

Young Lions

Wynton Marsalis	Terence Blanchard
Roy Hargrove	Wallace Roney
Philip Harper	Marlon Jordan
Ryan Kisor	Nicholas Payton

Other Fine Trumpeters of the 1980s/'90s

Marcus Belgrave	Randy Brecker
Ted Curson	Cecil Bridgewater
Rolf Ericson	Jon Faddis
Maynard Ferguson	Jerry Gonzalez
Eddie Henderson	Terumasa Hino
Steve Huffstetter	Tiger Okoshi
Chuck Mangione	James Morrison
Bobby Shew	Arturo Sandoval
Jack Sheldon	Don Sickler
Lew Soloff	Marvin Stamm
Ira Sullivan	Byron Stripling
Charles Tolliver	Jack Walrath

excellent advanced hard bop records in the mid-'60s, played with Gerald Wilson's Orchestra in Los Angeles (1966–67) and was a member of Max Roach's group at the same time (1967–69) as the compatible Gary Bartz. In 1969 Tolliver formed a quartet called Music Inc. that often featured pianist Stanley Cowell and was on a few occasions expanded to a big band. Tolliver and Cowell founded the Strata-East label in 1971, which released many fine records in the 1970s. Although it was an era when there was a serious shortage of talented young trumpeters (prior to the rise of Wynton Marsalis), Tolliver after the mid-'70s maintained a low profile and was thereafter overshadowed by the Young Lions. Charles Tolliver, whose fat tone was influenced by Freddie Hubbard while his ideas display bits of John Coltrane, has recorded as a leader for Impulse! (two songs from a 1965 concert), Black Lion, Enja and Strata East, most recently in 1988. —*Scott Yanow*

Paper Man / Jul. 2, 1968 / Black Lion ◆◆◆◆

★ **The Ringer** / Jun. 2, 1969 / Freedom ◆◆◆◆
Includes five Tolliver originals with the Stanley Cowell Trio. All the cuts are important, but "Plight" and "On the Nile" are particularly gripping. Cowell solos marvelously. —*Michael G. Nastos*

Live at Slugs, Vol. 1 / May 1, 1970 / Strata East ◆◆◆◆◆
Strata East recordings are quite difficult to acquire, which is unfortunate considering their high quality. Charles Tolliver was one of the great trumpeters to emerge during the late '60s yet has always been vastly underrated. On this quartet set with pianist Stanley Cowell, bassist Cecil McBee and drummer Jimmy Hopps, Tolliver has a real chance to stretch out. The 17-minute "Orientale" is particularly memorable. The music straddles the boundary between advanced hard bop and the avant-garde and rewards repeated listenings. —*Scott Yanow*

Live at Slugs, Vol. 2 / May 1, 1970 / Strata East ◆◆◆◆◆
Trumpeter in live club session with Cecil McBee (b), Stanley Cowell (p) and Jimmy Hopps (d). Modal jazz played with a real genuine honesty. Extended compositions let the band stretch out. —*Michael G. Nastos*

Music, Inc. Big Band / Nov. 11, 1971 / Strata East ◆◆◆◆
First document of progressive big band. Seventeen pieces. Famous works "Ruthie's Heart," "On the Nile" and "Departure." —*Michael G. Nastos*

Impact / Mar. 23, 1972 / Enja ◆◆◆◆

Live at the Loosdrecht Jazz Festival / Aug. 9, 1972 / Strata East ◆◆◆◆

Live in Tokyo / Dec. 7, 1973 / Strata East ◆◆◆◆

★ **Impact** / Jan. 17, 1975 / Strata East ◆◆◆◆◆
Six spectacular performances from trumpeters. twenty-three-piece plus eight-piece string section orchestra. Great solos from Tolliver and pianist Stanley Cowell on "Plight" and throughout by James Spaulding (as), George Coleman (ts), Charles McPherson (sax) and Harold Vick (ts). As powerful a record as you're likely to hear. —*Michael G. Nastos*

Live in Berlin at the Quasimodo, Vol. 1 / Jul. 21, 1988–Jul. 22, 1988 / Strata East ◆◆◆◆
A quartet recording from 1988, this features a stunning elongated version of "Ruthie's Heart" among four originals. There is great group interplay. —*Michael G. Nastos*

Mel Tormé

b. Sep. 13, 1925, Chicago, IL
Vocals / Bop, Swing
At the age of three, he was singing in public; at four, he was on

the radio; at nine, he was acting professionally, and at 15, he published his first composition—an instrumental. After playing drums and singing in Chico Marx's band (1942-1943), he formed a vocal ensemble, the Mel-Tones, for which he wrote exceptional arrangements; it performed with Artie Shaw's band. From the late '40s on, Tormé has pursued a career as solo singer with consistent success, also acting in films and on television and writing songs ("The Christmas Song" and "Born to Be Blue" have become standards). He has published a novel, a reminiscence of Judy Garland, an autobiography, and a biography of his friend and frequent coworker, Buddy Rich. Tormé is clearly a man of exceptional gifts; his voice has remained an astonishingly consistent and accurate instrument, and his upper range—always a special feature of his style—remains intact in his seventh decade of performing. Although somewhat overlooked as musical tastes changed in the 1960s, Tormé emerged in the late 1970s as a superb jazz singer and his string of Concord recordings (starting in the early 1980s) are among the finest of his career. Amazingly enough his voice has grown stronger with age (holding long unwavering notes on ballads with apparent ease), and as he passed his 70th birthday, Mel Tormé was at the peak of his powers. —*Ron Wynn and Dan Morgenstern*

A Foggy Day / 1945-1947 / Musicraft ✦✦✦

There's No One But You / 1945-1947 / Musicraft ✦✦✦

It Happened in Monterey / 1946 / Musicraft ✦✦✦✦
Brilliant harmonies, arrangements with the Mel-Tones. —*Ron Wynn*

Easy to Remember / 1946-1947 / Glendale ✦✦✦
This brief Hindsight CD (under 36 minutes) alternates Mel Tormé performances from 1953 with those from 1963; the backing personnel is not known in both cases. The previously unreleased material mostly emphasizes ballads and only three of the 16 selections are over 2 minutes. Tormé sounds fine, sticking primarily to the melody, but since he has continued to grow through the years (the singer's later Concord recordings find him at his peak) this nice middle-of-the-road set is not essential for anyone but true Mel Tormé fanatics. —*Scott Yanow*

Spotlight On Great Gentlemen Of Song / Jan. 17, 1949-Oct. 4, 1951 / Capitol ✦✦✦✦
This very interesting CD gives listeners a cross section of Mel Tormé's Capitol recordings. Caught fairly early in his career, Tormé's voice was already quite recognizable and appealing. Ballads alternate with occasional romps including several arranged by Frank DeVol in 1949 that are surprisingly boppish; Pete Rugolo, Nelson Riddle and Sonny Burke take care of the other charts. Highlights of the 18 cuts (four of which were previously unreleased) include a wild "Oh, You Beautiful Doll," "Stompin' at the Savoy," "Blue Moon," a spirited "Sonny Boy" and "You're a Heavenly Thing" (which finds Mel Tormé playing piano in a quartet with guitarist Mary Osborne). —*Scott Yanow*

California Suite / Nov. 1949 / Discovery ✦✦✦

In Hollywood / Dec. 15, 1954 / GRP/Decca ✦✦✦
This is an intriguing CD containing 20 performances (seven previously unissued) from one night in the life of Mel Tormé. Recorded live at the Crescendo in Hollywood, Tormé not only sings but also plays piano with a quartet comprised of clarinetist/pianist Al Pellegrini, bassist James Dupre and drummer Richard Shanahan. Although not quite as strong a jazz singer as he would later be, Tormé is consistently swinging on a well-rounded set highlighted by "That Old Black Magic," "My Shining Hour," "The Christmas Song," "Moonlight in Vermont," "Bernie's Tune," "Mountain Greenery" and "Get Happy." —*Scott Yanow*

★ **Tormé Touch** / Jan. 1956 / Bethlehem ✦✦✦✦✦
This Bethlehem LP (last reissued in 1978 and originally known as *Lulu's Back in Town*) is a classic. Singer Mel Tormé was matched for the first time with arranger Marty Paich's ten piece group which was called the Dek-tette. Among the sidemen are trumpeters Pete Candoli and Don Fagerquist, valve trombonist Bob Enevoldsen, Bud Shank on alto and flute and either Bob Cooper or Jack Montrose on tenors; in addition Paich uses both a French horn and a tuba. The arranged ensembles and cool-toned soloists match perfectly with Tormé's warm voice and there are many highpoints to this essential date. In particular "Lulu's Back in Town," "When the Sun Comes Out," "Fascinatin' Rhythm," "The Lady Is a Tramp" and "Lullaby of Birdland" are standouts, but all

dozen selections are excellent. This is one of Mel Tormé's finest records of the 1950s. —*Scott Yanow*

Round Midnight: A Retrospective / 1956-1962 / Stash ✦✦✦✦
This is a highly recommended set for Mel Tormé fans. The singer is heard on radio transcriptions (released for the first time in 1985) that compare favorably with his studio recordings of the period. Four selections are with the Marty Paich Dek-tette of 1956-57 while the other ten numbers (including instrumental versions of "Sugar Loaf" and "Marie") feature Tormé accompanied by a nonet headed by trumpeter Shorty Rogers. With such songs as "When the Sun Comes Out," "The Lady Is a Tramp," "The Surrey with the Fringe on Top," a "Porgy and Bess Medley" and two versions (with different arrangements) of "Lulu's Back in Town," this is a delightful set of cool but swinging jazz. —*Scott Yanow*

Back in Town / Apr. 23, 1959-Aug. 10, 1959 / Verve ✦✦✦✦
Mel Tormé had artistic–if not commercial–success with his vocal group the Mel-Tones in the mid-'40s. After its breakup in 1946, when Tormé was persuaded to go solo, the Mel-Tones were occasionally regrouped by Tormé for special projects. These 1959 dates, which have been reissued in full on a Verve CD, were the group's final recordings, and they make for an interesting comparison with their earlier sessions. In addition to remakes of their two hits, "What Is This Thing Called Love" and "It Happened in Monterey," the arrangements (mostly by Marty Paich) have many quotes from jazz songs and are heavily influenced by Count Basie's Orchestra of the 1950s. The Mel-Tones, which at the time also included Sue Allen, Ginny O'Connor, Bernie Parke and Tom Kenny, swing throughout and sing attractive harmonies without really improvising. However, the concise solos of Art Pepper on both alto and tenor and trumpeter Jack Sheldon work well with the singers, making this a recommended set to fans of jazz vocal groups, of which the relatively short-lived Mel-Tones ranked near the top. —*Scott Yanow*

I Dig the Duke, I Dig the Count / Dec. 12, 1960+Feb. 2, 1961 / Verve ✦✦✦✦✦

London Sessions / 1977 / DCC ✦✦✦
Mel Tormé had recorded relatively few rewarding albums in the decade before this set, originally put out by Gryphon before being reissued on CD by DCC Jazz. However, his voice had improved with time, his range had widened, and he had become an even stronger jazz singer than before. Since Tormé is joined here by the largely anonymous Chris Gunning Orchestra, with guest altoist Phil Woods, on a set of generally "contemporary" pop songs (including "All in Love Is Fair," "New York State of Mind," "Send in the Clowns" and "The First Time Ever I Saw Your Face"), this set is not too essential. However, Tormé's professionalism and ability to swing makes this an interesting outing anyway, and launched his "comeback." —*Scott Yanow*

Together Again: For the First Time / Jan. 1978 / Century ✦✦✦✦
Mel Tormé and Buddy Rich had been friends for decades prior to finally getting around to recording together. Although largely a Tormé vocal record, the Buddy Rich Orchestra, with guest altoist Phil Woods, is in top form, and the drummer/leader has several solos. Most memorable is Tormé's tribute to Ella Fitzgerald on "Lady Be Good" and a remarkable tour-de-force on "Blues in the Night." This enjoyable and somewhat historic LP, put out by Gryphon, deserves to be reissued on CD. —*Scott Yanow*

Encore at Marty's, New York / Mar. 27, 1982 / DCC ✦✦✦✦✦
This CD reissues a full set of music from Mel Tormé with his 1982 trio: pianist Mike Renzi, bassist Jay Leonhart and drummer Donny Osborne. No editing took place except for the excision of some chatter yet the music is consistently rewarding. Torme, who was already 56, was amazingly just entering his musical prime! His well-paced set mixes together older songs (highlighted by a Fred Astaire medley) with some newer but worthy pieces (including the debut of Tormé's own "I'm Gonna Miss You"), alternating scat-filled romps with lyrical ballad interpretations. Throughout it all Tormé succeeds at everything he tries with a humorous rendition of "I Like to Recognize the Tune" and some heated scatting on "Day in, Day Out" being among the memorable moments. This CD reissue of an album originally put out on the Flair label is recommended. —*Scott Yanow*

Evening with George Shearing / Apr. 15, 1982 / Concord Jazz ✦✦✦✦✦

Top Drawer / Mar. 1983 / Concord Jazz ✦✦✦✦✦

Evening at Charlie's / Oct. 1983 / Concord Jazz ✦✦✦✦✦
Mel Tormé and pianist George Shearing had recorded together

twice for Concord prior to this live set; both dates (*An Evening with George Shearing and Mel Tormé* and *Top Drawer*) gave Shearing top billing. For their third outing, the dynamic duo are up to their usual high level, with assistance from bassist Don Thompson and drummer Donny Osborne. Among the high points are "Nice's Dream," "Love Is Just Around the Corner" and a medley of "Just One of Those Things" and "On Green Dolphin Street." — *Scott Yanow*

Elegant Evening / May 1985 / Concord Jazz ✦✦✦✦

★ **Mel Tormé, Rob McConnell and the Boss Brass** / May 20, 1986 / Concord Jazz ✦✦✦✦✦
This was a very logical matchup that came out as well on record as it looked on paper. Valve trombonist/arranger Rob McConnell has long led one of the top mainstream jazz big bands, while Mel Tormé blossomed into one of the truly great jazz singers in the 1980s. McConnell's charts suited Tormé perfectly, and the result is this consistently enjoyable and swinging album. The singer is quite enthusiastic and in top form on "Just Friends," a touching "September Song," "Don'cha Go 'Way Mad," "A House Is Not a Home," "The Song Is You," a whimsical "Cow Cow Boogie," a "Stars" medley and an exciting six-song Duke Ellington medley. Highly recommended. — *Scott Yanow*

Vintage Year / Aug. 1987 / Concord Jazz ✦✦✦✦
Singer Mel Tormé and pianist George Shearing make a perfect team, bringing out the best in each other. With the assistance of bassist John Leitham and drummer Donny Osborne, the swinging, witty duo perform a variety of standards, including Noel Coward's "Someday I'll Find You," "The Way You Look Tonight" and "Anyone Can Whistle," and a couple of medleys highlighted by a humorous six-song "New York, New York Medley." All of the Torme/Shearing collaborations are quite enjoyable and highly recommended as some of their best work of the 1980s. — *Scott Yanow*

Reunion / Aug. 1988 / Concord Jazz ✦✦✦✦
In the 1950s, Mel Tormé recorded several memorable LPs on which he was joined by arranger Marty Paich and his Dek-tette (an all-star ten-piece band). For this long-overdue reunion, Paich utilized an 11-piece outfit (not counting two percussionists), adding a second trombone and a baritone to the original instrumentation while dropping the French horn. The results are quite enjoyable, with Torme, remarkably still improving with age, in peak form on such songs as "Sweet Georgia Brown," "More Than You Know," and several medleys, including one of bossa nova tunes and a combination of "For Whom the Bell Tolls" and Chick Corea's "Spain." The singer even attempts a couple of Steely Dan tunes with less success, since they are not that flexible; and Tormé seems to be in good spirits throughout this enjoyable set. — *Scott Yanow*

In Concert in Tokyo / Dec. 11, 1988 / Concord Jazz ✦✦✦✦✦
Mel Tormé and arranger Marty Paich (leading his ten-piece Dek-tette) recorded several classic albums in the late '50s. On *Reunion* earlier in 1988 they had an enjoyable collaboration and this live set was a follow-up. In general these in-concert performances are livelier with Tormé sounding quite exuberant at times. Highlights include "Just in Time," "When the Sun Comes Out," "The Carioca," "The Christmas Song" and an instrumental version of "Cotton Tail" featuring clarinetist Ken Peplowski and Tormé on drums. A joyful outing. — *Scott Yanow*

Night at the Concord Pavilion / Aug. 1990 / Concord Jazz ✦✦✦✦✦
This spontaneous set finds Mel Tormé in typically fine form. The first seven selections, which find Tormé backed by pianist John Campbell, bassist Bob Maize and drummer Donny Osborne, have three medleys, including three songs having "Sing" in their title and a definitive eight-theme "Guys and Dolls Medley." As if that were not enough, Tormé is joined at this concert from the 1990 Concord Jazz Festival by the all-star Frank Wess-Harry Edison Orchestra for "Down for Double" and rollicking renditions of "You're Driving Me Crazy" and "Sent for You Yesterday and Here You Come Today." Mel Tormé fans will have to get this delightful session. — *Scott Yanow*

Mel and George Do WWII / Sep. 2, 1990-Sep. 3, 1990 / Concord Jazz ✦✦✦✦
All of the Mel Torme-George Shearing collaborations are well worth acquiring, for the singer and the pianist constantly inspire each other. For this live concert, Tormé and Shearing perform a variety of songs popular during World War II. Shearing and bassist Neil Swainson duet on "Lilt Marlene" and "I've Heard That Song Before"; Shearing takes "I Know Why and So Do You" unaccompanied, and the duo is joined by drummer Donny Osborne and Tormé for a wide-ranging and consistently enjoyable set. Although "This Is the Army Mister Jones" is a bit dated, a four-song Duke Ellington medley, "I Could Write a Book" and a touching "We Mustn't Say Goodbye" are memorable. Recommended. — *Scott Yanow*

★ **Fujitsu-Concord Festival (1990)** / Nov. 11, 1990 / Concord Jazz ✦✦✦✦✦
A few months earlier in 1990, Mel Tormé recorded a set with his trio at the Concord Jazz Festival, which climaxed with three songs with the Frank Wess-Harry Edison Orchestra. This particular CD is similar and just as enjoyable. With the assistance of pianist John Campbell, bassist Bob Maize and drummer Donny Osborne, Tormé is swinging on "Shine on Your Shoes" and a medley of "Don't 'Cha Go 'Way Mad" and "Come to Baby Do." But it is his remarkable ballad renditions of "Star Dust" (during which Frank Wess sits in on tenor) and a definitive "A Nightingale Sang in Berkeley Square" that are most memorable; no other vocalist can hold notes so long. This time the big band is led by Wess only, and in addition to vocal versions of "You're Driving Me Crazy" and "Sent for You Yesterday," Tormé happily sits in on drums for "Swingin' the Blues," which has a trumpet solo by Joe Newman. Virtually everything Mel Tormé has recorded for Concord is quite rewarding; this is one of his best all-around sets. — *Scott Yanow*

Nothing Without You / Mar. 12, 1991-Mar. 13, 1991 / Concord Jazz ✦✦
Mel Tormé is in typically fine form on this Concord set; the problem is his musical partner Cleo Laine. Although often classified as a jazz singer, Laine, who has a tremendous range and a lovely voice, seems incapable of improvising. Backed by a 12-piece group led by Laine's husband John Dankworth, the duo perform a variety of mostly superior standards, but nothing unexpected happens—except for a somewhat disastrous "Two Tune Medley." On the latter, Tormé and Laine sing 20 songs, generally two at a time, in less than five minutes; it is quite annoying. Otherwise, Torme, who seems to have enjoyed the date, is weighed down and restricted by Cleo Laine's nonswinging style. Skip this one. — *Scott Yanow*

The Great American Songbook: Live at Michael's Pub / Oct. 1992 / Telarc ✦✦✦✦
Mel Torme, 67 at the time of this recording, proves to still be very much in his musical prime. His range remains impressive, his creative abilities have grown through the years and his breath control is remarkable; as proof Tormé holds some very long notes at the conclusion of some of the ballads. This live set finds Tormé backed by what he dubbed "the Great American Songbook Orchestra," his usual trio plus a dozen horns. The band gets "Ya Gotta Try" as an instrumental and Tormé sits in on drums on "Rockin' in Rhythm," but otherwise the orchestra sticks to its anonymous role in the background. The singer wrote ten of the 15 arrangements and programmed plenty of variety in moods and tempos for his voice including a seven-song Duke Ellington mini-set. His masterful interpretation of "Stardust" is a highpoint. Recommended — *Scott Yanow.*

Sing Sing Sing / Nov. 1992 / Concord Jazz ✦✦✦✦
Although 14 minutes of this CD is a specific "Tribute to Benny Goodman," actually the entire release is at least an indirect homage to the King of Swing. Tormé and his trio (pianist John Colianni, bassist John Leitham and drummer Donny Osborne) are joined by clarinetist Ken Peplowski and vibraphonist Peter Appleyard (who are very reminiscent of Goodman and Lionel Hampton) and the emphasis is on swing-era standards. Tormé is in typically fine form on such tunes as "It's All Right with Me," "These Foolish Things," "Three Little Words" and the closing "Ev'ry Time We Say Goodbye." The singer even has some additional fun during this live in Japan concert by switching to drums for a rousing "Sing, Sing, Sing" that climaxes the Goodman medley. — *Scott Yanow.*

Velvet & Brass / Jul. 5, 1995-Jul. 6, 1995 / Concord Jazz ✦✦✦✦

A Tribute to Bing Crosby / Concord Jazz ✦✦✦
As with most singers of his generation, Mel Tormé's early idol was Bing Crosby. On this set he is backed by 20 strings, his regular rhythm section (pianist John Colianni, bassist John Leitham and

drummer Donny Osborne) and three guests: guitarist Howard Alden, Ken Peplowski (on clarinet and tenor) and trumpeter Randy Sandke. Unfortunately the string arrangements (mostly by Bob Krogstad, Alan Broadbent and Angela Morley) weigh the music down and Tormé is content to stick almost exclusively to slow ballads. Crosby introduced a countless number of standards, but Tormé mostly takes the songs fairly straight, swinging and improvising in only selected spots. His voice sounds consistently beautiful, but the lack of mood variation and the heavy strings keep the music from reaching the heights of Mel Tormé's other Concord recordings. —*Scott Yanow*

Jean Toussaint

b. Jul. 27, 1960, St. Thomas, Virgin Islands
Tenor Sax / Hard Bop

Thus far Jean Toussaint's claim to fame is his period (1982-86) with Art Blakey's Jazz Messengers. After playing calypso locally in St. Thomas, he attended the Berklee College of Music, toured with an R&B band in 1979 and formed a quintet with Wallace Roney. He was with Blakey during the same period as Terence Blanchard and Donald Harrison. After leaving the Jazz Messengers, Toussaint began teaching in London and ever since has been based in London, mostly playing with English musicians although also gigging with Wynton Marsalis, McCoy Tyner and the Gil Evans Orchestra. Influenced by Wayne Shorter and Joe Henderson, Jean Toussaint's potential so far outweighs his accomplishments. —*Scott Yanow*

Ralph Towner

b. Mar. 1, 1940, Chehalis, WA
Guitar / Post-Bop

One of the founders of Oregon, Ralph Towner is one of the few modern jazz musicians to specialize on acoustic guitar. His playing often stretches beyond the boundaries of conventional jazz into world music and is quite distinctive. He started playing piano when he was three and trumpet at five, performing in a dance band when he was 13. Towner studied classical guitar in Vienna and played with classical chamber groups in the mid-'60s. After moving to New York in 1969, Towner worked with Jimmy Garrison, Jeremy Steig and Paul Winter's Winter Consort (1970-71). In the latter group Towner first met up with Collin Walcott, Glen Moore and Paul McCandless and in 1971 they broke away to form Oregon, a highly versatile group that ranges from jazz and free improvisations to folk music. Towner (who guested with Weather Report in 1971 and played with Gary Burton a bit during 1974-75) has performed and recorded with Oregon extensively since its formation in addition to recording as a leader and with many other artists on the ECM label. —*Scott Yanow*

Trios / Solos / Nov. 27, 1972-Nov. 28, 1972 / ECM ◆◆◆◆
Diary / Apr. 4, 1973-Apr. 5, 1973 / ECM ◆◆◆◆◆
Solo guitar and piano. —*Michael G. Nastos*
Matchbook / Jul. 26, 1974-Jul. 27, 1974 / ECM ◆◆◆◆◆
Definitive duets with vibist Gary Burton and Ralph Towner (g). —*Michael G. Nastos*
Solstice / Dec. 1974 / ECM ◆◆◆◆◆
Not only sounds wonderful, it has Jan Garbarek (ts). —*Ron Wynn*
Sounds and Shadows / Feb. 1977 / ECM ◆◆◆◆
Batik / Jan. 1978 / ECM ◆◆◆◆
Old Friends, New Friends / Jul. 1979 / ECM ◆◆◆◆◆
Excellent group work with trumpeter Kenny Wheeler. —*Michael G. Nastos*
★ **Solo Concert** / Oct. 1979 / ECM ◆◆◆◆◆
This very well-recorded album features Ralph Towner playing 12-string and classical guitar on "Nardis," two pieces by John Abercrombie and four of his own originals. The interpretations are typically sensitive, thoughtful and often introspective but also show off Towner's impressive technique. —*Scott Yanow*
Five Years Later / Mar. 1981 / ECM ◆◆◆◆
Blue Sun / Dec. 1982 / ECM ◆◆◆
Slide Show / May 1985 / ECM ◆◆◆
City of Eyes / Jan. 1988-Nov. 1988 / ECM ◆◆◆◆
Open Letter / Jul. 1991 / ECM ◆◆◆

Travelin' Light

Group / Swing

Formed in 1991, Travelin' Light is co-led by Frank Vignola (dou-

bling on banjo and acoustic guitar) and the fluent tuba player Sam Pilafian. With occasional guest stars (including Ken Peplowski), Travelin' Light has recorded several swinging and often-witty sets for Concord and Telarc. —*Scott Yanow*

● **Makin' Whoopee: Travelin' Light** / Jul. 15, 1992 / Telarc ◆◆◆◆◆
Christmas with Travelin' Light / Jul. 15, 1992 / Telarc ◆◆◆◆
This is a melodic and often-entertaining set of Christmas-related songs as performed by Travelin' Light (Sam Pilafian on tuba and Frank Vignola doubling on guitar and banjo) with guests: clarinetist Ken Peplowski, guitarist Don Keiling, drummer Joe Ascione and percussionist Andy Kubiezewski. The interpretations range from Dixielandish to folk with a nutty version of "The Twelve Days of Christmas" thrown in as a surprise. A happy program. —*Scott Yanow*
Cookin' With Frank & Sam / Jan. 5, 1995-Jan. 6, 1995 / Concord Jazz ◆◆◆◆

Lennie Tristano

b. Mar. 19, 1919, Chicago, IL, d. Nov. 18, 1978, New York, NY
Piano, Leader / Cool

There aren't many mavericks in any musical form, and even fewer people whose work represents a legitimate alternative. Pianist Lennie Tristano's was a definite departure from established jazz tradition. It emphasized the same instrumental and harmonic mastery as bebop but included many other unrelated elements. These included complex time signature changes, even rhythmic backgrounds rather than irregular cross-accents, carefully measured dissonance, and quite jarring polytonal effects. Tristano's music even veered into what would later be considered "free" collective improvisation, and he also was a pioneer in multi-track dubbing and recording. Tristano insisted his students, who included everyone from Bud Freeman to Art Pepper, thoroughly investigate the work of jazz greats from Louis Armstrong to Parker, and he put a premium on advanced ear training. Tristano's mother was an amateur pianist and opera singer, and he first studied music with her. He continued his studies at a school for the blind, spending 10 years there learning piano, wind instruments and music theory. Tristano then entered the American Conservatory in Chicago, graduating in 1943. He played piano and various instruments in jazz contexts and did some private teaching on the side while attending the Conservatory. By the mid-'40s, Tristano was attracting such musicians as Billy Bauer, Lee Konitz and Bill Russo. He made his first solo and trio recordings during this period. He moved to New York, performing with Charlie Parker and Dizzy Gillespie in concerts and on broadcasts, and doing arrangements for the Metronome All Stars. He was Metronome's "Musician of the Year" in 1947 and occasionally wrote for the magazine. Warne Marsh became his pupil in 1948, then Konitz and Bauer returned, helping form a sextet. This group recorded in 1949. Tristano founded a school in 1951, and hired as teachers such pupils as Konitz, Marsh and Sal Mosca. He steadily withdrew from public view, sporadically issuing some recordings. Various pupils and teachers left the fold, and Tristano closed the school in 1956, becoming a private teacher on Long Island. He made periodic appearances at the Half Note between 1958 and 1965, had a European tour in 1965, then made his last American public appearance in 1968. There was a French documentary interview about his life, times and work in 1973. After his death in 1978, there was a deluge of reissued and newly released Tristano recordings. There are a few Tristano sessions from the '40s and '50s available on CD. —*Ron Wynn and Dan Morgenstern*

Lost Session / May 1945-1946 / Phontastic ◆◆◆
This LP contains some real rarities. Side one has four selections and three alternates taken from a previously unknown session in which pianist Lennie Tristano teams up with the talented but now forgotten tenor Emmett Carls and several members of Woody Herman's Orchestra (trumpeter Shorty Rogers, trombonist Earl Swope, bassist Chubby Jackson and drummer Don Lamond). Although Tristano was not as well known as the others at the time, his unique playing really influences the sound of the ensembles. The flip side has four early and formerly rare piano solos plus a pair of trio outings with guitarist Billy Bauer and bassist Leonard Gaskin. Tristano collectors will have to acquire this European LP to fill some gaps in the pianist's relatively slim discography. —*Scott Yanow*
Live at Birdland (1949) / 1945-1949 / Jazz ◆◆◆◆
The Jazz label has made available several previously unknown Lennie Tristano sessions. The bulk of this LP features the pianist with tenor saxophonist Warne Marsh, guitarist Billy Bauer, bassist

Arnold Fishkin and drummer Jeff Morton, performing five selections that utilize common chord changes. Tristano and Marsh in particular are in creative form. The final four numbers must rank as among Lennie Tristano's earliest recordings for those unaccompanied solos were cut in 1945. Even at that early date, the pianist had his very unique style together. Although not as boppish as his playing would become, the basic principles are in place with long melodic lines and constant improvising being emphasized. —*Scott Yanow*

★ **Complete Lennie Tristano on Keynote** / Oct. 8, 1946-Oct. 23, 1947 / Mercury ✦✦✦✦✦

Rarest Trio / Quartet Sessions (1946-1947) / 1946-Dec. 31, 1947 / Raretone ✦✦✦✦✦
This collector's LP (from an Italian label) lives up to its name. These are among the rarest studio recordings of the remarkable pianist/teacher Lennie Tristano. He is heard on a dozen trio performances with guitarist Billy Bauer and either Leonard Gaskin John Levy or John LaPorta (who was avant-garde for his time) joins Lennie for four explorative quartet pieces. The music is utterly fascinating overall and shows that Tristano was already well past bebop, which was considered a revolutionary music itself at the time. —*Scott Yanow*

★ **Crosscurrents** / Mar. 4, 1949-Nov. 2, 1949 / Capitol ✦✦✦✦✦
Even though the music on this LP has yet to be made available on CD, it gets the highest rating because the performances are so unique. Pianist Lennie Tristano is heard with his finest group, a sextet with altoist Lee Konitz, tenor saxophonist Warne Marsh, guitarist Billy Bauer, bassist Arnold Fishkin and either Harold Granowsky or Denzil Best on drums. Their seven selections include some truly remarkable unisons on "Wow," memorable interplay by the horns on "Sax of a Kind" and the earliest examples of free improvisation in jazz: "Intuition" and "Digression." In addition, the set features clarinetist Buddy DeFranco with vibraphonist Teddy Charles in a sextet on three numbers and backed by a big band for two others; the radical "A Bird in Igor's Yard" was composed and arranged by George Russell. This essential LP (which is subtitled *Capitol Jazz Classics Vol. 14*) concludes with a feature for trombonist Bill Harris on Neal Hefti's "Opus 96." Consistently brilliant and advanced music. —*Scott Yanow*

Wow / 1950 / Jazz ✦✦✦✦✦
As is true of the Jazz label's CDs, there are no liner notes on this release and the total time falls into the range of an LP, but this is a rare live performance by pianist Lennie Tristano's finest group. The identities of the bassist and drummer (who are both relegated to quiet timekeeping) are unknown, but the other musicians are quite distinctive. With altoist Lee Konitz, tenor saxophonist Warne Marsh and guitarist Billy Bauer contributing their voices, Tristano explores a variety of common chord changes, a brief Fugue by Bach and his remarkable title cut. Well worth acquiring. —*Scott Yanow*

Live in Toronto (1952) / Jul. 17, 1952 / Jazz ✦✦✦✦
By 1952, pianist Lennie Tristano was starting to withdraw from public performances, spending most of his time teaching. This formerly unknown recording matches him with four of his best students: altoist Lee Konitz, tenor saxophonist Warne Marsh, bassist Peter Ind and drummer Al Levitt. Together they explore six common chord changes, five of them given new titles. Although not essential, this music is quite enjoyable and a good example of Lennie Tristano's unique approach to jazz improvisation. —*Scott Yanow*

Descent into the Maelstrom / 1952-1966 / Inner City ✦✦✦✦✦
This hard-to-find LP starts off with the utterly unique title cut. On this completely atonal track (which predates Cecil Taylor by a few years), Lennie Tristano overdubbed several pianos and created picturesque and extremely intense music. The remainder of this album is mostly comprised of leftovers and rehearsal tracks which, considering Tristano's slim discography, is quite welcome. The pianist is heard solo in 1961 and 1965, in a trio with bassist Peter Ind and drummer Roy Haynes in 1952 and (in what might be his last recordings) performing a pair of originals with bassist Sonny Dallas and drummer Nick Stabulas in 1966. Tristano fans can consider this important release to be essential. —*Scott Yanow*

Lennie Tristano Quartet / Jun. 11, 1955 / Atlantic ✦✦✦✦✦
These are previously unreleased performances from the Sing Song Room date....Here pianist Tristano presented his music in more refined terms with alto saxophonist Lee Konitz' interplay

both in the Tristano tradition and on his own personal terms. This was a set of excellent vintage, which remains remarkably stimulating. —*Bob Rusch, Cadence*

★ **Requiem** / Jun. 11, 1955-Aug. 1962 / Atlantic ✦✦✦✦✦
This two-LP set reissues the complete contents of pianist Lennie Tristano's two Atlantic studio albums, which were originally titled *Lennie Tristano* and *The New Tristano*. The first album was considered very controversial for on four selections Tristano overdubbed several pianos and altered the tape, speeding up and slowing down the individual tracks. The results are quite listenable but received a lot of negative comments at the time. The remainder of the first album matches Tristano with altoist Lee Konitz, bassist Gene Ramey and drummer Art Taylor, and although more conventional, are quite individual; the quartet takes apart and evaluates five standards. The second album features Tristano's solo piano (without any overdubbing) in 1961, years after he had stopped performing regularly in public. He has rarely played better than on these originals, making this set quite essential for all serious jazz collections. —*Scott Yanow*

New York Improvisations / 1955-1956 / Elektra ✦✦✦✦
By the mid-'50s pianist Lennie Tristano was pretty much a recluse, enthusiastically teaching his approach to jazz but rarely performing in public. This album has nine of his improvisations that were performed in his studio with the assistance of bassist Peter Ind and drummer Tom Weyburn. Tristano was one of the most talented jazz pianists in history, so practically every recording of his is worth savoring, especially considering that there are relatively few. These spontaneous solos (over common chord patterns) are no exception. —*Scott Yanow*

Continuity / Oct. 1958+Jun. 1964 / Jazz ✦✦✦✦
These valuable recordings document the great pianist Lennie Tristano during his later years, when public appearances were rare and recordings only an infrequent event. Tristano is heard playing at the Half Note on two separate occasions. Warne Marsh is on tenor, altoist Lee Konitz is a major asset to the selections from 1964, and the rhythm sections include either Henry Grimes or Sonny Dallas on bass and Paul Motian or Nick Stabulas on drums. The recording quality is decent if not admirable, but it is the music (six explorations of common chord changes and a 50-second "Everything Happens to Me") that is wonderful. Tristano, Marsh and Konitz constantly create new melody lines and make highly original music. —*Scott Yanow*

Note to Note / 1964-Mar. 12, 1993 / Jazz ✦✦
This LP-length CD contains five improvisations by pianist Lennie Tristano and bassist Sonny Dallas on "originals" based closely on common chord patterns and melodies. It was Tristano's wish that drums be added to these tapes at a later date so his daughter Carol Tristano overdubbed her rather basic timekeeping in 1993. Tristano collectors and completists will be interested in acquiring this CD, but in reality the music is just average and nothing all that surprising occurs. —*Scott Yanow*

Lennie Tristano Memorial Concert / Jan. 28, 1979-Jan. 29, 1980 / Jazz ✦✦✦
After his death, pianist/teacher Lennie Tristano was paid tribute to at a lavish Town Hall concert. This five-LP set has all of the music, plus a seven-minute drum solo recorded by Max Roach a year later. Many of Tristano's top students (although not Lee Konitz) are heard from including pianists Liz Gorrill, Lloyd Lifton, Virg Dzurinko, Sal Mosca and Connie Crothers, the solo guitar of Larry Meyer, unaccompanied flute performances by both Fran Canisius and Nomi Rosen, and six a cappella vocals from Lynn Anderson. Lennie Tristano was worshiped as a guru by some of these players (which sometimes results in overly precious performances), but in general the music is pretty rewarding. Not too surprisingly tenor saxophonist Warne Marsh (with a pianoless trio) and singer Sheila Jordan emerge as the solo stars. —*Scott Yanow*

Bobby Troup

b. Oct. 18, 1918, Harrisburg, PA
Piano, Vocals, Lyricist / Swing, Middle-of-the-Road Pop
Bobby Troup is not strictly a jazz performer, but he has made several important contributions to the music. As a composer he has written "Daddy," "Snooty Little Cutie," "Baby, Baby All the Time" and the major hit "Route 66." Troup has long been a fine pianist (having a regular jazz trio in the 1950s), a personable singer (although some of his early records were overly mannered) and an actor, and during 1956-58 he moderated a legendary television

series (*Stars of Jazz*) that featured a who's who of jazz players. He also produced some best-selling records for his wife Julie London. —*Scott Yanow*

Bobby / Aug. 1953-May 1954 / Capitol ✦✦

● **The Feeling of Jazz** / Sep. 17, 1955-Jun. 23, 1967 / Star Line ✦✦✦✦✦
Bobby Troup has long been a multitalented individual. This Star Line CD, which contains previously unissued performances from several settings, features Troup singing and playing a variety of high-quality songs, many of which he wrote. Highlights include Troup's lyrics to "Walkin' Shoes" and his hits "Daddy," "The Three Bears," "Girl Talk" and "Route 66" along with some cheerful novelties and standards. Singing in a style that is both gentle and forceful (and somehow hip for the period without sounding dated today), Bobby Troup is in excellent form throughout this definitive release. —*Scott Yanow*

Bobby Swings Tenderly / 1957 / VSOP ✦✦✦
This is one of pianist/vocalist/composer Bobby Troup's few (and possibly only) all-instrumental dates. Accompanied by cool-toned horns (valve trombonist Bob Enevoldsen, trumpeter Stu Williamson, tenor saxophonist Ted Nash and baritonist Ronnie Lang) along with bassist Buddy Clark and drummer Mel Lewis, Troup explores eight familiar standards plus his own "I See Your Bass Before Me." The easy-listening music that is heard on this VSOP LP (not yet out on CD) is fine if not overly stimulating. The emphasis is on ballads and mellow playing. —*Scott Yanow*

Big Joe Turner

b. May 18, 1911, Kansas City, MO, **d.** Nov. 24, 1985, Inglewood, CA
Vocals / Swing, Blues
Big Joe Turner enjoyed stardom in two related, but quite different eras. The Big Chill generation appreciates Turner for his contribution to rock & roll; those who know pre-rock history cherish his vocal contributions to the boogie-woogie and Kansas City jazz eras. He was among the greatest, most vociferous shouters ever, able to holler and roar above a striding big band, yet also fit his huge sound into situations with boogie-woogie players relying on timing and pace. Turner was tending bar and singing at age 14 in Kansas City. Known as "the singing bartender," the youth attracted the attention of such bandleaders as Bennie Moten, Andy Kirk and Count Basie. He and pianist Pete Johnson became great friends and a popular touring act in the late '30s and the '40s. After his appearance with Johnson at the "Spirituals to Swing" Carnegie Hall concert in 1938, Turner made his first recordings, notably the spectacular "Roll 'Em Pete." Turner's huge voice half shouts, half sings, with the piece's tension superbly developed via his use of repeated phrases and Johnson's rumbling, churning riffs and accompaniment. Turner was an equally gifted slow blues and ballad stylist, and his work with pianists and bands reflected his fluidity, knowledge of inflections and ability to develop themes and embellish lyrics. He recorded with Joe Sullivan, Benny Carter and Art Tatum among others. But his early '50s R&B hits "Still in the Dark," "Chains of Love" and "Sweet Sixteen" were forerunners of a new era. "Honey Hush" and "Shake, Rattle and Roll" marked Joe Turner's move to the pop arena, even though cover versions of both songs did better sales wise than his originals. But after his rock success ebbed, Turner returned to the jazzy blues he'd always done; he made fine dates in the '70s with Count Basie, the Trumpet Kings, Cleanhead Eddie Vinson, and Jimmy Witherspoon. In 1983, two years before his death, Turner recorded with Roomful of Blues. —*Ron Wynn and John Floyd*

★ **Big, Bad & Blue: The Big Joe Turner Anthology** / Dec. 30, 1938-Jan. 26, 1983 / Rhino ✦✦✦✦
A comprehensive, three-CD collection, *Big, Bad & Blue* is the only truly definitive Joe Turner compilation available, complete with stunning audio and terrific liner notes; it stands as a testament to the lasting influence of this seminal jump blues/R&B shouter. New fans will want to stick with the single-disc *Greatest Hits*, because the sheer weight of *Big, Bad & Blue* is a little intimidating. —*Stephen Thomas Erlewine*

★ **Complete 1940-1944** / Nov. 11, 1940-Nov. 13, 1944 / Official ✦✦✦✦✦
Big Joe Turner's 25 Decca recordings are all included on this excellent set. The music is consistently exciting and finds the blues singer in prime form. His accompaniment is quite varied and always colorful with such pianists as Art Tatum, Pete Johnson, Willie "the Lion" Smith (a perfect match), Sam Price and the sur-

prisingly effective Freddie Slack all getting their spots. Turner had a remarkably long and commercially successful career considering that he never changed his basic approach; he just never went out of style. —*Scott Yanow*

Every Day in the Week / Sep. 9, 1941-Apr. 13, 1967 / GRP ✦✦✦✦✦

Tell Me Pretty Baby / 1948-1949 / Arhoolie ✦✦✦✦
Nice late-'40s compilation with Pete Johnson's Boogie 88s. —*Bill Dahl*

Rhythm & Blues Years / Apr. 17, 1951-Sep. 29, 1959 / Atlantic ✦✦✦✦
Big Joe Turner, who started out as a singing bartender in 1930s Kansas City, is best known to jazz listeners for his early dates with the Boogie Woogie trio, his collaborations with Pete Johnson ("Roll 'Em Pete") and his much later albums for Pablo in the '70s, but the general public best remembers the shouting blues singer for his string of Atlantic hits ("Shake, Rattle and Roll," "Corrine Corrina" and others) in the 1950s. The two-fer *Rhythm & Blues Years* does not include the biggest sellers but featured selections from some of the same sessions, 32 cuts in all. Turner sings in a timeless blues style that dominated these performances and easily communicates to a large audience during this period. The back-up is generally pretty anonymous with the brief tenor solos all sounding a bit like Gene Ammons and the accompanying pianists emphasizing triplets. There are some familiar names in the groups (including Budd Johnson, Taft Jordan, Al Sears, Red Tyler, Sam the Man Taylor, Earle Warren, Jerome Richardson, Hilton Jefferson, King Curtis, Jesse Stone, George Barnes, Panama Francis and even Connie Kay), but they are virtually unrecognizable in this setting. Ray Charles sits in on piano for "Wee Baby Blues." —*Scott Yanow*

★ **Greatest Hits** / Apr. 19, 1951-Jan. 22, 1958 / Atlantic ✦✦✦✦✦
These are Turner's finest early-rock-era recordings, including his best (and best-known) hits and some tasty obscurities. A must-have. —*John Floyd*

★ **Boss of the Blues** / Mar. 6, 1956-Mar. 7, 1956 / Atlantic ✦✦✦✦✦
This Big Joe Turner set is a good one, particularly since there had been, at the time, some success in packaging and pushing Turner into an R&B cum rock and roll SENSATION. Here he is backed by a compatible and sympathetic group. Turner is in good voice and there is the added plus of Pete Johnson's piano, a legendary Kansas City artist in his own right, and other capable soloists—particularly tenor saxophonist Frank Wess and alto saxophonist Ray Brown. Ernie Wilkins' arrangements were a perfect match for the music and open, rolling shouts of Turner. —*Bob Rusch, Cadence*

Big Joe Rides Again / Sep. 9, 1959-Sep. 10, 1959 / Atlantic ✦✦✦✦

Singing the Blues / 1967 / Mobile Fidelity ✦✦✦✦

Texas Style / Apr. 26, 1971 / Evidence ✦✦✦
Big Joe Turner was well beyond his prime when he recorded these eight tracks for the Black and Blue label in 1971, but even at less than peak strength he could still shout, roar, and wail the blues with resonance and presence. This Evidence CD reissue features him backed by a small combo with the great "Papa" Jo Jones striding on drums, Milt Buckner adding rollicking piano licks, and bassist Slam Stewart keeping things steadily moving. Turner's treatment of "TV Mama" was not as majestic as the original with Elmore James; nor were "Cherry Red" or "Rock Me Baby" definitive versions. But they were nonetheless emphatic, rugged and rocking, with Turner's projection, delivery and tone alternately defiant, menacing (in a showman-like way) and suggestive. —*Ron Wynn*

Life Ain't Easy / Jun. 3, 1974 / Pablo ✦✦✦✦

Trumpet Kings Meet Joe Turner / Sep. 19, 1974 / Original Jazz Classics ✦✦✦✦

Everyday I Have the Blues / Mar. 3, 1975 / Original Jazz Classics ✦✦✦✦

Nobody in Mind / Aug. 27, 1975 / Original Jazz Classics ✦✦✦✦✦
Blues singer Big Joe Turner is in good form on this late-period session. In addition to his usual rhythm section (featuring guitarist Pee Wee Crayton), Turner is joined by two notable soloists: trumpeter Roy Eldridge (whose determination makes up for his occasional misses) and vibraphonist Milt Jackson. Other than "Red Sails in the Sunset" (which is largely turned into a blues), the music is fairly typical for Turner, but the spirit and sincerity of the

singer and his sidemen make this CD reissue worth picking up.
—*Scott Yanow*

Things That I Used to Do / Feb. 8, 1977 / Original Jazz Classics ✦✦✦✦

Blues Train / Jan. 26, 1983 / Muse ✦✦✦

Kansas City Here I Come / Feb. 14, 1984 / Original Jazz Classics ✦✦✦

Patcha, Patcha All Night Long / Apr. 11, 1985 / Pablo ✦✦

Norris Turney

b. Sep. 8, 1921, Wilmington, OH
Alto Saxophone / Swing

One of Ellington's most lyrical soloists, Norris Turney has a fine sound and style on alto sax, flute and clarinet. His alto combines swing era urgency and fluidity with bebop era exactness and technical expertise. Turnery played with A.B. Townsend in Ohio before working with Jeter-Pillars orchestra in the '40s. He later played with Tiny Bradshaw. Turney was in Billy Eckstine's orchestra in 1945 and 1946, then returned to Ohio. He moved to Philadelphia and played with Elmer Snowden in 1951, and in the late '60s toured Australia with the Ray Charles orchestra. Turney joined Ellington as a substitute for Johnny Hodges in 1969, then became a full-time member the next year. He remained until 1973, then worked in pit orchestras in New York the remainder of the decade. Turney joined Panama Francis' Savoy Sultans in 1980 and also toured and recorded with George Wein's Newport All Stars in the '80s and '90s. —*Ron Wynn*

● **Big, Sweet 'N Blue** / Apr. 5, 1993-Mar. 6, 1993 / Mapleshade ✦✦✦✦

Since there are not that many alumni of Duke Ellington's Orchestra still active, it is surprising that altoist Norris Turney (who was with Ellington from 1969-74 and eventually replaced the unreplaceable Johnny Hodges) has not been recorded all that extensively during the 20 years since. In fact his Mapleshade debut is the 72-year-old's first session at the head of a quartet and the music's obvious success is even more impressive when one realizes that Turney had never played with the other musicians (pianist Larry Willis, bassist Walter Booker and drummer Jimmy Cobb) before. Norris Turney is a melodic swing player with a large tone, and since the rhythm section is quite supportive and sympathetic, these renditions of blues, ballads and standards (including his own "Checkered Hat" and three Ellington/-Strayhorn pieces) came together rather quickly. Highlights include the lengthy "Blues for Edward," "Blood Count" and "Come Sunday." —*Scott Yanow*

Steve Turre

b. Sep. 12, 1948, Omaha, NE
Trombone, Conch Shells / Bop, Latin Jazz, Hard Bop

One of the finest trombonists of the 1980s and '90s, Steve Turre also introduced the conch shells to jazz. After a brief period on violin he switched to trombone when he was ten. Turre worked locally from age 13, played with Rahsaan Roland Kirk off and on from 1968, recorded with Santana in 1970 and in 1972 toured with Ray Charles. Turre had many diverse musical experiences in the 1970s including tours with Art Blakey's Jazz Messengers and the Thad Jones-Mel Lewis Orchestra (both in 1973), an opportunity to play trombone and electric bass regularly with Chico Hamilton (1974-76) and recording with Woody Shaw and Rahsaan Roland Kirk. Kirk inspired Turre to play exotic shells and his ability to get a wide range of clear tones is quite impressive. Since that time Turre toured with McCoy Tyner, Dexter Gordon, Slide Hampton, Poncho Sanchez, Hilton Ruiz and Tito Puente among others. In 1987 he joined Dizzy Gillespie's United Nations Orchestra and he has also played regularly with Lester Bowie's Brass Fantasy, the Leaders and the Timeless All-Stars. Turre performed with his Sanctified Shells (a group featuring four trombonists doubling on shells, trumpeter E.J. Allen, bass, drums and several percussionists) at the 1995 Monterey Jazz Festival and has recorded as a leader for Stash, Antilles and Verve. —*Scott Yanow*

Viewpoint / Feb. 7, 1987-Feb. 8, 1987 / Stash ✦✦✦✦✦

Steve Turre covers a lot of styles on his debut as a leader; from tributes to Kid Ory and Duke Ellington to bop, a bit of free form and Latin jazz. The trombonist proves that he is comfortable in all of those idioms, making this a rather impressive set. His supporting cast consists of pianist Mulgrew Miller, bassist Peter

Washington, drummer Idris Muhammed, occasionally cellist Akua Dixon, extra percussion and (on the Dixielandish piece) clarinetist Haywood Henry, trumpeter Jon Faddis and the tuba of Bob Stewart. Everything works. —*Scott Yanow*

Fire and Ice / Feb. 5, 1988-Feb. 6, 1988 / Stash ✦✦✦✦✦

Steve Turre is one of the most versatile and talented trombonists to emerge during the past 15 years. For his second Stash recording, Turre (who also plays his conch shells on two of the ten songs) utilizes a superb rhythm section (pianist Cedar Walton, bassist Buster Williams and drummer Billy Higgins) plus a jazz string quartet (Quartette Indigo) on six of the selections. The music ranges from standards (including "When Lights Are Low," Monk's "Well You Needn't" and "Mood Indigo") to some memorable originals and one complex piece played by the strings alone. Stimulating music with more than its share of variety. —*Scott Yanow*

Right There / Mar. 30, 1991-Apr. 10, 1991 / Antilles ✦✦✦✦

Sanctified Shells / Jan. 31, 1992-May 11, 1992 / Antilles ✦✦✦✦✦

★ **Rhythm Within** / 1995 / Verve ✦✦✦✦✦

Stanley Turrentine

b. Apr. 5, 1934, Pittsburgh, PA
Tenor Saxophone / Soul Jazz, Hard Bop

While highly regarded in soul jazz circles, Stanley Turrentine is one of the finest tenor saxophonists in any style in modern times. He excels at uptempo compositions, in jam sessions, interpreting standards, playing the blues or on ballads. His rich, booming and huge tone, with its strong swing influence, is one of the most striking of any tenor stylist, and during the '70s and '80s made otherwise horrendous mood music worth enduring. Turrentine toured with R&B and blues bands led by Ray Charles, Lowell Fulson and Earl Bostic in the early '50s; he replaced John Coltrane in Bostic's band. He later played with Max Roach in 1959 and 1960, cutting his first recordings with him. Turrentine started recording as a leader on Blue Note in 1959 and 1960, while also participating in some landmark Jimmy Smith sessions such as *Midnight Special, Back at the Chicken Shack* and *Prayer Meeting*. His decade plus association with Shirley Scott was both professional and personal, as they were married most of the time they were also playing together. They frequently recorded, with the featured leader's name often depending on the session's label affiliation. When they divorced and split musically in the early '70s, Turrentine became a crossover star on CTI. Several of his CTI, Fantasy, Elektra and Blue Note albums in the '70s and '80s made the charts. Though their jazz content became proportionally lower, Turrentine's playing remained consistently superb. He returned to straight-ahead and soul jazz in the '80s, cutting more albums for Fantasy and Elektra, then returning to Blue Note. He's currently on the Musicmasters label. Almost anything Turrentine's recorded, even albums with Stevie Wonder cover songs, are worth hearing for his solos. Many of his classic dates, as well as recent material, is available on CD. —*Ron Wynn and Bob Porter*

Stan the Man Turrentine / 1959-1960 / Bainbridge ✦✦✦

His earliest album. Uptempo mainstream. Lacks the distinctive Turrentine sound that later albums show. —*Michael Erlewine*

Look Out / Jun. 18, 1960 / Blue Note ✦✦✦✦

Blue Hour / Dec. 16, 1960 / Blue Note ✦✦✦✦✦

Recorded in Englewood Cliffs, NJ. with the Three Sounds, a small group. A beautiful album of relaxed, bluesy sound. —*Michael Erlewine*

● **Up at Minton's** / 1961 / Blue Note ✦✦✦✦✦

This is a particularly solid double CD featuring tenor saxophonist Stanley Turrentine, guitarist Grant Green, pianist Horace Parlan, bassist George Tucker and drummer Al Harewood during a frequently exciting live set. Although recorded early in the careers of Turrentine and Green, both lead voices are easily recognizable with Green actually taking solo honors on several of the pieces. Standards and a couple of blues make up the repertoire, giving listeners a definitive look at the soulful Mr. T. near the beginning of his productive musical life. —*Scott Yanow*

Comin' Your Way / Jan. 20, 1961 / Blue Note ✦✦✦✦

Recorded at Englewood Cliffs, NJ. Small group. 1988 reissue of sumptuous '60s soul-jazz date. Horace Parlan (p) at his bluesy best. —*Ron Wynn*

Up at Minton's, Vol. 1 / Feb. 23, 1961 / Blue Note ✦✦✦✦✦
Up at Minton's, Vol. 2 / Feb. 23, 1961 / Blue Note ✦✦✦✦✦
Dearly Beloved / Jun. 8, 1961 / Blue Note ✦✦✦✦
Z.T.'s Blues / Sep. 13, 1961 / Blue Note ✦✦✦✦✦
● That's Where It's at / Jan. 2, 1962 / Blue Note ✦✦✦✦✦
Jubilee Shout / Oct. 18, 1962 / Blue Note ✦✦✦✦
Never Let Me Go / Jan. 18, 1963+Feb. 13, 1963 / Blue Note ✦✦✦
A Chip off the Old Block / Oct. 21, 1963 / Blue Note ✦✦✦✦
Hustlin' / Jan. 24, 1964 / Blue Note ✦✦✦
In Memory Of / Jun. 3, 1964 / Blue Note ✦✦✦✦✦
Mr. Natural / Sep. 4, 1964 / Blue Note ✦✦✦✦
● Let It Go / Sep. 21, 1964+Apr. 15, 1966 / GRP/Impulse! ✦✦✦✦✦
Recorded in Englewood Cliffs, NJ. Small group. Some recorded on
Sep. 21, 1964. Husband and wife team Turrentine and Shirley
Scott (organ) produce one lovely album—blues/jazz, funky. —
Michael Erlewine
Joyride / Apr. 14, 1965 / Blue Note ✦✦✦✦
Rough 'n Tumble / Jul. 1, 1966 / Blue Note ✦✦✦✦
Easy Walker / Jul. 8, 1966 / Blue Note ✦✦✦✦
The Spoiler / Sep. 22, 1966 / Blue Note ✦✦✦✦
Ain't No Way / May 10, 1968 / Blue Note ✦✦✦
Common Touch! / Aug. 30, 1968 / Blue Note ✦✦✦
Look of Love / Sep. 29, 1968-Oct. 6, 1968 / Blue Note ✦✦✦✦
Always Something There / Oct. 14, 1968+Oct. 28, 1968 / Blue
Note ✦✦
Another Story / Mar. 3, 1969 / Blue Note ✦✦✦✦
★ Sugar / Nov. 1970 / CTI ✦✦✦✦✦
Recorded at Englewood Cliffs, NJ. Larger group. By far the best
thing he ever made on CTI. Among the handful of genuine jazz
albums that were cut on that label. —*Ron Wynn*
The Salt Song / Jul. 1971-Sep. 1971 / CTI ✦✦✦
Cherry / May 17, 1972 / Columbia ✦✦✦✦
Don't Mess with Mister T. / Jun. 7, 1973 / CTI ✦✦✦✦✦
Pieces of Dreams / May 30, 1974-May 31, 1974 / Original Jazz
Classics ✦✦
Tenor saxophonist Stanley Turrentine's recording of Michel
Legrand's "Pieces of Dreams" is quite memorable and made the
song into a standard. There are two versions of that song on this
CD reissue, but unfortunately, the other six numbers and the two
added alternate takes are all quite commercial. Turrentine's tenor
is joined by electric keyboards, up to three guitarists, a few back-
ground vocalists and strings, all arranged by Gene Page. None of
the other then-recent material is up to the level of "Pieces of
Dreams," making this a disc that can be safely passed by. —*Scott
Yanow*
In the Pocket / Jan. 1975 / Fantasy ✦
Have You Ever Seen the Rain / Jul. 1975 / Fantasy ✦✦
Everybody Come on Out / Mar. 1976 / Fantasy ✦
Man with the Sad Face / Aug. 25, 1976-Sep. 28, 1976 / Bainbridge
✦✦✦
Nightwings / Jun. 1977+Jul. 1977 / Fantasy ✦✦
West Side Highway / Jun. 1977+Jul. 1977 / Fantasy ✦✦
What About You! / Jun. 1978+Jul. 1978 / Fantasy ✦
Betcha / May 1979-Jun. 1979 / Elektra ✦✦
Tender Togetherness / Apr. 1981 / Elektra ✦✦
Straight Ahead / Nov. 24, 1984 / Blue Note ✦✦✦
Recorded at Power Play Studios, Long Island City, NY. Small
group. Same great combination of musicians as on earlier cook-
ers, but here it does not come off. Pleasant enough but lacks high
spots. —*Michael Erlewine*
Wonderland / Dec. 1986 / Blue Note ✦✦✦✦
L.A. Place / 1989 / Blue Note ✦✦✦
More Than a Mood / 1992 / Music Masters ✦✦✦✦
For this quartet date with pianist Cedar Walton, bassist Ron Carter
and drummer Billy Higgins (trumpeter Freddie Hubbard sits in on
two numbers), Turrentine is in top form on a variety of standards
plus Tommy Turrentine's "Thomasville" and Rahsaan Roland
Kirk's "Spirits up Above." A fine session. —*Scott Yanow*

If I Could / May 10, 1993-May 12, 1993 / Music Masters ✦✦✦✦
This session from tenor saxophonist Stanley Turrentine often
sounds like a CTI recording from the 1970s although Creed Taylor
had nothing to do with it. Backed by Don Sebesky's arrangements
and assisted by a strong rhythm section and Hubert Laws' flute,
Turrentine's solos are stronger than the melodies and he generally overcomes the unimaginative use of strings on the ballads. Mr.
T. is in fine form and he makes the most of each selection (particularly on the two blues "June Bug" and "A Luta Continua")
while Laws comes across much more creative than he does on
most of his own recordings. Recommended. —*Scott Yanow*

Tommy Turrentine
b. Apr. 12, 1928, Pittsburgh, PA
Trumpet / Hard Bop
Stanley Turrentine's older brother, Tommy had a parallel career
for a while. His most significant early gigs were with Benny
Carter (1946), Earl Bostic (1952-55) and Charles Mingus (1956) in
addition to big band work with Billy Eckstine, Dizzy Gillespie and
Count Basie. Turrentine received some recognition playing next to
his brother during a well-documented stint with Max Roach
(1959-60). In the early '60s he recorded his lone session as a leader
(for Time) and appeared on dates led by Horace Parlan, Jackie
McLean, Sonny Clark, Lou Donaldson and Stanley Turrentine
before retiring from music and falling into obscurity. Tommy
Turrentine was a fine hard loop-oriented trumpeter who had the
talent to go much further. —*Scott Yanow*
● Tommy Turrentine / Jan. 19, 1960 / Bainbridge ✦✦✦✦
It seems strange that trumpeter Tommy Turrentine (the brother of
the great tenor Stanley) never really made it for, at the time of this
release (his only session as a leader), he played on the level of a
Donald Byrd. A fine straight-ahead soloist, Turrentine is heard in a
sextet with his brother, trombonist Julian Priester, pianist Horace
Parlan, bassist Bob Boswell and his employer of the time drummer
Max Roach. The music is typical hard bop of the era with plenty
of soul and swing. Despite his talents, little has been heard of
Tommy Turrentine during the past 25 years. —*Scott Yanow*

Twenty-Ninth Street Saxophone Quartet
Group / Hard Bop
Formed in 1982 and comprised of altoists Bobby Watson and Ed
Jackson, Rich Rothenberg on tenor and baritonst Jim Hartog, the
29th Street Saxophone Quartet is hard bop's answer to the World
Saxophone Quartet. Actually within the straight-ahead tradition,
this part-time unit (which has recorded several sets for Red and
Antilles) is fairly adventurous. —*Scott Yanow*
Pointilistic Groove / Oct. 1985 / Osmosis ✦✦✦✦
Watch Your Step / 1985 / Antilles ✦✦✦✦
● The Real Deal / Jan. 1987 / Antilles ✦✦✦✦✦
The 29th Street Saxophone Quartet (which consists of Bobby
Watson and Ed Jackson on altos, Rich Rothenberg on tenor and
baritonist Jim Hartog) is much more conservative in style than the
other main a cappella sax groups (the World Saxophone Quartet
and Rova), but although based in the hard bop tradition, it does
have its free and explorative moments. Highlights of this general-
ly stimulating CD include Thelonious Monk's "I Mean You," Bud
Powell's "Un Poco Loco," Charlie Parker's "Confirmation" and
Watson's "Wheel Within a Wheel." —*Scott Yanow*
Live / Jul. 1988 / Red ✦✦✦✦✦
Underground / 1991 / Antilles ✦✦✦✦
Your Move / 1992 / Antilles ✦✦✦

Charles Tyler
b. Jul. 20, 1941, Cadiz, KY, d. Jun. 27, 1992, Toulon, France
Alto Saxophone, Baritone Saxophone / Avant-Garde, Free Jazz
One of the freer, more flamboyant baritone saxophonists as well
as a capable alto stylist, Charles Tyler unfortunately never
attained widespread recognition. He had complete command of
the baritone, was expressive in every register and played with
speed, lyricism or energy. Tyler studied clarinet and alto sax as a
child before playing baritone in an Army band. He moved to
Cleveland in 1960, where he played with Albert Ayler. Tyler later
moved to New York, where he became involved in the city's free
jazz scene, recording and working extensively with Ayler. He was
featured on the albums *Bells* and *Spirits Rejoice*, and also played
C-melody sax on a bootleg album with Ayler and Ornette

Coleman on trumpet. He made his recording debut as a leader on ESP in the late '60s. Tyler also played with Sunny Murray and others. He moved to California, teaching music for four years at Merritt College and working with Arthur Blythe, David Murray and Bobby Bradford. Tyler was featured on a Stanley Crouch album in 1973. When he returned to New York in 1976, Tyler began leading his own groups. He recorded for Ak-Ba, Nessa and Adelphi in the '70s and Sonet, Storyville, Silkheart, Mustevic and Nessa in the '80s. He worked with Dave Baker, Dewey Redman, Frank Lowe, Steve Reid and Cecil Taylor, and recorded and played with the Billy Bang Ensemble in 1981 and 1982. —*Ron Wynn*

First Album / Feb. 4, 1966 / ESP ◆◆◆◆◆

Second Album / Jan. 2, 1967 / ESP ◆◆◆◆

Saga of the Outlaws / May 20, 1976 / Nessa ◆◆◆◆

Sixty Minute Man / May 1979 / Adelphi ◆◆◆◆◆

★ **Definite, Vol. 1** / 1981 / Storyville ◆◆◆◆◆
For the first of two albums taken from an engagement in Stockholm, Charles Tyler (playing two songs apiece on alto and baritone) teams up with trumpeter Earl Cross, bassist Kevin Ross and drummer Steve Reid for some heated freebop. The expressive solos and explorative nature of the music hold one's interest throughout. —*Scott Yanow*

● **Definite, Vol. 2** / Oct. 20, 1981-Oct. 21, 1981 / Storyville ◆◆◆◆◆
This is the second of two albums that document a Charles Tyler club gig in Stockholm. Splitting his time between alto and baritone, Tyler (in a quartet with trumpeter Earl Cross, bassist Kevin Ross and drummer Steve Reid) has a real chance to stretch out on these five freebop originals. The compositions are strong, but it is the spirited and fairly free improvisations that make both of these volumes an excellent purchase for listeners with ears open toward the jazz avant-garde. —*Scott Yanow*

Autumn in Paris / Jun. 2, 1988 / Silkheart ◆◆◆◆

McCoy Tyner

b. Dec. 11, 1938, Philadelphia, PA
Piano, Leader / Post-Bop
It is to McCoy Tyner's great credit that his career after John Coltrane has been far from anti-climatic. Along with Bill Evans, Tyner has been the most influential pianist in jazz of the past 35 years with his chord voicings being adopted and utilized by virtually every younger pianist. A powerful virtuoso and a true original (compare his playing in the early '60s with anyone else from the time!), Tyner (like Thelonious Monk) has not altered his style all that much from his early days, but he has continued to grow and become even stronger.

McCoy Tyner grew up in Philadelphia where Bud Powell and Richie Powell were neighbors. As a teenager he gigged locally and met John Coltrane. He made his recording debut with the Art Farmer-Benny Golson Jazztet but after six months left the group to join Coltrane in what (with bassist Jimmy Garrison and drummer Elvin Jones) would become the classic quartet. Few other pianists of the period had both the power and the complementary open-minded style to inspire Coltrane, but Tyner was never overshadowed by the innovative saxophonist. During the Coltrane years (1960-65), the pianist also led his own record dates for Impulse.

After leaving Coltrane, McCoy Tyner struggled for a period, working as a sideman (with Ike and Tina Turner) and leading his own small groups; his recordings were consistently stimulating even during the lean years. After he signed with Milestone in 1972, Tyner began to finally be recognized as one of the greats, and he has never been short of work since. Although there have been occasional departures (such as a 1978 all-star quartet tour with Sonny Rollins and duo recordings with Stephane Grappelli), Tyner has mostly played with his own groups during the past 25 years, which have ranged from a quartet with Azar Lawrence and a big band to his current trio. —*Scott Yanow*

Inception / Nights of Ballads and Blues / Jan. 10, 1962+Apr. 3, 1963 / Impulse! ◆◆◆◆◆
1962 & 1963 trio albums on one CD. —*Michael G. Nastos*

Reaching Fourth / Nov. 14, 1962 / Impulse! ◆◆◆◆◆

Today and Tomorrow / Jun. 4, 1963 / Impulse! ◆◆◆◆
1991 release, reissue from limited Jazz Masters Series of '70s reissues. Superb music throughout. —*Ron Wynn*

Music Map

Tuba

1920s

Cyrus St. Clair	Pete Briggs
Joe Tarto	Ralph Escudero
June Cole	

The tuba was completely replaced by the string bass by the early 1930s.

New Orleans Revival
Dick Lammi (with Yerba Buena Jazz Band)

Modern Soloists

Red Callender	Bill Barber
Ray Draper	Laymon Jackson
Don Butterfield	Joe Daley
Bob Stewart	Howard Johnson

Live at Newport / Jul. 5, 1963 / Impulse! ◆◆◆◆

McCoy Tyner Plays Ellington / Dec. 2, 1964-Dec. 8, 1964 / Impulse! ◆◆◆◆

● **The Real McCoy** / Apr. 21, 1967 / Blue Note ◆◆◆◆◆
With Joe Henderson (sax). —*Michael G. Nastos*

Tender Moments / Dec. 1, 1967 / Blue Note ◆◆◆◆◆
Small big band. Some extraordinary music. —*Michael Erlewine*

Time for Tyner / May 17, 1968-May 17, 1969 / Blue Note ◆◆◆◆
Tyner and Bobby Hutcherson (vib) have some sparkling exchanges and dialogs. —*Ron Wynn*

Expansions / Aug. 23, 1968 / Blue Note ◆◆◆◆

Cosmos / Apr. 4, 1969-Jul. 21, 1970 / Blue Note ◆◆◆◆

● **Extensions** / Feb. 9, 1970 / Blue Note ◆◆◆◆◆

Asante / Sep. 10, 1970 / Blue Note ◆◆◆◆
The final McCoy Tyner Blue Note album found the innovative pianist during a lowpoint in his career. His records were not selling that well, his mentor John Coltrane had passed away three years earlier and it was not obvious that Tyner would be able to continue struggling successfully to make a living out of music. Fortunately his fortunes would soon rise when he signed with Milestone in 1972 and the critics began to rediscover him. *Asante* is a bit unusual for the emphasis is on group interplay rather than individual solos. The four originals feature Tyner with altoist Andrew White, guitarist Ted Dunbar, bassist Buster Williams, drummer Billy Hart, Mtume on congas and two spots for the voice of Songai. Worth investigating. —*Scott Yanow*

★ **Sahara** / Jan. 1972 / Original Jazz Classics ◆◆◆◆◆

★ **Echoes of a Friend** / Nov. 11, 1972 / Original Jazz Classics ◆◆◆◆◆

Song for My Lady / Nov. 27, 1972 / Original Jazz Classics ◆◆◆◆

Song of the New World / Apr. 6, 1973-Apr. 9, 1973 / Original Jazz Classics ◆◆◆◆
This set gave pianist McCoy Tyner his first opportunity to write music for a larger group that included brass, flutes and on two of the five songs, a string section. The powerful pianist is in fine form and the main soloist throughout (although there are spots for trumpeter Virgil Jones and the flute of Sonny Fortune). Most

memorable is the title cut and a reworking of "Afro Blue." —*Scott Yanow*

★ **Enlightenment** / Jul. 7, 1973 / Milestone ✦✦✦✦✦
This is one of the great McCoy Tyner recordings. The powerful, percussive and highly influential pianist sounds quite inspired throughout his appearance at the 1973 Montreux Jazz Festival. Azar Lawrence (on tenor and soprano) is also quite noteworthy (why didn't he ever become famous?) and there is plenty of interplay with bassist Juney Booth and drummer Alphonse Mouzon. But Tyner is the main star, whether it be on his three-part "Enlightenment Suite," "Presence," "Nebula" or the 25-minute "Walk Spirit, Talk Spirit." —*Scott Yanow*

Sama Layuca / Mar. 26, 1974-Mar. 28, 1974 / Milestone ✦✦✦✦✦
Pianist McCoy Tyner is heard at the height of his powers throughout this rewarding set. He contributed all five compositions and has a colorful and diverse group of major players at his disposal to interpret them: vibraphonist Bobby Hutcherson, altoist Gary Bartz, Azar Lawrence on tenor and soprano, John Stubblefield doubling on oboe and flute, bassist Buster Williams, drummer Billy Hart and both Mtume and Guillherme Franco on percussion. The results (which include a brief Tyner-Hutcherson duet on "Above the Rainbow") are quite rewarding and serve as a strong example of McCoy Tyner's music. —*Scott Yanow*

Atlantis / Aug. 31, 1974+Sep. 1, 1974 / Milestone ✦✦✦✦

● **Trident** / Feb. 18, 1975-Feb. 19, 1975 / Original Jazz Classics ✦✦✦✦✦
Pianist McCoy Tyner's first full-length trio album since 1964 was one of his most popular. Accompanied by bassist Ron Carter and Elvin Jones, Tyner (who uses harpsichord and/or celeste for flavoring on three of the six pieces) shows why he was considered the most influential acoustic pianist of the era (before Bill Evans began to surpass him in that category). Whether it be Jobim's "Once I Loved," "Impressions," "Ruby, My Dear" or Tyner's three powerful originals, this set finds Tyner in peak form. —*Scott Yanow*

Fly with the Wind / Jan. 19, 1976-Jan. 21, 1976 / Original Jazz Classics ✦✦✦✦

Focal Point / Aug. 4, 1976+Aug. 7, 1976 / Milestone ✦✦✦✦

★ **Supertrio** / Apr. 9, 1977-Apr. 12, 1977 / Milestone ✦✦✦✦✦
This album features the great pianist McCoy Tyner with two separate trios, either bassist Ron Carter and drummer Tony Williams or bassist Eddie Gomez and drummer Jack DeJohnette. The former session, which has a Tyner/Williams duet on "I Mean You" and a collaboration between Tyner and Carter on "Prelude to a Kiss," is the more interesting of the two, with the pianist interacting with Miles Davis' former rhythm section on six high-quality songs. But the Gomez-DeJohnette date (which includes four Tyner compositions plus "Stella by Starlight" and "Lush Life") also has its classic moments. Throughout, the percussive and highly influential pianist sounds inspired by the opportunity to create music with his peers. Recommended. —*Scott Yanow*

Inner Voices / Sep. 1, 1977-Sep. 8, 1977 / Milestone ✦✦✦

The Greeting / Mar. 17, 1978-Mar. 18, 1978 / Milestone ✦✦✦✦

Passion Dance / Jul. 28, 1978 / Milestone ✦✦✦✦

Together / Aug. 31, 1978+Sep. 3, 1978 / Milestone ✦✦✦✦

Horizon / Apr. 24, 1979-Apr. 25, 1979 / Milestone ✦✦✦✦

4 x 4 / Mar. 3, 1980-May 29, 1980 / Milestone ✦✦✦✦✦
This set matches the McCoy Tyner Trio (which includes bassist Cecil McBee and drummer Al Foster) with four different guests. Altoist Arthur Blythe and vibraphonist Bobby Hutcherson fare best, but both trumpeter Freddie Hubbard and guitarist John Abercrombie also have their strong moments. In addition to four Tyner compositions, there is one song apiece from McBee, Abercrombie and Hutcherson in addition to four jazz standards. This collection is a fine all-around showcase for the brilliant pianist even if no new ground is broken. —*Scott Yanow*

La Leyenda De La Hora / 1981 / Columbia ✦✦✦✦
There are no weak McCoy Tyner albums and this relative obscurity is better than average. The great pianist is heard with an all-star nonet that includes Hubert Laws on flute, vibraphonist Bobby Hutcherson, altoist Paquito D'Rivera, Chico Freeman on tenor and trumpeter Marchus Belgrave plus a seven-piece string section. The music (five Tyner originals) is highly rhythmic and generally quite stimulating. A strong effort. —*Scott Yanow*

13th House / 1981 / Milestone ✦✦✦✦

Looking Out / 1982 / Columbia ✦✦✦

Dimensions / Oct. 1983 / Elektra ✦✦✦✦

Just Feelin' / 1985 / Quicksilver ✦✦✦✦

It's About Time / Apr. 6, 1985-Apr. 7, 1985 / Blue Note ✦✦✦

Double Trios / Jun. 7, 1986-Jun. 9, 1986 / Denon ✦✦✦✦✦

Bon Voyage / Jun. 1987 / Timeless ✦✦✦✦

Tribute to John Coltrane / Jul. 9, 1987 / MCA/Impulse! ✦✦✦✦✦

Live at Musicians Exchange Cafe / Jul. 1987 / Who's Who in Jazz ✦✦✦

Revelations / Oct. 25, 1988, Oct. 27, 1988 / Blue Note ✦✦✦✦

Uptown-Downtown / Nov. 25, 1988-Nov. 26, 1988 / Milestone ✦✦✦✦✦
Live date at the Blue Note in NYC. Quintessential Tyner big band. —*Michael G. Nastos*

★ **Live at Sweet Basil** / May 19, 1989-May 20, 1989 / Evidence ✦✦✦✦
This double CD (originally recorded for King in 1989) finds the great pianist McCoy Tyner stretching out with bassist Avery Sharpe and drummer Aaron Scott on five standards, a pair of songs apiece by John Coltrane and Thelonious Monk, and two of his own originals. Tyner has continued to grow in density and power through the years and by this time possessed a technique nearly on the level of an Art Tatum; his version of "Yesterdays," although different, somehow recalls Tatum. With other highpoints including "Monk's Dream," "Don't Blame Me" and "Just in Time," this two-fer gives one a definitive look at McCoy Tyner in the late '80s. —*Scott Yanow*

Things Ain't What They Used to Be / Nov. 2, 1989 / Blue Note ✦✦✦✦

Remembering John / Feb. 1991 / Enja ✦✦✦✦
A trio session that's mainly Tyner extrapolations on Coltrane compositions matches his peerless keyboard improvisation with the equally adventuous bass work of Avery Sharpe and good drum support from Aaron Scott. —*Ron Wynn, Rock & Roll Disc.*

Soliloquy / Feb. 19, 1991-Feb. 21, 1991 / Blue Note ✦✦✦✦

New York Reunion / Apr. 3, 1991-Apr. 4, 1991 / Chesky ✦✦✦✦✦
Pianist McCoy Tyner and tenor saxophonist Joe Henderson were youthful improvisers seeking a foothold in jazz circles when they first worked together on Henderson's debut *Page One*. Some 28 years later, they reunited on the fine *New York Reunion*. Tyner's spinning two-handed phrases, rhythmic forays, and probing solos are among the most influential and imitated of any modern pianist. He proved both a sympathetic accompanist and first-rate interpreter, while Henderson's lush tone, dips, honks and flourishes are a familiar and welcome sound to any jazz fan. This was another of the many tremendous sessions recorded for independent labels that are ignored except by the faithful few. —*Ron Wynn*

44th St.Suite / May 11, 1991 / Red Baron ✦✦✦✦
Slashing solos from David Murray (ts), Arthur Blythe (as). Fine Tyner. —*Ron Wynn*

The Turning Point / Nov. 19, 1991-Nov. 20, 1991 / Verve ✦✦✦✦✦
This recording may not have been an actual "turning point" in pianist McCoy Tyner's productive career, but its success gave momentum to his big band. Although only a part-time affair, Tyner's orchestra (seven brass, four reeds and a four-piece rhythm section) is considered one of the major jazz big bands of the 1990s, a perfect outlet for the leader's percussive and modal-oriented piano. With arrangements by Tyner, Dennis Mackrel, Slide Hampton, Steve Turre and Howard Johnson, many of these performances are quite powerful. It is a pity though that the liners do not identify the soloists since there are several that are quite colorful. Recommended. —*Scott Yanow*

Journey / 1993 / Verve ✦✦✦✦
While this isn't among Tyner's greatest recordings, it's still a rigorous, often exciting big-band date. The repertoire includes familiar Tyner compositions "Peresina" and "Blues on the Corner," originals from trombonist Steve Turre ("Juanita") and bassist Avery Sharpe ("January In Brazil"), plus other numbers by Angel Rangelov, Dennis Mackrel and the interesting "You Taught My Heart to Sing," co-written by Tyner and legendary Broadway lyricist/tunesmith Sammy Cahn. Although Tyner doesn't play with

the ferocity or unpredictable edge that's characterized his finest sessions, he solos crisply, easily moving through hard bop, Afro-Latin and even swing-oriented big band settings. There's a comfortable feel but not a staid one. —*Ron Wynn*

Manhattan Moods / Dec. 3, 1993-Dec. 4, 1993 / Blue Note ✦✦✦

Prelude and Sonata / Nov. 26, 1994-Nov. 27, 1994 / Milestone ✦✦✦

★ **Infinity** / Apr. 12, 1995-Apr. 14, 1995 / Impulse! ✦✦✦✦✦

It seems only fitting that the initial new release on the latest revival of the Impulse! label features McCoy Tyner and Michael Brecker. When Impulse! started out in 1960, John Coltrane and Tyner were the first artists to be signed, and when Impulse! was briefly brought back by MCA in the 1980s, two of its most important albums were recordings by Brecker. There are not a lot of surprises on this quartet match-up (with bassist Avery Sharpe and drummer Aaron Scott) except perhaps for how well Tyner and Brecker mesh together. The music is somewhat similar to a set by the pianist's regular trio with a solo piece ("Blues Stride"), a generous amount of Tyner originals and colorful versions of Thelonious Monk's "I Mean You" and "Good Morning Heartache," but Brecker's presence and consistently powerful playing does inspire Tyner and his sidemen. For a strong example as to why today's saxophonists have such a high opinion of Michael Brecker, his roaring statement on the extended "Impressions" will suffice. Highly recommended. —*Scott Yanow*

U

James Blood Ulmer

b. Feb. 2, 1942, St. Matthews, SC
Guitar, Vocals / Free Funk, Avant-Garde, Crossover
One of the most individual and intense jazz guitarists, James "Blood" Ulmer has been a controversial figure ever since he started playing with Ornette Coleman. As a child he sang with the Southern Sons (a gospel group) but it was as a guitarist that he began performing professionally in 1959 in Pittsburgh. He spent a few years playing funky jazz with organ groups and during 1967–71 was based in Detroit. In 1971 Ulmer moved to New York where he worked regularly at Minton's Playhouse and played briefly with Art Blakey, Paul Bley, Larry Young and Joe Henderson. The turning point of his career came in 1974 when he studied with Ornette Coleman; soon he would be in Ornette's free funk band Prime Time. By the time he made his debut as a leader for Artist's House, Ulmer had a style that mixed together the power and sound of rock with Coleman's harmolodics and free-form approach. He recorded with Arthur Blythe, was in groups called Phalanx and the Music Revelation Ensemble and led his own rather abstract bands. Ulmer's recordings have been inconsistent and erratic, both primitive and futuristic while often being quite noisy; an acquired taste! —*Scott Yanow*

Tales of Cpt Black / Dec. 5, 1978 / Artists House ✦✦✦✦

Are You Glad to Be in America? / Jan. 17, 1980 / Rough Trade ✦✦✦✦✦
Visionary guitarist with a unique sound. His best. —*Michael G. Nastos*

Freelancing / 1981 / Columbia ✦✦✦✦

Black Rock / 1982 / Columbia ✦✦✦✦✦

Odyssey / 1983 / Columbia ✦✦✦

Part Time / 1984 / Rough Trade ✦✦✦

Got Something Good for You / Sep. 1985 / Moers ✦✦✦

● **America: Do You Remember the Love** / 1986 / Blue Note ✦✦✦✦✦
A 1987 release, uneven but lots of excitement. —*Ron Wynn*

Live at the Caravan of Dreams / 1986 / Caravan of Dreams ✦✦✦✦

In Touch / Feb. 1987+Feb. 1988 / DIW ✦✦✦

Blues All Night / May 1989 / In + Out ✦✦✦

Blues Preacher / Sep. 1992–Nov. 1992 / DIW/Columbia ✦✦
This effort from controversial guitarist James Blood Ulmer sticks to a harsh blues-rock groove with many of the one-chord vamps sounding like they are leftovers from John Lee Hooker's repertoire. There are no harmolodics (and little jazz) to be heard on the CD and this rather primitive music is to be recommended only to fans of Ulmer's shouting vocals. —*Scott Yanow*

Uptown String Quartet

Group / Post Bop
The Uptown String Quartet really began as part of the Max Roach Double Quartet. Their 1985 joint recording had John Williams and Cecelia Hobbs on violins, Maxine Roach (Max's daughter) on viola and cellist Eileen Folson. By 1986 the string quartet had its name and the personnel of violinists Diana Monroe and Lesa Terry, Maxine Roach and cellist Zela Terry. By the time they debuted in 1989 on record as a separate entity of their own, Monroe, Lesa Terry and Roach were joined by Eileen Folson; the personnel has remained the same up to now. One of the very first string quartets to improvise (they were preceded by Turtle Island), the group's repertoire on their two releases (for Philips and Bluemoon) ranges from bop standards and traditional folk songs to new advanced originals. —*Scott Yanow*

Max Roach Presents . . . / Apr. 19, 1989–Apr. 22, 1989 / Philips ✦✦✦✦✦
Neo-classical jazz flavors from string quartet. Very nice. —*Michael G. Nastos*

● **Just Wait a Minute!** / Aug. 1991 / Blue Moon ✦✦✦✦✦

Michael Urbaniak

b. Jan. 22, 1943, Warsaw, Poland
Violin, Tenor Saxophone / Avant-Garde, Fusion
Polish violinist, tenor saxophonist and bandleader Michael Urbaniak was a breath of fresh air when he first appeared on the American music scene in the mid-'70s. His violin playing had warmth, wit and flair, and Urbaniak's electric violin, and violectra (an electronic bowed string instrument with an octave lower sound than the violin) were both a curiosity and a different sound and voice. His sawing, bluesy phrases and interesting, if at times raw sax playing, coupled with his wife Urzula Dudziak's scatting and vocal gymnastics added welcome unpredictability and edge to what was already becoming a dreary landscape as jazz-rock's promise was fading into fusion's profitability. But Urbaniak never fulfilled that initial potential, and has enjoyed a very successful, but aesthetically uneven career. He studied violin as a child, as well as soprano sax; Urbaniak later played tenor. He experimented with traditional jazz and swing, then concentrated on bebop. He played with Zbigniew Namyslowski, Andrzej Trzaskowski and Krzysztof Komeda in the early and mid-'60s while working as a classical violinist. Urbaniak led a group in Scandananvia in 1965, then returned to Poland in 1969. He formed Constellation with Dudziak, Adam Makowicz, Czeslaw Bartkowski and Pawel Jarzebski (later Roman Dylag). Urbaniak and Dudziak came to America in 1974, and he formed Fusion. They performed and recorded until 1977, and made some compelling albums blending Dudziak's vocals and vocal effects, Polish folk melodies and irregular meters plus Urbaniak's scintillating violin solos. Urbaniak worked and recorded with Larry Coryell and Dudziak in the '80s, and also led his own bands. His albums became less free-wheeling and more restrained and overproduced. Urbaniak also did sessions with Archie Shepp. He has recorded as a leader for Columbia, Muza, Jazz America Marketing, Milan, Rykodisc and Steeplechase. Urbaniak, who has played everything from bop to free jazz, has in recent times been leading a fusion group called Urbanator. —*Ron Wynn*

Super Constellation / 1973 / Columbia ✦✦

Fusion / 1975 / Columbia ✦✦✦✦

Body English / Dec. 1976 / Arista ✦✦✦

Urbaniak / Aug. 1977 / Inner City ✦✦✦✦✦

Daybreak / 1980 / PA/USA ✦✦✦✦

Music for Violin and Jazz Quartet / Dec. 17, 1980–Dec. 18, 1980 / Jam ✦✦✦✦

My One and Only Love / Jul. 1981 / SteepleChase ✦✦✦✦

● **Take Good Care of My Heart** / Aug. 21, 1984 / SteepleChase ✦✦✦✦✦

Cinemode / 1988 / Rykodisc ✦✦✦✦
Polish violinist and saxophonist Michael Urbaniak was a fresh

voice on the horizon when he arrived here in the early '70s and began recording. Unfortunately, Urbaniak's once-vital sound was quickly absorbed into the trendy fabric of fusion, and his music was diluted to the point where it was indistinguished and empty. This 1988 solo set, with Urbaniak free from commercial pressures and considerations, ranks as his most accomplished, intriguing release. He plays violin, saxes and keyboards, and his solos are fierce, extensive and joyous. —*Ron Wynn*

Songbird / Oct. 1990 / SteepleChase ✦✦✦
Manhattan Man / 1992 / Milan ✦✦

Phil Urso

b. Oct. 2, 1925, Jersey City, NJ
Tenor Saxophone / Cool
A no-frills, almost prototype cool tenor saxophonist, Phil Urso has never modified his original Lester Young-influenced sound. His tone, style, phrasing and approach are his own, but they reflect the floating tone and lush, striding Young sound. Urso played clarinet at 13, then studied tenor sax in high school. He moved to New York in the late '40s, and played with Elliot Lawrence and Woody Herman until the early '50s. Urso played with many leaders during the '50s, among them Jimmy Dorsey and Miles Davis. He recorded with Don Elliott, Terry Gibbs and Oscar Pettiford, while leading his own bands. Urso co-led a band with Bob Brookmeyer that also included Horace Silver, Kenny Clarke and Percy Heath. He played with Chet Baker in 1955, and also recorded with him in 1956 and again in 1965. Urso moved back to Denver in the late '50s and contined to play in Denver during the '70s and '80s. He has no sessions currently available as a leader on CD. —*Ron Wynn and Michael G. Nastos*

● **Philosophy of Urso** / Apr. 14, 1953–Apr. 30, 1954 / Savoy
✦✦✦✦✦
Urso-Brookmeyer Quintet / 1954 / Savoy ✦✦✦✦
Sentimental Journey / Mar. 27, 1956 / Regent ✦✦✦

V

Warren Vache

b. Feb. 21, 1951, Rahway, NJ
Cornet, Fluegelhorn / Dixieland, Swing
Several years before Wynton Marsalis gained headlines for helping to revive hard bop, Warren Vache (along with Scott Hamilton) was among the few young jazz musicians who were reviving small-group swing. Vache, who always had a beautiful tone and a chancetaking style, is the son of a fine bassist (Warren Vache, Sr.) and the brother of clarinetist Allen Vache. He studied music with Pee Wee Erwin, gained early experience playing with Benny Goodman, Vic Dickenson and Bob Wilber, and has been a leader since the mid-'70s. Often teamed in his early years with tenorman Scott Hamilton, Vache has recorded regularly for Concord since the late '70s (and more recently Muse) and has been a regular at jazz parties and swing-oriented festivals ever since. —*Scott Yanow*

Jersey Jazz at Midnight / Dec. 31, 1975 / New Jersey Jazz Society ◆◆◆

First Time Out / Nov. 22, 1976+Dec. 6, 1976 / Monmouth ◆◆◆◆◆

Blues Walk / Nov. 1977 / Dreamstreet ◆◆◆◆◆

Jillian / Nov. 1978 / Concord Jazz ◆◆◆◆

★ **Polished Brass** / 1979 / Concord Jazz ◆◆◆◆◆

Iridescence / Jan. 1981 / Concord Jazz ◆◆◆◆◆

★ **Midtown Jazz** / Feb. 1982 / Concord Jazz ◆◆◆◆◆

Easy Going / Dec. 1986 / Concord Jazz ◆◆◆◆◆

Warm Evenings / Jun. 1989 / Concord Jazz ◆◆◆◆
Wonderful sound quality, production, and solos. Good production and arrangements, strings kept in right balance with Vache's trumpet. —*Ron Wynn*

Horn Of Plenty / Sep. 8, 1993+Oct. 5, 1993 / Muse ◆◆◆◆

Bebo Valdes

b. 1918, Quivican, Cuba
Piano / Afro-Cuban Jazz
A top-notch pianist/composer/arranger, Bebo Valdes (father of pianist Chucho Valdes) was the musical director of night club shows at the Tropicana in Havana by 1948. Very active in the 1950s, Valdes was considered one of the giants of Cuban music, arranging many recordings, composing mambos and organizing Afro-Cuban jazz jam sessions. He defected from Cuba in 1960 and by 1963 had settled in Stockholm. In 1994 after 34 years off records he cut *Bebo Rides Again* for the Messidor label, not only playing piano but also composing eight numbers and arranging 11 songs in the 36 hours before the first session; he was 76 at the time! —*Scott Yanow*

★ **Bebo Rides Again** / Nov. 1994 / Messidor ◆◆◆◆◆
This CD is both historic and quite exciting. Bebo Valdes (father of Chucho, the leader of Irakere) was one of the giants of Cuban jazz and popular music until he fled the country in 1960. Amazingly enough he had not recorded since despite living peacefully in Sweden. This recording is also significant in that it is one of the first times that Cuban exiles had recorded with Cubans still living under Castro (guitarist Carlos Emilio Morales and percussionist Amadito Valdes). Paquito D'Rivera (who organized this set) deserves a lot of credit for its success but Bebo Valdes is the real star. He composed eight new selections in the 36 hours before the

recordings began although he was 76 years old at the time! Although Valdes claimed that with the lack of sleep and excess of writing (he also arranged ten of the 11 songs) his fingers felt a bit stiff, he plays quite well throughout the very enjoyable music. The final results are full of strong melodies, stirring rhythms, exciting ensembles and lots of variety. The instrumentation differs on each track with plenty of solo space for D'Rivera (on both alto and clarinet), trombonist Juan-Pablo Torres (who takes "Veinte Anos" as a duet with Valdes), trumpeter Diego Urcola and the pianist. The percussionists work together quite well behind the lead voices and every selection is well worth hearing. This is one of the finest Afro-Cuban jazz recordings of recent times. Highly recommended. —*Scott Yanow*

Chucho Valdes

b. Oct. 9, 1941, Quivican, Cuba
Piano, Leader / Afro-Cuban Jazz
The son of the noted musician Bebo Valdes, Chucho began playing piano when he was three, and by the time he was 16, he was leading his own group. In 1960 his father defected from Cuba but Chucho stayed behind. In 1967 he formed the Orquesta Cubana de Musica Moderna and in 1973 he founded Irakere, the top Cuban jazz orchestra; among its original members were Arturo Sandoval and Paquito D'Rivera. Valdes has been Irakere's musical director almost from the start and has recorded with the full band, in small groups and as an impressive solo pianist. He remains one of the top jazz musicians living in Cuba. —*Scott Yanow*

Lucumbi: Piano Solo / Nov. 15, 1986 / Messidor ◆◆◆◆

● **Solo Piano** / Sep. 1991 / Blue Note ◆◆◆◆◆
The leader and founder of Irakere, Chucho Valdes is also a brilliant pianist who may be on the same level as Gonzalo Rubalcaba. He has a very impressive classical technique and is able to hint at such players as McCoy Tyner, Lennie Tristano and Cecil Taylor without watering down his Cuban heritage. This dazzling set covers a lot of ground with highlights including "Blue Yes" (which is based on the chords of Charlie Parker's "Confirmation"), a sensitive Bill Evans tribute and several nearly free explosions. Despite the CD's title, the final two of the ten selections add bass, drums and percussion and feature Valdes closely interacting with and pushing his sidemen. Highly recommended. —*Scott Yanow*

Dave Valentin

b. 1954, Bronx, NY
Flute / Latin Jazz, Crossover
Dave Valentin, who has recorded over 15 albums for GRP, combines together the influence of pop, R&B and Brazilian music with Latin-jazz to create a slick and accessible form of crossover jazz. At age nine, Valentin enjoyed playing bongos and congas. He gigged at Latin clubs in New York from age 12 and it was not until he was 18 that he seriously started studying flute. Valentin's teacher Hubert Laws suggested that he not double on saxophone because of his attractive sound on the flute. In 1977 he made his recording debut with Ricardo Marrero's group and he was also on a Noel Pointer album. Discovered by Dave Grusin and Larry Rosen, Valentin was the first artist signed to GRP and he has been a popular attraction ever since. —*Scott Yanow*

Legends / 1979 / GRP ✦✦
Kalahari / 1984 / GRP ✦✦✦✦
Jungle Garden / 1985 / GRP ✦✦✦
Light Struck / 1986 / GRP ✦✦
Mind Time / 1987 / GRP ✦✦✦
Earl Klugh plays nicely, as does Valentin on this session. —*Ron Wynn*

★ **Live at the Blue Note** / May 31, 1988–Jun. 1, 1988 / GRP ✦✦✦✦✦
Two Amigos / 1990 / GRP ✦✦✦✦
With Herbie Mann. —*Ron Wynn*
Musical Portraits / Jul. 10, 1990 / GRP ✦✦✦
Red Sun / 1992 / GRP ✦✦✦
This was flutist Dave Valetin's 15th release for GRP and, as with his previous ones, it features impeccable musicianship, subtle funk grooves, some heated Latin rhythms and rather lightweight melodies. Despite some passionate moments, the music always sounds a bit controlled, never exceeding prescribed time limits or emotional boundaries. There are some strong moments of interest on this relatively pleasing CD, particularly a restrained melodic statement by trumpeter Arturo Sandoval on "We'll Be Together Again" and a groovin' version of "With a Little Help from My Friends." —*Scott Yanow*

● **Tropic Heat** / 1993 / GRP ✦✦✦✦✦
Flutist Dave Valentin's 16th album for GRP is one of his best. His regular group (a quartet with pianist Bill O'Connell, bassist Lincoln Goines and drummer Robbie Ameen) is augmented by two percussionists and an excellent seven-member horn section that consists of the reeds of Dick Oatts, Mario Rivera and David Sanchez, trombonist Angel "Papo" Vasquez and three trumpeters including Charlie Sepulveda. All of the horns get their opportunities to solo and the result is a particularly strong Latin jazz session. Valentin continues to grow as a player and he cuts loose on several of these tracks. —*Scott Yanow*

Tom Varner

b. Jun. 17, 1957, NJ
French Horn / Post Bop
There have been few French horn soloists in jazz but, even if there had been dozens, chances are that Tom Varner would rank near the top. He started on piano at age ten and a few years later switched to French horn, discovering his predecessor Julius Watkins' recordings when he was 17. He graduated from New England Conservatory and in 1979 moved to New York. Since that time Varner has recorded several albums (mostly for Soul Note) as a leader and has worked with such players as Dave Liebman, Bobby Watson, George Gruntz (with his Concert Jazz Band), John Zorn, Steve Lacy, Lee Konitz and Bobby Previte. Varner has almost singlehandedly made the difficult French horn a viable jazz instrument for the 1990s. —*Scott Yanow*

Tom Varner Quartet / Aug. 29, 1980 / Soul Note ✦✦✦✦✦
Tom Varner turned heads and opened eyes on the jazz scene in the early '80s. There weren't, and still aren't, many French horn players who improvise and play with the facility he demonstrated on this 1980 session. There were five tracks, two of them over 10 minutes, and Varner displayed impressive speed and fire, playing with distinction while matching alto saxophonist Ed Jackson in range, control through every register, phrasing and tonal quality. —*Ron Wynn*

Motion / **Stillness** / Mar. 19, 1982 / Soul Note ✦✦✦✦
★ **Jazz French Horn** / Oct. 8, 1985–Oct. 9, 1985 / New Note ✦✦✦✦✦
Contains the parody on "What Is This Thing Called Love?" titled "What Is This Thing Called First Strike Capability?" Uplifting jazz. —*Michael G. Nastos*

Covert Action / Jan. 22, 1987–Jan. 23, 1987 / New Note ✦✦✦✦
The Mystery of Compassion / Mar. 5, 1992–Mar. 7, 1992 / Soul Note ✦✦✦✦✦

Johnny Varro

Piano / Swing
One of the top swing-oriented pianists since the 1950s, Johnny Varro has long been a fixture in the trad circuit even if the greater jazz world does not seem to know that he exists. He considers his influences to be Jess Stacy, Teddy Wilson and Eddie Miller. Varro's first professional job was with Bobby Hackett. In

1957 he replaced Ralph Sutton as the intermission pianist at Eddie Condon's club and was associated with Condon througout the first half of the 1960s. He worked with many top trad and swing players during that era before moving to Miami in 1964; in the late '70s he relocated to Southern California. The veteran pianist has kept up a busy schedule playing at clubs, jazz parties and festivals where his impeccable swing style is appreciated. In recent times Varro has made several recordings for Arbors. —*Scott Yanow*

Sittin' In / Oct. 8, 1985 / Too Cool ✦✦✦✦
Pianist Johnny Varro and Don Nelson (the latter on soprano sax and vocals) perform a set of duets on this enjoyable LP. In addition to six veteran swing standards, Nelson contributes five originals (and Varro one); the fresh material results in some inspired playing. Varro has long been one of the top swing pianists (most influenced by Teddy Wilson) and the more obscure Nelson has an attractive tone and a personable singing style. Even if all of the newer lyrics are not necessarily classic, the performances are consistently excellent and swinging. —*Scott Yanow*

● **Everything I Love** / Sep. 8, 1992–Sep. 9, 1992 / Arbors ✦✦✦✦✦

Nana Vasconcelos

b. Aug. 2, 1944, Recife, Brazil
Percussion / World Fusion
An excellent percussionist known for creating amazing melodies and rhythms, Brazilian percussion ace Nana Vasconcelos had the misfortune to make his American debut during the same era as Airto Moreira. Moreira has had a larger profile, but Vasconcelos need not take a back seat to anyone. His playing on the berimbau and cuica can be mesmerizing in its beauty and flair, and Vasconcelos can also dazzle on bongos, maracas and drums.

He played bongos and maracas in his father's band as a 12-year-old. Vasconcelos later was a drummer in Rio de Janeiro, and mastered several traditional Brazilian rhythm instruments while playing with Milton Nascimento. He came to America with Gato Barbieri in the early '70s, as well as Argentina and Europe. His berimbau playing and percussive support were featured on several Barbieri Flying Dutchman albums. Vasconcelos later lived for two years in Paris, working primarily with handicapped children and doing some dates in Sweden with Don Cherry. He toured and co-led a group with Egberto Gismonti in the mid-'70s, then co-founded the trio Codona with Don Cherry and Collin Walcott in the late '70s. This group combined African, Asian, and South American ethnic styles, playing them in an improvisatory, but not necessarily jazz-based manner. They disbanded after Walcott's death in 1984, but made some fine ECM albums during their tenure.

Vasconcelos also played with Pat Metheny's band in the early '80s and then was in Don Cherry's group Mu in 1984. In the late '80s, Vasconcelos recorded with The Bushdancers and made duet sessions with Gismonti for ECM and Antonello Salis for Soul Note. His albums with Codona, and the duets with Gismonti and Salis, are available on CD, as are his earlier dates with Gismonti. —*Ron Wynn*

★ **Saudades** / Mar. 1979 / ECM ✦✦✦✦✦
This 1979 recording is probably Afro-experimentalist Vasconcelos' finest. It presents his various facets—berimbao playing, intricate overlain vocals, fine percussion, even gorgeous guitar—simply and almost overwhelmingly. This is one of those performances that remind one to never let natural dogmatism get too out of hand. —*John Storm Roberts, Original Music*

Lester / Dec. 9, 1985–Dec. 10, 1985 / Soul Note ✦✦✦✦
Bush Dance / 1986 / Antilles ✦✦✦✦✦
Rain Dance / Oct. 1988 / Antilles ✦✦✦

Sarah Vaughan

b. Mar. 27, 1924, Newark, NJ, **d.** Apr. 3, 1990, Los Angeles, CA
Vocals / Bop, Standards
Bop's greatest diva, Sarah Vaughan was among jazz and popular music's supreme vocalists. She treated her voice as an instrument, improvising melodic and rhythmic embellishments, using her contralto range to make leaps and jumps, changing a song's mood or direction by enunciation and delivery, and altering her timbre. She turned sappy novelty tunes and light pop into definitive, jazz-based treatments. She had a distinctive swinging quality and intensity in her style and was also a great scat singer. Vaughan

was a dominant performer from the late '40s until the '80s, when illness forced her to cut back her appearances. Vaughan's recorded legacy stands with anyone in modern jazz history.

She sang in the Mt. Zion Baptist Church choir as a child and became its organist at 12. Vaughan won the famous Amateur Night at the Apollo talent contest in 1942, and by April of the next year had joined Earl Hines' band as a second pianist and vocalist. When Billy Eckstine left Hines and formed his own band in 1944, Vaughan soon joined and made her recording debut with his orchestra at the end of December.

She went solo a year later, and remained that way the rest of her career, except for a brief stint with John Kirby in 1945 and 1946. She became a star by performing pop ballads and show tunes, though she made numerous jazz anthems. Eckstine was a frequent duet partner, and the two collaborated on a fine Irving Berlin repertory record in the mid-'50s. Vaughan showed her jazz capabilities early in her solo career, recording a remarkable version of "Lover Man" with Dizzy Gillespie and Charlie Parker in 1945. But from 1949 to 1954, when she was with Columbia, she made hit albums with studio orchestras and cut only one jazz date with Miles Davis and Budd Johnson.

When Vaughan switched labels to Mercury in 1954 she won the right to make light pop and straight jazz recordings. She did jazz material for EmArcy, recording with Clifford Brown, Cannonball Adderley and Count Basie's sidemen, while cutting pop tracks for Mercury. These included the 1958 smash "Broken-hearted Melody." Vaughan maintained similiar relationships with Roulette, Mercury and Columbia from 1960 to 1967. After a five year break, she returned to recording in 1971, this time with Norman Granz's Pablo label. Granz made many sessions with Vaughan through the '70s, some excellent, others not so good. She made a *Duke Ellington Songbook*, worked with Count Basie and Oscar Peterson and even did an album of Afro-Latin and Brazilian material. There was a marvelous two-record live set recorded in Japan.

Her health worsened in the '80s, but she recorded an album of Gershwin songs with the Los Angeles Philharmonic in 1982 and an interesting concept/vocal album *The Planet Is Alive: Let It Live!* in 1985 on Gene Lees Jazzletter label. This was an album of poems by Pope John Paul II adapted by Lees with music by Tito Fontana and Sante Palumbo. It featured Vaughan's vocals backed by an orchestra that included such jazz veterans as Art Farmer, Benny Bailey and Sahib Shihab. When Vaughan died in 1990, there were tributes and worldwide outpourings of grief. Her albums are being steadily reissued, from the formative '40s dates to the '70s sets. Mercury has issued the mammoth *Complete Sarah Vaughan on Mercury* collection, which breaks down her career at the label into eras with multi-disc packages for each period. The songbooks have been reissued, and Columbia has a two-disc package of material from the late '40s and early '50s. Single album reissues are also available from the '50s, '60s, and '70s. —*Ron Wynn and Dan Morgenstern*

Time After Time / Dec. 31, 1944–Dec. 29, 1947 / Drive Archive ✦✦✦
This CD skips around a lot but it gives one a decent overview of Sarah Vaughan during her first three years on records. Best are "East of the Sun" (from her first session as a leader), "September Song" (even if she was a bit too young to make its words fully believable), "The One I Love," her hit "Tenderly" and effective versions of "The Lord's Prayer" and "Motherless Child." Lots of variety on this disc. —*Scott Yanow*

Sarah Vaughan / Dec. 31, 1944–Dec. 18, 1954 / Musica Jazz ✦✦✦✦
This hard-to-find Italian LP has some of the highlights of Sarah Vaughan's early years. Its main significance is that it has the four songs ("Singing Off," "Interlude," "No Smoke" and "East of the Sun") recorded at Vaughan's first session as a leader. Those rare titles have not been reissued in a long time and feature Dizzy Gillespie on trumpet, Georgie Auld on tenor and Leonard Feather on piano; "Interlude" is the first commercially recorded version of "Night in Tunisia" and one of the very few vocal renditions. The remainder of this valuable LP features Sassy with Billy Eckstine's Orchestra, with Dizzy and Charlie Parker, singing with Tony Scott's septet and performing two titles apiece from 1946 (including "If You Could See Me Now"), 1949 and 1954 (the latter has trumpeter Clifford Brown on "Lullaby of Birdland"). —*Scott Yanow*

The Man I Love / Oct. 1, 1945–Apr. 8, 1948 / Musicraft ✦✦✦✦
This LP has 11 selections featuring the magnificent singer Sarah

Vaughan during her period on Musicraft. On all but two of the selections (which mostly date from 1947) Sassy is backed by a commercial orchestra, but she excels on such songs as "Trouble Is a Man," "The Man I Love," "The One I Love" and "I Get a Kick out of You." In addition Vaughan is joined by a fine quartet on "Once in a While" while "Time and Again" (her very first record for the label which served as her audition) is with violinist Stuff Smith. —*Scott Yanow*

Divine Sarah / May 7, 1946–Oct. 10, 1947 / Mercury ✦✦✦✦✦
This Musicraft LP (which was released in 1980) has 14 titles from the early period of Sarah Vaughan. There are several classics here including "If You Could See Me Now," "You're Not the Kind" (the latter two songs have rare solos from trumpeter Freddie Webster), "Everything I Have Is Yours," "Body and Soul" and the earliest ever recording of "Tenderly" which was Vaughan's first hit. The last two performances, "The Lord's Prayer" and "Motherless Child," show just how powerful a singer (even beyond jazz) Sassy was from the start. Worth searching for. —*Scott Yanow*

Columbia Years (1949–1953) / Jan. 20, 1949–Jan. 5, 1953 / Columbia ✦✦✦✦✦
This attractive double LP has the best 28 recordings that Sarah Vaughan cut for the Columbia label during 1949–53. On most of the selections (including memorable versions of "Black Coffee," "Just Friends," "I Cried for You," "Perdido" and "After Hours") the great singer is backed by fairly commercial orchestras. However there are eight jazz selections from May 18–19, 1950 that match her beautiful voice with an all-star octet that includes trumpeter Miles Davis, Budd Johnson on tenor, trombonist Benny Green and clarinetist Tony Scott. Of the latter performances, her versions of "It Might as Well Be Spring," "Mean to Me," "Nice Work If You Can Get It" and "Ain't Misbehavin'" are true classics. Recommended. —*Scott Yanow*

I'll Be Seeing You / 1949 / Vintage Jazz Classics ✦✦✦✦
Shortly after Sarah Vaughan's death in 1990, this CD of previously unreleased live and radio performances was put out by Vintage Jazz Classics. The singer is heard in several different settings and excels in all of them. She sings two songs with a studio orchestra in 1949 (including Duke Ellington's "Tonight I Shall Sleep"), jams with her trio around 1961–62 (Woody Herman guests on clarinet for four songs), performs two short selections with Duke Ellington in 1951 and shares the vocal spotlight on "Love You Madly" with Nat King Cole and with Joe Williams on "Teach Me Tonight." Sassy's fans will want this very interesting release. —*Scott Yanow*

Perdido! Live (1953) / 1951 / Natasha ✦✦✦✦
Most of this CD features Sarah Vaughan on radio broadcasts from Birdland during March and April 1953. She is top form on the varied material (which is highlighted by "I Get a Kick out of You," "Tenderly" and "Perdido"), her trio is quite supportive and Dizzy Gillespie sits in on a few numbers, backing Sassy with respect. The CD concludes with a couple of fairly primitively recorded but impressive songs from a 1951 Apollo Theatre concert. Overall this release is quite valuable for it features Vaughan in her early prime; her voice is quite beautiful throughout. —*Scott Yanow*

★ **Complete Sarah Vaughan on Mercury, Vol. 1** / Feb. 10, 1954–Jun. 21, 1956 / Mercury ✦✦✦✦✦
Sarah Vaughan's years on Mercury (and its subsidiary EmArcy) feature inspired jazz performances, commercial recordings with string orchestras and big-band sides that fall in between jazz and middle-of-the-road pop music. All of her recordings for Mercury are on four impressive box sets that add up to 22 CDs. The first set (six CDs) is the best overall of the four for it has a full set with her trio, the famous session with trumpeter Clifford Brown, a date with the Ernie Wilkins Orchestra (featuring altoist Cannonball Adderley) and a variety of orchestral sides. As with all of these sets, there are many previously unissued performances included too. More selective fans may want to get some of Sassy's individual packages instead (particularly the Clifford Brown date) but completists and true Sarah Vaughan fanatics will consider these four perfectly done sets to be essential. —*Scott Yanow*

The George Gershwin Songbook, Vol. 1 / Apr. 2, 1954–1957 / EmArcy ✦✦✦✦
With the exception of three songs recorded earlier, all of this set (the first of two CDs) dates from 1957 and finds the great Sarah Vaughan accompanied by her regular pianist Jimmy Jones plus a studio orchestra arranged by Hal Mooney. Since these 15 selec-

tions are fairly concise (two to five minutes apiece), the emphasis is on the melody and the original lyrics without all that much improvising taking place. Sassy, who had a wondrous voice, is in excellent form on the superior material, making this CD a fine complement to Ella Fitzgerald's better-known *Gershwin Songbook.* —*Scott Yanow*

★ **Sarah Vaughan** / Dec. 18, 1954 / EmArcy ♦♦♦♦♦
This CD reissue features a classic (but unfortunately one-time only) collaboration between singer Sarah Vaughan and trumpeter Clifford Brown. In addition to Brownie, there is worthy solo space for flutist Herbie Mann and Paul Quinichette on tenor who both fit in perfectly. Highlights include "Lullaby of Birdland," "He's My Guy," "You're Not the Kind" and "September Song." It is a special joy to hear Sarah Vaughan romping with her contemporaries in such a spontaneous yet coherent setting, swinging up a storm. All of the music on this CD is also included in *Vol. 1* of the box set titled *The Complete Sarah Vaughan on Mercury Vol. 1* (and also in a Clifford Brown box) but, for those listeners who just want a strong sampling of Sassy at her best, this is highly recommended. —*Scott Yanow*

● **In the Land of Hi-Fi** / Oct. 25, 1955–Oct. 27, 1955 / EmArcy ♦♦♦♦♦
This single CD (whose contents are also included in the box set *The Complete Sarah Vaughan on Mercury Vol. 1*) has one of the great singer's best jazz dates for EmArcy. Accompanied by an all-star orchestra arranged by Ernie Wilkins and featuring altoist Cannonball Adderley (who was near the beginning of his career), Vaughan is in superior form during these concise (around three minutes apiece) performances, particularly on "Soon," "Cherokee," "I'll Never Smile Again" and "An Occasional Man." A strong session. —*Scott Yanow*

George Gershwin Songbook, Vol. 2 / Oct. 26, 1955–Aug. 15, 1964 / EmArcy ♦♦♦♦

Complete Sarah Vaughan on Mercury, Vol. 2: Sings Great American Songs (1956–1957) / Oct. 29, 1956–Jul. 12, 1957 / Mercury ♦♦♦♦♦
This five-CD box set, the second of four volumes that reissue all of Sarah Vaughan's recordings for Mercury and EmArcy (plus many previously unissued performances) contains her exploration of Gershwin songs, 13 vocal duets with her close friend Billy Eckstine and just five jazz numbers with her trio; all of the other selections feature Vaughan backed by large studio orchestras, usually led by Hal Mooney. Most of the material is a bit commercial (certainly the arrangements tend to be) but Sarah Vaughan generally uplifts the songs and overcomes her surroundings. Still, listeners strictly interested in her jazz performances are advised to get some of her single CD collections instead. —*Scott Yanow*

Complete Sarah Vaughan on Mercury, Vol. 3: Great Show on Stage (1954–1956) / Aug. 6, 1957–1959 / Mercury ♦♦♦♦♦
The third of four Sarah Vaughan Mercury box sets (this one has six CDs) traces her career during the last two and a half years of the 1950s. There are several very interesting sessions (expanded greatly by the inclusion of many previously unissued performances) on this box including 21 numbers from a gig at Mister Kelly's in Chicago with her trio (led by pianist Jimmy Jones), a meeting with the Count Basie Orchestra that resulted in the album *No Count Sarah* and a live set with a septet (which includes cornetist Thad Jones and the tenor of Frank Wess) at the London House in Chicago. In addition, there are quite a few commercial sides with large orchestras (including some sessions arranged by Quincy Jones), so overall this box lets one hear the many sides of Sarah Vaughan; a special highlight is her first recorded version of "Misty." The reissue (and the other three volumes) is a must for Sarah Vaughan's greatest fans although more general listeners may want to acquire one of the less expensive single CDs instead. —*Scott Yanow*

★ **At Mister Kelly's** / Aug. 8, 1957 / EmArcy ♦♦♦♦♦

No Count Sarah / Dec. 1958 / EmArcy ♦♦♦♦♦
Sarah Vaughan recorded in a variety of settings while with Mercury and EmArcy in the 1950s but this particular matchup with the Count Basie Orchestra (pianist Ronnell Bright substitutes for Count, thus the title) is pure jazz. During the classic encounter, Sassy fits in comfortably with the band, whether singing lyrics (such as "Darn That Dream," "Cheek to Cheek" or "Doodlin'") or scatting sensuously on "No Count Blues." The wit and constant swing (in addition to the spontaneous creativity), makes this one

Music Map

Vibraphone

Xylophone Pioneers
Charles Hamilton Green (studio player in 1920s)
Jimmy Bertrand (occasional jazz solos in 1920s)

Xylophone Master
Red Norvo (switched permanently to vibes in 1944)

First Vibraphone Virtuoso
Lionel Hampton

1930s
Adrian Rollini

Bop Innovator
Milt Jackson

1940s/1950s
Terry Gibbs	Margie Hyams
Tyree Glenn	Don Elliott
Cal Tjader	Teddy Charles

Two Modern Vibraphone Giants
Bobby Hutcherson	Gary Burton

1960s
Lem Winchester	Eddie Costa
Victor Feldman	Gary McFarland
Buddy Montgomery	Dave Pike
Roy Ayers	
(switched to commercial music in the 1970s)	

Avant-Garde
Walt Dickerson
Gunter Hampel
Karl Berger

Other Recent Vibraphonists
Charlie Shoemake	David Friedman
Khan Jamal	Jay Hoggard
Steve Nelson	Steve Hobbs
Joe Locke	
Mike Mainieri (leader of Steps Ahead)	
David Samuels (featured with Spyro Gyra)	

of the best of all Sarah Vaughan recordings. Highly recommended, either on this CD or as part of the six-CD set *The Complete Sarah Vaughan on Mercury, Vol. 3.* —*Scott Yanow*

The Singles Sessions / May 5, 1960–Feb. 1962 / Roulette ✦✦
During Sarah Vaughan's period with Roulette there were several attempts to come up with a hit record; none succeeded. This rather brief CD (around 35 minutes) has 14 songs but despite some moments of interest (such as cover versions of "Don't Go to Strangers," "Love" and "Mama, He Treats Your Daughter Mean," the latter two being previously unissued), little memorable occurs. Although of some interest to Sarah Vaughan completists, there are many more essential sets around than this one. —*Scott Yanow*

The Roulette Years / 1960 / Roulette ✦✦✦
This CD contains 24 selections so one cannot complain about its brevity, but it would have been preferable to have Sarah Vaughan's Roulette albums reissued in full (a few have been) rather than putting out this sampler. For the beginner there are many fine performances on the jazz-oriented set with Sassy's accompaniment ranging from guitar-bass duets and the Count Basie Big Band to string orchestras. Exact recording dates are not given (which is rather inexcusable) but the music is consistently enjoyable with some of the highpoints being "Just in Time," "Have You Met Miss Jones," "Perdido," "'Round Midnight," "I'll Be Seeing You" and "Spring Can Really Hang You up the Most." —*Scott Yanow*

Sarah Slightly Classical / May 1963–Jul. 1963 / Roulette ✦✦✦
Again, its value is in relation to appreciation of the concept. She sings wonderfully. CD 1991 reissue, six bonus cuts. —*Ron Wynn*

Sassy Swings the Tivoli / Jul. 18, 1963–Jul. 21, 1963 / Mercury ✦✦✦✦✦
Sassy Swings the Tivoli was an even, swinging live jazz set with backing by Kirk Stuart (piano), Charles Williams (bass) and George Hughes (drums). Stuart joined Vaughan briefly on vocals, but besides that this was not all that an usual date for the singer. It was, however, one of her jazz dates. —*Bob Rusch, Cadence*

Complete Sarah Vaughan on Mercury, Vol. 4, Pts. 1 and 2: (1963–1967) / Jul. 19, 1963–Jan. 1967 / Mercury ✦✦✦✦✦
The fourth of four box sets reissuing every recording Sarah Vaughan made for the Mercury and EmArcy labels (including many previously unreleased performances) starts off (after four orchestra tracks) with its strongest selections, no less than 32 songs recorded during a live four-day engagement in Copenhagen during which the singer is accompanied by the Kirk Stuart Trio. Everything else on this six-CD set is somewhat anticlimactic in comparison, for Vaughan is otherwise hindered a bit by string orchestras, a big band and/or a choir. Better to get the live sessions (released as *Sassy Swings the Tivoli* in addition to a Japanese set by the same name that has extra material) instead although lovers of Vaughan's voice will want to pick up this large reissue anyway. —*Scott Yanow*

Jazz Fest Masters / Jul. 1969 / Scotti Bros. ✦✦✦✦
Sarah Vaughan made no studio recordings between Jan. 1967 and Nov. 1971, which makes her live performance from 1969 (first released on this 1992 CD) of historic interest. More importantly the singer is in excellent form during these three different settings from the 1969 New Orleans Jazz Festival. She performs nine numbers with a quintet that includes fluegelhornist Clark Terry (who scats along with her on "Sometimes I'm Happy"), the tenor of Zoot Sims and pianist Jaki Byard, is accompanied by the University of Illinois Big Band on three Benny Carter arrangements and (during the most unusual track) collaborates with a Dixieland group and a gospel choir on "A Closer Walk with Thee." Overall the recording quality is decent and these lively performances add to the recorded legacy of the remarkable singer. —*Scott Yanow*

Sarah Vaughan with Michel Legrand / 1972–1974 / Mainstream ✦✦✦✦

★ **Complete: Live in Japan** / Sep. 24, 1973 / Mobile Fidelity ✦✦✦✦✦
This two-CD set contains all of the music that Sarah Vaughan recorded during her Tokyo concert for Mainstream. The 49-year-old singer is heard at the height of her powers, really digging into the standards and making magic out of such numbers as "Poor" "'Round Midnight," "Willow Weep," "My Funny Valentine," "Summertime" and "Bye Bye Blackbird." This two-fer (which finds Sassy accompanied by pianist Carl Schroeder, bassist John

Gianelli and drummer Jimmy Cobb) gives one a definitive look at the brilliant (and sometimes miraculous) singer. —*Scott Yanow*

I Love Brazil / Nov. 3, 1977–Nov. 7, 1977 / Pablo ✦✦✦
Sarah Vaughan's debut for the Pablo label is a bit of an acquired taste for the jazz fan. She is accompanied by a variety of Brazilian all-stars (including Milton Nascimento, Dori Caymmi and on two numbers Antonio Carlos Jobim himself) and Sassy (whose voice was still in tremendous form) fares quite well but few of the performances are all that memorable and none of the dozen songs entered her permanent repertoire. This set is really more for fans of contemporary Brazilian music than for jazz collectors. —*Scott Yanow*

How Long Has This Been Going on / Apr. 25, 1978 / Pablo ✦✦✦✦✦
This CD reissue features the great Sarah Vaughan in a typically spontaneous Norman Granz Pablo production with pianist Oscar Peterson, guitarist Joe Pass, bassist Ray Brown and drummer Louie Bellson. Sassy sounds wonderful stretching out on such songs as "Midnight Sun," "More Than You Know," "Teach Me Tonight" and "Body and Soul" among others. All ten of the melodies are veteran standards that she knew backward but still greeted with enthusiasm. A very good example of late-period Sarah Vaughan. —*Scott Yanow*

Duke Ellington Songbook, Vol. 1 / Aug. 15, 1979–Sep. 13, 1979 / Pablo ✦✦✦✦✦
Sarah Vaughan interprets ten Duke Ellington-associated songs on the first of two sets; *Song Book Two* was recorded at the same two sessions as this CD reissue. Vaughan is accompanied by a variety of jazz all-stars including trumpeter Waymon Reed, trombonist J.J. Johnson and the tenors of Frank Foster, Frank Wess and Zoot Sims. Bill Byers contributed the arrangements for the larger band performances. The emphasis is on ballads with the highlights including "I'm Just a Lucky So and So," "I Didn't Know About You," "All Too Soon" and "Lush Life." Sassy's voice is in typically wondrous form throughout. —*Scott Yanow*

Duke Ellington Songbook, Vol. 2 / Aug. 15, 1979–Sep. 13, 1979 / Pablo ✦✦✦✦
The second of two Pablo CDs featuring Sarah Vaughan interpreting Duke Ellington-associated material shows that the veteran singer never did decline. With assistance from trumpeter Waymon Reed, flutist Frank Wess, Eddie "Cleanhead" Vinson on alto and a surprise vocal and several overlapping rhythm sections, Sassy sounds in top form throughout this date. Highlights include "I Ain't Got Nothing but the Blues," "Chelsea Bridge," "Rocks in My Bed," "I Got It Bad" and "Mood Indigo," but all 11 numbers are well worth hearing. Both of these well-conceived sets are easily recommended. —*Scott Yanow*

Copacabana / Oct. 1979 / Pablo ✦✦

Send in the Clowns / Feb. 16, 1981–May 16, 1981 / Pablo ✦✦✦
Sarah Vaughan is accompanied by her regular rhythm section of the early '80s (with pianist George Gaffney, bassist Andy Simpkins and drummer Harold Jones), guitarist Freddie Green, and the Count Basie horn sections on this enjoyable date which has been reissued on CD. The arrangements by Sammy Nestico and Allyn Ferguson unfortunately do not leave much room for any of the Basie sidemen to solo but Sassy is in superb form. She is at her best on "I Gotta Right to Sing the Blues," a remake of "If You Could See Me Now" and a rapid "When Your Lover Has Gone" although some listeners may enjoy her overly dramatic rendition of "Send in the Clowns." —*Scott Yanow*

Gershwin Live! / 1982 / Columbia ✦✦✦
1982 date with LA Philharmonic. Lots of bombast, some good vocals. —*Ron Wynn*

Crazy and Mixed Up / Mar. 1, 1982+Mar. 2, 1982 / Pablo ✦✦✦✦✦
Sarah Vaughan had complete control over the production of this album (which would be her last small-group recording) and, even if the results are not all that unique, her voice is often in near-miraculous form. With fine backup work from pianist Roland Hanna, guitarist Joe Pass, bassist Andy Simpkins and drummer Harold Jones, Sassy sounds in prime form, on such songs as "I Didn't Know What Time It Was," "Autumn Leaves," "The Island" and "You Are Too Beautiful." It is hard to believe, listening to her still-powerful voice on this CD reissue, that she had already been a recording artist for 48 years. —*Scott Yanow*

The Mystery of Man / Jun. 30, 1984 / Kokopelli ✦✦
This CD reissue brings back the music from an unusual project.

Gene Lees was hired to translate the philosophical poems of Pope John II into English and match them to music. The project climaxed in a performance and recording by Sarah Vaughan who was backed by a huge orchestra and chorus conducted by Lalo Schifrin. Unfortunately, despite the best efforts of everyone involved, the results often sound rather ponderous. The best pieces are the two original ones by Lees ("The Mystery of Man" and "Let It Live") but otherwise this is a difficult set to sit through, not only from the jazz standpoint (the impressive all-stars who are in the orchestra are largely wasted) but musically; everything is too serious and a bit pompous. Skip. —*Scott Yanow*

Charlie Ventura

b. Dec. 2, 1916, Philadelphia, PA, **d.** Jan. 17, 1992, Pleasantville, NJ
Tenor Saxophone, Leader / Bop, Swing
Charlie Ventura was an extroverted and sometimes explosive tenor saxophonist whose solos could be tasteless but were rarely dull. He came to fame with the Gene Krupa big band (1942–43 and 1944–46) during which he was often featured with Krupa in a trio; their wild rendition of "Dark Eyes" was a favorite. Ventura first recorded as a leader in 1945 and, after an attempt at leading a big band in 1946, he cut back to a highly successful septet which by 1949 featured trumpeter Conte Candoli, the vocal duo of Jackie and Roy (Roy Kral also played piano), trombonist Benny Green and the leader's tenor. During the bop fad of that year Ventura termed his music "Bop for the People." After that quickly ran its course, Ventura recorded with a dance band during 1949–50 and then he cut back to a quartet (sometimes doubling on baritone or bass sax), making occasional records and having some concert reunions with Krupa. After 1957 Ventura only made one further record (a 1977 date for Famous Door) but continued playing in his largely unchanged style into the 1980s. —*Scott Yanow*

Euphoria / Aug. 15, 1945–Oct. 1948 / Savoy ◆◆◆◆◆
Charlie Ventura, who rose to fame with Gene Krupa's Orchestra and Trio, was a fine tenor saxophonist who could get rather silly at times in his playing. There is little of the latter on this definitive two-LP set. Ventura is heard with a sextet in 1945 that co-stars trumpeter Buck Clayton, heads a fine quartet, tries to sound modern in a septet with trumpeter Charlie Shavers and trombonist Bill Harris, shares a frontline with trombonist Kai Winding and jams with his septet in 1948. Some of the later selections with Jackie Cain and Roy Kral on the vocals are dated (check out their odd version of "I'm Forever Blowing Bubbles") as Ventura tried to get "with it" and take over the modern jazz movement with his "Bop for the People" music. However in general the music is quite rewarding and this two-fer gives one a strong look at his early dates as a leader. —*Scott Yanow*

Charlie Boy / Jan. 27, 1946–May 1946 / Phoenix ◆◆◆◆
★ **Charlie Ventura Concert Featuring the Charlie Ventura Septet** / May 9, 1949 / MCA ◆◆◆◆◆
Septet. Good high-energy concert reissue with Jackie & Roy, Bennie Green (tb). —*Ron Wynn*

★ **Charlie Ventura in Concert** / May 9, 1949 / GNP ◆◆◆◆◆
Charlie Ventura Plays Hi Fi Jazz / 1956 / Tops ◆◆◆
Chazz / 1977 / Famous Door ◆◆◆◆

Joe Venuti (Giuseppi Venuti)

b. Sep. 16, 1903, Philadelphia, PA, **d.** Aug. 14, 1978, Seattle, WA
Violin / Dixieland, Swing, Classic Jazz
Although renowned as one of the world's great practical jokers (he once called a couple dozen bass players with an alleged gig and asked them to show up with their instruments at a busy corner so he could view the resulting chaos!), Joe Venuti's real importance to jazz is as improvised music's first great violinist. He was a boyhood friend of Eddie Lang (jazz's first great guitarist) and the duo teamed up in a countless number of settings during the second half of the 1920s, including recording influential duets. Venuti moved to New York in 1925 and immediately he and Lang were greatly in demand for jazz recordings, studio work and club appearances. Venuti seemed to play with every top white jazz musician during the segregated era and in 1929 he and Lang joined Paul Whiteman's Orchestra, appearing in the film *The King of Jazz*.

Lang's premature death in 1933 was a major blow to Venuti who gradually faded away from the spotlight. In 1935 after visit-

ing Europe, the violinist formed a big band and, although it survived quite a while and helped introduce both singer Kay Starr and drummer Barrett Deems, it was a minor-league orchestra that only recorded four songs (which Venuti characteristically titled "Flip," "Flop," "Something" and "Nothing"!). His brief stint in the military during World War II ended the big band, and when he was discharged, Venuti stuck to studio work in Los Angeles. He was regularly featured on Bing Crosby's early-'50s radio show but in reality the 1936–66 period was the Dark Ages for Venuti as he drifted into alcoholism and was largely forgotten by the jazz world.

However in 1967 Joe Venuti began a major comeback, playing at the peak of his powers at Dick Gibson's Colorado Jazz Party. His long-interrupted recording career resumed with many fine sessions (matching his violin with the likes of Zoot Sims, Earl Hines, Marian McPartland, George Barnes, Dave McKenna and Bucky Pizzarelli among others) and, despite his increasingly bad health, Venuti's final decade was a triumph. —*Scott Yanow*

Joe Venuti And Eddie Lang 1926–1930 / Sep. 29, 1926–Oct. 7, 1930 / Swaggie ◆◆◆◆◆
The first of two Swaggie LPs to document some of the classic performances of violinist Joe Venuti and guitarist Eddie Lang, this is filled with exciting performances that mostly do not duplicate the recordings on the Columbia two-LP set *Stringing the Blues*. Venuti and Lang (sometimes with the assistance of pianist Frank Signorelli) are heard on all of the takes that exist of "Black and Blue Bottom," "Stringing the Blues," "Doin' Things" and "Wild Cat." In addition, Venuti's Blue Four (with either Jimmy Dorsey on trumpet, clarinet, alto and baritone, C-melody saxophonist Frankie Trumbauer, bass saxophonist Adrian Rollini or baritonist Pete Pumiglio) are heard on nine additional selections. The music is wonderful small-group New York jazz of the late '20s, played with high musicianship and plenty of spirit. —*Scott Yanow*

★ **Joe Venuti and Eddie Lang, Vol. 1** / Sep. 1926–Sep. 1928 / JSP ◆◆◆◆◆
Joe Venuti and Eddie Lang (1926–1933) / Nov. 8, 1926–May 8, 1933 / ABC ◆◆◆
This somewhat random sampling of the recordings of violinist Joe Venuti and guitarist Eddie Lang contains a variety of gems but will at least partly duplicate most other Venuti collections from the era. Common selections alternate with rarities (such as Red McKenzie's "My Baby Came Home"). In addition to numbers from Venuti and Lang sessions, there are selections taken from dates led by Red Nichols, Frankie Trumbauer ("Krazy Kat" which also has a short solo from Bix Beiderbecke) and Lang. Robert Parker's inventive engineering gives these selections a slight echo and the feel of stereo; collectors vary as to their liking of his methods. —*Scott Yanow*

Stringin' the Blues / 1926 / Sony ◆◆◆◆◆
1920-1930s. Classic, formative cuts on two-disc set. —*Ron Wynn*

Violin Jazz 1927–1934 / Jun. 28, 1927–Sep. 20, 1934 / Yazoo ◆◆◆◆
This hodgepodge sampler contains 14 of violinist Joe Venuti's better recordings from the 1927–34 period, many of them also featuring guitarist Eddie Lang. The performances are mostly drawn from sessions by Venuti's Blue Four with some of the soloists including Jimmy Dorsey (switching between clarinet, alto, trumpet and baritone), Frankie Trumbauer (on C-melody sax and bassoon), bass saxophonist Adrian Rollini and, on "Sweet Lorraine," clarinetist Benny Goodman. The music is consistently exciting although serious collectors will want to acquire releases from the more complete European series instead. —*Scott Yanow*

Big Bands Of Joe Venuti, Vol. 1 / May 25, 1928–Sep. 6, 1930 / JSP ◆◆◆◆◆
In contrast to the hot small groups that violinist Joe Venuti led during the 1927–34 period, his big-band recordings were generally commercial with middle-of-the-road pop vocals, dance-band arrangements and melodic solos. Still, the two-volume JSP series contains a great deal of worthwhile music. The musicianship is top notch, there are some good solo spots (particularly from Venuti and Jimmy Dorsey on clarinet and alto) and the music is pleasing if not too adventurous. 1920s collectors should pick up these two sets. —*Scott Yanow*

★ **Joe Venuti and Eddie Lang, Vol. 2** / Jun. 1928–Sep. 1931 / JSP ◆◆◆◆◆
Big Bands Of Joe Venuti, Vol. 2 / May 22, 1930–Oct. 13, 1933 / JSP ◆◆◆◆
There are many rarities on this dance-band album, the second of

two LPs in JSP's valuable series. The music is not as essential as violinist Joe Venuti's small-group sides of the period but there are some strong moments and the English JSP label wisely reissued everything. Five of these titles are from 1930 while the remaining eleven are from 1933. The personnel on the latter titles are mostly unknown but the musicianship is first rate. Overall this is not an essential acquisition but fans of the era will want to get this anyway. —*Scott Yanow*

Joe Venuti And Eddie Lang 1930–1933 / Nov. 12, 1930–Feb. 28, 1933 / Swaggie ✦✦✦✦✦
In Swaggie's second volume of small-group sides by violinist Joe Venuti and guitarist Eddie Lang, five sessions are reissued in full. The first ten titles match the pair with Jimmy Dorsey (who switches between clarinet, alto and baritone) on some delightful performances; composer Harold Arlen takes vocals on four of the numbers. In addition the Venuti-Lang All-Star Orchestra (with trumpeter Charlie Teagarden, trombonist Jack Teagarden and clarinetist Benny Goodman) performs classic versions of four standards ("Beale Street Blues," "After You've Gone," "Farewell Blues" and "Someday Sweetheart") and Venuti welcomes both Jimmy Dorsey and bass saxophonist Adrian Rollini to a particularly wild four-song session in 1933. Essential and timeless music. —*Scott Yanow*

★ **Fiddlesticks** / Oct. 22, 1931–Jan. 25, 1939 / Conifer ✦✦✦✦✦
This CD combines together five complete sessions, some of violinist Joe Venuti's finest recordings from the 1930s. Venuti, guitarist Eddie Lang, trumpeter Charlie Teagarden, trombonist Jack Teagarden and clarinetist Benny Goodman team together for four classics ("Beale Street Blues," "After You've Gone," "Farewell Blues" and "Someday Sweetheart"), Jimmy Dorsey and Adrian Rollini constantly switch instruments on their wild meeting with Venuti and Lang, the violinist is heard on two obscure but worthy dates from 1935 and the only four recordings made by his unsuccessful big band (titled "Flip," "Flop," "Something" and "Nothing") wrap up this essential CD. Venuti would spend 30 years in obscurity (due partly to his alcoholism) but he is heard very much at the peak of his powers throughout this essential CD. —*Scott Yanow*

Pretty Trix / Dec. 26, 1934–Dec. 28, 1934 / IAJRC ✦✦✦✦
This very interesting CD from the collectors' IAJRC label contains previously unknown performances from late 1934. Violinist Joe Venuti is heard with a large studio group that sometimes features such musicians as trumpeter Louis Prima, xylophonist Red Norvo, trombonist Jerry Colonna (yes, the same person as the comedian), guitarist Frank Victor and Larry Binyon on tenor and flute. The music is essentially swing with a few elements of Dixieland, and although some of the performances (which were radio transcriptions) have their share of flubs (these were all first takes), the results on a whole are quite musical and swinging. —*Scott Yanow*

The Mad Fiddler from Philly / 1952–1953 / Shoestring ✦✦✦
Violinist Joe Venuti was in obscurity during the 1939-69 period, an alcoholic whose music was out of style and whose bands were filled mostly with minor leaguers. In the early '50s he renewed his friendship with Bing Crosby and for a while became an important part of his radio show. Typically the pair would have some humorous dialogue and then Venuti would take a featured number. This Shoestring LP has a dozen of his performances (plus the preceding verbal banter), filling in an important historical gap in the violinist's career. Worth searching for. —*Scott Yanow*

Once More with Feeling / Jun. 1969 / Ovation ✦✦✦

The Daddy of the Violin / Mar. 29, 1971 / MPS ✦✦✦
Super playing at late stage in his career. —*Ron Wynn*

Joe Venuti In Milan / May 3, 1971 / Vanguard ✦✦✦
Violinist Joe Venuti's comeback after 30 years of obscurity began in earnest in 1969. By 1971 and his visit to Italy, he was fully back on the scene and would record quite frequently during his final seven years. This LP matches Venuti with a group of Italians on spirited versions of standards. The slightly unusual instrumentation includes guitarist Lino Patruno, baritone, trombone and a rhythm section and works perfectly on the material. An enjoyable outing. —*Scott Yanow*

Dutch Swing College Band Meets Joe Venuti / Nov. 15, 1971+Jan. 25, 1972 / Everest ✦✦✦
Violinist Joe Venuti is actually only on half of this LP, playing

three songs from his earlier days, two standards and a blues with the Dutch septet. The remaining five selections are between Dixieland and swing and feature fine playing by leader Peter Schilperoort and Bob Kaper on reeds, cornetist Bert De Kort and trombonist Dick Kaart. Last available as a budget LP from Everest. —*Scott Yanow*

★ **Joe and Zoot** / Sep. 27, 1973 / Chiaroscuro ✦✦✦✦✦
This is a very exciting LP. The veteran violinist Joe Venuti really hit it off with tenor great Zoot Sims (who is also heard here on soprano) and the results were three very memorable albums. Their first recorded encounter finds the two principal voices joined by the stride piano master Dick Wellstood, bassist George Duvivier and drummer Cliff Leeman. They perform a variety of familiar and high-quality standards including such romps as "I've Found a New Baby," "The Wild Cat," "It's the Girl" and "Lady Be Good." Wonderful and consistently hard-swinging music. —*Scott Yanow*

The Joe Venuti Blue Four / May 20, 1974 / Chiaroscuro ✦✦✦✦✦
The second of violinist Joe Venuti's three recordings with tenor saxophonist Zoot Sims (who is actually only on four of the 12 selections) also features the legendary bass saxophonist Spencer Clark, either Dick Hyman or Dill Jones on piano, guitarist Bucky Pizzarelli, bassist Milt Hinton and drummer Cliff Leeman in different combinations. This Chiaroscuro album (along with the other Venuti-Sims sessions) is long overdue to be reissued on CD. —*Scott Yanow*

Jazz Violin / Sep. 13, 1974–Sep. 14, 1974 / Vanguard ✦✦✦✦
Violinist Joe Venuti's second recording with Italian guitarist Lino Patruno's group follows the initial one by three years. The standards (which includes a Gershwin medley) are all quite familiar, but these versions are full of enthusiasm and interesting ideas. Venuti was in top form throughout his final period (1969–77) and seemed to enjoy interacting with the five other horns on this happy session, not yet reissued on CD. —*Scott Yanow*

Joe Venuti and Zoot Sims / Jul. 1975 / Chiaroscuro ✦✦✦✦✦
Violinist Joe Venuti's three recordings with tenor great Zoot Sims are all quite joyful and exciting. This Chiaroscuro LP matches the pair with pianist John Bunch, bassist Milt Hinton, drummer Bobby Rosengarden and, on "Don't Take Your Love from Me," trombonist Spiegel Wicox who was then 73. The small-group swing performances have plenty of life and more often than not are hard swinging. —*Scott Yanow*

Gems / Aug. 28, 1975 / Concord ✦✦✦✦
This matchup between violinist Joe Venuti and guitarist George Barnes works quite well. With fine accompaniment from rhythm guitarist Bob Gibbons, bassist Herb Mickman and drummer Jake Hanna, the lead voices are free to romp on the ten standards. There are many highpoints including "I Want to Be Happy," "Oh Baby," "Hindustan" and "Lady Be Good." Hot swing music. —*Scott Yanow*

Hot Sonatas / Oct. 1975 / Chiaroscuro ✦✦✦✦
This is an unusual and frequently exciting album of duets between the two great veterans Joe Venuti and Earl Hines; despite both being active for over a half-century, they had never played together before. The interplay between the violinist and the pianist is consistently unpredictable and they communicate quite well on these swing standards (three of which were composed by Hines long ago). This unique encounter deserves to be reissued on CD. —*Scott Yanow*

'S Wonderful: 4 Giants of Swing / 1976 / Flying Fish ✦✦✦✦
For this session, the veteran jazz violinist Joe Venuti is teamed with a top-notch group of country players including mandolinist Jethro Burns, Curley Chalker on steel guitar and guitarist Eldon Shamblin. The repertoire is strictly jazz and these diverse players (who are backed by a conventional rhythm section) find plenty of common ground on the veteran standards, most of them from the pens of Ellington or Gershwin. Venuti sounds inspired by the unusual setting. —*Scott Yanow*

Venuti-Barnes Live (At the Concord Summer Festival) / Jul. 30, 1976 / Concord Jazz ✦✦✦✦
Violinist Joe Venuti and guitarist George Barnes (joined by pianist Ross Tompkins, bassist Ray Brown and drummer Jake Hanna) make for a very complementary team on this live session. Tompkins is featured on "Too Close for Comfort," Barnes is showcased on "I Can't Get Started," the ensemble romps on "Sweet

Georgia Brown" and the full group plays a lengthy five-song Duke Ellington/Billy Strayhorn medley. Few surprises occur, but there are enough fireworks to justify this album's acquisition, even by those who already own 20 Joe Venuti albums. —*Scott Yanow*

Sliding By / Apr. 15, 1977 / Sonet ✦✦✦✦
Violinist Joe Venuti, 73 at the time of this recording and only a little more than a year away from his death, was in typically swinging form for this quintet set with Dick Hyman (who doubles on piano and organ), guitarist Bucky Pizzarelli, bassist Major Holley and drummer Cliff Leeman. In addition to the six standards, there are four lesser-known Venuti compositions performed by this fine group. The music alternates between romantic ballads and stomps such as "Sweet Georgia Brown" and "Clarinet Marmalade." —*Scott Yanow*

Alone at the Palace / Apr. 27, 1977–Apr. 28, 1977 / Chiaroscuro ✦✦✦✦✦
For one of violinist Joe Venuti's final recording sessions, he engages in a set of duets with the talented swing pianist Dave McKenna. The original LP had a dozen performances and the reissue CD adds seven more. In addition to the usual standards, there are several Dixieland tunes (including three versions of "At the Jazz Band Ball") and four Venuti originals. McKenna (with his rolling basslines) was a perfect partner for the violinist, making this set one of the best of Venuti's later years. —*Scott Yanow*

Live at Concord '77 / Aug. 1977 / Concord ✦✦✦✦

Marlene Ver Planck

Vocals / Cabaret, Standards
A melodic singer with a beautiful voice and a surprisingly wide range, Marlene Ver Planck's singing swings while falling between jazz and cabaret. She recorded an excellent album for Savoy in 1955, spent much of the next 20 years as a studio singer, recorded with her husband (the excellent arranger Billy Ver Planck) on their own Mounted Records label in the 1960s (some of which have been reissued by Audiophile) and has recorded many fine albums for Audiophile since 1976 in settings ranging from a trio to a big band and a collaboration with the French group Saxomania. She is at the peak of her powers in the 1990s. —*Scott Yanow*

With Every Breath I Take / Nov. 29, 1955 / Savoy ✦✦✦✦✦
Loves Johnny Mercer / Sep. 19, 1978 / Audiophile ✦✦✦✦
Pure And Natural / Jun. 1987–1992 / Audiophile ✦✦✦
A Quiet Storm / 1989 / Audiophile ✦✦✦✦
● **Meets Saxomania** / Jan. 29, 1993–Mar. 6, 1994 / Audiophile ✦✦✦✦✦
Marlene Ver Planck possesses one of the world's great voices; every note she hits is perfectly in tune. Despite this talent, she is a subtle improviser who goes out of her way to bring out the beauty of the lyrics she interprets. Occasionally she will throw in a high note (as if to remind listeners of her wide range) but it is all in the service of uplifting the song. Her husband/arranger Billy Ver Planck wrote colorful charts on this CD for the French seven-piece four-reed unit called Saxomania to accompany her. He left plenty of room for solos and gave the ensembles the feel of a big band despite the absence of any brass instruments. Marlene Ver Planck is in peak form, and even if a few of the newer songs ("Sooner or Later" from the *Dick Tracy* film and the overrated "Here's to Life") are not worthy of her, she is particularly delightful on "You Turned the Tables on Me," "Close Your Eyes," "Speak Low" and a quartet of Ellington and Strayhorn tunes. —*Scott Yanow*

Live! In London / Apr. 1993–May 1993 / Audiophile ✦✦✦✦✦
Marlene Ver Planck, a wonderful singer whose style falls somewhere between jazz and cabaret, is in fine form on this live CD. Ver Planck, although her improvisations are quite subtle, always swings and manages to find beauty in each song she interprets. This set has a wide variety of material which ranges from such classics as "Body and Soul" and "Let's Face the Music" to the potentially sticky "So in Love" and even a medley from "Doctor Doolittle." Backed by a solid if somewhat anonymous English rhythm section, Ver Planck (who is virtually the whole show) uplifts each song and surprises listeners with her occasional jumps into the stratosphere (her range is remarkable) although she mostly vocalizes in her warm middle register. Recommended. —*Scott Yanow*

Harold Vick

b. Apr. 3, 1936, Rocky Mount, NC, d. Nov. 13, 1987, New York, NY
Tenor Saxophone / Soul Jazz, Hard Bop
An excellent thick-toned tenor, Harold Vick sounded quite at home in hard bop and soul jazz settings. His uncle Prince Robinson (a reed player from the 1920s) gave him a clarinet when he was 13 and three years later Vick switched to tenor. He rose to prominence playing with organ combos in the mid-'60s, recording and performing with Jack McDuff, Jimmy McGriff and Big John Patton among others. He started recording as a leader in 1966 and among his other associations were Jack DeJohnette's unusual group Compost (1972), Shirley Scott in the mid-'70s and Abbey Lincoln, with whom he recorded two Billie Holiday tributes for Enja just a short time before his death. —*Scott Yanow*

● **Steppin' Out** / May 21, 1963 / Blue Note ✦✦✦✦✦
Commitment / Jun. 1966 / Muse ✦✦✦
Don't Look Back / Nov. 1974 / Strata East ✦✦✦✦

Leroy Vinnegar

b. Jul. 13, 1928, Indianapolis, IN
Bass / Cool
A great "walking" bassist who's a self-taught player, Leroy Vinnegar was a prolific player on the '50s and '60s West Coast recording scene who remains active. He's most famous for his dynamic accompaniment and "walking" lines. Vinnegar plucked open strings with the left hand, adding heavier accents. He doesn't take that many solos, but the ones he delivers are outstanding. Vinnegar and pianist Carl Perkins attended school together in Indianapolis and later became colleagues on the West Coast. Vinnegar worked in Chicago during the early '50s, serving as house bassist at the Beehive, and playing with Sonny Stitt and Charlie Parker. He moved to Los Angeles in 1954, and eventually recorded with Stan Getz, Shorty Rogers, Herb Geller, Chet Baker, Gerald Wilson and Serge Chaloff. He, Shelly Manne and Andre Previn formed a popular trio that did jazz adaptions of Broadway songs and scores. They enjoyed a huge hit album with *My Fair Lady* in 1956. Vinnegar began cutting his own record ings in 1957, and his "walking" trademark was featured on the Contemporary albums *Leroy Walks* and *Leroy Walks Again*. He worked often with Joe Castro and Teddy Edwards, co-leading groups and even touring Europe with them. Vinnegar made some seminal recordings with Sonny Rollins, Phineas Newborn, the Jazz Crusaders and Kenny Dorham. He remained in demand during the '60s, doing several sessions. Perhaps the most successful was another smash album, *Swiss Movement* with Les McCann and Eddie Harris in 1969. Vinnegar was in a quintet co-led by Howard McGhee and Edwards in the '70s and worked in the Panama Hats, a quasi-Dixieland band that backed actor George Segal and often appeared on late night television during the '80s. Health problems resulted in Vinnegar becoming less active in the late 1980s and moving to Portland, Oregon. —*Ron Wynn*

Leroy Walks! / Jul. 15, 1957–Sep. 23, 1957 / Original Jazz Classics ✦✦✦✦✦
This was bassist Leroy Vinnegar's sextet (Vic Feldman, Gerald Wilson, Teddy Edwards, Carl Perkins, Tony Bazley) date from 1957. …It wasn't Vinnegar's best. —*Bob Rusch, Cadence*

● **Leroy Walks Again** / Aug. 1, 1962–Mar. 5, 1963 / Original Jazz Classics ✦✦✦✦✦
This was a bop session that was for the most part music of the moment. …It's notable for being Freddy Hill's recorded debut (at 28 years old) and for Roy Ayers' solid solos. —*Bob Rusch, Cadence*

Walkin' the Basses / Mar. 1992 / Contemporary ✦✦✦✦
Bassist Leroy Vinnegar was a familiar figure on the West Coast scene of the late '50s and early '60s and drew praises for his entertaining, yet musically sophisticated "walking" bass lines. Vinnegar has not lost his prowess, and this album features him heading a group with pianist Geoff Lee, drummer Mel Brown and percussionist Curtis Craft. While it is Vinnegar's date, he doesn't dominate, but sets the table. Vinnegar produced the session and arranged nine of the 11 songs, co-arranging a tenth with Lee. It isn't so much easy listening as nice, sophisticated material from four established pros who enjoy working with each other. —*Ron Wynn*

Eddie "Cleanhead" Vinson

b. Dec, 18, 1917, Houston, TX, d. Jul. 2, 1988, Los Angeles, CA
Alto Saxophone, Vocals / Bop, Blues, Early R&B
Eddie "Cleanhead" Vinson was in reality two performers in one.

An excellent bop altoist influenced by Charlie Parker (whose tone he could come very close to duplicating), Vinson was also an animated blues singer in the tradition of Big Joe Turner who wrote the lyrics to "Kidney Stew" and "Alimony Blues." The actual composer of both "Tune Up" and "Four" (Miles Davis was wrongly credited) Vinson performed his bop/blues hybrid from the '30s to the '80s. He joined Arnett Cobb and Illinois Jacquet in Chester Boone's big band one year after he'd begun playing alto sax. He stayed in that band from 1935 until 1941 while it changed leaders to Milt Larkin in 1936 and Floyd Ray in 1940. Vinson toured the South with blues vocalists Big Bill Broonzy and Lil Green, then went to New York, joining Cootie Williams' band. He had a huge hit in 1944 with "Cherry Red Blues." He recorded with Williams' band on Okeh, Hit and Capitol.

Vinson led a big band in 1946 and 1947, and a septet with John Coltrane, Red Garland and Johnny Coles in 1948. There were sessions with Mercury and King in the late '40s and early '50s, then later for such labels as Bethlehem, Riverside, Delmark and Blues Way. He kept working and recording but didn't enjoy renewed popularity until 1969, when a European tour with Jay McShann and recording of "Wee Baby Blues" alerted old and new generations about Vinson. This band also recorded for Black and Blue. Vinson played and recorded frequently in the '70s and '80s, working with Count Basie, Johnny Otis, Arnett Cobb and Buddy Tate, even Roomful of Blues. He did sessions in the '70s and '80s for Muse, Fantasy, Circle and Pablo. Vinson's playing strongly influenced Cannonball Adderley; a healthy amount of Vinson dates are available on CD. —*Ron Wynn and Scott Yanow*

Eddie Cleanhead Vinson / 1946–1947 / Trip ✦✦✦
Mercury jump blues material swings hard. —*Bill Dahl*

Cleanhead's Back in Town / Sep. 1957 / Bethlehem ✦✦✦
Although he had achieved a certain amount of popularity in the late '40s with his blues vocals and boppish alto, Eddie Cleanhead Vinson's Bethlehem album was one of only two recordings he made as a leader between 1956–66. With arrangements by Ernie Wilkins, Manny Albam and Harry Tubbs, and his sidemen including several members (past and present) of the Count Basie Orchestra, the blues-oriented music (which gives Vinson a chance to sing such material as "It Ain't Necessarily So," "Is You Is or Is You Ain't My Baby" and "Caledonia") is quite enjoyable and really rocks; pity that this record did not catch on. —*Scott Yanow*

Cleanhead & Cannonball / Sep. 19, 1961+Feb. 14, 1962 / Landmark ✦✦✦
During these two sessions, Eddie Cleanhead Vinson was joined by the Cannonball Adderley Quintet. Five of the ten selections were previously unissued altogether until this album came out in 1988. On Vinson's vocal numbers he is backed by altoist Cannonball Adderley, cornetist Nat Adderley, pianist Joe Zawinul, bassist Sam Jones and drummer Louis Hayes. Unfortunately on the instrumentals and the one vocal tune ("Kidney Stew") in which he plays, Vinson is the only altoist as Cannonball sits out; it's a pity that the two very different stylists did not have a chance to trade off. Despite that missed opportunity, the music on this release is quite worthy with Cleanhead in top form on such numbers as "Person to Person," "Just a Dream" and the three instrumentals. —*Scott Yanow*

Cherry Red / Mar. 1967 / Bluesway ✦✦✦

Kidney Stew Is Fine / Mar. 28, 1969 / Delmark ✦✦✦
Although its programming has been juggled a bit and the CD has been given liner notes, this Delmark release is a straight reissue of the original LP. Clocking in at around 38 minutes, the relatively brief set is the only recording that exists of Vinson, pianist Jay McShann and guitarist T-Bone Walker playing together; the sextet is rounded out by the fine tenor Hal Singer, bassist Jackie Sampson and drummer Paul Gunther. Vinson, whether singing "Please Send Me Somebody to Love," "Just a Dream" and "Juice Head Baby" or taking boppish alto solos, is the main star throughout this album (originally on Black & Blue), a date that helped launch Vinson's commercial comeback. —*Scott Yanow*

You Can't Make Love Alone / Jun. 18, 1971 / Mega ✦✦✦
Eddie Cleanhead Vinson was in inspired form at the 1971 Montreux Jazz Festival. He stole the show when he sat in with Oliver Nelson's big band during their "Swiss Suite" and played a brilliant blues alto solo. The same day, he recorded this Mega album but, due to its extreme brevity (under 24 minutes), perhaps this label should have changed its name to "Mini." Despite the low

quantity, the quality of his performance (on which Vinson is joined by the guitars of Larry Coryell and Cornell Dupree, pianist Neal Creque, bassist Chuck Rainey and drummer Pretty Purdie) makes this album still worth acquiring although preferably at a budget price. Vinson takes "Straight No Chaser" as an instrumental and does a fine job of singing "Cleanhead Blues," "You Can't Make Love Alone," "I Had a Dream" and "Person to Person." —*Scott Yanow*

Jamming the Blues / Jul. 2, 1974 / Black Lion ✦✦✦

Kidney Stew / Apr. 17, 1976 / Riff ✦✦✦✦
Eddie Cleanhead Vinson plays and sings his usual material in this meeting with Ted Easton's five-piece Dutch jazz band. The group is enthusiastic and Vinson, even though he had performed such material as "Kidney Stew," "Just a Dream" and "Somebody Sure Has Gotta Go" a countless number of times by 1976, was still able to come up with something fresh to say on this blues-oriented set. —*Scott Yanow*

The Clean Machine / Feb. 22, 1978 / Muse ✦✦✦✦✦
What makes this album different from many of Eddie Cleanhead Vinson's is that four of the seven selections are taken as instrumentals. Vinson's alto playing has long been underrated due to his popularity as a blues singer, so this release gives one the opportunity to hear his bop-influenced solos at greater length. With the assistance of a strong rhythm section led by pianist Lloyd Glenn and some contributions from trumpeter Jerry Rusch and Rashid Ali on tenor, Vinson is in excellent form throughout this enjoyable set. —*Scott Yanow*

● **Hold It Right There!** / Aug. 25, 1978–Aug. 26, 1978 / Muse ✦✦✦✦✦
After years of neglect, Eddie Cleanhead Vinson was finally receiving long overdue recognition at the time of this live session—one of six albums recorded during a week at Sandy's Jazz Revival. Two of these albums featured tenors Arnett Cobb and Buddy Tate in lead roles. While Vinson has fine blues vocals on "Cherry Red" and "Hold It," it is his boppish alto solos on "Cherokee, "Now's the Time" and "Take the 'A' Train" (the latter also having spots for Cobb and Tate) that make this set recommended to blues and bop fans alike. —*Scott Yanow*

Live at Sandy's / Aug. 25, 1978–Aug. 26, 1978 / Muse ✦✦✦✦✦
Muse recorded six albums during one week at Sandy's Jazz Revival, a club in Beverly, MA; two of them (this one and *Hold It Right There!*) feature the blues vocals and alto solos of Eddie Cleanhead Vinson. Some of the songs also have the tenors of Arnett Cobb and Buddy Tate in a supporting role, but this album is largely Vinson's show. Backed by a superb rhythm section (pianist Ray Bryant, bassist George Duvivier and drummer Alan Dawson), Vinson takes four fine vocals and plays many swinging alto solos including one on "Tune Up," a song he wrote that has been mistakenly credited to Miles Davis for decades. —*Scott Yanow*

★ **I Want a Little Girl** / Feb. 10, 1981 / Original Jazz Classics ✦✦✦✦✦
Eddie Cleanhead Vinson, 64 at the time of this Pablo recording, is in superior form on the blues-oriented material. With Art Hillery (on piano and organ) and guitarist Cal Green leading the rhythm section, and trumpeter Martin Banks and the tenor of Rashid Ali offering contrasting solo voices, this is a particularly strong release. It is true that Vinson had sung such songs as "I Want a Little Girl," "Somebody's Got to Go," and "Stormy Monday" a countless number of times previously, but he still infuses these versions with enthusiasm and spirit, making this set a good example of Cleanhead's talents in his later years. —*Scott Yanow*

★ **And Roomful of Blues** / Jan. 27, 1982 / Muse ✦✦✦✦✦
If there were justice in the world, Eddie Cleanhead Vinson would have been able to tour with this type of group throughout much of his career. Roomful of Blues, a popular five-horn nonet, has rarely sounded more exciting than on this musical meeting with the legendary singer/altoist. Vinson himself is exuberant on some of the selections, particularly "House of Joy," one of five instrumentals among the eight selections. Whether one calls it blues, bebop or early rhythm & blues, this accessible music is very enjoyable and deserves to be more widely heard. Among the supporting players, tenorman Greg Piccolo, trumpeter Bob Enos and guitarist Ronnie Earl (in one of his earliest recordings) win honors. —*Scott Yanow*

Miroslav Vitous

b. Dec. 6, 1947, Prague
Bass / Fusion, Post Bop

Czechoslavakian bassist Miroslav Vitous is one of the greatest European players in modern jazz history. Besides being a magnificent bowed player, Vitous had the ability and flair to make the bass a lead rather than a support instrument. He has flourished in bebop, hard bop, free, jazz-rock, pop, classical and international sessions, displaying stunning tone, solo and accompaniment abilities.

Vitous studied violin and piano before turning to bass; his father was a saxophonist. Vitous won a scholarship to Berklee while studying at the Prague Conservatory in the '60s. He moved to New York in 1967, playing with Art Farmer, Freddie Hubbard and the Clark Terry-Bob Brookmeyer quintet. He later worked with two extremely popular jazz-rock groups of the late '60s and early '70s, Miles Davis' and Herbie Mann's. Vitous recorded with Donald Byrd, Chick Corea, Jack DeJohnette, Wayne Shorter and Larry Coryell in the '60s and early '70s.

He toured with Stan Getz in the early '70s, played with Mann again, and was a founding member of Weather Report with Shorter and Joe Zawinul. He left Weather Report in the mid-'70s, and for a time in the '70s experimented with electric guitar.

He returned to the bass and joined the faculty of the New England Conservatory in 1979. Vitous headed its jazz department during the mid-'80s. He also lead a group with John Surman, either Kenny Kirkland or John Taylor, and Jon Christensen in the late '70s and early '80s, and played in Chick Corea's Trio music with Roy Haynes in the '80s. Vitous also recorded for Storyville, ECM and Freedom. —*Ron Wynn*

★ **Mountain in the Clouds** / Oct. 8, 1969 / Atco ✦✦✦✦
A groundbreaking LP for fusioneers—pre-Weather Report—with John McLaughlin, Joe Henderson, Herbie Hancock, Jack DeJonette, and Joe Chambers. All Vitous originals except "Freedom Jazz Dance," clocking in at 11 minutes. Originally "Infinite Search." —*Michael G. Nastos*

Purple / Aug. 25, 1970 / Epic ✦✦✦✦

Miroslav / Dec. 1976-Jul. 1977 / Freedom ✦✦
1976–1977 sessions with Don Alias and Armen Halburian on percussion. Vitous overdubs bass and keyboards. A stunning musical trip through Afro-jazz texture music. "Tiger in the Rain" is absolutely captivating. —*Michael G. Nastos*

Magical Shepherd / 1976 / Warner Brothers ✦✦

Majesty Music / 1977 / Arista ✦✦✦

Guardian Angels / Nov. 9, 1978–Nov. 11, 1978 / Evidence ✦✦✦✦
Miroslav Vitous has long been one of Europe's premier jazz bassists, while John Scofield is a great American guitarist. Their team-up yields music that is immaculately presented but often deficient in the energy and soul departments. That seems by design; such numbers as "Inner Peace" and "Shinkansen" have subdued arrangements, and the players carefully solo without ever straining or exerting themselves. At other times, Vitous and company move into more of a funk or upbeat style and seem even less sure. Vitous' bass work, especially his acoustic bowing, is marvelous, while Scofield plays in a sharp, concise, impressive manner although without the characteristic edge and rock/blues stylings. —*Ron Wynn*

First Meeting / May 1979 / ECM ✦✦✦✦
Seven pieces written by Vitous. With John Surman (sax, b, cl), a very young Kenny Kirkland (p) and stellar Jon Christenson (d). This is very listenable music, rooted in freedom of expression. —*Michael G. Nastos*

Miroslav Vitous Group / Jul. 1980 / ECM ✦✦✦✦✦

Journey's End / Jul. 1982 / ECM ✦✦✦✦

Emergence / Sep. 1985 / ECM ✦✦✦

Atmos / Feb. 1992 / ECM ✦✦✦
Bassist Miroslav Vitous and Jan Garbarek (on soprano and tenor) are featured throughout this ECM CD on a set of introspective duets. Garbarek does emit some passion on soprano and tenor and Vitous augments the music at times with some percussive sounds made by hitting his bass; once in a while he also adds brief samples from what he calls "the Miroslav Vitous Symphony Orchestra

Music Map

Violin

The Three Most Significant Pre-Bop Violinists
Joe Venuti
Stephane Grappelli
Stuff Smith

Other Early Violinists

Eddie South	Michel Warlop
Svend Asmussen	Ray Nance
Emilio Caceres	Claude Williams

Major Bop Violinists
None

Fusion
Jean Luc Ponty
Jerry Goodman (with the Mahavishnu Orchestra)
Didier Lockwood
Michel Urbaniak

Blues-Oriented
Don "Sugar Cane" Harris
Papa John Creech

Avant-Garde

Ornette Coleman	Leroy Jenkins
Zbigniew Seifert	Ramsey Ameen
Billy Bang	Charles Burnham
Mark Feldman	

Other Modern Violinists

Johnny Frigo	Michael White
John Blake	Marc O'Connor
Pierre Blanchard	L. Shankar
L. Subramaniam	Darol Anger

Sound Library." But in general this is a stereotypical ECM date, recommended to fans of that genre. —*Scott Yanow*

Roseanna Vitro

b. 1951
Vocals / Bop, Standards

Although underrated, Roseanna Vitro's versatility, sense of swing and highly appealing voice have made her one of the most consistently interesting jazz singers of the 1990s. She started her career in Houston in the mid-'70s (originally singing blues and rock) where she had a two-year engagement at the Green Room while hosting a weekly live radio broadcast. Shortly after moving to New York in 1980 she worked with Lionel Hampton. Vitro has recorded for the private labels Texas Rose Music and Skyline plus the Chase Music Group and more recently Concord; she deserves much greater recognition. —*Scott Yanow*

Listen Here / Oct. 4, 1982 / Texas Rose ✦✦✦✦
A Quiet Place / 1988 / Skyline ✦✦
An absolutely romantic statement and a pure delight. Poppy but pure, with pianist Fred Hersch. Desert-island music, if you get to pick the island. —*Michael G. Nastos*
Reaching for the Moon / 1991 / Chase Music Group ✦✦✦✦
A solid effort from a most expressive and emotional singer. Jazz, Brazilian, and pop flavored music with pianist Ken Werner. She is one of the best. Highly recommended. —*Michael G. Nastos*

● **Softly** / 1993 / Concord ✦✦✦✦✦
Singer Roseanna Vitro is expert at interpreting lyrics and scats with a strong sense of adventure. Ballads predominate on her excellent Concord CD but there are also a few cookers (including a surprisingly rapid "I'm Through with Love"). The singer covers a wide variety of material (some of it of recent vintage) with a touching version of "So Many Stars" being a highpoint. Vitro is greatly assisted by a fine trio starring pianist Fred Hersch; the tenors of Tim Ries and George Coleman help out on some selections. This rewarding CD gives one a fine example of Roseanna Vitro's talents. —*Scott Yanow*
Passion Dance / Jul. 19, 1994–Jan. 1995 / Telarc ✦✦✦✦✦

W

Abdul Wadud

b. Apr. 30, 1947, Cleveland, OH
Cello / Avant-Garde
An outstanding cellist, Abdul Wadud has concentrated solely on the instrument since the age of nine, and never decided to double on bass. His plucking and bowed solos have been featured in jazz and symphonic/classical settings, and Wadud's easily the finest cellist to emerge from the '60s and '70s generation. He studied at Youngstown State and Oberlin in the late '60s and early '70s. He played in the Black Unity Trio at Oberlin and met Julius Hemphill; the two subsequently worked together well through the '80s. Wadud played in the New Jersey Symphony Orchestra in the '70s and earned his master's degree in 1972. He played with Arthur Blythe for the first time in '76, and has since maintained a working relationship with him. He also worked and recorded with Frank Lowe, George Lewis, Oliver Lake, Sam Rivers, Cecil Taylor, David Murray, Chico Freeman, Anthony Davis and James Newton in the '70s and '80s. Wadud, Newton and Davis were in both the octet Episteme and a trio from 1982 to 1984. Wadud recorded as a leader for Bishara and Gramavision in the '70s and '80s and in a duo with Jenkins for Red in the '70s. —*Ron Wynn*

Freddie Waits

b. Apr. 27, 1943, Jackson, MS
Drums / Hard Bop
He began playing blues and soul, but Freddy Waits eventually became an excellent hard bop, bebop and free jazz drummer, as well as a charter member of the percussive group M'Boom Re. Waits worked with Memphis Slim and John Lee Hooker as well as Motown vocalists in the late '50s and early '60s. He then moved from Mississippi to New York. Waits recorded and played with Ray Bryant, Johnny Hodges, Andrew Hill and McCoy Tyner during the '60s, Richard Davis, Ella Fitzgerald, Lee Morgan, Bennie Maupin, Teddy Edwards, Curtis Fuller and Tyner during the '70s and Bill Dixon in the '80s. Waits, Horacee Arnold and Billy Hart formed Colloquium III in the late '70s. He played with Cecil Taylor in the late '80s. —*Ron Wynn*

Collin Walcott

b. Apr. 24, 1945, New York, NY, **d.** Nov. 8, 1984, Magdeburg, East Germany
Percussion, Sitar / World Fusion, Post Bop
One of the first Western musicians to master both sitar and tabla, Collin Walcott also played violin, snare drum and timpani. He was among the most gifted and knowledgeable percussionists in recent jazz history. Walcott studied sitar with Ravi Shankar and tabla with Alla Rakha. As a teen he was resident percussionist at the Yale Summer School of Music in Norfolk, CT. Walcott graduated from Indiana University in 1966, and later traveled to Los Angeles. After moving to New York, he worked and recorded with Tony Scott in the late '60s; they played bebop and a wide range of ethnic musics. Walcott recorded with Miles Davis on sitar in 1972. He played with the Paul Winter Consort in the early '70s, then Oregon and Codona in the mid-'70s and the '80s. Walcott was killed in an accident in then East Germany while on tour with Oregon. He recorded as a leader for ECM. Walcott has a compilation *Works* available, and also can be heard on various discs by Oregon and Codona. —*Ron Wynn and David Nelson McCarthy*

Cloud Dance / Mar. 1975 / ECM ✦✦✦✦
● Grazing Dreams / Feb. 1977 / ECM ✦✦✦✦✦
With Don Cherry, John Abercrombie. Group music based around Walcott's sitar and tabla work. —*Michael G. Nastos*
Dawn Dance / Jan. 1981 / ECM ✦✦✦✦

Terry Waldo

b. 1944, Ironton, Ohio
Piano / Ragtime, Classic Jazz
One of the finest trad jazz pianists from the 1970s to the present and an interpreter who really brings new life to classic jazz and ragtime, Terry Waldo has often labored in near-anonymity yet has recorded quite a few highly enjoyable records. He took three years of classical piano lessons starting at age six before discovering ragtime and Dixieland. He also learned to play trumpet, tuba, banjo, cello and bass to various degrees and led a group (the Fungus Five) on the Ted Mack Original Amateur Hour in 1962. In Ohio, Waldo played with Gene Mayl's Dixieland Rhythm Kings, he spent time freelancing on various instruments in New Orleans and San Francisco, graduated from Ohio State and played tuba during his military service. He taught a history of jazz, blues and ragtime class at Denison University during 1971–78, hosted in 1972 a series for National Public Radio called *This Is Ragtime* and in 1976 wrote a definitive book on ragtime that used the same name. In the 1980s Waldo led the Gotham City Stompers, worked with the show *One Mo' Time*, toured with Leon Redbone and worked with Woody Allen. Terry Waldo has recorded for several labels including GHB (in 1969), Fat Cat Records, Stomp Off (with his Gutbucket Syncopators) and the Musical Heritage Society. —*Scott Yanow*

Ragtime Classics, Vol. 2 / Oct. 24, 1978–Jun. 24, 1983 / Musical Heritage Society ✦✦✦✦
New Orleans Jazz Echoes / Oct. 15, 1979–Jun. 8, 1989 / Musical Heritage Society ✦✦✦✦
Ragtime Classics, Vol. 1 / Jul. 22, 1980–Jun. 24, 1983 / Musical Heritage Society ✦✦✦
● Footlight Varieties / Jun. 23, 1985–Mar. 2, 1989 / Stomp Off ✦✦✦✦✦
This CD is a bit of a grab bag since its material was recorded at four different sessions from a four-year period. However with such talented soloists as cornetist Peter Ecklund, trombonist Dan Barrett, clarinetists Joe Muranyi and Ken Peplowski, guitarist Howard Alden and the leader/pianist, the mixture of complete obscurities and classic standards generally works quite well. There are vocals (of various quality) from Waldo, Muranyi, Susan LaMarche and even Leon Redbone and highlights include "Good Old New York," "I Need Some Pettin," "Some Sweet Day" and "Exit Gloom." Fans of traditional and classic jazz will enjoy this one. —*Scott Yanow*

Mal Waldron

b. Aug. 16, 1926, NYC
Piano / Hard Bop, Post Bop
Mal Waldron's piano playing has a pinched, angular sound, as he's among the artists not simply influenced by Thelonious Monk's unorthodox style, but able to incorporate it into their own work in an individualized way. Waldron isn't quite as idiosyncratic and scattershot as Monk but utilizes the identical sparse approach, unusual voicings and rhythms. He's written compositions for large

and small groups, backed vocalists, and done film and ballet scores. Waldron originally only played jazz on alto sax, preferring to play classical on piano, but switched while at Queens College. Waldron earned his degree in composition, then worked with various New York bands. He made his recording debut in the late '40s with Ike Quebec. Waldron played with Della Reese, then joined Charles Mingus in 1954, playing at the Newport Jazz Festival in 1955 and 1956. He then formed his own group with Gigi Gryce and Idrees Sulieman. Waldron was on a countless number of sessions for Prestige in the mid-to-late 50s, often supplying many originals including one ("Soul Eyes") that became a standard. He was Billie Holiday's accompanist from 1957 until her death in 1959, then he worked with Abbey Lincoln and did studio dates. Waldron was part of the remarkable Eric Dolphy quintet with Booker Little that played at the Five Spot in 1961. He also did a studio session with Dolphy. Waldron composed the film scores "The Cool World" in 1963, plus "Three Bedrooms in Manhattan" and "Sweet Love Bitter" in 1965. But he had to relearn the piano after suffering a nervous breakdown in the mid-'60s. Waldron partly did this by listening to his own recordings. He moved to Europe in 1965 to do more film work, settling in Munich in 1967. A trio album Waldron recorded was one of the first issued on the then new label ECM. He recorded and worked frequently with Steve Lacy and Archie Shepp in the '70s, toured Japan and began making return visits to America in 1975. Waldron was featured on numerous Enja releases in the '70s with trios, quartets and solo. He continued recording in the '80s on Enja, Palo Alto, Muse, Projazz, Hat Art and Soul Note. Waldron has a full slate of past and present sessions available on CD. — Ron Wynn

Mal 1 / Nov. 9, 1956 / Original Jazz Classics ✦✦✦✦

One and Two / Nov. 9, 1956–May 17, 1957 / Prestige ✦✦✦✦
Two of pianist Mal Waldron's first three albums as a leader are combined on this two-LP set. Waldron is heard in a quintet with trumpeter Idrees Sulieman and altoist Gigi Gryce, leading a sextet with trumpeter Bill Hardman, altoist Jackie McLean and tenor saxophonist John Coltrane and with a different sextet that also stars Sulieman, Coltrane and altoist Sahib Shihab. Many of the Prestige sessions from the era were essentially jam sessions, but Waldron's dates were better organized and had more challenging material. Five of the pianist's originals are among the dozen selections on this two-fer which also includes five standards and two obscurities. These hard bop performances are among Coltrane's lesser-known recordings and show that, even in his early days, Mal Waldron had his style. — Scott Yanow

Mal 2 / Apr. 19, 1957+May 17, 1957 / Original Jazz Classics ✦✦✦✦✦

Mal 3: Sounds / Jan. 31, 1958 / Original Jazz Classics ✦✦✦
This is an unusual set by pianist Mal Waldron. He utilizes a sextet with trumpeter Art Farmer, flutist Eric Dixon, cellist Calo Scott, bassist Julian Euell and drummer Elvin Jones on three of his picturesque originals and his wife Elaine Waldron contributes vocals to the wordless "Portrait of a Young Mother" and Harold Arlen's "For Every Man There's a Woman." The music is not essential but holds one's interest throughout the straight CD reissue of the original LP. — Scott Yanow

Mal 4 / Sep. 26, 1958 / Original Jazz Classics ✦✦✦✦✦
It seems strange that this, pianist Mal Waldron's seventh session as a leader, was his first with a group as small as his trio. With the assistance of bassist Addison Farmer and drummer Kenny Dennis, Waldron performs four standards and three of his moody originals. His sometimes-brooding style was already quite recognizable and his inventive use of repetition was quite impressive. This CD reissue of the original LP gives listeners a definitive look at the early style of Mal Waldron. — Scott Yanow

Impressions / Mar. 20, 1959 / Original Jazz Classics ✦✦✦✦

★ **The Quest** / Jun. 27, 1961 / New Jazz ✦✦✦✦✦

Free at Last / Nov. 24, 1969 / ECM ✦✦✦✦

First Encounter / Mar. 8, 1971 / Catalyst ✦✦✦

Black Glory / Jun. 29, 1971 / Enja ✦✦✦✦✦
One among many superb trio dates. Waldron's playing is alternately expressive, bluesy, and exacting. — Ron Wynn

Blues for Lady Day / Feb. 5, 1972 / Black Lion ✦✦✦✦

Up Popped the Devil / Dec. 28, 1973 / Enja ✦✦✦✦✦
Pianist Mal Waldron's music is characterized by a heavily brooding rhythmic quality, with the left hand usually carrying the theme at one repetitious tempo while the right hammers away in juxtaposition with a counter tempo (usually faster). Such was the case with "Up Popped the Devil," "Snake Out" and "Changachangachang," three very Waldronian pieces in both structure and execution, the latter deriving its melody from the whole-tone scale. Aside from Waldron, the record's strongest points were bassist Reggie Workman and drummer Billy Higgins, their work being sensitive and supportive throughout. — Bob Rusch, Downbeat

Hard Talk / May 4, 1974 / Enja ✦✦✦✦

One-Upmanship / Feb. 12, 1977 / Enja ✦✦✦✦

Moods / May 6, 1978+May 8, 1978 / Enja ✦✦✦✦
1990 reissue of a solid set. Wonderful sextet with Steve Lacy (sax) and Cameron Brown (b). — Ron Wynn

One Entrance, Many Exits / Jan. 4, 1982 / Palo Alto ✦✦✦✦

You and the Night and the Music / Dec. 9, 1983 / Projazz ✦✦✦✦
Trio. High-caliber lineup. With Reggie Workman (b), Ed Blackwell (d). — Ron Wynn

Encounters / Mar. 18, 1984 / Muse ✦✦
Though not with enough jazz edge, first-rate duets with David Friesen. — Ron Wynn

Sempre Amore / Feb. 17, 1986 / Soul Note ✦✦✦✦

★ **Left Alone '86** / Sep. 1, 1986 / Evidence ✦✦✦✦✦
Although he cannot maintain the same nonstop pace he had in the early '60s, Jackie McLean still plays magnificently. He demonstrated that repeatedly on this 1986 duo date with pianist Mal Waldron, whose lovely countermelodies, complementary solos, darting phrases, and supporting accompaniment proved a perfect contrast to McLean's forays. He is lyrical and engaging on some tracks; his explosive side emerges on others, where McLean, whose alto seemed ready to disintegrate on such sets as Action or A Fickle Sonance, charges to the fore, hitting upper register home runs and ripping through the notes. It's good to know that McLean could still summon that drive. — Ron Wynn

Live at the Village Vanguard / Sep. 16, 1986 / Soul Note ✦✦✦✦✦
This is a high-caliber quartet set, with Woody Shaw (tpt) triumphant. — Ron Wynn

Seagulls of Kristiansundi: Live at the Village Vanguard / Sep. 16, 1986 / Soul Note ✦✦✦✦✦

Our Colline's a Treasure / Apr. 28, 1987+Apr. 30, 1987 / Soul Note ✦✦✦
Trio. Fine interpretations and solos. — Ron Wynn

Crowd Scene / 1989 / Soul Note ✦✦✦✦
For this quintet session, Mal Waldron contributed two somewhat episodic originals (titled "Crowd Scene" and "Yin and Yang") that are used as the basis for extended improvisations by altoist Sonny Fortune, tenor saxophonist Ricky Ford, bassist Reggie Workman, drummer Eddie Moore and the pianist/leader. Despite the obvious talents of these very individual players, there are some rambling moments on these lengthy performances, both of which clock in at over 25 minutes. Still, it is often fascinating to hear what the musicians come up with during these go-for-broke improvisations. — Scott Yanow

Where Are You? / 1989 / Soul Note ✦✦✦
Mal Waldron's mellow and sentimental side is tapped on this session recently issued by Soul Note. It's spotlighted on the unaccompanied second take of the title track, where Waldron's opening and major solo are played with a somber, introspective flair, as he slowly constructs his statement. There are elegant left-hand movements and answering right-hand rhythms, and his interpretation is ultimately satisfying and memorable. A less demonstrative, but still quite enjoyable, Mal Waldron date. — Ron Wynn

Bennie Wallace

b. Nov. 18, 1940, Chattanooga, TN
Tenor Saxophone / Post Bop
Bennie Wallace has long had his own unique style, combining together the raspy tone of Ben Webster with the frequent wide interval jumps of Eric Dolphy. He has an explorative style that soundwise looks back toward the swing era. Wallace started on clarinet when he was 12 and a few years later switched to tenor. He graduated from the University of Tennessee in 1968 and in 1971 moved to New York where he debuted with Monty

Alexander. Wallace gigged with Sheila Jordan, played with many avant-garde musicians, was in George Gruntz's Concert Jazz Band in 1979 and led his own trio/quartet on-and-off throughout the 1970s and '80s. He recorded frequently prior to 1985 for Enja but his mid-to-late-'80s Blue Note recordings are more memorable for they find him infusing his appealing sound with touches of New Orleans R&B and a healthy dose of humor. In recent times Wallace has been writing music for films including *White Men Can't Jump*. —*Scott Yanow*

The Fourteen Bar Blues / Jan. 23, 1978 / Enja ◆◆◆

Live at the Public Theater / May 26, 1978 / Enja ◆◆◆◆
Surging, often frenetic live set by a saxophonist whose style merges hard bop, blues, and gospel influences. Bennie Wallace has a low-down tone, good skills on tenor, alto, and flute, and has played with both hard boppers and Dr. John. His versatility and fluidity are in evidence throughout this fine date. —*Ron Wynn*

The Free Will / Jan. 31, 1980–Feb. 1, 1980 / Enja ◆◆◆◆
1990 reissue, consistently strong playing by Wallace. —*Ron Wynn*

● **Plays Monk** / Mar. 4, 1981–Mar. 5, 1981 / Enja ◆◆◆◆◆
Recorded a year before pianist/composer Thelonious Monk's death, this tribute by Bennie Wallace features the dynamic tenor in trios with bassist Eddie Gomez and drummer Dannie Richmond plus three quartets with the addition of trombonist Jimmy Knepper. Wallace's eccentric interval jumps and very expressive sound (along with his advanced harmonic knowledge) made him a natural to explore Monk's music and he pours plenty of passion into these improvisations. In addition to seven of Monk's compositions, Wallace contributes his own "Prelude"; the CD reissue adds a second version of "'Round Midnight" to the original program. This colorful and chancetaking session can act as an introduction to both Bennie Wallace and Monk's music. —*Scott Yanow*

Bennie Wallace Trio & Chick Corea / May 4, 1982–May 5, 1982 / Enja ◆◆

Big Jim's Tango / Nov. 30, 1982–Dec. 1, 1982 / Enja ◆◆◆◆◆

Sweeping through the City / Mar. 1984–Apr. 1984 / Enja ◆◆◆◆◆
Large group date: blues and gospel element. Unwieldy at times, but effective overall. —*Ron Wynn*

★ **Twilight Time** / 1985 / Blue Note ◆◆◆◆◆

Brilliant Corners / Sep. 1986 / Denon ◆◆◆◆
A wonderful, overlooked 1986 session with the Japanese pianist Yosuke Yamashita. —*Ron Wynn*

The Art of the Saxophone / Feb. 7, 1987–Feb. 8, 1987 / Denon ◆◆◆◆◆
Incendiary Tennessean Wallace joins four other saxophonists—one at a time—on each track. Duelers include Oliver Lake (as), Jerry Bergonzi (ts), Harold Ashby (ts), and Lew Tabackin (ts). Six by Wallace, two by Ellington, one by Gillespie. Great playing and a unique idea fully realized. —*Michael G. Nastos*

★ **Border Town** / Jun. 1987 / Blue Note ◆◆◆◆◆
Top mix of blues and jazz. Dr. John (p) and John Scofield (g) are first rate. —*Ron Wynn*

Old Songs / 1993 / AudioQuest ◆◆◆◆
Much of this date features Bennie Wallace's distinctive tenor in a pianoless trio with bassist Bill Hunington and drummer Alvin Queen. Although it could be said that Wallace combines the sound of Ben Webster with the interval jumps of Eric Dolphy (a very potent combination), he has had his own style for over a decade. These eight standards (along with an original blues "At Lulu White's") are taken at a variety of tempos and Wallace really digs into these fertile chord changes after showing respect for the melodies. —*Scott Yanow*

Fats Waller (Thomas Wright Waller)

b. May 21, 1904, New York, NY, d. Dec. 15, 1943, Kansas City, MO
Organ, Vocals, Composer / Stride, Classic Jazz, Swing
Thomas "Fats" Waller was a larger than life figure, a multi-talented individual who was not only one of the great stride pianists of all time but an underrated singer, an often-hilarious personality, jazz's first organist and a brilliant songwriter. In addition, he had a constantly partying lifestyle full of food, liquor, women and heated music that was great fun while it lasted. Waller's skill as a melodic creator was unmatched, and he collaborated with lyricist partner Andy Razaf on dozens of classics, among them "Ain't Misbehavin'," "Honeysuckle Rose" and "Black and Blue." He was

the first pianist to swing the light, graceful fashion that's now associated with modern jazz. Waller influenced such pianists as Count Basie, Art Tatum and Dave Brubeck. He made hundreds of records, had his own radio programs and appeared in three films plus a handful of shorts. His father was a Baptist preacher who conducted open air religious services in Harlem at which the young Waller played reed organ. He played piano at school and by 15 was house organist at Lincoln Theatre. After his mother died in 1920, Waller moved in with pianist Russell Broooks' family, dashing his father's hopes he'd become a religious organist. Brooks introduced Waller to James P. Johnson, who became a tutor and mentor. Waller began making piano rolls in 1922, and made his recording debut as a soloist for the Okeh label, cutting "Muscle Shoals Blues" and "Birmingham Blues." Waller has claimed he studied piano with Leopold Godowsky and composition with Carl Bohm at the Juilliard School during this early period; this has not been fully verified. During the early '20s, Waller recorded with such blues vocalists as Sara Martin, Alberta Hunter and Maude Mills. He collaborated with Clarence Williams in 1923, an effort that led to his song "Wild Cat Blues" being published and recorded by Williams' Blue Five with Sidney Bechet. This song and the composition "Squeeze Me," issued that same year, helped make Waller's initial reputation as a songwriter. He made his radio debut in 1923 on a local Newark station, then began regular appearances on WHN in New York, while still playing organ regularly at both the Lincoln and Lafayette theaters. He began recording with the Victor company in 1926, cutting the organ solos "St. Louis Blues" and "Lenox Avenue Blues,"; he'd do most of his sessions for the label the rest of his career. Waller recorded his song "Whiteman Stomp" with Fletcher Henderson's orchestra in 1927; Henderson added other Waller songs like "Crazy 'Bout My Baby" and "Stealin' Apples" to the band's book. While working with other groups like Morris' Hot Babes, McKinney's Cotton Pickers and his own Fats Waller's Buddies (one of the earliest interracial groups to record), Waller turned heads with a string of marvelous solo recordings in 1929; these included "Handful of Keys," "Smashing Thirds," "Numb Fumblin'" and "Valentine Stomp." But he was attaining equal fame for his collaborations with lyricists. He and Razaf did much of the music for the 1928 black Broadway musical "Keep Shufflin," and a year later did songs for the shows "Load of Coal" and "Hot Chocolates," which marked the debut of "Ain't Misbehavin'." Waller made his own debut at Carnegie Hall in 1928, serving as piano soloist in Johnson's "Yamekraw," a fantasy for piano and orchestra. In the '30s, Waller did sessions with Ted Lewis, Jack Teagarden and Billy Banks Rhythmakers, before starting a lengthy recording series with the six-piece group Fats Waller and his Rhythm. Participants included Al Casey, Gene Sedric or Rudy Powell and either Herman Autrey, Bill Coleman or John Hamilton. Waller appeared in the films "Hooray for Love!" and "King of Burlesque" in 1935, while on the West Coast with Les Hite's band. Waller soon formed his own big band, and recorded with a unit that mixed some members of the Rhythm with additional personnel. Waller toured Europe in 1938 and 1939, and cut solo pipe organ tracks for HMV. He recorded "London Suite," an extended series of six related solo piano pieces, during his '39 London visit. This was his longest single composition. Waller returned to Hollywood in 1943, making the film "Stormy Weather" with Lena Horne and Bill Robinson. He led an all-star unit for the movie that included Benny Carter and Zutty Singleton. Waller also toured extensively that year, and collaborated with lyricist George Marion, Jr. on the score for the theatrical production "Early to Bed" that had its Boston opening May 24, 1943. A lifetime of overeating and alcohol abuse, plus financial pressures from many years of legal controversy over alimony payments took its toll. Waller became ill during another visit to the West Coast where he was solo pianist at the Zanzibar room in Hollywood. He died of pneumonia while returning to New York with his manager Ed Kirkeby. A volume of articles, plus several books have been written about Waller; there are many valuable reissues of his work available, while "Ain't Misbehavin'" has become an oft-recorded classic, cut by everyone from Nell Carter to Hank Williams, Jr. —*Ron Wynn, Dan Morgenstern and Scott Yanow*

★ **Piano Masterworks, Vol. 1** / Oct. 21, 1922–Sep. 24, 1929 / EPM ◆◆◆◆◆
Although he would become well-known in the '30s for his comic vocals and memorable personality, Fats Waller was always first and foremost a pianist. During the '20s he was purely an instrumentalist, one of the greatest and most powerful stride pianists of all time. This CD has all of Waller's early piano solos, including

every one of the alternate takes (two versions of many titles and a very rare third take of "I've Got a Feeling I'm Falling"). With the exception of his initial two sides from 1922 and 1927's "Blue Black Bottom," all of these titles are from 1929, including the original version of "Ain't Misbehavin.'" —*Scott Yanow*

Fats Waller in London / Oct. 21, 1922–Jun. 13, 1939 / Disques Swing ✦✦✦✦
Other than Fats Waller's first two recorded piano solos (from 1922), this double LP concentrates on the recordings he made while in London during 1938–39. Doubling on piano and organ, Waller romps and sings with a fine English octet, takes six comparatively somber organ solos (featuring Black spirituals) and backs singer Adelaide Hall on a delightful version of "I Can't Give You Anything but Love." In addition, Waller (backed by drummer Max Lewin) performs one of his few long works, the six-part "London Suite." Excellent music with plenty of variety on this fine two-fer. —*Scott Yanow*

Giants of Jazz / Oct. 21, 1922–Jan. 23, 1943 / Time Life ✦✦✦✦
Although now difficult to find, this three-LP box set gives listeners a perfect summation of Fats Waller's career and hits most of the highpoints. —*Scott Yanow*

Classic Jazz From Rare Piano Rolls / Mar. 1923–Jan. 1929 / Music Masters ✦✦✦
During 1922–27 Waller made 19 piano rolls, solos that could be reproduced by running marked paper through player pianos. 11 of these are on this CD, along with a duet with his teacher James P. Johnson ("If I Could Be with You") and a version of Waller's "Ain't Misbehavin'" from 1929 by J. Lawrence Cook. Piano rolls always come a distant second to recorded piano solos since the unchanging tempos and steady rhythms generally come across as mechanical. His piano rolls are as rollicking and swinging as it is possible to get and this interesting CD gives listeners versions of several tunes that Waller never did record. —*Scott Yanow*

★ **Turn on the Heat: The Fats Waller Piano Solos** / Feb. 16, 1927–May 13, 1941 / Bluebird ✦✦✦✦✦
With the exception of a third take of "I've Got a Feeling I'm Falling" and his two earliest records from 1922, all of Fats Waller's recorded piano solos are on this superior double-CD set. Over half of these recordings are from 1929, but fortunately he also cut three sessions of piano solos after he became much more famous as a comedy personality with his Rhythm sides. Highlights include the virtuosic "Handful of Keys," the earliest version of "Ain't Misbehavin,'" "Clothes Line Ballet," "I Ain't Got Nobody" and "Honeysuckle Rose." A special bonus is a pair of piano duets with Bennie Payne ("St. Louis Blues" and "After You've Gone"). Classic music. —*Scott Yanow*

★ **Fats Waller and His Buddies** / May 20, 1927–Dec. 18, 1929 / Bluebird ✦✦✦✦
This CD has most of Fats Waller's best band recordings of the '20s, including eight selections by his "Buddies" (highlighted by "The Minor Drag" and "Harlem Fuss"), six (counting two alternate takes) from the Louisiana Sugar Babes (an odd quartet featuring Waller's organ and James P. Johnson's piano) and seven selections on which Waller sits in with cornetist Thomas Morris' Hot Babies in 1927. Surprisingly, other than his scat vocal on "Red Hot Dan," Fats Waller is heard strictly as a pianist, but his talents were so giant as an instrumentalist that one never minds. With trombonists Charlie Irvis and Jack Teagarden and trumpeters Red Allen and Jabbo Smith among the strong supporting cast, the one word for this superior CD is hot. —*Scott Yanow*

Here 'Tis / Oct. 14, 1929–Dec. 1943 / Jazz Archives ✦✦✦
This long out-of-print LP is a real collector's item, featuring seven rare alternate takes and a few real Fats Waller oddities. Among the latter is an excerpt from the legendary production *Hot Chocolate* in 1929; Waller backs some of the dialogue. In addition, this LP has his final recordings, a broadcast from Los Angeles in Dec. 1943 with the pianist/singer performing "Your Feet's Too Big" and "Handful of Keys" one last time just a short while before his premature death. This LP is well worth acquiring but will take a long search. —*Scott Yanow*

Piano Masterworks, Vol. 2 (1929–1943) / 1929–1943 / Hot and Sweet ✦✦✦✦✦

Breakin' the Ice, The Early Years, Pt. 1 / May 16, 1934–May 6, 1935 / Bluebird ✦✦✦✦✦

The Definitive Fats Waller, Vol. 1: His Piano His Rhythm / Mar. 11, 1935–Aug. 7, 1939 / Stash ✦✦✦✦
In addition to his many studio recordings for Victor, the popular

pianist/singer/composer Fats Waller recorded two extensive sessions of radio transcriptions which could be used to fill in time between radio shows. These have now been reissued in full on two CDs. The first volume finds Waller performing seven songs in 1935 (two duets with the reeds of Rudy Powell and five solos with some vocals) in addition to 23 performances from 1939 (17 with his Rhythm, an excerpt from an organ solo and five unaccompanied piano solos). Throughout, Waller, who never really needed an audience, is in exuberant form, playing material that was generally superior than the dog tunes he was often handed at recording sessions. A fun set. —*Scott Yanow*

The Definitive Fats Waller, Vol. 2: Hallelujah / Mar. 11, 1935–Apr. 3, 1939 / Stash ✦✦✦✦✦
This second volume of rare Fats Waller items includes 24 selections performed at a marathon radio transcription session in 1935 (there were actually 31 pieces played, seven of which are on *Volume 1*). Waller is heard solo, singing and playing piano without the assistance of his sidemen, and he is in top form on a wide variety of material. This CD concludes with previously unreleased items from three different occasions: a 1936 solo broadcast from Bluefield, WV, two selections privately recorded in London in 1939, and Waller's appearance on *The George Jessel Show* during the same year. A superior release from the great stride pianist, vocalist, composer and personality. —*Scott Yanow*

● **I'm Gonna Sit Right Down . . . The Early Years, Part 2** / May 6, 1935–Dec. 24, 1936 / Bluebird ✦✦✦✦✦

● **Fats Waller and His Rhythm: The Middle Years, Pt. 1 (1936–1938)** / Dec. 24, 1936–Apr. 12, 1938 / Bluebird ✦✦✦✦✦
This particular three-CD set (which follows "The Last Years") picks up around where *Volume 4* of the *Complete* LP series ended and includes no less than 70 recordings from Fats Waller's "Middle Years." —*Scott Yanow*

A Good Man Is Hard To Find, The Middle Years: Part II / Apr. 12, 1938–Jan. 12, 1940 / Bluebird ✦✦✦✦✦
Subtitled "The Middle Years, Part 2," this three-CD set contains all of pianist/vocalist Fats Waller's Victor recordings from a nearly two-year period including all of the alternate takes. In fact the first five selections (the only ones contained here from his short-lived big band) are all alternate takes to the selections that close "The Middle Years, Part 1." Otherwise these performances are by Waller's septet with either Herman Autrey or John Hamilton on trumpet and Gene Sedric (who doubled on tenor and clarinet); Chauncey Graham filled in for Sedric on one date. Waller's great popularity resulted in the large number of recordings from this era (68 are on this set) and they range from hits ("Two Sleepy People," "Yacht Club Swing," an amazing version of "Hold Tight," "Your Feet's Too Big" and a new rendition of "Squeeze Me") to fresh originals and novelties to trash that Waller did his best (often through satirization) to uplift. Nearly every selection has a liberal dose of his classic piano and taken as a whole these much-maligned recordings are quite listenable, enjoyable and historical. —*Scott Yanow*

Jugglin' Jive of Fats Waller and His Orchestra / Jul. 16, 1938–Oct. 18, 1938 / Sandy Hook ✦✦✦✦
This very enjoyable CD contains three radio broadcasts featuring Fats Waller and his Rhythm in 1938. Despite some dated chatter (and not-so-subtle racism) from a radio announcer, the music on these live performances is quite spirited with Waller singing and playing heated stride piano with his sextet. While trumpeter Herman Autrey and Gene Sedric's reeds are major assets, Fats Waller is virtually the whole show, really driving his sidemen and stimulating both a memorable party atmosphere and creative swinging jazz. —*Scott Yanow*

Fine Arabian Stuff / Nov. 20, 1939 / Muse ✦✦✦
The music on this LP was all recorded in one day and finds an unaccompanied Fats Waller dealing with a variety of folk songs and spirituals, much of it out of character with the stereotype of Waller as a happy-go-lucky partying extrovert. He plays piano on the first six numbers while performing in a much more somber mood on organ for the last seven songs. Not essential music but Fats Waller collectors will want this unusual set. —*Scott Yanow*

Last Testament: 1943 / Jan. 23, 1943–Sep. 23, 1943 / Alamac ✦✦✦
This out-of-print budget LP contains some of Waller's last recordings, mostly V-Discs in which he sings and plays piano solo (although "That Ain't Right" is from the soundtrack of the film

Stormy Weather). Waller, who died at the age of 39 on Dec. 15, 1943, never had a chance to decline. One wonders how he would have handled the emergence of bebop and television in the years following his death. In at least his music was creative, spirited and joyful up until the end. —*Scott Yanow*

Fats at the Organ / Feb. 19, 1981–Feb. 21, 1981 / ASV/Living Era ✦✦✦

This is a rather unusual LP, for it features Fats Waller's player-piano rolls (dating from 1923–27) being pumped through a pipe organ. The liner notes go into detail about the difficulties involved (for example the organ has 61 notes while the piano has 88) but the results are quite successful. Since Waller's piano solos tended to be much more jubilant and harder-swinging than his comparatively somber organ playing, it is fascinating to hear him suddenly romping on the organ. —*Scott Yanow*

George Wallington (Giacinto Figlia)

b. Oct. 27, 1924, Palermo, Sicily, Italy, **d.** Feb. 15, 1993, New York, NY
Piano / Bop
George Wallington was one of the first and best bop pianists, ranking up there with Al Haig just below Bud Powell. He was also the composer of two bop standards that caught on for a time: "Lemon Drop" and "Godchild." Born in Sicily, Wallington and his family moved to the U.S. in 1925. He arrived in New York in the early '40s and was a member of the first bop group to play on 52nd Street, Dizzy Gillespie's combo of 1943–44. After spending a year with Joe Marsala's band, Wallington played with the who's who of bop during 1946–52 including Charlie Parker, Serge Chaloff, Allan Eager, Kai Winding, Terry Gibbs, Brew Moore, Al Cohn, Gerry Mulligan, Zoot Sims and Red Rodney. He toured Europe with Lionel Hampton's ill-fated big band of 1953 and during 1954–60 he led groups in New York that included among its up-and-coming sidemen Donald Byrd and Jackie McLean (the latter succeeded by Phil Woods). Then in 1960 Wallington gave up on the music business altogether and retired to work in his family's air-conditioning company. Twenty-four years later he re-emerged, recording two albums of original material before time ran out. —*Scott Yanow*

The George Wallington Trio / May 1949–Nov. 1951 / Savoy Jazz ✦✦✦✦

Live: at Cafe Bohemia / Sep. 9, 1955 / Original Jazz Classics ✦✦✦✦✦

This live set, although led by pianist George Wallington, is most significant for giving listeners early examples of the playing of trumpeter Donald Byrd and altoist Jackie McLean; bassist Paul Chambers and drummer Art Taylor complete the quintet. The music, although comprised mostly of group originals (other than "Johnny One Note" and Oscar Pettiford's "Bohemia After Dark"), is essentially a bebop jam, and it is particularly interesting to hear just how much McLean was influenced by Charlie Parker at this point (although his sound was already quickly recognizable). This was a solid if short-lived group and their brand of hard bop will be enjoyed by straight-ahead jazz fans. The CD reissue adds a second version of "Minor March" to the original program. —*Scott Yanow*

● Jazz for the Carriage Trade / Jan. 20, 1956 / Original Jazz Classics ✦✦✦✦✦

This was a Jan. 20, 1956 date with Donald Byrd (trumpet), Phil Woods (alto sax), Teddy Kotick (bass) and Art Taylor (drums), and it was also reissued as part of a two-fer. The session had a lasting hard bop edge and closely parallels what the Messengers were sounding like at the time. It was an exemplary sample of New York style bop. —*Bob Rusch, Cadence*

The New York Scene / Mar. 1, 1957 / Original Jazz Classics ✦✦✦✦✦

Before he retired from music in 1960, pianist George Wallington led a series of excellent bop-based quintet albums. For this particular CD (a reissue of a date originally put out by New Jazz), Wallington heads a group featuring altoist Phil Woods, trumpeter Donald Byrd, bassist Teddy Kotick and drummer Nick Stabulas. With the exception of the standard "Indian Summer," the repertoire is pretty obscure (with now-forgotten originals by Byrd, Woods and Mose Allison in addition to "Graduation Day") but of a consistent high quality. The emphasis is on hard-swinging and this set should greatly please straight-ahead jazz fans. —*Scott Yanow*

Leonard Feather Presents / Jul. 1957–Sep. 1957 / VSOP ✦✦✦

The sessions on this LP reissue were originally organized by Leonard Feather to pay tribute to the bop era. The 11 selections (all dating from the mid-to-late '40s) feature pianist George Wallington (who is actually the set's leader), altoist Phil Woods, either Idrees Sulieman or Thad Jones on trumpet, bassist Curley Russell and either Denzil Best or Art Taylor on drums. About the only surprise occurs on "Salt Peanuts" which has an off-key "vocal" from five-year-old Baird Parker, son of the late Charlie Parker. Otherwise the playing of Woods makes this a worthwhile session for bop fans. —*Scott Yanow*

Dance of the Infidels / Nov. 14, 1957 / Savoy ✦✦✦✦

Bebop is the main focus on this fine Savoy session. A young and not fully developed Donald Byrd is on trumpet, altoist Phil Woods is in exuberant form and the pianist/leader is accompanied by bassist Knobby Totah and drummer Nick Stabulas. In addition to Bud Powell's "Dance of the Infidels" and Dizzy Gillespie's "Ow," the group plays two of Wallington's pieces and Byrd's "'S Make 'T." Strangely enough, considering the consistent quality of his recordings, this would be George Wallington's final session as a leader for quite some time. He retired from music in 1960 and did not return until 1984. This LP (which is sure to be reissued on CD in Denon's massive *Savoy* series) is worth picking up for the playing of Wallington and Woods. —*Scott Yanow*

Virtuoso / 1984 / Interface ✦✦✦

Pleasure of a Jazz Inspiration / Aug. 19, 1985 / VSOP ✦✦✦✦✦

Pianist George Wallington, who retired from jazz in 1960, returned in the mid-'80s and recorded three solo albums; he passed away in 1993. This CD, which contains eight originals (which are subtitled *A Jazz Tone Poem*), is not as adventurous as one might think. Actually a lot of the songs are based on fairly common chord changes. Wallington plays quite well (mixing in his dominant Bud Powell influence with touches of Teddy Wilson), making one regret that the important bop-based pianist took so many years off. At least his final efforts were impressive, and this CD offers some fine examples of his playing after his "comeback." —*Scott Yanow*

Jack Walrath

b. May 5, 1946, Stuart, FL
Trumpet / Post Bop
An often exciting, thoughtful trumpeter and good arranger, Jack Walrath has steadily gained attention and exposure through his contributions to outstanding sessions. Walrath began playing trumpet at nine and studied at Berklee in the mid and late '60s while working with other students and backing up R&B vocalists. He moved to the West Coast in 1969, and co-led the bands Change with Gary Peacock and Revival with Glenn Ferris. Walrath also toured a year with Ray Charles. Walrath relocated to New York in the early 70's and worked with Latin bands before playing with Charles Mingus from 1974 to 1979, an association that gave him a certain amount of recognition. Walrath contributed some arrangements and orchestrations to Mingus' final recordings. In the 1980s and 90s he led his own bands, toured Europe with Dannie Richmond and the British group Spirit Level, worked with Charlie Persip's Superband and Richard Abrams, and helped keep the music of Charles Mingus alive by playing with Mingus Dynasty. He's recorded as a leader for Gatemouth, Stash, Blue Note and Muse. —*Ron Wynn*

Demons in Pursuit / Aug. 21, 1979–Aug. 22, 1979 / Gatemouth ✦✦✦✦

Trumpeter Jack Walrath has long been best known for his important association with Charles Mingus. For his debut as a leader, Walrath mixed together a wide variety of different stylists including Mingus' drummer Dannie Richmond, the harmonically advanced Jim McNeely on both piano and organ, the unique guitarist John Scofield and bassist Ray Drummond. Together they perform six of Walrath's quirky originals which, with titles such as "King Duke," "Ray Charles on Mars," "Spliptzill Rohenusi" and "Demons in Pursuit," lets one know that the music will not be all that predictable. Not everything works (the organ sounds dated) but overall this adventurous set is a successful effort. —*Scott Yanow*

Revenge of the Fat People / May 23, 1981 / Stash ✦✦✦✦✦

In Europe / Jul. 1982 / SteepleChase ✦✦✦

A Plea for Sanity / Sep. 1982 / Stash ✦✦✦✦

Drummerless trio with pianist Michael Cochran and bassist Anthony Cox. All originals. A delight. —*Michael G. Nastos*

At the Umbria Jazz Festival, Vol. 1 / Jul. 18, 1983 / Red ✦✦✦
Wholly Trinity / Mar. 1986–Apr. 1986 / Muse ✦✦✦✦✦
Killer Bunnies / May 12, 1986–May 13, 1986 / Spotlite ✦✦✦✦
★ Master of Suspense / Sep. 19, 1986 / Blue Note ✦✦✦✦✦
Septet cuts, exceptional playing by Walrath, Steve Torre (tb), and James Williams (p). —*Ron Wynn*

Neohippus / Aug. 19, 1988–Aug. 24, 1988 / Blue Note ✦✦✦✦✦
John Abercrombie slashes away on guitar. Rick Margitza (reeds), saxophonist for Miles Davis at the time, is an effective soloist. —*Ron Wynn*

Out of the Tradition / May 7, 1990 / Muse ✦✦✦✦
Gut Feelings / Sep. 10, 1990 / Muse ✦✦✦
Serious Hang / 1992 / Muse ✦✦✦✦
Jack Walrath and his Masters of Suspense turn to an idiom that was once among jazz's more popular, but in recent years has been almost ignored—funk/soul-jazz. Besides a decent remake of James Brown's "Get on the Good Foot," the group opens with "Anya and Liz on the Veranda" and also does Charles Mingus' "Better Get Hit in Your Soul." Walrath's trumpet and fluegelhorn solos are always intense and occasionally exciting; only the Brown remake falters, mainly because it was a textbook funk piece and doesn't translate well to a straight instrumental setting. Otherwise, the Masters of Suspense do a good job of displaying their soul-jazz chops. —*Ron Wynn*

Portraits In Ivory & Brass / Jun. 25, 1992–Jun. 26, 1992 / Mapleshade ✦✦✦✦✦

Cedar Walton

b. Jan. 17, 1934, Dallas, TX
Piano / Hard Bop
A classy, sophisticated, but hard bop expressive and skilled pianist, Cedar Walton has proved the ideal accompanist for numerous combos. He's never been a "star" but has provided tasteful, challenging backing and concise, impressive solos in many situations. Walton learned piano from his mother and later studied music at the University of Denver in the early '50s. He went to New York in 1955 but was drafted by the Army. He played with Leo Wright, Don Ellis and Eddie Harris while stationed in Germany. Walton recorded with Kenny Dorham after returning to New York then played in J.J. Johnson's group (1958–60) and took McCoy Tyner's place with the Jazztet (1960–61). Walton played in Art Blakey's Jazz Messengers during a peak period (1961–64). He replaced Bobby Timmons and was in the very strong edition that also included Wayne Shorter and Freddie Hubbard. Walton was Abbey Lincoln's accompanist (1965–66) then became Prestige's house pianist during 1967–69. Walton played in a group with Hank Mobley in the early 1970s, rejoined Blakey in the mid-1970s for a tour of Japan and started a quartet that in the 70s and 80s included Clifford Jordan, George Coleman or Bob Berg on tenors and fellow rhythm section mates Sam Jones and Billy Higgins. The group took the name Eastern Rebellion in 1975. Walton had a brief fling with fusion and jazz-rock in the early '70s, heading a group called Soundscapes that featured electric instrumentation, funk, fusion and rock rhythms and compositions. He also did some dates for RCA under the label of Mobius. Walton toured Europe, Japan and the United States in the late '70s in a trio with Higgins, and in the 1980s, Walton has been a member of the Timeless All-Stars. He has also played with J.J. Johnson's quintet and toured with his own trios. Walton, who remains greatly in demand, has recorded for many labels through the years including Blue Note, Prestige, Muse, Timeless, Steeplechase, CBS, Clean Cuts and Red. —*Ron Wynn and Scott Yanow*

Cedar! / Jul. 10, 1967 / Original Jazz Classics ✦✦✦✦
Excellent 1967 session with Kenny Dorham (tpt) and Junior Cook (ts). Typically no-frills, emphatic pieces and solos. —*Ron Wynn*

Spectrum / May 24, 1968 / Prestige ✦✦✦
Two of pianist Cedar Walton's lesser-known Prestige albums (*Spectrum* and *The Electric Boogaloo Song*) are combined on this single CD reissue. With strong assistance from trumpeter Blue Mitchell, tenor saxophonist Clifford Jordan and one of two rhythm sections (either Richard Davis or Bob Cranshaw on bass and Jack DeJohnette or Mickey Roker on drums), Walton performs six of his originals ("Ugetsu" is best known while "The Electric Boogaloo Song" was an attempt at a hit), two standards, Clifford Jordan's "Impressions of Scandinavia" and Calvin Massey's "Lady

Charlotte." The music, essentially advanced hard bop with a few odd twists, is well played if not essential. —*Scott Yanow*

Soul Cycle / Jul. 25, 1969 / Original Jazz Classics ✦✦
Half of this Prestige set by Cedar Walton, which has been reissued on CD in the OJC series, is frankly commercial, with the pianist switching to electric keyboard; "My Cherie Amour" is a low point. However, there are a couple of acoustic trio features with bassist Reggie Workman and drummer Albert "Tootie" Heath, and some worthwhile if not particularly essential solos from James Moody on tenor and flute. Walton was trying to widen his audience a bit at the time—not a bad goal, except that he felt he had to water down his music on a few of these numbers. A mixed bag. —*Scott Yanow*

★ Breakthrough / Feb. 22, 1972 / Muse ✦✦✦✦✦
As strong as pianist Cedar Walton plays on his session, the main honors are taken by two of his sidemen. Tenor saxophonist Hank Mobley, whose career was about to go into a complete eclipse, is in brilliant form, showing how much he had grown since his earlier days. Baritonist Charles Davis, who too often through the years has been used as merely a section player, keeps up with Mobley and engages in a particularly memorable tradeoff on the lengthy title cut. Mobley is well showcased on "Summertime," Davis switches successfully to soprano on "Early Morning Stroll" and Walton (with the trio) somehow turns the "Theme from *Love Story*" into jazz. Highly recommended. —*Scott Yanow*

A Night at Boomer's, Vol. 1 / Jan. 4, 1973 / Muse ✦✦✦✦✦
A Night at Boomer's, Vol. 2 / Jan. 4, 1973 / Muse ✦✦✦✦✦
Firm Roots / Apr. 1974 / Muse ✦✦✦✦
Eastern Rebellion, Vol. 1 / 1975 / Timeless ✦✦✦✦
George Coleman (ts) at his peak, brilliant playing. —*Ron Wynn*
Mobius / 1975 / RCA ✦✦✦
The Pentagon / May 17, 1976 / Inner City ✦✦✦✦
First Set / Jan. 1977+Oct. 1, 1977 / SteepleChase ✦✦✦
Second Set / Jan. 1977+Oct. 1, 1977 / SteepleChase ✦✦✦
Third Set / Jan. 1977+Oct. 1, 1977 / SteepleChase ✦✦✦
Animation / 1978 / Columbia ✦✦✦
The Maestro / Dec. 15, 1980 / Muse ✦✦✦✦
Piano Solos / Aug. 1981 / Clean Cuts ✦✦✦✦
● Among Friends / Jul. 1982 / Evidence ✦✦✦✦✦
Cedar Walton is one of jazz's great accompanists and session pianists, but he is even more accomplished in trio situations, where he gets the space to fully develop ideas and offer insightful interpretations. This set includes superb reworkings of the Thelonious Monk classics "Ruby My Dear" and "Off Minor," plus his own mid-tempo gem "Midnight Waltz" and the lushly performed "My Foolish Heart" that includes a nice vibes solo from special guest Bobby Hutcherson. Walton works with a thoroughly experienced rhythm section in bassist Buster Williams and drummer Billy Higgins. These are three longtime musical associates demonstrating what polished, distinctive jazz is all about. —*Ron Wynn*

The Trio, Vol. 1 / Mar. 1985 / Red ✦✦✦✦
The Trio, Vol. 2 / Mar. 1985 / Red ✦✦✦✦
The Trio, Vol. 3 / Mar. 1985 / Red ✦✦✦✦
Cedar Walton / Apr. 19, 1985 / Timeless ✦✦✦✦✦
Bluesville Time / Apr. 21, 1985 / Criss Cross ✦✦✦✦
Blues for Myself / Feb. 1986 / Red ✦✦✦✦
Plays / Sep. 29, 1986–Sep. 30, 1986 / Delos ✦✦✦✦✦
Up Front / Oct. 31, 1986 / Timeless ✦✦✦✦
Lush Life / Plays the Music of Billy Strayhorn / Sep. 29, 1988–Sep. 30, 1988 / Discovery ✦✦✦✦
As Long As There's Music / Jul. 1990 / Muse ✦✦✦✦✦
My Funny Valentine / Feb. 1991 / Evidence ✦✦✦✦
Live at Maybeck Recital Hall / Aug. 1992 / Concord Jazz ✦✦✦✦✦
Manhattan Afternoon / Dec. 26, 1992 / Criss Cross ✦✦✦✦

Carlos Ward

b. May 1, 1940, Ancon, Panama Canal Zone
Alto Saxophone, Tenor Saxophone / Post Bop
A versatile alto tenor saxophonist and flutist, Carlos Ward's played African music, hard bop, disco and R&B with fine jazz bands and

chart-topping funk groups. He moved from the Panama Canal Zone where he was born to Seattle in the '50s, and began playing clarinet. Ward switched to sax in the mid-'50s, and worked in various rock bands. He played in a military band during Army service in the early '60s, at one point being stationed in Germany. Ward remained in Europe after his discharge, and worked with Abdullah Ibrahim, Don Cherry and Karl Berger. He returned to Seattle in 1965 and worked with John Coltrane in concert that fall. He moved to New York and played with Coltrane again as well as Sunny Murray and Sam Rivers. Ward traveled to the West Coast with Murray in 1967, settling in San Francisco. He came back to New York in 1969 and recorded with B.T. Express, while also playing with Murray at the Newport Jazz Festival, and working with Rashied Ali. He later joined the Jazz Composer's Orchestra Association and worked with a group that included David Izenzon, Berger, Gato Barbieri and Barry Altschul. Ward played in bands led by Carla Bley, Ibrahim and Cherry in the 1980s, and in 1986 he was the first replacement for Jimmy Lyons in the Cecil Taylor unit. —*Ron Wynn and Michael G. Nastos*

● **Lito** / Jul. 9, 1988 / Leo ✦✦✦✦✦
Live date at the North Sea Jazz Festival for saxophonist/flutist with quartet featuring trumpeter Woody Shaw. Extended work. Excellent. —*Michael G. Nastos*

David S. Ware

b. Nov. 7, 1949, Plainfield, NJ
Tenor Saxophone / Avant-Garde, Free Jazz
A powerhouse tenor saxophonist, David S. Ware's swirling solos with their overblowing, energized screams and intensity make him one of the few current players willing to display ties to the '60s free style. Ware also smartly employs multiphonics and false fingerings. He played baritone, alto and tenor sax as a teen, and attended Berklee from 1967 to 1969. Ware formed the group Apogee in 1970 and played in Boston until they relocated to New York. Ware played in Cecil Taylor's orchestra during his 1974 Carnegie Hall concert. He spent two years with Andrew Cyrille in the mid-'70s, while also working in a trio with trumpeter Ralphe Malik and toured Europe with Taylor. Ware and Barry Harris made a duet album in 1977, and Ware and Cyrille rejoined forces, recording in 1978 and 1980. Ware recorded as a leader in the 1980s and 90s, most notably for DIW/Columbia and Silkheart. —*Ron Wynn*

Passage to Music / Apr. 4, 1988–Apr. 5, 1988 / Silkheart ✦✦✦✦✦
Great Bliss, Vol. 1 / Jan. 1990 / Silkheart ✦✦✦✦
★ **Flight of I** / Dec. 1991 / Columbia ✦✦✦✦✦
Third Ear Recitation / Oct. 14, 1992–Oct. 15, 1992 / DIW ✦✦✦✦

Wilbur Ware

b. Sep. 8, 1923, Chicago, IL, **d.** Sep. 9, 1979, Philadelphia, PA
Bass / Hard Bop
A wonderful, exciting bassist. Wilbur Ware managed to overcome some stylistic limitations by his ability to break up the beats, and substitute tones and notes in his solos. He could sometimes befuddle others on the bandstand by this method, but he always managed to link his statements thematically and resolve things to the success of the composition. He had great touch and articulation but didn't approach or roam over the instrument like some other players, preferring to emphasize the lower end in his playing. Ware was a self-taught banjo player and his foster father made him a bass. He played in string bands around Chicago, then worked in groups led by Stuff Smith, Roy Eldridge and Sonny Stitt in the late 40s. During the 50s he periodically had his own bands, while working with Eddie "Cleanhead" Vinson, Art Blakey, Buddy DeFranco, Thelonious Monk, and J.R. Monterose. He returned to Chicago from New York in 1959, went back to New York in the '60s, and reunited with Monk in 1970. The last part of his life he played with Clifford Jordan and Paul Jeffrey, led a group that recorded on Fantasy in the late-'50s and included Johnny Griffin, John Jenkins and Junior Mance. —*Ron Wynn*

● **Chicago Sound** / Oct. 16, 1957–Nov. 10, 1957 / Original Jazz Classics ✦✦✦✦✦
Legendary bassist. With Johnny Griffin (ts) and John Jenkins (as). A classic. —*Michael G. Nastos*

Butch Warren

b. Sep. 8, 1939, Washington, D.C.
Bass / Hard Bop
A prolific bassist who began his career at 14, Butch Warren has

played in swing, bebop, and hard bop sessions, working with musicians as diverse as Gene Ammons and Thelonious Monk. He's one of the great accompanists, known for the creative use of walking lines and tight, bluesy phrases as well as nicely placed accents. Warren played bass in his father's band as a teen, then worked in the Washington D.C. area with Gene Ammons and Stuff Smith in the late '50s. He moved to New York to play with Kenny Dorham in 1958, and served as house musician at Blue Note in the early '60s. Warren recorded with Jackie McLean, Donald Byrd, Herbie Hancock, Joe Henderson, Sonny Clark and Dexter Gordon, while he also played in New York clubs. He was Monk's bassist in 1963 and 1964, appearing on various recordings and touring Japan and Europe. Warren appeared on television in Washington upon his return and backed R&B vocal groups like the Platters. Illness forced a temporary retirement in the late '60s and early '70s, but he returned in the mid-'70s, playing with Howard McGhee and Richie Cole, and continued part-time. Warren's bass can be heard on CD reissues of such classics as *Miles and Monk at Newport, It's Monk's Time,* Sonny Clark's *Leapin' and Lopin'* and Herbie Hancock's *Takin' Off.* —*Ron Wynn*

Earle Warren

b. Jul. 1, 1914, Springfield, OH, **d.** 1995
Alto Saxophone / Swing
Earle Warren was Count Basie's longtime lead altoist and occasional pop ballad singer. He played piano, banjo and ukulele in a family band before taking up the saxophone, eventually settling on the alto. He led bands in the Midwest during part of the 1930s before joining Basie in 1937. Until the breakup of the band at the end of 1949, Warren was a strong presence in the saxophone section even though he rarely was given a full solo. In later years he worked as manager for a variety of R&B acts, had opportunities to solo with Buck Clayton's groups, was featured in the 1970s film *Born to Swing* and headed the Countsmen starting in 1973. —*Scott Yanow*

● **The Count's Men** / Jul. 9, 1985 / Muse ✦✦✦✦
Three of Count Basie's alumni (altoist Earle Warren, trombonist Eddie Durham and bassist Jimmy Lewis) team together with pianist Don Coates and drummer Clarence "Tootsie" Bean for a set of music dominated by Count Basie-associated material. It is a particular pleasure to hear Warren and Durham at this late stage in their careers. It had been quite a while since Warren (who takes five vocals) had recorded as a singer and Durham had been off records for a long time. Nothing that unusual occurs (one wishes that they had added a trumpeter, say Harry "Sweets" Edison) but this historical set always swings. —*Scott Yanow*

Washboard Rhythm Kings

Group / Classic Jazz
This recording group changed personnel from session to session although it always featured a washboard player and usually a couple of horns along with spirited group vocals. The emphasis was on basic goodtime music that fell between Dixieland and swing. It debuted as the Alabama Washboard Stompers in 1930, became the Washboard Rhythm Kings in 1931 and by 1934-35 was known as the Georgia Washboad Stompers. Some of the personnel have never been identified but among the known players are guitarist Teddy Bunn, trumpeters Taft Jordan and Valaida Snow, singer Leo Watson and such regulars as singer Jake Fenderson, Steve Washington on banjo and vocals and Ben Smith on clarinet and alto. —*Scott Yanow*

● **Washboard Rhythm Kings, Vol. 1** / Apr. 2, 1931–Mar. 1, 1932 / Collectors Classics ✦✦✦✦✦
The Washboard Rhythm Kings (whose personnel changed from session to session) was an unusual group to be on records during the early part of the Depression for it was a goodtime band usually featuring a washboard, spirited vocals, an occasional kazoo and a few horns. There were no major soloists in the group (guitarist Teddy Bunn, who is on ten of the 24 selections on this first volume, comes the closest), and they mostly covered current hits from other artists (including on this CD "Minnie the Moocher," "Walkin' My Baby Back Home," "You Rascal You," "I'm Crazy 'Bout My Baby," "Stardust" and "Georgia on My Mind") but they were always a fun band to hear. This Swedish import CD has the Washboard Rhythm Kings' first two dozen recordings. —*Scott Yanow*

Dinah Washington (Ruth Lee Jones)

b. Aug. 29, 1924, Tuscaloosa, AL, d. Dec. 14, 1963, Detroit, MI
Vocals / Blues, Standards

One of the most versatile and gifted vocalists in American popular music history, Dinah Washington made extraordinary recordings in jazz, blues, R&B and light pop contexts and could have done the same in gospel had she chosen to record in that mode. But the former Ruth Jones didn't believe in mixing the secular and spiritual, and once she'd entered the non-religious music world professionally, refused to include gospel in her repertoire. Washington's penetrating, high-pitched voice, incredible sense of drama and timing, crystal clear enunciation and equal facility with sad, bawdy, celebratory or rousing material enabled her to sing any and everything with distinction. Washington played piano and directed her church choir growing up in Chicago. For a while she did split her time between clubs and singing and playing piano in Salle Martin's gospel choir as Ruth Jones. There's some dispute about the origin of her name. Some sources say the manager of the Garrick Stage Bar gave her the name Dinah Washington; other say it was Hampton who selected it. It is undisputed Hampton heard and was impressed by Washington, who'd been discovered by manager Joe Glaser. She worked in Hampton's band from 1943 to 1946. Some of her biggest R&B hits were written by Leonard Feather, the distinguished critic who was a successful composer in the '40s. Washington dominated the R&B charts in the late '40s and '50s, but also did straight jazz sessions for EmArcy and Mercury, with horn accompanists including Clifford Brown, Clark Terry and Maynard Ferguson, and pianists Wynton Kelly, a young Joe Zawinul and Andrew Hill. She wanted to record what she liked, regardless of whether it was considered suitable, and in today's market would be a crossover superstar.

"What a Diff'rence a Day Makes." From that point forward nearly all of her recordings were slow ballads with accompaniment from faceless orchestras that would not have been out of place on a country record! Although she did have a few more hits (including some duets with Brook Benton), Washington's post-1958 output has not dated well at all, unlike the music from her first 15 years of recordings. However she was only 39 and still in peak musical form when she died from an accidental overdose of diet pills and alcohol in 1963. Dinah Washington remains the biggest influence on most Black female singers (particularly in R&B and soul) who have come to prominence since the mid-1950s. Virtually all of her recordings are currently in print on CDs including a massive reissue series of her Mercury and EmArcy sessions. —*Ron Wynn and Dan Morgenstern*

Slick Chick: R&B Years / Dec. 29, 1943–Nov. 17, 1954 / EmArcy ✦✦✦✦✦

This double LP has the cream of Dinah Washington's early recordings. She recorded extensively for Mercury and EmArcy and all of the performances are available on multi-disc sets but, for those listeners who want just a sampling of Dinah Washington at her best, this two-fer is the one to get. All 16 of her R&B hits from 1949–54 are here plus her very first recording session (which is highlighted by the original version of "Evil Gal Blues") and seven other selections. Whether backed by the Gerald Wilson Orchestra, Tab Smith, Cootie Williams, an all-star unit headed by drummer Jimmy Cobb or studio orchestras, she is in superb form. —*Scott Yanow*

Wise Woman Blues / 1943–Aug. 26, 1963 / Rosetta ✦✦✦✦

This Rosetta LP draws its material from three sources. Eight of the 15 recordings are from Dinah Washington's Apollo sessions of December 1945 (all of which are included on Delmark's CD). Six songs are taken from live performances with Lionel Hampton's orchestra during 1943–63 and "Do Nothing Till You Hear from Me" is a real rarity with Washington backed by Duke Ellington's Orchestra in 1963. The extensive liner notes (which have ten pictures of the singer from various stages of her career) are a major plus. —*Scott Yanow*

Mellow Mama / Dec. 10, 1945–Dec. 13, 1945 / Delmark ✦✦✦✦✦

Dinah Washington's first solo recordings (with the exception of a session supervised by Lionel Hampton in 1943) are included on this Delmark repackaging of her Apollo sides. Recorded in Los Angeles during a three-day period, the 12 selections feature the singer with a swinging jazz combo that has tenor saxophonist Lucky Thompson, trumpeter Karl George, vibraphonist Milt Jackson and bassist Charles Mingus among its eight members. The 21-year-old Washington was already quite distinctive at this

early stage and easily handles the blues and jive material with color and humor. Recommended despite the brevity (34 minutes) of the CD. —*Scott Yanow*

★ **The Complete Dinah Washington on Mercury, Vol. 1 (1946–1949)** / Jan. 14, 1946–Sep. 27, 1949 / Mercury ✦✦✦✦✦

All of Dinah Washington's studio recordings from 1946-61 have been reissued in definitive fashion by Polygram on seven three-CD sets. *Vol. 1* finds the youthful singer (who was 21 on the earliest sessions) evolving from a little-known but already talented singer to a best-selling R&B artist. Ranging from jazz and spirited blues to middle-of-the-road ballads, this set (as with the others in the *Complete* series) includes both gems and duds but fortunately the great majority fall into the former category. The backup groups include orchestras led by Gerald Wilson, Tab Smith, Cootie Williams, Chubby Jackson and Teddy Stewart, and there are a dozen strong numbers with just a rhythm section. The first five volumes in this series are highly recommended. —*Scott Yanow*

★ **The Complete Dinah Washington on Mercury, Vol. 2 (1950–1952)** / Feb. 7, 1950–May 6, 1952 / Mercury ✦✦✦✦✦

Dinah Washington was a best-selling artist on the R&B charts during this period, but she was also a very versatile singer who could easily handle swinging jazz, schmaltzy ballads, blues and novelties with equal skill. The second of these seven three-CD sets in Mercury's *Complete* program mostly finds Washington being accompanied by studio orchestras although the Ravens join her on two numbers and drummer Jimmy Cobb heads a couple of jazz groups (including one with both Ben Webster and Wardell Gray on tenors). Not every selection is a classic but the quality level is quite high and the packaging is impeccable. Recomended. —*Scott Yanow*

★ **Complete Dinah Washington on Mercury, Vol. 3 (1952–1954)** / 1952–Aug. 14, 1954 / Mercury ✦✦✦✦✦

Of the seven three-CD sets in Mercury's *Complete* series of Dinah Washington recordings, this is the most jazz-oriented one. The versatile singer participates in a very memorable jam session with an all-star group (featuring Clifford Brown, Maynard Ferguson and Clark Terry on trumpets!), meets up with Terry and tenor saxophonist Eddie Lockjaw Davis on another spontaneous date (highlighted by uptempo romps on "Bye Bye Blues" and "Blue Skies") and has several classic collaborations with the warm Lester Youngish tenor of Paul Quinichette. There are a few commercial sides with studio orchestras that are included (since they took place during the same period) but those are in the great minority on this essential volume. —*Scott Yanow*

★ **Dinah Jams** / Aug. 15, 1954 / EmArcy ✦✦✦✦✦

★ **Complete Dinah Washington on Mercury, Vol. 4 (1954–1956)** / Nov. 2, 1954–Apr. 25, 1956 / Mercury ✦✦✦✦✦

The fourth of seven three-CD sets in Mercury's *Complete* series alternates between strong swinging jazz with the likes of trumpeter Clark Terry, tenor saxophonist Paul Quinichette, pianist Wynton Kelly and altoist Cannonball Adderley, and middle-of-the-road pop performances with studio orchestras. The third volume is the strongest in this series but the first five sets all contain more than enough jazz to justify their purchase. *Vol. 4* really attests to Dinah Washington's versatility. —*Scott Yanow*

★ **Complete Dinah Washington on Mercury, Vol. 5 (1956–1958)** / Jun. 25, 1956–Jul. 6, 1958 / Mercury ✦✦✦✦✦

Mercury has given the great singer Dinah Washington the complete treatment with seven three-CD sets that contain all of her recordings during the 1946-61 period, practically her entire career. *Vol. 5* is the final volume to be highly recommended, since it has her final jazz recordings. On many of these performances she is backed by orchestras led by Quincy Jones, Ernie Wilkins (including a tribute to Fats Waller) or Eddie Chamblee in arrangements that often leave room for short statements from some of the sidemen; one of the albums with Chamblee has a full set of songs associated with Bessie Smith. *Vol. 5* (which contains only a few commercial sides) concludes with her strong performance at the 1958 Newport Jazz Festival. —*Scott Yanow*

The Swingin' Miss D / Dec. 4, 1956–Dec. 6, 1956 / EmArcy ✦✦✦✦✦

Dinah Washington Sings Fats Waller / 1957 / EmArcy ✦✦✦✦

The Bessie Smith Songbook / Dec. 30, 1957–Jan. 20, 1958 / EmArcy ✦✦✦

It was only natural that the "Queen of the Blues" should record songs associated with the "Empress of the Blues." The performances by the septet/octet do not sound like the 1920s and the purposely ricky-tick drumming is insulting, but Dinah Washington sounds quite at home on this music. "Trombone Butter" (featuring trombonist Quentin Jackson in Charlie Green's role), "You've Been a Good Ole Wagon," "After You've Gone" and "Back Water Blues" are highpoints as she overcomes the cornball arrangements. — *Scott Yanow*

What a Diff'rence a Day Makes! / Feb. 19, 1959–Aug. 1959 / Mercury ✦✦✦✦

Dinah Washington's career reached a turning point with this album. A very talented singer who could interpret jazz, blues, pop, novelties and religious songs with equal skill, Washington had an unexpected pop hit with her straightforward version of "What a Diff'rence a Day Makes." From then on she would only record with commercial studio orchestras and stick to middle-of-the-road pop music. This 1959 set is not as bad as what would follow, with such songs as "I Remember You," "I Thought About You," "Manhattan" and "A Sunday Kind of Love" all receiving tasteful melodic treatment (although no chances are taken) by Washington and an orchestra conducted and arranged by Belford Hendricks. — *Scott Yanow*

Complete Dinah Washington on Mercury, Vol. 6 (1958–1960) / Feb. 19, 1959–Nov. 12, 1960 / Mercury ✦✦

Up until 1959, Dinah Washington was able to excel in every musical setting that she found herself. A strong jazz/blues vocalist who had many R&B hits, Washington always sounded confident and soulful even when backed by insipid studio orchestras. However after her Feb. 19, 1959 recording of "What a Diff'rence a Day Makes" became a major hit and she gained fame, Dinah Washington stuck to safely commercial pop music. Even when she was singing superior songs during the 1959–63 period, Washington was always backed by large orchestras outfitted with extremely commercial charts better suited to country pop stars. The sixth in Mercury's series of three-CD sets starts with the Feb. 19 session and covers 21 months in Dinah Washington's career. Most of the 73 performances are difficult to sit through. *Scott Yanow*

Unforgettable / Aug. 1959–Jan. 15, 1961 / Mercury ✦✦

After her hit of "What a Diff'rence a Day Makes" in 1959, Dinah Washington largely discarded her blues and jazz roots (at least on recordings) and played the role of a pop star. This CD (which has the original LP program of 12 songs joined by six others) finds Washington singing brief (mostly under three-minute) versions of standards in hopes of gaining another hit. The backing is strictly commercial and, although some may enjoy "This Bitter Earth," "The Song Is Ended" and "A Bad Case of the Blues," the music is consistently predictable and disappointingly forgettable. — *Scott Yanow*

Complete Dinah Washington on Mercury, Vol. 7 (1961) / 1961 / Mercury ✦✦

The seventh and final volume in Mercury's *Complete* series of Dinah Washington's recordings has impeccable packaging and largely inferior music, at least from the jazz standpoint. After recording a surprising hit version of "What a Diff'rence a Day Makes" in 1959, the singer stuck exclusively to middle-of-the-road pop music with large string orchestras on her recordings. This three-CD set (which contains Washington's final 67 recordings for Mercury plus a recently discovered alternate take from 1947) is often difficult to sit through for it totally lacks surprises, suspense or spontaneity. For completists only, but get the first five volumes. — *Scott Yanow*

In Love / May 1962–Aug. 1962 / Roulette ✦✦

Dinah Washington's final four years of recordings (1959–63) were purely commercial. Even her mannerisms and phrasing leaned closer to middle-of-the-road pop than to her roots in jazz and blues. For this so-so Roulette CD, Washington interprets standards and current pop tunes in very predictable fashion. Everything has the impression of being planned in advance and the accompanying orchestra (arranged by Don Costa) is quite anonymous. Pass on this and get Dinah Washington's earlier jazz sides instead. — *Scott Yanow*

Dinah '63 / 1963 / Roulette ✦✦

It is fairly easy to evaluate Dinah Washington's recordings. Before 1959 virtually everything she recorded (even when in a commercial setting) is worth acquiring but the opposite is true of the

records from her final period (1959–63). As a pop artist, Washington was better than many but only a shadow of what she had been. Her pre-planned emotions and exaggerated mannerisms on her Roulette recordings (of which *Dinah '63* was one of her last) get tiring very fast. — *Scott Yanow*

Grover Washington, Jr.

b. Dec. 12, 1943, Buffalo, NY
Tenor Saxophone, Alto Saxophone, Soprano Saxophone / Soul Jazz, Crossover

Washington is one of the most commercially successful saxophonists in jazz history. A versatile reed specialist, he is equally at home on soprano, alto or tenor sax and has recorded on flute and baritone sax. A much more creative improviser than his hit-making saxophone competitors, Washington has had hits with almost everything he has done since his first album (*Inner City Blues*) for Kudu in 1971. His biggest albums, *Mister Magic* (Kudu) and *Winelight* (Elektra), have also spawned hit singles. His recordings for Kudu, Motown, Elektra and Columbia are mostly commercial in content but, given that, Washington's saxophone work is always first-rate and a good distance in front of his closest fusion rivals. — *Bob Porter*

Inner City Blues / Sep. 1971 / Motown ✦✦✦✦✦

Definitive early-'70s soul-jazz date. Washington has seldom been more convincing. — *Ron Wynn*

All the King's Horses / May 19, 1972–Jun. 1972 / Kudu ✦✦✦

★ **Mister Magic** / 1975 / Motown ✦✦✦✦✦

Feels So Good / May 1975+Jul. 1975 / Motown ✦✦✦

Reed Seed / 1979 / Motown ✦✦

Skylarkin' / Oct. 1979 / Motown ✦✦

Come Morning / 1980 / Elektra ✦✦

Background singers, synthesizers. This is more programmed mood music than jazz. Smooth and nice. Gold album. — *Michael Erlewine*

★ **Winelight** / Jun. 1980 / Elektra ✦✦✦✦✦

Grover Washington, Jr., has long been one of the leaders in what could be called rhythm & jazz, essentially R&B-influenced jazz. *Winelight* is one of his finest albums and not primarily because of the Bill Withers hit "Just the Two of Us." It is the five instrumentals that find Washington (on soprano, alto and tenor) really stretching out. If he had been only interested in sales, Washington's solos could have been half as long and he would have stuck closely to the melody. Instead he really pushes himself on some of these selections, particularly the title cut. A memorable set of high-quality and danceable soul jazz. — *Scott Yanow*

Inside Moves / Mar. 1984–Jun. 1984 / Elektra ✦✦✦✦

Strawberry Moon / 1987 / Columbia ✦✦✦

Then and Now / 1988 / Columbia ✦✦✦✦

This is one of Grover Washington, Jr.'s, occasional strays away from R&B-oriented jazz to play in a more straight-ahead setting. Switching between soprano, alto and tenor, Grover is accompanied by either Tommy Flanagan or Herbie Hancock on piano during five of the eight selections and he performs such numbers as Ron Carter's "Blues for D.P.," "Stolen Moments" and "Stella by Starlight" with swing and taste. Tenor saxophonist Igor Butman also helps out on three songs. Worth acquiring. — *Scott Yanow*

Time Out of Mind / 1989 / Columbia ✦✦✦

Next Exit / 1992 / Columbia ✦✦

All My Tomorrows / 1994 / Columbia ✦✦✦

Kazumi Watanabe

b. Oct. 14, 1953, Tokyo, Japan
Guitar / Fusion

Kazumi Watanabe has for the past 15 years been one of the top guitarists in fusion, a rock-oriented player whose furious power does not mask a creative imagination. Watanabe studied guitar at Tokyo's Yamaha Music School, and he was a recording artist while still a teenager. In 1979 he formed the group Kylyn and in 1983 he put together the Mobo band. Several of his recordings have been made available by Gramavision and they show that he ranks up with Al DiMeola (when he is electrified) and Scott Henderson among the pacesetters in the idiom. — *Scott Yanow*

Mermaid Boulevard / Dec. 17, 1977+Dec. 29, 1977 / Inner City ◆◆◆

Mobo, Vol. 1 / Aug. 14, 1983–Sep. 9, 1983 / Gramavision ◆◆◆◆
Mobo, Vol. 2 / Aug. 14, 1983–Sep. 9, 1983 / Gramavision ◆◆◆◆
Mobo Splash / Aug. 1985 / Gramavision ◆◆◆◆◆

★ **Spice of Life** / Oct. 1986–Nov. 1986 / Gramavision ◆◆◆◆◆
This album is a fusion-lover's dream. Bill Bruford (d) and Jeff Berlin (b) drive Watanabe. —*Paul Kohler*

Spice of Life Too / Feb. 1988–Mar. 1988 / Gramavision ◆◆◆◆
A continuation of *Spice of Life* with stronger compositions and a hint of softer tones, it's very nice! —*Paul Kohler*

Kilowatt / 1989 / Gramavision ◆◆◆
This release picks up where *Spice of Life Too* left off. Bunny Brunel's bass work shines. —*Paul Kohler*

Sadao Watanabe

b. Feb. 1, 1933, Utsunomiya, Japan
Alto Saxophone / Instrumental Pop, Bop
Sadao Watanabe has long had a split musical personality. He alternates excellent bebop dates with weak pop albums that pale next to the leaders of the idiom (such as Grover Washington, Jr., and David Sanborn). Watanabe learned clarinet and alto in high school, and in the 1950s he moved to Tokyo, joining Toshiko Akiyoshi's bop-oriented group in 1953. When the pianist moved to the U.S. in 1956, Watanabe took over the band. He attended Berklee during 1962–65 and had the opportunity to work with Gary McFarland, Chico Hamilton and Gabor Szabo. However Watanabe has remained mostly based in Japan throughout his career where he is a major influence on younger players. He has recorded steadily through the years, most notably with Chick Corea in New York (1970) and with the Galaxy All-Stars (1978). Watanabe's bop records are inspired by Charlie Parker but his Brazilian-flavored pop dates are instantly forgettable. —*Scott Yanow*

Nabasada and Charlie / Jun. 27, 1967 / Catalyst ◆◆◆◆
An excellent date with fellow saxophonist Charlie Mariano. Standards played with verve. —*Michael G. Nastos*

Round Trip / Jul. 15, 1974 / Vanguard ◆◆◆◆
With Chick Corea (k), Miroslav Vitous (b), and Jack DeJohnette (d). —*Michael G. Nastos*

☆ **I'm Old Fashioned** / May 22, 1976 / Inner City ◆◆◆◆◆
Most of the recordings of Japanese altoist Sadao Watanabe that have been made available in the U.S. through the years have been aimed at the so-called contemporary market. This one is one of the exceptions. Watanabe, joined by pianist Hank Jones, bassist Ron Carter and drummer Tony Williams, sticks to bebop. Three of the eight selections are Watanabe's but the other five include two Billy Strayhorn tunes and three other standards. This LP features Sadao Watanabe at his best. —*Scott Yanow*

My Dear Life / Apr. 16, 1977+Jun. 28, 1977 / Pro Arte ◆◆◆
Bird of Paradise / May 4, 1977 / Elektra ◆◆◆◆◆
Altoist Sadao Watanabe is considered one of Japan's top jazzmen. Some of his recordings are quite commercial but this particular one finds him paying tribute to Charlie Parker with what was called "the great jazz trio": pianist Hank Jones, bassist Ron Carter and drummer Tony Williams. The seven selections (four Bird compositions and three standards often played by Parker) are all given strong treatment by the quartet. Watanabe's true love is bebop and his solos here are very much in that tradition yet displaying a personality of his own. This LP will be difficult to find. —*Scott Yanow*

Autumn Blow / Oct. 23, 1977 / Inner City ◆◆◆
California Shower / Mar. 1978 / JVC ◆◆◆
Morning Island / Mar. 1979 / JVC ◆◆
Orange Express / Apr. 1981–May 1981 / Columbia ◆◆
Fill up the Night / Mar. 1983 / Elektra ◆◆◆
Rendezvous / Feb. 1984–Apr. 1984 / Elektra ◆◆◆
● **Parker's Mood** / Jul. 13, 1985 / Elektra ◆◆◆◆◆
Close to his best, both on his merit and thanks to aid from James Williams (p) and Jeff Watts (d). —*Ron Wynn*

Benny Waters

b. Jan. 23, 1902, Brighton, MD
Clarinet, Alto Saxophone, Tenor Saxophone / Swing
At the age of 94 in early 1996, Benny Waters was not only the old-

est active jazz musician but also a powerful altoist who would be considered impressive if he were only 50. Waters' personal history covers virtually the entire history of recorded jazz although he never really became a major name. He worked with Charlie Miller from 1918–21, studied at the New England Conservatory and became a teacher; one of his students was Harry Carney! Waters played, arranged for and recorded with Charlie Johnson's Paradise Ten (1925–32) an underrated group that also for a time included Benny Carter and Jabbo Smith. Waters, who was primarily a tenor saxophonist and an occasional clarinetist during this period, was influened to an extent by Coleman Hawkins, and he recorded with both Clarence Williams and King Oliver in the 1920s. Durng the next two decades Waters played in many groups including those led by Fletcher Henderson (for a few months), Hot Lips Page, Claude Hopkins and Jimmie Lunceford. He led his own unit during part of the 1940s, played with Roy Milton's R&B band and in 1949 went to France with the Jimmy Archey Dixieland group. Waters settled in Paris, working steadily although he was largely forgotten at home. By the 1980s he was visiting the U.S. more frequently and Waters is heard in brilliant form on a 1987 quartet set for Muse on which he plays tenor, alto and clarinet in addition to taking some effective vocals. A short time later he went blind and stuck exclusively to playing alto (on which he plays in a jump style reminiscent of Tab Smith that shows the occasional influence of John Coltrane!). The seemingly ageless Benny Waters has continued recording and performing with a remarkable amount of energy, touring with the Statesmen of Jazz in 1995 and creating some miraculous music. —*Scott Yanow*

And Traditional Jazz Studio, Prague / Jan. 12, 1976–Jan. 14, 1976 / I Giganti Del Jazz ◆◆◆◆

When You're Smiling / Aug. 28, 1980–Aug. 29, 1980 / Hep ◆◆◆◆◆

On the Sunny Side of the Street / Apr. 1981 / JSP ◆◆◆

★ **From Paradise (Small's) to Shangrila** / Jun. 26, 1987 / Muse ◆◆◆◆◆

Memories of the Twenties, Stomp Off / Sep. 22, 1988–Nov. 15, 1988 / Stomp Off ◆◆◆◆

Benny Waters: Freddy Randall Jazz Band / Dec. 5, 1992–Dec. 11, 1992 / Jazzology ◆◆◆

Swinging Again / May 4, 1993 / Jazzpoint ◆◆◆◆◆
Few people listening to this CD would guess that Benny Waters (heard exclusively on alto) was 91. Waters (a veteran of the 1920s) plays with such power and confidence throughout the standards and blues that he could pass for 51. With an excellent European rhythm section (pianist Thilo Wagner, bassist Jan Jankeje and drummer Gregor Beck) helping him out, the underrated but distinctive swing stylist is heard in top form, making this European import CD from Germany highly recommended. —*Scott Yanow*

Plays Songs Of Love / Jul. 28, 1993 / Jazzpoint ◆◆◆◆◆
The remarkable Benny Waters (who sticks here exclusively to alto) was 91 at the time of this recording yet still displays a strong tone and creative ideas. Assisted by guitarist Vic Juris and three nearly ancient veterans (pianist Red Richards, bassist Johnny Williams, Jr., and drummer Jackie Williams), Waters performs ten standards which have love as their main topic (including "What Is This Thing Called Love," "When Your Lover Has Gone," "Always," "Taking a Chance on Love," etc.) but fortunately varies the tempos (not every selection is taken at a ballad pace) and comes up with fresh ideas on these songs. Along with his other Jazzpoint release from the same period (*Swinging Again*), this CD is recommended. —*Scott Yanow*

Ethel Waters

b. Oct. 31, 1896, Chester, PA, **d.** Sep. 1, 1977, Chatsworth, CA
Vocals / Blues, Classic Jazz, Swing
Ethel Waters had a long and varied career and was one of the first true jazz singers to record. Defying racism with her talent and bravery, Waters became a stage and movie star in the 1930s and '40s without leaving the U.S. She grew up near Philadelphia and, unlike many of her contemporaries, developed a clear and easily understandable diction. Originally classified as a blues singer (and she could sing the blues almost on the level of a Bessie Smith), Waters' jazz-oriented recordings of 1921-28 swung before that term was even coined. A star early on at theatres and nightclubs, Waters introduced such songs as "Dinah," "Am I Blue" (in a 1929 movie) and "Stormy Weather." She made a smooth transition from

jazz singer of the 1920s to a pop music star of the '30s, and she was a strong influence on many vocalists including Mildred Bailey, Lee Wiley and Connee Boswell. Waters spent the latter half of the 1930s touring with a group headed by her husband, trumpeter Eddie Mallory, and appeared on Broadway (*Mamba's Daughter* in 1939) and in the 1943 film *Cabin in the Sky;* in the latter she introduced "Taking a Chance on Love," "Good for Nothing Joe" and the title cut. In later years Waters was seen in nonmusical dramatic roles and after 1960 she mostly confined her performances to religious work for the evangelist Billy Graham. The European Classics label has reissued all of Ethel Waters' prime recordings, and they still sound fresh and lively today. —*Scott Yanow*

1921–1923 / Mar. 21, 1921–Mar. 1923 / Classics ✦✦✦✦✦
Ethel Waters was one of the few singers from the early '20s whose early recordings are still quite listenable. This CD from the Classics label has her first 22 sides (many previously rare including five interesting instrumentals by Waters' band) and, although not on the same level as her performances from a few years later, the music is quite good for the time period. The sidemen are mostly obscure but include pianist Fletcher Henderson and cornetists Gus Aiken and Joe Smith with the highlights being "The New York Glide," "Down Home Blues," "There'll Be Some Changes Made" and "Midnight Blues." —*Scott Yanow*

1923–1925 / Mar. 1923–Jul. 28, 1925 / Classics ✦✦✦✦✦
The European Classics label's Ethel Waters program completely wipes out all of the other Waters reissues, for it reissues all of her recordings from her prime years in chronological order. Since the singer was very consistent, there are very few duds and many gems in these sets. This particular CD traces Ethel Waters during a two-year period; both the recording quality and her accompaniment greatly improve during this time; cornetist Joe Smith is a standout and pianist Fats Waller is present on "Pleasure Mad" and "Back-Bitin' Mamma." Highlights includes "You Can't Do What My Last Man Did," "Sweet Georgia Brown," "Go Back Where You Stayed Last Night" and "Sympathetic Dan." —*Scott Yanow*

Cabin in the Sky / 1923 1955 / Milan ✦✦✦

Ethel Waters' Greatest Years / Apr. 29, 1925–Mar. 30, 1934 / Columbia ✦✦✦✦✦
When this two-LP set was originally released, it was the definitive Ethel Waters reissue although now it has been succeeded by Classics' more complete CD program. However this two-fer is still the best single package ever released of the singer. The first album (covering 1925–28) focuses on her jazz years and has particularly strong contributions from cornetist Joe Smith and pianist James P. Johnson among others; "Sweet Georgia Brown," "Go Back Where You Stayed Last Night," "You Can't Do What My Last Man Did," "Sweet Man," "I've Found a New Baby," "Sugar," "Guess Who's in Town" and "My Handy Man" all qualify as classics. The second album mostly dates from 1929–34 and finds Waters joined by studio orchestras on most tracks. The emphasis is on ballads and sweet melodies, but Waters still excels, particularly on "Waiting at the End of the Road," "Porgy" and "A Hundred Years from Today." This set is highly recommended to listeners who do not have the Classics CDs. —*Scott Yanow*

★ **1925–1926** / Aug. 25, 1925–Jul. 29, 1926 / Classics ✦✦✦✦
This CD in the Classics complete Ethel Waters series contains plenty of gems including "You Can't Do What My Last Man Did," the original version of "Dinah," "Shake That Thing," "I've Found a New Baby" (which has some memorable cornet playing from Joe Smith), "Sugar" and "Heebies Jeebies." On "Maybe Not at All" Ethel Waters does eerie imitations of both Bessie Smith and Clara Smith. She had few competitors as a jazz singer during this era, and the mostly intimate recordings (12 of the 23 tracks find her backed by just a pianist) feature Waters at her best. —*Scott Yanow*

Ethel Waters on Stage/Screen (1925–1940) / Oct. 20, 1925–Nov. 7, 1940 / Columbia ✦✦✦✦
The Columbia LP features Ethel Waters performing 16 songs that debuted in shows or movies. With the exception of "Dinah" (this 1925 version is the original one) and "I'm Coming Virginia," all of the music dates from the 1929–40 era when Waters was better known as a musical comedy star than as a jazz singer. However, although the backing is generally a bit commercial, her performances of such numbers as "You're Lucky to Me," "Stormy Weather," "Taking a Chance on Love" and "Cabin in the Sky" are consistently memorable and definitive. —*Scott Yanow*

Music Map

Vocal Groups

Although there have been many jazz-influenced vocal groups, there have beenrelatively few that consistently sing jazz.

Early Innovators
Boswell Sisters
Rhythm Boys
Mills Brothers

1930s/'40s
Spirits Of Rhythm
The Cats And A Fiddle
Slim & Slam
Mel-Tones

1950s/'60s
Lambert, Hendricks And Ross
Lambert, Hendricks And Bavan
Jackie & Roy

1980s/'90s
Manhattan Transfer (also performs pop music)
Take Six (a gospel group using jazz harmonies)
Hendricks Family
New York Voices
Beachfront Property

★ **1926–1929** / Sep. 14, 1926–May 14, 1929 / Classics ✦✦✦✦
Few female jazz singers were on Ethel Waters' level during this period, just Bessie Smith and Annette Hanshaw, and all three were quite different from each other. Waters has rarely sounded better than on the four numbers in which she is backed rather forcefully by pianist James P. Johnson (particularly "Guess Who's in Town" and "Do What You Did Last Night") but she is also in fine form on the other small-group sides. "I'm Coming Virginia," "Home," "Take Your Black Bottom Outside," "Someday Sweetheart" and "Am I Blue" (which she introduced) are among the many gems on this highly recommended entry in Classics' complete series. —*Scott Yanow*

1929–1931 / Jun. 6, 1929–Jun. 16, 1931 / Classics ✦✦✦✦✦
During the period covered in this CD from Classics' complete Ethel Waters series, the singer was quickly developing into a top musical comedy and Broadway star. Although her backup was not as jazz-oriented as previously (despite the presence of such players as clarinetist Benny Goodman, trombonist Toomy Dorsey, Jimmy Dorsey on clarinet and alto and trumpeter Manny Klein), Waters' renditions of many of these future standards are definitive, particularly "True Blue Lou," "Waiting at the End of the Road," "Porgy," "You're Lucky to Me" and "When Your Lover Has Gone." Superior jazz-oriented singing from one of the very best. —*Scott Yanow*

1931–1934 / Aug. 10, 1931–Sep. 5, 1934 / Classics ✦✦✦✦✦
Ethel Waters was one of the very few Black performers who was able to keep working in music during the early years of the Depression; in fact her fame grew during the period covered by this excellent CD from Classics' complete series. Among her back-

up musicians on these consistently excellent sides are violinist Joe Venuti, the Dorsey Brothers, trumpeter Bunny Berigan, trombonist Jack Teagarden, clarinetist Benny Goodman, members of the Chick Webb big band and the entire Duke Ellington orchestra (the latter on "I Can't Give You Anything but Love" and "Porgy"). High points include the Ellington tracks, "St. Louis Blues" (with the Cecil Mack Choir), the original version of "Stormy Weather," "A Hundred Years from Today" and a remake of "Dinah." Highly recommended as are all of the Ethel Waters classics discs. —*Scott Yanow*

Foremothers, Vol. 6 / Nov. 9, 1938–Aug. 15, 1939 / Rosetta ✦✦✦✦
This very attractive Rosetta LP (which has definitive liner notes and numerous pictures) includes all of singer Ethel Waters' 16 Bluebird recordings of 1938-39. She is accompanied by two different bands led by her husband (trumpeter Eddie Mallory) with Benny Carter on alto and clarinet and trombonist Tyree Glenn (doubling on vibes) among the sidemen. Waters was not a major part of the swing era but her own career (on stage and in films) was booming around this period. Her voice is heard in its prime on a variety of period pieces which are highlighted by "Old Man Harlem," "Georgia on My Mind," "Jeepers Creepers" and "They Say." —*Scott Yanow*

Performing In Person Highlights From Her Illustrious Career / 1957 / Monmouth-Evergreen ✦✦✦
Ethel Waters is heard at the twilight of her career during this live performance. Recorded a decade after her last studio recordings, this was the singer's final nonreligious album. Accompanied by pianist Reginald Beane, Waters revisits most of her hits ("Am I Blue," "Dinah," "Porgy," "Supper Time," "Stormy Weather" and a medley from "Cabin in the Sky") and shows that, even at this late stage, her voice was still quite expressive. This is an LP that her many fans will want to search for. —*Scott Yanow*

Doug Watkins

b. Mar. 2, 1934, Detroit, MI, d. Feb. 5, 1962, Holbrook, AZ
Bass / Hard Bop
A top-flight bassist who was extremely active during the '50s, Doug Watkins had established himself as a first-rate accompanist and tasteful soloist on several recordings with Prestige and through many associations with major players. His career was cut short by an automobile accident in 1962. Watkins worked in the early '50s with James Moody, then came back to his native Detroit to play with Barry Harris' trio. In that role, Watkins worked with Stan Getz, Charlie Parker and Coleman Hawkins. He moved to New York in 1954, and during the remainder of the decade played with Horace Silver, Kenny Dorham and Hank Mobley, worked at Minton's and was an original member of Art Blakey's Jazz Messengers. He began doing sessions with Prestige in the mid-'50s, and appeared on recordings by Gene Ammons, Sonny Rollins, Phil Woods, Art Farmer, Donald Byrd, Kenny Burrell and Mobley. He substituted for Charles Mingus when Mingus moved to piano on performances and recording sessions of the Jazz Workshop in 1960 and 1961. Watkins also did a couple of recordings as a leader for Transition and New Jazz. These are not available on CD, but he can be heard on reissues by Blakey, Rollins, Ammons, Mingus and others. —*Ron Wynn*

Watkins at Large / Dec. 8, 1956 / Transition ✦✦✦✦
● **Soulnik** / May 17, 1960 / Original Jazz Classics ✦✦✦✦✦

Julius Watkins

b. Oct. 10, 1921, Detroit, MI, d. Apr. 4, 1977, Short Hills, NJ
French Horn / Hard Bop
Julius Watkins was virtually the father of the jazz French horn. He started playing French horn at the age of nine although he worked with the Ernie Fields orchestra on trumpet (1943-46). In the late '40s he took some French horn solos on records by Kenny Clarke and Babs Gonzales and spent 1949 as a member of the Milt Buckner big band. After three years of study at the Manhattan School of Music, Watkins started appearing on small-group dates including a pair of notable sessions led by Thelonious Monk in 1953-54. He co-led Les Jazz Modes with Charlie Rouse in 1956-59, toured with Quincy Jones' big band (1959-61) did plenty of studio work (including the Miles Davis-Gil Evans collaborations) and recorded with Charles Mingus (in 1965 and 1971), Freddie Hubbard, John Coltrane (the *Africa* sessions) and the Jazz Composer's Orchestra among many others. —*Scott Yanow*

Bill Watrous

b. Jun. 8, 1939, Middletown, CT
Trombone, Leader / Bop
One of the finest bop-oriented trombonists of the past 25 years, Bill Watrous has had a low profile since moving to Los Angeles in the 1980s despite remaining quite active. Possessor of a beautiful tone and remarkable technique, Watrous has been constantly overlooked in jazz popularity polls of the past decade. His father was a trombonist and introduced Bill to music. He played in traditional jazz bands as a teenager and studied with Herbie Nichols while in the military. Watrous made his debut with Billy Butterfield and was one of the trombonists in Kai Winding's groups during 1962-67. He was a busy New York-based studio musician during the 1960s, working and recording with Quincy Jones, Maynard Ferguson, Johnny Richards and Woody Herman, playing in the television band for Merv Griffin's show (1965-68) and working on the staff of CBS (1967-69). After playing with the jazz-rock group Ten Wheel Drive in 1971, Watrous led his own big band (the Manhattan Wildlife Refuge) during 1973-77, recording two superb albums for Columbia. After moving to Los Angeles in the late '70s, Watrous continued working in the studios, appearing at jazz parties, playing in local clubs and leading an occasional big band. He has recorded as a leader for Columbia, Famous Door, Soundwings and GNP/Crescendo although only the latter releases are currently available on CD. —*Scott Yanow*

Bone Straight Ahead / Dec. 15, 1972–Jan. 4, 1973 / Famous Door ✦✦✦✦

Manhattan Wildlife Refuge / May 1, 1974–May 3, 1974 / Columbia ✦✦✦✦✦

★ **Tiger of San Pedro** / 1975 / Columbia ✦✦✦✦✦
Trombonist Bill Watrous' second and final big-band album for Columbia is the equal of his first. With such soloists as Watrous, trumpeter Danny Stiles and either Tom Garvin or Derek Smith on keyboards, this well-rounded set (which includes ballads, Latin pieces, the rockish "T.S., T.S." and some heated workouts) well deserves to be reissued on CD, along with the earlier *Manhattan Wildlife Refuge.* —*Scott Yanow*

I'll Play for you / May 19, 1980 / Famous Door ✦✦✦✦
Coronary Trombossa / Dec. 1980 / Famous Door ✦✦✦✦
Bill Watrous in London / Mar. 1982 / Mole ✦✦✦✦
Roarin' Back into New York, New York / Jul. 1982 / Famous Door ✦✦✦✦✦
Someplace Else / 1986 / Soundwings ✦✦
Reflections / 1987 / Soundwings ✦✦
● **Bone-Ified** / 1992 / GNP ✦✦✦✦
Time for Love / 1993 / GNP Crescendo ✦✦✦
Bill Watrous has long had one of the prettiest tones of any trombonist, especially in his impressive upper register. It is Watrous' beautiful sound that is emphasized during the nine Johnny Mandel compositions that comprise this CD. Watrous is accompanied by a big band and on some selections a string section but, other than pianist Shelly Berg (who along with Sammy Nestico contributed all of the arrangements), the backup crew is never allowed to rise above its anonymous supportive role. Watrous tries to vary the program a little with the inclusion of some earlier (and hotter) Mandel pieces such as the swinging "Low Life" and "Not Really the Blues" but otherwise this is a ballad showcase, highlighted by "Emily" and "The Shadow of Your Smile." —*Scott Yanow*

Bobby Watson

b. Aug. 23, 1953, Lawrence, KS
Alto Saxophone, Leader / Post Bop, Hard Bop
Bobby Watson has long been one of the top altoists in jazz, a flexible player able to play swing (he once recorded a tribute to Johnny Hodges), hard bop and free jazz. He started playing the alto when he was 13 and was soon arranging and composing for his school bands. After graduating from the University of Miami in 1975 Watson moved to New York, hitting the big time by joining (and soon becoming the musical director of) Art Blakey's Jazz Messengers during 1977-81, participating in what were Wynton Marsalis' first recordings. In the 1980s Watson co-led groups with Curtis Lundy (with whom he formed the New Note label) and played with the George Coleman Octet, Charlie Persip's big band, Louis Hayes, Sam Rivers, Dameronia, the 29th Street Saxophone Quartet and the Savoy Sultans; quite a wide range of jazz styles!

Watson also began leading his own regular bands in the mid-'80s and the following decade he headed a regular hard bop quintet known as Horizon. His many recordings (for Enja, Red, New Note, Blue Note and Columbia) are always stimulating and worth investigating. —*Scott Yanow*

E.T.A / 1977 / Roulette ◆◆◆

Jewel / Apr. 1983 / Evidence ◆◆◆◆◆
Bobby Watson had not inked a major label recording pact and was not a finished improviser when he cut these songs in 1983. What he did not lack was intensity, passion and drive, and those served him well. His solos and playing are spirited, and he builds and completes ideas impressively. Likewise, pianist Mulgrew Miller and vibist Steve Nelson were also growing young players and sometimes tried to cram too much into their solos. Drummer Marvin "Smitty" Smith, on the other hand, capably held things together rhythmically, along with bassist Curtis Lundy and percussionist Dom Um Romao. This was a pivotal session for Watson; he established his identity in the post-Blakey era and went on to become the star everyone felt he would be when they initially heard him in the Messengers. —*Ron Wynn*

Gumbo / Dec. 1983 / Evidence ◆◆◆◆◆
At the time of this recording, Watson was still building his reputation, playing in a group co-led by bassist Curtis Lundy. This was an outstanding band bolstered by the booming baritone sax of Hamiett Bluiett and featuring a strong rhythm section with pianist Mulgrew Miller and drummer Marvin "Smitty" Smith alongside Lundy. Special guest trumpeter Melton Mustafa provided sparkling lines and fiery solos, interacting smoothly with Watson and Bluiett in a solid frontline. Watson has since recorded more impressively engineered and mastered dates, but few have been musically superior to this early-'80s session. —*Ron Wynn*

Advance / Aug. 8, 1984 / Enja ◆◆◆◆

Appointment in Milano / Feb. 5, 1985 / Red ◆◆◆◆

Round Trip / Feb. 6, 1985 / Red ◆◆◆◆

Love Remains / Nov. 13, 1986 / Red ◆◆◆◆◆

● **The Year of the Rabbit** / Feb. 7, 1987 / New Note ◆◆◆◆◆

No Question About It / May 1, 1988 / Blue Note ◆◆◆◆◆

The Inventor / 1990 / Blue Note ◆◆◆◆

Post-Motown Bop / Sep. 17, 1990–Sep. 18, 1990 / Blue Note ◆◆◆◆◆
Despite the title, this is an excellent and traditional set. Watson is sparkling. —*Ron Wynn*

This Little Light of Mine / 1991 / Red ◆◆◆◆

Present Tense / Dec. 9, 1991–Dec. 11, 1991 / Columbia ◆◆◆◆

Tailor Made / Dec. 9, 1992–Dec. 11, 1992 / Columbia ◆◆◆◆
This CD was altoist Bobby Watson's first as the leader of a big band. He leads the orchestra through a dozen of his compositions, none of which they had performed together before meeting up in the studio. But due to the high caliber of the players, the music came together smoothly. In performances ranging from modern hard bop to Latin with subtle hints of freer styles of jazz, Watson is the main soloist (although there are a few short spots for trumpeter Terell Stafford), making the album a sort of "concerto for alto and orchestra." Even if the backup musicians have little opportunity to star, the music is consistently enjoyable and recommended to fans of modern mainstream jazz. —*Scott Yanow*

Midwest Shuffle / 1993 / Columbia ◆◆◆◆◆
Alto saxophonist Bobby Watson has greatly benefited from his pact with Columbia Records, getting the wider profile and publicity punch possible only through the resources of a major label; plus, his albums have been excellently engineered, tightly produced forums for his growing compositional and playing talents. This date was designed to give audiences an example of the Watson sound in concert. Not only did it feature several intense and explosive selections, but it also included background snippets and dialogue showing the musicians interacting with audience members and each other off stage and between songs. The results are ideal; it's more evidence that Bobby Watson is a major force on the jazz scene. —*Ron Wynn*

Urban Renewal / 1995 / Kokopelli ◆◆

Lu Watters (Lucious Watters)

b. Dec. 19, 1911, Santa Cruz, CA, **d.** Nov. 5, 1989, Santa Rosa, CA
Trumpet, Bandleader / Dixieland
It would be difficult to overestimate the importance of Lu Watters

in the Dixieland revival movement. When he organized the two-trumpet Yerba Buena Jazz Band in late 1939, the New Orleans jazz of King Oliver and Jelly Roll Morton was considered not only old hat but also worthy of extinction. Over 55 years later there are a countless number of trad bands patterned after the two-beat Watters group, which like its predecessor King Olivers' Creole Jazz Band is now considered classic. Lu Watters formed his first jazz band in 1925, but he spent most of the 1930s playing in San Francisco in his own big band. By 1939 (at the height of the swing era) he had met fellow trumpeter Bob Scobey, trombonist Turk Murphy and pianist Wally Rose and was planning to bring back the music of the 1920s which had been largely neglected for quite a few years. In December 1939 his new band started playing regularly at the Dawn Club and by 1941 when they made their first recordings, the Yerba Buena Jazz Band was building up a large following in San Francisco. The records kept the band's legacy alive when some of their members were drafted; Watters spent 1942-45 in the navy, leading a 20-piece band in Hawaii. In 1946 when the band regrouped at the Dawn Club on Annie Street, it was more successful than ever, and its records from 1946-47 find the group at its height. In June 1947 the band's base of operations moved to Hambone Kelly's in El Cerrito. The eventual departure of Bob Scobey and Turk Murphy (who would soon lead important groups of their own) weakened the Yerba Buena Band slightly but the vocals of its banjoist Clancy Hayes were a crowd-pleaser and the band remained a powerful force. However when business fell off in 1950, Lu Watters broke up the band at the end of the year (feeling that its time had passed) and retired from music to be a cook and a geologist. Watters said later that he could see the eventual commercialization of Dixieland coming. He continued following the music scene closely but did not pick up his trumpet again until 1963 when a utility company in Northern California announced plans to build a nuclear power plant on an earthquake fault. Watters appeared at a couple of protest rallies with Turk Murphy's band (playing as well as ever) and recorded one last record before permanently retiring; the power plant was never built! —*Scott Yanow*

★ **The Complete Good Time Jazz Recordings** / Dec. 19, 1941–Aug. 16, 1947 / Good Time Jazz ◆◆◆◆
Lu Watters' Yerba Buena Jazz Band was one of the most influential Dixieland groups of all time. With Watters and Bob Scobey on trumpets, trombonist Turk Murphy, clarinetist Bob Helm, pianist Wally Rose, banjo, tuba (or bass) and drums, this band had a lot of power and enthusiasm. At a time when swing dominated jazz and bebop was ready to take over, Watters' successful extension of 1920s jazz was a major force in fueling the Dixieland revival movement. This four-CD set has all of the group's studio recordings plus live broadcasts from 1946-47 and six rare performances by the wartime version of the YBJB featuring the talented but ill-fated trumpeter Benny Strickler. This reissue is absolutely essential for all traditional jazz fans and historians. The heated ensembles and joyous solos are great fun to hear. —*Scott Yanow*

● **San Francisco Style, Vol. 1** / Apr. 15, 1946–May 27, 1946 / Good Time Jazz ◆◆◆◆
The repertoire that turned San Francisco "trad crazy"—Morton's "New Orleans Joys," Richard M. Jones' "Jazzin' Babies Blues" and "Ory's Creole Trombone," among others, are done in revival style. —*Bruce Boyd Raeburn*

San Francisco Style, Vol. 2 / Apr. 15, 1946–May 27, 1946 / Good Time Jazz ◆◆◆◆
It's especially notable for originals by Watters such as "Big Bear Stomp," "Emperor Norton's Hunch" and "Annie Street Rock," as well as Turk Murphy's "Trombone Rag." —*Bruce Boyd Raeburn*

San Francisco Style, Vol. 3 / Apr. 15, 1946–May 27, 1946 / Good Time Jazz ◆◆◆◆

Together Again / Jul. 28, 1963 / Merry Makers ◆◆◆◆◆
Trumpeter Lu Watters came out of his 12-year retirement to help lead a successful protest against a proposed nuclear power plant being built near the San Andreas Fault. After getting his "chops" back in shape, Watters appeared with Turk Murphy's band on three separate occasions and recorded a studio album for Fantasy before permanently quitting. This CD (the music was released for the first time in 1994) documents the second rally and is quite exciting. Watters and trombonist Turk Murphy are heard with a group also including cornetist Bob Neighbor, clarinetist Bob Helm, either Wally Rose or Pete Clute on piano, banjoist Dave Weirbach, Bob Short on tuba, drummer Thad Vandon and on

some tracks bassist Squire Girsback. The music is comprised of Dixieland standards and songs from the repertoire of Lu Watters' Yerba Buena Jazz Band of the 1940s and is played with high musicianship, creativity and plenty of spirit. Well worth searching for, this set is essential for Dixieland fans. —*Scott Yanow*

Blues over Bodega / Nov. 1964 / Fantasy ✦✦✦✦

Charlie Watts

b. Jul. 2, 1941, London, England
Drums / Rock, Bop
On first glance Charlie Watts would seem to be a funny choice to include in a jazz book for he is the longtime drummer of the Rolling Stones. However jazz was Watts' first love and in the 1980s he toured worldwide with a huge big band that included many of England's top musicians (giving one a chance to hear Evan Parker play "Lester Leaps In!"). In 1991 he organized an excellent bop quintet (featuring altoist Peter King) that paid tribute to Charlie Parker, justifying Watts' place in any jazz history book. —*Scott Yanow*

Live at Fulham Town Hall / Mar. 23, 1986 / Columbia ✦✦✦✦✦
Rolling Stones drummer makes a go with a big band and succeeds. —*Michael G. Nastos*

From One Charlie / Feb. 26, 1991–Feb. 27, 1991 / Continuum ✦✦✦
This is a rather unusual package. Inside the box is a single CD, an illustrated childrens' book on Charlie Parker by Charlie Watts and a frameable photo of Bird. This expensive set does contain some excellent music on the CD, hot bop performances from a quintet featuring the great altoist Peter King and trumpeter Gerard Presencer in addition to Watts on drums, but unfortunately it is also rather brief (under 28 minutes). If there had been twice as much music, this set would get a much higher rating, for the straightforward music is quite strong and the Bird tributes heartfelt. —*Scott Yanow*

● **Tribute to Charlie Parker With Strings** / 1992 / Continuum ✦✦✦✦✦

Warm & Tender / 1993 / Continuum ✦✦✦✦

Ernie Watts

b. Oct. 23, 1945, Norfolk, VA
Tenor Saxophone / Instrumental Pop, Post Bop
Because he was involved in many commercial recording projects from the mid-'70s through the early '80s and on an occasional basis ever since, some observers wrote Ernie Watts off prematurely as a pop/R&B tenorman. Actually Watts' main hero has always been John Coltrane, and his more recent work reveals him to be an intense and masterful jazz improviser who has developed his own sheets of sound approach along with a distinctive and soulful sound. After attending Berklee, he had an important stint with Buddy Rich's big band (1966–68) before moving to Los Angeles. Watts worked in the big bands of Oliver Nelson and Gerald Wilson, recorded with Jean-Luc Ponty in 1969 and became a staff musician for NBC, performing with the Tonight Show Band on a regular basis. His own records of the 1970s and early '80s were generally poppish (1982's *Chariots of Fire* was a big seller) and Watts played frequently with Lee Ritenour and Stanley Clarke in addition to recording with Cannonball Adderley (one of his idols) in 1972. However Ernie Watts' work became much more interesting from a jazz standpoint starting in the mid-'80s when he joined Charlie Haden's Quartet West and started recording no-nonsense quartet dates for JVC. —*Scott Yanow*

Look in Your Heart / Oct. 19, 1981–Oct. 31, 1981 / Elektra ✦✦

Chariots of Fire / 1982 / Qwest ✦✦

Ernie Watts Quartet / Dec. 1987 / JVC ✦✦✦✦✦
After years of being heard primarily in commercial settings, Ernie Watts finally had an opportunity to record exactly what he wanted as a leader on this JVC CD. Watts, in a quartet with pianist Pat Coil, bassist Joel DiBartolo and drummer Bob Leatherbarrow, features his Coltrane-influenced tenor and a bit of alto and soprano on some group originals and standards (including "My One and Only Love," "Skylark" and "Body and Soul"). One of his finest recordings to date. —*Scott Yanow*

Project: Activation Earth / 1989 / Amherst ✦✦
Jazz saxophonist Watts teams with the fusion band Gamalon with nice results! —*Paul Kohler*

Afoxe / 1991 / CTI ✦✦

★ **Reaching Up** / Oct. 7, 1993–Oct. 8, 1993 / JVC ✦✦✦✦✦
For this quartet set with pianist Mulgrew Miller, bassist Charles Fambrough and drummer Jack DeJohnette, Ernie Watts definitely came to play. Virtually all of his solos are high powered and even his ballad statements are filled with clusters of passionate notes. Trumpeter Arturo Sandval has two appearances and makes the music even more hyper. In addition, the rhythm section keeps the proceedings consistently stimulating. The main focus on these standards and originals is generally on Watts' tenor and, even though there isn't all that much variety, this CD is a strong example of his jazz talents. —*Scott Yanow*

Unity / Dec. 13, 1994–Dec. 14, 1994 / JVC ✦✦✦✦
The most unusual aspect to Ernie Watts' latest recording is that the great tenor is joined by a two-bass quartet. Eddie Gomez on acoustic and Steve Swallow on electric blend together quite well, are featured in a delightful version of Oscar Pettiford's "Tricotism" and (with pianist Geri Allen and drummer Jack DeJohnette) keep the accompaniment consistently stimulating. Ernie Watts is in top form throughout this fine modern mainstream date, playing with both passion and lyricism on a variety of standards and originals (which, in addition to four songs from the leader, include one apiece from DeJohnette and Swallow). There is just enough variety to keep the proceedings from ever getting predictable, making this one of Watts' finest sessions. —*Scott Yanow*

Jeff Watts

b. Jan. 20, 1960, Pittsburgh, PA
Drums / Post Bop
Jeff Watts came to fame as drummer with the early Wynton Marsalis band. He has been greatly in-demand ever since, playing and recording with such musicians as Geri Allen, Ricky Ford, Robin Eubanks, Betty Carter, McCoy Tyner, Gary Thomas and Branford Marsalis among others. He made his debut as a leader for the Sunnyside label in 1991 and became a member of the Tonight Show Band when Branford Marsalis became its leader. Jeff Watts is both a virtuosic and a subtle drummer who is versatile enough to fit into many settings. —*Scott Yanow*

● **Megawatts** / Jul. 1991 / Sunnyside ✦✦✦✦

Weather Report

Group / Fusion
Weather Report was among the earliest and most influential of all jazz-rock bands. The original unit was co-founded by Wayne Shorter and Joe Zawinul in the early '70s. It equaled the original Mahavishnu Orchestra, Tony Williams Lifetime, the original Return to Forever and Dreams (minus vocals), as bands that stretched the boundaries and created a fresh hybrid really blending jazz and rock. Shorter and Zawinul had learned from years of playing with Miles Davis how to combine rock energy, funk rhythms and a jazz sensibility. Their early lineup included bassist Miroslav Vitous and drummer Alphonze Mouzon. Their self-titled debut and second release *I Sing the Body Electric* remain seminal jazz-rock classics. Even as they began the game of rotating personnel that would continue until they disbanded in 1986, they continued making intriguing releases into the early '80s. Dom Um Romao, Eric Gravitt and Alphonso Johnson were in the band during the mid-'70s. But its greatest lineup was the late '70s contingent that included Jaco Pastorius and Peter Erskine. These were virtuosos on their instruments and excellent contributors able to hold their own in any situation besides being superb accompanists. The last great Weather Report albums were issued by this group, among them *Black Market*, *Heavy Weather* and *Mr. Gone*. But things detable when Pastorius, then Erskine left in the early '80s. Their replacements Victor Bailey and Omar Hakim were excellent musicians but neither the flamboyant soloists nor imaginative thinkers of their predecessors. Shorter and Zawinul also began to coast and grew tired of working in the group concept. The final albums were the detached, polished and extremely professional output of topflight musicians anxious to finish the gig and move on. Percussionists Jose Rossey, then Mino Cineliu, were in and out

of the band and Erskine returned from Steps Ahead for their final dates. Shorter first took an extended leave of absence, then he and Zawinul called it quits. *—Ron Wynn and Stephen Aldrich*

Weather Report / Feb. 16, 1971–Mar. 17, 1971 / Columbia ✦✦✦✦✦

★ **I Sing the Body Electric** / Nov. 1971–Jan. 13, 1972 / Columbia ✦✦✦✦✦

Live in Tokyo / Jan. 13, 1972 / Columbia ✦✦✦✦✦

Sweetnighter / 1972–1973 / Columbia ✦✦✦✦
Funkier and more rock-directed. *—Michael Erlewine*

Mysterious Traveller / 1973–1974 / Columbia ✦✦✦✦✦
Weather Report's fourth recording finds Wayne Shorter (on soprano and tenor) taking a lesser role as Joe Zawinul begins to really dominate the group's sound. Most selections also include bassist Alphonso Johnson and drummer Ishmael Wilburn although the personnel shifts from track to track. "Nubian Sundance" adds several vocalists while "Blackthorn Rose" is a Shorter-Zawinul duet. Overall the music is pretty stimulating and sometimes adventurous; high-quality fusion from 1974. *—Scott Yanow*

Tale Spinnin' / 1974 / Columbia ✦✦✦✦

Black Market / 1976 / Columbia ✦✦✦✦✦

★ **Heavy Weather** / 1977 / Columbia ✦✦✦✦✦
One of their best-selling albums. *—Michael Erlewine*

Mr. Gone / 1978 / Columbia ✦✦

8:30 / Dec. 1979 / Columbia ✦✦✦✦✦
This double LP gives one a fine retrospective of Weather Report from the vantage point of 1979 with the first three sides being taken up with live performances. There are remakes of such memorable selections as "Black Market," "Teen Town," "A Remark You Made" and Weather Report's big hit "Birdland." Not everything works (Wayne Shorter's unaccompanied tenor solo on "Thanks for the Memory" is merely odd) and the new studio recordings on Side Four are not at the same level but in general the music throughout this two-fer is quite rewarding. Keyboardist Joe Zawinul, Shorter, bassist Jaco Pastorius and drummer Peter Erskine are all in top form. *—Scott Yanow*

Night Passage / 1980 / Columbia ✦✦✦✦

Record / 1982 / Columbia ✦✦✦✦

Procession / Jun. 1983 / Columbia ✦✦✦

Domino Theory / 1983–1984 / Columbia ✦✦✦

Sportin' Life / 1984 / Columbia ✦✦

This Is This! / 1985 / Columbia ✦✦

Chick Webb (William Henry Webb)

b. Feb. 10, 1909, Baltimore, MD, **d.** Jun. 16, 1939, Baltimore, MD
Drums, Leader / Swing
His career was short, and Chick Webb seemed cursed with only bad luck. He was a hunchback and died at 30 from TB of the spine. But during his short lifetime, Webb was a propulsive, dominating figure behind the drums. He was a dynamo, whose speed, power and rhythmic skills were never fully captured on record according to many who saw him repeatedly triumph in head-to-head battles with swing era royalty. Gene Krupa reportedly was in awe of Webb and spoke in shell-shocked tones after being blown away at the Savoy in legendary combat that occured only a few months before Webb died. Webb overcame being unable to read music by memorizing the arrangements. He led the band from a raised platform in the center, cuing sections via his drumming. He ranged over a huge kit with specially constructed pedals and cymbal holders and was an imaginative stylist who shoved drum technique ahead through dashing fills and crashing cymbals. He came to New York in 1924 and formed a band two years later. Webb cut his first record in 1927. After a period of struggle by the early 1930s, Webb had solidified the personnel in his big band and was playing regularly at the Savoy. By 1933 his orchestra was recording regularly and with fine soloists in trumpeters Taft Jordan (who also sang) and Bobby Stark, trombonist Sandy Williams, Elmer Williams (and later Teddy McRae) on tenor, pioneer flutist Wayman Carver and most importantly arranger Edgar Sampson (who wrote "Stompin at the Savoy," "If Dreams Come True" and "Blue Lou" for the orchestra). Webb had

one of the better big bands of the 1930s; other members of the ensemble included bassist John Kirby (early on) and future star Louis Jordan on alto. The turning point occurred when Webb added Ella Fitzgerald to his band in 1935. She soon became a major attraction (her 1938 recording of "A-Ticket, A-Tasket" became a huge hit) and from 1937 on the majority of the orchestra's recordings were vocal features. Tragically Webb started becoming seriously ill in 1938 and his death in June 1939 was mourned by millions of swing fans; his final words were "I'm sorry, I've got to go." Ella Fitzgerald headed the orchestra for the next two years before the big band finally broke up. *—Ron Wynn and Scott Yanow*

★ **Chick Webb (1929–1934)** / Jun. 14, 1929–Nov. 19, 1934 / Classics ✦✦✦✦✦

Spinnin the Web / Jun. 14, 1929–Feb. 17, 1939 / Decca ✦✦✦✦✦
When Chick Webb mounted the bandstand, he created a percussive magic surpassed by none and equaled by only a handful of swing era drummers. His band played short, jubilant, exciting numbers that captivated listeners and motivated dancers. This recent disc features 20 Webb numbers, including sensational versions of "Blue Lou," "Heebie Jeebies" and "Blue Minor." Although he seldom took the spotlight, and when he did, did so only for brief interludes, Webb's presence kept the band moving and music driving. *—Ron Wynn*

Immortal Chick Webb: Stompin' at the Savoy / Dec. 20, 1933–Mar. 17, 1936 / Columbia ✦✦✦✦

★ **Chick Webb (1935–1938)** / Jun. 12, 1935–May 3, 1938 / Classics ✦✦✦✦✦
To a large extent the Chick Webb big band is now chiefly remembered as the launching pad for Ella Fitzgerald, but during its peak years it was one of the top swing bands. This 25-song CD from the European Classics label reissues all of the band's recordings from a three-year period that did not feature Fitzgerald as a solo singer; she does make a brief appearance on "Wake up and Live." Although there are nine vocals on this set (including three from a young Louis Jordan), the emphasis is very much on the band's instrumental talents. Such soloists as trumpeters Taft Jordan and Bobby Stark, trombonist Sandy Williams, Elmer Williams and Ted McRae on tenors and altoist Edgar Sampson are heard from while the drummer/leader propels the ensembles. A special highlight are the four numbers by Chick Webb's Little Chicks, an unusual quintet featuring the pioneering jazz flutist Wayman Carver and clarinetist Chauncey Haughton. This CD is highly recommended to swing fans. *—Scott Yanow*

Eberhard Weber

b. Jan. 22, 1940, Stuttgart, Germany
Bass / New Age, World Fusion, Post Bop
Though not strictly a jazz bassist and certainly one of the least flamboyant improvisers, Eberhard Weber is among Europe's finest bassists. His style doesn't embrace either a bluesy orientation or animated, energetic approach. Weber's influences are primarily European, notably contemporary classical and new music. His technique of using contrasting ostinato patterns in different voices was taken from composer Steve Reich. He's also made innovations in bass design. Weber added an extra string to his electric bass at the top in the early '70s; this extended its range and gave it a deeper, more striking sound. He added yet another string above that in the late '70s. Weber once doubled on cello, but dropped it to concentrate on acoustic and electric bass. Weber's father taught him cello at six, and he began to play bass at 16. He worked in school orchestras, dance bands and local jazz groups. He met Wolfgang Dauner while participating in the Dusseldorf Amateur Jazz Festival in the early '60s; they worked together over the next eight years, both as a duo and in the group Et Cetera. Weber worked with Dave Pike in the early '70s and co-led the band Spectrum with Volker Kriegel. His early-'70s album *The Colours of Chloe* was one of ECM's most acclaimed. He formed the group Colours in 1974 and toured America in 1976, '78 and '79, heading it until 1981. Weber also played from the mid-'70s to the early '80s with the United Jazz & Rock Ensemble. During the '80s, Weber worked and recorded with Jan Garbarek and also wrote film scores and gave solo concerts. He continued recording with ECM, both with his group and with other musicians such as Gary Burton. Weber has several ECM titles available on CD. *—Ron Wynn*

★ **The Colours of Chloe** / Dec. 1973 / ECM ✦✦✦✦✦
Yellow Fields / Sep. 1975 / ECM ✦✦✦✦
Following Morning / Aug. 1976 / ECM ✦✦✦
Silent Feet / Nov. 1977 / ECM ✦✦✦
Fluid Rustle / Jan. 1979 / ECM ✦✦✦✦✦
Little Movements / Jul. 1980 / ECM ✦✦✦
Later That Evening / Mar. 1982 / ECM ✦✦✦✦
Chorus / Sep. 1984 / ECM ✦✦
Orchestra / May 1988–Aug. 1988 / ECM ✦✦
Pendulum / 1993 / ECM ✦✦✦✦✦
Although this is essentially a solo bass date, Eberhard Weber's use of overdubbing and an echo unit turns his bass into an orchestra of sorts. Since he is a strong composer, covering a wide span of moods during this set of melodic originals and avoiding the use of his effects as gimmickry, Weber creates an introverted but accessible program whose appeal should stretch beyond just lovers of bass solos. —Scott Yanow

Ben Webster

b. Mar. 27, 1909, Kansas City, MO, d. Sep. 20, 1973, Amsterdam
Tenor Saxophone / Swing
Ben Webster was considered one of the "big three" of swing tenors along with Coleman Hawkins (his main influence) and Lester Young. He had a tough, raspy and brutal tone on stomps (with his own distinctive growls) yet on ballads he would turn into a pussy cat and play with warmth and sentiment. After violin lessons as a child, Wesbter learned how to play rudimentary piano (his neighbor Pete Johnson taught him to play blues). But after Budd Johnson showed him some basics on the saxophone, Webster played sax in the Young Family Band (which at the time included Lester Young). He had stints with Jap Allen and Blanche Calloway (making his recording debut with the latter) before joining Bennie Moten's Orchestra in time to be one of the stars on a classic session in 1932. Webster spent time with quite a few orchestras in the 1930s (including Andy Kirk, Fletcher Henderson in 1934, Benny Carter, Willie Bryant, Cab Calloway and the short-lived Teddy Wilson big band). In 1940 (after short stints in 1935 and 1936), Ben Webster became Duke Ellington's first major tenor soloist. During the next three years he was on many famous recordings including "Cotton Tail" (which in addition to his memorable solo had a saxophone ensemble arranged by Webster) and "All Too Soon." After leaving Ellington in 1943 (he would return for a time in 1948–49), Webster worked on 52nd Street, recorded frequently as both a leader and a sideman, had short periods with Raymond Scott, John Kirby and Sid Catlett, and toured with Jazz at the Philharmonic during several seasons in the 1950s. Although his sound was considered out-of-style by that decade, Webster's work on ballads became quite popular and Norman Granz recorded him on many memorable sessions. Webster recorded a classic set with Art Tatum and generally worked steadily, but in 1964 he moved permanently to Copenhagen where he played when he pleased during his last decade. Although not all that flexible, Webster could swing with the best and his tone was a later influence on such diverse players as Archie Shepp, Lew Tabackin, Scott Hamilton and Bennie Wallace. —Scott Yanow

Tribute To A Great Jazzman / Nov. 25, 1936–Feb. 19, 1945 / Jazz Archives ✦✦✦✦
This LP contains many very valuable live performances. The great tenor Ben Webster is heard on seven selections with Duke Ellington's Orchestra from the 1941–43 period, jamming with pianist Teddy Wilson's pickup septet on "I Got Rhythm" in 1936 (a band also including violinist Stuff Smith and trumpeter Jonah Jones), guesting with the Woody Herman All-Stars in 1945, sitting in with Mezz Mezzrow on "Lady Be Good" and performing four numbers with a little-known version of John Kirby's Sextet (featuring either Charlie Shavers or Hot Lips Page on trumpet, clarinetist Buster Bailey and the underrated altoist George Johnson). The recording quality is generally decent and there are many inspired solos on this strong collection of previously unknown material. —Scott Yanow

He Played It That Way / Apr. 4, 1943–Mar. 10, 1969 / IAJRC ✦✦✦✦✦
The collector's label IAJRC uncovered some real rarities for this LP. The great tenor Ben Webster is heard accompanying the vocals

of Al Hibbler (with some Ellington sidemen) and Walter Brown; the latter also features pianist Jay McShann. "Hayfoot, Strawfoot" is a 1943 aircheck with Duke Ellington's Orchestra, Webster sits in with Raymond Scott's Orchestra for "Powerhouse" and is also showcased on two longer selections apiece with trumpeter Roy Eldridge in 1954 and both McShann and altoist Eddie "Cleanhead" Vinson in 1969. Overall the recording quality is good and the solos up to the high level one would expect. Ben Webster fans in particular are advised to search out this LP. —Scott Yanow

Alternate and Incomplete Takes / Feb. 8, 1944 / Circle ✦✦
Circle 41 (and Jazz Archives 35) has the master takes of the eight selections recorded on Feb. 8, 1944, by a quintet comprised of tenor saxophonist Ben Webster, trumpeter Hot Lips Page, pianist Clyde Hart, bassist Charlie Drayton and drummer Denzil Best. Circle 42, in contrast, contains all nine of the alternate takes plus six false starts and one incomplete performance. Obviously this set will be of greatest interest to collectors rather than general listeners although there are some strong moments on the swing session. —Scott Yanow

Ben and the Boys / Feb. 8, 1944–May 3, 1958 / Jazz Archives ✦✦✦✦
This is the second of two Jazz Archives LPs that are comprised of rare Ben Webster performances. The first side has the eight selections recorded in 1944 by a hot quintet that stars the great tenor, trumpeter Hot Lips Page and pianist Clyde Hart; these strong swing sides were also reissued on the Circle label. The flip side has four oddities. Two other numbers are taken from a loose 1945 jam session and are of interest mainly because of the personnel, which includes pianist Duke Ellington, violinist Stuff Smith and both Don Byas and Dexter Gordon on tenors (along with Webster). Webster is also heard with an all-star group backing Woody Herman's vocal on "Somebody Loves Me" and jamming "Flying Home" in 1958 with trumpeter Buck Clayton; the latter is taken from a television show. There is a lot of exciting music on this unusual and diverse set. —Scott Yanow

The Complete Ben Webster on EmArcy (1951–1953) / Dec. 19, 1951–Apr. 7, 1953 / EmArcy ✦✦✦✦✦
The early '50s briefly found tenor saxophonist Ben Webster moving to Kansas City for a while before settling in Los Angeles. He recorded in several different settings for EmArcy during this time (prior to signing with Norman Granz's Verve label) and all of the music (19 songs plus 14 alternate takes) were released on this valuable two-LP set. In addition to a set with an all-star sextet that includes altoist Benny Carter and trumpeter Maynrd Ferguson and four numbers backed by Johnny Richard's septet, Webster is heard as a featured sideman with Jay McShann, Johnny Otis, Dinah Washington, Marshall Royal and even the Ravens. The tenorman, whose sound had continued to grow in emotional depth since leaving Duke Ellington, excels in all of these contexts although the large number of alternate takes makes this two-fer of primary interest to collectors. —Scott Yanow

● **King of the Tenors** / Dec. 8, 1953 / Norgran ✦✦✦✦✦
This 1953 date matched Webster with such peers as alto saxophonist Benny Carter, trumpeter Harry Edison and pianist Oscar Peterson for a series of elegant yet soulful and exuberant small group dates. With no cut longer than four and a half minutes, the players didn't have time for excess statements or overkill; they had to quickly get to the heart of the matter in their solos, make their points and return to the head. The original session has been enlarged by the addition of two previously unissued tracks, plus an alternate version of "That's All" that was later issued as a single. Label head Norman Granz excelled in producing swing-oriented, crisply played mainstream dates. Although this date is more than four decades old, Ben Webster's solos have a freshness and vitality that make them quite relevant to contemporary events. —Ron Wynn

Music with Feeling / Ben Webster with Strings / Sep. 9, 1955 / Verve ✦✦✦✦

The Soul of Ben Webster / Mar. 5, 1957–Jul. 1958 / Verve ✦✦✦✦
Although tenor saxophonist Ben Webster gets top billing, this two-CD set actually contains an LP apiece by Webster, trumpeter Harry "Sweets" Edison and altoist Johnny Hodges. Webster is on all of the recordings, but really only stars on the first date, a septet outing with trumpeter Art Farmer and fellow tenor Harold Ashby. The great tenor is at his best on a beautiful version of "Chelsea Bridge" and "When I Fall in Love." The Edison session is a sextet

outing with Webster, the Oscar Peterson Trio and drummer Alvin Stoller mixing blues and swing standards; Edison's usually muted trumpet is quite effective. The final set puts the focus on altoist Hodges, who sounds beautiful on "Don't Take Your Love from Me," although the many blues performances also give solo space to trumpeter Roy Eldridge (literally explosive on "Honey Hill") and trombonist Vic Dickenson. A total of three previously unissued performances have been added to the program, and all three of these sessions had been long out of print; they add to the legacy of Norman Granz's Verve label, showing that many top swing all-stars were actually at their prime in the 1950s. Recommended. —*Scott Yanow*

Trav'lin Light / Sep. 1957–Oct. 14, 1963 / Milestone ✦✦✦✦✦
Most of this two-LP set is an expanded version of a 1963 album co-led by tenor saxophonist Ben Webster and the young pianist Joe Zawinul; at the time Zawinul was a regular member of Cannonball Adderley's band. The eight selections are joined by three alternate takes, and four of the songs find cornetist Thad Jones making the quartet a quintet. In addition this two-fer has most of a 1957 session that teamed Webster with the personable trombonist Bill Harris. Throughout the set, the music is essentially mainstream swing with Webster heard in top form. —*Scott Yanow*

★ **Soulville** / Oct. 15, 1957 / Verve ✦✦✦✦✦
The veteran tenor saxophonist Ben Webster met up with the Oscar Peterson Trio on this CD. Other than two fairly basic originals, the great tenor is showcased on durable standards and the ballads in particular are quite memorable. Peterson, bassist Ray Brown, guitarist Herb Ellis and drummer Stan Levey are superior in support of the masterful saxophonist. —*Scott Yanow*

Tenor Giants / Oct. 16, 1957–Apr. 9, 1959 / Verve ✦✦✦✦✦
Coleman Hawkins has always been Ben Webster's idol. They finally shared a record date on Oct. 16, 1957, and it was reissued as half of this two-LP set. With the backing of the Oscar Peterson Trio plus drummer Alvin Stoller, Webster and Hawk match wits and ideas on seven standards and two of Hawkins's originals. Webster was really no match for the elder tenor (and he knew it), particularly harmonically (Hawk was a master of chords), but he had the advantage of a huge emotional tone. Although Hawkins wins honors, it is not a runaway. The second album also features the two tenor greats plus the tenor of Budd Johnson, trumpeter Roy Eldridge and a four-piece rhythm section. Webster wrote three songs for the date (including tributes to Hawk and Budd) and there is a 20-minute version of "In a Mellow Tone" to wrap up the proceedings. The results are a dead heat except on "Time After Time" where Webster's beautiful sound is well featured. Recommended, but it will take a search to locate this two-fer. —*Scott Yanow*

Meets Gerry Mulligan / Nov. 3, 1959 / Verve ✦✦✦✦✦

Ben Webster Meets Oscar Peterson / Nov. 6, 1959 / Verve ✦✦✦✦

Warm Moods / Jan. 18, 1960+Jan. 19, 1960 / Discovery ✦✦✦
The veteran tenor Ben Webster had a very warm tone on ballads that contrasted with the aggressive biting sound he used on faster material. For this 1960 set Webster is joined by a string quartet (arranged by Johnny Richards) and a rhythm section for his melodic interpretations of a dozen standards. Even when simply stating the melody, Webster brings out unexpected beauty in the songs. His tone has never been accurately duplicated and is the main reason to search for this out-of-print LP originally recorded for Reprise. —*Scott Yanow*

At the Renaissance / Oct. 14, 1960 / Original Jazz Classics ✦✦✦✦
This live set features tenor great Ben Webster playing with pianist Jimmy Rowles, guitarist Jim Hall, bassist Red Mitchell and drummer Frank Butler in a club, and the music is consistently wonderful. Whether showing warmth and sentimentality on "Georgia on My Mind" and "Stardust" or growling and roaring on "Caravan" and "Ole Miss Blues," Webster (who was then somewhat taken for granted) is in superior and creative form. Recommended. —*Scott Yanow*

Ben and Sweets / Jun. 6, 1962+Jun. 7, 1962 / Columbia ✦✦✦
Tenor saxophonist Ben Webster and trumpeter Harry "Sweets" Edison, both veterans of the swing era (although associated with different orchestras), had long wanted to record a full album together. The results, a swinging quintet set with pianist Hank Jones, bassist George Duvivier and drummer Clarence Johnston, are quite rewarding. There are two ballad features for the tenor

("How Long Has This Been Going On" and a beautiful version of "My Romance") and one for Edison ("Embraceable You") along with three medium-tempo collaborations. Nothing unexpected occurs but the melodic music is quite enjoyable. —*Scott Yanow*

Soulmates / Sep. 20, 1963+Oct. 14, 1963 / Riverside ✦✦✦✦
This is some of Zawinul's (k) best playing outside of his work in Miles bands, Weather Report or his days with the Adderleys. —*Ron Wynn*

Live at Pio's / 1963 / Enja ✦✦✦✦
Some rollicking piano by Junior Mance. —*Ron Wynn*

★ **Meet You At The Fair** / Mar. 11, 1964–Nov. 10, 1964 / Impulse! ✦✦✦✦✦
Ben Webster's final American recording was one of his greatest. At 55, the tenor saxophonist was still very much in his prime but considered out of style in the U.S. He would soon permanently move to Europe where he was better appreciated. This CD has the nine selections originally included on the LP of the same name, a quartet set with either Hank Jones or Roger Kellaway on piano, bassist Richard Davis and drummer Osie Johnson. Webster's tone has rarely sounded more beautiful than on "Someone to Watch over Me" and "Our Love Is Here to Stay." In addition one song from the same session (but originally released on a sampler) and two tunes featuring Webster on an Oliver Nelson date (*More Blues and the Abstract Truth*) wrap up this definitive CD. —*Scott Yanow*

Stormy Weather / Jan. 30, 1965 / Black Lion ✦✦✦✦✦
Recorded around a month after the veteran tenor Ben Webster moved to Europe, this high-quality set with pianist Kenny Drew, bassist Neils Pederson and drummer Alex Riel features Webster stretching out on the traditional "Londonderry Air," two originals and seven familiar but fresh standards. Webster, although neglected in the U.S., was still in peak form in the mid-'60s as witness this and his other Black Lion CDs covering the period. —*Scott Yanow*

Gone with the Wind / Jan. 31, 1965 / Black Lion ✦✦✦✦✦
A companion to *Stormy Weather* (which was recorded the day before), this "Live at the Montmartre" set finds tenor saxophonist Ben Webster in excellent form on two versions of his "Set Call" and nine veteran standards. Webster's repertoire did not evolve or change much during his final decade but he always was able to come up with strong statements on songs such as "Perdido," "Sunday" and "Gone with the Wind." Recommended as an example of Webster's continuing creativity during his later years. —*Scott Yanow*

There Is No Greater Love / Sep. 5, 1965 / Black Lion ✦✦✦✦
Ben Webster is reunited with pianist Kenny Drew, bassist Niels Pedersen and drummer Alex Riel for this fine studio recording. He had used the same sidemen earlier in the year at the Montmartre, resulting in two other Black Lion CDs. The emphasis here is on ballads and slower tempos for a very lyrical effort. Webster's tone sounds typically beautiful on the eight standards, highlighted by "Stardust," "There Is No Greater Love," "I Got It Bad" and "Autumn Leaves." —*Scott Yanow*

The Jeep Is Jumping / Sep. 13, 1965–Sep. 21, 1965 / Black Lion ✦✦✦✦
One of four Ben Webster Black Lion CDs from 1965, this is the only one in which he is matched with other horn players. The great tenor interacts happily with trumpeter Arnved Meyer's mainstream quintet with the resulting music sometimes a bit reminiscent of Duke Ellington's small-group recordings of the 1930s. In addition to his warm versions of "Nancy with the Laughing Face," "My Romance" and "Days of Wine and Roses," it is a pleasure to hear Webster romping on "Stompy Jones" and "The Jeep Is Jumping" over 20 years after he originally left Ellington's band. —*Scott Yanow*

Swingin' In London / Apr. 27, 1967 / Black Lion ✦✦✦✦
Tenor saxophonist Ben Webster, who had moved permanently to Europe in 1965, meets up with the veteran trumpeter Bill Coleman (a resident of Europe since the late '40s) for this happy swing session. In addition to three collaborations, they perform four standards with Coleman having a feature on "But Not for Me" and taking a pair of vocals. The music is quite enjoyable and swinging, a good outing for all concerned. —*Scott Yanow*

Plays Ballads / Jul. 14, 1967–Nov. 22, 1971 / Storyville ✦✦✦✦
Ben Webster had a perfect tone for playing ballads, full of sentiment and emotion. On this Storyville release he caresses seven timeless melodies in a variety of settings including trios with

either Teddy Wilson, Ole Kock Hansen or Kenny Drew on piano, backing by the Danish Radio Big Band (on "Cry Me a River") or a version of "Greensleeves" with a string orchestra. Although largely forgotten in the United States (he had moved to Europe in 1965), Ben Webster was still in fine form this late in his career. — *Scott Yanow*

Plays Duke Ellington / Jul. 14, 1967–Nov. 22, 1971 / Storyville ✦✦✦✦✦
Although he was only a member of Duke Ellington's Orchestra for three years, tenor saxophonist Ben Webster was linked with Duke Ellington throughout his career. This Storyville release features the great tenor playing nine songs associated with Ellington. The music is drawn from five separate sessions including trio gigs with pianists Kenny Drew and Teddy Wilson and three with the Danish Radio Big Band. The emphasis is on uptempo pieces such as "Perdido," "Rockin' in Rhythm" and "Stompy Jones"; a special highlight are the two very different versions of "Cottontail." — *Scott Yanow*

Ben Meets Don Byas / Feb. 1, 1968–Feb. 2, 1968 / Saba ✦✦✦✦
Masters of Jazz, Vol. 5 / 1968–Sep. 25, 1970 / Storyville ✦✦✦✦
This entry in Storyville's *Masters of Jazz* series (which does not duplicate his *Plays Duke Ellington* and *Plays Ballads* albums) alternates ballads and stomps to give listeners a well-rounded picture of Ben Webster during his last period. Webster is joined by trios led by pianists Kenny Drew and Teddy Wilson, interacts with a drumless piano-bass duo, plays with a Scandinavian quartet, romps with the Danish Radio Big Band on two numbers and is accompanied on "Going Home" and "Come Sunday" by a string orchestra. These Copenhagen recordings find the great tenor in consistently fine form. — *Scott Yanow*

At Work in Europe / May 26, 1969 / Prestige ✦✦✦✦
The most widely available recordings (other than the Black Lions) from Ben Webster's European period, this double LP gives the veteran tenor saxophonist an opportunity to stretch out on five Ellington songs (plus his original "One for the Guv'nor") with a trio led by pianist Cees Slinger in addition to performing four fairly basic numbers ("The Preacher," "Straight No Chaser," "Work Song" and "John Brown's Body") with an unusual quartet featuring both Kenny Drew and Frans Wieringa on pianos. Throughout Webster sounds quite relaxed, warm and swinging. He no longer had to prove himself, and he clearly enjoyed himself on these performances. — *Scott Yanow*

No Fool, No Fun / Oct. 27, 1970 / Spotlite ✦✦
This unusual LP features the great tenorman Ben Webster at a rehearsal with the Denmark Radio Big Band and singers Matty Peters and Freddy Albeck. Webster often calls out instructions to the group and at various times sound humorous, instructive and impatient. There is not a great amount of music on this set with its many breakdowns and interruptions, but Webster fans will find these candid and certainly spontaneous moments to be of interest. — *Scott Yanow*

Live at the Haarlemse Jazzclub / May 9, 1972 / Cat ✦✦✦
There are many CDs available from tenor saxophonist Ben Webster's period in Europe that were recorded live during club performances. Virtually all are worth hearing even though the veteran tenor's style was no longer evolving. This set, recorded in Holland with pianist Tete Montoliu and a pair of Dutch players, finds Webster playing six veteran standards including such standbys as "Sunday," "How Long Has This Been Going On" and "Perdido." The music is quite enjoyable and swinging if not all that essential. — *Scott Yanow*

Makin' Whoopee / Jun. 5, 1972 / Spotlite ✦✦✦✦
Due to the fresher than usual repertoire (which is highlighted by "Johnny Come Lately," "I Want a Little Girl" and two of his originals), this is one of Ben Webster's better recordings from his later years. Recorded just 15 months before his death, the veteran tenor is in excellent form. The French rhythm section (led by pianist Georges Arvanitas) is also excellent and the swinging music is given creative treatment. — *Scott Yanow*

Did You Call / Nov. 28, 1972 / Nessa ✦✦✦✦
The great tenor Ben Webster is in suprisingly solid form this late in his career for a quartet set. With the virtuosic pianist Tete Montoliu heading the rhythm section, Webster alternates standards with his riffing originals, showing that his memorable tone was still very much intact on what would be his final studio recording. — *Scott Yanow*

My Man / Jan. 1973–Apr. 1973 / SteepleChase ✦✦✦
Just months before his death, the great tenor Ben Webster shows that even with an occasional shortness of breath, he never really declined musically. The six selections (five standards and his "Set Call") are all familiar (one wonders how many times Webster recorded "Sunday") but he still sounds enthusiastic and emotional. Joined by pianist Ole Kock Hansen, bassist Bo Stief and drummer Alex Riel for these appearances at the Montmartre in Copenhagen, Webster's warm ballad renditions and hard-driving romps are as always quite enjoyable to hear. — *Scott Yanow*

Freddy Webster

b. 1916, Cleveland, OH, **d.** April, 1947, Chicago, IL
Trumpet / Bop
Evaluating the lyrical Freddie Webster (as with Freddie Keppard in the 1920s) can be a frustrating exercise due to his relatively few recordings. Miles Davis considered him a major influence and Dizzy Gillespie often praised his tone. After working with Earl Hines and Erskine Tate in 1938, Wesbter moved to New York and in his short career he played with many top big bands including those led by Benny Carter, Eddie Durham (1940), Lucky Millinder, Jimmy Lunceford (1942–43) and Cab Calloway. He had a few memorable solos with Miss Rhapsody, Frankie Socolow and Sarah Vaughan ("You're Not the Kind") and can be heard on broadcasts with Lucky Millinder but never led a session of his own. After playing with John Kirby's sextet, Dizzy Gillespie's big band and Sonny Stitt, drugs did him in at age 31. — *Scott Yanow*

George Wein

b. Oct. 3, 1925, Boston, MA
Piano, Vocals / Dixieland
George Wein's main importance to jazz has been his work at organizing and booking festivals including Newport (which he helped found in 1954) and his own Storyville club in the 1950s. However Wein has long been a fine Earl Hines-inspired pianist (and an occasional vocalist), quite comfortable in swing and Dixieland-oriented settings. On an irregular basis since the 1950s he has toured and recorded with his Newport All Stars, which has included cornetist Ruby Braff, clarinetist Pee Wee Russell and tenorman Bud Freeman; more recently Scott Hamilton on tenor and cornetist Warren Vache. — *Scott Yanow*

Wein, Women and Song / Apr. 11, 1955 / Atlantic ✦✦✦✦
★ **George Wein and the Newport All Stars** / Oct. 12, 1962 / Impulse! ✦✦✦✦✦
George Wein Is Alive and Well in Mexico / Feb. 12, 1967–Dec. 14, 1967 / Columbia ✦✦✦✦✦
Newport All Stars / Feb. 26, 1969+Feb. 27, 1969 / Atlantic ✦✦✦✦
Swing That Music / Aug. 24, 1993–Aug. 25, 1993 / Columbia ✦✦✦
With a lineup comprised of fluegelhornist Clark Terry, trumpeter Warren Vache, trombonist Al Grey, tenors Illinois Jacquet and Flip Phillips, guitarist Howard Alden, bassist Eddie Jones and drummer Kenny Washington, one would expect a lot of fireworks from the 1993 version of George Wein's Newport All Stars. Unfortunately the music does not quite live up to one's expectations. Phillips and Jacquet (two veterans of Jazz at the Philharmonic) never trade off, C.T. and Vache get in each other's way during ensembles and Grey's uptempo blues ("Open Wider Please") ends quite inconclusively. There are some exciting moments, such as Clark Terry's mumbles vocal on "Tain't What You Do," a ballad medley ("Tears" and "Nuages") by the duo of Phillips and Alden and a passionate R&Bish alto solo by Jacquet on a blues. The music is full of good humor but more planning would have made this enjoyable session into a great one. — *Scott Yanow*

Dicky Wells (William Wells)

b. Jun. 10, 1907, Centerville, TN, **d.** Nov. 12, 1985, NYC
Trombone / Swing
One of the more erratic trombonists of the swing era, the distinctive Dicky Wells was somewhat innovative, playing his horn in a speechlike style filled with a great deal of color, humor and swing. Although he came to fame with Count Basie in 1938, Wells had been a major-league player for a decade before that. After moving to New York in 1926 he recorded with Cecil Scott (to hilarious effect on "In a Corner") and Spike Hughes in addition to

working with Fletcher Henderson, Benny Carter and Teddy Hill; during a European tour with Hill he recorded extensively. The Basie years (1938-45 and 1947-50) gave him some fame and his playing behind singer Jimmy Rushing was particularly memorable. His later years were somewhat anticlimactic but there were engagements with Rushing, reunions with Basie sidemen, European tours with Buck Clayton, a stint (1961-63) with Ray Charles and occasional appearances (including on the classic TV special *The Sound of Jazz* in 1957). After about 1965 Wells' alcoholism and declining musicianship forced him to get a day job as a messenger although he did write his memoirs (*The Night People*) and resurfaced for a final album in 1982. *— Scott Yanow*

★ **Dickie Wells in Paris** / Jul. 7, 1937-Jul. 12, 1937 / Prestige ✦✦✦✦

Bones for the King / Feb. 3, 1958-Feb. 4, 1958 / Felsted ✦✦✦✦

Trombone Four in Hand / Apr. 21, 1959 / Felsted ✦✦✦

Lonesome Road / Apr. 8, 1981-Apr. 29, 1981 / Uptown ✦✦
This is a difficult LP to rate. Compared to the trombonist's best work, it is a weak effort, but considering that Dicky Wells (who had been in poor health) hadn't recorded for years and his extroverted personality still shines through (and he continues taking wild chances), this is certainly a colorful album. Joined by pianist Dick Katz, either George Duvivier or Michael Moore on bass, drummer Oliver Jackson and, on five of the nine songs, Buddy Tate on tenor and clarinet, Wells (on his final recording) mostly explores standards and blues with spirit, determination and swing. *— Scott Yanow*

Dick Wellstood

b. Nov. 25, 1927, Greenwich, CT, **d.** Jul. 24, 1987, Palo Alto, CA
Piano / Stride, Classic Jazz
One of the two great stride pianists (along with Ralph Sutton) to emerge during the 1940s when members of their generation were generally playing bebop, Wellstood kept an open mind toward later styles (he loved Monk) while sounding at his best playing classic jazz. A little more subtle than Sutton, Wellstood was also a powerful pianist who was a superb interpreter of the music of James P. Johnson and his contemporaries. He came to New York with Bob Wilber's Wildcats in 1946 and caught on in the trad jazz scene quickly. By 1947 he was playing with Sidney Bechet and in the 1950s he mostly worked with veteran players including trumpeters Roy Eldridge, Rex Stewart and Charlie Shavers and the Eddie Condon gang. He was in the intermission band at Condon's starting in 1956 and later was house pianist at the Metropole and Nick's. After a period with Gene Krupa's quartet, he toured with the World's Greatest Jazz Band. Wellstood remained active throughout his all-too-short life, playing solo concerts, performing at jazz parties and recording quite a few memorable albums. *— Scott Yanow*

Dick Wellstood Alone / Nov. 1970-Mar. 1971 / Jazzology ✦✦✦✦✦

From Ragtime on / Dec. 1971 / Chiaroscuro ✦✦✦

Dixie to Swing / 1972 / Classic Jazz ✦✦✦✦

★ **Dick Wellstood and His Famous Orchestra Featuring Kenny** / Jul. 1973-Dec. 1973 / Chiaroscuro ✦✦✦✦✦
Dick Wellstood was (along with Ralph Sutton), the top stride pianist of the 1970s and '80s. Two of his most exciting recordings are combined on this definitive CD with eight of the ten tracks originally on the Chiaroscuro LP *Dick Wellstood and His Famous Orchestra Featuring Kenny Davern* and nine of the ten songs from the Chaz Jazz release *the Blue Three* comprising the program. Kenny Davern sticks to soprano on the earlier set (their "Famous Orchestra" is actually a duet) and switches to clarinet for The Blue Three sides with Wellstood and drummer Bobby Rosengarden. The music ranges from Dixieland standards to swing tunes (and even "Blue Monk") but mostly falls into the genre of hot small-group swing. Highly recommended. *— Scott Yanow*

At the Cookery / 1975 / Chiaroscuro ✦✦✦✦

★ **Live at Hanratty's** / 1981 / Chaz Jazz ✦✦✦✦✦
Dick Wellstood, a versatile stride pianist who was at the top of the field in the 1970s and '80s, is heard playing solo on this definitive double LP. Whether it be "Jingle Bells" (an exquisite version), three medleys of unrelated songs, standards or jazz obscurities, Wellstood is in superb form throughout this highly enjoyable release. This music is long overdue to be reissued on CD. *— Scott Yanow*

Diane / Feb. 18, 1981-Feb. 19, 1981 / Swingtime ✦✦✦

I Wish I Were Twins / Mar. 8, 1983-Mar. 13, 1983 / Swingtime ✦✦✦✦✦

Frank Wess

b. Jan. 4, 1922, Kansas City, MO
Flute, Alto Saxophone, Tenor Saxophone / Bop, Swing
A pioneering jazz flutist, Frank Wess has blended a swinging style with bebop influences and nuances. He was an ideal partner to Frank Foster in the Basie band of the mid-'50s and early '60s, playing a softer, smoother and lighter sound to Foster's harder and more aggressive mode. Wess' flute work with its full, upbeat lines and expressive tones upgraded the instrument's role in jazz. Wess began on alto sax and even played some alto solos with Count Basie, but became better known for his playing on tenor. He worked with Blanche Calloway before World War II, then served in Army bands. After his discharge, Wess had a brief stint in Billy Eckstine's band and worked short periods with Eddie Heywood, Lucky Millinder and Bull Moose Jackson. Wess began playing flute in 1949, then joined Count Basie in 1953. He remained until 1964. Wess played alto at Basie's request with the band from the late '50s until the mid-'60s. He became active doing commercials and playing in pit and studio bands for plays and television shows. Wess was in the New York Jazz Quartet during the '70s and the repertory group Dameronia in the '80s, as well as the Toshiko Akiyoshi and Woody Herman big bands. He's performed and recorded with old friend Frank Foster in the '80s and '90s. Some recent Wess dates on Concord and Progressive are available on CD, while earlier material has been reissued on Savoy and Fresh Sound. *—Ron Wynn and Michael G. Nastos*

Opus in Swing / Jun. 20, 1956 / Savoy ✦✦✦

● **Jazz for Playboys** / Dec. 26, 1956+Jan. 5, 1957 / Savoy Jazz ✦✦✦✦✦

I Hear Ya' Talkin' / Dec. 8, 1959 / Savoy ✦✦✦✦
This lightly swinging session is very much in the Count Basie style of blues and swing. Frank Wess (switching between flute, tenor and alto) heads the septet, but it is trumpeter Thad Jones (who wrote three of the five numbers) who often takes solo honors. Trombonist Curtis Fuller, baritonist Charlie Fowlkes and pianist Hank Jones are also heard from on this enjoyable session that for some obscure reason was not released until 1984. *— Scott Yanow*

Flute Juice / Apr. 8, 1981 / Progressive ✦✦✦✦✦

Two at the Top / Jun. 8, 1983-Jun. 9, 1983 / Uptown ✦✦✦✦
With Johnny Coles on trumpet and the Kenny Barron Trio, these are all standards with the emphasis on hard- and cool-bop from Kenny Dorham (tpt), Gigi Gryce (as) and Benny Golson (ts). Wess plays alto and tenor sax only. The arrangements are by Don Sickler. *—Michael G. Nastos*

Dear Mr. Basie / Nov. 1989 / Concord Jazz ✦✦✦

Entre Nous / Nov. 11, 1990 / Concord Jazz ✦✦✦✦

Tryin' To Make My Blues Turn Green / Sep. 7, 1993-Sep. 8, 1993 / Concord ✦✦✦✦
Frank Wess has always been a steady, reliable swinger, able to play swaggering blues and soulful ballads with equal facility and hold his own on more challenging bop pieces. The 12 tracks on his release range from his own swing-tinged originals to the inevitable standards and fine reworkings of jazz pieces by Kenny Burrell and Horace Parlan. Highly professional, nicely played blues-swing material from an often overlooked, dependable improviser. *—Ron Wynn*

Going Wess / Sep. 20, 1993-Sep. 21, 1993 / Town Crier ✦✦✦✦✦
This CD gave Frank Wess (doubling on tenor and flute) his first opportunity to record with an organ and he is in top form on this trio outing with organist Bobby Forrester and drummer Clarence "Tootsie" Bean. Burners alternate with warm ballads and Wess (whether on his tough tenor or fluid flute) matches very well with Forrester's light pre-Jimmy Smith organ style. In fact, this session swings so naturally that it could have been recorded in 1958. The ten superior standards are all given very favorable treatment, making this a highly recommended outing. *— Scott Yanow*

Randy Weston

b. Apr. 6, 1926, Brooklyn, NY
Piano, Composer / Post Bop, Hard Bop
Randy Weston has pioneered a compositional and playing style

that merges the influence of Thelonious Monk's unconventional concepts with the multiple rhythms and accents of African music. Weston's also utilized bebop, blues and funk, mixing all this into an arresting, energetic style with simple melodies and creative uses of dissonance, Carribean themes and gospel/blues riffs. Monk's impact on Weston extends to his early years, when Monk informally trained him on piano during visits to his apartment. Weston started professionally in R&B bands, then worked in bebop groups with Kenny Dorham and Cecil Payne. He played with Art Blakey in the late '40s, and became Riverside's first bebop signee in 1954. Weston began leading bands with Ahmed Abdul-Malik, Ray Copeland, Payne, Booker Ervin and Melba Liston in the late '50s. He also gained fame as a composer, with such works as "Hi-Fly," "Little Niles" and "African Cookbook." Weston worked on the West Coast before heading to Nigeria in the early '60s. He returned to Africa on a tour in 1967, settling in Morocco and remaining there until the early '70s. Weston established a nightclub and led a trio. He continued traveling in the early '70s, appearing at the 1974 Montreaux Jazz Festival. Weston started recording in the '50s, and has been featured on sessions for United Artists, Jubilee, Dawn, Roulette, Bakton (his own label), Riverside, Trip, Arista/Freedom, Polydor, CTI, Atlantic, Owl, Inner City, Enja, Verve and Antilles. After undergoing a recording drought in the early '80s, there's now an ample amount of Weston sessions available on CD. —*Ron Wynn*

Cole Porter: In a Modern Mood / Apr. 27, 1954 / Riverside ✦✦✦

Get Happy / Aug. 29, 1955–Aug. 31, 1955 / Original Jazz Classics ✦✦✦✦

With These Hands / Mar. 14, 1956+Mar. 21, 1956 / Riverside ✦✦✦✦

● **Jazz á la Bohemia** / Oct. 25, 1956 / Original Jazz Classics ✦✦✦✦✦
Randy Weston, who was more under Thelonious Monk's influence back in 1956 then he would be in the near future, is in top form during this live set. His quartet features the rarely heard but talented baritonist Cecil Payne, bassist Ahmed Abdul-Malik and drummer Al Dreares. High points of the straight-ahead set (which has been reissued on CD) include the calypso "Hold 'Em Joe" (recorded almost a decade before Sonny Rollins), "It's All Right with Me" (one of two trio tracks) and the lone Weston original on the date, the stimulating "Chessman's Delight." —*Scott Yanow*

How High the Moon / Nov. 21, 1956–Jan. 19, 1957 / Biograph ✦✦✦✦✦

Piano a La Mode / 1957 / Jubilee ✦✦✦✦

Little Niles / Oct. 1958–Oct. 26, 1959 / United Artists ✦✦✦✦✦
This attractive two-LP set has selections drawn from three of pianist Randy Weston's most interesting sessions of the late '50s. Seven songs (taken from the original album Little Niles) feature Weston in a sextet with tenor saxophonist Johnny Griffin and either Ray Copeland or Idrees Sulieman on trumpet while four other selections (drawn from *Destry Rides Again*) match the pianist with four trombonists. However it is the second disc (originally issued as *Live at the Five Spot*) that is of greatest interest because Weston heads an all-star quintet (given Melba Liston's arrangements) that includes tenor saxophonist Coleman Hawkins and trumpeter Kenny Dorham. Overall the music is advanced bop with a strong nod toward African music. Well worth searching for. —*Scott Yanow*

★ **Uhuru Africa / Highlife** / Nov. 1960–Apr. 1963 / Roulette ✦✦✦✦✦
Futuristic exploration of link between Africa and jazz. Many of this pianist's best compositions. —*Michael G. Nastos*

Monterey '66 / Sep. 18, 1966 / Verve ✦✦✦✦

Blue Moses / Mar. 1972–Apr. 1972 / CTI ✦✦✦✦

Tanjah / May 21, 1973–May 22, 1973 / Verve ✦✦✦✦✦
Originally on the Polydor label, this lesser-known classic (reissued on CD) teams together pianist/composer Randy Weston and arranger Melba Liston (his musical soulmate) on seven of Weston's originals. The fairly large band is filled with distinctive soloists including trumpeter Jon Faddis (19 at the time), trombonist Al Grey, Billy Harper on tenor, altoist Norris Turney (heard on three versions of "Sweet Meat," two of which were previously unreleased) and several percussionists among others. The weak points are Weston's use of the Fender Rhodes on a few songs (it waters down his personality) and Candido's chanting during an otherwise exciting version of "Hi-Fly," but those are easily compensated for by the infectious calypso "Jamaican East" and

Liston's inventive reworking of "Little Niles." Recommended. —*Scott Yanow*

● **Carnival** / Jul. 5, 1974 / Freedom ✦✦✦✦✦

Blues to Africa / Aug. 14, 1974 / Freedom ✦✦✦✦✦

African Nite / Sep. 21, 1975 / Inner City ✦✦✦✦

Portraits of Monk / Jun. 3, 1989 / Verve ✦✦✦✦

Portraits of Duke Ellington / Jun. 4, 1989 / Verve ✦✦✦✦

Self Portraits / Jun. 5, 1989 / Verve ✦✦✦

● **The Spirits of Our Ancestors** / May 20, 1991–May 22, 1991 / Verve ✦✦✦✦✦
Weston with 11-piece band and guests Pharoah Sanders and Dizzy Gillespie. The stellar arrangements are by Melba Liston. Familiar themes are "The Healers," "Blue Moses," "African Cookbook" and "African Village/Bedford Stuyvesant." Most of the ten tracks are extended on this two-CD set. —*Michael G. Nastos*

Splendid Master Gnawa Musicians of Morocco / Sep. 17, 1992 / Verve Antilles ✦✦✦✦

Volcano Blues / Feb. 1993 / Antilles ✦✦✦✦✦
Pianist Randy Weston and trombonist/arranger Melba Liston have collaborated successfully for many years. This pairing was on a series of blues numbers, with Weston doubling as session producer and pianist while giving Liston almost total arranging control, except for three numbers. The results were an intriguing twist on standard 12-bar blues, as Weston's muscular piano lead the way through rigorous performances of Count Basie's "Volcano" and his own "Blues for Strayhorn," "Sad Beauty Blues" and "In Memory Of." Liston's arrangements required disciplined solos, and Weston's steady hand generated impressive cohesion and interaction during the unison segments. A superb example of the African/African-American musical continuum. —*Ron Wynn*

George Wettling

b. Nov. 28, 1907, Topeka, KS, **d.** Jun. 6, 1968, NYC
Drums / Dixieland
The definitive Dixieland drummer, George Wettling (who also appeared in swing settings) was heard at his best on a series of trios with Bud Freeman and Jess Stacy in 1938. He was also a critic who contributed to Downbeat and an artist whose work was featured on album sleeves of sessions by Eddie Condon and Joe Sullivan. Wettling was known for inventive breaks and a declarative, striking sound, plus sympathetic accompaniment and exuberant solos in those rare times he got the spotlight. Wettling worked in several Chicago bands during the '20s, then played and recorded with Paul Mares in the mid-'30s. He toured with Jack Hylton's band and played in several cities with Wingy Manone. Wettling recorded with Jimmy McPartland in 1936 and with Manone, then worked in the orchestras of Artie Shaw, Bunny Berigan, Red Norvo and Paul Whiteman in the late '30s and early '40s. He recorded frequently with groups assembled and/or led by Condon. During the '40s, Wettling played with Bobby Hackett and Muggsy Spanier, Benny Goodman, Miff Mole and Chico Marx as well as McPartland. He was an ABC staff musician in the '40s and early '50s and made regular appearances at Condon's club. Wettling made numerous recordings in the '40s and '50s with Yank Lawson, Dick Cary, Billie Holiday, Pee Wee Russell, Jack Teagarden, Hackett, Spanier, Bud Freeman, Joe Sullivan, Sidney Bechet and Ralph Sutton. He led his own band in the mid-'50s, and played throughout the decade with McPartland, Condon and Spanier. He kept working with Condon in the '60s and worked with Clarence Hutchenrider. Wettling recorded as a leader for Decca, Keynote, Commodore, World Pacific and Weathers Industries. He can be heard on CD reissues by McPartland, Holiday, Lawson, Bechet and several others, plus the Keynote Collection. —*Ron Wynn*

● **George Wettling's Jazz Band** / Mar. 2, 1951–May 4, 1951 / Columbia ✦✦✦✦

Kirk Whalum

b. Memphis, TN
Tenor Saxophone / Instrumental Pop, Crossover
From the jazz standpoint, Kirk Whalum's career has thus far been a consistent disappointment. Although obviously a talented player, he has thus far been satisfied to make a good living by performing R&B and pop music while keeping well hidden any individuality that he might possess. Whalum debuted on record for

Music Map

Vocalists – Male

First Important Jazz Singer and the Most Influential
Louis Armstrong

Pre-Bop Instrumentalists Who Also Sang

Don Redman (Took first recorded scat vocal in 1924)	
Jack Teagarden	Fats Waller
Red Allen	Hot Lips Page
Wingy Manone	Louis Prima
Nat Gonella	Jelly Roll Morton
Woody Herman	Jay McShann
Nat King Cole	Danny Barker
Clancy Hayes	Louis Jordan

Middle-of-he-Road Pop Singers Who Have Influenced Jazz

Bing Crosby • Frank Sinatra

Kansas City Swing/Blues Tradition

Jimmy Rushing	Big Joe Turner
Jimmy Witherspoon	Big Miller
Joe Williams	Ernie Andrews
Bill Henderson	

Two Other Influential Swing Vocalists

Cab Calloway • Billy Eckstine

Jive Singers

Slim Gaillard • Leo Watson
Harry "The Hipster" Gibson

Bop and Vocalese

Dizzy Gillespie	Joe Carroll
Babs Gonzales	Jackie Paris
Eddie Jefferson	King Pleasure
Buddy Stewart	Dave Lambert
Jon Hendricks	

R&B

Ray Charles • Charles Brown • Al Jarreau

More Recent Instrumentalists Who Also Sing

Chet Baker	Clark Terry
Richard Boone	George Adams
Grady Tate	George Benson

1960s to the Present

Mel Torme	Johnny Hartman
Earl Coleman	Bob Dorough
Oscar Brown, Jr.	Mose Allison
Leon Thomas	Mark Murphy
Dave Frishberg	Bobby McFerrin
Kevin Mahogany	Kurt Elling

Columbia in 1984 (on a Bob James record) and has been a popular attraction ever since. —*Scott Yanow*

Floppy Disk / 1985 / Columbia ✦✦

And You Know That! / 1988 / Columbia ✦✦✦✦
Light pop/fusion though Whalum's a very good player. —*Ron Wynn*

The Promise / 1989 / Columbia ✦✦✦

● **Cache** / 1993 / Columbia ✦✦✦✦

In This Life / 1995 / Columbia ✦✦✦

Kenny Wheeler

b. Jan. 14, 1930, Toronto, Canada
Trumpet, Fluegelhorn / Avant-Garde, Post Bop
Kenny Wheeler has long been one of the most technically proficient of the avant-garde trumpeters. He started on cornet when he was 12, studied at the Toronto Conservatory and then in 1952 moved to England. He worked in many big bands during the next decade (including with John Dankworth during 1959–65) and became an excellent hop-based soloist. However by the mid '60s his musical curiosity led him to freer forms of jazz and he did important work with John Stevens' Spontaneous Music Ensemble, Tony Oxley's sextet, the Mike Gibbs Orchestra, the Globe Unity Orchestra (starting in 1972), Anthony Braxton's Quartet and Azimuth. Wheeler has been a regular on ECM since the mid-'70s and during 1983–87 he was with the Dave Holland quintet. A thoughtful trumpeter with a wide range, Wheeler's playing is always stimulating yet generally introspective. —*Scott Yanow*

Windmill Tilter / Mar. 1968 / Fontana ✦✦✦✦

Song for Someone / 1973 / Incus ✦✦✦✦

★ **Gnu High** / Jun. 1975 / ECM ✦✦✦✦✦

Deer Wan / Jul. 1977 / ECM ✦✦✦✦
Kenny Wheeler's beautiful sound on trumpet and his wide range are well displayed on his four compositions, three of which are performances over ten minutes long. With the assistance of ECM regulars Jan Garbarek (on tenor and soprano), guitarist John Abercrombie, bassist Dave Holland, drummer Jack DeJohnette and (on one song) guitarist Ralph Towner, Wheeler emphasizes lyricism and romantic moods on this fine set of original music. —*Scott Yanow*

Around 6 / Aug. 1979 / ECM ✦✦✦✦✦

● **Double, Double You** / May 1983 / ECM ✦✦✦✦✦
Quintet set. Some good playing by Mike Brecker (sax). —*Ron Wynn*

Welcome / Mar. 26, 1986 / Soul Note ✦✦✦

Flutter By, Butterfly / May 1987 / Soul Note ✦✦✦✦

Music for Large and Small Ensembles / Jan. 1990 / ECM ✦✦✦✦✦

★ **The Widow in the Window** / Feb. 1990 / ECM ✦✦✦✦✦

Arthur Whetsol

b. 1905, Punta Gorda, FL, d. Jan. 5, 1940, New York, NY
Trumpet / Classic Jazz, Swing
Arthur Whetsol, one of the original members in Duke Ellington's

Washingtonians, had an attractive tone, impressive technique and a very lyrical style that set a standard for Ellington; in future years Harold "Shorty" Baker filled a similar role with Duke. A childhood friend of Ellington, Whetsol came to New York with Duke to join Elmer Snowden's group in 1923 but left a year later to study medicine at Howard University. He eventually returned to music and was a fixture in Duke's orchestra during 1928-36 until a brain disorder forced him to permanently retire. Featured prominently in Ellington's 1929 film short *Black and Tan*, Whetsol took many fine solos in the late '20s when his melodic style was a contrast to that of Bubber Miley and (a little later) Cootie Williams, most notably on "Mood Indigo," "Black and Tan Fantasy" and "Black Beauty"; his role became less prominent in the 1930s. —*Scott Yanow*

Brian White

Clarinet / Dixieland
Leader of the Magna Jazz Band in London since the mid-'50s, Brian White is a fine veteran clarinetist who (along with trumpeter Alan Gresty) was responsible for the rewarding tribute to Muggsy Spanier titled *Muggsy Remembered;* he has recorded a couple of easily available CDs for Jazzology. —*Scott Yanow*

Pleasure Mad / Apr. 24, 1982+Feb. 4, 1984 / Jazzology ◆◆◆◆

★ **Muggsy Remembered** / 1986+Oct. 30, 1993 / Jazzology ◆◆◆◆◆
In 1939 cornetist Muggsy Spanier recorded 16 selections with his four-horn seven-piece Ragtime Band that helped define Dixieland. Unfortunately he was just a little early, for gigs soon became difficult to find, and he had to break up the group before the year ended. In 1986, the English clarinetist Brian White decided to feature cornetist Alan Gresty on a dozen of the 16 numbers at a recording session because Gresty's sound and style (particularly when muted) uncannily resembled Muggsy Spanier's. This CD, which reissues that complete program, also has four additional tracks recorded in 1993. The music as a whole is quite enjoyable, hinting strongly at Spanier's band without actually copying any solos. Highlights include such numbers as "That Da Da Strain," "Lonesome Road," "Monday Date," "Relaxin' at the Touro" and "Sunday." The musicianship is high and the soloists (which also include trombonist Geoff Cole and the tenor of Goff Dubber) are consistently colorful and swinging. This is a highly recommended set for Dixieland fans. —*Scott Yanow*

Carla White

b. Oakland, CA
Vocals / Post Bop, Bop
Although she has not recorded enough (and there are long gaps between some of her recordings), Carla White has been one of the better jazz singers of the past decade. Raised in New York, her original goal was to be an improvising jazz dancer. However in high school she started singing and becoming involved in acting. After spending two years at the Webber-Douglas Academy of Dramatic Art in London (1969-71) and some time traveling overseas, White studied with Lennie Tristano for four years and later with Warne Marsh. In the late '70s she started collaborating with trumpeter Manny Duran, co-leading a band and recording for Stash. An expert scat singer, White started concentrating more on interpreting lyrics by the time she recorded two albums for Milestone and her 1991 Evidence set is one of her best to date. —*Scott Yanow*

Orient Express / Dec. 20, 1985-Jul. 1986 / Milestone ◆◆◆◆

Mood Swings / Apr. 4, 1988-Apr. 6, 1988 / Milestone ◆◆◆◆◆

● **Listen Here** / Sep. 4, 1991-Sep. 5, 1991 / Evidence ◆◆◆◆◆
Seven years after the release of singer Carla White's previous Milestone album (*Mood Swings*), she finally emerges with a new gem. True, her voice on *Listen Here* sounds as if she has experienced a great deal of life in the meantime, but it has lost none of its power, flexibility, optimism or sensuality. Joined by tenor great Lew Tabackin and a strong rhythm section, White really stretches herself on the diverse program which ranges from wild scatting and long vamps to ballad interpretations that would do credit to Susannah McCorkle. Whether it be an eccentric calypso duet with bassist Dean Jackson on "It's Only a Paper Moon," a touching "Lotus Blossom" or an unusual vocal rendition of "Harlem Nocturne," Carla White takes plenty of chances throughout her very satisfying release. Jazz needs more singers like her. —*Scott Yanow*

Paul Whiteman

b. Mar. 28, 1890, Denver, CO, d. Dec. 29, 1967, Doylestown, PA
Leader / Pop, Classic Jazz
Because press agents dubbed him "The King of Jazz" in the 1920s, Paul Whiteman has always been considered a controversial figure in jazz history. Actually his orchestra was the most popular during the era and at times (despite its size) it did play very good jazz; perhaps "King of the Jazz Age" would have been a better title.

Originally a classically trained violinist, Paul Whiteman led a large navy band during World War I and always had a strong interest in the popular music of the day. In 1918 he organized his first dance band in San Francisco and, after short periods in Los Angeles and Atlantic City, he settled in New York in 1920. His initial recordings ("Japanese Sandman" and "Whispering") were such big sellers that Whiteman was soon a household name. His superior dance band used some of the most technically skilled musicians of the era in a versatile show that included everything from pop tunes and waltzes to semi-classical works and jazz. Trumpeter Henry Busse (featured on "Hot Lips" and "When Day Is Done") was Whiteman's main star during the 1921-26 period. Seeking to "make a lady out of jazz," Whiteman's symphonic jazz did not always swing, but at Aeolian Hall in 1924 he introduced "Rhapsody in Blue" (with its composer George Gershwin on piano) in what was called "An Experiment in Modern Music." Red Nichols and Tommy Dorsey passed through the band but it was in 1927 with the addition of Bix Beiderbecke, Frankie Trumbauer and Bing Crosby (the latter originally featured as part of a vocal trio called the Rhythm Boys) that Whiteman began to finally have an important jazz band. Joe Venuti and Eddie Lang soon joined up and many of Whiteman's recordings of 1927-30 (particularly the ones with Bill Challis arrangements) are among his finest.

After Beiderbecke left the band in 1929 and Whiteman filmed the erratic but fascinating movie *The King of Jazz* in 1930, the Depression forced the bandleader to cut back on his personnel (which at one time included two pianos, tuba, bass sax, string bass, banjo and guitar in its rhythm section!). Although his orchestra in the 1930s at times featured Bunny Berigan, Trumbauer and both Jack and Charlie Teagarden, Whiteman's music was considered old hat by the time of the swing era, and he essentially retired (except for special appearances) by the early '40s. Many of his recordings (particularly those with Beiderbecke) have been reissued numerous times and are more rewarding than his detractors would lead one to believe. In the 1970s Dick Sudhalter for a time organized and led "The New Paul Whiteman Orchestra" which recorded a couple of fine recreation records. —*Scott Yanow*

★ **Jazz A La King (1920-1936)** / Aug. 23, 1920-Jun. 2, 1936 / RCA ◆◆◆◆

Paul Whiteman and His Orchestra with Bing Crosby / May 17, 1928-Oct. 18, 1929 / Columbia ◆◆◆◆
Of the 16 selections included on this LP, only two or three are regularly reissued. Paul Whiteman's large orchestra played first-class dance music with some spots for brief jazz solos. The legendary cornetist Bix Beiderbecke is heard from on six of the selections (not always the ones credited) but the main emphasis is on the early vocals of Bing Crosby (who is heard from on all but one number) and the distinctive ensembles. 1920s collectors will want to pick this album up due to the rarity of some of the recordings. —*Scott Yanow*

The Complete Capitol Recordings / Jun. 5, 1942-Oct. 26, 1951 / Capitol ◆◆◆
Although he had been the most popular bandleader of the 1920s, by the '40s Paul Whiteman was considered a bit of a has-been. This CD has his last significant recordings. There are eight songs from June 1942 (with vocals by Martha Tilton, Larry Neil, the Mellowaires, on "The Old Music Master" Johnny Mercer and Jack Teagarden and for the most famous selection, "Trav'lin Light," Billie Holiday) that find Whiteman doing his best to emulate Glenn Miller without outright copying him; a swinging "I've Found a New Baby" featuring pianist Buddy Weed is best. Two selections from 1945 really close the book on Whiteman: remakes of "San" (originally recorded with Bix Beiderbecke in 1928) and 1920's "Wang Wang Blues" (Whiteman's very first recording). The CD concludes with routine concert versions of "An American in Paris" and "Rhapsody in Blue" from 1951. Whiteman collectors and historians may find this set of interest but it pales next to his performances of the 1920s. —*Scott Yanow*

Mark Whitfield

b. 1967, Syosset, NY
Guitar / Soul Jazz, Hard Bop
A talented guitarist influenced by George Benson and versatile enough to play straight-ahead jazz or R&B, Mark Whitfield was originally a bassist. At 15 he switched to guitar and soon won a scholarship to Berklee. After graduating from Berklee in 1987 Whitfield temporarily moved to Brooklyn and appeared at many sessions. George Benson suggested he work for Jack McDuff and that association was a big break for Whitfield. He has since recorded as a leader for Warner Bros. and Verve and as a sideman with many players including Jimmy Smith, Nicholas Payton, Ray Brown and Courtney Pine. *—Scott Yanow*

The Marksman / 1990 / Warner Brothers ✦✦✦✦
Good young guitarist swings hard in the tradition. *—Michael G. Nastos*

Patrice / 1991 / Warner Brothers ✦✦✦✦

Mark Whitfield / 1993 / Warner Brothers ✦✦✦✦✦

● True Blue / 1994 / Verve ✦✦✦✦✦

7th Ave. Stroll / 1995 / Verve ✦✦✦✦✦

Sebastian Whittaker

b. Sep. 12, 1966, Houston, TX
Drums / Hard Bop
A fine musician, Sebastian Whittaker models his drumming and bandleading after his idol Art Blakey. Blind since the age of one, Whittaker began playing drums when he was three. After extensive musical study (he also took lessons on piano and composition), Whittaker resettled in Houston and has in recent times led a few dates for the Justice label. *—Scott Yanow*

First Outing / 1990 / Justice ✦✦✦✦

Searchin' for the Truth / 1991 / Justice ✦✦✦✦

● And The Creators / 1992 / Justice ✦✦✦✦✦
The word is out about drum sensation Sebastian Whittaker, and he justifies it on this sensational set. Whittaker takes the spotlight at the end of "Cherokee" for some whiplash licks and drumming, but otherwise provides steady, often explosive beats, support and rhythms. He's just as effective playing with subtlety as aggression; sometimes he's spurring on the soloists, and other times meshing behind them. He heads a superb trio that sounds like a revamped '90s version of Art Blakey's Jazz Messengers at times; then they'll switch modes and become a funky R&B horn section and blues-tinged gutbucket ensemble. This music has a vibrant quality, and shows that Sebastian Whittaker is ready to make his mark on the jazz and blues scene. *—Ron Wynn*

One for Bu!! / 1992 / Justice ✦✦✦✦
Drummer Sebastian Whittaker's Justice CD is an effective tribute to Art Blakey and his Jazz Messengers even though none of the sidemen in his septet (which includes trumpeter Barrie Lee Hall, altoist Jesse Davis and pianist Jacky Terasson) actually played with Blakey and all but two standards are group originals. The swinging hard bop date has many concise but colorful solos from a wide variety of talented stylists and a few surprises. The melancholy "Present State of Mind" (which has some fine bowed bass from David Craig) gets away a bit from the Messengers tribute and the minor blues "Mopac at Midnight" ends up with a ragged Dixielandish section (with altoist Shelley Carroll switching to clarinet) that reminds one of the presence of trumpeter Hall, arguably the last great Ellingtonian. Strangely enough some of the tracks also have G.T. Hogan on drums but, due to the lack of liner notes, it is difficult to know which songs. In any case Sebastian Whittaker demonstrates throughout this CD that he deserves to be ranked as one of the more promising of the younger bandleaders. *—Scott Yanow*

Gerald Wiggins

b. May 12, 1922, New York, NY
Piano / Bop, Swing
A veteran pianist who's backed many extraordinary performers, Gerald Wiggins has a swinging style and accomplished technique that's enabled him to adjust in swing, bebop, blues and hard bop situations, as well as with different vocalists. Wiggins toured with comedian Stepin Fechit in the early '40s, then worked in Les Hite's orchestra and with Louis Armstrong and Benny Carter. He moved to the West Coast in the early '50s, where he backed Lena

Horne and accompanied Kay Starr, Eartha Kitt and Helen Humes. He was a music director and film coach in the studios during the '60s, while leading and recording with various trios. During the '70s, '80s, and '90s Wiggins has done sessions for Muse, Hemisphere, Trend, Palo Alto, Specialty, Challenge, Black and Blue and Concord. *—Ron Wynn and Michael G. Nastos*

Gerald Wiggins Trio / Oct. 1956 / VSOP ✦✦✦✦
Due to his skills as an accompanist and his work in Hollywood, Gerald Wiggins has always been a bit underrated, but the pianist has long had his own style within the swing/bop tradition. For this trio date (originally out on Tampa and reissued on LP by VSOP), Wig is teamed with bassist Joe Comfort and drummer Bill Douglas for a set of seven standards and two originals. The music swings with both subtlety and soul, and the overall results are quite enjoyable. Highlights include "Love for Sale," Duke Ellington's "I Don't Know What Kind of Blues I Got," "Surrey with the Fringe on Top" and "The Man That Got Away." *—Scott Yanow*

Around the World in 80 Days / 1956 / Original Jazz Classics ✦✦✦

Relax and Enjoy It / 1961 / Original Jazz Classics ✦✦✦✦✦
Pianist Gerald Wiggins led this trio date (1961) with Joe Comfort (bass) and Jackie Mills (drums). While most people have probably heard Wiggins in support, here is a record that spotlights him (he's made numerous recordings under his name but most for very obscure labels). *—Bob Rusch, Cadence*

Wig is Here / Mar. 25, 1974 / Classic Jazz ✦✦✦✦

● Live at Maybeck Recital Hall, Vol. 8 / Aug. 1990 / Concord Jazz ✦✦✦✦✦

Bob Wilber

b. Mar. 15, 1928, New York, NY
Clarinet, Alto Saxophone, Soprano Saxophone / Swing, Dixieland
Throughout his long career Bob Wilber has done a lot to keep classic jazz alive. A bit misplaced (most jazz players of his generation were much more interested in bop and hard bop), Wilber (along with Kenny Davern, Ralph Sutton and Dick Wellstood) was one of the few in his age group to stick to prebop music. In high school he formed a band that included Wellstood and as a teenager he sat in at Jimmy Ryan's club in New York. Early on he became Sidney Bechet's protege and led his own young group the Wildcats (with whom he made his recording debut). The close association with the dominant Bechet led to a bit of a personality crisis in the 1950s as Wilber sought to find his own voice. He studied with Lennie Tristano and formed the Six, a group that tried to modernize early jazz. When that ended, he played Dixieland with Eddie Condon and in 1957 joined Bobby Hackett's band for a year. Wilber freelanced throughout the 1960s, in 1968 became a founding member of the World's Greatest Jazz Band and in 1973 formed Soprano Summit with Kenny Davern, one of the top swing-oriented groups of the decade. A few years later the band broke up and Wilber teamed up with his wife, singer Pug Horton, in Bechet Legacy (which also featured either Glenn Zottola or Randy Sandke on trumpet). In addition Bob Wilber has worked with the New York Jazz Repertory Company, released music on his own Bodeswell label, wrote the authentic soundtrack to the movie *The Cotton Club* (1984), in 1988 led a band at Carnegie Hall to celebrate the 50th anniversary of Benny Goodman's famous concert and authored his frank memoirs *Music Was Not Enough*. Influenced on soprano, clarinet and alto by respectively Bechet, Goodman and Johnny Hodges, Wilber has long had his own sound on each of his instruments. He has recorded frequently through the years for many labels, most recently Arbors. *—Scott Yanow*

Bob Wilber Jazz Band / Apr. 28, 1949 / Circle ✦✦✦✦✦

Spreadin' Joy / 1957 / Classic Jazz ✦✦✦✦

The Music of Hoagy Carmichael / Jun. 1969 / Monmouth ✦✦✦✦✦

Soprano Summit / Dec. 17, 1973–Dec. 22, 1973 / World Jazz ✦✦✦✦✦
The debut album by Soprano Summit features co-leaders Bob Wilber and Kenny Davern doubling on sopranos and clarinets while accompanied by pianist Dick Hyman, guitarist Bucky Pizzarelli, either George Duvivier or Milt Hinton on bass, and drummer Bobby Rosengarden. The music is often quite heated,

particularly on the numbers associated with Sidney Bechet. The style falls between hot swing and Dixieland with the interplay between the reeds being a constant delight. —*Scott Yanow*

Bob Wilber & The Scott Hamilton Quartet / Jun. 30, 1977–Jul. 1, 1977 / Chiaroscuro ✦✦✦✦

Music of King Oliver / May 10, 1981 / Bodeswell ✦✦✦

● **Ode to Bechet** / 1982 / Jazzology ✦✦✦✦✦

Reflections / Jun. 8, 1983+Jun. 10, 1983 / Bodeswell ✦✦✦

The Cotton Club / 1983–1984 / Geffen ✦✦

★ **Bob Wilber & Bechet Legacy** / Jan. 29, 1984 / Challenge ✦✦✦✦✦
After the breakup of Soprano Summit in the early '80s, Bob Wilber formed a group dedicated to reviving the music of his teacher, Sidney Bechet. Wilber (who triples here on soprano, clarinet and alto) is heard with his intimate quartet (which also includes trumpeter Randy Sandke, guitarist Mike Peters and bassist John Goldsby) during a live performance on nine selections associated with Bechet. This CD (its contents were released for the first time in 1995) has plenty of passionate and heated swing with the high points including "Down in Honky Tonk Town," "Promenade Aux Champs-Elysees," "China Boy" and "Lady Be Good." Quite enjoyable. —*Scott Yanow*

Recorded Live at Bechet's New York City / Apr. 1987 / Jazzology ✦✦✦✦

Horns A-Plenty / Mar. 14, 1994 / Arbors ✦✦✦✦✦

Lee Wiley

b. Oct. 9, 1915, Fort Gibson, OK, **d.** Dec. 11, 1975, New York, NY
Vocals / Swing, Standards
Lee Wiley occupies her own place in jazz history. Although a cooltoned and sophisticated singer, her interpretations of superior standards were often quite sensuous and, even if she did not improvise much, she was a favorite of many musicians, particularly Eddie Condon. She came to New York in the early '30s and at age 17 was singing and recording with Leo Reisman's orchestra. She spent most of the that decade singing with commercial radio orchestras (including Victor Young and Johnny Green) but eventually also appeared at clubs backed by small jazz groups, having a close relationship with Bunny Berigan. Starting in 1939 Lee Wiley became the first singer to devote an entire album to the music of one composer; her George Gershwin, Cole Porter, Harold Arlen and Rodgers & Hart sessions are considered classic and the high points of her career. Wiley married Jess Stacy in 1943 but after five years both their big band and marriage were history. She appeared at a few of Eddie Condon's Town Hall concerts but from the late '40s on Wiley performed and recorded less frequently. After some sessions for Columbia during 1950–51, Storyville in 1954 and Victor during 1956–57, all that remained was a final record for Monmouth-Evergreen in 1971. By then she was forgotten to all but veteran record collectors but Lee Wiley had made her mark decades earlier. —*Scott Yanow*

Complete Young Lee Wiley (1931–37) / Jun. 30, 1931–Feb. 10, 1937 / Vintage Jazz Classics ✦✦✦

★ **Sings the Songs of Ira and George Gershwin ...** / Nov. 13, 1939–Apr. 1940 / Audiophile ✦✦✦✦✦

Sings the Songs of Rodgers and Hart & Harold Arlen / Feb. 1940–Apr. 1943 / Audiophile ✦✦✦✦✦

Night in Manhattan / Dec. 12, 1950+Dec. 14, 1950 / Columbia Special Products ✦✦✦✦

Lee Wiley Sings Irving Berlin / Nov. 19, 1951+Dec. 4, 1951 / Columbia ✦✦✦

Lee Wiley Sings Vincent Youmans / Dec. 5, 1951+Dec. 7, 1951 / Columbia ✦✦✦

Duologue / Jul. 7, 1954 / Black Lion ✦✦✦✦

As Time Goes By / Jun. 12, 1956–Jul. 25, 1957 / Bluebird ✦✦✦✦✦

Back Home Again / Sep. 30, 1971–Oct. 11, 1971 / Monmouth ✦✦✦

Ernie Wilkins

b. Jul. 20, 1922, Saint Louis, MO
Tenor Saxophone, Arranger / Bop, Swing
A good saxophonist, but better arranger and composer, Ernie Wilkins has been providing fine compositions and arrangements for big bands since the early '50s. He learned piano and violin in his youth, then studied music at Wilberforce University. Wilkins played in a military band under Willie Smith's leadership in the service, then worked in the late '40s with the Jeters-Pillars Orchestra and Earl Hines' final big band. He joined Count Basie in the early '50s, playing alto and tenor and supplying compositions and arrangements. Wilkins also wrote tunes and arrangements for Dizzy Gillespie's mid-'50s band that toured the Middle East and South America. He later wrote arrangements for Tommy Dorsey and was staff composer for Harry James in the early '60s, and wrote pieces for his brother Jimmy Wilkins' band. Wilkins joined Clark Terry's B-A-D band in the late '60s as music director and principal composer but left to form his own band after they appeared at the Montreaux Jazz Festival. He supplied more compositions to Count Basie, then became head of Mainstream Records' A&R department in the early '70s. Wilkins toured Europe with Terry in the late '70s and settled in Copenhagen in 1979. He organized the Almost Big Band in 1980. —*Ron Wynn*

● **Here Comes the Swingin' Mr. Wilkins** / Dec. 9, 1959–Jan. 11, 1960 / Fresh Sound ✦✦✦✦✦

The Big New Band of the '60s / Mar. 11, 1960–Apr. 28, 1960 / Everest ✦✦✦✦✦

And the Almost Big Band / Oct. 30, 1980–Nov. 2, 1980 / Storyville ✦✦✦✦

Montreux / Jul. 1983 / SteepleChase ✦✦✦

Jack Wilkins

b. Jun. 3, 1944
Guitar / Hard Bop
A masterful, in-demand guitarist, Jack Wilkins might be the finest mainstream player on the New York scene. A New York native, Wilkins has a expressive, light style with great warmth and melodic integrity. He's famous for using classical guitar techniques in his playing and achieving a similiar approach to a pianist in his chording. But he's also a superb blues player. Wilkins had formal training with jazz education pioneer John Mghegan, and also studied vibes, piano and classical guitar. He's toured and recorded with Buddy Rich, and performed in concert with Stan Getz, Dizzy Gillespie, Morgana King and Pearl Bailey. Wilkins has recorded with Jack DeJohnette, Eddie Gomez, Randy and Mike Brecker, Phil Woods and Harvie Swartz among others. —*Ron Wynn and David Nelson McCarthy*

Windows / 1973 / Mainstream ✦✦✦✦

● **Merge** / Feb. 1977 / Chiaroscuro ✦✦✦✦✦
These two recordings originally released as two separate albums have been reissued on CD. *Merge* features Randy Brecker, Eddie Gomez, and Jack DeJohnette. "You Can't Live Without It" features Michael Brecker, Phil Markowitz, Jon Burr and Al Foster. —*Paul Kohler*

Call Him Reckless / May 1989 / Music Masters ✦✦✦✦

Alien Army / Jun. 13, 1990–Jun. 15, 1990 / Music Masters ✦✦✦✦

Mexico / 1992 / CTI ✦✦✦

Buster Williams (Charles Anthony Williams)

b. Apr. 17, 1942, Camden, NJ
Bass / Post Bop, Hard Bop
Here's one bassist who prefers the background to the spotlight and regards his role as a supportive rather than starring one. Buster Williams has made subtle swing, precise rhythms, a startling tone and impeccable technique the hallmark of his playing with numerous bands since the early '60s. He learned both bass and drums from his father, opting for bass after being impressed by recordings featuring Oscar Pettiford solos. Williams studied harmony, composition and theory at Combs College of Music in Philadelphia in the late '50s, then worked with Jimmy Heath. He toured and recorded with the Gene Ammons/Sonny Stitt quintet in 1960 and 1961. Williams played with vocalists Dakota Staton, Betty Carter, Sarah Vaughan and Nancy Wilson in the mid and late '60s, recording with Vaughan and Wilson. Williams moved to Los Angeles while with Wilson, playing and recording with the Jazz Crusaders, Prince Lasha and the Bobby Hutcherson-Harold Land quintet while also working with Miles Davis. He moved to New York in 1969 and joined Herbie Hancock, playing with him until 1972. He worked regularly with Mary Lou Williams (1973–75) and Ron Carter's Quartet (1977–78) and in the early 1980s was a member of both Sphere and the Timeless All Stars.

Although opportunities to lead his own sessions are rare (thus far for Muse and Buddah), Williams has appeared as a sideman on a countless number of sessions with the who's who of jazz and remains in great demand in the 1990s. —*Ron Wynn and Scott Yanow*

Crystal Reflections / Aug. 30, 1976 / Muse ◆◆◆◆
Excellent set. No reed or brass soloist but Kenny Barron (p) and Jimmy Rowles (p) are super. One of the last times Roy Ayers plays vibes in jazz context on record. —*Ron Wynn*

Tokudo / Jan. 7, 1978 / Denon ◆◆◆

Heartbeat / Mar. 28, 1978–Apr. 3, 1978 / Muse ◆◆◆◆
A diverse session of jazz touches by pop guests on the four originals by bassist Williams, one standard, and one by Jimmie Rowles. Includes Rowles (p), Kenny Barron (p), Ben Riley (d), vocalist Suzanne Klewan and strings from Pat and Gayle Dixon. —*Michael G. Nastos*

Dreams Come True / Sep. 1978–Oct. 1978 / Buddah ◆◆◆

● **Something More** / Mar. 1989 / In + Out ◆◆◆◆◆

Clarence Williams

b. 1896, Plaquemine, LA, d. Nov. 6, 1965, New York, NY
Piano, Vocals, Leader / Classic Jazz, Blues
Organization and consistency were what made Clarence Williams a key figure among early jazz musicians. He rivaled Fletcher Henderson for being the most recorded Black performer during the '20s and published and promoted the work of such seminal stars as Fats Waller, James P. Johnson, Willie "The Lion" Smith and Spencer Williams while co-writing major songs like "Royal Garden Blues," "Squeeze Me," "Baby, Won't You Please Come Home" and "Tain't Nobody's Business If I Do." In addition, his groups, especially the Blue Five, were an important repertory ensemble and backing band for several vocalists. Williams' piano playing and vocals were merely effective at best, but the 300 Williams songs issued between 1921 and 1938 included many extraordinary performances. Williams was part Creole and part Choctaw; at one time due to both his widow and his death certificate Williams' birth date was given as 1898, but further research now shows it was 1893. His childhood included periods where he worked in a hotel and sang in a street band. He came to New Orleans in 1906 and traveled with a ministrel show as an emcee, singer and dancer until 1911. Williams began managing a cabaret in 1913, then started a music publishing venture with A.J. Piron. Williams moved to Chicago later in the decade before relocating permanently to New York City in 1920. Prior to going to Chicago, he toured with Piron. Williams cut his first records in 1921, singing with a White band. By 1923, he'd become Okeh's "race music" A&R director, and in that capacity, as well as being a bandleader, became a conduit for the jazz community. The careers of Louis Armstrong, Sidney Bechet, Buster Bailey, King Oliver, Don Redman, Coleman Hawkins, Lonnie Johnson, Bubber Miley, Tommy Ladnier and Jimmy Harrison were aided either by him employing them or getting them recording sessions. Williams played on Bessie Smith sessions, and she cut several of his songs; he also backed vocalists Butterbeans & Susie, Sara Martin, Sippie Wallace and Eva Taylor (whom he married in 1921). The original Blue Five included Thomas Morris, Charlie Irvis or John Mayfield, Sticky Elliott or Bechet and Buddy Christian. Armstrong was a member in 1924 and 1925, and later came Bailey, Aaron Thompson, Hawkins, Redman and Miley. They continued recording through 1927. Williams later made nearly 100 recordings for Okeh, Vocalion and Victor from 1927–1939 with "washboard" bands that included Ed Allen, Bailey or Cecil Scott and Floyd Casey. Williams concentrated on writing after the late '30s but led a final Blue Five session in 1941 with James P. Johnson, Wellman Braud and Taylor doing vocals then sold his catalog to Decca in 1943. He was a shop owner in Harlem but went blind after being hit by a taxi in 1956. Nearly 11 years after his death, a comprehensive bio-discography "Clarence Williams" by Tom Lord put his accomplishments into perspective. —*Ron Wynn*

Clarence Williams 1921–1924 / Oct. 11, 1921–Nov. 6, 1924 / Classics ◆◆◆◆◆
Although this is not the most essential of the Clarence Williams CDs released in the complete Classics series, all of the releases are highly recommended to fans of early jazz. Many of these titles are quite rare and historical. First Williams is heard as a singer on five period numbers from 1921 ("The Dance They Call the Georgia

Hunch" is the most memorable) and has a vocal duet with Daisy Martin on "Brown Skin (Who You For)." Williams also takes four piano solos and on most of the other titles features the great soprano saxophonist Sidney Bechet (heard in his earliest recordings); "Wild Cat Blues" and "Kansas City Man Blues" are classics. In addition Louis Armstrong joins the group on three numbers, two of which have vocals from Eva Taylor. —*Scott Yanow*

The Complete Sessions, Vol. 1 (1923–1926) / Jul. 30, 1923–Nov. 12, 1923 / Hot and Sweet ◆◆◆
This imported CD has all of Clarence Williams' recordings from a 3-1/2 month period, not only the Blue Five performances but also Williams' work with blues singers Sara Martin, Mamie Smith, Rosetta Crawford and Margaret Johnson in addition to his wife Eva Taylor. Most valuable are the eight instrumentals, for they feature the great soprano saxophonist Sidney Bechet on his earliest recordings along with trumpeter Thomas Morris. Highlights include "Wild Cat Blues," "Kansas City Man Blues" and "Oh! Daddy Blues" although "I've Got the 'Yes We Have No Bananas' Blues" is amusing! The Classics reissues series bypasses the sometimes so-so blues singers. —*Scott Yanow*

The Complete Sessions, Vol. 2 (1923–1931) / Nov. 14, 1923–Mar. 4, 1925 / Hot 'N Sweet ◆◆◆
The second Clarence Williams CD from the French Hot 'N Sweet label has not only all of the performances by the pianist's Blue Five during a 16-month period (featuring Louis Armstrong and Sidney Bechet) but also lesser-known sides backing blues singers Virginia Liston (on which Bechet allegedly plays guitar), Maureen Englin, Margaret Johnson, Sippie Wallace and Eva Taylor. Although it is nice to have those rarities, the selections that match Armstrong and Bechet (particularly the explosive "Cake Walkin' Babies from Home" and "Mandy Make up Your Mind," which has an odd sarrusophone solo from Bechet) are the most memorable performances and those are also available on the Classics label. —*Scott Yanow*

Clarence Williams 1924–1926 / Dec. 17, 1924–Feb. 1926 / Classics ◆◆◆◆◆
The second CD in the Classics label's "complete" Clarence Williams series traces the pianist/bandleader's recordings during a 14-month period. The first six titles feature soprano great Sidney Bechet (who has a unique sarrusophone solo on "Mandy Make up Your Mind") while the first 13 also have Louis Armstrong. The pairing of these two classic and competitive greats is at its zenith on a brilliant version of "Cake Walking Babies from Home"; Satch gets the edge. In addition there are notable contributions on these 23 performances by trombonist Charlie Irvis, tenor saxophonist Coleman Hawkins, cornetists Joe Smith, Bubber Miley and Ed Allen, clarinetist Buster Bailey and singer Eva Taylor among others. Williams' series of hot performances really epitomized small-group 1920s jazz and every entry in this Classics series is highly recommended. Other highlights include "Coal Cart Blues," "Shake That Thing," "Dinah" (which features Hawkins on baritone), "I've Found a New Baby" and two versions of "Santa Claus Blues." —*Scott Yanow*

Clarence Williams And Eva Taylor 1925–1926 / Dec. 15, 1925–Dec. 10, 1926 / Swaggie ◆◆◆◆
This excellent Swaggie LP has 17 titles featuring pianist Clarence Williams and his various groups (known during this period as his Blue Five, Blue Seven, Morocco Five or Stompers). Eva Taylor sings on ten of the songs, six of which were originally issued under her name. Taylor's easy-going style fit the music well and Williams was wise enough to always use the best musicians available. For this album such top players as trumpeters Bubber Miley, Thomas Morris and Tommy Ladnier, trombonists Charlie Irvis and Jimmy Harrison, the reeds of Buster Bailey, Don Redman and Coleman Hawkins, the great tuba player Cyrus St. Clair and even violinist Eddie South. The easily enjoyable performances are highlighted by "Shake That Thing," "Get It Fixed," "Dinah," "Jackass Blues" and "Senegalese Stomp." The Eva Taylor sides are rare but those under Clarence Williams' name have been reissued on CD by Classics. —*Scott Yanow*

Clarence Williams 1926–1927 / Mar. 7, 1926–Jan. 29, 1927 / Classics ◆◆◆◆◆
The third CD in the Classics label's Clarence Williams program reissues all of the pianist/bandleader's dates from a ten-month period, 23 selections in all. Such groups as Joe Jordan's Ten Sharps and Flats (performing a memorable version of "Morocco Blues"), the Dixie Washboard Band, The Blue Grass Foot Warmers and

Clarence Williams' Stompers (or Blue Seven or Jazz Kings or Washboard Four!). Williams uses some of the top musicians of the era (including cornetists Bubber Miley, Tommy Ladnier and Ed Allen, trombonist Jimmy Harrison, clarinetist Buster Bailey, Coleman Hawkins on tenor, Cyrus St. Clair on tuba and Jasper Taylor on washboard among others) for the heated and free-wheeling performances. Highlights include "Jackass Blues," "I Found a New Baby," "Senegalese Stomp" and a truly classic version of "Candy Lips" (which features two clarinets in hot pursuit). All of the CDs in this valuable series are highly recommended to classic jazz fans. — *Scott Yanow*

Clarence Williams (1927–1934) / Jan. 25, 1927–1933 / ABC ◆◆◆
Engineer Robert Parker is famous (or in some minds infamous) for remastering early jazz recordings and making them sound as if they were originally made for stereo. This CD from the Australian Broadcasting Corporation, made available domestically through DRG, has 16 performances by the bandleader and occasional pianist Clarence Williams. Most of the selections are quite enjoyable, but the programming, jumping back and forth over a seven-year period, is pretty random and lowers this sampler's value. Still, there are quite a few enjoyable tracks, including "Candy Lips," "You're Bound to Look like a Monkey When You Get Old," "Close Fit Blues" and "He Wouldn't Stop Doin' It," with many all stars getting a chance to solo during the heated small-group jams. — *Scott Yanow*

Clarence Williams 1927 / Mar. 8, 1927–Sep. 23, 1927 / Classics ◆◆◆◆◆
Pianist/bandleader Clarence Williams was at the height of his productivity in 1927; the 22 numbers on this CD were recorded within a 6-1/2 month period. With the exception of the Dixie Washboard Band, all of the performances were originally released under Clarence Williams' name but the personnel and instrumentation often differ from session to session. The fourth in Classics' complete reissuance of Williams' recordings features such top sideman as Ed Allen and Louis Metcalf, trumpeter Red Allen (in what was probably his earliest recording), trombonist Charlie Irvis, clarinetist Buster Bailey and a variety of lesser-known players with some of the best performances being "Cushion Foot Stomp" (which is heard three different times), "Shooting the Pistol," "Baby, Won't You Please Come Home" and Williams' solo version of "When I March in April with May." Highly recommended to collectors of vintage jazz. — *Scott Yanow*

Clarence Williams 1927–1928 / Oct. 1927–Aug. 1, 1928 / Classics ◆◆◆◆◆
The fifth CD in Classics' "complete" Clarence Williams program (all are highly recommended to collectors of 1920s jazz) has 22 selections from 11 separate recording sessions, all of the pianist/bandleader's dates for a ten-month period. There are a pair of piano solos, two numbers in which Williams' vocals (including an eccentric "Farm Hand Papa") are backed by the great pianist James P. Johnson and band performances featuring cornetists Ed Allen and King Oliver, clarinetists Buster Bailey and Arville Harris, trombonist Ed Cuffee, Coleman Hawkins and Benny Waters on tenors, Cyrus St. Clair on tuba and the washboard of Floyd Casey. Highlights include "Jingles," "Church Street Sobbin' Blues," "Sweet Emmalina," and "Mountain City Blues." — *Scott Yanow*

Clarence Williams 1928–1929 / Aug. 1928–Jan. 1929 / Classics ◆◆◆◆◆
The sixth volume in the very valuable Classics Clarence Williams reissue program contains 22 numbers in its attractive CD, mostly from a four-month period. There is a lot of variety on these sessions with many of the best tracks featuring both King Oliver and Ed Allen on cornets along with tenorman Benny Waters. There are also numbers by Clarence Williams' Washboard Five, his Novelty Four (a quartet with Oliver and guitarist Eddie Lang) and a larger orchestra. Throughout all of the selections there are spirited ensembles, heated but coherent solos and plenty of joy and swing. The high points include "Organ Grinder Blues," "Have You Ever Felt That Way," "Wildflower Rag," "Bozo," "Bimbo" and "Beau-Koo Jack" (which is closely based on the Louis Armstrong recording). — *Scott Yanow*

● **Clarence Williams 1929** / Jan. 1929–May 28, 1929 / Classics ◆◆◆◆◆
The seventh volume in the European Classics label's complete reissuance of bandleader Clarence Williams' very valuable recordings documents his music during a four-month period. Included

are two Williams piano solos, his sessions leading the Barrelhouse Five Orchestra, Jazz Kings and the Memphis Jazzers, and quite a bit of superior small-group jazz. Among the sidemen are cornetist Ed Allen, trombonist Ed Cuffee, Arville Harris and Albert Socarras on reeds, banjoist Leroy Harris, pianist James P. Johnson (on two songs), the exuberant tuba of Cyrus St. Clair, Floyd Casey on drums and washboard and Williams himself on piano and occasional vocals. Highlights include "Endurance Stomp," "If You Like Me Like I Like You," "Steamboat Days," "Baby, Won't You Please Come Home," "In Our Cottage of Love" and the original version of "Breeze." All of the CDs in this enjoyable series are easily recommended to 1920s collectors. — *Scott Yanow*

Clarence Williams 1929–1930 / Jun. 21, 1929–Apr. 23, 1930 / Classics ◆◆◆◆◆
The eighth CD in the European Classics series that is reissuing complete and in chronological order all of the recordings led by pianist/composer Clarence Williams documents his activity from a ten-month period. During this era Williams varied his personnel and instrumentation from session to session and the results are quite varied yet consistently hot. Williams' groups feature such sidemen as cornetist Ed Allen, trumpeter Charlie Gaines, the reeds of Arville Harris and Russell Procope, the enthusiastic tuba of Cyrus St. Clair, Floyd Casey on drums and washboard, two excellent vocals apiece by Margaret Webster (her "You've Got to Give Me Some" is a near-classic) and Eva Taylor and, on eight selections, the masterful pianist James P. Johnson. The highpoints are "How Could I Be Blue?" and "I've Found a New Baby," performances taken as piano duets by Johnson and Williams that include some humorous conversation. All of the CDs in this very valuable series are highly recommended to collectors of 1920s jazz. — *Scott Yanow*

● **Clarence Williams 1930–1931** / May 22, 1930–Feb. 19, 1931 / Classics ◆◆◆◆◆
This CD is the ninth in an extensive series that reissues all of the recordings led by pianist/composer Clarence Williams. Since Williams headed a wide variety of exciting small groups in the 1920s and '30s that utilized the playing of many top jazz players, all of the CDs are worth acquiring by collectors of classic jazz. The 22 selections on this particular CD range from novelty Williams solo performances to groups featuring trumpeters Red Allen and Ed Allen, Albert Socarras on several reeds (including flute), clarinetists Buster Bailey and Cecil Scott, Prince Robinson doubling on clarinet and tenor, pianist Herman Chittison, Ikey Robinson on banjo, the great tuba player Cyrus St. Clair, singer Eva Taylor, Floyd Casey on washboard, the Bingie Madison big band and Williams himself on vocals, piano and jug. Highlights of this spirited program include "You're Bound to Look like a Monkey When You Get Old," "High Society Blues," "Hot Lovin,'" "Baby, Won't You Please Come Home" and four different versions of "Shout Sister Shout." — *Scott Yanow*

Claude Williams

b. Feb. 22, 1908, Muskogee, OK
Guitar, Violin / Swing
Bad luck kept Claude Williams from ever gaining the fame he deserved, but late in his life he finally achieved some notoriety. Early on Williams worked with the family band of Oscar Pettiford, and in 1928 he joined Terrence Holder's territory band, a group that soon became Andy Kirk's 12 Clouds of Joy. The violinist made his recording debut with Kirk in 1929 but had departed before the band finally made it big in 1936. By then Williams (after a stint with Alphonso Trent) was playing rhythm guitar and occasional violin with Count Basie's Orchestra. Unfortunately producer John Hammond did not care for Williams' violin playing and shortly after the band had relocated to New York and was on the verge of making it, Hammond persuaded Basie to replace Williams; Freddie Green filled the spot for the next 50 years. Claude Williams returned to Kansas City and decades of obscurity although he generally worked and had a stint with Roy Milton in the early '50s. However, starting in 1972 (due to his association with Jay McShann and some new recordings), Williams began to be discovered and tour more often. He recorded both as a leader and as a sideman and in 1994-95 played with the Statesmen of Jazz. A month younger than Stephane Grappelli, Claude Williams was still in his musical prime as he entered his late 80s. — *Scott Yanow*

★ **Call for the Fiddler** / Feb. 1976 / SteepleChase ✦✦✦✦
Fiddler's Dream / Jul. 1981 / Classic Jazz ✦✦✦✦
Live at J's, Pt. 1 / Apr. 24, 1989+May 1, 1989 / Arhoolie ✦✦✦✦
Violinist Claude Williams, one of the last surviving links to the swing era, had important stints with the big bands of Andy Kirk and Count Basie that were just barely documented. Unjustly obscure for decades, he is in excellent form on a live quintet date with guitarist James Chirillo, pianist Ron Mathews, bassist Al McKibbon and either Akira Tana or Grady Tate on drums. Williams fiddles and occasionally sings on a variety of swing standards and blues, showing that in 1989 he still very much had it. This is the first of two CDs from this engagement. —*Scott Yanow*

Live at J's, Pt. 2 / Apr. 24, 1989+May 1, 1989 / Arhoolie ✦✦✦✦
On the second of two volumes, veteran swing violinist Claude Williams (81 at the time of this live recording) proves that he is still in top form. The repertoire is primarily swing standards and (with the assistance of guitarist James Chirillo, pianist Ron Mathews, bassist Al McKibbon and either Akira Tana or Grady Tate on drums), Williams is easily the main star of this swinging set. His violin solos are excellent (a little rougher in tone but near the level of a Stephane Grappelli) while his occasional vocals show plenty of personality. This is fine music that helps to put the focus on a much neglected swing stylist. —*Scott Yanow*

Swingtime In New York / Sep. 5, 1994 / Progressive ✦✦✦✦✦
Violinist Claude Williams, at the age of 86, shows that he is still in his musical prime during this quintet date with Bill Easley (who switches between tenor, clarinet and flute), pianist Sir Roland Hanna, bassist Earl May and drummer Joe Ascione. Williams was with both Andy Kirk and Count Basie shortly before they made it big but has spent most of his long career in Kansas City in obscurity. Fortunately he has made several worthy recordings in his later years and this is one of his best, a well-rounded set ranging in repertoire from one of the first songs he ever learned ("You've Got to See Your Mama Ev'ry Night or You Can't See Mama at All") to Ellington, Monk ("Straight No Chaser") and even Stevie Wonder ("You Are the Sunshine of My Life"). The emphasis is on swing and Claude Williams is heard near the peak of his powers. —*Scott Yanow*

Cootie Williams (Charles Melvin Williams)

b. Jun. 24, 1910, Mobile, AL, d. Sep. 14, 1985, New York, NY
Trumpet / Swing
Cootie Williams, one of the finest trumpeters of the 1930s, expanded upon the role originally formed by Bubber Miley with Duke Ellington's Orchestra. Renowned for his work with the plunger mute, Cootie was also a fine soloist when playing open. Starting as a teenager, Cootie Williams played with a variety of local bands in the South, coming to New York with Alonzo Ross' Syncopators. He played for a short time with the orchestras of Chick Webb and Fletcher Henderson (recording with the latter) before joining Duke Ellington as Miley's replacement in February 1929. He was a fixture with Duke's band during the next 11 years, not only recording many classics with Ellington (including "Echoes of Harlem" and "Concerto for Cootie") but also leading some of his own sessions and recording with Lionel Hampton, Teddy Wilson and Billie Holiday in addition to being a guest at Benny Goodman's Carnegie Hall Concert in 1938. His decision to leave Ellington and join Goodman's Orchestra in 1940 was considered a major event in the jazz world. During his year with BG, Williams was well featured with both the big band and Goodman's sextet. The following year he became a bandleader, heading his own orchestra, which at times in the 1940s featured such up-and-coming players as pianist Bud Powell, tenorman Eddie "Lockjaw" Davis, altoist-singer Eddie "Cleanhead" Vinson and even Charlie Parker. Although he had a hit (thanks to Willis Jackson's honking tenor) on "Gator," by 1948 Cootie had cut his group back to a sextet. Playing R&B-oriented music, he worked steadily at the Savoy but by the 1950s was drifting into obscurity. However in 1962, after a 22-year absence, Cootie Williams rejoined Duke Ellington, staying even beyond Duke's death in 1974 as a featured soloist. By then his solos were much simpler and more primitive than earlier (gone was the Louis Armstrong-inspired bravado) but Cootie remained the master with the plunger mute. He was semi-retired during his final decade, taking a final solo in 1978 on a Teresa Brewer record and posthumously serving as an inspiration for Wynton Marsalis' own plunger playing. —*Scott Yanow*

● **Sextet and Orchestra: 1944 Recordings** / Jan. 6, 1944–Aug. 22, 1944 / Phoenix ✦✦✦✦✦
Typhoon / Feb. 26, 1945–1950 / Swingtime ✦✦✦✦✦
Cootie Williams in Hi Fi / Mar. 5, 1958–Apr. 8, 1958 / RCA ✦✦✦✦
The Solid Trumpet of Cootie Williams / Apr. 4, 1962 / Moodsville ✦✦✦

James Williams

b. Mar. 8, 1951, Memphis, TN
Piano / Hard Bop
One of the most consistent and reliable pianists in what could be called modern mainstream jazz, James Williams has made many rewarding recordings through the years. He started playing piano when he was 13, primarily gospel and soul music at first (influences that can still be felt in his solos). He studied at Memphis State University and taught at Berklee during 1972–77. While based in Boston, Williams played regularly with such visiting all-stars as Woody Shaw, Art Farmer, Clark Terry and Joe Henderson. He came to fame during his period with Art Blakey's Jazz Messengers (1977–81) and since then has performed and recorded frequently with a wide variety of players including Sonny Stitt, Bobby Hutcherson, Tom Harrell, his own trios and the very interesting Contemporary Piano Ensemble. —*Scott Yanow*

Everything I Love / Apr. 17, 1979 / Concord Jazz ✦✦✦
Images (of Things to Come) / Jun. 1980 / Concord Jazz ✦✦✦✦
Arioso Touch / Feb. 1982 / Concord Jazz ✦✦✦
Wonderful 1982 date; great solos, blues influences. Buster Williams (b) and Billy Higgins (d) are great. —*Ron Wynn*
● **Alter Ego** / Jul. 19, 1984+Jul. 20, 1984 / Sunnyside ✦✦✦✦✦
Pianist James Williams learned a great deal from his stint with Art Blakey's Jazz Messengers and, when he emerged from the group, he was perfectly qualified to be a bandleader. His Sunnyside session features such up-and-coming players as guitarist Kevin Eubanks, the reeds of Billy Pierce and Bill Easley, bassist Ray Drummond and drummer Tony Reedus on a set of original material. Five of the seven songs were composed by Williams while the other two (including the memorable "Waltz for Monk") were contributed by Donald Brown. The frequently exciting music (high-quality modern hard bop) still sounds fresh. —*Scott Yanow*

Progress Report / May 22, 1985–May 24, 1985 / Sunnyside ✦✦✦✦✦
Progress Report featured three Art Blakey alumni: James Williams (keyboards), Billy Pierce (reeds) and guitarist Kevin Eubanks (a member of Blakey's short-lived 1980 big band). None of the six originals (half by the leader, one from Eubanks and a pair by Donald Brown, Williams' successor with Blakey) had memorable melodies, but all contained plenty of room for explorative chord-based improvisations. —*Scott Yanow*

Magical Trio 1 / Jun. 26, 1987 / EmArcy ✦✦✦✦✦
With Art Blakey (d) and Ray Brown (b). —*Michael G. Nastos*
Magical Trio 2 / Nov. 23, 1987–Nov. 24, 1987 / EmArcy ✦✦✦
Elvin Jones (d) in driver's chair this time. —*Ron Wynn*
Meet the Magical Trio / Sep. 2, 1988 / EmArcy ✦✦✦✦
I Remember Clifford / 1989 / DIW ✦✦✦
Meets the Saxophone Masters / Sep. 23, 1991 / DIW/Columbia ✦✦✦✦
Pianist James Williams picked three of the top tenor players of the 1990s (Joe Henderson, George Coleman and Billy Pierce) to participate in a jam session-type set. The sextet (with bassist James Genus and drummer Tony Reedus) performs six selections, all but one of which are over 9 minutes long. Each of the saxophonists have plenty of solo space and many chances to trade off. The material is generally pretty basic, with two blues, a runthrough on rhythm changes, the folk song "Calgary" and a pair of standards being performed. The tenors are quite aware of each other's presence so the playing is of a consistently high quality even if no real explosions occur. An enjoyable set. —*Scott Yanow*

Talkin' Trash / Mar. 4, 1993 / DIW/Columbia ✦✦✦✦
Although pianist James Williams is the nominal leader of this CD and there is also room for many concise solos from Billy Pierce (mostly on tenor), vibraphonist Steve Nelson and the remarkable bassist Christian McBride, the star throughout is actually fluegel-

hornist Clark Terry. Seventy-two at the time but showing no sign of decline, Terry contributed three of the numbers, sings in his famous Mumbles voice on two humorous pieces (including a preacher routine on "The Orator") and plays quite well throughout. High points of this straight-ahead session include the boppish "Serenade to a Bus Seat," the uptempo blues "Chuckles" and Terry's spectacular solo on "Moonglow." —*Scott Yanow*

Jessica Williams

b. Mar. 17, 1948, Baltimore, MD
Piano / Bop, Post Bop

Due to her being based in Northern California, Jessica Williams is a bit underrated but (on evidence of her recent sets for Jazz Focus and Hep) she is one of the top jazz pianists of the 1990s. Williams is a powerful virtuoso whose complete control of the keyboard, wit, solid sense of swing and the influence of Thelonious Monk have combined to make her a particularly notable player. She started taking piano lessons when she was four and was gigging as a teenager. Williams took extensive classical lessons but also gigged with Philly Joe Jones in Philadelphia before moving to San Francisco in 1977. She was the house pianist at Keystone Korner for a time and made a few interesting recordings (some as Jessica Jennifer Williams) during the period, sometimes utilizing electronics. Although she appeared on Charlie Rouse's final record and gigged steadily, Williams was largely off record (outside of her own private Quanta label) until re-emerging in the late '80s as a brilliant solo acoustic player. She is a giant whose many dates for Jazz Focus (five of its first ten releases feature Williams) and Hep are consistently brilliant. —*Scott Yanow*

Nothin' But the Truth / Feb. 26, 1986 / Delos ✦✦✦✦

And Then, There's This / Feb. 1, 1990 / Timeless ✦✦ ✦✦✦

Live at Maybeck Recital Hall, Vol. 21 / Feb. 16, 1992 / Concord Jazz ✦✦✦✦✦
One of the happiest events of the 1990s has been the emergence of Jessica Williams as one of the most talented pianists in jazz. Her Maybeck Recital Hall solo concert is as good a place as any to discover her abilities. She explores a variety of standards and four of her originals (along with Dave Brubeck's fairly obscure "Summer Song") with creativity and wit. Sometimes Williams shows off the influence of Thelonious Monk, but she rarely stays predictable for long, and her sense of humor is quite original. This is an impressive outing with her interpretations of "Why Do I Love You?," "I'm Confessin'" and "It's Easy to Remember" being among the highlights. —*Scott Yanow*

★ Next Step / Apr. 6, 1993 / Hep ✦✦✦✦✦
Jessica Williams, although hardly a household name, is actually one of the finest jazz pianists of the 1990s and her Hep CD gives listeners ample proof. She does a brilliant imitation of Thelonious Monk on the first half of "Easter Parade" (before displaying her own strong musical personality, capturing not only Monk's unique chord patterns, but his touch and his wit. Throughout the rest of her colorful solo set, Williams also hints at Art Tatum and Lennie Tristano and yet comes across as a true original. Her creative interpretations of such standards as "Taking a Chance on Love," "Like Someone in Love" and a medium-tempo "I Got It Bad" are quite memorable and full of more than their share of surprises including some funny quotes from other songs. The polyrhythms on "Bongo's Waltz" are worthy of Dave Brubeck, whose tender "I Didn't Know Till You Told Me" Williams also revives. Highly recommended. —*Scott Yanow*

★ Arrival / Oct. 29, 1993 / Jazz Focus ✦✦✦✦✦
Jessica Williams is such an impressive pianist that Philip Barker originally started the Jazz Focus label primarily to record her. This solo outing (the debut of the label) is one of Williams' finest. She digs into a wide variety of material ranging from a traditional "Japanese Folk Song" and "The Creator Has a Master Plan" to compositions by Thelonious Monk, Dizzy Gillespie, Randy Weston and Duke Ellington ("Mood Indigo"). Having mastered the musical vocabulary of Monk, Williams is able to quote from Monk at will, but she uses his language to humorous effect (although respectfully) rather than allowing it to dominate her own individual style. "Lulu's Back in Town" and "Wrap Your Troubles in Dreams" are among the high points of this very stimulating (and often witty) outing. Highly recommended. —*Scott Yanow*

Momentum / Feb. 7, 1994 / Jazz Focus ✦✦✦✦✦
Cedar Walton on the back of this CD writes "Jessica has few peers

on the jazz scene today" and, although she remains a bit underrated, the statement is quite true. This trio set with bassist Jeff Johnson and drummer Dick Berk has many exciting moments with the pianist finding plenty of fresh ideas on such songs as "We Kiss in a Shadow," Thelonious Monk's "Shuffle Boil," "It's Easy to Remember" and "Autumn Leaves" in addition to four of her own originals. The music is quite unpredictable while remaining consistently exciting. Jessica Williams really is one of the best. —*Scott Yanow*

Joe Williams (Joseph Goreed)

b. Dec. 12, 1918, Cordele, GA
Vocals / Blues, Swing, Standards

Joe Williams was possibly the last great big band singer, following in the tradition of Jimmy Rushing but carving out his own unique identity. Equally skilled on blues (including double entendre ad-libs), ballads and standards, Williams has always been a charming and consistently swinging performer. In the late '30s he performed regularly with Jimmie Noone. Williams gigged with Coleman Hawkins and Lionel Hampton in the early '40s and toured with Andy Kirk during 1946–47. After stints with Red Saunders and Hot Lips Page and recordings with King Kolax (including a 1951 version of "Every Day I Have the Blues"), Williams joined Count Basie's Orchestra in 1954. During the next seven years he and Basie had a mutually satisfying relationship, both making each other more famous! His version of "Every Day" with Count became his theme song while many other pieces (such as "Goin' to Chicago" and "Smack Dab in the Middle") became permanent parts of Williams' repertoire. After leaving Basie in 1961, the singer worked with the Harry Edison quintet for a couple of years and has freelanced as a leader ever since, having occasional reunions with the Basie band. His collaborations with Cannonball Adderley and George Shearing were successful as was an album with the Thad Jones-Mel Lewis Orchestra. Joe Williams has remained one of the most popular and talented singers in jazz. —*Scott Yanow*

Everyday I Have the Blues / 1951–Sep. 28, 1953 / Savoy ✦✦✦✦
From the Roulette catalog, this superior Joe Williams/Count Basie collaboration finds the singer concentrating on the blues with consistently excellent results. In addition to a remake of the title cut, Williams is heard at his best on the classic "Going to Chicago" and such numbers as "Just a Dream," "Cherry Red" and "Good Mornin' Blues." This LP is well worth searching for. —*Scott Yanow*

★ Count Basie Swings / Joe Williams Sings / Jul. 17, 1955–Jul. 26, 1955 / Verve ✦✦✦✦✦
This is the definitive Joe Williams record, cut shortly after joining Count Basie's orchestra. Included are his classic versions of "Every Day I Have the Blues," "The Comeback," "Alright, Okay, You Win," "In the Evening" and "Teach Me Tonight." Williams' popularity was a major asset to Basie and getting to sing with that swinging big band on a nightly basis certainly did not harm the singer. This gem belongs in everyone's jazz collection. —*Scott Yanow*

A Swingin' Night at Birdland / Jun. 1962 / Roulette ✦✦✦✦
In 1961, after six years as one of the main attractions of Count Basie's orchestra, Williams (with Basie's blessing) went out on his own. One of his first sessions was this live recording cut at Birdland with a strong quintet that featured trumpeter Harry "Sweets" Edison and Jimmy Forrest on tenor. Williams mostly sings standards and ballads but also tosses in a few of his popular blues (including "Alright, OK, You Win" and "Goin' to Chicago") during a well-rounded and thoroughly enjoyable set. —*Scott Yanow*

● The Overwhelmin' / Feb. 6, 1963–Jun. 18, 1965 / Bluebird ✦✦✦✦✦
A CD sampler taken from five former LPs, this fine CD features Joe Williams doing three songs from Duke Ellington's play *Jump for Joy*, five numbers at the 1963 Newport Jazz Festival (during which he is joined by trumpeters Clark Terry and Howard McGhee and tenor greats Coleman Hawkins, Zoot Sims and Ben Webster), four blues backed by an all-star jazz group and five ballads in front of an orchestra. Although it would be preferable to have each of the five original albums intact, this superb collection features Joe Williams on a wide variety of material, and he is heard close to his peak throughout. —*Scott Yanow*

★ And The Thad Jones/Mel Lewis Orchestra / Sep. 1966 / Blue Note ✦✦✦✦✦
This CD reissues one of Joe Williams' finest recordings, Accompanied by the Thad Jones/Mel Lewis Orchestra, the singer is heard at the peak of his powers. The big band primarily func-

tions as an ensemble (Snooky Young gets off some good blasts on "Nobody Knows the Way I Feel This Morning") but the inventive Thad Jones arrangements ensure that his illustrious sidemen have plenty to play. Many of the selections (half of which have been in the singer's repertoire ever since) are given definitive treatment on this set (particularly a humorous "Evil Man Blues," "Gee Baby Ain't I Good to You?" and "Smack Dab in the Middle") and Williams scats at his best on "It Don't Mean a Thing." Get this one. — *Scott Yanow*

Live In Vegas / 1971 / Monad ✦✦✦✦
This previously unreleased set features Joe Williams at a late-night performance in Las Vegas. Very well recorded, the music offers few surprises but finds the singer in prime form. Although the Count Basie Orchestra backs him on most selections, the personnel is not listed, there are no significant solos and Basie himself is probably not on most of the tracks. The breezy liner notes say that "John Young, pianist extraordinaire" sat in during "Midnight Medley" (four ballads and "Thou Swell") and "Going to Chicago"; is this the Chicago-based player of the early '60s? Highlights include an animated "Nobody Loves You When You're Down & Out" (during which Williams really tells a story with the words), "Going to Chicago" (on this version he sings all of the famous big-band riffs along with his regular vocal) and the joyous "Smack Dab in the Middle." This is an excellent recording, easily recommended to Joe Williams fans. — *Scott Yanow*

Joe Williams Live / Aug. 7, 1973 / Original Jazz Classics ✦✦✦✦
Williams meets the Cannonball Adderley Septet on this rather interesting session. The expanded rhythm section (which includes keyboardist George Duke and both acoustic bassist Walter Booker and the electric bass of Carol Kaye) gives funky accompaniment to Williams while altoist Cannonball and cornetist Nat have some solo space. Actualy the singer easily steals the show on a rather searing version of "Goin' to Chicago Blues," his own "Who She Do" and a few unusual songs, including Duke Ellington's "Heritage." — *Scott Yanow*

Prez Conference / 1979 / GNP ✦✦✦✦✦
Dave Pell's Prez Conference was to Lester Young what Supersax is to Charlie Parker. Pell's short-lived group featured harmonized Lester Young solos recreated by three tenors and a baritone; their matchup with singer Joe Williams is quite enjoyable. Since Young was in Count Basie's orchestra when Jimmy Rushing was the vocalist, Joe Williams has a rare opportunity to give his own interpretation to Rushing and Billie Holiday classics like "I May Be Wrong," "You Can Depend on Me," "If Dreams Come True" and "Easy Living." A delightful and swinging date. — *Scott Yanow*

Nothin' But the Blues / Nov. 16, 1983–Nov. 17, 1983 / Delos ✦✦✦✦
Sticking to blues, Joe Williams is in prime form on this special session. His backup crew includes such all stars as tenor saxophonist Red Holloway, organist Brother Jack McDuff and (on alto and one lone vocal) the great Eddie "Cleanhead" Vinson. The many blues standards are familiar but these versions are lively and fresh. — *Scott Yanow*

I Just Wanna Sing / Jun. 29, 1985–Jun. 30, 1985 / Delos ✦✦✦✦
For this session, Joe Williams is backed by such master jazzmen as trumpeter Thad Jones, the contrasting tenors of Eddie "Lockjaw" Davis and Benny Golson and guitarist John Collins. The material varies from the dated humor of "It's Not Easy Being White" to classic versions of "Until I Met You" and "I Got It Bad." Joe Williams is in prime form and this is one of his better sessions from his later years. — *Scott Yanow*

Every Night: Live at Vine St. / May 7, 1987–May 8, 0987 / Verve ✦✦✦✦✦
The focus is entirely on Joe Williams (who is backed by a standard four-piece rhythm section) during this live session from Vine Street. Then 69, Williams had not lost a thing and his voice has rarely sounded stronger. This version of "Every Day I Have the Blues" is transformed into Miles Davis' "All Blues," Williams revives Euble Blake's "A Dollar for a Dime" and sounds wonderful on such songs as "Too Marvelous for Words," "I Want a Little Girl" and "Roll 'Em Pete." This is the best of Joe Williams' records from the '80s. — *Scott Yanow*

Ballad and Blues Master / May 7, 1987–May 8, 1987 / Verve ✦✦✦✦
Taken from the same sessions that had previously resulted in *Every Night*, the identical adjectives apply. Joe Williams was in

superior form for this live date, putting a lot of feeling into such songs as "You Can Depend on Me," "When Sunny Gets Blue" and "Dinner for One Please, James." A closing blues medley is particularly enjoyable and the backup by a quartet that includes pianist Morman Simmons and guitarist Henry Johnson is tasteful and swinging. — *Scott Yanow*

In Good Company / Jan. 19, 1989–Jan. 21, 1989 / Verve ✦✦✦✦
A bit of a grab bag, this CD finds Joe Williams joined by Supersax on two numbers, doing a pair of vocal duets with Marlena Shaw ("Is You Is or Is You Ain't My Baby" is excellent), teaming up with vocalist/pianist Shirley Horn for two ballads and being joined by the Norman Simmons Quartet for the remainder. Sticking mostly to standards, Joe Williams shows that at 70 he still had the magic. — *Scott Yanow*

Live at Orchestra . . . / Nov. 20, 1992 / Telarc ✦✦✦✦
Joe Williams is so closely associated with the Count Basie Orchestra that it is difficult to believe that this Telarc CD was his first recording with jazz's great institution in over 30 years. Williams (in generally fine form despite an occasionally raspy voice) performs a well-rounded set of blues, ballads and standards with the Frank Foster-led Basie orchestra, combining some of his older hits with a few newer songs such as Grady Tate's "A Little at a Time" and "My Baby Upsets Me." Foster's sidemen are mostly heard in an ensemble role with all of the instrumental solos being rather brief; there is little interaction with the vocalist. That fault aside, this is one of Joe Williams' better recordings of the past decade. — *Scott Yanow*

Here's to Life / Aug. 1993 / Telarc ✦✦
Joe Williams loves the string arrangements of Robert Farnon and the sappy ballad "Here's to Life" but in truth the charts border on muzak and the slow tempos on this Telarc CD have little variety. Reminiscent a bit of Nat King Cole's string sessions of the 1950s with Gordon Jenkins, there is little jazz content to this set. Williams is in particularly strong form, interpreting the ballads in dramatic and sensitive fashion, but, despite his charm, this is one of his lesser recordings. — *Scott Yanow*

Feel The Spirit / Sep. 20, 1994–Sep. 23, 1994 / Telarc ✦✦✦
Joe Williams had been wanting to record an album of spirituals since 1957 and this is it. The veteran singer gives a blues feeling and swing to the traditional pieces which range from the rollicking title cut to "Go Down Moses," "I Couldn't Hear Nobody Pray" and "The Lord's Prayer." He is assisted by Marlena Shaw (a particularly effective partner on three of the numbers) and a five-piece chorus on four other songs. The backing usually features Patrice Rushen getting organ sounds out of her synthesizer. Despite the one-message content, the music has more variety than one might expect and Joe Williams acquits himself very well on this sincere and heartfelt effort. — *Scott Yanow*

Mary Lou Williams

b. May 8, 1910, Atlanta, GA, **d.** May 28, 1981, Durham, NC
Piano / Swing, Stride, Bop, Post Bop
A superb pianist, Mary Lou Williams was among jazz's more progressive and forward-looking stylists. Her early playing fused stride and boogie-woogie elements; she adapted to bop, and by the '60s her solos had become more complex, creatively incorporating dissonance without sacrificing blues feeling or emotional intensity. She was a vital composer and arranger, from pivotal works for Andy Kirk's swing band in the '30s to 1946's "Waltz Boogie," in which Williams adapted jazz to @non-duple meters and her sacred works of the '60s and '70s, masses and a cantata. Williams grew up in Pittsburgh, where she was playing by ear as a six-year-old and working carnival and vaudeville shows at 13. She started performing as Mary Lou Burley, joining a group led by John Williams in 1925. The two married shortly afterward. She became Andy Kirk's deputy pianist and arranger in 1929 after he took over Terrence Holden's band in which Williams was a member. By 1930, she was a full member. Her arrangements, compositions and outstanding solos helped make the Kirk band one of the decade's finest. She was also writing arrangements for Benny Goodman, Earl Hines and Tommy Dorsey. "Froggy Bottom," "Walkin' and Swingin'," and "Little Joe from Chicago" were among songs for Kirk's orchestra, while she penned "Camel Hop" and "Roll 'Em" for Goodman. Williams stayed with Kirk until 1942, then formed her own band in New York with trumpeter Shorty Baker, who'd become her second husband. There was a brief stint as a staff arranger for Duke Ellington in the '40s, and she con-

tributed "Trumpet No End" to his orchestra's book in 1946. One year after Williams played "Zodiac Suite" at Town Hall, the New York Philharmonic performed three movements from it at Carnegie Hall, one of the first times a major symphony orchestra recognized a jazz composer's works. Williams contributed scores to Dizzy Gillespie's big band and continued writing influential songs. "In the Land Of Oo-Bla-Dee," which she co-wrote and recorded for King with Pancho Hagood's vocals in 1949, was subsequently recorded by Gillespie. "Satchel-Mouth Baby" in 1947 on Asch was turned into "Pretty Eyed Baby" for Frankie Laine and Jo Stafford in 1951. She played briefly with Goodman in 1948, then moved to Europe from 1952 to 1954. She left the music world in 1954, became a Catholic and formed a foundation to help musicians with personal problems. Williams returned in 1957, playing with Gillespie at the Newport Festival. She divided her time in the '60s and '70s between leading groups in New York clubs, recording and composing sacred pieces for jazz orchestras and voices. These included "Black Christ of the Andes" in 1963 and "Mary Lou's Mass" in 1970, which Alvin Ailey later choreographed. There were memorable '70s albums with Buster Williams, Mickey Roker, Buddy Tate and the controversial, sometimes compelling but ultimately uneven Embraced in 1977, which paired her with Cecil Taylor. Williams also became an busy educator. She recorded The History of Jazz in 1970, an elaborate project featuring her solo piano and commentary. After getting several honorary doctorates, Williams joined Duke University's faculty in 1977, staying with them until her death in 1981. — Ron Wynn and Dan Morgenstern

★ **1927–40** / Jan. 1927–Nov. 18, 1940 / Classics ✦✦✦✦✦
This CD features the great pianist Mary Lou Williams during her earliest period. She is heard in 1927 on six selections with the Synco Jazzers (a small group that included her then-husband John Williams on alto) and then on the first 19 selections ever recorded under her own name. Performed during the long period when she was the regular pianist with Andy Kirk's 12 Clouds of Joy, Williams is featured on two hot stride solos in 1930, leading trios in 1936 and 1938, playing "Little Joe from Chicago" unaccompanied in 1939 and heading septets in 1940; among her sidemen were trumpeter Harold "Shorty" Baker and the legendary tenor Dick Wilson. Many of the compositions were written by Williams including "Night Life," "New Froggy Bottom," "Mary's Special," and "Scratchin' the Gravel;" her version of Jelly Roll Morton's "The Pearls" is a high point. — Scott Yanow

First Ladies of Jazz / Jan. 26, 1940–Feb. 1954 / Savoy ✦✦✦✦✦
Three female pianists are well showcased on this Muse-sponsored CD reissue of Savoy material. The great Mary Lou Williams leads a septet of musicians from Andy Kirk's Orchestra (including the legendary tenor Dick Wilson) on four numbers, the interesting but now somewhat forgotten pianist Jutta Hipp heads a quartet with tenor saxophonist Hans Koller, and Beryl Booker is featured in a quartet that also includes Don Byas on tenor. The high-quality music overall ranges from swing to bop and these rarities are well worth hearing. — Scott Yanow

Roll 'Em / 1944 / Audiophile ✦✦✦
Pianist Mary Lou Williams, in a trio with bassist Al Lucas and drummer Jack "The Bear" Parker, is heard playing nine numbers for radio transcriptions on this LP. In addition to the regular takes, all of the music she performed that day is here including five false starts, five alternate takes and two incomplete versions. Because of the odd programming, it is a bit difficult to follow the evolution of some of these performances but the finished results are generally quite good. Highlights include "Limehouse Blues," "Froggy Bottom" and "Roll 'Em." — Scott Yanow

Asch Recordings, 1944–1947 / Mar. 12, 1944–1947 / Smithsonian/Folkways ✦✦✦✦✦
Mary Lou Williams recorded exclusively for Asch during this period, and most of her performances are included on this two-LP boxed set. Williams' style was in a state of transition as she was gradually discarding stride piano and developing a much more boppish approach. She is heard here in a wide variety of settings ranging from piano solos to small groups and even a big band. Among her sidemen are trumpeters Frankie Newton, Dick Vance, Bill Coleman (who is well featured) and Kenny Dorham, clarinetist Edmund Hall, trombonist Vic Dickenson and tenors Don Byas and Coleman Hawkins. This very valuable set is well worth an extensive search and will hopefully be put out on CD eventually by Folkways. — Scott Yanow

Town Hall (1945): The Zodiac Suite / Dec. 31, 1945 / Smithsonian/Folkways ✦✦✦✦
Mary Lou Williams' Zodiac Suite, a 12-piece work with a different theme made for each of the signs of the zodiac (and keeping in mind the personalities of a few jazz musicians born during each period), was composed and first recorded in 1945. With the assistance of bassist Al Lucas and drummer Jack "The Bear" Parker, pianist Williams performs these moody and often-introspective (but occasionally playful) sketches in a forward-looking swing style. Five alternate takes have been added to the original program on this CD reissue which, although not quite essential, has its interesting moments. — Scott Yanow

The First Lady of the Piano / Jan. 23, 1953 / Inner City ✦✦✦✦
Mary Lou Williams, who had started her career as a stride pianist, was one of the few early jazz players who successfully made the transition to more modern styles. On this Inner City LP (drawn from recordings made for Vogue), Williams and her trio (with clarinetist Toiiy Scott sitting in on bongos) performs such standards as "'Round Midnight," Tadd Dameron's "Lady Bird" and Wild Bill Davis' "Titoros" in convincing fashion, very much in a bop vein. Excellent music. — Scott Yanow

A Keyboard History / Mar. 8, 1955+Mar. 10, 1955 / Jazztone ✦✦✦
This LP contains Mary Lou Williams' last recording sessions before she retired for a period to devote herself to the Catholic religion. A bit of a retrospective, Mary Lou Williams on this trio set with bassist Wendell Marshall and drummer Osie Johnson plays some blues, stride and boogie-woogie along with "Taurus" from her Zodiac Suite and some more recent modern originals. This set will be very difficult to find. — Scott Yanow

Zoning / 1974 / Smithsonian/Folkways ✦✦✦✦
Mary Lou Williams emerged in the early '70s after a long period in which she worked with the Catholic church to resume her always-stimulating career as a jazz pianist. On this CD reissue, one of her finest recordings of her later years has been brought back and augmented by two previously unissued performances. Williams performs in duos and trios with bassist Bob Cranshaw and drummer Mickey Roker, uses Zita Carno on second piano during a couple of the more avant-garde pieces and performs some trios with bassist Milton Suggs and Tony Waters on congas. Rather than sounding like a veteran of the 1920s, Mary Lou Williams sounds 40 years younger, shows the influence of McCoy Tyner and hints at free jazz in spots. An often-surprising set of modern jazz. — Scott Yanow

Free Spirits / Jul. 8, 1975 / SteepleChase ✦✦✦
Includes great trio cuts with Buster Williams (b) and Mickey Roker (d). — Ron Wynn

● **Live at the Cookery** / Nov. 1975 / Chiaroscuro ✦✦✦✦✦
This CD gives one a definitive look at the talented pianist Mary Lou Williams in her later years. In these duets with bassist Brian Torff, Williams essentially takes listeners on a trip through the history of jazz from hymns and blues to stride, swing and bop (including "All Blues"). The CD reissue adds three fine performances to the original program. Recommended. — Scott Yanow

Embraced / Apr. 17, 1977 / Original Jazz Classsics ✦
This encounter is a disaster. Mary Lou Williams, who always prided herself on being open-minded, arranged to perform a duo piano concert with the avant-garde master Cecil Taylor. She wanted them to go through her usual history-of-jazz program but neglected to gain Taylor's consent and, since he never compromises his atonal music, the lack of communication between the two players is laughable. While Williams tries to demonstrate blues, ragtime, stride and swing, Taylor plays in his usual dense and dissonant style on top of her. The result is a complete mess that is almost impossible to listen to. — Scott Yanow

My Mama Pinned a Rose on Me / Dec. 27, 1977 / Pablo ✦✦✦
In this studio set with bassist Buster Williams and the occasional vocals of Cynthia Tyson, pianist Mary Lou Williams performs a full set of original blues. A certain sameness is heard after a while but in general the music is quite stimulating, showing that Williams (even this late in her career) had not lost her power and authority at the keyboard. — Scott Yanow

Mary Lou Williams Solo Recital / Jul. 16, 1978 / Pablo ✦✦✦✦✦
Mary Lou Williams' final recording (performed three years before her death) gives one a strong retrospective of her career. This solo concert at the 1978 Montreux Jazz Festival has a medley encompassing spirituals, ragtime, blues and swing. Other highlights

include Williams' reworkings of "Tea for Two," "Honeysuckle Rose" and her two compositions "Little Joe from Chicago" and "What's Your Story Morning Glory." Recommended. —*Scott Yanow*

Richard Williams

b. May 4, 1931, Galveston, TX, **d.** Nov. 5, 1985, New York, NY
Trumpet / Hard Bop
Richard Williams, although inspired by Fats Navarro, had developed his own sound (along with an impressive technique) on the trumpet by the 1960s and is best remembered for his occasional work with Charles Mingus. He was originally a tenor player, even gigging on the instrument with local bands. By the time he completed his time in the Air Force, Williams was a trumpeter and he toured Europe with Lionel Hampton in 1956. He had off-and-on associations with many top players including Mingus (1959–64), Gigi Gryce, Quincy Jones, Roland Kirk, Eric Dolphy, Duke Ellington and the Thad Jones-Mel Lewis Orchestra (1966–69). He worked with Gil Evans, played in some Broadway musicals, gigged with Clark Terry's big band in the mid-'70s and performed with Mingus Dynasty in 1982 but never did gain much recognition. Williams' lone set as a leader (which was cut for Candid in 1960) is available on CD. —*Scott Yanow*

● **New Horn in Town** / Sep. 27, 1960 / Candid ✦✦✦✦✦
Considering how well trumpeter Richard Williams plays on this session, it is hard to believe that this was the only record he ever led. Best known for his association with Charles Mingus, Williams was a strong bop improviser with a wide range. For this album (which is split between standards and originals) Williams and his quintet (altoist Leo Wright, pianist Richard Wyands, bassist Reggie Workman and drummer Bobby Thomas) are in fine form performing a set of strong hard bop. —*Scott Yanow*

Tony Williams

b. Dec. 12, 1945, Chicago, IL
Drums / Post Bop, Hard Bop, Fusion
Although he turned 40 in late 1995, Tony Williams has been a major drummer in jazz for 22 years. The open style that he created while with the Miles Davis Quintet in the mid-to-late '60s remains quite influential, and he has had a long list of accomplishments during the past couple of decades. Williams' father, a saxophonist, took his son out to clubs that gave him an opportunity to sit in; at 11 the youngster already showed potential. He took lessons from Alan Dawson and at 15 was apearing at Boston area jam sessions. During 1959–60 Williams often played with Sam Rivers and in December 1962 (when he was barely 17), the drummer moved to New York and played regularly with Jackie McLean. Within a few months he joined Miles Davis where his ability to imply the beat while playing quite freely influenced and inspired the other musicians; together with Herbie Hancock and Ron Carter he was part of one of the great rhythm sections. Williams, who was 18 when he appeared on Eric Dolphy's classic *Out to Lunch* album, stayed with Davis into 1969, leading his own occasional sessions and becoming a household name in the jazz world. In addition to his interest in avant-garde jazz, Tony Williams was a fan of rock music, and when he left Davis he formed the fusion band Lifetime, a trio with Larry Young and John McLaughlin. After leading other versions of Lifetime (one of them starring Allan Holdsworth), Williams stuck to freelancing for a time, studied composition and toured with Herbie Hancock's VSOP band. By the mid-'80s he was heading his own all-star hard bop group which featured Wallace Roney as a surrogate Miles Davis and a repertoire dominated by the drummer's originals (including the standard "Sister Cheryl"). With the breakup of the group recently after nearly a decade, Tony Williams has left his options open and his future directions should be well worth following. —*Scott Yanow*

● **Life Time** / Aug. 21, 1964–Aug. 24, 1964 / Blue Note ✦✦✦✦✦
One of his best solo albums of the '60s. '80s reissue. —*Ron Wynn*

Spring / Aug. 12, 1965 / Blue Note ✦✦✦✦✦

★ **Emergency** / May 26, 1969+May 28, 1969 / Polydor ✦✦✦✦✦

Turn It Over / 1970 / Polydor ✦✦✦✦

Ego / 1970 / Polydor ✦✦✦

The Old Album's Rush / 1972 / Polydor ✦✦

Believe It / 1975 / Columbia ✦✦✦✦
This is a hard-edged fusion quartet with guitarist Allan Holdsworth. —*Michael G. Nastos*

Million Dollar Legs / 1976 / Columbia ✦✦✦

Joy of Flying / 1978 / Columbia ✦✦✦✦
It would be an understatement to say that there was a fair amount of variety on this set. Drummer Tony Williams is heard in two duets with keyboardist Jan Hammer, with a quartet also including keyboardist Herbie Hancock, Tom Scott (who unfortunately sticks to lyricon) and bassist Stanley Clarke and he welcomes rock guitarist Ronnie Montrose, keyboardist Brian Auger, guitarist George Benson, Hammer and tenorman Michael Brecker on other tracks. Much of this music is closer to R&B than to jazz although there are many strong moments. But the most interesting selection is certainly "Morgan's Motion," which matches Williams with pianist Cecil Taylor in a powerful (and completely atonal) collaboration. —*Scott Yanow*

Foreign Intrigue / Jun. 18, 1985–Jun. 19, 1985 / Blue Note ✦✦✦✦
Williams had never led a straight-ahead recording session before and is a little higher in the mix than drummers usually rate. But despite the fact that he almost drowns out Bobby Hutcherson's vibes at times, Williams' playing is consistently colorful and would hold one's interest even if he were under-recorded. —*Scott Yanow*

Civilization / Nov. 24, 1986–Nov. 26, 1986 / Blue Note ✦✦✦✦
Good set, with Williams serving as mentor and leader for a good crop of "Young Lions." —*Ron Wynn*

Angel Street / Apr. 4, 1988–Apr. 6, 1988 / Blue Note ✦✦✦✦✦
1988 date, first class lineup for "Young Lions" fueled by red-hot Williams drumming. —*Ron Wynn*

Native Heart / Sep. 11, 1989–Sep. 13, 1989 / Blue Note ✦✦✦✦✦
Leading his by-now familiar band with Wallace Roney (tpt), Bill Pierce (reeds), and Mulgrew Miller (p). —*Ron Wynn*

The Story of Neptune / Nov. 29, 1991–Dec. 1, 1991 / Blue Note ✦✦✦✦
The Tony Williams Quintet has two obvious assets that put it ahead of most acoustic jazz bands: Williams' powerful and consistently creative drumming and his compositional talents. On this group's fifth Blue Note recording, the drummer contributed the three-part "Neptune," essentially a feature for his drums, a more memorable original, "Crime Scene" and arrangements of three standards. —*Scott Yanow*

★ **Tokyo Live** / Mar. 2, 1992–Mar. 8, 1992 / Blue Note ✦✦✦✦✦
Drummer Tony Williams recorded quite a few CDs with his modern hard bop quintet during 1986–93, a unit that also included trumpeter Wallace Roney, Bill Pierce on tenor and soprano, pianist Mulgrew Miller and bassist Ira Coleman. This double CD, their only live recording, is definitive of the band. With the exception of the Beatles' "Blackbird" all 12 selections are Williams' compositions including the classic "Sister Cheryl," heard here in a 14-minute version. Recommended. —*Scott Yanow*

Claude Williamson

b. Nov. 18, 1926, Brattleboro, VT
Piano / Bop, Cool
A classically trained pianist who became one of the most prolific and recorded players among '50s West Coast stylists, Claude Williamson began in the swing era. He later embraced bebop under the spell of Bud Powell. His swing playing was entertaining and enjoyable, but his bebop was stronger and more compelling, though he was more polished and elegant than the soloists he admired. Williamson worked in the late '40s with Charlie Barnet, and played briefly with Red Norvo. He led his own trio in the '50s, then toured and recorded with Bud Shank, playing in Africa and Europe in 1958. Williamson worked over 20 years in Hollywood, mostly with trios. He recorded for Capitol, Bethlehem, Criterion, Broadway International and Eastworld among others. In recent times Claude Williamson has returned to playing jazz full time, recording a well-received Bud Powell tribute on VSOP and performing regularly in the L.A. area. —*Ron Wynn*

Kenton Presents Jazz: Claude Williamson / Jun. 26, 1954–Jul. 29, 1954 / Capitol ✦✦✦✦

Key West / Dec. 14, 1955 / Capitol ✦✦✦✦

Claude Williamson / Jun. 27, 1956 / Bethlehem ✦✦✦✦

Theatre Party / 1962 / Fresh Sound ✦✦✦✦✦

★ **Hallucinations** / Feb. 28, 1995+Mar. 1, 1995 / VSOP ✦✦✦✦✦
For his VSOP release, veteran pianist Claude Williamson per-

forms six Bud Powell compositions plus six other standards that the innovative bop pianist enjoyed playing. With the assistance of bassist Dave Carpenter and drummer Paul Kreibich, Williamson displays both the Powell influence and his own approach to bebop piano. The music always swings, has enough surprises to hold on to one's interest and shows that Claude Williamson (who has been somewhat underrated through the years) was still in prime form four decades after his initial recognition. Highlights of this easily recommended disc include "Hallucinations," "Bud's Bubble," "Parisian Thoroughfare" and "Bouncing with Bud." — *Scott Yanow*

Stu Williamson

b. May 14, 1933, Brattleboro, VT
Trumpet, Valve Trombone / Cool
The younger brother of pianist Claude Williamson, Stu Williamson was a fixture on West Coast jazz dates of the 1950s. He moved to Los Angeles in 1949 and spent periods playing with Stan Kenton (1951), Woody Herman (1952–53) and Kenton again (1954–55) in addition to shorter stints with Billy May and Charlie Garnet. The mellow-toned Williamson, best known for his association with Shelly Manne (off and on during 1954–58), was on a countless number of sessions up until 1968 when he dropped out of the music scene; he passed away in the early '90s. — *Scott Yanow*

● **Stu Williamson Plays** / Jan. 18, 1955–Jan. 16, 1956 / Fresh Sound ✦✦✦✦✦
Stu Williamson led relatively few sessions in his career and over half of them are on this excellent Fresh Sound CD. The cool-toned trumpeter is mostly heard in a quintet with altoist Charlie Mariano, pianist Claude Williamson (his brother), either Max Bennett or Leroy Vinnegar on bass and Stan Levey or Mel Lewis on drums. The remaining four songs (all Bill Holman compositions) feature a sextet with Holman on tenor, baritonist Jimmy Giuffre, Claude, Vinnegar and Lewis. The music swings lightly but firmly with excellent solos from all concerned, making this CD a prime example of West Coast jazz from the 1950s. Recommended. — *Scott Yanow*

Cassandra Wilson

b. Dec. 1955, Jackson, MS
Vocals / Avant-Garde, Blues, Free Funk
Although her recording career has been somewhat erratic, Cassandra Wilson is one of the top jazz singers of the 1990s, a vocalist blessed with a distinctive and flexible voice who is not afraid to take chances. She began playing piano and guitar when she was nine and was working as a vocalist by the mid-'70s, singing a wide variety of material. Following a year in New Orleans, Wilson moved to New York in 1982 and began working with Dave Holland and Abbey Lincoln. After meeting Steve Coleman, she became the main vocalist with the M-Base collective. Although there was really no room for a singer in the overcrowded free funk ensembles, Wilson did as good a job of fitting in as is possible. She worked with New Air and recorded her first album as a leader in 1985. By her third record, a standards date, she was sounding quite a bit like Betty Carter. After a few more albums in which she mostly performed original and rather inferior material, Cassandra Wilson changed directions and performed an acoustic blues-oriented program for Blue Note called *Blue Light 'Til Dawn*. By going back in time, she had found herself and Wilson has continued interpreting in fresh and creative ways vintage country blues and folk music up until the present day. — *Scott Yanow*

Point of View / Dec. 14, 1985–Dec. 15, 1985 / JMT ✦✦✦✦
Bounces between jazz, R&B, funk, avant-garde, and rock. — *Ron Wynn*

Days Aweigh / May 1987 / JMT ✦✦✦

Blue Skies / Feb. 1988 / JMT ✦✦✦✦✦
Primarily associated with the M-Base school of creative funk, Cassandra Wilson was having a difficult time finding a place for her vocals in the dense ensembles that usually dominate that music. *Blue Skies* was a real change of pace, a set of nine standards in which Wilson is backed by a creative but conventional trio (pianist Mulgrew Miller, bassist Lonnie Plaxico and drummer Terri Lyne Carrington). Her voice in this setting (and her improvising style) sounds very much like Betty Carter but Wilson would

develop much more individuality during the next few years. — *Scott Yanow*

Jumpworld / Jul. 1989–Aug. 1989 / JMT ✦✦✦
She Who Weeps / Oct. 1990–Dec. 1990 / JMT ✦✦✦
Live / May 9, 1991 / JMT ✦✦✦
After The Beginning Again / Jul. 1991–Aug. 1991 / JMT ✦✦
Dance To The Drums Again / 1992 / DIW/Columbia ✦
It is obvious listening to this music in hindsight that vocalist Cassandra Wilson was at the crossroads of her career in 1992. She had spent several years often singing in a free funk M-Base setting, an idiom with little use for a vocalist. On this CD not only does she sound bored to death on her own unimaginative material but Wilson sings virtually everything in the same world-weary tone of voice. The rhythms are quite ponderous and annoying. Despite her best efforts, guitarist Jean-Paul Bourelly is unable to do much to uplift this fiasco. — *Scott Yanow*

★ **Blue Light Til Dawn** / 1993 / Blue Note ✦✦✦✦✦
Cassandra Wilson has steadfastly refused to be pigeonholed or confined to any stylistic formula. Her highly anticipated Blue Note debut may stir renewed controversy, as she is once again all over the place. She begins the set with her intriguing version of "You Don't Know What Love Is." Then she moves from two Robert Johnson covers ("Come On in My Kitchen" and "Hellhound on My Trail") to rock compositions from Van Morrison and Joni Mitchell, then to her own title track and blues cut "Redbone" and a piercing version of "I Can't Stand the Rain" that can hold up to comparisons with Ann Peebles' classic. She doesn't have Johnson's menacing quality (who does?) but does invoke an equally compelling air. Wilson has great timing, pacing and delivery and certainly has blues sensibility in her sound. — *Ron Wynn*

Garland Wilson

b. Jun. 13, 1909, Martinsburgh, WV, **d.** May 31, 1954, Paris, France
Piano / Stride
A fine stride pianist, Garland Wilson spent much of his career in Europe, which led to him being underrated. After studying at Howard University, he came to New York in 1929 and played regularly in Harlem for the next three years, recording as a soloist starting in 1931. The following year he went to France as singer Nina Mae McKinney's accompanist, and he played regularly overseas in both Great Britain and France, recording as a leader and with Nat Gonella. Due to World War II Wilson returned to the U.S. in 1939 where he worked in nightclubs until going back to Paris in 1951. — *Scott Yanow*

● **Garland Wilson 1931–1938** / May 18, 1931–Mar. 9, 1938 / Classics ✦✦✦✦✦
With the exception of five songs cut in 1951, this CD has every recording from the sessions led by Garland Wilson. The excellent swing pianist (who was influenced a bit by Earl Hines) is at his best on slower-to-medium material, for on the faster performances his ideas run a bit thin. On two numbers Wilson accompanies actress Nina Mae McKinney and two others are spirited duets with violinist Michel Warlop; the remaining 20 selections are all piano solos. This formerly rare music should be easily enjoyed by fans of the swing piano. — *Scott Yanow*

Gerald Wilson

b. Sep. 4, 1918, Shelby, MS
Trumpet, Arranger, Leader, Composer / Hard Bop
An outstanding bandleader and arranger as well as good trumpeter and composer, Gerald Wilson has updated and evolved his approach to big bands from the swing era to the present. His bands have been heralded for containing topflight, well-drilled musicians presenting immaculately played, superbly written and arranged material. Wilson studied music in high school after his family moved from Memphis to Detroit. He worked with Jimmie Lunceford's band from 1939 to 1942, where he replaced Sy Oliver and learned how to combine precision and flair in his roles as soloist, composer and arranger. Wilson moved to Los Angeles in the early '40s, and played with Benny Carter and Les Hite. He later worked with Clark Terry and Ernie Royal in Willie Smith's navy band, then organized his own big band. This intriguing group included Melba Liston and Snooky Young and played an aggressive, forward-looking blend of swing and bebop. Wilson

Music Map

Vocalists - Female

1920s Classic Blues Singers
Mamie Smith (1920, first blues recording)
Ma Rainey
Bessie Smith ("Empress of the Blues")
Ida Cox
Bertha "Chippie" Hill
Sippie Wallace
Alberta Hunter

Pacesetters of the Late 1920s
Ethel Waters
Annette Hanshaw
Connie Boswell

The Definitive Swing Singer
Billie Holiday

Swing Era
Mildred Bailey	Ivie Anderson
Helen Ward	Helen Forrest
Lee Wiley	Helen Humes
Maxine Sullivan	

Two Major Innovators
Ella Fitzgerald
Sarah Vaughan

1940s/'50s
Anita O'Day	June Christy
Dinah Washington	Peggy Lee
Helen Merrill	Chris Connor
Annie Ross	Betty Roche
Carmen McRae	

Avant-Garde
Betty Carter	Jeanne Lee
Patty Waters	Urszula Dudziak
Karin Krog	Jay Clayton
Norma Winstone	Maggie Nicols
Lauren Newton	Kate Hammett-Vaughan
Ann Dyer	

1960s to the Present
Abbey Lincoln	Sheila Jordan
Astrud Gilberto	Ernestine Anderson
Lorez Alexandria	Ruth Brown
Irene Kral	Etta Jones
Carol Sloane	Flora Purim
Janet Lawson	Dee Dee Bridgewater
Shirley Horn	Michele Hendricks
Dianne Reeves	Diane Schuur
Cassandra Wilson	Carmen Lundy
Vanessa Rubin	Nnenna Freelon
Banu Gibson	Roseanna Vitro
Diana Krall	Karlyn Allyson
Patricia Barber	Holly Cole
Stephanie Haynes	Madeline Eastman
Kitty Margolis	

kept it going from 1944 to 1947. He was off the scene for part of the '50s, then returned with a new band in 1952 in San Francisco. Among Wilson's studio duties in the '50s were sessions for Larry Williams on Specialty. He made several albums for World Pacific in the '60s that were highly successful, most notably *Moment of Truth* that featured Mel Lewis, Carmell Jones, Harold Land and Joe Pass. His band played at the 1963 Monterey Festival, and its roster included Land, Teddy Edwards and Pass. Wilson also did song arrangements on albums by Buddy Collette, Johnny Hartman, Nancy Wilson, Ella Fitzgerald, Al Hibbler, Julie London and Bobby Darin and played trumpet solos on Leroy Vinnegar's LP *Leroy Walks!* on Contemporary. He did a regular radio program, wrote for the symphony and did film and television scores. A little tune Wilson penned in 1970 titled "Viva Tirado" became a huge pop hit when recorded by the band El Chicano. He continued recording in the '80s for Discovery, World Pacific and Trend, and ran the house band for Redd Foxx's NBC shows. Gerald Wilson has been a fixture in Los Angeles since the 1940s as a bandleader, arranger, educator and radio broadcaster. He celebrated his 75th birthday by recording a new set for the MAMA Foundation, reviving some classic arrangements (including "Carlos") and writing some new ones. —*Ron Wynn*

You Better Believe It / Sep. 1961–Oct. 1961 / Pacific Jazz ✦✦✦✦

★ **Moment of Truth** / Sep. 1962 / Pacific Jazz ✦✦✦✦✦
Excellent reissue of fine '60s date with Harold Land, Teddy Edwards and Joe Pass. —*Ron Wynn*

Portraits / 1963 / Pacific Jazz ✦✦✦✦✦

Gerald Wilson on Stage / Jan. 13, 1965+Mar. 10, 1965 / Pacific Jazz ✦✦✦✦

Feelin' Kinda Blues / 1966 / Pacific Jazz ✦✦✦

The Golden Sword / 1966 / Discovery ✦✦✦✦✦

Live and Swinging / Apr. 1, 1967–Apr. 2, 1967 / Pacific Jazz ✦✦✦✦

Everywhere / 1967 / Pacific Jazz ✦✦✦

California Soul / 1968 / Pacific Jazz ✦✦✦

Eternal Equinox / 1969 / Pacific Jazz ✦✦✦✦✦

Lomelin / May 13, 1981–May 14, 1981 / Discovery ✦✦✦✦

Jessica / Nov. 29, 1982+Dec. 8, 1982 / Trend ✦✦✦✦✦
Super orchestra recordings. —*Ron Wynn*

Calafia / Nov. 29, 1984–Nov. 30, 1984 / Trend ✦✦✦✦
High-caliber orchestra arrangements and solos. —*Ron Wynn*

Jenna / Jun. 27, 1989–Jun. 28, 1989 / Discovery ✦✦✦✦✦

● **State Street Sweet** / 1994 / MAMA ✦✦✦✦✦
Bandleader/arranger Gerald Wilson's first recording in several years is a success. He revisits "Carlos" (featuring trumpeter Ron Barrows) and "Lighthouse Blues" and performs some newer originals including "State Street Sweet," "Lakeshore Drive" and "Jammin' in C." With such soloists as trumpeters Barrows, Bobby Shew, Tony Lujan and Snooky Young, altoist Randall Willis, tenors Louis Taylor, Plas Johnson (showcased on "Come Back to

Sorrento") and Carl Randall, pianist Brian O'Rourke and guitarists Anthony Wilson and Eric Otis, this edition of the Gerald Wilson Orchestra is quite strong, but it is the leader's colorful and distinctive arrangements that give the band its personality. Recommended. —*Scott Yanow*

Nancy Wilson

b. Feb. 20, 1937, Chillicothe, OH
Vocals / R&B, Pop, Standards
Nancy Wilson is continually called a jazz singer but in reality most of her work has been in the pop/R&B field. Never much of an improviser and overly mannered by her later years, Wilson's most valuable work can be found in early recordings with George Shearing and Cannonball Adderley (the latter is a classic). However very little of her post-1962 work can be considered relevant to jazz. —*Scott Yanow*

● **Swingin's Mutual** / Jun. 29, 1960–Jan. 7, 1961 / Capitol ✦✦✦✦✦
Singer Nancy Wilson has only made a few recordings throughout her career that are of any interest to jazz listeners. This CD reissue brings back her third album, an excellent collaboration with the George Shearing Quintet. Originally Wilson participated on six of the 12 selections but since five new tracks (with only one vocal) have been added, she is now on seven out of 17. Very much under the influence of Dinah Washington at this point, Nancy Wilson is in generally good form particularly on "The Nearness of You," "All Night Long" and "The Things We Did Last Summer." As far as the instrumentals by pianist Shearing's Quintet go, "I Remember Clifford," "Evansville," "Blue Lou" and "Lullaby of Birdland" are most memorable with short solos heard from vibraphonist Warren Chaisson and guitarist Dick Garcia. —*Scott Yanow*

★ **Nancy Wilson and Cannonball Adderley** / Sep. 1, 1962 / Capitol ✦✦✦✦✦

Lush Life / 1967 / Blue Note ✦✦
This CD does not belong in the Capitol Jazz reissue series, for it contains no jazz. Nancy Wilson's singing on the middle-of-the-road pop session from 1967 is consistently melodramatic, lacks subtlety, contains no improvisation and has enough preplanned cracks in her voice to irritate anyone; her version of "Lush Life" is a low point. The overblown string arrangements by Billy May and Oliver Nelson would have defeated most singers anyway, so this misfire does not deserve a second glance. —*Scott Yanow*

But Beautiful / 1969 / Capitol ✦✦✦
Valuable reissue of a late '60s set, when Nancy Wilson was still doing more jazz than pop. She was supported by a great combo that included Hank Jones, Grady Tate, Ron Carter and Gene Bertoncini. The original album didn't get the push it deserved, but the reissue market helped it reach a new audience. —*Ron Wynn*

Life, Love and Harmony / 1979 / Capitol ✦✦

Teddy Wilson (Theodore Shaw Wilson)

b. Nov. 24, 1912, Austin, TX, **d.** Jul. 31, 1986, New Britain, CT
Piano / Swing
Teddy Wilson was the definitive swing pianist, a solid and impeccable soloist whose smooth and steady style was more accessible to the general public than that of Earl Hines or Art Tatum. He picked up early experience playing with Speed Webb in 1929 and appearing on some Louis Armstrong recordings in 1933. Discovered by John Hammond, Willie joined Benny Carter's band and recorded with the Chocolate Dandies later that year. In 1935 he began leading a series of classic small-group recordings with swing all stars which on many occasions featured Billie Holiday. That was also the year that an informal jam session with Benny Goodman and Gene Krupa resulted in the formation of the Benny Goodman Trio (Lionel Hampton made the group a quartet the following year). Although he was a special added attraction rather than a regular member of the orchestra, Wilson's public appearances with Goodman broke important ground in the long struggle against segregation.

Between his own dates, many recordings with Benny Goodman's small groups and a series of piano solos, Teddy Wilson recorded a large number of gems during the second half of the 1930s. He left BG in 1939 to form his own big band but, despite some fine records, it folded in 1940. Wilson led a sextet at Cafe Society during 1940–44, taught music at Julliard during the summers of 1945–52, appeared on radio shows and recorded regular-

ly with a trio, as a soloist and with pick-up groups in addition to having occasional reunions with Goodman. Teddy Wilson's style never changed and he played very similar in 1985 to how he sounded in 1935; no matter, the enthusiasm and solid sense of swing were present up until the end. —*Scott Yanow*

Teddy Wilson (1934–1935) / May 1934–Dec. 1935 / Classics ✦✦✦✦✦

Too Hot for Words / Jan. 1935–Oct. 1935 / Hep ✦✦✦✦✦

Teddy Wilson (1935–1936) / Dec. 3, 1935–Aug. 24, 1936 / Classics ✦✦✦✦✦

Teddy Wilson, Vol. 2: Warmin' Up / Dec. 1935–Jun. 1936 / Hep ✦✦✦✦✦

Teddy Wilson (1936–1937) / Aug. 24, 1936–Feb. 18, 1937 / Classics ✦✦✦✦✦

Of Thee I Swing / Aug. 1936–Feb. 1937 / Hep ✦✦✦✦✦

Teddy Wilson (1937) / Mar. 31, 1937–Aug. 29, 1937 / Classics ✦✦✦✦✦

Teddy Wilson, Vol. 4: Fine and Dandy / Mar. 1937–Jul. 1937 / Hep ✦✦✦✦✦

Teddy Wilson, Vol. 5: Blue Mood / Aug. 1937–Jan. 1938 / Hep ✦✦✦✦✦

Teddy Wilson (1937–1938) / Sep. 5, 1937–Apr. 28, 1938 / Classics ✦✦✦✦✦

Teddy Wilson (1938) / Apr. 28, 1938–Nov. 28, 1938 / Classics ✦✦✦✦✦

Teddy Wilson (1938–1941) / Jul. 29, 1938–Apr. 11, 1941 / Tax ✦✦✦✦
This Tax LP contains an excellent cross section of pianist Teddy Wilson's work from the late '30s/early '40s. Wilson is heard with an all-star septet which includes trumpeter Jonah Jones, altoist Benny Carter and tenor saxophonist Ben Webster, backing four fine vocals from the forgotten but talented Nan Wynn, taking four piano solos in 1938–39, playing "Lady Be Good" and accompanying three fine Helen Ward vocals with an octet in 1940 and jamming with a trio in 1941. Throughout these lesser-known performances, Wilson is heard at his prime, setting the standard for swing piano. —*Scott Yanow*

Teddy Wilson (1939) / Jan. 27, 1939–Sep. 12, 1939 / Classics ✦✦✦✦✦

Teddy Wilson and His Big Band (1939–1940) / May 10, 1939–Jan. 18, 1940 / Tax ✦✦✦✦✦
Although he was one of the most popular and influential pianists of the swing era, Teddy Wilson (like Coleman Hawkins and Jack Teagarden) was unsuccessful at keeping a big band together. As with Hawkins and Teagarden, the reason Wilson's orchestra did not catch on is obvious when one hears its recordings; the band did not have a strong personality of its own or a purpose for its existence. This Tax LP contains 16 performances by this orchestra which, due to its strong soloists (including Wilson, trumpeter Shorty Baker and tenor saxophonist Ben Webster who is heard shortly before he joined Duke Ellington), high musicianship and a few memorable performances (including a version of "In the Mood" much different than Glenn Miller's), is well worth searching for. —*Scott Yanow*

Teddy Wilson (1939) / 1939 / Classics ✦✦✦✦✦

★ **And His All-Stars** / 1936–1940 / Columbia ✦✦✦✦✦
Pianist Teddy Wilson's most famous recordings of the 1930s as a leader are the ones in which he is joined by Billie Holiday, so it is a pleasure to have a double-LP dominated by the lesser-known— but often quite exciting—instrumentals performed by his all-star groups. Holiday is heard on six of these selections and Ella Fitzgerald on two others, but otherwise, the emphasis is on the hot soloing of such major swing stars as trumpeters Cootie Williams, Roy Eldridge, Jonah Jones, Frankie Newton., Buck Clayton, Harry James (heard at his best on "Just a Mood" and "Honeysuckle Rose") and Bill Coleman, clarinetists Benny Goodman, Buster Bailey and Pee Wee Russell, altoist Johnny Hodges, baritonist Harry Carney and the tenors of Ben Webster and Chu Berry among others. Until this music is reissued domestically on CD, this two-fer is well worth searching for. —*Scott Yanow*

B Flat Swing / 1944 / Jazz Archives ✦✦✦✦
One of pianist Teddy Wilson's lesser-known bands is the sextet he led during 1940–44, shortly after his orchestra broke up and before he cut back to a trio. This unit, well featured on this Jazz Archives LP, by 1944 featured trumpeter Emmett Berry, trom-

bonist Benny Morton and clarinetist Edmond Hall and played swinging versions of standards. The contents of this LP are taken from a session recorded for play on radio, and unlike the studio recordings of the era, many of these performances are over four minutes long. —*Scott Yanow*

Teddy Wilson Sextet: 1944, Vol. 2 / Jun. 15, 1944–Dec. 22, 1944 / Jazz Archives ✦✦✦✦
This Jazz Archives LP, a follow-up to *B Flat Swing*, features the great swing pianist Teddy Wilson in a variety of settings from the same time period. He is heard on four songs with the sextet that also performed on the latter LP, jamming with trumpeter Emmett Berry, trombonist Benny Morton and clarinetist Edmond Hall. However, seven other selections star either the fiery Roy Eldridge, the exciting Charlie Shavers or the great Cootie Williams on trumpet in Wilson's unit with vibraphonist Red Norvo, and "Sweet Lorraine" finds the pianist showcased as the lead voice with Paul Barron's radio orchestra. Timeless music. —*Scott Yanow*

Teddy Wilson All Star Sessions / Dec. 18, 1944–Aug. 14, 1945 / Musicraft ✦✦✦✦
Teddy Wilson, the definitive swing pianist, led a variety of interesting groups during 1940-45 before he reverted to touring with trios. In late 1944, he began to record for Musicraft, and this LP contains the earliest of that series. Eight selections feature the exciting unit that he had with trumpeter Charlie Shavers and vibraphonist Red Norvo; two numbers also have vocals by Maxine Sullivan. The remainder of this LP (four songs plus three alternate takes from August 14, 1945) finds Wilson heading an all-star group with trumpeter Buck Clayton and tenor saxophonist Ben Webster. Throughout this highly enjoyable set are many fine examples of high-quality swing. —*Scott Yanow*

Isn't It Romantic / 1944–1946 / Musicraft ✦✦✦

Sunny Morning / 1946 / Musicraft ✦✦✦✦
The third of four LPs released by Discovery that document Teddy Wilson's recordings for Musicraft, this set contains a dozen of his piano solos from 1946 when he was involved much more in teaching and performing on the radio than in making public appearances. These concise performances (all under three minutes) are melodic and swing lightly, showing why Wilson's influence reached beyond jazz and affected middle-of-the-road pianists such as Frankie Carle. —*Scott Yanow*

★ **Central Avenue Blues** / 1944–1945 / Vintage Jazz Classics ✦✦✦✦✦
Teddy Wilson was the definitive swing pianist, an influential stylist still best known for his association with Benny Goodman; however Wilson had a long career after his years with Goodman. This CD mostly features him with his brilliant sextet of 1944-45 which also includes trumpeter Charlie Shavers and vibraphonist Red Norvo playing concise versions of swing standards. Much of this music had previously been issued but never as complete as on this superb set. Also here are three Wilson performances from a V-Disc session that features trumpeter Joe Thomas and clarinetist Edmund Hall and two other numbers in which the pianist is backed by a radio orchestra. —*Scott Yanow*

Time After Time / 1945 / Musicraft ✦✦✦✦
The fourth and final LP put out by Discovery in a series that reissues the great bulk of Teddy Wilson's recordings for Musicraft during 1944-47 features the swing pianist with his 1945 sextet (which also stars trumpeter Charlie Shavers and vibraphonist Red Norvo), in a trio and on a couple of solos. The obscure but talented vocalist Kay Penton makes a few appearances, and throughout, Wilson, despite the fact that bebop was influencing most other musicians during this era, shows that his timeless style was unaffected by outside trends. —*Scott Yanow*

"Gypsy" in Jazz / Sep. 3, 1959 / Columbia ✦✦✦
Pianist Teddy Wilson interprets a dozen songs from the musical *Gypsy* with his 1959 trio (bassist Arvell Shaw and drummer Bert Dahlender). None of these songs became standards ("Everything's Coming up Roses" and "Let Me Entertain You" came close), but it is interesting to hear Wilson get away from his usual swing repertoire and uplift this music with his sparkling style. This long out-of-print LP is difficult to find! —*Scott Yanow*

Air Mail Special / Mar. 19, 1967–Jun. 1967 / Black Lion ✦✦✦✦
After several years of near-silence on records (only one album as a leader during 1960–66), Teddy Wilson recorded on a much more regular basis for the next 15 years. This Black Lion set (partly cut on the same day as the *Stomping at the Savoy* CD) matches the

great swing pianist with a few of London's best (clarinetist Dave Shepherd, vibraphonist Ronnie Gleaves, bassist Peter Chapman and drummer Johnny Richardson) on a variety of superior standards. The music, if a bit predictable, is quite enjoyable. —*Scott Yanow*

Stomping at the Savoy / Jun. 18, 1967 / Black Lion ✦✦✦✦
Strange as it seems, Teddy Wilson only made one record as a leader during 1960–66. His playing had not declined in the slightest, but the veteran swing pianist's style was overlooked in favor of newer players and, although still a household name in the jazz world, he was somewhat neglected. In 1967, with this excellent CD and its companion, *Air Mail Special*, Wilson returned to a more regular recording schedule. Recorded in London, this studio session finds Wilson joined by some fine English musicians (including clarinetist Dave Shepherd and vibraphonist Ronnie Gleaves) for a spirited runthrough of swing standards. Although the date on the CD says 1969, it is definitely 1967. —*Scott Yanow*

Masters of Jazz, Vol. 11 / Dec. 1968–Jun. 1980 / Storyville ✦✦✦✦
Storyville's Masters of Jazz series (which has since been reissued on CD) features swing stars playing material that has sometimes been released as part of other sets. In the case of Teddy Wilson, the two sessions that are included here are not on other releases. Wilson's swing piano style was unchanged through the years (at least since the mid-'30s) so these two dates (both recorded in Copenhagen) are equally rewarding, with fine backup from either Jesper Lundgard or Niels Pedersen on bass and Ed Thigpen or Biarne Rostvold on drums. —*Scott Yanow*

★ **With Billie in Mind** / May 1972 / Chiaroscuro ✦✦✦✦✦
The concept seemed so logical that it was surprising that no one else had thought of it earlier. Producer Hank O'Neal suggested to the veteran swing pianist Teddy Wilson that he record a set of Billie Holiday tunes since Lady Day had cut many of her greatest sides with Wilson in the 1930s. This solo CD, which was originally a 14-song LP, has been expanded with the release of six other solos cut at the same sessions. Wilson, who is in peak form, clearly enjoyed playing several tunes that he had not performed in years, and he is heard at the top of his game. Classic swing music. —*Scott Yanow*

Lionel Hampton Presents Teddy Wilson / 1973 / Who's Who In Jazz ✦✦✦✦
In the mid-to-late '70s, vibraphonist Lionel Hampton had the opportunity to record with some of his favorite jazz musicians on his Who's Who label. For his reunion with pianist Teddy Wilson, Hamp also utilized the fine clarinetist Jerry Fuller, bassist George Duvivier, Sam Turner on congas and Teddy Wilson, Jr., on drums, making this the only time that father and son recorded together. The music is a bit predictable with eight veteran swing standards, but the enthusiasm of Hampton makes the results more exciting than one might expect. —*Scott Yanow*

Runnin' Wild / Jul. 4, 1973 / Black Lion ✦✦✦✦✦
Black Lion has reissued several Teddy Wilson sessions on CD, but this one is by far the most exciting. Recorded live at the 1973 Montreux Jazz Festival, Wilson plays some surprisingly extroverted solos, even starting "One O'Clock Jump" off with some torrid boogie-woogie. The majority of the standards are taken at faster than usual paces with Wilson sounding very enthusiastic. Joined by bassist Kenny Baldock and drummer Johnny Richardson on eight of the nine selections, Wilson really inspires clarinetist Dave Shepherd during his four appearances to play what must have been some of the hottest solos of his career. This gem is highly recommended, showcasing the great swing pianist on a very good day. —*Scott Yanow*

Blues for Thomas Waller / Jan. 28, 1974+Jan. 31, 1974 / Black Lion ✦✦✦✦
Teddy Wilson, the definitive swing pianist, never really sounded like Fats Waller although his style was complementary. This solo session finds him swinging his way through 11 of Waller's compositions including two versions of "Honeysuckle Rose," along with two tributes—"Blues for Thomas Waller" and "Striding After Fats." Wilson's style was unchanged from 40 years earlier, but he still infused his solos with enthusiasm and melodic creativity, and this set is a pretty inspired effort. —*Scott Yanow*

Teddy Wilson in Tokyo / Dec. 1975 / Sackville ✦✦✦✦
The majority of pianist Teddy Wilson's recordings from his later period were recorded outside of the U.S. and later released domestically. This solo set, issued by the Canadian Sackville label, finds

the swing master melodically interpreting a dozen veteran standards, showing that his enthusiasm and creativity had not lessened, even on songs that he had already played regularly for more than 30 years! —*Scott Yanow*

Cole Porter Classics / 1977 / Black Lion ✦✦✦
The tasteful and lightly swinging pianist Teddy Wilson performs 11 well-known Cole Porter standards on this solo set. This generally relaxed session contains no new revelations (Wilson had solidified his swing style 40 years earlier) but should please Teddy Wilson's fans; it is always enjoyable to hear him play unaccompanied. —*Scott Yanow*

Marian McPartland's Piano Jazz with Guest Teddy Wilson / 1983 / Jazz Alliance ✦✦✦
Recorded a few years before Teddy Wilson's 1986 death (the exact date is not listed on this CD), this edition of Marian McPartland's *Piano Jazz* is quite valuable. Wilson talks about his early days, his practice routine, rambles a bit and plays a variety of swing standards. McPartland has "Marian's Motif" as her feature but best are the piano duets on "I'll Remember April" and a fun version of "Flying Home." This is a fine tribute to the much missed Teddy Wilson. —*Scott Yanow*

Lem Winchester

b. Mar. 19, 1928, Philadelphia, PA, **d.** Jan. 13, 1961, Indianapolis, IN
Vibes / Hard Bop
Lem Winchester had great potential as a vibraphonist but it was all cut short by a tragic accident. Influenced by Milt Jackson but developing a sound of his own, Winchester actually played tenor, baritone and piano before choosing to stick exclusively to vibes. A police officer in Wilmington, DE, he made a big impression at the 1958 Newport Jazz Festival and was soon recording regularly with such major players as Oliver Nelson, Benny Golson and Tommy Flanagan. Winchester resigned from the police force in 1960 so as to be a musician full time, but then on January 13, 1961, he unsuccessfully demonstrated a trick with a revolver! —*Scott Yanow*

Lem Winchester and the Ramsey Lewis Trio / Oct. 8, 1958 / Argo ✦✦✦✦

Winchester Special / Sep. 25, 1959 / Original Jazz Classics ✦✦✦✦✦
Solid set pairing Benny Golson (ts) and Lem Winchester. —*Ron Wynn*

Lem's Beat / Apr. 19, 1960 / Original Jazz Classics ✦✦✦✦
Lem Winchester, an ill-fated vibraphonist who was influenced musically by Milt Jackson, teams up with tenor saxophonist Oliver Nelson, altoist Curtis Peagler and a fine rhythm section for a good straight-ahead date that has been reissued on CD. Nelson emerges as the most distinctive solo voice and, since he contributed three of the six songs, the tenorman's musical personality dominates this set. Winchester shows much potential that, due to his untimely death in early 1961, was never fulfilled. Good bop-based music. —*Scott Yanow*

● **Another Opus** / Jun. 4, 1960 / Original Jazz Classics ✦✦✦✦✦
Vibraphonist Lem Winchester died on Jan. 13, 1961 after an accident with a gun. Although he did not stick around long enough to carve out his own original voice (remaining influenced to a large degree by Milt Jackson), Winchester did record several worthy albums during his final couple of years. This set, which has been reissued on CD in the OJC series, was one of his last and best. Winchester, in a quintet with flutist Frank Wess, pianist Hank Jones, bassist Eddie Jones and drummer Gus Johnson, is in swinging and creative form on three of his originals, Oliver Nelson's "The Meetin'" and the standard "Like Someone in Love." A "bonus cut" from Oct. 14, 1960 finds Winchester playing "Lid Flippin'" with a quintet that features organist Johnny "Hammond" Smith. Overall this CD is one of Lem Winchester's definitive sets. —*Scott Yanow*

Lem Winchester with Feeling / Oct. 7, 1960 / Moodsville ✦✦✦

Kai Winding

b. May 18, 1922, Aarhus, Denmark, **d.** May 6, 1983, Yonkers, NY
Trombone / Bop
One of the finest trombonists to emerge from the bebop era, Kai Winding was always to an extent overshadowed by J.J. Johnson and together they formed one of the most popular jazz groups of

the mid-'50s. Born in Denmark, Winding emigrated to the U.S. with his family when he was 12. He had short stints with the orchestras of Alvino Rey and Sonny Dunham and played in a service band in the Coast Guard for three years. Winding's first burst of fame occured during his year with Stan Kenton's Orchestra (1946-47) during which his phrasing influenced and was adopted by the other trombonists, leading to a permanent change in the Kenton sound. He also participated in some early bop sessions, played with Tadd Dameron (1948-49) and was on one of the Miles Davis' nonet's famous recording sessions. After playing with the big bands of Charlie Ventura and Benny Goodman, he formed a quintet with J.J. Johnson (1954-56); the two trombonists (who sounded nearly identical at the time) had occasional reunions after going their separate ways. Winding led a four-trombone septet off and on through the latter half of the 1950s and into the '60s, was music director for the Playboy clubs in New York and during 1971-72 worked with the Giants of Jazz (an all-star group with Dizzy Gillespie, Sonny Stitt and Thelonious Monk). Although he recorded frequently both as a leader and a sideman throughout his career, most of Winding's sessions are not currently available on CD. —*Scott Yanow*

The Swingin' States / Aug. 22, 1958-Aug. 29, 1958 / Columbia ✦✦✦

The Incredible Kai Winding Trombones / Nov. 17, 1960-Dec. 13, 1960 / Impulse! ✦✦✦✦
Great four-trombone set. —*Ron Wynn*

Kai Winding Solo / Jan. 23, 1963-Feb. 5, 1963 / Verve ✦✦✦✦✦
Israel / 1967 / A&M ✦✦✦

● **Lionel Hampton Presents Kai Winding** / Sep. 1, 1977 / Who's Who in Jazz ✦✦✦✦✦

Giant Bones / Nov. 23, 1979-Nov. 24, 1979 / Sonet ✦✦✦✦
Superior two-trombone set with Curtis Fuller (tb). —*Ron Wynn*

Paul Winter

b. Aug. 31, 1939, Altoona, PA
Soprano Saxophone, Alto Saxophone / Hard Bop, New Age
Environmental causes have been Paul Winter's concern as much as, if not more than, music since the '70s. He's joined Greenpeace expeditions, recorded accompanying whales and wolves, and formed an organization linking environmental issues with musical concerns. Winter's music has never been among the more soulful, hard-edged, funky or bluesy; he's utilized improvisation but also incorporated elements from ethnic, European folk, symphonic/classical and other sounds that gradually became known as "New Age," (now contemporary instrumental in some circles.) His alto and soprano sax playing is melodically enticing, but seldom harmonically or rhythmically challenging. Winter founded the Paul Winter sextet while a Northwestern University student. This group was a winner at the 1961 Intercollegiate Jazz Festival held at Notre Dame, where some judges on the panel included John Hammond and Dizzy Gillespie. Hammond got the Consort onto Columbia. They proved quite popular, and the State Department sponsored a Latin American tour for the band in 1962. But five years later, Winter broke from a strict jazz sound with the Winter Consort, a band blending ethnic influences from Africa and Latin America, as well as Europe and America. Ralph Towner, Glen Moore, Collin Walcott, Paul McCandless and David Darling at one time were all members, and the instrumentation included acoustic guitar, sitar, bass, cello and oboe. But the Consort eventually disbanded, with its core members forming a similiar, even more successful band, Oregon. Winter has blended music and environmental politics throughout the '80s and '90s. He's recorded as a leader for Columbia, A&M, Epic, and Living Music. Winter has several sessions available on CD. —*Ron Wynn and Linda Kohanov*

● **Winter Consort's Road** / 1969-1970 / A&M ✦✦✦✦
Icarus / Mar. 1973 / Epic ✦✦✦
Missa Gaia / Earth Mass / 1982 / Living Music ✦✦

Jimmy Witherspoon

b. Aug. 8, 1923, Gurdon, AK
Vocals / Blues, Swing
Swing Jimmy Witherspoon, an excellent singer versatile enough to fit into both the jazz and blues worlds, is a throwback to the styles of Jimmy Rushing and Big Joe Turner while looking for-

ward toward Joe Williams. As a child he sang in a church choir and he made his debut while overseas in the Navy singing with Teddy Weatherford in Calcutta! With Jay McShann during 1945-47, Witherspoon gained some fame and after he departed he became very popular; his rendition of "Tain't Nobody's Business If I Do" was a hit. The mid-'50s were a lean time (Witherspoon's style of shouting blues was temporarily out of fashion) but his appearance at the 1959 Monterey Jazz Festival (which was recorded by Fantasy) was a sensation and he has worked steadily ever since. He toured Europe in 1961 with Buck Clayton and toured overseas many times during the past 30 years. Despite throat cancer in the early '80s (which he recovered from), Jimmy Witherspoon has remained a popular attraction up to the present day. —*Scott Yanow*

● **Jimmy Witherspoon & Jay McShann** / 1947-1949 / Black Lion ✦✦✦✦✦
Vintage blues shouting, jump blues and boogie piano performed by two giants at their performance peaks. Vocalist Jimmy Witherspoon hollered, roared and strutted with authority, while pianist Jay McShann not only headed a superb combo and backed Weatherspoon stylishly, but when given the spotlight, he also supplied connecting riffs, offered emphatic solos and helped keep things roaring. There are 24 numbers on this 1992 CD reissue, and they illustrate the potency and appeal of Weatherspoon and McShann, while also revealing the links between swing, blues and early R&B. —*Ron Wynn*

★ **At Monterey Festival** / Oct. 2, 1959 / Hi Fi ✦✦✦✦✦

At the Renaissance / Dec. 2, 1959 / Hi Fi ✦✦✦✦✦

Baby Baby Baby / May 6, 1963 / Original Blues Classics ✦✦✦✦
Veteran singer Jimmy Witherspoon is in good voice on this CD reissue, performing a dozen two- to four-minute songs that include such blues standards as Duke Ellington's "Rocks in My Bed," "Bad Bad Whiskey," "One Scotch, One Bourbon, One Beer" and "It's a Lonesome Old World." He is joined by a quintet featuring altoist Leo Wright and guitarist Kenny Burrell on the first eight numbers and a background septet (with trumpeter Bobby Bryant and Arthur Wright on harmonica) for the remainder of the set. The music is enjoyable if not classic and should please Witherspoon's many fans. —*Scott Yanow*

Evenin' Blues / Aug. 15, 1963 / Original Blues Classics ✦✦✦✦

Blues Around the Clock / Nov. 5, 1963 / Original Blues Classics ✦✦✦✦
Veteran singer Jimmy Witherspoon (who bridges the gap between jazz and blues) mostly sticks to the latter on this spirited set. His backup group (organist Paul Griffin, guitarist Lord Westbrook, bassist Leonard Gaskin and drummer Herbie Lovelle) is fine in support, but the spotlight is almost entirely on Witherspoon throughout these ten concise performances, only one of which exceeds four minutes. Highlights include "No Rollin' Blues," "S.K. Blues" and "Around the Clock." Witherspoon is in fine voice and, even if nothing all that memorable occurs, the music is enjoyable. —*Scott Yanow*

Some of My Best Friends Are the Blues / Jun. 15, 1964 / Original Blues Classics ✦✦✦✦
Jimmy Witherspoon is accompanied by a large orchestra arranged by Benny Golson for a set emphasizing slow tempos (even on "And the Angels Sing" and "Who's Sorry Now"), ballads and blues. Nothing all that memorable occurs but the singer is in strong voice and his fans will want to pick up this interesting CD reissue. —*Scott Yanow*

Huhh / Sep. 15, 1969 / Bluesway ✦✦✦

Live / 1976 / MCA ✦✦✦✦
Jimmy Witherspoon sticks exclusively to the blues during this Los Angeles club date from 1976. Guitarist Robben Ford's fiery Chicago blues playing is consistently exciting and imaginative, often stealing the show from 'Spoon. This CD can easily be enjoyed by fans of both blues and swinging jazz. —*Scott Yanow*

Savoy Sultans / May 25, 1980 / Black & Blue ✦✦✦✦✦

Rockin' L.A. / Oct. 24, 1988-Oct. 25, 1988 / Fantasy ✦✦✦

Francis Wong

Flute, Tenor Saxophone / Post Bop
Long involved in the reparations movement to compensate Japanese Americans put in prison camps during World War II, Francis Wong has been a major force on the Asian Improv label

(which he co-founded in 1987 with Jon Jang), recording stimulating music both as a sideman and a leader. He has recorded with Jang, Fred Ho, Glenn Horiuchi, Mark Izu and with his own Great Wall Ensemble, being quite active in the San Francisco Bay area. —*Scott Yanow*

● **Ming** / Jul. 29, 1994 / Asian Improv ✦✦✦✦
On this CD tenor saxophonist Francis Wong sometimes plays with both the ferocity of an Albert Ayler and the thoughtfulness of Sonny Rollins. Although a few themes and specific moods are utilized, much of the music is quite free. It generally succeeds due to the close musical communication between Wong, pianist Glenn Horiuchi and percussionist Elliot Kaves even if Horiuchi's occasional vocal shouts are quite eccentric. Because Wong also plays a bit of flute and violin and Kaves uses a wide variety of percussion (including what is listed as "dishes, pots, pans, oven rack and kitchen sink"!), even the rambling moments tend to hold one's interest. A rewarding disc. —*Scott Yanow*

Rickey Woodard

b. 1956, Nashville, TN
Clarinet, Alto Saxophone, Tenor Saxophone / Hard Bop
Rickey Woodard picked up early experience playing in a family band. After attending Tennessee State University, Woodard joined Ray Charles in 1980. In 1988 he moved to Los Angeles and since then has recorded (both as a leader and as a sideman) for Concord Records, has led quartets and been a member of the Clayton/Hamilton Jazz Orchestra, the Juggernaut and the Cheathams in addition to making guest appearances. —*Scott Yanow*

California Cooking / Feb. 27, 1991 / Candid ✦✦✦✦✦

Night Mist / Oct. 22, 1991 / Fresh Sound ✦✦✦✦✦
Tenor saxophonist Rickey Woodard's many fans may be unaware of this particular CD. Recorded in 1991 for the Spanish Fresh Sound label, this somewhat obscure outing finds Woodard in top form heading a straight-ahead quartet comprised of pianist Eric Reed, bassist Tony Dumas and drummer Roy McCurdy. Together the Los Angeles all stars play a variety of standards plus Woodard's "Night Mist," the only song on which he switches to alto. The music consistently swings, features inventive solos within the boundaries of hard bop and is well-paced with the highlights including "Thou Swell," "Secret Love," "Billie's Bounce" and "My Shining Hour." Well worth searching for. —*Scott Yanow*

The Tokyo Express / Jun. 1992 / Candid ✦✦✦✦

● **Yazoo** / 1994 / Concord Jazz ✦✦✦✦✦

Britt Woodman

b. Jun. 4, 1920, Los Angeles, CA
Trombone / Swing
An extremely versatile trombone soloist, Britt Woodman led Duke Ellington's section in the '50s and was flexible enough to record with Charles Mingus and Miles Davis. Woodman had range, fire and the harmonic knowledge to handle sophisticated big band and swing dates, and Mingus' futuristic, challenging arrangements. Woodman and Mingus were boyhood friends as well as longtime musical associates. Woodman played with Phil Moore and Les Hite in the '30s, then with Boyd Raeburn and Eddie Heywood in the mid-'40s before joining Lionel Hampton in 1946. He studied music at Westlake College in Los Angeles from 1948 to 1950, then joined Ellington. Woodman replaced Lawrence Brown and remained with Ellington until 1960. In 1955 he also recorded in a band led by Miles Davis that included Mingus. Woodman worked in several Broadway shows in the '60s and recorded with Mingus on three sessions ranging from 1960 to 1963. He then returned to California in 1970, where he recorded, leading an octet, and played with the Akiyoshi-Tabackin, Capp-Pierce and Bill Berry bands. Woodman toured Japan twice with Benny Carter in the late '70s, then returned to New York in the '80s where he played with swing and bebop bands. —*Ron Wynn*

Chris Woods

b. Dec. 25, 1925, Memphis, TN, **d.** Jul. 4, 1985, New York, NY
Alto Saxophone / Bop, Early R&B
A fine altoist who was influenced by both bop and R&B, Chris Woods first played in Memphis and then after moving to St. Louis he performed with the Jeter-Pillars Orchestra and with George Hudson in the 1950s. Woods also recorded as a leader during the

era. Moving to New York in 1962, Woods played and recorded with Dizzy Gillespie and Clark Terry, worked with Sy Oliver (1970–73) and had a stint with Count Basie in 1983. He never became a major name but was an excellent player. —*Scott Yanow*

● **Somebody Done Stole My Blues** / Feb. 23, 1953 / Delmark ✦✦✦✦✦

Modus Operandi / 1978 / Delmark ✦✦✦✦

Jimmy Woods

b. Oct. 29, 1934, St. Louis, MS
Alto Saxophone / Avant-Garde, Post Bop
Not a great deal is known about Jimmy Woods, an explorative altoist who recorded two impressive albums for Contemporary during 1961-63 and then largely dropped out of the music scene. A passionate improviser, Woods joined Homer Carter's R&B band in 1951. After a period in the Air Force (1952–56) he worked in some other R&B groups including Roy Milton's. He played with Horace Tapscott in 1960, recorded with Joe Gordon the following year and spent a period playing with Gerald Wilson's big band and Chico Hamilton. However Jimmy Woods rarely made a living out of music and has been little heard from since the mid-'60s. —*Scott Yanow*

● **Awakening** / Aug. 1962 / Original Jazz Classics ✦✦✦✦✦
Altoist Jimmy Woods, whose style fell between hard bop and the avant-garde, only recorded two albums as a leader; this CD reissue brings back his first. The backup musicians include Joe Gordon or Martin Banks on trumpet, Amos Trice or Dick Whittington on piano, Jimmy Bond or Gary Peacock on bass and drummer Milt Turner, but Woods is by far the most advanced musician. On six of his originals, an obscurity and "Love for Sale," Jimmy Woods' original sound and passionate chance-taking style make one wonder why he was never able to really make it; his music has not really dated. —*Scott Yanow*
Conflict / Mar. 25, 1963–Mar. 26, 1963 / Contemporary ✦✦✦✦

Phil Woods

b. Nov. 2, 1931, Springfield, MA
Clarinet, Alto Saxophone / Bop, Hard Bop
One of bebop's most outspoken advocates and an admired alto saxophonist among numerous musicians, Phil Woods has fought the good fight since the '50s, even though he began playing in a time when other styles were challenging bebop's hegemony. Perhaps the fastest alto saxophonist currently active, Woods' technique, from its bright, shimmering tone to his dynamic interpretative abilities and insertion of humorous musical quotations into solos, is textbook bebop. He rivals Frank Morgan as the closest thing going to Charlie Parker in terms of sound and approach, and probably plays better in-tune than virtually any other modern jazz alto stylist. He could be considered a hard bopper, but his reverence for Parker makes it difficult to not associate Woods with this genre. He began playing sax at 12, and later attended Juilliard. While there he played briefly with Charlie Barnet. Woods then worked with George Wallington, Kenny Dorham and Friedrich Gulda, recorded with George Russell and toured the Near East and South America with Dizzy Gillespie during the mid-'50s. He began heading combos in the late '50s, while playing in Buddy Rich's band, touring Europe with Quincy Jones in 1959 and 1960 (he was a founding member of the big band) and the Soviet Union with Benny Goodman in 1962. There were sessions for Prestige in the late '50s and Candid in the early '60s, some with fellow saxophonist Gene Quill; *Phil and Quill with Prestige* and *Phil Talks with Quill* were the sax equivalent of the J.J. Johnson and Kai Winding collaborations. *Rights of Swing* in 1960 for Candid showcased his extended compositions. Woods turned to studio work for a while in the '60s, playing on several commercial, television and film dates. He played on the soundtracks for *The Hustler* and *Blow Up*. He recorded with Benny Carter in 1961, appearing on the *Further Definitions* album. During the summers from 1964 to 1967 he taught at the Ramblerny performing arts camp in Pennsylvania. Woods moved to France in 1968, and returned to straight jazz. He formed a combo called the European Rhythm Machine, with pianist George Gruntz, bassist Henri Texler and drummer Daniel Humair. They remained intact until 1972. Woods moved to Los Angeles and formed an electronic quartet that met with criticism and audience displeasure and soon disbanded. He relocated to the East Coast, and in 1973 started an acoustic group with pianist Mike Melillo, bassist Steve Gilmore and drummer Bill Goodwin. This band was critically acclaimed, and Woods won three Grammy awards in the

mid-'70s on the strength of such albums as *Images* and *Live from the Showboat*. He also was recognized for his work with pop and soul musicians; he did solos on vocal recordings by Billy Joel and Aretha Franklin among others. He made fine albums for Muse, Testament, Adelphi and Clean Cuts. Woods made personnel changes in the '80s, as Hal Galper replaced Melillo in 1981 and trumpeter Tom Harrell came on board in 1983. There were more solid dates for Palo Alto, Red Record, Blackhawk, Denon, Omnisound, and Antilles. Galper And Harrell eventually moved on to form their own bands, but Woods has continued recording and performing into the '90s. He's playing more clarinet and occasionally using synthesizer in his recordings. Woods' earlier albums have been steadily reissued, and he keeps making uncompromising music reflecting the influence of mentor Charlie Parker. He's also among the small corps of jazz saxophonists who continue to tour regularly. —*Ron Wynn*

Early Quintets / Aug. 11, 1954+Mar. 3, 1959 / Original Jazz Classics ✦✦✦✦
A pair of formerly rare quintet sets featuring altoist Phil Woods are combined on this CD reissue from the OJC series. One session was actually led by guitarist Jimmy Raney in 1954 (and also includes trumpeter John Wilson, bassist Bill Crow and drummer Joe Morello) while the other group (with trumpeter Howard McGhee, bassist Teddy Kotick and drummer Roy Haynes) was headed by pianist Dick Hyman in 1959. Both bop-oriented dates have their moments with the edge going to Hyman's session. —*Scott Yanow*

Woodlore / Nov. 25, 1955 / Original Jazz Classics ✦✦✦✦

● **Pairing Off** / Jun. 15, 1956 / Original Jazz Classics ✦✦✦✦✦
Septet/ First-rate '80s reissue of an excellent 1956 date with lots of heavy hitters—Kenny Dorham (tpt), Donald Byrd (tpt), Tommy Flanagan (p) and Woods. —*Ron Wynn*

Altology / Jun. 15, 1956–Mar. 29, 1957 / Original Jazz Classics ✦✦✦✦

The Young Bloods / Nov. 2, 1956 / Original Jazz Classics ✦✦✦✦
Fine reissue taken from days when Woods, Donald Byrd (tpt) and Teddy Kotick (b) were rising stars. —*Ron Wynn*

Four Altos / Feb. 9, 1957 / Original Jazz Classics ✦✦✦
Even with Phil Woods standing out, the "four altos" on this jam session all sound pretty similar. Few listeners will be able to consistently pick out which solos are by Gene Quill and which by Sahib Shihab, Hal Stein or Woods, and unfortunately there are no real liner notes (except basic information) on this budget LP. The solos (and the backup of pianist Mal Waldron, bassist Tommy Potter and drummer Louis Hayes) are generally hard swinging and well played but the strong influence of Charlie Parker makes all of the altoists sound alike. —*Scott Yanow*

Bird Feathers / Mar. 29, 1957 / Original Jazz Classics ✦✦✦
With Mclean/Jenkins/Mckusick. High-flying blowing/jam session from the 50s. —*Ron Wynn*

Phil and Quill with Prestige / Mar. 29, 1957 / Original Jazz Classics ✦✦✦✦

Sugan / Jul. 19, 1957 / Original Jazz Classics ✦✦✦✦
This CD from Fantasy's Original Jazz Classics series is essentially a bebop jam session. The quintet (altoist Phil Woods, trumpeter Ray Copeland, pianist Red Garland, bassist Teddy Kotick and drummer Nick Stabulas) performs three Charlie Parker compositions and three originals by Woods but the melodies are quickly discarded in favor of heated solos. Woods and the greatly underrated Copeland work together very well and Garland is a major asset both as a soloist and as an accompanist to the horns. This little-known date is quite enjoyable. —*Scott Yanow*

Bird's Night: a Celebration of the Music of Charlie Parker / Aug. 12, 1957 / Savoy ✦✦✦

Phil Talks with Quill / Sep. 11, 1957–Oct. 8, 1957 / Columbia ✦✦✦
Phil Woods and his fellow altoist Gene Quill had similar styles at the time of this quintet recording (in which they are accompanied by pianist Bob Corwin, bassist Sonny Dallas and drumer Nick Stabulas). They jam happily on five bop standards and Woods' "Hymn for Kim." Although not really essential, bebop fans may want to search for this hard-to-find LP. —*Scott Yanow*

★ **Rights of Swing** / Jan. 26, 1960 / Candid ✦✦✦✦✦
This Candid recording is such a major success that it is surprising that altoist Phil Woods has rarely recorded in this context. The all-

star octet not only features the altoist/leader but also trumpeter Benny Bailey, trombonist Curtis Fuller, baritonist Sahib Shihab, the innovative french horn player Julius Watkins (a major factor in this music), pianist Tommy Flanagan, bassist Buddy Catlett and drummer Osie Johnson. This set (reissued by Black Lion on CD) consists entirely of Woods' five-part "Rights of Swing" suite which clocks in around 38 minutes. The colorful arrangements use the distinctive horns in inventive fashion and the music (which leaves room for many concise solos) holds one's interest throughout. One of Phil Woods' finest recordings, it's a true gem. —*Scott Yanow*

The Birth of the ERM / Jun. 1968–Oct. 1968 / Philology ✦✦✦✦
At the Montreux Jazz Festival / Jun. 19, 1969 / Verve ✦✦✦✦✦
At the Frankfurt Jazz Festival / Mar. 21, 1970 / Atlantic ✦✦✦✦✦
Phil Woods Quartet / 1973 / Testament ✦✦✦
Musique Du Bois / Jan. 14, 1974 / Muse ✦✦✦✦
Images / Feb. 1975 / RCA ✦✦✦✦
New Phil Woods Album / Oct. 1975–Dec. 1975 / RCA ✦✦✦
Live from the Showboat / Nov. 1976 / RCA ✦✦✦✦✦
Song for Sisyphus / Nov. 9, 1977 / Gryphon ✦✦✦
I Remember / Mar. 1978 / Gryphon ✦✦
More Live / May 23, 1978–May 26, 1979 / Mobile Fidelity ✦✦✦
Crazy Horse / Jul. 1979 / Sea Breeze ✦✦✦✦
★ **Phil Woods/Lew Tabackin** / Dec. 10, 1980 / Omnisound ✦✦✦✦✦
Three for All / Jan. 6, 1981–Jan. 7, 1981 / Enja ✦✦✦✦✦
1990 reissue. This is an excellent trio date. With Tommy Flannagan (p). —*Ron Wynn*
Birds of a Feather / Aug. 11, 1981+Aug. 12, 1981 / Antilles ✦✦✦✦
At the Vanguard / Oct. 2, 1982 / Antilles ✦✦✦✦✦
Live from New York / Oct. 7, 1982 / Quicksilver ✦✦✦✦
Poor recording but excellent solos, especially Woods and Hal Galper (p). —*Ron Wynn*
Heaven / Dec. 1984 / Black Hawk ✦✦✦
Piper at the Gates of Dawn / 1984 / Rykodisc ✦✦✦✦
Gratitude / Jun. 19, 1986 / Denon ✦✦✦
Bouquet / Nov. 1987 / Concord Jazz ✦✦✦✦✦
● **Bop Stew** / Nov. 1987 / Concord Jazz ✦✦✦✦✦
Quintet. First in series of live dates from 1987 Concord Festival in Japan. Tom Harrell (tpt) and Woods emphatic. CD version has bonus track. —*Ron Wynn*
Evolution / May 1988 / Concord Jazz ✦✦✦✦✦
Here's to My Lady / Dec. 20, 1988–Dec. 21, 1988 / Chesky ✦✦✦✦
Flash / Apr. 1989 / Concord Jazz ✦✦✦✦✦
All Bird's Children / Jun. 1990 / Concord Jazz ✦✦✦✦✦
Real Life / Sep. 27, 1990–Sep. 28, 1990 / Chesky ✦✦✦✦
Flowers for Hodges / 1991 / Concord Jazz ✦✦✦✦✦
Full House / 1991 / Milestone ✦✦✦✦
Phil Woods Live / Oct. 1991 / Novus ✦✦✦
An Affair to Remember / 1993 / Evidence ✦✦✦✦✦

Reggie Workman

b. Jun. 26, 1937, Philadelphia, PA
Bass / Avant-Garde, Hard Bop
Reggie Workman has long been one of the most technically gifted of all bassists, a brilliant player whose versatile style fits into both hard bop and very avant-garde settings. He played piano, tuba and euphonium early on but settled on bass in the mid-'50s. After working regularly with Gigi Gryce (1958), Red Garland and Roy Haynes, he was a member of the John Coltrane Quartet for much of 1961, participating in several important recordings and even appearing with Coltrane and Eric Dolphy on a half hour West German television show that is currently available on video (*The Coltrane Legacy*). After Jimmy Garrison took his place with Coltrane, Workman became a member of Art Blakey's Jazz Messengers (1962–64) and was in the groups of Yusef Lateef (1964–65), Herbie Mann and Thelonious Monk (1967). He recorded frequently in the 1960s (including many Blue Note dates and Archie Shepp's classic *Four for Trane*). Since that time Workman has been an educator, played with everyone from Max Roach and

Art Farmer to Mal Waldron and David Murray and in 1989 recorded with Marilyn Crispell and Jeanne Lee. —*Scott Yanow*
Synthesis / Jun. 15, 1986 / Leo ✦✦✦✦✦
Images: The Reggie Workman Ensemble in Concert / Jan. 31, 1989–Jul. 1989 / Music & Arts ✦✦✦✦
● **Cerebral Caverns** / 1995 / Postcards ✦✦✦✦✦

World Saxophone Quartet

Group / Avant-Garde
The World Saxophone Quartet has long been an innovative group, an a capella saxophone group that originally consisted of altoists Julius Hemphill and Oliver Lake, David Murray on tenor and baritonist Hamiett Bluiett. Playing without a rhythm section, this band plays adventurous music that somehow always stays coherent; the baselines and rhythms provided by Bluiett help a great deal. In addition to their original music they have recorded tributes to Duke Ellington and 1960s R&B. However with Hemphill's departure in 1993 (replaced at times by Arthur Blythe, James Spaulding and Eric Person), the group has been weakened in recent years. —*Scott Yanow*
Point of No Return / Jun. 1977 / Moers ✦✦✦✦
Steppin' With / Dec. 1978 / Black Saint ✦✦✦✦✦
The second recording by the World Saxophone Quartet (which follows by a year their Moers Music release *Point of No Return*) gives one a well-rounded look at this powerful group. Comprised of altoist Julius Hemphill (who contributes four of the six group originals), altoist Oliver Lake, tenorman David Murray and baritonist Hamiett Bluiett, the explorative yet rhythmic group is heard in their early prime on this stimulating release. —*Scott Yanow*
W.S.Q. / Mar. 1980 / Black Saint ✦✦✦✦✦
★ **Revue** / Oct. 14, 1980 / Black Saint ✦✦✦✦✦
Prophet / 1980 / Black Saint ✦✦✦✦✦
Live in Zurich / Nov. 6, 1981 / Black Saint ✦✦✦✦✦
Live at Brooklyn Academy of Music / Dec. 6, 1985–Dec. 7, 1985 / Black Saint ✦✦✦✦
★ **Plays Duke Ellington** / Apr. 1986 / Elektra ✦✦✦✦✦
Brilliant adaption of Ellington catalog. —*Ron Wynn*
Dances and Ballads / Apr. 1987 / Elektra ✦✦✦✦
The Quartet extends its reach and scope to include danceable material. —*Ron Wynn*
Rhythm & Blues / Nov. 1988 / Elektra ✦✦✦✦
Metamorphosis / Apr. 1990 / Elektra ✦✦✦
You Don't Know Me / 1992 / Elektra ✦✦✦✦
Moving Right Along / 1993 / Black Saint ✦✦✦✦
This title applies to the World Saxophone Quartet's personnel as well as its music. Charter residents David Murray, Oliver Lake and Hamiett Bluiett were joined by special guest James Spaulding on two tracks, making it a quintet, and throughout by new member Eric Person. Person's composition "Antithesis," like several other selections, represented a change in the group's approach. Instead of their hallmark collectively improvised unison passages, most numbers had one or two featured soloists, with the others operating as harmony/contrast players. The WSQ did its usual array of material, from bubbling R&B and funk-tempered numbers to hard bop and swing-oriented tunes, plus two stirring renditions of "Amazing Grace." —*Ron Wynn*
Breath Of Life / 1995 / Elektra Nonesuch ✦✦✦

World's Greatest Jazz Band

Group / Dixieland
This all-star group was founded in 1968 by Dick Gibson at his sixth annual Jazz Party. Despite the impossibility of living up to its outrageous name, the band was indeed the finest in Dixieland/classic jazz. Co-led by Yank Lawson and Bob Haggart and also featuring Billy Butterfield, Bob Wilber and Ralph Sutton, the WGJB originally alternated standards with Dixiefied versions of current pop tunes like "Mrs. Robinson" but its finest album (*Live at Roosevelt Grill* on Atlantic) sticks to hot jamming. After the personnel changed a bit (Eddie Miller and Dick Wellstood passed through the band) the group broke up in 1978 although reunions by Lawson and Haggart in later years sometimes revived the name. Their recordings for Project 3, Atlantic and their own World Jazz label are pretty much all worth getting. —*Scott Yanow*

World's Greatest Jazz Band of Yank Lawson and Bob Haggart
/ Dec. 10, 1968 / Project 3 ++++

Extra! / Dec. 1968 / Project 3 ++++

★ **Live at Roosevelt Grill** / 1970 / Atlantic +++++

Century Plaza / Jan. 17, 1972–Jan. 19, 1972 / World Jazz ++++

Hark the Herald Angels Swing / Sep. 5, 1972–Sep. 7, 1972 / World Jazz ++++

At Massey Hall / Dec. 4, 1972 / World Jazz ++++
Anything from this delightful traditional jazz group is worth hearing. —*Ron Wynn*

On Tour, Vol. 1 / Oct. 1975 / World Jazz +++++

On Tour, Vol. 2 / Oct. 1975 / World Jazz ++++

In Concert at the Lawrenceville School / 1975 / Flying Dutchman ++++

Plays Rodgers and Hart / 1975 / World Jazz +++

Plays George Gershwin / Jun. 1, 1977–Jun. 3, 1977 / World Jazz +++

Frank Wright

b. Jul. 9, 1935, Grenada, MS, **d.** May 17, 1990, Germany
Tenor Saxophone / Avant-Garde, Free Jazz
Throughout his career Frank Wright always played free jazz with the emphasis on passionate sound explorations. Early on he was an electric bassist who played R&B. However upon meeting Albert Ayler he was inspired to switch to tenor and perform much more adventurous music. He moved to New York in the early '60s and played with many musicians including Larry Young, Sunny Murray and even briefly Cecil Taylor and John Coltrane. Wright recorded as a leader for ESP in 1967 and 1969 and then spent much of the rest of his career living and playing in Europe, touring with Cecil Taylor in the mid-'80s. —*Scott Yanow.*

Trio / Nov. 16, 1965 / ESP ++++
With Henry Grimes on bass, Tony Price on drums. Unafraid to explore new terrain. —*Michael G. Nastos*

● **Your Prayer** / May 1967 / ESP +++++
Quintet. More groundbreaking avant-garde music. Lengthy improvs and counterpoint. —*Michael G. Nastos*

Kevin, My Dear Son / Oct. 1978 / Chiaroscuro ++++

★ **Stove Man, Love Is the Word** / May 22, 1979 / Sandra +++++
Live at the Loft in Munich, Germany, with sextet. Rev. Wright is on the edge. This is an extension of Dolphy. Must have open ears. —*Michael G. Nastos*

Richard Wyands

b. Jul. 2, 1928, Oakland, CA
Piano / Hard Bop
A fine ballad and standards player, Richard Wyands is such a strong accompanist that his abilities as a soloist are overlooked. But he

plays with taste, delicacy and sophistication while never ignoring the blues nor lacking intensity in his solos. Wyands began playing professionally in the '40s, working with Oakland groups. He backed Ella Fitzgerald and Carmen McRae in the mid-'50s, then moved to New York. Wyands played with Roy Haynes, Charles Mingus, Jerome Richardson and Gigi Gryce in the late '50s, then was extremely active in the early '60s. He was featured on recordings by Oliver Nelson, Etta Jones, Eddie "Lockjaw" Davis, Lem Winchester, Gene Ammons, Willis Jackson, Taft Jordan and Gryce. Wyands toured and recorded with Kenny Burrell from 1965 to 1974, visiting England in 1969 and Japan in 1971. He also recorded with Freddie Hubbard in 1971. Wyands joined Budd Johnson's JPJ quartet in 1974, and recorded with Benny Bailey in 1978 and Zoot Sims in 1982. He has continued recording and touring through the '80s and '90s but has done few recordings as a leader. Wyands currently has no sessions available on CD, but can be heard on reissued discs by Burrell, Ammons, Hubbard and many others. —*Ron Wynn*

Then, Here and Now / Oct. 12, 1977 / Storyville +++++

Albert Wynn

b. Jul. 29, 1907, New Orleans, LA, **d.** May, 1973, Chicago, IL
Trombone / Classic Jazz, New Orleans Jazz
A first-rate blues and stomp trombonist who could also hold his own in jam sessions, Albert Wynn was quite active from the '20s until the '60s. He was well schooled in the "tailgate" style, but was also adept at low-down ballads. Wynn toured with Ma Rainey and led his own band in Chicago in the late '20s; he recorded and worked with Charlie Creath in St. Louis in 1927. He moved to Europe in 1928, and worked in 1929 with Sam Wooding and Harry Flemming. Upon returning to America, Wynn worked in New York with the New Orleans Feetwarmers and with Jesse Stone, Jimmie Noone, Richard M. Jones and Earl Hines in Chicago. He played with Fletcher Henderson in the late '30s, then joined Noone's big band. Wynn worked in Chicago with various musicians in the '40s and '50s, among them Floyd Campbell, Baby Dodds and Lil Armstrong. He later played with Franz Jackson and the Gold Coast Jazz Band in the late '50s and early '60s. He recorded for Riverside in the early '60s as part of their Living Legends series. But illness greatly restricted his playing from the mid-'60s until his death in 1973. Fantasy reissued his Riverside date in 1993 as part of a traditional reissue line. —*Ron Wynn*

● **Chicago: The Living Legends** / Sep. 5, 1961 / Fantasy +++++
Trombonist Albert Wynn's 1961 return to traditional jazz was a high point that year for New Orleans fans. He had not made a record in 33 years, yet his playing on the album *Chicago: The Living Legends* was joyous, vibrant, and exciting. Wynn also assembled a great group for the date, led by the outstanding clarinetist Darnell Howard. This long-out-of-print date has been newly reissued with two fine bonus cuts added and is a primer for the joys of traditional jazz and blues music. —*Ron Wynn*

Y

Yosuke Yamashita

b. Feb. 26, 1942, Tokyo, Japan
Piano / Avant-Garde, Free Jazz
One of the top Japanese jazz pianists, Yosuke Yamashita is a very adventurous and passionate improviser. After attending the Kunitachi Music University, Yamashita formed an avant-garde trio in 1969. Starting in 1974, Yamashita visited Europe most years. Since breaking up his trio in 1983, he has performed in a variety of settings ranging from a big band to solo. Most of Yamashita's recordings remain unavailable in the U.S. —*Scott Yanow*

Clay / Jun. 2, 1974 / Enja ✦✦✦✦
● **Chiasma** / Jun. 6, 1975 / MPS ✦✦✦✦✦
Trio recording. Influenced by Cecil Taylor. For special tastes only. —*Michael G. Nastos*

Banslikana / Jul. 1976 / Enja ✦✦✦✦✦
Inner Space / Jun. 24, 1977 / Enja ✦✦✦✦
Sakura (Cherry) / May 1, 1990–May 3, 1990 / Antilles ✦✦✦✦✦
● **Kurdish Dance** / 1993 / Antilles ✦✦✦✦✦
Tribute to Mal Waldron / 1994 / Enja ✦✦✦

Jimmy Yancey

b. 1894, Chicago, IL, **d.** Sep. 17, 1951, Chicago, IL
Piano / Boogie-Woogie, Blues
One of the pioneers of boogie-woogie piano, Jimmy Yancey was generally more subtle than the more famous Albert Ammons, Pete Johnson and Meade Lux Lewis, falling as much into the blues genre as in jazz. Yancey, who could romp as well as anyone, made many of his most memorable recordings at slower tempos. No matter what key he played in, Yancey ended every song in E flat, leading to some hilarious conclusions to some recordings. He worked in vaudeville as a singer and tap dancer starting at age six and in 1915 settled in Chicago as a pianist. But Yancey spent his last 26 years (from 1925 on) earning his living as a groundskeeper at Comiskey Park for the Chicago White Sox. He played part-time in local clubs and began recording in 1939, on a few occasions backing his wife, singer Mama Yancey. Jimmy Yancey never achieved the fame of his contemporaries but he remained a major influence on all practioners in the genre. —*Scott Yanow*

★ **Vol. 1 (1939–1940)** / May 4, 1939+Sep. 6, 1940 / Document ✦✦✦✦✦
Yancey's earliest and best sides for the Solo Art label. Beautiful and sensitive performances. —*Cub Koda*

★ **Complete Recorded Works, Vol. 2 (1939–1950)** / Feb. 23, 1940-Dec. 1943 / Document ✦✦✦✦
On the second of three CDs that trace virtually his entire recording career, pianist Jimmy Yancey is showcased on a variety of solo tracks. Two numbers from February 1940 are highlighted by the classic "Bear Trap Blues." There are a couple of numbers made for the tiny Art Center Jazz Gems label, a four-song (plus two alternate takes) definitive set cut for Bluebird (which includes "Death Letter Blues" and "Yancey's Bugle Call") and nine songs (five previously unissued) from 1943; on one version of "How Long Blues," Mama Yancey sings while Jimmy switches to the spooky sounding harmonium. This set also has Jimmy Yancey's only four recorded vocals, which are quite effective even though his voice is limited. All three volumes in this series are highly recommended

for the subtle pianist, who made expert use of space and ended every tune in E flat. —*Scott Yanow*

The Yancey-Lofton Sessions, Vol. 1 / Dec. 1943 / Storyville ✦✦✦✦
The Yancey-Lofton Sessions, Vol. 2 / Dec. 1943 / Storyville ✦✦✦✦
★ **Vol. 3 (1943–1950)** / Dec. 1943–Dec. 23, 1950 / Document ✦✦✦✦✦
The third of three CDs tracing the recording career of the unique boogie-woogie pianist Jimmy Yancey, whose subtlety could often result in some dramatic music, completes his December 1943 session and also has his December 23, 1950 solo set; his final recordings from July 1951 are available on an Atlantic release. The 1943 titles, three of which were previously unreleased, include two with Mama Yancey vocals (on one Jimmy switches to harmonium) and is highlighted by "White Sox Stomp," "Yancey Special" and two versions of "Pallet on the Floor." After the six fine titles from 1950, this CD finishes off with the only four numbers that Jimmy's older brother, the more ragtime-oriented Alonzo Yancey, ever recorded. Although his style was different, on "Ecstatic Rag" Alonzo does sound a bit like Jimmy. All three of these Document CDs, plus the Atlantic set, are highly recommended and preferable to the piecemeal domestic Bluebird reissues. —*Scott Yanow*

Chicago Piano, Vol. 1 / Jul. 18, 1951 / Atlantic ✦✦✦✦✦
Jimmy Yancey was one of the pioneer boogie-woogie pianists but, unlike many of the other pacesetters, he had a gentle and thoughtful style that also crossed over into the blues. This Atlantic CD, a straight reissue of the 1972 LP, contains Yancey's final recordings, cut just eight weeks before his death from diabetes. The pianist is in fine form on these introspective and often emotional performances which, with the exception of Meade Lux Lewis' "Yancey Special" and the traditional "Make Me a Pallet on the Floor," are comprised entirely of Yancey's originals. His wife Mama Yancey takes five memorable vocals on this memorable set of classic blues. —*Scott Yanow*

Yellowjackets

Group / Post Bop, Crossover
Although sometimes grouped with Spyro Gyra, the Yellowjackets are actually one of the most creative regular groups in the "rhythm and jazz" genre. Founded in 1981 as an R&B-oriented band that starred guitarist Robben Ford, the group took a giant step forward when after Ford's departure, altoist Marc Russo took his place. With original members Russell Ferrante on keyboards and electric bassist Jimmy Haslip in addition to drummer William Kennedy, the band found its own R&Bish sound, sometimes playing original compositions that sounded like Joe Zawinul at his most melodic. In recent times Russo chose to go out on his own and his replacement Bob Mintzer (on tenor and bass clarient) has added more jazz credibility to the group's music. Through the years the Yellowjackets have become quite popular, releasing excellent selling records for GRP and touring constantly. —*Scott Yanow*

Yellowjackets / 1981 / Warner Brothers ✦✦✦
Samurai Samba / 1984 / Warner Brothers ✦✦✦✦
Mirage a Trois / 1985 / Warner Brothers ✦✦✦✦
Shades / 1986 / MCA ✦✦✦✦
Four Corners / 1987 / MCA ✦✦✦✦✦
● **Politics** / 1988 / MCA ✦✦✦✦✦
Politics features the appealing sax of Marc Russo and the com-

positions of Russel Ferrante. Unpretentious, melodic and memorable, it has fine studio sound. —*David Nelson McCarthy*

★ **The Spin** / 1989 / MCA ✦✦✦✦✦

Green House / 1990 / GRP ✦✦✦✦✦
Included is guest sax by Bob Mintzer and fine orchestration for a real live string ensemble by Vince Mendoza. Very accessible, it has a high level of musicianship all around. —*David Nelson McCarthy*

Live Wires / Nov. 15, 1991–Nov. 16, 1991 / GRP ✦✦✦

Like a River / Apr. 1992 / GRP ✦✦✦✦✦
Other than the easy-listening pieces that appear near the beginning of the program, this is one of the Yellowjackets' strongest jazz dates. Bob Mintzer's creative reeds (switching between tenor, bass clarinet, soprano and the EWI) keep the music stimulating and keyboardist Russell Ferrante has come a long way as both an improviser (where he is most influenced by Herbie Hancock) and as the band's main composer. With bassist Jimmy Haslip and drummer William Kennedy in strong supporting roles, the ensemble plays intelligent funk grooves, some mood music and occasional sections of straight-ahead jamming. The inclusion of the Miles Davis-influenced trumpeter Tim Hagans on half of the selections adds variety to a particularly enjoyable set. —*Scott Yanow*

Run for Your Life / 1993 / GRP ✦✦✦✦✦
This is one of the Yellowjackets' most jazz-oriented sets. Roughly half of the music uses funky rhtyhms while the remainder is straight-ahead. "Jacket Town" sounds like it could have come from a good Eddie Harris record, Bob Mintzer's tenor is heard on a rapid run-through of rhythm changes on "Runferyerlife," keyboardist Russell Ferrante hints strongly at Chick Corea's acoustic playing on "Muhammed" and Mintzer's ballad "Sage" is memorable. This fine release is recommended both to the Yellowjackets' longtime fans and those listeners who mistakenly think that this popular group is a mundane fusion band. —*Scott Yanow*

Collection / 1995 / GRP ✦✦✦
Collection picks the best songs from the Yellowjackets' uneven albums for GRP, making it a good introduction to the group's mellow fusion. —*Stephen Thomas Erlewine*

Dreamland / 1995 / Warner ✦✦✦✦

Larry Young

b. Oct. 7, 1940, Newark, NJ, d. Mar. 30, 1978, New York, NY
Organ / Hard Bop, Post Bop, Fusion
Larry Young, also known as Khalid Yasin, offered as radical an approach on organ in the '60s as Jimmy Smith posed in the '50s. His free, swirling chords, surging lines and rock-influenced improvisations were an alternative to the groove-centered, blues and soul jazz sound that had become the organ's dominant direction. He brought John Coltrane's late '60s approach to the organ, generating waves of sound and greatly influencing any session he participated in during the '60s and '70s. Young studied piano rather than organ, though he later began playing organ in R&B bands in the '50s. He recorded in 1960 with Jimmy Forrest, and then did his first session for Blue Note as a leader. He worked and recorded with Grant Green in a hard bop vein in the mid-'60s, though he was beginning his experiments at that point. Young worked with Joe Henderson, Lee Morgan, Donald Byrd and Tommy Turrentine and toured Europe in 1964. His album *Into Something* in 1965 alerted everyone Young was heading a different way. He played with Coltrane, recorded with Woody Shaw and Elvin Jones, then joined Miles Davis' band in 1969. Young worked with John McLaughlin in 1970 and was in Tony Williams' Lifetime with McLaughlin and Jack Bruce among others in the early '70s. He only made a couple of other records for Perception and Arista, both of them uneven but with some intriguing moments. Neither label had the vaguest idea what Young was trying to do, nor how they could sell it. Sadly, he died in 1978 at 38. He'd only made a handful of recordings, and his labels never knew what to make of his music. Mosaic issued a superb boxed set of Young's Blue Note recordings, a six-CD (nine album) collection the *Complete Blue Note Recordings*. A very early session, *Testifying*, on New Jazz, was reissued by Fantasy in a limited edition in '92. Blue Note has an anthology package, *The Art of Larry Young*, available as well. —*Ron Wynn*

Testifying / Aug. 2, 1960 / Original Jazz Classics ✦✦✦
Organist Larry Young was 19 when he made this, his debut recording. Although he would become innovative later on, Young at this early stage was still influenced by Jimmy Smith even if he had a lighter tone; the fact that he used Smith's former guitarist, Thornel Schwartz, and a drummer whose name was coincidentally Jimmie Smith kept the connection strong. R&Bish tenor Joe Holiday helps out on two songs and the music (standards, blues and ballads) always swings. Easily recommended to fans of the jazz organ. —*Scott Yanow*

Young Blues / Sep. 30, 1960 / Original Jazz Classics ✦✦✦✦
Organist Larry Young's second recording (cut shortly before he turned 20) is the best from his early period before he completely shook off the influence of Jimmy Smith. With guitarist Thornel Schwartz in top form, and bassist Wendell Marshall and drummer Jimmie Smith excellent in support, Young swings hard on a few recent jazz originals, some blues and two standards ("Little White Lies" and "Nica's Dream"). Recommended as a good example of his pre-Blue Note work. —*Scott Yanow*

Groove Street / Feb. 27, 1962 / Original Jazz Classics ✦✦✦
Larry Young's third and final Prestige recording (reissued in the OJC series on CD) concludes his early period; he would next record as a leader two and a half years later on Blue Note, by which time his style would be much more original. For his 1962 outing, Young is joined by the obscure tenor Bill Leslie, guitarist Thornel Schwartz and drummer Jimmie Smith for some original blues and two standards ("I Found a New Baby" and "Sweet Lorraine"). Nothing all that substantial occurs but fans of Jimmy Smith will enjoy the similar style that Larry Young had at the time. —*Scott Yanow*

★ **Complete Blue Note Recordings** / Sep. 11, 1964–Feb. 7, 1969 / Mosaic ✦✦✦✦✦
Larry Young, one of the most significant jazz organists to emerge after the rise of Jimmy Smith, is heard on this limited-edition six-CD set at the peak of his creativity [The set comprises the following original albums: Grant Green *Talkin' About*, Larry Young *Into Somethin'*, Grant Green *Street of Dreams*, Grant Green *I Want to Hold Your Hand*, Larry Young *Unity*, Larry Young *Of Love and Peace*, Larry Young *Contrasts*, Larry Young *Heaven on Earth*, Larry Young *Mother Ship*, Larry Young *40 Years of Jazz, The History of Blue Note* (box 4 Dutch), Larry Young *The World of Jazz Organ* (Japanese), Larry Young *The Blue Note 50th Anniversary Collection Volume Two: The Jazz Message*]. Formerly available as nine LPs (three of which were actually under guitarist Grant Green's leadership), Young was still very much under Smith's influence on the first four sessions (which features a trio with Green and drummer Elvin Jones plus guests Sam Rivers or Hank Mobley on tenor and vibraphonist Bobby Hutcherson). However, starting with the monumental *Unity* session (a quartet outing with Joe Henderson on tenor, trumpeter Woody Shaw and Elvin Jones), Young emerged as a very advanced and original stylist in his own right. The final four dates are generally pretty explorative and feature such notable sidemen as altoist James Spaulding and Byard Lancaster, guitarist George Benson and trumpeter Lee Morgan along with some forgotten local players. This definitive Larry Young set is highly recommended. —*Scott Yanow*

Into Somethin' / Oct. 12, 1964 / Blue Note ✦✦✦✦✦

★ **Unity** / Nov. 10, 1965 / Blue Note ✦✦✦✦✦
Recorded at Englewood Cliffs, NJ. Innovative, far reaching organist. —*Ron Wynn*

Of Love and Peace / Jun. 28, 1966 / Blue Note ✦✦✦✦✦

Contrasts / Sep. 18, 1967 / Blue Note ✦✦✦✦

Heaven on Earth / Feb. 9, 1968 / Blue Note ✦✦✦
Organist Larry Young, who really found his own sound back in 1965 with the classic *Unity* album, is deep in the funk on this later Blue Note album (which has been included in the Mosaic box set *The Complete Blue Note Recordings of Larry Young*). With altoist Byard Lancaster, tenor saxophonist Herbert Morgan, guitarist George Benson and drummer Eddie Gladden completing the quintet, there are some explorative solos but the less imaginative funk rhythms lower the content of the music somewhat. Young's wife Althea Young has an effective vocal on "My Funny Valentine" but overall this is a lesser effort. —*Scott Yanow*

Mother Ship / Feb. 7, 1969 / Blue Note ✦✦✦
Lawrence of Newark / 1973 / Perception ✦✦
Spaceball / 1975 / Arista ✦✦
Fuel / 1975 / Arista ✦✦
The Art of Larry Young / Blue Note ✦✦✦✦✦

Lester Young

b. Aug. 27, 1909, Woodville, MS, **d.** Mar. 15, 1959, New York, NY
Tenor Saxophone, Clarinet / Swing
Lester Young was one of the true jazz giants, a tenor saxophonist who came up with a completely different conception in which to play his horn, floating over bar lines rather than adopting Coleman Hawkins' then-dominant forceful approach. A non-conformist, Young (nicknamed "Pres" by Billie Holiday) had the ironic experience in the 1950s of hearing many young tenors try to sound exactly like him!

Although he spent his earliest days near New Orleans, Lester Young lived in Minneapolis by 1920, playing in a legendary family band. He studied violin, trumpet and drums, starting on alto at age 13. Because he refused to tour in the South, Young left home in 1927 and instead toured with Art Bronson's Bostonians, switching to tenor. He was back with the family band in 1929 and then freelanced for a few years, playing with Walter Page's Blue Devils (1930), Eddie Barefield in 1931, back with the Blue Devils during 1932–33, Bennie Moten and King Oliver (1933). He was with Count Basie for the first time in 1934 but left to replace Coleman Hawkins with Fletcher Henderson. Unfortunately it was expected that Young would try to emulate Hawk and his laidback sound angered Henderson's sidemen, resulting in Young not lasting long. After a tour with Andy Kirk and a few brief jobs, Lester Young was back with Basie in 1936, just in time to star with the band as they headed East. Pres made history during his years with Basie, not only participating on Count's record dates but starring with Billie Holiday and Teddy Wilson on a series of classic small group sessions. In addition on his rare recordings on clarinet with Basie and the Kansas City Six, Young displayed a very original cool sound that almost sounded like altoist Paul Desmond in the 1950s. After leaving Count in 1940, Young's career became a bit aimless, not capitalizing on his fame in the jazz world. He co-led a low-profile band with his brother drummer Lee Young in Los Angles until rejoining Basie in December 1943. Young had a happy nine months back with the band, recorded a memorable quartet session with bassist Slam Stewart and starred in the short film *Jammin' the Blues* before he was drafted. His experiences dealing with racism in the military were horrifying, affecting his mental state of mind for the remainder of his life.

Although many critics have written that Lester Young never sounded as good after getting out of the military, despite erratic health he actually was at his prime in the mid-to-late '40s. He toured (and was well-paid by Norman Granz) with Jazz at the Philharmonic on-and-off through the '40s and '50s, made a wonderful series of recordings for Aladdin and worked steadily as a single. Young also adopted his style well to bebop (which he had helped pave the way for in the 1930s). But mentally he was suffering, building a wall between himself and the outside world and inventing his own colorful vocabulary. Although many of his recordings in the 1950s were excellent (showing a greater emotional depth than in his earlier days), Young was bothered by the fact that some of his White imitators were making much more money than he was. He drank huge amounts of liquor and nearly stopped eating with predictable results. 1956's *The Jazz Giants '56* album found him in peak form as did a well-documented engagement in Washington, D.C., with a quartet and a last reunion with Count Basie at the 1957 Newport Jazz Festival. But for the 1957 telecast *The Sound of Jazz* Young mostly played sitting down (although he stole the show with an emotional one-chorus blues solo played to Billie Holiday). After becoming ill in Paris in early 1959, Lester Young came home and essentially drank himself to death. Nearly 40 years after his death, Pres is still considered (along with Coleman Hawkins and John Coltrane) one of the three most important tenor saxophonists of all time. *—Scott Yanow*

Lester Young Story, Vol. 1 / Oct. 8, 1936–Jun. 15, 1937 / Columbia ✦✦✦✦
The idea of reissuing all of Lester Young's Columbia recordings on a series of five comprehensive two-LP sets is good in theory, until one realizes that the tenor did not lead any recording sessions for the label. These two-fers instead consist of all of Young's sideman appearances for Columbia on which he solos or is prominent in

the ensembles. *Vol. 1* starts off featuring Young with the Jones-Smith Inc. (Prez's recording debut) on four selections plus an alternate take of "Shoe Shine Boy." This quintet was actually taken from Count Basie's Orchestra and has a couple of Young's greatest solos, particularly his statement on "Lady Be Good." The remainder of the first volume features Young with Billie Holiday and on two instrumental versions of "I've Found a New Baby" with Teddy Wilson's Orchestra. The classic collaborations with Lady Day have since been reissued on CD but this set does offer the rare alternate takes of "Mean to Me," "Me, Myself and I" and "Without Your Love." *—Scott Yanow*

Young Lester Young / Oct. 8, 1936–Jun. 26, 1939 / Columbia ✦✦✦
This LP from French Columbia gathers together a variety of alternate takes and rare material usually featuring the great tenor of Lester Young. The word "usually" is used because the two selections by Jerry Kruger's Orchestra actually have Kermit Scott (not Young as listed) on tenor. Otherwise the LP includes the alternate takes of "Shoe Shine Boy" (from 1936), "Lester Leaps In" and two of "Dickie's Dream" by the Kansas City Seven in 1939, Young's solo on the jam session version of "Honeysuckle Rose" performed at Benny Goodman's famous Carnegie Hall concert and the six numbers cut by organist Glenn Hardman with an all star quintet in 1939. Excellent music, most of which is now available elsewhere. *—Scott Yanow*

Lester Young / Oct. 9, 1936–Dec. 5, 1957 / Time Life ✦✦✦✦
This three-LP box set gives one a good overview of the first half of tenor saxophonist Lester Young's career. Unfortunately it subscribes to the mistaken theory that his post-1945 output was pretty useless. By including only one selection from the last 13 years of his life, this set misses proving its point and gives an incomplete picture of the great tenor but, as an introduction to early Prez, it does have many of his best prewar recordings (most with either Count Basie or Billie Holiday) and includes an appealing booklet. *—Scott Yanow*

The Lester Young Story, Vol. 2 / Sep. 13, 1937–Sep. 15, 1938 / Columbia ✦✦✦✦
This series of five two-LP sets featuring Lester Young's recordings for Columbia is a bit odd because the great tenor did not lead any sessions for that label. *Vol. 2*, with the exception of his solo on "Honeysuckle Rose" from Benny Goodman's famous 1938 Carnegie Hall concert, consists entirely of Billie Holiday recordings. The main value to this set (since all of the master takes of Holiday's records are now out on CD) is that there are eight alternate takes included among these 24 performances, making this two-fer of greatest value to serious collectors who will want to hear these rare versions of "When You're Smiling," "If Dreams Come True" and "Back in Your Own Backyard." *—Scott Yanow*

The Lester Young Story, Vol. 3 / Oct. 31, 1938–Jun. 26, 1939 / Columbia ✦✦✦✦
The third of five two-LP sets that reissue all of Lester Young's sideman appearances for Columbia mostly consists of his recordings with Count Basie including two versions of the classic "Taxi War Dance" along with other performances that include Young tenor solos. In addition, one of the lesser sessions with Billie Holiday and two performances and one alternate take with organist Glenn Hardman's Hammond Five round out this set. Collectors in particular will want to acquire this series. *—Scott Yanow*

Lester Young Story, Vol. 4 / Jun. 26, 1939–Mar. 19, 1940 / Columbia ✦✦✦✦
This odd but valuable two-LP series features all of Lester Young's sideman appearances for Columbia in which he takes a solo. The fourth of five volumes features four selections with organist Glenn Hardman's Hammond Five and three numbers from Billie Holiday but the bulk of the set features Prez's tenor with Count Basie orchestra. There are several gems among the latter including "Clap Hands Here Comes Charley," "Ham 'N Eggs," four versions of "Dickie's Dream" and two of "Lester Leaps In." This out-of-print swing series will be of greatest interest to veteran collectors who will want the alternate takes not yet issued on CD. *—Scott Yanow*

Lester Young and Charlie Christian / 1939–Oct. 28, 1940 / Jazz Archives ✦✦✦✦✦
This LP from the collectors' label Jazz Archives starts out with rare radio appearances by the Count Basie Orchestra during

1939–40; star soloists include the great tenor saxophonist Lester Young, trumpeters Buck Clayton and Harry "Sweets" Edison and Basie himself. The Benny Goodman Sextet of 1939 (featuring Lionel Hampton and Charlie Christian, the pioneer of the electric guitar) is heard on three numbers and then comes five selections from a very special studio session. In late 1940 Benny Goodman was toying with the idea of breaking up his big band and touring with an octet comprised of these all stars: Clayton, Young, Basie, Christian, rhythm guitarist Freddie Green, bassist Walter Page and drummer Jo Jones. They actually got together for one recording date although the performances were not released until decades later. The results, heard on the latter half of this LP, are as brilliant as one might hope. — Scott Yanow

Lester Young Story, Vol. 5 / Mar. 19, 1940–Mar. 21, 1941 / Columbia ◆◆◆◆
The fifth and final two-fer in this unusual series (which reissued all of tenor saxophonist Lester Young's significant recordings as a sideman for Columbia) features him with Count Basie's Orchestra (nine songs and eight alternate takes) and on some memorable performances with Billie Holiday (five songs and four alternates). The Basie tracks include "Louisiana," "Blow Top" and "Broadway" while Young's collaborations with Lady Day include "Laughing at Life," "Let's Do It" and three excellent and contrasting versions of "All of Me." Since the alternate takes are mostly not available on CD, swing collectors will want to acquire this entire attractive series. — Scott Yanow

Historical Prez / 1940–May 20, 1944 / Everybody's ◆◆◆◆◆
This superior LP fills two important gaps in the discography of tenor saxophonist Lester Young. In 1940 after leaving Count Basie's Orchestra, Young led a band of his own with trumpeter Shad Collins and guitarist John Collins that, other than for a session backing singer Una Mae Carlisle, never recorded. Happily this LP has broadcast versions of "Tickle Toe" and "Taxi War Dance" by this excellent group, along with "Benny's Bugle" from the otherwise unrecorded unit that Prez co-led with his brother, drummer Lee Young, in 1941 on the West Coast. The remainder of this set features Young during his second (and also otherwise unrecorded) stint with Basie's Orchestra in 1944. Other soloists with Basie include trumpeters Harry "Sweets" Edison and Joe Newman, trombonist Dickie Wells and Basie himself. Recommended. — Scott Yanow

★ **The Complete Aladdin Sessions** / Jul. 15, 1942–Dec. 29, 1948 / Blue Note ◆◆◆◆◆
Although it has often been written that the cool-toned tenor saxophonist Lester Young's experiences with racism in the military during 1944–45 so scarred him that musically he never played at the same level as he had previously, the music on this essential two-CD reissue disproves that theory. It is true that his attitude toward life was affected and Young became somewhat self-destructive, but his post-war solos rank with the greatest work of his career. This two-fer, which has four selections from 1942 in which Young is heard in a trio with pianist Nat King Cole and bassist Red Callender and a rare 1945 session headed by singer Helen Humes (including a previously unknown instrumental "Riffin' Without Helen"), is mostly taken up with Lester Young's very enjoyable 1945–48 small-group dates. Highlights include "D.B. Blues," "Jumpin' with Symphony Sid" (which was a minor hit), "Sunday" and "New Lester Leaps In," among many others. Minor errors aside (trumpeter Snooky Young is left out of the personnel listing for the Humes date and Young's final Aladdin session is from 1948 not 1947), this is a well-conceived and brilliant set filled with exciting performances by one of the true greats of jazz. — Scott Yanow

★ **The Complete Lester Young on Keynote** / Dec. 28, 1943+Dec. 28, 1944 / Mercury ◆◆◆◆◆
This is an amazing compilation of powerhouse cuts fromthe '40s. — Ron Wynn

Master Takes / Apr. 18, 1944–Jun. 28, 1949 / Savoy ◆◆◆◆◆
Lester Young recorded for Savoy three separate times in four different settings. On Apr. 18, 1944 he performed as part of the Count Basie Orchestra (although Basie himself was absent) for three numbers and then cut four more songs with a septet that included trumpeter Billy Butterfield and pianist Johnny Guarnieri. A few weeks later he was featured on four selections in front of the Count Basie rhythm section. Prez made his final Savoy appearance in 1949, fronting a Young sextet that also included pianist Junior Mance and drummer Roy Haynes. All of those per-

formances are included on this CD minus the many alternate takes which can be heard (along with this entire program) on *Pres: The Complete Savoy Recordings*. — Scott Yanow

Pres: The Complete Savoy Recordings / Apr. 18, 1944–Jun. 28, 1949 / Savoy ◆◆◆◆
This set only has 15 selections but also 21 alternate takes. Most of the sessions date from 1944 when Lester Young was briefly back with Count Basie's Orchestra. He is heard with the Basie band (minus the pianist), in a septet with trumpeter Billy Butterfield and pianist Johnny Guarnieri and, best of all, on four titles ("Blue Lester," "Ghost of a Chance," "Indiana" and "Jump Lester Jump") with Basie and his rhythm section. The last part of the set finds Young in 1949 fronting a young sextet (which includes trumpeter Jesse Drakes, trombonist Jerry Elliot and pianist Junior Mance). Throughout, the cool-toned tenor is in excellent form. Pres collectors will have to get this set although most listeners would be satisfied with *Master Takes*. — Scott Yanow

Jammin' with Lester / 1944–Jun. 3, 1946 / Jazz Archives ◆◆◆◆
This LP from the collectors' label Jazz Archives includes the soundtrack of the award-winning short film *Jammin' the Blues*, which in 1944 gave Lester Young, Harry "Sweets" Edison and Illinois Jacquet an opportunity to be seen as well as heard. Not only are the three songs from the film on this set but also three other previously unheard performances from the same date that did not make it onto the screen. The second side of this enjoyable set features Young at a trio of different jam sessions: playing "Lady Be Good" with fellow tenors Coleman Hawkins and Illinois Jacquet, sharing the ballad "I Can't Get Started" with Hawk and trumpeter Buck Clayton, and romping on "Tea for Two" in a quintet with trumpeter Joe Guy. The music is frequently exciting and worth searching for. — Scott Yanow

Lester Swings / Dec. 1945–Mar. 8, 1951 / Verve ◆◆◆◆◆
Verve did such a fine job with their two-LP Lester Young sets of the late '70s that it is surprising that they have lagged behind in reissuing the material on CD. This two-fer is a real gem, featuring the Lester Young-Nat King Cole-Buddy Rich Trio in 1945, showcasing the great tenor with pianist Hank Jones, bassist Ray Brown and Buddy Rich in 1950 and matching Prez with pianist John Lewis and a pair of different rhythm sections during 1950–51. Young was in particularly top form for the matchup with Cole and Rich and, even if his cool brand of small-group swing was out of style by 1950, his tone had become extremely influential among younger players. Highly recommended. — Scott Yanow

● **Prez Conferences (1946–1958)** / Mar. 20, 1946–1958 / Jass ◆◆◆◆◆
The great tenor Lester Young is heard in a variety of different settings on this CD, chiefly taken from radio and television broadcasts. The best performances find Prez playing two songs with the Nat King Cole Trio and drummer Buddy Rich in 1946, jamming three standards with trumpeter Buck Clayton and fellow tenor Coleman Hawkins, sitting in with the Count Basie Orchestra in 1952 and performing three numbers with the Bill Potts Trio in 1956. Throughout this very interesting set, Lester Young is in excellent form, making this an excellent introductory CD for listeners not already familiar with Prez' music and a bonus for collectors who will probably not already have most of these rare performances. — Scott Yanow

Carnegie Blues / May 27, 1946–Oct. 19, 1957 / Verve ◆◆◆
The great tenor saxophonist Lester Young toured with Norman Granz's traveling jam session Jazz at the Philharmonic during 1949–53 and occasionally afterward. This in-concert LP contains three selections in which Young is backed by the Oscar Peterson Quartet in 1953, a pair of excerpts (all that survives) from jams in 1946, a ballad medley from 1957 (on which he plays "Polka Dots and Moonbeams") and, best yet, versions of "Tea for Two" (with trumpeter Joe Guy) and "Carnegie Blues" (which also features the trumpeter Buck Clayton and the tenors of Coleman Hawkins and Illinois Jacquet) in 1946. Although not essential music, this set is quite enjoyable and has its exciting moments. — Scott Yanow

Pres Lives! / Apr. 2, 1950 / Savoy ◆◆
Many of tenor saxophonist Lester Young's club performances of the early '50s were taped and came out on LP's posthumously (when he was not around to protest). In general they do little to

help his legacy for the crowd noises, distorted sound quality and sometimes routine solos are not up to the level of his studio sessions. This Savoy set, with an unknown rhythm section and the average trumpeter Jesse Drakes, falls into that general category although Young himself takes some fine solos. Mostly recommended to Lester Young fanatics. —*Scott Yanow*

Pres Is Blue / 1950–May 2, 1952 / Charlie Parker ♦♦
This LP claims that it has "Unprecedented Hi Fidelity." The streaky sound quality of these bootleg live recordings makes a joke out of that statement. Taken from a few club appearances during 1950–52 and featuring tenor saxophonist Lester Young, trumpeter Jesse Drakes and either Kenny Drew, John Lewis or Wynton Kelly on piano, these six standards have seen better days. Young has a few swinging solos but the crowd noise gets pretty distracting at times. —*Scott Yanow*

Masters of Jazz: Lester Young / May 19, 1951–Dec. 29, 1956 / Storyville ♦♦♦
This LP from the European Storyville label has some of tenor saxophonist Lester Young's better live performances from the 1950s. Trumpeter Jesse Drakes is on about half of the set and the young pianist Horace Silver is heard on three songs from 1951. However the better performances are from 1956 with Young joined by the Bill Potts Trio and, on four songs, the fine trumpeter Idrees Sulieman. Although Young's health declined gradually throughout the 1950s, his playing (when his strength did not give out) was generally at a fairly high level, actually superior emotionally to his earlier recordings. This is an excellent set of rarities. —*Scott Yanow*

★ **With the Oscar Peterson Trio** / Aug. 4, 1952 / Verve ♦♦♦♦♦
★ **Pres and Teddy and Oscar** / Aug. 4, 1952–Jan. 13, 1956 / Verve ♦♦♦♦♦
It has been said so often that Lester Young's playing declined after his terrible experience in the Army during World War II that it has almost become unanimously accepted as fact. Only trouble is that many of his recordings dispute that theory. In reality, although Young's health declined gradually throughout the 1950s (until his death in 1959), his solos were often at a high level. This two-LP set contains two of the great tenor's finest recordings, a set with the Oscar Peterson Quartet in 1952 and a reunion with Teddy Wilson in a trio in 1956. Young's performances of "All of Me," "Prisoner of Love," "Just You, Just Me" and melodic renditions of seven straight ballads (the latter from the date with Oscar Peterson) rank with some of the finest work of his career. Essential music for all jazz collections. —*Scott Yanow*

Pres and His Cabinet / Aug. 4, 1952–Feb. 8, 1958 / Verve ♦♦♦
A well-conceived sampling of tenor saxophonist Lester Young's Verve recordings of the 1950s, this long out-of-print LP contains "Just You, Just Me" with Oscar Peterson, "Lester Leaps In" with the Count Basie Orchestra in 1957, two numbers in a quintet with trumpeter Harry "Sweets" Edison, an explosive "Gigantic Blues" with trumpeter Roy Eldridge and trombonist Vic Dickenson, and a touching version of "They Can't Take That Away from Me" on which Prez takes a rare solo on clarinet. All of this wonderful mainstream music has since been reissued elsewhere. —*Scott Yanow*

Lester's Here / Dec. 11, 1953 / Verve ♦♦♦
Mean to Me / Dec. 10, 1954–Dec. 1, 1955 / Verve ♦♦♦♦
This double LP consists of two separate studio sessions featuring tenor saxophonist Lester Young. The first set has his regular working group of the mid-'50s with trumpeter Jesse Drakes, pianist Gildo Mahones, bassist John Ore and drummer Connie Kay (just prior to him joining the Modern Jazz Quartet). Although that session is decent, the other half of this two-fer (which matches Young with fellow Basie veteran Harry "Sweets" Edison on trumpet, the Oscar Peterson Trio and Buddy Rich) is the reason to search for this valuable out-of-print set. —*Scott Yanow*

Pres and Sweets / 1955 / Verve ♦♦♦♦♦
With Harry Edison. Brilliant duo work with Lester Young and Sweets Edison. —*Ron Wynn*

★ **Pres and Teddy** / 1956 / Verve ♦♦♦♦♦
With Teddy Wilson. Textbook music from two master improvisers. —*Ron Wynn*

★ **The Jazz Giants '56** / Jan. 12, 1956 / Verve ♦♦♦♦♦
Even critics who feel (against the recorded evidence to the con-

trary) that little of tenor saxophonist Lester Young's postwar playing is at the level of his earlier performances make an exception for this session. Young was clearly inspired by the other musicians (trumpeter Roy Eldridge, trombonist Vic Dickenson, pianist Teddy Wilson, guitarist Freddie Green, bassist Gene Ramey and drummer Jo Jones), which together made for a very potent band of swing all stars. The five songs on this LP include some memorable renditions of ballads and a fine version of "You Can Depend on Me," but it is the explosive joy of the fiery "Gigantic Blues" that takes honors. This set, a real gem, is highly recommended. —*Scott Yanow*

Prez in Europe / Oct. 1956–Jan. 2, 1957 / Onyx ♦♦♦
Although the veteran tenor saxophonist Lester Young was not in the best physical shape at the time of these club performances, he generally plays quite well throughout this LP. Five songs from Oct. 1956 find him in good form on some standards and blues with the assistance of pianist Horst ornimert, bassist Al King and drummer Lex Humphries. The final two tracks are a pair of short fragments from Jan. 1957. Overall the recording quality is quite streaky but the music deserved to be released although those just starting to investigate Lester Young's music should acquire his studio sessions first. —*Scott Yanow*

● **Lester Young in Washington, D.C., 1956, Vol. 1** / Dec. 7, 1956 / Pablo ♦♦♦♦♦
In December 1956 the great tenor saxophonist had a gig in Washington, D.C., playing at a club with the house rhythm section, the Bill Potts Trio. This engagement would have been long forgotten except that all of the music from one of the nights was recorded and released decades later on four LPs. The recording quality is excellent (studio quality) and, most importantly, Lester Young was in superb form throughout the night. Although there is nothing that distinctive about the trio, they are quite competent and evidently pleased Prez. The first volume of this highly enjoyable series features fine versions of five standards, a blues and Prez's "D.B. Blues." —*Scott Yanow*

Lester Young in Washington, D.C., 1956, Vol. 2 / Dec. 7, 1956 / Pablo ♦♦♦♦♦
The second of four volumes documenting a particularly strong musical night in the life of the great tenor saxophonist Lester Young features Prez with a very competent trio (led by pianist Bill Potts) performing five standards and Young's two most famous compositions: "Lester Leaps In" and "Jumpin' with Symphony Sid." The recording quality is excellent on this fine showcase for the swinging and emotionally deep style that Young developed in his later years. —*Scott Yanow*

Lester Young in Washington, D.C., 1956, Vol. 3 / Dec. 7, 1956 / Pablo ♦♦♦♦♦
The third of four volumes, as with its counterparts, features the great tenor saxophonist Lester Young sounding happy and quite comfortable playing in the company of the excellent trio that pianist Bill Potts led in 1956. Prez is near peak form on two of his originals and four veteran standards, bringing new life to "Indiana" and "Just You, Just Me." Those jazz fans who mistakenly feel that Young's post-1944 work is not worth bothering with are advised to purchase at least one of these volumes for proof to the opposite. —*Scott Yanow*

Lester Young in Washington, D.C., 1956, Vol. 4 / Dec. 7, 1956 / Pablo ♦♦♦♦♦
The fourth of four volumes, all presumably recorded the same night (the liners are a little vague on that matter although this quartet definitely only played together that week), documents tenor saxophonist Lester Young (only a little more than two years before his death) in excellent form with a complementary trio led by pianist Bill Potts. All four sets are recommended for Prez sounds quite happy, consistently swings and comes up with creative ideas on standards and fairly basic originals. Superior postwar Lester Young. —*Scott Yanow*

Going for Myself / Jul. 31, 1957–1958 / Verve ♦♦♦♦
Laughin' to Keep from Cryin' / Feb. 8, 1958 / Verve ♦♦♦♦
One of tenor saxophonist Lester Young's final studio sessions (he died a year later), this date apparently had a lot of difficulties but the recorded results are excellent. Prez was joined by two great swing trumpeters (Roy Eldridge and Harry "Sweets" Edison) and a fine rhythm section for two standards, two originals and the ballad "Gypsy in My Soul." Young takes rare clarinet solos on two of the selections with his emotional statement on "They Can't Take

That Away from Me" being one of the high points of his career. Recommended. —*Scott Yanow*

Lester Young in Paris / Mar. 4, 1959 / Verve ✦✦✦

Snooky Young

b. Feb. 3, 1919, Dayton, OH
Trumpet / Swing

If it's possible to be a star in the background, that's been the case with Snooky Young. He's one of the most famous section and session trumpeters, and has been a valued player in that role since his days with the Jimmie Lunceford orchestra. While able to play effectively in any situation, Young can provide dazzling high-note solos and blazing tempos, poignant ballads and outstanding blues interpretations. He was lead trumpeter in the Lunceford orchestra from 1939 to 1942. Young was featured on the soundtrack for the film "Blues in the Night." He worked with Count Basie in 1942 and Lionel Hampton in 1942 and 1943. Young played in California with Les Hite and Benny Carter, then joined Gerald Wilson's big band. He played with Basie again in the mid-'40s, and once more from 1957 to 1962 where he teamed with Wendell Culley and Thad Jones in a marvelous trumpet section. Young became a studio trumpeter with NBC in 1962, and was a founding member of the Thad Jones-Mel Lewis orchestra. He divided his time between that band and the Tonight Show orchestra until 1972, when he moved to California with the Tonight band. Young toured with the Basie Alumni band in 1981 and played on the Johnny Carson show until Carson left in '92 and the band was replaced. Young also did studio work in Los Angeles. He's recently played some dates with Doc Severinsen's orchestra. Young can be heard on many Count Basie reissued CDs. —*Ron Wynn*

Boys from Dayton / Aug. 26, 1971 / MJR ✦✦✦
Snooky & Marshall's Album / 1978 / Concord Jazz ✦✦✦

Fine, relaxed swing/mainstream affair. —*Ron Wynn*

★ **Horn of Plenty** / Mar. 1979 / Concord Jazz ✦✦✦✦✦
One of only three recording sessions led by the talented trumpeter Snooky Young and his only one as the lone horn, this Concord set (which includes pianist Ross Tompkins, guitarist John Collins, bassist Ray Brown and drummer Jake Hanna) features Snooky on four standards, an original blues and three compositions by saxophonist Tom Peterson. The music is essentially modern mainstream, allowing the leader to show off his wide range and swinging style. —*Scott Yanow*

Trummy Young

b. Jan. 12, 1912, Savannah, GA, **d.** Sep. 10, 1984, San Jose, CA
Trombone / Swing, Dixieland

Trummy Young was one of the finest trombonists to emerge during the swing era and, even though he was never really a star or a bandleader himself, he did have one hit with his version of "Margie" which he played and sang with Jimmy Lunceford's Orchestra. Growing up in Washington, Young was originally a trumpeter but by the time he debuted in 1928 he had switched to trombone. Extending the range and power of his instrument, Young was a major asset to Earl Hines' Orchestra during 1933–37 and really became a major influence in jazz while with Lunceford (1937–43). Young was a modern swing stylist with an open mind who fit in well with Charlie Parker and Dizzy Gillespie on a Clyde Hart-led session in 1945 and with Jazz at the Philharmonic. It was therefore a surprise when he joined the Louis Armstrong All-Stars in 1952 and stayed a dozen years. Trummy Young was a good foil for Armstrong (most memorably on their 1954 recording of "St. Louis Blues") but he simplified his style due to his love for the trumpet. In 1964 Young quit the road to settle in Hawaii, occasionally emerging for jazz parties and special appearances. —*Scott Yanow*

Z

Rachel Z (Rachel Nicolazzo)

b. New York, NY
Keyboards / Post Bop, Crossover
A keyboardist with great potential, Rachel Z worked closely with Wayne Shorter in 1995, arranging and soloing on his album and touring extensively with his group. Born and raised in Manhattan, Rachel Z had singing lessons when she was two and started studying piano at age seven. A summer session at Berklee College in 1979 gave her a strong interest in jazz. She studied with Joanne Brackeen, had a lesson with John Hicks, attended the New England Conservatory of Music (1980–84) and after graduation studied with Richie Beirach. She worked in the Boston area with a quartet that also included George Garzone and then moved to New York in 1988. In 1989 she toured with Najee and then joined Steps Ahead for a few years; leader/vibraphonist Mike Mainieri named her Rachel Z. Since that time she has recorded for Columbia and shown talent on both acoustic and electric keyboards. —*Scott Yanow*

● **Trust The Universe** / 1992 / Columbia ✦✦✦✦
Keyboardist Rachel Z divides her debut CD into "mainstream" and "contemporary" sections but in reality she plays basically the same in both sessions, emphasizing her acoustic work in a style most influenced by Chick Corea, Herbie Hancock and occasionally Bill Evans. The music is usually soulful enough for the jazz lite listeners and contains just enough chancetaking for more serious jazz collectors. Nothing too unexpected occurs but this enjoyable set has some fine solos from the leader and the contrasting saxophones of David Sanchez and David Mann. —*Scott Yanow*

Joe Zawinul

b. Jul. 7, 1932, Vienna, Austria
Leader, Piano, Keyboards / Soul Jazz, Fusion, Hard Bop
No one has ever been able to get a more human, funky sound out of electric keyboards and synthesizers than Joe Zawinul, Vienna's gift to the improvisational world. Zawinul began playing the accordion at six and started studying classical music a year later at the Vienna Conservatory. He worked with Austrian jazz saxophonist Hans Koller in 1952, then with various Austrian groups in the mid and late 50s, while also playing in France and Germany with his own trio. Zawinul won a scholarship to Berklee in 1959, and upon coming to America spent only a week at Berklee before joining Maynard Ferguson and touring with him for eight months. He became Dinah Washington's pianist after a brief stint with Slide Hampton in 1959 and stayed with her until 1961. After a month in Harry Edison's group, he joined Cannonball Adderley and remained with his band until 1970. There, Zawinul's skills flourished, and he become a sturdy blues player, good soloist and excellent accompanist. In 1969 and then throughout 1970 he worked in Miles Davis' electric units, gradually moving away from acoustic and concentrating on electric instruments. He co-founded Weather Report in 1971 with Wayne Shorter, and through the 70s and 80s made many influential recordings. Weather Report, especially in its early years, was a true jazz-rock band, able to make appealing, seminal work that had loose, adventurous foundations and energetic solos. Zawinul's synthesizer solos were never dry or dependent on gimmicks but showed it was possible to play with individuality and distinction on what many regarded as simply a technological tool. He and Shorter finally went their separate ways in 1986; since then Zawinul has worked with his own bands. Composer of such tunes as "Mercy, Mercy,

Mercy," "Rumplestiltskin," "Birdland" and "In a Silent Way," the masterful keyboardist (a perennial pollwinner) has in recent years led groups called Weather Update and Zawinul Syndicate. —*Ron Wynn*

The Rise and Fall of the Third Stream / Feb. 7, 1966–Dec. 12, 1967 / Rhino/Atlantic ✦✦✦✦
This CD collects two Zawinul solo projects from the late '60s, when he was laying the groundwork for concepts that were later highlighted during his Weather Report tenure. *The Rise and Fall of the Third Stream* featured Zawinul on acoustic and electric piano, where his funky, gospel and blues-drenched solos provided welcome relief in a setting where the large orchestra's arrangements were often ponderous and overly dense. *Money in the Pocket* also boasted a large group, but was a looser, more vibrant release. Neither release was flawless, but *Money in the Pocket* employed its group more creatively and provided tighter, yet less rhythmically and harmonically restrictive situations than *The Rise and Fall of the Third Stream*. However, both releases are important. —*Ron Wynn*

Money in the Pocket / Feb. 7, 1966 / Atco ✦✦✦

Concerto Retitled / Aug. 6, 1970 / Atlantic ✦✦✦✦

Zawinul / 1971 / Atlantic ✦✦✦✦✦
This is an interesting dual-keyboard effort. With Herbie Hancock (k). —*Ron Wynn*

Dialects / Jun. 1986 / Columbia ✦✦✦

The Immigrants / 1988 / Columbia ✦✦✦
Again, a wildly eclectic menu. Interest depends on how much you enjoy improvisatory music filtered through lots of styles rather than the straight-jazz approach. —*Ron Wynn*

Black Water / 1989 / Columbia ✦✦✦✦
His recent band has some strong players. This session is uneven by design, with Zawinul and crew going through many styles. —*Ron Wynn*

The Beginning / Dec. 1990 / Fresh Sound ✦✦✦

Lost Tribes / 1992 / Columbia ✦✦✦

Denny Zeitlin

b. Apr. 10, 1938, Chicago, IL
Piano / Post Bop, Hard Bop
Denny Zeitlin, a fine Bill Evans-inspired pianist, has throughout his life had a dual career as a psychiatrist and as a pianist. He had extensive classical training but found time to play jazz, even while a medical student at Johns Hopkins University. In 1964 he recorded his first album and has since maintained his two careers in San Francisco, recording and performing colorful and usually unpredictable jazz on an occasional basis. —*Scott Yanow*

Cathexis / Feb. 19, 1964–Mar. 6, 1964 / Columbia ✦✦✦✦

Carnival / Oct. 28, 1964 Oct. 30, 1964 / Columbia ✦✦✦✦✦

● **Live at the Trident** / Mar. 22, 1965–Mar. 24, 1965 / Columbia ✦✦✦✦✦
With Charlie Haden (b), Jerry Granelli (d). A great find. —*Michael G. Nastos*

Zeitgeist / Apr. 11, 1966–Mar. 18, 1967 / Columbia ✦✦✦✦
'60s trio recordings. Rare and wonderful. —*Michael G. Nastos*

● **Time Remembers One Time Once** / Jul. 1981 / ECM ✦✦✦✦✦
Live date at Keystone Korner in San Francisco with bassist Charlie

Haden. Extraordinary recording of compositions by Ornette Coleman, Coltrane and the participants. —*Michael G. Nastos*

Tidal Wave / Jan. 1983–Mar. 1983 / Quicksilver ✦✦✦✦

Trio / 1988 / Windham Hill ✦✦✦✦
1988 release containing five Zeitlin originals, plus standards by Mingus, Ornette Coleman, J.J. Johnson and Kern/Hammerstein. Quite enjoyable. —*Michael G. Nastos*

In the Moment / 1989 / Windham Hill ✦✦✦✦

● **Live at Maybeck Recital Hall** / Oct. 18, 1992 / Concord Jazz ✦✦✦✦✦

Attila Zoller

b. Jun. 13, 1927, Visegrad, Hungary
Guitar / Post Bop
Due to being based in Europe and having an introverted style, guitarist Attila Zoller has always had an underground reputation. He took violin lessons from his father when he was four and trumpet at nine but as a teenager after World War II he was playing guitar with jazz groups. Based in Vienna during 1948–54 and in Germany during 1954–59, Zoller worked with touring American jazzmen and such local players as Jutta Hipp and Hans Koller. Zoller came to the U.S. in 1959 to study at the Lenox School of Jazz, played with Chico Hamilton (1960), was a member of Herbie Mann's group during 1962–65 and worked with Benny Goodman (1967), Lee Konitz (on an occasional basis since 1968) and later a duo with Jimmy Raney (1979–80). Fame has thus far eluded him but his many recordings (most of which are difficult to find) attest to Attila Zoller's talent. —*Scott Yanow*

Zoller-Koller-Solal / Jan. 16, 1965 / German Saba ✦✦✦✦

Common Cause / May 6, 1979 / Enja ✦✦✦✦✦

Conjunction / Jan. 1982 / Enja ✦✦✦✦

● **Memories of Pannonia** / Jun. 1986 / Enja ✦✦✦✦✦

Overcome / Nov. 1986 / Enja ✦✦✦

When It's Time / Oct. 1995 / Enja ✦✦✦

John Zorn

b. Sep. 12, 1953, New York, NY
Alto Saxophone / Avant-Garde
The term *avant-garde* truly fits John Zorn; he falls into no easily definable category or school of playing or composition. His splaying, screaming alto sax solos, use of duck calls, and fondness for film soundtracks and mixing of rock, free, pop, and bop settings confound foes and friends alike. He's been identified with the New York "downtown" crowd, a tag he disdains. Zorn's work began to get wide attention in the mid '80s, especially the *Cobra* album on Hat Art, with its molecular system for 13 players, plus Zorn's live act which has included him blowing a mouthpiece under water. He's also worked with rockers the Golden Palaminos, the Kronos Quartet, been featured on tribute albums to Thelonious Monk and Sonny Clark, done solo, trio, duo, and combo recordings and utilized studio technology like multitrack dubbing quite creatively. Among more recent Zorn projects is an album mixing Klezmer and free jazz, plus sessions of pop and rock covers, and thrash/avant-garde material with the Naked City band. Zorn has many sessions of all styles available on CD. —*Ron Wynn*

Yankees / 1984 / Celluloid ✦✦✦✦
A collective improvisation by Derek Bailey, acoustic and electric guitars, George Lewis, trombone, John Zorn, alto and soprano saxes, clarinets, game calls. Subtle, droll, hilarious takes on the trivia of baseball sounds—Lewis speaks through the trombone "ball one, ball one…" there are snippets of a slipping and sliding version of "Take Me out to the Ball Game," and so on. Sections are titled "City City City," "The Legend of Enos Slaughter," "Who's On First," followed by "On Golden Pond"…tongue-in-cheek tone poem of the flora and fauna, mosquitos etc. and "The Warning Track"…about a very tiny railroad system(?). —*Blue Gene Tyranny*

Big Gundown / Sep. 1984–Sep. 1985 / Elektra/Nonesuch ✦✦✦✦✦
Music of Ennio Morricone. 1984–1985. Ambitious, rambling and reflective of Zorn's flirtations with rock and the New York downtown scene. —*Ron Wynn*

Classic Guide to Strategy / 1985 / Lumina ✦✦✦
Solo woodwind improvisations with gamecalls, parts of saxes and clarinets. Eccentric, pure Zorn. —*Blue Gene Tyranny*

Cobra / Oct. 21, 1985+May 9, 1986 / Hat Art ✦✦✦
A studio and live performance recording with many of NYC's "downtown" improvisors: Anthony Coleman, Bill Frisell, Wayne Horwitz, Bob James, Guy Klucesvek, Arto Lindsay, Christian Marclay, Zeena Parkins, Bobby Previte, Elliott Sharp, Jim Staley, David Weinstein, J.A. Deane and Carol Emanuel. —*Blue Gene Tyranny*

● **Voodoo: The Music of Sonny Clark** / Nov. 25, 1985–Nov. 26, 1985 / Black Saint ✦✦✦✦
Sonny Clark Memorial Quartet. This is not an album by Sonny Clark but a tribute to him by John Zorn. Essential Clark repertoire played by progressivists, with John Zorn on alto sax and Wayne Horvits on piano. —*Michael G. Nastos*

Classic Guide To Strategy, Vol. 2 / 1986 / Lumina ✦✦✦
More beautifully intense solo pieces with inflections like ancient Japanese music. Sections are named after various Japanese artists—Aoyama Michi, Enoken, Kazumi Shigeru, Kondo Toshinori, Yano Akiko, Togawa Jun and Mori Ikue. Cover art is calligraphy of the character for "water." —*Blue Gene Tyranny*

Spillane / Aug. 1986–Sep. 1987 / Elektra/Nonesuch ✦✦✦
An album of nice, dense and foreboding concept work, with everything from shuffle guitar by Albert Collins to the Kronos Quartet. —*Ron Wynn*

★ **News for Lulu** / Aug. 30, 1987 / Hat Hut ✦✦✦✦✦
This is a great power trio with George Lewis (tb), and Bill Frisell (g). —*Ron Wynn*

Spy vs. Spy: The Music of Ornette Coleman / Aug. 18, 1988–Aug. 19, 1988 / Elektra ✦✦✦✦
On *Spy vs. Spy,* John Zorn and his quintet play 17 Ornette Coleman tunes ranging chronologically from 1958's "Disguise" to four selections from 1987's *In All Languages.* The performances are concise with all but four songs being under three minutes and seven under two, but there is absolutely no variety in moods or routines. —*Scott Yanow, Cadence*

Naked City / 1989 / Elektra/Nonesuch ✦✦✦✦✦
His most intriguing, nicely conceived and executed date, with sparkling solos by Bill Frisell (g), Wayne Horovitz (k), and Joey Baron (d). CD has three bonus cuts. —*Ron Wynn*

More News for Lulu / Jan. 18, 1989–Jan. 19, 1989 / Hat Art ✦✦✦✦✦
Another CD of wonderful trio improvisations with John Zorn, George Lewis and, this time, Bill Frisell. Odd, humorous, melodic, dramatic. —*Blue Gene Tyranny*

John Zorn's Cobra Live at the Knitting Factory / 1992 / Knitting Factory ✦
Calling this set of performances bizarre would be an understatement. John Zorn inspired (through obscure game playing that is not explained anywhere on this CD) these 14 eccentric "tributes" to different types of cobras. Because many of the performances utilize samplers and voices (in addition to conventional instruments and miscellaneous devices), the wide range of sounds attained from the 87 musicians (heard in different combinations) is impressive if often quite unlistenable, ranging from humorous interludes to very obnoxious noise. For a few examples, "Cobra 4" has a man screaming over and over again, "Cobra 2" features a sound collage with a male opera singer repeating the same four notes continuously and "Cobra 5" has, among its many vocal noises, a man imitating a dog barking! There are some colorful segments, but in general, these self-indulgent performances would be much more interesting to see in person than to hear on record. Taken purely as a listening experience, one is surprised that this material has even been released! —*Scott Yanow*

VARIOUS ARTISTS

The 1930s Big Bands / Feb. 11, 1930–Dec. 14, 1939 / Columbia ✦✦✦
This excellent sampler contains 16 big-band performances, many of them formerly rare. Such orchestras as Casa Loma (playing "San Sue Strut"), Claude Hopkins, Duke Ellington, Don Redman, Cab Calloway, Fletcher Henderson, Chick Webb, Teddy Hill, the Blue Rhythm Band, Erskine Hawkins, Red Norvo, Ben Pollack ("Jimtown Blues" which features Harry James), Earl Hines, Jimmie Lunceford, Count Basie and Benny Goodman are heard on a selection apiece, making this a set of great interest to swing collectors. —*Scott Yanow*

The 1930s: Singers / Apr. 1, 1930–Nov. 23, 1937 / Columbia ✦✦✦

The 1930s: Small Combos / Apr. 4, 1930–Jul. 28, 1939 / Columbia ✦✦✦
Swing is the thing on this very enjoyable sampler which features 16 recordings by the same number of groups. Most of the combos are pickup bands but the quality of musicianship is so high that they sound like regularly working groups. Represented by a song apiece are Jack Purvis, the Chocolate Dandies, the Rhythmakers, Red Allen, Wingy Manone, Red Norvo, Jones-Smith Inc, Stuff Smith, Teddy Wilson, Roy Eldridge, Cootie Williams, the Gotham Stompers, Frankie Newton, Sidney Bechet, Chu Berry and John Kirby. Although one would prefer the complete sessions, this sampler serves as a perfect introduction to these brilliant players. —*Scott Yanow*

1940s: Singers / Feb. 9, 1940–Dec. 21, 1949 / Columbia ✦✦✦
A variety of different singers (most from the swing era) are heard on this excellent collection. The music is enjoyable, if generally not all that essential, although Mildred Bailey's "I'm Nobody's Baby" (with its advanced Eddie Sauter arrangement and Roy Eldridge's futuristic trumpet solo), Billie Holiday's "All of Me," Woody Hermans "Caldonia" and "Nat Meets June" from Nat King Cole and June Christy with the Metronome All-Stars are classics. Also heard from are Maxine Sullivan, Big Joe Turner, Jack Teagarden, Cab Calloway, Slim Gaillard, Anita O'Day, Jimmy Rushing, Peggy Lee, Roy Eldridge, Eddie "Cleanhead" Vinson, Hot Lips Page and Sarah Vaughan. —*Scott Yanow*

● **The 1940s: The Small Groups: New Directions** / Mar. 8, 1945–Nov. 3, 1947 / Columbia ✦✦✦✦
This is a particularly strong collection. Woody Herman's Woodchoppers, a nonet taken from his 1946 big band, is featured on ten selections (two of which were previously unissued) with solos from the leader-clarinetist, trumpeter Sonny Berman, trombonist Bill Harris, Flip Phillips on tenor and vibraphonist Red Norvo. In addition, drummer Gene Krupa and his 1945 trio (with Charlie Ventura on tenor and either Teddy Napoleon or George Walters on piano) play five songs (four previously unreleased) and, best of all, Harry James and his octet perform "Pagan Love Song" and a brilliant version of "Tuxedo Junction"; James takes a memorable boppish solo on the latter (which also features altoist Willie Smith and trombonist Ziggy Elmer). —*Scott Yanow*

The 1950s: Singers / Feb. 1, 1950–Aug. 6, 1959 / Columbia ✦✦✦
A variety of jazz singers are represented on this fine collection including Lee Wiley, Louis Armstrong (the original version of "Mack the Knife"), Billie Holiday, Jimmy Rushing, Sarah Vaughan ("Mean to Me" with a small group that co-stars Miles Davis), Hot Lips Page, Dolores Hawkins, Joe Williams, Betty Roche (a classic version of "Take the 'A' Train" with Duke Ellington), Babs Gonzales, Betty Carter, Lambert, Hendricks and Ross and surpris-

ingly enough Johnny Mathis on a jazz-oriented version of "Easy to Love." It's a good well-rounded set. —*Scott Yanow*

The 1986 Floating Jazz Festival / Oct. 15, 1986–Oct. 23, 1986 / Chiaroscuro ✦✦✦
This CD is a bit of a collector's item, a variety of interesting performances recorded during the S.S. Norway's Fourth Annual Jazz Cruise. The oddest selection is a long trumpet-drums duet by Dizzy Gillespie and Buddy Rich that is only partially successful. In addition to Joe Williams singing "I Want a Little Girl" with a big band and vibraphonist Gary Burton jamming with the Berklee Ensemble, such notables as Kenny Davern and Bob Wilber (who have a Soprano Summit reunion on "Moonglow"), violinist Svend Asmussen, pianist Mel Powell, fluegelhornist Clark Terry, trumpeter Warren Vache (jamming some Dixieland on "Jazz Me Blues") and (on "Flying Home") the tenors of Flip Phillips, Al Cohn, Buddy Tate and Scott Hamilton are heard from. Although a bit erratic, this CD has enough special moments to justify its acquisition. —*Scott Yanow*

25 Years of Prestige / Jan. 11, 1949–Jul. 26, 1970 / Prestige ✦✦✦
This is a two-LP set that really delighted collectors when it was released in 1974. To celebrate the 25th year of the Prestige label, unissued material, alternate takes and a few rarities were compiled for this two-fer. Starting out with the very first Prestige recording (Lee Konitz's "Progression"), the set is highlighted by performances featuring Stan Getz (with the similar-sounding tenors of Al Cohn, Allen Eager, Brew Moore and Zoot Sims), Fats Navarro, Wardell Gray, Miles Davis (the alternate take of "Blue Room", King Pleasure, Thelonious Monk, John Coltrane (jamming "Blue Calypso" with a Mal Waldron group), Benny Golson, Gene Ammons, Dexter Gordon and Eric Dolphy among others. Much of this material has since appeared on CD but the attractive set is still worth acquiring. —*Scott Yanow*

The '40s In Hollywood / Oct. 27, 1945–Jul. 6, 1946 / Jump ✦✦✦✦
This excellent LP reissues three four-song sessions from the 1945–46 era that feature Dixieland-style jazz as performed in Los Angeles by a variety of top-notch (if not overly famous) studio musicians. Yukl's Wabash Five (a septet!) has the leader on trombone, clarinetist Pate Legare and cornetist George Thow, Bob Anderson's Oshkosh Serenaders features Anderson's cornet, Joe Rushton on bass sax and clarinet and trombonist Warren Smith, and Mackey's Michigan Boulevard Gang has solos from trumpeter Mackey, trombonist Floyd O'Brien and clarinetist Matty Matlock. Forget the lack of major names; fans of this style of music would be well advised to pick up this increasingly rare LP. —*Scott Yanow*

50 Years of Jazz Guitar / Jul. 1921–Aug. 14, 1971 / Columbia ✦✦✦
27 performances by guitarists are included in this well-rounded two-LP sampler. Sam Moore is heard in 1921 taking a solo on the octocorda and there are examples of the talents of Lonnie Johnson, Eddie Lang, King Nawahi (playing Hawaiian guitar in 1929), Bobby Leecan, Teddy Bunn, Coco Heimal, Dick McDonough, Carl Kress, Leon McAuliffe, Buddy Woods, Joe Sodja, Charlie Christian, Slim Gailiard, Memphis Minnie, Django Reinhardt, George Van Eps, Hank Garland, Kenny Burrell, Eddie Durham, Herb Ellis, George Benson, Charlie Byrd and even John McLaughlin. Obviously not every jazz guitarist is represented (Wes Montgomery is absent and there is only one fusion performance and no real avant-garde) but there are quite a few rarities

on this two-fer, making this a set that collectors will want to look for. — *Scott Yanow*

52nd Street Swing / Sep. 11, 1934–Apr. 3, 1941 / GRP/Decca ✦✦✦

This fine CD includes performances from many of the most popular small jazz groups that played in New York's 52nd Street during the swing era. There are two hot numbers by the Delta Four (featuring trumpeter Roy Eldridge and clarinetist Joe Marsala), three from the goodtime ensemble the Spirits of Rhythm, a trio from violinist Stuff Smith's Onyx Club Band (which co-starred trumpeter Jonah Jones, three others from John Kirby's sextet, four numbers by Leonard Feather's All-Star Jam Band (with altoists Benny Carter and Pete Brown, cornetist Bobby Hackett and clarinetist Joe Marsala), three from trumpeter/vocalist Hot Lips Page and a pair of selections by pianist Sam Price's Texas Bluesicians including "Just Jivin' Around" which has a particularly rare solo from the great tenor Lester Young. Veteran collectors will have most of these performances in more complete fashion elsewhere but this is an excellent sampler for fans of small-group swing. — *Scott Yanow*

Afro-Cuban Jazz / Dec. 1948–Mar. 24, 1954 / Verve ✦✦✦✦

This double LP (which was released in 1977) has some of the most important early Afro-Cuban and Latin-jazz recordings. Machito's Orchestra welcomes guests Charlie Parker, Flip Phillips and Buddy Rich to such selections as "Tanga," "Mango Mangue" and Chico O'Farrill's five-part "Afro-Cuban Suite." In addition O'Farrill's own exciting big band (using some of the same personnel as Machito) in 1951 plays some of his originals, and Dizzy Gillespie's 1954 orchestra performs O'Farrill's four-part "Manteca Suite." The music (which belongs in all serious jazz collections) overall is quite exciting and historic; much of it has not yet been reissued on CD. — *Scott Yanow*

After Hours / Feb. 16, 1957+Jun. 21, 1957 / Prestige ✦✦✦

This two-LP set combines a pair of leaderless jam session albums: *Olio* and *After Hours*; the latter set has since been reissued on CD in the OJC series. The overlapping personnel features trumpeter Thad Jones, Frank Wess on tenor and flute, either vibraphonist Teddy Charles or guitarist Kenny Burrell, pianist Mal Waldron, Doug Watkins or Paul Chambers on bass and Elvin Jones or Art Taylor on drums. Waldron contributed six of the ten originals, Charles brought in three and the band also interprets "Embraceable You." This straight-ahead collection finds these young musicians playing quite well and uplifting the dates above the level of just a routine jam session. — *Scott Yanow*

All Star Swing Groups / Mar. 13, 1944–Jan. 31, 1946 / Savoy ✦✦✦✦✦

This double LP from 1977 (when Arista was reissuing recordings from the valuable Savoy catalog) has more than its share of gems. Drummer Cozy Cole's three 1944 sessions have overlapping personnel (including trumpeters Lamar Wright or Emmett Berry, trombonist Ray Coniff, the tenors of Ben Webster, Budd Johnson and Coleman Hawkins and pianist Johnny Guarnieri). Those classic musicians all get their solo space and play up to par with some exciting moments. In addition pianist Pete Johnson leads two bands that feature some great playing from trumpeter Hot Lips Page (who is quite memorable on the two versions of "Page Mr. Trumpet"), either J.C. Higginbotham or Clyde Bernhardt on trombone, clarinetist Albert Nicholas, Ben Webster or Budd Johnson on tenor, the underrated altoist Don Stovall and on a few numbers singer Etta Jones. The influence of the emerging bebop music is not felt at all on these highly enjoyable swing performances. Most of this music has not yet been reissued in coherent form on CD. — *Scott Yanow*

Almost Forgotten / Jun. 15, 1955–Dec. 10, 1962 / Columbia ✦✦✦

This LP (released by Columbia in 1983) contains eight previously "lost" recordings that were released for the first time. Many all stars appear and there are some historic performances. Drummer Dave Bailey leads a sextet in 1960 also featuring trumpeter Clark Terry, trombonist Curtis Fuller and Junior Cook on tenor. Terry interacts with the great tenor Coleman Hawkins on a 1962 version of "Ain't Misbehavin'," altoist Pony Poindexter performs an alternate take of his "Lanyop" in 1962 with five other saxophonists including Eric Dolphy, and Wes Montgomery is heard on "Love for Sale" in 1955, four years before his discovery. Side Two of this LP has trumpeter Johnny Coles leading a quartet with pianist Randy Weston, trombonist Slide Hampton at the head of an 11-piece group, the Engligh tenor Tubby Hayes in a quintet

with Clark Terry and a combo matching together trombonist J.J. Johnson and cornetist Nat Adderley in 1958. The bop-oriented music is consistently rewarding, making this an album well worth searching for. — *Scott Yanow*

Alto Summit / Jun. 2, 1968–Jun. 3, 1968 / Saba ✦✦✦

For this brainchild of Joachim Berendt, four top altoists (Lee Konitz, Pony Poindexter, Phil Woods and Leo Wright) team up with a fine rhythm section led by pianist Steve Kuhn to explore mostly originals. There are two quintets but otherwise all of the performances are by the full septet. A four-song ballad medley goes well until the ending when all of the saxophonists solo together quite chaotically to unintentionally hilarious effect. Much better is "Lee's Tribute to Bach and Bird," which goes from a Bach piece to Charlie Parker's solo on "Honeysuckle Rose." — *Scott Yanow*

Amarcord Nino Rota / May 1982 / Hannibal ✦✦✦✦

This tribute to the music of film composer Nino Rota was the first of Hal Willner's unusual multiartist projects and one of his more jazz-oriented ones. Such musicians as pianist Jaki Byard, vibraphonist Dave Samuels, guitarist Bill Frisell, soprano saxophonist Steve Lacy, trumpeter Wynton Marsalis and bands headed by Carla Bley, Muhal Richard Abrams and David Amram are heard from on these eccentric but very musical adaptations of Rota's themes from Fellini movies. — *Scott Yanow*

Americans In Europe / Jan. 3, 1960 / GRP/Impulse ✦✦✦

● **Anthology of Big Band Swing (1930–1955)** / Jan. 14, 1931–Aug. 1955 / GRP ✦✦✦✦✦

This two-CD set is an unusually successful sampler. Although there are a few hits among the 40 selections, many obscurities are also included and not all of the big bands represented are major names, such as Tiny Bradshaw, Noble Sissle, Spud Murphy, Teddy Powell and Jan Savitt. The emphasis is very much on jazz and this worthy reissue is overflowing with forgotten classics. Happily the music is programmed in chronological order so one can experience the evolution of big bands, from Duke Ellington, Fletcher Henderson and Luis Russell to postwar recordings from Artie Shaw, Tommy Dorsey and Benny Goodman. — *Scott Yanow*

Art Deco: Sophisticated Ladies / Apr. 5, 1929–Dec. 17, 1940 / Columbia/Legacy ✦✦✦✦

This is a very rewarding two-CD sampler that introduces listeners to a wide variety of singers who were active in the 1930s, ranging from jazz vocalists (Annette Hanshaw, Ethel Waters, Connie Boswell, the Boswell Sisters, Lee Wiley, Helen Ward, Ella Logan, Maxine Sullivan and Mildred Bailey) to cabaret and pop artists of the time (Ruth Etting, Helen Morgan, Greta Keller, Frances Langford, Alice Faye, Nan Wynn and Ginny Simms). This set has more than its share of rarities (including some previously unissued alternate takes) and there are many rewarding performances. The set is recommended to anyone with an interest in the singing stylists who rose to prominence between Bessie Smith and Billie Holiday. — *Scott Yanow*

Art Deco: The Crooners / Sep. 1926–Oct. 6, 1941 / Columbia/Legacy ✦✦✦✦

A wide span of styles is represented on this two-CD salute to the male singers of the 1930s, the "crooners." Some of the vocalists are quite enjoyable to hear while a few are very dated, but overall the 49 performances contain more than their share of highlights. There are selections featuring Willard Robison, Gene Austin, Seger Ellis, Smith Ballew, the completely forgotten Lew Bray, Bing Crosby, Harlan Lattimore, Russ Columbo, Red McKenzie, Cliff Edwards (who is heard on eight songs), Pinky Tomlin, Chick Bullock, Jack Teagarden, Harold Arlen ("You're a Builder-Upper"), Buddy Clark, Eddy Howard (a rare jazz session with an all-star group that includes trumpeter Bill Coleman, pianist Teddy Wilson and guitarist Charlie Christian), Frank Sinatra (with Harry James) and Dick Haymes. This set acts as a perfect introduction to these mostly very talented singers. — *Scott Yanow*

Art Of The Duo, Vol. 1 / Enja ✦✦✦

This is an unusual CD, nine duets taken from nine previous Enja releases. The music varies from modern hard bop to world music with six of the performances having bass and/or piano, two featuring drums and just one (a match-up between trombonist Albert Mangelsdorff and altoist Lee Konitz) with two horns; unfortunately the recording dates are not given for any of this material. Such notables as pianist Abdullah Ibrahim, tenor saxophonist Joe Henderson (who duets with bassist Wayne Darling), tenors

John Tchicai and Jim Pepper, singer Karin Krog (performing a haunting version of "'Round Midnight") and Joe Lovano (on soprano duetting with drummer Ed Blackwell) are heard from on a program dominated by originals. This interesting music serves well as an introduction to these fine artists. —*Scott Yanow*

At the Jazz Band Ball: Chicago/New York Dixieland / Feb. 8, 1929–Jul. 19, 1939 / Bluebird ✦✦✦✦✦
This 1988 CD contains what was originally called "the Great 16," the four 1939 recording sessions (16 songs in all) by cornetist Muggsy Spanier's hot Ragtime Band. All of that music (plus eight alternate takes) was reissued on CD by Bluebird in 1994 but this CD also contains two selections from Eddie Condon in 1929 and four songs from Bud Freeman's Summa Cum Laude Orchestra in 1939. For those listeners who do not need his alternates, this is a highly recommended set with plenty of exciting and heated Chicago jazz. —*Scott Yanow*

Atlantic Jazz: Best of the '50s / 1994 / Rhino ✦✦✦

Atlantic Jazz: Best of the '60s / 1994 / Rhino ✦✦✦✦✦

A Bag Of Sleepers, Vol. 1 / Oct. 28, 1927–Oct. 3, 1932 / Arcadia ✦✦✦
All three LPs in this series feature obscure jazz and hot dance bands from the 1927–32 period so these releases are highly recommended to collectors of early jazz who want to get beyond only hearing the most famous names. Hoagy Carmichael heads a group for three songs (including the earliest recorded version of "Star Dust" which is here taken as an uptempo instrumental) before the Emil Seidel, Johnny Burris and Howard Thomas Orchestras are featured. The Burris band would soon be reorganized as the Casa Loma Orchestra. —*Scott Yanow*

A Bag Of Sleepers, Vol. 2 / Sep. 15, 1927–Aug. 12, 1930 / Arcadia ✦✦✦
The second of three LPs in Arcadia's series of obscure but hot jazz and dance bands from the late '20s has recordings by groups even veteran collectors will most likely be unfamiliar with: Henry Lange's Orchestra, Clarie Hull's Boys, the original Atlanta Footwarmers, Hal Frazer's Georgians, Ruby Green's Manhattan Madcaps, Lew Weimer's Black and Gold Aces, Art Payne's Orchestra, Bob McGowanis Orchestra, Tommy Meyers' Gang, Ducky Yountz's Orchestra, Dick Coy's Racketeers and Dexter's Pennsylvanians. The music from these territory bands (most of whom were recorded in the Midwest) ranges from melodic jazz to hot dance arrangements, and this set has more than its share of interesting moments. —*Scott Yanow*

A Bag Of Sleepers, Vol. 3 / Jul. 19, 1927–Dec. 8, 1930 / Arcadia ✦✦✦
On the third of three LPs put out by Arcadia, there are two surprisingly hot numbers from an early edition of Lawrence Welk's Orchestra ("Spiked Beer" and "Doin' the New Lowdown") and jazz-oriented performances from a variety of obscure late-'20s groups including Bernie Schultz's Crescent Orchestra, the Cotton Pickers, Berlyn Baylor, Dick Kent, Joe Ward, Roy Wilson and Jack Davies' Kentuckians. None of the sidemen (except trumpeter Jack Purvis) went on to much, but this music should delight fans of the era. —*Scott Yanow*

● **Barrelhouse Boogie** / May 7, 1936–Jun. 17, 1941 / Bluebird ✦✦✦✦✦
The four most important boogie-woogie pianists are all represented on this easily enjoyable CD. Meade Lux Lewis performs a 1936 remake of his classic "Honky Tonk Train Blues" and accompanies himself on "Whistlin' Blues," the subtle Jimmy Yancey plays ten solos from 1939–40 and Pete Johnson and Albert Ammons (with drummer James Hoskins) jam on nine duets from 1940–41. Although there are more complete reissues of the pianists' work available from European labels, this Bluebird set gives listeners a strong sampling of boogie-woogie during its prime years. —*Scott Yanow*

Basie Reunion / Oct. 18, 1957+Sep. 5, 1958 / Prestige ✦✦✦✦✦
This double LP is a delight. Count Basie is nowhere in sight but a variety of his alumni team up for some solidly swinging and often-exciting performances. On the first date (originally issued as *For Basie*), tenor saxophonist Paul Quinichette (the main star of these sessions) heads a sextet with trumpeter Shad Collins, pianist Nat Pierce, guitarist Freddie Greene, bassist Walter Page (his last recording date) and drummer Jo Jones; the later session (*Basie Reunion*) utilizes the same group with Eddie Jones in Page's place and the additions of trumpeter Buck Clayton and baritonist Jack

Washington. The two-fer has ten performances of material associated with Basie's band of the late '30s and one gets a rare chance to hear Collins and Washington stretch out during this late period. Everyone sounds in prime form and very happy to get the opportunity to join in on the reunions. Unfortunately this music has yet to be reissued on CD but the two-LP set is quite attractive and worth picking up anyway. —*Scott Yanow*

Battle Of Tenor Saxes / Jul. 17, 1945–May 27, 1951 / IAJRC ✦✦✦
There is no actual tenor battle on this valuable IAJRC LP but a dozen different bop-based tenors are heard from on 16 studio selections, some of which were formerly rare. On Side One (which is titled "The Big Sound") Coleman Hawkins, Ben Webster, Gene Ammons, Ike Quebec, Paul Gonsalves and Illinois Jacquet (Quebec and Jacquet twice) are heard from while Side Two ("The Cool School") features Lester Young, Dexter Gordon, Allen Eager, Warne Marsh, James Moody and Wardell Gray; Young and Marsh pop up twice. Although this is very much a sampler (which unfortunately leaves out Teddy Edwards, Stan Getz and Zoot Sims), all of the diverse tenors play quite well; it is recommended to fans of the bop era. —*Scott Yanow*

The Be Bop Era / Feb. 27, 1946–Feb. 6, 1950 / RCA ✦✦✦✦
This LP gives listeners a strong cross-section of the better bop recordings that were made for Victor during 1946–50. Much of the material has since been reissued on CD but, taken as a whole, this is a fairly definitive set of the era. Coleman Hawkins lets his fellow tenor Allen Eager stretch out on "Allen's Alley," Illinois Jacquet romps on "Mutton Leg," Lucky Thompson plays "Boppin' the Blues," drummer Kenny Clarke leads an advanced nonet (with trumpeter Fats Navarro, saxophonist Sonny Stitt and pianist Bud Powell) on four numbers (including two by Thelonious Monk), Charlie Ventura's "Bop for the People" band jams on "Ha," Count Basie's 1950 sextet performs "Rat Race" and Dizzy Gillespie's big band plays five of its lesser-known songs. In addition the Metronome All-Stars of 1949 (with altoist Charlie Parker, pianist Lennie Tristano and the remarkable trumpet trio of Dizzy Gillespie, Miles Davis and Fats Navarro) perform "Overtime" (during which the three trumpeters trade off) and "Victory Ball." —*Scott Yanow*

The Bebop Boys / Aug. 23, 1946–Oct. 9, 1953 / Savoy ✦✦✦✦✦
This double LP is from the era when Arista (under the guidance of producers Bob Porter and Steve Backer) was doing a superlative job of reissuing music from the Savoy catalog. The emphasis is very much on bop with eight different groups heard from. The all-star quintet of trumpeter Kenny Dorham, altoist Sonny Stitt, pianist Bud Powell, bassist Al Hall and either Wally Bishop or Kenny Clarke on drums performs eight heated numbers from 1946, there is a session led by bassist Ray Brown that has Dizzy Gillespie and Milt Jackson among the sidemen and Gil Fuller has a rare opportunity to lead his own date. In addition vocalists Kenny-Hagood, Babs Gonzales and Eddie Jefferson (the latter's "Body and Soul" and "The Birdland Story" are among the highpoints of this two-fer) are heard from. This highly recommended and historic package concludes with a pair of dates headed by baritonist Leo Parker that also feature trumpeter Joe Newman, trombonist J.J. Johnson and the young tenor-great Dexter Gordon. Until Savoy's timeless recordings are reissued in more coherent form on CD, these Arista sets are worth a lengthy search. —*Scott Yanow*

★ **Bebop In Britain** / Jan. 13, 1948–Apr. 13, 1953 / Esquire ✦✦✦✦✦
England was not often thought of as a haven for bebop but once the records of Charlie Parker and Dizzy Gillespie started becoming common in 1947, many of the top swing players began to modernize their styles and record. This very interesting four-CD set contains many of the most significant English bop recordings, starring such important players as tenor saxophonist Ronnie Scott, Johnny Dankworth (on alto and clarinet), trumpeter Jimmy Deuchar, pianist Tommy Pollard and bandleaders Tito Burns and Vic Lewis among others. Even bop fanatics will probably not already own many of these rare recordings which, once they hit their stride, hold their own with their American counterparts. —*Scott Yanow*

Bebop Revisited, Vol. 1 / June 5, 1947–Nov. 29, 1948 / Xanadu ✦✦✦✦
The first of six LPs put out by the Xanadu label that reissues important but generally obscure bop sessions from the 1945–55 period has three very enjoyable dates. Tenor-great Dexter Gordon is teamed with trombonist Melba Liston in a 1947 quintet (they

perform two versions apiece of two songs), trumpeter Fats Navarro joins tenor saxophonist Don Lanphere in a backup group behind singer Earl Coleman (the sextet does get to play two takes of the instrumental "Move") and bassist Chubby Jackson leads a heated sextet that features trumpeter Conte Candoli, Frank Socolow on tenor and vibraphonist Terry Gibbs. There are many exciting moments on this LP; bop collectors will want the whole series. —*Scott Yanow*

Bebop Revisited, Vol. 2 / Jan. 9, 1945–Jun. 8, 1946 / Xanadu ✦✦✦✦
The second of six Xanadu LPs to reissue obscure bop sessions from the mid-'40s to mid-'50s has four interesting dates from very early in the bebop era. Bassist Oscar Pettiford leads a large band for four selections, three of which feature the so-so singer Rubberlegs Williams. However trumpeter Dizzy Gillespie's presence in this Jan. 1945 session gives it great historic value. In addition there are four selections apiece from groups led by trombonists Kai Winding (with a no-name septet) and J.J. Johnson (with a variety of Count Basie sidemen including tenorman Buddy Tate) and a quintet set by vibraphonist Terry Gibbs with clarinetist Aaron Sachs. This is historic and enjoyable music. —*Scott Yanow*

Bebop Revisited, Vol. 3 / Apr. 27, 1951–Dec. 29, 1953 / Xanadu ✦✦✦✦
On the third of six Xanadu LPs that reissue little-known early bop sessions, there are more than its share of highlights. Trombonist Kai Winding heads a quintet with tenor saxophonist Warne Marsh and pianist Billy Taylor; two of the four selections have fine vocals from the forgotten Melvin Moore. Trumpeter Tony Fruscella had one of his few opportunities to lead a session in 1952 and his septet (with altoist Herb Geller and Phil Urso on tenor) is in excellent form on four numbers. Probably the most memorable set is the one led by Sam Most (doubling on clarinet and flute) which also features trumpeter Doug Mettome, trombonist Urbie Green and Bob Dorough on piano. Most, one of the pioneers of the jazz flute, actually plays clarinet (which he rarely touched in later years) on five of the seven selections, showing off some virtuoso chops on "Notes to You" (a tribute to Benny Goodman). This LP (and the five others in the valuable series) is essential for bop collectors who want to expand their knowledge beyond the most famous recordings. —*Scott Yanow*

Bebop Revisited, Vol. 4 / Dec. 2, 1948–Aug. 13, 1950 / Xanadu ✦✦✦
For the fourth LP volume of six in a series, the focus is once again on early and obscure bebop sessions. tenor saxophonist James Moody leads a pair of sextets; the one from 1948 features the vocals of Babs Gonzales along with trumpeter Dave Burns and trombonist Bennie Green on such numbers as "A Lesson in Bopology" and "Honeysuckle Bop!" while the group from 1950 was recorded in France with trumpeter Ernie Royal (who gets a rare opportunity to stretch out). This LP is rounded out by a completely forgotten date led by trombonist Bennie Green that also features the tenor of Budd Johnson. Although the album on a whole is not essential, bop fans will want it. —*Scott Yanow*

Bebop Revisited, Vol. 5 / Apr. 17, 1957+Aug. 21, 1964 / Xanadu ✦✦✦✦
Unlike the other volumes in this six-LP series, *Vol. 5* does not feature music from the early bop years. As it turns out the music is very much in the bop vein even though recorded a decade later. Trumpeter Conte Candoli and tenor saxophonist Richie Kamuca really stretch out with a quintet on "Allen's Alley" and "Counting" in 1957; the two songs clock in at over 24 minutes. In addition a quartet set by trumpet-great Kenny Dorham with pianist Barry Harris from 1964 was released for the first time on this 1985 LP, and it finds Dorham in top form playing before a teenaged audience at a school. It's easily recommended (along with the other albums in this very valuable series) to bop collectors. —*Scott Yanow*

Bebop Revisited, Vol. 6 / May 2, 1945–Dec. 8, 1952 / Xanadu ✦✦✦✦
The sixth and final LP released by Xanadu in this valuable series from the mid-'40s has four rare bop sessions. The first set, a three-song date led by tenor saxophonist Frankie Socolow, features the rarely recorded (and legendary) trumpeter Freddy Webster and pianist Bud Powell in one of his earliest recordings. Although their playing is worth the price of this LP, there are also excellent performances by tenor saxophonist John Hardee (in a quartet), the fiery tenor Eddie "Lockjaw" Davis (during his early uninhibited

R&B days) and Lester Young-soundalike Paul Quinichette in 1952. Bop collectors will want all six of the consistently exciting LPs in this series. —*Scott Yanow*

Best Coast Jazz / Aug. 11, 1954 / EmArcy ✦✦✦✦
Best of the Jazz Pianos / 1957–1969 / Denon ✦✦
One of five CDs in Denon's series, this release has some interesting if hard-to-trace material. Bill Evans performs two numbers with his classic 1961 trio (which includes bassist Scott LaFaro and drummer Paul Motian), Bud Powell plays two lengthy songs with a quintet that features trumpeter Clark Terry in 1957, Teddy Wilson's trio runs through a pair of standards, Thelonious Monk and a quintet with Charlie Rouse on tenor and trumpeter Thad Jones play a version of "Light Blue" that is supposedly from a European tour in 1958 (doubtful) and Chick Corea is heard on the out-of-place and rather spacey "Sundance," a lengthy improvisation with a group of modernists in 1969. It's a mixed bag. —*Scott Yanow*

Best of the Big Bands / 1958–Jun. 1974 / Madacy ✦✦
This is one of five CDs (the others covering pianos, saxophones, singers and trumpets) put out by the Denon label and drawn partly from the catalog of Groove Merchant. A budget release, this set has a few numbers apiece from Benny Goodman (1958), Count Basie (early-'70s), Buddy Rich (one song from 1974), Woody Herman (1960), Harry James (a 1959 version of "Flying Home" with Jon Hendricks' vocal), Duke Ellington (1961) and Lionel Hampton (a 1974 runthrough on "Killer Joe"). None of this music is all that special; mostly worn out versions of greatest hits. —*Scott Yanow*

The Best of the Jazz Saxophones / 1958–1980 / Denon ✦✦✦
As with the other entries in this Denon series (which also include CDs devoted to big bands, pianos, singers and trumpets), the origin of the material on this set is difficult to trace. Stan Getz performs two numbers while in France during 1958–59, Gerry Mulligan and his quartet play "Jeru" in 1958 and the baritonist jams with tenorman Bud Freeman and trumpeter Ruby Braff on "Rose Room" from the same year. In addition, Zoot Sims leads a quartet in 1974 for two numbers, altoist Hank Crawford and Eddie Daniels (on tenor) team up in 1980, Eddie Lockjaw Davis jams in 1961, Sonny Stitt plays "My Little Suede Shoes" in 1972 and the tenors of Coleman Hawkins, Stan Getz and Don Byas team up for a rousing 1958 version of "Indiana." In general this is one of the most rewarding releases in the Denon series but the lack of any additional information (or liner notes) makes this a recommended set only if located at a budget price. —*Scott Yanow*

The Best of the Jazz Singers / 1954–1974 / Denon ✦✦
Only five singers appear on this sampler (part of a five-CD Denon series also including sets devoted to big bands, piano, saxophones and trumpets) but they are five of the best. Ella Fitzgerald and her trio in 1959 perform eight numbers (including "Air Mail Special"), Sarah Vaughan does a song apiece from 1954 and 1960, Carmen McRae is caught during 1972–73, Ruth Brown sings "Fine Brown Frame" with the assistance of the Thad Jones/Mel Lewis Orchestra And Dakota Staton in 1974 sings two numbers. There is nothing too essential on this set but, if seen at a budget price, it is worth picking up. —*Scott Yanow*

Best of the Jazz Trumpets / 1958–1976 / Denon ✦✦✦
One of five best-of CDs put out by Denon (along with collections featuring big bands, singers, saxophonists and pianists), this sampler features Chet Baker and Donald Byrd on one selection apiece from 1958, Dizzy Gillespie performing "Kush" in 1976, Freddie Hubbard on 1970's "Blues for Duane," three short numbers from Louis Armstrong in 1959, Maynard Ferguson's 1965 "Got the Spirit" and an unusual version of "The Theme" that features Thad Jones, Howard McGhee and Kenny Dorham. There is nothing all that essential on this release (some of whose material comes from the Groove Merchant catalog) but it does have its strong moments. —*Scott Yanow*

Big Band Hit Parade / Aug. 3, 1988 / Telarc ✦✦✦✦
This CD is a bit of an oddity but largely a success. A group of all-star jazzmen (trumpeter Doc Severinsen, trombonist Buddy Morrow, clarinetist Eddie Daniels, baritonist Gerry Mulligan, pianist Dave Brubeck, bassist Ray Brown and drummer Ed Shaughnessy) along with the great singer Cab Calloway team up with Erich Kunzel's Cincinnati Pops Big Band Orchestra to perform hits of the swing era; never mind that only Calloway was from that period. The arrangements (mostly by Jeff Tyzik and

Tommy Newsom) for the string orchestra are fortunately not recreations of the past but fresh and sometimes surprising reworkings of such songs as "One O'Clock Jump," "You Made Me Love You," "In the Mood" and "Artistry in Rhythm." Calloway gets to revisit "St. James Infirmary" and the episodic almost suite-like version of "When the Saints Go Marching In" is a near-classic. —*Scott Yanow*

The Big Beat / Sep. 4, 1958–Feb. 20, 1964 / Milestone ✦✦✦
This CD reissue brings back all of the music of the double LP of the same name except for Max Roach's version of "You Stepped out of a Dream." The sampler features four different drummer-led units in performances that are available on other Fantasy CDs. Art Blakey's 1962-64 Jazz Messengers (with trumpeter Freddie Hubbard, trombonist Curtis Fuller and tenor saxophonist Wayne Shorter) performs "Caravan," "The High Priest" and a brief "The Theme," Max Roach's 1958 Quintet (with trumpeter Booker Little and George Coleman on tenor) plays three selections including Roach's drum solo "Conversation," Elvin Jones meets up with his two brothers (cornetist Thad and pianist Hank) on some sextet sides and Philly Joe Jones heads two all-star groups which include such top musicians as trumpeters Lee Morgan and Blue Mitchell and flutist Herbie Mann. Because the performances are available elsewhere, this CD is not all that essential but it does serve as a good example of the talents of the four major drummers. —*Scott Yanow*

Billie, Ella, Lena, Sarah / Jul. 2, 1935–May 19, 1950 / Columbia ✦✦✦
This is a straight CD reissue of the original LP with four recordings apiece from Billie Holiday and Sarah Vaughan and two from Lena Horne and Ella Fitgerald. All of the performances are available elsewhere and this CD is rather brief in playing time (just 36 minutes, less than half of its capacity). The music is generally excellent with Lady Day heard during 1935–39, Fitzgerald's two songs being from a 1936 session with Teddy Wilson's Orchestra and Lena Horne also being backed by Wilson in 1941. However Sarah Vaughan takes honors for she is heard in prime form in 1950 on "Nice Work If You Can Get It," "East of the Sun," "Goodnight My Love" and a classic version of "Ain't Misbehavin'"; her all-star backup group includes Miles Davis. —*Scott Yanow*

Bird Feathers / Mar. 29, 1957–Dec. 27, 1957 / New Jazz ✦✦✦
Five different altoists are featured in three different quintets on this CD reissue. Meant to show off the influence of Charlie Parker on the younger players, these performances are (with the exception of Hal McKusick's "Interim") all bop standards. Phil Woods and Gene Quill team up for "Solar" and "Airegin," Jackie McLean meets John Jenkins on "Bird Feathers" and the three remaining selections ("Interim," "Don't Worry 'Bout me" and "Con Alma") feature McKusick with trombonist Billy Byers. Although full sessions did result from some of the dates, these particular selections were first issued in this format. It's recommended for fans of 1950s bop. —*Scott Yanow*

★ **Birdland All Stars at Carnegie Hall** / Sep. 25, 1954–Dec. 16, 1954 / Roulette ✦✦✦✦✦
There is a great deal of worthy and often historic music on this double CD. Most of the performances are taken from a Sept. 25, 1954 Carnegie Hall concert. Count Basie's Orchestra is in superb form on its seven selections; tenors Frank Foster and Frank Wess in particular blow up a storm. Billie Holiday (backed by the Basie band and pianist Carl Drinkard) is a bit out of it on her six numbers, sometimes getting remarkably far behind the beat. Charlie Parker, in a quartet with pianist John Lewis, bassist Percy Heath and drummer Kenny Clarke, is also a bit sub-par on his two numbers but Lester Young, having a rare reunion with the Basie orchestra, is wonderful on an emotional "Pennies from Heaven" and a cookin' "Jumpin' at the Woodside." The second half of the concert features Sarah Vaughan (backed at first by the Basie band and then by her trio) in wondrous form on a jazz-oriented set. She has rarely sounded better. This set concludes with the Basie band live at Birdland on Dec. 16, 1954 welcoming Stan Getz to sit in on five enjoyable numbers. —*Scott Yanow*

Birdology / Jun. 7, 1989 / Verve ✦✦✦✦
An all-star group (consisting of trumpeter Don Sickler, altoist Jackie McLean, tenor saxophonist Johnny Griffin, baritonist Cecil Payne, pianist Duke Jordan, bassist Ron Carter and drummer Roy Haynes) is heard performing five Charlie Parker compositions and McLean's "Bird Lives" at a Paris concert on this enjoyable CD. McLean in particular is in superior form and Sickler's transcrip-

tions (which sometimes feature the group playing excerpts from Charlie Parker and Duke Jordan recorded solos) lifts the set above the level of a jam session. —*Scott Yanow*

Birth of the Cool Vol. 2 / Jan. 23, 1951–Jan. 31, 1953 / Capitol ✦✦✦✦
Although its title might lead some to believe that this CD contains more "Birth of the Cool" recordings from Miles Davis, it actually consists of West Coast jazz performances that were influenced by those records. Trumpeter/arranger Shorty Rogers leads an octet that also features altoist Art Pepper and Jimmy Giuffre on tenor for six numbers; that date launched what became Shorty Rogers and his Giants. There are also eight performances by Gerry Mulligan's tentet (featuring trumpeter Chet Baker) and two selections from the 1951 Metronome All-Stars, an 11-piece unit that includes altoist Lee Konitz, Stan Getz on tenor, pianist George Shearing and Miles Davis himself. The music overall is both historically significant and quite enjoyable, making this a highly recommended set. —*Scott Yanow*

Black & White & Reeds All Over / Mar. 4, 1944–Sep. 1, 1944 / Pickwick ✦✦✦
One of six Pickwick CDs drawn from the Black & White catalog, this release has four complete sessions from 1944 that feature clarinetists in small groups. Rod Cless is heard with trumpeter Sterling Bose, the great pianist James P. Johnson and bassist Pops Foster, the obscure Bingie Madison plays tenor and clarinet with pianist Hank Duncan, the erratic Mezz Mezzrow interacts with pianist Gene Schroeder and drummer George Wettling and Pee Wee Russell takes solo honors with a group also including pianist Cliff Jackson. All of the releases in this short-lived series are recommended to collectors of '40s small-group jazz. —*Scott Yanow*

Black Legends Of Jazz / Apr. 20, 1926–Mar. 1 1959 / GRP/Decca ✦✦
This is a rather self-indulgent and ultimately pointless reissue although it does contain some timeless music. Thirty-eight jazz greats (all Blacks) are featured on 39 selections (Louis Armstrong gets two songs) that are programmed in alphabetical order according to the artist's name. Although professing to represent a full spectrum of jazz history, the great majority of the numbers feature swing stylists since the music is (with four exceptions) restricted to performances originally cut for the Decca label. There are some underrated classics (such as Coleman Hawkins' 1958 remake of "Body and Soul," Carmen McRae's "Something to Live For" and Hot Lips Page's "I Won't Be Here Long") but many of these songs (such as Nat King Cole's "Sweet Lorraine," Duke Ellington's "Mood Indigo" and Billie Holiday's "Good Morning Heartache," etc.) certainly did not need to be reissued again. And using Count Basie's original version of "One O'Clock Jump" as an example of Lester Young's playing is absurd. Skip. —*Scott Yanow*

Black Lion at Montreux / Jul. 4, 1973 / Black Lion ✦✦✦
This all-star concert from the 1973 Montreux Jazz Festival features a variety of top swing-oriented players. A septet with trumpeter Freddy Randall, trombonist Dave Hewitt, clarinetist Dave Shepherd and tenor saxophonist Danny Moss performs "I Surrender Dear" and trumpeter Bill Coleman and Guy Lafitte on tenor romp on a lengthy version of "I Want a Little Girl" and "I Know That You Know." The second side of the LP has the great pianist Teddy Wilson teaming up with clarinetist Shepherd for "Poor Butterfly," violinist Stephane Grappelli jamming "All God's Chillun Got Rhythm," guitarist Barney Kessel featured on "Old Devil Moon" and the duo of Grappelli and Kessel digging into "Tea for Two." This is an enjoyable and consistent program of fine straight-ahead swing music. —*Scott Yanow*

Blue Break Beats / Blue Note ✦✦✦✦✦
Blue Note released the two volume *Blue Break Beats* compilation in the early '90s. The music on *Blue Break Beats* dates from the late '60s and early '70s, when a large portion of Blue Note's soul-jazz artists began experimenting with funk and rock, creating dense electric fusions that concentrated on rhythm, not improvisation. None of this music has ever received much critical praise from jazz purists, but in the late '80s and early '90s, scores of hip-hop and dance DJs discovered these old records and began sampling the original tracks to use in new rap and dance songs. By the early '90s, this jazz/rap/funk fusion had become hip and profitable, which led Blue Note to assemble the *Blue Break Beats* compilations. All of the tracks on the two discs are rare tracks from out-of-print late '60s and early '70s albums, featuring multi-layered percussion, organs, and guitars. Every song on the two

discs—which are sold seperately—is hot, with a deep funky groove, and there are no dull spots on the albums. Though it's designed to appeal to fans of contemporary funk and rap, fans of rock-influenced soul-jazz will find *Blue Break Beats* a necessary purchase. —Stephen Thomas Erlewine

Blue Guitar / Feb. 5, 1941–Nov. 1989 / Blue Note ✦✦
This sampler contains music by 17 guitarists who recorded for Blue Note. Four (including Charlie Christian's acoustic feature on "Jammin' in Four" and the rare "Jimmy's Blues" by Jimmy Shirley) songs are from Blue Note's early days, seven are from its prime bop and hard bop years and the remaining six (ranging from Earl Klugh to Al DiMeola) are of more recent vintage. The CD gives one a good introduction to these talented players although this release is not too essential. —Scott Yanow

Blue Note Rare Grooves / Mar. 1996 / Blue Note ✦✦✦✦✦
Balancing previously unreleased tracks with obscure gems from out-of-print albums, *Blue Note Rare Grooves* is an excellent collection of extremely funky soul-jazz. All of the tracks were recorded between 1967 and 1971, with the majority dating between 1968 and 1969. Though some of the tracks on the disc have been featured on other Blue Note collections, none of the albums they were pulled from are easily available, which makes *Blue Note Rare Grooves* all the more valuable. A good cross-section of artists—featuring John Patton, Richard "Groove" Holmes, Larry Young, Stanley Turrentine, Jack McDuff, Jimmy McGriff, Donald Byrd, Candido, Reuben Wilson, and several others—are included and every single track has a raw, intoxicating groove. *Blue Note Rare Grooves* may not be for jazz purists, but for listeners looking for a first-rate jazz-funk sampler, it's essential. —Stephen Thomas Erlewine

Blue Piano, Vol. 1 / Jan. 6, 1939–Nov. 23, 1953 / Blue Note ✦✦✦
On this sampler there are 14 performances by a variety of pianists from the first 15 years of Blue Note Records. Few of the recordings are particularly rare but the CD does give one a fine sampling of boogie-woogie (Albert Ammons, Meade Lux Lewis and Pete Johnson), swing and stride (Earl Hines, James P. Johnson, Nat Cole, Art Tatum and Art Hodes) and bop (Bud Powell, Lennie Tristano, Thelonious Monk, Wynton Kelly, Al Haig and Horace Silver). The music is consistently excellent with none of the groups being larger than a quartet. —Scott Yanow

Blue Piano, Vol. 2 / Aug. 1, 1955– 1990 / Blue Note ✦✦✦
The second of two CDs containing a sampling of the many great pianists who recorded for Blue Note and its related labels, this program has performances from a dozen masters (Duke Ellington, Herbie Nichols, Cecil Taylor, Sonny Clark, Bill Evans, Herbie Hancock, Chick Corea, Michel Petruccinani, Benny Green, McCoy Tyner, Don Pullen and Andrew Hill) with three recordings from the 1950s, four dating from the '60s and five from 1987–90, after Blue Note's rebirth. Overall these two sets gives one a strong (if not really complete) sampling into the music of some of the great jazz pianists. —Scott Yanow

Blue Series: Female Vocals / Jan. 1945–Feb. 1990 / Blue Note ✦✦✦
Eighteen different female vocalists are heard from on one selection apiece during this CD reissue; *Volume One* dealt with the male singers. Some of the material is rarer than others but there are quite a worthy tracks from the likes of Anita O'Day, Billie Holiday ("Detour Ahead"), Kay Starr, Abbey Lincoln (during her earliest recording session), Annie Ross, Peggy Lee, Sheila Jordan, Sarah Vaughan, Carmen McRae and even Rachelle Ferrell. It's a good introduction to these diverse stylists. —Scott Yanow

Blue Series: Male Vocals / Jun. 12, 1942–Jan. 1989 / Blue Note ✦✦✦
This has vocals from 19 different male vocalists including Louis Armstrong and Bing Crosby (collaborating on "Now You Has Jazz"), Nat King Cole, Charles Brown, a previously unreleased item from Mel Torme, Chet Baker, Mark Murphy, King Pleasure, Jon Hendricks, Joe Williams, Tony Bennett (how did he get here—) and Billy Eckstein. The emphasis is very much on the swing and bop stylists and, once one eliminates Lou Rawls' 1989 outing, all of the music is from 1942–62. —Scott Yanow

The Bop Session / May 19, 1975–May 20, 1975 / Sonet ✦✦✦
This LP matches together trumpeter Dizzy Gillespie and Sonny Stitt (on alto and tenor) with an all-star rhythm section (John Lewis or Hank Jones on piano, bassist Percy Heath and drummer Max Roach) for six classic bop standards. Gillespie was near the

end of his prime but is in generally good form while Stitt typically eats the material (songs such as "Confirmation," "Groovin' High" and "All the Things You Are") with no difficulty. Bop fans should enjoy this date despite the lack of surprises. —Scott Yanow

British Dance Bands / Feb. 12, 1926–Dec. 13, 1935 / ABC ✦✦✦
This entry from the Robert Parker collection is comprised of 16 selections from as many British big bands. Some of the performances are more jazz-oriented than others (particularly Fred Elizalde's "Singapore Sorrows," the Arcadian Dance Orchestra's version of "'Leven Thirty Saturday Night" and Billy Cotton's "Somebody Stole My Gal") while most of the remainder is more commercial although usually using a reasonably swinging rhythm section. Even veteran collectors will not have had all of these formerly rare tracks, which on a whole give one a good idea as to how the English were coping musically during the Depression. —Scott Yanow

California Concert / Jul. 18, 1971 / CBS ✦✦✦✦✦
This double LP (whose contents are long overdue to appear on CD) is a classic. For a concert held at the Hollywood Palladium in 1971, Creed Taylor gathered together most of his top stars and demonstrated why CTI was one of the most significant labels of the era. On lengthy renditions of "Fire and Rain," "Red Clay," "Sugar," "Blues West" and "Leaving West," the all-star lineup (trumpeter Freddie Hubbard, tenor saxophonist Stanley Turrentine, altoist Hank Crawford, flutist Hubert Laws, guitarist George Benson, keyboardist Johnny Hammond, bassist Ron Carter, drummer Billy Cobham and percussionist Airto) is in inspired form, particularly Hubbard and Turrentine. This wonderful music belongs in every serious jazz collection. —Scott Yanow

Capitol Jazz Sings The Gershwin Songbook / Jul. 23, 1946–May, 1976 / Blue Note ✦✦✦
The music of George Gershwin (and in most cases the lyrics of Ira Gershwin) is interpreted by 16 fine singers on a sampler CD taken from sessions currently owned by Capitol and its related labels. The music jumps around chronologically and is not programmed with all that much coherence but the music is consistently enjoyable with such notable vocalists as Nat King Cole, Carmen McRae, Chet Baker, Sarah Vaughan, Annie Ross, Sarah Vaughan, Mel Torme, Peggy Lee, Johnny Hartman and Nina Simone ("Summertime") being among the stars. With one exception, all of the music is from the 1946–63 period. —Scott Yanow

The Caribbean Jazz Project / Apr. 1995 / Heads Up ✦✦✦✦✦
Altoist Paquito D'Rivera teams up with the great steel drummer Andy Narell and Dave Samuels (who doubles on marimba and vibes) to create music that is both easy-listening and stimulating on this CD. Influenced by the rhythms of the Caribbean, the attractive blend between the co-leaders, the strong melodic solos and the fine backup by the four-piece rhythm section make this a very accessible release that should appeal to a large audience while still interesting jazz fans. —Scott Yanow

Jazz Masters: Verve at 50 / 1994 / Verve ✦✦✦
Verve Records celebrated the 50th anniversary of Norman Granz's first Jazz at the Philharmonic concert with an all-star get-together at Carnegie Hall. Different groups of top players from Verve's legacy (both past and present) had opportunities to perform and this CD has many of the highlights. Pianist Peter Delano plays "Tangerine" with a trio, Dee Dee Bridgewater sings "Shiny Stockings" with the Carnegie Hall Jazz Band, Hank Jones pays tribute to Art Tatum, Abbey Lincoln sings "I Must Have That Man," Joe Henderson meets up with Antonio Carlos Jobim (who made his final concert appearance) on "Desafinado," "Manteca" features trumpeter Roy Hargrove and trombonist Steve Turre, pianist Yosuke Yamashita pays tribute to Bud Powell, Betty Carter scats on "How High the Moon," Herbie Hancock and John McLaughlin play a restrained acoustic version of Bill Evans' "Turn out the Stars," Hargrove teams up with altoist Jackie McLean and guitarist Pat Metheny for "The Eternal Triangle," organist Jimmy Smith revisits Oliver Nelson's arrangement of "Down by the Riverside," Art Porter and Jeff Lorber play some crossover and J.J. Johnson contributes a few trombone solos. Not that many special moments occur (too many of the original Verve stars had long since passed away) but jazz historians and bop fans may want to get this one. —Scott Yanow

Celebration of Duke / Sep. 12, 1979–May 13, 1980 / Original Jazz Classics ✦✦✦✦
Although Sarah Vaughan gets top billing on this set, she takes

vocals on just two of the ten songs. Four different groupings of Pablo's All-Star musicians are heard from during a tribute to Duke Ellington, and there are many strong moments. Guitarist Joe Pass, vibraphonist Milt Jackson, bassist Ray Brown and drummer Mickey Roker make for a potent quartet on three songs, fluegelhornist Clark Terry heads a quintet, Zoot Sims is featured on his lyrical soprano during memorable versions of "Rockin' in Rhythm" and the beautiful "Tonight I Shall Sleep," and Sassy (backed by just pianist Mike Wofford and guitarist Joe Pass) comes up with fresh interpretations of "I Ain't Got Nothin' but the Blues" and "Everything but You." This is a well-rounded and easily enjoyable set with plenty of variety. —*Scott Yanow*

Chartbusters! / Jan. 3, 1995–Jan. 4, 1995 / NYC ++++
For this unusual CD, eight songs from the prime years of Blue Note (compositions by Horace Silver, Hank Mobley, Bobby Timmons, Sonny Clark, Kenny Dorham, Freddie Hubbard, McCoy Tyner and the standard "If Ever I Would Leave You") are revisited. What is different from the original versions are not the styles of the solos but the instrumentation. Although tenor saxophonist Craig Handy is on six of the songs (two of which find trombonist Papo Vazquez blending with Handy to create a Jazz Crusaders feel), the dominant forces are organist Lonnie Smith (who with drummer Lenny White is on every selection) and a variety of guitarists. There are no trumpeters, and it is the guitarists (either John Scofield, David Fiuczynski or Hiram Bullock) who make it obvious that these recordings are not from 1965; they generally take solo honors, particularly Scofield. Organist Smith happily avoids getting into the clichéd boogaloo rhythm that he often played on his Blue Note recordings of the late '60s and the overall music is quite satisfying and swinging in its own way. —*Scott Yanow*

Chicago In The Twenties / Sep. 16, 1926–Oct. 4, 1928 / Arcadia ++++
In the mid-to-late '70s the Arcadia label came out with a variety of significant compilations of '20s jazz and dance music, much of it formerly rare. This particular LP has all of the recordings from Elgar's Creole orchestra (four titles plus two alternate takes), the four numbers recorded by Carroll Dickerson's Savoy Orchestra (including two with Louis Armstrong in 1928) and four songs from Sammy Stewart's Orchestra. On a whole these performances show there were plenty of big bands active in jazz years before the swing era. Elgar's "Nightmare" (heard in two versions) is quite eerie, the Dickerson sides are classics and Stewart's band holds its own. It's recommended to 1920s collectors. —*Scott Yanow*

Chicago In The Twenties, Vol. 2 / Sep. 1924–1932 / Arcadia +++
The second of two LPs put out by Arcadia in this series has a set of true obscurities. Elmer Kaiser's Ballroom Orchestra from 1924 plays "Monkey Business," the modestly titled "Super Syncopators" jams on four songs, Charley Straight's Orchestra is excellent on two numbers, Husk O'Hare's Footwarmers, the Midnight Serenaders, Bill Haid's Cubs and the Manhattan Entertainers are all heard from, and there are previously unknown versions of "China Boy" and "Nobody's Sweetheart" taken from a 1932 jam session that might include pianist Jess Stacy. This set is not essential but fans of early jazz will find it quite interesting. —*Scott Yanow*

★ **Chicago Jazz Summit** / Jun. 22, 1986 / Atlantic +++++
Trad jazz fans can consider this set to be essential, for in reality it was the last Eddie Condon record (even though Condon had passed away several years earlier). While Vince Giordano's Nighthawks (a group including the then-unknown clarinetist Ken Peplowski and trumpeter Randy Sandke) act as the "house band," such classic jazz veterans as trumpeters Wild Bill Davison, Yank Lawson, Max Kaminsky and Jimmy McPartland (the latter two making their final recordings), the tenors of Eddie Miller and Franz Jackson, clarinetists Clarence Hutchenrider, Frank Chace and Kenny Davern, trombonist George Masso, guitarist Ikey Robinson, pianists Art Hodes, Marian McPartland and George Wein, bassists Truck Parham and Milt Hinton and drummer Barrett Deems all have their moments. This historic and spirited set of Dixieland standards could have been titled "We're All Together Again for the Last Time." —*Scott Yanow*

Chicago Style / Apr. 18, 1932–Jan. 14, 1942 / Jazz Archives ++++
This LP launched the Jazz Archives label, a company whose releases of early jazz put an emphasis on alternate takes and unusual performances. This excellent album has eight exciting performances by the Rhythmakers, most of which match togeth-

er trumpeter Henry Red Allen and clarinetist Pee Wee Russell in 1932; their four versions of "Oh! Peter" are classic. In addition there are selections from Eddie Condon's groups in 1938 and 1940 (featuring trombonist Jack Teagarden, trumpeter Marty Marsala, clarinetist Russell and pianist Fats Waller), a Joe Sullivan piano solo and a version of "Honeysuckle Rose" that was the high point of Fats Waller's erratic 1942 Carnegie Hall concert. This album is worth searching for by prebop fans. Fortunately many of the Jazz Archives releases have been reissued on CD by a European label using the same name. —*Scott Yanow*

Christmas Cookies / Dec. 2, 1992–Dec. 3, 1992 / Arbors +++
Most of the selections on this upbeat Christmas jazz CD feature the trio of trumpeter Charlie Bertini, pianist Randy Morris and drummer Ed Metz; a few selections add violinist Renee Dover while the tuba of Dave Gannett helps out on "A Child Is Born." In addition Morris has a few piano solos. There is plenty of good humor, Xmas cheer and swinging music on this easily enjoyable trad jazz-oriented release of Christmas music. —*Scott Yanow*

Christmas Jubilee / Aug. 8, 1945–1953 / Vintage Jazz Classics +++
This enjoyable collector's CD contains two complete Christmas radio shows (one from 1947 and the other one performed in 1945, on August 8!), a brief Frank Sinatra Christmas program and a couple of miscellaneous items. Such performers as Count Basie's Orchestra, the Delta Rhythm Boys, Lena Horne, Bing Crosby (singing "Gotta Be This or That"), Duke Ellington, Art Tatum, Louis Armstrong, the Nat King Cole Trio, Kay Starr and Les Brown make notable appearances. Overall the results are an interesting variety of mid-'40s music that will be easily enjoyed by fans of the swing era. —*Scott Yanow*

☆ **Classic Jazz** / Smithsonian +++++
The Smithsonian Collection of Classic Jazz is itself somewhat of a classic, referred to in many books, and used as the main learning source in at least one. If you don't know what you like in jazz and are looking for a well-put-together introduction, this set is a good bet. It starts with ragtime's Scott Joplin, and proceeds through Bessie Smith, Louis Armstrong, Art Tatum, Duke Ellington...all the way up to and including the free jazz of Ornette Coleman, and even the World Saxophone Quartet. Of course John Coltrane, Thelonious Monk, Miles Davis, and all the other big guns are there—even Horace Silver and Lennie Tristano. This five-CD set (94 tracks) contains classic cuts in most cases. This set is a great place to begin. —*Michael Erlewine*

★ **Classic Tenors** / Dec. 8, 1943–Dec. 23, 1943 / Doctor Jazz +++++
"Classic" is an accurate description of the music on this LP. The great tenor Coleman Hawkins is heard in peak form on a quartet set with pianist Eddie Heywood, bassist Oscar Pettiford and drummer Shelly Manne, particularly during a brilliant version of "The Man I Love." Hawk is almost as creative on a septet date with trumpeter Bill Coleman and pianist Ellis Larkins, roaring on "Hawkins' Barrel House" and "Stumpy." The other four selections feature the equally great tenor Lester Young, interacting with trumpeter Bill Coleman and trombonist Dickie Wells. "I Got Rhythm" finds Prez at his best and Wells' high-note work on "I'm Fer It Too" is both humorous and memorable. This classic set has since been reissued on CD. —*Scott Yanow*

Classic Tenors, Vol. 2 / Dec. 18, 1943–Dec. 1950 / Doctor Jazz +++
Some of the music on this LP duplicates the Doctor Jazz album titled *The Big Three* (the two Coleman Hawkins and Lester Young selections) but it is completely different from the first volume of *Classic Tenors*. Hawkins is heard on an obscure two-song set with a quintet featuring pianist Ellis Larkins ("Lover Come Back to Me" and "Blues Changes") while Lester Young (in a septet with trumpeter Bill Coleman and trombonist Dickie Wells) plays the alternate versions of "Hello Babe" and "I'm Fer It Too." Julian Dash (best known as a sideman with Erskine Hawkins' Orchestra) heads a combo for four rare titles from 1950 while Edie "Lockjaw" Davis is heard during one of his earliest sessions (from May 1946) interpreting four heated songs including one ("Lockjaw") that gave him his nickname. The music on this album might not be in the "classic" category, but the four different approaches to playing swing tenor are interesting to compare and easy to enjoy. —*Scott Yanow*

Colorado Jazz Party / Sep. 5, 1971–Sep. 6, 1971 / MPS +++++
It is surprising that the music on this double LP has not been reis-

sued yet on CD for there are many exciting performances. Taken from Dick Gibson's 1971 Colorado Jazz Party, there are mini-sets from four separate groups. Trumpeters Clark Terry and Harry "Sweets" Edison lead a six-horn nonet (which includes Zoot Sims' tenor) for spirited versions of "On the Trail" and "The Hymn." Terry gets a chance to stretch out with tenor saxophonist Flip Phillips in a quintet while a similar-sized group showcases the underrated trombonist Carl Fontana and James Moody on tenor. Finally there is a four-trombone septet (with Fontana, Kai Winding, Urbie Green and an effective Trummy Young) performing long versions of "Undecided" and "Lover, Come Back to Me." Fans of straight-ahead jazz who run across this two-fer will not need to be told twice to get it. *— Scott Yanow*

☆ **Complete Blue Note Recordings of Hall/Johnson/Deparis/-Dickenson** / Feb. 5, 1941–Jun. 24, 1952 / Mosaic ✦✦✦✦✦
To say that this limited-edition six-LP Mosaic box is overflowing with classics is an understatement. Included are a variety of small-group sessions (with overlapping personnel) from the early days of Blue Note. The Edmond Hall Celeste Quartet has five songs that are the only examples that exist of Charlie Christian playing acoustic guitar; clarinetist Hall, Meade Lux Lewis (on celeste) and bassist Israel Crosby complete the unique group. The king of stride piano, James P. Johnson, is heard on eight solos and other combos are led by Johnson, Hall (who heads four groups in all), trumpeter Sidney DeParis and trombonist Vic Dickenson (heard in a 1952 quartet with organist Bill Doggett). Among the other key soloists are vibraphonist Red Norvo, pianist Teddy Wilson, tenor great Ben Webster, baritonist Harry Carney, clarinetist Omer Simeon and trombonist Benny Morton. But more important than the all-star personnel is the fact that the musicians are consistently inspired and that the performances (ranging from Dixieland to advanced swing) are well planned yet spontaneous. The accompanying 26-page booklet is a major plus too. Essential music; get this box while you can. *— Scott Yanow*

☆ **Complete Commodore Jazz Recordings, Vol. 1** / Apr. 1929–Dec. 21, 1943 / Mosaic ✦✦✦✦✦
The punchline for this 23-LP limited-edition box set is in its title, *Vol. 1*. On a total of 66 albums, Mosaic has reissued the entire jazz output of Milt Gabler's Commodore label, one of the most important jazz record companies of all time. There is an incredible amount of music included on this first set (the most essential of the three). After five early titles that Commodore acquired from other labels (featuring Cow Cow Davenport, Fletcher Henderson and Django Reinhardt), one hears the birth of Commodore with the exciting Jan. 17, 1938 outing by Eddie Condon. In addition to a lot more of Condon's freewheeling sessions (much of his best work was for Commodore), there are dates led by Bud Freeman, the Kansas City Five and Six (with Lester Young), Teddy Wilson, Jess Stacy, Chu Berry, Willie the Lion Smith, Billie Holiday, Stuff Smith, Jelly Roll Morton, Jack Teagarden, Art Hodes, Joe Marsala, Joe Bushkin, Coleman Hawkins, Lee Wiley, Pee Wee Russell, Bunk Johnson, Mel Powell (with Benny Goodman), Wild Bill Davison, George Brunies and Edmond Hall. There are many previously unissued performances (not just alternate takes) and literally dozens of classics. Fans of Chicago jazz and small-group swing should bid as much as necessary to acquire this out-of-print box (along with the other two volumes). *— Scott Yanow*

☆ **Complete Commodore Jazz Recordings, Vol. 2** / Feb. 5, 1944–Mar. 16, 1943 / Mosaic ✦✦✦✦
The second of three "volumes" put out by Mosaic that reissues the entire Commodore catalog is, like the first, a 23-LP set; all of the music in this massive box was recorded within 13 months. The limited-edition series is a must (although it will be quite difficult to locate) for collectors of Chicago jazz and small-group swing for it is literally overflowing with classics. The first box is the most essential but *Volume 2* is pretty close with recording sessions led by Sidney and Wilbur DeParis, Albert Ammons, Eddie Heywood, Hot Lips Page, Sic Catlett, Billie Holiday, the Kansas City Six with Lester Young, George Zack, Muggsy Spanier, Miff Mole, Joe Bushkin, Max Kaminsky, Edmond Hall, George Wettling, Bobby Hackett, Hot Lips Page, Pee Wee Russell, Red McKenzie, Jess Stacy, Jack Teagarden and Wild Bill Davison. In addition to the usual performances (many of which were previously hard-to-find), there are quite a few previously unissued alternate takes and some selections (including an entire Joe Bushkin Trio date) that were never out before. This set (if it can be found) will be expensive but worth it. *— Scott Yanow*

☆ **Complete Commodore Jazz Recordings, Vol. 3** / Jul. 12, 1938–Jul. 9, 1957 / Mosaic ✦✦✦✦✦
The third and final Mosaic box set that reissues all of the valuable recordings from Milt Gabler's Commodore label is the smallest of these reissues, a mere 20-LP set. All three of the volumes (which total 66 albums) are wonderful but since they were originally limited-edition releases (just 2500 copies apiece) and have gone out-of-print, they will be difficult to locate and expensive to acquire; buy them anyway if you have any interest in small-group swing and Chicago Dixieland. *Volume 3* starts out with some recently discovered alternate takes by Bud Freeman, Chu Berry, Bunk Johnson and Billie Holiday from 1938–44 before concentrating mostly on the 1945–46 period. There are sessions led by Red Norvo, Bill Coleman, Gene Krupa, Stuff Smith, Teddy Wilson and the duo of Don Byas and Slam Stewart (all of those are from a legendary 1945 Town Hall concert) plus dates headed by George Zack, Jonah Jones, Wild Bill Davison, Eddie Edwards, George Brunies and Mel Powell; in addition there are later sets by Bob Wilber, Ralph Sutton, Sidney Bechet, Johnny Wiggs, Willie the Lion Smith, Frank Wess and Peck Kelley. One exhausts superlatives when discussing this remarkable project. *— Scott Yanow*

☆ **The Complete Keynote Collection** / Mar. 14, 1941–May 23, 1947 / Polygram ✦✦✦✦✦
This is an incredible set, a 21-LP box that has all of the jazz recordings ever made for Harry Lim's Keynote label. Much of this music has been reissued in piecemeal fashion on CD by Polygram but this is the way to get it, complete and in chronological order with all of the alternate takes. Lim had impeccable taste and recorded Chicago jazz, small-group swing and bop by many of the top musicians of the period; all but the first session (George Hartman Dixieland sides from 1941) are from Dec. 1943 to May 1947. This box has dates by Lester Young, Dinah Washington, Roy Eldridge, Coleman Hawkins, Cozy Cole, the Kansas City Seven, Charlie Shavers with Earl Hines, Benny Morton, Rex Stewart, the Keynoters, Pete Brown, Red Norvo, bassist Billy Taylor, Jonah Jones, George Wettling, Chubby Jackson, Barney Bigard, Bill Harris, Willie Smith, Corky Corcoran, Milt Hinton, J.C. Heard, Irving Fazola, Bud Freeman, Ted Nash, Babe Russin, Manny Klein, Herbie Haymer, Clyde Hurley, Arnold Ross, Juan Tizol, Benny Carter, Marie Bryant, Bernie Leighton, Ann Hathaway, Joe Thomas, George Barnes, Lennie Tristano, Danny Hurd, Dave Lambert and Buddy Stewart, Gene Sedric, Neal Hefti and Red Rodney, and that is only the leaders. There is so much music (334 performances including 115 that were not previously released) that in addition to the 21 LPs included is a 45 with an extra Lennie Tristano song. This box will be very difficult to locate but fans of small-group swing and historic jazz should get it at any price. *— Scott Yanow*

The Complete Master Jazz Piano Series / Mar. 11, 1969–Jan. 9, 1974 / Mosaic ✦✦✦✦✦
During a five-year period the Master Jazz label recorded 11 swing-based pianists in solo settings. Although the label went under later in the decade, the recordings were treasured by collectors. Mosaic, on this four-CD set, brought back all of the music from the original five-volume Master Jazz Piano series, adding two unissued selections and a full album released separately of Ram Ramirez's playing. In addition to Ramirez (who is heard on 13 numbers), there are 13 performances by Earl Hines, four apiece from Claude Hopkins, Cliff Jackson, Keith Dunham, Sonny White, Teddy Wilson, Cliff Smalls and the obscure Gloria Hearn, eight by Jay McShann and two from Sir Charles Thompson. Most of the pianists (other than Hines and Wilson) rarely recorded during this period in their careers, making this box very important both musically and historically. *— Scott Yanow*

Concert in Argentina / Nov. 1974 / Jazz Alliance ✦✦✦
Although this double LP has been reissued by the Jazz Alliance label on CD, the LP version is preferable because it contains more performances. Pianists Marian McPartland, Teddy Wilson, Ellis Larkins and Earl Hines all play about 20 minutes apiece during a swing-oriented solo set. McPartland (whose performance is highlighted by a Duke Ellington medley), Wilson (who plays a couple of Gershwin medleys), and Larkins (sticking as usual to quiet ballads) are all in fine form, but it was wise to put Hines on last for he cuts everyone with his chancetaking set. *— Scott Yanow*

Concord Jazz Festival: Live 1990 / Aug. 18, 1990 / Concord Jazz ✦✦✦
The first of three CDs taken from the 1990 Concord Jazz Festival

features three trombonists (Rob McConnell, Al Grey and Benny Powell), trumpeter Harry "Sweets" Edison and a fine rhythm section (guitairst Ed Bickert, pianist Gene Harris, bassist Neil Swainson and drummer Alan Dawson) playing straight-ahead jazz. Edison, Powell, Harris, Grey and Bickert have individual features, the full group plays "Cottontail" and the trombonists (without Edison) get to stretch out on "Undecided." Nothing too surprising occurs but the good-humored music (Grey's "St. James Infirmary" is a high-point) is fun and swinging. —*Scott Yanow*

Live at the 1990 Concord Jazz Festival: Second Set / Aug. 18, 1990 / Concord Jazz ✦✦✦
The second of three Concord CDs documenting this 1990 festival matches together four veteran horn soloists (Frank Wess on tenor and flute, altoist Marshal Royal, Rick Wilkins on tenor and fluegelhornist Pete Minger) with a fine rhythm section (pianist Gerry Wiggins, bassist Lynn Seaton and drummer Harold Jones) for a variety of jazz standards. Wess, Royal and Minger each have features (Royal's outing on "Don't Get Around Much Anymore" is a high-point), Seaton sings "Just Squeeze Me" in humorous fashion and the full group jams on "The Blues Walk" and "Broadway." Few surprises occur but fans of straight-ahead jazz should enjoy this music. —*Scott Yanow*

Concord Jazz Festival: Live 1990, Third Set / Aug. 18, 1990 / Concord Jazz ✦✦✦✦✦
Although there is no official leader on the CD, this is really an Ernestine Anderson date. Pianist Gene Harris and his quartet (with guitarist Ed Bickert, bassist Lynn Seaton and drummer Harold Jones) romp through Oscar Pettiford's "Blues in the Closet" and then the singer takes over for the final six numbers; Frank Wess guests on tenor during "I Should Care" and altoist Marshall Royal is heard from on "Skylark." Ernestine Anderson is in top form during her well-rounded set with highlights including the lengthy "I Should Care," a swinging "There Is No Greater Love," "On My Own" and a definitive 15-minute version of "Never Make Your Move Too Soon." —*Scott Yanow*

Cool Whalin' / 1948–1970 / Spotlite ✦✦✦✦
Six different bop-oriented vocalists are heard on rare recordings on this LP, an English import from Spotlite, Joe Carroll performs "I Don't Want Love" and "Gambler's Blues" with a quartet led by trumpeter Howard McGhee in 1970, the forgotten Kenny "Pancho" Hagood sings four numbers with the Joe Sample Trio in 1967 and Babs Gonzales jams two songs with his usual enthusiasm in 1952. Side two has what might be Eddie Jefferson's earliest recordings ("Bless My Soul" and "Beautiful Memories" from 1948–49), Pancho Hagood and Earl Coleman are heard in 1948 and the obscure Frankie Passions sings "Especially to You" and "Nobody Knows" with a late '50s group that surprisingly includes pianist Thelonious Monk. This is an album that lovers of bop singing will have to get. —*Scott Yanow*

Cotton Club Stars / Feb. 9, 1927–Apr. 1945 / Stash ✦✦✦✦
This double LP pays tribute to the legacy of the Cotton Club on 30 mostly rare recordings by a wide variety of jazz-oriented performers. Taken more or less in chronological order, this collection has among its many highlights "I Found a New Baby" by Andy Preer's Cotton Club Orchestra from 1927, "A Night at the Cotton Club Medley" by Duke Ellington and selections by the Missourians, Bill Bojangles Robinson, Cab Calloway (including a Cotton Club radio broadcast from 1932), Harold Arlen, Buck and Bubbles, Ethel Waters, the Nicholas Brothers, Ella Fitgerald, Lena Horne and Louis Armstrong with the Mills Brothers. Even veteran collectors will probably not have all of these performances, making this attractive two-fer from 1984 worth picking up. —*Scott Yanow*

Danish Jazz In The '50s, Vol. 1 / Jun. 25, 1956–Mar. 10, 1957 / Olufsen ✦✦✦✦
While Sweden became known for its talented cool jazz performers during the 1950s, Denmark's interesting scene of the period has long been neglected. On the first of two Olufsen LPs to document the era, there are broadcasts by groups led by musicians unfamiliar to most Americans: tenor saxophonist Max Bruel, trumpeter Jorgen Ryg, pianists Otto Francker and Bertrand Bech and big bands headed by Peter Rasmussen and Ib Glindemann. Along with a few originals, the players perform bop and swing standards with subtle creativity and a surprising amount of individuality. The two LPs are worth checking out by bop fans who think they have heard everything. —*Scott Yanow*

Danish Jazz In The '50s, Vol. 2 / Mar. 10, 1957–May 30, 1959 / Olufsen ✦✦✦✦
The second of two Olufsen LPs shows off some of the top jazz talents to be found in Denmark during the 1950s. These radio broadcasts feature the Ib Glindemann big band on eight selections along with combos headed by vibraphonist Louis Hjulmand, pianist Paul Godske and tenor saxophonist Frank Jensen. No household names appear (pianist Bent Axen and trumpeter Allan Botchinsky are the best known in the U.S.), but the music is generally quite rewarding, emphasizing bop and swing standards. —*Scott Yanow*

Dr. Jazz Sampler / Dec. 20, 1951–May 25, 1952 / Storyville ✦✦✦
For seven months during 1951–52, announcer Aime Gauvin (as "Dr. Jazz") hosted a weekly half-hour radio show that spotlighted many of the Dixieland groups then performing nightly in New York clubs. Storyville has released quite a few CDs from these previously unissued broadcasts, focusing on individual bands. This sampler has 11 selections not included on the other sets, featuring bands headed by Eddie Condon, Wilbur DeParis, Buck Clayton, Bobby Hackett, Ralph Sutton, Red Allen, Pee Wee Erwin, Hot Lips Page and Jimmy Archey. The music is straight-ahead Dixieland including two versions of "Sweet Georgia Brown" and Buck Clayton's reworking of "Jingle Bells." With sidemen taken from the who's who of classic jazz, this CD gives one a fine sampler of the early-'50s Dixieland scene. —*Scott Yanow*

Dylan Jazz / 1967 / GNP Crescendo ✦✦
This is a most unusual record. Five studio musicians (including saxophonist Jim Horn and a then-unknown guitarist named Glenn Campbell) play jazz versions of ten Bob Dylan songs. This LP mostly finds the players sticking fairly close to the melodies (including such tunes as "Blowin' in the Wind," "Hey Mr. Tambourine Man" and "Like a Rolling Stone") in renditions that are generally under three minutes long. It's a very interesting novelty record. —*Scott Yanow*

Early Black Swing: the Birth of Big Band Jazz: 1927–1934 / Apr. 27, 1927–Aug. 4, 1936 / Bluebird ✦✦✦
The music on this CD is quite historic but available in more complete fashion elsewhere. However listeners wishing to acquire an overview of early swing (mostly prior to the rise of Benny Goodman) could certainly do much worse than these 22 performances. Included are strong examples of the big band music of Fletcher Hederson, Duke Ellington, Bennie Moten, McKinney's Cotton Pickers, Earl Hines, Charlie Johnson's Paradise Ten, the Missourians, Red Allen, Jimmie Lunceford and Louis Armstrong. —*Scott Yanow*

East Coast Jive / Aug. 9, 1946–Dec. 17, 1947 / Delmark ✦✦✦
The music varies on this collection but nearly all of the 21 performances are fun. Taken from the Apollo catalog, the Delmark CD has rare selections from singers Babs Gonzales, Loumell Morgan, Artie Simms, Babe Wallace, the Four Blues and Ben Smith. Ranging from swing to bop with many of the singers being influenced by the style of the Nat King Cole Trio, this "jive music" may not be all that original but it is quite accessible and full of joy. —*Scott Yanow*

Echoes of The Thirties / Jan. 4, 1930–Nov. 1, 1939 / Columbia ✦✦✦✦✦
This five-LP box set goes in chronological order from 1930–39 and amazingly enough nearly all of its 70 performances are rare. The music ranges from dance bands and swing to personalities and vocal groups but the emphasis is largely on jazz with plenty of previously unreleased recordings and alternate takes along with some very obscure items. There are many highlights with everyone from the California Ramblers, Fletcher Henderson, Ruth Etting, Red Nichols and Bing Crosby to Phil Harris, the Four Blackbirds, Red Allen, Raymond Scott (with Jerry Colonna), Cab Calloway and Benny Goodman being heard. Collectors of music from the era will want to search for this box which was originally issued in 1977. —*Scott Yanow*

★ **Exciting Battle: JATP Stockholm '55** / Feb. 2, 1955 / Pablo ✦✦✦✦✦
This is one of the great JATP recordings. Norman Granz's traveling jam session was at its height whenever trumpeter Roy Eldridge and Dizzy Gillespie teamed up. The octet heard on this CD reissue also includes trombonist Bill Harris, tenorsaxophonist Flip Phillips, pianist Oscar Peterson, guitarist Herb Ellis, bassist Ray Brown and drummer Louie Bellson. They all play well on the

jam "Birks" and a four-song ballad medley; "Ow" is a drum feature for Bellson. However it is the blues "Little David" that is quite classic for Oscar Peterson sets the groove with a masterful solo and then (after the other horns have their say) Roy Eldridge has one of the finest improvisations of his career. He builds up his solo ever so gradually and dramatically through chorus after chorus and, while the other players riff, Eldridge makes every sound fit, climaxing with some perfectly placed notes in the upper register. It is one of the great moments in recorded jazz history and enough of a reason by itself to acquire this CD. —*Scott Yanow*

★ **The First Esquire All-American Jazz Concert** / Jan. 18, 1944 / Radiola ✦✦✦✦✦
This set has one of the great jazz concerts of all time, one that features the who's who of the jazz world of 1944. In 1943 *Esquire* magazine held the first Critics Poll and sponsored a concert featuring many of the winners (those in first or second place); the results are released on this two-fer in its entirety. The high point is a remarkable version of "I Got Rhythm" that has Louis Armstrong and Roy Eldridge on trumpets, trombonist Jack Teagarden, clarinetist Barney Bigard, Coleman Hawkins on tenor, xylophonist Red Norvo, pianist Art Tatum, guitarist Al Casey, bassist Oscar Pettiford and drummer Sid Catlett. In addition there are individual features and notable appearances by clarinetist Benny Goodman, Lionel Hampton on vibes and drums, pianists Teddy Wilson and Jess Stacy, bassist Sid Weiss, drummer Morey Feld (the latter three on "Rachel's Dream" with Benny Goodman) and vocals from Billie Holiday and Mildred Bailey. The recording quality of the performances (some of which were broadcast over the radio), is generally quite good and getting to hear Tatum backing Louis Armstrong and Coleman Hawkins' playing on "Basin Street Blues" are two of the many reasons to acquire this unique set. —*Scott Yanow*

Four French Horns / Apr. 14, 1957 / Savoy ✦✦✦
This is an unusual session. Accordionist Mat Mathews came up with the idea of utilizing four French horns as the leading voices on a jazz date so, with guitarist Joe Puma, bassist Milt Hinton and drummer Osie Johnson, Mathews welcomed the French horns of Julius Watkins, David Amram, Fred Klein and Tony Miranda. Watkins has the lion's share of the solo space on this CD reissue but all of the horns are heard from both as soloists and in the colorful (and sometimes imaginative) ensembles. This is a moody bop-oriented date that succeeds beyond its novelty value. —*Scott Yanow*

Fourtune / Dec. 5, 1980–Dec. 6, 1980 / Drive Archive ✦✦✦
Originally released on the RealTime label as a double LP, this CD (which contains 11 of the 14 selections) is quite notable for containing some brilliant playing by Ernie Watts (during a period when his own recordings were very commercial). Chick Corea (sticking to acoustic piano) is also in excellent form as are bassist Andy Simpkins and drummer John Dentz (who was the actual leader). Although a few of the shorter numbers have their free moments, the high points are "My One and Only Love," "Night and Day," "Invitation," "Blues for John C.," "Bud Powell" and "Oleo," intense straight-ahead explorations that allow Watts and Corea opportunities to stretch out. —*Scott Yanow*

Friends In Need: 1991 Triangle Jazz Partyboys / Sep. 29, 1991 / Friends In Need ✦✦✦
Recorded as a fundraiser for Friends in Need, an organization working to provide health care equipment for people with serious diseases, this CD (released through Arbors) has some heated Dixieland and swing from a septet featuring trombonist Dan Barrett, trumpeter Randy Sandke, clarinetist Chuck Hedges, Rick Fay on tenor and soprano, and pianist Ralph Sutton; the final four of the 15 selections are by a sextet led by trumpeter Dick Gable. The music is quite joyous and easily recommended to fans of classic jazz. —*Scott Yanow*

From Spirituals to Swing: Carnegie Hall Concerts, 1938–1939 / 1938–1939 / Vanguard ✦✦✦✦✦
During a pair of Carnegie Hall concerts in late 1938 and late 1939, producer John Hammond had an opportunity to present many of his favorite artists, tracing the evolution of music (as its title said) from spirituals to swing. This double CD is a reissue of the previous double LP and features quite a few historic performances. Featured in good form are the Benny Goodman Sextet (with vibraphonist Lionel Hampton and guitarist Charlie Christian), the Count Basie Orchestra with singer Helen Humes and guest Hot Lips Page (the latter is wonderful on "Blues with

Lips"), the Kansas City Six (an all-star group with Lester Young, Buck Clayton and Charlie Christian), pianist James P. Johnson, the hot New Orleans Feetwarmers which features the soprano of Sidney Bechet, the Golden Gate Quartet, blues singer Ida Cox, the blues harmonica of Sonny Terry, Big Bill Broonzy, Mitchell's Christian Singers, singer Joe Turner with boogie-woogie pianists Pete Johnson, Meade Lux Lewis and Albert Ammons and a jam session version of "Lady Be Good" that includes many of these musicians. The recording quality is decent for the period and the music is generally quite timeless. It's an essential acquisition for all serious jazz collections. —*Scott Yanow*

From the Newport Jazz Festival: Tribute to Charlie Parker / Jul. 1964+Feb. 15, 1967 / Bluebird ✦✦✦✦✦
Although it is not apparent from the outside of this CD, these performances are actually taken from two separate occasions. Trumpeter Howard McGhee, trombonist J.J. Johnson, Sonny Stitt (sticking to tenor), pianist Harold Mabern, bassist Arthur Harper, Jr., and drummer Max Roach are heard at the 1964 Newport Jazz Festival jamming on three songs in tribute to Charlie Parker: "Buzzy," "Now's the Time" and "Wee." In addition the MC, Father Norman O'Connor, gets a few of the veterans to say a few words about Bird. The remainder of the CD features altoist Jackie McLean with his quartet at a studio session in 1967 performing searing ballad versions of "Embraceable You" and "Old Folks." A very interesting and well-rounded program, worth picking up. —*Scott Yanow*

Fujitsu-Concord 25th Jazz Festival: Silver Anniversary Set / Jul. 1993 / Concord Jazz ✦✦✦
This two-CD set has three sets from the 25th-annual Concord Jazz Festival. Guitarist Howard Alden performs five songs with his trio, pianist Gene Harris' quartet swings soulfully on four tunes and welcomes the fine swing tenor Scott Hamilton on three others, and pianist Marian McPartland's Trio plays swinging and sensitive versions of three standards. However it is the young tenor Chris Potter (jamming with McPartland on the final three pieces) who takes solo honors, raising this set above the predictably excellent with some intense and creative solos. —*Scott Yanow*

Fujitsu-Concord 26th Jazz Festival / Aug. 12, 1994 / Concord Jazz ✦✦✦
Recorded at the 26th-annual Concord Jazz Festival, this two-CD set features music from three different performances. The first disc has a well-rounded set with guitarist Charlie Byrd, Hendrik Meurkens on harmonica, clarinetist Ken Peplowski and a fine rhythm section paying tribute to the music of Antonio Carlos Jobim. A group billed as "Seven Sensational Saxophones" is good but not all that sensational with four altos being featured on two songs, four tenors on two others and six of the saxes soloing on "Tryin' to Make My Blues Turn Green"; the horns are altoists Jesse Davis, Gary Foster, tenors Ken Peplowski, Chris Potter and Frank Wess, Bill Ramsay on alto and baritone and Rickey Woodard doubling on tenor and alto. The remainder of this two-fer has eight numbers from what was dubbed "the Gene Harris/Rob McConnell/Frank Wess Concord Jazz All-Star Big Band." The three leaders are the main soloists and Jeannie Cheatham takes a couple of spirited guest vocals. Overall, this set should easily please fans of Concord's usual mainstream output. —*Scott Yanow*

Fun on the Frets: Early Jazz Guitar / 1936–1949 / Yazoo ✦✦✦✦
This Yazoo LP has many rather rare acoustic guitar performances. Carl Kress, a great chordal player, is heard on ten duets with fellow guitarist Tony Mottola in 1941, a couple of hot numbers with Dick McDonough (1934's "Danzon" and "I've Got a Feeling You're Fooling" from 1936) and two 1939 solos. In addition the seven-string guitar pioneer George Van Eps is featured on four numbers with a trio from 1949. Those listeners who have only heard of Django Reinhardt and Charlie Christian among early guitarists are well-advised to search for this fascinating LP. —*Scott Yanow*

A GRP Christmas Collection / 1988 / GRP ✦✦
Most of the notables on GRP's roster in 1988 participated in this pleasing Christmas CD. There is one selection apiece from guitarist Daryl Stuermer, Tom Scott, David Benoit, Diane Schuur, Dave Valentin, Lee Ritenour, Gary Burton, Yutaka, Chick Corea's Elektric Band ("God Rest Ye Merry Gentlemen"), Szakcsi, Eddie Daniels, Mark Egan, Special EFX, Kevin Eubanks and Dave Grusin. This relaxed set will be enjoyed by fans of those artists. — *Scott Yanow*

GRP Super Live in Concert / Oct. 8, 1987 / GRP ✦✦✦
This double CD is most notable for its second half which has a

strong outing from Chick Corea's Elektric Band, his pacesetting fusion band with guitarist Frank Gambale, altoist Eric Marienthal, bassist John Patitucci and drummer Dave Weckl. The first CD is of lesser interest since it contains three routine vocals by Diane Schuur and some dull R&B jams with guitarist Lee Ritenour, keyboardist Dave Grusin and saxophonist Tom Scott. This set is worth buying for Corea's contributions if seen at a budget price. —Scott Yanow

Giants of Small Band Swing, Vol. 1 / 1946 / Riverside ✦✦✦
The first of two CDs reissuing material originally on the H.R.S. label has generally strong performances by a variety of small swing-oriented bands from 1946. The personnel overlaps in five groups headed by pianist Billy Kyle, altoist Russell Procope, trombonist Sandy Williams, pianist Jimmy Jones and trombonist Dicky Wells; the sidemen include such veteran greats as trumpeters Dick Vance, Harold Baker and Pee Wee Erwin, trombonist Trummy Young, clarinetist Buster Bailey, altoists Lem Davis and Tab Smith and the tenors of John Hardee and Budd Johnson. Although the music overall is not that essential (the bop recordings of the period are much more significant), there are some memorable performances on this well-conceived set. —Scott Yanow

Giants of Small Band Swing, Vol. 2 / Nov. 5, 1945–Jun. 3, 1946 / Riverside ✦✦✦
The second of two CDs put out in the Original Jazz Classics series that reissues material originally on the H.R.S. label, this volume has fine performances from bands led by three trombonists (Dicky Wells, Sandy Williams and J.C. Higginbotham) and trumpeter Joe Thomas; among the sidemen are Budd Johnson and Ted Nash on tenors, altoists Tab Smith, Lem Davis and Johnny Hodges, trumpeters Pee Wee Erwin and Sidney DeParis and baritonist Harry Carney. Although none of the recordings are classic and one can argue that the music is slightly behind the times, the solos are quite enjoyable and will be savored by small-group swing fans. —Scott Yanow

Giants of Traditional Jazz / Mar. 21, 1944–Aug. 21, 1952 / Savoy ✦✦✦
The emphasis is on Dixieland throughout this historical and very enjoyable two-LP set put out by Arista in 1980. The primitive trumpeter Mutt Carey is heard on his only two sessions as a leader performing some jazzy versions of ragtime along with a couple of veteran tunes; Carey's band includes trombonist Jimmy Archey, either Albert Nicholas or Edmond Hall on clarinet and Cliff Jackson or Hank Duncan on piano. English trumpeter Humphrey Littleton welcomes the great soprano Sidney Bechet to his septet ("Some of These Days" is a highlight), cornetists Bobby Hackett and Wild Bill Davison star on a few Dixieland standards, drummer Ben Pollack features trombonist Jack Teagarden on "Mighty Like a Rose" and there are eight selections by Edmond Hall with a sextet that also stars trumpeter Ruby Braff and trombonist Vic Dickenson. Dixieland fans should bemoan the fact that most of this music has yet to be reissued on CD. —Scott Yanow

Giants of the Blues Tenor Sax / Nov. 7, 1958–Mar. 25, 1969 / Prestige ✦✦✦
This two-LP set (which has been reissued as part of a similarly titled three-CD set) has a dozen performances from a variety of great tenor saxophonists who recorded for Prestige during the period: Buddy Tate, Jimmy Forrest, Coleman Hawkins, Arnett Cobb, Eddie "Lockjaw" Davis, Hal Singer, Al Sears, Illinois Jacquet, King Curtis, Frank Foster and Jimmy Forrest. In addition to the later CD reissue, virtually all of the music is also available in its original context, making this two-fer far from essential, but it serves as a good introduction to these many bop-oriented and full-toned tenors. —Scott Yanow

Great Ladies of Jazz / K-Tel ✦✦
This sampler from the K-Tel label has 11 recordings from the same number of female jazz singers. Unfortunately the budget release does not list personnel or recording dates (inexcusable omissions) and most of the music is available elsewhere. Sarah Vaughan, June Christy, Dakota Staton ("The Late Late Show"), Billie Holiday ("God Bless the Child"), Anita O'Day, Gloria Lynne ("I Wish You Love"), Peggy Lee, Nancy Wilson, Dinah Washington, the unknown Kitty Lester and Carmen McRae are all heard from. —Scott Yanow

Great Ladies of Jazz, Vol. 2 / K-Tel ✦✦
The second of two CDs in this K-Tel series has one song apiece from ten different female jazz-oriented singers. The lack of a per-

sonnel or date listing is inexcusable and all of the music is readily available elsewhere. Still, if found at a budget price, the release might be worth picking up since it does have music from Ella Fitzgerald, Peggy Lee ("Fever"), Sarah Vaughan, Anita O'Day, Carmen McRae, Julie London ("Cry Me a River"), Dinah Washington, Billie Holiday, Morgana King and an out-of-place Nancy Wilson. —Scott Yanow

The Greatest Jazz Concert in the World / Mar. 26, 1967+Jul. 1, 1967 / Pablo ✦✦✦✦✦
In addition to having a somewhat immodest title, this three-CD set was not actually one single concert but two. That reservation aside, the music on the reissue is often quite special. There is a jam session in the Jazz at the Philharmonic vein with fluegelhornist Clark Terry, altoist Benny Carter, the tenors of Zoot Sims and Paul Gonsalves and the Oscar Peterson Trio with the all stars playing a ballad medley and heated runthroughs of a few familiar standards. In addition the Oscar Peterson Trio has a few features, an aging Coleman Hawkins does what he can on two numbers, Hawk teams up with altoists Benny Carter and Johnny Hodges on "C Jam Blues" and special guest T-Bone Walker sings and plays a couple of blues with assists from C.T., Gonsalves, Hodges and Peterson. But that's not all. The Duke Ellington Orchestra is in prime form performing a great deal of new material plus having guest spots for Sims (along with fellow tenors Gonsalves and Jimmy Hamilton on "Very Tenor"), Oscar Peterson (who gets to lead the band through a unique version of "Take the 'A' Train) and Carter; Johnny Hodges is also well-showcased. Ella Fitgerald completes the memorable set with her usual classy performance (accompanied by the Jimmy Jones Trio and sometimes the Ellington Orchestra), finishing the show with some hot scatting on "Cotton Tail." Maybe this really was "the Greatest Jazz Concert" after all. —Scott Yanow

Greenwich Village Jazz / Sep. 29, 1944–Jan. 5, 1945 / Pickwick ✦✦✦
One of six Pickwick CDs drawn from the mid-'40s Black & White catalog, this set has a lot of valuable swing and Dixieland-oriented performances. Clarinetist Barney Bigard leads two dates, one with trumpeter Joe Thomas and tenorman George Auld and the other one with Thomas, a tenor player by the same name and the great pianist Art Tatum. Pianist Willie "The Lion" Smith heads a spirited Dixieland set with trumpeter Max Kaminsky and clarinetist Rod Cless while pianist Cliff Jackson's Village Cats is a particularly impressive group with trumpeter Sidney DeParis, trombonist Wilbur DeParis, Gene Sedric on tenor and the unique Sidney Bechet on soprano. There is plenty of enjoyable music on this easily recommended set. —Scott Yanow

Greenwich Village Sound / Nov. 29, 1944–Jan. 12, 1945 / Pickwick ✦✦✦✦
Of the six Pickwick CD reissues drawn from the Black & White catalog of the mid-'40s, this one is the most valuable. Clarinetist Joe Marsala leads ten of the 14 performances. The first six songs feature his septet with trumpeter Joe Thomas and the brilliant jazz harpist Adele Girard who happily has a fair amount of solo space. However, it is the other four selections that really grab one's attention for the swing-oriented Marsala is matched with stride pianist Cliff Jackson and bebop innovator and trumpeter Dizzy Gillespie. On "My Melancholy Baby" all three of the stylists are heard in uncompromising fashion first in individual solos and then (much too briefly) battling it out in a unique ensemble. This CD is rounded out by singer Etta Jones (backed by a Barney Bigard combo) interpreting four blues from Dinah Washington's repertoire. This is a highly recommended set. —Scott Yanow

A GRP Artists' Celebration Of The Songs Of The Beatles / 1995 / GRP ✦✦

The Guitar Album / Aug. 14, 1971 / Columbia ✦✦✦✦
This double LP has a lot of interesting performances from a Town Hall concert that puts the emphasis on a variety of guitarists. Charlie Byrd, Joe Beck and Chuck Wayne are featured in trios, swing stylist Tiny Grimes has a rare opportunity to record, Bucky Pizzarelli and George Barnes team up for some delightful duets and John McLaughlin (who is a bit out of place) backs his wife Eve's vocal. This set is now a collector's item and is worth searching for. —Scott Yanow

The Guitarists / 1927–Oct. 1, 1941 / Time Life ✦✦✦✦
Despite its title, this three-LP boxed set from Time Life focuses only on jazz guitarists up to and including Charlie Christian, but

it does a definitive job. Eddie Lang (six songs including a duet with fellow guitarist Carl Kress), Django Reinhardt (six), Oscar Aleman (one), Charlie Christian (six), Lonnie Johnson (five including a duet with Lang), Bernard Addison (two), Teddy Bunn (three), Dick McDonough (two), Eddie Durham (two), Carmen Mastren (two), Carl Kress (two), George Van Eps (one) and Al Casey (two) are all featured in a wide variety of settings ranging from unaccompanied solos to large bands. The swing-oriented music is often classic, some of the performances are fairly rare and the 56-page booklet is excellent. This is one of the best of the Time Life jazz reissues but long out of print. —*Scott Yanow*

Halloween Stomp / May 21, 1929–1950 / Jass ✦✦✦
This collection of "spooky" performances is dominated by songs dealing with ghosts and monsters, everything from "Mysterious Mose" and "Got the Jitters" to "Zombie," "Skeleton in the Closet," "The Ghost of Smokey Joe" and "With Her Head Tucked Underneath Her Arm." Most of the music is from the swing era with such bands as those led by Red Nichols, Don Redman, Glen Gray, Louis Prima, Ozzie Nelson, Cab Calloway, Tommy Dorsey and even Rudy Vallee alternating with much more obscure groups. The producers at Jass have also "enhanced" the music by inserting odd sound effects between songs. This CD certainly qualifies as the definitive (and also only) Halloween jazz album. —*Scott Yanow*

Happy Anniversary Charlie Brown / 1987 / GRP ✦✦✦
The 40th anniversary of the Charlie Brown comic strip is celebrated on this 1987 CD by performances of songs used on the cartoon series (most of which were originally composed by Vince Guaraldi). A variety of artists participated in the project including David Benoit, B.B. King (singing "Joe Cool"), Dave Grusin, Chick Corea ("The Great Pumpkin Waltz"), Joe Williams, Gerry Mulligan, Lee Ritenour, Patti Austin and even Kenny G ("Breadline Blues") and Dave Brubeck ("Benjamin"). The results are pleasing if lightweight. —*Scott Yanow*

Highlights In Jazz / 1985 / Stash ✦✦✦
Jack Kleinsinger's series of concerts titled *Highlights In Jazz* gave New Yorkers an opportunity to see swing-oriented veteran all stars in fresh settings. Performances from his 12th-anniversary concert comprise this interesting LP which has features for clarinetist Phil Bodner ("After You've Gone"), singer Carrie Smith, pianist Marty Napoleon, tenor saxophonist Loren Schoenberg and multi-instrumentalist Glenn Zottola. However it is trumpeter Doc Cheatham, who is heard on "Sweet Georgia Brown" and a delightful version of "You're Lucky to Me," who takes honors. —*Scott Yanow*

Hill & Dale Rarities / Oct. 2, 1924–Jun. 1, 1928 / IAJRC ✦✦✦
Thomas Edison was a genius but he did not care much for jazz. His Edison label did not record much jazz before the company folded in 1929; many of the more interesting examples are included on this IAJRC LP. The music ranges from jazz to dance music and blues with performances from the Charleston Seven (which includes cornetist Red Nichols and trombonist Miff Mole), singers Josie Miles, Rosa Henderson and Viola McCoy and such bands as those led by Ross Gorman, B.A. Rolfe and Joe Herlihy. Interesting music, it's worth checking out by '20s collectors. —*Scott Yanow*

★ **History of Classic Jazz** / May 1921–Dec. 1953 / Riverside ✦✦✦✦✦
This three-CD reissue of an earlier Riverside five-LP set gives listeners a perfect introduction to early jazz. The 60 selections are divided into ten categories: Backgrounds (including African music, a sermon and marching music), Ragtime (both piano rolls and solo recordings), Blues, New Orleans Style, Boogie Woogie, South Side Chicago, Chicago Style, Harlem, New York Style and New Orleans Revival. The performances contain many highlights (nearly every selection is a gem) and, although emphasizing the 1920s, they do not neglect later developments in Dixieland. The informative booklet is also a major asset. It's a highly recommended acquisition even to collectors who may already have the majority of these recordings. —*Scott Yanow*

Homemade Jam, Vol. 1 / Nov. 19, 1935–Jul. 2, 1936 / World ✦✦✦✦
Virtually no English musician could make a living during the 1930s from playing exclusively jazz but fortunately quite a few had opportunities to record it. On the first of two LPs put out by the English World label (a subsidiary of EMI), there are 18 selections from 1935–36 featuring such interesting soloists as violinist

Hugo Rignold, trumpeters Norman Payne and Duncan Whyte, trombonist Lew Davis, clarinetist Jack Miranda, tenorman Buddy Featherstonaugh and Freddy Gardner (who played clarinet, alto and baritone). The repertoire is primarily American swing standards and these now somewhat forgotten players acquit themselves quite well. Highly recommended to swing collectors. —*Scott Yanow*

Homemade Jam, Vol. 2 / Sep. 19, 1936–Jan. 24, 1938 / World ✦✦✦✦
The second of two LPs released by the British label World in the late '70s continues reissuing some of the best jazz recordings cut in England during the mid-to-late '30s. This generous album has 20 selections (an hour of music) and features such strong soloists as Freddy Gardner (on clarinet, alto, tenor and baritone), trumpeter Duncan Whyte, trombonist George Chisholm and violinist Eric Siday among others. This rare music (primarily Dixieland and swing standards) is consistently enjoyable and full of surprises including a version of "Tiger Rag" featuring the violins of Eric Siday and Reg Leopold. Both of the valuable *Homemade Jam* sets are highly recommended to collectors of '30s jazz. —*Scott Yanow*

★ **Hot British Dance Bands** / Oct. 7, 1925–Jul. 8, 1937 / Timeless ✦✦✦✦✦
When one thinks of British music of the '30s, it is of polite society dance bands and sappy vocalists. This 22-song CD gives one a very different picture of the scene overseas. Twenty-two different bands (including those led by Fred Elizalde, Jack Hylton, Spike Hughes, Billy Cotton, Ray Noble and Ambrose) are represented by some of their hottest recordings. The music ranges from Dixieland-oriented tracks to sophisticated swing and, whether it be the Devonshire Restaurant Dance Band's rendition of "Sugar Foot Stomp," the Rhythm Maniacs' "That's a Plenty" or Ambrose's classic "Cotton Pickers' Congregation," this is a historic and very enjoyable reissue, made available by the Dutch Timeless label. Highly recommended to fans of swing who are tired of hearing the same familiar bands all the time. —*Scott Yanow*

Hot Jazz for Cool Nights / Sep. 12, 1990–Jun. 29, 1992 / Music Masters ✦✦✦
A cross-section of top musicians who have recorded for Music Masters are heard on these 14 Christmas-related songs, including Vincent Herring, Jim Hall, Loren Schoenberg, Marvin Stamm, Dave Brubeck ("We Three Kings"), Stanley Turrentine, Kenny Davern (jamming "Jingle Bells" in a duet with Howard Alden), the Vanguard Jazz Sextet, Benny Carter (playing "A Child Is Born" while backed by Hank Jones), Jack Wilkins, Eastern Rebellion, Dick Hyman (a solo "White Christmas"), Rebecca Parris and Louie Bellson. A happy and swinging Yuletide collection of Christmas jazz. —*Scott Yanow*

I Like Jazz / 1926–Oct. 13, 1954 / Columbia ✦✦✦
Many listeners were introduced to jazz through this well-conceived sampler LP from the late '50s. The dozen selections range from the ragtime of Wally Rose and the blues of Bessie Smith through the various forms of Dixieland and swing. Oddly enough bop is bypassed but there is "Progressive Jazz" from Pete Rugolo and "Modern Jazz" from Dave Brubeck. A much more recent *I Like Jazz* Columbia set on CD has a completely different program that is much less memorable. —*Scott Yanow*

In Performance At The Playboy Jazz Festival / Jun. 1982 / Elektra Musician ✦✦✦
The Playboy Jazz Festival was established as a yearly institution in Los Angeles in 1979. This double LP, the only recordings thus far to emanate from the marathon two-day festival, has some of the highlights from the 1982 edition. "Pieces of a Dream" (tackling "Take the 'A' Train" and "Pop Rock") are in above average form and Grover Washington, Jr., pleases the crowd with "Winelight." Tenor-great Dexter Gordon (in a quintet with trumpeter Woody Shaw) performs a pair of fine numbers, Weather Report romps on "Volcano for Hire" and is joined by Manhattan Transfer for a smoldering version of "Birdland." The Art Farmer/Bennie Golson Quintet is fine on five numbers although Nancy Wilson (who guests) is out-of-place. This two-fer concludes with three performances from an all-star quartet comprised of trumpeter Freddie Hubbard, pianist McCoy Tyner, bassist Ron Carter and drummer Elvin Jones. It is surprising that this well-rounded set has not yet been reissued on CD. —*Scott Yanow*

Jam Session in Swingville / Apr. 14, 1961+May 19, 1961 / Prestige ✦✦✦
This single CD has all of the music reissued in the mid-'70s on a

two-LP set. Although sometimes issued under the names of Coleman Hawkins and Pee Wee Russell, the two great jazzmen actually do not appear together. The music in general (which is performed by two all-star groups with arrangements by either Jimmy Hamilton or Al Sears) is modern swing. Hawkins' band is comprised of trumpeter Joe Newman, trombonist J.C. Higginbotham, clarinetist Hamilton, altoist Hilton Jefferson and a four-piece rhythm section, pianist Cliff Jackson plays "I Want to Be Happy" and clarinetist Russell's outfit also features trumpeter Joe Thomas, trombonist Vic Dickenson and both Al Sears and Buddy Tate on tenors. Nothing all that memorable or innovative occurs but the performances are enjoyable. — *Scott Yanow*

The Jam Sessions / Jul. 13, 1977–Jul. 14, 1977 / Pablo ✦✦✦✦
Norman Granz and his Pablo label took over a large part of the 1977 Montreux Jazz Festival (as they had done in 1975) and there were quite a few albums released that documented his all-star groups caught live and in spontaneous form. This double LP (six of the nine selections have since been issued as a single CD with the same title) has performances not included on the other albums. A who's who of veteran jazz greats are heard from including trumpeters Dizzy Gillespie, Clark Terry, Jon Faddis and Roy Eldridge, tenors Eddie "Lockjaw" Davis, Zoot Sims and Ronnie Scott, altoist Benny Carter, trombonists Vic Dickenson and Al Grey, pianists Oscar Peterson, Count Basie and Monty Alexander, guitarist Joe Pass, bassists Niels Pedersen and Ray Brown, and drummers Bobby Durham and Jimmie Smith. The tunes they perform (in five overlapping groups) are generally fairly basic, but the playing has its share of surprising moments and this two-fer gives one a strong overview of the Pablo label in the 1970s. — *Scott Yanow*

The Jam Sessions: Montreux '77 / Jul. 13, 1977–Jul. 14, 1977 / Original Jazz Classics ✦✦✦
This is a rare case where the CD reissue is inferior to the original LP. Put out in 1977 as a double LP that included nine performances from five different all-star groups playing at that year's Montreux Jazz Festival, this single CD just has six of the selections (the remaining tracks have been reissued as "bonus cuts" on other reissues). However what is here is excellent. There are bands headed by pianist Oscar Peterson, vibraphonist Milt Jackson with co-leader bassist Ray Brown, Dizzy Gillespie (teaming up with his protege Jon Faddis) and Count Basie in addition to one called the Pablo All-Stars; among the sidemen are trumpeters Clark Terry and Roy Eldridge, the tenors of Eddie "Lockjaw" Davis, Zoot Sims and Ronnie Scott, altoist Benny Carter, trombonists Vic Dickenson and Al Grey, guitarist Joe Pass and pianist Monty Alexander. There are lots of fine solos on these fairly basic tunes but get the original double LP if possible. — *Scott Yanow*

James Moody/Frank Foster In Paris / Jul. 13, 1951–Apr. 4, 1954 / Vogue ✦✦✦
On this Vogue CD there are three different sessions, none of which have been available domestically in many years. James Moody plays alto with a French quintet (which includes trumpeter Roger Guerin and pianist Raymond Fol) on six standards and two of his originals; "This Is Always" and "That's My Desire" are particularly memorable. Moody is also heard doubling on tenor and alto while backed by a string section on six French melodies. The emphasis is on ballads and there is little on that date to grab one's attention. This CD concludes with a 1954 hard bop set from tenor Frank Foster in which he is backed by a quiet French trio led by pianist Henri Renaud. Overall this is a CD that bop collectors will want because unlike many of the Vogue reissues, this music did not appear on the American Inner City label in the 1970s. — *Scott Yanow*

The Jazz Age/New York In The Twenties / Feb. 11, 1927–Oct. 7, 1930 / Bluebird ✦✦✦✦✦
Although other releases cover this music in greater depth, this is an excellent CD filled with some classic (if generally overlooked) performances from the late '20s. Red and Miff's Stompers (a sextet/septet with cornetist Red Nichols, trombonist Miff Mole and either Jimmy Dorsey or Pee Wee Russell on clarinet) perform six complex and unpredictable numbers, the Ben Pollack Orchestra gives some future-greats (clarinetist Benny Goodman, cornetist Jimmy McPartland and trombonist Glenn Miller) a few early opportunities to solo, Phil Napoleon's Emperors from 1929 feature the Dorsey Brothers and violinist Joe Venuti, and Venuti stars on four numbers with his own groups. This enjoyable set gives proof

(if it were needed) that '20s jazz was not all Dixieland. — *Scott Yanow*

Jazz Arranger, Vol. 1 (1928–1940) / 1928–1940 / Columbia ✦✦✦
A good overview of early jazz sides and the arrangers who made them work for such groups as the Dorseys, Cab Calloway, and Ellington. —Ron Wynn

Jazz Arranger, Vol. 2 (1946–1963) / 1945–1970 / Columbia ✦✦✦
A variety of odds and ends are tossed together in this sampler which inexcusably leaves off specific recording dates and personnel. Some of the selections (Neal Hefti's chart of "The Good Earth" for Woody Herman, Gerry Mulligan's "How High the Moon" for Gene Krupa and Oliver Nelson's "Trinkle Tinkle" for a Thelonious Monk big-band date) are common while some of the others (such as George Russell's "All About Rosie" and John Lewis' "Three Little Feelings") have otherwise been long out-of-print. Excellent music, dumb packaging. — *Scott Yanow*

● **Jazz at Santa Monica Civic '72** / Aug. 2, 1972 / Pablo ✦✦✦✦✦
The Pablo label (and Norman Granz's return as a full-time producer) was launched with this wonderful package, first released as a three-LP set and now available as a three-CD reissue. The 1972 concert was originally supposed to only feature the Count Basie Orchestra and Ella Fitzgerald but Granz surprised everyone by inviting some "guests": trumpeters Roy Eldridge and Harry "Sweets" Edison, the tenors of Stan Getz and Eddie "Lockjaw" Davis, pianist Oscar Peterson and bassist Ray Brown! Together with Basie-trombonist Al Grey they formed the Jazz at the Philharmonic All-Stars and play wonderfully on three jams (listen to Elridge's break on "In a Mellow Tone") and a ballad medley. In addition there are four selections from Basie's band (featuring the tenor of Jimmy Forrest, trumpeter Pete Minger and altoist Curtis Peagler), a full set from Fitzgerald and a Peterson-Brown duet on "You Are My Sunshine." The high point of the concert however is the final song, a classic version of "C Jam Blues" which finds Fitzgerald trading off in very humorous fashion with Grey, Getz, Sweets, Lockjaw and Eldridge; each of the encounters has at least one remarkable moment. This gem is highly recommended. — *Scott Yanow*

Jazz Band Ball / Dec. 24, 1947–May 5, 1951 / Good Time Jazz ✦✦✦✦
Four different New Orleans jazz bands are heard from on three or four selections apiece on this CD, a straight reissue of the original LP; none of the music is available elsewhere. Clarinetist George Lewis and his 1950 group (with Elmer Talbert on trumpet and the reliable trombonist Jim Robinson), Turk Murphy's 1947 band (recorded shortly after he left Lu Watters and featuring trumpeter Bob Scobey), trombonist Kid Ory's 1951 Creole Jazz Band (with trumpeter Teddy Buckner and clarinetist Joe Darensbourg) and the 1947 edition of trumpeter Pete Daily's Rhythm Kings are all in excellent form. This set offers listeners a good sampling of their work and, considering that Lewis, Murphy and Ory led three of the most popular traditional jazz bands of the 1950s (although each sounded quite different from each other), this CD is well worth picking up. — *Scott Yanow*

Jazz Classics in Digital Stereo, Vol. 1: New Orleans / Jul. 17, 1918–Sep. 12, 1934 / ABC ✦✦✦
As with the other CDs in the Robert Parker series, this release contains a variety of early jazz performances that have been enhanced to sound closer to stereo. The music is consistently enjoyable although programmed in an almost random fashion. There are selections from Jelly Roll Morton, King Oliver, Johnny Dodds, Louis Armstrong, Freddie Keppard, Oscar Celestin, the New Orleans Owls, Louis Dumaine's Jazzola Eight, the New Orleans Rhythm Kings, Red Allen, the Jones-Collins Astoria Hot Eight, Monk Hazel, Sidney Bechet and the Original Dixieland Jazz Band. Virtually all of the music is currently available elsewhere but listeners not already familiar with 1920s jazz will find this CD of interest. — *Scott Yanow*

Jazz Classics in Digital Stereo, Vol. 2: Chicago / Sep. 17, 1926–Sep. 12, 1934 / ABC ✦✦✦
All of the CDs in the BBC Robert Parker series (which has been made available at times through different sources) contain remastered and sonically improved recordings from the early days of jazz. Unfortunately the 20 selections on this set are rather randomly programmed and, although this set has a few rare items (such as Richard M. Jones' "African Hunch," the Mound City Blue Blowers' "What Do I Care What Somebody Said," and Omer

Simeon's "Beau Koo Jack"), there are also many familiar recordings (including Jelly Roll Morton's "Sidewalk Blues," Frankie Trumbauer's "Singin' the Blues" and Earl Hines' "Maple Leaf Rag") that are easily available elsewhere. It's a good acquisition for newcomers to early jazz. —*Scott Yanow*

Jazz Classics in Digital Stereo, Vol. 3: New York / May 29, 1925–Aug. 26, 1935 / ABC ✦✦✦
On the third of four CDs in the Robert Parker series that reissues a cross section of early jazz recordings from a regional area, the music ranges from the famous (Jelly Roll Morton, Fletcher Henderson, Bessie Smith and Duke Ellington) to the lesser known (Charlie Johnson's Paradise Ten, Lloyd Scott and Freddy Jenkins). Veteran collectors will prefer to skip this sampler and get the complete sessions elsewhere but listeners just beginning to explore early jazz should find these early recordings (which range from pre-swing to some heated jams) worth investigating. —*Scott Yanow*

Jazz Classics in Digital Stereo, Vol. 4: Hot Town / Feb. 27, 1927–Dec. 4, 1933 / ABC ✦✦✦
This CD sampler in the Robert Parker series mostly features territory bands from cities other than New York, Chicago and New Orleans. Other than a selection apiece from Jimmie Lunceford (1930s "In Dat Mornin'"), Duke Ellington, Andy Kirk and Benny Moten, all of the groups are quite obscure (such as those led by Alonzo Ross, Charley Williamson, Troy Floyd and Slatz Randall), making this release of greater than usual interest although unfortunately complete sessions are not reissued. Excellent music most highly recommended to listeners who want a general sampling of early rarities. —*Scott Yanow*

A Jazz Gumbo 1 / Apr. 18, 1993+Apr. 21, 1993 / Jazz Crusade ✦✦✦
For this very spirited CD, trombonist Big Bill Bissonnette utilized 18 musicians (mostly obscure names other than clarinetist/altoist Sammy Rimington) in a variety of settings. The music is a rambunctious and often-erratic but always sincere variety of New Orleans jazz. Not everything works but listeners who enjoy classic jazz and do not mind tonal variations (not everyone is in tune at all times) will find the unusual set of interest. —*Scott Yanow*

Jazz In L.A.: The 1940s / Sep. 1, 1941–1949 / KLON ✦✦✦✦✦
This CD, issued by radio station KLON in anticipation of presenting the Hollywood Jazz Festival (a major event that never occurred due to the L.A. riots), will be a tough one to find but is worth the search. Most of its material (all recorded in Los Angeles in the 1940s) is extremely rare. Its contents include a medley from the play "Jump for Joy" that features Duke Ellington, Herb Jeffries, Ivie Anderson and Joe Turner, a jam from a broadcast by the Lee and Lester Young band, live performances by Cee Pee Johnson's Orchestra, Benny Carter's big band, Dizzy Gillespie with Charlie Parker, the Nat King Cole Trio, Howard McGhee's Sextet and Boyd Raeburn's Orchestra plus mostly obscure studio sides by Lucky Thompson, the orchestras of Gerald Wilson, Earle Spencer and Lyle Griffin, Teddy Edwards, Dexter Gordon with Wardell Gray ("The Chase") and Charles Mingus (in 1949). The program traces the evolution of bop in Los Angeles and nearly every selection is quite successful. Historic music that deserves much better distribution. —*Scott Yanow*

Jazz Ltd., Vol. 1 / Feb. 1949–1951 / Delmark ✦✦✦✦✦
Starting in 1947 and continuing throughout the 1950s, Bill Reinhardt and his wife Ruth ran Jazz Ltd, a Chicago club that served as a haven for Dixieland. Reinhardt (a fine clarinetist) led the house band, a unit that invariably left a spot open for guest artists. This Delmark CD features the Jazz Ltd. group on 13 selections with such all stars as soprano great Sidney Bechet, cornetist Muggsy Spanier, trumpeter Doc Evans, trombonist Miff Mole and pianist Don Ewell; the disc is rounded off by an informative five-minute interview with the Reinhardts from the 1960s. The freewheeling music is quite enjoyable; Dixieland fans are advised to pick up this exciting disc. —*Scott Yanow*

Jazz Piano / Apr. 1924–Jan. 1972 / Smithsonian ✦✦✦
This four-CD boxed set attempts to trace the history of jazz piano through 68 recordings by 42 pianists. Actually the avant-garde is largely ignored (with no examples of the playing of Cecil Taylor, Paul Bley or Don Pullen) but otherwise the various acoustic styles are fairly well covered, even with the absence of Ralph Sutton and Dick Wellstood. One can argue with the individual choices but the music is generally quite excellent. There are one or two selections

from each of these players: Jelly Roll Morton, James P. Johnson, Willie "the Lion" Smith, Fats Waller, Earl Hines (who gets four songs), Teddy Wilson, Jimmy Yancey, Meade Lux Lewis, Pete Johnson, Avery Parrish, Count Basie, Billy Kyle, Mary Lou Williams, Art Tatum (five performances), Duke Ellington, Jess Stacy, Nat King Cole, Erroll Garner, Jimmy Jones, Bud Powell, Lennie Tristano, Dodo Marmarosa, Ellis Larkins, Dave McKenna, Al Haig, Oscar Peterson, Jimmy Rowles, Thelonious Monk, Phineas Newborn, Jr., Horace Silver, Martial Solal, Herbie Nichols, Hank Jones, Tommy Flanagan, John Lewis, Randy Weston, Ray Bryant, Bill Evans, McCoy Tyner, Chick Corea, Keith Jarrett and Herbie Hancock. —*Scott Yanow*

★ **Jazz Scene** / Mar. 1946–Feb. 4, 1955 / Verve ✦✦✦✦✦
In 1949 producer Norman Granz released a remarkable album of 78s that consisted of a dozen selections (many of them specially recorded for the occasion) that perfectly summed up the modern jazz scene of the time. The deluxe set consisted of two Duke Ellington features for baritonist Harry Carney with strings, a pair of complex Neal Hefti arrangements, small-group sides by Lester Young, Charlie Parker, Bud Powell and altoist Willie Smith, Machito's "Tanga," major works by arrangers Ralph Burns and George Handy and, as the piece-de-resistance, Coleman Hawkins' pioneering unaccompanied tenor solo "Picasso." Now all of this music has been reissued on a very attractive double-CD set that also contains five alternate takes plus three previously unknown Billy Strayhorn piano solos, further examples of Lester Young and Willie Smith, an obscure Hawkins session with J.J. Johnson from 1949, a few numbers from a forgotten Flip Phillips session and three selections by Ralph Burns in 1955, two of which feature explosive trumpet work from Roy Eldridge. The new packaging is magnificent with many Gjon Mili photographs of the top jazzmen of the era and extensive liner notes. This was one of the top reissues of 1994 and is essential for all serious historical jazz collections. —*Scott Yanow*

Jazz Sketches on Sondheim / Sony ✦✦✦
With so few major composers still alive by the mid-'90s, it was logical that jazz musicians would try to expand their repertoire by exploring the works of non-jazz writers. None of Stephen Sondheim's compositions have thus far become jazz standards but that may change after the release of this CD. Three of the tracks unfortunately feature vocals by the overdramatic Nancy Wilson and the R&Bish Peabo Bryson but Holly Cole (on two numbers) fares much better. The most interesting moments are provided by the all-star musicians which include such players as tenors Joshua Redman and Grover Washington, Jr., guitarist Jim Hall, pianist Herbie Hancock, Wayne Shorter on soprano and trumpeter Terence Blanchard among others. Sondheim himself makes a guest appearance in a piano duet with Hancock on "They Ask Me Why I Believe in You." And best of all, there is no version here of "Send in the Clowns." This varied set has its memorable performances. —*Scott Yanow*

Jazz at Lincoln Center Presents: The Fire of The Fundamentals / Aug. 8, 1991–Feb. 14, 1993 / Columbia ✦✦✦
This CD, which actually features The Lincoln Center Jazz Orchestra on only two selections, has highlights from a variety of concerts held at Lincoln Center during 1991-93. A fine octet with clarinetist Michael White, trumpeter Wynton Marsalis and pianist Marcus Roberts do an effective re-interpretation of Jelly Roll Morton's "Jungle Blues," pianist Kenny Barron strides enthusiastically on a solo version of Thelonious Monk's "Trinkle Tinkle" and Jimmy Heath's soprano playing is showcased on "Ellington's Stray-Horn." Pianist/vocalist Jay McShann recreates "Hootie Blues," pianist Marcus Roberts romps through Monk's "Bolivar Blues" and then "Dahomey Dance" offers particularly strong solos from a septet with Marsalis and tenorman Todd Williams. Betty Carter sings a spacey version of "You're Mine You," Marcus Roberts returns for a solo rendition of Morton's "The Crave," Marsalis' Sextet interprets Miles Davis' moody "Flamenco Sketches" and vocalist Milt Grayson finishes the CD anti-climactically with the ballad "Multi Colored Blue." It's an interesting if not essential set with plenty of variety and many worthwhile performances. —*Scott Yanow*

Jazz at the Hollywood Bowl / Aug. 15, 1956 / Verve ✦✦✦✦
This double LP was the first jazz concert ever recorded at the Hollywood Bowl (and only the second one held at that L.A. institution). Although not an official Jazz at the Philharmonic concert, it has the same basic format and was also produced by Norman

Granz. Trumpeters Roy Eldridge and Harry "Sweets" Edison, tenors Flip Phillips and Illinois Jacquet, the Oscar Peterson Trio and drummer Buddy Rich all jam on "Honeysuckle Rose" and "Jumpin' at the Woodside," and there is also a ballad medley and a drum solo by Rich. In addition the Oscar Peterson Trio plays two numbers, the remarkable pianist Art Tatum (in one of his final appearances) has four, Ella Fitzgerald sings six songs (including a scat-filled "Airmail Special") and collaborates with Louis Armstrong on two others. For the grand finale nearly everyone returns to the stage for "When the Saints Go Marching In" which Armstrong sings and largely narrates, cheerfully introducing all of the participants. This is a historic and very enjoyable release featuring more than its share of classic greats. —*Scott Yanow*

Jazz at the Pawnshop, Vol. 1 / Dec. 6-7, 1976 / Proprius ✦✦✦✦
Jazz at the Pawnshop Vol. 2 / Dec. 6, 1976 / Proprius ✦✦✦✦
Jazz at the Pawnshop, Vol. 3 / Dec. 7, 1976 / Proprius ✦✦✦✦
Jazz at the Pawnshop, Vol. 4 / Dec. 6-7, 1976 / Proprius ✦✦✦✦
★ **Jazz in the Thirties** / Feb. 28, 1933–Dec. 13, 1935 / Disques Swing ✦✦✦✦✦
There is a great deal of remarkable music included on this two-hour two-CD set. Among the 40 selections (all dating from the early years of swing) are sessions led by violinist Joe Venuti, bass saxophonist Adrian Rollini, Benny Goodman (in an all-star group with trombonist Jack Teagarden), Bud Freeman, trumpeter Bunny Berigan, Gene Krupa and piano solos by Joe Sullivan and Jess Stacy. The recording sessions are all complete and the music is quite rewarding and often very exciting. It's highly recommended as is the companion set *Ridin' in Rhythm*. —*Scott Yanow*

Jazznost / 1989 / Mapleshade ✦✦✦✦
Jazz has long since ceased to be an exclusively American music; top-flight foreign musicians live in all corners of the world, so no one should be surprised that there are some in what used to be the Soviet Union. This 1989 affair linked the talents of gifted pianist Walter Davis, Jr., and exciting drummer Bobby Battle with expert Russian improvisers, the best of whom turns out to be saxophonist Igor Butman. They handle some songs ("Blue 'N Green") better than others ("Blue Monk"), but do everything with sufficient cohesion, showing that music remains the universal language. —*Ron Wynn*

The John Reid Collection 1940–1944 / Jun. 17, 1940–Jun. 24, 1944 / American Music ✦✦
This is a very unusual CD which will be of greatest interest to collectors of New Orleans jazz of the Bunk Johnson variety. A radio broadcast from 1944 features trumpeter Peter Bocage and the clarinets of Big Eye Louis Nelson and Alphone Picou in a septet. In addition there are two piano solos from Burnell Santiago, a "talking record" from 1944 (in which one can hear the voices of Sidney Bechet, Manuel Perez, Nelson, Picou and Santiago), a couple of unaccompanied Bechet solos, his "Message to Bunk" in which he urges the veteran trumpeter to come up north and a 1940 performance by clarinetist George Bacquet in a small group; Bechet guests on one selection. This is a very historical (if "low-fi") release that fills a few gaps in the story of the New Orleans jazz revival. —*Scott Yanow*

The Joy Of Christmas Past / 1948–1968 / GRP ✦✦✦
The Christmas jazz recordings heard on this varied sampler CD are drawn from the catalogs of ABC-Paramount, Decca, Chess and Argo. Such artists as Louis Armstrong (how did "What a Wonderful World" become a Xmas song?), Les Brown, Mel Torme, Ramsey Lewis, Peggy Lee, Kenny Burrell, Ahmad Jamal, Al Hibbler, Duke Ellington ("Silent Night") and Gene Ammons are heard from and, even with the emphasis on ballads, this is a well-rounded set. —*Scott Yanow*

Krupa & Rich / May 16, 1955+Nov. 1, 1955 / Verve ✦✦✦✦
Although drummers Gene Krupa and Buddy Rich are pictured together on this CD's cover, they actually only play together on one selection, a lengthy "Bernie's Tune." The first five performances (with two songs apiece for Rich and Krupa) also feature short solos from trumpeters Dizzy Gillespie and Roy Eldridge, tenors Flip Phillips and Illinois Jacquet and pianist Oscar Peterson; Rich is reasonably restrained on his numbers but has his explosive moments. "Bernie's Tune" is far superior to the in-concert Rich/Krupa drum battles that were recorded at other times. The final two performances find Rich leading a different all-star group with consistently excellent solos from trumpeters Thad Jones and Joe Newman and tenors Ben Webster and Frank

Wess. This swinging set (which contains formerly rare recordings) is easily recommended to fans of straight-ahead and bop-oriented jazz. —*Scott Yanow*

Last Night When We Were Young / 1994 / Classical Action ✦✦✦✦
Pianist Fred Hersch organized this jazz project, a fundraiser in the fight against AIDS. All 13 performances are ballads and some of them (most notably Jane Ira Bloom's rendition of "In the Wee Small Hours") are quite touching. In addition to Hersch and Bloom, such artists as altoist Bobby Watson, the late pianist Dave Catney, vibraphonist Gary Burton, Toots Thielemans on harmonica, vocalists Janis Siegel and Mark Murphy, pianist George Shearing and Phil Woods (heard here on clarinet) all get to make contributions. The mood is consistently melancholy but rarely downbeat, superior music recorded for a noble cause. —*Scott Yanow*

The Legendary Big Band Singers / Mar. 3, 1931–Jan. 24, 1951 / GRP/Decca ✦✦
Twenty-one different singers from the swing era are mostly heard backed by big bands on this interesting but not essential sampler. Generally the performances give one a good idea as to the vocalist's abilities (such as Cab Calloway's "Minnie the Moocher," Louis Armstrong's "Thanks a Million," Jimmy Rushing's "Sent for You Yesterday" and Sister Rosetta Tharpe's "Trouble in Mind") and some of the singers (particularly June Richmond, Bon Bon, and Ella Johnson who is heard on the original version of "Since I Fell for You") deserve the recognition. On the minus side, the decision not to list the personnel of the many orchestras may lead one to wonder who is playing various tenor, trumpet and piano solos, information that should have been provided. —*Scott Yanow*

Live At Newport 1960 / Jul. 1960 / Omega ✦✦✦
The music is predictable but pleasing on this consistent CD, recorded at the 1960 Newport Jazz Festival. Cannonball Adderley's Quintet (with trumpeter Nat Adderley) swings hard on "Work Song" and "Stay on It," Gerry Mulligan's Concert Jazz Band sounds fine on three songs (although this version of "Blueport" does not quite compare to Mulligan's classic match up with fluegelhornist Clark Terry), the Oscar Peterson Trio jams two numbers and Dizzy Gillespie's three song miniset is highlighted by "Night in Tunisia." Nothing that unusual occurs in any of the performances but the playing is up-to-par and occasionally exciting. —*Scott Yanow*

Live At The Festival / 1970–1973 / Enja ✦✦✦
This very interesting CD contains four unrelated performances from three editions of Yugoslavia's Ljubljana Jazz Festival. The Bill Evans Trio (with bassist Eddie Gomez and a slightly out-of-place Tony Oxley on drums) plays "Nardis," "'Round Midnight" is explored by the duo of Karin Krog (who half-speaks her vocal) and bassist Arild Andersen, tenor saxophonist Archie Shepp and his quintet romp through the uptempo blues "Sonny's Back" in fairly straight-ahead if ragged fashion and, best of all, the 1970 Bobby Hutcherson-Harold Land quintet explores an original in 7/8; Land in particular is outstanding. This CD offers listeners four examples of the jazz modern mainstream of the early '70s. —*Scott Yanow*

The Magnificent VII: Live At The Hilton / Dec. 6, 1992 / Arbors ✦✦✦
Arbors in the 1990s has become one of the top Dixieland labels around, generally focusing on all-star groups. This spirited set has an interesting cast of players: trumpeter Jon-Erik Kellson, trombonist Dan Barrett, clarinetist Chuck Hedges, Rick Fay on tenor and soprano, pianist Johnny Varro, bassist Bob Haggart and drummer Gene Estes. Together they romp through ten Dixieland and swing standards along with a lengthy "Blues for an Unknown Gypsy." Highlights include "Mandy, Make up Your Mind," "Sensation," and "Nobody's Sweetheart." Fans of these musicians and of trad jazz in particular are advised to get this fine CD. —*Scott Yanow*

Masters Of Regional Jazz / Feb. 1, 1935–Sep. 18, 1937 / Harrison ✦✦✦
With one exception (four numbers from a Clarence Williams led group from 1935 titled the Birmingham Serenaders) all of the music on this collectors' LP features bands from the South. The original Yellow Jackets (no relation to the Yellowjackets of the 1990s), Jimmy Luverte's Society Troubadours and Ted Mays' Band are long forgotten but two numbers from the Carolina Cotton

Pickers in 1937 are notable for being the recording debut of both trumpeter Cat Anderson and pianist Cliff Smalls. It's an interesting if now difficult-to-find LP that is recommended to specialists of the era. —*Scott Yanow*

Masters Of Regional Jazz, Vol. 2 / Jan. 29, 1935+Aug. 14, 1935 / Harrison ✦✦✦
Even collectors of 1930s jazz will be unfamiliar with the two San Antonio-based groups heard on this collectors' LP: the KXYZ Novelty Band and Joe Kennedy's Rhythm Orchestra. Both groups are two-horn sextets that mostly stick to swing and Dixieland standards of the era; none of the sidemen succeeded in becoming famous later on. This is interesting and rare music that is unlikely to be reissued on CD anytime soon. —*Scott Yanow*

Masters Of Regional Jazz, Vol. 3 / Jan. 2, 1931–Apr. 6, 1938 / Harrison ✦✦✦
Harrison's series of obscure and mostly unheard hot dance and jazz band recordings from the 1920s and '30s (which numbers around 25 LPs) includes three volumes in a miniseries of *Regional Jazz* recordings. Nine of the 16 recordings on this LP are by Boots and His Buddies, a spirited if sometimes out-of-tune San Antonio band; all of its music has since been reissued on CD. In addition there are five good numbers from the Original St. Louis Crackerjacks and a song apiece from Leon Rene's Orchestra and Williams' Purple Knights. The overall results are not too essential but collectors of the era's music who do not have the Boots sides elsewhere (and who can locate this hard-to-find album) may want to get the Harrison LP. —*Scott Yanow*

Mercury 40th Anniversary / Dec. 5, 1945–Mar. 27, 1965 / Mercury ✦✦✦✦
To celebrate its 40th birthday and revival, Mercury came up with this attractive and valuable four-LP box set which is comprised of material largely unreleased at the time. The performances (mostly from the 1950s) feature such greats as Erroll Garner, Arnett Cobb, Clark Terry, Dinah Washington, Paul Quinichette, Junior Mance, Paul Bley, Helen Merrill, Clifford Brown, John Williams, Herb Geller, Maynard Ferguson, Jimmy Cleveland, Cannonball Adderley, the Quincy Jones Orchestra, Billy Taylor, the Jazztet, Bob James (as an acoustic pianist in 1962) and Dizzy Gillespie. Some but not all of this material has resurfaced on CD, and virtually all of the music is quite enjoyable. —*Scott Yanow*

Metronome All-Stars 1956 / Jun. 26, 1956–Jul. 18, 1956 / Verve ✦✦✦
This LP features a variety of great jazz players (the 1956 Metronome All-Stars) performing together. Count Basie's Orchestra plays their hit "April in Paris" with Ella Fitzgerald in what was the first meeting on records between Basie and Fitzgerald. "Everyday I Have the Blues" not only has the duo but also Joe Williams, the orchestra goes solo on "Basie's Back in Town" and on "Party Blues" Basie and the two singers have fun with a small group taken from the big band. In addition George Wallington performs a piano solo ("Lady Fair") and a 21-minute "Billie's Bounce" has solos by an impressive assortment of individualists: trumpeter Thad Jones, altoist Lee Konitz, Al Cohn and Zoot Sims on tenors, clarinetist Tony Scott, baritonist Serge Chaloff, trombonist Eddie Bert, vibraphonist Teddy Cohen, guitarist Tal Farlow, pianist Billy Taylor, bassist Charles Mingus and drummer Art Blakey. This would be the final recording by the Metronome All-Stars (a series that started in the late '30s) and the music on this LP still sounds exciting and joyful. —*Scott Yanow*

The Mills Brothers—The Boswell Sisters—The Inkspots / SMS ✦✦✦
This is a budget CD from England but, despite the very chintzy playing time (under 35 minutes) and the lack of liner notes, personnel listing or even recording dates, collectors will want it. There are four selections apiece from the Mills Brothers, the Boswell Sisters and the Inkspots and these rare items are presumably taken from radio shows. While the Boswell Sisters are heard late in their career (around 1935 as shown by the inclusion of "The Music Goes Round and Round") and the Mills Brothers are featured doing their classic imitations of instruments ("Caravan" is a gem), the Inkspots are showcased before they found their ballad style, when they were a hot group that was closely emulating the Mills Brothers; "Christopher Columbus" and "With Plenty of Money and You" is the type of jazz-oriented material that they did not perform after hitting it big. This is a set for the group's greatest fans; hopefully the enjoyable music will be reissued in a more coherent form some day. —*Scott Yanow*

Milton Jazz Concert 1963 / Apr. 26, 1963 / IAJRC ✦✦✦
Released on CD by the collector's label IAJRC, this concert features an all-star frontline (cornetist Bobby Hackett, trombonist Vic Dickenson and clarinetist Edmond Hall) with a local rhythm section. Together they perform a blues, a ballad medley and ten hot Dixieland/swing standards (including "Struttin' with Some Barbecue," "Indiana," "Fidgety Feet" and "China Boy"). The recording quality is decent, all of the principals are in fine form and one can consider this to be a predecessor of the quintet that Hackett and Dickenson would co-lead at the tail-end of the decade. —*Scott Yanow*

Milton Jazz Concert 1964 / Apr. 24, 1964 / IAJRC ✦✦✦
For a concert put on in Milton, MA (and released for the first time on this 1995 CD), several classic jazz veterans were teamed with some solid local musicians for a variety of Dixieland standards. Trumpeter Yank Lawson, trombonist Vic Dickenson, clarinetist Edmond Hall and pianist Dick Wellstood appear in a sextet for four songs (highlighted by Dickenson's witty growls on "Basin Street Blues" and a spirited "Hello Dolly" while trumpeter Buck Clayton stars on four other warhorses. High points of the CD are on the two numbers ("At the Jazz Band Ball" and "Struttin' with Some Barbecue") on which the two bands are combined; in both cases Yank and Buck get to trade off hot phrases. It's a worthy release by the collector's club IAJRC. —*Scott Yanow*

New Orleans 1924–1925 / Mar. 15, 1924–Jan. 23, 1925 / Rhapsody ✦✦✦
This interesting LP has the first jazz records ever made in New Orleans. Okeh Records conducted two field trips (one during March 15–16, 1924 and the other during Jan. 22–23, 1925) and the results were excellent recordings by Johnny De Droit, two blues from singer Lola Bolden, disappointingly primitive performances by Fate Marable (his band's only two recordings), a pair of vaudevillian numbers from Billy & Mary Mack, one song apiece from Russ Papalia and the New Orleans Rhythm Kings and three fine numbers by Oscar Celestin's Original Tuxedo Jazz Orchestra. This worthy English import contains some music not yet reissued on CD. —*Scott Yanow*

New Orleans Collective / Dec. 28, 1992 / Evidence ✦✦✦✦
Trumpeter Nicholas Payton is teamed up with Wessell Anderson (who doubles on sopranino and alto), pianist Peter Martin, bassist Christopher Thomas and drummer Brian Blade for an unusual set of music that shifts between hard bop and New Orleans jazz. While "Rhonda Mile" (which uses the chord changes to "Indiana") is pure bop, other selections combine the two idioms and "Four or Five Times" (listed as an Anderson original but actually a standard from the 1920s) is strictly Dixieland. A high point is the 16-minute "He Was a Good Man, Oh Yes He Was" which musically depicts a New Orleans funeral. Throughout, Anderson (particularly on the sopranino which he plays like a clarinet) and Payton work together quite well in the exciting ensembles and show impressive knowlege of earlier forms of jazz while carving out their own individual voices. —*Scott Yanow*

New Orleans Jazz Giants: 1936–1940 / Jan. 15, 1936–Jun. 5, 1940 / JSP ✦✦✦✦
There are 26 recordings on this imported CD from the English JSP label. These interesting and often historical performances feature a variety of New Orleans veterans, particularly clarinetists Jimmie Noone and Johnny Dodds. Noone is heard on 14 performances including a session with trumpeter Guy Kelly and trombonist Preston Jackson, a particularly strong outing with trumpeter Charlie Shavers and altoist Pete Brown, and on two songs with a group that includes the erratic cornetist Natty Dominique. Dodds' final session uses the same Dominique group but his earlier sextet set with Shavers is much more rewarding. In addition there are two songs apiece from trumpeter Red Allen and drummer Zutty Singleton, both recorded the same day in 1940 with the identical personnel. In general the music is quite enjoyable and, Dominique excepted, the veterans and relative youngsters (Shavers was 20) play quite well. —*Scott Yanow*

New Orleans Trumpets / Nov. 1, 1950–May 16, 1954 / Storyville ✦✦✦
On ten LPs (and reissued as ten CDs), the European Storyville label came out with a variety of rare performances recorded in New Orleans during the 1950s. None of the 13 selections on this particular volume were included in the other entries in this series. The focus is very much on trumpeters and there are selections featuring Ernie Cagnolatti, Alvin Alcorn, Lee Collins, Papa

Celestin ("The Saints"), Percy Humphrey, Lee Collins, Johnny Wiggs (who gets two songs), Sharkey Bonano, George Hartman, the forgotten Johnny Bayersdorffer (who is unfortunately not in good shape), Sharkey Bonano and the ill-fated but talented George Girard. These mostly live and freewheeling performances (a few are previously unreleased alternate takes) are generally quite rewarding and easily recommended to lovers of New Orleans jazz. —*Scott Yanow*

The New Wave in Jazz / Mar. 28, 1965 / Impulse ✦✦✦
On March 28, 1965 several of the top "New Thing" artists who were then recording for Impulse performed at a heated concert at the Village Gate that was fully documented. This CD reissue adds two selections to the original LP while dropping an Albert Ayler performance that will be included in an Ayler reissue in the future. There is plenty of fire on the release including a searing version of "Nature Boy" from the John Coltrane Quartet, a workout on "Hambone" by tenor saxophonist Archie Shepp's Septet and two numbers apiece from trumpeter Charles Tolliver (with altoist James Spaulding) and trombonist Grachan Moncur III (with a young Bobby Hutcherson on vibes). Some of the performances are free and ferocious while other tracks are on the advanced side of bop. Over 30 years later the music still sounds adventurous and full of life. —*Scott Yanow*

New York Horns / Sep. 1924–Oct. 19, 1928 / Hot 'N Sweet ✦✦✦
This European import CD has a variety of rare early performances. Cornetist Bubber Miley is heard in his pre-Duke Ellington period performing four odd duets with organist Arthur Ray (under the title of the Texas Blue Destroyers) and jamming with the interesting if erratic Kansas City Five. In addition there are three numbers from the Blue Rhythm Orchestra (a sextet with trombonist Jimmy Harrison and clarinetist Buster Bailey), three titles by the similar Gulf Coast Seven (although its 1928 selection includes several Ellingtonians), three songs from the Five Musical Blackbirds (a quintet with cornetist Thomas Morris) and, best of all, two full numbers from the Roy Williams Band. Even for 1920s collectors this CD is not really essential but it does have its interesting moments. —*Scott Yanow*

New York Jazz In The Roaring Twenties / Apr. 16, 1926–Jan. 27, 1928 / Biograph ✦✦✦
This CD is subtitled "Tommy Dorsey—Red Nichols—Jimmy Dorsey" but in reality the Dorsey Brothers are only heard as sidemen. Included on the enjoyable set are four selections from Red & Miff's Stompers (co-led by cornetist Nichols and trombonist Miff Mole), seven selections by the California Ramblers, two featuring the obscure Joe Herlihy's Orchestra and one by Phil Napoleon. The music ranges from hot (if complicated) '20s jazz to some jazz-oriented dance music. An improvement on Biograph's LP of the same name (due to the inclusion of a couple of extra tracks), these performances (originally released by the Edison label) are longer than the usual recordings of the era, often over four (as opposed to three) minutes long. Fans of '20s jazz will want to get this one. —*Scott Yanow*

New York Stories / 1992 / Blue Note ✦✦✦✦
This interesting outing by an all-star group (guitarist Danny Gatton, altoist Bobby Watson, trumpeter Roy Hargrove, Joshua Redman on tenor, pianist Franck Amsallem, bassist Charles Fambrough and drummer Yuron Israel) is most notable for featuring the brilliant Gatton in a jazz setting. Together the septet performs nine originals by group members and Gatton and Watson emerge as the main solo stars. Despite its somewhat generic name, this advanced hard bop date is quite memorable. — *Scott Yanow*

Newport Jazz Festival: Live / Jul. 7, 1956–Jul. 7, 1963 / Columbia ✦✦✦✦
At the time of the release of this 1982 double LP, all of its performances (which are taken from the 1956, 1958 and 1963 Newport Jazz Festival) were previously unissued. Quite a variety of musicians are featured and most of the music is quite enjoyable. Louis Armstrong pops up in three different settings, Rex Stewart leads an all-star group comprised of Duke Ellington alumni and there are selections from Ellington himself, Ben Webster, Willie "The Lion" Smith, Jimmy Rushing, Benny Goodman, Teddy Wilson, Dave Brubeck, the Miles Davis Quintet with John Coltrane ("Bye Bye Blackbird"), Thelonious Monk, Sonny Stitt, Gerry Mulligan and three all-star groups that include the likes of Bud Freeman, Ruby Braff, Buck Clayton, Jack Teagarden, Pee Wee Russell, Lester Young and Coleman Hawkins. Since the music (with a few excep-

tions) has not yet been reissued on CD, this two-LP set (which will be hard to find) is quite valuable both musically and historically. —*Scott Yanow*

Obscure And Neglected Chicagoans / 1925–Dec. 21, 1929 / IAJRC ✦✦✦✦✦
This CD from the International Association of Jazz Record Collectors (IAJRC) is one of their most exciting, particularly for collectors of 1920s jazz. Even fanatics of the era will probably not have the great majority of the 25 selections included on this very valuable disc. Released for the first time anywhere are two numbers from a demonstration record by Dud Mecum's Wolverines in 1925 that feature the remains of the group that launched the career of Bix Beiderbecke; it is miraculous that these well-recorded performances (starring the tenor of George Johnson) still exist. Also included on this set are six numbers from the Original Wolverines in 1927–28 with cornetist Jimmy McPartland, eleven selections by Ray Miller's hot dance orchestra from 1928–29 (some of which have cornet solos from Muggsy Spanier) and six songs from the totally forgotten but enjoyable band Thelma Terry and Her Boyfriends, a group that also includes a young Gene Krupa. Highly recommended to serious collectors of vintage jazz. —*Scott Yanow*

● **One Night With Blue Note Preserved** / Feb. 22, 1985 / Blue Note ✦✦✦✦✦
This four-LP set, whose material was also made available as single LPs and single CDs, not only extensively documented a historic concert that paid tribute to the Blue Note label's legacy but was also the start of that important record company's comeback. *Vol. 1* features veterans Herbie Hancock on piano, trumpeter Freddie Hubbard, tenor saxophonist Joe Henderson, bassist Ron Carter, drummer Tony Williams and vibraphonist Bobby Hutcherson on remakes of "Canteloupe Island" and "Recorda Me" and a pair of Hutcherson pieces but flutist James Newton takes honors with his version of Eric Dolphy's "Hat and Beard." The second set features strong advanced hard bop music from an all-star quintet (pianist McCoy Tyner, altoist Jackie McLean, trumpeter Woody Shaw, bassist Cecil McBee and drummer Jack DeJohnette), a trio workout by tenor Bennie Wallace and a typically intense piano solo from Cecil Taylor. The third album has an Art Blakey reunion band playing "Moanin'," numbers featuring either tenor Stanley Turrentine or altoist Lou Donaldson with organist Jimmy Smith, guitarist Kenny Burrell and drummer Grady Tate, and two songs in which Grover Washington, Jr. (on soprano) plays with Burrell, Tate and bassist Reggie Workman. The final set has five numbers by Charles Lloyd (on tenor and flute at the beginning of a successful comeback), pianist Michel Petrucciani, bassist Cecil McBee and drummer Jack DeJohnette but saves the best for last, two amazing guitar solos from Stanley Jordan. Obviously this music on a whole is highly recommended for all jazz collections. —*Scott Yanow*

The Original Sound Of "The Twenties" / Jul. 29, 1922–Aug. 9, 1932 / Columbia ✦✦✦✦
One of many valuable box sets released by Columbia in the mid-'60s, this particular three-LP reissue has 47 selections that range from jazz and dance music to pop vocals and piano solos. Paul Whiteman's Orchestra is well-represented and such major names of the 1920s as Duke Ellington, Bing Crosby, Joe Venuti, Louis Armstrong, Ted Lewis, Ruth Etting, Ethel Waters, Sophie Tucker, Rudy Vallee and Kate Smith are also heard from, in addition to lesser knowns such as Cass Hagan's Park Central Hotel Orchestra, Red McKenzie (a great version of "From Monday On"), Blossom Seely and Lee Morse. Although not quite essential, there are enough rarities on the set (in addition to a very attractive booklet) to make this box worth searching for. —*Scott Yanow*

Original V-Disc Collection / Jun. 1943–Dec. 30, 1944 / Pickwick ✦✦✦
This two-CD set contains 40 selections taken from V-Discs, special recordings made specifically for servicemen abroad during World War II. Since a Musicians Union recording strike was taking place during the period, these performances are even more valuable than usual because they document musicians at a time when they were not on commercial records. Nearly all of the music was previously included in Time/Life's four-CD V-Disc set but those collectors who do not have that reissue will find the selections of great interest. Not all of the performances are jazz (Marian Anderson, Perry Como, Andre Kostelanetz, Josh White, Paul Robeson and Kay Kyser make appearances) but most are and the

highlights are many: Hot Lips Page's "The Sheik of Araby," Pee Wee Russell's strange vocal on "Pee Wee Speaks," Louis Jordan's "Is You Is or Is You Ain't My Baby," Tony Pastor's alternate lyrics to "Makin' Whoopee," Johnny Long's "In a Shanty in Old Shantytown," a re-creation of the Original Dixieland Jazz Band's version of "Tiger Rag," Woody Herman's early rendition of "Apple Honey" and Art Tatum's reworking of "Liza." —*Scott Yanow*

The Pablo All-Stars Jam: Montreux '77 / Jul. 14, 1977 / Original Jazz Classics ✦✦✦
This CD reissue expands upon the original Pablo LP by adding a fifth song ("Sweethearts on Parade") to the original fourtune program. This jam session differs from Pablo's other recordings in that it includes the great English tenor Ronnie Scott along with the regular all-star personnel (vibraphonist Milt Jackson, flugehornist Clark Terry, guitarist Joe Pass, pianist Oscar Peterson, bassist Niels Pedersen and drummer Bobby Durham). Everyone plays well on the standards but Terry takes honors with a beautiful statement on "God Bless the Child." —*Scott Yanow*

The Pete Johnson/Earl Hines/Teddy Bunn Blue Note Sessions / Jul. 29, 1939–Mar. 28, 1940 / Mosaic ✦✦✦✦
One of Mosaic's pet projects was the complete reissue of all of the Blue Note label's early prebop recordings. This single LP has three unrelated but enjoyable small-group sessions originally cut for Blue Note. Pete Johnson is heard on two piano solos and in a trio for four other songs with guitarist Ulysses Livingston and bassist Abe Bolar. Earl Hines takes a couple of typically miraculous piano solos ("The Father's Getaway" and "Reminiscing at Blue Note") and guitarist Teddy Bunn is featured unaccompanied on four cuts plus an alternate take, one of his very rare opportunities to lead a recording session. Although this set is now out of print, swing fans will want to go out of their way to find it if they do not have the music elsewhere. —*Scott Yanow*

A Piano Anthology / Apr. 20, 1926–Mar. 8, 1968 / GRP/Decca ✦✦✦
This CD contains selections from 20 pianists, all but two (Dodo Marmarosa and Bill Evans) who play in pre-bop styles. Taken mostly from the Decca catalog, the collection has many fine performances highlighted by Jelly Roll Morton's "The Pearls," Fats Waller and James P. Johnson playing together on Johnny Dunn's "What's the Use of Being Alone," Joe Sullivan's "Little Rock Getaway," an alternate take of Art Tatum's "Deep Purple" and rare performances from Frank Melrose, Billy Kyle, Clarence Profit and Ralph Sutton. Not essential but this reissue has plenty of enjoyable music for fans of swing piano. —*Scott Yanow*

Piano Players & Significant Others (Jazz in July Live at the 92nd Street Y) / Jul. 31, 1985–Jul. 20, 1988 / Music Masters ✦✦✦✦
This is a fun CD. The 13 performances are taken from Dick Hyman's Jazz in July series and, as the title implies, the emphasis is on the pianists which in this case include Hyman, Derek Smith, Jay McShann, Ralph Sutton, Dick Wellstood, Marian McPartland and Roger Kellaway. There are a pair of wonderful Ralph Sutton solos, duets by Hyman with Wellstood and Smith and a closing "Nagasaki" that finds Hyman, Sutton and Smith all battling it out on three pianos. In addition cornetist Ruby Braff is on two numbers and Carrie Smith sings "Fine and Mellow." Excellent swing-based music. —*Scott Yanow*

Piano Playhouse / Sep. 13, 1957 / VSOP ✦✦✦
The recordings on this LP were originally supposed to be released by the Mode label in the late '50s but the company went defunct before it could come out. Released for the first time by VSOP in 1986, these 10 selections (all recorded the same day) feature five different pianists (Carl Perkins, Jimmy Rowles, Paul Smith, Gerald Wiggins and Lou Levy) in fine form on three or four songs apiece. It is interesting to compare the players' similar but individual styles and to see how they adapt their bop-based approaches to the demands of playing solo. —*Scott Yanow*

Piano Singer's Blues / Nov. 15, 1926–Mar. 14, 1962 / Rosetta ✦✦✦
The hook for this typically attractive Rosetta LP is that the 16 selections all feature female singers accompanying themselves on piano. Many of the performances are a bit rare and such diverse artists as Georgia White, Gladys Bentley, Edith Johnson, Billie Pierce, Arizona Dranes, Fannie May Goosby, Cleo Brown, Hociel Thomas, Julia Lee, Bernice Edwards, Hazel Scott, Nellie Lutcher, Una Mae Carlisle, Victoria Spivey, Hadda Brooks and Lil Armstrong are all heard in fine form. Recommended to fans of classic jazz. —*Scott Yanow*

Piano Summit / Oct. 30, 1965 / Philology ✦✦✦
This must have been a very interesting concert to attend. On "Blues in D" bassist Niels Pedersen and drummer Alan Dawson accompany six pianists: Earl Hines, Teddy Wilson, John Lewis, Lennie Tristano, Bill Evans and Jaki Byard. In addition there are individual features for each of the pianists in a trio and Hines performs "All of Me" with Wilson and "Rosetta" with Byard. Released by an Italian label but available through mail order, this unique outing (which has some of Tristano's final concert performances) lives up to its potential. —*Scott Yanow*

Playboy's 40th Anniversary: Four Decades of Jazz 1953–1993 / Jul. 1953–1993 / Verve ✦✦✦
To celebrate the 40th anniversary of *Playboy* magazine, this four-CD boxed set was compiled and released. The music is drawn from many catalogs (in addition to Verve) and is a sampler of some of the jazz styles from the 40-year period with the emphasis on greatest hits. From Charlie Parker's "Now's the Time," Errol Garner's "Misty," Dave Brubeck's "Take Five," John Coltrane's "Giant Steps," Astrud Gilberto's "The Girl from Ipanema" and Lee Morgan's "Sidewinder" to Donald Byrd's "Black Byrd," Grover Washington, Jr.'s, "Mister Magic," Kenny G's "Songbird" and Bobby McFerrin's "Don't Worry, Be Happy," many famous numbers are included although Dixieland, the avant-garde and creative fusion are completely ignored. The general collector may want to pick up this set as an introduction to some of these jazz artists, but they should be warned that this reissue does not give listeners the entire picture of the jazz world. —*Scott Yanow*

Playing For Keeps / Jan. 4, 1992 / GM ✦✦✦
This CD matches together three under-recorded veterans: trumpeter Joe Wilder (69 at the time of the 1992 session), trombonist Britt Woodman and tenor saxophonist John LaPorta (the latter two were both 71). Although Wilder and Woodman both show their age at times, the trumpeter's tone remains one of the prettiest ones around while Woodman (wa-waaing his way through "Britt's Blues") often steals the show with his spirited solos. LaPorta, doubling between tenor and clarinet, was never a major stylist but his fairly complex playing still sounds quite viable. Guitarist Jack Wilkins (along with bassist Ed Schuller and drummer George Schuller) does a fine job but this set would have swung harder and been more versatile had a pianist also been included. Even with a few adventurous pieces (most notably "While You Were Out"), the majority of the performances are fairly straightforward renditions of standards. An interesting set, both musically and historically. —*Scott Yanow*

Pre-Bop / Feb. 26, 1944–Sep. 7, 1946 / Bob Thiele Music ✦✦✦
These often-reissued performances (originally cut for Bob Thiele's Signature label) are worth acquiring in one form or another. This LP has three unrelated sessions: a Fats Waller tribute date by pianist Earl Hines' trio (with guitarist Al Casey and bassist Oscar Pettiford), four numbers from an all-star swing group headed by trumpeter Shorty Sherock and (most memorably) a set in which the eccentric vocalist Leo Watson interacts with trombonist Vic Dickenson; their version of "Jingle Bells" is a classic of its kind. —*Scott Yanow*

RCA Victor Jazz Workshop: the Arrangers / Mar. 3, 1956–Jul. 8, 1965 / Bluebird ✦✦✦✦
A lot of unusual music appears on this Bluebird CD. Altoist Hal McKusick (with arrangeents contributed by George Russell and Gil Evans) performs five numbers (including a version of "Blues for Pablo" that was cut a year before Miles Davis' recording) with a variety of musicians including trumpeter Art Farmer and trombonist Jimmy Cleveland. Arranger John Carisi (heard here on trumpet) interprets seven previously unreleased numbers with an octet and trombonist Rod Levitt performs five of his arrangements with his own advanced octet. Although these performances would have little influence on future developments in jazz (the free jazz movement of the 1960s overshadowed the trend toward using elements of modern classical music in charts), the music still sounds quite fresh and unpredictable today. —*Scott Yanow*

Rags To Rhythms / Jan. 24, 1906–Jul. 15, 1926 / Memphis Archives ✦✦
This is an interesting but odd reissue CD. The first 11 selections are mostly rarities from the ragtime era (1906–1913) including Jim Europe's Society Orchestra ("Down Home Rag"), three banjo showcases, two piano solos and a xylophone feature on "Dill Pickles Rag." However, the remaining seven recordings are from the 1920s and, although "Rag" appears in all of their titles, the

music (by the likes of King Oliver, Jelly Roll Morton and the New Orleans Rhythm Kings) is actually early jazz and mostly available elsewhere. This project would have been more significant if it had stuck exclusively with pre-1915 material. —*Scott Yanow*

The Rare Dawn Sessions / May 12, 1949–Sep. 1956 / Biograph ✦✦✦

This CD reissue, which features four classic tenor saxophonists, brings back material released by Biograph on LPs in the 1980s. Stan Getz jams on four songs with a five-piece rhythm section that includes pianist Al Haig and guitarist Jimmy Raney in 1949, Wardell Gray uses a similar group on his two pieces, Paul Quinichette does his impressions of Lester Young on two songs in a quintet with trumpeter Gene Roland and pianist Nat Pierce and Zoot Sims swings on six pieces with a quintet including trumpeter Jerry Lloyd. The music should satisfy straight-ahead jazz fans and, although no longer all that rare, it serves as a good introduction to the work of the four fine tenors. —*Scott Yanow*

RCA Victor Jazz: the First Half-Century—the Twenties through the Sixties / Mar. 25, 1918–Aug. 18, 1967 / Bluebird ✦✦✦✦

RCA has long had an up-and-down relationship with jazz and that is reflected in this very interesting five-CD boxed set drawn completely from their archives. Each disc focuses on a specific decade and the producers did an excellent job of picking representative recordings. The 1920s and '30s are covered particularly well (with 23 selections on each disc); virtually every major name is heard at their prime. The 1940s disc also contains many valuable recordings (although RCA had been slow to record bop), but by the '50s and '60s RCA was not in the forefront of discovering up-and-coming artists; there are only hints of the avant-garde and many of the giants (Miles Davis, John Coltrane and Thelonious Monk to name three) never made it into the label's studios. However, even in the later decades, a variety of great veterans and modernists did make significant recordings for the label and there is not a loser among the 96 recordings. Overall this reissue gives one a superb overview of RCA jazz activities through the years (from Coleman Hawkins' "Body and Soul" to Sonny Rollins' "The Bridge") and is recommended to all jazz historians along with beginners just starting to explore this classic music. —*Scott Yanow*

Recorded in New Orleans, Vol. 1 / Mar. 24, 1956–Apr. 28, 1956 / Good Time Jazz ✦✦✦✦

In 1956 the Good Time Jazz label traveled to New Orleans and recorded eight different regularly working bands for three songs apiece, releasing the results on two LPs; both volumes have been reissued on CD. The musicianship is quite high throughout this series and there are many fine soloists in addition to spirited ensembles. *Vol. 1* has music from trumpeter Sharkey Bonano's Kings of Dixieland (a sextet that includes a young Pete Fountain on clarinet) along with bands headed by drummer Paul Barbarin, trombonist Bill Matthews and the late great trumpeter George Girard. It's recommended as is *Vol. 2*. —*Scott Yanow*

Recorded in New Orleans, Vol. 2 / Mar. 10, 1956–May 26, 1956 / Good Time Jazz ✦✦✦✦

The Good Time Jazz label in 1956 ventured to New Orleans and recorded eight working bands for three songs apiece, giving listeners a good overview of the then-contemporary New Orleans jazz scene. The two LPs that were released at the time have been reissued on CDs and both are highly recommended to fans of New Orleans jazz. *Vol. 2* has performances from bands led by cornetist Johnny Wiggs, trombonist Eddie Pierson and trombonist Santo Pecora in addition to pianist Armand Hug's trio. The high-quality music has impressive musicianship and plenty of spirit. —*Scott Yanow*

Red, White & Blues / Aug. 23, 1928–Nov. 26, 1961 / Rosetta ✦✦✦

The LPs released by Rosetta generally feature pre-bop female jazz vocalists dealing with a particular subject matter. The 15 performances on this set all have a city, state or some aspect of a town in its title. There are consistently strong performances from Billie Holiday, Ethel Waters, Lillian Glinn, Ivie Anderson, Victoria Spivey, Rosetta Howard, Mildred Bailey, Bessie Smith ("St. Louis Blues" from the film of the same name), Blue Lou Barker, Ella Fitgerald, Helen Humes, Bertha "Chippie" Hill, Betty Roche (a rare broadcast version of "Take the 'A' Train" with Duke Ellington), Julia Lee, Lil Armstrong and Blossom Seeley. Although the LP is not really essential, the very appealing packaging and high-quality music makes it difficult to resist. —*Scott Yanow*

★ **Ridin' in Rhythm** / Feb. 15, 1933–May 26, 1939 / Disques Swing ✦✦✦✦✦

This two-hour two-CD set (a companion to *Jazz in the Thirties*) has more than its share of classic performances. There are big-band sessions by Duke Ellington, Mills Blue Rhythm Band, Benny Carter, Fletcher Henderson and Horace Henderson, piano solos from Buck Washington and Meade Lux Lewis plus quite a few selections from tenor saxophonist Coleman Hawkins just prior to his decision to move to Europe (in addition to a 1939 date with Jack Hylton's Orchestra). High points include "Sophisticated Lady," "Six Bells Stampede," "Nagasaki," "The Day You Came Along," "Symphony in Riffs," "Honky Tonk Train Blues" and many others. —*Scott Yanow*

Riverboat Shuffle / 1926–1936 / Memphis Archives ✦✦✦

The 18 songs on this unusual sampler all have something to do with the Mississippi River. With such titles as "Steamboat Bill," "Mississippi Mud," "River Stay Away from My Door" and "Floating down to Cotton Town," the plot of the CD is obvious. Some of the material is rare while other cuts are fairly common. Highlights include the Boswell Sisters' "Roll On, Mississippi, Roll On," Paul Whiteman's "Selections from *Showboat*," Paul Robeson singing "Ol' Man River" and two titles from Wingy Manone. —*Scott Yanow*

● **Saturday Night Swing Club** / Jun. 12, 1937 / Memphis Archives ✦✦✦✦✦

This double CD brings back an entire radio broadcast, the first anniversary show of the legendary *Saturday Night Swing Club*. The many performances are often classic, the recording quality is excellent (except for three songs by Django Reinhardt and Stephane Grappelli that were performed live in France and are very full of static) and even the announcing by Paul Douglas is lively. Such musicians as Duke Ellington, harpist Casper Reardon, vibraphonist Adrian Rollini, trumpeter Bunny Bergian, the Raymond Scott Quintet, the Casa Loma Orchestra, pianist Claude Thorhill, the Benny Goodman Trio and Quartet, the guitar duo of Carl Kress and Dick McDonough and an impressive house band are all in excellent form. To use a cliché, it is almost like being there. One can truly feel the excitement of the swing era during this highly recommended release. —*Scott Yanow*

Sax Appeal / 1954–1956 / Vee-Jay ✦✦✦✦

The corny cover photo (a female model allegedly playing a saxophone), the hodgepodge nature of the program and the barely adequate liner notes mask the fact that this CD contains a great deal of interesting music. Most of the 24 performances (nine previously unissued) put the emphasis on its tenor soloists and the music generally falls somewhere between bop and early rhythm & blues. Included are complete sessions by Julian Dash, bassist David Shipp (whose sidemen include altoist Porter Kilbert and pianist Andrew Hill), keyboardist Tommy Dean (one of his songs features altoist Oliver Nelson), the great tenor Wardell Gray (the four numbers from his final session), honker Big Jay McNeely ("Big Jay's Hop"), Al Smith (featuring the tenor of Red Holloway), Arnett Cobb and Noble "Thin Man" Watts. Collectors in particular will want to pick up this very interesting set. —*Scott Yanow*

Small Band Jazz / Mar. 8, 1936–Jan. 10, 1943 / Fanfare ✦✦✦

The collector's label Fanfare released some very valuable LPs in the late '70s that contained radio aircheck performances. On this album the 1936 Red Norvo Octet (with trumpeter Stew Pletcher and tenor saxophonist Herbie Haymer) perform two songs, Miff Mole's Nicksieland Six jams on two of their own (including "Peg of My Heart") and Raymond Scott's Captivators (its personnel is unknown) is fine on four pieces. However it is the music on Side Two that is most memorable for showcased is Bud Freeman's Summa Cum Laude Orchestra of 1940. The tenor's all-star group features such fine soloists as trumpeter Max Kaminsky, valve trombonist Brad Gowans, clarinetist Pee Wee Russell and Freeman. Their broadcast includes hot swing, dance music and a three-song Bix Beiderbecke tribute. Trad jazz historians will want this album, if they can find it. —*Scott Yanow*

Small Band Jazz, Vol. 2 / Feb. 11, 1940–Jan. 27, 1941 / Fanfare ✦✦✦

This LP has performances taken from some of the broadcasts of the Chamber Society of Lower Basin Street, a program that satirized the pretentiousness of some classical music shows while featuring notable jazz artists. On this album Jelly Roll Morton is heard during his last recorded appearance and there are spots for Charlie and Jack Teagarden, pianist Joe Sullivan, clarinetist Pee

Wee Russell, cornetist Bobby Hackett, vibraphonist Lionel Hampton, soprano saxophonist Sidney Bechet (in exciting form), the Count Basie rhythm section, drummer Zutty Singleton and trumpeter Roy Eldridge. Most of the guests sat in with the fine house band led by trumpeter Hot Lips Levine and many of these performances are quite memorable. Highly recommended. — *Scott Yanow*

Some Other Time: Tribute to Chet Baker / Apr. 17, 1989–Apr. 18, 1989 / Triloka ✦✦✦
Recorded a year after Chet Baker's death, this tribute album (which was organized by pianist Richie Beirach) features trumpeter Randy Brecker, tenor-great Michael Brecker, guitarist John Scofield, Beirach, bassist George Mraz and drummer Adam Nussbaum on material associated with Baker. Actually Beirach contributed five of the ten songs and, since Baker rarely if ever performed three of them, this session's purpose gets watered down a bit. However the solos are generally of high quality and the music of this modern mainstream session holds one's interest throughout. — *Scott Yanow*

Songposts, Vol. 1 / Mar. 14, 1987–Sep. 10, 1991 / Word of Mouth ✦✦✦
This CD sampler features a wide variety of adventurous singers. Most memorable are two duets by the great Sheila Jordan and bassist Harvie Swartz, Kate Hammett-Vaughan with Garbo's Hat on "The Oft Repeated Dream" and Jeanne Lee's unaccompanied "Journey to Edaneres." Also included are performances by Georgia Ambros, Paula Owen, Jeannette Lambert, Irene Aebi (in duet with Steve Lacy's piano), Corry Sobol with bassist Dave Young, Jay Clayton with pianist Kirk Nurock, the Anne LeBaron Ensemble and David Drain. Although not everything works, this release from the Canadian label Word of Mouth gives listeners a taste of many different singers, some of whom are barely known in the U.S. — *Scott Yanow*

☆ **The Sound of Chicago** / Jun. 23, 1923–May 8, 1940 / Columbia ✦✦✦✦✦
The second of three three-LP box sets released by Columbia in their Jazz Odyssey series of the early '60s is as highly recommended (and as rare) as the New Orleans and Harlem sets. Among the many bands featured on the 48 selections are those of King Oliver, Jelly Roll Morton, Carroll Dickerson, Mckenzie and Condon's Chicagoans, Bud Freeman, a few blues singers, Jimmie Noone, Paul Mares, Earl Hines, Roy Eldridge and Horace Henderson. The attractive booklet (which is full of interesting information) is a strong asset and, although some of the music has since been reissued on CD, much of it hasn't. This set will be difficult to find so it should not be passed by; it serves as an excellent introduction to 1920s and early '30s jazz. — *Scott Yanow*

☆ **The Sound of Harlem** / Aug. 10, 1920–Apr. 1, 1942 / Columbia ✦✦✦✦✦
The third of three three-LP box sets released by Columbia in the early '60s in their Jazz Odyssey series, as with the New Orleans and Chicago samplers, contains some common selections but quite a few rarities among its 48 performances. In addition to such major names as Mamie Smith (her pioneering 1920 recording of "Crazy Blues"), James P. Johnson, Fletcher Henderson, Louis Armstrong, Ethel Waters, Fats Waller, Cab Calloway and Billie Holiday, there are numbers from Edith Wilson, Thomas Morris, Leroy Tibbs, Mattie Hite, Lena Wilson, Buck and Bubbles and the Hokum Trio. Most of the first two LPs stick to the 1920s and early '30s while the last one goes up to Cootie Williams' 1942 recording of "Epistrophy." Highly recommended although this set is very difficult to find. — *Scott Yanow*

☆ **The Sound Of New Orleans** / Jan. 24, 1917–Sep. 23, 1947 / Columbia ✦✦✦✦✦
The first of three three-LP box sets put out by Columbia in the early '60s in their Jazz Odyssey series is (as is true of the Chicago and Harlem entries) a perfect introduction to early jazz. The 48 selections range from the Original Dixieland Jazz Band ("Darktown Strutters Ball," the first jazz record ever made) and Clarence Williams to Wingy Manone, Bunk Johnson, King Oliver, Louis Armstrong, Fate Marable, the New Orleans Rhythm Kings and all eight titles cut by Sam Morgan's Jazz Band. Most of the music is from the mid-to-late '20s and many rarities are included along with just a few familiar items. The large and very informative booklet included in the box is a major plus too. — *Scott Yanow*

Spirituals to Swing / Jan. 1967 / Columbia ✦✦✦
Although this John Hammond-produced concert was billed as the "30th Anniversary," it actually took place 28 years after his original Spirituals to Swing concert. Count Basie, Big Joe Turner and an obviously ill Pete Johnson were back from the earlier event. The two-LP set has spirituals (Marion Williams), blues (Big Mama Thornton and Turner), new stars (George Benson and John Handy) and a few swing all stars (including trumpeter Buck Clayton, clarinetist Edmond Hall and tenor saxophonist Buddy Tate). The spirited program certainly holds one's interest, making this a two-fer worth acquiring. — *Scott Yanow*

● **Stars Of Jazz, Vol. 1** / 1972 / Jazzology ✦✦✦✦✦
On the first of two CDs (and originally released on three LPs), pianist Art Hodes leads a particularly strong all-star group through a variety of familiar Dixieland standards. Presented to the audience in an informative and educational way, this music is often quite exciting, no surprise when one considers the lineup: cornetist Wild Bill Davison (in peak form), trombonist Jim Beebe, clarinetist Barney Bigard, guitarist Eddie Condon, bassist Rail Wilson and drummer Hillard Brown. This CD would be worth getting if only to hear Davison's highly expressive (and sometimes sarcastic) playing on "Just a Closer Walk with Thee." Traditional jazz fans should consider the two volumes in this series to be essential. — *Scott Yanow*

● **Stars of Jazz, Vol. 2** / 1972 / Jazzology ✦✦✦✦✦
The second of two CDs taken from a single concert (which was originally released as three LPs) features pianist Art Hodes leading a brilliant Chicago-style jazz group (with cornetist Wild Bill Davison in top form, trombonist Jim Beebe, clarinetist Barney Bigard, guitarist Eddie Condon, bassist Rail Wilson and drummer Hillard Brown) on a variety of mostly familiar Dixieland and swing standards. Hodes presents the music in an entertaining and educational fashion for the audience, and this concert is rounded out by a version of "Kansas City Blues," which was recorded before the concert, at the group's soundcheck. Both of the volumes in this short series are highly recommended, particularly for Davison's emotional and often-humorous solos. — *Scott Yanow*

Stars of The Apollo / Mar. 31, 1927–Jan. 7, 1965 / Columbia/Legacy ✦✦✦
This double CD is a straight reissue of the original double LP. Its 28 selections mostly focus on singers and bands from the swing era that performed at one time or another at the Apollo; all but eight of the numbers are from the 1927–42 period. Highpoints of this hodgepodge collection include Bessie Smith's "Gimme a Pigfoot," the Mills Brothers' "Sweet Sue," Bill "Bojangles" Robinson's "Doin' the New Lowdown," Slim Gaillard's "Sploghm," Sarah Vaughan's "Ain't Misbehavin'," Screamin' Jay Hawkins' remarkable "I Put a Spell on You" and Aretha Franklin's "Evil Gal Blues." — *Scott Yanow*

Straight No Chaser / 1994 / Blue Note ✦✦✦✦✦
Blue Note keeps the "concept" packages coming with this two-disc set presenting catalog tracks sampled by the hip-hop/jazz ensemble Us3. The 15 selections include dialogue snippets from Birdland's irrepressible Pee Wee Marquette and the great Art Blakey, with the other material divided between hard bop and soul-jazz and Herbie Hancock, Horace Silver and Donald Byrd getting two tracks each. John Patton, Reuben Wilson, Grant Green, Lou Donaldson, Thelonious Monk, Blakey and Bobby Hutcherson are other featured artists. The songs are first-rate, but Blue Note could have also included the recording years of the tracks as an additional service to listeners, particularly those coming from rap with little knowledge of the label's accomplishments or legacy. — *Ron Wynn*

The Sullivan Years: Big Band All-Stars / Feb. 10, 1957–Jun. 4, 1967 / TVT ✦✦
The performances on this CD are taken from the soundtrack of several episodes of *The Ed Sullivan Show*. The orchestras of Harry James, Woody Herman, Lionel Hampton, Benny Goodman, Count Basie along with the Glenn Miller ghost band are heard from during a ten-year period. The music in general is quite predictable with Herman's "Apple Honey" and Goodman's "Sing Sing Sing" providing the best moments; when are videos from these programs going to become available. — *Scott Yanow*

● **Sunset Swing** / Mar. 1, 1945–Nov. 12, 1945 / Black Lion ✦✦✦✦✦
This CD contains 22 generally exciting performances from jazz's transitional years. While the music technically falls into the swing

idiom, one can often hear the influence of bop (and even early rhythm & blues) creeping in. Nine different groups are heard from. Trumpeter Howard McGhee and tenor saxophonist Charlie Ventura head a sextet, the 16-year old pianist Andre Previn makes his recording debut on a trio version of "California Clipper" and joins trumpeter Buddy Childers, altoist Willie Smith and the tenor of Vido Musso in a sextet, McGhee, Willie Smith and tenor great Lucky Thompson join forces on another date, guitarist Les Paul is heard in a sextet with trumpeter Harry Edison, pianist Arnold Ross duets with bassist Red Callender, trumpeter Emmett Berry, trombonist Vic Dickenson and altoist Lem Davis swing in a sextet and drummer Ray Bauduc leads an unidentified group. Recommended. —Scott Yanow

● **Swing Time! (1925–1955)** / May 14, 1925–Feb. 15, 1955 / Columbia ✦✦✦✦
This three-disc box set does an excellent job of covering the big-band era through 66 recordings (by almost as many orchestras) owned by Columbia. The selections (programmed in chronological order), although emphasizing the 1934–45 era, also include 18 earlier and six later recordings. Although the package has some of the familiar hits (such as Glenn Miller's "In the Mood" and Tommy Dorsey's "Marie"), there are also many lesser-known performances, and such forgotten bands as those led by Eddie Stone, Fred Elizalde and Jack Jenney are represented along with Benny Goodman, Duke Ellington and Count Basie. Perfect for beginners, this set should also interest collectors who will probably find several "new" gems that they had been unfamiliar with. The accompanying booklet is also excellent. —Scott Yanow

Swingin' Britain: The Thirties / Feb. 1, 1935–Nov. 10, 1938 / Decca ✦✦✦✦
This double LP from British Decca will be difficult to find but it is worth the search for fans of swing music. The two-fer has 32 jazz-oriented recordings (most of them rare) by a variety of English groups: Danny Polo's Swing Stars, George Chisholm's Jive Five, the Embassy Rhythm Eight, Leonard Feather and Ye Old English Swynge Band, Lew Davis' Trombone Trio and Tiny Winters' Bogey Seven. Although the stereotype of British bands of the 1930s is of polite dance music, these performances show that the English had several very impressive swing stylists. Most notable, in addition to the American clarinetist Danny Polo (a bit of a ringer), are trumpeters Tommy McQuater, Max Goldberg and Dave Wilkins, trombonists George Chisholm and Lew Davis, Benny Winestone on clarinet and tenor and the tenors of Don Barrigo and Buddy Featherstonhaugh. This very worthy reissue is a collector's item. —Scott Yanow

Swinging Big Band Christmas / Laserlight ✦✦✦
This budget CD release from LaserLight does not give recording dates but the ten selections (totalling only around 36 minutes of music) mostly are from the 1940s. Such performers as Claude Thornhill ("Snowfall"), Gene Krupa, Larry Clinton, Jack Teagarden, Bob Crosby, the Glenn Miller Army Air Force Orchestra (playing a Christmas medley), Les Brown and even Guy Lombardo are all heard in fine form. The results as a whole are a satisfying and rather atmospheric set of nostalgic Christmas jazz. —Scott Yanow

Tar Heel Jazz / Jun. 18, 1936 / IAJRC ✦✦✦
This CD from the collector's label IAJRC contains the complete output of three obscure bands plus seven of the ten sides cut by the Hod Williams Orchestra. All of these sessions were recorded in the same building in Charlotte, NC, during 1936–37 and feature territory bands with their own strong and weak qualities. Jimmie Gunn's band is excellent on its three instrumentals but plagued by bad vocalists on the other three tracks. The Frankie and Johnny orchestra is more consistent and often often quite hot. The Hod Williams Orchestra took its inspiration (and to an extent its arrangements) from the sophisticated swing style of the Hudson-DeLange Orchestra while the recordings of the Frankie Reynolds Orchestra are swinging if not particularly distinctive. 1930s collectors should consider this set of rare material to be essential. —Scott Yanow

The Territories Vol. 1 / Oct. 14, 1927–Jun. 1931 / Arcadia ✦✦✦✦✦
This enjoyable LP puts the focus on five long-forgotten but talented territory bands of the late '20s and early '30s. All eight selections recorded by Curtis Mosby's Dixieland Blue Blowers (an excellent group from Los Angeles) fill up Side One while one of the two songs cut by Maynard Baird's Orchestra (a band from Knoxville, TN), three of the four sides performed by Red Perkins'

Dixie Ramblers and both of the titles recorded by singer Victoria Spivey with Hunter's Serenaders (which like Perkins was from Omaha, NE) and Grant Moore's New Orleans Black Devils (from Arkansas) are on the flip side. It is surprising that none of the sidemen became well known because these are excellent bands with Mosby's being most memorable on titles such as "Whoop 'Em up Blues," "Tiger Stomp" and "Blue Blowers Blues." Recommended. —Scott Yanow

The Territories, Vol. 2 / 1927–Jun. 14, 1933 / Arcadia ✦✦✦✦✦
There is quite a variety of performances on this interesting LP, much of it quite valuable. It starts off with all of the recordings of the important Kansas City band George E. Lee's Novelty Singing Orchestra (two titles from 1927 and four from 1929) plus the two songs on which the band backs the vocals of its pianist, the legendary (and future star) Julia Lee ("He's Tall, Dark and Handsome" and "Won't You Come over to My House"). In addition there are four songs from the spirited if primitive Alex Jackson's Plantation Orchestra (their "Jackass Blues" is a classic), a number by Curtis Mosby's Dixieland Blue Blowers that is taken from a movie and the complete output (two songs) by the completely obscure Erwing Brothers Orchestra in 1933. Collectors of early jazz should consider this music (most of which has not yet been reissued on CD) to be essential. —Scott Yanow

The Territories, Vol. 3: The South / Oct. 6, 1926–Jul. 15, 1936 / Arcadia ✦✦✦
The third of three LPs put out by Arcadia in their mini-series has a variety of rare recordings cut in the South mostly during the 1926–30 period. Eddie Heywood, Sr., (the father of the famous pianist) is heard on his only two band sides, Williamson's Beale Street Frolic Orchestra romps on four songs, the primitive Black Birds of Paradise struggle through "Muddy Water," the Triangle Harmony Boys do what they can on three songs, pianist Sammy Price's Four Quarters play "Blue Rhythm Stomp" (their only recording) and there is music by Ben Tobier's California Cyclones and Edgewater Crows; the latter from 1936. Interesting performances overall, most are highly recommended to connoisseurs of the era. —Scott Yanow

That Newport Jazz / Jul. 4, 1963+Jul. 6, 1963 / Columbia ✦✦✦✦✦
There is over an hour's worth of music on this generous LP which features two different all-star groups at the 1963 Newport Jazz Festival. One band (with trumpeters Clark Terry and Howard McGhee, tenors Coleman Hawkins and Zoot Sims, pianist Joe Zawinul, bassist Wendell Marshall and drummer Roy Haynes) could be considered more boppish than the other (which has trumpeter Ruby Braff, trombonist Al Grey, tenor Bud Freeman, pianist George Wein, bassist Wendell Marshall and drummer Haynes) but in reality the groups overlap stylistically. The jam sessions (eight standards including ballad features for Hawkins and Terry plus the original blues "Chasin' at Newport") are quite fun and generate plenty of heat. Historic and easily enjoyable music from quite a few classic greats. —Scott Yanow

★ **That's the Way I Feel Now: Tribute to T. Monk** / Oct. 1984 / A&M ✦✦✦✦✦

Thesaurus of Classic Jazz / Sep. 1926–Feb. 6, 1930 / Columbia ✦✦✦✦
In the early '60s, Columbia started digging into its vaults and coming out with box sets of valuable music from the 1920s. This four-LP set has 13 selections from Miff Mole's Molers, a dozen by the Charleston Chasers, eight apiece from the Redheads And the Arkansas Travellers, two by the Dorsey Brothers, three from Frankie Trumbauer, one apiece from the Goofus Five and Joe Venuti and four featuring Eddie Lang's Orchestra. Overall this superior collection gives one a large sampling of the White small groups of the era with plenty of solos from cornetists Red Nichols and (on three songs) Bix Beiderbecke, trombonists Tommy Dorsey and Miff Mole, Jimmy Dorsey on clarinet and alto and clarinetist Pee Wee Russell among others. The accompanying booklet is quite informative too. Recommended but this will be a hard set to find. —Scott Yanow

Tin Pan Alley Blues / May 4, 1916–Mar. 1925 / Memphis Archives ✦✦✦
The Memphis Archives label has mixed together some fairly common blues performances with some real oddities, blues as performed by vaudevillian performers. In addition to the original Dixieland Jazz Band ("Home Again Blues"), Trixie Smith, Bessie Smith and Edith Wilson, there is Marie Cahill singing "The Dallas

Blues" (from 1917), the very early "Homesickness Blues" from Nora Bayes in 1916 and even a rare example of Eddie Cantor singing blues. Obviously the music is not for everyone's taste but collectors of early American music will find this CD to be quite interesting. —*Scott Yanow*

Town Hall Jazz Concert 1945 / Jun. 9, 1945 / Atlantic ✦✦✦✦
There is nearly two hours of music on this double LP, all taken from a historic Town Hall concert. The swing-oriented performances (which have been reissued by Mosaic in their massive Commodore reissue series) are often quite exciting with strong appearances by such greats as vibraphonist Red Norvo, tenors Flip Phillips and Charlie Ventura, pianist Teddy Wilson, bassist Slam Stewart, tenor saxophonist Don Byas (who has a pair of classic duets with Stewart on "Indiana" and "I Got Rhythm"), trumpeter Bill Coleman, drummer Gene Krupa and violinist Stuff Smith. Although a couple of selections (particularly a 16-minute "In a Mellotone") go on a bit too long, there are plenty of memorable moments during this highly recommended set which deserves to be reissued in full on CD. —*Scott Yanow*

Jazz Fest Masters / 1969 / Scotti Bros. ✦✦✦
This is one of five CDs taken from the 1969 New Orleans Jazz Festival and released by Scott Bros. in 1992. The set consists of fine Dixieland from groups led by trombonist Jim Robinson, trumpeter Johnny Wiggs, drummer Barry Martyn and trombonist Papa Bue; sidemen include clarinetist Louis Cottrell, drummer Zutty Singleton, Danny Barker on banjo and clarinetist Raymond Burke. There are plenty of heated moments from these similar but distinctive groups and the music is consistently joyful and swinging. —*Scott Yanow*

Tribute to John Coltrane: Live under the Sky / Jul. 26, 1987 / Columbia ✦✦✦
With the assistance of a rhythm section comprised of pianist Richie Beirach, bassist Eddie Gomez and drummer Jack Dejohnette, Dave Liebman and Wayne Shorter really stretch out on their sopranos, playing two medleys ("India/Impressions" and "After the Rain/Naima") in addition to an intense version of "Mr. P.C." This Coltrane tribute concert (all of the compositions are by the great saxophonist) has strong playing by everyone concerned; it is also available on Laser disc. —*Scott Yanow*

A Tribute To Lee Morgan / Dec. 3, 1994–Dec. 4, 1994 / NYC ✦✦✦✦
Unlike many of the other recent tribute albums, this program of the music of the late trumpeter Lee Morgan casts his compositions in familiar surroundings not all that different from the original recordings. Trumpeter Eddie Henderson, who was influenced by Morgan but found his own voice, is a good choice for the lead role and his muted outing on the one non-Morgan piece, "You Don't Know What Love Is," is a strong feature. Tenorman Joe Lovano, who can sound like Joe Henderson at times and hints at the passion of Coltrane on the date's most advanced piece "Search for the New Land," has a strong personality of his own and matches well with Eddie Henderson. The solid rhythm section (pianist Cedar Walton, bassist Peter Washington and drummer Billy Higgins) is a major asset while guest Grover Washington, Jr., makes a pair of guest appearances on soprano and shows once again that he can play swinging soulful jazz; pity that he never seems to play tenor in this type of setting. The eight Lee Morgan songs heard on this recommended CD are interpreted in the same basic hard bop style that the trumpeter spent most of his career playing, an idiom that serves as the modern jazz mainstream of today. Highlights include "Sidewinder," "Ceora," "Speedball" (which has some heated tradeoffs by the horns) and the infectious "Ca-Lee-So." —*Scott Yanow*

A Tribute to Duke / 1977 / Concord Jazz ✦✦✦
For this tribute to Duke Ellington, Rosemary Clooney (making her debut on Concord) and Tony Bennett take two vocals apiece, Woody Herman plays "In a Sentimental Mood" and Bing Crosby guests on "Don't Get Around Much Anymore." Actually the three instrumentals are most significant, for the quintet (which includes pianist Nat Pierce, trumpeter Bill Berry, bassist Monty Budwig and drummer Jake Hanna) helped introduce the young tenor Scott Hamilton. The CD is a straight reissue of the original LP, a historic if not all that essential release. —*Scott Yanow*

Tribute to Miles / 1992 / Qwest ✦✦✦
This Miles Davis tribute set brings back four-fifths of his second classic quintet with Wallace Roney the logical choice to fill in for

the late trumpeter. Roney comes across as a sideman and is not as forceful here as one would have hoped. Wayne Shorter, Herbie Hancock, Ron Carter and Tony Williams had all grown with time and this reunion has Hancock and Williams taking on more prominent leadership roles than in the earlier days. With the exception of the drummer's "Elegy," all of the music ("So What," "RJ," "Little One," "Pinocchio," "Eighty One" and "All Blues") was regularly performed by the quintet back in the 1960s. In general this reunion is a success even if it contains no new revelations. It is particularly nice to hear Wayne Shorter in this setting again. —*Scott Yanow*

Lennie Tristano Memorial Concert / Jan. 28, 1979–Jan. 29, 1980 / Jazz ✦✦✦
After his death, pianist/teacher Lennie Tristano was paid tribute to at a lavish Town Hall concert. This five-LP set has all of the music, plus a seven-minute drum solo recorded by Max Roach a year later. Many of Tristano's top students (although not Lee Konitz) are heard from including pianists Liz Gorrill, Lloyd Lifton, Virg Dzurinko, Sal Mosca and Connie Crothers, the solo guitar of Larry Meyer, unaccompanied flute performances by both Fran Canisius and Nomi Rosen, and six a cappella vocals from Lynn Anderson. Lennie Tristano was worshiped as a guru by some of these players (which sometimes results in overly precious performances) but in general the music is pretty rewarding. Not too surprisingly tenor saxophonist Warne Marsh (with a pianoless trio) and singer Sheila Jordan emerge as the solo stars. —*Scott Yanow*

The Trumpet Summit Meets The Oscar Peterson Big 4 / Mar. 10, 1980 / Original Jazz Classics ✦✦✦✦
To call this CD (a reissue of a Pablo date) an all-star session would be an understatement. Joining pianist Oscar Peterson, guitarist Joe Pass, bassist Ray Brown and drummer Bobby Durham are three classic trumpeters: Dizzy Gillespie, Clark Terry and Freddie Hubbard. They clearly inspire each other (Gillespie flew in from the East Coast specifically for this date) and the music ("Daahoud," "Just Friends," the new blues "Chicken Wings" and a torrid version of "The Champ") has plenty of exciting moments. Other performances from the same date can be heard on *The Alternate Blues*, an LP overdue to be reissued on CD. —*Scott Yanow*

The Trumpets–Jazz Fest Masters / 1969 / Scotti Bros. ✦✦✦
A lot of classic greats are heard on this CD, taken from the 1969 New Orleans Jazz Festival. Roy Eldridge performs four songs while backed by pianist Jaki Byard, bassist Richard Davis and drummer Alan Dawson; on "Perdido" fellow trumpeters Bobby Hackett and Clark Terry sit in. Dizzy Gillespie plays two obscure numbers with his quintet of the time (with James Moody on tenor and flute) while Buck Clayton heads an octet on "St. Louis Blues" that also includes Buddy (not Bunny as it says in the scanty liner notes) Tate and trombonist Dickie Wells. The performances are quite enjoyable, obscure and well-recorded. This CD is worth getting for Roy Eldridge's playing by itself. —*Scott Yanow*

Trumpets In Modern Jazz / Feb. 1981–Jun. 1993 / Enja ✦✦✦
With the exception of an alternate take of Dusko Goykovich's "Adriatica," all of the dozen performances on this CD sampler are taken from previously released Enja albums. Of the trumpeters featured, Clark Terry, Woody Shaw (in a duet with drummer Roy Brooks) and the obscure Reiner Winterschladen are heard in cameos, Dizzy Gillespie is past his prime on 1989's "Kush" and Chet Baker plays a forgettable ballad "For Now." However Art Farmer, Benny Bailey, Goykovich, John D'Earth, Franco Ambrosetti and Jerry Gonzalez are in excellent form while young Nicholas Payton steals solo honors on "Body and Soul." Overall this CD gives one an interesting overview of a variety of trumpeters. —*Scott Yanow*

The 20th Concord Festival All Stars / Aug. 1988 / Concord Jazz ✦✦✦
To celebrate the 20th Concord Jazz Festival, an all-star quintet of veterans was gathered together to play swinging jazz. With trumpeter Harry "Sweets" Edison, Red Holloway on tenor, pianist Gene Harris, bassist Ray Brown and drummer Jeff Hamilton comprising the group, it is not a surprise that this session is quite successful. Standards and ballads (along with a Ray Brown blues) make up the program and the results are satisfying. —*Scott Yanow*

Unreleased Edison Laterals / Feb. 10, 1928–Apr. 6, 1929 / Diamond Cut Productions ✦✦✦
This CD contains 21 formerly rare performances originally

recorded for the Edison label during 1928–29. The music covers a wide variety of styles from dance bands (including The California Ramblers) and pop vocalists to the New York Military Band; some titles were previously unreleased. Lovers of 1920s music (as opposed to jazz collectors) will enjoy this sampler the most. — *Scott Yanow*

USA All Stars In Berlin / Feb. 1955 / Jazz Band ✦✦✦

The Jazz at the Philharmonic All Stars are featured on this enjoyable if not quite essential CD imported fron England. Trumpeters Dizzy Gillespie and Roy Eldridge, trombonist Bill Harris, tenor saxophonist Flip Phillips, pianist Oscar Peterson, guitarist Herb Ellis, bassist Ray Brown and drummer Louis Bellson stretch out on two fairly exciting jams and play a ballad medley. In addition Bellson has a drum feature, the Oscar Peterson Trio romps on two songs, clarinetist Buddy DeFranco is showcased with Peterson on "Billie's Bounce" and Ella Fitzgerald sings the happy "Papa Loves Mambo" and scats throughout a brief "Perdido." — *Scott Yanow*

● V-Disc: The Songs That Went To War / Aug. 27, 1943–Jul. 1948 / Time-Life ✦✦✦✦

During World War II a strike by the Musicians Union kept professional players off records for a long period. To fill the gap, a special "V-Disc" program was instituted to provide new music for military personnel serving overseas. This attractive four-CD box set from Time-Life contains 79 performances by a wide variety of artists from the period. Most of the music is jazz but there are some numbers from pop performers; such notables as Benny Goodman, Woody Herman, San Kenton, Lionel Hampton, Glenn Miller, the Nat King Cole Trio, Muggsy Spanier, Hoagy Carmicahel, Ella Fitzgerald, Roy Eldridge, Paul Robeson, Hot Lips Page, Stan Kenton, Marian Anderson, Jack Teagarden, Louis Armstrong, Bunk Johnson, Les Paul and even Ethel Merman make strong appearances. There is a lot of valuable music on this well-conceived reissue. — *Scott Yanow*

Violin Summit / Sep. 30, 1966 / Verve/MPS ✦✦✦✦

This album is a jazz collector's dream come true. Four of the greatest jazz violinists of all time (Stuff Smith, Stephane, Grappelli, Svend Asmussen and Jean-Luc Ponty) met up one day in the recording studio and recorded these swing-oriented performances. Accompanied by pianist Kenny Drew, bassist Niels Pedersen and drummer Axel Riel, the fiddle players all take solos on "It Don't Mean a Thing" and are well featured on the standards with "Pent up House" (which showcases Grappelli and Ponty) being a high point. This unique outing (which will hopefully be reissued on CD eventually) is highly recommended. — *Scott Yanow*

Warner Jams, Vol. 1 / 1995 / Warner Brothers ✦✦✦

On this CD some of the top young jazz players from the Warner Brothers roster (trumpeter Wallace Roney, altoist Kenny Garrett, Joshua Redman on tenor, guitarist Peter Bernstein, organist Larry Goldings, pianist Brad Mehldau, bassist Clarence Seay and drummer Brian Blade) are featured both individually and collectively. There are five showcases (for the three horns and the two keyboards), three songs in which a different duo of horns gets to extensively trade off and three looser numbers including an opening medium-up blues ("Blue Grass") that sounds like an outtake from a Jimmy Smith jam session. In general Kenny Garrett and Larry Goldings come across best. Garrett is the most advanced soloist on the date (sometimes hinting at the ideas of the M-Base players) while Goldings constantly pushes the horns in the ensembles and drives the rhythm section. Joshua Redman and Wallace Roney (the latter at his best on "Nature Boy") also have their strong moments. Although nothing all that innovative occurs during the hard bop-oriented performances, the straight-ahead music from these Young Lions is enjoyable and consistently swinging. — *Scott Yanow*

West Coast Hot / Jan. 3, 1969–Apr. 1, 1969 / Novus ✦✦✦✦✦

The music on this CD reissue is a bit historic and also stands as proof that there was a healthy (artistically if not commercially) avant-garde jazz scene in Los Angeles in the late '60s. John Carter (here switching between clarinet, tenor and alto) teams up with trumpeter Bobby Bradford in a pianoless quartet for four numbers while the masterful pianist/composer Horace Tapscott leads a two-bass quintet on four other songs (including the over-17-minute "The Giant Is Awakened") that also features the then-unknown altoist Arthur Blythe. The performances still sound explorative and have not really dated at all in the quarter-century since. — *Scott Yanow*

West Coast Jazz, Vol. 1 / Jun. 1922–Aug. 1931 / Arcadia ✦✦✦✦✦

The collector's label Arcadia found a niche by reissuing obscure recordings from territory bands of the 1920s and early '30s. On this LP, their first release, all of the music is by Los Angeles-based bands. Included are the two titles by Kid Ory's 1921 or 1922 band (which went by the odd title of "Spikes Seven Pods of Pepper Orchestra") along with various groups led by pianist Sonny Clay, Reb Spikes' Majors and Minors, the Dixie Serenaders and the excellent Curtis Mosby and his Dixieland Blue Blowers, including the soundtrack of their appearance in the 1929 film *Hallelujah*. This historic music is easily recommended to collectors of 1920s jazz. — *Scott Yanow*

West Coast Jazz, Vol. 2 / Feb. 1925–1931 / Arcadia ✦✦✦

The second of two LPs by the Arcadia label to reissue obscure recordings from West Coast groups in the 1920s features several bands from Hollywood and San Francisco. Included are long-forgotten performances by the Wilshire Dance Orchestra, Eddie Frazier's Plantation Orchestra, Carlyle Stevenson, Fred Elizade (his first two sides before moving to England), the Rhythm Makers, Tom Gerunovitch, Jack Danford's Ben Franklin Hotel Orchestra (which includes trumpeter Lu Watters in its personnel), Claude Sweeten's R.K. Olians and the Mezzanine Melodies. The hot dance music (often influenced by Red Nichols' Five Pennies) should delight 1920s collectors although this set is not too essential for more general listeners. — *Scott Yanow*

What Is Jazz / 1955 / Columbia ✦✦✦

This LP is a real collector's item. Leonard Bernstein talks about jazz and, with the assistance of vintage recordings and an all-star group assembled by trumpeter Buck Clayton, demonstrates various jazz styles. Most memorable are several examples of the standard "Sweet Sue" being played in different styles including a recording by the Miles Davis Quintet. Most of Bernstein's talking on this mid-'50s recording is surprisingly undated and collectors will find the album quite interesting. — *Scott Yanow*

World's Greatest Jazz Concert #1 / Feb. 22, 1947 / Jazzology ✦✦✦✦✦

With a title such as this one, it is impossible for the music to quite live up to the billing. However the performances (released for the first time on this Jazzology CD) are often quite special. On the first of two volumes (the second set was recorded at a different concert two months later), cornetist Wild Bill Davison, clarinetist Albert Nicholas and trombonist George Brunies (with the assistance of pianist Joe Sullivan, bassist Pops Foster and drummer Baby Dodds) form a very potent frontline on three songs. Brunies and Davison also have individual features, veteran blues singer Bertha "Chippie" Hill takes a vocal, trumpeter Muggsy Spanier leads a group (with Brunies, pianist Art Hodes and clarinetist Cecil Scott) on two songs and trumpeter-vocalist Hot Lips Page heads a hard-charging septet with clarinetist Tony Parenti. With all of those classic players, the music (not too surprisingly) is very enjoyable and spirited. Recommended. — *Scott Yanow*

World's Greatest Jazz Concert #2 / Apr. 26, 1947 / Jazzology ✦✦✦✦

The second of two CDs in this series was recorded two months after the earlier Jazzology release. This all-star concert is almost up to the level of the first. Trumpeter Mugsy Spanier, trombonist George Brunies and the great soprano-saxophonist Sidney Bechet are heard on five spirited numbers, trombonist Jack Teagarden teams up in separate performances with Spanier and trumpeter Johnny Windhurst, Windhurst is heard with pianist Dick Wellstood in a quartet, Bechet has a couple of features, the Two Gospel Keys sing a couple of traditional numbers and finally Spanier, Windhurst, Brunies and clarinetist Bob Wilber team up for the closing "Dippermouth Blues." Dixieland and New Orleans jazz are urged to pick up both of these Jazzology sets. — *Scott Yanow*

Young Lions / Apr. 25, 1960 / Vee-Jay ✦✦✦

A sextet of young talents (including trumpeter Lee Morgan, altoist Frank Strozier and tenor saxophonist Wayne Shorter) play a set of then-recent Shorter compositions on this CD which includes five songs plus three previously unissued alternate takes. The music fits the modern mainstream of the period while avoiding imitation of the past. This was one of Shorter's first recordings and, although none of his originals caught on, the set is an impressive early outing by all concerned. — *Scott Yanow*

The Young Lions / Jun. 30, 1982 / Elektra Musician ✦✦✦✦✦

This two-LP set documents a very interesting and historic concert. While the term "Young Lions" later came to be applied to young hard bop-oriented soloists who were intent on playing swinging jazz, many of the 17 musicians heard during this concert came to be associated with the avant-garde. Performing in different combinations ranging from solo vibes to a version of "Nigerian Sunset" that includes everyone, the talented musicians (many of whom were only slightly known at the time) are trumpeter Wynton Marsalis (then just 21), vocalist Bobby McFerrin, the reeds of Paquito D'Rivera, John Purcell and Chico Freeman, trombonist Craig Harris, baritonist Hamiet Bluiett, flutist James Newton, guitarist Kevin Eubanks, violinist John Blake, vibraphonist Jay Hoggard, cellist Abdul Wadud, pianist Anthony Davis, bassists Avery Sharpe and Fred Hopkins, drummer Ronnie Burrage and percussionist Daniel Ponce. A strong highlight is "B 'N' W," which features the trio of McFerrin, Marsalis and Sharpe, but quite a few

of the selections are memorable. This two-fer, a near-classic, obviously deserves to be reissued on CD. —*Scott Yanow*

Yule Struttin' / Oct. 27, 1953–Jul. 20, 1990 / Blue Note ✦✦✦
This CD has ten performances of Christmas songs from 1990 plus a few earlier recordings (Chet Baker's "Winter Wonderland," Count Basie's "Jingle Bells," Dexter Gordon's "Have Yourself a Merry Little Christmas" and Stanley Jordan's 1986 version of "Silent Night." With such top stars as Bobby Watson, Lou Rawls, Eliane Elias, Benny Green (who has two piano solos), Dianne Reeves, John Hart, John Scofield, Joey Calderazzo and Rick Margitza playing music not available elsewhere, this melodic CD is worth picking up. A particular highlight are two versions of "A Merrier Christmas," a previously unknown Thelonious Monk composition here performed separately by Benny Green and Dianne Reeves.
—*Scott Yanow*

A BRIEF HISTORY OF JAZZ

One of the major questions that will go forever unanswered is "How did jazz start?" The first jazz recording was in 1917, but the music existed in at least primitive forms for 20 years before that. Influenced by classical music, marches, spirituals, work songs, ragtime, blues and the popular music of the period, jazz was already a distinctive form of music by the time it was first documented.

The chances are that the earliest jazz was played by unschooled musicians in New Orleans marching bands. Music was a major part of life in New Orleans from at least the 1890s with brass bands hired to play at parades, funerals, parties and dances. It stands to reason that the musicians (who often did not read music) did not simply play the melodies continuously but came up with variations to keep the performances interesting.

Since cornetist Buddy Bolden (the first famous musician to be considered a jazz player) formed his band in 1895, one can use that year as a symbolic birthdate for jazz. During the next two decades the undocumented music progressed but probably at a slow pace. Bolden (whose worsening mental illness led to his being committed in 1906) was succeeded by Freddie Keppard as the top New Orleans cornetist and Keppard was eventually surpassed by King Oliver. Although some New Orleans musicians traveled up North, jazz remained strictly a regional music until the World War I years.

On Jan. 30, 1917 a White group immodestly called the Original Dixieland Jazz Band recorded "Darktown Strutters' Ball" and "Indiana" for Columbia. The often-riotous music was considered too radical to be released at the time, so on Feb. 26 the ODJB went to Victor and recorded "Livery Stable Blues" and "The Original Dixieland One Step." The latter performances were immediately released. "Livery Stable Blues" (which featured the horns imitating animals!) became a best-seller and jazz was discovered, sort of. Within a short period of time other groups were recorded playing in a similar all-ensemble style (the ODJB had virtually no solos). Jazz became a fad for a few years (as promoters rushed to make money off of the new music) and the Original Dixieland Jazz Band in 1919 was a sensation in London. However it would be a few years before Black jazz musicians were recorded, leading some observers the time to the false conclusion that whites (and the ODJB in particular) had invented the music! A backlash later on led to others feeling that only Blacks could play jazz and that all of the White players were poor imitations. Obviously both beliefs have been proven false many times since then.

In 1920 Mamie Smith recorded the first blues, "Crazy Blues," and the jazz fad was soon supplanted by a blues craze. However jazz continued to progress and the New Orleans Rhythm Kings (one of the first groups to feature short solos) in 1922 sounded a decade ahead of the ODJB. 1923 was a key year for jazz because during that year King Oliver's Creole Jazz Band (which had among its sidemen cornetist Louis Armstrong and clarinetist Johnny Dodds), blues singer Bessie Smith and pianist-composer Jelly Roll Morton all made their recording debuts. While King Oliver's band would be considered the definitive ensemble-oriented New Orleans group, Louis Armstrong would soon permanently change jazz.

In the early 1920s Chicago was the center of jazz. When Louis Armstrong joined Fletcher Henderson's big band in New York in 1924, he found that the Big Apple's musicians (although technically superior) often played with a staccato feeling and without much blues feeling. Armstrong, through his explosive, dramatic and swinging solos with Henderson, was extremely influential in changing the way that jazz musicians phrased and in opening up possibilities for improvisers. In fact it could be argued that Louis Armstrong was chiefly responsible (although it probably would have happened eventually) for jazz's emphasis shifting from collective improvisation to individual solos, setting the stage for the swing era.

The 1920s became known as the Jazz Age (although as much for its liberal social attitudes as for its music). Jazz began to greatly influence dance bands and even the most commercial outfits started having short solos and a syncopated rhythm section. Louis Armstrong's remarkable series of Hot Five and Hot Seven recordings inspired other musicians to stretch themselves while his popularization of scat singing and a relaxed vocal phrasing influenced Bing Crosby (who in turn influenced everyone else!). Such players as cornetist Bix Beiderbecke (who had a cooler sound than Armstrong), pianist Jelly Roll Morton (both in solos and with his Red Hot Peppers), pianist James P. Johnson (the king of stride pianists), arranger-composer Duke Ellington and the up-and-coming tenor Coleman Hawkins became important forces in the jazz world.

By the latter half of the decade, larger jazz-based orchestras had become popular and the collective improvisation to be found in Dixieland was going out of style and restricted to smaller groups. When the Depression hit, it pushed Dixieland almost completely underground for a decade. The general public did not want to be reminded of the carefree days of the 1920s and instead for a few years preferred ballads and dance music. However when Benny Goodman suddenly became popular in 1935, the newer generation showed that they were interested in doing what they could to overlook the Depression by having a good time and dancing to hard-swinging orchestras. The 1935-46 period was accurately known as the big band era for the large orchestras dominated the pop music charts. During this decade jazz was a large part of popular music, not just an influence as it had been earlier. Glenn Miller and Artie Shaw had million sellers and Benny Goodman, Count Basie and Duke Ellington were household names and celebrities.

During those years jazz developed in several ways. New soloists (such as pianists Art Tatum and Teddy Wilson, tenor saxophonist Lester Young and trumpeters Roy Eldridge and Bunny Berigan) came up with alternative styles, big band arranging became more sophisticated, Dixieland was revived and rediscovered (Lu Watters' Yerba Buena Jazz Band was a major force) and jazz was celebrated for the first time as an important part of America. However this golden age of popularity would not last.

Due to jazz's continual evolution, it was perhaps inevitable that it would eventually advance far ahead of what the general public preferred in its popular music. In the early 1940s many of the younger musicians sought to move beyond swing music (which was bogging down in clichéd arrangements and novelties) and develop their own conception of playing. Altoist Charlie Parker and trumpeter Dizzy Gillespie were the main founders of the new music called bebop or bop but they were not alone and were soon joined by dozens of other musicians. The ideas were often quickly discarded as the soloists indulged in more advanced chordal improvisations (leading some critics to ask, "Where's the melody?"), harmonies and rhythms became much more complicated and, most seriously of all, the music was performed less and less for dancers. A recording strike during 1942-44, a prohibitive entertainment tax (which closed many dance halls) and the growing popularity of pop singers doomed the big bands, and the elim-

Music Map

Jazz Innovators

Throughout the history of jazz there have been literally thousands of talented improvisers and hundreds who have developed their own individual voices and approaches. There are six, however, whose accomplishments, originality, innovations and influence tower above the rest; each one of the six greatly altered the vocabulary of jazz and permanently changed the music:

Louis Armstrong (trumpet, vocals)
Duke Ellington (composer, arranger, bandleader, piano)
Charlie Parker (alto sax)
Dizzy Gillespie (trumpet)
Miles Davis (trumpet, bandleader)
John Coltrane (tenor sax, soprano sax)

Here is a list of the second level of jazz greats, artists whose music also greatly enhanced jazz. The categories are meant as a guide and do not necessarily sum up the musicians' entire careers:

New Orleans Jazz

Jelly Roll Morton (piano, composer)
King Oliver (cornet)
Kid Ory (trombone)
Johnny Dodds (clarinet)
Sidney Bechet (soprano, clarinet)
Red Allen (trumpet)

Classic Jazz

Bix Beiderbecke (cornet)
Jack Teagarden (trombone, vocals)
Pee Wee Russell (clarinet)
Bud Freeman (tenor)
James P. Johnson (piano)
Fats Waller (piano, composer, vocals)
Earl Hines (piano)
Joe Venuti (violin)
Bessie Smith (vocals)
Eddie Condon (bandleader)

Swing

Roy Eldridge (trumpet)
Bunny Berigan (trumpet)
Charlie Shavers (trumpet)
Clark Terry (fluegelhorn)
Benny Goodman (clarinet, bandleader)
Artie Shaw (clarinet, bandleader)
Coleman Hawkins (tenor)
Lester Young (tenor)
Ben Webster (tenor)
Johnny Hodges (alto)
Benny Carter (alto, arranger)
Harry Carney (baritone)
Art Tatum (piano)

Teddy Wilson (piano)
Count Basie (piano, bandleader)
Nat King Cole (piano, vocals)
Django Reinhardt (guitar)
Charlie Christian (guitar)
Lionel Hampton (vibes)
Stephane Grappelli (violin)
Jimmy Blanton (bass)
Gene Krupa (drums)
Buddy Rich (drums)
Louis Bellson (drums)
Billie Holiday (vocals)
Ella Fitzgerald (vocals)

Bop

Howard McGhee (trumpet)
Fats Navarro (trumpet)
J.J. Johnson (trombone)
Buddy DeFranco (clarinet)
Dexter Gordon (tenor)
Bud Powell (piano)
Thelonious Monk (piano, composer)
Oscar Peterson (piano)
Erroll Garner (piano)
Milt Jackson (vibes)
Joe Pass (guitar)
Oscar Pettiford (bass)
Max Roach (drums, bandleader)
Sarah Vaughan (vocals)
Lambert, Hendricks & Ross (vocal group)

Cool Jazz

Gerry Mulligan (baritone)
Lennie Tristano (piano, bandleader)
Chet Baker (trumpet)
Shorty Rogers (arranger, trumpet, leader)
Lee Konitz (alto)
Paul Desmont (alto)
Dave Brubeck (piano, leader)
Stan Getz (tenor)
Shelly Manne (drums, leader)

Hard Bop

Clifford Brown (trumpet)
Lee Morgan (trumpet)
Freddie Hubbard (trumpet)
Cannonball Adderley (alto)
Phil Woods (alto)
Art Pepper (alto)
Sonny Rollins (tenor)
Rahsaan Roland Kirk (tenor, stritch, manzello, flutes)
Wes Montgomery (guitar)
Horace Silver (piano, composer)
Jimmy Smith (organ)
Art Blakey (drums, bandleader)

Music Map

Jazz Innovators – *continued*

Avant-Garde

Charles Mingus (bass, bandleader)
Eric Dolphy (alto, bass clarinet, flute)
Ornette Coleman (alto, composer)
Anthony Braxton (alto, composer)
Cecil Taylor (piano)
Don Cherry (trumpet)
Albert Ayler (tenor)
Archie Shepp (tenor)
Julius Hemphill (alto)
Paul Bley (piano)
David Murray (tenor, bass clarinet)

Post Bop

Woody Shaw (trumpet)
Jackie McLean (alto)
Joe Henderson (tenor)
Wayne Shorter (tenor, soprano, composer)
Bill Evans (piano)

McCoy Tyner (piano)
Elvin Jones (drums)
Tony Williams (drums)
Gil Evans (arranger)
John McLaughlin (guitar)

Fusion

Chick Corea (piano, keyboards)
Herbie Hancock (piano, keyboards)
Joe Zawinul (keyboards)
Jaco Pastorius (electric bass)

Modern Mainstream/1990s Jazz

Wynton Marsalis (trumpet, leader)
Eddie Daniels (clarinet, tenor)
Keith Jarrett (piano)
Pat Metheny (guitar)
John Scofield (guitar)
Bill Frisell (guitar)

ination of dance floors at many clubs made jazz into a music strictly for listening. By being uplifted to the level of an art music, jazz was isolated from the pop music world and saw its audience shrink drastically as other simpler styles rushed in to fill the gap.

However its commercial decline did not slow down jazz's artistic growth. Bop, once considered a radical music (the recording strike stopped many listeners from hearing its gradual growth), became a large part of the jazz mainstream by the 1950s. Cool jazz (or West Coast jazz), which put a greater emphasis on softer tones and arrangements and was at its height in popularity in the mid-50s, and hard bop (which brought out more soulful elements of jazz that were sometimes discarded in bop) were outgrowths of bebop and had their fans. But it was with the rise of the avant-garde (sometimes called free jazz) that improvised music moved a giant step forward, leaving even more listeners behind!

When Ornette Coleman and his quartet were featured at the Five Spot in New York in 1959, many listeners who were just beginning to accept the music of Thelonious Monk were bewildered. Ornette and his sidemen quickly stated a theme in unison and then improvised very freely without using chords at all! During the same period John Coltrane who had taken bop to its extreme with the endless number of chords he used in "Giant Steps," began to jam passionately over simple repetitive vamps. Pianist Cecil Taylor's percussive atonality owed as much to contemporary classical music as to earlier jazz stylists and Eric Dolphy's wide interval jumps were completely unpredictable. Avant-garde jazz had arrived!

By the mid-1960s free jazz was filled with high-energy improvisers who explored sounds as much as notes. Within a few years with the rise of the Art Ensemble of Chicago and Anthony Braxton, space was utilized much more liberally in the music and by the 1970s many avant-garde artists were spending much of their time integrating improvisations with complex compositions. The music was no longer continuously free form but musicians had complete freedom in their solos to create whatever sounds they felt fit. Although this music has been overshadowed by other styles since the 1970s, it is still a viable option for creative improvisers, and its innovations continue to indirectly influence the modern mainstream of jazz.

The 1970s are best remembered as the fusion era, when many jazz musicians integrated aspects of rock, R&B and pop into their music. Until the late '60s, the jazz and rock worlds had stayed pretty much separate but, with the rise of electric keyboards, a great deal of experimentation took place. Miles Davis, who was

an innovator in bop, cool jazz, hard bop and his own brand of the avant-garde, became a pacesetter in fusion when he recorded *In a Silent Way* and *Bitches Brew*. Groups began to be formed that combined together the improvising and musicianship of jazz with the power and rhythms of rock; most notable were Return to Forever, Weather Report and the Mahavishnu Orchestra. By 1975 this movement began to run out of gas artistically but due to its moneymaking potential it has continued up to the present time, often in watered-down form as crossover or instrumental pop and given the inaccurate name of "contemporary jazz."

The history of jazz from 1920-75 was a constant rush forward with new styles considered out of date within five or ten years. In the 1980s it suddenly became acceptable to honor the past and to look back before bop for inspiration. While Dixieland had remained quite active as an underground music for decades (it was at its height of popularity in the 1950s), few in the jazz modern mainstream acknowledged its existence and importance before the '80s. Wynton Marsalis, who symbolized the decade, began as a trumpeter greatly inspired by the playing of Miles Davis of the mid-'60s. He eventually found his own sound by going back in time and exploring the music of the pre-bop masters, and the result was that (even when he played modern new music) Marsalis was able to come up with fresh approaches by borrowing and adapting ideas from the distant past.

Many of the young players that have followed Marsalis ignore fusion and even most of the innovations of the avant-garde to use hard bop as the basis for their music. It was a rather unusual development to have so many musicians in their twenties playing in a style that was at its prime before their birth, but by the 1990s many of these "Young Lions" were finally developing their own sounds and starting to build on the earlier innovations.

Nearly all styles of jazz are still active in the 1990s including Dixieland, classic jazz, mainstream (essentially small group swing), bop, hard bop, post bop, the avant garde and various forms of fusion. Very much an international music (some of the most stimulating sounds of recent times have come from Europe), the evolution of jazz has definitely slowed down during the past 20 years. At this point in time it is not apparent which direction jazz will go in the future (some cynics even think the music has essentially reached the end of its development), but one can bet that as long as recordings exist (along with the need for self-expression), jazz will survive.

Ragtime

Important events

1892 - Tom Turpin composes the earliest-known rag ("Harlem Rag") although it is not published until 1897.

1895 - Scott Joplin's first two songs are published.

1897 - William Krell's "Mississippi Rag" is the first rag to appear in print.

1899 - Scott Joplin's "Maple Leaf Rag" is published and becomes ragtime's biggest seller, launching ragtime craze.

1902 - Scott Joplin writes "The Entertainer," "The Ragtime Dance" and "Elite Syncopations."

1904 - St. Louis World's Fair holds ragtime contest.

1906 - James Scott's "Frog Legs Rag" is his first to be published.

1907 - Joseph Lamb meets Scott Joplin and Joplin helps Lamb get his music published.

1911 - Scott Joplin completes his ragtime opera "Treemonisha." Irving Berlin has much better luck with his pop hit "Alexander's Ragtime Band."

1914 - Joplin writes his last two rags.

1917 - Scott Joplin dies and the classic ragtime era is officially over.

1921 - Zez Confrey records "Kitten on the Keys," the most famous composition from the brief novelty ragtime period.

1938 - James Scott dies in obscurity.

1941 - Wally Rose records "Black and White Rag." His ragtime features with the Yerba Buena Jazz Band start a mini-revival of interest in ragtime.

1950 - Rubi Blesh and Harriet Janis write their classic book *They All Played Ragtime.*

1955 - Johnny Maddox as "Crazy Otto" has hit as honky-tonk piano is at the height of its popularity.

1959 - Joseph Lamb records an album a year before his death.

1970 - Joshua Rifkin records the first of three albums of Scott Joplin rags.

1973 - The release of *The Sting,* which liberally used Scott Joplin's music in the soundtrack, starts a major ragtime revival which has lasted to an extent to the present day.

1986 - Eubie Blake, the last of the original ragtime pianist composers, dies at age 100.

New Orleans Jazz (1895-1940)

Important events

1895 - Buddy Bolden forms his first band.

1902 - Jelly Roll Morton, then just 12, starts playing piano in Storyville. Later he would claim that he invented jazz that year.

1906 - Buddy Bolden, suffering from mental illness, is committed to an institution. Freddie Keppard, Bolden's successor, stars with the Olympia Orchestra.

1908 - Bassist Bill Johnson travels to Los Angeles, introducing New Orleans Jazz to the West Coast.

1914 - Freddie Keppard leaves New Orleans to join the Original Creole Band.

1917 - The Original Dixieland Jazz Band make first jazz recordings. Jelly Roll Morton settles in Los Angeles. Storyville closes.

1918 - King Oliver moves to Chicago.

1919 - Sidney Bechet travels overseas with Will Marion Cook's Orchestra, introducing jazz to the European continent.

1922 - Kid Ory records two titles in Los Angeles. The New Orleans Rhythm Kings make their first recordings. King Oliver forms Creole Jazz Band.

1923 - King Oliver, Jelly Roll Morton, Johnny Dodds, Sidney Bechet and Louis Armstrong make their debuts on record.

1924 - Louis Armstrong stars with the Fletcher Henderson Orchestra, shows New York musicians how to swing. Muggsy Spanier makes recording debut. Fate Marable records his only session.

1925 - Louis Armstrong starts series of Hot Five recordings including "Cornet Chop Suey.

1926 - Jelly Roll Morton records with his Red Hot Peppers in Chicago. Freddie Keppard cuts his best recording. King Oliver records with his Dixie Syncopators.

Music Map

Significant Ragtime Players

Ragtime Composers from Classic Era
Scott Joplin
Joseph Lamb
James Scott
Tom Turpin
Eubie Blake

Transitional Composers from Ragtime to Early Jazz
Jelly Roll Morton
James P. Johnson

Early Ragtime Banjoists
Vess Ossman
Fred Van Eps

Drums
James I. Lent (recorded "The Ragtime Drummer" in 1904)

Recent Composers
David Thomas Roberts
Reginald Robinson

Ragtime Pianists from 1940s On
Wally Rose	Dick Hyman
Max Morath	Joshua Rifkin
Scott Kirby	David Thomas Roberts
Reginald Robinson	

Music Map

Significant Early New Orleans Jazz Players

Cornet/Trumpet

Buddy Bolden	Freddie Keppard
Manuel Perez	King Oliver
Louis Armstrong	Paul Mares
Oscar Celestin	Lee Collins
Punch Miller	Tommy Ladnier
Muggsy Spaniel	Wingy Manone
Louis Prima	Sidney DeParis
Red Allen	

Trombone

Kid Ory	George Brunies
Charlie Green	Roy Palmer
J.C. Higginbottham	

Clarinet

Sidney Bechet	Leon Rappolo
Johnny Dodds	Jimmy Noone
Buster Bailey	Albert Nicholas
Barnney Bigard	Omer Simeon

Soprano

Sidney Bechet

Banjo

Johnny St. Cyr

Piano

Jelly Roll Morton	Tony Jackson
Lil Harden	Luis Russell

Bass

Bill Johnson	Ed Garland
John Lindsay	Pops Foster

Drums

Tony Sbarbaro	Baby Dodds
Zutty Singleton	Paul Barbarin

Vocals

Louis Armstrong

1927 - Red Allen joins King Oliver's band. Louis Armstrong records with his Hot Seven.

1928 - Louis Armstrong teams up with Earl Hines, most notably for "West End Blues" and "Weatherbird."
Jimmy Noone records with his Apex Club Orchestra.

1929 - Louis Armstrong begins recording exclusively with big bands.
Luis Russell band makes finest recordings.
Red Allen leads first record dates.
New Orleans jazz goes underground as Depression hits.

1931 - The long forgotten Buddy Bolden dies.

1932 - Sidney Bechet records a session with his New Orleans Feetwarmers.

1933 - Freddie Keppard dies.

1935 - The Bob Crosby Orchestra is formed, features New Orleans-flavored jazz in a swing setting.

1938 - Jelly Roll Morton records extensively for the Library of Congress. King Oliver dies.
Johnny Dodds records for the first time since 1930.

1940 - Johnny Dodds dies. Louis Armstrong and Sidney Bechet team up on a record date.

1941 - Jelly Roll Morton dies as New Orleans revival starts to take off.

Classic Jazz (Jazz from the 1920s)

Important events

1917 - The Original Dixieland Jazz Band (ODJB) cuts the first jazz recordings. "Livery Stable Blues" is a best-seller.

1919 - The ODJB visits England and is a big sensation.

1920 - Mamie Smith records the first blues record, "Crazy Blues."

1922 - Kid Ory's band records in Los Angeles, under the name of "Spikes' Seven Pods of Pepper Orchestra!"
The New Orleans Rhythm Kings debuts on record.

1923 - King Oliver's Creole Jazz Band (with Louis Armstrong and Johnny Dodds) is the band of the year, playing nightly in Chicago.
Bessie Smith and Sidney Bechet make their first recordings.

1924 - Bix Beiderbecke records with the Wolverines.
Louis Armstrong joins Fletcher Henderson's Orchestra.
Paul Whiteman seeks to "make a lady out of jazz" and presents a watered-down version at Aeolian Hall.

1925 - Louis Armstrong's classic series of Hot Five recordings begins.

1926 - Jelly Roll Morton records his first Hot Peppers sessions.

1927 - Duke Ellington wins a regular gig at the Cotton Club.
Bix Beiderbecke, during his finest period, splits the year between the orchestras of Jean Goldkette and Paul Whiteman.

1928 - Louis Armstrong records "West End Blues" and "Weather Bird Rag"; the latter as a duet with Earl Hines.

1929 - Cootie Williams replaces Bubber Miley with Duke Ellington. Jabbo Smith records with his Rhythm Aces.

1930 - Paul Whiteman's Orchestra films *The King of Jazz*.

1931 - King Oliver's last recordings.
Bix Beiderbecke dies.

Swing

Important events

1923 - Don Redman, the first important jazz arranger, becomes a regular member of the Fletcher Henderson Orchestra.
Duke Ellington visits New York for the initial time with little success.

Music Map

Significant Classic Jazz Players

Louis Armstrong - cornet/trumpet, vocals
Bix Beiderbecke - cornet
Jelly Roll Morton - piano, composer
Johnny Dodds - clarinet
James P. Johnson - piano
Duke Ellington - bandleader, composer,
arranger, piano
Bessie Smith - vocals

Other Significant Players in 1920s

Alto Saxophone
Jimmy Dorsey

Banjo
Johnny St. Cyr

Bass
Steve Brown
Wellman Braud
Pops Foster

Bass Saxophone
Adrian Rollini

Clarinet
Leon Rappolo	Sidney Bechet
Jimmy Noone	Frankie Teschemacher
Omer Simeon	Benny Goodman
Jimmy Dorsey	

Cornet/Trumpet
King Oliver	Bubber Miley
Phil Napoleon	Red Nichols
Jabbo Smith	Red Allen

Drums
Tony Sbarbaro
Baby Dodds
Vic Berton
Zutty Singleton

Guitar
Eddie Lang
Lonnie Johnson

Piano
Fats Waller
Earl Hines

Soprano Saxophone
Sidney Bechet

Tenor Saxophone
Coleman Hawkins
Bud Freeman

Trombone
Kid Ory
Miff Mole
Jimmy Harrison
Tricky Sam Nanton
Jack Teagarden

Violin
Joe Venuti

Vocals - Male
Bing Crosby
Jack Teagarden

Vocals - Female
Ethel Waters
Annette Hanshaw
Boswell Sisters

Big Bands
Paul Whiteman
Fletcher Henderson
Duke Ellington
McKinney's Cotton Pickers

Bennie Moten's Kansas City Orchestra makes debut on records.

1924 - Fletcher Henderson's big band (featuring Louis Armstrong) begins its longtime residency at the Roseland Ballroom.

1927 - Don Redman leaves Fletcher Henderson to become leader of McKinney's Cotton Pickers.
Duke Ellington wins regular job at the Cotton Club.

1928 - Johnny Hodges joins Duke Ellington's Orchestra.
Earl Hines first plays with his big band at the Grand Terrace in Chicago.

1929 - The influential Casa Loma Orchestra makes its first recordings.
Count Basie joins Bennie Moten's Orchestra.

Louis Armstrong begins recording regularly with big bands.

1930 - Cab Calloway takes over the Missourians and begins playing at the Cotton Club.

1931 - Don Redman forms his own big band.

1932 - Duke Ellington with Ivie Anderson records "It Don't Mean a Thing If It Ain't Got That Swing."

1933 - Duke Ellington's Orchestra visits Europe.
Art Tatum makes his debut on records.
Billie Holiday records her first two songs.

Music Map

Significant Swing Players

Trumpet

Louis Armstrong	Roy Eldridge
Bunny Berigan	Charlie Shavers
Hot Lips Page	Buck Clayton
Harry "Sweets" Edison	Harry James
Ziggy Elman	Cootie Williams
Rex Stewart	Ray Nance
Taft Jordan	Erskine Hawkins
Bill Coleman	Jonah Jones
Frankie Newton	Yank Lawson
Billy Butterfield	Bobby Hackett

Trombone

Jack Teagarden	Tommy Dorsey
Dickie Wells	Trummy Young
Tricky Sam Nanton	Lawrence Brown
Jack Jenney	

Clarinet

Benny Goodman	Artie Shaw
Jimmy Dorsey	Woody Herman
Barney Bigard	Edmond Hall

Tenor

Coleman Hawkins	Lester Young
Chu Berry	Ben Webster
Charlie Barnet	Herschel Evans
Buddy Tate	Dick Wilson
Georgie Auld	Illinois Jacquet
Flip Phillips	Don Byas

Alto

Johnny Hodges	Benny Carter
Willie Smith	Jimmy Dorsey
Woody Herman	Tab Smith

Baritone

Harry Carney

Piano

Art Tatum	Fats Waller
Earl Hines	Teddy Wilson
Duke Ellington	Mary Lou Williams
Joe Sullivan	Jess Stacy
Count Basie	Billy Kyle
Johnny Guarnieri	Mel Powell
Nat King Cole	Jay McShann

Vibes

Lionel Hampton
Red Norvo

Violin

Stephane Grappelli
Stuff Smith

Guitar

Django Reinhardt	Charlie Christian
Carl Kress	Dick McDonough
Freddie Green	Al Casey
Oscar Moore	Tiny Grimes

Bass

Walter Page	Israel Crosby
John Kirby	Milt Hinton
Bob Haggart	Slam Stewart
Jimmy Blanton	

Drums

Gene Krupa	Chick Webb
Jo Jones	Dave Tough
Big Sid Catlett	Cozy Cole
Buddy Rich	

Vocals, Male

Louis Armstrong	Cab Calloway
Jimmy Rushing	Big Joe Turner
Jack Teagarden	Fats Waller
Hot Lips Page	Wingy Manone
Louis Prima	Billy Eckstine
Nat King Cole	

Vocals, Female

Billie Holiday	Ella Fitzgerald
Ethel Waters	Mildred Bailey
Ivie Anderson	Helen Ward
Helen Forrest	Helen Humes
Maxine Sullivan	

Arrangers

Duke Ellington	Don Redman
Fletcher Henderson	Benny Carter
Sy Oliver	Edgar Sampson
Mary Lou Williams	Horace Henderson
Jimmy Mundy	Glenn Miller
Eddie Sauter	

Significant Big Bands of the Swing Era

Duke Ellington	Benny Goodman
Count Basie	Glenn Miller
Fletcher Henderson	Bennie Moten
McKinney's Cotton Pickers	Earl Hines
Luis Russell	Casa Loma Orchestra
Cab Calloway	Jimmy Lunceford
Chick Webb	Andy Kirk
Tommy Dorsey	Jimmy Dorsey
Artie Shaw	Charlie Barnet
Bob Crosby	Harry James
Erskine Hawkins	Jay McShann
Gene Krupa	Lionel Hampton
Stan Kenton	Woody Herman

Music Map

Significant Bebop Players

Charlie Parker - alto
Dizzy Gillespie trumpet
Bud Powell - piano
Thelonious Monk - piano, composer
J.J. Johnson - trombone
Max Roach - drums
Tadd Dameron - composer, arranger

Other Significant Players of Classic Bop

Alto Saxophone

Sonny Criss	Sonny Stitt
Phil Woods	Lou Donaldson
Richie Cole	Charles McPherson

Bass

Oscar Pettiford
Charles Mingus
Ray Brown
Percy Heath

Clarinet

Buddy DeFranco

Drums

Kenny Clarke
Art Blakey
Roy Haynes

Guitar

Charlie Christian	Barney Kessel
Tal Farlow	Herb Ellis
Kenny Burrell	Joe Pass

Percussion

Chano Pozo

Piano

Al Haig	Dodo Marmarosa
Duke Jordan	John Lewis
Barry Harris	

Tenor Saxophone

Don Byas	Dexter Gordon
Wardell Gray	Teddy Edwards
Gene Ammons	Sonny Stitt

Trombone

Kai Winding
Jimmy Cleveland

Trumpet

Howard McGhee
Fats Navarro
Jon Faddis

Vibes

Milt Jackson
Terry Gibbs

Vocals - Male

Dave Lambert	Eddie Jefferson
King Pleasure	Jon Hendricks

Vocals - Female

Ella Fitzgerald	Sarah Vaughan
Anita O'Day	Annie Ross

Big Bands

Billy Eckstine
Dizzy Gillespie
Woody Herman's First Two Herds
Stan Kenton

1934 - Coleman Hawkins leaves Fletcher Henderson's Orchestra after a decade, moves to Europe.
Jimmy Lunceford makes his first important recordings.
Benny Goodman's orchestra begins appearing on the "Let's Dance" radio show.
Chick Webb records "Stompin' at the Savoy." Ella Fitzgerald joins band.
Fats Waller's extensive series of recordings with his Rhythm start.

1935 - Benny Goodman's Orchestra becomes a surprise sensation, launching the swing era.
Fletcher Henderson breaks up band, contributes arrangements to Benny Goodman.
Bennie Moten dies.
Count Basie soon forms own orchestra.
Billie Holiday starts recording with Teddy Wilson.
Tommy and Jimmy Dorsey have a public argument, break up Dorsey Brothers Orchestra and form their own separate big bands.

1936 - Woody Herman takes over the remains of the Isham Jones Orchestra and forms his first big band.
Fletcher Henderson's new orchestra has a hit in "Christopher Columbus" but his group would break up three years later.
Count Basie is discovered by John Hammond over the radio.
Lester Young makes his debut on records.
Artie Shaw puts together his first orchestra, but it flops.
Andy Kirk's Twelve Clouds of Joy become popular.

1937 - Tommy Dorsey records "Marie" and "Song of India" featuring trumpeter Bunny Berigan.
Berigan forms his own big band, records "I Can't Get Started."
Count Basie's Orchestra makes its first recordings.
Chu Berry joins Cab Calloway.
Glenn Miller forms an orchestra that quickly fails.

1938 - Benny Goodman has a historic concert at Carnegie Hall.
Gene Krupa soon leaves Goodman to form his own big band.

Artie Shaw has a major hit with "Begin the Beguine."
John Kirby's Sextet debuts on record.

1939 - Arranger Sy Oliver quits Jimmy Lunceford's Orchestra to join Tommy Dorsey.
Charlie Barnet's band catches on.
Artie Shaw, at the height of his popularity, breaks up his orchestra and flees to Mexico.
Harry James leaves Benny Goodman to form his own big band.
Glenn Miller's Orchestra becomes the most popular in the world.
Jimmy Blanton and Ben Webster join Duke Ellington.
Chick Webb dies; Ella Fitzgerald takes over band.
Coleman Hawkins, back from Europe after five years, records "Body and Soul."
Charlie Christian joins Benny Goodman.

1940 - Artie Shaw returns to U.S. and has major hit in "Frenesi."
Cootie Williams leaves Duke Ellington and joins Benny Goodman for a year.
Lester Young quits the Count Basie Orchestra.

1941 - Charlie Parker records with the Jay McShann big band.
Gene Krupa has several hits with Anita O'Day and Roy Eldridge.
Stan Kenton forms his first orchestra.
Chu Berry dies.

1942 - Glenn Miller and Artie Shaw break up their big bands to enlist in the military.
A disastrous recording strike starts the beginning of the end of the big band era.
Harry James' Orchestra succeeds Glenn Miller's as the most popular.
Bunny Berigan, Fats Waller, Jimmy Blanton and Charlie Christian die.
Lionel Hampton records "Flying Home."

1943 - Duke Ellington's Orchestra has debut at Carnegie Hall, introducing "Black, Brown & Beige."

1944 - Willie Smith, formerly with Jimmy Lunceford, joins Harry James.
Woody Herman's Orchestra becomes known as the Herd.
Glenn Miller dies.

1945 - Harry James ("It's Been a Long Long Time") and Les Brown ("Sentimental Journey") have major hits but the big bands are being replaced in popularity by vocalists.

1946 - Benny Goodman, Woody Herman, Harry James, Tommy Dorsey and Jack Teagarden are among many who break up their big bands.

1947 - Jimmy Lunceford dies.
Louis Armstrong breaks up orchestra, forms All-Stars.

Bebop

Important events

1937 - Dizzy Gillespie makes initial recordings with Teddy Hill.

1939 - Gillespie joins Cab Calloway's Orchestra.
Charlie Parker visits New York for the first time.

1940 - Dizzy Gillespie and Charlie Parker meet.
Parker makes first recordings with Jay McShann.

1941 - Late night jam sessions at Minton's Playhouse and Monroe's Uptown House feature Thelonious Monk and Kenny Clarke in the house bands with frequent guests Charlie Christian, Charlie Parker and Dizzy Gillespie among others.

1942 - Gillespie plays bop solo with Lucky Millinder on "Little John Special."

1943 - Earl Hines' big band features both Parker (on tenor) and Gillespie, but recording strike keeps association from being documented.
Gillespie co-leads early bop group with Oscar Pettiford.

1944 - Billy Eckstine forms bebop big band that for a time includes Charlie Parker and Dizzy Gillespie.
Coleman Hawkins leads earliest bop record date; group features Gillespie.
Charlie Parker heard on Tiny Grimes combo session.
Thelonious Monk composes "'Round Midnight" which is recorded by Cootie Williams orchestra with Bud Powell on piano.

1945 - Charlie Parker and Dizzy Gillespie make many recordings that stun the jazz world.
Howard McGhee (traveling with Coleman Hawkins) helps bring bebop to Los Angeles.
Gillespie leads his first big band but it fails.
Bird and Diz make trip to West Coast.
J.J. Johnson is with Count Basie's orchestra.

1946 - Dizzy Gillespie forms his second big band which is much more successful than the first.
Parker spends half year at Camarillo State Hospital.
J.J. Johnson's first recordings as a leader are so fluent that some suspect he is playing valve trombone!
Fats Navarro leaves Billy Eckstine's orchestra and starts recording many classic small group sides.

1947 - Gillespie adds innovative conga player Chano Pozo to big band.
Parker returns to New York and puts together his strongest regular quintet, a group featuring Miles Davis and Max Roach.
Thelonious Monk makes first sessions for Blue Note.
Billy Eckstine reluctantly breaks up his big band.
Bud Powell cuts his first trio sides.
Dexter Gordon and Wardell Gray record "The Chase."

1948 - Second recording strike keeps most artists off records but Charlie Parker still records "Parker's Mood."

1949 - Bop is everywhere; even Benny Goodman, Gene Krupa and Charlie Barnet record it.
Dizzy Gillespie signs with Capitol as larger record companies seek to make a fad out of bop.
Charlie Parker records with strings.
All-Star bop concert at Carnegie Hall on Christmas Day.

1950 - Bebop "fad" ends abruptly.
Fats Navarro dies.
Dizzy Gillespie breaks up big band.

Post 1950 - Despite pronouncements of bop's "death," the once radical music becomes part of the jazz mainstream, greatly influencing all future styles and surviving in many forms up to the present day.

Dixieland and New Orleans Jazz Revival

Important events

1929 - Freewheeling Dixieland goes out of style.
Louis Armstrong begins recording with big bands.

1932 - Sidney Bechet gets a single recording session with his New Orleans Feetwarmers.

1934 - Wingy Manone and Louis Prima both start recording frequently as singing Dixieland trumpeter bandleaders.
Fats Waller and His Rhythm began their popular series of Bluebird records.

1935 - Tommy Dorsey starts extensive series of good-natured Dixieland recordings with his Clambake Seven.

1937 - Bob Crosby's Dixieland-oriented swing big band and his Bobcats begin to become popular.

Music Map

Significant Dixieland Revival Players

Louis Armstrong trumpet, vocals
Eddie Condon bandleader
Jack Teagarden - trombone, vocals
Lu Watters - trumpet, bandleader
Kid Ory - trombone, bandleader

Other Significant Dixieland Players

Alto Saxophone
Captain John Handy

Baritone Saxophone
Ernie Caceres

Bass
Pops Foster
Bob Haggart

Bass Saxophone
Joe Rushton

Clarinet
Pee Wee Russell	Barney Bigard
Edmond Hall	George Lewis
Peanuts Hucko	Matty Matlock
Pete Fountain	Bob Wilber
Kenny Davern	Ken Peplowski

Drums
Baby Dodds
George Wettling
Nick Fatool
Ray Bauduc
Paul Barbarin

Guitar
Danny Barker
Marty Grosz
Howard Alden

Piano
Earl Hines	Joe Sullivan
Jess Stacy	Art Hodes
Wally Rose	Ralph Sutton
Dick Wellstood	Dick Hyman
Dave McKenna	James Dapogny
Judy Carmichael	

Tenor Saxophone
Bud Freeman
Eddie Miller

Trombone
George Brunies	Trummy Young
Vic Dickenson	Lou McGarity
Jim Robinson	Turk Murphy
Wilbur DeParis	Dan Barrett

Trumpet
Red Allen	Hot Lips Page
Wingy Manone	Sidney DeParis
Louis Prima	Yank Lawson
Billy Butterfield	Muggsy Spanier
Bobby Hackett	Max Kaminsky
Jimmy McPartland	Wild Bill Davison
Bob Scobey	Red Nichols
Ruby Braff	Warren Vache
Peter Ecklund	Jim Cullum, Jr.
Doc Cheatham	

Vocals - Male
Red Allen	Wingy Manone
Louis Prima	Jelly Roll Morton
Clancy Haynes	Danny Barker
Marty Grosz	

Vocals - Female
Lee Wiley	Alberta Hunter

1938 - Jelly Roll Morton records extensively for the Library of Congress but his attempt at a comeback (which ended with his death in 1941) is largely unsuccessful.
Eddie Condon records several classics for the new Commodore label.

1939 - Cornetist Muggsy Spanier records "The Great 16" with his Ragtime Band. Despite the major influence of this music on future Dixieland bands, Spanier's group cannot get a regular job and soon break up.

1940 - Sidney Bechet records for Bluebird.

1941 - The Dixieland revival really gets going full force with the first recordings of Lu Watters Yerba Buena Jazz Band.

1942 - Bunk Johnson emerges from retirement to make an unlikely comeback.

1943 - Wild Bill Davison records the definitive version of "That's a Plenty" for Commodore.

1944 - Kid Ory, who had spent the 1930s running a chicken farm, comes out of retirement and forms his Creole Jazz Band.
Eddie Condon's Town Hall Concerts feature all-star integrated jazz groups broadcasting over the radio on a weekly basis.

1945 - Mezz Mezzrow launches his King Jazz label.

1946 - Louis Armstrong stars in the fictional but entertaining movie *New Orleans*.

1947 - Louis Armstrong breaks up his big band and forms his All-Stars with Jack Teagarden and Barney Bigard.
Turk Murphy and Bob Scobey leave the Yerba Buena Jazz Band and soon form their own successful groups.
Rudi Blesh's hosts the legendary *This Is Jazz* radio series.

1949 - Firehouse Five Plus Two makes first recordings, helps launch Good Time Jazz label.
Sidney Bechet moves to France and soon becomes national hero.
Eddie Condon's Floor Show, a pioneering half-hour jam session series, is televised each week.

1950 - George Lewis' band begins to record and soon starts touring the world.
Lu Watters breaks up the Yerba Buena Jazz Band and retires.

1955 - Wilbur DeParis and his "New New Orleans Jazz Band" make their first recording for Atlantic.

1958 - *The Five Pennies*, a hit movie, features Danny Kaye in the fictional role of Red Nichols along with Louis Armstrong; Nichols himself plays on the soundtrack.

1959 - Pete Fountain, featured Dixieland clarinetist with the

Music Map

Significant Cool Jazz Players

Lester Young - tenor
Miles Davis - trumpet
Lennie Tristano - piano
Shorty Rogers - trumpet, arranger
Shelly Manne - drums, leader
Gerry Mulligan - baritone, arranger
Chet Baker - trumpet
Dave Brubeck - piano
Paul Desmond - alto
Stan Getz - tenor
Art Pepper - alto
Lee Konitz - alto
Gil Evans - arranger

Other Significant Cool Players

Alto Saxophone
Bud Shank

Baritone Saxophone
Lars Gullin

Bass
Red Callender   Percy Heath
Red Mitchell   Monty Budwig
Leroy Vinnegar

Clarinet
Jimmy Giuffre
Tony Scott

Drums
Chico Hamilton
Connie Kay
Stan Levey

Flute
Frank Wess
Bud Shank
Buddy Collette

Guitar
Billy Bauer
Jimmy Raney

Johnny Smith
Jim Hall

Piano
John Lewis   Russ Freeman
Claude Williamson   Pete Jolly
Lou Levy

Tenor Saxophone
Zoot Sims   Al Cohn
Jimmy Giuffre   Bob Cooper
Bill Perkins   Richie Kamuca
Jack Montrose

Trombone
Frank Rosolino
Bob Brookmeyer
Carl Fontana

Trumpet
Conte Candoli
Jon Eardley
Don Fagerquist

Vocals - Female
June Christy
Chris Connor
Helen Merrill

Big Bands
Claude Thornhill
Woody Herman's Second Herd

Groups
Miles Davis Birth of the Cool Nonet
Lennie Tristano Sextet
Dave Brubeck Quartet
Modern Jazz Quartet
Lighthouse All-Stars
Shorty Rogers & His Giants
Shelly Manne & His Men
The Dave Pell Octet
Jimmy Giuffre 3
Chico Hamilton Quintet

Lawrence Welk Show, leaves the series and begins his own lucrative career.

1961 - Kenny Ball has big hit with "Midnight in Moscow." Preservation Hall opens in New Orleans. Dukes of Dixieland sign with Columbia where they will make their finest recordings.

1964 - "Hello Dolly" becomes a huge hit for Louis Armstrong. Lu Watters returns to music briefly (sounding in fine form on his one recording) before retiring again.

1968 - Yank Lawson and Bob Haggart team up to form "The World's Greatest Jazz Band."

1971- Louis Armstrong dies.

1974 - The first Sacramento Dixieland Jubilee is held and the huge annual event attests to the continuing artistic (if not commercial) health of Dixieland.

1979 - Stomp Off label is formed and extensively documents the classic jazz scene of the 1980s and '90s.

Cool Jazz (West Coast Jazz)

Important events

1936 - Lester Young makes recording debut with a small group out of Count Basie's band, introducing to the jazz world a new softer sound for the tenor.

1938 - John Kirby forms his cool-toned swing sextet.

1942 - Claude Thornhill adds two french horns to his big band. One of his main arrangers is Gil Evans.

1945 - Miles Davis makes his recording debut.

1946 - Lennie Tristano cuts his first records.

1947 - Miles Davis joins the Charlie Parker Quintet. Woody Herman forms his Second Herd, an orchestra that features Stan Getz, Zoot Sims and Herbie Steward (later Al Cohn) on tenors and baritonist Serge Chaloff playing Jimmy Giuffre's "Four Brothers."

1948 - Miles Davis forms a nonet whose twelve very influential Capitol recordings of 1949-50 are later billed as "The Birth of the Cool." Despite the participation of Lee Konitz, Gerry Mulligan, John Lewis and Gil Evans, this band was only able to secure one gig! Dave Brubeck plays concerts with an octet.

1949 - Lennie Tristano records with his sextet, a group featuring altoist Lee Konitz and tenor saxophonist Warne Marsh. Tenors Stan Getz, Zoot Sims, Al Cohn, Allan Eager and Brew Moore record four songs together; it is impossible to tell any of the cool-toned players apart!

1950 - The Dave Brubeck Trio is popular on the West Coast.

1951 - Shorty Rogers' first recordings as a leader utilizes an octet similar in style to Miles Davis' famous nonet. Dave Brubeck forms his quartet with altoist Paul Desmond. Many former Stan Kenton and Woody Herman sidemen settle in Los Angeles to work in the studios.

1952 - First recordings by the Modern Jazz Quartet. Gerry Mulligan and Chet Baker team up in a very popular pianoless quartet. Miles Davis' recordings show a direct turn away from cool jazz toward what would be hard bop. Howard Rumsey's Lighthouse All-Stars is featured on the first of a series of records that would last until 1957.

1953 - Shorty Rogers settles in Los Angeles and has a busy and influential studio and recording career (both playing and arranging) throughout the remainder of the decade. Chet Baker forms his own quartet with pianist Russ Freeman. Shelly Manne begans a long series of recordings for Contemporary. The Dave Pell Octet debuts on record.

1954 - Bob Brookmeyer tours with Gerry Mulligan's Quartet.

1955 - The Chico Hamilton Quintet (with cellist Fred Katz and flutist Buddy Collette) is formed. Connie Kay replaces Kenny Clarke as drummer with the Modern Jazz Quartet.

1956 - The Shelly Manne Trio's recording of songs from "My Fair Lady" (featuring pianist Andre Previn) becomes a major hit.

1957 - West successfully meets East as altoist Art Pepper records a classic album with members of the Miles Davis Quintet titled *Art Pepper Meets the Rhythm Section.*

1958 - The Jimmy Giuffre 3 consists of the leader's clarinet, valve trombonist Bob Brookmeyer and guitarist Jim Hall.

1959 - The Dave Brubeck Quartet records "Take Five."

1960 - Gerry Mulligan forms his Concert Jazz Band.

1961 - The Jimmy Giuffre 3 becomes avant-garde. Dave Pell's Octet make their last recordings of the era. Chico Hamilton drops the cello from his quintet so as to get a harder sound. West Coast Jazz is essentially extinct as a separate style although it would remain an influence.

Hard Bop

Important events

1949 - The young Sonny Rollins records with J.J. Johnson.

1950 - Horace Silver is discovered by Stan Getz in Boston.

1951 - Miles Davis records his first hard bop records with Sonny Rollins and Jackie McLean.

1954 - Clifford Brown and Max Roach form their quintet. Miles Davis records "Walkin'." J.J. Johnson and Kai Winding team up for a two-trombone quintet.

1955 - Cannonball Adderley sits in with Oscar Pettiford's group at the Cafe Bohemia and becomes "new Bird." Art Blakey and Horace Silver form the Jazz Messengers.

1956 - Horace Silver leaves the Jazz Messengers to form his own quintet; records "Senor Blues." Jimmy Smith makes his first recordings and is an immediate sensation. Sonny Rollins and John Coltrane have a battle on "Tenor Madness." Clifford Brown dies. Lee Morgan makes his debut as a leader.

1957 - Jimmy Smith records ten albums for Blue Note, including five in a three-day period!

1958 - Booker Little joins Max Roach's pianoless quartet. The Jazz Messengers introduce "Moanin'" and "Blues March." Wes Montgomery records his first full-length album. Gene Harris and the Three Sounds start to catch on.

1959 - Bobby Timmons' "This Here" is major hit for Cannonball Adderley.

Music Map

Significant Hard Bop Players

Regular Working Groups
Art Blakey's Jazz Messengers
Horace Silver Quintet
The Jazztet
Clifford Brown-Max Roach Quintet
Cannonball Adderley Quintet
The Three Sounds

Trumpet
Miles Davis	Clifford Brown
Art Farmer	Lee Morgan
Freddie Hubbard	Woody Shaw
Donald Byrd	Blue Mitchell
Kenny Dorham	Nat Adderley

Trombone
J.J. Johnson	Kai Winding
Jimmy Cleveland	Curtis Fuller
Jimmy Knepper	Julian Priester

Alto Saxophone
Cannonball Adderley	Jackie McLean
Oliver Nelson	James Spaulding
Gary Bartz	

Tenor Saxophone
Sonny Rollins	Benny Golson
Johnny Griffin	Harold Land
Junior Cook	Hank Mobley
Jimmy Heath	Yusef Lateef
Clifford Jordan	Joe Henderson
George Coleman	Stanley Turrentine
Eddie Harris	Houston Person

Baritone Saxophone
Pepper Adams

Piano
Horace Silver	Red Garland
Wynton Kelly	Bobby Timmons
Les McCann	Gene Harris
Mal Waldron	Randy Weston
Phineas Newborn	Kenny Drew
Walter Bishop, Jr.	Walter Davis

Organ
Jimmy Smith	Charles Earland
Groove Holmes	Jack McDuff
Jimmy McGriff	Lonnie Smith
Johnny Hammond Smith	

Guitar
Wes Montgomery
Grant Green
Kenny Burrell

Bass
Paul Chambers	Doug Watkins
Sam Jones	Wilbur Ware
Richard Davis	Ron Carter
Buster Williams	

Drums
Max Roach	Art Blakey
Philly Joe Jones	Art Taylor
Jimmy Cobb	Louis Hayes
Roy Brooks	Grady Tate
Roy Haynes	

Composers & Arrangers
Horace Silver	Benny Golson
Bobby Timmons	Sonny Rollins
Kenny Dorham	Thad Jones
Randy Weston	Melba Liston
Oliver Nelson	Duke Pearson
Wayne Shorter	

Jackie McLean's *Jackie's Bag* is the first hard bop album to show influence of the avant-garde.
Wayne Shorter joins the Jazz Messengers.
Sonny Rollins retires for three years.
Blue Mitchell joins the Horace Silver Quintet.

1960 - Max Roach's quintet includes both Stanley and Tommy Turrentine.
Wes Montgomery records *The Incredible Jazz Guitar*.
Les McCann makes his first of many albums for Pacific Jazz.
The Jazztet debuts and introduces "Killer Joe."
Freddie Hubbard leads his first record date, *Open Sesame*.

1961 - Eddie Harris records "Exodus."
Oliver Nelson records classic album *Blues and the Abstract Truth*.

Lee Morgan leaves the Jazz Messengers and is succeeded by Freddie Hubbard.
Grant Green records five albums as a leader for Blue Note.

1962 - The Jazztet breaks up.

1963 - Lee Morgan records "The Sidewinder."

1964 - Horace Silver records "Song for My Father."
Freddie Hubbard leads quintet featuring James Spaulding.

1965 - Wes Montgomery switches to pop music with "Goin' Out of My Head."
Lee Morgan introduces "Ceora."

1966 - "Mercy, Mercy, Mercy" is a hit for Cannonball Adderley who moves away from playing hard bop.

Music Map

Significant Latin Jazz Players

Bandleaders

Machito	Tito Puente
Cal Tjader	Mongo Santamaria
Poncho Sanchez	Chuco Valdes (Irakere)
Jerry Gonzalez	

Percussion/Drums

Chano Pozo	Jack Costanzo
Tito Puente	Mongo Santamaria
Willie Bobo	Carlos Vidal
Candido	Armando Peraza
Potato Valdez	Ray Baretto
Poncho Sanchez	Ignacio Berroa
Giovanni Hidalgo	Jerry Gonzalez

Piano

Eddie Palmieri	Hilton Ruiz
Danilo Perez	Gonzalo Rubalcaba
Chucho Valdes	

Bass

Cachao

Alto/Clarinet

Paquito D'Rivera

Flute

Herbie Mann
Dave Valentin

Soprano Saxophone/Flute

Jane Bunnett

Trumpet

Arturo Sandoval

Vibes

Cal Tjader

1967 - Blue Note is sold to Liberty. The classic hard bop era begins to end.
Jackie McLean makes his final Blue Note album.
Eddie Harris records "Listen Here."

1968 - Wes Montgomery dies.

1970 - Woody Shaw records *Blackstone Legacy* and tries his best to keep hard bop alive in the 1970s.
Freddie Hubbard records *Red Clay* and *Straight Life* for CTI but soon switches to pop music.

1972 - Lee Morgan is killed.

1978 - Horace Silver, the final jazz artist on Blue Note, finally leaves the label.

Bossa-Nova

Important events

1954 - Laurindo Almeida and Bud Shank team up for two Pacific Jazz recordings that hint strongly at bossa-nova years before the term was coined.

1958 - Joao Gilberto records Antonio Carlos Jobim's "Chega De Saudade" in Brazil.

1959 - The film *Black Orpheus* features an exciting score by Antonio Carlos Jobim and Luiz Bonfa.

1960 - Joao Gilberto and Antonio Carlos Jobim record the little-known Capitol album *Samba De Uma Note So*.

1962 - Stan Getz and Charlie Byrd team up for *Jazz Samba* which features the hit "Desafinado" and really launches the bossa-nova movement.
Herbie Mann records in Brazil with Baden Powell, Sergio Mendes and Antonio Carlos Jobim.

1963 - Bossa-nova has become a fad in danger of quickly dying out but then *Getz/Gilberto* (featuring Stan Getz, Antonio Carlos Jobim, Joao Gilberto and, on the major hit "The Girl from Ipanema," Astrud Gilberto) is recorded and immediately recognized as a classic.
Laurindo Almeida records with the Modern Jazz Quartet

1964 - Joao Gilberto records with Stan Getz at Carnegie Hall.
Stan Getz and Astrud Gilberto perform "The Girl from Ipanema" in the movie *Get Yourself a College Girl* but Getz soon turns away from bossa-nova.

1965 - Astrud Gilberto records her definitive albums.
Bossa-Nova, no longer a fad, becomes a permanent part of American popular music.

Latin (Afro-Cuban) Jazz

Important events

1923 - Jelly Roll Morton uses a Latin rhythm (which he called a "Spanish tinge") on his solo piano recording of "New Orleans Joys."

1937 - Duke Ellington's valve trombonist Juan Tizol composes "Caravan."

1939 - Mario Bauza recommends Dizzy Gillespie to Cab Calloway.

1940 - Machito forms the "Afro-Cubans."

1941 - Mario Bauza joins Machito's band as musical director and begins hiring jazz arrangers for the influential group.

1943 - Mario Bauza writes "Tanga."

1947 - Afro-Cuban jazz is born as Chano Pozo joins the Dizzy Gillespie big band. Together they record "Manteca," Cubana Be" and "Cubana Bop."
Stan Kenton adds guitarist Laurindo Almeida and bongo player Jack Costanzo to his orchestra, using Machito on maraccas for recordings of "Cuban Carnival" and "The Peanut Vendor."

1948 - Chano Pozo is killed.
Charlie Parker, Flip Phillips and Buddy Rich record with Machito's Orchestra.

1949 - Jack Costanzo makes the Nat King Cole Trio a Quartet when he joins on bongos.
Chico O'Farrill contributes arrangements to both the Stan Kenton and Benny Goodman Orchestras.

Music Map

Significant Avant-Garde/
Free Jazz Players

John Coltrane - tenor, soprano
Ornette Coleman - alto, composer
Cecil Taylor - piano
Eric Dolphy - alto, flute, bass clarinet
Sun Ra - keyboards, arranger, bandleader
Anthony Braxton - alto, clarinet, composer

Other Important Players

Alto Saxophone

Roscoe Mitchell	Jimmy Lyons
Sonny Simmons	Joseph Jarman
Oliver Lake	Julius Hemphill
Henry Threadgill	Arthur Blythe
Tim Berne	John Zorn

Baritone Saxophone

Hamiet Bluiett

Bass

Charlie Haden	Gary Peacock
Reggie Workman	Jimmy Garrison
David Izenzon	Malachi Favors
Dave Holland	Cecil McBee
William Parker	Barry Guy

Bass Clarinet

David Murray

Clarinet

John Carter
Perry Robinson
Marty Ehrlich
Don Byron

Drums

Ed Blackwell	Elvin Jones
Rashied Ali	Charles Moffett
Andrew Cyrille	Sunny Murray
Don Moye	Beaver Harris
Barry Altschul	Paul Motian
Gerry Hemingway	Joey Baron
Han Bennink	

Flute

James Newton

Guitar

Sonny Sharrock
James "Blood" Ulmer
Derek Bailey

Piano

Paul Bley	Andrew Hill
Ran Blake	Mulah Richard Abrams
Don Pullen	Marilyn Crispell
Myra Melford	

Soprano Saxophone

Steve Lacy
Evan Parker

Tenor Saxophone

Archie Shepp	Pharoah Sanders
Albert Ayler	Sam Rivers
Evan Parker	David Murray
Peter Brotzmann	Charles Gayle
James Carter	

Trombone

Roswell Rudd	Grachan Moncur III
Albert Mangelsdorff	George Lewis
Craig Harris	Ray Anderson

Trumpet

Booker Little	Don Cherry
Lester Bowie	Bobby Bradford
Kenny Wheeler	Leo Smith

Violin

Leroy Jenkins
Billy Bang
Mark Feldman

Vocals, Female

Betty Carter
Jeanne Lee
Jay Clayton
Kate Hammett-Vaughan

1951 - Cal Tjader leaves the Dave Brubeck trio and records as a leader playing drums and bongos.

1954 - Cal Tjader makes his first full-fledged Latin jazz records.

1956 - Two of the most interesting records of the year are the Stan Kenton Orchestra's interpretations of Johnny Richards' *Cuban Fire* and Tito Puente's *Puente Goes Jazz*.

1958 - Cal Tjader cuts *Latin Concert* with his sextet featuring pianist Vince Guaraldi and both Willie Bobo and Mongo Santamaria on percussion.

1959 - Mongo Santamaria records his "Afro Blue" for the first time. Herbie Mann puts together a successful Afro-Cuban band.

1961 - Ray Barretto makes his first album as leader.

Music Map

Significant Fusion Players

Guitar

Larry Coryell	John McLaughlin
Al DiMeola	Steve Khan
Allan Holdsworth	Kazumi Watanabe
Hiram Bullock	Mike Stern
Frank Gambale	Scott Henderson

Keyboards

Joe Zawinul	Chick Corea
Herbie Hancock	Jan Hammer
Lyle Mays	Russell Ferrante
Jeff Lorber	

Electric Bass

Jaco Pastorius	Stanley Clarke
Marcus Miller	John Patitucci
Alphonso Johnson	Jamaaladeen Tacuma
Gerald Veasley	Mark Egan

Drums

Billy Cobham	Lenny White
Alphonse Mouzon	Steve Gadd
Jack DeJohnette	Tony Williams
Peter Erskine	Ronald Shannon Jackson
Dave Weckl	Bill Bruford

Composers

Joe Zawinul	Chick Corea
Herbie Hancock	Jaco Pastorius

Soprano Saxophone

Wayne Shorter

Tenor Saxophone

Michael Brecker

Trumpet

Miles Davis
Eddie Henderson
Randy Brecker

Vibes

Mike Mainieri

Violin

Jean Luc Ponty
Jerry Goodman
Didier Lockwood
Michael Urbaniak

1963 - Mongo Santamaria has a hit with his version of Herbie Hancock's "Watermelon Man."

1974 - Chucho Valdes becomes the musical director of Irakere.

1976 - Cal Tjader's group includes Poncho Sanchez

1978 - Irakere (with Arturo Sandoval and Paquito D'Rivera) performs and records at the Montreux Jazz Festival.

1982 - Cal Tjader dies.
Both Tito Puente and Poncho Sanchez begin recording regularly for the Concord Picante label.
Arturo Sandoval collaborates with Dizzy Gillespie on *To a Finland Station.*
Jerry Gonzalez's Fort Apache Band debuts on record.

1983 - Willie Bobo dies.

1984 - Dave Valetin makes his first record for GRP.

1988 - Jerry Gonzalez records *Rumba Para Monk,* a Latinized version of Thelonious Monk tunes.

1989 - Dizzy Gillespie tours and records with his United Nation Band.

1990 - Arturo Sandoval defects to the United States.
Gonzalo Rubalcaba plays at the Montreux Jazz Festival with Charlie Haden and Paul Motian.

1991 - Mario Bauza's Afro-Cuban Jazz orchestra records *Tanga.*
Jane Bunnett records *Spirits of Havana in Cuba.*

1992 - Tito Puente cuts his 100th album.

1993 - Dizzy Gillespie and Mario Bauza die.

Avant-Garde/Free Jazz

Important events

1949 - Lennie Tristano and his sextet record "Intuition" and "Digression," the first jazz free improvisations.

1954 - Shelly Manne, Shorty Rogers and Jimmy Giuffre form an unusual trio at a recording session and perform a couple of free pieces.

1955 - Pianist Cecil Taylor makes his recording debut.
John Coltrane joins the Miles Davis Quintet.
Sun Ra makes first recordings as a bandleader.

1956 - Charles Mingus records "Pithecanthropus Erectus" and starts to greatly free up his music.

1957 - John Coltrane spends a few months with the Thelonious Monk Quartet.

1958 - Eric Dolphy joins the Chico Hamilton Quintet.
Ornette Coleman makes his recording debut for Contemporary.

1959 - Ornette Coleman's Quartet with cornetist Don Cherry, bassist Charlie Haden and drummer Billy Higgins records for Atlantic. Their stint at the Five Spot splits the jazz world.

1960 - John Coltrane forms his "classic quartet" with pianist McCoy Tyner, drummer Elvin Jones and eventually bassist Jimmy Garrison. Coltrane begins doubling on soprano and his recording of "My Favorite Things" becomes very influential.
Ornette Coleman records "Free Jazz."
Charles Mingus leads a quartet with Eric Dolphy, Ted Curson and Dannie Richmond.
Archie Shepp records with Cecil Taylor.

1961 - Jimmy Lyons joins the Cecil Taylor Unit.
Eric Dolphy spends a few months with the John Coltrane Quintet.

Richard Abrams forms the Experimental Band in Chicago.

1962 - Ornette Coleman retires for several years.
Albert Ayler makes his recording debut in Europe.
Sun Ra and his Arkestra resettle in New York.

1963 - Charles Mingus records "The Black Saint and the Sinner Lady."

1964 - Eric Dolphy tours Europe with Charles Mingus just months before his death.
John Coltrane records *A Love Supreme*.
Pharoah Sanders makes recording debut.
Albert Ayler records for ESP and Debut.
Bill Dixon stages four-day "October Revolution in Jazz" and 20 groups participate.

1965 - John Coltrane's music becomes atonal and he records the monumental "Ascension."
Ornette Coleman returns with a new trio featuring bassist David Izenzon and drummer Charles Moffett.
Archie Shepp emerges as major force recording for Impulse. AACM formed in Chicago.

1966 - John Coltrane forms a new quintet with Alice Coltrane, Pharoah Sanders, Jimmy Garrison and Rashied Ali.
Roscoe Mitchell and his Art Ensemble (soon to be the Art Ensemble of Chicago) make first recordings.

1967 - John Coltrane dies.

1968 - Anthony Braxton makes first records as a leader.

1969 - Pharoah Sanders and Leon Thomas team up for surprising avant-garde pop hit "The Creator Has A Master Plan."

1971 - Albert Ayler dies.

Post-1971 - Too many events to list. The avant-garde has remained an important (if often underground) force in modern jazz.

Fusion, Crossover and Instrumental Pop

Important events

1967 - Miles Davis uses electric piano (Herbie Hancock) in quintet for first time.
Blues/rock guitarist Larry Coryell joins Gary Burton's quartet to form one of first fusion groups.

1968 - Chick Corea replaces Herbie Hancock with Miles Davis; plays electric piano for the first time.
Blood, Sweat and Tears uses a horn section in a rock setting.

1969 - Miles Davis records early fusion classics *In a Silent Way* and *Bitches Brew* with expanded bands of young all stars.
Tony Williams heads Lifetime, a trio with John McLaughlin and Larry Young.

1971 - Joe Zawinul and Wayne Shorter team up to form Weather Report.
John McLaughlin forms Mahavishnu Orchestra.

1972 - The first edition of Chick Corea's Return to Forever records two albums.

1973 - Chick Corea teams up with Bill Connors, Stanley Clarke and Lenny White in Return to Forever; they record *Hymn of the Seventh Galaxy*.
Herbie Hancock forms the Headhunters and has a big hit with "Chameleon."
Ornette Coleman founds "free funk" with formation of Prime Time.

1974 - Al DiMeola replaces Bill Connors with Return To Forever.

Music Map

Significant Crossover/Instrumental Pop Players

Alto Saxophone

David Sanborn	Sadao Watanabe
Jay Beckenstein	Brandon Fields
Marc Russo	

Tenor Saxophone

Michael Brecker	Grover Washington, Jr.
Tom Scott	Ernie Watts
Bill Evans	John Klemmer
Wilton Felder	

Trumpet

Chuck Mangione
Tom Browne
Rick Braun

Soprano Saxophone

Grover Washington, Jr.	George Howard
Kenny G.	Bill Evans

Guitar

Earl Klugh
Lee Ritenour
Larry Carlton, George Benson

Keyboards

David Benoit	Joe Sample
George Winston	George Duke
Patrice Rushen	Bob James

Arranger

Don Sebesky
Bob James
Dave Grusin

Grover Washington, Jr., a major influence in combining R&B with jazz, records "Mr. Magic."

1975 - Due to bad health Miles Davis retires for six years. David Sanborn records first album as leader.
John McLaughlin switches to acoustic guitar and performs with World Music group Shakti.
The Brecker Brothers record their first joint album.

1976 - Jaco Pastorius joins Weather Report.
"Birdland" is a huge hit for Weather Report.
Return To Forever breaks up. Al DiMeola begins his solo career.
George Benson has pop vocal hit with "This Masquerade."

1977 - Spyro Gyra records first album.
Jeff Lorber forms the Jeff Lorber Fusion, a group that would soon feature Kenny G. on saxophones.
Chuck Mangione has a big hit in "Feels So Good."

1978 - Pat Metheny makes his first recording with his Group.

1979 - Mike Mainieri forms Steps (later Steps Ahead).
Ronald Shannon Jackson forms his Decoding Society.

1980 - Grover Washington, Jr. records his famous *Winelight* album.

1981 - Miles Davis returns to active playing.
The Yellowjackets are formed.

1982 - New Age fad starts to catch on with release of George Winston piano solos.

1983 - Herbie Hancock scores with "Rockit."

1985 - Marc Russo is Robben Ford's replacement with the Yellowjackets.

1986 - Weather Report releases final album *This Is This* and then breaks up.
Chick Corea teams up with bassist John Patitucci and soon forms his Elektric Band.
Kenny G. becomes instrumental pop superstar with release of "Songbird."

1987 - Jaco Pastorius dies.

1991 - Miles Davis dies.
Bob Mintzer joins the Yellowjackets in Marc Russo's place.

1995 - Spyro Gyra releases 17th album.
Jean-Luc Ponty, Al DiMeola and Stanley Clarke team up to form the Rite of Strings.
Fusion, crossover and instrumental pop are continually lumped together as contemporary jazz.

–Scott Yanow

150
RECOMMENDED BOOKS

There are literally hundreds of jazz books currently available including biographies, autobiographies, essays, comprehensive histories and reprints of older classics. Although this list could have had 250 rather than 150 entries, suffice it to say that anyone acquiring all of these books will have a very strong jazz library! Although a few ragtime histories are included, I have otherwise stuck exclusively to jazz (leaving out blues books and most discographies except massive ones on Benny Goodman and John Coltrane). Also I have refrained from giving individual ratings in this section since all of these books deserve either four or five stars. ("Ed." means that the contents are a collection of essays and articles edited and organized by the person listed.)

Ain't Misbehavin' *by Ed Kirkeby with Duncan P. Schiedt and Sinclair Traill.* (Da Capo Press, 1966, 248 pages, 16 of photos.)

Fats Waller was a legendary character of many parts: a brilliant stride pianist, a very likable vocalist, an often-hilarious speaker, a very talented composer and a pioneering jazz organist who accomplished everything while constantly partying! Ed Kirkeby was Waller's manager during his final eight years and this biography (put together with the assistance of two top English writers) recreates the unique genius' life and times quite lovingly. The first 14 chapters (dealing with Fats' earlier years) are in the third person; in the final four Kirkeby writes in the first person. There are many recreated conversations that may not always be completely accurate but the end results are informative and entertaining. This paperback edition is rounded out by a discography that was excellent for the time.

American Musicians *by Whitney Balliett.* (Oxford Univ. Press, 1986, 415 pages.)

Whitney Balliett is the most picturesque of jazz writers, able to capture the joy and complexity of jazz, its creative process, the unique musicians and the music itself in words. This highly recommended book collects together 49 of his best portraits, focusing on the life of 56 musicians in all. Although the majority of the stories deal with classic jazz, swing or mainstream players (as befits Balliett's taste), there are intriguing articles on Ornette Coleman and Cecil Taylor. In nearly all cases, Balliett interviewed the subject and, even when it was impossible, associates were tracked down; trombonist Clyde Bernhardt's tales of life with King Oliver are utterly fascinating. Actually all of the chapters are of that level, giving readers a countless number of fresh anecdotes and insight into what drives these creative musicians. This is Whitney Balliett's most rewarding book.

American Popular Song *by Alec Wilder.* (Oxford Univ. Press, 1972, 536 pages.)

This book has long been considered a classic of its kind. Alec Wilder discusses the songs written by the top American pop composers of 1920-50 including full chapters on six writers (Jerome Kern, Irving Berlin, George Gershwin, Richard Rodgers, Cole Porter and Harold Arlen) plus substantial space for the work of 17 others. He writes technically about how individual songs were constructed (sometimes using musical notation) and points out what was most unusual or colorful about most pieces. Although it helps to be able to read music, Wilder's writing is more accessible than expected and his book is never boring. An excellent scholarly work.

American Singers *by Whitney Balliett.* (Oxford Univ. Press, 1988, 244 pages.)

Whitney Balliett has the very rare ability to turn the experience of playing, living and creating jazz into words. His book *American*

Musicians is highly recommended and *American Singers* (27 portraits in 25 chapters) is of the same quality. Not everyone covered in this book exclusively performed jazz (including Ray Charles, Tony Bennett, Mabel Mercer, Bobby Short, Hugh Shannon and Julie Wilson) and one (Alec Wilder) is not even a singer. However each chapter is well worth reading since Balliett does a definitive and colorful job of capturing his subjects. Some of these interviews are priceless.

The Art of Jazz *by Martin Williams.* (Da Capo Press, 1959, 253 pages, 4 of photos.)

Martin Williams collected together 19 articles plus two of his own in this interesting book which is subtitled "Ragtime to Bebop." Covering different aspects and personalities from jazz history that range from blues harmonica Sonny Terry and Jelly Roll Morton up to hard bop, this was a good all-around jazz book for 1959 although many of these topics have been discussed more definitively since then. Among the highlights are Ernest Ansermet's acclaimed and insightful assessment of Sidney Bechet in 1919, George Avakian's liner notes for Bix Beiderbecke and Bessie Smith reissues, William Russell's assessment of three boogie-woogie pianists, Andre Hodeir's provocative essay on Art Tatum and Ross Russell's discussion of bebop.

Bass Line *by Milt Hinton & David Berger.* (Temple Univ. Press, 1988, 28 pages, and countless number of photos.)

One of the most recorded jazz musicians of all time (who is possibly in first place), bassist Milt Hinton has been a fixture on the scene since the late 1920s. Little known to most until the last decade was the fact that he has long been an equally talented photographer and has been snapping pictures constantly since the 1930s. This wonderful oversize book is really two in one. The very well-written text (essentially Hinton's autobiography) has many interesting stories about his life and the remarkable musicians he knew. But even if there were no anecdotes, this book would be highly recommended because the photos are consistently interesting, historic and sometimes quite moving.

The Sidney Bechet - Wizard of Jazz *by John Chilton.* (Oxford Univ. Press, 1987, 331 pages, 32 of photos.)

This is an amazingly detailed biography, tracing the life of soprano-saxophonist Sidney Bechet nearly week-by-week throughout his busy career. Bechet, one of the masters of New Orleans jazz, had a fiery and occasionally erratic personality that was not absent of jealousy and pettiness. Through Chilton's very well-written narrative, the life of Bechet (from early New Orleans and his sometimes tumultuous tours overseas in the '20s through the Depression and his years in Paris in the 1950s when he was considered a national hero) is traced in colorful fashion. This book would (which ranks second to *Bix–Man and Legend* as the best jazz biography ever written) would be worth getting if only to read about the up and mostly down relationship that Bechet had with Louis Armstrong. An essential acquisition for all jazz libraries.

Bunny Berigan - Elusive Legend of Jazz *by Robert Dupuis.* (Louisiana University Press, 1993, 368 pages, 22 of photos.)

The ill-fated Bunny Berigan was arguably the top trumpeter in jazz during 1935-39 and a dramatic soloist who had an adventurous spirit and full control over his horn. His alcoholism resulted in quite a few colorful episodes before his premature death in 1942 at age 33. Although this book was completed over a half-century after Bunny's passing, author Robert Dupuis was able to track down many of Berigan's surviving relatives, friends (including some from childhood) and musical associates to piece together a very compelling story. In addition to his musical career, one learns about Berigan's family life, friendships, personality and difficulties with alcohol. Many more descriptions of Berigan's recordings (particularly his obscure sessions) and a more detailed discography would have improved the results, but this book is quite definitive and holds one's interest throughout.

The Best of Jazz *by Humphrey Lyttelton.* (Crescendo/Taplinger , 1978, 214 pages, 8 of photos.)

Humphrey Lyttelton, in addition to being a top trumpeter from Great Britain since the late 1940s, is a talented writer. In this first of two volumes (preceding *The Best of Jazz II*), Lyttelton contributes profiles on what he calls "Jazz Masters and Masterpieces, 1917-1930." His chapters (on the Original Dixieland Jazz Band, James P. Johnson, King Oliver, Sidney Bechet, Bessie Smith, Jelly Roll Morton, Fletcher Henderson, Louis Armstrong, Bix Beiderbecke, Duke Ellington, the Chicagoans, Johnny Dodds/Jimmy Noone, Louis Armstrong/Earl Hines, and Luis Russell) are filled with concise and easily understandable musical analysis of their styles and recordings. This book, which has more than its share of fresh ideas, will be most enjoyed by readers already a bit familiar with 1920s jazz.

The Best of Jazz II *by Humphrey Lyttelton.* (Taplinger Publ., 1981, 239 pages, 8 of photos.)

Trumpeter Humphrey Lyttelton, whose writing talents are on the same high level as his playing abilities, came out with this second book in 1981, three years after *The Best Of Jazz*. While the first focused on musicians from the 1920s, this volume (subtitled "Enter the Giants, 1931-1944") has chapters on Louis Armstrong, Fats Waller, Coleman Hawkins, Jack Teagarden, Art Tatum, Johnny Hodges/Benny Carter, Dickie Wells, Lester Young, Billie Holiday and Roy Eldridge. Lyttelton concentrates on musical analysis of styles and recordings but his book is quite readable, avoids clichés and will be found quite thought-provoking by listeners who already have strong knowledge of the swing era.

The Big Bands *by George T. Simon.* (Collier Books Editions, 1974, 584 pages.)

First published in 1967 and enlarged a couple times since, this is considered the most comprehensive of all the reference books on the swing era. George T. Simon, who was on the staff of Metronome during much of the 1930s and '40s, witnessed virtually all of the big bands in action and his summaries of the orchestras (which sometimes quote from his own reports of the time) are evenhanded, consistent and quite informative. There are a variety of essays on aspects of the era (including chapters on the public, the vocalists, arrangers, businessmen, recordings, radio, movies and the press), chapters on 72 of the bands and a paragraph apiece on hundreds of others. The book concludes with interviews of surviving bandleaders Count Basie, Benny Goodman, Woody Herman, Harry James, Stan Kenton, Guy Lombardo and Artie Shaw conducted in 1971. Essential.

Billie's Blues *by John Chilton.* (Da Capo Press, 1975, 264 pages, numerous photos.)

This interesting book covers the life of Billie Holiday from the time of her first recording in 1933 up until her death in 1959. Not as detailed as John Chilton's magnificent Sidney Bechet book and purposely skipping Holiday's childhood, the narrative gives readers all of the usual details about the public life of Lady Day, what was known at the time of her distressing private affairs and in four chapters discusses her recordings. Although not as definitive as Donald Clarke's *Wishing on the Moon*, *Billie's Blues* is a useful introductory book to Billie Holiday and puts the emphasis where it belongs, on her music.

Bird – The Legend of Charlie Parker *by Robert Reisner.* (Da Capo Press , 1962, 256 pages, numerous photos.)

Even decades later, this is one of the better books on Charlie Parker. Robert Reisner, an acquaintance of the great altoist during his final two years, interviewed 81 people that knew Bird (including Miles Davis, Kenny Dorham, Dizzy Gillespie, Earl Hines, Charles Mingus, Anita O'Day, two of Parker's wives, Max Roach and Lennie Tristano) and their responses are full of interesting stories. Because the interviews are put in alphabetical order, this book jumps around chronologically quite a bit (although Reisner did contribute a 20-page introduction titled "I Remember Bird"). Taken as a whole this book gives one a good idea as to what

Parker was like as a person; despite his excesses he comes across quite well.

Bird Lives *by Ross Russell* (Quartet Books, 1972, 405 pages, 16 of photos.)

Due to the fanciful (and sometimes inaccurate) nature of some of the stories told in this book, *Bird Lives* has often been put down as purely fiction. Actually it is one of the better books on Charlie Parker, written by Ross Russell who ran the Dial label. There are a few self-serving tales told but one gets a full picture of what Russell called "The High Life and Hard Times of Charlie 'Yardbird' Parker." The innovative altoist led an exciting if tumultuous life (actually several lives) before his death at age 34, and all aspects of this genius' crazy and self-destructive lifestyle are covered in this continually fascinating work.

Bix–Man and Legend *by Richard Sudhalter and Philip Evans with William Dean Myatt.* (Schirmer Books, 1974, 512 pages, numerous photos.)

This is the finest jazz biography written to date. Bix Beiderbecke was a legendary cornetist from the 1920s whose early death (at age 28 in 1931) led to him being considered one of jazz's first martyrs. Richard Sudhalter, Philip Evans and William Dean Myatt independently began research on Bix in 1957-58 and eventually joined forces, completing this remarkable work 16 years later. Beiderbecke's life is fully explored and discussed, many myths about him are disproved, a very complete chronology of his life (containing all kinds of trivial detail) is offered as one of the appendixes and there is a full discography. Due to the enormous amount of interviews conducted, the biography is full of fresh stories that explain many of the paradoxes of the legend's life. This is everything a jazz biography should be; it reads like a novel!

Black Beauty, White Heat *by Frank Driggs & Harris Lewine* (Morrow, 1982, 360 pages, infinite number of pictures.)

Frank Driggs owns what must be the largest jazz memorabilia collection in the world. This very impressive oversize book has over 1,500 rare photographs, advertisements and pictures of record labels dating from 1920-50. After a fine article by Paul Bacon about the joys of being a record collector in the 1940s and 50s, there are nine chapters that arrange the photos according to geography and time period, ranging from early New Orleans jazz to the bop era. A page or two of text introduces each chapter and the captions identify all of the musicians. *Black Beauty, White Heat* is the ultimate coffee table jazz book and will thrill early jazz collectors for dozens of hours.

Blues People *by LeRoi Jones.* (Morrow, 1963, 44 pages)

A bit of a classic although aspects of it are a little dated now, *Blues People* was the first important jazz book written by a black author. Dealing as much with the sociological aspects of being Black in the United States of the 19th and 20th century as it is about jazz, this highly original book has a lot of valuable information about early pre-jazz Black music and gives readers a different tilt toward aspects of jazz history and the struggle that Black creative musicians have had through the decades, from Congo Square up to Ornette Coleman.

Boogie, Pete & The Senator *by Mark Miller.* (Nightwood Editions, 1987, 312 pages, 47 of photos.)

Through this book and *Jazz in Canada: Fourteen Lives*, Mark Miller has documented the often overlooked world of Canadian jazz. While the earlier book covered the history of jazz up North, this second effort concentrates on Canadian musicians who were active in the 1980s. Forty different musicians are portrayed including Ed Bickert, Paul They, Terry Clarke, Jim Galloway, Linton Garner, Sonny Greenwich, Oliver Jones, Fraser MacPherson, Rob McConnell, Phil Nimmons, Oscar Peterson, Paul Plimley, Bill Smith, Don Thompson and Kenny Wheeler along with lesser-known talents. This is a particularly valuable book for modern jazz followers who wish to expand their knowledge beyond knowing just the top American players.

Celebrating Bird *by Gary Giddins.* (Beechtree Books, 1987, 128 pages, many photos.)

This is a particularly attractive book on Charlie Parker. Gary Giddins' text is concise, colorful, accessible and filled with original ideas and stories, many gained by interviewing the great altoist's first wife Rebecca Parker Davis. In addition, this slightly oversized book has many rare (and some famous) photographs which by themselves would justify its purchase. Although it came out as a companion to a documentary film of the same title, the book is quite enjoyable independent of the movie. This is one that all Charlie Parker fans should get!

Celebrating the Duke *by Ralph Gleason.* (Da Capo Press, 1975, 280 pages, 9 of photos.)
Ralph Gleason's final book is one of his best. His portraits of the jazz artists who he called his "heroes" (Bessie Smith, Louis Armstrong, Jimmie Lunceford, Billie Holiday, Lester Young, Charlie Parker, Dizzy Gillespie, the Modern Jazz Quartet, Carmen McRae, John Coltrane, Miles Davis and Albert Ayler) are full of insight and open-minded ideas; the Louis Armstrong chapter in particular has plenty of surprises. Gleason, one of the very few writers to love both Dixieland and rock (some of the portraits originally appeared in *Rolling Stone*), finishes off this fine book with a 114-page discussion of Duke Ellington, tracing his experiences seeing and talking with the genius during 1952-74. Although now over 20 years old, many of the opinions expressed in *Celebrating The Duke* are still relevant.

Ornette Coleman *by John Litweiler.* (Da Capo Press, 1992, 258 pages, 8 of photos.)
For the first biography ever written about one of jazz music's major innovators (nearly 40 years after his recording debut, some in the jazz audience still dismiss altoist Ornette Coleman's accomplishments), John Litweiler gathered all of the known information about Ornette, used a 1981 interview he had with Coleman, talked to most of Ornette's important sidemen and associates and added his own musical analysis. Although not quite definitive, this is an excellent effort that makes Coleman's unusual life and unique music more understandable; all future books on Ornette Coleman will have to deal with this one first. The discography, which goes up to 1991, is an added plus.

John Coltrane – A Discography and Musical Biography *by Yasubiro Fujicka with Lewis Porter and Yoh-Ichi Hamada* (Scarecrow Press, 1995, 377 pages, many photos.)
This hardback book is the best John Coltrane discography compiled thus far. A major help to collectors in sorting out the many European CD's that document the great saxophonist's tours overseas (where his quartet frequently broadcast on the radio), this easy-to-use book not only lists both released and unreleased recordings but all the tapes known to exist; even the music played at Coltrane's funeral! Actually the book is much more than just a discography, for there are around 110 photos (mostly unpublished) of Coltrane, 700 small photos of LP cover art and enough information to know where John Coltrane was at practically any night during his last 12 years. This is definitely an essential book for fans of John Coltrane.

Cool Blues *by Mark Miller.* (Nightwood Editions, 1989, 115 pages, 18 of photos.)
For this fairly slim paperback, Mark Miller fully documents Charlie Parker's two visits to Canada in 1953. One resulted in the famous Massey Hall concert with Dizzy Gillespie, Bud Powell, Charles Mingus and Max Roach while the other trip resulted in Bird being booked to play in Montreal and appear on a television show; Paul They made his recording debut during the latter. Both visits had more than their share of suspense (would Parker show up to play?) and the Massey Hall date involved so many difficult personalities that it is miraculous that it worked out. Miller's narrative is very informative and suspenseful, tracing Parker's adventures and leaving one with some sadness that there was so little time left; Bird would die two years later. Recommended.

Crazeology *by Bud Freeman and Robert Wolf.* (Univ. of Illinois Press, 1989, 104 pages, 8 of photos.)
Tenor saxophonist Bud Freeman, like altoist Paul Desmond of a later generation, was an excellent writer who wrote too little during his life. His autobiography has plenty of interesting stories (with a large dose of humor) and is quite colorful but it should have been three times as long! This is well worth picking up even though the slim volume (which also has a selective discography, leaves one wanting more.

Miles Davis *by Ian Carr* (Quill, 1982, 310 pages, 16 of photos.)
This book, which traces Miles Davis' very productive and often stormy career up to his comeback in the early 1980s, is an excel-

lent single volume that can be used as an introduction to the innovative trumpeter. Although Ian Carr (himself a fine trumpeter) did not get to interview Davis, he talked to many of his sidemen, put together the known facts of Miles' life in a coherent and easily readable fashion and does a fine job of analyzing his music. A few musical examples and a selective discography round out this fine book.

Different Drummers–Jazz in the Culture of Nazi Germany *by Michael Kater.* (Oxford Univ. Press, 1992, 291 pages, 14 of photos.)
This is an utterly fascinating book that answers the question "What happened to Swing music and its musicians in Germany during the Nazi years?" Michael Kater has put together a very well detailed narrative that discusses jazz in Germany prior to the Nazis, the persecution that occurred as the Nazis gradually declared war on the decadent music (turning teenagers who liked to dance into potential criminals), the Germans' attempts to use Swing as propaganda during the war years and the rebirth of jazz in Germany after 1945. Even jazz historians will not have heard many of these tales before and Kater's extensive research (and ability to tie together many unrelated stories) makes this a very valuable book.

The Baby Dodds Story *by Baby Dodds & Larry Gara.* (Louisiana State Univ. Press, 1959, 105 pages, 12 of photos.)
Until this book was republished (with a new introduction) in 1992, few jazz historians knew of its existence. Baby Dodds was one of the first significant jazz drummers; many would consider him the top drummer of the 1920s. In the 1950s he was extensively interviewed by Larry Gara and his tales about New Orleans in the teens, Chicago in the 1920s and his later experiences are often priceless. There are not too many people around anymore who can give firsthand accounts of playing with King Oliver, Fate Marable, Jelly Roll Morton and Johnny Dodds (Baby's brother)! Although the book is a bit short, there are a lot of memorable tales that should greatly interest fans of New Orleans jazz.

Eric Dolphy *by Vladimir Simosko and Barry Tepperman* (Da Capo Press, 1971, 132 pages, 11 of photos.)
This was the first book written about the unique multireedist Eric Dolphy, who had a unique style on alto, bass clarinet (which he virtually introduced as a jazz instrument) and flute. Vladimir Simosko wrote essays on Dolphy musical development and his life story (corresponding with Eric's parents and a few fellow musicians) while Barry Tepperman put together a discography that, although ideal for the time, has become a bit out of date. Overall this is an excellent first effort, but a new and more extensive Eric Dolphy biography is long overdue.

Drummin' Men *by Burt Korall.* (Schirmer Books, 1990, 381 pages, many photos.)
This is one of the finest jazz books to come out in the 1990s. Burt Korall contributed full-length portrayals of seven of the top drummers of the swing era (Chick Webb, Gene Krupa, Ray McKinley, Jo Jones, Sid Catlett, Dave Tough and Buddy Rich) along with shorter sketches about seven others (Sonny Greer, George Wettling, Cozy Cole, Jimmy Crawford, O'Neil Spencer, Cliff Leeman and Ray Bauduc). Not only does Korall cover these musicians' lives (complete with many interviews of their associates), but he also intelligently discusses their styles in an accessible fashion that will be of great interest both to other drummers and to nonmusician jazz fans. Highly recommended.

Early Jazz *by Gunther Schuller.* (Oxford Univ. Press, 1968, 401 pages.)
The first of two massive works by the near-genius Gunther Schuller (the other is simply called *The Swing Era*) goes into great depth about jazz of the 1920s. The emphasis is on analysis of the music (rather than historical anecdotes) yet always holds on to one's interest. Schuller has chapters on such topics as rhythm form, harmony, melody, timbre and improvisation, the beginnings of the music, Louis Armstrong, Jelly Roll Morton, the virtuoso performers of the decade, the big bands (including territory bands) and early Duke Ellington. This important book will be most enjoyed by connoisseurs of the 1920s who may not agree with all of Schuller's opinions but will certainly find them stimulating.

Duke Ellington–Beyond Category *by John Edward Hasse.* (Simon & Schuster, 1993, 480 pages, many pictures.)
In 1988 the Smithsonian Institution acquired tens of thousands

of pages of music, scrapbooks and documents from Mercer Ellington pertaining to his father Duke. John Edward Hasse drew liberally from this precious archive to put together a definitive biography that augments what was already known about the remarkable pianist-composer-arranger-bandleader with many new details. Combining together stories about his musical career and personal life with concise reviews of his recordings, this is a superlative portrait of America's greatest composer. Although Duke Ellington's life cannot be fully covered in just one book, this one comes as close as any to summarizing his accomplishments.

Ellington–The Early Years *by Mark Tucker.* (Univ. of Illinois Press, 1991, 344 pages, 7 of photos.)
Duke Ellington seemed to spring out of nowhere when he debuted at the Cotton Club in 1927, preceding over 46 years of remarkable musical accomplishments. Mark Tucker's well researched book ends with Ellington gaining the Cotton Club job! He fully explores Duke's beginnings in Washington D.C. and his struggles in New York during 1923-27, analyzes his first recordings and compositions, lists everything he could find about Ellington's early activities and tries (somewhat in vain) to explain where Duke got his musical genius from. Fans of Duke Ellington's music will find this definitive book about his beginnings quite interesting.

The Duke Ellington Reader *by Mark Tucker.* (Oxford Univ. Press, 1993, 536 pages.)
This is a book that all followers of Duke Ellington will have to have. Mark Tucker gathered together 101 articles on the phenomenal pianist-composer-arranger-bandleader ranging from reviews (including one from 1923!), essays and interviews to analysis and pieces by Duke himself. Some of the articles are quite famous and historic while many are obscure and have been out-of-print since they were first published. Arranged more or less in chronological order, this large book has a huge amount of interesting information, sometimes-conflicting but always thought-provoking opinions and plenty of variety.

The Encyclopedia of Jazz *by Leonard Feather.* (Da Capo Press, 1960, 527 pages, 80 of photos.)
Arguably Leonard Feather's greatest accomplishment, *The Encyclopedia of Jazz* (which was later followed by editions focusing on the 1960s and '70s) was the first book to fully cover jazz of the 1900-60 period. Although Feather had his weak points (not caring much for Dixieland and downgrading the piano playing of both Jelly Roll Morton and Thelonious Monk), most of the over 2,000 biographical entries are quite evenhanded and (even with a few inevitable errors) quite accurate. In addition to interesting but unnecessary "appreciations" by Duke Ellington, Benny Goodman and John Hammond, this book has an overview of the preceding 60 years, a chronology of important events, articles on the anatomy of jazz, jazz in American society (which is mostly about racism and drugs), jazz overseas, jazz and classical music (the latter written by Gunther Schuller), excerpts from Feather's famed blindfold test and a list of musicians' birthdays and birthplaces. However the bulk of the book is taken up by the invaluable entries, making this (over 35 years later) still a primary jazz reference book.

The Encyclopedia of Jazz in the Sixties *by Leonard Feather.* (Da Capo Press, 1966, 312 pages, 80 of photos.)
The second in Leonard Feather's monumental Encyclopedia of Jazz series appeared only six years after his revised first Encyclopedia. The 1,100 biographies focus on the participants' activities during the first half of the 1960s except in cases where the musician did not have an entry in the original book. In addition there are excerpts from Feather's famous blindfold test, an article by Pete Welding on "The Blues and Folk Scene" and an overview of the important events of the past six years. Although not as essential as the original Encyclopedia, this book is quite valuable and very much reflects the time period from which it originated.

The Encyclopedia of Jazz in the Seventies *by Leonard Feather* and Ira Gitler. (Da Capo Press, 1976, 393 pages, 48 of photos.)
The third of Leonard Feather's Encyclopedia of Jazz books came out a decade after the second, so the focus in its 1,000 plus biographical entries is on events of the past ten years and musicians who have emerged since then. All three of the Encyclopedias are quite valuable and this one stuffs a great deal of information (compiled by both Feather and Ira Gitler) into a

short amount of space. Although Leonard Feather did not care for Dixieland, the avant-garde or fusion (and his prejudices are often felt throughout the book), most of the entries are quite evenhanded and fair. In addition there are humorous and interesting excerpts from Feather's blindfold tests, lists of poll winners and articles on jazz education and jazz films (the latter by Leonard Maltin).

52nd Street *by Arnold Shaw.* (Da Capo Press, 1971, 378 pages, photos.)
52nd Street in New York during its prime (1935-47) was a truly remarkable place, an area where one club after another (which were sometimes next door to each other) featured the top names in jazz. It was possible in one night to see Coleman Hawkins, Art Tatum, Billie Holiday, Charlie Parker and Eddie Condon; every night was a jazz festival. Arnold Shaw in this entertaining and very informative book goes club-by-club through the Street. He interviewed musicians, singers, club owners and even a stripper to get a well-rounded picture of this very special (and never duplicated) center of jazz.

Ella Fitzgerald by Stuart Nicholson. (DaCapo Press, 1993, 334 pages, 16 of photos.)
Ella Fitzgerald's life will never be the topic of a movie. After a short period of struggle she became a success at the age of 18 in 1935 singing with Chick Webb's Orchestra, and she never looked back. Until the start of her decline 40 years later due to advancing age, she had one success after another. Also, despite giving a countless number of public performances, Ella was a very private person and a clean liver. Stuart Nicholson was unable to get an interview with the great singer for this book (the first biography of her) but he talked to practically everyone else including childhood friends and pieced together a very complete portrayal of "the First Lady of Jazz." There are only a few revelations (such as the fact that Ella is a year older than expected and that she was homeless before joining Webb) but the story is fairly interesting; Ella Fitzgerald comes across as a wonderful (if somewhat lonely) human being. A lengthy discography concludes the well-conceived book.

Forces in Motion *by Graham Lock.* (Da Capo Press, 1988, 412 pages, 16 of photos.)
Because his complex music is quite original and his liner notes tend to be very difficult to understand, multireedist Anthony Braxton's contributions to jazz are sometimes misunderstood, underrated and somewhat forbidding. Graham Lock has done the jazz world a major service with the release of this book for it portrays Braxton as a likable, down-to-earth and sometimes humorous human being. Lock accompanied Braxton's quartet (which included the brilliant pianist Marilyn Crispell, bassist Mark Dresser and drummer Gerry Hemingway) on a tour in 1985 and conducted extensive and wide-ranging interviews with each of the musicians. Braxton talks with great detail not only about his music but also about his history and any other topics that come up. Readers come away from this continually interesting book feeling that they have joined Lock, Braxton and the musicians on the journey and with a much deeper understanding as to what makes Anthony Braxton tick.

Four Lives in the Bebop Business *by A.B. Spellman.* (Limelight, 1966, 241 pages.)
This was an extraordinary book when it came out and it has retained its freshness and significance through the decades. A.B. Spellman's lengthy portraits of Cecil Taylor, Ornette Coleman, Herbie Nichols and Jackie McLean (each of whom he interviewed) are still definitive. All four musicians had to struggle to play the adventurous music they felt; Nichols did not make it but the other three are still major forces in modern jazz. There is a great deal of interesting information about the early days of Taylor and Coleman (both of whom did not record until their styles were almost fully formed) and Nichols has still not been fully discovered by much of the jazz world. This book is a gem.

The Freedom Principle–Jazz After 1958 *by John Litweiler.* (Da Capo Press, 1984, 324 pages, 11 of photos.)
There have been many books on jazz but relatively few dealing with an overview of the avant-garde movement of the 1960s. John Litweiler conducted a few interviews for this project (including the members of the Art Ensemble of Chicago, Derek Bailey, Ornette Coleman, Oliver Lake, Leo Smith and Charles Tyler) but

most of the book consists of intelligent musical analysis that ably details the innovations and unusual aspects of the particular recordings. There are full chapters on Ornette Coleman, Eric Dolphy, John Coltrane, Sun Ra, Albert Ayler and Cecil Taylor, the beginnings of the avant-garde, modal jazz and the players from Chicago and St. Louis. This is an excellent acquisition for free jazz collectors who wish to learn more about the music.

Free Jazz by Ekkehard Jost. (Da Capo Press, 1974, 214 pages.)
This is a pioneering book, the first full-length book to give an overview of the avant-garde jazz scene. The German author Ekkehard Jost does an excellent job of summing up and analyzing the music of John Coltrane, Charles Mingus, Ornette Coleman, Cecil Taylor, Archie Shepp, Albert Ayler, Don Cherry, Sun Ra and the AACM players. Although this book has been superseded to an extent by John Litweiler's *The Freedom Principle* (which was written a decade later) and its discography is out of date, Jost's comments and analysis are still relevant and accurate.

From Satchmo to Miles by Leonard Feather. (Da Capo Press, 1972, 258 pages, 13 of photos.)
Leonard Feather was unique among jazz critics in that, in addition to reporting on jazz history, he was a part of the history himself. *From Satchmo to Miles* profiles 13 important artists who Feather knew quite well: Louis Armstrong, Duke Ellington, Billie Holiday, Ella Fitzgerald, Count Basie, Lester Young, Charlie Parker, Dizzy Gillespie, producer Norman Granz, Oscar Peterson, Ray Charles (who arguably does not belong in a jazz book), Don Ellis and Miles Davis. Feather's stories are often quite personal and have much more to do with the artists' private lives than with mere musical analysis, making this the most accessible of all of Leonard Feather's books. Some of the stories are quite riveting.

The Golden Age of Jazz by William Gottlieb. (Da Capo Press, 1995, 162 pages, countless photos.)
This new edition of William Gottlieb's 1979 book revises and expands his original release. Gottlieb was a busy jazz photographer during 1939-48, taking classic photos of nearly every top jazz musician active during that era. This very attractive collection covers Dixieland and New Orleans jazz, swing, vocalists and the early days of bop with everyone from Leadbelly to Dizzy Gillespie being profiled. Some of the photos are quite famous while others (often equally as interesting) are lesser known. Gottlieb's excellent text gives backgrounds to the musicians and identifies the subjects. A delightful book that really captures the spirit and joy of the era.

Benny Goodman–Listen to His Legacy by D. Russell Connor. (Scarecrow Press, 1988, 357 pages, 32 of photos.)
This is a massive book that every Benny Goodman fanatic can consider essential. D. Russell Connor had been BG's discographer for a couple of decades and this 1988 work was his final version. All of the clarinetist's recordings are listed in great detail along with radio appearances and unissued tapes of his live performances. It is possible to trace his whereabouts throughout every year of his long career and, when one considers the huge amount of recordings that Goodman made, it becomes clear that this oversized book (which has superb photos) is not only Benny Goodman's legacy but D. Russell Connor's too.

The Great Jazz Pianists by Len Lyons. (Quill, 1983, 322 pages, 27 of photos.)
For this book, Len Lyons interviewed 27 top pianists who were still active in the early 1980s: Teddy Wilson, Mary Lou Williams, John Lewis, Sun Ra, George Shearing, Dave Brubeck, Ahmad Jamal, Horace Silver, Oscar Peterson, Red Garland, Jimmy Rowles, Paul They, Marian McPartland, Billy Taylor, Jaki Byard, Ran Blake, Ramsey Lewis, Randy Weston, Bill Evans, Steve Kuhn, McCoy Tyner, Toshiko Akiyoshi, Chick Corea, Herbie Hancock, Joe Zawinul, Keith Jarrett and Cecil Taylor. In addition to an interview, each chapter has an introduction that sums up the pianist's career and concludes with a (now-dated) selected discography. In addition Lyons contributed a 40-page summary of the history of the jazz piano that is well balanced and comprehensive. This book is worth searching for.

The Great Jazz Revival by Jim Goggin & Pete Clute. (Ewald Publ., 1994, 160 pages, countless photos.)
This attractive book pays tribute to the New Orleans jazz revival that took place in the 1940s and still continues up to the present time. In what is essentially a picture book with many per-

formance photos and shots of memorabilia from the era, the text is informative and nostalgic, giving readers a history of the movement. Highly recommended to fans of Lu Watters, Turk Murphy, Louis Armstrong and San Francisco-style Dixieland.

Hear Me Talkin' to Ya by Nat Hentoff & Nat Shapiro. (Peter Davies, 1955, 383 pages.)
This out-of-print book is the main one that needs to be reissued. In 1955 Nat Hentoff and Nat Shapiro conducted a series of interviews with active jazz musicians and also gathered together significant quotes and anecdotes that had previously been printed. Through the words of the musicians (from Jelly Roll Morton to Dave Brubeck) the two editors essentially told the history of jazz. All of the classic and colorful stories are here covering early New Orleans (including Buddy Bolden, Storyville, Bunk Johnson and King Oliver), the 1920s (the ODJB, Bix Beiderbecke, Louis Armstrong, the Chicago jazz scene), Harlem, the swing era, the Kansas City jam sessions, Minton's Playhouse, bop, West Coast jazz and the Dixieland revival. In all 150 musicians and important people in the jazz world are heard from, making this one of the great jazz history books.

High Times, Hard Times by Anita O'Day & George Ellis. (Berkley Publ., 1981, 386 pages.)
In her very honest autobiography, singer Anita O'Day details her colorful up-and-down life. One learns what it was like to be a frequent contestant in marathon dances and walkathons, a successful singer with the Gene Krupa and Stan Kenton Orchestras, a star and eventually a drug addict who almost died from her habits. The very frank memoirs contain many memorable episodes and the book concludes with O'Day making a successful comeback in the early 1980s. This is one of the best jazz autobiographies.

His Eye Is on the Sparrow by Ethel Waters & Charles Samuels. (Da Capo Press, 1950, 278 pages, 10 of photos.)
Ethel Waters' 1950 memoirs detail a difficult but mostly rewarding life. Growing up poor and in terrible conditions, Waters (through perseverance and talent) rose to become one of the top blues and jazz singers in the 1920s, a major pop vocalist and actress in the 1930s and the star of "Cabin in the Sky" in the early 1940s. Her autobiography contains some brutal and scary episodes along with tales of her success, and they help one to understand this complex women. A major plus of the 1992 Da Capo Press paperback reissue is the inclusion of an 11 page preface by Donald Bogle that tells of the events in Ethel Waters' life during the 26 years that followed the close of her autobiography. Recommended.

Hot Man by Art Hodes & Chadwick Hansen. (Univ. of Illinois Press, 1992, 160 pages, 16 of photos.)
Art Hodes was a talented pianist in the Dixieland/Chicago jazz style who was also a fine writer and a strong propagandist for the music. For his autobiography (published just a year before his death), Hodes brings back to life Chicago of the 1920s, Wingy Manone, the no-win moldy fig vs. bebop jazz wars of the 40s, 52nd Street, Eddie Condon, Bunk Johnson, Pee Wee Russell and many others. Chadwick Hansen, who transcribed Hodes' reminiscences, also added some historical background to each chapter while Howard Rye contributed a valuable (and very comprehensive) discography of the distinctive pianist.

Alberta Hunter by Frank Taylor & Gerald Cook (McGraw-Hill, 1987, 311 pages, 32 of photos.)
Alberta Hunter had a remarkable life. A talented blues performer in the 1920s who was quite successful as a stage actress and a cabaret performer in Europe during the 1930s, Hunter became a nurse while in her early 60s and worked until she was involuntarily retired at the age of 82; it was believed that she had just turned 70! At that point in time (1977), Alberta Hunter returned to singing and again became a hit until her death in 1984 at the age of 89. This biography (which was written by Frank Taylor with the assistance of Hunter's accompanist Gerald Cook) is a definitive and very readable work that details not only Hunter's public life but also her well-hidden and sometimes difficult private life too. An excellent book which is rounded out by a good discography.

The Imperfect Art by Ted Gioia. (Portable Stanford, 1988, 161 pages, 9 of photos.)

Subtitled "Reflections on Jazz and Modern Culture," Ted Gioia's slim but high-quality book is filled with original ideas and different angles in which to view jazz, its history and its future. The seven chapters (which have such provocative titles as "Louis Armstrong and Furniture Music," "Jazz and the Primitivist Myth" and "Boredom and Jazz") are accessible without being obvious, fresh without being radical and both educational and thought-provoking. Recommended.

In Search of Buddy Bolden *by Donald Marquis.* (Da Capo Press, 978, 76 pages, 18 of photos.)
This is a remarkable book. Donald Marquis did everything he could to find out about cornetist Buddy Bolden, the very important jazz pioneer who played his last notes in 1907. Since Bolden had been a legend for 70 years, Marquis had to deal first with the myth and, through intense detective work, find out what was and what was not true about the man who in 1895 put together what could be considered the first jazz band. He uncovered a previously unknown drawing of Bolden (which is reproduced in the book) and enough fresh and accurate details to make this a definitive work, dispelling part of the legend (Bolden was never a barber nor an editor of a scandal sheet) and uncovering details that fill in the gaps. The finished product is perfectly done!

Inside Jazz *by Leonard Feather.* (Da Capo Press, 1949, 103 pages, 27 of photos.)
Originally titled *Inside Bebop,* this important book (reissued by Da Capo Press in 1977 with a new introduction) was the first to intelligently discuss bop. Leonard Feather discusses the beginnings of the music, the lives of Dizzy Gillespie and Charlie Parker (at least up until 1949), explains in technical detail how bop differs from swing and, in a section that preceded the Encyclopedia of Jazz, gives biographical data about a variety of "modern" jazz players. Even over 45 years later, the book still reads quite well.

In the Mainstream *by Chip Deffaa.* (Scarecrow Press, 1992, 390 pages, photos scattered throughout book.)
Chip Deffaa's third book profiles 19 musicians (in 18 chapters) who had not been covered in his previous *Voices of the Jazz Age* and *Swing Legacy.* Focusing once again on artists who play music that could be considered pre-bop, Deffaa gives readers the colorful life stories of Doc Cheatham, Bill Challis, Andy Kirk, Ray McKinley, Bob Haggart, Erskine Hawkins, Bill Dillard, Johnny Mince, Buddy Morrow, George Kelly, Mahlon Clark, Sonny Igoe, Joe Wilder, Oliver Jackson, Buck and John Pizzarelli, Ken Peplowski, Dick Hyman and Jake Hanna. Several of these players have since passed on and Deffaa has done a major service to the jazz world (just as Stanley Dance had a couple decades earlier with his "World of" series) by getting down on paper priceless anecdotes and details about the early days. Because Deffaa really knows his subjects well, these are not merely oral histories but definitive portraits. Highly recommended, as are his two previous books.

Jaco *by Bill Milkowski.* (Miller Freeman Books, 1995, 264 pages, photos.)
Jaco Pastorius was the world's top electric bassist, the first on his instrument to develop a truly distinctive voice. Writer Bill Milkowski was a friend of Jaco's during the later years of his life and in this superlative biography he not only gives readers the details of Pastorius's glory years with Weather Report but also the previously obscure details of his rise to fame plus an insightful look at Jaco's sad and fairly rapid decline (caused mostly by his untreated mental illness). The bassist definitely comes alive throughout this book, for Milkowski contacted virtually all of Jaco's associates, friends and relatives and adds some personal stories of his own to the legacy of Jaco Pastorius.

Jazz *by John Fordham.* (Dorling Kindersley, 1993, 216 pages, countless photos.)
This is one of the most colorful books to ever come out on jazz. John Fordham breezily discusses the history of jazz, the instruments used, the careers of 20 jazz giants and some of the classic recordings, but it is the pictures (of album jackets, instruments and musicians) that are most appealing. Although published in England, this book is readily available domestically and serves as a very accessible (and rather informative) introduction to jazz.

Jazz *by Nat Hentoff & Albert McCarthy.* (Da Capo Press, 1959, 387 pages, 8 of photos.)

Unlike most other jazz anthologies, this book's 14 articles (written by Ernest Borneman, Charles Edward Smith, Guy Waterman, Martin Williams, Paul Oliver, Max Harrison, John Steiner, Hsio Wen Shih, Frank Driggs, Gunther Schuller, Albert McCarthy and Nat Hentoff) were all commissioned specifically for the project. The essays, which cover all styles of jazz that were around at the time of the mid-1950s including New Orleans, ragtime, swing, boogie-woogie, bop and the revival of Dixieland, contains plenty of information, analysis and interesting opinions. Although now over 35 years old, most of the essays have not dated much and are still stimulating.

Jazz – A History of the New York Scene *by Samuel Charters & Leonard Kunstadt* (Da Capo Press, 1962, 382 pages.)
This book does an excellent job of summing up and documenting the many styles of jazz that were prominent in New York during 1900-60 Although there are chapters on Chick Webb, Count Basie, and Dizzy Gillespie, this book is at its strongest in covering the 1920s and earlier times with prominence given to Scott Joplin (shown trying unsuccessfully to produce his ragtime opera *Treemonisha*), Jim Europe, the blues craze and some of the lesser-known classic jazz bands. In fact it might have made more sense for the authors to concentrate exclusively on the 1900-40 period since a lot less space is given to the 52nd Street nightly jazz festivals than one might hope. However this book is continually interesting and well worth picking up for fans of early jazz.

Jazz Anecdotes *by Bill Crow.* (Oxford Univ. Press, 1990, 350 pages.)
For this book (which is as humorous as one might hope), bassist Bill Crow collected together stories from previously printed material, unpublished oral histories and his own experiences. The tales, arranged by topics (such as teachers and students, hiring and firing, cutting contests, prejudice, nicknames and such musicians as Louis Armstrong, Benny Goodman, Joe Venuti and Charles Mingus) are sometimes hilarious, sometimes poignant and mostly quite fresh. This book is a perfect gift jazz fans.

Jazz Band *by Max Kaminsky & V.E. Hughes.* (Da Capo Press, 1963, 242 pages, 8 of photos.)
This is a very successful and mostly entertaining autobiography. Max Kaminsky was a fine trumpeter often associated with Dixieland and Eddie Condon. A veteran of the 1920s, his stories about Bix Beiderbecke, Billie Holiday, Pee Wee Russell, Louis Armstrong, Artie Shaw, Condon and the many other musicians he played with are quite special and colorful. Kaminsky kept an open mind towards more modern styles of jazz (although it did not influence his style) and his book is both valuable and enjoyable.

The Jazz Book *by Joachim Berendt.* (Lawrence Hill Books, 1992, 541 pages.)
Ever since its first edition in 1953, Joachim Berendt's *The Jazz Book* has done an expert job of summing up all aspects of jazz history along with the current scene. Because the number of important names have multiplied several times since the '50s, the individual notations have become briefer and briefer and in this information-packed volume, some musicians are only mentioned for a sentence or two. However Berendt manages to still cover just about everyone and his book remains invaluable. There are overviews of the styles of jazz, some of the key musicians (including David Murray and Wynton Marsalis), the elements of jazz, the history of each instrument, vocalists, big bands and combos. Kevin Whitehead contributed an interesting if erratic selective discography. Recommended.

Jazz Changes *by Martin Williams.* (Oxford Univ. Press, 1992, 317 pages.)
Martin Williams was one of the most stimulating of all jazz writers, a journalist who somehow could make musical analysis seem colorful. This particular book (one of his last) is a collection of interviews, eye-witness accounts of recording sessions, rehearsals and concert performances and portraits dating from the 1950s to the late 80s. Among the many musicians featured are Earl Hines, Bob Wilber, Billie Holiday, Ruby Braff, producer Ross Russell, John Lewis, Thelonious Monk, Ornette Coleman and Pharoah Sanders. In addition there is an extensive reprint of Williams' liner notes for the Jelly Roll Morton Library of Congress recordings, a variety of other liner notes and some dated record reviews. In this, his third book, one gets a good all-round feel for Martin Williams' writing style and open-minded opinions.

The Jazz Crusade by Big Bill Bissonnette. (Special Request Books, 1992, 344 pages, lots of photos.)

Big Bill Bissonnette crusaded for New Orleans jazz in the 1960s, running his own record label (Jazz Crusade), playing trombone with his Easy Riders Jazz Band and sponsoring dozens of tours by ancient New Orleans jazzmen. This frank and continually interesting book details his adventures with such musicians as George Lewis, Jim Robinson, Kid Thomas Valentine, Sammy Rimington and Capt. John Handy among others. The stories (sometimes heartwarming, occasionally quite humorous) hold one's interest and add to the legacy of 1960s New Orleans jazz. The deluxe edition of this book includes a CD of music from the period including six previously unreleased selections.

Jazz Giants by K. Abe. (Billboard Publ., 1986, 280 pages, countless photos.)

This large oversized book is one of the most attractive of the jazz photo books that have been released. In addition to K. Abe, the work of 13 other photographers (along with a few that are anonymous shots) are represented including Ray Avery, trombonist Eddie Bert, William Claxton, William Gottlieb, Milt Hinton and Charles Stewart. Most of the photos are from the 1940s to the '60s although there are some of earlier and later vintage. Beautifully reproduced, this coffee table edition will give jazz fans many hours of enjoyment; Gottlieb's classic shot of 52nd Street at night is here in color and rightfully gets the centerfold position. Also check out the 1960 photo of Dizzy Gillespie sitting in with Ornette Coleman!

Jazz in Canada by Mark Miller. (Nightwood Editions, 1982, 245 pages.)

This is a very valuable book. Prior to its publication, relatively little was known about the history of jazz in Canada, particularly since few recordings were made prior to 1960. Mark Miller did what he could to correct the major oversight by portraying 14 important Canadian players: Trump & Teddy Davidson, Paul & P.J. Perry, Chris Gage, Herbie Spanier, Wray Downes, Larry Dubin, Nelson Symonds, Guy Nadon, Claude Ranger, Soony Greenwich, Brian Barley and Ron Park. Although a few of these players are reasonably well known today (P.J. Perry, Spanier, Downes and Greenwich) most of the others are forgotten legends. Jazz followers who think they know all about jazz history are particularly advised to pick up this well-written and important book.

The Jazz Life by Nat Hentoff. (Da Capo Press, 1961, 255 pages.)

This is Nat Hentoff's most important book. Not only does Hentoff accurately portray what it was like to be a jazz musician in the 1950s (both the glory and the potential hazards) but his writings about Count Basie, John Lewis and particularly Charles Mingus, Miles Davis, Thelonious Monk and Ornette Coleman were also among the first honest appraisals of these masterful musicians' lives. The Monk section contains all kinds of information previously unknown about the introverted genius. This book is one of the finest of the period.

The Jazz Makers by Nat Shapiro & Nat Hentoff. (Da Capo Press, 1957, 368 pages, 12 of photos.)

This excellent work contains chapters on 21 top jazzmen; all but Charlie Parker and Dizzy Gillespie fall into the prebop era (including Jelly Roll Morton, Baby Dodds, Louis Armstrong, Bix, Bessie Smith, Art Tatum, Benny Goodman, Duke Ellington, Lester Young and Billie Holiday). The writers (Orrin Keepnews, George Avakian, Charles Edward Smith, John S. Wilson, George Hoefer, Leonard Feather and Bill Simon in addition to Nat Shapiro and Nat Hentoff) were some of the finest of the writers of the time. The essays/biographies, although written from the standpoint of the 1950s, were generally definitive (especially Bill Simon's chapter on Charlie Christian) for the period and have been "borrowed" from often.

Jazz Masters of New Orleans by Martin Williams. (Da Capo Press, 1967, 287 pages.)

The first book chronologically in the valuable Jazz Masters series gave Martin Williams an opportunity to stretch out and examine (in a chapter apiece) the lives and music of Buddy Bolden, the Original Dixieland Jazz Band, Jelly Roll Morton, King Oliver, the New Orleans Rhythm Kings, Sidney Bechet, early Louis Armstrong, Zutty Singleton, Kid Ory, Bunk Johnson and Red Allen. Although some of the stories have become dated or been disproved (the Bolden chapter has been succeeded by the

definitive book In Search of Buddy Bolden), the portrayals give today's readers a strong introduction into the creators of the joyous music called New Orleans Jazz.

Jazz Masters of the Twenties by Richard Hadlock. (Da Capo Press, 1965, 255 pages, 12 of photos.)

The second in the valuable Jazz Masters series focuses on the innovators of the 1920s. Richard Hadlock contributed a chapter apiece on Louis Armstrong (the 1924-31 period), Earl Hines, Bix Beiderbecke, the Chicagoans, Fats Waller and James P. Johnson, Jack Teagarden, Fletcher Henderson and Don Redman, Bessie Smith, and Eddie Lang (but not Joe Venuti!). One of the best books on these important early players (although full-length biographies on Bix and Bessie are obviously more definitive), Hadlock's analysis of the music of the Chicagoans and Fletcher Henderson in particular is quite rewarding. Recommended.

Jazz Masters of the Thirties by Rex Stewart. (Da Capo Press, 1972, 223 pages, 8 of photos.)

One of the first jazz history books written by a musician that is not autobiographical, this entry in the valuable Jazz Masters series has particularly colorful chapters contributed by cornetist Rex Stewart. Although he does not cover all of the main innovators of the 1930s, since he largely wrote about musicians he knew, the stories are quite insightful. Stewart portrays the Jean Goldkette Orchestra, Fletcher Henderson, Louis Armstrong, Jimmy Harrison, Coleman Hawkins, Red Norvo, Duke Ellington, Tricky Sam Nanton, Barney Bigard, Ben Webster, Harry Carney, John Kirby, Sid Catlett, Benny Carter and Art Tatum. In addition there are appendixes by other writers on Count Basie and Rex Stewart himself. Since the book was published posthumously, there is not much on Benny Goodman, Lester Young and Roy Eldridge but Stewart's picturesque and knowledgeable articles are consistently a joy to read.

Jazz Masters of the Forties by Ira Gitler. (Da Capo Press, 1966, 290 pages, 10 of photos.)

This is one of the strongest books in the Jazz Masters series for not only does Ira Gitler (who really loves bebop) portray the leading players (Charlie Parker, Dizzy Gillespie, Bud Powell, J.J. Johnson, Oscar Pettiford, Kenny Clarke, Max Roach, Dexter Gordon, Lennie Tristano, Lee Konitz and Tadd Dameron) but each chapter also has shorter sketches on some of the other top bop stars to play the particular instruments (with chapters titled "J.J. Johnson and the Trombonists," "Oscar Pettiford and the Bassists," etc.). This is strictly a bop book so the title (which implies that one would also get information on the second half of the swing era) is not completely accurate but this collection (along with Gitler's later work From Swing to Bop) is highly recommended.

Jazz Masters of the Fifties by Joe Goldberg. (Da Capo Press, 1965, 246 pages, 8 of photos.)

The fifth in the Jazz Masters series (following books on New Orleans Jazz, the Twenties, Thirties and Forties), Joe Goldberg's work has chapters on a wide variety of top artists: Gerry Mulligan, Thelonious Monk, Art Blakey, Miles Davis, Sonny Rollins, the Modern Jazz Quartet, Charles Mingus, Paul Desmond (but not Dave Brubeck!), Ray Charles, John Coltrane, Cecil Taylor and Ornette Coleman. What is here is excellent (the Cecil Taylor chapter is particularly interesting) but Goldberg ignores West Coast Jazz almost completely and in portraying Taylor, Ornette and Coltrane (the latter was still alive at the time), he slips into the early 1960s so this book really covers 1955-65 rather than 1950-60. That reservation aside, the portrayals are well written and informative, making this a recommended book along with the others in the valuable series.

Jazz Matters by Doug Ramsey. (Univ. of Arkansas Press, 1989, 314 pages.)

Doug Ramsey, one of the better jazz writers of the past 20 years, collected together a grab bag of reviews, liner notes, essays and articles for his first book. In most cases the material had been previously published but it does give one a good overview of Ramsey's writing style, musical tastes and ideas. Among the musicians discussed are Clark Terry, Art Farmer, Miles Davis, John Coltrane, Bud Powell, Woody Herman, Thelonious Monk, Charles Mingus, Phil Woods, Gerry Mulligan, Chet Baker, Duke Ellington and (most memorably) Dave Brubeck and Paul Desmond.

Jazzmen by Frederic Ramsey & Charles Edward Smith.

(Harvest/HBJ Books, 1939, 360 pages, 32 of photos.)

This 1967 reissue brought back the first great jazz book (since Hugues Panassie's slightly earlier *Le Jazz Hot* is greatly flawed). Most of the top jazz writers of the 1930s contributed historical articles, covering such topics as early New Orleans jazz, King Oliver, the blues, Louis Armstrong, Bix Beiderbecke, the Five Pennies, collecting jazz records and even reviews of the earlier jazz books. It was indirectly due to the focus that *Jazzmen* put on Bunk Johnson that the veteran trumpeter was able to come out of retirement. This is a classic work that still reads well today.

Jazz People *by Valerie Wilmer.* (Da Capo Press, 1977, 168 pages, 14 of photos.)

In sketches usually lasting a mere seven pages apiece, Valerie Wilmer colorfully portrays 14 top jazz musicians (Art Farmer, Cecil Taylor, Eddie "Lockjaw" Davis, Thelonious Monk, Billy Higgins, Jimmy Heath, Randy Weston, Babs Gonzales, Clark Terry, Jackie McLean, Buck Clayton, Howard McGhee, Big Joe Turner and Archie Shepp). Each interview tells at least several interesting stories and gives readers a good idea as to the personality of the artist, his philosophy, and his then-current situation in music and in life. This is a particularly memorable book, making one wish that Valerie Wilmer had written dozens more.

The Jazz Scene *by Francis Newton.* (Weidenfeld & Nicolson, 1961, 298 pages.)

This classic look at the sociology of the contemporary jazz scene of 1961 was actually written by British historian E.J. Hobsbawm under the pseudonym Francis Newton. In 1989 it was reprinted and happily Hobsbawm was present to write a new introduction that summarizes the changes in jazz during the prior three decades. Otherwise the text is the same as the original and it serves as a superb time capsule. With such chapters as "How to Recognize Jazz," "The Jazz Business," "The Public" and "Jazz as a Protest" (in addition to looks at jazz's history, instruments and musical qualities), this is a very intelligent book that discusses many rare topics pertaining to the jazz world.

The Jazz Scene *by W. Royal Stokes.* (Oxford Univ. Press, 1991, 261 pages, 16 of photos.)

W. Royal Stokes during his career as a jazz journalist interviewed approximately 500 musicians from the 1970s up to 1990. He tied together many of the best stories to form what he accurately calls "An Informal History from New Orleans to 1990." By arranging the quotes and anecdotes into chapters ranging from "New Orleans," "The Big Bands" and "California" to "Post Bebop Developments" and "The Contemporary Scene," Stokes essentially gives readers a new history of jazz with fresh stories, some never previously published. This book is particularly recommended to readers who think they know everything about jazz history! The photos are great too.

Jazz Singing *by Will Friedwald.* (Charles Scribners & Sons, 1990, 477 pages, 16 of photos.)

Will Friedwald's massive look at jazz singers is continually interesting, even when one disagrees with him! A very inclusive critic, Friedwald stretches the meaning of jazz a bit (Sinatra, Bobby Darren, Doris Day?) but he also appreciates the undeservedly obscure talents such as Annette Hanshaw and the Boswell Sisters, and he clearly knows his stuff. This occasionally eccentric (and often witty) book will cause many listeners to rethink their positions, and (due to its huge amount of information) it is essential for any serious jazz library.

Jazz Spoken Here *by Wayne Enstice & Paul Rubin.* (Louisiana State Univ. Press, 1992, 316 pages, 22 of photos.)

This well-conceived book consists of 22 interviews that radio hosts Wayne Enstice and Paul Rubin conducted between 1975-81. Each chapter has a photo, an up-to-date introduction, the interview and a selected discography. Because the jazz greats represent a wide variety of idioms and are placed in alphabetical order rather than stylistically, it is refreshing to have such different players next to each other (such as Ruby Braff and Anthony Braxton!). The questions are often quite original and the responses include fresh stories and some surprises. The subjects are Mose Allison, Art Blakey, Ruby Braff, Anthony Braxton, Bob Brookmeyer, Dave Brubeck, Ray Bryant, Larry Coryell, Mercer Ellington, Bill Evans, Gil Evans, Tommy Flanagan, Dizzy Gillespie, Chico Hamilton, Lee Konitz, Charles Mingus, Joe Pass, Sonny Stitt, Gabor Szabo, Clark

Terry, Henry Threadgill and Bill Watrous; fans of any of these top musicians are advised to get this enjoyable book.

Jazz - The 1980s Resurgence *by Stuart Nicholson.* (Da Capo Press, 1990, 402 pages, photos.)

This is the type of jazz book that should be written for each decade. Stuart Nicholson essentially tells what nearly every top jazz musician (how could he miss Marian McPartland?) happened to be doing in the 1980s. Each chapter deals with a different style or aspect of the jazz field, from "Past Masters and Keepers of the Faith" and "Big Bands" to "Miles and the Fusion Junta" and "European Dreams and the Global Democracy." The narrative moves smoothly from one musician to another, from Wild Bill Davison to Steve Coleman, giving one a real feel for the decade. Highly recommended.

Jazz - The Rough Guide *by Ian Carr, Digby Fairweather & Brian Priestley.* (Penguin Group, 1995, 754 pages, photos.)

This is the best of all the current jazz reference books. Co-written by three English musicians, there are over 1,600 (!) biographies of jazz musicians that, while giving the usual important information, also have enough space for color, stories and analysis; the writers are not shy to show their wit when it fits! The entries conclude by reviewing a few of the better available recordings by the artist and at the book's end there is an extensive glossary. More complete than the Grove Dictionary of Jazz and more up-to-date than Leonard Feather's Encyclopedia of Jazz, this is an essential book for all jazz collections.

The Jazz Years *by Leonard Feather.* (Da Capo Press, 1987, 310 pages, 16 of photos.)

Of all of the jazz critics, Leonard Feather had the most remarkable life. A writer steadily from 1934 until his death sixty years later in 1994, Feather was the most famous of all jazz journalists but was probably proudest of his ability as a songwriter. This particular book is a sort of autobiography, what he subtitled "Earwitness to an Era." Feather talks extensively about his life in jazz and, although he dishes some dirt and settles a few scores, he is honest about his own life and provides many new stories about the jazz greats he knew. Although there is little here that takes place after 1960 (when the former musical radical reluctantly became a defender of the status quo), this continually interesting book is recommended.

Scott Joplin *by James Haskins & Kathleen Benson.* (Doubleday, 1978, 248 pages, 8 of photos.)

The best biography on Scott Joplin at the time (although somewhat eclipsed by 1994's *King Of Ragtime*), this book gives one a definitive portrait of the most important ragtime composer. James Haskins begins logically with a prologue about the rediscovery of Joplin's music after decades of neglect, and then in eight well-written chapters covers his accomplishments and his eventual sad decline. This is a perfect introduction to the life of the innovative composer.

Stan Kenton *by Carol Easton.* (Da Capo Press, 1973, 252 pages, 16 of photos.)

Rather than presenting a standard musical biography, Carol Easton in this book focuses on the unique personal life and personality of Stan Kenton, a man full of contradictions and accomplishments. Kenton's marriages and many bands are covered in detail and with honesty, giving readers an idea what it was like to travel constantly on the road with his band. Kenton comes across (despite his flaws) as rather admirable and one imagines that after reading this book he gave Carol Easton grudging respect. Recommended to all Stan Kenton fans, particularly those who feel he could do no wrong!

King of Ragtime *by Edward A. Berlin.* (Oxford Univ. Press, 1994, 334 pages, photos.)

This is the most thorough biography of Scott Joplin written to date. Edward Berlin did a great deal of digging through old newspapers and came up with some gap filling information that helps to give one a more complete picture of the innovative ragtime composer. Not only a biography but also a summary of the ragtime era, this definitive book is highly recommended to anyone with an interest in the music of 1900-1920.

Lady Sings the Blues *by Billie Holiday & William Dufty.* (Avon Books, 1956, 192 pages.)

Much of this book (Billie Holiday's ghost-written memoirs) is a bit fanciful but the picturesque episodes are often quite memorable. Considered very frank (and a bit ground breaking) at the time, Lady Day's autobiography is half true, half semi-fictional but always colorful. Donald Clarke's more recent Holiday biography *Wishing on the Moon* analyzes this book in great detail. However *Lady Sings the Blues* (which would have made a great movie if someone had had the wisdom to stick to reality!) is essential for it lets the reader inside Billie Holiday's mind late in her life.

Laughter from the Hip *by Leonard Feather & Jack Tracy.* (Da Capo Press, 1963, 175 pages.)

This was the first jazz comedy book, preceding *Jazz Anecdotes* by 27 years. Leonard Feather and Jack Tracy put together a series of funny essays (including Feather's fantasy on what Hollywood would have come up with for *The Duke Ellington Story*), anecdotes about practical jokes (with extra space reserved for Joe Venuti stories!), tales about drunk musicians, and so on. A few of the chapters are trivial but it is good to have all of these humorous incidents (including those involving Benny Goodman, Dizzy Gillespie, Eddie Condon and Wingy Manone among many others) available in one place. An enjoyable if purposely lightweight read.

A Life in Jazz *by Danny Barker & Alyn Shipton.* (Oxford Univ. Press, 1986, 223 pages, 16 of photos.)

Danny Barker, a fine guitarist, banjoist, singer, jazz educator and humorist, put together his entertaining memoirs eight years before his death. Barker was always full of stories and he tells many of the best ones in his book, starting in his early days in New Orleans through his experiences with Jelly Roll Morton and Cab Calloway and then more skimpily through the 1960s and '70s and his return home. Barker's experiences in the classic jazz, swing and New Orleans revival worlds are well worth reading; his writing style is quite colorful and often laced with humor. A fine discography rounds out this recommended book.

A Life In Ragtime *by Reid Badger.* (Oxford Univ. Press, 1995, 328 pages, 16 of photos.)

Although he was not active in jazz (and his murder in 1919 took away any chance he had of being a leader in the Jazz Age), James Reese Europe was important in the music of the teens. The first Black bandleader to record, Europe's dance band and later military orchestra was influenced by ragtime and employed some future jazz musicians. This well-researched book is quite definitive with 75 pages of footnotes (!), a discography (which shows that over half of Europe's recordings have never been reissued) and a very readable text. This book is well worth getting by readers interested in the early days of jazz and ragtime.

Louis *by Max Jones & John Chilton.* (Da Capo Press, 1971, 302 pages, 32 of photos.)

This excellent book (reissued on paperback by Da Capo in 1988) does a fine job of summarizing Louis Armstrong's colorful life, bringing out some information new at the time along with some fresh angles and including an often-revealing interview with Armstrong that was conducted late in his life. Although the emphasis is on Louis' work in the 1920s and '30s, to the author's credit they do not write off his years with the All-Stars. A 40-page discussion of his recordings, a chronology and a film list round out this work which serves as a good introduction to the musical magic of the brilliant trumpeter-singer.

Louis' Children *by Leslie Gourse.* (Morrow, 1984, 366 pages, 24 of photos.)

Although there is a chapter on Louis Armstrong, the main emphasis in this consistently interesting book (arguably Leslie Gourse's finest) is on the many jazz-oriented singers who were influenced by Satch. A writer who is able to bring out the personal side of each subject, Gourse portrays a wide variety of talents including Cousin Joe, Ethel Waters, Cab Calloway, Billie Holiday, Etta Jones, Helen Merrill, Billy Eckstine, Jon Hendricks, Mel Torme, Nat King Cole, Joe Williams, Dinah Washington, Sarah Vaughan, Ella Fitzgerald, Carmen McRae, Annie Ross, Rosemary Clooney, Betty Carter, Janet Lawson and Tania Maria among others. Although some of the singers that she predicted greatness for did not live up to their potential, this book holds one's interest and gives a bit of information about a lot of different vocalists.

The Man in the Green Shirt *by Richard Williams.* (Henry Holt and Co., 1993, 192 pages, many pictures.)

Although the most notable aspect to this attractive oversized book are the many photos (quite a few of which are rare), this portrait of Miles Davis also has an insightful narrative by Richard Williams. Other than dismissing Davis' work from the 1970s, Williams' writing is quite even handed and does an excellent job of summarizing in concise fashion Miles Davis' productive and crowded life. However it is the photos (many of which are in color) that really make this an essential acquisition for the trumpeter's fans.

Miles *by Miles Davis and Quincy Troupe.* (Simon & Schuster, 1989, 431 pages, 32 of photos.)

Miles Davis' somewhat infamous autobiography has far too many obscenities (especially in the first twenty pages), should have been more tightly edited (one-third could have been cut out) and was probably never read by the trumpeter himself. However the many fresh stories, the honesty (Miles does not always come across too well) and the rare opportunity to get at least partly into his mind make this a unique and essential book. He comments on nearly all of his recording sessions, tells anecdotes about everyone from Charlie Parker to John Coltrane and constantly explains (but does not excuse) some of his unusual behavior. A must.

Milestones 1 *by Jack Chambers.* (Beech Tree Books, 1983, 345 pages, 12 of photos.)

In the first of his two comprehensive biographies of trumpeter Miles Davis, Jack Chambers covers Miles' career up to 1960. Although he did not interview Davis (or it seems anyone else), Jack Chambers does a superior job of organizing all of the known facts about Miles (the bibliography is quite extensive) and analyzing all of Davis' recordings (at least all of the ones released by 1983). The results are quite complete and very informative; the trumpeter's autobiography *Miles* (which came out six years later) helped fill in the remaining gaps. Recommended.

Milestones 2 *by Jack Chambers.* (Beech Tree Books, 1985, 416 pages, 21 of photos.)

In the second of two books on the life of Miles Davis, Jack Chambers expertly traces the events in the remarkable trumpeter's life and musical career during the 1960-85 period. Since he did not interview anyone, Chambers relies on previously printed material (which he expertly organized together) and concise musical analysis. Although the period on Davis' retirement has been succeeded by Miles' autobiography of four years later, this book has dated quite well. Chambers gives the music of Miles Davis' "difficult" period (1969-75) an even handed approach, and his two books are quite informative and educational. Recommended.

Glenn Miller & His Orchestra *by George Simon.* (Da Capo Press, 1974, 473 pages, many photos.)

George Simon is uniquely qualified to write a biography on Glenn Miller for he was a top jazz journalist for Metronome during the Swing era and knew Miller quite well. Although he was obviously a fan of Miller's, Simon is quite fair about evaluating aspects of the bandleader's career. He covers with great detail Miller's early life, his unsuccessful attempt to make it with his new big band of 1937, his eventual rise to fame and the glory years, and his years in the military heading his Army Air Force Band. This is the definitive work on Glenn Miller and even over 20 years later it remains irreplaceable.

Mingus *by Brian Priestley.* (Da Capo Press, 1982, 308 pages, 16 of photos.)

The emphasis is on musical analysis during this interesting book on the great bassist-bandleader Charles Mingus. Until the definitive work on the volatile genius is written, this remains the top Mingus book; it discusses the usual biographical information but also goes into great detail about Mingus' music (including ten notated examples) and contains a complete discography of his work as both a leader and as a sideman. Recommended to his fans.

Mister Jelly Roll *by Alan Lomax.* (Pantheon Books, 1950, 392 pages.)

Alan Lomax's biography of Jelly Roll Morton, which is drawn from Morton's colorful interviews with Lomax for the Library of Congress in 1938 (and in reality the results are mostly an autobiography), is quite definitive. Reissued by Pantheon Books in 1993 with a new foreword by Lomax (who rightfully blasts the hideous play *Jelly's Last Jam*), this classic book is full of fanciful but probably true stories by Morton about early New Orleans, Storyville and Chicago in the 1920s. Lomax filled in some of the gaps with interludes and details about Morton's last years. In addition there are appendixes that discuss Morton's tunes, records and discography.

Music on My Mind *by Willie "The Lion" Smith & George Hoefer.* (Da Capo Press, 1964, 318 pages.)
Willie "The Lion" Smith was considered one of the "big three" of stride pianists in the 1920's. Unlike James P. Johnson and Fats Waller, he survived long enough to dictate his autobiography. Smith could be a bit of a braggart but most of his story (which is particularly valuable for describing the music heard on the East Coast during 1915-25) rings true. He mostly focuses on the pre-1950 era and there are a lot of colorful tales of life in the 1920s and '30s and of his contemporaries (from Jelly Roll Morton and Clarence Williams to Fats Waller and Sidney Bechet). Unfortunately he does not comment at all about bop or even much about swing but what is here is often quite fascinating, bringing attention to a lot of musicians who would otherwise be forgotten.

Music Was Not Enough *by Bob Wilber & Derek Webster.* (Oxford Univ. Press, 1987, 216 pages, 16 of photos.)
Bob Wilber, a talented clarinetist and soprano saxophonist, had an identity crisis throughout much of his career. A student of Sidney Bechet's, Wilber spent much of the 1950s and '60s doing his best to escape from Bechet's dominant influence and develop his own voice. His memoirs are primarily about his struggle to find himself both musically and personally. In this very honest autobiography, many top musicians (including Bechet, Louis Armstrong and Duke Ellington) make appearances and Wilber proves to be an expert story teller. His memoirs (which have a happy ending) are rounded out by a selective discography of the clarinetist's favorite sessions.

The New Grove Dictionary of Jazz *by Barry Kernfeld.* (St. Martin's Press, 1988, 1358 pages, pictures.)
Originally issued as two large books and then in 1994 combined into this one giant encyclopedia, the Grove Dictionary is quite impressive quantity-wise with over 4,500 entries and 1,800 discographies. Because so many different writers worked on it and the quality varies greatly, this book does have quite a few flaws with many major names (including Dorothy Donegan) being omitted altogether and some entries (such as Pete Fountain's whose biography essentially ends in 1959) being very incomplete. Still, this book (which has accurate birth and death dates) does have its value although it falls short of being truly definitive.

Oh Didn't He Ramble *by Lee Collins with Mary Collins.* (Univ. of Illinois Press, 1974, 165 pages, 16 of photos.)
The legendary New Orleans trumpeter Lee Collins (who passed away in 1960) informally began writing his memoirs in 1943 and, with the assistance of his wife, his book was finally published in 1974. Collins was one of the few musicians around in the 1950s who could write with firsthand knowledge about such early players as Chris Kelly, Buddy Petit and Manuel Perez. His tales of the early days in New Orleans are very valuable as are his stories about New Orleans in the 1920s, Chicago in the '30s and his two European tours. In fact Collins even talks about what would be his final illness! A fascinating and rather unique book.

Outcats *by Francis Davis.* (Oxford Univ. Press, 1990, 261 pages.)
Francis Davis is one of the finest jazz writers of his generation. This entertaining and informative book has essays written in the 1980s on such artists as Duke Ellington, Sun Ra, Gil Evans, Cecil Taylor, Henry Threadgill, Doc Cheatham, Miles Davis (an often-humorous piece), Frank Morgan, Steve Lacy, Ran Blake, Susannah McCorkle, Harry Conick, Jr., Steve Coleman and even Bobby Darin! No matter what style is being represented by his subject, Davis does justice to the artist and brings up some new points and fresh angles. This is a thought-provoking and highly recommended collection.

Oscar Peterson *by Gene Lees.* (Prima Publishing, 1990, 294 pages, 8 of photos.)
On first glance, pianist Oscar Peterson would seem to be a poor subject for a biography. A brilliant player with a quiet personal life, Peterson has been a very consistent performer throughout his productive career and he early on developed a style, that has

changed very little during the past four decades. However as Gene Lees shows in this book (possibly his finest), Peterson's personal life and growth are more interesting than expected and even in Canada he had to battle racism. One gets a good idea as to what the Canadian jazz scene was like in the 1940s, the difference between each of Peterson's groups and what motivates and inspires the great pianist. Recommended.

A Pictorial History of Jazz *by Orrin Keepnews & Bill Grauer Jr.* (Bonanza Books, 1966, 297 pages, infinite number of photos.)
This wonderful book, reprinted in 1981, lives up to its title. Most of the more famous jazz photos are here along with many lesser-known shots. Although the emphasis is on jazz's early days (the first 12 of the 20 chapters stick primarily to the years before 1930), this book does reach up to Ornette Coleman and Archie Shepp. Orrin Keepnews' text is concise and insightful but it is the photos (compiled by Keepnews and his partner in running Riverside Records Bill Grauer, Jr.) that are especially memorable. This delightful book belongs in every jazz collection.

Raise Up off Me *by Hampton Hawes & Don Asher.* (Da Capo Press, 1974, 179 pages.)
This was possibly the first important jazz autobiography from a member of the bebop generation. Pianist Hampton Hawes tells about the excitement of exploring new music and his problems with drugs. These very frank memoirs discuss many of Hawes' associates (including Charlie Parker, Miles Davis, Thelonious Monk and Billie Holiday), his time in jail, his pardon from President Kennedy and before ending optimistically. Hawes would pass away only two years later at the age of 49. Gary Giddins' fine introduction (written in 1979) fills in the gaps in the life of the talented pianist.

Really the Blues *by Mezz Mezzrow & Bernard Wolf.* (Doubleday, 1946, 348 pages.)
Mezz Mezzrow had his heart in the right place, at least musically. An erratic clarinetist who was best on the blues, Mezzrow was a propagandist for New Orleans jazz who probably made more money from selling marijuana than he ever did from music. His 1946 memoirs still are a bit sensational with many memorable tales of the jazz life including friendships with Sidney Bechet and Fats Waller, adventures with gangsters in Chicago, an opium addiction and eventual recovery, jail sentences and glorious jam sessions. Mezz might not have been much of a musician but he had a colorful story to tell!

Red & Hot–The Fate Of Jazz in the Soviet Union *by S. Frederick Starr.* (Limelight Editions, 1983, 368 pages, 24 of photos.)
This is a consistently fascinating book, the type that should be written about each country's relationship with jazz. S. Frederick Starr's history of jazz in the Soviet Union often reads like a novel with plenty of scary (and sometimes tragic) adventures. Through extensive research, Starr is able to tell about the beginnings of jazz in Russia, the brief period in the 1920s when jazz was accepted, the repression felt under Stalin, the use of jazz as propaganda during World War II, a major backlash against jazz in the second half of the 1940s and the gradual acceptance of the music during the '60s and '70s. One learns about many obscure but important heroes who kept the music alive under Communism.

Django Reinhardt *by Charles Delaunay.* (Da Capo Press, 1961, 248 pages, 12 of photos.)
Django Reinhardt was one of the all-time great jazz guitarists and a true original, both musically and in his very spontaneous personal life. French writer Charles Delaunay did an excellent job of summarizing Django's life; it helped that he knew both Reinhardt and violinist Stephane Grappelli. Although not definitive (the text is around 160 pages while a discography takes up 80 pages), this is still the only full-length Django Reinhardt biography to ever be published in English.

The Reluctant Art *by Benny Green.* (Da Capo Press, 1962 and 1976, 210 pages.)
Benny Green's thought-provoking essays on Bix Beiderbecke, Benny Goodman, Lester Young, Billie Holiday, Charlie Parker and Art Tatum (the latter was written as liner notes in 1976) have held up pretty well over the decades. Sometimes he puts a bit too much emphasis on the importance of recorded solos (which after all were generally improvised on the spot) and gets overly analytical but his ideas (such as Bix's happiness not despair at being

in Paul Whiteman's Orchestra) were fresh at the time and have often become accepted.

Reminiscing in Tempo *by Teddy Reig & Edward Berger.* (Scarecrow Press, 1990, 204 pages, 17 of photos.)

Teddy Reig was an insightful jazz record producer who worked extensively with Savoy (highlighted by the Charlie Parker sessions), Roost (his own label) and Roulette (including the Count Basie records). He was also a bit nuts, which helped him to deal with such characters as Herman Lubinsky of Savoy (a legendary cheapskate), uncaring executives and erratic but brilliant musicians. Reig was interviewed by Edward Berger but died before this project could be completed. The first 75 pages of the book are his memoirs (which are full of hilarious stories and revelations), Berger also interviewed ten people who knew Reig and wraps up the work with a selected discography of the albums Reig worked on. Despite its brevity, this book is recommended to fans of 1940s and '50s jazz.

Rhythm-A-Ning *by Gary Giddins.* (Oxford Univ. Press, 1985, 291 pages.)

With the exception of fusion (which he has never embraced), Gary Giddins is one of the open-minded and consistently talented jazz journalists of the past 20 years. This book (a bit of a time capsule) collects together many of his best articles from the first half of the 1980s, 61 pieces in all. Among the subjects covered are Jaki Byard, Jack DeJohnette, Sarah Vaughan, comparisons of different versions of "Body and Soul," Teddy Wilson, Lester Young, Miles Davis, Arthur Blythe, obituaries on Art Pepper and Sonny Stitt, pieces on Woody Herman, Illinois Jacquet, Thelonious Monk and even Frank Sinatra, Tony Bennett and Jackie Wilson. In general Giddin's articles (some of which are quite brief) will hold the reader's interest and make one think.

Pee Wee Russel *by Robert Hilbert.* (Oxford Univ. Press, 1993, 300 pages, 16 of photos.)

Robert Hilbert, who would sadly pass away just a year after completing this book, put together a memorable portrait of the colorful (and utterly unique) clarinetist Pee Wee Russell, interviewing every possible person and tying together information from previously published sources to fill in the gaps. Russell emerges as likable if a bit self-destructive and one gets the full story behind his early rise to fame, his successful flirtation with "modernism" in the early 1960s and his swift decline after his wife's death. Hilbert's *Pee Wee Speaks* (Scarecrow Press) completes the picture with a full discography.

Satchmo *by Gary Giddins.* (Anchor Books, 1988, 240 pages, countless photos.)

The many wonderful photos (which are beautifully reproduced), many of which were formerly unpublished, to an extent overshadow the enlightening text of Gary Giddins. Giddins punctuates the myths long surrounding Louis Armstrong because they are not needed; he was larger than life and a true hero anyway! This superb book will delight both beginners (who will get a strong introduction to the magic of Louis' life) and veteran collectors (who will find much to learn). Highly recommended to all.

Selections From the Gutter *by Art Hodes & Chadwick Hansen.* (Univ. of California Press, 1977, 233 pages, photos.)

During 1943-47, pianist Art Hodes edited *The Jazz Record*, an extremely valuable jazz magazine that often told about the lives of jazz artists through the musician's own words. The emphasis is principally on vintage jazz. In addition to standard interviews and portraits, there are articles written by the likes of Cow Cow Davenport, Little Brother Montgomery, Big Bill Broonzy, Mezz Mezzrow, Zutty Singleton, Kaiser Marshall, Omer Simeon, Baby Dodds, Pops Foster, George Wettling, Doc Evans and many others. Hodes himself sets the stage by describing various aspects of the jazz scene of the mid-1940s. Overall the 79 articles included in this very enjoyable book are consistently colorful, informative and timeless.

Self-Portrait of a Jazz Artist *by David Liebman.* (Advance Music, 1988, 96 pages.)

In this slim volume, soprano saxophonist David Liebman does a masterful job of summing up his life's experiences, his musical evolution, how he creates music and why he plays jazz. He not only lists a discography of his recordings up to 1988 but also a sampling of his personal favorite books and records. There is a lot

of variety in this volume, making the book of great interest to anyone who collects Liebman's recordings.

The Song of the Hawk *by John Chilton.* (Univ. of Michigan Press, 1990, 429 pages, 16 of photos.)

Although not quite at the same level as his remarkable Sidney Bechet biography, John Chilton's study of the great tenor Coleman Hawkins is very well researched and complete. Hawkins was not really all that interesting a personality (unlike the volatile Bechet) and was a very private person but Chilton did the best with what was available (although a discography would have been an asset). Even if his account of Hawk's childhood is a mere seven pages, the remainder of Hawkins' musical career, its evolution and what could be found about his private life is covered quite definitively.

Stormy Weather *by Linda Dahl.* (Limelight Editions, 1984, 372 pages, a few photos.)

This is the first truly definitive book on women in jazz. Linda Dahl divided her important work into five parts: 1890s-1920s, Women Instrumentalists, Women Vocalists, 1960s-1980s and Profiles (the latter has chapters on Willene Barton, Carla They, Clora Bryant, Dottie Dodgion, Helen Humes, Sheila Jordan, Helen Keane, Melba Liston, Mary Osborne and Ann Patterson). In addition, an appendix briefly discusses "More Women in Jazz" and there is a discography. Nearly every important female jazz singer and musician (although Annette Hanshaw is missing) is discussed and Dahl did a masterful job of putting together a unified narrative out of the many individual stories. Recommended.

The Story of Jazz *by Marshall Stearns.* (Oxford Univ. Press, 1956, 379 pages, 16 of photos.)

This early jazz history book is most significant for logically discussing the pre-history of jazz (pre-1900) and where jazz probably came from. In addition, despite the lack of recordings, Stearns was able to cover with authority the music of early New Orleans, the work song, the early blues, minstrel shows, spirituals and ragtime. In fact, the book is nearly half finished before Stearns reaches 1920! After quickly covering the swing era, bop and Afro-Cuban jazz, Stearns makes a sincere attempt to explain what jazz is and to come up with a definition although the latter is somewhat dated due to the rise of the avant-garde and fusion. But four decades later this book still reads quite well and is recommended for its discussion of jazz's roots.

The Story of the Original Dixieland Jazz Band *by H.O. Brunn* (Louisiana State Univ. Press, 1960, 268 pages, 8 of photos.)

This book is flawed since H.O. Brunn was a partisan for the Original Dixieland Jazz Band, but it is nevertheless still quite intriguing and informative. Brunn, who accepted without much question all of cornetist Nick LaRocca's assertions as to the importance of the ODJB, effectively traces the evolution of the group, the events that occurred during its prime years (1917-23), the band's brief comeback in 1936 and the activities of the group's members up until 1960. Some of Brunn's opinions are offbase but this book reads quite well and does uncover a lot of information as to the lives of these jazz pioneers.

Straight Life *by Art Pepper & Laurie Pepper.* (Da Capo Press, 1979, 558 pages, 36 of photos.)

This is one of the major jazz autobiographies. Art Pepper is extremely honest in his stories about life as both a great alto saxophonist and a destructive drug addict. Some of the episodes are scary and Pepper is not shy to paint himself in a bad light. The early chapters about his days with the Stan Kenton Orchestra are fairly happy, in striking contrast to the tales of his years in prison. Laurie Pepper, who largely saved Art's life and made his successful comeback (before his death in 1982) possible, collaborated with him on the book and contributed in 1993 a 29-page "Afterword" that talks about Pepper's final three years and how the success of the book helped his career. The forward by Gary Giddins and a lengthy discography sandwich the fascinating narrative.

Sweet Swing Blues on the Road *by Wynton Marsalis & Frank Stewart.* (W.W. Norton, 1994, 192 pages, many photos.)

Throughout this well-conceived and colorful book, trumpeter Wynton Marsalis talks about what it is like to go on the road (both the glamour and the drudgery), the joys of jazz and his personal philosophy. The many anecdotes are often quite humorous (Marsalis does not mind being the occasional butt of jokes) and he constantly shows the creative process in action. There are sketches of his band members and a few "heavy" discussions but most of the text is fairly breezy while remaining quite intelligent. The many photographs by Frank Stewart are a perfect complement to Wynton's text.

The Swing Era *by Gunther Schuller.* (Oxford Univ. Press, 1989, 919 pages.)

This is a massive work by the versatile near-genius Gunther Schuller. Focusing on the 1930-45 period, Schuller examines in depth the recordings of every major (and many minor) swing era musician and bands in ten chapters: Benny Goodman, Duke Ellington, Louis Armstrong, Jimmie Lunceford/Count Basie, the Great Black Bands, the Great Soloists, the White Bands, the Territory Bands, Small Groups and Things to Come. Although sometimes quite technical, Schuller's summaries are quite interesting, particularly since he is not afraid to criticize popular bands. The countless number of hours that he spent listening to swing era records is obvious and, even when one does not agree with him, his opinions are well worth reading.

Swing Era – New York *by W. Royal Stokes & Charles Peterson.* (Temple Univ. Press, 1994, 220 pages, countless photos.)

The photos of the late Charles Peterson (many of which were previously unpublished) and the informative text of W. Royal Stokes are combined in this very attractive book. The candid photos (from 1935-42, 1945 and 1950-51) are often quite fascinating and worth close looks; in fact, in some of the shots one can almost hear the music! The photos are arranged into chapters titled "Harlem," "52nd Street," "Nick's, the Village Vanguard, Cafe Society and Other Venues," "Jam Sessions," "The Recording Scene" and "The Big Bands." The emphasis is generally on small group swing and the Eddie Condon-style of Dixieland, perfectly capturing the magic and joy of many of the classic musicians from the golden age of jazz.

Swing Legacy *by Chip Deffaa.* (Scarecrow Press, 1989, 379 pages, many photos.)

In this consistently interesting and well-written collection Chip Deffaa has interview/profiles with many of the top musicians who were helping to keep swing-styled jazz alive in the 1980s: Artie Shaw, Chris Griffin, Buck Clayton, Johnny Blowers, Maxine Sullivan, John Williams, Jr, Maurice Purtill, Lee Castle, Panama Francis, Stephane Grappelli, Mel Torme, Harold Asby, Thad Jones, Frank Foster, Mercer Ellington, Warren Vache, Scott Hamilton and Woody Herman. Each of these musicians had an important story to tell and Deffaa draws out from his subjects fresh anecdotes, insights and opinions. Highly recommended as are Deffaa's other important books.

Swing Swing Swing *by Ross Firestone.* (W.W. Norton, 1993, 522 pages, photos.)

There has been a great deal written about clarinetist Benny Goodman through the decades but this biography is the definitive work. Rather than just focus on BG's glory years or his personal eccentricities, Ross Firestone gives readers the full story of Goodman's childhood, his unlikely rise to fame and his life after 1945 when Goodman suddenly found his music being considered old fashioned. There is plenty of fresh material in this book (which includes new interviews with Goodman's associates) and, even when Firestone recounts familiar stories, he gives the tales fresh angles and additional information. A perfectly done biography of the King of Swing.

Swing to Bop *by Ira Gitler* (Oxford Univ. Press, 1985, 331 pages.)

This oral history is remarkable in that virtually all of the stories (dealing with the well documented transition of jazz in the 1940s) are new and fresh. Gitler, whose true love has long been bebop, interviewed 66 major figures who were around during the era (including many who have since passed on) about every aspect of the period from life in the big bands, the legendary sessions at Minton's and Monroe's, 52nd Street, the underrated scene in California, the bop era and the death of the brief "bop fad." Whether it be about drug abuse, life on the road, the public's indifference and the difficulty of older musicians to adjust to the new music, Ira Gitler (through the musicians' memories) does a superlative job of summing up the volatile time period.

Talking Jazz *by Ben Sidran.* (Da Capo Press, 1995, 509 pages, 16 of photos.)

Ben Sidran for the National Public Radio show *Sidran On Record* interviewed over 100 jazz musicians. The 43 interviews included in this excellent book are taken from the 1984-90 period. Because Sidran is himself a musician, he was able to get these very interesting subjects to open up and discuss their music and their lives on a higher level than they might have if he were a typical journalist. Among the artists who interact with Sidran (reproduced in a question and answer format) are Miles Davis, Dizzy Gillespie, Max Roach, Betty Carter, Jackie McLean, Mose Allison, Sonny Rollins, Phil Woods, Archie Shepp, Keith Jarrett, Wynton Marsalis, Don Cherry, Bobby McFerrin and Bob James; each has an interesting story to tell and Sidran skillfully inspires them to express themselves in an intelligent and coherent fashion.

Jack Teagarden *by Jay Smith & Len Guttridge.* (Da Capo Press, 1960, 208 pages, 16 of photos.)

This underrated book, written four years before trombonist Jack Teagarden's death and with his cooperation (a short preface by Martin Williams was added to the 1987 reissue) colorfully tells the Jack Teagarden story. From his early days in Texas with Peck Kelly and his discovery in the 1920s to his days with Paul Whiteman, leading his own unsuccessful big band and gigs with the Louis Armstrong All-Stars, the narrative never loses one's interest. The 1950s are sped through very quickly before the book concludes with details about Teagarden's extensive tour of the Orient. A fairly complete discography (which has become a bit dated) concludes this worthwhile book.

They All Played Ragtime *by Rudi Blesh & Harriet Janis.* (Oak Publ., 1950, 347 pages, 26 of photos.)

Although revised slightly (mostly the discography) upon its reissue in 1971, this is essentially the same magnificent book that came out in 1950. For what would be the first ever full-length book on ragtime (a style that had been neglected for 30 years at the time), Blesh and Janis interviewed scores of survivors (including Scott Joplin's widow and the great ragtime composer Joseph Lamb), consulted with musicians active in the revivalist movement and did an enormous amount of research. The results (which include 16 complete scores of rags) are still quite definitive 45 years later. All ragtime books written since 1950 have had to deal first with this admirable and accurate work which essentially tells fans and scholars alike nearly everything they need to know about ragtime.

This Is Ragtime *by Terry Waldo* (Da Capo Press, 1976, 244 pages, photos scattered throughout book.)

Rudi Blesh's *They All Played Ragtime* is the definitive book about that very likable music but Terry Waldo's 1976 book (reissued with an additional introduction in 1991) is also valuable. In addition to covering most areas of classic ragtime, Waldo (himself a talented pianist) has separate chapters on novelty ragtime of the 1920s, and the ragtime revivals of the 1940s (in jazz groups), 1950s (honky tonk), 1960s and 1970s (the latter fueled by the release of *The Sting*). Waldo's even handed account is colorful, entertaining and informative, bringing classic ragtime history's up to nearly the present day. A good selective discography concludes this fine work.

To Be or Not to Bop *by Dizzy Gillespie & Al Fraser.* (Doubleday, 1979, 552 pages, 56 of photos.)

Dizzy Gillespie's memoirs are extensive, educational and colorful although once it hits 1960 details become much more sparse; Jon Faddis is not mentioned once! This book is at its strongest when covering the innovative trumpeter's early years and the gradual formation of bebop. In addition to the 150 interviews that he conducted with Gillespie, Al Fraser gathered extensive quotes from dozens of Dizzy's associates (including relatives, Roy Eldridge, Kenny Clarke, Cab Calloway, Thelonious Monk, Mary Lou Williams, Billy Eckstine, Earl Hines, Sarah Vaughan, Max Roach, Ella Fitzgerald and even Miles Davis among many others), including them in the relevant chapters (even when they occasionally contradict Gillespie's version of a story). This is a very valuable book as one might expect, highly recommended to fans of bop.

Too Marvelous for Words *by James Lester* (Oxford Univ. Press, 1994, 240 pages, 8 of photos.)

Art Tatum, one of the most remarkable musicians (not just in jazz) of all time, was a rather private person. As James Lester discovered in researching for his definitive book, Tatum rarely did any interviews and did not have much of a life outside of his music; although married twice, his women always played second fiddle to his piano. Lester did talk to everyone possible (including Art's childhood friends and many musicians) about Tatum and was able to piece together a fairly complete picture even though there are still some mysteries. This is a well-conceived book about one of the immortals, the only one ever written on Art Tatum.

Traditionalists & Revivalists in Jazz by Chip Deffaa. (Scarecrow Press, 1993, 391 pages, 50 of photos.)
For his fourth book, Chip Deffaa includes 14 portraits of musicians who play or sing vintage jazz in the 1990s. Unlike in his first three books, Deffaa sticks (with a couple of exceptions) to younger players rather than ancient veterans; only Marty Grosz had previously been profiled in a book. Each of the subjects (Vince Giordano, Terry Waldo, Eddy Davis, Peter Ecklund, Marty Grosz, Joe Muranyi, Richard Sudhalter, Dan Barrett, Ed Polcer, Stan Rubin, Carrie Smith, Sandra Reaves-Phillips, Orange Kellin and Vernel Bagneris) have interesting stories to tell with many previously unknown details and anecdotes about classic jazz, a truly underground form of jazz in the 90s. Recommended.

Traps—The Drum Wonder by Mel Tormé. (Oxford Univ. Press, 1991, 233 pages, 16 of photos.)
Mel Tormé, a talented writer as well as singer, was a longtime friend of Buddy Rich and was asked by Rich back in 1975 to write his biography. This consistently fascinating book has a great deal of inside information about the amazing drummer along with many humorous stories. Rich, a true genius who was a top drummer in vaudeville by the time he was 18 months old (!), expected greatness at all times from his sidemen and was quite difficult to work for; Tormé is quite fair in evaluating Buddy's personality and temper. But when it came to drumming, Buddy Rich still ranks at the top and Tormé never shies away from the fact that Rich really was the world's greatest drummer. Highly recommended.

Treat It Gentle by Sidney Bechet with Desmond Flower. (Da Capo Press, 1960, 245 pages, 16 of photos.)
The great New Orleans pioneer Sidney Bechet's autobiography is one of the most picturesque in jazz history. Some of his stories are more legendary than fact (particularly the chapter on his grandfather) but there is a great deal of valuable information in these memoirs. Unfortunately the masterful soprano saxophonist died in 1959, a year before the book was published, and he had run out of time before saying much about his last decade when he was adopted as a national hero in France, but what is here is generally memorable. This book is recommended as a complement to John Chilton's much more thorough Bechet biography The Wizard Of Jazz.

Unfinished Dream by Red Callender and Elaine Cohen. (Quartet Jazz, 1985, 239 pages, 16 of photos.)
Red Callender, the only musician to turn down jobs with both the Louis Armstrong All-Stars and Duke Ellington's Orchestra (working in the studios of Los Angeles was more lucrative), was a versatile and talented bassist and tuba player who recorded extensively between 1937-84. Fortunately he had a very good memory and his interesting (if generally little-known) life story is full of intricate details, particularly up through the 1950s. This biography is easily recommended.

Voices of the Jazz Age by Chip Deffaa. (Univ. Of Illinois Press, 1990, 256 pages, 30 of photos.)
Just as Stanley Dance in the early 1960s did the jazz world a major service by interviewing veteran jazzmen while they were still around, Chip Deffaa in his first book captured seven jazzmen before it was too late; only 93-year old Benny Waters is still around. Deffaa's portraits of Waters, Sam Wooding (who was on his deathbed!), Joe Tarto, Bud Freeman, Jimmy McPartland, Freddie Moore, Jabbo Smith and his tribute to Bix Beiderbecke are all pretty definitive with lots of new information. Deffaa brought to the interviews both enthusiasm and vast knowledge, and the results are consistently memorable. This appealing book is highly recommended to fans of classic jazz.

We Called It Music by Eddie Condon and Thomas Sugrue. (Da Capo Press, 1947, 357 pages.)
This book (which was reissued in 1992 with a foreword by Gary Giddins and a chapter added for the 1962 reprint) is a classic. Eddie Condon (bandleader, rhythm guitarist and propagandist for Chicago Dixieland) was one of the great wits of jazz. His colorful memoirs (which cover the first half of his career) are filled with memorable stories about the great early legends of jazz (including Bix Beiderbecke) and are augmented by Thomas Sugrue's "narration" which puts the anecdotes into historical perspective. One comes away from this entertaining book fully understanding why some jazzmen enjoy playing this freewheeling music and also with an appreciation for Eddie Condon's unique place in jazz history.

Who's Who of Jazz by John Chilton. (Chilton Book Co., 1978, 370 pages.)
This is one of the great jazz reference books. John Chilton has a biographical entry on virtually every important jazz musician (many of whom are little known today) born before 1920. Although Dizzy Gillespie makes the book, the emphasis is on vintage and swing musicians. Chilton largely avoids commenting on the subject's musical significance, sticking to facts and providing a major service to historians and early jazz fans alike. There is a lot of information in this book that can not be found elsewhere.

Wishing on the Moon by Donald Clarke. (Viking, 1994, 468 pages, 24 of photos.)
Billie Holiday is one of the great jazz legends and has been written about steadily for the past four decades. Donald Clarke interviewed many of Lady Day's associates who had rarely been spoken to by biographers and he also had access to the files of Linda Kuehl (who had interviewed nearly 150 people before her death in the 1970s). The result is a truly definitive book that successfully separates facts from myths. Clarke disproves much of what was thought to be true about Holiday's early life (her Lady Sings the Blues memoirs are mostly fanciful) and shows that Billie brought a lot of her troubles on herself while still painting her as a largely sympathetic character. This is a masterful work that is a must for anyone wanting to know the true story of Billie Holiday.

The World of Count Basie by Stanley Dance. (Charles Scribner's Sons, 1980, 400 pages, 24 of photos.)
For the fourth book in his very valuable the World of series, Stanley Dance focused on Count Basie and his legacy. As with the prior books, Dance emphasizes oral histories mostly taken in the 1960s and early '70s. The Lester Young chapter (an interview from a different source and a 1956 appreciation) is an exception. Heard from telling colorful stories in this enjoyable book are such Basie alumni as Jimmy Rushing, Buck Clayton, Jo Jones, Eddie Durham, Earle Warren, Dicky Wells, Harry "Sweets" Edison, Buddy Tate, Helen Humes, Snooky Young, Joe Newman, Preston Love, Marshall Royal, Eddie "Lockjaw" Davis, Frank Wess, Frank Foster, Joe Williams, Al Grey, Sonny Cohn, Eric Dixon, Bobby Plater, Richard Boone, Paul Quinichette and Basie himself. In addition there are interviews with such Basie associates as Nat Pierce, Jay McShann, Gene Ramey, Gus Johnson, Paul Quinichette, Jimmy Witherspoon, Eddie Barefield, Snub Mosley, Sir Charles Thompson and Melvin Moore. All four of Dance's books are well worth acquiring by fans of swing-oriented jazz.

The World of Duke Ellington by Stanley Dance. (Da Capo Press, 1970, 311 pages, photos.)
Stanley Dance's interviews with veteran swing musicians in his four the World of books are extremely valuable, saving stories and information for posterity that would otherwise be permanently lost. This important work starts off with a few interviews with Duke Ellington and then there are oral histories of many of his top associates including Billy Strayhorn, Mercer Ellington, Otto Hardwick, Sonny Greer, Harry Carney, Barney Bigard, Johnny Hodges, Cootie Williams, Juan Tizol, Lawrence Brown, Ben Webster, Ray Nance, Jimmy Hamilton, Cat Anderson, Russell Procope, Shorty Baker, Paul Gonsalves, Willie Cook, Clark Terry, Sam Woodyard, Booty Wood, Aaron Bell, Buster Cooper, Jimmy Jones, Jeff Castleman, Alice Babs, Harold Ashby and Wild Bill Davis. When one considers how few of these musicians are still around, it quickly become apparent just how valuable this project was. In addition Dance reports on some of the Ellington tours and festivals on which he was fortunate enough to attend. This book

is not a standard biography nor is there much information on Duke's offstage life, but it is quite memorable anyway!

The World of Earl Hines *by Stanley Dance.* (Da Capo Press, 1977, 324 pages, many photos.)

This entry in Stanley Dance's unique World of series is the best book thus far written about pianist Earl "Fatha" Hines. In addition to extensive interviews with Hines that take up 100 pages, Dance includes oral histories of Hines' manager Charlie Carpenter plus 20 musicians including Lois Deppe (Hines' first boss), Walter Fuller, Teddy Wilson, Milt Hinton, Jimmy Mundy, Budd Johnson, Trummy Young, Billy Eckstine, Dizzy Gillespie and Dicky Wells among others. In addition there is a chapter on road stories, capsule biographies of Hines' 1946 band (taken from publicity material) and a chronology of his life. A superior effort.

The World of Swing *by Stanley Dance.* (Da Capo Press, 1974, 436 pages, photos.)

In the second of Stanley Dance's very valuable World of series of books, rather than focusing on one individual (as in his Duke Ellington, Count Basie and Earl Hines books), Dance covers a wider spectrum. His profiles (most of which contain timeless interviews filled with unique anecdotes) include pieces on Claude Hopkins, Sandy Williams, Taft Jordan, Willie Smith, Sy Oliver, Benny Carter, Coleman Hawkins, Roy Eldridge, Jonah Jones, Stuff Smith, Cozy Cole, Charlie Holmes, Benny Goodman, Lionel Hampton, Vic Dickenson, Doc Cheatham, Eddie Heywood, Al Casey, Tiny Grimes, Milt Hinton, Chick Webb, Mildred Bailey and Billie Holiday among others. Fans of the swing era (particularly the many talented Black bands) are well advised to pick up this very interesting book.

You Just Fight for Your Life *by Frank Buchmann-Moller.* (Greenwood Press, 1990, 282 pages, 4 of photos.)

Lester Young was always a legendary figure with his own unusual personality, language and playing style. In this definitive book, Danish writer Frank Buchmann-Moller clears up some of the mysteries about the great tenor, he includes a great deal of previously unknown information that partly explains Young's eventual decline and he pieces together a very complete portrait. A valuable appendix lists all of Lester Young's known musical jobs. For readers who really want to study Young's playing, Buchmann-Moller's companion book *You Got to Be Original, Man* has a discussion of all of Lester's solos but more general collectors will be satisfied with this fine biography.

A Lester Young Reader *by Lewis Porter.* (Smithsonian Institution Press, 1991, 323 pages, 8 of photos.)

This very valuable book from the Smithsonian's Reader series has 14 articles on tenor saxophonist Lester Young's life, nine interviews and 13 essays on his music; overall these are among the most rewarding articles ever written on the great tenor. The wide range of opinions (particularly about Young's playing during the 1950s) is contradictory but very interesting and the various critiques (which sometimes use different assumptions) on a whole present a fairly complete portrayal of Prez. Best are Young's interviews where he gets to speak for himself. Highly recommended to Lester Young fans.

–Scott Yanow

VENUES

52nd Street

Like Storyville in New Orleans, 52nd Street in New York wasn't a club but an entity and spawning ground for superb talent. When the center of jazz headed downtown from Harlem, 52nd Street was for many years the city's jazz mecca and main headquarters. It offered diverse clubs and incredible talent at numerous locations. The Onyx opened first, followed by the Famous Door, then the Hickory House, Downbeat, Three Deuces and Jimmy Ryan's. The styles ranged from traditional New Orleans to bebop, and the roster of stars included Art Tatum, Coleman Hawkins, Erroll Garner, Charlie Parker, Billie Holiday, Hot Lips Page, Count Basie, Woody Herman, Buddy Rich, Charlie Barnet, and Fats Waller. The street reigned supreme in the '30s and early '40s, but began coming undone after World War II ended. Gradually, strip bars and clip joints replaced the jazz clubs. Today there are some commemorative signs and sidewalk plaques that recognize past achievements and heroes.

Alhambra

Though not as well known as some other New York clubs, the Alhambra has a special place in the hearts of jazz fans. It was here that the 16-year-old John Hammond, supposedly out to practice music with his friends, slipped instead into the Alhambra and heard Bessie Smith. The club opened in the '20s under the direction of Milton Gosdorfer. He presented variety shows with major blues and jazz stars. In addition to Smith, Cab Calloway performed there in the '30s, as did Billie Holiday. Edgar Hayes was the resident bandleader from 1927 to 1930 and then the Emmett Mathews band was employed. It is currently an office building of the New York Department of Motor Vehicles.

Ali's Alley

Drummer Rashied Ali opened Ali's Alley in New York at North Green Street between Spring Street and Broome Street in 1973. It was located in a loft in Greenwich Village that was formerly named Studio 77. Ali was initially the principal performer, and later such musicians as Archie Shepp and Gunter Hampel were featured with their bands. It closed in 1979.

Apollo Theater

The greatest entertainment venue in African-American cultural history and one of the most significant in popular music annals, the Apollo Theater opened in New York in 1913. Frank Schiffman and Leo Brecher had earlier operated the Lafayette Theatre. The Apollo had some jazz presentations in the '20s but came of age in the '30s. Sidney Cohen bought and renovated the building in 1933 and reopened in January of 1934. The club then evolved into the premier facility for jazz and African-American popular music. Big bands from Count Basie and Duke Ellington to Chick Webb, as well as classic blues vocalists; jazz, R&B and soul singers; tap and jazz dancers, comedians; and gospel acts appeared there. Only down-home and urban blues vocalists found the going a bit rough at the Apollo, where the audiences were known as the nation's toughest—and most loyal once they were on an act's side. The weekly amateur competitions were a launching pad for many great careers. The Apollo's importance as a jazz center dimmed after the '40s, was limited in the '50s

and '60s, and almost nil after that, though some jazz performers still appeared there out of loyalty and a desire to remain close to the black community. R&B, soul, and gospel flourished there. Contrary to the film *The Buddy Holly Story*, White bandleader Johnny Otis appeared there long before Holly. Jerry Lee Lewis and Wayne Cochran were other White acts who headlined there and were a big success. Though threatened with extinction many times, the club has been saved through ventures with Inner City Broadcasting and with the help of national appeals to famous African-American entertainers. Television specials have been held at the refurbished and restored center in the '80s and '90s, and a syndicated program reprising the old Amateur Night contests also aired for a number of seasons.

Baby Grand

Once a great cabaret club, the Baby Grand at 319 W. 125th Street, on what is now Frederick Douglass Boulevard in New York City, operated for over 40 years as a hot spot where musicians like Joe Turner and Jimmy Butts were featured, as well as comedians like Nipsey Russell and Manhattan Paul. It opened its doors in the mid '40s, and kept going until 1989. Ruth Brown taped a nationally televised birthday special there in 1988. It is now a clothing store.

Beale Street

While it can be debated whether Beale Street in Memphis was ever as much the national center of African-American cultural activities as its admirers claim, its importance as a business and musical mecca for Blacks in the South is indisputable. Much as Storyville in New Orleans and Central Avenue in Los Angeles were much more than places to simply hear music, Beale Street was a thriving, constantly busy hub for Black financial, social, and political affairs throughout the mid-South. W.C. Handy arrived there in the '20s, and through the '30s, '40s, and into the '50s, jazz, followed closely by blues and later rhythm and blues and soul, seemed to constantly be in the air. Legendary names from Furry Lewis to B.B. King to Rufus Thomas and even Elvis Presley put in their time on Beale. Memphis' longtime political ruler and mayor, E. H. "Boss" Crump, the subject of many a great blues tune, essentially left the street alone. As a result it had the good (banks, numerous businesses, clubs), the bad (prostitution, gambling), and the ugly (a sky-high murder rate long before discussions about so-called Black-on-Black crime were in vogue). When Crump began closing down certain establishments in the '50s, legitimate businesses gradually faded away. A combination of urban renewal, neglect from city administrations, and the pall cast over Memphis by Dr. Martin Luther King Jr.'s assassination in 1968 left the old Beale Street dead and almost completely abandoned at one point. But today the area is a historic district, with small reminders of what life was like in the glory years.

Bee Hive

The Bee Hive opened in 1948, right when jazz activity in Chicago was at its peak. It was located at East 55th Street and South Harper Avenue. Many of the city's greatest musicians such as Sonny Stitt, Johnny Griffin, and Eddie "Lockjaw" Davis played there, while Charlie Parker and the Clifford Brown-Max Roach quartet, among other national headliners, also appeared there. (A two-album set of performances by the Brown/Roach quartet at the Bee Hive was issued by Columbia but hasn't been reissued on CD.) It was also known for featuring jazz veterans like Chippie Hill, Miff Mole, Baby Dodds, and Lester Young. Norman Simmons was the house pianist in the mid '50s. The Bee Hive closed in 1956.

Birdland

One of several clubs near 52nd Street in New York, Birdland opened on Broadway in 1949 as a shrine to Charlie Parker, complete with his nickname as its signature. Morris Levy, not exactly an altar boy, operated it; and many top bebop and swing stars regularly appeared there. The club initially had parakeets in cages, but they soon died from the smoke and air conditioning. It also had tables on the dance floor, bleachers for anyone who only wanted, or could only afford, to pay the cover charge, and a milk bar for nondrinkers. Count Basie used the club as his New York headquarters in the '50s, and it had its own radio wire, broadcast booth, and eventually an NBC affiliation. Symphony Sid Torin held court there, and many Birdland shows were recorded and issued on labels owned by Boris Rose. Impulse released a 1963 John Coltrane concert, and Count Basie's 1955 recording of George Shearing's "Lullaby of Birdland" was also issued. Art Blakey recorded some superb Blue Note dates at Birdland. The pint-sized emcee Pee Wee Marquette can be heard shouting out calls for applause and announcing acts on various albums. Unfortunately, the club was just as famous for some unsavory events as for musical ones. Miles Davis was savagely beaten by two policemen outside the club one night for "loitering," an incident that led to his being jailed and needing five stitches. The club got massive unfavorable publicity before the charges were dropped. Charlie Parker had a number of horrible encounters, including one that turned into a suicide attempt. He was ultimately banned from the place bearing his nickname. The club declined in the '60s and was eventually taken over by R&B vocalist Lloyd Price. The great place that was immortalized in song by Joe Zawinul in 1976 with the composition "Birdland" was finally replaced by a strip joint.

Blackhawk

A principal San Francisco spot for hard bop and bebop in the '50s and early '60s, the Blackhawk was the site where Art Tatum had one of his last extended engagements in 1955 and the location for a pair of famous Miles Davis albums in the early '60s, *Friday and Saturday Nights at the Blackhawk*. It didn't have a long run, opening in the '50s and closing in the '60s.

Boomer's

A hard bop, bebop, and soul-jazz center in New York in the '70s, Boomer's began in 1971 at 340 Bleecker Street at Christopher Street. Cedar Walton recorded there for Muse in 1973; others who appeared included Barry Harris, Junior Mance, Joe Newman, Junior Cook and Woody Shaw. It closed six years later in 1977.

Bottom Line

This has never been exclusively or even mainly a jazz club, but it has certainly presented its share of great jazz performers since it opened in 1974. More so than the Fillmore East or West or any other major rock and pop club, the Bottom Line has featured top jazz stars like Charles Mingus, Sun Ra, Dexter Gordon, Sonny Rollins, Ralph Towner, John Abercrombie, Andrew Cyrille, and Lester Bowie. It is still in operation at 15 West Fourth Street at Mercer Street in Greenwich Village in New York.

Cafe Bohemia

Jimmy Garofolo owned and operated the Cafe Bohemia at 15 Barrow Street. This New York spot opened in 1955 and had the great bassist/cellist Oscar Pettiford as its music director, doubling as a bandleader. Cannonball Adderley made his New York debut here in 1955. Kenny Clarke immortalized it on his album *Bohemia After Dark* for Savoy. It is now a residential building.

Cafe Carlyle

This isn't a jazz club, but it possesses a special significance as the New York home for noted cabaret artist Bobby Short for well over two decades. Located in the Hotel Carlyle, Madison Avenue at

East 76th Street, it enjoys an elegant, old-fashioned, intimate setting. Other top pianists such as George Shearing, Marian McPartland, and Joe Bushkin have had extended residencies there.

Cafe Society

Before he began operating the Cookery, Barney Josephson blazed some social trails with his Cafe Society clubs. The downtown New York location opened in 1939 at 2 Sheridan Square with another venue in midtown New York at 128 East 58th Street starting in October of 1940. Josephson ran a truly integrated operation in every sense of the word, right down to being unfazed by interracial couples dancing and openly associating in public during the '40s. Billie Holiday helped get the downtown club going, as did the boogie-woogie trio of Albert Ammons, Pete Johnson, and Meade "Lux" Lewis, who made their New York debut there. Lena Horne followed Holiday and remained until 1941. James P. Johnson, Teddy Wilson, Art Tatum, and Sarah Vaughan were others who played there, while Fletcher Henderson held his final gig there in 1950. George Simon and Leonard Feather directed jam sessions there in 1941. Edmond Hall, Mary Lou Williams, and several others played at both Cafe Society clubs, but others like John Kirby, Mildred Bailey, and Count Basie only appeared at the midtown spot. Both clubs closed in 1950, but Josephson would go on to run the Cookery in the '70s.

Carnegie Hall

Carnegie Hall has been in business on West 57th Street and Seventh Avenue in New York since 1891 and has featured many magnificent jazz concerts in its array of showcase entertainment. James Reese Europe organized a series of events from 1912 to 1914 to assist the Clef Club, an organization that promoted African-American artists. A 1928 tribute to W.C. Handy featured performances by James P. Johnson and Fats Waller, while the immortal 1938 "Spirituals to Swing" concert organized by John Hammond in memory of Bessie Smith featured Sidney Bechet, Jo Jones, Meade "Lux" Lewis, Albert Ammons, Pete Johnson, and Tommy Ladnier. Benny Goodman also had a famous 1938 concert there, and he returned in 1978 to celebrate that concert's 40th anniversary. Duke Ellington's *Black, Brown and Beige* suite debuted in 1943, and he presented six more concerts between 1943 and 1948. There was also Woody Herman's *Ebony Concerto* debut in 1946, Charlie Parker's late '40s and mid-'50s concerts and '60s appearances by Miles Davis, Charles Mingus, and John Coltrane. The Newport Jazz Festival has been presenting shows there since the '70s, and many other major stars have appeared in the last three decades.

Central Avenue

In its heyday, Central Avenue was the Los Angeles counterpart to New York's 52nd Street or New Orleans' Storyville, though not quite that wide open. It was not a site or a club but a lifestyle and environment. It had dozens of clubs and, with its 100-block radius, featured numerous musicians going from place to place seeking a chance to play. There were also dance halls, theaters, and other diverse forms of entertainment, some legitimate, some not so legitimate. When Los Angeles disbanded the Red Car trolley system, it spelled the doom of Central Avenue. Currently, one blues club plus the Hotel Dunbar and Lincoln Theater remain of what was once a creative oasis.

Condon's

A traditional New Orleans jazz impresario and jack-of-all-trades, Eddie Condon opened the original Condon's in New York in 1945 at 47 West Third Street. Condon co-operated the club with Pete Pesci. Its specialty was Chicago jazz of the vintage (and predominantly White) variety, though Condon certainly did not adopt any color-conscious booking policies. Sammy Price, James P. Johnson, and Walter Page also often played there along with George Wettling, Pee Wee Russell, Herb Hall, Tony Parenti, Yank Lawson, and Wild Bill Davison, though not all appeared at the same location. Condon moved the club in 1957 to 330 East 56th Street. The second club closed in 1967. A third club bearing Condon's name was opened after his death in 1975 on West 54th Street next to Jimmy Ryan's. Red Balaban led the house band and they recorded a combination tribute/live album at the newly opened club that Concord Records later issued. This club closed in 1985. A fourth Condon's opened in 1990 at 117 East 15th Street. This club has featured a more diverse lineup with Jimmy Witherspoon, Ernestine Anderson, and Harry "Sweets" Edison among its earliest performers.

Cookery

Barney Josephson, who at one time ran the Cafe Society clubs, owned and operated the Cookery in New York at 21 University Place at East Eighth Street. It began as a restaurant and then started offering music in the early '70s. It featured either solo or small combo acts. Mary Lou Williams's early '70s appearances there rekindled memories of her past achievements among some critics, while Alberta Hunter was "rediscovered" performing there in the late '70s. Teddy Wilson, Blossom Dearie, Helen Humes, and Jimmy Rowles are some of the artists who appeared there in the '70s and '80s.

Cotton Club

Jack Johnson, the first undisputed African-American heavyweight boxing champion, was the owner of the Club Deluxe in New York. This club was overrun and taken over by Owney Madden's gang in 1922. Madden hired Andy Preer's Cotton Club syncopators, complete with a chorus line composed exclusively of light-skinned Black women, all of whom had to be under 21 and at least five feet, six inches tall. It was Madden who recruited Duke Ellington to replace Preer after Preer's death in 1927. The small matter of a contract Ellington had in Philadelphia was considered of no consequence. Ellington became a hit at the Cotton Club, and his "jungle band" sound with its inspired arrangements and creative use of mutes and plungers was on its way to glory. Ellington made it his home base as did Cab Calloway. Ethel Waters, Louis Armstrong, and many other seminal figures also appeared there. The Cotton Club relocated to West 48th Street from Lenox Avenue in 1936 following the bloody Harlem riots but failed to generate the same excitement and buzz in its new headquarters. It closed a few years later and was torn down in the '50s to make room for a housing project. A fictional film about the Cotton Club starring Richard Gere was made in 1986. It won Bob Wilber a Grammy award for his music.

Earle

Another now defunct Philadelphia nightclub, the Earle was famous for both traditional jazz and bebop performers, among them Louis Armstrong, Jack Teagarden, and Lucky Millinder with Dizzy Gillespie. It stood at the Southeast corner of 11th and Market streets; now in its place stands a Woolworth's.

Five Spot

Joe and Iggy Termini opened the original Five Spot on the edge of the Bowery in the early '50s and made it a showcase for every style. But the Five Spot was most famous for on-the-edge performances. Cecil Taylor had a residency there in 1956, and that same year an all-star tribute to Charlie Parker featuring Phil Woods, Duke Jordan, Art Taylor, and Cecil Payne was recorded at the club. Thelonious Monk played and recorded there in the late '50s with John Coltrane, and Ornette Coleman made his controversial New York debut at the Five Spot. Eric Dolphy's incendiary club performances with a quintet that included Booker Little, Mal Waldron, Richard Davis, and Ed Blackwell were recorded in 1961. Charles Mingus also played there in both the '50s and mid '60s and was famous for reportedly destroying a $20,000 bass in response to heckling from some partisans. Monk returned in 1963 after the club had moved to Third Avenue and East Seventh Street. The Five Spot changed both its name and its booking policies when it opened at St. Marks Place east of Seventh Avenue in 1972. Now called the Two Saints, the club booked jazz-rock and fusion acts. But the old Five Spot name and entertainment style returned in 1975. Art Blakey's Jazz Messengers were the opening act, and later came Jackie McLean and Coleman again. The Termini brothers lost their

cabaret license and had to close the Five Spot. A horribly anti-Semitic characterization of two Jewish club owners featured in Spike Lee's film *Mo' Better Blues* may have been based on them though, wisely, no one admitted that for the record.

Hi-Hat

The Hi-Hat was located at Columbus and Mass. Ave., right at the two streets' intersection. It was the first club to present bebop to Boston audiences. Charlie Parker did several concerts there, which were broadcast, and selections were later issued in an album on the Phoenix Jazz label. They were reissued on CD in 1993 by Blue Note. The club closed in the late '50s.

Jazz Workshop/Paul's Mall

The Jazz Workshop opened in 1964 at 733 Boylston Street in Boston and was originally managed by Fred Taylor and Tony Mauriello. There was a separate club in an adjacent room in the same basement called Paul's Mall. While they both featured jazz, the Workshop was more of a mainstream and exclusive jazz venue, while Paul's Mall also presented fusion, jazz-rock, and various types of popular music. Charles Mingus, Rahsaan Roland Kirk, Miles Davis, and many others appeared at the Workshop until both clubs closed in 1978.

Keystone Korner

During the '70s, the Keystone Korner on Vallejo Street at Stockton in San Francisco was a top West Coast attraction. Todd Barkan directed its booking and also doubled as a liner note writer and producer. It was famous for great acoustics, knowledgeable audiences, and a good environment. Many jazz acts recorded there, among them Art Blakey, Tete Montoliu, and Bobby Hutcherson. It was from this locale that National Public Radio broadcast during New Year's Eve celebrations for several years. It closed in 1982.

Lafayette Theater

The Lafayette opened in New York in 1915 and became most famous for its great variety shows and revues in the '20s. The Coleman brothers were its original owners, followed by Frank Schiffman and Leo Brecher, who also took over the Apollo Theater and Harlem Opera House in the '30s. The Lafayette made one of Harlem's two biggest theaters, and Duke Ellington made his New York debut there in 1923 playing with Wilbur Sweatman's band. Fats Waller also played there, while *Shuffle Along*, the first major African-American theatrical presentation to make it to Broadway, was initially produced at the Lafayette. Sissle and Blake presented *The Chocolate Dandies* there, and Lew Leslie's *Blackbyrds* and *The Plantation Revue* with Florence Mills were also staged at the Lafayette. Fletcher Henderson, Bennie Moten, Chick Webb, Zutty Singleton, and Ellington, this time leading a band, were among other major performers who played the Lafayette. It was turned into a full-time film theater in 1935.

Lighthouse

It is now a rock and pop outlet, but for over 20 years the Lighthouse was the center for recurring jam and recording sessions in Hermosa Beach, CA. Bandleader Howard Rumsey began the Lighthouse in 1949, and its Sunday jam sessions ran from two in the afternoon until two the next morning and sometimes longer. Shorty Rogers, Art Pepper, Hampton Hawes, Sonny Criss, Teddy Edwards, and Shelly Manne were among the musicians who regarded it as home, and a group of regulars known as the Lighthouse All-Stars cut several records in the '50s. Many are currently available on reissued CDs.

Lincoln

The Lincoln had a short but influential run. Marie Downs built a small theater at 58 West 135th Street in New York in 1909. Her theater was demolished and replaced by the Lincoln in 1915. Frank Schiffman and Leo Brecher operated it for a short time before moving on to the Lafayette and eventually the Apollo. This theater catered to an African-American audience from its inception and included many jazz performers on its variety bills. Fats Waller served as house organist in the '20s, and a young Count Basie was a regular visitor, occasionally getting some free organ lessons. Victoria Spivey was also a resident vocalist there in 1927. It is now a church.

Lincoln Theater

Though not in operation today, Philadelphia's Lincoln Theater was a busy nightspot in the '30s. It wasn't so much a jazz club as a site for variety acts that included jazz musicians. Fletcher Henderson, Noble Sissle, Duke Ellington, Jimmie Lunceford, and Don Redman were among the bands that appeared on various Lincoln Theater bills. It was located across the street from the Showboat at South Broad Street and Lombard Street.

Lulu White's

A much-beloved though short-lived institution, Lulu White's began in the late '70s on 3 Appleton Street in Boston.. It mixed both bebop and adventurous free music during its brief tenure and was one of the few places in the city that had no problems booking Dizzy Gillespie, Harry Edison, the Art Ensemble of Chicago, and Air. It closed in 1980.

Lulu White's Mahogany Hall

Both an expensive brothel and home of superb pianists, Lulu White's Mahogany Hall was operated by Lulu White, Storyville's reigning madam. White was the aunt of composer Spencer Williams and was known either as "The Queen of Demimonde" or "The Queen of Diamonds." Among the great players White employed to provide suitable "background" music were Kid Ross, Tony Jackson, and Jelly Roll Morton. The building was demolished in the '50s, though the saloon still stands.

Maybeck Recital Hall

Concord Records has made the Maybeck Recital Hall a status symbol with its series of solo piano concerts recorded there at 1537 Euclid Avenue in Berkeley, California. The hall's acoustics, coupled with the company's choice of artists and exquisite recorded results, have generated massive favorable publicity. In some cases, players who lack big reputations, like Buddy Montgomery and Gerry Wiggins, have turned in stunning performances. The 30th volume in the series was issued in 1993. Architect Bernard Maybeck built the hall in 1914 for a classical piano teacher who used it for student recitals. Nonpianists like Dizzy Gillespie and Joe Henderson have also played the intimate building. Weekly jazz concerts are now held there on Sundays, with room for only 50 guests.

Metropole

It did not begin offering jazz until the '50s, but the Metropole made up for its absence with a full slate of performers. Tony Scott, Max Kaminsky, and Sol Yaged were among the early attractions at the Metropole, located at Seventh Avenue and 48th Street in New York. Red Allen served as emcee and resident musician from 1954 until 1967. The club presented trios in the afternoon and bands at night as well as occasional featured performances by single acts like Louis Armstrong or Gene Krupa or periodic big band concerts with such bands as Lionel Hampton or Woody Herman. Zutty Singleton and Tony Parenti led groups there for long periods, and Allen headed one evening band, Coleman Hawkins and Roy Eldridge the other. Cozy Cole, Claude Hopkins, and Buster Bailey were among the resident players. The club continued presenting jazz through the '60s and for a short time also featured more modern fare. It is currently called the Metropole à Go-Go.

Minton's

Tenor saxophonist Henry Minton opened this club at 210 West 118th Street in New York in 1938. It was located in a hotel named the Cecil. Teddy Hill took over its operation two years later, and the Monday night jam sessions were widely regarded as bebop incubators in the '40s. Dizzy Gillespie, Charlie Parker, Hot Lips Page, Roy Eldridge, Charlie Christian, and Don Byas were among

the guest performers, while Thelonious Monk, Kenny Clarke, Rudy Williams, and Joe Guy played in the house band. The jam sessions and late-night after-hours dates provided opportunities for major woodshedding and exchanges of ideas. Tony Scott and Jerome Richardson were some of the musicians featured at Minton's in the '50s. The old club is now a tourist attraction in the restored Cecil, and rumors abound that it will be reopened as a music facility.

Monroe's

Clark Monroe opened Monroe's Uptown House at 198 West 134th Street in New York in the '30s. The Theatrical Grill had previously occupied the location. It was a premier swing and bebop venue in the '30s and '40s with Billie Holiday performing there in 1937. The jam sessions in the '40s rivaled those at Minton's, and Charlie Parker was a featured soloist in 1943. Monroe opened a second club, Spotlite, for a couple of years in the mid '40s but eventually ran into financial difficulties with both operations. Monroe's is currently a deli.

Nick's

Nick Rongetti turned Nick's Tavern at 140 Seventh Avenue South into New York's mainline traditional jazz center beginning in the mid '30s. Bobby Hackett led the house band and regulars included Eddie Condon, Pee Wee Russell, and Zutty Singleton, while Russell and Singleton also brought in their own bands. Sidney Bechet was a bandleader there in the late '30s and early '40s. George Brunies, Meade "Lux" Lewis, Muggsy Spanier, Wild Bill Davison, Miff Mole, Billy Butterfield, Phil Napoleon, and Kenny Davern were among those who had extended club residences in the '30s, '40s, '50s, and early '60s. Nick's closed in 1963.

Palace

Once Memphis' predominant nightspot, the Palace had an importance to the local Black community that transcended its musical role, though it did occasionally feature jazz musicians. It was located at 318 Beale Street near Hernando and had a Wednesday night amateur contest, which was initially hosted by influential newspaper columnist and radio disc jockey Nat D. Williams and later by the great musician and fellow disc jockey Rufus Thomas. B.B. King, Johnny Ace, and Bobby "Blue" Bland were among the stars who got their start at the Palace. It was also the site of many spectacular concerts. It is now demolished.

Paradise Theater

The Paradise Theater is still operational in Detroit, though it encountered rough going in the '70s. Originally called Orchestra Hall, it opened in 1919 at 3711 Woodward Avenue. The place was built for the Detroit Symphony Orchestra but was renamed the Paradise Theater in recognition of the fact that it had become the prime venue for touring African-American acts that came to the city in the '40s and '50s. Count Basie and the Earl Hines band with Charlie Parker as well as many Detroit greats like Kenny Burrell, Hank Jones, and Yusef Lateef played at the Paradise. It closed temporarily in the '70s, then reopened in the late '80s with its old name again. The Detroit Symphony Orchestra, which vacated the premises in 1939, returned with the renovations in the '80s.

Plugged Nickel

Another club that did not have a long existence but burned brightly while it was active was the Plugged Nickel on North Wells Street in Chicago, a major hard bop and bebop venue in the '60s. Miles Davis recorded there during a two-week residency from December 21, 1965, to January 2, 1966, but for reasons known only to the company, Columbia did not issue the recordings until the mid '70s and then only in limited form. They have finally been made available in the CD era. Gene Ammons also appeared there when he returned to public dates in 1969. The club closed in the '70s.

Preservation Hall

Larry Borenstein had been presenting informal performances by veteran New Orleans musicians in a location directly adjacent to his art gallery. He opened Preservation Hall at 726 Peter Street in June of 1961 along with Grayson Mills and Allan and Sandra Jaffe. Preservation Hall is now a shrine to traditional New Orleans music where such venerable players as Kid Thomas, Punch Miller, and George Lewis have led the band. There have also been many albums recorded there by both small jazz independents and major operations like Columbia. A Preservation Hall Jazz Band has also periodically toured nationally and internationally.

Regal Theatre

The Midwestern version of the Apollo, the Regal opened in 1928. Situated at 4719 South Parkway Boulevard in Chicago, it was a theater with a grand architecture and huge capacity. It could seat 3,500 with room in the foyer for 1,500. During the '30s and '40s, Louis Armstrong, Duke Ellington, Count Basie, Jimmie Lunceford, Lucky Millinder, and many others appeared at the Regal, which was also the site of several major concerts in the '50s and '60s by Miles Davis, Dizzy Gillespie, and Sonny Stitt. It also had its own tradition of amateur contests, which helped launch almost as many careers as those at the Apollo. Ken Blewett was manager from 1939 to 1959. While it is equally famous for its blues shows, particularly a '60s B.B. King concert that was recorded and released by ABC/Bluesway, the Regal had its share of remarkable jazz concerts. A new Regal Theatre was opened in 1987, built along the same architectural lines as the original, but it is otherwise unconnected. The original building was demolished in the '70s.

Roseland

While two places used this name, the one that is most synonymous with jazz was opened in 1919 on New Year's Day by Louis J. Brecker. It was one of New York's largest ballrooms and was lavishly designed and maintained, then refurbished in 1930. Like the Cotton Club, Roseland attracted White customers but began hiring Black bands in the early '20s. A.J. Piron appeared in 1924, and Fletcher Henderson began a residency that same year and stayed until 1941. The best White musicians also played at the ballroom, notably Bix Beiderbecke, who appeared with Jean Goldkette's band from 1926 to 1931. The Goldkette and Henderson bands battled in 1926. Other famous orchestras such as McKinney's Cotton Pickers, the Casa Loma orchestra, Marion Hardy's Alabamians, and the bands of Luis Russell, Cab Calloway, Chick Webb, Andy Kirk, and Benny Carter also appeared there. Roseland had regular live broadcasts transmitted throughout the country by landline. The ballroom remained open until 1955 and was demolished shortly after closing. A new, larger Roseland opened at 239 West 52nd Street a few months later. Count Basie's was one of many bands that played there in the '60s and '70s. A second Roseland ballroom opened in Brooklyn during the '30s; Woody Herman's band played there in 1936.

Ryles

Cambridge's oldest jazz club and the second oldest in the Greater Boston area, Ryles has been a boon for local talent, particularly Berklee students. But it has also welcomed national headliners like Pat Metheny, Robben Ford, and Grover Washington, Jr. It is located at 212 Hampshire Street in the Inman Square area. Ryles has not completely filled the void left by the disappearance of such places as Paul's Mall and the Jazz Workshop, but at least it is still active.

Savoy

Moses Galewski, better known as Moe Gale, along with Charles Galewski and Charles Buchanan, opened the Savoy Ballroom in New York on West 140th Street in March of 1926. It occupied the entire second floor of a building extending along the entire block between 140th and 141st streets in New York. There was a huge dance floor, two bandstands, and a retractable stage. The Savoy became Harlem's hottest club and the site where many dance crazes were launched in the '20s and '30s. It was also famous for

its band battles, with the ballroom engaging two bands playing alternate sets. On special occasions they would book three or more bands for all-out warfare. A 1927 duel pitted King Oliver's Dixie Syncopators against resident performers Fess Williams and His Royal Flush Orchestra and Chick Webb's Harlem Stompers. During the '30s, Webb's band was linked with the Savoy on a long-running basis. Others with similiar arrangements were Al Cooper's Savoy Sultans and Erskine Hawkins's Orchestra. Many other landmark bands and performers made regular appearances, among them Coleman Hawkins, Count Basie, the Mills Brothers, Andy Kirk, Sidney Bechet, and Benny Carter, whose big band debuted there in 1939. The Savoy had its own radio line and several concerts were broadcast as well as recorded during its heyday. A Woolworth's now occupies the spot where the Savoy once stood.

Showboat

The Showboat was Philadelphia's reigning jazz club in the '50s. The club at 1409 Lombard Street near South Broad Street featured entertainment by John Coltrane, Thelonious Monk, Sonny Rollins, and Dizzy Gillespie, among others. It is now a mental health facility.

Slugs

Despite having a short tenure, Slugs was a hard bop haven from the mid '60s until 1972. It was located at 242 East Third Street in New York and featured performances from Jackie McLean, Joe Henderson, Philly Joe Jones, Yusef Lateef, Stanley Turrentine, Charles Lloyd, Ornette Coleman, Freddie Hubbard, Sun Ra, Art Blakey, and many others. Charles Tolliver's 1972 date there was recorded and issued on the Strata-East label. Slugs also has a tragic place in jazz annals: trumpeter Lee Morgan was shot and killed there by a distraught woman in a bizarre incident that may or may not have been a case of mistaken identity. The club closed shortly after that, ending a bright but quick chapter in hard bop and jazz club history.

Smalls' Paradise

Ed Smalls opened Smalls' Paradise at 2294½ Seventh Avenue, at West 135th Street, in 1925. The New York basement club featured music and dancing and was one of Harlem's most successful clubs even during the Depression. It was one of New York's main jazz centers in the '20s and '30s, with such legendary figures as Willie "The Lion" Smith, Jimmy Archey, Fletcher Henderson, and Charlie Johnson playing there, and Smith and Johnson having lengthy extended tours. Elmer Snowden served as bandleader of the Smalls' Paradise Orchestra in the early '30s and made the film Smash Your Baggage in 1932. James P. Johnson led a revised, scaled-down band in the mid 30s, but Hot Lips Page was back at the helm of a big band by 1937. Gene Sedric, Harry Dial, Happy Caldwell, and Gus Aitken were resident bandleaders in the '40s and '50s. Smalls' finally ceased operation in 1986.

Sportsmen Lounge

The Sportsmen Lounge in Baltimore still remains a perennial nightspot for both local and visiting music fans, though not as prominent now in the '90s as it was in the '50s and '60s. As one of the relatively few jazz clubs still in the heart of an African-American neighborhood, it has a cultural status as important as its legacy of great performances by such names as Gene Ammons, Gary Bartz, Count Basie, and Sonny Stitt. National Football League great and ex-Baltimore Colt Lenny Moore owned the club in the '60s, when its entertainment roster would be headline material in national Black newspapers.

Storyville

Not to be confused with the relatively new Storyville Jazz Hall which opened in the mid '80s at 1104 Decatur Street, Storyville was once a 16-block district of New Orleans located adjacent to the French Quarter. It was created January 1, 1898, out of the notion that if prostitution could not be eliminated it could be confined. But by forging this monument to hedonism, the New Orleans power brokers created both a mini-empire of vice and an area where musical creativity flourished. While full-time pimp and part-time state legislator Tom Anderson operated as mayor and principal flesh broker, the multitude of dance halls and night clubs all needed entertainment. An array of great musicians from Jelly Roll Morton to King Oliver and Clarence Williams regularly played Storyville. The district was finally shut down by the Secretary of the Navy in 1917. There are some who claim jazz got its name from the Storyville/whorehouse connection. Other insist there is little, if any, direct link.

Storyville

Longtime concert promoter and part-time musician George Wein opened Storyville in Boston in 1950. It was located initially in Kenmore Square and featured traditional jazz and swing. The club was later situated in the Copley Square Hotel. Sidney Bechet worked there extensively in 1951 and 1953. Wein also did several recording sessions there, using such musicians as Wild Bill Davison, Bechet, Ruby Braff, and Pee Wee Russell. Duke Ellington, Count Basie, Billie Holiday, and Charlie Parker were among others who appeared there.

Studio Rivbea

Multi-instrumentalist and composer Sam Rivers opened the doors of the loft Studio Rivbea, named after his wife Bea Rivers, in 1970 in New York City. It soon became one of the principal homes of what was deemed "loft jazz," free jazz played in loft apartments and clubs. The high point was a series of concerts recorded there by Douglas Records in the late '70s featuring the movement's biggest names. Unfortunately, the "Wildflowers" concert series has yet to be issued on CD and was poorly promoted and distributed during its vinyl lifetime. Sam Rivers kept the club going untl 1980.

Subway

It has been demolished for many years, but Kansas City swing veterans have fond memories of the Subway Club at 18th and Vine streets. Felix Payne and Piney Brown managed it in the '30s, and it was the haven for all the top touring big bands. It was also the spot of some savage band battles; drummer Jessie Price is reported to have once played a hour-long-plus solo (over 100 choruses) of *Nagasaki* in response to a challenge from two out-of-town drummers.

Theresa

Not a club but a hotel, the Theresa was formerly Harlem's largest and most famous hotel. Lena Horne, Lester Young, Joe Louis, and Fidel Castro were among its residents at various times. Cab Calloway's band once resided there, and Andy Kirk was its manager in the '50s. The grand edifice at 2090 Adam Clayton Powell Boulevard at 125th Street is now an office building.

Tipitina's

Though not exclusively or even predominantly a jazz club, Tipitina's is a special place for anyone who loves great piano and/or great music. It was founded in 1977 by some local New Orleans citizens who wanted a place in the area for venerable Crescent City musicians, regardless of idiom, to play. Professor Longhair, whose rumbling, yodeling vocals immortalized the song "Tipitina," was among the acts who appeared at the club on 500 Napoleon Avenue. It is the home base for the Neville Brothers as well as Dr. John and the Radiators. Longhair was a part owner and frequent guest during his lifetime. Tipitina's also has a colorful past: it was once a bordello and also a meeting place for the New Orleans chapter of the Ku Klux Klan.

Village Gate

One of the New York jazz club mainstays that has survived, the Village Gate opened in 1958 at 160 Bleecker Street at Thompson Street. Numerous bebop and hard bop greats have appeared there as well as many great blues artists. Miles Davis, Erroll Garner, Cecil Taylor, Horace Silver, Lee Konitz, Rahsaan Roland Kirk, McCoy Tyner, and Art Blakey are among musicians who have worked the club. Over 60 albums have been recorded at the Village Gate over the years; Herbie Mann cut one of his finest straight jazz dates there, while B.B. King was welcomed in one of his first engagements before a predominantly White audience. Otis Rush, John Lee Hooker, Memphis Slim, and Thelonious Monk are others who have given historic Village Gate performances. The club instituted a Monday night Latin music policy in the '70s, and it is currently still in effect. The series was initially straight salsa but is now called "Salsa Meets Jazz." Willie Colón and Tito Puente have been among featured performers. While the original Village Gate was part of a decrepit, dilapidated flophouse, it is now in a luxury apartment building.

Village Vanguard

The Village Vanguard became a jazz mecca despite its tiny size and dingy look. It has operated since the early '30s and was run for many years by Max Gordon, who started it as a place for writers and artists. Gordon gradually altered the club's live entertainment policy from folk, comedy, and poetry to exclusively jazz. Many spectacular albums were recorded there, including a pair of remarkable dates by John Coltrane and Sonny Rollins. The Thad Jones-Mel Lewis orchestra, later the Mel Lewis orchestra, performed there Monday nights for over 20 years. The first Village Vanguard was located in a basement on Charles Street in Greenwich Village. Gordon was denied a cabaret license when he wanted to introduce music there because the place was deemed unsuitable. He had previously opened the Village Fair on Sullivan Street and moved the Vanguard to Seventh Avenue in a location formerly owned by a speakeasy called the Golden Triangle. From Sidney Bechet and Mary Lou Williams to Dizzy Gillespie, Art Blakey, Thelonious Monk, and Charles Mingus, headlining at the Vanguard signaled "making it" as a top jazz artist. Major folk acts such as the Weavers, Woody Guthrie, and Leadbelly; comedians like Lenny Bruce; and other miscellaneous performers such as Eartha Kitt and Burl Ives also appeared at the Vanguard at various times. It continues today as a jazz club mainstay and is now operated by Max's widow Lorraine Gordon, who is credited with the club's initial booking of Monk. It will mark its 60th anniversary in 1995. Gordon wrote a combination club history and memoir *Live at the Village Vanguard* in 1980.

—Ron Wynn

RECOMMENDED VIDEOS & MAGAZINES

50 Recommended Jazz Videos

Starting in the 1980s it became possible to view jazz greats on one's television screen at will through the magic of videos. Although some legendary artists (such as Jelly Roll Morton, King Oliver, Charlie Christian and Fats Navarro) were not filmed at all while others (Django Reinhardt, Charlie Parker and Bessie Smith) barely made it onto film, most of the more valuable documented jazz performances (along with many historical documentaries and more recent concerts) have been made available to the public. Here are reviews of 50 of the best videos.

After Hours (Rhapsody Films, 27 minutes.) This 1959 pilot for a television series that never ran is supposed to show what it is like to attend an after-hours jam session. The narration is dated but the music (featuring tenor saxophonist Coleman Hawkins and trumpeter Roy Eldridge in a quintet) is often quite exciting. Highlights include Hawk's feature on "Lover Man" and a heated "Sunday."

The Art Ensemble of Chicago– Live from the Jazz Showcase (Rhapsody Films, 50 minutes.) This enjoyable tape captures a lengthy performance by the Art Ensemble of Chicago from Nov. 1, 1981. During the set the Art Ensemble (featuring trumpeter Lester Bowie, Joseph Jarman and Roscoe Mitchell on reeds, bassist Malachi Favors and drummer Don Moye) cover a lot of ground from free jazz to bop and funk with a touch of New Orleans parade rhythms. This time capsule gives one a good idea as to how unique the adventurous group was in its prime.

At the Jazz Band Ball (Yazoo Video, 60 minutes.) This essential video has 16 clips of early jazz from the 1925-33 period, most of which were previously unavailable. The highlights include Duke Ellington's Orchestra in 1930 playing "Old Man Blues," the Boswell Sisters in wonderful form on a 1931 rendition of "Heebie Jeebies," the full 1933 clip of Louis Armstrong in Europe performing "I Cover The Waterfront," "Dinah" and "Tiger Rag," a long excerpt from Bessie Smith's lone film *St. Louis Blues*, the superior 1928 dance band of Tommy Christian playing two songs and Ben Bernie (in an extremely rare sound film from 1925) in hot form on "Sweet Georgia Brown." The most notable discovery, a newsreel excerpt that finds Bix Beiderbecke playing "My Ohio Home" with Paul Whiteman (!), is a bit of a disappointment since Bix does not solo but it is fascinating to watch. Other performers include the Dorsey Brothers (a brief but colorful song from 1929), Bill Robinson, Duke Ellington's band from 1929's *Black & Tan* and a few lesser singers and dancers. Overall, this video is a real collector's item; very highly recommended!

Count Basie–Whirly-Bird (Vintage Classics, 45 minutes.) The Count Basie Orchestra is in particularly fine form on ten numbers performed in London for a television show on Sept. 18, 1965. Although this edition of the Basie band mostly recorded commercial albums, live in concert it was as strong as ever. Highlights include "All of Me" (featuring the leader-pianist), the usual enthusiastic versions of the band's hits (such as "Jumpin' at the Woodside" with Eddie Lockjaw Davis' tough tenor, "April in Paris" and "Li'l Darlin'"), a showcase for altoist Marshall Royal (on "The Midnight Sun Never Sets") and occasional solo work from trumpeter Al Aarons, Eric Dixon on flute and tenor and (on "I Needs to Be Bee'd With") trombonist Al Grey. But the most notable track is a very intense runthrough of "Whirly-Bird" which

after Lockjaw's solo has a very powerful spot for the remarkable drummer Rufus "Speedy" Jones, who certainly lives up to his nickname!

Bird (Warner Home Video, 161 minutes.) Clint Eastwood's 1988 biography of Charlie Parker may be partly fictional, a bit downbeat (emphasizing his decline) and an incomplete picture of the genius but it is one of the finest Hollywood films ever made about jazz. Forest Whitaker is excellent in the title role, his fingering during saxophone solos exactly fit the notes and Charlie Parker's own playing is heard throughout the film. A few scenes (the view of 52nd Street, Bird riding a horse and his relationship with Chan) ring true while some others (his crackup in 1946) are a little off the mark. Overall this well-intentioned film is a success.

Art Blakey–The Jazz Messenger (Rhapsody Films, 78 minutes.) This 1987 film is quite fascinating, for a camera follows drummer-bandleader Art Blakey around for most of a year. Trumpeter Terence Blanchard and altoist Donald Harrison were on the verge of leaving the Jazz Messengers during this period so Blakey is seen auditioning various young musicians. In addition to lots of hard bop music, some of the alumni comment on the importance of their period with Blakey, Art jams with Courtney Pine, has some sequences backing dance groups and gives the listeners quite a bit of his philosophy towards both jazz and life. If only a camera had followed Art Blakey for the 30 previous years too!

Buck Clayton All-Stars (Shanachie, 54 minutes.) Two half-hour Swiss television shows from 1961 feature trumpeter Buck Clayton with such swing all stars as fellow trumpeter Emmett Berry, altoist Earle Warren, tenorman Buddy Tate, trombonist Dickie Wells, pianist Sir Charles Thompson, bassist Gene Ramey, drummer Oliver Jackson and singer Jimmy Witherspoon. There are 11 complete songs in all and each of the musicians has plenty of space to stretch out during the series of informal but hard-swinging performances.

Ornette Coleman - David, Moffett & Ornette (Rhapsody Films, 26 minutes.) This is a rather unusual film. In 1966 the innovative Ornette Coleman (along with bassist David Izenzon and drummer Charles Moffett) was in Paris to improvise the soundtrack to a film titled *Who's Crazy?* The movie does appear to be a bit nuts, and it is fascinating to see the trio (with Ornette switching between alto, trumpet and violin) performing while watching the film. The musicians' verbal comments about their lives at the time are also quite interesting and this video (which is probably the earliest example of Ornette Coleman on film) has quite a few memorable moments.

John Coltrane – The Coltrane Legacy (Video Artists Int., 61 minutes.) The bulk of John Coltrane's film appearances are on this essential video. First he is seen playing his solo from "So What" with Miles Davis in 1959 and then there are two complete half-hour television shows. Coltrane teams up with Eric Dolphy (who doubles on alto and flute), pianist McCoy Tyner, bassist Reggie Workman and drummer Elvin Jones on a 1961 West German show playing "Every Time We Say Goodbye," a burning version of "Impressions" and "My Favorite Things." The second half of the video is from 1964 (a PBS program produced by Ralph Gleason) that features Coltrane, Tyner, bassist Jimmy Garrison and Jones in prime form on intense renditions of "Afro Blue," "Impressions" and a melancholy "Alabama." This is a video that belongs in every jazz collection for the power of Coltrane's music really comes through.

Miles Davis–In Paris (Warner/Reprise Video, 60 minutes) Caught at the Paris Jazz Festival on Nov. 3, 1989 (less than two years before his death), Miles Davis is in generally excellent form playing five songs with his septet of the time (comprised of altoist Kenny Garrett, keyboardist Kei Akagi, Foley and Benjamin Rietveld on basses, drummer Ricky Wellman and percussionist John Bigham). There are a few brief interview segments and a bit too much stop-action photography but in general this set gives one a good idea as to how the innovative trumpeter sounded during his final period. Best is "New Blues" and a brief "Mr. Pastorius."

Miles Davis–Live at Montreux (Warner/Reprise Video, 75 minutes.) In the summer of 1991 Miles Davis did what he said he would never do, revisit the past. Joined by a large orchestra conducted by Quincy Jones at that year's Montreux Jazz Festival (only a couple months before his death), Miles is seen performing Gil Evans arrangements from the Birth of the Cool band and the three famous albums *Miles Ahead, Porgy and Bess* and *Sketches of Spain*. Miles generally plays pretty well although his decision to allocate some of his solo space to his chief imitator Wallace Roney and altoist Kenny Garrett was unfortunate. But overall this is a pretty successful effort that ranks historically as Miles Davis' last hurrah.

Duke Ellington (Video Artists Int., 25 minutes.) In 1962 the Goodyear Tire Company sponsored several half-hour jazz films to be shown on television. This particular entry features the Duke Ellington Orchestra performing "Take the 'A' Train," "Satin Doll," "Blow by Blow" (a feature for tenorman Paul Gonsalves), "Things Ain't What They Used to Be" (altoist Johnny Hodges' showcase), "VIP Boogie/Jam with Sam" and a short workout for the rhythm section on "Kinda Dukish." Although nothing all that unusual occurs, it is enjoyable to see the Ellington band near their peak; the video reproduction of this color film is excellent.

Duke Ellington –- Memories Of Duke (A Vision Entertainment, 85 minutes.) This is a particularly interesting film for trumpeter Cootie Williams and clarinetist Russell Procope are seen in the mid-1970s watching and commenting on lengthy clips from Duke Ellington's 1968 tour of Mexico. There is quite a bit of strong music on this video with highlights including the medley of "Creole Love Call," "Black and Tan Fantasy" and "The Mooch," the obscure "Mexican Suite," "It Don't Mean a Thing" and "Mood Indigo." This is one of the best Duke Ellington videos currently available.

Bill Evans–Jazz at the Maintenance Shop (Shanachie, 59 minutes.) Pianist Bill Evans' last trio (a particularly strong one with bassist Marc Johnson and drummer Joe LaBarbera) is seen during a live performance from 1979 (only a year before the pianist's death) that was filmed for Iowa Public Television. The group performs eight numbers with the highlights including "The Peacocks," "The Theme from Mash," "In Your Own Sweet Way" and "My Romance." The musicians' close musical communication is as impressive as one would expect from a Bill Evans group.

Talmage Farlow (Rhapsody Films, 58 minutes.) This 1986 film is delightful. Guitarist Tal Farlow, one of the giants of bop, has long been semi-retired, preferring the easy-going life of a New England sign painter over having to constantly travel for gigs. This video expertly summarizes his career, shows what his day-to-day lifestyle is like, includes an exciting version of "Fascinatin' Rhythm" which features Farlow in a trio with pianist Tommy Flanagan and bassist Red Mitchell and finds him preparing for (and playing at) a New York engagement. Director Lorenzo De Stefano, who put this labor of love together, certainly did an admirable job.

Five Guys Named Moe (Vintage Classics, 55 minutes.) This easily enjoyable video is a must for fans of Louis Jordan and his Tympany Five. Jordan, a fine altoist, was a particularly talented singer and personality who still appears "hip" forty years later. This video features him performing 21 songs, all but one from the 1942-46 period. The clips are taken from films, shorts and Soundies and they find Jordan doing most of his hits. Highlights include "Five Guys Named Moe," "Caldonia," "Let the Good Times

Roll," "Beware," "Choo Choo Ch'Boogie," "Reef, Petite and Gone" and "Is You Is or Is You Ain't Ma Baby."

Stephane Grappelli–Live In San Francisco (Rhapsody Films, 60 minutes.) Already in his late '70s at the time of the two 1985 concerts that are on this video, violinist Stephane Grappelli proves to still be in prime form. Assisted by guitarist Diz Disley and bassist Jack Sewing, Grappelli swings hard on a variety of veteran standards including such old standbys as "Fascinating Rhythm," "Minor Swing," "Them There Eyes" and even Stevie Wonder's "You Are the Sunshine of My Life." Toward the end of this video, mandolinist David Grisman and his group join Grappelli and the heat is turned up even more on "Sweet Georgia Brown" and "Honeysuckle Rose."

Herbie Hancock–Hurricane (View Video, 60 minutes.) Herbie Hancock is so versatile that one never knows what he will do next. On this set (performed in Switzerland in 1984) the music is purely acoustic. With fine work from bassist Ron Carter and drummer Billy Cobham, Hancock performs seven selections including his "Eye of the Hurricane," "Dolphin Dance," the lengthy "Princess" and the blues "Walkin.'" Excellent modern straightahead (and sometimes impressionistic) jazz.

Alberta Hunter–My Castle's Rockin' (View Video, 60 minutes.) This documentary (narrated by Billy Taylor) traces the remarkable life of singer Alberta Hunter who had a major comeback (after 20 years out of the music business) when she was 82. There are some brief interviews but the bulk of the film features Hunter performing at the Cookery in the early 1980s. She is quite appealing and seemingly ageless on such tunes as "My Castle's Rockin'," "Downhearted Blues," "Handy Man" and "The Love I Have for You."

Jazz on a Summer's Day (New Yorker Video, 84 minutes.) This is considered a classic. The beautifully photographed color film documents the 1958 Newport Jazz Festival and there are many musical highlights. The camerawork holds one's interest even though it occasionally wanders way from the music; Thelonious Monk's performance of "Blue Monk" becomes the background for an irrelevant if colorful America's Cup yacht race (one never learns who won!) and there are many distracting shots of the audience. Among the most memorable performers are Anita O'Day (her inventive rendition of "Tea for Two" was one of the high points of her career), Dinah Washington (quite strong and humorous on "All of Me" with Terry Gibbs), the Jimmy Giuffre Three, Chico Hamilton's Quintet with Eric Dolphy, Sonny Stitt, Gerry Mulligan, Mahalia Jackson, Louis Armstrong (doing "Rockin' Chair" with Jack Teagarden) and an out-of-place but rocking number by Chuck Berry. Highly recommended.

Jazz Scene USA–Cannonball Adderley/Teddy Edwards (Shanachie, 60 minutes.) In 1962 *Jazz Scene USA* was a short-lived but imaginative half-hour jazz series shown on some syndicated television channels. Each week Oscar Brown, Jr., (as host) would introduce a major group or musician, conduct a short interview and provide segues between the performances. Eight of the shows (two per tape) have been made available by Shanachie on four videos; all are well worth acquiring. On this particular tape Cannonball Adderley is seen leading his finest group, the sextet with cornetist Nat Adderley, pianist Joe Zawinul and Yusef Lateef on tenor, flute and oboe. They perform short but strong versions of "Jessica's Birthday," "Primitivo," "Jive Samba" and "Work Song." Tenor saxophonist Teddy Edwards dominates his episode, leading a sextet that also has trumpeter Freddie Hill and trombonist Richard Boone on five of his originals including "Sunset Eyes." Overall, this tape is quite valuable, showing the state of hard bop in 1962.

Jazz Scene USA - Shelly Manne/Shorty Rogers (Shanachie, 60 minutes.) In 1962 half-hour episodes of *Jazz Scene USA* (an intelligent program hosted by Oscar Brown Jr.) were shown on some television channels before passing into history as a legendary series. Shanachie has happily released eight of the shows on four video tapes. This particular one features two West Coast jazz groups at what was the tail-end of the cool jazz era. Drummer Shelly Manne's quintet was a particularly strong since it was comprised of trumpeter Conte Candoli, Richie Kamuca on tenor, pianist Russ Freeman and bassist Monty Budwig. Although the material it performs ("Speak Low," a Freeman original and two songs from the forgotten series *Checkmate*) is not all that memorable, it is fun to get to see these players perform together. Fluegelhornist Shorty Rogers, who would soon retire for a long time from active playing to concentrate on writing, heads a quintet with the tenor of Gary LeFebvre and a strong rhythm section (pianist Lou Levy, bassist Gary Peacock and drummer Larry Bunker). Their repertoire is more imaginative: "Greensleeves," "Time Was," LeFebvre's "The Outsider" and the near-classic "Martians Go Home." Recommended.

Jazz Scene USA - Phineas Newborn/Jimmy Smith (Shanachie, 60 minutes.) Shanachie has thus far released four videos that contain two shows apiece from the legendary 1962 half-hour series *Jazz Scene USA*. One of the first attempts to feature jazz on television in an intelligent way (and with respect), these programs (hosted by Oscar Brown, Jr.) still communicate well today. This particular tape gives one a rare opportunity to see the great pianist Phineas Newborn, Jr. (in a trio with bassist Al McKibbon and drummer Kenny Dennis). He performs three originals (including "Blues Theme for Left Hand Only") and a pair of standards, showing off his ability to swing creatively at any tempo. Organist Jimmy Smith's set (with guitarist Quentin Warren and drummer Donald Bailey) is of lesser interest since he seems to be fooling around a lot but his versions of "Walk on the Wild Side," "Mack the Knife" and "The Champ" are reasonably enjoyable. All four videos in this valuable series are recommended.

Jazz Scene USA - Frank Rosolino/Stan Kenton (Shanachie, 60 minutes.) This is one of the most enjoyable of the four videos released to date by Shanachie in this important series. *Jazz Scene USA* was an attempt to intelligently feature jazz on television in 1962; naturally it only lasted a year! These legendary shows still look fine today with excellent camerawork, fine commentary by Oscar Brown, Jr., and well-played music. Trombonist Frank Rosolino performs a rapid "Yesterdays," "Mean to Me," "Lover Man," "Well You Needn't" and "Please Don't Bug Me" while accompanied by pianist Mike Melvoin, bassist Bob Bertaux and drummer Nick Martinis. The Stan Kenton Orchestra during their half hour mostly emphasizes ensemble work from the mellophonium band (highlights include "Limehouse Blues," "Malaguena" and "Maria") although there are short spots for trumpeter Marvin Stamm and Don Menza on tenor. Recommended.

Eddie Jefferson–Live from the Jazz Showcase (Rhapsody Films, 50 minutes.) This performance by singer Eddie Jefferson (with a quartet that includes altoist Richie Cole and pianist John Campbell) was performed May 6, 1979, two days before he was shot to death! Ironically Jefferson is heard in top form doing a retrospective of his career with such pieces as "Moody's Mood For Love," his vocalese version of "I Cover the Waterfront," the humorous "Bennies from Heaven," "Jeannine," "Body and Soul" and "Freedom Jazz Dance"; 14 songs in all. If one can put the tragic and senseless tragedy of his murder out of their minds, this definitive film is quite enjoyable.

Barney Kessel - Rare Performances 1962-91 (Vestapol, 60 minutes.) The fine loop-based guitarist Barney Kessel is seen and heard on several different occasions during this well-rounded video. He is first interviewed in 1987, performs two songs on an episode of the 1962 TV show *Jazz Scene USA*, plays in Sweden in 1967 and 1973, in England in 1974, and in Switzerland five years later. In all circumstances he is featured performing with a trio except for three numbers jammed in 1979 with fellow guitarists Herb Ellis and Charlie Byrd in a quintet. This valuable tape concludes with him making a speech in 1991 at the Oklahoma Jazz Hall of Fame during which he speaks about the importance of improvised music; soon afterward Kessel's playing days would end when he suffered a serious stroke. Barney Kessel is in consistently fine form throughout these performances (it is interesting to observe the hair and clothes styles change!) and this video serves as a fine introduction to his music.

Lee Konitz - Portrait of an Artist as Saxophonist (Rhapsody Videos, 83 minutes.) From 1988, this documentary features six duets by altoist Lee Konitz and pianist Harold Danko (including "Struttin' with Some Barbecue," "Hi Beck" and "Subconscious-Lee") along with a great deal of talk. Konitz discusses his life and music at a workshop with students and is seen in several different settings. His wit and intelligence come across well and one

learns a great deal about Lee Konitz's personality and attitudes. His fans will find this tape riveting at times.

Gene Krupa - Jazz Legend (DCI Video, 60 minutes.) Gene Krupa, a colorful figure who was the first drummer to become a national celebrity, is profiled throughout this well-done retrospective. Steve Allen narrates, there is an interview with Krupa and lots of footage including his Soundies from the 1940s and later television appearances. The results are quite fun and fairly definitive of the great legend.

Steve Lacy - Lift the Bandstand (Rhapsody Films, 50 minutes.) This is one of the better jazz documentaries. The virtuosic soprano saxophonist Steve Lacy talks about his entire career including his periods in Dixieland and his experiences with Cecil Taylor, exploring Thelonious Monk's music and forming his longtime sextet. Lacy also performs with his group and "Gay Paree Bop" is a high point. Listeners new to Lacy's scalar music will learn a great deal about his history and his motivation by viewing this excellent video.

The Ladies Sing the Blues (View Video, 60 minutes.) A variety of historical clips (all featuring female singers) are included on this worthy video; 16 selections in all. Unfortunately there is little information included about dates but the quality of the music overrides any packaging faults. Bessie Smith performs "St. Louis Blues" from the film of the same name, Ethel Waters is on two lesser clips, Billie Holiday sings "Fine and Mellow" from *The Sound of Jazz* telecast, Ida Cox is seen in her only film appearance and there are generally memorable clips featuring Sister Rosetta Tharpe, Connee Boswell, Dinah Washington, Ruth Brown, Lena Horne, Sarah Vaughan, Helen Humes and Peggy Lee (her "I Cover the Waterfront" is haunting).

Lady Day–The Many Faces of Billie Holiday (Kulter, 60 minutes.) This is a fine documentary that covers the difficult and erratic life of Billie Holiday. There are interviews with such associates as Carmen McRae, Annie Ross, Buck Clayton and Harry "Sweets" Edison among others. Although Ruby Dee's readings from Lady Day's largely fictional memoirs are a bit frivolous, the clips (particularly the rare ones taken from 1958 and '59 television shows) are quite fascinating. Overall this interesting tribute is quite even handed and worth acquiring by Billie Holiday collectors and admirers.

Legends of Jazz Guitar Vol. 1 (Vestapol, 60 minutes.) The first of three samplers of the music of various loop-based guitarists put out by Vestapol is most notable for three performances ("Twisted Blues," "Jingles" and "Yesterdays") by Wes Montgomery in 1965, taken from an appearance on English television. In addition there are a pair of unaccompanied solos from Joe Pass, two selections apiece featuring Herb Ellis and Barney Kessel and a collaboration by the pair on 1979's "A Slow Burn." All of the performances are complete and worth seeing.

Legends of Jazz Guitar Vol. 2 (Vestapol, 60 minutes.) The second of three videos in this valuable Vestapol series starts out with the most interesting performance, a blues ("Blue Mist") from 1969 featuring Barney Kessel, Kenny Burrell and Grant Green; the latter guitarist was hardly ever on film. Although the other tracks are to an extent anti-climactic, there are two numbers from Wes Montgomery in 1965 ("Full House" and "Round Midnight") that are of great interest along with performances featuring Joe Pass, Burrell, Kessel and Charlie Byrd that make this well-rounded set a worthwhile purchase for fans of loop-based guitar.

Legends of Jazz Guitar Vol. 3 (Vestapol, 60 minutes.) The third of three videos in this valuable Vestapol series has several intriguing selections by a variety of guitarists. Jim Hall in 1964 is featured on "I'm Getting Sentimental Over You" and shares the spotlight with fluegelhornist Art Farmer on "Valse Hot"; he also pops up in a lyrical 1986 duet with pianist Michel Petrucciani on "My Funny Valentine." In addition there are numbers featuring Tal Farlow, Pat Martino (in 1987) and Barney Kessel (the latter sometimes in collaborations with Herb Ellis and Charlie Byrd). All three entries in this program are worth picking up.

Les McCann Trio (Rhapsody Films, 28 minutes.) This valuable video features pianist-vocalist Les McCann and his trio (with bassist Jimmy Rowser and drummer Donald Dean) at the legendary Los Angeles club Shelly's Manne Hole sometime in the late 1960s/early '70s. McCann, at the top of his form, plays "Right On," "Sunny," "With These Hands" and his big hit "Compared To What" with spirit, power and soul.

Jackie McLean–Dynasty (Triloka Video, 58 minutes.) This video is essentially a filmed version of a live recording from Nov. 5, 1988 released by Triloka on CD. Fortunately this is a very exciting session with altoist Jackie McLean (who is joined by his son Rene McLean on tenor, soprano, flute and alto, pianist Hotep Idris Galeta, bassist Nat Reeves and drummer Carl Allen) playing at his most intense and creative. Most of the selections are group originals but Jackie's searing rendition of Burt Bacharach's "A House Is Not a Home" is one of the many highlights. The music bridges the gap between hard bop and the avant-garde and is consistently burning with passion.

Jackie McLean on Mars (Rhapsody Films, 31 minutes.) Despite the odd title, this is a very coherent if overly brief portrait of Jackie McLean from the early 1980s. McLean talks with his students about jazz, drugs, the difficulties of surviving in the music business and the joys of the music itself. There is not enough playing by the great altoist but there are glimpses of his style (trumpeter Woody Shaw has a cameo) and this film increases one's understanding of his creativity and motivation; it certainly holds one's interest.

Charles Mingus Sextet (Shanachie, 59 minutes.) For his European tour of 1964, bassist Charles Mingus led what was arguably his greatest band: a sextet with Eric Dolphy (tripling on alto, flute and bass clarinet), tenor saxophonist Clifford Jordan, trumpeter Johnny Coles, pianist Jaki Byard and drummer Dannie Richmond. Miraculously this band was featured on a Norwegian television show and the results have survived and been released by Shanachie. The solos on "So Long Eric" are very exciting and the performances of "Orange Was the Color of Her Dress" and a medley of "Ow" and "Take the 'A' Train" are also memorable. Just getting an opportunity of seeing Mingus and Richmond at work (their constant changing of grooves keeps the horns from ever getting too comfortable) and of observing Dolphy (who died a few months later) at the peak of his powers are reasons enough to acquire this essential film.

Thelonious Monk in Oslo (Rhapsody, 33 minutes.) Taken from a Norwegian television show, this half-hour video features the Thelonious Monk Quartet which at the time (April 15, 1966) consisted of the pianist-leader, tenor saxophonist Charlie Rouse, bassist Larry Gales and drummer Ben Riley. This straight performance film gives one an opportunity to see Monk in action on versions of "Lulu's Back in Town," "Blue Monk" and "'Round Midnight." The musicians all play quite well although the lack of an applauding audience results in a few awkward pauses between songs! Recommended.

Thelonious Monk–Straight No Chaser (Warner Home Video, Approx. 120 minutes.) This is a remarkable film. In 1968 Michael and Christian Blackwood shot extensive footage of Thelonious Monk not only onstage but also off. Twenty years later Bruce Ricker edited the priceless film and used other clips and new interviews to put together a pretty full portrait of the unique pianist-composer. In some of the more memorable scenes Monk is seen lying in bed ordering room service, arguing with producer Teo Macero at a recording session and appearing on stage with an under-rehearsed (and visibly struggling) octet; fortunately the latter group quickly improves after a rough start. Tenorman Charlie Rouse is often prominent but also seen are fluegelhornist Clark Terry, altoist Phil Woods and Johnny Griffin on tenor. However the main focus is on Monk and there are many extraordinary moments. This is a consistently intriguing and informative film that all bop and modern jazz followers should see!

Joe Pass in Concert (Vestapol, 40 minutes.) Joe Pass revitalized and uplifted the art of playing unaccompanied jazz guitar. Unlike Stanley Jordan (who developed a radically new approach to playing guitar with his tapping technique), Pass' approach was conventional but at such a high level that it amazed fellow guitarists. On this video, the late guitarist is seen at a concert in Wales playing three Gershwin tunes, Dizzy Gillespie's "That's Earl Brother," "All the Things You Are" and his own "Joe's Blues." Pass, who played fast single-note lines in a bebop-oriented style yet always at least implied chords and baselines, was in his own category.

Buddy Rich, Part 1 1917-1970 (DCI Music Video, 67 minutes.) This is the first of two videos that trace the career of the amazing Buddy Rich, who did deserve the title of the "world's greatest drummer." His formative years are traced through interviews, still pictures and lots of film clips; there is a wonderful example of him playing a four-bar drum break with Eddie Condon in the 1940s that is absolutely ferocious. Mel Torme does the narration and sometimes there is talking over the music but there are quite a few stunning performances. Rich, who is seen with the bands of Artie Shaw, Tommy Dorsey (in one instance dueting with trumpeter Ziggy Elman) and Harry James (the latter in the 1960s) also has a drum battle with Gene Krupa (no contest!). The video (which also contains plenty of interesting and often-humorous stories) concludes with Rich leading his own big band in 1970. Highly recommended, as is the second volume.

Buddy Rich, Part 2 1970-1987 (DCI Music Video, 80 minutes.) The second of two full-length videos on the amazing drummer Buddy Rich mostly features him with his various big bands in live performances. Highlights include fairly incredible solos on "Channel One Suite" and "West Side Story." There is also a lot of storytelling from Rich, narrator Mel Torme, Buddy's daughter Cathy and some fellow drummers. Although the first volume (due to the greater variety) gets the edge, both of these videos are easily recommended to viewers who love to see memorable drum solos.

The Sound of Jazz (Vintage Jazz Classics, 58 minutes.) It would not be an overstatement or an exaggeration to say that *The Sound of Jazz* is the greatest of all jazz films. Many of the top swing stylists were featured in a variety of very informal settings, playing live for a large audience. This show was only broadcast once on CBS but it is so full of excitement, suspense and spontaneity that it rewards repeated viewings. The most famous performance is Billie Holiday's touching rendition of "Fine and Mellow" on which she is joined by trumpeter Roy Eldridge and tenors Lester Young (who takes a remarkably emotional one chorus solo), Coleman Hawkins and Ben Webster, but there is much more. On "Wild Man Blues" and "Rosetta" trumpeter Red Allen leads an extraordinary group that includes clarinetist Pee Wee Russell (who on the former song makes a squeak a logical part of his very speechlike solo) cornetist Rex Stewart (who satirizes Russell and challenges Allen with a high note), Hawkins and trombonist Vic Dickenson. When Thelonious Monk plays "Blue Monk," he gets very different facial expressions from Coleman Hawkins (pride at having discovered him 13 years earlier), Count Basie (who looks happily surprised) and Jimmy Rushing (he looks up to the heavens as if Monk is nuts!). In addition, Basie leads an all-star big band, Rushing gets to sing, the Jimmy Giuffre Three plays "The Train and the River" and Giuffre teams up with Russell for a closing blues. This video is truly essential.

The String Trio of New York–Built by Hand (Rhapsody Films, 30 minutes.) Although only a half-hour long, this video has a lot of music and information about the avant-garde String Trio of New York. The trio was comprised at the time of violinist Charles Burnham, guitarist James Emery and bassist John Lindberg. Each of the musicians outline their hopes and goals and together they perform six originals, starting out with a fairly accessible blues and gradually evolving into the intense "Seven Vice." A thought-provoking and stimulating film.

Tenor Legends–Coleman Hawkins/Dexter Gordon (Shanachie, 57 minutes.) This video is comprised of two unrelated films. The great tenor Coleman Hawkins is featured in Brussels in 1962 with a group that includes pianist Georges Arvanitas, guitarist Mickey Baker, bassist Jimmy Woode and drummer Kansas Fields. Highlights include Hawkins' opening (and unaccompanied!) "Blowing for Adolphe Sax" and a heated "Disorder at the Border." The second half of this tape has the talented tenor Dexter Gordon at the Club Montmartre in 1969 with pianist Kenny Drew, bassist Niels Pedersen and drummer Makaya Ntshoko. Although the camerawork starts off overly hyper, it eventually settles down and Dexter sounds in fine form, particularly on "Those Were the Days" and "Fried Bananas." But Hawkins takes honors on this recommended tape.

Things to Come (Vintage Jazz Classics, 55 minutes.) Two historical films from the bebop era are included on this valuable tape. Billy Eckstine's legendary big band is seen in 1946's *Rhythm in* *a Riff* performing ten numbers. The appealing singer, after large-ly getting rid of the plot, sings a few ballads and turns his band loose on such numbers as "Rhythm in a Riff," "Taps Miller" and "Our Delight." Among the prominent sidemen are tenor saxo-phonist Gene Ammons, Frank Wess (also on tenor) and drummer Art Blakey who even back then was quite explosive. Also on this video is the classic Dizzy Gillespie short film *Jivin' in Bebop* which features his 1947 orchestra on such numbers as "Salt Peanuts," "Oop Bop Sh'Bam," "One Bass Hit" (a showcase for bassist Ray Brown) and the still-futuristic "Things to Come." Fortunately all of the dated comedy by other acts has been cut out although this print (and maybe all of the ones that exist) is not too clean and the sound is fuzzy. Still, the opportunity to see the leader-trumpeter when he was only 30 (along with glimpses of James Moody, John Lewis, Milt Jackson, Ray Brown and singer Helen Humes) certainly compensates.

Trumpet Kings (Video Artists Int., 72 minutes.) Wynton Marsalis hosts this series of clips featuring great trumpeters in loosely chronological order. Highlights include Louis Armstrong on two songs from 1933, Bunny Berigan in his only film appearance (1936's "Until Today"), Muggsy Spanier's "Someday Sweetheart," a trumpet battle by Charlie Shavers and Buck Clayton, Miles Davis on "So What," Lester Bowie in 1981 jamming freely over the chord changes of "I Got Rhythm" and the only joint appear-ance of Dizzy Gillespie and Louis Armstrong. Other trumpeters seen include Red Allen, Red Nichols, Freddie Jenkins, Cootie Williams, Harry James, Rex Stewart, Roy Eldridge, Lee Morgan, Art Farmer, Shorty Rogers, Clark Terry, Nat Adderley, Freddie Hubbard and Wynton himself. Some of the excerpts are more common than others but overall this video is well worth getting.

Vintage Collection Vol. 2 (A-Vision Entertainment, 45 minutes.) While the first volume of A-Vision's *Vintage Collection* is largely a rip-off version of *The Sound of Jazz* (which is available in its complete form elsewhere), *Vol. 2* is much more valuable despite the inaccurate dates given on the cover. The Ahmad Jamal Trio (probably in 1959) with bassist Israel Crosby and drummer Vernel Fournier shows off their distinctive style and close interplay on "Darn That Dream" and "Ahmad's Blues." Tenor great Ben Webster (with pianist Hank Jones, bassist George Duvivier and drummer Jo Jones) follows up by being featured on the ballad "Chelsea Bridge" and he welcomes trumpeter Buck Clayton and trombonist Vic Dickenson to a stomping version of "Duke's Place." However it is the second half of the tape that is most mem-orable for it is Miles Davis' famous 1959 television half-hour spe-cial (his earliest appearance on film). Miles, tenor saxophonist John Coltrane, pianist Wynton Kelly, bassist Paul Chambers and drummer Jimmy Cobb play a renowned version of "So What" before Davis (backed by the Gil Evans Orchestra) performs three lyrical numbers. This is classic music that was luckily captured for posterity.

Lester Young - Song Of The Spirit (Song of the Spirit, 110 min-utes.) Bruce Fredericksen's decision to make a documentary on the life of the great tenor Lester Young was a difficult decision because there is so little footage of Prez. However by utilizing still photos and including a lot of interviews (by the likes of Norman Granz, John Hammond, Dizzy Gillespie, Count Basie, Harry "Sweets" Edison and Jo Jones among others), the Lester Young story is very capably told. A special bonus is the complete inclu-sion of the three-song 1944 short *Jammin' the Blues* (which fea-tures Young, Edison and Illinois Jacquet) at the end of this defin-itive video.

Jazz Magazines

Cadence *Cadence* is a monthly founded in 1976 that is edited and published by Bob Rusch. No other magazine in the world reviews as many jazz recordings and their coverage ranges from bop and the avant-garde to Dixieland, blues, reissues, imports and more commercial jazz-related genres. Its subtitle is "The Review of Jazz & Blues Creative Improvised Music" and *Cadence* lives up to the billing. No matter what label a recording comes out on, it receives equal consideration based purely on the quality of the music. In each issue, in addition to hundreds of reviews of CDs, books and videos, *Cadence* generally has two or three oral history interviews

(some of them quite lengthy) with jazz and blues artists, both obscure and famous. The middle third of the approximately 112 pages has thousands of recordings for sale through *Cadence* at reasonable prices and fortunately there is no correlation between what is offered and whether a review is favorable or not. In fact *Cadence* is proud of its noncommercial status and even releases put out by Cadence Records have received negative reviews now and then. This magazine is essential for the true jazz record col-lector who wants to be informed as to what is available and its value from the jazz standpoint. Unfortunately *Cadence* is found on few newsstands so a subscription ($30 per year in the US, $35 outside) is essential. Its address is Cadence, Cadence Building, Redwood, NY 13679.

Coda A consistent force in the jazz scene since 1958, *Coda* (which is co-run by John Norris and Bill Smith) has been Canada's top jazz magazine for decades. A bi-monthly, *Coda* has an inter-esting (if sometimes out-of-date) news section, extensive coverage of the Canadian scene, many CD reviews (which are packaged together as articles) and interviews. Its coverage ranges from vet-eran bop and swing stars to the avant-garde with little notice taken of fusion or so-called contemporary jazz. Along with *Cadence*, *Coda* is the least commercial of all the jazz magazines and consistently makes for stimulating reading. Subscriptions are available for $24 annually in the U.S., $25.68 in Canada and $30 elsewhere. Its address is Coda Publications, Box 1002, Station O, Toronto, Ontario M4A 2N4 CANADA.

Down Beat Founded in 1934, *Down Beat* remains the most famous jazz magazine in the world. Its prime years were from about the mid-'40s up until the late '60s (some of its older articles and controversies are fascinating to read now) when its only com-petitor (at least up until 1960) was *Metronome*. However when it opened the door to covering rock in 1967, *Down Beat* alienated some of its audience who did not feel that the Beatles and the Rolling Stones should be covered in a jazz magazine. Even today its motto, "Jazz, Blues & Beyond" keeps it from being taken com-pletely seriously in the jazz community. However *Down Beat*'s articles and interviews are consistently excellent and its CD reviews are generally quite informative if occasionally erratic. There are also transcriptions and articles geared toward student musicians. *Down Beat* does not cover the jazz world with as much depth as *Jazz Times* (and virtually ignores the West Coast) but the two-thirds of each issue that deals with jazz is well worth reading. Subscription rates are $29 for one year, $40.50 for foreign sub-scribers. Its mailing address is Down Beat, P.O. Box 906, Elmhurst, IL 60126-0906.

Jazz Now Founded in 1991 by its editor/publisher Haybert Houston, *Jazz Now* (originally called *California Jazz Now*) is based in the Bay Area and seems to be attempting to fill the gap caused by the demise of *Jazz Forum*. It calls itself "The Jazz World Magazine" and *Jazz Now* has correspondents and regular columns from America, the United Kingdom, Poland and New York but it remains primarily a West Coast publication. Published 11 times a year (every month but January), this interesting magazine features news and reviews from a variety of cities, emphasizes noncom-merical jazz and generally has a few major interviews along with some CD and book reviews. An unusual innovation is a series of articles focusing on jazz fans who frequent Bay Area clubs. This magazine's progress during the next few years will be worth watching. Subscriptions are $21.65 in California and $20 for the rest of the U.S. Their offices are located at the Jazz Now Building, 3733 California Street, Oakland, CA 94619-1413.

The Jazz Report Second to *Coda* among Canadian jazz maga-zines, the *Jazz Report* is a promising quarterly that was founded in 1988 by publisher Bill King and editor Greg Sutherland. Boasting slick paper and interesting photos, the *Jazz Report* gen-erally has around three interviews per issue along with some CD and book reviews and news. Subscription rates are $18 in the U.S. and overseas and $15 in Canada. Its address is The Jazz Report, 14 London St, Toronto, Ontario M6G 1M9 CANADA.

Jazz Times Founded in 1970 by Ira Sabin as *Radio Free Jazz* and published ten times a year (every month but January and August), *Jazz Times* has become what is arguably the number one jazz magazine in the world. Certainly when it comes to its news sec-tion and keeping on top of the latest developments, *Jazz Times* has surpassed *Down Beat* and stayed ahead of *Jazziz*, retaining its credibility and becoming an influential force. Most issues have around 100 CD reviews (second to *Cadence*), six or seven major articles, up to ten shorter interviews and a few live reviews. *Jazz Times*'s weaknesses include a general neglect of the West Coast, an occasional tendency to copy *Down Beat* and an inconsistent coverage of fusion and so-called "contemporary" jazz, perhaps in reaction to *Jazziz*. All jazz followers can consider *Jazz Times* and *Cadence* to be the two essential monthly purchases. Yearly subscription rates are $21.95 in the U.S., $35.95 in Canada and $59.95 overseas. Its address is Jazz Times, 7961 Eastern Avenue, Suite 303, Silver Spring, MD 20910-4898.

Jazziz The most improved jazz magazine of the past two years, *Jazziz* still confuses many readers. Its coverage of the jazz scene through probing interviews, columns and individual CD reviews is quite impressive but it has a tendency to praise nearly everything. Because its publishers Michael and Lori Fagien (both of whom founded *Jazziz* in 1983) have always enjoyed pop music and crossover, the monthly stretches in coverage from Henry Threadgill to Paul Simon, featuring profiles on world music, and pop and ethnic music pacesetters in addition to jazz artists (most of whom have recent releases out). A very attractive-looking magazine with quite a few unusual and unique articles, *Jazziz* is both innovative and a bit inconsistent, a very useful tool in opening up one's musical horizons. *Jazziz*'s subscriptions are $7.77 per issue (which includes a special CD compilation each month) or $3.98 on the newsstand. Its mailing address is 3620 N.W. 43rd Street, Gainesville, FL 32606.

The Mississippi Rag Founded in 1973 by editor/publisher Leslie Johnson, the *Mississippi Rag* (which is actually located in Minnesota) has been the top classic jazz monthly ever since. Full of interesting interviews, CD reviews and news dealing with Dixieland, New Orleans jazz and swing, this newspaper is quite informative, even handed and both historical and up-to-date. Fans of early jazz will find lots of valuable information in this important paper. Subscriptions are $18 in the U.S., $20 elsewhere, and its mailing address is The Mississippi Rag, P.O. Box 19068, Minneapolis, MN 55419.

The West Coast Rag Since its formation in 1989, the *West Coast Rag* has attracted a growing audience with its lively mixture of classic jazz news, festival listings, nostalgic articles, a growing CD review section and a bit of corn. Founded by Woody Laughnan (who retired in 1995) and now run by Don Jones, the Dixieland-oriented *West Coast Rag* is generally less serious than the *Mississippi Rag* but informative when it comes to listing upcoming festivals and is becoming a bit more national in scope. It accurately describes itself as "An independent, write-it-yourself newspaper concerned with vintage jazz, ragtime and other early American music forms as well as some Americana and period humor." It is published 11 times a year (no January issue), subscriptions are $18 in the U.S. ($20 in Canada and $25 elsewhere) and its mailing address is West Coast Rag, P.O. Box 4127, Fresno, CA.

JAZZ RECORDINGS:
A BEGINNER'S GUIDE

For the beginner, going into a large record store and looking through the jazz section can be a bewildering experience. Jazz history is an endless series of names, most of them quite talented, and with a nonstop series of releases coming out on a daily basis, there is almost too much to absorb. Where does one start?

We have compiled this list of 300+ recommended CDs for listeners who are just beginning to collect jazz recordings. Rather than take the easy way out and simply include some of the huge and very complete sets that are currently available (such as Mosaic's 18-CD Nat King Cole trio box), many of which are limited-editions or beyond the budget of the beginner who wishes to simply get a taste of jazz, we have instead concentrated on variety, giving the reader a sampling of the many styles and major players from all

eras of jazz history (although due to space ragtime has been excluded). Not that many listeners will immediately enjoy every one of these records (the range of styles is quite vast) but by listening to all of this music with an open mind, its beauty and excitement will be gradually appreciated.

The emphasis is on smaller CD sets (with a few exceptions all are one or two CDs), domestic releases (also with a few exceptions) and music that is available as of this writing. Nearly every significant musician is represented somewhere on the list (for example Scott Hamilton is on Dave McKenna's *No Bass Hit*). Although we would never claim that these are the 300 "best" jazz recordings of all time, listeners should feel free to acquire as many of these releases as possible; no two are identical and all are good.

Cannonball Adderley/John Coltrane, *Cannonball And Coltrane*, Emarcy
Cannonball Adderley, *Cannonball Adderley Quintet in San Francisco*, Original Jazz Classics (OJC)
Cannonball Adderley, *Mercy, Mercy, Mercy!*, Capitol
Cannonball Adderley, *Somethin' Else*, Blue Note
Cannonball Adderley, *Things Are Getting Better*, OJC
Air, *Air Lore*, RCA/Bluebird
Howard Alden/Dan Barrett Quintet, *ABQ Salutes Buck Clayton*, Concord Jazz
Geri Allen, *In The Year Of The Dragon*, Verve
Henry "Red" Allen, *Henry Allen Collection, Vol. 1 (1929-1930)*, JSP
Henry "Red" Allen, *World On A String*, Bluebird
Mose Allison, *I Don't Worry About A Thing*, Rhino/Atlantic
Albert Ammons/Meade Lux Lewis, *The First Day*, Blue Note
Gene Ammons, *Boss Tenors*, OJC
Gene Ammons, *The Happy Blues*, OJC
Gene Ammons/Sonny Stitt, *Boss Tenors*, OJC
Ray Anderson, *Big Band Record*, Gramavision
Louis Armstrong/King Oliver, *Louis Armstrong and King Oliver*, Milestone
Louis Armstrong, *Hot Fives, Vol. 1*, Columbia
Louis Armstrong, *Hot Fives & Sevens, Vol. 2*, Columbia
Louis Armstrong, *Hot Fives & Sevens, Vol. 3*, Columbia
Louis Armstrong, *The Louis Armstrong Collection, Vol. 4: Louis Armstrong and Earl Hines*, Columbia
Louis Armstrong, *Pops: 1940's Small Band Sides*, RCA/Bluebird
Art Ensemble Of Chicago, *Live*, Delmark
Albert Ayler, *Love Cry*, Impulse
Chet Baker, *Chet Baker & Crew*, Pacific Jazz
Chet Baker, *My Favorite Songs, Vol. 1 and 2: The Last Great Concert*, Enja
Charlie Barnet, *Drop Me Off In Harlem*, Decca
Count Basie, *The Complete Decca Recordings (1937-1939) (3 CDs)*, GRP
Count Basie, *April In Paris*, Verve
Count Basie/Joe Williams, *Count Basie Swings, Joe Williams Sings*, Verve
Count Basie, *Count Basie at Newport*, Verve

Count Basie/Zoot Sims, *Basie and Zoot*, OJC
Sidney Bechet, *Master Takes: Victor Sessions (1932-1943) (3 CDs)*, Bluebird
Bix Beiderbecke, *Singin' The Blues*, Drive Archive
Bix Beiderbecke, *Bix Lives*, RCA
George Benson, *Body Talk*, Columbia
George Benson, *Breezin'*, Warner Brothers
Bunny Berigan, *The Pied Piper*, Bluebird
Art Blakey, *Moanin': Art Blakey and the Jazz Messengers*, Blue Note
Art Blakey, *A Night In Tunisia*, Blue Note
Art Blakey, *Keystone 3*, Concord Jazz
Boswell Sisters, *Boswell Sisters, Vol. 1*, Collector's Classics
Ruby Braff, *A Sailboat In The Moonlight*, Concord Jazz
Anthony Braxton, *Dortmund (Quartet 1976)*, Hat Art
Michael Brecker, *Michael Brecker*, MCA/Impulse!
Clifford Brown, *Brown and Roach, Inc.*, EmArcy
Clifford Brown, *At Basin Street*, EmArcy
Dave Brubeck, *Jazz Goes To College*, Columbia
Dave Brubeck, *Time Out*, Columbia
Jane Bunnett, *Spirits of Havana*, Denon
George Cables, *Cables' Vision*, OJC
Benny Carter, *All Of Me*, Bluebird
Benny Carter, *Benny Carter 4: Montreux 1977*, OJC
James Carter, *Jurassic Classics*, DIW/Columbia
Doc Cheatham, *The Eighty-Seven Years Of Doc Cheatham*, Columbia
Charlie Christian, *The Genius Of The Electric Guitar*, Columbia
June Christy, *Something Cool*, Capitol
Nat King Cole, *Nat King Cole*, Capitol
Nat King Cole, *Jazz Encounters*, Blue Note
Richie Cole, *Hollywood Madness*, Muse
Ornette Coleman, *At The "Golden Circle" in Stockholm, Vol. 1*, Blue Note
Ornette Coleman, *Free Jazz (A Collective Improvisation)*, Atlantic
Ornette Coleman, *The Shape Of Jazz To Come*, Atlantic
John Coltrane, *Blue Train*, Blue Note
John Coltrane, *Giant Steps*, Atlantic
John Coltrane, *John Coltrane and Johnny Hartman*, GRP/Impulse!

John Coltrane, *Live At Birdland*, Impulse
John Coltrane, *Meditations*, MCA
John Coltrane, *My Favorite Things*, Atlantic
Eddie Condon, *Dixieland All Stars*, GRP/Decca
Bob Cooper, *Coop! The Music of Bob Cooper*, OJC
Chick Corea, *Now He Sings, Now He Sobs*, Blue Note
Chick Corea, *Light As A Feather*, Polydor
Chick Corea, *My Spanish Heart*, Polydor
Marilyn Crispell, *Live In San Francisco*, Music & Arts
Sonny Criss, *Crisscraft*, Muse
Bob Crosby, *Bob Crosby & His Orchestra (1952-1953)*, Hindsight
Eddie Daniels, *Breakthrough*, GRP
Eddie Lockjaw Davis, *All Of Me*, SteepleChase
Miles Davis, *Birth Of The Cool*, Capitol
Miles Davis, *Miles Ahead*, Columbia
Miles Davis, *Milestones*, Columbia
Miles Davis, *Kind Of Blue*, Columbia
Miles Davis, *The Complete Concert: 1964 (My Funny Valentine)* (2 CDs), Columbia
Miles Davis, *Miles Smiles*, Columbia
Miles Davis, *Bitches Brew* (2 CDs), Columbia
Miles Davis, *Sketches of Spain*, Columbia
Wild Bill Davison, *Showcase*, Jazzology
Jack DeJohnette, *Special Edition*, ECM
Johnny Dodds, *Blue Clarinet Stomp*, Bluebird
Eric Dolphy, *Outward Bound*, OJC
Eric Dolphy, *Out There*, OJC
Eric Dolphy, *Out To Lunch*, Blue Note
Lou Donaldson, *Blues Walk*, Blue Note
Kenny Dorham, *Jazz Contrasts*, OJC
Kenny Dorham, *Una Mas*, Blue Note
Tommy Dorsey, *Yes Indeed!*, Bluebird
Roy Eldridge, *Little Jazz*, Columbia
Roy Eldridge, *Montreux 1977*, OJC
Duke Ellington, *Early Ellington (1927-1934)*, Bluebird
Duke Ellington, *Okeh Ellington* (2 CDs), Columbia
Duke Ellington, *Blanton-Webster Band* (3 CDs), Bluebird
Duke Ellington, *Fargo, ND, November 7, 1940* (2 CDs), Vintage Jazz Classics
Duke Ellington, *The Carnegie Hall Concerts (January 1943)* (2 CDs), Prestige
Duke Ellington, *The Far East Suite (Special Mix)*, Bluebird
Duke Ellington, *Seventieth Birthday Concert* (2 CDs), Blue Note
Herb Ellis, *Nothing But The Blues*, Verve
First Esquire All-American Jazz Concert, Radiola
Bill Evans, *Portrait In Jazz*, OJC
Bill Evans, *Undercurrent*, Blue Note
Gil Evans, *New Bottle, Old Wine*, Blue Note
Gil Evans, *Out of the Cool*, MCA
Art Farmer, *Meet The Jazztet*, MCA/Chess
Maynard Ferguson, *The Birdland Dream Band*, Bluebird
Ella Fitzgerald, *Pure Ella*, GRP/Decca
Ella Fitgerald, *The Complete Ella in Berlin*, Verve
Dave Frishberg, *Can't Take You Nowhere*, Fantasy
Erroll Garner, *Concert By The Sea*, Columbia
Stan Getz, *Bossa Nova Years (Girl from Ipanema)*, DCC
Stan Getz, *Stan Getz and J.J. Johnson at the Opera House*, Verve
Stan Getz, *Getz and Gilberto*, Mobile Fidelity
Dizzy Gillespie, *Shaw Nuff*, Musicraft
Dizzy Gillespie, *Complete RCA Victor Recordings 1947-1979* (2 CDs), Bluebird
Dizzy Gillespie/Roy Eldridge, *Dizzy Gillespie with Roy Eldridge*, Verve
Dizzy Gillespie At Newport, Verve
Jerry Gonzalez, *Rhumba Para Monk*, Sunnyside
Benny Goodman, *Sing, Sing, Sing*, Bluebird
Benny Goodman, *The Birth of Swing*, Bluebird

Benny Goodman, *Benny Goodman Carnegie Hall Concert* (2 CDs), Columbia
Dexter Gordon, *Swiss Nights, Vol. 1*, Inner City
Stephane Grappelli, *Young Django*, Verve
Stephane Grappelli, *Stephane Grappelli and David Grisman Live*, Warner Bros.
Grant Green, *Complete Blue Note with Sonny Clark*, Mosaic
Grant Green, *Matador*, Blue Note
Johnny Griffin, *The Congregation*, Blue Note
George Gruntz Concert Jazz Band, *First Prize*, Enja
Vince Guaraldi, *Jazz Impressions of "Black Orpheus"*, OJC
Lionel Hampton, *Midnight Sun*, GRP
Herbie Hancock, *Maiden Voyage*, Blue Note
Herbie Hancock, *Mwandishi: The Complete Warner Bros. Recordings* (2 CDs), Warner Archives
Roy Hargrove, *Of Kindred Souls*, Novus
Eddie Harris, *Exodus To Jazz*, Vee-Jay
Eddie Harris, *Swiss Movement*, Atlantic
Coleman Hawkins, *Body and Soul*, RCA/Bluebird
Erskine Hawkins, *The Original Tuxedo Junction*, Bluebird
Fletcher Henderson, *A Study In Frustration/Thesaurus of Classic Jazz* (4 CDs), Columbia
Joe Henderson, *Page One*, Blue Note
Joe Henderson, *Lush Life*, Verve
Woody Herman, *Blues On Parade*, GRP
Woody Herman, *Thundering Herds*, Columbia
Woody Herman, *Keeper Of The Flame: Complete Capitol Recordings*, Capitol
Andrew Hill, *Point Of Departure*, Blue Note
Earl Hines, *Spontaneous Explorations* (2 CDs), Contact
Billie Holiday, *Billie Holiday: The Legacy Box* (3 CDs), Columbia
Shirley Horn, *Close Enough For Love*, Verve
Freddie Hubbard, *Breaking Point*, Blue Note
Freddie Hubbard, *Red Clay*, CTI
Helen Humes, *Songs I Like To Sing!*, OJC
Dick Hyman, *Live From Toronto's Cafe Des Copains*, Music & Arts
Willis Jackson, *Bar Wars*, Muse
Illinois Jacquet, *The Black Velvet Band*, Bluebird
Keith Jarrett, *Koln Concert*, ECM
Keith Jarrett, *My Song*, ECM
Jazz At The Philharmonic, *The First Concert*, Verve
Jazz At The Philharmonic, *Live At The Nichigeki Theatre 1953* (2 CDs), Pablo
Jazz At The Philharmonic, *The Stockholm '55–The Exciting Battle*, Pablo
Bunk Johnson/Lu Watters, *Bunk And Lu*, Good Time Jazz
James P. Johnson, *Snowy Morning Blues*, GRP
Louis Jordan, *The Best Of Louis Jordan*, MCA
Sheila Jordan, *Portrait Of Sheila*, Blue Note
Stan Kenton, *Retrospective* (4 CDs), Capitol
Freddie Keppard, *The Complete Freddie Keppard 1923/27*, King Jazz
John Kirby, *John Kirby 1938-1939*, Classics
Andy Kirk, *The 1936*, Classics
Rahsaan Roland Kirk, *Bright Moments* (2 CDs), Rhino
Lee Konitz, *Subconscious-Lee*, OJC
Gene Krupa, *Uptown*, Columbia
Steve Lacy, *Evidence*, OJC
Steve Lacy, *Live At Sweet Basil*, Novus
Bireli Lagrene, *Routes To Django: Live*, Antilles
Lambert, Hendricks & Ross, *Sing A Song Of Basie*, GRP/Impulse!
George Lewis, *Hot Creole Jazz 1953*, DCC
Lighthouse All-Stars, *Music for Lighthousekeeping*, OJC
Abbey Lincoln, *Straight Ahead*, Candid
Abbey Lincoln, *Abbey Sings Billie*, Enja
Joe Lovano, *Rush Hour*, Blue Note
Jimmie Lunceford, *Stomp It Off*, Decca

Machito, *Mucho Macho Machito*, Pablo
Shelly Manne, *Vol. 1: The West Coast Sound*, OJC
Shelly Manne, *My Fair Lady*, OJC
Branford Marsalis, *Trio Jeepy (2 CDs)*, Columbia
Wynton Marsalis, *Black Codes (From The Underground)*, Columbia
Wynton Marsalis, *In This House, On This Morning (2 CDs)*, Columbia
Les McCann, *Les McCann Ltd. In New York*, Pacific Jazz
Susannah McCorkle, *I'll Take Romance*, Concord Jazz
Bobby McFerrin, *Spontaneous Inventions*, Blue Note
Dave McKenna, *No Bass Hit*, Concord Jazz
McKinney's Cotton Pickers (1928-1929), *Classics*
Jackie McLean, *Let Freedom Ring*, Blue Note
Jackie McLean, *Dynasty*, Triloka
Carmen McRae, *Carmen Sings Monk*, Novus
Jay McShann, *Blues From Kansas City*, GRP
Pat Metheny, *1980-1981 (2 CDs)*, ECM
Pat Metheny, *Letter From Home*, Geffen
Glenn Miller, *A Legendary Performer*, Bluebird
Charles Mingus, *Charles Mingus Presents Charles Mingus*, Candid
Charles Mingus, *Mingus at Antibes*, Atlantic
Charles Mingus, *Mingus, Mingus, Mingus, Mingus, Mingus*, Impulse
Mingus Big Band, *Mingus Big Band 93: Nostalgia in Times Square*, Dreyfus
Blue Mitchell, *The Thing To Do*, Blue Note
Hank Mobley, *Workout*, Blue Note
Modern Jazz Quartet, *Django*, OJC
Thelonious Monk, *Brilliant Corners*, OJC
Thelonious Monk, *Big Band And Quartet In Concert (2 CDs)*, Columbia
Wes Montgomery, *The Incredible Jazz Guitar of Wes Montgomery*, OJC
Wes Montgomery, *So Much Guitar*, OJC
Lee Morgan, *Candy*, Blue Note
Lee Morgan, *The Sidewinder*, Blue Note
Jelly Roll Morton, *Jelly Roll Morton Centennial: His Complete Victor Recordings (5 CDs)*, Bluebird
Bennie Moten, *South (1926-1929)*, Bluebird
Bennie Moten, *Basie Beginnings (1929-1932)*, Bluebird
Gerry Mulligan, *What Is There to Say*, Columbia
Gerry Mulligan, *Best Of Mulligan Quartet With Chet Baker*, Pacific Jazz
Turk Murphy, *Jazz Band Favorites*, Good Time Jazz
David Murray Hope Scope, *Black Saint*
Fats Navarro And Tadd Dameron (2 CDs), Blue Note
Buell Neidlinger, *Blue Chopsticks*, K2B2
The New Orleans Rhythm Kings And Jelly Roll Morton, Milestone
James Newton, *The African Flower*, Blue Note
Red Norvo, *Dance Of The Octopus* Hep
Anita O'Day, *Anita Sings The Most*, Verve
King Oliver, *Sugar Foot Stomp*, GRP
Original Dixieland Jazz Band, *75th Anniversary*, Bluebird
Kid Ory, *Kid Ory's Creole Jazz Band (1954)*, Good Time Jazz
Charlie Parker, *The Complete Dial Sessions (4 CDs)*, Stash
Charlie Parker, *Charlie Parker & Stars of Modern Jazz at Carnegie Hall (Christmas 1949)*, Jass
Charlie Parker, *The Jazz At Massey Hall*, OJC
Joe Pass, *Virtuoso, Vol. 1*, Pablo
Art Pepper, *Meets The Rhythm Section*, OJC
Art Pepper, *Straight Life*, OJC
Art Pepper, *Landscape*, OJC
Oscar Peterson, *At The Stratford Shakespearean Festival*, Verve
Oscar Peterson/Clark Terry, *Oscar Peterson Trio + One*, Verve
Oscar Peterson, *My Favorite Instrument*, Verve
Oscar Peterson, *The Trio*, Verve

King Pleasure/Annie Ross, *King Pleasure Sings with Annie Ross*, OJC
Bud Powell, *The Complete Blue Note And Roost Recordings (4 CDs)*, Blue Note
Tito Puente, *Goza Me Timbal*, Concord Picante
Django Reinhardt, *Django's Music*, Hep
Max Roach, *Freedom Now Suite*, Columbia
Max Roach, *To The Max (2 CDs)*, Blue Moon
Luckey Roberts & Willie The Lion Smith, *Good Time Jazz*
Sonny Rollins, *Saxophone Colossus and More*, OJC
Sonny Rollins, *Way Out West*, OJC
Gonzalo Rubalcaba, *The Blessing*, Blue Note
Poncho Sanchez, *A Night At Kimball's East*, Concord Picante
Pharoah Sanders, *Karma*, Impulse
John Scofield, *Hand Jive*, Blue Note
Artie Shaw, *Personal Best*, Bluebird
Woody Shaw, *Solid*, Muse
George Shearing, *I Hear a Rhapsody: Live at the Blue Note*, Telarc
Archie Shepp, *Fire Music*, Impulse
Wayne Shorter, *Native Dancer*, Columbia
Wayne Shorter, *Speak No Evil*, Blue Note
Horace Silver, *Song For My Father*, Blue Note
Zoot Sims, *Zoot Sims and the Gershwin Brothers*, OJC
Bessie Smith, *The Complete Recordings, Vol. 3 (2 CDs)*, Columbia
Jimmy Smith, *Back at the Chicken Shack*, Blue Note
Jimmy Smith, *The Sermon*, Blue Note
Jimmy Smith/Wes Montgomery, *The Dynamic Duo*, Verve
Muggsy Spanier, *The Ragtime Band Sessions*, Bluebird
Sonny Stitt, *Tune-Up!*, Muse
Supersax, *Supersax Plays Bird*, Capitol
Art Tatum, *Piano Starts Here*, Columbia/Legacy
Cecil Taylor, *Jazz Advance*, Blue Note
Cecil Taylor, *Silent Tongues*, Freedom
Jack Teagarden, *The Indispensable (2 CDs)*, RCA
Claude Thornhill, *Best Of Big Bands*, Columbia
Cal Tjader, *Latin Concert*, OJC
Mel Torme, *In Concert in Tokyo*, Concord Jazz
Lennie Tristano, *The Complete Lennie Tristano on Keynote*, Mercury
Stanley Turrentine, *Comin' Your Way*, Blue Note
Stanley Turrentine, *Sugar*, CTI
McCoy Tyner, *Enlightenment*, Milestone
McCoy Tyner, *Supertrio*, Milestone
Sarah Vaughan, *Complete: Live in Japan (2 CDs)*, Mobile Fidelity
Joe Venuti, *Fiddlesticks*, Conifer
Bennie Wallace, *Twilight Time*, Blue Note
Fats Waller, *Fats Waller and His Buddies*, Bluebird
Dinah Washington, *Dinah Jams*, EmArcy
Grover Washington, Jr., *Mister Magic*, Motown
Weather Report, *Heavy Weather*, Columbia
Chick Webb, *Chick Webb (1929-1934)*, Classics
Ben Webster, *Meet You At The Fair*, Impulse
Randy Weston, *Uhuru Afrika/Highlife*, Roulette
Kenny Wheeler, *Gnu High*, ECM
Clarence Williams, *Clarence Williams 1926-1927*, Classics
Tony Williams, *Emergency*, Polydor
Teddy Wilson, *With Billie In Mind*, Chiaroscuro
Phil Woods, *Rights Of Swing*, Candid
World's Greatest Jazz Band, *Live at Roosevelt Grill*, Atlantic
Yellowjackets, *Four Corners*, MCA
Larry Young, *Unity*, Blue Note
Lester Young, *The Complete Aladdin Sessions (2 CDs)*, Blue Note
Lester Young, *The Jazz Giants '56*, Verve
Various Artists, *Jazz In The Thirties (2 CDs)*, Disques Swing
Various Artists, *Ridin' In Rhythm (2 CDs)*, Disques Swing
Various Artists, *Jazz Scene (2 CDs)*, Verve

PRODUCERS

Steve Backer

Steve Backer moved from the unemployment line to the jazz front line in the late '60s. Backer had a business degree from Hofstra and at one point was running a travel firm in France. When the business went under, Backer turned toward music, having once entertained a desire to be a jazz musician. He initially worked for MGM and Verve as a promotion executive and later for Elektra, where he helped start the Elektra/Musician series in the early '70s. Then Backer moved to Impulse where he served as the label's general manager from 1971 to 1974. He put several marquee label artists on tour and introduced Alice Coltrane, Sam Rivers, Pharoah Sanders, Keith Jarrett, and others to new and larger-than-usual audiences before he departed for Arista in 1974. There, Backer got the chance to run three different labels: one division reissued classic free jazz material from several labels as well as some new dates; another issued exclusively new free jazz; a third issued jazz-rock, fusion, and instrumental pop. Backer was even able to land the GRP label and for a while issued its recordings, coordinating and spearheading the efforts of four operations. But the wheels came off the entire automobile in 1980, and Backer soon left the company. He is currently at RCA, working with the Novus label that he previously founded at Arista.

Rudi Blesh

(1899-1985) Rudi Blesh's interest in jazz began when he was a Dartmouth College student. He became jazz critic for the *San Francisco Chronicle* in the early '40s, then for the *New York Herald Tribune* when he moved to New York in the mid '40s. Blesh promoted concerts while on the West Coast, presenting events featuring New Orleans veterans Bunk Johnson and Kid Ory, among others. He wrote one of the first comprehensive jazz histories, *Shining Trumpets*, in 1946 and cowrote with Harriet Janis in 1950 *They All Played Ragtime*, that music's first legitimate history. Blesh and Janis cofounded Circle Records, the first label to issue Jelly Roll Morton's Library of Congress recordings. He wrote and narrated a series of radio broadcasts on jazz and American vernacular music, "This Is Jazz," from 1947 to 1950 and in 1964. Blesh was an instructor in jazz history during the '50s at Queens College and New York University and contributed liner notes for ragtime recordings in the '70s while helping to rediscover ragtime musicians Eubie Blake and Joseph Lamb and compiling ragtime collections. Blesh was also an art and film critic.

Richard Bock

(1927-1988) Richard Bock was among the early producers and record company owners to fully exploit the roster of available talent on the West Coast, along with Lester Koenig of Contemporary. Bock coformed Pacific Jazz in 1952 with drummer Roy Harte. He eventually became its sole owner and built the label through astute signings even though many of the artists he inked eventually left for bigger companies. Bock signed and produced some of the earliest dates by Chet Baker, Clare Fischer, Jim Hall, Art Pepper, Les McCann, and many others. He also started World Pacific in 1958, recording Indian sitar master Ravi Shankar. Bock began this subsidiary label feeling Shankar's music did not fit on Pacific Jazz. He would later issue other types of jazz on World Pacific, but it was a short-lived label. Bock sold it and Pacific to Liberty in 1965. He remained as an advisor until 1970, when he left music production completely and entered the world of film. But Bock later become a producer for Koenig's Contemporary label after it had been acquired by Fantasy and produced sessions by George Cables, Bud Shank, Frank Morgan, Art Farmer, and Barney Kessel until his death in 1988.

Dr. George Butler

The current head of jazz at Columbia Records and the person credited (or blamed) in many circles for instituting the "Young Lions" furor of the '80s through his signing and promotion of Wynton Marsalis, Dr. George Butler has been a controversial figure since his days at Blue Note. He was the impetus behind such albums as Donald Byrd's *Ethiopian Nights* and *Black Byrd*. *Black Byrd* became the biggest-selling album in Blue Note history, and the former bastion of traditionalism subsequently issued pop-oriented dates by Bobbi Humphrey, Ronnie Foster, Noel Pointer, Ronnie Laws, Alphonse Mouzon, and Earl Klugh. Butler moved to Columbia in the '80s and was the person who signed Wynton and Branford Marsalis to the label and helped drum up the publicity for a "Young Lions" movement (though Butler denies ever using that term). Columbia also inked deals with Marlon and Kent Jordan, Monte Croft, Terence Blanchard, and Ryan Kisor, among others in the 20-30 age group. Butler eventually rose to become head of the jazz division and has generated equal furor in the other direction during the '90s launching of a "Pioneers of Jazz" series. Some signings include Doc Cheatham and Alvin Batiste. Butler is also a trustee at LeMoyne-Owen University in Memphis.

Ozzie Cadena

The head of jazz Artists and Repertory (A&R) at Savoy in the mid and late '50s, Ozzie Cadena oversaw the debut sessions of Cannonball Adderley, Donald Byrd, Yusef Lateef, and Charlie Byrd and produced dates by Hank Jones, Kenny Clarke, and Milt Jackson. Cadena left Savoy in 1959 and later produced dates at Prestige for Brother Jack McDuff, Eddie "Lockjaw" Davis, Etta Jones, Shirley Scott, Willis Jackson, Frank Wess, and many others.

Willis Conover

(b. 1920) A voice better known to generations of foreign listeners than to many Americans, Willis Conover began broadcasting both jazz and classical music in Washington, D.C., and Manhattan in 1939. He started doing jazz worldwide via the Voice of America in 1954 and traveled to more than 40 countries. Conover presented concerts at Washington, D.C., nightclubs and insisted on integrated seating in the '40s at a time when segregation was not merely policy but actual law. He also instituted a midnight concert series on Saturday nights at the Howard Theater. Conover served as emcee of the Newport Jazz Festival for over 10 years in the '50s and '60s and produced and narrated the New Orleans International Jazz Festival in 1969. He produced and narrated Duke Ellington's 70th birthday concert at the White House in 1969 and established and chaired the jazz panel for the National Endowment for the Arts, raising the annual allotment to $250,000 in the early '70s. Conover also taught summer courses in jazz appreciation for elementary and secondary school teachers at the University of Maryland in the '70s and '80s.

Michael Cuscuna

(b. 1948) Currently the co-owner with Charlie Lourie and executive producer of the fantastic Mosaic reissue label, Michael Cuscuna began playing drums at 12 and, later, sax and flute. He attended the Wharton School at the University of Pennsylvania in the mid '60s with an eye on eventually establishing a jazz label. Soon he had a nightly jazz program on radio station WXPN and later worked part-time for ESP-Disk. Cuscuna was a critic for *Jazz and Pop* and *Down Beat* magazines and later produced a date by guitarist George Freeman that was issued by Delmark. He was a disc jockey for stations in Philadelphia and New York and helped launch a mixed musical approach that was eventually known as "progressive" rock, sans playlists and restrictive formats. Cuscuna left radio in the early '70s subsequent to the institution of demographic charting, consultants, and rigid formatting. He became a producer for Atlantic, doing sessions with Dave Brubeck and the Art Ensemble before going on to work with Motown for a short while, and then began a reissue line for ABC, which had the Impulse catalog in the '70s. Cuscuna also produced sessions for Arista and Muse. He coproduced with Alan Douglas the extensive late '70s loft jazz "Wildflowers," a magnificent, now-deleted five-volume set of performances recorded at Sam Rivers's Studio Rivbea. Cuscuna produced Anthony Braxton in the '70s and '80s, helped establish the Freedom and Novus labels, and provided a U.S. recording outlet for Cecil Taylor, Oliver Lake, Julius Hemphill, and Henry Threadgill, among others.

Cuscuna gained access to Blue Note's vaults after a five-year campaign and released nearly 100 albums of unissued classic material between 1975 and 1981. He teamed with Charlie Lourie, another jazz producer with extensive credentials, to begin Mosaic in 1983. Mosaic's operation differed markedly from that of standard jazz companies, even great ones. It did all business by mail-order and specialized in deluxe, multialbum (now multidisc) boxed sets focusing on the complete sessions of a designated artist on a particular label. Each set contained lavishly illustrated and annotated booklets, and the series has spotlighted many neglected or underrated artists such as Herbie Nichols, Tina Brooks, and Ike Quebec along with familiar giants like Charles Mingus and Thelonious Monk. Mosaic has expanded into blues with exquisite sets by T-Bone Walker and Lightnin' Hopkins, issued three massive sets dedicated to the complete output of Commodore Records, and released Nat "King" Cole's complete trio sessions. Cuscuna was voted *Down Beat's* "Producer of the Year" in 1979 and remained high in its rankings for several years afterward. He participated in the reactivation of Blue Note in 1984 and has produced new sessions by McCoy Tyner, Tony Williams, and Don Pullen. Mosaic continued its exploits in 1993 with two huge sets devoted to live and studio recordings by Count Basie and other packages on Louis Armstrong, Serge Chaloff, Mingus, Buck Clayton, Don Cherry, Jackie McLean, and Benny Goodman.

Tom Dowd

A staff engineer at Atlantic Records for more than 25 years, Tom Dowd is best known for his exploits on behalf of R&B, soul, and rock groups, but he also engineered numerous jazz dates by Ornette Coleman, Charles Mingus, John Coltrane, the Modern Jazz Quartet, and Ray Charles, among others. Dowd did landmark work with multitracking, helping Atlantic become one of the nation's best facilities in the early days of eight-track and stereo recording. Both a knowledgeable musician and a physics and electronics master, Dowd understood sound from the technical and performance aspects. He later went on to craft hit albums as a producer for Eric Clapton, Rod Stewart, Lynyrd Skynyrd, Chicago, Meat Loaf, and the James Gang.

Manfred Eicher

German bassist Manfred Eicher formed ECM in 1969 in Cologne, Germany. Initially, the label was known for free music, issuing dates by Marion Brown, Paul Bley, and Dave Holland. But it has evolved to the point of being regarded as almost a midwife to new age, with many sessions of atmospheric, minimally improvised dates by Jan Garbarek, Ralph Towner, Terje Rypdal,

Eberhard Weber, and other Europeans. Eicher's dense, expertly engineered productions have always ensured great sound. The knock on ECM is not completely fair; Jack DeJohnette, Chick Corea, Gary Burton, Keith Jarrett, Pat Metheny, Ralph Towner, Egberto Gismonti, Old and New Dreams, and Codona are among the acts who have either previously recorded or are still recording ECM dates—certainly a mixed bag. The label is still among the most prolific in recent jazz history and a place where unusual and ambitious projects often happen.

Nesuhi Ertegun

(1917-1989) The brother of Ahmet Ertegun, Nesuhi Ertegun began his involvement with jazz as a concert promoter in Washington, D.C. during the early '40s. After moving to the West Coast, Ertegun and his wife organized a band led by Kid Ory and cofounded the Crescent label in Hollywood to record it. The pair owned and operated the Jazzman label in the mid '40s and early '50s, while Ertegun was also a writer for *Clef* and record editor of *Record Changer*. He was an instructor in American music history at UCLA during the early '50s and has been cited as giving the first lectures on jazz history for college credit anywhere in the United States. Ertegun was also working part-time for both Good Time Jazz and Contemporary. He moved to New York in 1955, becoming head of Artists and Repertory (A&R) for his brother's label and started steering Atlantic toward jazz. Under Ertegun, the company at one point had John Coltrane, Charles Mingus, Milt Jackson, the Modern Jazz Quartet, Hank Crawford, David Newman, Ornette Coleman, and numerous other legendary figures under contract. He produced many Modern Jazz Quartet sessions and also helped Atlantic develop a reputation as a cutting-edge company in the '50s and '60s, while still making lucrative pop-jazz dates like Herbie Mann's *Memphis Underground* and Les McCann and Eddie Harris's *Swiss Movement*. Atlantic albums were famous for their inner sleeves, which were filled with pictures of other albums that were either available or forthcoming. Ertegun was a vice president of Atlantic until 1971 when he became president and chief executive officer under the newly merged Warner/Elektra/Atlantic situation. He helped launch Atlantic's 1976 "That's Jazz" reissue program and in 1985 became chair and co-chief executive of the joint company. He died in 1989.

Leonard Feather

(b. 1914) Best known as a syndicated critic and columnist, Leonard Feather has also been a composer, arranger, writer for radio and television, college professor, and producer. Feather attended St. Paul's School and later University College in London in the '20s and '30s, formally studying piano and clarinet and teaching himself arranging. He produced sessions in London for Benny Carter and George Chisholm and also wrote compositions. Feather came to America in the mid '30s and soon produced dates for Duke Ellington and Louis Armstrong as well as organizing jazz concerts at Carnegie Hall in the '40s. He was producer for the earliest recording dates by Dinah Washington, George Shearing, and Sarah Vaughan. Washington recorded such Feather songs as "Evil Gal Blues," "Salty Papa Blues," and "Blowtop Blues." Cleo Laine, Vaughan, Phil Woods, Sonny Stitt, Andre Previn, Cannonball Adderley, and Yusef Lateef are other noted jazz musicians who have recorded Feather numbers. Feather taught in the '70s and '80s at Loyola Marymount, the University of California at Riverside, California State University at Northridge, and UCLA. He is also a longtime columnist for the *Los Angeles Times,* the inventor of *Down Beat* magazine's blindfold test, and the compiler of several editions of *The Encyclopedia of Jazz* in various decades (a '90s edition is reportedly slated to be issued in either '94 or '95). Feather has also written several books and had numerous articles published in magazines ranging from *Metronome* to *Jazz Times.* He was an early advocate for women in jazz, helping such artists as Jutta Hipp, Yma Sumac, and others, at one point trying to establish a label devoted to recording women artists.

Joe Fields

Joe Fields established his first label, Cobblestone, in 1972 in New York as a Buddah subsidiary . He hired Don Schlitten as executive producer and the duo moved on after a few months to establish Muse and then Onyx in 1973. After dissolving the partnership when he and Schlitten had a dispute in the late '70s, Fields not only managed the company but began producing sessions himself as well as hiring Michael Cuscuna, Herb Wong, Bob Porter, and other name producers to do some sessions and having some musicians produce themselves. Muse acquired the Savoy catalog from Arista in 1985 and launched a reissue series before selling the catalog to Denon in 1993. It acquired the Landmark catalog from Fantasy and the Trix blues masters from former owner and producer Pete Lowry that same year. Muse has also distributed Enja and Sunnyside at various times.

Milt Gabler

(b. 1911) Milt Gabler's father got him involved in the music business at an early age. The senior Gabler owned a record store, the Commodore Music Shop, at 144 East 42nd Street in New York City. Milt took over the operation in the '30s and initially sold sporting goods and novelty items in addition to records. His habit of playing records all day attracted many top journalists and researchers to the store. After convincing major record labels to reissue rare out-of-print items by guaranteeing orders prior to sales, Gabler founded Commodore Records in 1938 with the assistance of Eddie Condon. Coleman Hawkins, Hot Lips Page, the Kansas City Five, and Edmond Hall were among early signees. Billie Holiday issued "Strange Fruit" on Commodore, one of four songs she cut in 1939. With Condon Gabler also started a series of jam sessions at Jimmy Ryan's on 52nd Street, and he eventually opened a second store across the street from Ryan's. Commodore was among the first companies to issue material on 12-inch 78 rpm discs, and Gabler operated Commodore until the mid '40s. He then joined Decca, where he remained until the late '70s. Louis Jordan, Holiday, and Lionel Hampton were among the artists Gabler helped bring to Decca before it was acquired by the Music Corporation of America (MCA) in 1959. Mosaic issued three massive multialbum volumes in 1992 comprising the entire Commodore output. Previously, Commodore reissues appeared on Mainstream in the '60s and overseas on London in the '70s. Columbia reissued Commodore sessions Gabler prepared when he revived the label in the '70s after retiring from Decca. There was also a German Commodore series in the late '80s.

Ira Gitler

(b. 1928) An acclaimed and extremely knowledgeable critic whose writings on jazz have been published in numerous magazines, Ira Gitler was also a staff producer for Prestige from 1950 to 1955. He produced dates by Thelonious Monk, the Modern Jazz Quartet, Miles Davis, Billy Taylor, Art Farmer, and Teddy Charles, among others. He collaborated with Leonard Feather and served as assistant writer and editor on the 1955 edition of The Encyclopedia of Jazz as well as The Encyclopedia of Jazz in the Sixties and coauthored with Feather The Encyclopedia of Jazz in the Seventies. Gitler was an associate editor of Down Beat, has written for such publications as Metronome, Jazz Magazine, and Jazz Times, produced film scripts on Louis Armstrong and Lionel Hampton for the United States Information Service, and been a host and commentator at radio station WBAI in New York. He has also been an instructor at CUNY in New York and wrote Swing to Bop: an Oral History of the Transition in Jazz in the 1940s in 1985.

Norman Granz

(b. 1918) A record producer, longtime concert promoter, and manager, Norman Granz has been associated with jazz since the '40s. He attended UCLA and, following army service in World War II, worked as a film editor. Granz began a series of concerts at the Los Angeles Philharmonic Auditorium in 1944; the response was so great, he took the shows on the road, completing the tour in Canada. From this emerged the "Jazz at the Philharmonic" series, a legacy of fervent, flamboyant, and intense jam sessions that became world famous. Numerous classic live albums were recorded at JATP shows. That same year Granz supervised production of the classic film Jammin' the Blues. It received an Oscar nomination. He established Clef and Norgran in the late '40s and early '50s and also temporarily leased records to Mercury during that time. Hank Jones, Charlie Parker, Lester Young, Flip Phillips, Johnny Hodges, Artie Shaw, Stan Getz, Charlie Barnet, and Illinois Jacquet were some of the artists Granz recorded and produced on Clef, while Don Byas, Charlie Ventura, Bud Powell, George Wallington, and Buddy Rich cut Norgran sessions. Granz eventually bought all rights to his recordings and formed the Verve label in 1956, then moved to Switzerland in 1960 and has resided in Europe ever since. He has managed Ella Fitzgerald, Oscar Peterson, and Duke Ellington, while Roy Eldridge, Dizzy Gillespie, Art Tatum, Joe Pass, Young, Parker, and Fitzgerald have ranked among his favorite artists. Granz finally sold Verve to Polygram, but began a new label, Pablo, in 1973. He maintained it into the late '80s before selling it to Fantasy.

Dave Grusin

While best known as a pianist, composer, arranger, and bandleader (see bio), Dave Grusin has also been a producer and record executive. He started GRP records with partner Larry Rosen (Grusin-Rosen Productions) in 1974 and procured a deal with Arista a few years later. MCA has owned GRP since the mid '80s and the roster has included both fusion and instrumental pop acts like Chick Corea's Elektric Band, Spyro Gyra, Lee Ritenour, the Yellowjackets, Dave Weckl, and David Benoit and also more conventional jazz performers like Gary Burton, Michael Brecker, Kenny Kirkland, and Afro-Latin trumpeter Arturo Sandoval. GRP is now also responsible for Impulse and Decca reissues through MCA.

John Hammond

(1910-1987) A legendary producer as well as talent scout, promoter, and advocate for social causes, John Hammond was drawn to the music of African Americans as a teenager listening to Bessie Smith in Harlem. The fact that he came from a wealthy family enabled Hammond to purchase jazz and blues records early and often and to become intimately familiar with the styles, nuances, and tendencies of jazz. His very first production was pianist Garland Wilson on a 12-inch 78 rpm. Some of his earliest sessions included producing and recording a series for Columbia in England featuring Fletcher Henderson, Benny Carter, and Benny Goodman. Hammond produced Bessie Smith's final session and Billie Holiday's first, and he later supervised several Teddy Wilson dates with Holiday as soloist in the late '30s and organized the classic "Spirituals to Swing" concerts in 1938 and 1939. Hammond's many other exploits include introducing guitarist Charlie Christian to Goodman, overcoming Goodman's initial skepticism, and getting some fabulous music recorded as a result.

Hammond served as executive producer or president at various times for Brunswick/Vocalion, Keynote, Majestic, Mercury, and Vanguard in addition to his longtime affiliation with Columbia. He was also an officer in the NAACP and wrote several nonmusical articles on political injustices dating back to the Scottsboro Boys atrocity in 1931. Hammond was responsible for the casting in the all-Black opera Carmen Jones. He was also a prolific critic of both jazz and popular music. Count Basie, Mildred Bailey, George Benson, Pete Seeger, Carolyn Hester, Leonard Cohen, Aretha Franklin (one of the few great artists with whom he had relatively little popular success), Bob Dylan, and Bruce Springsteen are only a few of the many great artists Hammond worked with throughout his exemplary career. He was given a special Grammy in 1971, and Dylan broke an embargo on television appearances to be on one of the Public Broadcasting System's "The World of John Hammond" specials in 1975. His son John Hammond (also known as John Hammond, Jr.) is a longtime blues guitarist. His autobiography John Hammond on Record, cowritten with Irving Townsend in 1977, outlined the triumphs of a remarkable lifetime.

Nat Hentoff

(b. 1925) Today an award-winning columnist on political and educational issues for the *Village Voice* specializing in First Amendment cases, Nat Hentoff was a distinguished writer and producer of jazz in the '50s. Hentoff attended Northeastern University and Harvard in the '40s and was a disc jockey at WMEX radio station in the '40s and '50s. He was the author of several profiles that were later issued in the book *The Jazz Life* and coeditor with Nat Shapiro of *Hear Me Talkin' To Ya: The Story of Jazz by the Men Who Made It* in 1955. This book was one of the earliest jazz oral histories told by the musicians. He coedited *Jazz: New Perspectives on the History of Jazz by Twelve of the World's Foremost Jazz Critics and Scholars* with A.J. McCarthy in 1959. Hentoff also cowrote *Jazz Street* with D. Stock in 1960 and wrote *Jazz Maker* in 1957. He was coeditor of the *Jazz Review* in the late '50s and early '60s and associate editor of *Down Beat* in the mid and late '50s. Hentoff was also executive and principal producer for the Candid record label in the early '60s, producing sessions by Cecil Taylor, Charles Mingus, Lightnin' Hopkins, and Otis Spann, among others. His notes have appeared on numerous albums as well.

Carl Jefferson

Carl Jefferson established the Concord record label in 1973. The company became a prime outlet for swing-influenced, mainstream, and bebop dates by jazz veterans, although it had its own version of the "Young Lions" movement as well with several contemporary musicians like Scott Hamilton and Warren Vaché playing in an older style. Jefferson has developed the company into an independent power that now has separate divisions for Latin (Concord Picante), classical (Concord Concerto), fusion/contemporary jazz and pop (Concord Crossover), and reissues (Collector's series) and has issued 30 volumes of solo piano dates recorded at the Maybeck Recital Hall in Berkeley, California. The roster ranges from George Shearing, Mel Torme, and Dave McKenna to relative newcomers like Jesse Davis, Eden Atwood, and even some individuals with thin jazz connections like Lucie Arnaz or minimal jazz importance like Steve Allen. While it has never issued any free sessions, Jefferson's label has released dates by Marvin "Smitty" Smith, Art Blakey and the Jazz Messengers, and the duo of Donald Harrison and Terence Blanchard.

Quincy Jones

(b. 1933) A multitalented individual who has been a successful instrumentalist, composer, arranger, and record label executive, Quincy Jones possesses production credentials that are equally impressive. He was a producer for Barclay Records in Paris during the late '50s and produced sessions for Lesley Gore and Frank Sinatra in the '60s. He also produced his own successful albums for A&M like *Walking In Space* and *Gula Matari*. Jones did the scores and production for soundtracks of more than 40 films and numerous television programs during the '60s and '70s. During the '70s and early '80s, Jones produced the biggest-selling album of all time, Michael Jackson's *Thriller*, and the top-selling single, "We Are The World," as well as sessions for Al Jarreau, Chaka Khan, and other soul, R&B, and pop acts. Jones produced dates for his own Qwest label in the '80s including *Patti Austin*, the Sinatra comeback album *L.A. Is My Lady*, and tracks on a George Benson date, plus his own hit releases. He produced a Ray Charles date in the '90s and the session *Miles and Quincy at Montreux* in 1993. Jones's list of performances, arrangements, compositions, and productions is among the most extensive in popular music history.

Orrin Keepnews

(b. 1923) A critic before he became a producer, Orrin Keepnews produced numerous seminal albums by Thelonious Monk and Bill Evans, among many others. A native New Yorker, Keepnews graduated from Columbia University in the early '40s. By the late '40s he was writing for the *Record Changer*, a magazine published by former Columbia classmate Bill Grauer. They started a reissue series of 10-inch albums for RCA Victor's X label featuring classic dates by Jelly Roll Morton, King Oliver, and others.

The pair cofounded Riverside Records in 1953 and initially specialized in similiar reissues. But they quickly ventured into new material, and Riverside became one of the places to hear bebop and other adventurous styles of the day. Keepnews personally produced all of Monk's dates for the label and most of Evans's. By the mid '60s, Keepnews was in charge of both the Riverside and Milestone labels, a position he held until 1972. He then became director of jazz productions for Fantasy, and when Fantasy acquired the Riverside, Milestone, and Prestige catalogs, he was in charge of reissuing a series of acclaimed two-record sets that laid the groundwork for the reissue boom of the '80s and '90s. Keepnews resigned as vice president of Fantasy in 1980 and returned to producing. He established a new company, Landmark, in 1985 and doubled as owner and producer of many dates by such musicians as Mulgrew Miller and Buddy Montgomery. Keepnews sold the Landmark masters to Muse in 1993. His book *The View from Within*, a critically praised collection of various writings, was issued in the late '80s.

Lester Koenig

(1918-1977) Lester Koenig established the Contemporary record label in 1951 and maintained it until 1977. While it earned the reputation in some circles as a "cool" label because of the predominance of such artists as Art Pepper and Chet Baker, Koenig was a fair-minded, open individual who did not close his doors to anyone. Hampton Hawes made many tremendous albums for the label and Ornette Coleman made his debut there. Koenig was the principal producer for such artists as Coleman, Pepper, Phineas Newborn, Sonny Rollins, Art Farmer, Baker, Shelly Manne, and Hawes while also establishing a subsidiary label, Good Time Jazz, for traditional material. Koenig's son took over the operation after his death, until it was acquired by Fantasy.

Bob Koester

Bob Koester established Delmark Records in 1953 in St. Louis. It was known then as Delmar and was one of the first companies that issued entire 10-inch albums of traditional New Orleans jazz rather than 7-inch or 12-inch singles. Koester moved to Chicago in 1959 and changed the label's name to Delmark. The company had a threefold strategy: Koester released traditional New Orleans jazz by people like George Lewis, Art Hodes, Albert Nicholas, and Earl Hines; expanded into modern material with releases from Ira Sullivan, Sonny Stitt, and Jimmy Forrest; and then put a foot into the free arena with albums by Sun Ra and many members of the Association for the Advancement of Creative Musicians (AACM) in the late '60s and early '70s. Delmark issued albums by The Art Ensemble and individual members including Roscoe Mitchell and Joseph Jarman, plus Muhal Richard Abrams, Anthony Braxton, Kalaparusha Maurice McIntyre, and others. Its series of brilliant blues dates in the '60s by Junior Wells, Magic Sam, Otis Rush, J.B. Hutto, and early stars like Big Joe Williams and Sleepy John Estes were justly celebrated, as were its free releases. During the '70s, Koester acquired the rights to the United label as well as two pioneering Black-owned companies, Pearl and States, and reissued sessions by J.T. Brown, Robert Nighthawk, Paul Bascomb, and Johnny Wicks. During the '90s, Delmark began an Apollo reissue line with titles from Coleman Hawkins, Willis Jackson, and Sir Charles Thompson. It has also issued new jazz by Malachi Thompson, Brad Goode, Frank Walton, and others. Koester operates the Jazz Record Mart as well, one of the nation's premier mail-order and retail record stores. Delmark has actively entered the CD reissue market.

Bill Laswell

(b. 1950) Still an active musician, Bill Laswell has also been a prominent producer in pop/rock and improvisational circles, though he's never done bebop, hard bop, or soul-jazz dates. A one-time guitarist who later switched to bass, Laswell hit the big time with his '84 production of Herbie Hancock's album *Future Shock*, notably the smash single "Rockit." He also produced a less successful followup *Sound System*, but at that point his reputation had already been established. Laswell produced releases by Mick Jagger, Laurie Anderson, Fela Kuti, Gil Scott-Heron, Manu Dibango, Yoko Ono, Nona Hendryx, James "Blood" Ulmer (arguably his best major label effort with 1987's *America–Do You Remember The Love*), and Public Image, Ltd. Some artists have been less than thrilled by Laswell productions, despite his reputation for being a musicians' rather than a company advocate. He erased Kuti's sax solos on "Army Arrangement" and substituted organ parts, a decision that outraged world music purists. Laswell defended it, saying Fela couldn't play and it was obvious. Scott-Heron was also unhappy about Laswell's productions and said so publicly. But Laswell remains a prime producer and doubles as a periodic member of the group Last Exit with Peter Brotzmann, Sonny Sharrock, and Ronald Shannon Jackson. He also established the record labels OAO and Celluloid and had previously organized the bands Material and Curlew.

Harry Lim

(b. 1919) Harry Lim learned about many things, including jazz, in the Netherlands. He was hooked by the music and pursued this love when he returned to his native Batavia in what was then the Dutch East Indies (now Jakarta, Indonesia). Lim followed the muse to the United States in 1939. After working as a producer in New York and Chicago, he produced dates for Keynote in the mid '40s, doing sessions by Lester Young, Coleman Hawkins, and Red Norvo as well as Milt Hinton's earliest recordings, Lennie Tristano's first commercial sessions, a date by a Charlie Shavers-led band with Earl Hines, and another composed of musicians from Woody Herman's first band with bandleader Chubby Jackson. Dave Lambert and Buddy Stewart recorded some of the first scat singing on record during a Lim production. He supervised sessions in New York, Chicago, New Orleans, and Los Angeles. Keynote later replaced Lim with another legendary figure, John Hammond, in 1947. Lim formed his own short-lived label, HL, in 1949 and produced and recorded Al Haig. He did a few sessions for Seeco, including a date by Wardell Gray, before reviving Keynote in 1955 to record material for Nat Pierce. Lim later founded Famous Door, named for the New York nightclub, in 1972. It issued sessions by George Barnes, Bill Watrous, Mundell Lowe, Zoot Sims, Red Norvo, Eddie Barefield, Scott Hamilton, George Masso, and others in the '70s and early '80s. Lim was the jazz advisor and expert for Sam Goody's record store in New York from 1956 until 1973. *The Complete Keynote Collection*, an elaborate boxed set, was issued in 1986, as well as some subsequent special collections culled from the main package.

Alfred Lion

(1908-1987) The founder of one of jazz's greatest all-time labels fell in love with the music after hearing Sam Woodling's band in Berlin in the '20s. Alfred Lion came to the United States in 1938 and attended John Hammond's "Spirituals to Swing" concert that December. The next month Lion cofounded Blue Note with Francis Wolff. The label was initially famous for great swing and traditional jazz sessions. James P. Johnson, Art Hodes, Edmond Hall, and Sidney Bechet were among their earliest artists. One of Lion's innovations was the use of 12-inch 78 rpm discs to accommodate longer sessions. Lion owned Blue Note until he sold it to Liberty in 1966. He worked another year for the new label, then retired for health reasons. Lion was honored at EMI's ceremonies reviving Blue Note in 1985 and attended a Blue Note festival in Japan the next year. (See also Blue Note in the Labels section.)

Herman Lubinsky

(1896-1974) A record dealer, electronics parts salesman, and operator of the first radio station in New Jersey, Herman Lubinsky nevertheless is a major name in jazz history as the founder of Savoy Records. Lubinsky devoted himself to the business side, leaving the production and musical decisions to his staff of A&R professionals. He was responsible for Savoy being one of the earliest labels to embrace and actively issue 12-inch albums and began the MG 1200 series, an extremely influential move. Lubinsky was sole owner until his death in 1974, and Savoy was sold the next year to Arista, which began a reissue campaign. Muse operated a similar line in the '80s, and Denon currently owns the masters and has been reissuing classic titles on a single-item basis.

Teo Macero

(b. 1925) He had an extensive performing career long before turning to production (see bio), but Teo Macero's fortunes took a major turn when he joined the CBS staff as a music editor in 1957. Among his earliest exploits was working with Charles Mingus on the great *Mingus Ah Um* and *Mingus Dynasty* releases (the eventual debacle with Mingus's material cannot be blamed on Macero). He produced Thelonious Monk during his stay on the label, though Monk's tenure was marred by the company's failure to understand his talents and refusal to issue quality material when it was fresh. Macero became Miles Davis's producer in 1959, replacing George Avakian. He and Davis worked together through the '60s and '70s, making many landmark sessions despite frequent personality clashes. His production imprint and hand in editing on numerous albums from *Sketches of Spain* to *Bitches Brew* was immense. Macero finally left Columbia in 1980 and has since issued albums on American Clave and Palo Alto and produced a date for Loose Tubes in 1987.

Sid McCoy

Although he is much better known for his radio stints as a soul music disc jockey and also an announcer on the "Soul Train" program, Sid McCoy was the principal jazz producer for Vee Jay. He produced dates by Wayne Shorter, Wynton Kelly, Lee Morgan, Eddie Harris, and others on Vee Jay from the late '50s to the early '60s.

Chuck Nessa

Michigan native Charles T. Nessa started his Chicago-based company in 1967. He produced and recorded formative sessions by Roscoe Mitchell and Lester Bowie before they became members of the Art Ensemble of Chicago, which he produced and recorded in turn. Nessa's releases were among the finest produced, packaged, and mastered of their day, and he was among the earliest sources for recordings by Bobby Bradford, John Stevens, Leo Smith, Hal Russell, Charles Tyler, and Fred Anderson. But Nessa did not restrict himself to free material; he also issued fine dates by Von Freeman, Warne Marsh, Lucky Thompson, and Ben Webster. His label was dormant for a time in the early '70s, though it kept everything in print. It became active again in the late '70s, with new dates by Marsh and Freeman. Nessa issued a limited-edition boxed set of Art Ensemble recordings, including several previously unissued tracks, in 1993.

Hughes Panassie

(1912-1974) Without question the first great non-American jazz critic, Hughes Panassie studied saxophone and began writing about the music at 18. He was a founder and later president of "The Hot Club De France" and edited *Jazz Hot* from 1936 to 1947. He also wrote the book *Le jazz Hot*, a mid-'30s treatise that was a leader in addressing the music as a serious art form. Panassie organized a series of small-group recording sessions in 1938 with Mezz Mezzrow, Tommy Ladnier, and Sidney Bechet that reportedly led to Eddie Condon's famous comment that "he didn't go over there (to France) and tell him how to stomp a grape." Count Basie recorded *Panassie Stomp* that same year. Panassie recorded and produced a swing date led by Frankie Newton in 1939. But he was an avowed, unrepentant anti-bebop scribe, repeatedly denouncing the form as the antithesis of jazz. He continued the charges until his death in the mid '70s. Panassie's extensive private collection now resides in the Discothèque Municipale at Villefranche-de-Rougergue.

Duke Pearson

Though also well known as a musician and a bandleader, Duke Pearson had an equally important role as an A&R head and codirector of Blue Note in the '60s and early '70s. During Pearson's run from 1963 to 1971, Blue Note issued pivotal sessions by Herbie Hancock, Wayne Shorter, McCoy Tyner, Andrew Hill, Joe Henderson, and Bobby Hutcherson, among others. After Francis Wolff died in 1971 and the label began issuing jazz-rock, fusion, and instrumental pop, Pearson departed.

Ike Quebec

(1918-1963) Besides having an extensive recording career (see bio), Ike Quebec played a pivotal role in the evolution of Blue Note Records from being mainly a swing and traditional jazz company into its involvement in soul-jazz, hard bop, and even some free music. Quebec began recording for Blue Note in the mid '40s and was one of only four artists to issue an album in the 78 rpm format complete with artwork and photos. He became a close friend of label owner Alfred Lion and encouraged him to pay attention to intriguing, fresh developments coming from such then-unheralded artists as Bud Powell and Thelonious Monk. Quebec soon became a combination Artists and Repertory (A&R) head, talent scout, writer (he provided the song "Suburban Eyes," which appeared on the first Monk Blue Note date), and de facto producer. Quebec remained in this role for the rest of his life, helping the label become the premier hard bop and soul-jazz company with landmark dates by Horace Silver, Art Blakey and the Jazz Messengers, Lee Morgan, Johnny Griffin, and many more. Quebec battled heroin addiction and recovered enough to resume his recording career until his death in 1963.

Teddy Reig

Teddy Reig ranks among the greatest Artists and Repertory (A&R) people in modern music history. He was a staff producer and A&R man at Savoy and Roulette. Reig produced sessions for Charlie Parker, Miles Davis, Sonny Stitt, Kenny Dorham, Kai Winding, and Leo Parker among others at Savoy. He also played a major role in the explosion of instrumental R&B by producing and in some cases actually discovering such artists as Hal Singer, Paul Williams, and Wild Bill Moore. Reig founded the (Royal) Roost label before returning to Savoy, then moved on to Roulette in the '50s and '60s. He produced early sessions by Stan Getz, and Roost reissued Charlie Parker tracks made for Dial and Bud Powell material originally recorded for Deluxe in the late '40s. Coleman Hawkins, Billy Taylor, Seldon Powell, and Gene Quill were other acts that recorded for Roost. Reig also reissued some Roost sessions through Roulette while overseeing major issue dates by Count Basie, Joe Williams, Maynard Ferguson, Harry Edison, Jack Teagarden, Randy Weston, and Sarah Vaughan.

Larry Rosen

The partner of pianist Dave Grusin and cofounder of GRP Records in 1974.

Bob Rusch

(b. 1945) A former drummer who played in '70s workshops with Jaki Byard and Cedar Walton, Bob Rusch was a writer for such publications as Down Beat, Jazz Journal, and Jazz Forum before he established Cadence magazine in 1975. It has become perhaps the nation's premier jazz journal, with loads of reviews covering independent and small jazz labels and also extensive oral interviews, histories, and commentary. In 1980 Rusch formed Cadence Jazz Records, which distributes jazz and blues recordings for hundreds of small labels. Rusch also operates North County Audio, one of the nation's finest audio/video outlets. The book Jazz Talk: The Cadence Interviews (1984) is a collection of several of his interviews in book form. Rusch has also donated his exhaustive indexed collection of periodicals on jazz and blues literature to the Schomburg Center for Research in Black Culture of the New York Public Library.

Bill Russell

(b. 1905) A musician, composer, and historian in addition to being a producer, Bill Russell began collecting jazz records in the '30s. He resold them through the Hot Record Exchange, a business he co-operated with painter Steve Smith. Russell helped rediscover Bunk Johnson in the early '40s and recorded him in 1942. He later recorded Baby Dodds, Dink Johnson, George Lewis, Wooden Joe Nicholas, and others in Los Angeles, New Orleans, and New York for his American Music label. Russell was later curator of Tulane University's jazz archive from 1958 to 1965 and co-interviewed dozens of musicians for its oral history project with Richard B. Allen. He also played in the New Orleans ragtime festival through

the '60s, '70s, and '80s. The William Ransom Hogan Jazz Archive at Tulane has a collection of Russell's published and unpublished writings as well as other materials.

Ross Russell

(b. 1920) Ross Russell's exploits in jazz include involvement in the entrepreneurial, production, journalistic, and management ends. Russell founded Dial Records in 1946 and was Charlie Parker's manager for a couple of years in the late '40s. He was also a journalist who wrote for Down Beat and the Jazz Review, among others. His book The High Life and Hard Times of Charlie "Yardbird" Parker, which was issued in 1973, was quite controversial, with some critics disputing the accuracy of accounts and validity of his contentions. Russell also penned the less-disputed Jazz Style in Kansas City and the South and was an instructor in African-American music history at the University of California and Palomar College in the '60s and '70s. The University of Texas purchased the Russell collection in 1981.

Don Schlitten

(b. 1932) Don Schlitten's experiences and credentials in jazz are extensive and varied. He cofounded Signal Records in New York with Jules Colomby and Harold Goldberg in 1955. Signal had a reputation for superbly engineered sessions with comprehensive liner notes and attractive packaging. The roster featured such artists as Duke Jordan, Cecil Payne, Red Rodney, and Gigi Gryce. After the label folded and its catalog was sold to Savoy, Schlitten became executive producer for Joe Fields's Cobblestone label, a subsidiary of Buddah, in New York in the early '70s. Schlitten produced dates by Jimmy Heath, Sonny Stitt, and Pat Martino and was responsible for a six-album series featuring highlights from the 1972 Newport in New York Jazz Festival, covering the first season the storied event moved to New York from Newport. Cobblestone also issued a previously unreleased date by Grant Green with Big John Patton. Schlitten departed Cobblestone for Muse in 1972, joining Fields in the same capacity as executive producer. The duo also formed Onyx in 1973, and during the mid '70s, Schlitten produced dates by Stitt, Kenny Barron, Willis Jackson, Woody Shaw, Kenny Burrell, and Red Rodney before a dispute between Fields and him escalated into an unsolvable feud. Their partnership was dissolved and Schlitten established Xanadu, turning it into one of the late '70s and '80s' finest hard bop, bebop, and historical labels. Xanadu issued over 200 albums, with Schlitten producing new dates by Al Cohn, Barry Harris, Bob Mover, Frank Butler, and others on the Xanadu Silver series and reissuing vintage sessions on the Gold line, including seminal material by Billy Eckstine, Sonny Criss, and others. Schlitten designed all album liners, took every photograph, and wrote most of the notes for the newer Xanadu sessions. While the company has not issued any new material since the late '80s, it has kept most of its catalog in print, though it had not entered the CD reissue market as of 1993.

Bob Shad

(1920-1985) Bob Shad was not only an outstanding jazz producer, but he supervised several major blues, pop, rock, and R&B dates as well. Shad started his production career with Savoy in the '40s, producing jazz sessions for Charlie Parker and blues and R&B albums for National. He founded the Sittin' In With label in 1948 and produced albums by Lightnin' Hopkins, Sonny Terry and Brownie McGhee, Smokey Hogg, Peppermint Harris, and Curley Weaver as well as jazz and R&B albums. Shad became director of Artists and Repertory (A&R) for Mercury in 1951 and launched its EmArcy division, producing dates by Sarah Vaughan, Maynard Ferguson, the Clifford Brown/Max Roach Quintet, and Dinah Washington, among many others. Shad produced Washington's first album with strings, which proved a huge hit. He also supervised pop dates by Patti Page and Vic Damone, R&B by the Platters, and blues sessions by Hopkins, Big Bill Broonzy, and several others. Shad founded Mainstream in the '60s after leaving Mercury and reissued several Sittin' In With albums as well as new dates by Shelly Manne, Dizzy Gillespie, Roy Haynes, Buddy Terry, Pete Yellin, and others. He continued at Mainstream through the '70s and also served as a producer for the debuts of Ted Nugent and Janis Joplin.

Nat Shapiro

(1922-1983) Nat Shapiro was not only a talented and influential writer but a longtime producer and record executive. He was Mercury Records' national director of promotion from 1948 to 1950 and the public relations representative for Broadcast Music Incorporated (BMI) in 1954 and 1955 as well as head of Columbia Records Artists and Repertory (A&R) from 1956 to 1966. Shapiro produced albums for Columbia, Philips, Vanguard, Epic, and RCA, among other companies, doing over 100 sessions by everyone from Miles Davis to Michel Legrand. Shapiro coedited *Hear Me Talkin' to Ya: The Story of Jazz by the Men Who Made It* and *The Jazz Masters* with Nat Hentoff in 1953 and 1957, respectively, and also compiled and revised *An Annotated Index of American Popular Songs* from 1964 until 1979.

John Snyder

John Snyder got his start working for CTI in the early '70s. A music education major and law school graduate, Snyder worked with such artists as Jim Hall and Paul Desmond. He then moved to A&M, where he created Horizon, a label famed for its great sound, exhaustively annotated albums, and eclectic roster. Snyder produced and issued sessions by Ornette Coleman, Charlie Haden, Dave Brubeck and Paul Desmond, Jim Hall, the Revolutionary Ensemble, and the Thad Jones-Mel Lewis orchestra. He was reportedly dismissed from A&M for presenting a company executive with a present of a clock made from a Revolutionary Ensemble record. Snyder then began the Artists House series, another acclaimed but low-selling label. This time, in addition to retaining all the things that made Horizon such a great label, Snyder also gave the musicians partial ownership and creative control of the sessions, as well as paying them 67½ cents per record pressed. He used virgin vinyl and generally operated on behalf of the music and musicians, rather than strictly for profit. Unfortunately, Artists House did not succeed either. Snyder is currently a freelance producer.

Creed Taylor

(b. 1929) One of jazz's most commercially successful and controversial producers, Creed Taylor was a trumpeter in the Duke Ambassadors Dance Orchestra in the early '50s before moving into the production end of the business. A psychology major and Duke graduate, Taylor became head of A&R at Bethlehem Records in 1954. Charlie Mariano, Chris Connor, Oscar Pettiford, Bobby Scott, Ruby Braff, Carmen McRae, Charlie Shavers, Jack Teagarden, Charles Mingus, Herbie Mann, and the duo of J.J. Johnson and Kai Winding were some artists who recorded Bethlehem sessions during Taylor's two-year stay. He joined ABC-Paramount in 1956 and started the Impulse division in 1960. Taylor signed John Coltrane and produced the *Africa/Brass* sessions. He launched the label with an album by the Johnson/Winding duo but left to go to Verve in 1962. Taylor produced the Charlie Byrd/Stan Getz hit LP *Jazz Samba* that topped the charts in 1962 and launched the bossa nova trend. He also produced the Grammy-winning smash hit album *Getz/Gilberto* that was number two on the pop charts in 1964 and included the top-five single *The Girl from Ipanema*. After so much success at Verve, Taylor moved to A&M in 1967 where he enjoyed more commercial winners with Wes Montgomery, although the results were extremely controversial. Taylor's productions for Montgomery on such albums as *A Day in the Life, Down Here on the Ground*, and *Road Song* immersed the guitarist in arrangements with large orchestras and featured an exclusive diet of light pop and rock covers with minimal solo space and short playing times. Montgomery was supposedly so disillusioned by these albums that he refused to play them for friends at home. They certainly did well on the charts.

But Taylor wanted his own operation and got that in 1970, starting CTI, Kudu, and Salvation Records. CTI became the '70s' dominant pop jazz label, with a lineup that at one point included Freddie Hubbard, Hubert Laws, George Benson, Stanley Turrentine, Chet Baker, Deodato, and Joe Farrell. Kudu issued

more funk/soul and pop material by such artists as Esther Phillips, Johnny "Hammond" Smith, and Lonnie Smith. CTI was famous for its cover art, and at one time their albums included ads for separate purchases of cover illustrations. Some releases like Turrentine's *Sugar, Cherry*, and *Don't Mess with Mister T*, Hubbard's *Red Clay, Straight Life*, and *Sky Dive*, Benson's *White Rabbit*, Laws's *Afro-Classic* and *The Rite of Spring*, and Milt Jackson's *Sunflower* were fine releases in their genre. Grover Washington became an instrumental pop superstar through Kudu albums *Inner City Blues* and *Mister Magic*, while Esther Phillips scored her last hit with a disco version of *What a Difference a Day Makes* from her '75 Kudu album. But the productions became increasingly predictable and boring even to the legions who had earlier embraced them. That, coupled with financial problems, finally caused the labels to go into bankruptcy. At one point they were owned by Motown. But CTI has resurfaced in the '90s as both a new and reissue label through a tie-in with Sony/Columbia. Columbia has reissued '70s CTI dates as part of their Contemporary Masters and Associated labels line. Bassist Charles Fambrough, a former member of Art Blakey's Jazz Messengers, has three releases on CTI including *Blues At Bradley's* in 1993.

Bob Thiele

(b. 1922) Bob Thiele's involvement in the music industry dates back to his days as a radio announcer in the '30s. Thiele was the leader of a 14-piece dance band and editor/publisher of *Jazz* magazine from 1939 to 1941. He was the first person to record pianist Erroll Garner on his Signature label, which began in 1939 and continued until 1948. Thiele also produced sessions by Coleman Hawkins, Lester Young, Eddie "Lockjaw" Davis, Julian Dash, Flip Phillips, and Anita O'Day. He joined Decca in 1952 and was responsible for productions on the Coral and Brunswick labels. Some of the artists Thiele produced were Teresa Brewer, Pearl Bailey, the McGuire Sisters, Johnny and Dorsey Burnette, and even Lawrence Welk. Thiele signed Buddy Holly after Decca rejected him, and he helped launch the careers of Jackie Wilson, Henry Mancini, Eydie Gorme, and Steve Lawrence. Thiele moved to Dot in 1959 where he produced the Mills Brothers, recorded the Clara Ward Singers live at the Apollo Theater, and did sessions with Pat Boone. He edited the soundtrack for a Red Nichols film. When Dot head Randy Wood nixed the release of a Jack Kerouac album with comedian/writer Steve Allen on piano, Thiele quit and took the session with him. He and Allen coformed the short-lived Hanover-Signature label. Thiele produced another Kerouac session with special guests Zoot Sims and Al Cohn. Others on the label included Ray Bryant, who scored a 1960 R&B hit with "Little Susie," and the team of Don Elliot and Sascha Burland, who had a novelty smash under the guise of the Nutty Squirrels. Thiele produced a classic album for Roulette starring Louis Armstrong performing Duke Ellington selections with the Duke on piano.

Thiele moved to ABC-Impulse in 1961 and remained there until 1969, producing and recording more than 100 albums that were some of the turbulent '60s' greatest jazz statements. These included landmark sessions by Charles Mingus, Archie Shepp, Pharoah Sanders, Oliver Nelson, Albert Ayler, Charlie Haden's Liberation Music Orchestra, and, of course, John Coltrane. Thiele took little credit for his Coltrane productions, often saying he gave Coltrane his head in the studio and recorded the results. He also produced fine dates by Earl Hines, Johnny Hodges, Quincy Jones, Count Basie, Coleman Hawkins, and Duke Ellington, devising inspired pairings of Ellington and Coltrane, Ellington and Hawkins, and Coltrane and Johnny Hartman. Thiele also launched the Bluesway label, with remarkable albums by B.B. King, T-Bone Walker, and John Lee Hooker, and produced Frankie Laine, Della Reese, and other pop acts for ABC. In addition to all this, he composed lyrics for the song "Duke's Place" (with the melody for *C-Jam Blues*) and wrote "Bean's Place" and "Dear John C." Thiele started the Flying Dutchman, BluesTime, and Amsterdam labels after leaving ABC-Impulse. Among his activities there were Armstrong's final sessions, co-writing "What A Wonderful World," producing albums by Gato Barbieri, Eddie "Cleanhead" Vinson, Nelson, Otis Spann, Big Joe Turner, and Count Basie. Thiele helped turn poet/musician Gil Scott-Heron into a '70s campus hero by issuing his early albums of poetry and music on Flying Dutchman. He formed the Mysterious Flying Orchestra that included Larry Coryell and Lonnie Liston Smith, which wasn't one of his stellar accomplishments, though it recorded for RCA. Thiele did productions for CBS in the '70s, among them Smith and Arthur Blythe. He married Teresa Brewer in 1972 and has frequently recorded her with everyone from Count Basie to Stephane Grappelli, Hines, and Oily Rags. He started more new labels in the '80s, including Dr. Jazz and the revived Signature. He produced dates by Arnie Lawrence and Smith and issued vintage unreleased material by Ellington and Basie, plus other items from the early Signature days on Dr. Jazz. Thiele has continued his production/label exploits in the '90s with the Red Baron company. At the end of '93 the label issued new releases by David Murray, Jackie Cain and Roy Kral, Clark Terry, Thiele's own collective all-star band, and reissues featuring Paul Desmond with the Modern Jazz Quartet and Al Cohn backed by a big band led by Al Porcino. He is still active as a producer, performer, and composer.

Rudy Van Gelder

Rudy Van Gelder is perhaps modern jazz's greatest engineer. He began engineering Blue Note sessions in 1953 and was famous for clean, sonically impeccable, and sharp recordings that were expertly balanced and ideal for jazz fans, critics, and anyone eager to hear accurate sound reproduction. Van Gelder initially juggled an optometry business and engineering before becoming a full-time sound man in 1959. He initially operated in his home studio in Hackensack, New Jersey, before moving to Englewood Cliffs in 1959. There he designed a home and studio intended for optimum recording production. Van Gelder was Blue Note's surrogate producer as well as engineering mainstay throughout its greatest days in jazz. He has remained active in jazz as a freelance engineer and continues recording at his Englewood Cliffs home; among his most recent dates are a '93 session by trumpeter Wallace Roney. Many of Van Gelder's vintage Blue Note sessions have been reissued on CD with little or no remastering other than conversion from analog to digital. Amazingly, many ostensibly comprehensive jazz reference guides carry little or no mention of his role in jazz history, an astonishing oversight.

George Wein

(b. 1925) He studied classical piano at seven with Serge Chaloff's mother and took lessons from Sam Saxe and Teddy Wilson, but George Wein's ultimate greatness came in the promotional, not the performance end of jazz. He was the first director and ultimate impresario of the Newport Jazz Festival and numerous other related festivals across the nation and around the world. The Newport Jazz Festival has been in operation since 1954 and survived fiascoes in the '60s and '70s that could have brought it to a permanent end. Wein formed a 13-piece jazz band and led it until 1941. As a teen, he played several Boston nightclubs, working with Max Kaminsky, Edmond Hall, and Wild Bill Davison before graduating from Boston University in 1950. Wein initially organized and presented groups at the Savoy in New York, then opened his own club, Storyville, featuring famous traditional jazz musicians. During the early '50s, Wein played with Bobby Hackett and recorded with Ruby Braff, Pee Wee Russell, Vic Dickenson, Jimmy McPartland, and Papa Jo Jones. He opened a second traditional jazz club, Mahogany Hall, and later recorded with the Mahogany Hall All-Stars including Doc Cheatham and Vic Dickenson.

But all those achievements take second place to his role in helping to establish the Newport Jazz Festival in 1954, serving as its director. With the financial impetus of Louis and Elaine Lorillard,

Wein initiated the festival at Newport. It became so successful that it led to the inception of many other related events ranging from the Boston Globe Jazz & Heritage Festival to the Grande Parade Du Jazz. The Newport Jazz Festival was featured in the film *Jazz on a Summer's Day* in 1958. The Newport City Council canceled it in 1961 due to unruly crowds, but it returned the next season. Wein also began a Newport Jazz Festival in Europe in 1962. A 1971 riot caused its premature end and subsequent move to New York, where it has remained ever since. The festival has grown in scope to the point that it now utilizes multiple venues, presents many special events and concerts, and remains a premier event despite continual grousing each year over conservative policies regarding invited performers and overall musical direction. Its sponsorship affiliation has changed from Kool cigarettes in the early '80s to its current JVC. Wein has also produced adjacent festivals held under the Newport banner in many cities and returned to Newport with a scaled-down version of the original. The festival's 25th anniversary was celebrated at the White House in 1978. But while he has remained busy as the head and director of Festival Productions, Inc., Wein's performing career has not ended. As early as the late '50s he was touring with a handpicked group of top musicians called the Newport Festival All-Stars. He formed the New York Jazz Repertory Company in 1974 and created another edition of the Newport Jazz Festival All-Stars in the '80s with such musicians as Scott Hamilton, Oliver Jackson, Harold Ashby, Slam Stewart, Norris Turney, and Warren Vaché. They have recorded for Concord in the '80s and '90s. Wein has also been a jazz history instructor at Boston University since the mid '50s.

Bob Weinstock

Bob Weinstock founded Prestige Records in 1949 at 446 West 50th Street in New York. Under his leadership the label evolved into a premier outlet for cool, hard bop, and soul-jazz dates. Prestige sessions were produced by Chris Albertson, Ozzie Cadena, Esmond Edwards, Ira Gitler, Cal Lampley, Bob Porter, and Don Schlitten, and mainly engineered by Rudy Van Gelder. Weinstock also produced many sessions by such musicians as Sonny Rollins, Miles Davis, the Modern Jazz Quartet, Art Farmer, James Moody, and several other individuals and groups. Prestige was sold to Fantasy, along with subsidiary companies Bluesville, Swingville, and Moodsville, in 1971.

Martin Williams

(1924-1992) While he was first and foremost one of the greatest and most knowledgeable critics in jazz history, Martin Williams was also director of the Smithsonian's jazz program and an acquisitions editor at the Smithsonian Institution Press. He was the person who selected and helped to sequence and/or annotate the sessions included in several notable releases through the '70s, '80s, and '90s. These include *The Smithsonian Collection of Classic Jazz* and other valuable releases by Duke Ellington, Fletcher Henderson, Dizzy Gillespie, and Jelly Roll Morton and anthologies of jazz piano and American popular song. He coprogrammed and annotated *Big Band Jazz: From the Beginnings to the Fifties* with Gunther Schuller; it was issued in 1993. Williams also wrote many valuable books and wrote commentaries on jazz for the Encyclopedia Britannica. He died in 1992.

—Ron Wynn

LABELS

Aladdin

Jim and Edward Mesner formed Aladdin Records in Los Angeles in the mid '40s. The company's original name was actually Philco, and the first sessions were issued under that name in 1946. The name changed shortly after to eliminate confusion with Philco products. Aladdin's early importance was as a jazz and blues label, though it subsequently became among the most prominent R&B companies in operation during the '50s and also had some major gospel releases. Lester Young, Illinois Jacquet, Billie Holiday, Louis Jordan, Art Pepper, Lawrence Marable, Harry Edison, Helen Humes, Howard McGhee, and Jay McShann were among the jazz artists who recorded for Aladdin and its late '50s subsidiary operation Jazz West (1956-1957). The company also leased some jazz masters by Erroll Garner and Howard McGhee from the Black and White label. Aladdin jazz sessions by Young, Pepper, and a few other artists have been reissued by United Artists and EMI. Aladdin's masters were purchased by Imperial in 1961 and were passed on to the Minit label in 1963. Liberty eventually purchased Aladdin as well as Imperial and Minit. Liberty was in turn absorbed in 1969 by United Artists, which later became part of EMI, the current holders of the Aladdin masters.

American

Bill Russell founded the American Music company in the early '40s, operating it at various times from homes in Pittsburgh, Chicago, New Orleans, and Canton, Missouri. Bunk Johnson was its first featured recording artist with the initial sessions issued in 1944. George Lewis, Dink Johnson, and Wooden Joe Nicholas were among the artists spotlighted by the label. It issued over 50 records on 78 rpm and continued into the 12-inch LP era of the '50s, finally ceasing production in 1957. The company also reissued Paramount blues and jazz dates from the '20s. Storyville reissued American sessions, and the Japanese label Dan started a reissue line in 1973.

Argo/Cadet

The jazz wing of the Chess empire, Argo was established by Leonard and Phil Chess in the mid '50s as a separate division. It represented an expansion into jazz by a company that up to that point was almost exclusively known for blues and R&B. Chess had previously recorded a few sessions by Leo Parker, Gene Ammons, and Al Hibbler, but now Argo signed James Moody, Ahmad Jamal, and Ramsey Lewis. Lewis's dates were among the best-selling in jazz history, though with controversial jazz output. Barry Harris and Ira Sullivan made their debuts on Argo, and Illinois Jacquet, Budd Johnson, Kenny Burrell, Max Roach, and Red Rodney were other label artists. Argo's name was changed to Cadet in 1965, after the Argo company in England raised objections and pointed to its longer history with the name. After Leonard Chess died in 1971, a series of misadventures with the total Chess catalog affected Argo/Cadet. It was bought and mismanaged by GRT, which sold it to All Platinum in 1975. It was then bought by Sugar Hill. MCA now owns all Chess, Checker, and Argo/Cadet material but has not been as exhaustive in mining its jazz resources as it has been with Chess blues and R&B material. MCA has reissued specific titles by Jamal, Lewis, and a few others.

Arista

Clive Davis, who had formerly been with many other labels including Columbia, formed Arista in New York in 1974. The company had three jazz divisions with Steve Backer directing each one and issuing material on separate labels. The Arista/Freedom wing reissued free jazz originally released on the labels Freedom, Black Lion, Fontana, Polydor, and Debut as well as new sessions. Anthony Braxton, Albert Ayler, Charles Tolliver, Cecil Taylor, Randy Weston, Archie Shepp, and Oliver Lake were among artists with titles on this label. Arista/Novus began in 1978 with new material by free jazz players like Air, Muhal Richard Abrams, and Henry Threadgill. The company also acquired the rights to the Savoy catalog and started a reissue series from its masters. Backer even began issuing jazz-rock dates from the GRP catalog. But everything crumbled in the '80s. New recording ended, Arista sold Savoy to Muse in 1985, and RCA acquired the Novus line along with Backer's services. MCA eventually purchased GRP. Arista has kept its foot in the jazz market, albeit in the fusion/contemporary pop category, thanks to Kenny G.

Artists House

John Snyder established Artists House in the late '70s and modeled it after his previously acclaimed Horizon operation. He signed Ornette Coleman, Paul Desmond, Charlie Haden, Jim Hall, Thad Jones, and Mel Lewis. Artists House was also the company that issued James "Blood" Ulmer's debut jazz session. Snyder allowed musicians maximum creative input and quality control and once again included extensive biographical and musical information with each release as well as exhaustive liner notes. The featured musicians also retained ownership of the rights to the music, giving musicians a chance to earn much more than was usual in the standard contract and royalty percentage. Sadly, this label did not last any longer than Horizon. Snyder issued about 10 albums over a two-year period and nothing was recorded after 1978.

Atlantic

The Atlantic legacy in R&B and jazz is unsurpassed among American labels, though a few others have been its equal. Herb Abramson and Ahmet Ertegun founded Atlantic in 1947, with Tiny Grimes and Erroll Garner among their earliest signees. They leased sessions from the French company Blue Star for Wilbur de Paris, Jimmy Yancey, Sidney Bechet, Don Byas, and Dizzy Gillespie in the early '50s. While Jerry Wexler became justifiably famous for his production work with Joe Turner, Ray Charles, and Aretha Franklin, Ertegun's brother Nesuhi became just as prominent for his efforts in the jazz division. As head of Artists and Repertory (A&R) for the album catalog, he was responsible for sessions by Lennie Tristano, Lee Konitz, Charles Mingus, the Modern Jazz Quartet, Ornette Coleman, John Coltrane, Phineas Newborn, Eddie Harris, Charles Lloyd, Yusef Lateef, Herbie Mann, and Rahsaan Roland Kirk among many others. Mann's sessions in the '60s were often pop/crossover hits. The company established some subsidiary operations in the '50s and '60s that issued many notable jazz dates. Atco (1955) featured sessions by Herb Geller, Helen Merrill, Betty Carter, Vi Redd, and Roland Hanna. It also distributed the Flying Dutchman label in the mid '70s. Vortex (1966) was a jazz operation that issued the recording debuts of Keith Jarrett and Chick Corea and released albums by Robin Kenyatta, Dave Pike, Byard Lancaster, Von Freeman, and Clifford Jordan. For a brief time in the late '60s and early '70s Herbie Mann served as a producer and operated Embryo Records, which issued albums by Ron Carter, Sonny Sharrock, Miroslav Vitous, and Attila Zoller.

Atlantic was purchased by Warner Bros. in 1967 and is now part of the Warner/Elektra/Atlantic combine within the greater Warner Communications conglomerate. Things got a bit bleak from a cutting-edge and jazz standpoint in the late '70s and early '80s, as fusion and instrumental pop artists dominated. But Atlantic initiated a "Just Jazz" reissue campaign in 1986 and began an ambitious cross-company reissue campaign with Rhino Records in 1993. The results were impressive: two-disc anthologies by Les McCann, Coltrane, Kirk, Mingus, David Newman, and Eddie Harris; single re-issues of prime Mingus, McCann, and Newman dates; and the four-disc gem *The Complete Recordings of Ornette Coleman* were among '93 releases. The company also hired Michele Taylor with great fanfare at the end of '93 to oversee the revamping of its jazz division.

Bethlehem

Though it was absorbed by King in the early '60s, Bethlehem was a prominent label through the '50s. It began operations in 1953 and issued albums in the 10-inch format during its first two years before converting to 12-inch in 1955. Carmen McRae made her debut for Bethlehem, while Chris Connor was the first artist to record for it in 1953. The label had a diverse catalog of hard bop and cool West Coast performers, among them Dexter Gordon, Frank Rosolino, Charlie Mariano, Duke Ellington, Oscar Pettiford, Art Blakey, Booker Ervin, Herbie Nichols, Claude Williamson, Conte Candoli, Johnny Hartman, and Mel Torme. By having both New York and Hollywood offices, Bethlehem was able to line up prime talent on both coasts. Creed Taylor and Teddy Charles were among its producers. The company's original jazz sessions came to a standstill after the purchase by King. Bethlehem reissue campaigns have been conducted frequently in the '70s, '80s, and '90s. Some Bethlehem sessions have been reissued by Affinity in England, and others are currently coming via Evidence.

Black & Blue

This was a French company that began operations in 1968 and focused on blues and jazz. Black & Blue started as a reissue company but soon started recording original sessions as well. Buddy Tate, Papa Jo Jones, Milt Buckner, Sammy Price, Jay McShann, Illinois Jacquet, and Ray Bryant were among the jazz acts that recorded for Black & Blue. The label finally ceased operation in the late '80s. Evidence now owns the catalog and has been reissuing selected titles since 1992.

Black Jazz

Producer and musician Gene Russell started Black Jazz in Glenview, Illinois, in 1971. It was one of the rare companies owned and operated by African Americans that specialized in jazz during the '70s. The roster included Doug and Jean Carn, Walter Bishop, Jr., Harold Vick, and a group called the Awakening. It unfortunately had a short life, ending operations before the end of the decade. But in December 1993, former Arista Artist and Repertory (A&R) representative Erik Nuri bought the Black Jazz holdings and announced plans to both start a reissue campaign and issue new releases in the mainstream, contemporary/fusion, and acid-jazz mode using the original Black Jazz title and logo.

Black Lion

Alan Bates started Black Lion in 1968. The London-based label issued new material by a diverse roster that ranged from Stephane Grappelli and Barney Kessel to Philly Joe Jones, Abdullah Ibrahim (then known as Dollar Brand), Thelonious Monk, and even Sun Ra. It reissued recordings originally released on the Sunset label, V-discs from Art Tatum, and European dates recorded by American jazz artists like Ben Webster, Earl Hines, Bud Freeman, and Bud Powell. Black Lion also issued sessions by British musicians such as Chris Barber, Freddy Randall, and Humphrey

Lyttelton. It had a subsidiary wing, Freedom, that concentrated on free jazz and was purchased in 1975 by Arista, which also bought some Black Lion dates as well. DA music currently owns and distributes Black Lion reissues.

Black Saint

A critically acclaimed label that has emerged as perhaps the finest foreign jazz outlet, Black Saint began in 1975. Giacomo Pellicciotti started the company in Milan and established its prime concentration on free jazz. In 1978 Giovanni Bonandrini became executive producer and helped expand the operation. Soul Note was established for recordings by bebop and hard bop musicians. The releases were distributed in America by many companies, among them Rounder, but are now part of the Sphere marketing group, along with Red, DIW, Avant, and others. David Murray, Air, Anthony Braxton, the World Saxophone Quartet, Old and New Dreams, Max Roach, the String Trio of New York, Muhal Richard Abrams, Julius Hemphill, Oliver Lake, Hamiet Bluiett, the Saxophone Choir, and many others are among the wide array of artists recording for the Black Saint/Soul Note family.

Black Swan

Black Swan, the nation's first record label owned and operated by African Americans, began in 1921. It was part of the Pace Phonograph Corporation, with president and general manager Harry H. Pace, the former partner of W. C. Handy in the music publishing firm Pace & Handy. The company took its name from opera singer Elizabeth Taylor Greenfield, nicknamed "The Black Swan." Fletcher Henderson was house accompanist, and he not only backed vocalists like Ethel Waters and Trixie Smith and led his own band but also played with and for classical musicians as the label issued jazz, blues, and classical works. Pace bought the Olympic Disc Record Corporation in 1922 with John Fletcher, reorganized it as the Fletcher Record Corporation and made its Brooklyn plant a pressing and production outlet of Black Swan. Black Swan got lots of mileage by claiming loudly and often that they were run solely by Blacks and only issued recordings by race artists, but they fudged those claims by issuing sessions by such white bands as the Original Memphis Five and others from the Olympic catalog, trying to mask this practice by releasing them as "Henderson's Dance Orchestra." The Pace Phonograph Corporation was renamed the Black Swan Phonograph Company in 1923. By May of 1924, Pace and Paramount had made an arrangement: Paramount would reissue Black Swan dates with the company logo on the records as part of Paramount's race line. Paramount absorbed Black Swan's artist contracts and made monthly payments to the musicians. This arrangement lasted until 1926, with Black Swan then getting back its masters but going out of business. Jazzology started a Black Swan reissue series in the late '80s, featuring previously issued material from Paramount.

Blue Note

The company many consider the greatest modern jazz label began in 1939. Alfred Lion established Blue Note Records and subsequently teamed with childhood friend Francis Wolff to make it a prime player in traditional jazz, swing, hard bop, and soul jazz, making later forays into free music, jazz-rock, and fusion. Blue Note was among the earliest labels to move to the 12-inch format for 78 rpm discs, providing additional recording space. Sidney Bechet, Earl Hines, Albert Ammons, Meade "Lux" Lewis, James P. Johnson, Art Hodes, and Edmond Hall were some early Blue Note artists. Lion and Wolff made Blue Note famous for everything from sound, with engineering great Rudy Van Gelder, to album cover art, thanks to the designs of Paul Bacon, Gil Melle, and John Hermansader. Under the direction of A&R heads and musicians Ike Quebec and Duke Pearson, Blue Note expanded into bebop, hard bop, and soul jazz. Thelonious Monk, Jimmy Smith, Grant Green, Stanley Turrentine, Jackie McLean, Lou Donaldson, Hank Mobley, Lee Morgan, Miles Davis, Sonny Rollins, Art Blakey & The Jazz Messengers, Freddie Hubbard, and Horace Silver, who recorded for the label over 25 years, were among the stars of the second wave. Artists who made Blue Note dates in the '60s included Bobby Hutcherson, Andrew Hill, Herbie Hancock, Joe Henderson, Wayne Shorter, McCoy Tyner, and even Ornette Coleman.

Things changed in the '70s as jazz-rock, fusion, and instrumental pop were produced under the influence of George Butler with Larry Mizell, Wayne Henderson, and the Dave Grusin-Larry Rosen team. Donald Byrd's *Black Byrd* was a milestone. It was the company's best-selling record of all time but one that was markedly different from those it had become famous for making. Noel Pointer, Bobbi Humphrey, Byrd, Ronnie Foster, and Ronnie Laws were among the artists during this period. The team of Michael Cuscuna and Charlie Lourie began a reissue program in 1975, and their efforts would lead to the creation of the ultimate reissue company Mosaic in the '80s. Blue Note was sold to Liberty in 1967. EMI distributed Liberty at that time, and Blue Note reissue lines appeared throughout Europe and Japan. EMI then purchased Liberty in 1980 and passed Blue Note on to Manhattan in 1985. The label was reactivated that year with a gala series of events and later commemorative album reissues and concert recordings. The current Blue Note includes contemporary names like the newly signed Cassandra Wilson, Benny Green, Kevin Eubanks, Bobby McFerrin, Stanley Jordan, Don Pullen, and Michel Petrucciani. Mosaic continues to issue the best of the classic items, and Blue Note has also been reissuing many titles itself, from single sessions to anthologies, compilations, and boxed sets.

Bluebird

RCA Victor established the subsidiary label Bluebird in 1932 to issue 8-inch discs that were first sold in drugstores. The next year it began releasing 10-inch discs and continued until 1950. Bluebird was the company's "race" label in the '30s, with discs numbered differently from those on RCA Victor. Earl Hines, Fats Waller, Jelly Roll Morton, and Artie Shaw, as well as blues, folk, and gospel acts, recorded on Bluebird. It was also used to reissue some traditional jazz material and sessions not originally issued. RCA revived Bluebird in the late '70s for reissues and has since periodically released several classics on Bluebird.

Cadence

Writer/historian Bob Rusch started Cadence Jazz Records in 1980. The record label is still in operation, with sessions by such artists as Bill Dixon, Chet Baker, and Beaver Harris. Cadence Distribution distributes recordings by hundreds of small jazz and blues independents.

Candid

This company has had a distinctive history. Originally owned and operated by Nat Hentoff in the early '60s, it issued recordings by Charles Mingus, Cecil Taylor, Abbey Lincoln, Lightnin' Hopkins, Otis Spann, Steve Lacy, and the Newport Rebels among others. The company was later purchased by Andy Williams, and there was a Candid reissue series in the '70s that was operated by his Barnaby label. Candid albums were also reissued in Japan and Europe. Mosaic has compiled deluxe boxed sets of classic Candid dates by Mingus, Taylor, Hopkins, and Spann. Candid currently operates as a contemporary jazz label under DA Music and has issued recordings by Gary Bartz, Larry Gales, Greg Abate, and many others.

Capitol

A team consisting of songwriting great Johnny Mercer, record store executive Glenn Wallichs, and Paramount Pictures representative Buddy de Sylvia began Capitol in Los Angeles in 1942. Originally called Liberty, the label changed its name to Capitol in two months. Under the Artists and Repertory (A&R) direction of Dave Dexter, Capitol's jazz importance zoomed. Nat "King" Cole's trio, Stan Kenton, Benny Goodman, Marian McPartland, George Shearing, Jonah Jone, and Miles Davis were among the acts who recorded for Capitol in the '40s, '50s, and '60s. But in the '70s the company's prominence and jazz activity diminished. Capitol was purchased by EMI in 1979 and has been reissuing several classic sessions since the '80s. A 40th anniversary boxed set was issued in 1992.

Charlie Parker

Doris Parker, the widow of Charlie Parker, and Aubrey Mayhew founded Charlie Parker Records in 1961 in New York. They intended to issue previously unreleased Parker dates and did release two albums of new Parker as well as three albums initially released by Le Jazz Cool. They also reissued a Red Norvo record originally made for Comet and put into circulation for the first time air checks of sessions by Lester Young and Billie Holiday. The company cut new recordings by Cecil Payne, Duke Jordan, Sadik Hakim, Joe Carroll, Barry Miles, Mundell Lowe, Teddy Wilson, and Slide Hampton. Charlie Parker Records only lasted a couple of years; Audiofidelity Enterprises purchased the masters and began reissuing some dates in 1981 for a brief period.

Chiaroscuro

Hank O'Neal started Chiaroscuro in New York in 1970. The label emphasized mostly bebop and swing sessions, with Joe Venuti, Teddy Wilson, Mary Lou Williams, and Earl Hines among its roster. But in 1976 and 1977 it also issued compelling free and more adventurous material by Hamiet Bluiett, Abdullah Ibrahim, Perry Robinson, and others. O'Neal was the primary producer, coproducing the first album with John Hammond in 1969. He sold the label in 1978 to Audiophile, which issued original albums using the Chiaroscuro banner and also reissued material by Louis Armstrong, Elmo Hope, and others. O'Neal and Andrew Sordoni formed SOS Productions in Pennsylvania in 1987 and reacquired the Chiaroscuro catalog. They are currently issuing new and reissued material.

Circle

Rudi Blesh and Harriet Janis began Circle in 1946. They recorded more than 500 masters over a six-year span in several cities, featuring such artists as Baby Dodds, Chippie Hill, George Lewis, and Albert Nicholas, and also issued recordings from Blesh's radio series "This Is Jazz" in 1947. Circle was the first label to issue Jelly Roll Morton's Library of Congress sessions on 12 albums of 78 rpm discs. The label blended old and new material in 1951 and 1952. Riverside had the Circle catalog for a while, then it was sold to George H. Buck's Jazzology label in the mid '60s. Some reissues were released on the GHB label.

Columbia

A legendary label and recording company, Columbia counted among its innovations the first LPs in the late '40s, subsidiaries in various European companies to issue Columbia material available in America, and reissues in the '60s. Columbia actually recorded the Original Dixieland Jazz Band before Victor in 1917 but did not issue the sessions until after Victor. It also recorded W.C. Handy's Orchestra of Memphis, Wilbur Sweatman's Original Jazz Band, the Louisiana Five, and other dance bands before starting a "race" series in the early '20s. The first recordings of Bessie Smith, Clara Smith, and Johnny Dunn's Original Jazz Hounds were not among "race" entries, but were part of Columbia's general catalog. The company went into receivership in 1922, then started its "race" line in 1923. Four Bessie Smith titles and one by King Oliver appeared among the initial eight issued. The line started again later in the year with material from Bessie and Clara Smith and Ethel Waters. This time Columbia maintained it with a series of recordings by Clarence Williams and New Orleans dates from Oscar Celestin and Sam Morgan. There were also sessions by Paul Whiteman, Jack Teagarden, and Red Norvo in the general line, along with Atlanta recordings by white territory bands. The company was owned for a time by British interests in the mid '20s and acquired Okeh in 1926.

By the early '30s, through various worldwide financial machinations, Victor ended up owning the American branch of Columbia. Fearing antitrust action, the owners shuffled Columbia around, and, when the maneuvering ended, the American Record Company and Brunswick (ARC-BRC) were its owners in 1933. For a time during the mid '30s, no American branch of Columbia existed—it was operated overseas. The Columbia Broadcasting System purchased ARC-BRC in 1938 and revived Columbia in 1939. Operations at Brunswick ceased in 1940. George Avakian and John Hammond became production heads, and Columbia emerged as one of the nation's finest jazz labels. Benny Goodman, Count Basie, Woody Herman, and Duke Ellington were among acts creating classics during the '40s, while the company reinstituted a "race" line in 1945 that continued into the '50s. CBS severed its affiliation with the non-American branches of Columbia in the mid '50s due to these companies' reluctance to enter the album market. Columbia inked an agreement with the Dutch company Phillips and its subsidiaries to sell its records in Europe and overseas.

Meanwhile, the company continued to grow in scope with Dave Brubeck, Louis Armstrong, Miles Davis, Ellington, Charles Mingus, and others joining it. Unfortunately, as it grew so did its reputation for artistic mismanagement. The experiences of Thelonious Monk, Mingus, Ornette Coleman, and many others were not positive; Mingus's late '50s sessions were not properly released, while much of Monk's best music in the '60s was not issued until he had left the company. There were more misadventures in the '70s and '80s: mass firings of such acts as the Heath Brothers and Coleman, incredible hype centered around Arthur Blythe that hindered every Columbia release he made in the '80s, and controversial reissues of seminal dates like *Miles Ahead* by their premier modern artist, Miles Davis. Dr. George Butler's coming in the '80s and the signing of Wynton Marsalis helped trigger the "young lions" and "neobeop/neoconservative" controversies of the '80s and '90s. Columbia has tried to reclaim some luster with extensive reissue programs, and its Jazz Masterpieces line has helped ease some image problems, as has its 1993 "Pioneers of Jazz" line. But the company's legacy was hurt by the '60s, '70s, and '80s fiascos (another was the sabotaging of the Portrait label), and it has not been completely forgiven by knowledgeable jazz fans.

Commodore

Milt Gabler began Commodore in 1938 from his New York Commodore Music Shop. Commodore was the label that issued some of Jelly Roll Morton's final dates and was also one of the pioneers in 12-inch 78 rpm discs. It released plenty of swing material by such acts as Coleman Hawkins and Hot Lips Page and was the label that issued Billie Holiday's "Strange Fruit" composition. Commodore has been reissued many times by Mainstream, Columbia, and PPI in America and by London and Telefunken in Germany. Mosaic reissued the entire Commodore catalog in three huge boxed sets during the early '90s.

Concord

Carl Jefferson established Concord in 1973 in Concord, California. The label was initially and is still primarily an outlet for swing and veteran bebop players, though it has also issued recordings by Marvin "Smitty" Smith and Jesse Davis. It was the label that helped make media sensations out of young swing-influenced types like Scott Hamilton and Warren Vaché in the '70s, but it has grown into a multifaceted operation with separate divisions for Latin (Concord Picante), fusion/jazz-rock (Concord Crossover) and classical (Concord Concerto). The company is also famous for a solo piano series recorded at the Maybeck Recital Hall; the 30th volume in this line appeared in 1993.

Debut

A company established jointly by musicians Charles Mingus and Max Roach, Debut was intended to give jazz greats an alternative to the major labels. Debut began in 1952 and continued until 1955. Many of the early sessions by Mingus's Jazz Workshop were issued by Debut, as well as the first releases by Teo Macero, Kenny Dorham, Paul Bley, John LaPorta, and Sam Most. In 1992 Fantasy issued a 16-disc set, *The Complete Debut Sessions*, that featured virtually the entire output of the label.

Decca

Decca was begun in England in 1929 by Edward Lewis, and he soon acquired British rights to recordings by the American Record Company (ARC) and issued them on the subsidiary Brunswick label. Jack Kapp helped establish an American branch in 1934, and soon it began issuing "race" records. J. Mayo Williams served as a

talent scout, and the company purchased part of Gennett's catalog plus the Champion label in 1935. Decca bought the early catalogs of Brunswick and Vocalion from CBS in 1938 and was soon reissuing classic titles plus new dates from Louis Armstrong, Woody Herman, Andy Kirk, Billie Holiday, Johnny Dodds, Count Basie, Louis Jordan, and Lionel Hampton through the '40s and '50s. The American branch of Decca split from its British counterpart in the '40s. It was affiliated with Coral and Brunswick in the '40s and '50s but was acquired in 1959 by the Music Corporation of America (MCA). MCA has since reissued many Decca titles.

Delmark

Bob Koester established Delmark in 1953 in St. Louis. He originally named it Delmar after the street where the company was located and began issuing 10-inch LPs of traditional jazz by local musicians. When Delmar moved to Chicago in 1959 the name was changed to Delmark. The company's roster included urban and traditional blues musicians ranging from Junior Wells and Magic Sam to Big Joe Williams and Sleepy John Estes; free jazz types like the Art Ensemble of Chicago, Anthony Braxton, and Muhal Richard Abrams; and traditional jazz musicians George Lewis and Earl Hines. Delmark also released the earliest material by Ira Sullivan, had soul jazz from Jimmy Forrest and Sonny Stitt, and even issued some Sun Ra dates. It acquired the masters from the United, States, Pearl, and Apollo labels in the '70s, '80s, and '90s and has reissued several titles. The company has also released new jazz dates by Jodie Christian, Malachi Thompson, Brad Goode, and others.

Dial

Ross Russell founded Dial Records in Hollywood in 1946. Russell owned the Tempo Music Shop and received financial support from Marvin Freeman. When Dial recorded Charlie Parker, its status within the jazz world zoomed. Parker did seven sessions for Dial in the late '40s, and the company also recorded dates by Dizzy Gillespie, Howard McGhee, Dodo Marmarosa, Dexter Gordon, James Moody, Erroll Garner, and Don Lanphere. It acquired a Red Norvo session with Gillespie and Parker from Comet, recordings by Art Tatum, and sessions from Woody Herman's sidemen. The company shifted locales to New York in 1947 and released more dates by Parker and McGhee. Dial scored with tenor sax "battle" sessions matching Dexter Gordon/Wardell Gray on *The Chase* and Gordon/Teddy Edwards on *The Duel*. It also had recordings by Earl Hines, Sidney Bechet, Roy Eldridge, and Willie "The Lion" Smith in its "historical jazz" catalog and issued dates that were fragments, such as Parker's "The Famous Alto Break" in 1946. Dial innovations included being among the earliest companies to issue 33⅓ rpm recordings and pioneering in the 12-inch album format. Dial recorded most of its releases on pure vinyl and cut jazz sessions on 16-inch lacquer discs, producing masters from these and keeping a second set for protection in the pretape era. Russell ended jazz production in 1949 and sold some Dial masters to Concert Hall in 1955. Other items were sporadically reissued by various labels until the late '60s when Russell helped English owner Tony Williams initiate a coherent Dial reissue series on vinyl for his Spotlite label in the late '60s. Warner Bros. briefly released an unimpressive Parker Dial "best of" reissue in the late '80s. Stash reissued the full Parker Dial sessions on CD in 1993.

EmArcy

Longtime jazz producer and Artists and Repertory (A&R) head Bob Shad launched the EmArcy division of Mercury in 1954 as the company's prime jazz wing. Shad produced dates by the Clifford Brown/Max Roach quintet, Dinah Washington, Cannonball Adderley, Rahsaan Roland Kirk, and Sarah Vaughan, among others. Jack Tracy replaced Shad as EmArcy's head in 1958 but was unable to keep it active as Mercury began funneling jazz talent to the main label. EmArcy folded altogether in the early '60s, though there was a reissue series in the '80s.

FMP

Free Music Production (FMP) Records emerged from the brief New Artists Guild organization, a group of European musicians that included Manfred Schoof, Alex Von Schlippenbach, Peter Brotzmann, and Peter Kowald. In Berlin in 1968 the guild sponsored an alternative festival to the Berliner Jazztage that featured free performers. The next year the organization took the name FMP and began recording free sessions, notably by the Globe Unity Orchestra. It has continued issuing them into the '90s with two types of sessions. Those produced by individual musicians remain their property. Others that are produced in collaboration with other participating labels, such as Bvhaast or Claxion, remain the properties of those companies with the musicians being paid only once for the recording, as on a session.

Fantasy

Max and Sol Weiss established Fantasy in 1949. Some of its earliest artists were Dave Brubeck, Gerry Mulligan, Cal Tjader, Vince Guaraldi, and Earl Hines. Later came Duke Ellington, Cannonball Adderley, Kenny Burrell, Bill Evans, and Flora Purim. The label also issued comedy recordings by Lenny Bruce in the late '50s and reaped dividends in the pop/rock market of the '60s and '70s with Creedence Clearwater Revival. But Fantasy's greatest role was as a pioneer in the reissue field. Saul Zaentz joined the company in 1955. He was a co-owner of Debut with his wife, Charles Mingus, and Max Roach. Fantasy soon acquired the Debut catalog, and Zaentz eventually became head of Fantasy in 1967 after he formed an investment team that purchased it and the Galaxy subsidiary label it had started in 1964 .

Fantasy purchased Prestige and Riverside in 1971 and 1972 and bought Milestone in 1973. The company has since acquired Contemporary, Good Time Jazz, and Stax. Orrin Keepnews, who was formerly the sole owner of Milestone and a joint owner of Riverside, became head of jazz productions for Fantasy in 1972. He began a series of double and occasionally triple reissue albums spotlighting classic titles and artists. The success of this venture led to the establishment of the Original Jazz Classics series in 1983. This series presented reissues of vintage titles but reproduced the original cover art and liner notes. It supplanted the "twofer" line and sparked a reissue boom that has yet to subside through the '90s. It also spawned the subsidiary lines, Original Blues Classics and Limited Edition. Fantasy has not only reissued Stax items but has also reactivated the Volt division and released new albums by the Dramatics and Dorothy Moore. It has also issued deluxe boxed sets featuring complete Prestige, Milestone, or Riverside recordings by John Coltrane, Miles Davis, Thelonious Monk, Bill Evans, and Wes Montgomery.

Flying Dutchman

One of Bob Thiele's many labels, Flying Dutchman began operation in 1969 and continued until 1975. Thiele had a roster ranging from Gato Barbieri, Leon Thomas, and Oliver Nelson to Bobby Hackett, Groove Holmes, Shelly Manne, and the World's Greatest Jazz Band. Flying Dutchman issued some of Louis Armstrong's final recordings and helped launch the career of poet/musician Gil Scott-Heron. Atco acquired the label in 1971, then RCA distributed and issued material from Flying Dutchman sessions until 1984.

GNP Crescendo

GNP Crescendo was founded by West Coast producer and promoter Gene Norman in 1947. He had organized a series of concerts called Just Jazz, and that was the company's original focus. It expanded into regular studio sessions in the '50s, featuring dates by Dizzy Gillespie, Charlie Ventura, Lionel Hampton, Gerry Mulligan, Teddy Buckner, and Frank Morgan. The label was the earliest to record the Clifford Brown/Max Roach quintet. GNP Crescendo also issued recordings by Cajun and Afro-Latin artists such as Bobby Enriquez and Queen Ida in the '60s and '70s. GNP Crescendo releases are currently available via reissue.

GRP

Pianist, film score composer, and bandleader Dave Grusin teamed with producer Larry Rosen to form the GRP record label in the early '70s. The label quickly established its reputation as the company of choice for jazz-rock, instrumental pop, and fusion. Arista began issuing GRP sessions in the late '70s but then severed the arrangement in the '80s. MCA now owns GRP and has continued its jazz-rock and fusion practice but also used GRP to oversee and maintain its Impulse reissue line. GRP's most popular acts include Chick Corea's Elektric Band, Eric Marienthal, David Benoit, and Grusin.

Hat Hut/Hat Art

Werner Uehlinger established the Hat Hut label in 1974 in Therwil, Switzerland. Hat Hut featured free jazz by such musicians as Cecil Taylor, Anthony Braxton, the Vienna Art Orchestra, and, most notably, Steve Lacy and Joe McPhee. Uehlinger expanded the operation during the '80s, adding Hat Art and Hat Musics. Max Roach also made a pair of two-record duo recordings with Braxton and Archie Shepp. The older dates, as well as new sessions, are now being issued on CD.

Horizon

Horizon was among the finest '70s labels. It was a subsidiary of A&M and established by producer John Snyder in 1975. Snyder's roster had a good mixture of styles and artists, with Ornette Coleman and Charlie Haden representing more outside material; Dave Brubeck, Paul Desmond, and the Thad Jones/Mel Lewis orchestra holding down the mainstream; and Andrew Hill and Hampton Hawes somewhere between the poles. Snyder divided settings between studio and live dates, and each release included comprehensive information about musical compositions, solo transcriptions, and other discographical material. Recordings were also issued in gatefold packages with elaborate designs and photographs and extensive liner notes. Horizon albums were famous for high-quality sound and were pressed on virgin vinyl. Unfortunately, the label lasted only two years, after which Snyder left A&M.

Improvising Artists

Pianist Paul Bley along with artist Carol Goss founded Improvising Artists Incorporated in 1974. The company issued recordings by such artists as Dave Holland and Sam Rivers, Sun Ra playing solo piano, Lee Konitz, and Bley. Emphasizing mainly acoustic free dates, it continued through the '70s and into the early '80s before folding. But it resurfaced in 1993 as a CD-reissue label.

Impulse

Creed Taylor helped create Impulse as a subsidiary outlet of ABC-Paramount in 1960. An album by the duo of Kai Winding and J.J. Johnson officially launched the label in 1961, and Taylor signed John Coltrane and produced the *Africa/Brass* album before departing. Bob Thiele became major producer and Impulse became the voice of the new jazz sound, recording releases by Archie Shepp, Cecil Taylor, Marion Brown, and Coltrane. But the label did not restrict itself to free material; it issued albums by Coleman Hawkins, Gil Evans, Duke Ellington, Oliver Nelson, Gary McFarland, Paul Gonsalves, Curtis Fuller, Terry Gibbs, and many others. The label was active into the '70s, with several posthumous Coltrane recordings coming in its last years. Impulse material was reissued haphazardly for several years by both domestic and foreign companies; MCA's recent decision to put the Impulse reissue campaign in the hands of its GRP subsidiary has resulted in the albums finally being reissued the right way.

Incus

Musicians Derek Bailey, Evan Parker, and Tony Oxley started Incus in London in 1970. They have primarily issued dates by English free jazz players, particularly Bailey and Parker, but also have issued dates by Alan Skidmore, John Surman, and others, plus sessions with American and international guest stars.

Jazzology

George H. Buck owned and operated Jazzology, which was initially conceived in 1949 solely to issue sessions by Tony Parenti. Nothing further came of Jazzology for several years. In 1954 Buck started GHB, a label for traditional New Orleans music. Jazzology was later activated, at first as a label for vintage Chicago-style jazz, but it began purchasing and reissuing dates from other labels in the '60s. Jazzology bought the catalogs of Icon, Mono, Southland, Jazz Crusade, and Circle. It soon revived Circle to reissue swing and big band dates from the World label and items from the Lang-Worth catalog. Jazzology took over Paramount in 1970 but was inactive from 1973 to 1975 as it moved from South Carolina to Atlanta. A debacle occurred when RCA, in the midst of shutting down its pressing plant, destroyed Jazzology's masters. While recovering from that disaster, Jazzology purchased Audiophile's catalog but then used the label to issue popular music rather than jazz. The company also acquired the Jazz Record and Lang-Worth catalogs in the early '80s and took over Bob Wilber's Bodeswell company and Monmouth-Evergreen in the mid '80s. It purchased Progressive from Gus Statiras in 1984. GHB currently reissues numerous materials.

Keynote

When Eric Bernay, a record store owner, founded Keynote in 1940, it was a folk music label. Paul Robeson and the Almanac Singers were some of the early artists. But when Harry Lim began recording artists in 1943, the focus shifted to jazz. Lester Young, Count Basie, Coleman Hawkins, Nat "King" Cole, and many others were recorded on Keynote. The company suffered through problems getting quality pressings after Capitol became too busy to continue with them. Mercury took over the label in 1948 but soon closed it down. A spectacular 21-album boxed set was issued in 1986 featuring over 330 tracks, among them 115 previously unissued cuts plus booklets with notes by Bob Porter, Dan Morgenstern, and Lim, plus rare photographs. Special sets have since been culled from this massive reissue.

Leo

Leo Feigin began Leo in London in 1980. Feigin had emigrated to England from Russia in 1973. His catalog has become one of Europe's finest for free jazz, featuring both American and international musicians like Anthony Braxton, Sun Ra, and Marilyn Crispell, and also 20 albums of the Russian trio the Ganelin Ensemble.

Limelight

Limelight replaced EmArcy as the jazz subsidiary of Mercury in 1962 with Jack Tracy as its main producer and head. The company featured Dizzy Gillespie, Art Blakey, Earl Hines, Milt Jackson, Rahsaan Roland Kirk, Gerry Mulligan, and Oscar Peterson among its artists. Limelight albums also contained expensively produced, elaborate folds and cuts plus odd liners. The label only made new recordings from 1962 to 1966, though there were albums issued until 1970. Polydor and Trip reissued Limelight dates in the '70s, and an '80s line appeared in Japan under the original company name.

Mercury

A premier label for both jazz and popular music, Mercury began operation in 1945 with Irv Green as president. Erroll Garner and both Albert and Gene Ammons were among early company signees. Mercury distributed recordings by Norman Granz's Clef label in the '40s and early '50s and acquired the Keynote label in 1948. Bob Shad began the EmArcy division, which was devoted to jazz, in 1954, but there was no rigid separation between the labels. Only Sarah Vaughan was contractually bound to do pop for Mercury and jazz for EmArcy. Quincy Jones came on board as a staff arranger, composer, bandleader, and producer in 1956 and remained 10 years. He became head of Artists and Repertory (A&R) in 1961. Ernestine Anderson, Al Cohn, Buddy Rich, and Cannonball Adderley and Dinah Washington from EmArcy were among jazz acts on Mercury. EmArcy folded in the early '60s, replaced by Limelight, but that did not last long either. Mercury

was acquired by Polydor in the '70s, with Trip reissuing much of its catalog. *Mercury 40th Anniversary V.S.O.P.* was issued in 1985.

Metronome

Sweden's major source for jazz in the '50s, Metronome was started by Lars Burman, Borje Ekberg, and Anders Burman. It issued both 78 rpm releases and EPs, drawing some material from Prestige and Atlantic but also recording several of Sweden's top stars. Arne Domnerus, Bengt Hallberg, Lars Gullin, Rolf Ericson, Jan Johansson, and Eje Thelin recorded for Metronome as well as Zoot Sims, Toots Thielemans, Alice Babs, Svend Asmussen, and Stephane Grappelli. It continued until the mid '60s.

Mosaic

The greatest American reissue company in recent history evolved from the efforts of veteran producers Charlie Lourie and Michael Cuscuna to maintain Blue Note's heritage and tradition. Cuscuna and Lourie had jointly spearheaded a Blue Note reissue series from the mid '70s until 1981, issuing two-album sets by artists from the Jazz Crusaders to Art Pepper, Herbie Nichols, and Thelonious Monk. They designed an operation that differed in many ways from the conventional record company, making albums available only by mail order and only producing a certain number and only one edition. Each boxed set contained an expertly annotated, comprehensively prepared booklet with exacting discographical and personnel information. Mosaic spotlighted many deserving artists deemed of little or no importance by their original labels, though it also presented major names like Charles Mingus, Thelonious Monk, Count Basie, Art Blakey, Chet Baker, Gerry Mulligan, Nat "King" Cole, and T-Bone Walker. The company issued magnificent sets by Tina Brooks, Larry Young, Buddy DeFranco, Ike Quebec and John Hardee, Freddie Redd, and Shorty Rogers. It released the complete output of the Commodore label in three volumes and the full Nat "King" Cole trio sessions.

Though it began in Santa Monica, California, Mosaic has been located for several years at 35 Melrose Place, Stamford, Connecticut. Unfortunately, some of the earlier sets are now out of print and others are soon slated to disappear. In addition, major labels that once sat by and gladly made material available to Mosaic with a "good riddance" attitude are now being much tougher about what they will issue and how long they will allow it to be licensed. But Mosaic continues fighting the good fight; its most recent series in 1993 included superb sets from Jackie McLean, Benny Goodman, and Count Basie.

Norgran

Norman Granz established Norgran in Los Angeles in the early '50s and used it to both reissue and issue new material. He rereleased some Clef dates on Norgran and also new sessions by swing and bebop players, among them Johnny Hodges, Louis Bellson, Benny Carter, and Ben Webster. Granz absorbed both Norgran and Clef into Verve in 1956.

Okeh

The General Photograph Corporation founded Okeh in 1916 to manage the American holdings of Carl Lindstrom's German company. It began releasing recordings two years later. The New Orleans Jazz Band was the first group to begin recording for Okeh, but it was Mamie Smith's "Crazy Blues" that made the label a power in the newly evolving "race" recordings market. Okeh established a line originally called "The Colored Catalog," then the "race" series. Clarence Williams handled the Artists and Repertory (A&R) duties in New York and Richard M. Jones in Chicago. Williams and His Blue Five, King Oliver, Louis Armstrong's Hot Five and Hot Seven, Bennie Moten, Bix Beiderbecke, Eddie Lang, and Lonnie Johnson were among the groups and musicians who recorded for Okeh. Columbia began operating Okeh in 1926. By the mid '30s, ARC BRC had acquired Okeh and dropped the "race" series and the name. Columbia purchased the company and revived it in 1938, using the vintage 8,000 "race" series designation and Okeh labels for Vocalion material. When Danny Kessler became head of A&R in 1950, Okeh's direction became predominantly R&B, though it maintained a jazz catalog as well. A two-record reissue, *Okeh Jazz*, was released in the '80s.

Prestige

Bob Weinstock founded Prestige Records in 1949. The original offices were at 446 West 50th Street in New York, and the company used several New York studios for sessions, though most recordings were done during the '50s at Rudy Van Gelder's studios in Hackensack, New Jersey. The label moved to Bergenfield, New Jersey, in 1967. It was sold in 1971 to Fantasy, a San Francisco Bay Area company. Everything moved to Berkeley, California. Prestige continued recording new dates until the late '70s, then began reissuing classic items in two-album sets. In the label's heyday, the roster included Lennie Tristano, Lee Konitz, Stan Getz, Thelonious Monk, Miles Davis, John Coltrane, Art Farmer, Red Garland, Jackie McLean, Sonny Rollins, Booker Ervin, and many others. Prestige issued cool, hard bop, and soul jazz dates and also maintained subsidiary operations Bluesville, Swingville, and Moodsville in the '60s. All the masters on Prestige and its subsidiary labels are now property of Fantasy.

Progressive

Gus Statiras started Progressive in New York in 1950. It has had a spotty history, issuing dates by Al Cohn and George Wallington in the '50s, then closing up shop in 1955. Several Progressive masters were sold to Savoy, which reissued many dates in the '60s. Prestige issued a Cohn session from 1954 in 1970, then a George Wallington date was reissued in the late '70s through the Japanese company Baybridge with some bonus unissued cuts from the original mid '50s date. J.R. Monterose, Al Haig, and Tommy Flanagan were among artists who cut new sessions for the temporarily revived Progressive. Statiras did the productions, wrote the liners, and took the photographs, using the original '50s cover art and logs for the new dates. There are currently Progressive sessions being reissued through the Collector's Record Club (CRC) of the GHB Music Foundation.

RCA Victor

Eldridge R. Johnson founded the Victor Talking Machine Corporation in Camden, New Jersey, in 1901. It was initially linked with Emile Berliner's Gramophone Company and shared the rights to use the dog-and-gramophone logo that became the trademark of His Master's Voice. The company issued recordings of James Reese Europe's Society Orchestra in 1913 and 1914 and released the first jazz record, which was recorded by the Original Dixieland Jazz Band. But Victor abandoned both jazz and the emerging "race" market during the Artists and Repertory (A&R) reign of Edward T. King. Victor tried a "race" series in the '20s, but it lapsed after a few releases by such performers as Lizzie Miles and Rosa Henderson. It did issue sessions by Paul Whiteman and A.J. Piron's New Orleans orchestra. When Nat Shikret took over, the company began emphasizing jazz and became a force in the late '20s and the '30s. Jelly Roll Morton, Bennie Moten, Duke Ellington, and King Oliver were pivotal in establishing Victor's jazz line. It also did extensive recordings of the Memphis Jug Band and restarted a "race" series in 1929. Victor soon split the series into vocal and instrumental divisions.

The Radio Corporation of America (RCA) bought Victor in 1932 and while it initially trimmed recording activity, the company was soon back at full strength in both the jazz and "race" markets. Fats Waller, Lionel Hampton, and Benny Goodman were among big sellers in the '30s and '40s. It also established subsidiary labels for cheap releases, like the short-lived Elektradisk and Sunrise and far more substantial Bluebird. During the '40s, Sidney Bechet and Ellington were among the prime sellers. Victor began using vinyl rather than shellac in the mid '40s and issued the first 45 rpm single in 1949. The company name was officially changed that year to RCA Victor. The label has consistently maintained its jazz interest since then, and has reissued through its French RCA wing material on the Black & White and Treasury of Jazz labels. The main company briefly ran a reissue label, X, in the early '50s for traditional jazz. During the mid '70s it distributed and manufactured Flying Dutchman releases and in the late '80s revived the Novus label. RCA Victor has issued new

titles by James Moody, Antonio Hart, Chris Hollyday, and others on Novus in the '80s and '90s.

Riverside

Orrin Keepnews and Bill Grauer, Jr., established Riverside in 1953 in New York. They began issuing classic sessions from the Paramount catalog as well as recordings from Champion, Gennett, the Hot Record Society, QRS, Circle, and others. Randy Weston was the company's first contemporary artist; a pair of 10-inch albums featuring Weston was released in 1954. Keepnews was the main producer, and the Riverside roster included Thelonious Monk, Bill Evans, Cannonball Adderley, Johnny Griffin, Wes Montgomery, and Barry Harris among its main stars. Riverside began the subsidiary labels Judson and Jazzland in the late '50s and early '60s. It started a Living Legends series of traditional artists in the early '60s, recording Lil Hardin Armstrong, Albert Wynn, and others in either New Orleans or Chicago. Grauer died in 1963 and Riverside went bankrupt in 1964. Keepnews eventually resurfaced at Fantasy, and the current Riverside holdings are now part of the Fantasy empire. Many Riverside sessions, including most of the Living Legends series as well as various Judson and Jazzland dates, have been reissued on CD as part of Fantasy's Original Jazz Classics line.

Roulette

Morris Levy was the head of a group of directors that founded Roulette Records in New York in 1957. The most significant jazz releases were issued on the Birdland series. These included sessions from Count Basie, Joe Williams, Maynard Ferguson, Harry Edison, Jack Teagarden, Randy Weston, and Sarah Vaughan in the late '50s and early and mid '60s. Many were produced by Teddy Reig, who signed several of the premier artists at Roulette in its prime period. The company continued recording into the '70s with Betty Carter, Art Blakey, and Lee Konitz performing on some of its final new dates. Currently, CEMA is reissuing Roulette material via Blue Note, while Mosaic issued the complete studio and live Roulette recordings of Count Basie in two massive boxed-set packages in 1993.

Sackville

John Norris and Bill Smith, the editor and publisher of *Coda* magazine, Canada's finest jazz publication, started Sackville in Toronto in 1968. The company has issued both sessions by Canadian musicians and dates recorded there by American players. Ralph Sutton, Sir Charles Thompson, Sammy Price, Jay McShann, and Willie "The Lion" Smith are among pianists who have done Sackville dates, and it has also issued sessions by Frank Rosolino, Buddy Tate, Doc Cheatham, Archie Shepp, and Bill Holman's big band. Sackville's recordings can also be ordered through *Coda*, as well as found in stores.

Saturn

Herman "Sonny" Blount, aka Sun Ra, operated the Saturn label as a conduit for his recordings in the '50s, '60s, and early '70s. It was one of many labels Sun Ra recorded on; other labels include Transition, Delmark, Steeplechase, ESP, Inner City, Improvising Artists Incorporated, Savoy, ABC/Impulse, BASF/MPS, Actuel/BYG, and Black Saint/Soul Note. Evidence acquired the Saturn masters in 1992 and reissued 15 CDs through 1993. Most were two-in-one discs covering studio and live material recorded in both Chicago and New York.

Savoy

Herman Lubinsky founded the Savoy label in Newark, New Jersey, in 1942. Its first releases were 1939 sessions recorded by the Savoy Dictators. Artists and Repertory (A&R) head Teddy Reig arranged, recorded, and/or produced releases by Charlie Parker, Dexter Gordon, Miles Davis, Fats Navarro, J.J. Johnson, and others in the mid and late '40s and early '50s, making the company one of the strongest in bebop. It also issued swing and early R&B. Ralph Bass would become a legendary R&B producer and A&R head, but he was also the person who signed Erroll Garner to Savoy. Savoy purchased Regent from Fred Mendelsohn in 1948, getting subsidiary labels National, Bop, and Discovery in the process. The company leased material from Century and Crown and reissued recordings from Jewell. While Lee Magid turned Savoy's focus more toward R&B during his A&R tenure, Ozzie Cadena put renewed focus on jazz in the mid and late '50s. He signed Kenny Clarke, Cannonball Adderley, Yusef Lateef, and Hank Jones, and Savoy established the subsidiary label Worldwide in 1958. It also did some free dates by Sun Ra, Bill Dixon, and Archie Shepp in the '60s. After Lubinsky's death in 1974, Arista purchased the Savoy catalog in 1975. Muse bought it 10 years later; both companies maintained reissue lines while they owned the masters. The current holder, Denon, started a reissue campaign in 1993.

Signal

The team of Don Schlitten, Jules Colomby, and Harold Goldberg established Signal Records in New York in 1955. The company issued dates by Duke Jordan, Cecil Payne, Red Rodney, and Gigi Gryce, plus an all-star sextet that recorded a Charlie Parker tribute at the Five Spot. Signal also started a Jazz Laboratory series with particular albums featuring music by quartets with a saxophonist and rhythm section on one side and rhythm section sans sax on the other. Savoy purchased part of the Signal catalog in the mid '50s and issued several titles. Shortly after that operations ceased.

Signature

The Signature label was the very first company started by longtime producer and label executive Bob Thiele, in 1939. Erroll Garner made his recording debut on Signature, and the company also had Coleman Hawkins, Lester Young, Julian Dash, Flip Phillips, Anita O'Day, and Eddie "Lockjaw" Davis on its roster. Thiele operated Signature until 1948. He later reissued vintage Signature sessions on his Dr. Jazz label in the '80s and temporarily revived Signature as well.

Strata-East

Trumpeter Charles Tolliver and pianist Stanley Cowell founded the Strata-East record label in 1971. Amid much publicity about being owned and operated by African Americans, Strata-East was designed to be a cooperative venture, with musicians getting larger shares of royalties and maintaining part ownership of publishing and copyrights. Some Strata-East artists included Cecil Payne, Charles Brackeen, the Piano Choir, Pharoah Sanders, Keno Duke, Mtume, and the co-owners themselves. The label continued until near the end of the decade, then ran into financial problems and ceased production. A reissue campaign has recently begun.

Timeless

Wim Wigt founded Timeless in the Netherlands in 1975 as a label devoted mainly to hard bop. The company has also recorded Lionel Hampton and Machito but has been an outlet for such players as Cedar Walton, Curtis Fuller, Buster Williams, Harold Land, and Bobby Hutcherson. It issued many remarkable sessions by the George Adams/Don Pullen combo in the late '70s and early '80s and also some of the final recordings by Art Blakey and the Jazz Messengers. Timeless has also regularly recorded and released sessions by a group known as the Timeless All-Stars that includes Walton, Land, Fuller, Hutcherson, Williams, and Billy Higgins. It has a subsidiary line devoted to traditional jazz by such acts as Chris Barber and Peanuts Hucko.

United Artists

United Artists Records was established as a subsidiary of the United Artists film company in 1958. The label was one of the finest of its time with such individuals as George Wein, Jack Lewis, Tom Wilson, and Alan Douglas serving as producers. Duke Ellington, Charles Mingus, Max Roach, Art Blakey, Count Basie, Ruby Braff, Gerry Mulligan, Betty Carter, the Modern Jazz Quartet, Booker Little, Oliver Nelson, Teddy Charles, Zoot Sims, and Bud Freeman were among those who recorded for United Artists. A subsidiary company, Solid State, was formed in 1966 and was the label that issued many fine Thad Jones-Mel Lewis dates. EMI took

over United Artists in the '80s and has subsequently reissued much of its catalog.

United/States

United and States were co-owned by African-American postman Leonard Allen and Lew Simpkins in Chicago during the early '50s. These two labels issued a wide range of sessions, many of them R&B and blues, but they also featured jazz dates by Tab Smith, Paul Bascomb, and Jimmy Forrest. Forrest's initial recording of "Night Train" was the company's biggest hit in 1951. Simpkins died in 1953, but Allen maintained the labels until 1957. Delmark acquired the masters in 1975 and initiated a combination reissue and new release program of classic material.

Vee Jay

Vivian and James Bracken, along with Calvin Carter, started Vee Jay Records in Chicago as a gospel operation in 1952. Maceo Smith and the Staples Singers were their first artists. They were best known for extraordinary R&B, blues, and gospel, but Vee Jay also had an active jazz division. Lee Morgan, Wynton Kelly, Eddie Harris, Wayne Shorter, Frank Strozier, Bill Henderson, Ira Sullivan, Louis Hayes, and many others recorded for Vee Jay from the late '50s to the mid '60s. Big Sid McCoy, who later became famous as a disc jockey and then as the voice introducing Don Cornelius on "Soul Train," produced many of the sessions. Vee Jay was among the premier labels owned and operated by African Americans in the '50s and '60s until it ran into money problems. The company also produced hits by the Four Seasons and, indeed, was the first American company to issue material by the Beatles. That coup probably hastened Vee Jay's demise, as it was unable to come up with the pressings required to meet the demand the recordings generated, due to slow pay from distributors.

Verve

Norman Granz established Verve in 1956 after having purchased the rights to all the recordings he had previously issued on prior labels Norgran and Clef. Granz folded these into Verve and also issued new recordings of swing and bebop, though what the label issued was solely dependent on Granz's taste. Ella Fitzgerald, Louis Armstrong, Duke Ellington, Count Basie, Sarah Vaughan, and many other major names appeared on Verve. Granz sold the company to MGM in 1960, but it continued issuing new material through 1967 while also having sessions issued in England by Columbia and HMV and in France by Barclay and Blue Star. Polydor purchased Verve from MGM in 1967 and it ceased operation. Polydor reissued many dates through the '70s and into the '80s, then reactivated Verve, both in its domestic and foreign operations, for new dates in the '80s and '90s as well as continuing reissues.

Vocalion

Vocalion was part of the Aeolian Company, a piano manufacturing firm in New York. It began releasing records in 1916 and released a series by the Original Dixieland Jazz Band in 1917. These were vertically cut releases; the company switched to lateral-cut discs in 1920 and dropped the Aeolian part of the name in 1924. (In early recordings sounds were directed into a large horn, which was connected to a cutting stylus at its tapered end. This stylus cut a spiral groove in the thick wax coating of a cylinder or disc in response to the vibrations af air in the horn. The stylus was rotated by a crank. If the stylus moved up and down in the cutting process it was termed "vertical-cut"; if the stylus moved side to side, it was termed "lateral-cut.") Vocalion was sold that same year to Brunswick, and the Brunswick-Balke-Callendar firm that owned both labels operated them separately but intermingled personnel and material. Vocalion started a formal "race" series in 1926 with Jack Kapp serving as producer and issued sessions by King Oliver, Jimmy Noone, and Duke Ellington. Warner Bros. took over Vocalion in 1930, then sold it to Consolidated Film Industries in 1931. It temporarily stopped marketing "race" records but resumed in 1933. Billie Holiday and Duke Ellington's combos recorded on Vocalion in the early '30s. CBS eventually purchased Vocalion as well as ARC and Brunswick. Vocalion kept issuing dates until 1940. Then it was phased out in favor of the Okeh name and logo, with many Vocalion dates being reissued as Okeh but with their original Vocalion numbers.

Vogue

This label began in France in 1948, with Charles Delaunay in charge of its Artists and Repertory (A&R). Henri Renaud, Sidney Bechet, Clifford Brown, Bobby Jaspar, and Art Farmer were among the acts who recorded on Vogue, which also reissued American dates. It distributed recordings in France from the King, Coral, Contemporary, Good Time Jazz, Hot Record Society, Blue Note, and Fantasy labels. In 1951 a subsidiary Vogue branch in Britain began, which England's Decca took over in 1956. The Vogue trademark reverted to the parent company in 1962. Decca absorbed the label, and French Vogue found a new British subsidiary via the Pye companies. Vogue has continued issuing jazz in France and had a reissue series called Jazz Legacy in the '80s. It has also periodically reissued blues and gospel titles from American labels.

Xanadu

Veteran producer Don Schlitten started Xanadu in the mid '70s, shortly after a dispute with Joe Fields at Muse led to a dissolution of their partnership agreement. Schlitten made Xanadu one of the finest bebop, cool, hard bop, and mainstream labels of the '70s and '80s, issuing over 200 albums by such artists as Al Cohn, Dolo Coker, Barry Harris, Sonny Criss, Bob Mover, and Frank Butler, among others. He also issued a series of live dates recorded at the 1978 Montreux International Jazz Festival and a reissue line that included the first recordings by Billy Eckstine and vintage dates from the '30s. Xanadu sponsored tours of Japan and West Africa in the late '70s and early '80s, respectively, and was among the first to feature American jazz acts in Africa and also to record African jazz performers for distribution and sales overseas. Xanadu has not been active since the late '80s, but its catalog remains in print. However, it had not entered the reissue market as of 1993.

—Ron Wynn

MAIL ORDER SOURCES

For those millions of us unlucky enough to reside in places outside the realm of superstores (in other words, most folks), trying to find even the latest hyped major-label jazz item in a mall store, standard retail outlet, or neighborhood mom-and-pop one-stop can be disastrous. Assuming the clerk even knows what you're talking about ("Duke who?"), you've got a better chance of striking oil in the back yard than you do of finding much jazz. Thus, you're forced to the option of mail order. Granted, there are many disadvantages to this. For one, unless you're a preferred customer, by the time you find out about sales, most of the prime items are gone. Frequently, you send the money in for six titles and two weeks later get four, with either a refund check or an inquiry asking if you want to backorder. Plus, nothing's preferable to walking in to a store, browsing, winnowing down a pile of potential buys, and finally walking out with records (discs/tapes) in hand. Anyway, here are a few places that we've personally dealt with over the years with no problems. This means they have reasonable shipping rates and will actually send you what you order, the product arrives in playable shape, and they issue catalogs in a timely manner. By no means are these the only options available: such magazines as *Goldmine, Record Collector,* and *Discoveries* are full of ads for stores that deal in jazz mail order; there are also many collectors nationwide who regularly hold auctions and set sales. But if you have never ventured into the wild world of mail order, here are some good places to start.

Cadence Mail Order

Among its many other functions, each month *Cadence* magazine also conducts monthly sales of CDs, books, and records. It carries numerous labels, including many European imports and American independents. The address is *Cadence,* Cadence Building, Redwood, New York 13679.

Coda Sales

Canada's premier jazz publication also sells records, videos, and books. Specific price information may be obtained by contacting Coda Publications, P.O. Box 1002, Station O, Toronto, Ontario M4A 2N4, Canada.

Record Roundup

Though not a jazz specialty operation, Rounder's mail-order service, Roundup, can help you find several independent-label current and classic sessions. It publishes a newsletter periodically that lists current specials, and also prints a catalog each year with more detailed listings. The address is Roundup Records, One Camp Street, Cambridge, Massachusetts 02140.

Roots and Rhythm

For many years known as Down Home Music, Inc., this operation is now Roots and Rhythm. Otherwise, nothing has changed. It remains among the finest and most diverse mail-order services in the world. It has plenty of domestic and foreign label/import jazz, though some of the import prices are a bit to the high side. It also publishes periodic newsletters and has catalogs for many categories, though surprisingly it hasn't as yet (March 1994) issued a strictly jazz catalog. The address: Roots and Rhythm, 10341 San Pablo Avenue, El Cerrito, California 94530.

Stash-Daybreak Express

For pure jazz, the number of labels carried by Stash-Daybreak Express rivals any mail operation. It also carries blues, R&B, soul, and doo-wop, but jazz is its specialty and it is very impressive in the caliber and volume that is available. Stash-Daybreak Express, 140 W. 22nd Street, 12th Floor, New York, New York 10011.

I.M.D.

If you haven't yet disposed of your records, or are looking for recent and/or reissued items that have been deleted and/or cut out, here is a great source. I.M.D. carries both cutout vinyl LPs and records and is particularly good for such treasured items as Smithsonian and Arista/Freedom albums. It also has a free catalog available. I.M.D., 160 Hanford Street, Columbus, Ohio 43206.

Audiophile Imports

Yes, even fusion has its champions, and Audiophile Imports offers an extensive variety of fusion and jazz-rock titles. It is a great source for Miles Davis Japanese imports for one, and Jaco Pastorius titles for another. Audiophile, Dept. JT, P.O. Box 4801, Lutherville, Maryland 21094-4801.

Double-Time Jazz

Double-Time can compete with any mail-order service for volume in old and new titles. It handles domestic independent and major-label products, as well as reissues, cutouts, and imports, while also carrying albums and videos in addition to CDs. Double-Time, P.O. Box 1244, New Albany, Indiana 47151-1244.

Worlds Records

If you're a fan of big band or blues, Worlds may prove your best bet for mail-order service. It also carries a full line of major-label, domestic independent, and foreign import titles. Worlds Records, P.O. Box 1922, Novato, California 94948.

Jaybee Jazz

Another excellent source for cutouts and deleted titles, Jaybee is quite strong with big-band items, records, CDs, and cassettes, as well as other styles. Jaybee Jazz, P.O. Box 411004, Creve Coeur, Missouri 63141.

Rick Ballard Imports

If your tastes run predominantly to styles that are mostly available on imports, here is a good source. Rick Ballard Imports carries an extensive number of titles for such labels as Black Saint/Soul Note, DIW, Philology, Timeless, and many others. Rick Ballard Imports, P.O. Box 5063, Dept DB, Berkeley, California 94705.

Descarga

A great Afro-Latin mail-order service. Here is a major option for Latin jazz and salsa that is on the myriad labels out of the American major-label/independent loop. Descarga carries contemporary and classic titles, publishes a newsletter, and qualifies as a first-class operation. Descarga Records, 328 Flatbush Avenue, Suite 180-L, Brooklyn, New York 11238.

Africassette

While world music is its bailiwick, Africassette does also carry quite a bit of Afro-Latin material, including Latin jazz and salsa. It also periodically gets in jazz titles from Africa and the Caribbean, which adds other ingredients to the mix. Africassette, P.O. Box 24941, Detroit, Michigan 48224.

Original Music

While not jazz specialists, Original Music boasts a roster that includes many Afro-Latin titles. It is the company founded and still operated by John Storm Roberts. If there is anyone who knows more about "world" music and its permutations, combinations, hybrids, and multiple genres, I'd sure like to know who it is. Original Music, R.D. 1, P.O. Box 190, Lasher Road, Tivoli, New York 12583

—Ron Wynn

INDEX

When it comes to music, we wrote the book

All Music Guide to Rock
The Best CDs, Albums & Tapes—Rock, Pop, Soul, R&B, and Rap
Edited by Michael Erlewine, et. al.

This is the ultimate guide to rock recordings. For 15,500 CDs, albums and tapes by 2,500 artists—everything from doo-wop to hip-hop—you get concise reviews, expert ratings and revealing career profiles, plus historical music maps and dozens of essays on rock styles and influences.

Softcover, 970pp, 6-1/8 x 9-1/4, ISBN 0-87930-376-X, $24.95

All Music Guide
The Best CDs, Albums & Tapes
Third Edition • Edited by Michael Erlewine, with Chris Woodstra and Vladimir Bogdanov

This fascinating reference leads readers to the best recordings of 6,000-plus artists and groups. From rock to rap, classical to country and everything in between, more than 23,000 recordings in 22 categories are reviewed and rated by 150 top music critics. Includes artist bios, music timelines, and more. *Available 10/97*

Softcover, 1,417pp, 6-1/8 x 9-1/4, ISBN 0-87930-423-5, $27.95

All Music Guide to The Blues
The Experts' Guide to the Best Blues Recordings
Edited by Michael Erlewine, with Chris Woodstra, Vladimir Bogdanov, and Cub Koda

The essential reference for starting, expanding, or fine-tuning a prime collection of the best in blues recordings. Noted critics profile the lives and work of hundreds of key artists, and review and rate thousands of top recordings. *Available 9/97*

Softcover, 400pp, 6-1/8 x 9-1/4, ISBN 0-87930-424-3, $17.95

All Music Book of Hit Albums
The Top 10 US & UK Album Charts from 1960 to the Present Day
Compiled by Dave McAleer

From the birth of album charts in 1960, this unique book lists the Top 10 albums in both the US and the UK through the present. Also filled with photos and fascinating trivia. *Softcover, 352pp, 8 x 9-1/2, ISBN 0-87930-393-X, $22.95*

All Music Book of Hit Singles
Top Twenty Charts from 1954 to the Present Day
Compiled by Dave McAleer

This musical time capsule compares U.S. and U.K. Top 20 charts for the past 40 years. The book is studded with photos, trivia and chartfacts featuring the stars and styles of pop music. *Softcover, 432pp, 8 x 9-1/2, ISBN 0-87930-330-1, $22.95*

Jaco
The Extraordinary and Tragic Life of Jaco Pastorius, "The World's Greatest Bass Player"
By Bill Milkowski

This is a fitting tribute to the talented but tormented genius who revolutionized the electric bass and single-handedly fused jazz, classical, R&B, rock, reggae, pop, and punk—all before the age of 35, when he met his tragic death.

Hardcover, 264pp, 6 x 9, ISBN 0-87930-361-1, $22.95

Secrets from the Masters
40 Great Guitar Players
Edited by Don Menn

Featuring the most influential guitarists of the past 25 years: Jimi Hendrix, Les Paul, Eric Clapton, Eddie Van Halen, Chuck Berry, Andrés Segovia, Pete Townshend and many more. Combines personal biography, career history, and playing techniques. *Softcover, 300 pp, 8-1/2 x 11, ISBN 0-87930-260-7, $19.95*

Blues Guitar • The Men Who Made the Music
Second Edition • Edited by Jas Obrecht

Readers get a look inside the lives and music of thirty great bluesmen, through interviews, articles, discographies, and rare photographs. Covers Buddy Guy, Robert Johnson, John Lee Hooker, Albert King, B.B. King, Muddy Waters, and more. *Softcover, 280pp, 8-1/2 x 11, ISBN 0-87930-292-5, $19.95*

Bass Heroes
Styles, Stories & Secrets of 30 Great Bass Players
Edited by Tom Mulhern

Thirty of the world's greatest bass players in rock, jazz, studio/pop, and blues & funk share their musical influences, playing techniques, and opinions. Includes Jack Bruce, Stanley Clarke, James Jamerson, Paul McCartney, and more. *Softcover, 208pp, 8-1/2 x 11, ISBN 0-87930-274-7, $17.95*

1000 Great Guitarists
By Hugh Gregory

Profiling the world's outstanding guitarists from A to Z, this inviting "encyclopedia" covers all kinds of guitar music. Superstars and lesser-knowns are listed with full details on their styles, guitars, best recordings, and more. *Softcover, 164pp, 7-1/4 x 9-1/2, ISBN 0-87930-307-7, $19.95*

How to Play Guitar
The Basics & Beyond—Chords, Scales, Tunes & Tips
By the Editors of Guitar Player

For anyone learning to play acoustic or electric guitar, this book and CD set is packed with music, licks, and lessons from the pros. The CD guides readers through nine lessons. *Softcover, 80 pp, 8-1/2 x 11, ISBN 0-87930-399-9, $14.95*

Hot Guitar
Rock Soloing, Blues Power, Rapid-Fire Rockabilly, Slick Turnarounds, Hot Country, and Cool Licks
By Arlen Roth

Drawing on ten years of the "Hot Guitar" column from *Guitar Player*, this book covers string bending, slides, picking and fingering techniques, soloing, and rock, blues, and country licks. *Softcover, 160pp, 8-1/2 x 11, ISBN 0-87930-276-3, $19.95*

Guitar Player Repair Guide
How to Set Up, Maintain, and Repair Electrics and Acoustics • By Dan Erlewine—Second Edition

Whether you're a player, collector, or repairperson, this hands-on guide provides all the essential information on caring for guitars and electric basses. Includes hundreds of photos and drawings detailing techniques for guitar care and repair. *Softcover, 309pp, 8-1/2 x 11, ISBN 0-87930-291-7, $22.95*

Miller Freeman Books

Available at fine book and music stores, or contact:

Miller Freeman Books , 6600 Silacci Way, Gilroy, CA 95020
Phone (800) 848-5594 • Fax (408) 848-5784 • E-Mail: mfbooks@mfi.com
World Wide Web: http://www.mfi.com/mf-books/